VideoHound's
GOLDEN
MOVIE
RETRIEVER

Also available from Visible Ink Press

VideoHound's Video Premieres: The Only Guide to Video Originals and Limited Releases
Mike Mayo. 431 pages. $17.95 ISBN: 0-7876-0825-4

VideoHound's Independent Film Guide
Monica Sullivan. Foreword by Mare Winningham. 575 pages. $17.95 ISBN: 1-57859-018-3

VideoHound's Soundtracks: Music from the Movies, Broadway, and Television
Didier Deutch. 800 pages. $24.95 ISBN: 1-57859-025-6

VideoHound's Vampires on Video
J. Gordon Melton. Foreword by Jeanne Keyes Youngson. 335 pages. $17.95 ISBN: 1-57859-002-7

VideoHound's Sci-Fi Experience: Your Quantum Guide to the Video Universe
445 pages. $17.95 ISBN: 0-7876-0615-4

VideoHound's Complete Guide to Cult Flicks and Trash Pics
438 pages. $17.95 ISBN: 1-7876-0616-2

VideoHound's Family Video Guide, 2nd Edition
Edited by Martin F. Kohn. Foreword by Brian Henson. 760 pages. $17.95 ISBN: 0-7876-0984-6

VideoHound's GOLDEN MOVIE RETRIEVER

Martin Connors and Jim Craddock, Editors

VISIBLE INK PRESS

Detroit New York Toronto London

VideoHound®'s Golden Movie Retriever® 1998

Copyright © 1991, 1993, 1994, 1995, 1996, 1997, 1998 by Visible Ink Press™

Published by Visible Ink Press, a division of Gale Research, 835 Penobscot Building, Detroit, MI 48226-4094

Visible Ink Press, VideoHound, the VideoHound logo, Golden Movie Retriever, and A Cunning Canine Production are trademarks of Gale Research

Most Visible Ink Press books are available at special quantity discounts when purchased in bulk by corporations, organizations, or groups. Customized printings, special imprints, messages, and excerpts can be produced to meet your needs. For more information, contact Special Markets Manager, Gale Research, 835 Penobscot Bldg., Detroit, MI 48226-4094.

ISBN 1-57859-024-8

Printed in the United States of America

All rights reserved

10 9 8 7 6 5 4 3 2 1

Credits

DIRECTED BY:
MARTIN CONNORS

STARRING:
JAMES CRADDOCK

CO-STARRING:
MICHELLE BANKS
CHRISTA BRELIN
DEAN DAUPHINAIS
BETH FHANER
JUDY GALENS
BRAD MORGAN
CHRISTOPHER SCANLON
CAROL SCHWARTZ
DEVRA SLADICS

FEATURING:
MARTIN CRADDOCK
HILARY WEBER

WITH A SPECIAL APPEARANCE BY:
JULIA FURTAW

AND INTRODUCING:
AMBER FOULKROD
HOLLY MONACELLI

SPECIAL GUEST STAR:
JIM OLENSKI

CASTING:
TERRI SCHELL

RESEARCH & SITE SELECTION:
CHRISTINE TOMASSINI

DIGITAL FX:
WAYNE FONG

TITLES AND OPTICALS:
MICHAEL BOYD, ATLIS PUBLISHING SERVICES, INC.

SET DECORATION:
MARY KRZEWINSKI

ART DIRECTION:
CYNTHIA BALDWIN

FRONTMATTER BEST BOY:
MARCO DI VITA, GRAPHIX GROUP

VIDEOHOUND'S PERSONAL ILLUSTRATOR:
STEPHEN DUERR

KEY GRIPS:
MARY BETH TRIMPER
DOROTHY MAKI
EVI SEOUD
DEBORAH MILLIKEN
WENDY BLURTON

HAIR STYLIST TO THE STARS:
ROBERT RUFFER

ASSISTANT TO MR. HOUND:
JANE P. CONNORS

HYPE:
MARYLOU CARLIN

MARKETING:
KIM INTINDOLA
BETSY ROVEGNO

KOPYKAT:
SUE STEFANI

IMPATIENT SHORTWAVE OPERATOR:
DAN SKAGGS

FIRST BODY IN THE MUD:
MARK FLEEMAN

SECOND BODY IN THE MUD:
KEVIN COSTELLO

LITTLE NEL:
JEANNIE DUNHAM

VOICES OF THE SINGING MICE:
ROGER MOSS
TED WEDEL
JERRY STROUD

CINEMATOGRAPHY:
BOB ARNOLD

SOUND:
DON STURTZ

COSTUMES:
KEN ROTHMAN

LICENSING/SPECIAL MARKET GUYS:
TOBY LEITH
ROGER JANECKE

MR. PITT'S STUNT DOUBLE:
MICHAEL GORLEY

CATERING CREW:
TRICIA COSTELLO
RANDY SPURGIN
ROBIN BELL

BASED ON A STORY AS TOLD TO:
BILL HOAR

ENDLESS BACKGROUND GUITAR STRUMMING:
RICHARD DETRANO

STUNTS:
NICOLE FORTIER

MR. PITT'S DRIVER:
KEN HILL

MR. JACKSON'S DRIVER:
John Little

A Cunning Canine Production™

Contents

Introduction

Reader writes:

"It [VideoHound] is the ephemeral spark which ignites the collective truths embedded deep in all of us. It is poignant yet lighthearted. Mysterious yet user-friendly. Action-packed, yet in its quietest moments exudes more feelings, more descriptive paragraphs, more explosions than Stephen King in his wildest fantasies." Irene From the Land of Those with Far Too Much Time.

Goodnight Irene Who Dances with Video-Hound and welcome to the 1998 edition of *VideoHound's Golden Movie Retriever*, our gala 7th anniversary edition (note the special cover design, which in the right light, reflects a hologram of Brad Pitt running around naked as a jaybird. Or, on other special editions, Demi Moore appears with her clothes on, an equally rare treat). What do we have in store this time?

VideoHound now covers DVD (which stands for Digital Vegetable Debutante, and is reputed to be the video and music format of the next 10 minutes) to the extent permitted under the law. While more than 100 movies are now on DVD, many more will become available before the next edition. A complete list is available within the Digital Formats Index (DVI), which used to be the Alternate Formats Index (AFI), until we changed the name and screwed around with the content. This, we call job security (JS).

In our spare time we added nominees to the awards index, so you can discover who lost as well as who won (and as we all know, the losers are often more noteworthy, particularly when you're talking Oscars). This index is now four times as large, and we're very

impressed. The awards index is handy to use as a tool for recommended watching, since *VideoHound*, alone among all the video guides, covers awards worldwide, including those handed out in places like Australia and Britain and Canada and France and even Los Angeles. And speaking of awards, did you know that *VideoHound* helped the Detroit Red Wings win the Stanley Cup? It's true. Honest. Ask Brendan Shanahan. Go ahead. We dare you.

Responding to the many cards and letters we received on the subject, *VideoHound* has added content warnings to the *NC-17, R*, and *PG-13* movies. These warnings speak of the coming apocalypse, where movies will be the only currency available, and your children will live in the mountains and hunt wild goats and barter Pauly Shore videos in order to survive. These MPAA cautions will guide the morally prudent to good choices, and allow everyone else to lock in on flicks with nudity, foul language, and violence. *Vive la difference!*

In order to make room for these home improvements, we've eliminated the Song Title Index. The song titles are still in the reviews themselves, but the index is no longer with us. Sometimes an index just has to follow its own path. It did receive a nice severance package and a swell turnout at the farewell party. For those of you looking for more authoritative information on movie soundtracks, might we suggest a fine chardonnay and *VideoHound's Soundtracks: Movies from the Movies, Broadway, and Television*, available at better bookstores everywhere, and even some that are not so better.

More than 1,000 new reviews have been added to *VideoHound*. So, the existing indexes have gotten bigger, and continue to threaten to blow out of the back of the book. These indexes have also developed something of an attitude problem, believing (we think unjustly) that they are being ignored in favor of the "new stuff". We beg their pardon. The older indexes are some of our favorite indexes, unlike say, the Song Title Index. For instance, the Category Index, always near and dear, has a number of new categories, including "Scared 'Chuteless" which covers those movies making use of the naked jump from an airplane. Or, "Terminal Confusion" which covers that classic scene in too many movies to count (the answer is four or five) where parcels are switched at the airport, bus station, etc. And in honor of Dolly the Cloned Sheep, we proudly announce "Cloning Around" which covers those instances of exact genetic duplication in the movies (not sequels). The cast, director, writer, and composer indexes are all much larger, befitting those sections now at the Darwinian peak of their evolution.

These changes are all self-inflicted, although at your request. Some things have been done *to* us. Horrible, awful things. Like *Speed 2*, although we did enjoy the homage to the Dangerfield boat scene in *Caddyshack* and would like Sandra Bullock to call us. A new batch of videos always brings with it a variety of emotions. Surprise, happiness, joy, disappointment, sorrow, anger, a deep-seated sense of betrayal, nausea, and finally, acceptance. Who can forget endearing cinematic moments like *The Relic* or *The Cable Guy* or *The Glimmer Man* or *Batman and Robin*? Movies that make you yearn for the good old days when it only took $100 million to make a movie. On the budget side, *VideoHound* hails the ascent of the Independent Movie, and we salute the Independent Director and His/Her Independent Crew, many of whom are currently on staff and grumbling about their day jobs.

You, the movie watcher, deserve more variety, and frankly, quality could improve. *VideoHound* is proof that there is more to the cinematic experience than the latest loud crash boom at the box office. Although we have nothing against the loud crash boom if it's done with style. Dozens of new movies with a heart and soul are released every year, some straight to video, some for extremely limited theatrical runs before reaching video. *VideoHound* covers all the flicks that are new to video, and is the only guide that continues to do so. Plus, we publish a variety of Hound puppies, including *VideoHound's Premieres*, covering the wonderful world of direct to video, and the brand spanking new *VideoHound's Independent Film Guide*, reviewing those movies made outside the studio system.

One last check to make sure we've mentioned our name enough. Okay, now we're very interested in knowing what you think of the coming year in video; write us with your nominations for the best and worst of 1998. We'll probably let you know ours in next year's introduction, thus avoiding the always popular "What should we write about in the Intro?" discussion. In the meantime, enjoy the book. Hope it helps.

Reader writes again:

"VideoHound's Golden Movie Retriever is, in a word, life. And my only question or comment is, where can I get more, if there can ever be enough? I give it four bones, two thumbs up, a lifetime supply of kudos, a cup of hot soup and a pony."

When do we get the pony?

Using VideoHound

Alphabetization

Titles are arranged on a word-by-word basis, including articles and prepositions. Leading articles (A, An, The) are ignored in English-language titles. The equivalent foreign articles are not ignored, however: The Abyss appears under "A" while Les Miserables appears under "L." **Other points to keep in mind:**

- Acronyms appear alphabetically as if regular words. For example C.H.U.D. is alphabetized as "Chud"; M*A*S*H as "Mash."

- Common abbreviations in titles file as if they are spelled out, so St. Elmo's Fire will be found under "Saint Elmo's Fire" and Mr. Holland's Opus will be alphabetized as "Mister Holland's Opus."

- Proper Names in titles are alphabetized beginning with the individual's first name; for instance, Monty Python's The Meaning of Life is under "M;" Eddie Murphy: Raw under "E."

- Titles with numbers (2001: A Space Odyssey) are alphabetized as if the number was spelled out under the appropriate letter, in this case "Two Thousand One." When numeric titles gather in close proximity to each other (2000 Year Old Man, 2001, 2069: A Sex Odyssey), the titles will be arranged in a low (2000) to high (2069) numeric sequence.

Indexes

Alternate Title Index A number of videos, particularly older or B-type releases, may have variant titles. Alternate titles are listed alphabetically and refer the reader to the title under which the entry is listed. The alternate titles are also noted within the review.

Category Index Subject categories ranging from the orthodox to slightly eccentric permit you to video sleuth from broad type to significant themes to signature scenes. The mix, arranged alphabetically by category, includes hundreds of traditional film genres and sub-genres as well as a feast of VideoHound exclusives. Integrated into the index are cross references, while preceding the index is a list of definitions. **A tipped triangle indicates a movie rated three bones or above.**

Kibbles and Series Index Not your everyday categories, Kibbles span the literary side of movie-making (adapted from a play, Hemingway on video) as well as pointing out key producers and special effects masters. Yearly box-office winners (that are now on video) since 1939 are listed, along with classic movies, four-bone delights, trash films, modern Shakespeare, Disney fare, and of course, bottom of the barrel Woof! features, some of which are terrible enough to provide an amusing evening.

The index formerly known as Series, now combined with the Kibbles, provides listings of major movie series, ranging from James Bond to National Lampoon to Indiana Jones. Recurring cinematic collaborations and partnerships of note are also listed, including Hope & Crosby, Abbott & Costello, De Niro & Scorsese, and Rafelson & Nicholson. A complete list of the categories precedes the index. **As in the Category Index, tipped triangles indicate quality views.**

Awards Index The Awards Index lists almost 7,000 films honored by 20 national and international award bodies, representing some 90 categories of competition. Nomination information is now included. This information is also contained in the review following the credits. **Only features available on video and reviewed in the main section are listed in this index; movies not yet released on video are not covered.**

As award-winning and nominated films find their way to video, they will be added to the review section and covered in this index. Awards listed include the American Academy Awards; Australia Film Institute; British Academy of Film and Television Arts; Cannes Film Festival; French Cesar; Canadian Genie; Golden Globe; Directors Guild of America; Independent Spirit; Montreal Film Festival; and the MTV Awards.

Foreign Film Index Here the Hound classifies movies by the country/countries of record in which the feature was financed (but not necessarily where they were filmed). Since the producers of a specific film may hail from more than one country, some videos will be listed under more than one country. **The foreign codes also appear in the review immediately following the color or black and white designation. A**

tipped triangle following the title indicates a three bone or above endeavor.

Cast/Director Indexes The Cast Index provides full videographies for all actors and actresses listed in <u>VideoHound</u> with more than one movie on their resume. The Director Index lists the works of any director who has made it to video and to <u>VideoHound</u>. Although listed in a first name, last name sequence, the names are alphabetized by last name. Film titles, complete with initial year of release, are arranged in chronological order, starting with their most recent.

Writer Index Scriptwriters and script doctors are listed with their vital works. Names are arranged alphabetically by last name. Works are arranged chronologically.

Cinematographer Index Directors of Photography are listed alphabetically by last name, along with their work, which is arranged chronologically. Cinematography is often a starting point for feature directors.

Composer Index Videographies of movie music composers, arrangers, lyricists, and so on are listed. Arranged alphabetically by last name.

Digital Formats Index. Laserdisc, CD-I, and the new DVD format are included. This index will now focus on non-videotape alternatives for home viewing, concentrating on current (as well as any future) digital-based technologies. Movies are listed alphabetically after each format subheading.

Distributor Guide Each video review has at least one and as many as three distributor codes. In the reviews, these are located at the bottom of the review. The full address and phone, toll-free, and fax numbers of the 340 distributors listed can be found in the Distributor Guide. For added convenience and less confusion, the distributors are split into wholesale and retail subheads. In some cases the distributors did not indicate which market they served. These distributors are listed in a straight alphabetical sort at the beginning of the index. **Caution: a small number of distributors adhere to a nomadic life-style that includes frequent address changes. A tiny minority on the list in any given year will also go out of business. An extra caution: Studio distributors do not sell to the general public, they generally act as wholesalers, selling only to retail outlets.** Up to three distributors are listed in order to give you more choice. A Distributor List, preceding the Guide, provides an alphabetical list of the distributor codes which will refer the reader to the proper distributor.

In the main section, those reviews with the code **OM** are on moratorium (distributed at one time, though not currently). Since a title enjoying such status was once distributed, it may well linger on your local video store shelf. When the distributor is not known, the code **NO** appears. For new releases to the theater that have not yet made it to video (but likely will in the coming year), the code **NYR** (not yet released) appears.

Web Site Guide Lists Internet web sites for popular actors, actresses and directors, studio movie sites, general entertainment information, filmmaker resources, as well as sites for gossip and trivia. Actor and movie sites list the URLs after the main citation. The more popular the personality, the more URLs. Sites with more generalized information contain text after the URL to help you decide if they are worth a visit.

Sample Review

Each *VideoHound* review contains up to 19 items, ranging from title to the review to awards received to the distributor code. The information in these reviews is designed to help you choose a video you'll like, increase your enjoyment of a movie as you watch (especially by answering that nagging question of "What else have I seen that guy in?"), and increase your knowledge of movie trivia.

1 Sling Blade 2 ♫♫♫⩊ **3** *Some Call It a Sling Blade* **4 1996 5 (R) 6** Mildly retarded killer Karl (Thornton, making his feature directorial debut) is released from a mental hospital, where he was placed after killing his mother and her lover, after 25 years. Returning to his hometown, he befriends a boy (Black) with problems of his own. His mother is living with a mean, bullying drunkard (Yoakam, in a brilliant performance) who has no use for anyone, least of all mom's openly gay co-worker (Ritter). Thornton's excellent script moves at the slow pace of its hero, providing the superb cast plenty of opportunity to explore the rich characterization and dialogue. Filmed in Thornton's home state of Arkansas. **7** *CW:* Some violence and language. **8** _ Slice of Life; I Lahk the Way Yew Talk; Sling Blade Blues. **9&10 134m/C 11 VHS. 12** *GB* **13** Billy Bob Thornton, Dwight Yoakam, John Ritter, Lucas Black, Natalie Canerday, James Hampton, Robert Duvall, J.T. Walsh, Rick Dial, Brent Briscoe, Christy Ward, Col. Bruce Hampton, Vic Chesnutt, Mickey Jones, Jim Jarmusch, Ian Moore; **14** *D:* Billy Bob Thornton; **15** *W:* Billy Bob Thornton; **16** *C:* Barry Markowitz; **17** *M:* Daniel Lanois. **18** Academy Awards '96: Best Adapted Screenplay; Independent Spirit Awards '97: Best First Feature; Writers Guild of America '96: Best Adapted Screenplay; Nominations: Academy Awards '96: Best Actor (Thornton); Screen Actors Guild Award '96: Best Actor (Thornton), Cast. **19** *TOU*

1	Title
2	One-to-four bone rating (or *Woof!*)
3	Alternate Title
4	Year released
5	MPAA Rating
6	Description/review
7	Content Warning (new)
8	Songs (we made these up, too)
9	Length (in minutes)
10	Black and White (B) or Color (C)
11	Format (VHS, Beta, LV-Laserdisc, or 8mm)
12	Country produced in (made it up)
13	Cast (V: indicates voiceovers; also includes cameos)
14	Director
15	Writers
16	Cinematographer(s)
17	Composers/Lyricists
18	Awards and Nominations
19	Distributor code

Mail Order
Video Sources

Some of the movies reviewed in this book may be difficult to find using conventional devices such as the neighborhood video rental chain. Many independent and mail order video outlets specialize in rare or hard-to-find movies. We have included a small list of such outlets to assist you in your search.

Thomas Video
122 S. Main St.
Clawson, MI 48017
(248) 280-2833
fax: (248) 280-4463
http://www.thomasvideo.com

Video Vision
Attn: Chris Hendlin
4603 Bloomington Ave.
Minneapolis, MN 55407
(612) 728-0000

Luminous Film & Video
PO Box 1047, Dept. AC
Medford, NY 11763
(516) 289-1644
E-mail: LFVW@aol.com

House of Monsters
2038 N. Clark St., No. 348
Chicago, IL 60614
fax: (312) 929-7205

Video Vault
323 S. Washington
Alexandria, VA 22314
(800) VAULT66

A Million and One World-Wide Videos
PO Box 349
Orchard Hill, GA 30266
(800) 849-7309; (770) 227-7309
fax: (800) 849-0873; (770) 227-0873
E-mail: barbara@wwvideo.com
http://www.wwvideos.com

Video Oyster
145 W. 12th St.
New York, NY 10011
(212) 989-3300
fax: (212) 989-3533
E-mail: video@VideoOyster.com

China West Video
PO Box 291655, Dept. 8
Los Angeles, CA 90029

Facets Video
1517 Fullerton Ave.
Chicago, IL 60614
(800) 331-6197

Movies Unlimited
3015 Darnell Rd.
Philadelphia, PA 19154
(800) 4-MOVIES

The **Alternate Titles Index** provides variant and foreign titles for movies with more than one name. Titles are listed in alphabetical order, followed by a cross-reference to the appropriate entry in the main video review section. If you don't find a movie you're looking for in the main section, this is the best place to look next.

A-009 Missione Hong Kong *See* Code Name Alpha (1967)

A Bout de Souffle *See* Breathless (1959)

Abar, the First Black Superman *See* In Your Face (1977)

Abbott and Costello in the Navy *See* In the Navy (1941)

Abbott and Costello Meet the Ghosts *See* Abbott and Costello Meet Frankenstein (1948)

ABC Murders *See* The Alphabet Murders (1965)

Abdullah's Harem *See* Abdulla the Great (1956)

Abismos de Pasion *See* Wuthering Heights (1953)

Absent-Minded *See* The Daydreamer (1975)

Absinthe *See* Madame X (1966)

The Accused *See* The Mark of the Hawk (1957)

Ace *See* The Great Santini (1980)

Ace Ventura Goes to Africa *See* Ace Ventura: When Nature Calls (1995)

Acla *See* Acla's Descent into Floristella (1987)

Across Five Aprils *See* Civil War Diary (1990)

Act of Violence *See* Deadline Assault (1990)

Acts of Love *See* Carried Away (1995)

Adam Wants to Be a Man *See* Adomas Nori Buti Zmogumi (1959)

Addict *See* Born to Win (1971)

Addio, Fratello, Crudele *See* 'Tis a Pity She's a Whore (1973)

Adorable Idiot *See* Ravishing Idiot (1964)

The Adventure *See* L'Avventura (1960)

Adventure for Two *See* The Demi-Paradise (1943)

The Adventure of Lyle Swan *See* Timerider (1983)

Adventures at Rugby *See* Tom Brown's School Days (1940)

The Adventures of Chatran *See* The Adventures of Milo & Otis (1989)

The Adventures of Galgameth *See* Galgameth (1996)

The Adventures of Hercules *See* Hercules 2 (1985)

The Adventures of Jack London *See* Jack London (1944)

The Adventures of the Great Mouse Detective *See* The Great Mouse Detective (1986)

The Adventuress *See* I See a Dark Stranger (1946)

Aelita: The Revolt of the Robots *See* Aelita: Queen of Mars (1924)

Aerobicide *See* Killer Workout (1986)

An Affair of the Heart *See* Body and Soul (1947)

An Affair of the Heart *See* The Love Affair, or The Case of the Missing Switchboard Operator (1967)

AFO *See* Air Force One (1997)

African Fury *See* Cry, the Beloved Country (1951)

After Jenny Died *See* Revenge (1971)

Afurika Monogatari *See* Green Horizon (1983)

Agaguk: Shadow of the Wolf *See* Shadow of the Wolf (1992)

Against All Odds *See* Kiss and Kill (1968)

Agatha Christie's Endless Night *See* Endless Night (1971)

Agatha Christie's Miss Marple: A Murder Is Announced *See* A Murder Is Announced (1987)

Agatha Christie's Miss Marple: A Pocketful of Rye *See* A Pocketful of Rye (1987)

Agatha Christie's Miss Marple: The Body In the Library *See* The Body in the Library (1987)

Agatha Christie's Ten Little Indians *See* Ten Little Indians (1989)

The Age of Beauty *See* Belle Epoque (1992)

Age of Gold *See* L'Age D'Or (1930)

Agent 38-24-36 *See* Ravishing Idiot (1964)

The Agitators *See* The Fix (1984)

Agoniya *See* Rasputin (1985)

Agostino di Ippona *See* Augustine of Hippo (1972)

Aimez-Vous Brahms *See* Goodbye Again (1961)

Aiqing Wansui *See* Vive L'Amour (1994)

Airport '79 *See* The Concorde: Airport '79 (1979)

Akage *See* Red Lion (1969)

Akahige *See* Red Beard (1965)

Akasen Chitai *See* Street of Shame (1956)

Al Di La Della Legge *See* Beyond the Law (1968)

Al-Ris-Alah *See* Mohammed: Messenger of God (1977)

Alas de Mariposa *See* Butterfly Wings (1991)

Alem Da Paixao *See* Happily Ever After (1986)

Alfie Darling *See* Oh, Alfie (1975)

Alfred Hitchcock's Bon Voyage & Aventure Malgache *See* Alfred Hitchcock's Aventure Malgache (1944)

Alfred Hitchcock's Bon Voyage & Aventure Malgache *See* Alfred Hitchcock's Bon Voyage (1944)

Ali Baba et les Quarante Voleurs *See* Ali Baba and the 40 Thieves (1954)

Alias Bulldog Drummond *See* Bulldog Jack (1935)

Alien P.I. *See* Alien Private Eye (1987)

Badkonake Sefid *See* The White Balloon (1995)

The Bailiff *See* Sansho the Bailiff (1954)

Baisers Voles *See* Stolen Kisses (1968)

The Bait *See* L'Appat (1994)

The Baited Trap *See* The Trap (1959)

Bakushu *See* Early Summer (1951)

The Banana Monster *See* Schlock (1973)

Bande a Part *See* Band of Outsiders (1964)

The Bandit *See* Crossfire (1967)

Banditi a Orgosolo *See* Bandits of Orgosolo (1961)

Bang Bang *See* Bang Bang Kid (1967)

Bangiku *See* Late Chrysanthemums (1954)

The Bank Detective *See* The Bank Dick (1940)

Banner in the Sky *See* Third Man on the Mountain (1959)

The Bar Sinister *See* It's a Dog's Life (1955)

Barbados Quest *See* Murder on Approval (1956)

Barbarella, Queen of the Galaxy *See* Barbarella (1968)

The Barbarians and Co. *See* The Barbarians (1987)

The Barbaric Beast of Boggy Creek, Part II *See* Boggy Creek II (1983)

Bargain Basement *See* Department Store (1935)

Baron Blood *See* Torture Chamber of Baron Blood (1972)

Batman: The Animated Movie *See* Batman: Mask of the Phantasm (1993)

Batmen of Africa *See* Darkest Africa (1936)

Battle Beyond the Stars *See* The Green Slime (1968)

The Battle for Anzio *See* Anzio (1968)

Battle of the Astros *See* Godzilla vs. Monster Zero (1968)

The Battle of the Mareth Line *See* Battleforce (1978)

The Battle of the River Plate *See* Pursuit of the Graf Spee (1957)

Battle Stripe *See* The Men (1950)

Battletruck *See* Warlords of the 21st Century (1982)

The Battling Bellhop *See* Kid Galahad (1937)

Battling Hoofer *See* Something to Sing About (1936)

Bawang Bie Ji *See* Farewell My Concubine (1993)

Bay of Blood *See* Twitch of the Death Nerve (1971)

The Bay of Saint Michel *See* Pattern for Plunder (1962)

Bayou *See* Poor White Trash (1957)

Be Beautiful but Shut Up *See* Just Another Pretty Face (1958)

Be My Valentine, Or Else... *See* Hospital Massacre (1981)

Be Roringen *See* The Touch (1971)

The Beans of Egypt, Maine *See* Forbidden Choices (1994)

The Bear Hunt *See* Bare Hunt (1963)

The Beast Must Die *See* Black Werewolf (1975)

The Beast of War *See* The Beast (1988)

Beasts *See* Twilight People (1972)

Beatlemania *See* Beatlemania! The Movie (1981)

Beatsville *See* The Rebel Set (1959)

Beautiful But Dangerous *See* She Couldn't Say No (1952)

Beautiful But Deadly *See* The Don Is Dead (1973)

A Beautiful Place to Kill *See* Paranoia (1969)

Beethoven's Great Love *See* Beethoven (1936)

Beggars' Opera *See* The Threepenny Opera (1931)

The Beginners *See* The First Time (1969)

The Beginners Three *See* The First Time (1969)

Behind Enemy Lines *See* The P.O.W. Escape (1986)

Behind Locked Doors *See* Human Gorilla (1948)

Behind the Blue *See* L'Enfant d'Eau (1995)

Behind the Iron Mask *See* The Fifth Musketeer (1979)

Believe Me *See* Hollow Reed (1995)

Bells *See* Murder by Phone (1982)

The Beloved *See* Restless (1972)

Berry Gordy's The Last Dragon *See* The Last Dragon (1985)

The Best Way to Walk *See* The Best Way (1976)

Bethune, The Making of a Hero *See* Dr. Bethune (1990)

Betrayal *See* Trahir (1993)

Between Us *See* Entre-Nous (1983)

Beware! The Blob *See* Son of Blob (1972)

Bewitching Scatterbrain *See* Ravishing Idiot (1964)

The Beyond *See* Seven Doors of Death (1982)

Beyond Bedlam *See* Nightscare (1993)

Beyond Justice *See* Guardian Angel (1994)

Beyond Obsession *See* Beyond the Door (1975)

Beyond the Fog *See* Tower of Evil (1972)

Beyond the Living *See* Hospital of Terror (1978)

Beyond the Living Dead *See* The Hanging Woman (1972)

Beyond the Rising Moon *See* Star Quest (1989)

Bez Konca *See* No End (1984)

Bez Znieczulenia *See* Without Anesthesia (1978)

The Big Bankroll *See* The King of the Roaring '20s: The Story of Arnold Rothstein (1961)

The Big Boss *See* Fists of Fury (1973)

The Big Day *See* Jour de Fete (1948)

Big Deal at Dodge City *See* A Big Hand for the Little Lady (1966)

Big Duel in the North *See* Godzilla vs. the Sea Monster (1966)

Big Enough and Old Enough *See* Savages from Hell (1968)

The Big Heart *See* Miracle on 34th Street (1947)

The Big Lobby *See* Rosebud Beach Hotel (1985)

The Big Payoff *See* Win, Place, or Steal (1972)

Big Time Operators *See* The Smallest Show on Earth (1957)

The Biggest Right on Earth *See* Ghidrah the Three Headed Monster (1965)

Biggles: Adventures in Time *See* Biggles (1985)

Bijo to Ekitainigen *See* H-Man (1959)

Bikini Genie *See* Wildest Dreams (1990)

Billy the Kid's Fighting Pals *See* Trigger Men (1941)

Bio-Force I *See* Mutant Species (1995)

Birds of a Feather *See* The Birdcage (1995)

Birds of Prey *See* Beaks: The Movie (1987)

Birthmark *See* The Omen (1976)

Birumano Tategoto *See* The Burmese Harp (1956)

The Bitch *See* La Chienne (1931)

Bittere Ernte *See* Angry Harvest (1985)

Black Angels *See* Black Bikers from Hell (1970)

Black Arrow Strikes *See* Black Arrow (1948)

The Black Book *See* Reign of Terror (1949)

The Black Bounty Killer *See* Boss (1974)

The Black Buccaneer *See* The Black Pirate (1926)

Black Eliminator *See* Kill Factor (1978)

Black Flowers for the Bride *See* Something for Everyone (1970)

Black Frankenstein *See* Blackenstein (1973)

Black Gauntlet *See* Black Starlet (1974)

Black Jack *See* Captain Blackjack (1951)

Black Love, White Love *See* Sweet Love, Bitter (1967)

Black Rider *See* Joshua (1976)

Black Rose of Harlem *See* Machine Gun Blues (1995)

Black Valor *See* Savage! (1973)

Blade of Steel *See* The Far Pavilions (1984)

Blake Edwards' Son of the Pink Panther *See* Son of the Pink Panther (1993)

Blast-Off *See* Those Fantastic Flying Fools (1967)

Blazing Arrows *See* Fighting Caravans (1931)

Blazing Magnums *See* Strange Shadows in an Empty Room (1976)

Bless 'Em All *See* The Act (1982)

Blind Alley *See* Perfect Strangers (1984)

The Blind Dead *See* Tombs of the Blind Dead (1972)

Blind Man's Bluff *See* Cauldron of Blood (1967)

Blind Terror *See* See No Evil (1971)

Blonde Bombshell *See* Bombshell (1933)

The Blonde From Peking *See* The Peking Blond (1968)

A Blonde in Love *See* Loves of a Blonde (1965)

Blondie Has Servant Trouble *See* Blondie Has Trouble (1940)

Blood and Sand *See* Sand and Blood (1987)

Blood Bath *See* Track of the Vampire (1966)

Blood Beast from Outer Space *See* Night Caller from Outer Space (1966)

Blood Brides *See* Hatchet for the Honeymoon (1970)

The Blood Brother *See* Texas Pioneers (1932)

Blood Castle *See* The Blood Spattered Bride (1972)

Blood Ceremony *See* The Legend of Blood Castle (1972)

Blood Couple *See* Black Vampire (1973)

Blood Creature *See* Terror Is a Man (1959)

The Blood Crowd *See* The McMasters (1970)

The Blood Cult of Shangri-La *See* The Thirsty Dead (1974)

Blood Demon *See* The Torture Chamber of Dr. Sadism (1969)

Blood Doctor *See* Mad Doctor of Blood Island (1969)

Campsite Massacre *See* The Final Terror (1983)

A Candle for the Devil *See* It Happened at Nightmare Inn (1970)

Canicule *See* Dog Day (1983)

Cannibal Orgy, or the Maddest Story Ever Told *See* Spider Baby (1964)

Cannibals in the City *See* Invasion of the Flesh Hunters (1982)

Cannibals in the Streets *See* Invasion of the Flesh Hunters (1982)

Capitaine Conan *See* Captain Conan (1996)

Capitaine Morgan *See* Morgan the Pirate (1960)

Capitalismo Salvaje *See* Savage Capitalism (1993)

Captain Mephisto and the Transformation Machine *See* Manhunt of Mystery Island (1945)

Captain Midnight *See* On the Air Live with Captain Midnight (1979)

Captain Yankee *See* Jungle Raiders (1985)

Captive *See* Sex and the Other Man (1995)

Captive Women 3: Sweet Sugar *See* Sweet Sugar (1972)

Caravans West *See* Wagon Wheels (1934)

The Card *See* The Promoter (1952)

Cardigan's Last Case *See* State's Attorney (1931)

Care of the Spitfire Grill *See* The Spitfire Grill (1995)

Carlo Collodi's Pinocchio *See* The Adventures of Pinocchio (1996)

Carnage *See* Twitch of the Death Nerve (1971)

Carnival of Fools *See* Death Wish Club (1983)

Carnival of Thieves *See* Caper of the Golden Bulls (1967)

Carquake *See* Cannonball (1976)

Carry On Follow That Camel *See* Follow That Camel (1967)

The Cars That Eat People *See* The Cars That Ate Paris (1974)

Cartagine in Fiamme *See* Carthage in Flames (1960)

Cartes sur Table *See* Attack of the Robots (1966)

Carthage en Flammes *See* Carthage in Flames (1960)

The Case of Jonathan Drew *See* The Lodger (1926)

The Case of the Hillside Stranglers *See* The Hillside Strangler (1989)

Case of the Missing Switchboard Operator *See* The Love Affair, or The Case of the Missing Switchboard Operator (1967)

Cash *See* If I Were Rich (1933)

Cassanova and Co. *See* Sex on the Run (1978)

Castle in the Sky *See* Yidl Mitn Fidl (1936)

Castle of Doom *See* Vampyr (1931)

Castle of Terror *See* Castle of Blood (1964)

Castle of Terror *See* The Virgin of Nuremberg (1965)

The Castle of the Spider's Web *See* Throne of Blood (1957)

Castle of the Walking Dead *See* The Torture Chamber of Dr. Sadism (1969)

The Cat *See* Le Chat (1975)

C.A.T. Squad *See* Stalking Danger (1986)

C.A.T. Squad: Python Wolf *See* Python Wolf (1988)

Catacombs *See* Curse 4: The Ultimate Sacrifice (1990)

Catastrophe 1999 *See* Last Days of Planet Earth (1974)

Catchfire *See* Backtrack (1989)

Catholic Boys *See* Heaven Help Us (1985)

Cathy Tippel *See* Keetje Tippel (1975)

Cauchemares *See* Cathy's Curse (1977)

Cavalleria Commandos *See* Cavalry Command (1963)

The Cave Dwellers *See* One Million B.C. (1940)

Cave Man *See* One Million B.C. (1940)

Cavegirl *See* Cave Girl (1985)

C.C. & Company *See* Chrome Hearts (1970)

Cell Block Girls *See* Women's Prison Escape (19??)

Cemetary Girls *See* The Vampire Hookers (1978)

Cemetary Girls *See* The Velvet Vampire (1971)

Cento Dollari D'Odio *See* Uncle Tom's Cabin (1969)

Ceremonia Sangrienta *See* The Legend of Blood Castle (1972)

A Certain Mr. Scratch *See* The Devil & Daniel Webster (1941)

Cet Obscur Objet Du Desir *See* That Obscure Object of Desire (1977)

Chaingang Girls *See* Sweet Sugar (1972)

The Challenge *See* It Takes a Thief (1959)

Chamber of Fear *See* The Fear Chamber (1968)

Champ d'Honneur *See* Field of Honor (1987)

Champion Charlie *See* The Champion/His New Job (1915)

Changes *See* Danielle Steel's Changes (1991)

Chaos-Kaos *See* Kaos (1985)

Charlie's Ghost Story *See* Charlie's Ghost: The Secret of Coronado (1994)

Charterhouse at Parma *See* La Chartreuse de Parme (1948)

Chastnaya Zhizn *See* Private Life (1982)

The Chautauqua *See* The Trouble with Girls (and How To Get Into It) (1969)

Che? *See* Diary of Forbidden Dreams (1973)

Cheaters *See* Tricheurs (1984)

Chernobyl: The Final Warning *See* Final Warning (1990)

Cheun Gwong Tsa Sit *See* Happy Together (1996)

Chevy Van *See* The Van (1977)

The Chief Wants No Survivors *See* No Survivors, Please (1963)

Chikamatsu Monogatari *See* The Crucified Lovers (1954)

Chikyu Boelgun *See* The Mysterians (1958)

The Child *See* Kill and Go Hide (1976)

Child of Satan *See* To the Devil, A Daughter (1976)

Child of the Night *See* What the Peeper Saw (1972)

Childish Things *See* Confessions of Tom Harris (1972)

Children of the Dust *See* A Good Day to Die (1995)

China 9, Liberty 37 *See* Gunfire (1978)

Chinchero *See* The Last Movie (1971)

Christmas Evil *See* Terror in Toyland (1985)

A Christmas Memory *See* ABC Stage 67: Truman Capote's A Christmas Memory (1966)

The Christmas Tree *See* When Wolves Cry (1969)

Christmas Vacation *See* National Lampoon's Christmas Vacation (1989)

Chuck Norris vs. the Karate Cop *See* Slaughter in San Francisco (1981)

Chungon Satluk Linggei *See* Organized Crime & Triad Bureau (1993)

Ciao! Manhattan *See* Edie in Ciao! Manhattan (1972)

Cica Tomina Koliba *See* Uncle Tom's Cabin (1969)

The Circle *See* The Vicious Circle (1957)

The Circle *See* Woman in Brown (1948)

Circuitry Man 2 *See* Plughead Rewired: Circuitry Man 2 (1994)

Citadel of Crime *See* Wheel of Fortune (1941)

Citizen's Band *See* FM (1978)

The City Jungle *See* The Young Philadelphians (1959)

The City of the Dead *See* Horror Hotel (1960)

City of the Living Dead *See* Gates of Hell (1983)

The Clairvoyant *See* The Evil Mind (1934)

The Clairvoyant *See* Killing Hour (1984)

The Clansman *See* The Birth of a Nation (1915)

Class of '86 *See* National Lampoon's Class of '86 (1986)

Class Reunion *See* National Lampoon's Class Reunion (1982)

Claude *See* The Two of Us (1968)

Clean Slate *See* Coup de Torchon (1981)

Cleo de 5 a 7 *See* Cleo from 5 to 7 (1961)

Clickety Clack *See* Dodes 'ka-den (1970)

Clinton & Nadine *See* Blood Money: The Story of Clinton and Nadine (1988)

Clive Barker's Lord of Illusions *See* Lord of Illusions (1995)

The Closest of Kin *See* All the Lovin' Kinfolk (1989)

Club Dead *See* Terror at Red Wolf Inn (1972)

Coast of Terror *See* Summer City (1977)

Coastwatcher *See* The Last Warrior (1989)

Cobweb Castle *See* Throne of Blood (1957)

Code Name: Operation Crossbow *See* Operation Crossbow (1965)

Code Name: Trixie *See* The Crazies (1973)

Code 645 *See* G-Men Never Forget (1948)

Codename: The Soldier *See* The Soldier (1982)

Coffin of Terror *See* Castle of Blood (1964)

Colin Nutley's House of Angels *See* House of Angels (1992)

Collision Course *See* The Bamboo Saucer (1968)

Colonel Blimp *See* The Life and Death of Colonel Blimp (1943)

Colorado Ranger *See* Guns of Justice (1950)

Come Back to Me *See* Doll Face (1946)

Come Dance with Me *See* Voulez-Vous Danser Avec Moi? (1959)

Come 'n' Get It *See* Lunch Wagon (1981)

Coming Attractions *See* Loose Shoes (1980)

Comizi d'Amore *See* Love Meetings (1964)

Communion *See* Alice Sweet Alice (1976)

D'Artagnan *See* The Three Musketeers (1916)

Das Bildness des Dorian Gray *See* Dorian Gray (1970)

Das Blaue Licht *See* The Blue Light (1932)

Das Phantom von Soho *See* The Phantom of Soho (1964)

Das Schlangenei *See* The Serpent's Egg (1978)

Das Schloss *See* The Castle (1968)

Das Ungeheuer von London City *See* The Monster of London City (1964)

Das Versprechen *See* The Promise (1994)

Dashiell Hammett's The Dain Curse *See* The Dain Curse (1978)

The Daughter of Frankenstein *See* Lady Frankenstein (1972)

David Lynch's Hotel Room *See* Hotel Room (1993)

Day of the Woman *See* I Spit on Your Grave (1977)

The Day the Hot Line Got Hot *See* The Hot Line (1969)

The Day the Screaming Stopped *See* The Comeback (1977)

The Day They Gave the Babies Away *See* All Mine to Give (1956)

A Day to Remember *See* Two Bits (1996)

Daybreak *See* Le Jour Se Leve (1939)

De Aanslag *See* The Assault (1986)

De Eso No Se Habla *See* I Don't Want to Talk About It (1994)

De la Part des Copains *See* Cold Sweat (1974)

De Sable et de Sang *See* Sand and Blood (1987)

De Stilte Rond Christine M *See* Question of Silence (1983)

De Wisselwachter *See* The Pointsman (1986)

Dead Aim *See* Born in America (1990)

Dead Drop *See* Chain Reaction (1996)

Dead Kids *See* Strange Behavior (1981)

Dead Man's Walk *See* Larry McMurtry's Dead Man's Walk (1996)

Dead of Night *See* Deathdream (1972)

Dead on Course *See* Wings of Danger (1952)

Dead or Alive *See* A Minute to Pray, A Second to Die (1967)

Dead or Alive *See* The Tracker (1988)

Dead People *See* Messiah of Evil (1974)

Dead Tired *See* Grosse Fatigue (1994)

Deadlocked: Escape from Zone 14 *See* Deadlock 2 (1994)

Deadly Companion *See* The Double Negative (1980)

Deadly Desire *See* Maybe I'll Be Home in the Spring (1970)

Deadly Desires *See* Home for the Holidays (1972)

Deadly Encounter *See* The Meal (1975)

Deadly Is the Female *See* Gun Crazy (1949)

The Deadly Rays From Mars *See* Flash Gordon: Mars Attacks the World (1938)

Deadly Rivals *See* Rivals (1972)

The Deadly Spawn *See* Return of the Aliens: The Deadly Spawn (1983)

Deadly Sting *See* Evil Spawn (1987)

The Deadly Three *See* Enter the Dragon (1973)

The Deadly Tower *See* Sniper (1975)

Deadly Treasure of the Piranha *See* Killer Fish (1979)

Dear Diary *See* Caro Diario (1993)

Dear Inspector *See* Dear Detective (1977)

Death and the Green Slime *See* The Green Slime (1968)

Death Bite *See* Spasms (1982)

Death Collector *See* Family Enforcer (1976)

Death Corps *See* Shock Waves (1977)

Death Dimension *See* Kill Factor (1978)

Death From Outer Space *See* The Day the Sky Exploded (1957)

Death Game *See* Seducers (1977)

Death House *See* Silent Night, Bloody Night (1973)

Death of a Hooker *See* Who Killed Mary What's 'Er Name? (1971)

Death of Her Innocence *See* Our Time (1974)

Death Ride to Osaka *See* Girls of the White Orchid (1985)

Death Scream *See* The Deadly Trap (1971)

Death Train *See* Detonator (1993)

Death Trap *See* Eaten Alive (1976)

Death Vengeance *See* Fighting Back (1982)

The Death Wheelers *See* Psychomania (1973)

Deathshead Vampire *See* Blood Beast Terror (1967)

Deathstalker 3: The Warriors From Hell *See* Deathstalker 3 (1989)

Debajo del Mundo *See* Under the Earth (1986)

The Debt *See* Veronico Cruz (1987)

Decoy for Terror *See* Playgirl Killer (1966)

Dedee *See* Dedee d'Anvers (1949)

Delirios de Um Anormal *See* Hallucinations of a Deranged Mind (1970)

Dellamorte Delamore *See* Cemetery Man (1995)

Delta Pi *See* Mugsy's Girls (1985)

Dem Khann's Zindl *See* The Cantor's Son (1937)

Demanty Noci *See* Diamonds of the Night (1964)

Dementia *See* Daughter of Horror (1955)

Demolition Day *See* Captain Nuke and the Bomber Boys (1995)

Demon *See* God Told Me To (1976)

The Demon *See* Onibaba (1964)

Demon Keeper *See* Tales from the Crypt Presents Demon Knight (1994)

Demon Knight *See* Tales from the Crypt Presents Demon Knight (1994)

Demon Master *See* Craze (1974)

The Demon Planet *See* Planet of the Vampires (1965)

Demoni *See* Demons (1986)

Demonios En El Jardin *See* Demons in the Garden (1982)

The Deputy *See* El Diputado (1978)

Der Amerikanische Soldat *See* The American Soldier (1970)

Der Bewegte Mann *See* Maybe...Maybe Not (1994)

Der Blaue Engel *See* The Blue Angel (1930)

Der Chef Wuenscht Keine Zeugen *See* No Survivors, Please (1963)

Der Fluch der Gruenen Augen *See* Cave of the Living Dead (1965)

Der Fussgaenger *See* The Pedestrian (1973)

Der Hauptmann von Koepenick *See* The Captain from Koepenick (1956)

Der Henker Von London *See* The Mad Executioners (1965)

Der Himmel Uber Berlin *See* Wings of Desire (1988)

Der Joker *See* Lethal Obsession (1987)

Der Kongress Tanzt *See* Congress Dances (1931)

Der Letzte Mann *See* The Last Laugh (1924)

Der Morder Dimitri Karamasoff *See* The Brothers Karamazov (1958)

Der Prozess *See* The Trial (1963)

Der Schweigende Stern *See* First Spaceship on Venus (1960)

Der Toderspringer *See* The Jumper (1985)

Der Verlone *See* The Lost One (1951)

Der Vilner Shtot Khazn *See* Overture to Glory (1940)

Deranged *See* Idaho Transfer (1973)

Des Enfants Gates *See* Spoiled Children (1977)

Desert Patrol *See* Sea of Sand (1958)

The Deserter *See* Ride to Glory (1971)

Desire in Motion *See* Mouvements du Desir (1994)

Desperate Siege *See* Rawhide (1950)

The Destroyers *See* Devastator (1985)

Destruction, Inc. *See* Just for the Hell of It (1968)

Det Sjunde Inseglet *See* The Seventh Seal (1956)

Det Stora Aventyret *See* The Great Adventure (1953)

Detective Geronimo *See* The Mad Bomber (1972)

The Detective Kid *See* The Gumshoe Kid (1989)

Deutschland im Herbst *See* Germany in Autumn (1978)

Deux ou Trois Choses Que Je Sais d'Elle *See* Two or Three Things I Know About Her (1966)

The Devil and the Nun *See* Mother Joan of the Angels (1960)

The Devil Walks at Midnight *See* The Devil's Nightmare (1971)

The Devil Within Her *See* I Don't Want to Be Born (1975)

The Devil Woman *See* Onibaba (1964)

The Devil's Bride *See* Velnio Nuotaka (1975)

Devil's Doll *See* The Devil's Hand (1961)

The Devil's Envoys *See* Les Visiteurs du Soir (1942)

Devil's Express *See* Gang Wars (1975)

The Devil's Men *See* Land of the Minotaur (1977)

Devil's Odds *See* The Wild Pair (1987)

The Devil's Plot *See* Counterblast (1948)

The Devil's Undead *See* Nothing But the Night (1972)

The Devil's Weed *See* Wild Weed (1949)

The Diabolical Dr. Mabuse *See* The Thousand Eyes of Dr. Mabuse (1960)

Diabolik *See* Danger: Diabolik (1968)

Diaboliquement Votre *See* Diabolically Yours (1967)

Dial 999 *See* The Way Out (1956)

Diamond Alley *See* Little Ladies of the Night (1977)

Diamond Earrings *See* The Earrings of Madame De... (1954)

Diamond Skulls *See* Dark Obsession (1990)

Earth Defense Forces *See* The Mysterians (1958)

The Earth Will Tremble *See* La Terra Trema (1948)

East of Shanghai *See* Rich and Strange (1932)

East of the Bowery *See* Follow the Leader (1944)

East of the Rising Sun *See* Malaya (1949)

Easy Go *See* Free and Easy (1930)

Eaten Alive by Cannibals *See* Emerald Jungle (1980)

Ebirah, Terror of the Deep *See* Godzilla vs. the Sea Monster (1966)

Eboli *See* Christ Stopped at Eboli (1979)

Edgar Allan Poe's Conqueror Worm *See* The Conqueror Worm (1968)

Edgar Allen Poe's House of Usher *See* The House of Usher (1988)

Edgar Allen Poe's The Oblong Box *See* The Oblong Box (1969)

The Edge of Hell *See* Rock 'n' Roll Nightmare (1985)

Edipo Re *See* Oedipus Rex (1967)

Ein Mann wie Eva *See* A Man Like Eva (1983)

Ein Toter Hing im Netz *See* Horrors of Spider Island (1959)

Eine Liebe in Deutschland *See* A Love in Germany (1984)

Einer Frisst den Anderen *See* Dog Eat Dog (1964)

Ekstase *See* Ecstasy (1933)

El Ataud Del Coffin *See* The Vampire's Coffin (1958)

El Ataud Del Vampiro *See* The Vampire's Coffin (1958)

El Buque Maldito *See* Horror of the Zombies (1974)

El Cazador de la Muerte *See* Deathstalker (1983)

El Cobra *See* The Cobra (1968)

El Coleccionista de Cadaveres *See* Cauldron of Blood (1967)

El Dedo En El Gatillo *See* Finger on the Trigger (1965)

El Espiritu de la Colmena *See* Spirit of the Beehive (1973)

El Grito de la Muerte *See* The Living Coffin (1958)

El la Nave Va *See* And the Ship Sails On (1983)

El Lazarillo de Tormes *See* Lazarillo (1959)

El Mariachi 2 *See* Desperado (1995)

El Mas Fabulosi Golpe del Far West *See* The Boldest Job in the West (1971)

El Patrullero *See* Highway Patrolman (1991)

El Rapto de las Sabinas *See* The Rape of the Sabines (1961)

El Retorno de la Walpurgis *See* Curse of the Devil (1973)

El Robot Humano *See* The Robot vs. the Aztec Mummy (1959)

El Rublo de las dos Caras *See* The Hot Line (1969)

El Sonido de la Muerte *See* Sound of Horror (1964)

El Tesoro del Amazones *See* The Treasure of the Amazon (1984)

El Verano de la Senora Forbes *See* The Summer of Miss Forbes (1988)

Electric Boogaloo "Breakin' 2" *See* Breakin' 2: Electric Boogaloo (1984)

The Electric Monster *See* The Electronic Monster (1957)

Elena et les Hommes *See* Elena and Her Men (1956)

Elevator to the Gallows *See* Frantic (1958)

Elisa, My Life *See* Elisa, Vida Mia (1977)

Elisa, My Love *See* Elisa, Vida Mia (1977)

Emergency Landing *See* Robot Pilot (1941)

Emil Und Die Detektive *See* Emil and the Detectives (1964)

Emma Mae *See* Black Sister's Revenge (1976)

The Emperor of Peru *See* The Odyssey of the Pacific (1982)

Empire of Passion *See* In the Realm of Passion (1980)

The Empress Yang Kwei Fei *See* Princess Yang Kwei Fei (1955)

En Compagnie d'Antonin Artaud *See* My Life and Times with Antonin Artaud (1993)

En Effeuillant la Marguerite *See* Mademoiselle Striptease (1957)

En Enda Natt *See* Only One Night (1942)

En Kvinnas Ansikte *See* A Woman's Face (1938)

En Lekiton i Karlek *See* Lesson in Love (1954)

End of the Rainbow *See* Northwest Outpost (1947)

End of the World *See* Panic in the Year Zero! (1962)

End of the World (in Our Usual Bed in a Night Full of Rain) *See* A Night Full of Rain (1978)

Enemies of the Public *See* Public Enemy (1931)

Enemy from Space *See* Quatermass 2 (1957)

Enemy Round-Up *See* Hillbilly Blitzkrieg (1942)

The Engagement *See* Fiances (1963)

The Enigma of Kaspar Hauser *See* Every Man for Himself & God Against All (1975)

Enormous Changes at the Last Minute *See* Enormous Changes (1983)

Enormous Changes at the Last Minute *See* Trumps (1983)

Ensayo de un Crimen *See* The Criminal Life of Archibaldo de la Cruz (1955)

Entebbe: Operation Thunderbolt *See* Operation Thunderbolt (1977)

Entre Tinieblas *See* Dark Habits (1984)

Episoda Del Mare *See* La Terra Trema (1948)

Ercole al Centro Della Terra *See* Hercules in the Haunted World (1964)

Ercole Alla Conquista di Atlantide *See* Hercules and the Captive Women (1963)

Ercole Contro Molock *See* Conquest of Mycene (1963)

Ercole e la Regina di Lidia *See* Hercules Unchained (1959)

Erik the Conqueror *See* The Invaders (1963)

Ernest Hemingway's the Killers *See* The Killers (1964)

Escapade *See* Utopia (1951)

Escape from the Dark *See* The Littlest Horse Thieves (1977)

Escape If You Can *See* St. Benny the Dip (1951)

The Escape of Megagodzilla *See* Terror of Mechagodzilla (1978)

Escape Route *See* I'll Get You (1953)

Escape to Freedom *See* Judgment in Berlin (1988)

Escapement *See* The Electronic Monster (1957)

The Escort *See* L'Escorte (1996)

Escort Girl *See* Half Moon Street (1986)

The Escorts *See* La Scorta (1994)

Espiritismo *See* Spiritism (1961)

Et Dieu Crea la Femme *See* And God Created Woman (1957)

Et Mourir de Plaisir *See* Blood and Roses (1961)

Etat de Siege *See* State of Siege (1973)

Etz Hadomim Tafus *See* Under the Domim Tree (1995)

European Vacation *See* National Lampoon's European Vacation (1985)

Every Day's a Holiday *See* Seaside Swingers (1965)

Every Home Should Have One *See* Think Dirty (1970)

Every Man For Himself *See* The Ruthless Four (1970)

Every Woman's Man *See* The Prizefighter and the Lady (1933)

Everybody's Cheering *See* Take Me Out to the Ball Game (1949)

Evil Angels *See* A Cry in the Dark (1988)

Evil Dead 3 *See* Army of Darkness (1992)

Evil Eden *See* Death in the Garden (1956)

Evil in the Swamp *See* All the Kind Strangers (1974)

Ewiger Walzer *See* The Eternal Waltz (1954)

Except For Me and Thee *See* Friendly Persuasion (1956)

Expedition Moon *See* Rocketship X-M (1950)

Exploring the Kinsey Report *See* One Plus One (1961)

Expose *See* The House on Straw Hill (1976)

Exquisite Tenderness *See* The Surgeon (1994)

Extase *See* Ecstasy (1933)

Extenuating Circumstances *See* Circonstances Attenuantes (1936)

Extreme Close-Up *See* Sex Through a Window (1972)

An Eye for an Eye *See* Psychopath (1973)

An Eye for an Eye *See* Talion (1966)

Eyes of Hell *See* The Mask (1961)

Eyes Without a Face *See* The Horror Chamber of Dr. Faustus (1959)

Eyewitness *See* Sudden Terror (1970)

Fabula de la Bella Palomera *See* The Fable of the Beautiful Pigeon Fancier (1988)

The Fabulous Baron Munchausen *See* The Original Fabulous Adventures of Baron Munchausen (1961)

Face of a Stranger *See* The Promise (1979)

Face the Music *See* Black Glove (1954)

The Faceless Monsters *See* Nightmare Castle (1965)

Fairytales *See* Fairy Tales (1976)

Fakebook *See* American Blue Note (1989)

Falcon's Gold *See* Robbers of the Sacred Mountain (1983)

Fall Break *See* The Mutilator (1985)

The Fall Guy *See* What's Up Front (1963)

The Fall of the House of Usher *See* La Chute de la Maison Usher (1928)

Falltime *See* Fall Time (1994)

False Face *See* Scalpel (1976)

False Faces *See* Let 'Em Have It (1935)

Falstaff *See* Chimes at Midnight (1967)

Fanatic *See* Die! Die! My Darling! (1965)

The Fanatic *See* The Last Horror Film (1982)

Fanfan the Tulip *See* Fanfan la Tulipe (1951)

Fangelse *See* Devil's Wanton (1949)

Fanny by Gaslight *See* Man of Evil (1948)

Fanny Och Alexander *See* Fanny and Alexander (1983)

Fan's Video *See* Otaku no Video (1991)

The Far Country *See* Nevil Shute's The Far Country (1985)

Farewell, Friend *See* Honor Among Thieves (1968)

Farewell, My Love *See* Murder, My Sweet (1944)

Farinelli Il Castrato *See* Farinelli (1994)

Farinelli the Castrato *See* Farinelli (1994)

The Farm *See* The Curse (1987)

Farm Girl *See* The Farmer's Other Daughter (1965)

Farm of the Year *See* Miles from Home (1988)

Fashions *See* Fashions of 1934 (1934)

Fast Fortune *See* 11 Harrowhouse (1974)

Fatal Assassin *See* African Rage (1978)

Fatal Woman *See* Femme Fatale (1990)

The Father *See* Baba (1973)

Father & Son: Dangerous Relations *See* Dangerous Relations (1993)

Father Brown *See* The Detective (1954)

Father Damien: The Leper Priest *See* Damien: The Leper Priest (1980)

Father Goose *See* Fly Away Home (1996)

The Father Kino Story *See* Mission to Glory (1980)

Father Master *See* Padre Padrone (1977)

Father, Son and the Mistress *See* For Richer, For Poorer (1992)

Faustrecht der Freiheit *See* Fox and His Friends (1975)

The FBI Murders *See* In the Line of Duty: The FBI Murders (1988)

Fear *See* Night Creature (1979)

The Fear *See* Gates of Hell (1983)

Fear Eats the Soul *See* Ali: Fear Eats the Soul (1974)

Fear in the City of the Living Dead *See* Gates of Hell (1983)

Fear in the Night *See* Dynasty of Fear (1972)

Fearless Little Soldier *See* Fanfan la Tulipe (1951)

Feast of Flesh *See* Blood Feast (1963)

Federico Fellini's 8 1/2 *See* 8 1/2 (1963)

Federico Fellini's Intervista *See* Intervista (1987)

Feel the Heat *See* Catch the Heat (1987)

Female *See* The Violent Years (1956)

The Female Butcher *See* The Legend of Blood Castle (1972)

Feng Yue *See* Temptress Moon (1996)

A Few Days in the Life of I.I. Oblomov *See* Oblomov (1981)

The Fiend with the Atomic Brain *See* Blood of Ghastly Horror (1972)

The Fiend with the Electronic Brain *See* Blood of Ghastly Horror (1972)

Fiendish Ghouls *See* Mania (1960)

Fierce *See* Fighting Mad (1977)

The Fifth Chair *See* It's in the Bag (1945)

The Fighting Phantom *See* The Mysterious Rider (1933)

The Fighting Pimpernel *See* The Elusive Pimpernel (1950)

The Fighting Seventh *See* Little Big Horn (1951)

Film d'Amore et d'Anarchia *See* Love and Anarchy (1973)

Filofax *See* Taking Care of Business (1990)

The Final Crash *See* Steelyard Blues (1973)

Finally, Sunday *See* Confidentially Yours (1983)

Fine and Dandy *See* The West Point Story (1950)

Fire Festival *See* Himatsuri (1985)

Fire in Eden *See* Tusks (1989)

The First and the Last *See* 21 Days (1937)

The First Great Train Robbery *See* The Great Train Robbery (1979)

The First Hello *See* High Country (1981)

The First of the Few *See* Spitfire (1942)

The First Rebel *See* Allegheny Uprising (1939)

First Strike *See* Jackie Chan's First Strike (1996)

The First Time *See* The Fighter (1952)

First Woman Into Space *See* Space Monster (1964)

A Fist Full of Chopsticks *See* They Call Me Bruce? (1982)

Fist of Fury *See* Chinese Connection (1973)

Fist Right of Freedom *See* Fox and His Friends (1975)

Five Angles on Murder *See* The Woman in Question (1950)

Five Bloody Days to Tombstone *See* Gun Riders (1969)

Five Bloody Graves *See* Gun Riders (1969)

The Five Day Lover *See* Time Out for Love (1961)

Five Days *See* Paid to Kill (1954)

Five Minutes to Live *See* Door to Door Maniac (1961)

Five Women Around Utamaro *See* Utamaro and His Five Women (1946)

Fixing the Shadow *See* Beyond the Law (1992)

The Flame of Torment *See* Enjo (1958)

Flash Gordon's Trip to Mars *See* Flash Gordon: Mars Attacks the World (1938)

Flatbed Annie *See* Flatbed Annie and Sweetiepie: Lady Truckers (1979)

The Flesh and the Fiends *See* Mania (1960)

The Flesh Creatures *See* Horror of the Blood Monsters (1970)

Flesh Creatures of the Red Planet *See* Horror of the Blood Monsters (1970)

Flesh for Frankenstein *See* Andy Warhol's Frankenstein (1974)

The Flight *See* The Taking of Flight 847: The Uli Derickson Story (1988)

Flight of the Dove *See* The Spy Within (1994)

The Flight of the White Stallions *See* The Miracle of the White Stallions (1963)

Flipper and the Pirates *See* Flipper's New Adventure (1964)

Floating Weeds *See* Drifting Weeds (1959)

Flying Aces *See* The Flying Deuces (1939)

Flying Wild *See* Fly Away Home (1996)

Fog *See* A Study in Terror (1966)

Folies Bourgeoises *See* Twist (1976)

The Folks at Red Wolf Inn *See* Terror at Red Wolf Inn (1972)

Follow That Bird *See* Sesame Street Presents: Follow That Bird (1985)

Follow the Hunter *See* Fangs of the Wild (1954)

Follow Your Dreams *See* Independence Day (1983)

Fontane Effi Briest *See* Effi Briest (1974)

For a Few Bullets More *See* Any Gun Can Play (1967)

For Better or For Worse *See* Honeymoon Academy (1990)

For Love or Money *See* If I Were Rich (1933)

For Men Only *See* Tall Lie (1953)

For We Too Do Not Forgive *See* Death Is Called Engelchen (1963)

Forbidden Alliance *See* The Barretts of Wimpole Street (1934)

Forbidden Love *See* Freaks (1932)

Forbidden Paradise *See* Hurricane (1979)

Forbidden Passions *See* The Sensuous Teenager (1970)

Forbidden Son *See* Bulldance (1988)

The Forbin Project *See* Colossus: The Forbin Project (1970)

Forbrydelsens Element *See* The Element of Crime (1984)

Ford Fairlane *See* The Adventures of Ford Fairlane (1990)

The Forest Primeval *See* The Final Terror (1983)

Forgotten Prisoners: The Amnesty Files *See* Forgotten Prisoners (1990)

The Forsyte Saga *See* That Forsyte Woman (1950)

Fortune in Diamonds *See* The Adventurers (1951)

47 Samurai *See* 47 Ronin, Part 1 (1942)

Forward March *See* Doughboys (1930)

The Four Just Men *See* The Secret Four (1940)

A Fourth for Marriage *See* What's Up Front (1963)

4...3...2...1...Morte *See* Mission Stardust (1968)

F.P. 1 Antwortet Nicht *See* F.P. 1 Doesn't Answer (1933)

Fra Diavolo *See* The Devil's Brother (1933)

Frameup *See* Jon Jost's Frameup (1993)

Francis *See* Francis the Talking Mule (1949)

Frankenstein *See* Mary Shelley's Frankenstein (1994)

Frankenstein '88 *See* The Vindicator (1985)

Frankenstein Meets the Spacemen *See* Frankenstein Meets the Space Monster (1965)

Frasier the Lovable Lion *See* Frasier the Sensuous Lion (1973)

Fraternally Yours *See* Sons of the Desert (1933)

The Freak From Suckweasel Mountain *See* Geek Maggot Bingo (1983)

Freddie as F.R.O.7 *See* Freddie the Frog (1992)

Free to Live *See* Holiday (1938)

Freefall *See* Firefall (1994)

The Freeze Bomb *See* Kill Factor (1978)

Frenzy *See* Torment (1944)

Fresa y Chocolate *See* Strawberry and Chocolate (1993)

Fresh Bait *See* L'Appat (1994)

Freylekhe Kabtsonim *See* The Jolly Paupers (1938)

Friend of the Family *See* Elke (1995)

The Fright *See* Visiting Hours (1982)

The Frightened Lady *See* The Case of the Frightened Lady (1939)

Frightmare 2 *See* Frightmare (1974)

Friz Freleng's Looney Looney Looney Bugs Bunny Movie *See* Looney Looney Looney Bugs Bunny Movie (1981)

The Frog Prince *See* The French Lesson (1986)

From a Whisper to a Scream *See* The Offspring (1987)

From Broadway to Cheyenne *See* Broadway to Cheyenne (1932)

From the Mixed-Up Files of Mrs. Basil E. Frankweiler *See* The Hideaways (1973)

Fruhlingssinfonie *See* Spring Symphony (1986)

The Fruit Machine *See* Wonderland (1988)

F.T.W. *See* The Last Ride (1994)

Fukkatsu no Hi *See* Virus (1982)

The Fulfillment of Mary Gray *See* Fulfillment (1989)

The Fun House *See* Last House on Dead End Street (1977)

Fun Loving *See* Quackser Fortune Has a Cousin in the Bronx (1970)

Fungus of Terror *See* Attack of the Mushroom People (1963)

Funny Little Dirty War *See* Funny, Dirty Little War (1983)

Fuoco Fatuo *See* The Fire Within (1964)

Furankenshutain No Kaijusanda Tai Gailah *See* War of the Gargantuas (1970)

The Further Adventures of Ma and Pa Kettle *See* Ma and Pa Kettle (1949)

Fury of Samson *See* The Fury of Hercules (1961)

Fury of the Succubus *See* Demon Rage (1982)

Fury of the Vikings *See* The Invaders (1963)

Future Cop *See* Trancers (1984)

Gallery of Horror *See* Alien Massacre (1967)

Gambara vs. Barugon *See* Gamera vs. Barugon (1966)

Gamblin' Man *See* Cockfighter (1974)

Gamera *See* Gamera, the Invincible (1966)

Gamera Tai Barugon *See* Gamera vs. Barugon (1966)

Gamera Tai Gaos *See* Gamera vs. Gaos (1967)

Gamera Tai Guiron *See* Gamera vs. Guiron (1969)

Gamera Tai Shinkai Kaiju Jigara *See* Gamera vs. Zigra (1971)

Gamera Tai Uchukaiju Bairasu *See* Destroy All Planets (1968)

Gamera Tai Viras *See* Destroy All Planets (1968)

Gamera vs. Gyaos *See* Gamera vs. Gaos (1967)

Gamera Vs. Outer Space Monster Viras *See* Destroy All Planets (1968)

Gamera vs. the Deep Sea Monster Zigra *See* Gamera vs. Zigra (1971)

Gamera Vs. Viras *See* Destroy All Planets (1968)

Gamma Sango Uchu Daisakusen *See* The Green Slime (1968)

Gamma 693 *See* The Chilling (1989)

Gamma 693 *See* Night of the Zombies (1981)

Gammera *See* Gamera, the Invincible (1966)

Gang War *See* Odd Man Out (1947)

Gangs of Sonora *See* Western Double Feature 6: Rogers & Trigger (1950)

Gangster *See* Hoodlum (1996)

Ganja and Hess *See* Black Vampire (1973)

The Gardener *See* Seeds of Evil (1976)

The Gargon Terror *See* Teenagers from Outer Space (1959)

Garou Garou le Passe Muraille *See* Mr. Peek-A-Boo (1950)

Gas-s-s-s... or, It May Become Necessary to Destroy the World in Order to Save It *See* Gas-s-s-s! (1970)

Gasu Ningen Daiichigo *See* The Human Vapor (1968)

A Gathering of Old Men *See* Murder on the Bayou (1991)

Gatto Rossi In Un Labirinto Do Vetro *See* Eyeball (1978)

The Gay Divorce *See* The Gay Divorcee (1934)

The Gay Mrs. Trexel *See* Susan and God (1940)

The Gaze of Ulysses *See* Ulysses' Gaze (1995)

Gazon Maudit *See* French Twist (1995)

Gebroken Spiegels *See* Broken Mirrors (1985)

Geheimecode Wildganse *See* Codename: Wildgeese (1984)

A Gentle Creature *See* A Gentle Woman (1969)

The Gentleman Tramp *See* La Collectionneuse (1967)

Gentlemen Don't Eat Poets *See* Grave Indiscretions (1996)

Georgia's Friends *See* Four Friends (1981)

Gestapo *See* Night Train to Munich (1940)

Get Down and Boogie *See* Darktown Strutters (1974)

Get Well Soon *See* Visiting Hours (1982)

Getting Even *See* Utilities (1983)

Gharbar *See* The Householder (1963)

Ghare Baire *See* The Home and the World (1984)

Ghidora, The Three-Headed Monster *See* Ghidrah the Three Headed Monster (1965)

Ghidorah Sandai Kaiju Chikyu Saidai No Kessan *See* Ghidrah the Three Headed Monster (1965)

Ghidrah *See* Ghidrah the Three Headed Monster (1965)

The Ghost Creeps *See* Boys of the City (1940)

The Ghost of John Holling *See* Mystery Liner (1934)

The Ghost Steps Out *See* The Time of Their Lives (1946)

Ghost Story *See* Madhouse Mansion (1974)

Ghosts from the Past *See* Ghosts of Mississippi (1996)

The Ghoul in School *See* Werewolf in a Girl's Dormitory (1961)

The Giant Leeches *See* Attack of the Giant Leeches (1959)

Gigantis, the Fire Monster *See* Godzilla Raids Again (1959)

Gilbert Grape *See* What's Eating Gilbert Grape (1993)

Gill Woman *See* Voyage to the Planet of Prehistoric Women (1968)

Gill Women of Venus *See* Voyage to the Planet of Prehistoric Women (1968)

Gingerbread House *See* Who Slew Auntie Roo? (1971)

Gion Bayashi *See* A Geisha (1953)

Gion Festival Music *See* A Geisha (1953)

Girl in Pawn *See* Little Miss Marker (1934)

Girl in the Leather Suit *See* Hell's Belles (1969)

Girl in the Moon *See* Woman in the Moon (1929)

Girl in the Park *See* Sanctuary of Fear (1979)

Girl in the Street *See* London Melody (1937)

The Girl Was Young *See* Young and Innocent (1937)

The Girl You Want *See* Boys (1995)

The Girls *See* Les Bonnes Femmes (1960)

Girls For Rent *See* I Spit on Your Corpse (1974)

Girls in Uniform *See* Maedchen in Uniform (1931)

Giro City *See* And Nothing But the Truth (1982)

Giu la Testa *See* A Fistful of Dynamite (1972)

Giulietta Degli Spiriti *See* Juliet of the Spirits (1965)

Gladiatorerna *See* The Gladiators (1970)

The Glass Cage *See* Glass Tomb (1955)

Gli Indifferenti *See* Time of Indifference (1964)

Gli Invasori *See* The Invaders (1963)

Glorious Sacrifice *See* The Glory Trail (1936)

Glory at Sea *See* The Gift Horse (1952)

The Glove: Lethal Terminator *See* The Glove (1978)

Glump *See* Please Don't Eat My Mother (1972)

G'mar Giviya *See* Cup Final (1992)

Gnaw: Food of the Gods 2 *See* Food of the Gods: Part 2 (1988)

A Gnome Named Gnorm *See* The Adventures of a Gnome Named Gnorm (1993)

Go and See *See* Come and See (1985)

The Goat *See* La Chevre (1981)

God's Gift *See* Wend Kuuni (1982)

Godzilla Fights the Giant Moth *See* Godzilla vs. Mothra (1964)

Godzilla Versus the Bionic Monster *See* Godzilla vs. the Cosmic Monster (1974)

Godzilla vs. Gigan *See* Godzilla on Monster Island (1972)

Godzilla vs. Hedora *See* Godzilla vs. the Smog Monster (1972)

Godzilla vs. Mechagodzilla *See* Godzilla vs. the Cosmic Monster (1974)

Godzilla vs. the Giant Moth *See* Godzilla vs. Mothra (1964)

Godzilla vs. the Thing *See* Godzilla vs. Mothra (1964)

Godzilla's Counter Attack *See* Godzilla Raids Again (1959)

Going Ape *See* Where's Poppa? (1970)

Gojira *See* Godzilla, King of the Monsters (1956)

Gojira no Musuko *See* Son of Godzilla (1966)

Gojira Tai Hedora *See* Godzilla vs. the Smog Monster (1972)

Gojira Tai Megaro *See* Godzilla vs. Megalon (1976)

Gojira Tai Meka-Gojira *See* Godzilla vs. the Cosmic Monster (1974)

Goke, Body Snatcher from Hell *See* Body Snatcher from Hell (1969)

Goke the Vampire *See* Body Snatcher from Hell (1969)

Gokiburi *See* Twilight of the Cockroaches (1990)

Golden Hands of Kurigal *See* Federal Agents vs. Underworld, Inc. (1949)

The Golden Heist *See* Inside Out (1975)

The Golden Hour *See* Pot O' Gold (1941)

Golden Ivory *See* White Huntress (1957)

Golden Marie *See* Casque d'Or (1952)

The Golden Trail *See* Riders of the Whistling Skull (1937)

Golden Virgin *See* The Story of Esther Costello (1957)

Goldy 3 *See* The Magic of the Golden Bear: Goldy 3 (1994)

Goliat Contra Los Gigantes *See* Goliath Against the Giants (1963)

Goliath and the Giants *See* Goliath Against the Giants (1963)

Goliath and the Golden City *See* Samson and the 7 Miracles of the World (1962)

Goliath Contro I Giganti *See* Goliath Against the Giants (1963)

Gomar the Human Gorilla *See* Night of the Bloody Apes (1968)

The Good Girls *See* Les Bonnes Femmes (1960)

Good Luck, Miss Wyckoff *See* The Shaming (1971)

A Good Marriage *See* Le Beau Mariage (1982)

Good Morning Babilonia *See* Good Morning, Babylon (1987)

Good to Go *See* Short Fuse (1988)

Goodbye Bruce Lee: His Last Game of Death *See* Game of Death (1979)

Goodbye, Children *See* Au Revoir Les Enfants (1987)

Goodbye Gemini *See* Twinsanity (1970)

Goodbye to the Hill *See* Paddy (1970)

Gordon il Pirata Nero *See* The Black Pirate (1926)

Gorilla *See* Nabonga (1944)

Gosta Berling's Saga *See* The Atonement of Gosta Berling (1924)

Gotter der Pest *See* Gods of the Plague (1969)

Grace Under Pressure *See* Something to Talk About (1995)

The Grail *See* Lancelot of the Lake (1974)

Gran Amore del Conde Dracula *See* Dracula's Great Love (1972)

The Grand Highway *See* Le Grand Chemin (1987)

The Grand Maneuvers *See* Les Grandes Manoeuvres (1955)

The Grass is Singing *See* Killing Heat (1984)

The Grasshopper *See* The Passing of Evil (1970)

Grave Desires *See* Brides of the Beast (1968)

Grave Robbers from Outer Space *See* Plan 9 from Outer Space (1956)

Graveyard Tramps *See* Invasion of the Bee Girls (1973)

The Great Adventure *See* The Adventurers (1951)

Great American Bugs Bunny-Road Runner Chase *See* The Bugs Bunny/Road Runner Movie (1979)

The Great Balloon Adventure *See* Olly Olly Oxen Free (1978)

The Great Day *See* A Special Day (1977)

Great Friends *See* Grandes Amigos (197?)

The Great Georgia Bank Hoax *See* Great Bank Hoax (1978)

The Great Lester Boggs *See* Hootch Country Boys (1975)

The Great Manhunt *See* The Doolins of Oklahoma (1949)

Great Monster Yongkari *See* Yongkari Monster of the Deep (1967)

The Great Schnozzle *See* Palooka (1934)

The Great Spy Mission *See* Operation Crossbow (1965)

The Great Wall is a Great Wall *See* A Great Wall (1986)

The Greatest Battle *See* Battleforce (1978)

The Greatest Battle on Earth *See* Ghidrah the Three Headed Monster (1965)

The Greatest Love *See* Europa '51 (1952)

The Greeks Had a Word for Them *See* Three Broadway Girls (1932)

The Green Carnation *See* The Trials of Oscar Wilde (1960)

Green Monkey *See* Blue Monkey (1987)

The Green Ray *See* Summer (1986)

The Greenhouse *See* The Green House (1996)

Greta the Mad Butcher *See* Ilsa, the Wicked Warden (1978)

Grey Matter *See* Mind Warp (1972)

Gridlock *See* Great American Traffic Jam (1980)

Grijpstra and de Gier *See* Fatal Error (1983)

Grine Felder *See* Green Fields (1937)

Gringo *See* Gun Fight at Red Sands (1963)

The Grip of the Strangler *See* The Haunted Strangler (1958)

The Grotesque *See* Grave Indiscretions (1996)

Gruner Felder *See* Green Fields (1937)

Gruppo di Famiglia in un Interno *See* Conversation Piece (1975)

Guardian of the Wilderness *See* Mountain Man (1977)

Guilty Assignment *See* Big Town (1947)

Gun Man from Bodie *See* Gunman from Bodie (1941)

Gun Moll *See* Get Rita (1975)

Gun Moll *See* Jigsaw (1949)

Guney's The Wall *See* The Wall (1983)

Gunpoint *See* At Gunpoint (1955)

Guns in the Afternoon *See* Ride the High Country (1962)

Guns, Sin and Bathtub Gin *See* Lady in Red (1979)

Gwendoline *See* The Perils of Gwendoline (1984)

Gycklarnas Afton *See* Sawdust & Tinsel (1953)

Haakon Haakonsen *See* Shipwrecked (1990)

Hab Og Karlighed *See* Twist & Shout (1984)

Habricha el Hashemesh *See* Escape to the Sun (1972)

Hadaka No Shima *See* The Island (1961)

Hail to the Chief *See* Hail (1973)

Half Slave, Half Free 2 *See* Charlotte Forten's Mission: Experiment in Freedom (1985)

Hallelujah, I'm a Tramp *See* Hallelujah, I'm a Bum (1933)

Hallucination Generation *See* Hallucination (1967)

Ham Ham *See* Jamon, Jamon (1993)

Ha'Matarah Tiran *See* Sinai Commandos (1968)

The Hammond Mystery *See* The Undying Monster (1942)

Hand of Night *See* Beast of Morocco (1966)

Handgun *See* Deep in the Heart (1983)

Handle With Care *See* Citizens Band (1977)

Hands of a Killer *See* Planets Against Us (1961)

The Hands of Orlac *See* Mad Love (1935)

Hands of the Strangler *See* The Hands of Orlac (1960)

Hands Off the Loot *See* Grisbi (1953)

Handsome Serge *See* Le Beau Serge (1958)

The Hangover *See* The Female Jungle (1956)

Hans Christian Andersen's Thumbelina *See* Thumbelina (1994)

Happiness *See* Le Bonheur (1965)

Happiness *See* Le Bonheur Est Dans le Pre (1995)

Happiness Is In the Fields *See* Le Bonheur Est Dans le Pre (1995)

Happy Go Lucky *See* Hallelujah, I'm a Bum (1933)

Happy Mother's Day, Love, George *See* Run, Stranger, Run (1973)

The Happy New Year Caper *See* Happy New Year (1974)

Happy Times *See* The Inspector General (1949)

Hard Driver *See* The Last American Hero (1973)

Hard Stick *See* A Real American Hero (1978)

Hard to Die *See* Crime Story (1993)

The Hardcore Life *See* Hardcore (1979)

Harem Holiday *See* Harum Scarum (1965)

Harlem Hot Shot *See* The Black King (1932)

Harlequin *See* Dark Forces (1983)

Harold Robbins' The Betsy *See* The Betsy (1978)

Harp of Burma *See* The Burmese Harp (1956)

Harrison Bergeron *See* Kurt Vonnegut's Harrison Bergeron (1995)

Harry Black *See* Harry Black and the Tiger (1958)

Harry Tracy—Desperado *See* Harry Tracy (1983)

Harry's Machine *See* Hollywood Harry (1986)

Hasta Cierto Punto *See* Up to a Certain Point (1983)

The Hatchet Murders *See* Deep Red: Hatchet Murders (1975)

Hatred *See* Hate (1995)

The Haunted and the Hunted *See* Dementia 13 (1963)

The Haunting of Hamilton High *See* Hello Mary Lou: Prom Night 2 (1987)

The Haunting of Julia *See* Full Circle (1977)

Haus Der Tausend Freuden *See* The House of 1000 Dolls (1967)

Haxan *See* Witchcraft Through the Ages (1922)

He Lived to Kill *See* Night of Terror (1933)

He Loved an Actress *See* Mad About Money (1930)

He or She *See* Glen or Glenda: Confessions of Ed Wood (1953)

He, She or It *See* The Doll (1962)

Head On *See* Fatal Attraction (1980)

Head Over Heels *See* Chilly Scenes of Winter (1979)

The Head That Wouldn't Die *See* The Brain That Wouldn't Die (1963)

A Heart in Winter *See* Un Coeur en Hiver (1993)

The Heart of New York *See* Hallelujah, I'm a Bum (1933)

Heartbeat *See* Danielle Steel's Heartbeat (1993)

Heartbeat *See* Le Schpountz (1938)

Hearts and Minds *See* Master Touch (1974)

Heartstone *See* Demonstone (1989)

Heavenly Pursuits *See* The Gospel According to Vic (1987)

Hector Servadac's Ark *See* On the Comet (1968)

Hei Ma *See* A Mongolian Tale (1994)

The Heir to Genghis Khan *See* Storm over Asia (1928)

The Heist *See* Dollars (1971)

Heldorado *See* Helldorado (1946)

Hell Bent for Glory *See* Lafayette Escadrille (1958)

Hell Fire *See* They (1977)

Hell in Normandy *See* Special Forces (1968)

Hell of the Living Dead *See* Night of the Zombies (1983)

Hell to Macao *See* The Corrupt Ones (1967)

Hellborn *See* The Sinister Urge (1960)

Hellcamp *See* Opposing Force (1987)

Hellfire *See* Primal Scream (1987)

Hellfire on Ice, Part 2: Escape from Hell *See* Escape from Hell (1989)

Hello Elephant *See* Pardon My Trunk (1952)

Hellraiser 2 *See* Hellbound: Hellraiser 2 (1988)

Her Mad Night *See* Held for Murder (1932)

Hercules and the Conquest of Atlantis *See* Hercules and the Captive Women (1963)

Hercules and the Haunted Women *See* Hercules and the Captive Women (1963)

Hercules and the Hydra *See* The Loves of Hercules (1960)

Hercules Goes Bananas *See* Hercules in New York (1970)

Hercules: The Movie *See* Hercules in New York (1970)

Here Come the Tigers *See* Manny's Orphans (1978)

Here Is a Man *See* The Devil & Daniel Webster (1941)

Here Lies Love *See* Second Woman (1951)

Here We Go Again *See* Pride of the Bowery (1941)

The Hero of Pine Ridge *See* Yodelin' Kid From Pine Ridge (1937)

Heroes Die Hard *See* Mr. Kingstreet's War (1971)

Herzbube *See* King, Queen, Knave (1972)

The Heterosexuals *See* Les Biches (1968)

Hets *See* Torment (1944)

Hex *See* The Shrieking (1973)

Hidden Face *See* Jail Bait (1954)

The Hidden Room of 1,000 Horrors *See* The Tell-Tale Heart (1962)

Hidden Vision *See* Night Eyes (1990)

Hide and Shriek *See* American Gothic (1988)

Hifazaat *See* In Custody (1994)

High Rolling *See* High Rolling in a Hot Corvette (1977)

The Highest Bidder *See* Woman Hunt (1972)

Highlander 2: Renegade Version *See* Highlander 2: The Quickening (1991)

Highlander 3: The Magician *See* Highlander: The Final Dimension (1994)

Highlander 3: The Sorcerer *See* Highlander: The Final Dimension (1994)

Highway to Hell *See* Running Hot (1983)

Him *See* Only You (1994)

The Hindu *See* Sabaka (1955)

His Other Woman *See* Desk Set (1957)

Histoires Extraordinaires *See* Spirits of the Dead (1968)

Hitler's Gold *See* Inside Out (1975)

Hitman *See* American Commandos (1984)

HMS Defiant *See* Damn the Defiant (1962)

Hol Volt, Hol Nem Volt *See* A Hungarian Fairy Tale (1987)

Holiday *See* Jour de Fete (1948)

Hollow Point *See* The Wild Pair (1987)

Hollow Triumph *See* The Scar (1948)

Hollyweird *See* Flicks (1985)

Hollywood Cowboy *See* Hearts of the West (1975)

Hollywood Hoodlum *See* Hollywood Mystery (1934)

The Hollywood Strangler *See* Don't Answer the Phone (1980)

Hollywood Stunt Man *See* Movie Stuntmen (1953)

Hollywood Thrillmakers *See* Movie Stuntmen (1953)

Holocaust 2000 *See* The Chosen (1977)

Holy Terror *See* Alice Sweet Alice (1976)

Hombre Mirando Al Sudeste *See* Man Facing Southeast (1986)

Home Front *See* Morgan Stewart's Coming Home (1987)

Home In Oklahoma *See* Big Show (1937)

Home is Where the Heart Is *See* Square Dance (1987)

Home on the Range *See* Western Double Feature 2: Wayne & Hale (198?)

L'Homme du Minnesota *See* Minnesota Clay (1965)

Honeymoon in Bali *See* My Love For Yours (1939)

Honeymoon of Fear *See* Dynasty of Fear (1972)

The Honeymooners: The Lost Episodes *See* Honeymooners Hidden Episodes, Vol. 1 (1953)

The Honorary Consul *See* Beyond the Limit (1983)

Honour Among Thieves *See* Grisbi (1953)

Hoodlum Girls *See* Youth Aflame (1959)

Hoods *See* Hoodlum (1996)

The Hooker Cult Murders *See* The Pyx (1973)

Hopalong Cassidy Enters *See* Hopalong Cassidy (1935)

The Hopeless Ones *See* The Round Up (1966)

A Hora Da Estrela *See* The Hour of the Star (1985)

The Horrible House on the Hill *See* Devil Times Five (1974)

The Horrible Mill Women *See* Mill of the Stone Women (1960)

Horror Castle *See* The Virgin of Nuremberg (1965)

Horror Convention *See* Nightmare in Blood (1975)

Horror Creatures of the Prehistoric Planet *See* Horror of the Blood Monsters (1970)

Horror High *See* Twisted Brain (1974)

Horror Hotel Massacre *See* Eaten Alive (1976)

Horror in the Midnight Sun *See* Invasion of the Animal People (1962)

Horror Maniacs *See* The Greed of William Hart (1948)

Horror of the Stone Women *See* Mill of the Stone Women (1960)

Horror on Snape Island *See* Tower of Evil (1972)

Horse, My Horse *See* The Horse (1982)

A Horse Named Comanche *See* Tonka (1958)

Horsie *See* Queen for a Day (1951)

Hostage *See* Savage Attraction (1983)

Hostage: Dallas *See* Getting Even (1986)

Hostage: The Christine Maresch Story *See* Savage Attraction (1983)

Hot and Cold *See* Weekend at Bernie's (1989)

Hot Car Girl *See* Hot Rod Girl (1956)

Hot Lead *See* Run of the Arrow (1956)

The Hot One *See* Corvette Summer (1978)

Hot Seat *See* The Chair (1987)

Hot Spot *See* I Wake Up Screaming (1941)

Hot Sweat *See* Keetje Tippel (1975)

Hotel Sorrento *See* Sorrento Beach (1995)

The Houghland Murder Case *See* Murder by Television (1935)

The Hounds of Zaroff *See* The Most Dangerous Game (1932)

Hour of Glory *See* The Small Back Room (1949)

The Hour of the Pig *See* The Advocate (1993)

House 3 *See* The Horror Show (1989)

House by the Lake *See* Death Weekend (1976)

House in Nightmare Park *See* Night of the Laughing Dead (1975)

House of Crazies *See* Asylum (1972)

House of Doom *See* The Black Cat (1934)

House of Evil *See* Dance of Death (1968)

House of Evil *See* The House on Sorority Row (1983)

The House of Exorcism *See* Lisa and the Devil (1975)

House of Fear *See* Fearmaker (1989)

House of Fright *See* The Two Faces of Dr. Jekyll (1960)

House of Insane Women *See* Exorcism's Daughter (1974)

House of Mortal Sin *See* The Confessional (1975)

House of Mystery *See* Night Monster (1942)

House of Pleasure *See* Le Plaisir (1952)

House of Terror *See* Face of the Screaming Werewolf (1959)

House of the Damned *See* Spectre (1996)

House of the Dark Stairway *See* A Blade in the Dark (1983)

House of Usher *See* The Fall of the House of Usher (1960)

The House Where Death Lives *See* Delusion (1984)

The Incredibly Strange Creatures *See* Incredibly Strange Creatures Who Stopped Living and Became Mixed-Up Zombies (1963)

An Indian in the City *See* Little Indian, Big City (1995)

Indian Love Call *See* Rose Marie (1936)

Indiscretion *See* Christmas in Connecticut (1945)

Indiscretion *See* Indiscretion of an American Wife (1954)

The Infernal Idol *See* Craze (1974)

Infested *See* Ticks (1993)

The Infra Superman *See* Infra-Man (1976)

Inn of the Frightened People *See* Revenge (1971)

Innocence is Bliss *See* Miss Grant Takes Richmond (1949)

The Innocent and the Damned *See* Girls' Town (1959)

The Insect *See* The Insect Woman (1963)

Inseminoid *See* Horror Planet (1980)

L'Insoumis *See* Fight for Us (1989)

Interlude *See* Intermezzo (1936)

Intermezzo: A Love Story *See* Intermezzo (1939)

Intruder *See* Intruso (1993)

The Intruder *See* Shame (1961)

The Invader *See* Old Spanish Custom (1936)

The Invaders *See* The Forty-Ninth Parallel (1941)

Invasion Earth 2150 A.D. *See* Daleks—Invasion Earth 2150 A.D. (1966)

Invasion Force *See* Hangar 18 (1980)

Invasion from Inner Earth *See* They (1977)

Invasion of Planet X *See* Godzilla vs. Monster Zero (1968)

Invasion of the Astro-Monsters *See* Godzilla vs. Monster Zero (1968)

Invasion of the Astros *See* Godzilla vs. Monster Zero (1968)

Invasion of the Flying Saucers *See* Earth vs. the Flying Saucers (1956)

Invasion of the Zombies *See* Horror of Party Beach (1964)

An Investigation of Murder *See* The Laughing Policeman (1974)

The Invisible Horror *See* The Invisible Dr. Mabuse (1962)

Io Speriamo Che Me La Cavo *See* Ciao, Professore! (1994)

The Iron Hand *See* Chinese Connection (1973)

The Iron Kiss *See* Naked Kiss (1964)

Irving Berlin's Alexander's Ragtime Band *See* Alexander's Ragtime Band (1938)

Irving Berlin's Second Fiddle *See* Second Fiddle (1939)

Island of Monte Cristo *See* Sword of Venus (1953)

Island of Shame *See* The Young One (1961)

Island of the Burning Damned *See* Island of the Burning Doomed (1967)

Island of the Fishmen *See* Screamers (1980)

Island of the Living Horror *See* Brides of the Beast (1968)

Isle of Lost Women *See* 99 Women (1969)

Isle of the Living Dead *See* The Snake People (1968)

Isle of the Snake People *See* The Snake People (1968)

Isn't Life A Bitch? *See* La Chienne (1931)

Istanbul, Keep Your Eyes Open *See* Istanbul (1990)

It Comes Up Murder *See* The Honey Pot (1967)

It Happened at Lakewood Manor *See* Ants (1977)

It Happened in Paris *See* The Lady in Question (1940)

It Happened One Summer *See* State Fair (1945)

It Hurts Only When I Laugh *See* Only When I Laugh (1981)

It Lives By Night *See* The Bat People (1974)

It Only Take Five Minutes *See* Five Minutes to Love (1963)

It Runs in the Family *See* My Summer Story (1994)

It Stalked the Ocean Floor *See* Monster from the Ocean Floor (1954)

It! The Vampire From Beyond Space *See* It! The Terror from Beyond Space (1958)

It Won't Rub Off, Baby *See* Sweet Love, Bitter (1967)

The Italian Connection *See* Hired to Kill (1973)

The Italian Connection *See* Manhunt (1973)

It's Hot in Hell *See* Un Singe en Hiver (1962)

It's Hot in Paradise *See* Horrors of Spider Island (1959)

It's My Life *See* My Life to Live (1962)

It's Only Money *See* Double Dynamite (1951)

Ivan's Childhood *See* My Name is Ivan (1962)

Jack London's Klondike Fever *See* Klondike Fever (1979)

Jackals *See* American Justice (1986)

Jackie Chan's Police Story *See* Jackie Chan's Police Force (1985)

Jack's Wife *See* Season of the Witch (1973)

Jacqueline Susann's Once is Not Enough *See* Once is Not Enough (1975)

Jacquot de Nantes *See* Jacquot (1991)

J'ai Pas Sommeil *See* I Can't Sleep (1993)

Jail Birds *See* Pardon Us (1931)

Jailbirds' Vacation *See* Les Grandes Gueules (1965)

James A. Michener's Texas *See* Texas (1994)

James Clavell's Shogun *See* Shogun (1980)

Jane Austen's Emma *See* Emma (1997)

The Janitor *See* Eyewitness (1981)

Japan Sinks *See* Tidal Wave (1975)

Jatszani Kell *See* Lily in Love (1985)

Jaws 3-D *See* Jaws 3 (1983)

Jayne Mansfield: A Symbol of the '50s *See* The Jayne Mansfield Story (1980)

J.C. *See* Iron Horsemen (1971)

Je Vous Salue Marie *See* Hail Mary (1985)

Jealousy *See* L'Enfer (1993)

Jean de Florette 2 *See* Manon of the Spring (1987)

Jeder fur Sich und Gott Gegen Alle *See* Every Man for Himself & God Against All (1975)

Jekyll's Inferno *See* The Two Faces of Dr. Jekyll (1960)

Jennie *See* Portrait of Jennie (1948)

Jennifer (The Snake Goddess) *See* Jennifer (1978)

The Jester *See* Der Purimshpiler (1937)

Jesus de Montreal *See* Jesus of Montreal (1989)

Jette un Sort *See* Rough Magic (1995)

Jeu de Massacre *See* The Killing Game (1967)

Jew Suss *See* Power (1934)

The Jewish Jester *See* Der Purimshpiler (1937)

The Jezebels *See* Switchblade Sisters (1975)

Jigokumen *See* Gate of Hell (1954)

Jim Buck *See* Portrait of a Hitman (1977)

Job Lazadasa *See* The Revolt of Job (1984)

Joe Palooka *See* Palooka (1934)

John Carpenter Presents Body Bags *See* Body Bags (1993)

John Carpenter's Escape from L.A. *See* Escape from L.A. (1996)

John Le Carre's A Perfect Spy *See* A Perfect Spy (1988)

John Travis, Solar Survivor *See* Omega Cop (1990)

Johnnie Mae Gibson: FBI *See* Johnnie Gibson F.B.I. (1987)

Johnny Vagabond *See* Johnny Come Lately (1943)

Johnny Zombie *See* My Boyfriend's Back (1993)

A Joke of Destiny *See* A Joke of Destiny, Lying in Wait Around the Corner Like a Bandit (1984)

Joker's Wild *See* Body Trouble (1992)

Jonas—Qui Aura 25 Ans en l'An 2000 *See* Jonah Who Will Be 25 in the Year 2000 (1976)

Joseph Conrad's Nostromo *See* Nostromo (1996)

Joseph Conrad's The Secret Agent *See* The Secret Agent (1996)

Joseph Sold by His Brothers *See* Joseph & His Brethren (1960)

Journey into Autumn *See* Dreams (1955)

Journey of the Hyena *See* Touki Bouki (1973)

Joyous Laughter *See* Passionate Thief (1960)

J.R. *See* Who's That Knocking at My Door? (1968)

Jude the Obscure *See* Jude (1996)

A Judgement in Stone *See* The Housekeeper (1986)

A Judgment in Stone *See* La Ceremonie (1995)

Jules et Jim *See* Jules and Jim (1962)

Jules Verne's Rocket to the Moon *See* Those Fantastic Flying Fools (1967)

Julie Darling *See* Daughter of Death (1982)

July Pork Bellies *See* For Pete's Sake (1974)

Jumbo *See* Billy Rose's Jumbo (1962)

Jungfrauenmaschine *See* Virgin Machine (1988)

Jungfrukallan *See* The Virgin Spring (1959)

The Jungle Book *See* Rudyard Kipling's The Jungle Book (1994)

Jungle Book 2 *See* Rudyard Kipling's the Second Jungle Book: Mowgli and Baloo (1997)

Jungle Gold *See* Perils of the Darkest Jungle (1944)

Jungle Woman *See* Nabonga (1944)

Juninatten *See* June Night (1940)

Jurassic Park 2 *See* The Lost World: Jurassic Park 2 (1997)

Jury Duty *See* The Great American Sex Scandal (1994)

Just Another Day at the Races *See* Win, Place, or Steal (1972)

Libido See The Sensuous Teenager (1970)

Licensed to Kill See Second Best Secret Agent in the Whole Wide World (1965)

The Lie Detector See Le Polygraphe (1996)

The Life and Adventures of Nicholas Nickleby See Nicholas Nickleby (1946)

The Life and Loves of Beethoven See Beethoven (1936)

Life at Stake See The Key Man (1957)

Life in the Food Chain See Age Isn't Everything (1991)

Life is Rosy See La Vie est Belle (1987)

Life of Brian See Monty Python's Life of Brian (1979)

The Life of Jack London See Jack London (1944)

Lifesavers See Mixed Nuts (1994)

The Light Fantastic See Love Is Better Than Ever (1952)

Lights of Variety See Variety Lights (1951)

Like a Crow on a June Bug See Sixteen (1972)

Like Father, Like Son See The Executioner (1978)

Lila See Mantis in Lace (1968)

Lilacs in the Spring See Let's Make Up (1955)

L'Inafferrabile Invincible See Mr. Superinvisible (1973)

Lincoln See Gore Vidal's Lincoln (1988)

L'Innocente See The Innocent (1976)

The Lion's Den See La Boca del Lobo (1989)

L'Isola Degli Uomini Pesce See Screamers (1980)

The Little Martyr See The Children Are Watching Us (1944)

The Little Mermaid See La Petite Sirene (1980)

Little Mother See Mamele (1938)

Little Pal See Healer (1936)

Little Panda See The Amazing Panda Adventure (1995)

The Little Sister See The Tender Age (1984)

Live a Little, Steal a Lot See Murph the Surf (1975)

Live Bait See L'Appat (1994)

Live to Love See The Devil's Hand (1961)

The Liver Eaters See Spider Baby (1964)

Ljubarni Slucaj See The Love Affair, or The Case of the Missing Switchboard Operator (1967)

Lo Chiamavano Trinita See They Call Me Trinity (1972)

Lo Que Vendra See Times to Come (1981)

Lo Sbarco di Anzio See Anzio (1968)

Lo Scatenato See Catch as Catch Can (1968)

Lo Sceicco Bianco See The White Sheik (1952)

Lo Spettro See The Ghost (1963)

Lo Strano Vizio Della Signora Wardh See The Next Victim (1971)

Lo Zio Indegno See The Sleazy Uncle (1989)

Loaded Weapon 1 See National Lampoon's Loaded Weapon 1 (1993)

Lock Your Doors See The Ape Man (1943)

The Lodger: A Case of London Fog See The Lodger (1926)

L'Oeuvre au Noir See The Abyss (1989)

The Lone Troubador See Two-Gun Troubador (1937)

Lone Wolf and Cub: Baby Cart at the River Styx See Baby Cart at the River Styx (1972)

Lone Wolf and Cub: Sword of Vengeance See Baby Cart 1: Lend a Child...Lend an Arm (1972)

The Lonely Hearts Killers See Honeymoon Killers (1970)

Lonely Man See Gun Riders (1969)

The Loner See Ruckus (1981)

The Long Arm See The Third Key (1957)

The Long, Dark Night See The Pack (1977)

Long John Silver Returns to Treasure Island See Long John Silver (1953)

The Long Ride See Brady's Escape (1984)

The Long Shot See African Rage (1978)

Look Down and Die See Steel (1980)

The Look of Ulysses See Ulysses' Gaze (1995)

Loonies On Broadway See Zombies on Broadway (1944)

Loose Joints See Flicks (1985)

Looters See Trespass (1992)

L'Opera De Quat'Sous See The Threepenny Opera (1931)

Lorca and the Outlaws See Starship (1987)

Lords of Treason See Secret Honor (1985)

L'Oro Di Napoli See The Gold of Naples (1954)

L'Orribile Segreto Del Dr. Hichcock See The Horrible Dr. Hichcock (1962)

Los Ambiciosos See Fever Mounts at El Pao (1959)

Los Despiadados See Hellbenders (1967)

Los Ojos Azules de la Muneca Rota See House of Psychotic Women (1973)

Los Santos Inocentes See The Holy Innocents (1984)

Loser Take All See Strike It Rich (1990)

The Lost Glory of Troy See The Avenger (1962)

The Lost Illusion See The Fallen Idol (1949)

Lost Island of Kioga See Hawk of the Wilderness (1938)

Lost Women See Mesa of Lost Women (1952)

Lost Women of Zarpa See Mesa of Lost Women (1952)

The Loudest Whisper See The Children's Hour (1961)

Louis L'Amour's Conagher See Conagher (1991)

Louis L'Amour's "The Shadow Riders" See The Shadow Riders (1982)

Louis 19, le Roi des Ondes See King of the Airwaves (1994)

Love and Death in Saigon See A Better Tommorow, Part 3 (1989)

Love and Hate: The Story of Colin and Joanne Thatcher See Love and Hate: A Marriage Made in Hell (1990)

The Love Cage See Joy House (1964)

Love Eternal See Eternal Return (1943)

The Love Factor See Alien Women (1969)

Love in Las Vegas See Viva Las Vegas (1963)

Love is Blind See Love at First Sight (1976)

Love Lessons See All Things Fair (1995)

The Love Maniac See Blood of Ghastly Horror (1972)

Love, the Magician See El Amor Brujo (1986)

Love Trap See Curse of the Black Widow (1977)

Love You to Death See Deadly Illusion (1987)

Lover of the Great Bear See Smugglers (1975)

Lover, Wife See Wifemistress (1979)

Lovers From Beyond the Tomb See Nightmare Castle (1965)

Lovers Must Learn See Rome Adventure (1962)

The Lovers of Montparnasse See Modigliani (1958)

Loves of a Scoundrel See Death of a Scoundrel (1956)

The Loves of Isadora See Isadora (1968)

Loving Moments See Bleak Moments (1971)

The Loyal 47 Ronin See 47 Ronin, Part 1 (1942)

L'Ucello dalle Plume di Cristallo See The Bird with the Crystal Plumage (1970)

Luci Del Varieta See Variety Lights (1951)

The Lucifer Project See Barracuda (1978)

Lucky Boots See Gun Play (1936)

Lucky Break See Paperback Romance (1996)

Lucky 13 See Running Hot (1983)

The Lullaby See The Sin of Madelon Claudet (1931)

L'Ultimo Uomo Della Terra See The Last Man on Earth (1964)

Lunch on the Grass See Picnic on the Grass (1959)

Lunch Wagon Girls See Lunch Wagon (1981)

L'Une Chante, L'Autre Pas See One Sings, the Other Doesn't (1977)

L'Uomo Dalle Due Ombre See Cold Sweat (1974)

L'Uomo di Rio See That Man from Rio (1964)

Lust for Evil See Purple Noon (1960)

Lust och Fagring Stor See All Things Fair (1995)

Lust of the Vampires See The Devil's Commandment (1956)

Lycanthropus See Werewolf in a Girl's Dormitory (1961)

M. Hire See Monsieur Hire (1989)

Ma and Pa Kettle Go to Paris See Ma and Pa Kettle on Vacation (1953)

Ma Nuit Chez Maud See My Night at Maud's (1969)

Macabra See Demonoid, Messenger of Death (1981)

Macabre Serenade See Dance of Death (1968)

Maccheroni See Macaroni (1985)

Maciste Alla Corte Del Gran Khan See Samson and the 7 Miracles of the World (1962)

Maciste at the Court of the Great Khan See Samson and the 7 Miracles of the World (1962)

Maciste la Regina di Samar See Hercules Against the Moon Men (1964)

Maciste, L'Eroe Piu Grande Del Mondo See Goliath and the Sins of Babylon (1964)

Maciste Nella Terra dei Ciclopi See Atlas in the Land of the Cyclops (1961)

Mad Dog See Mad Dog Morgan (1976)

Mad Dog Time See Trigger Happy (1996)

Mad Dogs and Englishmen See Shameless (1994)

The Mad Hatter See Breakfast in Hollywood (1946)

Mad Magazine's Up the Academy See Up the Academy (1980)

Mad Trapper of the Yukon See Challenge To Be Free (1976)

Milagro en Roma *See* Miracle in Rome (1988)

Milczaca Gwiazda *See* First Spaceship on Venus (1960)

Mile a Minute Love *See* Roaring Speedboats (1937)

Milou en Mai *See* May Fools (1990)

Milou in May *See* May Fools (1990)

Mind Games *See* The Agency (1981)

Mind Ripper *See* Wes Craven Presents Mind Ripper (1995)

Mindwarp: An Infinity of Terror *See* Galaxy of Terror (1981)

The Miracle of Fatima *See* Miracle of Our Lady of Fatima (1952)

Miracle of Life *See* Our Daily Bread (1934)

Miracolo a Milano *See* Miracle in Milan (1951)

Miss Europe *See* Prix de Beaute (1930)

Miss Muette *See* The Diabolical Dr. Z (1965)

Miss Shumway *See* Rough Magic (1995)

Mrs. Parker and the Round Table *See* Mrs. Parker and the Vicious Circle (1994)

Mr. Ashton was Indiscreet *See* The Senator was Indiscreet (1947)

Mr. Bug Goes to Town *See* Hoppity Goes to Town (1941)

Mr. Celebrity *See* Turf Boy (1942)

Mr. Forbush and the Penguins *See* Cry of the Penguins (1971)

Mr. Fox of Venice *See* The Honey Pot (1967)

Mr. Invisible *See* Mr. Superinvisible (1973)

Mr. Quilp *See* The Old Curiosity Shop (1975)

Mr. Sebastian *See* Sebastian (1968)

Mr. 247 *See* A Modern Affair (1994)

Mister V *See* Pimpernel Smith (1942)

Mr. Wrong *See* Dark of the Night (1985)

Misterios del Ultratumba *See* Black Pit of Dr. M (1947)

Mit Eva Fing Die Sunde An *See* The Bellboy and the Playgirls (1962)

Mitt Liv Som Hund *See* My Life As a Dog (1985)

The Model Killer *See* The Hollywood Strangler Meets the Skid Row Slasher (1979)

Model Massacre *See* Color Me Blood Red (1964)

A Modern Bluebeard *See* Boom in the Moon (1946)

A Modern Hero *See* Knute Rockne: All American (1940)

Modigliani of Montparnasse *See* Modigliani (1958)

Mogliamante *See* Wifemistress (1979)

The Mogul *See* Ratings Game (1984)

Molly Louvain *See* The Strange Love of Molly Louvain (1932)

Mondo Pazzo *See* Mondo Cane 2 (1964)

A Monkey in Winter *See* Un Singe en Hiver (1962)

Monkey Shines: An Experiment in Fear *See* Monkey Shines (1988)

Monsieur Hulot's Holiday *See* Mr. Hulot's Holiday (1953)

Monster *See* Humanoids from the Deep (1980)

The Monster Baran *See* Varan the Unbelievable (1961)

Monster from a Prehistoric Planet *See* Gappa the Trifibian Monster (1967)

Monster Maker *See* Monster from the Ocean Floor (1954)

Monster of Monsters *See* Ghidrah the Three Headed Monster (1965)

Monster of Terror *See* Die, Monster, Die! (1965)

The Monster Show *See* Freaks (1932)

The Monster Walked *See* The Monster Walks (1932)

The Monster with Green Eyes *See* Planets Against Us (1961)

Monster Yongkari *See* Yongkari Monster of the Deep (1967)

Monster Zero *See* Godzilla vs. Monster Zero (1968)

The Monsters Are Loose *See* The Thrill Killers (1965)

Monsters From the Moon *See* Robot Monster (1953)

Monsters from the Unknown Planet *See* Terror of Mechagodzilla (1978)

Monstrosity *See* The Atomic Brain (1964)

Montana Justice *See* Man from Montana (1941)

Monte Carlo or Bust *See* Those Daring Young Men in Their Jaunty Jalopies (1969)

Montenegro—Or Pigs and Pearls *See* Montenegro (1981)

Montparnasse 19 *See* Modigliani (1958)

Morgan: A Suitable Case for Treatment *See* Morgan! (1966)

Morgan il Pirata *See* Morgan the Pirate (1960)

Morgen Grauen *See* Time Troopers (1989)

The Mormon Peril *See* Trapped by the Mormons (1922)

Morning Terror *See* Time Troopers (1989)

Mortal Sins *See* Dangerous Obsession (1988)

Morte a Venezia *See* Death in Venice (1971)

Moscow Distrusts Tears *See* Moscow Does Not Believe in Tears (1980)

Moscow Nights *See* I Stand Condemned (1936)

Moskwa Sljesam Nje Jerit *See* Moscow Does Not Believe in Tears (1980)

The Most Desired Man *See* Maybe...Maybe Not (1994)

Mosura Tai Goira *See* Godzilla vs. Mothra (1964)

Motel *See* Pink Motel (1982)

Motel Vacancy *See* Talking Walls (1985)

Mother Goose A Go-Go *See* The Unkissed Bride (1966)

Mother Riley Meets the Vampire *See* My Son, the Vampire (1952)

Mothra vs. Godzilla *See* Godzilla vs. Mothra (1964)

Mountain of Cannibal Gods *See* Slave of the Cannibal God (1979)

Movie Struck *See* Pick a Star (1937)

The Moving Target *See* Harper (1966)

Mowgli and Baloo: Jungle Book 2 *See* Rudyard Kipling's the Second Jungle Book: Mowgli and Baloo (1997)

Mud *See* The Stick-Up (1977)

Muhomatsu no Issho *See* Rikisha-Man (1958)

Mujeres al Borde de un Ataque de Nervios *See* Women on the Verge of a Nervous Breakdown (1988)

Mumsy, Nanny, Sonny, and Girly *See* Girly (1970)

Munkbrogreven *See* The Count of the Old Town (1934)

Murder by Mail *See* Schizoid (1980)

Murder by Proxy *See* Blackout (1954)

The Murder in Thorton Square *See* Gaslight (1944)

Murder, Inc. *See* The Enforcer (1951)

Murder on Diamond Row *See* The Squeaker (1937)

Murder One *See* Death Sentence (1974)

The Murderer Dmitri Karamazov *See* The Brothers Karamazov (1958)

Muriel, Or the Time of Return *See* Muriel (1963)

Muriel, Ou le Temps d'Un Retour *See* Muriel (1963)

The Murri Affair *See* La Grande Bourgeoise (1974)

Music in Darkness *See* Night Is My Future (1947)

Mussolini: The Decline and Fall of Il Duce *See* Mussolini & I (1985)

Mutant *See* Forbidden World (1982)

The Mutation *See* The Freakmaker (1973)

Mutations *See* The Freakmaker (1973)

The Mutilator *See* The Dark (1979)

The Mutineers *See* Pirate Ship (1949)

Mutter Kusters Fahrt Zum Himmel *See* Mother Kusters Goes to Heaven (1976)

My Brother, the Outlaw *See* My Outlaw Brother (1951)

My Crazy Life *See* Mi Vida Loca (1994)

My Darling Shiksa *See* Over the Brooklyn Bridge (1983)

My Father, My Master *See* Padre Padrone (1977)

My Favorite Season *See* Ma Saison Preferee (1993)

My Favourite Year *See* My Favorite Year (1982)

My Girlfriend's Boyfriend *See* Boyfriends & Girlfriends (1988)

My Gun is Jammed *See* Bare Hunt (1963)

My Hero *See* A Southern Yankee (1948)

My Love Letters *See* Love Letters (1983)

My Name is John *See* The Legend of Hillbilly John (1973)

My Night with Maud *See* My Night at Maud's (1969)

My Posse Don't Do Homework *See* Dangerous Minds (1995)

My Son Alone *See* American Empire (1942)

My Teenage Daughter *See* Teenage Bad Girl (1959)

My Uncle *See* Mon Oncle (1958)

My Uncle, Mr. Hulot *See* Mon Oncle (1958)

Mystere Alexina *See* The Mystery of Alexina (1986)

Mysterious Invader *See* The Astounding She-Monster (1958)

The Mysterious Satellite *See* Warning from Space (1956)

The Mystery of Kaspar Hauser *See* Every Man for Himself & God Against All (1975)

Mystery of the Black Jungle *See* The Black Devils of Kali (1955)

The Mystery of the Marie Celeste *See* The Mystery of the Mary Celeste (1937)

Mystique *See* Circle of Power (1983)

Nybyggarna *See* The New Land (1973)

Nyoka and the Lost Secrets of Hippocrates *See* Nyoka and the Tigermen (1942)

O Estranho Mundo de Ze do Caixao *See* Strange World of Coffin Joe (1968)

Obch Od Na Korze *See* The Shop on Main Street (1965)

Obecna Skola *See* The Elementary School (1991)

Oblivion 2 *See* Backlash: Oblivion 2 (1995)

Obsession *See* The Hidden Room (1949)

Occhi Senza Volto *See* The Horror Chamber of Dr. Faustus (1959)

Ochoa *See* 8-A (1992)

Oci Ciornie *See* Dark Eyes (1987)

October *See* Ten Days That Shook the World (1927)

Odio le Bionde *See* I Hate Blondes (1983)

Of a Thousand Delights *See* Sandra of a Thousand Delights (1965)

Of Death, Of Love *See* Cemetery Man (1995)

Office Party *See* Hostile Takeover (1988)

The Official History *See* The Official Story (1985)

The Official Version *See* The Official Story (1985)

Oh, Charlie *See* Hold That Ghost (1941)

Oh Woe is Me *See* Helas Pour Moi (1994)

Okasan *See* Mother (1952)

The Old and the New *See* The General Line (1929)

The Old Corral *See* Song of the Gringo (1936)

Old Greatheart *See* Way Back Home (1932)

Old Heidelberg *See* The Student Prince in Old Heidelberg (1927)

Old Man *See* William Faulkner's Old Man (1997)

The Old Man and the Boy *See* The Two of Us (1968)

Old Mother Riley Meets the Vampire *See* My Son, the Vampire (1952)

Old Shatterhand *See* Apaches Last Battle (1964)

Olelkezo Tekintetek *See* Another Way (1982)

Omar Mukhtar *See* Lion of the Desert (1981)

The Omen 3 *See* The Final Conflict (1981)

On the Great White Trail *See* Renfrew on the Great White Trail (1938)

On the Road Again *See* Honeysuckle Rose (1980)

Once Upon a Texas Train *See* Texas Guns (1990)

Once Upon a Time There Was a Country *See* Underground (1995)

One Born Every Minute *See* Flim-Flam Man (1967)

One Cup of Coffee *See* Pastime (1991)

One For All *See* The President's Mystery (1936)

One for Sorrow, Two for Joy *See* Signs of Life (1989)

One Horse Town *See* Small Town Girl (1953)

One Hundred Percent Pure *See* The Girl from Missouri (1934)

One-Man Mutiny *See* The Court Martial of Billy Mitchell (1955)

One Plus One *See* Sympathy for the Devil (1970)

Onkel Toms Hutte *See* Uncle Tom's Cabin (1969)

Only the French Can! *See* French Can-Can (1955)

Onna Ga Kaidan O Agaru Toki *See* When a Woman Ascends the Stairs (1960)

Oopsie Poopsie *See* Get Rita (1975)

Operacione Paura *See* Kill, Baby, Kill (1966)

Operation Cicero *See* Five Fingers (1952)

Operation Kid Brother *See* Secret Agent 00 (1967)

Operation Overthrow *See* Power Play (1981)

Operation Serpent *See* Fer-De-Lance (1974)

Operation Snafu *See* On the Fiddle (1961)

Operation Undercover *See* Report to the Commissioner (1974)

Operation Warhead *See* On the Fiddle (1961)

Operazione Goldman *See* Lightning Bolt (1967)

Opium Connection *See* The Poppy Is Also a Flower (1966)

The Oracle *See* The Horse's Mouth (1958)

Orazi e Curiazi *See* Duel of Champions (1961)

Orca—Killer Whale *See* Orca (1977)

Order of Death *See* Corrupt (1984)

Orfeu Negro *See* Black Orpheus (1958)

Orgasmo *See* Paranoia (1969)

Orkobefogadas *See* Adoption (1975)

Orloff Against the Invisible Man *See* The Invisible Dead (1970)

Orphee *See* Orpheus (1949)

Oru Kaiju Daishingeki *See* Godzilla's Revenge (1969)

Osenny Marafon *See* Autumn Marathon (1979)

Other People's Business *See* Way Back Home (1932)

The Other Side of Paradise *See* Foxtrot (1976)

Otto E Mezzo *See* 8 1/2 (1963)

Our Daily Bread *See* City Girl (1930)

Our Girl Friday *See* The Adventures of Sadie (1955)

Ourselves Alone *See* River of Unrest (1937)

Out of Rosenheim *See* Bagdad Cafe (1988)

Out of the Darkness *See* Night Creature (1979)

Out of the Darkness *See* Teenage Caveman (1958)

Out of the Night *See* Strange Illusion (1945)

Out of the Shadow *See* Murder on the Campus (1952)

Out on Probation *See* Daddy-O (1959)

The Outcast *See* Man in the Saddle (1951)

The Outcry *See* Il Grido (1957)

Outer Reach *See* Spaced Out (1980)

Outlaw Gun *See* A Minute to Pray, A Second to Die (1967)

Outomlionnye Solntsem *See* Burnt by the Sun (1994)

Outside In *See* Red, White & Busted (1975)

The Outsider *See* Fatal Error (1983)

The Outsider *See* The Guinea Pig (1948)

Outsider in Amsterdam *See* Fatal Error (1983)

The Outsiders *See* Band of Outsiders (1964)

Over Her Dead Body *See* Enid Is Sleeping (1990)

The Pace That Kills *See* Cocaine Fiends (1936)

Palomino *See* Danielle Steel's Palomino (1991)

Pamela Principle 2 *See* Seduce Me: Pamela Principle 2 (1994)

Pane e Cioccolata *See* Bread and Chocolate (1974)

Panga *See* Curse 3: Blood Sacrifice (1990)

Panic *See* Panique (1947)

Panic at Lakewood Manor *See* Ants (1977)

Panic on the Trans-Siberian Express *See* Horror Express (1972)

Panico en el Transiberiano *See* Horror Express (1972)

Panny z Wilka *See* Maids of Wilko (1979)

Paoda Shuang Deng *See* Red Firecracker, Green Firecracker (1993)

Paper Bullets *See* Gangs, Inc. (1941)

The Parasite Murders *See* They Came from Within (1975)

Pardon Me, Your Teeth are in My Neck *See* The Fearless Vampire Killers (1967)

Paris Brule-t-il? *See* Is Paris Burning? (1966)

Paris Does Strange Things *See* Elena and Her Men (1956)

Paris is Ours *See* Paris Belongs to Us (1960)

Paris Nous Appartient *See* Paris Belongs to Us (1960)

Paris Qui Dort *See* The Crazy Ray (1922)

Paris vu Par *See* Six in Paris (1968)

Park Plaza *See* Norman Conquest (1953)

Paroxismus *See* Venus in Furs (1970)

Parts: The Clonus Horror *See* The Clonus Horror (1979)

Party Girls *See* Party Incorporated (1989)

Pasazerka *See* Passenger (1961)

Pasqualino Settebellezze *See* Seven Beauties (1976)

Pasqualino: Seven Beauties *See* Seven Beauties (1976)

Passages from "Finnegans Wake" *See* Finnegan's Wake (1963)

Passages from James Joyce's "Finnegans Wake" *See* Finnegan's Wake (1963)

The Passerby *See* La Passante (1983)

The Passion Flower Hotel *See* Boarding School (1983)

Passion Play *See* Love Letters (1983)

Passione d'Amore *See* Passion of Love (1982)

Passions *See* The Passing of Evil (1970)

Passport to Shame *See* Room 43 (1958)

The Patsy *See* L'Addition (1985)

Patterns of Power *See* Patterns (1956)

Patton: A Salute to a Rebel *See* Patton (1970)

Patton—Lust for Glory *See* Patton (1970)

Paul Bowles: Halbmond *See* Halfmoon (1995)

Pauline a la Plage *See* Pauline at the Beach (1983)

Paura Nella Citta Dei Morti Viventi *See* Gates of Hell (1983)

P.D. James: A Mind to Murder *See* A Mind to Murder (1996)

P.D. James' Devices & Desires *See* Devices and Desires (1991)

The Peace Game *See* The Gladiators (1970)

Peacemaker *See* The Ambassador (1984)

Peau d'Ane *See* Donkey Skin (1970)

The Peking Medallion *See* The Corrupt Ones (1967)

Penn of Pennsylvania *See* The Courageous Mr. Penn (1941)

Pensionat Oskar *See* Like It Never Was Before (1995)

People Toys *See* Devil Times Five (1974)

People's Enemy *See* Prison Train (1938)

Pepi, Luci, Bom y Otras Chicas del Monton *See* Pepi, Luci, Bom and Other Girls on the Heap (1980)

Percy's Progress *See* It's Not the Size That Counts (1974)

Peril en la Demeure *See* Peril (1985)

Perils from Planet Mongo *See* Flash Gordon: Rocketship (1936)

The Perils of Gwendoline in the Land of the Yik-Yak *See* The Perils of Gwendoline (1984)

Perils of Nyoka *See* Nyoka and the Tigermen (1942)

Persecution *See* The Graveyard (1974)

Persecution and Assassination of Jean-Paul Marat as Performed by the Inmates of the Asylum of Charenton Under the Direction of the Marquis De Sade *See* Marat/Sade (1966)

Perseus the Invincible *See* Medusa Against the Son of Hercules (1962)

Peter Rabbit and Tales of Beatrix Potter *See* Tales of Beatrix Potter (1971)

Petersen *See* Jock Petersen (1974)

Petroleum Girls *See* Legend of Frenchie King (1971)

Phantom Fiend *See* The Return of Dr. Mabuse (1961)

The Phantom of Terror *See* The Bird with the Crystal Plumage (1970)

Phantom of the Air *See* The Phantom Broadcast (1933)

Phantom of the Plains *See* Western Double Feature 7: Wild Bill & Crabbe (1945)

The Phantom Ship *See* The Mystery of the Mary Celeste (1937)

Phar Lap: Heart of a Nation *See* Phar Lap (1984)

Phenomena *See* Creepers (1985)

Philo Vance Returns *See* Infamous Crimes (1947)

Phoebe *See* Zelly & Me (1988)

The Phoenix *See* War of the Wizards (1981)

Pickup on 101 *See* Where the Eagle Flies (1972)

Pigsty *See* Porcile (1969)

Pilgrimage to Rome *See* L'Anne Sainte (1978)

The Pilot *See* Danger in the Skies (1979)

Pinball Pick-Up *See* Pick-Up Summer (1979)

Pinball Summer *See* Pick-Up Summer (1979)

Pinocchio *See* The Adventures of Pinocchio (1996)

Pioneers *See* Pioneer Woman (1973)

Pippi Langstrump Pa de Sju Haven *See* Pippi in the South Seas (1974)

Piranha 2: Flying Killers *See* Piranha 2: The Spawning (1982)

Pirate's Fiancee *See* A Very Curious Girl (1969)

Pirate's Harbor *See* Haunted Harbor (1944)

The Pizza Connection *See* The Sicilian Connection (1985)

The Plains of Heaven *See* Panic Station (1982)

Planet of Horrors *See* Galaxy of Terror (1981)

Planet of Love *See* Galaxies Are Colliding (1992)

Planet of the Lifeless Men *See* Battle of the Worlds (1961)

The Plants Are Watching *See* The Kirlian Witness (1978)

Players *See* The Club (1981)

Playgirl Gang *See* Switchblade Sisters (1975)

The Playgirls and the Bellboy *See* The Bellboy and the Playgirls (1962)

Playing for Keeps *See* Lily in Love (1985)

Please! Mr. Balzac *See* Mademoiselle Striptease (1957)

Plein Soleil *See* Purple Noon (1960)

Plein Sud *See* Heat of Desire (1984)

Pluck of the Irish *See* Great Guy (1936)

Po Dezju *See* Before the Rain (1994)

Pocomania *See* The Devil's Daughter (1939)

Poe's Tales of Terror *See* Tales of Terror (1962)

Poisoned by Love: The Kern County Murders *See* Murder So Sweet (1993)

Pokayaniye *See* Repentance (1987)

Police Connection *See* The Mad Bomber (1972)

Police Force *See* Jackie Chan's Police Force (1985)

The Police Story *See* Jackie Chan's Police Force (1985)

Police Story 3: Supercop *See* Supercop (1992)

Police Story 4 *See* Jackie Chan's First Strike (1996)

Poncomania *See* The Devil's Daughter (1939)

Pony Express *See* Peter Lundy and the Medicine Hat Stallion (1977)

Pookie *See* The Sterile Cuckoo (1969)

Poopsie *See* Get Rita (1975)

Poor Albert and Little Annie *See* I Dismember Mama (1974)

The Poor Outlaws *See* The Round Up (1966)

The Pope Must Die *See* The Pope Must Diet (1991)

Popiol i Diament *See* Ashes and Diamonds (1958)

Poppies Are Also Flowers *See* The Poppy Is Also a Flower (1966)

Porte Aperte *See* Open Doors (1989)

Portrait of a Woman, Nude *See* Nudo di Donna (1983)

Portrait of Alison *See* Postmark for Danger (1956)

Portrait of Maria *See* Maria Candelaria (1946)

Potemkin *See* The Battleship Potemkin (1925)

Potop *See* The Deluge (1973)

Practice Makes Perfect *See* Le Cavaleur (1978)

Prairie Outlaws *See* Wild West (1946)

Prairie Rustlers *See* Western Double Feature 7: Wild Bill & Crabbe (1945)

Pratldwandi *See* The Adversary (1971)

Precious *See* Citizen Ruth (1996)

The Prehistoric Sound *See* Sound of Horror (1964)

Prehistoric World *See* Teenage Caveman (1958)

Prenom: Carmen *See* First Name: Carmen (1983)

Preparez Vous Mouchoirs *See* Get Out Your Handkerchiefs (1978)

Preppies *See* Making the Grade (1984)

The President's Women *See* Foreplay (1975)

Pret-a-Porter *See* Ready to Wear (1994)

Pride of Kentucky *See* The Story of Seabiscuit (1949)

Priority Red One *See* Delta Force Commando 2 (1990)

Prison *See* Devil's Wanton (1949)

The Prisoner *See* Cold Room (1984)

Prisoner of the Caucasus *See* Prisoner of the Mountains (1996)

The Private Life of Paul Joseph Goebbels *See* Enemy of Women (1944)

The Private Lives of Elizabeth and Essex *See* Elizabeth, the Queen (1968)

Private Snuffy Smith *See* Snuffy Smith, Yard Bird (1942)

The Private Wore Skirts *See* Never Wave at a WAC (1952)

Profession: Reporter *See* The Passenger (1975)

The Profile of Terror *See* The Sadist (1963)

Profumo di Donna *See* The Scent of a Woman (1975)

Profundo Rosso *See* Deep Red: Hatchet Murders (1975)

Project Shadowchaser 2 *See* Night Siege Project: Shadowchaser 2 (1994)

Prom Night 2 *See* Hello Mary Lou: Prom Night 2 (1987)

Promise Her Anything *See* Promises! Promises! (1963)

Prophecies of Nostradamus *See* Last Days of Planet Earth (1974)

A Proposito Luciano *See* Lucky Luciano (1974)

Prorva *See* Moscow Parade (1992)

The Protectors, Book One *See* Angel of H.E.A.T. (1982)

Proud, Damned, and Dead *See* The Proud and the Damned (1972)

Przesluchanie *See* The Interrogation (1982)

Psycho a Go Go! *See* Blood of Ghastly Horror (1972)

Psycho-Circus *See* Circus of Fear (1967)

Psycho Killers *See* Mania (1960)

Psycho Puppet *See* Delirium (1977)

Psycho Sisters *See* The Sibling (1972)

Psychotic *See* Driver's Seat (1973)

Ptang, Yang, Kipperbang *See* Kipperbang (1982)

Public Be Damned *See* The World Gone Mad (1933)

The Public Be Hanged *See* The World Gone Mad (1933)

Puo Una Morta Rivivere Per Amore? *See* Venus in Furs (1970)

The Pupil *See* L'Eleve (1995)

The Purim Player *See* Der Purimshpiler (1937)

Purple Death from Outer Space *See* Flash Gordon Conquers the Universe (1940)

The Purple Riders *See* Purple Vigilantes (1938)

Pursuit *See* Apache Blood (1975)

Putyovka V Zhizn *See* The Road to Life (1931)

Q Planes *See* Clouds Over Europe (1939)

Qiuyue *See* Autumn Moon (1992)

Quai des Orfevres *See* Jenny Lamour (1947)

Qualcosa di Biondo *See* Aurora (1984)

Quando De Donne Avevando La Coda *See* When Women Had Tails (1970)

Que He Hecho Yo Para Merecer Estol? *See* What Have I Done to Deserve This? (1985)

Que La Bete Meure *See* This Man Must Die (1970)

Queen of Blood *See* Planet of Blood (1966)

Queen of Broadway *See* Kid Dynamite (1943)

Queen of the Cannibals *See* Doctor Butcher M.D. (1980)

Queen of the Gorillas *See* The Bride & the Beast (1958)

The Queen's Husband *See* The Royal Bed (1931)

Quei Temerari Sulle Loro Pazze, Scatenate, Scalcinate Carriole *See* Those Daring Young Men in Their Jaunty Jalopies (1969)

Quella Villa Accanto Al Cimitero *See* The House by the Cemetery (1983)

Quelqu' Un Derriere la Porte *See* Someone Behind the Door (1971)

Quemimada! *See* Burn! (1970)

The Quest *See* The Longest Drive (1976)

Qui Ju Da Guansi *See* The Story of Qui Ju (1991)

Quien Sabe? *See* A Bullet for the General (1968)

A Quiet Little Neighborhood, A Perfect Little Murder *See* A Perfect Little Murder (1990)

A Quiet Place to Kill *See* Paranoia (1969)

Quoi De Neuf, Pussycat? *See* What's New Pussycat? (1965)

Race for the Yankee Zephyr *See* Treasure of the Yankee Zephyr (1983)

The Radical *See* Katherine (1975)

Radio Ranch *See* The Phantom Empire (1935)

Radon *See* Rodan (1956)

Radon the Flying Monster *See* Rodan (1956)

Rafferty and the Highway Hustlers *See* Rafferty & the Gold Dust Twins (1975)

Rage *See* Rabid (1977)

Rage of the Buccaneers *See* The Black Pirate (1926)

Ragewar *See* Dungeonmaster (1983)

Ragged Angels *See* They Shall Have Music (1939)

The Raging Moon *See* Long Ago Tomorrow (1971)

Raging Waters *See* The Green Promise (1949)

Rags to Riches *See* Callie and Son (1981)

Raiders of the Doomed Kingdom *See* After the Fall of Saigon (1988)

Rainbow on the River *See* It Happened in New Orleans (1936)

Raise Ravens *See* Cria (1976)

Ramblin' Man *See* The Concrete Cowboys (1979)

Ramrodders *See* The Ramrodder (1969)

The Ranger, the Cook and a Hole in the Sky *See* Hole in the Sky (1995)

Ransom *See* Maniac (1977)

Rape of Innocence *See* Dupont Lajoie (1974)

The Rape of Richard Beck *See* Broken Badge (1985)

Rape Squad *See* Act of Vengeance (1974)

Rasputin: The Mad Monk *See* Rasputin and the Empress (1933)

The Rats *See* Deadly Eyes (1982)

The Raven *See* Le Corbeau (1943)

RE: Lucky Luciano *See* Lucky Luciano (1974)

The Reader *See* La Lectrice (1988)

The Rebel *See* The Bushwackers (1952)

Rebel of the Road *See* Hot Rod (1979)

Rebel with a Cause *See* The Loneliness of the Long Distance Runner (1962)

Rece do Gory *See* Hands Up (1981)

Record of a Living Being *See* I Live in Fear (1955)

Red *See* Trois Couleurs: Rouge (1994)

Red Dragon *See* Code Name Alpha (1967)

Red Dragon *See* Manhunter (1986)

The Red Hangman *See* The Bloody Pit of Horror (1965)

The Red Head *See* Poil de Carotte (1931)

Red Hot Tires *See* Racing Luck (1935)

Red Hot Wheels *See* To Please a Lady (1950)

Red-Light District *See* Street of Shame (1956)

Red on Red *See* Scarred (1984)

The Red Tide *See* Blood Tide (1982)

Redheads *See* Desperate Prey (1994)

Redneck County *See* Hootch Country Boys (1975)

Reflections on a Crime *See* Reflections in the Dark (1994)

The Refugee *See* Three Faces West (1940)

Rehearsal for a Crime *See* The Criminal Life of Archibaldo de la Cruz (1955)

Rejuvenatrix *See* The Rejuvenator (1988)

Rekopis Znaleziony W Saragossie *See* The Saragossa Manuscript (1965)

The Remarkable Mr. Kipps *See* Kipps (1941)

Remembrance of Love *See* Holocaust Survivors...Remembrance of Love (1983)

Remorques *See* Stormy Waters (1941)

Renegade Girls *See* Caged Heat (1974)

Renfrew of the Royal Mounted on the Great White Trail *See* Renfrew on the Great White Trail (1938)

Reprieved *See* Sing Sing Nights (1935)

Requiem fur Dominic *See* Requiem for Dominic (1991)

The Rescue *See* Let's Get Harry (1987)

The Resurrection Syndicate *See* Nothing But the Night (1972)

Retaliator *See* Programmed to Kill (1986)

Retik, the Moon Menace *See* Radar Men from the Moon (1952)

Return from the Past *See* Alien Massacre (1967)

The Return of Captain America *See* Captain America (1944)

The Return of Maxwell Smart *See* The Nude Bomb (1980)

The Return of Mr. H. *See* They Saved Hitler's Brain (1964)

Return of the Blind Dead *See* Return of the Evil Dead (1975)

The Return of the Giant Monsters *See* Gamera vs. Gaos (1967)

Return of the Living Dead *See* Messiah of Evil (1974)

Return of the Magnificent Seven *See* Return of the Seven (1966)

Return of the Zombies *See* The Hanging Woman (1972)

Reunion *See* Reunion in France (1942)

Revenge *See* Blood Feud (1979)

The Revenge of Dracula *See* Dracula vs. Frankenstein (1971)

The Revenge of Milady *See* The Four Musketeers (1975)

The Revenge of the Blood Beast *See* The She-Beast (1965)

Revenge of the Dead *See* Night of the Ghouls (1959)

Revenge of the Innocents *See* South Bronx Heroes (1985)

Revenge of the Living Dead *See* Children Shouldn't Play with Dead Things (1972)

Revenge of the Screaming Dead *See* Messiah of Evil (1974)

Revenge Squad *See* Hit & Run (1982)

Rhodes of Africa *See* Rhodes (1936)

Rhosyn A Rhith *See* Coming Up Roses (1987)

Rhythm on the Ranch *See* Rootin' Tootin' Rhythm (1938)

Rice, Beans and Ketchup *See* Manhattan Merenque! (1995)

Rich, Young, and Deadly *See* Platinum High School (1960)

Riches and Romance *See* Amazing Adventure (1937)

The Richest Man in the World: The Story of Aristotle Onassis *See* Onassis (1988)

Richie *See* The Death of Richie (1976)

Rickshaw Man *See* Rikisha-Man (1958)

Ride a Dark Horse *See* Man & Boy (1971)

Riders *See* Guerilla Brigade (1939)

Riffraff *See* Riff Raff (1935)

The Right Man *See* Her First Romance (1940)

Ripped Off *See* Counter Punch (1971)

Risate de Gioia *See* Passionate Thief (1960)

The Rise of Catherine the Great *See* Catherine the Great (1934)

The Rise of Helga *See* Susan Lenox: Her Fall and Rise (1931)

Rising to Fame *See* Susan Lenox: Her Fall and Rise (1931)

Riso Amaro *See* Bitter Rice (1949)

Riten *See* The Rite (1969)

Rites of Summer *See* White Water Summer (1987)

The Ritual *See* The Rite (1969)

Ritual Dos Sadicos *See* Awakenings of the Beast (1968)

Ritual of the Maniacs *See* Awakenings of the Beast (1968)

The Road *See* La Strada (1954)

Road to Avonlea *See* Tales from Avonlea, Vol. 1: The Journey Begins (1990)

The Road to Frisco *See* They Drive by Night (1940)

Roaring Timber *See* Come and Get It (1936)

Rob Roy *See* Rob Roy—The Highland Rogue (1953)

Robert A. Heinlein's The Puppet Masters *See* The Puppet Masters (1994)

Robinson Crusoeland *See* Utopia (1951)

Rocco et Ses Freres *See* Rocco and His Brothers (1960)

Rocket to the Moon *See* Cat Women of the Moon (1953)

Rocky Mountain Mystery *See* The Fighting Westerner (1935)

Senior Trip *See* National Lampoon's Senior Trip (1995)

Sensations *See* Sensations of 1945 (1944)

Sensuous Vampires *See* The Vampire Hookers (1978)

Separate Beds *See* The Wheeler Dealers (1963)

Sept Fois Femme *See* Woman Times Seven (1967)

Sergeant Steiner *See* Breakthrough (1978)

The Serpent *See* Night Flight from Moscow (1973)

Seryozha *See* A Summer to Remember (1961)

Sette Volte Donna *See* Woman Times Seven (1967)

Seven Bad Men *See* Rage at Dawn (1955)

Seven Different Ways *See* Quick, Let's Get Married (1971)

Seven Graves for Rogan *See* Time to Die (1983)

Seven Sisters *See* The House on Sorority Row (1983)

Seven Waves Away *See* Abandon Ship (1957)

The Sex of the Stars *See* Le Sexe des Etoiles (1993)

Sex Play *See* Games Girls Play (1975)

The Sex Racketeers *See* Man of Violence (1971)

The Shadow Versus the Thousand Eyes of Dr. Mabuse *See* The Thousand Eyes of Dr. Mabuse (1960)

The Shadow Warrior *See* Kagemusha (1980)

Shadows in an Empty Room *See* Strange Shadows in an Empty Room (1976)

Shadows of Our Ancestors *See* Shadows of Forgotten Ancestors (1964)

Shadows of Our Forgotten Ancestors *See* Shadows of Forgotten Ancestors (1964)

Shadows of the Peacock *See* Echoes of Paradise (1986)

Shalimar *See* Deadly Thief (1978)

Shame of the Sabine Women *See* The Rape of the Sabines (1961)

Shark Reef *See* She Gods of Shark Reef (1956)

Shatter *See* Call Him Mr. Shatter (1974)

Shatterhand *See* Apaches Last Battle (1964)

She Demons of the Swamp *See* Attack of the Giant Leeches (1959)

She Devil *See* Drums O'Voodoo (1934)

She Drives Me Crazy *See* Friends, Lovers & Lunatics (1989)

She Got What She Asked For *See* Yesterday, Today and Tomorrow (1964)

She Knew No Other Way *See* Last Resort (1986)

She Monster of the Night *See* Frankenstein's Daughter (1958)

She Shoulda Said No *See* Wild Weed (1949)

Sheba *See* The Graveyard (1974)

She'll Be Sweet *See* Magee and the Lady (1978)

Shenanigans *See* Great Bank Hoax (1978)

Sheriff of Wichita *See* Western Double Feature 4: Rogers & Evans (194?)

Sherlock Holmes *See* The Adventures of Sherlock Holmes (1939)

Sherlock Holmes and the Prince of Crime *See* Hands of a Murderer (1990)

Sherlock Holmes and the Scarlet Claw *See* Scarlet Claw (1944)

Sherlock Holmes and the Spider Woman *See* Spider Woman (1944)

Sherlock Holmes and the Woman in Green *See* The Woman in Green (1945)

Sherlock Holmes Grosster Fall *See* A Study in Terror (1966)

Sherlock Holmes in The Hound of London *See* The Hound of London (1993)

Sherlock Holmes Und Das Halsband des Todes *See* Sherlock Holmes and the Deadly Necklace (1962)

She's De Lovely *See* She's So Lovely (1997)

Shichinin No Samurai *See* Seven Samurai (1954)

Shinju Ten No Amijima *See* Double Suicide (1969)

The Ship was Loaded *See* Carry On Admiral (1957)

Shivers *See* They Came from Within (1975)

Shizuka Naru Ketto *See* A Quiet Duel (1949)

Shock *See* Beyond the Door 2 (1979)

Shocked *See* Mesmerized (1984)

Shockwave *See* The Arrival (1996)

Shogun Island *See* Raw Force (1981)

Shoot the Pianist *See* Shoot the Piano Player (1962)

The Shooter *See* Hidden Assassin (1994)

The Shop on High Street *See* The Shop on Main Street (1965)

Shuban *See* Scandal (1950)

The Shuttered Room *See* Blood Island (1968)

Sidney Sheldon's Windmills of the Gods *See* Windmills of the Gods (1988)

Siegfried's Death *See* Siegfried (1924)

Siegfrieds Tod *See* Siegfried (1924)

Signe Charlotte *See* Sincerely Charlotte (1986)

Significant Other *See* When a Man Loves a Woman (1994)

The Silence of the Sea *See* La Silence de la Mer (1947)

A Silent Duel *See* A Quiet Duel (1949)

The Silent Flute *See* Circle of Iron (1978)

Silent Night, Evil Night *See* Black Christmas (1975)

Silken Skin *See* The Soft Skin (1964)

Silver Blaze *See* Murder at the Baskervilles (1937)

The Silver Brumby *See* The Silver Stallion: King of the Wild Brumbies (1993)

Silver Devil *See* Wild Horse (1931)

The Sin *See* The Shaming (1971)

Sinai Commandos: The Story of the Six Day War *See* Sinai Commandos (1968)

The Singing Musketeer *See* The Three Musketeers (1939)

Sinister House *See* Who Killed Doc Robbin? (1948)

Sista Dansen *See* The Last Dance (1993)

Sisters *See* Some Girls (1988)

Sitting Bull's History Lesson *See* Buffalo Bill & the Indians (1976)

The Sixth of June *See* D-Day, the Sixth of June (1956)

Sizzle Beach U.S.A. *See* Malibu Hot Summer (1974)

Skate! *See* Blades of Courage (1988)

Ski Lift to Death *See* Snowblind (1978)

Skipper *See* The Todd Killings (1971)

Skyggen af Emma *See* Emma's Shadow (1988)

The Slammer *See* Short Eyes (1979)

The Slasher *See* Cosh Boy (1961)

Slasher in the House *See* Home Sweet Home (1980)

The Slaughterers *See* Invasion of the Flesh Hunters (1982)

Slave Girls *See* Prehistoric Women (1950)

Slaves of the Invisible Monster *See* The Invisible Monster (1950)

Slay It Again, Sam *See* Codename: Foxfire (1985)

Slip Slide Adventures *See* Water Babies (1979)

Small Town Massacre *See* Strange Behavior (1981)

Smart Alec *See* Movie Maker (1986)

Smokey and the Bandit Ride Again *See* Smokey and the Bandit, Part 2 (1980)

Smorgasbord *See* Cracking Up (1983)

Smultron-Stallet *See* Wild Strawberries (1957)

Snake Eyes *See* Dangerous Game (1993)

Snow White and the Three Clowns *See* Snow White and the Three Stooges (1961)

Snuffy Smith *See* Snuffy Smith, Yard Bird (1942)

So Evil, My Sister *See* The Sibling (1972)

Sodome et Gomorrhe *See* Sodom and Gomorrah (1962)

Soldier Duroc *See* Soldat Duroc...Ca Va Etre Ta Fete! (196?)

Soldier in Skirts *See* Triple Echo (1977)

The Soldier Who Declared Peace *See* Tribes (1970)

The Soldiers *See* Les Carabiniers (1963)

Solomon Northrup's Odyssey *See* Half Slave, Half Free (1985)

Sombra, the Spider Woman *See* The Black Widow (1947)

Some Like It Cool *See* Sex on the Run (1978)

Someone is Killing the Great Chefs of Europe *See* Who Is Killing the Great Chefs of Europe? (1978)

Someone's Killing the World's Greatest Models *See* She's Dressed to Kill (1979)

Something Fishy *See* Pas Tres Catholique (1993)

Something is Out There *See* Day of the Animals (1977)

Something Like the Truth *See* The Offence (1973)

Something to Hide *See* Shattered (1972)

Something Waits in the Dark *See* Screamers (1980)

Somewhere in France *See* The Foreman Went to France (1942)

Sommarlek *See* Summer Interlude (1950)

Sommarnattens Leende *See* Smiles of a Summer Night (1955)

Son of My Life *See* Hijazo de Mi Vidaza (197?)

The Song of the Road *See* Pather Panchali (1954)

Song of the Sierra *See* Springtime in the Sierras (1947)

Sons and Warriors *See* Some Mother's Son (1996)

Sons of the Legion *See* Sons of the Desert (1933)

Super Dragon *See* Secret Agent Super Dragon (1966)

Super Fly T.N.T. *See* Superfly T.N.T. (1973)

The Super Inframan *See* Infra-Man (1976)

Superargo the Giant *See* Superargo (1967)

Superfantagenio *See* Aladdin (1986)

Superman and the Strange People *See* Superman & the Mole Men (1951)

Supersnooper *See* Super Fuzz (1981)

Surf 2: The End of the Trilogy *See* Surf 2 (1984)

Surf Warriors *See* Surf Ninjas (1993)

Suspected Alibi *See* Suspended Alibi (1956)

Swamp Diamonds *See* Swamp Women (1955)

Sweeney Todd: The Demon Barber of Fleet Street *See* Demon Barber of Fleet Street (1936)

Sweet Candy *See* Candy Stripe Nurses (1974)

Sweet Dirty Tony *See* The Mercenaries (1980)

Sweet Kill *See* The Arousers (1970)

Sweet Revenge *See* Code of Honor (1984)

Sweet Smell of Woman *See* The Scent of a Woman (1975)

Sweet Violence *See* Sweet Ecstasy (1962)

Sweetheart! *See* Canada's Sweetheart: The Saga of Hal C. Banks (1985)

Swept Away...By an Unusual Destiny in the Blue Sea of August *See* Swept Away... (1975)

Swing it Buddy *See* Swing It, Professor (1937)

Swing, Teacher, Swing *See* College Swing (1938)

Switchboard Operator *See* The Love Affair, or The Case of the Missing Switchboard Operator (1967)

Swordkill *See* Ghostwarrior (1986)

Swords of Blood *See* Cartouche (1962)

Sylvia and the Ghost *See* Sylvia and the Phantom (1945)

Sylvia Kristel's Beauty School *See* Beauty School (1993)

Symphony of Love *See* Ecstasy (1933)

Szegenylegenyek Nehezeletuck *See* The Round Up (1966)

T & A Academy *See* H.O.T.S. (1979)

T & A Academy 2 *See* Gimme an F (1985)

Tacones Lejanos *See* High Heels (1991)

Tainted Money *See* Show Them No Mercy (1935)

A Tale of Africa *See* Green Horizon (1983)

Tale of the Cock *See* Confessions of Tom Harris (1972)

A Talent for Loving *See* Gun Crazy (1969)

Tales from the Crypt II *See* Vault of Horror (1973)

Tales of the City *See* Armistead Maupin's Tales of the City (1993)

Ta'm e Guilass *See* The Taste of the Cherry (1996)

Tangled Trails *See* Sands of Sacrifice (1921)

Tanner: A Political Fable *See* Tanner '88 (1988)

Target: Embassy *See* Embassy (1972)

Target in the Sun *See* The Man Who Would Not Die (1975)

Target of an Assassin *See* African Rage (1978)

Tartu *See* The Adventures of Tartu (1943)

Taste of Cherries *See* The Taste of the Cherry (1996)

Taste of Fear *See* Scream of Fear (1961)

Tears in Florence *See* Traenen in Florenz (1984)

Teen Kanya *See* Two Daughters (1961)

Teenage Monster *See* Meteor Monster (1957)

The Teenage Psycho Meets Bloody Mary *See* Incredibly Strange Creatures Who Stopped Living and Became Mixed-Up Zombies (1963)

Tell It To the Marines *See* Here Come the Marines (1952)

Tell Your Children *See* Reefer Madness (1938)

Tema *See* The Theme (1979)

Tempo di Uccidere *See* Time to Kill (1989)

Tender Love *See* L'Amour en Herbe (1977)

The Tenderfoot *See* Bushwhacked (1995)

Tenderfoots *See* Bushwhacked (1995)

Tendre Poulet *See* Dear Detective (1977)

Tenebrae *See* Unsane (1982)

Tengoku To Jigoku *See* High & Low (1962)

Tenue de Soiree *See* Menage (1986)

Terminal Station Indiscretion *See* Indiscretion of an American Wife (1954)

Terminus Station *See* Indiscretion of an American Wife (1954)

Terra em Transe *See* Earth Entranced (1966)

Terreur dans l'Espace *See* Planet of the Vampires (1965)

Terror Castle *See* The Virgin of Nuremberg (1965)

Terror Eyes *See* Night School (1981)

Terror From the Sun *See* Hideous Sun Demon (1959)

Terror Hospital *See* Hospital of Terror (1978)

Terror House *See* The Night Has Eyes (1942)

Terror House *See* Terror at Red Wolf Inn (1972)

Terror in Space *See* Planet of the Vampires (1965)

Terror in the Midnight Sun *See* Invasion of the Animal People (1962)

Terror of Sheba *See* The Graveyard (1974)

The Terror Strikes *See* The War of the Colossal Beast (1958)

Terror under the House *See* Revenge (1971)

The Testament of Dr. Mabuse *See* Das Testament des Dr. Mabuse (1933)

Texas Desperadoes *See* Drift Fence (1936)

Texas in Flames *See* She Came to the Valley (1977)

Texas Road Agent *See* Road Agent (1926)

Texas Serenade *See* Old Corral (1936)

Teyve der Milkhiker *See* Tevye (1939)

That Man Mr. Jones *See* The Fuller Brush Man (1948)

That They May Live *See* J'Accuse (1937)

That's the Way of the World *See* Shining Star (1975)

Therese Und Isabell *See* Therese & Isabelle (1968)

These Dangerous Years *See* Dangerous Youth (1958)

These Foolish Things *See* Daddy Nostalgia (1990)

They *See* They Watch (1993)

They Call Me Hallelujah *See* Guns for Dollars (1973)

They Don't Wear Pajamas at Rosie's *See* The First Time (1969)

They Loved Life *See* Kanal (1956)

They Made Me a Fugitive *See* They Made Me a Criminal (1939)

They Passed This Way *See* Four Faces West (1948)

They're Coming to Get You *See* Dracula vs. Frankenstein (1971)

Thieves *See* Les Voleurs (1996)

Thin Air *See* Invasion of the Body Stealers (1969)

The Thing From Another World *See* The Thing (1951)

Thinner *See* Stephen King's Thinner (1996)

Thirst *See* Three Strange Loves (1949)

The Thirteen Chairs *See* 12 Plus 1 (1970)

The Thirty-Sixth Chamber *See* Master Killer (1984)

This Strange Passion *See* El (1952)

Thomas Crown and Company *See* The Thomas Crown Affair (1968)

Thoroughbred *See* Run for the Roses (1978)

Those Were the Happy Times *See* Star! (1968)

Thou Shall Not Kill *See* Avenging Conscience (1914)

Thou Shalt Honour Thy Wife *See* Master of the House (1925)

Three Bad Men in the Hidden Fortress *See* The Hidden Fortress (1958)

Three Colors: Blue *See* Trois Couleurs: Bleu (1993)

Three Colors: Red *See* Trois Couleurs: Rouge (1994)

Three Colors: White *See* Trois Couleurs: Blanc (1994)

Three Crazy Legionnaires *See* Three Legionnaires (1937)

Three For the Money *See* Win, Place, or Steal (1972)

Three Rascals in the Hidden Fortress *See* The Hidden Fortress (1958)

Three Steps to the Gallows *See* White Fire (1953)

The Three Stooges Go Around the World in a Daze *See* Around the World in a Daze (1963)

The Threepenny Opera *See* Mack the Knife (1989)

Through the Looking Glass *See* The Velvet Vampire (1971)

Thunder *See* Thunder Warrior (1985)

Thunder Mountain *See* Shadow of Chikara (1977)

Thunder on the Trail *See* Thundering Trail (1951)

Thursday the 12th *See* Pandemonium (1982)

Tianguo Niezi *See* The Day the Sun Turned Cold (1994)

Tidal Wave *See* Portrait of Jennie (1948)

The Tiger *See* Tiger Warsaw (1987)

Tiger in the Sky *See* The McConnell Story (1955)

Tiger of Bengal *See* Journey to the Lost City (1958)

The Tiger Woman *See* Perils of the Darkest Jungle (1944)

Tigers Don't Cry *See* African Rage (1978)

Tight Little Island *See* Whiskey Galore (1948)

'Til Christmas *See* Breathing Room (1996)

Til Dawn Do Us Part *See* Dressed for Death (1974)

Tim Burton's The Nightmare Before Christmas *See* The Nightmare Before Christmas (1993)

Timber Tramps *See* The Big Push (1975)

Time Flyers *See* The Blue Yonder (1986)

A Time For Caring *See* Generation (1969)

The Time of Return *See* Muriel (1963)

Time of the Beast *See* Mutator (1990)

Time Raiders *See* Warriors of the Apocalypse (1985)

Time Trap *See* The Time Travelers (1964)

Time Warp Terror *See* Bloody New Year (1987)

Timeslip *See* The Atomic Man (1956)

Timewarp *See* Day Time Ended (1980)

Tini Zabutykh Predkiv *See* Shadows of Forgotten Ancestors (1964)

Tintorera *See* Tintorera...Tiger Shark (1978)

Tintorera...Bloody Waters *See* Tintorera...Tiger Shark (1978)

Tirez sur le Pianiste *See* Shoot the Piano Player (1962)

Titan Find *See* Creature (1985)

To Be a Man *See* Cry of Battle (1963)

To Catch a Spy *See* Catch Me a Spy (1971)

To Die For *See* Heaven's a Drag (1994)

To Elvis, With Love *See* Touched by Love (1980)

To Have and to Hold *See* When a Man Loves a Woman (1994)

To Live *See* Ikiru (1952)

To Love a Vampire *See* Lust for a Vampire (1971)

To Vlemma Tou Odyssea *See* Ulysses' Gaze (1995)

Today We Live *See* The Day and the Hour (1963)

A Toi De Faire *See* Your Turn Darling (1963)

Tomb of the Cat *See* Tomb of Ligeia (1964)

Tomb of the Living Dead *See* Mad Doctor of Blood Island (1969)

The Tommyknockers *See* Stephen King's The Tommyknockers (1993)

The Tomorrow Man *See* 984: Prisoner of the Future (1984)

Ton Kero Ton Hellinon *See* When the Greeks (1981)

Tong Nien Wang Shi *See* A Time to Live and a Time to Die (1985)

Too Many Chefs *See* Who Is Killing the Great Chefs of Europe? (1978)

Topio Stin Omichli *See* Landscape in the Mist (1988)

Torment *See* L'Enfer (1993)

Torture Zone *See* The Fear Chamber (1968)

Toto the Hero *See* Toto le Heros (1991)

The Touch of Melissa *See* The Touch of Satan (1970)

Touchez Pas Au Grisbi *See* Grisbi (1953)

Tower of Terror *See* Assault (1970)

Tower of Terror *See* Hard to Die (1990)

A Town Called Bastard *See* A Town Called Hell (1972)

The Town That Cried Terror *See* Maniac (1977)

T.R. Sloane *See* Death Ray 2000 (1981)

Trackers *See* Space Rage (1986)

Trail of the Royal Mounted *See* Mystery Trooper (1932)

Train of Terror *See* Terror Train (1980)

Train 2419 *See* The Return of Casey Jones (1934)

Traitement de Choc *See* Shock Treatment (1981)

Trancers *See* Future Cop (1976)

Transport Z Raje *See* Transport from Paradise (1965)

The Transvestite *See* Glen or Glenda: Confessions of Ed Wood (1953)

Tras el Cristal *See* In a Glass Cage (1986)

Trauma *See* Dario Argento's Trauma (1993)

Travels with Anita *See* Lovers and Liars (1981)

The Tree of Hands *See* Innocent Victim (1990)

Tree of Liberty *See* The Howards of Virginia (1940)

Trial by Combat *See* Choice of Weapons (1976)

Trick of the Eye *See* Primal Secrets (1994)

Trigger, Jr. *See* Western Double Feature 6: Rogers & Trigger (1950)

A Trip with Anita *See* Lovers and Liars (1981)

Triple Trouble *See* Kentucky Kernels (1934)

Tristan and Isolde *See* Lovespell (1979)

Trois Hommes et un Couffin *See* Three Men and a Cradle (1985)

The Trollenberg Terror *See* The Crawling Eye (1958)

Tromba *See* Tromba, the Tiger Man (1952)

Trop Belle Pour Toi *See* Too Beautiful for You (1988)

Trop Jolie pour Etre Honette *See* Too Pretty to Be Honest (1972)

Tropicana *See* The Heat's On (1943)

Trottie True *See* The Gay Lady (1949)

Trouble at 16 *See* Platinum High School (1960)

Trouble Chaser *See* Li'l Abner (1940)

The Trout *See* La Truite (1983)

Truman Capote's A Christmas Memory *See* ABC Stage 67: Truman Capote's A Christmas Memory (1966)

Truman Capote's The Glass House *See* The Glass House (1972)

Try and Find It *See* Hi Diddle Diddle (1943)

Tsarskaya Nevesta *See* The Tsar's Bride (1966)

Tsubaki Sanjuro *See* Sanjuro (1962)

Tsvet Granata *See* The Color of Pomegranates (1969)

Tudor Rose *See* Nine Days a Queen (1936)

Tueur de Ch Icago *See* Scarface Mob (1962)

Tulitkkutehtaan Tytto *See* The Match Factory Girl (1990)

The Tunnel *See* Transatlantic Tunnel (1935)

Turkey Shoot *See* Escape 2000 (1981)

Turn Your Pony Around *See* Mortal Danger (1994)

Turtle Beach *See* The Killing Beach (1992)

Twelve Miles Out *See* Second Woman (1951)

Twenty-One Days Together *See* 21 Days (1937)

Twice Bitten *See* The Vampire Hookers (1978)

Twilight of the Dead *See* Gates of Hell (1983)

Twinkle, Twinkle, Killer Kane *See* The Ninth Configuration (1979)

Twinky *See* Lola (1969)

Twisted *See* Medusa (1974)

The Twisted Road *See* They Live by Night (1949)

2 Cries in the Night *See* Funeral Home (1982)

Two Guys Talkin' About Girls *See* At First Sight (1995)

Two Minds for Murder *See* Someone Behind the Door (1971)

2002: The Rape of Eden *See* Bounty Hunter 2002 (1994)

Two Weeks in September *See* A Coeur Joie (1967)

Tystnaden *See* The Silence (1963)

U-238 and the Witch Doctor *See* Jungle Drums of Africa (1953)

Uccellacci e Uccellini *See* The Hawks & the Sparrows (1967)

Uccidero Un Uomo *See* This Man Must Die (1970)

Uchu Daikaiiju Dogora *See* Dagora, the Space Monster (1965)

Uchudai Dogora *See* Dagora, the Space Monster (1965)

Uchujin Tokyo Ni Arawaru *See* Warning from Space (1956)

Ugetsu Monogatari *See* Ugetsu (1953)

Ukigusa *See* Drifting Weeds (1959)

Ulisse *See* Ulysses (1955)

The Ultimate Chase *See* The Ultimate Thrill (1974)

Ultimate Desires *See* Beyond the Silhouette (1990)

The Ultimate Solution of Grace Quigley *See* Grace Quigley (1984)

Ultimi Giorni di Pompeii *See* The Last Days of Pompeii (1960)

The Umbrella Woman *See* The Good Wife (1986)

Un Amour De Swann *See* Swann in Love (1984)

Un Amour En Allemagne *See* A Love in Germany (1984)

Un Angelo e Sceso a Brooklyn *See* The Man Who Wagged His Tail (1957)

Un Arma de Dos Filos *See* Shark! (1968)

Un Autre Homme, Une Autre Chance *See* Another Man, Another Chance (1977)

Un Chapeau de Paille d'Italie *See* Italian Straw Hat (1927)

Un Complicato Intrigo Di Donne, Vicoli E Delitti *See* Camorra: The Naples Connection (1985)

Un Condamne a Mort s'est Echappe *See* A Man Escaped (1957)

Un, Deux, Trois, Quatre! *See* Black Tights (1960)

Un Dimanche a la Campagne *See* A Sunday in the Country (1984)

Un Divan a New York *See* A Couch in New York (1995)

Un Elephant a Trompe Enormement *See* Pardon Mon Affaire (1976)

Un Grand Amour de Beethoven *See* Beethoven (1936)

Un Homme Amoureux *See* A Man in Love (1987)

Un Homme Est Mort *See* The Outside Man (1973)

Un Homme et Un Femme *See* A Man and a Woman (1966)

Un Homme Et Une Femme: Vingt Ans Deja *See* A Man and a Woman: 20 Years Later (1986)

Un Indien dans la Ville *See* Little Indian, Big City (1995)

Un Minuto Per Pregare, Un Istante Per Morire
See A Minute to Pray, A Second to Die (1967)

Un Senor Muy Viejo Con Unas Alas Enormes
See A Very Old Man with Enormous Wings (1988)

Un Trem Para as Estrelas See Subway to the Stars (1987)

Un Uomo da Rispettare See Master Touch (1974)

Un Week-end sur Deux See Every Other Weekend (1991)

Un Zoo, La Nuit See Night Zoo (1987)

Una Bruja Sin Escoba See A Witch Without a Broom (1968)

Una Giornata Speciale See A Special Day (1977)

Una Hacka Para la Luna de Miel See Hatchet for the Honeymoon (1970)

Una Pura Formalita See A Pure Formality (1994)

Una Ragione Per Vivere e Una Per Morire See A Reason to Live, A Reason to Die (1973)

Una Sombra Ya Pronto Seras See A Shadow You Soon Will Be (1994)

Unagi See The Eel (1996)

Unakrsna Vatra See Operation Cross Eagles (1969)

Uncle Harry See The Strange Affair of Uncle Harry (1945)

Uncle Silas See Inheritance (1947)

Unconventional Linda See Holiday (1938)

Under California Skies See Under California Stars (1948)

Under the Clock See The Clock (1945)

Under the Olive Trees See Through the Olive Trees (1994)

Under the Sun of Satan See Under Satan's Sun (1987)

Underground See The Lower Depths (1936)

An Underwater Odyssey See Neptune Factor (1973)

Underworld See Transmutations (1985)

Underworld After Dark See Big Town After Dark (1947)

Une Affaire de Femmes See The Story of Women (1988)

Une Femme a sa Fentre See A Woman at Her Window (1977)

Une Femme Douce See A Gentle Woman (1969)

Une Femme Est Une Femme See A Woman is a Woman (1960)

Une Femme ou Deux See One Woman or Two (1985)

Une Histoire Simple See A Simple Story (1979)

Une Partie de Campagne See A Day in the Country (1946)

Une Pure Formalite See A Pure Formality (1994)

Unknown Satellite Over Tokyo See Warning from Space (1956)

Untel Pere et Fils See Heart of a Nation (1943)

The Unvanquished See Aparajito (1958)

Uomo Dalla Pelle Dura See Counter Punch (1971)

L'Uomo delle Stelle See The Star Maker (1995)

Up in the Cellar See Three in the Cellar (1970)

Up the Chastity Belt See Naughty Knights (1971)

Up to a Point See Up to a Certain Point (1983)

The Upstate Murders See Savage Weekend (1980)

Urga See Close to Eden (1990)

Ursus See Ursus in the Valley of the Lions (1962)

The Usual Unidentified Thieves See Big Deal on Madonna Street (1958)

Utamaro O Meguru Gonin No Onna See Utamaro and His Five Women (1946)

Utvandrarna See The Emigrants (1972)

Vacation See National Lampoon's Vacation (1983)

Vagabond Violinist See Broken Melody (1934)

Vaghe Stelle Dell'Orsa See Sandra of a Thousand Delights (1965)

Valborgmassoafton See Walpurgis Night (1941)

The Valdez Horses See Chino (1975)

Valdez the Half Breed See Chino (1975)

Valley of Fear See Sherlock Holmes and the Deadly Necklace (1962)

Valley of the Swords See The Castilian (1963)

The Vampire See Vampyr (1931)

The Vampire and the Robot See My Son, the Vampire (1952)

The Vampire-Beast Craves Blood See Blood Beast Terror (1967)

Vampire Men of the Lost Planet See Horror of the Blood Monsters (1970)

Vampire Over London See My Son, the Vampire (1952)

The Vampire's Niece See Fangs of the Living Dead (1968)

Vampire's Night Orgy See Orgy of the Vampires (1973)

Vampyr, Der Traum des David Gray See Vampyr (1931)

Vampyr, Ou L'Etrange Aventure de David Gray See Vampyr (1931)

Vampyres, Daughters of Dracula See Vampyres (1974)

The Varrow Mission See Teen Alien (1988)

Vasectomy See Vasectomy: A Delicate Matter (1986)

The Veil See Haunts (1977)

Velvet House See Crucible of Horror (1969)

Vendetta: Secrets of a Mafia Bride See A Family Matter (1991)

Vengeance See The Brain (1962)

Vengeance: The Story of Tony Cimo See Vengeance (1989)

Venus in Peltz See Venus in Furs (1970)

The Venusian See The Stranger from Venus (1954)

Vesnicko Ma Strediskova See My Sweet Little Village (1986)

Vessel of Wrath See Beachcomber (1938)

The Veteran See Deathdream (1972)

The Vicious Circle See Woman in Brown (1948)

Victims of the Beyond See Sucker Money (1934)

Vindicator See Wheels of Fire (1984)

Violence et Passion See Conversation Piece (1975)

Violent Journey See The Fool Killer (1965)

Violent Midnight See Psychomania (1963)

Violent Rage See Fearmaker (1989)

Violent Streets See Thief (1981)

Violette Noziere See Violette (1978)

Virgin Hunters See Test Tube Teens from the Year 2000 (1993)

The Virtuous Tramps See The Devil's Brother (1933)

Virus See Invasion of the Flesh Hunters (1982)

Viskingar Och Rop See Cries and Whispers (1972)

Vita Privata See A Very Private Affair (1962)

Vitelloni See I Vitelloni (1953)

Vivement Dimanche! See Confidentially Yours (1983)

Viviamo Oggi See The Day and the Hour (1963)

Vivre Savie See My Life to Live (1962)

Vogues See Vogues of 1938 (1937)

Voodoo Blood Bath See I Eat Your Skin (1964)

Vortex See Day Time Ended (1980)

Voyage Beyond the Sun See Space Monster (1964)

Voyage to a Prehistoric Planet See Voyage to the Prehistoric Planet (1965)

Vrazda Po Cesky See Murder Czech Style (1966)

Vredens Dag See Day of Wrath (1943)

Vulcan, Son of Jupiter See Vulcan God of Fire (1962)

Vzlomschik See Burglar (1987)

Wages of Fear See Sorcerer (1977)

Waiting Women See Secrets of Women (1952)

Waldo Warren: Private Dick Without a Brain See Maximum Thrust (1988)

The Wandering Kid See Urotsukidoj 1: Legend of the Overfiend (1993)

Wannseekonferenz See The Wannsee Conference (1984)

Want a Ride, Little Girl? See Impulse (1974)

Wanted Women See Jessie's Girls (1975)

The Wanton Contessa See Senso (1954)

War Between the Planets See Planet on the Prowl (1965)

War Games See Suppose They Gave a War and Nobody Came? (1970)

The War of the Monsters See Gamera vs. Barugon (1966)

War of the Planets See Cosmos: War of the Planets (1980)

War Shock See Battle Shock (1956)

Ward 13 See Hospital Massacre (1981)

Warlock See Skullduggery (1979)

The Warm-Blooded Spy See Ravishing Idiot (1964)

Warnung Vor Einer Helligen Nutte See Beware of a Holy Whore (1970)

Warrior's Rest See Le Repos du Guerrier (1962)

Warum Lauft Herr R Amok? See Why Does Herr R. Run Amok? (1969)

Washington, B.C. See Hail (1973)

Water Child See L'Enfant d'Eau (1995)

Water Cyborgs See Terror Beneath the Sea (1966)

The Watts Monster See Dr. Black, Mr. Hyde (1976)

The Way Ahead See Immortal Battalion (1944)

The Way of Life See They Call It Sin (1932)

Ways of Love See The Miracle (1948)

We Will All Meet in Paradise See Pardon Mon Affaire, Too! (1977)

Wedding Bells See Royal Wedding (1951)

Wedding Breakfast *See* The Catered Affair (1956)

Wednesday's Child *See* Family Life (1971)

Weekend Babysitter *See* Weekend with the Babysitter (1970)

Welcome Home Brother Charles *See* Soul Vengeance (1975)

Welcome to Jericho *See* Last Man Standing (1996)

Welcome to Oblivion *See* Ultra Warrior (1992)

The Well-Made Marriage *See* Le Beau Mariage (1982)

Wendy Cracked a Walnut *See* ...Almost (1990)

We're In the Army Now *See* Pack Up Your Troubles (1932)

The Werewolf and the Yeti *See* Night of the Howling Beast (1975)

What? *See* Diary of Forbidden Dreams (1973)

What a Chassis! *See* Belle Americaine (1961)

What a Drag *See* Pedale Douce (1996)

What a Man *See* Never Give a Sucker an Even Break (1941)

What Changed Charley Farthing *See* Bananas Boat (1978)

What Lola Wants *See* Damn Yankees (1958)

The Wheelchair *See* El Cochecito (1960)

Wheels of Terror *See* The Misfit Brigade (1987)

When Knighthood Was in Flower *See* The Sword & the Rose (1953)

When Michael Calls *See* Shattered Silence (1971)

When the Girls Meet the Boys *See* Girl Crazy (1943)

When Youth Conspires *See* Old Swimmin' Hole (1940)

Where is the Friend's Home? *See* Where is My Friend's House? (1987)

Where the Hell's the Gold? *See* Dynamite and Gold (1988)

Where the River Bends *See* Bend of the River (1952)

While Plucking the Daisy *See* Mademoiselle Striptease (1957)

The Whipping Boy *See* Prince Brat and the Whipping Boy (1995)

White *See* Trois Couleurs: Blanc (1994)

White Paws *See* Pattes Blanches (1949)

White Trash on Moonshine Mountain *See* Moonshine Mountain (1964)

A White White Boy *See* The Mirror (1975)

Who? *See* Roboman (1975)

Who Dares Wins *See* The Final Option (1982)

Who Fears the Devil *See* The Legend of Hillbilly John (1973)

Who Is Killing the Stuntman *See* Stunts (1977)

Who Murdered Joy Morgan? *See* Killjoy (1981)

Who Shot Patakango? *See* Who Shot Pat? (1992)

Whoever Slew Auntie Roo? *See* Who Slew Auntie Roo? (1971)

Why Not? *See* Eijanaika (1981)

Wide-Eyed and Legless *See* The Wedding Gift (1993)

The Widow and the Gigolo *See* Roman Spring of Mrs. Stone (1961)

Wild Beds *See* Tigers in Lipstick (1980)

Wild Drifters *See* Cockfighter (1974)

Wild Flower *See* Fiorile (1993)

Wild Flower *See* Flor Silvestre (1958)

Wild For Kicks *See* Beat Girl (1960)

Wild Geese *See* Mistress (1953)

Wild Horses of Fire *See* Shadows of Forgotten Ancestors (1964)

Wild Oats *See* The Errors of Youth (1978)

The Wild Pack *See* Defiant (1970)

The Wild Side *See* Suburbia (1983)

Wild Youth *See* Naked Youth (1959)

Wildcat *See* Great Scout & Cathouse Thursday (1976)

Wilderness Family, Part 2 *See* Further Adventures of the Wilderness Family, Part 2 (1977)

Willy Milly *See* Something Special (1986)

Wilt *See* The Misadventures of Mr. Wilt (1990)

The Wind Bloweth Where it Listeth *See* A Man Escaped (1957)

A Window in London *See* Lady in Distress (1939)

A Window to the Sky *See* The Other Side of the Mountain (1975)

Wings of the Apache *See* Fire Birds (1990)

Winter Rates *See* Out of Season (1975)

The Wistful Widow *See* The Wistful Widow of Wagon Gap (1947)

The Witch *See* Superstition (1982)

Witch Doctor *See* Men of Two Worlds (1946)

Witchcraft 8 *See* Salem's Ghost (1995)

The Witches of Salem *See* The Crucible (1957)

Witchfinder General *See* The Conqueror Worm (1968)

Witchkill *See* The Witchmaker (1969)

Witch's Curse *See* Maciste in Hell (1960)

With Words and Music *See* The Girl Said No (1937)

Wit's End *See* G.I. Executioner (1971)

The Wizard of Mars *See* Horrors of the Red Planet (1964)

Wo Die Grunen Ameisen Traumen *See* Where the Green Ants Dream (1984)

Wo Do I Gotta Kill? *See* Me and the Mob (1994)

Wolf Larsen *See* The Legend of the Sea Wolf (1958)

Woman Alone *See* Sabotage (1936)

A Woman Destroyed *See* Smash-Up: The Story of a Woman (1947)

Woman, Forty *See* Summer Snow (1994)

The Woman in His House *See* The Animal Kingdom (1932)

Woman of Antwerp *See* Dedee d'Anvers (1949)

Woman of Dolwyn *See* The Last Days of Dolwyn (1949)

Woman of Osaka *See* Osaka Elegy (1936)

Woman of Summer *See* The Stripper (1963)

Woman of the Dunes *See* Woman in the Dunes (1964)

A Woman Scorned: The Betty Broderick Story *See* Till Murder Do Us Part (1992)

A Woman's Devotion *See* Battle Shock (1956)

A Woman's Revenge *See* La Vengeance d'une Femme (1989)

Women in Cages *See* The Big Doll House (1971)

Women in Prison *See* Ladies They Talk About (1933)

Women of Nazi Germany *See* Hitler (1962)

Women without Names *See* Women in Prison (1949)

Women's Penitentiary 1 *See* The Big Doll House (1971)

Women's Penitentiary 2 *See* The Big Bird Cage (1972)

Women's Penitentiary 4 *See* Caged Women (1984)

Wonder Women *See* The Deadly and the Beautiful (1973)

The Word *See* Ordet (1955)

The World and His Wife *See* State of the Union (1948)

The World of Yor *See* Yor, the Hunter from the Future (1983)

The Worlds of Gulliver *See* The Three Worlds of Gulliver (1959)

Worthy Deceivers *See* Big Bluff (1955)

The Wounded Man *See* L'Homme Blesse (1983)

Wrong Bet *See* Lionheart (1990)

The Wrong Kind of Girl *See* Bus Stop (1956)

Wuya Yu Maque *See* Crows and Sparrows (1949)

X *See* X: The Man with X-Ray Eyes (1963)

X-Ray *See* Hospital Massacre (1981)

Xiyan *See* The Wedding Banquet (1993)

Xochimilco *See* Maria Candelaria (1946)

The XYZ Murders *See* Crimewave (1985)

...Y No Se Lo Trago La Tierra *See* ... And the Earth Did Not Swallow Him (1994)

Yangtse Incident *See* Battle Hell (1956)

A Yank In London *See* I Live in Grosvenor Square (1946)

A Yankee in King Arthur's Court *See* A Connecticut Yankee in King Arthur's Court (1949)

The Year of the Jellyfish *See* L'Annee des Meduses (1986)

Yellow Faced Tiger *See* Slaughter in San Francisco (1981)

Yellow Hair and the Pecos Kid *See* Yellow Hair & the Fortress of Gold (1984)

Yiddle with a Fiddle *See* Yidl Mitn Fidl (1936)

Yingxiong Bense *See* A Better Tomorrow (1986)

Yo, la Peor de Todas *See* I, the Worst of All (1990)

Yokihi *See* Princess Yang Kwei Fei (1955)

Yosei Gorasu *See* Gorath (1964)

You Better Watch Out *See* Terror in Toyland (1985)

You Can't Steal Love *See* Murph the Surf (1975)

You Don't Need Pajamas at Rosie's *See* The First Time (1969)

The Young and the Damned *See* Los Olvidados (1950)

The Young and the Immortal *See* The Sinister Urge (1960)

The Young and the Passionate *See* I Vitelloni (1953)

Young Commandos *See* Delta Force 3: The Killing Game (1991)

The Young Cycle Girls *See* Cycle Vixens (1979)

Young Dracula *See* Andy Warhol's Dracula (1974)

Young Dracula *See* Son of Dracula (1943)

Young Hearts *See* Promised Land (1988)

Young Hellions *See* High School Confidential (1958)

Young Invaders *See* Darby's Rangers (1958)

The Young Ladies of Wilko *See* Maids of Wilko (1979)

Young Scarface *See* Brighton Rock (1947)

The Youngest Spy *See* My Name is Ivan (1962)

Your Past is Showing *See* The Naked Truth (1958)

Your Red Wagon *See* They Live by Night (1949)

Your Witness *See* Eye Witness (1949)

Youth Takes a Hand *See* Behind Prison Walls (1943)

Yukinojo Henge *See* An Actor's Revenge (1963)

Zabudnite na Mozarta *See* Forget Mozart (1985)

Zamri Oumi Voskresni *See* Freeze-Die-Come to Life (1990)

Zato Ichi To Yojimbo *See* Zatoichi vs. Yojimbo (1970)

Zatoichi Meets Yojimbo *See* Zatoichi vs. Yojimbo (1970)

Zayn Vaybs Lubovnik *See* His Wife's Lover (1931)

Zazie in the Subway *See* Zazie dans le Metro (1961)

Zazie in the Underground *See* Zazie dans le Metro (1961)

Zee & Co. *See* X, Y & Zee (1972)

Zeisters *See* Fat Guy Goes Nutzoid (1986)

Zemlya *See* Earth (1930)

Zendegi Va Digar Hich ... *See* Life and Nothing More ... (1992)

Zerkalo *See* The Mirror (1975)

Zero de Conduit *See* Zero for Conduct (1933)

Zero Degrees Kelvin *See* Zero Degrees Kelvin (1995)

Zeta One *See* Alien Women (1969)

Ziemia Obiecana *See* Land of Promise (1974)

Zire Darakhtan Zeyton *See* Through the Olive Trees (1994)

Zombie *See* I Eat Your Skin (1964)

Zombie Creeping Flesh *See* Night of the Zombies (1983)

Zombie Flesh Eaters *See* Zombie (1980)

Zombie ja Kummitusjuna *See* Zombie and the Ghost Train (1991)

Zombies *See* I Eat Your Skin (1964)

Zormba *See* Zorba the Greek (1964)

Z.P.G. *See* Zero Population Growth (1972)

Zuckerbaby *See* Sugarbaby (1985)

Zycie Rodzinne *See* Family Life (1971)

A la Mode 🎬🎬½ *In Fashion* **1994 (R)** It's Paris in the '60s as shy 17-year-old orphan Fausto (Higelin) is apprenticed to fatherly Jewish tailor Mietek (Yanne). But Fausto is transfixed by lovely mechanic Tonie (Darel) and decides what he really wants (besides the girl) is to design women's fashions. Very frothy coming-of-age tale, anchored by Yanne's veteran charm. Based on the novel "Fausto" by Richard Morgieve. French with subtitles.**CW:** Some language and nudity. **89m/C VHS, LV.** *FR* Ken Higelin, Jean Yanne, Florence Darel, Francois Hautesserre; *D:* Remy Duchemin; *W:* Remy Duchemin, Richard Morgieve; *M:* Denis Barbier. *MAX*

A Nos Amours 🎬🎬🎬 **1984 (R)** Craving the attention she is denied at home, a young French girl searches for love and affection from numerous boyfriends in hopes of eradicating her unhappy home. Occasional lapses in quality and slow pacing hamper an otherwise excellent effort. The characterization of the girl Suzanne is especially memorable. In French with English subtitles. **99m/C VHS, Beta, LV.** *FR* Sandrine Bonnaire, Dominique Besnehard, Maurice Pialat, Evelyne Ker; *D:* Maurice Pialat. *COL*

A Nous la Liberte 🎬🎬🎬🎬 **1931** Two tramps encounter industrialization and automation, making one into a wealthy leader, the other into a nature-loving iconoclast. A poignant, fantastical masterpiece by Clair, made before he migrated to Hollywood. Though the view of automation may be dated, it influenced such films as Chaplin's "Modern Times." In French with English subtitles. **87m/B VHS, Beta, 8mm.** *FR* Henri Marchand, Raymond Cordy, Rolla France, Paul Olivier, Jacques Shelly, Andre Michaud; *D:* Rene Clair; *W:* Rene Clair; *C:* Georges Perinal. National Board of Review Awards '32: 5 Best Foreign Films of the Year; Nominations: Academy Awards '32: Best Interior Decoration.*NOS, MRV, VYY*

Aaron Loves Angela 🎬🎬 **1975 (R)** Puerto Rican girl falls in love with a black teen amidst the harsh realities of the Harlem ghetto. "Romeo and Juliet" meets "West Side Story" in a cliched comedy drama. **99m/C VHS, Beta.** Kevin Hooks, Irene Cara, Moses Gunn, Robert Hooks, Jose Feliciano; *D:* Gordon Parks Jr.; *M:* Jose Feliciano. *COL*

Abandon Ship 🎬🎬½ *Seven Waves Away* **1957** A luxury liner hits a derelict mine and sinks within minutes, leaving 27 survivors clinging to one tiny lifeboat. Ship's officer Alex Holmes (Power) knows that the amount of food and water they have is limited, the waters are shark-infested, and the injured stand little chance, so he must decide who will survive. **97m/B VHS.** *GB* Tyrone Power, Mai Zetterling, Lloyd Nolan, Stephen Boyd, Moira Lister, James Hayter, Marie Lohr, Gordon Jackson, Finlay Currie, John Stratton, Victor Maddern, Eddie Byrne, Noel Willman, Ralph Michael, David Langton, Ferdinand "Ferdy" Mayne, Austin Trevor, Moultrie Kelsall, Jill Melford; *D:* Richard Sale; *W:* Richard Sale; *C:* Wilkie Cooper; *M:* Arthur Bliss. *COL*

Abbott and Costello Go to Mars 🎬½ **1953** Poor parody of sci-fi films finds the frantic duo aboard a rocket ship and accidentally heading off into outer space. They don't land on Mars, but Venus, which is populated by lots of pretty women and no men. Even this duo looks good to the ladies. Cheapie production and uninspired buffoonery. **77m/B VHS, Closed Caption.** Bud Abbott, Lou Costello, Mari Blanchard, Robert Paige, Martha Hyer, Horace McMahon, Jack Kruschen, Anita Ekberg; *D:* Charles Lamont; *W:* John Grant, D.D. Beauchamp. *USH*

Abbott and Costello in Hollywood 🎬🎬 *Bud Abbott and Lou Costello In Hollywood* **1945** Bud and Lou appear as a barber and porter of a high class tonsorial parlor in Hollywood. A rather sarcastic look at backstage Hollywood, Abbott & Costello style. Ball makes a guest appearance. **111m/B VHS, Beta.** Bud Abbott, Lou Costello, Frances Rafferty, Warner Anderson, Lucille Ball; *D:* Sylvan Simon; *M:* George Bassman. *MGM, CCB*

Abbott and Costello in the Foreign Legion 🎬🎬½ **1950** Fight promoters Jonesy and Max trail their runaway fighter to Algiers where they're tricked into joining the French Foreign Legion. They have to cope with a sadistic sargeant, a sexy spy, and still find their man. Most amusement comes from Lou's wild desert mirages. **80m/B VHS, Closed Caption.** Bud Abbott, Lou Costello, Walter Slezak, Patricia Medina, Douglass Dumbrille, Leon Belasco, Marc Lawrence, Tor Johnson; *D:* Charles Lamont; *W:* John Grant, Martin Ragaway, Leonard Stern. *USH*

Abbott and Costello Meet Captain Kidd 🎬🎬 **1952** With pirates led by Captain Kidd on their trail, Abbott and Costello follow a treasure map. Bland A&C swashbuckler spoof with a disinterested Laughton impersonating the Kidd. One of the duo's few color films. **70m/C VHS, Beta, LV.** Bud Abbott, Lou Costello, Charles Laughton, Hillary Brooke, Fran Warren, Bill Shirley, Leif Erickson; *D:* Charles Lamont. *NOS*

Abbott and Costello Meet Dr. Jekyll and Mr. Hyde 🎬🎬 **1952** Abbott and Costello take on evil Dr. Jekyll, who has transformed himself into Mr. Hyde, and is terrorizing London. A lame attempt at recapturing the success of "Abbott and Costello Meet Frankenstein." **77m/B VHS, Beta.** Bud Abbott, Lou Costello, Boris Karloff, Craig Stevens, Helen Westcott, Reginald Denny; *D:* Charles Lamont. *USH*

Abbott and Costello Meet Frankenstein 🎬🎬🎬 *Abbott and Costello Meet the Ghosts* **1948** Big-budget A&C classic is one of their best efforts and was rewarded handsomely at the box office. Two unsuspecting baggage clerks deliver a crate containing the last but not quite dead remains of Dracula and Dr. Frankenstein's monster to a wax museum. The fiends are revived, wreaking havoc with the clerks. Chaney makes a special appearance to warn the boys that trouble looms. Last film to use the Universal creature pioneered by Karloff in 1931. **83m/B VHS, Beta, LV.** Bud Abbott, Lou Costello, Lon Chaney Jr., Bela Lugosi, Glenn Strange, Lenore Aubert, Jane Randolph; *D:* Charles T. Barton; *V:* Vincent Price. *USH*

Abbott and Costello Meet the Invisible Man 🎬🎬🎬 **1951** Abbott and Costello play newly-graduated detectives who take on the murder case of a boxer (Franz) accused of killing his manager. Using a serum that makes people invisible, the boxer helps Costello in a prizefight that will frame the real killers, who killed the manager because the boxer refused to throw a fight. Great special effects and hilarious gags make this one of the best from the crazy duo. **82m/B VHS.** Bud Abbott, Lou Costello, Nancy Guild, Adele Jergens, Sheldon Leonard, William Frawley, Gavin Muir, Arthur Franz, Frederic Rinaldo, John Grant; **D:** Charles Lamont; **W:** Robert Lees; **C:** George Robinson. *USH*

Abbott and Costello Meet the Keystone Kops 🐾🐾½ 1954
It's 1912 and the boys are bilked into buying a fake movie studio by a clever con man. When they find out they've been tricked, the duo head to Hollywood to track him down and find out the crook is trying to cheat Sennett's film company. Sennett himself trained A&C and the new Keystone Kops in their recreations of his silent screen routines. Good final chase sequence but the earlier work is tired. **79m/B VHS, Closed Caption.** Bud Abbott, Lou Costello, Fred Clark, Lynn Bari, Mack Sennett, Maxie "Slapsie" Rosenbloom, Frank Wilcox, Harold Goodwin; **D:** Charles Lamont; **W:** John Grant; **M:** Henry Mancini. *USH*

Abbott and Costello Meet the Killer, Boris Karloff 🐾🐾 1949
Unremarkable Abbott and Costello murder mystery. Karloff plays a psychic who tries to frame Lou for murder. Pleasant enough but not one of their best. **84m/B VHS, Beta, LV, Closed Caption.** Bud Abbott, Lou Costello, Boris Karloff, Lenore Aubert, Gar Moore, Donna Martell, Alan Mowbray, James Flavin, Roland Winters; **D:** Charles T. Barton. *USH*

Abbott and Costello Meet the Mummy 🐾🐾½ 1955
Okay comedy from the duo has them stranded in Egypt with a valuable medallion which will lead to secret treasure and the mummy who guards the tomb. The last of the films the twosome made for Universal. **90m/B VHS.** Bud Abbott, Lou Costello, Marie Windsor, Michael Ansara, Dan Seymour, Kurt Katch, Richard Deacon, Mel Welles, Edwin Parker; **D:** Charles Lamont; **W:** John Grant. *USH, FCT*

ABC Stage 67: Truman Capote's A Christmas Memory
Truman Capote's A Christmas Memory; A Christmas Memory 1966 A television drama special narrated by Capote about his remembered childhood experience of baking dozens of fruitcakes for friends at Christmas with his elderly distant cousin, Miss Sook Faulk (Page). She is quiet, lovely and true in this sensitive portrait of why we give and what we have to be thankful for. Adapted from a Capote short story by Capote and Eleanor Perry. **51m/B VHS, Beta, 8mm.** Geraldine Page, Donnie Melvin; **D:** Frank Perry. *MOV, VYY*

ABC's of Love & Sex, Australia Style 🐾 1986
An Australian-made sex-education parody. **87m/C VHS, Beta.** *AU* Brigittia Almsrom, Rettima Borer, Ian Broadbent. *ACA*

Abducted 🐾½ 1986 (PG)
A woman jogger is abducted by a crazed mountain man in the Canadian Rockies. Weird and unbelievably tedious film is nevertheless highlighted by some spectacular wilderness footage of the Vancouver area, a travelogue bonus for those in the mood. **87m/C VHS, Beta.** *CA* Dan Haggerty, Roberta Weiss, Lawrence King Phillips; **D:** Boon Collins. *PSM*

Abducted 2: The Reunion 🐾½ 1994 (R)
Three girlfriends decide to go camping for their reunion trip. Oops—psycho mountain man alert! **CW:** Language; brief nudity; violence. **91m/C VHS.** Dan Haggerty, Jan-Michael Vincent, Donna Jason, Raquel Bianca, Debbie Rochon, Lawrence King; **D:** Boon Collins; **W:** Boon Collins; **C:** Danny Nowak. *AVI*

Abduction 🐾½ 1975 (R)
Exploitative account of the Patty Hearst kidnapping, loosely adapted from the Harrison James novel written before the kidnapping. A young woman from a wealthy capitalist family is kidnapped by black radicals and held for an unusual ransom. Oh, and she tangles with lesbians, too. **100m/C VHS, Beta.** Judith-Marie Bergan, David Pendleton, Gregory Rozakis,

Leif Erickson, Dorothy Malone, Lawrence Tierney; **D:** Joseph Zito. *MED*

The Abduction of Allison Tate 🐾½ 1992 (R)
Rich developer takes land belonging to a group of Native Americans. Three young tribe members retaliate by kidnapping the developer's daughter. But when their plans go awry and one of the trio is killed, Allison finds herself sympathizing more with them than with her father's ambitions. **CW:** Language and one sex scene. **95m/C VHS.** Leslie Hope, Bernie White; **D:** Paul Leder. *NO*

The Abduction of Kari Swenson 🐾½ 1987
An account of the true-life (it really happened) kidnapping of Olympic biathalon hopeful Swensen by a pair of mischievous Montana mountain men with matrimony in mind. The movie details the abduction of Swenson by the scruffy father and son duo and the massive manhunt. As the put-upon Kari, Pollan exceeds script expectations in this made-for-television exercise in stress avoidance. **100m/C VHS.** Joe Don Baker, M. Emmet Walsh, Ronny Cox, Michael Bowen, Geoffrey Blake, Dorothy Fielding, Tracy Pollan; **D:** Stephen Gyllenhaal. *THV*

Abduction of St. Anne 🐾🐾 1975
An almost interesting made-for-television mystical thriller about a detective and a bishop trying to track down a gangster's daughter, who may have nifty supernatural healing powers the Church would be very interested in having documented. **78m/C VHS, Beta.** Robert Wagner, E.G. Marshall, William Windom, Lloyd Nolan; **D:** Harry Falk; **M:** George Duning. *WOV, GKK*

The Abductors 🐾 1972 (R)
Caffaro's super-agent takes on international white slavery, a worthy target for any exploitation effort. While the novelty is a tough and intelligent on-screen heroine, sufficient sleaze and violence bring it all down to the proper level of swampland video. Sequel to the never-to-be-forgotten "Ginger." **90m/C VHS, Beta.** Cheri Caffaro, William Grannell, Richard Smedley, Patrick Wright, Jennifer Brooks; **D:** Don Schain. *MON*

Abdulla the Great 🐾🐾 1956
Abdullah's Harem A dissolute Middle Eastern monarch falls for a model, who spurns him for an army officer. While distracted by these royal shenanigans, the king is blissfully unaware of his subjects' disaffection—until they revolt. Dares to lampoon Egypt's dead King Farouk, going against conventional Hollywood wisdom ("Farouk in film is box office poison"). **89m/C VHS, Beta.** *GB* Gregory Ratoff, Kay Kendall, Sydney Chaplin; **D:** Gregory Ratoff. *VYY*

Abe Lincoln in Illinois 🐾🐾🐾🐾 Spirit of the People 1940
Massey considered this not only his finest film but a part he was "born to play." Correct on both counts, this Hollywood biography follows Lincoln from his log cabin days to his departure for the White House. The Lincoln-Douglass debate scene and Massey's post-presidential election farewell to the citizens of Illinois are nothing short of brilliant. Written by Sherwood from his Pulitzer-Prize winning play. Contrasted with the well-known "Young Mr. Lincoln" (Henry Fonda), its relative anonymity is perplexing. **110m/B VHS, Beta.** Raymond Massey, Gene Lockhart, Ruth Gordon, Mary Howard, Dorothy Tree, Harvey Stephens, Minor Watson, Alan Baxter, Howard da Silva, Maurice Murphy, Clem Bevans, Herbert Rudley; **D:** John Cromwell; **W:** Robert Sherwood; **C:** James Wong Howe. Nominations: Academy Awards '40: Best Actor (Massey), Best Black and White Cinematography. *MED, TTC*

The Abe Lincoln of Ninth Avenue 🐾🐾½ Streets of New York 1939
All-American tale of a poor young man making good in New York. His role model is Abraham Lincoln. Cooper is exceptional, supported by effective performances by the rest of the cast. **68m/B VHS, Beta, 8mm.** Jackie Cooper, Martin Spelling, Marjorie Reynolds, Dick Purcell, George Cleveland, George Irving; **D:** William Nigh. *VYY*

Abigail's Party 🐾🐾 1977
Steadman plays the hostess for a very ill-fated dinner party, especially when she realizes her husband has just died on her new carpet. Made for British television. **105m/C VHS.** *GB* Alison Steadman; **D:** Mike Leigh. *WBF, BTV*

Abilene Town 🐾🐾🐾 1946
In a post-Civil War Kansas town far from the freeway, Scott is the tough marshal trying to calm the conflict between cattlemen and homesteaders. He also finds time to participate in a romantic triangle with dance hall vixen Dvorak and heart-of-gold Fleming. Snappy pace keeps it interesting. Based on a novel by Ernest Haycox. **90m/B VHS, Beta.** Randolph Scott, Ann Dvorak, Edgar Buchanan, Rhonda Fleming, Lloyd Bridges; **D:** Edwin L. Marin. *MRV, NOS, PSM*

The Abominable Dr. Phibes 🐾🐾🐾 1971 (PG)
After being disfigured in a freak car accident that killed his wife, an evil genius decides that the members of a surgical team let his wife die and shall each perish by a different biblical plague. High camp with the veteran cast in top form. **90m/C VHS, Beta, LV.** *GB* Vincent Price, Joseph Cotten, Hugh Griffith, Terry-Thomas, Virginia North, Susan Travers, Alex Scott, Caroline Munro; **D:** Robert Fuest. *VES, LIV, ORI*

The Abomination 🐾 1988 (R)
After a 5,000-year-old creature possesses him during a nightmare, a boy goes on an eye-gouging frenzy. Only the audience gets hurt. **100m/C VHS, Beta.** Van Connery, Victoria Chaney, Gaye Bottoms, Suzy Meyer, Jude Johnson, Blue Thompson, Scott Davis; **D:** Max Raven. *DMP*

About Last Night... 🐾🐾🐾 1986 (R)
Semi-realistic comedy-drama which explores the ups and downs of one couple's relationship. Mostly quality performances, especially Perkins and Belushi as friends of the young lovers. Based on David Mamet's play "Sexual Perversity in Chicago," but considerably softened so that more people would buy tickets at the box office, the film acts as a historical view of contemporary mating rituals before the onset of the AIDS crisis. **113m/C VHS, Beta, LV.** Rob Lowe, Demi Moore, Elizabeth Perkins, James Belushi, George DiCenzo, Robin Thomas, Michael Alldredge; **D:** Edward Zwick; **W:** Tim Kazurinsky, Denise DeClue; **M:** Miles Goodman. *COL*

Above and Beyond 🐾🐾🐾 1953
Good performance by Taylor as Col. Paul Tibbets, the man who piloted the Enola Gay, which dropped the atomic bomb on Hiroshima. Focuses on the secrecy of the mission and the strain this puts on Tibbets marriage. Exciting action sequences of the mission itself. **122m/B VHS.** Robert Taylor, Eleanor Parker, James Whitmore, Larry Keating, Larry Gates, Robert Burton, Jim Backus; **D:** Melvin Frank, Norman Panama; **W:** Melvin Frank, Norman Panama, Beirne Lay Jr. Nominations: Academy Awards '53: Best Story, Original Dramatic/Comedy Score. *MGM*

Above Suspicion 🐾🐾🐾 1943
MacMurray and Crawford are American honeymooners (poor Fred!) asked to assist an international intelligence organization. They engage the Nazis in a tense battle of wits. Well-made and engaging. **91m/B VHS.** Joan Crawford, Fred MacMurray, Conrad Veidt, Basil Rathbone, Reginald Owen; **D:** Richard Thorpe. *MGM*

Above Suspicion 🐾🐾 1995 (R)
Dempsey Cain (Reeve) seems to be the perfect cop, as well as a loving husband and father and a mentor to his younger brother. But when Cain is paralyzed by a drug dealer's bullet, he begins to notice just how close his wife (Cattrall) and brother (Kerr) are. There's adultery, there's murder, and there's the cop who just may be a cold-blooded killer. Unnervingly, Reeve plays a paraplegic in the last movie he made before his own paralyzing riding accident. Made for cable. **CW:** Strong sex scenes, language and violence. **92m/C VHS.** Christopher Reeve, Kim Cattrall, Joe Mantegna, Edward Kerr; **D:** Steven Schachter. *HBO*

Above the Law ♂♂ 1988 (R) In his debut, Seagal does his wooden best to portray a tough Chicago police detective planning an enormous drug bust of one of the biggest felons in the state. Unfortunately, the FBI has ordered him to back off and find another bust. The reasons are almost as complex as Seagal's character, and like most details of the flick, stupid. However, people don't watch these movies for the acting or the plot, but for the fight scenes, which are well-choreographed and violent. Watch it with someone you love. **99m/C VHS, Beta, LV, 8mm, Closed Caption.** Steven Seagal, Pam Grier, Henry Silva, Sharon Stone, Ron Dean, Daniel Faraldo, Chelcie Ross; **D:** Andrew Davis; **W:** Andrew Davis, Steven Pressfield; **C:** Robert Steadman. **WAR, TLF**

Above the Rim ♂♂½ 1994 (R) Vulgar, violent hoopster drama about a fiercely competitive inner-city playground game. Kyle-Lee Watson (Martin), a self-involved high school star raised by a saintly single mom (Pinkins), is torn between the lure of the streets and his college recruiting chances. His odds aren't made any easier by homeboy hustler Birdie (Shakur), who wants to improve his chances of making money on the local games by making sure Watson plays for his team. Energetic b-ball sequences, strong performances lose impact amid formulaic melodrama and the usual obscenities. Debut for director Pollack.**CW:** Pervasive strong language and violence. **97m/C VHS, LV, Closed Caption.** Duane Martin, Tupac Shakur, Leon, Marlon Wayans, Tonya Pinkins, Bernie Mac; **D:** Jeff Pollack; **W:** Jeff Pollack, Barry Michael Cooper; **M:** Marcus Miller. Nominations: MTV Movie Awards '95: Best Song ("Regulate"). **NLC**

Above Us the Waves ♂♂♂ 1956 During WWII, the British navy immobilizes a huge German battleship off the coast of Norway. Effectively dramatizes the British naval preparations for what seemed a suicidal mission: using midget submarines to plant underwater explosives on the hull of the German vessel and detonating them before the Germans could detect the danger. **92m/C VHS. GB** John Mills, John Gregson, Donald Sinden, James Robertson Justice, Michael Medwin, James Kenney, O.E. Hasse, Thomas Heathcote, Lee Patterson, Theodore Bikel, Lyndon Brook, Anthony Newley; **D:** Ralph Thomas. **REP**

Abraham ♂♂½ 1994 Made for cable Biblical epic chronicling the Old Testament story of humble shepherd Abraham (Harris), who's commanded by God to lead his family into the promised land of Canaan. Among his family's many trials will be God's command that Abraham sacrifice his son Isaac as a test of faith and obedience. Filmed on location in Morocco with a commanding performance by Harris that somewhat redeems the film's dullness. **?m/C VHS.** Richard Harris, Barbara Hershey, Maximilian Schell, Vittorio Gassman, Caroline Rosi, Gottfried John, Kevin McNally; **D:** Joseph Sargent. **TTC**

Abraham Lincoln ♂♂½ 1930 Griffith's first feature movie takes Abraham Lincoln from his birth through his assassination. This restored version includes the original slavery sequences which were believed to be lost, but obviously were not. Musical score included. **97m/B VHS, Beta, LV.** Walter Huston, Una Merkel, Kay Hammond, E. Alyn Warren, Hobart Bosworth, Fred Warren, Henry B. Walthall, Russell Simpson; **D:** D.W. Griffith; **C:** Karl Struss. **NOS, MRV, CCB**

Abraxas: Guardian of the Universe ♂½ 1990 (R) Good space cop versus bad space cop with an ecological twist. Goodguy Abraxas (Ventura) has the task of stopping planets from destroying their environments and fighting senseless wars. His ex-partner Secundas (Ole-Thorsen) has his own mission, seeking an anti-life power which could destroy the universe. They decide to fight it out, using Earth as the battleground. Also available in an edited PG-13 version. **90m/C VHS.** Jesse Ventura, Sven Ole-Thorsen; **Cameos:** James Belushi. **PSM**

Abroad with Two Yanks ♂♂ 1944 Two Marine buddies on furlough exhibit slapstick tendencies while competing for the same girl. Along the way a big chase ensues with the two soldiers in drag. Typical wartime shenanigans likely to incite only weak chuckling or inspired snoozing. **81m/B VHS, Beta.** William Bendix, Dennis O'Keefe, Helen Walker, John Loder, George Cleveland, Janet Lambert, James Flavin, Arthur Hunnicutt; **D:** Allan Dwan. **LIV**

Absence of Malice ♂♂½ 1981 (PG) High-minded story about the harm that the news media can inflict. Field is the earnest reporter who, after being fed some facts by an unscrupulous federal investigator, writes a story implicating Newman in a murder he didn't commit. Field hides behind journalistic confidentiality privilege to put off the outraged Newman, who loses a friend to suicide during the debacle. Interesting performances by Field and Newman. **116m/C VHS, Beta, LV.** Paul Newman, Sally Field, Bob Balaban, Melinda Dillon, Luther Adler, Barry Primus, Josef Sommer, John Harkins, Don Hood, Wilford Brimley; **D:** Sydney Pollack; **W:** Kurt Luedtke; **C:** Owen Roizman; **M:** Dave Grusin. Nominations: Academy Awards '81: Best Actor (Newman), Best Original Screenplay, Best Supporting Actress (Dillon). **COL**

The Absent-Minded Professor ♂♂♂½ 1961 Classic dumb Disney fantasy of the era. A professor accidentally invents an anti-gravity substance called flubber, causing inanimate objects and people to become airborne. Great sequence of the losing school basketball team taking advantage of flubber during a game. MacMurray is convincing as the absent-minded genius in this newly colored version. Followed by "Son of Flubber." **97m/C VHS, Beta, LV.** Fred MacMurray, Nancy Olson, Keenan Wynn, Tommy Kirk, Leon Ames, Ed Wynn; **D:** Robert Stevenson; **C:** Edward Colman; **M:** George Bruns. Nominations: Academy Awards '61: Best Art Direction/Set Decoration (B & W), Best Black and White Cinematography. **DIS, BTV**

Absent Without Leave ♂♂½ 1995 Ed (McLachlan) marries his pregnant girlfriend Daisy (Hobbs) in 1942 before joining the army. When Daisy miscarries, Ed pledges to take her home even though it means leaving the army without permission. As the newlyweds travel across the New Zealand countryside, they struggle with the new demands of their relationship. **104m/C VHS. NZ** Craig McLachlan, Katrina Hobbs; **D:** John Laing. **LEO**

Absolute Beginners ♂♂ 1986 (PG) Fervently stylish camp musical exploring the lives of British teenagers in the 1950s never quite gets untracked, although MTV video moments fill out a spare plot line. Based on a novel by Colin MacInnes. ♫Absolute Beginners; That's Motivation; Volare; Killer Blow; Have You Ever Been Blue?; Quiet Life; Having It All; Selling Out; Va Va Voom. **107m/C VHS. GB** David Bowie, Ray Davies, Mandy Rice-Davies, James Fox, Eddie O'Connell, Patsy Kensit, Anita Morris, Sade Adu, Sandie Shaw; **D:** Julien Temple; **W:** Richard Burridge, Don MacPherson. **NO**

Absolute Power ♂♂½ 1997 (R) Eastwood is "In the Line of Fire," (against the very agents he previously glorified) as an expert thief being pursued by rogue Secret Service men in this fast-paced thriller. While looting a Washington official's place, Luther (Eastwood) inadvertently witnesses a murder committed by none other than U.S. President Richmond (Hackman) and his goons. Immediately, a cover-up is organized by his unbalanced chief-of-staff (Davis) and Luther becomes the prime suspect. Harris gives his usual good performance as the homicide detective. Eastwood's simple directorial style keeps up the suspense and propels the film steadily forward, alongside a generally solid plot that gets a bit improbable near the end. Based on the novel by David Baldacci.**CW:** Violence, sexuality, and language. **120m/C VHS, LV, Closed Caption, DVD.** Clint Eastwood, Gene Hackman, Ed Harris, Laura Linney, Judy Davis, Scott Glenn, Dennis Haysbert, E.G. Marshall, Melora

Hardin; **D:** Clint Eastwood; **W:** William Goldman; **C:** Jack N. Green; **M:** Lennie Niehaus. **WAR**

Absolutely Fabulous: The Last Shout ♂♂♂½ 1996 The first TV movie from the British comedy series finds Edina (Saunders) selling her fashion PR business after a near-death experience and doing some soul-searching—AbFab style, which involves shopping, travel, and champagne. Naturally, Patsy (Lumley) goes along for the ride. The duo's favorite designer Christian LaCroix even has a cameo. **90m/C VHS. GB** Jennifer Saunders, Joanna Lumley; **Cameos:** Marianne Faithfull. **PGV, VIF**

Absolution ♂♂ 1981 (R) Two English boys trapped in a Catholic boarding school conspire to drive a tyrannical priest over the edge of sanity. As a result, bad things (including murder) occur. Burton is interesting in sadistic character study. Not released in the U.S. until 1988 following Burton's death, maybe due to something written in the will. **105m/C VHS, Beta, LV. GB** Richard Burton, Dominic Guard, Dai Bradley, Andrew Keir, Billy Connolly, Willoughby Gray; **D:** Anthony Page. **SIM, TWE, FCT**

Abuse ♂♂ 1982 Fourteen-year-old Tommy (Sbarge) is the victim of child abuse. After a beating causes convulsions, his parents rush him to a New York hospital where the intern on duty phones his student filmmaker friend Larry (Ryder), who's doing a documentary on child abuse as his master thesis. When Tommy learns that Larry is also gay, he agrees to discuss his problems but their continuing contact leads the duo to fall in love and Larry to worry about exploiting Tommy's affections. Interspersed with their story are interviews and photos of child abuse victims and their abusers. Not necessarily for the squeamish. **93m/B VHS.** Richard Ryder, Raphael Sbarge; **D:** Arthur J. Bressan Jr.; **W:** Arthur J. Bressan Jr.; **C:** Douglas Dickinson; **M:** Shawn Phillips. **CCN**

The Abyss ♂♂♂ L'Oeuvre au Noir 1989 (PG-13) Underwater sci-fi adventure about a team of oil-drilling divers pressed into service by the navy to locate and disarm an inoperative nuclear submarine. A high-tech thriller with fab footage underwater and pulsating score. The laserdisc version contains 27 extra minutes of footage. **140m/C VHS, Beta, LV, Closed Caption.** Ed Harris, Mary Elizabeth Mastrantonio, Todd Graff, Michael Biehn, John Bedford Lloyd, J.C. Quinn, Leo Burmester, Kidd Brewer Jr., Kimberly Scott, Adam Nelson, George Robert Kirk, Chris Elliott, Jimmie Ray Weeks; **D:** James Cameron; **W:** James Cameron; **C:** Mikael Salomon; **M:** Alan Silvestri. Academy Awards '89: Best Visual Effects; Nominations: Academy Awards '89: Best Art Direction/Set Decoration, Best Cinematography, Best Sound. **FXV**

Accatone! ♂♂♂ 1961 Accatone (Citti), a failure as a pimp, tries his luck as a thief. Hailed as a return to Italian neo-realism, this is a gritty, despairing, and dark look at the lives of the street people of Rome. Pasolini's first outing, adapted by the director from his novel, "A Violent Life." Pasolini served as mentor to Bernardo Bertolucci, listed in the credits as an assistant director. **116m/B VHS. IT** Franco Citti, Franca Pasut, Roberto Scaringelli, Adele Cambria, Paolo Guidi, Silvana Corsini; **D:** Pier Paolo Pasolini; **C:** Tonino Delli Colli. **WBF, APD**

Acceptable Risks ♂½ 1986 (R) Toxic disaster strikes when a plant manager is ordered to cut costs and sacrifice safety at the Citichem plant. Predictable plot stars Dennehy as the plant manager who risks all and fights politicians to reinstate the safety standards. Meanwhile, Tyson is the city manager who tries to warn the town of a possible chemical accident that could have devastating effects on the community. Made for television drama that shamelessly preys on audience fears. **97m/C VHS, Beta, Closed Caption.** Brian Dennehy, Cicely Tyson, Kenneth McMillan, Christine Ebersole, Beah Richards, Richard Gilliland; **D:** Rick Wallace. **PSM**

Access Code 🎞 1984 Government agents attempt to uncover a private organization that has gained control of nuclear weapons for the purpose of world domination. A ragged patchwork of disconnected scenes meant to test the virtue of patience. 90m/C VHS, Beta. Martin Landau, Michael Ansara, MacDonald Carey; *D:* Mark Sobel. *PSM*

Accident 🎞🎞½ 1967 A tangled web of guilt, remorse, humor and thwarted sexuality is unravelled against the background of the English countryside in this complex story of an Oxford love triangle. An inside view of English repression at the university level adapted for the screen by Pinter from the novel by Nicholas Mosley. Long-winded but occasionally engrossing character study with interesting performances. 100m/C VHS, Beta. *GB* Dirk Bogarde, Michael York, Stanley Baker, Jacqueline Sassard, Delphine Seyrig, Alexander Knox, Vivien Merchant, Freddie Jones, Harold Pinter; *D:* Joseph Losey; *W:* Harold Pinter. Cannes Film Festival '67: Grand Jury Prize; National Board of Review Awards '67: 10 Best Films of the Year. *NO*

Accident 🎞½ 1983 Skate for your life. A hockey game turns into a nightmare when the roof over the arena collapses under the weight of too much ice and snow. One of the few hockey disaster films. 104m/C VHS, Beta. Terence Kelly, Fiona Reid, Frank Perry; *D:* Donald Britlain. *TWE*

Accidental Meeting 🎞🎞½ 1993 (R) A female version of "Strangers on a Train." Two women meet because of an auto accident and wind up talking about their lives. The main topic is man trouble and both "jokingly" plot to murder each other's man. Only, one woman does the deed and the other soon finds herself on the murderess' hit list. 91m/C VHS, Beta, Closed Caption. Linda Gray, Linda Purl, Leigh McCloskey, David Hayward, Ernie Lively, Kent McCord; *D:* Michael Zinberg; *W:* Pete Best; Christopher Horner. *PAR*

The Accidental Tourist 🎞🎞🎞½ 1988 (PG) A bittersweet and subtle story, adapted faithfully from Anne Tyler's novel, of an introverted, grieving man who learns to love again after meeting an unconventional woman. After his son's death and subsequent separation from wife Turner, Macon Leary (Hurt) avoids emotional confrontation, burying himself in routines with the aid of his obsessive-compulsive siblings. Kooky dog-trainer Muriel Pritchett (an exuberant Davis) wins his attention, but not without struggle. Hurt effectively uses small gestures to describe Macon's emotional journey, while Davis grabs hearts with her open performance. Outstanding supporting cast. 121m/C VHS, Beta, LV, 8mm, Closed Caption. William Hurt, Geena Davis, Kathleen Turner, Ed Begley Jr., David Ogden Stiers, Bill Pullman, Amy Wright; *D:* Lawrence Kasdan; *W:* Lawrence Kasdan; *C:* John Bailey; *M:* John Williams. Academy Awards '88: Best Supporting Actress (Davis); New York Film Critics Awards '88: Best Film; Nominations: Academy Awards '88: Best Adapted Screenplay, Best Picture, Best Original Score. *WAR, BTV*

Accidents 🎞½ 1989 (R) A scientist discovers that his invention has been stolen and is going to be used to cause worldwide havoc. He becomes concerned and spends the remainder of the movie trying to relieve himself of anxiety. 90m/C VHS, Beta. Edward Albert, Leigh Taylor-Young, Jon Cypher; *D:* Gideon Amir. *TWE*

The Accompanist 🎞🎞½ 1993 (PG) Centers around a Parisian diva Irene's (Safonova) relationship with her talented pianist Sophie (Romane Bohringer), amidst the clamor of WWII Europe. Sophie impresses Irene with her musical abilities, and takes on additional work as her housekeeper. Meanwhile, Charles (Richard Bohringer), Irene's husband, schmoozes with the Nazis to line his own pockets while she helps the war effort by having an affair with a member of the resistance (Labarthe). Unfortunately, Sophie starts to resent living in Irene's shadow. Adapted from the novel by Nina Berberouva. The Bohringers are father and daughter. French with subtitles. 111m/C VHS. *FR* Elena Safonova, Romane Bohringer,

Richard Bohringer, Samuel Labarthe, Nelly Borgeaud, Julien Rassam; *D:* Claude Miller; *W:* Claude Miller, Luc Beraud; *M:* Alain Jomy. *COL*

Accomplice 🎞½ 1946 Plodding whodunit with Arlen as a shy, bookish private eye hired by his old flame to locate her missing husband. His investigations uncover several murders and long after the viewers have put 2 + 2 together, the P.I. smells a rat. The missing husband was a ruse to divert him from the real scam-a bank heist. Painfully low-level excitement. 66m/B VHS. Richard Arlen, Veda Ann Borg, Tom Dugan, Francis Ford; *D:* Walter Colmes. *NOS*

Accused 🎞🎞½ 1936 Married dancers Fairbanks and Del Rio are working in a Parisian revue when the show's sultry leading lady (Desmond) makes a pass at Fairbanks. Though he's turned her down, through a series of misunderstandings Del Rio believes the worst and the two women get into a vicious argument. When the star is found dead guess who gets the blame? Del Rio is lovely, Desmond is spiteful, and Fairbanks serves as a fine object of two women's affections. 83m/B VHS. *GB* Douglas Fairbanks Jr., Dolores Del Rio, Florence Desmond, Basil Sydney, Athole Stewart, Esme Percy, Googie Withers, Cecil Humphreys; *D:* Thornton Freeland. *HCV*

The Accused 🎞🎞½ *Strange Deception* 1948 Young is cast against character in this story of a college professor who is assaulted by one of her students and kills him in self-defense. A courtroom drama ensues, where Young is defended by the dead man's guardian. Film noir with nice ensemble performance. 101m/B VHS, Beta. Loretta Young, Robert Cummings, Wendell Corey, Sam Jaffe, Douglas Dick, Sara Allgood, Ann Doran; *D:* William Dieterle; *C:* Milton Krasner. *PAR*

The Accused 🎞🎞🎞 1988 (R) Provocative treatment of a true story involving a young woman gang raped in a bar while onlookers cheer. McGillis is the assistant district attorney who takes on the case and must contend with the victim's questionable past and a powerful lawyer hired by a wealthy defendant's parents. As the victim with a past, Foster gives an Oscar-winning performance that won raves for its strength and complexity. 110m/C VHS, Beta, LV, 8mm, Closed Caption. Jodie Foster, Kelly McGillis, Bernie Coulson, Leo Rossi, Ann Hearn, Carmen Argenziano, Tom O'Brien, Peter Van Norden, Woody Brown; *D:* Jonathan Kaplan; *W:* Tom Topor; *C:* Ralf Bode; *M:* Brad Fiedel. Academy Awards '88: Best Actress (Foster); Golden Globe Awards '89: Best Actress—Drama (Foster); National Board of Review Awards '88: Best Actress (Foster). *PAR, FCT, BTV*

Ace Crawford, Private Eye 🎞🎞 19?? Bumbling private eye struggles with confusing murder and somehow manages to solve the case. 71m/C VHS. Tim Conway, Billy Barty, Bill Henderson. *MCG*

Ace Drummond 🎞🎞 *Squadron of Doom* 1936 The complete 13-chapter serial about a murder organization that tries to stop several countries from forming a worldwide clipper ship air service and government troubleshooter Ace Drummond who's out to stop them. 260m/B VHS, Beta. John "Dusty" King, Jean Rogers, Noah Beery Jr.; *D:* Ford Beebe. *GPV, HHT, VCN*

Ace High 🎞½ 1968 Spaghetti western about a ruthless outlaw named Cat Stevens trying to save himself from the noose. Patterned after the famous Sergio Leone-Clint Eastwood westerns, with less of a budget and more camp tendencies. 120m/C VHS, Beta. *IT* Eli Wallach, Terence Hill, Bud Spencer, Brock Peters, Kevin McCarthy; *D:* Giuseppe Colizzi. *PAR, FCT*

Ace of Aces 🎞🎞 1933 An American sculptor is reviled, particularly by his girlfriend, when he does not join fellows in enlisting in what becomes WWI. Out to prove he's not lacking testosterone, he becomes a pilot in France, but is embittered by his experiences. Dated but well-acted war melodrama. 77m/B VHS, Beta. Richard Dix, Elizabeth Allan, Theodore Newton, Ralph Bellamy, Joseph Sawyer, Frank Conroy, William Cagney; *D:* J. Walter Ruben; *M:* Max Steiner. *TTC*

Ace of Hearts 🎞 1985 A seedy story about a rich guy in the South Pacific who pays heavily to have himself killed. 90m/C VHS, Beta. Mickey Rooney, Chris Robinson, Pilar Velasquez. *VCD*

Ace Ventura: Pet Detective 🎞🎞 1993 (PG-13) Shamelessly silly comedy casts human cartoon Carrey, he of the rubber limbs and spasmodic facial muscles, as Ace, the guy who'll find missing pets, big or small. When the Miami Dolphins' mascot Snowflake is kidnapped, he abandons his search for an albino pigeon to save the lost dolphin just in time for the Super Bowl. This is brain candy, running full throttle with juvenile humor, some charm, and the hyper-energetic Carrey, not to mention Young as the police chief with a secret. Critically trashed box office smash catapulted Carrey into nearly instant stardom after seven seasons as the geeky white guy on "In Living Color." *CW:* Off-color humor and some nudity. 87m/C VHS, LV, 8mm, Closed Caption. Jim Carrey, Dan Marino, Courteney Cox, Sean Young, Tone Loc; *D:* Tom Shadyac; *W:* Jim Carrey, Tom Shadyac, Jack Bernstein; *M:* Ira Newborn. Blockbuster Entertainment Awards '95: Male Newcomer, Video (Carrey), Comedy Actor, Video (Carrey); Nominations: MTV Movie Awards '94: Best Comedic Performance (Carrey). *WAR*

Ace Ventura: When Nature Calls 🎞🎞 *Ace Ventura Goes to Africa* 1995 (PG-13) Ace is back on the case as the pet dick (Carrey) ventures to Africa to restore peace among rival tribes by finding an albino bat that's M.I.A. Plot is secondary, however, to multi-million dollar man Carrey's outrageous brand of physical comedy combined with his unique ability to deliver junior high level lines with pseudo-suave savoir-faire. Contains only a handful of outstanding gags, the best with Ace and a mechanical rhino. Mainly for Carrey aficionados (of which there are many) and original "Ace" fans—the low-brow humor runs a bit thin by the end. *CW:* Crude humor. 94m/C VHS, LV, Closed Caption. Jim Carrey, Ian McNeice, Simon Callow, Maynard Eziashi, Bob Gunton, Sophie Okonedo, Tommy Davidson; *D:* Steve Oedekerk; *W:* Steve Oedekerk; *C:* Donald E. Thorin; *M:* Robert Folk. MTV Movie Awards '96: Best Male Performance (Carrey), Best Comedic Performance (Carrey); Blockbuster Entertainment Awards '96: Comedy Actor, Theatrical (Carrey); Nominations: MTV Movie Awards '96: Best Kiss (Jim Carrey/Sophie Okonedo). *WAR*

Aces and Eights 🎞🎞½ 1936 Gambler McCoy catches a fellow cardsharp cheating and the marshal runs the varmint out of town. When the cheater is murdered, the lawman suspects McCoy, who sets out to prove his innocence. Title refers to the "death hand" held by Wild Bill Hickok, killed while playing poker. Film opens with a shot of Hickok and a speech about gambler's luck. 62m/B VHS. Tim McCoy, Jimmy Aubrey, Luana Walters, Wheeler Oakman, Earle Hodgins, Frank Glennon, Rex Lease, Charles Stevens, Joseph Girard, John Merton; *D:* Sam Newfield. *NOS, DVT, RXM*

Aces: Iron Eagle 3 🎞🎞 1992 (R) Colonel "Chappy" Sinclair returns once again in this air adventure. He's been keeping busy flying in air shows when he stumbles across the nefarious activities of a Peruvian drug baron working out of a remote village. Sinclair recruits a team of maverick air circus pilots and they "borrow" a fleet of WWII vintage aircraft to raid the village, coming up against a fellow Air Force officer who turns out to be another villain. Lots of action and a stalwart cast. *CW:* War violence. 98m/C VHS, LV, Closed Caption. Louis Gossett Jr., Rachel McLish, Paul Freeman, Horst Buchholz, Christopher Cazenove, Sonny Chiba, Fred Dalton Thompson, Mitchell Ryan, Robert Estes, J.E. Freeman; *D:* John Glen. *COL*

Aces Wild 🎞½ 1937 Another poker title. Outlaws menace an honest newspaper until the lawmen show up and send them on their way. 62m/B VHS, Beta, LV. Harry Carey Sr., Gertrude Messinger, Edward Cassidy, Roger Williams; *D:* Harry Fraser. *NO*

The Acid Eaters 🎬 1967 Straight-laced desk jockeys spend their weekends exploring the realm of the senses. Includes nudity. **62m/C VHS.** Buck Kartalian, Pat Barringer; **D:** B. Ron Elliott; **W:** B. Ron Elliott, Carl Monson; **M:** Billy Allen. *SMW, TPV*

Acla's Descent into Floristella 🎬🎬 *Acla* 1987 Twelve-year-old Acla (Cusimano) is sold by his father to work underground in the sulfur mines for eight years. Repeatedly beaten by his owner, Acla runs away, but there are dire consequences for him and his family. Set in 1930s Sicily. Italian with subtitles. **86m/C VHS. IT** Francesco Cusimano, Tony Sperandeo; **D:** Aurelio Grimaldi; **W:** Aurelio Grimaldi; **C:** Maurizio Calvesi; **M:** Dario Lucantoni. *FCT*

Acorn People 🎬🎬 1982 An unemployed teacher takes a summer job at a camp for handicapped children and learns sensitivity. Made-for-television weeper adapted by Tewkesbury from the book by Ron Jones. **97m/C VHS, Beta.** Ted Bessell, Cloris Leachman, LeVar Burton, Dolph Sweet, Cheryl Anderson; **D:** Joan Tewkesbury. *TLF*

Acqua e Sapone 🎬½ 1983 (PG) A young innocent model goes to Rome under the watchful eyes of an appointed priest-chaperon, but finds love, fun and other sinful things. Sudsy/romantic comedy. **100m/C VHS, Beta. IT** Carlo Verdone, Natasha Hovey, Florinda Bolkan, Elena Bolkan; **D:** Carlo Verdone. *NO*

Across 110th Street 🎬🎬 1972 (R) Gritty, violent cop thriller in the blaxploitation genre. Both the Mafia and the cops hunt down three black hoods who, in a display of extremely bad judgement, knocked over a mob-controlled bank while disguised as police. Lots of bullets create buckets of blood. Filmed on location in Harlem. **102m/C VHS, Beta.** Anthony Quinn, Yaphet Kotto, Anthony (Tony) Franciosa, Paul Benjamin, Ed Bernard, Antonio Fargas, Tim O'Connor, Lewis Gilbert, Richard Ward; **D:** Barry Shear; **W:** Luther Davis; **C:** Jack Priestley. *MGM, FOX*

Across the Bridge 🎬🎬½ 1957 A man on the run from Scotland Yard for stealing a fortune flees to Mexico, in the process killing a man and assuming his identity. An ironic twist and his love for a dog seal his final destiny. Steiger's psychological study as the fugitive is compelling. Based on a novel by Graham Greene. **103m/B VHS, Beta. GB** Rod Steiger, David Knight, Marla Landi, Noel William, Bernard Lee; **D:** Ken Annakin; **M:** James Bernard. *LCA*

Across the Great Divide 🎬🎬½ 1976 (G) Two orphans must cross the rugged snow-covered Rocky Mountains in 1876 in order to claim their inheritance — a 400-acre plot of land in Salem, Oregon. Pleasant coming-of-age tale with majestic scenery. **102m/C VHS, Beta.** Robert F. Logan, George Flower, Heather Rattray, Mark Hall; **D:** Stewart Raffill; **W:** Stewart Raffill; **M:** Angelo Badalamenti. *MED, VTR*

Across the Moon 🎬🎬 1994 (R) A road trip to the desert takes Carmen and Kathy away from their incarcerated boyfriends but into troubles with cowboys and prospectors. **CW:** Strong language; some sexuality. **88m/C VHS.** Elizabeth Pena, Christina Applegate, Tony Fields, Peter Berg, James Remar, Michael McKean, Burgess Meredith, Jack Nance; **D:** Lisa Gottlieb; **C:** Andrzej Sekula; **M:** Christopher Tyng, Exene Cervenka. *HMD*

Across the Pacific 🎬🎬🎬½ 1942 Classic Bogie/Huston vehicle made on the heels of "The Maltese Falcon." Bogie is an American Army officer booted out of the service on false charges of treason. When no other military will accept him, he sails to China (via the Panama Canal) to offer his services to Chiang Kai-Shek. On board, he meets a variety of seedy characters who plan to blow up the canal. Huston again capitalizes on the counterpoint between the rotundly acerbic Greenstreet, who plays a spy, and stiff-lipped, Bogart, who's wooing Astor. Great Bogie moments and fine direction make this an adventure classic. When he departed for the service just prior to filming the final scenes, Huston turned over direction to Vincent Sherman. Also available

colorized. **97m/B VHS.** Humphrey Bogart, Mary Astor, Sydney Greenstreet, Charles Halton, Victor Sen Yung, Roland Got, Keye Luke, Richard Loo; **D:** John Huston. *MGM, FCT*

Across the Plains 🎬½ 1939 Predictable oater about two brothers who are raised separately after their parents are murdered by outlaws. One is brought up by Indians, the other by the outlaws responsible for wiping out the folks, who tell the boy that Indians did in his ma and pa. Eventually the brothers meet and fight. Odds favor the good one winning, aided by Indian pals. **59m/B VHS, Beta.** Jack Randall, Frank Yaconelli, Joyce Bryant, Hal Price, Dennis Moore, Glenn Strange, Bud Osborne; **D:** Spencer Gordon Bennet. *NOS, GPV, DVT*

Across the Tracks 🎬🎬 1989 (PG-13) Two brothers, Billy (Schroder), a juvie-home rebel, and Joe (Pitt), a straight-A jock, are at odds when the black sheep is pressured into selling drugs. In an attempt to save his brother from a life of crime, saintly Joe convinces Billy to join him on the school track team, and the brothers are forced to face off in a big meet. Fairly realistic good guy/bad guy who's really a good guy teen drama. **101m/C VHS.** Rick Schroder, Brad Pitt, Carrie Snodgress; **D:** Sandy Tung; **W:** Sandy Tung; **C:** Michael Delahoussaye; **M:** Joel Goldsmith. *MPI*

Across the Wide Missouri 🎬🎬½ 1951 Pioneer epic stars Gable as a rugged fur trapper who marries an Indian woman (Marques) so he can trap beaver pelts on her people's rich land. On the journey to the Indian territory however, the trapper truly falls in love with his bride. Superior historical drama is marred slightly by the use of narration (provided by Howard Keel). Look for lively performances from Menjou as a French tippler and Naish as the quirky Indian Chief. Beautiful scenery filmed in the spectacular Rocky Mountains. **78m/C VHS, Beta.** Clark Gable, Ricardo Montalban, John Hodiak, Adolphe Menjou, Maria Elena Marques, J. Carrol Naish, Jack Holt, Alan Napier; **D:** William A. Wellman; **C:** William Mellor. *MGM, CCB*

The Act 🎬🎬 *Bless 'Em All* 1982 (R) A muddled satire about political double dealing and union corruption further muddled by a twangy musical score manufactured by folksy Sebastian. **90m/C VHS, Beta.** Jill St. John, Eddie Albert, Pat Hingle, Robert Ginty, Sarah Langenfeld, Nicolas Surovy; **D:** Sig Shore; **M:** John Sebastian. *VES*

Act of Aggression 🎬🎬 1973 (R) When a Parisian man finds his wife and daughter murdered at a summer resort, he takes the law into his own hands, with predictable results. **100m/C VHS, Beta. FR** Jean-Louis Trintignant, Catherine Deneuve, Claude Brasseur. *FCT*

Act of Passion: The Lost Honor of Kathryn Beck 🎬🎬½ 1983 A woman meets a man at a party and has the proverbial one-night stand. Her privacy is shattered when she discovers that he's a terrorist under surveillance by the police and press. Strong performances by Thomas and Kristofferson help turn this into an interesting American television remake of the German "Lost Honor of Katharina Blum," based loosely on a novel by Heinrich Boll. **100m/C VHS, Beta.** Marlo Thomas, Kris Kristofferson, George Dzundza, Jon DeVries; **D:** Simon Langton. *THV*

Act of Piracy 🎬½ 1989 (R) A bankrupt contractor reunites with his estranged wife to track down the brutal terrorists who have kidnapped their son. **105m/C VHS, Beta, LV.** Ray Sharkey, Gary Busey. *WAR*

Act of Vengeance 🎬🎬 *Rape Squad* 1974 (R) A group of women band together to hunt down and exact revenge on the man who raped them. Exploitative action-filled thriller. **90m/C VHS, Beta.** Jo Ann Harris, Peter Brown, Jennifer Lee, Lisa Moore, Connie Strickland, Pat Estrin; **D:** Bob Kelljan. *NO*

Act of Vengeance 🎬🎬½ 1986 Drama about Jock Yablonski, a United Mine Workers official who challenged the president, Tony Boyle. Made for cable, based on fact, showing the

events that led up to the murder of Yablonski and his family. Intriguing story lacking cinematic drive. **97m/C VHS, Beta, Closed Caption.** Charles Bronson, Ellen Burstyn, Wilford Brimley, Hoyt Axton, Robert Schenkkan, Ellen Barkin, Keanu Reeves; **D:** John MacKenzie; **W:** Scott Spencer. *NO*

Acting on Impulse 🎬🎬 1993 (R) Impulsive, troublemaking movie star (Fiorentino) becomes a murder suspect when her producer is killed. This doesn't slow her down. She checks into a hotel with a major party attitude and manages to seduce a conservative businessman (Howell) and his junior exec (Allen) into helping her forget her troubles. And then the businessman's fiance turns up dead. Any connection? Made for cable television. **94m/C VHS.** Linda Fiorentino, C. Thomas Howell, Nancy Allen, Adam Ant, Judith Hoag, Patrick Bachau, Isaac Hayes, Paul Bartel, Donny Most, Miles O'Keeffe, Dick Sargent, Charles Lane, Mary Woronov, Zelda Rubinstein, Nicholas Sadler, Peter Lupus, Kim McGuire, Cassandra Peterson, Brinke Stevens, Michael Talbot, Robert Alan Golub, Cliff Dorfman, Craig Shoemaker, Scott Thompson Stevens; **D:** Sam Irvin; **W:** Mark Pittman, Alan Moskowitz; **C:** Dean Lent; **M:** Daniel Licht. *ACA*

Action for Slander 🎬🎬½ 1938 A British army officer sporting the typical stiff upper lip is accused of cheating during a card game, and the slander mars his reputation until the case is taken to court. Dryly earnest and honest in its depiction of class differences in pre-war England. Based on a novel by Mary Borden. **84m/B VHS, Beta, 8mm. GB** Clive Brook, Ann Todd, Margaretta Scott, Ronald Squire, Francis L. Sullivan, Felix Aylmer, Googie Withers; **D:** Tim Whelan. *VYY*

Action in Arabia 🎬🎬 1944 A newsman uncovers a Nazi plot to turn the Arabs against the Allies while investigating a colleague's murder in Damascus. The desert teems with spies, double agents, and sheiks as suave Sanders goes about his investigative business. Quintessential wartime B-movie. **75m/B VHS, Beta.** George Sanders, Virginia Bruce, Lenore Aubert, Gene Lockhart, Robert Armstrong, H.B. Warner, Alan Napier, Michael Ansara; **D:** Leonide Moguy. *TTC*

Action in the North Atlantic 🎬🎬 1943 Massey and Bogart are the captain and first mate of a Merchant Marine vessel running the lone supply route to the Soviet Union. Eventually they wind up locking horns with a Nazi U-boat. Plenty of action and strenuous flag waving in this propagandorama. Gordon fans won't want to miss her as Massey's wife. Also available colorized. **126m/B VHS.** Humphrey Bogart, Raymond Massey, Alan Hale, Julie Bishop, Ruth Gordon, Sam Levene, Dane Clark; **D:** Lloyd Bacon. Nominations: Academy Awards '43: Best Story. *MGM, FCT*

Action Jackson 🎬🎬 1988 (R) Power-hungry auto tycoon Nelson tries to frame rebellious black police sergeant Weathers for murder. Being a graduate of Harvard and a tough guy, the cop doesn't go for it. Nelson eats up the screen as the heavy with no redeeming qualities, while Weathers is tongue-in-cheek as the resourceful good guy who keeps running afoul of the law in spite of his best efforts. Lots of action, violence, and a few sexy women help cover the plot's lack of common sense. **96m/C VHS, Beta, LV, Closed Caption.** Carl Weathers, Vanity, Craig T. Nelson, Sharon Stone; **D:** Craig R. Baxley; **W:** Robert Reneau; **M:** Herbie Hancock, Michael Kamen. *ORI, WAR*

Action U.S.A. 🎬½ 1989 A young woman witnesses the murder of her boyfriend by gangsters, who then pursue her to make sure she will never tell what she saw. Throughout Texas she rambles with the mob sniffing at her heels, grateful for the opportunity to participate in numerous stunts and car crashes. **90m/C VHS, Beta.** Barri Murphy, Greg Cummins, William Knight, William Smith, Cameron Mitchell; **D:** John Stewart; **W:** David Reskin; **C:** Thomas Callaway. *IMP*

Actor: The Paul Muni Story 🐾🐾

1978 Musical biography of Paul Muni, from his beginnings as a traveling actor in Hungary to his New York theatre and movie career. **105m/C VHS, Beta.** Herschel Bernardi, Georgia Brown, Harold Gould. *LIV*

Actors and Sin 🐾🐾½ 1952

Two-part film casting a critical eye toward actors and Hollywood. "Actor's Blood" is the melodramatic story of Shakespearean actor Robinson and his unhappy actress daughter. She commits suicide and he sets out to prove it was murder. Heavy going. Lighter and more entertaining is "Woman of Sin," which relates a Hollywood satire involving a theatrical agent and his newest client, a precocious nine-year-old. **82m/B VHS, LV.** Edward G. Robinson, Eddie Albert, Marsha Hunt, Alan Reed, Dan O'Herlihy, Tracey Roberts, Rudolph Anders, Paul Guilfoyle, Alice Key, Douglas Evans, Rick Roman, Jenny Hecht, Jody Gilbert, John Crawford; *D:* Lee Garmes, Ben Hecht; *W:* Ben Hecht; *C:* Lee Garmes; *M:* George Antheil. *COL*

An Actor's Revenge 🐾🐾 *Yukinojo Henge*

1963 In the early 19th century, a female impersonator in a Kabuki troupe takes revenge on the three men who killed his parents. Fascinating study of opposites—male/female, stage/life, love/hate. In Japanese with English subtitles. **110m/C VHS.** *JP* Kazuo Hasegawa, Fujiko Yamamoto, Ayako Wakao, Ganjiro Nakamura; *D:* Kon Ichikawa; *W:* Teinosuke Kinugasa, Daisuke Ito, Natto Wada; *M:* Yashushi Akutagawa. *NYF, ING*

Adam 🐾🐾🐾½ 1983

Television docu-drama based on a tragic, true story. John and Reve Williams (Travanti and Williams) desperately search for their 6-year-old son abducted during an outing. During their long search and struggle, they lobby Congress for use of the FBI's crime computer. Eventually their efforts led to the creation of the Missing Children's Bureau. Sensitive, compelling performances by Travanti and Williams as the agonized, courageous parents. **100m/C VHS, Beta, Closed Caption.** Daniel J. Travanti, JoBeth Williams, Martha Scott, Richard Masur, Paul Regina, Mason Adams; *D:* Michael Tuchner. *NO*

Adam at 6 a.m. 🐾🐾 1970 (PG)

Douglas is a young college professor who decides to spend a summer laboring in Missouri, where life, he thinks, is simpler. Of course, he learns that life in the boonies has its own set of problems, but unfortunately it takes him the entire movie before he catches the drift. **100m/C VHS, Beta.** Michael Douglas, Lee Purcell, Joe Don Baker, Charles Aidman, Marge Redmond, Louise Latham, Grayson Hall, Dana Elcar, Meg Foster, Richard Derr, Anne Gwynne; *D:* Robert Scheerer. *FOX*

Adam Had Four Sons 🐾🐾½ 1941

Satisfying character study involving the typical turn-of-the-century family nearly consumed by love, jealousy, and hatred. In the early part of the century, a goodly governess (Bergman in her second U.S. film) watches sympathetically over four sons of an American businessman after their mother dies. Economic necessity separates Bergman from the family for several years. Upon her return, she tangles with scheming bride-to-be Hayward, a bad girl intent on dividing and conquering the family before walking down the aisle with one of the sons. Based on a novel by Charles Bonner. **81m/B VHS, Beta.** Ingrid Bergman, Warner Baxter, Susan Hayward, Fay Wray, Richard Denning, June Lockhart, Robert Shaw; *D:* Gregory Ratoff. *COL*

Adam's Rib 🐾🐾🐾🐾 1950

Classic war between the sexes cast Tracy and Hepburn as married attorneys on opposite sides of the courtroom in the trial of blonde bombshell Holliday, charged with attempted murder of the lover of her philandering husband. The battle in the courtroom soon takes its toll at home as the couple is increasingly unable to leave their work at the office. Sharp, snappy dialogue by Gordon and Kanin with superb direction by Cukor. Perhaps the best of the nine movies pairing Tracy and Hepburn. Also available colorized. **101m/B VHS, Beta, LV.** Spencer Tracy, Katharine Hepburn, Judy Holliday, Tom Ewell, David Wayne, Jean Hagen, Hope Emerson, Polly Moran, Marvin Kaplan, Paula Raymond, Tommy Noonan; *D:* George Cukor; *W:* Garson Kanin, Ruth Gordon; *M:* Miklos Rozsa. Nominations: Academy Awards '50: Best Story & Screenplay. *MGM, HMV*

The Addams Family 1964

The positively ooky family, based on the characters created by cartoonist Charles Addams, appear in the original, uncut television episodes. Two episodes per tape. This volume includes "The Addams Family Goes to School" and "Morticia and the Psychiatrist." **50m/B VHS.** John Astin, Carolyn Jones, Jackie Coogan, Ted Cassidy, Blossom Rock, Ken Weatherwax, Lisa Loring, Felix Silla. *WOV, MOV*

The Addams Family 🐾🐾 1991 (PG-13)

Everybody's favorite family of ghouls hits the big screen, but something is lost in the translation. An imposter claiming to be long-lost Uncle Fester (Lloyd), who says he was in the Bermuda Triangle for 25 years, shows up at the Addams' home to complete a dastardly deed—raid the family's immense fortune. Although Fester's plan is foiled, a series of plot twists highlight the ghoulish family's eccentricities. Darkly humorous but eventually disappointing: Julia, Huston, and Ricci are great in their roles and the sets look good, but the plot is thin. Much closer to the original comic strip by Charles Addams than the popular TV show ever was. **102m/C VHS, Beta, LV, Closed Caption.** Anjelica Huston, Raul Julia, Christopher Lloyd, Dan Hedaya, Elizabeth Wilson, Judith Malina, Carel Struycken, Dana Ivey, Paul Benedict, Christina Ricci, Jimmy Workman, Christopher Hart, John Franklin; *Cameos:* Marc Shaiman; *D:* Barry Sonnenfeld; *W:* Caroline Thompson, Larry Thompson; *C:* Owen Roizman; *M:* Marc Shaiman. Golden Raspberry Awards '91: Worst Song ("Addams Groove"); Nominations: Academy Awards '91: Best Costume Design. *PAR*

Addams Family Values 🐾🐾½ 1993 (PG-13)

The creepy Addams' are back, but this time they leave the dark confines of the mansion to meet the "real" world. New baby Pubert causes homicidal jealousy in sibs Wednesday and Pugsley, causing Mom and Dad to hire a gold-digging, serial-killing nanny (Cusack) with designs on Uncle Fester to watch over the tot. A step above its predecessor, chock full of black humor, sub-plots, and one-liners. Cusack fits right in with an outrageously over the top performance and Ricci nearly steals the show again as the deadpan Wednesday. *CW:* Macabre humor. **93m/C VHS, Beta, LV, Closed Caption.** Anjelica Huston, Raul Julia, Christopher Lloyd, Joan Cusack, Carol Kane, Christina Ricci, Jimmy Workman, Kaitlyn Hooper, Kristen Hooper, Carel Struycken, David Krumholtz, Christopher Hart, Dana Ivey, Peter MacNicol, Christine Baranski, Mercedes McNab; *D:* Barry Sonnenfeld; *W:* Paul Rudnick; *M:* Marc Shaiman. Golden Raspberry Awards '93: Worst Song ("WHOOMP! There It Is"); Nominations: Academy Awards '93: Best Art Direction/Set Decoration; Golden Globe Awards '94: Best Actress—Musical/Comedy (Huston). *PAR*

Addicted to Love 🐾🐾½ 1996 (R)

Warning: Do not rent this movie with your significant other if you're thinking about breaking up with them. After they're both dumped, mild-mannered Sam (Broderick) and wild woman Maggie (Ryan) discover they have a lot in common. First of all, their exes Linda (Preston) and Anton (Karyo) are dating each other. Secondly, they're both stalkers! Yep! A romantic comedy about stalking. Sam wants nothing more than to reclaim Linda as his own. Maggie wants nothing less than Anton's head on a plate. Interesting comedy wavers between dark and light moments, aided by the rather murky sets and lighting. Directorial debut for Dunne, who makes his father eat a bug in one scene. *CW:* Sexual content. **100m/C VHS.** Meg Ryan, Matthew Broderick, Kelly Preston, Tcheky Karyo, Maureen Stapleton, Remak Ramsay, Nesbitt Blaisdell, Dominick Dunne; *D:* Griffin Dunne; *W:* Robert Gordon; *C:* Andrew Dunn; *M:* Rachel Portman. *NYR*

The Addiction 🐾🐾½ 1995 (R)

Ph.D. candidate Kathleen Conklin (Taylor, in a haunting performance) gets bitten by more than the philosophy bug while attending university in Manhattan. When attacked by a female vampire (Sciorra), Kathleen quickly becomes driven by a ferocious blood need, beginning with an attack that parallels drug addiction when she stabs a derelict with a hypodermic needle and injects his blood into her own veins. Bitingly pretentious, themes experiment with the philosophy of Kirkegaard, Nietzche, and Sarte, and exploitative glimpses of the Holocaust and the My Lai massacre attempt to connect Kathleen's struggle to resist evil to historical atrocities. *CW:* Contains scenes of bloody vampire assaults. **82m/B VHS.** Lili Taylor, Christopher Walken, Annabella Sciorra, Edie Falco, Paul Calderone, Fredro Star, Kathryn Erbe, Michael Imperioli; *D:* Abel Ferrara; *W:* Nicholas St. John; *M:* Joe Delia. Nominations: Independent Spirit Awards '96: Best Actress (Taylor), Best Film. *PGV*

Address Unknown 🐾🐾½ 1996 (PG)

A ten-year-old letter and a priceless stamp provide a teenager with clues to dad's mysterious death. **92m/C VHS.** Kyle Howard, Johna Stewart, Patrick Renna, Corbin Allred, Michel Flynn; *D:* Shawn Levy. *WAR*

Adios Amigo 🐾🐾 1975 (PG)

Offbeat western comedy has ad-libbing Pryor hustling as a perennially inept con man. Script and direction (both provided by Williamson) are not up to Pryor's level, although excessive violence and vulgarity are avoided in a boring attempt to provide good clean family fare. **87m/C VHS, LV.** Fred Williamson, Richard Pryor, Thalmus Rasulala, James Brown, Robert Philip, Mike Henry; *D:* Fred Williamson; *W:* Fred Williamson. *SIM, THV*

Adios Gringo 🐾½ 1965

Routine oater in which a young rancher is swindled in a cattle deal and forced to kill in self defense. **?m/C VHS.** Montgomery Wood, Evelyn Stewart. *SNC*

Adios, Hombre 🐾 1968

An innocent man who was imprisoned for murder escapes from prison and seeks revenge. You'll be saying adios as well. **90m/C VHS, Beta.** *IT* Craig Hill, Giulia Rubini; *D:* Mario Caiano. *UNI*

The Adjuster 🐾🐾½ 1991 (R)

Critics either loved or hated this strange film. Insurance adjuster Noah Render's clients look to him for all sorts of comfort, so much so that his own identity becomes a blurred reflection of their tragedies. Wife Hera is a film censor who secretly tapes the pornographic videos she watches at work. Their carefully organized lives are invaded by Bubba and Mimi, a wealthy couple who pass themselves off as filmmakers who want to use the Render house as a movie set. They are instead looking to involve the Renders in their latest and most elaborate erotic fantasy. Lots of symbolism, but little substance. *CW:* Language and sensuality. **102m/C VHS.** *CA* Elias Koteas, Arsinee Khanjian, Maury Chaykin, Gabrielle Rose, David Hemblen, Jennifer Dale, Don McKellar, Raoul Trujillo; *D:* Atom Egoyan; *W:* Atom Egoyan; *C:* Paul Sarossy; *M:* Mychael Danna. Toronto-City Award '91: Best Canadian Feature Film. *ORI*

The Admiral Was a Lady 🐾🐾 1950

Four ex-GIs try to get by in life without going to work. Hendrix walks into their lives as a winning ex-Wave gifted with a knack for repartee who is disgusted by their collective lack of ambition. Nevertheless, she is pursued by the zany quartet with predictable results. **87m/B VHS, Beta.** Edmond O'Brien, Wanda Hendrix, Rudy Vallee, Steve Brodie; *D:* Albert Rogell. *NOS, FRH, VHE*

Adomas Nori Buti Zmogumi 🐾🐾

Adam Wants to Be a Man **1959** Soviet Lithuanian feature in its original form, with dialogue in Lithuanian. A young worker scrapes together money for a ticket to Buenos Aires, but the money is stolen by the manager of the travel office. **90m/B VHS.** *RU LI* **D:** V. Zhalakyavichus. *IHF*

Adoption 🐾🐾🐾 *Orkobefogadas* **1975** The third of Meszaros's trilogy, involving a middle-aged Hungarian woman who longs for a child and instead forms a deep friendship with a 19-year-old orphan. In Hungarian with English subtitles. **89m/B VHS, Beta. HU** Kati Berek, Laszlo Szabo, Gyongyver Vigh, Dr. Arpad Perlaky; **D:** Marta Meszaros; **W:** Marta Meszaros, Gyula Hernadi; **C:** Lajos Koltai; **M:** Gyorgy Kovacs. Berlin International Film Festival '75: Golden Berlin Bear. *KIV*

The Adorable Cheat 🐾🐾 **1928** A low-budget, late-silent melodrama about a young woman who tries to get involved in the family business, despite her father's refusal of her help. Once in the business, she finds love. **76m/B VHS, Beta, 8mm.** Lila Lee, Cornelius Keefe, Burr McIntosh; **D:** Burton King. *GPV, VYY*

Adorable Julia 🐾🐾 **1962** When an actress takes on a lover many years younger than herself, the laughs begin to fly in this sex comedy based on W. Somerset Maugham's novel. **97m/C VHS. FR** Lilli Palmer, Charles Boyer; **D:** Alfred Weidenmann. *FCT, VEC*

Adrenalin: Fear the Rush 🐾 **1996 (R)** Dull future thriller in the deadly virus category. In 2007, a plague in Eastern Europe causes those that survive to turn into cannabalistic killers. The U.S. has started quarantine camps, one of which is in Boston, and two cops (Henstridge and Lambert) must track down an infected killer who's escaped. Not worth your time. **CW:** Gruesome violence and gore, strong language. **77m/C VHS, LV, Closed Caption.** Christopher Lambert, Natasha Henstridge, Norbert Weisser, Craig Davis, Elizabeth Barondes, Xavier DeClie; **D:** Albert Pyun; **W:** Albert Pyun; **C:** George Mooradian; **M:** Tony Riparetti. *TOU*

Adrift 🐾🐾½ **1993** Yet another couple-in-terror-from-psychos-on-the-high-seas flick. Katie and Guy Nast (Jackson and Welsh) are on an anniversary sailing adventure intended to shore up their shaky marriage. They discover a boat adrift with two survivors (Greenwood and Rowan) who have a suspicious story but they help them nonetheless. Big mistake. Made for television. **92m/C VHS, Closed Caption.** Kate Jackson, Kenneth Welsh, Bruce Greenwood, Kelly Rowan; **D:** Christian Duguay. *WOV*

The Adultress 🐾 **1977 (R)** When a husband and wife cannot satisfy their desire to have a family, they hire a young man to help them in this dumb made-for-television melodrama. **85m/C VHS, Beta.** Tyne Daly, Eric (Hans Gudegast) Braeden, Gregory Morton; **D:** Norbert Meisel. *NO*

Adventure 🐾🐾 **1945** Gable's first postwar film has him as a roughneck sailor romancing a shy and reserved librarian (Garson). Dull and disappointing—both stars deserve better. However, there is a touching scene of Gable with newborn child that might be of interest to some. Based on the novel by Clyde Brion Davis. **130m/B VHS.** Clark Gable, Greer Garson, Joan Blondell, Thomas Mitchell, Tom Tully, John Qualen, Richard Haydn, Lina Romay; **D:** Victor Fleming; **W:** Vincent Lawrence, Frederick Hazlitt Brennan; **C:** Joseph Ruttenberg. *MGM*

Adventure Island 🐾½ **1947** En route to Australia, a small ship stops at a remote island for supplies. The crew is greeted by a crazed, tyrannical leader who makes their lives difficult. Dull low-budget remake of 1937's "Ebb Tide." **66m/C VHS, Beta.** Rory Calhoun, Rhonda Fleming, Paul Kelly, John Abbott; **D:** Sam Newfield. *SNC*

Adventure of the Action Hunters 🐾 **1987 (PG)** A dying sailor leaves a tourist couple a message leading to a treasure, and they vie for it along with gangsters, mercenaries and other unsavory types. **81m/C VHS, Beta.** Ronald Hunter, Sean Murphy, Joe Cimino; **D:** Lee Bonner. *NO*

The Adventurer 🐾🐾½ **1917** An escaped convict saves two wealthy women from death. They mistake him for a gallant sportsman and bring him home. Early Chaplin silent with music track. **20m/B VHS, Beta.** Charlie Chaplin, Charles Halton; **D:** Charlie Chaplin. *CAB*

The Adventurers 🐾🐾 *Fortune in Diamonds; The Great Adventure* **1951** At the turn of the century, two Boers and an English officer set out to recover stolen jewels hidden in the jungles of South Africa. On the way, greed and anger take their toll a la "The Treasure of Sierra Madre," only on a less convincing scale. **82m/B VHS, Beta. GB** Dennis Price, Jack Hawkins, Siobhan McKenna, Peter Hammond, Bernard Lee; **D:** David MacDonald. *NOS*

The Adventurers WOOF! **1970 (R)** Sleazy Harold Robbins novel retains its trashy aura on film. Unfortunately, this turkey is also long and boring. Set in South America, it tells the tale of a rich playboy who uses and destroys everyone who crosses his path. His vileness results from having seen his mother murdered by outlaws, but his obsession is to avenge his father's murder. Blood, gore, revolutions, and exploitive sex follow him everywhere. Watch and be amazed at the big-name stars who signed on for this one. **171m/C VHS, Closed Caption.** Candice Bergen, Olivia de Havilland, Bekim Fehmiu, Charles Aznavour, Alan Badel, Ernest Borgnine, Leigh Taylor-Young, Fernando Rey, Thommy Berggren, John Ireland, Sydney Tafler, Rossano Brazzi, Anna Moffo, Christian Roberts, Yorgo Voyagis, Angela Scoular, Yolande Donlan, Ferdinand "Ferdy" Mayne, Jaclyn Smith, Peter Graves, Roberta Haynes; **D:** Lewis Gilbert. *PAR*

Adventures Beyond Belief 🐾 *Neat and Tidy* **1987** An irreverent motorcyclist is chased across Europe for a murder he didn't commit. Firmly within the boundaries of belief. **95m/C VHS, Beta.** Elke Sommer, Jill Whitlow, Graham Stark, Stella Stevens, Larry Storch, Thick Wilson, Skyler Cole, Edie Adams, John Astin; **D:** Marcus Thompson. *NO*

Adventures in Babysitting 🐾🐾½ **1987 (PG-13)** Pleasant comedy has its moments when a babysitter and her charges leave peaceful suburbia for downtown Chicago to rescue a friend in trouble. After a flat tire strands them on the freeway, trouble takes on a new meaning. Shue is charming as the hapless sitter, unexpectedly dateless, who finds herself doing a lot more than just watching the kids. Ludicrous at times, but still fun to watch. **102m/C VHS, Beta, LV, 8mm, Closed Caption.** Elisabeth Shue, Keith Coogan, Maia Brewton, Anthony Rapp, Calvin Levels, Vincent D'Onofrio, Penelope Ann Miller, George Newbern, John Ford Noonan, Lolita Davidovich, Albert Collins; **D:** Chris Columbus; **W:** David Simkins; **M:** Michael Kamen. *TOU*

Adventures in Dinosaur City 🐾🐾 **1992 (PG)** Expect to see lots of movies riding on the coattails of the dino mania sweeping the land. Some will be good, others will not. "Adventures" falls into the latter category. Modern-day pre-teen siblings are transported back in time to the stone age. There they meet their favorite TV characters (they're dinosaurs) and help them solve prehistoric crimes. Family film may amuse kids, but adults should stick to "Jurassic Park." **88m/C VHS, LV, Closed Caption.** Omri Katz, Shawn Hoffman, Tiffanie Poston, Pete Koch, Megan Hughes, Tony Doyle, Mimi Maynard; **D:** Brett Thompson; **W:** Willie Baronet, Lisa Morton; **M:** Fredric Teetsel. *REP*

Adventures in Spying 🐾🐾 **1992 (PG-13)** Brian McNichols is just trying to enjoy his summer vacation when he discovers that a notorious drug lord is living in his neighborhood. After realizing there is a $50,000 reward for his capture, he enlists the help of his friend (Schoelen) to get the man's picture for the police. Action-packed film is geared towards the junior high set, but relies too heavily on coincidence and other plot connivances to compete with espionage flicks directed at an older market. **92m/C VHS, Closed Caption.** Jill Schoelen, Bernie Coulson, Seymour Cassel, G. Gordon Liddy, Michael Emil; **D:** Hil Covington; **W:** Hil Covington; **M:** James Stemple. *NLC*

The Adventures of a Gnome Named Gnorm 🐾🐾½ *A Gnome Named Gnorm* **1993 (PG)** Silly cop caper finds LAPD detective Casey (Hall) stuck with a very strange new partner—a bark-wearing gnome named Gnorm. The two team up to go after a diamond smuggling ring. The special-effects creature may hold the kiddies interest. **86m/C VHS.** Anthony Michael Hall, Jerry Orbach, Claudia Christian; **D:** Stan Winston. *PGV*

Adventures of a Private Eye 🐾 **1987** A self-mocking British detective farce about an inept private eye who takes his time tracking down a beautiful girl's blackmailer, bedding down with all the women he meets along the way. **96m/C VHS, Beta. GB** Christopher Neil, Suzy Kendall, Irene Handl; **D:** Stanley Long. *ACA*

Adventures of a Taxi Driver WOOF! **1976** Cabbie finds sex, crime, sex, adventure and sex on the road in this off-duty comedy. **89m/C VHS, Beta. GB** Barry Evans, Judy Geeson, Adrienne Posta, Diana Dors, Liz Fraser; **D:** Stanley Long. *ACA*

The Adventures of Baron Munchausen 🐾🐾🐾½ **1989 (PG)** From the director of "Time Bandits," "Brazil," and "The Fisher King" comes an ambitious, imaginative, chaotic, and under-appreciated marvel based on the tall (and often confused) tales of the Baron. Munchausen encounters the King of the Moon, Venus, and other odd and fascinating characters during what might be described as an circular narrative in which flashbacks dovetail into the present and place is never quite what it seems. Wonderful special effects and visually stunning sets occasionally dwarf the actors and prove what Gilliam can do with a big budget. **126m/C VHS, Beta, LV, 8mm, Closed Caption.** John Neville, Eric Idle, Sarah Polley, Valentina Cortese, Oliver Reed, Uma Thurman, Sting, Jonathan Pryce, Bill Paterson, Peter Jeffrey, Alison Steadman, Charles McKeown, Dennis Winston, Jack Purvis; **Cameos:** Robin Williams; **D:** Terry Gilliam; **W:** Terry Gilliam; **C:** Giuseppe Rotunno; **M:** Michael Kamen. Nominations: Academy Awards '89: Best Art Direction/Set Decoration, Best Costume Design, Best Makeup. *COL, CRC*

The Adventures of Buckaroo Banzai Across the Eighth Dimension 🐾🐾🐾 *Buckaroo Banzai* **1984 (PG)** A man of many talents, Buckaroo Banzai (Weller) travels through the eighth dimension in a jet-propelled Ford Fiesta to battle Planet 10 aliens led by the evil Lithgow. Buckaroo incorporates his vast knowledge of medicine, science, music, racing, and foreign relations to his advantage. Offbeat and often humorous cult sci-fi trip. **100m/C VHS, Beta, LV, Closed Caption.** Peter Weller, Ellen Barkin, Jeff Goldblum, John Lithgow, Lewis Smith, Rosalind Cash, Robert Ito, Pepe Serna, Vincent Schiavelli, Dan Hedaya, Yakov Smirnoff, Jamie Lee Curtis; **D:** W.D. Richter; **C:** Fred W. Koenekamp; **M:** Michael Boddicker. *VES, LIV*

The Adventures of Bullwhip Griffin 🐾🐾½ **1966** A rowdy, family-oriented comedy-adventure set during the California Gold Rush. Light Disney farce catches Russell at the tail end of his teenage star days. Pleshette and McDowall embark upon an ocean trip from Boston to San Francisco to find her brother, Russell, who's out west digging for gold. Assorted comedic adventures take place. **110m/C VHS, Beta.** Roddy McDowall, Suzanne Pleshette, Karl Malden, Harry Guardino, Kurt Russell; **D:** James Neilson; **C:** Edward Colman; **M:** George Bruns. *DIS*

Adventures of Captain Fabian 🐾½ **1951** When the captain of the "China Sea" learns that a beautiful woman has been falsely imprisoned, he comes to her rescue. Not one of Flynn's better swashbucklers, with typically low-quality Republic production. **100m/B VHS, Beta.** Errol Flynn, Vincent Price, Agnes Moorehead, Micheline Presle; **D:** William Marshall. *NO*

The Adventures of Captain Marvel 🎬🎬½ 1941

A 12-episode cliff-hanging serial based on the comic book character. Details the adventures of klutzy Billy Batson, who transforms into superhero Captain Marvel by speaking the magic word, "Shazam!" 240m/B VHS, LV. Tom Tyler, Frank "Junior" Coghlan, Louise Currie; **D:** William Witney. *VCN, REP, MLB*

Adventures of Don Juan 🎬🎬🎬½

The New Adventures of Don Juan 1949 Flynn's last spectacular epic features elegant costuming and loads of action. Don Juan saves Queen Margaret from her evil first minister. He then swashbuckles his way across Spain and England in an effort to win her heart. Grand, large-scale fun and adventure with Flynn at his self-mocking best. Special laserdisc edition includes the original trailer. 111m/C VHS, Beta, LV. Errol Flynn, Viveca Lindfors, Robert Douglas, Romney Brent, Alan Hale, Raymond Burr, Aubrey Mather, Ann Rutherford; **D:** Vincent Sherman; **M:** Max Steiner. Academy Awards '49: Best Costume Design (Color); Nominations: Academy Awards '49: Best Art Direction/Set Decoration (Color). *MGM, MLB*

Adventures of Eliza Fraser 🎬½ 1976

A young shipwrecked couple move from bawdy pleasures to cannibalism after being captured by aborigines. 114m/C VHS, Beta, LV. Susannah York, Trevor Howard, Leon Lissek, Abigail, Noel Ferrier, Carole Skinner; **D:** Tim Burstall. *NWV*

The Adventures of Ford Fairlane woof!

Ford Fairlane 1990 (R) The Diceman plays an unusual detective specializing in rock 'n' roll cases. When a heavy metal singer dies on stage, he takes the case in his own inimitable fashion, pursuing buxom gals, sleazy record executives and even his ex-wife. Not surprisingly, many of his stand-up bits are worked into the movie. Clay, the ever-so-controversial comic in his first (and likely last) starring role haplessly sneers his way through this rock 'n roll dud of a comedy thriller. A quick effort to cash in on Clay's fading star. Forget about it. 101m/C VHS, Beta, LV, Closed Caption. Andrew Dice Clay, Wayne Newton, Priscilla Presley, Morris Day, Lauren Holly, Maddie Corman, Gilbert Gottfried, David Patrick Kelly, Brandon Call, Robert Englund, Ed O'Neill, Sheila E, Kari Wuhrer, Tone Loc; **D:** Renny Harlin; **W:** David Arnott, Daniel Waters, James Cappe. Golden Raspberry Awards '90: Worst Picture, Worst Actor (Clay), Worst Screenplay. *FXV*

The Adventures of Frank and Jesse James 1948

The bad brothers of the Wild West are trying to make good for rip-offs committed in their names, so they're hoping to hit pay-dirt with a silver mine. A 13-episode serial on two cassettes. 180m/B VHS. Steve Darrell, Clayton Moore, Noel Neill, Stanley Andrews; **D:** Yakima Canutt. *REP, MOV*

The Adventures of Frontier Fremont 🎬🎬 1975

A rough and tumble story of a man who leaves the city, grows a beard, and makes the wilderness his home (and the animals his friends). Mountain life, that's the life for me. Almost indistinguishable from Haggerty's "Grizzly Adams," with the usual redeeming panoramic shots of majestic mountains. 95m/C VHS, Beta. Dan Haggerty, Denver Pyle; **D:** Richard Friedenberg. *NO*

The Adventures of Gallant Bess 🎬🎬 1948

The time-honored story of a rodeo man torn between his girl and his talented horse (the Bess of the title). 73m/C VHS. Cameron Mitchell, Audrey Long, Fuzzy Knight, James Millican; **D:** Lew (Louis Friedlander) Landers. *HEG*

The Adventures of Hairbreadth Harry 192?

Three short spoofs of the early melodramas cranked out by the movie industry. Includes "Sawdust Baby," "Fearless Harry," and "Rudolph's Revenge." 65m/B VHS, Beta. Billy West. *GPV*

The Adventures of Huck Finn 🎬🎬🎬 1993 (PG)

Decent Disney attempt at adapting an American favorite by Mark Twain. Mischievious Huck and runaway slave Jim travel down the muddy Mississippi, working on life and friendship and getting into all sorts of adventures in the pre-Civil War era. Fast-paced and amusing with good performances by Wood (in the title role) and Broadway trained Vance (as Jim). Racial epithets and minstrel show dialect have been eliminated in this version. Some material, including Jim's close call with a lynch mob and Huck's drunken, brutal father may be too strong for immature children. 108m/C VHS, Beta, LV, Closed Caption. Elijah Wood, Courtney B. Vance, Robbie Coltrane, Jason Robards Jr., Ron Perlman, Dana Ivey, Anne Heche, James Gammon, Paxton Whitehead, Tom Aldredge, Curtis Armstrong, Mary Louise Wilson, Frances Conroy; **D:** Stephen Sommers; **W:** Stephen Sommers; **C:** Janusz Kaminski; **M:** Bill Conti. *DIS, BTV*

The Adventures of Huckleberry Finn 🎬🎬🎬 1939

Mark Twain's classic story about a boy who runs away and travels down the Mississippi on a raft, accompanied by a runaway slave, is done over in MGM-style. Rooney is understated as Huck (quite a feat), while the production occasionally floats aimlessly down the Mississippi. An entertaining follow-up to "The Adventures of Tom Sawyer." 89m/B VHS, Beta. Mickey Rooney, Lynne Carver, Rex Ingram, William Frawley, Walter Connolly; **D:** Richard Thorpe. *MGM, HMV*

The Adventures of Huckleberry Finn 🎬🎬½ 1960

A lively adaptation of the Twain saga in which Huck and runaway slave Jim raft down the Mississippi in search of freedom and adventure. Miscasting of Hodges as Huck hampers the proceedings, but Randall shines as the treacherous King. Strong supporting cast includes Keaton as a lion-tamer and boxing champ Moore as Jim. 107m/C VHS, Beta. Tony Randall, Eddie Hodges, Archie Moore, Patty McCormack, Neville Brand, Mickey Shaughnessy, Judy Canova, Andy Devine, Sherry Jackson, Buster Keaton, Finlay Currie, Josephine Hutchinson, Parley Baer, John Carradine, Royal Dano, Sterling Holloway, Harry Dean Stanton; **D:** Michael Curtiz. *MGM, FCT*

The Adventures of Huckleberry Finn 🎬🎬 1978

The classic adventure by Mark Twain of an orphan boy and a runaway slave done again as a TV movie and starring "F-Troop" regulars Tucker and Storch. Lacks the production values of earlier versions. 100m/C VHS, Beta. Forrest Tucker, Larry Storch, Kurt Ida, Mike Mazurki, Brock Peters; **D:** Jack B. Hively. *NO*

The Adventures of Huckleberry Finn 🎬🎬½ 1985

An adaptation of the Mark Twain story about the adventures encountered by Huckleberry Finn and a runaway slave as they travel down the Mississippi River. Top-notch cast makes this an entertaining version. Originally made for television in a much longer version for PBS's "American Playhouse." 121m/C VHS, Beta. Sada Thompson, Lillian Gish, Richard Kiley, Jim Dale, Barnard Hughes, Patrick Day, Frederic Forrest, Geraldine Page, Butterfly McQueen, Samm-Art Williams; **D:** Peter H. Hunt. *USH, MON*

The Adventures of Ichabod and Mr. Toad 🎬🎬🎬½ 1949

Disney's wonderfully animated versions of Kenneth Grahame's "The Wind in the Willows" and "The Legend of Sleepy Hollow" by Washington Irving. Rathbone narrates the story of Mr. Toad, who suffers from arrogance and eventually must defend himself in court after being charged with driving a stolen vehicle (Disney did take liberties with the story). Crosby provides all the voices for "Ichabod," which features one of the all-time great animated sequences—Ichabod riding in a frenzy through the forest while being pursued by the headless horseman. A treat for all ages. 68m/C VHS, LV. **D:** Clyde Geronimi, James Algar; **V:** Jack Kinney, Bing Crosby. *DIS*

Adventures of Kit Carson 1951

Television western, which ran from 1951-1955, set in the 1880s about the famed frontiersman who kept the peace with the help of Mexican sidekick El Toro. Two episodes per tape. 50m/C VHS, Beta. Bill Williams, John Hamilton, Don Diamond. *MOV, MVC*

The Adventures of Marco Polo 🎬🎬½ 1938

Lavish Hollywood production based on the exploits of 13th-century Venetian explorer Marco Polo (Cooper). He becomes the first white man to record his visit to the Eastern court of Kublai Khan, where he falls for a beautiful princess also desired by the evil Rathbone. Lots of action, though its hard to picture the laconic Cooper in the title role. 100m/B VHS. Gary Cooper, Sigrid Gurie, Basil Rathbone, Ernest Truex, George Barbier, Binnie Barnes, Alan Hale, H.B. Warner; **D:** Archie Mayo; **W:** Robert Sherwood; **M:** Hugo Friedhofer. *FCT*

The Adventures of Mark Twain 🎬🎬🎬 1944

March stars as Mark Twain, the nom de plume of Samuel Clemens, the beloved humorist and writer. His travels and adventures along the Mississippi and on to the California gold rush would later result in the books and stories which would make him so well-known. March attains a quiet nobility as he goes from young man to old sage, along with Smith, who plays Olivia, Twain's beloved wife. 130m/B VHS, Beta. Fredric March, Alexis Smith, Donald Crisp, Alan Hale, Sir C. Aubrey Smith, John Carradine, William Henry, Robert Barrat, William Hampden, Percy Kilbride; **D:** Irving Rapper; **W:** Alan LeMay, Harry Chandlee; **M:** Max Steiner. Nominations: Academy Awards '44: Best Interior Decoration, Best Special Effects, Original Dramatic/Comedy Score. *MGM, FCT, BTV*

The Adventures of Mark Twain 🎬🎬🎬 1985 (G)

A clay-animated fantasy based on, and radically departing from, the life and work of Mark Twain. Story begins with Twain flying into outer space in a blimp with stowaways Huck Finn, Tom Sawyer and Becky Thatcher and takes off from there. Above average entertainment for kids and their folks. 86m/C VHS, Beta, LV. **D:** Will Vinton; **W:** Susan Shadburne; **V:** James Whitmore, Chris Ritchie, Gary Krug, Michele Mariana. *BAR*

The Adventures of Milo & Otis 🎬🎬🎬

Koneko Monogatari; The Adventures of Chatran 1989 (G) Delightful Japanese children's film about a farm-dwelling dog and cat and their odyssey after the cat is accidentally swept away on a river. Notable since no humans appear in the film. A record-breaking success in its homeland. Well received by U.S. children. Narrated by Dudley Moore. 76m/C VHS, Beta, LV, Closed Caption. **JP D:** Masanori Hata; **W:** Mark Saltzman; **M:** Michael Boddicker. *COL, RDG, HMV*

The Adventures of Nellie Bly 🎬 1981

Made for television "Classics Illustrated" story of Nellie Bly, a strong-willed female reporter doing her best to expose wrongdoings in the late 19th century. A decent performance by Purl is overshadowed by the general lack of direction. 100m/C VHS, Beta. Linda Purl, Gene Barry, John Randolph, Raymond Buktenica, J.D. Cannon, Elayne Heilveil, Cliff Osmond; **D:** Henning Schellerup. *NO*

The Adventures of Ozzie & Harriet 195?

Each volume in this 12-set series contains 4 episodes of the Nelsons' hit TV show from 1953-1964. Vol. 1 features 17-year-old Mary Tyler Moore doing the commercials. Vol. 2 features Mamie Van Doren as the housemother of Ricky's fraternity (some housemother!). The program was the prototype of family sitcoms. Original commercials included. Tapes are available for purchase individually. 56m/B VHS. Ozzie Nelson, Harriet Hilliard Nelson, Ricky Nelson, David Nelson; **D:** Ozzie Nelson. *MOV*

The Adventures of Picasso 🎬🎬 1980

A Swedish satire on the life of Picasso, dubbed in English. Don't look for art or facts here, or, for that matter, many laughs. 88m/C VHS, Beta. SW Gosta Ekman, Lena Nyman, Hans Alfredson, Margareta Krook, Bernard Cribbins, Wilfrid Brambell; **D:** Tage Danielsson. *NO*

The Adventures of Pinocchio 🎬🎬½

Pinocchio; Carlo Collodi's Pinocchio 1996 (G) Live-action version of Carlo Collodi's story about woodcarver Gepetto (Landau) who carves himself a puppet son (Thomas) who longs to be a real boy. Story differs from the Disney cartoon version in that it's a little darker and the cat, the fox, and the cricket have larger roles. Jim Henson's Creature Shop provided the animatronic magic to bring Pinocchio to life. His head alone was jammed with wiring and 18 tiny motors to give the "boy" a full range of facial expressions. It took as many as five puppeteers at a time to animate the character. So lifelike was the puppet that some of the crew actually spoke to it as they did the human actors. **88m/C VHS, LV, Closed Caption.** Martin Landau, Jonathan Taylor Thomas, Rob Schneider, Bebe Neuwirth, Udo Kier; **D:** Steven Barron; **W:** Steven Barron, Tom Benedek, Sherry Mills; **C:** Juan Ruiz-Anchia; **M:** Rachel Portman. *NLC*

The Adventures of Priscilla, Queen of the Desert ⚔⚔⚔ 1994 (R) Quirky down-under musical-comedy follows two drag queens and a transsexual across the Australian Outback on their way to a gig in a small resort town. They make the drive in a pink bus nicknamed Priscilla. Along the way they encounter, and perform for, the usual unusual assortment of local characters. Scenes depicting homophobic natives play out as expected. Finest moments occur on the bus or onstage (all hail ABBA). Strong performances, especially by usually macho Stamp as the widowed Bernadette, rise above the cliches in what is basically a bitchy, cross-dressing road movie, celebrating drag as art and the nonconformity of its heroes. Costumes (by Lizzy Gardner and Tim Chappel) are a lark, the photography's surreal, and the soundtrack fittingly campy.**CW:** Language and sex-related situations. **102m/C VHS, LV.** *AU* Terence Stamp, Hugo Weaving, Guy Pearce, Bill Hunter, Sarah Chadwick, Mark Holmes, Julia Cortez; **D:** Stephan Elliott; **W:** Stephan Elliott; **C:** Brian J. Breheny; **M:** Guy Gross. Academy Awards '94: Best Costume Design; Australian Film Institute '94: Best Costume Design; Nominations: Australian Film Institute '94: Best Actor (Stamp), Best Actor (Weaving), Best Cinematography, Best Director (Elliott), Best Film, Best Screenplay; Golden Globe Awards '95: Best Actor—Musical/Comedy (Stamp), Best Film—Musical/Comedy; Writers Guild of America '94: Best Original Screenplay. *PGV*

Adventures of Red Ryder ⚔⚔ 1940 The thrills of the rugged West are presented in this twelve-episode serial. Based on the then-famous comic strip character. **240m/B VHS, Beta.** Donald (Don "Red") Barry, Noah Beery Sr.; **D:** William Witney. *MLB*

The Adventures of Rex & Rinty ⚔⚔ 1935 An adventure serial in 12 chapters, featuring Rin-Tin-Tin, Jr. **156m/B VHS, Beta.** Kane Richmond, Harry Woods, Smiley Burnette; **D:** Ford Beebe, B. Reeves Eason. *NOS, VCN, DVT*

The Adventures of Rin Tin Tin ⚔⚔½ 1947 Chronicles the adventures of that crime-fighting dog, Rin-Tin-Tin. **65m/B VHS.** Robert (Bobby) Blake. *CCB*

The Adventures of Robin Hood ⚔⚔⚔⚔ 1938 Rollicking Technicolor tale of the legendary outlaw, regarded as the swashbuckler standard-bearer. The justice-minded Saxon knight battles the Normans, outwits evil Prince John, and gallantly romances Maid Marian. Grand castle sets and lush forest photography display ample evidence of the huge (in 1938) budget of $2 million plus. Just entering his prime, Flynn enthusiastically performed most of his own stunts, including intricate sword play and advanced tree and wall climbing. His Robin brims with charm and bravura, the enthusiastic protector of poor Saxons everywhere and the undeclared king of Sherwood forest. The rest of the cast likewise attacks with zest: de Havilland, a cold but eventually sympathetic Maid Marian; Rains' dastardly Prince John (the predecessor to Alan Rickman's over-the-top spin as the Sheriff in Costner's remake); and Rathbone's conniving Sir Guy to Robin's band of very merry men. Based on various Robin Hood legends as well as Sir Walter Scott's "Ivanhoe" and the opera "Robin Hood" by

De Koven-Smith. Also available in letter-box format. **102m/C VHS, Beta, LV, Closed Caption.** Errol Flynn, Olivia de Havilland, Basil Rathbone, Alan Hale, Una O'Connor, Claude Rains, Patric Knowles, Eugene Pallette, Herbert Mundin, Melville Cooper, Ian Hunter, Montagu Love; **D:** Michael Curtiz; **W:** Norman Reilly Raine, Seton I. Miller; **M:** Erich Wolfgang Korngold. Academy Awards '38: Best Film Editing, Best Interior Decoration, Best Original Score; Nominations: Academy Awards '38: Best Picture. *MGM, FOX, CRC*

The Adventures of Robin Hood 1955 Filmed on location in England and starring Greene as the legendary outlaw/hero, with Pleasance as the evil Prince John. Two episodes per tape. Volume 1 features "The Highlander" and "Tables Turned." Additional episodes are available. **60m/C VHS, Beta.** Richard Greene, Donald Pleasence. *MVC, MOV*

The Adventures of Rusty ⚔⚔½ 1945 Forties family film series begins with this classic boy-meets-dog story. Danny's dog dies in an accident and his widowed father has just remarried so the kid's feeling pretty bad. Then he meets neglected German Shepherd Rusty, a former police dog with an undeservedly bad rep. Naturally, boy and dog bond and even capture a couple of escaped convicts (and Danny learns to love his stepmom too). **67m/B VHS.** Ted Donaldson, Margaret Lindsay, Conrad Nagel, Gloria Holden; **D:** Paul Burnford; **W:** Aubrey Wisberg. *COL*

The Adventures of Sadie ⚔⚔½ *Our Girl Friday* 1955 Collins is stranded on a desert island with three men, two of whom continuously chase her around. Naturally, she falls for the guy who ignores her. Obvious sex comedy which plays on Collins' scantily-clad physical assets. Based on the novel "The Cautious Amorist" by Norman Lindsay. **87m/C VHS.** *GB* Joan Collins, George Cole, Kenneth More, Robertson Hare, Hermione Gingold, Walter Fitzgerald; **D:** Noel Langley; **W:** Noel Langley. *NO*

The Adventures of Sherlock Holmes ⚔⚔½ *Sherlock Holmes* 1939 The immortal Sherlock Holmes and his assistant Dr. Watson conflict with Scotland Yard as they both race to stop arch-criminal Professor Moriarty. The Yard is put to shame as Holmes, a mere amateur sleuth, uses his brilliant deductive reasoning to save the damsel in distress and to stop Moriarty from stealing the Crown Jewels. Second in the series. **83m/B VHS, Beta, Closed Caption.** Basil Rathbone, Nigel Bruce, Ida Lupino, George Zucco, E.E. Clive, Mary Gordon; **D:** Alfred Werker; **W:** Edwin Blum; **C:** Leon Shamroy. *FOX*

The Adventures of Sherlock Holmes: Hound of the Baskervilles 1989 Holmes tackles the mysterious and long-lived curse of the Baskervilles. Made for British television. Fine acting, detailed production. A pleasure. **120m/C VHS.** *GB* Jeremy Brett, Edward Hardwicke. *MPI*

The Adventures of Sherlock Holmes' Smarter Brother ⚔⚔⚔ 1978 (PG) The unknown brother of the famous Sherlock Holmes takes on some of his brother's more disposable excess cases and makes some hilarious moves. Moments of engaging farce borrowed from the Mel Brooks school of parody (and parts of the Brooks ensemble as well). **91m/C VHS, Beta.** Gene Wilder, Madeline Kahn, Marty Feldman, Dom DeLuise, Leo McKern, Roy Kinnear, John Le Mesurier, Douglas Wilmer, Thorley Walters; **D:** Gene Wilder; **W:** Gene Wilder. *FOX*

Adventures of Smilin' Jack 1943 WWII flying ace Smilin' Jack Martin comes to life in this action-packed serial. Character from the Zack Mosley comic strip about air force fighting over China. **90m/B VHS, Beta.** Tom Brown, Sidney Toler; **D:** Ray Taylor. *SNC, NOS, VAN*

The Adventures of Tartu ⚔⚔½ *Tartu* 1943 A British secret agent, sent to blow up a Nazi poison gas factory in Czechoslovakia, poses as a Romanian. One of Donat's lesser films, in the

style of "The 39 Steps." **103m/C VHS, Beta.** *GB* Robert Donat, Valerie Hobson, Glynis Johns; **D:** Harold Bucquet. *HHT, TIM, VEC*

The Adventures of Tarzan ⚔⚔ 1921 The screen's first Tarzan in an exciting jungle thriller. Silent. **153m/B VHS, Beta.** Elmo Lincoln. *VYY, GVV*

The Adventures of the Flying Cadets ⚔½ 1944 Early aerial war adventure serial in thirteen complete chapters. **169m/B VHS, Beta.** Johnny Downs, Regis Toomey; **D:** Ray Taylor, Lewis D. Collins. *VYY, VCN, NOS*

The Adventures of the Masked Phantom ⚔½ 1938 The adventures of the Masked Phantom. **56m/B VHS, Beta.** Monte Rawlins, Betty Burgess, Larry Mason, Sonny Lamont, Jack Ingram; **D:** Charles Abbott. *NOS, VYY, RXM*

The Adventures of the Wilderness Family ⚔⚔ 1976 (G) The story of a modern-day pioneer family who becomes bored with the troubles of city life and heads for life in the wilderness. There, they find trouble in paradise. Family-oriented adventure offering pleasant scenery. Followed by "The Wilderness Family, Part 2." **100m/C VHS, Beta, LV.** Robert F. Logan, Susan Damante Shaw; **D:** Stewart Raffill; **W:** Stewart Raffill. *MED, VTR*

The Adventures of Tom Sawyer ⚔⚔⚔ 1938 The vintage Hollywood adaptation of the Mark Twain classic, with art direction by William Cameron Menzies. Not a major effort from the Selznick studio, but quite detailed and the best Tom so far. **91m/C VHS, Beta, LV.** Tommy Kelly, Walter Brennan, Victor Jory, May Robson, Victor Kilian, Jackie Moran, Donald Meek, Ann Gillis, Marcia Mae Jones, Clara Blandick, Margaret Hamilton; **D:** Norman Taurog; **C:** James Wong Howe; **M:** Max Steiner. Nominations: Academy Awards '38: Best Interior Decoration.*FOX, FCT, MLB*

The Adventures of Tom Sawyer ⚔⚔½ 1973 Tom Sawyer is a mischievous Missouri boy who gets into all kinds of trouble in this white-washed, made for TV adaptation of the Mark Twain classic. **76m/C VHS, Beta.** Jane Wyatt, Buddy Ebsen, Vic Morrow, John McGiver, Josh Albee, Jeff Tyler. *USH*

The Adventurous Knights woof! 1935 An athlete learns he is the heir to a Transylvanian throne. **60m/B VHS, Beta, LV.** David Sharpe, Mary Kornman, Mickey Daniels, Gertrude Messinger; **D:** Edward Roberts. *NO*

The Adversary ⚔⚔½ *Pratldwandi* 1971 A young man must quit college because of his father's death. He struggles to find employment in Calcutta but his hardships are magnified by the impersonal society. In Bengali with English subtitles. **110m/C VHS.** *IN D:* Satyajit Ray; **W:** Satyajit Ray. *FCT*

Advise and Consent ⚔⚔⚔ 1962 An interesting political melodrama with a fascinating cast, based upon Allen Drury's novel. The President chooses a candidate for the Secretary of State position which divides the Senate and causes the suicide of a senator. Controversial in its time, though somewhat turgid today. Laughton's last film. **139m/B VHS, Beta.** Don Murray, Charles Laughton, Henry Fonda, Walter Pidgeon, Lew Ayres, Burgess Meredith, Gene Tierney, Franchot Tone, Paul Ford, George Grizzard, Betty White, Peter Lawford, Edward Andrews; **D:** Otto Preminger; **W:** Wendell Mayes; **C:** Sam Leavitt. National Board of Review Awards '62: Best Supporting Actor (Meredith). *WAR, KAR, VTR*

The Advocate ⚔⚔⚔ *The Hour of the Pig* 1993 (R) Bizarre black comedy about 15th-century Paris lawyer Richard Courtois (Firth) who decides to ply his trade in the country, only to find things stranger than he can imagine. His first case turns out to be defending a pig that's accused of murdering a child. And the pig is owned by beautiful gypsy Samira (Annabi), so the idealistic lawyer can fall in love (or lust). There's religion and superstition, there's power struggles, there's ignorance versus knowledge— things sound very modern indeed.**CW:** Strong sexuality; nudity; violence; profanity. 102m/C VHS, LV, **Closed Caption.** *GB* Colin Firth, Amina Annabi, Nicol Williamson, Ian Holm, Lysette Anthony, Donald Pleasence, Michael Gough, Harriet Walter, Jim Carter; ***D:*** Leslie Megahey; ***W:*** Leslie Megahey. *MAX, TOU*

Aelita: Queen of Mars 🎬🎬 *Aelita: The Revolt of the Robots* 1924 Though the title has blockbuster potential, "Aelita" is a little-known silent Soviet sci-fi flick destined to remain little known. After building a rocket to fly to Mars, a Russian engineer finds its no Martian holiday on the fourth planet from the sun, with the Martians in the midst of a revolution. Silent, with a piano score. 113m/B VHS, LV. *RU* Yulia Solntseva, Nikolai Batalov, Igor Illinski, Nikolai Tseretelli, Vera Orlova, Pavel Poi, Konstantin Eggert, Yuri Zavadski, Valentina Kuindzi, N. Tretyakova; ***D:*** Yakov Protazanov; ***W:*** Fedor Ozep, Aleksey Fajko; ***C:*** Yuri Zhelyabuzhsky, Emil Schoenemann. *KIV, FCT, SNC*

The Affair 🎬🎬🎬 1973 Songwriter/polio victim Wood falls in love for the first time with attorney Wagner. Delicate situation handled well by a fine cast in this television movie. 74m/C VHS, Beta. Natalie Wood, Robert Wagner, Bruce Davison, Kent Smith, Frances Reid, Pat Harrington; ***D:*** Gilbert Cates. *NO*

The Affair 🎬🎬½ 1995 (R) It's 1944 in a small English town, where a troop of black American soldiers are billeted prior to the D-Day invasion. Travis (Vance) falls for the married Maggie (Fox)—whose husband, Edward (Hinds), is supposed to be away at sea—and they begin an affair. Unfortunately, Edward arrives home unexpectedly and accuses Travis of raping his wife. If Maggie denies the accusation, she'll lose her home and family but if she confirms it, Travis, according to Army law, will be condemned to death. Made for cable TV.**CW:** Strong sexuality, some language and drug use. 105m/C VHS. *GB* Courtney B. Vance, Kerry Fox, Ciaran Hinds, Beatie Edney, Leland Gantt, Bill Nunn, Ned Beatty; ***D:*** Paul Seed; ***W:*** Pablo F. Fenjves, Bryan Goluboff; ***C:*** Ivan Strasburg; ***M:*** Christopher Gunning. *HBO*

An Affair in Mind 🎬🎬 1989 British television movie about a professional writer who falls in love with a beautiful woman who tries to convince him to assist her in murdering her husband. 88m/C VHS, Beta, **Closed Caption.** *GB* Amanda Donohoe, Stephen Dillon, Matthew Marsh, Kean-Laurent Cochot; ***D:*** Michael Baker.

Affair in Trinidad 🎬🎬 1952 Fun in the tropics as nightclub singer Hayworth enlists the help of brother-in-law Ford to find her husband's murderer. The trail leads to international thieves and espionage in a romantic thriller that reunites the stars of "Gilda." Hayworth sings (with Jo Ann Greer's voice) "I've Been Kissed Before." 98m/B VHS, LV. Rita Hayworth, Glenn Ford, Alexander Scourby, Torin Thatcher, Valerie Bettis, Steve Geray; ***D:*** Vincent Sherman. Nominations: Academy Awards '52: Best Costume Design (B & W). *COL, CCB*

The Affair of the Pink Pearl 🎬½ 1984 The husband-and-wife private investigation team of Tommy and Tuppence must find within 24 hours the culprit who stole a valuable pink pearl. Based on the Agatha Christie series of short stories. Made for British television. 60m/C VHS, Beta. *GB* James Warwick, Francesca Annis. *TPV*

An Affair to Remember 🎬🎬🎬½ 1957 McCarey remakes his own "Love Affair," with less success. Nightclub singer Kerr and wealthy bachelor Grant discover love on an ocean liner and agree to meet six months later on top of the Empire State Building to see if their feelings are the same. Not as good as the original, but a winner of a fairy tale just the same. Notable for causing many viewers to sob uncontrollably. "Affair" was gathering dust on store shelves until "Sleepless in Seattle" used it as a plot device and rentals skyrocketed. In 1994 real life couple Warren Beatty and Annette Bening attempted a third "Love Affair" remake. 115m/C VHS, Beta, LV, **Closed Caption.** Cary Grant, Deborah Kerr, Richard Denning, Cathleen Nesbitt, Neva Patterson, Robert Q. Lewis, Fortunio Bonanova,

Matt Moore, Nora Marlowe, Sarah Selby; ***D:*** Leo McCarey; ***W:*** Leo McCarey, Delmer Daves; ***C:*** Milton Krasner; ***M:*** Hugo Friedhofer. Nominations: Academy Awards '57: Best Cinematography, Best Costume Design, Best Song ("An Affair to Remember"), Best Score. *FOX*

The Affairs of Annabel 🎬🎬½ 1938 The first of the popular series of Annabel pictures Lucy made in the late 1930s. Appealing adolescent is zoomed to movie stardom by her press agent's stunts. A behind-the-scenes satire on Hollywood, stars, and agents. 68m/B VHS, Beta, LV. Lucille Ball, Jack Oakie, Ruth Donnelly, Fritz Feld, Bradley Page; ***D:*** Ben Stoloff. *CCB, IME, MLB*

The Affairs of Dobie Gillis 🎬🎬½ 1953 Light musical-comedy about a group of college kids and their carefree antics. Complete with big-band tunes, dance numbers, and plenty of collegiate shenanigans, this '50s classic inspired a hit TV series, "The Many Loves of Dobie Gillis." ♫I'm Through with Love; All I Do Is Dream of You; You Can't Do Wrong Doing Right; Those Endearing Young Charms. 72m/B VHS. Debbie Reynolds, Bobby Van, Barbara Ruick, Bob Fosse, Lurene Tuttle, Hans Conried, Charles Lane; ***D:*** Don Weis; ***W:*** Max Shulman; ***C:*** William Mellor. *MGM*

Afraid of the Dark 🎬🎬 1992 (R) Convoluted psycho-thriller from a child's point of view. Young Lucas is fearful for his blind mother. It seems a vicious slasher has been attacking blind women and Lucas' father, a policeman, has yet to apprehend the criminal. But...Lucas it seems has a problem with reality. With his fantasies and realities mixed, all the people in his life also play entirely different roles. Characters are so detached and unreal that a viewer is prevented from a clear understanding of anything that may, or may not, be going on. Directorial debut of Peploe.**CW:** Violence and one scene of sensuality. 91m/C VHS, LV, **Closed Caption.** Ben Keyworth, James Fox, Fanny Ardant, Paul McGann, Clare Holman, Robert Stephens; ***D:*** Mark Peploe. *COL, NLC*

Africa Screams 🎬🎬½ 1949 Abbott and Costello go on an African safari in possession of a secret map. Unheralded independent A&C film is actually quite good in the stupid vein, with lots of jungle slapstick, generally good production values and a supporting cast of familiar comedy faces. 79m/B VHS, Beta, LV. Lou Costello, Bud Abbott, Shemp Howard, Hillary Brooke, Joe Besser, Clyde Beatty; ***D:*** Charles T. Barton. *KAR, MRV, CNG*

Africa Texas Style 🎬🎬 1967 An East African rancher hires an American cowboy and his Navajo sidekick to help run his wild game ranch. Decent family adventure which served as the pilot for the short-lived TV series "Cowboy in Africa." Features lots of wildlife footage and a cameo appearance by Hayley Mills. 109m/C VHS. Hugh O'Brian, John Mills, Nigel Green, Tom Nardini; ***Cameos:*** Hayley Mills; ***D:*** Andrew Marton; ***M:*** Malcolm Arnold. *REP*

An African Dream 🎬½ 1990 (PG) A period tale about a black man and a white woman fighting against repression in South Africa. 94m/C VHS, Beta, LV. Kitty Aldridge, John Kani, Dominic Jephcott, John Carson, Richard Haines, Joy Stewart Spence; ***D:*** John Smallcombe. *HMD, IME, FCT*

African Journey 1989 A moving, cross-cultural drama of friendship. A young black American goes to Africa for the summer to be with his divorced father who is working in the diamond mines. There he meets a young black African like himself; they overcome cultural clashes and learn respect for one another. Beautiful scenery, filmed in Africa. Part of the "Wonderworks" series. 174m/C VHS, **Closed Caption.** Jason Blicker, Pedzisai Sithole. *PME, HMV, BTV*

The African Queen 🎬🎬🎬🎬 1951 After Bible-thumping spinster Hepburn's missionary brother is killed in WWI Africa, hard-drinking, dissolute steamer captain Bogart offers her safe passage. Not satisfied with sanctuary, she persuades him to destroy a German gunboat blocking the

British advance. The two spend most of their time battling aquatic obstacles and each other, rather than the Germans. Time alone on a African river turns mistrust and aversion to love, a transition effectively counterpointed by the continuing suspense of their daring mission. Classic war of the sexes script adapted from C.S. Forester's novel makes wonderful use of natural dialogue and humor. Shot on location in Africa. 105m/C VHS, Beta, LV. *GB* Humphrey Bogart, Katharine Hepburn, Robert Morley, Theodore Bikel, Peter Bull, Walter Gotell, Peter Swanwick, Richard Marner; ***D:*** John Huston; ***W:*** John Huston, James Agee; ***C:*** Jack Cardiff. Academy Awards '51: Best Actor (Bogart); Nominations: Academy Awards '51: Best Actress (Hepburn), Best Director (Huston), Best Screenplay. *FOX, FCT, TLF*

African Rage 🎬🎬 *Tigers Don't Cry; The Long Shot; Target of an Assassin; Fatal Assassin* 1978 Little known release about an aging male nurse (yes, Quinn) who discovers he's dying of an incurable disease. With nothing left to lose, he plans the kidnapping of an African leader, hoping that the ransom will support his family. Meanwhile, another man is plotting the same leader's death. Decent performances help move along the improbable plot. 90m/C VHS, Beta. *SA* Anthony Quinn, John Phillip Law, Simon Sabela, Ken Gampu, Marius Weyers, Sandra Prinsloo; ***D:*** Peter Collinson. *HBO*

Afrita Hanen 🎬🎬🎬 1947 A rare Egyptian fantasy starring the famous Mid-Eastern actor, Farrid El Atrache. In Arabic with titles. 97m/B VHS, Beta. Farrid El Atrache. *FCT*

After Dark, My Sweet 🎬🎬🎬 1990 (R) A troubled young man in search of a little truth ends up entangled in a kidnapping scheme. Muddled direction is overcome by above average performances and gritty realism. Based on the novel by Jim Thompson. 114m/C VHS, LV, **Closed Caption.** Jason Patric, Rachel Ward, Bruce Dern, George Dickerson, James Cotton, Corey Carrier, Rocky Giordani; ***D:*** James Foley; ***W:*** Robert Redlin, James Foley; ***M:*** Maurice Jarre. *LIV*

After Darkness 🎬 1985 Slow-moving psycho-suspenser about a man obsessed with trying to remedy his twin brother's schizophrenia. 104m/C VHS, Beta. *SI GB* John Hurt, Julian Sands, Victoria Abril, Pamela Salem; ***D:*** Dominique Othenin-Girard. *CEL*

After Hours 🎬🎬🎬½ 1985 (R) An absurd, edgy black comedy that's filled with novel twists and turns and often more disturbing than funny. An isolated uptown New York yuppie (Dunne) takes a late night stroll downtown and meets a sexy woman in an all-night coffee shop. From there he wanders through a series of threatening and surreal misadventures, leading to his pursuit by a vigilante mob stirred by ice cream dealer O'Hara. Something like "Blue Velvet" with more Catholicism and farce. Or similar to "Something Wild" without the high school reunion. Great cameos from the large supporting cast, including Cheech and Chong as burglers. A dark view of a small hell-hole in the Big Apple. 97m/C VHS, Beta, LV, **Closed Caption.** Griffin Dunne, Rosanna Arquette, John Heard, Teri Garr, Catherine O'Hara, Verna Bloom, Linda Fiorentino, Dick Miller, Bronson Pinchot, Will Patton, Rockets Redglare; ***Cameos:*** Richard "Cheech" Marin, Thomas Chong, Martin Scorsese; ***D:*** Martin Scorsese; ***C:*** Michael Ballhaus; ***M:*** Howard Shore. Cannes Film Festival '86: Best Director (Scorsese); Independent Spirit Awards '86: Best Director (Scorsese), Best Film. *WAR*

After Julius 🎬🎬 1978 Twenty years after Julius Grace's death, his memory still hovers over his wife's and daughters' lives. British soap opera moves with glacier-like speed. Adapted from the book by Elizabeth Jane Howard. 150m/C VHS. *GB* Faith Brook, John Carson, Cyd Hayman; ***D:*** John Glenister. *NO*

After Midnight 🎬 *I Have Lived* 1933 An aspiring playwright tries to get his work produced, only to meet with dead ends. Eventually, he hooks up with a talented young actress with whom he finds romance and success. 69m/B VHS, Beta, Closed

Caption. Alan Dinehart, Anita Page, Allen Vincent, Gertrude Astor; **D:** Richard Thorpe. SNC

After Midnight 🎬🎬 1989 (R) Suspended in a central story about an unorthodox professor who preys upon the deepest fears of his students, a trio of terror tales come to life. From the writers of "The Fly II" and "Nightmare on Elm Street, Part IV." Some chills, few thrills. 90m/C VHS, Beta, Closed Caption. Marg Helgenberger, Marc McClure, Alan Rosenberg, Pamela Segall, Nadine Van Der Velde, Ramy Zada, Jillian McWhirter, Billy Ray Sharkey; **D:** Jim Wheat. FOX, MGM

After Pilkington 🎬🎬 1988 British television thriller about an uptight Oxford professor who runs into his bewitching childhood sweetheart after many years. She persuades him to help search for a missing archaeologist. 100m/C VHS, Beta, Closed Caption. GB Bob Peck, Miranda Richardson, Barry Foster; **D:** Christopher Morahan. FOX

After the Fall of New York woof! 1985 (R) Dim-witted post-apocalyptic tale set in New York after the fall of the "Big Bomb." A man, driven to search for the last normal woman, has reason to believe she is frozen alive and kept in the heart of the city. His mission: locate her, thaw her, engage in extremely limited foreplay with her, and repopulate the planet. A poorly dubbed dating allegory. 95m/C VHS, Beta. IT FR Michael Sopkiw, Valentine Monnier, Anna Kanakis, Roman Geer, Edmund Purdom, George Eastman; **D:** Martin Dolman. VES, LIV

After the Fall of Saigon 🎬 Raiders of the Doomed Kingdom 1988 Soldiers in Vietnam go on a killing rampage. Dubbed; country of origin isn't known. 100m/C VHS, Beta. Danny Aswatep, Peter Ramwa, Rayak Ramnate, Krao Spartacus. NO

After the Fox 🎬🎬 Caccia alla Volpe 1966 Sellers is a con artist posing as a film director to carry out a bizarre plan to steal gold from Rome. Features occasional backhand slaps at Hollywood, with Mature turning in a memorable performance as the has-been actor starring in Sellers' movie. Though the screenplay was co-written by Neil Simon, the laughs are marginal. 103m/C VHS, Beta. GB IT Peter Sellers, Victor Mature, Martin Balsam, Britt Ekland; **D:** Vittorio De Sica; **W:** Neil Simon; **M:** Burt Bacharach. MGM, FOX

After the Promise 🎬🎬 1987 During the Depression, a poor carpenter tries to regain custody of his four sons following the death of his wife. Maudlin television melodrama based on a true story. 100m/C VHS. Mark Harmon, Diana Scarwid, Rosemary Dunsmore, Donnelly Rhodes, Mark Hildreth, Trey Ames, Richard Billingsley; **D:** David Greene; **M:** Ralph Burns. VTR, NWV

After the Rehearsal 🎬🎬🎬 1984 (R) Two actresses, one young, the other at the end of her career, challenge their director with love and abuse. Each questions his right to use them on stage and off. A thoughtful discussion of the meaning and reason for art originally made for Swedish television. Swedish with English subtitles. 72m/C VHS, Beta. SW Erland Josephson, Ingrid Thulin, Lena Olin; **D:** Ingmar Bergman; **W:** Ingmar Bergman; **C:** Sven Nykvist. COL

After the Revolution 🎬🎬 1990 A struggling novelist decides to write his next book from the viewpoint of his cat. In Hungarian with English subtitles. 82m/C VHS. HU D: Andras Szirtes. FCT

After the Shock 🎬🎬 1990 (PG) Documentary-like dramatization of the San Francisco-Oakland earthquake of October, 1989 and, of course, its aftermath. Incorporates actual footage of the disaster. Made for cable. 92m/C VHS, Beta, Closed Caption. Yaphet Kotto, Rue McClanahan, Jack Scalia, Scott Valentine; **D:** Gary Sherman; **W:** Gary Sherman. PAR

After the Thin Man 🎬🎬🎬 1936 Second in a series of six "Thin Man" films, this one finds Nick, Nora and Asta, the lovable terrier, seeking out a murderer from Nora's own blue-blooded relatives. Fast-paced mystery with a witty script and the popular Powell/Loy charm. Sequel to "The Thin Man," followed by "Another Thin Man." 113m/B VHS, Beta. William Powell, Myrna Loy, James Stewart, Elissa Landi, Joseph Calleia, Jessie Ralph, Alan Marshal; **D:** Woodbridge S. Van Dyke. Nominations: Academy Awards '36: Best Screenplay. MGM

Afterburn 🎬🎬🎬 1992 (R) When Ted, her Air Force pilot husband, is killed in a crash of his F-16 fighter, Janet Harduvel learns the official explanation is pilot error. Convinced that something was wrong with his plane, Janet sets out to investigate, and eventually sue, military contractor General Dynamics. Dern turns in a great performance as the tough widow determined to clear her husband's name. Based on a true story; made for cable television. **CW:** Language. 103m/C VHS, LV, Closed Caption. Laura Dern, Robert Loggia, Vincent Spano, Michael Rooker, Andy Romano; **D:** Robert Markowitz; **W:** Elizabeth Chandler. HBO, FCT

Aftermath 🎬1/2 1985 Three astronauts return to Earth and are shocked to discover that the planet has been ravaged by a nuclear war. Quickly they make new plans. 96m/C VHS, Beta. Steve Barkett, Larry Latham, Lynne Margulies, Sig Haig, Forrest J. Ackerman; **D:** Ted V. Mikels. PSM

Aftershock 🎬1/2 1988 (R) A beautiful alien and a mysterious stranger battle the Earth's repressive, evil government. 90m/C VHS, Beta. Jay Roberts Jr., Elizabeth Kaitan, Chris Mitchum, Richard Lynch, John Saxon, Russ Tamblyn, Michael Berryman, Chris De Rose, Chuck Jeffreys; **D:** Frank Harris. PSM

Afterward 🎬 1985 Made-for-British-television horror story about a family that moves into a supposedly haunted house with deadly results. 60m/C VHS, Beta. GB Michael J. Shannon, Kay Harper, John Grillo. PSM

Against A Crooked Sky 🎬🎬 1975 (G) A young boy sets out with an elderly trapper to find his sister, who was captured by the Indians. Similiar story to "The Searchers," but no masterpiece. 89m/C VHS, Beta. Richard Boone, Stewart Peterson, Clint Ritchie, Geoffrey Land, Jewel Blanch; **D:** Earl Bellamy. LIV, VES

Against All Flags 🎬🎬🎬 1952 An enjoyable Flynn swashbuckler about a British soldier slashing his way through the Spanish fleet at the turn of the 18th century. Though the story has been told before, tight direction and good performances win out. O'Hara is a tarty eyeful as a hot-tempered pirate moll. 81m/C VHS, Beta, LV. Errol Flynn, Maureen O'Hara, Anthony Quinn, Mildred Natwick; **D:** George Sherman. BAR, USH

Against All Odds 🎬🎬1/2 1984 (R) An interesting love triangle evolves when an ex-football player, played by Bridges, travels to Mexico to find his good friend's girlfriend. Contains complicated plot, numerous double crosses, sensual love scenes, and a chase scene along Sunset Boulevard. As the good friend sans conscience, Woods stars. A remake of 1947's "Out of the Past." 122m/C VHS, Beta, LV, 8mm, Closed Caption. Jeff Bridges, Rachel Ward, James Woods, Alex Karras, Jane Greer, Richard Widmark, Dorian Harewood, Swoosie Kurtz, Bill McKinney, Saul Rubinek; **D:** Taylor Hackford; **C:** Donald E. Thorin; **M:** Michel Colombier, Larry Carlton. Nominations: Academy Awards '84: Best Song ("Against All Odds (Take a Look at Me Now)"). COL

Against the Drunken Cat Paws 🎬 1975 A blind young martial arts student seeks to regain his sight and avenge the death of his father. 94m/C VHS, Beta. Chia Ling, Ou-Yang Ksiek. UNI

Against the Wall 🎬🎬🎬 1994 Compelling and tense dramatization of the 1971 Attica, New York prison uprising in which 10 guards were held hostage and state troopers and the National Guard killed 29 prisoners before regaining control. Partially fictionalized version of the story told from the viewpoints of a young prison guard (MacLachlan) and a politicized prisoner (Jackson). Filmed at a prison in Clarksville, Tennessee. Made for cable television. 115m/C VHS, LV. Kyle MacLachlan, Samuel L. Jackson, Clarence Williams III, Frederic Forrest, Harry Dean Stanton, Tom Bower, Philip Bosco,

Anne Heche, David Ackroyd; **D:** John Frankenheimer; **W:** Ron Hutchinson; **M:** Gary Chang. HBO

Against the Wind 🎬🎬1/2 1948 A motley crew is trained for a mission into Nazi Germany to blow up records and rescue a prisoner. The first half of the film focuses on the group's training, but despite its intensity they win only a pyrrhic victory. A well-done production with solid performances from the cast. 96m/B VHS. Robert Beatty, Jack Warner, Simone Signoret, Gordon Jackson, Paul Dupuis, Peter Illing; **D:** Charles Crichton. NOS, VEC

Against the Wind 🎬🎬 Contra el Viento 1990 Juan (Banderas) takes refuge in a remote area of Andalusia in an effort to get away from a mutually obsessive love. But his exile is in vain when his lover appears—his sister (Suarez). Spanish with subtitles. 117m/C VHS. SP Antonio Banderas, Emma Suarez; **D:** Paco Perinan. FCT

Agatha 🎬🎬1/2 1979 (PG) A speculative period drama about Agatha Christie's still unexplained disappearance in 1926, and a fictional American reporter's efforts to find her. Beautiful but lackluster mystery. Unfortunately, Hoffman and Redgrave generate few sparks. 98m/C VHS, Beta. Dustin Hoffman, Vanessa Redgrave, Timothy Dalton, Helen Morse, Tony Britton, Timothy West, Celia Gregory; **D:** Michael Apted. Nominations: Academy Awards '79: Best Costume Design. WAR

Agatha Christie's Miss Marple 198? Elderly, proper Jane Marple hardly seems the sort to get involved in murder and mayhem but her prim exterior hides a razor-sharp mind and intuitive understanding of criminal behavior. Two boxed collections. 65m/C VHS. GB Joan Hickson. VCO, AAE, NEW

Age Isn't Everything 🎬 Life in the Food Chain 1991 (R) An appalling clumsy comedy about a recent college graduate who abruptly becomes an old man while retaining his youthful exterior. He looks the same, but walks slowly and talks with a thick Yiddish accent, get it? The cast just marks time until an inexplicable ending. **CW:** Language. 91m/C VHS. Jonathan Silverman, Robert Prosky, Rita Moreno, Paul Sorvino, Rita Karin, Robert Cicchini, Brian Williams, Dee Hoty; **Cameos:** Dr. Joyce Brothers, Bella Abzug; **W:** Douglas Katz. VES

The Age of Innocence 🎬🎬🎬 1993 (PG) Magnificently lavish adaptation of Edith Wharton's novel of passion thwarted by convention is visually stunning, but don't expect action since these people kill with a word or gesture. Lead performances are strong though perhaps miscast, with Ryder an exception. Outwardly docile and conventional, she nevertheless holds on to her husband with steely manipulation. Woodward's narration of Wharton's observations helps sort out what goes on behind the proper facades. Although slow, see this one for the beautiful period authenticity, thanks to Scorsese, who obviously labored over the small details. He shows up as a photographer; his parents appear in a scene on a train. 138m/C VHS, LV, 8mm, Closed Caption. Daniel Day-Lewis, Michelle Pfeiffer, Winona Ryder, Richard E. Grant, Alec McCowen, Miriam Margolyes, Sian Phillips, Geraldine Chaplin, Stuart Wilson, Mary Beth Hurt, Michael Gough, Alexis Smith, Jonathan Pryce, Robert Sean Leonard; **Cameos:** Martin Scorsese; **D:** Martin Scorsese; **W:** Jay Cocks, Martin Scorsese; **C:** Michael Ballhaus; **M:** Elmer Bernstein. Academy Awards '93: Best Costume Design; British Academy Awards '93: Best Supporting Actress (Margolyes); Golden Globe Awards '94: Best Supporting Actress (Ryder); National Board of Review Awards '93: Best Director (Scorsese), Best Supporting Actress (Ryder); Nominations: Academy Awards '93: Best Adapted Screenplay, Best Art Direction/Set Decoration, Best Supporting Actress (Ryder), Best Original Score; British Academy Awards '94: Best Supporting Actress (Ryder); Directors Guild of America Awards '93: Best Director (Scorsese); Golden Globe Awards '94: Best Actress—Drama (Pfeiffer), Best Director (Scorsese), Best Film—Drama. COL

Age Old Friends ✓✓✓½ 1989 Crusty octogenarian Cronyn must choose. His daughter (played by real-life offspring Tandy) wants him to move out of a retirement home and into her house. But he's struggling to keep neighbor and increasingly senile friend Gardenia from slipping into "zombieland." An emotional treat with two fine actors deploying dignity and wit in the battle against old age. Originally adapted for HBO from the Broadway play, "A Month of Sundays" by Bob Larbey. 89m/C VHS, Beta, Closed Caption. Vincent Gardenia, Hume Cronyn, Tandy Cronyn, Esther Rolle, Michelle Scarabelli; D: Allen Kroeker. HBO

The Agency ✓✓ *Mind Games* 1981 (R) An advertising agency attempts to manipulate public behavior and opinion through the use of subliminal advertising. A good premise is bogged down by a dull script and plodding performances by all concerned. Based on a Paul Gottlieb novel. 94m/C VHS, Beta. CA Robert Mitchum, Lee Majors, Valerie Perrine, Saul Rubinek, Alexandra Stewart, George Kaczender; D: George Kaczender; M: Lewis Furey. VES, MTX, VTR

Agent on Ice ✓✓ 1986 (R) Hockey team is stalked by lawyers. No, wait. An ex-CIA agent is stalked for cover-up purposes by the agency and the mob. One slippery fellow. 96m/C VHS, Beta. Tom Ormeny, Clifford David, Louis Pastore, Matt Craven; D: Clark Worswick. VTR, NWV

Aggie Appleby, Maker of Men ✓✓½ *Cupid in the Rough* 1933 A wimpy society boy transforms himself into a tough guy, all for the love of a dame. Based on a play by Joseph O. Kesselring. Very slight comedy. 73m/B VHS. Charles Farrell, Wynne Gibson, William Gargan, ZaSu Pitts; D: Mark Sandrich; M: Max Steiner. FCT

Agnes of God ✓✓ 1985 (PG-13) Stage to screen translation of John Pielmeier's play loses something in the translation. Coarse chain-smoking psychiatrist Fonda is sent to a convent to investigate whether young nun Tilly is fit to stand trial. Seems that the nun may have given birth to and then strangled her baby, although she denies ever having sexual relations and knows nothing about an infant. Naive Tilly is frightened by probing Fonda, while worldly mother-superior Bancroft is distrusting. Melodramatic stew of Catholicism, religious fervor, and science features generally good performances, although Fonda often seems to be acting (maybe it's the cigarettes). 99m/C VHS, Beta, LV, Closed Caption. Jane Fonda, Anne Bancroft, Meg Tilly, Anne Pitoniak, Winston Reckert, Gratien Gelinas; D: Norman Jewison; W: John Pielmeier; C: Sven Nykvist; M: Georges Delerue. Golden Globe Awards '86: Best Supporting Actress (Tilly); Nominations: Academy Awards '85: Best Actress (Bancroft), Best Supporting Actress (Tilly), Best Original Score. COL

The Agony and the Ecstasy ✓✓½ 1965 Big-budget (for 1965 anyway at $12 million) adaptation of the Irving Stone novel recounts the conflict between Michelangelo and Pope Julius II after His Holiness directs the artist to paint the Sistine Chapel. Follow the tortured artist through his unpredictable creative process and the hours (it seems literal due to movie length) of painting flat on his back. Heston exudes quiet strength in his sincere interpretation of the genius artist, while Harrison has a fling as the Pope. Slow script is not up to the generally good performances. Disappointing at the box office, but worth a look on the small screen for the sets alone. 136m/C VHS, Beta, LV. Charlton Heston, Rex Harrison, Harry Andrews, Diane Cilento, Alberto Lupo, Adolfo Celi; D: Carol Reed; W: Philip Dunne; C: Leon Shamroy; M: Jerry Goldsmith, Alex North. National Board of Review Awards '65: Best Supporting Actor (Andrews); Nominations: Academy Awards '65: Best Art Direction/Set Decoration (Color), Best Color Cinematography, Best Costume Design (Color), Best Sound, Best Original Score. FOX, IGP

Agony of Love 1966 An unhappy homemaker rents a nearby apartment to live out her wildest fantasies and bring some excitement into her otherwise dull life. ?m/C VHS. SMW, TPV

Aguirre, the Wrath of God ✓✓✓½ 1972 Herzog at his best, combining brilliant poetic images and an intense narrative dealing with power, irony, and death. Spanish conquistadors in 1590 search for the mythical city of gold in Peru. Instead, they descend into the hell of the jungle. Kinski is fabulous as Aquirre, succumbing to insanity while leading a continually diminishing crew in this compelling, extraordinary drama shot in the jungles of South America. Both English- and German-language versions available. 94m/C VHS. GE Klaus Kinski, Ruy Guerra, Del Negro, Helena Rojo, Cecilia Rivera, Peter Berling, Danny Ades; D: Werner Herzog; W: Werner Herzog. National Society of Film Critics Awards '77: Best Cinematography. NYF, APD

Ah, Wilderness! ✓✓✓½ 1935 Delightful tale of a teen boy coming of age in small town America. Watch for the hilarious high school graduation scene. Based on the play by Eugene O'Neill. Remade in 1948 as "Summer Holiday," a musical with Mickey Rooney in the lead. 101m/B VHS. Wallace Beery, Lionel Barrymore, Aline MacMahon, Eric Linden, Cecilia Parker, Spring Byington, Mickey Rooney, Charley Grapewin, Frank Albertson; D: Clarence Brown; C: Clyde De Vinna. MGM, BTV

Ain't No Way Back ✓ 1989 Two hunters stumble upon a feudin' bunch of moonshiners and must leave their city ways behind if they plan to survive. 90m/C VHS, Beta. NO

Air America ✓✓ 1990 (R) It's the Vietnam War and the CIA is operating a secret drug smuggling operation in Southeast Asia to finance the effort. Flyboys Gibson and Downey drop opium and glib lines all over Laos. Big-budget Gibson vehicle with sufficient action but lacking much of a story, which was adapted from a book by Christopher Robbins. 113m/C VHS, Beta, LV, Closed Caption. Mel Gibson, Robert Downey Jr., Marshall Bell, Nancy Travis, David Marshall Grant, Tim Thomerson, Lane Smith; D: Roger Spottiswoode; W: Richard Rush; C: Roger Deakins. LIV, IME

Air Bud ✓✓½ 1997 Buddy's a basketball-playing golden retriever (no relation) who befriends a lonely misfit (Zegers) and teaches him the nuances of the layup, fade-away J, and pick-and-roll. It's good to see dog athletes getting to stretch beyond the usual frisbee and stick-fetching roles. Teaming animals (especially canines) with kids usually adds up to success. This one's no exception, especially for the grade school crowd. ?m/C VHS. Kevin Zegers, Michael Jeter, Bill Cobbs, Cynthia Stevenson; D: Charles Martin Smith. NYR

Air Force ✓✓✓½ 1943 One of the finest of the WWII movies, Hawks' exciting classic has worn well through the years, in spite of the Japanese propaganda. It follows the hazardous exploits of a Boeing B-17 bomber crew who fight over Pearl Harbor, Manila, and the Coral Sea. Extremely realistic dogfight sequences and powerful, introspective real guy interfacing by the ensemble cast are masterfully combined by Hawks. 124m/B VHS, Closed Caption. John Garfield, John Ridgely, Gig Young, Arthur Kennedy, Charles Drake, Harry Carey Sr., George Tobias; D: Howard Hawks; C: James Wong Howe. Academy Awards '43: Best Film Editing; Nominations: Academy Awards '43: Best Black and White Cinematography, Best Original Screenplay. FOX

Air Force One ✓✓✓ *AFO* 1997 (R) Ford stars as a U.S. President who is not only tough on crime but tough, period. His policy is to not negotiate with terrorists. Then Air Force One, with him, the First Lady and their daughter aboard is hijacked by Russian nationalists, led by ice cold Oldman. Close is the first woman Veep, stuck in D.C. coping with the situation. Ford is in fine form as the President who's forced to kick some Commie butt to save the day. Director Petersen ("In The Line of Fire") is becoming a master of building tension in confined places and puts his strong cast to good use. Nail-biting suspense and breath-taking action sequences cap off tour-de-force adventure. ?m/C VHS. Harrison Ford, Gary Oldman, Glenn Close, Juergen Prochnow, Dean Stockwell, J.A.

Preston, Wendy Crewson, Xander Berkeley; D: Wolfgang Petersen; W: Andrew Marlowe; C: Michael Ballhaus; M: Jerry Goldsmith. NYR

Air Hawk ✓ 1984 Australian made for TV release details the adventures of an outback pilot involved with stolen diamonds. 90m/C VHS, Beta. AU Eric Oldfield, Louise Howitt, Ellie MacLure, David Robson, David Baker; D: David Baker. VCD

Air Raid Wardens ✓✓½ 1943 Laurel & Hardy play a couple of small-town failures who become the local air raid wardens during WWII. They even manage to make a mess of this but redeem themselves when they overhear a spy plot and save the town's munitions factory from a German spy ring. A so-so effort from the comic duo. 67m/B VHS. Stan Laurel, Oliver Hardy, Edgar Kennedy, Jacqueline White, Stephen McNally, Russell Hicks, Howard Freeman, Donald Meek, Henry O'Neill; D: Edward Sedgwick. MGM

The Air Up There ✓✓ 1994 (PG) Assistant basketball coach Jimmy Dolan (Bacon) heads to the African village of Winabi to recruit talented (and tall) Saleh (Maina) to play b-ball in the U.S. But Saleh is next in line to be the tribe's king and doesn't want to leave. Stupid American in foreign country learning from the natives story is lighthearted, but relies heavily on formula—and borders on the stereotypical, though climatic game is a lot of fun. 108m/C VHS, LV, Closed Caption. Kevin Bacon, Charles Gitona Maina, Sean McCann, Dennis Patrick; D: Paul Michael Glaser; W: Max Apple; C: Elliot Davis; M: David Newman. HPH

Airborne ✓½ 1993 (PG) Cool California rollerblade dude gets transplanted to Cincinnati for a school year, and has to prove himself when those good ol' midwestern boys come after him. Nothing short of a skate vehicle appealing largely, if not solely, to the high school contingent. 91m/C VHS, Beta, LV, Closed Caption. Shane Maclewary, Seth Green, Brittney Powell, Edie McClurg; D: Rob Bowman; W: Bill Apablasa; M: Stewart Copeland. WAR

Airheads ✓✓ 1994 (PG-13) "Wayne's World" meets "Dog Day Afternoon." Silly farce has three metal heads (Buscemi, Fraser, Sandler) holding a radio station hostage in order to get their demo tape played. Events snowball and they receive instant fame. Cast and crew rich with subversive comedic talents, including Sandler and Farley from "Saturday Night Live." Soundtrack authenticity supplied by White Zombie and The Galatic Cowboys. 81m/C VHS, LV, Closed Caption. Brendan Fraser, Steve Buscemi, Adam Sandler, Chris Farley, Michael McKean, Judd Nelson, Joe Mantegna, Michael Richards, Ernie Hudson, Amy Locane, Nina Siemaszko, John Melendez; D: Michael Lehmann; W: Rich Wilkes; M: Carter Burwell. FXV

Airplane! ✓✓✓½ 1980 (PG) Classic lampoon of disaster flicks is stupid but funny and launched a bevy wanna-be spoofs. A former pilot who's lost both his girl (she's the attendant) and his nerve takes over the controls of a jet when the crew is hit with food poisoning. The passengers become increasingly crazed and ground support more surreal as our hero struggles to land the plane. Clever, fast-paced, and very funny parody mangles every Hollywood cliche within reach. The gags are so furiously paced that when one bombs it's hardly noticeable. Launched Nielsen's second career as a comic actor. And it ain't over till it's over: don't miss the amusing final credits. Followed by "Airplane 2: The Sequel." 88m/C VHS, Beta, 8mm. Robert Hays, Julie Hagerty, Lloyd Bridges, Peter Graves, Robert Stack, Kareem Abdul-Jabbar, Leslie Nielsen, Stephen Stucker; Cameos: Ethel Merman, Barbara Billingsley; D: Jerry Zucker, Jim Abrahams, David Zucker; W: Jerry Zucker, Jim Abrahams, David Zucker; C: Joseph Biroc; M: Elmer Bernstein. Writers Guild of America '80: Best Adapted Screenplay. PAR

Airplane 2: The Sequel ✓✓ 1982 (PG) Not a Zucker, Abrahams and Zucker effort, and sorely missing their slapstick and script finesse. The first passenger space shuttle has taken off for the moon and there's a mad bomber on board.

Given the number of stars mugging, it's more of a loveboat than a fitting sequel to "Airplane." Nonetheless, some funny laughs and gags. 84m/C VHS, Beta, LV. Robert Hays, Julie Hagerty, Lloyd Bridges, Raymond Burr, Peter Graves, William Shatner, Sonny Bono, Chuck Connors, Chad Everett, Stephen Stucker, Rip Torn, Ken Finkleman, Sandahl Bergman; **D:** Ken Finkleman; **C:** Joseph Biroc; **M:** Elmer Bernstein. PAR

Airport 🐾🐾🐾 1970 (G) Old-fashioned disaster thriller built around an all-star cast, fairly moronic script, and an unavoidable accident during the flight of a passenger airliner. A box-office hit that paved the way for many lesser disaster flicks (including its many sequels) detailing the reactions of the passengers and crew as they cope with impending doom. Considered to be the best of the "Airport" series; adapted from the Arthur Hailey novel. 137m/C VHS, Beta, LV. Dean Martin, Burt Lancaster, Jean Seberg, Jacqueline Bisset, George Kennedy, Helen Hayes, Van Heflin, Maureen Stapleton, Barry Nelson, Lloyd Nolan; **D:** George Seaton; **W:** George Seaton; **C:** Ernest Laszlo. Academy Awards '70: Best Supporting Actress (Hayes); Golden Globe Awards '71: Best Supporting Actress (Stapleton); Nominations: Academy Awards '70: Best Adapted Screenplay, Best Art Direction/Set Decoration, Best Cinematography, Best Costume Design, Best Film Editing, Best Picture, Best Sound, Best Supporting Actress (Stapleton), Best Original Score. USH, BTV

Airport '75 🐾🐾 1975 (PG) After a mid-air collision, a jumbo 747 is left pilotless. Airline attendant Black must fly da plane. She does her cross-eyed best in this absurd sequel to "Airport" built around a lesser "all-star cast." Safe on the ground, Heston tries to talk the airline hostess/pilot into landing, while the impatient Kennedy continues to grouse as leader of the foam-ready ground crew. A slick, insincere attempt to find box office magic again (which unfortunately worked, leading to two more sequels). 107m/C VHS, Beta. Charlton Heston, Karen Black, George Kennedy, Gloria Swanson, Helen Reddy, Sid Caesar, Efrem Zimbalist Jr., Susan Clark, Dana Andrews, Linda Blair, Myrna Loy; **D:** Jack Smight. GKK

Airport '77 🐾🐾 1977 (PG) Billionaire Stewart fills his converted passenger jet with priceless art and sets off to Palm Beach for a museum opening, joined by an uninvited gang of hijackers. Twist to this in-flight disaster is that the bad time in the air occurs underwater, a novel (and some might say, desperate) twist to the old panic in the plane we're all gonna die formula. With a cast of familiar faces, some of them stars and some of them just familiar faces, this is yet another sequel to "Airport" and another box-office success, leading to the last of the tired series in 1979. 114m/C VHS, Beta, LV. Jack Lemmon, James Stewart, Lee Grant, Brenda Vaccaro, Joseph Cotten, Olivia de Havilland, Darren McGavin, Christopher Lee, George Kennedy, Kathleen Quinlan; **D:** Jack Smight. Nominations: Academy Awards '77: Best Art Direction/Set Decoration, Best Costume Design. USH

Akermania, Vol. 1 🐾🐾🐾 1992 This compilation of director Akerman's shorter works includes "I'm Hungry, I'm Cold," the story of two Belgian girls on the loose in Paris, and "Saute Ma Ville," Akerman's first film. Both are in French with English subtitles. Also included is "Hotel Monterey," a silent experimental film. 89m/C VHS. FR Maria De Medeiros, Pascale Salkin, Chantal Akerman; **D:** Chantal Akerman. WAC

Akira 🐾🐾 1989 Secret government experiments on children with ESP go awry, resulting in an cataclysmic explosion on Tokyo. The city in turn builds itself up into a Megalopolis and the experiments continue. Animated; in Japanese with English subtitles or dubbed. 124m/C VHS, LV. JP 🐾: Katsuhiro Otomo, Sheldon Renan; **W:** Katsuhiro Otomo, Izo Hashimoto; **C:** Katsuji Misawa. STP, CRC

Akira Kurosawa's Dreams 🐾🐾½ Dreams 1990 (PG) An anthological lesson regarding the simultaneous loss of humanity and nature that threatens us all from the renowned Japanese director. Although the startling and memorable im-

agery is still present, Kurosawa's lessons are strangely trite and consequently lack the power that is normally associated with his work. Watch for Scorsese as Van Gogh. With English subtitles. 120m/C VHS, LV. JP Akira Terao, Mitsuko Baisho, Meiko Harada, Chishu Ryu, Hisashi Igawa, Mitsunori Isaki, Toshihiko Nakano, Yoshitaka Zushi, Toshie Negishi, Martin Scorsese; **D:** Akira Kurosawa; **W:** Akira Kurosawa; **M:** Shinichiro Ikebe. WAR, FCT

Al Capone 🐾🐾🐾 1959 Film noir character study of one of the most colorful gangsters of the Roaring Twenties. Sort of an underworld "How to Succeed in Business." Steiger chews scenes and bullets as they fly by, providing the performance of his career. Plenty of gangland violence and mayhem and splendid cinematography keep the fast-paced period piece sailing. 104m/C VHS, Beta. Rod Steiger, Fay Spain, Murvyn Vye, Nehemiah Persoff, Martin Balsam, James Gregory, Joe De Santis; **D:** Richard Wilson. FOX, FCT

Alabama's Ghost 🐾½ 1972 (PG) Musician steals a dead master magician's secrets, incurring the wrath of the paranormal underworld. 96m/C VHS, Beta. Christopher Brooks, E. Kerrigan Prescott; **D:** Fredric Hobbs. LIV

Aladdin 🐾 Superfantagenio 1986 (PG) A comedic Italian modernization of the Aladdin fable. 97m/C VHS, Beta, Closed Caption. IT Bud Spencer, Luca Venantini, Janet Agren, Julian Voloshin, Umberto Raho; **D:** Bruno Corbucci. MED

Aladdin 🐾🐾🐾½ 1992 (G) Boy meets princess, loses her, finds her, wins her from evil vizier and nasty parrot. Superb animation triumphs over average songs and storyline by capitalizing on Williams' talent for ad-lib with lightning speed genie changes, lots of celebrity spoofs, and even a few pokes at Disney itself. Adults will enjoy the 1,001 impersonations while kids will get a kick out of the big blue genie and the songs, three of which are the late Ashman's legacy. Kane and Salonga are responsible for the singing voices of Aladdin and Jasmine; Gottfried is a riot as the obnoxious parrot sidekick. Be forewarned: small children may be frightened by some of the scarier sequences. ♫A Whole New World; Prince Ali; Friend Like Me; One Jump Ahead; Arabian Nights. 90m/C VHS, Beta, LV, Closed Caption. **D:** Ron Clements, John Musker; **W:** Ron Clements, John Musker, Ted Elliot, Terry Rossio; **M:** Alan Menken, Howard Ashman, Tim Rice; **V:** Robin Williams, Scott Weinger, Linda Larkin, Jonathan Freeman, Frank Welker, Gilbert Gottfried, Douglas Seale, Brad Kane, Lea Salonga. Academy Awards '92: Best Song ("A Whole New World"), Best Original Score; Golden Globe Awards '93: Best Song ("A Whole New World"); MTV Movie Awards '93: Best Comedic Performance (Williams); Nominations: Academy Awards '92: Best Song ("Friend Like Me"), Best Sound, Best Sound Effects Editing. DIS, BTV

Aladdin and His Wonderful Lamp 🐾🐾½ 1984 The story of Aladdin, a young man who finds a magical oil lamp when he is trapped in a tiny cave. From the "Faerie Tale Theatre" series and director of "Beetlejuice" and "Batman" Tim Burton. 60m/C VHS, Beta, Closed Caption. Valerie Bertinelli, Robert Carradine, Leonard Nimoy, James Earl Jones; **D:** Tim Burton. KUI, FOX, FCT

Aladdin and the King of Thieves 1996 Second-direct-to-video saga (following "The Return of Jafar") once again features Williams as the voice of the genie (after settling a dispute with Disney). On the eve of Aladdin's marriage to Jasmine, thieves try to steal a magic talisman, sending Aladdin on a mission to find the thieves—and his father. Disney had such terrific success with"Return" that it was inevitable they would try again. 82m/C VHS, Closed Caption. **D:** Ted Stones; **W:** Mark McCorkle, Robert Schooley; **M:** Mark Watters; **V:** Robin Williams, Scott Weinger, Jerry Orbach, John Rhys-Davies, Gilbert Gottfried, Linda Larkin, CCH Pounder, Frank Welker. DIS

Alakazam the Great! 1961 Japanese animated film about an arrogant monkey who is sent on a mission to learn about life. 84m/C VHS. **D:** Lee Kresel; **M:** Les Baxter; **V:** Frankie Avalon, Dodie Stevens, Jonathan Winters, Arnold Stang, Sterling Holloway. CNG

The Alamo 🐾🐾🐾 1960 Old-fashioned patriotic battle epic recounts the real events of the 1836 fight for independence in Texas. The usual band of diverse and contentious personalities, including Wayne as a coonskin-capped Davy Crockett, defend a small fort against a very big Mexican raiding party outside of San Antonio. Before meeting mythic death, they fight with each other, learn the meaning of life, and ultimately come to respect each other. Just to make it more entertaining, Avalon sings. Big-budget production features an impeccable musical score by Tiomkin and an impressive 7,000 extras for the Mexican army alone. Wayne reportedly received directorial assistance from John Ford, particularly during the big massacre finale. 161m/C VHS, Beta, LV, Closed Caption. John Wayne, Richard Widmark, Laurence Harvey, Frankie Avalon, Richard Boone, Carlos Arruza, Chill Wills, Veda Ann Borg; **D:** John Wayne; **C:** William Clothier; **M:** Dimitri Tiomkin. Academy Awards '60: Best Sound; Golden Globe Awards '61: Best Score; Nominations: Academy Awards '60: Best Color Cinematography, Best Film Editing, Best Picture, Best Song ("The Green Leaves of Summer"), Best Supporting Actor (Wills), Original Dramatic/Comedy Score.MGM, FOX, TLF

Alamo Bay 🐾🐾½ 1985 A slow-moving but sincere tale of contemporary racism. An angry Vietnam veteran and his red-neck buddies feel threatened by Vietnamese refugees who want to go into the fishing business. Set in Texas, filled with Texas-sized characters, and based on a true Texas story, as interpreted by the French Malle. 99m/C VHS, Beta, LV, Closed Caption. Ed Harris, Ho Nguyen, Amy Madigan, Donald Moffat, Cynthia Carle, Truyen V. Tran, Rudy Young; **D:** Louis Malle; **W:** Alice Arlen; **M:** Ry Cooder. COL

The Alamo: Thirteen Days to Glory 🐾🐾 1987 The legendary Davy Crockett (Keith), Colonel William Travis (Baldwin), and Jim Bowie (Arness) overcome personal differences to unite against the Mexican Army, vowing to hold down the fort or die. It takes a true Texan to fully appreciate the merits of this rather pedestrian retelling of a familiar story, but the battle scenes are pretty heady (although they lose some of their froth on the small screen). If nothing else, the ever-versatile Julia is worth seeing as Santa Anna in this made-for-TV rendering of J. Lon Tinkle's "Thirteen Days to Glory." You may not want to remember the Alamo this way. 180m/C VHS, Beta, Closed Caption. James Arness, Lorne Greene, Alec Baldwin, Brian Keith, Raul Julia; **D:** Peter Werner; **M:** Peter Bernstein. FRH

Alamut Ambush 🐾 1986 A federal agent is stalked by assassins, and decides to hunt them in return. Sequel to "Cold War Killer." 94m/C VHS, Beta. GB Terence Stamp, Michael Culver; **D:** Ken Grieve. NO

Alan & Naomi 🐾🐾½ 1992 (PG) In 1944, 14-year-old Alan Silverman is more concerned with his Brooklyn stickball team than the war raging across Europe. This changes when his upstairs neighbor offers refuge to a French-Jewish mother and her young daughter and he is asked to befriend the girl. Naomi witnessed the brutal death of her father by the Nazis and retreated into a world of her own. Together the two build a sweet, if unlikely, friendship. Fine performances save this average coming of age tale. Based on the novel by Myron Levoy. 95m/C VHS, LV. Lukas Haas, Vanessa Zaoui, Michael Gross, Amy Aquino, Kevin Connolly, Zohra Lampert; **D:** Sterling Van Wagenen; **W:** Jordan Horowitz; **M:** Dick Hyman. COL

Alaska 🐾🐾½ 1996 (PG) Fourteen-year-old Vincent Barnes (Kartheiser) and his 12-year-old sister Jessie (Birch) try to rescue their bush pilot father Jake (Benedict) whose plane has crashed in the wilderness. They also rescue an orphaned polar bear cub from an evil poacher (Heston) that manages to help them out along the way. See this flick if only to enjoy the lush backdrop of Alaska and British Columbia and, of course, the absolutely adorable polar cub. Director Fraser C. Heston directs dad Charlton, appropriate payback for landing him the role as the infant Moses in "The Ten Commandments." **109m/C VHS, LV, Closed Caption.** Thora Birch, Vincent Kartheiser, Dirk Benedict, Charlton Heston; **D:** Fraser Heston; **W:** Andy Burg, Carol Fuchs; **C:** Tony Westman. COL

The Alaska Wilderness Adventure 🐾🐾 1978 The tale of a family struggling for survival in the Arctic wilderness. Baby, it's cold out there. **90m/C VHS, Beta.** NO

Alberto Express 🐾🐾½ 1992 Black comedy explores the debts children owe their parents—literally. Alberto's family has a peculiar tradition. It seems that now he's married and about to become a father, he's expected to pay back every cent spent on his own upbringing. Cash poor (and panicky) Alberto hops a train from Paris to Rome and frantically tries to raise the necessary cash by preying, in a series of increasingly bizarre ways, on his fellow passengers before he faces his father once again. In French and Italian with English subtitles. **90m/C VHS.** FR Sergio Castellitto, Nino Manfredi, Marie Trintignant, Jeanne Moreau, Michel Aumont, Dominique Pinon, Marco Messeri, Eugenia Marruzzo; **D:** Arthur Joffe; **W:** Arthur Joffe. FXL

Albino woof! 1976 (R) Albino chief leads African terrorists to murder white settlers, one of whom is an ex-policeman's fiancee. So the ex-cop pursues the bad guys, who are fairly easy to identify (just look for the big group hanging with the albino). Danning, Lee, and Howard only briefly show faces and collect checks. **85m/C VHS, Beta.** Christopher Lee, Trevor Howard, Sybil Danning, Horst Frank, James Faulkner; **D:** Jurgen Goslar. MED

Albino Alligator 🐾🐾 1996 (R) Three small-time crooks bungle a robbery and inadvertently run down a federal officer in Academy Award-winning actor Spacey's directorial debut. The trio, consisting of leader Dova (Dillon), brains Milo (Sinise) and brawn Law (Fichtner) hole up in a seedy bar and grab the occupants as hostages. The police soon surround the dive, and the crooks begin arguing among themselves and with brash barmaid Janet (Dunaway) about their chances and means for escape. All, however, is not as it seems. The claustrophobic setting seems more suitable for the stage than the screen, and the plot twists don't bend very far from predictable. Screenwriter Forte is the son of 60s teen idol Fabian. **CW:** Strong violence and language. **94m/C VHS, LV, Closed Caption.** Matt Dillon, Gary Sinise, Faye Dunaway, William Fichtner, Joe Mantegna, Viggo Mortensen, John Spencer, Skeet Ulrich, M. Emmet Walsh; **D:** Kevin Spacey; **W:** Christian Forte; **C:** Mark Plummer; **M:** Michael Brook. TOU

The Alchemist woof! 1981 (R) See humans transformed into murderous zombies! A bewitched man seeks revenge upon the evil magician who placed a curse on him, causing him to live like an animal. Painfully routine, with a few chills along the way. Amonte is an alias for Charles Band. Filmed in 1981 and released four years later. **86m/C VHS, Beta.** Robert Ginty, Lucinda Dooling, John Sanderford, Viola Kate Stimpson, Bob Glaudini; **D:** James Amonte; **W:** Alan J. Adler; **M:** Richard Band. VES, LIV

Alex 🐾🐾½ 1992 Inspirational story about 15-year-old New Zealand swimmer Alex Archer (Jackson), who is working towards a spot at the 1960 Rome Olympics. But her goal is threatened by an accident and a new rival and Alex struggles to overcome her obstacles with the help of her boyfriend (Picker) and her coach (Heywood). Based on the novel by Tessa Duder. **92m/C VHS, LV.** AU Lauren Jackson, Chris Haywood, Josh Picker, Catherine Godbold, Elizabeth Hawthorne; **D:** Megan Simpson. ORI

Alex in Wonderland 🐾🐾½ 1970 (R) A semi-autobiographical and satirical look at Hollywood from the standpoint of a young director who's trying to follow up his recent hit (in real life, "Bob & Carol & Ted & Alice") with a picture of some integrity that will keep the mass audience away. The confused plot provides obvious parallels to Fellini (who appears in a cameo) and some sharp, often bitter insights into the Hollywood of the early '60s. Strong performances by Sutherland and Burstyn compensate somewhat for the patience-trying self-indulgent arty whining of the script. **109m/C VHS, Beta.** Donald Sutherland, Ellen Burstyn, Jeanne Moreau, Paul Mazursky; **Cameos:** Federico Fellini; **D:** Paul Mazursky; **W:** Larry Tucker, Paul Mazursky. MGM, FCT

Alexander Nevsky 🐾🐾🐾½ 1938 A story of the invasion of Russia in 1241 by the Teutonic Knights of Germany and the defense of the region by good old Prince Nevsky. Eisenstein's first completed project in nearly ten years, it was widely regarded as an artistic disappointment upon release and as pro-war propaganda for the looming conflict with the Nazis. Fabulous Prokofiev score illuminates the classic battle scenes, which used thousands of Russian army regulars. Russian with subtitles. **110m/B VHS, LV.** RU Nikolai Cherkassov, N.P. Okholopkov, Al Abrikossov; **D:** Sergei Eisenstein; **M:** Sergei Prokofiev. National Board of Review Awards '39: 5 Best Foreign Films of the Year. BMG, MRV, NOS

Alexander the Great 🐾🐾½ 1955 A lavish epic about the legendary Greek conqueror of the fourth century B.C., which provides Burton a rare chance at an adventure role. Here we find Alexander is the product of a dysfunctional royal family who hopes to create an idealized world modeled after Greek culture to make up for the love he lacks from daddy. This he does by conquering everything before dying at the age of 33. The great cast helps to overcome the sluggish pacing of the spectacle, while numerous battle scenes featuring loads of spears and arrows are staged effectively. **135m/C VHS, Beta, LV.** Richard Burton, Fredric March, Claire Bloom, Harry Andrews, Peter Cushing, Danielle Darrieux, Helmut Dantine; **D:** Robert Rossen; **C:** Robert Krasker. MGM, FCT

Alexander: The Other Side of Dawn 🐾🐾 1977 Tired made-for-television sequel to the television movie "Dawn: Portrait of a Teenage Runaway." A young man turns to prostitution to support himself on the street of Los Angeles. **100m/C VHS.** Leigh McCloskey, Eve Plumb, Earl Holliman, Juliet Mills, Jean Hagen, Lonny Chapman; **D:** John Erman. MOV

Alexander's Ragtime Band 🐾🐾🐾
Irving Berlin's Alexander's Ragtime Band 1938 Energetic musical that spans 1915 to 1938 and has Power and Ameche battling for Faye's affections. Power is a society nabob who takes up ragtime. He puts together a band, naming the group after a piece of music (hence the title), and finds a singer (Faye). Ameche is a struggling composer who brings a Broadway producer to listen to their performance. Faye gets an offer to star in a show and becomes an overnight success. Over the years the trio win and lose success, marry and divorce, and finally end up happy. Corny but charming. 🎵Alexander's Ragtime Band; All Alone; Blue Skies; Easter Parade; Everybody's Doin' It; Everybody Step; For Your Country and My Country; Heat Wave; I Can Always Find a Little Sunshine at the YMCA. **105m/B VHS.** Tyrone Power, Alice Faye, Don Ameche, Ethel Merman, Jack Haley, Jean Hersholt, Helen Westley, John Carradine, Paul Hurst, Joe King, Ruth Terry; **D:** Henry King; **W:** Kathryn Scola, Lamar Trotti; **M:** Irving Berlin, Irving Berlin. Academy Awards '38: Best Score; Nominations: Academy Awards '38: Best Film Editing, Best Interior Decoration, Best Picture, Best Song ("Now It Can Be Told"), Best Story. FXV

Alfie 🐾🐾🐾 1966 (PG) What's it all about, Alfie? Caine, in his first starring role, plays the British playboy out of control in mod London. Alfie is a despicable, unscrupulous and vile sort of guy who uses woman after woman to fulfill his basic

needs and then casts them aside until...tragedy strikes. Though this box office hit was seen as a sophisticated take on current sexual mores upon release, it now seems a dated but engaging comedy, notable chiefly for its performances. From the play from Bill Naughton. The title song "Alfie", sung by Dionne Warwick, was a top ten hit. **113m/C VHS, Beta.** GB Michael Caine, Shelley Winters, Millicent Martin, Vivien Merchant, Julia Asher; **D:** Lewis Gilbert. Cannes Film Festival '67: Grand Jury Prize; Golden Globe Awards '67: Best Foreign Film; National Board of Review Awards '66: 10 Best Films of the Year, Best Supporting Actress (Merchant); National Society of Film Critics Awards '66: Best Actor (Caine); Nominations: Academy Awards '66: Best Actor (Caine), Best Adapted Screenplay, Best Picture, Best Song ("Alfie"), Best Supporting Actress (Merchant). PAR

Alfred Hitchcock's Aventure Malgache *Madagascar Landing; Alfred Hitchcock's Bon Voyage & Aventure Malgache* 1944 Hitchcock worked with the Moliere Players on this propaganda piece about the French Resistance. He based this story on the experiences of the actor Clarousse. Working for the Resistance in occupied Madagascar, Clarousse is betrayed and sent to prison by the Vichy government. Rescued by the British he returns to resume his work. In French with English subtitles. **31m/B VHS.** **D:** Alfred Hitchcock. MIL

Alfred Hitchcock's Bon Voyage *Alfred Hitchcock's Bon Voyage & Aventure Malgache* 1944 One of director Hitchcock's short propaganda pieces filmed as a tribute to the French Resistance. In London an RAF pilot is interrogated by the Free French about his escape from France. He was aided by a Polish agent who was actually working for the Gestapo to learn about the Resistance's movements. Flashbacks show the pilot's adventures from the spy's point-of-view. In French with English subtitles. **26m/B VHS.** John Blythe; **D:** Alfred Hitchcock. MIL

Alfredo, Alfredo 🐾🐾 1972 (R) Hoffman plays a mild-mannered bank clerk who regrets marrying a sexy woman. Lightweight domestic comedy. In Italian with English subtitles (Hoffman's voice was dubbed). **97m/C VHS, Closed Caption.** IT Dustin Hoffman, Stefania Sandrelli, Carla Gravina, Clara Colosimo, Daniela Patella, Dulio Del Prete; **D:** Pietro Germi. PAR

Algiers 🐾🐾🐾 1938 Nearly a scene-for-scene Americanized remake of the 1937 French "Pepe Le Moko" about a beautiful rich girl (Lamarr) who meets and falls in love with a notorious thief (Boyer, then a leading sex symbol). Pursued by French police and hiding in the underworld-controlled Casbah, Boyer meets up with Lamarr in a tragically fated romance done in the best tradition of Hollywood. Boyer provides a measured performance as Le Moko, while Lamarr is appropriately sultry in her American film debut (which made her a star). Later remade as the semi-musical "Casbah." **96m/B VHS, Beta.** Charles Boyer, Hedy Lamarr, Sigrid Gurie, Gene Lockhart, Joseph Calleia, Alan Hale; **D:** John Cromwell; **C:** James Wong Howe. Nominations: Academy Awards '38: Best Actor (Boyer), Best Cinematography, Best Interior Decoration, Best Supporting Actor (Lockhart). CNG, MRV, NOS

Ali Baba and the Forty Thieves 🐾🐾½ 1943 Ali Baba and his gang of thieves do battle against Hulogn Khan, leader of the Mongols, to save Baghdad and its citizens from ruin and death. **87m/C VHS, Closed Caption.** Jon Hall, Turhan Bey, Maria Montez, Andy Devine, Kurt Katch, Frank Puglia, Fortunio Bonanova, Moroni Olsen, Scotty Beckett; **D:** Arthur Lubin; **W:** Edmund Hartmann; **C:** William Howard Greene. USH, FCT

Ali Baba and the 40 Thieves 🐾🐾🐾 1954 French adaptation of the popular novel "A Thousand and One Nights." Servant boy Ali Baba discovers the magic cave holding the stolen treasure of Abdul and his 40 thieves. Shot on location in Morocco. Also available dubbed. **92m/C VHS.** FR Samia Gamal, Dieter

Borsche, Henri Vilbert; **D:** Jacques Becker; **W:** Jacques Becker. *FRA, FCT*

Ali: Fear Eats the Soul ⅅⅅⅅ *Fear Eats the Soul* 1974 A widow cleaning woman in her sixties has a love affair with a Moroccan man 30 years her junior. To no one's surprise, both encounter racism and moral hypocrisy in West Germany. Serious melodrama from Fassbinder, who wrote it and appears as the squirmy son-in-law. In German with English subtitles. **68m/C VHS.** *GE* Brigitte Mira, El Hedi Ben Salem, Irm Hermann; **D:** Rainer Werner Fassbinder. *NYF, FCT*

Alias Billy the Kid ⅅⅅ 1946 Western adventure with Carson posing as a famous outlaw to find out who's behind the scam involving the Denton City cattle trade. **54m/B VHS, Closed Caption.** Sunset Carson. *REP*

Alias Jesse James ⅅⅅ 1959 (PG) Insurance agent Milford Farnsworth (Hope) is an eastern tenderfoot who holds a policy on Jesse James (Corey). So he heads west to make certain the outlaw doesn't get killed. Only Jesse sets Milford up as himself, hoping to collect on his own policy. Fleming's the local beauty. A number of western stars have cameos, coming to Hope's rescue. **92m/C VHS, Closed Caption.** Bob Hope, Rhonda Fleming, Wendell Corey, Jim Davis, Gloria Talbott, William Wright, Mary Young, Joseph Vitale; **Cameos:** Hugh O'Brian, Ward Bond, James Arness, Roy Rogers, Fess Parker, Gail Davis, James Garner, Gene Autry, Jay Silverheels, Bing Crosby, Gary Cooper; **D:** Norman Z. McLeod; **W:** William Bowers, D.D. Beauchamp; **C:** Lionel Lindon. *MGM*

Alias John Law ⅅ 1935 The Good Guy fights for oil rights against the bad guys. Confused program western with an especially convoluted plot. **54m/B VHS, Beta.** Bob Steele; **D:** Robert North Bradbury. *NO*

Alias John Preston ⅅ½ 1956 Yet another one of those pseudo-psychological to sleep perchance to dream movies. Lee plays a man haunted by dreams in which he's a murderer, and soon starts to question whether his dreams might not imitate life. It's been done before, it's been done since, and it's been done better. **66m/B VHS.** *GB* Betta St. John, Alexander Knox, Christopher Lee, Sandra Dorne, Patrick Holt, Betty Ann Davies, John Longden, Bill Fraser, John Stuart; **D:** David MacDonald. *SNC*

Alias, La Gringa ⅅ 1991 Follows the adventures of La Gringa, a likeable criminal capable of escaping from any Peruvian jail. After being aided in his latest escape by a political prisoner, La Gringa decides to return in disguise to pay back the favor. But the prison is rocked by rioting and La Gringa finds himself in a situation out of his control. Spanish with subtitles. **100m/C VHS. D:** Alberto Durant. *FCT*

Alice ⅅ 1986 A twist on the "Alice in Wonderland" tale. Alice witnesses an attempted murder, faints, and awakens in a weird, yet strangely familiar environment. Adapted from the stage production. **80m/C VHS, Beta.** Sophie Barjae, Susannah York, Jean-Pierre Cassel, Paul Nicholas. *ORI, WAR*

Alice ⅅⅅⅅ½ 1988 An acclaimed surreal version of Lewis Carroll's already surreal "Alice in Wonderland," with the emphasis on Carroll's obsessiveness. Utilizing animated puppets and a live actor for Alice, Czech director Svankmajer injects grotesque images and black comedy into Wonderland. Not for the kids. **84m/C VHS.** *GB* Kristina Kohoutova; **D:** Jan Svankmajer. *ICA, TPV*

Alice ⅅⅅ 1990 (PG-13) Farrow is "Alice," a woman plagued with doubts about her lifestyle, her religion, and her happiness. Her perfect children, husband, and apartment don't prevent her backaches, and she turns to an Oriental "herbalist" for aid. She finds his methods unusual and the results of the treatments surprising. Lightweight fairytale of Yuppiedom gone awry. Fine performances, but superficial and pointed story that may leave the viewer looking for more. (Perhaps that's Allen's point.) Farewell performance from character actor Luke, unbilled cameo from

Judith Ivey, and first time out for Dylan O'Sullivan Farrow, adopted daughter of Allen and Farrow, as Kate. **106m/C VHS, Beta, LV, Closed Caption.** Mia Farrow, William Hurt, Joe Mantegna, Keye Luke, Alec Baldwin, Cybill Shepherd, Blythe Danner, Gwen Verdon, Bernadette Peters, Judy Davis, Patrick O'Neal, Julie Kavner, Caroline Aaron, Holland Taylor, Robin Bartlett, David Spielberg, Bob Balaban, Dylan O'Sullivan Farrow, Elle Macpherson; **D:** Woody Allen; **W:** Woody Allen; **C:** Carlo DiPalma. National Board of Review Awards '90: Best Actress (Farrow); Nominations: Academy Awards '90: Best Original Screenplay. *ORI, FCT*

Alice Adams ⅅⅅ½ 1935 Based on the classic Booth Tarkington novel about a poor girl from a small Midwestern town who falls in love with a man from the upper level of society. She tries desperately to fit in and nearly alienates her family and friends. The sets may be dated, but the insight on human behavior is timeless. **99m/B VHS, Beta, LV.** Katharine Hepburn, Fred MacMurray, Evelyn Venable, Hattie McDaniel, Fred Stone; **D:** George Stevens; **M:** Max Steiner. National Board of Review Awards '35: 10 Best Films of the Year; Nominations: Academy Awards '35: Best Actress (Hepburn), Best Picture. *CCB, MED, NOS*

Alice Doesn't Live Here Anymore ⅅⅅ½ 1974 (PG) Scorsese marries road opera with pseudo-feminist semi-realistic melodrama and produces uneven but interesting results. When Alice's husband dies suddenly, leaving her with their eleven-year-old son, she leaves for California, but finds herself stranded in Phoenix, down to her last few bucks. There she lands a job as a waitress in a diner where she meets kindly rancher Kristofferson. Notable for its female point of view, it was also the basis for the once popular TV show "Alice." Burstyn and Ladd lend key performances, while Kristofferson is typically wooden. **105m/C VHS, Beta, LV.** Ellen Burstyn, Kris Kristofferson, Diane Ladd, Jodie Foster, Harvey Keitel, Vic Tayback, Billy Green Bush; **D:** Martin Scorsese; **W:** Robert Getchell. Academy Awards '74: Best Actress (Burstyn); British Academy Awards '75: Best Actress (Burstyn), Best Film, Best Screenplay, Best Supporting Actress (Ladd); National Board of Review Awards '75: 10 Best Films of the Year; Nominations: Academy Awards '74: Best Original Screenplay, Best Supporting Actress (Ladd). *WAR, FCT, BTV*

Alice in the Cities ⅅⅅⅅ½ 1974 American and German culture are compared and contrasted in this early Wenders road work about a German journalist in the USA on assignment who suddenly finds himself custodian to a worldly nine-year-old girl abandoned by her mother. Together they return to Germany and search for the girl's grandmother. Along the way they learn about each other, with many distinctive and graceful Wenders moments. **110m/B VHS, Beta.** Ruediger Vogler, Yella Rottlaender, Elisabeth Kreuzer, Edda Kochi; **D:** Wim Wenders; **W:** Wim Wenders. *FCT, APD, GLV*

Alice in Wonderland ⅅⅅ½ 1950 Another version of the Lewis Carroll classic which combines the usage of Lou Bunin's puppets and live action to tell the story. Released independently to cash in on the success of the Disney version. Takes a more adult approach to the story and is worth viewing on its own merits. **83m/C VHS, Beta.** *FR* Carol Marsh, Stephen Murray, Pamela Brown, Felix Aylmer, Ernest Milton; **D:** Dallas Bower. *MON*

Alice in Wonderland ⅅⅅⅅ 1951 (G) Classic Disney dream version of Lewis Carroll's famous children's story about a girl who falls down a rabbit hole into a magical world populated by strange creatures. Beautifully animated with some startling images, but served with a strange dispassion warmed by a fine batch of songs. Wynn's Mad Hatter and Holloway's Cheshire Cat are among the treats in store. ♫Alice in Wonderland; I'm Late; A Very Merry Un-Birthday. **75m/C VHS, Beta, LV, Closed Caption. D:** Clyde Geronomi; **V:** Kathryn Beaumont, Ed Wynn, Sterling Holloway, Jerry Colonna, Hamilton Luske, Wilfred Jackson. Nominations: Academy Awards '51: Scoring of a Musical. *DIS, FCT, KUI*

Alice in Wonderland ⅅⅅ½ 1982 Musical version of the Lewis Carroll's classic tale performed by the Children's Theatre Company and School. **81m/C VHS, Beta.** Annie Enneking, Solveig Olsen, Wendy Lehr, Jason McLean, Gary Briggle, Elizabeth Fink. *USH*

Alice Sweet Alice ⅅ½ *Holy Terror; Communion* 1976 (R) Mediocre, gory who-killed-her, best remembered as the debut of Shields (in a small role). **112m/C VHS, Beta.** Brooke Shields, Linda Miller, Paula Sheppard; **D:** Alfred Sole. *VTR, MRV, BTV*

Alice Through the Looking Glass 1966 Based on Lewis Carroll's classic adventure. Follows the further adventures of young Alice. After a chess piece comes to life, it convinces Alice that excitement and adventure lie through the looking glass. **72m/C VHS, Beta.** Judi Rolin, Ricardo Montalban, Nanette Fabray, Robert Coote, Agnes Moorehead, Jack Palance, Jimmy Durante, Tom Smothers, Roy Castle, Richard Denning; **D:** Alan Handley. *KAR*

Alice to Nowhere ⅅⅅ 1986 Concerns a running argument in the Outback over a fortune in gems unknowingly carried by a young woman. Made for Australian television and based on a novel by Evan Green. **210m/C VHS, Beta.** *AU* Rosie Jones, Steve Jacobs, John Waters, Ruth Cracknell; **D:** John Power. *PAR*

Alice's Adventures in Wonderland 1972 Musical adaptation of Lewis Carroll's timeless fantasy of a young girl who meets new friends when she falls into a rabbit hole. **96m/C VHS, Beta.** *GB* Fiona Fullerton, Michael Crawford, Ralph Richardson, Flora Robson, Peter Sellers, Robert Helpmann, Dudley Moore, Michael Jayston, Spike Milligan, Michael Hordern; **D:** William Sterling; **W:** William Sterling; **C:** Geoffrey Unsworth; **M:** John Barry. *VES*

Alice's Restaurant ⅅⅅ½ 1969 (PG) Based on the popular and funny 20-minute Arlo Guthrie song "Alice's Restaurant Massacre" about a Flower Child during the Last Big War who gets hassled for littering, man. Step back in time and study the issues of the hippie era, including avoiding the draft, dropping out of college, and dealing with the local pigs. Sort of a modern movie in the cinematic ambling genre, in that nothing really happens. **111m/C VHS, Beta.** Arlo Guthrie, James Broderick, Pat Quinn, Geoff Outlaw; **D:** Arthur Penn. Nominations: Academy Awards '69: Best Director (Penn). *MVD, MGM*

Alien ⅅⅅⅅ½ 1979 (R) Terse direction, stunning sets and special effects, and a well-seasoned cast save this from being another "Slimy monster from Outerspace" story. Instead it's a grisly rollercoaster of suspense and fear (and a huge box office hit). Intergalactic freighter's crew is invaded by an unstoppable carnivorous alien intent on picking off the crew one by one. While the cast mostly bitches and banters while awaiting the horror of their imminent departure, Weaver is exceptional as Ripley, a self-reliant survivor who goes toe to toe with the Big Ugly. Futuristic, in the belly of the beast visual design creates a vivid sense of claustrophobic doom enhanced further by the ominous score. Oscar-winning special effects include the classic baby alien busting out of the crew guy's chest routine, a rib-splitting ten on the gore meter. Successfully followed by "Aliens" and "Alien 3." **116m/C VHS, Beta, LV.** Tom Skerritt, Sigourney Weaver, Veronica Cartwright, Yaphet Kotto, Harry Dean Stanton, Ian Holm, John Hurt; **D:** Ridley Scott; **W:** Dan O'Bannon; **M:** Jerry Goldsmith. Academy Awards '79: Best Visual Effects; Nominations: Academy Awards '79: Best Art Direction/Set Decoration. *FOX*

Alien 3 ⅅⅅ 1992 (R) Picks up where "Aliens" left off as Ripley crash lands on Fiorina 161, a planet that serves as a penal colony for 25 celibate but horny men who smell bad. Ripley is forced to shave her head because of the planet's lice problem, and she sets out to survive on the cold, unfriendly planet until a rescue ship can come for her. Fending off sexual advances from the men, Ripley soon discovers she wasn't the only survivor of the crash—the alien survived too and has somehow implanted her with an alien of her own. Dark and disturbing, filled with religious allegories, and a universe removed from the two earlier Aliens. Intended as the final installment of the series. *CW:* Language and monster violence. **135m/C VHS, LV, Closed Caption.** Sigourney Weaver, Charles S. Dutton, Charles Dance, Paul McGann, Brian Glover, Ralph Brown, Danny Webb, Christopher John Fields, Holt McCallany, Lance Henriksen; *D:* David Fincher; *M:* Elliot Goldenthal. Nominations: Academy Awards '92: Best Visual Effects. *FXV*

Alien Chaser 🎬🎬 **1996 (R)** Alien android Zagarino, who crashed in the African desert 5000 years ago, returns to life thanks to the unwitting aid of archeologists Jensen and MacDonald. They literally hold the key to stopping his destruction of mankind. **95m/C VHS, LV.** Frank Zagarino, Todd Jensen, Jennifer MacDonald; *D:* Mark Roper; *W:* B.J. Nelson; *C:* Rod Stewart; *M:* Robert O. Ragland. *APX*

Alien Contamination woof! *Contamination* **1981 (R)** Tale of two astronauts who return to Earth from an expedition on Mars carrying some deadly bacterial eggs. Controlled by a Martian intent on conquering the world, the eggs squirt a gloppy juice that makes people explode on contact (a special effect). A cheap and sloppy attempt to cash in on the success of "Alien." Dubbed. **90m/C VHS, Beta.** *IT* Ian McCulloch, Louise Monroe, Martin Mase, Samuel Rauch, Lisa Hahn; *D:* Lewis (Luigi Cozzi) Coates; *W:* Lewis (Luigi Cozzi) Coates. *NO*

Alien Dead 🎬 **1985 (R)** The teenage victims of a bizarre meteor crash reincarnate as flesh-eating ghouls anxious for a new supply of human food in this extremely low-budget sleep inducer. **87m/C VHS, Beta.** Buster Crabbe, Linda Lewis, Ray Roberts; *D:* Fred Olen Ray. *ACA, GHV*

The Alien Factor 🎬🎬 **1978 (PG)** Another low-budget crazed critter from outerspace dispatch, this one featuring multiple aliens, one of whom is good, who have the misfortune of crash landing near Baltimore. The grotesque extraterrestrials jolt a small town out of its sleepy state by wreaking havoc (except for the good one, of course). Decent special effects. **82m/C VHS, Beta.** Don Leifert, Tom Griffith, Mary Mertens, Dick Dyszel; *D:* Donald M. Dohler. *NO*

Alien from L.A. woof! **1987 (PG)** Awesomely inept comedy about a California girl who unwittingly stumbles onto the famed continent of Atlantis and can't find a yogurt stand. Like, really. **88m/C VHS, Beta, LV.** Kathy Ireland, Thom Mathews, Don Michael Paul, Linda Kerridge, William R. Moses, Richard Haines; *D:* Albert Pyun; *W:* Albert Pyun, Debra Ricci, Regina Davis; *C:* Tom Fraser. *MED*

Alien Intruder 🎬🎬 **1993 (R)** What happens when an evil demon appears before the soldiers of the future in the guise of a beautiful woman? Futuristic trash B-movie emerges from the depths. *CW:* Language, violence, and strong sexuality. **90m/C VHS, LV, Closed Caption.** Billy Dee Williams, Tracy Scoggins, Maxwell Caulfield; *D:* Ricardo Jacques Gale. *PMH*

Alien Massacre woof! *Dr. Terror's Gallery of Horrors; Return from the Past; The Blood Suckers; Gallery of Horror* **1967** One of the worst films of all time—five short horror stories about zombies and vampires. Goes by many names—stinks in all of them. **90m/C VHS, Beta.** Lon Chaney Jr., John Carradine, Rochelle Hudson, Roger Gentry, Mitch Evans; *D:* David L. Hewitt. *ACA, MRV*

Alien Nation 🎬🎬½ **1988 (R)** A few hundred thousand alien workers land accidentally on Earth and slowly become part of its society, although widely discriminated against. One of the "newcomers" teams with a surly and bigoted human cop to solve a racially motivated murder. An inconsistent and occasionally transparent script looks at race conflicts and includes some humorous parallels with contemporary American life. Basis for the television series. Producer Hurd was

also the force behind "The Terminator" and "Aliens." **89m/C VHS, Beta, LV, Closed Caption.** James Caan, Mandy Patinkin, Terence Stamp, Kevyn Major Howard, Peter Jason, Jeff Kober, Leslie Bevins; *D:* Graham Baker; *W:* Rockne S. O'Bannon; *M:* Curt Sobel. *FOX*

Alien Nation: Dark Horizon 🎬🎬½ **1994 (PG)** The alien Newcomers have successfully adapted to life on Earth but face continuing dangers when a human-supremacy group develops a virus to wipe them out and an alien infiltrator is plotting to return them to slavery on Tencton. Naturally, it's up to detectives Sykes and Francisco to save the day. Based on the TV series. **90m/C VHS, Closed Caption.** Gary Graham, Eric Pierpont, Scott Patterson, Terri Treas, Michelle Scarabelli, Lee Bryant, Sean Six, Lauren Woodland, Ron Fassler, Jeff Marcus; *D:* Kenneth Johnson; *W:* Diane Frolov, Andrew Schneider; *M:* David Kurtz. *FXV*

Alien Predators woof! **1980 (R)** Three friends encounter a malevolent alien in this dull reworking of the plot of "The Andromeda Strain" with laughable special effects tossed in for those outwitted by the script. **92m/C VHS, Beta.** Dennis Christopher, Martin Hewitt, Lynn-Holly Johnson, Luis Prendes; *D:* Deran Sarafian. *VTR*

Alien Prey 🎬½ **1983 (R)** Two lesbians are making love when they are unexpectedly devoured by a hungry and indiscreet alien. No safe sex there. Graphic sex, violence, and cannibalism abound. Interesting twist to the old eat 'em and leave 'em genre. **85m/C VHS, Beta.** Barry Stokes, Sally Faulkner; *D:* Norman J. Warren. *NO*

Alien Private Eye 🎬🎬 *Alien P.I* **1987** An extraterrestrial detective searches Los Angeles for a missing magic disk while investigating an intergalactic crime ring. **90m/C VHS.** Nikki Fastinetti; *D:* Nik Rubenfeld. *NO*

Alien Seed 🎬 **1989** Aliens kidnap a woman and impregnate her. Estrada is the government scientist hot on her trail. (How far could a woman carrying alien offspring wander?) **88m/C VHS.** Erik Estrada, Heidi Paine, Steven Blade; *D:* Bob James. *AIP*

Alien Space Avenger 🎬½ *Space Avenger* **1991** A spaceship piloted by four alien convicts crash lands in New York City. Stalked by an intergalatic bounty hunter whose job is to kill them, the aliens attack and hide inside human bodies to avoid discovery. It's a race against time as the preservation of the human race depends on the avenger's ability to seek and destroy the alien invaders. Bland ripoff of "Aliens" is reminiscent of old-time "B" sci-fi flicks, with more gore and violence. Shot with the old 3-strip Technicolor method. **88m/C VHS.** Robert Prichard, Mike McClerie, Charity Staley, Gina Mastrogiacomo, Kick Fairbanks Fogg, Angela Nicholas, Marty Roberts, James Gillis; *D:* Richard W. Haines; *W:* Richard W. Haines, Linwood Sawyer; *M:* Richard Fiocca. *AIP*

Alien Terminator 🎬 **1995 (R)** Scientists experimenting with DNA find themselves creating an organism capable of instant regeneration that also likes to nosh on living flesh. To make matters worse, the scientists are trapped in their lab complex, which happens to be located five miles below Los Alamos. **95m/C VHS.** Maria Ford, Kevin Alber, Rodger Halstead, Cassandra Leigh, Emile Levisetti; *D:* Dave Payne. *NHO*

Alien Warrior woof! **1985 (R)** An extraterrestrial fights a street pimp to save a crime-ridden Earth neighborhood. Low-brain rip-off of Superman. **92m/C VHS, Beta.** Brett Clark, Pamela Saunders; *D:* Edward Hunt. *VES, LIV*

Alien Women 🎬 *Zeta One; The Love Factor* **1969 (R)** A soft-core British science fiction yarn about scantily clad alien babes and the special agent who's trying to uncover their secret. It's all very sketchy, silly and campy, though pleasantly cast with plenty of lovely British actresses. **86m/C VHS, Beta.** *GB* James Robertson Justice, Charles Hawtrey, Robin Hawdon, Anna Gael, Brigitte Skay, Dawn Addams, Valerie Leon, Yutte Stensgaard, Wendy Lingham, Rita Webb, Caroline Hawkins; *D:* Michael Cort. *PSM, SNC*

Alienator 🎬 **1989 (R)** In the improbable future, an unstoppable android killer is sent after an intergalactic villain. An intentional "Terminator" rip-off. **93m/C VHS, Beta, LV.** Jan-Michael Vincent, John Phillip Law, Ross Hagen, Dyana Ortelli, Dawn Wildsmith, P.J. Soles, Teagan Clive, Robert Clarke, Leo Gordon, Robert Quarry, Fox Harris, Hoke Howell, Jay Richardson; *D:* Fred Olen Ray. *PSM*

Aliens 🎬🎬🎬½ **1986 (R)** The bitch is back, some 50 years later. Popular sequel to "Alien" amounts to non-stop, ravaging combat in space. Contact with a colony on another planet has mysteriously stopped. Fresh from deep space sleep, Ripley and a slew of pulsar-equipped Marines return to confront the mother alien at her nest, which is also inhabited by a whole bunch of the nasty critters spewing for a fight. Something's gotta give, and the Oscar-winning special effects are especially inventive (and messy) in the alien demise department. Dimension (acting biz talk) is given to our hero Ripley, as she discovers maternal instincts lurking within her space suit while looking after a young girl, the lone survivor of the colony. Tension-filled gore blaster. Followed by "Aliens 3." *CW:* Language and monster violence. **138m/C VHS, Beta, LV, Closed Caption.** Sigourney Weaver, Michael Biehn, Lance Henriksen, Bill Paxton, Paul Reiser, Carrie Henn, Jenette Goldstein; *D:* James Cameron; *W:* James Cameron, Walter Hill; *M:* James Horner. Academy Awards '86: Best Sound Effects Editing, Best Visual Effects; Nominations: Academy Awards '86: Best Actress (Weaver), Best Art Direction/Set Decoration, Best Film Editing, Best Sound, Best Original Score. *FOX*

Aliens Are Coming 🎬½ **1980** A spaceship crash lands on Earth, and its devious denizens begin invading human bodies. TV movie that's a dull echo of "Invasion of the Body Snatchers." **100m/C VHS, Beta.** Tom Mason, Melinda Fee, Max Gail, Eric (Hans Gudegast) Braeden, Matthew Laborteaux; *D:* Harvey Hart; *M:* William Goldstein. *WOV, GKK*

Aliens from Spaceship Earth 🎬½ **1977** Are strange, celestial forces invading our universe? If they are, is man prepared to defend his planet against threatening aliens of unknown strength? Lame docudrama featuring the Hurdy Gurdy man himself, Donovan. **107m/C VHS, Beta.** Donovan, Lynda Day George; *D:* Don Como. *GEM*

Alison's Birthday 🎬🎬 **1979** A teenage girl learns that some of her family and friends are Satan worshipers at a terrifying birthday party. Meanwhile, the ghost of her dad hovers about, asking for more lines. **99m/C VHS, Beta.** *AU* Joanne Samuel, Lou Brown, Bunny Brooke; *D:* Ian Coughlan. *NO*

Alive 🎬🎬½ **1993 (R)** Recounts the true-life survival story of a group of Uruguayan rugby players in 1972. After their plane crashes in the remote, snowy Andes (in a spectacular sequence) they're forced to turn to cannibalism during a 10-week struggle to stay alive. Marshall doesn't focus on the gruesome idea, choosing instead to focus on all aspects of their desperate quest for survival. The special effects are stunning, but others parts of the film are never fully realized, including the final scene. Based on the nonfiction book by Piers Paul Read. *CW:* Psychological intensity. **127m/C VHS, Beta, LV, Closed Caption.** Ethan Hawke, Vincent Spano, Josh Hamilton, Bruce Ramsay, John Haymes Newton, David Kriegel, Kevin Breznahan, Sam Behrens, Illeana Douglas, Jack Noseworthy, Christian Meoli, Jake Carpenter; *Cameos:* John Malkovich; *D:* Frank Marshall; *W:* John Patrick Shanley; *C:* Peter James; *M:* James Newton Howard. *TOU*

Alive: 20 Years Later **1993** With the release of the big-screen fictional version comes this follow-up documentary with the survivors of the 1972 mountain plane crash telling their own story. **51m/C VHS, Beta, LV, Closed Caption.** *D:* Jill Fullerton-Smith. *TOU*

All About Eve 🎬🎬🎬🎬 **1950** One of the wittiest (and most cynical) flicks of all time follows aspiring young actress Baxter as she ingratiates herself with a prominent group of theater people so she can become a Broadway star without the usual years of work. The not-so-innocent babe becomes secretary to aging star Davis and ruthlessly uses everyone in her climb to the top, much to Davis' initial disbelief and eventual displeasure. Satirical, darkly funny view of the theater world features exceptional work by Davis, Sanders, and Ritter. Based on "The Wisdom of Eve" by Mary Orr. Later staged as the musical "Applause." **138m/B VHS, Beta, LV.** Bette Davis, Anne Baxter, George Sanders, Celeste Holm, Gary Merrill, Thelma Ritter, Marilyn Monroe, Hugh Marlowe, Gregory Ratoff, Eddie Fisher; **D:** Joseph L. Mankiewicz; **W:** Joseph L. Mankiewicz; **C:** Milton Krasner. Academy Awards '50: Best Costume Design (B & W), Best Director (Mankiewicz), Best Picture, Best Screenplay, Best Sound, Best Supporting Actor (Sanders); British Academy Awards '50: Best Film; Cannes Film Festival '51: Best Actress (Davis), Grand Jury Prize; Directors Guild of America Awards '50: Best Director (Mankiewicz); Golden Globe Awards '51: Best Screenplay; National Board of Review Awards '50: 10 Best Films of the Year; New York Film Critics Awards '50: Best Actress (Davis), Best Director (Mankiewicz), Best Film; Nominations: Academy Awards '50: Best Actress (Baxter), Best Actress (Davis), Best Art Direction/Set Decoration (B & W), Best Black and White Cinematography, Best Supporting Actress (Holm, Ritter), Original Dramatic/Comedy Score. **FOX, BTV, HMV**

All-American Murder 🎬🎬 1991 (R)
A rebellious young man is enrolled in a typical, all-American college for one last shot at mainstream life. Things start out okay, as he meets an attractive young coed. Hours later, he finds himself accused of her grisly murder. The youth is then given 24 hours to prove his innocence by a canny homicide detective. Average performances highlight this film, which isn't able to rise above the mediocre. **CW:** Language, violence, and sexual scenes. **94m/C VHS, Beta, LV, Closed Caption.** Christopher Walken, Charlie Schlatter, Josie Bissett, Joanna Cassidy, Richard Kind, Woody Watson, J.C. Quinn, Amy Davis; **D:** Anson Williams; **W:** Barry Sandler. **PSM**

All Creatures Great and Small 🎬🎬🎬 1974
Taken from James Herriot's best selling novels, this is a delightful, quiet drama of a veterinarian's apprentice in rural England. Fine performance by Hopkins. Followed by "All Things Bright and Beautiful" and a popular British television series. **92m/C VHS, Beta, Closed Caption.** GB Simon Ward, Anthony Hopkins, Lisa Harrow, Brian Stirner, Freddie Jones, T.P. McKenna; **D:** Claude Whatham. **RDG, FOX, HMV**

All Dogs Go to Heaven 🎬🎬 1989 (G)
Somewhat heavy-handed animated musical (Reynolds sings) about a gangster dog who is killed by his partner in business. On the way to Heaven, he discovers how to get back to Earth to seek his revenge. When he returns to Earth, he is taken in by a little girl and learns about something he missed in life the first time around: Love. Expertly animated, but the plot may not keep the grown-ups engrossed, and the kids may notice its lack of charm. **85m/C VHS, Beta, LV, 8mm, Closed Caption.** **D:** Don Bluth; **W:** Don Bluth, David A. Weiss; **M:** Ralph Burns; **V:** Burt Reynolds, Judith Barsi, Dom DeLuise, Vic Tayback, Charles Nelson Reilly, Melba Moore, Candy Devine, Loni Anderson. **MGM, RDG**

All Dogs Go to Heaven 2 🎬🎬½
1995 (G) Animated musical finds lovable scamp Charlie (Sheen) the dog discovering that the afterlife is not all it's cracked up to be and pining for dysfunction aplenty back on earth. He gets his chance when Gabriel's Horn is stolen and Charlie is assigned to retrieve it. Charlie teams up again with old buddy Itchy (Deluise) as the two come down from Dog Heaven to stop the villainous Carface (Borgnine) and demonic cat Red (Hearn). Along the way, Charlie falls in love with sexy Irish Setter Sasha (Easton), and finds a chance for redemption by helping a little boy in trouble. Animation not outstanding, but should keep the attention of small children. **82m/C VHS, LV, Closed Caption.** **D:** Paul Sabella, Larry Leker; **W:** Arne Olsen, Kelly Ward, Mark Young; **M:** Mark Watters, Barry Mann, Cynthia Weil; **V:** Charlie Sheen, Sheena Easton, Ernest Borgnine,

Dom DeLuise, George Hearn, Bebe Neuwirth, Hamilton Camp, Wallace Shawn, Bobby DiCicco, Adam Wylie. **MGM**

All Fall Down 🎬🎬½ 1962
A young man (de Wilde) idolizes his callous older brother (Beatty) until a tragedy forces him to grow up. Saint plays the older woman taken in by the brothers' family, who is seduced and abandoned. When she finds herself pregnant and alone, she commits suicide causing the younger brother, who loved her from afar, to vow to kill his older sibling. A well-acted melodrama. Also available colorized. **111m/B VHS.** Eva Marie Saint, Brandon de Wilde, Warren Beatty, Karl Malden, Angela Lansbury, Constance Ford, Barbara Baxley; **D:** John Frankenheimer; **W:** William Inge; **C:** Lionel Lindon; **M:** Alex North. **MGM**

All God's Children 🎬🎬½ 1980
Made for television drama about the controversial forced busing issue and two families who must face it. Top-notch cast is occasionally mislead by meandering script attempting to stay true to a sensitive issue. **100m/C VHS, Beta.** Richard Widmark, Ned Beatty, Ossie Davis, Ruby Dee, Mariclare Costello, George Spell, Trish Van Devere, Ken Swofford; **D:** Jerry Thorpe; **M:** Billy Goldenberg. **NO**

All I Desire 🎬🎬½ 1953
Estranged wife and mother (Stanwyck) returns to her hometown after fleeing years ago to pursue a stage career. She desires a new beginning with her family, but finds things have changed in her absence. The story examines the will of a strong woman and small town values. Director Sirk disagreed with the happy ending demanded by producers, but the drama is still noteworthy. **80m/B VHS, Closed Caption.** Barbara Stanwyck, Richard Carlson, Lyle Bettger, Maureen O'Sullivan; **D:** Douglas Sirk; **W:** James Gunn, Robert Blees, Carl Guthrie, Gina Kaus; **M:** Joseph Gershenson. **USH**

All I Want for Christmas 🎬🎬 1991
(G) Low-budget, sappy holiday tale of a young girl (Birch) who wants to reunite her divorced parents. Determined to fulfill her Christmas wish, Hallie seeks out the Santa Claus at Macy's department store to tell him the one thing she truly wants for Christmas. Birch is charming as are Bacall as her grandmother and Nielsen as Santa but the story is too squishy and bland to be believable. **92m/C VHS, LV.** Thora Birch, Leslie Nielsen, Lauren Bacall, Jamey Sheridan, Harley Jane Kozak, Ethan Randall, Kevin Nealon, Andrea Martin; **D:** Ron Lieberman; **W:** Richard Kramer, Thom Eberhardt, Neal Israel, Gail Parent; **C:** Robbie Greenberg; **M:** Bruce Broughton. **PAR**

All in a Night's Work 🎬🎬½ 1961
The founder of a one-man publishing empire is found dead with a smile on his face. His nephew inherits the business and finds himself caught in a series of big and small business misunderstandings. He's also falling in love with the woman he suspects was responsible for his uncle's grin. Nicely paced sex and business comedy with warm performances. **94m/C VHS, Beta.** Dean Martin, Shirley MacLaine, Cliff Robertson, Charlie Ruggles; **D:** Joseph Anthony; **W:** Sidney Sheldon; **M:** Andre Previn. **FOX**

All Mine to Give 🎬🎬½ The Day They Gave
the Babies Away 1956 Sad saga of a Scottish family of eight who braved frontier hardships, epidemics, and death in the Wisconsin wilderness more than a century ago. Midway through, mom and dad die, leaving the oldest child struggling to keep the family together. A strange, though often effective, combination of pioneer adventures and tearjerking moments that avoids becoming hopelessly soapy due to fine performances. Unless you're pretty weathered, you'll need some hankies. Based on the reminiscences of Dale and Katherine Eunson as detailed in a "Cosmopolitan" magazine article. **102m/C VHS, Beta.** Glynis Johns, Cameron Mitchell, Rex Thompson, Patty McCormack, Ernest Truex, Hope Emerson, Alan Hale Jr., Royal Dano, Reta Shaw, Rita Johnson, Ellen Corby, Jon Provost; **D:** Allen Reisner; **M:** Max Steiner. **NO**

All My Good Countrymen 🎬🎬½ All
Good Citizens 1968 A lyrical, funny film about the eccentric denizens of a small Moravian village soon after the socialization of Czechoslovakia in 1948. Completed during the Soviet invasion of 1968 and immediately banned. In Czech with English subtitles. **115m/C VHS, Beta.** CZ Vladimir Mensik, Radoslav Brozobohaty, Pavel Pavlovsky; **D:** Vojtech Jasny. Cannes Film Festival '69: Best Director (Jasny). **FCT**

All My Sons 🎬🎬🎬 1986
A wealthy family is distraught when their eldest son is listed as missing-in-action during WWII. They must cope with guilt, as well as grief, because the father's business reaped profits from the war. Adapted for television from the acclaimed Arthur Miller play. **122m/C VHS, Beta.** James Whitmore, Aidan Quinn, Joan Allen, Michael Learned; **D:** John Power. **USH**

All Night Long 🎬🎬🎬 1981 (R)
Offbeat middle-age crisis comedy about a burned-out and recently demoted drugstore executive in L.A. who leaves his wife, takes up with his fourth cousin by marriage, and begins a humorous rebellion, becoming an extremely freelance inventor while joining the drifters, weirdos and thieves of the night. An obscure, sometimes uneven little gem with Hackman in top form and an appealing supporting performance by Streisand. Highlighted by delightful malapropisms and sataric inversion of the usual cliches. **100m/C VHS, Beta.** Gene Hackman, Barbra Streisand, Diane Ladd, Dennis Quaid, Kevin Dobson, William Daniels; **D:** Jean-Claude Tramont; **M:** Ira Newborn. **GKK**

All Night Long/Smile Please 1924
Two classic comedies by the most overlooked of the great silent clowns, both produced by slapstick progenitor Mack Sennett. **66m/B VHS, Beta.** Harry Langdon, Natalie Kingston, Jack Cooper, Alberta Vaughn. **VYY**

All of Me 🎬🎬½ 1984 (PG)
A wealthy woman (Tomlin) dies and her guru accidentally transfers her soul to the right side of her lawyer's body, a modern version of existential hell. Lawyer Martin indulges in some funny slapstick as he discovers that his late client is waging an internal war for control of his body. Flat and cliched at times, but redeemed by the inspired clowning of Martin and witty Martin/Tomlin repartee. Based on the novel "Me Too" by Ed Davis. **93m/C VHS, Beta, LV.** Steve Martin, Lily Tomlin, Victoria Tennant, Madolyn Smith, Richard Libertini, Dana Elcar, Selma Diamond; **D:** Carl Reiner; **W:** Phil Alden Robinson. New York Film Critics Awards '84: Best Actor (Martin); National Society of Film Critics Awards '84: Best Actor (Martin). **FCT**

All Over Town 🎬🎬½ 1937
Two vaudevillians with a trained seal find themselves involved in a murder when they are kidnapped by a gang of thugs. A lesser Olsen and Johnson comedy with scattered funny moments. **52m/B VHS, Beta.** Ole Olsen, Chic Johnson, Mary Howard, Franklin Pangborn, James Finlayson; **D:** James W. Horne; **W:** Jack Townley, Jerome Chodorov. **NOS, MRV, VYY**

All Quiet on the Western Front 🎬🎬🎬🎬 1930
Extraordinary and realistic anti-war epic based on the novel by Erich Maria Remarque. Seven patriotic German youths go together from school to the battlefields of WWI. They experience the horrors of war first-hand, stuck in the trenches and facing gradual extermination. Centers on experiences of one of the young men, Paul Baumer, who changes from enthusiastic war endorser to battle-weary veteran in an emotionally exact performance by Ayres. Boasts a gigantic budget (for the time) of $1.25 million, and features more than 2,000 extras swarming about battlefields set up on ranchland in California. Relentless anti-war message is emotionally draining and startling with both graphic shots and haunting visual poetry. Extremely controversial in the U.S. and Germany upon release, the original version was 140 minutes long (some versions are available with restored footage) and featured ZaSu Pitts as Ayres mother

(later reshot with Mercer replacing her). Remarque, who had fought and been wounded on the Western Front, was eventually forced to leave Germany for the U.S. due to the film's ongoing controversy. **103m/B VHS, Beta, LV.** Lew Ayres, Louis Wolheim, John Wray, Slim Summerville, Russell Gleason, Raymond Griffith, Ben Alexander, Beryl Mercer; **D:** Lewis Milestone. Academy Awards '30: Best Director (Milestone), Best Picture; National Board of Review Awards '30: 10 Best Films of the Year; Nominations: Academy Awards '30: Best Cinematography, Best Writing. *USH, FCT, GLV*

All Quiet on the Western
Front 🐾🐾½ 1979 A big-budget television remake of the 1930 masterpiece starring John Boy. Sensitive German youth Thomas plunges excitedly into WWI and discovers its terror and degradation. Nowhere near the original's quality. **150m/C VHS, Beta, LV.** Richard Thomas, Ernest Borgnine, Donald Pleasence, Patricia Neal; **D:** Delbert Mann. *FOX, FCT*

All Screwed Up 🐾🐾🐾 *All in Place; Nothing in Order* 1974 A group of young immigrants come to Milan and try to adjust to city life; they soon find that everything is in its place, but nothing is in order. Wertmuller in a lighter vein than usual. **104m/C VHS, Beta.** *IT* Luigi Diberti, Lina Polito; **D:** Lina Wertmuller; **W:** Lina Wertmuller. *FOX*

All That Jazz 🐾🐾🐾½ 1979 (R) Fosse's autobiographical portrait with Scheider fully occupying his best role as the obsessed, pill-popping, chain-smoking choreographer/director dancing simultaneously with love and death. But even while dying, he creates some great dancing. Vivid and imaginative with exact editing, and an eerie footnote to Fosse's similar death almost ten years later. Egocentric and self-indulgent for sure, but that's entertainment. ♫On Broadway; Everything Old is New Again; After You've Gone; There'll Be Some Changes Made; Some of These Days; Bye Bye Love. **120m/C VHS, Beta, LV, Closed Caption.** Roy Scheider, Jessica Lange, Ann Reinking, Leland Palmer, Cliff Gorman, Ben Vereen, Erzebet Foldi, John Lithgow, Wallace Shawn, Sandahl Bergman, Nicole Fosse, Keith Gordon, Ben Masters, Theresa Merritt; **D:** Bob Fosse; **C:** Giuseppe Rotunno; **M:** Ralph Burns. Academy Awards '79: Best Art Direction/Set Decoration, Best Costume Design, Best Film Editing, Original Song Score and/or Adaptation; Cannes Film Festival '80: Best Film; Nominations: Academy Awards '79: Best Actor (Scheider), Best Cinematography, Best Director (Fosse), Best Original Screenplay, Best Picture. *FOX, OM*

All the Brothers Were
Valiant 🐾🐾½ 1953 Brothers Taylor and Granger are New England whaling captains but Granger decides to treasure hunt instead. He finds a priceless cache of black pearls on an island but angers the locals who regard the gems as sacred. When Taylor rescues him, Granger promptly turns his brother's crew into mutineers in order to return to the island and retrieve his prize. Lots of brawling and there's an incidental love story with Blyth desired by both men (she's married Taylor and just happens to be aboard). Last role for Stone. Based on the novel by Ben Ames Williams. **101m/C VHS.** Robert Taylor, Stewart Granger, Ann Blyth, Betta St. John, Keenan Wynn, James Whitmore, Kurt Kasznar, Lewis Stone, Robert Burton, Peter Whitney, John Lupton, Billie Dove; **D:** Richard Thorpe; **W:** Harry Brown; **M:** Miklos Rozsa. Nominations: Academy Awards '53: Best Color Cinematography. *MGM*

All the Kind Strangers 🐾🐾 *Evil in the Swamp* 1974 Traveling photographer Keach picks up a young hitchhiker and takes him to the boy's home. He discovers six other children there who want him as a father, his alternative being death. He and "Mother" Eggar plot their escape from the dangerous orphans. Made-for-television thriller short on suspense. **72m/C VHS, Beta, Closed Caption.** Stacy Keach, Robby Benson, John Savage, Samantha Eggar; **D:** Burt Kennedy. *FOX*

All the King's Men 🐾🐾🐾🐾 1949 Grim and graphic classic set in the Depression follows the rise of a Louisiana farm-boy from angry and honest political hopeful to powerful but corrupt governor. Loosely based on the life (and death) of Huey Long and told by a newsman who's followed his career (Ireland). Willy Stark (Crawford, in his break-through role) is the politician who, while appearing to improve the state, rules dictatorially, betraying friends and constituents and proving once again that power corrupts. In her first major role, McCambridge delivers a powerful performance as the cunning political aide. Potent morality play based on the Robert Penn Warren book. **109m/B VHS, Beta, LV.** Broderick Crawford, Mercedes McCambridge, John Ireland, Joanne Dru, John Derek, Anne Seymour, Shepperd Strudwick; **D:** Robert Rossen; **W:** Robert Rossen; **C:** Burnett Guffey. Academy Awards '49: Best Actor (Crawford), Best Picture, Best Supporting Actress (McCambridge); Golden Globe Awards '50: Best Actor—Drama (Crawford), Best Director (Rossen), Best Film—Drama, Best Supporting Actress (McCambridge); New York Film Critics Awards '49: Best Actor (Crawford), Best Film; Nominations: Academy Awards '49: Best Director (Rossen), Best Film Editing, Best Screenplay, Best Supporting Actor (Ireland). *COL, BTV*

All the Lovin' Kinfolk 🐾 *Kin Folk; Kinfolk; The Closest of Kin* 1989 (R) Two recent Hillbilly High graduates decide to take on the big city, but find themselves in dire situations. For those with time to kill. **80m/C VHS.** Mady Maguire, Jay Scott, Anne Ryan, John Denis, Donna Young; **D:** John Hayes. *NO*

...All the Marbles 🐾🐾 *The California Dolls* 1981 (R) A manager of two beautiful lady wrestlers has dreams of going to the top. Aldrich's last film, and an atypical one, with awkward pacing and a thin veil of sex exploitation. Falk provides needed grace and humor as the seedy manager, with Young contributing his usual competent bit as a hustling promoter dabbling in criminal activity. One of the few tag-team women wrestling pictures, it builds to a rousing finale match in the "Rocky" tradition, although the shift in tone and mounting cliches effectively body slam the intent. **113m/C VHS, Beta, LV.** Peter Falk, Burt Young, Richard Jaeckel, Vicki Frederick; **D:** Robert Aldrich; **C:** Joseph Biroc. *MGM, OM*

All the President's Men 🐾🐾🐾½ 1976 (PG) True story of the Watergate break-in that led to the political scandal of the decade, based on the best-selling book by Washington Post reporters Bob Woodward and Carl Bernstein. Intriguing, terse thriller is a nail-biter even though the ending is no secret. Expertly paced by Pakula with standout performances by Hoffman and Redford as the reporters who slowly uncover and connect the seemingly isolated facts that ultimately lead to criminal indictments of the Nixon Administration. Deep Throat Holbrook and Robards as executive editor Ben Bradlee lend authenticity to the endeavor, a realistic portrayal of the stop and go of journalistic investigations. **135m/C VHS, Beta, LV.** Robert Redford, Dustin Hoffman, Jason Robards Jr., Martin Balsam, Jane Alexander, Hal Holbrook, F. Murray Abraham, Stephen Collins, Lindsay Crouse; **D:** Alan J. Pakula; **W:** William Goldman; **C:** Gordon Willis; **M:** David Shire. Academy Awards '76: Best Adapted Screenplay, Best Art Direction/Set Decoration, Best Sound, Best Supporting Actor (Robards); National Board of Review Awards '76: 10 Best Films of the Year, Best Director (Pakula), Best Supporting Actor (Robards); New York Film Critics Awards '76: Best Director (Pakula), Best Film, Best Supporting Actor (Robards); National Society of Film Critics Awards '76: Best Film, Best Supporting Actor (Robards); Writers Guild of America '76: Best Adapted Screenplay; Nominations: Academy Awards '76: Best Director (Pakula), Best Film Editing, Best Picture, Best Supporting Actress (Alexander). *WAR, BTV*

All the Right Moves 🐾🐾½ 1983 (R) Cruise is the high school football hero hoping for a scholarship so he can vacate pronto the dying Pennsylvania mill town where he grew up. At least he thinks that's what he wants to do. Further mixing up his own mixed feelings are his pushy, ambitious coach (Nelson, doing what he does best), his understanding dad (Cioffi) and supportive girlfriend (Thompson, in a notable early role). Strong performances push the relatively cliched melodrama into field goal range. Cinematographer Chapman's directorial debut. **90m/C VHS, Beta, LV, Closed Caption.** Tom Cruise, Lea Thompson, Craig T. Nelson, Christopher Penn; **D:** Michael Chapman; **W:** Michael Kane; **C:** Jan De Bont. *FOX, FXV*

All the Rivers Run 1984 First made-for-cable miniseries. A young Australian girl spends her inheritance on a river boat and becomes the first female river captain in Australian history. Directed by George Miller of "Man from Snowy River" fame. Four parts. **400m/C VHS.** *AU* Sigrid Thornton, John Waters, Diane Craig, Charles Tingwell, Gus Mercurio; **D:** George Miller, Pino Amenta; **C:** David Connell. *HBO*

All the Vermeers in New
York 🐾🐾🐾½ 1991 A stressed-out Wall Street broker flees to the soothing recesses of the Metropolitan Museum's Vermeer Room. There he meets a beautiful, manipulative French actress dreaming of success in Manhattan. Amidst the opulent art world of New York, the two pursue their relationship to an ultimately tragic end. Jost offers an inside look at the collision of commerce and art and the corrupt underside of New York in this elegant contemporary film. **87m/C VHS, LV.** Emmanuelle Chaulet, Stephen Lack, Grace Phillips, Katherine Bean, Laurel Lee Kiefer, Gracie Mansion, Gordon Joseph Weiss, Roger Ruffin; **D:** Jon Jost; **W:** Jon Jost. *WAC*

All the Way, Boys 🐾½ 1973 (PG) Two inept adventurers crash-land a plane in the Andes in the hope of discovering slapstick, but find none. "Trinity" cast up to no good. **105m/C VHS, Beta.** *IT* Terence Hill, Bud Spencer, Cyril Cusack, Michel Antoine; **D:** Giuseppe Colizzi.

All the Young Men 🐾🐾🐾 1960 Fairly powerful men-uniting-in-battle story with an interesting cast, highlighted by Poitier in an early role. A tiny marine squadron overrun by the Chinese in the Korean War attempts to resist the numerous attackers. In their spare time, the men confront racial prejudice when a black man (guess who) takes command. **86m/B VHS, Beta.** Alan Ladd, Sidney Poitier, James Darren, Glenn Corbett, Mort Sahl; **D:** Hall Bartlett; **W:** Hall Bartlett; **C:** Daniel F. Fapp. *COL*

All Things Fair 🐾🐾½ *Lust och Fagring Stor; Love Lessons; Laererinden* 1995 Coming of age story set in neutral Sweden in 1943. Fifteen-year-old Stig (Widerberg, the director's son) has just arrived in Malmo to begin classes at his all-male school—a situation filled with sexual curiosity and repression. Stig is attracted to his beautiful teacher Viola (Lagercrantz), whose marriage to alcoholic traveling salesman Frank (von Bronssen) is less than ideal, and the duo begin an affair. Frank not only seems not to care but befriends his wife's youthful lover, although the situation is ripe for tragedy. Excellent performances, sensual air, though somewhat lacking in logical narrative. Swedish with subtitles. **128m/C VHS.** *DK SW* Johan Widerberg, Marika Lagercrantz, Tomas von Bromssen, Bjorn Kjellman, Charles A. Palmer; **D:** Bo Widerberg; **W:** Bo Widerberg; **C:** Morten Bruus. Nominations: Academy Awards '95: Best Foreign Language Film. *NYR*

All This and Heaven Too 🐾🐾🐾 1940 When a governess arrives at a Parisian aristocrat's home in the 1840s, she causes jealous tension between the husband and his wife. The wife is soon found murdered. Based on Rachel Field's best-seller. **141m/B VHS, Beta.** Charles Boyer, Bette Davis, Barbara O'Neil, Virginia Weidler, Jeffrey Lynn, Helen Westley, Henry Daniell, Harry Davenport; **D:** Anatole Litvak; **M:** Max Steiner. Nominations: Academy Awards '40: Best Black and White Cinematography, Best Picture, Best Supporting Actress (O'Neil). *MGM*

All Through the Night 🐾🐾🐾 1942 A very funny spy spoof as well as a thrilling crime story with Bogart playing a gambler who takes on a Nazi spy ring. Features memorable double-talk and a great auction scene that inspired the one with Cary Grant in "North by Northwest." Suspense builds throughout the film as Lorre appears in a sinister role as Pepi and Veidt gives a fine performance as the spymaster. **107m/B VHS,**

Closed Caption. Humphrey Bogart, Conrad Veidt, Karen Verne, Jane Darwell, Frank McHugh, Peter Lorre, Judith Anderson, William Demarest, Jackie Gleason, Phil Silvers, Barton MacLane, Martin Kosleck; **D:** Vincent Sherman. *MGM*

All Tied Up 🎬🎬½ 1992 (R) Ladies man Brian (Galligan) thinks he's found true love with Linda (Hatcher) but that doesn't mean he's stopped seeing other women. And when Linda finds out, she breaks it off. So Brian goes over to her house to work things out and gets tied up—literally—by Linda and her girlfriends. Talk about teaching a guy a lesson. 90m/C VHS. Zach Galligan, Teri Hatcher, Tracy Griffith, Lara Harris; **D:** John Mark Robinson; **W:** Robert Madero, I. Markie Lane; **M:** Bernardo Bonazzi. *COL*

All You Need Is Cash 🎬🎬🎬 *The Rutles* 1978 "The Rutles" star in this parody of The Beatles' legend, from the early days of the "Pre-Fab Four" in Liverpool to their worldwide success. A marvelous pseudo-documentary, originally shown on NBC-TV and with various SNL alumni (including Weiss), that captures the development of the Beatles and '60s rock with devastating effect. Served as the inspiration for "This Is Spinal Tap." 70m/C VHS, Beta, LV. Eric Idle, Neil Innes, Ricky Fataar, Dan Aykroyd, Gilda Radner, John Belushi, George Harrison, Paul Simon, Mick Jagger, John Halsey; **D:** Eric Idle, Gary Weis. *MVD, MLT*

Allan Quatermain and the Lost City of Gold 🎬½ 1986 (PG) While trying to find his brother, Quatermain discovers a lost African civilization, in this weak adaptation of an H. Rider Haggard adventure. An ostensible sequel to the equally shallow "King Solomon's Mines." 100m/C VHS, Beta, Closed Caption. Richard Chamberlain, Sharon Stone, James Earl Jones; **D:** Gary Nelson; **W:** Gene Quintano, Lee Reynolds; **C:** Frederick Elmes. *FHE, MED, VTR*

Allegheny Uprising 🎬🎬½ *The First Rebel* 1939 Set in 1759, the story of a frontiersman who clashes with a British military commander in order to stop the sale of firearms to Indians. The stars of "Stagecoach" are back on board in this lesser effort. Also available colorized. 81m/B VHS, Beta, LV, Closed Caption. John Wayne, Claire Trevor, George Sanders, Brian Donlevy, Chill Wills, Moroni Olsen; **D:** William A. Seiter. *CCB, TTC*

Allegro Non Troppo 🎬🎬🎬 1976 (PG) An energetic and bold collection of animated skits set to classical music in this Italian version of Disney's "Fantasia." Watch for the evolution of life set to Ravel's Bolero, or better yet, watch the whole darn movie. Features Nichetti (often referred to as the Italian Woody Allen, particularly by people in Italy) in the non-animated segments, who went on to write, direct, and star (he may have sold concessions in the lobby as well) in "The Icicle Thief." 75m/C VHS, LV. *IT* Maurizio Nichetti; **D:** Bruno Bozzetto. *BMG, IME, BTV*

Alley Cat 🎬 1984 (R) Woman uses martial arts to fight back against a street gang that attacked her. 82m/C VHS, Beta. Karin Mani, Robert Torti, Brit Helfer, Michael Wayne, Jon Greene; **D:** Edward Victor. *VES, LIV*

Alligator 🎬🎬🎬 1980 (R) Dumped down a toilet 12 long years ago, lonely alligator Ramon resides in the city sewers, quietly eating and sleeping. In addition to feasting on the occasional stray human, Ramon devours the animal remains of a chemical plant's experiment involving growth hormones and eventually begins to swell at an enormous rate. Nothing seems to satisfy Ramon's ever-widening appetite: not all the people or all the buildings in the whole town, but he keeps trying, much to the regret of the guilt-ridden cop and lovely scientist who get to know each other while trying to nab the gator. Mediocre special effects are only a distraction in this witty eco-monster take. 94m/C VHS, Beta. Robert Forster, Robin Riker, Jack Carter, Henry Silva, Robin Riker, Dean Jagger; **D:** Lewis Teague; **W:** John Sayles, Frank Ray Perilli. *LIV*

Alligator 2: The Mutation 🎬🎬 1990 (PG-13) Not a sequel to 1980's surprisingly good "Alligator," but a bland rehash with a decent cast. Once again a toxic alligator grows to enormous size and menaces a community. A Donald-Trump-like villain and pro wrestlers (!) bring this up to date, but it's all on the level of a TV disaster movie; even the PG-13 rating is a bit too harsh. 92m/C VHS, LV. Steve Railsback, Dee Wallace Stone, Joseph Bologna, Woody Brown, Bill Daily, Brock Peters; **W:** Curt Allen. *COL, NLC*

Alligator Alley 🎬 1972 When two young divers witness a major drug deal, they become entangled in a web of danger they never expected. 92m/C VHS, Beta. Steve Alaimo, John Davis Chandler, Willie Pastrano, Jeremy Slate, Cece Stone; **D:** William Grefe. *PSM*

Alligator Eyes 🎬🎬½ 1990 (R) Stranger wearing trouble like a cheap perfume enters the midst of a vacationing trio of New Yorkers. Their vulnerabilities are exposed by a young hitchhiker sporting a slinky polka dot ensemble and way cool sunglasses who insinuates herself into their vacation plans (not to mention their private lives), before the three realize she's blind and full of manipulative and vindictive tricks, thanks to the usual brutal childhood. Psycho-sexo-logical thriller may have some fine performances and a promising beginning, before fizzling into celluloid cotton candy. 101m/C VHS. Annabelle Larsen, Roger Kabler, Mary McLain, Allen McCullough, John MacKay; **D:** John Feldman; **W:** John Feldman; **M:** Sheila Silver. *ACA*

The Allnighter 🎬 1987 (PG-13) A college coed searches through the hypersexed beach-party milieu of her senior year for Mr. Right. Bangle Hoffs is directed by her mom, to no avail. 95m/C VHS, Beta. Susanna Hoffs, John Terlesky, Joan Cusack, Michael Ontkean; **D:** Tamar Simon Hoffs; **M:** Charles Bernstein. *USH*

Allonsanfan 🎬🎬🎬½ 1973 Early Taviani, in which a disillusioned Jacobin aristocrat in 1816, after Napoleon has fallen, struggles with his revolutionary ideals and his accustomed lifestyle. Exciting score. In Italian with English subtitles. 115m/C VHS, Beta. *IT* Marcello Mastroianni, Laura Betti, Renato de Carmine, Lea Massari, Mimsy Farmer, Claudio Cassinelli, Bruno Cirino; **D:** Paolo Taviani, Vittorio Taviani; **W:** Paolo Taviani, Vittorio Taviani; **C:** Giuseppe Ruzzolini; **M:** Ennio Morricone. *FCT, WBF*

All's Fair 🎬 1989 Silly and predictable comedy about executives who take on their spouses at weekend war games. An unfortunate waste of a good cast. 89m/C VHS, Beta, LV, Closed Caption. George Segal, Sally Kellerman, Robert Carradine, Jennifer Edwards, Jane Kaczmarek, John Kapelos, Lou Ferrigno; **D:** Rocky Lane; **W:** Peter Collister. *MED*

Almanac of Fall 🎬🎬 19?? Set in a claustrophic apartment, where the occupants reveal all their deepest hostilities, fears, and obsessions. In Hungarian with English subtitles. 119m/C VHS. *HU* Hedi Temessy, Erika Bodnar, Miklos B. Szekely, Pal Hetenyi, Janos Dersi; **D:** Bela Tarr; **W:** Bela Tarr. *FCT*

...Almost 🎬🎬 *Wendy Cracked a Walnut* 1990 (PG) Arquette plays a curiously giddy bookworm with a vivid imagination. When her husband disappears on their anniversary, the man of her dreams shows up to sweep her off her feet. Is he real or is he simply another daydream? Almost a good time. 87m/C VHS, LV. *AU* Rosanna Arquette, Bruce Spence; **D:** Michael Pattinson. *NO*

Almost an Angel 🎬½ 1990 (PG) Another in a recent spat of angels and ghosts assigned back to earth by the head office. A life-long criminal (Hogan) commits a heroic act and finds himself a probationary angel returned to earth to gain permanent angel status. He befriends a wheelchair-bound man, falls in love with the guy's sister, and helps her out at a center for potential juvenile delinquents. Melodramatic and hokey in places, relying too much on Hogan's crocodilian charisma. 98m/C VHS, LV, Closed Caption. Paul Hogan, Linda Kozlowski, Elias Koteas, Doreen Lang, Charlton Heston; **D:** John Cornell; **W:** Paul Hogan; **C:** Russell Boyd. *PAR*

Almost Angels 🎬🎬 1962 Two boys romp in Austria as members of the Vienna Boys Choir. Lesser sentimental Disney effort that stars the actual members of the Choir; not much of a draw for today's Nintendo-jaded young viewers. 85m/C VHS, Beta. Vincent Winter, Peter Weck, Hans Holt; **D:** Steve Previn. *DIS*

Almost Blue 🎬½ 1993 (R) A gigantic, slow-moving, movie cliche. Madsen is a sulky, hard-living sax player going off the deep end because of his wife's death. Walden is the good woman who comes along to save him from himself. Tenor saxman Ernie Watts doubles for Madsen. Do yourself a favor—skip the movie and listen to some good jazz instead. 98m/C VHS, LV. Michael Madsen, Lynette Walden, Garrett Morris, Gale Mayron, Yaphet Kotto; **D:** Keoni Waxman. *LIV*

Almost Dead 🎬🎬½ 1994 Psychiatrist Katherine Roshak's (Doherty) mother committed suicide four years ago and suddenly her corpse is appearing to Katherine. When she visits Mom's grave, Katherine finds an empty coffin. So she teams up with a skeptical cop (Mandylor) to figure out what's going on. Lots of loose ends. Based on the novel "Resurrection" by William Valtos. 92m/C VHS. Shannen Doherty, Costas Mandylor, John Diehl, William R. Moses; **D:** Ruben Preuss; **W:** Miguel Tejada-Flores; **C:** Zoran Hochstatter. *MNC*

Almost Human woof! *The Kidnap of Mary Lou* 1979 (R) An Italian Mafia gorefest about a second-class don who kidnaps a businessman's daughter, and then has trouble trying to collect a ransom. For aficionados of Italian Mafia gorefests only (check your weapons at the door). 90m/C VHS, Beta. *IT* Henry Silva, Tomas Milian, Laura Belli; **D:** Umberto Lenzi; **M:** Ennio Morricone. *PSM*

Almost Partners 1987 Grandpa's ashes are in trouble. His urn and remains have been stolen. Fortunately, his teenage granddaughter and a detective are on the case. From the PBS "Wonderworks" television series. 58m/C VHS, Closed Caption. Paul Sorvino, Royana Black, Mary Wickes; **D:** Alan Kingsberg. *PME, HMV, FCT*

An Almost Perfect Affair 1979 (PG) Taxing romantic comedy about an ambitious independent American filmmaker who, after finishing a movie about an executed murderer, travels to the Cannes festival and proceeds to fall in love or lust with the wife of an Italian producer. Numerous inside jokes and capable performances nearly overcome script lethargy. 92m/C VHS, Beta. Keith Carradine, Monica Vitti, Raf Vallone, Christian de Sica, Dick Anthony Williams; **D:** Michael Ritchie; **W:** Walter Bernstein; **M:** Georges Delerue. *PAR*

Almost Pregnant 🎬🎬½ 1991 (R) Linda Anderson (Roberts) desperately wants a baby, but her husband, Charlie (Conaway) is unable to get her pregnant. Dead set against artificial insemination, Linda decides to take a lover. Charlie doesn't want to lose her, so he goes along with her idea. Linda falls in love with the new guy; discovers he's had a vasectomy and takes yet another lover while continuing to see the other two guys. Hilarious complications abound in her outrageous quest for a baby. An unrated version containing explicit scenes is also available. **CW:** Sexual dialogue and sexual content. 90m/C VHS, LV, Closed Caption. Tanya Roberts, Jeff Conaway, Joan Severance, Dom DeLuise; **D:** Michael DeLuise; **W:** Fred Stroppel. *COL*

Almost Royal Family 🎬 1984 All kinds of problems arise when a family inherits an island on the St. Lawrence River embargoed by the United States and Canada. 52m/C VHS, Beta. Sarah Jessica Parker, John Femia. *WAR*

Almost You 🎬🎬 1985 (R) Normal marital conflicts and uncertainties grow exponentially when a wealthy New York City thirty-something couple hires a lovely young nurse to help care for the wife after a car accident. An unsentimental marital comedy with a good cast that still misses. **91m/C VHS, Beta, Closed Caption.** Brooke Adams, Griffin Dunne, Karen Young, Marty Watt, Christine Estabrook, Josh Mostel, Laura Dean, Dana Delany, Miguel Pinero, Joe Silver, Suzzy Roche, Spalding Gray; **D:** Adam Brooks; **M:** Jonathan Elias. *FOX*

Aloha, Bobby and Rose 🎬🎬½ 1974
(PG) A mechanic and his girlfriend in L.A. become accidentally involved in an attempted robbery and murder and go on the run for Mexico, of course. Semi-satisfying drama in the surf, with fine location photography. **90m/C VHS, Beta.** Paul LeMat, Dianne Hull, Robert Carradine, Tim McIntire, Edward James Olmos, Leigh French; **D:** Floyd Mutrux. *MED*

Aloha Summer 🎬🎬 1988 (PG)
Six surfing teenagers of various ethnic backgrounds learn of love and life in 1959 Hawaii while riding the big wave of impending adulthood, with a splash of Kung Fu thrown in for good measure. Sensitive and bland. **97m/C VHS, Beta, LV.** Chris Makepeace, Lorie Griffin, Don Michael Paul, Sho Kosugi, Yuji Okumoto, Tia Carrere; **D:** Tommy Lee Wallace; **W:** Robert Benedetto. *WAR, ORI*

Alone Against Rome 🎬½ 1962
A muscle-bound warrior takes on the forces of Rome to avenge himself against a scornful woman. **100m/B VHS, Beta.** *IT* Lang Jeffries, Rossana Podesta, Phillippe LeRoy; **D:** Herbert Wise. *SNC*

Alone in the Dark 🎬🎬 1982 (R)
Slash and dash horror attempt featuring four escaped patients from a mental hospital who decide that they must kill their doctor because they don't like him. Conveniently, a city-wide blackout provides the opportunity, as the good doctor defends home and family against the aging stars intent on chewing up as much scenery as possible. **92m/C VHS, Beta.** Jack Palance, Donald Pleasence, Martin Landau, Dwight Schultz; **D:** Jack Sholder. *NLC, COL*

Alone in the Neon Jungle 🎬🎬 1987
A glamorous big-city police captain is assigned to clean up the most corrupt precinct in town. Pleshette is untypically cast but still manages to make her role believable in a serviceable TV cop drama with more dialogue than action. **90m/C VHS.** Suzanne Pleshette, Danny Aiello, Georg Stanford Brown, Frank Converse, Joe Morton; **D:** Georg Stanford Brown. *NLC*

Alone in the T-Shirt Zone 🎬 1986
A maniacal T-shirt designer lands in a mental institution. **81m/C VHS, Beta.** Michael Barrack, Taylor Gilbert, Bill Barron. *NWV*

Along Came Jones 🎬🎬🎬 1945
Cowboy Cooper, who can't handle a gun and is saddled with grumpy sidekick Demarest, is the victim of mistaken identity as both the good guys and the bad guys pursue him thinking he is a vicious killer. Young is the woman who rides to his defense. Offbeat and charming western parody based on a novel by Alan le May. **93m/B VHS, Beta.** Gary Cooper, Loretta Young, Dan Duryea, William Demarest; **D:** Stuart Heisler; **W:** Nunnally Johnson; **C:** Milton Krasner. *MGM, FCT*

Along the Great Divide 🎬🎬 1951
A U.S. marshal and his deputy battle pursuing vigilantes and the untamed frontier to bring a falsely accused murderer to trial (and of course, find the real bad guy). Douglas' first western has the usual horse opera cliches supported by excellent cinematography. **88m/B VHS, Beta.** Kirk Douglas, John Agar, Walter Brennan, Virginia Mayo; **D:** Raoul Walsh. *WAR, TLF*

Along the Sundown Trail 🎬½ 1942
Standard western escapades as cowboy G-men round up the villains. **59m/B VHS, Beta.** William Boyd, Art Davis, Lee Powell, Julie Duncan, Kermit Maynard, Charles "Blackie" King; **D:** Sam Newfield. *GPV, VCN*

Alpha Beta 🎬🎬½ 1973
A stage production set to film studying the break-up of a marriage, where all the husband and wife have in common is the children. Finney and Roberts efficiently carry the load. **70m/C VHS, Beta.** Albert Finney, Rachel Roberts; **D:** Anthony Page. *NO*

The Alpha Incident 🎬½ 1976 (PG)
Time-worn doomsday drama about an alien organism with the potential to destroy all living things. Government works hard to cover up. **86m/C VHS, Beta.** Ralph Meeker, Stafford Morgan, John Goff, Carol Irene Newell, John Alderman; **D:** Bill Rebane. *MED*

Alphabet City 🎬🎬 1984 (R)
A drug kingpin who runs New York's Lower East Side has decided to turn over a new leaf, but first he must survive his last night as a criminal while figuring out a way to pay off his large debts. Very stylish and moody, but light on content and plot. **85m/C VHS, Beta.** Vincent Spano, Michael Winslow, Kate Vernon, Jami Gertz, Zohra Lampert, Raymond Serra, Kenny Marino, Daniel Jordano, Miguel Pinero; **D:** Amos Poe; **W:** Amos Poe. *FOX*

The Alphabet Murders 🎬🎬 ABC Murders 1965
Picture this: Randall playing Agatha Christie's famous Belgian sleuth, Hercule Poirot, and Rutherford—in a cameo—as Miss Marple. As if that wouldn't be enough to make Dame Agatha roll over in her grave, there's plenty of cloying wisecracking and slapsticking throughout. An adaptation of "The ABC Murders" in which Poirot stalks a literate killer who snuffs out his victims in alphabetical order. Hardly a must-see, unless you're hellbent on viewing the entire Randall opus. **90m/B VHS, Beta.** Tony Randall, Anita Ekberg, Robert Morley, Maurice Denham, Guy Rolfe, Sheila Allen; **Cameos:** Margaret Rutherford; **D:** Frank Tashlin. *MGM, FCT*

Alphaville 🎬🎬🎬 Alphaville, a Strange Case of Lemmy Caution; Alphaville, Une Etrange Aventure de Lemmy Caution 1965
Engaging and inimitable Godard attempt at science fiction mystery. P.I. Lemmy Caution searches for a scientist in a city (Paris as you've never seen it before) run by robots and overseen by a dictator. The futuristic techno-conformist society must be upended so that Caution may save the scientist as well as nonconformists everywhere. In French with subtitles. **100m/B VHS, Beta.** *FR* Eddie Constantine, Anna Karina, Akim Tamiroff; **D:** Jean-Luc Godard; **W:** Jean-Luc Godard. Berlin International Film Festival '65: Golden Berlin Bear. *HMV, SNC, MRV*

Alpine Fire 🎬🎬½ 1989 (R)
Coming of age story about an adolescent girl and her deaf-mute brother living an isolated life in the Swiss Alps. When life on the mountain overwhelms them, they turn to each other for love. Sharply observed with a naturalistic style, elevating the proceedings above mere voyeurism. **119m/C VHS, Beta, LV.** *SI* Thomas Knock, Johanna Lier, Dorothea Moritz, Rolf Illig; **D:** Fredi M. Murer. *VES, LIV*

Alsino and the Condor 🎬🎬🎬 1982 (R)
An acclaimed Nicaraguan drama about a young boy, caught in war-torn Nicaragua between the Somoza government and the Sandinista rebels, who dreams of flying above the human strife. In Spanish with English subtitles. **89m/C VHS, Beta, LV.** *NI* Dean Stockwell, Alan Esquivel; **D:** Miguel Littin. Nominations: Academy Awards '82: Best Foreign Language Film. *FCT, TPV*

Altered States 🎬🎬🎬 1980 (R)
Obsessed with the task of discovering the inner man, Hurt's ambitious researcher ignores his family while consuming hallucinogenic drugs and floating in an immersion tank. He gets too deep inside, slipping way back through the evolutionary order and becoming a menace in the process. Confusing script based upon Chayefsky's (alias Sidney Aaron) confusing novel is supported by great special effects and the usual self-indulgent and provocative Russell direction. Chayefsky eventually washed his hands of the project after artistic differences with the producers. Others who departed from the film include initial director William Penn and special effects genius John Dykstra (relieved ably by Bran Ferren). Hurt's a solemn hoot in his first starring role. **103m/C VHS, Beta, LV.** William Hurt, Blair Brown, Bob Balaban, Charles Haid, Dori Brenner, Drew Barrymore, Miguel Godreau, John Larroquette; **D:** Ken Russell; **W:** Paddy Chayefsky; **C:** Jordan Cronenweth.

Nominations: Academy Awards '80: Best Sound, Best Original Score. *WAR*

Alternative 🎬🎬 1976
A female magazine editor finds herself unmarried and quite pregnant. She is caught in a tug-of-war between the baby's father and her current lover. Dated liberated woman and career snoozer. **90m/C VHS, Beta.** Wendy Hughes, Peter Adams, Mary Mackie, Carla Hoogeveen, Tony Bonner. *NO*

Alvarez Kelly 🎬🎬½ 1966
Offbeat western with Holden as the Mexican-Irish Kelly who has just sold a herd of cattle to the North during the Civil War. Confederate officer Widmark kidnaps Holden in an effort to have the cattle redirected to the South. Aided by the traditional women in the midst of men intent on double-crossing each other, a fierce hatred develops between the two, erupting into violence. Sleepy performance by Holden is countered by an intensive Widmark. Based on a true Civil War incident, the script occasionally wanders far afield with the cattle, who cleverly heighten the excitement by stampeding. **109m/C VHS, Beta.** William Holden, Richard Widmark, Janice Rule, Patrick O'Neal, Harry Carey Jr.; **D:** Edward Dmytryk. *COL, GKK*

Alvin Purple 🎬½ 1973 (R)
Pedestrian comedy about a Mr. Purple, an ordinary Aussie who sells waterbeds and is for some reason constantly being pursued by throngs of sexually insatiable women. Fortunately, he too enjoys sex, even though complications abound. Sexual situations, double entendres, and a script that aims for cleverness (but rarely attains it) somehow made the lust romp a hit in its native Australia, while worldwide it helped establish a market for Down Under cinema. Shot in Melbourne, and followed by "Alvin Rides Again." **97m/C VHS, Beta, LV.** *AU* Graeme Blundell, George Whaley, Ellie MacLure, Jacki Weaver; **D:** Tim Burstall; **W:** Alan Finney, Alan Hopgood, Tim Burstall. *NWV*

Alvin Rides Again 🎬🎬 1974
The sexually insatiable Alvin Purple is asked to impersonate an American gangster who was accidentally killed. Another Aussie sex farce from the original writers, who conspire to create a decent sequel to "Alvin Purple," with much of the same cast and crew. **89m/C VHS, Beta.** *AU* Graeme Blundell, Alan Finney, Brionny Behets, Frank Thring Jr., Jeff Ashby, Robin Copping; **D:** David Bilcock; **W:** Tim Burstall, Alan Finney, Alan Hopgood. *NWV*

Always 🎬🎬🎬 1985 (R)
Jaglom fictionally documents his own divorce and reconciliation with Patrice Townsend: set in the director's home and starring his friends and family, the film provides comic insight into the dynamics of married/about-to-be-married/and used-to-be-married relationships. Set at a Fourth of July barbecue, this bittersweet romantic comedy is a veritable feast for Jaglom fans, but not everyone will find the director's free-form narrative to their taste. **105m/C VHS, Beta, LV, Closed Caption.** Henry Jaglom, Patrice Townsend, Bob Rafelson, Melissa Leo, Andre Gregory, Michael Emil, Joanna Frank, Alan Rachins, Jonathan Kaufer; **D:** Henry Jaglom; **W:** Henry Jaglom; **C:** Hanania Baer. *VES, LIV*

Always 🎬🎬½ 1989 (PG)
A hotshot pilot (Dreyfuss) meets a fiery end and finds that his spirit is destined to become a guardian angel to the greenhorn fire-fighting flyboy (Johnson) who steals his girl's heart. Warm remake of "A Guy Named Joe," one of Spielberg's favorite movies. Sparks between Dreyfuss and Hunter eventually ignite, and Goodman delivers the most heat. Hepburn makes an appearance as the angel who guides Dreyfuss. An old-fashioned tree-burner romance that includes actual footage of the 1988 Yellowstone fire. **123m/C VHS, Beta, LV, Closed Caption.** Holly Hunter, Richard Dreyfuss, John Goodman, Audrey Hepburn, Brad Johnson, Marg Helgenberger, Keith David, Roberts Blossom; **D:** Steven Spielberg; **W:** Jerry Belson; **C:** Mikael Salomon; **M:** John Williams. *USH, FCT*

Amadeus ✓✓✓½ 1984 (PG) Entertaining adaptation by Shaffer of his play about the intense rivalry between 18th century composers Antonio Salieri and Wolfgang Amadeus Mozart. Abraham's Salieri is a man who desires greatness but is tortured by envy and sorrow. His worst attacks of angst occur when he comes into contact with Hulce's Mozart, an immature, boorish genius who, despite his gifts, remains unaffected and delighted by the beauty he creates while irking the hell out of everyone around him. Terrific period piece filmed on location in Prague; excellent musical score, beautiful sets, nifty billowy costumes, and realistic American accents for the 18th century Europeans. ♫Concert No. 27 for Pianoforte and Orchestra in B Flat Major; Ave Verum Corpus; A Quintet For Strings in E Flat; A Concerto for Clarinet and Orchestra in A Major; Number 39 in E Flat Major; Number 40 in G Minor; Number 41 in C Major. 158m/C VHS, Beta, LV. F. Murray Abraham, Tom Hulce, Elizabeth Berridge, Simon Callow, Roy Dotrice, Christine Ebersole, Jeffrey Jones, Kenny Baker, Cynthia Nixon, Vincent Schiavelli; *D:* Milos Forman; *W:* Peter Shaffer. Academy Awards '84: Best Actor (Abraham), Best Adapted Screenplay, Best Art Direction/Set Decoration, Best Costume Design, Best Director (Forman), Best Makeup, Best Picture, Best Sound; Cesar Awards '85: Best Foreign Film; Directors Guild of America Awards '84: Best Director (Forman); Golden Globe Awards '85: Best Actor—Drama (Abraham), Best Director (Forman), Best Film—Drama, Best Screenplay; Los Angeles Film Critics Association Awards '84: Best Director (Forman), Best Film, Best Screenplay; Nominations: Academy Awards '84: Best Actor (Hulce), Best Cinematography, Best Film Editing; Los Angeles Film Critics Association Awards '84: Best Actor (Abraham), Best Director (Forman), Best Screenplay. REP, GLV, BTV

Amanda and the Alien ✓½ 1995 (R) Dumb cable TV saga finds flaky Californian Amanda (Eggert) taking care of a sex-starved, shape-changing extraterrestrial (Meneses) while a couple of feds hunt him down. Based on a story by Robert Silverberg. *CW:* Sexuality and language. 94m/C VHS, Closed Caption. Alex Meneses, Nicole Eggert, Michael Dorn, Stacy Keach, Michael C. Bendetti; *D:* Jon Kroll; *W:* Jon Kroll. REP

Amarcord ✓✓✓½ 1974 (R) Semi-autobiographical Fellini fantasy which takes place in the village of Rimini, his birthplace. Focusing on the young Zanin's impressions of his town's colorful slices of life, Fellini takes aim at facism, family life, and religion in 1930's Italy. Visually ripe, delivering a generous, occasionally uneven mix of satire, burlesque, drama, and tragicomedic lyricism. Considered by people in the know as one of Fellini's best films and the topic of meaningful discussions among art film students everywhere. 124m/C VHS. *IT* Magali Noel, Bruno Zanin, Pupella Maggio, Armando Brancia; *D:* Federico Fellini; *W:* Federico Fellini, Tonino Guerra; *M:* Nino Rota. Academy Awards '74: Best Foreign Language Film; National Board of Review Awards '74: 5 Best Foreign Films of the Year; New York Film Critics Awards '74: Best Director (Fellini), Best Film; Nominations: Academy Awards '75: Best Director (Fellini), Best Original Screenplay. HMV

The Amateur ✓½ 1982 (R) Computer technologist for the CIA dives into a plot of international intrigue behind the Iron Curtain when he investigates the death of his girlfriend, murdered by terrorists. Confused and ultimately disappointing spy drama cursed with a wooden script written by Littell, based on his novel. 112m/C VHS, Beta. John Savage, Christopher Plummer, Marthe Keller, Arthur Hill, Ed Lauter; *D:* Charles Jarrott; *W:* Robert Littell. FOX

Amateur ✓✓✓ 1994 (R) Former nun Huppert, trying to make a living writing pornography, hooks up with an amnesiac (Donovan) who turns out to have a criminal past and a porno actress wife (Lowensohn) who wants him dead. Blackmail plot has oddball characters racing through dark and evocative settings while unfolding a tale loaded with offbeat oppositions and an irresistibly bizarre romantic triangle. Lively and playful without becoming pretentious, Hartley's self-described

"action thriller... with one flat tire" evokes his typical deadpan subtle style. *CW:* Contains obscene language. 105m/C VHS, LV, Closed Caption. Isabelle Huppert, Martin Donovan, Elina Lowensohn, Damian Young, Chuck Montgomery, David Simonds, Pamela Stewart; *D:* Hal Hartley; *W:* Hal Hartley; *M:* Jeff Taylor, Ned Rifle. COL

Amateur Night ✓ 1985 Sloppy musical comedy about the backstage bickering occuring during the amateur night at a famous nightclub. 91m/C VHS, Beta. Geoffrey Deuel, Dennis Cole, Allen Kirk. VES, LIV

Amazing Adventure ✓✓ *Romance and Riches; The Amazing Quest of Ernest Bliss; Riches and Romance* 1937 A millionaire wins a bet when he rises from a chauffeur's position to the executive board room without using his wealth. Though not particularly amazing, lightweight English comedy has Grant working hard to charm over and above the demands of the dated formula, a performance he undertook during a vacation from Hollywood. Adapted from a novel by E. Phillips Oppenheim. 63m/C VHS, Beta. Cary Grant, Mary Brian, Henry Kendall, Leon M. Lion, Ralph Richardson; *D:* Alfred Zeisler. NOS, BAR, DVT

The Amazing Colossal Man ✓✓ 1957 A standard '50s sci-fi film about atomic radiation. Colonel Manning is exposed to massive doses of plutonium when an experiment backfires (literally). The former good-guy grows to seventy feet and starts taking out his anger on a helpless Las Vegas. Can anything stop his murderous rampages? Followed by "War of the Colossal Beast." 79m/B VHS. Glenn Langan, Cathy Downs, William Hudson, James Seay, Russ Bender, Lyn Osborn; *D:* Bert I. Gordon; *C:* Joseph Biroc. COL, FUS

The Amazing Dobermans ✓✓ 1976 (G) Family-oriented pooch performance piece featuring Astaire in one of his lesser roles. Ex-con man Daniel and his five trained Dobermans assist an undercover agent in foiling a small-time criminal's gambling and extortion racket. The last in a series that includes "The Daring Dobermans" and "The Doberman Gang." 96m/C VHS, Beta. Fred Astaire, Barbara Eden, James Franciscus, Jack Carter, Billy Barty; *D:* Byron Ross Chudnow; *M:* Alan Silvestri. MED

Amazing Grace ✓✓ 1974 Some righteous mothers led by Moms Mabley go up against corrupt city politics in this extremely dated comedy that was cast with a sense of the absurd. 99m/C VHS. Moms Mabley, Slappy (Melvin) White, Moses Gunn, Rosalind Cash, Dolph Sweet, Butterfly McQueen, Stepin Fetchit; *D:* Stan Lathan. NO

Amazing Grace ✓✓ 1992 Eighteen-year-old Jonathan leaves home to share his friend Mickey's apartment. He meets Thomas, who has just returned to Israel after years in New York, and they begin a tentative relationship. But Thomas is hiding the fact that he may be HIV-positive and tries to keep a distance from the eager Jonathan. Hebrew with subtitles. 95m/C VHS. *IS* Rivka Michaely, Sharon Alexander, Gal Hoyberger, Hina Rozovska; *D:* Amos Gutman. CCN

Amazing Grace & Chuck ✓✓ 1987 (PG) Perhaps the only anti-war/sports fantasy ever made. After a visit to a Minuteman missile site in Montana, 12-year-old Little Leaguer Chuck learns of the dangers of nuclear arms. He begins a protest by refusing to play until the nations come to a peace agreement. In a sudden surge of social conscience, athletes worldwide put down their equipment and join in droves, starting with pro-basketball star Amazing Grace Smith (Denver Nugget English). Capra-like fantasy has good intentions but ultimately lacks two key elements: coherency and plausibility. 115m/C VHS, Beta, LV, Closed Caption. Jamie Lee Curtis, Gregory Peck, William L. Petersen, Joshua Zuehlke, Alex English; *D:* Mike Newell; *C:* Robert Elswit; *M:* Elmer Bernstein. HBO

The Amazing Howard Hughes ✓✓½ 1977 Reveals the full story of the legendary millionaire's life and career, from daring test pilot to inventor to Hollywood film producer to isolated wealthy paranoiac with a germ phobia. Lingers on the rich guy with big problems theme. Big-budget, made for television drama with a nice performance by Jones. 119m/C VHS, Beta. Tommy Lee Jones, Ed Flanders, James Hampton, Tovah Feldshuh, Lee Purcell; *D:* William A. Graham. FCT

Amazing Mr. Blunden ✓✓½ 1972 (G) Solid kidvid about two youngsters aided by a ghost who travel back in time to save the lives of two murdered children. Adapted by Jeffries from Antonia Barber's novel, "The Ghosts." 100m/C VHS, Beta. Laurence Naismith, Lynne Frederick, Garry Miller, Marc Granger, Rosalyn London, Diana Dors; *D:* Lionel Jeffries; *M:* Elmer Bernstein. MED

The Amazing Mr. X ✓✓½ *The Spiritualist* 1948 When a woman's husband dies, she tries to contact him via a spiritualist. Things are not as they seem however, and the medium may just be part of an intricate scheme to defraud the woman. 79m/B VHS, Beta. Turhan Bey, Lynn Bari, Cathy O'Donnell, Richard Carlson, Donald Curtis, Virginia Gregg; *D:* Bernard Vorhaus. NOS, SNC, RXM

The Amazing Panda Adventure ✓✓½ *Little Panda; The Amazing Panda Rescue* 1995 (PG) Ryan (Slater) is off to China during his spring break to visit dad Michael (Lang), who's working on a project to rescue the dwindling panda population. But there's poacher trouble and Ryan and young translator Ling (Ding) decide to rescue the preserve's panda cub, which has been animal-napped (where's Ace Ventura when you need him). Family fare, with a mixture of totally adorable real and animatronic pandas; filmed in the Sichuan province of China, home to the Wolong Nature Reserve which is famous for its successful breeding of the endangered giant pandas. Slater, in his first starring role, is the younger brother of Christian. 84m/C VHS, LV, Closed Caption. Ryan Slater, Stephen Lang, Yi Ding, Wang Fei; *D:* Christopher Cain; *W:* Laurice Elehwany, Jeff Rothberg; *C:* Jack N. Green; *M:* William Ross. WAR

The Amazing Spider-Man ✓✓ *Spider-Man* 1977 The Marvel Comics superhero's unique powers are put to the test when he comes to the rescue of the government by preventing an evil scientist from blackmailing the government for big bucks. The wall-walking web-slinger has his origins probed (a grad student bit by a radioactive spider develops super-human powers) in his live-action debut, which was made for television and led to a short-lived series. 94m/C VHS, Beta, LV, Closed Caption. Nicholas Hammond, David White, Lisa Eilbacher, Michael Pataki; *D:* E.W. Swackhamer. FOX, IME

Amazing Stories 1985 From the Steven Spielberg produced television series. "The Mission" sees a WWII tail gunner trapped in an unusual predicament. In "The Wedding Ring," a man gives his wife a strange ring and bizarre situations ensue. Additional episodes available. 70m/C VHS, LV. Kevin Costner, Casey Siemaszko, Kiefer Sutherland, Danny DeVito, Rhea Perlman; *D:* Danny DeVito, Steven Spielberg. USH, FCT, MOV

The Amazing Transparent Man woof! 1960 A mad scientist makes a crook invisible in order to steal the radioactive materials he needs. The crook decides to rob banks instead. Shot at the Texas State Fair for that elusive futuristic look. For Ulmer fans only. 58m/B VHS. Douglas Kennedy, Marguerite Chapman, James Griffith, Ivan Triesault; *D:* Edgar G. Ulmer. NOS, SNC

The Amazing Transplant woof! 1970 A sleaze-bag psycho has a "love enhancing" transplant, much to the pleasure of his sexual partners. Much to their and our dismay, however, he then kills them and bores us. 90m/C VHS, Beta. Juan Fernandez, Linda Southern; *D:* Doris Wishman. TPV

Amazon ⅊⅊ **1990 (R)** An adventure movie filmed in the Brazilian rainforest with an environmental message. A businessman being chased by the police in the Amazon jungle is rescued by a bush pilot who dreams of mining the Amazon's riches. A Brazilian woman enters the picture and persuades the businessman to help save the rainforest. Portions of the proceeds from the sale of this film go to the Rainforest Action Network. **88m/ C VHS, LV, Closed Caption.** Kari Vaananen, Robert Davi, Rae Dawn Chong; **D:** Mika Kaurismaki. *LIV*

Amazon Jail ⅊ **1985** Scantily clad women go over the wall and promptly get caught by devil worshiping men in the jungle. They should have known better. Redeemed only by lingerie selection. **94m/C VHS, Beta.** Elisabeth Hartmann, Mauricio Do Valle, Sondra Graffi; **D:** Oswald De Oliveira. *NO*

Amazon Women on the Moon ⅊⅊ **1987 (R)** A plotless, irreverent media spoof, depicting the programming of a slipshod television station as it crams weird commercials and shorts around a comical '50s' science fiction film. Inconsistent, occasionally funny anthology hangs together very loosely. Produced by Landis, with the usual amount of in-joke cameos and allusions to his other works of art. **85m/C VHS, Beta, LV.** Rosanna Arquette, Steve Guttenberg, Steve Allen, B.B. King, Michelle Pfeiffer, Arsenio Hall, Andrew Dice Clay, Howard Hesseman, Lou Jacobi, Carrie Fisher, Griffin Dunne, Sybil Danning, Henny Youngman, Monique Gabrielle, Paul Bartel, Kelly Preston; **D:** John Landis, Joe Dante, Carl Gottlieb, Peter Horton, Robert Weiss; **W:** Michael Barrie, Jim Mulholland; **M:** Ira Newborn. *USH*

The Amazons ⅊½ **1984** Goofy made for television drama about a beautiful doctor who discovers an underground organization of Amazon-descended women bent on taking over the world or at least making life hard for men while investigating a Congressman's mysterious death. **100m/ C VHS, Beta.** Tamara Dobson, Jack Scalia, Stella Stevens, Madeleine Stowe, Jennifer Warren; **D:** Paul Michael Glaser; **M:** Basil Poledouris. *NO*

Amazons ⅊ **1986 (R)** Tall, strong women who occasionally wander around nude search for a magical talisman that will overthrow an evil magician. **76m/C VHS, Beta.** Windsor Taylor Randolph, Penelope Reed, Joseph Whipp, Willie Nelson, Danitza Kingsley; **D:** Alex Sessa. *MGM*

The Ambassador ⅊⅊½ *Peacemaker* **1984** An American ambassador (Mitchum) is sent to the Middle East to try to solve the area's deep political problems. He quickly becomes the target of terrorist attacks, and is blamed for the nation's unrest. To make matters worse, his wife is having an affair with a PLO leader. The President ignores him, forcing the ambassador to fend for himself. Talk about your bad days. Hudson's last feature. Based on Elmore Leonard's "52 Pickup," and remade a year later under its own title. **97m/C VHS, Beta.** Robert Mitchum, Ellen Burstyn, Rock Hudson, Fabio Testi, Donald Pleasence; **D:** J. Lee Thompson. *MGM*

Ambassador Bill ⅊⅊ **1931** An Oklahoma rancher is appointed ambassador to a country in revolt. Rogers, of course, saves the day with his rustic witticisms. Based on the story "Ambassador from the United States" by Vincent Sheean. **68m/B VHS.** Will Rogers, Marguerite Churchill, Greta Nissen; **D:** Sam Taylor. *FOX, FCT*

The Ambassador's Daughter ⅊⅊ **1956** The Parisian adventures of an American ambassador's daughter De Havilland and soldier Forsythe, who, unaware of her position, falls in love with her. Faltering comedy is supported by an expert cast (although nearly 40, De Havilland is charming as the young woman) with especially good performances from Menjou and Loy. **102m/C VHS.** Olivia de Havilland, John Forsythe, Myrna Loy, Adolphe Menjou, Edward Arnold, Francis Lederer, Tommy Noonan, Minor Watson; **D:** Norman Krasna; **W:** Norman Krasna. *MOV*

Amber Waves ⅊⅊½ **1982** Credible made for television drama about a generation-gap conflict between a Midwestern farmer (Weaver) and an irresponsible male model (Russell) who has coasted through life on con and charm. **98m/C VHS, Beta.** Dennis Weaver, Kurt Russell; **D:** Joseph Sargent. *TLF*

Ambition ⅊½ **1991 (R)** Scriptwriter/star Phillips gets a bone for chutzpah by taking an unsavory lead role; his character torments a paroled psycho so that the killer will kill again and inspire a true-crime bestseller. The plot looks good on paper, but onscreen it's padded and unconvincing. **CW:** Language, violence, and sensuality. **99m/ C VHS, Beta, LV, Closed Caption.** Lou Diamond Phillips, Clancy Brown, Cecilia Peck, Richard Bradford, Willard Pugh, Grace Zabriskie, Katherine Armstrong, John Cullum, Haing S. Ngor; **D:** Scott Goldstein; **W:** Lou Diamond Phillips; **M:** Leonard Rosenman. *FXV, MED, VTR*

The Ambulance ⅊⅊½ **1990 (R)** A New York cartoonist witnesses a mysterious ambulance at work and decides to investigate. His probings uncover a plot to sell the bodies of dying diabetics. A surprisingly good no-money feature from low-budget king Cohen. Includes an appearance by Marvel Comics' Stan Lee as himself. **95m/ C VHS, LV, Closed Caption.** Eric Roberts, James Earl Jones, Megan Gallagher, Richard Bright, Janine Turner, Eric (Hans Gudegast) Braeden, Red Buttons, Laurene Landon, Jill Gatsby, Nicholas Chinlund; **D:** Larry Cohen; **W:** Larry Cohen. *COL, EPC*

Ambush at Tomahawk Gap ⅊⅊ **1953** Three released prisoners go in search of hidden loot and tempers rise when the goods don't turn up. Then the Apaches show up. **73m/C VHS, Beta.** John Hodiak, John Derek, David Brian, Maria Elena Marques, Ray Teal; **D:** Fred F. Sears. *GKK*

The Ambush Murders ⅊⅊½ **1982** True story of a stalwart white attorney defending a black activist accused of killing two cops. Not the compelling television it could be, but still enjoyable. From Ben Bradlee, Jr.'s novel. **100m/C VHS, Beta.** James Brolin, Dorian Harewood, Alfre Woodard, Louis Giambalvo, John McLiam, Teddy Wilson, Antonio Fargas, Amy Madigan; **D:** Steven Hilliard Stern. *FRH, LIV*

Ambush Trail ⅊⅊ **1946** Stranger-in-town Steele metes out justice to help local ranchers while sidekick Saylor leaves 'em laughing. **60m/B VHS.** Bob Steele, Syd Saylor, I. Stanford Jolley, Lorraine Miller, Charles "Blackie" King, Kermit Maynard; **D:** Harry Fraser. *NOS, GPV*

The Ambushers woof! **1967** Martin's third Matt Helm farce finds him handling a puzzling case involving the first United States spacecraft. When the craft is hijacked with Rule on board, it's Matt to the rescue, regaining control before unfriendly forces can take it back to Earth. Tired formula seems to have worn Martin out while the remainder of the cast goes to camp. Followed by "The Wrecking Crew." **102m/C VHS, Beta, LV.** Dean Martin, Janice Rule, James Gregory, Albert Salmi, Senta Berger; **D:** Henry Levin. *COL*

Amelia Earhart: The Final Flight ⅊⅊½ **1994** Investigates the mysterious disappearance of pioneering aviatrix Amelia Earhart's 1937 flight to become the first pilot to circumnavigate the globe. Earhart (Keaton) and her navigator Fred Noonan (Hauer) disappeared over the Pacific Ocean and their fate has never been determined. Dern plays Earhart's husband, publisher George B. Putnam, who served as Amelia's manager and publicist. Based on the biography by Doris L. Rich. Made for television. **95m/C VHS, LV, Closed Caption.** Diane Keaton, Rutger Hauer, Bruce Dern, Paul Guilfoyle, Denis Arndt, David Carpenter, Diana Bellamy; **D:** Yves Simoneau; **W:** Anna Sandor; **M:** George S. Clinton. *TTC*

America ⅊⅊½ **1924** Young patriot Nathan Holden (Hamilton) is torn between his political beliefs and his love for the daughter of a Virginia Tory (Dempster). Meanwhile, evil redcoat Captain Butler (Barrymore) and his band of murderous Mohawks ruthlessly attack the colonists. **141m/B VHS.** Neil Hamilton, Carol Dempster, Lionel Barrymore; **D:** D.W. Griffith. *KIV*

America ⅊½ **1986 (R)** New York cable station receives worldwide fame when their signal bounces off the moon. Uninspired piece of fluff from otherwise talented director Downey. **83m/C VHS.** Zack Norman, Tammy Grimes, Michael J. Pollard, Monroe Arnold, Richard Belzer, Liz Torres, Howard Thomashefsky, Laura Ashton, Robert Downey Jr.; **D:** Robert Downey. *NO*

America at the Movies ⅊⅊½ **1976** Scenes from more than 80 of the finest American motion pictures fly by in an effort to tell the story of the cinema and provide a portrait of America as it has been seen on screen for half a century. Scenes from "The Birth of a Nation," "Citizen Kane," "Dr. Strangelove," "East of Eden," "The French Connection," and "From Here to Eternity," are among the many included. Some black and white scenes; produced by the American Film Institute. **116m/C VHS, Beta, LV.** John Wayne, Orson Welles, Peter Sellers, James Dean, Gene Hackman, Burt Lancaster, Julie Harris, Deborah Kerr, Al Pacino, Robert De Niro. *COL, IME*

America First ⅊½ **1970** A group of seven travelers try to build an "Eden" with the inhabitants of an Appalachian hollow. **90m/C VHS, Beta.** Michael Kennedy, Walter Keller, Pat Estrin, Lois McGuire. *NO*

America/The Fall of Babylon ⅊⅊⅊ **1924** A double feature containing abridged versions; in "America," a Boston patriot and the daughter of an aristocratic Virginia Tory fall in love during the Revolutionary War; "The Fall of Babylon" is one of the stories in D.W. Griffith's "Intolerance." Silent. **56m/B VHS, Beta.** Neil Hamilton, Lionel Barrymore, Constance Talmadge, Elmer Clifton, Alfred Paget. *CCB*

America 3000 ⅊ **1986 (PG-13)** Hundreds of years in the holocaust-torn future, men rebel against a brutal, overpowering race of women, with predictable results. **94m/C VHS, Beta.** Chuck Wagner, Laurene Landon; **D:** David Engelbach. *MGM*

The American Angels: Baptism of Blood ⅊ **1989 (R)** Three beautiful young women, each with a personal dream, strive to make it in the world of professional wrestling. Hackneyed plot devices, but those simply watching for the wrestling scenes won't be disappointed. **99m/C VHS, Beta, LV, Closed Caption.** Jan MacKenzie, Tray Loren, Mimi Lesseos, Trudy Adams, Patricia Cavoti, Susan Sexton, Jean Kirkland, Jeff Lundy, Lee Marshall; **D:** Beverly Sebastian, Ferd Sebastian. *PAR*

American Anthem ⅊ **1986 (PG-13)** A young gymnast must choose between family responsibilities or the parallel bars. Olympic gymnast Gaylord makes his movie debut but doesn't get the gold. Good fare for young tumblers, but that's about it. Followed by two of the films' music videos and tape-ads featuring Max Headroom. **100m/C VHS, Beta, LV, Closed Caption.** Mitch Gaylord, Janet Jones, Michelle Phillips, Michael Pataki; **D:** Albert Magnoli; **W:** Evan P. Archerd, Jeff Benjamin; **M:** Alan Silvestri. *ORI, WAR*

American Aristocracy ⅊⅊½ **1917** A silent comic romp in which Fairbanks, an old moneyed dandy, wreaks havoc on an island resort whose clientele is composed of the nouveau well-to-do. **52m/B VHS, Beta.** Douglas Fairbanks Sr., Jewel Carmen, Albert Parker; **D:** Lloyd Ingraham. *GPV*

American Autobahn ⅊½ **1984** A low-budget independent actioner about a journalist who discovers an underworld weapons ring that hits the highway in pursuit of him. **90m/C VHS, Beta.** Jan Jalenak, Michael von der Goltz, Jim Jarmusch; **D:** Andre Degas. *NO*

American Blue Note ⅊⅊ *Fakebook* **1989 (PG-13)** Loosely plotted, bittersweet account of a struggling jazz quartet in the early 1960s, as its leader (MacNicol) must decide if their fruitless tours of sleazy bars and weddings are still worth it. The debut of director Toporoff. **96m/C VHS, LV.** Peter MacNicol, Carl Capotorto, Tim Guinee, Bill Christopher-Myers, Jonathan Walker, Charlotte d'Amboise, Louis Guss, Zohra Lampert, Trini Alvarado, Sam Behrens; *D:* Ralph Toporoff; *W:* Gilbert Girion, Larry Schanker. COL, BTV

American Born 🐾½ 1989 Murder Inc. returns to the dismay of one idealist who embarks on a battle he doesn't intend to lose. The mob had better look out. **90m/C VHS.** Joey Travolta, Andrew Zeller; *D:* Raymond Martino; *W:* Raymond Martino. PMH

American Boyfriends 🐾🐾 1989 (PG-13) An ostensible sequel to "My American Cousin," in which two Canadian girls go to California and discover innocent romance and friendship. **90m/C VHS, Beta, LV.** CA Margaret Langrick, John Wildman, Jason Blicker, Lisa Repo Martell; *D:* Sandy Wilson; *W:* Sandy Wilson. LIV

American Buffalo 🐾🐾½ 1995 (R) Somewhat lackluster but decent screen adaptation of a classic American drama. Franz's junk shop owner Donny plans to steal back a rare Buffalo-head nickel that he feels he was swindled out of, with the help of his protege Bobby (Nelson). Hoffman's ferret-like Teach, one of Donny's card-playing buddies and an arrogant opportunist, tries to weasel in on the plan that never comes to fruition. Set in Corrente's hometown of Pawtucket, the director's reverence for the material is obvious and he plays it too safe. Top-notch performances raise the level. Mamet adapts his play for the screen.**CW:** Language. **88m/C VHS, Closed Caption.** Dustin Hoffman, Dennis Franz, Sean Nelson; *D:* Michael Corrente; *W:* David Mamet; *C:* Richard Crudo; *M:* Thomas Newman. EVE

American Chinatown 🐾½ 1996 Orphaned tough guy is taken in by a powerful Chinatown mob family but gets into trouble when he falls for the head man's sister. He has a chance to redeem himself when he learns about a plot to overthrow the triad clan but will he take it? **90m/C VHS.** Henry Lee, Robert Z'Dar, Liat Goodson; *D:* Richard W. Park. HVF

An American Christmas Carol 🐾🐾 1979 Charles Dickens' classic story is retold with limited charm in a made for television effort. This time a greedy American financier (Winkler) learns about the true meaning of Christmas. **98m/C VHS, Beta.** Henry Winkler, David Wayne, Dorian Harewood; *D:* Eric Till; *M:* Hagood Hardy. VES, LIV

American Cinema 1994 Ten-part series covering the roughly 100 years of cinema history through a look at the Hollywood film. Lots of clips and interviews with each part providing an overview of a particular feature of the movie industry from stars to studios to independent filmmakers. Available as a five-tape boxed set or individually. **500m/C VHS.** FOX

American Commandos 🐾 Hitman 1984 (R) An ex-Green Beret slaughters the junkies who killed his son and raped his wife, and then joins his old buddies for a secret, Rambo-esque mission in Vietnam providing a tired rehash of Vietnam movie cliches. **96m/C VHS, Beta.** Chris Mitchum, John Phillip Law, Franco Guerrero; *D:* Bobby Suarez. LIV

American Cop 🐾½ 1994 (PG-13) Elmo LaGrange is an ordinary cop taking a vacation, when his layover in the Moscow airport becomes a lesson in mistaken identities. He teams up with the pre-requisite beautiful woman to outwit and outrun the Russian mafia.**CW:** Action violence. **91m/C VHS, LV.** Wayne Crawford, Ashley Laurence, Daniel Quinn, William Katt, Olga Vodin, Vlaimir Shpoudeiko, Nickolai Nedovodin; *D:* Wayne Crawford; *W:* Carlos Brooks; *C:* Nicholas Von Sternberg. APX

American Cyborg: Steel Warrior 🐾🐾½ 1994 (R) Basic evil-machine-bent-on-mankind's-destruction movie—with a hero bent on rescuing the world. **95m/C VHS, LV.** Joe Lara, John P. Ryan; *D:* Boaz Davidson; *W:* Bill Crounse. CAN

American Dream 🐾🐾🐾 1981 A midwestern family leaves the suburbs and moves into a Chicago inner-city neighborhood. Good TV-movie pilot for the short-lived series that was Emmy nominated for direction and writing. **90m/C VHS, Beta.** Stephen Macht, Karen Carlson, John Karlen, Andrea Smith, John Malkovich, John McIntire; *D:* Mel Damski; *M:* Artie Butler. UNI

American Dreamer 🐾🐾 1984 (PG) A housewife wins a trip to Paris as a prize from a mystery writing contest. Silly from a blow on the head, she begins living the fictional life of her favorite literary adventure. Sporadic comedy with a good cast wandering about courtesy of a clumsy screenplay. **105m/C VHS, Beta, Closed Caption.** JoBeth Williams, Tom Conti, Giancarlo Giannini, Coral Browne, James Staley; *D:* Rick Rosenthal; *M:* Lewis Furey. FOX

American Eagle 🐾½ 1990 (R) A veteran goes crazy and seeks sadistic, bloody revenge on his war buddies. Now his war buddies are the only ones who can stop him. **92m/C VHS, LV.** Asher Brauner, Robert F. Lyons, Vernon Wells, Kai Baker; *D:* Robert J. Smawley. THV

American Empire 🐾🐾½ My Son Alone 1942 Two Civil War heroes struggle to build a cattle empire in Texas and are hampered by rustlers, one of whom was their partner. A fine, veteran cast and a tight script keep things moving, including the cattle. **82m/B VHS, Beta.** Preston Foster, Richard Dix, Frances Gifford, Leo Carrillo; *D:* William McGann. NOS, MRV, DVT

American Fabulous 🐾🐾½ 1992 The posthumously released autobiography of an eccentric homosexual who lived life in the fast lane. Jeffrey Strouth performs his monologue from the back seat of a 1957 Cadillac, where the images of small-town America are seen to contrast sharply with his flamboyant style. His grotesque and candid recollections include his alcoholic Elvis-impersonator father, a stint as a teenage prostitute, drag queen friends, and drug addiction in New York. Strouth puts a comic twist on even the most brutal of his memories. He died of AIDS at the age of 33 in 1992. **105m/C VHS.** Jeffrey Strouth; *D:* Reno Dakota; *W:* Jeffrey Strouth. FRF

American Flyers 🐾🐾½ 1985 (PG-13) Two competitive brothers train for a grueling three-day bicycle race in Colorado while tangling with personal drama, including the spector that one of them may have inherited dad's tendency for cerebral aneurisms and is sure to drop dead during a bike race soon. Written by bike movie specialist Tesich ("Breaking Away") with a lot of the usual cliches (the last bike ride, battling bros, eventual understanding), which are gracefully overridden by fine bike-racing photography. Interesting performances, especially Chong as a patient girlfriend and Amos the trainer. **113m/C VHS, Beta, LV, Closed Caption.** Kevin Costner, David Marshall Grant, Rae Dawn Chong, Alexandra Paul, John Amos, Janice Rule, Robert Townsend, Jennifer Grey, Luca Bercovici; *D:* John Badham; *W:* Steve Tesich; *M:* Lee Ritenour, Greg Mathieson. WAR

The American Friend 🐾🐾🐾½ 1977 Tribute to the American gangster film helped introduce Wenders to American moviegoers. Young Hamburg picture framer thinks he has a terminal disease and is set up by American expatriate Hopper to become a hired assassin in West Germany. The lure is a promise of quick money that the supposedly dying man can then leave his wife and child. After the first assasination, the two bond. Hopper is the typical Wenders protagonist, a strange man in a strange land looking for a connection. Great, creepy thriller adapted from Patricia Highsmith's novel "Ripley's Game." Fuller and Ray (better known as directors) appear briefly as gangsters. **127m/C VHS, Beta, LV.** FR GE Bruno Ganz, Dennis Hopper, Elisabeth Kreuzer, Gerard Blain, Jean Eustache, Samuel Fuller, Nicholas Ray, Wim Wenders; *D:* Wim Wenders; *W:* Wim Wenders. National

Board of Review Awards '77: 5 Best Foreign Films of the Year. FCT, GLV, TPV

American Friends 🐾🐾 1991 (PG) Genteel story masquerades as high comedy. Palin is a fussy middle-aged Oxford classics tutor. On a holiday he meets American Hartley (Booth) and her adopted daughter, Elinor (Alvarado). Both women are immensely attracted to the don (for reasons that are unclear) and follow him back to Oxford, where he's engaged in a battle of succession with his rival Molina. Dismal screenplay lacks logic and urgency, making it difficult to care about the story or the characters. Script is said to have been inspired by an incident in the life of Palin's great-grandfather. If this sounds like your cup of tea, save your time and watch a Merchant Ivory film instead. **95m/C VHS, LV.** GB Michael Palin, Connie Booth, Trini Alvarado, Alfred Molina; *D:* Tristam Powell; *W:* Michael Palin, Tristam Powell; *M:* Georges Delerue. THV, FCT

The American Gangster 1992 Documentary look at the beginnings of organized crime and the rise of the gangster in American society. Includes vintage film and photographs. Profiles include Bugsy Siegel, Al Capone, John Dillinger, Pretty Boy Floyd, and Lucky Luciano. **45m/C VHS.** COL

American Gigolo 🐾🐾 1979 (R) A Los Angeles loner who sexually services the rich women of Beverly Hills becomes involved with the wife of a California state senator and is then framed for a murder he did not commit. A highly stylized but empty view of seamy low lives marred by a contrived plot, with decent romp in the hay readiness displayed by Gere. **117m/C VHS, Beta, LV.** Richard Gere, Lauren Hutton, Hector Elizondo, Paul Schrader; *D:* Paul Schrader; *W:* Paul Schrader; *C:* John Bailey. PAR

American Gothic woof! Hide and Shriek 1988 (R) Three couples headed for a vacation are instead stranded on an island and captured by a demented family headed by Steiger and De Carlo, a scary enough proposition in itself. Even worse, Ma and Pa have three middle-aged moronic offspring who still dress as children and are intent on killing the thwarted vacationers (who are none too bright themselves) one by one by bloody one. A stultifying career low for all involved. **89m/C VHS, Beta, LV.** Rod Steiger, Yvonne De Carlo, Michael J. Pollard, Sarah Torgov, Fiona Hutchinson; *D:* John Hough. THV

American Graffiti 🐾🐾🐾½ 1973 (PG) Atmospheric, episodic look at growing up in the innocence of America before the Kennedy assassination and the Vietnam War. It all takes place on one hectic but typical night in the life of a group of recent California high school grads unsure of what the next big step in life is. So they spend their time cruising, listening to Wolfman Jack, and meeting at the drive-in. Slice of '60s life boasts a prudent script, great set design, authentic soundtrack, and consistently fine performances by the young cast. Catapulted Dreyfuss, Ford, and Somers to stardom, branded Lucas a hot directorial commodity with enough leverage to launch "Star Wars," and steered Howard and Williams towards continued age-of-innocence nirvana on "Happy Days." **112m/C VHS, Beta, LV.** Richard Dreyfuss, Ron Howard, Cindy Williams, MacKenzie Phillips, Paul LeMat, Charles Martin Smith, Suzanne Somers, Candy Clark, Harrison Ford, Bo Hopkins, Joe Spano, Kathleen Quinlan, Wolfman Jack; *D:* George Lucas; *W:* George Lucas, Gloria Katz, Willard Huyck. Golden Globe Awards '74: Best Film—Musical/Comedy; New York Film Critics Awards '73: Best Screenplay; National Society of Film Critics Awards '73: Best Screenplay; Nominations: Academy Awards '73: Best Director (Lucas), Best Film Editing, Best Picture, Best Story & Screenplay, Best Supporting Actress (Clark). USH, FCT

American Heart 🐾🐾🐾½ 1992 (R) Jack (Bridges) is a suspicious ex-con, newly released from prison, with few prospects and little hope. He also has a teenage son, Nick (Furlong), he barely remembers but who desperately wants to have his father back in his life. Jack is reluctantly persuaded to let Nick stay with him in his cheap hotel where Nick befriends fellow resident, Molly, a teenage hooker, and other castoff street kids. Superb performances by both male leads—Furlong, both yearning and frustrated as he pursues his dream of having a family, and Bridges as the tough parolee, unwilling to open his heart. Hard-boiled, poignant, and powerful. **114m/C VHS, LV.** Jeff Bridges, Edward Furlong, Lucinda Jenney, Tracey Kapisky, Don Harvey, Margaret Welsh; **D:** Martin Bell; **W:** Peter Silverman; **M:** James Newton Howard. Independent Spirit Awards '94: Best Actor (Bridges); Nominations: Independent Spirit Awards '94: Best Cinematography, Best First Feature, Best Supporting Actor (Furlong), Best Supporting Actress (Jenney). *LIV, BTV*

An American in Paris 🎬🎬🎬🎬 1951
Lavish, imaginative musical features a sweeping score, and knockout choreography by Kelly. Ex-G.I. Kelly stays on in Paris after the war to study painting, supported in his efforts by rich American Foch, who hopes to acquire a little extra attention. But Kelly loves the lovely Caron, unfortunately engaged to an older gent. Highlight is an astonishing 17-minute ballet which holds the record for longest movie dance number—and one of the most expensive, pegged at over half a million for a month of filming. For his efforts, the dance king won a special Oscar citation. While it sure looks like Paris, most of it was filmed in MGM studios. ♫S'Wonderful; I Got Rhythm; Embraceable You; Love Is Here To Stay; Tra-La-La; I'll Build a Stairway to Paradise; Nice Work If You Can Get It; By Strauss; Concerto in F (3rd Movement). **113m/C VHS, Beta, LV, 8mm.** Gene Kelly, Leslie Caron, Oscar Levant, Nina Foch, Georges Guetary; **D:** Vincente Minnelli; **W:** Alan Jay Lerner; **C:** John Alton; **M:** George Gershwin, Ira Gershwin. Academy Awards '51: Best Art Direction/Set Decoration (Color), Best Color Cinematography, Best Costume Design (Color), Best Picture, Best Story & Screenplay, Scoring of a Musical; Golden Globe Awards '52: Best Film—Musical/Comedy; National Board of Review Awards '51: 10 Best Films of the Year; Nominations: Academy Awards '51: Best Director (Minnelli), Best Film Editing. *MGM, TLF, BTV*

American Justice 🎬🎬 *Jackals* 1986 (R)
Two cops, one of whom looks suspiciously like a Simon of "Simon and Simon" fight political corruption and white slavery near the Mexican border. The chief white slaver bears a full resemblance to the other Simon. Sufficient action but less than enough. **96m/C VHS, Beta.** Jameson Parker, Gerald McRaney, Wilford Brimley, Jack Lucarelli; **D:** Gary Grillo. *LIV*

American Kickboxer 1 🎬½ 1991 (R)
Barrett stars as B.J. Quinn, a down on his luck kickboxing champion who spends much of his time onscreen aimlessly wandering (apparently searching for the meaning of his life.) Lackluster script and performances will make this one trying —even for kickboxing fans. Barrett is Chuck Norris' former workout partner, bu t there isn't enough action often enough for him to show off his formidable skills. **CW:** Language and kickboxing violence. **93m/C VHS, Beta.** John Barrett, Keith Vitali, Brad Morris, Terry Norton, Ted Leplat; **D:** Frans Nel; **W:** Emil Kolbe; **M:** Frank Becker. *CAN*

American Kickboxer 2: To the Death 🎬½ 1993 (R)
Lillian must find a way to get her cop ex-husband and her kickboxer ex-lover to work together to save her kidnapped daughter's life. **CW:** Language, continous violence, and some sexuality. **91m/C VHS, LV, Closed Caption.** Dale "Apollo" Cook, Evan Lurie, Kathy Shower, Ted Markland; **D:** Jeno Hodl. *THV*

American Madness 🎬🎬½ 1932
Benevolent banker Dickson (Huston) has been making loans without sufficient collateral. The bank's board of directors give him a warning and then a robbery causes a run on the bank. The directors are ready to oust Dickson when the small businessmen he's helped rally to his defense. Tedious romantic subplot has Dickson's unhappy wife (Johnson) accusing him of neglect and dallying with unscrupulous bank clerk Cluett (Gordon). **75m/B VHS.** Walter Huston, Pat O'Brien, Kay Johnson,

Gavin Gordon, Constance Cummings, Robert Ellis, Walter Walker, Arthur Hoyt; **D:** Frank Capra; **W:** Robert Riskin; **C:** Joseph Walker. *COL*

American Matchmaker 🎬🎬½ *Amerikaner Shadkhn* 1940
Nat Silver decides to go into the matchmaking business, after his own marriages fail miserably, hoping to experience happiness vicariously. However, he soon begins to realize that one of his clients is a better match for him than the man he chose for her. In Yiddish with English subtitles. **87m/B VHS.** Leo Fuchs, Judith Abarbanel, Rosetta Bialis, Yudel Dubinsky, Abe Lax; **D:** Edgar G. Ulmer. *ERG*

American Me 🎬🎬🎬 1992 (R)
Violent and brutal depiction of more than thirty years of gang wars and drugs in East Los Angeles. Santana founded a street as a teenager, but has spent the last 18 years in prison, where he's the boss of the so-called Mexican Mafia, which oversees the drugs, scams, murders, and violence that are an everyday fact of prison life. Released from Folsom, Santana goes back to his old neighborhood and attempts to distance himself from his old life but finds his gang ties are stronger than any other alliance. Unsparing and desolate directorial debut from Olmos. **CW:** Language, strong violence and drug content, and sexuality. **119m/C VHS, LV, Closed Caption.** Edward James Olmos, William Forsythe, Pepe Serna, James Victor, Evelina Fernandez, Sal Lopez, Daniel Villarreal, Cary-Hiroyuki Tagawa; **D:** Edward James Olmos; **W:** Floyd Mutrux, Desmond Nakano; **C:** Reynaldo Villalobos; **M:** Dennis Lambert. *USH*

American Nightmare 🎬½ 1981
Young man searches for his missing sister against a background of pornography, drug peddling, and prostitution in the slums of a city. The usual titillating squalid urban drama. **85m/C VHS, Beta.** Lawrence S. Day, Lora Staley, Lenore Zann, Michael Ironside, Alexandra Paul; **D:** Don McBrearty. *MED*

American Ninja 🎬🎬 *American Warrior* 1985 (R)
American Dudikoff is G.I. Joe, a martial-arts expert stationed in the Philippines who alienates most everyone around him (he's a rebel). Deadly black-belt war begins with Joe confronting the army which is selling stolen weapons to the South American black market. Aided by one faithful pal, Joe uses his head-kicking martial arts skills to stop hundreds of ninja combatants working for the corrupt arms dealer. In his spare time he romances the base chief's daughter. Efficient rib-crunching chop-socky action wrapped in no-brainer plot and performed by nonactors. Cannon epic mercilessly followed by at least three sequels. **96m/C VHS, Beta, Closed Caption.** Michael Dudikoff, Guich Koock, Judie Aronson, Steve James; **D:** Sam Firstenberg; **W:** Gideon Amir; **C:** Hanania Baer; **M:** Michael Linn. *MGM*

American Ninja 2: The Confrontation 🎬🎬 1987 (R)
Soldiers Dudikoff and James are back again using their martial arts skills (in lieu of any acting) to take on a Caribbean drug-lord. Apparently he has been kidnapping Marines and taking them to his island, where he genetically alters them to become fanatical ninja assassins eager to do his dirty work. The script hardly gets in the way of the rib-crunching action, but is an improvement upon Ninja Number One. **90m/C VHS, Beta, LV, Closed Caption.** Michael Dudikoff, Steve James, Gary Poindexter, Gary Conway; **D:** Sam Firstenberg; **W:** Gary Conway, James Booth. *MED, VTR*

American Ninja 3: Blood Hunt woof! 1989 (R)
Second sequel in the American Ninja series. Bradley replaces Dudikoff as the martial arts good guy fighting the martial arts bad guys on a Caribbean island. He's pursued by ex-evangelist Marjoe, who wants to inject him with a nasty ninja virus before unloading the germs to bad buys worldwide. Less ninjitsu; more uninspired martial arts. **90m/C VHS, Beta, LV.** David Bradley, Steve James, Marjoe Gortner, Michele Chan, Calvin Jung; **D:** Cedric Sundstrom; **W:** Paul DeMielche, Gary Conway; **M:** George S. Clinton. *MGM, CAN*

American Ninja 4: The Annihilation woof! 1991 (R)
Dudikoff returns after noticeable absence in last sequel. He should have stayed away from #4—it's a rehash of tired ideas that never gets off the ground. Forget this and see "American Ninja 2: The Confrontation," the best of this series. **99m/C VHS, Beta, LV, Closed Caption.** Michael Dudikoff, David Bradley, James Booth, Dwayne Alexandre, Robin Stille, Ken Gampu; **D:** Cedric Sundstrom; **W:** David Geeves; **M:** Nicolas Tenbroek. *CAN*

American Pluck 🎬🎬 1925
Before he can inherit anything, a playboy millionaire's son must go out into the world and prove he can make his own way. He meets a beautiful princess, who is pursued by a villainous count. Walsh, as the dashing hero, was the younger brother of director Raoul. Silent with original organ music. **91m/B VHS, Beta, 8mm.** George Walsh, Wanda Hawley, Frank Leigh, Sidney De Grey; **D:** Richard Stanton. *VYY*

The American President 🎬🎬🎬 1995 (PG-13)
Widower president Andrew Shepherd (Douglas) decides it's time to get back into the dating game. But just what woman wants to find her romance in the public eye? Well, it turns out to be feisty environmental lobbyist Sydney Wade (the ever-charming Bening). But the Prez also has to put up with nasty opponent Bob Rumson (Dreyfuss), who's using their courtship as political fodder, approval ratings, and a nosy press. Glossy fairytale material expertly handled by both cast and director. **CW:** Contains sexual situations and some strong language. **114m/C VHS, LV, Closed Caption.** Michael Douglas, Annette Bening, Martin Sheen, Michael J. Fox, David Paymer, Samantha Mathis, John Mahoney, Anna Deavere Smith, Nina Siemaszko, Wendie Malick, Shawna Waldron, Richard Dreyfuss; **D:** Rob Reiner; **W:** Aaron Sorkin; **C:** John Seale; **M:** Marc Shaiman. Nominations: Academy Awards '95: Best Original Score; Golden Globe Awards '96: Best Actor—Musical/Comedy (Douglas), Best Actress—Musical/Comedy (Bening), Best Director (Reiner), Best Film—Musical/Comedy, Best Screenplay; Writers Guild of America '95: Best Original Screenplay. *COL*

American Roulette 🎬 1988 (R)
Garcia is the exiled president of a Latin American country living in London in this thin political thriller. A plot riddled with weaknesses and poor direction make this potentially interesting film dull and lifeless. **102m/C VHS, LV.** *GB AU* Andy Garcia, Kitty Aldridge, Robert Stephens, Al Matthews, Susannah York; **D:** Maurice Hatton; **M:** Michael Gibbs. *NO*

American Samurai 🎬½ 1992 (R)
Drew is the adopted son of a Japanese samurai, who gives him the family's sacred sword. This gesture angers his stepbrother who gets involved with Japanese gangsters and illegal live-blade fighting, and who also vows revenge on this American upstart. Lots of sword play to go with the chop-socky action. **CW:** Violence. **89m/C VHS, LV, Closed Caption.** David Bradley, Mark Dacascos, John Fujioka, Valarie Trapp; **D:** Sam Firstenberg; **W:** John Corcoran. *WAR, PMS, CAN*

The American Scream 🎬½ 198?
An innocent family vacationing in the mountains stumbles on to a satanic cult. And that can really ruin a vacation. **85m/C VHS, Beta.** Jennifer Darling, Pons Marr, Blackie Cammett, Kimberly Kramer, Jean Sapienza, Kevin Kaye, Matt Borlenghi, James Cooper; **D:** Mitchell Linden. *GHV*

American Shaolin: King of the Kickboxers 2 🎬½ 1992 (PG-13)
When Drew gets his butt kicked in a karate tournament he decides to head to China and learn some fight-winning moves from a group of warrior monks. **CW:** Martial arts violence. **103m/C VHS, Closed Caption.** Reese Madigan, Trent Bushy, Daniel Dae Kim, Billy Chang, Cliff Lenderman, Zhang Shi Yen, Kim Chan, Alice Zhang Hung; **D:** Lucas Lowe. *ACA*

The American Soldier 🎬🎬½ *Der Amerikanische Soldat* 1970
Fassbinder's homage to the American gangster film tells the story of Ricky, a charismatic hit man. Ricky always wears a gun in a shoulder holster, sports a fedora and a white

double-breasted suit, and drinks Scotch straight from the bottle. He also carries out his assigned murders with complete efficiency and no emotion. In German with English subtitles. **80m/C VHS. GE** Karl Scheydt, Elga Sorbas, Jan George; **D:** Rainer Werner Fassbinder; **W:** Rainer Werner Fassbinder; **M:** Peer Raben. *NYF*

An American Story 🎞️🎞️½ 1992 **(PG)** Earnest but predictable story based on an actual incident. Six WWII vets return to their small Texas town as heroes. But when they find a corrupt mayor and a brutal sheriff running things they decide to campaign to unseat the local politicos, in spite of some dire warnings. Meade (Johnson), their commanding officer in Europe, is the designated leader in the plan but his ambitious wife and father-in-law want him to align himself with the status quo instead. Hallmark Hall of Fame production is enjoyable and better than most made for TV movies, but fails to reach the heights of many other HHF offerings. **97m/C VHS, Closed Caption.** Brad Johnson, Kathleen Quinlan, Tom Sizemore, Josef Sommer, Patricia Clarkson, Lisa Blount, G.W. Bailey, John M. Jackson; **D:** John Gray; **W:** John Gray; **C:** Johnny E. Jensen. *REP*

American Strays 🎞️½ 1996 **(R)** Episodic black comedy about various oddballs (most of them violent) who cross paths (usually in Kane's roadside diner) in an isolated desert town. There's a masochist who wants help committing suicide, an unemployed family man on the verge of a breakdown, a serial killer, and more—mostly strange. **CW:** Strong language, some violence and sexuality. **97m/C VHS.** Carol Kane, Jennifer Tilly, Eric Roberts, John Savage, Luke Perry, Joe Viterelli, James Russo, Vonte Sweet, Sam Jones, Brion James, Toni Kalem, Melora Walters; **D:** Michael Covert; **W:** Michael Covert; **C:** Sead Mutarevic; **M:** John Graham. *APX*

American Streetfighter 🎞️🎞️ 1996 Martial arts expert Jake Tanner gets involved with an illegal streetfighting ring to rescue his brother, Randy, who's the target of a drug courier. But what happens when his next opponent is his sibling? **80m/C VHS.** Gary Daniels, Ian Jacklin, Tracy Dali; **D:** Steve Austin. *SCP*

An American Summer 🎞️🎞️ 1990 A Chicago kid spends a summer with his aunt in beach-rich Los Angeles in this coming-of-age tale filled with '90s teen idols. **100m/C VHS, Closed Caption.** Brian Austin Green, Joanna Kerns, Michael Landes, Tony Crane. *NO*

An American Tail 🎞️🎞️½ 1986 **(G)** While emigrating to New York in the 1880s, a young Russian mouse (Fievel) is separated from his family. He matures as he learns to live on the Big Apple's dirty boulevards. The bad guys are of course cats. Excellent animation and a high-minded (though sentimental and stereotypical) plot keep it interesting for adults. Produced by Spielberg and the first big hit for the Bluth factory, a collection of expatriate Disney artists. Knowing better than to let a money-making mouse tale languish, Bluth followed with "An American Tale: Fievel Goes West." **81m/C VHS, Beta, LV, Closed Caption. D:** Don Bluth; **M:** James Horner; **V:** Dom DeLuise, Madeline Kahn, Phillip Glasser, Christopher Plummer, Nehemiah Persoff, Will Ryan, John Finnegan, Cathianne Blore. Nominations: Academy Awards '86: Best Song ("Somewhere Out There"). *USH, APD*

An American Tail: Fievel Goes West 🎞️🎞️ 1991 **(G)** Fievel and the Mousekewitz family continue their pursuit of the American dream by heading West, where the intrepid mouse seeks to become a famous lawman while his sister looks to make it big as a dance hall singer. The score is performed by the London Symphony Orchestra. Unfortunately released at the same time as "Beauty and the Beast," "Fievel Goes West" suffers from comparison. Worthwhile viewing for the whole family, but it won't ever reach the heights of "B&B." The laser edition is letterboxed and features chapter stops. **75m/C VHS, Beta, LV, Closed Caption. D:** Phil Nibbelink, Simon

Wells; **W:** Flint Dille; **M:** James Horner; **V:** John Cleese, Dom DeLuise, Phillip Glasser, Amy Irving, Jon Lovitz, Cathy Cavadini, Nehemiah Persoff, Erica Yohn, James Stewart. *USH*

American Tickler *Draws* 1976 **(R)** A thigh-slappin' (or is it head-whacking?) series of satirical pastiches in the grand style of "Kentucky Fried Movie," only more sophomoric. A tasteless collection of yearning to be funny sketches about American institutions. **77m/C VHS, Beta.** W.P. Dremak, Joan Sumner, Marlow Ferguson, Jeff Alin; **D:** Chuck Vincent. *GEM*

American Tiger 🎞️🎞️ *American Rickshaw* 1989 **(R)** The collegiate hero of "American Tiger" is, like so many college students, framed for murder, and he applies himself to clearing his sullied name. Somewhere during this process, he finds himself in the middle of a battle between good and evil on a football field. About what you'd expect from a supernatural kung-fu teen-action drama. **CW:** Some language, violence, and sensuality. **93m/C VHS.** Mitch Gaylord, Donald Pleasence, Daniel Greene, Victoria Prouty; **D:** Martin Dolman. *ACA*

An American Werewolf in London 🎞️🎞️🎞️ 1981 **(R)** Strange, darkly humorous version of the classic man-into-wolf horror tale became a cult hit, but never clicked with most American critics. Two American college students (Naughton and Dunne) backpacking through England are viciously attacked by a werewolf one foggy night. Dunne is killed, but keeps appearing (in progressively decomposed form) before the seriously wounded Naughton, warning him of impending werewolfdom when the moon is full; Dunne advises suicide. Seat-jumping horror and gore, highlighted by intensive metamorphosis sequences orchestrated by Rick Baker, are offset by wry humor, though the shifts in tone don't always work. Great moon songs permeate the soundtrack, including CCR's "Bad Moon Rising" and Van Morrison's "Moondance." **97m/C VHS, Beta, LV.** David Naughton, Griffin Dunne, Jenny Agutter, Frank Oz, Brian Glover, David Schofield; **D:** John Landis; **W:** John Landis; **M:** Elmer Bernstein. Academy Awards '81: Best Makeup. *LIV, VES*

American Yakuza 🎞️🎞️ 1994 **(R)** FBI agent Nick Davis (Mortensen) is sent to L.A. to infiltrate the American arm of the Yakuza, Japan's dangerous criminal underworld. He rises through the ranks and is adopted into the powerful Tendo family. Now Davis finds himself caught between the FBI, the Yakuza, and the vengeful American mafia. **95m/C VHS, Closed Caption.** Viggo Mortensen, Michael Nouri; **D:** Frank Cappello; **W:** Max Strom, John Allen Nelson. *COL*

Americana 🎞️🎞️½ 1981 **(PG)** A troubled Vietnam vet tries to restore himself by rebuilding a merry-go-round in a small midwestern town, while dealing with opposition from the local residents. Offbeat, often effective post-Nam editorial that was produced and directed in 1973 by Carradine and then shelved. Hershey and Carradine were a couple back then. **90m/C VHS, Beta.** David Carradine, Barbara Hershey, Bruce Carradine, John Blythe Barrymore Jr., Michael Greene; **D:** David Carradine; **W:** Richard Carr. *VES, LIV*

The Americanization of Emily 🎞️🎞️🎞️ 1964 A happy-go-lucky American naval officer (Garner) with no appetite for war discovers to his horror that he may be slated to become the first casualty of the Normandy invasion as part of a military PR effort in this black comedy-romance. Meanwhile, he spreads the charisma in an effort to woo and uplift Emily (Andrews), a depressed English woman who has suffered the loss of her husband, father, and brother during the war. A cynical, often funny look at military maneuvers and cultural drift that was adapted by Paddy Chayefsky from William Bradford Huie's novel. Also available colorized. **117m/B VHS, LV.** James Garner, Julie Andrews, Melvyn Douglas, James Coburn, Joyce Grenfell, Keenan Wynn, Judy Carne, Liz Fra-

ser, Edward Binns; **D:** Arthur Hiller; **W:** Paddy Chayefsky. Nominations: Academy Awards '64: Best Art Direction/Set Decoration (B & W), Best Black and White Cinematography. *MGM*

The Americano 🎞️🎞️½ 1917 Ever-suave Fairbanks frees a South American politician locked in a dungeon, returns him to political success, and captures the heart of his beautiful daughter. Based on Eugene P. Lyle, Jr.'s "Blaze Derringer." **58m/B VHS, Beta.** Douglas Fairbanks Sr., Alma Rubens, Spottiswoode Aitken, Lillian Langdon, Carl Stockdale, Tom Wilson; **D:** John Emerson. *GPV*

Americano 🎞️🎞️ 1955 A cowboy travelling to Brazil with a shipment of Brahma bulls discovers the rancher he's delivering them to has been murdered. An odd amalgam of western cliches and a South American setting. **85m/C VHS.** Glenn Ford, Frank Lovejoy, Abbe Lane, Cesar Romero; **D:** William Castle. *REP*

The Americano/Variety 1925 The two silent classics in abridged form: "The Americano," (1917) about a soldier-of-fortune who aids a revolt-ridden Caribbean country, and "Variety," (1925) a classic German masterpiece about the career of a trapeze artist. **54m/B VHS, Beta.** Douglas Fairbanks Sr., Emil Jannings; **D:** John Emerson, E.A. Dupont. *CCB*

America's Deadliest Home Video 🎞️🎞️ 1991 Camp spoof about America's obsession with videotaping everything in sight. Video enthusiast Doug is taken hostage by the Clint Dryer gang who want him to tape their crime spree. Every aspect is only seen through the lens of the video camera. **90m/C VHS.** Danny Bonaduce, Mick Wynhoff, Mollena Williams, Melora Walters; **D:** Jack Perez; **W:** Jack Perez. *FCT*

America's Dream 🎞️🎞️🎞️ 1995 **(PG-13)** Trilogy of short stories covering black life from 1938 to 1958. In "Long Black Song," based on a short story by Richard Wright, Alabama farmer Silas (Glover) lives with lonely wife Sarah (Tifford), who succumbs to the charms of white travelling salesman, David (Donovan). "The Boy Who Painted Christ Black" is young Aaron (Golden), who gives the drawing to his teacher, Miss Williams (Calloway). But the portrait causes a great deal of controversy in Aaron's 1948 Georgia school, especially for ambitious principal George Du Vaul (Snipes). Based on a story by John Henrich Clarke. The last story is Maya Angelou's "The Reunion," about Chicago jazz pianist Philomena (Toussaint), who encounters her childhood nemesis, Beth Ann (Thompsn), the daughter of the white family who employed her parents as servants. **CW:** Scene of sexuality. **87m/C VHS.** Danny Glover, Tina Lifford, Tate Donovan, Dan Kamin, Wesley Snipes, Jasmine Guy, Vanessa Bell Calloway, Norman D. Golden II, Timothy Carhart, Yolanda King, Rae'ven Kelly, Lorraine Toussaint, Susanna Thompson, Carl Lumbly, Phyllis Cicero; **D:** Bill Duke, Kevin Rodney Sullivan, Paris Barclay; **W:** Ron Stacker Thompson, Ashley Tyler; **C:** Karl Herrmann; **M:** Patrice Rushen. *HBO*

Americathon woof! 1979 **(PG)** It is the year 1998 and the United States is almost bankrupt, so President Chet Roosevelt decides to stage a telethon to keep the country from going broke. Interesting satiric premise with a diverse cast, but a poor script and slack pacing spoil all the fun. The soundtrack features music by The Beach Boys and Elvis Costello while the narration is by George Carlin. **85m/C VHS, Beta.** Peter Riegert, John Ritter, Nancy Morgan, Harvey Korman, Fred Willard, Meat Loaf, Elvis Costello, Chief Dan George, Howard Hesseman, Jay Leno; *Cameos:* Tommy Lasorda, Peter Marshall; **D:** Neal Israel; **W:** Monica Johnson; **M:** Earl Brown Jr. *ORI, WAR*

Amin: The Rise and Fall woof! 1982 Excessively violent and ultimately pointless dramatization of Idi Amin's eight-year reign of terror in Uganda, which resulted in the deaths of a half million people and the near ruin of a nation. **101m/C VHS, Beta.** Joseph Olita, Geoffrey Keen; **D:** Sharad Patel. *EMI*

The Amityville Horror 🎬🎬 1979 (R)

Sometimes a house is not a home. Ineffective chiller that became a box-office biggie, based on a supposedly real-life occurrence in Amityville, Long Island. The Lutz family moves into the house of their dreams only to find it full of nightmares. Once the scene of a grisly mass murder, the house takes on a devilish attitude, plunging the family into supernatural terror. Pipes and walls ooze icky stuff, flies manifest in the strangest places, and doors mysteriously slam while exorcist Steiger staggers from room to room in scene-chewing prayer. Based on the Jay Anson book and followed by a number of sequels. 117m/C **VHS, Beta, LV.** James Brolin, Margot Kidder, Rod Steiger, Don Stroud, Murray Hamilton, Helen Shaver, Amy Wright; **D:** Stuart Rosenberg; **W:** Sandor Stern; **C:** Fred W. Koenekamp; **M:** Lalo Schifrin. Nominations: Academy Awards '79: Best Original Score. *WAR, OM*

Amityville 2: The Possession woof!

1982 (R) More of a prequel than a sequel to "The Amityville Horror" (1979). Relates the story of the house's early years as a haven for demonic forces intent on driving a father to beat the kids, a mother to prayer, and a brother to lust after his sister (before he murders them all). Young etc. portray an obnoxious family that you're actually glad to see wasted by the possessed son. A stupid, clumsy attempt to cash in on the success of the first film, which was also stupid and clumsy but could at least claim novelty in the bad housing development genre. Followed by "Amityville III: The Demon" in 1983. 110m/C **VHS, Beta, LV.** James Olson, Burt Young, Andrew Prine, Moses Gunn, Rutanya Alda; **D:** Damiano Damiani; **C:** Franco Di Giacomo; **M:** Howard Blake.

Amityville 3: The Demon 🎬½ Amityville 3-D

1983 (R) America's worst real-estate value dupes another funky buyer. The infamous Amityville house is once again restless with terror and gore, though supported with even less plot than the usual smidgin. Cynical reporter Roberts moves in while trying to get to the bottom of the story by way of the basement. Courtesy of 3-D technology, monsters sprang at theater patrons but the video version is strictly two-dimensional, forcing the viewer to press his or her face directly onto the television screen in order to derive similar effect. 98m/C **VHS, Beta, LV.** Tony Roberts, Tess Harper, Robert Joy, Candy Clark, John Beal, Leora Dana, John Harkins, Lori Loughlin, Meg Ryan; **D:** Richard Fleischer; **W:** David Ambrose; **M:** Howard Blake. *VES, LIV*

Amityville 4 🎬½ The Amityville Horror: The Evil Escapes, Part 4

1989 (R) It's an unusual case of house-to-house transference as the horror from Amityville continues, now lodged in a Californian residence. The usual good house gone bad story has the place creating a lot of unusual creaks and rattles before deciding to use its inherited powers to attack and possess a little girl. Special effects from Richard Stutsman ("The Lost Boys" and "Jaws"). Made for television. 95m/C **VHS.** Patty Duke, Jane Wyatt, Norman Lloyd, Frederic Lehne, Brandy Gold; **D:** Sandor Stern; **M:** Rick Conrad. *THV*

Amityville: A New Generation 🎬½

1993 (R) And the bad sequels just go on and on and on. Terry is a young photographer who's given an old mirror by a crazy homeless man (tell me why he took it). He shares a loft with three friends and all begin experiencing vivid and terrifying dreams of murder. Seems the mirror is tied to Amityville and its evil legacy and Terry is the designated inheritor. 92m/C **VHS, LV, Closed Caption.** Ross Partridge, Julia Nickson-Soul, David Naughton, Richard Roundtree, Terry O'Quinn; **D:** John Murlowski; **W:** Christopher DeFaria, Antonio Toro. *REP*

The Amityville Curse woof! 1990 (R)

The possessed house is yet again purchased by a pathetically uninformed family. The usual ghostly shenanigans occur with low-budget regularity in this fifth film in the series. Never released theatrically, for good reason. 91m/C **VHS, LV.** *CA* Kim Coates, Dawna Wightman, Helen Hughes, David Stein, Anthony Dean Rubes, Cassandra Gava, Jan Rubes; **D:** Tom Berry. *VTR, THV*

Amityville Dollhouse 🎬½ 1996 (R)

Family moves into their Victorian dream home in Amityville, which comes complete with a replica dollhouse that charms the daughter. But the Amityville curse inhabits the plaything and soon the poltergeists make their nasty appearance. **CW:** Horror violence, sensuality, and some language. 97m/C **VHS, Closed Caption.** Robin Thomas, Starr Andreeff; **D:** Steve White. *REP*

Amityville 1992: It's About Time 🎬🎬 1992 (R)

Time is of the essence in the sixth installment of the Amityville flicks. A vintage clock (from Amityville, of course), causes creepy goings-on in a family's house. Actually a halfway decent horror film with high-grade special effects, and much, much better than previous Amityville sequels, which isn't saying much. **CW:** Language, horror violence, and sensuality. 95m/C **VHS, LV, Closed Caption.** Stephen Macht, Shawn Weatherly, Megan Ward, Damon Martin, Nita Talbot, Dick Miller; **D:** Tony Randel. *REP*

Among the Cinders 🎬🎬 1983

Sometimes interesting coming of age drama about a sixteen-year-old New Zealand boy who runs away to his grandfather's farm to forget about his friend's accidental death. At the farm, he meets an older woman and compromises his virtue. 103m/C **VHS, Beta, LV.** *GE NZ* Paul O'Shea, Derek Hardwick, Rebecca Gibney, Yvonne Lawley, Amanda Jones; **D:** Rolf Haedrich. *NWV, VTR*

Amongst Friends 🎬🎬 1993 (R)

Three boyhood buddies, Trevor (McGaw), Billy (Lindsey), and Andy (Parlavecchio), from a nice Long Island neighborhood turn to crime out of boredom. Trevor gets busted and goes to prison for two years. Upon getting out, he finds his old cronies still share the taste for crime and general aimlessness but also still want that one big score. Trevor finally agrees to join Andy and Billy in a drug deal but the jealous Billy, who wants Trevor's old girlfriend Laura (Sorvino), plans a double-cross that will affect them all. Filled with cutting attacks on the society that spawns aimless youth. Debut of then 26-year-old writer/director Weiss. **CW:** Pervasive strong language, violence and drug use, and sexuality. 88m/C **VHS, LV, Closed Caption.** Patrick McGaw, Steve Parlavecchio, Joseph Lindsey, Mira Sorvino, David Stepkin, Michael Artura; **D:** Rob Weiss; **W:** Rob Weiss; **C:** Michael Bonvillain; **M:** Mick Jones. *COL*

Amor Bandido 🎬🎬½ 1979

When cab drivers in Rio are turning up dead, a young prostitute is torn between her detective father and her prime suspect boyfriend. Drama based on a true story. In Portuguese with English subtitles. 95m/C **VHS, LV.** *BR* Paulo Gracindo, Cristina Ache, Paulo Guarniero; **D:** Bruno Barreto. *FXL, IME, FCT*

Amore 🎬🎬🎬 1948

Rossellini's tribute to actress Magnani consists of the short films "The Human Voice" and "The Miracle." In "The Human Voice," Magnani is shown alone, speaking to her lover on the telephone. Based on Jean Cocteau's one-act drama. In "The Miracle," she is a simple peasant girl who believes her illegitimate child is acutally the new Messiah. In Italian with English subtitles. 78m/B **VHS.** *IT* Anna Magnani; **D:** Roberto Rossellini. *FCT, CVC*

Amore! 🎬🎬½ 1993 (PG-13)

Wealthy investment banker Saul Schwartz (Scalia) hates his job, his wife, and his life. The only way he loses himself is by watching movies starring Italian matinee idol Rudolfo Carbonera (Hamilton). So Saul gets divorced and decides to change his life—by going to Hollywood and becoming an actor like his debonair idol. With the help of some newfound friends he transforms himself into suave leading man material (under the name of Salvatore Guiliano III) but promptly winds up falling for a writer (Ireland), who couldn't care less. **CW:** Sex-related scenes and dialogue. 93m/C **VHS, LV, Closed Caption.** Jack Scalia, Kathy Ireland, Elliott Gould, George Hamilton, Brenda Epperson, James Doohan, Katherine Helmond, Betsy Russell, Norm Crosby, Frank Gorshin; **D:** Lorenzo Doumani; **W:** Lorenzo Doumani. *PMH*

The Amorous Adventures of Moll Flanders 🎬🎬 1965

An amusing romp set in 18th century England focusing on a poor orphan girl who seeks wealth. Moll plots to get ahead through an advantageous series of romances and marriages. Her plan is ruined when she falls in love and he turns out to be a wanted highwayman, landing her in prison. Not surprisingly, love (and money) conquers all. Based on the novel by Daniel Defoe. Novak tries in this female derivative of "Tom Jones," but this period piece isn't her style. 126m/C **VHS.** Kim Novak, Richard Johnson, Angela Lansbury, Vittorio De Sica, Leo McKern, George Sanders, Lilli Palmer; **D:** Terence Young; **C:** Ted Moore; **M:** John Addison. *PAR*

Amos 🎬🎬½ 1985

Douglas is Amos, an aging baseball coach confined most reluctantly to a nursing home. He's disturbed by recent suspicious events there, his concern causing him to take on Montgomery, the staunch head nurse. Well-acted drama produced by Douglas's son Peter, offering an echo of "One Flew Over the Cuckoo's Nest," which Dad starred in on Broadway and son Michael helped produced as a movie classic. 100m/C **VHS.** Kirk Douglas, Elizabeth Montgomery, Dorothy McGuire, Noriyuki "Pat" Morita, James Sloyan, Ray Walston; **D:** Michael Tuchner; **M:** Georges Delerue. *NO*

Amos and Andrew 🎬½ 1993 (PG-13)

Embarrassing attempt at comedy stops short of endorsing the stereotypes it tries to parody. Prizewinning African-American author Andrew Sterling (Jackson) is seen moving into a house on an island previously reserved for the uptight white, and the neighbors call the cops, assuming he's a thief. Chief of police (Coleman) eagerly gets into the act, then exploits drifter Amos (Cage) in a cover-up attempt when he realizes his mistake. Talented cast can't overcome lame jokes and transparent plot that serves as an opportunity to bring black and white together for a "see how much we have in common" bonding session. **CW:** Some language, drug content; mock violence, and sexual reference. 96m/C **VHS, LV, Closed Caption.** Nicolas Cage, Samuel L. Jackson, Michael Lerner, Margaret Colin, Giancarlo Esposito, Dabney Coleman, Bob Balaban, Aimee Graham, Brad Dourif, Chelcie Ross, Jodi Long; **D:** E. Max Frye; **W:** E. Max Frye; **M:** Richard Gibbs. *COL, IME, NLC*

The Amphibian Man 🎬🎬 1961

What does a scientist do once he's created a young man with gills? Plunge him in the real world of aqua pura to experience life and love, albeit underwater. Trouble is, the protagonist, who's come to be known as the Sea Devil, takes a dive for a young pretty he's snatched from the jaws of death. A 60's Soviet sci-fi romance originally seen on American television. 96m/C **VHS.** *RU* K. Korieniev, M. Virzinskaya; **D:** Y. Kasancki. *SNC*

The Amsterdam Connection 🎬 197?

Film company acts as a cover for prostitution and drug smuggling, with the girls acting as international couriers. 90m/C **VHS, Beta.** *HK* Chen Shing, Kid Sherrif, Yeung Sze, Jason Pai Piu, Fang Mui San; **D:** Fang Mui San, Lo Ke. *NO*

The Amsterdam Kill 🎬🎬 1978 (R)

A washed-up ex-agent of the U.S. Drug Enforcement Agency is hired by a desperate U.S. Drug Enforcement Agency to hunt down the kingpin of a narcotics syndicate in Hong Kong. Tedious pace with occasional spells of violence fails to awaken somnambulent Mitchum. Shot on location in Hong Kong. 93m/C **VHS, Beta, LV.** *HK* Robert Mitchum, Richard Egan, Keye Luke, Leslie Nielsen, Bradford Dillman; **D:** Robert Clouse; **W:** Robert Clouse. *GKK*

Amsterdamned 🎬🎬 1988 (R)

A crime thriller taking place on the canals of Amsterdam featuring a serial skindiver killer who surfaces periodically to slash and splash. A steely detective fishes for clues. Dubbed. **114m/C VHS, Beta, LV.** *NL* Monique Van De Ven, Huub Stapel; *D:* Dick Maas. *VES, LIV*

Amy �ましま½ **1981 (G)** Set in the early 1900s, the story follows the experiences of a woman after she leaves her well-to-do husband to teach at a school for the deaf and blind. Eventually she organizes a football game between the handicapped kids and the other children in the neighborhood. Good Disney family fare. **100m/C VHS, Beta.** Jenny Agutter, Barry Newman, Kathleen Nolan, Margaret O'Brien, Nanette Fabray, Chris Robinson, Lou Fant; *D:* Vincent McEveety; *M:* Robert F. Brunner. *DIS*

The Amy Fisher Story ✋✋ **1993** Amy Fisher wishes she looked this good. Perhaps if she did, she could be acting in made-for-television movies like Barrymore instead of providing fodder for them. The ABC account draws from a variety of sources to dramatize the relationship between Amy and her married, ahem, friend, and Amy's subsequent attack on his wife. Although it tries not to take sides, it does include some pretty hot sex scenes which could be why this docudrama garnered the highest ratings of the three network productions released on TV. See also: "Casualties of Love: The 'Long Island Lolita' Story" and "Lethal Lolita—Amy Fisher: My Story." **96m/C VHS.** Drew Barrymore, Anthony John Denison, Harley Jane Kozak, Tom Mason, Laurie Paton, Ken Pogue, Linda Darlow; *D:* Andy Tennant; *W:* Janet Brownell. *ABC*

Anaconda ✋✋½ **1996 (PG-13)** Snakes—lots and lots of snakes. Teeny baby snakes, little snakes, medium-sized snakes, large snakes, and one gigantic 40-foot long snake that likes to swallow people and then vomit them up again (the better to have room to swallow somebody else). Oh yeah, the minimal plot concerns a documentary film crew traveling the Amazon River looking for a legendary Indian tribe. They not only have to contend with the snakes but with crazy, snake-obsessed fugitive guide Paul Sarone (Voight). The actors react appropriately to becoming snake food. *CW:* Intense adventure violence, and for brief language and sensuality. **90m/C VHS.** Jon Voight, Jennifer Lopez, Ice Cube, Eric Stoltz, Owen C. Wilson, Kari Wuhrer, Jonathan Hyde, Vincent Castellanos; *D:* Luis Llosa; *W:* Jim Cash, Jack Epps Jr., Hans Bauer; *C:* Bill Butler; *M:* Randy Edelman. *NYR*

Anastasia ✋✋✋½ **1956** Bergman won her second Oscar, and deservedly so, for her classic portrayal of the amnesia victim chosen by Russian expatriate Brynner to impersonate Anastasia, the last surviving member of the Romanoff dynasty. As such, she becomes part of a scam to collect millions of rubles deposited in a foreign bank by her supposed father, the now-dead Czar. But is she just impersonating the princess? Brynner as the scheming White General and Hayes as the Grand Duchess who needs to be convinced turn in fine performances as well. Based on Marcelle Maurette's play. **105m/C VHS, LV.** Ingrid Bergman, Yul Brynner, Helen Hayes, Akim Tamiroff; *D:* Anatole Litvak; *W:* Arthur Laurents; *C:* Jack Hildyard. Academy Awards '56: Best Actress (Bergman); Golden Globe Awards '57: Best Actress—Drama (Bergman); New York Film Critics Awards '56: Best Actress (Bergman); Nominations: Academy Awards '56: Original Dramatic/Comedy Score. *TCF*

Anastasia: The Mystery of Anna ✋✋½ **1986** Irving stars as Anna Anderson, a woman who claimed to be the Grand Duchess Anastasia, the sole surviving daughter of Russian Czar Nicholas II. A powerful epic reliving her experience of royalty, flight from execution, and struggle to retain her heritage. The story of Anastasia remains as one of the greatest dramatic mysteries of the 20th century. Adapted from the book "Anastasia: The Riddle of Anna Anderson" by Peter Kurth; originally broadcast on cable television. **190m/C VHS, LV.** Amy Irving, Olivia de Havilland, Jan Niklas, Nicolas Surovy, Susan Lucci, Elke Sommer, Edward Fox, Claire Bloom, Omar Sharif, Rex Harrison; *D:* Marvin J. Chomsky; *W:* James Goldman. *CAF, PBS, FUS*

Anatomy of a Murder ✋✋✋✋ **1959** Considered by many to be the best courtroom drama ever made. Small-town lawyer in northern Michigan faces an explosive case as he defends an army officer who has killed a man he suspects was his philandering wife's rapist. Realistic, cynical portrayal of the court system isn't especially concerned with guilt or innocence, focusing instead on the interplay between the various courtroom characters. Classic performance by Stewart as the down home but brilliant defense lawyer who matches wits with Scott, the sophisticated prosecutor; terse and clever direction by Preminger. Though tame by today's standards, the language used in the courtroom was controversial. Filmed in upper Michigan; based on the bestseller by judge Robert Traver. **161m/B VHS, Beta, LV.** James Stewart, George C. Scott, Arthur O'Connell, Ben Gazzara, Lee Remick, Eve Arden, Orson Bean, Kathryn Grant, Murray Hamilton, Joseph Welch; *Cameos:* Duke Ellington; *D:* Otto Preminger; *W:* Wendell Mayes; *C:* Sam Leavitt; *M:* Duke Ellington. National Board of Review Awards '59: 10 Best Films of the Year; New York Film Critics Awards '59: Best Actor (Stewart), Best Screenplay; Nominations: Academy Awards '59: Best Actor (Stewart), Best Adapted Screenplay, Best Black and White Cinematography, Best Film Editing, Best Picture, Best Supporting Actor (O'Connell, Scott). *COL*

Anatomy of a Psycho ✋ **1961** A man plans to avenge his gas chambered brother by committing mass murder. Very cheaply and poorly produced. **75m/B VHS, Beta.** Ronnie Burns, Pamela Lincoln, Darrell Howe, Russ Bender; *D:* Brooke L. Peters. *SNC*

Anatomy of a Seduction ✋✋ **1979** Television formula melodrama of a middle-aged divorcee's affair with her son's best friend. Age knows no boundaries when it comes to television lust. **100m/C VHS, 8mm.** Susan Flannery, Jameson Parker, Rita Moreno, Ed Nelson, Michael Le Clair; *D:* Steven Hilliard Stern; *M:* Hagood Hardy. *HBO*

Anatomy of Terror ✋ **1974** A made for television drama about an army vet going bonkers (what? really?) and revealing espionage secrets in his home life. **73m/C VHS, Beta.** Paul Burke, Polly Bergen, Dinsdale Landen, Basil Henson. *LIV*

Anchors Aweigh ✋✋✋ **1945** Snappy big-budget (for then) musical about two horny sailors, one a girl-happy dancer and the other a shy singer. While on leave in Hollywood they return a lost urchin to his sister. The four of them try to infiltrate a movie studio to win an audition for the girl from maestro Iturbi. Kelly's famous dance with Jerry the cartoon Mouse (of "Tom and Jerry" fame) is the second instance of combining live action and animation. The young and handsome Sinatra's easy crooning and Grayson's near operatic soprano are blessed with music and lyrics by Styne and Cahn. Lots of fun, with conductor-pianist Iturbi contributing and Hollywood-style Little Mexico also in the brew. ♫We Hate to Leave; I Fall in Love Too Easily; The Charm of You; The Worry Song; Jalousie; All of a Sudden My Heart Sings; I Begged Her; What Makes the Sun Set?; Waltz Serenade. **139m/C VHS, Beta, LV, Closed Caption.** Frank Sinatra, Gene Kelly, Kathryn Grayson, Jose Iturbi, Sharon McManus, Dean Stockwell, Carlos Ramirez, Pamela Britton; *D:* George Sidney; *M:* Jule Styne, Sammy Cahn. Academy Awards '45: Scoring of a Musical; Nominations: Academy Awards '45: Best Actor (Kelly), Best Color Cinematography, Best Picture, Best Song ("I Fall in Love Too Easily"). *MGM*

And a Nightingale Sang ✋✋½ **1991** WWII England is the scene of this sweet romance, a sad and humorous tale of a woman who gives everything for the war effort. Stunning recreation of the final days of the Blitzkreig. Originally produced for Masterpiece Theatre. **90m/C VHS, Closed Caption.** Joan Plowright, Tom Watt, Phyllis Logan, John Woodvine. *PBS, FUS, VIF*

And Baby Makes Six ✋✋½ **1979** An unexpected pregnancy creates new challenges for a couple with grown children. Dewhurst is excellent as usual. Made for television. Followed by "Baby Comes Home." **100m/C VHS, 8mm.** Colleen Dewhurst, Warren Oates, Maggie Cooper, Mildred Dunnock, Timothy Hutton, Allyn Ann McLerie; *D:* Waris Hussein; *W:* Shelley List. *NO*

And God Created Woman ✋✋½ *And Woman...Was Created; Et Dieu Crea la Femme* **1957 (PG)** Launching pad for Bardot's career as a sex siren, as she flits across the screen in a succession of scanty outfits and hangs out at the St. Tropez beach in what is euphemistically known as a swimsuit while turning up the heat for the males always in attendance. The plot concerns an 18-year-old nymphomaniac who is given a home by a local family with three handsome young sons. A cutting-edge sex film in its time that was boffo at the box office. In French with English subtitles. **93m/C VHS, Beta.** *FR* Brigitte Bardot, Curt Jurgens, Jean-Louis Trintignant, Christian Marquand; *D:* Roger Vadim; *W:* Roger Vadim. *NO*

And God Created Woman ✋½ **1988 (R)** Loose, dull remake by Vadim of his own 1957 softcore favorite about a free-spirited woman dodging men and the law while yearning for rock and roll stardom. DeMornay is a prisoner who hopes to marry one of the local hunks (Spano) so she can be paroled. They marry, she strips, he frets, while political hopeful Langella smacks his lips in anticipation. Available in an unrated 100-minute version. **98m/C VHS, Beta, LV.** Rebecca DeMornay, Vincent Spano, Frank Langella, Donovan Leitch, Judith Chapman, Thelma Houston; *D:* Roger Vadim; *M:* Tom Chase, Steve Rucker. *VES, LIV*

And God Said to Cain ✋ **196?** Another Biblically titled western from the prolific Kinski, about a put-upon gunman who must fight for his life. **95m/C VHS, Beta.** Klaus Kinski. *UNI, CNG*

...And God Spoke ✋✋ **1994 (R)** Low budget spoof takes on both religion and moviemaking with two schlockmeisters filming a biblical epic. Since the duo have no budget and are basic hacks with pretensions, they have to settle...so Sales plays Moses, "The Incredible Hulk" Ferrigno gets cast as Cain, while Plumb ("Jan" on "The Brady Bunch") does Mrs. Noah. Has some lulls but also covers very recognizable territory. Directorial debut of Borman. *CW:* Language. **82m/C VHS.** Michael Riley, Stephen Rappaport, Soupy Sales, Lou Ferrigno, Eve Plumb, Andy Dick, R.C. Bates, Fred Kaz, Daniel Tisman; *D:* Arthur Borman; *W:* Gregory S. Malins, Michael Curtis. *WEA*

And Hope to Die ✋✋½ **1972** Moody, muddled crime drama with a good cast about a fleeing Frenchman who joins a gang of hardened criminals in Canada. They go ahead with their plans to kidnap a retarded girl even though she is already dead. Standard caper film is enhanced by arty camera work and some unusual directorial touches. **95m/C VHS, Beta.** *FR* Robert Ryan, Jean-Louis Trintignant, Aldo Ray, Tisa Farrow; *D:* Rene Clement. *NO*

And I Alone Survived ✋✋ **1978** Made-for-television adaptation of the true story of a woman who survives a leisure-plane crash in the Sierra Nevadas and her struggle to get to the village below. Brown does her best to elevate the proceedings above the usual I-hope-I-don't-die cliches. **90m/C VHS, Beta.** Blair Brown, David Ackroyd, Vera Miles, G.D. Spradlin; *D:* William A. Graham; *C:* Jordan Cronenweth. *PSM*

And Justice for All ✋✋½ **1979 (R)** Earnest attorney Pacino questions the law and battles for justice in and out of the courtroom. He's hired to defend a detested judge from a rape charge, while dealing with a lost-soul caseload of eccentric and tragedy-prone clients. Overly melodramatic, an odd mix of satire, cynicism, and seemingly sincere drama that hits a club when a stick will do. Jewison aims for black surrealism, permitting both Pacino and Warden (as a judge losing his sanity) to veer into histrionics, to the detriment of what is essentially a gripping behind-the-scenes story. Excellent cast creates sparks, including Lahti in her film debut. And Baltimore never looked lovelier. **120m/C VHS, Beta, LV, 8mm.** Al Pacino, Jack Warden, Christine Lahti, Thomas G. Waites, Craig T. Nelson, John Forsythe, Lee Strasberg; **D:** Norman Jewison; **W:** Barry Levinson, Valerie Curtin; **M:** Dave Grusin. Nominations: Academy Awards '79: Best Actor (Pacino), Best Original Screenplay. COL

And Nothing But the Truth 🐾🐾½
Giro City 1982 A multinational corporation is out to ruin the investigative television report team trying to do a story on the company. **90m/C VHS, Beta.** GB Glenda Jackson, Jon Finch, Kenneth Colley, James Donnelly; **D:** Karl Francis. NO

And Now for Something Completely Different 🐾🐾🐾
1972 (PG) A compilation of skits from BBC-television's "Monty Python's Flying Circus" featuring Monty Python's own weird, hilarious brand of humor. Sketches include "The Upper Class Twit of the Year Race," "Hell's Grannies" and "The Townswomen's Guild Reconstruction of Pearl Harbour." A great introduction to Python for the uninitiated, or a chance for the converted to see their favorite sketches again. **89m/C VHS, Beta, LV.** GB John Cleese, Michael Palin, Eric Idle, Graham Chapman, Terry Gilliam, Terry Jones; **D:** Ian McNaughton; **W:** John Cleese, Michael Palin, Graham Chapman, Terry Gilliam, Terry Jones. COL, TVC

And Now Miguel 🐾🐾
1966 Plodding tale of a young boy who wants to take over as head shepherd of his family's flock. Filmed in New Mexico, but the over-long outdoor shots make it drag a bit in spite of Cardi's competent performance. **95m/C VHS.** Pat Cardi, Michael Ansara, Guy Stockwell, Clu Gulager, Joe De Santis, Pilar Del Rey, Buck Taylor; **D:** James B. Clark. NOS

And Now My Love 🐾🐾½
1974 (PG) A French couple endeavor to maintain their romance despite interfering socio-economic factors—she's a millionaire and he's an ex-con filmmaker. Keller plays three roles spanning three generations, as Lelouch invests autobiographical details to invent a highly stylized, openly sentimental view of French folks in love with love. Along the way he comments on social mores and changing attitudes through the years. Dubbed in English. **121m/C VHS, Beta.** FR Marthe Keller, Andre Dussollier, Carla Gravina; **D:** Claude Lelouch; **W:** Claude Lelouch. Los Angeles Film Critics Association Awards '75: Best Foreign Film; Nominations: Academy Awards '75: Best Original Screenplay. COL

And Now the Screaming Starts 🐾🐾½
1973 (R) The young bride-to-be of the lord of a British manor house is greeted by bloody faces at the window, a severed hand, and five corpses. Then Cushing shows up to investigate. Good-looking, sleek production with genuine chills. **87m/C VHS, Beta.** GB Peter Cushing, Herbert Lom, Patrick Magee, Ian Ogilvy, Stephanie Beacham, Geoffrey Whitehead, Guy Rolfe; **D:** Roy Ward Baker. PSM, MED

And Soon the Darkness 🐾🐾
1970 (PG) One of two vacationing young nurses disappears in France where a teenager was once murdered and the search is on. Predictable, ineffective suspenser. **94m/C VHS, Beta.** GB Pamela Franklin, Michele Dotrice, Sandor Eles, John Nettleton, Claire Kelly, Hanna-Marie Pravda; **D:** Robert Fuest; **W:** Brian Clemens. NO

And the Band Played On 🐾🐾🐾
1993 (PG-13) Randy Shilts' monumental, and controversial, 1987 book on the AIDS epidemic comes to television in an equally controversial made for cable movie. Details the intricate medical research undertaken by doctors in France and the U.S. who fought to isolate and identify the mystery virus despite governmental neglect, red tape, clashing egos, and lack of funding. Various aspects of gay life are shown objectively, without sensationalizing. Celebrity cameos are somewhat distracting though most acquit themselves well.

The script went through numerous rewrites; director Spottiswoode reportedly objected to HBO interference at the editing stage. **CW:** Subject matter. **140m/C VHS, LV, Closed Caption.** Matthew Modine, Alan Alda, Ian McKellen, Lily Tomlin, Glenne Headly, Richard Masur, Saul Rubinek, Charles Martin Smith, Patrick Bauchau, Nathalie Baye, Christian Clemenson; **Cameos:** Richard Gere, David Clennon, Phil Collins, Alex Courtney, David Dukes, David Marshall Grant, Ronald Guttman, Anjelica Huston, Ken Jenkins, Richard Jenkins, Tcheky Karyo, Swoosie Kurtz, Jack Laufer, Steve Martin, Dakin Matthews, Peter McRobbie, Lawrence Monoson, B.D. Wong, Donal Logue, Jeffrey Nordling, Stephen Spinella; **D:** Roger Spottiswoode; **W:** Arnold Schulman; **C:** Paul Elliott; **M:** Carter Burwell. HBO

And the Children Shall Lead
1985 A young black girl is moved by the coming of the civil rights movement to her small Mississippi town. Part of the "Wonderworks" series. **60m/C VHS.** Danny Glover, LeVar Burton, Pam Potillo, Denise Nicholas, Andrew Prine; **D:** Michael Pressman. PME, PTB, HMV

... And the Earth Did Not Swallow Him 🐾🐾½
...Y No Se Lo Trago La Tierra 1994 Family trials of migrant farm workers from the perspective of 12-year-old Marcos, who travels with his parents on their annual (it's 1952) move from Texas throughout the midwest during harvest season. Balances their struggles with the strong family bonds that allow them to endure. Based on the semi-autobiographical novel by Tomas Rivera. **99m/C VHS.** Jose Alcala, Rose Portillo, Marco Rodriguez; **D:** Severo Perez; **W:** Severo Perez; **C:** Virgil Harper; **M:** Marcos Loya. KIV, FCT

And the Ship Sails On 🐾🐾🐾
El la Nave Va 1983 (PG) On the eve of WWI, a group of devoted opera lovers take a luxury cruise to pay their respects to a recently deceased opera diva. Also on board is a group of fleeing Serbo-Croation freedom fighters. A charming and absurd autumnal homage-to-life by Fellini shot entirely in the studio. **130m/C VHS, Beta, LV.** IT Freddie Jones, Barbara Jefford, Janet Suzman, Peter Cellier; **D:** Federico Fellini; **W:** Federico Fellini, Tonino Guerra. COL, APD

And Then There Were None 🐾🐾🐾½
1945 An all-star cast makes up the ten colorful guests invited to a secluded estate in England by a mysterious host. What the invitations do not say, however, is the reason they have been specifically chosen to visit—to be murdered, one by one. Cat and mouse classic based on Agatha Christie's book with an entertaining mix of suspense and black comedy. Remade in 1966 and again in 1975 as "Ten Little Indians," but lacking the force and gloss of the original. **97m/C VHS, Beta, LV.** Louis Hayward, Barry Fitzgerald, Walter Huston, Roland Young, Sir C. Aubrey Smith, Judith Anderson, Mischa Auer, June Duprez; **D:** Rene Clair. NOS, VCI

And Then You Die 🐾🐾🐾
1988 (R) An intense crime drama about a Canadian drug lord who amasses a fortune from the cocaine and marijuana trade. His empire is threatened as the Mafia, Hell's Angels, and the police try to bring him down. **115m/C VHS, Beta.** CA Kenneth Welsh, R.H. Thomson, Wayne Robson, Tom Harvey, George Bloomfield, Graeme Campbell; **D:** Francis Mankiewicz. THV

And You Thought Your Parents Were Weird! 🐾🐾½
1991 (PG) A pair of introverted, whiz kid brothers invent a lovable robot to provide fatherly guidance as well as companionship for their widowed mother. Surprisingly charming, sentimental film is only slightly hampered by low-budget special effects. **92m/C VHS, Closed Caption.** Marcia Strassman, Joshua Miller, Edan Gross, John Quade, Sam Behrens, Susan Gibney, Gustav Vintas, Eric Walker; **D:** Tony Cookson; **W:** Tony Cookson; **C:** Paul Elliott; **M:** Randy Miller; **V:** Alan Thicke, Richard Libertini. THV

The Anderson Tapes 🐾🐾🐾
1971 (PG) Newly released from prison, an ex-con assembles his professional pals and plans the million-dollar robbery of an entire luxury apartment house on NYC's upper east side. Of course, he's unaware

that a hoard of law men from federal, state, and local agencies are recording their activities for a wide variety of reasons, though none of the surveillance is coordinated and it has nothing to do with the planned robbery. Based on the novel by Lawrence Sanders, the intricate caper is effectively shaped by Lumet, who skillfully integrates broad satire with suspense. Shot on location in New York City. Walken is The Kid, his first major role. **100m/C VHS, Beta, LV.** Sean Connery, Dyan Cannon, Martin Balsam, Christopher Walken, Alan King, Ralph Meeker, Garrett Morris, Margaret Hamilton; **D:** Sidney Lumet; **W:** Frank Pierson; **M:** Quincy Jones. GKK, COL

Andersonville 🐾🐾🐾
1995 Andersonville was an infamous Confederate prison camp in Georgia that by August, 1864 contained more than 32,000 Union POWs—and was planned to hold 8,000 men. One in four soldiers died in the camp. The story is told through the eyes of Massachusetts Corporal Josiah Day (Emick), who is captured in 1864 and struggles to survive the hellish conditions. The commander of the Andersonville was a deranged German-Swiss captain named Wirz (Triska)—who became the only Civil War soldier to be hanged for war crimes (depicted in "The Andersonville Trial"). The TV miniseries was filmed some 150 miles from the original site. **168m/C VHS.** Jarrod Emick, Frederic Forrest, Ted Marcoux, Jan Triska, Cliff DeYoung, Tom Aldredge, Frederick Coffin, Justin Henry, Kris Kamm, William H. Macy, Gabriel Olds, William Sanderson, Bud Davis, Carmen Argenziano, Peter Murnik; **D:** John Frankenheimer; **W:** David W. Rintels; **C:** Ric Waite; **M:** Gary Chang. TTC

The Andersonville Trial 🐾🐾🐾½
1970 Details the atrocities experienced by captured Union soldiers who were held in the Confederacy's notorious Andersonville prison during the American Civil War. Provides an interesting account of the war-crimes trial of the Georgia camp's officials, under whom more than 14,000 prisoners died. Moving, remarkable television drama based on the Pulitzer-honored book by MacKinlay Kantor. **150m/C VHS, Beta, LV.** Martin Sheen, William Shatner, Buddy Ebsen, Jack Cassidy, Richard Basehart, Cameron Mitchell; **D:** George C. Scott. LIV

Andre 🐾🐾½
1994 (PG) More human-animal interaction from the director of "The Man from Snowy River," telling the true story of an orphaned seal that was adopted by the local Maine harbormaster (Carradine) and his family. As they raise their houseguest, the question arises whether Andre should be returned to the wild. It'll remind you of "Free Willy" with an appealing smaller sea mammal and the equally appealing Majorino, as the youngster who befriends Andre. For those who are sticklers for accuracy, Andre is actually portrayed by a sea lion and not a seal. **94m/C VHS, Beta, Closed Caption.** Keith Carradine, Tina Majorino, Chelsea Field, Keith Szarabajka, Shane Meier; **D:** George Miller; **W:** Dana Baratta; **C:** Thomas Burstyn; **M:** Bruce Rowland. PAR

Andrei Rublev 🐾🐾🐾🐾
1966 A 15th-century Russian icon painter must decide whether to record history or participate in it as Tartar invaders make life miserable. During the black and white portion, he becomes involved in a peasant uprising, killing a man in the process. After a bout of pessimism and a vow of silence, he goes forth to create artistic beauty as the screen correspondingly blazes with color. A brilliant historical drama censored by Soviet authorities until 1971. In Russian with English subtitles. **185m/C VHS, LV.** RU Anatoli Solonitzin, Ivan Lapikov, Nikolai Grinko, Nikolai Sergueiev; **D:** Andrei Tarkovsky; **W:** Andrei Tarkovsky, Andrei Konchalovsky. FXL, NOS, FCT

Androcles and the Lion 🐾🐾½
1952 Stage-bound Hollywood version of the George Bernard Shaw story about a tailor in Imperial Rome who saves Christians from a hungry lion he had previously befriended. Sharp dialogue and a plot that's relatively (within the bounds of Hollywood) faithful help a great play become a semi-satisfying cinematic morsel. Harpo Marx was orig-

inally cast as Androcles, but was fired by producer Howard Hughes five weeks into the shooting. **105m/B VHS, Beta.** Jean Simmons, Alan Young, Victor Mature, Robert Newton, Maurice Evans; **D:** Chester Erskine; **C:** Harry Stradling. COL

Android 🐾🐾½ 1982 (PG) When an android who has been assisting a quirky scientist in space learns that he is about to be permanently retired, he starts to take matters into his own synthetic hands. Combines science fiction, suspense and cloned romance. A must for Kinski fans. **80m/C VHS, Beta, LV.** Klaus Kinski, Don Opper, Brie Howard; **D:** Aaron Lipstadt. MED

The Android Affair 🐾🐾½ 1995 (PG-13) Karen Garrett (Kozak) is studying at the Institute for Surgical Research where doctors practice experimental techniques on lifelike androids. Her next patient is William (Dunne), a handsome and charming android with a heart defect, who doesn't want to "die" during Karen's risky surgical procedure. What's worse is Karen finds this 'droid all too humanly appealing and decides to help him escape the Institute. From a story by Isaac Asimov and screenwriter Kletter. **CW:** Some sensuality and violence. **90m/C VHS, LV, Closed Caption.** Harley Jane Kozak, Griffin Dunne, Ossie Davis, Saul Rubinek, Peter Outerbridge, Natalie Radford; **D:** Richard Kletter; **W:** Richard Kletter; **C:** Bernhard Salzmann; **M:** Simon Boswell. USH

The Andromeda Strain 🐾🐾½ 1971 (G) A satellite falls back to earth carrying a deadly bacteria that must be identified in time to save the population from extermination. The tension inherent in the bestselling Michael Crichton novel is talked down by a boring cast. Also available in letter-box format. **131m/C VHS, Beta, LV.** Arthur Hill, David Wayne, James Olson, Kate Reid, Paula Kelly; **D:** Robert Wise. Nominations: Academy Awards '71: Best Art Direction/Set Decoration, Best Film Editing. USH

Andy and the Airwave Rangers 🐾🐾 *Andy Colby's Incredibly Awesome Adventure* 1989 Andy is whisked into the TV!! He finds adventure and excitement—car chases, intergalactic battles, and cartoons. **75m/C VHS, LV.** Dianne Kay, Vince Edwards, Bo Svenson, Richard Thomas, Erik Estrada, Randy Josselyn, Jessica Puscas, Chuck Kovacic; **D:** Deborah Brock. COL

Andy Griffith Show 1960 Life in Mayberry with smalltown sheriff Andy (Griffith), inept deputy Barney Fife (Knotts), Andy's son Opie (Howard), Aunt Bee (Bavier) and all the other townsfolk in the first of the rural comedy series. Two episodes: "Barney's Sidecar" and "The Darlings Are Coming." Additional episodes are available. **52m/B VHS, Beta.** Andy Griffith, Don Knotts, Ron Howard, Jim Nabors, Frances Bavier, George Lindsey, Howard McNear, Hal Smith, Howard Morris. MOV

Andy Hardy Gets Spring Fever 🐾🐾 1939 Andy falls for a beautiful acting teacher, and then goes into a funk when he finds she's engaged. Judge Hardy and the gang help heal the big wound in his heart. A lesser entry (and the seventh) from the popular series. **88m/B VHS, Beta.** Mickey Rooney, Lewis Stone, Ann Rutherford, Fay Holden, Cecilia Parker, Sara Haden, Helen Gilbert; **D:** Woodbridge S. Van Dyke. MGM

Andy Hardy Meets Debutante 🐾🐾½ 1940 Seems like there should be an article in that title. Garland's second entry in series, wherein Andy meets and falls foolishly for glamorous debutante Lewis with Betsy's help while family is on visit to New York. Judy/Betsy sings "I'm Nobody's Baby" and "Singing in Rain." Also available with "Love Finds Andy Hardy" on laser disc. **86m/B VHS, Beta, LV, Closed Caption.** Mickey Rooney, Judy Garland, Lewis Stone, Ann Rutherford, Fay Holden, Sara Haden, Cecilia Parker, Diana Lewis, Tom Neal; **D:** George B. Seitz. MGM

Andy Hardy's Double Life 🐾🐾½ 1942 In this entertaining installment from the Andy Hardy series, Andy proposes marriage to two girls at the same time and gets in quite a pickle when

they both accept. Williams makes an early screen splash. **91m/B VHS, Beta.** Mickey Rooney, Lewis Stone, Ann Rutherford, Fay Holden, Sara Haden, Cecilia Parker, Esther Williams, William Lundigan, Susan Peters, Robert (Bobby) Blake; **D:** George B. Seitz. MGM, MLB

Andy Hardy's Private Secretary 🐾🐾 1941 After Andy fails his high school finals he gets help from a sympathetic faculty member. As the secretary, Grayson makes a good first impression in one of her early screen appearances. The Hardy series was often used as a training ground for new MGM talent. **101m/B VHS, Beta.** Mickey Rooney, Kathryn Grayson, Lewis Stone, Fay Holden, Ian Hunter, Gene Reynolds, Sara Haden; **D:** George B. Seitz. MGM

Andy Warhol's Bad 🐾🐾🐾 1977 (R) In the John Waters' school of "crime is beauty," a Queens housewife struggles to make appointments for both her home electrolysis clinic and her all-female murder-for-hire operation, which specializes in children and pets (who are thrown out of windows and knived, respectively). Her life is further complicated by a boarder (King) who's awaiting the go-ahead for his own assignment, an autistic child unwanted by his mother. One of Warhol's more professional-appearing films, and very funny if your tastes run to the tasteless. **100m/C VHS, Beta, LV.** Perry King, Carroll Baker, Susan Tyrrell, Stefania Cassini; **D:** Jed Johnson. MLB

Andy Warhol's Dracula 🐾🐾🐾 *Blood for Dracula; Young Dracula* 1974 (R) Sex and camp humor, as well as a large dose of blood, highlight Warhol's treatment of the tale. As Dracula can only subsist on the blood of pure, untouched maidens ("were-gins"), gardener Dallesandro rises to the occasion in order to make as many women as he can ineligible for Drac's purposes. Very reminiscent of Warhol's "Frankenstein," but with a bit more spoofery. Look for Roman Polanski in a cameo peek as a pub patron. **CW:** Horror violence and sexuality. **106m/C VHS, Beta.** IT FR Udo Kier, Arno Juergling, Maxine McKendry, Joe Dallesandro, Vittorio De Sica; **Cameos:** Roman Polanski; **D:** Paul Morrissey; **W:** Paul Morrissey. TRI, GEM

Andy Warhol's Frankenstein 🐾🐾½ *Flesh for Frankenstein* 1974 (R) A most outrageous parody of Frankenstein, featuring plenty of gore, sex, and bad taste in general. Baron von Frankenstein (Kier) derives sexual satisfaction from his corpses (he delivers a particularly thought-provoking philosphy on life as he lustfully fondles a gall bladder); his wife seeks her pleasure from the monster himself (Dallesandro). Originally made in 3-D, this is one of Warhol's campiest outings. **CW:** Language, bizarre violence, and bizarre sexuality. **95m/C VHS, Beta.** GE FR IT Udo Kier, Dalia di Lazzaro, Monique Van Vooren, Joe Dallesandro; **D:** Paul Morrissey; **W:** Paul Morrissey. TRI, MLB

Angel 🐾🐾½ 1937 Melodrama finds Maria Barker (Dietrich) the bored wife of British diplomat Sir Frederick (Marshall). So she heads off to Paris to visit a friend and meets the dashing Anthony Halton (Douglas), with whom she has a fling. Too bad Halton's next stop is jolly old England where he runs into an old military chum (Sir Fred, of course). High gloss but no heart. **91m/B VHS.** Marlene Dietrich, Herbert Marshall, Melvyn Douglas, Edward Everett Horton, Laura Hope Crews; **D:** Ernst Lubitsch; **W:** Guy Bolton, Samson Raphaelson, Russell Medcroft; **C:** Charles B(ryant) Lang; **M:** Friedrich Hollander. USH

Angel 🐾½ 1984 (R) Low-budget leerer about a 15-year-old honor student who attends an expensive Los Angeles private school during the day and by night becomes Angel, a streetwise prostitute making a living amid the slime and sleaze of Hollywood Boulevard. But wait, all is not perfect. A psycho is following her, looking for an opportunity. **94m/C VHS, Beta.** Donna Wilkes, Cliff Gorman, Susan Tyrrell, Dick Shawn, Rory Calhoun, John Diehl, Elaine Giftos, Ross Hagen; **D:** Robert Vincent O'Neil; **W:** Joseph M. Cala. VTR

Angel 3: The Final Chapter woof! 1988 (R) Former hooker Angel hits the streets to save her newly discovered sister from a life of prostitution. Trashy sequel with a better cast to tepid "Avenging Angel," which was the inept 1985 follow-up to 1984's tasteless "Angel." **100m/C VHS, Beta, LV.** Maud Adams, Mitzi Kapture, Richard Roundtree, Mark Blankfield, Kin Shriner, Tawny Fere, Toni Basil; **D:** Tom De Simone; **M:** Eric Allaman. VTR, NWV, IME

Angel and the Badman 🐾🐾🐾 1947 When notorious gunslinger Wayne is wounded during a shoot-out, a pacifist family takes him in and nurses him back to health. While he's recuperating, the daughter in the family (Russell) falls for him. She begs him not to return to his previous life. But Wayne, though smitten, thinks that a Duke's gotta do what a Duke's gotta do. And that means finding the dirty outlaw (Cabot) who killed his pa. Predictable but nicely done, with a good cast and script. Wayne provides one of his better performances (and also produced). **100m/B VHS, LV.** John Wayne, Gail Russell, Irene Rich, Harry Carey Sr., Bruce Cabot; **D:** James Edward Grant; **W:** James Edward Grant; **C:** Archie Stout. REP, CNG, MRV

An Angel at My Table 🐾🐾🐾🐾 1989 (R) New Zealand television mini-series chronicling the life of Janet Frame, New Zealand's premiere writer/poet. At once whimsical and tragic, the film tells of how a mischievious, free-spirited young girl was wrongly placed in a mental institution for eight years, yet was ultimately able to cultivate her incredible storytelling gifts, achieving success, fame and happiness. Adapted from three of Frame's novels: "To the Is-land," "An Angel at My Table," and "The Envoy From Mirror City." Highly acclaimed the world over, winner of over 20 major international awards. **CW:** Language and sensuality. **157m/C VHS.** NZ Kerry Fox, Alexia Keogh, Karen Fergusson, Iris Churn, K.J. Wilson, Martyn Sanderson; **D:** Jane Campion; **W:** Laura Jones; **C:** Stuart Dryburgh. Chicago Film Critics Awards '91: Best Foreign Film; Independent Spirit Awards '92: Best Foreign Film. COL, NLC

Angel Baby 🐾🐾½ 1961 A mute girl struggles to re-define her faith when she is cured by preacher, but then sees him fail with others. Fine performances all around, notably Reynolds in his screen debut, with cinematography by Haskell Wexler. Adapted from "Jenny Angel" by Elsie Oaks Barber. **97m/B VHS.** George Hamilton, Salome Jens, Mercedes McCambridge, Joan Blondell, Henry Jones, Burt Reynolds; **D:** Paul Wendkos, Hubert Cornfield; **C:** Haskell Wexler. NO

Angel Baby 🐾🐾🐾 1995 (R) Psychiatric out patients Kate (McKenzie) and Harry (Lynch) fall in love and move in together despite some misgivings from family and the medical bureaucracy. When Kate becomes pregnant, they decide to stop taking their medication so the baby has a better chance of being born healthy. Kate's doctors believe she's not capable of dealing with a child, although she is equally determined to have her baby, while Harry struggles to make a life for all of them. Strong performances and an assured debut by writer/director Rymer. Film won all 7 of the Australian Film Institute Awards for which it was nominated. **CW:** Strong sexuality and a traumatic childbirth. **101m/C VHS, LV, Closed Caption.** AU John Lynch, Jacqueline McKenzie, Colin Friels, Deborra-Lee Furness, Robyn Nevin; **D:** Michael Rymer; **W:** Michael Rymer; **C:** Ellery Ryan; **M:** John Clifford Ryan. Australian Film Institute '95: Best Actor (Lynch), Best Actress (McKenzie), Best Cinematography, Best Director (Rymer), Best Film, Best Film Editing, Best Original Screenplay. REP

Angel City 🐾🐾½ 1980 A Florida labor camp is the setting for this made-for-TV drama. A family of rural West Virginia migrant workers find themselves trapped inside the camp and exploited by the boss-man. Adapted from Patricia Smith's book. **90m/C VHS.** Ralph Waite, Paul Winfield, Jennifer Warren, Jennifer Jason Leigh, Mitchell Ryan; **D:** Philip Leacock; **W:** James Lee Barrett. XVC

Angel City *🗡🗡* **1984** An experimental parody of film mysteries where a detective investigates the nature of visual truth in and about Hollywood. 75m/C VHS, Beta. Bob Glaudini; **D:** Jon Jost. *FCT*

Angel Dust *🗡🗡* **1996** Nightmare noir about a serial killer who haunts Tokyo's subways. Setsuko (Minami) is a criminal psychologist investigating the murders of several young women, all committed during rush hour at various commuter stops. Each victim has been killed with a poisonous injection. Setsuko learns the first victim was psychologically deprogrammed after leaving a religious cult and contacts her ex-lover, Rei (Wakamatsu), who runs a clinic specializing in such deprogramming. But Rei also becomes the chief suspect when he begins to play sadistic mind games with Setsuko. Is she paranoid or truly in danger? Japanese with subtitles. 116m/C VHS. *JP* Kaho Minami, Takeshi Wakamatsu; **D:** Sogo Ishii; **W:** Sogo Ishii, Yorozu Ikuta; **C:** Norimichi Kasamatsu; **M:** Hiroyuki Nagashima. *NYF*

An Angel for Satan *🗡½* **1966** Steele plays a dual role in her last major, Italian horror film. She gives a strong performance as a woman obsessed by the spirit of a statue. In Italian with no subtitles. ?m/C VHS. *IT* Barbara Steele, Anthony Steffen. *SNC*

Angel Heart *🗡🗡½* **1987 (R)** Exotic, controversial look at murder, voodoo cults, and sex in 1955 New Orleans. Bonet defiantly sheds her image as a young innocent (no more Cosby Show for you, young lady). Rourke is slimy as marginal NYC private eye Angel, hired by the devilish De Niro to track a missing big band singer who violated a "contract." His investigation leads him to the bizarre world of the occult in New Orleans, where the blood drips to a different beat. Visually stimulating, with a provocative sex scene between Bonet and Rourke, captured in both R-rated and unrated versions. Adapted by Parker from "Falling Angel" by William Hjortsberg. 112m/C VHS, Beta, LV. Mickey Rourke, Robert De Niro, Lisa Bonet, Charlotte Rampling, Michael Higgins, Charles Gordone, Kathleen Wilhoite, Stocker Fountelieu, Brownie McGhee; **D:** Alan Parker; **W:** Alan Parker; **M:** Trevor Jones. *LIV, FCT*

Angel in a Taxi *🗡🗡* **1959** A six-year-old boy in an orphanage decides to choose his own mother, a beautiful ballerina he sees in a magazine, when an ugly couple try to adopt him. Italian film dubbed in English. 89m/B VHS, Beta, 8mm. *IT* Wera Cecova, Ettore Manni, Vittorio De Sica, Marietto, Gabriele Ferzetti. *VYY, FCT*

Angel of Death woof! **1986 (R)** A small mercenary band of Nazi hunters attempt to track down Josef Mengele in South America. Stupid entry in the minor "let's find the darn Nazi before he really causes trouble" genre. Director Franco is also known as A. Frank Drew White. 92m/C VHS, Beta. Chris Mitchum, Fernando Rey, Susan Andrews; **D:** Jess (Jesus) Franco. *VTR, NWV*

Angel of Destruction *🗡½* **1994 (R)** Undercover cop is assigned to protect controversial rock star from psycho fan. Cop gets killed and cop's sister decides to go after the killer. **CW:** Language, violence, and sexuality. 80m/C VHS, LV. Maria Ford, Charlie Spradling; **D:** Charles Philip Moore. *NHO*

Angel of Fury *🗡🗡½* **1993 (R)** Rothrock plays the head of security of a computer corporation who must battle terrorists after the company's top-secret computer. And there's no one she can trust. Lots of martial arts action with the competent Rothrock. 91m/C VHS, LV, Closed Caption. Cynthia Rothrock, Christopher Barnes, Peter O'Brien; **D:** Ackyl Anwary. *IMP*

Angel of H.E.A.T. woof! *The Protectors, Book One* **1982 (R)** Porn-star Chambers is Angel, a female super-agent on a mission to save the world from total destruction. Sex and spies abound with trashy nonchalance. 90m/C VHS, Beta, LV. Marilyn Chambers, Mary Woronov, Steve Johnson; **D:** Helen Sanford, Myrl A. Schreibman. *VES*

Angel on My Shoulder *🗡🗡🗡* **1946** A murdered convict makes a deal with the Devil (Rains) and returns to earth for revenge as a respected judge who's been thinning Hell's waiting list. Occupying the good judge, the murderous Muni has significant problems adjusting. Amusing fantasy with Muni in a rare and successful comic role. Co-written by Segall, who scripted "Here Comes Mr. Jordan," in which Rains played an angel. Remade in 1980. 101m/B VHS, Beta. Paul Muni, Claude Rains, Anne Baxter, Onslow Stevens; **D:** Archie Mayo; **W:** Harry Segall. *MRV, NOS, HHT*

Angel on My Shoulder *🗡🗡* **1980** A small-time hood wrongfully executed for murder comes back as district attorney. He owes the devil, but he's finding it tough to be evil enough to repay his debt. Okay television remake of the better 1946 film starring Paul Muni. 96m/C VHS, Beta. Peter Strauss, Richard Kiley, Barbara Hershey, Janis Paige; **D:** John Berry; **M:** Artie Butler.

Angel Square *🗡🗡* **1992** A Canadian production from the director of the acclaimed "Bye Bye Blues." When the father of a neighborhood boy is brutally attacked, the community bands together to search for the culprit. 106m/C VHS. *CA* Ned Beatty; **D:** Anne Wheeler; **W:** James DeFelice. *NO*

Angel Town *🗡* **1989 (R)** A foreign exchange student, who happens to be a champion kick-boxer, is forced into combat with LA street gangs. 90m/C VHS, Beta, LV. Olivier Gruner, Theresa Saldana, Frank Aragon, Tony Valentino, Peter Kwong, Mike Moroff; **D:** Eric Karson. *IMP*

Angel Unchained *🗡½* **1970** Typical biker exploitation flick has bikers and hippies joining together to fend off small-town redneck hostility. 92m/C VHS. Don Stroud, Tyne Daly, Luke Askew, Larry Bishop, Aldo Ray, Bill McKinney; **D:** Lee Madden; **W:** Jeffrey Alladin Fiskin. *ORI*

Angel with the Trumpet *🗡🗡* **1950** Depressing character study of a woman who marries to please her family, rather than herself. When the Gestapo finds out about her Jewish ancestry, she must make the most important decision of her life. 98m/B VHS. *GB* Eileen Herlie, Basil Sydney, Norman Wooland, Maria Schell, Olga Edwards, Oskar Werner, Anthony Bushell, Wilfrid Hyde-White; **D:** Anthony Bushell. *NOS*

Angela *🗡* **1977** Twisted love story about a young man (Railsback) who jumps the bones of an older woman, unaware that she is the mother he's been separated from for 23 long years. Seems that way back when, the boy was kidnapped by crime boss Huston from mom Loren, an ex-prostitute, who then turned in the boy's dad, who was something of a criminal. Mom thought son was dead, dad vowed revenge from prison, and son went about his unwitting business. It all comes together insipidly, at the expense of the cast and viewer. 91m/C VHS, Beta. *CA* Sophia Loren, Steve Railsback, John Huston, John Vernon; **D:** Boris Sagal; **M:** Henry Mancini. *SIM*

Angela *🗡🗡* **1994** Exceedingly mystical film focuses on religiously obsessed 10-year-old Angela (Rhyne), who tells her 6-year-old sister Ellie (Blythe) that unless they are very good the Devil will come to take them away. Meanwhile, she tries to cope with volatile family relationships, including their unstable mother. Good performances in a sometimes sluggish and abstract drama. 105m/C VHS. Miranda Stuart Rhyne, Charlotte Blythe, Anna Thomson, John Ventimiglia, Vincent Gallo; **D:** Rebecca Miller; **W:** Rebecca Miller; **C:** Ellen Kuras; **M:** Michael Rohatyn. Sundance Film Festival '95: Best Cinematography, Filmmakers Trophy. *NYR*

Angele *🗡🗡🗡* **1934** A lovely, naive country girl is lured to the city by a cunning pimp who knows that she wants to escape her oppressive father. With her illegitimate baby, she's discovered in a whorehouse and taken in disgrace back home to dad, who promptly locks her in the barn. One special guy, however, appreciates her purity and plots to rescue her. What he lacks in material resources he makes up for in character. An overlong but moving story of lost innocence and intolerence. In French with English subtitles. Based on the novel "Un de Baumugnes" by Jean Giono. 130m/B VHS. *FR* Orane Demazis, Fernandel, Henri Poupon, Edouard Delmont; **D:** Marcel Pagnol. *INT*

Angelo My Love *🗡🗡🗡* **1983 (R)** Compassionate docudrama about New York's modern gypsy community. Follows the adventures of 12-year-old Angelo Evans, the streetwise son of a fortune teller, who, with a fresh view, explores the ups and downs of his family's life. Duvall financed the effort and cast non-professional actors in this charming tale of reality and fairy-tale. 91m/C VHS, Beta, LV. Angelo Evans, Michael Evans, Steve "Patalay" Tsiginoff, Cathy Kitchen, Millie Tsiginoff; **D:** Robert Duvall; **M:** Michael Kamen. *COL*

Angels and Insects *🗡🗡🗡* **1995 (R)** Very strange Victorian-era romantic drama is definitely an acquired taste. The mysteries of nature are nothing compared to the mysteries of human life as naturalist William Adamson (Rylance) comes to discover when he takes up a position at the home of amateur insect collector, Sir Harald Alabaster (Kemp). He falls in love and quickly marries blondly beautiful Eugenia (Kensit), whose outward propriety hides a sensual nature and some decadent family secrets. Based on A.S. Byatt's novella "Morpho Eugenia." Take particular note of the costumes by Paul Brown, which mimic the exoticness of insects. **CW:** Heavy sexual content, nudity. 116m/C VHS. *GB* Mark Rylance, Patsy Kensit, Kristin Scott Thomas, Jeremy Kemp, Douglas Henshall, Chris Larkin, Annette Badland, Anna Massey, Saskia Wickham; **D:** Philip Haas; **W:** Belinda Haas, Philip Haas; **C:** Bernard Zitzermann; **M:** Alexander Balanescu. Nominations: Academy Awards '96: Best Costume Design. *HMK*

Angel's Brigade *🗡🗡* **1979 (PG)** Seven models get together to stop a big drug operation. Drive-in vigilante movie fare fit for a rainy night. 97m/C VHS, Beta. Jack Palance, Peter Lawford, Jim Backus, Arthur Godfrey; **D:** Greydon Clark; **W:** Greydon Clark; **C:** Dean Cundey. *LIV*

Angels Die Hard *🗡🗡* **1984 (R)** Novel biker story with the cyclists as the good guys intent on helping a town during a mining disaster. Grizzly Adams makes an early film appearance. 86m/C VHS, Beta, LV. Tom Baker, R.G. Armstrong, Dan Haggerty, William Smith; **D:** Richard Compton. *NWV*

Angels from Hell *🗡* **1968** Early application in the nutso 'Nam returnee genre. Disillusioned Vietnam veteran forms a massive biker gang for the sole purpose of wreaking havoc upon the Man, the Establishment and anyone else responsible for sending him off to war. The big gang invades a town, with predictably bloody results. Sort of a follow-up to "Hell's Angels on Wheels." 86m/C VHS. Tom Stern, Arlene Martel, Ted Markland, Stephen Oliver, Paul Bertoya, James Murphy, Jack Starrett, Pepper Martin, Luana Talltree; **D:** Bruce Kessler. *NO*

Angels Hard as They Come *🗡🗡* **1971 (R)** Opposing Hell's Angels leaders clash in a hippie-populated ghost town. A semi-satiric spoof of the biker genre's cliches features an early Glenn appearance and Busey's film debut. 86m/C VHS, Beta. Gary Busey, Scott Glenn, James Iglehart, Gary Littlejohn, Sharon Peckinpah; **D:** Joe Viola; **W:** Jonathan Demme.

Angels in the Outfield *🗡🗡🗡* **1951** Enjoyable comedy fantasy about the lowly Pittsburgh Pirates who get a little celestial help in their race for the pennant. Great performances all around, especially Douglas as the gruff manager of the losing baseball team. Based on a story by Richard Conlin. 102m/C VHS. Paul Douglas, Janet Leigh, Keenan Wynn, Donna Corcoran, Lewis Stone, Spring Byington, Bruce (Herman Brix) Bennett, Marvin Kaplan, Ellen Corby, Jeff Richards; **D:** Clarence Brown; **W:** Dorothy Kingsley, George Wells; **C:** Paul Vogel. *MGM*

Angels in the Outfield 🎬🎬½ 1994 (PG)
Remake of the 1951 fantasy about a lowly baseball team who, along with some heavenly animated help find themselves on a winning streak. The new lineup includes Glover as manager of the hapless California Angels, Danza as a washed-up pitcher, and Lloyd as captain of the celestial spirits. Gordon-Levitt plays the foster child who believes he'll get his family back together if the Angels win the pennant. Familar ground still yields good, heartfelt family fare. Oakland A's third baseman Carney Lansford served as technical advisor, molding actors into fair semblance of baseball team. 105m/C VHS, Closed Caption. Danny Glover, Tony Danza, Christopher Lloyd, Brenda Fricker, Ben Johnson, Joseph Gordon-Levitt, Jay O. Sanders; **D:** William Dear; **W:** Holly Goldberg Sloan. *DIS*

Angels of the City 🎬🎬 1989 What's a
girl got to do to join a sorority? A house prank turns vicious when two coeds take a walk on the wild side and accidentally observe a murder, making them the next targets. Credible exploitation effort, if that's not an oxymoron. 90m/C VHS, Beta. Lawrence-Hilton Jacobs, Cynthia Cheston, Kelly Galindo, Sandy Gershman; **D:** Lawrence-Hilton Jacobs; **W:** Lawrence-Hilton Jacobs, Raymond Martino, Joseph Merhi. *PMH*

Angels One Five 🎬🎬 1954 A worm's-
eye view of British air power in WWII. What little "excitement" there is, is generated by flashing lights, plotting maps and status boards. Hawkins and Denison are the only bright spots. 97m/B VHS. Jack Hawkins, Michael Denison, Dulcie Gray, John Gregson, Cyril Raymond, Veronica Hurst, Geoffrey Keen, Vida Hope. *NOS*

Angels Over Broadway 🎬🎬🎬 1940
Slick, fast-paced black comedy about con man Fairbanks, who plans to hustle suicidal thief Qualen during a poker game, but has a change of heart. With the help of call-girl Hayworth and drunken playwright Mitchell, he helps Qualen turn his life around. Ahead of its time with an offbeat morality, but a delight in the '90s. 80m/B VHS, LV. Douglas Fairbanks Jr., Rita Hayworth, Thomas Mitchell, John Qualen, George Watts; **D:** Ben Hecht, Lee Garmes; **C:** Lee Garmes. Nominations: Academy Awards '40: Best Original Screenplay. *FCT, COL*

Angels' Wild Women woof! 1972 From
the man who brought you "Dracula vs. Frankenstein" comes an amalgamation of hippies, motorcycle dudes, evil desert gurus and precious little plot. 85m/C VHS. Kent Taylor, Regina Carrol, Ross Hagen, Maggie Bemby, Vicki Volante; **D:** Al Adamson. *NO*

Angels with Dirty Faces 🎬🎬🎬🎬
1938 Rousing classic with memorable Cagney twitches and the famous long walk from the cell to the chair. Two young hoods grow up on NYC's lower East Side with diverse results—one enters the priesthood and the other opts for crime and prison. Upon release from the pen, famed gangster Cagney sets up shop in the old neighborhood, where Father O'Brien tries to keep a group of young toughs (the Dead End Kids) from following in his footsteps. Bogart's his unscrupulous lawyer and Bancroft a crime boss intent on double-crossing Cagney. Reportedly they were blasting real bullets during the big shootout, no doubt helping Cagney's intensity. Adapted from a story by Rowland Brown. 97m/B VHS, Beta, LV. James Cagney, Pat O'Brien, Humphrey Bogart, Ann Sheridan, George Bancroft, Billy Halop, Leo Gorcey, Huntz Hall, Bobby Jordan, Dan Jesse, Gabriel Dell, J. Frank Burke, William Tracy, Bernard Punsley; **D:** Michael Curtiz; **W:** John Wexley, Warren Duff; **M:** Max Steiner. New York Film Critics Awards '38: Best Actor (Cagney); Nominations: Academy Awards '38: Best Actor (Cagney), Best Director (Curtiz), Best Story. *MGM, FOX, MLB*

Angie 🎬🎬 1994 (R) Brassy Angie finds herself pregnant and unmarried. Tired of the advice and criticism she receives from her close knit neighborhood she strikes out of Brooklyn to find a new life for herself. Average "woman's movie" wrought with messages of pregnancy, childbirth, friendship, love, and family has far too much going on and relies too heavily on formula soap. Davis, in what could have been a juicy (read "Oscar") role is strong, but her performance is drowned by all the melodrama. Madonna was originally cast as Angie, but was bounced when the filming of "Snake Eyes" conflicted. Adapted from the book "Angie, I Says" by Avra Wing. **CW:** Language. 108m/C VHS, LV, Closed Caption. Geena Davis, Aida Turturro, Stephen Rea, Philip Bosco, James Gandolfini, Jenny O'Hara; **D:** Martha Coolidge; **W:** Todd Graff. *HPH*

AngKor: Cambodia Express 🎬 1981
An American journalist travels back to Vietnam to search for his long lost love. 96m/C VHS, Beta. Robert Walker Jr., Christopher George; **D:** Lek Kitiparaporn. *VES, LIV*

Angry Harvest 🎬🎬🎬 Bittere Ernte 1985
During the WWII German occupation of Poland, a gentile farmer shelters a young Jewish woman on the run, and a serious, ultimately interdependent relationship forms. Acclaimed; Holland's first film since her native Poland's martial law imposition made her an exile to Sweden. In German with English subtitles. Contains nudity and violence. 102m/C VHS, Beta. Armin Mueller-Stahl, Elisabeth Trissenaar, Wojciech Pszoniak, Margit Carstensen, Kurt Raab, Kathe Jaenicke, Hans Beerhenke, Isa Haller; **D:** Agnieszka Holland; **W:** Agnieszka Holland. Montreal World Film Festival '85: Best Actor (Mueller-Stahl); Nominations: Academy Awards '85: Best Foreign Language Film. *CTL, FCT, TPV*

Angry Joe Bass 🎬 1976 Contemporary
Native American Joe Bass faces government officials who continually usurp his fishing rights. Something like "Billy Jack" without the intelligence. 82m/C VHS, Beta. Henry Bal, Molly Mershon; **D:** Thomas G. Reeves. *NO*

The Angry Red Planet 🎬🎬 1959 An
unintentionally amusing sci-fi adventure about astronauts on Mars fighting off aliens and giant, ship-swallowing amoebas. Filmed using bizarre "Cinemagic" process, which turns almost everything pink. Wild effects have earned the film cult status. 83m/C VHS, Beta. Gerald Mohr, Les Tremayne, Jack Kruschen; **D:** Ib Melchior. *NO*

Anguish 🎬🎬½ 1988 (R) Well-done horror
thriller about a lunatic who, inspired to duplicate the actions of an eyeball-obsessed killer in a popular film, murders a movie audience as they watch the movie. Violence and gore abound. 85m/C VHS, Beta, LV, Closed Caption. SP Zelda Rubinstein, Michael Lerner, Talia Paul, Clara Pastor; **D:** Bigas Luna; **W:** Bigas Luna; **M:** J.M. Pagan. *FOX*

Angus 🎬🎬 1995 (PG-13) Dull teen comedy
about self-esteem revolves around the overweight Angus (Talbert), a friendly kid tormented by the usual school bullies. His best bud is twerp Troy (Owen), who tries to help Angus out with his crush on cute blonde Melissa (Ariana). There's even a schmaltzy prom scene. The profanity, though mild, and the boys sexual interests make this questionable for the pre-teen audience that could actually enjoy it. **CW:** Some coarse adolescent language. 87m/C VHS. Charlie Talbert, Kathy Bates, George C. Scott, Chris Owen, Ariana Richards, Lawrence Pressman, Rita Moreno, James Van Der Beek, Anna Thompson; **D:** Patrick Read Johnson; **W:** Jill Gordon; **C:** Alexander Grusynski; **M:** David E. Russo. *TTC*

Animal Behavior 🎬 1989 (PG) An animal
researcher and a music professor fall in love on a college campus. Bowen's (she actually released it under the alias Riley H. Anne) comedy was filmed in 1985 and edited/shelved for over 4 years, with good reason. 79m/C VHS, Beta, LV. Karen Allen, Armand Assante, Holly Hunter, Josh Mostel, Richard Libertini; **D:** Jenny Bowen; **W:** Susan Rice; **C:** Richard Bowen; **M:** Cliff Eidelman. *HBO*

Animal Called Man 🎬 1987 Two
crooked buddies join a big western gang in pillaging a small town and get in too deep. 83m/C VHS, Beta. Vassilli Karis, Craig Hill. *TWE*

Animal Crackers 🎬🎬🎬½ 1930 (G) The
second and possibly the funniest of the thirteen Marx Brothers films, "Animal Crackers" is a screen classic. Groucho is a guest at the house of wealthy matron Margaret Dumont and he, along with Zeppo, Chico, and Harpo, destroy the tranquility of the estate. Complete with the Harry Ruby music score—including Groucho's "Hooray for Captain Spaulding" with more quotable lines than any other Marx Brothers film: "One morning I shot an elephant in my pajamas. How he got into my pajamas, I'll never know." Based on a play by George S. Kaufman. 98m/B VHS, Beta, LV. Groucho Marx, Chico Marx, Harpo Marx, Zeppo Marx, Lillian Roth, Margaret Dumont, Louis Sorin, Hal Thompson, Robert Greig; **D:** Victor Heerman; **W:** Morrie Ryskind. *USH, FCT*

Animal Farm 🎬🎬🎬 1955 An animated
version of George Orwell's classic political satire about a barnyard full of animals who parallel the growth of totalitarian dictatorships. Not entirely successful, but probably best translation of Orwell to film. 73m/C VHS, Beta, LV, 8mm. **D:** John Halas, Joy Batchelor; **V:** Maurice Denham, Gordon Heath. *VYY, KUI, VTR*

Animal Instincts 🎬🎬 1992 (R) A woman
takes a prescription drug that makes her a nymphomaniac, and her police officer husband discovers that he's turned on by videotaping her in bed with other men and women. One of the many in her constant stream of lovers is a politician whose campaign is based on shutting down all the town's sex clubs. Another in the string of sexual thrillers riding on the coattails of "Basic Instinct." **CW:** Strong language and strong sexuality. 94m/C VHS, Closed Caption. Maxwell Caulfield, Jan-Michael Vincent, Mitch Gaylord, Shannon Whirry, Delia Sheppard, John Saxon, David Carradine; **D:** Alexander Gregory Hippolyte. *ACA*

Animal Instincts 2 🎬🎬 1994 (R) Joanna
leaves her overbearing husband and moves into a supposedly quiet community. Neighbor Steve is a security expert—and a voyeur. He's hidden a camera in Joanna's bedroom but she knows he's watching. **CW:** Language, nudity, and sexual situations. 92m/C VHS, Beta, LV, Closed Caption. Shannon Whirry, Woody Brown, Elizabeth Sandifer, Al Sapienza; **D:** Alexander Gregory Hippolyte. *ACA*

Animal Instincts 3: The
Seductress 🎬½ 1995 (R) Woman finds a new kind of sexual excitement when she gets involved with a blind rock music promoter. The unrated version contains 12 more minutes of footage. **CW:** Strong sexuality, and for language and some violence. 92m/C VHS. Wendy Schumacher, James Matthew; **D:** Alexander Gregory Hippolyte. *APX*

The Animal Kingdom 🎬🎬🎬 The Woman in His House 1932 A romantic triangle develops when Howard, married to Loy, has an affair with Harding. The problem is Harding acts more like a wife and Loy a mistress. Intelligently written and directed, with a marvelous performance from veteran character actor Gargan. 95m/B VHS. Ann Harding, Leslie Howard, Myrna Loy, Neil Hamilton, William Gargan, Henry Stephenson, Ilka Chase; **D:** Edward H. Griffith; **W:** Horace Jackson. *FCT, HEG*

Anita, Dances of Vice 🎬🎬 Anita-
Tanze des Lasters 1987 German avant-garde film celebrates Anita Berber, the "most scandalous woman in 1920s Berlin." Berber was openly bisexual, used drugs, and danced nude in public. In von Praunheim's film, she rises from the dead and creates yet more scandal. 85m/C VHS, Beta. GE Lotti Huber, Ina Blum, Mikhael Honesseau; **D:** Rosa von Praunheim. *FRF, GLV, TPV*

The Ann Jillian Story 🎬½ 1988 Jillian
stars as herself in this television melodrama recounting her battle with breast cancer. Several musical numbers are included. 96m/C VHS, Beta. Ann Jillian, Tony LoBianco, Viveca Lindfors, Leighton Bewley; **D:** Corey Allen. *NO*

Ann Vickers ✓✓½ 1933 A dashing young army captain wins over the heart of a dedicated social worker. Okay adaptation of a Sinclair Lewis novel, with Dunne suffering more than usual. **76m/ B VHS, Beta.** Irene Dunne, Walter Huston, Bruce Cabot, Conrad Nagel, Edna May Oliver; **D:** John Cromwell; **M:** Max Steiner. *TTC*

Anna ✓✓ 1951 Novitiate nun Anna (Mangano) is forced to confront her sordid past (as a nightclub entertainer), and her love for two very different men, when her seriously injured former fiancee is brought to the hospital where she is a nurse. Anna must finally deal with her feelings and decide which path her life will take. Dubbed in English. **111m/B VHS.** *IT* Silvana Mangano, Raf Vallone, Vittorio Gassman; **D:** Alberto Lattuada; **C:** Otello Martelli; **M:** Nino Rota. *FCT*

Anna ✓✓✓ 1987 (PG-13) Age, envy, and the theatrical world receive their due in an uneven but engrossing drama about aging Czech film star Anna, making a sad living in New York doing commercials and trying for off-Broadway roles. She takes in Krystyna, a young Czech peasant girl who eventually rockets to model stardom. Modern, strongly acted "All About Eve" with a story partially based on a real Polish actress. Kirkland drew quite a bit of flak for shamelessly self-promoting for the Oscar. She still lost. **101m/C VHS, Beta, LV, Closed Caption.** Sally Kirkland, Paulina Porizkova, Robert Fields, Stefan Schnabel, Larry Pine, Ruth Maleczech; **D:** Yurek Bogayevicz; **W:** Yurek Bogayevicz, Agnieszka Holland; **C:** Bobby Bukowski; **M:** Greg Hawkes. Golden Globe Awards '88: Best Actress—Drama (Kirkland); Independent Spirit Awards '88: Best Actress (Kirkland); Los Angeles Film Critics Association Awards '87: Best Actress (Kirkland); Nominations: Academy Awards '87: Best Actress (Kirkland). *VES, LIV*

Anna and the King of Siam ✓✓✓½ 1946 Splendid adaptation, from the book by Margaret Landon, about the true life adventures of 33-year-old English widow Anna Leonowens. In 1862 Anna and her son travelled to the exotic kingdom of Siam to educate the harem and children of the king. Dunne is splendid as the strong-willed governess as is Harrison (in his first American film) as the authoritarian eastern ruler. Remade as the musical "The King and I." **128m/B VHS.** Irene Dunne, Rex Harrison, Linda Darnell, Lee J. Cobb, Gale Sondergaard, Mikhail Rasumny, Dennis Hoey, Richard Lyon, John Abbott; **D:** John Cromwell; **W:** Sally Benson, Talbot Jennings; **C:** Arthur C. Miller; **M:** Bernard Herrmann. Academy Awards '46: Best Art Direction/Set Decoration (B & W), Best Black and White Cinematography; Nominations: Academy Awards '46: Best Screenplay, Best Supporting Actress (Sondergaard), Original Dramatic/Comedy Score. *FXV*

Anna Christie ✓✓✓½ 1923 Silent production of Eugene O'Neill's play that even he liked. A young girl is sent away by her father, a seaman, and finds her way to Chicago, where she becomes a prostitute. Later she visits her father's barge and falls for a sailor. She shares her past life story, hoping they will understand. This film was acclaimed when it was released, and still remains a touching work of art. Remade in 1930. **75m/B VHS, Beta.** Blanche Sweet, George F. Marion Sr., William Russell, Eugenie Besserer, Chester Conklin, George Siegmann, Victor Potel, Fred Kohler Sr.; **D:** John Wray. *GPV, FCT*

Anna Christie ✓✓½ 1930 Garbo is the ex-prostitute who finds love with sailor Bickford. Bickford is unaware of his lover's tarnished past and she does her best to keep it that way. Garbo's first sound effort was advertised with the slogan "Garbo Talks." Adapted from the classic Eugene O'Neill play, the film is a slow but rewarding romantic drama. **90m/B VHS, Beta.** Greta Garbo, Marie Dressler, Charles Bickford, George F. Marion Sr.; **D:** Clarence Brown; **C:** William H. Daniels. Nominations: Academy Awards '30: Best Actress (Garbo), Best Cinematography, Best Director (Brown).*MGM*

Anna Karenina ✓✓✓½ 1935 Cinematic Tolstoy with Garbo as the sad, moody Anna willing to give up everything to be near Vronsky (March), the cavalry officer she's obsessed with. A classic Garbo vehicle with March and Rathbone providing excellent support. Interestingly, a remake of the Garbo and John Gilbert silent, "Love." **85m/B VHS, Beta.** Greta Garbo, Fredric March, Freddie Bartholomew, Maureen O'Sullivan, May Robson, Basil Rathbone, Reginald Owen, Reginald Denny; **D:** Clarence Brown; **C:** William H. Daniels. New York Film Critics Awards '35: Best Actress (Garbo). *NOS, MGM, HEG*

Anna Karenina ✓✓½ 1948 Stiff version of Tolstoy's passionate story of illicit love between a married woman and a military officer. In spite of exquisite costumes, and Leigh and Richardson as leads, still tedious. **123m/C VHS, LV.** *GB* Vivien Leigh, Ralph Richardson, Kieron Moore; **D:** Julien Duvivier. *MON, FCT, MRV*

Anna Karenina ✓✓½ 1985 (PG) Made for television version of Tolstoy's novel of betrayal, intrigue, and forbidden love. Anna, defying all social practices of the time, falls into the arms of a dashing count. Features an excellent performance from Paul "A Man For All Seasons" Scofield. **96m/C VHS, Beta, LV.** Jacqueline Bisset, Christopher Reeve, Paul Scofield, Ian Ogilvy, Anna Massey, Judi Bowker; **D:** Simon Langton. *VES*

Anna to the Infinite Power ✓✓½ 1984 Sci fi based on the book of the same name follows a young girl with telepathic powers. When the girl discovers that she has sisters as the result of a strange scientific experiment, she sets out to find them, drawing on her own inner strength. **101m/C VHS, Beta.** Dina Merrill, Martha Byrne, Mark Patton; **D:** Robert Wiemer. *COL*

Annabel Takes a Tour/Maid's Night Out 1938 A delightful comedy double feature. In "Annabel Takes a Tour," a fading movie star falls in love with a writer while on a tour to boost her career, and in "Maids Night Out," an heiress and a millionaire fall in love. **131m/B VHS, Beta.** Lucille Ball, Jack Oakie, Ruth Donnelly, Joan Fontaine, Allan "Rocky" Lane, Hedda Hopper, Alice White; **D:** Lew (Louis Friedlander) Landers. *MLB, TTC*

Annapolis ✓ 1928 Life's in the pink for two guys at the U.S. naval academy until jealousy rears its loathsome head when they fall for the same gal. Just when it's beginning to look like love and honor is an either-or proposition, the lovelorn rivals find that although love transcends all, a guy's gotta do what a guy's gotta do, even if it means sticking up for his romantic nemesis. Lots of sub-par male bonding. **63m/B VHS, Beta.** Johnny Mack Brown, Hugh Allan, Hobart Bosworth, William "Billy" Bakewell, Charlotte Walker, Jeanette Loff; **D:** Christy Cabanne. *GPV, FCT*

The Annapolis Story ✓½ *Blue and the Gold* 1955 Cliche-ridden WWII drama about two naval cadets romancing the same lucky girl. Low-rent time for director Siegel which wastes a decent cast. **81m/C VHS, Beta.** John Derek, Kevin McCarthy, Diana Lynn, Pat Dooley, L.Q. Jones; **D:** Donald Siegel. *FOX*

Anne of Avonlea ✓✓✓½ *Anne of Green Gables: The Sequel* 1987 Equally excellent mini-series sequel to "Anne of Green Gables" in which the romantic heroine grows up and discovers romance. The same cast returns and Sullivan continues his tradition of lavish filming on Prince Edward Island and beautiful costumes. Based on the characters from L.M. Montgomery's classic novels "Anne of Avonlea," "Anne of the Island," and "Anne of Windy Poplars." CBC, PBS, and Disney worked together on this WonderWorks production. On two tapes. **224m/C VHS, LV, Closed Caption.** *CA* Megan Follows, Colleen Dewhurst, Wendy Hiller, Frank Converse, Patricia Hamilton, Schuyler Grant, Jonathan Crombie, Rosemary Dunsmore; **D:** Kevin Sullivan; **W:** Kevin Sullivan; **M:** Hagood Hardy. *KUI, TOU, DIS*

Anne of Green Gables ✓✓✓ 1934 A lonely Canadian couple adopts an orphan who keeps them on their toes with her animated imagination, and wins a permanent place in their hearts. Warm (but loose) adaptation of Lucy Maud Montgomery's popular novel is entertaining although 1985 remake is far superior. Followed by "Anne of Windy Poplars." **79m/B VHS, Beta.** Anne Shirley, Tom Brown, O.P. Heggie; **D:** George Nicholls Jr.; **M:** Max Steiner. *TTC*

Anne of Green Gables ✓✓✓½ 1985 Splendid production of the famous Lucy Maud Montgomery classic about a young orphan girl growing to young adulthood with the help of a crusty brother and sister duo. The characters come to life under Sullivan's direction, and the movie is enhanced by the beautiful Prince Edward Island scenery and wonderful costumes. One of the few instances where an adaptation lives up to (if not exceeds) the quality of the original novel. A WonderWorks presentation that was made with the cooperation of the Disney channel, CBC, and PBS. Followed by "Anne of Avonlea." On two tapes. **197m/C VHS, Beta, LV, Closed Caption.** *CA* Megan Follows, Colleen Dewhurst, Richard Farnsworth, Patricia Hamilton, Schuyler Grant, Jonathan Crombie, Marilyn Lightstone, Charmion King, Rosemary Radcliffe, Jackie Burroughs, Robert Collins, Joachim Hansen, Cedric Smith, Paul Brown, Miranda de Pencier, Jennifer Inch, Wendy Lyon, Christiane Krueger, Trish Nettleton, Morgan Chapman; **D:** Kevin Sullivan; **W:** Kevin Sullivan, Joe Weisenfeld; **C:** Rene Ohashi; **M:** Hagood Hardy. *KUI, TOU, IGP*

Anne of the Thousand Days ✓✓✓½ 1969 (PG) Lavish re-telling of the life and loves of Henry the VIII. Henry tosses aside his current wife for the young and devastatingly beautiful Anne Boleyn. Burton's performance of the amoral king garnered him an Oscar nomination. Watch for Elizabeth Taylor as a masked courtesan at the costume ball. **145m/C VHS.** Richard Burton, Genevieve Bujold, Irene Papas, Anthony Quayle, John Colicos, Michael Hordern; **D:** Charles Jarrott; **M:** Georges Delerue. Academy Awards '69: Best Costume Design; Directors Guild of America Awards '70: Best Director (Jarrott); Golden Globe Awards '70: Best Actress—Drama (Bujold), Best Director (Jarrott), Best Film—Drama, Best Screenplay; Nominations: Academy Awards '69: Best Actor (Burton), Best Actress (Bujold), Best Adapted Screenplay, Best Art Direction/Set Decoration, Best Cinematography, Best Picture, Best Sound, Best Supporting Actor (Quayle), Best Original Score. *USH*

Annie ✓✓ 1982 (PG) Stagy big-budget adaption of the Broadway musical, which was an adaptation of the comic strip. A major financial disaster upon release, still it's an entertaining enterprise curiously directed by Huston and engagingly acted by Finney and Quinn. ♫ Tomorrow; It's the Hard Knock Life; Maybe; I Think I'm Gonna Like It Here; Little Girls; We Got Annie; Let's Go to the Movies; You're Never Fully Dressed Without a Smile; Easy Street. **128m/C VHS, Beta, LV, 8mm, Closed Caption.** Aileen Quinn, Carol Burnett, Albert Finney, Bernadette Peters, Ann Reinking, Tim Curry; **D:** John Huston; **W:** Thomas Meehan; **M:** Ralph Burns. Golden Raspberry Awards '82: Worst Supporting Actress (Quinn); Nominations: Academy Awards '82: Best Art Direction/Set Decoration, Original Song Score and/or Adaptation. *COL, FCT, MLT*

Annie: A Royal Adventure ✓✓½ 1995 TV sequel to "Annie" finds the red-haired heroine (Johnson) traveling to England with her Daddy Warbucks (Hearn), who's about to be knighted in London. But the evil Lady Edwina Hogbottom (played to a high-camp hilt by Collins) has a plan to blow up Buckingham Palace and take over as queen. Naturally, it's up to Annie to defeat her and have a happy ending. **92m/C VHS.** Ashley Johnson, George Hearn, Joan Collins, Emily Ann Lloyd, Camilla Bell, Ian McDiarmid. *COL*

Annie Hall ✓✓✓✓ 1977 (PG) Acclaimed coming-of-cinematic-age film for Allen is based in part on his own life. His love affair with Hall/Keaton is chronicled as an episodic, wistful comedy commenting on family, love, loneliness, communicating, maturity, driving, city life, careers, and various other topics. Abounds with classic scenes, including future star Goldblum and his mantra at a cocktail party; Allen and the lobster pot; and Allen, Keaton, a bathroom, a tennis racket, and a spider. The film operates on many levels, as does Keaton's wardrobe, which started a major fashion trend. Don't blink or you'll miss several future stars in bit parts. Expertly shot by Gordon Willis. **94m/C VHS, Beta, LV.** Woody Allen, Diane Keaton, Tony Roberts, Paul Simon, Shelley Duvall, Carol Kane, Colleen Dewhurst, Christopher Walken, Janet Margolin, John Glover, Jeff Goldblum, Sigourney Weaver, Marshall McLuhan, Beverly D'Angelo, Shelley Hack; **D:** Woody Allen; **W:** Woody Allen, Marshall Brickman; **C:** Gordon Willis. Academy Awards '77: Best Actress (Keaton), Best Director (Allen), Best Original Screenplay, Best Picture; British Academy Awards '77: Best Actress (Keaton), Best Director (Allen), Best Film, Best Screenplay; Directors Guild of America Awards '77: Best Director (Allen); Golden Globe Awards '78: Best Actress—Musical/Comedy (Keaton); Los Angeles Film Critics Association Awards '77: Best Screenplay; National Board of Review Awards '77: 10 Best Films of the Year, Best Supporting Actress (Keaton); New York Film Critics Awards '77: Best Actress (Keaton), Best Director (Allen), Best Film, Best Screenplay; National Society of Film Critics Awards '77: Best Actress (Keaton), Best Film, Best Screenplay; Writers Guild of America '77: Best Original Screenplay; Nominations: Academy Awards '77: Best Actor (Allen). *MGM, FOX, CRC*

Annie O ✶✶½ 1995 (PG) 15-year-old girl runs into problems when she joins the boys' basketball team. Her teammates are jealous and so are her brother and boyfriend. **93m/C VHS, Closed Caption.** Coco Yares, Chad Willet, Robert Stewart; **D:** Michael McClary. *HMK*

Annie Oakley ✶✶✶ 1935 Energetic biographical drama based on the life and legend of sharpshooter Annie Oakley and her on-off relationship with Wild Bill Hickok. Stanwyck makes a great Oakley. Later musicalized as "Annie Get Your Gun." **90m/B VHS, Beta.** Barbara Stanwyck, Preston Foster, Melvyn Douglas, Pert Kelton, Andy Clyde; **D:** George Stevens. *MED, NOS, TTC*

Annie Oakley 1985 This biography of the acclaimed shooting star covers her career from age 15 to retirement, including some actual silent footage of Miss Oakley filmed by Thomas Edison in 1923. Made for television. From the "Tall Tales & Legends" series by Shelley Duvall. **52m/C VHS, Beta, Closed Caption.** Jamie Lee Curtis, Cliff DeYoung, Brian Dennehy; **D:** Michael Lindsay-Hogg. *FOX*

The Annihilators woof! 1985 (R) A group of Vietnam vets band together in an extremely violent manner to protect their small town from a gang of thugs. **87m/C VHS, Beta.** Gerrit Graham, Lawrence-Hilton Jacobs, Paul Koslo, Christopher Stone, Andy Wood, Sid Conrad, Dennis Redfield; **D:** Charles E. Sellier. *NWV, VTR*

The Anniversary ✶✶ 1968 One-eyed monster mom Mrs. Taggart (Bette at her baddest) gives new meaning to the word "possessive." Thoroughly cowing her three grown sons, she manages to get them to come home each year on the wedding anniversary to the husband she despised. Only this time, the trio tell her they're going to live their own lives. Hah—not if mom has anything to do with it. Based on the play by Bill MacIlwraith. **93m/C VHS.** *GB* Bette Davis, Jack Hedley, James Cossins, Christian Roberts, Sheila Hancock, Elaine Taylor; **D:** Roy Ward Baker; **W:** Jimmy Sangster; **C:** Henry Waxman; **M:** Philip Martell. *FXV*

Another Chance ✶✶ 1988 (R) Girl-crazy bachelor is returned from heaven for a second chance and has to choose between a "bad" girl and a "good" girl. What a choice! **99m/C VHS, LV.** Bruce Greenwood, Frank Annese, Jeff East, Anne Ramsey, Barbara Edwards; **D:** Jerry Vint. *REP*

Another Country ✶✶½ 1984 Julian Mitchell's adaptation of his play about the true story of two English boarding school friends who wind up as spies for the Soviet Union. Based on

the lives of Guy Burgess and Donald MacLean, whose youth is rather fancifully depicted in this loving recreation of 1930s English life. Although the film is inferior to the award-winning play, director Kanievska manages to transform a piece into a solid film, and Everett's performance as Burgess is outstanding. **90m/C VHS, Beta, LV.** *GB* Rupert Everett, Colin Firth, Michael Jenn, Robert Addie, Anna Massey, Betsy Brantley, Rupert Wainwright, Cary Elwes, Arthur Howard, Tristan Oliver, Frederick Alexander, Adrian Ross-Magenty, Geoffrey Bateman, Philip Dupuy, Jeffrey Wickham, Gideon Boulting, Ivor Howard, Charles Spencer; **D:** Marek Kanievska; **W:** Julian Mitchell; **C:** Peter Biziou; **M:** Michael Storey.

Another 48 Hrs. ✶½ 1990 (R) Continuing chemistry between Nolte and Murphy is one of the few worthwhile items in this stodgy rehash. Any innovation by Murphy seems lost, the story is redundant of any other cop thriller, and violence and car chases abound. Pointlessly energetic and occasionally fun for only the true devotee. **98m/C VHS, Beta, LV, 8mm, Closed Caption.** Eddie Murphy, Nick Nolte, Brion James, Kevin Tighe, Bernie Casey, David Anthony Marshall, Ed O'Ross; **D:** Walter Hill; **W:** Jeb Stuart; **M:** James Horner. *PAR*

Another Man, Another Chance ✶✶ *Un Autre Homme, Une Autre Chance* 1977 (PG) Remake of Lelouch's "A Man and a Woman," set in the turn-of-the-century American West, pales by comparison to the original. Slow-moving tale casts widow Bujold and widower Caan as lovers. **132m/C VHS, Beta.** *FR* James Caan, Genevieve Bujold, Francis Huster, Jennifer Warren, Susan Tyrrell; **D:** Claude Lelouch; **W:** Claude Lelouch. *NO*

Another Pair of Aces: Three of a Kind ✶✶✶ 1991 Nelson and Kristofferson team up to clear the name of Torn, a Texas Ranger accused of murder. Made for television; some scenes deemed too racy for TV were added to the video version. Sequel to "A Pair of Aces." **93m/C VHS.** Willie Nelson, Kris Kristofferson, Joan Severance, Rip Torn, Dan Kamin, Ken Farmer; **D:** Bill Bixby. *THV*

Another Stakeout ✶✶½ *Stakeout 2* 1993 (PG-13) Sequel six years after the original finds Dreyfuss and Estevez partnered again for another stakeout, this time to keep an eye on Moriarty, a reluctant witness against the Mob. The two spying detectives find themselves in an upscale neighborhood where blending in is a hard thing to do. O'Donnell is a breath of fresh air as a wisecracking assistant district attorney. Stowe briefly reprises her role as Dreyfuss' girlfriend. Writer Kouf reportedly had difficulty penning the script, surprising since there isn't much new here.**CW:** Comic action violence. **109m/C VHS, LV, Closed Caption.** Richard Dreyfuss, Emilio Estevez, Rosie O'Donnell, Cathy Moriarty, Madeleine Stowe, John Rubinstein, Marcia Strassman, Dennis Farina, Miguel Ferrer; **D:** John Badham; **W:** Jim Kouf; **C:** Roy Wagner. *TOU*

Another Thin Man ✶✶½ 1939 Powell and Loy team up for the third in the delightful "Thin Man" series. Slightly weaker series entry takes its time, but has both Powell and Loy providing stylish performances. Nick Jr. is also introduced as the newest member of the sleuthing team. Sequel to "After the Thin Man;" followed by "Shadow of the Thin Man." **105m/B VHS, Closed Caption.** William Powell, Myrna Loy, Virginia Grey, Otto Kruger, Sir C. Aubrey Smith, Ruth Hussey; **D:** Woodbridge S. Van Dyke. *MGM*

Another Time, Another Place ✶✶ 1958 Sappy melodrama about an American journalist who suffers an emotional meltdown when her married British lover is killed during WWII. So she heads for Cornwall to console the widow and family. **98m/B VHS, Beta.** *GB* Lana Turner, Barry Sullivan, Glynis Johns, Sean Connery, Terence Longdon; **D:** Lewis Allen; **C:** Jack Hildyard. *BAR, PAR*

Another Time, Another Place ✶✶✶ 1983 (R) Bored young Scottish housewife married to an older fella falls in love with an Italian prisoner-of-war who works on her farm during WWII. Occasionally quirky, always finely crafted view of

wartime Britain and the little-known life of POWs in England. **101m/C VHS, Beta, LV, Closed Caption.** *GB* Phyllis Logan, Giovanni Mauriello, Gian Luca Favilla, Paul Young, Tom Watson; **D:** Michael Radford; **C:** Roger Deakins.

Another Way ✶✶✶ *Olelkezo Tekintetek* 1982 The director of 1971's much-lauded "Love" sets this politically charged love story in Hungary in 1958. Opening with a view of a female corpse, the story flashes backward to look at the woman's journalistic career and her relationship with a women colleague. Candid love scenes between women in Hungary of 1958, considered a cinematic novelty in many places outside Hungary. In Hungarian with English subtitles. **100m/C VHS, Beta.** *HU* Jadwiga Jankowska Cieslak, Grazyna Szapolowska, Josef Kroner, Hernadi Judit, Andorai Peter; **D:** Karoly Makk. Cannes Film Festival '82: Best Actress (Cieslak). *NYF, FCT, EVD*

Another Woman ✶✶✶ 1988 (PG) The study of an intellectual woman whose life is changed when she begins to eavesdrop. What she hears provokes her to examine every relationship in her life, finding things quite different than she had believed. Heavy going, with Rowlands effective as a woman coping with an entirely new vision of herself. Farrow plays the catalyst. Although Allen's comedies are more popular than his dramas, this one deserves a look. **81m/C VHS, Beta, LV, Closed Caption.** Gena Rowlands, Gene Hackman, Mia Farrow, Ian Holm, Betty Buckley, Martha Plimpton, Blythe Danner, Harris Yulin, Sandy Dennis, David Ogden Stiers, John Houseman, Philip Bosco, Frances Conroy, Kenneth Welsh, Michael Kirby; **D:** Woody Allen; **W:** Woody Allen; **C:** Sven Nykvist. *ORI*

Another You ✶ 1991 (R) Con man Wilder takes pathological liar Pryor under his care and decides to use his talents to his fullest advantage. Posing as successful businessmen, the duo initiate a scam so complicated that they may end up being double-crossed or worse yet, dead! Can the pair see their plan through without losing their lives? Sad to see how far these two gifted comedians have fallen. Their collaboration is tired and the movie generally dreadful. **98m/C VHS, LV, 8mm, Closed Caption.** Richard Pryor, Gene Wilder, Mercedes Ruehl, Vanessa Williams, Stephen Lang, Kevin Pollak; **D:** Maurice Phillips. *COL*

Antarctica ✶✶ 1984 Due to unfortunate circumstances, a group of scientists must leave their pack of huskies behind on a frozen glacier in the Antarctic. The film focuses on the dogs' subsequent struggle for survival. Dubbed. **112m/C VHS, Beta, Closed Caption.** *JP* Ken Takakura, Masako Natsume, Keiko Oginome; **D:** Koreyoshi Kurahara; **M:** Vangelis. *FOX*

Anthony Adverse ✶✶½ 1936 March is a young man in the 19th century who searches for manhood across America and Mexico. He grows slowly as he battles foes, struggles against adversity and returns home to find his lover in this romantic swashbuckler. A star-studded cast, lush costuming, and an energetic musical score. Highly acclaimed in its time, but now seems dated. Based on the novel by Hervey Allen. **141m/B VHS, Beta.** Fredric March, Olivia de Havilland, Anita Louise, Gale Sondergaard, Claude Rains, Louis Hayward, Scotty Beckett; **D:** Mervyn LeRoy; **C:** Gaetano Antonio "Tony" Gaudio. Academy Awards '36: Best Cinematography, Best Film Editing, Best Supporting Actress (Sondergaard), Best Score; Nominations: Academy Awards '36: Best Interior Decoration, Best Picture. *MGM, BTV, FHE*

Antonia and Jane ✶✶✶ 1991 (R) Enjoyable film tells the story of a longstanding, heavily tested friendship between two women. From the very beginning, they are a study in contrasts—Jane as rather plain, frumpy, and insecure; Antonia as glamorous, elegant, and successful. Both believe that each other's lives are more interesting and exciting than their own. Kidron, who directed this smart witty comedy for British television, offers an honest look into the often complex world of adult friendships.**CW:** Language and sensuality. **75m/C VHS, Beta, Closed Caption.** *GB* Imelda Staunton, Saskia Reeves, Patricia Leventon, Alfred Hoffman, Maria Charles, John Bennett, Richard Hope, Alfred Marks, Lila Kaye, Bill Nighy, Brenda Bruce; *D:* Beeban Kidron; *W:* Marcy Kahan; *M:* Rachel Portman. *PAR*

Antonia's Line ♂♂½ 1995 (R) 90-year-old Antonia (Van Ammelrooy) has decided that she is going to die today and so begins a 50-year-long flashback of her nonconformist life in a Dutch village. Her lesbian daughter Danielle (Dottermans) wants a child without bothering about a husband and Antonia obliging arranges a brief interlude that produces child prodigy Therese (Van Overloop), who eventually has her own daughter, Sarah (Ravesteijn). Lots of female bonding (the male characters are mostly on the periphery of the action) and a certain magic realism abound. Dutch with subtitles.*CW:* Strong sexual content and some violence, including a rape scene. **102m/C VHS.** *NL* Willeke Van Ammelrooy, Els Dottermans, Veerle Van Overloop, Thyrza Ravesteijn, Jan Decleir, Mil Seghers, Jan Steen, Marina De Graaf; *D:* Marleen Gorris; *W:* Marleen Gorris; *C:* Willy Stassen; *M:* Ilona Seckaz. Academy Awards '95: Best Foreign Language Film; Nominations: British Academy Awards '96: Best Foreign Film. *BMG*

Antonio ♂♂ 1973 A Texas millionaire on the run from his wife and her divorce lawyer alights in a small Chilean village and turns it upside down. **89m/C VHS, Beta.** Larry Hagman, Trini Lopez, Noemi Guerrero, Pedro Becker; *D:* Claudio Guzman. *HHE*

Antonio Das Mortes ♂♂½ 1968 Antonio is a savage mercenary hired to kill rebels against the Brazilian government. Belatedly he realizes he sympathizes with the targets and turns his guns the other way for an incredible shootout finale. A visually lavish political polemic, espousing revolutionary guerrilla action within the format of a South American western. In Portuguese with English subtitles. **100m/C VHS.** *BR* Mauricio Do Valle, Odete Lara; *D:* Glauce Rocha; *W:* Glauce Rocha. *FCT*

Antony and Cleopatra ♂♂ 1973 (PG) Heston wrote, directed, and starred in this long, dry adaptation of the Shakespeare play that centers on the torrid romance between Mark Antony and Cleopatra. **150m/C VHS, Beta.** Charlton Heston, Hildegarde Neil, Fernando Rey, Eric Porter; *D:* Charlton Heston.

Ants ♂½ *Panic at Lakewood Manor; It Happened at Lakewood Manor* 1977 A mad bug parable for the planet-obsessed 90s. Insecticide-infected ants turn militant and check into a local hotel to vent their chemically induced foul mood on the unsuspecting clientele. The guest register includes a gaggle of celebrities who probably wish they'd signed on the Love Boat instead. Made for television (an ant farm would probably be just too horrible on the big screen). **100m/C VHS, Beta.** Suzanne Somers, Robert Foxworth, Myrna Loy, Lynda Day George, Gerald Gordon, Bernie Casey, Barry Van Dyke, Karen Lamm, Anita Gillette, Moosie Drier, Steve Franken, Brian Dennehy, Bruce French, Stacy Keach, Rene Enriquez, James Storm; *D:* Robert Scheerer. *LIV*

Any Gun Can Play ♂ *For a Few Bullets More* 1967 Typical spaghetti western. Three men (banker, thief, and bounty hunter) compete for a treasure of gold while wandering about the Spanish countryside. **103m/C VHS.** *IT SP* Edd Byrnes, Gilbert Roland, George Hilton, Kareen O'Hara, Pedro Sanchez, Gerard Herter; *D:* Enzo G. Castellari. *HHE*

Any Man's Death ♂♂ 1990 (R) Savage is a globe-trotting reporter on the trail of a worldwide conspiracy who accidentally uncovers a Nazi war criminal in Africa. Well-meaning but confused tale. **105m/C VHS, Beta, LV.** John Savage, William Hickey, Mia Sara, Ernest Borgnine, Michael Lerner; *D:* Tom Clegg. *PSM*

Any Number Can Play ♂♂½ 1949 Fast-moving drama about an ailing gambler who faces a series of crises. Gable gives a commanding performance as the noble dice-roller. Based on the novel by Edward Harris Heath. **102m/B VHS.** Clark Gable, Alexis Smith, Wendell Corey, Audrey Totter,

Frank Morgan, Mary Astor, Lewis Stone, Barry Sullivan; *D:* Mervyn LeRoy; *W:* Richard Brooks. *MGM*

Any Place But Home ♂♂½ 1997 (PG-13) Cable movie finds Lando and Keller unexpectedly rescuing the kidnapped son of powerful businessman Thicke, only to discover the boy doesn't want to return to his abusive father.*CW:* Thematic elements including child abuse and kidnapping, and for violence and brief sensuality. **90m/C VHS.** Joe Lando, Mary Page Keller, Alan Thicke, Dale Midkiff, Cristie Conway, Richard Roundtree. *USH*

Any Wednesday ♂♂½ *Bachelor Girl Apartment* 1966 Okay sex farce about powerful industrialist Robards' use of his mistress's apartment as a tax write-off. When a young company executive learns of the "company" apartment, he meets Robards' nonchalant wife for a tryst of their own. Based on Muriel Resnik's Broadway play; similar to the 1960 "The Apartment." **110m/C VHS, Beta.** Jane Fonda, Jason Robards Jr., Dean Jones, Rosemary Murphy; *D:* Robert Ellis Miller; *W:* Julius J. Epstein, Philip C. Epstein; *M:* George Duning. *WAR*

Any Which Way You Can ♂♂ 1980 (PG) Bad brawler Philo Beddoe and his buddy Clyde, the orangutan, are back again in the sequel to "Every Which Way But Loose." This time Philo is tempted to take part in a big bout for a large cash prize. Clyde steals scenes, brightening up the no-brainer story. **116m/C VHS, Beta, LV.** Clint Eastwood, Sondra Locke, Ruth Gordon, Harry Guardino; *D:* Buddy Van Horn. *WAR*

Anything for a Thrill ♂ 1937 Two kids save a cameraman's career, make friends with a millionairess, and foil some crooks. **59m/B VHS.** Frankie Darro, Kane Richmond; *D:* Leslie Goodwins. *NOS, DVT, HEG*

Anything for Love ♂½ 1993 Teen musician is the object of a school bully's rage so he decides to dress up as a girl to escape the guy's fists. **90m/C VHS.** Corey Haim. *THV*

Anzacs: The War Down Under ♂ 1985 Well-made Australian TV miniseries about the Australian & New Zealand Army Corps during WWI. Follows the men from the time they enlist to the campaigns in Gallipoli and France. **165m/C VHS, Beta.** *AU* Paul Hogan, Andrew Clarke, Jon Blake, Megan Williams; *D:* George Miller. *CEL*

Anzio ♂♂ *The Battle for Anzio; Lo Sbarco di Anzio* 1968 The historic Allied invasion of Italy during WWII as seen through the eyes of American war correspondent Mitchum. Fine cast waits endlessly to leave the beach, though big battle scenes are effectively rendered. Based on the book by Wynford Vaughan Thomas. **117m/C VHS, Beta.** Robert Mitchum, Peter Falk, Arthur Kennedy, Robert Ryan, Earl Holliman, Mark Damon, Reni Santoni, Patrick Magee; *D:* Edward Dmytryk. *NO*

Apache ♂♂½ 1954 Lancaster is the only Indian in Geronimo's outfit who refuses to surrender in this chronicle of a bitter battle between the Indians and the U.S. cavalry in the struggle for the West. First western for Aldrich is a thoughtful piece for its time that had the original tragic ending reshot (against Aldrich's wishes) to make it more happy. Adapted from "Bronco Apache" by Paul I. Wellman. **91m/C VHS, Beta.** Burt Lancaster, John McIntire, Jean Peters; *D:* Robert Aldrich; *C:* Ernest Laszlo. *MGM, FOX, FCT*

Apache Blood ♂½ *Pursuit* 1975 (R) An Indian Brave, the lone survivor of an Indian massacre by the U.S. Army, squares off with a cavalry scout in the forbidding desert. **92m/C VHS.** Ray Danton, DeWitt Lee, Troy Neighbors, Diane Taylor, Eva Kovacs, Jason Clark; *D:* Thomas Quillen. *PSM*

Apache Chief ♂ 1950 Two Apache tribe leaders, one good, the other evil clash. Ultimately, and perhaps predictably, they face each other in hand-to-hand combat and peace prevails. **60m/B VHS, Beta, LV.** Alan Curtis, Tom Neal, Russell Hayden, Carol Thurston; *D:* Frank McDonald. *NO*

Apache Kid's Escape ♂ 1930 The Apache Kid leads the cavalry on a wild chase across the plains in this saga of the old west. **60m/B VHS, Beta.** Jack Perrin, Buzz Barton. *NOS, DVT, RXM*

Apache Rose ♂♂ 1947 Gambling boat owner plots to gain control of oil found on Vegas Ranch. Roy and Dale oppose the idea. First of the series in color; the original, unedited version of the film. **75m/B VHS, Beta, LV.** Roy Rogers, Dale Evans, Olin Howlin, George Meeker; *D:* William Witney. *FOX, NOS, VCN*

Apache Uprising ♂½ 1966 A standard western with Calhoun as the lawman up against gunfighters and stagecoach robbers as well as the usual Indians. **60m/C VHS, Closed Caption.** Rory Calhoun, Corinne Calvet, DeForest Kelley, John Russell, Lon Chaney Jr., Gene Evans, Richard Arlen, Robert Harris, Arthur Hunnicutt, Jean Parker, Johnny Mack Brown; *D:* R.G. Springsteen. *PAR*

Apache Woman ♂½ 1955 Bridges stars as a government agent sent to investigate some crimes committed by a group of Apache Indians. As he tries to calm the townspeople, Bridges discovers that the group is made up of white people led by an educated half-breed. He instigates the help of the half-breed's sister (and also Bridges' love interest) to stop the gang. Some good action, but lots of dull spots. **82m/C VHS.** Lloyd Bridges, Joan Taylor, Lance Fuller, Morgan Jones, Paul Birch, Jonathan Haze, Paul Dubov, Lou Place; *D:* Roger Corman. *COL, FCT*

Apaches Last Battle ♂♂ *Old Shatterhand; Shatterhand* 1964 A boundary scout discovers the ward of an Apache chief has been framed for murder by a cavalry officer who wants to start an Indian war in this exciting Euro western. **?m/C VHS.** Lex Barker, Guy Madison, Pierre Brice. *SNC*

Aparajito ♂♂♂½ *The Unvanquished* 1958 The second of the Apu trilogy, about a boy growing up in India, after "Pather Panchali," and before "The World of Apu." Apu is brought to Benares and his education seriously begins. The work of a master; in Bengali with English subtitles. **108m/B VHS, Beta.** *IN* Pinaki Sen Gupta, Karuna Banerjee, Kanu Banerjee, Ramani Sen Gupta; *D:* Satyajit Ray. National Board of Review Awards '59: 5 Best Foreign Films of the Year; Venice Film Festival '57: Best Film. *FCT, MRV, TIM*

Apart from Hugh ♂♂ 1994 Collin and Hugh have been living together for a year and to celebrate the occasion, Hugh decides to plan an anniversary party. Unfortunately, Collin hasn't told Hugh he's having second thoughts about their relationship. Directorial debut of FitzGerald. **87m/B VHS.** *D:* Jon FitzGerald. *WBF*

The Apartment ♂♂♂½ 1960 A lowly insurance clerk tries to climb the corporate ladder by "loaning" his apartment out to executives having affairs. Problems arise, however, when he unwittingly falls for the most recent girlfriend of the boss. Highly acclaimed social satire. **125m/B VHS, Beta, LV.** Jack Lemmon, Shirley MacLaine, Fred MacMurray, Ray Walston, Jack Kruschen, Joan Shawlee, Edie Adams, Hope Holiday, David Lewis; *D:* Billy Wilder; *W:* I.A.L. Diamond, Billy Wilder; *C:* Joseph LaShelle. Academy Awards '60: Best Art Direction/Set Decoration (B & W), Best Director (Wilder), Best Film Editing, Best Picture, Best Story & Screenplay; British Academy Awards '60: Best Actor (Lemmon), Best Actress (MacLaine), Best Film; Directors Guild of America Awards '60: Best Director (Wilder); Golden Globe Awards '61: Best Actor—Musical/Comedy (Lemmon), Best Actress—Musical/Comedy (MacLaine), Best Film—Musical/Comedy; National Board of Review Awards '60: 10 Best Films of the Year; New York Film Critics Awards '60: Best Director (Wilder), Best Film, Best Screenplay; Nominations: Academy Awards '60: Best Actor (Lemmon), Best Actress (MacLaine), Best Black and White Cinematography, Best Sound, Best Supporting Actor (Kruschen). *MGM, BTV*

Apartment Zero ♂♂♂½ 1988 (R) A decidedly weird, deranged psychological drama about the parasite/host-type relationship between two roommates in downtown Buenos Aires: one, an obsessive British movie nut, the other, a sexually mesmerizing stud who turns out to be a cold-blooded psycho. **124m/C VHS, Beta, LV.** *GB* Hart Bochner, Colin Firth, Fabrizio Bentivoglio, Liz Smith; **D:** Martin Donovan; **W:** Martin Donovan, David Koepp. *ACA, FCT, IME*

The Ape 🐾🐾 **1940** When his daughter dies of a crippling disease, Karloff becomes fixated with the mission to cure paralysis. Obviously distraught, he begins donning the hide of an escaped circus ape whose spinal fluid is the key to the serum. Hide-bedecked, he slays unknowing townspeople to tap them of their spinal fluid and cure his latest patient. **62m/B VHS, Beta.** Boris Karloff, Maris Wrixon, Henry Hall, Gertrude Hoffman; **D:** William Nigh. *NOS, SNC, VYY*

A*P*E* woof! **1976 (PG)** A*P*E* is thirty-six feet tall and ten tons of animal fury who destroys anything that comes between him and the actress he loves. Cheap rip-off of Kong. **87m/C VHS, Beta.** Rod Arrants, Joanna DeVarona, Alex Nicol; **D:** Paul Leder. *NWV*

The Ape Man 🐾🐾 *Lock Your Doors* **1943** With the aid of a secret potion, a scientist turns himself into a murderous ape. The only way to regain his human side is to ingest human spinal fluid. Undoubtedly inspired by Boris Karloff's 1940 film, "The Ape." **64m/B VHS, Beta.** Wallace Ford, Bela Lugosi; **D:** William Beaudine. *NOS, MRV, SNC*

A.P.E.X. 🐾🐾 **1994 (R)** Nicholas Sinclair (Keats), a researcher from 2073, time travels back to 1973 to retrieve a faulty robot probe called A.P.E.X. (Advanced Prototype Extermination Unit). Unwittingly he has been infected with a mysterious virus and when he returns it's to a version of his own time where humans are dying from the virus and robots are sent to eradicate the few survivors. It also seems Sinclair is now a guerilla in an anti-robot army. Yes, it sounds like "The Terminator" but the action moves and though the budget is limited the special effects are still impressive. **103m/C VHS, LV, Closed Caption.** Richard Keats, Mitchell Cox, Lisa Ann Russell, Marcus Aurelius, Adam Lawson; **D:** Phillip J. Roth; **W:** Phillip J. Roth, Ronald Schmidt; **M:** Jim Goodwin. *REP*

Apocalypse Now 🐾🐾🐾🐾 **1979 (R)** Coppola's $40 million epic vision of the Vietnam War was inspired by Joseph Conrad's novella "Heart of Darkness," and continues to be the subject of debate. Disillusioned Army captain Sheen travels upriver into Cambodia to assassinate overweight renegade colonel Brando. His trip is punctuated by surrealistic battles and a terrifying descent into a land where human rationality seems to have slipped away. Considered by some to be the definitive picture of war in its overall depiction of chaos and primal bloodletting; by others, overwrought and unrealistic. May not translate as well to the small screen, yet worth seeing if for nothing more than Duvall's ten minutes of scenery chewing as a battle-obsessed major ("I love the smell of napalm in the morning!"), a study in manic machismo. Stunning photography by Vittorio Storaro, awe-inspiring battle scenes, and effective soundtrack montage. Both Sheen and Coppola suffered emotional breakdowns during the prolonged filming, and that's a very young Fishburne in his major film debut. Available in widescreen format on laserdisc and in a remastered version in letterbox on VHS with a remixed soundtrack that features Dolby Surround stereo. In 1991 a documentary detailing the making of the film, "Hearts of Darkness: A Filmmaker's Apocalypse," was released. **153m/C VHS, Beta, LV, CD-I.** Marlon Brando, Martin Sheen, Robert Duvall, Frederic Forrest, Sam Bottoms, Scott Glenn, Albert Hall, Laurence "Larry" Fishburne, Harrison Ford, G.D. Spradlin, Dennis Hopper, Colleen Camp, Tom Mason; **D:** Francis Ford Coppola; **W:** Francis Ford Coppola, John Milius; **M:** Carmine Coppola. Academy Awards '79: Best Cinematography, Best Sound; British Academy Awards '79: Best Director (Coppola), Best Supporting Actor (Duvall); Cannes Film Festival '79: Best Film; Golden Globe Awards '80: Best Director (Coppola), Best Supporting Actor (Duvall), Best Score; National Board of Review Awards '79: 10 Best Films of the Year; National Society of Film Critics Awards '79: Best Supporting Actor

(Forrest); Nominations: Academy Awards '79: Best Adapted Screenplay, Best Art Direction/Set Decoration, Best Director (Coppola), Best Film Editing, Best Picture, Best Supporting Actor (Duvall). *PAR*

Apollo 13 🐾🐾🐾½ **1995 (PG)** Realistic big-budget reenactment of the 1970 Apollo lunar mission that ran into a "problem" 205,000 miles from home reunites Hanks and Sinese from "F. Gump" and Howard and Hanks from "Splash." And an enjoyable reunion it is. Explosion in one of two oxygen tanks helping power the spacecraft leaves the three astronauts (lead by Hanks) tumbling through space. With the electrical system kaput and oxygen running low, the men seek refuge in the Lunar Excursion Module. Since it's based on the real event and the outcome is known, director Howard concentrates on the personalities and the details of the seven-day adventure at Mission Control and in space, in the process delivering the dramatic payload. Weightless shots are the real deal as crew filmed for ten days and made 600 parabolic loops in a KC-135 jet, NASA's "Vomit Comet," the long plunge creating 25 seconds of weightlessness. Special effects (by James Cameron's Digital Domain) and set design do the rest; no NASA footage is used, though original TV footage is used to dramatic effect. Script, with an uncredited rewrite by John Sayles, is based on the 1994 book, "Lost Moon," written by 13's Jim Lovell (who has a cameo as the Navy captain welcoming the astronauts aboard the recovery ship), while Apollo 15 commander David Scott served as a consultant. **140m/C VHS, LV, Closed Caption.** Tom Hanks, Kevin Bacon, Bill Paxton, Gary Sinise, Ed Harris, Kathleen Quinlan, Brett Cullen, Emily Ann Lloyd, Miko Hughes, Max Elliott Slade, Jean Speegle Howard, Tracy Reiner, Michelle Little, David Andrews, Mary Kate Schellhardt; **D:** Ron Howard; **W:** William Broyles Jr., Al Reinert; **C:** Dean Cundey; **M:** James Horner. Academy Awards '95: Best Film Editing, Best Sound; Directors Guild of America Awards '95: Best Director (Howard); Screen Actors Guild Award '95: Best Supporting Actor (Harris), Cast; Blockbuster Entertainment Awards '96: Drama Actor, Theatrical (Hanks); Nominations: Academy Awards '95: Best Adapted Screenplay, Best Art Direction/Set Decoration, Best Picture, Best Supporting Actor (Harris), Best Supporting Actress (Quinlan), Original Dramatic/Comedy Score; British Academy Awards '95: Best Cinematography; Golden Globe Awards '95: Best Director (Howard), Best Film—Drama, Best Supporting Actor (Harris), Best Supporting Actress (Quinlan); MTV Movie Awards '96: Best Film, Best Male Performance (Hanks); Writers Guild of America '95: Best Adapted Screenplay. *USH*

Apology 🐾🐾 **1986** A psychotic killer stalks Warren, an experimental artist, in Manhattan while a detective stalks the killer. Made for cable, so expect a little more sex and violence than network TV movies. Written by Medoff, author of "Children of a Lesser God." **98m/C VHS.** Lesley Ann Warren, Peter Weller, John Glover, George Loros, Jimmie Ray Weeks, Christopher Noth, Harvey Fierstein; **D:** Robert Bierman; **W:** Mark Medoff; **M:** Maurice Jarre. *NO*

The Appaloosa 🐾🐾½ *Southwest to Sonora* **1966** A lamenting loner who decides to begin anew by breeding Appaloosas is ripped off by a desperate woman who steals his horse in order to get away from her abusive amour. Brando falls in love with the girl and the two amazingly survive a wealth of obstacles in their battle against Mexican bandits. **99m/C VHS, Beta, LV.** Marlon Brando, Anjanette Comer, John Saxon; **D:** Sidney J. Furie; **W:** James Bridges; **C:** Russell Metty. *USH*

Applause 🐾🐾🐾 **1929** Morgan plays a down-and-out burlesque star trying to protect her fresh from the convent daughter. Definitely dated, but a marvelous performance by Morgan. Film buffs will appreciate this early talkie. **78m/B VHS.** Helen Morgan, Joan Peers, Fuller Mellish Jr., Henry Wadsworth, Dorothy Cumming; **D:** Rouben Mamoulian. *PAR*

The Apple 🐾½ **1980 (PG)** Futuristic musical filmed in Berlin that features a young, innocent, folk-singing couple who nearly become victims of the evil, glitzy record producer who tries to recruit the couple into a life of sex and drugs. **90m/C VHS,**

Beta. Catherine Mary Stewart, Alan Love, Grace Kennedy, Joss Ackland; **D:** Menahem Golan. *NO*

The Apple Dumpling Gang 🐾🐾 **1975 (G)** Three frisky kids strike it rich and trigger the wildest bank robbery in the gold-mad West. Unmistakably Disney, a familial subplot and a wacky duo are provided. Mediocre yet superior to its sequel, "The Apple Dumpling Gang Rides Again." **100m/C VHS, Beta, Closed Caption.** Bill Bixby, Susan Clark, Don Knotts, Tim Conway, David Wayne, Slim Pickens, Harry (Henry) Morgan; **D:** Norman Tokar; **M:** Buddy Baker. *DIS*

The Apple Dumpling Gang Rides Again 🐾🐾 **1979 (G)** Two lovable hombres terrorize the West in their bungling attempt to go straight. Fans of Conway or Knotts may appreciate this sequel to Disney's "The Apple Dumpling Gang." **88m/C VHS, Beta.** Tim Conway, Don Knotts, Tim Matheson, Kenneth Mars, Harry (Henry) Morgan, Jack Elam; **D:** Vincent McEveety; **M:** Buddy Baker. *DIS*

The Applegates 🐾🐾½ *Meet the Applegates* **1989 (R)** Ecologically correct Amazonian beetles are more than a little miffed about the slash-and-burn tactics in their home and decide to establish a kinder, gentler habitat. Bug Begley and his brood transform themselves into average Americans, but then don't want to leave their decadent life: even insects aren't immune to the lure of sex, drugs, and cable shopping networks. Imaginative, often quite funny one-joke flick should've been shorter. Fits quite well as a double feature with Lehmann's earlier "Heathers." **90m/C VHS, Beta, LV, Closed Caption.** Ed Begley Jr., Stockard Channing, Dabney Coleman, Cami Cooper, Bobby Jacoby, Glenn Shadix, Susan Barnes, Adam Biesk, Savannah Smith Boucher; **D:** Michael Lehmann; **W:** Michael Lehmann, Redbeard Simmons. *MED, FOX, VTR*

The Appointment woof! **1982** A supernatural force enters the bodies and minds of people and suddenly everyone begins going crazy. **90m/C VHS, Beta, 8mm.** Edward Woodward, Jane Merrow; **D:** Lindsey C. Vickers; **C:** Carlo DiPalma. *NO*

Appointment in Honduras 🐾🐾 **1953** An adventurer goes on a dangerous trek through the Central American jungles to deliver funds to the Honduran President. **79m/C VHS, Beta.** Glenn Ford, Ann Sheridan, Zachary Scott; **D:** Jacques Tourneur. *NO*

Appointment with Crime 🐾🐾½ **1945** After serving a prison sentence, an ex-con sets out to avenge himself against the colleagues who double crossed him. Well done, highlighted by superior characterizations. Based on the story by Michael Leighton. **91m/B VHS, Beta.** *GB* William Hartnell, Raymond Lovell, Robert Beatty, Herbert Lom, Joyce Howard, Alan Wheatley, Cyril Smith; **D:** John Harlow; **W:** John Harlow. *SNC*

Appointment with Death 🐾½ **1988 (PG)** Disappointing Agatha Christie mystery with Hercule Poirot solving the murder of a shrewish widow in 1937 Palestine. **103m/C VHS, Beta, LV, Closed Caption.** Peter Ustinov, Lauren Bacall, Carrie Fisher, John Gielgud, Piper Laurie, Hayley Mills, Jenny Seagrove, David Soul; **D:** Michael Winner; **W:** Anthony Shaffer, Peter Buckman, Michael Winner; **M:** Pino Donaggio. *WAR, FCT*

Appointment with Fear 🐾 **1985 (R)** A tough detective investigates a murder and all of the clues lead him mysteriously to a comatose asylum inmate. **95m/C VHS, Beta, LV.** Michael Wyle, Michelle Little, Garrick Dowhen; **D:** Alan Smithee. *LIV*

Apprentice to Murder 🐾🐾 **1988 (PG-13)** A small Pennsylvania Dutch town is shaken by a series of murders, thought to be associated with a bizarre local mystic and healer. Based on a true story, sort of. **97m/C VHS, Beta, LV, Closed Caption.** Donald Sutherland, Mia Sara, Chad Lowe, Eddie Jones; **D:** Ralph L. Thomas; **W:** Allan Scott, Wesley Moore. *VTR, NWV, HHE*

The Apprenticeship of Duddy Kravitz 🎬🎬🎬½ 1974 (PG) Young Jewish man in Montreal circa 1948 is driven by an insatiable need to be the "somebody" everyone has always told him he will be. A series of get-rich-quick schemes backfire in different ways, and he becomes most successful at driving people away. Young Dreyfuss is at his best. Made in Canada with thoughtful detail, and great cameo performances. Script by Richler, from his novel. 121m/C **VHS, Beta. CA** Richard Dreyfuss, Randy Quaid, Denholm Elliott, Jack Warden, Micheline Lanctot, Joe Silver; **D:** Ted Kotcheff; **W:** Mordecai Richler, Lionel Chetwynd. Berlin International Film Festival '74: Golden Berlin Bear; Writers Guild of America '74: Best Adapted Screenplay; Nominations: Academy Awards '74: Best Adapted Screenplay. **PAR**

April Fool 🎬🎬½ 1926 A man makes a fortune in the umbrella business and then discovers his daughter has fallen in love with the son of a nouveaux riche neighbor, resulting in all sorts of complications. 63m/B **VHS.** Alexander Carr, Mary Alden, Raymond Keane, Snitz Edwards; **D:** Nat Ross; **W:** Zion Myers. **GPV, FCT**

April Fools 🎬🎬 1969 (PG) A bored stockbroker falls in love with a beautiful woman who turns out to be married to his boss. 95m/C **VHS, Beta.** Jack Lemmon, Catherine Deneuve, Sally Kellerman, Peter Lawford, Charles Boyer, Myrna Loy, Harvey Korman; **D:** Stuart Rosenberg; **M:** Marvin Hamlisch. **FOX**

April Fool's Day 🎬 1986 (R) Rich girl Foreman invites eight college friends to spend the April Fool's weekend with her at her family's isolated island mansion. Everyone is subjected to an endless series of practical jokes when things apparently turn deadly and several of the kids begin disappearing. Lame spoof of "Friday the 13th" and other teenagers-in-peril slasher films. 90m/C **VHS, Beta, LV, Closed Caption.** Deborah Foreman, Jay Baker, Pat Barlow, Lloyd Berry, Deborah Goodrich, Ken Olandt, Griffin O'Neal, Tom Heaton, Mike Nomad, Leah K. Pinsent, Clayton Rohner, Amy Steel, Thomas F. Wilson; **D:** Fred Walton; **M:** Charles Bernstein. **PAR**

April In Paris 🎬🎬 1952 Dynamite Jackson (Day), a chorus girl accidentally sent by the State Department to perform in Paris, meets S. Winthrop Putnam (Bolger), a timid fellow trapped in an unpleasant marriage. They eventually sing and dance their way to warm feelings as they begin a lifelong romance and live happily ever after. 100m/C **VHS.** Doris Day, Ray Bolger, Claude Dauphin, Eve Miller, George Givot, Paul Harvey; **D:** David Butler; **W:** Jack Rose, Melville Shavelson. **WAR, CCB, MVD**

The Arab Conspiracy 🎬🎬 The Next Man; Double Hit 1976 (R) Sharpe plays a hit-woman conspiring with assassins from all over the world to kill Arab leaders. One problem—she falls in love with Saudi Arabian ambassador Connery as he tries to gain peace with Palestine. 108m/C **VHS.** Sean Connery, Cornelia Sharpe, Albert Paulsen, Adolfo Celi, Charles Cioffi; **D:** Richard Sarafian; **W:** Alan R. Trustman; **C:** Michael Chapman; **M:** Michael Kamen. **SIM, QVD**

Arabesque 🎬🎬½ 1966 A college professor is drawn into international espionage by a beautiful woman and a plot to assassinate an Arab prince. Stylish and fast moving. From the novel "The Cipher" by Gordon Cotler. 105m/C **VHS, Beta.** Gregory Peck, Sophia Loren, George Coulouris; **D:** Stanley Donen; **M:** Henry Mancini. **USH, FCT**

Arabian Nights 🎬🎬 1942 Two brothers fight for the throne of Turkey and the affection of the sultry dancing girl Scheherazade. Enchanting costumes and lavish sets augment the fantasy atmosphere. 87m/C **VHS, Closed Caption.** Jon Hall, Maria Montez, Sabu, Leif Erickson, Edgar Barrier, Richard Lane, Turhan Bey; **D:** John Rawlins; **W:** Michael Hogan; **C:** Milton Krasner. Nominations: Academy Awards '42: Best Color Cinematography, Best Sound, Original Dramatic/Comedy Score. **USH, FCT**

Arabian Nights 🎬🎬🎬 1974 The third of Pasolini's epic, explicit adaptations of classic portmanteau, featuring ten of the old Scheherazade favorites adorned by beautiful photography, explicit sex scenes and homoeroticism. In Italian with English subtitles; available dubbed. 130m/C **VHS, Beta, LV.** *IT* Ninetto Davoli, Franco Merli, Ines Pellegrini, Luigina Rocchi; **D:** Pier Paolo Pasolini; **M:** Ennio Morricone. **WBF, APD**

Arachnophobia 🎬🎬½ 1990 (PG-13) Big-budget big-bug horror story has a few funny moments as lots and lots of spiders wreak havoc in a white picket fence community somewhere off the beaten track. Lethal South American spider makes a trek to sunny California, meets up with local spiders, and rapidly multiplies. Utterly arachnophobic (read: totally scared of spiders) town doctor Daniels pairs with gung-ho exterminator Goodman to try and track down the culprits. The script's a bit yawn-inspiring but the cast and effects will keep you from dozing off. Directorial debut for Marshall, a longtime friend and producer for Spielberg. 109m/C **VHS, Beta, LV, Closed Caption.** Jeff Daniels, John Goodman, Harley Jane Kozak, Julian Sands, Roy Brocksmith, Stuart Pankin, Brian McNamara, Mark L. Taylor, Henry Jones, Peter Jason, James Handy; **D:** Frank Marshall; **W:** Wesley Strick, Don Jakoby; **C:** Mikael Salomon; **M:** Trevor Jones. **HPH**

Arcade 🎬½ 1993 (R) All the kids in town are desperate to play the new virtual reality game Arcade, only the game is just a little too real. Seems it can transport you into another world with its stunning graphics and sound effects but you really put your life on the line. Only Alex (Ward) worries when kids start to disappear and she decides to battle the game for their lives.**CW:** Violence. 85m/C **VHS, Beta, Closed Caption.** Megan Ward, Peter Billingsley, John de Lancie, Sharon Farrell, Seth Green, Humberto Ortiz, Jonathan Fuller, Norbert Weisser; **D:** Albert Pyun; **W:** David S. Goyer; **M:** Alan Howarth. **PAR**

Arcadia of My Youth 🎬 1982 In the 30th century the evil Illumidus Empire has conquered Earth and only the heroic Captain Harlock and his friends can battle their tyranny. Based on Matsumoto Leiji's comic book series. Draws parallels to the post-WWII occupation of Japan. Animated; in Japanese with English subtitles. 130m/C **VHS.** *JP* **ANI**

Arch of Triumph 🎬🎬🎬 1948 In Paris, an Austrian refugee doctor falls in love just before the Nazis enter the city. Big-budget box-office loser featuring fine cast but sluggish pace. Based on the Erich Maria Remarque novel and remade for television. 120m/B **VHS.** Ingrid Bergman, Charles Boyer, Charles Laughton, Louis Calhern; **D:** Lewis Milestone; **W:** Harry Brown, Lewis Milestone; **C:** Russell Metty. **REP**

Arch of Triumph 🎬🎬½ 1985 A refugee doctor falls in love with a mystery woman as the Nazis enter Paris. Made for television remake of the 1948 film. 95m/C **VHS.** Anthony Hopkins, Lesley-Anne Down, Donald Pleasence, Frank Finlay; **D:** Waris Hussein; **W:** Charles Israel; **M:** Georges Delerue. **FCT**

Archer: The Fugitive from the Empire 🎬 1981 A young warrior battles the forces of evil in this television movie. Lots of strange names to learn even if you already know who's going to win the final battle. 97m/C **VHS, Beta.** Lane Caudell, Belinda Bauer, George Kennedy, Victor Campos, Kabir Bedi, George Innes, Marc Alaimo, Allen Rich, John Hancock, Priscilla Pointer, Sharon Barr; **D:** Nick Corea. **USH**

Archer's Adventure 🎬½ 1985 An Australian family film based on a true story. A horse-trainer's young apprentice delivers a prize racehorse to Melbourne, through 600 miles of tough frontier, devious bush rangers, and disaster. 120m/C **VHS, Beta.** *AU* Brett Climo, Nicole Kidman; **D:** Denny Lawrence. **NWV, VTR, TVC**

Arctic Blue 🎬½ 1993 (R) Alaskan biologist Walsh gets stuck being the local lawman when he's the only one willing to escort Hauer, a homicidal trapper, to a Fairbanks jail. But nothing's that easy—their plane crashes atop a glacier and the duo must battle each other and the elements to survive, while Hauer's brutal partners hunt Walsh. 95m/C **VHS, LV, Closed Caption.** Dylan Walsh, Rutger Hauer, Richard Bradford; **D:** Peter Masterson; **W:** Ross LaManna. **COL**

Are Parents People? 🎬🎬 1925 Lighthearted silent comedy about a young girl's successful attempts to reunite her feuding parents. It all begins as she runs away and spends the night in the office of a doctor she has grown to like. After a frantic night of searching, her parents are reunited through their love for her. 60m/B **VHS.** Betty Bronson, Adolphe Menjou, Florence Vidor. **GPV, PAR**

Are You in the House Alone? 🎬🎬 1978 Made for television adaptation of Richard Peck's award-winning novel. Story of a high school coed who becomes the target of a terror campaign. 100m/C **VHS, Beta.** Blythe Danner, Kathleen Beller, Tony Bill, Scott Colomby; **D:** Walter Grauman; **M:** Charles Bernstein. **WOV, GKK**

Are You Lonesome Tonight 🎬🎬½ 1992 (PG-13) Suspense thriller casts Seymour as a wealthy socialite who discovers her husband is having an affair with a phone-sex girl. His sudden and mysterious disappppearance forces her to hire a private detective (Stevenson) to track him down, with only the taped conversations as clues. Average made for cable television fare. 91m/C **VHS, Beta, Closed Caption.** Jane Seymour, Parker Stevenson, Beth Broderick, Joel Brooks, Robert Pine; **D:** E.W. Swackhamer; **W:** Wesley Moore. **PAR**

Arena 🎬🎬 1989 (PG-13) Remember old boxing melodramas about good-natured palookas, slimy opponents, gangsters and dames? This puts those cliches in a garish sci-fi setting, with handsome Steve Armstrong battling ETs and the astro-mob to be the first human pugilistic champ in decades. A really cute idea (from the screenwriters of "The Rocketeer"), but it conks out at the halfway point. Worth a look for buffs. 97m/C **VHS, LV, Closed Caption.** *IT* Paul Satterfield, Claudia Christian, Hamilton Camp, Marc Alaimo, Armin Shimerman, Shari Shattuck, Jack Carter; **D:** Peter Manoogian; **W:** Danny Bilson, Paul DeMeo; **M:** Richard Band. **COL**

Aria 🎬🎬 1988 (R) Ten directors were given carte blanche to interpret ten arias from well-known operas. Henry and D'Angelo star in Julian Temple's rendition of Verdi's "Rigoletto." In Fonda's film debut, she and her lover travel to Las Vegas and eventually kill themselves in the bathtub, just like "Romeo & Juliet." Jarman's piece (a highlight) shows an aged operatic star at her last performance remembering an early love affair. "I Pagliacci" is the one aria in which the director took his interpretation in a straightforward manner. 90m/C **VHS, Beta.** *GB* Theresa Russell, Anita Morris, Bridget Fonda, Beverly D'Angelo, Buck Henry, John Hurt; **D:** Ken Russell, Charles Sturridge, Robert Altman, Bill Bryden, Jean-Luc Godard, Bruce Beresford, Nicolas Roeg, Franc Roddam, Derek Jarman, Julien Temple. **ACA, FCT, LTY**

Ariel 🎬🎬🎬 1989 Refreshing, offbeat Finnish comedy by highly praised newcomer Kaurismaki. Hoping to find work in Southern Finland, an out-of-work miner from Northern Finland (Pajala) jets off in his white Cadillac convertible given to him in a cafe by a friend, who promptly shoots himself. There's no linear progression toward a happy ending, although antiheroic subject does find employment and romances a meter maid. Mostly, though, he's one of those it's hell being me guys who wouldn't have any luck if it weren't for bad luck. Strange slice-of-life sporting film noir tendencies, although essentially anti-stylistic. 74m/C **VHS.** *FI* Susanna Haavisto, Turo Pajala, Matti Pellonpaa; **D:** Aki Kaurismaki; **W:** Aki Kaurismaki. National Society of Film Critics Awards '90: Best Foreign Film. **KIV, FCT**

The Aristocats 🎬🎬🎬 1970 Typically entertaining Disney animated story about pampered pussy Duchess (Gabor) and her three kittens, who are left a fortune in their mistress' will. The fortune goes to the butler if the cats don't survive, so he dumps them in the country hoping they won't find their way home. The cats are aided by tough alley denizen O'Malley (Harris)—it's kind of the feline version of "Lady and the Tramp." Maurice Chevalier sings the title tune. 78m/C **VHS. D:**

Wolfgang Reitherman; **M:** George Bruns; **V:** Eva Gabor, Phil Harris, Sterling Holloway, Roddy Maude-Roxby, Bill Thompson, Hermione Baddeley, Carol Shelley, Pat Buttram, Nancy Kulp, Paul Winchell. *DIS*

Arizona 🖋🖋½ 1940 Arthur is a hellion in wild 1860 Tucson who falls for the wandering Holden. He's headed for California and she can't keep him in town so Arthur throws herself into business by establishing a freight line. Only warring Apaches try to burn her out and Holden rides in to save the day (with the cavalry and a stampeding cattle herd). Holden's first western is lively but long. 121m/B VHS. Jean Arthur, William Holden, Warren William, Porter Hall, Paul Harvey, George Chandler, Regis Toomey, Edgar Buchanan; **D:** Wesley Ruggles; **W:** Claude Binyon; **M:** Victor Young. Nominations: Academy Awards '40: Best Original Score. *COL*

Arizona 🖋½ 1986 A group of illegal aliens struggle for survival after they cross the border into the harsh desert. 94m/C VHS, Beta. MX Roberto "Flaco" Guzman, Juan Valentin. *MED*

Arizona Badman 🖋½ 1935 There is a bad man in Arizona, and he must be gotten rid of. 60m/B VHS, Beta. Reb Russell; **D:** S. Roy Luby. *NOS, DVT*

Arizona Bound 🖋 1941 Mesa City is infested with a villain and our "Rough Rider" trio must rid the town of him. 57m/B VHS, Beta. Buck Jones, Tim McCoy, Raymond Hatton, Dennis Moore, Luana Walters; **D:** Spencer Gordon Bennet. *NOS, VCN, DVT*

Arizona Bushwackers 🖋½ 1967 Routine western that has Confederate spy Keel taking job as sheriff in small Arizona town. Once there, he has to straighten out a few bad guys who have been selling weapons to the Apaches. Notable for presence of old western-movie veterans Ireland, Donlevy, Brady, and MacLane. Based on a story by Steve Fisher. 87m/C VHS, LV. Howard Keel, Yvonne De Carlo, John Ireland, Marilyn Maxwell, Scott Brady, Brian Donlevy, Barton MacLane; **D:** Lesley Selander. *PAR*

Arizona Cowboy 🖋 1949 An ex-G.I., now the rodeo's big attraction, gets involved in a robbery. 57m/B VHS, Beta. Rex Allen, Gordon Jones, Roy Barcroft; **D:** R.G. Springsteen. *DVT*

Arizona Days 🖋½ 1937 Cowboys join a minstrel group and rescue the show when a group of toughs try to break it up. 56m/B VHS, Beta. Tex Ritter, Eleanor Stewart, Syd Saylor, Snub Pollard; **D:** John English. *NOS, VCI, VDM*

Arizona Dream 🖋🖋 1994 (R) Alex (Depp) is a New York drifter who gets stuck working for his uncle's (Lewis) car dealership in a small Arizona town. He meets an eccentric older woman (Dunaway) with a homemade plane and some dreams of her own. Tends toward the surreal and confusing. **CW:** Language; sexuality. 119m/C VHS, Closed Caption. Johnny Depp, Faye Dunaway, Jerry Lewis, Lili Taylor, Paulina Porizkova, Tricia Leigh Fisher, Vincent Gallo; **D:** Emir Kusturica; **W:** Emir Kusturica, David Atkins; **C:** Vilko Filac. *WAR*

Arizona Gangbusters 🖋 1940 Below-average oater has real-life cowboy McCoy fighting city hall in order to fight other baddies. Newfield created the pseudonym "Peter Stewart." 57m/B VHS. Tim McCoy, Pauline Hadden, Forrest Taylor, Julian Rivero, Curly Dresden; **D:** Sam Newfield. *DVT, HEG*

Arizona Gunfighter 🖋 1937 A young cowhand seeks revenge against the man who murdered his father in this western. 60m/B VHS, Beta. Bob Steele, Ted Adams; **D:** Sam Newfield. *NOS, DVT*

Arizona Heat 🖋🖋 1987 (R) A violent cop is teamed up with a tough, but tender female cop in this all-too-familiar tale of two cops chasing a cop killer. 91m/C VHS. Michael Parks, Denise Crosby, Hugh Farrington; **D:** John G. Thomas. *REP*

Arizona Kid 🖋 1939 Another sagebrush saga featuring Roy in singin' and fightin' action. 54m/B VHS, Beta. Roy Rogers; **D:** Joseph Kane. *NOS, DVT, TIM*

Arizona Mahoney 🖋 1936 Weird mixture of circus adventure and serious western doesn't work too well. Confused film with farfetched reasons for having the paths of circus performers and cowboys cross. Based on a Zane Grey novel. 58m/B VHS. Joe Cook, Robert Cummings, June Martel, Marjorie Gateson, John Miljan, James Mason; **D:** James Hogan; **W:** Robert Yost, Stuart Anthony. *MOV*

Arizona Raiders 🖋 1965 Arizona rangers hunt down killers who have been terrorizing the territory. 88m/C VHS, Beta. Audie Murphy, Buster Crabbe, Gloria Talbott; **D:** William Witney. *NOS, VCI, VCN*

Arizona Roundup 🖋½ 1942 Good vs. bad amid tumbleweed, bleached-white chaps, bloodless shoot-outs and happy endings. 54m/B VHS, Beta. Tom Keene, Sugar Dawn, Jack Ingram; **D:** Robert Emmett Tansey. *NOS, VDM*

Arizona Stagecoach 🖋 1942 The Range Busters set out to bust a notorious, guiltless, devil-may-care outlaw gang. 58m/B VHS, Beta. Ray Corrigan, Max Terhune, Kermit Maynard, Charles "Blackie" King, John "Dusty" King; **D:** S. Roy Luby. *NOS*

Arizona Terror 🖋½ 1931 Our hero is on a quest for vengeance, seeking the posse that killed his partner. 64m/B VHS, Beta. Ken Maynard. *VCN*

Arizona Whirlwind 🖋 1944 Our intrepid heroes must battle torrents of gunfire in order to prevent a stage hold-up in this western saga. 59m/B VHS, Beta. Ken Maynard, Hoot Gibson, Bob Steele. *NOS, DVT*

Ark of the Sun God 🖋 1982 Another adventurer battles the Nazis and nutsies for a 2000-year-old ark buried in the Sahara. 95m/C VHS, Beta. David Warbeck, John Steiner, Susie Sudlow, Alan Collins, Riccardo Palacio; **D:** Anthony (Antonio Margheriti) Dawson. *TWE*

Armageddon: The Final Challenge 🖋½ 1994 After a nuclear holocaust, evil forces rule the Earth in the guise of "The Future Bank." They send out Fear-Permutator Clones to keep order and kill undesirables but naturally there's a rebel ready to do battle. 85m/C VHS. Todd Jensen, Graham Clarke, Tony Caprari, Joanna Rowlands; **D:** Michael Garcia; **W:** George Garcia, Michael Garcia; **M:** Johan Lass. *YHV*

Armed and Dangerous 🖋🖋 1986 (PG-13) Candy and Levy are incompetent security guards assigned to a do-nothing job. Things get spiced up when a mobster tries to run a crime ring under their nose. Candy catches on and winds up in a full-fledged chase. Not as funny as it sounds, though occasionally has moments of genuine comedy. 88m/C VHS, Beta, LV, Closed Caption. John Candy, Eugene Levy, Kenneth McMillan, Brion James, Robert Loggia, Meg Ryan, Don Stroud, Jonathan Banks, Steve Railsback, Bruce Kirby, Tony Burton, Larry Hankin, Judy Landers, David Wohl; **D:** Mark L. Lester; **W:** Harold Ramis, Peter Torokvei, James Keach, Brian Grazer. *COL*

Armed for Action 🖋🖋 1992 Routine action thriller casts Estevez as Sgt. Phil Towers who gets more than he bargained for when his prisoner, Mafia kingpin David Montel, escapes while en route from New York to Los Angeles. When he finally catches up with them, Towers leads a small army of locals on a brutal assault. 88m/C VHS, Closed Caption. Joe Estevez, Rocky Patterson, Barri Murphy, David Harrod, J. Scott Guy; **D:** Shane Spaulding. *AIP*

Armed Response 🖋🖋 1986 (R) Carradine leads a group of mercenaries in a battle against Chinatown mobsters. They race to locate a priceless jade statue before it can fall into the wrong hands. 86m/C VHS, Beta, LV. David Carradine, Lee Van Cleef, Mako, Lois Hamilton, Ross Hagen, Brent Huff; **D:** Fred Olen Ray; **C:** Paul Elliott. *NO*

Armistead Maupin's Tales of the City 🖋🖋½ *Tales of the City* 1993 Carefree '70s San Francisco is the setting for the interconnected stories of the inhabitants of 28 Barbary Lane. There's mysterious landlady Mrs. Madrigal (Dukakis); free-spirit Mona Ramsey (Webb); her gay roomie, Michael "Mouse" Tolliver (D'Amico); hetero lawyer-turned-waiter Brian (Gross); nerdy, se-

cretive Norman (DeSantis); and the naively sweet Mary Ann Singleton (Linney). Definite time-warp factor in this pre-AIDS depiction of sex and drugs, but also the timeless search for love and happiness. Maupin first wrote the stories as an ongoing serial for the *San Francisco Chronicle* and they were later turned into 6 novels. Made for British TV. 360m/C VHS. *GB* Olympia Dukakis, Donald Moffat, Chloe Webb, Laura Linney, Marcus D'Amico, Paul Gross, Stanley DeSantis, Bill Campbell, Cynda Williams, Barbara Garrick, Thomas Gibson, Nina Foch, Paul Dooley, Belita Morena; *Cameos:* Karen Black, Edie Adams, Michael Jeter, Ian McKellen, Rod Steiger, Paul Bartel; **D:** Alastair Reid; **W:** Richard Kramer. *PGV*

Armored Car Robbery 🖋🖋 1950 Talman and his buddies plot to rob an armored car but are foiled by McGraw and his crimefighters. Surprisingly good B-crime drama. 68m/B VHS. Charles McGraw, Adele Jergens, William Talman, Steve Brodie; **D:** Richard Fleischer. *NO*

Armored Command 🖋🖋½ 1961 A beautiful German spy infiltrates an American outpost during the Battle of the Bulge. Tepid WWII fare made too long after the fact. 105m/B VHS, Beta. Burt Reynolds, Tina Louise, Howard Keel, Earl Holliman, Warner Anderson, Carleton Young; **D:** Byron Haskin. *FOX, FCT*

The Armour of God 🖋 1986 Chan plays an adventurous thief who steals and sells pieces of a prized medieval armour set to collectors. When a criminal gang kidnaps his girl to get the entire set, Chan must come up with some spectacular saves of both the armour and the girl. In Cantonese with English subtitles. 100m/C VHS. CH Jackie Chan; **D:** Jackie Chan. *TAI, FCT*

Army Brats 🖋½ 1984 In this Dutch film a military family goes bloodily and comically to war with itself. Even in a welfare state, parents can't control their wee ones. 105m/C VHS, Beta. NL Akkemay, Frank Schaafsma, Peter Faber; **D:** Ruud Van Hemert. *WAR*

Army of Darkness 🖋🖋🖋 *Evil Dead 3* 1992 (R) Campbell returns for a third "Evil Dead" round as the square-jawed, none too bright hero, Ash in this comic book extravaganza. He finds himself hurled back to the 14th-century through the powers of an evil book. There he romances a babe, fights an army of skeletons, and generally causes all those Dark Age knights a lot of grief, as he tries to get back to his own time. Raimi's technical exuberance is apparent and, as usual, the horror is graphic but still tongue-in-cheek. **CW:** Violence and horror. 77m/C VHS, Beta, LV, Closed Caption. Bruce Campbell, Embeth Davidtz, Marcus Gilbert, Ian Abercrombie, Richard Grove, Michael Earl Reid, Tim Quill, Patricia Tallman, Theodore (Ted) Raimi, Ivan Raimi; *Cameos:* Bridget Fonda; **D:** Sam Raimi; **W:** Ivan Raimi, Sam Raimi; **M:** Danny Elfman, Joseph Lo Duca. *USH, FCT*

Army of One 🖋½ 1994 (R) Santee (Lundgren) and his pal are hauling stolen cars across the desert when a cop pulls them over. Soon there's two dead bodies and Santee's in big trouble. An unrated version is also available. 102m/C VHS, LV. Dolph Lundgren, George Segal, Kristian Alfonso, Geoffrey Lewis, Michelle Phillips; **D:** Vic Armstrong; **W:** Steven Pressfield, Joel Goldsmith. *LIV*

Arnold 🖋🖋½ 1973 (PG) Outrageous black comedy involving a woman who marries a cadaver to gain his large inheritance. Lots of bizarre and creative deaths in this horror spoof. Unusual wedding scene is a must-see. 96m/C VHS, Beta. Stella Stevens, Roddy McDowall, Elsa Lanchester, Victor Buono, Bernard Fox, Farley Granger, Shani Wallis; **D:** Georg Fenady; **W:** Jameson Brewer; **M:** George Duning. *LIV*

Around the World 🖋½ 1943 Kyser leads a USO-like tour to entertain troops. Interesting only in a historical sense. ♫Doodle-Ee-Doo; He's Got a Secret Weapon; Candlelight and Wine; Great News in the Making; They Chopped Down the Old Apple Tree; A Moke from Shamokin. 80m/B VHS, Beta. Kay Kyser, Ish Kabibble, Ginny Simms, Joan Davis, Mischa Auer; **D:** Allan Dwan. *TTC*

Around the World in a Daze 🎬🎬½ *The Three Stooges Go Around the World in a Daze* 1963 The Stooges are servants for Phileas Fogg's great-grandson, who has decided to repeat his ancestor's famous feat. Mayhem ensues when the three help out in their usual efficient, competent way. 93m/B VHS. Moe Howard, Larry Fine, Joe DeRita, Jay Sheffield; *D:* Norman Maurer. COL

Around the World in 80 Days 🎬🎬🎬 1956 (G) Niven is the unflappable Victorian Englishman who wagers that he can circumnavigate the earth in four-score days. With his faithful manservant Cantinflas they set off on a spectacular journey. A perpetual favorite providing ample entertainment. Star-gazers will particularly enjoy the more than 40 cameo appearances by many of Hollywood's biggest names. Adapted from the novel by Jules Verne. 178m/C VHS, LV, Closed Caption. David Niven, Shirley MacLaine, Cantinflas, Robert Newton, Charles Boyer, Joe E. Brown, Martine Carol, John Carradine, Charles Coburn, Ronald Colman; *Cameos:* Melville Cooper, Noel Coward, Andy Devine, Reginald Denny, Fernandel, Marlene Dietrich, Hermione Gingold, Cedric Hardwicke, Trevor Howard, Glynis Johns, Buster Keaton, Evelyn Keyes, Peter Lorre, Mike Mazurki, Victor McLaglen, John Mills, Robert Morley, Jack Oakie, George Raft, Cesar Romero, Gilbert Roland, Red Skelton, Frank Sinatra, Ava Gardner; *D:* Michael Anderson Sr.; *W:* James Poe, John Farrow, S.J. Perelman; *C:* Lionel Lindon; *M:* Victor Young. Academy Awards '56: Best Adapted Screenplay, Best Color Cinematography, Best Film Editing, Best Picture, Original Dramatic/Comedy Score; Golden Globe Awards '57: Best Actor—Musical/Comedy (Cantinflas), Best Film—Drama; National Board of Review Awards '56: 10 Best Films of the Year; New York Film Critics Awards '56: Best Film, Best Screenplay; Nominations: Academy Awards '56: Best Art Direction/Set Decoration (Color), Best Costume Design (Color), Best Director (Anderson). WAR, BTV, HMV

Around the World in 80 Days 🎬🎬½ 1989 TV adaptation of the Jules Verne adventure novel that finds Victorian gentleman Phineas Fogg (Brosnan) wagering that he can circle the globe in 80 days. He's pursued by private detective Fix (Ustinov), who suspects him of a daring bank robbery, and faces many trials and much excitement along the way. On 2 cassettes. 270m/C VHS. Pierce Brosnan, Peter Ustinov, Eric Idle, Arielle Dombasle, Henry Gibson, John Hillerman, Jack Klugman, Christopher Lee, Patrick Macnee, Roddy McDowall, Darren McGavin, John Mills, Robert Morley, Lee Remick, Pernell Roberts, James B. Sikking, Jill St. John, Robert Wagner, Julia Nickson-Soul; *D:* Buzz Kulik. BFV

Around the World in 80 Ways 🎬🎬½ 1986 (R) Sometimes clever, sometimes crude Australian comedy about an aging man rescued from a nursing home and taken on a phony trip around the world by his sons. Odd, but genuinely funny at times. 90m/C VHS, LV. AU Philip Quast, Alan Penney, Diana Davidson, Kelly Dingwall, Gosia Dobrowolska; *D:* Stephen MacLean; *W:* Stephen MacLean, Paul Leadon; *M:* Chris Neal. NLC

Around the World Under the Sea 🎬🎬 1965 Bunch of men and one woman scientist plunge under the ocean in an experiment to predict earthquakes. They plant earthquake detectors along the ocean floor and discover the causes of tidal waves. They have men-women battles. They see big sea critters. 111m/C VHS, Beta. David McCallum, Shirley Eaton, Gary Merrill, Keenan Wynn, Brian Kelly, Lloyd Bridges; *D:* Andrew Marton. MGM

Aroused 🎬 1966 Hollister is an apparently dedicated policeman who commits a number of blunders in the pursuit of a serial killer, including leaving his wife with the sociopath while he cavorts with the prostitute assigned to his protection. Director Holden's psychothriller was gorily ahead of its time. Includes heart-stopping castration sequence. 78m/B VHS. Janine Lenon, Steve Hollister, Fleurette Carter, Joanna Mills, Tony Palladino, Ted Gelanza; *D:* Anton Holden. SMW, TPV

The Arousers 🎬🎬½ *Sweet Kill; A Kiss from Eddie* 1970 (R) Cult item starring hunk Hunter as a handsome California psycho. Tab travels the coast searching for a woman he is able to make love to; those who fail to arouse him come to tragic, climactic ends. Definitely underground and moderately interesting. 85m/C VHS, Beta. Tab Hunter, Nadyne Turney, Roberta Collins, Isabel Jewell, John Aprea, Angel Fox; *D:* Curtis Hanson.

The Arrangement 🎬½ 1969 (R) Veteran advertising executive Douglas attempts suicide and then sets out to search for the meaning of life. Along the way he attempts to patch up his "arrangements" with his wife, his mistress and his father. Forced, slow, and self-conscious, though well acted. Adapted by Kazan from the director's own novel. 126m/C VHS, Beta. Kirk Douglas, Faye Dunaway, Deborah Kerr, Richard Boone, Hume Cronyn, Elia Kazan; *D:* Elia Kazan; *C:* Robert L. Surtees; *M:* David Amram. WAR

Arrest Bulldog Drummond 🎬🎬 1938 Captain Drummond is accused of killing the inventor of a futuristic detonator machine and must track down the real killers. Part of the "Bulldog Drummond" series. 57m/B VHS, Beta. John Howard, Heather Angel, George Zucco, H.B. Warner, E.E. Clive, Reginald Denny, John Sutton; *D:* James Hogan. PAR, RXM, SNC

The Arrival 🎬 1990 (R) An never-seen alien parasite turns an old man into a vampiric young stud after female blood. Plot and characterizations never do arrive. Horror director Stuart Gordon cameos as a hairy biker. *CW:* Language, violence, and sensuality. 107m/C VHS, LV. John Saxon, Joseph Culp, Robert Sampson, Michael J. Pollard; *Cameos:* David Schmoeller; *D:* David Schmoeller; *W:* David Schmoeller; *M:* Richard Band. PSM

The Arrival 🎬🎬½ *Shockwave* 1996 (PG-13) Radio astronomer Zane (Sheen) picks up a message from deep space and discovers a planned alien invasion. When he brings evidence of such to his boss Gordian (Silver) he finds himself on the run from both government operatives and morphing aliens. Starts off slow, but an intelligent script and premise makes this is a grade above cheesy. The aliens, with their kooky flaps of skin and back bending knees, are fun to watch. Directorial debut for Twohy. *CW:* Some sci-fi violence and terror, and for brief language. 109m/C VHS, LV, Closed Caption, DVD. Charlie Sheen, Ron Silver, Lindsay Crouse, Teri Polo; *D:* David N. Twohy; *W:* David N. Twohy; *C:* Hiro Narita; *M:* Arthur Kempel. LIV

Arrivederci, Baby! 🎬 1966 An unfunny sex comedy with Curtis as a modern Bluebeard who weds rich women and kills them for their money. His last mate plans to turn the tables and kill him first. 100m/C VHS, Closed Caption. Tony Curtis, Rosanna Schiaffino, Lionel Jeffries, Zsa Zsa Gabor, Nancy Kwan, Fenella Fielding, Anna Quayle, Warren Mitchell, Mischa Auer; *D:* Ken Hughes; *W:* Ken Hughes. PAR

Arrowhead 🎬🎬½ 1953 A long-running argument between a tough Cavalry scout and an Apache chief pits the cowboys against the Indians in this western fantasy. The personal battles that become all-out wars turn back to fist-fights before the matter is finally settled. 105m/C VHS, Beta, LV, Closed Caption. Charlton Heston, Jack Palance, Katy Jurado, Brian Keith, Milburn Stone; *D:* Charles Marquis Warren; *C:* Ray Rennahan. PAR

Arrowsmith 🎬🎬½ 1932 A small-town medical researcher battles his conscience as he juggles his selfish and unselfish motivations for the work he does. He travels to the West Indies to confront the issues of his life and come to terms with himself once and for all. A talented cast takes their time. Based on the classic Sinclair Lewis novel. Two edited versions available (99 and 89 minutes), both of which delete much of Loy. 95m/B VHS, Beta. Ronald Colman, Helen Hayes, Myrna Loy; *D:* John Ford. Nominations: Academy Awards '32: Best Adapted Screenplay, Best Cinematography, Best Interior Decoration, Best Picture.

Arsenal 🎬🎬🎬 1929 Classic Russian propagandist drama about strikes affecting the Russian home front during WWI, marking Dovzhenko's first great achievement in the realm of Eisenstein and Pudovkin. Silent. 70m/B VHS, Beta. RU Semyon Svashenko; *D:* Alexander Dovzhenko. NOS, MRV, IHF

The Arsenal Stadium Mystery 🎬🎬½ 1939 Inspector Banks of Scotland Yard tracks down the killer of a football star in this clever but unassuming murder mystery. 85m/B VHS. GB Leslie Banks, Greta Gynt, Ian MacLean, Liane Linden, Anthony Bushell, Esmond Knight; *D:* Thorold Dickinson. SNC

Arsenic and Old Lace 🎬🎬🎬½ 1944 Set-bound but energetic adaptation of the classic Joseph Kesselring play. Easy-going drama critic Grant is caught in a sticky situation when he learns of his aunts' favorite pastime. Apparently the kind, sweet, lonely spinsters lure gentlemen to the house and serve them elderberry wine with a touch of arsenic, then they bury the bodies in the cellar—a cellar which also serves as the Panama Canal for Grant's cousin (who thinks he's Theodore Roosevelt). Massey and Lorre excel in their sinister roles. One of the best madcap black comedies of all time—a must-see. Shot in 1941 and released a wee bit later. Available colorized. 158m/B VHS, Beta, LV, Closed Caption. Cary Grant, Josephine Hull, Jean Adair, Raymond Massey, Jack Carson, Priscilla Lane, John Alexander, Edward Everett Horton, John Ridgely, James Gleason, Peter Lorre; *D:* Frank Capra; *W:* Julius J. Epstein, Philip C. Epstein; *M:* Max Steiner. MGM, FOX, HMV

Art for Teachers of Children 🎬🎬 1995 Autobiographical account of 14-year-old Jennifer (McDonnell) who becomes a model for married photographer John (Hannah), who's also her boarding school dorm advisor. He's well-known for his nude portraits of young women as well as his affairs with his models and Jennifer's both confused and excited by her emerging sexuality as she and John become lovers. Remarkably detached considering the provocative subject matter. 82m/B VHS. Caitlin Grace McDonnell, Duncan Hannah, Coles Burroughs, Bryan Keane; *D:* Jennifer Montgomery; *W:* Jennifer Montgomery; *C:* Jennifer Montgomery. ZGI

The Art of Crime 🎬🎬½ 1975 A gypsy/detective is drawn into a homicide case when one of his fellow antique dealers is charged with murder. Maintains an atmospheric edge over others of the crime art genre. A pilot for a prospective television series based on the novel "Gypsy in Amber." 72m/C VHS. Ron Leibman, Jose Ferrer, David Hedison, Jill Clayburgh, Martin Smith; *D:* Richard Irving; *W:* Bill Davidson, Martin Smith. MOV

The Art of Dying 🎬🎬🎬 1990 A loony videophile decides to start staging productions of his all-time favorite scenes. Trouble is, his idea of a fabulous film moment calls for lots of blood and bile as he lures teenage runaways to his casting couch. Director Hauser stars as the cop who's none too impressed with the cinematic remakes, while cult favorite Pollard is his partner. If you like a little atmosphere and psychological depth in your slashers, you'll find this to be the stuff that populates film noir nightmares. 90m/C VHS, LV. Wings Hauser, Michael J. Pollard, Sarah Douglas, Kathleen Kinmont, Sydney Lassick; *D:* Wings Hauser. PMH

Arthur 🎬🎬🎬 1981 (PG) Spoiled, alcoholic billionaire Moore stands to lose everything he owns when he falls in love with a waitress. He must choose between wealth and a planned marriage, or poverty and love. Surprisingly funny, with an Oscar for Gielgud as Moore's valet, and great performance from Minnelli. Arguably the best role Moore's ever had, and he makes the most of it, taking the one-joke premise to a nomination for Oscar actor. ♫ Arthur's Theme; Blue Moon; If You Knew Susie; Santa Claus is Coming to Town. 97m/C VHS, Beta, LV, 8mm, Closed Caption. Dudley Moore, Liza Minnelli, John Gielgud, Geraldine Fitzgerald,

Stephen Elliott, Jill Eikenberry, Lou Jacobi, Ted Ross, Barney Martin; **D:** Steve Gordon; **M:** Burt Bacharach. Academy Awards '81: Best Song ("Arthur's Theme"), Best Supporting Actor (Gielgud); Golden Globe Awards '82: Best Actor—Musical/Comedy (Moore), Best Film—Musical/Comedy, Best Song ("Arthur's Theme"), Best Supporting Actor (Gielgud); Los Angeles Film Critics Association Awards '81: Best Supporting Actor (Gielgud); New York Film Critics Awards '81: Best Supporting Actor (Gielgud); Writers Guild of America '81: Best Original Screenplay; Nominations: Academy Awards '81: Best Actor (Moore), Best Original Screenplay. *WAR, FCT, BTV*

Arthur 2: On the Rocks 🐾½ 1988 (PG) When Arthur finally marries his sweetheart, it may not be "happily ever after" because the father of the girl he didn't marry is out for revenge. When Arthur discovers that he is suddenly penniless, a bit of laughter is the cure for the blues and also serves well when the liquor runs out. A disappointing sequel with few laughs. 113m/C VHS, Beta, LV, 8mm, Closed Caption. Dudley Moore, Liza Minnelli, John Gielgud, Geraldine Fitzgerald, Stephen Elliott, Ted Ross, Barney Martin, Jack Gilford; **D:** Bud Yorkin; **W:** Andy Breckman; **C:** Stephen Burum; **M:** Burt Bacharach. Golden Raspberry Awards '87: Worst Actress (Minnelli). *WAR, FCT*

Arthur's Hallowed Ground 🐾 1984 A cricket field caretaker battles the board of directors over the fate of his favorite plot of sod. 75m/C VHS, Beta. Jimmy Jewel, Jean Bolt, Michael Elphick; **D:** Frederick A. (Freddie) Young. *MGM*

Article 99 🐾🐾 1992 (R) Doctors in a Kansas City Veteran's Administration hospital try to heal patients while putting up with bureaucratic red tape and a stingy administrator. When rogue physician Sturgess (Liotta) is dismissed, the patients hold a siege. Sort of son of "M.A.S.H." (Big Daddy Sutherland did Hawkeye) that gets its title from a fictional rule that says veterans can be treated only for conditions related to military service. Erstwhile cast labors to combine comedic and dramatic intentions of script. 100m/C VHS, LV, Closed Caption. Ray Liotta, Kiefer Sutherland, Forest Whitaker, Lea Thompson, John C. McGinley, John Mahoney, Keith David, Kathy Baker, Eli Wallach, Noble Willingham, Julie Bovasso, Troy Evans, Lynne Thigpen, Jeffrey Tambor, Rutanya Alda; **D:** Howard Deutch; **W:** Ron Cutler; **C:** Rick Bota; **M:** Danny Elfman. *ORI*

Artists and Models 🐾🐾½ 1955 Martin is a struggling comic book artist and Lewis his idiot roommate. The pair become mixed up in both romance and intrigue when Lewis begins talking in his sleep about spies and such. One of the duo's more pleasant cinematic outings. 🎵Inamorata; Lucky Song; You Look So Familiar; Why You Pretend. 109m/C VHS, Closed Caption. Dean Martin, Jerry Lewis, Shirley MacLaine, Dorothy Malone, Eddie Mayehoff, Eva Gabor, Anita Ekberg, George Winslow, Jack Elam, Herbert Rudley, Nick Castle; **D:** Frank Tashlin; **W:** Frank Tashlin, Hal Kanter, Herbert Baker; **C:** Daniel F. Fapp. *PAR, MLB*

Artist's Studio Secrets 🐾 *The Story of an Artist's Studio Secrets; Artist Nude Secrets* 1964 An artist from Greenwich Village only gets aroused by clothed models, so his wife jealously arranges for him to only work with nude women. 78m/B VHS, Beta. *VDM, TPV*

As Good as Dead 🐾🐾½ 1995 (PG-13) A young woman allows her sick friend to assume her identity but when her friend is murdered, she realizes the killer was really after her.**CW:** Violence. 88m/C VHS, Beta, Closed Caption. Crystal Bernard, Traci Lords, Judge Reinhold; **D:** Larry Cohen; **W:** Larry Cohen. *PAR*

As If It Were Raining 🐾🐾 1963 Constantine gets involved in an embezzlement scheme in Spain in this espionage thriller. 85m/C VHS. **FR** Eddie Constantine, Henri Cogan, Elisa Montes, Jose Nieto, Silvia Solar; **D:** Jose Monter. *SNC*

As Is 🐾2½ 1985 Two gay New Yorkers deal with a troubled romance and AIDS. A cable television adaptation from the William M. Hoffman play. 86m/C VHS, Beta. Jonathan Hadary, Robert Carradine; **D:** Michael Lindsay-Hogg. *ORI, WAR*

As Summers Die 🐾🐾 1986 Louisiana attorney Glenn fights in the late 1950s to protect the rights of a black family, against the wishes of a powerful local clan. Glenn finds support in surprising places, though. From Winston Groom's acclaimed novel. A cable television movie. 100m/C VHS, Beta. Scott Glenn, Jamie Lee Curtis, Penny Fuller, Bette Davis, John Randolph, Beah Richards, Ron O'Neal, John McIntire; **D:** Jean-Claude Tramont. *CNG*

As You Desire Me 🐾🐾 1932 Garbo plays an amnesia victim who returns to a husband she doesn't even remember after an abusive relationship with a novelist. An interesting, if not down-right bizarre movie, due to the pairing of the great Garbo and the intriguing von Stroheim. An adaption of Luigi Pirandello's play. 71m/B VHS, Beta. Greta Garbo, Melvyn Douglas, Erich von Stroheim, Owen Moore, Hedda Hopper; **D:** George Fitzmaurice. *MGM, FCT*

As You Like It 🐾🐾½ 1936 A Duke's banished daughter poses as a man to win the attentions of one of her father's attendants in this highly stylized Shakespearean comedy adapted by J.M. Barrie and Robert Cullen. Early Shakespearean Olivier. 96m/B VHS, Beta, LV. **GB** Elisabeth Bergner, Laurence Olivier, Henry Ainley, Felix Aylmer; **D:** Paul Czinner; **W:** J.M. Barrie, Robert Cullen. *NOS, MRV, VYY*

As You Were 🐾 1951 A girl with a photographic memory enlists in the Army, becoming both a nuisance and comedic victim to her sergeant. 57m/B VHS, Beta, LV. Joseph Sawyer, William Tracy, Sondra Rogers, Joan Vohs. *NO*

As Young As You Feel 🐾🐾🐾 1951 A 65-year-old man is forced to retire from his job. He poses as the head of the conglomerate and convinces them to repeal their retirement policy. He then gains national publicity when he makes a speech about the dignity of man. Watch for Monroe as the boss's secretary. Fine comic performances enhance the script; based on a story by Chayefsky. 77m/C VHS. Monty Woolley, Thelma Ritter, David Wayne, Jean Peters, Constance Bennett, Marilyn Monroe, Allyn Joslyn, Albert Dekker, Clinton Sundberg, Minor Watson; **D:** Harmon Jones; **W:** Paddy Chayefsky. *FXV*

The Ascent 🐾🐾½ 1994 (PG) Based on the true story of Franco (Spano) a WWII Italian POW who's held in a camp in Africa. The prisoners enjoy making fun of the camp commander (Cross), who consistently fails at his attempts to climb the 15,500 peak of Mt. Kenya. Meanwhile, Franco decides to escape and climb the mountain himself—with the commander right behind. Beware if you suffer from vertigo. 96m/C VHS, Closed Caption. Vincent Spano, Ben Cross, Tony LoBianco, Rachel Ward; **D:** Donald Shebib; **C:** David Connell. *CAF*

Ash Wednesday 🐾 1973 (R) Taylor endures the pain of cosmetic surgery in an effort to rescue her floundering union with Fonda. Another undistinguished performance by Liz. Fonda is especially slimy as the philandering husband, but only appears in the latter stages of the film. 99m/C VHS, Closed Caption. Elizabeth Taylor, Henry Fonda, Helmut Berger, Keith Baxter, Margaret Blye, Maurice Teynac, Monique Van Vooren; **D:** Larry Peerce; **M:** Maurice Jarre. *PAR, CCB*

Ashanti, Land of No Mercy 🐾🐾 *Ashanti* 1979 Caine of the week movie with Michael portraying a doctor acting as a missionary in South Africa who finds himself alone in a battle to rescue his wife from a band of slave traders. The chase spans many Middle Eastern countries and begins to look bleak for our man. Talented cast and promising plot are undone by slow pace. Based on the novel "Ebano" by Alberto Vasquez-Figueroa. 117m/C VHS, Beta. Michael Caine, Omar Sharif, Peter Ustinov, Rex Harrison, William Holden, Beverly Johnson; **D:** Richard Fleischer. *TWE*

Ashes and Diamonds 🐾🐾🐾½ *Popiol i Diament* 1958 In the closing days of WWII, a Polish resistance fighter assassinates the wrong man, tries to find love with the right women, and questions the meaning of struggle. A seminal Eastern

European masterpiece that defined a generation of pre-solidarity Poles. Available in Polish with English subtitles or dubbed into English. The last installment of the trilogy that includes "A Generation" and "Kanal" and based on a novel by Jerzy Andrzewski. 105m/B VHS, Beta, LV. **PL** Zbigniew Cybulski, Eva Krzyzewska, Adam Pawlikowski, Bogumil Kobiela, Waclaw Zastrzezynski; **D:** Andrzej Wajda. Venice Film Festival '59: International Critics Award. *ING, MRV, NLC*

Ashes and Embers 🐾🐾 1982 A black Vietnam vet in Los Angeles has trouble fitting into society, eventually running afoul of the police. Ethiopian-born director Gerima endows vital subject matter with a properly alienated mood. 120m/C VHS. John Anderson, Evelyn Blackwell; **D:** Haile Gerima. *FCT*

Ashik Kerib 🐾🐾🐾 1988 Ashik Kerib is a wandering minstrel who is rejected by a rich merchant as his daughter's suitor. He then journeys for 1,000 days trying to earn enough money to marry his beloved. Along the way he's imprisoned by an evil sultan and rides a flying horse, among other adventures. Wonderful use of exotic makeup and costumes highlight this Arabian Nights tale. Adapted from a story by Mikhail Lermontov. Paradjanov's last film. In Russian with English subtitles. 75m/C VHS. **RU** Yiur Mgoyan, Veronika Metonidze, Levan Natroshvili, Sofiko Chiaureli; **D:** Dodo Abashidze, Sergei Paradjanov; **W:** Giya Badridze; **M:** Djavashir Kuliev. *KIV, FCT*

Ask Any Girl 🐾🐾½ 1959 Lighthearted fluff about a small-town girl who moves to Manhattan. MacLaine plays the bright Meg who gets a job at an ad agency and decides to set her sights on marrying her boss (Young). She asks her older brother's (Niven) help in her quest and the inevitable happens. 101m/C VHS. Shirley MacLaine, David Niven, Gig Young, Rod Taylor, Jim Backus, Claire Kelly, Elisabeth Fraser; **D:** Charles Walters. British Academy Awards '59: Best Actress (MacLaine). *MGM, MOV*

Aspen Extreme 🐾 1993 (PG-13) Former Aspen ski instructor writes and directs a movie on (what else?) ski instructors in (where?) Aspen! Long on ski shots and short on plot, this movie never leaves the bunny hill. Two Detroiters leave Motown for Snowtown to pursue a life on the slopes. T.J (Gross) soon has his hands full with two beautiful women (Polo and Hughes) who encourage his dream of becoming a writer. His friend Dexter (Berg), however, acquires a few bad habits, and the whole movie just goes downhill from there.**CW:** Language, nudity, and drug content. 128m/C VHS, Beta, LV, Closed Caption. Paul Gross, Peter Berg, Finola Hughes, Teri Polo, Martin Kemp, Nicolette Scorsese, William Russ; **D:** Patrick Hasburgh; **W:** Patrick Hasburgh; **M:** Michael Convertino. *HPH, TOU*

The Asphalt Jungle 🐾🐾🐾🐾 1950 An aging criminal emerges from his forced retirement (prison) and assembles the old gang for one final heist. A very realistic storyline and a superb cast make this one of the best crime films ever made. Highly acclaimed; based on the work of W.R. Burnett. 112m/B VHS, Beta, LV. Sterling Hayden, Louis Calhern, Jean Hagen, James Whitmore, Sam Jaffe, John McIntire, Marc Lawrence, Barry Kelley, Anthony Caruso, Teresa Celli, Marilyn Monroe; **D:** John Huston; **W:** Ben Maddow; **M:** Miklos Rozsa. Edgar Allan Poe Awards '50: Best Screenplay; National Board of Review Awards '50: 10 Best Films of the Year, Best Director (Huston); Venice Film Festival '50: Best Actor (Hayden); Nominations: Academy Awards '50: Best Black and White Cinematography, Best Director (Huston), Best Screenplay, Best Supporting Actor (Jaffe). *MGM*

The Asphyx 🐾🐾🐾 *Spirit of the Dead* 1972 (PG) Nineteenth century doctor Stephens is studying death when he discovers The Asphyx, an aura that surrounds a person just before they die. Stephens delves deeper into his research and finds the keys to immortality. However, his irresponsibility in unleashing the obscure supernatural power on the world brings a swarm of unforeseen and irreversible troubles. High-class sci fi. 98m/C VHS, Beta. **GB** Robert Stephens, Robert Powell, Jane Lapotaire, Alex Scott, Ralph Arliss, Fiona Walker, John Lawrence; **D:** Peter Newbrook; **C:** Frederick A. (Freddie) Young. *MED*

Assassin *&* 1979 Athletic karate fighter poses as an underworld figure and infiltrates the largest gang in Japan where he is hired as a hit man. 86m/C **VHS, Beta.** Sonny Chiba. *FOX*

Assassin *& &* 1986 (PG-13) Made for TV drama about a mad scientist who creates a bionic killer for a bizarre plot to take over the world. He programs the cyborg to assassinate the President and other key people to help carry out his plan. A retired CIA operative emerges to stop the scientist by trying to destroy the robot. 94m/C **VHS, Beta.** Robert Conrad, Karen Austin, Richard Young, Jonathan Banks, Robert Webber; **D:** Sandor Stern. *ACA*

Assassin *& &* 1989 (R) Fairly lame thriller about a CIA agent protecting a Senator who falls under suspicion when his charge is shot by an assassin. In investigating the killing the agent discovers the usual governmental conspiracy. 92m/C **VHS, Beta, LV.** Steve Railsback, Nicholas Guest, Xander Berkeley, Elpidia Carrillo; **D:** Jon Hess. *NO*

Assassin of Youth *&½* 1935 Girl is introduced to marijuana and soon becomes involved in "the thrills of wild parties," and the horrors of the "killer weed." Camp diversion. 70m/B **VHS, Beta.** Luana Walters, Arthur Gardner; **D:** Elmer Clifton. *SNC, NOS, DVT*

Assassination *&* 1987 (R) A serious threat has been made to First Lady Ireland and no one is taking it lightly. Secret Service agent Bronson has been called as Ireland's personal bodyguard and suddenly they are both the target of terrorist attacks. Strangely though, the attacks seem to be directed from inside the White House. Bronson as you've seen him many times before. 93m/C **VHS, Beta, LV, Closed Caption.** Charles Bronson, Jill Ireland, Stephen Elliott, Michael Ansara; **D:** Peter Hunt; **C:** Hanania Baer. *MED, VTR*

The Assassination Bureau *& & &* 1969 Set in Victorian-era London, this amusing farce concerns a society of international assassins led by the charming Reed. Rigg is an intrepid reporter who pays Reed to have his own organization try to kill him. Reed in turn will try to get them first. A cross-European chase ends in a battle aboard a Zeppelin. Tongue-in-cheek whimsey with a fine cast. Based on a short story by Jack London. 106m/C **VHS, LV, Closed Caption.** *GB* Oliver Reed, Diana Rigg, Telly Savalas, Curt Jurgens, Philippe Noiret, Warren Mitchell, Beryl Reid, Clive Revill, Kenneth Griffith, Vernon Dobtcheff, Annabella Incontrera; **D:** Basil Dearden; **C:** Geoffrey Unsworth. *PAR*

The Assassination Game *&* 1992 (R) Rookie CIA agent teams up with a veteran KGB agent to prevent the assassination of a world leader. 90m/C **VHS.** Robert Rusler, Theodore Bikel, Doug Wert, Denise Bixler; **D:** Jonathan Winfrey. *NHO*

Assassination of Trotsky *&* 1972 Middling attempt to dramatize the last days of the Russian Revolutionary leader in Mexico before he's done in with an ice pick. 113m/C **VHS, Beta, LV.** *FR GB IT* Richard Burton, Alain Delon, Romy Schneider, Valentina Cortese, Jean Desailly; **D:** Joseph Losey; **C:** Pasquale De Santos. *REP, FCT*

The Assassination Run *&* 1984 A retired British spy is involved against his will in an intricate plot of terrorism, counter-terrorism and espionage. 111m/C **VHS, Beta.** *GB* Malcolm Stoddard, Mary Tamm; **D:** Ken Hannam. *FOX*

Assassins *& &½* 1995 (R) Stallone gets to play elder statesman in the very deadly rivalry between two contract killers. Robert Rath (Stallone) is the man—number one with a bullet—whose reputation has caught up with him. Hot-headed Miguel Bain (the ever-smoldering Banderas) wants to off Rath and assume the position of top hitman. Caught in the middle of this macho posturing is surveillance expert—and potential murderee—Electra (Moore). It's Stallone to the rescue but his character pays more attention to Pearl, Electra's pampered Persian cat than to the

lovely lady herself. But then romance isn't what this film is about—and director Donner does know his action.**CW:** Violence and language. 132m/C **VHS.** Sylvester Stallone, Antonio Banderas, Julianne Moore, Anatoly Davydov; **D:** Richard Donner; **W:** Brian Helgeland, Andy Wachowski, Larry Wachowski; **C:** Vilmos Zsigmond; **M:** Mark Mancina. Nominations: Golden Raspberry Awards '95: Worst Actor (Stallone). *WAR*

Assault *&½* *In the Devil's Garden; Tower of Terror; The Creepers* 1970 Violent sex murders in a girl's school have the police baffled. The school's pretty art teacher offers to act as bait in order to catch the murderer. 89m/C **VHS, Beta.** *GB* Suzy Kendall, Frank Finlay, Freddie Jones, James Laurenson, Lesley-Anne Down, Tony Beckley; **D:** Sidney Hayers.

The Assault *& & &½* *De Aanslag* 1986 (PG) Powerful and disturbing drama about a Dutch boy who witnesses the arbitrary murder of his family by Nazis. The memory tortures him and leaves him empty as he matures. Years later he meets other victims and also the perpetrators of the incident, each of them changed forever by it. Thought-provoking consideration of WWII and the horrors of living in Nazi Germany from many points of view. Based on a novel by Harry Mulisch. Dutch language dubbed into English. 149m/C **VHS, Beta.** *NL* Derek De Lint, Marc Van Uchelen, Monique Van De Ven; **D:** Fons Rademakers. Academy Awards '86: Best Foreign Language Film; Golden Globe Awards '87: Best Foreign Film. *MGM, SWC*

Assault and Matrimony *&½* 1987 Real-life married people Tucker and Eikenberry play a married couple fighting tooth and nail. Lots of slapstick and general nonsense. Television film based on James Anderson's novel. 100m/C **VHS, Beta, LV, Closed Caption.** John Hillerman, Michelle Phillips, Joe Cortese, Michael Tucker, Jill Eikenberry; **D:** James Frawley. *THV*

Assault at West Point: The Court-Martial of Johnson Whittaker *& &½* 1994 (PG-13) In 1880, Johnson C. Whittaker, a black West Point cadet, is found beaten, mutilated, and tied to his bed. Instead of seeking his attackers, the Academy sets up a court martial to expel Whittaker, claiming he faked his own attack. Clashes also ignite between Whittaker's defense counsel—white abolitionist lawyer Chamberlain, whose own racism is thinly disguised—and black lawyer Greener, who originally encouraged Whittaker to enroll at the Point. Interesting case but a shallow production. Based on a true story and adapted from the book by John Marszalek. Made for television. 98m/C **VHS, Closed Caption.** Seth Gilliam, Samuel L. Jackson, Sam Waterston, John Glover, Al Freeman Jr.; **D:** Harry Moses; **W:** Harry Moses; **M:** Terence Blanchard. *REP*

Assault of the Killer Bimbos *&½* 1988 (R) A show girl gets framed for the murder of her boss and takes off for the border with a couple of girlfriends. On the way they get pursued by the expected dumb cops and meet up with horny, clean-cut hunks. In Mexico they encounter the villain and extract comic vengeance. Watchable mainly due to the likable female leads and pleasant, lightly camp execution, although it might prove too tame for most of its target audience. 85m/C **VHS, Beta.** Patti Astor, Christina Whitaker, Elizabeth Kaitan, Griffin O'Neal, Nick Cassavetes, Clayton Landey, Eddie Deezen, Arell Blanton, David Marsh, Tammara Souza, Jamie Bozian, Mike Muscat, Jeffrey Orman, John Quern; **D:** Patti Astor; **W:** Patti Astor, Anita Rosenberg; **C:** Thomas Callaway; **M:** Fred Lapides, Marc Ellis. *AFE*

Assault of the Party Nerds *&* 1989 (R) Nerds throw a wild party to try and attract new members to their fraternity, while a jock frat plots against them. Sound familiar? Little more than a ripoff of "Revenge of the Nerds" made especially for video. 82m/C **VHS, Beta.** Linnea Quigley, Troy Donahue, Richard Gabai, C. Paul Demsey, Marc Silverberg, Robert Mann, Richard Rifkin, Deborah Roush; **D:** Richard Gabai. *PSM*

Assault of the Party Nerds 2: Heavy Petting Detective *&* 1995 Detective tries to save a beauty from her scheming husband. 87m/C **VHS.** Linnea Quigley, Richard Gabai, Michelle (McClellan) Bauer, Arte Johnson, Burt Ward. *VCI*

Assault of the Rebel Girls *&½* *Cuban Rebel Girls; Attack of the Rebel Girls* A reporter gets involved with smuggling in Castro's Cuba. Flynn's last film, saving the worst for last. 66m/B **VHS, Beta.** Errol Flynn, Beverly Aadland, John McKay, Jackie Jackler, Marie Edmund; **D:** Barry Mahon; **W:** Errol Flynn. *MED*

Assault on a Queen *&* 1966 Stupid Sinatra vehicle about a group of con men who plot together to rob the Queen Mary on one of her trips. Their attack vessel is a renovated WWII German U-boat. The producers tried to capitalize on the popularity of "Ocean's Eleven," but they didn't even come close. Based on a novel by Jack Finney. 106m/C **VHS, Closed Caption.** Frank Sinatra, Virna Lisi, Anthony (Tony) Franciosa, Richard Conte, Reginald Denny; **D:** Jack Donohue; **W:** Rod Serling; **C:** William H. Daniels. *PAR*

Assault on Agathon *& &* 1975 (PG) Amid the scenic Greek isles, an "executed" WWII guerilla leader returns to lead a revolution, and bloodshed and bombings ensue. 95m/C **VHS, Beta.** *GB IT* Nina Van Pallandt, Marianne Faithfull, John Woodvine, Nico Minardos; **D:** Laslo Benedek. *GEM, MRV, PSM*

Assault on Precinct 13 *& & &* 1976 Urban horror invades LA. A sleepy police station in Los Angeles is suddenly under siege from a violent youth gang. Paranoia abounds as the police are attacked from all sides and can see no way out. Carpenter's musical score adds much to the setting of this unique police exploitation story that somehow stands as Carpenter's adaptation of Howard Hawks' "Rio Bravo." Semi-acclaimed and very gripping. 91m/C **VHS, Beta, LV.** Austin Stoker, Darwin Joston, Martin West, Tony Burton, Nancy Loomis, Kim Richards, Henry Brandon; **D:** John Carpenter; **W:** John Carpenter; **M:** John Carpenter. *MED*

Assault with a Deadly Weapon *&* 1982 When the police budget is cutback, crime runs rampant in an unnamed American city. 86m/C **VHS, Beta.** Sandra Foley, Richard Holliday, Lamont Jackson; **D:** Arthur Kennedy. *LIV*

The Assignment *& &* 1978 The assassination of a high-ranking officer in an uneasy Latin American nation spurs violence and political instability. A Swedish diplomat is assigned the tremendous task of restoring peace and stability between the political factions. 92m/C **VHS, Beta.** *SW* Christopher Plummer, Thomas Hellberg, Carolyn Seymour, Fernando Rey; **D:** Mats Arehn. *NWV*

Assignment Outer Space *&* *Space Men* 1961 A giant spaceship with bytes for brains is on a collision course with Earth. A team of astronauts is sent to save the world from certain peril. Seems they take the task lightly, though, and their mission (and hence the plot) revolves more around saving sexy sultress Farinon from certain celibacy. If you're into stultifying Italian space operas with a gratuitous sex sub-plot then look up this assignment, but don't say we didn't warn you. Narrated by Jack Wallace; director Margheriti is also known as Anthony Dawson, not to be confused with the actor of the same name. 79m/B **VHS.** *IT* Rik von Nutter, Gabriella Farinon, Archie Savage, Dave Montresor, Alan Dijon; **D:** Anthony (Antonio Margheriti) Dawson. *NOS, SNC*

Assignment Skybolt *&½* 198? When terrorists get their hands on a hydrogen bomb, a special mission is detached to stop them before they start WWIII. 109m/C **VHS, Beta.** **D:** Greg Tallas. *BFV*

The Assisi Underground *& &* 1984 True but boringly told story of how the Catholic Church helped to save several hundred Italian Jews from being executed by the Nazis during the 1943 German occupation of Italy. Edited from 178 minutes, a good-will gesture from the producers.

115m/C **VHS, Beta.** James Mason, Ben Cross, Maximilian Schell, Irene Papas; *D:* Alexander Ramati; *M:* Pino Donaggio. *MGM, IGP*

The Associate 🎬🎬 *L'Associe* 1979 (R) French farce about penniless financial consultant Julien Pardot (Serrault) who invents a fictitious partner, Mr. Davis, in order to get his business rolling. When his clients, his wife, and even his mistress are all more intrigued by the partner than Julien, he becomes so jealous he decides to "murder" his creation. Based on the novel "My Partner, Mr. Davis" by Jenaro Prieto. French with subtitles; remade in 1996 with Whoopi Goldberg. 93m/C **VHS.** *FR* Michel Serrault, Claudine Auger, Catherine Alric, Matthieu Carriere; *D:* Rene Gainville; *W:* Jean-Claude Carriere. *FRF*

The Associate 🎬🎬 1996 (PG-13) Whoopi drags a 20-minute premise over almost two hours when she invents an elderly, white, male business partner to give her fledgling financial consulting business some prestige. After having all her moneymaking ideas appropriated by male colleagues, Laurel Ayres (Goldberg) starts her own business, only to find that no one wants to hire her. She creates the genius and the money comes rolling in. Everyone clamors to meet the mystery man, so she goes undercover as the elusive Robert S. Cutty. The sight of Goldberg in old white guy garb and makeup is jarring, and the payoff doesn't merit the overlong build up. Based on the French film "L'Associe" and the Jenaro Prieto novel "El Socio." *CW:* Sensuality and an exotic dance club scene. 113m/C **VHS.** Whoopi Goldberg, Timothy Daly, Bebe Neuwirth, Dianne Wiest, Eli Wallach; *D:* Donald Petrie; *W:* Nick Thiel; *C:* Alex Nepomniaschy; *M:* Christopher Tyng. *TOU*

The Association 🎬½ 198? A man and a woman go undercover to bust an international white slavery ring. 92m/C **VHS, Beta.** *TW* Carter Huang, Angela Mao; *D:* Cheung Wo Chang. *NO*

Assunta Spina 🎬 1915 A very early, very rare Italian epic about ancient Rome, the prototype for the Italian silent epics to come. 70m/B **VHS, Beta.** *IT FCT*

The Astounding She-Monster woof! *Mysterious Invader* 1958 How can you not love a movie with a title like this? A bad script and snail-paced plot are a good start. A geologist wanting only to be left alone with his rocks survives a brush with the kidnappers of a wealthy heiress only to happen upon an alien spacecraft that's crashed nearby. At the helm is a very tall, high-heeled fem-alien in an obligatory skintight space outfit. Excellent, our rock jock thinks, but it seems she kills with the slightest touch. For connoisseurs of truly bad movies. 60m/B **VHS.** Robert Clarke, Kenne Duncan, Marilyn Harvey, Jeanne Tatum, Shirley Kilpatrick, Ewing Miles Brown; *D:* Ronnie Ashcroft. *SNC, MRV, CNM*

The Astro-Zombies woof! 1967 A contender as one of the worst movies of all time. Carradine plays a mad scientist creating zombies who eat people's guts. Cult favorite Satana stars. Co-written and co-produced by Rogers of "M*A*S*H" fame. 83m/C **VHS, Beta.** Tura Satana, Wendell Corey, John Carradine, Tom Pace, Joan Patrick, Rafael Campos; *D:* Ted V. Mikels; *W:* Ted V. Mikels, Wayne Rogers. *NO*

Asylum 🎬🎬½ *House of Crazies* 1972 (PG) Four strange and chilling stories weave together in this film. A murderer's victim seeks retribution. A tailor seems to be collecting his bills. A man who makes voodoo dolls...only to become one later on. A woman plagued by a double. A doctor visiting the asylum tells each tale. Horrifying and grotesque, not as humorless as American horror films. 100m/C **VHS, Beta, LV.** *GB* Peter Cushing, Herbert Lom, Britt Ekland, Barbara Parkins, Patrick Magee, Barry Morse; *D:* Roy Ward Baker. *PSM, MED*

Asylum of Satan 🎬 1972 A beautiful concert pianist is savagely tortured by a madman in the Asylum of Satan. Filmed on location in Louisville, Kentucky. 87m/C **VHS, Beta.** Charles Kissinger,

Carla Borelli, Nick Jolly, Sherry Steiner; *D:* William Girdler; *W:* William Girdler. *VCI*

At Close Range 🎬🎬🎬 1986 (R) Based on the true story of Bruce Johnston Sr. and Jr. in Brandywine River Valley, Pennsylvania. Father, Walken, tempts his teen-aged son, Penn, into pursuing criminal activities with talk of excitement and high living. Penn soon learns that his father is extremely dangerous and a bit unstable, but he's still fascinated by his wealth and power. Sometimes overbearing and depressing, but good acting and fancy camera work. A young cast of stars includes Masterson as the girl Penn tries to impress. Features Madonna's "Live to Tell." 115m/C **VHS, Beta, LV, Closed Caption.** Sean Penn, Christopher Walken, Christopher Penn, Mary Stuart Masterson, Crispin Glover, Kiefer Sutherland, Candy Clark, Tracey Walter, Millie Perkins, Alan Autry, David Strathairn, Eileen Ryan; *D:* James Foley; *W:* Nicholas Kazan; *C:* Juan Ruiz-Anchia; *M:* Patrick Leonard. *VES, LIV*

At First Sight 🎬½ *Two Guys Talkin' About Girls* 1995 (R) Yakky pedestrian comedy about schleppy Lenny (Silverman) and his best friend, macho Joey (Cortese), trying to help each other out with their romantic crises. Lenny meets cute when he picks up Rhonda (Smith) at the planetarium while Joey beds a string of girls, all of whom are named Cindy, in an effort to get over the first Cindy who broke his heart. It's been done before—and better. *CW:* Crude sexuality and language. 90m/C **VHS.** Jonathan Silverman, Dan Cortese, Allison Smith, Monte Markham, Kathleen Freeman, Susan Walters; *D:* Steven Pearl; *W:* Ken Copel; *C:* Glenn Kershaw; *M:* Richard Gibbs. *THV*

At Gunpoint 🎬🎬 *Gunpoint* 1955 A store owner becomes the town hero when, by accident, he shoots and kills a bank robber. 81m/C **VHS, Beta.** Fred MacMurray, Dorothy Malone, John Qualen, Walter Brennan; *D:* Alfred Werker; *C:* Ellsworth Fredericks. *REP, HHE*

At Gunpoint 🎬½ 1990 A no-account bank robber spends his six year stint in the slammer plotting his revenge. Having gone thoroughly stir-crazy, the vengeful criminal stalks the lawman who put him away, like so many vengeful criminals before him. Run of the mill addition to big list of bad-guy-hunting-for-revenge flicks. 90m/C **VHS.** Frank Kanig, Tain Bodkin, Scott Claflin; *D:* Steven Harris; *W:* Steven Harris. *CAF*

At Home with the Webbers 🎬🎬 1994 (R) Gerald, Emma, Johnny, and Miranda Webber win a contest to star in a cable TV series about their lives. What they don't expect is that the series will become a hit or that all the family idiosyncrasies will be exaggerated by stardom (the manipulative TV producer doesn't help). Over-the-top comedy requires tolerance but does have some amusing performances. 109m/C **VHS, LV, Closed Caption.** Jeffrey Tambor, Rita Taggart, Jennifer Tilly, David Arquette, Robby Benson, Brian Bloom, Caroline Goodall; *D:* Brad Marlowe; *W:* Brad Marlowe. *LIV*

At Midnight, I'll Take Your Soul 🎬 *A Meia-Noite Levarei Sua Alma* 1963 Brazilian import about sadistic gravedigger Coffin Joe (alter ego of director Jose Mojica Marins), who wanders the streets of his hometown in order to meet a desirable woman. His mission is to sire a son to continue his legacy and wiggle his lips at screaming women. A study in psycho-sexual horror, this makes "Apocalypse Now" look like a beach party. Coffin Joe, or "Ze do Caixao," is a kind of South American Freddy or Jason; Mojica Marin's movies—which are graphically sadistic—were banned by the Brazilian government. In Portugese with English subtitles. Followed by "Tonight I'll Be Incarnated in Your Corpse." ?m/B **VHS.** *BR* Jose Mojica Marins; *D:* Jose Mojica Marins. *SMW, FCT, TPV*

At Play in the Fields of the Lord 🎬🎬🎬 1991 (R) A thoughtful epic that never quite lives up to its own self-importance—or length. Two yankee missionary couples try to evangelize a fearsome tribe of Brazilian rain-for-

est dwellers. One of the Christian families suffers a crisis of faith that's well-acted but not as powerful as a co-plot regarding a modern American Indian (Berenger) who joins the jungle natives with calamitous results. Based on the novel by Peter Matthiessen. *CW:* Language and sensuality. 186m/C **VHS, Beta, LV, Closed Caption.** Tom Berenger, Aidan Quinn, Kathy Bates, John Lithgow, Daryl Hannah, Tom Waits, Stenio Garcia, Nelson Xavier, Jose Dumont, Niilo Kivirinta; *D:* Hector Babenco; *W:* Hector Babenco, Jean-Claude Carriere; *M:* Zbigniew Preisner. *USH*

At Sword's Point 🎬🎬 *Sons of the Musketeers* 1951 Adventure tale based on Alexandre Dumas' "The Three Musketeers," wherein the sons of the musketeers vie to save their queen from the evil plots of Duke Douglas. 81m/C **VHS, Beta, LV.** Cornel Wilde, Maureen O'Hara, Robert Douglas, Dan O'Herlihy, Alan Hale Jr., Blanche Yurka; *D:* Lewis Allen. *MED, TTC, FCT*

At the Circus 🎬🎬½ *The Marx Brothers at the Circus* 1939 Marx Brothers invade the circus to save it from bankruptcy and cause their usual comic insanity, though they've done it better before. Beginning of the end for the Marxes, a step down in quality from their classic work, though frequently darn funny. ♫Lydia the Tattooed Lady; Step Up and Take a Bow; Two Blind Loves; Blue Moon. 87m/B **VHS, Beta, LV.** Groucho Marx, Chico Marx, Harpo Marx, Margaret Dumont, Kenny L. Baker, Florence Rice, Eve Arden, Nat Pendleton, Fritz Feld; *D:* Edward Buzzell. *MGM*

At the Earth's Core 🎬🎬 1976 (PG) A Victorian scientist invents a giant burrowing machine, which he and his crew use to dig deeply into the Earth. To their surprise, they discover a lost world of subhuman creatures and prehistoric monsters. Based on Edgar Rice Burrough's novels. 90m/C **VHS, Beta.** *GB* Doug McClure, Peter Cushing, Caroline Munro, Cy Grant, Godfrey James, Keith Barron; *D:* Kevin Connor. *WAR, OM*

At War with the Army 🎬🎬 1950 Serviceable comedy from Martin and Lewis in their first starring appearance, as the recruits get mixed up in all kinds of wild situations at their army base. Based on the play by James Allardice. 93m/B **VHS, Beta.** Dean Martin, Jerry Lewis, Polly Bergen, Mike Kellin; *D:* Hal Walker. *NOS, MRV, CAB*

Atalia 🎬🎬 1985 Relates the love between Atalia, a war widow, and the younger man she loves. The problem stems from the fact that she lives in a Kibbutz, and the lifestyle contradicts sharply from that of her beliefs in love, forcing her to eventually make a momentous decision. 90m/C **VHS.** Michal Bat-Adam, Yftach Katzur, Dan Toren; *D:* Akiva Tevet. *ERG*

Athena 🎬🎬½ 1954 Two sisters (Powell and Reynolds) from an eccentric, health-faddist family fall in love with their opposites. Purdom is the stuffy Boston lawyer who goes off with Powell and Reynolds entices a TV crooner (Damone). Routine romance with routine songs. Reeves, who would become a star as a movie muscleman, appears in a brief role. ♫Love Can Change the Stars; The Girl Next Door; Imagine; Venezia; Chacun le Sait; I Never Felt Better; Vocalize. 96m/C **VHS.** Jane Powell, Debbie Reynolds, Edmund Purdom, Vic Damone, Louis Calhern, Evelyn Varden, Linda Christian, Virginia Gibson, Nancy Kilgas, Dolores Starr, Jane Fischer, Cecile Rogers, Steve Reeves; *D:* Richard Thorpe; *W:* William Ludwig, Leonard Spigelgass; *M:* Hugh Martin, Ralph Blane. *MGM*

Atlantic City 🎬🎬🎬½ *Atlantic City U.S.A* 1981 (R) A small-time, aging Mafia hood falls in love with a young clam bar waitress, and they share the spoils of a big score against the backdrop of Atlantic City. Wonderful character study that becomes something more, a piercing declaration about a city's transformation and the effect on the people who live there. Lancaster, in a sterling performance, personifies the city, both of them fading with time. 104m/C **VHS, Beta, LV.** *FR CA* Burt Lancaster, Susan Sarandon, Kate Reid, Michel Piccoli, Hollis McLaren; *D:* Louis Malle. British Academy Awards

'81: Best Actor (Lancaster), Best Director (Malle); Genie Awards '81: Best Supporting Actress (Reid); Los Angeles Film Critics Association Awards '81: Best Actor (Lancaster), Best Film, Best Screenplay; New York Film Critics Awards '81: Best Actor (Lancaster), Best Screenplay; National Society of Film Critics Awards '81: Best Actor (Lancaster), Best Director (Malle), Best Film, Best Screenplay; Nominations: Academy Awards '81: Best Actor (Lancaster), Best Actress (Sarandon), Best Director (Malle), Best Original Screenplay, Best Picture. *PAR*

Atlantis, the Lost Continent 🎬 1961
If anything could sink the fabled lost continent of Atlantis it's this cheap fantasy flick. A greek sailor saves a princess and takes her back to her Atlantis home where he's promptly enslaved by the island's evil ruler. But this hero won't put up with any nonsense so he leads his fellow slaves in a revolt and gains his freedom before sinking both evil ruler and island (using atomic power no less!). **90m/C VHS.** Anthony Hall, Joyce Taylor, John Dall, Bill Smith, Edward Platt, Frank De Kova; **D:** George Pal. *MGM, FCT*

Atlas 🎬 1960
The mighty Atlas takes on massive armies, one of which includes director Corman, in a bid to win the hand of a princess. About as cheap as they come, although it is one of the few Sword & Sandal epics that isn't dubbed. **84m/C VHS.** Michael Forest, Frank Wolff, Barboura Morris, Walter Maslow; **D:** Roger Corman; **W:** Charles B. Griffith. *DVT, SNC, HEG*

Atlas in the Land of the Cyclops woof!
Atlas Against the Cyclops; Maciste Nella Terra dei Ciclopi 1961 Atlas takes on a hideous one-eyed monster to save a baby from an evil queen. Not a divorce custody drama. **100m/C VHS.** *IT* Mitchell Gordon, Chelo Alonso, Vira Silenti; **D:** Antonio Leoniuola. *SNC*

Atom Age Vampire woof! 1961
Mad scientist doing research on Japanese nuclear bomb victims falls in love with a woman disfigured in an auto crash. To remove her scars, he treats her with a formula derived from the glands of freshly killed women. English dubbed. Not among the best of its kind (a low-rent district if ever there was one), but entertaining in a mischievous, boy-is-this-a-stupid-film sort of way. **71m/B VHS, Beta.** *IT* Alberto Lupo, Susanne Loret, Sergio Fantoni; **D:** Albert Magnoli. *SNC, NOS, VYY*

Atom Man vs. Superman 1950
Superman saves Metropolis from the machinations of his deadly foe, Atom Man, in this long-unseen second theatrical serial. Contains all 15 episodes on two tapes. **251m/B VHS, Beta.** Kirk Alyn, Lyle Talbot, Noel Neill, Tommy "Butch" Bond, Pierre Watkin; **D:** Spencer Gordon Bennet. *WAR, MLB*

Atomic Attack 🎬 1950
Nuclear bomb is dropped on New York City and a family living 50 miles away must escape. Gentlemen, start your engines. **50m/B VHS.** Walter Matthau. *IHF*

The Atomic Brain woof!
Monstrosity 1964 An old woman hires a doctor to transplant her brain into the body of a beautiful young girl. Of the three girls who are abducted, two become homicidal zombies and the third starts to act catty when she is given a feline brain. A must-see for bad-brain movie fans. **72m/B VHS.** Frank Gerstle, Erika Peters, Judy Bamber, Marjorie Eaton, Frank Fowler, Margie Fisco; **D:** Joseph Mascelli. *NOS, SNC*

The Atomic Cafe 🎬🎬🎬 1982
A chillingly humorous compilation of newsreels and government films of the 1940's and 1950's that show America's preoccupation with the A-Bomb. Some sequences are in black and white. Includes the infamous training film "Duck and Cover," which tells us what to do in the event of an actual bombing. **92m/C VHS, Beta.** **D:** Kevin Rafferty. *FRF*

The Atomic City 🎬🎬½ 1952
Barry plays a nuclear physicist at Los Alamos whose son is kidnapped by terrorists who want his bomb-making formulas. The bad guys hide out in the nearby mountains which at least makes for some pleasant scenery in this average thriller. **84m/B VHS,**

Closed Caption. Gene Barry, Lee Aaker, Michael Moore, Lydia Clarke, Nancy Gates, Milburn Stone; **D:** Jerry Hopper. Nominations: Academy Awards '52: Best Story & Screenplay. *PAR*

The Atomic Kid 🎬½ 1954
A man survives an atomic blast because of a peanut butter sandwich he was eating. As a result, he himself becomes radioactive and discovers that he has acquired some strange new powers which get him into what pass for hilarious predicaments. **86m/B VHS.** Mickey Rooney, Robert Strauss, Elaine Davis, Bill Goodwin; **D:** Leslie Martinson; **W:** Blake Edwards; **M:** Van Alexander. *REP*

The Atomic Man 🎬½
Timeslip 1956 Owing to radioactive experimentation, a scientist exists for a short time in the future. Once there, both good and evil forces want to use him for their own purposes. **78m/B VHS.** *GB* Gene Nelson, Faith Domergue, Joseph Tomelty, Peter Arne; **D:** Ken Hughes. *NOS, SNC*

Atomic Submarine 🎬🎬 1959
Futuristic sci fi plots government agents against alien invaders. The battle, however, takes place in the ocean beneath the Arctic and is headed by an atomic-powered submarine clashing with a special alien underwater saucer. We all live on the atomic submarine: fun for devotees. **80m/C VHS, Beta.** Arthur Franz, Dick Foran, Bob Steele, Brett Halsey, Joi Lansing, Tom Conway, Paul Dubov; **D:** Spencer Gordon Bennet; **W:** Orville H. Hampton; **C:** Gilbert Warrenton. *SNC*

The Atonement of Gosta Berling 🎬🎬🎬
Gosta Berling's Saga; The Legend of Gosta Berling; The Story of Gosta Berling; The Saga of Gosta Berling 1924 A priest, forced to leave the priesthood because of his drinking, falls in love with a young married woman. Garbo shines in the first role which brought her critical acclaim; Hanson's performance also makes this a memorable drama. Adapted from the novel by Selma Lagerlof. **91m/B VHS.** *SW* Lars Hanson, Greta Garbo, Ellen Cederstrom, Mona Martenson, Jenny Hasselquist, Gerda Lundequist; **D:** Mauritz Stiller. *VYY, MRV, DVT*

Ator the Fighting Eagle woof! 1983
(PG) Styled after "Conan The Barbarian" this mythical action fantasy stars O'Keeffe as Ator, son of Thorn. Ator must put an end to the tragic Dynasty of the Spiders, thereby fulfilling the legend of his family at the expense of the viewer. Goofy low-budget sword and sandal stuff. Followed by "The Blade Master." **98m/C VHS, Beta.** *IT* Miles O'Keeffe, Sabrina Siani, Ritza Brown, Edmund Purdom, Laura Gemser; **D:** David Hills. *NO*

Attack Force Z 🎬🎬 1984
An elite corps of Australian military is Force Z. Volunteers are chosen for a dangerous mission: find the plane that crashed somewhere in the South Pacific and rescue the defecting Japanese government official on board, all before the end of WWII and the feature. Talented cast is effectively directed in low-key adventure featuring young Gibson. **84m/C VHS, Beta.** *AU* Mel Gibson, Chris Haywood, Mel Gibson, John Phillip Law, John Waters; **D:** Tim Burstall. *MCG, MTX*

Attack of the Beast Creatures woof! 1985
The survivors of a wrecked ocean liner are stranded on a desert island overrun by savage creatures. This makes them anxious. **82m/C VHS, Beta.** Robert Nolfi, Robert Langvel, Julia Rust, Lisa Pak; **D:** Michael Stanley. *NO*

Attack of the 50 Foot Woman 🎬🎬½ 1958
A beautiful, abused housewife has a frightening encounter with a giant alien, causing her to grow to an enormous height. Then she goes looking for hubby. Perhaps the all-time classic '50s sci fi, a truly fun movie highlighted by the sexy, 50-foot Hayes in a bikini. Has intriguing psychological depth and social commentary done in a suitably cheezy manner. Also available with "House on Haunted Hill" on laser disc. **72m/B VHS, Beta, LV.** Allison Hayes, William Hudson, Roy Gordon; **D:** Nathan (Hertz) Juran. *FOX, FCT*

Attack of the 50 Ft. Woman 🎬🎬½
1993 Campy remake of the 1958 sci-fi cult classic features the statuesque Hannah in the title role. Nancy's a put-upon hausfrau with zero self-esteem thanks to her domineering father (Windom) and loutish hubby (Baldwin). They should have been sweet to her because after an encounter with a flying saucer Nancy starts to grow...and grow...and grow. And then she decides to get some revenge. Made for television. **90m/C VHS, LV.** Daryl Hannah, Daniel Baldwin, William Windom, Frances Fisher, Cristi Conaway, Paul Benedict, Lewis Arquette, Xander Berkeley, Hamilton Camp, Richard Edson, Victoria Haas, O'Neal Compton; **D:** Christopher Guest; **W:** Joseph Dougherty; **M:** Nicholas Pike. *HBO*

Attack of the Giant Leeches 🎬
The Giant Leeches; She Demons of the Swamp 1959 Cheapo Corman fare about giant leeches in a murky swamp who suddenly decide to make human flesh their new food supply. Perturbed inn keeper plays along by forcing his wife and lover into the murk. Leeches frolic. Sometimes tedious, sometimes chilling, always low budget and slimy. Although the special effects aren't top notch, this might be a fine choice for a late night scare/laugh. **62m/B VHS.** Ken Clark, Yvette Vickers, Gene Roth, Bruno Ve Sota, Michael Emmet; **D:** Bernard L. Kowalski; **W:** Leo Gordon; **C:** John M. Nickolaus Jr. *VYY, SNC, NOS*

Attack of the Killer Refrigerator woof! 1990
Chiller featuring a group of sleazy college students having a wild party. In the process, they abuse a hapless refrigerator. Fed up, the vengeful appliance goes on a rampage of murder and destruction. Certain to make you view kitchen appliances in a new light. Planned sequels in the newfound kitchen-utility horror genre include "Refrigerator II: Brutally Defrosted" and "Bloody, Bloody Coffee Maker." **?m/C VHS.** *BFA*

Attack of the Killer Tomatoes woof! 1977
(PG) Candidate for worst film ever made, deliberate category. Horror spoof that defined "low budget" stars several thousand ordinary tomatoes that suddenly turn savage and begin attacking people. No sci-fi cliche remains untouched in this dumb parody. A few musical numbers are performed in lieu of an actual plot. Followed by "Return of the Killer Tomatoes." Originally released at 87 minutes. **100m/C VHS, Closed Caption.** George Wilson, Jack Riley, Rock Peace, Eric Christmas; **D:** John DeBello; **W:** John DeBello. *TOU*

Attack of the Mayan Mummy woof!
1963 A greedy doctor gets his patient to channel her former self so that she can show him where to find an ancient tomb that is filled with treasure. Good idea. **77m/B VHS.** *MX* Richard Webb, Nina Knight, Norman Burton, Steve Conte; **D:** Jerry Warren. *NOS, LOO, SNC*

Attack of the Mushroom People 🎬🎬
Matango; Fungus of Terror; Curse of the Mushroom People 1963 Secluded island is the site where people eating mysterious mushrooms have been turning into oversized, killer 'shrooms' themselves. Trouble is, the only witness to this madness has gone insane. Will anyone believe him before it's too late? **70m/B VHS.** *JP* Akira Kubo, Kenji Sahara, Yoshio Tsuchiya, Hiroshi Koizumi, Kumi Mizuno, Miki Yashiro; **D:** Inoshiro Honda. *SMW*

Attack of the Robots 🎬½
Cartes sur Table 1966 Silly spy spoof about powerful government officials who are being killed off by a mad scientist's robots. Interpol agent Lemmy Caution comes to the rescue. **88m/B VHS, Beta.** *FR SP* Eddie Constantine, Fernando Rey; **D:** Jess (Jesus) Franco; **W:** Jean-Claude Carriere. *VYY*

Attack of the 60-Foot Centerfold 🎬½ 1995
(R) Angel Grace wants to be Centerfold of the Year so badly that she gets a doctor to enhance her endowments even more through a mystery formula. Only there's a little complication. Cheesy, with pretty women and

no discernable acting (and a spoof of that '58 gem "Attack of the 50 Ft. Woman").*CW:* Nudity; sexual situations; mild violence. **83m/C VHS.** J.J. North, Tammy Parks, John Lazar; *Cameos:* Russ Tamblyn, Michelle (McClellan) Bauer; *D:* Fred Olen Ray. *NHO*

Attack of the Swamp Creature woof! 1975 A deranged scientist transforms himself into a swamp critter and terrorizes a small town. **96m/C VHS, Beta.** Frank Crowell, David Robertson; *D:* Arnold Stevens. *LIV*

Attack Squadron 🐾½ *Kamakazi* 197? Story of Japan's suicidal WWII pilots. **105m/C VHS, Beta.** *JP NO*

The Attic 🐾🐾½ 1980 (R) Psycho-drama about an overbearing invalid father and his insecure and unmarried daughter. The girl learns to escape her unhappy life by hiding in the attic. Not horrifying, but a clear analytical look into the game of control. **92m/C VHS, Beta.** Carrie Snodgress, Ray Milland, Rosemary Murphy, Ruth Cox, Francis Bay, Marjorie Eaton; *D:* George Edwards. *FOX*

The Attic: The Hiding of Anne Frank 🐾🐾½ 1988 Steenburgen is wonderful in the true story of Miep Gies, the Dutch woman who hid Otto Frank, her employer, and his family from the Nazis. Unusual because it is told from Gies' perspective, rather than from the more familiar Anne Frank story. Based on Gies' book, "Anne Frank Remembered." Made for television. **95m/C VHS, LV, Closed Caption.** Mary Steenburgen, Paul Scofield, Huub Stapel, Eleanor Bron, Miriam Karlin, Lisa Jacobs, Ronald Pickup; *D:* John Erman; *W:* William Hanley; *M:* Richard Rodney Bennett. *CAF*

Attica 🐾🐾🐾 1980 Tense made for television depiction of the infamous Attica prison takeover in 1971 and the subsequent bloodbath as state troops were called in. Although edited due to the searing commentary by Nelson Rockefeller, it remains powerful and thought-provoking. Adapted from the Tom Wicker bestseller "A Time to Die." **97m/C VHS, Beta.** George Grizzard, Charles Durning, Anthony Zerbe, Roger E. Mosley; *D:* Marvin J. Chomsky. *NLC*

Au Revoir Les Enfants 🐾🐾🐾🐾 *Goodbye, Children* 1987 (PG) During the Nazi occupation of France in the 1940s, the headmaster of a Catholic boarding school hides three Jewish boys among the other students by altering their names and identities. Two of the students, Julien (Manesse) and Jean (Fejto), form a friendship that ends tragically when Jean and the other boys are discovered and taken away by the Gestapo. Compelling and emotionally wrenching coming of age tale based on an incident from director Malle's childhood is considered to be his best film to date and quite possibly the best he will ever make. In French with English subtitles. Other 1987 movies with similar themes are "Hope and Glory" and "Empire of the Sun." **104m/C VHS, Beta, LV.** FR Gaspard Manesse, Raphael Fejto, Francine Racette, Stanislas Carre de Malberg, Philippe Morier-Genoud, Francois Berleand, Peter Fitz, Francois Negret, Irene Jacob; *D:* Louis Malle; *C:* Renato Berta; *M:* Franz Schubert, Camille Saint-Saens. British Academy Awards '88: Best Director (Malle); Cesar Awards '88: Best Art Direction/Set Decoration, Best Cinematography, Best Director (Malle), Best Film, Best Sound, Best Writing; Los Angeles Film Critics Association Awards '87: Best Foreign Film; Venice Film Festival '87: Best Film; Nominations: Academy Awards '87: Best Foreign Language Film, Best Original Screenplay.*ORI, FCT, HMV*

Audrey Rose 🐾🐾 1977 (PG) Parents of a young girl are terrified when their darling daughter is having dreadful dreams. Mysterious friend Hopkins cements their fears when he declares that his dead daughter has been reincarnated in their child. The nightmares continue suggesting that none other than Lucifer could be at work. Good cast is hampered by slow-moving take-off on "The Exorcist" with a weak staged ending. Adapted by DeFelitta from his novel. **113m/C VHS, Beta.** Marsha Mason, Anthony Hopkins, John Beck, John Hillerman; *D:* Robert Wise; *W:* Frank de Felitta. *MGM*

August 🐾🐾½ 1995 (PG) Yet another version of Chekov's "Uncle Vanya," this time transported to 1890s Wales. Hopkins (who makes his directorial debut and composed the score) stars as Ieuan Davies, a bitter drinker who manages the estate of brother-in-law Alexander Blathwaite (Phillips). Blathwaite arrives for his annual summer stay with unhappy, young second wife Helen (Burton), who's the object of desire for both Ieuan and the local doctor, Michael Lloyd (Grainger). It's a perfectly adequate rendition but offers little that's new except a change of scenery. **93m/C VHS.** GB Anthony Hopkins, Kate Burton, Leslie Phillips, Gawn Grainger, Rhian Morgan, Hugh Lloyd, Rhoda Lewis, Menna Tussler; *D:* Anthony Hopkins; *W:* Julian Mitchell; *C:* Robin Vidgeon; *M:* Anthony Hopkins. *HMK*

Augustin 🐾🐾 1995 Very short comedy about aspiring actor Augustin (Sibertin-Blanc), who may just get his break when he hears about a part for a room-service waiter and prepares himself rigorously by actually getting a job in a Paris hotel. Pathetically earnest and dignified, at the actual audition he bewilders actor Lhermitte, when instead of just reading the scene, Augustin proceeds to act it out in detail. Very slight but charming thanks to a deadpan performance by Sibertin-Blanc (who's also director Fontaine's brother). French with subtitles. **61m/C VHS.** FR Jean-Chretien Sibertin-Blanc, Thierry Lhermitte; *D:* Anne Fontaine; *W:* Anne Fontaine; *C:* Jean-Marie Dreujou. *KIV*

Augustine of Hippo 🐾🐾🐾 *Agostino di Ippona* 1972 One of Rossellini's later historical epics, depicting the last years of St. Augustine and how they exemplify the growing conflicts between Church and State, Christian ethic and societal necessity. In Italian with subtitles. **120m/C VHS, Beta.** IT *D:* Roberto Rossellini. *FCT*

Auntie woof! 1980 (R) Entertainer must dress and act like his madam aunt who has died, in order to fool her former employees in a house of prostitution. **85m/C VHS, Beta.** *NO*

Auntie Lee's Meat Pies 🐾½ 1992 (R) Auntie Lee's meat pie business is booming thanks to her five beautiful nieces. They help keep their aunt supplied with the secret ingredient—gorgeous young men! Four Playboy Playmates are featured in this cannibalistic horror comedy.*CW:* Language, horror violence, and sexuality. **100m/C VHS, LV.** Karen Black, Noriyuki "Pat" Morita, Pat Paulsen, Huntz Hall, Michael Berryman, David Parry, Stephen Quadros; *D:* Joseph F. Robertson; *C:* Arledge Armenaki. *COL*

Auntie Mame 🐾🐾🐾 1958 A young boy is brought up by his only surviving relative—flamboyant and eccentric Auntie Mame. Mame is positive that "life is a banquet and most poor suckers are starving to death." Based on the Patrick Dennis novel about his life with "Auntie Mame." Part of the "A Night at the Movies" series, this tape simulates a 1958 movie evening, with a Road Runner cartoon, "Hook, Line and Stinker," a newsreel and coming attractions for "No Time for Sergeants" and "Chase a Crooked Shadow." **161m/C VHS, Beta, LV.** Rosalind Russell, Patric Knowles, Roger Smith, Peggy Cass, Forrest Tucker, Coral Browne; *D:* Morton DaCosta; *W:* Betty Comden, Adolph Green; *C:* Harry Stradling. Golden Globe Awards '59: Best Actress—Musical/Comedy (Russell); Nominations: Academy Awards '58: Best Actress (Russell), Best Art Direction/Set Decoration, Best Color Cinematography, Best Film Editing, Best Picture, Best Supporting Actress (Cass). *WAR*

Aurora 🐾🐾½ *Aurora by Night; Qualcosa di Biondo* 1984 Single mom Aurora (Loren) will do anything for her blind son Ciro (played by Loren's son Edoardo Ponti). When she discovers that there's a possible operation that could restore his sight, Aurora decides to call up all Ciro's possible fathers and get them to finance the surgery. This plan also reunites Aurora with the one man she truly loved. Made for Italian TV. **91m/C VHS.** IT Sophia Loren, Daniel J. Travanti, Ricardo Tognazzi, Philippe Noiret, Anna Strasberg, Franco Fabrizi; *D:* Maurizio Ponzi; *M:* Georges Delerue. *FCT*

The Aurora Encounter 🐾🐾 1985 (PG) Aliens surreptitiously infiltrate a small town in 1897, and spread benevolence everywhere. Family fare. **90m/C VHS, Beta.** Jack Elam, Peter Brown, Carol Bagdasarian, Dottie West, George "Spanky" McFarland; *D:* Jim McCullough. *NWV, VTR, HHE*

Austin Powers: International Man of Mystery 🐾🐾🐾 1997 (PG-13) Hilarious spoof of '60s spy and babe movies. Groovy '60s spy Austin Powers (Myers) discovers that his arch-enemy, Dr. Evil (Myers again) has frozen himself in order to elude capture, so the swingin' dentally challenged Brit decides to do the same. They awaken thirty years later in the same state: woefully out of touch. Dr. Evil is attempting to blackmail the British government and deal with his Gen-X son, Scott Evil (Green), who wants more quality time and less world conquest. Austin, on the other hand, is trying to "shag" every "groovy bird" he sees. He is teamed with Vanessa (Hurley), the daughter of his former partner, and they try to stop the evil machinations of...well..Evil. A festival of crushed velvet, political incorrectness and female robots with lethal breasts. Myers revels in playing the fool, and he may step over the line once in a while, but he gets plenty of mileage out of the one-joke premise.*CW:* Nudity, sex-related dialogue and humor. **88m/C VHS.** Mike Myers, Elizabeth Hurley, Michael York, Seth Green, Mimi Rogers, Christian Slater, Tom Arnold, Carrie Fisher, Robert Wagner, Fabiana Udenio, Paul Dillon, Charles Napier; *D:* Jay Roach; *W:* Mike Myers; *C:* Peter Deming; *M:* George Clinton. *NLC*

Author! Author! 🐾🐾½ 1982 (PG) Sweet, likable comedy about playwright Pacino who is about to taste success with his first big hit. Suddenly his wife walks out, leaving him to care for her four children and his own son. His views shift as he begins to worry about, among other things, who will watch the obnoxious kids on opening night. **100m/C VHS, Beta.** Al Pacino, Tuesday Weld, Dyan Cannon, Alan King, Andre Gregory; *D:* Arthur Hiller; *W:* Israel Horovitz; *M:* Dave Grusin. *FOX*

Autobiography of a Princess 🐾🐾 1975 A brief character study shot by Merchant-Ivory in six days. An East Indian princess, living in self-enforced exile in London, invites her father's former tutor to tea. They watch old movie footage of royal India together and dream of a happier past. **59m/C VHS, LV.** James Mason, Madhur Jaffrey; *D:* James Ivory; *W:* Ruth Prawer Jhabvala. *FCT, LUM, CVC*

The Autobiography of Miss Jane Pittman 🐾🐾🐾½ 1974 The history of blacks in the South is seen through the eyes of a 110-year-old former slave. From the Civil War through the Civil Rights movement, Miss Pittman relates every piece of black history, allowing the viewer to experience the injustices. Tyson is spectacular in moving, highly acclaimed television drama. Received nine Emmy awards; adapted by Tracy Keenan Wynn from the novel by Ernest J. Gaines. **110m/C VHS, Beta.** Cicely Tyson, Odetta, Joseph Tremice, Richard Dysart, Michael Murphy, Katherine Helmond; *D:* John Korty. *PSM*

Automatic 🐾½ 1994 (R) Renegade RobGen Industries android Gruner saves Ashbrook from the loathsome sexual advances of the boss but kills the scum in the process. So the duo are targeted for death by company head Glover with killers, lead by Kober, sent to do the mopping up.*CW:* Strong violence; language; a scene of nudity. **90m/C VHS, LV, Closed Caption.** Olivier Gruner, Daphne Ashbrook, John Glover, Jeff Kober, Dennis Lipscomb; *D:* John Murlowski; *W:* Susan Lambert, Patrick Highsmith. *REP*

Autopsy 🐾½ 1978 (R) Rash of unexplainable, spontaneous suicides cause a college student to become emotionally upset. **89m/C VHS, Beta.** IT Mimsy Farmer, Barry Primus, Angela Goodwin, Ray Lovelock; *D:* Armando Crispino; *M:* Ennio Morricone. *MPI, PSM*

Autopsy 🎬 197? A young gold-digger and a millionaire marry, and then cheat on each other, provoking blackmail and murder. 90m/C VHS, Beta. Fernando Rey, Gloria Grahame, Christian Hay. NO

Autopsy 🎬½ 1986 A war correspondent in Vietnam discovers the gruesome secret behind the doctors' autopsy methods at a military hospital. 90m/C VHS, Beta. NO

Autopsy of a Ghost 🎬½ 1967 Comedy/horror film stars Rathbone and Mitchell as a mad scientist. Notable as Rathbone's last screen appearance. In Spanish with no subtitles. ?m/C VHS. SP Basil Rathbone, John Carradine, Cameron Mitchell. SNC

An Autumn Afternoon 🎬🎬🎬½ 1962 Ozu's final film is a beautiful expression of his talent. In postwar Tokyo, an aging widower loses his only daughter to marriage and begins a life of loneliness. A heart-wrenching tale of relationships and loss. In Japanese with English subtitles. 112m/C VHS. JP Chishu Ryu, Shima Iwashita, Shin-Ichiro Mikami, Mariko Okada, Keiji Sada; D: Yasujiro Ozu; W: Yasujiro Ozu. NYF

Autumn Born 🎬½ 1979 (R) Young heiress is abducted by her guardian and imprisoned while she's taught to obey his will. Ill-fated ex-Playmate Dorothy Stratton's first film. 76m/C VHS, Beta. Dorothy Stratton. NO

Autumn Leaves 🎬🎬½ 1956 Crawford plays a middle-aged typist grasping at her last chance for love. She marries a younger man who's been romancing her, then finds him more and more unstable and violent. Weak story material that could turn melodramatic and tawdry, but doesn't because of Crawford's strength. 108m/B VHS, Beta. Cliff Robertson, Joan Crawford, Vera Miles, Lorne Greene; D: Robert Aldrich; W: Robert Blees, Lewis Meltzer, Hugo Butler, Jean Rouveral; C: Charles B(ryant) Lang. Berlin International Film Festival '56: Best Director (Aldrich). GKK

Autumn Marathon 🎬🎬½ Osenny Marafon 1979 To say that this is one of the better Russian movies of the past three decades is sort of faint praise, given the state of Soviet cinema. Written by playwright Volodin, it's just another paint-by-number version of the philandering man who's really an OK Joe who loves his kids comedy. In Russian with English subtitles. 100m/C VHS. RU Oleg Basilashvili, Natalia Gundareva, Marina Neyelova; D: Georgi Daniela; W: Alexander Volodin. KIV, AUD

Autumn Moon 🎬🎬 Qiuyue 1992 Young Japanese tourist (Nagase) travels to Hong Kong to enjoy some sexual fun but instead he befriends a 15-year-old girl (Wai), who's afraid of her family's impending emigration to Canada. Not much happens but the Hong Kong setting is eye-catching. English and Cantonese with subtitles. 108m/C VHS. HK Masatoshi Nagase, Li Pui Wai; D: Clara Law. FRF

Autumn Sonata 🎬🎬🎬 1978 Nordic family strife as famed concert pianist Bergman is reunited with a daughter she has not seen in years. Bergman's other daughter suffers from a degenerative nerve disease and had been institutionalized until her sister brought her home. Now the three women settle old scores, and balance the needs of their family. Excellent performance by Bergman in her last feature film. 97m/C VHS, Beta, LV. SW Ingrid Bergman, Liv Ullmann, Halvar Bjork, Lena Nyman, Gunnar Bjornstrand; D: Ingmar Bergman; W: Ingmar Bergman; C: Sven Nykvist. Golden Globe Awards '79: Best Foreign Film; National Board of Review Awards '78: 5 Best Foreign Films of the Year, Best Actress (Bergman), Best Director (Bergman); New York Film Critics Awards '78: Best Actress (Bergman); National Society of Film Critics Awards '78: Best Actress (Bergman); Nominations: Academy Awards '78: Best Actress (Bergman), Best Original Screenplay. FOX

Avalanche 🎬½ 1978 (PG) Disasterama as vacationers at a new winter ski resort find themselves at the mercy of a monster avalanche leaving a so-called path of terror and destruction in its wake. Talented cast is buried by weak material,

producing a snow-bound adventure yawn. 91m/C VHS, Beta. Rock Hudson, Mia Farrow, Robert Forster, Rick Moses; D: Corey Allen; W: Corey Allen.

Avalanche Express 🎬 1979 (PG) Marvin is a CIA agent who uses a defector (Shaw) to lure a scientist (Schell), specializing in biological warfare, aboard a European train. Marvin wants to eliminate Schell but all plans go awry when the snow begins to fall. Ineffective thriller. Director Robson's and actor Shaw's last film—much of Shaw's dialogue was dubbed due to his death before the film's soundtrack was completed. Based on a novel by Colin Forbes. 89m/C VHS. Lee Marvin, Robert Shaw, Maximilian Schell, Linda Evans, Mike Connors, Joe Namath, Horst Buchholz, David Hess; D: Mark Robson; W: Abraham Polonsky; C: Jack Cardiff. WAR

Avalon 🎬🎬🎬 1990 (PG) Powerful but quiet portrait of the break-up of the family unit as seen from the perspective of a Russian family settled in Baltimore at the close of WWII. Initally, the family is unified in their goals, ideologies and social lives. Gradually, all of this disintegrates; members move to the suburbs and television replaces conversation at holiday gatherings. Levinson based his film on experiences within his own family of Russian Jewish immigrants. 126m/C VHS, Beta, LV, 8mm, Closed Caption. Armin Mueller-Stahl, Aidan Quinn, Elizabeth Perkins, Joan Plowright, Lou Jacobi, Leo Fuchs, Eve Gordon, Kevin Pollak, Israel Rubinek, Elijah Wood, Grant Gelt, Bernard Hiller; D: Barry Levinson; W: Barry Levinson; C: Allen Daviau; M: Randy Newman. Writers Guild of America '90: Best Original Screenplay; Nominations: Academy Awards '90: Best Cinematography, Best Costume Design, Best Original Screenplay, Best Original Score. COL, FCT

Avanti! 🎬🎬½ 1972 (R) Stuffy businessman Wendell Armbruster (Lemmon) heads to Italy to claim his father's body when the old man dies while on vacation. Then he discovers dad has been visiting his mistress lo these many years. While trying to get through mountains of red tape, Wendell finds himself romancing the woman's daughter (Mills). Too long but still amusing. 144m/C VHS. Jack Lemmon, Juliet Mills, Clive Revill, Edward Andrews, Gianfranco Barra, Franco Angrisano; D: Billy Wilder; W: I.A.L. Diamond, Billy Wilder. USH

Ava's Magical Adventure 🎬🎬½ 1994 (PG) Ten-year-old Eddie decides to take Ava on a little adventure. Too bad she's a 2-ton elephant he's stolen from the circus. Based on the Mark Twain story "The Stolen White Elephant." 97m/C VHS, LV. Timothy Bottoms, Georg Stanford Brown, Patrick Dempsey, Priscilla Barnes, David Lander, Kaye Ballard, Remi Ryan; D: Patrick Dempsey, Rocky Parker; W: Susan D. Nimm; M: Mark Holden. PSM

The Avenger 🎬🎬½ 1960 The story of a criminal who cuts off the heads of people and mails them off makes for a shocker. Graphic violence will appeal to those who like a good mail-order gorefest and are not employed by the post office. 102m/B VHS. GE Ingrid van Bergen, Heinz Drache, Ina Duscha, Mario Litto, Klaus Kinski; D: Karl Anton. SNC

The Avenger 🎬 The Lost Glory of Troy 1962 This time muscleman Reeves plays Aeneas and leads the Trojans in battle against the Greeks. It's supposedly an adaptation of "The Aeneid" by Virgil. 108m/C VHS. FR IT Steve Reeves, Giacomo "Jack" Rossi-Stuart, Carla Marlier, Gianni "John" Garko, Liana Orfei; D: Giorgio Rivalta. SNC, NOS, VYY

The Avenging 🎬🎬 1992 (PG) Horse comes home from college to run the family ranch but has problems with his two resentful brothers. 100m/C VHS, Closed Caption. Michael Horse, Efrem Zimbalist Jr., Sherry Hursey, Joseph Runningfox, Taylor Lacher; D: Lyman Dayton; W: Lyman Dayton. IMP

Avenging Angel woof! 1985 (R) Law student Molly "Angel" Stewart is back on the streets to retaliate against the men who killed the policeman who saved her from a life of prostitution. Worthless sequel to 1984's "Angel," exploiting the original's exploitative intent. Followed listlessly by "Angel III: The Final Chapter." 94m/C VHS, Beta, LV, Closed Caption. Betsy Russell, Rory Calhoun,

Susan Tyrrell, Ossie Davis, Barry Pearl, Ross Hagen, Karin Mani, Robert Tessier; D: Robert Vincent O'Neil; W: Joseph M. Cala; C: Peter Collister; M: Paul Antonelli. NWV, VTR

The Avenging Angel 🎬🎬½ 1995 Unusual take on religion and western justice. Brigham Young (Heston) and his Mormon sect have established themselves in Utah—with the aid of some sharpshooting vigilantes, including Miles Utley (Berenger). When an assassination attempt is made on Young's life, Utley finds he's stumbled into an ever-widening church conspiracy that threatens to consume him. Based on the novel by Gary Stewart. 100m/C VHS. Tom Berenger, Charlton Heston, James Coburn, Kevin Tighe, Jeffrey Jones, Tom Bower, Joanna Miles; D: Craig R. Baxley; W: Dennis Nemec; C: Mark Irwin; M: Gary Chang. TTC

Avenging Conscience 🎬🎬 Thou Shall Not Kill 1914 An early eerie horror film, based on tales of Edgar Allan Poe. D.W. Griffith's first large-scale feature. Silent. 78m/B VHS, Beta. Henry B. Walthall, Blanche Sweet; D: D.W. Griffith. GPV, VYY, LSV

Avenging Disco Godfather 🎬½ Avenging Godfather; Disco Godfather 1976 (R) Moore parodies the "Godfather" and martial arts movies. 99m/C VHS, Beta. Rudy Ray Moore, Lady Reed, Carol Speed, Jimmy Lynch; D: Rudy Ray Moore. XVC

Avenging Force 🎬🎬 1986 (R) Okay actioner about retired CIA agent Dudikoff returning to the force to help colleague James run for political office. A group of right-wing terrorists called "Pentangle" threatens James, so Dudikoff adds his name to their wanted list. Conflict leads to a forest manhunt where the avenging force does its avenging. 104m/C VHS, Beta, LV, Closed Caption. Michael Dudikoff, Steve James, John P. Ryan; D: Sam Firstenberg; W: Mercer Ellington, James Booth; M: George S. Clinton. MED, VTR

The Avenging Hand 🎬½ 1943 Leaden suspense story about a hotel filled with thieves all searching for stolen loot. 56m/B VHS. Noah Beery Jr., Kathleen Kelly, Louis Borell, James Harcourt, Charles Oliver, Reginald Long; D: Victor Hanbury. HCV

The Average Woman 🎬🎬 1924 Gritty journalist consults plain Jane for "Modern Woman" story and finds a major rewrite in order when he falls with a thud for Miss Jane. 52m/B VHS, Beta. Pauline Garon, David Powell, Burr McIntosh, Harrison Ford, De Sacia Mooers; D: Christy Cabanne. GPV, GVV

The Aviator 🎬🎬 1985 (PG) Pilot Reeve, haunted by the memory of a fatal crash, tries to find a new line of work. Large sums of money persuade him to transport spoiled Arquette to Washington. When the biplane crashes in the mountain wilderness, the two fall in love between scavenging for food and fighting wild animals. From the director of "Man From Snowy River." 98m/C VHS, Beta. Christopher Reeve, Rosanna Arquette, Jack Warden, Tyne Daly, Marcia Strassman, Sam Wanamaker, Scott Wilson; D: George Miller; W: Marc Norman; C: David Connell. MGM

The Awakening 🎬½ 1980 (R) An archeologist discovers the tomb of a murderous queen, but upon opening the coffin, the mummy's spirit is transferred to his baby daughter, born at that instant. They call that bad luck. 101m/C VHS, Beta. Charlton Heston, Susannah York, Stephanie Zimbalist; D: Mike Newell; W: Allan Scott, Chris Bryant; C: Jack Cardiff; M: Claude Bolling. WAR

Awakening of Candra woof! 1981 Based on a real 1975 incident, a young couple honeymooning in the mountains is assaulted by a lunatic fisherman. The psycho kills the husband and rapes the girl, then he brainwashes poor Candra into thinking it was all an accident. Intense subject matter should be horrifying, but falls short of the mark in this television flop. 96m/C VHS, Beta. Blanche Baker, Cliff DeYoung, Richard Jaeckel; D: Paul Wendkos. GEM

Awakenings 🎬🎬🎬½ 1990 (PG-13) Marshall's first dramatic effort is based on the true story of Dr. Oliver Sacks, from his book of the same title. It details his experimentation with the drug L-dopa which inspired the "awakening" of a number of catatonic patients, some of whom had been "sleeping" for as long as thirty years. Occasionally over-sentimental, but still providing a poignant look at both the patients—who find themselves confronted with lost opportunities and faded youth—and at Sacks, who must watch their exquisite suffering as they slip away. De Niro's performance as the youngest of the group is heart-rending, while Williams offers a subdued, moving performance as the doctor. **120m/C VHS, Beta, LV, 8mm, Closed Caption.** Robin Williams, Robert De Niro, John Heard, Julie Kavner, Penelope Ann Miller, Max von Sydow, Anne Meara; **D:** Penny Marshall; **W:** Steven Zaillian; **M:** Randy Newman. National Board of Review Awards '90: Best Actor (De Niro), Best Actor (Williams); National Society of Film Critics Awards '90: Best Actor (De Niro); Nominations: Academy Awards '90: Best Actor (De Niro), Best Adapted Screenplay, Best Picture. COL, FCT

Awakenings of the Beast *♂* *Ritual Dos Sadicos; Ritual of the Maniacs* 1968 Documents the protracted sufferings of an LSD drug user who is beset with hallucinatory visions and is prone to fits of frenzied violence. Director Jose Mojica Marins (AKA Coffin Joe) steps out of his Ze do Ciaxia character in this disjointed mix of drugs and sex intercut with Mojica Marins himself on trial for his offensive movies, followed by a case study on drugs and sexual behavior. By the end of the movie, there is a point—that drugs aren't the cause of evil behavior—but it's very painful getting there. In Portugese with English subtitles. **?m/B VHS.** **BR** Jose Mojica Marins; **D:** Jose Mojica Marins. SMW, FCT

Away All Boats *♂♂½* 1956 The true story of one Captain Hawks, who led a crew of misfits to victory in WWII Pacific aboard transport USS Belinda. Battle scenes are well done; look for early (and brief) appearance by young Clint Eastwood. **114m/B VHS, Beta.** Jeff Chandler, George Nader, Richard Boone, Julie Adams, Keith Andes, Lex Barker; **D:** Joseph Pevney. USH

The Awful Dr. Orloff *♂* 1962 Set in a bygone era, Dr. Orloff (Vernon) is a retired prison physician who needs unblemished skin to remedy the horrible disfigurement of his daughter Melissa (Lorys), ravaged by fire. He abducts promising young women candidates with the help of his blind zombie henchman Morpho (Valle), who simply cannot be trusted with a scalpel. After several surgical mishaps, they kidnap the perfect specimen, a woman who bears an uncanny resemblance to Melissa. Unfortunately, she is engaged to suspicious police inspector Tanner (San Martin). French version with English subtitles that includes more explicit gore is also available. **86m/B VHS.** Howard Vernon, Diana Lorys, Frank Wolff, Riccardo Valle, Conrado San Martin; **D:** Jess (Jesus) Franco; **M:** Jose Pagan, Antonio Ramirez Angel. SMW, VSM, TPV

The Awful Truth *♂♂♂♂* 1937 Classic screwball comedy. Young couple discards their marriage made in heaven and go their separate ways in search of happiness. Meticulously sabotaging each others' new relationships, they discover they really were made for each other. First on-screen pairing for Grant and Dunne: Grant is at his most charming with dead-on comic timing while Dunne is brilliant as his needling ex. The scene where Dunne poses as Grant's prodigal fan-dancing sister who pays a surprise cocktail-hour visit to the family of his stuffy, upper-class bride-to-be is among the most memorable screwball vignettes of all time. And don't miss the custody battle they have over the family dog (Asta of "The Thin Man" fame). Based on Arthur Richman's play. Preceded by 1925 and 1929 versions; remade in 1953 as "Let's Do it Again." **92m/B VHS, Beta, LV.** Irene Dunne, Cary Grant, Ralph Bellamy, Alexander D'Arcy, Cecil Cunningham, Molly Lamont, Esther Dale, Joyce Compton, Robert Allen, Robert Warwick, Mary Forbes; **D:** Leo McCarey; **W:** Vina Delmar. Academy Awards '37: Best Director (McCarey); Nominations: Academy Awards '37: Best Actress (Dunne), Best Film Editing,

Best Picture, Best Screenplay, Best Supporting Actor (Bellamy). MLB, BTV, COL

An Awfully Big Adventure *♂♂* 1994 **(R)** Coming-of-age saga set in postwar Liverpool around a provincial reperatory company. Stage-struck 16-year-old Stella (Cates) gets work as a company apprentice, immediately getting a crush on arch, callous theater manager Meredith Potter (a deliciously nasty Grant), who enjoys degrading everyone around him. The company's chance for success rests on a production of "Peter Pan," with visiting actor P.L. O'Hara (dashing Rickman), who immediately seduces Stella and has more than a few secrets of his own. Theatrically exaggerated; based on the novel by Beryl Bainbridge.**CW:** Sexuality; some language. **113m/C VHS, LV, Closed Caption. GB** Georgina Cates, Hugh Grant, Alan Rickman, Peter Firth, Alun Armstrong, Prunella Scales, Rita Tushingham, Alan Cox, Edward Petherbridge, Nicola Pagett, Carol Drinkwater, Clive Merrison, Gerard McSorley; **D:** Mike Newell; **W:** Charles Wood; **C:** Dick Pope; **M:** Richard Hartley. NLC

Ay, Carmela! *♂♂♂* 1990 During the Spanish Civil War, two vaudevillians with strong anti-Franco views are captured by Franco forces and sentenced to execution. They are reprieved when a theater-loving Lieutenant offers to spare their lives if they will entertain the troops. Clever and entertaining farce, with poignant undertones. **105m/C VHS. SP IT** Carmen Maura, Andres Pajares, Gabino Diego, Maurizio De Razza, Miguel Rellan, Edward Zentara, Jose Sancho, Antonio Fuentes; **D:** Carlos Saura; **W:** Rafael Azcona; **C:** Jose Luis Alcaine. HBO

Baba *♂♂♂* *The Father* 1973 A poor boatman agrees to be the fall guy in a murder in exchange for the actual murderer supporting his family. But after 24 years in prison, the boatman finds all his sacrificing has been in vain. His daughter has become a prostitute and his son is working as one of the murderer's henchman. In Turkish with English subtitles. **95m/C VHS. TU D:** Yilmaz Guney. FCT, HEG

Babar: The Movie *♂♂½* 1988 **(G)** The lovable Babar, king of the elephants, must devise a plan to outwit an angry hoard of attacking rhinos. Based on the characters of Jean and Laurent de Brunhoff. **75m/C VHS, Beta, LV, 8mm. CA FR D:** Alan Bunce; **W:** Alan Bunce, John deKlein; **V:** Gavin Magrath, Gordon Pinsent, Sarah Polley, Chris Wiggins, Elizabeth Hanna. FHE, IME

Babe! *♂♂♂½* 1975 A fine television movie about the life of one of America's most famous woman athletes, Babe Didrickson. Adapted by Joanna Lee from Didrickson's autobiography, "The Life I've Led." The movie was nominated for Outstanding Special of 1975-76 and Clark won an Emmy for her work. **120m/C VHS.** Susan Clark, Alex Karras, Slim Pickens, Jeanette Nolan, Ellen Geer, Ford Rainey; **D:** Buzz Kulik; **M:** Jerry Goldsmith. NO

The Babe *♂♂½* 1992 **(PG)** Follows the life of legendary baseball player Babe Ruth, portrayed as a sloppy drunkard whose appetites for food, drink, and sex were as large as he was. Alvarado and McGillis do well as the Babe's first and second wives, but this is Goodman's show from start to finish. He's excellent as Ruth, and looks the part, but his fine performance can't make up for a lackluster script filled with holes. **115m/C VHS, LV, Closed Caption.** John Goodman, Kelly McGillis, Trini Alvarado, Bruce Boxleitner, Peter Donat, J.C. Quinn, Richard Tyson, James Cromwell, Joe Ragno, Bernard Kates, Michael McGrady, Stephen Caffrey; **D:** Arthur Hiller; **W:** John Fusco; **C:** Haskell Wexler; **M:** Elmer Bernstein. USH

Babe *♂♂♂½* *Babe, the Gallant Pig* 1995 **(G)** Totally charming fable has intelligent piglet Babe being raised by matriarch sheepdog Fly, and learning the art of sheep herding along with his new canine brothers. Farmer Hoggett (Cromwell), Babe's owner by virtue of a winning raffle ticket, sees that he's more than just a ham, and enters them in the world sheepdog herding championship. Whimsy that never crosses the line into treacle. Four different special effects houses were

used to make the barnyard animals talk and walk. Filmed on location in Australia; based on Dick King-Smith's book "The Sheep-Pig." **91m/C VHS, LV, Closed Caption. AU** James Cromwell, Magna Szubanski; **D:** Chris Noonan, George Miller; **C:** Andrew Lesnie; **M:** Nigel Westlake; **V:** Christine Cavanaugh, Miriam Margolyes, Danny Mann, Hugo Weaving. Academy Awards '95: Best Visual Effects; Golden Globe Awards '96: Best Film—Musical/Comedy; National Society of Film Critics Awards '95: Best Film; Nominations: Academy Awards '95: Best Adapted Screenplay, Best Art Direction/Set Decoration, Best Director (Noonan), Best Film Editing, Best Picture, Best Supporting Actor (Cromwell); British Academy Awards '95: Best Adapted Screenplay, Best Film; Writers Guild of America '95: Best Adapted Screenplay. USH

Babe Ruth Story *♂♂* 1948 An overly sentimental biography about the famed baseball slugger. Bendix is miscast as the Bambino, but the actual film clips of the Babe are of interest. A movie to be watched during those infrequent bouts of sloppy baseball mysticism. **107m/B VHS, Beta, Closed Caption.** William Bendix, Claire Trevor, Charles Bickford, William Frawley, Sam Levene, Gertrude Niesen; **D:** Roy Del Ruth. NO

Babes in Arms *♂♂½* 1939 The children of several vaudeville performers team up to put on a show to raise money for their financially impoverished parents. Loosely adapted from the Rodgers and Hart Broadway musical of the same name; features some of their songs as well as new additions. ♫Babes in Arms; I Cried for You; Good Morning; You Are My Lucky Star; Broadway Rhythm; Where or When; Daddy Was a Minstrel Man; I'm Just Wild About Harry; God's Country. **91m/B VHS, Beta, LV.** Judy Garland, Mickey Rooney, Charles Winninger, Guy Kibbee, June Preisser; **D:** Busby Berkeley; **M:** George Bassman, Richard Rodgers, Lorenz Hart. Nominations: Academy Awards '39: Best Actor (Rooney), Best Score. MGM

Babes in Toyland *♂♂* 1961 A lavish Disney production of Victor Herbert's timeless operetta, with Toyland being menaced by the evil Barnaby and his Bogeymen. Yes, Annette had a life after Mickey Mouse and before the peanut butter commercials. Somewhat charming, although the roles of the lovers seem a stretch for both Funicello and Kirk. But the flick does sport an amusing turn by Wynn. **105m/C VHS, Beta.** Annette Funicello, Ray Bolger, Tommy Sands, Ed Wynn, Tommy Kirk; **D:** Jack Donohue; **C:** Edward Colman; **M:** George Bruns. Nominations: Academy Awards '61: Best Costume Design (Color), Scoring of a Musical.DIS

Babes in Toyland *♂½* 1986 Young girl must save Toyland from the clutches of the evil Barnaby and his monster minions. Bland TV remake of the classic doesn't approach the original. **96m/C VHS, LV.** Drew Barrymore, Noriyuki "Pat" Morita, Richard Mulligan, Eileen Brennan, Keanu Reeves, Jill Schoelen, Googy Gress; **D:** Clive Donner; **M:** Leslie Bricusse. ORI

Babes on Broadway *♂♂½* 1941 Mickey and Judy put on a show to raise money for a settlement house. Nearly the best of the Garland-Rooney series, with imaginative numbers staged by Berkeley. ♫Babes on Broadway; Anything Can Happen in New York; How About You?; Hoe Down; Chin Up! Cheerio! Carry On!; Mama Yo Quiero; F.D.R. Jones; Waiting for the Robert E. Lee. **118m/B VHS, Beta, LV.** Mickey Rooney, Judy Garland, Fay Bainter, Richard Quine, Virginia Weidler, Ray Macdonald, Busby Berkeley; **D:** Busby Berkeley; **M:** George Bassman. Nominations: Academy Awards '42: Best Song ("How About You?"). MGM

Babette's Feast *♂♂♂½* 1987 A simple, moving pageant-of-life fable. A group of religiously zealous villagers are taught love and forgiveness through a lavish banquet prepared by one of their housemaids, who turns out to be a world-class chef. Adapted from a tale by Isak Dinesen. In French and Danish with English subtitles. **102m/C VHS, Beta, LV. DK FR** Stephane Audran, Bibi Andersson, Bodil Kjer, Birgitte Federspiel, Jean-Philippe LaFont, Ebbe Rode, Jarl Kulle; **D:** Gabriel Axel; **W:** Gabriel Axel.

Academy Awards '87: Best Foreign Language Film; British Academy Awards '88: Best Foreign Film. *ORI, FCT, APD*

The Baby 🎬🎬 **1972 (PG)** Bizarre story of a social worker who resorts to swinging an ax to cut the apron strings of "baby," a retarded man-child, from his over-protective and insane (bad combination) mother and sisters. Low-budget production looks and feels like a low-budget production, but any movie featuring a grown man wandering about in diapers can't be all bad. **85m/C VHS, Beta.** Anjanette Comer, Ruth Roman, Marianna Hill, Suzanne Zenor, David Manzy, Michael Pataki; **D:** Ted Post. *NO*

The Baby and the Battleship 🎬🎬½ **1956** The old baby out of (on the?) water plot. While on liberty in Italy, a sailor, after a series of complications, becomes custodian of a baby and attempts to hide the tyke aboard his battleship (hence the title). More complications ensue. Some funny moments. Great cast. **96m/C VHS.** *GB* John Mills, Richard Attenborough, Andre Morell, Bryan Forbes, Lisa Gastoni, Michael Hordern, Lionel Jeffries, Gordon Jackson, John Le Mesurier; **D:** Jay Lewis. *NOS, MOV, VEC*

Baby Boom 🎬🎬½ **1987 (PG)** When a hard-charging family executive becomes the reluctant mother of a baby girl (a gift from a long-lost relative), she adjusts with great difficulty to motherhood and life outside the rat race and New York City (and Sam Shepard as the love interest). A fairly harmless collection of cliches bolstered by Keaton's usual nervous performance as a power-suited yuppie ad queen saddled with a noncareer-enhancing baby, moving from manic yuppie ad maven to jelly-packing Vermont store-owner/ mom. To best appreciate flick, see it with a bevy of five- and six-year-olds (a good age for applauding the havoc that a baby creates). **103m/C VHS, Beta, LV, Closed Caption.** Diane Keaton, Sam Shepard, Harold Ramis, Sam Wanamaker, James Spader, Pat Hingle, Mary Gross, Victoria Jackson, Paxton Whitehead, Annie Golden, Dori Brenner, Robin Bartlett, Christopher Noth, Britt Leach; **D:** Charles Shyer; **W:** Charles Shyer, Nancy Meyers; **M:** Bill Conti. *MGM, FCT, FOX*

Baby Cart 1: Lend a Child...Lend an Arm 🎬 *Lone Wolf and Cub: Sword of Vengeance* **1972** First in a series of six from the sword-wielding samurai genre. Chronicles the events leading up to a samurai warrior's (Wakayama) expulsion from his native village along with his infant son (Tomikawa). Father's intense rivalry with the evil Shogun whom he was ousted by becomes an epic struggle of good vs. evil. The adorable baby "Lone Cub" provides an effective counterpoint for Dad's sideline excursion into a local brothel. In Japanese with English subtitles in a letterbox format. **83m/C VHS, LV.** *JP* Tomisaburo Wakayama, Akihiro Tomikawa; **D:** Kenji Misumi. *ANI, VSM*

Baby Cart 4: Heart of a Parent...Heart of a Child 🎬 **1972** Fourth in a series of six. A man (Wakayama) pushes his son (Tomikawa) across Japan in a baby cart loaded with deadly accessories including built-in guns and switchblades. Copious amounts of bloodshed. In Japanese with English subtitles in a letterbox format. **80m/C VHS.** *JP* Tomisaburo Wakayama, Akihiro Tomikawa; **D:** Buichi Sato. *VSM*

Baby Cart at the River Styx 🎬 *Lone Wolf and Cub: Baby Cart at the River Styx; Baby Cart 2* **1972** Second of six parts in the "Kozure Ohkami" ("Sword of Vengeance") series about a man who wheels his motherless infant through the Chinese countryside in a baby cart armed with secret weapons, plotting his revenge on the warlord who expelled him. This one features the intro of Sayka and her fellow female assassins. Subtitled in English. **80m/C VHS.** *JP* Tomisaburo Wakayama, Akihiro Tomikawa; **D:** Kenji Misumi. *MOV*

Baby Cart to Hades 🎬 **1972** The third "Kozure Ohkami" ("Sword of Vengeance") film once again finds samurai Itto Ogami and his son Diagoro embroiled in a power struggle between a regional landlord and a governor in feudal Japan.

Subtitled in English. **88m/C VHS.** *JP* Tomisaburo Wakayama, Akihiro Tomikawa; **D:** Kenji Misumi. *VSM*

Baby Doll 🎬🎬🎬 **1956** Suggestive sex at its best, revolving around the love of cotton in Mississippi. Nubile Baker is married to slow-witted Malden, who runs a cotton gin. His torching of Wallach's cotton gin begins a cycle of sexual innuendo and tension, brought to exhilarating life on screen, without a single filmed kiss. Performers and sets ooze during the steamy exhibition, which was considered highly erotic when released. Excellent performances from entire cast, with expert pacing by director Kazan. Screenplay is based on Tennessee Williams' "27 Wagons Full of Cotton." **115m/B VHS, Beta.** Eli Wallach, Carroll Baker, Karl Malden, Mildred Dunnock, Rip Torn; **D:** Elia Kazan; **W:** Tennessee Williams; **C:** Boris Kaufman. Golden Globe Awards '57: Best Director (Kazan); Nominations: Academy Awards '56: Best Actress (Baker), Best Adapted Screenplay, Best Black and White Cinematography, Best Supporting Actress (Dunnock). *WAR, FCT*

The Baby Doll Murders 🎬🎬 **1992 (R)** Someone in L.A. is killing beautiful young women and then leaving a broken baby doll at the scene of the crime. The gruesome murderer manages to elude everyone, until Detective Benz discovers a link between the victims and a pattern begins to form. He also discovers that his partner's wife is going to be the next victim unless he can stop this ruthless serial killer from striking again. **CW:** Language, violence, and sexuality. **90m/C VHS, Closed Caption.** Jeff Kober, Melanie Smith, John Saxon, Tom Hodges; **D:** Paul Leder; **W:** Paul Leder. *REP*

Baby Face 🎬🎬 **1933** A small town girl moves to the city when her father dies. There she gets a job at a bank and sleeps her way to the top of the business world, discarding used men left and right. The Hays Office was extremely upset with the then risque material and forced Warner to trim the first cut. **70m/B VHS, Beta.** Barbara Stanwyck, George Brent, Donald Cook, John Wayne, Henry Kolker, Margaret Lindsay, Douglass Dumbrille, James Murray; **D:** Alfred E. Green. *MGM, FCT*

Baby Face Harry Langdon 🎬🎬½ **1926** Two silent shorts by the limpid-eyed comedian: "Saturday Afternoon" (1926), and "Lucky Stars" (1925). **60m/B VHS, Beta, 8mm.** Harry Langdon, Alice Ward, Natalie Kingston, Vernon Dent, Harry Edwards; **D:** Harry Edwards; **W:** Frank Capra, Arthur Ripley. *VYY*

Baby Face Morgan 🎬🎬 **1942** Poor comedy about gangsters who attempt to take advantage of the FBI's preoccupation with saboteurs and spies by muscling in on an insurance firm. **60m/B VHS.** Mary Carlisle, Richard Cromwell, Robert Armstrong, Chick Chandler, Charles Judels, Warren Hymer, Vince Barnett, Ralf Harolde; **D:** Arthur Dreifuss. *SNC*

Baby Girl Scott 🎬🎬½ **1987** Hurt and Lithgow play the parents of an extremely premature infant who is being kept alive by technology. They make a heartrending decision and then must battle doctors and the system to let their daughter die with dignity. Made for television. **97m/C VHS.** John Lithgow, Mary Beth Hurt, Linda Kelsey; **D:** John Korty. *LIV*

Baby It's You 🎬🎬🎬 **1982 (R)** In New Jersey in the '60s, the relationship between a smart, attractive Jewish girl who yearns to be an actress and a street-smart Catholic Italian boy puzzles their family and friends. It all works due to Arquette's strong acting and Sayles' script, which explores adolescent dreams, the transition to adulthood, class differences, and the late 1960s with insight and humor. Interesting period soundtrack (Woolly Bully and, for some reason, Bruce Springsteen) helps propel the film, a commercial job which helped finance Sayles' more independent ventures. **105m/C VHS, Closed Caption.** Rosanna Arquette, Vincent Spano, Jack Davidson, Joanna Merlin, Nick Ferrari, Leora Dana, Robert Downey Jr., Tracy Pollan, Matthew Modine; **D:** John Sayles; **W:** John Sayles; **C:** Michael Ballhaus. *PAR*

Baby Love woof! **1969 (R)** A softcore fluff-fest about a trollop seducing a doctor's family. The doctor may or may not be her father. Hayden tantalizes the doctor, the doctor's son, and the doctor's wife, as well as the neighbors, leaving only those in adjoining communities untouched. Based on the novel by Tina Chad Christian. **98m/C VHS, Beta.** *GB* Ann Lynn, Keith Barron, Linda Hayden, Derek Lamden, Diana Dors, Patience Collier; **D:** Alastair Reid. *NLC*

Baby Love woof! **1983** Nerds get revenge against the freshmen who run the local frat house. **80m/C VHS, Beta.** *MGM*

The Baby Maker 🎬🎬 **1970 (R)** A couple who cannot have children because the wife is sterile decides to hire a woman to have a child for them. However, the relationship between the husband and the surrogate progresses beyond what either of them wanted. Hershey stars as the free-love surrogate mama (just before she underwent the supreme 60s transformation into Barbara Seagull) and Bridges makes his directorial debut. Flick is interesting as a combo critique/exploitation of those wild and groovy 1960s. **109m/C VHS.** Barbara Hershey, Collin Wilcox-Horne, Sam Groom, Scott Glenn, Jeannie Berlin; **D:** James Bridges; **W:** James Bridges. Nominations: Academy Awards '70: Original Song Score and/or Adaptation. *WAR*

Baby of the Bride 🎬🎬½ **1991** Follow-up to "Children of the Bride," has McClanahan settling into wedded bliss with younger husband Shackleford when she discovers she's pregnant. Not only is she unsure about wanting to be a mom again at her age but then grown—and single—daughter McNichol announces she is also pregnant. The sheer silliness of this made-for-television fare makes it fun to watch. **93m/C VHS, Closed Caption.** Rue McClanahan, Ted Shackleford, Kristy McNichol, John Wesley Shipp, Anne Bobby, Conor O'Farrell; **D:** Bill Bixby; **W:** Bart Baker. *TTC*

Baby on Board 🎬🎬 **1992 (PG)** Kane plays the wife of a Mafia bookkeeper who is accidentally killed in a gangland murder. Out for revenge, she tracks her husband's killer to JFK airport with her four-year old daughter in tow. Just as she pulls the loaded gun from her purse and takes aim, a pickpocket snatches her purse, accidentally firing the gun. Now she's on the run and she jumps into the first cab she can find, driven by Reinhold. New York City is turned upside down as mother, daughter, and cabbie try to elude the mob in this funny but predictable comedy. **90m/C VHS, Beta, LV, Closed Caption.** Carol Kane, Judge Reinhold, Geza Kovacs, Errol Slue, Alex Stapley, Holly Stapley; **D:** Francis Schaeffer. *PSM*

Baby ... Secret of the Lost Legend 🎬🎬 **1985 (PG)** A sportswriter and his paleontologist wife risk their lives to reunite a hatching brontosaurus with its mother in the African jungle. Although this Disney film is not lewd in any sense, beware of several scenes displaying frontal nudity and some violence. **95m/C VHS, Beta, LV.** William Katt, Sean Young, Patrick McGoohan, Julian Fellowes; **D:** Bill W.L. Norton. *TOU*

The Baby-Sitters Club 🎬🎬½ **1995 (PG)** Centering on the summer vacation of seven enterprising Connecticut 13-year-olds and their teen trials with parents, boys, and babysitting, this film is sure to hit home with a crowd that is rarely featured, pre-teen girls. Director Mayron claims, "It's the 'Mystic Pizza' of their age." Young girls and girls young at heart should enjoy this touching look at the fragile years of our youth, leaving baby dolls behind and heading towards dating. Based on the best-selling book series by Ann Martin. Fisk, who plays club leader Kristy, is the daughter of actress Sissy Spacek and director Jack Fisk. **92m/C VHS, LV, Closed Caption.** Schuyler Fisk, Bre Blair, Rachel Leigh Cook, Larisa Oleynik, Tricia Joe, Stacey Linn Ransower, Zelda Harris, Brooke Adams, Peter Horton, Bruce Davison, Ellen Burstyn, Austin O'Brien, Aaron Michael Metchik; **D:** Melanie Mayron; **W:** Dalene Young; **C:** Willy Kurant; **M:** David Michael Frank. *COL*

Baby Snakes: The Complete Version 1979 Concert footage of Zappa is interspersed with clay animation by Bruce Bickford. 166m/C VHS, Beta. Frank Zappa; **D:** Frank Zappa. MVD

Baby, Take a Bow 🎬🎬 1934 (PG) Temple's first starring role. As a cheerful Pollyanna-type she helps her father, falsely accused of theft, by finding the true thief. 76m/B VHS, Beta, Closed Caption. Shirley Temple, James Dunn, Claire Trevor, Alan Dinehart; **D:** Harry Lachman. FXV

Baby, the Rain Must Fall 🎬🎬 1964 A rockabilly singer, paroled from prison after serving time for a knifing, returns home to his wife and daughter, but his outbursts of violence make the reunion difficult. Unsentimental with realistic performances, but script is weak (although written by Foote, based on his play, "The Traveling Lady"). Theme song was a Top 40 hit. 100m/B VHS, Beta, LV. Steve McQueen, Lee Remick, Don Murray; **D:** Robert Mulligan; **W:** Horton Foote; **C:** Ernest Laszlo; **M:** Elmer Bernstein. COL, MOV

Babycakes 🎬🎬½ 1989 A marshmellow romance between an overweight mortuary attendant who decides to follow her heart when she falls for a hunky ice skater. Can she make him appreciate her inner beauty instead of just her not-the-normal-beauty-standard outward appearance? (Happy ending guaranteed.) A made for television remake of the darker German film "Sugarbaby." 94m/C VHS, Closed Caption. Ricki Lake, Craig Sheffer, Paul Benedict, Betty Buckley, John Karlen, Nada Despotovich; **D:** Paul Schneider. TTC

Babyfever 🎬🎬½ 1994 (R) Women gather at a baby shower and tell stories about motherhood and related topics. May be viewed as a babblefest with video accompaniment or as an overdue cinematic exploration of a fairly important aspect of life (where would we be without mom?). That said, pace of the comedy drama is less than feverish, although director Jaglom captures the essence of the stories without disturbing their flow. Foyt, Jaglom's wife and co-screenwriter, makes her acting debut. 110m/C VHS. Matt Salinger, Eric Roberts, Frances Fisher, Victoria Foyt, Zack Norman, Dinah Lenney, Elaine Kagan; **D:** Henry Jaglom; **W:** Victoria Foyt, Henry Jaglom; **C:** Hanania Baer. FXL

The Babylon Story from "Intolerance" 🎬🎬🎬½ 1916 Lavishly produced vignette from Griffith's film "Intolerance" as it was released on its own in 1919, in order to recoup the studio losses incurred by that grandest of cinematic follies. Silent with organ score, tinted color. 25m/C VHS, Beta. Constance Talmadge, Alfred Paget; **D:** D.W. Griffith. VYY

Baby's Day Out 🎬🎬½ 1994 (PG) Poor man's "Home Alone" refits tired Hughes formula using little tiny baby for original spin. Adorable Baby Bink crawls his way onto the city streets, much to his frantic mother's dismay, and unwittingly outsmarts his would-be kidnappers. As in "HA I and II," the bad guys fall victim to all sorts of cataclysmic Looney Tunes violence. Small kids will get a kick out of this one. Particular problem for the moviemakers was that the nine-month old Worton twins were past the year mark by the end of the shoot, a world of difference in infantdom. Blue screens and out-of-sequence shooting were used to overcome the developmental gap. 99m/C VHS, Closed Caption. Adam Worton, Jacob Worton, Joe Mantegna, Lara Flynn Boyle, Joe Pantoliano, Fred Dalton Thompson, John Neville, Brian Haley, Matthew Glave; **D:** Patrick Read Johnson; **W:** John Hughes; **C:** Thomas Ackerman; **M:** Bruce Broughton. FXV

The Babysitter 🎬🎬 1980 A family hires the mysterious but ingratiating Johanna (Zimbalist) as live-in help without checking on her references (who'd all checked out). The babysitter is the answer to all their problems—Mom's an alcoholic, Dad's a workaholic, and their daughter's just plain maladjusted—but once Johanna's gained their trust (or, in Dad's case, lust), she sets out to manipulate and exploit the family for her

own psychotic purposes. Houseman plays the nosy neighbor who's on to her evil plan. Fair made-for-TV treatment of a common suspense plot. 96m/C VHS, Beta, LV. William Shatner, Patty Duke, Stephanie Zimbalist, Quinn Cummings, John Houseman, David Wallace; **D:** Peter Medak. NO

The Babysitter 🎬🎬½ 1995 (R) All-American teen Jennifer (Silverstone) becomes the unexpected object of desire for family man Harry (Walsh), whose wife Dolly (Garlington) is fantasizing about having an affair with a neighbor (Segal). But then Jennifer's boyfriend (London) gets caught up in a malicious prank that turns bad for everyone involved. Based on a short story by Robert Coover.**CW:** Brief nudity, violence, adult situations, language. 90m/C VHS, LV, Closed Caption. Alicia Silverstone, Jeremy London, J.T. Walsh, Lee Garlington, Nicky Katt, Lois Chiles, George Segal; **D:** Guy Ferland; **W:** Guy Ferland; **M:** Loek Dikker. REP

The Bacchantes 🎬🎬 1963 Poorly dubbed account of a ballerina, her life and loves. Based on the play by Euripides. 100m/B VHS. IT Taina Elg, Pierre Brice, Alessandra Panaro, Alberto Lupo, Akim Tamiroff; **D:** Giorgio Ferroni. FCT

Bach: Mass in B Minor 199? Features Bach scholar Helmuth Rilling, soprano Arleen Auger, alto Anne Sophie von Otter, tenor Aldo Baldin, tenor Aldo Baldin, Gachinger Kantorei, and Bach-Collegium Stuttgart as they perform the Johann Sebastian Bach classic at the International Bach Festival in Stuttgart, Germany. m/C VHS. PRS

The Bachelor 🎬🎬🎬 1993 Beautiful, seductive period drama about a shy and solitary physician who is forced into a new life when a family tragedy changes everything he once took for granted. Richardson and Carradine give brilliant performances in this provocative story of one man's sexual awakening. Based on a novel by Arthur Schnitzler. 105m/C VHS. Keith Carradine, Miranda Richardson, Mari Torocsik, Max von Sydow, Kristin Scott Thomas, Sarah-Jane Fenton, Franco Diogene; **D:** Roberto Faenza; **W:** Roberto Faenza, Ennio de Concini, Hugh Fleetwood; **M:** Ennio Morricone. TRI

The Bachelor and the Bobby-Soxer 🎬🎬🎬 Bachelor Knight 1947 Playboy Grant is brought before Judge Loy for disturbing the peace and sentenced to court her teen-age sister Temple. Cruel and unusual punishment? Maybe, but the wise Judge hopes that the dates will help Temple over her crush on handsome Grant. Instead, Loy and Grant fall for each other. 95m/B VHS, Beta, LV. Cary Grant, Myrna Loy, Shirley Temple, Rudy Vallee, Harry Davenport, Ray Collins, Veda Ann Borg; **D:** Irving Reis; **W:** Sidney Sheldon. Academy Awards '47: Best Original Screenplay. CCB, MED, MLB

Bachelor Apartment 🎬🎬½ 1931 Once at the leading edge of the bachelor on the loose genre, this one's hopelessly dated. The scandalous womanizing of a wealthy thirties Lothario just doesn't have the same impact on the men just don't understand generation. Nevertheless, as vintage if-the-walls-could-talk fluff, it's good for a giggle. 77m/B VHS. Lowell Sherman, Irene Dunne, Norman Kerry, Claudia Dell, Noel Francis, Charles Coleman; **D:** Lowell Sherman. TTC, FCT

Bachelor Bait 🎬½ 1934 A marriage license clerk who's tired of just handing out licenses opens a matrimonial service for men. 75m/B VHS, Beta. Stuart Erwin, Rochelle Hudson, Pert Kelton, Richard "Skeets" Gallagher; **D:** Max Steiner. FCT

Bachelor in Paradise 🎬🎬½ 1969 Silly tale starring Hope as a writer of books to the lovelorn who decides to do firsthand research on the sexual goings-on of a suburban California community. All the married ladies find him charming (much to their husbands' disgust) and the lone single woman, Turner, isn't single by the end of the movie. 109m/C VHS, Closed Caption. Bob Hope, Lana Turner, Janis Paige, Jim Hutton, Paula Prentiss, Don Porter, Virginia Grey, Agnes Moorehead, John McGiver; **D:** Jack Arnold; **W:** Hal Kanter, Valentine Davies; **M:** Henry

Mancini. Nominations: Academy Awards '61: Best Song ("Bachelor in Paradise"). MGM, FCT

Bachelor Mother 🎬🎬🎬 1939 A single salesgirl causes a scandal when she finds an abandoned baby and is convinced by her boss to adopt the child. Smart, witty comedy with nice performance by Rogers. 82m/B VHS, Beta, LV. Ginger Rogers, David Niven, Charles Coburn; **D:** Garson Kanin. Nominations: Academy Awards '39: Best Story. CCB, MED, FCT

Bachelor of Hearts 🎬½ 1958 Sophomoric British comedy set at Cambridge University, with a German exchange student whose difficulty with English brings him to date several women in one evening. Notable for horror fans as the debut of femme fright fave Barbara Steele. 94m/C VHS. GB Hardy Kruger, Sylvia Syms, Ronald Lewis; **D:** Wolf Rilla; **W:** Frederic Raphael, Leslie Bricusse. NOS

Bachelor Party 🎬🎬 1984 (R) He's silly, cute, and poor. She's intelligent, beautiful, and rich. It must be a marriage made in heaven, because no one in their right mind would put these two together. All is basically well, except that her parents hate him and his friends dislike her. Things are calm until right before the big event, when bride-to-be Kitaen objects to Hank's traditional pre-nuptial partying. Light and semi-entertaining with scattered laughs. 105m/C VHS, Beta, LV, Closed Caption. Tom Hanks, Tawny Kitaen, Adrian Zmed, George Grizzard, Robert Prescott, William Tepper, Wendie Jo Sperber, Barry Diamond, Michael Dudikoff, Deborah Harmon, John Bloom, Toni Alessandra, Monique Gabrielle, Angela Aames, Rosanne Katon; **D:** Neal Israel; **W:** Pat Proft; **M:** Robert Folk. FXV, FOX

Back Door to Heaven 🎬🎬🎬½ 1939 Traces the path of a young boy who is born into a poor family and the reasons for his turning to a life of crime. A grim and powerful drama with many convincing performances. 85m/B VHS. Wallace Ford, Aline MacMahon, Stuart Erwin, Patricia Ellis, Kent Smith, Van Heflin, Jimmy Lydon; **D:** William K. Howard. NOS, MOV

Back from Eternity 🎬🎬 1956 Eleven survivors of a plane crash are stranded in a headhunter region of South America's jungle. Remake of "Five Came Back" (1939), which was also directed by Farrow. 97m/B VHS, Beta, LV. Robert Ryan, Rod Steiger, Anita Ekberg, Phyllis Kirk, Keith Andes, Gene Barry; **D:** John Farrow; **W:** William Mellor. NO

Back Home 🎬🎬½ 1990 A family reunion movie with pure Disney sentiment. A 12-year-old English girl, who has been living in America during WWII, is reunited with her family in postwar England. Made for cable television. 103m/C VHS, Closed Caption. Hayley Carr, Hayley Mills, Jean Anderson, Rupert Frazer, Brenda Bruce, Adam Stevenson, George Clark; **D:** Piers Haggard. DIS

Back in Action 🎬½ 1994 (R) Veteran LA detective Rossi (Piper) is out to bust the ruthless drug gang who gunned down his partner. But he's got company—martial-arts expert Billy (Blanks) whose young sister has fallen prey to the same gang. So the two action junkies reluctantly team up to cause some major damage. 93m/C VHS, LV, Closed Caption. Roddy Piper, Billy Blanks, Bobbie Phillips, Matt Birman, Nigel Bennett, Damon D'Oliveira, Kai Soremekun; **D:** Paul Ziller, Steve DiMarco; **W:** Karl Schiffman. USH

Back in Business 🎬🎬 1996 (R) Joe Elkhart's (Bosworth) life is down the drain. After failing to expose a fellow police officer as corrupt, he's kicked off the force, abandoned by his friends, and divorced by his wife. Now working as a mechanic, Joe gets pulled back into the action when his ex-partner, Tony (Torry), goes undercover to bring down a major drug dealer and Joe discovers the corrupt cops that framed him are also behind the current heroin deal.**CW:** Strong violence and language, and for sexuality. 93m/C VHS, Closed Caption. Brian Bosworth, Joe Torry; **D:** Philippe Mora; **W:** Ed Decatur, Ash Staley. COL

Back in the USSR ⚔️½ 1992 (R) Danger follows two lovers caught up in the Moscow underworld. When young American touring Russia unwittingly gets involved with a beautiful art thief. Lots of fast-paced action in an otherwise muddled film. The first American film shot entirely on location in Moscow. **CW:** Language, violence, and one scene of sensuality. 87m/C VHS. Frank Whaley, Natalia Negoda, Roman Polanski, Claudia Robinson, Dey Young, Andrew Divoff, Brian Blessed, Ravil Issyanov; **D:** Deran Sarafian; **C:** Yuri Neyman. FXV

Back of Beyond ⚔️⚔️ 1995 (R) Spectacular setting in the Australian outback can't make up for unfocused plot and characters with little impact. Tom (Mercutio) ran a remote desert gas station with his sister, Susan (Elmalogulou), before she was killed on his motorbike. When Connor's (Friels) car breaks down by the derelict station, he, girlfriend Charlie (Smart), and sidekick Nick (Polson) must wait while Tom tries to fix it. Only Connor is a diamond thief and patience isn't one of his virutes, especially when he notices the unhappy Charlie making friends with Tom. Mystical/supernatural elements involving ghosts and Aboriginal sites only add to the confusion. **CW:** Language and a scene of sexual assault. 85m/C VHS. AU Paul Mercurio, Colin Friels, Dee Smart, John Polson, Rebekah Elmaloglou, Bob Maza, Terry Serio; **D:** Michael Robertson; **W:** Paul Leadon, A.M. Brooksbank, Richard I. Sawyer; **C:** Stephen Dobson; **M:** Mark Moffatt, Wayne Goodwin. LIV

Back Roads ⚔️⚔️ 1981 (R) Southern hooker meets a down-on-his-luck boxer and both head out for a better life in California, finding love along the way. Ritt road trip lacks any comedic rhythm and survives on Field and Jones working to entertain. 94m/C VHS, Beta. Sally Field, Tommy Lee Jones, David Keith; **D:** Martin Ritt; **W:** Gary De Vore; **C:** John A. Alonzo; **M:** Henry Mancini. FOX

Back Street ⚔️⚔️ 1961 The forbidden affair between a married man and a beautiful fashion designer carries on through many anxious years to a tragic end. The lavish third film version of the Fannie Hurst novel. 107m/C VHS, Beta. Susan Hayward, John Gavin, Vera Miles; **D:** David Miller; **C:** William H. Daniels. Nominations: Academy Awards '61: Best Costume Design (Color). USH, MLB

Back to Back ⚔️ 1990 (R) A beautiful young vigilante embarks on a rampage to clear her family's name and make her town's redneck crooks pay for their crimes. Never released in theaters. 95m/C VHS, Beta. Bill Paxton, Todd Field, Apollonia, Luke Askew, Ben Johnson, David Michael-Standing, Susan Anspach, Sal Landi; **D:** John Kincade; **C:** James L. Carter. MGM

Back to Back ⚔️⚔️½ 1996 Ex-cop Malone (Rooker) must team up with hitman Koji (Ishibashi), who's holding Malone's daughter hostage, to double-cross a corrupt cop and stay alive while being hunted by the Mafia. 95m/C VHS, **Closed Caption.** Michael Rooker, Ryo Ishibashi, John Laughlin, Danielle Harris, Bob(cat) Goldthwait, Vincent Schiavelli; **D:** Roger Nygard; **W:** Lloyd Keith; **C:** Mark W. Gray; **M:** Walter Werzowa. BMG

Back to Bataan ⚔️⚔️½ 1945 Colonel forms guerrilla army to raid Japanese in the Philippines and to help Americans landing on Leyte. Also available in a colorized version. 95m/B VHS, Beta, LV, **Closed Caption.** John Wayne, Anthony Quinn, Beulah Bondi, Fely Franquelli, Richard Loo, Philip Ahn, Lawrence Tierney; **D:** Edward Dmytryk. TTC

Back to Hannibal: The Return of Tom Sawyer and Huckleberry Finn ⚔️⚔️½ 1990 Mark Twain's characters Tom Sawyer and Huckleberry Finn are reunited as adults to solve a murder mystery. Tom is a lawyer, Finn a newspaper man, and it's Becky Thatcher's husband who's been murdered. Did a freed slave really commit the crime? Made for television. 92m/C VHS. Raphael Sbarge, Mitchell Anderson, Megan Follows, William Windom, Ned Beatty, Paul Winfield; **D:** Paul Krasny; **M:** Lee Holdridge. DIS

Back to School ⚔️⚔️½ 1986 (PG-13) Dangerfield plays an obnoxious millionaire who enrolls in college to help his wimpy son, Gordon, achieve campus stardom. His motto seems to be "if you can't buy it, it can't be had." At first, his antics embarrass his wimp son, but soon everyone is clamoring to be seen with the pair as Gordon develops his own self confidence. 96m/C VHS, Beta, LV, **Closed Caption.** Rodney Dangerfield, Keith Gordon, Robert Downey Jr., Sally Kellerman, Burt Young, Paxton Whitehead, Adrienne Barbeau, M. Emmet Walsh, Severn Darden, Ned Beatty, Sam Kinison, Kurt Vonnegut Jr., Robert Picardo, Terry Farrell, Edie McClurg, Jason Hervey; **D:** Alan Metter; **W:** Will Aldis, Steven Kampmann, Harold Ramis, Peter Torokvei; **C:** Thomas Ackerman; **M:** Danny Elfman. NO

Back to the Beach ⚔️½ 1987 (PG) Frankie and Annette return to the beach as self-parodying, middle-aged parents with rebellious kids, and the usual run of sun-bleached, lover's tiff comedy ensues. Plenty of songs and guest appearances from television past. Tries to bring back that surf, sun, and sand feel of the orignal "Beach Party" movies, but fails. ♫Absolute Perfection; California Sun; Catch a Ride; Jamaica Sky; Papa-Oom-Mow-Mow; Sign of Love; Sun, Sun, Sun, Sun, Sun; Surfin' Bird; Wooly Bully. 92m/C VHS, Beta, LV, **Closed Caption.** Frankie Avalon, Annette Funicello, Connie Stevens, Jerry Mathers, Bob Denver, Barbara Billingsley, Tony Dow, Paul (Pee Wee Herman) Reubens, Edd Byrnes, Dick Dale, Don Adams, Lori Loughlin; **D:** Lyndall Hobbs; **C:** Bruce Surtees; **M:** Stephen Dorff. PAR

Back to the Future ⚔️⚔️⚔️ 1985 (PG) When neighborhood mad scientist Doc Brown constructs a time machine from a DeLorean, his youthful companion Marty accidentally transports himself to 1955. There, Marty must do everything he can to bring his parents together, elude the local bully, and get back...to the future. Solid fast-paced entertainment is even better due to Lloyd's inspired performance as the loony Doc while Fox is perfect as the boy completely out of his element. Soundtrack features Huey Lewis and the News. Followed by two sequels. 116m/C VHS, Beta, LV, **Closed Caption.** Michael J. Fox, Christopher Lloyd, Lea Thompson, Crispin Glover, Wendie Jo Sperber, Marc McClure, Thomas F. Wilson, James Tolkan, Casey Siemaszko, Billy Zane, George DiCenzo, Courtney Gains, Claudia Wells, Jason Hervey, Harry Waters Jr., Maia Brewton, J.J. Cohen; **Cameos:** Huey Lewis; **D:** Robert Zemeckis; **W:** Robert Zemeckis, Bob Gale; **C:** Dean Cundey; **M:** Alan Silvestri. People's Choice Awards '86: Best Film; Nominations: Academy Awards '85: Best Original Screenplay, Best Song ("The Power of Love"), Best Sound. USH, FCT, TLF

Back to the Future, Part 2 ⚔️⚔️½ 1989 (PG) Taking up exactly where Part 1 left off, Doc Brown and Marty time-hop into the future (2015 to be exact) to save Marty's kids, then find themselves returning to 1955 to retrieve a sports almanac that causes havoc for the McFly family. Clever editing allows for Marty Part 2 to see Marty Part 1 at the school dance. Most of the cast returns, although Glover appears only in cuts from the original and Shue steps in as girlfriend Jennifer. Not up to the original, but still satisfying. Cliffhanger ending sets up Part 3, which was shot simultaneously with this. 107m/C VHS, Beta, LV, **Closed Caption.** Michael J. Fox, Christopher Lloyd, Lea Thompson, Thomas F. Wilson, Harry Waters Jr., Charles Fleischer, Joe Flaherty, Elisabeth Shue, James Tolkan, Casey Siemaszko, Jeffrey Weissman, Flea, Billy Zane, J.J. Cohen, Darlene Vogel, Jason Scott Lee, Crispin Glover, Ricky Dean Logan; **D:** Robert Zemeckis; **W:** Robert Zemeckis, Bob Gale; **C:** Dean Cundey; **M:** Alan Silvestri. USH

Back to the Future, Part 3 ⚔️⚔️⚔️ 1990 (PG) Picks up where Part 2 climaxed a la cliffhanger. Stuck in 1955, time-traveling hero Marty frantically searches for Doc Part 1 so he can return to 1985. Instead, he finds himself in the Wild West circa 1885, trying to save Doc's life. Plot is related to earlier BTTFs, so first time viewers might be confused. For those who've seen previous incarnations, the clever interconnections

are really nifty. Nearly matches the original for excitement and offers some snazzy new special effects. Supposedly the last installment, though don't be surprised if another sequel follows. The complete trilogy is available as a boxed set. 118m/C VHS, Beta, LV, **Closed Caption.** Michael J. Fox, Christopher Lloyd, Mary Steenburgen, Thomas F. Wilson, Lea Thompson, Elisabeth Shue, Matt Clark, Richard Dysart, Pat Buttram, Harry Carey Jr., Dub Taylor, James Tolkan, Marc McClure, Wendie Jo Sperber, J.J. Cohen, Ricky Dean Logan, Jeffrey Weissman; **D:** Robert Zemeckis; **W:** Robert Zemeckis, Bob Gale; **C:** Dean Cundey; **M:** Alan Silvestri. USH

Back to the Wall ⚔️⚔️ 1956 Moreau is an adulterous wife whose web of deceit results in a suspenseful tale of murder and blackmail. 94m/B VHS. FR Jeanne Moreau, Gerard Oury, Claire Maurier; **D:** Edouard Molinaro. FCT

Backbeat ⚔️⚔️⚔️ 1994 (R) Backed by the beat of early Beatle tunes as rendered by some of today's top alternative musicians, the debut for director Softley explores the Fab Four's beginnings in Hamburg's underground music scene. Storyline is driven by the complications of a romantic triangle between John Lennon, Astrid Kirchherr (the photographer who came up with the band's signature look) and Stu Sutcliffe, Lennon's best friend and the original bass player for the Beatles. Hart's dead-on as Lennon, playing him a second time (check out "The Hours and Times"). Energetic and enjoyable, particularly when the Was-produced music takes center stage. **CW:** Strong language, nudity, and sexuality. 100m/C VHS, LV, **Closed Caption.** GB Stephen Dorff, Sheryl Lee, Ian Hart, Gary Bakewell, Chris O'Neill, Scot Williams, Kai Wiesinger, Jennifer Ehle; **D:** Iain Softley; **W:** Michael Thomas, Stephen Ward, Iain Softley; **M:** Don Was. PGV

Backdraft ⚔️⚔️½ 1991 (R) High action story of Chicago firemen has some of the most stupendous incendiary special effects ever filmed. But then there's that plot, B-movie hokum about a mystery arsonist torching strategic parts of the community with the finesse of an expert and a brother-against-brother conflict. Straight-forward performances from most of the cast in spite of the weak storyline. Writer Widen wrote from experience—he used to be a fireman; real-life Chicago firefighters were reportedly very happy with the realistic and intense fire scenes. Forget the plot and just watch the fires. Also available in a letterboxed version. **CW:** Language and scene of sensuality. 135m/C VHS, Beta, LV, **Closed Caption.** Kurt Russell, William Baldwin, Robert De Niro, Donald Sutherland, Jennifer Jason Leigh, Scott Glenn, Rebecca DeMornay, Jason Gedrick, J.T. Walsh, Tony Mockus Sr., Clint Howard, David Crosby; **D:** Ron Howard; **W:** Gregory Widen; **C:** Mikael Salomon; **M:** Hans Zimmer. Nominations: Academy Awards '91: Best Sound, Best Visual Effects. USH

Backfield in Motion ⚔️⚔️½ 1991 Silly but harmless comedy about a widowed mom who tries to get closer to her high-schooler son by organizing a mother-son football game. But it's the boys' football coach who really wants to get close—to mom. Made for television movie debut of both Arnolds. 95m/C VHS, Beta, **Closed Caption.** Roseanne, Tom Arnold, Colleen Camp, Conchata Ferrell, Johnny Galecki, Kevin Scannell; **D:** Richard Michaels. TTC

Backfire ⚔️ 1922 If you're gonna rob a bank, you shouldn't let anyone hear you plan it, and if you're not gonna rob a bank, you shouldn't let anyone hear you plan one. This vintage "Lightning" Carson crime western has Carson and friend suspected of bank robbery because someone heard them planning one. The sheriff follows their every footstep as they search for the real perpetrators. 56m/B VHS, Beta. Jack Hoxie, George Sowards, Lew Meehan, Florence Gilbert; **D:** Alan James. GPV

Backfire ⚔️⚔️ 1988 (R) A mysterious stranger enters the lives of a disturbed 'Nam vet and his discontented wife, setting a pattern of murder and double-cross in motion. 90m/C VHS, Beta, LV. Karen Allen, Keith Carradine, Jeff Fahey, Bernie Casey, Dinah

Manoff, Dean Paul Martin; **D:** Gilbert Cates; **W:** Larry Brand; **M:** David Shire. *THV*

Backfire! 🎬½ **1994 (PG-13)** Silly spoof finds Jeremy (Mosby) wanting to join New York City's all-female fire brigade who are trying to stop an arsonist from blowing up the city's toilets. Mitchum is the fire marshal and Ireland the mayor's charming assistant.**CW:** Sensuality; crude humor. **88m/C VHS.** Josh Mosby, Kathy Ireland, Robert Mitchum, Shelley Winters; **D:** A. Dean Bell. *APX*

Background to Danger 🎬🎬🎬 **1943** A suspenseful WWII actioner about American agent Raft who travels to Turkey to receive secret documents from the soon-to-be-murdered Massen. Greenstreet is the Nazi master spy who also wants the documents as do Russian spies, Lorre and Marshall. Somewhat confusing plot but fastpaced. Based on the thriller "Uncommon Danger" by Eric Ambler. This film was Warner Brothers' follow-up to "Casablanca" with Raft in the Bogie role he had turned down in that cinema classic. **80m/B VHS.** George Raft, Sydney Greenstreet, Peter Lorre, Brenda Marshall, Osa Massen, Turhan Bey, Kurt Katch; **D:** Raoul Walsh. *MGM, MOV*

Backlash 🎬🎬½ **1986 (R)** An aborigine barmaid is raped. When her assailant turns up dead, she's charged with murder and winds up in the custody of two police officers on a trip across the outback. Holes in the plot undermine this interesting, although graphic, drama with racial overtones. **88m/C VHS, Beta.** *AU* David Argue, Gia Carides, Lydia Miller, Brian Syron, Anne Smith; **D:** Bill Bennett; **W:** Bill Bennett; **M:** Michael Atkinson, Michael Spicer. *MCG*

Backlash: Oblivion 2 🎬🎬½ *Oblivion 2* **1995 (PG-13)** Galactic supervillainess Lash stakes her claim to a rare derconium mine on the remote space outpost of Oblivion. Will cave monsters thwart her evil plan before space cowboys come to the town's rescue?**CW:** Some violence and sexual material. **82m/C VHS, LV, Closed Caption.** Andrew Divoff, Meg Foster, Isaac Hayes, Julie Newmar, Carel Struycken, George Takei, Musetta Vander, Jimmie F. Skaggs, Irwin Keyes, Maxwell Caulfield; **D:** Sam Irvin; **W:** Peter David; **M:** Pino Donaggio. *FLL*

Backstab 🎬🎬½ **1990 (R)** A spellbinding tale of work, lust, and murder. Architect Brolin finds himself unable to get over the death of his wife, until a seductive and mysterious woman helps him over his grief. They spend the night together, engulfed in passion, but in the morning he wakes to find himself sleeping with the corpse of his boss. Only the first twist in this intriguing thriller. **91m/C VHS, LV, Closed Caption.** James Brolin, Meg Foster, Isabelle Truchon; **D:** Jim Kaufman. *MED, VTR*

Backstairs 🎬🎬 **1921** An obscure German silent film about urban degradation and familial strife. **44m/B VHS.** *GE* Henny Porten, Fritz Kortner, William Dieterle; **D:** Leopold Jessner. *NOS, DVT, GLV*

Backstreet Dreams 🎬🎬 **1990 (R)** The young parents of an autistic child find themselves torn apart due to their feelings of guilt. The father has an affair with a specialist hired to help the boy, causing further strife. Interesting story possibilities never get far. **104m/C VHS, LV.** Brooke Shields, Jason O'Malley, Sherilyn Fenn, Tony Fields, Burt Young, Anthony (Tony) Franciosa, Nick Cassavetes, Ray "Boom Boom" Mancini; **D:** Rupert Hitzig; **M:** Bill Conti. *PSM*

Backstreet Justice 🎬🎬½ **1993 (R)** Pittsburgh PI Keri Finnegan (Kozlowski) is investigating a series of murders in her neighborhood when she uncovers ties to police corruption dating back 30 years. This doesn't make her popular since it involves her dead cop father and a number of old friends (and enemies). Kozlowski is appropriately feisty and the plot twists will hold your attention. **91m/C VHS, LV.** Linda Kozlowski, Hector Elizondo, John Shea, Paul Sorvino, Viveca Lindfors, Tammy Grimes; **D:** Chris McIntyre; **W:** Chris McIntyre. *PSM*

Backtrack 🎬🎬🎬 *Catchfire* **1989 (R)** Foster costars in this thriller about an artist who accidentally witnesses a mob hit. The mob puts a hitman (Hopper) on her trail, and after studying her back-

ground and listening to audio tapes she recorded, he finds himself falling in love. Originally intended for a theatrical release, it hit the European screens in a different cut as "Catchfire;" Hopper restored his original version and it was released on cable TV in the U.S . **102m/C VHS, Closed Caption.** Dennis Hopper, Jodie Foster, Dean Stockwell, Vincent Price, John Turturro, Fred Ward, G. Anthony Sirico, Julie Adams, Frank Gio, Sy Richardson, Helena Kallianiotes, Bob Dylan; **Cameos:** Charlie Sheen, Joe Pesci; **D:** Dennis Hopper; **W:** Ann Louise Bardach; **M:** Michel Colombier. *LIV*

Backwoods 🎬 **1987 (R)** Two campers wish they had never encountered a mountain man when he begins to stalk them with murder in mind. **90m/C VHS, Beta.** Jack O'Hara, Dick Kreusser, Brad Armacot; **D:** Dean Crow. *NO*

The Bad and the Beautiful 🎬🎬🎬½ **1952** The story of a Hollywood producer, told from the eyes of an actress, a writer, and a director. Featuring what some consider Turner's best performance ever. Winner of five Oscars, a splendid drama. **118m/B VHS, LV, Closed Caption.** Kirk Douglas, Lana Turner, Dick Powell, Gloria Grahame, Barry Sullivan, Walter Pidgeon, Gilbert Roland; **D:** Vincente Minnelli; **C:** Robert L. Surtees. Academy Awards '52: Best Art Direction/ Set Decoration (B & W), Best Black and White Cinematography, Best Costume Design (B & W), Best Screenplay, Best Supporting Actress (Grahame); Nominations: Academy Awards '52: Best Actor (Douglas). *MGM, BTV*

Bad Attitude 🎬🎬 **1993 (R)** Leon is a narcotics officer on a mission to restore his badge after his careless pistol work gets him booted off the force. The quick-tempered cop relentlessly pursues druglord Finque with the help of an openminded preacher (De Veaux) and his sexy, streetwise assistant (Lim). **87m/C VHS.** Leon, Gina Lim, Nathaniel DeVeaux, Susan Lill; **D:** Bill Cummings. *XVC*

Bad Behavior 🎬🎬½ **1992 (R)** Unscripted character-driven drama. Gerry and Ellie McAllister are an Irish couple living in North London. He's tired of working for the local planning commission, she's bored being just a mum at home, and both are still a little uneasy living in England. When they decide to remodel the family bath, the unexpected problems lead to an emotional shakeup. Don't expect a lot of drama, the film works only if you accept the decency of the characters and the small moments of recognizable daily life. Director Blair wrote a basic script outline and had the actors improvise their dialogue, in character, over a long rehearsal period to develop their roles.**CW:** Language. **103m/C VHS, Closed Caption.** *GB* Stephen Rea, Sinead Cusack, Philip Jackson, Clare Higgins, Phil Daniels, Saira Todd; **D:** Les Blair; **M:** John Altman. *THV*

Bad Blood 🎬🎬 **1987** The true story of Stan Graham, who went on a killing spree in the New Zealand bush when his farm was foreclosed and his life ruined. **104m/C VHS, Beta.** *NZ* Jack Thompson, Carol Burns, Dennis Lill; **D:** Mike Newell. *ACA*

Bad Blood 🎬½ **1994 (R)** Travis Blackstone (Lamas) will use any methods to protect his brother Franklin, who's targeted for death by a ruthless drug lord. Lots of action and violence.**CW:** Language, violence, nudity, sexual situations. **90m/C VHS, LV, Closed Caption.** Lorenzo Lamas, Hank Cheyne, Frankie Thorn, Kimberley Kates, Joe Son; **D:** Tibor Takacs; **W:** Neil Ruttenberg; **C:** Berhard Salzmann. *WEA, LIV*

Bad Boy 🎬½ *Branded* **1939** A country boy goes to the big city, and succumbs to urban evils and temptations, but is eventually saved by motherly love. **60m/B VHS, Beta, LV.** Johnny Downs, Helen MacKellar, Rosalind Keith, Holmes Herbert; **D:** Kurt Neumann. *NO*

Bad Boy Bubby 🎬🎬 **1993** Bizarre black comedy about the extremely maladjusted Bubby (Hope), who becomes a pop culture phenomena. The 35-year-old childlike Bubby has been kept a virtual prisoner by his monstrous mom, who has told him the world outside is filled with poisonous gas. Wondering how his cat survived, Bubby wraps it in plastic wrap and is puzzled when it

dies. Still, this gives Bubby an idea—he wraps mom in plastic and escapes outside, where he's soon adopted by a struggling rock band that writes a cult song hit about his experiences. It's even stranger than it sounds. **114m/C VHS.** *IT AU* Nicholas Hope, Claire Benito, Carmel Johnson, Ralph Cotterill, Norman Kaye, Paul Philpot, Graham Duckett, Bridget Walters; **D:** Rolf de Heer; **W:** Rolf de Heer; **M:** Graham Tardiff. Australian Film Institute '94: Best Actor (Hope), Best Director (de Heer), Best Film Editing, Best Original Screenplay; Nominations: Australian Film Institute '94: Best Cinematography, Best Film.*NYR*

Bad Boys 🎬🎬🎬 **1983 (R)** When a gang member's little brother is killed in a rumble, the teen responsible (Penn, who else?) goes to a reformatory, where he quickly (though somewhat reluctantly) takes charge. Meanwhile, on the outside, his rival attacks Penn's girlfriend (Sheedy, in her feature film debut) in retaliation, is incarcerated, and ends up vying with Penn for control of the cell block. Backed into a corner by their mutual hatred and escalating peer pressure, the two are pushed over the brink into a final and shattering confrontation. Not as violent as it could be, to its credit; attempts to communicate a message. **104m/C VHS, Beta, LV.** Sean Penn, Esai Morales, Reni Santoni, Jim Moody, Eric Gurry, Ally Sheedy, Clancy Brown; **D:** Rick Rosenthal; **C:** Donald E. Thorin; **M:** Bill Conti. *REP*

Bad Boys 🎬🎬½ **1995 (R)** And you thought the old buddy-cop formula was played out. Well, Hollywood sticks with what works, and pairing the two television personalities definitely works at the minimalist level required. Mike (Smith) and Marcus (Lawrence) are Miami cops who must track down $100 million dollars worth of heroin stolen from their evidence room before internal affairs shuts down the precinct. The case leads them to a vicious thief and a beautiful female witness to his murderous handiwork. Plot lacks depth, but high energy and dazzling action sequences keep things moving. Loud adventure is made louder still by cranking soundtrack. Satisfying addition to the odd-couple cops genre with potential to spawn a "Lethal Weapon"-type franchise. Feature film debut for director Bay.**CW:** Intense violent action; pervasive strong language. **118m/C VHS, LV, Closed Caption, DVD.** Martin Lawrence, Will Smith, Tcheky Karyo, Tea Leoni, Theresa Randle, Marg Helgenberger, Joe Pantoliano, John Salley; **D:** Michael Bay; **W:** Michael Barrie, Jim Mulholland; **C:** Howard Atherton. Blockbuster Entertainment Awards '96: Male Newcomer, Theatrical (Smith); Nominations: MTV Movie Awards '96: Best On-Screen Duo (Martin Lawrence/Will Smith), Best Action Sequence. *COL*

Bad Bunch 🎬🎬 **1976** A white liberal living in Watts tries to befriend a ruthless black street gang, but is unsuccessful. **82m/C VHS, Beta.** Greydon Clark, Tom Johnigam, Pamela Corbett, Jacqulin Cole, Aldo Ray, Jock Mahoney; **D:** Greydon Clark. *VCI*

B.A.D. Cats 🎬 **1980** Two members of a police burglary auto detail team chase after a group of car thieves who are planning a million-dollar gold heist. **74m/C VHS, Beta, LV.** Asher Brauner, Michelle Pfeiffer, Vic Morrow, Jimmie Walker, Steve Hanks, LaWanda Page; **D:** Bernard L. Kowalski. *ORI*

Bad Channels 🎬🎬 **1992 (R)** Radio goes awry when female listeners of station KDUL are shrunk and put into speciman jars by a way-out disc jockey, and a visiting alien, who plans to take the women back to his planet. Mildly amusing comedy features ex-MTV VJ Quinn and score by Blue Oyster Cult. Also available with Spanish subtitles.**CW:** Language. **88m/C VHS, Beta, Closed Caption.** Paul Hipp, Martha Quinn, Aaron Lustig, Ian Patrick Williams, Charlie Spradling, Tim Thomerson; **D:** Ted Nicolaou; **W:** Jackson Barr. *PAR*

Bad Charleston Charlie woof! **1973 (PG)** Dud of a gangster comedy with terrible acting. A comedy? **91m/C VHS.** Ross Hagen, John Carradine; **D:** Ivan Nagy. *NO*

Bad Company 🎬🎬🎬½ 1972 (PG)
Thoughtful study of two very different Civil War draft dodgers roaming the Western frontier and eventually turning to a fruitless life of crime. Both the cast and script are wonderful in an entertaining film that hasn't been given the attention it's due. 94m/C VHS, Beta, LV. Jeff Bridges, Barry Brown, Jim Davis, John Savage; **D:** Robert Benton; **W:** Robert Benton, David Newman; **C:** Gordon Willis. PAR

Bad Company 🎬🎬 1994 (R) Cynical thriller pits the bad against the worst. Vic Grimes (Langella) and Margaret Wells (Barkin) run a company of former secret agents who specialize in corporate dirty work. Nelson Crowe (Fishburne) is an ex-CIA agent who's their latest recruit. But maybe he's not so ex and maybe Margaret doesn't like sharing power and maybe the cold-blooded duo will get together to make some changes. Everything is stylish, including the leads, but there's a definite chill in the air. **CW:** Violence; sexual situations; some language. 118m/C VHS, LV, Closed Caption. Ellen Barkin, Laurence "Larry" Fishburne, Frank Langella, Michael Beach, Gia Carides, David Ogden Stiers, Spalding Gray, James Hong, Daniel Hugh-Kelly; **D:** Damian Harris; **W:** Ross Thomas; **C:** Jack N. Green; **M:** Carter Burwell. TOU

Bad Day at Black Rock 🎬🎬🎬½ 1954
Story of a one-armed man uncovering a secret in a Western town. Wonderful performances from all concerned, especially Borgnine. Fine photography, shot using the new Cinemascope technique. Based on the novel by Howard Breslin. 81m/C VHS, LV. Spencer Tracy, Robert Ryan, Anne Francis, Dean Jagger, Walter Brennan, John Ericson, Ernest Borgnine, Lee Marvin; **D:** John Sturges; **C:** William Mellor; **M:** Andre Previn. Cannes Film Festival '55: Best Actor (Tracy); Nominations: Academy Awards '55: Best Actor (Tracy), Best Director (Sturges), Best Screenplay. MGM, CRC, FCT

Bad Dreams 🎬½ 1988 (R) The only surviving member of a suicidal religious cult from the '60s awakens in 1988 from a coma. She is pursued by the living-dead cult leader, who seeks to ensure that she lives up (so to speak) to the cult's pact. Blood begins flowing as her fellow therapy group members begin dying, but the only bad dreams you'd get from this flick would be over the money lost on the video rental. 84m/C VHS, Beta, LV, Closed Caption. Bruce Abbott, Jennifer Rubin, Richard Lynch, Harris Yulin, Dean Cameron, Elizabeth Daily, Susan Ruttan, Charles Fleischer; **D:** Andrew Fleming; **W:** Andrew Fleming, Steven E. de Souza; **M:** Jay Michael Ferguson. FOX

Bad Georgia Road 🎬½ 1977 (R) A New Yorker inherits a moonshine operation from her uncle, and fights off the syndicate for its profits. 85m/C VHS, Beta. Gary Lockwood, Carol Lynley, Royal Dano, John Wheeler, John Kerry; **D:** John Broderick. VCI

Bad Girls 🎬🎬½ 1994 (R) Latest in the current western craze turns the tables as women take their turns being the gunslingers. Four hooker chums hastily flee town after one kills a nasty customer—only to find the bank where their cash was stashed was robbed by baddies Loggia and Russo. Wearing stylish duds and with each hair perfectly in place the beauties manage to recover their loot. Unexciting script leaves a lot to be desired, but a strong performance from Stowe makes this nearly worthwhile. Lots of off-set drama with original director Tamra Davis fired, and the actresses reportedly having a less-than-bonding experience. **CW:** Mild profanity, brief nudity, western violence; suggested rape, and references to prostitution. 99m/C VHS, LV, Closed Caption. Andie MacDowell, Madeleine Stowe, Mary Stuart Masterson, Drew Barrymore, James Russo, Dermot Mulroney, Robert Loggia, James LeGros; **D:** Jonathan Kaplan; **W:** Ken Friedman, Yolande Finch; **M:** Jerry Goldsmith. FXV

Bad Girls Do Cry woof! 1954 Unbelievably bad exploitation film. Idiotic plot with long scenes of girls stripping down to their undies. Although an American film, the voice track was dubbed in later. ?m/C VHS. Bill Page, Misty Ayers, Heather English, Ben Frommer. SNC, TPV

Bad Girls Dormitory 🎬🎬 1984 (R) At the New York Female Juvenile Reformatory, suicide seems a painless and welcome escape. Utilizes standard genre identifiers, including rape, drugs, soapy showers, bad docs, and desperate young women trapped in a web of frustration and desire. Cheap and mindless titillation. 95m/C VHS, Beta. Carey Zuris, Teresa Farley; **D:** Tim Kincaid. AHV

Bad Girls from Mars woof! 1990 (R) "B" movie sleaze-o-rama in which everyone is murdered, either before, after, or during sex, just like in real life. When the director of the film within this film hires an actress who is, shall we say, popular, to be the heroine of his latest sci-fier, the fun, slim as it is, begins. **CW:** Strong language, frontal nudity, and sensuality. 86m/C VHS. Edy Williams, Brinke Stevens, Jay Richardson, Oliver Darrow; **D:** Fred Olen Ray; **W:** Sherman Scott, Mark Thomas McGee. THV

Bad Girls Go to Hell woof! 1965 From the sultana of sleaze, Wishman, comes this winning entry into Joe Bob Briggs' "Sleaziest Movies in the History of the World" series. A ditsy-but-sexy housewife accidentally commits murder and what follows is a plethora of perversion involving hirsute men and gender-bending women who are hell-bent on showing her how hot it is where bad girls go. 98m/B VHS. **D:** Doris Wishman; **W:** Doris Wishman. VTR

Bad Girls in the Movies 🎬 1986 A compilation of film clips depicting sleazy, criminal, female characters from women's prison films and other seedy sub-genres. 56m/C VHS, Beta. David Carradine, Gene Autry, Yvonne De Carlo. LIV

Bad Guys 🎬🎬 1979 A goulash western about the outlaw days of Hungary in the 1860s. A gang of bandits terrorizes the Transdanubian countryside. In Hungarian with English subtitles. For those seeking the Eastern European Wild West experience. 93m/C VHS. HU Janos Derzsi, Djoko Rosic, Mari Kiss, Gyorgy Dorner, Laszlo Szabo, Miklos Benedek; **D:** Gyorgy Szomjas. EVD, FCT

Bad Guys 🎬 1986 (PG) An inane comedy about two ridiculous policemen who decide to take the wrestling world by storm after being kicked off the police force. Featuring scenes with many of the world's most popular wrestlers. 86m/C VHS. Adam Baldwin, Mike Jolly, Michelle Nicastro, Ruth Buzzi, James Booth, Gene LeBell, Norman Burton; **D:** Joel Silberg; **C:** Hanania Baer; **M:** William Goldstein. VTR

Bad Influence 🎬½ 1990 (R) A lackluster effort in the evil-doppelganger school of psychological mystery, where a befuddled young executive (Spader) is led into the seamier side of life by a mysterious stranger (Lowe). 99m/C VHS, Beta, LV. Rob Lowe, James Spader, Lisa Zane, Christian Clemenson, Kathleen Wilhoite; **D:** Curtis Hanson; **C:** Robert Elswit; **M:** Trevor Jones. COL

Bad Jim 🎬½ 1989 (PG) A cowpoke buys Billy the Kid's horse and, upon riding it, becomes an incorrigible outlaw himself. First feature film for Hollywood legend Clark Gable's son. 110m/C VHS, Beta, LV. James Brolin, Richard Roundtree, John Clark Gable, Harry Carey Jr., Ty Hardin, Pepe Serna, Rory Calhoun; **D:** Clyde Ware. COL

Bad Lands 🎬🎬½ 1939 A small cowboy posse finds themselves trapped by a band of Apache Indians in the Arizona desert. A remake of "The Lost Patrol." 70m/B VHS, Beta. Robert Barrat, Guinn "Big Boy" Williams, Douglas Walton, Andy Clyde, Addison Richards, Robert Coote, Paul Hurst, Noah Beery Jr.; **D:** Lew (Louis Friedlander) Landers. TTC

Bad Lieutenant 🎬🎬🎬 1992 (NC-17) Social chaos and degeneration characterize story as well as nameless loner lieutenant Keitel, who is as corrupt as they come. Assigned to a case involving a raped nun, he's confronted by his own lagging Catholic beliefs and the need for saving grace. From cult filmmaker Ferrara ("Ms. 45") and filled with violence, drugs, and grotesque sexual situations. Tense, over-the-top, urban drama is not intended for seekers of the subtle. Rent it with "Reservoir Dogs" and prepare yourself for a long tense evening of top-rated Keitel and screen-splitting violence. "R" rated version is also available at 91 minutes. **CW:** Language, nudity, violence, and sensuality. 98m/C VHS, LV, Closed Caption. Harvey Keitel, Brian McElroy, Frankie Acciario, Peggy Gormley, Stella Keitel, Victor Argo, Paul Calderone, Leonard Thomas, Frankie Thorn; **D:** Abel Ferrara; **W:** Zoe Tamerlaine Lund, Abel Ferrara; **M:** Joe Delia. Independent Spirit Awards '93: Best Actor (Keitel). LIV, FCT

Bad Love 🎬🎬½ 1995 (R) Unlucky Eloise (Gridley) stays true to nature when she falls for loser Lenny (Sizemore), who decides the big score lies with robbing the fading movie star (O'Neill) Eloise works for. Naturally, things go badly. Slick production for anyone who likes fringe romances. **CW:** Nudity, language, violence, sexual situations. 93m/C VHS. Tom Sizemore, Pamela Gidley, Debi Mazar, Jennifer O'Neill, Margaux Hemingway, Richard Edson, Seymour Cassel; **D:** Jill Goldman. APX

Bad Man of Deadwood 🎬 1941 A man-with-a-past joins a circus as a sharp-shooter, and is threatened with disclosure. 54m/B VHS, Beta. Roy Rogers, George "Gabby" Hayes. DVT, NOS, RXM

Bad Manners 🎬 1984 (R) When an orphan is adopted by a wealthy but entirely selfish couple, a group of his orphan friends try to free him from his new home and lifestyle. 85m/C VHS, Beta. Martin Mull, Karen Black, Anne DeSalvo, Murphy Dunne, Pamela Segall, Edy Williams, Susan Ruttan, Richard Deacon; **D:** Bobby Houston; **C:** Jan De Bont. VTR

Bad Man's River 🎬🎬 1972 A Mexican revolutionary leader hires a gang of outlaws to blow up an arsenal used by the Mexican Army. 92m/C VHS, Beta. IT SP Lee Van Cleef, James Mason, Gina Lollobrigida; **D:** Gene Martin; **W:** Philip Yordan. NO

Bad Medicine woof! 1985 (PG-13) A youth who doesn't want to be a doctor is accepted by a highly questionable Latin American school of medicine. Remember that it was for medical students like these that the U.S. liberated Grenada. 97m/C VHS, Beta, Closed Caption. Steve Guttenberg, Alan Arkin, Julie Hagerty, Bill Macy, Curtis Armstrong, Julie Kavner, Joe Grifasi, Robert Romanus, Taylor Negron, Gilbert Gottfried; **D:** Harvey Miller; **W:** Harvey Miller. FOX

Bad Men of the Border 🎬½ 1945 Routine oater has Kirby posing as a bandit in order to infiltrate an outlaw band passing counterfeit money. He rounds up the bad guys and finds time to romance Armida too. 56m/B VHS. Kirby Grant, Fuzzy Knight, Armida, John Eldridge, Francis McDonald; **D:** Wallace Fox; **W:** Adele Buffington. MOV

Bad Moon 🎬½ 1996 (R) Let's put it this way, the werewolf in this movie is not the only thing that bites. Shortest (mercifully) studio release in recent history is a horror (in more ways than one) film with Pare leading the pack as Ted, a photojournalist who comes back from the Amazon a different, more nocturnally hirsute man. Fleeing from the site of his nightly gore, Ted takes refuge with his loving sister Janet (Hemingway) and her son Brett (Gamble). The real hero (and best actor) is a German shepherd named Thor (Primo) who discovers that Ted's a werewolf. Dog steals the show paws down (naturally). Decent special FX. Adapted from Wayne Smith's novel "Thor." **CW:** Horror violence and gore, brief language and a scene of sexuality. 79m/C VHS, Closed Caption. Mariel Hemingway, Michael Pare, Mason Gamble, Ken Pogue; **D:** Eric Red; **W:** Eric Red; **C:** Jan Kiesser; **M:** Daniel Licht. WAR

The Bad News Bears 🎬🎬🎬 1976 (PG) Family comedy about a misfit Little League team that gets whipped into shape by a cranky, sloppy, beer-drinking coach who recruits a female pitcher. O'Neal and Matthau are top-notch. The kids' language is rather adult, and very titillating for younger viewers. Spawned two sequels and a television series. 102m/C VHS, Beta, LV, 8mm. Walter Matthau, Tatum O'Neal, Vic Morrow, Joyce Van Patten, Jackie Earle Haley; **D:** Michael Ritchie; **C:** John A. Alonzo. Writers Guild of America '76: Best Original Screenplay. PAR

The Bad News Bears Go to Japan ✗ 1978 (PG) The second sequel, in which the famed Little League team goes to the Little League World Series in Tokyo. Comic adventure features Curtis as a talent agent out to exploit the team's fame. 102m/C VHS, Beta, LV. Tony Curtis, Jackie Earle Haley, Tomisaburo Wakayama, George Wyner; *D:* John Berry. *PAR*

The Bad News Bears in Breaking Training ✗½ 1977 (PG) With a chance to take on the Houston Toros for a shot at the little league baseball Japanese champs, the Bears devise a way to get to Texas to play at the famed Astrodome. Disappointing sequel to "The Bad News Bears"; followed by "The Bad News Bears Go to Japan" (1978). 105m/C VHS, Beta, LV. William Devane, Clifton James, Jackie Earle Haley, Jimmy Baio; *D:* Michael Pressman; *W:* Paul Brickman. *PAR*

Bad Ronald ✗✗✗ 1974 No, not a political biography of Ronald Reagan... Fascinating thriller about a disturbed teenager who kills a friend after being harassed repeatedly. The plot thickens after the boy's mother dies, and he is forced to hide out in a secret room when an unsuspecting family with three daughters moves into his house. The story is accurately recreated from the novel by John Holbrook Vance. 78m/C VHS. Scott Jacoby, Pippa Scott, John Larch, Dabney Coleman, Kim Hunter, John Fiedler; *D:* Buzz Kulik. *LIV*

The Bad Seed ✗✗½ 1956 A mother makes the tortuous discovery that her cherubic eight-year-old daughter harbors an innate desire to kill. Based on Maxwell Anderson's powerful Broadway stage play. Remade for television in 1985. 129m/B VHS, Beta. Patty McCormack, Nancy Kelly, Eileen Heckart, Henry Jones, Evelyn Varden, Paul Fix; *D:* Mervyn LeRoy; *M:* Alex North. Golden Globe Awards '57: Best Supporting Actress (Heckart); Nominations: Academy Awards '56: Best Actress (Kelly), Best Black and White Cinematography, Best Supporting Actress (Heckart, McCormack). *WAR*

The Bad Seed ✗✗ 1985 Television remake of the movie with the same name. Story about a sadistic little child who kills for her own evil purposes. Acting is not up to par with previous version. 100m/C VHS. Blair Brown, Lynn Redgrave, David Carradine, Richard Kiley, David Ogden Stiers, Carrie Wells; *D:* Paul Wendkos. *NO*

The Bad Sleep Well ✗✗✗½ 1960 Japanese variation of the 1940 Warner Brothers crime dramas. A tale about corruption in the corporate world as seen through the eyes of a rising executive. 135m/B VHS, Beta. *JP* Toshiro Mifune, Masayuki Kato, Masayuki Mori, Takashi Shimura, Akira Nishimura; *D:* Akira Kurosawa. *COL, APD*

Bad Taste ✗✗✗ 1988 A definite pleaser for the person who enjoys watching starving aliens devour the average, everyday human being. Alien fast-food manufacturers come to earth in hopes of harvesting all of mankind. The earth's fate lies in the hands of the government who must stop these rampaging creatures before the whole human race is gobbled up. Terrific make-up jobs on the aliens add the final touch to this gory, yet humorous cult horror flick. 90m/C VHS, LV. *NZ* Peter Jackson, Pete O'Herne, Mike Minett, Terry Potter, Craig Smith, Doug Wren, Dean Lawrie; *D:* Peter Jackson. *FCT*

Badge of the Assassin ✗✗ 1985 A television movie based on the true story of a New York assistant DA who directed a campaign to catch a pair of cop-killers from the '70s. 96m/C VHS, Beta, LV. James Woods, Yaphet Kotto, Alex Rocco, David Harris, Pam Grier, Steven Keats, Richard Bradford, Rae Dawn Chong; *D:* Mel Damski. *THV*

Badge 373 ✗½ 1973 (R) In the vein of "The French Connection," a New York cop is suspended and decides to battle crime his own way. 116m/C VHS, Beta. Robert Duvall, Verna Bloom, Eddie Egan; *D:* Howard W. Koch. *PAR*

The Badlanders ✗✗✗ 1958 A western remake of the crime drama "The Asphalt Jungle." Ladd and Borgnine plan a gold robbery against Smith, who cheated them out of their share in a gold mine. Cross and double-cross follow the partners as does romance. 85m/C VHS. Alan Ladd, Ernest Borgnine, Kent Smith, Katy Jurado, Claire Kelly, Nehemiah Persoff, Adam Williams; *D:* Delmer Daves. *MGM*

Badlands ✗✗✗ 1974 (PG) Based loosely on the Charlie Starkweather murders of the 1950s, this impressive debut by director Malick recounts a slow-thinking, unhinged misfit's killing spree across the midwestern plains, accompanied by a starry-eyed 15-year-old schoolgirl. Sheen and Spacek are a disturbingly numb, apathetic, and icy duo. 94m/C VHS, Beta, LV. Martin Sheen, Sissy Spacek, Warren Oates; *D:* Terence Malick; *W:* Terence Malick. *WAR*

Badman's Territory ✗✗✗ 1946 A straight-shooting marshal has to deal with such notorious outlaws as the James and Dalton boys in a territory outside of government control. 79m/B VHS, Beta. Randolph Scott, Ann Richards, George "Gabby" Hayes, Steve Brodie; *D:* Tim Whelan. *TTC*

Badmen of Nevada ✗✗½ 1933 Badmen roam Nevada in the early days before law and order. 57m/B VHS, Beta. Kent Taylor, Gail Patrick. *VCN*

Baffled ✗✗½ 1972 Nimoy is a race car driver who has visions of people in danger. He must convince an ESP expert (Hampshire) of the credibility of his vision, and then try to save the lives of the people seen with his sixth sense. Made for television. 90m/C VHS. Leonard Nimoy, Susan Hampshire, Vera Miles, Rachel Roberts, Jewel Blanch, Christopher Benjamin; *D:* Philip Leacock. *FOX*

Bagdad ✗✗ 1949 Arabian nights story with the lovely O'Hara starring as Princess Marjan, the daughter of a sheik. She returns from England to find her father murdered and Hassan (Christian), the leader of a suspicious group known as The Black Riders, the main suspect. But then there's Turkish Pasha Al Nadim (Price) lurking sinisterly, as well. 83m/C VHS. Maureen O'Hara, Paul Christian, Vincent Price, John Sutton, Jeff Corey, Frank Puglia, David Wolfe, Fritz Leiber; *D:* Charles Lamont; *C:* Russell Metty. *USH*

Bagdad Cafe ✗✗✗ *Out of Rosenheim* 1988 (PG) A large German woman, played by Sagebrecht, finds herself stranded in the Mojave desert after her husband dumps her on the side of the highway. She encounters a rundown cafe where she becomes involved with the off-beat residents. A hilarious story in which the strange people and the absurdity of their situations are treated kindly and not made to seem ridiculous. Spawned a short-lived TV series with Whoopi Goldberg. 91m/C VHS, LV, Closed Caption. *GE* Marianne Saegebrecht, CCH Pounder, Jack Palance, Christine Kaufmann, Monica Calhoun, Darron Flagg; *D:* Percy Adlon; *W:* Percy Adlon, Eleonore Adlon; *M:* Bob Telson. Cesar Awards '89: Best Foreign Film; Nominations: Academy Awards '88: Best Song ("Calling You"). *PGV, FCT*

Bahama Passage ✗✗½ 1942 Trite story of one lady's efforts to win the affection of a macho Bahamas stud. 83m/C VHS. Madeleine Carroll, Sterling Hayden, Flora Robson, Leo G. Carroll; *D:* Edward H. Griffith. *PAR, MLB*

Bail Jumper ✗✗ 1989 A story of love and commitment against incredible odds; some of which happen to be a swarm of locusts, a tornado, and falling meteorites. Joe and Elaine are small-time hoods escaping their dreary lives in Murky Springs Missouri by heading for that great bastion of idyllism and idealism—New York City. But even as the world starts to crumble around them, get the message that love prevails. 96m/C VHS, Beta. Eszter Balint, B.J. Spalding, Tony Askin, Joie Lee; *D:* Christian Faber. *FXL*

Bail Out ✗ 1990 (R) Three bounty hunters, armed to the teeth, run a car-trashing police gauntlet so they may capture a valuable crook. 88m/C VHS, Beta, LV. David Hasselhoff, Linda Blair, John Vernon, Tom Rosales, Charlie Brill; *D:* Max Kleven. *VES, LIV*

Bail Out at 43,000 ✗✗ 1957 Movie about the lifestyles and love affairs of your average, everyday parachutist. 80m/B VHS. John Payne, Karen Steele, Paul Kelly; *D:* Francis D. Lyon; *W:* Paul Monash. *MGM*

Baja ✗✗ 1995 (R) Bebe (Ringwald) hides out in Baja with her beau Alex (Logue) after a drug deal goes bad. They hold up in a sleazy motel while Bebe waits for dad, John (Bernsen), to bail her out. But instead, John persuades estranged hubby Michael (Nickles) to track down the runaways and Michael finds out that hitman Tom (Henriksen) is hunting for Alex. Must be the desert heat causing all the ensuing commotion. *CW:* Language, violence and brief strong sexuality. 92m/C VHS, LV, Closed Caption. Molly Ringwald, Lance Henriksen, Michael A. Nickles, Donal Logue, Corbin Bernsen; *D:* Kurt Voss; *W:* Kurt Voss; *C:* Denis Maloney; *M:* Reg Powell. *REP*

Baja Oklahoma ✗ 1987 A made-for-cable-television film about a country barmaid with dreams of being a country singer. Songs by Willie Nelson, Emmylou Harris and Billy Vera. 97m/C VHS, Beta, LV. Lesley Ann Warren, Peter Coyote, Swoosie Kurtz, Willie Nelson, Julia Roberts; *D:* Bobby Roth; *W:* Bobby Roth; *C:* Michael Ballhaus. *WAR, ORI*

Baker's Hawk ✗✗ 1976 A young boy befriends a red-tailed hawk and learns the meaning of family and caring. 98m/C VHS, Beta. Clint Walker, Diane Baker, Burl Ives; *D:* Lyman Dayton. *HHE*

The Baker's Wife ✗✗✗½ *La Femme du Boulanger* 1933 There's a new baker in town, and he brings with him to the small French village an array of tantalizing breads, as well as a discontented wife. When she runs off with a shepherd, her loyal and naive husband refuses to acknowledge her infidelity; however, in his loneliness, the baker can't bake, so the townspeople scheme to bring his wife back. Panned as overly cute Marcel Pagnol peasant glorification, and hailed as a visual poem full of wit; you decide. In French with subtitles. Also available for French students without subtitles; a French script booklet is also available. 101m/B VHS, Beta. *FR* Raimu, Ginette LeClerc, Charles Moulton, Charpin, Robert Vattier; *D:* Marcel Pagnol. National Board of Review Awards '40: 5 Best Foreign Films of the Year; New York Film Critics Awards '40: Best Foreign Film. *INT, MRV, DVT*

Bakery/Grocery Clerk ✗✗ 1921 A package of shorts featuring crazy comedian Larry Semon, getting tangled up in mayhem and molasses. Silent with piano score. 55m/B VHS, Beta. Larry Semon, Oliver Hardy, Lucille Carlisle; *D:* Larry Semon. *CCB*

Balalaika ✗✗ 1939 Rather dull operetta about the Russian revolution with Eddy playing a Russian prince. Eddy masquerades as a member of the proletariat in order to romance Massey, who was expected to become the next Garbo. Didn't happen, though. Eddy's rendition of "Stille Nacht" ("Silent Night") is highlight of film. Based on the operetta by Eric Maschwitz, George Ponford, and Bernard Gruen. 102m/B VHS. Nelson Eddy, Ilona Massey, Charlie Ruggles, Frank Morgan, Lionel Atwill, Sir C. Aubrey Smith, Joyce Compton; *D:* Reinhold Schunzel; *W:* Leon Gordon, Charles Bennett, Jacques Deval; *C:* Karl Freund. Nominations: Academy Awards '39: Best Sound. *MGM*

Balance of Power ✗½ 1996 (R) Martial arts master Mako prepares fighter Blanks for a death match against a former student who's gone bad. *CW:* Strong violence and some language. 92m/C VHS, Closed Caption. Billy Blanks, Mako, James Lew; *D:* Rick Bennet; *W:* Phil Good, Rick Bennet; *C:* Gilles Corbeil. *ITP*

Balboa WOOF! 1982 Set on sun-baked Balboa Island, this is a melodramatic tale of high-class power, jealousy, and intrigue. Never-aired pilot for a television mini-series, in the night-time soap tradition (even features Steve Kanaly from TV's "Dallas"). Special appearance by Cassandra Peterson, also known as horror hostess Elvira; and if that interests you, look for Sonny Bono, as well. **92m/C VHS, Beta.** Tony Curtis, Carol Lynley, Chuck Connors, Sonny Bono, Steve Kanaly, Jennifer Chase, Lupita Ferrer, Martine Beswick, Henry Jones, Cassandra Peterson; *D:* James Polakof. VES, LIV

The Balcony 🎬🎬🎬 1963 A film version of the great Jean Genet play about a surreal brothel, located in an unnamed, revolution-torn city, where its powerful patrons act out their fantasies. Scathing and rude. **87m/B VHS, Beta, LV.** Peter Falk, Shelley Winters, Lee Grant, Kent Smith, Peter Brocco, Ruby Dee, Jeff Corey, Leonard Nimoy, Joyce Jameson; *D:* Joseph Strick. Nominations: Academy Awards '63: Best Black and White Cinematography.MFV

Ball of Fire 🎬🎬🎬 1941 A gang moll hides out with a group of mundane professors, trying to avoid her loathsome boyfriend. The professors are busy compiling an encyclopedia and Stanwyck helps them with their section on slang in the English language. Cooper has his hands full when he falls for this damsel in distress and must fight the gangsters to keep her. Stanwyck takes a personal liking to naive Cooper and resolves to teach him more than just slang. **111m/B VHS, Beta, LV.** Gary Cooper, Barbara Stanwyck, Dana Andrews, Gene Krupa, Oscar Homolka, Dan Duryea, S.Z. Sakall, Henry Travers; *D:* Howard Hawks; *W:* Billy Wilder, Charles Brackett; *C:* Gregg Toland. Nominations: Academy Awards '41: Best Actress (Stanwyck), Best Sound, Best Story, Original Dramatic/Comedy Score.

Ballad in Blue 🎬🎬 Blues for Lovers 1966 Real life story of Ray Charles and a blind child. Tearjerker also includes some of Charles' hit songs. 🎵I Got a Woman; What'd I Say? **89m/B VHS, Beta.** GB Ray Charles, Tom Bell, Mary Peach, Dawn Addams, Piers Bishop, Betty McDowall; *D:* Paul Henreid. LIV

Ballad of a Gunfighter 🎬 1964 A feud between two outlaws reaches the boiling point when they both fall in love with the same woman. **84m/C VHS, Beta.** Marty Robbins, Bob Barron, Joyce Redd, Nestor Paiva, Laurette Luez; *D:* Bill Ward. FHE, PSM

Ballad of a Soldier 🎬🎬 1960 As a reward for demolishing two German tanks, a nineteen-year-old Russian soldier receives a six-day pass so he can see his mother; however, he meets another woman. Well directed and photographed, while avoiding propaganda. Russian with subtitles. **88m/B VHS.** RU Vladimir Ivashov, Shanna Prokhorenko; *D:* Grigori Chukrai. British Academy Awards '61: Best Film; Nominations: Academy Awards '61: Best Story & Screenplay. NYF, NOS, HHT

Ballad of Cable Hogue 🎬🎬🎬 1970 (R) A prospector, who had been left to die in the desert by his double-crossing partners, finds a waterhole. A surprise awaits his former friends when they visit the remote well. Not the usual violent Peckinpah horse drama, but a tongue-in-cheek comedy romance mixed with tragedy. Obviously offbeat and worth a peek. **122m/C VHS, Beta, LV.** Jason Robards Jr., Stella Stevens, David Warner, L.Q. Jones, Strother Martin, Slim Pickens; *D:* Sam Peckinpah; *C:* Lucien Ballard; *M:* Jerry Goldsmith. WAR

Ballad of Gregorio Cortez 🎬🎬🎬 1983 (PG) Tragic story based on one of the most famous manhunts in Texas history. A Mexican cowhand kills a Texas sheriff in self-defense and tries to elude the law, all because of a misunderstanding of the Spanish language. Olmos turns in a fine performance as Cortez. **105m/C VHS, Beta, LV.** Edward James Olmos, James Gammon, Tom Bower, Alan Vint, Barry Corbin, Rosana De Soto, Bruce McGill, Brion James, Pepe Serna, William Sanderson; *D:* Robert M. Young; *W:* Robert M. Young; *C:* Reynaldo Villalobos. NLC

The Ballad of Little Jo 🎬🎬½ 1993 (R) Inspired by a true story set during the 1866 gold rush. Easterner Josephine Monaghan is cast out of her wealthy family after she has a baby out of wedlock. Heading west, she passes herself off as a man—Little Jo—in an attempt to forestall harrasssment. Solemn and overly-earnest attempt that Greenwald to demystify the old west and bring a

feminist viewpoint to a familiar saga.*CW:* Some violence and sexuality. **110m/C VHS, Closed Caption.** Suzy Amis, Bo Hopkins, Ian McKellen, Carrie Snodgress, David Chung, Rene Auberjonois, Heather Graham, Anthony Heald, Sam Robards, Ruth Maleczech; *D:* Maggie Greenwald; *W:* Maggie Greenwald; *M:* David Mansfield. Nominations: Independent Spirit Awards '94: Best Actress (Amis). COL

The Ballad of Narayama 🎬🎬🎬🎬 *Narayama-Bushi-Ko* 1983 Director Imamura's subtle and vastly moving story takes place a vague century ago. In compliance with village law designed to control population among the poverty-stricken peasants, a healthy seventy-year-old woman must submit to solitary starvation atop a nearby mountain. We follow her as she sets into motion the final influence she will have in the lives of her children and grandchildren, a situation described with detachment and without imposing a tragic perspective. In Japanese with English subtitles. **129m/C VHS.** JP Ken Ogata, Sumiko Sakamota, Takejo Aki, Tonpei Hidari, Shoichi Ozawa; *D:* Shohei Imamura; *W:* Shohei Imamura. Cannes Film Festival '83: Best Film. HMV, FCT, KIV

The Ballad of Paul Bunyan 1972 The good-humored, legendary American giant is pitted against a powerful lumber camp boss who likes to pick on the little guy. **30m/C VHS.** *D:* Arthur Rankin Jr., Jules Bass. VTR, PSM

The Ballad of the Sad Cafe 🎬🎬½ 1991 (PG-13) Unusual love story set in a small Southern town during the Depression. The everyday lives of its townspeople are suddenly transformed when a distant relation of the town's outcast (Redgrave) unexpectedly shows up. A moving story that tries to portray both sides of love and its power to enhance and destroy simultaneously. Emotion never seems to come to life in a movie that's nice to watch, but is ultimately disappointing. Adapted from the play by Edward Albee, which was based on the critically acclaimed novella by Carson McCullers. A British/U.S. co-production. **100m/C VHS, LV, Closed Caption.** GB Vanessa Redgrave, Keith Carradine, Cork Hubbert, Rod Steiger, Austin Pendleton, Beth Dixon, Lanny Flaherty, Mert Hatfield, Earl Hindman, Anne Pitoniak; *D:* Simon Callow; *W:* Michael Hirst; *C:* Walter Lassally; *M:* Richard Robbins. NO

Ballbuster 19?? Cops take on gangs in an all-out high-stakes battle to win back the streets. **100m/C VHS.** Ivan Rogers, Bonnie Paine, W. Randolph Galvin, Bill Shirk, Brenda Banet; *D:* Eddie Beverly Jr.; *W:* Eddie Beverly Jr. XVC

Ballet Shoes 🎬🎬½ 19?? The classic children's tale of three sisters living a very sheltered life with their guardian Sylvia, who is working to support all four of them. A story of hope and possibilities. From the BBC Television network. **120m/C VHS.** GB VCO, HMV

Ballistic 🎬½ 1994 (R) L.A. cop Jesse Gavin (Holden) gets in trouble when the government witness she's supposed to be protecting gets murdered. So she teams up with her ex-con father and her boyfriend to track the mobster responsible for the hit.*CW:* Language; violence; nudity. **86m/C VHS, LV, Closed Caption.** Marjean Holden, Richard Roundtree, Sam Jones, Joel Beeson, Charles Napier; *D:* Kim Bass. IMP, IME

The Balloonatic/One Week 1923 "The Balloonatic" (1923) features Keaton in several misadventures. In "One Week" (1920), Keaton and his new bride, Seely, receive a new home as a wedding gift—the kind you have to assemble yourself. Silent. **48m/B VHS, Beta.** Buster Keaton, Phyllis Haver, Sybil Seely; *D:* Buster Keaton. CCB

Baltic Deputy 🎬🎬🎬½ 1937 An early forerunner of Soviet historic realism, where an aging intellectual deals with post-revolution Soviet life. In Russian with subtitles. **95m/B VHS, Beta.** RU Nikolai Cherkassov; *D:* Yosif Heifitz. National Board of Review Awards '37: 10 Best Films of the Year. FCT, IHF

The Baltimore Bullet 🎬🎬 1980 (PG) Two men make their living traveling through the country as pool hustlers, bilking would-be pool sharks. Features ten of the greatest pool players in the world. **103m/C VHS, Beta.** James Coburn, Omar Sharif, Bruce Boxleitner, Ronee Blakley, Jack O'Halloran; *D:* Robert Ellis Miller; *W:* Robert Vincent O'Neil, John F. Brascia. NLC

Balto 🎬🎬½ 1995 (G) Animated adventure, based on a true story, of a half-husky, half-wolf sled dog, Balto, who faces overwhelming odds to bring life-saving medicine to Nome, Alaska. It's 1925, there's a diptheria epidemic, and Balto is the lead team dog on the final leg of the race to get the serum to Nome in time. Balto and the rest of the team dogs became instant heroes and even journeyed to Hollywood to star in their own silent film "Balto's Race to Nome." **78m/C VHS, LV, Closed Caption.** *D:* Simon Wells; *W:* Cliff Ruby, Elana Lesser, David Steven Cohen, Roger S.H. Schulman; *M:* James Horner; *V:* Kevin Bacon, Bob Hoskins, Bridget Fonda, Jim Cummings, Phil Collins, Juliette Brewer, Danny Mann, Miriam Margolyes. USH

Bambi 🎬🎬🎬🎬 1942 (G) A true Disney classic, detailing the often harsh education of a newborn deer and his friends in the forest. Proves that Disney animation was—and still is—the best to be found. Thumper still steals the show and the music is delightful, including "Let's Sing a Gay Little Spring Song," "Love is a Song," "Little April Shower," "The Thumper Song," and "Twitterpated." Stands as one of the greatest children's films of all time; a genuine perennial from generation to generation. Based very loosely on the book by Felix Salten. **69m/C VHS, Beta, LV, Closed Caption.** *D:* David Hand; *W:* Larry Morey; *M:* Frank Churchill, Edward Plumb; *V:* Bobby Stewart, Peter Behn, Stan Alexander, Cammie King, Donnie Dunagan, Hardie Albright, John Sutherland, Tim Davis, Sam Edwards, Sterling Holloway, Ann Gillis, Perce Pearce. Nominations: Academy Awards '42: Best Song ("Love Is a Song"), Best Sound, Original Dramatic/Comedy Score. DIS

The Bamboo Saucer 🎬½ Collision Course 1968 Russian and American scientists race to find a U.F.O. in Red China. **103m/C VHS.** Dan Duryea, John Ericson, Lois Nettleton, Nan Leslie; *D:* Frank Telford. REP

Bananas 🎬🎬🎬 1971 (PG-13) Intermittently hilarious pre-"Annie Hall" Allen fare is full of the director's signature angst-ridden philosophical comedy. A frustrated product tester from New York runs off to South America, where he volunteers his support to the revolutionary force of a shaky Latin-American dictatorship and winds up the leader. Don't miss cameos by Stallone and Garfield. Witty score contributes much.*CW:* Comic sexuality including some pin-up nudity, some drug use and crude language. **82m/C VHS, Beta, LV.** Woody Allen, Louise Lasser, Carlos Montalban, Howard Cosell, Charlotte Rae, Conrad Bain; *Cameos:* Sylvester Stallone, Allen (Goorwitz) Garfield; *D:* Woody Allen; *W:* Woody Allen; *M:* Marvin Hamlisch. MGM, FCT, FOX

Bananas Boat woof! What Changed Charley Farthing 1978 A captain takes a man and his daughter away from the collapsing government of their banana republic. The cast and director take a few risks but fail in this would-be comedy. **91m/C VHS.** GB Doug McClure, Hayley Mills, Lionel Jeffries, Dilys Hamlett, Warren Mitchell; *D:* Sidney Hayers. VCI

Band of Angels 🎬🎬½ 1957 Orphaned Amantha (De Carlo) learns she has African-American blood and since it's the pre-Civil War era she promptly winds up on the auction block. She becomes both the property and the mistress of mysterious New Orleans landowner Hamish Bond (Gable). Then the Civil War comes along bringing threats and revelations. De Carlo looks properly sultry but this is a weak attempt at costume drama. Based on the novel by Robert Penn Warren. **127m/C VHS.** Clark Gable, Yvonne De Carlo, Sidney Poitier, Efrem Zimbalist Jr., Rex Reason, Patric Knowles, Torin Thatcher, Andrea King, Ray Teal; *D:* Raoul Walsh; *W:* John Twist, Ivan Goff; *M:* Max Steiner. WAR, MOV

Band of Gold 🎬🎬🎬 **1995** Unflinching British miniseries follows the lives of Yorkshire prostitutes Rosie (James), Carol (Tyson), and Gina (Gemmell). They try to survive the streets of Bradford while a serial killer is targeting the local hookers. On six cassettes. **312m/C VHS.** *GB* Geraldine James, Cathy Tyson, Ruth Gemmell, Barbara Dickson, David Schofield, Richard Moore, Rachel Davies, Samantha Morton; **D:** Richard Standeven, Richard Laxton; **W:** Kay Mellor; **C:** Peter Jessop; **M:** Hal Lindes. *CCB*

Band of Outsiders 🎬🎬½ *Bande a Part; The Outsiders* **1964** A woman hires a pair of petty criminals to rip off her aunt; Godard vehicle for exposing self-reflexive comments on modern film culture. In French with English subtitles. **97m/ B VHS, Beta.** *FR* Sami Frey, Anna Karina, Claude Brasseur, Louisa Colpeyn; **D:** Jean-Luc Godard; **W:** Jean-Luc Godard. *HTV, NOS, MRV*

Band of the Hand 🎬 **1986 (R)** A "Miami Vice" type melodrama about five convicts who are trained to become an unstoppable police unit. The first feature film by Glaser, last seen as Starsky in "Starsky & Hutch." **109m/C VHS, Beta, LV.** Stephen Lang, Michael Carmine, Lauren Holly, Leon Robinson; **D:** Paul Michael Glaser; **W:** Jack Baran, Leo Garen. *NO*

The Band Wagon 🎬🎬🎬 **1953** A Hollywood song-and-dance man finds trouble when he is persuaded to star in a Broadway musical. Charisse has been called Astaire's most perfect partner, perhaps by those who haven't seen Rogers. ♫That's Entertainment; Dancing in the Dark; By Myself; A Shine On Your Shoes; Something to Remember You By; High and Low; I Love Louisa; New Sun in the Sky; I Guess I'll Have to Change My Plan. **112m/C VHS, Beta, LV.** Fred Astaire, Cyd Charisse, Oscar Levant, Nanette Fabray, Jack Buchanan, Bobby Watson; **D:** Vincente Minnelli; **W:** Betty Comden; **M:** Arthur Schwartz, Howard Dietz. Nominations: Academy Awards '53: Best Costume Design (Color), Best Story & Screenplay, Scoring of a Musical, Best Original Score. *MGM, FCT*

Bandit King of Texas 🎬🎬½ **1949** A varmint is swindling unsuspecting settlers in a land scheme and then robbing and murdering them when they go to visit their supposed property. Rocky and friends come to the rescue. **60m/B VHS, Closed Caption.** Allan "Rocky" Lane, Eddy Waller, Helene Stanley, Robert Bice, Harry Lauter, Jim Nolan, John Hamilton, Lane Bradford; **D:** Fred Brannon; **W:** Olive Cooper. *REP, GPV*

Bandit Queen 🎬½ **1951** Spanish girl forms a band to stop seizure of Spanish possessions by lawless Californians. **71m/B VHS, Beta.** Barbara Britton, Willard Parker, Philip Reed, Jack Perrin; **D:** William (Lester Williams) Berke. *RXM*

Bandit Queen 🎬🎬 **1994** Phoolan Devi (Biswas) is a female Robin Hood in modern-day India. A lower-caste woman, Devi is sold into marriage at 11, brutalized by her husband (and many others throughout the film), and eventually winds up with an equally brutal group of hill bandits. Only this time around, Devi takes action by aiding the group in robbing, kidnapping (and murdering) the rich and higher castes. Devi surrendered to authorities in 1983 and spent 11 years in jail. Based on screenwriter Sen's biography "India's Bandit Queen: The True Story of Phoolan Devi" and Devi's diaries. In Hindi with subtitles. **119m/C VHS, LV.** *GB IN* Seema Biswas, Nirmal Pandey, Manoj Bajpai, Raghubir Yadav, Rajesh Vivek, Govind Namdeo; **D:** Shekhar Kapur; **W:** Mala Sen; **C:** Ashok Mehta. *HMK*

Bandits 🎬½ **1973** Three cowboys team up with a band of Mexican outlaws to fight a Mexican traitor. **83m/C VHS, Beta.** Robert Conrad, Jan-Michael Vincent, Roy Jenson; **D:** Robert Conrad, Alfredo Zacharias. *UNI*

Bandits 🎬🎬½ **1986** Simon Verini (Yanne), a sophisticated recluse, is given the loot from a 10 million dollar Cartier heist to exchange for cash by Mozart (Bruel) the leader of the thieves. But two of Mozart's gang want to keep the jewels instead and kidnap Verini's wife as ransom. She's killed, even after he returns the goods, and Verini is then

framed for the theft and spends 10 years in prison. He's sent his daughter Marie-Sophie to a Swiss boarding school and upon his release works to both establish a relationship with her and to find those responsible for his wife's death. Director Lelouch's wife portrays the adult Marie-Sophie. In French with English subtitles. **98m/C VHS.** *FR* Jean Yanne, Marie-Sophie L(elouch), Patrick Bruel, Charles Gerard, Corinne Marchand, Christine Barbelivien; **D:** Claude Lelouch; **W:** Pierre Uytterhoeven, Claude Lelouch. *FXL, FCT*

Bandits of Orgosolo 🎬🎬½ *Banditi a Orgosolo* **1961** An acclaimed, patient drama about a Sardinian shepherd who shelters a band of thieves from the police. When one of the cops is killed the shepherd panics and flees into the hills for survival. Dubbed in English. **98m/B VHS, Beta.** *IT* Michele Cossu, Peppeddu Cuccu; **D:** Vittorio de Seta. *NOS, FCT, VYY*

Bandolero! 🎬🎬½ **1968 (PG)** In Texas, Stewart and Martin are two fugitive brothers who run into trouble with their Mexican counterparts. **106m/C VHS, Beta, Closed Caption.** James Stewart, Raquel Welch, Dean Martin, George Kennedy, Will Geer, Harry Carey Jr., Andrew Prine; **D:** Andrew V. McLaglen; **C:** William Clothier; **M:** Jerry Goldsmith. *FOX*

Bang Bang Kid 🎬🎬 *Bang Bang* **1967 (G)** A western spoof about a klutzy gunfighter defending a town from outlaws. **78m/C VHS, Beta.** Tom Bosley, Guy Madison, Sandra Milo; **D:** Stanley Prager. *NO*

Bang the Drum Slowly 🎬🎬 **1956** The original television adaptation of a Mark Harris novel about baseball. A ball player stricken by a terminal illness strikes an unlikely friendship with a teammate. Interesting role for an actor (Newman) who claims to have been driven to acting by running away from the sporting goods business. **60m/B VHS.** Paul Newman, George Peppard, Albert Salmi. *NOS*

Bang the Drum Slowly 🎬🎬🎬 **1973 (PG)** The touching story of a major league catcher who discovers that he is dying of Hodgkins disease and wants to play just one more season. De Niro is the weakening baseball player and Moriarty is the friend who helps him see it through. Based on a novel by Mark Harris. **97m/C VHS, Beta, LV.** Robert De Niro, Michael Moriarty, Vincent Gardenia, Phil Foster, Ann Wedgeworth, Heather MacRae, Selma Diamond, Danny Aiello; **D:** John Hancock. National Board of Review Awards '73: 10 Best Films of the Year; New York Film Critics Awards '73: Best Supporting Actor (De Niro); Nominations: Academy Awards '73: Best Supporting Actor (Gardenia). *PAR, FCT*

The Bank Dick 🎬🎬🎬🎬 *The Bank Detective* **1940** Fields wrote the screenplay (using an alias) and stars in this zany comedy about a man who accidentally trips a bank robber and winds up as a guard. Fields' last major role is a classic, a worthy end to his great career. Side two of the laserdisc is in CAV format, which allows single frame access to the frenetic cops and robbers chase sequence. **73m/B VHS, Beta, LV.** W.C. Fields, Cora Witherspoon, Una Merkel, Evelyn Del Rio, Jack Norton, Jessie Ralph, Franklin Pangborn, Shemp Howard, Grady Sutton, Russell Hicks, Richard Purcell, Reed Hadley; **D:** Eddie Cline; **W:** W.C. Fields; **C:** Milton Krasner. *USH*

Bank Robber 🎬🎬 **1993 (R)** Billy (Dempsey) is a thief who will retire after one final bank heist, if only he hadn't forgotten to break that surveillance camera. Holed up in a New York hotel he's subjected to extortion schemes and finds himself a new outlaw celebrity to newshounds. Bonet is a sweet hooker who falls in love with him. Satire on crooks and fame is too mild-mannered for its own good but not without charm. Directorial debut of Mead. Unedited NC-17 version also available. **CW:** Explicit sex scenes. **94m/C VHS, LV, Closed Caption.** Patrick Dempsey, Lisa Bonet, Olivia D'Abo, James Garde, Forest Whitaker, Judge Reinhold, Michael Jeter, Joe Alaskey, John Chappoulis; **D:** Nick Mead; **W:** Nick Mead; **M:** Stewart Copeland. *LIV*

Bank Shot 🎬🎬🎬 **1974** Hilarious comedy about a criminal who plans to rob a bank by stealing the entire building. Based on the novel by Donald Westlake, and the sequel to "The Hot Rock." **83m/C VHS.** George C. Scott, Joanna Cassidy, Sorrell Booke, G. Wood, Clifton James, Bob Balaban, Bibi Osterwald; **D:** Gower Champion; **W:** Wendell Mayes; **C:** Harry Stradling Jr. *NO*

The Banker 🎬🎬 **1989 (R)** A cop, played by Forster, suspects a wealthy, highly influential banker of brutal serial killings. **90m/C VHS, Beta, LV.** Robert Forster, Jeff Conaway, Leif Garrett, Duncan Regehr, Shanna Reed, Deborah Richter, Richard Roundtree, Teri Weigel, E.J. Peaker; **D:** William Webb. *NO*

Banzai Runner 🎬🎬 **1986** A cop whose brother was killed in an exclusive desert-highway race decides to avenge by joining the race himself. **88m/C VHS, Beta.** Dean Stockwell, John Shepherd, Charles Dierkop; **D:** John G. Thomas; **M:** Joel Goldsmith. *THV*

B.A.P.'s 🎬½ **1997 (PG-13)** Ghetto to riches story about Georgia waitresses Nisi (Berry) and Mickey (Desselle) who dream about opening their own business—a combo restaurant and hair salon. An L.A. audition offering $10,000 gets them to the sunny coast and eventually into the Beverly Hills mansion of Mr. Blakemore (Landau), where Nisi's persuaded to pose as the granddaughter of his lost love by Blakemore's money-grubbing nephew, Isaac (Fried). Everybody bonds and butler Manley (Richardson) instructs the women in taste and etiquette. Good cast is wasted and the comedy's lame when not offensive. **CW:** Brief strong language. **91m/C VHS.** Halle Berry, Natalie Desselle, Martin Landau, Ian Richardson, Troy Beyer, Luigi Amodeo, Jonathan Fried, A.J. Johnson; **D:** Robert Townsend; **W:** Troy Beyer; **C:** Bill Dill; **M:** Stanley Clarke. *NYR*

Bar Girls 🎬🎬 **1995 (R)** Mating rituals, set in L.A. wateringhole "The Girl Bar," finds usually tough cookie Loretta (Wolfe) spotting new face Rachael (D'Agostino) and deciding she likes what she sees. There's various mind games as they chart a rocky course to true love—with jealousy, possessiveness, and past romance all playing their parts. Hoffman adapted from her play and the staginess remains; film debut for director Giovanni. **CW:** Strong sexuality; nudity; language. **95m/C VHS, Closed Caption.** Nancy Allison Wolfe, Liza D'Agostino, Justine Slater, Paula Sorge, Camila Griggs, Pam Raines; **D:** Marita Giovanni; **W:** Lauran Hoffman; **C:** Michael Ferris. *ORI*

Bar-20 🎬½ **1943** Stage hold-ups and jewel robberies abound in this Hopalong Cassidy western. **54m/B VHS, Beta.** George Reeves, Douglas Fowley, William Boyd, Andy Clyde, Robert Mitchum, Victor Jory; **D:** Lesley Selander. *NOS, MRV, GVV*

Barabbas 🎬🎬½ **1962** Barabbas, a thief and murderer, is freed by Pontius Pilate in place of Jesus. He is haunted by this event for the rest of his life. Excellent acting, little melodrama, lavish production make for fine viewing. Based on the novel by Lagerkvist. **144m/C VHS, Beta, LV.** Anthony Quinn, Silvana Mangano, Arthur Kennedy, Jack Palance, Ernest Borgnine, Katy Jurado; **D:** Richard Fleischer. National Board of Review Awards '62: 5 Best Foreign Films of the Year. *COL*

Baraka 🎬🎬🎬 **1993** Time-lapse photography transforms a fascinating array of scenic panoramas into a thought-provoking experience. No dialogue, but the captivating visuals, shot in 24 countries, are a feast for the eyes. Points of interest include Iguacu Falls in Argentina, Ayers Rock in Australia, the temples of Angkor Wat in Cambodia, and the Grand Canyon. Also tours Auschwitz and the streets of Calcutta, in an effort to warn the viewer of the planet's fragility. Filmed in 70mm. **96m/C VHS, LV.** *D:* Ron Fricke; **W:** Ron Fricke, Mark Magidson, Bob Green; **C:** Ron Fricke; **M:** Michael Stearns. *MPI*

Barb Wire 🎬½ **1996 (R)** "Don't call me babe!" That'll be difficult when the figure in question is Anderson Lee's big-screen take on Dark Horse comic book heroine Barb Wire. Barb runs the sleazy Hammerhead Bar & Grille in Steel Harbor, the only neutral city in an America torn by a second civil war, and reluctantly agrees to aid hunky resistance leader Axel (Morrison) on a dangerous peace mission. Pambo gives Stallone a fight for the action title—fetching in high heels and black leather—with lots of fire power and a take-no-prisoners attitude. Plot's secondary to pulchritude but, unfortunately, the movie's just not a lotta fun. *CW:* Violence and nudity/sexuality. **98m/C VHS, LV, Closed Caption.** Pamela Anderson Lee, Temuera Morrison, Jack Noseworthy, Victoria Rowell, Xander Berkeley, Udo Kier, Steve Railsback, Clint Howard, Tony Bill; *D:* David Hogan; *W:* Ilene Chaiken, Chuck Pfarrer; *C:* Rick Bota; *M:* Michel Colombier. Golden Raspberry Awards '96: Worst New Star (Anderson Lee); Nominations: MTV Movie Awards '97: Best Fight (Pamela Lee/A Guy); Golden Raspberry Awards '96: Worst Picture, Worst Screenplay, Worst Song ("Welcome to Planet Boom!"). *PGV.*

Barbarella 🐾🐾½ *Barbarella, Queen of the Galaxy* **1968 (PG)** Based on the popular French sci-fi comic strip drawn by Jean-Claude Forest, this cult classic details the bizarre adventures of a space nymphette (Fonda) encountering fantastic creatures and super beings. You'll see sides of Fonda you never saw before (not even in the workout videos). Notorious in its day; rather silly, dated camp now. Don't miss the elbow-sex scene. Terry Southern contributed to the script. **98m/C VHS, Beta, LV. FR IT** Jane Fonda, John Phillip Law, David Hemmings, Marcel Marceau, Anita Pallenberg, Milo O'Shea; *D:* Roger Vadim; *W:* Terry Southern; *C:* Claude Renoir; *M:* Charles Fox. *FUS, PAR*

Barbarian and the Geisha 🐾🐾 **1958** The first US diplomat in Japan undergoes culture shock as well as a passionate love affair with a geisha, circa 1856. **104m/C VHS, Beta, Closed Caption.** John Wayne, Eiko Ando, Sam Jaffe, So Yamamura; *D:* John Huston; *M:* Hugo Friedhofer. *FOX*

Barbarian Queen 🐾 **1985 (R)** Female warriors led by beauteous babe seek revenge for the capture of their men in this sword-and-sorcery epic. Low-budget rip-off "Conan the Barbarian" is laughable. Also available in an unrated version. Followed by "Barbarian Queen 2: The Empress Strikes Back." **71m/C VHS, Beta, LV. IT** Lana Clarkson, Frank Zagarino, Katt Shea Ruben, Dawn Dunlap, Susana Traverso; *D:* Hector Olivera. *VES, LIV*

Barbarian Queen 2: The Empress Strikes Back 🐾 **1989 (R)** Apparently one movie wasn't enough to tell the beautiful Princess Athalia's story. This time she fights her evil brother Ankaris. He throws her in prison, she escapes, joins a band of female rebels, and leads them into battle. No better than the first attempt. **87m/C VHS. IT** Lana Clarkson, Greg Wrangler, Rebecca Wood, Elizabeth Jaegen, Roger Cundy; *D:* Joe Finley. *LIV*

The Barbarians 🐾 *The Barbarians and Co* **1987 (R)** Two bodybuilder siblings in animal skins battle wizards and warlords in this dumb-but-fun U.S./Italian production. **88m/C VHS, Beta, LV. IT** David Paul, Peter Paul, Richard Lynch, Eva LaRue, Virginia Bryant, Sheeba Alahani, Michael Berryman; *D:* Ruggero Deodato; *M:* Pino Donaggio. *MED, VTR*

Barbarians at the Gate 🐾🐾🐾½ **1993 (R)** In the "greed is good" financial climate of the 80's, this made-for-cable movie chronicles the $25 billion dollar battle in 1988 for RJR Nabisco, which at the time was working on developing a "smokeless cigarette." Garner is CEO F. Ross Johnson, who is confident that their "smokeless cigarette" will boost the stock's value—until he gets the test-marketing results. Unwilling to risk the product's failure, Johnson decides to buy the company and is challenged by master dealer Kravis (Pryce). Fascinating social commentary on the nastiest mega-deal in history. Based on the book by Bryan Burrough and John Helyar. *CW:* Language. **107m/C VHS, Closed Caption.** James Garner, Jonathan Pryce, Peter Riegert, Joanna Cassidy, Fred Dalton Thompson, Leilani Sarelle Ferrer, Matt Clark, Jeffrey DeMunn; *D:* Glenn Jordan; *W:* Larry Gelbart; *M:* Richard

Gibbs. Golden Globe Awards '94: Best Movie/Miniseries. *HBO, FCT, BTV*

Barbarosa 🐾🐾🐾 **1982 (PG)** Offbeat western about an aging, legendary outlaw constantly on the lam who reluctantly befriends a naive farmboy and teaches him survival skills. Nelson and Busey are a great team, solidly directed. Lovely Rio Grande scenery. **90m/C VHS, Beta, LV.** Willie Nelson, Gilbert Roland, Gary Busey, Isela Vega; *D:* Fred Schepisi; *C:* Ian Baker; *M:* Bruce Smeaton. *FOX*

Barbary Coast 🐾🐾🐾 **1935** A ruthless club owner tries to win the love of a young girl by building her into a star attraction during San Francisco's gold rush days. **90m/B VHS, Beta, LV.** Edward G. Robinson, Walter Brennan, Brian Donlevy, Joel McCrea, Donald Meek, David Niven, Miriam Hopkins; *D:* Howard Hawks. Nominations: Academy Awards '35: Best Cinematography. *NO*

The Barbary Coast 🐾🐾 **1974** A turn-of-the-century detective sleuths the streets of San Francisco in this average made-for-television movie. **100m/C VHS, Beta.** William Shatner, Dennis Cole, Lynda Day George, John Vernon, Charles Aidman, Michael Ansara, Neville Brand, Bill Bixby; *D:* Bill Bixby. *ORI*

The Barber Shop 🐾🐾 **1933** Fields portrays the bumbling, carefree barber Cornelius O'Hare, purveyor of village gossip and problem solver. Havoc begins when a gangster enters the shop and demands that Cornelius change his appearance. **21m/B VHS, Beta.** W.C. Fields, Elise Cavanna, Harry Watson, Dagmar Oakland, Frank Yaconelli. *CCB*

Barcelona 🐾🐾🐾 **1994 (PG-13)** Old-fashioned talkfest about two neurotic Americans experiencing sibling rivalry in Spain. Serious Ted (Nichols) is an American sales rep, posted to Barcelona, who can't quite get into the city's pleasure-loving rhythm. This is not a problem for Ted's cousin Fred (Eigeman), an obnoxious naval officer, with whom Ted has had a rivalry dating back to their boyhood. Set in the 1980s, the two must also deal with anti-Americanism, which leads both to violence and romantic developments. Tart dialogue, thoughtful performances, and exotic locales prove enticing in low-budget sleeper that effectively mixes drama and dry comedy. Watch for Eigeman in Tom Cruise's uniform from "A Few Good Men." **102m/C VHS, LV.** Taylor Nichols, Christopher Eigeman, Tushka Bergen, Mira Sorvino, Pep Munne, Francis Creighton, Thomas Gibson, Jack Gilpin, Nuria Badia, Hellena Schmied; *D:* Whit Stillman; *W:* Whit Stillman; *M:* Tom Judson, Mark Suozzo. Independent Spirit Awards '95: Best Cinematography. *NLC, TTC, IME*

The Barcelona Kill 🐾½ **1977** When a journalist and her boyfriend get in too deep with the Barcelona mob, their troubles begin. **86m/C VHS, Beta.** Linda Hayden, John Astin, Simon Andrew, Maximo Valverde; *D:* Jose Antonio De La Loma. *NO*

Bare Essentials 🐾 **1991 (PG)** Made for TV yuppie Club Med nightmare in which a high-strung couple from New York find themselves marooned on a desert isle with only two other inhabitants. With no cellular telephoning ability and an absence of large-ticket consumer goods to purchase, the two turn their reluctant sights on each other, focusing on the bare essentials, as it were. Great soul-searching scenes for the inarticulate. **94m/C VHS, Closed Caption.** Gregory Harrison, Lisa Hartman Black, Mark Linn-Baker, Charlotte Lewis; *D:* Martha Coolidge. *REP*

Bare Hunt 🐾 *My Gun is Jammed; The Bear Hunt* **1963** Detective Max T. Unimportant is dragged into the underground world of prospective nude actresses in this supposedly funny "nudie." **69m/B VHS, Beta.** *VDM, TPV*

Bare Knees 🐾🐾 **1928** A woman causes a scandal in her family when she arrives at her sister's birthday party with bare knees, cigarettes, and other flapper items. The quintessential flapper movie. **61m/B VHS, Beta.** Virginia Lee Corbin, Donald Keith, Jane Winton, Johnnie Walker, Forrest Stanley, Maude Fulton; *D:* Erle C. Kenton. *GPV*

Bare Knuckles 🐾 **1977 (R)** The adventures of a low-rent bounty hunter. **90m/C VHS, Beta.** Robert Viharo, Sherry Jackson, Michael Heit, Gloria Hendry, John Daniels; *D:* Don Edmunds; *C:* Dean Cundey. *TWE*

The Barefoot Contessa 🐾🐾🐾 **1954** The story, told in flashback, of a Spanish dancer's rise to Hollywood stardom, as witnessed by a cynical director. Shallow Hollywood self-examination. **128m/C VHS, Beta.** Ava Gardner, Humphrey Bogart, Edmond O'Brien, Valentina Cortese, Rossano Brazzi; *D:* Joseph L. Mankiewicz; *W:* Joseph L. Mankiewicz; *C:* Jack Cardiff. Academy Awards '54: Best Supporting Actor (O'Brien); Golden Globe Awards '55: Best Supporting Actor (O'Brien); Nominations: Academy Awards '54: Best Story & Screenplay. *MGM, FOX, FCT*

The Barefoot Executive 🐾🐾 **1971** A mailroom boy who works for a national television network finds a chimpanzee that can pick hit shows in this Disney family comedy. **92m/C VHS, Beta.** Kurt Russell, John Ritter, Harry (Henry) Morgan, Wally Cox, Heather North, Joe Flynn; *D:* Robert Butler; *M:* Robert F. Brunner. *DIS, OM*

Barefoot in Athens 🐾🐾 **1966** Television presentation from "George Schaefer's Showcase Theatre" chronicles the last years of the philosopher Socrates who, barefoot and unkempt, an embarrassment to his wife, and a dangerous critic to the corrupt Athenian leaders, nevertheless believes that democracy and truth are all-important in his city. **76m/C VHS, Beta.** Peter Ustinov, Geraldine Page, Anthony Quayle; *D:* George Schaefer. *FHS*

Barefoot in the Park 🐾🐾🐾 **1967** Neil Simon's Broadway hit translates well to screen. A newly wedded bride (Fonda) tries to get her husband (Redford, reprising his Broadway role) to loosen up and be as free-spirited as she is. **106m/C VHS, Beta, LV.** Robert Redford, Jane Fonda, Charles Boyer, Mildred Natwick; *D:* Gene Saks; *W:* Neil Simon; *C:* Joseph LaShelle. Nominations: Academy Awards '67: Best Supporting Actress (Natwick). *PAR*

Barfly 🐾🐾🐾 **1987 (R)** Bukowski's semi-autobiographical screenplay is the story of a talented writer who chooses to spend his time as a lonely barfly, hiding his literary abilities behind glasses of liquor. Dunaway's character is right on target as the fellow alcoholic. **100m/C VHS, Beta, LV, 8mm, Closed Caption.** Mickey Rourke, Faye Dunaway, Alice Krige, Frank Stallone, J.C. Quinn, Jack Nance; *D:* Barbet Schroeder; *W:* Charles Bukowski. *WAR, FCT*

The Bargain 🐾½ **1915** Hart's first feature, in which he portrays a bandit desperately trying to go straight. Original titles with musical score. **50m/B VHS, Beta.** William S. Hart. *NOS, GPV, DVT*

Baritone 🐾🐾 **1985** Concerned Polish drama about a prominent opera singer who promises to deliver a grand concert upon returning to his small town, only to lose his voice just before the show is to start. Proof positive that the opera ain't over 'til the fat lady sings. **100m/C VHS. PL** Zbigniew Zapasiewicz; *D:* Janusz Zaorski. *FCT*

Barjo 🐾🐾 **1993** In a bland and isolated French suburb lives willful housewife Fanfan (Bouchet) with her older businessman husband Charles (Bohringer) and her eccentric twin brother Barjo (Girardot). Barjo is obsessed with lists and extraterrestrials and his sister's affair with their next-door neighbor, which he likes to spy on. Her husband naturally begins to go crazy. Deadpan satire based on the novel "Confessions of a Crap Artist" by Philip K. Dick. The post-WWII American setting of the novel makes a decidedly uneasy transistion to contemporary French life. In French with English subtitles. **85m/C VHS. FR** Anne Brochet, Hippolyte Girardot, Richard Bohringer, Consuelo de Haviland, Renaud Danner, Nathalie Boutefeu; *D:* Jerome Boivin; *W:* Jerome Boivin, Jacques Audiard; *M:* Hugues LeBars. *FXL*

The Barkleys of Broadway 🐾🐾🐾 **1949** The famous dancing team's last film together; they play a quarreling husband/wife showbiz team. ♫ They Can't Take That Away From Me; The Sabre Dance; Swing Trot; Manhattan Downbeat; A Weekend in the Country; My One and Only Highland Fling; You'd Be Hard to Replace; Bouncin' the Blues; Shoes With Wings On. **109m/C VHS, Beta, LV.** Fred Astaire, Ginger Rogers, Gale Robbins, Oscar Levant, Jacques Francois, Billie Burke; **D:** Charles Walters; **W:** Adolph Green, Betty Comden; **C:** Harry Stradling; **M:** Ira Gershwin, Harry Warren. Nominations: Academy Awards '49: Best Color Cinematography. *MGM*

Barn of the Naked Dead woof! 1973 Prine plays a sicko who tortures women while his radioactive monster dad terrorizes the Nevada desert. Rudolph's first film, directed under the pseudonym Gerald Comier. Also on video as "Terror Circus" and "Nightmare Circus." **86m/C VHS.** Andrew Prine, Manuela Thiess, Sherry Alberoni, Gylian Roland, Al Cormier, Jennifer Ashley; **D:** Alan Rudolph. *NO*

Barnaby and Me 🐾🐾 1977 Australian star Barnaby the Koala Bear joins an international con-man in this romantic adventure. The mob is chasing the con-man when he meets and falls for a lovely young woman and her daughter. **90m/C VHS, Beta.** *AU* Sid Caesar, Juliet Mills, Sally Boyden; **D:** Norman Panama. *ACA*

Barnum 🐾🐾½ 1986 P.T. Barnum's life is focused upon in this biography about the man who helped to form "The Greatest Show On Earth." **100m/C VHS, Beta, LV.** Burt Lancaster, Hanna Schygulla, Jenny Lind, John Roney; **D:** Lee Philips. *ACA*

The Baron 🐾½ 1988 Vengeance is the name of the game when an underworld boss gets stiffed on a deal. Fast-paced no-brainer street drama. **88m/C VHS.** Calvin Lockhart, Charles McGregor, Joan Blondell, Richard Lynch, Marlene Clark; **D:** Philip Fently. *NO*

The Baron and the Kid 🐾 1984 A pool shark finds out that his opponent at a charity exhibition game is his long-lost son. Based on Johnny Cash's song. Made for TV. **100m/C VHS, Beta, Closed Caption.** Johnny Cash, Darren McGavin, June Carter Cash, Richard Roundtree; **D:** Gary Nelson; **M:** Brad Fiedel. *FOX*

Baron Munchausen 🐾🐾🐾 1943 The German film studio UFA celebrated its 25th anniversary with this lavish version of the Baron Munchausen legend, starring a cast of top-name German performers at the height of the Third Reich. Filmed in Agfacolor; available in English subtitled or dubbed versions. **120m/C VHS, Beta.** *GE* Hans Albers, Kaethe Kaack, Hermann Speelmanns, Leo Slezak; **D:** Josef von Baky. *VCD, GLV, TPV*

Baron of Arizona 🐾🐾🐾 1951 Land office clerk almost succeeds in convincing the U.S. that he owned the state of Arizona. **99m/B VHS, Beta.** Vincent Price, Ellen Drew, Beulah Bondi, Reed Hadley, Vladimir Sokoloff; **D:** Samuel Fuller; **W:** Samuel Fuller; **C:** James Wong Howe. *RXM*

Barracuda woof! *The Lucifer Project* 1978 (R) Lots of innocent swimmers are being eaten by crazed killer barracudas. **90m/C VHS, Beta.** Wayne Crawford, Jason Evers, Roberta Leighton; **D:** Harry Kerwin. *NO*

The Barretts of Wimpole Street 🐾🐾🐾 *Forbidden Alliance* 1934 The moving, almost disturbing, account of poetess Elizabeth Barrett, an invalid confined to her bed, with only her poetry and her dog to keep her company. She is wooed by poet Robert Browning, in whose arms she finds true happiness and a miraculous recovery. Multi-faceted drama expertly played by all. **110m/B VHS, LV.** Fredric March, Norma Shearer, Charles Laughton, Maureen O'Sullivan, Katherine Alexander, Una O'Connor, Ian Wolfe; **D:** Sidney Franklin; **C:** William H. Daniels. Nominations: Academy Awards '34: Best Actress (Shearer), Best Picture. *MGM, CCB*

Barry Lyndon 🐾🐾🐾½ 1975 (PG) Ravishing adaptation of the classic Thackeray novel about the adventures of an Irish gambler moving from innocence to self-destructive arrogance in the aristocracy of 18th Century England. Visually opulent. Kubrick received excellent performances from all his actors, and a stunning display of histo-

ry, but the end result still overwhelms. O'Neal has seldom been better. **185m/C VHS, Beta, LV.** Ryan O'Neal, Marisa Berenson, Patrick Magee, Hardy Kruger, Guy Hamilton; **D:** Stanley Kubrick. Academy Awards '75: Best Art Direction/Set Decoration, Best Cinematography, Best Costume Design, Original Song Score and/or Adaptation; British Academy Awards '75: Best Director (Kubrick); Los Angeles Film Critics Association Awards '75: Best Cinematography; National Board of Review Awards '75: 10 Best Films of the Year, Best Director (Kubrick); National Society of Film Critics Awards '75: Best Cinematography; Nominations: Academy Awards '75: Best Adapted Screenplay, Best Director (Kubrick), Best Picture. *WAR*

Barry McKenzie Holds His Own 🐾🐾 1974 In this sequel to "The Adventures of Barry McKenzie," we find that after a young man's aunt is mistaken for the Queen of England, two emissaries of Count Plasma of Transylvania kidnap her to use as a Plasma tourist attraction. Based on the 'Private Eye' comic strip, this crude Australian film is as disappointing as the first of the Barry McKenzie stories. **93m/C VHS, Beta.** *AU* Barry Humphries, Barry Crocker, Donald Pleasence; **D:** Bruce Beresford; **W:** Barry Humphries, Bruce Beresford. *NO*

Bartleby 🐾🐾½ 1970 A new version of the classic Herman Melville short story. McEnery is Bartleby the clerk, who refuses to leave his job even after he's fired; Scofield is his frustrated boss. **79m/C VHS, LV.** Paul Scofield, John McEnery, Colin Jeavons, Thorley Walters; **D:** Anthony Friedman; **W:** Rodney Carr-Smith. *WST, TVC*

Barton Fink 🐾🐾🐾 1991 (R) This eerie comic nightmare comes laden with awards (including the Palme D'Or from Cannes) but only really works if you care about the time and place. Fink is a trendy New York playwright staying in a seedy Hollywood hotel in the 1940s, straining to write a simple B-movie script. Macabre events, both real and imagined, compound this writer's block. Superb set design from Dennis Gassner complements an unforgettable cast of grotesques. **CW:** Language and some violence. **116m/C VHS.** John Turturro, John Goodman, Judy Davis, Michael Lerner, John Mahoney, Tony Shalhoub, Jon Polito, Steve Buscemi, David Warrilow, Richard Portnow, Christopher Murney; **D:** Joel Coen; **W:** Joel Coen, Ethan Coen; **C:** Roger Deakins; **M:** Carter Burwell. Cannes Film Festival '91: Best Actor (Turturro), Best Director (Coen), Best Film; Los Angeles Film Critics Association Awards '91: Best Cinematography, Best Supporting Actor (Lerner); New York Film Critics Awards '91: Best Cinematography, Best Supporting Actress (Davis); National Society of Film Critics Awards '91: Best Cinematography; Nominations: Academy Awards '91: Best Art Direction/Set Decoration, Best Costume Design, Best Supporting Actor (Lerner). *FXV, CCB*

Baseball 1994 Ken Burns' follow-up to "The Civil War" is an equally epic history of the great American pastime, spanning 150 years. 9 tapes released in a collector's edition or individually. **1080m/C VHS. D:** Ken Burns. *WAR, PBS*

Based on an Untrue Story 🐾🐾½ 1993 Campy spoof of popular "true story" television docudramas in which powerful Satin Chau (Fairchild), a perfume mogul, loses her sense of smell. Satin leaves her mentor Varda (Cannon) to discovery herself but finds that only her two separated-at-birth sisters, Velour (Lake) and Corduroy (Jackson), hold the secrets to the past. It's hard to spoof a genre that's become a cliche but this television movie does its best. **90m/C VHS, Closed Caption.** Morgan Fairchild, Dyan Cannon, Victoria Jackson, Ricki Lake, Harvey Korman, Robert Goulet, Dan Hedaya; **D:** Jim Drake. *FXV*

The Bashful Bachelor 🐾🐾 1942 Yokel joker Abner trades his delivery car for a race horse, hoping to win a big race. **78m/B VHS.** Chester Lauck, Norris Goff, ZaSu Pitts, Grady Sutton, Louise Currie, Irving Bacon, Earle Hodgins, Benny Rubin; **D:** Malcolm St. Clair. *NOS, RXM*

Basic Instinct 🐾🐾½ 1992 (R) Controversial thriller had tongues wagging months before its theatrical release. Burnt-out detective Douglas falls for beautiful, manipulative murder suspect Stone, perfectly cast as a bisexual ice queen who may or may not have done the deed. Noted for highly erotic sex scenes and an expensive (3 million bucks) script; ultimately the predictable plot is disappointing. Gay activists tried to interrupt filming because they objected to the depiction of Stone's character but only succeeded in generating more free publicity. The American release was edited to avoid an "NC-17" rating, but an uncut, unrated video version is also available. **CW:** Language, strong violence and drug use, and strong sensuality. **123m/C VHS, Beta, Closed Caption, DVD.** Michael Douglas, Sharon Stone, George Dzundza, Jeanne Tripplehorn, Denis Arndt, Leilani Sarelle Ferrer, Bruce A. Young, Chelcie Ross, Dorothy Malone, Wayne Knight, Stephen Tobolowsky; **D:** Paul Verhoeven; **W:** Joe Eszterhas; **C:** Jan De Bont; **M:** Jerry Goldsmith. MTV Movie Awards '93: Best Female Performance (Stone), Most Desirable Female (Stone); Nominations: Academy Awards '92: Best Film Editing, Best Original Score. *LIV, PMS*

Basic Training woof! 1986 (R) Three sexy ladies wiggle into the Pentagon in their efforts to clean up the government. **85m/C VHS, Beta.** Ann Dusenberry, Rhonda Shear, Angela Aames, Walter Gotell; **D:** Andrew Sugarman. *LIV, VES*

Basileus Quartet 🐾🐾🐾 1982 The replacement for a violinist in a well-established quartet creates emotional havoc. Beautiful music, excellent and evocative photography. **118m/C VHS, LV.** *FR IT* Pierre Malet, Hector Alterio, Omero Antonutti, Michel Vitold, Alain Cuny, Gabriele Ferzetti, Elisabeth Kreuzer; **D:** Fabio Carpi. *TPV*

Basket Case 🐾🐾🐾 1982 A gory horror film about a pair of Siamese twins—one normal, the other gruesomely deformed. The pair is surgically separated at birth, and the evil disfigured twin is tossed in the garbage. Fraternal ties being what they are, the normal brother retrieves his twin—essentially a head atop shoulders—and totes him around in a basket (he ain't heavy). Together they begin twisted and deadly revenge, with the brother-in-a-basket in charge. Very entertaining, if you like this sort of thing. Followed by two sequels, if you just can't get enough. **89m/C VHS, Beta, LV.** Kevin Van Hentenryck, Terri Susan Smith, Beverly Bonner; **D:** Frank Henenlotter. *MED*

Basket Case 2 🐾🐾½ 1990 (R) Surgically separated teenage mutant brothers Duane and Belial are back! This time they've found happiness in a "special" family—until they're plagued by the paparazzi. Higher production values make this sequel slicker than its low-budget predecessor, but it somehow lacks the same charm. **CW:** Language, graphic monster violence, and sensuality. **90m/C VHS, Beta, LV, Closed Caption.** Kevin Van Hentenryck, Annie Ross, Kathryn Meisle, Heather Rattray, Jason Evers, Ted Sorel, Matt Mitler; **D:** Frank Henenlotter; **W:** Frank Henenlotter. *VTR, IME, SGE*

Basket Case 3: The Progeny 🐾🐾½ 1992 (R) In this sequel to the cult horror hits "Basket Case" and "Basket Case 2," Belial is back and this time he's about to discover the perils of parenthood as the mutant Mrs. Belial delivers a litter of bouncing mini-monsters. Everything is fine until the police kidnap the little creatures and chaos breaks out as Belial goes on a shocking rampage in his newly created mechanical body. Weird special effects make this a cult favorite for fans of the truly outrageous. **90m/C VHS, Closed Caption.** Annie Ross, Kevin Van Hentenryck, Gil Roper, Tina Louise Hilbert, Dan Biggers, Jim O'Doherty; **D:** Frank Henenlotter; **W:** Robert Martin, Frank Henenlotter; **M:** Joe Renzetti. *USH, SGE*

The Basketball Diaries 🐾🐾 1994 (R) Disappointing adaptation of underground writer/musician Jim Carroll's 1978 cult memoirs, with DiCaprio starring as the teen athlete whose life spirals into drug addiction and hustling on the New York streets. Carroll and friends Mickey

(Wahlberg), Neutron (McGaw), and Pedro (Madio), form the heart of St. Vitus' hot hoopster team. But the defiant quartet really get their kicks from drugs, dares, and petty crime—leading to an ever-downward turn. The book takes place in the '60s but the film can't make up its mind what the decade is, although DiCaprio (and Wahlberg) are particularly effective in a self-conscious first effort from Kalvert.**CW:** Graphic depiction of drug addiction with related strong violence, sexuality and language. 102m/C VHS. Leonardo DiCaprio, Mark Wahlberg, Patrick McGaw, James Madio, Bruno Kirby, Ernie Hudson, Lorraine Bracco, Juliette Lewis, Josh Mostel, Michael Rapaport, Michael Imperioli; *Cameos:* Jim Carroll; *D:* Scott Kalvert; *W:* Bryan Goluboff; *C:* David Phillips; *M:* Graeme Revell. *PGV*

Basquiat 🎬🎬🎬 *Build a Fort Set It on Fire* 1996 (R) First-time writer/director and reknowned 80's pop artist Schnabel paints a celluloid portrait of African-American artist Jean Michel Basquiat, who went from grafitti artist to overnight sensation in the mid-1980s before dying of a drug overdose at 27. Schnabel's first-hand knowledge provides details of the painters, the dealers, and the patrons of the whirlwind New York art scene of the time using an all-star cast (no mean feat on a $3 million budget). Making the move from stage to screen, Wright is an aptly deep and elusive Basquiat and Bowie stands out in a marvelously conceived portrayal of Basquiat's pseudo-mentor, the equally sensational Warhol. Features authentic works of the artists portrayed and some very convincing Basquiat reproductions done by Schnabel.*CW:* Drug use and strong language. 108m/C VHS, LV, Closed Caption. Jeffrey Wright, David Bowie, Dennis Hopper, Gary Oldman, Christopher Walken, Michael Wincott, Benicio Del Toro, Parker Posey, Elina Lowensohn, Courtney Love, Claire Forlani, Willem Dafoe, Paul Bartel, Tatum O'Neal, Chuck Pfeiffer; *D:* Julian Schnabel; *W:* Julian Schnabel; *C:* Ron Fortunato; *M:* John Cale. Independent Spirit Awards '97: Best Supporting Actor (Del Toro); Nominations: Independent Spirit Awards '97: Debut Performance (Wright). *MAX*

The Bastard 🎬🎬½ *The Kent Chronicles* 1978 Dashing (but alas, illegitimate) nomads roams Europe on futile, Roots-like search, then settles for America during the Revolutionary War in this longwinded television adaptation of John Jakes' equally cumbersome bestseller (part of his popular Bicentennial series). Stevens stars, along with many supporting performers merely keeping active. Followed by "The Rebels" and "The Seekers." 189m/C VHS, Closed Caption. Andrew Stevens, Tom Bosley, Kim Cattrall, Buddy Ebsen, Lorne Greene, Olivia Hussey, Cameron Mitchell, Harry (Henry) Morgan, Patricia Neal, Eleanor Parker, Donald Pleasence, William Shatner, Barry Sullivan, Noah Beery Jr., William Daniels, Keenan Wynn; *D:* Lee H. Katzin; *M:* John Addison. *USH*

Bastard out of Carolina 🎬🎬 1996 (R) Huston's steeped-in-controversy directorial debut tells the story of young mom Anney (Leigh), who lives a hardscrabble life in Greenville, South Carolina, with an illegitimate daughter nicknamed Bone (Malone). Working as a waitress, Anney's eager to find love and succumbs to the charms of laborer Glen (Eldard), despite his nasty temper. Eleven-year-old Bone and Glen are immediately at odds and he begins to beat her, with Anney unwilling to face the truth, until a final horrific event. Based on the 1992 semiautobiographical novel by Dorothy Allison, the film was originally made for Ted Turner's TNT network but was rejected as unsuitable because of its graphic depiction of child abuse.*CW:* Strong depiction of sexual and violent abuse, including a rape scene involving a young girl. 97m/C VHS. Jennifer Jason Leigh, Jena Malone, Ron Eldard, Glenne Headly, Lyle Lovett, Dermot Mulroney, Christina Ricci, Michael Rooker, Diana Scarwid, Susan Traylor, Grace Zabriskie; *D:* Anjelica Huston; *W:* Anne Meredith; *C:* Anthony B. Richmond; *M:* Van Dyke Parks. Nominations: Independent Spirit Awards '97: Debut Performance (Malone). *BMG*

The Bat 🎬🎬🎬 1926 A bat-obsessed killer stalks the halls of a spooky mansion in this early film version of the Mary Roberts Rinehart novel. 81m/B VHS, Beta. Andre de Beranger, Charles Herzinger, Emily Fitzroy, Louise Fazenda, Arthur Housenan, Robert McKim, Jack Pickford, Jewel Carmen; *D:* Roland West; *W:* Roland West. *SNC, FUS*

The Bat 🎬🎬 1959 A great plot centering around a murderer called the Bat, who kills hapless victims by ripping out their throats when he isn't busy searching for a million dollars worth of securities stashed in the old house he is living in. Adapted from the novel by Mary Roberts Rinehart. 80m/B VHS, Beta. Vincent Price, Agnes Moorehead, Gavin Gordon, John Sutton, Lenita Lane, Darla Hood; *D:* Crane Wilbur. *NOS, SNC, DVT*

The Bat People 🎬 *It Lives By Night* 1974 (R) Less-than-gripping horror flick in which Dr. John Bech is bitten by a bat while on his honeymoon. He then becomes a sadistic bat creature, compelled to kill anyone who stumbles across his path. The gory special effects make for a great movie if you've ever been bitten by that sort of thing. 95m/C VHS, Beta. Stewart Moss, Marianne McAndrew, Michael Pataki, Paul Carr; *D:* Jerry Jameson. *HBO*

Bat 21 🎬🎬 1988 (R) Hackman, an American officer, is stranded in the wilds of Vietnam alone after his plane is shot down. He must rely on himself and Glover, with whom he has radio contact, to get him out. Glover and Hackman give solid performances in this otherwise average film. 112m/C VHS, Beta, LV, Closed Caption. Gene Hackman, Danny Glover, Jerry Reed, David Marshall Grant, Clayton Rohner, Erich Anderson, Joe Dorsey; *D:* Peter Markle; *W:* Marc Norman, William C. Anderson. *MED, VTR*

The Bat Whispers 🎬🎬½ 1930 A masked madman is stalking the halls of a creepy mansion; eerie tale that culminates in an appeal to the audience to keep the plot under wraps. Unusually crafted film for its early era. Comic mystery based on the novel and play by Mary Roberts Rinehart and Avery Hopwood. 82m/B VHS, LV. Chester Morris, Chance Ward, Richard Tucker, Wilson Benge, DeWitt Jennings, Una Merkel, Spencer Charters; *D:* Roland West; *W:* Roland West. *NOS, DVT, MLB*

Bataan 🎬🎬½ 1943 A rugged war-time combat drama following the true story of a small platoon in the Philippines endeavoring to blow up a pivotal Japanese bridge. Also available in a colorized version. 115m/B VHS, Beta. Robert Taylor, George Murphy, Thomas Mitchell, Desi Arnaz Sr., Lee Bowman, Lloyd Nolan, Robert Walker; *D:* Tay Garnett. *MGM, TLF*

Bathing Beauty 🎬🎬½ 1944 This musical stars Skelton as a pop music composer who the hots for college swim teacher Williams. Rathbone is a music executive who sees the romance as a threat to Skelton's career and to his own profit margin. Full of aquatic ballet, Skelton's shtick, and wonderful original melodies. The first film in which Williams received star billing. 🎵 I Cried for You; Bim, Bam, Boom; Tico-Tico; I'll Take the High Note; Loch Lomond; By the Waters of Minnetonka; Magic is the Moonlight; Trumpet Blues; Hora Staccato. 101m/C VHS, LV. Red Skelton, Esther Williams, Basil Rathbone, Bill Goodwin, Jean Porter, Carlos Ramirez, Donald Meek, Ethel Smith, Helen Forrest; *D:* George Sidney; *C:* Harry Stradling; *M:* Xavier Cugat. *MGM, TTC, FCT*

Batman 🎬🎬½ 1966 Holy television camp, Batman! Will the caped crusader win the Bat-tle against the combined forces of the Joker, the Riddler, the Penguin, and Catwoman? Will Batman and Robin save the United World Security Council from dehydration? Will the Bat genius ever figure out that Russian journalist Miss Kitka and Catwoman are one and the same? Biff! Thwack! Socko! Not to be confused with the Michael Keaton version of the Dark Knight, this is the pot-bellied Adam West Batman, teeming with Bat satire and made especially for the big screen. 104m/C VHS, Beta, LV, Closed Caption. Burt Ward, Adam West, Burgess Meredith, Cesar Romero, Frank Gorshin, Lee Meriwether; *D:* Leslie Martinson. *FOX*

Batman 🎬🎬🎬½ 1989 (PG-13) The blockbuster fantasy epic that renewed Hollywood's faith in media blitzing. The Caped Crusader is back in Gotham City, where even the criminals are afraid to walk the streets alone. There's a new breed of criminal in Gotham, led by the infamous Joker. Their random attacks via acid-based make-up are just the beginning. Keaton is surprisingly good as the dual personality hero though Nicholson steals the show. Marvelously designed and shot. Much better on the big screen. Followed in 1992 by "Batman Returns." 126m/C VHS, Beta, LV, Closed Caption, DVD. Michael Keaton, Jack Nicholson, Kim Basinger, Robert Wuhl, Tracey Walter, Billy Dee Williams, Pat Hingle, Michael Gough, Jack Palance, Jerry Hall; *D:* Tim Burton; *W:* Sam Hamm, Warren Skaaren; *M:* Danny Elfman, Prince. Academy Awards '89: Best Art Direction/Set Decoration; People's Choice Awards '90: Best Film—Drama. *FOX, WAR*

Batman and Robin 🎬🎬 1997 (PG-13) Lots of flash but, as usual, not much substance in this fourth adventure, which features a less angst-ridden caped crusader in the charming persona of Clooney. O'Donnell, who apparently knows a good gig when he's got one, returns as Robin. They must battle evil industrialist, Mr. Freeze (an impressively costumed Schwarzenegger), and his partner-with-the-deadly-kiss (but what a way to go!), Poison Ivy (Thurman), who have plans to freeze Gotham City. Our heroes have some additional help in the person of Batgirl (Silverstone), who's now butler Alfred's (Gough) ward (she was Commissioner Gordon's daughter in the comics). Story's simplified but the secondary characters still get lost in the crowd. Director Schumacher's already agreed to helm a fifth film although the comic book hero's more fanatic followers keep complaining about the films' camp, high-gloss tone.*CW:* Strong stylized action and some innuendos. 130m/C VHS. George Clooney, Chris O'Donnell, Arnold Schwarzenegger, Uma Thurman, Alicia Silverstone, Michael Gough, Pat Hingle, John Glover, Elle Macpherson, Vivica A. Fox, Vendela Thommessen, Jeep Swenson; *D:* Joel Schumacher; *W:* Joel Schumacher, Akiva Goldsman; *C:* Stephen Goldblatt; *M:* Elliot Goldenthal. *NYR*

Batman Forever 🎬🎬🎬 1995 (PG-13) Holy franchise, Batman! Third-time actioner considerably lightens up Tim Burton's dark vision for a more family-oriented Caped Crusader (now played by Kilmer, who fills out lip requirement nicely). The Boy Wonder also makes a first-time appearance in the bulked-up form of O'Donnell, a street-smart Robin with revenge on his mind. Naturally, the villains still steal the show in the personas of maniacal Carrey (the Riddler) and the sartorially splendid Jones as Harvey "Two-Face" Dent. Rounding out this charismatic cast is Kidman's slinky psychologist Chase Meridian, who's eager to find the man inside the bat (and who can blame her). Lots of splashy toys for the boys and awe-inspiring sets to show you where the money went. A Gotham City gas that did $53 million at it's opening weekend box office—breaking the "Jurassic Park" record, testimony to the power of aggressive marketing.*CW:* Strong stylized action. 121m/C VHS, LV, Closed Caption, DVD. Val Kilmer, Tommy Lee Jones, Jim Carrey, Chris O'Donnell, Nicole Kidman, Drew Barrymore, Debi Mazar, Michael Gough, Pat Hingle; *D:* Joel Schumacher; *W:* Janet Scott Batchler, Akiva Goldsman, Lee Batchler; *C:* Stephen Goldblatt; *M:* Elliot Goldenthal. Blockbuster Entertainment Awards '96: Action Actress, Theatrical (Kidman); Nominations: Academy Awards '95: Best Cinematography, Best Sound; Golden Globe Awards '96: Best Song ("Hold Me, Thrill Me, Kiss Me, Kill Me"); MTV Movie Awards '96: Most Desirable Male (Kilmer), Best Villain (Carrey, Jones), Best Song ("Kiss from a Rose", "Hold Me, Thrill Me, Kiss Me, Kill Me"). *WAR*

Batman: Mask of the Phantasm 🎬🎬½ *Batman: The Animated Movie* 1993 (PG) Based on the Fox television series with the animated Batman fending off old enemy the Joker, new enemy the Phantasm, and dreaming of his lost first love. Cartoon film noir set in the 1940's but filled with '90s sarcasm. Complicated storyline with a stylish dark look may be lost on the kiddies but adults will stay awake. **77m/C VHS, LV, Closed Caption. D:** Eric Radomski, Bruce W. Timm; **W:** Michael Reeves, Alan Burnett, Paul Dini, Martin Pako; **M:** Shirley Walker; **V:** Kevin Conroy, Dana Delany, Mark Hamill, Stacy Keach, Hart Bochner, Abe Vigoda, Efrem Zimbalist Jr., Dick Miller. *WAR*

Batman Returns 🦇🦇½ 1992 (PG-13)
More of the same from director Burton, with Batman more of a supporting role overshadowed by provocative villains. DeVito is the cruely misshapen Penguin who seeks to rule over Gotham City; Pfeiffer is the exotic and dangerous Catwoman— who has more than a passing purr-sonal interest in Batman; Walken is the maniacal tycoon Max Shreck. Pfeiffer fares best in her wickedly sexy role and second-skin costume (complete with bullwhip). Plot is secondary to special effects and nightmarish settings. Despite a big budget, this grandiose sequel is of the love it or leave it variety. **126m/C VHS, Closed Caption.** Michael Keaton, Danny DeVito, Michelle Pfeiffer, Christopher Walken, Michael Gough, Michael Murphy, Cristi Conaway, Pat Hingle, Vincent Schiavelli, Jan Hooks, Paul (Pee Wee Herman) Reubens, Andrew Bryniarski; **D:** Tim Burton; **W:** Daniel Waters; **C:** Stefan Czapsky; **M:** Danny Elfman. Nominations: Academy Awards '92: Best Makeup, Best Visual Effects. *WAR*

Baton Rouge 🦇🦇 1988
Gigolo Banderas gets together with psychiatrist Abril in a scheme to seduce one of her patients, the wealthy Maura, who suffers from terrible nightmares. They plan to kill her husband and accuse her of the crime in order to get her fortune. The plan backfires. The spanish trio, all veterans of director Pedro Almodovar's films, certainly know how to steam up the screen. Spanish with subtitles. **90m/C VHS.** *SP* Antonio Banderas, Victoria Abril, Carmen Maura; **D:** Rafael Moleon; **W:** Rafael Moleon, Augustin Diaz Yanes. *NYF, FCT*

*batteries not included 🦇🦇½ 1987
(PG) As a real estate developer fights to demolish a New York tenement, the five remaining residents are aided by tiny metal visitors from outer space in their struggle to save their home. Each resident gains a renewed sense of life in this sentimental, wholesome family film produced by Spielberg. Cronyn and Tandy keep the schmaltz from getting out of hand. Neat little space critters. **107m/C VHS, Beta, LV.** Hume Cronyn, Jessica Tandy, Frank McRae, Michael Carmine, Elizabeth Pena, Dennis Boutsikaris; **D:** Matthew Robbins; **W:** Matthew Robbins; Brad Bird, Brent Maddock, S.S. Wilson; **M:** James Horner. *USH*

Battle Beneath the Earth 🦇🦇 1968
The commies try to undermine democracy once again when American scientists discover a Chinese plot to invade the U.S. via a series of underground tunnels. Perhaps a tad jingoistic. **112m/C VHS, Beta.** *GB* Kerwin Mathews, Peter Arne, Viviane Ventura, Robert Ayres; **D:** Montgomery Tully.

Battle Beyond the Stars 🦇🦇½ 1980
(PG) The planet Akir must be defended against alien rapscallions in this intergalactic Corman creation. Sayles authored the screenplay and co-authored the story on which it was based. **105m/C VHS, Beta, LV.** Richard Thomas, Robert Vaughn, George Peppard, Sybil Danning, Sam Jaffe, John Saxon, Darlanne Fluegel; **D:** Jimmy T. Murakami; **W:** John Sayles; **M:** James Horner. *VES, LIV*

Battle Beyond the Sun 🦇🦇 1963
Former Russian movie "Nebo Zowet" is Americanized. Everyone is trying to send a mission to Mars. Roger Corman was the producer, Thomas Colchart is a pseudonym for Francis Ford Coppola. **75m/C VHS.** Edd Perry, Arla Powell, Bruce Hunter, Andy Stewart; **D:** Francis Ford Coppola; **M:** Les Baxter. *NOS, SNC*

Battle Circus 🦇½ 1953
Sappy drama casts Bogart as a surgeon at a M*A*S*H unit during the Korean War. Allyson is a combat nurse who finds love amongst the harsh reality of a war zone. Bogart was badly miscast and his performance proves it. Weak script and uninspired performances don't help this depressing story. **90m/B**

VHS, Closed Caption. Humphrey Bogart, June Allyson, Keenan Wynn, Robert Keith, William Campbell; **D:** Richard Brooks; **W:** Richard Brooks; **C:** John Alton. *MGM*

Battle Cry 🦇🦇🦇 1955
A group of U.S. Marines train, romance, and enter battle in WWII. Based on the novel by Leon Uris. Part of the "A Night at the Movies" series, this tape simulates a 1955 movie evening, with a cartoon, "Speedy Gonzales," a newsreel, and coming attractions for "Mr. Roberts" and "East of Eden." **169m/C VHS, Beta, LV, Closed Caption.** Van Heflin, Aldo Ray, Mona Freeman, Tab Hunter, Dorothy Malone, Anne Francis, James Whitmore, Raymond Massey; **D:** Raoul Walsh. Nominations: Academy Awards '55: Original Dramatic/Comedy Score. *WAR*

Battle for the Planet of the Apes 🦇🦇 1973 (G)
A tribe of human atomic bomb mutations are out to make life miserable for the peaceful ape tribe. The story is told primarily in flashback with the opening and closing sequences taking place in the year 2670 A.D. Final chapter in the five-movie simian saga. **96m/C VHS, Beta, Closed Caption.** Roddy McDowall, Lew Ayres, John Huston, Paul Williams, Claude Akins, Severn Darden, Natalie Trundy; **D:** J. Lee Thompson; **W:** John W. Corrington, Joyce H. Corrington. *FOX*

Battle Hell 🦇🦇 *Yangtse Incident* 1956
The true story of how a British ship was attacked by the Chinese Peoples Liberation Army on the Yangtze River in 1949. **112m/B VHS, Beta.** *GB* Richard Todd, Akim Tamiroff, Keye Luke; **D:** Michael Anderson Sr. *NO*

Battle Hymn 🦇🦇½ 1957
After accidentally bombing an orphanage as a WWII fighter pilot, Dean Hess (Hudson) becomes a minister. He returns to the Air Force in 1950 to train Korean pilots in Seoul and winds up building a home for the local orphans. True story on which the real Hess served as technical advisor. **109m/C VHS, Closed Caption.** Rock Hudson, Dan Duryea, Martha Hyer, Anna Kashfi, Don DeFore, Jock Mahoney, Carl Benton Reid, Alan Hale Jr., Richard Loo, Philip Ahn; **D:** Douglas Sirk; **W:** Charles Grayson, Vincent B. Evans; **C:** Russell Metty; **M:** Frank Skinner. *USH*

The Battle of Algiers 🦇🦇🦇½ 1966
Famous, powerful, award-winning film depicting the uprisings against French Colonial rule in 1954 Algiers. A seminal documentary-style film which makes most political films seem ineffectual by comparison in its use of non-professional actors, gritty photography, realistic violence, and a boldly propagandistic sense of social outrage. **123m/B VHS, Beta, LV.** *AL IT* Yacef Saadi, Jean Martin, Brahim Haggiag, Tommaso Neri, Samia Kerbash, Fawzia el Kader, Michele Kerbash, Mohamed Ben Kassen; **D:** Gillo Pontecorvo; **W:** Franco Solinas; **M:** Ennio Morricone. Venice Film Festival '66: Best Film; Nominations: Academy Awards '66: Best Foreign Language Film; Academy Awards '68: Best Director (Pontecorvo), Best Story & Screenplay. *IHF, TPV*

The Battle of Austerlitz 🦇🦇 *Austerlitz* 1960 (PG)
Ambitious but numbing costume drama about the events leading up to the epic battle between Napoleon and the overwhelming forces of the Czar and the Austrian Emperor at Austerlitz. Napoleon won. Film has been drastically cut from original 166 minute release. Watch director Gance's silent version, "Napoleon," for a truly epic experience. **123m/C VHS.** *FR IT YU* Claudia Cardinale, Martine Carol, Leslie Caron, Vittorio De Sica, Jean Marais, Ettore Manni, Jack Palance, Orson Welles; **D:** Abel Gance. *LIV, TPV*

The Battle of Blood Island 🦇 1960
Two G.I.s, one Christian and one Jewish, face death at the hands of the Japanese during WWII. Still, they bicker incessantly before finally pulling together to save themselves. **64m/B VHS, Beta.** Richard Devon, Ron Kennedy; **D:** Joel Rapp. *NOS, SNC*

Battle of Britain 🦇🦇½ 1969 (G)
A powerful retelling of the most dramatic aerial combat battle of WWII, showing how the understaffed Royal Air Force held off the might of the German Luftwaffe. **132m/C VHS, Beta, LV, Closed Caption.** Michael Caine, Laurence Olivier, Trevor Howard, Kenneth More, Christopher Plummer, Robert Shaw, Susannah York,

Ralph Richardson, Curt Jurgens, Michael Redgrave, Nigel Patrick, Edward Fox; **D:** Guy Hamilton; **C:** Frederick A. (Freddie) Young. *MGM, FOX*

Battle of China 1944
A look at the people, culture, and industry of China, and Japan's total commitment to conquer the country during WWII, through authentic newsreel footage. **67m/B VHS, Beta. D:** Frank Capra. *MPI, MRV, HHT*

The Battle of El Alamein 🦇🦇 1968
Action filled movie about the alliance of Italy and Germany in a war against the British, set in a North African desert in the year 1942. **105m/C VHS, Beta.** *IT FR* Frederick Stafford, Ettore Manni, Robert Hossein, Michael Rennie, George Hilton, Ira Furstenberg; **D:** Calvin Jackson Padget. *CNG, MRV, GEM*

Battle of Elderbush Gulch 1913
An ancient pioneering western short famous for innocently employing the now-established cliches of bad guy, good guy, and helpless frontier heroine. One of Gish's first films. **22m/B VHS, Beta.** Lillian Gish; **D:** D.W. Griffith. *VCN, PYR, GVV*

Battle of Neretva 🦇🦇 1969
During WWII, Yugoslav partisans are facing German and Italian troops and local Chetniks as they battle for freedom. Big budget war film lost continuity with U.S. cut. **106m/C VHS.** *YU* Yul Brynner, Curt Jurgens, Orson Welles, Hardy Kruger, Franco Nero, Sergei Bondarchuk; **D:** Veljko Bulajic. Nominations: Academy Awards '69: Best Foreign Language Film. *REP*

The Battle of Russia 1944
Hitler's forces are victorious in Moscow and Leningrad but are thoroughly defeated at the battle of Stalingrad. Authentic newsreel footage. **83m/B VHS, Beta. D:** Frank Capra. *HHT, MRV, CCB*

The Battle of San Pietro 1944
John Huston's powerful documentary about the famous battle in Italy's Liri Valley, stressing the number of losses sustained in taking this military objective. The film was almost suppressed by the U.S. government, because it was considered to be too strong for general release. **43m/B VHS, Beta.** John Huston. *IHF, WFV, FUS*

Battle of the Bulge 🦇🦇 1965
A recreation of the famous offensive by Nazi Panzer troops on the Belgian front during 1944-45, an assault that could have changed the course of WWII. **141m/C VHS, Beta, LV, Closed Caption.** Henry Fonda, Robert Shaw, Robert Ryan, Dana Andrews, Telly Savalas, Ty Hardin, Pier Angeli, George Montgomery, Charles Bronson; **D:** Ken Annakin; **W:** Philip Yordan; **C:** Jack Hildyard. *WAR*

Battle of the Bullies woof! 1985
A made-for-television special about an unsalvageable nerd who plots a high-tech revenge upon a slew of high school bullies. **45m/C VHS, Beta.** Manny Jacobs, Christopher Barnes, Sarah Inglis. *NWV*

Battle of the Commandos 🦇 *Legion of the Damned* 1971
A tough Army colonel leads a group of convicts on a dangerous mission to destroy a German-built cannon before it's used against the Allied Forces. **94m/C VHS.** *IT* Jack Palance, Curt Jurgens, Thomas Hunter, Robert Hunter; **D:** Umberto Lenzi. *REP*

Battle of the Eagles 🦇½ 1981
Follows the true adventures of the "Partisan Squadron," the courageous airmen known as the "Knights of the Sky" during WWII in Yugoslavia. **102m/C VHS, Beta.** Bekim Fehmiu, George Taylor, Gloria Samara, Frank Phillips; **D:** Tom Raymonth. *NO*

The Battle of the Japan Sea 🦇🦇 1970 (G)
A Japanese epic, dubbed in English, centering around the historic WWII battle between Japan and Russia. **120m/C VHS, Beta.** *JP* Toshiro Mifune. *VCD*

The Battle of the Sexes 🦇🦇🦇 1960
Sophisticated British comedy has mild-mannered Sellers trying to prevent a business takeover by the brash American Cummings. A good supporting cast and the impeccable Sellers make this one unique. Adapted from the James Thurber short story "The Catbird Seat." **88m/B VHS, Beta.**

GB Peter Sellers, Robert Morley, Constance Cummings, Jameson Clark, Ernest Thesiger, Donald Pleasence, Moultrie Kelsall, Alex Mackenzie, Roddy McMillan, Michael Goodliffe, Norman MacOwen, William Mervyn; *D:* Charles Crichton; *W:* Monja Danischewsky; *C:* Freddie Francis; *M:* Stanley Black. *MRV*

Battle of the Worlds ✓ *Il Pianeta Degli Uomini Spenti; Planet of the Lifeless Men* 1961 Typical low-budget science fiction. A scientist tries to stop an alien planet from destroying the Earth. Even an aging Rains can't help this one. Poorly dubbed in English. **84m/C VHS.** *IT* Claude Rains, Maya Brent, Bill Carter, Marina Orsini, Jacqueline Derval; *D:* Anthony (Antonio Margheriti) Dawson. *SNC, MRV*

Battle of Valiant ✓ 1963 Thundering hordes of invading barbarians trample the splendor of ancient Rome beneath their grimy sandals. **90m/C VHS, Beta.** Gordon Mitchell, Ursula Davis, Massimo Serato; *D:* John Gentil. *NO*

Battle Shock ✓½ *A Woman's Devotion; War Shock* 1956 Painter is accused of murdering a cantina waitress while on his honeymoon in Mexico. **88m/C VHS.** Ralph Meeker, Janice Rule, Paul Henreid; *D:* Paul Henreid; *W:* Robert Hill. *REP*

Battleforce ✓ *The Battle of the Mareth Line; The Greatest Battle* 1978 Exciting battle scenes lose their power in the confusion of this mixed-up WWII film about Rommel's last days. Dubbed sequences, news-reel vignettes and surprise performances by big name stars are incomprehensibly glued together. **97m/C VHS, Beta.** *GE YU* Henry Fonda, Stacy Keach, Helmut Berger, Samantha Eggar, Giuliano Gemma, John Huston; *D:* Umberto Lenzi. *QVD, TLF*

Battleground ✓✓✓ 1949 A tightly-conceived post-WWII character drama, following a platoon of American soldiers through the Battle of the Bulge. Available in a Colorized version. **118m/B VHS, Beta, LV, Closed Caption.** Van Johnson, John Hodiak, James Whitmore, George Murphy, Ricardo Montalban, Marshall Thompson, Jerome Courtland, Don Taylor, Bruce Cowling, Leon Ames, Douglas Fowley, Richard Jaeckel, Scotty Beckett; *D:* William A. Wellman; *W:* Robert Pirosh; *C:* Paul Vogel. Academy Awards '49: Best Black and White Cinematography, Best Story & Screenplay; Golden Globe Awards '50: Best Screenplay, Best Supporting Actor (Whitmore); Nominations: Academy Awards '49: Best Director (Wellman), Best Film Editing, Best Picture, Best Supporting Actor (Whitmore). *MGM*

The Battleship Potemkin ✓✓✓✓ *Potemkin; Bronenosets Potemkin* 1925 Eisenstein's best work documents mutiny aboard the Russian battleship Potemkin in 1905 which led to a civilian uprising against the Czar in Odessa, and the resulting crackdown by troops loyal to the Czar. Beautiful cinematography, especially the use of montage sequences, changed filmmaking. In particular, a horrifying sequence depicting the slaughter of civilians on an Odessa beach by soldiers coming down the stairs leading to it is exceptional; many movies pay homage to this scene including "The Untouchables" and "Love and Death." Viewers should overlook obvious Marxist overtones and see this film for what it is: a masterpiece. **71m/B VHS, Beta, LV.** *RU* Alexander Antonov, Vladimir Barsky, Grigori Alexandrov, Mikhail Gomorov, Sergei Eisenstein; *D:* Sergei Eisenstein; *M:* Eric Allaman. *REP, MRV, NOS*

Battlestar Galactica ✓✓½ 1978 **(PG)** Plot episode of the sci-fi television series which was later released in the theaters. The crew of the spaceship Galactica must battle their robot enemies in an attempt to reach Earth. Contains special effects designed by John "Star Wars" Dykstra. Individual episodes of the series are also available. **125m/C VHS, Beta, LV.** Lorne Greene, Dirk Benedict, Maren Jensen, Jane Seymour, Patrick Macnee, Terry Carter, John Colicos, Richard A. Colla, Laurette Spang, Richard Hatch; *D:* Richard A. Colla. *USH, MOV*

Battling Bunyon ✓✓½ 1924 A wily youngster becomes a comedy boxer for profit, and eventually gets fed up and battles the champ. Silent. **71m/B VHS, Beta.** Chester Conklin, Wesley Barry, Mollie Malone, Jackie Fields. *GPV, VYY*

Battling Butler ✓✓½ 1926 Rich young Keaton tries to impress a young lady by impersonating a boxer. All goes well until he has to fight the real thing. Mostly charming if uneven; one of Keaton's more unusual efforts, thought to be somewhat autobiographical. Silent. **70m/B VHS.** Buster Keaton, Sally O'Neil, Snitz Edwards, Francis McDonald, Mary O'Brien, Tom Wilson, Walter James; *D:* Buster Keaton. *NO*

Battling for Baby ✓✓ 1992 It's the war of the Grandmas. New mother Katherine decides to return to work and both her mother and mother-in-law want to look after the little tyke. Silly made-for-TV fluff. **93m/C VHS, Closed Caption.** Courteney Cox, Suzanne Pleshette, Debbie Reynolds, John Terlesky, Doug McClure, Leigh Lawson, Mary Jo Catlett; *D:* Art Wolff; *W:* Walter Lockwood, Nancy Silvers. *TTC*

Battling Marshal ✓½ 1948 Fast-moving action western starring Carson. **52m/B VHS, Beta.** Sunset Carson, Lee Roberts; *D:* Oliver Drake. *VCN*

Battling Orioles 1924 The once scrappy baseball team is now a bunch of grumpy old men, that is until Glenn whips them into shape. Silent. **58m/B VHS, Beta, 8mm.** Glenn Tryon, Blanche Mehaffey, Noah Young; *D:* Ted Wilde, Fred Guiol. *GVV*

Battling Outlaws ✓½ 194? Western featuring the American cowboy Bob Steele. **64m/B VHS, Beta.** Bob Steele. *NOS, VCN*

Battling with Buffalo Bill 1931 Twelve episodes of the vintage serial concerning the exploits of the legendary Indian fighter. **180m/B VHS, Beta.** Tom Tyler, Rex Bell, Franklyn Farnum. *VCN*

The Bawdy Adventures of Tom Jones ✓½ 1976 **(R)** An exploitive extension of the Fielding novel about the philandering English lad, with plenty of soft-core skin and lewdness. **89m/C VHS, Beta.** *GB* Joan Collins, Trevor Howard, Terry-Thomas, Arthur Lowe, Murray Melvin; *D:* Cliff Owen. *USH*

Baxter ✓✓½ 1989 A bull terrier lives his life with three different sets of masters. He examines all of humankind's worst faults and the viewer quickly realizes that Baxter's life depends on his refusal to obey like a good dog should. Based on the novel by Ken Greenhall. Funny, sometimes erotic, quirky comedy. In French with English subtitles. **82m/C VHS, LV.** *FR* Lisa Delamare, Jean Mercure, Jacques Spiesser, Catherine Ferran, Jean-Paul Roussillon, Sabrina Leurquin; *D:* Jerome Boivin; *W:* Jerome Boivin, Jacques Audiard; *M:* Marc Hillman, Patrick Roffe. *FXL, PMS*

The Bay Boy ✓✓½ 1985 **(R)** Set in the 1930s in Nova Scotia, this period piece captures the coming-of-age of a rural teenage boy. Young Sutherland's adolescent angst becomes a more difficult struggle when he witnesses a murder, and is tormented by the secret. **107m/C VHS, Beta, LV, Closed Caption.** *CA* Liv Ullmann, Kiefer Sutherland, Peter Donat, Matthieu Carriere, Joe MacPherson, Isabelle Mejias, Alan Scarfe, Chris Wiggins, Leah K. Pinsent; *D:* Daniel Petrie; *M:* Claude Bolling. Genie Awards '85: Best Film, Best Supporting Actor (Scarfe). *ORI*

Bayou Romance ✓ 1986 Painter inherits a Louisiana plantation, moves in, and falls in love with a young gypsy. **90m/C Beta.** Annie Potts, Michael Ansara, Barbara Horan. *PSM*

Baywatch the Movie: Forbidden Paradise ✓½ 1995 **(PG)** The "Baywatch" babes and their fellow lifesaving hunks-in-trunks head off to Hawaii to study the latest search and rescue techniques from the state's premier lifeguard team. **90m/C VHS.** David Hasselhoff, Pamela Anderson Lee, Alexandra Paul, Yasmine Bleeth, David Charvet, Gregory Alan-Williams, Jeremy Jackson; *D:* Douglas Schwartz. *LIV*

Be My Valentine, Charlie Brown 1975 The Peanuts gang endures the follies of the heart on St. Valentine's Day. Animated. **30m/C VHS, Beta.** *D:* Phil Roman. *MED*

Beach Babes from Beyond Infinity ✓ 1993 **(R)** "HOT. TAN. ALIEN." Three words that would send shivers through the body of any red-blooded American boy. And as if

alien silicone isn't enough to draw a crowd, this piece of fluff also features the relatives of big name stars hoping to cash in on the family name. Typical Hollywood cheese and sleaze should be fun for those who still can't get this kind of quality entertainment on cable. *CW:* Nudity and stong sexuality. **78m/C VHS, Closed Caption.** Joe Estevez, Don Swayze, Joey Travolta, Burt Ward, Jacqueline Stallone, Linnea Quigley, Sara Bellomo, Tamara Landry, Nicole Posey; *D:* Ellen Cabot. *PAR*

Beach Blanket Bingo ✓✓✓ 1965 Fifth entry in the "Beach Party" series (after "Pajama Party") is by far the best and has achieved near-cult status. Both Funicello and Avalon are back, but this time a very young Evans catches Avalon's eye. Throw in a mermaid, some moon-doggies, skydiving, sizzling beach parties, and plenty of nostalgic golly-gee-whiz fun and you have the classic '60s beach movie. Totally implausible, but that's half the fun when the sun-worshipping teens become involved in a kidnapping and occasionally break into song. Followed by "How to Stuff a Wild Bikini." ♬ Beach Blanket Bingo; The Cycle Set; Fly Boy; The Good Times; I Am My Ideal; I Think You Think; It Only Hurts When I Cry; New Love; You'll Never Change Him. **96m/C VHS, Beta, LV.** Frankie Avalon, Annette Funicello, Linda Evans, Don Rickles, Buster Keaton, Paul Lynde, Harvey Lembeck, Deborah Walley, John Ashley, Jody McCrea, Marta Kristen, Timothy Carey, Earl Wilson, Bobbi Shaw; *D:* William Asher; *W:* William Asher, Sher Townsend, Leo Townsend; *M:* Les Baxter. *NO*

Beach Girls ✓ 1982 **(R)** Three voluptuous coeds intend to re-educate a bookish young man and the owner of a beach house. **91m/C VHS, Beta, LV.** Debra Blee, Val Kline, Jeana Tomasina, Adam Roarke; *D:* Patrice Townsend. *PAR*

The Beach Girls and the Monster ✓ 1965 Here's one on the cutting edge of genre bending: while it meticulously maintains the philosophical depth and production values of sixties beach bimbo fare, it manages to graft successfully with the heinous critter from the sea genre to produce a hybrid horror with acres o'flesh. **70m/B VHS.** Jon Hall, Sue Casey, Walker Edmiston; *D:* Jon Hall; *M:* Frank Sinatra Jr. *SNC*

Beach House ✓ 1982 In this boring comedy, adolescents frolic on the beach, get inebriated, and listen to rock 'n' roll. **76m/C VHS, Beta.** Kathy McNeil, Richard Duggan, Ileana Seidel, John Cosola, Spence Waugh, Paul Anderson, John A. Gallagher; *W:* Marino Amaruso. *NO*

Beach Party ✓✓ 1963 Started the "Beach Party" series with the classic Funicello/Avalon combo. Scientist Cummings studying the mating habits of teenagers intrudes on a group of surfers, beach bums, and bikers, to his lasting regret. Typical beach party bingo, with sand, swimsuits, singing, dancing, and bare minimum in way of a plot. Followed by "Muscle Beach Party." ♬ Beach Party; Don't Stop Now; Promise Me Anything; Secret Surfin' Spot; Surfin' and a-Swingin'; Treat Him Nicely. **101m/C VHS, Beta.** Frankie Avalon, Annette Funicello, Harvey Lembeck, Robert Cummings, Dorothy Malone, Morey Amsterdam, Jody McCrea, John Ashley, Candy Johnson, Dolores Wells, Yvette Vickers, Eva Six; *D:* William Asher; *W:* Lou Rusoff; *M:* Les Baxter. *NO*

Beachcomber ✓✓✓ *Vessel of Wrath* 1938 Comedy set in the Dutch East Indies about a shiftless beachcomber (Laughton) who falls in love with a missionary's prim sister (Lanchester), as she attempts to reform him. The real-life couple of Laughton and Lanchester are their usual pleasure to watch. Remade in 1954. Story by W. Somerset Maugham. **88m/B VHS, Beta.** *GB* Charles Laughton, Elsa Lanchester, Robert Newton, Tyrone Guthrie; *D:* Erich Pommer. *NOS, MRV, DVT*

Beaches ✓✓✓½ 1988 **(PG-13)** Based on the novel by Iris Rainer Dart about two girls whose friendship survived the test of time. The friendship is renewed once more when one of the now middle-aged women learns that she is dying slowly of a fatal disease. **123m/C VHS, Beta, LV, 8mm.** Bette Midler, Barbara Hershey, John Heard, Spalding Gray, Lainie Kazan, James Read, Mayim Bialik; **D:** Garry Marshall; **W:** Mary Agnes Donoghue; **C:** Dante Spinotti; **M:** Georges Delerue. Nominations: Academy Awards '88: Best Art Direction/Set Decoration. *TOU*

Beaks: The Movie woof! *Birds of Prey* **1987 (R)** Two television reporters try to figure out why birds of prey are suddenly attacking humans. Owes nothing to Hitchcock's "The Birds." **86m/C VHS, Beta.** Christopher Atkins, Michelle Johnson; **D:** Rene Cardona Jr. *LIV*

Beanstalk 𝒵𝒵½ **1994 (PG)** Modern-day version of the fairytale finds young Jack Taylor (Daniels) scheming to make it big to help his hardworking single mom. He meets up with a wacky scientist (Kidder), who gives Jack some recently discovered seeds that naturally grow into an enormous beanstalk. And what does Jack find when he climbs the beanstalk—why an entire family of silly giants. **80m/C VHS, Beta, Closed Caption.** J.D. Daniels, Margot Kidder, Richard Moll, Amy Stock-Poynton, Patrick Renna, Richard Paul, David Naughton, Stuart Pankin, Cathy McAuley; **D:** Michael Paul Davis; **W:** Michael Paul Davis; **M:** Kevin Bassinson. *PAR*

The Bear 𝒵𝒵𝒵 **1989 (PG)** Breathtaking, effortlessly entertaining family film about an orphaned bear cub tagging after a grown male and dealing with hunters. The narrative is essentially from the cub's point of view, with very little dialogue. A huge money-maker in Europe. Based on a novel by James Oliver Curwood. **92m/C VHS, Beta, LV, Closed Caption.** FR Jack Wallace, Tcheky Karyo, Andre Lacombe; **D:** Jean-Jacques Annaud; **W:** Gerard Brach, Michael Kane; **C:** Philippe Rousselot; **M:** Bill Conti. Nominations: Academy Awards '89: Best Film Editing. *COL, RDG, HMV*

Bear Island 𝒵½ **1980 (PG)** Group of secret agents cleverly disguising themselves as U.N. weather researchers converge upon Bear Island in search of a Nazi U-Boat. Looks like rain. **118m/C VHS, Beta.** Donald Sutherland, Richard Widmark, Barbara Parkins, Vanessa Redgrave, Christopher Lee, Lloyd Bridges; **D:** Don Sharp. *NO*

The Bears & I 𝒵𝒵 **1974 (G)** A young Vietnam vet helps Indians regain their land rights while raising three bear cubs. Beautiful photography in this Disney production. **89m/C VHS.** Patrick Wayne, Chief Dan George, Andrew Duggan, Michael Ansara; **D:** Bernard McEveety; **M:** Buddy Baker. *DIS*

The Beast 𝒵𝒵½ *The Beast of War* **1988 (R)** Violent and cliche-driven war drama notable for its novel twist: wild Russian tank officer becomes lost in the Afghanistan wilderness while being tracked by Afghan rebels with revenge in mind. Filmed in the Israel desert and adapted by William Mastrosimone from his play. **93m/C VHS, Beta, Closed Caption.** George Dzundza, Jason Patric, Steven Bauer, Stephen Baldwin, Don Harvey, Kabir Bedi, Erik Avari, Haim Gerafi; **D:** Kevin Reynolds; **W:** William Mastrosimone; **M:** Mark Isham. *COL*

The Beast from Haunted Cave 𝒵𝒵 **1960** Gold thieves hiding in a wilderness cabin encounter a spiderlike monster. Surprisingly good performances from Sinatra (Frank's nephew) and Carol. Produced by Gene Corman, Roger's brother. **64m/B VHS.** Michael Forest, Sheila Carol, Frank Wolff, Richard Sinatra, Wally Campo; **D:** Monte Hellman; **W:** Charles B. Griffith. *DVT, MRV, SNC*

The Beast from 20,000 Fathoms 𝒵𝒵½ **1953** Atomic testing defrosts a giant dinosaur in the Arctic; the hungry monster proceeds onwards to its former breeding grounds, now New York City. Oft-imitated saurian-on-the-loose formula is still fun, brought to life by Ray Harryhausen special effects. Based loosely on the Ray Bradbury story "The Foghorn." **80m/B VHS, Beta, LV.** Paul Christian, Paula Raymond, Cecil Kellaway, Kenneth Tobey, Donald Woods, Lee Van Cleef, Steve Brodie, Mary Hill; **D:** Eugene Lourie; **W:** Fred Freiberger, Louis Morheim. *WAR, FCT, MLB*

Beast in the Cellar 𝒵½ *Are You Dying Young Man?* **1970 (R)** Every family has something to hide, and in the case of two spinster sisters, it's their murderous inhuman brother, whom they keep chained in the cellar. Like all brothers, however, the "beast" rebels against his sisters' bossiness and escapes to terrorize their peaceful English countryside. The sisters' (Reid and Robson) performances aren't bad, but rest of effort is fairly disappointing. **85m/C VHS, Beta.** GB Beryl Reid, Flora Robson, T.P. McKenna; **D:** James Kelly. *NO*

Beast of Morocco 𝒵𝒵 *Hand of Night* **1966** Interesting vampire film about a Morrocan vampire princess who sets her sights on seducing a noted archaeologist. Of course his girlfriend ends up being abducted by the vampire's servant. **88m/C VHS.** GB William Sylvester, Alizia Gur, Terence de Marney. *SNC*

Beast of the Yellow Night woof! **1970 (R)** A dying soldier sells his soul to Satan at the close of WWII. Years later, existing without aging, he periodically turns into a cannibal monster. Although the first half is tedious, the monster turns things around when he finally shows up. Decent gore effects. **87m/C VHS, Beta.** PH John Ashley, Mary Wilcox, Eddie Garcia, Vic Diaz; **D:** Eddie Romero. *NOS, VCI, INC*

The Beast of Yucca Flats woof! **1961** A really cheap, quasi-nuclear protest film. A Russian scientist is chased by communist agents into a nuclear testing area and is caught in an atomic blast. As a result, he turns into a club-weilding monster. Voice over narration is used in lieu of dialogue as that process proved too expensive. **53m/B VHS.** Tor Johnson, Douglas Mellor, Larry Aten, Barbara Francis; **D:** Coleman Francis; **W:** Coleman Francis. *SNC, CNM, MLB*

The Beast that Killed Women 𝒵𝒵½ **1965** Colonists at a sunny Florida nudist camp have their beach party interrupted by an escaped gorilla. Director Mahon, in his first color effort, stretches this panicky moment into an hour of fleshy fun and games. **60m/C VHS.** **D:** Barry Mahon. *SMW, TPV*

The Beast with Five Fingers 𝒵𝒵½ **1946** After a pianist mysteriously dies and leaves his fortune to his private nurse, the occupants of his villa are terrorized by a creature that turns out to be the pianist's hand which was severed by his personal secretary (Lorre). Lorre is also terrorized by hallucinations of the hand, and no matter what he does to stop it (nail it to a desk, throw it in the fire, etc.), nothing can keep the hand from carrying out its mission. A creepy thriller with inventive shots of the severed hand. **88m/B VHS, Closed Caption.** Robert Alda, Andrea King, Peter Lorre, Victor Francen, J. Carrol Naish, Charles Dingle; **D:** Robert Florey; **M:** Max Steiner. *MGM*

The Beast Within 𝒵𝒵 **1982 (R)** Young woman has the misfortune of being raped by an unseen creature in a Mississippi swamp. Seventeen years later, her son conceived from that hellish union begins to act quite strange, developing a penchant for shedding his skin before turning into an insect-like critter with a cannibalistic appetite. First film to use the air "bladder" type of prosthetic make-up popularized in later, and generally better, horror films. Contains some choice cuts in photo editing: the juxtaposition of hamburger and human "dead meat" is witty. Based on Edward Levy's 1981 novel. **98m/C VHS, Beta.** Ronny Cox, Bibi Besch, L.Q. Jones, Paul Clemens, Don Gordon; **D:** Philippe Mora; **W:** Tom Holland; **M:** Les Baxter. *MGM*

Beastmaster 𝒵𝒵 **1982 (PG)** Adventure set in a wild and primitive world. The Beastmaster is involved in a life-and-death struggle with overwhelming forces of evil. Campy neanderthal flesh flick. **119m/C VHS, Beta, LV.** Marc Singer, Tanya Roberts, Rip Torn, John Amos, Josh Milrad, Billy Jacoby; **D:** Don A. Coscarelli; **W:** Don A. Coscarelli; **C:** John Alcott. *MGM*

Beastmaster 2: Through the Portal of Time 𝒵𝒵½ **1991 (PG-13)** This time the laughs are intentional as the Beastmaster follows an evil monarch through a dimensional gate to modern-day L.A., where the shopping is better for both trendy clothes and weapons. Fun for genre fans, with a behind-the-scenes featurette on the tape. **107m/C VHS, LV, Closed Caption.** Marc Singer, Kari Wuhrer, Sarah Douglas, Wings Hauser, James Avery, Robert Fieldsteel, Arthur Malet, Robert Z'Dar, Michael Berryman; **D:** Sylvio Tabet; **M:** Robert Folk. *REP*

Beastmaster 3: The Eye of Braxus 𝒵𝒵½ **1995 (PG)** Heroic hunk Dar the Beastmaster (Singer) returns to battle evil. Lord Agon (Warner) needs to obtain a jeweled eye that will bring the demon Braxus back to life—and he'll stop at nothing, including kidnapping Dar's brother King Tal (Van Dien), to reach his terrifying goal. But Dar isn't alone—he's got the bewitching sorceress Morgana (Down), tempting warrioress Shada (Hess), and loyal advisor Seth (Todd) to help him out. **92m/C VHS, LV, Closed Caption.** Marc Singer, David Warner, Lesley-Anne Down, Tony Todd, Caspar Van Dien, Keith Coulouris, Sandra Hess, Patrick Kilpatrick; **D:** Gabrielle Beaumont; **W:** David Wise; **C:** Barbara Claman; **M:** Jan Hammer. *USH*

Beasts 𝒵 **1983** A young couple's plans for a romantic weekend in the Rockies are slightly changed when the pair are savagely attacked by wild beasts. **92m/C VHS, Beta.** Tom Babson, Kathy Christopher, Vern Potter. *PSM*

The Beat 𝒵 **1988** Unrealistic film about a bookish new kid who intercedes in the tension between two rival street gangs, changing their lives in his literary way. **101m/C VHS, Beta, LV.** John Savage, Kara Glover, Paul Dillon, David Jacobson, William McNamara; **D:** Peter Mones; **W:** Peter Mones; **M:** Carter Burwell. *LIV, VES*

Beat Girl 𝒵𝒵 *Wild For Kicks* **1960** An architect's rebellious teenage daughter sinks to the bottom and gets involved in murder along the way. **85m/B VHS.** GB David Farrar, Noelle Adam, Christopher Lee, Gillian Hills, Shirley Anne Field, Oliver Reed; **D:** Edmond T. Greville; **M:** John Barry. *SNC, FCT, HEG*

Beat Street 𝒵𝒵½ **1984 (PG)** Intended as a quick cash-in on the break dancing trend, this essentially plotless musical features kids trying to break into local show biz with their rapping and dancing skills. Features the music of Afrika Bambaata and the Soul Sonic Force, Grand Master Melle Mel and the Furious Five, and others. ♫Beat Street Breakdown; Baptize the Beat; Stranger in a Strange Land; Beat Street Strut; Us Girls; This Could be the Night; Breakers Revenge; Tu Carino (Carmen's Theme); Frantic Situation. **106m/C VHS, Beta, LV.** Rae Dawn Chong, Leon Grant, Saundra Santiago, Guy Davis, Jon Chardiet, Duane Jones, Kadeem Hardison; **D:** Stan Lathan; **W:** Andrew Davis. *VES, LIV*

Beat the Devil 𝒵𝒵𝒵 **1953** Each person on a slow boat to Africa has a scheme to beat the other passengers to the uranium-rich land that they all hope to claim. An unusual black comedy which didn't fare well when released, but over the years has come to be the epitome of spy-spoofs. **89m/C VHS, Beta, LV, Closed Caption.** Humphrey Bogart, Gina Lollobrigida, Peter Lorre, Robert Morley, Jennifer Jones, Edward Underdown, Ivor Barnard, Bernard Lee, Marco Tulli; **D:** John Huston; **W:** John Huston, Truman Capote; **C:** Oswald Morris. *MRV, NOS, COL*

Beatlemania! The Movie 𝒵 *Beatlemania* **1981** Boring look at the Fab Four. Not the real Beatles, but impersonators who do a very inadequate job. Based on the equally disappointing stage show. **86m/C VHS, Beta, LV.** Mitch Weissman, Ralph Castelli, David Leon, Tom Teeley; **D:** Joseph Manduke. *IME*

The Beatniks 𝒵 **1960** Story about the dark secrets of the beat generation in which a man is promised fame and fortune by an agent, but his dreams are dashed when his friend commits murder. A big waste of time. **78m/B VHS.** Tony Travis,

Peter Breck, Karen Kadler, Joyce Terry; **D:** Paul Frees. *SNC, TPV*

Beatrice ♬♬♬½ *La Passion Beatrice* **1988 (R)** In France during the Middle Ages, a barbaric soldier of the Hundred Years' War returns to his estate that his daughter has maintained, only to brutalize and abuse her. In French with English subtitles. **132m/C VHS, Beta, LV.** *FR* Julie Delpy, Barnard Pierre Donnadieu, Nils Tavernier; **D:** Bertrand Tavernier; **W:** Colo Tavernier O'Hagan; **C:** Bruno de Keyzer; **M:** Lili Boulanger. Cesar Awards '88: Best Costume Design. *NO*

Beau Brummel ♬♬½ **1924** The famous silent adaptation of the Clyde Fitch play about an ambitious English dandy's rise and fall. **80m/B VHS, Beta.** John Barrymore, Mary Astor, Willard Louis, Irene Rich, Carmel Myers, Alec B. Francis, William Humphreys; **D:** Harry Beaumont. *NOS, HHT, VYY*

Beau Brummel ♬♬♬ **1954** Lavish production casts Granger in the role of the rags-to-riches dandy and chief adviser to the Prince of Wales. Born into a life of poverty, George Bryan Brummel uses wit and intelligence to meet the vain Prince and ingratiate himself to the future king (George IV). He also manages to catch the eye of Taylor, who falls in love with him. Outstanding period piece cinematography, sets, and costumes. Shot on location in England's beautiful countryside, many of the interior shots are from a 15th-century mansion, Ockwell Manor, located near Windsor Castle. Remake of the 1924 silent film starring John Barrymore. Based on the play by Clyde Fitch. **113m/C VHS.** Stewart Granger, Elizabeth Taylor, Peter Ustinov, Robert Morley, James Donald, James Hayter, Rosemary Harris, Paul Rogers, Noel Willman, Peter Dyneley, Charles Carson; **D:** Curtis Bernhardt; **W:** Karl Tunberg; **C:** Oswald Morris. *MGM*

Beau Geste ♬♬♬½ **1939** The classic Hollywood adventure film based on the Percival Christopher Wren story about three brothers who join the Foreign Legion after nobly claiming responsibility for a jewel theft they didn't commit. Once enlisted, they must face desert wars and the most despicable commanding officer ever, before clearing their family name. A rousing, much-copied epic. **114m/B VHS, Beta.** Gary Cooper, Ray Milland, Robert Preston, Brian Donlevy, Donald O'Connor, J. Carrol Naish, Susan Hayward, James Stephenson; **D:** William A. Wellman. Nominations: Academy Awards '39: Best Interior Decoration, Best Supporting Actor (Donlevy). *USH*

Beau Pere ♬♬♬ *Stepfather* **1981** Bittersweet satiric romp from Blier about the war zone of modern romance, wherein a 30-year-old widower falls madly in love with his 14-year-old stepdaughter. Sharp-edged and daring. In French with subtitles. **125m/C VHS, Beta.** *FR* Patrick Dewaere, Nathalie Baye, Ariel Besse, Maurice Ronet; **D:** Bertrand Blier; **W:** Bertrand Blier; **C:** Sacha Vierny. *MED*

Beau Revel ♬♬♬½ **1921** Critically acclaimed romantic drama of the silent era. A passionate dancing girl played by Vidor, one of the twenties' more prolific romantic leads (and erstwhile wife of director King Vidor), is the object of romantic interest of a father and son, which leaves the threesome lovelorn, suicidal, and emotionally scarred. You might recognize Stone from his later role as Judge Hardy in the MGM "Hardy Family" series. **70m/B VHS, Beta.** Lewis Stone, Florence Vidor, Lloyd Hughes, Katherine Kirkham, William Conklin; **D:** John Wray. *GPV, FCT*

The Beautician and the Beast ♬♬ **1997 (PG)** Evita meets Lucille Ball when TV's "Nanny" enters Eastern Europe whining to conquer fictional "Slovetzia" royalty. Camp comedy casts Drescher as Joy, a beautician who becomes a local hero after a fire in her beauty class and is subsequently hired by a visiting emissary to tutor the children of despotic dictator Pochenko (Dalton). Overridingly well-known caricatures, loosely based on the fairy tale "Beauty and the Beast," as well as a host of old-time, culture clash movies ("The King and I," "Sound of Music"), where the humble nanny attempts to bring joy

(get it?) into the life of a man who carries the weight of the world on his shoulders. Lensed in Prague inside a Gothic, 17th-century castle. Pleasant enough, if not original, time-killer. **105m/C VHS.** Fran Drescher, Timothy Dalton, Ian McNeice, Patrick Malahide, Lisa Jakub, Michael Lerner, Phyllis Newman, Todd Graff; **D:** Ken Kwapis; **W:** Todd Graff; **C:** Peter Collister; **M:** Cliff Eidelman. *PAR*

Beauties of the Night ♬♬ *Night Beauties; Les Belles de Nuit* **1952** Dreamy fantasy finds a shy music teacher (Philipe) escaping from his boring life into romantic adventures with beautiful women. But his dreams slowly turn nightmarish and he's forced to deal with reality—and real love. French with subtitles. **89m/B VHS.** *FR* Gerard Philipe, Gina Lollobrigida, Martine Carol, Magali Vendeuil, Paolo Stoppa, Raymond Bussieres, Raymond Cordy; **D:** Rene Clair; **W:** Rene Clair; **C:** Armand Thirard; **M:** Georges Van Parys. *WBF*

The Beautiful Blonde from Bashful Bend ♬♬½ **1949** Charming comedy-western gets better with age. Grable is the pistol packing mama mistaken for the new school teacher. Fun performances by all, especially Herbert. **77m/C VHS, LV, Closed Caption.** Betty Grable, Cesar Romero, Rudy Vallee, Olga San Juan, Hugh Herbert, Porter Hall, Sterling Holloway, El Brendel; **D:** Preston Sturges. *FOX*

Beautiful Dreamers ♬½ **1992 (PG-13)** Maurice Bucke is a young Canadian physician who runs the London Insane Asylum. After a chance meeting with poet Walt Whitman, both men discover their mutual outrage for current treatment of the mentally ill. Bucke persuades Whitman to visit his asylum in order to try Whitman's theory of human compassion on the asylum's inmates. However, Bucke runs into opposition from the local townspeople, scandalized by Whitman's radical reputation. Fairly humdrum with a larger-than-life performance by Torn as Whitman. Based on Whitman's visit to Canada in 1880. **108m/C VHS, LV, Closed Caption.** *CA* Rip Torn, Colm Feore, Wendel Meldrum, Sheila McCarthy, Colin Fox; **D:** John Kent Harrison; **W:** John Kent Harrison. *HMD, FCT*

Beautiful Girls ♬♬½ **1996 (R)** Slow but easy-going film highlights the differences between men, women, and relationships. A 10-year high school reunion brings together buddies Tommy (Dillon), Kev (Perlich), Paul (Rappaport), and Willie (Hutton). They ice-fish, drink, and talk about women (about whom they haven't a clue). All are smitten by Andera (Thurman), the gorgeous visiting cousin of another friend, and Willie becomes intrigued by Marty (Portman), his precociously tantalizing 13-year-old neighbor. The guys whining gets annoying and the women are strictly secondary characters, but O'Donnell's tirade about fake femininity is amusing. The Afghan Whigs are featured as the bar band. **CW:** Strong language and nude pin-ups. **110m/C VHS, LV, Closed Caption.** Matt Dillon, Timothy Hutton, Michael Rapaport, Max Perlich, Noah Emmerich, Lauren Holly, Uma Thurman, Natalie Portman, Mira Sorvino, Martha Plimpton, Rosie O'Donnell, Annabeth Gish, Pruitt Taylor Vince, Sam Robards, David Arquette, Anne Bobby, Richard Bright; **D:** Ted Demme; **W:** Scott Rosenberg; **C:** Adam Kimmel; **M:** David A. Stewart. *TOU*

The Beautiful, the Bloody and the Bare ♬ **1969** Sordid screamer in the Herschell Gordon Lewis tradition. Set in New York City in the sixties, a depraved artist kills the nude models who pose for him. **?m/C VHS.** *MOV*

Beautiful Thing ♬♬♬ **1995 (R)** Sweet, fairytalish, gay coming-of-age story set in a working-class southeast London housing estate. Shy teenager Jamie (Berry) lives with his barmaid mum, Sandra (Henry), and her lover, Tony (Daniels). Next-door is his best mate, the stoic Ste (Neal), who's regularly abused by his father and brother. But when things get too bad, he sleeps over with Jamie. And one night, nature hesitantly takes its course. Their tart-tongued, Mama Cass fanatic, friend Leah (Empson) starts rumors about the twosome that lead to some uneasy (but ulti-

mately conciliatory) confrontations. Fine performances; Harvey adapted from his play. **CW:** Sexuality, pervasive strong language and some drug content. **89m/C VHS, Closed Caption.** *GB* Glen Berry, Scott Neal, Linda Henry, Tameka Empson, Ben Daniels; **D:** Hettie Macdonald; **W:** Jonathan Harvey; **C:** Chris Seager. *COL*

Beauty and the Beast ♬♬♬♬ *La Belle et Laete* **1946** The classic medieval fairy tale is brought to life on the big screen for the first time. Beauty takes the place of her father after he is sentenced to die by the horrible Beast and falls in love with him. Cocteau uses the story's themes and famous set-pieces to create a cohesive and captivating surreal hymn to romantic love that is still the definitive version of B&B. In French with subtitles. **90m/B VHS, Beta, LV.** *FR* Jean Marais, Josette Day, Marcel Andre, Mila Parely, Nane Germon, Michel Auclair, Georges Auric; **D:** Jean Cocteau. *HMV, MLB, CRC*

Beauty and the Beast ♬♬♬ **1983** From "Faerie Tale Theatre" comes the story of a Beauty who befriends a Beast and learns a lesson about physical appearance and true love. **60m/C VHS, Beta, LV, Closed Caption.** Susan Sarandon, Anjelica Huston, Klaus Kinski, Stephen Elliott; **D:** Roger Vadim. *FOX, FCT*

Beauty and the Beast ♬♬♬♬ **1991 (G)** Wonderful Disney musical combines superb animation, splendid characters, and lively songs about a beautiful girl, Belle, and the fearsome disagreeable Beast. Supporting cast includes the castle servants (a delightful bunch of household objects). Notable as the first animated feature to be nominated for the Best Picture Oscar. Destined to become a classic. The deluxe video version features a work-in-progress rough film cut, a compact disc of the soundtrack, a lithograph depicting a scene from the film, and an illustrated book. ♫Beauty and the Beast; Belle; Something There; Be Our Guest. **84m/C VHS, LV.** **D:** Kirk Wise, Gary Trousdale; **M:** Alan Menken, Howard Ashman; **V:** Paige O'Hara, Robby Benson, Rex Everhart, Richard White, Jesse Corti, Angela Lansbury, Jerry Orbach, David Ogden Stiers, Bradley Michael Pierce, Jo Anne Worley, Kimmy Robertson. Academy Awards '91: Best Song ("Beauty and the Beast"), Best Original Score; Golden Globe Awards '92: Best Film—Musical/Comedy; Nominations: Academy Awards '91: Best Picture, Best Song ("Belle," "Be Our Guest"), Best Sound. *DIS, OM*

Beauty and the Beast, Episode 1: Once Upon a Time in New York 1987 When socialite attorney Catherine Chandler is brutally attacked in New York, Vincent, a mysterious man/beast, rescues and befriends her, taking her to his fantastical subterranean world. Pilot for the popular television series. Additional episodes are available. **48m/C VHS, LV.** Ron Perlman, Linda Hamilton, Roy Dotrice, Ray Wise. *MOV*

Beauty and the Beast: Though Lovers Be Lost 1989 The love affair of Vincent and Catherine takes a tragic turn when she is kidnapped by a crime lord. Feature-length drama from the television series. **90m/C VHS, LV, Closed Caption.** Linda Hamilton, Ron Perlman. *REP*

Beauty and the Devil ♬♬ *La Beaute du Diable* **1950** Ambitious retelling of the Faust legend finds old Faust (Simon) willing to sell his soul to the Devil, courtesy of his agent Mephistopheles (Philipe), in return for youth and beauty to pursue the beautiful woman he loves. Clair has his actors trade roles midway through as Faust makes his bargain. French with subtitles. **97m/B VHS.** *FR* Michel Simon, Gerard Philipe, Simone Valere, Raymond Cordy, Gaston Modot, Paolo Stoppa, Nicole Besnard; **D:** Rene Clair; **W:** Rene Clair, Armand Salacrou; **C:** Michel Kelber; **M:** Roman Vlad. *WBF*

Beauty for the Asking ♬ **1939** It sounds like a workable Lucille Ball vehicle—a beautician develops a bestselling skin cream—and even the title sounds like something you'd like to love Lucy in. But somehow the numerous plot implausibilities managed to get by the story's five writers, and the idea of a jilted woman making millions while being financed by her ex's wife just doesn't fly (perhaps it was an idea ahead of its time). Die-hard Lucy fans may find this interesting. **68m/B VHS.** Lucille Ball, Patric Knowles, Donald Woods, Frieda Inescort, Frances Mercer; **D:** Glenn Tryon. *TTC, FCT*

Beauty on the Beach ♂ 196? A comedy about a mad psychologist, his bizarre experiments with women, and his eventual descent into insanity. In Italian with English subtitles. **90m/C VHS, Beta.** *IT* Valeria Fabrizi. *NO*

Beauty School ♂ *Sylvia Kristel's Beauty School* 1993 (R) The promise of an advertising contract pits the owners of rival beauty schools against each other. **95m/C VHS, LV.** Sylvia Kristel, Kevin Bernhardt, Kimberly Taylor, Jane Hamilton; **D:** Ernest G. Sauer; **W:** Mike MacDonald, Merrill Friedman; **M:** Jonathan Hannah. *IMP*

Beavis and Butt-Head Do America ♂♂½ 1996 (PG-13) Moronic MTV metalheads go on the road in search of their stolen TV and are somehow mistaken for criminal masterminds. Okay, enough about plot. If you're thinking of renting this one, you don't care about that stuff anyway. Director/writer/voice of B&B Judge is smart enough not to change our "heroes" just because they're on a bigger screen. They're still stupid, obsessed with chicks (Yeah! Chicks are cool!) and blissfully unaware of what's happening around them. The opening sequence, a parody of 70s cop shows, is hilarious (and cool). For those who like the show, and for people who just don't admit that they do, the boys' movie debut (he said "but") doesn't suck. **CW:** Continuous crude sex-related humor and language, and a drug-related scene. **82m/C VHS, Beta, Closed Caption. D:** Mike Judge; **W:** Mike Judge, Joe Stillman; **M:** John Frizzell; **V:** Mike Judge, Robert Stack, Cloris Leachman, Demi Moore, Eric Bogosian, Richard Linklater. Nominations: MTV Movie Awards '97: Best On-Screen Duo (Beavis/Butt-head). *PAR*

Bebe's Kids ♂♂½ 1992 (PG-13) When ladies' man Robin falls for the lovely Jamika, he gets some unexpected surprises when he takes her out on a first date to an amusement park—and she brings along four kids. Animated comedy takes some funny pot-shots at both black and white culture and Disneyland. The children are amusing, especially baby PeeWee, a tot with chronically dirty diapers and Tone Loc's gravelly voice. Based on characters created by the late comedian Robin Harris. The video includes the seven-minute animated short "Itsy Bitsy Spider." **74m/C VHS, Beta, LV, Closed Caption. D:** Bruce Smith; **W:** Reginald Hudlin; **M:** John Barnes; **V:** Faizon Love, Vanessa Bell Calloway, Wayne Collins, Jonell Green, Marques Houston, Tone Loc, Nell Carter, Myra J. *PAR*

Because of the Cats ♂½ 1974 Police inspector uncovers an evil cult within his seaside village while investigating a bizarre rape and burglary. **90m/C VHS, Beta.** Bryan Marshall, Alexandra Stewart, Alex Van Rooyen, Sylvia Kristel, Sebastian Graham Jones; **D:** Fons Rademakers. *PSM*

Because You're Mine ♂♂ 1952 Lanza plays an opera star who is drafted and falls in love with Morrow, his top sergeant's sister. Plenty of singing—maybe too much at times, but Lanza's fans will enjoy it nonetheless. ♫All the Things You Are; Because You're Mine; Be My Love; Granada; Lee-Ah-Loo; The Lord's Prayer; The Song Angels Sing; You Do Something to Me. **103m/C VHS.** Mario Lanza, James Whitmore, Doretta Morrow, Dean Miller, Rita (Paula) Corday, Jeff Donnell, Spring Byington; **D:** Alexander Hall. Nominations: Academy Awards '52: Best Song ("Because You're Mine"). *MGM*

Becket ♂♂♂♂ 1964 Adaptation of Jean Anouilh's play about the tumultuous friendship between Henry II of England and the Archbishop of Canterbury Thomas Becket. Becket views his position in the church of little relation to the sexual and emotional needs of a man, until he becomes archbishop. His growing concern for religion and his shrinking need of Henry as friend and confidant eventually cause the demise of the friendship and the resulting tragedy. Flawless acting from every cast member, and finely detailed artistic direction make up for the occasional slow moment. **148m/C VHS, Beta, LV.** Richard Burton, Peter O'Toole, John Gielgud, Donald Wolfit; **D:** Peter Glenville; **W:** Edward Anhalt; **C:** Geoffrey Unsworth. Academy Awards '64: Best Adapted Screenplay; Golden Globe Awards '65: Best Actor—Drama (O'Toole), Best Film—Drama; National Board of Review Awards '64: 10 Best Films of the Year; Nominations: Academy Awards '64: Best Actor (Burton), Best Actor (O'Toole), Best Art Direction/Set Decoration (Color), Best Color Cinematography, Best Costume Design (Color), Best Director (Glenville), Best Film Editing, Best Picture, Best Sound, Best Supporting Actor (Gielgud), Best Original Score. *MPI, TVC*

Becky Sharp ♂♂½ 1935 This premiere Technicolor film tells the story of Becky Sharp, a wicked woman who finally performs one good deed. **83m/C VHS, Beta.** Miriam Hopkins, Frances Dee, Cedric Hardwicke, Billie Burke, Nigel Bruce, Pat Nixon; **D:** Rouben Mamoulian; **C:** Ray Rennahan. Nominations: Academy Awards '35: Best Actress (Hopkins). *NOS, MRV, HEG*

Becoming Colette ♂♂ 1992 (R) Tedious flashbacking bio of French writer Colette, from her innocent days in the country to her (bad) marriage to writer/publisher Willy and on and on to her own growing career as a writer. She begins writing stories, using an alter-ego character, Claudine, which detail her sexual escapades. Lots of naked flesh but little passion. A postscript notes that Colette wrote "Gigi" and was the first woman to receive the French Legion of Honor. **CW:** Strong sexuality. **97m/C VHS, Closed Caption.** Mathilda May, Klaus Maria Brandauer, Virginia Madsen, Paul Rhys, Jean-Pierre Aumont, John van Dreelen, Lucienne Hamon; **D:** Danny Huston; **W:** Ruth Graham; **M:** John Scott. *ACA*

Bed & Breakfast ♂♂½ 1992 (PG-13) Three generations of women lead quiet lives while running a failing Nantucket bed and breakfast. When a mystery man washes up on their beach, he charms them all, but it seems that he has a past that could endanger everyone. Lightweight final role for Dewhurst, though she provides some sparks as the strong and loving matriarch. Gentle romantic comedy skims the surface, but is still enjoyable. **97m/C VHS, LV, Closed Caption.** Roger Moore, Talia Shire, Colleen Dewhurst, Nina Siemaszko, Ford Rainey, Stephen Root, Jamie Walters, Victor Slezak; **D:** Robert Ellis Miller; **W:** Cindy Myers; **M:** David Shire. *HMD*

Bed and Sofa ♂♂♂½ 1927 Adultery, abortion, and women's rights are brought about by a housing shortage which forces a man to move in with a married friend. Famous, groundbreaking Russian silent. **73m/B VHS, Beta.** *RU* Nikolai Batalov, Vladimar Fogel; **D:** Abram Room. *IHF*

Bed of Roses ♂♂½ *Amelia and the King of Plants* 1995 (PG) Wistful romance finds workaholic investment banker Lisa Walker (Masterson) receiving lavish floral tributes from an unknown admirer. When Lisa tracks her giver down, it turns out to be lovestruck widowed florist Lewis Farrell (Slater), who noticed Lisa crying through her apartment window and sent the flowers to cheer her up. Best friend Kim (Seagall) urges Lisa to go for Lewis but a problematic past has Lisa distrusting her emotions and their romantic path has a few bumps (easily overcome). Appealing leads, lots of cliches. Goldenberg's debut. **88m/C VHS, LV, Closed Caption.** Christian Slater, Mary Stuart Masterson, Pamela Segall, Josh Brolin, Ally Walker, Debra Monk; **D:** Michael Goldenberg; **W:** Michael Goldenberg; **C:** Adam Kimmel; **M:** Michael Convertino. *NLC*

Bedazzled ♂♂♂ 1968 (PG) In the process of hanging himself, Stanley, a short-order cook is approached by the devil with an offer: seven wishes in exchange for his soul. Each of Stanley's wishes is granted with surprising consequences. Cult comedy is a sometimes uneven, but thoroughly entertaining and funny retelling of the Faustian story. **107m/C VHS, Beta, LV.** *GB* Dudley Moore, Peter Cook, Eleanor Bron, Michael Bates, Raquel Welch, Bernard Spear, Parnell McGarry, Howard Goorney, Daniele Noel, Barry Humphries, Robert Russell, Lockwood West, Robin Hawdon, Evelyn Moore, Charles Lloyd Pack; **D:** Stanley Donen; **W:** Dudley Moore, Peter Cook; **C:** Austin Dempster; **M:** Dudley Moore. *FOX*

Bedford Incident ♂♂½ 1965 The U.S.S. Bedford discovers an unidentified submarine in North Atlantic waters. The Bedford's commander drives his crew to the point of exhaustion as they find themselves the center of a fateful controversy. **102m/B VHS, Beta, LV.** Richard Widmark, Sidney Poitier, James MacArthur, Martin Balsam, Wally Cox, Donald Sutherland, Eric Portman; **D:** James B. Harris. *COL, IME*

Bedknobs and Broomsticks ♂♂½ 1971 (G) A novice witch and three cockney waifs ride a magic bedstead and stop the Nazis from invading England during WWII. Celebrated for its animated art. **117m/C VHS, Beta, LV.** Angela Lansbury, Roddy McDowall, David Tomlinson, Bruce Forsyth, Sam Jaffe; **D:** Robert Stevenson. Academy Awards '71: Best Visual Effects; Nominations: Academy Awards '71: Best Art Direction/Set Decoration, Best Costume Design, Best Song ("The Age of Not Believing"), Original Song Score and/or Adaptation. *DIS*

Bedlam ♂♂♂ 1945 Creeper set in the famed asylum in 18th-century London. A woman, wrongfully committed, tries to stop the evil doings of the chief (Karloff) of Bedlam, and endangers herself. Fine horror film co-written by producer Lewton. **79m/B VHS, Beta, LV.** Jason Robards Sr., Ian Wolfe, Glenn Vernon, Boris Karloff, Anna Lee, Billy House, Richard Fraser; **D:** Mark Robson. *TTC, MED, FCT*

Bedroom Eyes ♂♂ 1986 (R) A successful businessman becomes a voyeur by returning nightly to a beautiful woman's window, until she is killed and he is the prime suspect. Part comic, part disappointing thriller. **90m/C VHS, Beta, LV.** Kenneth Gilman, Dayle Haddon, Christine Cattall; **D:** William Fruet. *FOX*

Bedroom Eyes 2 ♂♂ 1989 (R) After discovering his wife has had an affair, a stockbroker takes a lover. When she turns up dead, he and his wife become murder suspects. Provides some suspenseful moments. **85m/C VHS, LV.** Wings Hauser, Kathy Shower, Linda Blair, Jane Hamilton, Jennifer Delora; **D:** Chuck Vincent. *THV, IME*

The Bedroom Window ♂♂½ 1987 (R) Guttenberg is having an illicit affair with his boss' wife (Huppert), who witnesses an assault on another woman (McGovern) from the bedroom window. To keep the affair secret Guttenberg reports the crime, but since it is secondhand, the account is flawed and he becomes a suspect. Semi-tight thriller reminiscent of Hitchcock mysteries isn't always believable, but is otherwise interesting. **113m/C VHS, Beta, LV, Closed Caption.** Steve Guttenberg, Elizabeth McGovern, Isabelle Huppert, Wallace Shawn, Paul Shenar, Carl Lumbly, Frederick Coffin, Brad Greenquist; **D:** Curtis Hanson; **W:** Curtis Hanson; **M:** Patrick Gleeson, Michael Shrieve, Felix Mendelssohn. *FHE, VES, LIV*

Bedtime for Bonzo ♂♂½ 1951 A professor adopts a chimp to prove that environment, not hereditary, determines a child's future. Fun, lighthearted comedy that stars a future president. Followed by "Bonzo Goes to College." **83m/B VHS, Beta.** Ronald Reagan, Diana Lynn, Walter Slezak, Jesse White, Bonzo the Chimp; **D:** Fred de Cordova. *USH, FCT*

Bedtime Story ♂♂ 1963 Two con artists attempt to fleece an apparently wealthy woman and each other on the French Riviera. Re-made in 1988 as "Dirty Rotten Scoundrels." One of Brando's thankfully few forays into comedy. **99m/C VHS, Beta.** Marlon Brando, David Niven, Shirley Jones, Dody Goodman, Marie Windsor; **D:** Ralph Levy. *USH*

Beer ♂ 1985 (R) A female advertising executive devises a dangerous sexist campaign for a cheap beer, and both the beer and its nickname become nationwide obsessions. Not especially amusing. **83m/C VHS, Beta, Closed Caption.** Loretta Swit, Rip Torn, Dick Shawn, David Alan Grier, William Russ,

Kenneth Mars, Peter Michael Goetz; **D:** Patrick Kelly; **C:** Bill Butler; **M:** Bill Conti. *NO*

The Bees woof! **1978 (PG)** Sting of a poor movie is painful. A strain of bees have ransacked South America and are threatening the rest of the world. The buzz is that no one is safe. Cheap rip-off of "The Swarm," which is saying something. **93m/C VHS, Beta.** John Saxon, John Carradine, Angel Tompkins, Claudio Brook, Alicia Encinas; **D:** Alfredo Zacharias. *WAR*

Beethoven *Beethoven's Great Love; The Life and Loves of Beethoven; Un Grand Amour de Beethoven* **1936** Startling biography of the musical genius, filled with opulent, impressionistic visuals. **116m/B VHS.** *FR* Harry Baur, Jean-Louis Barrault, Marcel Dalio; **W:** Abel Gance. *CVC, TPV*

Beethoven 🐾🐾½ **1992 (PG)** Adorable St. Bernard puppy escapes from dognappers and wanders into the home of the Newtons, who, over dad's objections, adopt him. Beethoven grows into a huge, slobbering dog who sorely tries dad's patience. To make matters worse, two sets of villains also wreak havoc on the Newton's lives. Evil veterinarian Dr. Varnick plots to steal Beethoven for lab experiments, and yuppie couple Brad and Brie plot to take over the family business. Enjoyable cast, particularly Grodin as dad and Chris as Beethoven enable this movie to please more than the milk and cookies set. Followed by "Beethoven's 2nd." **89m/C VHS, LV, Closed Caption.** Charles Grodin, Bonnie Hunt, Dean Jones, Oliver Platt, Stanley Tucci, Nicholle Tom, Christopher Castile, Sarah Rose Karr, David Duchovny, Patricia Heaton, Laurel Cronin; **D:** Brian Levant; **W:** John Hughes, Amy Holden Jones. *USH, FCT*

Beethoven Lives Upstairs 🐾🐾½ **1992** In 19th century Vienna 10 year-old Christoph's life is turned upside-down when the family's eccentric new tenant turns out to be composer Ludwig Van Beethoven. In time, Christoph comes to appreciate the beauty of the music and the tragedy of the composer's deafness. Features more than 25 excerpts of Beethoven's works. **52m/C VHS, Closed Caption.** Neil Munro, Illya Woloshyn, Fiona Reid, Paul Soles, Sheila McCarthy, Albert Schultz; **D:** David Devine; **W:** Heather Conkie. *BMG, MVD*

Beethoven's Nephew 🐾½ *Le Neveu de Beethoven* **1988** A tepid pseudo-historical farce about Beethoven's strange obsession with his only nephew. Directed by erstwhile Warhol collaborator Morrissey. **103m/C VHS, Beta, LV.** *FR* Wolfgang Reichmann, Ditmar Prinz, Jane Birkin, Nathalie Baye; **D:** Paul Morrissey; **W:** Paul Morrissey, Matthieu Carriere. *NWV, VTR*

Beethoven's 2nd 🐾🐾½ **1993 (PG)** Sequel has awwww factor going for it as new daddy Beethoven slobbers over four adorable and appealing St. Bernard pups and his new love Missy. Same basic evil subplot as the first, with wicked kidnappers replacing evil vet. During the upheaval, the Newtons take care of the little yapping troublemakers, providing the backdrop for endless puppy mischief and exasperation on Grodin's part. Silly subplots and too many human moments tend to drag, but the kids will find the laughs (albeit stupid ones). **87m/C VHS, LV, Closed Caption.** Charles Grodin, Bonnie Hunt, Nicholle Tom, Christopher Castile, Sarah Rose Karr, Debi Mazar, Christopher Penn, Ashley Hamilton; **D:** Rod Daniel; **W:** Len Blum; **C:** Bill Butler; **M:** Randy Edelman. Nominations: Academy Awards '93: Best Song ("The Day I Fall in Love"); Golden Globe Awards '94: Best Song ("The Day I Fall in Love"). *USH*

Beetlejuice 🐾🐾🐾½ **1988 (PG)** The after-life is confusing for a pair of ultra-nice novice ghosts who are faced with chasing an obnoxious family of post-modern art lovers who move into their house. Then they hear of a poltergeist who promises to rid the house of all trespassers for a price. Things go from bad to impossible when the maniacal Keaton (as the demonic "Betelgeuse") works his magic. The calypso scene is priceless. A cheesy, funny, surreal farce of life after death with inventive set designs popping continual surprises. Ryder is striking as the misunderstood teen with a

death complex, while O'Hara is hilarious as the yuppie art poseur. **92m/C VHS, Beta, LV, 8mm, Closed Caption, DVD.** Michael Keaton, Geena Davis, Alec Baldwin, Sylvia Sidney, Catherine O'Hara, Winona Ryder, Jeffrey Jones, Dick Cavett; **D:** Tim Burton; **W:** Michael McDowell, Warren Skaaren; **C:** Thomas Ackerman; **M:** Danny Elfman. Academy Awards '88: Best Makeup; National Society of Film Critics Awards '88: Best Actor (Keaton). *WAR, FCT, TLF*

Before and After 🐾½ **1995 (PG-13)** Disjointed drama depicts well-off suburban couple, Carolyn (Streep) and Ben (Neeson), who are thrown into chaos when their teenaged son Jacob (Furlong) is accused of murdering his girlfriend. Upon notification by the police that his son is the prime suspect and on the lam, Ben finds what seems to be bloody evidence in the family's car, which he destroys. The story loses steam from there. Based on the novel by Rosellen Brown, the focus is on the effect the death has on this picture book Massachusetts family. Neeson and Streep fall short of usually deliverable goods and director Schroeder takes the middle-of-the-road sentimental approach. *CW:* Some disturbing images of violence, brief strong language and some sensuality. **107m/C VHS, LV, Closed Caption.** Meryl Streep, Liam Neeson, Edward Furlong, Alfred Molina, John Heard, Julia Weldon, Daniel von Bargen, John Heard, Ann Magnuson, Alison Folland, Kaiulani Lee; **D:** Barbet Schroeder; **W:** Ted Tally; **C:** Luciano Tovoli; **M:** Howard Shore. *TOU*

Before I Hang 🐾🐾🐾 **1940** When a doctor invents a youth serum from the blood of a murderer, he'll stop at nothing to keep his secret. Karloff himself stands the test of time, and is satisfying as the mad scientist, giving this horror flick its appeal. **60m/B VHS, Beta.** Boris Karloff, Evelyn Keyes, Bruce (Herman Brix) Bennett, Edward Van Sloan; **D:** Nick Grinde. *COL*

Before Morning 🐾½ **1933** Police officer poses as a blackmailer to find out which of the two women in the murder victim's life are guilty. **68m/B VHS, Beta, LV.** Leo Carrillo, Lora Baxter, Taylor Holmes. *NO*

Before Sunrise 🐾🐾½ **1994 (R)** Light, "getting-to-know-you," romance unfolds as two twenty-somethings share an unlikely 14-hour date. Gen-Xer Jesse (Hawke) and French beauty (Delpy) meet on the Eurail and he convinces her to join him in exploring Vienna and their mutual attraction before he heads back to the States in the morning. The two exchange life experiences and philosophies in the typical Linklater conversational fashion, but the film strays from the comical accounts of earlier works "Slacker" and "Dazed and Confused". Cinematographer Daniel captures the Old World with finesse, especially in the inevitable "first kiss" atop the Ferris wheel made famous in Orson Welles' "The Third Man". *CW:* Some strong language. **101m/C VHS, LV, Closed Caption.** Ethan Hawke, Julie Delpy; **D:** Richard Linklater; **W:** Richard Linklater, Kim Krizan; **C:** Lee Daniel. Berlin International Film Festival '94: Best Director (Linklater); Nominations: MTV Movie Awards '95: Best Kiss (Ethan Hawke/ Julie Delpy). *COL*

Before the Rain 🐾🐾🐾 *Po Dezju* **1994** War-torn Macedonia is the backdrop for Manchevski's first film (and first made in the newly declared republic of Macedonia). Powerful circular narrative joins three stories about the freedom of love and the pervasiveness of violence. "Words" finds young Macedonian monk Kiril (Colin) distracted from his spiritual duties by young Albanian Muslim Zamira (Mitevska), who takes refuge in his monastery. In "Faces," pregnant picture editor Anne (Cartlidge) is torn between her estranged husband and her lover, Aleksander (Serbedzija), a London-based war photographer who left his native Macedonia years before. "Pictures" finds Aleksandar returning to his old village—now torn by ethnic strife. In Macedonian, Albanian, and English, with subtitles. **120m/C VHS.** *GB FR MA* Rade Serbedzija, Katrin Cartlidge, Gregoire Colin, Labina Mitevska; **D:** Milcho Manchevski; **W:** Milcho Man-

chevski; **C:** Manuel Teran; **M:** Anastasia. Independent Spirit Awards '96: Best Foreign Film; Venice Film Festival '94: Golden Lion; Nominations: Academy Awards '94: Best Foreign Language Film. *PGV*

Before the Revolution 🐾🐾 **1965** One of Bertolucci's first films. Love and politics are mixed when the young Fabrizio, who is dabbling in communism, is also flirting with his young aunt. Striking and powerful film that has yet to lose its effect despite the times. Italian with subtitles. **115m/C VHS.** *IT* Francesco Barilli, Adrianna Asti, Alain Midgette, Morando Morandini, Domenico Alpi; **D:** Bernardo Bertolucci; **W:** Bernardo Bertolucci; **M:** Ennio Morricone, Gato Barbieri. *NYF*

Beggars in Ermine 🐾🐾 **1934** A handicapped, impoverished man organizes all the beggars in the world into a successful corporation. Unusual performance from Atwill. **70m/B VHS, Beta.** Lionel Atwill, Henry B. Walthall, Betty Furness, Jameson Thomas, James Bush, Astrid Allwyn, George "Gabby" Hayes; **D:** Phil Rosen. *VYY, SNC*

Beginning of the End 🐾½ **1957** Produced the same year as "The Deadly Mantis," Gordon's effort adds to 1957's harvest of bugs on a rampage "B"-graders. Giant, radiation-spawned grasshoppers attack Chicago causing Graves to come to the rescue. Easily the best giant grasshopper movie ever made. **73m/B VHS, Beta.** Peggy Castle, Peter Graves, Morris Ankrum, Richard Benedict, James Seay; **D:** Bert I. Gordon. *NO*

The Beguiled 🐾🐾🐾 **1970 (R)** During the Civil War a wounded Union soldier is taken in by the women at a girl's school in the South. He manages to seduce both a student and a teacher, and jealousy and revenge ensue. Decidedly weird psychological melodrama from action vets Siegel and Eastwood. **109m/C VHS, Beta, LV.** Clint Eastwood, Geraldine Page, Elizabeth Hartman, Jo Ann Harris; **D:** Donald Siegel; **C:** Bruce Surtees; **M:** Lalo Schifrin. *USH*

Behave Yourself! 🐾½ **1952** A married couple adopts a dog who may be the key for a million-dollar hijacking setup by a gang of hoodlums. **81m/B VHS, Beta.** Shelley Winters, Farley Granger, William Demarest, Lon Chaney Jr., Hans Conried, Elisha Cook Jr., Francis L. Sullivan; **D:** George Beck. *NOS*

Behind Enemy Lines 🐾½ **1985 (R)** Special Forces soldier goes on a special mission to eliminate a possible Nazi spy. Made for television. **83m/C VHS, Beta.** Hal Holbrook, Ray Sharkey, David McCallum, Tom Isbell, Anne Twomey, Robert Patrick; **D:** Sheldon Larry. *MED*

Behind Locked Doors 🐾🐾½ **1948** A journalist fakes mental illness to have himself committed to an asylum, where he believes a crooked judge is in hiding. A superior "B" mystery/suspense feature, with some tense moments. **61m/B VHS.** Lucille Bremer, Richard Carlson, Tor Johnson, Douglas Fowley, Herbert Heyes, Ralf Harolde; **D:** Budd Boetticher. *VDM*

Behind Office Doors 🐾🐾 **1931** Astor stars as the secretarial "power behind the throne" in this look at who really wields power in an office. Her boss takes her for granted until things go wrong. **82m/B VHS.** Mary Astor, Robert Ames, Ricardo Cortez, Charles Sellon; **D:** Melville Brown. *NOS, HEG*

Behind Prison Walls 🐾🐾 *Youth Takes a Hand* **1943** A steel tycoon and his son are sent to prison, and the son tries to convert his dad to socialism. A fun, light hearted film, the last for veteran Tully. **64m/B VHS.** Alan Baxter, Gertrude Michael, Tully Marshall, Edwin Maxwell, Jacqueline Dalya, Matt Willis; **D:** Steve Sekely. *SNC*

Behind the Front 🐾🐾½ **1926** Two friends tumble in and out of trouble in this comic Army film. One of the most profitable films of the late twenties. **60m/B VHS.** Wallace Beery, Raymond Hatton, Richard Arlen, Mary Brian, Chester Conklin; **D:** Edward Sutherland. *GPV*

Behind the Mask 🐾🐾½ **1946** Lamont Cranston, better known as do-gooder "The Shadow," finds himself accused of murdering a blackmailing newspaper reporter. Based on the radio serial. **68m/C VHS.** Kane Richmond, Barbara Read, George Chandler, Dorothea Kent, Robert Shayne, June Clyde; *D:* Phil Karlson. *GPV, ADL*

Behind the Rising Sun 🎞🎞½ 1943 A
Japanese publisher's political views clash with those of his American-educated son in 1930s Japan. Well done despite pre-war propaganda themes. **88m/B VHS, Beta.** Tom Neal, J. Carrol Naish, Robert Ryan, Mike Mazurki, Margo, Gloria Holden, Don Douglas; *D:* Edward Dmytryk. *NO*

Behold a Pale Horse 🎞🎞½ 1964 A
Spanish police captain attempts to dupe Peck into believing that his mother is dying and he must visit her on her deathbed. Loyalist Spaniard Peck becomes privy to the plot against him, but goes to Spain anyway in this post Spanish Civil War film. **118m/B VHS, Beta.** Gregory Peck, Anthony Quinn, Omar Sharif, Mildred Dunnock; *D:* Fred Zinnemann; *M:* Maurice Jarre. *GKK*

The Being 🎞 1983 (R) People in Idaho are
terrorized by a freak who became abnormal after radiation was disposed in the local dump. Another dull monster-created-by-nuclear-waste non-event. Of limited interest is Buzzi. However, you'd be more entertained (read: amused) by Troma's "The Toxic Avenger," which takes itself much (much!) less seriously. **82m/C VHS, Beta.** Ruth Buzzi, Martin Landau, Jose Ferrer; *D:* Jackie Kong. *NO*

Being at Home with Claude 🎞🎞
1992 Yves (Godin) is a 22-year-old Montreal hustler being interrogated by a nameless inspector (Dupuis) for the murder of his lover, Claude (Pichette). Yves has admitted his guilt but the inspector wants to reconstruct the event and determine a motive. Lots of black-and-white flashbacks as Yves dwells on his work and his psychologically love-death relationship with Claude. Rather pretentious and long-winded. Based on the play by Rene-Daniel DuBois. In French with English subtitles. **86m/C VHS.** *CA* Roy Dupuis, Jacques Godin, Jean-Francois Pichette, Gaston Lepage; *D:* Johanne Boisvert; *W:* Jean Boudin. Genie Awards '92: Best Score. *ACA, FCT*

Being Human 🎞🎞½ 1994 (PG-13) Ambi-
tious comedy drama promises more than it delivers, and shackles Williams in the process. Hector (Williams) is a regular guy continuously reincarnated throughout the millennia. He plays a caveman, a Roman slave, a Middle Ages nomad, a crew member on a 17th century new world voyage, and a modern New Yorker in separate vignettes that echo and/or extend the main themes of family, identity, and random fate. But he manages to emerge from each sketch as an unassuming everyman who never learns his lesson. One of Williams' periodic chancy ventures away from his comedic roots occasionally strikes gold, but often seems overly restrained. *CW:* Language, elements of violence, and elements of sensuality. **122m/C VHS, LV, Closed Caption.** Robin Williams, John Turturro, Anna Galiena, Vincent D'Onofrio, Hector Elizondo, Lorraine Bracco, Lindsay Crouse, Kelly Hunter, William H. Macy, Grace Mahlaba, Theresa Russell, Charles Miller, Helen Miller; *D:* Bill Forsyth; *W:* Bill Forsyth; *C:* Michael Coulter; *M:* Michael Gibbs. *WAR*

Being There 🎞🎞🎞½ 1979 (PG) A feeble-
minded gardener, whose entire knowledge of life comes from watching television, is sent out into the real world when his employer dies. Equipped with his prize possession, his remote control unit, the gardener unwittingly enters the world of politics and is welcomed as a mysterious sage. Sellers is wonderful in this satiric treat adapted by Jerzy Kosinski from his novel. **130m/C VHS, Beta, LV, Closed Caption.** Peter Sellers, Shirley MacLaine, Melvyn Douglas, Jack Warden, Richard Dysart, Richard Basehart; *D:* Hal Ashby; *C:* Caleb Deschanel. Academy Awards '79: Best Supporting Actor (Douglas); British Academy Awards '90: Best Screenplay; Golden Globe Awards '80: Best Actor—Musical/Comedy (Sellers), Best Supporting Actor (Douglas); Los Angeles Film Critics Association Awards '79: Best Supporting Actor (Douglas); National Board of Review Awards '79: 10 Best Films of the Year, Best Actor

(Sellers); New York Film Critics Awards '79: Best Supporting Actor (Douglas); National Society of Film Critics Awards '79: Best Cinematography; Writers Guild of America '79: Best Adapted Screenplay; Nominations: Academy Awards '79: Best Actor (Sellers). *FOX, FCT, WAR*

Being Two Isn't Easy 🎞🎞½ 1962 Di-
rector Ichikawa shows the world through the eyes of a two-year-old as a young couple struggle to raise their son. In Japanese with English subtitles. **88m/C VHS.** *JP* Fujiko Yamamoto, Eiji Funakoshi; *D:* Kon Ichikawa. *HMV, FCT*

Bela Lugosi Meets a Brooklyn
Gorilla woof! *The Boys from Brooklyn* 1952 Two
men who look like Dean Martin and Jerry Lewis (but aren't) get lost in the jungle, where they meet mad scientist Lugosi. Worse than it sounds. Real Jerry sued for unflattering imitation. **74m/B VHS, Beta.** Bela Lugosi, Duke Mitchell, Sammy Petrillo; *D:* William Beaudine. *NOS, SNC, AOV*

Belfast Assassin 🎞 1984 A British anti-
terrorist agent goes undercover in Ireland to find an IRA assassin who shot a British cabinet minister. **130m/C VHS, Beta.** Derek Thompson, Ray Lonnen. *PSM*

The Believers 🎞🎞½ 1987 (R) Tense hor-
ror mystery set in New York city about a series of gruesome, unexplained murders. A widowed police psychologist investigating the deaths unwittingly discovers a powerful Santeria cult that believes in the sacrifice of children. Without warning he is drawn into the circle of the "Believers" and must free himself before his own son is the next sacrifice. Gripping (and grim), unrelenting horror. **114m/C VHS, Beta, LV, Closed Caption.** Martin Sheen, Helen Shaver, Malick Bowens, Harris Yulin, Robert Loggia, Jimmy Smits, Richard Masur, Harley Cross, Elizabeth Wilson, Lee Richardson; *D:* John Schlesinger; *W:* Mark Frost; *M:* J. Peter Robinson. *HBO*

Belizaire the Cajun 🎞🎞½ 1986 (PG)
19th-century Louisiana love story. White prejudice against the Cajuns is rampant and violent, but that doesn't stop sexy faith healer Assante from falling in love with the inaccessible Cajun wife (Youngs) of a rich local. Made with care on a tight budget. Worthwhile, though uneven. **103m/C VHS, Beta, Closed Caption.** Armand Assante, Gail Youngs, Will Patton, Stephen McHattie, Michael Schoeffling, Robert Duvall, Nancy Barrett; *D:* Glen Pitre; *W:* Glen Pitre; *C:* Richard Bowen; *M:* Michael Doucet, Howard Shore. *FOX*

Bell, Book and Candle 🎞🎞½ 1958 A
young witch makes up her mind to refrain from using her powers. When an interesting man moves into her building, she forgets her decision and enchants him with a love spell. **106m/C VHS, Beta, LV, Closed Caption.** James Stewart, Kim Novak, Jack Lemmon, Elsa Lanchester, Ernie Kovacs, Hermione Gingold; *D:* Richard Quine; *W:* Daniel Taradash; *C:* James Wong Howe; *M:* George Duning. Nominations: Academy Awards '58: Best Art Direction/Set Decoration, Best Costume Design. *COL, FCT, MLB*

Bell Diamond 🎞🎞 1981 A study by the ex-
perimental filmmaker of a Vietnam vet surviving in a bankrupt mining town. Created without a script using non-professional actors. **96m/C VHS, Beta.** *D:* Jon Jost. *FCT*

Bell from Hell 🎞🎞 1974 A tale of insanity
and revenge, wherein a young man, institutionalized since his mother's death, plots to kill his aunt and three cousins. **80m/C VHS, Beta.** Viveca Lindfors, Renaud Verley, Alfredo Mayo; *D:* Claudio Guerin Hill. *UNI*

The Bell Jar 🎞½ 1979 (R) Based on poet
Sylvia Plath's acclaimed semi-autobiographical novel, this is the story of a young woman who becomes the victim of mental illness. Not for the easily depressed and a disjointed and disappointing adaptation of Plath's work. **113m/C VHS, Beta.** Marilyn Hassett, Julie Harris, Barbara Barrie, Anne Bancroft, Robert Klein, Anne Jackson; *D:* Larry Peerce. *VES*

Bell Ringer of Antigua 🎞🎞 1946 In-
spirational story by Royer, one of Hollywood's pioneering women. Shot on location in Guatemala. **?m/C VHS.** *D:* Fanchon Royer; *W:* Fanchon Royer. *LOO*

Bellamy 🎞 1980 Murderous madman massa-
cres masseuses, and Bellamy is the cop out to get him. **92m/C VHS, Beta.** John Stanton, Timothy Elston, Sally Conabere; *D:* Colin Eggleston, Pino Amenta. *NO*

The Bellboy 🎞🎞½ 1960 Lewis makes his
directorial debut in this plotless but clever outing. He also stars as the eponymous character, a bellboy at Miami's Fountainbleau Hotel. Cameos from Berle and Winchell are highlights. **72m/B VHS, Beta, LV.** Jerry Lewis, Alex Gerry, Bob Clayton, Sonny Sands; *Cameos:* Milton Berle, Walter Winchell; *D:* Jerry Lewis; *W:* Jerry Lewis. *LIV*

The Bellboy and the
Playgirls woof! *The Playgirls and the Bellboy; Mit*
Eva Fing Die Sunde An 1962 Early Coppola effort adds new film footage to a 1958 German movie. Stars Playboy playmate June "The Body" Wilkinson, with other centerfolds of the time. **93m/C VHS.** June Wilkinson; *D:* Francis Ford Coppola; *W:* Francis Ford Coppola. *NO*

Belle Americaine 🎞🎞 *What a Chassis!* 1961
Title refers to the Cadillac car young Parisian factory worker Dhery buys at a suspiciously bargain price. Naturally, his deal is too good to be true and trouble follows. Dubbed in English. **97m/C VHS.** *FR* Robert Dhery, Louis de Funes, Collette Brosset, Alfred Adam, Bernard Lavelette, Annie Ducaux; *D:* Robert Dhery; *W:* Robert Dhery, Alfred Adam, Pierre Tchernia; *C:* Ghislan Cloquet; *M:* Gerard Calvi. *FCT*

Belle de Jour 🎞🎞🎞 1967 (R) Based on
Joseph Kessel's novel, one of director Bunuel's best movies has all his characteristic nuances: the hypocrisy of our society; eroticism; anti-religion. Deneuve plays Severine, a chic, frigid Parisian newlywed, who decides to become a daytime prostitute, unbeknownst to her husband. Bunuel blends reality with fantasy, and the viewer is never sure which is which in this finely crafted movie. French with subtitles. *CW:* Language, sensuality, nudity, violence. **100m/C VHS, LV.** *FR* Catherine Deneuve, Jean Sorel, Genevieve Page, Michel Piccoli, Francesco Rabal, Pierre Clementi, Georges Marchal, Francoise Fabian; *D:* Luis Bunuel; *W:* Luis Bunuel, Jean-Claude Carriere; *C:* Sacha Vierny. Venice Film Festival '67: CINE Golden Eagle. *TOU*

Belle Epoque 🎞🎞🎞 *The Age of Beauty* 1992
(R) Young army deserter Fernando (Sanz) embarks on a personal voyage of discovery when he meets Manolo (Gomez), an eccentric old man, and father to four beautiful daughters. Fernando can't believe his luck—and the sisters share his interest, resulting in an amusing round of musical beds. Lighthearted romp set in 1930's Spain with a terrific screenplay that tastefully handles the material without stooping to the obvious leering possibilities. In addition to Oscar, won 9 Spanish Goyas, including best picture, director, actress (Gil), and screenplay. Spanish with English subtitles or dubbed. *CW:* Brief nudity and sexual situations. **108m/C VHS, LV.** *SP* Jorge Sanz, Fernando Gomez, Ariadna Gil, Maribel Verdu, Penelope Cruz, Miriam Diaz-Aroca, Mary Carmen Ramirez, Michel Galabru, Gabino Diego; *D:* Fernando Trueba; *W:* Rafael Azcona. Academy Awards '93: Best Foreign Language Film. *COL*

The Belle of New York 🎞🎞 1952 A
turn-of-the-century bachelor falls in love with a Salvation Army missionary in this standard musical. ♫Naughty But Nice; Baby Doll; Oops; I Wanna Be a Dancin' Man; Seeing's Believing; Bachelor's Dinner Song; When I'm Out With the Belle of New York; Let a Little Love Come In. **82m/C VHS, Beta.** Fred Astaire, Vera-Ellen, Marjorie Main, Keenan Wynn, Alice Pearce, Gale Robbins, Clinton Sundberg; *D:* Charles Walters. *MGM, FHE*

Belle of the Nineties 🎞🎞½ 1934 West
struts as a 1890s singer who gets involved with a boxer. Her trademark sexual innuendos were already being censored but such lines as "It's better to be looked over than overlooked," done in West style, get the point across. **73m/B VHS.** Mae West, Roger Pryor, Johnny Mack Brown, John Miljan, Katherine DeMille, Harry Woods, Edward Gargan; *D:* Leo McCarey; *W:* Mae West; *C:* Karl Struss. *USH, BTV*

Belle Starr 🎬½ **1979** The career of Wild West outlaw Belle Starr is chronicled in this strange western pastiche about lawlessness and sexual agression. Wertmuller directed under the pseudonym Nathan Wich. Dubbed in English. **90m/C VHS, Beta.** *IT* Elsa Martinelli, Robert Wood, George Eastman, Dan Harrison; **D:** Lina Wertmuller. *FCT*

The Belles of St. Trinian's 🎬🎬🎬 **1953** Sim is priceless in a dual role as the eccentric headmistress of a chaotic, bankrupt girls' school and her bookie twin brother who scheme the school into financial security. The first in a series of movies based on a popular British cartoon by Ronald Searles about a girls' school and its mischievous students. Followed by "Blue Murder at St. Trinian's," "The Pure Hell of St. Trinian's," and "The Great St. Trinian's Train Robbery." **86m/B VHS, Beta.** *GB* Alastair Sim, Joyce Grenfell, Hermione Baddeley, George Cole, Eric Pohlmann, Renee Houston, Beryl Reid, Balbina, Jill Braidwood, Annabelle Covey, Betty Ann Davies, Diana Day, Jack Doyle, Irene Handl, Arthur Howard, Sidney James, Lloyd Lamble, Jean Langston, Belinda Lee, Vivian Martin, Andree Melly, Mary Merrall, Guy Middleton, Joan Sims, Jerry Verno, Richard Wattis; **D:** Frank Launder; **W:** Frank Launder, Sidney Gilliat, Val Valentine; **C:** Stanley Pavey; **M:** Malcolm Arnold, Malcolm Arnold. *REP*

Bellhop/The Noon Whistle **1922** Two comedic shorts back to back, separately featuring the famous comics Laurel and Hardy. **46m/B VHS, Beta.** Stan Laurel, Oliver Hardy. *CCB*

Bellissima 🎬🎬🎬 **1951** A woman living in an Italian tenement has unrealistic goals for her plain baby but endearing daughter when a famous director begins casting a role designed for a child. The mother's maternal fury and collision with reality highlight a poignant film. Italian with subtitles. **130m/B VHS.** *IT* Anna Magnani; **D:** Luchino Visconti; **W:** Luchino Visconti, Cesare Zavattini, Francesco Rosi, Suso Cecchi D'Amico. *CIG, APD*

Bellman and True 🎬🎬½ **1988 (R)** Rewarding, but sometimes tedious character study of a mild mannered computer whiz who teams with a gang of bank robbers. Fine performances, especially subtle dangerous gang characters. **112m/C VHS, Beta.** *GB* Bernard Hill, Kieran O'Brien, Richard Hope, Frances Tomelty, Derek Newark, John Kavanagh, Ken Bones; **D:** Richard Loncraine; **M:** Colin Towns. *MGM, CAN, VES*

Bells are Ringing 🎬🎬🎬 **1960** A girl who works for a telephone answering service can't help but take an interest in the lives of the clients, especially a playwright with an inferiority complex. Based on Adolph Green and Betty Comden's Broadway musical. Special letterboxed edition along with the original trailer available on laserdisc format. 🎵Just in Time; The Party's Over; It's a Perfect Relationship; Do It Yourself; It's a Simple Little System; Better Than a Dream; I Met a Girl; Drop That Name; I'm Going Back. **126m/C VHS, Beta, LV.** Judy Holliday, Dean Martin, Fred Clark, Eddie Foy Jr., Jean Stapleton; **D:** Vincente Minnelli; **W:** Betty Comden, Adolph Green; **C:** Milton Krasner; **M:** Andre Previn. Nominations: Academy Awards '60: Scoring of a Musical. *MGM*

Bells of Coronado 🎬🎬 **1950** Rogers and Evans team up to expose the murderer of the owner of a profitable uranium mine. A gang of smugglers trying to trade the ore to foreign powers is thwarted. The usual thin storyline, but filled with action and riding stunts. **67m/B VHS.** Roy Rogers, Dale Evans, Pat Brady, Grant Withers; **D:** William Witney. *REP*

Bells of Death 🎬½ **1990** A young martial arts student infiltrates the gang that killed his family and kidnapped his sister, finishing them off one by one. **91m/C VHS.** Chun Ping, Chang Yi, Chao Hsin Yen; **D:** Yueh Fung. *HMD*

Bells of Rosarita 🎬🎬½ **1945** Roy helps foil an evil plan to swindle Evans out of the circus she inherited. All-star western cast under the big top. **54m/B VHS, Beta.** Roy Rogers, Dale Evans, George "Gabby" Hayes, Sunset Carson, Adele Mara, Grant Withers, Roy Barcroft, Addison Richards; **D:** Frank McDonald. *NOS, MRV, VCN*

The Bells of St. Mary's 🎬🎬🎬½ **1945** An easy-going priest finds himself in a subtle battle of wits with the Mother Superior over how the children of St. Mary's school should be raised. It's the sequel to "Going My Way." Songs include the title tune and "Aren't You Glad You're You?" Also available in a colorized version. **126m/B VHS, Beta, LV, Closed Caption.** Bing Crosby, Ingrid Bergman, Henry Travers; **D:** Leo McCarey; **C:** George Barnes. Academy Awards '45: Best Sound; Golden Globe Awards '46: Best Actress—Drama (Bergman); New York Film Critics Awards '45: Best Actress (Bergman); Nominations: Academy Awards '45: Best Actor (Crosby), Best Actress (Bergman), Best Director (McCarey), Best Film Editing, Best Picture, Best Song ("Aren't You Glad You're You"), Original Dramatic/Comedy Score. *REP, IGP*

Bells of San Angelo 🎬 **1947** Roy foils thieves' attempts to steal a girl's inherited ranch. **54m/C VHS, Beta.** Roy Rogers, Dale Evans; **D:** William Witney. *NOS, DVT, TIM*

Bells of San Fernando 🎬 **1947** An Irish seaman wanders into California during early Spanish rule and confronts a cruel overseer in this lackluster Western drama. Scripted by "Cisco Kid" Renaldo. **75m/B VHS.** Donald Woods, Gloria Warren, Byron Foulger; **D:** Terry Morse; **W:** Jack DeWitt, Duncan Renaldo. *MOV*

The Belly of an Architect 🎬🎬🎬½ **1991 (R)** A thespian feast for the larger-than-life Dennehy as blustering American architect whose personal life and health both crumble as he obsesssively readies an exhibition in Rome. A multi-tiered, carefully composed tragicomedy from the ideosyncratic filmmaker Greenaway, probably his most accessible work for general audiences. **119m/C VHS, LV.** *GB IT* Brian Dennehy, Chloe Webb, Lambert Wilson; **D:** Peter Greenaway; **W:** Peter Greenaway; **C:** Sacha Vierny. *NO*

Beloved Enemy 🎬🎬🎬 **1936** A romantic tragedy set in Civil War-torn Ireland in the 1920s. A rebel leader and a proper English lady struggle to overcome the war's interference with their burgeoning relationship. **86m/B VHS, Beta.** David Niven, Merle Oberon, Brian Aherne, Karen Morley, Donald Crisp; **D:** H.C. Potter; **C:** Gregg Toland. *NOS, CAB*

Beloved Infidel 🎬🎬½ **1959** Sudsy, lavish romancer, based on the book by gossip queen Sheila Graham, about her brief romance with novelist F. Scott Fitzgerald. Fitzgerald (a badly miscast Peck) was in Hollywood trying to write screenplays when he meets young, English, aspiring writer Graham (an equally miscast Kerr). She becomes his mistress, putting up with Fitzgerald's drinking and insults, while he interferes with her career. Story is slanted towards Graham nobly trying to rescue Fitzgerald from himself (he did actually die from a heart attack while with Graham). **123m/C VHS, Beta.** Gregory Peck, Deborah Kerr, Eddie Albert, Philip Ober, Herbert Rudley, John Sutton, Karin Booth; **D:** Henry King; **W:** Sy Bartlett; **C:** Leon Shamroy; **M:** Franz Waxman. *FXV*

The Beloved Rogue 🎬🎬🎬 **1927** Crosland—who gained a reputation for innovation, having directed "Don Juan" the previous year (noted for the debut of synchronized music), and "The Jazz Singer" the following year (noted for the first talkie bits)—mounted this well-designed and special effect-laden medieval costumer. Barrymore is in high profile as a swashbuckling caricature of French poet Francois Villon, who battles mightily (and verbally) with Louis XI (played by Veidt, in his first US film). Marked by the excesses typical of Barrymore's prestige days, it flouts history, taking generous poetic license when the facts ain't fab enough. In short, it's great entertainment. **110m/B VHS, Beta, LV.** John Barrymore, Conrad Veidt, Marceline Day, Henry Victor, Mack Swain, Slim Summerville; **D:** Alan Crosland. *GPV, FCT, CRC*

Below the Belt 🎬🎬 **1980 (R)** Almost interesting tale of street-smart woman from New York City who becomes part of the blue-collar "circus" of lady wrestlers. Ex-wrestling champ Burke plays herself. **98m/C VHS, Beta.** Regina Baff, Mildred Burke, John C. Becher; **D:** Robert Fowler. *TPV*

Below the Border 🎬½ **1942** The Rough Riders go undercover to straighten out some cattle rustlers. **57m/B VHS, Beta.** Buck Jones, Tim McCoy, Raymond Hatton, Linda Brent, Roy Barcroft, Charles "Blackie" King; **D:** Howard Bretherton. *NOS, DVT, VDM*

Below the Deadline 🎬🎬 **1929** A man framed for embezzlement is set free and allowed to clear his name by a sympathetic detective. **79m/B VHS.** Frank Leigh, Barbara Worth, Arthur Rankin, Walter Merrill; **D:** J.P. McGowan. *SNC, VYY*

The Belstone Fox 🎬🎬 **1973** Orphaned fox goes into hiding, and is hunted by the hound he has befriended and his former owner. **103m/C VHS, Beta.** Eric Porter, Rachel Roberts, Jeremy Kemp; **D:** James Hill.

Ben 🎬½ **1972 (PG)** Sequel to "Willard" finds police Detective Kirtland still on the hunt for a killer rat pack led by Ben, king of the rodents. Title song by young Michael Jackson hit the top of the charts. **95m/C VHS, Beta, LV.** Joseph Campanella, Lee Montgomery, Arthur O'Connell, Rosemary Murphy, Meredith Baxter; **D:** Phil Karlson; **C:** Russell Metty. Golden Globe Awards '73: Best Song ("Ben"); Nominations: Academy Awards '72: Best Song ("Ben"). *PSM, PAR*

Ben-Hur 🎬🎬🎬🎬 **1926** Second film version of the renowned story of Jewish and Christian divisiveness in the time of Jesus. Battle scenes and chariot races still look good, in spite of age. Problems lingered on the set and at a cost of over $4,000,000 it was the most expensive film of its time and took years to finish. A hit at the box office, it still stands as the all-time silent classic. In 1931, a shortened version was released. Based on the novel by Lewis Wallace. **148m/B VHS, Beta, LV.** Ramon Novarro, Francis X. Bushman, May McAvoy, Betty Bronson, Claire McDowell, Carmel Myers, Nigel de Brulier, Ferdinand P. Earle; **D:** Fred Niblo; **C:** Clyde De Vinna. *MGM*

Ben-Hur 🎬🎬🎬🎬 **1959** The third film version of the Lew Wallace classic stars Heston in the role of a Palestinian Jew battling the Roman empire at the time of Christ. Won a record 11 Oscars. The breathtaking chariot race is still one of the best screen races today. Perhaps one of the greatest pictures of all time. Also available in letterbox format. **212m/C VHS, Beta, LV, Closed Caption.** Charlton Heston, Jack Hawkins, Stephen Boyd, Haya Harareet, Hugh Griffith, Martha Scott, Sam Jaffe, Cathy O'Donnell, Finlay Currie; **D:** William Wyler; **W:** Karl Tunberg; **C:** Robert L. Surtees; **M:** Miklos Rozsa. Academy Awards '59: Best Actor (Heston), Best Art Direction/Set Decoration (Color), Best Color Cinematography, Best Costume Design (Color), Best Director (Wyler), Best Film Editing, Best Picture, Best Sound, Best Special Effects, Best Supporting Actor (Griffith), Original Dramatic/Comedy Score; British Academy Awards '59: Best Film; Directors Guild of America Awards '59: Best Director (Wyler); Golden Globe Awards '60: Best Director (Wyler), Best Film—Drama, Best Supporting Actor (Boyd); New York Film Critics Awards '59: Best Film; Nominations: Academy Awards '59: Best Adapted Screenplay. *MGM, APD, BTV*

Ben Turpin: An Eye for an Eye **1924** Two silent Ben Turpin comedies: "He Looked Crooked, or Why Ben Bolted" (1917) and "Ten Dollars or Ten Days" (1924). **77m/B VHS, Beta, 8mm.** Ben Turpin, Harry Gribbon. *VYY*

Bend of the River 🎬🎬🎬 *Where the River Bends* **1952** A haunted, hardened guide leads a wagon train through Oregon territory, pitting himself against Indians, the wilderness and a former comrade-turned-hijacker. **91m/C VHS, Beta.** James Stewart, Arthur Kennedy, Rock Hudson, Harry (Henry) Morgan, Royal Dano; **D:** Anthony Mann. *USH*

Beneath Arizona Skies/Paradise Canyon 🎬½ **1935** A package of John Wayne westerns filled with lots of rumble tumble action. **109m/B VHS, Beta.** John Wayne. *REP*

Beneath the Planet of the Apes 🐾🐾½ 1970 (G) In the first sequel, another Earth astronaut passes through the same warp and follows the same paths as Taylor, through Ape City and to the ruins of bomb-blasted New York's subway system, where warhead-worshipping human mutants are found. The strain of sequelling shows instantly, and gets worse through the next three films; followed by "Escape from the Planet of the Apes." 108m/C VHS, Beta, LV, Closed Caption. Charlton Heston, James Franciscus, Kim Hunter, Maurice Evans, James Gregory, Natalie Trundy, Jeff Corey, Linda Harrison, Victor Buono; D: Ted Post; C: Milton Krasner. FOX, FUS

Beneath the 12-Mile Reef 🐾🐾 1953 Two rival groups of divers compete for sponge beds off the Florida coast. Lightweight entertainment notable for underwater photography and early Cinemascope production, as well as Moore in a bathing suit. 102m/C VHS, Beta, LV. Robert Wagner, Terry Moore, Gilbert Roland, Richard Boone, Peter Graves, J. Carrol Naish; D: Robert D. Webb. Nominations: Academy Awards '53: Best Color Cinematography. NOS, FCT, GEM

Beneath the Valley of the Ultra-Vixens 🐾 1979 Sex comedy retread directed by the man with an obsession for big. Scripted by Roger Ebert, who also scripted the cult classic "Beyond the Valley of the Dolls." Explicit nudity. 90m/C VHS. Francesca "Kitten" Natividad, Ann Marie, Ken Kerr, Stuart Lancaster; D: Russ Meyer; W: Roger Ebert. RMF

Benefit of the Doubt 🐾🐾 1993 (R) Ex-con Sutherland, released from prison after 22 years, attempts to repaint his family a la Norman Rockwell. Grown-up daughter Irving, who testified against him in her mother's murder, wants to put a crimp in those plans since daddy's new vision of family fondness frankly makes her stomach turn. Aside from the sexual shenanigans, and the haunting Monument Valley backdrop, an extended chase scene would seem to be the film's only hope of salvation. Unfortunately, it fails to deliver, being both implausible and boring. Based on a story by Michael Lieber. CW: Language, violence, and sexuality. 92m/C VHS, Beta, Closed Caption. Donald Sutherland, Amy Irving, Christopher McDonald, Rider Strong, Graham Greene, Theodore Bikel, Gisele Kovach, Ferdinand "Ferdy" Mayne; D: Jonathan Heap; W: Jeffrey Polman, Christopher Keyser; M: Hummie Mann. PAR

The Beniker Gang 🐾🐾½ 1983 (G) Five orphans, supported by the eldest who writes a syndicated advice column, work together as a family. A made-for-television film. 87m/C VHS, Beta. Andrew McCarthy, Jennie Dundas, Danny Pintauro, Charlie Fields; D: Ken Kwapis. WAR

Benji 🐾🐾🐾 1974 (G) In the loveable mutt's first feature-length movie, he falls in love with a female named Tiffany, and saves two young children from kidnappers. Kiddie classic that was a box office hit when first released. Followed by "For the Love of Benji." 87m/C VHS, Beta. Benji, Peter Breck, Christopher Connelly, Patsy Garrett, Deborah Walley, Cynthia Smith; D: Joe Camp; W: Joe Camp; M: Euel Box. Golden Globe Awards '75: Best Song ("I Feel Love"); Nominations: Academy Awards '74: Best Song ("Benji's Theme (I Feel Love)"). VES, FCT, APD

Benji the Hunted 🐾½ 1987 (G) The heroic canine, shipwrecked off the Oregon coast, discovers a litter of orphaned cougar cubs, and battles terrain and predators to bring them to safety. 89m/C VHS, Beta, LV, Closed Caption. Benji, Red Steagall, Frank Inn; D: Joe Camp; W: Joe Camp; M: Euel Box. DIS

Benji's Very Own Christmas Story 1983 Benji and his friends go on a magic trip and meet Kris Kringle and learn how Christmas is celebrated around the world. Also included: "The Phenomenon of Benji," a documentary about Benji's odyssey from the animal shelter to international stardom. 60m/C VHS, Beta. BFV

Benny & Joon 🐾🐾½ 1993 (PG) Depending on your tolerance for cute eccentrics and whimsy this will either charm you with sweetness or send you into sugar shock. Masterson is Joon, a mentally disturbed young woman who paints and has a habit of setting fires. She lives with overprotective brother Benny (Quinn). Sam (Depp) is the outsider who charms Joon, a dyslexic loner who impersonates his heroes Charlie Chaplin and Buster Keaton with eery accuracy. Depp is particularly fine with the physical demands of his role, but the film's easy dismissal of Joon's mental illness is a serious flaw. The laserdisc version is letterboxed. 98m/C VHS, Beta, LV, Closed Caption. Johnny Depp, Mary Stuart Masterson, Aidan Quinn, Julianne Moore, Oliver Platt, CCH Pounder, Dan Hedaya, Joe Grifasi, William H. Macy, Eileen Ryan; D: Jeremiah S. Chechik; W: Barry Berman; M: Rachel Portman. Nominations: Golden Globe Awards '94: Best Actor—Musical/Comedy (Depp); MTV Movie Awards '94: Best On-Screen Duo (Johnny Depp/Mary Stuart Masterson), Best Comedic Performance (Depp), Best Song ("I'm Gonna Be 500 Miles"). MGM

The Benny Goodman Story 🐾🐾 1955 The life and music of Swing Era bandleader Benny Goodman is recounted in this popular biopic. Covering Benny's career from his child prodigy days to his monumental 1938 Carnegie Hall Jazz Concert, the movie's soggy plot machinations are redeemed by a non-stop music track featuring the real Benny and an all-star lineup. ♫ Don't Be That Way; Memories of You; Sing, Sing, Sing; Slipped Disc. 116m/C VHS, Beta. Steve Allen, Donna Reed, Gene Krupa, Lionel Hampton, Kid Ory, Ben Pollack, Harry James, Stan Getz, Teddy Wilson, Martha Tilton; D: Valentine Davies; M: Henry Mancini. USH, FCT

Benny Hill's Crazy World 1974 The British comedian delivers some of his best material with the help of "Hill's Angels." 55m/C VHS, Beta. GB Benny Hill. HBO

Beretta's Island 🐾🐾 1992 (R) When Interpol operative Beretta comes out of retirement to track his friend's killer, the chase leads him to back to his homeland of Sardinia, which has been overrun by drugs. CW: Some nudity and violence and drug use. 97m/C VHS. Franco Columbu, Ken Kercheval; Cameos: Arnold Schwarzenegger. LIV

Bergonzi Hand 🐾 1970 Drama about two art scoundrels who are astonished when an immigrant admits to painting a forged "Bergonzi." 62m/C VHS, Beta. Keith Mitchell, Gordon Jackson, Martin Miller. VYY

The Berlin Affair 🐾🐾 1985 (R) A sordid tale from "The Night Porter" director about a Japanese woman seducing various parties in pre-WWII Germany. 97m/C VHS, Beta. IT GE Mio Takaki, Gudrun Landgrebe, Kevin McNally; D: Liliana Cavani; M: Pino Donaggio. MGM

Berlin Alexanderplatz 🐾🐾🐾½ 1980 Fassbinder's 15 1/2-hour epic follows the life, death, and resurrection of Franz Biberkof, a former transit worker who has just finished a lengthy prison term and must learn to adjust in the harsh social atmosphere of Berlin in the 1920s. Melodramatic parable with Biblical overtones considered by some to be a masterpiece. Based on the novel by Alfred Doblin; originally aired as a miniseries on German television. On eight tapes. 930m/C VHS, Beta. Gunter Lamprecht, Hanna Schygulla, Barbara Sukowa, Gottfried John, Elisabeth Trissenaar, Brigitte Mira, Karin Baal, Ivan Desny; D: Rainer Werner Fassbinder. FCT, MGM

Berlin Blues 1989 (PG-13) A nightclub singer is torn between two men. 90m/C VHS, LV. Julia Migenes-Johnson, Keith Baxter; D: Richardo Franco. CAN

The Berlin Conspiracy 🐾🐾 1991 (R) Espionage/action potboiler does an imaginative job of setting its action against the fall of the Berlin Wall and the end of the Cold War. A CIA agent forms a shaky alliance with his East German spymaster rival to prevent germ warfare technology

from falling into terrorist hands. CW: Violence and sensuality. 83m/C VHS, LV. Marc Singer, Mary Crosby, Stephen Davies, Richard Leparmentier, Terence Henry; D: Terence H. Winkless. COL

Berlin Express 🐾🐾🐾½ 1948 Battle of wits ensues between the Allies and the Nazis who are seeking to keep Germans divided in post-WWII Germany. Espionage and intrigue factor heavily. 86m/B VHS, Beta, LV. Robert Ryan, Merle Oberon, Paul Lukas, Charles Korvin; D: Jacques Tourneur. MED, TTC, FCT

Berlin Tunnel 21 🐾½ 1981 Based on the novel by Donald Lindquist, five American soldiers attempt a daring Cold War rescue of a beautiful German girl. The plan is to construct a tunnel under the Berlin Wall. A better-than-average film that was made for television. 150m/C VHS, Beta. Richard Thomas, Jose Ferrer, Horst Buchholz; D: Richard Michaels. NO

Bernadette 🐾🐾½ 1990 A French-made version of the legend of St. Bernadette, who endured persecution after claiming to have seen the Virgin Mary. Beautiful in its simplicity, but overly long. 120m/C VHS, Beta. FR Sydney Penny, Roland LeSaffre, Michele Simonnet, Bernard Dheran, Arlette Didier; D: Jean Delannoy. IGP

Bernard and the Genie 🐾🐾½ 199? (G) It seems Bernard Bottle is not going to have a happy Christmas—he's been fired from his job and his girlfriend has left him. But things take a turn for the better when he discovers an antique lamp and its resident Genie. But with the Genie granting his every wish, Bernard's sudden wealth is causing some suspicions among both his greedy ex-employer and the police. Meanwhile, the Genie discovers the delights of modern-day England and poses as a department store Santa to truly fulfill a child's Christmas wish. Amusing family fare. 70m/C VHS, Closed Caption. GB Alan Cumming, Lenny Henry, Rowan Atkinson; D: Paul Weiland. FOX, BTV, VCO

Berserk! 🐾½ 1967 A seedy traveling circus is beset by a series of murders. Not heralded as one of Crawford's best pieces. 95m/C VHS, Beta. Joan Crawford, Diana Dors, Judy Geeson, Ty Hardin; D: James O'Connolly. COL

Berserker 🐾 1987 (R) Six camping college students are attacked by a bloodthirsty psychotic out of a Nordic myth, who takes the shape of a badder-than-the-average bear. 85m/C VHS, Beta. Joseph Alan Johnson, Valerie Sheldon, Greg Dawson; D: Jef Richard. PSM

Bert Rigby, You're a Fool 🐾🐾½ 1989 (R) A starstruck British coal miner finds his way to Hollywood singing old showtunes, only to be rebuffed by a cynical industry. Available with Spanish subtitles. 94m/C VHS, Beta, LV, Closed Caption. Robert Lindsay, Robbie Coltrane, Jackie Gayle, Bruno Kirby, Cathryn Bradshaw, Corbin Bernsen, Anne Bancroft; D: Carl Reiner; W: Carl Reiner; C: Jan De Bont; M: Ralph Burns. WAR, MVD

Best Buns on the Beach woof! 1987 Sexploitation movie about 10 beautiful girls in a bikini contest, that ends up with them going topless. Ridiculous plot, for mature (??) audiences. 60m/C VHS, LV. IME

The Best Christmas Pageant Ever 1986 The meanest kids in town just decided to participate in the town's Christmas pageant and something special happens when the curtain finally goes up. 60m/C VHS. Dennis Weaver, Karen Grassle. RHV

Best Defense 🐾 1984 (R) A U.S. Army tank operator is sent to Kuwait to test a new state-of-the-art tank in a combat situation. Although the cast is popular, the movie as a whole is not funny and the story frequently is hard to follow. 94m/C VHS, Beta, LV, Closed Caption. Dudley Moore, Eddie Murphy, Kate Capshaw, George Dzundza, Helen Shaver; D: Willard Huyck; W: Willard Huyck, Gloria Katz. PAR

Best Enemies 🎞️½ **1986** An English film about a man suffering the trials of the 1960s, including Vietnam, and how it affects his relationships with his friends and wife. **96m/C VHS, Beta.** *GB* Sigrid Thornton, Paul Williams, Judy Morris, Brandon Burke; *D:* David Baker. *ACA*

Best Foot Forward 🎞️🎞️½ **1943** Vintage musical about a movie star who agrees to accompany a young cadet to a military ball. Based on the popular Broadway show. The film debuts of Walker, Allyson, and DeHaven. ♫Buckle Down, Winsocki; The Three B's (Barrelhouse, Boogie Woogie, and the Blues); Alive and Kicking; Two O'Clock Jump; Ev'ry Time; Three Men on a Date; Wish I May; Shady Lady; My First Promise. **95m/C VHS, Beta.** Lucille Ball, June Allyson, Tommy Dix, Nancy Walker, Virginia Weidler, Gloria De Haven, William Gaxton, Harry James; *D:* Edward Buzzell; *W:* Irving Brecher; *M:* George Bassman. *MGM*

Best Friends 🎞️🎞️ **1982 (PG)** A pair of screenwriters decide to marry after years of living and working together. Story based on the lives of screenwriters Barry Levinson and Valerie Curtin. **109m/C VHS, Beta, LV.** Goldie Hawn, Burt Reynolds, Jessica Tandy, Barnard Hughes, Audra Lindley, Keenan Wynn, Ron Silver; *D:* Norman Jewison; *W:* Valerie Curtin, Barry Levinson; *C:* Jordan Cronenweth. Nominations: Academy Awards '82: Best Song ("How Do You Keep the Music Playing?"). *WAR*

The Best Intentions 🎞️🎞️🎞️½ **1992** Ingmar Bergman wrote the screenplay chronicling the early years of the stormy relationship of his parents. Set in Sweden at the turn of the century, the film focuses on the class differences that divide his mother and father, while portrayal of little Bergy is limited to a bundle under his mother's maternity dress. Inspired performances and directing illuminates the emotionally complex relationship, revealing truths about the universal human condition along the way. Six-hour version was shot for television in Europe and Japan. Director August and actress August met and married during filming. In Swedish with English subtitles. **182m/C VHS.** *SW* Samuel Froler, Pernilla August, Max von Sydow, Ghita Norby, Mona Malm, Lena Endre, Bjorn Kjellman; *D:* Bille August; *W:* Ingmar Bergman. Cannes Film Festival '92: Best Actress (August), Best Film. *ACA, FCT*

Best Kept Secrets 🎞️🎞️½ **1988** A feisty woman discovers corruption and blackmail in the police department where her husband is an officer. **104m/C VHS, Beta.** Patty Duke, Frederic Forrest, Peter Coyote; *D:* Jerrold Freedman. *THV*

Best Legs in the 8th Grade 🎞️🎞️ **1984** A handsome attorney bumps into the gorgeous homeroom angel who had ignored his nebbishly dull countenance in grade school. Lightweight made for TV comedy. **60m/C VHS, Beta.** Tim Matheson, James Belushi, Annette O'Toole, Kathryn Harrold; *D:* Tom Patchett. *NO*

The Best Little Girl in the World 🎞️🎞️🎞️ **1981** Exceptional made for TV tale of an apparently perfect teenager suffering from anorexia. Slow starvation is her only cry for help. Fine performances from Durning and Saint. **96m/C VHS, Beta.** Charles Durning, Eva Marie Saint, Jennifer Jason Leigh, Melanie Mayron, Viveca Lindfors, Jason Miller, David Spielberg, Lisa Pelikan, Ally Sheedy; *D:* Sam O'Steen; *M:* Billy Goldenberg. *NO*

The Best Little Whorehouse in Texas 🎞️🎞️ **1982 (R)** Parton is the buxom owner of The Chicken Ranch, a house of ill-repute that may be closed down unless Sheriff-boyfriend Reynolds can think of a way out. Strong performances don't quite make up for the erratically comic script. Based on the long-running Broadway musical, in turn based on a story by Larry McMurtry. Available in a letterboxed edition on laserdisc. **115m/C VHS, Beta, LV.** Dolly Parton, Burt Reynolds, Dom DeLuise, Charles Durning, Jim Nabors, Lois Nettleton; *D:* Colin Higgins. Nominations: Academy Awards '82: Best Supporting Actor (Durning). *USH, FCT*

The Best Man 🎞️🎞️🎞️½ **1964** An incisive, darkly satiric political tract, based on Gore Vidal's play, about two presidential contenders who vie for the endorsement of the aging ex-president, and trample political ethics in the process. **104m/B VHS, Beta.** Henry Fonda, Cliff Robertson, Lee Tracy, Margaret Leighton, Edie Adams, Kevin McCarthy, Ann Sothern, Gene Raymond, Shelley Berman, Mahalia Jackson; *D:* Franklin J. Schaffner; *W:* Gore Vidal; *C:* Haskell Wexler. Nominations: Academy Awards '64: Best Supporting Actor (Tracy). *MGM*

The Best of Abbott & Costello Live 1954 A compilation of vintage live-television routines by the duo, naturally including "Who's on First," along with their other celebrated bits. **58m/B VHS, Beta.** Bud Abbott, Lou Costello, George Raft, Charles Laughton. *WAR*

The Best of Bogart 🎞️🎞️🎞️ **1943** A two-cassette gift pack of the Bogie classics "The Maltese Falcon" and "Casablanca." **204m/B VHS, Beta.** Humphrey Bogart, Ingrid Bergman, Mary Astor, Sydney Greenstreet. *MGM*

Best of Bugs Bunny & Friends 1940 This collection includes classics from great cartoon stars Bugs Bunny, Daffy Duck, Tweetie Pie and Porky Pig. Includes "Duck Soup to Nuts," "A Feud There Was" and "Tweetie Pie." **53m/C VHS, Beta.** *D:* Isadore "Friz" Freleng, Chuck Jones, Robert McKimson. Academy Awards '47: Best Animated Short Film ("Tweetie Pie"). *MGM*

The Best of Chaplin 1918 Three Chaplin comedies when he worked with Mutual. Includes "The Rink," "One A.M.," and "The Floorwalker." **60m/B VHS.** Charlie Chaplin; *D:* Charlie Chaplin. *MVC, VRS*

The Best of Cracker Mysteries 🎞️🎞️🎞️ **1993** Coltrane stars as brilliant-but-abrasive forensic psychologist Dr. Eddie Fitzgerald. His insatiable desires for smoking, drinking, and gambling have blown apart his marriage and caused him grief at work. But Fitz's brilliant at "cracking" cases by reading clues (and people) to nail wrongdoers. In "The Mad Woman in the Attic," a murder suspect, claiming to have amnesia, may be a serial killer. "To Say I Love You," finds a loan shark gettting murdered and a recently paroled hijacker and his girlfriend being involved. And in "One Day a Lemming Will Fly," a teen suicide turns out to be murder. On 3 cassettes. **350m/C VHS.** *GB* Robbie Coltrane, Andrew Tiernan, Susan Lynch, Christopher Eccleston, Beryl Reid, Adrian Dunbar, Barbara Flynn, Geraldine Sommerville, Lorcan Cranitch, Frances Tomelty; *D:* Simon Cellan Jones, Michael Winterbottom, Andy Wilson; *W:* Jimmy McGovern. *PBS, AAE, TVC*

Best of Eddie Murphy 🎞️½ **1989** A compilation of Murphy's funniest bits from his three seasons on "Saturday Night Live," including appearances as Stevie Wonder, Buckwheat, Bill Cosby and Little Richard. **78m/C VHS, Beta, Closed Caption.** Eddie Murphy, Joe Piscopo, Robin Duke, Tim Kazurinsky, Mary Gross, Gary Kroeger, Brad Hall, Julia Louis-Dreyfus. *PAR*

Best of Ernie Kovacs 1956 A compilation of some of the best moments from Ernie Kovacs' television programs that features such memorable characters as Percy Dovetonsils and the Nairobi Trio. **60m/B VHS, Beta.** Ernie Kovacs, Edie Adams, Ernie Hatrak, Bill Wendell, Peter Hanley. *WST, DVT, TVC*

The Best of Everything 🎞️🎞️🎞️ **1959** Trashy sexist soap opera about women seeking success and love in the publishing world of N.Y.C. Several stories take place, the best being Crawford's hard-nosed editor who's having an affair with a married man. Look for Evans as a philandering playboy (he went on to become the producer of "Chinatown," among others.) Based on the novel by Rona Jaffe. **121m/C VHS, Closed Caption.** Hope Lange, Stephen Boyd, Suzy Parker, Diane Baker, Martha Hyer, Joan Crawford, Brian Aherne, Robert Evans, Louis Jourdan; *D:* Jean Negulesco; *W:* Edith Sommer, Mann Rubin; *C:* William Mellor; *M:* Alfred Newman.

Nominations: Academy Awards '59: Best Costume Design (Color), Best Song ("The Best of Everything"). *FXV*

The Best of John Candy on SCTV 198? Some of Candy's most memorable characters, including Johnny LaRue, Yosh Schmenge, and the grown up Theodore "Beaver" Cleaver, are featured on this compilation of his years on SCTV (Second City Television). **62m/C VHS, LV.** John Candy, Eugene Levy, Rick Moranis, Catherine O'Hara, Harold Ramis, Martin Short. *COL*

The Best of Lovejoy Mysteries 1993 Four-tape series features the best adventures of irrepressible (if untrustworthy) antiques dealer Lovejoy (McShane). What he usually discovers are forgeries, dirty dealing, and other assorted mayhem. Based on the mysteries by Jonathan Gash; made for British TV. **200m/C VHS.** *GB* Ian McShane, Phyllis Logan, Dudley Sutton, Chris Jury. *TVC, AAE*

The Best of Soap: Jessica's Wonderful Life 197? From the camp TV sitcom comes this take-off on "It's a Wonderful Life." Jessica Tate (Helmond) finds herself at the stairway to heaven, pleading with an angel (Arthur) to return to aid her very dysfunctional family. **70m/C VHS.** Katherine Helmond, Beatrice Arthur, Robert Mandan, Cathryn Damon, Richard Mulligan, Billy Crystal. *REP*

The Best of Soap: Who Killed Peter? 1977 From the outrageous comedy TV series, featuring the eccentric and rich Tate family and the equally eccentric, but working-class, Campbell family. When Jessica Tate (Helmond) is convicted of murdering her tennis pro, brother-in-law Burt (Mulligan) decides to investigate. Crystal gained attention as gay son Jodie Dallas. **72m/C VHS.** Katherine Helmond, Richard Mulligan, Diana Canova, Robert Urich, Robert Mandan, Ted Wass, Billy Crystal, Robert Guillaume. *REP*

Best of the Badmen 🎞️🎞️½ **1950** A whole bunch of outlaws, although seemingly quite nice, are brought together by an ex-Union general who is being framed. Too much talk, not enough action. **84m/B VHS, Beta.** Robert Ryan, Claire Trevor, Jack Buetel, Robert Preston, Walter Brennan, Bruce Cabot, John Archer, Lawrence Tierney; *D:* William D. Russell. *TTC*

Best of the Best 🎞️½ **1989 (PG-13)** An interracial kick-boxing team strives to win a world championship. **95m/C VHS, Beta, LV.** Eric Roberts, Sally Kirkland, Christopher Penn, Phillip Rhee, James Earl Jones, John P. Ryan, John Dye, David Agresta, Tom Everett, Louise Fletcher, Simon Rhee; *D:* Robert Radler. *COL*

Best of the Best 2 🎞️½ **1993 (R)** The Coliseum is a notorious martial-arts venue owned by the champion fighter Brackus and his manager Weldon. No rules death matches are the norm and when their friend is killed Tommy and Alex set up a grudge match with Brackus. *CW:* Strong martial arts violence. **100m/C VHS, LV, Closed Caption.** Eric Roberts, Phillip Rhee, Christopher Penn, Ralph Moeller, Wayne Newton, Edan Gross, Sonny Landham, Meg Foster, Simon Rhee, Claire Stansfield, Betty Carvalho; *D:* Robert Radler; *W:* John Allen Nelson, Max Strom; *M:* David Michael Frank. *FXV*

Best of the Best 3: No Turning Back 🎞️🎞️ **1995 (R)** Tommy Lee (Rhee) discovers a band of racist vigilantes are trying to take over the rural community of Liberty, where his sister lives. But with the help of the sheriff (McDonald) and the school teacher (Gershon), Tommy is going to fight back. *CW:* Shootings and martial arts violence. **102m/C VHS, LV, Closed Caption.** Phillip Rhee, Gina Gershon, Christopher McDonald; *D:* Phillip Rhee. *TOU*

The Best of the Kenny Everett Video Show 1981 Scenes from the popular British late-night television show combining new wave rock music, outrageous dancing and innovative video special effects. **104m/C VHS, Beta.** Kenny Everett. *NO*

The Best of the Kids in the Hall
1993 Features some of the best clips of the hot Canadian comedy ensemble "The Kids in the Hall." Executive producer Lorne Michaels is best known for producing "Saturday Night Live." **120m/C VHS.** *CA* Dave Foley, Bruce McCulloch, Kevin McDonald, Mark McKinney, Scott Thompson. COL

The Best of the Two Ronnies 197?
A selection of skits from the well-loved BBC comedy series. **45m/C VHS, Beta, Closed Caption.** *GB* Ronnie Barker, Ronnie Corbett. FOX

The Best of Times ✍️✍️ 1986 (PG)
Slim story of two grown men who attempt to redress the failures of the past by reenacting a football game they lost in high school due to a single flubbed pass. With this cast, it should have been better. **105m/C VHS, Beta, LV, 8mm, Closed Caption.** Robin Williams, Kurt Russell, M. Emmet Walsh, Pamela Reed, Holly Palance, Donald Moffat, Margaret Whitton, Kirk Cameron; *D:* Roger Spottiswoode; *W:* Ron Shelton. NLC

Best of W.C. Fields 1933
Three of W.C. Field's Mack Sennett shorts are presented in their complete, uncut form: "The Dentist," "The Fatal Glass of Beer," and "The Golf Specialist." **58m/B VHS.** W.C. Fields, Elise Cavanna. REP

Best Revenge ✍️✍️ 1983 (R)
Two aging hippies engage in a Moroccan drug deal in order to free a kidnapped friend from a sleazy gangster. They get caught by the police, but escape, searching for the engineers of the frame-up. **92m/C VHS.** John Heard, Levon Helm, Alberta Watson, John Rhys-Davies, Moses Znaimer; *D:* John Trent; *M:* Keith Emerson. ORI, WAR

Best Seller ✍️✍️✍️ 1987 (R)
Interesting, subtext-laden thriller about a cop/bestselling author with writer's block, and the strange symbiotic relationship he forms with a slick hired killer, who wants his own story written. Dennehy is convincing as the jaded cop, and is paired well with the psychotic Woods. **112m/C VHS, Beta, LV.** James Woods, Brian Dennehy, Victoria Tennant, Paul Shenar, Seymour Cassel, Allison Balson, George Coe, Anne Pitoniak; *D:* John Flynn; *W:* Larry Cohen; *M:* Jay Michael Ferguson. VES

The Best Way ✍️✍️½ The Best Way to Walk;
La Meilleure Facon de Marcher 1976 Two summer camp counselors discover they might be gay and desirous of each other. Miller's first film; in French with English subtitles. **85m/C VHS, Beta.** *FR* Patrick Dewaere, Patrick Bouchitey, Christine Pascal, Claude Pieplu; *D:* Claude Miller; *W:* Luc Beraud, Claude Miller; *C:* Bruno Nuytten; *M:* Alain Jomy. FCT

The Best Years of Our Lives ✍️✍️✍️✍️ 1946
Three WWII vets return home to try to pick up the threads of their lives. A film that represented a large chunk of American society and helped it readjust to the modern postwar ambience is now considered an American classic. Supporting actor Russell, an actual veteran, holds a record for winning two Oscars for a single role. In addition to his Best Supporting Actor award, Russell was given a special Oscar for bringing hope and courage to fellow veterans. Based on the novella by MacKinlay Kantor. Remade for television in 1975. **170m/B VHS, Beta, LV.** Fredric March, Myrna Loy, Teresa Wright, Dana Andrews, Virginia Mayo, Harold Russell, Hoagy Carmichael, Gladys George, Roman Bohnen, Steve Cochran, Charles Halton; *D:* William Wyler; *W:* Robert Sherwood; *C:* Gregg Toland; *M:* Hugo Friedhofer. Academy Awards '46: Best Actor (March), Best Director (Wyler), Best Film Editing, Best Picture, Best Screenplay, Best Supporting Actor (Russell), Original Dramatic/Comedy Score; British Academy Awards '47: Best Film; Golden Globe Awards '47: Best Film—Drama; National Board of Review Awards '46: 10 Best Films of the Year, Best Director (Wyler); New York Film Critics Awards '46: Best Director (Wyler), Best Film; Nominations: Academy Awards '46: Best Sound. HBO, FCT, BTV

Bethune ✍️✍️½ 1977
The life story of a Canadian doctor who started a practice in Communist China. **88m/C VHS, Beta.** Donald Sutherland, Kate Nelligan, David Gardner, James Hong; *D:* Eric Till. TWE

Betrayal ✍️ 1974
Psycho-thriller pits an unhappy widow against her seemingly innocent hired companion. Seems this girl has a boyfriend who has a plan to murder the lonely lady for her money. Routine and predictable. **78m/C VHS.** Amanda Blake, Dick Haymes, Tisha Sterling, Sam Groom; *D:* Gordon Hessler; *M:* Ernest Gold. JEF

Betrayal ✍️½ 1978
Telefilm based on the book by Lucy Freeman and Julie Roy about a historic malpractice case involving a psychiatrist and one of his female patients. The doctor convinced the female patient that sex with him would serve as therapy. **95m/C VHS, Beta.** Lesley Ann Warren, Rip Torn, Ron Silver, Richard Masur, Stephen Elliott, John Hillerman, Peggy Ann Garner; *D:* Paul Wendkos. NO

Betrayal ✍️✍️½ 1983 (R)
An unusual adult drama, beginning at the end of a seven-year adulterous affair and working its way back in time to finally end at the start of the betrayal of a husband by his wife and his best friend. Kingsley and Irons make Pinter's adaptation of his own play work. **95m/C VHS, Beta.** *GB* Ben Kingsley, Patricia Hodge, Jeremy Irons; *D:* David Jones; *W:* Harold Pinter. Nominations: Academy Awards '83: Best Adapted Screenplay. FOX

Betrayal from the East ✍️✍️ 1944
A carnival barker saves the Panama Canal from the vicious Japanese war machine in this rather silly wartime drama. **82m/B VHS, Beta.** Lee Tracy, Nancy Kelly, Richard Loo, Abner Biberman, Regis Toomey, Philip Ahn, Addison Richards, Victor Sen Yung, Drew Pearson; *D:* William (Lester Williams) Berke. TTC

Betrayal of the Dove ✍️✍️ 1992 (R)
Slater stars as a divorced woman set-up on a blind date by her best friend Le Brock. Zane is the dashing doctor who sweeps Slater off her feet but things are never quite what they seem. He may not be Mr. Right and the best friend has her own hidden agenda. *CW:* Language, violence, and sexuality. **93m/C VHS.** Helen Slater, Kelly Le Brock, Billy Zane, Alan Thicke, Harvey Korman, Stuart Pankin, David Lander; *D:* Strathford Hamilton; *W:* Robby Benson. PSM

Betrayed ✍️✍️✍️ 1954
Bombshell Turner and strongman Gable star in this story of WWII intrigue. Suspected of being a Nazi informer, Turner is sent back to Holland for a last chance at redemption. Her cover as a sultry nightclub performer has the Nazis drooling and ogling (can you spell h-o-t?), but her act may be blown by an informant. Can luscious Lana get out of this one intact? **107m/C VHS, Beta.** Clark Gable, Lana Turner, Victor Mature, Louis Calhern, O.E. Hasse, Wilfrid Hyde-White, Ian Carmichael, Niall MacGinnis, Nora Swinburne, Roland Culver; *D:* Gottfried Reinhardt; *C:* Frederick A. (Freddie) Young. MGM, CCB

Betrayed ✍️✍️ 1988 (R)
A rabid political film, dealing with an implausible FBI agent infiltrating a white supremacist organization via her love affair with a handsome farmer who turns out to be a murderous racist. Winger is memorable in her role as the FBI agent, despite the film's limitations, and admirers of Costa-Gavras's directorial work and political stances will want to see how the director botched this one. **112m/C VHS, Beta, LV, Closed Caption.** Tom Berenger, Debra Winger, John Mahoney, John Heard, Albert Hall, Jeffrey DeMunn; *D:* Constantin Costa-Gavras; *W:* Joe Eszterhas; *C:* Patrick Blossier. MGM

The Betsy ✍️✍️ Harold Robbins' The Betsy 1978
(R) A story of romance, money, power, and mystery centering around the wealthy Hardeman family and their automobile manufacturing business. Loosely patterned after the life of Henry Ford as portrayed in the Harold Robbins' pulp-tome. Olivier is the redeeming feature. **132m/C VHS, Beta.** Laurence Olivier, Kathleen Beller, Robert Duvall, Lesley-Anne Down, Edward Herrmann, Tommy Lee Jones, Katharine Ross, Jane Alexander; *D:* Daniel Petrie; *W:* William Bast, Walter Bernstein; *M:* John Barry. FOX

Betsy's Wedding ✍️✍️½ 1990 (R)
Betsy wants a simple wedding, but her father has other, grander ideas. Then there's the problem of paying for it, which Dad tries to take care of in a not-so-

typical manner. Alda at his hilarious best. **94m/C VHS, Beta, LV, Closed Caption.** Alan Alda, Joey Bishop, Madeline Kahn, Molly Ringwald, Catherine O'Hara, Joe Pesci, Ally Sheedy, Burt Young, Anthony LaPaglia, Julie Bovasso, Nicolas Coster, Bibi Besch, Dylan Walsh; *D:* Alan Alda; *W:* Alan Alda; *M:* Bruce Broughton. TOU

Better Late Than Never ✍️✍️ 1979
Fun television tale of senior citizens in revolt at an old-age home. Fine characters portrayed by some of the best in the business. **100m/C VHS.** Harold Gould, Tyne Daly, Strother Martin, Harry (Henry) Morgan, Victor Buono, George Gobel, Lou Jacobi, Donald Pleasence, Larry Storch; *D:* Richard Crenna; *M:* Charles Fox. FOX

Better Late Than Never ✍️✍️½ 1983
Two penniless old fools vie for the acceptance of a bratty 10-year-old millionairess, who must choose one as her guardian. Niven's last film. **95m/C VHS, Beta.** David Niven, Art Carney, Maggie Smith, Kimberly Partridge, Catherine Hicks, Melissa Prophet; *D:* Bryan Forbes; *M:* Henry Mancini. FOX

Better Off Dead ✍️✍️½ 1985 (PG)
A compulsive teenager's girlfriend leaves him and he decides to end it all. After several abortive attempts, he decides instead to out-ski his ex-girlfriend's obnoxious new boyfriend. Uneven but funny. **97m/C VHS, Beta, LV, Closed Caption.** John Cusack, Curtis Armstrong, Diane Franklin, Kim Darby, David Ogden Stiers, Dan Schneider, Amanda Wyss, Taylor Negron, Vincent Schiavelli, Demian Slade, Scooter Stevens; *D:* Steve Holland; *W:* Steve Holland; *M:* Rupert Hine. FOX

Better Off Dead ✍️✍️½ 1994
Preachy, manipulative TV movie redeemed by good performances. Kit (Winningham) is an unrepentant white-trash thief who kills a black police officer and is sentenced to death. Cutter Dubuque (Ferrell) is the ambitious black district attorney who prosecuted the case but comes to doubt the wisdom of the death penalty and slowly begins to try to help Kit. **91m/C VHS.** Mare Winningham, Tyra Ferrell, Kevin Tighe, Don Harvey; *D:* M. Neema Barnette; *W:* Marlane X. Meyer; *C:* Ueli Steiger; *M:* John Barnes. TTC

A Better Tomorrow ✍️½ Yingxiong Bense 1986
Gangster movie with the requisite bloodletting and male bonding. Film captured a big box-office. In Cantonese with English subtitles. **95m/C VHS.** *CH* Chow Yung Fat, Leslie Cheung, Ti Lung; *D:* John Woo. REP, FCT

A Better Tomorrow, Part 2 ✍️½ 1988
A smooth-talking gangster, who was killed in Part I, returns in Part II as the dead man's twin brother (unmentioned in Part I). He teams up with a cop and a reformed gangster to fight the forces of evil. In Cantonese with English subtitles. **100m/C VHS.** *HK* Chow Yung Fat, Leslie Cheung; *D:* John Woo. FCT

A Better Tommorow, Part 3 ✍️✍️
Love and Death in Saigon 1989 Prequel set in 1974 finds detective Mark Gor (Fat) and his cousin (Leung) seeking to escape from Saigon. Unfortunately, they both fall for the same sultry babe (Mui), who's also a gangster's moll. Mandarin with subtitles. **114m/C VHS.** *HK* Chow Yung Fat, Tony Leung, Anita Mui; *D:* Tsui Hark. FCT

Betty ✍️✍️ 1992
Sulky, drunken Betty (Trintignant) is doing her best to destroy her bourgeois life, escaping from her marriage into adultery and debasement. She meets the concerned middle-aged widow Laure (Audran), who inexplicably takes her to her hotel room, cleans her up, and spends the remainder of the movie as Betty's sounding-board. Betty's passive personality offers little to explain her appeal to either Laure or the viewer. Based on the novel by Georges Simenon. French with subtitles. **103m/C VHS.** *FR* Marie Trintignant, Stephane Audran, Jean-Francoise Garreau, Yves Lambrecht, Christiane Minazolli, Pierre Vernier; *D:* Claude Chabrol; *W:* Claude Chabrol; *M:* Matthieu Chabrol. NYF

Betty Blue ✍️✍️✍️ 1986 (R)
A vivid, intensely erotic film about two young French lovers and how their inordinately strong passion for each other destroys them, leading to poverty, violence, and insanity. English subtitles. From the director of "Diva." Based on the novel "37.2 Le Matin" by

Philippe Djian. **121m/C VHS, Beta, LV, Closed Caption.** *FR* Beatrice Dalle, Jean-Hugues Anglade, Gerard Darmon, Consuelo de Haviland, Clementine Celarie, Jacques Mathou, Vincent Lindon; *D:* Jean-Jacques Beineix; *W:* Jean-Jacques Beineix; *M:* Gabriel Yared. Nominations: Academy Awards '86: Best Foreign Language Film; Cesar Awards '86: Best Actor (Anglade). *FOX*

Between Fighting Men 🎬½ **1932** The orphaned daughter of a shepherd is adopted by the cowpoke who caused her father's death. The cowpoke's sons fall in love with, and compete for, the love of the girl. **62m/B VHS.** Ken Maynard, Ruth Hall, Josephine Dunn, Wallace MacDonald; *D:* Forrest Sheldon. *NOS, DVT*

Between Friends 🎬🎬½ **1983** Two women with only their respective divorces in common, meet and become fast friends. The rapport between Burnett and Taylor makes for a touching drama. Adapted for cable television from the book "Nobody Makes Me Cry," by Shelley List, one of the producers. **105m/C VHS, Beta.** Elizabeth Taylor, Carol Burnett; *D:* Lou Antonio; *M:* James Horner. *VES*

Between God, the Devil & a Winchester 🎬 **1972** Violent western with plenty of shooting and dust. Lots of cowboys are hot on the trail of some stolen loot from a church but apparently God isn't on their side since the majority bite the dust and become a snack for the vultures. **98m/C VHS, Beta.** Gilbert Roland, Richard Harrison; *D:* Dario Silvester. *UNI*

Between Heaven and Earth 🎬🎬 **1993** Maria (Maura) is an ambitious television journalist, prone to surreal dreams, who becomes pregnant after a one-night stand. After witnessing a violent protest, Maria becomes convinced that she can communicate with her unborn baby and that the child is unwilling to be born into such a violent world. So Maria must try to convince her baby otherwise. In French with English subtitles. **80m/C VHS.** *BE FR SP* Carmen Maura, Jean-Pierre Cassel, Didier Bezace, Samuel Mussen, Andre Delvaux; *D:* Marion Hansel; *W:* Marion Hansel. *FCT*

Between Heaven and Hell 🎬🎬🎬 **1956** Prejudiced Southern gentleman Wagner finds how wrong his misconceptions are, as he attempts to survive WWII on a Pacific Island. Ebsen is exceptional, making this rather simplistic story a meaningful classic. **94m/C VHS.** Robert Wagner, Terry Moore, Broderick Crawford, Buddy Ebsen, Robert Keith, Brad Dexter, Mark Damon, Kenneth Clark, Harvey Lembeck, Frank Gorshin, Scatman Crothers; *D:* Richard Fleischer. Nominations: Academy Awards '56: Original Dramatic/Comedy Score. *FXV*

Between Men 🎬🎬 **1935** A father kills a man he believes killed his son and flees. Later in life, the son meets his father. For father and son, this causes some major concern. **59m/B VHS.** Johnny Mack Brown, Beth Marion, William Farnum, Earl Dwire, Lloyd Ingraham, Milburn Morante; *D:* Robert North Bradbury. *NOS, DVT, GPV*

Between the Lines 🎬🎬🎬½ **1977 (R)** A witty, wonderfully realized ensemble comedy about the staff of a radical post-'60s newspaper always on the brink of folding, and its eventual sell-out. **101m/C VHS, Beta.** John Heard, Lindsay Crouse, Jeff Goldblum, Jill Eikenberry, Stephen Collins, Lewis J. Stadlen, Michael J. Pollard, Marilu Henner, Bruno Kirby; *D:* Joan Micklin Silver; *W:* Fred Barron; *M:* Michael Kamen. *VES*

Between Two Women 🎬🎬 **1986** A television movie about a wife's rocky relationship with her bossy mother-in-law, until the latter has a stroke and needs care. Dewhurst won an Emmy for her portrayal of the mother-in-law. **95m/C VHS, Beta.** Farrah Fawcett, Michael Nouri, Colleen Dewhurst, Steven Hill, Bridgette Anderson, Danny Corkill; *D:* Jon Avnet. *WAR*

Between Wars 🎬🎬 **1974** Young doctor in Australia's Medical Corps encounters conflict when he tries to introduce Freud's principles into his work. **97m/C VHS, Beta.** *AU* Corin Redgrave, Arthur Dignam, Judy Morris, Patricia Leehy, Gunter Meisner; *D:* Michael Thornhill. *NO*

Beulah Land 🎬½ **1980** A television miniseries about 45 years in the lives of a Southern family, including the Civil War. Based on the novels "Beulah Land" and "Look Away, Beulah Land" by Lonnie Coleman. **267m/C VHS, Beta, LV.** Lesley Ann Warren, Michael Sarrazin, Don Johnson, Meredith Baxter, Dorian Harewood, Eddie Albert, Hope Lange, Paul Rudd; *D:* Virgil W. Vogel, Harry Falk. *COL, TVC*

The Beverly Hillbillies **1962** The successful sitcom series, which ran from 1962-1971, features Jed Clampett and his Ozark clan striking oil, getting rich, and heading for the good life in California. Two episodes per tape. **51m/B VHS.** Buddy Ebsen, Irene Ryan, Donna Douglas, Max Baer Jr., Nancy Kulp, Raymond Bailey, Phil Silvers; *Cameos:* John Wayne. *FXV, MOV*

The Beverly Hillbillies 🎬🎬½ **1993 (PG)** Big-screen transfer of the long-running TV show may appeal to fans. Ozark mountaineer Jed Clampett discovers oil, becomes an instant billionaire, and packs his backwoods clan off to the good life in California. Minimal plot finds dim-bulb nephew Jethro and daughter Elly May looking for a bride for Jed. Not that any of it matters. Everyone does fine by their impersonations, particularly Varney as the good-hearted Jed and Leachman as stubborn Granny. Ebsen, the original Jed, reprises another of his TV roles, detective Barnaby Jones. And yes, the familiar strains of the "Ballad of Jed Clampett" by Jerry Scoggins starts this one off, too. **93m/C VHS, LV, Closed Caption.** Jim Varney, Erika Eleniak, Diedrich Bader, Cloris Leachman, Dabney Coleman, Lily Tomlin, Lea Thompson, Rob Schneider, Linda Carlson, Penny Fuller, Kevin Connolly; *Cameos:* Buddy Ebsen, Zsa Zsa Gabor, Dolly Parton; *D:* Penelope Spheeris; *W:* Larry Konner, Mark Rosenthal, Jim Fisher, Jim Staahl; *C:* Robert Brinkmann; *M:* Lalo Schifrin. *FXV*

Beverly Hills Bodysnatchers 🎬½ **1989 (R)** A mad scientist and a greedy mortician plot to get rich, but their plan backfires when they bring a Mafia godfather back to life and he terrorizes Beverly Hills. **85m/C VHS, LV.** Vic Tayback, Frank Gorshin, Brooke Bundy, Seth Jaffe, Art Metrano; *D:* Jonathan Mostow. *IME*

Beverly Hills Brats 🎬 **1989 (PG-13)** A spoiled, rich Hollywood brat hires a loser to kidnap him, in order to gain his parents' attention, only to have both of them kidnapped by real crooks. **90m/C VHS, Beta, LV, Closed Caption.** Martin Sheen, Burt Young, Peter Billingsley, Terry Moore; *D:* Dimitri Sotirakis; *M:* Barry Goldberg. *LIV, IME, VTR*

Beverly Hills Cop 🎬🎬½ **1984 (R)** When a close friend of smooth-talking Detroit cop Axle Foley is brutally murdered in L.A., he traces the murderer to the posh streets of Beverly Hills. There he must stay on his toes to keep one step ahead of the killer and two steps ahead of the law. Better than average Murphy vehicle. **105m/C VHS, Beta, LV, 8mm, Closed Caption.** Eddie Murphy, Judge Reinhold, John Ashton, Lisa Eilbacher, Ronny Cox, Steven Berkoff, James Russo, Jonathan Banks, Stephen Elliott, Bronson Pinchot, Paul Reiser, Damon Wayans, Rick Overton; *D:* Martin Brest; *W:* Danilo Bach, Dan Petrie Jr.; *C:* Bruce Surtees; *M:* Harold Faltermeyer. People's Choice Awards '85: Best Film; Nominations: Academy Awards '84: Best Original Screenplay. *PAR*

Beverly Hills Cop 2 🎬½ **1987 (R)** The highly successful sequel to the first profitable comedy, with essentially the same plot, this time deals with Foley infiltrating a band of international munitions smugglers. **103m/C VHS, Beta, LV, 8mm, Closed Caption.** Eddie Murphy, Judge Reinhold, Juergen Prochnow, Ronny Cox, John Ashton, Brigitte Nielsen, Allen (Goorwitz) Garfield, Paul Reiser, Dean Stockwell; *D:* Tony Scott; *W:* Larry Ferguson, Warren Skaaren; *M:* Harold Faltermeyer. Golden Raspberry Awards '87: Worst Song ("I Want Your Sex"); Nominations: Academy Awards '87: Best Song ("Shakedown"). *PAR*

Beverly Hills Cop 3 🎬½ **1994 (R)** Yes, Detroit cop Axel Foley (Murphy) just happens to find another case that takes him back to his friends on the Beverly Hills PD. This time he uncovers a criminal network fronting WonderWorld,

an amusement park with a squeaky-clean image. Fast-paced action, lots of gunplay, and Eddie wisecracks his way through the slow spots. Reinhold returns as the still impossibly naive Rosewood, with Bronson briefly reprising his role as Serge of the undeterminable accent. Critically panned box office disappointment relies too heavily on formula and is another disappointing follow-up.*CW:* Language and some violence. **105m/C VHS, Beta, Closed Caption.** Eddie Murphy, Judge Reinhold, Hector Elizondo, Timothy Carhart, Stephen McHattie, Theresa Randle, John Saxon, Alan Young, Bronson Pinchot; *Cameos:* Al Green, Gil Hill; *D:* John Landis; *W:* Steven E. de Souza; *C:* Mac Ahlberg; *M:* Nile Rodgers. *PAR*

Beverly Hills Knockouts **1989** A bevy of beautiful boxers pummel each other with both fists. **60m/C VHS, Beta.** *CEL*

Beverly Hills Madam 🎬 **1986 (PG-13)** In this routine plot, a stable of elite call girls struggle with their lifestyle and their madam, played by Dunaway. Made for television. **97m/C VHS, Beta, LV.** Faye Dunaway, Louis Jourdan, Donna Dixon, Robin Givens, Marshall Colt, Melody Anderson, Terry Farrell; *D:* Harvey Hart. *ORI*

Beverly Hills 90210 **1990** In the pilot episode for the immensely popular series, the world is introduced to the exciting teens who wander the halls of West Beverly High. Join Brandon and Brenda Walsh as they move from Minneapolis to Beverly Hills and experience all the trials and tribulations that come with the new zip code. Includes 25 minutes of previously unseen footage. **90m/C VHS, LV, Closed Caption.** Jason Priestley, Shannen Doherty, Jennie Garth, Brian Austin Green, Tori Spelling, Ian Ziering, Gabrielle Carteris. *WOV, MOV*

Beverly Hills 90210: The Graduation **1993** The 1993 end-of-the-season episode of the hit TV series finds the group finally getting out of Beverly Hills High. As they graduate the friends share plans for the summer (and the future) and you'll see lots of flashbacks as well as their final graduation prank. Includes interviews with the cast and music videos from the series soundtrack. **90m/C VHS.** Jason Priestley, Shannen Doherty, Luke Perry, Jennie Garth, Brian Austin Green, Tori Spelling, Ian Ziering, Gabrielle Carteris. *WOV*

Beverly Hills Ninja 🎬½ **1996 (PG-13)** Farley plays Haru, a pathetically inept adopted son of a ninja, who is, nevertheless, sent to Beverly Hills on a rescue mission to break up an international counterfeiting ring. There, second-time spoof siren Sheridan hires the "great white ninja" to follow her no-good boyfriend and becomes the object of Haru's desire. Farley's extraordinary gift for physical comedy is exploited to the hilt, and the increase in Haru's tripping and stumbling (and in one harrowing scene, stripping) usually coincides with the fumbling of the plot. Rock's talents are squandered on a poorly conceived bellboy character. Farley's first feature sans fellow SNL alumni Spade suffers for his absence. Director Duggan, who also helmed Adam Sandler's "Happy Gilmore," might want to start screening his calls.*CW:* Sex-related humor, martial arts violence and a humorous drug related scene. **88m/C VHS, LV, Closed Caption.** Chris Farley, Nicolette Sheridan, Robin Shou, Nathaniel Parker, Chris Rock, Soon-Teck Oh, Francois Chau, Keith Cooke Hirabayashi; *D:* Dennis Dugan; *M:* Mark Feldberg, Mitch Klebenoff; *C:* Arthur Albert; *M:* George S. Clinton. Nominations: MTV Movie Awards '97: Best Comedic Performance (Farley). *COL*

Beverly Hills Vamp 🎬🎬 **1988 (R)** A madame and her girls are really female vampires with a penchant for hot-blooded men. **88m/C VHS, Beta.** Britt Ekland, Eddie Deezen, Debra Lamb; *D:* Fred Olen Ray. *THV*

Beware 🎬½ **1946** A black singer saves a college from bankruptcy and makes off with the gym teacher. The photography may be a bit harsh, but the all-black cast made this a pioneering but impressive film. **64m/B VHS.** Louis Jordan, Frank Wilson, Emory Richardson, Valerie Black, Milton Woods; *D:* Bud Pollard. *NOS, RXM*

Beware! Children at Play woof! 1995 (R) Cult leader kidnaps kids and introduces them to cannibalism. Bleech! As if this didn't sound grim enough, there's also an unrated version.*CW:* Violence and gore, and for some sexuality. 90m/C VHS. *TTV*

Beware, My Lovely 🐾🐾½ 1952 Taut chiller. Lonely widow Lupino hires a new handyman. He's great with screen doors and storm windows, but has a problem with sharp tools. Intense and gripping with fine performances. 77m/B VHS, LV. Ida Lupino, Robert Ryan, Taylor Holmes, O.Z. Whitehead, Barbara Whiting, Dee Pollock; *D:* Harry Horner. *REP*

Beware of a Holy Whore 🐾🐾 *Warnung Vor Einer Helligen Nutte* 1970 German film crew sits around a Spanish resort—complaining, drinking, and making love—as they wait for financial support from Bonn. Provocative and self-indulgently honest look at filmmaking. Filmed on location in Sorrento, Italy; German with subtitles. 103m/C VHS. *GE* Lou Castel, Eddie Constantine, Hanna Schygulla, Marquard Bohm, Ulli Lommel, Margarethe von Trotta, Kurt Raab, Ingrid Caven, Werner Schroeter, Rainer Werner Fassbinder; *D:* Rainer Werner Fassbinder; *W:* Rainer Werner Fassbinder; *C:* Michael Ballhaus; *M:* Peer Raben. *ORI*

Beware of Pity 🐾🐾½ 1946 A crippled baroness thinks she's found true love with a military officer, but it turns out his marriage proposal grew out of pity for her, not passion. A quality but somber British-made historical drama, based on a novel by Stefan Zweig. 129m/B VHS. Lilli Palmer, Albert Lieven, Cedric Hardwicke, Gladys Cooper, Ernest Thesiger, Freda Jackson, Linden Travers, Ralph Truman, Peter Cotes, Jenny Laird, Emrys Jones, Gerhard Kempinski, John Salew, Kenneth Warrington; *D:* Maurice Elvey; *W:* W.P. Lipscomb, Elizabeth Barron, Margaret Steen. *HMK*

Bewitched 1985 A made-for-British-television horror story about an elderly couple ostensibly plagued by the witch-like conniving of a dead woman. 60m/C VHS, Beta. *GB* Eileen Atkins, Alfred Lynch; *D:* Edmund Oboler. *PSM*

Beyond a Reasonable Doubt 🐾🐾 1956 In order to get a behind-the-scenes glimpse at the judicial system, a man plays the guilty party to a murder. Alas, when he tries to vindicate himself, he is the victim of his own folly. Not as interesting as it sounds on paper. 80m/B VHS. Dana Andrews, Joan Fontaine, Sidney Blackmer, Philip Bourneuf, Barbara Nichols, Shepperd Strudwick, Arthur Franz, Edward Binns; *D:* Fritz Lang; *W:* Douglas S. Morrow. *NO*

Beyond Atlantis woof! 1973 (PG) An ancient underwater tribe is discovered when it kidnaps land-lubbin' women with which to mate. 91m/C VHS, Beta. *PH* John Ashley, Patrick Wayne, George Nader; *D:* Eddie Romero. *VCI*

Beyond Darkness 🐾½ 1992 (R) When Peter and his family move into their New England home they are immediately beset by some unknown terror. With the help of Father George, Peter learns his house was built upon the graves of twenty witches burned for heresy. The witches have decided to seek revenge by kidnapping Peter's young son and sacrificing him to an evil demon. Can Peter destroy the evil spirits before they destroy his son?*CW:* Horror violence. 111m/C VHS, LV, Closed Caption. Gene Le Brock, David Brandon, Barbara Bingham, Michael Stephenson, Stephen Brown; *D:* Clyde Anderson. *IMP*

Beyond Desire 🐾🐾½ 1994 (R) Con released after 14 years in prison gets picked up by a corvette-driving Las Vegas prostitute but more than sex is on both their minds.*CW:* Strong sexuality, violence, and language. 87m/C VHS, Closed Caption. William Forsythe, Kari Wuhrer, Leo Rossi, Sharon Farrell; *D:* Dominique Othenin-Girard. *LIV*

Beyond Dream's Door 🐾 1988 A young, All-American college student's childhood nightmares come back to haunt him, making dreams a horrifying reality. 86m/C VHS, Beta. Nick Baldasare, Rick Kesler, Susan Pinsky, Norm Singer; *D:* Jay Woelfel. *NO*

Beyond Erotica 1979 After being cut out of his father's will, a sadistic young man takes out his rage on his mother and a peasant girl. 90m/C VHS. David Hemmings, Alida Valli, Andrea Rau. *PSM*

Beyond Evil woof! 1980 (R) Relatively dim-witted newlywed couple moves into an old island mansion despite rumors that the house is haunted. Sure enough, wife George becomes possessed by the vengeful spirit of a woman murdered 200 years earlier, and a reign of pointless terror begins. Poor rip-off of hybrid Amityville/Exorcist paranormality. 98m/C VHS, Beta. John Saxon, Lynda Day George, Michael Dante, Mario Milano; *D:* Herb Freed; *W:* Herb Freed; *M:* Pino Donaggio. *MED*

Beyond Fear 🐾🐾½ 1975 Compelling drama about a man forced to aid a gang in robbery while they hold his wife and son captive. 92m/C VHS, Beta. Michael Boquet. *PSM*

Beyond Fear 🐾🐾½ 1993 (R) Tipper Taylor (Lesseos) is a wilderness tour guide who's also a martial arts expert. This is going to come in handy when her tour group is stalked by two men who are after a videotape innocently filmed by someone in Tipper's group. It seems the tape shows the men committing a murder. 84m/C VHS. Mimi Lesseos. *MNC*

Beyond Forgiveness 🐾🐾½ 1994 (R) Basic maverick cop goes after his brother's killers and winds up involved in an international black market in transplantable human organs. 95m/C VHS, LV, Closed Caption. Thomas Ian Griffith, Roger Hauer, John Rhys-Davies; *D:* Bob Misiorowski; *W:* Charles Cohen. *REP*

Beyond Innocence 🐾 1987 A 17-year-old lusts after a mature married woman. Ostensibly based on Raymond Radiguet's "Devil in the Flesh." 87m/C VHS, Beta. Keith Smith, Katia Caballero, John Morris; *D:* Scott Murray; *C:* Andrzej Bartkowiak. *NO*

Beyond Justice 🐾🐾 1992 (PG-13) High action-adventure with the prolific Hauer starring as an ex-CIA agent who is hired to rescue the kidnapped son of a beautiful executive.*CW:* Action violence. 113m/C VHS, LV, Closed Caption. Rutger Hauer, Carol Alt, Omar Sharif, Elliott Gould; *M:* Ennio Morricone. *THV*

Beyond Obsession 🐾🐾 1982 The strange relationship between a political prisoner, his daughter, and her obsession with a mysterious American is provocatively explored. 116m/C VHS. *IT* Marcello Mastroianni, Elenora Giorgi, Tom Berenger, Michel Piccoli; *D:* Liliana Cavani. *FCT*

Beyond Rangoon 🐾🐾½ 1995 (R) Sisters Laura (Arquette) and Andy (McDormand) Bowman travel to Burma to unwind, only to have political unrest and a repressive regime spoil the holiday. Dr. Laura (yeah, right) loses her passport and must flee from trigger-happy soldiers with a political dissident (Ko, a real-life exiled Burmese activist) who befriends her. The search for her passport soon becomes a imperiled trek of survival and self-discovery. Tense, well-crafted action sequences hint at a potential for excitement and intrigue; too bad Arquette isn't the least bit convincing. Filmed in Malaysia.*CW:* Depiction of violent political oppression. 100m/C VHS, LV, Closed Caption. Patricia Arquette, Frances McDormand, Spalding Gray, U Aung Ko, Victor Slezak; *D:* John Boorman; *W:* Alex Lasker, Bill Rubenstein; *C:* John Seale; *M:* Hans Zimmer. *COL*

Beyond Reason 🐾 1977 A psychologist uses unorthodox methods by treating the criminally insane with dignity and respect. 88m/C VHS, Beta. Telly Savalas, Laura Johnson, Diana Muldaur, Marvin Laird, Priscilla Barnes; *D:* Telly Savalas; *C:* John A. Alonzo. *MED*

Beyond Reasonable Doubt 🐾🐾½ 1980 Chilling true-life murder mystery which shattered the peaceful quiet of a small New Zealand town and eventually divided the country. An innocent farmer (Hargreaves) was convicted of a grisly double murder based on evidence planted by a local cop (Hemmings, in a superb role). It wasn't

until Yallop's book questioned the facts of the case that it was reopened. Yallop also wrote the screenplay. 127m/C VHS, Beta. *NZ* David Hemmings, John Hargreaves, Martyn Sanderson, Grant Tilly, Diana Rowan, Ian Watkin; *D:* John Laing; *W:* David Yallop. *NO*

Beyond the Bermuda Triangle 🐾½ 1975 Unfortunate and flat television flick. Businessman MacMurray, now retired, doesn't have enough to do. He begins an investigation of the mysterious geometric island area when his friends and fiancee disappear. Silly. 78m/C VHS. Fred MacMurray, Sam Groom, Donna Mills, Suzanne Reed, Dana Plato, Woody Woodbury; *D:* William A. Graham. *NO*

Beyond the Call 🐾🐾½ 1996 (R) Connecticut housewife Pam O'Brien (Spacek) learns from the paper that her high-school sweetheart Russell Cates (Strathairn) is on death row in South Carolina for killing a cop and his execution has been scheduled within weeks. Pam writes Russell and then hears from his sister Fran (Wright), who urges Pam to visit her brother and get him to apply for a clemency hearing. Husband Keith (Howard) becomes angry and alarmed as Pam gets more involved with Russell and his case, which hinges on Russell's Vietnam experiences and post-traumatic shock syndrome. Cable movie.*CW:* Strong language and some violence. 101m/C VHS, LV, Closed Caption. David Strathairn, Sissy Spacek, Arliss Howard, Janet Wright; *D:* Tony Bill; *W:* Doug Magee; *C:* Jean Lepine; *M:* George S. Clinton. *HMK*

Beyond the Call of Duty 🐾½ 1992 (R) Renegade U.S. Army Commander Len Jordan (Vincent) is after a particularly deadly Vietcong enemy. Aided by the head of a special forces naval unit he tracks his quarry through the notorious Mekong River Delta. But Jordan's mission may be hindered, both personally and professionally, by a beautiful American journalist after a hot story.*CW:* Language and war violence. 92m/C VHS, LV. Jan-Michael Vincent, Eb Lottimer, Jillian McWhirter; *D:* Cirio H. Santiago. *NHO*

Beyond the Carribean 🐾🐾 1936 Bizarre jungle thriller featuring voodoo and native crucifixion. Also known as "Manhunters of the Carribean." 56m/B VHS. Andre Roosevelt. *SNC*

Beyond the Door woof! *Beyond Obsession* 1975 (R) San Francisco woman finds herself pregnant with a demonic child. One of the first "Exorcist" ripoffs; skip this one and go right to the sequel, "Beyond the Door 2." In Italian; dubbed. 97m/C VHS, Beta, LV, Closed Caption. *IT* Juliet Mills, Richard Johnson, David Colin Jr.; *D:* Oliver Hellman. *MED, COL*

Beyond the Door 2 🐾🐾 *Shock* 1979 (R) Better treatment of the possession theme, but this time the door is to the home of a new family: Colin (from the original) plays a boy possessed by his dead father, who seeks revenge on his widow and her new husband. Director Bava's last feature. 90m/C VHS, Beta. *IT* John Steiner, Daria Nicolodi, David Colin Jr., Ivan Rassimov; *D:* Mario Bava; *W:* Lamberto Bava, Franco Barbieri. *MED*

Beyond the Door 3 woof! 1991 (R) Fool American students in Yugoslavia board a hellish locomotive which speeds them toward a satanic ritual. Demonic disaster-movie stuff (with poor miniatures) isn't as effective as the on-location filming; Serbian scenery and crazed peasants impart an eerie pagan aura. What this has to do with earlier "Beyond the Door" movies only the marketing boys can say. Some dialogue in Serbo-Croat with English subtitles. 94m/C VHS, LV, Closed Caption. Mary Kohnert, Sarah Conway Ciminera, William Geiger, Renee Rancourt, Alex Vitale, Victoria Zinny, Savina Gersak, Bo Svenson; *D:* Jeff Kwitny. *COL*

Beyond the Forest 🐾½ 1949 Camp diva Davis, in her last role for Warner Bros., really turns on the histrionics as a big-city gal married to a small-town guy (Cotten) and bored out of her mind. Although the most memorable line, "What a dump," has become larger-than-life, the film itself is rather small and muddled (interestingly, Vidor directed "The Fountainhead" the same year). A trashy melodrama full of ennui, envy, unwanted pregnancy, and murder, it's definitely high on camp and low on art. **96m/B VHS.** Bette Davis, Joseph Cotten, David Brian, Ruth Roman, Minor Watson, Regis Toomey; **D:** King Vidor; **C:** Robert Burks; **M:** Max Steiner. Nominations: Academy Awards '49: Original Dramatic/Comedy Score. *MGM, FCT*

Beyond the Law 🐾🐾 *Bloodsilver; Al Di La Della Legge*
1968 Spaghetti western with Van Cleef as the too smart bad guy. He becomes sheriff, picks up the stack of silver at the depot, and disappears. Humorous and clever, with fine location photography. **91m/C VHS.** *IT* Lee Van Cleef, Antonio Sabato, Lionel Stander, Bud Spencer, Gordon Mitchell, Ann Smyrner; **D:** Giorgio Stegani. *IMP, QVD*

Beyond the Law 🐾½ *Fixing the Shadow*
1992 (R) Ex-undercover cop Danny Saxon (Sheen) is recruited by the FBI to infiltrate a biker gang involved in drugs and gun smuggling. But Saxon finds himself drawn too close into the unconventional biker lifestyle and into an uneasy friendship with leader Blood (Madsen). Clumsy and exploitative. **CW:** Pervasive strong language, violence and drug use, and sexuality. **101m/C VHS, LV.** Charlie Sheen, Michael Madsen, Linda Fiorentino, Courtney B. Vance, Leon Rippy, Rip Torn; **D:** Larry Ferguson; **W:** Larry Ferguson; **M:** John D'Andrea, Cory Lerios. *LIV*

Beyond the Limit 🐾🐾½ *The Honorary Consul*
1983 (R) The story of an intense and darkly ominous love triangle which takes place in the South American coastal city of Corrientes. Based on Graham Greene's novel "The Honorary Consul." **103m/C VHS, Beta.** Michael Caine, Richard Gere, Bob Hoskins, Elpidia Carrillo; **D:** John MacKenzie; **W:** Christopher Hampton; **C:** Phil Meheux. *PAR*

Beyond the Next Mountain 🐾 1987
(PG) A missionary in China attempts to convert all those he meets. Thin plot and marginal acting will likely make viewers fall asleep. **97m/C VHS, Beta.** Alberto Isaac, Jon Lormer, Bennett Ohta, Richard Lineback, Edward Ashley, Barry Foster; **D:** James F. Collier, Rolf Forsberg. *NO*

Beyond the Poseidon Adventure 🐾
1979 (PG) A sequel to the 1972 film in which salvage teams and ruthless looting vandals compete for access to the sunken ocean liner. Sinking ships should be abandoned. **115m/C VHS, Beta.** Michael Caine, Sally Field, Telly Savalas, Peter Boyle, Jack Warden, Slim Pickens, Shirley Knight, Shirley Jones, Karl Malden, Mark Harmon; **D:** Irwin Allen; **C:** Joseph Biroc. *WAR*

Beyond the Rockies 🐾🐾½ 1932
Keene and a group of cowboys battle cattle rustlers in this action-packed sagebrush saga. Solid script with good direction by Allen. **55m/B VHS.** Tom Keene, Rochelle Hudson, Ernie Adams, Julian Rivero, Hank Bell, Tom London; **D:** Fred Allen; **W:** John P. McCarthy. *MOV*

Beyond the Silhouette 🐾 *Ultimate Desires*
1990 It starts out as another sleazy video sex thriller, as the lawyer heroine discovers her sensuality and poses a lot in her underclothes. Then in the third act it become a hyper-paranoid political-conspiracy assassination-o-rama. Pretty weird junk. **90m/C VHS, Beta.** *CA* Tracy Scoggins, Marc Singer, Brion James; **D:** Lloyd A. Simanol. *NO*

Beyond the Stars 🐾 1989
A sci-fi adventure directed by the author of "Cocoon," wherein a whiz-kid investigates the NASA cover-up of a deadly accident that occurred on the moon during the Apollo 11 landing. Unfortunately, the interesting cast can't make up for the script. **94m/C VHS, Beta, LV.** Martin Sheen, Christian Slater, Olivia D'Abo, F. Murray Abraham, Robert Foxworth, Sharon Stone; **D:** David Saperstein. *LIV*

Beyond the Time Barrier 🐾🐾½ 1960
Air Force test pilot gets more than he bargained for when his high speed plane carries him into the future. There he sees the ravages of an upcoming plague, to which he must return. **75m/B VHS, Beta.** Robert Clarke, Darlene Tompkins, Arianne Arden, Vladimir Sokoloff; **D:** Edgar G. Ulmer. *SNC, CNM*

Beyond the Trail 1926
One of Bill Patton's most entertaining and funny films. In this comedic Western adventure he must face Black Mike and his gang and rescue Mary from their clutches. **50m/C VHS.** Bill Patton, Sheldon Lewis, Stuart Holmes, Eric Wayne, Janet Dawn, Clara Horton, James F. Fulton; **D:** Al(bert) Herman. *GPV*

Beyond the Valley of the Dolls 🐾🐾½ 1970 (NC-17)
Sleazy, spirited non-sequel to "Valley of the Dolls." Meyer ("Faster, Pussycat! Kill! Kill!") directed this Hollywood parody ("BVD," as it came to be known) about an all-girl rock combo and their search for stardom. Labeled the first "exploitation horror camp musical"—how can you pass that up? Screenplay by film critic Ebert, from an original story by Ebert and Meyer. Mondo trasho. **109m/C VHS, Beta, LV.** Edy Williams, Dolly Reed; **D:** Russ Meyer; **W:** Roger Ebert. *FXV, BTV*

Beyond the Walls 🐾🐾½ *Meachorei Hasoragim*
1984 (R) The opposing factions of a hellish Israeli prison unite to beat the system. Brutal with good characterizations. Available in both subtitled and dubbed versions. **104m/C VHS, Beta.** *IS* Arnon Zadok, Muhamad Bakri; **D:** Uri Barbash; **W:** Benny Barbash. Venice Film Festival '85: Best Film; Nominations: Academy Awards '84: Best Foreign Language Film. *WAR*

Beyond Therapy 🐾½ 1986 (R)
A satire on modern psychotherapy, from the play by Christopher Durang, about a confused, crazily neurotic couple and their respective, and not any saner, analysts. Unfortunately, comes off as disjointed and confused. **93m/C VHS, Beta, Closed Caption.** Jeff Goldblum, Tom Conti, Julie Hagerty, Glenda Jackson, Christopher Guest; **D:** Robert Altman; **W:** Robert Altman. *VTR, NWV*

Beyond Tomorrow 🐾🐾 1940
Young romance is guided from the spirit world during the Christmas season, as two "ghosts" come back to help young lovers. **84m/B VHS, Beta.** Richard Carlson, Sir C. Aubrey Smith, Jean Parker, Charles Winninger, Harry Carey Sr., Maria Ouspenskaya, Rod La Rocque; **D:** Edward Sutherland. *SNC, NOS, DVT*

Bhaji on the Beach 🐾🐾½ 1994 (R)
Amusing comedy-drama about a group of Indian women who organize a bus outing from Birmingham to the seaside resort town of Blackpool. They range from sari-clad elders to feminist Gen Xers and a couple of teenagers looking for romance. There's bonding and gossiping and secrets galore before the story is tidily wrapped up. **CW:** Language; scene of domestic abuse. **100m/C VHS, Closed Caption.** *GB* Kim Vithana, Jimmi Harkishin, Sarita Khajuria, Mo Sesay, Lalita Ahmed, Shaheen Khan; **D:** Gurinder Chadha; **W:** Meera Syal; **C:** John Kenway; **M:** John Altman, Craig Preuss. *COL*

Bhowani Junction 🐾🐾 1956
A half-Indian, half-English woman is torn between her country and the British officer she loves in post-colonial India. Great cinematography. Based on a book by John Masters. **110m/C VHS, LV.** Ava Gardner, Stewart Granger, Bill Travers, Abraham Sofaer, Francis Matthews, Marne Maitland, Peter Illing, Edward Chapman, Freda Jackson, Lionel Jeffries; **D:** George Cukor; **C:** Frederick A. (Freddie) Young; **M:** Miklos Rozsa. *MGM*

The Bible 🐾 1966
Bloated, even by religious epic standards, Huston's drama covers the first 22 chapters of Genesis. So you get the Creation, Adam and Eve, Noah and the ark, the flood, the Tower of Babel, and Abraham, among other would-be spectacles. **174m/C VHS.** Michael Parks, Ulla Bergryd, Richard Harris, Stephen Boyd, George C. Scott, Ava Gardner, Peter O'Toole, Franco Nero, John Huston; **D:** John Huston; **W:** Christopher Fry, Vittorio Bonicelli; **C:** Giuseppe Rotunno; **M:** Toshiro Mayuzumi. Nominations: Academy Awards '66: Best Original Score. *TCF*

The Bible...In the Beginning 🐾🐾🐾
1966 The book of Genesis is dramatized, including the stories of Adam and Eve, Cain and Abel, and Noah and the flood. **155m/C VHS, Beta, LV.** *IT* George C. Scott, Richard Harris, Stephen Boyd, John Huston, Peter O'Toole, Franco Nero, Ava Gardner; **D:** John

Huston; **C:** Giuseppe Rotunno. National Board of Review Awards '66: 10 Best Films of the Year. *FOX*

The Bicycle Thief 🐾🐾🐾🐾 *Ladri di Biciclette*
1948 A world classic and indisputable masterpiece about an Italian workman who finds a job, only to have the bike he needs for work stolen; he and his son search Rome for it. A simple story that seems to contain the whole of human experience, and the masterpiece of Italian neo-realism. Based on the book by Luigi Bartolini. In Italian with English subtitles. **90m/B VHS, Beta, LV.** *IT* Lamberto Maggiorani, Lianella Carell, Enzo Staiola, Elena Altieri, Vittorio Antonucci, Gino Saltamerenda, Fausto Guerzoni; **D:** Vittorio De Sica; **W:** Cesare Zavattini. Academy Awards '49: Best Foreign Language Film; British Academy Awards '49: Best Film; Golden Globe Awards '50: Best Foreign Film; National Board of Review Awards '49: 5 Best Foreign Films of the Year, Best Director (De Sica); New York Film Critics Awards '49: Best Foreign Film; Nominations: Academy Awards '49: Best Screenplay. *NOS, MRV, FCT*

Big 🐾🐾🐾½ 1988 (PG)
A 13-year-old boy makes a wish at a carnival fortune-teller to be "big." When he wakes up the next morning he finds that he suddenly won't fit into his clothes and his mother doesn't recognize him. Until he finds a cure, he must learn to live in the adult world—complete with job, apartment, and romance. Perkins is wonderful as a warming cynic while Hanks is totally believable as the little boy inside a man's body. Marshall directs with authority and the whole thing clicks from the beginning. **98m/C VHS, Beta, LV.** Tom Hanks, Elizabeth Perkins, John Heard, Robert Loggia, Jared Rushton, David Moscow, Jon Lovitz, Mercedes Ruehl; **D:** Penny Marshall; **W:** Gary Ross; **M:** Howard Shore. Golden Globe Awards '89: Best Actor—Musical/Comedy (Hanks); Los Angeles Film Critics Association Awards '88: Best Actor (Hanks); People's Choice Awards '89: Best Film—Musical/Comedy; Nominations: Academy Awards '88: Best Actor (Hanks), Best Original Screenplay. *FOX, HMV*

Big Bad John 🐾½ 1990 (PG-13)
Some good ol' boys ride around in trucks as they get into a variety of shootouts. The soundtrack includes music by Willie Nelson, The Charlie Daniels Band, and others. **91m/C VHS, Beta, LV.** Jimmy Dean, Ned Beatty, Jack Elam, Bo Hopkins, Romy Windsor, Doug English. *IME*

Big Bad Mama 🐾🐾½ 1974 (R)
Tough and sexy machine-gun toting mother moves her two nubile daughters out of Texas during the Depression, and they all turn to robbing banks as a means of support while creating sharp testosterone increases among the local men. "Wild Palm" Dickinson has notable nude scene with Captain Kirk. "Big Bad Mama 2" arrived some 13 years later. **83m/C VHS, Beta.** Angie Dickinson, William Shatner, Tom Skerritt, Susan Sennett, Robbie Lee, Sally Kirkland, Noble Willingham, Royal Dano, Dick Miller; **D:** Steve Carver; **W:** William W. Norton Sr. *NHO*

Big Bad Mama 2 🐾½ 1987 (R)
Belated Depression-era sequel to the 1974 Roger Corman gangster film, where the pistol-packin' matriarch battles a crooked politician with the help of her two daughters. **85m/C VHS, Beta.** Angie Dickinson, Robert Culp, Danielle Brisebois, Julie McCullough; **D:** Jim Wynorski; **W:** Jim Wynorski, R.J. Robertson. *MGM*

The Big Bet 🐾 1985 (R)
High school sex comedy about a guy who is challenged by the school bully to get the gorgeous new girl into bed. Energetic romp is for adults. **CW:** Language and strong sexuality. **90m/C VHS, Beta.** Sylvia Kristel, Kimberly Evenson, Ron Thomas; **D:** Bert I. Gordon. *NO*

The Big Bird Cage 🐾🐾 *Women's Penitentiary 2*
1972 (R) Prison spoof sequel to "The Big Doll House." Horny females incarcerated in a rural jail decide to defy their homosexual guards and plan an escape. They are aided by revolutionaries led by a Brooklynese expatriate and his lover. **93m/C VHS, Beta.** Pam Grier, Sid Haig, Anitra Ford, Candice Roman, Teda Bracci, Carol Speed, Karen McKevic; **D:** Jack Hill. *WAR*

The Big Blue ⅆ½ *Le Grand Bleu* 1988 (PG) Vapid, semi-true tale about competing free-divers, who descend deep into the big blue without the aid of any kind of breathing apparatus. Arquette is the ditz who makes them come up for air. **122m/C VHS, Beta, LV, Closed Caption.** Rosanna Arquette, Jean Reno, Jean-Marc Barr, Paul Shenar, Sergio Castellitto, Marc Duret, Griffin Dunne; **D:** Luc Besson; **W:** Luc Besson; **M:** Bill Conti. Cesar Awards '89: Best Sound, Best Score. COL

Big Bluff ⅆⅆ *Worthy Deceivers* 1955 Disappointing result from an interesting premise: fatally ill woman finds love, but when she surprisingly recovers, her new husband decides to help her back along the path to death. Uneven and melodramatic. **70m/B VHS.** SI John Bromfield, Martha Vickers, Robert Hutton, Rosemary Bowe; **D:** W. Lee Wilder. NOS, MOV, HEG

Big Boss ⅆ½ 1977 (R) A hoodlum climbs to the top of a crime syndicate. An Italian film previously titled "Mr. Scarface." **90m/C Beta.** IT Jack Palance, Edmund Purdom, Al Cliver, Harry Baer, Gisela Hahn. NO

The Big Broadcast of 1938 ⅆ½ 1938 Fields is the owner of an ocean liner which he enters in a race. Supposedly, the ship can convert the electricity from radio broadcasts into power for the propellers. No, it doesn't make sense, as it's just an excuse for various radio stars to show off their routines in the ship's entertainment room. Hope, in his first feature, gets to sing his Oscar-winning signature tune "Thanks for the Memories." **94m/B VHS.** W.C. Fields, Martha Raye, Dorothy Lamour, Shirley Ross, Russell Hicks, Bob Hope, Ben Blue, Leif Erickson; **D:** Mitchell Leisen; **W:** Walter DeLeon, Francis Martin. Academy Awards '38: Best Song ("Thanks for the Memories"). USH

The Big Brawl ⅆ½ 1980 (R) Chicago gangster recruits a martial arts expert to fight in a free-for-all match in Texas. **95m/C VHS, Beta.** Jackie Chan, Jose Ferrer, Mako, Rosalind Chao; **D:** Robert Clouse; **W:** Robert Clouse; **M:** Lalo Schifrin. WAR

The Big Broadcast of 1938 ⅆ½ 1938 Fields is the owner of an ocean liner which he enters in a race. Supposedly, the ship can convert the electricity from radio broadcasts into power for the propellers. No, it doesn't make sense, as it's just an excuse for various radio stars to show off their routines in the ship's entertainment room. Hope, in his first feature, gets to sing his Oscar-winning signature tune "Thanks for the Memories." **94m/B VHS.** W.C. Fields, Martha Raye, Dorothy Lamour, Shirley Ross, Russell Hicks, Bob Hope, Ben Blue, Leif Erickson; **D:** Mitchell Leisen; **W:** Walter DeLeon, Francis Martin. Academy Awards '38: Best Song ("Thanks for the Memories"). USH

Big Bully ⅆⅆ 1995 (PG) David Leary (Moranis) is an aspiring novelist who moves back to the town where he was picked on as a kid. His son immediately starts bullying a smaller child, whose father happens to be Roscoe "Fang" Bigger (Arnold), David's former tormentor. The timid henpecked Roscoe's sadistic streak is awakened with the reappearance of his old prey, leading to a barrage of wet willies and indian burns. The slapstick quickly escalates to danger before all is tied up in a syrupy sweet ending. With Moranis playing the nerdy bespectacled underdog and Arnold playing the loud obnoxious guy (although that might not be acting), it may be time to call the typecasting cops. Don Knotts (looking very un-Barney-like) makes an appearance as the high school principal. **93m/C VHS.** Tom Arnold, Rick Moranis, Julianne Phillips, Don Knotts, Carol Kane, Jeffrey Tambor, Curtis Armstrong, Faith Prince, Tony Pierce, Blake Bashoff; **D:** Steve Miner; **W:** Mark Steven Johnson; **C:** Daryn Okada; **M:** David Newman. Golden Raspberry Awards '96: Worst Actor (Arnold). WAR

The Big Bus ⅆⅆ 1976 (PG) The wild adventures of the world's first nuclear-powered bus as it makes its maiden voyage from New York to Denver. Clumsy disaster-movie parody. **88m/C VHS, Beta.** Joseph Bologna, Stockard Channing, Ned Beat-

ty, Ruth Gordon, Larry Hagman, John Beck, Jose Ferrer, Lynn Redgrave, Sally Kellerman, Stuart Margolin, Richard Mulligan, Howard Hesseman, Richard B. Shull; **D:** James Frawley; **W:** Lawrence J. Cohen; **C:** Harry Stradling Jr.; **M:** David Shire. PAR

Big Business ⅆⅆ 1988 (PG) Strained high-concept comedy about two sets of identical twins, each played by Tomlin and Midler, mismatched at birth by a near-sighted country nurse. The city set of twins intends to buy out the factory where the country set of twins work. So the country twins march up to the big city to stop the sale and destruction of their beloved home. Both set of twins stay in the Plaza Hotel and zany consequences ensue. Essentially a one-joke outing with some funny moments, but talented comediennes Midler and Tomlin are somewhat wasted. Great technical effects. **98m/C VHS, Beta, LV, 8mm, Closed Caption.** Bette Midler, Lily Tomlin, Fred Ward, Edward Herrmann, Michele Placido, Barry Primus, Michael Gross, Mary Gross, Daniel Gerroll, Roy Brocksmith; **D:** Jim Abrahams; **C:** Dean Cundey. TOU

Big Business Girl ⅆⅆ 1931 Less than remarkable comedy starring Young as a corporate climber who must dodge her boss' advances and save her troubled marriage when her jazz singer husband is called away to perform in Paris. Based on a story by Patricia Reilly and Harold N. Swanson. **72m/B VHS.** Loretta Young, Frank Albertson, Ricardo Cortez, Joan Blondell, Dorothy Christy; **D:** William A. Seiter; **W:** Robert Lord. MGM

The Big Bust Out woof! 1973 (R) Several female convicts escape from prison only to be sold into slavery and face additional torture. Nothing redeeming about this exploitative film. **75m/C VHS, Beta.** Vonetta McGee, Monica Taylor, Linda Fox, Karen Carter, Gordon Mitchell; **D:** Karen Carter.

Big Calibre ⅆ 1935 A rancher is inches away from being lynched for his dad's murder before he is found to be innocent. **59m/B VHS, Beta.** Bob Steele, Bill Quinn, Earl Dwire, Peggy Campbell, John Elliott, Georgia O'Dell; **D:** Robert North Bradbury. SNC, DVT, HEG

The Big Cat ⅆⅆ 1949 Mountain valley in Utah is ravaged by a cougar, while two ranchers fuss and feud. Big cat, bickering, help make okay adventure. **75m/C VHS, Beta.** Lon McCallister, Peggy Ann Garner, Preston Foster, Forrest Tucker; **D:** Phil Karlson; **C:** William Howard Greene. NOS, MRV, DVT

Big Chase ⅆ 1954 A rookie cop chases down a mob of payroll thieves in this early action film. **60m/B VHS, Beta, LV.** Glenn Langan, Adele Jergens, Lon Chaney Jr., Jim Davis. NO

The Big Chill ⅆⅆⅆ½ 1983 (R) Seven former '60s radicals, now coming upon middle age and middle class affluence, reunite on the occasion of an eighth friend's suicide and use the occasion to re-examine their past relationships and commitments. A beautifully acted, immensely enjoyable ballad to both the counter-culture and its Yuppie descendants. Great period music. Kevin Costner is the dead man whose scenes never made it to the big screen. **108m/C VHS, Beta, LV, 8mm, Closed Caption.** Tom Berenger, Glenn Close, Jeff Goldblum, William Hurt, Kevin Kline, Mary Kay Place, Meg Tilly, JoBeth Williams; **D:** Lawrence Kasdan; **W:** Lawrence Kasdan, Barbara Benedek; **C:** John Bailey. Writers Guild of America '83: Best Original Screenplay; Nominations: Academy Awards '83: Best Original Screenplay, Best Picture, Best Supporting Actress (Close). COL, CRC

The Big Clock ⅆⅆⅆ 1948 George Stroud (Milland) is the editor of the successful Crimeways magazine, owned by tyrannical publisher Earl Janoth (Laughton). Forced to miss a vacation with his wife Georgette (O'Sullivan), George winds up spending time with lovely Pauline (Johnson), whom he inadvertently discovers is the boss' mistress. Pauline's murdered and George is quick to realize all the clues are deliberately pointed in his direction. Classic crime melodrama adapted from Kenneth Fearing's novel. Remade as "No Way Out" (1987). **95m/B VHS, Closed Caption.** Ray Milland, Charles Laughton, Maureen

O'Sullivan, George Macready, Rita Johnson, Dan Tobin, Elsa Lanchester, Harry (Henry) Morgan; **D:** John Farrow; **W:** Jonathan Latimer; **C:** John Seitz; **M:** Victor Young. USH

Big Combo ⅆⅆⅆ 1955 A gangster's ex-girlfriend helps a cop to smash a crime syndicate. Focuses on the relationship between Wilde's cop and the gangster Conte in an effective film noir, with some scenes of torture that were ahead of their time. **87m/B VHS, Beta.** Cornel Wilde, Richard Conte, Jean Wallace, Brian Donlevy, Earl Holliman, Lee Van Cleef, Helen Walker; **D:** Joseph H. Lewis; **W:** Philip Yordan; **C:** John Alton. PSM

The Big Country ⅆⅆ½ 1958 (R) Ex-sea captain Peck heads west to marry fiance Baker and live on her father's (Bickford) ranch. Peck immediately clashes with ranch foreman Heston and finds out there's a vicious feud with neighbor Ives. Then Peck decides he and Baker aren't meant to be and he falls for schoolmarm Simmons instead. It's too long but if you like sprawling western sagas, this one has its moments. **168m/C VHS, Beta.** Gregory Peck, Charlton Heston, Burl Ives, Jean Simmons, Carroll Baker, Chuck Connors; **D:** William Wyler. Academy Awards '58: Best Supporting Actor (Ives); Golden Globe Awards '59: Best Supporting Actor (Ives); Nominations: Academy Awards '58: Original Dramatic/Comedy Score. MGM, BTV

The Big Crimewave ⅆⅆ 1986 A cast of unknowns in a comedy about a loner who takes a bus to Kansas City (Kansas City?) to become a screenwriter, with comic adventures along the way. A feast of jabs at genre films. **80m/C VHS, Beta.** CA John Paizs, Eva Covacs, Darrel Baran; **D:** John Paizs. HHE

Big Deadly Game ⅆ½ 1954 A vacationing American gets caught up in a complicated espionage plot by helping a mysterious wartime buddy. **63m/B VHS, Beta, LV.** Lloyd Bridges, Simone Silva, Finlay Currie. NO

Big Deal on Madonna Street ⅆⅆⅆ *The Usual Unidentified Thieves* 1958 A band of inept crooks plan to make themselves very rich when they attempt to rob a jewelry store. Their elaborate plans cause numerous (and hilarious) disasters. In Italian with English subtitles. Remade as "Crackers." **90m/B VHS, Beta.** IT Marcello Mastroianni, Vittorio Gassman, Claudia Cardinale; **D:** Mario Monicelli. Nominations: Academy Awards '58: Best Foreign Language Film. CVC, MRV, DVT

The Big Dis ⅆⅆ 1989 An interracial comedy about a young black soldier on a weekend pass who's looking for a willing sexual partner. His confidence is shattered when 12 possibilities turn him down. Feature debut of Eriksen and O'Brien. **88m/B VHS.** **D:** Gordon Eriksen, John O'Brien. FCT, FRF

The Big Doll House ⅆⅆ *Women's Penitentiary 1; Women in Cages* 1971 (R) Roger Corman-produced prison drama about a group of tormented female convicts who decide to break out. Features vintage Grier, and a caliber of women's-prison sleaziness that isn't equalled in today's films. **93m/C VHS, Beta.** Judy Brown, Roberta Collins, Pam Grier, Brooke Mills, Pat Woodell, Sid Haig, Christianne Schmidtmer, Kathryn Loder; **D:** Jack Hill; **M:** Les Baxter. NLC

The Big Easy ⅆⅆⅆ½ 1987 (R) A terrific thriller. A slick New Orleans detective uncovers a heroin-based mob war while romancing the uptight assistant DA who's investigating corruption on the police force. An easy, Cajun-flavored mystery, a fast-moving action-comedy, a very sexy romance, and a serious exploration of the dynamics of corruption. **101m/C VHS, Beta, LV, Closed Caption.** Dennis Quaid, Ellen Barkin, Ned Beatty, John Goodman, Ebbe Roe Smith, Charles Ludlam, Lisa Jane Persky, Tom O'Brien, Grace Zabriskie, Marc Lawrence; **D:** Jim McBride; **W:** Dan Petrie Jr.; **C:** Alfonso Beato; **M:** Brad Fiedel. Independent Spirit Awards '88: Best Actor (Quaid). HBO, FCT

The Big Fix 🎬🎬🎬 **1978 (PG)** Private investigator Moses Wine finds himself in an ironic situation: searching for a fugitive alongside whom he'd protested in the 60s. Based on a Roger Simon novel. **108m/C VHS, Beta.** Richard Dreyfuss, Susan Anspach, Bonnie Bedelia, John Lithgow, F. Murray Abraham, Fritz Weaver, Mandy Patinkin; **D:** Jeremy Paul Kagan; **M:** Bill Conti. *USH*

Big Foot woof! **1972** Even genre devotees will be disappointed with this one. Sasquatch, who has procreation on his mind, searches rather half-heartedly for a human mate. A horror flick that forgot to include the horror. **92m/C VHS, Beta.** Chris Mitchum, Joi Lansing, John Carradine, John Mitchum; **D:** Bob Slatzer. *NO*

The Big Gag 🎬 **1987 (R)** An international group of comedians travel the world and pull gags on people. Lame. **84m/C VHS, Beta.** *TWE, HHE*

Big Girls Don't Cry...They Get Even 🎬½ **1992 (PG)** A teenage girl decides to run away from home after she's driven crazy by her eccentric new stepfamily. Comic confusion ensues as various family members set out to find her. Hackneyed script and annoying characters hinder this comedy. **98m/C VHS, LV, Closed Caption.** Hillary Wolf, Griffin Dunne, Margaret Whitton, David Strathairn, Ben Savage, Adrienne Shelly, Patricia Kalember; **D:** Joan Micklin Silver. *COL, NLC*

The Big Grab 🎬🎬½ **1963** A dark big caper thriller about a couple of aging French thugs determined to rip off a casino at Cannes. In French with English subtitles. Also called "Any Number Can Win." **118m/B VHS, Beta.** *FR* Jean Gabin, Alain Delon, Viviane Romance, Maurice Biraud, Carla Marlier; **D:** Henri Verneuil. *FCT*

The Big Green 🎬½ **1995 (PG)** British teacher Anna Montgomery (D'Abo) blows into a small Texas town determined to give the deprived kiddies a boost of self-esteem. With help from the town sheriff (Guttenberg), Anna organizes a soccer team that's supposed to give the kids a reason to live. Problems abound when the star player disappears just before the face-off with the biggest, nastiest team in the league. Sound familiar? This is the soccer version of "The Bad News Bears," "The Little Giants," and "The Mighty Ducks." The formula is less successful in this case, but some mildly amusing moments and a few fresh performances from the kids offer minor bright spots in this tired scenario. **100m/C VHS, LV, Closed Caption.** Olivia D'Abo, Steve Guttenberg, Jay O. Sanders, John Terry, Chauncey Leopardi, Patrick Renna, Billy L. Sullivan, Yareli Arizmendi, Bug Hall; **D:** Holly Goldberg Sloan; **W:** Holly Goldberg Sloan; **C:** Ralf Bode; **M:** Randy Edelman. *TOU*

A Big Hand for the Little Lady 🎬🎬½ *Big Deal at Dodge City* **1966** Fonda and Woodward, playing two West-headed country bumpkins, get involved in a card game in Laredo against high rollers Robards and McCarthy. Fonda risks his savings, finds himself stuck with a losing hand, and has a bit of heart trouble; that's where the little lady comes in. Fine performances and a nifty twist ending don't entirely compensate for the overly-padded script (which evolved from a 48-minute TV play drafted by Sydney Carroll). **95m/C VHS, Beta.** Henry Fonda, Joanne Woodward, Jason Robards Jr., Charles Bickford, Burgess Meredith, Kevin McCarthy; **D:** Fielder Cook; **C:** Lee Garmes. *WAR, FCT*

The Big Hangover 🎬🎬 **1950** Odd story about a man whose allergy to alcohol makes him drunk at the most inopportune moments. Johnson stars as the attorney with the peculiar problem and Taylor plays the boss' daughter who helps him overcome the allergy. Good supporting cast can't help this otherwise boring and predictable film. **82m/B VHS.** Van Johnson, Elizabeth Taylor, Percy Waram, Fay Holden, Leon Ames, Edgar Buchanan, Selena Royle, Gene Lockhart; **D:** Norman Krasna; **W:** Norman Krasna. *MGM*

The Big Heat 🎬🎬🎬½ **1953** When detective Ford's wife (played by Jocelyn Brando, sister of Marlon) is killed in an explosion meant for him, he pursues the gangsters behind it and uncovers a police scandal. His appetite is whetted after this discovery and he pursues the criminals even more vigorously with the help of gangster moll Gloria Grahame. Definitive film noir. **90m/B VHS, Beta, LV.** Glenn Ford, Lee Marvin, Gloria Grahame, Jocelyn Brando, Alexander Scourby, Carolyn Jones; **D:** Fritz Lang; **C:** Charles B(ryant) Lang. Edgar Allan Poe Awards '53: Best Screenplay. *COL*

The Big House 🎬🎬🎬 **1930** Prison melodrama at its best follows top con Beery as he plans a big breakout—and is betrayed. Life in the pen is depicted as brutal and futile, with sadistic guards and a hapless warden. Spawned numerous imitators. **80m/B VHS.** Wallace Beery, Chester Morris, Robert Montgomery, Lewis Stone, Leila Hyams, George F. Marion Sr., Karl Dane, DeWitt Jennings; **D:** George Hill; **W:** Frances Marion. Academy Awards '30: Best Writing; Nominations: Academy Awards '30: Best Actor (Beery), Best Picture. *MGM*

The Big Hurt 🎬½ **1987 (R)** A reporter investigating a bizarre double murder discovers a secret government agency involved in torture and mind-control. **90m/C VHS, Beta, LV.** *AU* David Bradshaw, Lian Lunson, Simon Chilvers, Nick Wateres; **D:** Barry Peak. *NO*

Big Jake 🎬🎬 **1971 (PG)** An aging Texas cattle man who has outlived his time swings into action when outlaws kidnap his grandson and wound his son. He returns to his estranged family to help them in the search for Little Jake. O'Hara is once again paired up with Wayne and the chemistry is still there. **90m/C VHS, Beta, LV, Closed Caption.** John Wayne, Richard Boone, Maureen O'Hara, Patrick Wayne, Chris Mitchum, Bobby Vinton; **D:** George Sherman; **C:** William Clothier; **M:** Elmer Bernstein. *FOX*

Big Jim McLain 🎬🎬 **1952** Wayne and Arness are federal agents working on behalf of the House Un-American Activities Committee to eliminate communist terrorism in Hawaii. And there's a suspicious psychiatrist, too: Wayne falls for a babe whose boss is a shrink who doesn't quite seem on the level. Definitely not a highpoint in the Duke's career. **90m/C VHS, LV, Closed Caption.** John Wayne, Nancy Olson, James Arness, Veda Ann Borg; **D:** Edward Ludwig; **C:** Archie Stout. *WAR, FCT*

The Big Knife 🎬🎬🎬 **1955** Palance plays a Hollywood superstar who refuses to renew his studio contract, which enrages studio boss Steiger. It seems Steiger knows a very damaging secret about the star and is willing to go to any lengths to have Palance re-sign or wind up destroying himself. A ruthless, emotional look at fame and power, with excellent performances by all. Based on the play by Clifford Odets. **113m/B LV.** Jack Palance, Rod Steiger, Ida Lupino, Shelley Winters, Wendell Corey, Jean Hagen, Ilka Chase, Everett Sloane, Wesley Addy, Paul Langton; **D:** Robert Aldrich; **C:** Ernest Laszlo. *FCT*

The Big Lift 🎬🎬½ **1950** Two G.I.'s assigned to the Berlin airlift ally themselves in counter-intelligence when they discover that their mutual girlfriend is a spy. **119m/B VHS, Beta.** Montgomery Clift, Paul Douglas, Cornell Borchers, Bruni Lobel, O.E. Hasse; **D:** George Seaton. *NOS, MRV, DVT*

The Big Man: Crossing the Line 🎬🎬🎬 *Crossing the Line* **1991 (R)** Neeson shines as a down on his luck Scottish miner who loses his job during a union strike. Desperate for cash and unable to resolve his bitterness at being unable to support his family, he's enticed by a Glasgow hood to fight in an illegal bare-knuckled boxing match. What follows is an overlong and extremely brutal fight. Good performances from a talented cast overcome a rather preachy script that doesn't disguise its contempt for the Thatcher government, but also allows a glimpse into the tough times that many Brits suffered during the '80s. Based on the novel by William McIlvanney. **93m/C VHS, LV.** *GB* Liam Neeson, Joanne Whalley, Ian Bannen, Billy Connolly, Hugh Grant, Maurice Roeves, Rob Affleck; **D:** David Leland; **W:** Don MacPherson; **M:** Ennio Morricone. *COL*

Big Man on Campus 🎬 **1989 (PG-13)** A modern-day Quasimodo makes his home in an affluent university's belltower. Of course he falls in love with one of the pretty young co-eds and races out of his tower only to be captured by the psychology department. Really, really bad. **102m/C VHS, Beta, LV.** Tom Skerritt, Corey Parker, Allan Katz, Cindy Williams, Melora Hardin, Jessica Harper; **D:** Jeremy Paul Kagan; **C:** Bojan Bazelli. *VES*

Big Meat Eater 🎬🎬 **1985** A musical gore-comedy about extraterrestrials using radioactive butcher's discards for ship fuel. Deliberate camp that is so bad its funny! **81m/C VHS, Beta.** *CA* George Dawson, Big Miller, Andrew Gillies; **D:** Chris Windsor. *MED*

Big Mo 🎬🎬 *Maurie* **1973 (G)** True story of the friendship that developed between Cincinnati Royals basketball stars Maurice Stokes and Jack Twyman after a strange paralysis hit Stokes. **110m/C VHS, Beta.** Bernie Casey, Bo Svenson, Stephanie Edwards, Janet MacLachlan; **D:** Daniel Mann. *VES*

Big Mouth 🎬 **1967** A dopey fisherman gets ahold of a treasure map and is pursued by cops and gangsters. Standard Lewis fare, with the requisite infantile histrionics; must be French to appreciate. **107m/C VHS, Beta.** Jerry Lewis, Jeannine Riley, Harold J. Stone, Charlie Callas, Buddy Lester, Susan Bay; **D:** Jerry Lewis; **W:** Jerry Lewis; **M:** Harry Betts. *COL*

Big News 🎬🎬 **1929** Based on the play "For Two Cents" by George S. Brooks, this early talkie uses sound to great advantage. Fired for going after a gangster who's a big advertiser (Hardy), reporter Armstrong nevertheless keeps after the crook. When the intrepid reporter pushes too far, murder enters the picture. **75m/B VHS.** Robert Armstrong, Carole Lombard, Tom Kennedy, Warner Richmond, Wade Boteler, Sam Hardy, Lew Ayres; **D:** Gregory La Cava. *NOS*

Big Night 🎬🎬½ **1995 (R)** Set in '50s New Jersey, film provides an Old World/New World look at Italian brothers Primo (Shalhoub) and Secondo (Tucci) Pilaggi and their elegant but failing restaurant. Primo is the perfectionist chef who hates compromise while Secondo wants to Americanize the place in an effort to make it a success. (He knows the customer is always right even if they can't appreciate Primo's exquisitely authentic Italian dishes). In order to get attention, Secondo arranges a special night in honor of jazz great Louis Prima, with Primo out to cook the feast of a lifetime—if they can pull it off. Another food film guaranteed to make you hungry. **CW:** Language. **109m/C VHS, LV, Closed Caption.** Tony Shalhoub, Stanley Tucci, Ian Holm, Minnie Driver, Campbell Scott, Isabella Rossellini, Mark Anthony, Allison Janney; **D:** Stanley Tucci, Campbell Scott; **W:** Stanley Tucci, Joseph Tropiano; **C:** Ken Kelsch. National Society of Film Critics Awards '96: Best Supporting Actor (Shalhoub); Sundance Film Festival '96: Best Screenplay; Nominations: Independent Spirit Awards '97: Best First Feature, Best First Feature (Shalhoub, Tucci). *COL*

The Big Parade 🎬🎬🎬🎬 **1925** Wonderful WWI silent, considered to be one of the best war flicks of all time. Gilbert and Adoree are exceptional as lovers torn apart by the conflict. Interesting and thoughtful picture of the trauma and trouble brought to men and their loved ones in wartime. Battle scenes are compelling and intense; Vidor's masterpiece. **141m/B VHS, LV.** John Gilbert, Renee Adoree, Hobart Bosworth, Claire McDowell, Claire Adams, Karl Dane; **D:** King Vidor. *MGM*

The Big Picture 🎬🎬½ **1989 (PG-13)** A hilarious, overlooked comedy by and starring a variety of Second City/National Lampoon alumni, about a young filmmaker who is contracted to a big studio, only to see his vision trampled by formula-minded producers, crazed agents, hungry starlets, and every other variety of Hollywood predator. **95m/C VHS, Beta, LV, Closed Caption.** Kevin Bacon, Jennifer Jason Leigh, Martin Short, Michael McKean, Emily Longstreth, J.T. Walsh, Eddie Albert, Richard Belzer,

John Cleese, June Lockhart, Stephen Collins, Roddy McDowall, Kim Miyori, Teri Hatcher, Dan Schneider, Jason Gould, Tracy Brooks Swope; **D:** Christopher Guest; **W:** Christopher Guest, Michael McKean, Michael Varhol; **M:** David Nichtern. COL

The Big Push 🎞️½ *Timber Tramps* 1975 (PG) Motley bunch of Alaskan lumberjacks get together to save a poor widow's logging camp from a pair of greedy mill owners. 98m/C VHS, Beta. Joseph Cotten, Claude Akins, Cesar Romero, Tab Hunter, Roosevelt Grier, Leon Ames, Stubby Kaye, Patricia Medina; **D:** Tay Garnett. GEM

Big Red 🎞️🎞️½ 1962 Set amid the spectacular beauty of Canada's Quebec Province, an orphan boy protects a dog which later saves him from a mountain lion. 89m/C VHS, Beta. Walter Pidgeon, Gilles Payant; **D:** Norman Tokar; **C:** Edward Colman. DIS

The Big Red One 🎞️🎞️🎞️½ 1980 (PG) Fuller's harrowing, intense semi-autobiographical account of the U.S. Army's famous First Infantry Division in WWII, the "Big Red One." A rifle squad composed of four very young men, led by the grizzled Marvin, cut a fiery path of conquest from the landing in North Africa to the liberation of the concentration camp at Falkenau, Czechoslovakia. In part a tale of lost innocence, the film scores highest by bringing the raw terror of war down to the individual level. 113m/C VHS, Beta, LV. Lee Marvin, Robert Carradine, Mark Hamill, Stephane Audran; **D:** Samuel Fuller; **W:** Samuel Fuller. FOX, WAR

The Big Scam 🎞️🎞️½ *A Nightingale Sang in Berkeley Square; The Mayfair Bank Caper* 1979 Criminal mastermind Niven recruits ex-con Jordan to pull off a massive bank heist. 102m/C VHS. Richard Jordan, David Niven, Oliver Tobias, Elke Sommer, Gloria Grahame, Hugh Griffith, Richard Johnson; **D:** Ralph Thomas. SIM

Big Score 🎞️ 1983 (R) When a policeman is falsely accused and dismissed from the Chicago Police Department, he goes after the men who really stole the money from a drug bust. Script was originally intended to be a Dirty Harry flick; too bad it wasn't. 88m/C VHS, Beta. Fred Williamson, John Saxon, Richard Roundtree, Nancy Wilson, Ed Lauter, Ron Dean, D'Urville Martin, Michael Dante, Joe Spinell; **D:** Fred Williamson; **C:** Joao Fernandes. VES

Big Shots 🎞️ 1987 (PG-13) Two kids, one naive and white, the other black and streetwise, search for a stolen watch. 91m/C VHS, Beta, LV, **Closed Caption.** Ricky Busker, Darius McCrary, Robert Joy, Paul Winfield, Robert Prosky, Jerzy Skolimowski; **D:** Robert Mandel; **W:** Joe Eszterhas; **M:** Bruce Broughton. ORI, WAR

Big Show 🎞️🎞️ *Home In Oklahoma* 1937 A western adventure about the making of a western adventure. Autry jangles spurs aplenty in duel role. 54m/B VHS, Beta. Gene Autry, Smiley Burnette; **D:** Mack V. Wright. NOS, VCN, VDM

The Big Sky 🎞️🎞️🎞️ 1952 It's 1830, and a rowdy band of fur trappers embark upon a back breaking expedition up the uncharted Missouri River. Based on the A.B. Guthrie Jr. novel, it's an effortlessly enjoyable and level-headed Hawksian American myth, with a streak of gentle gallows humor. Also available colorized. 122m/C VHS, Beta, **Closed Caption.** Kirk Douglas, Dewey Martin, Arthur Hunnicutt, Elizabeth Threatt, Buddy Baer, Steve Geray, Jim Davis; **D:** Howard Hawks. Nominations: Academy Awards '52: Best Black and White Cinematography, Best Supporting Actor (Hunnicutt). FCT, TTC

The Big Sleep 🎞️🎞️🎞️🎞️ 1946 Private eye Philip Marlowe, hired to protect a young woman from her own indiscretions, falls in love with her older sister while uncovering murders galore. A dense, chaotic thriller that succeeded in defining and setting a standard for its genre. The very best Raymond Chandler on film combining a witty script with great performances, especially from Bogart and Bacall. 114m/B VHS, Beta, LV. Humphrey Bogart, Lauren Bacall, John Ridgely, Martha Vickers, Louis Jean Heydt, Regis Toomey, Peggy Knudsen, Dorothy Malone, Bob Steele, Elisha Cook Jr.; **D:** Howard Hawks; **W:**

William Faulkner, Jules Furthman, Leigh Brackett; **M:** Max Steiner. MGM, FOX, TLF

The Big Sleep 🎞️🎞️ 1978 (R) A tired remake of the Raymond Chandler potboiler about exhausted Los Angeles private dick Marlowe and his problems in protecting a wild young heiress from her own decadence and mob connections. Mitchum appears to need a rest. 99m/C VHS, Beta, LV. Robert Mitchum, Sarah Miles, Richard Boone, Candy Clark, Edward Fox, Joan Collins, John Mills, James Stewart, Oliver Reed, Harry Andrews, James Donald, Colin Blakely, Richard Todd; **D:** Michael Winner; **W:** Michael Winner. COL

The Big Slice 🎞️½ 1990 (R) Two would-be crime novelists want to improve their fiction. One masquerades as a cop, the other as a crook, and they infiltrate the underworld from both ends. Clever comedy premise, but vaudeville-level jokes fall flat. **CW:** Sexual dialogue. 86m/C VHS, LV. Casey Siemaszko, Leslie Hope, Justin Louis, Heather Locklear, Kenneth Welsh, Nicholas Campbell, Henry Ramer; **D:** John Bradshaw; **W:** John Bradshaw; **M:** Mychael Danna, Jeff Danna. ACA

The Big Sombrero 🎞️🎞️½ 1949 Autry takes a stand against the marriage between an unsuspecting, wealthy Mexican girl and her fortune-seeking bridegroom who wants her land. 77m/C VHS. Gene Autry, Elena Verdugo, Steve Dunne, George Lewis; **D:** Frank McDonald. NO

The Big Squeeze 🎞️🎞️½ 1996 (R) Married bartender Tanya (Boyle) is displeased to find out her born-again hubby Henry (Bercovici) has been holding out a large wad of cash from an insurance settlement, apparently about to donate it to a local Spanish mission. Enter Benny (Dobson), a cocky con man willing to help Tanya get her share of the dough for his own cut; sweet bartender Jesse (Nucci), who's secretly in love in Tanya; and fellow barmaid Cece (Dispina), who catches Benny's wandering eye. All get caught up in the frantic double-dealing. **CW:** Sexuality and some language. 100m/C VHS, LV. Lara Flynn Boyle, Peter Dobson, Luca Bercovici, Danny Nucci, Teresa Dispina, Sam Vlahos, Valente Rodriguez; **D:** Marcus De Leon; **W:** Marcus De Leon; **C:** Jacques Haitkin; **M:** Mark Mothersbaugh. BMG

Big Stakes 🎞️ 1922 Extremely rare Western feature that has a Texas cowboy falling for a Mexican senorita. Plenty of action as complications ensue. ?m/B VHS. H.B. Warner, Elinor Fair, Les Bates; **D:** Clifford S. Elfelt; **W:** Frank Howard Clark. GVV

The Big Stampede 🎞️🎞️ 1932 Twenty-five year old Wayne stars in this action-packed Western that was a remake of "Land Beyond the Law" from Ken Maynard's silent. Based on a story by Marion Jackson. 63m/B VHS, **Closed Caption.** John Wayne, Noah Beery Sr., Luis Alberni, Berton Churchill, Paul Hurst, Lafe McKee, Frank Ellis, Hank Bell; **D:** Tenny Wright; **W:** Kurt Kempler. MGM, GPV

Big Steal 🎞️🎞️🎞️ 1949 An Army officer recovers a missing payroll and captures the thieves after a tumultuous chase through Mexico. 72m/B VHS, Beta, LV. Robert Mitchum, William Bendix, Jane Greer, Ramon Novarro, Patric Knowles; **D:** Donald Siegel. MED

Big Store 🎞️🎞️½ 1941 Late Marx Brothers in which they are detectives in a large metropolitan department store, foiling a hostile takeover and preventing a murder. Their last MGM effort, with some good moments between the Tony Martin song numbers which include "If It's You" and the immortal "Tenement Symphony." Groucho also leads the "Sing While You Sell" number. 96m/B VHS, Beta. Groucho Marx, Harpo Marx, Chico Marx, Tony Martin, Margaret Dumont, Virginia Grey, Virginia O'Brien; **D:** Charles Riesner; **M:** George Bassman. MGM, CCB

Big Street 🎞️🎞️½ 1942 A timid busboy, in love with a disinterested nightclub singer, gets to prove his devotion when she is crippled in a fall. Based on a Damon Runyon story, "Little Pinks." 88m/B VHS, Beta, LV. Henry Fonda, Lucille Ball, Agnes Moorehead, Louise Beavers, Barton MacLane, Eugene Pallette, Ozzie Nelson; **D:** Irving Reis. MED, TTC

The Big Sweat 🎞️ 1990 Maybe you've heard this one before: a man who has been framed by the mob escapes from prison and heads for Mexico. But first, he's got to get past the mobsters and police who are hot on his trail. And maybe you've seen some of it before: some of the same stock footage appears in Lommel's "Cold Heat." Not surprisingly, this one bypassed theaters and went straight to video. 85m/C VHS, LV. Robert Z'Dar, Steve Molone, Kevin McBride, William Roebuck, Cheri Caspari, David Rushing, Joanne Watkins, Ken Letner; **D:** Ulli Lommel; **W:** Max Bolt; **M:** John Massari. AIP

The Big Switch 🎞️½ *Strip Poker* 1970 (R) Gambler is framed for murder and becomes embroiled in a plot to reinstate an old gangster kingpin. 68m/C VHS, Beta. Sebastian Breaks, Virginia Wetherell, Erlka Raffael; **D:** Pete Walker. NO

Big Top Pee Wee 🎞️🎞️ 1988 (PG) Pee Wee's second feature film following the success of "Pee Wee's Big Adventure." This time Pee Wee owns a farm, has a girlfriend (!) and lives the good life until a weird storm blows a traveling circus onto his property. Cute, but not the manic hilarity the first one was. 86m/C VHS, Beta, LV, 8mm, **Closed Caption.** Paul (Pee Wee Herman) Reubens, Kris Kristofferson, Susan Tyrrell, Penelope Ann Miller; **D:** Randal Kleiser; **W:** Paul (Pee Wee Herman) Reubens; **C:** Steven Poster; **M:** Danny Elfman. PAR

Big Town 🎞️ *Guilty Assignment* 1947 A newspaper is saved by a new editor who brings integrity to the once scandalous paper. The editor and his reporters also solve a series of murders. Some action, but weak dialogue and direction hold it back. Based on the radio program of the same name. 59m/B VHS. Philip Reed, Hillary Brooke, Robert Lowery, Byron Barr, Veda Ann Borg, Nana Bryant, Charles Arnt; **D:** William C. Thomas. SNC

Big Town 🎞️🎞️ 1987 (R) A farmboy, lucky with dice, hits Chicago to claim his fortune where he meets floozies, criminals, and other streetlife. Look for Lane's strip number. 109m/C VHS, Beta, LV. Matt Dillon, Diane Lane, Tommy Lee Jones, Bruce Dern, Tom Skerritt, Lee Grant, Suzy Amis; **D:** Ben Bolt; **C:** Ralf Bode. VES, LIV

Big Town After Dark 🎞️🎞️ *Underworld After Dark* 1947 Daring journalists search for the bottom-line story on a gang of criminals. They find themselves caught behind the firing lines when the sun goes down. Slightly better than average thriller. 69m/B VHS. Philip Reed, Hillary Brooke, Richard Travis, Ann Gillis; **D:** William C. Thomas. NOS, SNC, RXM

Big Trail 🎞️🎞️🎞️ 1930 This pioneering effort in wide-screen cinematography was Wayne's first feature film. A wagon train on the Oregon trail encounters Indians, buffalo, tough terrain, and romantic problems. 110m/B VHS, Beta, **Closed Caption.** John Wayne, Marguerite Churchill, El Brendel, Tully Marshall, Tyrone Power Sr., Ward Bond, Helen Parrish; **D:** Raoul Walsh. FOX

Big Trees 🎞️🎞️🎞️ 1952 A ruthless lumberman attempts a takeover of the California Redwood Timberlands that are owned by a group of peaceful homesteaders. 89m/C VHS, Beta. Kirk Douglas, Patrice Wymore, Eve Miller, Alan Hale Jr.; Edgar Buchanan; **D:** Felix Feist. NOS, MRV, DVT

Big Trouble 🎞️🎞️ 1986 (R) An insurance broker endeavors to send his three sons to Yale by conspiring with a crazy couple in a fraud scheme that goes awry in every possible manner. Look for the cameo by screenwriter Bergman as Warren Bogle. 93m/C VHS, Beta, LV. Alan Arkin, Peter Falk, Beverly D'Angelo, Charles Durning, Robert Stack, Paul Dooley, Valerie Curtin, Richard Libertini; **Cameos:** Andrew Bergman; **D:** John Cassavetes; **W:** Andrew Bergman; **C:** Bill Butler; **M:** Bill Conti. COL

Big Trouble in Little China 🎞️🎞️½ 1986 (PG-13) A trucker plunges beneath the streets of San Francisco's Chinatown to battle an army of spirits. An uproarious comic-book-film parody with plenty of action and a keen sense of sophomoric sarcasm. 99m/C VHS, Beta, LV, **Closed Caption.** Kurt Russell, Suzze Pai, Dennis Dun, Kim Cattrall, James Hong,

Victor Wong, Kate Burton; **D:** John Carpenter; **W:** Gary Goldman, W.D. Richter; **C:** Dean Cundey; **M:** John Carpenter, Alan Howarth. *FXV, FOX*

Big Valley 1968 The western television series's two feature-length episodes: "Explosion," and "Legend of a General." 90m/C VHS, Beta. Richard Long, Linda Evans, Barbara Stanwyck, Lee Majors. *NO*

Big Wednesday 🎬🎬½ *Summer of Innocence* 1978 **(PG)** Three California surfers from the early sixties get back together after the Vietnam war to reminisce about the good old days and take on the big wave. 120m/C VHS, Beta, LV. Jan-Michael Vincent, Gary Busey, William Katt, Lee Purcell, Patti D'Arbanville; **D:** John Milius; **W:** John Milius; **M:** Basil Poledouris. *WAR*

The Big Wheel 🎬🎬½ 1949 Old story retold fairly well. Rooney is young son determined to travel in his father's tracks as a race car driver, even when dad buys the farm on the oval. Good acting and direction keep this a cut above average. 92m/B VHS. Mickey Rooney, Thomas Mitchell, Spring Byington, Mary Hatcher, Allen Jenkins, Michael O'Shea; **D:** Edward Ludwig. *GPV*

Big Zapper 🎬½ 1973 Violent P.I. Marlowe and masochistic assistant Rock work together in this British comic strip film. 94m/C VHS. GB Linda Marlowe, Gary Hope, Sean Hewitt, Richard Monette, Penny Irving; **D:** Lindsay Shonteff. *VCD*

The Bigamist 🎬½ 1953 Have you heard the one about the traveling salesman in this movie? He has one wife in Los Angeles, another in San Francisco, and they inevitably find out about each other. A maudlin soap opera with a do-it-yourself ending, only shows why bigamy was done better as farce in the later "Micki and Maude." 79m/B VHS. Edmond O'Brien, Joan Fontaine, Ida Lupino, Edmund Gwenn, Jane Darwell, Kenneth Tobey; **D:** Ida Lupino. *DVT, NOS, HEG*

Bigfoot: The Unforgettable Encounter 🎬🎬½ 1994 **(PG)** Young boy heads off into the woods, comes face to face with Bigfoot, and sets off a media frenzy and a band of ruthless bounty hunters determined to capture his hairy friend. 89m/C VHS, Closed Caption. Zachery Ty Bryan, Matt McCoy, Barbara Willis Sweete, Clint Howard, Rance Howard, David Rasche; **D:** Corey Michael Eubanks; **W:** Corey Michael Eubanks; **M:** Shimon Arama. *REP*

Biggles 🎬🎬 *Biggles: Adventures in Time* 1985 **(PG)** Time-travel fantasy in which a young businessman from present-day New York City is inexplicably transferred into the identity of a 1917 WWI flying ace. He suddenly finds himself aboard a fighter plane over Europe during WWI. 100m/C VHS, Beta, LV, Closed Caption. GB Neil Dickson, Alex Hyde-White, Peter Cushing; **D:** John Hough. *VTR, NWV*

Bikers, Blondes, and Blood 1993 A montage of the sleaze genre's greatest moments including a clip from Jayne Mansfield's "Single Room Furnished." Suitable for dorm keggers, frat parties or any other venue where the audience wants supplementary amusements of some kind. Some clips in black and white. 90m/B VHS. *SMW, TPV*

Bikini Beach 🎬🎬½ 1964 Surfing teenagers of the "Beach Party" series follow up "Muscle Beach Party" with a third fling at the beach and welcome a visitor, British recording star "Potato Bug" (Avalon in a campy dual role). But, golly gee, wealthy Wynn wants to turn their sandy, surfin' shores into a retirement community. What to do? Sing a few songs, dance in your bathing suits, and have fun. Classic early '60s nostalgia is better than the first two efforts; followed by "Pajama Party." 🎵Because You're You; Love's a Secret Weapon; Bikini Drag. 100m/C VHS, Beta. Annette Funicello, Frankie Avalon, Martha Hyer, Harvey Lembeck, Don Rickles, Stevie Wonder, John Ashley, Keenan Wynn, Jody McCrea, Candy Johnson, Danielle Aubry, Meredith MacRae, Dolores Wells, Donna Loren, Timothy Carey; **D:** William Asher; **W:** William Asher, Leo Townsend, Robert Dillon; **C:** Floyd Crosby; **M:** Les Baxter.

Bikini Bistro 🎬 1994 **(R)** A boring vegetarian cafe gets turned into a gourmet restaurant but, faced with an eviction notice, the female owners decide to increase business by waitressing in bikinis. Also available in an unrated version at 84 minutes. **CW:** Numerous sex-related situations. 80m/C VHS. Marilyn Chambers, Amy Lynn Baxter, Joan Gerardi, Isabelle Fortea, John Altamura, Joseph Pallister; **D:** Ernest G. Sauer; **W:** Matt Unger. *AVI*

The Bikini Car Wash Company woof! *California Hot Wax* 1990 **(R)** Babes in bikinis in Los Angeles. A young man is running his uncle's carwash when he meets a business major who persuades him to let her take over the business for a cut of the profits. She decides that a good gimmick would be to dress all the female employees in the tiniest bikinis possible. The story is of course secondary to the amount of flesh on display. Also available in an unrated version. **CW:** Language, nudity, and sexuality. 87m/C VHS, Closed Caption. Joe Dusic, Neriah Napaul, Suzanne Browne, Kristie Ducati; **D:** Ed Hansen. *IMP*

The Bikini Car Wash Company 2 🎬 1992 **(R)** Entrepreneur Melissa and the other lovely ladies of the Bikini Car Wash Co. find themselves a big success, so much so that a greedy businessman wants to buy them out. In order to get money to fight the takeover, the ladies take to the airwaves of a cable-access station. Their new business adventure involves selling sexy lingerie which means the flesh quotient is as great as ever. An unrated version is also available. **CW:** Nudity and sexual situations. ?m/C VHS, LV, Closed Caption. Kristie Ducati, Suzanne Browne, Neriah Napaul, Rikki Brando, Greg Raye, Larry De Russy; **D:** Gary Orona; **W:** Bart B. Gustis; **M:** Michael Smith. *IMP*

Bikini Drive-In 🎬½ 1994 **(R)** Babe (Rhey) inherits grandad's decrepit drive-in, which is wanted by a mall mogul, but she refuses to sell. So to raise some cash, Rhey stages a B-movie marathon with in-person, bikini-clad scream queens. **CW:** Strong sexual content. 85m/C VHS. Ashlie Rhey, Richard Gabai, Ross Hagen, Sara Bellomo, Steve Barkett, Conrad Brooks; **D:** Fred Olen Ray. *AVI*

Bikini Island 🎬 1991 **(R)** Beautiful swimsuit models gather on a remote tropical island for a big photo shoot, each vying to be the next cover girl of the hottest swimsuit magazine. Before long, scantily clad lovelies are turning up dead and full out madness ensues. Will the mystery be solved before they run out of models, or will the magazine have no choice but to grace its cover with a bikinied cadaver? Low-budget trash that has few, if any, redeeming qualities. **CW:** Violence and sensuality. 85m/C VHS, Beta. Holly Floria, Alicia Anne, Jackson Robinson, Shannon Stiles, Cyndi Pass, Sherry Johnson; **D:** Anthony Markes; **W:** Emerson Bixby; **M:** Marc David Deeker. *PSM*

Bikini Summer 🎬½ 1991 Laughs, music, and skin are the order of the day as two nutty guys and a few beautiful girls form an unlikely friendship on the beach. Konop was Julia Roberts's "Pretty Woman" body double. Sort of the 90's version of the old 60's Frankie and Annette beach parties. 90m/C VHS, LV. David Millburn, Melinda Armstrong, Jason Clow, Shelley Michelle, Alex Smith, Kent Lipham, Kelly Konop, Carmen Santa Maria; **D:** Robert Veze; **W:** Robert Veze, Nick Stone; **M:** John Gonzalez. *PMH*

Bikini Summer 2 🎬 1992 **(R)** An eccentric family decides to stage a bikini contest to raise money to help the homeless. 94m/C VHS, LV. Jeff Conaway, Jessica Hahn, Melinda Armstrong, Avalon Anders; **D:** Jeff Conaway; **M:** Jim Halfpenny. *PMH*

Bilitis 🎬½ 1977 **(R)** A young girl from a private girls' school is initiated into the pleasures of sex and the unexpected demands of love. One of director Hamilton's exploitative meditations on nudity. 95m/C VHS, Beta. FR Patti D'Arbanville, Bernard Giraudeau, Mona Kristensen; **D:** David Hamilton. *MED*

Bill 🎬🎬🎬 1981 A made-for-television movie based on a true story about a mentally retarded man who sets out to live independently after 44 years in an institution. Rooney gives an affecting performance as Bill and Quaid is strong as the filmmaker who befriends him. Awarded Emmys for Rooney's performance and the well written script. Followed by "Bill: On His Own." 97m/C VHS, Beta. Mickey Rooney, Dennis Quaid, Largo Woodruff, Harry Goz; **D:** Anthony Page. *LIV*

Bill and Coo 🎬🎬 1947 An unusual love story with a villian and hero using an all bird cast. 61m/C VHS, Beta, 8mm. **D:** Dean Riesner. *VYY, MRV, NOS*

Bill & Ted's Bogus Journey 🎬🎬 1991 **(PG)** Big-budget sequel to B & T's first movie has better special effects but about the same quota of laughs. Slain by lookalike robot duplicates from the future, the airhead heroes pass through heaven and hell before tricking the Grim Reaper into bringing them back for a second duel with their heinous terminators. Most excellent closing-credit montage. Non-fans still won't think much of it. 98m/C VHS, Closed Caption. Keanu Reeves, Alex Winter, William Sadler, Joss Ackland, Pam Grier, George Carlin, Amy Stock-Poynton, Hal Landon Jr., Annette Azcuy, Sarah Trigger, Chelcie Ross, Taj Mahal, Roy Brocksmith, William Shatner; **D:** Pete Hewitt; **W:** Chris Matheson, Edward Solomon; **M:** David Newman. *ORI*

Bill & Ted's Excellent Adventure 🎬🎬½ 1989 **(PG)** Excellent premise: when the entire future of the world rests on whether or not two '80s dudes pass their history final, Rufus comes to the rescue in his time-traveling telephone booth. Bill and Ted share an adventure through time as they meet and get to know some of history's most important figures. 105m/C VHS, Beta, LV, 8mm, Closed Caption. Keanu Reeves, Alex Winter, George Carlin, Bernie Casey, Dan Shor, Robert Barron, Amy Stock-Poynton, Ted Steedman, Terry Camillieri, Rod Loomis, Al Leong, Tony Camilieri; **D:** Stephen Herek; **W:** Chris Matheson, Edward Solomon; **M:** David Newman. *COL, NLC*

A Bill of Divorcement 🎬🎬½ 1932 Hepburn's screen debut, as the daughter of a shell-shocked WWI vet, who requires her care after her mother decides to divorce him. Creaky early talker. 76m/B VHS, Beta, LV, Closed Caption. John Barrymore, Katharine Hepburn, Billie Burke, Henry Stephenson, David Manners, Paul Cavanagh, Elizabeth Patterson; **D:** George Cukor; **M:** Max Steiner. National Board of Review Awards '32: 10 Best Films of the Year. *FOX*

Bill: On His Own 🎬🎬🎬 1983 Rooney is again exceptional in this sequel to the Emmy-winning TV movie "Bill." After 44 years in an institution, a mentally retarded man copes more and more successfully with the outside world. Fine supporting cast and direction control the melodramatic potential. 100m/C VHS. Mickey Rooney, Helen Hunt, Teresa Wright, Dennis Quaid, Largo Woodruff, Paul Leiber, Harry Goz; **D:** Anthony Page. *LIV*

Billie 🎬½ 1965 Duke stars as a tomboy athlete who puts the boys' track team to shame. Some amusing but very predictable situations, plus a few songs from Miss Duke. Based on Ronald Alexander's play "Time Out for Ginger." 86m/C VHS, Beta, LV. Patty Duke, Jim Backus, Jane Greer, Warren Berlinger, Billy DeWolfe, Charles Lane, Dick Sargent, Susan Seaforth Hayes, Ted Bessell, Richard Deacon; **D:** Don Weis; **W:** Ronald Alexander. *MGM*

The Billion Dollar Hobo 🎬½ 1978 **(G)** Poor, unsuspecting heir of a multimillion dollar fortune must duplicate his benefactor's experience as a hobo during the Depression in order to collect his inheritance. Slow-moving family stuff. 96m/C VHS, Beta. Tim Conway, Will Geer, Eric Weston, Sydney Lassick; **D:** Stuart E. McGowan. *FOX*

A Billion for Boris 🎬🎬½ 1990 Boris' TV gives a sneak preview of the future and Boris plans to make some money off of it. Zany comedy in the vein of "Let It Ride." 89m/C VHS, Beta. Lee

Grant, Tim Kazurinsky; **D:** Alex Grasshof; **W:** Mary Rogers. *IMP*

Billionaire Boys Club 🐾🐾½ 1987 Chilling look at greed in the '80s. Nelson plays Joe Hunt, who gets together with a group of rich, preppie friends to manipulate investments in the commodities markets. When a slick con man (Silver) gets in their way he's murdered to keep their schemes intact. Based on a true story and adapted from the book by Sue Horton. Originally shown on television in two parts, the video version is considerably pared down. **94m/C VHS.** Judd Nelson, Frederic Lehne, Brian McNamara, Raphael Sbarge, John Stockwell, Barry Tubb, Stan Shaw, Jill Schoelen, Ron Silver, James Sloyan, James Karen; **D:** Marvin J. Chomsky. *LIV*

Billy Bathgate 🐾🐾½ 1991 (R) Uneven but well acted drama set in 1935 New York. A streetwise young man decides getting ahead during the Depression means gaining the attention of mobster Dutch Schultz and joining his gang. As Billy becomes the confidant of the racketeer he learns the criminal life is filled with suspicion and violence; in order to stay alive he must rely on every trick he's learned. Willis has a small role as a rival mobster who gets fitted for cement overshoes. Kidman does well as Dutch's girlfriend with Hill fine as the gang's number man. Based on the novel by E.L. Doctorow. **CW:** Language and gangster violence. **107m/C VHS, Beta, LV, Closed Caption.** Dustin Hoffman, Nicole Kidman, Loren Dean, Bruce Willis, Steven Hill, Steve Buscemi, Stanley Tucci, Tim Jerome, Billy Jaye, Katharine Houghton, Mike Starr, John Costelloe, Moira Kelly; **D:** Robert Benton; **W:** Tom Stoppard; **C:** Nestor Almendros; **M:** Mark Isham. Nominations: Golden Globe Awards '91: Best Supporting Actress (Kidman). *TOU*

Billy Budd 🐾🐾🐾 1962 The classic Melville good-evil allegory adapted to film, dealing with a British warship in the late 1700s, and its struggle between evil master-at-arms and innocent shipmate. Stamp's screen debut as the naive Billy who is tried for the murder of the sadistic first mate. Well directed and acted. **123m/B VHS, Beta, LV.** **GB** Terence Stamp, Peter Ustinov, Robert Ryan, Melvyn Douglas, Paul Rogers, John Neville, Ronald Lewis, David McCallum, John Meillon; **D:** Peter Ustinov; **W:** Peter Ustinov, Robert Rossen; **C:** Robert Krasker. Nominations: Academy Awards '62: Best Supporting Actor (Stamp). *FOX*

Billy Galvin 🐾🐾½ 1986 (PG) A bullheaded ironworker tries to straighten out the turbulent relationship he has with his rebellious son. **95m/C VHS, Beta.** Karl Malden, Lenny Von Dohlen, Joyce Van Patten, Toni Kalem, Keith Szarabajka, Alan North, Paul Guilfoyle, Barton Heyman; **D:** John Gray; **W:** John Gray; **M:** Joel Rosenbaum. *LIV, VES*

Billy Jack 🐾🐾 1971 (PG) On an Arizona Indian reservation, a half-breed ex-Green Beret with pugnacious martial arts skills (Laughlin) stands between a rural town and a school for runaways. Laughlin stars with his real-life wife Taylor. Features the then-hit song "One Tin Soldier," sung by Coven. The movie and its marketing by Laughlin inspired a "Billy Jack" cult phenomenon. A Spanish-dubbed version of this film is also available. Followed by a sequel in 1974, "Trail of Billy Jack," which bombed. **112m/C VHS, Beta, LV.** Tom Laughlin, Delores Taylor, Clark Howat; **D:** Tom Laughlin; **W:** Tom Laughlin. *WAR*

Billy Liar 🐾🐾🐾 1963 A young Englishman dreams of escaping from his working class family and dead-end job as an undertaker's assistant. Parallels James Thurber's story, "The Secret Life of Walter Mitty." **94m/B VHS, Beta.** **GB** Tom Courtenay, Julie Christie, Finlay Currie; **D:** John Schlesinger; **M:** Richard Rodney Bennett. *REP*

Billy Madison 🐾½ 1994 (PG-13) Wealthy slacker Billy (Sandler) must prove to Dad he is capable of running the family hotel business by undertaking the obvious challenge of repeating grades 1-12 in six months. Ponder a few bodily function gags, and you'll have exhausted the humor in this lame attempt at creating a feature-length movie out of what would barely pass as a

Saturday Night Live sketch. For only the most die-hard fans of Sandler's silly shtick. **CW:** Language; crude humor. **90m/C VHS, LV, Closed Caption.** Adam Sandler, Darren McGavin, Brigitte Wilson, Bradley Whitford, Josh Mostel, Norm MacDonald, Mark Beltzman, Larry Hankin, Theresa Merritt; **Cameos:** Chris Farley, Steve Buscemi; **D:** Tamra Davis; **W:** Adam Sandler; **M:** Randy Edelman. Nominations: MTV Movie Awards '95: Best Comedic Performance (Sandler). *USH*

Billy: Portrait of a Street Kid 🐾🐾 1977 A ghetto youngster tries to pry himself up and out of his bleak surroundings through education, but complications arise when he gets his girlfriend pregnant. **96m/C VHS, Beta.** LeVar Burton, Tina Andrews, Ossie Davis, Michael Constantine; **D:** Steven Gethers. *WOV*

Billy Rose's Jumbo 🐾🐾🐾 *Jumbo* 1962 Better-than-average update of the circus picture. Durante and Raye are terrific, as are the Rodgers and Hart songs. Fun, with lively production numbers in the inimitable Berkeley style. 🎵 Over and Over Again; Circus on Parade; Why Can't I?; This Can't Be Love; The Most Beautiful Girl in the World; My Romance; Little Girl Blue; What is a Circus; Sawdust, Spangles and Dreams. **125m/C VHS, LV.** Doris Day, Stephen Boyd, Jimmy Durante, Martha Raye, Dean Jagger; **D:** Charles Walters; **W:** Sidney Sheldon. Nominations: Academy Awards '62: Best Adapted Score. *MGM*

Billy the Kid 🐾🐾½ 1941 Billy Bonney joins up with a group of outlaws in a Southwest town where he bumps into his old friend Jim Sherwood, now the marshal. Attempting to change his ways, he falls back into the life of a bandit when an outlaw friend is murdered. Although an entertaining western, the story bears no resemblance to the actual last days of Billy the Kid. Based on a story by Howard Emmett Rogers and Bradbury Foote, suggested by the book "The Saga of Billy the Kid" by Walter Noble Burns. **94m/C VHS, Closed Caption.** Robert Taylor, Brian Donlevy, Ian Hunter, Mary Howard, Gene Lockhart, Lon Chaney Jr., Guinn "Big Boy" Williams, Cy Kendall, Henry O'Neill, Ted Adams, Frank Puglia, Mitchell Lewis, Dick Curtis, Grant Withers, Joe Yule, Eddie Dunn, Kermit Maynard, Chill Wills, Olive Blakeney, Carl Pitti; **D:** David Miller; **W:** Gene Fowler Jr.; **M:** David Snell. Nominations: Academy Awards '41: Best Color Cinematography. *MGM*

Billy the Kid in Texas 🐾½ 1940 The famed outlaw takes on trouble and makes sure the Texans never forget that he has been there. **52m/B VHS, Beta.** Bob Steele. *NOS, VCN*

Billy the Kid Returns 🐾½ 1938 While trying to clean up a town of its criminal element, Rogers is mistaken for the legendary Billy. Complications ensue. **60m/B VHS, Beta.** Roy Rogers, George "Gabby" Hayes, Smiley Burnette, Lynn (Mary Hart) Roberts; **D:** Joseph Kane. *NOS, HHT, VCN*

Billy the Kid Trapped 🐾½ 1942 Billy and his partner are rescued from hanging by an outlaw band. **59m/B VHS.** Buster Crabbe, Al "Fuzzy" St. John, Bud McTaggart, Anne Jeffreys, Glenn Strange; **D:** Sam Newfield. *NOS, MRV, DVT*

Billy the Kid Versus Dracula 🐾🐾 1966 The title says it all. Dracula travels to the Old West, anxious to put the bite on a pretty lady ranch owner. Her fiance, the legendary outlaw Billy the Kid, steps in to save his girl from becoming a vampire herself. A Carradine camp classic. **95m/C VHS, Beta.** Chuck Courtney, John Carradine, Melinda Plowman, Walter Janovitz, Harry Carey Jr., Roy Barcroft, Virginia Christine, Bing Russell; **D:** William Beaudine. *NOS, VYY*

Billy Two Hats 🐾🐾½ *The Lady and the Outlaw* 1974 (PG) Grizzled Scottish bandit Deans (Peck) teams up with young half-breed Billy (Arnaz Jr.) to pull off a robbery that results in an accidental death and Billy's capture. Deans is shot while breaking the kid out of jail and must rely on Billy to get them through, while being pursued by the law. It ain't happy. Mainly notable as the first western shot in Israel. **139m/C VHS.** Gregory Peck, Desi Arnaz Jr., Jack Warden, Sian Barbara Allen,

David Huddleston; **D:** Ted Kotcheff; **W:** Alan Sharp; **C:** Brian West; **M:** John Scott. *MGM*

Billyboy 1979 Coming of age film with the world of boxing as background. Excellent fight scenes. **94m/C VHS, Beta.** Duane Bobrick, Kim Braden. *BFV*

Biloxi Blues 🐾🐾½ *Neil Simon's Biloxi Blues* 1988 (PG-13) Eugene Morris Jerome has been drafted and sent to boot camp in Biloxi, Mississippi where he encounters a troubled drill sergeant, hostile recruits, and a skillful prostitute. Walken is the drill sergeant from hell. Some good laughs from the ever-wry Broderick. A sequel to Neil Simon's "Brighton Beach Memoirs" and adapted by Simon from his play. Followed by "Broadway Bound." **105m/C VHS, Beta, LV.** Matthew Broderick, Christopher Walken, Casey Siemaszko, Matt Mulhern, Corey Parker, Penelope Ann Miller, Michael Dolan, Park Overall; **D:** Mike Nichols; **W:** Neil Simon; **C:** Bill Butler; **M:** Georges Delerue. *USH*

Bimini Code 🐾 1984 Two female adventurers accept a dangerous mission where they wind up on Bimini Island in a showdown with the mysterious Madame X. **95m/C VHS, Beta.** Vickie Benson, Krista Richardson, Frank Alexander, Rosanna Simanaitis; **D:** Barry Clark. *PSM*

Bingo 🐾🐾½ 1991 (PG) Mediocre spoof of hero-dog movies. The heroic title mutt roams from Denver to Green Bay in search of his absent-minded master, with numerous absurd adventures en route. Some cute moments, but sometimes Bingo is just lame-o. Good family fare. **90m/C VHS, LV, Closed Caption.** Cindy Williams, David Rasche, Robert J. Steinmiller Jr., David French, Kurt Fuller, Joe Guzaldo, Glenn Shadix; **D:** Matthew Robbins; **W:** Jim Strain; **M:** Richard Gibbs. *COL*

Bingo Long Traveling All-Stars & Motor Kings 🐾🐾🐾 1976 (PG) Set in 1939, this film follows the comedic adventures of a lively group of black ball players who have defected from the old Negro National League. The All-Stars travel the country challenging local white teams. **111m/C VHS, Beta.** Billy Dee Williams, James Earl Jones, Richard Pryor, Stan Shaw; **D:** John Badham; **W:** Matthew Robbins, Hal Barwood; **C:** Bill Butler; **M:** William Goldstein. *USH, FCT*

Bio-Dome 🐾 1996 (PG-13) Pauly Shore in a hermetically sealed environment separated from the rest of society? Great! Where do I sign? Unfortunately, it's only a movie, and a typically useless one, at that. Shore brings his lame schtick to a scientifically created "perfect environment" that he and his college (yeah, right) buddy Doyle (Baldwin) mistake for a mall and eventually destroy. In Bloom's not-too-auspicious directorial debut, bodily function jokes found in Jim Carrey's wastebasket masquerade as a script, while the supporting cast wanders aimlessly, perhaps pondering a switch in agents. **CW:** Crude language, sex-related material and some drug content. **94m/C VHS, LV, Closed Caption.** Pauly Shore, Stephen Baldwin, William Atherton, Henry Gibson, Joey Lauren Adams, Teresa Hill, Kylie Minogue, Kevin West, Denise Dowse, Dara Tomanovich; **D:** Jason Bloom; **W:** Kip Koenig, Scott Marcano; **C:** Phedon Papamichael; **M:** Andrew Gross. Golden Raspberry Awards '96: Worst Actor (Shore). *MGM*

Bio Hazard 🐾 1985 (R) A toxic monster needs human flesh to survive and consequently goes on a rampage. **84m/C VHS, Beta.** Angelique Pettyjohn, Carroll Borland, Richard Hench, Aldo Ray; **D:** Fred Olen Ray. *MTX*

Biohazard: The Alien Force 🐾½ 1995 (R) Reptilian mutant, the result of a genetic experiment gone awry, must be hunted down before it can reproduce. Sounds like a rip-off of "Species." **CW:** Sci-fi violence and gore, and for some sexuality and language. **88m/C VHS.** Steve Zurk, Chris Mitchum, Susan Fronsoe, Tom Ferguson, Patrick Moran, John Maynard; **D:** Steve Latshaw. *THV*

The Bionic Woman 🦝🦝 1975 Sky-diving accident leaves tennis pro Jaimie Somers crippled and near death. Her bionic buddy, Steve Austin, gets his friends to rebuild her and make her better than she was before. The pilot for the television series. **96m/C VHS, Beta.** Lindsay Wagner, Lee Majors, Richard Anderson, Alan Oppenheimer; **D:** Richard Moder. *USH*

The Birch Interval 🦝🦝 1978 (PG) A chronicle of a young Amish girl growing up and experiencing adult passions and fears when she visits her kin in their isolated Pennsylvania community. **104m/C VHS, Beta.** Eddie Albert, Rip Torn, Ann Wedgeworth; **D:** Delbert Mann; **W:** Joanna Crawford. *MED*

Bird 🦝🦝🦝 1988 (R) The richly-textured, though sadly one-sided biography of jazz sax great Charlie Parker, from his rise to stardom to his premature death via extended heroin use. A remarkably assured, deeply imagined film from Eastwood that never really shows the Bird's genius of creation. The soundtrack features Parker's own solos re-mastered from original recordings. **160m/C VHS, Beta, LV, Closed Caption.** Forest Whitaker, Diane Venora, Michael Zelniker, Samuel E. Wright, Keith David, Michael McGuire, James Handy, Damon Whitaker, Morgan Nagler, Peter Crook; **D:** Clint Eastwood; **W:** Joel Oliansky; **C:** Jack N. Green; **M:** Lennie Niehaus. Academy Awards '88: Best Sound; Cannes Film Festival '88: Best Actor (Whitaker); Golden Globe Awards '89: Best Director (Eastwood); New York Film Critics Awards '88: Best Supporting Actress (Venora). *MVD, WAR, FCT*

Bird of Paradise 🦝🦝½ 1932 An exotic South Seas romance in which an adventurer is cast onto a remote Polynesian island when his yacht haphazardly sails into a coral reef. There he becomes enamored of an exotic island girl, and nature seems to disapprove. **80m/B VHS, Beta, 8mm.** Joel McCrea, Dolores Del Rio, Lon Chaney Jr.; **D:** King Vidor; **M:** Max Steiner. *NOS, MRV, VYY*

Bird of Prey 🦝🦝½ 1995 (R) Nick Milev (Milushev) has just been released from a Bulgarian prison for attacking Jonathan Griffith (Chamberlain), the drugs-and-arms dealer who was responsible for the death of Milev's policeman father. But Milev still wants revenge, though matters get complicated by Kily (Tilly), Griffith's naive daughter, with whom he falls in love. Plot's so-so but characters make up for some of the routiness. Filmed on location in Sofia, Bulgaria. **102m/C VHS, Closed Caption.** Boyan Milushev, Jennifer Tilly, Richard Chamberlain, Lenny Von Dohlen, Robert Carradine, Lesley Ann Warren; **W:** Boyan Milushev; **C:** David Knaus. *CAF*

Bird on a Wire 🦝🦝 1990 (PG-13) After suddenly being forced to emerge from a prolonged period under the Witness Protection Program, an ex-hood and his ex-girlfriend are pursued by old enemies. **110m/C VHS, Beta, LV, Closed Caption.** Mel Gibson, Goldie Hawn, David Carradine, Bill Duke, Stephen Tobolowsky; **D:** John Badham; **W:** David Seltzer; **C:** Robert Primes; **M:** Hans Zimmer. *USH*

The Bird with the Crystal Plumage 🦝🦝½ *L'Ucello dalle Plume di Cristallo; The Phantom of Terror* 1970 (PG) An American writer living in Rome witnesses a murder. He becomes involved in the mystery when the alleged murderer is cleared because the woman believed to be his next victim is shown to be a psychopathic murderer. Vintage Argento mayhem. **98m/C VHS, Beta, LV.** *IT* Tony Musante, Suzy Kendall, Eva Renzi; **D:** Dario Argento; **W:** Dario Argento; **M:** Ennio Morricone. *VCI, MRV*

The Birdcage 🦝🦝🦝 *Birds of a Feather* 1995 (R) Somewhat overlong but well-played remake of "La Cage aux Folles" features Williams suppressing his usual manic schtick to portray Armand, the subdued half of a longtime gay couple living in Miami. His partner is the ever-hysterical-but-loving drag queen Albert (Lane), whose presence provides a distinct challenge when Armand's son Val (Futterman) announces his engagement to the daughter of family values, right-wing senator Kevin Keeley (Hackman). When the Senator and family arrive for dinner, Armand tries to play it straight while Albert opts for a matronly mom impersonation (think Barbara Bush). Highlights include Armand's initial attempts to teach Albert to be butch (walk like John Wayne) and Hackman congoing in drag. *CW:* Language. **120m/C VHS, LV, Closed Caption, DVD.** Robin Williams, Nathan Lane, Gene Hackman, Dianne Wiest, Hank Azaria, Dan Futterman, Christine Baranski, Calista Flockhart, Tom McGowan; **D:** Mike Nichols; **W:** Elaine May; **C:** Emmanuel Lubezki. Screen Actors Guild Award '96: Cast; Nominations: Academy Awards '96: Best Art Direction/Set Decoration; Golden Globe Awards '97: Best Actor—Musical/Comedy (Lane), Best Film—Musical/Comedy; MTV Movie Awards '97: Best On-Screen Duo (Robin Williams/Nathan Lane), Best Comedic Performance (Williams); Screen Actors Guild Award '96: Best Supporting Actor (Azaria), Best Supporting Actor (Lane); Writers Guild of America '96: Best Adapted Screenplay. *MGM*

Birdman of Alcatraz 🦝🦝🦝 1962 Robert Stroud, convicted of two murders and sentenced to life imprisonment on the Island, becomes an internationally accepted authority on birds. Lovingly told, with stunning performance from Lancaster, and exceptionally fine work from the supporting cast. The confinement of Stroud's prison cell makes the film seem claustrophobic and tedious at times, just as the imprisonment must have been. Ritter played Stroud's mother, who never stops trying to get him out of prison. **143m/B VHS.** Burt Lancaster, Karl Malden, Thelma Ritter, Betty Field, Neville Brand, Edmond O'Brien, Hugh Marlowe, Telly Savalas; **D:** John Frankenheimer; **C:** Burnett Guffey, Robert Krasker; **M:** Elmer Bernstein. British Academy Awards '62: Best Actor (Lancaster); Nominations: Academy Awards '62: Best Actor (Lancaster), Best Black and White Cinematography, Best Supporting Actor (Savalas), Best Supporting Actress (Ritter). *COL, FCT*

The Birds 🦝🦝🦝½ 1963 (PG-13) Hitchcock attempted to top the success of "Psycho" with this terrifying tale of Man versus Nature, in which Nature alights, one by one, on the trees of Bodega Bay to stage a bloody act of revenge upon the civilized world. Only Hitchcock can twist the harmless into the horrific while avoiding the ridiculous; this is perhaps his most brutal film, and one of the cinema's purest, horrifying portraits of apocalypse. Based on a short story by Daphne Du Maurier; screenplay by novelist Evan Hunter (aka Ed McBain). **120m/C VHS, Beta, LV.** Rod Taylor, Tippi Hedren, Jessica Tandy, Veronica Cartwright, Suzanne Pleshette; **D:** Alfred Hitchcock; **C:** Robert Burks. *USH*

The Birds 2: Land's End woof! 1994 (R) Unfortunate rip-off of the Hitchcock fright classic. Killer seagulls begin attacking the inhabitants of east coast Gull Island. Seems they're tired of being oil slick victims. Hedren's the town shopkeeper in a role that's nothing like the one she played in the original. Definitely for the birds—even the director refuses to acknowledge it by officially using the film industry pseudonym "Alan Smithee." Made for TV. **87m/C VHS, LV, Closed Caption.** Brad Johnson, Chelsea Field, Tippi Hedren, James Naughton, Jan Rubes, Megan Gallagher; **D:** Rick Rosenthal; **W:** Jim Wheat, Ken Wheat. *USH*

Birds & the Bees 🦝🦝 1956 A millionaire falls in love with an alluring card shark, and then calls it all off when he learns of her profession, only to fall in love with her again when she disguises herself. A remake - and poor shade - of Preston Sturge's 1941 classic "The Lady Eve." **94m/C VHS, Beta.** Mitzi Gaynor, David Niven, George Gobel, Reginald Gardiner, Hans Conried; **D:** Norman Taurog; **W:** Sidney Sheldon. *BAR*

Birds of Prey 🦝🦝 1972 Made-for-television action film pits an ex-WWII army pilot against a group of kidnapping thieves in an airborne chopper chase. **81m/C VHS, Beta.** David Janssen, Ralph Meeker, Elayne Heilveil; **D:** William A. Graham; **C:** Jordan Cronenweth. *PSM*

Birdy 🦝🦝🦝½ 1984 (R) An adaptation of the William Wharton novel about two Philadelphia youths, one with normal interests, the other obsessed with birds, and their eventual involvement in the Vietnam War, wrecking one physically and the other mentally. A hypnotic, evocative film, with a compelling Peter Gabriel soundtrack. **120m/C VHS, Beta, LV, Closed Caption.** Matthew Modine, Nicolas Cage, John Harkins, Sandy Baron, Karen Young, Bruno Kirby; **D:** Alan Parker; **W:** Jack Behr, Sandy Kroopf; **M:** Peter Gabriel. Cannes Film Festival '85: Grand Jury Prize. *COL*

Birgitt Haas Must Be Killed 🦝🦝½ 1983 A ruthless secret agent (Noiret) plots to murder a German female terrorist and make it appear that her boyfriend was the killer. Never quite hits the mark, despite novel premise and strong cast. **105m/C VHS, Beta, LV.** Philippe Noiret, Jean Rochefort, Elisabeth Kreuzer; **D:** Laurent Heynemann. *GLV*

The Birth of a Nation 🦝🦝🦝🦝 *The Clansman* 1915 Lavish Civil War epic in which Griffith virtually invented the basics of film grammar. Gish and Walthall have some of the most moving scenes ever filmed and the masterful battle choreography brought the art of cinematography to new heights. Griffith's positive attitude toward the KKK notwithstanding, this was the first feature length silent, and it brought credibility to an entire industry. Based on the play "The Clansman" and the book "The Leopard's Spots" by Thomas Dixon, it is still a rouser, and of great historical interest. Silent with music score. Also available in a 124 minute version. **175m/B VHS, LV.** Lillian Gish, Mae Marsh, Henry B. Walthall, Robert "Bobbie" Harron, Wallace Reid, Joseph Henabery, Donald Crisp, Raoul Walsh, Erich von Stroheim, Eugene Pallette; **D:** D.W. Griffith. *VYY, MRV, REP*

Birth of the Blues 🦝🦝½ 1941 Songman Crosby starts a band in New Orleans in the midst of the jazz boom. Help from partner Martin and real-life trombonist Teagarden, with comic relief from Eddie "Rochester" Anderson, make for a fun-filled story. Plot is riddled with some unbelievable gangster scenes, but the music and laughs will keep you amused. In B&W with color segments. 🎵St. Louis Blues; St. James Infirmary; Melancholy Baby; Birth of the Blues. **76m/B VHS, Closed Caption.** Bing Crosby, Mary Martin, Brian Donlevy, Eddie Anderson, J. Carrol Naish, Cecil Kellaway, Warren Hymer, Horace McMahon, Carolyn Lee, Jack Teagarden; **D:** Victor Schertzinger; **W:** Harry Tugend, Walter DeLeon; **C:** William Mellor; **M:** Robert Emmett Dolan. Nominations: Academy Awards '41: Scoring of a Musical. *USH*

Birthday Boy 🦝 1985 A cable comedy about a buffoonish salesman's 30th birthday, on which he takes an ill-fated business trip. Written by Belushi. **33m/C VHS, Beta.** James Belushi; **D:** Claude Conrad; **W:** James Belushi. *VES, LIV*

The Bishop's Wife 🦝🦝🦝 1947 An angel comes down to earth at Christmas to help a young bishop, his wife and his parishioners. Excellent performances by the cast make this an entertaining outing. **109m/B VHS, Beta, LV.** Cary Grant, Loretta Young, David Niven, Monty Woolley, Elsa Lanchester, James Gleason, Gladys Cooper, Regis Toomey; **D:** Henry Koster; **C:** Gregg Toland. Academy Awards '47: Best Sound; Nominations: Academy Awards '47: Best Director (Koster), Best Film Editing, Best Picture, Original Dramatic/Comedy Score. *HBO, FCT, MLB*

The Bitch woof! 1978 (R) High-camp follies are the rule in this lustful continuation of "The Stud" as it follows the erotic adventures of a beautiful divorcee playing sex games for high stakes on the international playgrounds of high society. A collaborative effort by the sisters Collins: written by Jackie, with sister Joan well cast in the title role. **90m/C VHS, Beta.** *GB* Joan Collins, Kenneth Haigh, Michael Coby, Ian Hendry, Carolyn Seymour, Sue Lloyd, John Ratzenberger; **D:** Gerry O'Hara. *NO*

Bite the Bullet 🦝🦝🦝½ 1975 (PG) Moralistic western tells of a grueling 600-mile horse race where the participants reluctantly develop respect for one another. Unheralded upon release and shot in convincing epic style by Harry Stradling, Jr. Excellent cast. **131m/C VHS, Beta, LV.** Gene Hackman, James Coburn, Candice Bergen, Dabney Coleman, Jan-Michael Vincent, Ben Johnson, Ian Bannen, Paul Stewart, Sally Kirkland; **D:** Richard Brooks; **W:** Richard Brooks; **C:** Harry Stradling Jr.; **M:** Alex North. Nominations: Academy Awards '75: Best Sound, Best Original Score. *COL*

Bitter Harvest ⬥⬥⬥ 1981 Emmy-nominated made-for-television movie concerning a dairy farmer frantically trying to discover what is mysteriously killing off his herd. Howard is excellent as the farmer battling the bureaucracy to find the truth. Based on a true story. **98m/C VHS, Beta.** Ron Howard, Art Carney, Tarah Nutter, Richard Dysart, Barry Corbin, Jim Haynie, David Knell; **D:** Roger Young. *FRH, LIV*

Bitter Harvest ⬥⬥ 1993 (R) Rubin and Kensit are the femme fatales who turn their considerable wiles on the innocent Baldwin. He's more than happy to be their lover but does he want to be their victim as well? *CW:* Violent language, violent action, and strong sexual scenes. **98m/C VHS, Closed Caption.** Stephen Baldwin, Patsy Kensit, Jennifer Rubin, Adam Baldwin, M. Emmet Walsh; **D:** Duane Clark; **W:** Randall Fontana; **C:** Remi Adefarasin. *PSM*

Bitter Moon ⬥⬥ 1992 (R) Polanski effort looks promising, but ultimately disappoints. Bored British couple (Grant and Scott Thomas) meet up with sexual deviants (Coyote and Seigner, aka Mrs. Polanski) on a cruise and learn that passion and cruelty often share the same path to destruction. Masquerades as high class art, but whenever substance is lacking expect a silly, kinky sex scene. Needless to say, there isn't much substance, so erotic mischief abounds. Scott Thomas manages to hold her own, but Coyote is almost embarrassingly over the top. Based on the Pascal Bruckner novel "Lunes de Fiel." **139m/C VHS, LV.** Peter Coyote, Emmanuelle Seigner, Hugh Grant, Kristin Scott Thomas, Victor Banerjee; **Cameos:** Stockard Channing; **D:** Roman Polanski; **W:** Roman Polanski, Gerard Brach, John Brownjohn; **C:** Tonino Delli Colli; **M:** Vangelis. *COL*

Bitter Rice ⬥⬥⬥ *Riso Amaro* 1949 Mangano became a star with her sultry performance about survival in postwar Italy. She scrapes by, working in the rice fields of the Po Valley, loved by the down-to-earth Vallone, who provides her with little excitement. Gassman is the rotten-to-the-core thief who meets up with Mangano while he's running from the police. He mistreats her, she steals his money and betrays her friends, and both destroy each other. In Italian with English subtitles. **96m/C VHS.** *IT* Silvana Mangano, Vittorio Gassman, Raf Vallone; **D:** Guiseppe de Santis. Nominations: Academy Awards '50: Best Story.*FCT*

Bitter Sweet ⬥⬥½ 1933 Tragic tale of a woman who finally marries the man she loves, only to find that he is a compulsive gambler. Written by Coward, adapted from his operetta. **76m/B VHS.** Anna Neagle, Fernand Graavey, Esme Percy, Clifford Heatherly, Hugh Williams; **D:** Herbert Wilcox; **W:** Noel Coward. *NOS, MRV, DVT*

Bitter Sweet ⬥⬥ 1940 The second version of the Noel Coward operetta, about young romance in 1875 Vienna. Creaky and overrated, but the lush Technicolor and Coward standards help to compensate. ♫ Ziguener; I'll See You Again. **94m/C VHS, Beta.** Jeanette MacDonald, Nelson Eddy, George Sanders, Felix Bressart, Ian Hunter, Sig Rumann, Herman Bing, Fay Holden, Curt Bois, Edward Ashley; **D:** Woodbridge S. Van Dyke; **W:** Lesser Samuels, Noel Coward. Nominations: Academy Awards '40: Best Color Cinematography, Best Interior Decoration. *MGM*

The Bitter Tea of General Yen ⬥⬥⬥ 1933 Stanwyck arrives in Shanghai to marry a missionary (Gordon) during the threatening days of China's civil war. Unexpectedly swept into the arms of an infamous warlord (Asher), she becomes fascinated, although his attempts to seduce her fail. She even remains with

him while his enemies close in. Exotic and poetic, if melodramatic by today's standards. The interracial aspects were considered very daring for their time. Adapted from the book by Grace Zaring Stone. **89m/B VHS.** Barbara Stanwyck, Nils Asther, Gavin Gordon, Walter Connolly, Lucien Littlefield, Toschia Mori, Richard Loo, Clara Blandick; **D:** Frank Capra; **W:** Edward Paramore. *COL, FCT, BTV*

The Bitter Tears of Petra von Kant ⬥⬥½ *Die Bitteren Traenen der Petra von Kant* 1972 Dark German story of lesbian love, the fashion world, obsession and anger. Claustrophobic settings and slow pace may frustrate some viewers. In German with English subtitles. **124m/C VHS.** *GE* Margit Carstensen, Hanna Schygulla, Irm Hermann, Eva Mattes; **D:** Rainer Werner Fassbinder; **C:** Michael Ballhaus. *NYF, FCT*

Bitter Vengeance ⬥⬥ 1994 (R) Security guard Jack Westford (Greenwood) pulls off a bank heist with his lover Isabella (Hocking) and plans to frame his wife Annie (Madsen) for the crime. Only Annie finds out and sets out to get them before the police get her. Made for cable TV.*CW:* Some violence and sexuality. **90m/C VHS, Beta, Closed Caption.** Virginia Madsen, Bruce Greenwood, Kristen Hocking, Eddie Velez, Gordon Jump, Carlos Gomez, Tim Russ; **D:** Stuart Cooper; **W:** Pablo F. Fenjves; **M:** David Michael Frank. *PAR*

Bittersweet Love ⬥½ 1976 (PG) Two young people fall in love and marry, only to have the bride's mother and the groom's father confess a 30-year-old affair, disclosing that the two newlyweds are actually half-siblings. **92m/C VHS, Beta.** Lana Turner, Robert Lansing, Celeste Holm, Robert Alda, Meredith Baxter; **D:** David Miller.

Bix ⬥⬥ 1990 Based on the brief life of legendary Jazz Age cornetist Leon Bix Beiderbecke, who died at age 28. Story unfolds in flashbacks, through friend Joe Venuti memories of the dissipated genius and the music he created with Hoagy Carmichael, Pee Wee Russell, Paul Whiteman, and others. **100m/C VHS.** *IT* Bryant Weeks, Emile Levisetti, Mark Collver, Sally Groth; **D:** Pupi Avati; **W:** Pupi Avati, Antonio Avati, Lino Patruno. *RHP*

Bizarre ⬥ 1987 When a wife escapes her perverse, psychologically threatening marriage, she finds her husband still haunts her literally and figuratively, and plots psychological revenge. Dubbed. **93m/C VHS, Beta.** *IT* Florence Guerin, Luciano Bartoli, Robert Egon Spechtenhauser, Stefano Sabelli. *PSM*

Bizarre Bizarre ⬥⬥⬥ *Drole de Drama* 1939 A mystery writer is accused of murder and disappears, only to return in disguise to try to clear his name. Along the way, a number of French comedians are introduced along with a revue of comedy-farce sketches that include slapstick, burlesque, black humor, and comedy of the absurd. In French with English subtitles. **90m/B VHS, Beta.** *FR* Louis Jouvet, Michel Simon, Francoise Rosay; **D:** Marcel Carne. *NOS, HHT, DVT*

The Black Abbot ⬥⬥ 1963 A mysterious black-hooded figure is seen entering a ruined Abbey tower that leads to a country house with buried treasure. Based on an Edgar Wallace story. **95m/C VHS.** *GE* Joachim Fuchsberger, Dieter Borsche, Gritt Bottcher, Eva Scholtz, Franz Gottlieb; **D:** Franz Gottlieb. *SNC*

Black and White as Day and Night ⬥⬥ 1963 A man's talent for the game of chess becomes a destructive obsession. In German with English subtitles. **?m/C VHS.** Bruno Ganz. *SNC*

Black and White in Color ⬥⬥⬥ *La Victoire en Chantant* 1976 (PG) Award-winning satire about a French soldier at an African outpost, who, upon hearing the news of the beginning of WWI, takes it upon himself to attack a neighboring German fort. Calamity ensues. In French, with English subtitles. **100m/C VHS, Beta, LV.** *FR* Jean Carmet, Jacques Dufilho, Catherine Rouvel, Jacques Spiesser, Dora Doll, Jacques Perrin; **D:** Jean-Jacques Annaud; **W:** George

Conchon, Jean-Jacques Annaud; **M:** Pierre Bachelet. Academy Awards '76: Best Foreign Language Film. *ORI, WAR*

Black Arrow ⬥⬥⬥ *Black Arrow Strikes* 1948 Original adventure film of the famous Robert Louis Stevenson novel. Upon return from 16th century's War of the Roses, a young man must avenge his father's murder by following a trail of clues in the form of black arrows. Well made and fun. **76m/B VHS, Beta.** Louis Hayward, Janet Blair, George Macready, Edgar Buchanan, Paul Cavanagh; **D:** Gordon Douglas. *DIS*

The Black Arrow ⬥⬥ 1984 Exiled bowman returns to England to avenge the injustices of a villainous nobleman. Made-for-cable version of the Robert Louis Stevenson medieval romp is not as well done as the 1948 adaptation. **93m/C VHS, Beta.** Oliver Reed, Benedict Taylor, Georgia Slowe, Stephan Chase, Donald Pleasence; **D:** John Hough. *DIS*

Black Beauty ⬥⬥ 1946 In this adaptation of Anna Sewell's familiar novel, a young girl develops a kindred relationship with an extraordinary horse. **74m/B VHS, Beta.** Mona Freeman, Richard Denning, Evelyn Ankers; **D:** Max Nosseck. *CCB, MED, VTR*

Black Beauty ⬥⬥ 1971 (G) International remake of the classic horse story by Anna Sewell. **105m/C VHS, Beta, LV.** *GB GE SP* Mark Lester, Walter Slezak; **D:** James Hill; **C:** Chris Menges; **M:** Lionel Bart. *PAR, FCT*

Black Beauty ⬥⬥⬥ 1994 (G) Remake of the classic Anna Sewell children's novel about an oft-sold horse whose life has its shares of ups and downs. Timeless tale still brings children and adults to tears. Six-year-old quarterhorse named Justin gives a nuanced portrayal as the Black Beauty, recalling Olivier in "Hamlet." Directorial debut of "Secret Garden" screenwriter Thompson. **88m/C VHS, LV, Closed Caption.** Andrew Knott, Sean Bean, David Thewlis, Jim Carter, Alun Armstrong, Eleanor Bron, Peter Cook, Peter Davison, John McEnery, Nicholas Jones; **D:** Caroline Thompson; **W:** Caroline Thompson. *WAR*

Black Beauty/Courage of Black Beauty ⬥⬥ 1957 Two feature-length films based on Anna Sewell's novel about the love of a child for a black stallion. "Black Beauty" was first released in 1946; "Courage of Black Beauty" in 1957. Excellent for children who love horses, of course. **145m/C VHS, Beta.** Mona Freeman, Johnny Crawford; **D:** Max Nosseck, Harold Schuster. *MED*

Black Belt ⬥ 1992 (R) A private detective is hired to protect a rock star from a fanatic Vietnam vet. **80m/C VHS, Closed Caption.** Don "The Dragon" Wilson, Richard Beymer, Alan Blumenfeld, Matthias Hues; **D:** Charles Philip Moore; **W:** Charles Philip Moore. *NHO*

Black Belt Jones ⬥ 1974 (R) Martial arts expert fights the mob to save a school of self-defense in Los Angeles' Watts district. **87m/C VHS, Beta.** Jim Kelly, Gloria Hendry, Scatman Crothers; **D:** Robert Clouse. *WAR*

Black Bikers from Hell ⬥½ *Black Angels* 1970 (R) Black gang-members infiltrate and wreak havoc on their rivals. Who can stop these brutal young men? Cast with real bikers and biker chicks. **87m/C VHS, Beta.** King John III, Des Roberts, Linda Jackson, James Whitworth, James Young-El, Clancy Syrko, Beverly Gardner; **D:** Lawrence Merrick; **W:** Lawrence Merrick. *TPV, JEF*

Black Bird ⬥⬥ 1975 (PG) In this satiric "sequel" to "The Maltese Falcon," detective Sam Spade, Jr. searches for the mysterious black falcon statuette that caused his father such trouble. Features appearances by Elisha Cook Jr. and Lee Patrick, who starred in the 1941 classic "The Maltese Falcon" with Humphrey Bogart. **98m/C VHS, Beta.** George Segal, Stephane Audran, Lionel Stander, Lee Patrick, Elisha Cook Jr., Connie Kreski; **D:** David Giler. *GKK*

Black Box Affair ⬥½ 1966 An American secret agent must find a black box lost in a B-52 plane crash before it falls into the wrong hands. **95m/C VHS, Beta.** Craig Hill, Teresa Gimpera, Luis Martin, Jorge Rigaud. *NO*

Black Brigade 🎬🎬 **1969** Pryor and Williams star in this low budget movie as leaders of an all-black outfit assigned to a suicide mission behind Nazi lines during WWII. Their force wreaks havoc and earns them the respect of military higher-ups. Lots of action and climactic finish. **90m/C VHS.** Richard Pryor, Billy Dee Williams, Stephen Boyd. *QVD*

Black Caesar 🎬🎬 **1973 (R)** A small-time hood climbs the ladder to be the head of a Harlem crime syndicate. Music by James Brown. Followed by the sequel "Hell Up in Harlem." **92m/C VHS, Beta, LV.** Fred Williamson, Julius W. Harris, Val Avery, Art Lund, Gloria Hendry; **D:** Larry Cohen; **M:** James Brown. *ORI*

The Black Castle 🎬🎬 **1952** MacNally plays an 18th-century Austrian count whose guests tend to disappear after a visit. This happens to two of Greene's friends and he decides to investigate. Uninspired and melodramatic, not enough horror. Karloff doesn't have enough to do. **81m/B VHS, Beta.** Richard Greene, Boris Karloff, Stephen McNally, Rita (Paula) Corday, Lon Chaney Jr., John Hoyt; **D:** Nathan (Hertz) Juran. *USH*

The Black Cat 🎬🎬½ *House of Doom* **1934** The first of the Boris and Bela pairings stands up well years after release. Polished and taut, with fine sets and interesting acting. Confrontation between architect and devil worshiper acts as plot, with strange twists. Worth a look. Also available with "The Raven" (1935) on laserdisc. **65m/B VHS, LV.** Boris Karloff, Bela Lugosi, David Manners, Jacqueline Wells, Lucille Lund, Henry Armetta; **D:** Edgar G. Ulmer. *MED, MLB, USH*

The Black Cat woof! **1981** Spaghetti splatter-meister Fulci, best known for his unabashed ripoffs "Zombie" and "Gates of Hell," tones down the gore this time in a vaguely Poe-ish tale of a medium with some marbles loose (Magee) whose kitty provides the temporary habitat for spirits its master calls up. The dreary English village setting and the downright myopic camerawork add up to an oppressive viewing experience. **92m/C VHS.** *IT GB* Patrick Magee, Mimsy Farmer, David Warbeck, Al Cliver, Dagmar Lassander; **D:** Lucio Fulci; **W:** Lucio Fulci; **M:** Pino Donaggio. *MED, RHI*

Black Cat 🎬½ **1990** Filmmakers find lots of action in a haunted house. Chock full of references to the works of spaghetti horror dons Mario Bava and Dario Argento. **?m/C VHS, Beta.** *IT* Caroline Munro, Brett Halsey; **D:** Lewis (Luigi Cozzi) Coates; **W:** Lewis (Luigi Cozzi) Coates. *COL*

Black Christmas 🎬🎬½ *Silent Night, Evil Night; Stranger in the House* **1975 (R)** A college sorority is besieged by an axe-murderer over the holidays. **98m/C VHS, Beta.** *CA* Olivia Hussey, Keir Dullea, Margot Kidder, John Saxon; **D:** Bob (Benjamin) Clark. *WAR*

Black Cobra woof! **1983 (R)** A lesbian exacts revenge for her lover's snake-bite murder by trapping the guilty party with his own snakes. **97m/C VHS, Beta.** Laura Gemser, Jack Palance. *GEM*

The Black Cobra woof! **1987 (R)** After photographing a psychopath in the process of killing someone, a beautiful photographer seeks the help of a tough police sergeant to protect her. The members of the Black Cobras gang gives chase. **90m/C VHS, Beta.** *IT* Fred Williamson, Karl Landgren, Eva Grimaldi. *TWE*

Black Cobra 2 🎬🎬 **1989 (R)** A mismatched team of investigators tracks a notorious terrorist. They find him holding a school full of children as hostage. **95m/C VHS.** Fred Williamson. *HMD*

Black Cobra 3: The Manila Connection 🎬½ **1990 (R)** Interpol turns to police lieutenant Robert Malone (Williamson) when a team of high-tech weapons thieves threatens the world. Malone attacks like a cyclone on the terrorists' jungle haven. They won't know what hit 'em! **92m/C VHS.** Fred Williamson, Forry Smith, Debra Ward; **D:** Don Edwards. *HMD*

The Black Coin **1936** A 15-episode adventure serial about a cursed silver piece from the Middle Ages and the ill luck that has followed its possessors through the years. **316m/B VHS, Beta, LV.** Ralph Graves, Ruth Mix, Dave O'Brien, Matthew Betz. *VYY, NOS, MLB*

Black Day Blue Night 🎬🎬 **1995 (R)** Rinda (Forbes) and Hallie (Sara) take a road trip from Utah to Phoenix and pick up the handsome Dodge (Bellows). Turns out he's being pursued by cop John Quinn (Walsh) as a suspect in a murder/robbery. Women-in-peril-who-help-themselves type story. **CW:** Violence, sexuality, and language. **99m/C VHS, LV, Closed Caption.** Michelle Forbes, Mia Sara, Gil Bellows, J.T. Walsh, Tim Guinee, John Beck; **D:** J.S. Cardone; **W:** J.S. Cardone; **C:** Michael Cardone; **M:** Johnny Lee Schell, Joe Sublett. *REP*

Black Devil Doll from Hell 🎬 **1984** This shot-on-video movie deals with a nasty little voodoo doll that likes to kill its owners. **70m/C VHS, Beta.** Shirley Jones, Rickey Roach, Marie Sainvilvs; **D:** Chester Turner. *HHT*

The Black Devils of Kali 🎬 *Mystery of the Black Jungle* **1955** Adventurers in the Indian jungle discover a lost race of idol-worshipping primitives. Racist garbage produced near the end of Republic Pictures' existence. Based on a novel by Emillio Salgari. **72m/B VHS.** Lex Barker, Jane Maxwell, Luigi Tosi, Paul Muller; **D:** Ralph Murphy. *SNC, MLB*

Black Dragon 🎬 **1974 (R)** Young farm boy moves to the city and teams up with an undercover narcotics agent to infiltrate and destroy the underworld syndicate. **93m/C VHS.** Ron Van Cliff, Jason Rai Pow, Jorge Estraga, Nancy Veronica. *SUN*

The Black Dragons 🎬 **1942** Weird and fairly stupid war drama involving sabotage by the Japanese. Lugosi is the plastic surgeon who deftly cuts and pastes Japanese face parts to permit agents to pass as Americans. Also available colorized. **62m/B VHS, Beta.** Bela Lugosi, Joan Barclay, George Pembroke, Clayton Moore; **D:** William Nigh. *VYY, MRV, SNC*

Black Dragon's Revenge 🎬 **1975 (R)** The Black Dragon arrives in Hong Kong to investigate the death of a great kung fu master. **90m/C VHS.** Ron Van Cliff, Charles Bonet, Jason Rai Pow. *SUN*

Black Eagle 🎬 **1988 (R)** Pre-Glasnost, anti-Soviet tale of two high-kicking spies. CIA and KGB agents race to recover innovative equipment in the Mediterranean. **93m/C VHS, Beta, LV.** Bruce Doran, Jean-Claude Van Damme, Sho Kosugi; **D:** Eric Karson. *NO*

Black Eliminator 🎬 **197?** A black cop struggles to stop a maniacal secret agent who plans to destroy the world. **84m/C VHS, Beta.** Jim Kelly, George Lazenby, Harold Sakata, Bob Minos, Patch MacKenzie, Aldo Ray. *NO*

Black Eyes 🎬½ **1939** A lowly waiter, working in a Moscow restaurant, manages to overhear a number of stock tips from the wealthy patrons and makes a tidy pile of rubles to improve his daughter's life. The daughter already thinks he's a successful businessman and is disillusioned when she discovers dad's true profession. All comes out right in the end. **72m/B VHS.** *GB* Otto Kruger, Mary Maguire, Walter Rilla, George L. Baxt, Marie Wright; **D:** Herbert Brenon. *HCV*

Black Force 🎬🎬 **1975** Brothers who fight crime with violent actions, are called for assistance in the recovery of an African artifact. Originally known as "Force Four." **82m/C VHS, Beta.** Malachi Lee, Warhawk Tanzania, Owen Watson, Judie Soriano; **D:** Michael Fink. *NO*

Black Force 2 🎬🎬 **1978 (R)** The brothers are back on the scene in another violent, cartilage-shattering adventure. **90m/C VHS.** Terry Carter, James B. Sikking. *NO*

Black Fox: Blood Horse 🎬🎬½ **1994** Alan Johnson (Reeve) and Britt (Todd) try to maintain an uneasy peace with the local Kiowas until evil Ralph Holtz (Wiggins) tries to stir things up and have some vigilantes attack the tribe. The second episode in the three-part series. **90m/C VHS, Closed Caption.** Christopher Reeve, Raoul Trujillo, Tony Todd, Chris Wiggins; **D:** Steven Hilliard Stern; **C:** Frank Tidy, Eric N. Robertson. *CAF*

Black Fox: Good Men and Bad 🎬🎬½ **1994** Britt (Todd) accepts a job as a federal marshall while Alan (Reeve) goes after desperado Carl Glenn (Fox) and his gang. During a stagecoach robbery, the outlaws take Hallie (Rowan) hostage, thinking she's the wife of a tycoon and Alan manages to use her to get to Glenn. The third episode in the sagebrush series. **90m/C VHS, Closed Caption.** Christopher Reeve, David Fox, Tony Todd, Kim Coates, Kelly Rowan; **D:** Steven Hilliard Stern; **C:** Frank Tidy; **M:** Eric N. Robertson. *CAF*

Black Fox: The Price of Peace 🎬🎬½ **1994** Former plantation owner Alan Johnson (Reeve) and childhood friend Britt (Todd), whom he frees from slavery, try to forge a new life in 1860s Texas. But there's trouble when abusive bigot Ralph Holtz (Wiggins) threatens the peace between settlers and Indians when he goes after his wife delores (Holtz) who left him for a Kiowa warrior, Running Dog (Trujillo). Based on the novel by Matt Braun; made for TV. **90m/C VHS, Closed Caption.** Christopher Reeve, Raoul Trujillo, Tony Todd, Chris Wiggins, Cyndy Preston; **D:** Steven Hilliard Stern; **C:** Frank Tidy; **M:** Eric N. Robertson. *CAF*

Black Friday 🎬🎬½ **1940** Karloff is a surgeon who saves the life of his college professor friend (Ridges) by transplanting part of the brain of a gangster (involved in the same car crash) into the man's body. This results in a Jekyll/Hyde complex with the gangster's evil portion taking over and seeking revenge on rival mobster Lugosi. Horror stars Karloff and Lugosi never have any scenes together. **70m/B VHS, Closed Caption.** Boris Karloff, Stanley Ridges, Bela Lugosi, Anne Nagel, Anne Gwynne, Paul Fix, Virginia Brissac; **D:** Arthur Lubin; **W:** Curt Siodmak, Eric Taylor. *USH*

Black Fury 🎬🎬🎬 **1935** A coal miner's efforts to protest working conditions earn him a beating by the company goons who also kill his friend. He draws national attention to this brutal plight of the workers when he barricades himself inside the mine. Muni's carefully detailed performance adds authenticity to this powerful drama, but it proved too depressing to command a big box office. **95m/B VHS.** Paul Muni, Barton MacLane, Henry O'Neill, J. Carrol Naish; **D:** Michael Curtiz. *FOX*

Black Gestapo woof! **1975 (R)** Black-exploitation film about a vigilante army taking over a Los Angeles ghetto, first to help residents, but later to abuse them. Extremely violent. **89m/C VHS, Beta.** Rod Perry, Charles Robinson, Phil Hoover, Ed Gross. *UNI*

Black Glove 🎬 *Face the Music* **1954** A trumpet star defends himself against charges of murdering a Spanish singer by tracking down the real killer. **84m/B VHS, Beta, LV.** Alex Nicol, Eleanor Summerfield. *NOS*

Black God & White Devil 🎬🎬 **1964** Another Brazilan socio-political commentary by Rocha, an oft-incendiary filmmaker whose left-leaning works are steeped in mysticism, obscure folkore, and powerful images. An impoverished man transforms from a religious zealot to a bandit, his tale underscored by conflict between poor masses and wealthy landowners. Portuguese with subtitles. **102m/C VHS.** *BR* **D:** Glauce Rocha. *FCT*

Black Godfather 🎬 **1974 (R)** The grueling story of a hood clawing his way to the top of a drug-selling mob. Features an all-black cast. **90m/C VHS, Beta.** Rod Perry, Damu King, Don Chastain, Jimmy Witherspoon, Diane Summerfield; **D:** John Evans. *NO*

Black Gold 🎬 **1936** Oil field suspense thriller by "B" movie king Hopton. **57m/B VHS.** Frankie Darro, Leroy Mason; **D:** Russell Hopton. *SNC, VYY*

The Black Hand 🐾🐾🐾 1950 Kelly plays well against character in this atmospheric turn-of-the-century thriller. The evil society of the Black Hand murders his father, and he seeks revenge. Well-made drama. 93m/B VHS. Gene Kelly, J. Carrol Naish, Teresa Celli, Marc Lawrence, Frank Puglia; *D:* Richard Thorpe; *C:* Paul Vogel. NO

Black Hand 🐾½ 1976 Unemployed Italian immigrant is drawn into a web of murder and betrayal after he is attacked by an Irish gang. 90m/C VHS, Beta. Lionel Stander, Mike Placido. NO

Black Hills 🐾 1948 Dull oater with Dean and his sidekick Ates out to avenge the murder of a struggling ranch owner. 60m/B VHS. Eddie Dean, Roscoe Ates, Shirley Patterson, Terry Frost, Nina Bara, William "Bill" Fawcett; *D:* Ray Taylor. MOV

The Black Hole 🐾½ 1979 (G) A high-tech, computerized Disney space adventure dealing with a mad genius who attempts to pilot his craft directly into a black hole. Except for the top quality special effects, a pretty creaky vehicle. 97m/C VHS, Beta, LV. Maximilian Schell, Anthony Perkins, Ernest Borgnine, Yvette Mimieux, Joseph Bottoms, Robert Forster; *D:* Gary Nelson; *W:* Gerry Day; *M:* John Barry. Nominations: Academy Awards '79: Best Cinematography. DIS, OM

Black Ice 🐾🐾 1992 (R) After an affair with a popular politician ends violently, Vanessa (Pacula) realizes her boss set up her death—and she's next in line. She finds the nearest taxi and offers the driver plenty of cash if he can quickly get her out of the country. It's going to be the ride of her life. Also available in an unrated version. *CW:* Language, violence, and sexuality. 90m/C VHS, Beta, Closed Caption. Michael Nouri, Michael Ironside, Joanna Pacula; *D:* Neill Fearnley; *M:* Amin Bhatia. PSM

The Black King 🐾½ *Harlem Hot Shot* 1932 Prejudiced propaganda based on the life of Marcus Garvey, black leader of the '20s, who advocated black superiority and a return to Africa. A black con man takes advantage of fellow blacks by organizing a phony back-to-Africa movement, enriching himself in the process. When one man's girlfriend deserts him for the bogus leader, the jilted one blows the whistle. 70m/B VHS. A.B. Comethiere, Vivianne Baber, Knolly Mitchell, Dan Michaels, Mike Jackson; *D:* Bud Pollard. FCT, BTV, HEG

The Black Klansman 🐾 *I Crossed the Line* 1966 A black man masquerades as a white extremist in order to infiltrate the KKK and avenge his daughter's murder. In the interest of racial harmony, he seduces the Klan leader's daughter. As bad as it sounds. 88m/B VHS, Beta. Richard Gilden, Rima Kutner, Harry Lovejoy; *D:* Ted V. Mikels. UNI

The Black Lash 🐾 1952 Two lawmen go undercover to break a silver hijacking gang. 55m/B VHS, Beta. Lash LaRue, Al "Fuzzy" St. John, Peggy Stewart, Kermit Maynard; *D:* Ron Ormond. NOS, DVT, GPV

Black Lemons 🐾 198? While in prison, a convict is stalked by the Mafia because of what he knows. He eventually spills the beans to the cops, putting himself in unavoidable jeopardy. 93m/C VHS, Beta. IT Peter Carsten, Antonio Sabato, Florinda Bolkan; *D:* Camillo Bazzoni. UNI

Black Like Me 🐾½ 1964 Based on John Howard Griffin's successful book about how Griffin turned his skin black with a drug and traveled the South to experience prejudice firsthand. Neither the production nor the direction enhance the material. 107m/B VHS, Beta. James Whitmore, Roscoe Lee Browne, Will Geer, Walter Mason, John Marriott, Clifton James, Dan Priest; *D:* Carl Lerner. RHI, UND, PTB

Black Limelight 🐾½ 1938 Massey plays a fugitive from justice and Marion the loyal wife who clears her husband of the murder of his mistress. Distracting lead performance by Marion who insists on shouting her lines. Based on the play by Gordon Sherry. 60m/B VHS. GB Raymond Massey, Joan Marion, Walter Hudd, John Marriott; *D:* Paul Stein; *W:* Walter Summers. DVT

Black Lizard 🐾🐾 1968 A camp spectacle set in the Japanese underworld. The Lizard is the glamorous queen of Tokyo crime who plots to steal a famous diamond by first kidnapping the owner's daughter. Complications arise when she falls for a detective. The Lizard is played by female impersonator Maruyama. Mishima, who wrote the original drama and the screenplay, has a cameo as an embalmed corpse. Style is all. In Japanese with English subtitles. 112m/C VHS. JP Akihiro Maruyama, Isao Kimura; *Cameos:* Yukio Mishima; *D:* Kinji Fukasaku; *W:* Yukio Mishima. CCN

Black Magic 🐾🐾½ 1949 Cagliostro the magician becomes involved in a plot to supply a double for Marie Antoinette. 105m/B VHS, Beta. Orson Welles, Akim Tamiroff, Nancy Guild, Raymond Burr; *D:* Gregory Ratoff; *W:* Charles Bennett. MED

Black Magic 🐾🐾½ 1992 (PG-13) Insomniac Alex, haunted by the nightly appearances of his dead cousin Ross, goes to Ross' hometown to see if he can find a way to make the apparition disappear. On the way, he runs into his cousin's ex-girlfriend Lilian and falls in love. Problem is, Lilian's a witch, maybe. Lightweight made for cable TV fare. 94m/C VHS, LV, Closed Caption. Rachel Ward, Judge Reinhold, Brion James, Anthony LaPaglia; *D:* Daniel Taplitz; *W:* Daniel Taplitz. USH

Black Magic Terror 🐾 1979 Jilted by her lover, the old queen of black magic has everybody under her spell. Trouble starts, however, when she turns her back on one of her subjects. 85m/C VHS, Beta. JP Suzanna, W.D. Mochtar, Alan Nuary; *D:* L. Sudjio. TWE

Black Magic Woman woof! 1991 (R) An art gallery owner has an affair with a beautiful and exotic woman but starts to get cold feet when he's plagued by inexplicable phenomena. Seems that black magic woman has put a voodoo spell on him. Listless companion to director Warren's "Blood Spell" that gives away the ending, has a wretched script, and poor acting. *CW:* Violence and sensual scenes. 91m/C VHS, Closed Caption. Mark Hamill, Amanda Wyss, Apollonia, Abadah Viera, Larry Hankin, Victor Rivers, Bonnie Ebson; *D:* Deryn Warren; *W:* Gerry Daly; *M:* Randy Miller. THV

The Black Maid woof! 1974 A scantily-clad, sassy black maid cleans, cooks, cusses and drives her racist employer to the brink of insanity. 90m/C VHS, Beta. IT NO

The Black Marble 🐾🐾🐾 1979 (PG) A beautiful policewoman is paired with a policeman who drinks too much, is divorced, and is ready to retire. Surrounded by urban craziness and corruption, they eventually fall in love. Based on the Joseph Wambaugh novel. 110m/C VHS, Beta. Paula Prentiss, Harry Dean Stanton, Robert Foxworth, James Woods, Michael Dudikoff, Barbara Babcock, John Hancock, Judy Landers, Anne Ramsey, Christopher Lloyd; *D:* Harold Becker; *M:* Maurice Jarre. NLC

Black Market Rustlers 🐾½ 1943 The Range Busters are at it again. This time they break up a cattle rustling syndicate. 60m/B VHS, Beta. Ray Corrigan, Dennis Moore, Max Terhune; *D:* S. Roy Luby. VDM, RXM

Black Moon Rising 🐾½ 1986 (R) Based on an idea by John Carpenter ("Halloween"), this film deals with the theft of a new jet-powered car and its involvement in an FBI investigation. Solid performances and steady action enhance this routine effort. 100m/C VHS, Beta, LV, Closed Caption. Tommy Lee Jones, Linda Hamilton, Richard Jaeckel, Robert Vaughn; *D:* Harley Cokliss; *W:* John Carpenter; *M:* Lalo Schifrin. VTR, NWV

Black Narcissus 🐾🐾🐾½ 1947 A group of Anglican nuns attempting to found a hospital and school in the Himalayas confront native distrust and human frailties amid beautiful scenery. Adapted from the novel by Rumer Godden. Stunning cinematography. Crucial scenes were cut from the American release by censors. 101m/C VHS, Beta, LV. GB Deborah Kerr, David Farrar, Sabu, Jean Simmons, Kathleen Byron, Flora Robson, Esmond Knight,

Jenny Laird, Judith Furse, May Hallitt, Nancy Roberts; *D:* Michael Powell, Emeric Pressburger; *C:* Jack Cardiff. Academy Awards '47: Best Art Direction/Set Decoration (Color), Best Color Cinematography; New York Film Critics Awards '47: Best Actress (Kerr). MLB

Black Oak Conspiracy 🐾🐾 1977 (R) Based on a true story, this film deals with a mining company conspiracy discovered by an inquisitive stuntman. 92m/C VHS, Beta. Jesse Vint, Karen Carlson, Albert Salmi, Seymour Cassel, Robert F. Lyons; *D:* Bob Kelljan. NLC

Black Orchid 🐾🐾½ 1959 A businessman and a crook's widow fall in love and try to persuade their children it can work out. 96m/B VHS, Beta. Sophia Loren, Anthony Quinn, Ina Balin, Peter Mark Richman, Jimmie Baird; *D:* Martin Ritt; *W:* Joseph Stefano; *C:* Robert Burks. PAR

Black Orpheus 🐾🐾🐾½ *Orfeu Negro* 1958 The legend of Orpheus and Eurydice unfolds against the colorful background of the carnival in Rio de Janeiro. In the black section of the city, Orpheus is a street-car conductor and Eurydice, a country girl fleeing from a man sworn to kill her. Dancing, incredible music, and black magic add to the beauty of this film. Based on the play "Orfeu da Conceica." In Portuguese with English subtitles or dubbed. 103m/C VHS, Beta, LV. BR FR PT Breno Mello, Marpessa Dawn, Lea Garcia, Fausto Guerzoni, Lourdes De Oliveira; *D:* Marcel Camus; *C:* Jean Bourgoin; *M:* Antonio Carlos Jobim, Luis Bonfa. Academy Awards '59: Best Foreign Language Film; Cannes Film Festival '59: Best Film; Golden Globe Awards '60: Best Foreign Film. CVC, FOX, FCT

Black Out 🐾½ 1996 (R) Bosworth, who's suffering from amnesia after a car crash, becomes desperate to remember his life after his wife is murdered. 98m/C VHS. Brian Bosworth; *D:* Allan Goldstein. THV

Black Panther 🐾½ 1977 True story of psycho-killer Donald Neilson, who murdered heiress Lesley Whittle in England in the 1970s. 90m/C VHS, Beta. Donald Sumpter, Debbie Farrington; *D:* Ian Merrick; *W:* Michael Armstrong. VES, LIV

The Black Pirate 🐾🐾🐾 *Rage of the Buccaneers; The Black Buccaneer; Gordon il Pirata Nero* 1926 A shipwrecked mariner vows revenge on the pirates who destroyed his father's ship. Quintessential Fairbanks, this film features astounding athletic feats and exciting swordplay. Silent film with music score. Also available in color. 122m/B VHS, Beta, LV. IT Douglas Fairbanks Sr., Donald Crisp, Billie Dove; *D:* Albert Parker. KIV, MRV, REP

Black Pit of Dr. M 🐾 *Misterios del Ultratumba* 1947 The ghost of a doctor who has been unjustly executed for murder seeks revenge on employees of an insane asylum. The horror is not just confined to the asylum. 90m/B VHS, Beta. MX Gaston Santos, Rafael Bertrand, Mapita Cortes; *D:* Fernando Mendez; *W:* Ramon Obon. MAD, SMW

Black Rain 🐾🐾🐾 *Kuroi Ame* 1988 Erstwhile Ozu assistant Imamura directs this powerful portrait of a post-Hiroshima family five years after the bombing. Tanaka plays a young woman who, having been caught in a shower of black rain (radioactive fallout) on an ill-timed visit to Hiroshima, returns to her village to find herself ostracized by her peers and no longer considered marriageworthy. Winner of numerous awards (including five Japanese Academy Awards). In Japanese with English subtitles. 123m/B VHS. JP Kazuo Kitamura, Yoshiko Tanaka, Etsuko Ichihara, Shoichi Ozawa, Norihei Miki; *D:* Shohei Imamura. FXL, FCT

Black Rain 🐾🐾½ 1989 (R) Douglas portrays a ruthless American cop chasing a Japanese murder suspect through gang-controlled Tokyo. Loads of action and stunning visuals from the man who brought you "Blade Runner." 125m/C VHS, Beta, LV, 8mm, Closed Caption. Michael Douglas, Andy Garcia, Kate Capshaw, Ken Takakura, Yusaku Matsuda, John Spencer, Shigeru Koyama; *D:* Ridley Scott; *W:* Craig Bolotin, Warren Lewis; *C:* Jan De Bont; *M:* Hans Zimmer. Nominations: Academy Awards '89: Best Sound. PAR

Black Rainbow 🐾🐾🐾 1991 (R) Surprisingly good thriller that's relatively unknown, haunted by a menacing mood. Robards and Arquette are a father/daughter duo who perform clairvoyance scams at carnival sideshows. Suddenly, without warning, Arquette's former cons become real: she sees murder victims—before their demise. Quirky sleeper filmed on location in North Carolina. **CW:** Language, violence, and sensual scene. **103m/C VHS, Beta, LV, Closed Caption.** Rosanna Arquette, Jason Robards Jr., Tom Hulce, Ron Rosenthal, John Bennes, Linda Pierce, Mark Joy; **D:** Mike Hodges; **W:** Mike Hodges. *VTR, FXV, MED*

The Black Raven 🐾½ 1943 An action film that combines several plots into one. The Black Raven is an inn that sees more excitement than any other—not the least of which is murder! **64m/B VHS, Beta.** George Zucco, Wanda McKay, Glenn Strange, I. Stanford Jolley; **D:** Sam Newfield. *SNC, MLB, RXM*

Black Robe 🐾🐾🐾½ 1991 (R) In 1634 a young Jesuit priest journeys across the North American wilderness to bring the word of God to Canada's Huron Indians. The winter journey is brutal and perilous and he begins to question his mission after seeing the strength of the Indian's native ways. Stunning cinematography, a good script, and fine acting combine to make this superb. Portrays the Indians in a realistic manner, the only flaw being that Beresford portrays the white culture with very few redeeming qualities and as the only reason for the Indian's downfall. Moore adapted his own novel for the screen. **CW:** Violence and sensuality. **101m/C VHS, LV.** *AU CA* Lothaire Bluteau, Aden Young, Sandrine Holt, August Schellenberg, Tantoo Cardinal, Billy Two Rivers, Lawrence Bayne, Harrison Liu; **D:** Bruce Beresford; **W:** Brian Moore; **M:** Georges Delerue. Australian Film Institute '92: Best Cinematography; Genie Awards '91: Best Director (Beresford), Best Film. *THV*

The Black Room 🐾🐾🐾 1935 As an evil count lures victims into his castle of terror, the count's twin brother returns to fulfill an ancient prophecy. Karloff is wonderful in his dual role as the twin brothers. **70m/B Beta, LV.** Boris Karloff, Marian Marsh, Robert Allen, Katherine DeMille, John Buckler, Thurston Hall; **D:** Roy William Neill. *GKK, MLB*

The Black Room 🐾 1982 (R) Couples are lured to a mysterious mansion where a brother and his sister promise to satisfy their sexual desires. **90m/C VHS, Beta, LV.** Linnea Quigley, Stephen Knight, Cassandra Gaviola, Jim Stathis; **D:** Norman Thaddeus Vane. *VES, LIV*

Black Roses 🐾 1988 (R) A disgusting band of rockers shows up in a small town, and the local kids start turning into monsters. Coincidence? **90m/C VHS, Beta, LV.** Carmine Appice, Sal Viviano, Carla Ferrigno, Julie Adams, Ken Swofford, John Martin; **D:** John Fasano. *IMP*

Black Sabbath 🐾🐾🐾 *I Tre Volti della Paura* 1964 An omnibus horror film with three parts, climaxing with Karloff as a Wurdalak, a vampire who must kill those he loves. Also available with "Black Sunday" on laserdisc. **99m/C VHS, Beta.** *IT* Boris Karloff, Jacqueline Pierreux, Michele Mercier, Lidia Alfonsi, Susy Anderson, Mark Damon, Rika Dialina; **D:** Mario Bava; **M:** Les Baxter. *SNC*

Black Samurai 🐾 1977 (R) When his girlfriend is held hostage, a martial arts warrior will stop at nothing to destroy the organization that abducted her. **84m/C VHS, Beta.** Jim Kelly; **D:** Al Adamson. *NO*

The Black Scorpion 🐾½ 1957 Two geologists in Mexico unearth a nest of giant scorpions living in a dead volcano. Eventually one of the oversized arachnids escapes to wreak havoc on Mexico City. **85m/B VHS.** Richard Denning, Mara Corday, Carlos Rivas; **D:** Edward Ludwig; **W:** Robert Blees. *WAR, MLB, FRG*

Black Scorpion 🐾🐾½ *Roger Corman Presents: Black Scorpion* 1995 (R) Darcy Walker (Severance) is an ex-cop-turned-superhero (the scorpion is her symbol), who dons a mask and fetching (and tight) black vinyl to fight crime and avenge her dad's death. She's got the prerequisite sidekick—an ex-chop shop operator (Morris)—and a supervillain—the asthmatic Breathtaker (Siemaszko) who threatens to annihilate the city with toxic gas. Campy, schlock fun. **CW:** Violence, sexuality and some language. **92m/C VHS.** Joan Severance, Garrett Morris, Casey Siemaszko, Rick Rossovich; **D:** Jonathan Winfrey. *NHO*

Black Scorpion 2: Ground Zero 🐾🐾 1996 (R) Fetching crimefighter Darcy Walker (Severance) returns to battle villains Gangster Prankster and AfterShock, who are set on destroying the City of Angels by earthquake. Made for cable. **CW:** Sexuality, violence and some language. **85m/C VHS.** Joan Severance, Whip Hubley, Stoney Jackson; **D:** Jonathan Winfrey. *NHO*

Black Shampoo WOOF! 1976 A black hairdresser on the Sunset Strip fights the mob with a chainsaw. **90m/C VHS, Beta.** John Daniels, Tanya Boyd, Joe Ortiz; **D:** Greydon Clark. *VCI*

Black Sheep 🐾½ 1996 (PG-13) Isn't there a five-day waiting period for remakes? The previously viewed copies of "Tommy Boy" hadn't even hit the sale bin before Spade and Farley went in search of more property to destroy. The twist here? Spade is assigned to keep the oafish brother (not son) of a gubernatorial candidate (not auto parts dealer) out of trouble until after the election (not so he can save the family business). In an effort to provide humor, plot points, and character development, Farley falls out of, off of or onto every prop in sight while Spade smirks. **CW:** Crude language and humor, drug-related material and sexual innuendo. **87m/C VHS, Beta, Closed Caption.** Chris Farley, David Spade, Tim Matheson, Christine Ebersole, Gary Busey, Grant Heslov, Timothy Carhart, Bruce McGill; **D:** Penelope Spheeris; **W:** Fred Wolf; **C:** Daryn Okada; **M:** William Ross. *PAR*

Black Sister's Revenge 🐾🐾 *Emma Mae* 1976 Poorly selected video title mars this intelligent drama about a young black woman's struggle to adjust to the big city after growing up in the deep South. **100m/C VHS, Beta.** Jerri Hayes, Ernest Williams II, Charles D. Brook III, Eddie Allen; **D:** Jamaa Fanaka; **W:** Jamaa Fanaka. *UNI*

The Black Six 🐾 1974 (R) Six black Vietnam veterans are out to punish the white gang who killed the brother of one of the black men. **91m/C VHS, Beta.** Gene Washington, Carl Eller, Lem Barney, Mercury Morris, Joe "Mean Joe" Greene, Willie Lanier, Rosalind Miles, John Isenbarger, Ben Davidson, Maury Wills; **D:** Matt Cimber. *UNI*

Black Snow 🐾½ 1993 The mob is off on a violent search for fifty million bucks in cocaine. **90m/C VHS, LV.** Jane Badler, Peter Sherayko, Julia Montgomery, Randy Brooks; **D:** Frank Patterson. *AIP*

The Black Stallion 🐾🐾🐾 1979 (PG) A young boy and wild Arabian Stallion are the only survivors of a shipwreck, and they develop a deep affection for each other. When rescued, they begin training for an important race. Exceptionally beautiful first half. Rooney plays a horse trainer, again. Great for adults and kids. **120m/C VHS, Beta, LV, Closed Caption.** Kelly Reno, Mickey Rooney, Teri Garr, Clarence Muse; **D:** Carroll Ballard; **W:** William D. Wittliff, Melissa Mathison, Jeanne Rosenberg; **C:** Caleb Deschanel; **M:** Carmine Coppola. Academy Awards '79: Best Sound Effects Editing; Los Angeles Film Critics Association Awards '79: Best Cinematography; National Society of Film Critics Awards '79: Best Cinematography; Nominations: Academy Awards '79: Best Film Editing, Best Supporting Actor (Rooney). *MGM, FOX, TLF*

The Black Stallion Returns 🐾🐾½ 1983 (PG) Sequel to "The Black Stallion" follows the adventures of young Alec as he travels to the Sahara to search for his beautiful horse, which was stolen by an Arab chieftain. Unfortunately lacks much of the charm that was present in the first film. Adapted from the stories by Walt Farley. **103m/C VHS, Beta, LV, Closed Caption.** Kelly Reno, Teri Garr, Vincent Spano; **D:** Robert Dalva; **C:** Carlo DiPalma; **M:** Georges Delerue. *FOX*

Black Starlet 🐾½ *Black Gauntlet* 1974 (R) A girl from the projects of Chicago travels to Hollywood in search of fame. She winds her way through a world of sleaze and drugs in order to make it to the top. **90m/C VHS.** Juanita Brown, Eric Mason, Rockne Tarkington, Damu King, Diane Holden; **D:** Chris Munger. *GEM*

Black Sunday 🐾🐾🐾 1960 Executed one hundred years previously, a witch returns with her vampire servant to do the bidding of Satan. A must see for horror fans; firsts for Steele and Bava as director. Also available with "Black Sabbath" on laserdisc. **83m/B VHS.** *IT* Barbara Steele, John Richardson, Ivo Garrani, Andrea Checchi, Arturo Dominici; **D:** Mario Bava; **M:** Les Baxter. *SNC, MRV, MOV*

Black Sunday 🐾🐾½ 1977 (R) An Arab terrorist group plots to steal the Goodyear Blimp and load it with explosives. Their intent is to explode it over a Miami Super Bowl game to assassinate the U.S. president and to kill all the fans. Based on Thomas Harris' novel. **143m/C VHS, Beta, LV.** Robert Shaw, Bruce Dern, Marthe Keller, Fritz Weaver, Steven Keats, Michael V. Gazzo, William Daniels; **D:** John Frankenheimer; **W:** Ernest Lehman; **C:** John A. Alonzo; **M:** John Williams. *PAR*

The Black Swan 🐾🐾🐾 1942 Swashbuckling pirate film, based on the novel by Rafael Sabatini, stars Power as James Waring, compatriot of notorious buccaneer Henry Morgan (Cregar). Morgan is pardoned and sent to Jamaica as its new governor—if he can prevent his from associates from continuing their criminal ways. He enlists Waring to help him fight the renegades; meanwhile Waring falls in love with former governor's daughter Margaret (O'Hara). Lots of derring do. **85m/C VHS, Closed Caption.** Tyrone Power, Maureen O'Hara, Laird Cregar, Thomas Mitchell, George Sanders, Anthony Quinn, George Zucco, Edward Ashley, Fortunio Bonanova; **D:** Henry King; **W:** Ben Hecht, Seton I. Miller; **C:** Leon Shamroy; **M:** Alfred Newman. Academy Awards '42: Best Color Cinematography; Nominations: Academy Awards '42: Original Dramatic/Comedy Score. *FXV*

Black Terrorist 1985 Terrorists take over a ranch and slay the inhabitants. They keep a young boy alive and the mother tries to rescue him. **81m/C VHS, Beta.** Allan Granville, Vera Jones; **D:** Neil Hetherington. *NO*

Black Tide 🐾 *Stormy Crossing* 1958 Suspicions arise that a drowning may have actually been a murder. **69m/C VHS.** John Ireland, Derek Bond. *SNC, VYY*

Black Tights 🐾🐾½ *Un, Deux, Trois, Quatre!* 1960 Chevalier introduces four stories told in dance by Roland Petit's Ballet de Paris company: "The Diamond Crusher," "Cyrano de Bergerac," "A Merry Mourning," and "Carmen." A keeper for dance fans. Shearer's Roxanne in "Cyrano" was her last performance before retirement. **120m/C VHS, Beta.** *FR* Cyd Charisse, Zizi Jeanmaire, Moira Shearer, Dirk Sanders, Roland Petit; **D:** Terence Young. *VYY, NOS, VAI*

Black Tower 🐾🐾 1950 An interesting murder mystery telling the story of a desperately impoverished medical student. **54m/B VHS, Beta.** Peter Cookson, Warren William, Anne Gwynne, Charles Calvert. *VYY*

Black Vampire 🐾 *Blood Couple; Ganja and Hess; Double Possession* 1973 (R) Jones plays a professor of African studies who is turned into a vampire by another vampire. He then marries the villain's ex-wife, played by Clark, a veteran of Russ Meyer films. Not much of a story but the acting is actually quite good and there are some creepy moments thanks mainly to an interesting score. **83m/C VHS, Beta.** Duane Jones, Marlene Clark, Bill Gunn, Sam Waymon, Leonard Jackson, Candece Tarpley, Mabel King; **D:** Bill Gunn; **W:** Bill Gunn. *GEM*

A Black Veil for Lisa 🎬🎬 1968 A man attempts to exact revenge upon his unfaithful wife, but things go horribly awry. 87m/C **VHS**. *IT GE* John Mills, Luciana Paluzzi, Robert Hoffman; **D:** Massimo Dallamano. *REP*

The Black Velvet Gown 🎬🎬½ 1992 Riah Millican (McTeer) is a poor miner's widow living in rural 1834 England with her three children. She finds work as a housekeeper to the reclusive Miller (Peck), who agrees to educate her children and even gives Riah the titular gown, which was once his mother's. Now educated out of their working-class, the Millican's lives provide unexpected love and tragedy for all concerned. Based on the novel by Catherine Cookson; made for British TV. 103m/C **VHS**. *GB* Janet McTeer, Bob Peck, Geraldine Somerville; **D:** Norman Stone. *TVC*

Black Venus woof! 1983 (R) A soft-core epic, starring the former Miss Bahamas, Josephine Jacqueline Jones, about the 18th-century French aristocracy. Laughably based upon the stories of Balzac. European film dubbed in English. 80m/C **VHS, Beta**. Josephine Jacqueline Jones, Emiliano Redondo; **D:** Claude Mulot. *MGM*

Black Water 🎬🎬½ 1994 Tennessee fishing trip turns into a nightmare for an innocent man accused of murder. Based on the novel "Minnie" by Hans Werner Kettenbach. 105m/C **VHS, Closed Caption**. Julian Sands, Stacey Dash, Ned Beatty, Ed Lauter, Denise Crosby, Billy McNamara, Rod Steiger; **D:** Nicolas Gessner; **W:** Nicolas Gessner, Laird Koeing; **M:** Gabriel Yared. *ACA*

Black Water Gold 🎬🎬½ 1969 Television movie about a search for sunken Spanish gold. 75m/C **VHS**. Ricardo Montalban, Keir Dullea, Lana Wood, Bradford Dillman, France Nuyen; **D:** Alan Landsburg. *NO*

Black Werewolf 🎬🎬 *The Beast Must Die* 1975 (PG) A millionaire sportsman invites a group of men and women connected with bizarre deaths or the eating of human flesh to spend the cycle of a full moon at his isolated lodge. 93m/C **VHS, LV**. *GB* Peter Cushing, Calvin Lockhart, Charles Gray, Anton Diffring; **D:** Paul Annett; **M:** Jack Hildyard. *MED, PSM*

The Black Widow *Sombra, the Spider Woman* 1947 A fortune-teller plots to steal scientific secrets and take over the world. Serial in thirteen episodes. 164m/B **VHS**. Bruce Edwards, Carol Forman, Anthony Warde; **D:** Spencer Gordon Bennet. *VCN, REP, MLB*

Black Widow 🎬🎬🎬 1987 (R) A federal agent pursues a beautiful murderess who marries rich men and then kills them, making the deaths look natural. The agent herself becomes involved in the final seduction. The two women are enticing and the locations picturesque. 101m/C **VHS, LV, Closed Caption**. Debra Winger, Theresa Russell, Sami Frey, Nicol Williamson, Terry O'Quinn, Dennis Hopper, D.W. Moffett, Lois Smith, Mary Woronov, Rutanya Alda, James Hong, Diane Ladd; **Cameos:** David Mamet; **D:** Bob Rafelson; **W:** Ronald Bass; **C:** Conrad Hall; **M:** Michael Small. *FOX*

The Black Windmill 🎬🎬½ 1974 (PG) An English spy is caught between his service and the kidnapping of his family by rival spies. 102m/C **VHS, Beta**. Michael Caine, Donald Pleasence, Delphine Seyrig, Clive Revill, Janet Suzman, John Vernon; **D:** Donald Siegel. *USH*

Blackbeard the Pirate 🎬🎬 1952 The 18th-century buccaneer is given the full-blooded, Hollywood treatment. 99m/C **VHS, Beta, LV**. Robert Newton, Linda Darnell, Keith Andes, William Bendix, Richard Egan; **D:** Raoul Walsh. *TTC*

Blackbeard's Ghost 🎬🎬 1967 Disney comedy in which the famed 18th-century pirate's spirit is summoned to wreak havoc in order to prevent an old family home from being turned into a casino. 107m/C **VHS, Beta, LV**. Peter Ustinov, Dean Jones, Suzanne Pleshette, Elsa Lanchester, Richard Deacon; **D:** Robert Stevenson; **C:** Edward Colman; **M:** Robert F. Brunner. *DIS*

Blackbelt 2: Fatal Force 🎬½ 1993 (R) A man seeks to avenge his brother's murder by going after his killers. ?m/C **VHS**. Blake Bahner, Roxanne Baird, Michael Vlastas. *NHO*

Blackboard Jungle 🎬🎬🎬½ 1955 Well-remembered urban drama about an idealistic teacher in a slum area who fights doggedly to connect with his unruly students. Bill Hailey's "Rock Around the Clock" over the opening credits was the first use of rock music in a mainstream feature film. Based on Evan Hunter novel. 101m/B **VHS, Beta, Closed Caption**. Glenn Ford, Anne Francis, Louis Calhern, Sidney Poitier, Vic Morrow, Richard Kiley, Margaret Hayes, John Hoyt, Warner Anderson; **D:** Richard Brooks; **W:** Richard Brooks. Nominations: Academy Awards '55: Best Art Direction/Set Decoration (B & W), Best Black and White Cinematography, Best Film Editing, Best Screenplay. *MGM*

Blackenstein woof! *Black Frankenstein* 1973 (R) Doctor into nouveau experimentation restores a man's arms and legs. But a jealous assistant gives our man a bogus injection, causing him to become "Blackenstein," a large African American with chip on hulking shoulder who enjoys killing people and otherwise causing big trouble. Ripe blaxploitation. 87m/C **VHS, Beta**. John Hart, Ivory Stone, Andrea King, Liz Renay, Joe DiSue; **D:** William A. Levey. *MED*

Blackjack 🎬🎬 1978 (R) Las Vegas is the scene for action and excitement as the mob puts the hit on tough guy William Smith! 104m/C **VHS**. William Smith, Tony Burton, Paris Earl, Damu King, Diane Summerfield, Angela May; **D:** John Evans. *TPV*

Blackmail 🎬🎬🎬 1929 This first sound film for Great Britain and director Hitchcock features an early visualization of some typical Hitchcockian themes. The story follows the police investigation of a murder, and a detective's attempts to keep his girlfriend from being involved. Look for Hitchcock's screen cameo. Made as a silent, this was reworked to become a talkie. 86m/B **VHS, Beta, LV**. *GB* Anny Ondra, John Longden, Sara Allgood, Charles Paton, Cyril Ritchard, Donald Calthrop, Charles Paton, Hannah Jones, Percy Parsons, Johnny Butt, Harvey Braban, Phyllis Monkman; **Cameos:** Alfred Hitchcock; **D:** Alfred Hitchcock; **W:** Alfred Hitchcock, Charles Bennett, Benn W. Levy, Garnett Weston. *REP, MRV, NOS*

Blackmail 🎬🎬🎬 1991 (R) Familiar story is given new life in this suspenseful movie originally made for cable TV. Blakely is a lonely woman who succumbs to Midkiff's attentions. She doesn't suspect that he's conning her with the help of his lover, Toussaint. Engaging thriller adapted from a short story by Bill Crenshaw. *CW:* Violence and sensuality. 87m/C **VHS, Beta, LV, Closed Caption**. Susan Blakely, Dale Midkiff, Beth Toussaint, John Saxon, Mac Davis; **D:** Ruben Preuss. *PAR*

Blackout 🎬½ 1950 Blind man recovers his sight and finds that the brother of his girlfriend, once thought dead, is actually alive and well and running a smuggling ring. Routine. 73m/B **VHS, Beta**. *GB* Maxwell Reed, Dinah Sheridan, Patric Doonan, Eric Pohlmann; **D:** Robert S. Baker. *SNC*

Blackout 🎬🎬 *Murder by Proxy* 1954 A drunken private eye is offered a murder case, and is subsequently framed for the crime. 87m/B **VHS, Beta, LV**. Dane Clark, Belinda Lee, Betty Ann Davies; **D:** Terence Fisher. *MLB*

Blackout 🎬🎬 1978 (R) Four killers terrorize an office building during the 1977 New York electrical blackout. Soon the police enter, confront them, and the fun starts. Comic touches provide some relief from the violence here. 86m/C **VHS, Beta**. Jim Mitchum, Robert Carradine, Ray Milland, June Allyson, Jean-Pierre Aumont, Belinda J. Montgomery; **D:** Eddy Matalon; **W:** Joseph Stefano. *NLC*

Blackout 🎬🎬½ 1985 Made-for-cable-TV thriller. An aging police chief suspects a disfigured amnesiac is responsible for past killings, in spite of the fact that he now leads a subdued family life. 99m/C **VHS, Beta**. Richard Widmark, Keith Carradine, Kathleen Quinlan, Michael Beck, Gerald Hiken; **D:** Douglas Hickox; **W:** David Ambrose. *MED*

Blackout 🎬🎬 1988 (R) Strange memories from childhood come back to her as a woman fights for her life. 91m/C **VHS, Beta, LV**. Carol Lynley, Gail O'Grady, Michael Keys Hall, Joseph Gian, Joanna Miles; **D:** Doug Adams; **C:** Arledge Armenaki. *NO*

The Blacksmith/The Balloonatic 1923 Two Buster Keaton shorts: "The Blacksmith" (1922) features Buster as the local blacksmith's apprentice who suddenly finds himself in charge. "The Balloonatic" (1923) presents Buster trapped in a runaway hot air balloon. Both films include music score. 57m/B **VHS, Beta**. Buster Keaton, Virginia Fox, Phyllis Haver; **D:** Buster Keaton. *VYY*

The Blacksmith/The Cops 1922 "The Blacksmith" is a burlesque of Longfellow's famous poem "The Village Blacksmith." In "Cops" Buster tries a new business venture to win his girl's hand. Chaos ensues. Silent comedy at its most adroit. 38m/B **VHS, Beta**. Buster Keaton, Virginia Fox. *CCB*

Blacksnake! woof! 1973 (R) Overheated sex and race tale, set in 1835, finds a British lord travelling to a Caribbean island in search of his brother. What he finds is his sadistic sister-in-law and her evil overseer using violence to keep the slaves in line. *CW:* Nudity, violence, mature themes. 83m/C **VHS, Beta**. Anouska Hempel, David Warbeck, Percy Herbert, David Prowse; **D:** Russ Meyer. *RMF*

Blackwater Trail 🎬🎬 1995 (R) Novelist Matt Curran (Nelson) travels from L.A. to Michelton, Australia, to attend the funeral of his best friend Andy, a cop who supposedly committed suicide. But Andy's sister (and Matt's former lover) Cathy (Smart) thinks he was murdered because of a case involving a serial killer. Matt decides to snoop around and finds out the killer likes to leave behind body parts and biblical quotations. Contrived plotting but some good performances and some spectacular scenery. 100m/C **VHS, Closed Caption**. *AU* Judd Nelson, Dee Smart, Peter Phelps, Mark Lee, Brett Climo; **D:** Ian Barry; **W:** Andrew Russell; **C:** John Stokes; **M:** Stephen Rae. *WAR*

Blacula 🎬🎬 1972 (PG) The African Prince Mamuwalde stalks the streets of Los Angeles trying to satisfy his insatiable desire for blood. Mildly successful melding of blaxploitation and horror that spawned a sequel, "Scream, Blacula, Scream." 92m/C **VHS, Beta, LV**. William Marshall, Thalmus Rasulala, Denise Nicholas, Vonetta McGee; **D:** William Crain. *ORI*

Blade 🎬🎬 1972 (PG) An honest cop challenges a dirty cover-up in killer-stalked New York. 79m/C **VHS, Beta**. Steve Landesburg, John Schuck, Kathryn Walker; **D:** Ernie Pintoff. *GEM, MRV*

Blade in Hong Kong 🎬🎬½ 1985 Made-for-TV action outing. Investigator travels to Hong Kong, finds trouble and romance in the underbelly of the city. Pilot for un-sold series. 100m/C **VHS**. Terry Lester, Keye Luke, Mike Preston, Jean-Marie Hon, Leslie Nielsen, Nancy Kwan, Anthony Newley, Ellen Regan; **D:** Reza Badiyi. *NO*

A Blade in the Dark 🎬🎬 *La Casa Con La Scala Nel Buio; House of the Dark Stairway* 1983 A young man composing a score for a horror film moves into a secluded villa and is inspired and haunted by the mysterious murder he witnesses. 99m/C **VHS, Beta**. Andrea Occhipinti, Anny Papa; **D:** Lamberto Bava. *VES, LIV*

Blade Master 🎬½ *Ator the Invincible* 1984 (PG) In this sequel to "Ator the Fighting Eagle," O'Keeffe as Ator is back as the Blade Master. Ator defends his people and his family name in a battle against the "Geometric Nucleus": a primitive bomb. His quest leads him and his small band of men to the castle of knowledge. 92m/C **VHS, Beta**. Miles O'Keeffe, Lisa Foster; **D:** David Hills. *MED*

Blade of the Ripper woof! 1984 A madman armed with a razor slashes his way through the lovelies of the international jet set. 90m/C **VHS, Beta**. George Hilton, Edwige Fenech. *NO*

Blade Runner 🎬🎬🎬½ **1982 (R)** Los Angeles, the 21st century. World-weary cop tracks down a handful of renegade "replicants" (synthetically produced human slaves who, with only days left of life, search madly for some way to extend their prescribed lifetimes). Moody, beautifully photographed, dark thriller with sets from an architect's dream. Based on "Do Androids Dream of Electric Sheep" by Philip K. Dick. Laser edition features restored footage, information about special effects, and production sketches. Director's cut, released at 117 minutes, removes Ford's narration and the last scene of the film, which Scott considered too "up," and inserts several short scenes, including a dream sequence. **CW:** Violence. **122m/C VHS, Beta, LV, 8mm, DVD.** Harrison Ford, Rutger Hauer, Sean Young, Daryl Hannah, M. Emmet Walsh, Edward James Olmos, Joe Turkel, Brion James, Joanna Cassidy, William Sanderson; **D:** Ridley Scott; **W:** Hampton Fancher, David Peoples; **C:** Jordan Cronenweth; **M:** Vangelis. Los Angeles Film Critics Association Awards '82: Best Cinematography; Nominations: Academy Awards '82: Best Art Direction/Set Decoration. **COL, WAR, CRC**

Blades 🎬 **1989 (R)** Another junk heap from Troma, dealing with the efforts of three golfers who try to stop a maniacal power mower that's been grinding duffers with regularity. **101m/C VHS, Beta, LV.** Robert North, Jeremy Whelan, Victoria Scott, Jon McBride. **MED**

Blades of Courage 🎬🎬 *Skate!* **1988** A made-for-television biography of Olympic skater Lori Larouche. Choreographed by Debbi Wilkes. **98m/C VHS, Beta.** **CA** Lynn Nightingale, Christianne Hirt, Colm Feore, Rosemary Dunsmore; **D:** Randy Bradshaw. **ACA**

Blaise Pascal 🎬🎬🎬½ **1971** Another of Rossellini's later historical portraits, detailing the life and times of the 17th-century philosopher, seen as a man whose scientific ideas conflicted with his own religious beliefs. Made for Italian television. In Italian with subtitles. **131m/C VHS, Beta.** **IT D:** Roberto Rossellini. **FCT**

Blake of Scotland Yard **1936** Blake, the former Scotland Yard inspector, battles against a villain who has constructed a murderous death ray. Condensed version of the 15 episode serial (originally at 180 minutes). **70m/B VHS, Beta.** Ralph Byrd, Herbert Rawlinson, Joan Barclay, Lloyd Hughes; **D:** Robert F. "Bob" Hill. **VYY, DVT, NOS**

Blake's Seven **1978** Freedom-fighter Blake and his crew battle against a totalitarian superpower in this futuristic space adventure series from Great Britain. Created by Terry Nation of "Doctor Who" fame. Each volume contains two episodes and is available individually. **105m/C VHS.** **GB** Gareth Thomas, Sally Knyvette, Paul Darrow, Michael Keating, David Jackson, Jan Chappell; **D:** Michael E. Briant, Vere Lorrimer. **VCO, TVC, MOV**

Blame It on Rio 🎬🎬 **1984 (R)** A middle-aged man has a ridiculous fling with his best friend's daughter while on vacation with them in Rio de Janeiro. Caine and Johnson are amusing, but the script is somewhat weak. Remake of the French film "One Wild Moment." **90m/C VHS, Beta, LV.** Michael Caine, Joseph Bologna, Demi Moore, Michelle Johnson, Valerie Harper; **D:** Stanley Donen; **W:** Charlie Peters, Larry Gelbart. **VES, LIV**

Blame It on the Bellboy 🎬🎬½ **1992 (PG-13)** Wild farce set in Venice about a hotel bellboy who confuses three similarly named visitors—sending the wrong ones to meet corporate bigwigs, date women, or even kill. The brisk pace loses it towards the end and devolves into chase scenes. **79m/C VHS, Beta, Closed Caption.** Dudley Moore, Bryan Brown, Richard Griffiths, Andreas Katsulas, Patsy Kensit, Alison Steadman, Bronson Pinchot, Lindsay Anderson, Penelope Wilton; **D:** Mark Herman; **W:** Mark Herman; **M:** Trevor Jones. **HPH**

Blame It on the Night 🎬🎬 **1984 (PG-13)** A rock star gets to take care of the military cadet son he never knew after the boy's mother suddenly dies. Mick Jagger helped write the story.

Available in VHS and Beta Hi-Fi. **85m/C VHS, Beta.** Nick Mancuso, Byron Thames, Leslie Ackerman, Billy Preston, Merry Clayton; **D:** Gene Taft. **FOX**

Blanche Fury 🎬🎬½ **1948** Governess Blanche (Hobson) marries her wealthy widowed cousin but the man she truly desires is the illegitimate Philip Thorn (Granger), who manages the estate for her husband. So Blanche decides to get rid of the man she doesn't love. Based on England's 19th-century Rush murder and adapted from the novel by Joseph Shearing. **95m/C VHS.** **GB** Valerie Hobson, Stewart Granger, Walter Fitzgerald, Michael Gough, Maurice Denham, Sybilla Binder; **D:** Marc Allegret; **W:** Hugh Mills; **C:** Guy Green, Geoffrey Unsworth; **M:** Clifton Parker. **FCT**

Blank Check 🎬 *Disney's Blank Check* **1993 (PG)** Parents may want to verify the whereabouts of their checkbooks after this one. 11-year-old Preston receives a blank check from a mobster on the run, cashes it for a million bucks, and goes on a spending orgy under an assumed name. Where are his parents? Apparently they don't have a problem with a shadowy benefactor taking their son under his wing. Sound familiar? And who thought it would be a good idea to have the little twerp mooning after a comely bank teller? Formula aside, this blatant rip-off of "Home Alone" tries to throw in an ending moral but probably won't fool the kids either. **93m/C VHS, LV, Closed Caption.** Brian Bonsall, Miguel Ferrer, Michael Lerner, Tone Loc, Rick Ducommun, Karen Duffy; **D:** Rupert Wainwright; **W:** Colby Carr, Blake Snyder; **M:** Nicholas Pike. **DIS**

Blankman 🎬🎬 **1994 (PG-13)** Self-appointed superhero (Wayans), who makes up in creativity what he lacks in superpowers, fights crime in his underwear and a cape made from his grandmother's bathrobe. Life is simple, until an ambitious TV reporter (Givens) finds out about him. Silly one-joke premise is carried a little too far; didn't similar "Meteor Man" crash? Gifted comedian Wayans tries, but can't make this guy fly. **96m/C VHS, LV, Closed Caption.** Damon Wayans, Robin Givens, David Alan Grier, Jason Alexander, Jon Polito; **D:** Mike Binder; **W:** Damon Wayans, J.F. Lawton. **COL**

Blast 🎬🎬 **1996** Terrorists take a group of spectators hostage at the Atlanta Summer Olympics. **98m/C VHS.** Linden Ashby, Andrew Divoff, Rutger Hauer, Tim Thomerson; **D:** Albert Pyun. **WAR**

Blast-Off Girls 🎬 **1967** A scuzzball promoter sets out to avenge himself for being blacklisted by the rock 'n' roll industry. He discovers a fresh group, but without corporate backing he can only pay them with groovy clothes and mini-skirted girls. Trouble ensues when they unexpectedly hit the charts and want real money. **83m/C VHS.** Ray Sager, Dan Conway; **D:** Herschell Gordon Lewis. **MOV, SMW**

Blastfighter woof! **1985 (R)** After local hoodlums kill his daughter, an ex-con cop goes on a spree of violence and revenge. Director Bava uses the pseudonym "John Old, Jr.," as his father Mario Bava occasionally credited himself as John Old. Italian film shot in Atlanta. **93m/C VHS, Beta.** **IT** Michael Sopkiw, Valerie Blake, George Eastman; **D:** Lamberto Bava. **VES, LIV**

Blaze 🎬🎬½ **1989 (R)** The true story of Louisiana governor Earl Long who became involved with a stripper, Blaze Starr, causing a political scandal of major proportions. Robust, good-humored bio-pic featuring a fine character turn by Newman. **117m/C VHS, Beta, LV, Closed Caption.** Paul Newman, Lolita Davidovich, Jerry Hardin, Robert Wuhl, Gailard Sartain, Jeffrey DeMunn, Richard Jenkins, Garland Bunting; **D:** Ron Shelton; **W:** Ron Shelton; **C:** Haskell Wexler. Nominations: Academy Awards '89: Best Cinematography. **TOU**

Blazing Across the Pecos 🎬½ **1948** The Durango Kid (Starrett) is after Pecos Flats mayor Ace Brockaway (Wilson), who's secretly selling guns to the local Indian tribe so they'll attack the supply wagons of his business rivals.

54m/B VHS. Charles Starrett, Smiley Burnette, Charles C. Wilson, Chief Thundercloud; **D:** Ray Nazarro. **COL**

Blazing Guns 🎬 *Marshal of Heldorado* **1950** A marshal, masquerading inexplicably as a tenderfoot, enters a lawless town and is immediately hired as a deputy. **54m/B VHS, Beta, LV.** Raymond Hatton, Russell Hayden, Fuzzy Knight, Julie Adams. **NOS, HEG**

Blazing Saddles 🎬🎬🎬½ **1974 (R)** Wild, wacky spoof by Brooks of every cliche in the western film genre. Little is Black Bart, a convict offered a reprieve if he will become a sheriff and clean up a nasty frontier town; the previous recipients of this honor have all swiftly ended up in shallow graves. A crazy, silly film with a cast full of lovable loonies including comedy greats Wilder, Kahn, and Korman. Watch for the Count Basie Orchestra. A group writing effort, based on an original story by Bergman. Was the most-viewed movie in its first year of release on HBO cable. **90m/C VHS, Beta, LV, DVD.** Cleavon Little, Harvey Korman, Madeline Kahn, Gene Wilder, Mel Brooks, John Hillerman, Alex Karras, Dom DeLuise, Liam Dunn; **D:** Mel Brooks; **W:** Mel Brooks, Norman Steinberg, Andrew Bergman, Richard Pryor; **C:** Joseph Biroc; **M:** John Morris. Writers Guild of America '74: Best Original Screenplay; Nominations: Academy Awards '74: Best Film Editing, Best Song ("Blazing Saddles"), Best Supporting Actress (Kahn). **WAR**

Blazing Stewardesses woof! **1975 (R)** The Hound salutes the distributor for truth in advertising, as they stamped this as one of the world's worst videos. Lusty, busty stewardesses relax at a western guest ranch under siege from hooded riders and the aging gags of the Ritz Brothers. **95m/C VHS.** Yvonne De Carlo, Bob Livingston, Donald (Don "Red") Barry, Regina Carrol; **Cameos:** The Ritz Brothers; **D:** Al Adamson. **NO**

Bleak House 🎬🎬½ **1985** The British television mini-series adaptation of the Charles Dickens tome about an interminable lawsuit and the decadent, criminal ruling class of 19th-century England. On three tapes. **391m/C VHS, Beta, Closed Caption.** **GB** Denholm Elliott, Diana Rigg, Philip Franks, Peter Vaughan, T.P. McKenna; **D:** Ross Devenish; **M:** Geoffrey Burgon. **FOX, SIG, TVC**

Bleak Moments 🎬🎬 *Loving Moments* **1971** Bored secretary Sylvia (Raitt) tries to work her flirtatious charms on a repressed teacher (Allan) and an eccentric musician (Bradwell). **110m/C VHS.** **GB** Anne Raitt, Eric Allen, Mike Bradwell, Joolia Cappleman; **D:** Mike Leigh; **W:** Mike Leigh; **C:** Bahram Manocheri; **M:** Eric Allen. **WBF**

Bless the Beasts and Children 🎬🎬½ **1971 (PG)** A group of six teenage boys at a summer camp attempt to save a herd of buffalo from slaughter at a national preserve. Treacly Kramer drama. Based on the novel by Glendon Swarthout. **109m/C VHS, Beta.** Billy Mumy, Barry Robins, Miles Chapin, Darel Glaser, Bob Kramer, Ken Swofford, Jesse White; **D:** Stanley Kramer; **M:** Perry Botkin. Nominations: Academy Awards '71: Best Song ("Bless the Beasts and the Children"). **COL**

Blessed Event 🎬🎬🎬 **1932** Fast-moving, entertaining film about a Broadway gossip columnist with a poison pen. Tracy has the role of a lifetime as a Walter Winchell prototype who thinks no one is exempt from his juicy column. Powell makes film debut as a crooner after a brief career as a band singer. Based on a play by Manuel Seff and Forrest Wilson. **77m/B VHS, Closed Caption.** Lee Tracy, Mary Brian, Dick Powell, Allen Jenkins, Ruth Donnelly, Emma Dunn, Walter Miller, Tom Dugan, Isabel Jewell; **D:** Roy Del Ruth; **W:** Howard J. Green. **MGM**

Blessing 🎬🎬 **1994** It's an unhappy time down on the Wisconsin dairy farm in this tale of family life. Embittered patriarch Jack (Griffis) can barely make a go of it and takes his frustrations out by beating his cows and climbing to the top of the silo. Despairing wife Arlene (Glynn) enters newspaper lotteries and collects religious statues while daughter Randi (Griffis) keeps delaying leaving the farm because of a nagging sense of responsibility. Claustrophobic atmosphere. **94m/C**

VHS. Guy Griffis, Carlin Glynn, Melora Griffis, Gareth Williams, Clovis Siemon; **D:** Paul Zehrer; **W:** Paul Zehrer; **C:** Stephen Kazmierski; **M:** Joseph S. DeBeasi. Nominations: Independent Spirit Awards '95: First Screenplay. LEO

Blind Ambition 🎬🎬½ 1982
Television mini-series docu-drama traces the career of John Dean, special counsel to President Richard M. Nixon. Focuses on his fractured personal life and touches on virtually all of the Watergate headlines. 95m/C VHS, Beta. Martin Sheen, Rip Torn. TLF

Blind Date 🎬½ 1984 (R)
Blind man agrees to have a visual computer implanted in his brain in order to help the police track down a psychopathic killer. Violent scenes may be disturbing to some. 100m/C VHS, Beta, LV. Joseph Bottoms, Kirstie Alley, Keir Dullea, James Daughton, Lana Clarkson, Marina Sirtis; **D:** Nico Mastorakis; **W:** Nico Mastorakis. VES, LIV

Blind Date 🎬🎬 1987 (PG-13)
A blind date between a workaholic yuppie and a beautiful blonde starts off well, but when she drinks too much at dinner, things get out of hand. In addition to embarrassing her date and destroying the restaurant, she has a jealous ex-boyfriend who must be dealt with. 95m/C VHS, Beta, LV. Kim Basinger, Bruce Willis, John Larroquette, William Daniels, George Coe, Mark Blum, Phil Hartman, Stephanie Faracy, Alice Hirson, Graham Stark; **D:** Blake Edwards; **C:** Harry Stradling Jr.; **M:** Henry Mancini. COL

Blind Faith 🎬 1989 (R)
Action and adventure take a turn for the horrific when several men find themselves in captivity. ?m/C VHS. Eric Gunn, Kevin Yon, Lynne Browne; **D:** Dean Wilson; **W:** Dean Wilson. HHE

Blind Fear 🎬½ 1989 (R)
A blind woman is stalked by three killers in an abandoned country inn. 98m/C VHS, Beta, LV. Shelley Hack, Jack Langedijk, Kim Coates, Jan Rubes, Heidi von Palleske; **D:** Tom Berry; **W:** Sergio D. Altieri. ACA

Blind Fists of Bruce 🎬½ 197?
A rich, idle young man learns the techniques of kung fu from a former warrior. 92m/C VHS, Beta. Bruce Li; **D:** Kam Bo. NO

Blind Fools 🎬½ 1940
A scathing indictment of children neglected by ambitious parents. 66m/B VHS, Beta, LV. Herbert Rawlinson, Claire Whitney, Russell Hicks, Miriam Battista. NO

Blind Fury 🎬🎬½ 1990 (R)
A blind Vietnam vet enlists the aid of a Zen master and a sharpshooter to tackle the Mafia. Hauer works well in the lead, but unfortunately, the movie doesn't. 86m/C VHS, Beta, LV, Closed Caption. Rutger Hauer, Terry O'Quinn, Brandon Call, Lisa Blount, Randall "Tex" Cobb, Noble Willingham, Meg Foster, Sho Kosugi, Nick Cassavetes, Charles Cooper, Rick Overton; **D:** Phillip Noyce; **C:** Charles Robert Carner; **C:** Don Burgess; **M:** J. Peter Robinson. COL, FCT

Blind Husbands 🎬🎬🎬½ 1919
An Austrian officer is attracted to the pretty wife of a dull surgeon. Controversial in its day, this lurid, sumptuous melodrama instigated many stubborn Hollywood truths, including the stereotype of the brusque, jodhpur-clad Prussian officer. This was von Stroheim's first outing as director. 98m/B VHS, Beta. Erich von Stroheim, Fay Wray; **D:** Erich von Stroheim. VYY, GVV

Blind Justice 🎬🎬 1986
An innocent man is identified as a rapist, and the accusation ruins his life. Made for television. 94m/C VHS, Beta. Tim Matheson, Lisa Eichhorn, Mimi Kuzyk, Philip Charles MacKenzie, Tom Atkins; **D:** Rod Holcomb; **M:** Miles Goodman. FOX

Blind Justice 🎬🎬½ 1994 (R)
Gunfighter gets blinded in battle and rides into a small town where he's nursed back to health by an attractive lady doctor. While he recovers, he learns the town is trying to protect a cache of government silver from being stolen by bandits. Made for cable TV.**CW:** Some language; graphic western violence. 85m/C VHS. Armand Assante, Elisabeth Shue, Robert Davi; **D:** Richard Spence. HBO

Blind Man's Bluff 🎬🎬 1991 (PG-13)
A blind professor is accused of murdering his neighbor, but as he tries to solve the mystery, evidence points to his ex-girlfriend who may have framed him for the murder. Surprisingly suspenseful made for cable TV movie is hampered by a stock Hollywood ending. 86m/C VHS, Beta, Closed Caption. Robert Urich, Lisa Eilbacher, Patricia Clarkson, Ken Pogue, Ron Perlman; **D:** James Quinn; **W:** Joel Gross; **M:** Richard Bellis. PAR

Blind Rage 🎬 1978 (R)
When the United States government transports $15 million to the Philippines, five blind kung fu masters want a piece of the action. 81m/C VHS, Beta. PH D'Urville Martin, Leo Fong, Tony Ferrer, Dick Adair, Darnell Garcia, Leila Hermosa, Fred Williamson; **D:** Efren C. Pinon. MGM

Blind Side 🎬½ 1993 (R)
DeMornay and Silver are a married couple whose Mexican vacation turns into trouble when they get into a hit-and-run accident which they don't report. Back home, they're frightened by the sudden appearance of Hauer, who's also just back from Mexico. They think he's after blackmail but he's really just a run-of-the-mill psycho intrigued by DeMornay, who at least keeps her character in control. Silver and Hauer have a great time chewing scenery. Made for cable television. Also available in an unrated version which run 98 minutes.**CW:** Violence and terror and sexuality. 92m/C VHS. Rebecca DeMornay, Ron Silver, Rutger Hauer; **D:** Geoff Murphy; **W:** John Carlen. HBO

Blind Spot 🎬🎬½ 1993
Okay family drama which works because of the performances and not the script. Woodward stars as Nell Harrington, a take-charge U.S. Representative long married to Simon (Weaver). Her troubled, pregnant daughter Phoebe (Linney) is married to Nell's aide Charlie (Diamond). Charlie is killed and Phoebe injured in a car crash but the real tragedy is when Nell discovers what caused the accident—drugs—and that her daughter is a cocaine addict. Lots of suffering. Made for television. 99m/C VHS, Closed Caption. Joanne Woodward, Laura Linney, Fritz Weaver, Reed Edward Diamond, Cynthia Martells, Patti Yasutake, Patti D'Arbanville; **D:** Michael Toshiyuki Uno; **W:** Nina Shengold; **M:** Patrick Williams. REP

Blind Vengeance 🎬🎬 1990 (R)
A man whose son was murdered by white supremacists decides to take his own special revenge when they are acquitted by the local jury. But this isn't your usual bloodbath, instead he plays psychological games with the men, waiting for them to break. Made for cable television. 93m/C VHS. Gerald McRaney, Marg Helgenberger, Thalmus Rasulala, Lane Smith, Don Hood, Grand Bush; **D:** Lee Philips; **W:** Henri Simoun, Curt Allen. USH

Blind Vision 🎬½ 1991
Von Dohlen stars as William Dalton, a mail clerk who is in love with his beautiful neighbor Leanne (Shelton). Suffering from extreme shyness, Dalton can only spy on her through a telephoto lens. Things start to get complicated for him when one of Leanne's boyfriends turns up dead outside her apartment. Soon afterwards, their landlady and a local police detective uncover a shocking sexual secret that forces Dalton into a deadly game of obsession and desire. 92m/C VHS, LV, Closed Caption. Lenny Von Dohlen, Deborah Shelton, Ned Beatty, Robert Vaughn, Louise Fletcher; **D:** Shuki Levy. WOV

Blind Witness 🎬🎬½ 1989
Routine story about a blind woman who's the only witness to her husband's murder during a robbery. Made for television. 92m/C VHS, Closed Caption. Victoria Principal, Paul LeMat, Stephen Macht, Matt Clark, Tim Choate; **D:** Richard A. Colla; **M:** Robert Alcivar. WOV

Blinded by the Light 🎬🎬 1982
Young woman tries to save her brother from attachment to a quasi-religious cult, The Light of Salvation. Real-life brother and sister McNichol team up in this made-for-television drama, one of the earlier examinations of cult behavior. 90m/C VHS, Beta. Kristy McNichol, Jimmy McNichol, Anne Jackson, Michael McGuire; **D:** John Alonzo. TLF

Blindfold: Acts of Obsession 🎬🎬 1994 (R)
Madeline's (Doherty) marriage is boring so she consults therapist Jennings (Nelson). He suggests a number of sexual fantasies Madeline plays out with hubby Woods only to have murder enter the picture. Then Madeline's older sister Chris (Alfonso) is assigned to investigate and lets out lots of family secrets. Shannen in the buff, murder, infidelity, deception, and sex. An unrated version is also available.**CW:** Language, nudity, violence, and sexual situations. 93m/C VHS. Shannen Doherty, Judd Nelson, Michael Woods, Kristian Alfonso, Shell Danielson, Drew Snyder; **D:** Lawrence L. Simeone; **W:** Lawrence L. Simeone; **M:** Shuki Levy. AVE

Blindside 🎬🎬 1988 (R)
A surveillance hobbyist who owns a motel spies on his tenants until a murder involves him in a big-scale drug war. 98m/C VHS, Beta, LV. Harvey Keitel, Lori Hallier, Lolita Davidovich, Alan Fawcett, Michael Rudder; **D:** Paul Lynch. NLC

Blindsided 🎬🎬½ 1993 (PG-13)
A former police officer temporarily loses his sight when he plays the middle man in a bank robbery. Sight improving, he falls for a woman who draws him into another crime. 93m/C VHS, LV. Jeff Fahey, Mia Sara, Rudy Ramos, Jack Kehler, Ben Gazzara; **D:** Tom Donnelly. USH

Blink 🎬🎬½ 1993 (R)
Recent corneal transplants allow blind musician Emma (Stowe) to regain her sight, but until they "settle" what she sees may not register in her mind immediately, a phenomenon the script dubs "retroactive vision." This poses a problem for Chicago cop Quinn when he falls for Emma—the only one who can recognize a sadistic killer. Average thriller has been done better before, but adds two attractive leads, enough suspense, and a unique twist to the typical woman-in-jeopardy tale to keep things interesting. The distorted images in Stowe's blurry vision were created by computer. Stowe also learned fiddle for her place as the fictional member of the real-life Irish-American band, The Drovers.**CW:** Nudity, graphic violence, and sexual content. 106m/C VHS, LV, Closed Caption. Madeline Stowe, Aidan Quinn, Laurie Metcalf, James Remar, Bruce A. Young, Peter Friedman, Paul Dillon, Michael Kirkpatrick; **D:** Michael Apted; **W:** Dana Stevens; **C:** Dante Spinotti; **M:** Brad Fiedel. NLC

Blink of an Eye 🎬½ 1992 (R)
Special agent Sam Browning (Pare) must use his psychic powers and military skills against the terrorists who have kidnapped the CIA director's daughter.**CW:** Violence. 90m/C VHS, LV, Closed Caption. Michael Pare. THV

Bliss 🎬🎬🎬 1985 (R)
A savage, surreal Australian comedy about an advertising executive who dies suddenly for a few minutes, and upon his awakening he finds the world maniacally, bizarrely changed. Based on the Peter Carey novel, and one of the most inspired absurdist films of the decade. 112m/C VHS, Beta. AU Barry Otto, Lynette Curran, Helen Jones; **D:** Ray Lawrence; **W:** Peter Carey. Australian Film Institute '85: Best Film. NWV, VTR

Bliss 🎬½ 1996 (R)
Creepy feature-length sex-ed lecture delves deeply into sexual problems in modern society. So deeply, in fact, that it could've been called "Ouch, You're on my Hair." Clueless yuppies Joseph (Sheffer) and Maria's (Lee) sexual dysfunctions lead her to seek aid from unconventional therapist Baltazar (Stamp), who does things like compare women to violins (hint: they're not really the same. Unless you REALLY like wood). Joseph has his doubts, but soon becomes a chanting tantric goofball. Too clinical to be sexy, but too sexy to be used as an Army training film.**CW:** Graphic sex scenes with strong sex-related dialogue. 103m/C VHS. Sheryl Lee, Craig Sheffer, Terence Stamp, Casey Siemaszko, Spalding Gray, Leigh Taylor-Young, Lois Chiles; **D:** Lance

Young; **W:** Lance Young; **C:** Mike Molloy; **M:** Jan A.P. Kaczmarek. *NYR*

The Bliss of Mrs. Blossom 🎬🎬🎬
1968 Three's a crowd in this light-hearted romp through the machinations of a brassiere manufacturer (Attenborough) and his neglected wife (MacLaine). Mrs. Blossom finds sewing machine repairman Booth so appetizing that she hides him in the attic of the Blossom home. He reads books and redecorates, until, several plot twists later, Attenborough discovers the truth. Witty and wise, with fine supporting cast and excellent pacing. **93m/C LV, Closed Caption.** *GB* Shirley MacLaine, Richard Attenborough, James Booth, Freddie Jones, John Cleese; **D:** Joseph McGrath. *PAR, MOV*

Blithe Spirit 🎬🎬🎬½
1945 Charming and funny adaptation of Coward's famed stage play. A man re-marries and finds his long-dead wife is unhappy enough about it to come back and haunt him. Clever supporting cast, with Rutherford exceptional as the medium. Received Oscar for its Special Effects. **96m/C VHS.** *GB* Rex Harrison, Constance Cummings, Kay Hammond, Margaret Rutherford, Hugh Wakefield, Joyce Carey, Jacqueline Clarke; **D:** David Lean; **C:** Ronald Neame; **M:** Richard Addinsell. Academy Awards '46: Best Special Effects. *MLB, FCT*

The Blob 🎬🎬½
1958 Sci fi thriller about a small town's fight against a slimy jello invader from space. Slightly rebellious McQueen (in his first starring role) redeems himself when he saves the town with quick action. Low-budget, horror/teen-fantasy became a camp classic. Other names considered included "The Glob," "The Glob that Girdled the Globe," "The Meteorite Monster," "The Molten Meteorite," and "The Night of the Creeping Dead." Followed by a worthless sequel in 1972, "Son of Blob" and a worthwhile remake in 1988. Laserdisc contains an additional fifteen minutes of McQueen interviews and the trailers for both the original and the 1988 remake. **83m/C VHS, Beta, LV.** Steve McQueen, Aneta Corsaut, Olin Howlin, Earl Rowe; **D:** Irvin S. Yeaworth Jr.; **C:** Thomas E. Spalding. *COL, GEM, MLB*

The Blob 🎬🎬🎬
1988 (R) A hi-tech remake of the 1958 camp classic about a small town beset by a fast-growing, man-eating mound of glop shot into space by scientists, irradiated into an unnatural being, and then returned to earth. Well-developed characters make this an excellent tribute to the first film. **92m/C VHS, Beta, LV, Closed Caption.** Kevin Dillon, Candy Clark, Joe Seneca, Shawnee Smith, Donovan Leitch, Jeffrey DeMunn, Ricky Paull Goldin; **D:** Chuck Russell; **W:** Frank Darabont, Chuck Russell. *COL*

Block-heads 🎬🎬🎬
1938 Twenty years after the end of WWI, soldier Stan is found, still in his foxhole, and brought back to America, where he moves in with old pal Ollie. Also includes a 1934 Charley Chase short "I'll Take Vanilla." **75m/B VHS, Beta.** Stan Laurel, Oliver Hardy, Billy Gilbert, Patricia Ellis, James Finlayson, Charley Chase; **D:** John Blystone. *CCB, MED, MLB*

Blockhouse woof!
1973 Four men are entombed in a subterranean stronghold for six years after the D-Day invasion of Normandy. Encourages claustrophobic feeling in viewer. Based on Jean Paul Clebert's novel "Le Blockhaus." **88m/C VHS, Beta.** *GB* Peter Sellers, Charles Aznavour, Per Oscarsson, Peter Vaughan, Leon Lissek, Alfred Lynch, Jeremy Kemp; **D:** Clive Rees. *NO*

Blonde Blackmailer 🎬
1958 Boring story about an innocent man who serves time for the murder of a female blackmailer. When he's released, he searches for the real killer. **69m/B VHS.** *GB* Richard Arlen, Susan Shaw, Vincent Ball, Constance Leigh; **D:** Charles Deane; **W:** Charles Deane. *RXM*

Blonde Crazy 🎬🎬½
Larceny Lane 1931 A charming grifter hooks up with a gorgeous blonde as he works the territory of a big wheel criminal. Escapist fare, with fun performances from Cagney and Blondell. **81m/B VHS.** James Cagney, Joan Blondell, Louis Calhern, Ray Milland, Nat Pendleton; **D:** Roy Del Ruth. *MGM*

Blonde in Black Leather 🎬½
1977 A bored Italian housewife takes up with a leather-clad lady biker, and together they cavort about. **88m/C VHS, Beta.** Claudia Cardinale, Monica Vitti; **D:** Carlo DiPalma. *NLC*

Blonde Savage 🎬
1947 Charting African territories, an adventurer encounters a white jungle queen swinging amongst the vines. Essentially a cheap, distaff "Tarzan." **62m/B VHS, Beta.** Leif Erickson, Gale Sherwood, Veda Ann Borg, Douglass Dumbrille, Frank Jenks, Matt Willis, Ernest Whitman; **D:** Steve Sekely. *SNC*

Blonde Venus 🎬🎬🎬½
1932 A German cafe singer marries an Englishman, but their marriage hits the skids when he contracts radiation poisoning and she gets a nightclub job to pay the bills. Sternberg's and Dietrich's fourth film together, and characteristically beautiful, though terribly strange. Dietrich's cabaret number "Hot Voodoo," in a gorilla suit and blonde afro, attains new heights in early Hollywood surrealism. **94m/B VHS, Beta.** Marlene Dietrich, Herbert Marshall, Cary Grant, Dickie Moore, Hattie McDaniel, Sidney Toler; **D:** Josef von Sternberg. *USH*

Blondes Have More Guns 🎬🎬
1995 (R) Very dumb detective Harry Bates (McGaharin) is investigating a chainsaw murder and falls for the mysterious Montana (Key), who's possibly a serial killer, or maybe it's her half-sister, Dakota (Lusiak). Spoof of "Basic Instinct" and others of that ilk, done in the usual Troma fashion. **CW:** Language, nudity, sexual situations, violence. **90m/C VHS.** Michael McGahern, Elizabeth Key, Gloria Lusiak, Richard Neil; **D:** George Merriweather. *TTV*

Blondie 🎬🎬½
1938 Chic Young's famous comic strip debuted on the big screen with Singleton in the title role, Lake as the bumbling Dagwood, and Simms as Baby Dumpling (son Alexander, when he grows up). The couple are about to celebrate their 5th wedding anniversary when Dagwood loses his job and Blondie suspects him of infidelity. The series eventually contained 28 films. **68m/B VHS.** Penny Singleton, Arthur Lake, Larry Simms, Gene Lockhart, Ann Doran, Jonathan Hale, Gordon Oliver, Stanley Andrews; **D:** Frank Strayer; **W:** Richard Flournoy. *MOV*

Blondie Has Trouble 🎬🎬½
Blondie Has Servant Trouble 1940 Mr. Dithers has a property he just can't sell because of rumors that the house is haunted. So he offers to let the Bumsteads stay in it to prove that the rumors are false. The Bumsteads also find the creepy mansion comes complete with two equally creepy servants. 6th film in the series. **70m/B VHS.** Penny Singleton, Arthur Lake, Larry Simms, Danny Mummert, Jonathan Hale, Arthur Hohl, Esther Dale, Irving Bacon; **D:** Frank Strayer; **W:** Richard Flournoy. *MOV*

Blondie Hits the Jackpot 🎬½
1949 Dagwood is fired for the umpteenth time after he makes a mistake in a construction deal and tries frantically to get his job back. Meanwhile, Blondie wins the big prize on a radio quiz show. The 26th film in the series. **66m/B VHS.** Penny Singleton, Arthur Lake, Larry Simms, Marjorie Kent, Jerome Cowan, Lloyd Corrigan, Danny Mummert, James Flavin; **D:** Edward L. Bernds; **W:** Jack Henley. *MOV*

Blondie in Society 🎬½
1941 A weak entry (the ninth) in the comedic series. Dagwood brings home a pedigreed Great Dane and Blondie decides to enter the pooch in the local dog show. Then an important client of Dagwood's decides he wants the dog. **77m/B VHS.** Penny Singleton, Arthur Lake, Larry Simms, William Frawley, Edgar Kennedy, Jonathan Hale, Danny Mummert, Chick Chandler; **D:** Frank Strayer; **W:** Karen De Wolf. *MOV*

Blondie Knows Best 🎬½
1946 Dagwood impersonates his boss, Mr. Dithers, and causes all sorts of problems. Howard, one of the Three Stooges, has a cameo as a myopic process-server. The 18th film in the series. **66m/B VHS.** Penny Singleton, Arthur Lake, Larry Simms, Marjorie Kent, Jonathan Hale, Steve Geray, Jerome Cowan, Danny

Mummert; **Cameos:** Shemp Howard; **D:** Abby Berlin; **W:** Edward L. Bernds, Al Martin. *MOV*

Blondie Takes a Vacation 🎬🎬½
1939 Third in the series of fluff films adapted from Chic Young's comic strip. After the Bumstead family is snubbed at a snobby mountain resort they move to a friendlier nearby hotel where they try to help out the owners who are in danger of losing their investment. Baby Dumpling does his bit by unleashing a skunk in the ventilation system of the competing hotel. **68m/B VHS.** Penny Singleton, Arthur Lake, Larry Simms, Danny Mummert, Donald Meek, Donald MacBride, Thomas Ross, Robert Wilcox, Irving Bacon; **D:** Frank Strayer; **W:** Richard Flournoy. *MOV*

Blondie's Blessed Event 🎬🎬½
1942 Cookie is born, causing even more chaos in the Bumstead household. Meanwhile, Dagwood gets into trouble at work when he hires a cynical playwright to write an important speech for him. 11th entry in series. **69m/B VHS.** Penny Singleton, Arthur Lake, Larry Simms, Norma Jean Wayne, Donald Hale, Danny Mummert, Hans Conried, Irving Bacon, Stanley Brown, Mary Wickes, Paul Harvey, Arthur O'Connell; **D:** Frank Strayer; **W:** Richard Flournoy, Karen De Wolf, Connie Lee. *MOV*

Blood Alley 🎬🎬
1955 A seasoned Merchant Marine captain takes on a cargo of refugee Chinese to smuggle through enemy territory. Middling, mid-career Wayne vehicle. **115m/C VHS, Beta, LV, Closed Caption.** John Wayne, Lauren Bacall, Paul Fix, Joy Kim, Berry Kroeger, Mike Mazurki, Anita Ekberg; **D:** William A. Wellman; **C:** William Clothier. *WAR, FCT*

Blood and Black Lace 🎬
1964 Beautiful models are being brutally murdered and an inspector is assigned to the case, but not before more gruesome killings occur. Bava is, as usual, violent and suspenseful. Horror fans will enjoy this flick. **90m/C VHS, Beta.** *IT FR GE* Cameron Mitchell, Eva Bartok, Mary Arden; **D:** Mario Bava. *MED*

Blood & Concrete: A Love Story 🎬🎬
1990 (R) Bizarre, violent and stylish film-noir spoof, definitely not for all tastes. The innocent hero gets drawn into a maelstrom of intrigue over a killer aphrodisiac drug. Beals, an addicted punk rocker, gets to perform a few songs. **CW:** Language, violence and drug content, and sensuality. **97m/C VHS, LV.** Billy Zane, Jennifer Beals, Darren McGavin; **D:** Jeff Reiner; **W:** Jeff Reiner. *COL*

Blood & Donuts 🎬🎬
1995 (R) Hungry vampire Boya (Currie) is looking for a rat snack when he stumbles across an all-night donut shop where pretty cashier Molly (Clarkson) and friendly cabbie Earl (Louis) seek his help with a local crime boss. Mild horror mixed with comedy and limited gore. **CW:** Language, violence, sexual situations. **89m/C VHS, LV, Closed Caption.** *CA* Gordon Currie, Justin Louis, Helene Clarkson, Fiona Reid, Frank Moore; **Cameos:** David Cronenberg; **D:** Holly Dale; **W:** Andrew Rai Berzins; **C:** Paul Sarossy. Nominations: Genie Awards '96: Best Actress (Clarkson), Best Costume Design, Best Original Screenplay. *LIV*

Blood and Guns 🎬½
1979 (R) Romance, revenge, and action abound in post-revolutionary Mexico. **96m/C VHS, Beta.** Orson Welles, Tomas Milian, John Steiner; **D:** Giulio Petroni. *MRV*

Blood and Roses 🎬½
Et Mourir de Plaisir 1961 A girl who is obsessed with her family's vampire background becomes possessed by a vampire and commits numerous murders. The photography is good, but the plot is hazy and only effective in certain parts. Based on the book "Carmilla" by Sheridan LeFanu. Later remade as "The Vampire Lovers" and "The Blood-Spattered Bride." **74m/C VHS, Closed Caption.** Mel Ferrer, Elsa Martinelli, Annette Vadim, Marc Allegret; **D:** Roger Vadim; **W:** Roger Vadim. *PAR*

Blood and Sand 🎬🎬½
1922 Vintage romance based on Vicente Blasco Ibanez's novel about the tragic rise and fall of a matador, and the women in his life. The film that made Valentino a star. Remade in 1941. Silent. **87m/B VHS, Beta.** Ru-

dolph Valentino, Nita Naldi, Lila Lee, Walter Long; **D:** Fred Niblo. *REP, NOS, CAB*

Blood and Sand 🎞️🎞️🎞️ 1941 Director Mamoulian "painted" this picture in the new technicolor technique, which makes it a veritable explosion of color and spectacle. Power is the matador who becomes famous and then falls when he is torn between two women, forsaking his first love, bullfighting. Based on the novel "Sangre y Arena" by Vicente Blasco Ibanez. This movie catapulted Hayworth to stardom, primarily for her dancing, but also for her sexiness and seductiveness (and of course, her acting). Remake of the 1922 silent classic; remade again in 1989. **123m/C VHS, Beta, LV,** Tyrone Power, Linda Darnell, Rita Hayworth, Alla Nazimova, Anthony Quinn, J. Carrol Naish, John Carradine, George Reeves; **D:** Rouben Mamoulian; **W:** Jo Swerling; **C:** Ernest Palmer, Ray Rennahan; **M:** Alfred Newman. Academy Awards '41: Best Color Cinematography; Nominations: Academy Awards '41: Best Interior Decoration. *FXV*

Blood and Sand 🎞️🎞️ 1989 (R) A bullfighter on the verge of super-stardom risks it all when he falls under the spell of a sexy, seductive woman. Will she destroy his one opportunity for fame? Interesting for people who actually enjoy watching the "sport" of bullfighting. Originally made in 1922 and remade in 1941.**CW:** Drug use and strong sensuality. **96m/C VHS, LV,** Christopher Rydell, Sharon Stone, Ana Torrent, Jose-Luis De Villalonga, Simon Andrew; **D:** Javier Elorrieta. *THV*

Blood and Sand/Son of the Sheik 1926 A double feature containing two abridged versions; in "Blood and Sand," an idolized matador meets another woman just before his wedding; in "Son of the Sheik," a man believes he has been betrayed by a dancing girl, and he abducts her to seek revenge. Silent. **56m/B VHS, Beta,** Rudolph Valentino, Lila Lee, Vilma Banky. *CCB*

Blood and Steel 1925 The railroad tycoon's daughter and the construction foreman wind up together on an exciting train ride. Silent. **?m/B VHS, Beta, 8mm.** Helen Holmes, William Desmond; **D:** J.P. McGowan. *GVV*

Blood & Wine 🎞️🎞️½ 1996 (R) Miami wine merchant Alex (Nicholson) gets involved with terminally ill safecracker Victor (Caine) to steal a necklace worth a cool million. Meanwhile he must deal with his crumbling marriage to Suzanne (Davis) and the bitter relationship with his stepson Jason (Dorff), who has eyes for both the necklace and his Cuban mistress (Lopez). Characterizations and strong performances (particularly by Nicholson and Caine) haul the sometimes lumbering plot to its violent conclusion. Promoted as the third part of a "dysfunctional family trilogy" with "Five Easy Pieces" and "The King of Marvin's Gardens." Seventh time Nicholson has worked with director Rafelson.**CW:** Violence and language. **100m/C VHS.** Jack Nicholson, Michael Caine, Judy Davis, Stephen Dorff, Jennifer Lopez, Harold Perrineau Jr.; **D:** Bob Rafelson; **W:** Nick Villiars, Allison Cross; **C:** Newton Thomas Sigel; **M:** Stephen Cohen. *NYR*

Blood at Sundown 🎞️½ 1988 Routine oater where man returns home after the Civil War to find his wife kidnapped by a group of Mexican outlaws who have also taken over his village. **92m/C VHS, Beta,** Giuliano Gemma, Hally Hamond, Nieves Navarro, Antonio Casas, Fernando Sancho, Pajarito, George Martin; **D:** Duccio Tessari. *IMP*

Blood Beach woof! 1981 (R) A group of teenagers are devoured by menacing sand, which keeps people from getting to the water by swallowing them whole. Weak parody with some humorous moments; more silly than scary. **92m/C VHS, Beta,** David Huffman, Marianna Hill, John Saxon, Burt Young, Otis Young; **D:** Jeffrey Bloom; **W:** Jeffrey Bloom. *MED*

Blood Beast Terror 🎞️½ *The Vampire-Beast Craves Blood; Deathshead Vampire* 1967 An entomologist transforms his own daughter into a Deathshead Moth and she proceeds to terrorize

and drink innocent victims' blood. **81m/C VHS, Beta.** GB Peter Cushing, Robert Flemyng, Wanda Ventham, Vanessa Howard; **D:** Vernon Sewell. *MON*

Blood Bride 🎞️½ 19?? A lonely young woman finally finds happiness with her new husband but her world comes crashing about her with soul-mangling ferocity when she discovers he is actually a bloodthirsty maniac. **90m/C VHS, Beta.** Ellen Barber, Philip English. *NO*

Blood Brothers 🎞️🎞️ 1974 (R) A young man who dreams of becoming a lawyer is disturbed when he discovers that his family has mafia ties. **148m/C VHS, Beta.** IT Claudia Cardinale, Franco Nero, Lina Polito; **D:** Pasquale Squitieri. *NO*

Blood Brothers 1977 James Grizzly Adams, who lives in the mountains of the American wilderness, relives the story of how he met his Indian blood brother, Nakuma. Beautiful scenery. **50m/C VHS, Beta.** Dan Haggerty, Denver Pyle, Don Shanks. *MCG*

Blood Clan 🎞️½ 1991 (R) Based on the true story of Katy Bane, daughter of notorious Scottish cult leader, Sawney Bane, in whose lair were found the remains of over 1000 killed and cannibalized followers. When found, Bane's entire family was sentenced to death with the exception of Katy, who left to make a new start in Canada. When a rash of mysterious deaths break out in Katy's new home, she must defend herself from rumors that her father's murderous cult is resurfacing.**CW:** Violence and sensuality. **91m/C VHS.** Gordon Pinsent, Michelle Little, Robert Wisden; **D:** Charles Wilkinson. *FXL*

Blood Cult 🎞️ 1985 A bizarre series of murder-mutilations take place on a small midwestern campus. Contains graphic violence that is not for the squeamish. This film was created especially for the home video market. **92m/C VHS, Beta.** Chuck Ellis, Julie Andelman, Jim Vance, Joe Hardt; **D:** Christopher Lewis. *VCI*

Blood Debts 1983 A father is out for revenge after he saves his daughter from some hunters who raped her and also killed her boyfriend. **91m/C VHS, Beta.** Richard Harrison, Mike Manty, Jim Gaines, Anne Jackson, Anne Milhench; **D:** Teddy Page. *NO*

Blood Diner woof! 1987 Two spirit-possessed, diner-owning brothers kill countless young girls for demonic rituals, and serve their corpses as gourmet food in their restaurant. Some funny moments mixed in with the requisite gore. Cult potential. **88m/C VHS, Beta.** Rick Burks, Carl Crew; **D:** Jackie Kong. *VES, LIV*

Blood Feast 🎞️ *Feast of Flesh* 1963 The first of Lewis' gore-fests, in which a demented caterer butchers hapless young women to splice them together in order to bring back an Egyptian goddess. Dated, campy, and gross; reportedly shot in four days (it shows). **70m/C VHS, Beta.** Connie Mason, Thomas Wood, Malcolm Arnold; **D:** Herschell Gordon Lewis. *VTR, FCT*

Blood Feud 🎞️🎞️ *Revenge* 1979 (R) In Italy preceding Europe's entry into WWII, a young widow is in mourning over the brutal murder of her husband by the Sicilian Mafia. In the meantime she must contend with the rivalry between Mastroianni as a lawyer and Giannini as a small-time crook both vying for her affections. Dubbed. **112m/C VHS, Beta.** IT Sophia Loren, Marcello Mastroianni, Giancarlo Giannini; **D:** Lina Wertmuller; **W:** Lina Wertmuller. *FOX*

Blood for a Silver Dollar 🎞️½ 1966 Action-filled western, littered with murder, revenge and romance. **98m/C VHS, Beta.** Montgomery Wood, Evelyn Stewart. *VYY*

Blood for Blood 🎞️½ 1995 (R) Cop must take up the martial arts skills he learned in childhood in order to protect his family from assassination. **93m/C VHS, LV, Closed Caption.** Lorenzo Lamas, James Lew, Mako, Eric Pierpont, James Shigeta, James Callahan; **D:** John Weidner; **M:** Joel Goldsmith. *LIV*

Blood Freak woof! 1972 An absolutely insane anti-drug, Christian splatter film. A Floridian biker is introduced to drugs by a young woman and eventually turns into a poultry-monster who drinks the blood of junkies. Narrated by a chain smoker who has a coughing fit. Don't miss it. **86m/C VHS, Beta.** Steve Hawkes, Dana Culliver, Randy Grinter Jr., Tina Anderson, Heather Hughes; **D:** Steve Hawkes, Brad Grinter. *NO*

Blood Frenzy 🎞️ 1987 Psychologist's patients take a therapeutic trip to the desert. The sun and heat take their toll, and everyone gets violent. This kind of therapy we don't need, and the movie's a waste, as well. Made for video. Loring was Wednesday on TV's "The Addams Family." **90m/C VHS, Beta.** John Montero, Lisa Loring, Hank Garrett, Wendy MacDonald; **D:** Hal Freeman. *NO*

Blood Games woof! 1990 (R) Buxom baseball team bats 1000 against the home team and the winning babes find out just how poor losers can be. Diamonds aren't always a girl's best friend. **90m/C VHS, LV, Closed Caption.** Gregory Cummings, Laura Albert, Shelly Abblett, Luke Shay, Ross Hagen; **D:** Tanya Rosenberg. *COL*

Blood Hook 🎞️½ 1986 A self-parodying teenage-slasher film about kids running into a backwoods fishing tournament while on vacation, complete with ghouls, cannibalism and grotesquerie. **85m/C VHS, Beta.** Mark Jacobs, Lisa Todd, Patrick Danz; **D:** James Mallon. *PSM, PAR*

Blood In ... Blood Out: Bound by Honor 🎞️½ *Bound by Honor* 1993 (R) Three-hour epic about Chicano gang culture focuses on three buddies whose lives evolve into a drug-addicted artist, a narc, and a prison regular. Written by acclaimed poet Baca, the film touches on issues such as poverty, racism, drugs, and violence as they pertain to Hispanic life. Unfortunately, the extreme violence (shootings, stabbings, and garrotings) completely overwhelms the rest of the story. Contains profanity, nudity, and sexual innuendo. Based on a story by Ross Thomas.**CW:** Strong language, strong violence and drug content, and sexuality. **180m/C VHS, Beta, LV, Closed Caption.** Damian Chapa, Jesse Borrego, Benjamin Bratt, Enrique Castillo, Victor Rivers, Delroy Lindo, Tom Towles; **D:** Taylor Hackford; **W:** Floyd Mutrux, Jimmy Santiago Baca, Jeremy Iacone; **M:** Bill Conti. *HPH, TOU*

Blood Island 🎞️🎞️ *The Shuttered Room* 1968 A couple inherits an old house on a remote New England island where the woman grew up. They discover that this old house needs more than a paint job to make it livable; seems there's something evil in them there walls. Based on an H.P. Lovecraft story. Greene, who's best known for later directing "Godspell," and the solid cast fail to animate the inert script. **100m/C VHS.** GB Gig Young, Carol Lynley, Oliver Reed, Flora Robson; **D:** David Greene. *ACE*

Blood Legacy 🎞️🎞️ *Legacy of Blood* 1973 (R) Four heirs must survive a night in a lonely country estate to collect their money; what do you think happens? Average treatment of the haunted house theme. **77m/C VHS, Beta.** John Carradine, John Russell, Faith Domergue, Merry Anders; **D:** Carl Monson. *CNG, MRV, GEM*

Blood Mania 🎞️ 1970 (R) A retired surgeon's daughter decides to murder her father to collect her inheritance prematurely, but soon learns that crime doesn't pay as well as medicine. Low-budget, low-interest flick. **90m/C VHS, Beta.** Peter Carpenter, Maria de Aragon, Alex Rocco; **D:** Robert Vincent O'Neil. *NO*

Blood Money 🎞️½ 1980 (PG) A dying ex-criminal returns to Australia to redeem his name and die with dignity. **64m/C VHS, Beta.** AU Bryan Brown, John Flaus, Chrissie James; **D:** Christopher Fitchett. *NO*

Blood Money: The Story of Clinton and Nadine 🎞️🎞️½ *Clinton & Nadine* 1988 A confusing action/thriller with a good cast. Garcia is a small-time exotic bird smuggler whose gun-running brother has been murdered. He uses high-class hooker Barkin to get close to his brother's contacts, who turn out to be running guns to the Nicaraguan contras and involved in a dangerous government conspiracy. Made for cable television. 95m/C VHS, Beta. Andy Garcia, Ellen Barkin, Morgan Freeman; **D:** Jerry Schatzberg. *FCT*

The Blood of a Poet *Le Sang d'un Poete* 1930 Cocteau's first film, a practically formless piece of poetic cinema, detailing all manner of surreal events occurring in the instant a chimney falls. In French with English subtitles. **55m/B VHS, Beta.** Jean Cocteau; **D:** Jean Cocteau; **C:** Georges Perinal. National Board of Review Awards '33: 10 Best Films of the Year. *VYY, MRV, HHT*

Blood of Dracula ♂½ *Blood is My Heritage* 1957 They don't make 1950s rock'n'roll girls' school vampire movies like this anymore, for which we may be grateful. Hypnotism, an amulet, and a greasepaint makeup job turn a shy female student into a bloodsucker. 71m/B VHS. Sandra Harrison, Louise Lewis, Gail Ganley, Jerry Blaine, Heather Ames, Malcolm Atterbury; **D:** Herbert L. Strock. *COL, MLB*

Blood of Dracula's Castle ♂♂ *Dracula's Castle* 1969 Couple inherits an allegedly deserted castle but upon moving in, discover Mr. and Mrs. Dracula have settled there. The vampires keep young women chained in the dungeon for continual blood supply. Also present are a hunchback and a werewolf. Awesome Adamson production is highlighted by the presence of the gorgeous Volante. Early cinematography effort by the renowned Laslo Kovacs. **84m/C VHS, Beta.** John Carradine, Alexander D'Arcy, Paula Raymond, Ray Young, Vicki Volante, Robert Dix, John Cardos; **D:** Jean Hewitt, Al Adamson. *NO*

Blood of Ghastly Horror woof! *The Fiend with the Atomic Brain; Psycho a Go Go!; The Love Maniac; The Man with the Synthetic Brain; The Fiend with the Electronic Brain* 1972 A young man thinks he has a new lease on life when he is the happy recipient of a brain transplant, but his dreams are destroyed when he evolves into a rampaging killer. This movie is so awful it hides behind numerous but rather creative aliases. 87m/C VHS. John Carradine, Kent Taylor, Tommy Kirk, Regina Carrol; **D:** Al Adamson. *MOV*

The Blood of Heroes ♂♂ *The Salute of the Jugger* 1989 (R) A post-apocalyptic action flick detailing the adventures of a battered team of "juggers," warriors who challenge small village teams to a brutal sport (involving dogs' heads on sticks) that's a cross between jousting and football. **97m/C VHS, Beta, LV, Closed Caption.** Rutger Hauer, Joan Chen, Vincent D'Onofrio, Anna Katarina; **D:** David Peoples; **W:** David Peoples; **C:** David Eggby; **M:** Todd Boekelheide. *HBO*

Blood of Jesus ♂♂ 1941 A sinful husband accidentally shoots his newly-baptized wife, causing an uproar in their rural town. Williams later starred as Andy on the "Amos 'n' Andy" television series. 50m/C VHS. Spencer Williams Jr., Kathryn Craviness; **D:** Spencer Williams Jr.; **W:** Spencer Williams Jr. *FCT, HEG, BTV*

The Blood of Others ♂ 1984 A driveling adaptation of the Simone de Beauvoir novel about a young French woman at the outbreak of WWII torn between her absent boyfriend in the Resistance and a kind, wealthy German. Made for French television, it stars Jodie Foster and Michael Ontkean as the Gallic pair. 130m/C VHS, Beta. **FR** Jodie Foster, Sam Neill, Michael Ontkean, Stephane Audran, Lambert Wilson, John Vernon, Kate Reid, Jean-Pierre Aumont; **D:** Claude Chabrol; **W:** Brian Moore. *PSM*

Blood of the Hunter ♂♂½ 1994 (PG-13) Psycho-killer holds postman's wife captive in a remote cabin in the Canadian wilderness. Turns out hubby and psycho share a mysterious past. **CW:** Violence, scene of nudity. 92m/C VHS. Michael Biehn, Alexandra Vandernoot, Gabriel Arcand; **D:** Gilles Carle. *THV, FCT*

Blood of the Vampire ♂♂½ 1958 A Transylvanian doctor is executed for being a vampire and his hunchbacked assistant brings him back to life. 84m/C VHS, Beta. **GB** Donald Wolfit, Vincent Ball, Barbara Shelley, Victor Maddern; **D:** Henry Cass; **W:** Jimmy Sangster. *MPI, MLB*

The Blood on Satan's Claw ♂♂♂ *Satan's Skin; Satan's Claw* 1971 Graphic tale centering on the Devil himself. Townspeople in an English village circa 1670 find the spirit of Satan taking over their children, who begin to practice witchcraft. Well made with lots of attention to period details. Not for the faint-hearted. 90m/C VHS, Beta. **GB** Patrick Wymark, Linda Hayden, Barry Andrews, Michele Dotrice; **D:** Piers Haggard. *MGM, FCT*

Blood on the Badge ♂♂½ 1992 Illegal arms have been stolen from a military arsenal and fall into the hands of Libyan Nationalists who begin a terrorist campaign. Detective Neal Farrow is assigned to stop them. 92m/C VHS. Ramon Estevez, David Harrod, Rocky Patterson, Desiree Laforge, Dean Nolen, Melissa Deleon, Todd Everett; **D:** Bret McCormick. *AIP*

Blood on the Moon ♂♂½ 1948 Well-acted film about a cowboy's involvement in a friend's underhanded schemes. Based on a Luke Short novel, this dark film revolves around a western land dispute between cattlemen and homesteaders. 88m/B VHS, Beta, LV. Robert Mitchum, Robert Preston, Walter Brennan, Barbara Bel Geddes; **D:** Robert Wise. *MED, TTC*

Blood on the Mountain ♂ 1988 After escaping from prison, Jim plots revenge against his accomplice, only to kill an innocent man instead. 71m/C VHS. Stracker Edwards, Tim Jones, Paula Preston, Cliff Turknett, Rich Jury; **D:** Donald W. Thompson.

Blood on the Sun ♂♂½ 1945 Newspaperman in Japan uncovers plans for world dominance as propaganda, violence, and intrigue combine in this action-adventure. Also available colorized. 98m/B VHS, LV. James Cagney, Sylvia Sidney, Robert Armstrong, Wallace Ford; **D:** Frank Lloyd; **M:** Miklos Rozsa. Academy Awards '45: Best Interior Decoration. *NOS, MRV, HHT*

Blood Orgy of the She-Devils woof! 1974 (PG) Exploitative gore nonsense about female demons, beautiful witches, and satanic worship. Some movies waste all their creative efforts on their titles. 73m/C VHS, Beta. Lila Zaborin, Tom Pace, Leslie McRae, Ray Myles. *NO*

Blood Rage woof! *Nightmare at Shadow Woods* 1987 (R) A maniacal twin goes on a murderous rampage through his brother's neighborhood. AKA "Nightmare at Shadow Woods." Only for die-hard "Mary Hartman" fans. 87m/C VHS, Beta. Louise Lasser, Mike Soper; **D:** John Grissmer; **M:** Richard Einhorn. *PSM*

Blood Red ♂♂½ 1988 (R) In 1895 Northern California, an Italian immigrant and his family give bloody battle to a powerful industrialist who wants their land in wine-growing country. Watch for the scenes involving veteran Roberts and his then-newcomer sister, pretty woman Julia. 91m/C VHS, Beta, LV, 8mm. Eric Roberts, Dennis Hopper, Giancarlo Giannini, Burt Young, Carlin Glynn, Lara Harris, Susan Anspach, Julia Roberts, Elias Koteas, Frank Campanella, Aldo Ray, Horton Foote Jr.; **D:** Peter Masterson; **W:** Ron Cutler. *COL*

Blood Relations ♂♂½ 1987 (R) A woman is introduced to her fiance's family only to find out that they, as well as her fiance, are murdering, perverted weirdos competing for an inheritance. 88m/C VHS, Beta, LV. **CA** Jan Rubes, Ray Walston, Lydie Denier, Kevin Hicks, Lynne Adams; **D:** Graeme Campbell. *NLC*

Blood Relatives ♂ *Les Liens de Sang* 1977 Langlois admits she saw her brother kill her cousin, with whom he had been carrying on an incestuous relationship. But the discovery of the dead girl's diary by police inspector Sutherland reveals many more layers of intrigue than were initially evident. Based on a novel by Ed McBain. The French actors have been dubbed into English.

94m/C VHS. **CA** Lisa Langlois, Donald Sutherland, Stephane Audran, David Hemmings, Aude Landry; **D:** Claude Chabrol; **W:** Claude Chabrol. *NO*

Blood Ring ♂♂½ 1993 When Sue's boxer husband goes missing she enlists old friend Max to help find him. They uncover a gambling ring run by drug lords where the kickboxing matches are to the death. Naturally, Max decides to use his expert kickboxing skills to get a violent revenge. 90m/C VHS. Dale "Apollo" Cook, Andrea Lamatsch, Don Nakaya Neilsen, Steve Tartalia; **D:** Irvin Johnson; **W:** Ron Davies. *AIP*

Blood Salvage ♂ 1990 (R) A crazy junkman kidnaps beautiful girls, selling their organs to the highest bidder. He meets his match when a potential target refuses to become a victim in spite of her wheelchair. Interesting plot twists keep this Grade B thriller above average. 90m/C VHS, Beta, LV. Evander Holyfield, Lori Birdsong, Danny Nelson, John Saxon, Ray Walston; **D:** Tucker Johnson. *TTC*

Blood Screams woof! 1988 (R) Nosy people drop in on an old town in Mexico and attempt to uncover the secrets hidden there, but bizarre entities throw out the unwelcome mat and terrorize them. Lots of blood and screaming. 75m/C VHS, Beta. Ran Sands, James Garnett. *WAR*

Blood Simple ♂♂♂½ 1985 (R) A jealous husband hires a sleazy private eye to murder his adulterous wife and her lover. A dark, intricate, morbid morality tale that deviates imaginatively from the standard murder mystery thriller. First film scripted by the Coen brothers. 96m/C VHS, Beta, LV, Closed Caption. John Getz, M. Emmet Walsh, Dan Hedaya, Frances McDormand, Samm-Art Williams; **D:** Joel Coen; **W:** Joel Coen, Ethan Coen; **C:** Barry Sonnenfeld; **M:** Carter Burwell. Independent Spirit Awards '86: Best Actor (Walsh), Best Director (Coen); Sundance Film Festival '85: Grand Jury Prize. *USH*

Blood Sisters woof! 1986 (R) Sorority babes intend to spend a giggle-strewn night in a haunted house but end up decapitated, butchered, and cannibalized. 85m/C VHS, Beta. Amy Brentano, Marla MacHart, Brigete Cossu, Randy Mooers; **D:** Roberta Findlay. *COL*

Blood Song ♂ *Dream Slayer* 1982 A patient (yester-decade teen throb Frankie Avalon) escapes into the night from a mental institution after murdering an attendant. He takes his only possession with him, a carved wooden flute. A young woman sees him burying his latest victim, and now he's on a hunt to play his "blood song" for her. Pretty bad, but fun to see Avalon play a less-than-squeaky-clean role. 90m/C VHS, Beta. Frankie Avalon, Donna Wilkes, Richard Jaeckel, Dane Clark, Antoinette Bower; **D:** Alan J. Levi. *NO*

The Blood Spattered Bride ♂ *Blood Castle; La Novia Esangentada* 1972 Newlywed couple honeymoons in a remote castle in southern Spain. They are visited by a mysterious young woman who begins to influence the bride in the ways of lesbian bloodsucking. Okay '70s Euro-eroti-horror based on LeFanu's "Carmilla." 82m/C VHS, Beta. **SP** Simon Andrew, Maribel Martin, Alexandra Bastedo, Dean Selmier, Rosa Ma Rodriguez, Montserrat Julio; **D:** Vicente Aranda. *MPI*

Blood Thirst ♂♂ 1965 Obscure horror film about a woman who stays young by indulging in ritual killings and strange experiments. ?m/C VHS. Robert Winston, Yvonne Nielson; **D:** Newton Arnold. *SNC*

Blood Tide ♂ *The Red Tide* 1982 (R) A disgusting, flesh-eating monster disrupts a couple's vacation in the Greek isles. Beautiful scenery, good cast, bad movie. 82m/C VHS, Beta. James Earl Jones, Jose Ferrer; **D:** Richard Jeffries; **W:** Nico Mastorakis. *NO*

Blood Ties ♂♂½ 1987 An American naval engineer in Sicily gets involved with the Mob in order to save his father's life. 98m/C VHS, Beta. **IT** Brad Davis, Tony LoBianco, Vincent Spano, Barbara DeRossi, Maria Conchita Alonso; **D:** Giacomo Battiato. *TWE*

Blood Ties ✞✞½ 1992 Reporter Harry Martin belongs to an unusual family—modern-day vampires (who prefer to be known as Carpathian-Americans). But they have an age-old problem with a band of fanatical vampire hunters. This time around you'll root for the bloodsuckers. Made for television. 90m/C VHS. Harley Venton, Patrick Bauchau, Kim Johnston-Ulrich, Michelle Johnson, Jason London, Bo Hopkins, Grace Zabriskie; **D:** Jim McBride; **W:** Richard Shapiro. NHO

Blood Tracks ✞½ 1986 A woman kills her abusive husband, then hides out in the mountains with her kids until they turn into cannibalistic savages. Years later, people show up to shoot a music video. Blood runs in buckets. 82m/C Beta. Jeff Harding, Michael Fitzpatrick, Naomi Kaneda; **D:** Mike Jackson. NO

Blood Vows: The Story of a Mafia Wife ✞✞ 1987 TV's Laura Ingalls (Gilbert) leaps from the prairie to modern-day mafia in this warped Cinderella story. She meets the man of her dreams, whom she slowly finds is her worst nightmare as she becomes trapped within the confines of her new-found "family." Made for television soaper is way over the top in terms of melodrama. 100m/C VHS. Melissa Gilbert, Joe Penny, Eileen Brennan, Talia Shire, Anthony (Tony) Franciosa; **D:** Paul Wendkos; **M:** William Goldstein. FRH

Blood Voyage woof! 1977 (R) A crewman aboard a pleasure yacht must find out who is killing off his passengers one by one. 80m/C VHS, Beta. Jonathon Lippe, Laurie Rose, Midori, Mara Modair; **D:** Frank Mitchell. NO

Blood Warriors ✞½ 1993 An ex-Marine finds out a old buddy is leading a private army of mercenaries. When he refuses to join up their friendship turns violent. 93m/C VHS, LV, **Closed Caption.** David Bradley, Frank Zagarino; **D:** Sam Firstenberg. IMP, IME

Blood Wedding ✞✞✞ Bodas de Sangre 1981 A wonderfully passionate dance film from Saura and choreographed by Gades, based on the play by famed author Federico Garcia Lorca. A young bride runs off with her married lover on her wedding day and her jilted husband comes after them. If you like flamenco, there are two more: "Carmen" and "El Amor Brujo." In Spanish with English subtitles. 71m/C VHS, Beta. **SP** Antonio Gades, Christina Hoyos, Marisol, Carmen Villena; **D:** Carlos Saura. XVC, CTH, MED

Bloodbath 19?? Drugs, sex and terrorism—Hopper is typecast as an American degenerate who, along with his expatriate friends, is persecuted by local religious cults who need sacrifices. 89m/C VHS, Beta. Dennis Hopper, Carroll Baker, Richard Todd, Faith Brook, Win Wells; **D:** Silvio Narizzano. GHV, HHE

Bloodbath at the House of Death ✞✞ 1985 Price and his compatriots fight a team of mad scientists in this parody of popular horror films. Fun to see Price spoofing his own genre; die-hard horror camp fans will be satisfied. Best line: "Wanna fork?" 92m/C VHS, Beta. GB Kenny Everett, Pamela Stephenson, Vincent Price, Gareth Hunt; **D:** Ray Cameron. MED

Bloodbath in Psycho Town ✞ 1989 (R) A film crew is marked for death by a hooded man when it enters a remote little village. 87m/C VHS. Ron Arragon, Donna Baltron, Dave Elliott; **D:** Alessandro DeGaetano; **W:** Alessandro DeGaetano. NO

Bloodbeat ✞ 1985 A supernatural being terrorizes a family as they gather at their country home to celebrate Christmas. 84m/C VHS. Helen Benton, Terry Brown, Claudia Peyton; **D:** Fabrice A. Zaphiratos. TWE

Bloodbrothers ✞✞½ 1978 (R) Portrayal of working-class Italian men's lives—if that's possible without the benefit of Italian writers, producers, or director. Still, lots of cussing and general intensity, as Gere's character struggles between staying in the family construction business and doing what he wants to do—work with children.

Re-cut for television and re-titled "A Father's Love." 120m/C VHS. Richard Gere, Paul Sorvino, Tony LoBianco, Kenneth McMillan, Marilu Henner, Danny Aiello, Lelia Goldoni, Yvonne Wilder; **D:** Robert Mulligan; **C:** Robert L. Surtees; **M:** Elmer Bernstein. Nominations: Academy Awards '78: Best Adapted Screenplay. WAR

Bloodfight ✞ 1990 (PG-13) Exciting kick-boxing and martial arts tournament turns sour when champ offends the sense of honor of the master. Now the champ must battle the master, and only one will remain standing! ?m/C VHS. Bolo Yeung. IMP

Bloodfist ✞✞ 1989 (R) A kickboxer tears through Manila searching for his brother's killer. A Roger Corman production. 85m/C VHS, Beta. Don "The Dragon" Wilson, Rob Kaman, Billy Blanks, Kris Aguilar, Riley Bowman, Michael Shaner; **D:** Terence H. Winkless. MGM

Bloodfist 2 ✞✞½ 1990 (R) Six of the world's toughest martial artists find themselves kidnapped and forced to do the bidding of the evil Su. The mysterious recluse stages a series of incredible fights between the experts and his own army of drugged warriors. 85m/C VHS, Beta, Closed Caption. Don "The Dragon" Wilson, Maurice Smith, James Warring, Timothy Baker, Richard Hill, Rina Reyes; **D:** Andy Blumenthal. MGM

Bloodfist 3: Forced to Fight ✞½ 1992 (R) Just as long as nobody's forced to watch, real-life world champion kickboxer Wilson thrashes his way through another showdown-at-the-arena plot. Better-than-average fight choreography. **CW:** Language, violence, and sensuality. 90m/C VHS. Don "The Dragon" Wilson, Richard Roundtree, Laura Stockman, Richard Paul, Rick Dean, Peter "Sugarfoot" Cunningham; **D:** Oley Sassone; **W:** Allison Burnett; **C:** Rick Bota; **M:** Nigel Holton. NHO

Bloodfist 4: Die Trying ✞½ 1992 (R) To rescue his daughter, a fighter must do battle with the FBI, the CIA, and an international arms cartel. **CW:** Language and violence. 86m/C VHS, LV. Don "The Dragon" Wilson, Catya Sassoon, Amanda Wyss, James Tolkan, Liz Torres; **D:** Paul Ziller. NHO

Bloodfist 5: Human Target ✞½ 1993 (R) When undercover FBI agent Jim Roth (Wilson) attempts to unravel an international arms deal he's found out and left for dead. He comes to with no memory only to find himself caught between the arms dealers and the FBI, who think he's turned double-agent. Both sides want Roth dead. ?m/C VHS. Don "The Dragon" Wilson, Denice Duff, Yuji Okumoto, Don Stark, Danny Lopez, Steve James, Michael Yama; **D:** Jeff Yonis; **W:** Jeff Yonis. NHO

Bloodfist 6: Ground Zero ✞½ 1994 (R) Nick Corrigan (Wilson) must battle terrorists who have a nuclear missile aimed at New York City. **CW:** Violence; language; nudity. 86m/C VHS, LV. Don "The Dragon" Wilson, Cat Sasson, Steve Garvey; **D:** Rick Jacobson. NHO

Bloodhounds ✞✞ 1996 (R) Detective Harnos, who's skilled in the martial arts, reluctantly agrees to team up with writer Bersnen, whose specialty is criminal cases, to catch a killer. Made for cable. **CW:** Violent content. 86m/C VHS, Beta, **Closed Caption.** Corbin Bernsen, Christina Harnos, Marcus Flanagan, Gina Mastrogiacomo, James Pickens Jr., Kirk Baltz; **D:** Michael Katleman; **W:** Pablo F. Fenjves. PAR

Bloodhounds 2 ✞✞ 1996 (PG-13) True-crime writer Harrison Coyle (Bersen) teams up with PI Nikki Cruz (Peeples) to nab serial killer Matthew Standing (Tracey), who hunts down convicted rapists he thinks haven't been punished enough. Turns out the killer is also a fan of Coyle's and begins contacting him about them writing a book together. Made for cable. **CW:** Violence and thematic elements. ?m/C VHS. Corbin Bernsen, Nia Peeples, Ian Tracey, Amy Yasbeck, Jim Byrnes, Suki Kaiser, Tom Cavanagh. PAR

Bloodhounds of Broadway ✞✞½ 1989 (PG) A musical tribute to Damon Runyon, detailing the cliched adventures of an assortment of jazz-age crooks, flappers, chanteuses, and losers. 90m/C VHS, Beta, LV, Closed Caption. Madonna,

Rutger Hauer, Randy Quaid, Matt Dillon, Jennifer Grey, Julie Hagerty, Esai Morales, Anita Morris, Josef Sommer, William S. Burroughs, Ethan Phillips, Stephen McHattie, Dinah Manoff, Googy Gress, Tony Azito, Tony Longo, Madeleine Potter; **D:** Howard Brookner; **W:** Howard Brookner, Colman DeKay; **C:** Elliot Davis; **M:** Jonathan Sheffer. COL

Bloodknot ✞✞ 1995 (R) The Reaves' are devastated when their son Martin is killed in a military accident. So they're an easy target when Kaye (Vernon) shows up, claiming to be Martin's girlfriend. Mom Evelyn (Kidder) and brother Tom (Dempsey) are only too eager to welcome Kaye into the family but it wouldn't be a thriller if devious Kaye didn't have some deadly ulterior motives. Made for cable TV. **CW:** Strong sexuality, language, and some violence. 98m/C VHS, Beta, **Closed Caption.** Patrick Dempsey, Kate Vernon, Margot Kidder, Craig Sheffer; **D:** Jorge Montesi; **W:** Randy Kornfield; **C:** Philip Linzey; **M:** Ian Thomas. PAR

Bloodlink ✞½ 1986 (R) A well-to-do doctor has a recurring nightmare about killing an elderly woman. This prompts him to explore his past, discovering that he was separated at birth from a twin brother. Naturally, only by searching frantically for his long-lost sibling can the good doctor hope to solve the mystery of the recurring nightmare. A somnolent tale indeed. 98m/C VHS, Beta. Michael Moriarty, Penelope Milford, Geraldine Fitzgerald, Cameron Mitchell, Sarah Langenfeld; **D:** Alberto De Martino. VTR

Bloodlust ✞ 1959 More teenagers fall prey to yet another mad scientist, who stores their dead bodies in glass tanks. Low-budget ripoff of "The Most Dangerous Game" and other such films. A must for Mike Brady (Robert Reed) fans though. 89m/B VHS. Wilton Graff, June Kennedy, Robert Reed, Lilyan Chauvin; **D:** Ralph Brooke; **W:** Ralph Brooke. SNC, NOS

Bloodlust: Subspecies 3 ✞½ Subspecies 3 1993 (R) Equally gory followup to "Bloodstone: Subspecies 2." Sadistic vampire Radu is still battling for Michelle's soul, this time against Michelle's sister Becky, aided by his disgusting Mummy and the demonic Subspecies. Castle Vladislas is awash in blood and Becky discovers more than Michelle's fate is at risk. **CW:** Gory vampire violence and some sexuality. 83m/C VHS, Beta, LV, **Closed Caption.** Anders Hove, Kevin Blair, Denice Duff, Pamela Gordon, Ion Haiduc, Michael DellaFemina; **D:** Ted Nicolaou; **W:** Ted Nicolaou. PAR

Bloodmatch ✞ 1991 (R) A whodunit, martial-arts-style: the "sleuth" kidnaps all the suspects in a corruption case and kickboxes each to death until somebody confesses. Not exactly Agatha Christie, and artsy camera moves fail to exploit the fancy footwork. **CW:** Language, pervasive violence, and strong sex scene. 85m/C VHS, LV, **Closed Caption.** Thom Mathews, Michel Qissi, Benny "The Jet" Urquidez, Marianne Taylor, Hope Marie Carlton, Dale Jacoby, Thunder Wolf, Vincent Klyn, Peter "Sugarfoot" Cunningham, Hector Pena; **D:** Albert Pyun; **W:** K. Mannah; **M:** Tony Riparetti. HBO

Bloodmoon woof! 1990 The setting is Australia but the sleazy story's all too familiar: an insane killer employs knives and other sharp objects to prevent sex-crazed students from getting past third base. 104m/C VHS, Beta, LV. AU Leon Lissek, Christine Amor, Ian Patrick Williams, Helen Thomson, Hazel Howson, Craig Cronin, Anya Molina; **D:** Alec Mills; **W:** Richard Brennan; **M:** Brian May. LIV

Bloodshed ✞ 1983 (R) A psychotic harbors a girl's dead body, and systematically kills anyone who discovers his secret. 88m/C VHS, Beta. Laslo Papas, Beverly Ross; **D:** Richard Cassidy. NO

Bloodspell ✞ 1987 (R) A student with an evil power unleashes it on those who cross his path. 87m/C VHS, Beta. Anthony Jenkins, Aaron Teich, Alexandra Kennedy, John Reno; **D:** Deryn Warren. MCG

Bloodsport ✞✞ 1988 (R) American soldier Van Damme endeavors to win the deadly Kumite, an outlawed martial arts competition in Hong Kong. Lots of kick-boxing action and the sound of bones cracking. 92m/C VHS, Beta, LV, Closed Caption. Jean-Claude Van Damme, Leah Ayres, Roy Chiao, Donald Gibb, Bolo Yeung, Norman Burton, Forest Whitaker; **D:** Newton Arnold; **W:** Christopher Cosby. WAR, TLF

Bloodsport 2: The Next Kumite 🗡½ 1995 (R) Old-fashioned kickfest has Alex (Bernhardt) stealing antiquities in Thailand. He's left to take the fall by his partner in the theft of an ancient sword belonging to powerful businessman Leung (Morita) and is sent to a prison where sadistic head guard Demon (Han) takes an instant dislike to him. Alex learns about a sacred fighting competition, the Kumite, from wise prison sage Sun (Hong) and naturally, once Alex manages to get into the contest, his opponent is—you guessed it—Demon.**CW:** Non-stop martial arts violence. 87m/C VHS. Daniel Bernhardt, Ong Soo Han, Noriyuki "Pat" Morita, James Hong; **D:** Alan Mehrez. FEI

Bloodsport 3 🗡½ 1995 Alex must avenge the death of his mentor and regain the Kumite sword. 92m/C VHS. Daniel Bernhardt, John Rhys-Davies, James Hong, Noriyuki "Pat" Morita; **D:** Alan Mehrez; **W:** James Williams. FEI

Bloodstalkers woof! 1976 Two vacationers in Florida meet up with a band of slaughtering, swamp-based lunatics. 91m/C VHS, Beta. Kenny Miller, Celea Ann Cole, Jerry Albert; **D:** Robert W. Morgan. THV

Bloodstone 🗡🗡 1988 (PG-13) A couple honeymooning in the Middle East unexpectedly become involved in a jewel heist when they discover a valuable ruby amongst their luggage. Non-stop action and humor. 90m/C VHS, Beta. Charlie Brill, Christopher Neame, Jack Kehler, Brett Stimely; **D:** Dwight Little; **W:** Nico Mastorakis, Curt Allen. MCG

Bloodstone: Subspecies 2 🗡½ Subspecies 2 1992 (R) A gory sequel to "Subspecies" finds Radu the vampire pursuing the luscious Michelle. Radu gets some help from his ghoulish mother and yucky demonic spawn. Filmed on location in Romania.**CW:** Vampire violence. 107m/C VHS, LV, Closed Caption. Anders Hove, Denice Duff, Kevin Blair, Michael Denish, Pamela Gordon, Ion Haiduc; **D:** Ted Nicolaou; **W:** Ted Nicolaou. PAR

The Bloodsuckers 🗡🗡 Incense For the Damned; Doctors Wear Scarlet 1970 A British horror tale set on a Greek Island. An Oxford don is seduced into an ancient vampire cult. Director Michael Burrowes replaces Hartford-Davis in the credits due to a dispute over post-production editing. 90m/C VHS, Beta. GB Patrick Macnee, Peter Cushing, Patrick Mower, Edward Woodward; **D:** Robert Hartford-Davis. SNC

Bloodsuckers from Outer Space woof! 1983 Via an alien invasion, Texas farmers becoming bloodsucking zombies. 80m/C VHS, Beta. Thom Meyer, Laura Ellis, Billie Keller, Kim Braden; **D:** Glenn Coburn. ORI, WAR

Bloodsucking Freaks woof! The Incredible Torture Show 1975 (R) Virtually plotless Troma gagfest full of torture, cannibalistic dwarfs, and similar debaucheries, all played out on a Soho Grand Guignol stage (horror shows that allegedly contained real torture and death). Features "The Caged Sexoids," if that tells you anything (a cage of naked cannibal women tended by a dwarf). Not to mention the woman who has her brain sucked out through a straw. Filmed in "Ghoulovision" and originally rated X. Intolerable for most. 89m/C VHS, Beta. Seamus O'Brian, Niles McMaster; **D:** Joel M. Reed. VES

Bloodsucking Pharoahs of Pittsburgh woof! 1990 (R) Pittsburgh is plagued by crazed cannibals who think eternal life is in Pennsylvania. Two detectives on the case are mystified.**CW:** Language, strong violence, and sensuality. 89m/C VHS, Beta, Closed Caption. Jake Dengel, Joe Sharkey, Suzanne Fletcher, Beverly Penberthy, Shawn Elliott, Pat Logan, Jane Hamilton; **D:** Alan Smithee; **W:** Dean Tschetter. PAR, FCT

Bloody Avenger 🗡 198? A trio of detectives search for a murderer in the streets of Philadelphia. 100m/C VHS, Beta. Jack Palance, George Eastman, Jenny Tamburi; **D:** Al Bradley. THV

Bloody Birthday 🗡½ Creeps 1980 (R) Three youngsters, bound together by their eerie birth during an eclipse (you know what that means), kill everyone around them that ever gave them problems. Typical "and the fun continues" ending; standard fare. 92m/C VHS, Beta. Susan Strasberg, Jose Ferrer, Lori Lethin, Melinda Cordell, Joe Penny, Ellen Geer, Julie Brown, Michael Dudikoff, Billy Jacoby; **D:** Edward Hunt. PSM

The Bloody Brood woof! 1959 Really bad flick about a drug-dealing beatnik gang who commit nasty crimes, like feeding messenger boys hamburgers filled with ground glass. Yuck. 80m/C VHS. CA Jack Betts, Barbara Lord, Peter Falk, Robert Christie; **D:** Julian Hoffman. SNC, TPV

The Bloody Fight 🗡 197? Two young people learn the cost of courage and the high price of justice when they avenge a murderer. 90m/C VHS, Beta. Alan Tang, Yu In Yin, Tan Chin, Pai Ying, Lui Ran In; **D:** N.G. Tien Tsu. NO

Bloody Mama 🗡🗡½ 1970 (R) Corman's violent, trashy story of the infamous Barker Gang of the 30s, led by the bloodthirsty and sex-crazed Ma Barker (Winters, can't you just picture it?) and backed by her four perverted sons. De Niro is the space cadet sibling, Walden the homosexual excon, Stroud the sadistic mama lover, and Kimbrough the lady killer. They're joined by Walden's prison lover, Dern, who also has a thing for Ma Barker. Winters is a riot in this perverse stew of crime, violence, and, of course, sentimental blood bonding (the family that slays together, stays together). First of the Corman-produced (and sometimes directed) mama movies, followed by "Big Bad Mama" and "Crazy Mama." 90m/C VHS, Beta, LV. Shelley Winters, Robert De Niro, Don Stroud, Pat Hingle, Bruce Dern, Diane Varsi, Robert Walden, Clinton Kimbrough, Scatman Crothers; **D:** Roger Corman; **C:** John A. Alonzo. VES, LIV

Bloody Moon woof! 1983 Tourists are being brutally attacked and murdered during a small Spanish village's Festival of the Moon. 84m/C VHS, Beta. Olivia Pascal, Christopher Brugger; **D:** Jess (Jesus) Franco. TWE

Bloody New Year 🗡 Time Warp Terror 1987 (R) Corpses stalk the living as a group of teens happen upon an impromptu New Year's Eve party on a deserted island. Auld acquaintance shouldn't be forgot, just this flick. 90m/C VHS, Beta. **D:** Norman J. Warren. ACA

The Bloody Pit of Horror 🗡½ Crimson Executioner; The Red Hangman 1965 While wife Jayne Mansfield is in Italy filming "Primitive Love," bodybuilder Hargitay starred in this sado-horror epic. He owns a castle that is visited by a group of models for a special shoot. While in the dungeon, Hargitay becomes possessed by the castle's former owner, a sadist, and begins torturing the models. Supposedly based on the writings of the Marquis de Sade. 87m/B VHS. IT Mickey Hargitay, Louise Barrett, Walter Brandi, Moa Thai, Ralph Zucker, Albert Gordon; **D:** Max (Massimo Pupillo) Hunter. SNC

Bloody Trail 🗡 1972 A Union soldier who chooses the recently pummeled South as the venue for postwar R-and-R is, for some reason, pursued by Confederates. And his good ol' boy pursuers don't have a sudden change of heart when he teams up with a former slave. Lots of violence and nudity; little plot and entertainment. 91m/C VHS. Paul Harper, Rance Howard, John Mitchum; **D:** Richard Robinson. ACA

The Bloody Vampire 🗡½ 1962 Atmospheric and chilling Mexican vampire film. Sequel to "Invasion of the Vampires." ?m/C VHS. MX Carlos Agosti. SNC

Bloody Wednesday 🗡🗡½ 1987 It's sanity check-out time when a hotel caretaker is driven mad by tormentors...or is he driving himself mad? What is it about vacant hotels that make men lose their minds? If you can remove "The Shining" from yours, this flick's worthwhile. 89m/C VHS, Beta. Raymond Elmendorf, Pamela Baker, Navarre Perry; **D:** Mark Gilhuis; **W:** Philip Yordan; **M:** Al Sendry. PSM

Blossoms in the Dust 🗡🗡 1941 The true story of Edna Gladney is told as she starts the Texas Children's Home and Aid Society of Fort Worth. Major league Garson tear-jerker. 100m/B VHS, Beta, Closed Caption. Greer Garson, Walter Pidgeon, Felix Bressart, Marsha Hunt, Fay Holden, Samuel S. Hinds, Kathleen Howard; **D:** Mervyn LeRoy. Academy Awards '41: Best Interior Decoration; Nominations: Academy Awards '41: Best Actress (Garson), Best Color Cinematography, Best Picture. MGM

The Blot 🗡🗡 1921 A story about a poorly paid professor and his family, whose lifestyle contrasts with that of an affluent neighbor, a butcher. 55m/B VHS, Beta. Louis Calhern, Claire Windsor; **D:** Lois Weber. GPV, GVV, DVT

Blow Out 🗡🗡🗡 1981 (R) When a prominent senator is killed in a car crash, a sound effects engineer becomes involved in political intrigue as he tries to expose a conspiracy with the evidence he has gathered. An intricate mystery and homage to Antonioni's "Blow-Up." 108m/C VHS, Beta, LV. John Travolta, Nancy Allen, John Lithgow, Dennis Franz; **D:** Brian DePalma; **W:** Brian DePalma; **C:** Vilmos Zsigmond; **M:** Pino Donaggio. WAR, OM

Blow-Up 🗡🗡🗡½ 1966 A young London photographer takes some pictures of a couple in the park and finds out he may have recorded evidence of a murder. Though marred by badly dated 1960s modishness, this is Antonioni's most accessible film, a sophisticated treatise on perception and the film-consumer-as-voyeur, brilliantly assembled and wrought. 111m/C VHS, Beta, LV. GB IT David Hemmings, Vanessa Redgrave, Sarah Miles, Jane Birkin, Veruschka; **D:** Michelangelo Antonioni; **W:** Tonino Guerra, Michelangelo Antonioni; **C:** Carlo DiPalma; **M:** Herbie Hancock. Cannes Film Festival '67: Best Film; National Society of Film Critics Awards '66: Best Director (Antonioni), Best Film; Nominations: Academy Awards '66: Best Director (Antonioni), Best Story & Screenplay. MGM, FCT

Blowing Wild 🗡½ 1954 Filmed in Mexico, this Quinn-Stanwyck-Cooper love triangle, set in the early thirties, speaks of lust and vengeance, rashness and greed. Stanwyck, married to oil tycoon Quinn, lusts after one-time lover wildcatter Cooper. 92m/B VHS, LV. Gary Cooper, Barbara Stanwyck, Anthony Quinn, Ruth Roman, Ward Bond; **D:** Hugo Fregonese; **W:** Philip Yordan. REP, FCT

Blown Away 🗡 1990 (R) A mafia wife goes up against her husband in order to retrieve her kidnapped child.**CW:** Language, violence, and strong sexuality. 92m/C VHS, Beta. Loni Anderson, John Heard, James Naughton; **D:** Michael Miller. ACA

Blown Away 🗡½ 1993 (R) Haim and Feldman are brothers working at a ski resort where Haim falls for rich teenager Eggert. She's a young femme fatale who manages to get Haim all hot and bothered but she's actually using the unsuspecting dupe in a murder plot. Also available in an unrated version at 93 minutes. 91m/C VHS, LV, Closed Caption. Nicole Eggert, Corey Haim, Corey Feldman. LIV

Blown Away 🗡🗡 1994 (R) Boston Irish bomb-squad cop Jimmy Dove (Bridges) is after former compatriot Ryan Gaerity (Jones), an Irish radical who's taken his bombing expertise onto Jimmy's new turf. Meanwhile, Jimmy wants to keep his unsavory past from unsuspecting wife Amis. Real life dad Lloyd plays Jeff's uncle. While Jones seems adequately obsessed with making things go boom and Bridges significantly concerned that they don't, thriller moves on predictable path toward explosive climax. Special effects create the suspense, as everyday objects become lethal in Gaerity's knowledgeable hands.

The final explosion was more than even the special effects coordinator desired—windows were unintentionally blown out in nearby buildings. **CW:** Some language and violence. **121m/C VHS, LV, Closed Caption.** Jeff Bridges, Tommy Lee Jones, Suzy Amis, Lloyd Bridges, Forest Whitaker; **D:** Stephen Hopkins; **W:** Joe Batteer, John Rice; **C:** Gregory McClatchy. Nominations: MTV Movie Awards '95: Best Villain (Jones), Best Action Sequence. *MGM*

Blue 🐾 1968 A dull western about an American boy (Stamp) raised by Mexicans who doesn't trust another living soul until he finds himself face to face with his former gang, led by his adoptive father (Montalban). **113m/C VHS, Closed Caption.** Terence Stamp, Joanna Pettet, Karl Malden, Ricardo Montalban, Joe De Santis, Sally Kirkland; **D:** Silvio Narizzano; **W:** Ronald M. Cohen; **M:** Manos Hadjidakis. *PAR*

Blue 🐾 1993 (R) Meditation/memoir of director Jarman's deteriorating AIDS condition consists of narration and a soundtrack set against an unvaried white screen. Jarman ponders the associations with the color blue (sky, ocean, blindness, heaven, eternity) and his own physical problems, alternately expressed with dreamy vagueness or incendiary contempt. Limited in appeal, depending highly on boredom tolerance and ability to suspend visual expectations. **CW:** Some sexuality. **76m/C VHS.** **GB D:** Derek Jarman; **W:** Derek Jarman; **M:** Simon Fisher Turner. *KIV*

The Blue and the Gray 🐾🐾 1985 Epic television mini-series about love and hate inflamed by the Civil War. Keach plays a Pinkerton's secret service agent in this loosely based historical romance. The uncut version is available on three cassettes; the 295 minute version is on two cassettes. **398m/C VHS, Beta, LV.** Gregory Peck, Lloyd Bridges, Colleen Dewhurst, Stacy Keach, John Hammond, Sterling Hayden, Warren Oates; **D:** Andrew V. McLaglen; **M:** Bruce Broughton. *COL, TVC, FCT*

The Blue Angel 🐾🐾🐾🐾 *Der Blaue Engel* 1930 Tale of a man stripped of his dignity. A film classic filled with sensuality and decay, which made Dietrich a European star and led to her discovery in Hollywood. When a repressed professor (Jannings) goes to a nightclub hoping to catch some of his students in the wrong, he's taken by Lola, the sultry singer portrayed by Dietrich. After spending the night with her, losing his job, and then marrying her, he goes on tour with the troupe, peddling indiscreet photos of his wife. Versions were shot in both German and English, with the German version sporting English subtitles. ♫Falling in Love Again; They Call Me Wicked Lola. **90m/B VHS, Beta, 8mm.** **GE** Marlene Dietrich, Emil Jannings, Kurt Gerron, Rosa Valetti, Hans Albers; **D:** Josef von Sternberg; **W:** Karl Vollmoller, Robert Liebmann, Carl Zuckmayer; **M:** Friedrich Hollander. *NOS, FCT, BAR*

The Blue Bird 🐾🐾🐾 1940 (G) A weird, dark fantasy about two children who search for the blue bird of happiness in various fantasy lands, but find it eventually at home. Overlooked and impressively fatalistic. **98m/C VHS, Beta, Closed Caption.** Shirley Temple, Gale Sondergaard, John Russell, Eddie Collins, Nigel Bruce, Jessie Ralph, Spring Byington, Sybil Jason; **D:** Walter Lang; **C:** Arthur C. Miller. Nominations: Academy Awards '40: Best Color Cinematography. *FXV, MLB*

Blue Blazes Rawden 1918 Hart plays a lumberjack who gains control of a local saloon after shooting its villainous proprietor. **?m/B VHS, Beta, 8mm.** William S. Hart. *GPV, GVV*

Blue Blood 🐾 1973 A demonic butler inflicts nightmares upon a family to gain possession of its mansion. **90m/C VHS, Beta.** **GB** Oliver Reed, Derek Jacobi, Fiona Lewis; **D:** Andrew Sinclair. *NO*

Blue Canadian Rockies 🐾½ 1952 Autry's employer sends him to Canada to discourage his daughter from marrying a fortune hunter. The daughter has turned the place into a dude ranch and wild game preserve. When Autry arrives, he encounters some mysterious killings.

58m/B VHS, Beta. Gene Autry, Pat Buttram, Gail Davis, Ross Ford, Tom London; **D:** George Archainbaud. *CCB*

Blue Chips 🐾🐾½ 1994 (PG-13) Nolte does Bobby Knight in this saga of Western U basketball coach Pete Bell, suffering through his first losing season. What follows is a tug of war between rich alumni who want to win at any cost and his ethics as he recruits for a new season. Larger than life hoopster O'Neal's film debut. McDonnell and Woodard are merely afterthoughts, but look for cameos from many real life b-ballers, including Dick Vitale and Larry Bird. Average script is bolstered by exciting game footage, shot during real games for authenticity. **CW:** Profanity. **108m/C VHS, Beta, LV, Closed Caption.** Nick Nolte, Shaquille O'Neal, Mary McDonnell, Ed O'Neill, J.T. Walsh, Alfre Woodard; **Cameos:** Larry Bird, Bobby Knight, Rick Pitino; **D:** William Friedkin; **W:** Ron Shelton; **M:** Nile Rodgers, Jeff Beck, Jed Leiber. *PAR*

Blue City 🐾½ 1986 (R) A young man returns to his Florida hometown to find his father murdered, and subsequently vows to solve and avenge the matter. Based on a Ross MacDonald thriller. **83m/C VHS, Beta, LV, Closed Caption.** Judd Nelson, Ally Sheedy, Paul Winfield, Anita Morris, David Caruso, Julie Carmen, Scott Wilson; **D:** Michelle Manning; **W:** Walter Hill, Lukas Heller; **M:** Ry Cooder. *PAR*

Blue Collar 🐾🐾🐾 1978 (R) An auto assembly line worker, tired of the poverty of his life, hatches a plan to rob his own union. A study of the working class and the robbing of the human spirit. **114m/C VHS, Beta, LV.** Richard Pryor, Harvey Keitel, Yaphet Kotto, Ed Begley Jr.; **D:** Paul Schrader; **W:** Paul Schrader, Leonard Schrader; **M:** Jack Nitzsche. *USH, FCT*

Blue Country 🐾🐾½ *Le Pays Bleu* 1977 (PG) A joyful romantic comedy about a pair of free souls who leave their stagnant lives behind to seek out a more idyllic existence. Subtitled in English. **104m/C VHS, Beta.** **FR** Brigitte Fossey, Jacques Serres, Ginette Garcin, Armand Meffre, Ginette Mathieu, Roger Crouzet; **D:** Jean-Charles Tacchella; **W:** Jean-Charles Tacchella; **C:** Edmond Sechan; **M:** Gerard Anfosso. *COL*

The Blue Dahlia 🐾🐾🐾½ 1946 Classic film noir finds Navy vet Johnny Morrison (Ladd) returning home to discover his wife Helen (Dowling) has been keeping the home fires burning—with Eddie Harwood (Da Silva), owner of the Blue Dahlia nightclub. After a nasty fight, Johnny takes off and is picked up by sultry blonde Joyce (Lake). The next day Johnny discovers he's wanted by the cops for the murder of his wife and decides to hide out until he can find the real killer, with Joyce's help. Very stylish and fast-paced with excellent performances; Chandler's first original screenplay. **100m/B VHS, Closed Caption.** Alan Ladd, Veronica Lake, William Bendix, Howard da Silva, Doris Dowling, Tom Powers, Hugh Beaumont, Howard Freeman, Don Costello; **D:** George Marshall; **W:** Raymond Chandler; **C:** Lionel Lindon; **M:** Victor Young. Nominations: Academy Awards '46: Best Original Screenplay. *USH*

Blue De Ville 🐾🐾 1986 (PG) Two young women buy a '59 Cadillac and journey from St. Louis to New Mexico, having adventures on the way. The rambling, free-spirited movie was a pilot for a prospective series that never set sail—but when "Thelma & Louise" hit big this superficially similar item was hauled out on video. **96m/C VHS, Closed Caption.** Jennifer Runyon, Kimberly Pistone, Mark Thomas Miller, Alan Autry, Robert Prescott; **D:** Jim Johnston. *THV*

Blue Desert 🐾🐾🐾 1991 (R) Cox is strong in her performance as Lisa Roberts, a comic book artist who leaves New York City for small town Arizona life after surviving a traumatic rape. Once there, she's befriended by Sheffer and Sweeney, a local cop. Battersby does a good job of keeping the suspense level high (in his directorial debut) as Cox finds that there's danger in small towns, too. Fine performances keep this slightly above average. **CW:** Sexual scene. **98m/C VHS.** D.B. Sweeney, Courteney Cox, Craig Sheffer, Philip Baker Hall, Sandy

Ward; **D:** Bradley Battersby; **W:** Bradley Battersby, Arthur Collis; **M:** Jerry Goldsmith. *ACA*

Blue Fin 🐾🐾 1978 (PG) When their tuna boat is shipwrecked, and the crew disabled, a young boy and his father learn lessons of love and courage as the son tries to save the ship. **93m/C VHS, Beta.** **AU** Hardy Kruger, Greg Rowe; **D:** Carl Schultz; **C:** Geoff Burton.

Blue Fire Lady 🐾🐾 1978 The heartwarming story of a young girl and her love of horses which endures even her father's disapproval. Good family fare. **96m/C VHS, Beta.** Cathryn Harrison, Mark Holden, Peter Cummins. *MED*

Blue Flame 🐾🐾 1993 (R) Vigilante cop is hired to track down two humanoid aliens who have escaped captivity in futuristic L.A. They evade him by time-traveling through alternate realities, infiltrating the cop's mind, and using his fantasies against him. **88m/C VHS, Closed Caption.** Brian Wimmer, Ian Buchanan, Kerri Green, Cecilia Peck, Jad Mager; **D:** Cassian Elwes; **W:** Cassian Elwes. *COL*

Blue Hawaii 🐾🐾 1962 A soldier, returning to his Hawaiian home, defies his parents by taking a job with a tourist agency. Presley sings "Can't Help Falling in Love." For Elvis fans. **101m/C VHS, Beta, LV.** Elvis Presley, Angela Lansbury, Joan Blackman, Roland Winters, Iris Adrian, John Archer, Steve Brodie; **D:** Norman Taurog; **W:** Hal Kanter. *FOX, MVD*

Blue Heaven 🐾 1984 A couple struggles through problems with their marriage and alcohol abuse. **100m/C VHS, Beta.** Leslie Denniston, James Eckhouse; **D:** Kathleen Dowdey. *VES, LIV*

The Blue Hour 🐾🐾 1991 Theo is a Berlin hustler whose business is so good he can pick his clients. Marie, his next-door neighbor, lives with her boyfriend Paul until he just walks out one day. Marie is shattered and refuses to leave her apartment until Theo takes an interest in her plight. Just when it seems that the improbable couple could find true love, Paul comes back. In German with English subtitles. **87m/C VHS, Closed Caption.** **GE** Andreas Herder, Dina Leipzig, Cyrill Rey-Coquais; **D:** Marcel Gisler. *WBF, FCT*

Blue Ice 🐾🐾½ 1992 (R) Harry Anders (Caine) is an ex-spy with an eye for the ladies and a loyalty to his friends. When his friends start winding up dead, Harry decides to investigate—a very dangerous decision, especially when a mysterious woman (Young) takes an interest. Made for cable television. **CW:** Strong language, nudity, and violence. **96m/C VHS, LV, Closed Caption.** Michael Caine, Sean Young, Ian Bannen, Bob Hoskins; **D:** Russell Mulcahy; **W:** Ron Hutchinson; **M:** Michael Kamen. *HBO*

Blue Iguana 🐾🐾 1988 (R) An inept bounty hunter travels south of the border to recover millions from a crooked South American bank, and meets up with sexy women, murderous thugs, and corruption. **88m/C VHS, Beta, LV, Closed Caption.** Dylan McDermott, Pamela Gidley, James Russo, Dean Stockwell, Pamela Gidley, Tovah Feldshuh; **D:** John Lafia. *PAR*

Blue in the Face 🐾🐾½ 1995 (R) Wang and Auster's immediate follow-up to "Smoke," shot in five days, recycles the same Brooklyn cigar shop setting and contains a dozen fast-paced, loosely scripted or wholly improvised scenes that they couldn't cram into "Smoke," led by Reed's deadpan riff on eyewear, New York, and smoking. The action again centers around Auggie (Keitel), the shop manager, who hangs out with the mostly eccentric, and sometimes famous clientele. Harmusch idly waxes philosophic on smoking technique, while puffing on what he claims is his last. Scenes are woven together with videotaped interviews from actual Brooklyn residents, creating a tribute to life in the borough with a documentary feel. Improv lovers will enjoy watching what sometimes seems more like outtakes than finished performances. **CW:** Language; scene of nudity. **83m/C VHS, LV, Closed Caption.** Harvey Keitel, Lou Reed, Michael J. Fox, Roseanne, Jim Jarmusch, Lily Tomlin, Mel Gorham, Jared Harris, Giancarlo Esposito, Victor Argo, Madonna, Keith David, Mira Sorvino, Malik Yoba; **D:** Wayne Wang, Paul Auster; **W:** Wayne Wang, Paul Auster. TOU

Blue Jeans 🎬🎬½ 1978 A young French boy experiences sexual awakening and humiliation in a British school. In French with English subtitles. 80m/C VHS, Beta. FR **D:** Hugues des Roziers. FCT

Blue Jeans and Dynamite 🎬🎬 198? A stuntman is hired to lift the "Golden Mask of the Duct Tomb" and is followed on land, water, and air. Great chase scenes and action-filled finale. 90m/C VHS. Robert Vaughn, Simon Andrew, Katia Kristine. NO

The Blue Kite 🎬🎬🎬 1993 Fifteen years of political and cultural upheaval in China is shown through the eyes of young troublemaker Tietou, who certainly earns his nickname of "Iron Head" after his 1954 birth. Soon his father is sent to a labor reform camp and his mother remarries—only to be faced with more struggles as the years go by. The kite is Tietou's cherished toy, which keeps getting lost or destroyed but is always being rebuilt, offering one token of hope. Chinese with subtitles. 138m/C VHS. CH Lu Liping, Zhang Wenyao, Pu Quanxin; **D:** Tian Zhuangzhuang; **W:** Xiao Mao. Nominations: Independent Spirit Awards '95: Best Foreign Film. KIV

The Blue Knight 🎬🎬½ 1975 Kennedy brings energy and care to this basically standard story. Policeman waiting for retirement searches for his partner's killer. Unexceptional treatment made palatable by actors. Made for television movie. 72m/C VHS. George Kennedy, Alex Rocco, Glynn Turman, Verna Bloom, Michael Margotta, Seth Arnold; **D:** J. Lee Thompson. LIV

The Blue Lagoon WOOF! 1980 (R) Useless remake of 1949 film of the same name. An adolescent boy and girl marooned on a desert isle discover love (read: sex) without the restraints of society. Not too explicit, but nonetheless intellectually offensive. Gorgeous photography of island paradise is wasted on this Shields vehicle. 105m/C VHS, Beta, LV. Brooke Shields, Christopher Atkins, Leo McKern, William Daniels; **D:** Randal Kleiser; **C:** Nestor Almendros; **M:** Basil Poledouris. Golden Raspberry Awards '80: Worst Actress (Shields); Nominations: Academy Awards '80: Best Cinematography. COL

The Blue Lamp 🎬🎬🎬 1949 Action-adventure fans familiar with the hoary plot where a cop must avenge the wrongful death of his partner will appreciate this suspenseful British detective effort. It's one of the very first in the genre to explore buddy cop revenge in a very British sort of way. Also sports a concluding chase scene which has stood the test of time. Led to the long-running British TV series "Dixon of Dock Green." 84m/B VHS. GB Dirk Bogarde, Jimmy Hanley, Jack Warner, Bernard Lee, Robert Flemyng, Patric Doonan, Bruce Seton, Frederick Piper, Betty Ann Davies, Peggy Evans; **D:** Basil Dearden. British Academy Awards '50: Best Film. FCT

The Blue Light 🎬🎬🎬 Das Blaue Licht 1932 Fairy-tale love story, based on an Italian fable about a mysterious woman, thought to be a witch, and a painter. Riefenstahl's first film which brought her to the attention of Adolf Hitler, who requested she make films glorifying the Nazi Party. In German with English subtitles. 77m/B VHS, Beta. GE Leni Riefenstahl, Matthias Wieman, Max Holsboer; **D:** Leni Riefenstahl; **W:** Leni Riefenstahl. VYY, MRV, FCT

The Blue Lightning 🎬🎬½ 1986 Investigator Elliott travels to Australia to retrieve the priceless Blue Lightening gem. He must fight the crime lord in his Aussie encampment. Nice scenery, but unexceptional television story. 95m/C VHS. Sam Elliott, Rebecca Gilling, Robert Culp, John Meillon, Robert Coleby, Max Phipps; **D:** Lee Philips. FRH

The Blue Max 🎬🎬½ 1966 During WWI a young German, fresh out of aviation training school, competes for the coveted "Blue Max" flying award with other members of a squadron of seasoned flyers from aristocratic backgrounds.

Based on a novel by Jack D. Hunter. 155m/C VHS, Beta, LV. George Peppard, James Mason, Ursula Andress; **D:** John Guillermin; **M:** Jerry Goldsmith. FOX

Blue Money 🎬🎬 1984 A wild, comedic caper film about a cab-driving nightclub impressionist who absconds with a briefcase packed with cash and is pursued by everyone, even the I.R.A. Originally made for British television. 82m/C VHS, Beta. GB Tim Curry, Dabby Bishop, Billy Connolly, Frances Tomelty; **D:** Colin Bucksey. NO

Blue Monkey 🎬 Green Monkey 1987 (R) A mysterious alien plant impregnates a man, who gives birth to a huge, meat-eating insect larva. It subsequently grows up into a giant bug, and roams around a quarantined hospital looking for patients to eat. What made you think it had anything to do with monkeys? 97m/C VHS, Beta. Steve Railsback, Susan Anspach, Gwynyth Walsh, John Vernon, Joe Flaherty; **D:** William Fruet. COL

Blue Movies WOOF! 1988 (R) A couple of jerks try their hand at making porn films with predictable results. 92m/C VHS, Beta. Larry Linville, Lucinda Crosby, Steve Levitt, Darien Mathias, Larry Poindexter; **D:** Paul Koval. ACA

Blue Murder at St. Trinian's 🎬🎬🎬 1956 The second of the madcap British comedy series (based on cartoons by Ronald Searle) about an incredibly ferocious pack of schoolgirls. This time they travel to the European continent and make life miserable for a jewel thief. Highlight: fantasy sequence in ancient Rome showing the girls thrown to the lions—and scaring the lions. 86m/B VHS. GB Joyce Grenfell, Terry-Thomas, George Cole, Alastair Sim, Lionel Jeffries, Thorley Walters; **D:** Frank Launder; **M:** Malcolm Arnold. VYY, VDM, FUS

Blue Paradise WOOF! 1986 A depiction of Adam and Eve as they peruse the primal landscape and each other. 90m/C VHS, Beta. Mark Gregory, Andrea Goldman. TWE, MLB

Blue River 🎬🎬½ 1995 (PG-13) Flashbacks highlight this saga of a troubled family. Successful doctor Edward Sellers (McDonough) is dismayed when his derelict older brother Lawrence (O'Connell), whom he hasn't seen in 15 years, suddenly appears on his doorstep. A gifted teenager, Lawrence once built his world around science and logic after their father deserted the family but his only purpose turns out to be getting even with everyone he feels has betrayed him. Young Edward (Stahl) tried to be the "good" son, while Mom (Dey) retreated into religion and an affair with self-righteously nasty school principal Henry Howland (Elliott). TV adaptation of the novel by Ethan Canin. **CW:** Thematic material, sensuality and a scene of violence. 90m/C VHS. Jerry O'Connell, Nick Stahl, Susan Dey, Sam Elliott, Neal McDonough, Jean Marie Barnwell, Patrick Renna; **D:** Larry Elikann; **W:** Maria Nation; **C:** Eric Van Haren Noman; **M:** Lawrence Shragge. HMK

Blue Skies 🎬🎬🎬 1946 Former dancer turned radio personality Astaire flashes back to his friendship with singer Crosby and the gal (Caulfield) that came between them. Flimsy plot is just an excuse for some 20 Irving Berlin songs and Astaire's split-screen dance number, "Puttin' on the Ritz." 🎵 All By Myself; Always; Any Bonds Today?; Blue Skies; A Couple of Song and Dance Men; Everybody Step; Getting Nowhere; Heat Wave; I'll See You in C-U-B-A. 104m/C VHS, LV, Closed Caption. Fred Astaire, Bing Crosby, Joan Caulfield, Billy DeWolfe, Olga San Juan, Frank Faylen; **D:** Stuart Heisler; **W:** Arthur Sheekman; **C:** Charles B(ryant) Lang. Nominations: Academy Awards '46: Best Song ("You Keep Coming Back Like a Song"), Scoring of a Musical. USH

Blue Skies Again 🎬½ 1983 (PG) Spunky young woman determined to play major league baseball locks horns with the chauvinistic owner and the gruff manager of her favorite team. 91m/C VHS, Beta. Robyn Barto, Harry Hamlin, Mimi Rogers, Kenneth McMillan, Dana Elcar, Andy Garcia; **D:** Richard Michaels. WAR

Blue Sky 🎬🎬🎬 1991 (PG-13) Carly Marshall (Lange) is an irrepressible beauty, long married to adoring but uptight military scientist Hank (Jones). Things are barely in control when they're stationed in Hawaii but after Hank's transfer to a backwater base in Alabama, Carly's emotional mood swings go wildly out of control. Hell truly breaks loose when Carly attracts the attention of the camp's commander (Boothe), who's only too willing to take advantage. Set in 1962, a nuclear radiation subplot (Hank's new project) proves a minor distraction. Exceptional performance by Lange with Jones providing a quiet counterpoint as a man still deeply in love with his disturbed wife. Director Richardson's final film. Release date was delayed to 1994 due to Orion's financial problems. **CW:** Glimpse of nudity; strong language; sexual situations; some violence. 101m/C VHS, LV, Closed Caption. Jessica Lange, Tommy Lee Jones, Powers Boothe, Carrie Snodgress, Amy Locane, Chris O'Donnell, Mitchell Ryan, Dale Dye; **D:** Tony Richardson; **W:** Jerry Leichtling, Arlene Sarner, Rama Laurie Stagner; **M:** Jack Nitzsche. Academy Awards '94: Best Actress (Lange); Golden Globe Awards '95: Best Actress—Drama (Lange); Los Angeles Film Critics Association Awards '94: Best Actress (Lange); Nominations: Screen Actors Guild Award '94: Best Actress (Lange). ORI

Blue Steel 🎬🎬 1934 A young Wayne saves a town from financial ruin by leading the citizens to a gold strike. Also available with "Man From Utah" on Laser Disc. 59m/B VHS, Beta, LV. John Wayne, George "Gabby" Hayes; **D:** Robert North Bradbury. COL, NOS, MRV

Blue Steel 🎬🎬 1990 (R) Director Bigelow's much-heralded, proto-feminist cop thriller. A serious female rookie's gun falls into the hands of a Wall Street psycho who begins a killing spree. Action film made silly with over-anxious sub-text and patriarchy-directed rage. 102m/C VHS, Beta, LV, 8mm, Closed Caption. Jamie Lee Curtis, Ron Silver, Clancy Brown, Louise Fletcher, Philip Bosco, Elizabeth Pena, Tom Sizemore; **D:** Kathryn Bigelow; **W:** Kathryn Bigelow, Eric Red; **M:** Brad Fiedel. MGM

Blue Sunshine 🎬🎬½ 1978 (R) A certain brand of L.S.D. called Blue Sunshine starts to make its victims go insane. 94m/C VHS, Beta. Zalman King, Deborah Winters, Mark Goddard, Robert Walden, Charles Siebert, Ann Cooper, Ray Young, Alice Ghostley; **D:** Jeff Lieberman; **W:** Jeff Lieberman. VES

Blue Thunder 🎬🎬½ 1983 (R) Police helicopter pilot Scheider is chosen to test an experimental high-tech chopper that can see through walls, record a whisper, and level a city block. Seems anti-terrorist supercopter is needed to ensure security during 1984 Olympics. Bothered by Vietnam flashbacks, Scheider then battles wacky McDowell in the skies over L.A. High-techy police drama with satisfying aerial combat scenes nearly crashes with storyline. 110m/C VHS, Beta, LV, Closed Caption. Roy Scheider, Daniel Stern, Malcolm McDowell, Candy Clark, Warren Oates; **D:** John Badham; **W:** Dan O'Bannon, Don Jakoby; **C:** John A. Alonzo. Nominations: Academy Awards '83: Best Film Editing. COL

Blue Tiger 🎬🎬 1994 (R) Gina Hayes (Madsen) is shopping with her young son when a masked gunman enters the store and opens fire. When Gina realizes her son has been killed she becomes obsessed with finding the assailant. Her one clue—a blue tiger tattoo. **CW:** Language; some sexuality; strong, brutal violence. 88m/C VHS, LV, Closed Caption. Virginia Madsen, Toru Nakamura, Harry Dean Stanton, Ryo Ishibashi; **D:** Norberto Barba; **W:** Joel Soisson. COL

Blue Tornado 🎬 1990 (PG-13) An eerie bright light, emitted from a mountain, makes supersonic jets disappear into thin air. A beautiful researcher and a cocky pilot set out to solve the mystery. Better-than-average aerial sequences don't make up for goofy story and ludicrous dialogue. 96m/C VHS. Dirk Benedict, Patsy Kensit, Ted McGinley, David Warner; **D:** Tony B. Dobb. THV

Blue Velvet ⚉⚉⚉ **1986 (R)** Disturbing, unique exploration of the dark side of American suburbia, involving an innocent college youth who discovers a severed ear in an empty lot, and is thrust into a turmoil of depravity, murder, and sexual deviance. Brutal, grotesque, and unmistakably Lynch; an immaculately made, fiercely imagined film that is unlike any other. Mood is enhanced by the Badalamenti soundtrack. Graced by splashes of Lynchian humor, most notably the movie's lumber theme. Hopper is riveting as the chief sadistic nutcase and Twin Peaks' MacLachlan is a study in loss of innocence. Cinematography by Frederick Elmes. **121m/C VHS, Beta, LV, Closed Caption.** Brad Dourif, Kyle MacLachlan, Isabella Rossellini, Dennis Hopper, Laura Dern, Hope Lange, Jack Nance, Dean Stockwell, George Dickerson, Priscilla Pointer; *D:* David Lynch; *W:* David Lynch; *C:* Frederick Elmes; *M:* Angelo Badalamenti. Independent Spirit Awards '87: Best Actress (Rossellini); Los Angeles Film Critics Association Awards '86: Best Director (Lynch), Best Supporting Actor (Hopper); Montreal World Film Festival '86: Best Supporting Actor (Hopper); National Society of Film Critics Awards '86: Best Cinematography, Best Director (Lynch), Best Film, Best Supporting Actor (Hopper); Nominations: Academy Awards '86: Best Director (Lynch). WAR

The Blue Yonder ⚉½ *Time Flyers* **1986** In this made-for-video feature, a young boy travels back in time to meet the grandfather he never knew, risking historical integrity. **89m/C VHS, Beta, Closed Caption.** Art Carney, Peter Coyote, Huckleberry Fox; *D:* Mark Rosman. DIS

Bluebeard ⚉⚉½ **1944** Tormented painter with a psychopathic urge to strangle his models is the basis for this effective, low-budget film. One of Carradine's best vehicles. **73m/B VHS, Beta.** John Carradine, Jean Parker, Nils Asther; *D:* Edgar G. Ulmer. NOS, MRV, SNC

Bluebeard ⚉⚉⚉ *Landru* **1963** French biography of Henri-Desire Landru, who seduced and murdered eleven women and was subsequently beheaded. Dubbed into English. **108m/C VHS, Beta.** *FR* Charles Denner, Danielle Darrieux, Michele Morgan, Hildegarde Neff; *D:* Claude Chabrol. NLC

Bluebeard ⚉½ **1972 (R)** Lady killer Burton knocks off series of beautiful wives in soporific remake of the infamous story. **128m/C VHS.** Richard Burton, Raquel Welch, Joey Heatherton, Nathalie Delon, Virna Lisi, Sybil Danning; *D:* Edward Dmytryk; *M:* Ennio Morricone. LIV

Bluebeard's Eighth Wife ⚉⚉ **1938** Problematic comedy set on the French Riviera about a spoiled millionaire (Cooper) who's been married seven times and wants to go for eight with Colbert, the daughter of a destitute aristocrat. Good for a few laughs, but Coop seemed out of place in his role. Based on the play by Alfred Savoir, American version by Charlton Andrews. **86m/B VHS, Closed Caption.** Claudette Colbert, Gary Cooper, David Niven, Edward Everett Horton, Elizabeth Patterson, Herman Bing, William Hymer, Franklin Pangborn; *D:* Ernst Lubitsch; *W:* Charles Brackett, Billy Wilder. USH

Blueberry Hill ⚉½ **1988 (R)** While her mother struggles with the grief over husband's death, a young girl in a small town learns about life, music, and her late father from a jazz singer. Good soundtrack. **93m/C VHS, Beta.** Jennifer Rubin, Carrie Snodgress, Margaret Avery; *D:* Strathford Hamilton. FOX

The Blues Brothers ⚉⚉½ **1980 (R)** As an excuse to run rampant on the city of Chicago, Jake and Elwood Blues attempt to raise $5,000 for their childhood orphanage by putting their old band back together. Good music, and lots of cameos. **133m/C VHS, Beta, LV.** John Belushi, Dan Aykroyd, James Brown, Cab Calloway, Ray Charles, Henry Gibson, Aretha Franklin, Carrie Fisher, John Candy; *Cameos:* Frank Oz, Steven Spielberg, Twiggy, Paul (Pee Wee Herman) Reubens, Steve Lawrence, John Lee Hooker; *D:* John Landis; *W:* Dan Aykroyd, John Landis; *M:* Ira Newborn. USH

Blues Busters ⚉⚉½ **1950** Another entry in the "Bowery Boys" series. When Sach emerges from a tonsillectomy with the velvety voice of a crooner, Slip cashes in by turning Louie's Sweet Shop into a nightclub, the better to showcase his buddy's talents. Sach's singing voice provided by John Lorenz. **68m/B VHS.** Leo Gorcey, Huntz Hall, Adele Jergens, Gabriel Dell, Craig Stevens, Phyllis Coates, Bernard Gorcey, David Gorcey; *D:* William Beaudine. WAR

Bluffing It ⚉⚉ **1987** A made-for-television movie about an older man who has been disguising his illiteracy for years. **120m/C VHS.** Dennis Weaver, Janet Carroll, Michelle Little, Robert Sean Leonard, Cleavant Derricks, Victoria Wauchope; *D:* James Sadwith; *M:* Brad Fiedel. NO

The Blum Affair ⚉⚉ **1948** In post-WWI Germany, a Jewish man is framed for the murder of an accountant and uncovers in his capture and prosecution a rat's nest of corruption and anti-Semitism. In German with English subtitles. **109m/B VHS, Beta.** *GE* Hans-Christian Blech, Gisela Trowe, Kurt Ehrhardt, Paul Bildt, Klaus Becker; *D:* Erich Engel. NOS, FCT, APD

Blume in Love ⚉⚉⚉ **1973 (R)** An ironic comedy/drama about a man who falls hopelessly in love with his ex-wife who divorced him for cheating on her while they were married. **115m/C VHS, Beta.** George Segal, Susan Anspach, Kris Kristofferson, Shelley Winters, Marsha Mason; *D:* Paul Mazursky; *W:* Paul Mazursky; *C:* Bruce Surtees; *M:* Bill Conti. WAR

BMX Bandits ⚉⚉ **1983** Three adventurous Aussie teens put their BMX skills to the test when they witness a crime and are pursued by the criminals. Much big air. **92m/C VHS.** Nicole Kidman, David Argue, John Ley, Angelo D'Angelo; *D:* Brian Trenchard-Smith; *W:* Patrick Edgeworth. IMP

Boarding House ⚉ **1983 (R)** Residents of a boardinghouse discover sinister doings in the basement. It does not occur to any of them to move to another house. **90m/C VHS, Beta.** Hank Adly, Kalassu, Alexandra Day; *D:* John Wintergate. MRV

Boarding School ⚉⚉ *The Passion Flower Hotel* **1983 (R)** Basic teen sex comedy about students at a proper Swiss boarding school for girls who devise a plan to seduce the boys at a nearby school by posing as prostitutes. Kinski stars as the American girl who masterminds the caper. **100m/C VHS, Beta.** *GE* Nastassia Kinski; *D:* Andre Farwagi. VES, LIV

Boardinghouse Blues ⚉⚉ **1948** A showbiz musical centered around a boarding house with tenant troubles. It's an excuse for popular black entertainers of the day to perform, including Lucky Millinder, Bull Moose Jackson, Una Mae Carlisle, and Stumpy and Stumpy. **90m/C VHS.** Dusty Fletcher, Moms Mabley; *D:* Josh Binney. FCT, RXM

The Boat is Full ⚉⚉⚉ **1981** A group of refugees pose as a family in order to escape from Nazi Germany as they seek asylum in Switzerland. Available in German with English subtitles or dubbed into English. **104m/C VHS, Beta.** *SI* Tina Engel, Curt Bois, Renate Steiger, Mathias Gnaedinger; *D:* Markus Imhoof. Berlin International Film Festival '81: Best Director (Imhoof); Nominations: Academy Awards '81: Best Foreign Language Film. FRF, GLV, SWC

The Boatniks ⚉⚉½ **1970 (G)** An accident-prone Coast Guard ensign finds himself in charge of the "Times Square" of waterways: Newport Harbor. Adding to his already "titanic" problems is a gang of ocean-going jewel thieves who won't give up the ship! **99m/C VHS, Beta.** Robert Morse, Stefanie Powers, Phil Silvers, Norman Fell, Wally Cox, Don Ameche; *D:* Norman Tokar; *M:* Robert F. Brunner. DIS

Bob & Carol & Ted & Alice ⚉⚉½ **1969 (R)** Two California couples have attended a trendy therapy session and, in an attempt to be more in touch with sexuality, resort to applauding one another's extramarital affairs and swinging. Wacky and well-written, this is a farce on free love and psycho-speak. Mazursky's directorial debut. **104m/C VHS, Beta, LV.** Natalie Wood, Robert Culp, Dyan Cannon, Elliott Gould; *D:* Paul Mazursky; *W:* Paul Mazursky, Larry Tucker; *C:* Charles B(ryant) Lang; *M:* Quincy Jones. New York Film Critics Awards '69: Best Screenplay, Best Supporting Actress (Cannon); National Society of Film Critics Awards '69: Best Screenplay; Writers Guild of America '69: Best Original Screenplay; Nominations: Academy Awards '69: Best Cinematography, Best Story & Screenplay, Best Supporting Actor (Gould), Best Supporting Actress (Cannon). GKK

Bob Dylan: Don't Look Back ⚉⚉⚉ **1991** A famous documentary about Bob Dylan at the beginning of his career: on the road, in performance and during private moments. From the director of "Monterey Pop." **95m/B VHS, Beta, LV.** Bob Dylan, Joan Baez, Donovan; *D:* D.A. Pennebaker. WRV, MVD, PAR

Bob le Flambeur ⚉⚉⚉ *Bob the Gambler* **1955** Wonderful film noir of a compulsive gambler who decides to take a final fling by robbing the casino at Deauville. In French, subtitled in English. **106m/B VHS, Beta, LV.** *FR* Roger Duchesne, Isabel Corey, Daniel Cauchy; *D:* Jean-Pierre Melville. COL, ING, CVC

Bob Roberts ⚉⚉⚉ **1992 (R)** Pseudo-documentary satire about a 1990 Pennsylvania senatorial race between Robbins' right-wing folk singer/entrepreneur versus Vidal's aging liberal incumbent. Roberts seems like a gee-whiz kinda guy but he'll stop at nothing to get elected and he knows a lot about political dirty tricks and, even more important, manipulating the media to get what he wants. Robbins directorial debut turned out to be very timely in view of the 1992 presidential campaign. Features a number of cameos. Line to remember: "Vote first. Ask questions later."*CW:* Momentary language. **105m/C VHS, LV, Closed Caption.** Tim Robbins, Giancarlo Esposito, Ray Wise, Rebecca Jenkins, Harry J. Lennix, John Ottavino, Robert Stanton, Alan Rickman, Gore Vidal, Brian Doyle-Murray, Anita Gillette, David Strathairn; *Cameos:* Susan Sarandon, James Spader, John Cusack, Fred Ward, Pamela Reed; *D:* Tim Robbins; *W:* Tim Robbins; *M:* David Robbins. LIV, BTV

Bobbie Jo and the Outlaw ⚉½ **1976 (R)** Wonderwoman Carter is a bored carhop who yearns to be a country singer. She becomes involved with Marjoe, who fancies himself as a contemporary Billy the Kid. Together, they do their Bonnie and Clyde thing, to a significantly lesser dramatic effect than the original, though a glut of violence keeps the bodies dropping. **89m/C VHS, Beta.** Lynda Carter, Marjoe Gortner, Jesse Vint; *D:* Mark L. Lester. VES, LIV

Bobby Deerfield ⚉⚉ **1977 (PG)** Cold-blooded Grand Prix driver comes face to face with death each time he races, but finally learns the meaning of life when he falls in love with a critically ill woman. Even with race cars, soap opera stalls. **124m/C VHS, Beta.** Al Pacino, Marthe Keller, Anny Duperey, Romolo Valli; *D:* Sydney Pollack; *W:* Alvin Sargent; *C:* Henri Decae; *M:* Dave Grusin. WAR

Bobo ⚉½ **1967** Lousy bullfighter tries to lure a gorgeous woman into romance. Filmed in Spain and Italy. **103m/C VHS, Beta, LV.** *GB* Peter Sellers, Britt Ekland, Rossano Brazzi, Adolfo Celi; *D:* Robert Parrish. WAR, FCT

Boca ⚉⚉ **1994 (R)** American journalist J.J. (Chong) arrives in Rio during Carnival to investigate a story about random killings throughout the Brazilian streets. She gets stonewalled asking questions, until she meets an up-from-poverty crimelord named Boca De Ouro (Meira). Now, our noisy journalist may learn too much to keep her alive. Filmed in Rio de Janiero.*CW:* Strong violence and sexuality; language; some drug content. **92m/C VHS, Closed Caption.** Rae Dawn Chong, Martin Kemp, Tarcizio Meira, Martin Sheen; *D:* Sandra Werneck, Walter Avancini; *W:* Ed Silverstein. REP

Boccaccio '70 ⚉⚉ **1962** Three short bawdy/comedy/pageant-of-life films inspired by "The Decameron," each pertaining to ironically twisted sexual politics in middle class life. A fourth story,

"Renzo and Luciana," by Mario Monicelli, has been cut. Dubbed. **145m/C VHS, Beta.** *IT* Anita Ekberg, Romy Schneider, Tomas Milian, Sophia Loren; **D:** Vittorio De Sica, Luchino Visconti, Federico Fellini; **W:** Federico Fellini; **M:** Nino Rota. *FCT*

Bodies, Rest & Motion 🎬🎬 1993 (R) Stagnant twentysomething movie in which four young people basically do nothing in the sun-baked town of Enfield, Arizona. Similar to the movie "Singles," but without the Seattle grunge scene. The title's reference to Newton is fitting: "A body in rest or motion remains in that state unless acted upon by an outside force." Appealing cast is wasted in listless film that's content to just drift along. Based on the play by Roger Hedden. **CW:** Language and sexuality. **94m/C VHS, LV, Closed Caption.** Phoebe Cates, Bridget Fonda, Tim Roth, Eric Stoltz, Scott Frederick, Scott Johnson, Alicia Witt, Rich Wheeler, Peter Fonda; **D:** Michael Steinberg; **W:** Roger Hedden; **M:** Michael Convertino. *NLC, BTV*

Bodily Harm 🎬🎬 1995 (R) By-the-numbers neo-noir features Fiorentino as Vegas detective Rita Cates, who's investigating the murders of two women with ties to ex-cop Sam McKeon (Baldwin), not incidentally Rita's former lover. She rekindles their lust but then begins to have second thoughts about Sam's innocence. Unconvincing despite the expert cast. **CW:** Scenes of violence, sex and nudity, and for some language. **91m/C VHS.** Linda Fiorentino, Daniel Baldwin, Greg Henry, Bill Smitrovich, Troy Evans, Joe Regalbuto, Millie Perkins, Todd Susman, Shannon Kenny; **D:** James Lemmo; **W:** James Lemmo, Joseph Whaley, Ronda Barendse; **M:** Robert Sprayberry. *AVE*

Body and Soul 🎬🎬 1924 The first screen appearance of Robeson has him cast in a dual role as a conniving preacher and his good brother. The preacher preys on the heroine, making her life a misery. Objections by censors to the preacher's character caused him to be redeemed and become worthy of the heroine's love. **?m/C VHS.** Paul Robeson, Julia Theresa Russell, Mercedes Gilbert; **D:** Oscar Micheaux. *FCT*

Body and Soul 🎬🎬🎬½ *An Affair of the Heart* 1947 A young boxer fights his way unscrupulously to the top. Vintage '40s boxing film that defines the genre. Remade in 1981. **104m/B VHS, LV.** John Garfield, Lilli Palmer, Hazel Brooks, Anne Revere, William Conrad, Canada Lee; **D:** Robert Rossen; **W:** Abraham Polonsky; **C:** James Wong Howe. Academy Awards '47: Best Film Editing; Nominations: Academy Awards '47: Best Actor (Garfield), Best Original Screenplay. *REP*

Body & Soul 🎬🎬½ 1981 (R) Interesting remake of 1947 gem about a boxer who loses his perspective in the world of fame, fast cars, and women. **109m/C VHS, Beta.** Leon Isaac Kennedy, Jayne Kennedy, Peter Lawford, Muhammad Ali, Perry Lang; **D:** George Bowers. *MGM*

Body & Soul 🎬🎬🎬 1993 After spending 16 years as a cloistered nun in a Welsh convent, with vows of poverty, chastity, and obedience, Anna Gibson (Scott Thomas) must return to the outside world. Following her brother's suicide, Anna is forced to deal with his pregnant widow (Redman) and two children and her family's failing Yorkshire mill. Anna suffers a crisis of faith as both the secular and the religious exert their strong influences and she's drawn as well to two very different men—younger Hal (Mavers), the mill's supervisor, and divorced bank manager Daniel Stern (Bowe). Based on the 1991 novel by Marcelle Bernstein; British TV miniseries. **312m/C VHS.** *GB* Kristin Scott Thomas, Amanda Redman, Gary Mavers, Anthony Valentine, Sandra Voe, John Bowe, Dorothy Tutin, Patrick Allen; **D:** Moira Armstrong; **W:** Paul Hines; **C:** Peter Middleton; **M:** Jim Parker. *WMI, VIF*

Body Bags 🎬🎬½ *John Carpenter Presents Body Bags* 1993 (R) Three gory, though humorous, made for cable stories hosted by horrormeister Carpenter as your friendly local coroner. "The Gas Station" finds the young female overnight attendent menaced by a psycho. "Hair" is about a balding yuppie who'll do anything for a full head of

hair. Then he meets the sinister Dr. Lock and his magical new-hair growth treatment. The grisly "Eye" concerns a ballplayer who loses the aforementioned appendage and finds that his transplanted eyeball, taken from an executed serial killer, is subject to ghastly visions. Several fellow horror directors have cameos. **CW:** Horror violence and sexuality. **95m/C VHS, LV, Closed Caption.** Alex Datcher, Robert Carradine, Stacy Keach, David Warner, Mark Hamill, Twiggy, John Agar, Deborah Harry, Sheena Easton, David Naughton, John Carpenter; **Cameos:** Wes Craven, Sam Raimi, Roger Corman, Tobe Hooper; **D:** Tobe Hooper, John Carpenter; **W:** Billy Brown, Dan Angel; **M:** John Carpenter, Jim Lang. *REP*

Body Beat 🎬🎬 1988 (PG) Wild jazz and rock dancers are integrated into a previously classical ballet academy. While the students become fast friends, the teachers break off into two rival factions. **90m/C VHS, Beta.** Tony Fields, Galyn Gorg, Scott Grossman, Eliska Krupka. *THV*

The Body Beneath WOOF! 1970 A living-dead ghoul survives on the blood of innocents and is still preying on victims today. **85m/C VHS, Beta.** Gavin Reed, Jackie Skarvellis, Susan Heard, Colin Gordon; **D:** Andy Milligan. *NO*

Body Chemistry 🎬 1990 (R) A married sexual-behavior researcher starts up a passionate affair with his lab partner. When he tries to end the relationship, his female associate becomes psychotic. You've seen it all before in "Fatal Attraction." And you'll see it again in "Body Chemistry 2." **84m/C VHS, Beta, LV.** Marc Singer, Mary Crosby, Lisa Pescia, Joseph Campanella, David Kagen; **D:** Kristine Peterson; **W:** Jackson Barr, Thom Babbes; **C:** Phedon Papamichael. *COL*

Body Chemistry 2: Voice of a Stranger 🎬½ 1991 (R) An ex-cop (Harrison) obsessed with violent sex gets involved with a talk-radio psychologist (Pescia) whose advice could prove deadly in this erotic sequel. **CW:** Language, violence, and strong sensuality. **84m/C VHS, LV, Closed Caption.** Gregory Harrison, Lisa Pescia, Morton Downey Jr., Robin Riker; **D:** Adam Simon. *COL*

Body Chemistry 3: Point of Seduction 🎬🎬 1993 (R) TV producer Alan Clay (Stevens) finds himself caught in a business and sexual triangle when he okays the making of a movie about the life of a TV sex therapist (Shattuck). Seems the lady's lovers have a nasty habit of getting murdered which doesn't prevent Clay from getting personally involved. His actress wife (Fairchild), who wants to star in the movie, is not pleased. Lives up to its title. **CW:** Nudity and sexual situations. **90m/C VHS, LV.** Andrew Stevens, Morgan Fairchild, Shari Shattuck; **D:** Jim Wynorski. *NHO*

Body Chemistry 4: Full Exposure 🎬½ 1995 (R) When sex psychologist Claire Archer (Tweed) is accused of murder she hires Simon Mitchell (Poindexter), the best criminal defense attorney around. But Simon becomes just a little too closely involved with his possibly psycho client and it could cost him not only his career and marriage but his life. Also available unrated. **CW:** Strong graphic sex scenes, and some violence and language. **89m/C VHS, LV.** Shannon Tweed, Larry Poindexter, Andrew Stevens, Chick Vennera, Larry Manetti, Stella Stevens; **D:** Jim Wynorski; **W:** Karen Kelly; **C:** Zoran Hochstatter. *NHO*

Body Count 🎬½ 1987 A weird and wealthy family will stop at nothing, including murder and cannibalism, to enhance their fortune. Rather than bodies, count the minutes 'til the movie's over. Also titled "The 11th Commandment." **90m/C VHS, Beta.** Marilyn Hassett, Dick Sargent, Steven Ford, Greg Mullavey, Thomas Ryan, Bernie White; **D:** Paul Leder. *MCG*

Body Count 🎬½ 1995 (R) Professional killer Makoto (Chiba) and his female partner (Nielsen) seek revenge on the New Orleans cops who set them up. Opposing them are special crime unit partners, Eddie Cook (Davi) and Vinnie Rizzo (Bauer). Lots of shootouts and macho brava-

do. **CW:** Violence, sexuality and language. **93m/C VHS, LV.** Sonny Chiba, Brigitte Nielsen, Robert Davi, Steven Bauer; **D:** Talun Hsu. *APX*

Body Double 🎬🎬🎬 1984 (R) A voyeuristic unemployed actor peeps on a neighbor's nightly disrobing and sees more than he wants to. A grisly murder leads him into an obsessive quest through the world of pornographic films. **114m/C VHS, Beta, LV, Closed Caption.** Craig Wasson, Melanie Griffith, Greg Henry, Deborah Shelton, Guy Boyd, Dennis Franz, David Haskell, Rebecca Stanley, Barbara Crampton; **D:** Brian DePalma; **W:** Brian DePalma, Robert J. Avrech; **C:** Stephen Burum; **M:** Pino Donaggio. National Society of Film Critics Awards '84: Best Supporting Actress (Griffith). *COL*

Body Heat 🎬🎬🎬½ 1981 (R) During a Florida heat wave, a none-too-bright lawyer becomes involved in a steamy love affair with a mysterious woman and then in a plot to kill her husband. Hurt and Turner (in her film debut) became stars under Kasdan's direction (the three would reunite for "The Accidental Tourist"). Hot love scenes supplement a twisting mystery with a suprise ending. Rourke's arsonist and Danson's soft shoe shouldn't be missed. **113m/C VHS, Beta, LV.** William Hurt, Kathleen Turner, Richard Crenna, Ted Danson, Mickey Rourke; **D:** Lawrence Kasdan; **W:** Lawrence Kasdan; **M:** John Barry. *WAR*

The Body in the Library 🎬½ *Agatha Christie's Miss Marple: The Body In the Library* 1987 A British television-produced Miss Marple mystery, based on Agatha Christie's 1942 novel, involving the septuagenarian detective investigating the murder of a young woman in a wealthy British mansion. **155m/C VHS, Beta, Closed Caption.** *GB* Joan Hickson; **D:** Silvio Narizzano. *FOX, HMV, VCO*

Body Language 🎬🎬 1992 (R) A successful businesswoman, with a man problem, hires a super secretary with answers to all life's questions—and a deadly agenda all her own. **CW:** Violence. **93m/C VHS, Beta, Closed Caption.** Heather Locklear, Linda Purl, Edward Albert, James Acheson; **D:** Arthur Seidelman; **W:** Dan Gurskis, Brian Ross; **C:** Hanania Baer. *PAR*

Body Language 🎬🎬½ 1995 (R) Criminal defense attorney Gavin St. Claire (Berenger) falls for a topless dancer (Schanz), which leads him into all sorts of trouble, including murder. **CW:** Violence, language and strong sexuality. **95m/C VHS, Closed Caption.** Tom Berenger, Heidi Schanz, Nancy Travis; **D:** George Case. *HBO*

Body Melt 🎬🎬½ 1993 When a crazed doctor unleashes an experimental drug on an unsuspecting town, the residents begin to literally melt away. **82m/C VHS, LV.** *AU* Gerard Kennedy, Andrew Daddo, Ian Smith, Vincent Gil, Regina Gaigalas; **D:** Philip Brophy; **W:** Philip Brophy, Rod Bishop; **M:** Philip Brophy. *PSM*

Body Moves 🎬🎬 1990 (PG-13) Romantic entanglements heat up the competition when two couples enter a steamy dance contest. Not apt to move you. **98m/C VHS, Beta.** *IT* Kirk Rivera, Steve Messina, Diana Granger, Linsley Allen, Philip Spruce, Nicole Kolman, Susan Gardner; **D:** Gerry Lively; **W:** Daniel Steel. *PSM*

Body of Evidence WOOF! 1992 (R) Bad movie with pretensions takes "Basic Instinct" a step further. Instead of an ice pick and sex, sex itself is used as the weapon in a murder trial featuring Madonna as the defendant, Dafoe as her lawyer, and Mantegna as the prosecutor. The plot is, of course, secondary to the S&M sex scenes with Dafoe which feature hot wax and broken glass. Madonna's lack of performance is the least of the film's problems since everyone seems to have forgotten any acting talent they possess. Director Edel fails to direct—the film even looks bad. "Body" was the subject of another NC-17 ratings flap but this film shouldn't be seen by anybody. An unrated version is also available. **CW:** Language, violence, and strong sexuality. **99m/C VHS, Beta, LV, Closed Caption.** Madonna, Willem Dafoe, Joe Mantegna, Anne Archer, Michael Forest, Charles Hallahan, Mark Rolston, Richard Riehle, Julianne Moore, Frank Langella, Juergen Prochnow, Stan Shaw; **D:** Uli Edel; **W:**

Brad Mirman; **M:** Graeme Revell. Golden Raspberry Awards '93: Worst Actress (Madonna). *MGM*

Body of Influence ⅏⅏ 1993 (R) A Beverly Hills psychiatrist gets overly involved with a beautiful female patient. But she not only wants his love—she wants his life. Also available in an unrated version.**CW:** Strong language and strong language. 96m/C VHS, Closed Caption. Nick Cassavetes, Shannon Whirry, Sandahl Bergman, Don Swayze, Anna Karin, Catherine Parks, Steve Poletti, Jonathan Goldstein, Pat Brennan; **D:** Andrew Garroni; **W:** David Schreiber. *ACA*

Body of Influence 2 ⅏ 1996 (R) Shrink Dr. Benson (Anderson) finds he's using his couch for more than professional purposes with his latest patient, Leza (Fisher), whose seductive charms prove more than the doc can handle. The unrated version is 94 minutes. **CW:** Strong sexuality, language and some violence. 88m/C VHS. Daniel Anderson, Jodie Fisher, Steve Poletti, Jonathan Goldstein, Pat Brennan; **D:** Brian J. Smith; **W:** Brian J. Smith; **C:** Azusa Ohno; **M:** Ron Sures. *APX*

Body Parts ⅏ 1990 For fans of the demented dismemberer niche. Body Parts, a sleazy skin club, loses some of its star talent when the strippers start turning up in cameo video appearances. Seems there's a psycho killer on the loose who videotapes the dismemberment of his stripper-victims. The police decide they've got to meet this guy when he sends them a sample of his work. 90m/C VHS, LV. Teri Lee, Dick Monda, Johnny Mandel. *NO*

Body Parts ⅏⅏ 1991 (R) A crime psychologist loses his arm in an auto accident and receives a transplant from an executed murderer. Does the limb have an evil will of its own? Poorly paced horror goes off the deep end in gore with its third act. Based on the novel "Choice Cuts" by French writers Pierre Boileau and Thomas Narcejac, whose work inspired some of the greatest suspense films.**CW:** Language, violence and gore, and sensual scene. 88m/C VHS, Beta, LV, Closed Caption. Jeff Fahey, Kim Delaney, Lindsay Duncan, Peter Murnik, Brad Dourif, Zakes Mokae, Johnny Walsh, Gregg Benevictor; **D:** Eric Red; **W:** Eric Red, Norman Snider, Larry Gross; **M:** Loek Dikker. *PAR*

Body Rock woof! 1984 (PG-13) Brooklyn breakdancer Lamas deserts his buddies to work at a chic Manhattan nightclub. Watching Lamas as the emcee/breakdancing fool is a hoot. ♫Body Rock; Team Work; Why Do You Want to Break My Heart?; One Thing Leads to Another; Let Your Body Rock; Vanishing Point; Sharpshooter; The Jungle; Deliver. 93m/C VHS, Beta. Lorenzo Lamas, Vicki Frederick, Cameron Dye, Michelle Nicastro, Ray Sharkey, Grace Zabriskie, Carole Ita White; **D:** Marcelo Epstein. *NO*

The Body Shop woof! *Doctor Gore* 1972 Unorthodox love story in which a man decides to patch up his relationship with his dead wife by piecing together her dismembered body. For lovers only. Under "Doctor Gore" title the film includes an intro by horror director Herschell Gordon Lewis. 91m/C VHS. Pat Patterson, Jenny Driggers, Roy Mehaffey, Linda Faile, Candy Furr; **D:** Pat Patterson. *NO*

Body Shot ⅏⅏½ 1993 (R) Celebrity shutterbug Mickey Dane (Patrick) is fingered in the murder of a rock star after it turns out he did a kinky layout for a look-alike. When police find out he had an obsession for the dead woman, he employs his photographic expertise in the search for the real killer. Effective tension-builder with fast-paced chases through the seamy side of Los Angeles.**CW:** Language and nudity. 98m/C VHS, LV. Robert Patrick, Michelle Johnson, Ray Wise, Jonathan Banks, Kim Miyori; **D:** Dimitri Logothetis; **W:** Robert Strauss; **C:** Nicholas Von Sternberg. *TRI*

Body Slam ⅏½ 1987 (PG) A small-time talent monger hits it big with a rock and roll/ professional wrestling tour. Piper's debut; contains some violence and strong language. 100m/C VHS, Beta. Roddy Piper, Captain Lou Albano, Dirk Benedict, Tan-

ya Roberts, Billy Barty, Charles Nelson Reilly, John Astin, Wild Samoan, Tonga Kid, Barry Gordon; **D:** Hal Needham; **W:** Steven H. Burkow; **M:** John D'Andrea. *NLC*

The Body Snatcher ⅏⅏⅏½ 1945 Based on Robert Louis Stevenson's story about a grave robber who supplies corpses to research scientists. Set in Edinburgh in the 19th century, this Lewton production is superior. One of Karloff's best vehicles. 77m/B VHS, Beta, LV. Edith Atwater, Russell Wade, Rita (Paula) Corday, Boris Karloff, Bela Lugosi, Henry Daniell; **D:** Robert Wise. *MED, TTC*

Body Snatcher from Hell ⅏½ *Goke, Body Snatcher from Hell; Goke the Vampire; Kyuketsuki Gokemidoro* 1969 An airliner passes through a mysterious cloud and crashes in a desert. One by one, the passengers are turned into vampires. Some interesting special effects. 84m/C VHS. JP Hideo Ko, Teruo Yoshida, Tomomi Sato, Eizo Kitamura, Masay Takahashi, Cathy Horlan, Kazuo Kato, Yuko Kusunoki; **D:** Hajime Sato. *SNC*

Body Snatchers ⅏⅏ 1993 (R) Yet another version of "Invasion of the Body Snatchers." An innocent family arrive at an Army base which turns out to be infested with pod people. This time around the heroine is angst-ridden teenager Marti (Anwar) and the pods have something to do with a mysterious toxic spill. The 1978 remake was well done; this so-so version takes advantage of the advances in special effects (particularly in Anwar's bathtub scene) and sound technology but is slow-paced with few jolts of terror.**CW:** Nudity and violence. 87m/C VHS, LV, Closed Caption. Gabrielle Anwar, Meg Tilly, Terry Kinney, Forest Whitaker, Billy Wirth, R. Lee Ermey; **D:** Abel Ferrara; **W:** Stuart Gordon, Dennis Paoli, Nicholas St. John; **C:** Bojan Bazelli; **M:** Joe Delia. *WAR*

Body Strokes ⅏ 1995 Blocked artist Leo Kessler (Johnston) is aroused by the wild fantasies of his beautiful models Beth (Knittle) and Claire (Weber). But it's just fantasy and it also helps get Leo's marriage back on track when manager/wife Karen (Beck) gets jealous. Also available unrated. 99m/C VHS. Bobby Johnston, Dixie Beck, Kristen Knittle, Catherine Weber; **D:** Edward Holzman; **M:** Richard Bronskill. *APX*

Body Trouble ⅏½ *Joker's Wild* 1992 (R) After being attacked by sharks while vacationing in the Caribbean, a man washes ashore in Miami and then somehow makes his way to New York City. There he meets Vera Vin Rouge and her friends Cinnamon, Spice, Paprika, and Johnny Zero, a gangster. Zero decides he doesn't like the man, so he chases him back to the Caribbean. Supposedly this all happens in only one day. Hmmm...**CW:** Language and sexuality. 98m/C VHS. Dick Van Patten, Priscilla Barnes, Frank Gorshin, James Hong, Marty Rackham, Michael Unger, Jonathan Soloman, Brit Helfer, Leigh Clark, Patricia Cardell, Richie Barathy; **D:** Bill Milling; **W:** Bill Milling. *TRI*

The Body Vanished ⅏⅏ 1939 Murder mystery featuring a corpse that disappears from the scene of the crime. ?m/C VHS. *GB* Lewis Wilson, Frances Dubay, Dana Wilson. *SNC*

Body Waves ⅏½ 1992 (R) Beach comedy starring Calvert as a teenager who bets his father that he can raise money on his own. In typical teen movie fashion, he invents a sex cream that drives boys and girls wild. Brain candy featuring lots of skimpy bikinis.**CW:** Language, drug content, and sensuality. 80m/C VHS, Closed Caption. Bill Calvert, Leah Lail, Larry Linville, Dick Miller, Jim Wise; **D:** P.J. Pesce. *NHO*

The Bodyguard ⅏½ 1976 (R) The Yakuza, Japan's mafia, and New York's big crime families face off in this martial arts extravaganza. 89m/ C VHS, Beta. Sonny Chiba, Aaron Banks, Bill Louie, Judy Lee; **D:** Maurice Sarli. *MED*

The Bodyguard ⅏⅏ 1992 (R) Buttoned-down, ex-Secret Service agent turned private bodyguard reluctantly takes on a wildly successful singer/actress as a client. Houston, in her acting debut as the over-indulged diva, doesn't have to stretch too far but acquits herself well. Costner

has really bad hair day but easily portrays the tightly wound Frank. Critically trashed, a box office smash, and too long. Originally scripted by producer Kasdan over a decade ago, with Steve McQueen in mind. Predictable romantic melodrama is kept moving by the occasional sharp dialog and a few action pieces. Songs include the smash hit "I Will Always Love You," written and originally performed by Dolly Parton.**CW:** Language and violence. 130m/C VHS, LV, Closed Caption, DVD. Kevin Costner, Whitney Houston, Gary Kemp, Bill Cobbs, Ralph Waite, Tomas Arana, Michele Lamar Richards, Mike Starr, Christopher Birt, DeVaughn Nixon, Charles Keating, Robert Wuhl; **Cameos:** Debbie Reynolds; **D:** Mick Jackson; **W:** Lawrence Kasdan; **M:** Alan Silvestri. MTV Movie Awards '93: Best Song ("I Will Always Love You"); Nominations: Academy Awards '92: Best Song ("I Have Nothing"), Best Song ("Run to You"). *WAR, BTV*

Boeing Boeing ⅏⅏½ 1965 A dated but still amusing sex farce about a bachelor newspaperman (Curtis) in Paris, his three stewardess girlfriends, and the elaborate plots he resorts to in trying to keep them from finding out about each other. When the new Boeing jet makes air travel faster all Curtis' schemes may come crashing down. Ritter is fun as the exasperated housekeeper and Lewis amazingly subdued as Curtis' business rival. 102m/C VHS, LV, Closed Caption. Tony Curtis, Jerry Lewis, Dany Saval, Christianne Schmidtner, Suzanna Leigh, Thelma Ritter; **D:** John Rich; **W:** Edward Anhalt. *PAR*

Bog ⅏ 1984 (PG) Boggy beast from the Arctic north awakens to eat people. Scientists mount an anti-monster offensive. 90m/C VHS, Beta. Gloria De Haven, Marshall Thompson, Leo Gordon, Aldo Ray. *PSM*

Boggy Creek II ⅏½ *The Barbaric Beast of Boggy Creek, Part II* 1983 (PG) The continuing saga of the eight-foot-tall, 300 pound monster from Texarkana. Third in a series of low-budget movies including "The Legend of Boggy Creek" and "Return to Boggy Creek." 93m/C VHS, Beta, LV. Charles B. Pierce, Cindy Butler, Serene Hedin; **D:** Charles B. Pierce; **W:** Charles B. Pierce. *MED*

Bogie: The Last Hero 1980 Television biography of Humphrey Bogart, populated by almost-lookalikes who can almost act. 100m/C VHS, Beta. Kevin J. O'Connor, Kathryn Harrold, Ann Wedgeworth, Patricia Barry, Alfred Ryder, Donald May, Richard Dysart, Arthur Franz; **D:** Vincent Sherman; **M:** Charles Bernstein. *FRH*

Bogus ⅏⅏ 1996 (PG) Aptly-named fantasy-comedy has orphan Albert (Osment) sent to foster aunt Harriet (Goldberg) after his magician's assistant mom (Travis) dies in a car accident. He brings along an imaginary friend, the eponymous Bogus (Depardieu) to ease the transition. Harriet is your typical workaholic easterner and isn't too thrilled with the arrangement. Goldberg and Depardieu are fine, but predictability drains most of the magic. 112m/C VHS, LV, Closed Caption. Whoopi Goldberg, Gerard Depardieu, Haley Joel Osment, Nancy Travis, Andrea Martin, Denis Mercier, Ute Lemper, Sheryl Lee Ralph, Al Waxman, Fiona Reid, Don Francks; **D:** Norman Jewison; **W:** Alvin Sargent; **C:** David Watkin; **M:** Marc Shaiman. Nominations: Golden Raspberry Awards '96: Worst Actress (Goldberg). *WAR*

Bohemian Girl ⅏⅏⅏ 1936 The last of Laurel and Hardy's comic operettas finds them as guardians of a young orphan (Hood, famous for her roles in the Our Gang comedies), whom no one realizes is actually a kidnapped princess. 74m/B VHS, Beta. Stan Laurel, Oliver Hardy, Mae Busch, Darla Hood, Jacqueline Wells, Thelma Todd, James Finlayson; **D:** James W. Horne. *MED, CCB*

Boiling Point ⅏½ 1932 Lawman proves once again that justice always triumphs. 67m/B VHS, Beta. Hoot Gibson. *NOS, VCI, DVT*

Boiling Point ⅏⅏½ 1993 (R) Darkly-flavored action drama delves into the personalities of its two main characters before setting up a final confrontation. Treasury agent Jimmy Mercer (Snipes) is trying to solve his partner's murder, relentlessly pursuing the murderers in cold and methodical fashion. Sleazy Red Diamond (Hopper), just out of prison, owes the mob and has one week to pay them back. Lawman and crook both come home to women, (Davidovich and Perrine) graduates of the Hollywood school of female martyrdom, selflessly supportive of their men. Grim but cliched. Adapted from the Gerald Petievich novel "Money Men." *CW:* Language and violence. **93m/C VHS, Beta, LV.** Wesley Snipes, Dennis Hopper, Lolita Davidovich, Viggo Mortensen, Dan Hedaya, Valerie Perrine, Seymour Cassel, Jonathan Banks, Tony LoBianco, Christine Elise, James Tolkan, Paul Gleason; *D:* James B. Harris; *W:* James B. Harris; *M:* Cory Lerios, John D'Andrea. WAR

The Bold Caballero ✶✶½ *The Bold Cavalier* 1936 Rebel chieftain Zorro overthrows oppressive Spanish rule in the days of early California. **69m/B VHS, Beta.** Bob Livingston, Heather Angel, Sig Rumann, Robert Warwick; *D:* Wells Root. NOS, VDM, VCN

The Boldest Job in the West ✶ *El Mas Fabulosi Golpe del Far West* 1971 Italian western about bankrobbers who meet to divide their spoils. Problem is, the guys with the loot don't show. Dubbed in English. **200m/C VHS, Beta.** IT Frank Edwards, Frank Sancho, Carmen Sevilla; *D:* Joseph Loman. NO

Bolero ✶✶½ 1982 Beginning in 1936, this international epic traces the lives of four families across three continents and five decades, highlighting the music and dance that is central to their lives. **173m/C VHS, Beta.** James Caan, Geraldine Chaplin, Robert Hossein, Nicole Garcia, Jacques Villeret; *D:* Claude Lelouch; *W:* Claude Lelouch. VES

Bolero woof! *Bolero: An Adventure in Ecstasy* 1984 (R) What sounds like a wet dream come true is really just a good snooze: Bo Derek plays a beautiful young woman who goes on a trip around the world in hopes of losing her virginity; in Spain, she meets a bullfighter who's willing to oblige. Too bad Bo cannot act as good as she looks. **106m/C VHS, Beta.** Bo Derek, George Kennedy, Andrea Occhipinti, Anna Obregon, Olivia D'Abo; *D:* John Derek; *W:* John Derek; *M:* Peter Bernstein, Elmer Bernstein. Golden Raspberry Awards '84: Worst Picture, Worst Actress (Derek), Worst Director (Derek), Worst Screenplay, Worst New Star (D'Abo). LIV

Bomb at 10:10 ✶✶ 1967 An American pilot escapes from a German POW camp and plots to assassinate a camp commandant. **87m/C VHS, Beta.** George Montgomery, Rada Popovic, Peter Banicevic; *D:* Charles Damic. GEM

Bombardier ✶✶½ 1943 A group of cadet bombardiers discover the realities of war on raids over Japan during WWII. Also available colorized. **99m/B VHS, Beta.** Pat O'Brien, Randolph Scott, Robert Ryan, Eddie Albert, Anne Shirley, Barton MacLane; *D:* Richard Wallace. TTC

Bombay Talkie ✶✶½ 1970 (PG) A bored British writer (Kendal) heads to India to gather "experiences" and becomes involved with an Indian movie actor (Kapoor). Early clash-of-cultures film from Merchant Ivory has it's dull spots; the behind-the-scenes look at the Indian film industry is more interesting than the romance. **110m/C VHS, Beta.** IN Jennifer Kendal, Shashi Kapoor, Zia Mohyeddin, Aparna Sen; *D:* James Ivory; *W:* Ruth Prawer Jhabvala. NLC

Bombs Away! ✶ 1986 An atomic bomb is mistakenly shipped to a seedy war surplus store in Seattle, and causes much chicanery. **90m/C VHS, Beta.** Michael Huddleston, Pat McCormick; *D:* Bruce Wilson. COL, NLC

Bombshell ✶✶✶ *Blonde Bombshell* 1933 Wry insightful comedy into the Hollywood of the 1930s. Harlow plays a naive young actress manipulated by her adoring press agent. He thwarts her plans until she finally notices and begins to fall in love with him. Brilliant satire with Harlow turning in perhaps the best performance of her short career. **96m/B VHS, Beta.** Jean Harlow, Lee Tracy, Pat O'Brien, Una Merkel, Sir C. Aubrey Smith, Franchot Tone; *D:* Victor Fleming. MGM, BTV, FCT

Bon Voyage! ✶✶½ 1962 A family's long-awaited European "dream" vacation turns into a series of comic misadventures in this very Disney, very family, very predictable comedy. **131m/C VHS, Beta, LV.** Fred MacMurray, Jane Wyman, Deborah Walley, Michael Callan, Tommy Kirk, Jessie Royce Landis; *D:* James Neilson. Nominations: Academy Awards '62: Best Costume Design (Color), Best Sound. DIS

Bon Voyage, Charlie Brown ✶✶✶ 1980 (G) The "Peanuts" comic strip group becomes exchange students in Europe, led by Charlie Brown, Linus, Peppermint Patty, Marcie, and the irrepressible beagle, Snoopy. **76m/C VHS, Beta, LV.** *D:* Bill Melendez, Lee Mendelson; *W:* Charles M. Schulz; *M:* Ed Bogas; *V:* Arrin Skelley, Laura Planting, Casey Carlson, David Anderson, Annalisa Bartolin, Scott Beads. PAR

Bonanza 1964 This western series about the Cartwright clan and their Ponderosa ranch ran on TV from 1959-1973, second only to "Gunsmoke." Additional episodes available. In "The Pure Truth" Hoss escapes from jail after being unjustly accused of robbing the bank. An eccentric recluse comes to his aid. **50m/C VHS.** Lorne Greene, Pernell Roberts, Dan Blocker, Michael Landon, Glenda Farrell. REP, MOV

Bonanza: The Return ✶½ 1993 (PG) In 1905, the children of various members of the Cartwright clan work to see the Ponderosa is safe from an unscrupulous businessman. Lame update of the classic family western series. Made for television. **96m/C VHS, LV, Closed Caption.** Michael Landon Jr., Dirk Blocker, Emily Warfield, Alistair MacDougall, Brian Leckner, Dean Stockwell, Ben Johnson, Richard Roundtree, Linda Gray, Jack Elam. THV

Bonanza Town ✶½ 1951 Steve Ramsey (Starrett), aka The Durango Kid, and sidekick Smiley (Burnette) are hired to locate the loot stolen in a Dodge City hold-up. Marked money leads our heroes to Bonanza Town, where the Kid tracks down outlaws and corrupt officials. **56m/B VHS.** Charles Starrett, Smiley Burnette, Myron Healey, Fred F. Sears; *D:* Fred F. Sears; *C:* Henry Freulich. COL

The Bone Yard ✶ 1990 (R) A weird mortuary is the setting for strange goings on when a murder is investigated. **98m/C VHS, Beta.** Ed Nelson, Deborah Rose, Norman Fell, Jim Eustermann, Denise Young, Willie Stratford Jr., Phyllis Diller; *D:* James Cummins; *W:* James Cummins. PSM

The Bonfire of the Vanities ✶✶½ 1990 (R) If you liked Tom Wolfe's viciously satirical novel, chances are you won't like this version. If you didn't read the book, you probably still won't like it. Miscast and stripped of the book's gutsy look inside its characters, the film's sole attribute is Vilmos Zsigmond's photography. Hanks is all wrong as wealthy Wall Street trader Sherman McCoy who, lost in the back streets of the Bronx, panics and accidentally kills a young black kid. Willis' drunken journalist/narrator, Griffith's mistress, and Freeman's righteous judge are all awkward and thinly written. If you're still awake, look for F. Murray Abraham's cameo as the Bronx D.A. *CW:* Language. **126m/C VHS, Beta, LV, 8mm, Closed Caption.** Tom Hanks, Melanie Griffith, Bruce Willis, Morgan Freeman, Alan King, Kim Cattrall, Saul Rubinek, Clifton James, Donald Moffat, Richard Libertini, Andre Gregory, Robert Stephens; *Cameos:* F. Murray Abraham; *D:* Brian DePalma; *W:* Michael Cristofer; *C:* Vilmos Zsigmond; *M:* Dave Grusin. WAR, FCT

Bonjour Tristesse ✶✶✶ 1957 An amoral French girl conspires to break up her playboy father's upcoming marriage to her stuffy godmother in order to maintain her decadent freedom. Preminger attempted, unsuccessfully, to use this soaper to catapult Seberg to stardom. Based on the novel by Francoise Sagan. **94m/C VHS, Beta.** FR Deborah Kerr, David Niven, Jean Seberg, Mylene Demongeot, Geoffrey Horne, Walter Chiari, Jean Kent; *D:* Otto Preminger; *W:* Arthur Laurents; *C:* Georges Perinal. COL

Bonnie & Clyde ✶✶✶½ 1967 Based on the biographies of the violent careers of Bonnie Parker and Clyde Barrow, who roamed the Southwest robbing banks. In the Depression era, when any job, even an illegal one, was cherished, money, greed, and power created an unending cycle of violence and fury. Highly controversial and influential, with pronounced bloodshed that spurred mainstream cinematic proliferation. Established Dunaway as a star; produced by Beatty in one of his best performances. **111m/C VHS, Beta, LV, Closed Caption, DVD.** Warren Beatty, Faye Dunaway, Michael J. Pollard, Gene Hackman, Estelle Parsons, Denver Pyle, Gene Wilder, Dub Taylor; *D:* Arthur Penn; *W:* David Newman, Robert Benton; *C:* Burnett Guffey. Academy Awards '67: Best Cinematography, Best Supporting Actress (Parsons); New York Film Critics Awards '67: Best Screenplay; National Society of Film Critics Awards '67: Best Screenplay, Best Supporting Actor (Hackman); Writers Guild of America '67: Best Original Screenplay; Nominations: Academy Awards '67: Best Actor (Beatty), Best Actress (Dunaway), Best Costume Design, Best Director (Penn), Best Picture, Best Story & Screenplay, Best Supporting Actor (Hackman, Pollard). WAR, BTV

Bonnie Prince Charlie ✶✶½ 1948 Historical epic opening in 1745 and romanticizing the title pretender to the British throne, who united Scottish clans in a doomed campaign against King George. Talky and rather slow-moving except for stirring battle scenes. A notorious box-office flop in its native Britain, where the original running time was 140 minutes. **114m/C VHS, Closed Caption.** GB David Niven, Margaret Leighton, Judy Campbell, Jack Hawkins, Morland Graham, Finlay Currie, Elwyn Brook-Jones, John Laurie; *D:* Anthony Kimmins. NOS, REP

Bonnie Scotland ✶✶½ 1935 Laurel & Hardy accidentally join an India-bound Scottish regiment. Laughs aplenty. **81m/B VHS, Beta.** Stan Laurel, Oliver Hardy, James Finlayson, Daphne Pollard, June Lang; *D:* James W. Horne. MGM, MLB

Bonnie's Kids ✶½ 1973 (R) Two sisters become involved in murder, sex, and stolen money. **107m/C VHS, Beta.** Tiffany Bolling, Robin Mattson, Scott Brady, Alex Rocco; *D:* Arthur Marks. NO

The Boogey Man ✶✶ 1980 (R) Through the reflection in a mirror, a girl witnesses her brother murder their mother's lover. Twenty years later this memory still haunts her; the mirror is now broken, revealing its special powers. Who will be next? Murder menagerie; see footage from this flick mirrored in "The Boogey Man 2." **93m/C VHS, Beta, LV.** John Carradine, Suzanna Love, Ron James; *D:* Ulli Lommel. HHE

Boogey Man 2 woof! 1983 The story continues; same footage, new director but with Lommel, the director of the original "Boogey Man," co-writing the script and appearing in the film. **90m/C VHS, Beta.** John Carradine, Suzanna Love, Shannah Hall, Ulli Lommel, Sholto Von Douglas; *D:* Bruce Starr. VHE

Book of Love ✶✶ 1991 (PG-13) "Zany" hijinks as a teenager struggles with friendship, girls, and those all-important hormones when he moves to a new neighborhood in the mid-50's. Average rehash of every 50's movie and TV show cliche in existence. Surprise! There's a classic rock 'n' roll soundtrack. Adapted by Kotzwinkle from his novel "Jack in the Box." **88m/C VHS, LV, 8mm, Closed Caption.** Chris Young, Keith Coogan, Aeryk Egan, Josie Bissett, Tricia Leigh Fisher, Danny Nucci, Michael McKean, John Cameron Mitchell, Lewis Arquette; *D:* Robert Shaye; *W:* William Kotzwinkle; *M:* Stanley Clarke. COL

Boom in the Moon woof! *A Modern Bluebeard* 1946 Keaton fares poorly in this sci-fi comedy. He's trapped on a space ship to the moon. Poor production, with uneven direction and acting. **83m/C VHS.** Buster Keaton, Angel Garasa, Virginia Serret, Fernando Soto, Luis Barreiro; *D:* Jaime Salvador. NO

Boom Town ✶✶½ 1940 A lively vintage comedy/drama/romance about two oil-drilling buddies competing amid romantic mix-ups and fortunes gained and lost. **120m/B VHS, Beta, Closed**

Caption. Clark Gable, Spencer Tracy, Claudette Colbert, Hedy Lamarr, Frank Morgan, Lionel Atwill, Chill Wills, Curt Bois; *D:* Jack Conway. Nominations: Academy Awards '40: Best Black and White Cinematography.*MGM, CCB*

Boomerang 🐾🐾🐾 **1947** Film noir based on actual events features the murder of a Connecticut clergyman and the quick arrest of vagrant John Waldron (Kennedy). Prosecuting attorney Henry Harvey (Andrews) is told by his political bosses to get an equally quick conviction to stem public outrage. The evidence seems overwhelming but Harvey begins his own investigation and suddenly switches to the defense to prove Waldron's innocence in dramatic courtroom style. Kazan filmed on location in Bridgeport, CT in a successful semi-documentary style that heightened the tension. **88m/B VHS, Closed Caption.** Dana Andrews, Arthur Kennedy, Lee J. Cobb, Jane Wyatt, Cara Williams, Sam Levene, Ed Begley Sr., Karl Malden, Taylor Holmes, Robert Keith; *D:* Elia Kazan; *W:* Richard Murphy; *C:* Norbert Brodine; *M:* David Buttolph. Nominations: Academy Awards '47: Best Screenplay. *FXV*

Boomerang 🐾½ **1976** A father rescues his wrongly convicted son from prison. Dubbed. **101m/C VHS, Beta, Closed Caption.** *IT* Alain Delon, Carla Gravina, Dora Doll; *D:* Jose Giovanni. *UNI*

Boomerang 🐾🐾 **1992 (R)** Successful, womanizing marketing exec (Murphy) meets his match when he falls for a colleague (Givens) who is as vain and sexually predatory as he is. She treats him the way he treats women (as a sex object), and he's shocked into the arms of a nice girl (Berry). Although it's refreshing to see this sexual role reversal, the typical Murphy-style humor is in play with sexist jokes and a couple of vulgar female characters. Grier and Lawrence are great as Murphy's best friends. Blaustein and Sheffield are the same guys who wrote Murphy's "Coming to America."*CW:* Language and sexuality. **118m/C VHS, Beta, LV, Closed Caption.** Eddie Murphy, Halle Berry, Robin Givens, David Alan Grier, Martin Lawrence, Grace Jones, Geoffrey Holder, Eartha Kitt, Chris Rock, Tisha Campbell, John Witherspoon, Melvin Van Peebles; *D:* Reginald Hudlin; *W:* Barry W. Blaustein, David Sheffield. *PAR*

The Boost 🐾½ **1988 (R)** A feverish, messy melodrama about a young couple's spiraling decline from yuppie-ish wealth in a haze of cocaine abuse. **95m/C VHS, Beta, LV.** James Woods, Sean Young, John Kapelos, Steven Hill, Kelle Kerr, John Rothman, Amanda Blake, Grace Zabriskie; *D:* Harold Becker; *W:* Darryl Ponicsan; *C:* Howard Atherton. *HBO*

Boot Hill 🐾½ **1969 (PG)** Two guys mess with western baddies and wild women in spaghetti oater. **97m/C VHS, Beta.** *IT* Terence Hill, Bud Spencer, Woody Strode, Victor Buono, Lionel Stander; *D:* Giuseppe Colizzi. *NO*

Boot Hill Bandits 🐾🐾½ **1942** "Crash" Corrigan fights on the side of right in this classic western as he helps corral Wells Fargo bandits. **58m/B VHS.** Ray Corrigan, John "Dusty" King, Max Terhune, Jean Brooks, John Merton, Glenn Strange; *D:* S. Roy Luby. *NOS, HEG*

Boothill Brigade 🐾🐾 **1937** Former football player Brown rides to the rescue when criminals steal land from homesteaders. **58m/B VHS.** Johnny Mack Brown, Claire Rochelle, Dick Curtis, Horace Murphy, Frank LaRue, Edward Cassidy, Bobby Nelson, Frank Ball, Steve Clark; *D:* Sam Newfield. *NOS, MRV*

Bootleg 🐾🐾 **1989** A detective is on a case that leads to crooked politics and espionage. **82m/C VHS.** Ray Meagher; *D:* John Prescott. *AIP*

Boots & Saddles 🐾½ **1937** A young English lord wants to sell the ranch he has inherited but Autry is determined to make him a real Westerner. **54m/B VHS, Beta.** Gene Autry, Judith Allen, Smiley Burnette; *D:* Joseph Kane. *NOS, MRV, VYY*

Boots Malone 🐾🐾½ **1952** An old down-on-his-luck gambling addict and a young, rich kid fascinated by the sordid atmosphere of the racetrack stumble upon one another and form a symbiotic relationship. All goes well for while, but

there'd be no movie unless a collection of obstacles suddenly threatens their success, friendship, and even their lives. A rather melodramatic buddy tale, but Holden and Stewart hold interest. **103m/C VHS.** William Holden, John Stewart, Ed Begley Sr., Harry (Henry) Morgan, Whit Bissell; *D:* William Dieterle; *M:* Elmer Bernstein. *GKK*

Boots of Destiny 🐾 **1937** Cheap western with Maynard and his sidekick Barnett on the lam and coming to the aid of ranch owner Dell. Based on a story by E. Morton Hough. **59m/B VHS.** Ken Maynard, Claudia Dell, Vince Barnett, Edward Cassidy, Martin Garralaga; *D:* Arthur Rosson; *W:* Arthur Rosson. *MOV*

Booty Call 🐾🐾½ **1996 (R)** Reserved Rushon (Davidson) and conservative Nikki (Jones) have been dating for a couple of months and Rushon's decided they should consummate their relationship. Nikki's more ambivalent and first sets up a double date with her vivacious best friend Lysterine (Fox) and Rushon's bragging buddy Bunz (Foxx). The duos do pair up but since the "no glove, no love" rule prevails, first the guys have to find some condoms. Raunch rules as might be expected but it's an appealing cast.*CW:* Non-stop sexuality including sex-related dialogue and humor, and for strong language. **120m/C VHS, LV, Closed Caption.** Jamie Foxx, Tommy Davidson, Vivica A. Fox, Tamala Jones, Art Malik, Gedde Watanabe, Scott LaRose, Ammie Sin, Bernie Mac, David Hemblen; *D:* Jeff Pollack; *W:* Takashi Bufford; *C:* Ronald Orieux; *M:* Robert Folk. *COL*

Bopha! 🐾🐾🐾 **1993 (PG-13)** Father-son strife set against the anti-apartheid movement. In the Senior township police officer Mikah takes pride in his peaceful community, particularly in light of the growing unrest in the other townships. Son Zweli has become an activist and wife Rosie must be the family peacemaker. Then a prominent freedom movement member is arrested and two officers of the secret police make their sinister appearance. Well-acted; directorial debut of Freeman. Adapted from the play by Percy Mtwa, although the hopeful ending has been changed in the movie. The title, a Zulu word, stands for arrest or detention. Filmed on location in Zimbabwe. **121m/C VHS, Beta, LV, Closed Caption.** Danny Glover, Maynard Eziashi, Alfre Woodard, Malcolm McDowell, Marius Weyers, Malick Bowens, Robin Smith, Michael Chinyamurindi, Christopher John Hall, Grace Mahlaba; *D:* Morgan Freeman; *W:* Brian Bird, John Wierick; *M:* James Horner. *PAR*

Bordello 🐾 **1979** A made-for-television western spoof about cowboys and shady ladies. **90m/C VHS, Beta.** Chuck Connors, Michael Conrad, John Ireland, Isela Vega, George Rivero. *PSM*

The Border 🐾🐾🐾 **1982 (R)** A border guard faces corruption and violence within his department and tests his own sense of decency when the infant of a poor Mexican girl is kidnapped. Excellent cast, fine cinematography, unusual Nicholson performance. **107m/C VHS, Beta, LV.** Jack Nicholson, Harvey Keitel, Valerie Perrine, Warren Oates, Elpidia Carrillo; *D:* Tony Richardson; *W:* Deric Washburn, Walon Green; *M:* Ry Cooder. *USH*

Border Badmen 🐾½ **1945** It's just another tired old western, even if it does appropriate the classic mystery-thriller plot; following the reading of a silver baron's will, someone starts killing off the relatives. **59m/B VHS, Beta.** Buster Crabbe, Lorraine Miller, Charles "Blackie" King, Ray Bennett, Archie Hall, Budd Buster, Bud Osborne; *D:* Sam Newfield. *GPV, MRV*

Border Bandits 🐾 **1946** Plodding oater has Brown going after the bad guys. Not only is it a dirty job, but apparently pretty boring. **57m/B VHS.** Johnny Mack Brown, Raymond Hatton, John Merton, Frank LaRue, Steve Clark, Charles Stevens, Bud Osborne; *D:* Lambert Hillyer. *DVT, HEG*

Border Caballero 🐾½ **1936** Western star McCoy and lady cowpoke January shoot out the skies in this lackluster McCoy vehicle. Based on a story by Norman S. Hall. **57m/B VHS.** Tim McCoy, Lois

January, Ralph Byrd, Ted Adams; *D:* Sam Newfield; *W:* Joseph O'Donnell. *MOV*

Border Devils 🐾 **1932** A boy is pursued by a ruthless gang of outlaws, until he is saved by the good guys. **60m/B VHS, Beta, LV.** Harry Carey Sr., Art Mix, George "Gabby" Hayes; *D:* William Nigh. *NO*

Border Feud 🐾 **1947** LaRue endeavors to prevent someone who, by instigating a family feud, will claim large gold mine rights. **54m/B VHS, Beta.** Lash LaRue, Al "Fuzzy" St. John, Bob Duncan; *D:* Ray Taylor. *COL*

Border Law 🐾🐾½ **1931** Jones plays a heroic Texas Ranger who goes undercover to find the man who killed his brother. One of Jones' finest outings and far better than most B westerns. **62m/B VHS.** Buck Jones, Lupita Tovar, James Mason, Frank Rice, Glenn Strange; *D:* Louis King; *W:* Stuart Anthony. *MOV, GVV*

The Border Legion 🐾½ **1940** Sappy retelling of Grey's novel about an outlaw sacrificing himself for a pair of young lovers. This time Rogers is the outlaw with a heart of gold. Originally filmed in 1930 with Jack Holt, Richard Arlen, and Fay Wray. **58m/B VHS.** Roy Rogers, George "Gabby" Hayes, Carol Hughes, Joseph Sawyer, Maude Eburne, Jay Novello; *D:* Joseph Kane; *W:* Olive Cooper, Louis Stevens. *MOV*

Border Patrol 🐾🐾 **1943** Another installment in the Hopalong Cassidy series. This time there's a villainous owner of a silvermine to reckon with. A man so low he's abducting hapless Mexicans as they cross the border, forcing them to work his mines. Hoppy is saddled with the task of persuading him that the town ain't big enough for the both of them. Robert Mitchum makes his perfectly-forgettable film debut as one of the bad guys. Not one of the best in the series, but plenty of action. **63m/B VHS.** William Boyd, Andy Clyde, Jay Kirby, Russell Simpson, Claudia Drake, George Reeves, Duncan Renaldo; *D:* Lesley Selander. *NOS*

Border Phantom 🐾🐾 **1937** Steele (whom you might recognize as Canino in "The Big Sleep"), takes on a suave Chinese businessman who heads a mail order business: seems he's smuggling mail-order brides from Mexico in this vintage "B"-grade horse opera. **60m/B VHS.** Bob Steele, Harley Wood, Don Barclay, Karl Hackett, Horace Murphy, Miki Morita; *D:* S. Roy Luby. *NOS, MRV, VTR*

Border Radio woof! **1988** A rock singer decides to steal a car and try to outrun some tough thugs hot on his trail. **88m/B VHS, Closed Caption.** Chris D, Luana Anders; *D:* Allison Anders, Kurt Voss; *W:* Allison Anders, Kurt Voss; *M:* Dave Alvin. *FCT*

Border Rangers 🐾 **1950** A man joins the Rangers in order to avenge the murders of his brother and sister-in-law. **57m/B VHS, Beta, LV.** Robert Lowery, Donald (Don "Red") Barry, Lyle Talbot, Pamela Blake; *D:* William (Lester Williams) Berke. *NO*

Border Romance 🐾½ **1930** Three Americans have their horses stolen by bandits while riding through Mexico. Trouble with the locals follows in this early sound western. **58m/B VHS, Beta.** Don Terry, Armida, Marjorie Kane. *VYY*

Border Roundup 🐾 **1941** The "Lone Rider" uncovers a gang of thieving crooks. **57m/B VHS, Beta.** George Houston, Al "Fuzzy" St. John, Dennis Moore; *D:* Sam Newfield. *VDM*

Border Saddlemates 🐾 **1952** U.S. government veterinarian Allen is asked to sub for the local doc in the Canadian border town of Pine Rock. But he learns that a gang is using silver fox pelts to smuggle illegal goods into the U.S. and it's up to Allen and the Rhythm Riders to stop them. **67m/B VHS, Closed Caption.** Rex Allen. *REP*

Border Shootout 🐾🐾 **1990 (PG)** A trigger-happy sheriff battles a rich young cattle rustler. **110m/C VHS, Beta, Closed Caption.** Glenn Ford, Charlene Tilton, Jeff Kaake, Michael Horse, Russell Todd, Cody Glenn, Sergio Calderon, Michael Ansara; *D:* C.T. McIntyre. *TTC*

Border Vengeance ⅛⅛½ **1935** Reb is a member of a family of outlaws. He aims to improve himself and steer his family to the straight and narrow trail. **45m/B VHS.** Reb Russell, Mary Jane Carey, Kenneth MacDonald, Hank Bell, Glenn Strange, Norman Feusier, Charles "Slim" Whitaker; *D:* Ray Heinz. *GPV*

Border Vigilantes ⅛⅛ **1941** Hoppy and pals try to rid a town of outlaws that even the vigilantes can't run off. The big surprise comes when they find out who the leader of the outlaws is. **61m/B VHS.** William Boyd, Russell Hayden, Andy Clyde, Victor Jory, Morris Ankrum, Frances Gifford, Ethel Wales, Hal Taliaferro; *D:* Derwin Abrahams. *NOS*

Borderline ⅛⅛ **1950** MacMurray and Trevor play undercover agents trying to infiltrate a Mexican drug ring. With their real identities hidden, they fall for each other and make a run for the border. Although the leads work well together, they're hindered by an occasionally confusing script. Unfortunately, director Seiter never decides whether the material is of a comedic or dramatic nature. **88m/B VHS.** Fred MacMurray, Claire Trevor, Raymond Burr, Roy Roberts, Jose Torvay, Morris Ankrum, Charles Lane, Don Diamond, Nacho Galindo, Pepe Hern, Richard Irving; *D:* William A. Seiter. *HEG*

Borderline ⅛⅛ **1980 (PG)** Bronson is a border patrol guard in pursuit of a murderer in this action flick. Meanwhile, he gets caught up in trying to help an illegal alien and her young child. **106m/C VHS, Beta, Closed Caption.** Charles Bronson, Wilford Brimley, Bruno Kirby, Benito Morales, Ed Harris, Kenneth McMillan; *D:* Jerrold Freedman. *FOX*

Bordertown Gunfighters ⅛⅛½ **1943** A cowboy breaks up a vicious lottery racket and falls in love in the process. **56m/B VHS, Beta.** Wild Bill Elliott, Anne Jeffreys. *DVT*

Boris and Natasha: The Movie ⅛½ **1992 (PG)** The two inept spies from the classic television cartoon "The Adventures of Rocky and Bullwinkle" star in this mediocre live-action comedy. These nogoodniks are sent by "Fearless Leader" to America and encounter the usual misadventures. For true fun watch the original animated versions. Never released theatrically, it aired for the first time on cable television. **88m/C VHS, Closed Caption.** Sally Kellerman, Dave Thomas, Paxton Whitehead, Andrea Martin, Alex Rocco, Larry Cedar, Arye Gross, Christopher Neame, Anthony Newley; *Cameos:* John Candy, John Travolta, Charles Martin Smith; *D:* Charles Martin Smith. *ACA, NLC*

B.O.R.N. ⅛½ **1988 (R)** Hagen uncovers an underground network of doctors who kill people and sell the body parts and organs. **90m/C VHS, Beta.** Ross Hagen, P.J. Soles, William Smith, Hoke Howell, Russ Tamblyn, Amanda Blake, Clint Howard, Rance Howard, Debra Lamb; *D:* Ross Hagen. *PSM*

Born Again **1978** This is the filmed adaptation of Charles Colson's biography of when he became a born again Christian. **110m/C VHS, Beta.** Dean Jones, Anne Francis, Dana Andrews, George Brent; *D:* Irving Rapper; *C:* Harry Stradling Jr.; *M:* Les Baxter.

Born American ⅛ *Arctic Heat* **1986 (R)** Pre-Glasnost flick about teenagers vacationing in Finland who "accidentally" cross the Russian border. There they battle the Red Plague. Melodramatic and heavily politicized. Original release banned in Finland. **95m/C VHS, Beta.** Mike Norris, Steve Durham, David Coburn, Thalmus Rasulala, Albert Salmi; *D:* Renny Harlin. *NO*

Born Beautiful ⅛⅛½ **1982** Made for TV. Beautiful young women come to New York, hoping to strike it rich in the world of modeling. At the same time, a still beautiful, but older and overexposed model comes to grips with a change in her career. Well-told, but sugar-coated. **100m/C VHS.** Erin Gray, Ed Marinaro, Polly Bergen, Lori Singer, Ellen Barber, Judith Barcroft, Michael Higgins; *D:* Brad Fiedel. *WAR*

Born Free ⅛⅛⅛ **1966** The touching story of a game warden in Kenya and his wife raising Elsa the orphaned lion cub. When the cub reaches maturity, they work to return her to life in the wild. Great family entertainment based on Joy Adamson's book. Theme song became a hit. ♫Born Free. **95m/C VHS, Beta, LV.** Virginia McKenna, Bill Travers; *D:* James Hill; *W:* Lester Cole; *M:* John Barry. Academy Awards '66: Best Song ("Born Free"), Best Original Score; National Board of Review Awards '66: 10 Best Films of the Year. *COL, HMV*

Born in America ⅛ *Dead Aim* **1990** A young orphan is adopted by an undertaker. The boy grows up enveloped by his guardian's business and, when things are slow, works to bring in business himself. **90m/C VHS.** James Westerfield, Glen Lee, Virgil Frye, Venetia Vianello; *D:* Jose Antonio Bolanos. *NO*

Born in East L.A. ⅛⅛ **1987 (R)** Marin brings his Bruce Springsteen-parody song to life as he plays a mistakenly deported illegal alien who struggles to return to the U.S. Suprisingly resolute effort by the usually self-exploiting Mexican-American. Stern is the American expatriate who helps him get back and Lopez is the love interest who stalls him. **85m/C VHS, Beta, LV.** Richard "Cheech" Marin, Daniel Stern, Paul Rodriguez, Jan-Michael Vincent, Kamala Lopez, Tony Plana, Vic Trevino, A. Martinez; *D:* Richard "Cheech" Marin. *USH, FCT*

Born in Flames ⅛ **1983** An acclaimed futuristic feminist film about women who band together in an effort to gain control of the state owned media. **90m/C VHS.** *D:* Lizzie Borden; *W:* Lizzie Borden. *ICA*

Born Innocent ⅛½ **1974** As if "The Exorcist" weren't bad enough, Blair is back for more abuse-on-film, this time as a 14-year-old runaway from a dysfunctional family who lands in a reform school for girls. There, she must struggle to be as brutal as her peers in order to survive. Fairly tame by today's standards, but controversial at its made-for-TV premiere, chiefly due to a rape scene involving a broom handle. First trip up the river for Blair. **92m/C VHS, Beta.** Linda Blair, Joanna Miles, Kim Hunter, Richard Jaeckel; *D:* Donald Wrye. *NO*

Born Invincible ⅛ **1976** A Kung Fu master avenges the kick-death of a student by randomly kick-killing suspects. **90m/C VHS, Beta.** Lo Lieh, Carter Wong, Nancy Yan; *D:* Joseph Kuo. *GEM*

Born Killer ⅛ **1989** Teenagers in the woods meet up with murderous escaped convicts. **90m/C VHS, Beta.** Francine Lapensee, Fritz Matthews, Ted Prior, Adam Tucker; *D:* Kimberly Casey. *AIP*

Born Losers ⅛⅛ **1967 (PG)** The original "Billy Jack" film in which the Indian martial arts expert takes on a group of incorrigible bikers bothering some California babes and runs afoul of the law. Classic drive-in fare. **112m/C VHS, Beta, LV.** Tom Laughlin, Elizabeth James, Jeremy Slate, William Wellman Jr., Robert Tessier, Jane Russell; *D:* Tom Laughlin; *W:* Tom Laughlin. *VES, LIV*

Born of Fire ⅛½ **1987 (R)** A flutist investigating his father's death seeks the Master Musician; his search leads to the volcanic (and supernatural) mountains of Turkey. **84m/C VHS, Beta, LV.** Peter Firth, Susan Crowley, Stephan Kalipha; *D:* Jamil Dehlavi; *M:* Colin Towns. *THV*

Born on the Fourth of July ⅛⅛⅛½ **1989 (R)** A riveting meditation on American life affected by the Vietnam War, based on the real-life, bestselling experiences of Ron Kovic, though some facts are subtly changed. The film follows him as he develops from a naive recruit to an angry, wheelchair-bound paraplegic to an active antiwar protestor. Well-acted and generally lauded; Kovic co-wrote the screenplay and appears as a war veteran in the opening parade sequence. **145m/C VHS, Beta, LV, 8mm, Closed Caption.** Tom Cruise, Kyra Sedgwick, Raymond J. Barry, Jerry Levine, Tom Berenger, Willem Dafoe, Frank Whaley, John Getz, Caroline Kava, Bryan Larkin, Abbie Hoffman, Stephen Baldwin, Josh Evans; *D:* Oliver Stone; *W:* Oliver Stone; *C:* Robert Richardson; *M:* John Williams. Academy Awards '89: Best Director (Stone), Best Film Editing; Directors Guild of America Awards '89: Best Director (Stone); Golden Globe Awards '90: Best Actor—Drama (Cruise), Best Director (Stone), Best Film—Drama, Best Screenplay; Nominations:

Academy Awards '89: Best Actor (Cruise), Best Adapted Screenplay, Best Cinematography, Best Picture, Best Sound, Best Original Score. *USH, FCT, BTV*

Born Reckless ⅛½ **1959** Van Doren plays a singer working the rodeo circuit who falls for aging rider Richards. Not bad enough to be funny, however, Van Doren shows an incredible lack of talent while singing several tunes. ♫Song of the Rodeo; Born Reckless; A Little Longer; Home Type Girl; Separate the Men from the Boys; Something to Dream About; You, Lovable You. **79m/B VHS.** Mamie Van Doren, Jeff Richards, Arthur Hunnicutt, Carol Ohmart, Donald (Don "Red") Barry, Nacho Galindo; *D:* Howard W. Koch. *MOV*

Born to Be Bad ⅛⅛½ **1950** Fontaine, an opportunistic woman who was b-b-born to be b-b-bad, attempts to steal a wealthy business man away from his wife while carrying on an affair with a novelist. Ray's direction (he's best known for "Rebel Without a Cause," filmed five years later) prevents the film from succumbing to standard Hollywood formula. **93m/B VHS, Beta, LV.** Joan Fontaine, Robert Ryan, Zachary Scott, Joan Leslie, Mel Ferrer; *D:* Nicholas Ray. *TTC*

Born to Be Wild ⅛⅛ **1938** A pair of truck drivers are commissioned to deliver a shipment of dynamite. The dynamite will be used to destroy a dam, preventing the surrounding land from falling into the hands of unscrupulous land barons. Good action picture thanks to the cast. **66m/B VHS, Beta.** Ralph Byrd, Doris Weston, Ward Bond, Robert Emmett Keane, Bentley Hewlett, Charles Williams; *D:* Joseph Kane. *SNC, RXM*

Born to Be Wild ⅛½ **1995 (PG)** Rebellious teenager Rick (Hornoff) befriends Katie, the 3-year-old gorilla his behaviorial scientist mom (Shaver) is studying. When Katie's owner (Boyle) decides she would make a better sideshow attraction than science project, Rick busts her out and they head for the Canadian border. Animal slapstick and bodily function jokes ensue as the chase continues. "Free Willy"-inspired plot and primate hijinks should keep young kids interested, but anyone over the age of nine probably won't be too impressed. **98m/C VHS, LV, Closed Caption.** Wil Horneff, Helen Shaver, Peter Boyle, Jean Marie Barnwell, John C. McGinley, Marvin J. McIntyre; *D:* John Gray; *W:* John Bunzel, Paul Young; *C:* Donald M. Morgan. *WAR*

Born to Boogie ⅛⅛ **1972** A concert, a chronicle, and a tribute, "Born To Boogie" is about Marc Bolan and his band T. Rex. The film, which features concert footage from a 1972 concert at the Wembley Empire Pool in London, chronicles the glitter rock era and the next wave of British rock and roll, and pays tribute to Bolan, who died in 1977 just as he was starting a comeback. Ringo Starr and Elton John join T. Rex in the studio for "Children of the Revolution" and "Tutti-Frutti" as well as a psychadelic soiree where Bolan plays acoustic versions of his hits. This film was never released in the United States. **75m/C VHS.** Marc Bolan, Elton John, Ringo Starr; *D:* Ringo Starr. *MPI, MVD*

Born to Dance ⅛⅛½ **1936** A quintessential MGM 1930s dance musical, wherein a beautiful dancer gets a sailor and a big break in a show. Great songs by Cole Porter sung in a less than great manner by a gangly Stewart. Powell's first starring vehicle. ♫Love Me Love My Pekinese; I've Got You Under My Skin; Hey Babe Hey; Easy to Love; Rolling Home; Rap Tap on Wood; Entrance of Lucy James; Swingin' the Jinx Away. **108m/B VHS, Beta, LV.** Eleanor Powell, James Stewart, Virginia Bruce, Una Merkel, Frances Langford, Sid Silvers, Raymond Walburn, Reginald Gardiner, Buddy Ebsen; *D:* Roy Del Ruth; *M:* Cole Porter, Cole Porter. Nominations: Academy Awards '36: Best Song ("I've Got You Under My Skin"). *MGM, MLB*

Born to Kill ⅛⅛⅛ *Lady of Deceit* **1947** A ruthless killer marries a girl for her money. Minor tough-as-nails film noir exemplifying Tierney's stone-faced human-devil film persona. **92m/B VHS,**

Beta. Lawrence Tierney, Claire Trevor, Walter Slezak, Elisha Cook Jr.; **D:** Robert Wise. *TTC*

Born to Race 🎬 1988 **(R)** In the world of competitive auto racing, a beautiful engineer is kidnapped for her new controversial engine design. 95m/C VHS, Beta. Joseph Bottoms, George Kennedy, Marc Singer, Marla Heasly; **D:** James Fargo. *FOX*

Born to Ride 🎬🎬 1991 **(PG)** A biker rebel joins the Army prior to WWII in order to escape a prison term after a good ol' boy brush with the law. He shuns Army discipline, but proves himself in action as the leader of a scout troup for the Army's motorcycle cavalry brigade. Available with Spanish subtitles. 88m/C VHS, Beta, **Closed Caption.** John Stamos, John Stockwell, Teri Polo, Kris Kamm; **D:** Graham Baker. *WAR*

Born to Run 🎬🎬½ 1993 Nicky Donatello (Grieco) is a Brooklyn street drag racer who gets mixed up with the mob while trying to rescue his no-account brother. But he still finds time to fall for an uptown model who also happens to be the mobster's girlfriend. Made for television. 97m/C VHS, LV. Richard Grieco, Jay Acovone, Shelli Lether, Christian Campbell, Brent Stait, Martin Cummins, Wren Roberts, Joe Cortese; **D:** Albert Magnoli; **W:** Randall Badat. *FXV*

Born to Win 🎬🎬½ *Addict* 1971 **(R)** A New York hairdresser with an expensive drug habit struggles through life in this well made comedy drama. Excellent acting from fine cast, well-paced, and interestingly photographed. Not well received when first released, but worth a look. 90m/C VHS. George Segal, Karen Black, Paula Prentiss, Hector Elizondo, Robert De Niro, Jay Fletcher; **D:** Ivan Passer; **C:** Jack Priestley. *QVD, MGM*

Born Wild 🎬🎬½ 1995 **(PG)** Documentary filmmaker Christine Shaye (Shields) has just gotten her first important assignment from overbearing boss Dan Walker (Sheen), which is to capture the beauty of Africa. Christine arrives at the South African game preserve of Londolozi where she meets passionate conservationist John Varty (who plays himself). Varty has filmed one leopard family for 12 years but when the mother leopard is killed, he violates his own ethical code when he rescues her two orphaned cubs. 98m/C VHS, LV, **Closed Caption.** Brooke Shields, Martin Sheen, John Varty, David Keith; **D:** Duncan McLachlan; **W:** Duncan McLachlan, Andrea Buck. *COL*

Born Yesterday 🎬🎬🎬½ 1950 Ambitious junk dealer Harry Brock is in love with smart but uneducated Billie Dawn. He hires newspaperman Paul Verrall to teach her the finer points of etiquette. During their sessions, they fall in love and Billie realizes how she has been used by Brock. She retaliates against him and gets to deliver that now-famous line: "Do me a favor, drop dead." Based on the Broadway play. 103m/B VHS, Beta, LV, **Closed Caption.** Judy Holliday, Broderick Crawford, William Holden; **D:** George Cukor. Academy Awards '50: Best Actress (Holliday); Golden Globe Awards '51: Best Actress—Musical/Comedy (Holliday); Nominations: Academy Awards '50: Best Costume Design (B & W), Best Director (Cukor), Best Picture, Best Screenplay. *COL, FCT, BTV*

Born Yesterday 🎬🎬 1993 **(PG)** Remake of the 1950 classic suffers in comparison, particularly Griffith, who has the thankless task of surpassing (or even meeting) Judy Holliday's Oscar-winning mark as not-so-dumb blonde Billie Dawn. Her intellectual inadequacies are glaring when she hits the political world of D.C. with obnoxious tycoon boyfriend Goodman. To save face, he hooks her up with a journalist (Johnson) willing to coach her in Savvy 101, a la Eliza Doolittle. What worked well in post-WWII America seems sadly outdated today; stick with the original. 102m/C VHS, Beta, LV, **Closed Caption.** Melanie Griffith, John Goodman, Don Johnson, Edward Herrmann, Max Perlich, Fred Dalton Thompson, Nora Dunn, Benjamin C. Bradlee, Sally Quinn, Michael Ensign, William Frankfather, Celeste Yarnall, Meg Wittner; **D:** Luis Mandoki; **W:** Douglas McGrath; **C:** Lajos Koltai; **M:** George Fenton. *TOU, HPH*

The Borrower 🎬🎬 1989 **(R)** An exiled unstable mutant insect alien serial killer (you know the type) must switch heads with human beings regularly to survive. This colorful, garish gorefest has humor and attitude, but never develops behind the basic grossout situation. 97m/C VHS, LV. Rae Dawn Chong, Don Gordon, Antonio Fargas, Tom Towles; **D:** John McNaughton. *WAR, CAN*

The Borrowers 🎬🎬🎬 1993 Excellent made for television adaptation of the May Norton childrens classics "The Borrowers" and "The Borrowers Afield." This miniature family (about mouse-size) live beneath the floorboards of an English house and borrow what they need to survive from the normal-sized human inhabitants. Problems come when the teeny family are discovered and must make their way to a new home. Sweet and humorous. On two cassettes. 199m/C VHS, **Closed Caption.** *GB* Ian Holm, Penelope Wilton, Rebecca Callard; **D:** John Henderson; **W:** Richard Carpenter. *TTC*

Borsalino 🎬🎬🎬 1970 **(R)** Delon and Belmondo are partners in crime in this seriocomic film about gang warfare in 1930's Marseilles. The costumes, settings, and music perfectly capture the mood of the period. Followed by a sequel "Borsalino and Co." Based on "The Bandits of Marseilles" by Eugene Saccomano. **CW:** Strong gangster violence. 124m/C VHS. *FR* Jean-Paul Belmondo, Alain Delon, Michel Bouquet, Catherine Rouvel, Francoise Christophe, Corinne Marchand; **D:** Jacques Deray; **W:** Jacques Deray, Claude Sautet, Jean-Claude Carriere; **M:** Claude Bolling. *PAR*

Bosom Buddies 1980 Sitcom features best friends Hanks and Scolari who, desperate for cheap rent in New York City, dress in drag in order to move into the women-only Susan B. Anthony hotel. Naturally, this causes some confusion in their love lives. Two episodes per tape. 51m/C VHS, **Closed Caption.** Tom Hanks, Peter Scolari, Donna Dixon, Wendie Jo Sperber, Holland Taylor, Telma Hopkins. *PAR*

Boss 🎬½ *The Black Bounty Killer; Boss Nigger* 1974 **(PG)** Blaxploitation western parody with Williamson and Martin as a couple of bounty hunters tearing apart a town to find a fugitive. Relatively non-violent. 87m/C VHS. Fred Williamson, D'Urville Martin, R.G. Armstrong, William Smith, Carmen Hayworth, Barbara Leigh; **D:** Jack Arnold; **W:** Fred Williamson. *NO*

Boss Cowboy 🎬 1935 A cowboy shows who wears the chaps in his family when he kidnaps his girlfriend to prevent her from moving East. 51m/B VHS, Beta. Buddy Roosevelt, Frances Morris, Sam Pierce, Fay McKenzie, Lafe McKee; **D:** Victor Adamson. *GPV*

Boss Foreman **woof!** 1939 A languorous, entwining comedy of errors about a construction foreman and his misadventures with the mob. 58m/B VHS, Beta. Henry Armetta. *VYY*

The Boss Is Served 🎬🎬 196? A mother (Berger) and three daughters, racked with debt, are forced to take in boarders. The lascivious man and teenage son want to be more than just boarders to the lovely Berger. In Italian with English subtitles. 95m/C VHS, Beta. *IT* Senta Berger, Maurizio Arena, Bruno Zanin. *NO*

Boss of Big Town 🎬🎬 1943 Gangsters try to infiltrate the milk industry in this standard crime drama. 58m/B VHS, Beta. John Litel, Florence Rice, H.B. Warner, Jean Brooks, John Miljan, Mary Gordon, John Maxwell; **D:** Arthur Dreifuss. *SNC, RXM*

Boss of Bullion City 🎬½ 1941 A crooked sheriff is exposed by Brown and sidekick Knight in this sagebrush saga. Based on a story by Arthur St. Claire. 61m/B VHS. Johnny Mack Brown, Fuzzy Knight, Maria Montez, Earle Hodgins, Harry Woods; **D:** Ray Taylor; **W:** Victor McLeod, Arthur St. Claire. *MOV*

Boss of Rawhide 🎬 1944 The Texas Rangers fight for law and order in the old west despite odds against them. 60m/B VHS, Beta. Dave O'Brien, James Newill. *NOS, DVT*

Boss' Son 🎬🎬🎬 1978 Worthwhile coming-of-age tale about a young man who learns more than he bargained for about life when he goes to work for his father in the family carpet business. Dad feels he should work his way up through the ranks and makes him a delivery man. The young man meets reality head on and must deal with the injustices of the world around him. Independently filmed by director/writer Roth. 97m/C VHS, Beta. Rita Moreno, James Darren, Asher Brauner, Rudy Solari, Henry Sanders, Richie Havens, Piper Laurie, Elena Verdugo; **D:** Bobby Roth; **W:** Bobby Roth; **C:** Alfonso Beato. *VES, LIV*

The Boss' Wife 🎬🎬 1986 **(R)** A young stockbroker attempts to fix what's wrong with his life by maneuvering sexually with the boss' wife, and complications set in. 83m/C VHS, Beta, **Closed Caption.** Daniel Stern, Arielle Dombasle, Christopher Plummer, Martin Mull, Melanie Mayron, Lou Jacobi; **D:** Ziggy Steinberg; **M:** Bill Conti. *FOX*

Boston Kickout 🎬🎬 1995 A quartet of teenaged friends/losers struggle to grow up in a bleak concrete town outside London. There are neglected girlfriends, dysfunctional families, menial jobs, petty crime, emotional disasters—and some faint glimmer of hope for at least a couple of the lads. Title refers to a destructive game the boys play. 105m/C VHS. *GB* John Simm, Andrew Lincoln, Richard Hanson, Nathan Valente, Emer McCourt, Marc Warren, Derek Martin, Vincent Phillips, Natalie Davies; **D:** Paul Hills; **W:** Paul Hills, Diane Whitley, Roberto Troni; **C:** Roger Bonnici; **M:** Robert Hartshorne. *BMG*

The Boston Strangler 🎬🎬½ 1968 Based on Gerold Frank's bestselling factual book about the deranged killer who terrorized Boston for about a year and a half. Traces events from first killing to prosecution. Curtis, going against type, is compelling in title role. 116m/C VHS, Beta, **Closed Caption.** Tony Curtis, Henry Fonda, George Kennedy, Murray Hamilton, Mike Kellin, George Voskovec, William Hickey, James Brolin, Hurd Hatfield, William Marshall, Jeff Corey, Sally Kellerman; **D:** Richard Fleischer; **W:** Edward Anhalt. *FOX*

The Bostonians 🎬🎬½ 1984 **(PG)** A faith healer's daughter is forced to choose between the affections of a militant suffragette and a young lawyer in 19th Century Boston. Based on Henry James' classic novel. 120m/C VHS, Beta, LV. Christopher Reeve, Vanessa Redgrave, Madeleine Potter, Jessica Tandy, Nancy Marchand, Wesley Addy, Linda Hunt, Wallace Shawn; **D:** James Ivory; **W:** Ruth Prawer Jhabvala; **C:** Walter Lassally. National Society of Film Critics Awards '84: Best Actress (Redgrave); Nominations: Academy Awards '84: Best Actress (Redgrave), Best Costume Design. *VES, LIV*

Botany Bay 🎬🎬 1953 A rousing costumer about a convict ship in the 1700s that, after a trying voyage, lands in Australia, wherein a framed doctor conquers the local plague. From the novel by Charles Nordoff. 99m/C VHS, Beta. Alan Ladd, James Mason, Patricia Medina, Cedric Hardwicke; **D:** John Farrow. *BAR*

Bottle Rocket 🎬🎬½ 1995 **(R)** A trio of inexperienced but aspiring criminals attempt to make their mark on the world in suburban Dallas. Newcomers Wilson, who plays the group's ambitious leader Dignan, and Anderson penned this smart ensemble piece first as a 13-minute black and white short. A subsequent showing at the Sundance Film Festival got the attention of producer James L. Brooks ("Broadcast News"). Film got the backing to go feature length with Anderson directing, and deservedly so, with its fresh dialogue and surprising warmth. **CW:** Language. 91m/C VHS, LV, **Closed Caption.** Owen C. Wilson, Luke Wilson, Robert Musgrave, Lumi Cavazos, James Caan, Teddy Wilson, Andrew Wilson, Jim Ponds; **D:** Wes Anderson; **W:** Owen C. Wilson, Wes Anderson; **C:** Robert Yeoman; **M:** Mark Mothersbaugh. MTV Movie Awards '96: Best New Filmmaker Award (Anderson). *COL*

Bottoms Up woof! **1987** Three nympho-maniacs seduce a virginal mechanic and turn him into an insatiable womanizer. Skin aplenty. **90m/C VHS, Beta.** Adam Janas, Sparky Abbrams, Kathleen Johnson. *PSM*

Boudu Saved from Drowning *ɪɪɪ½ Boudu Sauve des Eaux* **1932** A suicidal tramp completely disrupts the wealthy household of the man that saves him from drowning. A gentle but sardonic farce from the master filmmaker. Remade in 1986 as "Down and Out In Beverly Hills." **87m/B VHS, Beta.** FR Michel Simon, Charles Granval, Jean Daste; **D:** Jean Renoir. *INT, MRV, DVT*

Boulevard *ɪ½* **1994 (R)** Jennefer (Wuhrer) is forced to give her baby up for adoption, after escaping from an abusive husband, and make her way on the city's mean streets. She meets prostitute Ola (Chong), who decides to look after the naif and protect Jennefer from violent pimp Hassan (Phillips). But Ola gets into trouble with tough cop Claren (Henriksen) and soon Jennefer must survive on her own—against both Hassan and her vengeful husband. Woman empowerment, complete with standard cliches.*CW:* Violence, sexual situations, nudity. **96m/C VHS, LV, Closed Caption.** Kari Wuhrer, Rae Dawn Chong, Lou Diamond Phillips, Lance Henriksen, Joel Bissonnette; **D:** Penelope Buitenhuis; **W:** Rae Dawn Chong; **M:** Ian Thomas. *LIV*

Boulevard Nights *ɪɪ* **1979 (R)** A young Latino man tries to escape his neighborhood's streetgang violence, while his older brother is sucked into it. Music by Schifrin, known for the "Mission: Impossible" theme. **102m/C VHS, Beta.** Richard Yniguez, Danny De La Paz, Marta DuBois, Carmen Zapata, Victor Millan; **D:** Michael Pressman; **C:** John Bailey; **M:** Lalo Schifrin. *WAR*

Boulevard of Broken Dreams *ɪɪ* **1988 (PG-13)** Successful Hollywood screenwriter Tom Garfield (Waters) returns to his native Australia to figure out how his life got so screwed up. His estranged wife is living with someone else and his daughter barely remembers him. Affecting look at personal priorities versus success. **95m/C VHS.** AU John Waters, Kim Gyngell, Penelope Stewart; **D:** Pino Amenta. *ACA*

Bound *ɪɪ* **1996 (R)** Ex-con Corky (Gershon) is busy fixing up her new apartment after serving five years for robbery. Her next-door neighbors are Caesar (Pantoliano), a neurotic, money-laundering mobster, and his sexy girlfriend, a seemingly dumb brunette named Violet (Tilly). The femme twosome hook up (in and out of bed) and hatch a plan to steal two million freshly-laundered dollars from Caesar, who goes ballistic when he discovers the money gone. It's a flashy—but not substantive—thriller. Directorial debut for the brothers Wachowski.*CW:* Strong sexuality, violence and language. **107m/C VHS, LV, Closed Caption.** Gina Gershon, Jennifer Tilly, Joe Pantoliano, John P. Ryan, Barry Kivel, Christopher Meloni, Peter Spellos, Richard Sarafian, Mary Mara, Susie Bright, Ivan Kane, Kevin M. Richardson, Gene Borkan; **D:** Andy Wachowski, Larry Wachowski; **W:** Andy Wachowski, Larry Wachowski; **C:** Bill Pope; **M:** Don Davis. Nominations: Independent Spirit Awards '97: Best Cinematography; MTV Movie Awards '97: Best Kiss (Jennifer Tilly/Gina Gershon). *REP*

Bound and Gagged: A Love Story *ɪ* **1993 (R)** For some reason, Elizabeth (Saltarelli), who is desperate for a husband, thinks that she might increase her chances of finding one if she kidnaps her friend Leslie (Allen) and goes on a weird wild goose chase through Minnesota with the hostage and her hopeless partner-in-crime, Cliff (Denton). Go figure.*CW:* Language and strong sexuality. **96m/C VHS, LV.** Ginger Lynn Allen, Karen Black, Chris Denton, Elizabeth Saltarelli, Mary Ella Ross, Chris Mulkey; **D:** Daniel Appleby; **W:** Daniel Appleby; **M:** William Murphy. *TRI*

Bound for Glory *ɪɪɪ½* **1976 (PG)** The award-winning biography of American folk singer Woody Guthrie set against the backdrop of the Depression. Superb portrayal of the spirit and feelings of the period featuring many of his songs encased in the incidents that inspired them. Haskell Wexler's award-winning camera work is superbly expressive. **149m/C VHS, Beta, LV.** David Carradine, Ronny Cox, Melinda Dillon, Randy Quaid; **D:** Hal Ashby; **W:** Robert Getchell; **C:** Haskell Wexler. Academy Awards '76: Best Cinematography, Original Song Score and/or Adaptation; Los Angeles Film Critics Association Awards '76: Best Cinematography; National Board of Review Awards '76: Best Actor (Carradine); National Society of Film Critics Awards '76: Best Cinematography; Nominations: Academy Awards '76: Best Adapted Screenplay, Best Costume Design, Best Film Editing, Best Picture. *MGM*

The Bounty *ɪɪɪ* **1984 (PG)** A new version of "Mutiny on the Bounty," with emphasis on a more realistic relationship between Fletcher Christian and Captain Bligh—and a more sympathetic portrayal of the captain, too. The sensuality of Christian's relationship with a Tahitian beauty also receives greater importance. **130m/C VHS, Beta, LV.** Mel Gibson, Anthony Hopkins, Laurence Olivier, Edward Fox, Daniel Day-Lewis, Bernard Hill, Philip Davis, Liam Neeson; **D:** Roger Donaldson; **W:** Robert Bolt; **M:** Vangelis. *VES, LIV*

Bounty Hunter **2002** *ɪ½ 2002: The Rape of Eden* **1994** A rogue virus kills most of the world's population and few of those remaining are completely immune. So slave trading in the capture and sale of immune survivors is a lucrative business and a bounty's hunter's last assignment is to bring in a beautiful but deadly woman. **90m/C VHS, LV.** Phil Nordell, Francine Lapensee, Vernon Wells, Jeff Conaway; **D:** Sam Auster; **W:** Sam Auster. *AIP*

Bounty Hunters *ɪɪ* **1989 (R)** A man hunts down his friend's killer. **91m/C VHS, Beta.** Robert Ginty, Bo Hopkins, Loeta Waterdown; **D:** Robert Ginty. *AIP*

The Bounty Man *ɪɪ* **1972** A bounty hunter brings an outlaw in, robbing him of his freedom and his girlfriend. **74m/C VHS, Beta.** Clint Walker, Richard Basehart, Margot Kidder, Arthur Hunnicutt, John Ericson, Gene Evans; **D:** John Llewellyn Moxey. *FOX*

Bounty Tracker *ɪ½* **1993 (R)** Johnny Damone (Lamas) is a bounty-hunter in pursuit of the killer-for-hire who murdered his brother. This personal vendetta leads to an action-packed martial arts showdown between Johnny and his cold-blooded prey. **90m/C VHS, LV, Closed Caption.** Lorenzo Lamas, Matthias Hues, Eugene Glazer. *REP*

Bouquet of Barbed Wire *ɪ½* **1976** Overlong soaper revolves around a weathly family and their hidden secrets: incest and infidelity. On three tapes. **330m/C VHS.** Frank Finlay, Susan Penhaligon, Deborah Grant, Sheila Allen, James Aubrey; **D:** Tom Wharmby. *NO*

The Bourne Identity *ɪɪɪ* **1988** Chamberlain stars as an amnesiac trying to piece together the fragments of his memory. Is he U.S. espionage agent Jason Bourne or an international terrorist? Aided by Smith (the kidnap victim who falls in love with her captor), the two traverse Europe trying to escape the spy network out to assassinate the mystery man who knows too little. Exciting adaptation of the Robert Ludlum thriller. Originally a two-part television miniseries. **185m/C VHS.** Richard Chamberlain, Jaclyn Smith, Denholm Elliott, Anthony Quayle, Donald Moffat, Yorgo Voyagis; **D:** Roger Young; **W:** Carol Sobieski. *WAR, BTV*

Bowery at Midnight *ɪ½* **1942** Lugosi plays a man who recycles criminals into zombies that commit crimes for his benefit. Bela and an intense mood can't quite save this pic. **60m/B VHS, Beta.** Bela Lugosi, Tom Neal, Dave O'Brien, Wanda McKay; **D:** Wallace Fox. *NOS, MRV, SNC*

Bowery at Midnight/Dick Tracy vs. Cueball **1942** On one tape, the vintage Lugosi grade-C thriller about zombies in the Bowery, and a standard Dick Tracy entry. **125m/B VHS, Beta.** Bela Lugosi, Morgan Conway, Dick Wessel, Skelton Knaggs. *AOV*

Bowery Blitzkrieg *ɪ Stand and Deliver* **1941** This lesser "East Side Kids" entry has Gorcey opting to enter the boxing ring rather than turn to crime. Needs more Huntz. **62m/B VHS.** Leo Gorcey, Huntz Hall, Bobby Jordan, Warren Hull, Charlotte Henry, Keye Luke; **D:** Wallace Fox. *NOS, VEC, HEG*

Bowery Boys Meet the Monsters **1954** The infamous Bowery Boys display their usual hilarious hijinks in this comedy in which they confront a group of transplant-happy scientists. **65m/C VHS.** Leo Gorcey, Huntz Hall, Bernard Gorcey, Bennie Bartlett, Lloyd Corrigan; **D:** Edward L. Bernds. *GPV*

Bowery Buckaroos *ɪɪ* **1947** The Bowery Boys take their act West in search of gold, meeting up with the usual amounts of goofy characters and hilarious misunderstandings. **66m/B VHS.** Leo Gorcey, Huntz Hall, Bobby Jordan, Gabriel Dell, Billy Benedict, David Gorcey, Julie Briggs, Bernard Gorcey, Chief Yowlachie, Iron Eyes Cody; **D:** William Beaudine. *WAR*

Boxcar Bertha *ɪɪ½* **1972 (R)** Scorsese's vivid portrayal of the South during the 1930s' Depression casts Hershey as a woman who winds up in cahoots with an anti-establishment train robber. Based on the book "Sister of the Road" by Boxcar Bertha Thomson. **90m/C VHS, Beta, LV.** Barbara Hershey, David Carradine, John Carradine; **D:** Martin Scorsese; **W:** John W. Corrington, Joyce H. Corrington. *VES, LIV*

Boxcar Blues *ɪ* **1990** Bird (Coufos) is a down and out fighter who decides to fight "The Man" (Ventura), a bare knuckle fighter who enjoys beating his opponents to death. On the way to the fight, in New Orleans, he meets up with his girl Casey (Langrick), along with some other shady characters, including a truck driving preacher. **96m/C VHS.** Paul Coufos, Margaret Langrick, Jesse Ventura, M. Emmet Walsh, Donny Lalonde; **D:** Damian Lee. *VHE, VTR*

The Boxer and Death *ɪɪɪ* **1963** A new-wave Czech film about a boxer in a Nazi concentration camp who interests the boxing-obsessed commandant in a match. In Czech with subtitles. **120m/B VHS, Beta.** Stefan Kvietik; **D:** Peter Solan. *NOS, FCT, DVT*

Boxing Helena *ɪɪ* **1993 (R)** Highly publicized as the film that cost Basinger almost $9 million in damages, the debut of director/writer Jennifer Lynch (daughter of David) explores the dark side of relationships between men and women. Sands is Dr. Nick Cavanaugh, a surgeon who becomes dangerously obsessed with the beautiful, yet unattainable Helena (Fenn). When she is hit by a car near his home, he performs emergency surgery and amputates her arms and legs, forcing her to be dependent on him. Metaphorically a situation, albeit an extreme one, that mirrors the power struggle in any sexual relationship. Problematic in some aspects, although equally fascinating as it is disturbing.*CW:* Strong language and strong sexuality. **107m/C VHS, LV, Closed Caption.** Julian Sands, Sherilyn Fenn, Bill Paxton, Kurtwood Smith, Betsy Clark, Nicolette Scorsese, Art Garfunkel; **D:** Jennifer Lynch; **W:** Jennifer Lynch; **M:** Graeme Revell. Golden Raspberry Awards '93: Worst Director (Lynch). *ORI*

A Boy and His Dog *ɪɪ½* **1975 (R)** In the post-holocaust world of 2024, a young man (Johnson) and his telepathic canine (McIntire supplies narration of the dog's thoughts) cohort search for food and sex. They happen upon a community that drafts Johnson to repopulate their largely impotent race; Johnson is at first ready, willing, and able, until he discovers the mechanical methods they mean to employ. Based on a short story by Harlan Ellison. The dog was played by the late Tiger of "The Brady Bunch."*CW:* Adult situations, brief nudity. **87m/C VHS, Beta, LV.** Don Johnson, Susanne Benton, Jason Robards Jr., Charles McGraw, Alvy Moore; **D:** L.Q. Jones; **V:** Tim McIntire. *FRF, MED, MRV*

A Boy Called Hate 🎬🎬 **1995 (R)** Troubled teen Steve (Caan)—whose nickname is "Hate" after his tattoo—lives with his divorced dad in an L.A. suburb. Steve's on a latenight motorcycle ride, taking potshots at billboards with his trusty handgun, when he stumbles onto what he thinks is an attempted rape. So Steve shoots at the rapist, Richard (Gould), and takes off with would-be victim Cindy (Crider). Turns out Richard is the assistant D.A. and he tells the cops he's been robbed, so the teen duo are now on the run. Familiar tale with some good twists and believable performances. Caan is the son of James (seen in a cameo as the dad). Debut for director Marcus.**CW:** Language; sexuality; violence. **98m/C VHS, Beta, Closed Caption.** Scott Caan, Missy Crider, Elliott Gould, Adam Beach; **Cameos:** James Caan; **D:** Mitch Marcus; **W:** Mitch Marcus; **C:** Paul Holahan. *PAR*

Boy, Did I Get a Wrong Number! 🎬 **1966** A real estate agent gets more than he bargained for when he accidentally dials a wrong number. Zany comedy persists as Hope gets entangled in the life of sexy starlet Sommer. **100m/C VHS, Beta.** Bob Hope, Phyllis Diller, Marjorie Lord, Elke Sommer, Cesare Danova; **D:** George Marshall. *MGM, FCT*

The Boy Friend 🎬🎬🎬 **1971 (G)** Russell pays tribute to the Busby Berkeley Hollywood musical. Lots of charming dance numbers and clever parody of plot lines in this adaptation of Sandy Wilson's stage play. Fun! 🎵The Boy Friend; I Could Be Happy; Won't You Charleston With Me?; Fancy Forgetting; Sur La Plage; A Room in Bloomsbury; Safety in Numbers; It's Never Too Late to Fall in Love; Poor Little Pierette. **135m/C VHS.** **GB** Twiggy, Christopher Gable, Moyra Fraser, Max Adrian, Vladek Sheybal, Georgina Hale, Tommy Tune; **D:** Ken Russell; **W:** Ken Russell; **C:** David Watkin. Golden Globe Awards '72: Best Actress—Musical/Comedy (Twiggy); Nominations: Academy Awards '71: Original Song Score and/or Adaptation. *MGM*

The Boy God 🎬 **1986** Rocco here describes his trials and everyday shenanigans; he the young demi-God, battling evil on a fantasy land. **100m/C VHS, Beta.** Nino Muhlach; **D:** Erastheo J. Navda. *VCD*

Boy in Blue 🎬🎬½ **1986 (R)** A "Rocky"-esque biography of Canadian speed-rower Ned Hanlan, who set aside lackluster pursuits to turn to rowing. **97m/C VHS, Beta, Closed Caption.** **CA** Nicolas Cage, Christopher Plummer, David Naughton; **D:** Charles Jarrott; **W:** Douglas Bowie. *FOX*

The Boy in the Plastic Bubble 🎬🎬½ **1976** Well-made, sensitive television drama about a young man born with immunity deficiencies who must grow up in a specially controlled plastic environment. Travolta is endearing as the boy in the bubble. **100m/C VHS, Beta.** John Travolta, Robert Reed, Glynnis O'Connor, Diana Hyland, Ralph Bellamy, Anne Ramsey; **D:** Randal Kleiser. *PSM*

Boy Meets Girl 🎬🎬🎬 **1938** Cagney and O'Brien play screenwriters whose every film is a variation on the boy meets girl theme. Trouble is they're running out of ideas and their scripts get increasingly outlandish. A fading cowboy actor is supposed to star in the duo's next film—if they can ever settle down to work. Then they get the idea to feature their friend Wilson's baby in the movie—and guess who becomes a new star. Good satire on moviemaking and movie moguls, which made fine use of the Warner studio back lots, sound stages, and offices. Based on the play by Bella and Samuel Spewack who also wrote the screenplay. **86m/B VHS, Beta.** James Cagney, Pat O'Brien, Ralph Bellamy, Dick Foran, Marie Wilson, Frank McHugh, Bruce Lester, Ronald Reagan, Penny Singleton, James Stephenson; **D:** Lloyd Bacon; **W:** Bella Spewack, Samuel Spewack. *MGM, FCT*

Boy Meets Girl 🎬🎬🎬 **1984** A French Holden Caulfield type character cruises the seamier side of Paris in this acclaimed film. Carax's directoral debut at age 22. In French with English subtitles. **100m/B VHS.** **FR** Denis Lavant, Mireille Perrier; **D:** Leos Carax; **W:** Jim Brady. *FCT, MGM*

A Boy Named Charlie Brown 🎬🎬🎬 **1970** Charlie Brown enters the National Spelling Bee in New York and makes the final rounds with one other contestant. Based on Charles Schultz's popular comic strip characters from "Peanuts." Music by the Vince Guaraldi trio is, as always, a treat. **86m/C VHS, Beta, LV, Closed Caption. D:** Bill Melendez; **W:** Charles M. Schulz; **M:** Vince Guaraldi, Rod McKuen. Nominations: Academy Awards '70: Original Song Score and/or Adaptation. *FOX*

Boy of Two Worlds 🎬½ **1970 (G)** Because of a lineage foreign to his late father's town, a boy is exiled to the life of a junior Robinson Crusoe. **103m/C VHS, Beta.** Jimmy Sternman, Edvin Adolphson; **D:** Astrid Henning Jensen. *GEM*

Boy Takes Girl 🎬🎬 **1983** A little girl finds it hard adjusting to life on a farming cooperative during a summer recess. **93m/C VHS, Beta.** Gabi Eldor, Hillel Neeman, Dina Limon; **D:** Michal Bat-Adam. *MGM*

Boy! What a Girl 🎬🎬 **1945** Moore (in drag) is mistaken for a woman, and is fought over by a couple of suitors. **60m/B VHS, Beta.** Tim Moore, Duke Williams, Sheila Guyse, Beth Mays, Elwood Smith; **D:** Arthur Leonard. *FCT, GVV, DVT*

The Boy Who Could Fly 🎬🎬🎬 **1986 (PG)** After a plane crash kills his parents, a boy withdraws into a fantasy land where he can fly. The young daughter of a troubled family makes friends with him and the fantasy becomes real. A sweet film for children, charming though melancholy for adults, too. Fine cast, including Savage, Dewhurst, and Bedelia keep this from becoming sappy. **120m/C VHS, Beta, LV, Closed Caption.** Lucy Deakins, Jay Underwood, Bonnie Bedelia, Colleen Dewhurst, Fred Savage, Fred Gwynne, Louise Fletcher, Jason Priestley; **D:** Nick Castle; **W:** Nick Castle; **C:** Steven Poster; **M:** Bruce Broughton. *WAR, ORI*

The Boy Who Left Home to Find Out About the Shivers **1981** From "Faerie Tale Theatre" comes this tale about a boy who learns about fear. **60m/C VHS, Beta, LV.** Peter MacNicol, Christopher Lee, David Warner, Dana Hill, Frank Zappa; **D:** Graeme Clifford; **V:** Vincent Price. *FOX*

The Boy Who Loved Trolls **1984** Paul's fantastic dreams come true when he meets Ofoeti, a real, live troll. The only problem is Ofeoti only has a day to live, and Paul must find a way to save him. Aired on PBS as part of the "Wonderworks" series. **58m/C VHS, Closed Caption.** Sam Waterston, Susan Anton, Matt Dill; **D:** Harvey Laidman. *PME, HMV, FCT*

The Boy with the Green Hair 🎬🎬🎬 **1948** When he hears that his parents were killed in an air raid, a boy's hair turns green. The narrowminded members of his community suddenly want nothing to do with him and he becomes an outcast. Thought-provoking social commentary. **82m/C VHS, Beta, LV.** Pat O'Brien, Robert Ryan, Barbara Hale, Dean Stockwell; **D:** Joseph Losey. *IME*

Boyfriends & Girlfriends 🎬🎬½ *My Girlfriend's Boyfriend; Ami de Mon Ami* **1988 (PG)** Another one of Rohmer's "Comedies and Proverbs," in which two girls with boyfriends fade in and out of interest with each, casually reshuffling their relationships. Typical, endless-talks-at-cafes Rohmer, the most happily consistent of the aging French New Wave. In French with subtitles. **102m/C VHS, Beta, LV.** **FR** Emmanuelle Chaulet, Sophie Renoir, Eric Viellard, Francois-Eric Gendron; **D:** Eric Rohmer; **W:** Eric Rohmer. *ORI*

Boys 🎬 *The Girl You Want* **1995 (PG-13)** Seems like only yesterday we saw Haas as that big-eared, doe-eyed Amish kid from "Witness," but now, in this dry love story, he has grown into a big-eared, doe-eyed teenager lusting after older woman Ryder. John (Haas) saves Patty (Ryder) after a riding accident leaves her unconscious near his New England prep school. Immediately taken by her beauty and mystery, John decides to hide her in his dorm room and a romance blossoms between the unlikely pair. But John isn't the only one hiding something. Patty has a terrible secret from her past (gasp!), but when it's finally revealed, you'll be too bored to care. Based on the short story "Twenty Minutes" by James Salter. **86m/C VHS, LV, Closed Caption.** Winona Ryder, Lukas Haas, John C. Reilly, William Sage, Skeet Ulrich; **D:** Stacy Cochran; **W:** Stacy Cochran; **C:** Robert Elswit; **M:** Stewart Copeland. *TOU*

The Boys Club 🎬🎬 **1996 (R)** Teens-in-trouble film is given a tough core by first time director Fawcett. Excitement-craving 14-year-olds Kyle (Zamprogna), Eric (Sawa), and Brad (Stone) spend all their free time at an abandoned shack at the outskirts of their small town. Only one day they discover it occupied by gun-pointing criminal Luke Cooper (Penn), who tells the boys he's actually a good cop who's been shot and is on the run from some bad cops. The boys are willing to buy into the story at first but Cooper is quick to show his psycho colors, taking Eric hostage, and precipitating a violent finale.**CW:** Violence including a scene of sexual intimidation, language and some nude pin-ups. **92m/C VHS.** **CA** Christopher Penn, Stuart Stone, Devon Sawa, Dominic Zamprogna, Nicholas Campbell, Jarred Blanchard; **D:** John Fawcett; **W:** Peter Wellington; **C:** Thom Best; **M:** Michael Timmins. Nominations: Genie Awards '96: Best Actor (Penn), Best Art Direction/Set Decoration, Best Director (Fawcett), Best Film Editing, Best Original Screenplay. *APX*

The Boys from Brazil 🎬🎬½ **1978 (R)** Based on Ira Levin's novel, a thriller about Dr. Josef Mengele endeavoring to reconstitute the Nazi movement from his Brazilian sanctuary by cloning a brood of boys from Hitler's genes. **123m/C VHS, Beta, LV.** Gregory Peck, James Mason, Laurence Olivier, Uta Hagen, Steve Guttenberg, Denholm Elliott, Lilli Palmer; **D:** Franklin J. Schaffner; **W:** Heywood Gould; **C:** Henri Decae; **M:** Jerry Goldsmith. National Board of Review Awards '78: Best Actor (Olivier); Nominations: Academy Awards '78: Best Actor (Olivier), Best Film Editing, Best Original Score. *FOX*

The Boys in Company C 🎬🎬 **1977 (R)** A frank, hard-hitting drama about five naive young men involved in the Vietnam War. **127m/C VHS, Beta, LV.** Stan Shaw, Andrew Stevens, James Canning, Michael Lembeck, Craig Wasson, R. Lee Ermey, James Whitmore Jr., Scott Hylands; **D:** Sidney J. Furie; **W:** Sidney J. Furie. *FOX*

Boys in Love 🎬🎬 **1995** Four gay shorts about young men in love. "Death in Venice, CA" finds a repressed academic drawn to his landlady's stepson. The animated "Achilles" features the Greek heros Achilles and Petroclus at the battle of Troy. A young man becomes determined to conquer "My Polish Waiter" and a rejected Latin lover finds love again (with some help from a dog) in "Miguel, Ma Belle." **83m/C VHS. D:** Barry Purves, P. David Ebersole. *FRF*

The Boys in the Band 🎬🎬½ **1970 (R)** A group of gay friends get together one night for a birthday party. A simple premise with a compelling depiction of friendship, expectations, and lifestyle. One of the first serious cinematic presentations to deal with the subject of homosexuality. The film was adapted from Mart Crowley's play using the original cast. **120m/C VHS, Beta, LV.** Frederick Combs, Cliff Gorman, Laurence Luckinbill, Kenneth Nelson, Leonard Frey; **D:** William Friedkin; **W:** Matt Crowley. *FOX*

Boys Life 🎬🎬 **1994** Three shorts about gay teenagers coming of age. "Pool Days" has 17-year-old Justin (Weinstein) taking a summer job as a lifeguard at a health spa. Still clueless as to his sexual preferences, Justin is flustered when cruised by a charming male swimmer but it does get him to thinking. "A Friend of Dorothy" finds NYU student Winston (O'Connell) seeking freedom in Greenwich Village as he looks for like-minded friends (and a little romance). "The Disco Years" takes place in California during the Nixon era as casually gay-bashing high-schooler Tom (Nolan) gradually realizes his true nature. 90m/C VHS. Josh Weinstein, Nick Poletti, Kimberly Flynn, Richard Salamanca, Raoul O'Connell, Kevin McClatchy, Greg Lauren, Anne Zupa, Matt Nolan, Russell Scott Lewis, Gwen Welles, Dennis Christopher; *D:* Brian Sloan, Raoul O'Connell, Robert Lee King; *W:* Brian Sloan, Raoul O'Connell, Robert Lee King. SHV, MOV

The Boys Next Door 🐾🐾½ 1985 (R)
Two California lads kill and go nuts during a weekend in Los Angeles. Sheen overacts as a budding psychotic, not an easy thing to do. Apparently is trying to show what a particular lifestyle can lead to. Violent. 90m/C VHS, Beta, LV. Maxwell Caulfield, Charlie Sheen, Christopher McDonald, Hank Garrett, Patti D'Arbanville, Moon Zappa; *D:* Penelope Spheeris; *W:* Glen Morgan, James Wong; *C:* Arthur Albert; *M:* George S. Clinton. VTR, NWV

The Boys Next Door 🐾🐾½ 1996 (PG)
Gentle comedy/drama, based on Tom Griffin's play, about four mentally disabled men—Norman (Lane), Barry (Leonard), Arnold (Jeter), and Lucien (Vance)—who share a house under the supervision of too-dedicated social worker Jack (Goldwyn). In fact, Jack's devotion is causing enough problems in his marriage to have him consider changing careers, even as each of "the boys" struggle with their daily lives. TV movie is overly sweet but the performances are very good. 99m/C VHS, Closed Caption. Nathan Lane, Tony Goldwyn, Robert Sean Leonard, Michael Jeter, Courtney B. Vance, Mare Winningham, Jenny Robertson, Elizabeth Wilson, Richard Jenkins, Lynne Thigpen; *D:* John Erman; *W:* William Blinn; *C:* Frank Tidy; *M:* John Kander. HMK

Boys' Night Out 🐾🐾🐾 1962 Amusing comedy about four businessmen who desperately want to escape the suburban doldrums by setting up an apartment equipped with plaything Novak. Little do they know, but Novak is a sociology student studying the American male, and they are merely her guinea pigs in an experiment beyond their control. Blair, Page, and Gabor provide comic relief. Based on a story by Marvin Worth and Arne Sultan. 113m/C VHS. Kim Novak, James Garner, Tony Randall, Howard Duff, Janet Blair, Patti Page, Jessie Royce Landis, Oscar Homolka, Zsa Zsa Gabor; *D:* Michael Gordon; *W:* Ira Wallach. MGM

The Boys of St. Vincent 🐾🐾🐾🐾
1993 Outstanding, and heartbreaking, story of sexual abuse by Catholic clergy that was inspired by actual events. Divided into two segments, the drama begins in 1975 with 10-year-old Kevin Reevey (Morina) living at the St. Vincent orphanage in an eastern Canadian town. The orphanage is run by charismatic and terrifying Brother Lavin (Czerny), who it turns out has a special fondness for "his boy" Kevin. Nor is Brother Lavin alone—a fact eventually revealed by a police investigation, although the matter is hushed up by both the church and the government. Until 15 years later. In 1990, the case is reopened and Lavin, having married and fathered two sons, is returned to face charges. Now the young men must open wounds that have never truly healed and confront their tormentors in a court of law, amidst a blaze of publicity. Czerny gives a truly inspired performance as the self-loathing monster. The emotional agony is excruciating to watch and be forewarned that the depiction of the sexual abuse is unflinching. Made for Canadian TV; on 2 cassettes. 186m/C VHS. *CA* Henry Czerny, Johnny Morina, Sebastian Spence, Brian Dodd, David Hewlett, Jonathan Lewis, Jeremy Keefe, Phillip Dinn, Brian Dooley, Greg Thomey, Michael Wade, Lise Roy, Timothy Webber, Kristine Demers, Ashley Billard, Sam Grana; *D:* John N. Smith; *W:* Sam Grana, John N. Smith, Des Walsh; *C:* Pierre Letarte; *M:* Neil Smolar. Nominations: Independent Spirit Awards '95: Best Foreign Film. NYF

Boys of the City 🐾🐾 *The Ghost Creeps*
1940 The East Side Kids run amuck in an eerie mansion while trying to solve the murder of a judge. 63m/B VHS, Beta. Leo Gorcey, Bobby Jordan; *D:* Joseph H. Lewis. NOS, SNC, DVT

Boys on the Side 🐾🐾½ 1994 (R) It's "Thelma & Louise" come to "Terms of Endearment" by way of "Philadelphia." Goldberg is Jane, an unemployed lesbian singer, who connects with Ms. Priss real estate agent Robin (Parker) for a road trip to California. The two become a female version of the Odd Couple as Jane tags Robin as "the whitest woman in America." They stop off to pick up adddle-brain friend Holly (Barrymore) who has just knocked her drug-crazed abusive beau in the head with a baseball bat. Holly's accident turns fatal and the threesome are on the run from cops. They bond like crazy glue and become a family as they face two huge setbacks—one's pregnant, another has AIDS. Strong performances by the lead actresses and a cool soundtrack may make up for this often trite movie of the week premise. *CW:* Strong language; some sexuality. 117m/C VHS, LV, Closed Caption. James Remar, Anita Gillette, Matthew McConaughey, Whoopi Goldberg, Mary-Louise Parker, Drew Barrymore; *D:* Herbert Ross; *W:* Don Roos; *C:* Donald E. Thorin. WAR

Boy's Reformatory 🐾½ 1939 Brothers are framed. One takes the rap, goes to the title institution, breaks out, and hunts the real bad guys. Creaky and antiquated. 62m/B VHS. Frankie Darro, Grant Withers, David Durand, Warren McCollum; *D:* Howard Bretherton. NOS, LOO

Boys Town 🐾🐾🐾½ 1938 Righteous portrayal of Father Flanagan and the creation of Boys Town, home for juvenile soon-to-be-ex-delinquents. 93m/B VHS, Beta, LV, Closed Caption. Spencer Tracy, Mickey Rooney, Henry Hull, Gene Reynolds, Sidney Miller, Frankie Thomas Jr.; *D:* Norman Taurog. Academy Awards '38: Best Actor (Tracy), Best Story; Nominations: Academy Awards '38: Best Director (Taurog), Best Picture. MGM, BTV, IGP

Boyz N the Hood 🐾🐾🐾½ 1991 (R) Singleton's debut as a writer and director is an astonishing picture of young black men, four high school students with different backgrounds, aims, and abilities trying to survive Los Angeles gangs and bigotry. Excellent acting throughout, with special nods to Fishburne and Gooding, Jr. Violent outbreaks outside theaters where this ran only proves the urgency of its passionately nonviolent, pro-family message. Hopefully those viewers scared off at the time will give this a chance in the safety of their VCRs. Singleton was the youngest director ever nominated for an Oscar. The laserdisc version includes two extra scenes and an interview with Singleton. *CW:* Language, violence, and sensuality. 112m/C VHS, Beta, LV, 8mm, Closed Caption. Laurence "Larry" Fishburne, Ice Cube, Cuba Gooding Jr., Nia Long, Morris Chestnut, Tyra Ferrell, Angela Bassett; *D:* John Singleton; *W:* John Singleton; *M:* Stanley Clarke. Chicago Film Critics Awards '91: Most Promising Actor (Ice Cube); MTV Movie Awards '92: Best New Filmmaker Award (Singleton); National Board of Review Awards '91: 10 Best Films of the Year; Nominations: Academy Awards '91: Best Director (Singleton), Best Original Screenplay. COL, CRC, FCT

Braddock: Missing in Action 3 🐾
1988 (R) The battle-scarred, high-kicking 'Nam vet battles his way into the jungles once more, this time to rescue his long-lost Vietnamese family. A family effort, Chuck co-wrote the script; his brother directed. 104m/C VHS, Beta, LV, 8mm, Closed Caption. Chuck Norris, Aki Aleong, Roland Harrah III; *D:* Aaron Norris; *W:* Chuck Norris, James Bruner; *C:* Joao Fernandes. MED, CCB, VTR

The Brady Bunch 1969 Relive classic moments with TV's grooviest family—two episodes per tape—including "The Honeymoon," the premiere episode explaining how Mike and his 3 boys get hitched to Carol and her 3 girls. Additional episodes available. 51m/C VHS, Closed Caption. Robert Reed, Florence Henderson, Ann B. Davis, Maureen McCormick, Barry Williams, Eve Plumb, Christopher Knight, Michael Lookinland, Susan Olsen. PAR

The Brady Bunch Movie 🐾🐾🐾 1995 (PG-13) Grunge and CDs may be the norm in the '90s, but the Bradys still live in the eight-track world of the '70s, where Davy Jones rocks and every day is a sunshine day. Then greedy developer McKean schemes to cash in on Mike and Carol's financial woes. (Hawaii! The Grand Canyon! What were they thinking?) Great ensemble cast capably fills the white platform shoes of the originals—Cole sounds just like Mr. Brady, Cox hilariously channels Jan's tormented middle child angst, and Taylor's self-absorbed Marcia, Marcia, Marcia is dead-on, right down to the frosty pursed lips. Look for neat-o cameos from some original Bradys and most of the Monkees. Followed by "A Very Brady Sequel." *CW:* Sly references to sex that most kids probably won't understand; Marcia's girlfriend has a crush on her, Alice wears a leather teddy during the final credits, and Jan hears inner voices. "Hey there, groovy chick" is about as offensive as the language gets. Cast wears dangerously high levels of bad polyester without much thought for taste. Florence Henderson says "crap!" 88m/C VHS, Beta, Closed Caption. Shelley Long, Gary Cole, Michael McKean, Jean Smart, Henriette Mantel, Christopher Daniel Barnes, Christine Taylor, Paul Sutera, Jennifer Elise Cox, Jesse Lee, Olivia Hack, David Graf, Jack Noseworthy, Shane Conrad, RuPaul; *Cameos:* Ann B. Davis, Florence Henderson, Davy Jones, Barry Williams, Christopher Knight, Michael Lookinland, Mickey Dolenz, Peter Tork; *D:* Betty Thomas; *W:* Bonnie Turner, Terry Turner, Laurice Elehwany, Rick Copp; *C:* Mac Ahlberg; *M:* Guy Moon. Nominations: MTV Movie Awards '95: Best Dance Sequence (The Brady Kids). PAR

Brady's Escape 🐾½ *The Long Ride* 1984 American WWII pilot is shot down in the Hungarian countryside and befriended by Hungarian csikos (cowboys) in this made-for-cable television movie. 92m/C VHS, Beta, LV. HU John Savage, Kelly Reno; *D:* Pal Gabor. CAF

The Brain 🐾🐾½ *Vengeance* 1962 A scientist learns that a mind isn't always a terrible thing to waste when he finds himself being manipulated by the brain of a dead man he's trying to keep alive. Remake of "Donovan's Brain" (1953). 83m/B VHS, Beta, LV. GB GE Anne Heywood, Peter Van Eyck, Bernard Lee, Cecil Parker, Jack MacGowran; *D:* Freddie Francis. NOS, SNC

The Brain 🐾🐾 *Le Cerveau* 1969 (G) Run of the mill comedy caper has Niven planning to heist millions from a NATO train. The caper begins when lots of other crooks decide to rob the same train. The cast holds this one together. 100m/C VHS, Closed Caption. FR David Niven, Jean-Paul Belmondo, Bourvil, Eli Wallach, Silvia Monti, Fernand Valois; *D:* Gerard Oury; *M:* Georges Delerue. PAR

The Brain 🐾½ 1988 (R) Dr. Blake, host of a popular TV talk-show, is in league with a power-hungry alien brain. Viewers of his show kill themselves and others in the midst of many special effects. The ratings go down. 94m/C VHS, Beta. Tom Breznahan, Cyndy Preston, David Gale; *D:* Edward Hunt. LIV

Brain Damage 🐾🐾 1988 (R) A tongue-in-bloody-cheek farce about a brain-sucking parasite. The parasite in question, Aylmer, addicts our dubious hero to the euphoria induced by the blue liquid the parasite injects into his brain, paving the way for the bloody mayhem that follows. Poor shadow of Henenlotter's far-superior "Basket Case." In fact, it even includes an inside-joke cameo by Van Hentenryck, reprising his "Basket Case" character; look for him on the subway. 89m/C VHS, Beta, Closed Caption. Rick Herbst, Gordon MacDonald, Jennifer Lowry; *Cameos:* Kevin Van Hentenryck; *D:* Frank Henenlotter. PAR

Brain Dead 🐾🐾🐾½ 1989 (R) Low-budget but brilliantly assembled puzzle-film about a brain surgeon who agrees to perform experimental surgery on a psychotic to retrieve some corporately valuable data—his first mistake, which begins a seemingly endless cycle of nightmares and identity alterations. A mind-blowing sci-fi feast from ex-"Twilight Zone" writer Charles Beaumont. **85m/C VHS, Beta.** Bill Pullman, Bill Paxton, Bud Cort, Patricia Charbonneau, Nicholas Pryor, George Kennedy; **D:** Adam Simon. MGM

Brain Donors 🐾🐾½ 1992 **(PG)** Goofy, uneven film starring Turturro as a sleazy lawyer trying to take over the Oglethorpe Ballet Company by sweet-talking its aged patronness. He is helped by two eccentric friends, and together the three crack a lot of bad but witty jokes. The film culminates into a hilarious ballet scene featuring someone giving CPR to the ballerina playing the dying swan, an actor in a duck suit, duck hunters, and a pack of hounds. This trio reminds us of second-rate Marx Brothers (or the Three Stooges) but the movie has enough funny moments to be worth a watch. **79m/C VHS, Beta, LV, Closed Caption.** John Turturro, Bob Nelson, Mel Smith, Nancy Marchand, John Savident, George de la Pena, Juli Donald, Spike Alexander, Teri Copley; **D:** Dennis Dugan; **W:** Pat Proft; **M:** Ira Newborn. PAR

The Brain Eaters 🐾🐾 1958 A strange ship from inside the Earth invades a small town, and hairy monsters promptly attach themselves to people's necks in a daring bid to control the planet. The imaginative story compensates somewhat for the cheap special effects. Watch for Nimoy before he grew pointed ears. **60m/B VHS.** Edwin Nelson, Alan Frost, Jack Hill, Joanna Lee, Jody Fair, Leonard Nimoy; **D:** Bruno Ve Sota. NOS, CNM

The Brain from Planet Arous 🐾 1957 Lassie meets Alien when an evil alien brain appropriates the body of a scientist in order to take over planet Earth. His plans are thwarted, however, by a good alien brain that likewise inhabits the body of the scientist's dog. High camp and misdemeanors. **80m/B VHS, Beta, LV.** John Agar, Joyce Meadows, Robert Fuller, Henry Travis; **D:** Nathan (Hertz) Juran. SNC, CNM, AOV

Brain of Blood woof! 1971 The Creature's Revenge Deals with a scientist who transplants the brain of a politician into the body of a deformed idiot. The change is minimal. **107m/C VHS, Beta.** Kent Taylor, John Bloom, Regina Carrol, Angelo Rossitto, Grant Williams, Reed Hadley, Vicki Volante, Zandor Vorkov; **D:** Al Adamson. NO

Brain Smasher...A Love Story 🐾 1993 **(PG-13)** A bouncer and a super model become the targets of a gang of killer ninjas who want the mysterious blood-red lotus the model's been given. Of course they do. What's the lovely Hatcher doing in such a stupid movie? **88m/C VHS, LV, Closed Caption.** Andrew Dice Clay, Teri Hatcher; **D:** Albert Pyun. THV

The Brain That Wouldn't Die 🐾🐾½ The Head That Wouldn't Die 1963 Love is a many-splattered thing when a brilliant surgeon keeps the decapitated head of his fiancee alive after an auto accident while he searches for a suitably stacked body onto which to transplant the head. Absurd and satiric (head talks so much that Doc tapes her/its mouth shut) adding up to major entry in trash film genre; much of the gore was slashed for the video, however. **92m/B VHS, Beta.** Herb Evers, Virginia Leith, Adele Lamont; **D:** Joseph Green. SNC, MRV, FCT

The Brainiac 🐾½ 1961 Sorcerer sentenced for black magic returns to strike dark deeds upon the descendants of those who judged him. He turns himself into a hideous monster, feeding on his victims' brains and blood. Yuck. **75m/B VHS, Beta.** MX Abel Salazar, Ariadne Welter, Mauricio Garces, Rosa Maria Gallardo. SNC, MRV, HHT

Brainscan 🐾 1994 **(R)** Teenage loner takes a trip in virtual reality and finds that murder is the first stop. Furlong ("Terminator 2") is the troubled youth whose voyage is led by Smith as Trickster, the Freddy Krueger meets David Bowie tour guide from virtual hell. Langella turns in a straight performance as a local cop hot on the trail. Hard-core

horror fans will be disappointed by the lack of on-screen violence, and special effects buffs won't see anything new. Lame effort tries to appeal to a wide audience and is bland as a result. The end is left wide open, so expect a sequel or two or three. **96m/C VHS, LV, Closed Caption.** Edward Furlong, Frank Langella, T. Ryder Smith, David Hemblen, Amy Hargreaves, Jamie Marsh, Victor Ertmanis; **D:** John Flynn; **W:** Andrew Kevin Walker; **M:** George S. Clinton. COL

Brainstorm 🐾🐾½ 1983 **(PG)** Husband-and-wife scientist team invents headphones that can record dreams, thoughts, and fantasies (VCR-style) and then allow other people to experience them by playing back the tape. Their marriage begins to crumble as the husband becomes more and more obsessed with pushing the limits of the technology; things get worse when the government wants to exploit their discovery. Special effects and interesting camerawork punctuate this sci-fi flick. Wood's last film; in fact, she died before production was completed. **106m/C VHS, Beta, LV.** Natalie Wood, Christopher Walken, Cliff Robertson, Louise Fletcher; **D:** Douglas Trumbull; **W:** Bruce Joel Rubin; **M:** James Horner. MGM

Brainwaves 🐾🐾 1982 **(R)** A young woman has disturbing flashbacks after her brain is electrically revived following a car accident. Curtis is the demented doctor who jump-starts her. **83m/C VHS, Beta.** Suzanna Love, Tony Curtis, Keir Dullea, Vera Miles; **D:** Ulli Lommel; **W:** Ulli Lommel.

Bram Stoker's Dracula 🐾🐾 Dracula 1992 **(R)** Coppola's highly charged view of the vampire classic is visually stunning, heavy on eroticism and violence, and weak in plot and performance. Oldman, in a number of amazing transformations, portrays the deadly bloodsucker as a lonely soul determined to reunite with his lost love, the innocent Ryder. Hopkins cheerfully chews the scenery as nemesis Van Helsing, newcomer Frost is fetching, Reeves is lightweight, and Ryder goes way over the top. Musician Waits is great as bug-eating madman Renfield. Filmed entirely on soundstages with beautiful costumes and some amazing visual effects and sets. Laserdisc includes "The Making of Bram Stoker's Dracula." **CW:** Horror violence and sexuality. **128m/C VHS, Beta, LV, Closed Caption, DVD.** Gary Oldman, Winona Ryder, Anthony Hopkins, Keanu Reeves, Richard E. Grant, Cary Elwes, Bill Campbell, Sadie Frost, Tom Waits; **D:** Francis Ford Coppola; **W:** Jim V. Hart; **C:** Michael Ballhaus. Academy Awards '92: Best Costume Design, Best Makeup, Best Sound Effects Editing; Nominations: Academy Awards '92: Best Art Direction/Set Decoration. COL

The Bramble Bush 🐾🐾½ 1960 Guy (Burton) is a doctor who returns to his New England hometown to care for a dying friend, Larry (Drake). Unfortunately, Guy falls for Larry's wife Mar (Rush) and they have an affair. When Guy pulls the plug on his friend's suffering, suspicious townspeople (who of course know what's going on) wonder just how "merciful" the doctor was really being and he's tried for murder. Tawdry "Peyton Place"-ish soap opera based on the novel by Charles Mergendahl. **104m/C VHS.** Richard Burton, Barbara Rush, Tom Drake, Jack Carson, Angie Dickinson, James Dunn, Henry Jones, Frank Conroy, Carl Benton Reid; **D:** Daniel Petrie; **W:** Philip Yordan. WAR

Bramwell 1995 British miniseries stars Redgrave as the determined Eleanor Bramwell. In 1895, she manages to follow in her physician father's footsteps but it's a battle to gain respect from her sexist colleagues and to overcome her own class prejudices as she works with London's poor. Seven episodes on four cassettes. **360m/C VHS.** GB Jemma Redgrave, David Calder, Kevin McMonagle, Keeley Gainey, Cliff Parisi, Ruth Sheen, Michele Dotrice, Robert Hardy; **D:** David Tucker, Laura Sims; **W:** Lucy Gannon. FCT, ATS

Brand New Life 🐾 1972 A childless couple in their 40s are unexpectedly confronted by the wife's first pregnancy. Both have careers and well-ordered lives that promise to be disrupted. **74m/C VHS, Beta.** Cloris Leachman, Martin Balsam, Wilfrid

Hyde-White, Mildred Dunnock; **D:** Sam O'Steen; **M:** Billy Goldenberg. LCA

Brand of Fear 🐾½ 1949 Crooning cowpoke Wakely puts down his guitar long enough to chase rustlers off the land of an innocent lady in this average oater. **56m/B VHS.** Jimmy Wakely, Dub Taylor, Gail Davis, Tom London; **D:** Oliver Drake; **W:** Basil Dickey. MOV

Brand of Hate 🐾 1934 A good cowboy rustles up a gang of rustlers. **61m/B VHS, Beta.** Bob Steele, George "Gabby" Hayes, Lucille Browne, James Flavin; **D:** Lewis D. Collins. NOS, RXM

Brand of the Outlaws 🐾 1936 A cowboy becomes an unwitting aid to rustlers in this early western. **56m/B VHS, Beta.** Bob Steele, Margaret Marquis, Virginia True Boardman, Jack Rockwell; **D:** Robert North Bradbury. NOS, DVT

Branded 🐾🐾½ 1950 Ladd (pre-"Shane") impersonates the long-gone son of rich rancher Bickford, with unusual results. Nicely balanced action and love scenes makes this old Max Brand story a better-than-average western. Filmed in Technicolor. **95m/C VHS, LV, Closed Caption.** Alan Ladd, Mona Freeman, Charles Bickford, Joseph Calleia, Milburn Stone; **D:** Rudolph Mate. PAR

Branded a Bandit 🐾 1924 Yakima must avoid the sheriff while tracking down the killers of an old miner so that he can clear himself of the crime. **58m/C VHS.** Yakima Canutt; **D:** Paul Hurst. GPV

Branded a Coward 🐾 1935 A man whose parents were killed seeks revenge via his trusty six-shooters. **56m/B VHS, Beta.** Johnny Mack Brown, Billie Seward, Yakima Canutt; **D:** Sam Newfield. NOS, DVT

Branded Men 🐾🐾 1931 A couple of oddballs become mixed up in a number of zany, western-type adventures. **60m/B VHS.** Ken Maynard, June Clyde, Irving Bacon, Billy Bletcher, Charles "Blackie" King, Donald Keith; **D:** Phil Rosen. NOS

Brannigan 🐾🐾½ 1975 **(PG)** The Duke stars in the somewhat unfamiliar role of a rough and tumble Chicago police officer. He travels across the Atlantic to arrest a racketeer who has fled the States rather than face a grand jury indictment. Humor and action abound. **111m/C VHS, Beta.** John Wayne, John Vernon, Mel Ferrer, Daniel Pilon, James Booth, Ralph Meeker, Lesley-Anne Down, Richard Attenborough; **D:** Douglas Hickox; **W:** Michael Butler, William W. Norton Sr. MGM, FOX

Brass 🐾½ 1985 **(PG)** First post-Archie Bunker role for O'Connor, who plods through this average police drama at a snail's pace, dragging everything else down with him. Made-for-TV pilot for a series that never aired. **94m/C VHS, LV.** Carroll O'Connor, Lois Nettleton, Jimmie Baird, Paul Shenar, Vincent Gardenia, Anita Gillette; **D:** Corey Allen. ORI

Brass Target 🐾½ 1978 **(PG)** Hypothetical thriller about a plot to kill George Patton in the closing days of WWII for the sake of $250 million in Nazi gold stolen by his staff. Interesting cast can't find story. **111m/C VHS, Beta, LV.** Sophia Loren, George Kennedy, Max von Sydow, John Cassavetes, Patrick McGoohan, Robert Vaughn, Bruce Davison, Edward Herrmann, Ed Bishop; **D:** John Hough; **W:** Alvin Boretz. MGM

Brassed Off 🐾🐾½ 1996 **(R)** Bittersweet tale of despair and hope in the fictional coal mining town of Grimly in Yorkshire, England. Set in 1992, when sweeping closures of British coal mines devastated the area, the sole respite of these workers is playing in the pit's brass band. Secretly suffering from black lung disease, the band's leader (Postlethwaite) dreams of winning a competition in Albert Hall. Fitzgerald plays the flugelhorn-tooting vixen who returns to the small town, inspiring the music (and virility) of the formerly all male band. She resumes her relationship with former flame MacGregor, but all is on shaky ground with the imminent closure of the mine. Fine performances brighten the generally gloomy proceedings. The band is played by the real-life Grimethorpe Colliery Brass Band. **CW:** Language.

109m/C VHS. *GB* Pete Postlethwaite, Ewan McGregor, Tara Fitzgerald, Jim Carter, Philip Jackson, Peter Martin, Stephen Tompkinson; *D:* Mark Herman; *W:* Mark Herman; *C:* Andy Collins; *M:* Trevor Jones. Nominations: British Academy Awards '96: Best Original Screenplay. *NYR*

The Bravados 🎬🎬🎬 1958 A rough, distressing Western revenge tale, wherein a man is driven to find the four men who murdered his wife. In tracking the perpetrators, Peck realizes that he has been corrupted by his vengeance. 98m/C VHS, **Beta, Closed Caption.** Gregory Peck, Stephen Boyd, Joan Collins, Albert Salmi, Henry Silva, Lee Van Cleef, George Voskovec, Barry Coe; *D:* Henry King; *W:* Philip Yordan; *C:* Leon Shamroy. National Board of Review Awards '58: Best Supporting Actor (Salmi). *FOX*

The Brave Bunch 🎬½ 1970 A courageous Greek soldier tries to save his men and country during WWII. 110m/C VHS. *GR* Peter Funk, John Miller; *D:* Costa Carayiannis. *LIV*

The Brave One 🎬🎬🎬 1956 A love story between a Spanish boy and the bull who saves his life. The animal is later carted off to the bullring. Award-winning screenplay by the then-blacklisted Trumbo, as "Robert Rich." 100m/C VHS, **Beta, LV.** Michel Ray, Rodolfo Hoyos, Joi Lansing; *D:* Irving Rapper; *W:* Dalton Trumbo; *C:* Jack Cardiff. Academy Awards '56: Best Story; Nominations: Academy Awards '56: Best Film Editing, Best Sound. *VCI*

Braveheart 1925 When a Native American adapts to the white man's world, he alienates his own people. He eventually chooses to renounce his love for a white woman, and returns to lead his people. Silent. 62m/B VHS, **Beta, 8mm.** Rod La Rocque; *D:* Alan Hale. *GVV, FCT*

Braveheart 🎬🎬🎬½ 1995 (R) Producer-director-star Gibson does it all in this bold, ferocious, reasonably accurate epic about the passion and cost of freedom. Charismatic 13th century Scottish folk hero William Wallace leads his desperate and outnumbered clansmen in revolt against British oppression. Sweeping, meticulous battle scenes fit suprisingly well with moments of stirring romance and snappy wit. Among the mostly unknown (in the States, anyway) cast, Marceau and McCormack are elegant as Wallace's lady loves, and McGoohan is positively hateful as King Edward I. Gory and excessively violent (as medieval warfare tends to be) and a bit too long (as historical epics tend to be), but rewarding entertainment for those who stick it out—where else can you see the king's army get mooned en masse? Script was based on 300 pages of rhyming verse attributed to a blind poet known as Blind Hally. Gibson put up $15 million of his own money to complete the film. *CW:* Brutal medieval warfare. 178m/C VHS, **Beta, Closed Caption.** Mel Gibson, Sophie Marceau, Patrick McGoohan, Catherine McCormack, Brendan Gleeson, James Cosmo, David O'Hara, Angus McFadyen, Peter Hanly; *D:* Mel Gibson; *W:* Randall Wallace; *John Toll; *M:* James Horner. Academy Awards '95: Best Cinematography, Best Director (Gibson), Best Makeup, Best Picture; British Academy Awards '95: Best Cinematography; Golden Globe Awards '95: Best Director (Gibson); MTV Movie Awards '96: Best Action Sequence; Writers Guild of America '95: Best Original Screenplay; Broadcast Film Critics Association Awards '95: Best Director (Gibson); Nominations: Academy Awards '95: Best Costume Design, Best Film Editing, Best Screenplay, Best Sound, Original Dramatic/Comedy Score; British Academy Awards '95: Best Director (Gibson), Best Score; Directors Guild of America Awards '95: Best Director (Gibson); Golden Globe Awards '96: Best Film—Drama, Best Screenplay, Best Score; MTV Movie Awards '96: Best Film, Best Male Performance (Gibson), Most Desirable Male (Gibson). *PAR*

Brazil 🎬🎬🎬½ 1985 (R) The acclaimed nightmare comedy about an Everyman trying to survive in a surreal paper-choked bureaucratic society. There are copious references to "1984" and "The Trial," fantastic mergings of glorious fantasy and stark reality, and astounding visual design. *CW:* Strong violence. 131m/C VHS, **Beta, LV, Closed Caption.** *GB* Jonathan Pryce, Robert De Niro, Michael Palin, Katherine Helmond, Kim Greist, Bob Hoskins, Ian Holm, Peter Vaughan, Ian Richardson; *D:* Terry Gilliam;

W: Terry Gilliam, Tom Stoppard; *M:* Michael Kamen. Los Angeles Film Critics Association Awards '85: Best Director (Gilliam), Best Film, Best Screenplay; Nominations: Academy Awards '85: Best Art Direction/Set Decoration, Best Original Screenplay. *USH, FCT*

Breach of Conduct 🎬½ 1994 (PG-13) Colonel Bill Case (Coyote) is the commander of the Fort Benton, Utah Army base where Helen Lutz's (Thorne-Smith) husband Tom (Verica) has just been transferred. At first there's a mutual attraction between Helen and Case, but then hubby is assigned a mission off base and, when Helen refuses Case's overtures, things turn very nasty. Made for cable TV. *CW:* Mature thematic material. 93m/C VHS, **LV, Closed Caption.** Peter Coyote, Courtney Thorne-Smith, Tom Verica, Beth Toussaint; *D:* Tim Matheson; *W:* Scott Abbott; *C:* Gideon Porath. *USH*

Breach of Trust 🎬🎬½ 1995 (R) Small-time crook Casey (Biehn) winds up in big trouble when he steals a computer disc with access codes to millions in drug cartel money. He goes on the lam and meets Madeline (Ferrer), an undercover cop who thinks that some police are on the cartel's payroll. So the daring duo decide to take on the drug lords and the dirty cops. *CW:* Violence, a scene of sexuality, language and some drug use. 96m/C VHS, **LV, Closed Caption.** Michael Biehn, Matt Craven, Leilani Sarelle Ferrer, Miguel Sandoval, Kim Coates, Ed Lauter; *D:* Charles Wilkinson; *W:* Gordon Basichis, Raul Inglis; *C:* Michael Slovis; *M:* Graeme Coleman. *REP*

Bread and Chocolate 🎬🎬🎬 *Pane e Cioccolata* 1974 Uneducated Italian immigrant Manfredi works a series of odd jobs in complacently bourgeois Switzerland and tries desperately to fit in and better himself (which he fails utterly to do). Culture clash satire, with an engaging everyman lead. Italian with subtitles. 109m/C VHS. *IT* Nino Manfredi, Anna Karina, Johnny Dorelli, Paolo Turco; *D:* Franco Brusati; *W:* Nino Manfredi, Franco Brusati, Iaia Fiastri; *C:* Luciano Tovoli; *M:* Daniele Patrucchi. New York Film Critics Awards '78: Best Foreign Film. *HTV*

The Break 🎬🎬 1995 (PG-13) Clumsy teen tennis hopeful Ben (Jorgensen) refuses to give up his dreams even after his bookie dad Robbins (Sheen) hires washed-up player Nick Irons (Van Patten) as a coach to show Ben the error of his game. *CW:* Some racy sexuality and brief strong language. 104m/C VHS. Vincent Van Patten, Martin Sheen, Ben Jorgensen, Rae Dawn Chong, Valerie Perrine; *W:* Vincent Van Patten, Dan Jenkins. *THV*

Break of Hearts 🎬🎬½ 1935 Hepburn marries Boyer, who becomes an alcoholic, and then more troubles arise. Very soapy, but well-made. 78m/B VHS, **Beta, LV.** Katharine Hepburn, Charles Boyer, Jean Hersholt, John Beal, Sam Hardy; *D:* Philip Moeller; *M:* Max Steiner. *TTC*

Breakaway 🎬 1995 (R) Myra (Thompson) decides to get away from her drop-woman job with $300,000 of mob money. Naturally, she's pursued by a hit man (Estevez) and then betrayed by a boyfriend (De Rose), who steals the cash and hides it in the apartment of the other woman he's seeing (Harding). Thompson does fine but to describe Harding's debut performance as wooden is to be very, very kind. *CW:* Sex scene, violence and some nudity. 94m/C VHS. Teri Thompson, Joe Estevez, Chris De Rose, Tonya Harding; *D:* Sean Dash; *W:* Sean Dash. *NYR*

Breakdown 🎬 1953 A boxer is set up by his girlfriend's father to take the rap for a murder. Lackluster effort. 76m/B VHS, **Beta.** Ann Richards, William Bishop, Anne Gwynne, Sheldon Leonard, Wally Cassell, Richard Benedict; *D:* Edmond Angelo. *NOS, SNC*

Breakdown 🎬🎬🎬 1996 (R) Jeff (Russell) and Amy (Quinlan) are high-falootin' Easterners on their way to San Diego when their car breaks down somewhere in the vast Southwest. When a trucker (Walsh) stops and offers to take Amy to the next stop while Jeff guards their yuppie treasure trove, they accept willingly. Inconvenience soon turns to terror when Jeff gets the car started,

drives to meet his wife and finds her nowhere in sight. Spotting the truck by the side of the road, he confronts the trucker with the cops only to have him deny ever having seen them before. Thus begins the frantic hunt. Russell's descent from dismay to panic to resolve is grippingly played. You may know where it's going, but the fun is in getting there. *CW:* Strong violence/terror and language. 93m/C VHS. Kurt Russell, Kathleen Quinlan, J.T. Walsh, M.C. Gainey, Jack Noseworthy, Rex Linn, Ritch Brinkley, Kim Robillard; *D:* Jonathan Mostow; *W:* Jonathan Mostow; *C:* Doug Milsome; *M:* Basil Poledouris. *NYR*

Breaker! Breaker! 🎬 1977 (PG) Convoy of angry truck drivers launch an assault on the corrupt and sadistic locals of a small Texas town. Goofy entry in "mad or sex-crazed trucker armed with a CB radio" genre. 86m/C VHS, **Beta.** Chuck Norris, George Murdock; *D:* Don Hulette.

Breaker Morant 🎬🎬🎬½ 1980 (PG) In 1901 South Africa, three Australian soldiers are put on trial for avenging the murder of several prisoners. Based on a true story which was then turned into a play by Kenneth Ross, this riveting, popular antiwar statement and courtroom drama heralded Australia's film renaissance. Rich performances by Woodward and Waters. 107m/C VHS, **Beta, LV, 8mm.** *AU* Edward Woodward, Jack Thompson, John Waters, Bryan Brown; *D:* Bruce Beresford; *W:* Jonathon Hardy, David Stevens, Bruce Beresford. Australian Film Institute '80: Best Actor (Thompson), Best Film; Nominations: Academy Awards '80: Best Adapted Screenplay. *CCB, COL, HMV*

Breakfast at Tiffany's 🎬🎬🎬½ 1961 Truman Capote's amusing story of an endearingly eccentric New York City playgirl and her shaky romance with a young writer. Hepburn lends Holly Golightly just the right combination of naivete and worldly wisdom with a dash of melancholy. A wonderfully offbeat romance. ♫ Moon River. 114m/C VHS, **Beta, LV, 8mm.** Audrey Hepburn, George Peppard, Patricia Neal, Buddy Ebsen, Mickey Rooney, Martin Balsam, John McGiver; *D:* Blake Edwards; *W:* George Axelrod; *M:* Henry Mancini. Academy Awards '61: Best Song ("Moon River"), Original Dramatic/Comedy Score; Nominations: Academy Awards '61: Best Actress (Hepburn), Best Adapted Screenplay, Best Art Direction/Set Decoration (Color). *PAR, FCT*

The Breakfast Club 🎬🎬🎬 1985 (R) Five students from different cliques at a Chicago suburban high school spend a day together in detention. Rather well done teenage culture study; these characters delve a little deeper than the standard adult view of adolescent stereotypes. One of John Hughes' best movies. Soundtrack features Simple Minds and Wang Chung. 97m/C VHS, **Beta, LV, Closed Caption.** Ally Sheedy, Molly Ringwald, Judd Nelson, Emilio Estevez, Anthony Michael Hall, Paul Gleason, John Kapelos; *D:* John Hughes; *W:* John Hughes; *M:* Gary Chang, Keith Forsey. *USH, FCT*

Breakfast in Hollywood 🎬½ *The Mad Hatter* 1946 Movie about the popular morning radio show of the 1940s hosted by Tom Breneman, a coast-to-coast coffee klatch. 93m/B VHS, **Beta.** Tom Breneman, Bonita Granville, Eddie Ryan, Beulah Bondi, Billie Burke, ZaSu Pitts, Hedda Hopper, Spike Jones; *D:* Harold Schuster. *NO*

Breakfast in Paris 🎬½ 1981 Two American professionals in Paris, both crushed from past failures in the love department, find each other. 85m/C VHS. *AU* Rod Mullinar, Barbara Parkins, Jack Lenoir; *D:* John Lamond. *NWV*

Breakheart Pass 🎬🎬 1976 (PG) A governor, his female companion, a band of cavalrymen, and a mysterious man travel on a train through the mountains of Idaho in 1870. The mystery man turns out to be a murderer. Based on a novel by Alistair MacLean. 92m/C VHS, **Beta, LV, Closed Caption.** Charles Bronson, Ben Johnson, Richard Crenna, Jill Ireland, Charles Durning, Ed Lauter, Archie Moore, Sally Kirkland; *D:* Tom Gries; *C:* Lucien Ballard; *M:* Jerry Goldsmith. *MGM, FOX*

Breakin' 🎬🎬 *Breakdance* **1984 (PG)** Dance phenomenon break dancing along with the hit songs that accompanied the fad. 🎵Tibetan Jam; Heart of the Beat; Breakin...There's No Stopping Us; Street People; Showdown; 99 1/2. **87m/C VHS, Beta, LV.** Lucinda Dickey, Adolfo "Shabba Doo" Quinones, Michael "Boogaloo Shrimp" Chambers, Ben Lokey, Christopher McDonald, Phineas Newborn III; *D:* Joel Silberg; *W:* Allen N. DeBevoise; *C:* Hanania Baer; *M:* Michael Boyd. *MGM*

Breakin' 2: Electric Boogaloo 🎬 *Breakdance 2: Electric Boogaloo; Electric Boogaloo "Breakin' 2"* **1984 (PG)** Breakdancers hold a benefit concert to preserve an urban community center. 🎵Electric Boogaloo; Radiotron; Action; When I.C.U. **94m/C VHS, Beta, LV.** Lucinda Dickey, Adolfo "Shabba Doo" Quinones, Michael "Boogaloo Shrimp" Chambers, Susie Bono; *D:* Sam Firstenberg; *C:* Hanania Baer. *MGM*

Breakin' Through 🎬 **1984** The choreographer of a troubled Broadway-bound musical decides to energize his shows with a troupe of street dancers. **73m/C VHS, Beta.** Ben Vereen, Donna McKechnie, Reid Shelton; *D:* Peter Medak. *DIS*

Breaking All the Rules 🎬½ **1985 (R)** Comedy about two teenage lovers who find themselves embroiled in a slapdash jewel robbery at an amusement park during the last day of summer break. **91m/C VHS, Beta.** *CA* Carolyn Dunn, Carl Marotte, Thor Bishopric, Rachel Hayward; *D:* James Orr; *W:* James Orr, Jim Cruickshank. *NWV, VTR*

Breaking Away 🎬🎬🎬½ **1979 (PG)** A lighthearted coming-of-age drama about a high school graduate's addiction to bicycle racing, whose dreams are tested against the realities of a crucial race. An honest, open look at present Americana with tremendous insight into the minds of average youth; shot on location at Indiana University. Great bike-racing photography. Quaid, Barrie, and Christopher give exceptional performances. Basis for television series. **100m/C VHS, Beta, LV.** Dennis Christopher, Dennis Quaid, Daniel Stern, Jackie Earle Haley, Barbara Barrie, Paul Dooley, Amy Wright; *D:* Peter Yates; *W:* Steve Tesich. Academy Awards '79: Best Original Screenplay; Golden Globe Awards '80: Best Film—Musical/Comedy; National Board of Review Awards '79: 10 Best Films of the Year, Best Supporting Actor (Dooley); New York Film Critics Awards '79: Best Screenplay; National Society of Film Critics Awards '79: Best Film, Best Screenplay; Writers Guild of America '79: Best Original Screenplay; Nominations: Academy Awards '79: Best Director (Yates), Best Picture, Best Supporting Actress (Barrie), Original Song Score and/or Adaptation. *FOX, HMV*

Breaking Free 🎬🎬½ **1995 (PG)** Teenaged loser forms an unlikely friendship with a bitter gymnast who's been blinded and forced to give up her dreams. **106m/C VHS.** Jeremy London, Gina Philips, Christine Taylor, Megan Gallagher. *AVE*

Breaking Glass 🎬🎬½ **1980 (PG)** A "New Wave" musical that gives an insight into the punk record business and at the same time tells of the rags-to-riches life of a punk rock star. **94m/C VHS, Beta.** *GB* Hazel O'Connor, Phil Daniels, Jon Finch, Jonathan Pryce; *D:* Brian Gibson. *PAR*

Breaking Home Ties 🎬🎬½ *Norman Rockwell's Breaking Home Ties* **1987** Norman Rockwell's illustration is the basis for this coming of age story set in a small Texas town. A young man is eager to be off to college and lessen his family ties but his mother's serious illness may prevent both. Good performances help overcome the sentimentality. Originally made for television. **95m/C VHS.** Jason Robards Jr., Eva Marie Saint, Doug McKeon, Claire Trevor, Erin Gray; *D:* John Wilder; *W:* John Wilder. *CAF*

Breaking In 🎬🎬🎬 **1989 (R)** A semi-acclaimed comedy about a professional thief who takes a young amateur under his wing and shows him the ropes. Under-estimated Reynolds is especially charming. Witty and innovative script, with intelligent direction from Forsyth. **95m/C VHS, Beta, LV, Closed Caption.** Burt Reynolds, Casey Siemaszko, Sheila Kelley, Lorraine Toussaint, Albert Salmi, Harry Carey Jr., Maury Chaykin, Stephen Tobolowsky, David Frishberg; *D:* Bill Forsyth; *W:* John Sayles; *C:* Michael Coulter; *M:* Michael Gibbs. *HBO, WAR*

Breaking Loose 🎬½ **1990 (R)** A surfer is on the run from a vicious motorcycle gang that kidnapped his girlfriend, but turns to fight eventually, board in hand. **88m/C VHS.** Peter Phelps, Vince Martin, Abigail, David Ngcombujarra; *D:* Rod Hay. *HMD*

Breaking Point 🎬🎬½ **1994 (R)** Ex-cop Dwight Meadows (Busey) retired from the force when he was nearly killed by a scalpel-wielding mass murderer known as "The Surgeon." Now the psycho is back and Meadows returns to active duty, paired with relentless officer Dana Preston (Fluegel), who wants the killer caught—at any cost. Vancouver, British Columbia fills in for the Seattle, Washington setting. *CW:* Language; violence; nudity. **95m/C VHS, LV, Closed Caption.** Gary Busey, Darlanne Fluegel, Jeff Griggs, Kim Cattrall; *D:* Paul Ziller; *M:* Graeme Coleman. *REP*

Breaking the Code 🎬🎬½ **1995** Alan Turing (Jacobi) is a British mathematical genius whose work leads to the birth of the digital computer and who is instrumental in enabling the allies to crack the German WWII Enigma code. An active homosexual when homosexuality was illegal, Turing's personal behavior was tolerated because of the importance of his war work but after the gay spy scare of the '50s, Turing was regarded as a security risk and his life increasingly restricted. British TV adaptation based on the play by Hugh Whitemore (Jacobi also played the role on stage) and the book "Alan Turing: The Enigma" by Andrew Hodges. **90m/C VHS.** *GB* Derek Jacobi, Amanda Root, Prunella Scales, Harold Pinter, Julian Kerridge, Richard Johnson; *D:* Herbert Wise; *W:* Hugh Whitemore. *VTR, VIF, WMI*

Breaking the Ice 🎬🎬 **1938** Unlikely mixture of Mennonites and a big city ice skating show. Young man leaves the farm to get a job singing at the rink. Musical numbers abound with backing by Victor Young and his Orchestra. **79m/B VHS, Beta.** Bobby Breen, Charlie Ruggles, Dolores Costello, Billy Gilbert, Margaret Hamilton. Nominations: Academy Awards '38: Best Original Score. *NOS, VYY, DVT*

Breaking the Rules 🎬🎬½ **1992 (PG-13)** Predictable buddy-road movie with a tearjerking premise and comedic overtones. Rob, Gene, and Phil were best buds growing up in Cleveland but young adulthood has separated them. They are reunited by Phil, who is dying of leukemia, and whose last wish is a cross-country road trip to California so he can appear as a contestant on "Jeopardy." Along the way they meet brassy waitress Mary, who impulsively decides to join them and winds up bringing the trio's shaky friendship back together. Potts does well as the big-haired, big-hearted Mary but the actors must work hard to maintain any dignity given the story's melodrama. **100m/C VHS, LV, Closed Caption.** Jason Bateman, C. Thomas Howell, Jonathan Silverman, Annie Potts, Kent Bateman, Shawn Phelan; *D:* Neal Israel; *W:* Paul Shapiro; *M:* David Kitay. *HBO*

Breaking the Waves 🎬🎬🎬 **1995 (R)** Sacrificial journey of shy, religious Beth (Watson), who's living in an austere northern Scotland coastal village in the '70s. Bess, who regularly talks to God, marries Jan (Skarsgard), an adventurer working on a North Sea oil rig. It must be a case of opposites attracting but the couple are happy until Jan is paralyzed from the neck down in a rig accident. Beth, who blames herself, begins sleeping around, believing her actions can somehow help Jan, and slides ever deeper into mental instability. Powerful story is divided into seven chapters and an epilogue. *CW:* Strong graphic sexuality, nudity, language and some violence. **152m/C VHS, Closed Caption.** *DK FR* Emily Watson, Stellan Skarsgard, Katrin Cartlidge, Adrian Rawlins, Jean-Marc Barr, Sandra Voe, Udo Kier, Mikkel Gaup; *D:* Lars von Trier; *W:* Lars von Trier; *C:* Robby Muller; *M:* Joachim Holbek. Cannes Film Festival '96: Grand Jury Prize; Cesar Awards '97: Best Foreign Film; New York Film Critics Awards '96: Best Actress (Watson), Best Cinematography, Best Director (von Trier); National Society of Film Critics Awards '96: Best Actress (Watson), Best Cinematography, Best Director (von Trier), Best Film; Nominations: Academy Awards '96: Best Actress (Watson); British Academy Awards '96: Best Actress (Watson); Golden Globe Awards '97: Best Actress—Drama (Watson), Best Film—Drama; Independent Spirit Awards '97: Best Foreign Film. *EVE*

Breaking Up 🎬🎬½ **1978** A woman fights to rediscover her personal identity after her fifteen-year marriage crumbles. Made for television. Emmy nominated. **90m/C VHS, Beta.** Lee Remick, Granville Van Dusen, David Stambaugh; *D:* Delbert Mann. *TLF*

Breaking Up Is Hard to Do 🎬 **1979** Six men leave their wives and shack up together on Malibu for a summer of partying and introspection. Made for television; edited down from its original 201 minute length. **96m/C VHS, Beta, LV.** Billy Crystal, Bonnie Franklin, Ted Bessell, Jeff Conaway, Tony Musante, Robert Conrad, Trish Stewart, David Ogden Stiers, George Gaynes; *D:* Lou Antonio; *M:* Richard Bellis. *THV*

Breakout 🎬🎬 **1975 (PG)** The wife of a man imprisoned in Mexico hires a Texas bush pilot (Bronson) to help her husband (Duvall) escape. **96m/C VHS, Beta, LV.** Charles Bronson, Jill Ireland, Robert Duvall, John Huston, Sheree North, Randy Quaid; *D:* Tom Gries; *C:* Lucien Ballard; *M:* Jerry Goldsmith. *COL*

Breakthrough 🎬🎬 *Sergeant Steiner* **1978 (PG)** German soldier, broken at the end of WWII, sets out to negotiate with the Allies. Average at best. **96m/C VHS, Beta.** Richard Burton, Robert Mitchum, Rod Steiger, Michael Parks, Curt Jurgens; *D:* Andrew V. McLaglen. *WOV*

Breath of Scandal 🎬🎬 **1960** An American diplomat in Vienna rescues a princess when she is thrown off a horse; he falls for her like a ton o' bricks. Viennese politics complicate things. Based on a play by Molnar. **98m/C VHS, Closed Caption.** Sophia Loren, John Gavin, Maurice Chevalier, Angela Lansbury; *D:* Michael Curtiz. *PAR, BAR*

Breathing Fire 🎬🎬 **1991 (R)** A Vietnamese teenager and his American brother find out their ex-GI father is behind an armed bank robbery and murder. They join together to protect the only eyewitness—a young girl—against the ruthless gang of criminals and their own father. Lots of kickboxing action for martial arts fans. *CW:* Martial arts violence. **86m/C VHS, Closed Caption.** Bolo Yeung, Jonathan Ke Quan, Jerry Trimble; *D:* Lou Kennedy. *IMP*

Breathing Lessons 🎬🎬🎬 **1994 (PG)** Sweet look at a long-term marriage that renews itself on a road trip. Flighty Maggie and pragmatic Ira have been married for 28 squabbling but loving years. They're driving from their Baltimore home to a funeral in Pennsylvania and the road stops provide some small adventures and a great deal of conversation. Drama rests easily on the capable shoulders of the veteran performers. Based on the novel by Anne Tyler. Made for TV. **98m/C VHS, Closed Caption.** James Garner, Joanne Woodward, Paul Winfield, Kathryn Erbe, Joyce Van Patten, Eileen Heckart, Tim Guinee, Henry Jones, Stephi Lineburg, Jean Louisa Kelly, John Considine; *D:* John Erman; *W:* Robert W. Lenski. *REP*

Breathing Room 🎬🎬 *'Til Christmas* **1996 (R)** New Yorker David (Futterman) has trouble with commitment to girlfriend Kathy (Floyd) and the duo break up again at Thanksgiving when he won't tell her he loves her. Kathy decides they need a break and refuses to see David until Christmas. She plays at seeing her boss, both get too much advice from friends and family, they attend the same holiday party—and the inevitable happens. Nothing new here. *CW:* Language and some sexuality. **90m/C VHS.** Dan Futterman, Susan Floyd, David Thornton; *D:* Jon Sherman; *W:* Jon Sherman; *C:* Jim Denault; *M:* Pat Irwin. *AVI*

Breathless 🐾🐾🐾🐾 *A Bout de Souffle* 1959 Godard's first feature catapulted him to the vanguard of French filmmakers. A carefree Parisian crook, who emulates Humphrey Bogart, falls in love with an American girl with tragic results. Wonderful scenes of Parisian life. Established Godard's Brechtian, experimental style. Belmondo's film debut. Mistitled "Breathless" for American release, the film's French title actually means "Out of Breath"; however, the fast-paced, erratic musical score leaves you breathless. French with English subtitles. Remade with Richard Gere in 1983 with far less intensity. **90m/B VHS, Beta.** *FR* Jean-Paul Belmondo, Jean Seberg, Daniel Boulanger, Jean-Pierre Melville, Liliane Robin; *D:* Jean-Luc Godard; *W:* Jean-Luc Godard. Berlin International Film Festival '60: Best Director (Godard). *NOS, MRV, CVC*

Breathless 🐾🐾 1983 (R) Car thief turned cop killer has a torrid love affair with a French student studying in Los Angeles as the police slowly close in. Glossy, smarmy remake of the Godard classic that concentrates on the thin plot rather than any attempt at revitalizing the film syntax. **105m/C VHS, Beta, LV.** Richard Gere, Valerie Kaprisky, Art Metrano, John P. Ryan, Lisa Jane Persky; *D:* Jim McBride; *W:* Jim McBride, L.M. Kit Carson; *M:* Jack Nitzsche. *VES*

A Breed Apart 🐾🐾 1984 (R) An on-going battle over a rare eagle's eggs strikes sparks between a reclusive conservationist and a scheming adventurer hired by a billionaire collector. **95m/C VHS, Beta.** Kathleen Turner, Rutger Hauer, Powers Boothe, Donald Pleasence, Brion James, John Dennis Johnston; *D:* Philippe Mora. *HMD*

Breed of the Border 🐾 *Speed Brent Wins* 1933 Tough-fisted cowboys must take the law into their own hands. **60m/B VHS, Beta.** Bob Steele, Marion Byron, George "Gabby" Hayes, Ernie Adams; *D:* Robert North Bradbury. *NOS, DVT*

Brenda Starr 🐾 1986 (PG) Amateurish adaptation of the comic strip by Dale Messick. Shields stars as girl reporter Brenda Starr, who is once again risking her life to get the scoop. She finds herself in the jungles of South America searching for a mad scientist who is creating a rocket fuel that could destroy the world. The most entertaining thing about this film is the costumes designed by Bob Mackie. **94m/C VHS.** Brooke Shields, Timothy Dalton, Tony Peck, Diana Scarwid, Nestor Serrano, Jeffrey Tambor, June Gable, Charles Durning, Eddie Albert, Henry Gibson, Ed Nelson; *D:* Robert Ellis Miller; *W:* James David Buchanan. *COL*

The Bretts 🐾🐾🐾 1988 Amusing two-part British miniseries follows the egos and eccentricities of the British theatrical dynasty, the Bretts. Part 1 is set in the '20s and introduces the family heads, Charles (Rodway) and Lydia (Murray), who enjoy performing off-stage almost as well as they enjoy performing on. Also introduced are their five children and loyal (if opinionated) servants. Part 2 follows the family into the 30s with son Edwin (Yelland) having become a film star, actress daughter Martha (Lang) falling for a politician, and son Tom (Winter) continuing to write his gloomy social dramas. Each part is on 6 cassettes. **600m/C VHS.** *GB* Barbara Murray, Norman Rodway, David Yelland, Belinda Lang, George Winter, Janet Maw, Tim Wylton, Bert Parnaby, Lysette Anthony, Clive Francis, Frank Middlemass, John Castle, Hugh Fraser, Patrick Ryecart, Sally Cookson, Billy Boyle; *W:* Rosemary Anne Sisson. *SIG, VCO*

Brewster McCloud 🐾🐾🐾½ 1970 (R) Altman's first picture after M*A*S*H reunites much of the cast and combines fantasy, black comedy, and satire in the story of a young man whose head is in the clouds or at least in the upper reaches of the Houston Astrodome. Brewster (Cort) lives covertly in the Dome and dreams of flying. He also has a guardian angel (Kellerman) who watches over him and may actually be killing people who give him a hard time. Murphy is a cop obsessed with catching the killer. And there's a circus allegory as well. Hard to figure what it all

means and offbeat as they come, but for certain tastes, exquisite. **101m/C VHS, Beta, LV.** Bud Cort, Sally Kellerman, Shelley Duvall, Michael Murphy, William Windom, Rene Auberjonois, Stacy Keach, John Schuck, Margaret Hamilton; *D:* Robert Altman; *W:* Doran William Cannon; *C:* Jordan Cronenweth. *MGM*

Brewster's Millions 🐾🐾½ 1945 If Brewster, an ex-GI, can spend a million dollars in one year, he will inherit a substantially greater fortune. Originally a 1902 novel, this is the fifth of seven film adaptations. **79m/B VHS, Beta.** Dennis O'Keefe, June Havoc, Eddie Anderson, Helen Walker, Gail Patrick, Mischa Auer; *D:* Allan Dwan. Nominations: Academy Awards '45: Original Dramatic/Comedy Score. *MED*

Brewster's Millions 🐾½ 1985 (PG) An aging minor league baseball player must spend 30 million dollars in order to collect an inheritance of 300 million dollars. He may find that money can't buy happiness. Seventh remake of the story. **101m/C VHS, Beta, LV, Closed Caption.** Richard Pryor, John Candy, Lonette McKee, Stephen Collins, Jerry Orbach, Pat Hingle, Tovah Feldshuh, Hume Cronyn, Rick Moranis; *D:* Walter Hill; *W:* Herschel Weingrod, Timothy Harris; *M:* Ry Cooder. *USH*

Brian's Song 🐾🐾🐾🐾 1971 (G) The story of the unique relationship between Gale Sayers, the Chicago Bears' star running back, and his teammate Brian Piccolo. The friendship between the Bears' first interracial roommates ended suddenly when Brian Piccolo lost his life to cancer. Made for television. Incredibly well-received in its time. **74m/C VHS, Beta, LV, Closed Caption.** James Caan, Billy Dee Williams, Jack Warden, Shelley Fabares, Judy Pace; *D:* Buzz Kulik; *C:* Joseph Biroc. *COL*

The Bride 🐾½ 1985 (PG-13) Re-telling of "The Bride of Frankenstein." Sting's Dr. Frankenstein has much more success in creating his second monster (Beals). She's pretty and intelligent and he may even be falling in love with her. When she begins to gain too much independence, though, the awful truth about her origins comes out. Fans of the two leads will want to see this one, but for a true classic see Elsa Lanchester's bride. **118m/C VHS, Beta, LV, Closed Caption.** Sting, Jennifer Beals, Anthony Higgins, David Rappaport, Geraldine Page, Clancy Brown, Phil Daniels, Veruschka; *D:* Franc Roddam; *C:* Stephen Burum; *M:* Maurice Jarre. *FOX*

The Bride & the Beast woof! *Queen of the Gorillas* 1958 While on an African safari honeymoon, a big game hunter's new bride is carried off by a gorilla. Ludicrous jungle tale. **78m/B VHS, Beta.** Charlotte Austin, Lance Fuller, William Justine; *D:* Adrian Weiss; *W:* Edward D. Wood Jr.; *M:* Les Baxter. *AOV*

The Bride Came C.O.D. 🐾🐾 1941 Rough'n'tough pilot Cagney is hired by a rich Texas oil man to prevent his daughter (the one with the Bette Davis eyes) from marrying cheesy bandleader Carson. The payoff: $10 per pound if she's delivered unwed. What a surprise when Cagney faces the timeworn dilemma of having to choose between love and money. A contemporary issue of "Time" magazine trumpeted: "Screen's most talented tough guy rough-houses one of screen's best dramatic actresses." That tells you right there it's a romantic comedy. Cagney and Davis—a likely pairing, you'd think—are essentially fish out of water, bothered and bewildered by a weak script. **92m/B VHS.** Bette Davis, James Cagney, Stuart Erwin, Jack Carson, George Tobias, Eugene Pallette, William Frawley; *D:* William Keighley; *W:* Julius J. Epstein, Philip G. Epstein; *M:* Max Steiner. *MGM, FCT*

The Bride Is Much Too Beautiful 🐾🐾½ 1958 Bardot, playing a French farm girl, becomes a renowned model. Dubbed. **90m/C VHS, Beta.** *FR* Brigitte Bardot, Louis Jourdan, Micheline Presle, Marcel Amont; *D:* Fred Surin. *NOS, FCT, HEG*

The Bride of Frankenstein 🐾🐾🐾🐾 1935 The classic sequel to the classic original in which Dr. F. seeks to build a mate for his monster. More humor than the first, but also more pathos,

including the monster's famous but short-lived friendship with a blind hermit. Lanchester plays both the bride and Mary Shelley in the opening sequence. **75m/B VHS, Beta, LV.** Boris Karloff, Elsa Lanchester, Ernest Thesiger, Colin Clive, Una O'Connor, Valerie Hobson, Dwight Frye, John Carradine, E.E. Clive, O.P. Heggie, Gavin Gordon, Douglas Walton; *D:* James Whale. Nominations: Academy Awards '35: Best Sound. *USH, MLB*

Bride of Killer Nerd 🐾 1991 Harold Kunkel, left over from the original "Killer Nerd," finds his opposite sex nirvana in the person of Thelma, also a nerd in mind, body, and soul. They relentlessly pursue revenge on the rockers who humiliate them at a campus beer bash. **75m/C VHS.** Toby Radloff, Wayne A. Harold, Heidi Lohr; *D:* Mark Steven Bosko. *TEM*

Bride of Re-Animator 🐾🐾½ 1989 Herbert West is back, and this time he not only re-animates life but creates life—sexy female life—in this sequel to the immensely popular "Re-Animator." High camp and blood curdling gore make this a standout in the sequel parade. Available in a R-rated version as well. **99m/C VHS, Beta, LV, Closed Caption.** Bruce Abbott, Claude Earl Jones, Fabiana Udenio, Jeffrey Combs, Kathleen Kinmont, David Gale; *D:* Brian Yuzna; *M:* Richard Band. *LIV*

Bride of the Gorilla 🐾🐾 1951 Burr travels to the jungle where he finds a wife, a plantation, and a curse in this African twist on the werewolf legend. Chaney is the local policeman on his trail. Burr's physical changes are fun to watch. **76m/B VHS.** Raymond Burr, Barbara Payton, Lon Chaney Jr., Tom Conway, Paul Cavanagh; *D:* Curt Siodmak; *W:* Curt Siodmak. *NOS, MRV, SNC*

Bride of the Monster woof! *Bride of the Atom* 1956 Lugosi stars as a mad scientist trying to create a race of giants. Classic Woodian badness. **70m/B VHS, Beta.** Bela Lugosi, Tor Johnson, Loretta King, Tony McCoy; *D:* Edward T. Wood Jr. *NOS, SNC, VYY*

The Bride Walks Out 🐾🐾 1936 Newlywed crisis: a woman with rich taste learns how to adjust to living on her husband's poor salary, but not before she samples the life of the wealthy. Interesting in a sociological sort of way. **81m/B VHS, Beta.** Barbara Stanwyck, Gene Raymond, Robert Young, Ned Sparks, Willie Best, Helen Broderick, Hattie McDaniel; *D:* Leigh Jason. *TTC*

The Bride with White Hair 🐾🐾 1993 Operatic martial arts fable based on a novel by Leung Yu-Sang. A young warrior revives a beautiful witch (also a champion warrior) who was killed by jealous Siamese twins. Now the duo, who have fallen in love, must battle the evil twins who rule the corrupt Mo Dynasty. Available dubbed or in Chinese with subtitles. **92m/C VHS.** *HK* Leslie Cheung, Brigitte Lin Ching Hsia; *D:* Ronny Yu. *TAI*

The Bride with White Hair 2 🐾🐾 1993 The magic saga continues with the massacre of the followers of the Eight Lineages. Powerful and obsessed with vengeance, the Bride can only be stopped by the one man who loves her. Chinese with subtitles or dubbed. **80m/C VHS, LV.** *HK* Brigitte Lin Ching Hsia, Leslie Cheung. *TAI*

The Bride Wore Black 🐾🐾🐾 *La Mariee Etait en Noir* 1968 Truffaut's homage to Hitchcock, complete with Bernard Herrmann score. A young woman exacts brutal revenge on the five men who accidentally killed her husband. Adapted from a novel by Cornell Woolrich. **107m/C VHS, LV.** *FR* Jeanne Moreau, Claude Rich, Jean-Claude Brialy, Michel Bouquet, Claude Rich; *D:* Francois Truffaut; *C:* Raoul Coutard; *M:* Bernard Herrmann. *MGM, MLB, FCT*

The Bride Wore Red 🐾🐾 1937 Crawford stars as a cabaret singer who masquerades as a socialite in an attempt to break into the upper crust. When a wealthy aristocrat invites her to spend two weeks at a posh resort in Tyrol, Crawford plays her part to the hilt, managing to charm both a rich gentleman and the village postman. Typical "love conquers all" melodrama. **103m/B VHS, Closed Caption.** Joan Crawford, Franchot Tone,

Robert Young, Billie Burke, Reginald Owen, Lynne Carver, George Zucco; **D:** Dorothy Arzner. *MGM*

Brides of Christ 🎬🎬½ 1991 Set in the Australian Santo Spirito Convent during the Vatican II upheaval of the 1960s. Explores the tensions between old and new religious ideas by focusing on novices, older nuns, and the Reverend Mother of the convent as they try to cope with a changing world. TV miniseries. **300m/C VHS.** Brenda Fricker, Sandy Gore, Josephine Byrnes, Lisa Hensley, Naomi Watts, Kym Wilson, Melissa Thomas; **D:** Ken Cameron; **W:** John Alsop, Sue Smith. *AAE, NEW*

The Brides of Dracula 🎬🎬½ 1960 A young French woman unknowingly frees a vampire. He wreaks havoc, sucking blood and creating more of the undead to carry out his evil deeds. One of the better Hammer vampire films. **86m/C VHS, LV.** *GB* Peter Cushing, Martita Hunt, Yvonne Monlaur, Freda Jackson, David Peel, Mona Washbourne; **D:** Terence Fisher. *USH, FCT*

Brides of the Beast woof! *Brides of Blood; Grave Desires; Island of the Living Horror* 1968 Filipino radiation monsters get their jollies by eating beautiful young naked women. Newly arrived research scientist and his bride oppose this custom. First in a series of "Blood Island" horrors. **85m/C VHS, Beta.** *PH* John Ashley, Kent Taylor, Beverly Hills, Eva Darren, Mario Montenegro; **D:** Eddie Romero, Gerardo (Gerry) De Leon. *NO*

Brideshead Revisited 🎬🎬🎬 1981 The acclaimed British miniseries based on the Evelyn Waugh classic about an Edwardian young man who falls under the spell of a wealthy aristocratic family and struggles to retain his integrity and values. On six tapes. **540m/C VHS, Beta, Closed Caption.** *GB* Jeremy Irons, Anthony Andrews, Diana Quick, Laurence Olivier, John Gielgud, Claire Bloom, Stephane Audran, Mona Washbourne, John Le Mesurier, Charles Keating; **D:** Charles Sturridge, Michael Lindsay-Hogg; **M:** Geoffrey Burgon. *MOV, FUS, FCT*

The Bridge 🎬🎬 *Die Brucke* 1959 In 1945, two days before the end of WWII, seven German schoolboys are drafted to defend an unimportant bridge from American tanks. Emotional anti-war film based on the autobiographical novel of Manfred Gregor. German with subtitles. **102m/B VHS.** *GE* Fritz Wepper, Volker Bohnet, Franz Glaubrecht, Karl Michael Balzer, Gunther Hoffman; **D:** Bernhard Wicki; **W:** Michael Mansfield, Karl-Wilhelm Vivier; **C:** Gerd Von Bonen; **M:** Hans-Martin Majewski. Nominations: Academy Awards '59: Best Foreign Language Film. *FCT*

The Bridge at Remagen 🎬🎬½ 1969 **(PG)** Based on the true story of allied attempts to capture a vital bridge before retreating German troops destroy it. For war-film buffs. **115m/C VHS, Beta.** George Segal, Robert Vaughn, Ben Gazzara, Bradford Dillman, E.G. Marshall; **D:** John Guillermin; **W:** William Roberts; **M:** Elmer Bernstein. *NO*

The Bridge of San Luis Rey 🎬🎬🎬 1944 A priest investigates the famous bridge collapse in Lima, Peru that left five people dead. Based upon the novel by Thornton Wilder. **89m/B VHS, Beta, LV.** Lynn Bari, Francis Lederer, Louis Calhern, Akim Tamiroff, Donald Woods, Alla Nazimova, Blanche Yurka; **D:** Rowland V. Lee. Nominations: Academy Awards '44: Original Dramatic/Comedy Score. *NWV, IME*

The Bridge on the River Kwai 🎬🎬🎬🎬 1957 Award-winning adaptation of the Pierre Bouelle novel about the battle of wills between a Japanese POW camp commander and a British colonel over the construction of a rail bridge, and the parallel efforts by escaped prisoner Holden to destroy it. Holden's role was originally cast for Cary Grant. Memorable too for whistling "Colonel Bogey March." Because the writers were blacklisted, Bouelle (who spoke no English) was originally credited as the screenwriter. **161m/C VHS, Beta, LV.** *GB* William Holden, Alec Guinness, Jack Hawkins, Sessue Hayakawa, James Donald, Geoffrey Horne, Andre Morell, Ann Sears; **D:** David Lean; **W:** Michael Wilson, Carl Foreman; **C:** Jack Hildyard; **M:** Malcolm Arnold. Academy Awards '57: Best Actor (Guinness), Best Adapted Screenplay, Best Cinematogra-

phy, Best Director (Lean), Best Film Editing, Best Picture, Best Score; British Academy Awards '57: Best Actor (Guinness), Best Film, Best Screenplay; Directors Guild of America Awards '57: Best Director (Lean); Golden Globe Awards '58: Best Actor—Drama (Guinness), Best Director (Lean), Best Film—Drama; National Board of Review Awards '57: 10 Best Films of the Year, Best Actor (Guinness), Best Director (Lean), Best Supporting Actor (Hayakawa); New York Film Critics Awards '57: Best Actor (Guinness), Best Director (Lean), Best Film; Nominations: Academy Awards '57: Best Supporting Actor (Hayakawa). *COL, BTV, HMV*

Bridge to Hell 🎬½ 1987 A group of allied P.O.W.s try to make their way to the American front during WWII in Yugoslavia. A heavily guarded bridge occupied by Nazi troops stands between them and freedom. A special introduction by Michael Dudikoff doing martial arts. **94m/C VHS.** Jeff Connors, Francis Ferre, Andy Forrest, Paky Valente; **D:** Umberto Lenzi. *CAN*

The Bridge to Nowhere 🎬🎬 1986 Five city kids go hunting and back-packing in the New Zealand wilderness, and are hunted by a maniacal backwoodsman. **82m/C VHS, Beta.** *NZ* Bruno Lawrence, Alison Routledge, Margaret Umbers, Philip Gordon; **D:** Ian Mune. *NLC*

Bridge to Silence 🎬🎬 1989 A young hearing-impaired mother's life begins to crumble following the death of her husband in a car crash. Her mother tries to get custody of her daughter and a friend applies romantic pressure. Made for TV melodrama features Matlin in her first television speaking role. **95m/C VHS, Closed Caption.** Marlee Matlin, Lee Remick, Josef Sommer, Michael O'Keefe, Allison Silva, Candice Brecker; **D:** Karen Arthur. *FRH*

Bridge to Terabithia 1985 An imaginative girl and a young boy learn the joys of friendship in a magic make-believe kingdom called Terabithia. Adapted from the novel by Katherine Paterson. Originally aired by PBS for the "Wonderworks" television series. **58m/C VHS, Closed Caption.** Annette O'Toole, Julian Coutts, Julie Beaulieu; **D:** Eric Till. *PME, HMV, FCT*

A Bridge Too Far 🎬🎬 1977 **(PG)** A meticulous recreation of one of the most disastrous battles of WWII, the Allied defeat at Arnhem in 1944. Misinformation, adverse conditions, and overconfidence combined to prevent the Allies from capturing six bridges that connected Holland to the German border. **175m/C VHS, Beta, LV, Closed Caption.** *GB* Sean Connery, Robert Redford, James Caan, Michael Caine, Elliott Gould, Gene Hackman, Laurence Olivier, Ryan O'Neal, Liv Ullmann, Dirk Bogarde, Hardy Kruger, Arthur Hill, Edward Fox, Anthony Hopkins; **D:** Richard Attenborough; **W:** William Goldman; **C:** Geoffrey Unsworth; **M:** John Addison. British Academy Awards '77: Best Supporting Actor (Fox); National Society of Film Critics Awards '77: Best Supporting Actor (Fox). *MGM, FOX*

The Bridges at Toko-Ri 🎬🎬🎬½ 1955 Based on the James A. Michener novel, the rousing war-epic about a lawyer being summoned by the Navy to fly bombing missions during the Korean War. A powerful anti-war statement. **103m/C VHS, Beta, LV.** William Holden, Grace Kelly, Fredric March, Mickey Rooney, Robert Strauss, Earl Holliman, Keiko Awaji, Charles McGraw; **D:** Mark Robson; **W:** Valentine Davies; **C:** Loyal Griggs. Academy Awards '55: Best Special Effects; Nominations: Academy Awards '55: Best Film Editing. *PAR*

The Bridges of Madison County 🎬🎬🎬 1995 **(PG-13)** Robert Kincaid (Eastwood) is on assignment in 1965 Iowa to photograph Madison County's scenic covered bridges. Only problem is he gets lost and stops for directions at Francesca Johnson's (Streep) farmhouse. There's an immediate attraction between the repressed Italian war-bride-turned-farm-wife and the charismatic world traveler, which they act on in four short days. Much of the treacle from Robert James Waller's novel has been fortunately abandoned but the mature romance remains. 64-year-old Eastwood exudes low-key sexiness while Streep (with a light Italian accent) is all earthy warmth. Fans of both book and stars should

be pleased, though the leisurely paced film takes too long to get started. **CW:** Some sexuality; brief strong language. **135m/C VHS, LV, Closed Caption, DVD.** Clint Eastwood, Meryl Streep, Victor Slezak, Annie Corley, Jim Haynie; **D:** Clint Eastwood; **W:** Richard LaGravenese; **C:** Jack N. Green; **M:** Lennie Niehaus. Nominations: Academy Awards '95: Best Actress (Streep); Golden Globe Awards '96: Best Actress—Drama (Streep), Best Film—Drama; Screen Actors Guild Award '95: Best Actress (Streep). *WAR*

Brief Encounter 🎬🎬🎬🎬 1946 Based on Noel Coward's "Still Life" from "Tonight at 8:30," two middle-aged, middle-class people become involved in a short and bittersweet romance in WWII England. Intensely romantic, underscored with Rachmaninoff's Second Piano Concerto. **86m/B VHS, Beta.** *GB* Celia Johnson, Trevor Howard, Stanley Holloway, Cyril Raymond, Joyce Carey, Everley Gregg, Margaret Barton, Dennis Harkin, Valentine Dyall, Marjorie Mars, Irene Handl; **D:** David Lean; **W:** Noel Coward; **C:** Robert Krasker. National Board of Review Awards '46: 10 Best Films of the Year; New York Film Critics Awards '46: Best Actress (Johnson); Nominations: Academy Awards '46: Best Actress (Johnson), Best Director (Lean), Best Screenplay. *PAR, HMV*

A Brief History of Time 🎬🎬🎬 1992 **(G)** A stunning documentary about physicist Stephen Hawking, the author of the popular book "Brief History of Time." Crippled by Lou Gehrig's Disease, Hawking narrates the film in the computer-synthesized voice he uses to speak. Interviews with family, friends, and colleagues, bring Hawking's scientific theories to light. **85m/C VHS, Beta, Closed Caption.** Stephen Hawking; **D:** Errol Morris; **W:** Stephen Hawking; **C:** John Bailey; **M:** Philip Glass. Sundance Film Festival '92: Filmmakers Trophy. *PAR, BTV, WSH*

The Brig 🎬🎬🎬 1964 A film by Jonas Mekas documenting the Living Theatre's infamous performance of Kenneth H. Brown's experimental play. Designed by Julian Beck. **65m/B VHS, Beta.** Adolfas Mekas, Jim Anderson, Warren Finnerty, Henry Howard, Tom Lillard, James Tiroff, Gene Lipton; **D:** John Mekas. Venice Film Festival '64: Best Documentary. *MFV, FCT, TPV*

Brigadoon 🎬🎬🎬 1954 The story of a magical, 18th century Scottish village which awakens once every 100 years and the two modern-day vacationers who stumble upon it. Main highlight is the Lerner and Loewe score. ♪Brigadoon; Almost Like Being in Love; I'll Go Home With Bonnie Jean; Wedding Dance; From This Day On; Heather on the Hill; Waitin' For My Dearie; Once in the Highlands. **108m/C VHS, Beta, LV, DVD.** Gene Kelly, Van Johnson, Cyd Charisse; **D:** Vincente Minnelli; **C:** Joseph Ruttenberg; **M:** Alan Jay Lerner, Frederick Loewe. Nominations: Academy Awards '54: Best Art Direction/Set Decoration (Color), Best Costume Design (Color), Best Sound. *MGM, TLF*

Brigham Young: Frontiersman 🎬🎬 1940 Somewhat interesting story about the pioneering Mormons and their founding of Salt Lake City. Under the leadership of Brigham Young (Jagger), they set out across the plains, battling hardships and starvation along the way. An emphasis was placed on the historical rather than the religious in an effort not to scare off moviegoers, but the picture failed at the box office anyway. Based on the story by Louis Bromfield. **114m/C VHS.** Tyrone Power, Linda Darnell, Dean Jagger, Brian Donlevy, John Carradine, Jane Darwell, Jean Rogers, Mary Astor, Vincent Price; **D:** Henry Hathaway; **W:** Lamar Trotti; **C:** Arthur C. Miller. *FXV*

Bright Angel 🎬🎬½ 1991 **(R)** Road movie pairs an unconventional team: George wants to visit his aunt to see if she's heard from his mother who ran off with another man; Luey is a free-spirit trying to free her brother from jail. Good performances by Mulroney, Taylor, & Pullman. Ford adapted two of his short stories, "Childern" and "Great Falls" for the gritty and uncompromising script of life in the modern west. **94m/C VHS, Closed Caption.** Dermot Mulroney, Lili Taylor, Sam Shepard, Valerie Perrine, Burt Young, Bill Pullman, Benjamin Bratt, Mary

Kay Place, Delroy Lindo, Kevin Tighe, Sheila McCarthy; **D:** Michael Fields; **W:** Richard Ford; **M:** Christopher Young. *HBO*

Bright Eyes 🎬🎬 1934 (PG)
Shirley Temple stars as an adorable orphan caught between foster parents. Submitted for an MPAA rating when the video was released. Also available colorized. **84m/B VHS, Beta, Closed Caption.** Shirley Temple, James Dunn, Lois Wilson, Jane Withers, Judith Allen; **D:** David Butler. *FOX, MLT*

Bright Lights, Big City 🎬🎬 1988 (R)
Based on Jay McInerney's popular novel, Fox plays a contemporary yuppie working in Manhattan as a magazine journalist. As his world begins to fall apart, he embarks on an endless cycle of drugs and nightlife. Fox is poorly cast, and his character is hard to care for as he becomes more and more dissolute. Although McInerney wrote his own screenplay, the intellectual abstractness of the novel can't be captured on film. **110m/C VHS, Beta, LV, Closed Caption.** Michael J. Fox, Kiefer Sutherland, Phoebe Cates, Frances Sternhagen, Swoosie Kurtz, Tracy Pollan, Jason Robards Jr., John Houseman, Dianne Wiest, Charlie Schlatter, William Hickey; **D:** James Bridges; **C:** Gordon Willis. *MGM*

Bright Smiler 🎬½ 1985
A made-for-British-television mystery about a writer who retires to her favorite spa and falls into the hands of a malevolent masseuse. **60m/C VHS, Beta.** *GB* Janet Suzman. *PSM*

Brighton Beach Memoirs 🎬🎬½ 1986
Neil Simon's Brighton Beach Memoirs (PG-13) The film adaptation of the popular (and semiautobiographical) Neil Simon play. Poignant comedy/drama about a young Jewish boy's coming of age in Depression-era Brooklyn. Followed by "Biloxi Blues" and "Broadway Bound." **108m/C VHS, Beta, LV, Closed Caption.** Blythe Danner, Bob Dishy, Judith Ivey, Jonathan Silverman, Brian Drillinger, Stacey Glick, Lisa Waltz, Jason Alexander; **D:** Gene Saks; **W:** Neil Simon; **C:** John Bailey; **M:** Michael Small. *USH, FCT*

Brighton Rock 🎬🎬🎬
Young Scarface 1947 Sterling performances highlight this seamy look at the British underworld. Attenborough is Pinkie Brown, a small-time hood who ends up committing murder. He manipulates a waitress to get himself off the hook, but things don't go exactly as he plans. Based on the novel by Graham Greene. **92m/B VHS.** *GB* Richard Attenborough, Hermione Baddeley, William Hartnell, Carol Marsh, Nigel Stock, Wylie Watson, Alan Wheatley, George Carney, Reginald Purdell; **D:** John Boulting. *DVT, HEG*

Brighton Strangler 🎬🎬 1945
An actor who plays a murderer assumes the role of the strangler after suffering from a concussion. Decent psychodrama. **67m/B VHS, Beta.** John Loder, June Duprez, Miles Mander; **D:** Max Nosseck. *NO*

The Brighton Strangler/Before Dawn 🎬🎬 1945
A mystery double feature: In "The Brighton Strangler," an actor takes his part too seriously as he murders Londoners at night; in "Before Dawn" a brilliant scientist turns to a life of murderous crime. **128m/B VHS, Beta.** John Loder, June Duprez, Miles Mander, Stuart Oland, Dorothy Wilson. *TTC*

Brighty of the Grand Canyon 🎬½ 1967
The spunky donkey Brighty roams across the Grand Canyon in search of adventure. He finds friendship with a gold-digging old prospector who hits pay dirt. **90m/C VHS, Beta.** Joseph Cotten, Pat Conway, Dick Foran, Karl Swenson; **D:** Norman Foster. *AHV, KAR*

A Brilliant Disguise 🎬½ 1993 (R)
Sportswriter gets involved with an artist who turns out to have multiple personality disorder and a sinister psychiatrist. Then his friends start to turn up dead but things aren't exactly what they seem. **97m/C VHS, LV.** Lysette Anthony, Anthony John Denison, Corbin Bernsen, Gregory McKinney, Robert Shafer; **D:** Nick Vallelonga; **W:** Nick Vallelonga. *PSM*

Brimstone & Treacle 🎬🎬🎬 1982 (R)
Weird, obsessive psychodrama in which a young rogue (who may or may not be an actual agent of the Devil) infiltrates the home of a staid British family caring for their comatose adult daughter. **85m/C VHS, Beta.** *GB* Sting, Denholm Elliott, Joan Plowright, Suzanna Hamilton; **D:** Richard Loncraine; **W:** Dennis Potter. Montreal World Film Festival '82: Best Film. *MGM*

Bring Me the Head of Alfredo Garcia 🎬🎬 1974 (R)
Peckinpah falters in this poorly paced outing. American piano player on tour in Mexico finds himself entwined with a gang of bloodthirsty bounty hunters. Bloody and confused. **112m/C VHS.** Warren Oates, Isela Vega, Gig Young, Robert Webber, Helmut Dantine, Emilio Fernandez, Kris Kristofferson; **D:** Sam Peckinpah; **W:** Sam Peckinpah, Gordon Dawson. *MGM*

Bring Me the Vampire 🎬 1961
A wealthy baron must endure a night of terror in order to receive an inheritance. **100m/B VHS.** *MX* Maria Eugenia San Martin, Hector Godoy, Joaquin Vargas. *SNC, MOV*

Bringing Up Baby 🎬🎬🎬🎬 1938
The quintessential screwball comedy, featuring Hepburn as a giddy socialite with a "baby" leopard, and Grant as the unwitting object of her affections. One ridiculous situation after another adds up to high speed fun. Hepburn looks lovely, the supporting actors are in fine form, and director Hawks manages the perfect balance of control and mayhem. From a story by Hagar Wilde, who helped Nichols with the screenplay. Also available in a colorized version. **103m/B VHS, Beta, LV.** Katharine Hepburn, Cary Grant, May Robson, Charlie Ruggles, Walter Catlett, Fritz Feld, Jonathan Hale, Barry Fitzgerald, Ward Bond; **D:** Howard Hawks; **W:** Dudley Nichols; **C:** Russell Metty. *TTC, HMV, BTV*

Brink of Life 🎬🎬½
Nara Livet 1957 Three pregnant women in a hospital maternity ward await the impending births with mixed feelings. Early Bergman; in Swedish with English subtitles. **82m/B VHS, Beta.** *SW* Eva Dahlbeck, Bibi Andersson, Ingrid Thulin, Barbro Ornas, Max von Sydow, Erland Josephson, Gunnar Sjoberg; **D:** Ingmar Bergman. Cannes Film Festival '58: Best Actress (Dahlbeck), Best Actress (Andersson, Thulin), Best Director (Bergman). *VYY*

Brink's Job 🎬🎬🎬 1978 (PG)
Recreates the "crime of the century," Tony Pino's heist of 2.7 million dollars from a Brink's truck. The action picks up five days before the statute of limitations is about to run out. **103m/C VHS, Beta.** Peter Falk, Peter Boyle, Warren Oates, Gena Rowlands, Paul Sorvino, Sheldon Leonard, Allen (Goorwitz) Garfield; **D:** William Friedkin; **W:** Walon Green; **M:** Richard Rodney Bennett. Nominations: Academy Awards '78: Best Art Direction/Set Decoration. *USH*

Britannia Hospital 🎬🎬½ 1982 (R)
This is a portrait of a hospital at its most chaotic: the staff threatens to strike, demonstrators surround the hospital, a nosey BBC reporter pursues an anxious professor, and the eagerly-anticipated royal visit degenerates into a total shambles. **111m/C VHS, Beta.** *GB* Malcolm McDowell, Leonard Rossiter, Graham Crowden, Joan Plowright, Mark Hamill, Alan Bates; **D:** Lindsay Anderson. *REP*

British Intelligence 🎬½ 1940
Silly American-made film about British espionage. Boris Karloff plays a butler (who is also a spy) trapped by an agent who visits the home of a British bureaucrat. Half-baked story that doesn't hold up. **62m/B VHS.** Boris Karloff, Margaret Lindsay, Maris Wrixon, Holmes Herbert, Leonard Mudie, Bruce Lester; **D:** Terry Morse. *NOS, SNC, MLB*

A Brivele der Mamen 🎬🎬🎬
A Letter to Mother; A Letter to Mama 1938 A Jewish mother does her best to hold her fragile family together, in spite of the ravages of war and poverty. Her travails take her and her family from the Polish Ukraine to New York City. In Yiddish with English subtitles. **90m/C VHS, Beta.** *PL* Berta Gersten, Lucy Gerhman, Misha Gerhman, Edmund Zayenda; **D:** Joseph Green. *ERG*

Broadcast News 🎬🎬🎬½ 1987 (R)
The acclaimed, witty analysis of network news shows, dealing with the three-way romance between a driven career-woman producer, an ace nebbish reporter, and a brainless, popular on-screen anchorman. Incisive and funny, though often simply idealistic. **132m/C VHS, Beta, LV, Closed Caption.** William Hurt, Albert Brooks, Holly Hunter, Jack Nicholson, Joan Cusack, Robert Prosky, Lois Chiles, Gennie James; **Cameos:** John Cusack; **D:** James L. Brooks; **W:** James L. Brooks; **C:** Michael Ballhaus; **M:** Bill Conti, Michael Gore. Los Angeles Film Critics Association Awards '87: Best Actress (Hunter); National Board of Review Awards '87: 10 Best Films of the Year, Best Actress (Hunter); New York Film Critics Awards '87: Best Actress (Hunter), Best Director (Brooks), Best Film, Best Screenplay; Nominations: Academy Awards '87: Best Actor (Hurt), Best Actress (Hunter), Best Cinematography, Best Film Editing, Best Original Screenplay, Best Picture, Best Supporting Actor (Brooks). *FOX*

Broadway Bill 🎬🎬🎬
Strictly Confidential 1934 A man decides to abandon his nagging wife and his job in her family's business for the questionable pleasures of owning a racehorse known as Broadway Bill. This racetrack comedy was also remade by Frank Capra in 1951 as "Riding High." **90m/C VHS, Beta, LV.** Warner Baxter, Myrna Loy, Walter Connolly, Helen Vinson, Margaret Hamilton, Frankie Darro; **D:** Frank Capra. *PAR*

Broadway Bound 🎬🎬½
Neil Simon's Broadway Bound 1992 The final film in Simon's trilogy (preceded by "Brighton Beach Memoirs" and "Biloxi Blues"). This time the playwright's alter ego, Eugene Morris Jerome, is ready to leave Brooklyn for good, hoping to make it as a comedy writer for a radio show. Meanwhile, his mother decides what to do about his unfaithful father. Made for television. **90m/C VHS, Closed Caption.** Jonathan Silverman, Anne Bancroft, Jerry Orbach, Corey Parker, Hume Cronyn, Michele Lee; **D:** Paul Bogart; **W:** Neil Simon. *ABC*

Broadway Danny Rose 🎬🎬🎬½ 1984 (PG)
One of Woody Allen's best films, a hilarious, heart-rending anecdotal comedy about a third-rate talent agent involved in one of his client's infidelities. The film magically unfolds as show business veterans swap Danny Rose stories at a delicatessen. Allen's Danny Rose is pathetically lovable. **85m/B VHS, Beta, LV.** Woody Allen, Mia Farrow, Nick Apollo Forte, Sandy Baron, Milton Berle, Howard Cosell; **D:** Woody Allen; **W:** Woody Allen; **C:** Gordon Willis. British Academy Awards '84: Best Original Screenplay; Writers Guild of America '84: Best Original Screenplay; Nominations: Academy Awards '84: Best Director (Allen), Best Original Screenplay. *VES*

The Broadway Drifter 🎬🎬 1927
A silent Jazz Age drama about a playboy who repents his decadent ways by opening a girls' health school. Complications ensue. **90m/B VHS, Beta, 8mm.** George Walsh, Dorothy Hall, Bigelow Cooper, Arthur Donaldson; **D:** Bernard McEveety Sr. *VYY*

Broadway Limited 🎬🎬
The Baby Vanishes 1941 Three aspiring actors head for the Great White Way with a baby to use as a prop. Thinking the baby kidnapped, the police make things tough for the trio. McLaglen was wasted on this one, which was apparently made to show off the considerable assets of Woodworth. **75m/B VHS.** Victor McLaglen, Marjorie Woodworth, Dennis O'Keefe, Patsy Kelly, ZaSu Pitts, Leonid Kinskey, George E. Stone; **D:** Gordon Douglas. *NOS*

Broadway Melody 🎬🎬½ 1929
Early musical in which two sisters hope for fame on Broadway, and encounter a wily song and dance man who traps both their hearts. Dated, but still charming, with a lovely score. Considered the great granddaddy of all MGM musicals; followed by three more melodies in 1935, 1937, and 1940. ♪Broadway Melody; Give My Regards to Broadway; Truthful Parson Brown; The Wedding of the Painted Doll; The Boy Friend; You Were Meant For Me; Love Boat; Broadway Babies. **104m/B VHS, Beta.** Bessie Love, Anita Page, Charles King, Jed Prouty, Kenneth Thomson, Edward Dillon, Mary Doran; **D:**

Harry Beaumont; **M:** Nacio Herb Brown, Arthur Freed. Academy Awards '29: Best Picture; Nominations: Academy Awards '29: Best Actress (Love), Best Director (Beaumont). *MGM, BTV*

Broadway Melody of 1936 🎬🎬🎬
1935 Exceptional musical comedy with delightful performances from Taylor and Powell. Benny is a headline-hungry columnist who tries to entrap Taylor by using Powell. ♫Broadway Melody; Broadway Rhythm; You Are My Lucky Star; I've Got a Feeling You're Fooling; All I Do Is Dream of You; Sing Before Breakfast; On a Sunday Afternoon. **110m/B VHS, Beta.** Jack Benny, Eleanor Powell, Robert Taylor, Una Merkel, Sid Silvers, Buddy Ebsen; **D:** Roy Del Ruth; **C:** Charles Rosher; **M:** Nacio Herb Brown, Arthur Freed. Nominations: Academy Awards '35: Best Picture, Best Story. *MGM, MLB, CCB*

Broadway Melody of 1938 🎬🎬½
1937 Third entry in the melody series lacks the sparkle of "Broadway Melody of 1936" despite the all-star cast. Lots of singing and dancing without much charm. Two bright spots: a young Garland singing the now famous "Dear Mr. Gable" and the always lovely Powell's dance numbers. ♫Broadway Rhythm; Dear Mr. Gable (You Made Me Love You); A New Pair of Shoes; Yours and Mine; I'm Feeling Like a Million; Everybody Sing; Follow in My Footsteps; Your Broadway and My Broadway; Sun Showers. **110m/B VHS, Beta, Closed Caption.** Eleanor Powell, Sophie Tucker, George Murphy, Judy Garland, Robert Taylor, Buddy Ebsen, Binnie Barnes; **D:** Roy Del Ruth; **C:** William H. Daniels; **M:** Nacio Herb Brown, Arthur Freed. *MGM*

Broadway Melody of 1940 🎬🎬½
1940 The last entry in the melody series features the only screen teaming of Astaire and Powell. The flimsy plot is just an excuse for a potent series of Cole Porter musical numbers. ♫I Concentrate on You; I've Got My Eye on You; Begin the Beguine; I am the Captain; Please Don't Monkey With Broadway; Between You and Me; Il Bacio. **103m/B VHS, Beta, LV.** Fred Astaire, Eleanor Powell, George Murphy, Frank Morgan, Ian Hunter; **D:** Norman Taurog. *MGM, TTC, FCT*

Broadway Rhythm 🎬🎬½ **1944** A too-long look at Broadway behind-the-scenes. Murphy plays a Broadway producer who hopes to land a Hollywood star for his new show. She rejects his offer in favor of a show being produced by his father. Just a chance to showcase a number of popular vaudeville acts, songs, and the music of Tommy Dorsey and his orchestra. ♫All the Things You Are; That Lucky Fellow; In Other Words; Seventeen; All In Fun; Brazilian Boogie; What Do You Think I Am?; Somebody Loves Me; Milkman Keep Those Bottles Quiet. **111m/C VHS.** George Murphy, Ginny Simms, Charles Winninger, Gloria De Haven, Nancy Walker, Ben Blue, Lena Horne, Eddie Anderson; **D:** Roy Del Ruth; **W:** Dorothy Kingsley, Harry Clork. *MGM*

Broadway Serenade 🎬🎬½ **1939** Melodramatic musical in which a songwriter (Ayres) and his wife, singer MacDonald, make career choices that destroy their marriage. ♫Broadway Serenade for the Lonely Heart; High Flyin'; One Look at You; Time Changes Everything; Un Bel Di; No Time to Argue; Italian Street Song; Les Filles de Cadiz; Musical Contract. **114m/B VHS.** Jeanette MacDonald, Lew Ayres, Ian Hunter, Frank Morgan, Wally Vernon, Rita Johnson, Virginia Grey, William Gargan; **D:** Robert Z. Leonard; **W:** Charles Lederer. *MGM*

Broadway to Cheyenne 🎬 *From Broadway to Cheyenne* **1932** A group of big city gangsters try to take over a small western town but are opposed by heroic cowboys. **53m/B VHS, Beta.** Rex Bell, George "Gabby" Hayes, Marceline Day, Robert Ellis, Alan Bridge, Matthew Betz; **D:** Harry Fraser. *GPV, RXM, VDM*

Broken Angel 🎬½ **1988** Jamie seemed to be such a nice girl, with good looks and great grades—and membership in a notorious street gang. When Jamie disappears, her family discovers her secret activities and dad tries to find his

wayward little girl. Melodramatic made for television goo. **94m/C VHS, Closed Caption.** William Shatner, Susan Blakely, Erika Eleniak, Roxann Biggs-Dawson; **D:** Richard T. Heffron. *MGM*

Broken Arrow 🎬🎬½ **1950** A U.S. scout befriends Cochise and the Apaches, and helps settlers and Indians live in peace together in the 1870s. Acclaimed as the first Hollywood film to side with the Indians, and for Chandler's portrayal of Cochise. Based on the novel "Blood Brother" by Elliot Arnold. **93m/C VHS, Beta, Closed Caption.** James Stewart, Jeff Chandler, Will Geer, Debra Paget, Basil Ruysdael, Arthur Hunnicutt, Jay Silverheels; **D:** Delmer Daves; **W:** Albert Maltz; **C:** Ernest Palmer. Nominations: Academy Awards '50: Best Color Cinematography, Best Screenplay, Best Supporting Actor (Chandler). *FOX*

Broken Arrow 🎬🎬 **1995 (R)** Air Force pilot Vic Deakins (Travolta) rips off a couple of nuclear weapons during a routine exercise over the Utah desert. Deakins' ex-co-pilot Riley Hale (Slater), with help from spunky park ranger Terry Carmichael (Mathis), sets out to find and retrieve the warheads before the big bang. Hong Kong action king Woo once again tries his hand at the big-budget Hollywood action extravaganza, with mixed results. Triple script whammy of cheesy dialogue, continuity problems, and predictability undercuts, but doesn't obscure, his talent for choreographing mayhem. Travolta plays the All-American Boy as creepily charming psychotic to great effect.**CW:** Contains strong action violence and language. **108m/C VHS, Closed Caption.** John Travolta, Christian Slater, Samantha Mathis, Delroy Lindo, Bob Gunton, Frank Whaley, Howie Long; **D:** John Woo; **W:** Graham Yost; **C:** Peter Levy; **M:** Hans Zimmer. Nominations: MTV Movie Awards '96: Best Villain (Travolta), Best Action Sequence. *FXV*

Broken Badge 🎬🎬🎬 *The Rape of Richard Beck* **1985** Crenna stars as a macho, chauvinistic cop whose attitude towards rape victims changes dramatically after he himself is raped by a couple of thugs. Excellent TV movie. **100m/C VHS.** Richard Crenna, Meredith Baxter, Pat Hingle, Frances Lee McCain, Cotter Smith, George Dzundza, Joanna Kerns; **D:** Karen Arthur; **W:** James G. Hirsch; **M:** Peter Bernstein. *SIM, VTR*

Broken Blossoms 🎬🎬🎬 **1919** One of Griffith's most widely acclaimed films, photographed by Billy Bitzer, about a young Chinaman in London's squalid Limehouse district hoping to spread the peaceful philosophy of his Eastern religion. He befriends a pitiful street waif who is mistreated by her brutal father, resulting in tragedy. Silent. Revised edition contains introduction from Gish and a newly-recorded score. **102m/B VHS, Beta, LV.** Lillian Gish, Richard Barthelmess, Donald Crisp; **D:** D.W. Griffith. *NOS, MRV, HHT*

The Broken Chain 🎬🎬½ **1993** In the mid 18th-century Joseph Brant (Schweig), a member of the Mohawk tribe, is sent away to be educated by the British. When he returns, his loyalties are divided between his Native American roots and his English mentor, Sir William Johnson (Brosnan). His boyhood friend Lohaheo (White Shirt) disdains Joseph's white man ways, leading to tragic consequences. Historical background features the French and Indian Wars, the splintering of the Iroquois Confederacy, and the coming of the American Revolution. Filmed on location in Virginia. Made for television. **93m/C VHS, Closed Caption.** Eric Schweig, Wes Studi, Buffy Saint Marie, Pierce Brosnan, J.C. White Shirt, Floyd "Red Crow" Westerman, Graham Greene, Elaine Bilstad, Kim Snyder; **D:** Lamont Johnson; **W:** Earl W. Wallace; **M:** Charles Fox. *TTC*

Broken English 🎬🎬½ **1996 (NC-17)** Ethnically diverse New Zealand is the setting for this story of young lovers and the parents who don't understand them. Croatian refugee Nina (Vujcic) and Maori cook Eddie (Arahanga) meet in the Chinese restaurant where they both work and quickly fall in love. Nina's menacing father Ivan (Serbedzija) objects to their passion, sometimes with a baseball bat. Film deals honestly with immigration and racial issues. Engaging debut for

Vujcic, a Croatian refugee director Nicholas met in a bar.**CW:** Strong sexual content. **90m/C VHS.** *NZ* Aleksandra Vujcic, Julian (Sonny) Arahanga, Rade Serbedzija, Marton Csokas, Jing Zhao, Yang Li, Madeline McNamara; **D:** Gregor Nicholas; **W:** Gregor Nicholas, Johanna Pigott, Jim Salter; **C:** John Toon. *NYR*

Broken Glass 🎬🎬½ **1996** Set in Brooklyn in 1938 and adapted from a play by Arthur Miller. Jewish housewife, Sylvia Gellberg (Leicester), has been stricken by a mysterious paralysis and Dr. Harry Hyman (Patinkin) is called in to treat her. Her illness is apparently psychosomatic and Sylvia gradually reveals her anxiety about her unhappy marriage and her obsessive fears with newspaper reports concerning Jewish persecution in Germany. Hyman and his wife Margaret (McGovern) soon find themselves drawn in deeper than could have imagined. Made for TV. **120m/C VHS, Closed Caption.** Mandy Patinkin, Margot Leicester, Henry Goodman, Elizabeth McGovern; **D:** David Thacker; **W:** David Thacker, David Holman. *PBS*

Broken Harvest 🎬🎬½ **1994** Jimmy O'Leary remembers his youth in rural 1950s Ireland when a poor wheat harvest led to his family's financial demise and a feud between his father (Lane) and neighbor Josie McCarthy (O'Brien) threatened to destroy their lives. The men fought side by side for Ireland's independence, but the friendship dissolved when they took different sides during the ensuing civil war, and fought over Jimmy's mother. Strong performances and the beautiful West Cork and Wicklow location shots provide a nice balance to the uneven narrative. The black and white scenes were actually filmed in the mid-'80s when the independently-financed project was begun. Adapted from O'Callaghan's own story "The Shilling." **101m/C VHS.** *IR* Colin Lane, Niall O'Brien, Marian Quinn, Darren McHugh, Joy Florish, Joe Jeffers, Pete O'Reilly, Michael Crowley; **D:** Maurice O'Callaghan; **W:** Maurice O'Callaghan; **C:** Jack Conroy; **M:** Patrick Cassidy. *KIT, FCT*

Broken Hearts of Broadway 🎬🎬
1923 Stories of heartbreak and success along the Great White Way. **85m/B VHS.** Colleen Moore, John Walker, Alice Lake, Tully Marshall, Creighton Hale; **D:** Irving Cummings. *GPV*

Broken Lance 🎬🎬🎬½ **1954** Western remake of "House of Strangers" that details the dissolution of a despotic cattle baron's family. Beautifully photographed. **96m/C VHS, Beta, LV, Closed Caption.** Spencer Tracy, Richard Widmark, Robert Wagner, Jean Peters, Katy Jurado, Earl Hoffman, Hugh O'Brian, E.G. Marshall; **D:** Edward Dmytryk; **W:** Philip Yordan. Academy Awards '54: Best Story; Nominations: Academy Awards '54: Best Supporting Actress (Jurado). *FOX*

The Broken Mask 🎬🎬 **1928** A doctor performs remarkable plastic surgery on a patient, but when the patient becomes attracted to his sweetheart, he throws the Hippocratic oath to the wind, and his patient's spiffy new look has got to go. A ground-breaker about plastic surgery-gone-amok pieces. **58m/B VHS, Beta.** Cullen Landis, Barbara Bedford, Wheeler Oakman, James Marcus; **D:** James Hogan. *GPV, FCT*

Broken Melody 🎬½ *Vagabond Violinist* **1934** An opera singer sent to prison by mistake must escape in order to return to the woman of his dreams. **62m/B VHS.** *GB* John Garrick, Margot Grahame, Merle Oberon, Austin Trevor, Charles Carson, Harry Terry; **D:** Bernard Vorhaus. *FCT*

Broken Mirrors 🎬🎬½ *Gebroken Spiegels* **1985** A disturbing film which intertwines two stories of violence against women: prostitutes go about their daily business in Amsterdam, while a twisted serial killer who imprisons, photographs, and ultimately destroys his victims, draws near. An independently made chiller with staunch feminist agenda. **110m/C NL.** Lineke Rijxman, Henriette Tol, Edda Barends, Eddie Brugman, Coby Stunnenberg; **D:** Marleen Gorris; **W:** Marleen Gorris. *ICA*

Broken Strings 🎞 1940 All-black musical in which a concert violinist must come to terms with himself after an auto accident limits the use of his left hand. 50m/B VHS, Beta. Clarence Muse, Sybil Lewis, William Washington, Matthew "Stymie" Beard; **D:** Bernard B. Ray. *VYY, NOS, VCN*

Broken Trust 🎞🎞 1993 Erica inherits her fabulously weathy uncle's estate but she has problems knowing who to trust now that she has all this money. Seems her husband is greedy and her sister resentful but just how far will they go to get what Erica has? 85m/C VHS. Kimberly Foster, Nick Cassavetes, Kathryn Harris, Don Swayze, Edward Albert, Wendy MacDonald; **D:** Rafael Portillo. *MNC*

Broken Trust 🎞🎞½ 1995 Municipal judge Timothy Nash (Selleck) is recruited for a sting operation, designed to ensnare fellow judges, by two slightly-less-than-ethical feds (Atherton and McGovern). When Nash decides he doesn't like what's going on he discovers it's not going to be so easy to get out. Selleck's stoic, McGovern provides attractive ornamentation, and Atherton excels as the smarmy villain. From the novel "Court of Honor" by William P. Wood; made for cable. 90m/C VHS. Tom Selleck, Elizabeth McGovern, William Atherton, Fritz Weaver, Marsha Mason, Charles Haid, Stanley DeSantis, Cynthia Martells; **D:** Geoffrey Sax; **W:** Joan Didion, John Gregory Dunne; **C:** Ronald Orieux; **M:** Richard Horowitz. *TTC*

Broken Vows 🎞🎞½ 1987 Made for TV thriller with Jones as ghetto priest Father Joseph, who has doubts about his calling. When he gives last rites to a murder victim, he decides to help the victim's girlfriend find his killers. Based on the novel "Where the Dark Secrets Go" by Dorothy Salisbury Davis. 95m/C VHS, Closed Caption. Tommy Lee Jones, Annette O'Toole, M. Emmet Walsh, Milo O'Shea, David Groh, Madeline Sherwood, Jean De Baer, David Strathairn; **D:** Jud Taylor; **C:** Thomas Burstyn. *CAF*

Bronco Billy 🎞🎞 1980 (PG) Eastwood stars as a New Jersey shoe clerk who decides to fulfill his dream of being a cowboy hero by becoming the proprietor of a rag-tag wild west show. Locke's one-note performance as a spoiled rich girl who joins up is a problem and the film's charm is as ragged as the acts. Good if you want to see Eastwood in something other than a shoot-'em-up. 117m/C VHS, Beta, LV. Clint Eastwood, Sondra Locke, Bill McKinney, Scatman Crothers, Sam Bottoms, Geoffrey Lewis, Dan Vadis, Sierra Pecheur; **D:** Clint Eastwood; **M:** Stephen Dorff. *WAR, TLF, RXM*

Bronson Lee, Champion 🎞 1978 (PG) Kung-fu and karate highlight this action adventure. 81m/C VHS, Beta. Tadashi Yamashita. *NO*

Bronson's Revenge 🎞½ 1979 (R) Two frontier soldiers face constant danger as they attempt to transport death row prisoners, a large quantity of gold, and a stranded woman across the Rocky Mountains territory. 90m/C VHS. Robert Hundar, Roy Hill, Emma Cohen. *SUN*

The Bronx Executioner 🎞 1986 Android, robot, and human interests clash in futuristic Manhattan and all martial arts hell breaks loose. Special introduction by martial arts star Michael Dudikoff. 88m/C VHS, Beta. Rob Robinson, Margie Newton, Chuck Valenti, Gabriel Gori; **D:** Bob Collins. *CAN*

A Bronx Tale 🎞🎞🎞 1993 (R) Vivid snapshot of a young Italian-American boy growing up in the '60s among neighborhood small-time wiseguys. As a 9-year-old Calogero witnesses mobster Sonny kill a man but doesn't rat to the police, so Sonny takes the kid under his wing. His upright bus-driving father Lorenzo doesn't approve but the kid is drawn to Sonny's apparent glamor and power. At 17, he's gotten both an education in school and on the streets but he needs to make a choice. Good period detail and excellent performances. Palminteri shows both Sonny's charisma and virulence and De Niro handles the less-showy father role with finesse. Based on Palminteri's one-man play; De Niro's directorial debut. **CW:**

Strong language and several scenes of violence. 122m/C VHS, LV, Closed Caption. Robert De Niro, Chazz Palminteri, Lillo Brancato, Francis Capra, Taral Hicks, Kathrine Narducci, Clem Caserta, Alfred Saucheli Jr., Frank Pietrangolare; **Cameos:** Joe Pesci; **D:** Robert De Niro; **W:** Chazz Palminteri. *HBO*

The Bronx War 🎞🎞 1990 (R) Rival gangs take to the streets in this film from the director of "Hangin' with the Homeboys." A malicious gang leader tricks his gang into going to war over a girl he wants. Very violent; an unrated version available. **CW:** Language, nudity, and gang violence and drug content. 91m/C VHS. Joseph B. Vasquez, Fabio Urena, Charmaine Cruz, Andre Brown, Marlene Forte, Francis Colon, Miguel Sierra, Kim West; **D:** Joseph B. Vasquez. *ACA*

Bronze Buckaroo 🎞🎞 1939 Horse opera in which a cowpoke seeks revenge for his pa's death. Commendable performances from the all-black cast and crew. 57m/B VHS. Herbert Jeffries, Artie Young, Rellie Hardin, Spencer Williams Jr., Clarence Brooks, F.E. Miller; **D:** Richard C. Kahn; **W:** Richard C. Kahn. *NOS, MRV, TPV*

The Brood 🎞🎞½ 1979 (R) Cronenberg's inimitable biological nightmares, involving an experimentally malformed woman who gives birth to murderous demon-children that kill every time she gets angry. Extremely graphic. Not for all tastes. 92m/C VHS, Beta, LV. CA Samantha Eggar, Oliver Reed, Art Hindle, Susan Hogan; **D:** David Cronenberg; **W:** David Cronenberg; **M:** Howard Shore.

Broth of a Boy 🎞🎞½ 1959 A hungry British producer decides to film a birthday party of the oldest man in the world. The old Irishman wants a portion of the profits. Well made and thought provoking. 77m/B VHS. IR Barry Fitzgerald, Harry Brogan, Tony Wright, June Thorburn, Eddie Golden; **D:** George Pollock. *NOS, HEG, FCT*

Brother Cadfael 🎞🎞½ 1994 Four episodic mysteries featuring a 12th-century Welsh soldier-turned-Benedictine monk (Jacobi), combining medieval atmosphere and politics with murder. Adapted from the novels by Ellis Peters. Hungary substitutes for the no-longer green and rural English setting of Shrewsbury. Made for British TV. Tapes available individually or as a boxed set. 300m/C VHS. GB Derek Jacobi, Sean Pertwee, Tara Fitzgerald, Jonathan Firth, Norman Eshley; **D:** Graham Theakston. *SIG, TVC*

Brother Cadfael 2 1995 Brother Cadfael (Jacobi), the medieval, mystery-solving, man-of-the-world turned man-of-the-cloth returns in three more adventures. "The Virgin in the Ice" finds the monk's novice accused of rape and murder. Cadfael also discovers a young squire is the son he never knew about. At "St. Peter's Fair" a disagreeable merchant is murdered but Cadfael doesn't believe greed is the motive. In "The Devil's Novice" a young man confesses to murder but is actually hiding family secrets. Based on the mystery series by Ellis Peters. On 3 cassettes. 75m/C VHS. GB Derek Jacobi. *ATS, FCT, VIF*

The Brother from Another Planet 🎞🎞🎞 1984 A black alien escapes from his home planet and winds up in Harlem, where he's pursued by two alien bounty hunters. Independently made morality fable by John Sayles before he hit the big time; features Sayles in a cameo as an alien bounty hunter. 109m/C VHS, Beta, Closed Caption. Joe Morton, Dee Dee Bridgewater, Ren Woods, Steve James, Maggie Renzi, David Strathairn; **Cameos:** John Sayles; **D:** John Sayles; **W:** John Sayles; **M:** Mason Daring. *FOX, FCT*

Brother Future 1991 T.J., a black, streetsmart city kid who thinks school and helping others is all a waste of time gets knocked out in a car accident. As he's lying unconscious, he is transported back in time to a slave auction block in the Old South. There the displaced urbanite is forced to work on a cotton plantation, and watch the stirrings of a slave revolt. T.J. sees the light and realizes just how much opportunity he's been wasting

in his own life. He comes to just a few moments later, but worlds away from who he was before. Part of the "Wonderworks" series. 110m/C VHS. Phill Lewis, Frank Converse, Carl Lumbly, Vonetta McGee. *PME, HMV, BTV*

Brother John 🎞🎞🎞 1970 (PG) An early look at racial tensions and labor problems. An angel goes back to his hometown in Alabama to see how things are going. 94m/C VHS, Beta. Sidney Poitier, Will Geer, Bradford Dillman, Beverly Todd, Paul Winfield; **D:** James Goldstone; **M:** Quincy Jones. *COL, FCT*

Brother of Sleep 🎞🎞 *Schlafes Bruder* 1995 (R) Elias (Eisermann), the illegitimate son of the local priest, is discovered to have perfect pitch, a beautiful voice, and a special symbiosis with nature. Which does nothing to endear him to the superstitious inhabitants of his 19th-century Austrian mountain village. Elias doesn't know whether his gift is a blessing or a curse but he'd give it up if he could win the love of his cousin Elspeth (Vavrova). Schneider scripted from his 1992 novel, which has previously been adapted as a ballet and opera. German with subtitles. **CW:** Violent and disturbing images, and for some sexuality. 133m/C VHS, LV. GE Andre Eisermann, Dana Vavrova, Ben Becker; **D:** Joseph Vilsmaier; **W:** Robert Schneider; **C:** Joseph Vilsmaier; **M:** Norbert J. Schneider. Nominations: Golden Globe Awards '96: Best Foreign Language Film. *COL*

Brother Orchid 🎞🎞🎞 1940 Mobster puts a henchman in charge of his gang while he vacations in Europe. Upon his return, he is deposed and wounded in an assassination attempt. Hiding out in a monastary, he plots to regain control of the gang, leading to fish outta water episodes and a change in his outlook on life. Fine cast fans through farce intelligently. 87m/B VHS, Beta. Edward G. Robinson, Humphrey Bogart, Ann Sothern, Donald Crisp, Ralph Bellamy, Allen Jenkins, Charles D. Brown, Cecil Kellaway; **D:** Lloyd Bacon; **C:** Gaetano Antonio "Tony" Gaudio. *MGM, CCB*

Brother Sun, Sister Moon 🎞🎞½ 1973 (PG) Post-'60s costume epic depicting the trials of St. Francis of Assisi as he evaluates his beliefs in Catholicism. 120m/C VHS, Beta. Graham Faulkner, Judi Bowker, Alec Guinness, Leigh Lawson, Kenneth Cranham, Lee Montague, Valentina Cortese; **D:** Franco Zeffirelli; **M:** Donovan. Nominations: Academy Awards '73: Best Art Direction/Set Decoration. *PAR, APD, TVC*

The Brotherhood 🎞🎞½ 1968 Two hotheaded brothers in a Mafia syndicate clash over old vs. new methods and the changing of the Family's guard. 96m/C VHS, Beta, LV. Kirk Douglas, Alex Cord, Irene Papas, Luther Adler, Susan Strasberg, Murray Hamilton; **D:** Martin Ritt; **W:** Lewis John Carlino; **C:** Boris Kaufman; **M:** Lalo Schifrin. *PAR*

Brotherhood of Death 🎞½ 1976 (R) Three black Vietnam veterans return to their southern hometown to get even with the Klansmen who slaughtered all of the townspeople. 85m/C VHS, Beta. Roy Jefferson, Larry Jones, Mike Bass, Le Tari, Haskell V. Anderson; **D:** Bill Berry. *MPI*

Brotherhood of Justice 🎞🎞 1986 Young men form a secret organization to rid their neighborhood of drug dealers and violence. As their power grows, their propriety weakens, until all are afraid of the "Brotherhood of Justice." Exciting made-for-television feature. 97m/C VHS. Keanu Reeves, Kiefer Sutherland, Billy Zane, Joe Spano, Darren Dalton, Evan Mirand, Don Michael Paul; **D:** Charles Braverman; **M:** Brad Fiedel. *THV, VTR*

The Brotherhood of Satan 🎞🎞½ 1971 (PG) In an isolated southern town, a satanic coven persuades children to join in their devil-may-care attitude. Worthwhile. 92m/C VHS, Beta, LV. Strother Martin, L.Q. Jones, Charles Bateman, Ahna Capri, Charles Robinson, Alvy Moore, Geri Reischl; **D:** Bernard McEveety. *GKK, IME*

The Brotherhood of the Rose 🎞½ 1989 (PG-13) Too many twists and turns mar the otherwise mediocre plot of this murky adaption of a book by David (First Blood) Morrell. Strauss and

Morse are the C.I.A. agents marked for death and running for their lives after uncovering their boss's (Mitchum) plot of world domination. Though almost every scene takes place in a different country, the movie was in fact filmed entirely in New Zealand. Convoluted and frustratingly difficult to follow. **103m/C VHS, Closed Caption.** Robert Mitchum, Peter Strauss, Connie Sellecca, James B. Sikking, David Morse, M. Emmet Walsh, James Hong; **D:** Marvin J. Chomsky. *THV*

Brotherly Love 🎬½ 1985 Good twin/bad twin made-for-TV mystery about an escaped psychopath who's out to get his businessman twin brother (Hirsch in both roles). **94m/C VHS, Beta, Closed Caption.** Judd Hirsch, Karen Carlson, George Dzundza, Barry Primus, Lori Lethin; **D:** Jeff Bleckner. *FOX*

Brothers in Arms 🎬🎬 1988 (R) Savage mountainmen have developed a weird religion that requires them to hunt down and mercilessly massacre human prey. **95m/C VHS, LV.** Todd Allen, Jack Starrett, Dedee Pfeiffer; **D:** George J. Bloom III. *REP*

Brothers in Law 🎬🎬½ 1957 Wry British humor in this tale of a rookie lawyer up against a veteran judge who forces him to sink or swim. **94m/B VHS.** GB Richard Attenborough, Ian Carmichael, Terry-Thomas, Miles Malleson, John Le Mesurier; **D:** Roy Boulting; **W:** Roy Boulting. *NOS*

The Brothers Karamazov 🎬🎬🎬 *Karamazov; The Murderer Dmitri Karamazov; Der Morder Dimitri Karamasoff* 1958 Hollywood adaptation of the classic novel by Dostoyevsky, in which four 19th-Century Russian brothers struggle with their desires for the same beautiful woman and with the father who brutalizes them. Incredible performances from every cast member, especially Cobb. Long and extremely intense, with fine direction from Brooks. Marilyn Monroe tried desperately to get Schell's part. **147m/C VHS, Beta.** Yul Brynner, Claire Bloom, Lee J. Cobb, William Shatner, Maria Schell, Richard Basehart; **D:** Richard Brooks; **W:** Richard Brooks; **C:** John Alton. Nominations: Academy Awards '58: Best Supporting Actor (Cobb). *MGM*

Brother's Keeper 🎬🎬🎬 1992 Filmmakers Berlinger and Sinofsky document the story of the eccentric and reclusive Ward brothers, four bachelor dairy farmers who shared the same two-room shack for more than 60 years in rural New York. When Bill Ward dies, brother Delbert is accused of murder and goes to trial. The film covers a year's span in preparation for the trial and how the media attention changed the Ward's lives. **104m/C VHS, LV.** **D:** Joe Berlinger, Bruce Sinofsky. National Board of Review Awards '92: Best Feature Documentary; New York Film Critics Awards '92: Best Feature Documentary; Sundance Film Festival '92: Audience Award. *FXL, BTV*

A Brother's Kiss 🎬🎬 1997 (R) Growing up in an East Harlem neighborhood with an alcoholic mother (Moriarty), two brothers are set on different paths that strain their brotherly love. Lex (Chinlund) is a never-was ex-basketball player with a bad marriage and an even worse drug problem. Mick (Raynor) is a tightly-wound, obsessive, and sexually dysfunctional cop. Both of their problems stem from a childhood trauma that neither is able or willing to discuss with the other. Starts out strong but runs out of energy by the second half. Expanded from a one-act play by director Rosenfeld. **CW:** Strong sexuality, pervasive strong language, drug use and violence. **92m/C VHS.** Nicholas Chinlund, Michael Raynor, Justin Pierce, Cathy Moriarty, Rosie Perez, Marisa Tomei, Joshua Danowsky; **D:** Seth Zvi Rosenfeld; **W:** Seth Zvi Rosenfeld; **C:** Fortunato Procopio; **M:** Frank London. *NYR*

Brothers Lionheart 🎬🎬½ 1985 (G) The Lion brothers fight for life, love and liberty during the Middle Ages. **120m/C VHS, Beta.** Staffan Gotestam, Lars Soderdahl, Allan Edwall; **D:** Olle Hellbron. *NO*

The Brothers McMullen 🎬🎬🎬 1994 (R) Slice of life drama finds three Irish-American brothers suddenly living under the same Long Island roof for the first time since childhood. Eld-est brother Jack (Mulcahy) is a stolid high-school basketball coach married to teacher Molly (Britton) who's pressing him to have children. Cynical middle brother Barry (Burns), a writer, has just broken up with free-spirited Ann (McKay), and earnest young Patrick (McGlone) is engaged to Jewish girlfriend Susan (Albert). All three find their romantic relationships, as well as their belief in each other, tested. Generally good performances and dialogue, with Burns proving himself a triple threat as actor/writer/director. **CW:** Language and some sexuality. **98m/C VHS, Closed Caption.** Edward Burns, Jack Mulcahy, Mike McGlone, Connie Britton, Shari Albert, Elizabeth P. McKay, Maxine Bahns, Jennifer Jostyn, Catharine Bolt, Peter Johansen; **D:** Edward Burns; **W:** Edward Burns; **M:** Seamus Egan. Independent Spirit Awards '96: Best First Feature; Sundance Film Festival '95: Grand Jury Prize. *FXV*

Brothers of the West 🎬½ 1937 Cowboy saves his brothers from being lynched by proving the guilt of the real outlaws. **56m/B VHS, Beta.** Tom Tyler, Bob Terry, Lois Wilde, Dorothy Short. *NOS, VCN, DVT*

Brothers O'Toole 🎬🎬 1973 (G) The misadventures of a pair of slick drifters who, by chance, ride into a broken-down mining town in the 1890s. **94m/C VHS, Beta.** John Astin, Steve Carlson, Pat Carroll, Hans Conried, Lee Meriwether; **D:** Richard Erdman. *NO*

The Browning Version 🎬🎬🎬½ 1951 A lonely, unemotional classics instructor at a British boarding school realizes his failure as a teacher and as a husband. From the play by Terrence Rattigan. **89m/B VHS, Beta.** GB Michael Redgrave, Jean Kent, Nigel Patrick, Wilfrid Hyde-White, Bill Travers; **D:** Anthony Asquith. Cannes Film Festival '51: Best Actor (Redgrave); National Board of Review Awards '51: 5 Best Foreign Films of the Year. *HMV, MOV, FUS*

The Browning Version 🎬🎬½ 1994 (R) Mediocre remake of the Terence Rattigan play, previously filmed in 1951. Austere classics professor (Finney) at prestigious British boys school is disillusioned with both his floundering career and marriage. His emotional chill drives his younger wife (Scacchi) into an affair with a visiting American science teacher (Modine). Unfortunately updated to contemporary times, which can't hide apparent mustiness. Worth seeing for Finney's superb work as the out-of-touch prof. **CW:** Some language. **97m/C VHS, Beta, Closed Caption.** Albert Finney, Greta Scacchi, Matthew Modine, Michael Gambon, Julian Sands, Ben Silverstone, Maryam D'Abo; **D:** Mike Figgis; **W:** Ronald Harwood; **M:** Mark Isham. *PAR*

Brubaker 🎬🎬🎬 1980 (R) A sanctimonious drama about a reform warden who risks his life to replace brutality and corruption with humanity and integrity in a state prison farm. Powerful prison drama. **131m/C VHS, Beta, LV.** Robert Redford, Jane Alexander, Yaphet Kotto, Murray Hamilton, David Keith, Morgan Freeman, Matt Clark, M. Emmet Walsh, Everett McGill; **D:** Stuart Rosenberg; **W:** W.D. Richter, Arthur Ross; **M:** Lalo Schifrin. Nominations: Academy Awards '80: Best Original Screenplay. *FOX*

Bruce Lee: Curse of the Dragon 🎬🎬🎬 *The Curse of the Dragon* 1993 A behind the scenes look at the continuing mystery surrounding the life and untimely death of the martial arts superstar who died in 1973 at the age of 32. Highlights the spectacular fight sequences from Lee's movies as well as footage from his funeral and an interview with his son Brandon Lee, whose own death in 1993 raised further comment about a Lee family curse. **90m/C VHS, Beta, LV.** *WAR, BTV*

Bruce Lee Fights Back From the Grave 🎬 1976 (R) Bruce Lee returns from the grave to fight the Black Angel of Death with his feet and to wreak vengeance on the evil ones who brought about his untimely demise. **97m/C VHS, Beta.** Deborah Chaplin, Anthony Bronson; **D:** Umberto Lenzi. *MED*

Bruce Lee's Ways of Kung Fu 🎬 198? Copious head-kicking film in honor of the long-dead star. Brings together the best from Shaolin: White Crane, Wu-Deng, Dragon-Fist, Kwun-Lun, Eagle Claws, Tiger, and Leopard in a fight against the Dragon. **87m/C VHS, Beta.** Bruce Lei, Philip Cheung, Pearl Lin. *UNI*

Bruce Le's Greatest Revenge 🎬 1980 (R) Bruce Le, one e. Kung-fu action and martial arts fighting occur when a martial arts student gets involved in a clash between Chinese and a discriminatory European Club. **94m/C VHS, Beta.** Bruce Le. *GEM*

Bruce Li in New Guinea 🎬 1980 (PG) Bruce Li, i, not ee. The tribe of a remote island worships the legendary Snake Pearl. Two masters of Kung-fu visit the isle and discover they must defend the daughter of the murdered chief against a cruel wizard. **98m/C VHS, Beta.** Bruce Li, Ho Chung Dao, Chen Sing; **D:** C.Y. Yang. *MGI, GEM, MRV*

Bruce Li the Invincible 🎬 1980 Cheng, the Kung-Fu killer, is pursued by the vengeance-minded Bruce. **93m/C VHS.** Bruce Li, Ho Chung Dao, Chen Sing; **D:** C.Y. Yang. *MGI, MRV, GEM*

Bruce the Superhero 🎬 1979 Chop-socky action as the coattails-riding Bruce Le takes on the Black Dragon Society. **88m/C VHS, Beta.** Bruce Le. *BFV, MRV*

Bruce's Deadly Fingers 🎬 1980 (R) Bruce Lee kept a book of deadly finger techniques for kung fu killing. When a vicious gangster kidnaps the Master's ex-girlfriend, one of his followers must rescue her and maintain the book's integrity. **90m/C VHS, Beta.** Bruce Le, Lo Lieh, Chan Wai, Nora Miao, Rose Marie, Yuen Man Chi, Chang Leih, Young Zee, Wuk Ma No Hans. *GEM*

Bruce's Fists of Vengeance 🎬 1984 Le and Lee guard master Bruce Lee's kicking secrets from an evil adversary. **87m/C VHS, Beta.** Bruce Le, Jack Lee, Ken Watanabe, Romano Kristoff, Don Gordon. *GEM*

Brussels Transit 🎬🎬🎬 1980 The story of a Yiddish family's arrival and adjustment to the new world of Brussels, Belgium, after WWII. In Yiddish with English subtitles. **80m/B VHS.** **D:** Samy Szlingerbaum. *NO*

Brutal Fury 🎬 1992 Detective Molly Griffin goes undercover at a local high school and discovers a secret female vigilante group, called the "Fury," which goes after the drug dealers and rapists preying on the school's students. Teenagers with an attitude. **97m/C VHS.** Tom Campitelli, Lisa-Gabrielle Greene, Annette Gerbon, Karen Eppers, Jennifer Winder, Allen Arkus; **D:** Frederick P. Watkins. *AIP*

Brutal Glory 🎬 1989 Set in New York City in 1918 and based on the true story of the boxer known as "The Real McCoy." Fascinating and detailed history of a period, a champion, and the man who made it happen. **96m/C VHS.** Robert Vaughn, Timothy Brantley, Leah K. Pinsent; **D:** Koos Roets. *NO*

The Brute Man 🎬🎬 1946 A young man who had been disfigured by his school mates goes out on a trail of revenge. Hatton is convincing in the title role, as in real life he was afflicted with acromegaly, an ailment that produces an enlargment of the bones in the face, hands, and feet. **62m/B VHS, Beta, LV.** Rondo Hatton, Tom Neal, Jane Adams; **D:** Jean Yarbrough. *AOV, MLB, COL*

The Buccaneer 🎬🎬 1958 A swashbuckling version of the adventures of pirate Jean LaFitte and his association with President Andrew Jackson during the War of 1812. Remake of Cecille B. DeMille's 1938 production. **121m/C VHS, Beta, LV, Closed Caption.** Yul Brynner, Charlton Heston, Claire Bloom, Inger Stevens, Charles Boyer, Henry Hull, E.G. Marshall, Lorne Greene; **D:** Anthony Quinn; **C:** Loyal Griggs; **M:** Elmer Bernstein. Nominations: Academy Awards '58: Best Costume Design. *BAR, FCT, RXM*

The Buccaneers 🎬🎬🎬 1995 Lavish adaptation of the Edith Wharton novel follows the adventures of four American girls in 1870s society. Nouveaux riche, the young ladies are unable to crack New York snobbery and, after vivacious Brazilian Conchita (Sorvino) manages to snag Lord Richard (Vibert), the others are encouraged by English governess Laura Testvalley (Lunghi) to try their luck in London. There, Virginia (Elliott), sister Nan (Gugino), their friend Lizzy (Kihlstedt), and Conchita all find hope and heartbreak among the English aristocracy. Wharton's novel was unfinished at her death and, though she left story notes, scripter Wadey concedes to changes. Made for TV. 288m/C VHS. *GB* Carla Gugino, Mira Sorvino, Alison Elliott, Rya Kihlstedt, Cherie Lunghi, Connie Booth, Mark Tandy, Ronan Vibert, Jenny Agutter, Richard Huw, Greg Wise, James Frain, Michael Kitchen, Sheila Hancock, Rosemary Leach, Elizabeth Ashley, Conchata Ferrell, Peter Michael Goetz, James Rebhorn, E. Katherine Kerr; *D:* Philip Saville; *W:* Maggie Wadey; *C:* Maggie Wadey; *M:* Colin Towns. FOX

Buck and the Preacher 🎬🎬½ 1972 (PG) A trail guide and a con man preacher join forces to help a wagon train of former slaves who are seeking to homestead out West. Poitier's debut as a director. 102m/C VHS, Beta. Sidney Poitier, Harry Belafonte, Ruby Dee, Cameron Mitchell, Denny Miller; *D:* Sidney Poitier. COL

Buck Privates 🎬🎬½ *Rookies* 1941 Abbott and Costello star as two dim-witted tie salesmen, running from the law, who become buck privates during WWII. The duo's first great success, and the film that established the formula for each subsequent film. 84m/B VHS, Beta, LV. Bud Abbott, Lou Costello, Shemp Howard, Lee Bowman, Alan Curtis, The Andrews Sisters; *D:* Arthur Lubin; *C:* Milton Krasner. Nominations: Academy Awards '41: Best Song ("Boogie Woogie Bugle Boy of Company B"), Scoring of a Musical. USH

Buck Privates Come Home 🎬🎬🎬 *Rookies Come Home* 1947 Abbott and Costello return to their "Buck Privates" roles as two soldiers trying to adjust to civilian life after the war. They also try to help a French girl sneak into the United States. Funny antics culminate into a wild chase scene. 77m/B VHS. Bud Abbott, Lou Costello, Tom Brown, Joan Shawlee, Nat Pendleton, Beverly Simmons, Don Beddoe, Don Porter, Donald MacBride; *D:* Charles T. Barton. USH

Buck Rogers Conquers the Universe 🎬🎬 1939 The story of Buck Rogers, written by Phil Nolan in 1928, was the first science fiction story done in the modern superhero space genre. Many of the "inventions" seen in this movie have actually come into existence—spaceships, ray guns (lasers), anti-gravity belts—a testament to Nolan's almost psychic farsightedness. 91m/B VHS, Beta. Buster Crabbe, Constance Moore, Jackie Moran; *D:* Ford Beebe, Saul Goodkind. FOX

Buck Rogers in the 25th Century 🎬🎬 1979 (PG) An American astronaut, preserved in space for 500 years, is brought back to life by a passing Draconian flagship. Outer space adventures begin when he is accused of being a spy from Earth. Based on the classic movie serial. Made for TV movie that began the popular series. Additional series episodes are available. 90m/C VHS, Beta, LV. Gil Gerard, Pamela Hensley, Erin Gray, Henry Silva; *D:* Daniel Haller; *V:* Mel Blanc. USH, MOV

A Bucket of Blood 🎬🎬🎬 1959 Cult favorite Dick Miller stars as a sculptor with a peculiar "talent" for lifelike artwork. Corman fans will see thematic similarities to his subsequent work, "Little Shop of Horrors" (1960). "Bucket of Blood" was made in just five days, while "Little Shop of Horrors" was made in a record breaking two days. Corman horror/spoof noted for its excellent beatnik atmosphere. 66m/B VHS, Beta. Dick Miller, Barboura Morris, Antony Carbone, Julian Burton, Ed Nelson, Bert Convy; *D:* Roger Corman. NOS, RHI, SNC

Buckeye and Blue 🎬½ 1987 (PG) A hero turned outlaw, his 14 year-old female sidekick, and a gang known as the McCoys are all on the lam from the law in this western adventure. 94m/C VHS, Beta. Robin Lively, Jeffery Osterhage, Rick Gibbs, Will Hannah, Kenneth Jensen, Patrick Johnston, Stuart Rogers, Michael Horse; *D:* J.C. Compton. ACA

Buckskin 🎬½ 1968 Slowmoving western about a marshall protecting townspeople from a greedy, land-grabbing cattle baron. 98m/C VHS, LV, Closed Caption. Barry Sullivan, Wendell Corey, Joan Caulfield, Lon Chaney Jr., John Russell, Barbara Hale, Barton MacLane, Bill Williams; *D:* Michael Moore. PAR

Buckskin Frontier 🎬½ 1943 Story is built around Western railroad construction and cattle empires in the 1860s. Cobb tries to stop the railroad from coming through by hiring Jory to do his dirty work. 75m/B VHS, Beta. Richard Dix, Jane Wyatt, Lee J. Cobb, Albert Dekker, Victor Jory, Lola Lane, Max Baer Sr.; *D:* Lesley Selander. NOS, MRV, GPV

Bucktown 🎬½ 1975 (R) A black man who reopens his murdered brother's bar fights off police corruption and racism in a Southern town. 95m/C VHS, Beta. Fred Williamson, Pam Grier, Bernie Hamilton, Thalmus Rasulala, Art Lund; *D:* Arthur Marks. ORI

Bud and Lou 🎬½ 1978 Comedy/drama recounts Abbott & Costello's rise in Hollywood. While the story, based on the book by Bob Thomas, is interesting, the two funnymen in the leads can't pull off the old classic skits. 98m/C VHS, Beta, LV. Harvey Korman, Buddy Hackett, Michele Lee, Arte Johnson, Robert Reed; *D:* Robert C. Thompson. JTC

Buddha Assassinator 🎬 1982 Young Kung-Fu enthusiast challenges a Ming dynasty lord to a duel to the death. 93m/C VHS, Beta. Hwang Jang Lee, Mang Hai, Lung Fei, Chien Yueh Sheng. WVE

The Buddha of Suburbia 🎬🎬🎬 1992 Satire set in late '70s suburban London follows the coming of age adventures of Karim (Andrews), the handsome son of an Indian father and English mother. His gleeful father Haroon (Seth) exploits the vogue for eastern philosophies he knows nothing about with lectures to the upper-middle classes while he carries on with devotee Eva (Fleetwood). When his mother finds out, Karim and his father move into central London with Eva, where Karim decides to take up acting in fringe theatre and sex while his friend, Eva's son Charlie (Mackintosh), experiments with the punk music scene. TV miniseries adapted by Kureishi from his novel. 220m/C VHS. *GB* Naveen Andrews, Roshan Seth, Susan Fleetwood, Steven Mackintosh, Brenda Blethyn, John McEnery, Janet Dale, David Bamber, Donald Sumpter, Jemma Redgrave; *D:* Roger Michell; *W:* Hanif Kureishi, Roger Michell; *C:* John McGlashan; *M:* David Bowie. FOX

Buddy 🎬🎬½ 1997 (PG) Animals run amok in the Lintz household. Mother hen Gertrude Lintz (Russo) raises just about everything from mischievous chimps to impressionable parrots on her estate. A baby gorilla (named Buddy, short for Budha) becomes part of the family, but as he grows in size, so does the difficulty in caring for him. Amiable tale of one woman's motherly bond with a gorilla includes convincing performances by Russo and an animatronic gorilla courtesy of Jim Henson's Creature Shop. Well-paced and very touching at moments, children will definitely enjoy the zany animal antics, and adults should be moved by the unusual relationship. Based on the book by Lintz. 84m/C VHS. Rene Russo, Robbie Coltrane, Irma P. Hall; *D:* Caroline Thompson; *W:* Caroline Thompson; *C:* Steve Mason; *M:* Elmer Bernstein. NYR

Buddy Buddy 🎬🎬½ 1981 (R) A professional hitman's well-ordered arrangement to knock off a state's witness keeps being interrupted by the suicide attempts of a man in the next hotel room. 96m/C VHS, Beta. Jack Lemmon, Walter Matthau, Paula Prentiss, Klaus Kinski; *D:* Billy Wilder; *W:* Billy Wilder, I.A.L. Diamond; *C:* Harry Stradling Jr.; *M:* Lalo Schifrin. MGM

The Buddy Holly Story 🎬🎬🎬½ 1978 (PG) An acclaimed biography of the famed 1950s pop star, spanning the years from his meteoric career's beginnings in Lubbock to his tragic early death in the now famous plane crash. Busey performs Holly's hits himself. 🎵 Rock Around the Ollie Vee; That'll Be the Day; Oh, Boy; It's So Easy; Well All Right; Chantilly Lace; Peggy Sue. 113m/C VHS, Beta, LV, Closed Caption. Gary Busey, Don Stroud, Charles Martin Smith, Conrad Janis, William Jordan; *D:* Steve Rash; *M:* Joe Renzetti. Academy Awards '78: Original Song Score and/or Adaptation; National Society of Film Critics Awards '78: Best Actor (Busey); Nominations: Academy Awards '78: Best Actor (Busey), Best Sound. COL

The Buddy System 🎬🎬 1983 (PG) A tale of contemporary love and the modern myths that outline the boundaries between lovers and friends. 110m/C VHS, Beta, Closed Caption. Richard Dreyfuss, Susan Sarandon, Jean Stapleton, Nancy Allen, Wil Wheaton, Ed Winter, Keene Curtis; *D:* Glenn Jordan; *W:* Mary Agnes Donoghue. FOX

Buddy's Song 🎬🎬 1991 (R) A '60s coming of age tale, only in this case it's the father and not the son who needs to grow up. Dad (Daltrey) is more interested in hanging out with his no-account musician friends than in looking after his family. Although he's not above meddling in his teenage son's musical career, which could be the success his father's never was. Based on the novel by Nigel Hinton who also did the screenplay. British teen idol Hawkes (in his film debut) had a top ten hit song from the film with "The One and Only." 106m/C VHS, LV, Closed Caption. *GB* Roger Daltrey, Chesney Hawkes; *W:* Nigel Hinton. THV, BTV

Buffalo Bill 🎬🎬 1944 A light, fictionalized account of the life and career of Bill Cody, from frontier hunter to showman. 89m/C VHS, Beta, Closed Caption. Joel McCrea, Maureen O'Hara, Linda Darnell, Thomas Mitchell, Edgar Buchanan, Anthony Quinn, Moroni Olsen, Sidney Blackmer; *D:* William A. Wellman; *C:* Leon Shamroy. FOX

Buffalo Bill & the Indians 🎬🎬🎬 *Sitting Bull's History Lesson* 1976 (PG) A perennially underrated Robert Altman historical pastiche, portraying the famous Wild West character as a charlatan and shameless exemplar of encroaching imperialism. Great all-star cast amid Altman's signature mise-en-scene chaos. 135m/C VHS, Beta. Paul Newman, Geraldine Chaplin, Joel Grey, Will Sampson, Harvey Keitel, Burt Lancaster, Kevin McCarthy; *D:* Robert Altman; *W:* Robert Altman, Alan Rudolph; *M:* Richard Baskin. FOX

Buffalo Bill Rides Again 🎬½ 1947 With an Indian uprising on the horizon, Buffalo Bill is called in. Mr. Bill finds land swindlers pitting natives against ranchers, but there's precious little action or interest here. 68m/C VHS, Beta. Richard Arlen, Jennifer Holt, Edward Cassidy, Edmund Cobb, Charles Stevens; *D:* Bernard B. Ray. GPV

Buffalo Girls 🎬🎬½ 1995 Western saga, set in the 1870s, tells of the lifelong friendship between hard-drinking, hard-living Calamity Jane (Huston—who's not exactly any plain Jane) and buxom, soft-hearted madam Dora DuFran (Griffith). Dora's in love (but refuses to marry) rancher Teddy Blue (Byrne) while Calamity has a daughter by Wild Bill Hickok (Elliott) that she gives up for adoption. There's lots of rambling and commiserating over the changing and civilizing of the west and various man trouble. Based on the novel by Larry McMurtry; originally a two-part TV miniseries. 180m/C VHS, Closed Caption. Anjelica Huston, Melanie Griffith, Gabriel Byrne, Peter Coyote, Jack Palance, Sam Elliott, Reba McEntire, Floyd "Red Crow" Westerman, Tracey Walter, Russell Means, Charlaine Woodard, John Diehl, Liev Schreiber, Andrew Bicknell, Paul Lazar; *D:* Rod Hardy; *W:* Cynthia Whitcomb; *C:* David Connell; *M:* Lee Holdridge. CAF

Buffalo Heart: The Pain of Death 🎬½ 1996 Buffalo Heart decides to avenge the rape and murder of his daughter by tracking down her killers. 85m/C VHS. Daniel Matmor,

Alex Wexo, Craig Eisner; *D:* Daniel Matmor; *W:* Daniel Matmor; *C:* Paul DeGruccio. *TPV*

Buffalo Jump ✍✍✍ **1990** An independent woman, working as a lounge singer in Toronto, returns to her home in Alberta when her father dies. To her surprise he has left her the family ranch and, to the surprise of everyone else, she decides to stay and run it. She hires a good-looking local man to help her out and they both discover that they want more than a working relationship. However, the fireworks really start when he proposes a marriage of convenience. Engaging performances and beautiful scenery help raise this romantic tale of opposites above the average. **97m/C VHS.** *CA* Wendy Crewson, Paul Gross, Marion Gilsenan, Kyra Harper, Victoria Snow; *D:* Eric Till. *ACA*

Buffalo Rider ✍½ **1978** An adventure film depicting the real-life experiences of C.J. "Buffalo" Jones who worked to save the American buffalo from extinction. **90m/C VHS, Beta.** Rick Guinn, John Freeman, Pricilla Lauris, George Sager, Rich Scheeland; *D:* George Lauris. *NO*

Buffalo Stampede ✍ **1933** Our heroes are involved in a plot to round up buffalo to sell for meat. **60m/B VHS, Beta.** Randolph Scott, Buster Crabbe, Harry Carey Sr., Noah Beery Sr., Raymond Hatton. *NOS, VCN, MRV*

Buffet Froid ✍✍✍½ **1979** Surreal black comedy about a group of bungling murderers. First rate acting and directing makes this film a hilarious treat. From the director of "Menage." In French with English subtitles. **95m/C VHS, LV.** *FR* Gerard Depardieu, Bernard Blier, Jean Carmet, Genevieve Page, Denise Gence, Carole Bouquet, Jean Benguigui, Michel Serrault; *D:* Bertrand Blier; *W:* Bertrand Blier. Cesar Awards '80: Best Writing.*INT, TPV*

Buffy the Vampire Slayer ✍✍✍ **1992 (PG-13)** Funny, near-camp teen genre spoof. Buffy is a typical mall gal concerned with shopping and cheerleading, until the mysterious Sutherland proclaims it her destiny to slay the vampires who have suddenly infested Los Angeles. Like, really. Buffy requires some convincing, but eventually takes up the challenge, fighting off the vamps and their seductive leader Hauer, aided by perpetual guy-in-distress Perry. "Pee Wee" Reubens is unrecognizable and terribly amusing as the vampire king's sinister henchman, engaging in one of the longer death scenes of film history. Check out Cassandra (Wagner), Natalie Wood's daughter. **98m/C VHS, LV.** Kristy Swanson, Donald Sutherland, Luke Perry, Paul (Pee Wee Herman) Reubens, Rutger Hauer, Michele Abrams, Randall Batinkoff, Hilary Swank, Paris Vaughan, David Arquette, Candy Clark, Natasha Gregson Wagner; *D:* Fran Rubel Kazui; *W:* Joss Whedon; *M:* Carter Burwell. *FXV, PMS*

Buford's Beach Bunnies ✍ **1992 (R)** Harry Buford has made a fortune selling barbecued rabbit sandwiches served by the sexiest waitresses around. Harry wants to leave the business to his son Jeeter—if Jeeter can overcome his overwhelming fear of women. So three of Harry's waitresses decide to show Jeeter a very good time. Lots of pretty girls in not much clothing.*CW:* Language, nudity, and sex scenes. **90m/C VHS, Closed Caption.** Jim Hanks, Rikki Brando, Monique Parent, Amy Page, Barrett Cooper, Ina Rogers, Charley Rossman, David Robinson; *D:* Mark Pirro; *W:* Mark Pirro. *IMP*

Bug woof! **1975 (PG)** The city of Riverside is threatened with destruction after a massive earth tremor unleashes a super-race of ten-inch megacockroaches that belch fire, eat raw meat, and are virtually impervious to Raid. Produced by gimmick-king William Castle, who wanted to install windshield wiper-like devices under theatre seats that would brush against the patrons' feet as the cockroaches crawled across the screen; unfortunately, the idea was squashed flat. **100m/C VHS, Beta.** Bradford Dillman, Joanna Miles, Richard Gilliland, Jamie Smith-Jackson, Alan Fudge, Jesse Vint, William Castle; *D:* Jeannot Szwarc; *W:* William Castle; *C:* Michael Hugo; *M:* Charles Fox. *PAR*

Bugged! ✍ **1996 (PG-13)** Flesh-eating insects attack a beautiful homemaker and a group of bumbling exterminators are her only hope.*CW:* Comic sci-fi violence/gore, and for brief strong language. **90m/C VHS.** Ronald K. Armstrong, Priscilla Basque, Jeff Lee, Derek C. Johnson, Billy Graham; *D:* Ronald K. Armstrong; *W:* Ronald K. Armstrong; *C:* S. Torriano Berry; *M:* Boris Elkis. *TTV*

Bugles in the Afternoon ✍✍ **1952** Life in the army during Custer's last days, with a love triangle, revenge and the Little Big Horn for added spice. **85m/C VHS.** Ray Milland, Hugh Marlowe, Helena Carter, Forrest Tucker, Barton MacLane, George Reeves; *D:* Roy Rowland. *REP, FCT*

Bugs & Daffy: The Wartime Cartoons **1945** A compilation of Daffy and Bugs classics made during WWII, often dominated by propaganda and Axis-baiting. **120m/C VHS, Beta, LV.** *D:* Robert McKimson, Chuck Jones, Isadore "Friz" Freleng. *MGM*

The Bugs Bunny/Road Runner Movie*Great American Bugs Bunny-Road Runner Chase* **1979 (G)** A compilation of classic Warner Brothers cartoons, starring Bugs Bunny, Daffy Duck, Elmer Fudd, the Road Runner, Wile E. Coyote, Porky Pig, and Pepe Le Pew, including some all-new animated sequences. Also available with Spanish dubbing. **98m/C VHS, Beta.** *D:* Chuck Jones, Phil Monroe; *V:* Mel Blanc. *WAR, APD*

Bugs Bunny Superstar **1975 (G)** A collection of nine animated classics starring everybody's favorite "wascally wabbitt." Includes fascinating interviews and behind the scenes moments featuring the men and women who brought Bugs to life. **91m/C VHS, LV.** *D:* Larry Jackson, Bob Clampett, Tex Avery, Isadore "Friz" Freleng; *V:* Mel Blanc. *MGM*

Bugsy ✍✍✍½ **1991 (R)** Beatty is Benjamin "Bugsy" Siegel, the 40s gangster who built the Flamingo Hotel in Las Vegas when it was still a virtual desert, before it became a gambling mecca. Bening is perfect as Bugsy's moll, Virginia Hill, who inspired him to carry out his dream of building the Flamingo (which was her nickname). Beatty and Bening heat up the screen and their off-screen relationship was no different. Fans anticipated their seemingly imminent marriage almost as much as the release of this movie. Almost nothing mars this film which Toback adapted from a novel by Dean Jennings, "We Only Kill Each Other: The Life and Bad Times of Bugsy Siegel."*CW:* Language, violence, and sensuality. **135m/C VHS, Beta, LV, 8mm, Closed Caption.** Warren Beatty, Annette Bening, Harvey Keitel, Ben Kingsley, Elliott Gould, Joe Mantegna, Richard Sarafian, Bebe Neuwirth, Wendy Phillips, Robert Beltran, Bill Graham, Lewis Van Bergen, Debrah Farentino; *D:* Barry Levinson; *W:* James Toback; *C:* Allen Daviau; *M:* Ennio Morricone. Academy Awards '91: Best Art Direction/Set Decoration, Best Costume Design; Chicago Film Critics Awards '91: Best Supporting Actor (Keitel); Golden Globe Awards '92: Best Film—Drama; Los Angeles Film Critics Association Awards '91: Best Director (Levinson), Best Film, Best Screenplay; National Board of Review Awards '91: 10 Best Films of the Year, Best Actor (Beatty); Nominations: Academy Awards '91: Best Actor (Beatty), Best Cinematography, Best Director (Levinson), Best Original Screenplay, Best Picture, Best Supporting Actor (Keitel, Kingsley), Best Original Score. *COL*

Bugsy Malone ✍✍½ **1976 (G)** Delightful musical features an all-children's cast highlighting this spoof of 1930s' gangster movies. **94m/C VHS, Beta, LV.** *GB* Jodie Foster, Scott Baio, Florrie Augger, John Cassisi, Martin Lev; *D:* Alan Parker; *W:* Alan Parker; *C:* Peter Biziou; *M:* Paul Williams. British Academy Awards '76: Best Screenplay; Nominations: Academy Awards '76: Best Original Score. *PAR*

Bull Durham ✍✍✍½ **1988 (R)** Lovable American romantic comedy, dealing with a very minor minor-league team and three of its current constituents: an aging baseball groupie that beds one player each season; a cocky, foolish new pitcher; and the older, weary catcher brought in to

wise the rookie up. The scene in which Sarandon tries poetry out on the banal rookie is a hoot. Highly acclaimed, the film sears with Sarandon and Costner's love scenes. **107m/C VHS, Beta, LV, Closed Caption.** Kevin Costner, Susan Sarandon, Tim Robbins, Trey Wilson, Robert Wuhl, Jenny Robertson; *D:* Ron Shelton; *W:* Ron Shelton; *M:* Michael Convertino. Los Angeles Film Critics Association Awards '88: Best Screenplay; New York Film Critics Awards '88: Best Screenplay; National Society of Film Critics Awards '88: Best Screenplay; Writers Guild of America '88: Best Original Screenplay; Nominations: Academy Awards '88: Best Original Screenplay. *ORI, HMV*

Bull of the West ✍½ **1989** Cattlemen battle for land in the wide open spaces of the old West. **90m/C VHS.** Charles Bronson, Lee J. Cobb, Brian Keith, George Kennedy, DeForest Kelley, Doug McClure. *NO*

Bulldance ✍ *Forbidden Son* **1988** At a gymnastic school in Crete, a girl's obsession with Greek mythological ritual leads to murder. **105m/C VHS, Beta.** Lauren Hutton, Cliff DeYoung, Renee Estevez; *D:* Zelda Barron. *ACA*

Bulldog Courage ✍✍ **1935** Young man is out to avenge his father's murder. **66m/B VHS, Beta.** Tim McCoy, Lois January, Joan Woodbury, John Elliott; *D:* Sam Newfield. *NOS, VCN, DVT*

Bulldog Drummond ✍✍½ **1929** The Bulldog Drummond character, created by "Sapper" (Herman Cyril McNeile), underwent a number of different incarnations from 20s silents through the 40s, and even occasionally in the 50s and 60s. A suave ex-British officer (a precursor to the glib shaken-not-stirred gentleman-spy variety), Bulldog has been played by the likes of Colman, Ralph Richardson, and Tom Conway, among others. In this, the first installment in the long-standing series, a WWI vet, bored with civilian life, is enlisted by a beautiful woman to help her father in various adventures. **85m/B VHS, Beta, LV.** Ronald Colman, Joan Bennett, Montagu Love; *D:* F. Richard Jones. Nominations: Academy Awards '30: Best Actor (Colman), Best Interior Decoration, Best Interior Decoration. *RXM*

Bulldog Drummond at Bay ✍ **1937** Drummond searches for a group of foreign agents who are trying to steal the plans for a top-secret warplane. Poor British entry to the "Bulldog Drummond" series. **63m/B VHS.** *GB* John Lodge, Dorothy Mackaill, Victor Jory, Claud Allister, Hugh Miller; *D:* Norman Lee. *SNC*

Bulldog Drummond Comes Back ✍✍ **1937** Drummond, aided by Colonel Nielson, rescues his fiancee from the hands of desperate kidnappers. **119m/B VHS, Beta.** John Howard, John Barrymore, Louise Campbell, Reginald Denny, Guy Standing; *D:* Louis King. *SNC, NOS, DVT*

Bulldog Drummond Escapes ✍✍ **1937** Drummond, aided by his side-kick and valet, rescues a beautiful girl from spies. He then falls in love with her. **67m/B VHS, Beta.** Ray Milland, Heather Angel, Reginald Denny, Guy Standing, Porter Hall, E.E. Clive; *D:* James Hogan. *SNC, NOS, VYY*

Bulldog Drummond in Africa/Arrest Bulldog Drummond ✍✍ **1938** Two midseries Bulldog Drummond films, with two new villains. **115m/B VHS, Beta.** John Howard, H.B. Warner, George Zucco. *RXM*

Bulldog Drummond's Bride ✍✍ **1939** Ace detective Bulldog Drummond has to interrupt his honeymoon in order to pursue a gang of bank robbers across France and England. The last of the Bulldog Drummond film series. **69m/B VHS, Beta.** John Howard, Heather Angel, H.B. Warner, E.E. Clive, Reginald Denny, Eduardo Ciannelli; *D:* James Hogan. *DVT, MRV, RXM*

Bulldog Drummond's Peril ✍✍ **1938** Murder and robbery drag the adventurous Drummond away from his wedding and he pursues the villains once they are behind bars. One in the film series. **77m/B VHS, Beta.** John Barrymore, John Howard,

Louise Campbell, Reginald Denny, E.E. Clive, Porter Hall; **D:** James Hogan. *SNC, RXM, MRV*

Bulldog Drummond's Revenge 🎬🎬½ 1937
Bulldog's "Revenge" was made during the series' heyday and was the second to star Howard as Drummond; Barrymore revels in the character of Inspector Neilson of Scotland Yard, and Denny is Algy. In this typically fast-paced installment, suave sleuth Drummond stalks the master criminal responsible for stealing the formula to an explosive. 55m/B VHS. John Howard, John Barrymore, Reginald Denny, Louise Campbell, Frank Puglia, Nydia Westman, Lucien Littlefield; **D:** Louis King. *SNC, MOV*

Bulldog Drummond's Revenge/ Bulldog Drummond's Peril 1938
Once again, Bulldog Drummond becomes entangled with diamond counterfeiters, secret explosives, and other crime and criminals. Two episodes in a series. 118m/B VHS, Beta. John Howard, John Barrymore, Louise Campbell, Reginald Denny, E.E. Clive, Porter Hall.

Bulldog Drummond's Secret Police 🎬🎬 1939
The 15th Drummond film, adapted from Herman Cyril McNeile's famed detective novels featuring a million-pound treasure stashed in the Drummond manor and the murderous endeavors to retrieve it. 54m/B VHS. John Howard, Heather Angel, H.B. Warner, Reginald Denny, E.E. Clive, Leo G. Carroll; **D:** James Hogan. *SNC, VYY, RXM*

Bulldog Edition 🎬🎬 1936
Two newspapers engage in an all-out feud to be number one in the city, even going so far as to employ gangsters for purposes of sabotage. 57m/B VHS, Beta. Ray Walker, Evalyn Knapp, Regis Toomey, Cy Kendall, Billy Newell, Oscar Apfel, Betty Compson, Robert Warwick; **D:** Charles Lamont. *SNC*

Bulldog Jack 🎬🎬🎬 *Alias Bulldog Drummond* 1935
Fine entry in the series has Drummond's colleague battling it out with Richardson, the leader of gang of jewel thieves. 62m/B VHS, Beta. *GB* Fay Wray, Jack Hulbert, Claude Hulbert, Ralph Richardson, Paul Graetz, Gibb McLaughlin; **D:** Walter Forde. *NOS, SNC*

The Bulldozer Brigade 🎬🎬½ 1985
Young friends fight city hall in an effort to save their secret wooded playground from land developers. 86m/C VHS, Closed Caption. *FHE, BTV*

Bullet 🎬½ 1994 (R)
Butch (Rourke) gets released from prison and immediately returns to his old drug and burglary ways on New York's mean streets. And he's got a score to settle with crazy drug kingpin Tank (Shakur). Has little to recommend it, except to those who like violence, with lackluster performances and a dull script.**CW:** Strong violence, drug use, pervasive language and a graphic sex scene. 96m/C VHS, LV, Closed Caption. Mickey Rourke, Tupac Shakur, Ted Levine, Adrien Brody, John Enos; **D:** Julien Temple; **W:** Bruce Rubenstein; **C:** Crescenzo G.P. Notarile. *NLC*

Bullet Code 🎬🎬 1940
It's quick-shooting shenanigans when O'Brien chases a pack of angry rustlers off his neighbor's land. 56m/B VHS. George O'Brien, Virginia Vale, Howard Hickman, Harry Woods, Charles "Slim" Whitaker; **D:** David Howard; **W:** Doris Schroeder. *MOV*

Bullet for Sandoval 🎬🎬 1970 (PG)
An ex-Confederate renegade loots and pillages the north Mexican countryside on his way to murder the grandfather of the woman he loves. 96m/C VHS, Beta. *SP IT* Ernest Borgnine, George Hilton; **D:** Julio Buchs. *VCI*

A Bullet for the General 🎬 *Quien Sabe?* 1968
An American mercenary joins with rebel forces during the Mexican Revolution. 95m/C VHS, Beta. *IT* Martine Beswick, Lou Castel, Gian Marie Volonte, Klaus Kinski; **D:** Damiano Damiani; **M:** Luis Bacalov. *COL, NLC*

A Bullet in the Head 🎬🎬🎬 1990
Violent (no surprise there) tale of friendship finds Frank (Cheung), Ben (Leung), and Paul (Lee) heading out of 1967 Hong Kong for Saigon, where they hope to make money selling contra-

band goods in the city. They wind up on the wrong side of the Vietnamese Army, steal a fortune in gold from a local crime lord, and end up the prisoners of the Viet Cong. There's betrayal and death and a final moral reckoning and—did we mention lots and lots of (over-the-top) violence? Chinese with subtitles. 85m/C VHS. *HK* Tony Leung, Jacky Cheung, Waise Lee; **D:** John Woo. *FCT*

A Bullet Is Waiting 🎬🎬 1954
A diligent sheriff finally catches his man only to be trapped in a blinding snowstorm with the hardened criminal. 83m/C VHS, Beta. Jean Simmons, Rory Calhoun, Stephen McNally, Brian Aherne; **D:** John Farrow. *GKK*

Bullet to Beijing 🎬🎬½ *Len Deighton's Bullet to Beijing* 1995 (R)
After some 30 years, Caine returns to his role as intelligence agent Harry Palmer. Forced into retirement, Harry finds himself privately recruited by a Russian businessman (Gambon) to locate a stolen chemical weapon. Now just who can Harry trust to help him out? Follows "The Ipcress File," "Funeral in Berlin," and "Billion Dollar Brain;" based on the novel by Len Deighton.**CW:** Violence, nudity and language. 105m/C VHS. *GB* Michael Caine, Michael Gambon, Jason Connery, Patrick Allen, Mia Sara, Burt Kwouk, Michael Sarrazin; **D:** George Mihalka; **W:** Peter Welbeck; **M:** Rick Wakeman. *NYR*

Bulletproof 🎬 1988 (R)
An unstoppable ex-CIA agent battles to retrieve a high-tech nuclear tank from terrorist hands. 93m/C VHS, Beta, LV. Gary Busey, Darlanne Fluegel, Henry Silva, Thalmus Rasulala, L.Q. Jones, R.G. Armstrong, Rene Enriquez; **D:** Steve Carver; **W:** Steve Carver. *COL*

Bulletproof 🎬 1996 (R)
Desperately trying to be a male buddy bonding movie, "Bulletproof" fails miserably in every respect. Keats (Wayans) and Moses (Sandler) are an unlikely pair of car thieves with an equally unlikely bond to each other. Turns out Keats is really undercover cop Jack Carter, who is trying to infiltrate a drug cartel via his pal Moses. When the bust goes bad, Carter must bring Moses in unharmed to testify. Meanwhile the two rejuvenate their tainted relationship amid many homoerotic innuendos. It's an embarrassment all around, especially for ex-Spike Lee cinematographer Dickerson on his first directing outing.**CW:** Strong violence and language, some sexuality and drug use. 85m/C VHS, LV, Closed Caption. Damon Wayans, Adam Sandler, James Caan, Kristen Wilson, James Farentino, Bill Nunn, Mark Roberts, Xander Berkeley, Alan Covert, Jeep Swenson, McCoy Larry; **D:** Ernest R. Dickerson; **W:** Joe Gayton, Lewis Colick; **C:** Steve Bernstein; **M:** Elmer Bernstein. Nominations: Golden Raspberry Awards '96: Worst Actor (Sandler). *USH*

Bulletproof Heart 🎬🎬🎬 *Killer* 1995 (R)
Mick (LaPaglia), a hit man with a severe case of burnout, is assigned to kill Fiona (Rogers), a beautiful socialite who, conveniently, wants to die. Despite being warned by his boss (Boyle) that Fiona has a habit of making men weak, he falls in love and can't bring himself to kill her. First-time director Malone takes great care to establish the noir look and feel, capitalizing on the all-in-one-night timeframe to raise the tension level. LaPaglia and Rogers turn in riveting performances, but can't stop the film from losing momentum when it becomes self-consciously melodramatic near the end.**CW:** Strong graphic sex scene; language. 95m/C VHS, LV, Closed Caption. Anthony LaPaglia, Mimi Rogers, Peter Boyle, Matt Craven, Monika Schnarre, Joseph Maher; **D:** Mark Malone; **W:** Gordon Melbourne, Mark Malone; **C:** Tobias Schliessler; **M:** Graeme Coleman. *REP*

Bullets or Ballots 🎬🎬 1938
Tough New York cop goes undercover to join the mob in order to get the goods on them. Old-fashioned danger and intrigue follow, making for some action-packed thrills. 82m/B VHS, Beta. Edward G. Robinson, Humphrey Bogart, Barton MacLane, Joan Blondell, Frank McHugh, Louise Beavers; **D:** William Keighley; **C:** Hal Mohr. *MGM, CCB*

Bullets Over Broadway 🎬🎬🎬½ 1994 (R)
Mediocre playwright David Shayne (Cusack, in the Allen role) talks up the virtues of artistic integrity to his pretentious hothouse contemporaries, then sells out to a gangster who agrees to finance his latest play provided his no-talent, brassy moll (Tilly) gets a part. And it's her hit-man bodyguard's (Palminteri) unexpected artistic touches that redeem Shayne's otherwise lousy work. Wiest as the eccentric diva, Ullman as the aging ingenue, Reiner as the Greenwich Village sage, and Broadbent as the increasingly plump matinee idol lead a collection of delicious, over-the-top performances in this smart and howlingly funny tribute to Jazz Age New York City that showcases Woody at his self-conscious best. 106m/C VHS, LV, Closed Caption. Dianne Wiest, John Cusack, Jennifer Tilly, Rob Reiner, Chazz Palminteri, Tracey Ullman, Mary-Louise Parker, Joe Viterelli, Jack Warden, Jim Broadbent, Harvey Fierstein, Annie-Joe Edwards; **D:** Woody Allen; **W:** Woody Allen, Douglas McGrath; **C:** Carlo DiPalma. Academy Awards '94: Best Supporting Actress (Wiest); Chicago Film Critics Awards '94: Best Supporting Actress (Wiest); Golden Globe Awards '95: Best Supporting Actress (Wiest); Independent Spirit Awards '95: Best Supporting Actor (Palminteri), Best Supporting Actress (Wiest); Los Angeles Film Critics Association Awards '94: Best Supporting Actress (Wiest); New York Film Critics Awards '94: Best Supporting Actress (Wiest); National Society of Film Critics Awards '94: Best Supporting Actress (Wiest); Screen Actors Guild Award '94: Best Supporting Actress (Wiest); Nominations: Academy Awards '94: Best Art Direction/Set Decoration, Best Costume Design, Best Director (Allen), Best Original Screenplay, Best Supporting Actor (Palminteri), Best Supporting Actress (Tilly); British Academy Awards '95: Best Original Screenplay; Independent Spirit Awards '95: Best Film, Best Screenplay; Writers Guild of America '94: Best Original Screenplay. *MAX*

Bullfighter & the Lady 🎬🎬½ 1950
An American goes to Mexico to learn the fine art of bullfighting in order to impress a beautiful woman. 87m/B VHS, LV. Robert Stack, Gilbert Roland, Virginia Grey, Katy Jurado; **D:** Budd Boetticher. Nominations: Academy Awards '51: Best Story.*REP*

Bullfighters 🎬🎬 1945
Stan and Ollie are in hot pursuit of a dangerous criminal which leads them to Mexico where Stan winds up in a bull ring. 61m/B VHS, Beta. Stan Laurel, Oliver Hardy, Margo Woode, Richard Lane; **D:** Malcolm St. Clair. *FOX, MLB*

Bullies woof! 1986 (R)
A woodland-transplanted young man decides to fight back against an ornery mountain clan who have raped his mother, tortured his father, and beat up his girlfriend. Brutal and unpalatable. 96m/C VHS, Beta, LV, Closed Caption. *CA* Janet-Laine Green, Dehl Berti, Stephen Hunter, Jonathan Crombie, Olivia D'Abo; **D:** Paul Lynch. *USH*

Bullitt 🎬🎬🎬 1968 (PG)
A detective assigned to protect a star witness for 48 hours senses danger; his worst fears are confirmed when his charge is murdered. Based on the novel, "Mute Witness" by Robert L. Pike, and featuring one of filmdom's most famous car chases. 105m/C VHS, Beta, LV. Steve McQueen, Robert Vaughn, Jacqueline Bisset, Don Gordon, Robert Duvall, Norman Fell, Simon Oakland; **D:** Peter Yates; **W:** Alan R. Trustman; **C:** William A. Fraker; **M:** Lalo Schifrin. Academy Awards '68: Best Film Editing; Edgar Allan Poe Awards '68: Best Screenplay; National Society of Film Critics Awards '68: Best Cinematography; Nominations: Academy Awards '68: Best Sound. *WAR*

Bullseye! 🎬½ 1990 (PG-13)
Knockabout farce is a letdown considering the talents involved. Shady scientists (Moore and Caine) pursue/are pursued by lookalike con-artists (Caine and Moore), who are pursued in turn by international agents. Full of inside jokes and celebrity cameos, but nothing exceptional. 95m/C VHS, LV. Michael Caine, Roger Moore, Sally Kirkland, Patsy Kensit, Jenny Seagrove, John Cleese, Lee Patterson, Deborah Barrymore, Mark Burns, Deborah Leng, Alexandra Pigg; **Cameos:** Lynn Nesbitt, Steffanie Pitt; **D:** Michael Winner; **W:** Michael Winner, Leslie Bricusse; **M:** John Du Prez. *COL*

Bullshot 🦴🦴½ **1983 (PG)** Zany English satire sends up the legendary Bulldog Drummond. In the face of mad professors, hapless heroines, devilish Huns and deadly enemies, our intrepid hero remains distinctly British. **84m/C VHS, Beta.** *GB* Alan Shearman, Diz White, Ron House, Frances Tomelty, Michael Aldridge, Ron Pember, Christopher Good; *D:* Dick Clement; *J:* John Du Prez. *NO*

Bullwhip 🦴🦴 **1958** A man falsely accused of murder saves himself from the hangman's noose by agreeing to a shotgun wedding. **80m/C VHS.** Guy Madison, Rhonda Fleming, James Griffith, Peter Adams; *D:* Harmon Jones. *REP*

Bummer woof! **1973 (R)** Rock band's wild party turns into tragedy when the bass player goes too far with two groupies. It's a bad scene, man. **90m/C VHS, Beta.** Kipp Whitman, Dennis Burkley, Carol Speed, Connie Strickland; *D:* William Allen Castleman. *NO*

Bums 🦴🦴 **1993** Sergeant Andrew Holloman is a military officer in search of his long lost brother. It turns out his brother was homeless and is now dead at the hands of a skid row killer. Holloman recruits a platoon of other homeless people to help him track the killer but what he discovers is a multimillion conspiracy behind the murders. **94m/C VHS.** Christopher McDonald, Dawn Evans; *D:* Andy Galler; *W:* Pat Allee, Ben Hurst. *MNC*

Bunco 🦴 **1983** Two policemen working for the Los Angeles Police Department's Bunco Squad discover a college for con artists complete with tape-recorded lessons and on-the-job training. **60m/C VHS, Beta.** Tom Selleck, Robert Urich, Donna Mills, Will Geer, Arte Johnson, Alan Feinstein. *ORI, WAR*

Bundle of Joy 🦴🦴½ **1956** Salesgirl who saves an infant from falling off the steps of a foundling home is mistaken for the child's mother. Remake of 1939's "Bachelor Mother." 🎵Bundle of Joy; I Never Felt This Way Before; Lullaby in Blue; Worry About Tomorrow; All About Love; Someday Soon; What's So Good About Morning?; You're Perfect In Every Departmant. **98m/C VHS, Beta, LV.** Debbie Reynolds, Eddie Fisher, Adolphe Menjou; *D:* Norman Taurog. *NO*

A Bunny's Tale 🦴🦴 **1985** The story of Gloria Steinem's undercover journey into the Playboy Club as a fledgling journalist. It is here that she discovered her dedication as a feminist. Based on the book by Steinem. **97m/C VHS, Closed Caption.** Kirstie Alley, Cotter Smith, Deborah Van Valkenburgh, Joanna Kerns, Delta Burke, Diana Scarwid; *D:* Karen Arthur. *PSM*

Buona Sera, Mrs. Campbell 🦴🦴½ **1968** The lovely Lollobridgida and some fast-paced plot moves are the main highlights of this comedy. Mrs. Campbell convinced her three American WWII lovers that each of them had fathered her daughter. All three have supported mother and child through the years, unbeknowst to each other and their wives. When their 20-year reunion brings them back to Italy, Mrs. Campbell must do some fast-thinking and some quick-stepping to keep everyone happy. **113m/C VHS, LV.** Gina Lollobrigida, Shelley Winters, Phil Silvers, Peter Lawford, Telly Savalas, Lee Grant, Janet Margolin, Marian Moses; *D:* Melvin Frank. *MGM*

The 'Burbs 🦴½ **1989 (PG)** A tepid satire about suburbanites suspecting their creepy new neighbors of murderous activities. Well-designed and sharp, but light on story. **101m/C VHS, Beta, LV.** Tom Hanks, Carrie Fisher, Rick Ducommun, Corey Feldman, Brother Theodore, Bruce Dern, Gale Gordon, Courtney Gains; *D:* Joe Dante; *M:* Jerry Goldsmith. *USH, CCB*

Burden of Dreams **1982** The landmark documentary chronicling the berserk circumstances behind the scenes of Werner Herzog's epic "Fitzcarraldo." Stuck in the Peruvian jungles, the film crew was subjected to every disaster imaginable while executing Herzog's vision, including disease, horrendous accident, warring local tribes and the megalomaniacal director himself. Considered better than "Fitzcarraldo," although

both films discuss a man's obsession. **94m/C VHS, Beta, LV.** Klaus Kinski, Mick Jagger, Jason Robards Jr., Werner Herzog; *D:* Les Blank. *TPV, FFM, BTV*

Bureau of Missing Persons 🦴🦴½ **1933** Comedy-drama about big-city bureau of missing persons, in which the hardened Stone is in charge. O'Brien plays a tough cop who is transferred to the bureau and Davis stars as the mystery woman with whom he gets involved. Although fast-paced and intriguing, the film is somewhat confusing and never stays in one direction for very long. **75m/B VHS, Closed Caption.** Bette Davis, Lewis Stone, Pat O'Brien, Glenda Farrell, Allen Jenkins, Ruth Donnelly, Hugh Herbert; *D:* Roy Del Ruth. *MGM*

Burglar 🦴🦴 **1987 (R)** A cat burglar moves to the right side of the law when she tries to solve a murder case. Whoopi's always a treat, but this movie's best forgotten; Goldberg's fans should watch "Jumpin' Jack Flash" again instead. Co-star Goldthwait elevates the comedic level a bit. **103m/C VHS, Beta, LV, Closed Caption.** Whoopi Goldberg, Bob(cat) Goldthwait, Lesley Ann Warren, John Goodman, G.W. Bailey, James Handy, Anne DeSalvo; *D:* Hugh Wilson; *W:* Hugh Wilson. *WAR, KIV*

Burglar 🦴🦴🦴 *Vzlomschik* **1987** Not to be confused with the Whoopi Goldberg vehicle, this Russian film relates a story no less American than apple pie and teenage angst. Senka and would-be punk star Kostya are two neglected and disaffected brothers whose father is a drunken womanizer best known for absentee paternalism. When Howmuch, a serious heavy metalloid, pressures Kostya to steal a synthesizer, brother Senka steps in to steal the Community Center's property himself. In Russian with English subtitles, the solid performances hold their own against the heavy musical content. **89m/C VHS.** *RU* Konstantin Kinchev, Oleg Yelykomov; *D:* Valery Orgorodnikov. *FCT, KIV*

Burial Ground 🦴 **1985** A classically grisly splatter film in which the hungry dead rise and proceed to kill the weekend denizens of an isolated aristocratic mansion. **85m/C VHS, Beta.** Karen Well, Peter Bark; *D:* Andrew Bianchi. *VES, LIV*

Burial of the Rats 🦴½ *Roger Corman Presents Burial of the Rats; Bram Stoker's Burial of the Rats* **1995 (R)** Based on a short story by Bram Stoker, this cable campiness features young Bram (Alber) himself being kidnapped while traveling in Eastern Europe. He's taken to the "Queen of Vermin" (Barbeau), who heads a bloodthirsty cult that hate men, worship rats, and live by violence. Fortunately, the Queen decides to spare Bram so he can write of their exploits and he falls for the fleshy charms of rat-woman Madeleine (Ford). *CW:* Nudity; a sex scene; horror violence/gore. **85m/C VHS.** Adrienne Barbeau, Marla Ford, Kevin Alber; *D:* Dan Golden. *NHO*

Buried Alive 🦴 **1939** A man is sent to prison on trumped up charges. Only the prison nurse believes he is innocent as a crooked politician strives to keep him behind bars. **74m/B Beta.** Beverly Roberts, Robert Wilcox, George Pembroke, Ted Osborn, Paul McVey, Alden Chase; *D:* Victor Halperin. *NOS, MRV, LOO*

Buried Alive 🦴🦴 **1981** Director d'Amato reaps his finest gore-fest to date, incorporating the well-established taxidermist gone loony motif in his repertoire of appalling bad taste. Not for the squeamish, this bloodier-than-thou spaghetti spooker is chock full of necrophilia, cannibalism, and more. **90m/C VHS.** *IT* Kieran Canter, Cinzia Monreale, Franca Stoppi; *D:* Joe D'Amato. *NO*

Buried Alive 🦴🦴 **1989 (R)** Once Ravenscroft Hall was an asylum for the incurably insane. Now, the isolated mansion is a school for troubled teenage girls, run by a charismatic politician psychiatrist. Captivated by his charm, a young woman joins the staff. Soon, she is tormented by nightmare visions of the long-dead victims of a nameless killer. When the students begin to disappear, she realizes he still lives...and she may be

his next victim. Carradine's last role. **97m/C VHS, LV.** Robert Vaughn, Donald Pleasence, Karen Witter, John Carradine, Ginger Lynn Allen; *D:* Gerard Kikoine. *COL*

Buried Alive 🦴🦴½ **1990 (PG-13)** One of the many horror flicks entitled "Buried Alive," this one is not bad, injecting a bit of levity into the time-worn genre. Schemestress Leigh and her paramour poison her husband. Or so they think, only to discover that he's not quite dead. Made for cable. **93m/C VHS.** Tim Matheson, Jennifer Jason Leigh, William Atherton, Hoyt Axton; *D:* Frank Darabont; *W:* Mark Patrick Carducci, Jake Clesi; *M:* Michel Colombier. *USH*

Burke & Wills 🦴🦴½ **1985 (PG-13)** A lush, big-budgeted true story of the two men who first crossed Australia on foot, and explored its central region. Popular Australian film. **120m/C VHS, Beta, LV, Closed Caption.** *AU* Jack Thompson, Nigel Havers, Greta Scacchi, Ralph Cotterill, Drew Forsythe, Chris Haywood, Matthew Fargher; *D:* Graeme Clifford; *W:* Michael Thomas; *C:* Russell Boyd; *M:* Peter Sculthorpe. *NLC*

Burlesque of Carmen 🦴🦴 **1916** A silent pastiche of the Bizet opera, with Charlie as Don Schmose. Interesting early work. **30m/B VHS, Beta.** Charlie Chaplin, Ben Turpin, Edna Purviance; *D:* Charlie Chaplin. *NOS, DVT, GVV*

The Burmese Harp 🦴🦴🦴🦴 *Harp of Burma; Birumana Tategoto* **1956** At the end of WWII, a Japanese soldier is spiritually traumatized and becomes obsessed with burying the masses of war casualties. A searing, acclaimed anti-war statement, in Japanese with English subtitles. Remade by Ichikawa in 1985. **115m/B VHS, Beta, LV.** *JP* Shoji Yasui, Rentaro Mikuni, Tatsuya Mihashi, Tanie Kitabayashi, Yunosuke Ito; *D:* Kon Ichikawa. Nominations: Academy Awards '56: Best Foreign Language Film. *CVC, APD, TPV*

Burn! 🦴🦴🦴½ *Quemimada!* **1970 (PG)** An Italian-made indictment of imperialist control by guerrilla-filmmaker Pontecorvo, depicting the efforts of a 19th century British ambassador to put down a slave revolt on a Portuguese-run Caribbean island. Great Brando performance. **112m/C VHS, Beta, LV.** *IT* Marlon Brando, Evarist Marquez, Renato Salvatori; *D:* Gillo Pontecorvo; *M:* Ennio Morricone. *MGM, CRC, FCT*

Burn 'Em Up Barnes **1934** Twelve episodes each depicting the adventures of "Burn'Em Up" Barnes, a racer, and his buddy, Bobbie. **40m/B VHS, Beta.** Frankie Darro, Lola Lane, Jack Mulhall. *SNC, NOS, VCN*

Burn Witch, Burn! 🦴🦴🦴 *Night of the Eagle* **1962** A college professor proudly finds himself rapidly rising in his profession. His pride turns to horror though when he discovers that his success is not due to his own abilities, but to the efforts of his witchcraft practicing wife. Excellent, atmospheric horror with a genuinely suspenseful climax. **87m/B VHS.** *GB* Peter Wyngarde, Janet Blair, Margaret Johnston, Anthony Nicholls, Colin Gordon, Kathleen Byron, Reginald Beckwith, Jessica Dunning; *D:* Sidney Hayers; *W:* Richard Matheson. *FRG*

Burndown 🦴 **1989 (R)** Victims of a serial killer in a town with a large nuclear reactor are themselves radioactive, which leads the Police Chief and a beautiful reporter to the truth and the hidden conspiracy. **97m/C VHS, Beta, LV.** Cathy Moriarty, Peter Firth; *D:* James Allen. *NO*

The Burning 🦴 **1982 (R)** Story of macabre revenge set in the dark woods of a seemingly innocent summer camp. **90m/C VHS, Beta.** Brian Matthews, Leah Ayres, Holly Hunter, Jason Alexander; *D:* Tony Maylam. *NO*

The Burning Bed 🦴🦴🦴½ **1985** A made for television dramatic expose (based on a true story) about wife-beating. Fawcett garnered accolades for her performance as the battered wife who couldn't take it anymore. Highly acclaimed and Emmy-nominated. **95m/C VHS, Beta, Closed Caption.** Farrah Fawcett, Paul LeMat, Penelope Milford, Richard Masur; *D:* Robert Greenwald. *FOX*

The Burning Court 🎬½ **1962** Unusual horror film involving occultism, possession, and family curses. Dubbed into English. Based on a story by John Dickson Carr. **102m/C VHS.** Nadja Tiller, Jean-Claude Brialy, Edith Scob. *SNC*

Burning Daylight 🎬🎬 **1928** Alaskan real estate baron loses everything to a group of San Francisco sharpies. Based on the story by Jack London. **72m/B VHS.** Milton Sills, Arthur Stone, Doris Kenyon, Guinn "Big Boy" Williams; *D:* Richard A. Rowland. *GPV*

The Burning Hills 🎬½ **1956** Unexceptional cow flick based on a Louis L'Amour novel. Hunter hides from cattle thieves in a barn and, eventually, in the arms of a half-breed Mexican girl (Wood). Tedious and unsurprising. **94m/C VHS.** Tab Hunter, Natalie Wood, Skip Homeier, Eduard Franz; *D:* Stuart Heisler. *WAR, MLB*

Burning Rage 🎬 **1984** A blazing, abandoned coal mine threatens to wreak havoc on the Appalachians. The government sends geologist Mandrell to help prevent a disaster. Made for television. **100m/C VHS, LV.** Barbara Mandrell, Tom Wopat, Bert Remsen, John Pleshette, Carol Kane, Eddie Albert; *D:* Gilbert Cates. *VTR*

The Burning Season 🎬🎬🎬 **1994** In one of his last performances, Julia inspires as Chico Mendes, a socialist union leader who fought to protect the homes and land of Brazilian peasants in the western Amazon rain forest. With Mendes' help the peasants form a union and struggle to prevent the building of a road that will provide easy access to forest land for speculators and cattlemen. Naturally, they are violently opposed by corruption-ridden capitalist powers in the government. Julia provides a haunting portrayal of the heroic figure who was assassinated in 1990. Based in part on the book by Andrew Revkin. Filmed on location in Mexico. **123m/C VHS, Closed Caption.** Raul Julia, Edward James Olmos, Sonia Braga, Luis Guzman, Nigel Havers, Kamala Dawson, Tomas Milian, Esai Morales, Tony Plana, Carmen Argenziano; *D:* John Frankenheimer; *W:* William Mastrosimone, Michael Tolkin, Ron Hutchinson; *M:* Gary Chang. *WAR*

Burning Secret 🎬🎬 *Brennendes Geheimnis* **1989 (PG)** After WWI, a widow in Austria (Dunaway) meets a baron (Brandauer) who has befriended her son. Mutual seduction ensues but the sparks don't fly. Adapted from Stefan Zweig story. **107m/C VHS, Beta, LV.** *GB* Faye Dunaway, Klaus Maria Brandauer, Ian Richardson, David Eberts; *D:* Andrew Birkin; *W:* Andrew Birkin; *M:* Hans Zimmer. *VES, IME, LIV*

The Burns and Allen Show **1950** George and Gracie's classic vaudeville routines are a highlight of this sitcom series, with George the perpetually harried husband to the scatterbrained Gracie. Additional episodes are available. **115m/B VHS, Beta, LV, Closed Caption.** Gracie Allen, George Burns. *SHO, COL, MOV*

Burnt by the Sun 🎬🎬🎬 *Outomlionnye Solntsem* **1994 (R)** Masterful evocation of '30's Stalinist Russia, covering a day in the life of Soviet revolutionary hero Serguei (Mikhalkov) and his family, far from the purges and gulags. Enjoying a country existence with wife Moroussia (Dapkounaite) and daughter Nadia (played by Mikhalkov's daughter), his idyll is disturbed by mystery man Dimitri (Menchikov), and Serguei realizes their fates are bound by the difference between their Communist dreams and reality. Symbolism is a little heavy but film delivers emotionally. Russian with subtitles. *CW:* Some language and sexuality. **134m/C VHS, LV.** *RU FR* Nikita Mikhalkov, Ingeborga Dapkounaite, Oleg Menshikov, Nadia Mikhalkov, Andre Oumansky, Viatcheslav Krioutchkov, Svetlana Krioutchkova, Vladimir Ilyine; *D:* Nikita Mikhalkov; *W:* Nikita Mikhalkov, Rustam Ibragimbekov; *M:* Eduard Artemyev. Academy Awards '94: Best Foreign Language Film; Cannes Film Festival '94: Grand Jury Prize; Nominations: Australian Film Institute '96: Best Foreign Film; British Academy Awards '95: Best Foreign Film. *COL*

Burnt Offerings 🎬🎬 **1976 (PG)** A family rents an old mansion for the summer and they become affected by evil forces that possess the house. Based on the novel by Robert Marasco. **116m/C VHS, Beta.** Oliver Reed, Karen Black, Bette Davis, Burgess Meredith; *D:* Dan Curtis; *W:* Dan Curtis. *MGM*

Bury Me an Angel 🎬 **1971** A female biker sets out to seek revenge against the men who killed her brother. **85m/C VHS, Beta, LV.** Dixie Peabody, Terry Mace, Clyde Ventura, Dan Haggerty, Stephen Whittaker, Gary Littlejohn; *D:* Barbara Peeters. *NWV, HHT*

Bury Me Not on the Lone Prairie 🎬🎬 **1941** When his brother is murdered in cold blood by claim jumpers, mining engineer Brown goes to avenge the dead. Based on a story by Sherman Lowe. **57m/B VHS.** Johnny Mack Brown, Fuzzy Knight, Nell O'Day, Frank O'Connor, Kermit Maynard; *D:* Ray Taylor; *W:* Sherman Lowe, Victor McLeod. *MOV*

The Bus Is Coming 🎬🎬 **1972** A love story entwined with the problems of blacks in a small town. **95m/C VHS, Beta.** Mike Sims, Stephanie Faulkner, Morgan Jones; *D:* Horace Jackson. *NO*

Bus Stop 🎬🎬🎬 *The Wrong Kind of Girl* **1956** Murray plays a naive cowboy who falls in love with Monroe, a barroom singer, and decides to marry her without his permission. Considered by many to be the finest performance by Marilyn Monroe; she sings "That Old Black Magic" in this one. Very funny with good performances by all. Based on the William Inge play. **96m/C VHS, Beta, LV.** Marilyn Monroe, Arthur O'Connell, Hope Lange, Don Murray, Betty Field, Max Casey Adams Showalter, Hans Conried, Eileen Heckart; *D:* Joshua Logan; *W:* George Axelrod; *C:* Milton Krasner. National Board of Review Awards '56: 10 Best Films of the Year; Nominations: Academy Awards '56: Best Supporting Actor (Murray). *FOX*

The Busby Berkeley Disc 🎬🎬 **1992** A collection of the innovative dance director's work at Warner Bros. studio covering 1933-37. Berkeley was known for his elaborate production numbers, beautiful women, military precision, and kaleidoscopic patterns in such films as "42nd Street," "Footlight Parade," and the "Gold Diggers" series. **176m/B LV.** *MGM*

Bush Mama 🎬🎬 **1976** A hallucinatory film about a black woman on welfare trying to care for her daughter in a Los Angeles ghetto. Street violence varies with fantasy scenes in a loose narrative filled with flashbacks. **100m/C VHS.** *D:* Haile Gerima. *FCT*

The Bushbaby 🎬½ **1970** The young Brooks is given a tiny bushbaby while visiting Africa with her father. Because of her pet she misses her ship home and finds herself with former servant Gossett, who agrees to take her to a family friend. Unfortunately, the authorities think he's kidnapped the girl and the two, along with the trouble-causing pet, are pursued by the police. Simple-minded safari fare. **100m/C VHS.** Margaret Brooks, Louis Gossett Jr., Donald Houston, Laurence Naismith, Marne Maitland, Geoffrey Bayldon, Jack Gwillim; *D:* John Trent. *MGM, FCT*

The Busher 🎬½ **1919** All-American pitcher's romance is interrupted by a gratuitous Mr. Moneybags. Minor-league conflict with little real hardball. **54m/B VHS, Beta.** Charles Ray, Colleen Moore, John Gilbert. *GPV, FCT, GVV*

The Bushido Blade 🎬🎬½ *The Bloody Bushido Blade* **1980** An action-packed samurai thriller of adventure and betrayal set in medieval Japan. **92m/C VHS, Beta.** *JP* Richard Boone, James Earl Jones, Frank Converse; *D:* Tom Kotani. *NO*

The Bushwackers 🎬½ *The Rebel* **1952** Ireland plays a veteran of the Confederate army who wishes only to put his violent past behind him. He is forced to reconsider his vow when old-west bullies threaten his family. **70m/B VHS.** Dorothy Malone, John Ireland, Wayne Morris, Lawrence Tierney, Jack Elam, Lon Chaney Sr., Myrna Dell; *D:* Rod Amateau. *NOS, LOO, SNC*

Bushwhacked 🎬🎬½ *Tenderfoots; The Tenderfoot* **1995 (PG-13)** Crude, rude, dim-witted, kidhating Max Grabelski (Stern) is falsely accused of murder and forced to become a fugitive. While not to be confused with Harrison Ford, he is mistaken for the leader of a group of Cub Scouts on their maiden camping trip and soon finds himself in an unlikely partnership with the boys. Together they encounter everything from grizzly bears to whitewater rapids. Light-hearted, goofy comedy continues Stern's tendency toward kid-intensive, family-oriented fare in the "Rookie of the Year" vein. *CW:* Crude dialogue. **85m/C VHS, Closed Caption.** Daniel Stern, Jon Polito, Brad Sullivan, Ann Dowd, Anthony Heald, Thomas Wood; *D:* Greg Beeman; *W:* Tommy Swerdlow, Michael Goldberg, John Jordan, Danny Byers; *M:* Bill Conti. *FXV*

A Business Affair 🎬🎬½ *D'Une Femme a L'Autre* **1993 (R)** Kate Swallow (the ravishing Bouquet), the neglected wife of temperamental author Alex Bolton (Pryce), begins an affair with his flamboyant American publisher Vanni Corso (Walken). While the men posture between themselves for her affections, Kate, who has literary aspirations, decides to strike out on her own. Based on the romantic triangle of British writers Barbara Skelton and Cyril Connolly and his publisher George Weidenfeld and taken from Skelton's memoirs "Tears Before Bedtime" and "Weep No More." *CW:* Language and some sexuality. **102m/C VHS.** Carole Bouquet, Jonathan Pryce, Christopher Walken, Sheila Hancock; *D:* Charlotte Brandstrom; *W:* William Stadiem; *C:* Willy Kurant; *M:* Didier Vasseur. *THV*

Business as Usual 🎬🎬 **1988 (PG)** A meek boutique manager in Liverpool defends a sexually harassed employee, is fired, fights back, and creates a national furor over her rights as a woman. **89m/C VHS, Beta, Closed Caption.** Glenda Jackson, Cathy Tyson, John Thaw, Craig Charles, Eamon Boland; *D:* Lezli-Ann Barrett; *W:* Lezli-Ann Barrett. *WAR*

Busted Up 🎬 **1986 (R)** A young, hard-luck urban street-fighter battles for the sake of his family and neighborhood against local crimelords. **93m/C VHS, Beta, Closed Caption.** *CA* Irene Cara, Paul Coufos, Tony Rosato, Stan Shaw, Gordon Judges; *D:* Conrad Palmisano; *M:* Charles P. Barnett. *USH*

Buster 🎬🎬½ **1988 (R)** The story of Buster Edwards, the one suspect in the 1963 Great Train Robbery who evaded being captured by police. Collins makes his screen debut as one of Britain's most infamous criminals. Collins also performs on the film's soundtrack, spawning two hit singles, "Two Hearts" and "Groovy Kind of Love." **102m/C VHS, Beta, LV, Closed Caption.** *GB* Phil Collins, Julie Walters, Larry Lamb, Stephanie Lawrence, Ellen Beaven, Michael Atwell, Ralph Brown, Christopher Ellison, Sheila Hancock, Martin Jarvis, Anthony Quayle; *D:* David Green; *M:* Anne Dudley. Nominations: Academy Awards '88: Best Song ("Two Hearts"). *HBO*

Buster and Billie 🎬½ **1974 (R)** Tragedy ensues when a popular high school student falls in love with the class tramp in rural Georgia in 1948. Serious, decently appointed period teen drama. **100m/C VHS, Beta.** Jan-Michael Vincent, Joan Goodfellow, Clifton James, Pamela Sue Martin, Robert Englund; *D:* Daniel Petrie. *COL*

Buster Keaton Rides Again/The Railrodder **1965** "The Railrodder" is a silent comedy short that returns Buster Keaton to the type of slapstick he made famous in his legendary 1920's films. "Buster Keaton Rides Again" (in black-and-white) is a documentary-style look at Keaton filmed during the making of "The Railrodder." Besides scenes of Keaton at work, there is also a capsule rundown of his career. **81m/C VHS, Beta, LV.** Buster Keaton. *GPV*

Bustin' Loose 🎬🎬🎬 **1981 (R)** A fast-talking ex-con reluctantly drives a bus load of misplaced kids and their keeper cross-country. **94m/C VHS, Beta, LV.** Richard Pryor, Cicely Tyson, Robert Christian, George Coe, Bill Quinn; *D:* Oz Scott; *W:* Richard Pryor, Lonne Elder III. *USH*

Busting 🎬🎬½ 1974 (R) Gould and Blake play a pair of slightly off-the-wall L.A. cops. The pair are forced "to bust" local addicts and prostitutes instead of the real crime bosses because much of the police department is on the take. Plenty of comedy and action as well as highly realistic drama. 92m/C VHS. Elliott Gould, Robert (Bobby) Blake, Allen (Goorwitz) Garfield, Antonio Fargas, Michael Lerner, Sid Haig, Cornelia Sharpe; **D:** Peter Hyams; **W:** Peter Hyams; **M:** Billy Goldenberg. MGM, USH

But Not for Me 🎬🎬½ 1959 Gable stars as a middle-aged entertainment executive who thinks he can forestall maturity by carrying on with his youthful secretary. 105m/B VHS, Closed Caption. Clark Gable, Carroll Baker, Lilli Palmer, Lee J. Cobb, Barry Coe, Thomas Gomez, Charles Lane; **D:** Walter Lang; **W:** John Michael Hayes; **C:** Robert Burks. PAR

But Where Is Daniel Wax? 🎬🎬 1974 At a class reunion, a doctor and a popular singing star reminisce about their youth and Daniel Wax, their one-time hero. Hebrew with English subtitles. 95m/C VHS, Beta. Lior Yaeni, Michael Lipkin, Esther Zevko; **D:** Avram Heffner. ERG

Butch and Sundance: The Early Days 🎬🎬½ 1979 (PG) Traces the origins of the famous outlaw duo. It contains the requisite shoot-outs, hold-ups, and escapes. A "prequel" to "Butch Cassidy and the Sundance Kid." 111m/C VHS, Beta. Tom Berenger, William Katt, John Schuck, Jeff Corey, Jill Eikenberry, Brian Dennehy, Peter Weller; **D:** Richard Lester; **W:** Allan Burns. Nominations: Academy Awards '79: Best Costume Design. FOX

Butch Cassidy and the Sundance Kid 🎬🎬🎬🎬 1969 (PG) Two legendary outlaws at the turn of the century take it on the lam with a beautiful, willing ex-school teacher. With a clever script, humanly fallible characters, and warm, witty dialogue, this film was destined to become a box-office classic. Featured the hit song, "Raindrops Keep Falling on My Head" and renewed the buddy film industry, as Newman and Redford trade insult for insult. Look for the great scene where Newman takes on giant Ted Cassidy in a fist fight. 🎵Raindrops Keep Fallin' on My Head; On a Bicycle Built for Joy. 110m/C VHS, Beta, LV. Paul Newman, Robert Redford, Katharine Ross, Jeff Corey, Strother Martin, Cloris Leachman, Kenneth Mars, Ted Cassidy, Henry Jones, George Furth, Sam Elliott; **D:** George Roy Hill; **W:** William Goldman; **C:** Conrad Hall; **M:** Burt Bacharach. Academy Awards '69: Best Cinematography, Best Song ("Raindrops Keep Fallin' on My Head"), Best Story & Screenplay, Best Original Score; British Academy Awards '70: Best Actor (Redford), Best Actress (Ross), Best Director (Hill), Best Film, Best Screenplay; Golden Globe Awards '70: Best Score; Writers Guild of America '69: Best Adapted Screenplay; Nominations: Academy Awards '69: Best Director (Hill), Best Picture, Best Sound. FXV, OM

The Butcher's Wife 🎬🎬 1991 (PG-13) Charming tale of a young psychic (Moore) who brings romance to a Greenwich Village neighborhood that never quite gets off the ground. Moore stars as the clairvoyant whose mystical powers bring magic into the lives of everyone around her, including the local psychiatrist (Daniels), who falls under her spell. Talented cast is virtually wasted with a script that is lightweight; excepting Steenburgen and Dzundza who shine. 107m/C VHS, Beta, LV, Closed Caption. Demi Moore, Jeff Daniels, George Dzundza, Frances McDormand, Margaret Colin, Mary Steenburgen, Max Perlich, Miriam Margolyes, Christopher Durang, Diane Salinger; **D:** Terry Hughes; **W:** Ezra Litwack, Marjorie Schwartz; **M:** Michael Gore. PAR

Butler's Dilemma 🎬🎬 1943 A jewel thief and a playboy both claim the identity of a butler who never existed, with humorous results. 75m/B VHS, Beta. GB Richard Hearne, Francis L. Sullivan, Hermione Gingold, Ian Fleming. VYY

Butterfield 8 🎬🎬🎬 1960 A seedy film of the John O'Hara novel about a prostitute that wants to go straight and settle down. Taylor won an Oscar, perhaps because she was ill and had lost in the two previous years in more deserving roles. 108m/C VHS, Beta, LV. Elizabeth Taylor, Laurence

Harvey, Eddie Fisher, Dina Merrill, Mildred Dunnock, Betty Field, Susan Oliver, Kay Medford; **D:** Daniel Mann; **W:** John Michael Hayes, Charles Schnee; **C:** Joseph Ruttenberg. Academy Awards '60: Best Actress (Taylor); Nominations: Academy Awards '60: Best Color Cinematography. MGM, BTV

Butterflies 1975 Ria, a middle-aged housewife with two lazy sons, is beginning to feel her age, and like a butterfly, feeling like she has too much to do and not enough time. Then Leonard appears in her life—divorced, lonely and romantic. Made for British television. 60m/C VHS. GB VCO

Butterflies Are Free 🎬🎬🎬 1972 (PG) Fast-paced humor surrounds the Broadway play brought to the big screen. Blind youth Albert is determined to be self-sufficient. A next-door-neighbor actress helps him gain independence from his over-protective mother (Heckart). 109m/C VHS, Beta. Goldie Hawn, Edward Albert, Eileen Heckart, Michael Glaser; **D:** Milton Katselas; **C:** Charles B(ryant) Lang; **M:** Robert Alcivar. Academy Awards '72: Best Supporting Actress (Heckart); Nominations: Academy Awards '72: Best Cinematography, Best Sound. GKK

Butterfly 🎬½ 1982 (R) Based on James M. Cain's novel about an amoral young woman (Pia, who'd you think?) who uses her beauty and sensual appetite to manipulate the men in her life, including her father. Set in Nevada of the 1930s, father and daughter are drawn into a daring and forbidden love affair by their lust and desperation. 105m/C VHS, Beta, LV. Pia Zadora, Stacy Keach, Orson Welles, Edward Albert, James Franciscus, Lois Nettleton, Stuart Whitman, June Lockhart, Ed McMahon; **D:** Matt Cimber; **W:** Matt Cimber; **M:** Ennio Morricone. Golden Raspberry Awards '82: Worst Actress (Zadora), Worst Supporting Actor (McMahon), Worst New Star (Zadora). VES, LIV

Butterfly Affair 🎬½ 1971 (PG) Beautiful singer, involved in a scheme to smuggle two million dollars worth of gems, plots to double-cross her partners in crime. 75m/C VHS, Beta. Claudia Cardinale, Henri Charriere, Stanley Baker; **D:** Jean Herman. NO

Butterfly Ball 🎬 1976 Retelling of the 19th century classic combines the rock music of Roger Glover, live action and animation by Halas and Batchelor. Only for the brain-cell depressed. 85m/C VHS, Beta. GB Twiggy, Ian Gillian, David Coverdale; **D:** Tony Klinger.

Butterfly Kiss 🎬🎬 1994 Strange psychodrama/road tale finds drifter Eunice (Plummer) wandering the motorways of northern England. At one service station she meets Miriam (Reeves)—the two, immediately drawn together, make love at Miriam's that night. When Eunice hitches a ride with a trucker next morning, Miriam decides to follow and discovers Eunice with the truck and the driver's dead body. It's soon not the only dead body Miriam encounters as she discovers Eunice is a serial killer—not that this seems to worry Miriam a great deal as she herself gets into the spirit of their crimes. Grim all the way 'round. 85m/C VHS. GB Amanda Plummer, Saskia Reeves, Paul Brown, Des McAleer, Ricky Tomlinson; **D:** Michael Winterbottom; **W:** Frank Cottrell Boyce; **M:** Seamus McGarvey; **M:** John Harle. TRI

Butterfly Wings 🎬🎬 Alas de Mariposa 1991 The tragedy of a dysfunctional family. Pregnant Carmen longs for a boy to carry on her husband's name but she's afraid to tell her shy six-year-old daughter Ami about the baby. Maybe with reason, since the child's brith triggers a series of nightmarish events. Spanish with subtitles. 105m/C VHS. SP D: Juanma Bajo Ulloa. FCT

Buy & Cell 🎬½ 1989 (R) A stockbroker attempts to set up a business while serving a prison sentence. An assortment of amusing inmates doesn't help matters much. Fans of Malcolm McDowell will enjoy his performance as the shady warden. 95m/C VHS, LV. Robert Carradine, Michael Winslow, Malcolm McDowell, Ben Vereen, Lise Cutter, Randall "Tex" Cobb, Roddy Piper; **D:** Robert Boris. NWV

Buying Time 🎬 1989 (R) Two teenagers are arrested when they try to pry their money away from a dishonest bookie, and the police use their connections to solve a drug-related murder. 97m/C VHS, Beta. Dean Stockwell, Jeff Schultz, Michael Rudder, Tony De Santis, Leslie Toth, Laura Cruickshank; **D:** Mitchell Gabourie. FOX

Buzzy Rides the Range 🎬🎬 1940 Average "B" western with a kid saving the day. 60m/C VHS. Robert "Buzzy" Henry, Dave O'Brien. LOO

By Dawn's Early Light 🎬🎬 1989 Made-for-cable-TV thriller about two Air Force pilots who must decide whether or not to drop the bombs that would begin WWIII. 100m/C VHS, Beta, LV. Powers Boothe, Rebecca DeMornay, James Earl Jones, Martin Landau, Rip Torn, Darren McGavin; **D:** Jack Sholder; **M:** Trevor Jones. HBO

By Design 🎬 1982 (R) Two cohabiting women want to have a baby, so they embark on a search for the perfect stud. Not one of Astin's better performances. 90m/C VHS, Beta. CA Patty Duke, Sara Botsford; **D:** Claude Jutra. NO

By Love Possessed 🎬🎬½ 1961 Can a seemingly typical, quiet, New England town stay quiet when Lana Turner is your neighbor? Vintage romantic melodrama about an attorney who is drawn into an affair when he realizes his home life is not all it could be. 115m/C VHS. Lana Turner, Efrem Zimbalist Jr., Jason Robards Jr., George Hamilton, Thomas Mitchell; **D:** John Sturges; **C:** Russell Metty; **M:** Elmer Bernstein. MGM

By the Blood of Others 🎬🎬🎬 1973 In a small French town, a psycho holds two women hostage in a farmhouse, and the townspeople try to figure out a solution without getting anyone killed. In French with English subtitles. 90m/C VHS, Beta. FR Mariangela Melato; **D:** Marc Simenon. FCT

By the Light of the Silvery Moon 🎬🎬½ 1953 The equally old-fashioned sequel to "On Moonlight Bay" finds Day engaged to MacRae, who's just returned from Army service in WWI. He wants to postpone their marriage until he gets financially secure and the waiting causes some jealous misunderstandings (naturally resolved by movie's end). Based on Booth Tarkington's "Penrod" stories. 🎵By the Light of the Silvery Moon; I'll Forget You; Your Eyes Have Told Me So; Be My Little Baby Bumble Bee; If You Were the Only Girl in the World; Ain't We Got Fun; King Chanticleer. 101m/C VHS, LV. Doris Day, Gordon MacRae, Leon Ames, Billy Gray, Rosemary DeCamp, Mary Wickes, Russell Arms, Maria Palmer; **D:** David Butler; **W:** Robert O'Brien, Irving Elinson; **M:** Max Steiner. WAR, MVD

By the Sword 🎬½ 1993 (R) Maximilian Suba (Abraham) is a one-time fencing whiz who has spent the last 25 years in prison for the murder of his mentor during a fencing match. Upon his release, Suba heads back to his old fencing grounds to see what's become of the murdered man's now-grown son and discovers Alexander (Roberts) is as ruthless and ambitious as Suba once was. Incoherent plot leaves both actors and viewers in the dark. **CW:** Vulgar language and some violence. 91m/C VHS, Closed Caption. F. Murray Abraham, Eric Roberts, Mia Sara, Christopher Rydell; **D:** Jeremy Paul Kagan; **W:** John McDonald, James Donadio; **C:** Arthur Albert; **M:** Bill Conti. COL

By Way of the Stars 🎬🎬½ 1992 (PG) Young man is pursued by a killer while he searches for his father on the 19th-century Canadian frontier. Made for TV. 150m/C VHS. CA Zachary Bennett, Tantoo Cardinal, Gema Zamprogna, Jan Rubes, Michal Mahonen; **D:** Allan King. HMK

Bye-Bye 🎬🎬 1996 Ismael (Bouajila), 25, and his 14-year-old brother Mouloud (Embarek) are French-born Arabs whose parents had abruptly returned to their Tunisian homeland after a family tragedy. The brothers have travelled from Paris to stay with their uncle (Ahourari) and his family in the port city of Marseilles. Their cousin Rhida (Mammeri), a petty criminal involved with drugs, takes the innocent Mauloud under his wing and hides him away so the boy won't be sent back to his parents. Ismael desperately roams the city trying to find his brother while he also struggles to make a fresh start amidst much societal hostility. French and Arabic with subtitles. 105m/C VHS. **FR** Sami Bouajila, Ouassini Embarek, Benhaissa Ahourari, Sofiane Mammeri, Jamila Darwich-Farah, Nozha Khouadra; **D:** Karim Dridi; **W:** Karim Dridi; **C:** John Mathieson; **M:** Jimmy Oihid, Steve Shehan. FXL

Bye Bye Baby 🐾 1988 (R) Two luscious young women cavort amid lusty Italian men on various Mediterranean beaches. 80m/C VHS, Beta, LV. **IT** Carol Alt, Brigitte Nielsen, Jason Connery, Luca Barbareschi; **D:** Enrico Oldoini; **M:** Manuel De Sica. PSM, PAR

Bye, Bye, Birdie 🐾🐾🐾 1963 Energized and sweet film version of the Broadway musical about a teen rock and roll idol (Pearson doing Elvis) coming to a small town to see one of his fans before he leaves for the army. The film that made Ann-Margret a star. ♫Bye Bye Birdie; The Telephone Hour; How Lovely to be a Woman; Honestly Sincere; One Boy; Put on a Happy Face; Kids; One Last Kiss; A Lot of Livin' to Do. 112m/C VHS, Beta, LV. Dick Van Dyke, Janet Leigh, Ann-Margret, Paul Lynde, Bobby Rydell, Maureen Stapleton, Ed Sullivan, Trudi Ames; **D:** George Sidney; **W:** Irving Brecher; **C:** Joseph Biroc. Nominations: Academy Awards '63: Best Adapted Score, Best Sound. COL

Bye Bye Blues 🐾🐾½ 1989 (PG) The lives of the Cooper family are disrupted when the husband is called to service during WWII and is then taken prisoner by the Japanese. In need of money, wife Daisy (Jenkins) joins a local swing band and begins charming all who watch her, especially the band's trombone player (Reilly). A sweet-spirited tale of love, loyalty, and the search for inner strength. Jenkins gives a strong performance as the shy wife who becomes an independent woman during her husband's absence. 110m/C VHS. **CA** Rebecca Jenkins, Michael Ontkean, Luke Reilly, Stuart Margolin, Robyn Stevan, Kate Reid, Wayne Robson; **D:** Anne Wheeler; **W:** Anne Wheeler; **M:** George Blondheim. Genie Awards '90: Best Actress (Jenkins), Best Supporting Actress (Stevan). MNC

Bye Bye Brazil 🐾🐾½ 1979 A changing Brazil is seen through the eyes of four wandering gypsy minstrels participating in a tent show traveling throughout the country. Lots of Brazilian charm. In Portuguese with English subtitles. 110m/C VHS, Beta, LV. **BR** Jose Wilker, Betty Faria, Fabio Junior, Zaira Zambello; **D:** Carlos Diegues; **W:** Carlos Diegues. FXL, TPV

Bye Bye, Love 🐾🐾½ 1994 (PG-13) Forty-eight hours in the lives of three divorced buddies starts at the local Mickey D's for the biweekly exchange of their kids. The dads don't offer any surprises: Donny (Reiser) still loves his ex, Vic (Quaid) hates his, and Dave (Modine) loves anything in a skirt. Sometimes witty, but just as often sadly poignant, the plot is as shallow as a TV sitcom, with an easy answer for every difficult question about divorce. The three leads are likeable enough, but Garofalo is the gem in an otherwise dull flick. She looks like she's having a blast, stealing scenes with abandon as Vic's blind date from hell. **CW:** Brief language; sensuality. 107m/C VHS, LV, Closed Caption. Matthew Modine, Randy Quaid, Paul Reiser, Rob Reiner, Janeane Garofalo, Ed Flanders, Lindsay Crouse, James Whitworth, Maria Pitillo; **D:** Sam Weisman; **W:** Gary David Goldberg, Brad Hall; **M:** J.A.C. Redford. FXV

The C-Man 🐾🐾 1949 Customs agent Jagger finds work isn't so dull after all. Murder and theft on an international scale make for a busy week as he follows jewel smugglers from Paris to New York. Docu-style though routine crime story. 75m/B VHS. Dean Jagger, John Carradine, Harry Landers, Rene Paul; **D:** Joseph Lerner. SNC

Cabaret 🐾🐾🐾½ 1972 (PG) Hitler is rising to power, racism and anti-Semitism are growing, and the best place to hide from it all is the cabaret. With dancing girls, androgynous master of ceremonies Grey and American expatriate and singer Minnelli, you can laugh and drink and pretend tomorrow will never come. Minnelli does just that. Face to face with the increasing horrors of Nazism, she persists in the belief that the "show must go on." Based on the John Kander's hit Broadway musical (taken from the Christopher Isherwood stories), the film is impressive, with excellent direction and cinematography. ♫Cabaret; Wilkommen; Mein Herr; Maybe This Time; Two Ladies; Money, Money; Hieraten; Tomorrow Belongs to Me; If You Could See Her. 119m/C VHS, Beta, LV, Closed Caption. Liza Minnelli, Joel Grey, Michael York, Marisa Berenson; **D:** Bob Fosse; **W:** Jay Presson Allen; **C:** Geoffrey Unsworth; **M:** Ralph Burns. Academy Awards '72: Best Actress (Minnelli), Best Art Direction/Set Decoration, Best Cinematography, Best Director (Fosse), Best Film Editing, Best Sound, Best Supporting Actor (Grey), Original Song Score and/or Adaptation; British Academy Awards '72: Best Actress (Minnelli), Best Director (Fosse), Best Film; Golden Globe Awards '73: Best Actress—Musical/Comedy (Minnelli), Best Film—Musical/Comedy, Best Supporting Actor (Grey); National Board of Review Awards '72: 10 Best Films of the Year, Best Director (Fosse), Best Supporting Actor (Grey); National Society of Film Critics Awards '72: Best Supporting Actor (Grey); Writers Guild of America '72: Best Adapted Screenplay; Nominations: Academy Awards '72: Best Adapted Screenplay, Best Picture. FOX, BTV, CCB

Cabeza de Vaca 🐾🐾🐾 1990 (R) In 1528, a Spanish expedition shipwrecks in unknown territory off the Florida coast. Only survivor Cabeza de Vaca is captured by the Iguase Indian tribe and made a slave to their shaman. He's later freed, but leaves with respect for their culture. Spanish soldiers find him and want his help in capturing the natives, but he is outraged by their cruelty and must confront his own people. Strong visual style easily brings the audience deeply into this uncharted world. Based on Cabeza de Vaca's book "Naufragios." Director Echevarria's feature film debut. Spanish and Indian with subtitles.**CW:** Nudity and violence. 111m/C VHS. **MX SP** Juan Diego, Daniel Gimenez Cacho, Roberto Sosa, Carlos Castanon, Gerardo Villarreal, Roberto Cobo, Jose Flores, Ramon Barragan; **D:** Nicolas Echevarria; **W:** Guillermo Sheridan, Nicolas Echevarria; **M:** Mario Lavista. NHO, FCT

Cabin Boy woof! 1994 (PG-13) Obnoxious "fancy lad" Elliott mistakenly boards the wrong boat and becomes the new cabin boy for a ridiculous bunch of mean, smelly sailors. Fish out of water saga is so bad it's — bad, a blundering attempt at parody that's just plain stupid. Surprisingly produced by Tim Burton, this effort will disappoint even diehard fans. Look for Chris' real life dad Bob as the lad's dad; good friend Letterman appears briefly as nasty "Old Salt," but uses the alias Earl Hofert in the final credits. As usual, the acerbic Letterman gets the best line, "Man, oh, man do I hate them fancy lads." We know how you feel Dave.**CW:** Strong language and sexual humor. 80m/C VHS, LV, Closed Caption. Chris Elliott, Ann Magnuson, Ritch Brinkley, James Gammon, Brian Doyle-Murray, Russ Tamblyn, Brion James, Ricki Lake, Bob Elliott; **Cameos:** David Letterman; **D:** Adam Resnick; **W:** Adam Resnick; **M:** Steve Bartek. TOU

The Cabin in the Cotton 🐾🐾½ 1932 Davis stars as a rich, ruthless Southern belle in this dated melodrama about sharecroppers. Barthelmess is cast as a poor sharecropper who is almost brought to ruin when he falls for the sexy Southern vamp. Contains Davis's most famous line, "Ah'd love t'kiss you, but ah jes washed mah hair." 77m/B VHS, Closed Caption. Bette Davis, Richard Barthelmess, Dorothy Jordan, Henry B. Walthall, Tully Marshall; **D:** Michael Curtiz; **W:** Paul Green. MGM

Cabin in the Sky 🐾🐾🐾 1943 A poor woman fights to keep her husband's soul out of the devil's clutches. Based on a Broadway show and featuring an all-Black cast. Lively dance numbers and a musical score with contributions from Duke Ellington. Minnelli's first feature film. ♫Cabin in the Sky; Happiness Is Just a Thing Called Joe; Taking a Chance on Love; Life's Full of Consequence; Li'l Black Sheep; Shine; Honey in the Honeycomb. 99m/C VHS, Beta, LV. Ethel Waters, Eddie Anderson, Lena Horne, Rex Ingram, Louis Armstrong, Duke Ellington; **D:** Vincente Minnelli; **M:** Duke Ellington, Harold Arlen, E.Y. Harburg, George Bassman. Nominations: Academy Awards '43: Best Song ("Happiness Is a Thing Called Joe"). MGM, MLB, FHE

The Cabinet of Dr. Caligari 🐾🐾🐾🐾 1919 A pioneering film in the most extreme expressionistic style about a hypnotist in a carnival and a girl-snatching somnambulist. Highly influential in its approach to lighting, composition, design and acting. Much imitated. Silent. 92m/B VHS, Beta, LV. **GE** Conrad Veidt, Werner Krauss, Lil Dagover; **D:** Robert Wiene. KIV, REP, MRV

Cabiria 🐾🐾½ 1914 The pioneering Italian epic about a Roman and a slave girl having a love affair in Rome during the Second Punic War. Immense sets and set-pieces; an important influence on Griffith and DeMille. Silent. 123m/B VHS, Beta, 8mm. **IT D:** Giovanni Pastrone. KIV, FCT

The Cable Guy 🐾🐾½ 1996 (PG-13) Carrey's first $20 million paycheck finds cable subscriber Broderick in for a comedic nightmare when he accepts the offer of free movie channels. The overeager installer (Carrey, naturally) turns his life upside down. A little darker humor than Carrey fans may be used to, and don't expect any bodily ventriloquism. Carrey (did we mention he's in it?) gets to act with real life people. Director Stiller does a nice job of reining in his more manic impulses when necessary. Broderick holds his own as the reluctant pal. Original scripter Holtz won a Writer's Guild arbitration for sole writing credit from producer-writer Judd Apatow.**CW:** Dark thematic elements and crude humor. 95m/C VHS, LV, 8mm, Closed Caption, DVD. Jim Carrey, Matthew Broderick, Leslie Mann, George Segal, Diane Baker, Jack Black, Janeane Garofalo, Andy Dick, Charles Napier; **D:** Ben Stiller; **W:** Judd Apatow, Lou Holtz Jr.; **C:** Robert Brinkmann; **M:** John Ottman. MTV Movie Awards '97: Best Villain (Carrey), Best Comedic Performance (Carrey); Nominations: MTV Movie Awards '97: Best Fight (Jim Carrey/Matthew Broderick). COL

Cabo Blanco 🐾🐾 1981 (R) A bartender and a variety of other characters, including an ex-Nazi and a French woman searching for her lover, assemble in Peru after WWII. Nazi Robards controls police chief Rey, while American Bronson runs the local watering hole and eyes French woman Sanda. Hey, this sounds familiar. Everyone shares a common interest: finding a missing treasure of gold, lost in a ship wreck. Remaking "Casablanca" via "The Treasure of Sierra Madre" is never easy. 87m/C VHS, Beta. Charles Bronson, Jason Robards Jr., Dominique Sanda, Fernando Rey, Gilbert Roland, Simon MacCorkindale; **D:** J. Lee Thompson; **M:** Jerry Goldsmith. MED

Cactus 🐾🐾½ 1986 Melodrama about a young French woman, separated from her husband, who faces the reality of losing her sight after a car accident. She experiences a growing relationship with a blind man and contemplates the thought of risky surgery which may improve her eyesight or cause complete blindness. Countering all that blindness and tangled romance is a camera that pans lush Australian landscapes and humorously focuses on the small telling details of daily life. 95m/C VHS, Beta. **AU** Isabelle Huppert, Robert Menzies, Monica Maughan, Sheila Florence, Norman Kaye, Banduk Marika; **D:** Paul Cox; **W:** Norman Kaye, Paul Cox, Bob Ellis; **M:** Giovanni Pergolese, Yannis Markopolous, Elsa Davis. ORI

Cactus Flower 🐾🐾 1969 (PG) Good cast doesn't quite suffice to make this adaptation of a Broadway hit work. A middle-aged bachelor dentist gets involved with a kookie mistress, refusing to admit his real love for his prim and proper receptionist. Hawn's big leap to stardom. 103m/C VHS, Beta, LV. Walter Matthau, Goldie Hawn, Ingrid Bergman, Jack Weston, Rick Lenz; **D:** Gene Saks; **C:** Charles B(ryant) Lang; **M:** Quincy Jones. Academy Awards '69: Best

Supporting Actress (Hawn); Golden Globe Awards '70: Best Supporting Actress (Hawn). *COL*

Cactus in the Snow 🎬½ 1972 A virginal Army private serving during the Vietnam War era tries to find sex on a 72-hour leave and instead discovers love. Some guys have all the luck. Melodrama never grabs where it ought to. **90m/C VHS, Beta, LV.** Richard Thomas, Mary Layne, Lucille Benson; *D:* Martin Zweiback. *NO*

Caddie 🎬🎬½ 1976 Based on an autobiographical story of a woman who leaves her unfaithful husband in 1930s Australia. Struggling to raise her two children, she works as a waitress in a bar where she finds romance with one of the regulars. Average script bolstered by Morse's performance. **107m/C VHS, Beta.** *AU* Helen Morse, Jack Thompson, Takis Emmanuel, Jacki Weaver; *D:* Donald Crombie; *W:* Joan Long; *C:* Peter James; *M:* Patrick Flynn. *NO*

The Caddy 🎬🎬 1953 Lewis plays frantic caddy prone to slapstick against Martin's smooth professional golfer with a bent toward singing. Mostly a series of Martin and Lewis sketches that frequently land in the rough. Introduces several songs, including a classic Martin and Lewis rendition of "That's Amore." Look for cameos by a host of professional golfers. **95m/C VHS, Beta.** Dean Martin, Jerry Lewis, Donna Reed, Barbara Bates, Joseph Calleia, Marshall Thompson, Fred Clark; *Cameos:* Ben Hogan, Sam Snead, Byron Nelson, Julius Boros, Jimmy Thomson, Harry E. Cooper; *D:* Norman Taurog; *W:* Danny Arnold. Nominations: Academy Awards '53: Best Song ("That's Amore"). *PAR*

Caddyshack 🎬🎬🎬½ 1980 (R) Inspired performances by Murray and Dangerfield drive this sublimely moronic comedy onto the green. The action takes place at Bushwood Country Club, where caddy O'Keefe is bucking to win the club's college scholarship. Characters involved in various sophomoric set pieces include obnoxious club president Knight, a playboy who is too laid back to keep his score (Chase), a loud, vulgar, and extremely rich golfer (Dangerfield), and Murray as a filthy gopher-hunting groundskeeper. Occasional dry moments are followed by scenes of pure (and tasteless) anarchy, so watch with someone immature. Does for golf what "Major League" tried to do for baseball. **99m/C VHS, Beta, LV, DVD.** Chevy Chase, Rodney Dangerfield, Ted Knight, Michael O'Keefe, Bill Murray, Sarah Holcomb, Brian Doyle-Murray; *D:* Harold Ramis; *W:* Brian Doyle-Murray, Doug Kenney, Harold Ramis. *WAR*

Caddyshack 2 🎬½ 1988 (PG) Obligatory sequel to "Caddyshack," minus Bill Murray who wisely avoided further encroachment of gopher holes and director Ramis who opted for the screenwriting chore. Mason is the star of the show as a crude self-made millionaire who tangles with the snobs at the country club. Although it occasionally earns a side-splitting chuckle, "Shack 2" has significantly fewer guffaws than the original, proving once again that funny guys are always undone by lousy scripts and weak direction. **103m/C VHS, Beta, LV, 8mm, Closed Caption.** Jackie Mason, Chevy Chase, Dan Aykroyd, Dyan Cannon, Robert Stack, Dina Merrill, Randy Quaid, Jessica Lundy, Jonathan Silverman, Chynna Phillips; *D:* Allan Arkush; *W:* Harold Ramis, Peter Torokvei; *C:* Harry Stradling Jr.; *M:* Ira Newborn. Golden Raspberry Awards '88: Worst Supporting Actor (Aykroyd), Worst Song ("Jack Fresh"). *WAR*

Cadence 🎬🎬 1989 (PG-13) The directorial debut of actor Martin Sheen, this fitful melodrama stars son Charlie as an unruly trooper on a 1960s army base. Placed in an all-black stockade for punishment, he bonds with his brother prisoners by defying the hardcase sergeant (played by Sheen the elder). Characters and situations are intriguing but not rendered effectively. Based on the novel "Count a Lonely Cadence" by Gordon Weaver. **97m/C VHS, LV, Closed Caption.** Charlie Sheen, Martin Sheen, Laurence "Larry" Fishburne, Michael Beach, Ramon Estevez; *D:* Martin Sheen; *M:* Georges Delerue. *REP*

Cadillac Girls 🎬½ 1993 Page is a self-destructive teenager who is arrested for car theft. To avoid jail, Page is placed in her single mom's custody and moves to her family's straitlaced hometown in Nova Scotia. Mom isn't exactly good at parenting and Page's adolescent anger extends to putting the moves on mom's potential new beau. **99m/C VHS.** Jennifer Dale, Gregory Harrison, Mia Kirshner. Genie Awards '93: Best Score. *MNC*

Cadillac Man 🎬🎬 1990 (R) Williams is the quintessential low-life car salesman in this rather disjointed comedy. A lesser comedic talent might have stalled and been abandoned, but Williams manages to drive away despite the flat script and direction. One storyline follows his attempt to sell 12 cars in 12 days or lose his job, while another follows his confrontation with a gun-toting, mad-as-hell cuckolded husband. Williams and Robbins are often close to being funny in a hyperkinetic way, but the situations are dumb enough to rob most of the scenes of their comedy. Watch for a movie-stealing bit by the spunky waitress at the local Chinese restaurant. **95m/C VHS, Beta, LV, Closed Caption.** Robin Williams, Tim Robbins, Pamela Reed, Fran Drescher, Zack Norman, Annabella Sciorra, Lori Petty, Paul Guilfoyle; *D:* Roger Donaldson; *W:* Ken Friedman. *ORI*

Cadillac Ranch 🎬🎬½ 1996 (R) CJ (Amis), Frances (Feeney), and Mary Katharine (Humphrey) Crowley are three squabbling Texas sisters who have reunited to celebrate Mary K.'s upcoming marriage. CJ works in a strip club owned by greedy ex-Texas Ranger Wood (Lloyd), who sent their long-gone daddy, Travis (Metzler), to prison for a heist Wood was involved in. When CJ gets fired, the threesome steal a key from Wood that will supposedly access money from the heist and the vengeful Wood goes after them. *CW:* Language and some nudity. **104m/C VHS.** Suzy Amis, Renee Humphrey, Caroleen Feeney, Christopher Lloyd, Jim Metzler, Linden Ashby; *D:* Lisa Gottlieb; *W:* Jennifer Cecil; *C:* Bruce Douglas Johnson; *M:* Christopher Tyng. *BMG*

Caesar and Cleopatra 🎬🎬½ 1946 Based on the classic George Bernard Shaw play. Caesar meets the beautiful Cleopatra in ancient Egypt and helps her gain control of her life. Remains surprisingly true to Shaw's adaptation, unlike many other historical films of the same era. **135m/C VHS.** *GB* Claude Rains, Vivien Leigh, Stewart Granger, Flora Robson, Francis L. Sullivan, Cecil Parker; *D:* Gabriel Pascal; *W:* Robert Krasker. Nominations: Academy Awards '46: Best Interior Decoration. *NO*

Cafe au Lait 🎬🎬🎬 *Metisse* 1994 Actor/director/writer Kassovitz scores in his debut feature about an interracial menage a trois. Beautiful mulatto Lola (Mauduech) is pregnant but she's not sure by which of her two contrasting lovers (who don't yet know about each other). It could be white, Jewish, easy-going bicycle messenger Felix (Kassovitz) or stuffy, wealthy, black Moslem student Jamal (Kounde). Both men desire the fatherhood role and both move in with Lola to share responsibility. This is not without complications. Generally light and frothy without ignoring racial tensions. French with subtitles. **94m/C VHS.** *FR* Mathieu Kassovitz, Julie Mauduech, Hubert Kounde, Vincent Cassel, Tadek Lokcinski, Jany Holt; *D:* Mathieu Kassovitz; *W:* Mathieu Kassovitz; *C:* Pierre Aim; *M:* Marie Daulne, Jean-Louis Daulne. *NYF*

Cafe Express 🎬🎬½ 1983 A con artist (he sells coffee illegally aboard an Italian train) stays one step ahead of the law as he raises money to help his ailing son. As in "Bread and Chocolate," Manfredi is again the put-upon working class hero comedically attempting to find a better way of life in this bittersweet tale. **90m/C VHS, Beta.** *IT* Nino Manfredi, Gigi Reder, Adolfo Celi, Vittorio Mezzogiorno; *D:* Nanni Loy. *NO*

Cafe Romeo 🎬🎬 1991 (R) Tale of twenty-something friendships forged in the neighborhood coffeehouse of a heavily Italian community. Lia (Stewart) is a waitress who dreams of becoming a fashion designer, but her marriage to a small time hood holds her back. Crombie, her cousin by marriage, is a dental student confused about his future, but very much in love with Lia. Quiet movie boasts average script that's helped along by strong performances. Originally broadcast on Canadian TV. *CW:* Language. **93m/C VHS, LV, Closed Caption.** *CA* Catherine Mary Stewart, Jonathan Crombie; *D:* Rex Bromfield. *REP*

The Cage 🎬 1989 (R) Gangsters enlist a brain-damaged Vietnam vet played by Ferrigno to participate in illegal "cage fights," enclosed wrestling matches fought to the death. Crude and annoying. **101m/C VHS, Beta, LV, Closed Caption.** Lou Ferrigno, Reb Brown, Michael Dante, Mike Moroff, Marilyn Tokuda, James Shigeta, Al Ruscio; *D:* Hugh Kelley. *ORI*

The Cage 🎬🎬🎬 1990 Sent to prison for murdering his girlfriend, Jive has no idea what the pen has in store for him. The inmates stage a mock trial, the defendant is found guilty and the sentence is too horrible to imagine. From a stage play by the San Quentin Drama Workshop and co-starring Hayes, author of "Midnight Express." **90m/C VHS, Beta.** Rick Cluchey, William Hayes; *D:* Rick Cluchey; *W:* Rick Cluchey. *NO*

Cage 2: The Arena of Death 🎬½ 1994 (R) Billy Thomas (Ferrigno) is kidnapped by a vicious mobster and forced to battle martial arts experts in a steel cage battle to the death. But his best friend (Brown) plans to infiltrate the show and put a stop to the carnage. *CW:* Violence; brief nudity; language. **94m/C VHS.** Lou Ferrigno, Reb Brown; *D:* Lang Elliott. *PAR*

Caged Fear 🎬½ 1992 (R) Young Krissie (Cloke) is mistakenly put behind bars in a brutal, high-security prison for a shootout caused by her outlaw husband Tommy (Keith) during their honeymoon. Tommy comes up with an outrageous scheme to rescue her. Not quite as bad as it sounds, but close. *CW:* Language, violence, and sexuality. **94m/C VHS, LV.** David Keith, Deborah May, Ray Sharkey, Loretta Devine, Karen Black, Kristen Cloke; *D:* Bobby Houston; *W:* Bobby Houston. *NLC*

Caged Fury 🎬 1980 (R) American women being held captive in Southeast Asia are brainwashed into becoming walking time bombs. Yes, that dame's gonna blow. Made in the Philippines with the best of intentions. **90m/C VHS, Beta.** *PH* Bernadette Williams, Taaffe O'Connell, Jennifer Laine; *D:* Cirio H. Santiago. *NO*

Caged Fury 🎬 1990 Two Los Angeles women allegedly commit sexual crimes and are sent to prison. Cheap, exploitive women's prison rehash. **85m/C VHS, Beta.** Erik Estrada, Richie Barathy, Roxanna Michaels, Paul Smith, James Hong, Greg Cummins; *D:* Bill Milling. *COL*

Caged Hearts 🎬 1995 (R) Chicks-behind-bars flick finds Kate (Genzel) and Sharon (McClure) framed for murder by a shady organization called "The Shield." Cliches abound. *CW:* Nudity; sexuality; violence; language. **87m/C VHS.** Tane McClure, Carrie Genzel, Taylor Leigh, Nick Wilder; *D:* Henri Charr. *PMH*

Caged Heat 🎬🎬 *Renegade Girls; Caged Females* 1974 Low-budget babes-behind-bars film touted as the best sexploitation film of the day. Demme's directorial debut is a genre-altering installment in Roger Corman's formulaic cellblock Cinderella cycle. Recycled plot—innocent woman is put behind bars, where she loses some of her innocence—boasts an updated treatment. These babes may wear hot pants and gratuitously bare their midriffs, but they're not brainless bimbos. They're strong individuals who work together to liberate themselves. Reached cult status. Cult diva Steele returned to the big screen after six years to play the wheelchair-ridden prison warden, written specifically for her. **83m/C VHS, LV.** Juanita Brown, Erica Gavin, Roberta Collins, Barbara Steele, Ella Reid, Cheryl "Rainbeaux" Smith; *D:* Jonathan Demme; *W:* Jonathan Demme. *NWV*

Caged Heat 2: Stripped of Freedom 🎬½ 1994 (R) Women-in-prison formula with a princess thrown into the pen following a political coup. CIA agent is sent undercover as an inmate to bust her out. Usual sadistic guards, rape, and revenge scenes. From Roger Corman's direct-to-video factory. *CW:* Language, nudity, violence, and sexual situations. 84m/C VHS, LV. Jewel Shepard, Chanel Akiko Hirai, Pamella D'Pella, Vic Diaz; *D:* Cirio H. Santiago. NHO

Caged Heat 3000 🎬 1995 (R) Yes, it's a sci-fi chicks-in-prison movie! Innocent Kira Murphy (Leigh) is wrongly condemned to an underground prison located 45 lightyears from Earth where there are lots of racial tensions and evil prison officials. Prerequisite shower scenes and sadistic guards also add to the standard exploitation. 84m/C VHS. Cassandra Leigh, Kena Land, Debra Beatty; *D:* Cirio H. Santiago; *W:* Paul Ziller. NHO

Caged in Paradiso 🎬½ 1989 (R) A convicted criminal and his wife are dumped onto a remote prisoner's isle to live out their lives. When Cara loses contact with her husband, she must fend for herself. Survival tale boringly told. 90m/C VHS, Beta, LV. Michael Snyder. THV, IME

Caged Terror woof! 1972 Two urbanites hit the countryside for a weekend and meet a band of crazy rapists who ravage the wife and set the husband raging with bloodthirsty revenge. Squalid stroll through the ruins. 76m/C VHS, Beta. Percy Harkness, Elizabeth Suzuki, Leon Morenzie. NWV

Caged Women 🎬 *Women's Penitentiary 4* 1984 (R) Undercover journalist enters a women's prison and gets the usual eyeful. 97m/C VHS, Beta. FR IT Laura Gemser, Gabriele Tinti, Lorraine De Selle, Maria Romano; *D:* Vincent Dawn. VES, LIV, DMP

Cahill: United States Marshal 🎬🎬 1973 (PG) The aging Duke in one of his lesser moments, portraying a marshal who comes to the aid of his sons. The boys are mixed up with a gang of outlaws, proving that no matter how good a parent you are, sometimes the kids just lean toward the wayward. Turns out, though, that the boys harbor a grudge against the old man due to years of workaholic neglect. Will Duke see the error of his ways and reconcile with the delinquent boys? Will he catch the outlaw leader? Will he go on to star in other Duke vehicles? 103m/C VHS, Beta, LV. John Wayne, Gary Grimes, George Kennedy, Neville Brand, Marie Windsor, Harry Carey Jr.; *D:* Andrew V. McLaglen; *M:* Elmer Bernstein. WAR, TLF

The Caine Mutiny 🎬🎬🎬🎬 1954 A group of naval officers revolt against a captain they consider mentally unfit. Bogart is masterful as Captain Queeg, obsessed with cleanliness while onboard and later a study in mental meltdown during the court-martial of a crew member who participated in the mutiny. Based on the Pulitzer-winning novel by Herman Wouk, the drama takes a close look at the pressure-filled life aboard ship during WWII. 125m/C VHS, Beta, LV, 8mm, Closed Caption. Humphrey Bogart, Jose Ferrer, Van Johnson, Fred MacMurray, Lee Marvin, Claude Akins, E.G. Marshall, Robert Francis, May Wynn, Tom Tully; *D:* Edward Dmytryk; *W:* Stanley Roberts; *M:* Max Steiner. Nominations: Academy Awards '54: Best Actor (Bogart), Best Film Editing, Best Picture, Best Screenplay, Best Sound, Best Supporting Actor (Tully), Original Dramatic/Comedy Score. COL, HMV

The Caine Mutiny Court Martial 🎬🎬🎬 1988 (PG) A young lieutenant is up for a court-martial after taking control of the U.S.S. Caine in the midst of a typhoon. In order to save him, his lawyer must discredit the paranoid Commander Queeg. As the events of the mutiny unfold, it becomes clear that Queeg's obsession with discipline had become a threat to everyone aboard. Good performances, particularly by Bogosian as the lawyer. Based on the Pulitzer Prize-winning novel by Herman Wouk. Made for television. 100m/C VHS, LV, Closed Caption. Jeff Daniels, Eric Bogosian, Brad Davis, Peter Gallagher, Michael Murphy,

Kevin J. O'Connor, Daniel H. Jenkins; *D:* Robert Altman. THV

Cain's Cutthroats 🎬 *Cain's Way; The Blood Seekers* 1971 (R) A former Confederate army captain and a bounty hunting preacher team up to settle the score with soldiers on a gang-raping, murdering spree. 87m/C VHS, Beta. Scott Brady, John Carradine, Robert Dix. GHV

Cairo 🎬🎬 1942 War correspondent Young lands in Cairo where he is supposed to pass along classified information to a Nazi spy posing as a Brit. He meets and falls in love with American movie queen thought to be enemy agent (MacDonald) and a race across the desert follows when Young is trapped in a pyramid. Catchy tunes can't save this cheesy WWII spy spoof that marked the end of MacDonald's MGM contract. 101m/B VHS. Jeanette MacDonald, Robert Young, Ethel Waters, Reginald Owen, Grant Mitchell, Lionel Atwill, Eduardo Ciannelli, Mitchell Lewis; *D:* Woodbridge S. Van Dyke; *W:* John McClain; *M:* Herbert Stothart. MGM

Cal 🎬🎬🎬 1984 (R) Cal (Lynch), a young Catholic man, is reluctantly recruited into the Irish Republican Army. He falls in love with the older Marcella (Mirren), the widow of a Protestant policeman whom he helped kill while acting as the getaway driver for his fellow Republicans. Thoughtful and tragic, with excellent performances; set in Northern Ireland. 104m/C VHS, Beta. IR Helen Mirren, John Lynch, Donal McCann, Kitty Gibson, Ray McAnally, John Kavanagh; *D:* Pat O'Connor; *W:* Bernard MacLaverty; *M:* Mark Knopfler. Cannes Film Festival '84: Best Actress (Mirren). WAR, FCT

Calamity Jane 🎬🎬🎬 1953 In one of her best Warner musicals, Day stars as the rip-snortin', gun-totin' Calamity Jane of Western lore, in an on-again, off-again romance with Wild Bill Hickok. ♫Secret Love; Just Blew in From the Windy City; The Black Hills of Dakota; The Deadwood Stage (Whip-Crack-Away!). 101m/C VHS, Beta, LV. Doris Day, Howard Keel, Allyn Ann McLerie; *D:* David Butler; *M:* Sammy Fain, Paul Francis Webster. Academy Awards '53: Best Song ("Secret Love"); Nominations: Academy Awards '53: Best Sound, Scoring of a Musical. WAR, FCT

Calamity Jane 🎬🎬½ 1982 A made-for-television biography of the famous lady crack shot. Alexander is cast as the tough-as-nails woman who considered herself on a par with any man. 96m/C VHS, Beta. Jane Alexander, Frederic Forrest, Ken Kercheval, Talia Balsam, David Hemmings; *D:* James Goldstone. FOX

Calendar 🎬🎬🎬 1993 A Canadian photographer (Egoyan) is hired to take pictures of ancient Armenian churches for a calendar. His wife (Egoyan's real-life spouse Khanjian) accompanies him, serving as a translator, and they hire a driver (Adamian) who turns out to be an architectural expert. Told in flashback, the film gradually reveals a romantic triangle—with the photographer becoming so caught up in his work that he fails to realize his wife, increasingly drawn to her ethnic heritage, and their driver are having an affair. This romantic puzzle also includes the photographer, having returned to Canada wifeless and apparently seeking a replacement, having dinner with a series of women he's meet through the personals. In English and Armenian. 78m/C VHS. CA Atom Egoyan, Arsinee Khanjian, Ashot Adamian; *D:* Atom Egoyan; *W:* Atom Egoyan; *C:* Norayr Kasper. KIV

Calendar Girl 🎬🎬½ 1993 (PG-13) In 1962 three high-school best friends borrow a convertible and travel from their Nevada homes to Hollywood to meet their pinup idol, Marilyn Monroe. Roy's (Priestley) a rebel, Ned's (Olds, in his film debut) sensitive, and Scott's (O'Connell) just a nice guy. They stay with Roy's Uncle Harvey (Pantoliano), an aspiring actor, and work to meet their dream girl. Which they finally do, in a notably weak sequence which fits in with this notably uninspired film. The three actors at least have enough comradery to make realistic buddies—

one of the few true touches in the film. *CW:* Language, nudity, and drug content. 86m/C VHS, LV, 8mm, Closed Caption. Jason Priestley, Gabriel Olds, Jerry O'Connell, Joe Pantoliano, Stephen Tobolowsky, Kurt Fuller, Steve Railsback, Emily Warfield, Stephanie Anderson; *Cameos:* Chubby Checker; *D:* John Whitesell; *W:* Paul Shapiro; *M:* Hans Zimmer. COL

Calendar Girl Murders 🎬🎬½ 1984 Minor mystery about the murder of some girlie magazine pinups. Made for television. 104m/C VHS. Robert Culp, Tom Skerritt, Barbara Parkins, Sharon Stone; *D:* William A. Graham; *M:* Brad Fiedel. EDV

California Casanova woof! 1989 (R) Mirthless, semi-musical farce about a nerdy stagehand learning to be a great lover to win a beautiful singer's heart who's being blackmailed by a cruel gangster. Nice cast; nobody's home. *CW:* Sensuality. 94m/C VHS. Jerry Orbach, Audrey Landers, Tyrone Power Jr., Bryan Genesse, Ken Kercheval, Ted Davis, Joyce Blair; *D:* Nathaniel Christian; *W:* Nathaniel Christian. ACA

California Dreaming 🎬🎬 1979 (R) Nerdy young man heads west to California where he tries to fit in with the local beach crowd. Reminiscent of the popular beach movies of the '60s. 93m/C VHS, Beta. Dennis Christopher, Tanya Roberts, Glynnis O'Connor, John Calvin, Seymour Cassel; *D:* John Hancock. VES, LIV

California Girls 🎬 1984 Radio station stages a beauty contest and three sexy ladies prove to be tough competition. Features women in little swimsuits, minimal plot, and a soundtrack by the Police, Kool & the Gang, Blondie, Queen, and 10cc. 83m/C VHS, Beta. Al Music, Mary McKinley, Alicia Allen, Lantz Douglas, Barbara Parks; *D:* Rick Wallace; *C:* Gil Hubbs. NO

California Gold Rush 🎬🎬 1981 Hays portrays young aspiring writer, Bret Harte, who, in search of adventure in 1849, arrives in Sutter's Fort and takes on a job at the local sawmill. When gold is found, Sutter's Fort is soon overrun with fortune hunters whose greed, violence and corruption threaten to tear apart the peaceful community. Made for television. 100m/C VHS, Beta. Robert Hays, John Dehner, Dan Haggerty, Ken Curtis; *D:* Jack B. Hively. NO

California Joe 🎬 1943 California is being eyed by Confederate sympathizers and also by their leader, who wants it for his own plans. Enter California Joe, a Union officer in disguise, who will save the day. Standard western. 55m/B VHS, Beta. Donald (Don "Red") Barry, Lynn Merrick, Helen Talbot. DVT

California Straight Ahead 🎬🎬 1925 Denny—whose niche in the twenties was silent action comedies, and who had teamed with director Pollard earlier in the decade to produce "The Leatherpushers" series—stars in this silent actioner which features a cross-country road trip, zoo animals-on-a-rampage, and a car-racing conclusion (sounds like an action formula ahead of its time). Audiences didn't realize until the talkies that the All-American manly man was in fact played by a Brit. For those who revel in trivia, Denny appeared in the 1961 "Batman." 77m/B VHS, Beta. Reginald Denny, Gertrude Olmsted, Tom Wilson, Lucille Ward, John Steppling; *D:* Harry Pollard. GPV, FCT

California Suite 🎬🎬🎬 1978 (PG) The posh Beverly Hills Hotel is the setting for four unrelated Neil Simon skits, ranging from a battling husband and wife to feuding friends. Simonized dialogue is crisp and funny. 103m/C VHS, Beta, LV. Alan Alda, Michael Caine, Bill Cosby, Jane Fonda, Walter Matthau, Richard Pryor, Maggie Smith, Elaine May; *D:* Herbert Ross; *W:* Neil Simon; *M:* Claude Bolling. Academy Awards '78: Best Supporting Actress (Smith); Golden Globe Awards '79: Best Actress—Musical/Comedy (Smith); Nominations: Academy Awards '78: Best Adapted Screenplay, Best Art Direction/Set Decoration. COL

Caligari's Cure 🐾🐾🐾 1982 Palazzolo's first film is a satiric, non-narrative stab at his Catholic upbringing via German expressionism and modern performance art. 70m/C VHS, Beta. **D:** Tom Palazzolo. *FCT*

Caligula woof! 1980 Infamous, expensive, extremely graphic, and sexually explicit adaptation of the life of the mad Roman emperor, Caligula. Scenes of decapitation, necrophilia, rape, bestiality, and sadomasochism abound. Biggest question is why Gielgud, O'Toole, and McDowell lent their talents to this monumentally abhorred film (not to mention Gore Vidal on the writing end, who didn't want the credit). Adult magazine publisher Bob Guccione coproduced and didn't particularly want to release it. Also available in a censored, "R" rated version. 143m/C VHS, Beta, LV. *IT* Malcolm McDowell, John Gielgud, Peter O'Toole, Helen Mirren; **D:** Tinto Brass; **W:** Gore Vidal. *NO*

Call Him Mr. Shatter 🐾 *Shatter* 1974 (R) A hired killer stalks a tottering Third World president and becomes embroiled in international political intrigue. 90m/C VHS, Beta. *GB* Stuart Whitman, Peter Cushing, Anton Diffring; **D:** Michael Carreras. *NLC*

Call Me 🐾🐾 1988 (R) Psycho-drama about a lusty young woman who responds positively to an obscene telephone caller until she witnesses him murder another person. Doubt creeps into the relationship. 98m/C VHS, Beta, LV. Patricia Charbonneau, Patti D'Arbanville, Sam Freed, Boyd Gaines, Stephen McHattie; **D:** Sollace Mitchell. *VES*

Call Me Bwana 🐾½ 1963 Pure cornpone with Hope as a bumbling explorer sent with CIA agent Adams to track down a lost American space capsule in deepest Africa. Enemy agents Ekberg and Jeffries try to make things difficult. 103m/C VHS. Bob Hope, Edie Adams, Anita Ekberg, Lionel Jeffries, Percy Herbert, Paul Carpenter, Orlando Martins; **D:** Gordon Douglas; **W:** Nate Monaster, Johanna Harwood. *MGM, FCT*

Call Northside 777 🐾🐾🐾½ *Calling Northside 777* 1948 Chicago reporter Stewart finds himself in the crux of a decade-old murder investigation when he follows up a newspaper ad offering $5,000 for any information leading to the arrest and conviction of a police killer. The cunning reporter discovers police coverups and missing evidence pointing to an imprisoned man's innocence. Powerful performance from Stewart directs this docu-drama based on the real-life story of Chicago's Joe Majczek, unjustly imprisoned for 11 years, and the Pulitzer Prize winning reporter Jim McGuire who, through a clever investigation, found enough evidence to have the case reopened. 111m/B VHS, Closed Caption. James Stewart, Richard Conte, Lee J. Cobb, Helen Walker, Betty Garde, Moroni Olsen, E.G. Marshall, Howard Smith, John McIntire, Paul Harvey, George Tyne, Michael Chapin, Addison Richards, Richard Rober, Eddie Dunn, Charles Lane, Walter Greaza, William Post Jr., George Melford, Charles Miller, Lionel Stander, Jonathan Hale; **D:** Henry Hathaway; **M:** Alfred Newman. *FXV*

Call of the Canyon 🐾½ 1942 A crooked agent for a local meat packer won't pay a fair price, so Gene goes off to talk to the head man to set him straight. 71m/B VHS, Beta. Gene Autry, Smiley Burnette, Ruth Terry, Thurston Hall, Pat Brady; **D:** Joseph Santley. *CCB, VCN, GPV*

Call of the Forest 🐾½ 1949 Bobby makes friends with a beautiful wild black stallion which is captured and tamed by his father. The father has found a goldmine, also desired by a villain, and Bobby and his horse must come to his father's aid. Black Diamond (the horse) has the best role. 74m/B VHS. Robert Lowery, Ken Curtis, Martha Sherrill, Chief Thundercloud, Charles Hughes; **D:** John F. Link. *NOS, DVT, VYY*

Call of the Rockies 🐾🐾 1944 Action-packed oater in which Carson and Burnette ride across country to save Placer City's mine from crooked townsmen. 54m/B VHS, Closed Caption. Sunset Carson, Smiley Burnette. *REP*

Call of the Wild 🐾🐾 1972 (PG) Jack London's famous story about a man whose survival depends upon his knowledge of the Alaskan wilderness almost comes to life. Filmed in Finland. 105m/C VHS, Beta. Charlton Heston, Michele Mercier, George Eastman; **D:** Ken Annakin. *KUI, SIM, MPI*

Call of the Wild 🐾🐾½ 1993 Another of Jack London's survival tales is dramatized for television. John Thornton (Schroder) is a rich greenhorn seeking adventure during the 1897 Klondike gold rush. Buck is a German shepherd, sold as a sled dog, who finds adventures of his own in the frozen North until man and dog are united to search for a legendary gold mine. The book is more exciting but the film is more violent. Filmed on location in British Columbia. 97m/C VHS, Closed Caption. Rick Schroder, Gordon Tootoosis, Mia Sara, Duncan Fraser, Richard Newman, Brent Stait. *CAF*

Call Out the Marines 🐾🐾 1942 A group of army buddies re-enlist to break up a spy ring. Two of the guys fall in love with the same girl, not realizing that she's one of the spies. McLaglen and Lowe's last comedy together. Mediocre outing isn't redeemed by below average musical numbers. ♫Call Out the Marines; Zana Zaranda; The Light of My Life; Beware; Hands Across the Border. 67m/B VHS, Beta. Edmund Lowe, Victor McLaglen, Binnie Barnes, Paul Kelly, Dorothy Lovett, Franklin Pangborn; **D:** William Hamilton, Frank Ryan. *NO*

Call to Glory 🐾🐾½ 1984 Pilot for the critically praised television series. An Air Force pilot and his family face turbulent times during the Cuban missile crisis. 96m/C VHS, Beta, LV. Craig T. Nelson, Cindy Pickett, Gabriel Damon, Keenan Wynn, Elisabeth Shue, G.D. Spradlin. *PAR*

The Caller 🐾 1987 (R) A strange man enters the house of a lone woman and sets off a long night of suspense and an almost longer evening of inept movie-making. 90m/C VHS, Beta. Malcolm McDowell, Madolyn Smith; **D:** Arthur Seidelman; **M:** Richard Band. *TWE*

Callie and Son 🐾🐾 *Rags to Riches* 1981 Details the sordid story of a waitress who works her way up to become a Dallas socialite and her obsessive relationship with her illegitimate son. Also known as "Rags to Riches." 97m/C VHS, VHS, Beta. Lindsay Wagner, Dabney Coleman, Jameson Parker, Andrew Prine, James Sloyan, Michelle Pfeiffer; **D:** Waris Hussein; **M:** Billy Goldenberg. *HBO*

Calling Dr. Death/Strange Confession 194? In 1943's "Calling Dr. Death," Chaney plays a neurologist with an unfaithful wife who gets herself murdered. Naturally, Chaney's the primary suspect. In 1944's "Strange Confession" idealistic writer Chaney made a fool of by publishing mogul Naish, who not only distorts his work but steals his wife. So Chaney plans an elaborate revenge. Based on the "The Inner Sanctum Mysteries" radio show. ?m/C VHS. Lon Chaney Jr., J. Carrol Naish, Brenda Joyce, Patricia Morrison, Ramsay Ames, David Bruce; **D:** Reginald Le Borg; **W:** Edward Dein. *USH*

Calling Paul Temple 🐾½ 1948 The wealthy patients of a nerve doctor have been dying and a detective is called in to investigate. 92m/B VHS, Beta. *GB* John Bentley, Dinah Sheridan, Margaretta Scott, Abraham Sofaer, Celia Lipton, Alan Wheatley, Wally Patch; **D:** Maclean Rogers. *SNC*

Calling Wild Bill Elliott 🐾½ 1943 The crooked territorial governor is exposed by hero Elliott and sidekick Hayes and justice is restored in this typical B-western. Elliott's first film for Republic; he went on to star in 16 Red Ryder films as well as other westerns for the studio. 55m/B VHS. Wild Bill Elliott, George "Gabby" Hayes, Herbert Heyes, Anne Jeffreys, Fred Kohler Jr., Roy Barcroft, Yakima Canutt; **D:** Spencer Gordon Bennet. *REP*

Calm at Sunset 🐾🐾½ 1996 (PG) James Pfeiffer (Facinelli) drops out of college to pursue his dream of becoming a commercial fisherman, much to the dismay of his parents (Moriarty, Nelligan) who already know how rough that life can be. But James gets his chance when he rescues a seaman (Conway) and the two become partners. Still, James must deal with secrets, a tragedy, and some hard decisions. TV drama with some solid performances. 98m/C VHS. Peter Facinelli, Michael Moriarty, Kate Nelligan, Kevin Conway, Gretchen Mol, Melvin Van Peebles; **D:** Daniel Petrie. *HMK*

Came a Hot Friday 🐾🐾 1985 (PG) Two cheap conmen arrive in a 1949 southern New Zealand town, run various scams and pursue women. 101m/C VHS, Beta, Closed Caption. *NZ* Peter Bland, Philip Gordon, Billy T. James; **D:** Ian Mune; **C:** Alun Bollinger. *NLC*

Camel Boy 🐾½ 1984 True story of a young Arabian boy who befriends a camel and their treacherous trek across the desert. 78m/C VHS, Beta. *AU* **D:** Yoram Gross; **V:** Michael Pate, Ron Haddrick, John Meillon. *VES, LIV*

Camelot 🐾🐾 1967 The long-running Lerner and Loewe Broadway musical about King Arthur, Guinevere, and Lancelot was adapted from T.H. White's book, "The Once and Future King." Redgrave and Nero have chemistry as the illicit lovers, Harris is strong as the king struggling to hold together his dream, but muddled direction undermines the effort. Laserdisc edition contains 28 minutes of previously edited footage, trailers and backstage info. ♫I Wonder What the King is Doing Tonight; The Simple Joys of Maidenhood; Camelot; C'est Moi; The Lusty Month of May; Follow Me; How To Handle a Woman; Then You May Take Me to the Fair; If Ever I Would Leave You. 150m/C VHS, Beta, LV, Closed Caption. Richard Harris, Vanessa Redgrave, David Hemmings, Franco Nero, Lionel Jeffries; **D:** Joshua Logan; **M:** Frederick Loewe, Alan Jay Lerner. Academy Awards '67: Best Adapted Score, Best Art Direction/Set Decoration, Best Costume Design; Golden Globe Awards '68: Best Actor—Musical/Comedy (Harris), Best Song ("If Ever I Should Leave You"), Best Score; Nominations: Academy Awards '67: Best Cinematography, Best Sound. *WAR, RDG, HMV*

Camera Buff 🐾🐾 *Amator* 1979 Satire on bureaucracy finds a factory worker buying a home-movie camera to film his new baby but becoming obsessed with his new toy. So he begins recording everything he sees—even things the authorities don't want shown. Polish with subtitles. 108m/C VHS. *PL* Jerzy Stuhr, Malgorzata Zajaczkowska, Ewa Pokas, Krzysztof Zanussi; **D:** Krzysztof Kieslowski; **W:** Jerzy Stuhr, Krzysztof Kieslowski; **M:** Krzysztof Knittel. *NYF*

The Cameraman 🐾🐾🐾🐾 1928 After moving to MGM, Keaton made his first feature with a major studio, giving up the artistic control he had enjoyed in his previous films. Spared from the vilification of studio politics (not the case with later Keaton films) "The Cameraman" enjoyed both critical and popular success. Keaton's inept tintype portrait-maker has a heart that pitter-patters for an MGM office girl. He hopes to impress her by joining the ranks of the newsreel photographers. Fortuitously poised to grab a photo scoop on a Chinese tong war, he is forced to return empty-handed when an organ-grinder's monkey absconds with his firsthand footage. Silent with a musical score. 78m/B VHS, LV. Buster Keaton, Marceline Day, Harold Goodwin, Harry Gribbon, Sidney Bracy, Edward Brophy, Vernon Dent, William Irving; **D:** Edward Sedgwick. *MGM, FCT*

Cameron's Closet 🐾½ 1989 (R) Every child's nightmare comes true. A young boy is convinced that a monster lives in his closet due to his perverse father's psychological tortures. Only this time the monster is real! 86m/C VHS, LV. Cotter Smith, Mel Harris, Scott Curtis, Chuck McCann, Leigh McCloskey, Kim Lankford, Tab Hunter; **D:** Armand Mastroianni; **W:** Gary Brandner; **C:** Russell Carpenter. *COL*

Camila 🐾🐾🐾 1984 The true story of the tragic romance between an Argentinean socialite and a Jesuit priest in 1847. The two lovers escape to a small provincial village where they live together as man and wife. Eventually they are recognized and condemned to death. Available in Spanish with English subtitles or dubbed into English. 121m/C

VHS, Beta. *AR SP* Susu Pecoraro, Imanol Arias, Hector Alterio, Elena Tasisto; *D:* Maria-Luisa Bemberg. Nominations: Academy Awards '84: Best Foreign Language Film. *COL, MFI*

Camilla 🐾🐾½ 1994 (PG-13) Tandy is delightful in her last starring role as a former violinist on the run with frustrated musician Fonda. Oafish son (Chaykin) and insensitive husband (Koteas) just don't understand, so its time to head to Toronto, site of a fondly, if perhaps incorrectly, remembered triumph. Sort of a May-December female-bonding roadtrip with lots of conversation and comic asides. An inevitably poignant pairing of Tandy and real-life husband Cronyn offers the chance to experience one of America's greatest acting teams one last time. Lack of stereotyping and fairly novel twist on the road movie keep this one on the highway. *CW:* Contains profanity, brief nudity, and some sensuality. 91m/C VHS, LV, Closed Caption. Jessica Tandy, Bridget Fonda, Hume Cronyn, Elias Koteas, Maury Chaykin, Graham Greene; *D:* Deepa Mehta; *W:* Paul Quarrington; *M:* Daniel Lanois. *MAX*

Camille 🐾🐾 1921 Dying courtesan falls in love with innocent young man in the Dumas classic. Valentino in his prime. 55m/B VHS. Rudolph Valentino, Alla Nazimova; *D:* Fred Niblo. *FCT*

Camille 🐾🐾🐾½ 1936 The classic Alexandre Dumas story about a dying French courtesan falling in love with a shallow young nobleman. A clean, romantic adaptation that somehow escapes the cliches and stands as one of the most telling monuments to Garbo's unique magic and presence on film. 108m/B VHS, Beta. Greta Garbo, Robert Taylor, Lionel Barrymore, Henry Daniell, Elizabeth Allan, Rex O'Malley, Lenore Ulric, Laura Hope Crews; *D:* George Cukor; *C:* William H. Daniels. National Board of Review Awards '37: 10 Best Films of the Year; New York Film Critics Awards '37: Best Actress (Garbo); Nominations: Academy Awards '37: Best Actress (Garbo). *MGM*

Camille Claudel 🐾🐾🐾 1989 (R) A lushly romantic version of the art world at the turn of the century, when art was exploding in new forms and independence for women was unheard of. Sculptor Claudel's tragic love for art, Auguste Rodin (for whom she modeled), and independence clash, costing her sanity. Very long, it requires an attentive and thoughtful viewing. In French with English subtitles. 149m/C VHS, Beta, LV. *FR* Isabelle Adjani, Gerard Depardieu, Laurent Grevill, Alain Cuny, Madeleine Robinson, Katrine Boorman; *D:* Bruno Nuytten; *W:* Bruno Nuytten, Marilyn Goldin; *M:* Gabriel Yared. Cesar Awards '89: Best Actress (Adjani), Best Art Direction/Set Decoration, Best Cinematography, Best Costume Design, Best Film; Nominations: Academy Awards '89: Best Actress (Adjani), Best Foreign Language Film. *ORI, IME*

Camorra: The Naples Connection 🐾🐾 *Un Complicato Intrigo Di Donne, Vicoli E Delitti* 1985 (R) A prostitute and an American drug dealer find themselves embroiled in the murders of Neapolitan Mafia heads. Violent, overblown, minor Wertmuller. 94m/C VHS, Beta. *IT* Harvey Keitel, Angela Molina, Lorraine Bracco, Francesco Rabal; *D:* Lina Wertmuller; *W:* Lina Wertmuller. *MGM*

Camp Cucamonga: How I Spent My Summer Vacation 🐾 1990 Zany antics at summer camp abound when Camp Cucamonga's owner mistakes the new handyman for the camp inspector. Well known stars from TV's "Cheers," "The Jeffersons," "The Wonder Years," and "The Love Boat" are featured in this silly made for television flick. 100m/C VHS. John Ratzenberger, Sherman Hemsley, Josh Saviano, Danica McKellar, Chad Allen, Dorothy Lyman, Lauren Tewes, G. Gordon Liddy; *D:* Roger Duchonwny. *GKK*

Camp Nowhere 🐾🐾 1994 (PG) Video fodder for the juniors in the household as kids turn tables on parents. Instead of trudging off to summer camp for the umpteenth time, a group of upscale kids create their own with the help of laid-off drama teacher Lloyd, who must first con their parents into believing that Camp Nowhere is legit. What follows is that very special summer camp in the Hollywood tradition with lots of junk food, vid-

eo games galore, and of course, no rules. Camp beserko formula good for a few laughs. 106m/C VHS, LV, Closed Caption. Christopher Lloyd, Wendy Makkena, M. Emmet Walsh, Peter Scolari, Peter Onorati, Ray Baker, Kate Mulgrew, Jonathan Jackson, Romy Walthall, Maryedith Burrell, Tom Wilson, Nathan Cavaleri, Andrew Keegan, Melody Kay; *D:* Jonathan Prince; *W:* Andrew Kurtzman, Eliot Wald; *C:* Sandi Sissel. *TOU*

The Campus Corpse 🐾 1977 (PG) Young man stumbles into deadly college frat hazing and discovers he and rest of cast are utterly devoid of acting ability. 92m/C VHS, Beta. Charles Martin Smith, Jeff East, Brad Davis; *D:* Douglas Curtis. *VES*

Campus Knights 🐾 1929 If you're a serious student of the campus caper film, this is one of the earliest (though not one of the best) of the genre (if such a distinction can be made). The story involves twin brothers—one a tweedy high-browed professor, the other a bon vivant man about town—who wreak fraternal chaos on the quads. 70m/B VHS, Beta. Raymond McKee, Shirley Palmer, Marie Quillen, Jean Laverty, Sybil Grove; *D:* Albert Kelly. *GPV, FCT*

Campus Man 🐾 1987 (PG) An entrepreneurial college student markets a beefcake calendar featuring his best friend, until the calendar's sales threaten his friend's amateur athletic status. 94m/C VHS, Beta, LV. John Dye, Steve Lyon, Kim Delaney, Miles O'Keeffe, Morgan Fairchild, Kathleen Wilhoite; *D:* Ron Casden; *W:* Geoffrey Baere; *M:* James Newton Howard. *PAR*

Can-Can 🐾🐾 1960 Lackluster screen adaptation of the Cole Porter musical bears little resemblance to the stage version. MacLaine is a cafe owner who goes to court to try and get the "Can-Can," a dance considered risque in gay Paree at the end of the nineteenth century, made legal. Love interest Sinatra happens to be a lawyer. ♫C'est Manifique; Let's Do It; I Love Paris; You Do Something to Me; It's All Right With Me; Live and Let Live; Come Along With Me; Just One of Those Things. 131m/C VHS, Beta, LV, Closed Caption. Frank Sinatra, Shirley MacLaine, Maurice Chevalier, Louis Jourdan, Juliet Prowse, Marcel Dalio, Leon Belasco; *D:* Walter Lang; *C:* William H. Daniels. Nominations: Academy Awards '60: Best Costume Design (Color), Scoring of a Musical. *FOX, FCT*

Can I Do It...Till I Need Glasses? WOOF! 1977 More to the point, can you stay awake till the end? Prurient juvenile junk. Brief Williams footage was grafted to this mess during 15 minutes of Mork fame. 72m/C VHS, Beta. Robin Williams, Roger Behr, Debra Klose, Moose Carlson, Walter Olkewicz; *D:* I. Robert Levy. *MED*

Can She Bake a Cherry Pie? 🐾🐾 1983 Two offbeat characters meet and fall in love in an odd sort of way. Slow-moving and talky but somewhat rewarding. One of Black's better performances. 90m/C VHS, Beta, Closed Caption. Karen Black, Michael Emil, Michael Margotta, Frances Fisher, Martin Frydberg; *D:* Henry Jaglom; *W:* Henry Jaglom; *M:* Karen Black. *PAR, FCT*

Can You Feel Me Dancing? 🐾🐾 1985 Family-happy lightweight entertainment co-produced by Kent Bateman and starring Bateman progeny Jason and Justine as brother and sister, a novel premise that only a father could love. A blind independence-impaired teenager tries to liberate herself from her overbearing family, and finds the secret to conquering her fears and to standing up for herself when she falls in love. Written by spouse-team Steven and J. Miyoko Hensley. 95m/C VHS. Jason Bateman, Justine Bateman; *D:* Michael Miller; *W:* Steven Hensley, J. Miyoko Hensley. *NO*

Can You Hear the Laughter? The Story of Freddie Prinze 🐾🐾 1979 Heartstring tugging biography of the late Puerto Rican comedian whose troubled life lead to suicide in spite of his apparent success. He was most noted for his starring role in "Chico and the Man." 100m/C VHS, Beta. Ira Angustain, Kevin Hooks,

Randee Heller, Devon Ericson, Julie Carmen, Stephen Elliott; *D:* Burt Brinckerhoff. *GEM*

Canada's Sweetheart: The Saga of Hal C. Banks 🐾🐾 *Sweetheart!* 1985 True story of Banks, hired by the Canadian government to break up a strike among the communist-led seaman's union which had put a stranglehold on Canadian commerce, and who was eventually convicted of strong-arm tactics. 115m/C VHS, Beta. *CA* Maury Chaykin. Toronto-City Award '85: Best Canadian Feature Film. *NO*

Canadian Bacon 🐾½ 1994 (PG) Regrettably amateurish satire (with some sharp observations) serves as the feature film debut for Moore, who irritated many with "Roger and Me." Title refers to the military code name for a campaign to whip up anti-Canadian hysteria and justify a U.S. invasion of its neighbor to the north. Evil political advisor Pollak convinces well-meaning but inept President Alda that it's just the thing to get the presidential popularity up and those defense industries humming. Ugly Americans abound, at expense of polite Canadians, eh? Filmed in Toronto, which is shown to good advantage. Candy in one of last roles is the superpatriotic sheriff of Niagara Falls, New York. 110m/C VHS. Alan Alda, Kevin Pollak, John Candy, Rhea Perlman, Rip Torn, Bill Nunn, Kevin J. O'Connor, Steven Wright, G.D. Spradlin; *Cameos:* Michael Moore; *D:* Michael Moore; *W:* Michael Moore; *C:* Haskell Wexler; *M:* Elmer Bernstein. *PGV*

Canadian Mounties vs. Atomic Invaders 🐾🐾½ 1953 Mountie Don Roberts and undercover agent Kay Conway chase foreign agents and face natural disasters (avalanches and reindeer stampedes) to keep atomic missiles away from Canada and the U.S. Part of "The Cliffhanger Serials" series. 12 chapters. 169m/B VHS. William Henry, Susan Morrow, Arthur Space. *REP, MOV*

Cancel My Reservation 🐾 1972 (G) New York talk show host Hope sets out for a vacation on an Arizona ranch, but winds up in trouble due to a mysterious corpse, a rich rancher, and an enigmatic mystic. Even more muddled than it sounds. Based on the novel "Broken Gun" by Louis L'Amour, with pointless cameos by Crosby, Wayne, and Wilson. 99m/C VHS, Beta. Bob Hope, Eva Marie Saint, Ralph Bellamy, Anne Archer, Forrest Tucker, Keenan Wynn, Flip Wilson, Noriyuki "Pat" Morita, Chief Dan George; *Cameos:* John Wayne, Bing Crosby, Doodles Weaver; *D:* Paul Bogart; *W:* Arthur Marx; *C:* Russell Metty. *COL, FCT*

The Candidate 🐾🐾🐾 1972 (PG) Realistic, satirical look at politics and political campaigning. A young, idealistic lawyer is talked into trying for the Senate seat and learns the truth about running for office. Ritchie's other efforts include "Downhill Racer" and "Bad News Bears". 105m/C VHS, Beta, LV. Robert Redford, Peter Boyle, Don Porter, Allen (Goorwitz) Garfield, Karen Carlson, Melvyn Douglas, Michael Lerner; *D:* Michael Ritchie; *W:* Jeremy Larner. Academy Awards '72: Best Story & Screenplay; National Board of Review Awards '72: 10 Best Films of the Year; Writers Guild of America '72: Best Original Screenplay; Nominations: Academy Awards '72: Best Sound. *WAR*

Candles at Nine 🐾½ 1944 An innocent showgirl must spend a month in her late uncle's creepy mansion in order to inherit it, much to the malevolent chagrin of the rest of the family who want the place and the loot for themselves. Uninspired. 84m/B VHS, Beta. *GB* Jessie Matthews, John Stuart, Reginald Purdell; *D:* John Harlow. *SNC, VYY, MLB*

Candleshoe 🐾🐾 1978 (G) A Los Angeles street urchin poses as an English matron's long lost granddaughter in order to steal a fortune hidden in Candleshoe, her country estate, where Niven butlers. Somewhat slapschticky Disney fare. 101m/C VHS, Beta, Closed Caption. Vivian Pickles, Helen Hayes, David Niven, Jodie Foster, Leo McKern; *D:* Norman Tokar. *DIS*

Candy Mountain 🎬🎬 1987 **(R)** Guitar playin' O'Connor roadtrips across America and Canada in search of a legendary guitar maker Yulin. Occasional interest derives from musician cameos from the likes of Buster Poindexter, Dr. John and Redbone. **90m/C VHS. FR SI CA** Kevin J. O'Connor, Harris Yulin, Tom Waits, Bulle Ogier, Roberts Blossom; **Cameos:** David Johansen, Leon Redbone, Joe Strummer, Rita MacNeil, Laurie Metcalf; **D:** Robert Frank; **W:** Rudy Wurlitzer. **REP, FCT**

Candy Stripe Nurses 🎬 Sweet Candy 1974 **(R)** Even hard-core Roger Corman fans might find his final installment in the nursing comedy pentad to be a lethargic exercise in gratuitous "sexual situations." Bet those uniforms don't meet hospital standards. The previous films in the series are: "The Student Nurses," "Private Duty Nurses," "Night Call Nurses," and "The Young Nurses." **80m/C VHS, Beta.** Candice Rialson, Robin Mattson, Maria Rojo, Kimberly Hyde, Dick Miller, Stanley Ralph Ross, Monte Landis, Tom Baker; **D:** Allan Holleb.

Candy Tangerine Man 🎬 1975 Respectable businessman leads a double life as loving father and LA pimp. **88m/C VHS, Beta.** John Daniels, Tom Hankerson, Eli Haines, Marva Farmer, George Flower; **D:** Matt Cimber. **UNI**

Candyman 🎬🎬 1992 **(R)** Terrifying tale from horror maven Clive Barker is an effective combination of American gothic, academia, and urban squalor. A search for dissertation material leads graduate student Helen Lyle (Madsen) into gang-infested housing. There she encounters the urban myth of Candyman, the son of a former slave who was lynched and is now back with a hook and a vendetta. Filled with the appropriate amount of yucky stuff, yet successfully employs subtle scare tactics and plausible characters. **CW:** Violence and gore. **98m/C VHS, Beta, LV, 8mm, Closed Caption.** Virginia Madsen, Tony Todd, Xander Berkeley, Kasi Lemmons, Vanessa Williams, DeJuan Guy, Michael Culkin, Gilbert Lewis, Stanley DeSantis; **D:** Bernard Rose; **W:** Bernard Rose; **M:** Philip Glass. **COL**

Candyman 2: Farewell to the Flesh 🎬 1994 **(R)** Explains the origins of the urban bogeyman called Candyman—the man, the hook and the bees. Rehashes the same old scare tactics from previous and better horror movies and uses cheesy special effects. The sensual background of New Orleans during Mardi Gras can't help this stale sequel. Embrace this "Farewell" from a distance. Based on stories by Clive Barker. **CW:** Violence and gore; some sexuality and language. **99m/C VHS.** Tony Todd, Kelly Rowan, Veronica Cartwright, Timothy Carhart, William O'Leary, Bill Nunn, Fay Hauser; **D:** Bill Condon; **W:** Rand Ravich, Mark Kruger; **C:** Tobias Schliessler; **M:** Philip Glass. **PGV**

Cannery Row 🎬🎬½ 1982 **(PG)** Baseball has-been Nolte lives anonymously among the downtrodden in the seamy part of town and carries on with working girl girlfriend Winger. Based on John Steinbeck's "Cannery Row" and "Sweet Thursday." **120m/C VHS, Beta.** Nick Nolte, Debra Winger, Audra Lindley, M. Emmet Walsh, Frank McRae, James Keane, Sunshine Parker; **D:** David S. Ward; **W:** David S. Ward; **C:** Sven Nykvist; **M:** Jack Nitzsche. **MGM**

Cannes Man 🎬🎬 1996 **(R)** Legendary Hollywood producer Sy Lerner (Cassel) vows to make unknown cabbie/screenwriter Frank Rhinoslavsky (Quinn) a star, all while being schmoozed at Cannes by stars who want to be in his latest epic, while he tries to find backers for his unwritten script. **CW:** Adult themes, language, brief nudity. **88m/C VHS.** Seymour Cassel, Francesco Quinn, Rebecca Broussard; **D:** Richard Martini. **ROC**

Cannibal Campout 🎬 1988 Crazed orphans with eating disorders make square meal of coed babes getting back to nature. **89m/C VHS, Beta.** Carrie Lindell, Richard Marcus, Amy Chludzinski, Jon McBride; **D:** Jon McBride, Tom Fisher. **DMP**

Cannibal! The Musical 🎬 1996 **(R)** Only those wacky people at Troma could make a horror/musical about a group of 1883 gold miners who get lost in the Colorado Rockies, have some strange adventures, and eventually wind up as dinner to cannibal Alfred Packer (who's telling his version of the story to a female reporter while in prison). Seven rather tedious musical numbers lead up to the gore-splashed finale. **CW:** Comic gore/violence and some language. **105m/C VHS.** Ian Hardin, Jason McHugh, Matt Stone, Trey Parker; **D:** Trey Parker; **W:** Trey Parker. **TTV**

Cannibal Women in the Avocado Jungle of Death 🎬🎬½ 1989 **(PG-13)** Tongue-in-cheek cult classic features erstwhile playmate Tweed as feminist anthropologist who searches with ditzy student and mucho macho male guide for lost tribe of cannibal women who dine on their mates. Lawton directed under the alias "J.D. Athens." **90m/C VHS, Beta, LV, Closed Caption.** Shannon Tweed, Adrienne Barbeau, Karen Mistal, Barry Primus, Bill Maher; **D:** J.F. Lawton; **W:** J.F. Lawton. **PAR**

Cannon Ball/Eyes Have It 🎬 1915 Conklin stars in "The Cannon Ball" (1915), as an explosives expert in the Boom Powder Factory. "The Eyes Have It" (1928), stars Turpin involved in another misunderstanding with wife and mother-in-law. Silent. **41m/B VHS, Beta.** Chester Conklin, Ben Turpin, Georgia O'Dell, Helen Gilmore, Jack Lipson. **CCB**

Cannon Movie Tales: Red Riding Hood 🎬🎬½ 1989 **(G)** Bright re-telling of the little girl in red and that nasty wolf. **84m/C VHS.** Craig T. Nelson, Isabella Rossellini; **D:** Adam Brooks. **WAR**

Cannon Movie Tales: Sleeping Beauty 🎬🎬½ 1989 **(G)** Fairchild stars in this version of the sleeping princess and the evil witch. **90m/C VHS.** Morgan Fairchild, Tracy Welch, Nicholas Clay, Sylvia Miles, Kenny Baker, David Holliday; **D:** David Irving. **WAR**

Cannon Movie Tales: The Emperor's New Clothes 🎬🎬½ 1989 Caesar stars in this version of vain despot and the crafty tailors. **85m/C VHS.** Sid Caesar, Robert Morse, Clive Revill; **D:** David Irving. **WAR**

Cannonball 🎬🎬 Carquake 1976 **(PG)** Assorted ruthless people leave patches of rubber across the country competing for grand prize in less than legal auto race. Not top drawer New World but nonetheless a cult fave. Inferior to Bartel's previous cult classic, "Death Race 2000." Most interesting for plethora of cult cameos, including Scorsese, Dante, and grandmaster Corman. **93m/C VHS, Beta.** David Carradine, Bill McKinney, Veronica Hamel, Gerrit Graham, Robert Carradine, Sylvester Stallone, Jonathan Kaplan; **Cameos:** Martin Scorsese, Roger Corman, Joe Dante; **D:** Paul Bartel; **W:** Paul Bartel; **M:** David A. Axelrod. **NO**

Cannonball/Dizzy Heights and Daring Hearts 🎬 1916 Two classic comedies featuring Conklin, the Keystone Kops, and wacky aeroplanes from the irrepressible Sennett. **71m/B VHS, Beta.** Chester Conklin; **D:** Mack Sennett. **VYY**

Cannonball Run 🎬½ 1981 **(PG)** So many stars, so little plot. Reynolds and sidekick DeLuise disguise themselves as paramedics to foil cops while they compete in cross-country Cannonball race. Shows no sign of having been directed by an ex-stuntman. One of 1981's top grossers—go figure. Followed by equally languid sequel "Cannonball Run II." **95m/C VHS, Beta, LV.** Burt Reynolds, Farrah Fawcett, Roger Moore, Dom DeLuise, Dean Martin, Sammy Davis Jr., Jack Elam, Adrienne Barbeau, Peter Fonda, Molly Picon, Bert Convy, Jamie Farr; **D:** Hal Needham. **VES**

Cannonball Run 2 🎬 1984 **(PG)** More mindless cross-country wheel spinning with gratuitous star cameos. Director Needham apparently subscribes to the two wrongs make a right school of sequels. **109m/C VHS, Beta, LV, Closed Caption.** Burt Reynolds, Dom DeLuise, Jamie Farr, Marilu Henner,

Shirley MacLaine, Jim Nabors, Frank Sinatra, Sammy Davis Jr., Dean Martin, Telly Savalas, Susan Anton, Catherine Bach, Jack Elam, Sid Caesar, Ricardo Montalban, Charles Nelson Reilly; **Cameos:** Henry Silva, Tim Conway, Don Knotts, Molly Picon; **D:** Hal Needham; **W:** Harvey Miller; **M:** Stephen Dorff. **WAR**

Can't Buy Me Love 🎬½ 1987 **(PG-13)** Unpopular high school nerd Dempsey buys a month of dates with teen babe Peterson for $1000 in order to win friends and influence people. Previously known as "Boy Rents Girl." **94m/C VHS, Beta, LV, Closed Caption.** Patrick Dempsey, Amanda Peterson, Dennis Dugan, Courtney Gains; **D:** Steve Rash; **C:** Peter Collister; **M:** Robert Folk. **TOU**

Can't Help Singing 🎬🎬½ 1945 In 1849, willful heiress Caroline (Durbin) ignores her senator father's (Collins) wishes and heads west to marry her Army sweetheart (Bruce). But on the wagon train she falls for wagon master Lawlor (Paige), who's a better guy anyway. Durbin's first color musical. **90m/C VHS.** Deanna Durbin, Robert Paige, David Bruce, Akim Tamiroff, Leonid Kinskey, Ray Collins, June Vincent, Thomas Gomez; **D:** Frank Ryan; **W:** Frank Ryan, Lewis R. Foster; **C:** Woody Bredell, William Howard Greene; **M:** Hans J. Salter, Jerome Kern, E.Y. Harburg. Nominations: Academy Awards '45: Best Song ("More and More"), Scoring of a Musical. **USH**

Can't Stop the Music woof! 1980 **(PG)** Retired model invites friends from Greenwich Village to a party to help the career of her roommate, an aspiring composer. Disco inferno that nearly reaches heights of surreal ineptness. Put it in a time capsule and let the people of the future decide what the heck was going on in the seventies. Features two of the top hits by the Village People. ♫Y.M.C.A.; Macho Man; Give Me a Break; The Sound of the City; Samantha; I'm a Singing Juggler; Sophistication; Liberation; I Love You to Death. **120m/C VHS, Beta.** Valerie Perrine, Bruce Jenner, Steve Guttenberg, Paul Sand, Leigh Taylor-Young, Village People; **D:** Nancy Walker; **W:** Allan Carr; **C:** Bill Butler. Golden Raspberry Awards '80: Worst Picture, Worst Screenplay. **REP**

A Canterbury Tale 🎬🎬🎬 1944 Writer-director team Powell and Pressburger have loosely modeled a retelling of Chaucer's famous tale of a pilgrimage to the cathedral in Canterbury. Set in Nazi-threatened Britain in 1944, the story follows the pilgrimage of three Brits and an American GI to the eponymous cathedral. Strange, effective, worth looking at. The 95-minute American version, with added footage of Kim Hunter, is inferior to the 124-minute original. **124m/B VHS. GB** Eric Portman, Sheila Sim, Dennis Price, Esmond Knight, Charles Hawtrey, Hay Petrie; **D:** Michael Powell, Emeric Pressburger. **HMV**

The Canterbury Tales 🎬🎬 1971 Four Chaucer tales, most notably "The Merchant's Tale" and "The Wife of Bath," are recounted by travelers, with director Pasolini as the bawdy poet. Deemed obscene by the Italian courts, it's the second entry in Pasolini's medieval "Trilogy of Life," preceded by "The Decameron" and followed by "The Arabian Nights." In Italian with English subtitles. **109m/C VHS, Beta. IT** Laura Betti, Ninetto Davoli, Pier Paolo Pasolini, Hugh Griffith, Josephine Chaplin, Michael Balfour, Jenny Runacre; **D:** Pier. Paolo Pasolini. Berlin International Film Festival '72: Golden Berlin Bear. **WBF, APD**

The Canterville Ghost 🎬🎬½ 1944 Laughton, a 300-year old ghost with a yellow streak, is sentenced to spook a castle until he proves he's not afraid of his own shadow. American troops stay at the castle during WWII and, as luck would have it, soldier Young is distantly related to spunky young keeper of the castle O'Brien, ghost Laughton's descendant. Once Young is acquainted with his cowardly ancestor, he begins to fear a congenital yellow streak, and both struggle to be brave despite themselves. Vaguely derived from an Oscar Wilde tale. **95m/B VHS, Beta, Closed Caption.** Charles Laughton, Robert Young, Margaret O'Brien, William Gargan, Reginald Owen, Rags Ragland,

Una O'Connor, Peter Lawford, Mike Mazurki; **D:** Jules Dassin; **W:** Edwin Blum; **M:** George Bassman. *MGM*

The Canterville Ghost 1991 During a family's vacation in an old English manor, they run into a ghost who is doomed to haunt the place until he can overcome his fears. Problems start when the family tries to scare him away. From the "Wonderworks" family movie series. 58m/C VHS. Richard Kiley, Mary Wickes. *PME, FCT*

The Canterville Ghost ♪♪½ 1996 (PG) Stewart is the highlight of this updated TV version of the Oscar Wilde short story. He's the cursed Elizabethan spirit of Sir Simon de Canterville, doomed to haunt the family mansion until a prophecy is fulfilled. But he's not happy with a family of American intruders, until teenager Virginia (Campbell) discovers Sir Simon and realizes she may hold the key to freeing the unhappy ghost. 91m/C VHS. Patrick Stewart, Neve Campbell, Ed Wiley, Cherie Lunghi, Donald Sinden, Joan Sims, Leslie Phillips, Ciaran Fitzgerald, Daniel Betts, Raymond Pickard; **D:** Syd Macartney; **W:** Robert Benedetto; **C:** Denis Lewiston; **M:** Ernest Troost. *HMK*

The Cantor's Son ♪½ *Dem Khann's Zindl* 1937 Real-life story based on Moishe Oysher's life, vaguely influenced by Jolson's "Jazz Singer." Runaway Oysher joins troupe of performers as a youth, travels to the shores of America, and finds fame once his beautiful voice is discovered. Returning to his mother country to celebrate his parents' golden anniversary, he encounters his childhood sweetheart and falls in love, but another woman is written into the plot to complicate matters. Poorly acted, laughable staging. In Yiddish with English subtitles. 90m/B VHS, Beta. Judith Abarbanel, Florence Weiss, Moishe Oysher, Isadore Cashier; **D:** Ilya Motyleff. *ERG, HEG*

Canvas: The Fine Art of Crime ♪♪ 1992 (R) A ruthless, underhanded art gallery owner recruits a desperate young artist into his art stealing schemes. The artist learns how to steal, but decides he wants out after his burglary partner has a brush with death. The gallery owner, however, wants one last job completed. **CW:** Language, violence and drug content, and some sexuality. 94m/C VHS. Gary Busey, John Rhys-Davies, Vittorio Rossi, Nick Cavaiola, Cary Lawrence; **D:** Alain Zaloum. *LIV*

Cape Fear ♪♪♪½ 1961 Former prosecutor turned small-town lawyer Peck and his family are plagued by the sadistic attentions of criminal Mitchum, who just finished a six year sabbatical at the state pen courtesy of prosecutor Peck. Taut and creepy; Mitchum's a consummate psychopath. Based on (and far superior to) John MacDonald's "The Executioners." Don't pass this one up in favor of the Scorsese remake. 106m/B VHS, Beta. Gregory Peck, Robert Mitchum, Polly Bergen, Martin Balsam, Telly Savalas, Jack Kruschen; **D:** J. Lee Thompson; **C:** Sam Leavitt. *USH*

Cape Fear ♪♪♪ 1991 (R) Scorsese takes on this terrifying tale of brutality and manipulation (previously filmed in 1961) and cranks it up a notch as a paroled convict haunts the lawyer who put him away. Great cast, a rollercoaster of suspense. Note the cameos by Mitchum, Peck, and Balsam, stars of the first version. Original source material was "The Executioners" by John D. MacDonald. Breath-taking rollercoaster of a film. Elmer Bernstein adapted the original score by Bernard Herrmann. **CW:** Language and strong violence. 128m/C VHS, LV, Closed Caption. Robert De Niro, Nick Nolte, Jessica Lange, Juliette Lewis, Joe Don Baker, Illeana Douglas, Fred Dalton Thompson; **Cameos:** Robert Mitchum, Gregory Peck, Martin Balsam; **D:** Martin Scorsese; **W:** Wesley Strick; **M:** Bernard Herrmann, Elmer Bernstein. Chicago Film Critics Awards '91: Most Promising Actress (Lewis); Nominations: Academy Awards '91: Best Actor (De Niro), Best Supporting Actress (Lewis). *USH*

Caper of the Golden Bulls ♪ *Carnival of Thieves* 1967 Former bank robber Boyd is blackmailed into joining a group of safecrackers who plan to assault the Royal Bank of Spain during the annual Santa Maria bull run. More like siesta of the golden bulls. 104m/C VHS, Beta. Stephen Boyd, Yvette Mimieux, Giovanna Ralli, Walter Slezak, Vito Scotti; **D:** Russel Rouse. *NLC*

Capital Punishment ♪♪½ 1996 Martial arts expert James Thayer (Daniels) is recruited by the DEA to go undercover and stop Nakata (Yamashita), the supplier of a new illegal drug. His operation turns up a corrupt police chief (Carradine), who frames him for murder, and lots of action. 90m/C VHS. Gary Daniels, Tadashi Yamashita, David Carradine, Mel Novak, Ian Jacklin, Ava Fabian; **D:** David Hue; **W:** David Hue; **C:** David Swett. *SCP*

Capone ♪♪½ 1989 (R) This is the story of the gangster after Elliot Ness put him in a Chicago jail. That didn't stop Capone from running his crime empire until a single FBI agent worked to sent the crime boss to Alcatraz, where his power would be useless. Exuberant performances from Sharkey and Carradine. Made for television. **CW:** Violence and sexuality. 96m/C VHS, LV, Closed Caption. Ray Sharkey, Keith Carradine, Debrah Farentino. *THV*

Capricorn One ♪♪♪ 1978 (R) Astronauts Brolin, Simpson and Waterston follow Mission Controller Holbrook's instructions to fake a Mars landing on a fabricated soundstage when their ship is discovered to be defective. When they find out they're supposed to expire in outer space so that the NASA scam won't become public knowledge, they flee to the desert, while reporter Gould sniffs out the cover up. Based on a pseudonymous novel by Ken Follett. 123m/C VHS, Beta, LV. Elliott Gould, James Brolin, Brenda Vaccaro, O.J. Simpson, Hal Holbrook, Sam Waterston, Karen Black, Telly Savalas; **D:** Peter Hyams; **W:** Peter Hyams; **C:** Bill Butler; **M:** Jerry Goldsmith. *FOX*

Captain America *The Return of Captain America* 1944 Captain America battles a mad scientist in this fifteen-episode serial based on the comic book character. 240m/B VHS, Beta. Dick Purcell, Adrian Booth, Lionel Atwill; **D:** John English; **W:** Elmer Clifton. *VCN, MLB, VTR*

Captain America ♪½ 1979 Marvel Comic character steps into feature film and flounders. The patriotic superhero son of WWII hero fights bad guy with contraband nuclear weapon. Made for television. Followed the same year with "Captain America II: Death Too Soon." 98m/C VHS, Beta. Reb Brown, Len Birman, Heather Menzies, Steve Forrest, Robin Mattson, Joseph Ruskin, Michael McManus; **D:** Rod Holcomb. *USH*

Captain America ♪½ 1989 (PG-13) Based on the Marvel Comics superhero. It's 1941 and Steve Rogers has just been recruited to join a top secret experimental government program after flunking his army physical. Injected with a serum, Steve becomes super strong, fast, and smart but is matched in all three by an evil Nazi counterpart, Red Skull. The two battle to a WWII standstill and while Red Skull goes on with his evil plots, the next 40 years finds Captain America fast frozen in the Alaskan tundra. Finally, our hero is thawed in time to do a final battle with his evil nemesis. This one is ridiculous even by comic book standards but it may amuse the kids. 103m/C VHS, LV. Matt Salinger, Scott Paulin, Ronny Cox, Ned Beatty, Darren McGavin, Melinda Dillon; **D:** Albert Pyun; **W:** Stephen Tolkin. *COL*

Captain America 2: Death Too Soon ♪ 1979 Terrorists hit America where it hurts, threatening to use age accelerating drug. Sequelized superhero fights chronic crow lines and series dies slow, painful death. Made for television. 98m/C VHS, Beta. Reb Brown, Connie Sellecca, Len Birman, Christopher Lee, Katherine Justice, Lana Wood, Christopher Carey; **D:** Ivan Nagy. *USH*

Captain Apache ♪ 1971 Union intelligence officer Van Cleef investigates murder of Indian commissioner and discovers fake Indian war landscam. As clever as the title. 95m/C VHS, Beta. Lee Van Cleef, Carroll Baker, Stuart Whitman; **D:** Alexander Singer; **W:** Philip Yordan. *MRV, PSM*

Captain Blackjack ♪♪ *Black Jack* 1951 All star cast craps out in wannabe thriller about drug smuggling on the French Riviera. Social butterfly Moorehead directs drug traffic, detective Marshall undercovers as doctor, and Sanders looks bored in a British sort of way. 90m/B VHS. *FR* George Sanders, Herbert Marshall, Agnes Moorehead, Patricia Roc, Marcel Dalio; **D:** Julien Duvivier. *NO*

Captain Blood ♪♪♪½ 1935 Sabatini adventure story launched then unknown 26-year old Flynn and 19-year old De Havilland to fame in perhaps the best pirate story ever. Exiled into slavery by a tyrannical governor, Irish physician Peter Blood is forced into piracy but ultimately earns a pardon for his swashbuckling ways. Love interest De Havilland would go on to appear in seven more features with Flynn, who took the part Robert Donat declined for health reasons. Cleverly budgeted using ship shots from silents, and miniature sets when possible. First original film score by composer Korngold. Also available colorized. 120m/B VHS, Beta, Closed Caption. Errol Flynn, Olivia de Havilland, Basil Rathbone, J. Carrol Naish, Guy Kibbee, Lionel Atwill; **D:** Michael Curtiz; **C:** Hal Mohr. Nominations: Academy Awards '35: Best Picture, Best Sound. *MGM, FCT, MLB*

Captain Boycott ♪♪½ 1947 In 1880 Ireland, Boycott (Parker) is the despised rent collector for an aristocratic English landlord. When the poor tenant farmers can't pay, he's quick to throw them off the land. The farmers then band together to get rid of Boycott. Granger and Ryan are the prerequisite young lovers. Adapted from the novel by Philip Rooney. 94m/B VHS. *GB* Cecil Parker, Stewart Granger, Kathleen Ryan, Niall McGinnis, Robert Donat, Mervyn Johns, Alastair Sim, Noel Purcell, Maurice Denham; **D:** Frank Launder; **W:** Frank Launder, Wolfgang Wilhelm; **C:** Wilkie Cooper, Oswald Morris; **M:** William Alwyn. *HMK*

Captain Caution ♪♪ 1940 Young girl throws caution to the wind when dad dies during the War of 1812, assisting young Mature to take over the old man's ship to do battle with the British. Watch for then unknown sailor Ladd. 84m/B VHS, Beta. Victor Mature, Louise Platt, Bruce Cabot, Alan Ladd, Robert Barrat, Vivienne Osborne; **D:** Richard Wallace. Nominations: Academy Awards '40: Best Sound. *MED*

Captain Conan ♪♪♪ *Capitaine Conan* 1996 On the Bulgarian border in 1918, during the last clashes of WWI, Conan (Torreton) is a fearless, impulsive warrior, reserving his respect only for his men. Although armistice is finally declared, the troops stationed in the Balkans are not demobilized and become increasingly fractious. This causes a rift between Conan and his educated friend Norbert (Le Bihan), who's been appointed a military legal representative. They are warily reunited in defense of a soldier (Val) charged with desertion, while still dealing with the ravages of the long conflict. Adapted from the book by Roger Vercel; French with subtitles. 129m/C VHS. *FR* Philippe Torreton, Samuel Le Bihan, Bernard Le Coq, Pierre Val, Francois Berleand, Claude Rich, Catherine Rich; **D:** Bertrand Tavernier; **W:** Bertrand Tavernier, Jean Cosmos; **C:** Alain Choquart; **M:** Oswald D'Andrea. Cesar Awards '97: Best Actor (Torreton), Best Director (Tavernier), Best Film. *NYR*

Captain from Castile ♪♪♪ 1947 Exciting saga finds 16th-century Spanish nobleman Pedro De Vargas (Power) forced to flee the wrath of Inquisition chief De Silva (Sutton). He takes peasant girl Cantana (Peters), who's helped him, and joins Cortez's expedition to Mexico and the search for Aztec riches. Lots of adventures and old-fashioned pageantry. Peters' screen debut. 141m/C VHS, Closed Caption. Tyrone Power, Jean Peters, Cesar Romero, Lee J. Cobb, John Sutton, Antonio Moreno, Thomas Gomez, Alan Mowbray; **D:** Henry King; **W:**

Lamar Trotti; **C:** Charles Clarke, Arthur E. Arling; **M:** Alfred Newman. Nominations: Academy Awards '47: Original Dramatic/Comedy Score. *FXV*

The Captain from Koepenick 🐾🐾½
Der Hauptmann von Koepenick 1956 Popular true life comedy about a Berlin cobbler in 1906 who rebels against military bureaucracy by impersonating a Prussian officer and wreaking havoc on his town, arresting authorities and capturing soldiers, only to enjoy folk herodom when his ruse is discovered. Remake of Richard Oswald's 1931 classic. In German with subtitles. **93m/B VHS, Beta.** *GE* Heinz Ruehmann, Hannelore Schroth, Martin Held, Erich Schellow; **D:** Helmut Kaeutner. *NOS, FCT*

Captain Horatio Hornblower 🐾🐾🐾
1951 A colorful drama about the life and loves of the British sea captain during the Napoleonic wars. Peck is rather out of his element as the courageous, swashbuckling hero (Errol Flynn was originally cast) but there's enough fast-paced derring-do to make this a satisfying saga. Based on the novel by C.S. Forester. **117m/C VHS, Beta, LV.** *GB* Gregory Peck, Virginia Mayo, Robert Beatty, Denis O'Dea, Christopher Lee; **D:** Raoul Walsh; **W:** Ivan Goff; **C:** Guy Green. *WAR*

Captain January 🐾🐾½ 1936 (G)
Crusty old lighthouse keeper rescues little orphan girl with curly hair from drowning and everyone breaks into cutesy song and dance, interrupted only when the authorities try to separate the two. Also available colorized. ♫At the Codfish Ball; Early Bird; The Right Somebody to Love. **81m/B VHS, Closed Caption.** Shirley Temple, Guy Kibbee, Buddy Ebsen, Slim Summerville, Jane Darwell, June Lang, George Irving, Si Jenks; **D:** David Butler. *FXV*

Captain Kidd 🐾🐾½ 1945
Laughton huffs and puffs and searches for treasure on the high seas, finds himself held captive with rest of cast in anemic swashbuckler. **83m/B VHS, Beta.** Charles Laughton, John Carradine, Randolph Scott, Reginald Owen, Gilbert Roland, Barbara Britton, John Qualen, Sheldon Leonard; **D:** Rowland V. Lee; **C:** Archie Stout. Nominations: Academy Awards '45: Original Dramatic/Comedy Score. *MRV, NOS, HHT*

Captain Kronos: Vampire Hunter 🐾🐾🐾
Kronos 1974 (R) Captain Kronos fences thirsty foes in Hammer horror hybrid. Artsy, atmospheric and atypical, it's written and directed with tongue firmly in cheek by Clemens, who penned many an "Avengers" episode. **91m/C VHS, Beta.** *GB* Horst Janson, John Carson, Caroline Munro, Ian Hendry, Shane Briant, Wanda Ventham; **D:** Brian Clemens; **W:** Brian Clemens. *PAR*

Captain Newman, M.D. 🐾🐾½ 1963
Three army guys visit stiff shrink Peck during the final months of WWII in VA ward for the mentally disturbed. Much guilt and agonizing, with comic relief courtesy of Curtis. Peck is sub par, the direction flounders and there's something unsettling about quicksilver shifts from pathos to parody. Nonetheless touching with fine performance from Darin as guilt ridden hero. Based on the novel by Leo Rosten. **126m/C VHS, Beta.** Gregory Peck, Bobby Darin, Tony Curtis, Angie Dickinson, Eddie Albert, James Gregory, Jane Withers, Larry Storch, Robert Duvall; **D:** David Miller. Nominations: Academy Awards '63: Best Adapted Screenplay, Best Sound, Best Supporting Actor (Darin). *USH*

Captain Nuke and the Bomber Boys 🐾½
Demolition Day 1995 (PG) Three teenagers, who've stumbled across an atomic bomb, decide to use the device to get school called off. Instead, they wind up with the FBI and a couple of crooks after them. **?m/C VHS, Closed Caption.** Joe Mantegna, Martin Sheen, Joe Piscopo, Joanna Pacula, Rod Steiger. *NHO*

Captain Ron 🐾½ 1992 (PG-13)
Harried couple Short and Place inherit a large boat and, with their two smart-mouthed kids, go to the Caribbean to sail the boat back to the U.S. Of course they know nothing about sailing, so they hire Captain Ron (Russell), a one-eyed, Long John Silver-talk-

ing boat captain. From there, numerous mishaps occur. Amusing sounding premise sinks like a stone. Russell looks great in his teeny-weeny bikini, and the scenery is beautiful, but that's about it. **CW:** Some language and sensual situations. **104m/C VHS, Beta, LV, Closed Caption.** Kurt Russell, Martin Short, Mary Kay Place, Meadow Sisto, Benjamin Salisbury; **D:** Thom Eberhardt; **W:** Thom Eberhardt. *TOU*

Captain Scarlett 🐾½ 1953
Formulaic swashbuckler has nobleman Greene and highway guy Young fighting nasty French Royalists who've been putting the pressure on impecunious peasants. Runaway Spanish damsel in distress courtesy of Amar. Most novel aspect of the production is that the post-Napoleon French terrain has that vaguely south of the border feel. **75m/C VHS, Beta.** Richard Greene, Leonora Amar, Isobel Del Puerto, Nedrick Young, Manolo Fabregas; **D:** Thomas Carr. *NOS, MRV, GEM*

Captain Sinbad 🐾🐾½ 1963
Captain Sinbad must destroy the evil El Kerim, but first he must tackle a many-headed ogre, man-eating fish and crocodiles, a large fist clad in a spiked glove, an invisible monster, and more. To kill the villain, Sinbad must destroy his heart, which is kept in a tower with no entrance. A huge, witty, epic production with lots of special effects. This one is fun. **85m/C VHS.** Guy Williams, Heidi Bruhl, Pedro Armendariz Sr., Abraham Sofaer, Bernie Hamilton, Helmut Schneider; **D:** Byron Haskin. *MGM*

Captain Swagger 🐾½ 1925
A man on the brink of thievery experiences some changes that keep him on the right side of the law. **50m/B VHS, Beta.** Rod La Rocque, Sue Carol, Richard Tucker, Victor Potel, Ullrich Haupt; **D:** Edward H. Griffith. *GPV*

Captains Courageous 🐾🐾🐾 1937
Rich brat Bartholomew takes a dip sans life jacket while leaning over an ocean liner railing to relieve himself of the half dozen ice cream sodas imprudently consumed at sea. Picked up by a Portuguese fishing boat, he at first treats his mandatory three month voyage as an unscheduled cab ride, but eventually, through a deepening friendship with crewman Tracy, develops a hitherto unheralded work ethic. The boy's filial bond with Tracy, of course, requires that the seaman meet with watery disaster. Based on the Rudyard Kipling novel. Director Fleming went on to "Gone With the Wind" and "The Wizard of Oz." **116m/B VHS, Beta.** Spencer Tracy, Lionel Barrymore, Freddie Bartholomew, Mickey Rooney, Melvyn Douglas, Charley Grapewin, John Carradine, Bobby Watson, Jack LaRue; **D:** Victor Fleming. Academy Awards '37: Best Actor (Tracy); National Board of Review Awards '37: 10 Best Films of the Year; Nominations: Academy Awards '37: Best Film Editing, Best Picture, Best Screenplay. *MGM, BMV, BTV*

Captains Courageous 🐾🐾½ 1995
TV adaptation of the 1897 novel by Rudyard Kipling finds pampered rich kid Vadas learning to become a man at the hands of stalwart sea captain Urich. **93m/C VHS.** Robert Urich, Kenny Vadas, Kaj-Erik Eriksen, Robert Wisden, Duncan Fraser; **D:** Michael Anderson Jr.; **W:** John McGreevey; **C:** Glen MacPherson; **M:** Eric N. Robertson, Claude Desjardins. *CAF*

Captains of the Clouds 🐾🐾½ 1942
Unabashedly patriotic film starring Cagney as a daredevil, independent Canadian bush pilot who makes his own flying rules. When WWII begins he joins the Royal Canadian Air Force but washes out when he can't follow orders. However, he finds a way to prove himself a hero as a civilian pilot ferrying a bomber to England. Cagney's first Technicolor film. **113m/C VHS.** James Cagney, Dennis (Stanley Morner) Morgan, Brenda Marshall, Alan Hale, George Tobias, Reginald Gardiner, Reginald Denny, Russell Arms, Paul Cavanagh, Charles Halton; **D:** Michael Curtiz; **M:** Max Steiner. Nominations: Academy Awards '42: Best Color Cinematography. *MGM, FCT*

Captain's Paradise 🐾🐾🐾 1953
Golden Fleece captain Guinness chugs between wives in Gibraltar and North Africa, much to the adulation of chief officer Goldner. While Gibraltar's little woman Johnson is homegrown homebody, little

woman de Carlo is paint the town red type, allowing Guinness to have cake and eat it too, it seems, except that he's inconveniently positioned in front of a firing squad at movie's start. **89m/B VHS, Beta.** *GB* Alec Guinness, Yvonne De Carlo, Celia Johnson, Miles Malleson, Nicholas Phipps, Ferdinand "Ferdy" Mayne, Sebastian Cabot; **D:** Anthony Kimmins; **M:** Malcolm Arnold. Nominations: Academy Awards '53: Best Story. *FCT*

The Captain's Table 🐾🐾 1960
Former cargo vessel captain Gregson is given luxury liner to command, and fails to revise his cargo captain style to fit new crew and clientele. British cast saves unremarkable script from mediocrity. **90m/C VHS.** *GB* John Gregson, Peggy Cummins, Donald Sinden, Nadia Gray; **D:** Jack Lee. *PAR*

Captive 🐾½ 1987 (R)
Spoiled heiress is kidnapped by terrorist trio and brainwashed into anti-establishment Hearst-like creature. **98m/C VHS, Beta.** Oliver Reed, Irina Brook, Xavier DeLuc, Hiro Arai; **D:** Paul Mayersberg. *VTR*

Captive Heart 🐾🐾🐾 1947
Czech soldier Redgrave assumes the identity of a dead British officer in order to evade Nazis in WWII. Captured and imprisoned in camp reserved for British POWs, his stalagmates think they smell a spy, but he manages to convince them he's an OK Joe. Meanwhile, he's been writing letters home to the little missus, which means he's got a little explaining to do when he's released from prison. Especially fine Redgrave performance. **86m/B VHS, Beta.** *GB* Michael Redgrave, Basil Radford, Jack Warner, Jimmy Hanley, Rachel Kempson, Mervyn Johns; **D:** Basil Dearden. *NOS, DVT, VEC*

Captive Hearts 🐾 1987 (PG)
Well frayed story holds cast captive in sushi romance. Two American flyers are shot down and taken prisoner in isolated Japanese mountain village, and one is shot by Cupid's arrow. **97m/C VHS, Beta, Closed Caption.** Noriyuki "Pat" Morita, Michael Sarrazin, Chris Makepeace; **D:** Paul Almond; **M:** David Benoit. *MGM, FOX*

A Captive in the Land 🐾½ 1991 (PG)
Routine survival pic pits two strangers against the frozen Arctic tundra. Potapov is a Soviet airman who's too injured to walk when he's discovered by American meteorologist Waterston. When a rescue seems unlikely, the two are forced to try for a trek to civilization. Based on the novel by James Aldridge. **96m/C VHS.** Sam Waterston, Alexander Potapov; **D:** John Berry; **M:** Bill Conti, Lee Gold. *LIV*

Captive Planet 🐾 1978
Bargain basement FX and really atrocious acting hold audience captive in routine earth on the verge of obliteration yarn. **95m/C VHS, Beta.** Sharon Baker, Chris Auram, Anthony Newcastle; **D:** Al Bradley. *NO*

Captive Rage 🐾 1988 (R)
South American general Reed hijacks planeful of girlies to encourage US to release his son, who's in trouble because he swaps money for white powder. Violence lives up to title, all else disappoints. **99m/C VHS, Beta.** Oliver Reed, Robert Vaughn, Claudia Udy; **D:** Cedric Sundstrom. *MCG*

The Captive: The Longest Drive 2 🐾🐾 1976 (PG-13)
Matheson and Russell play two recently reunited brothers in search of their sister, whom they believe is still a captive of the Cheyenne Indians who also raised Russell. Along the way the two come to the aid of a pioneer woman and her young son. This western was actually a brief television series known as "The Quest," and is a continuation of the pilot episode released on video as "The Longest Drive." **80m/C VHS, LV, Closed Caption.** Kurt Russell, Tim Matheson. *THV*

Captive Wild Woman 🐾🐾½ 1943
Mad scientist Dr. Sigmund Walters (Carradine) transforms an ape into the beautiful Paula Depress (Aquanetta), who promptly joins the circus as a mysterious animal trainer. Unfortunately, she falls in love with fellow trainer Fred (Stone), who already has a gal, bringing back the beast in the pretty Paula. Sequelled by "Jungle Captive" and

"Jungle Woman." **61m/B VHS, Closed Caption.** Acquanetta, John Carradine, Milburn Stone, Evelyn Ankers, Lloyd Corrigan, Vince Barnett, Paul Fix; **D:** Edward Dmytryk; **W:** Griffin Jay, Henry Sucher. *USH*

Captives 🐾🐾½ **1994 (R)** Middle-class dentist Rachel Clifford (Ormond), recently separated from her husband, takes a part-time job at a local prison where she becomes attracted to her patient, Cockney charmer Philip Chaney (Roth). He's coming to the end of a 10-year sentence and the lusty duo manage to consummate their relationship during one of Philip's day-releases. Only problem is fellow con Towler (Salmon) notices what's happening and blackmails and threatens Rachel—leading to a violent confrontation. Roth and Ormond click believably as opposites-attract partners though the script has some weak elements. *CW:* Strong sex scene, and for language and some violence. **100m/C VHS, LV, Closed Caption.** *GB* Tim Roth, Julia Ormond, Colin Salmon, Keith Allen, Siobhan Redmond, Peter Capaldi, Richard Hawley, Annette Badland, Jeff Nuttal; **D:** Angela Pope; **W:** Frank Deasy; **C:** Remi Adefarasin; **M:** Colin Towns. *TOU*

The Capture 🐾🐾🐾 **1950** Above-average story told in flashback has Ayres hiding out in Mexico because he thought he killed an innocent man. He seeks out the widow to question her about him and they wind up marrying. When he finds the real culprit, the man is killed and the evidence points to Ayres. Ayres and Wright are great, as is the native Mexican musical score. **67m/B VHS.** Lew Ayres, Teresa Wright, Victor Jory, Jacqueline White, Jimmy Hunt, Duncan Renaldo, William "Billy" Bakewell; **D:** John Sturges. *NOS*

The Capture of Bigfoot 🐾 **1979 (PG)** Barefoot monster tracks footprints around town after 25 years of peace, and evil businessman attempts to capture creature for personal gain. **92m/C VHS, Beta.** Stafford Morgan, Katherine Hopkins, Richard Kennedy, Otis Young, George Flower, John Goff; **D:** Bill Rebane. *AHV*

The Capture of Grizzly Adams 🐾½ **1982** Framed for murder, Adams and his ever-faithful companion Ben the bear must not only clear his name but outwit a band of outlaws who are holding his young daughter captive. Made for television. **96m/C VHS.** Dan Haggerty, Chuck Connors, June Lockhart, Kim Darby, Noah Beery Jr., Keenan Wynn. *WOV*

Captured in Chinatown 🐾 **1935** Dog chases bad guys in Chinatown. Bow wow. **53m/B VHS, Beta, LV.** Marion Shilling, Charles Delaney, Philo McCullough, Robert Ellis; **D:** Elmer Clifton. *SNC*

Car Crash 🐾 **19??** Organized crime hits stock car racing head on to produce crashing bore. **103m/C VHS.** Joey Travolta, Anna Obregon, Vittorio Mezzogiorno. *NO*

Car 54, Where Are You? **1961** The first situation comedy about police officers ran on television from 1961-1963. Join offbeat New York cops Gunther Toody and Francis Muldoon of the beleaguered 53rd Precinct. Each cassette contains two episodes. Eight cassettes. **50m/B VHS.** Fred Gwynne, Joe E. Ross, Nipsey Russell, Al Lewis; **D:** Stanley Prager, Nat Hiken. *REP, FCT, MOV*

Car 54, Where Are You? 🐾 **1994 (PG-13)** Exceedingly lame remake of the exceedingly lame television series, which ran for only two seasons, 1961-63. This time, Toody (Johansen) and Muldoon (McGinley) are protecting a mafia stool pigeon (Piven), while vampy Velma Velour (Drescher) sets her sights on Muldoon. Not many laughs and a waste of a talented cast. Sat on the shelf at Orion for three years (with good reason). *CW:* Language and sexual suggestiveness. **89m/C VHS, LV, Closed Caption.** David Johansen, Fran Drescher, Rosie O'Donnell, John C. McGinley, Nipsey Russell, Al Lewis, Daniel Baldwin, Jeremy Piven; **D:** Bill Fishman; **W:** Ebbe Roe Smith, Erik Tarloff, Peter McCarthy, Peter Crabbe; **M:** Bernie Worrell, Pray For Rain. Golden Raspberry Awards '94: Worst Supporting Actress (O'Donnell). *ORI*

Car Trouble 🐾🐾½ **1986 (R)** Young English husband buys new Jaguar and wife's not so minor car trouble causes major marital trouble. Funny-bone-tickling pairing of Walters and Charleson. **93m/C VHS, Beta, LV.** *GB* Julie Walters, Ian Charleson; **D:** David Green; **M:** Meat Loaf. *MCG*

Car Wash 🐾🐾½ **1976 (PG)** L.A. carwash provides a soap-opera setting for disjointed comic bits about owners of dirty cars and people who hose them down for a living. Econo budget and lite plot, but serious comic talent. A sort of disco carwash version of "Grand Hotel." **97m/C VHS, Beta.** Franklin Ajaye, Sully Boyer, Richard Brestoff, George Carlin, Richard Pryor, Melanie Mayron, Ivan Dixon, Antonio Fargas; **D:** Michael A. Schultz; **W:** Joel Schumacher. *USH, FCT*

Caravaggio 🐾🐾🐾 **1986** Controversial biography of the late Renaissance painter famous for his bisexuality, fondness for prostitute models, violence and depravity. Photography by Gabriel Beristain reproduces the artist's visual style. **97m/C VHS, Beta, LV.** *GB* Nigel Terry, Sean Bean, Tilda Swinton; **D:** Derek Jarman; **W:** Derek Jarman. *TPV, FCT, CCN*

Caravan to Vaccares 🐾 **1974 (PG)** French Duke hires young American to sneak Eastern European scientist into the States, and little suspense ensues. Based on Alistair MacLean novel. **98m/C VHS, Beta.** David Birney, Charlotte Rampling; **D:** Geoffrey Reeve. *MED*

The Caravan Trail 🐾🐾 **1946** A cowboy becomes marshal in order to bring to justice those who have stolen land and murdered his friend. This was shot in color, which was rare for the 1940s. **53m/C VHS.** Eddie Dean, Lash LaRue, Emmett Lynn, Jean Carlin, Charles "Blackie" King, Bob Barron, Lloyd Ingraham, Bud Osborne; **D:** Robert Emmett Tansey. *NOS, RXM, HEG*

Carbon Copy 🐾🐾 **1981 (PG)** Successful white executive has life turned inside out when his seventeen-year old illegitimate son, who happens to be black, decides it's time to look up dear old dad. Typical comedy-with-a-moral. **92m/C VHS, Beta, LV.** George Segal, Susan St. James, Jack Warden, Paul Winfield, Dick Martin, Vicky Dawson, Tom Poston, Denzel Washington; **D:** Michael A. Schultz; **W:** Stanley Shapiro; **M:** Bill Conti. *COL*

Cardiac Arrest 🐾 **1974 (PG)** Lunatic eviscerates victims in trolley town. They left their hearts in San Francisco. **95m/C VHS, Beta.** Garry Goodrow, Mike Chan, Max Gail; **D:** Murray Mintz. *MED*

The Cardinal 🐾🐾½ **1963** Priestly young Tryon rises through ecclesiastical ranks to become Cardinal, struggling through a plethora of tests of faith, none so taxing as the test of the audience's patience. Had Preminger excised some sixty minutes of footage, he might have had a compelling portrait of faith under fire, but as it stands, the cleric's life is epic confusion. Fine acting, even from Tryon, who later went on to bookish fame, and from Huston who's normally on the other side of the camera. McNamara's final performance. Based on the Henry Morton Robinson novel. **175m/C VHS, Beta, LV.** Tom Tryon, Carol Lynley, Dorothy Gish, Maggie McNamara, Cecil Kellaway, John Huston, John Saxon, Burgess Meredith; **D:** Otto Preminger; **C:** Leon Shamroy. Golden Globe Awards '64: Best Film—Drama, Best Supporting Actor (Huston); National Board of Review Awards '63: 10 Best Films of the Year; Nominations: Academy Awards '63: Best Art Direction/Set Decoration (Color), Best Color Cinematography, Best Costume Design (Color), Best Director (Preminger), Best Film Editing, Best Supporting Actor (Huston). *WAR, IME, VTR*

The Care Bears Movie 🐾🐾 **1984 (G)** The Care Bears leave their cloud home in Care-a-lot to try and teach earthlings how to share their feelings of love and caring for each other. **75m/C VHS, Beta, LV.** **D:** Arna Selznick; **V:** Mickey Rooney, Georgia Engel, Harry Dean Stanton. *LIV, VES, FCT*

The Care Bears Movie 2: A New Generation 🐾🐾 **1986 (G)** Sequel to the sweet adventures of the animated bear family and their new offspring. **77m/C VHS, Beta, Closed Caption.** **D:** Dale Schott; **V:** Maxine Miller, Pam Hyatt, Hadley Key. *COL*

Career 🐾🐾½ **1959** An overwrought, depressing drama about the trials and tribulations of an actor trying to make it on Broadway. He'll try anything to succeed. Good direction, but so-so acting. **105m/B VHS, LV, Closed Caption.** Dean Martin, Anthony (Tony) Franciosa, Shirley MacLaine, Carolyn Jones, Joan Blackman, Robert Middleton, Donna Douglas; **D:** Joseph Anthony; **C:** Joseph LaShelle. Golden Globe Awards '60: Best Actor—Drama (Franciosa); Nominations: Academy Awards '59: Best Art Direction/Set Decoration (B & W), Best Black and White Cinematography, Best Costume Design (B & W). *PAR*

Career Opportunities 🐾½ **1991 (PG-13)** "Home Alone" clone for teenagers from John Hughes' factory. Whaley is an unsuccessful con-artist who finally gets a job as the night janitor of the local department store. He fools around at company expense until he finds the town's beauty (Connelly) asleep in a dressing room. The pair then play make-believe until its time to thwart some small-time thieves. Unexciting and unrealistic in the worst way; no wonder Candy isn't billed—he probably didn't want to be. **83m/C VHS, LV, Closed Caption.** Frank Whaley, Jennifer Connelly, Dermot Mulroney, Kieran Mulroney, John M. Jackson, Jenny O'Hara, Noble Willingham, Barry Corbin, Denise Galik, William Forsythe; **Cameos:** John Candy; **D:** Bryan Gordon; **W:** John Hughes; **M:** Thomas Newman. *USH*

Carefree 🐾🐾🐾 **1938** Dizzy radio singer Rogers can't make up her mind about beau Bellamy, so he sends her to analyst Astaire. Seems she can't even dream a little dream until shrink Astaire prescribes that she ingest some funny food, which causes her to dream she's in love with the Fredman. Au contraire, says he, it's a Freudian thing, and he hypnotically suggests that she really loves Bellamy. The two line up to march down the aisle together, and Fred stops dancing just long enough to realize he's in love with Ginger. A screwball comedy with music. 🎵I Used to be Colorblind; The Night is Filled With Music; Change Partners; The Yam. **83m/B VHS, Beta, LV.** Fred Astaire, Ginger Rogers, Ralph Bellamy, Jack Carson, Franklin Pangborn, Hattie McDaniel; **D:** Mark Sandrich; **M:** Irving Berlin. Nominations: Academy Awards '38: Best Interior Decoration, Best Song ("Change Partners and Dance with Me"), Best Score. *TTC, IME, IME*

Careful 🐾🐾 **1994** Butler-in-training Neale courts Neville in an alpine mountain village where silence is golden, or at least being quiet will lessen the chance of an avalanche. Dig a little deeper and you find incest, repression and other nasty things. Highly individualistic black comedy parodies German Expressionism and Freudian psychology to the point of absurdity, dealing with snow, sex, sleep, spirits, and obsessive/compulsive personality disorders. Third film from Canadian cult director Maddin is awash in vivid primary colors when it suits the scene's mood and employs between-scenes titles in a homage to cinematic antiquity. **100m/C VHS.** Kyle McCulloch, Gosia Dobrowolska, Jackie Burroughs, Sarah Neville, Brent Neale, Paul Cox, Victor Cowie, Michael O'Sullivan, Vince Rimmer, Katya Gardner; **D:** Guy Maddin; **W:** Guy Maddin, George Toles; **M:** John McCulloch. *KIV*

Careful, He Might Hear You 🐾🐾🐾 **1984 (PG)** Abandoned by his father, six-year-old P.S. becomes a pawn between his dead mother's two sisters, one working class and the other wealthy, and his worldview is further overturned by the sudden reappearance of his prodigal father. Set in Depression-era Australia, Schultz's vision is touching and keenly observed, and manages a sort of child's eye sense of proportion. Based on a novel by Sumner Locke Elliott. **113m/C VHS, Beta, Closed Caption.** *AU* Nicholas Gledhill, Wendy Hughes, Robyn Nevin, John Hargreaves; **D:** Carl Schultz. Australian Film Institute '83: Best Actress (Hughes), Best Film. *FOX*

Caribe 🎬½ 1987 Caribbean travelogue masquerades as spy thriller. Arms smuggling goes awry, and neither voodoo nor bikinied blondes can prevent audience from dozing. Never released theatrically. 96m/C VHS, Beta, LV. John Savage, Kara Glover, Stephen McHattie, Sam Malkin; **D:** Michael Kennedy. *LIV, VES*

The Cariboo Trail 🎬🎬 1950 Two prospecting men seek their fortune in British Columbia, the golden West of Canada in the 1890s. But they find themselves opposed by a ruthless rancher and claim-jumpers. Actually filmed in Colorado with excellent cinematography and solid performances from some big names, it's still a run-of-the-mill entry. Made the same year that the Gabby Hayes' show first aired. 80m/C VHS, LV, **Closed Caption.** Randolph Scott, George "Gabby" Hayes, Bill Williams, Victor Jory; **D:** Edwin L. Marin. *FRH, IME*

Carlito's Way 🎬🎬🎬 1993 (R) Puerto Rican crime czar Carlito Brigante (Pacino) has just gotten out of jail and wants to go straight. But his drug underworld cohorts don't believe he can do it. Penn (barely recognizable) is great as a sleazy coked-out lawyer who's way out of his league. Remarkably subdued violence given DePalma's previous rep—it's effective without being gratuitous, especially the final shootout set in Grand Central Station. Pacino's performance is equally subdued, with controlled tension and lots of eye contact rather than grandiose emotions. Based on the novels "Carlito's Way" and "After Hours" by Edwin Torres. Pacino and DePalma previously teamed up for "Scarface."**CW:** Drug content and language, strong violence, and sexuality. 145m/C VHS, LV, **Closed Caption.** Al Pacino, Sean Penn, Penelope Ann Miller, Luis Guzman, John Leguizamo, Ingrid Rogers, James Rebhorn, Viggo Mortensen, Jorge Porcel, Joseph Siravo, Adrian Pasdar; **D:** Brian DePalma; **W:** David Koepp; **C:** Stephen Burum; **M:** Patrick Doyle. Nominations: Golden Globe Awards '94: Best Supporting Actor (Penn), Best Supporting Actress (Miller). *USH*

Carlton Browne of the F.O. 🎬🎬½ *Man in a Cocked Hat* 1959 Bumbling Brit diplomat Thomas visits tiny Pacific island of Gallardia, forgotten by the mother country for some fifty years, to insure tenuous international agreement after the island's king dies. Not sterling Sellers but some shining moments. 88m/C VHS, Beta. **GB** Peter Sellers, Terry-Thomas, Luciana Paluzzi, Ian Bannen; **D:** Roy Boulting, Jeffrey Dell; **W:** Roy Boulting; **M:** John Addison. *FCT*

Carmen 🎬🎬🎬 1983 (R) Choreographer casts Carmen and finds life imitates art when he falls under the spell of the hotblooded Latin siren. Bizet's opera lends itself to erotically charged flamenco context. Well acted, impressive scenes including cigarette girls' dance fight and romance between Carmen and Don Jose. In Spanish with English subtitles. 99m/C VHS, Beta. **SP** Antonio Gades, Laura Del Sol, Paco DeLucia, Christina Hoyos; **D:** Carlos Saura; **C:** Pasquale De Santos. British Academy Awards '84: Best Foreign Film; Nominations: Academy Awards '83: Best Foreign Language Film. *CTH, MED*

Carmen Jones 🎬🎬🎬 1954 Bizet's tale of fickle femme fatale Carmen heads South with an all black cast and new lyrics by Hammerstein II. Soldier Belafonte falls big time for factory working belle Dandridge during the war, and runs off with miss thang after he kills his C.O. and quits the army. Tired of prettyboy Belafonte, Dandridge's eye wanders upon prize pugilist Escamillo, inspiring ex-soldier beau to wring her throaty little neck. Film debuts of Carroll and Peters. More than a little racist undertone to the direction. Actors' singing is dubbed. 🎵Dat's Love; Dere's a Cafe on de Corner; Beat Out Dat Rhythm on a Drum; You Talk Just Like My Maw; Stand Up and Fight; Dis Flower; My Joe. 105m/C VHS, LV, **Closed Caption.** Dorothy Dandridge, Harry Belafonte, Pearl Bailey, Roy Glenn, Diahann Carroll, Brock Peters; **D:** Otto Preminger; **C:** Sam Leavitt. Golden Globe Awards '55: Best Film—Mu-

sical/Comedy; Nominations: Academy Awards '54: Best Actress (Dandridge), Scoring of a Musical. *FXV*

Carmilla 1989 An adaptation of the Sheridan Le Fanu lesbian vampire tale. From Shelley Duvall's cable television series "Nightmare Classics." 60m/C VHS, Beta. Meg Tilly, Ione Skye, Roddy McDowall, Roy Dotrice; **D:** Gabrielle Beaumont. *NO*

Carnage 🎬 1984 Hungry house consumes inhabitants. 91m/C VHS, Beta. Leslie Den Dooven, Michael Chiodo, Deeann Veeder; **D:** Andy Milligan. *MED*

Carnal Crimes 🎬½ 1991 (R) Well-acted upscale softcore trash about a sensuous woman, ignored by her wealthy middle-aged lawyer husband and drawn to a young stud photographer with a shady past and S&M tendencies. Available in a sexy unrated version also.**CW:** Language, violence, and strong sensuality. 103m/C VHS. Martin Hewitt, Linda Carol, Rich Crater, Alex Kubik, Yvette Stefens, Paula Trickey; **D:** Alexander Gregory Hippolyte; **W:** Jon Robert Samsel; **M:** Matthew Ross, Jeff Fishman. *NO*

Carnal Knowledge 🎬🎬🎬 1971 (R) Carnal knowledge of the me generation. Three decades in the sex-saturated lives of college buddies Nicholson and Garfunkel, chronicled through girlfriends, affairs and marriages. Controversial upon release, it's not a flattering anatomy of Y chromosome carriers. Originally written as a play. Kane's debut. 96m/C VHS, Beta, LV, 8mm. Jack Nicholson, Candice Bergen, Art Garfunkel, Ann-Margret, Rita Moreno, Carol Kane; **D:** Mike Nichols; **W:** Jules Feiffer; **C:** Giuseppe Rotunno. Golden Globe Awards '72: Best Supporting Actress (Ann-Margret); Nominations: Academy Awards '71: Best Supporting Actress (Ann-Margret). *COL, FOX, CRC*

Carnival in Flanders 🎬🎬🎬½ *La Kermesse Heroique* 1935 When Spanish invaders enter a small 17th century Flemish village they discover all the men have disappeared. So it's up to the women to save the town from destruction—and they decide to do it by seducing the invaders. Classic French costume farce with a witty script and fine performances. In French with English subtitles. 90m/B VHS, Beta. *FR* Francoise Rosay, Louis Jouvet, Jean Murat, Andre Aleme, Micheline Cheirel; **D:** Jacques Feyder; **C:** Harry Stradling. National Board of Review Awards '36: 5 Best Foreign Films of the Year; New York Film Critics Awards '36: Best Foreign Film; Venice Film Festival '36: Best Director (Feyder). *HTV, MRV, HHT*

Carnival Lady 🎬 1933 Silver spooner Vincent is scheduled to tie the knot until little lady-to-be discovers he's a bit out of pocket after the stock market takes a wee dip. Jilted and impecunious, he heads for the big top, where he horns in on the high diver's turf, and it's all downhill from there. 66m/B VHS, Beta. Patricia "Boots" Mallory, Allen Vincent. *VCN*

Carnival of Blood 🎬 1971 (PG) Boring talky scenes punctuated by Coney Island murder mayhem followed by more boring talky scenes. Young's debut, not released for five years. The question's not why they delayed release, but why they bothered at all. A carnival of cliches. 88m/C VHS, Beta. Earle Edgerton, Judith Resnick, Martin Barlosky, John Harris, Burt Young; **W:** Leonard Kirtman. *NO*

Carnival of Souls 🎬🎬🎬 1962 Cult-followed zero budget zombie opera has young Hilligoss and girlfriends take wrong turn off bridge into river. Mysteriously unscathed, Hilligoss rents room and takes job as church organist, but she keeps running into dancing dead people, led by director Harvey. Spooky, very spooky. Laserdisc version offers restored picture quality and a refined audio track, as well as introductory feature on the movie's background. 80m/B VHS, Beta, LV. Candace Hilligoss, Sidney Berger, Frances Feist, Stan Levitt, Art Ellison, Harold (Herk) Harvey; **D:** Harold (Herk) Harvey. *MRV, SNC, NOS*

Carnival Rock 🎬½ 1957 Story of love triangular in seedy nightclub. Club owner Stewart loves chanteuse Cabot who loves card playin' Hutton. Who cares? Maybe hard-core Corman devotees will. Good tunes from the Platters, the Blockbusters, Bob Luman and David Houston.

80m/B VHS, Beta. Susan Cabot, Brian Hutton, David J. Stewart, Dick Miller; **D:** Roger Corman. *RHI, AOV, FCT*

Carnival Story 🎬½ 1954 Yet another melodramatic cliche about love triangular under the big top. German girl joins American-owned carnival and two guys start acting out unbecoming territorial behavior. Filmed in Germany. 94m/C VHS, Beta. Anne Baxter, Steve Cochran, Lyle Bettger, George Nader; **D:** Kurt Neumann. *NOS, GEM, DVT*

Carnosaur 🎬🎬 1993 (R) Straight from the Corman film factory, this exploitive quickie about dinosaurs harkens back to '50s-style monster epics. Predictable plot with extremely cheap effects. Genetic scientist Dr. Jane Tiptree (Ladd) is hatching diabolic experiments with chickens when things go awry. The experiments result in a bunch of lethal prehistoric creatures wrecking havoc among the community.**CW:** Language and monster violence. 82m/C VHS. Diane Ladd, Raphael Sbarge, Jennifer Runyon, Harrison Page, Clint Howard, Ned Bellamy; **D:** Adam Simon; **W:** Adam Simon; **M:** Nigel Holton. *NHO*

Carnosaur 2 🎬½ 1994 (R) Technicians investigating a power shortage at a secret military mining facility encounter deadly dinos. Entertaining schlock.**CW:** Language; violence; gore. 90m/C VHS, LV. John Savage, Cliff DeYoung, Arabella Holzbog, Ryan Thomas Johnson; **D:** Louis Morneau. *NHO*

Carnosaur 3: Primal Species 🎬½ 1996 Terrorists get big surprise when the cargo they hijack turns out to be three very hungry dinos who make snacks out of them all. Then it's up to commando Valentine, scientist Gunn, and some soldiers to get rid of the beasts. 82m/C VHS. Scott Valentine, Janet Gunn, Rick Dean, Rodger Halstead, Tony Peck; **D:** Jonathan Winfrey. *NHO*

Carny 🎬🎬🎬 1980 (R) Hothead carnival bozo Busey and peacemaker Robertson experience friendship difficulties when runaway Foster rolls in hay with one and then other. Originally conceived as a documentary by "Derby" filmmaker Kaylor, it's a candid, unsavory, behind-the-scenes anatomy. Co-written by "The Band" member Robertson. 102m/C VHS, Beta. Gary Busey, Robbie Robertson, Jodie Foster, Meg Foster, Kenneth McMillan, Elisha Cook Jr., Craig Wasson; **D:** Robert Kaylor; **W:** Robbie Robertson, Thomas Baum; **C:** Harry Stradling Jr.; **M:** Alex North. *FOX, WAR*

Caro Diario 🎬🎬🎬 *Dear Diary* 1993 Three offbeat chapters from director Moretti's own life. "On My Vespa" has the director taking off on a personal tour of Rome, including its cinemas and their influence on him. In "Islands" Moretti and friend Gerardo travel to a series of island communities, including Salina, dominated by only children to whom their parents defer obsessively. "Doctors" finds Moretti experiencing a misdiagnosed medical crisis. Lots of charm and a certain shameless romanticism. Italian with subtitles. 100m/C VHS, LV. *IT* Renato Carpentieri; **D:** Nanni Moretti; **W:** Nanni Moretti; **M:** Nicola Piovani. Cannes Film Festival '94: Best Director (Moretti). *NLC*

Carolina Skeletons 🎬🎬 1992 (R) As a child in a small southern town Gossett, Jr. watched as his brother was accused of a vicious double murder and quickly tried and executed. Thirty years later, the ex-Green Beret returns home to find the real killer and clear his brother's name. But there are those in the town who will do anything to stop their secrets from being revealed.**CW:** Violence to children. 94m/C VHS, LV. Louis Gossett Jr., Bruce Dern, Melissa Leo, Paul Roebling, G.D. Spradlin, Bill Cobbs, Henderson Forsythe, Clifton James; **D:** John Erman; **W:** Tracy Keenan Wynn; **M:** John Morris. *TRI*

Caroline? 🎬🎬🎬 1990 (PG) A wealthy young woman is presumed dead in a plane crash. Now 15 years later a stranger appears at the family home claiming to be Caroline—and wanting her inheritance. Is it possible that what she says is true or is it all an elaborate ruse? An especially good performance by Zimbalist. Made for television as a "Hallmark Hall of Fame" presentation.

Based on the novel "Father's Arcane Daughter" by E.L. Konigsburg. **100m/C VHS, LV, Closed Caption.** Stephanie Zimbalist, Pamela Reed, George Grizzard, Dorothy McGuire, Patricia Neal, Shawn Phelan, Jenny Jacobs; **D:** Joseph Sargent; **M:** Charles Bernstein. *REP*

Caroline at Midnight ♂♂ 1993 (R) After a reporter's former girlfriend, Caroline, dies in a mysterious auto accident he winds up falling for her girlfriend Victoria. Then he discovers both women are connected to drug-dealing cops. Good cast in this atmospheric erotic thriller with plenty of puzzles.**CW:** Language, violence and drug content, and sexuality. **92m/C VHS, LV.** Clayton Rohner, Mia Sara, Timothy Daly, Judd Nelson, Virginia Madsen, Zach Galligan; **D:** Scott McGinnis. *NHO*

Carousel ♂♂♂ 1956 Much-loved Rodgers & Hammerstein musical based on Ferenc Molnar's play "Liliom" (filmed by Fritz Lang in 1935) about a swaggering carnival barker (MacRae) who tries to change his life after he falls in love with a good woman. Killed while attempting to foil a robbery he was supposed to help commit, he begs his heavenly hosts for the chance to return to the mortal realm just long enough to set things straight with his teenage daughter. Now indisputably a classic, the film lost $2 million when it was released. ♪If I Loved You; Soliloquy; You'll Never Walk Alone; What's the Use of Wond'rin; When I Marry Mister Snow; When the Children Are Asleep; A Real Nice Clambake; Carousel Ballet; Carousel Waltz. **128m/C VHS, Beta, LV, Closed Caption.** Gordon MacRae, Shirley Jones, Cameron Mitchell, Gene Lockhart, Barbara Ruick, Robert Rounseville, Richard Deacon, Tor Johnson; **D:** Henry King; **M:** Richard Rodgers, Oscar Hammerstein. *FOX, RDG, HMV*

The Carpathian Eagle ♂ 1981 Police wonder why murdered victims have hearts ripped out while audience wonders what weird title has to do with anything. Routine evisceration fest, part of Elvira's Thriller Video. **60m/C VHS, Beta.** Suzanne Danielle, Sian Phillips, Pierce Brosnan, Anthony Valentine; **D:** Francis Megahy. *LIV*

The Carpenter ♂ 1989 (R) Post-nervous breakdown woman receives nightly visits from guy who builds stuff with wood. Very scary stuff. Also available in slightly longer unrated version. **85m/C VHS, LV.** Wings Hauser, Lynne Adams, Pierce Lenoir, Barbara Ann Jones; **D:** David Wellington. *REP*

Carpet of Horror ♂♂ 1964 The city of London is terrorized by a small ball emitting poison gas in this schlock horror film. Death results when the ball is rolled into the living rooms of intended victims. **?m/C VHS.** Joachim Berger, Carl Lange, Karin Dor. *SNC*

The Carpetbaggers ♂♂ 1964 (PG) Uncannily Howard Hughesian Peppard wallows in wealth and women in Hollywood in the 1920s and 1930s. Spayed version of the Harold Robbins novel. Ladd's final appearance. Followed by the prequel "Nevada Smith." Introduced by Joan Collins. **150m/C VHS, Beta.** George Peppard, Carroll Baker, Alan Ladd, Elizabeth Ashley, Lew Ayres, Martha Hyer, Martin Balsam, Robert Cummings, Archie Moore, Audrey Totter; **D:** Edward Dmytryk; **W:** John Michael Hayes; **M:** Elmer Bernstein. National Board of Review Awards '64: Best Supporting Actor (Balsam). *PAR*

Carpool ♂♂ 1996 (PG) Dumb but amiable comedy finds harried dad Daniel Miller stuck driving a minivan filled with kids to school. Too bad he gets sidetracked and hijacked by bumbling would-be bank robber Franklin Laszlo (Arnold) who takes them hostage and on a really wild ride through the streets and shopping malls of Seattle (except it's filmed in Vancouver). **92m/C VHS, LV, Closed Caption.** Tom Arnold, David Paymer, Rhea Perlman, Rod Steiger, Kim Coates, Rachel Leigh Cook, Mikey Kovar, Micah Gardener, Blake Warkol; **D:** Arthur Hiller; **W:** Don Rhymer; **C:** David M. Walsh; **M:** John Debney. Golden Raspberry Awards '96: Worst Actor (Arnold). *MGM*

Carrie ♂♂♂ 1952 In a part turned down by Cary Grant, Olivier plays a married American who self destructs as the woman he loves scales the heights to fame and fortune. The manager of a posh epicurean mecca, Olivier deserts wife Hopkins and steals big bucks from his boss to head east with paramour Jones, a country bumpkin transplanted to Chicago. Once en route to thespian fame in the Big Apple, Jones abandons her erstwhile beau, who crumbles pathetically. Adapted from Theodore Dreiser's "Sister Carrie," it's mega melodrama, but the performances are above reproach. **118m/B VHS, Beta, LV, Closed Caption.** Laurence Olivier, Jennifer Jones, Miriam Hopkins, Eddie Albert, Basil Ruysdael, Ray Teal, Barry Kelley, Sara Berner, William Reynolds, Mary Murphy, Charles Halton; **D:** William Wyler; **C:** Victor Milner. Nominations: Academy Awards '52: Best Art Direction/Set Decoration (B & W), Best Costume Design (B & W). *PAR, FCT*

Carrie ♂♂♂ 1976 (R) Overprotected by religious fanatic mother Laurie and mocked by the in-crowd, shy, withdrawn high school girl Carrie White is asked to the prom. Realizing she's been made the butt of a joke, she unleashes her considerable telekinetic talents. Travolta, Allen, and Irving are teenagers who get what they deserve. Based on the Stephen King novel. Laserdisc version features the original movie trailer, an interview with screenwriter Lawrence D. Cohen, publicity shots, a study of De Palma's film-making techniques, and commentary by film expert Laurent Bouzereau. **98m/C VHS, Beta, LV.** Sissy Spacek, Piper Laurie, John Travolta, William Katt, Amy Irving, Nancy Allen, Edie McClurg, Betty Buckley; **D:** Brian DePalma; **W:** Lawrence D. Cohen; **M:** Pino Donaggio. National Society of Film Critics Awards '76: Best Actress (Spacek); Nominations: Academy Awards '76: Best Actress (Spacek), Best Supporting Actress (Laurie). *MGM, FOX, CRC*

Carried Away ♂♂ *Acts of Love* 1995 (R) Exposing his middle-aged bod, as well as the myth that he can play only psycho toughs, Hopper, as the Midwestern teacher Joseph, is seduced by a 17-year-old student (Locane) in their small conservative town. Based on Harrison's novel "Farmer," it's a sexually active slice of life with the injured Joseph limping through the care of his dying mother, the fate of the small country school where he teaches and his relationship with longtime lover Rosealee (Amy Irving). Hopper's not the only one playing against type, as Irving turns in a fine performance as the widowed schoolmarm. Director Barreto (and Irving's husband) pushes the envelope with full frontal nudity.**CW:** Nudity, strong sexuality, and language. **109m/C VHS, LV, Closed Caption.** Dennis Hopper, Amy Locane, Gary Busey, Hal Holbrook, Amy Irving, Julie Harris, Christopher Pettiet, Priscilla Pointer, Gail Cronauer; **D:** Bruno Barreto; **W:** Ed Jones; **C:** Declan Quinn; **M:** Bruce Broughton. *NLC*

The Carrier ♂♂ 1987 (R) Smalltown Sleepy Rock is ideal family-raising turf until plague mysteriously blights inhabitants, and townspeople are out to exterminate all potential carriers. Silverman is standout as local spiritual leader; well orchestrated crowd scenes. Best park your IQ before watching. Filmed on location in Manchester, Michigan. **99m/C VHS, Beta.** Gregory Fortescue, Steve Dixon, Paul Silverman; **D:** Nathan J. White. *NO*

Carrington ♂♂♂½ 1995 (R) England's artistic Bloomsbury group is examined through the eccentric relationship of artist Dora Carrington (Thompson) and her love for homosexual Lytton Strachey (Pryce), celebrated author of "Eminent Victorians." There's many a menage as the duo live together with Carrington's husband (Waddington), on whom Strachey has a crush, and both their various amours (though Carrington's heart is reserved for Lytton). Film is distractingly divided into titled segments (from 1915 to 1932) and, while Pryce gives a bravura performance, Thompson is merely enigmatic. Based on Michael Holroyd's biography "Lytton Strachey." Hampton's directorial debut.**CW:** Strong sexuality and

language, nudity. **120m/C VHS, LV. FR GB** Emma Thompson, Jonathan Pryce, Steven Waddington, Sam West, Rufus Sewell, Penelope Wilton, Jeremy Northam, Peter Blythe, Janet McTeer, Alex Kingston, Sebastian Harcombe, Richard Clifford; **D:** Christopher Hampton; **W:** Christopher Hampton; **C:** Denis Lenoir; **M:** Michael Nyman. Cannes Film Festival '95: Special Jury Prize, Best Actor (Pryce); National Board of Review Awards '95: Best Actress (Thompson); Nominations: British Academy Awards '95: Best Actor (Pryce), Best Film. *PGV*

Carrington, V.C. ♂♂♂ *Court Martial* 1954 British army major Niven is brought up for a court-martial on embezzlement charges because he arranges, without official permission, to be reimbursed for money owed to him. A former war hero, he decides to defend himself in court, and, once an affair comes to light, his vindictive wife joins the opposition. Good cast, superlative Niven performance. **100m/B VHS, Beta. GB** David Niven, Margaret Leighton, Noelle Middleton, Laurence Naismith; **D:** Anthony Asquith. *NO*

Carry Me Back ♂½ 1982 Two brothers carry dead dad back to Australian ranch in order to inherit mucho dinero. **93m/C VHS, Beta. AU** Grant Tilly, Kelly Johnson. *LIV*

Carry On Admiral ♂½ *The Ship was Loaded* 1957 Weak British comedy about two friends who get drunk and decide it would be fun to switch identities. One has an easy job as a public relations exec but the other is supposedly the captain of a ship. His lack of sea knowledge causes wacky catastrophes. Unrelated to the "Carry On" series of comedies. **85m/B VHS. GB** David Tomlinson, Brian Reece, Peggy Cummins, Eunice Gayson, A.E. Matthews, Lionel Murton, Joan Sims; **D:** Val Guest; **W:** Val Guest. *FUS*

Carry On at Your Convenience ♂½ 1971 Low-brow humor in and around a toilet factory. **86m/C VHS, Beta. GB** Sidney James, Kenneth Williams, Charles Hawtrey, Joan Sims, Kenneth Cope; **D:** Gerald Thomas. *NO*

Carry On Behind ♂♂ 1975 "Carry On" crew heads for archeological dig and find themselves sharing site with holiday caravan. **95m/C VHS, Beta. GB** Sidney James, Kenneth Williams, Elke Sommer, Joan Sims; **D:** Gerald Thomas. *NO*

Carry On Camping ♂½ 1971 Another entry in the silly series finds James and Bresslaw trying to persuade their girlfriends to go on a camping trip to what the men hope is a nudist colony. They don't find nudists but they do find a group of sex-starved schoolgirls. **88m/C VHS. GB** Sidney James, Bernard Bresslaw, Kenneth Williams, Joan Sims, Charles Hawtrey, Barbara Windsor; **D:** Gerald Thomas; **W:** Talbot Rothwell. *TVC*

Carry On Cleo ♂♂½ 1965 "Carry On" spoof of Shakespeare's "Antony and Cleopatra." **91m/C VHS, Beta. GB** Sidney James, Amanda Barrie, Kenneth Williams, Kenneth Connor, Jim Dale, Charles Hawtrey, Joan Sims; **D:** Gerald Thomas. *NO*

Carry On Cowboy ♂♂ *Rumpo Kid* 1966 "Carry On" Western parody of "High Noon." **91m/C VHS, Beta. GB** Sidney James, Kenneth Williams, Jim Dale. *NO*

Carry On Cruising ♂ 1962 "Carry On" gang attacks sailing world with low humor and raunchiness. **89m/C VHS, Beta.** Sidney James, Kenneth Williams, Liz Fraser; **D:** Gerald Thomas. *NO*

Carry On Dick ♂♂ 1975 What made the seemingly endless "Carry On" series of super-low-budget British farces such a hit is a mystery not to be solved. Low production values, scripts that peter out midway, and manifest humor don't normally a classic make; and yet the gang has its following. "Dick," a detective movie spoof, was preceded by some twenty-odd carryings on; suffice it to say that the series, which began in 1958 with "Carry on Sergeant," has not improved with age in subsequent incarnations. **95m/C VHS. GB** Sidney James, Joan Sims; **D:** Gerald Thomas. *NO*

Carry On Doctor 🎞🎞🎞 1968 British series continues as characters of questionable competence join the medical profession. Hospital staff gets caught in battle over secret weight loss formula. 95m/C VHS. **GB** Frankie Howerd, Kenneth Williams, Jim Dale, Barbara Windsor; **D:** Gerald Thomas. PAR

Carry On Emmanuelle 🎞 1978 Bedroom diplomat Emmanuelle enters international politics by taking on foreign legion. Part of the British "Carry On" series. **GB** Suzanne Danielle, Kenneth O'Connor, Kenneth Williams, Beryl Reid; **D:** Gerald Thomas. NO

Carry On England 🎞 1976 Mercifully, the gang didn't carry on much beyond this entry, in which a WWII antiaircraft fleet captain bumbles through the usual pranks and imbroglios. 89m/C VHS. **GB** Kenneth Connor, Patrick Mower, Judy Geeson; **D:** Gerald Thomas. NO

Carry On Henry VIII 🎞½ 1971 Slapstick sex humor with Henry marrying the French Marie of Normandie and having to deal with both her addiction to garlic and the fact that she's pregnant by her lover. 88m/C VHS. **GB** Sidney James, Kenneth Williams, Joan Sims, Charles Hawtrey, Barbara Windsor, Kenneth Connor, Julian Holloway; **D:** Gerald Thomas; **W:** Talbot Rothwell. TVC

Carry On Nurse 🎞🎞 1959 Men's ward in a British hospital declares war on nurses and the rest of the hospital. The second of the "Carry On" series. 86m/B VHS, Beta. **GB** Shirley Eaton, Kenneth Connor, Hattie Jacques, Wilfrid Hyde-White; **D:** Gerald Thomas. NOS, VYY, VDM

Carry On 'Round the Bend 🎞½ 1972 Williams, who played in the original ("Carry On Sergeant"), and Carry On regulars (charpei-mugged James and ever-zaftig Jacques), go 'round the bend in yet another installment of the British spoof. 89m/C VHS. **GB** Sidney James, Kenneth Williams, Hattie Jacques; **D:** Gerald Thomas. NO

Carry On Screaming 🎞🎞 1966 "Carry On" does horror. A pair of goofy detectives trail monsters suspected in kidnapping. 97m/C VHS. **GB** Harry H. Corbett, Kenneth Williams, Fenella Fielding, Joan Sims, Charles Hawtrey, Jim Dale, Angela Douglas, Jon Pertwee; **D:** Gerald Thomas. MOV

The Cars That Ate Paris 🎞🎞🎞 The Cars That Eat People 1974 (PG) Parasitic town in the Parisian (Australia) outback preys on car and body parts generated by deliberate accidents inflicted by wreck-driving wreckless youths. Weir's first film released internationally, about a small Australian town that survives economically via deliberately contriving car accidents and selling the wrecks' scrap parts. A broad, bitter black comedy with some horror touches. 91m/C VHS, Beta. **AU** Terry Camillieri, Kevin Miles, John Meillon, Melissa Jaffe; **D:** Peter Weir; **W:** Peter Weir. COL

Carson City Kid 🎞½ 1940 Typical western which has Rogers trying to exact revenge on the man who killed his brother. 54m/B VHS, Beta. Roy Rogers. NOS, VCN, MED

Cartel woof! 1990 (R) O'Keeffe, "B" actor extraordinaire, plays the wrong man to pick on in this rancid dope opera. Hounded by drug lord Stroud and framed for murder, pilot O'Keeffe decides the syndicate has gone too doggone far when they kill his sister. Exploitive and otherwise very bad. 106m/C VHS, LV. Miles O'Keeffe, Don Stroud, Crystal Carson, William Smith; **D:** John Stewart; **C:** Thomas Callaway. IME

Carthage in Flames 🎞🎞 Cartagine in Fiamme; Carthage en Flammes 1960 A graphic portrayal of the destruction of ancient Carthage in a blood and guts battle for domination of the known world. A tender love story is a welcome aside in this colorful Italian-made epic. 96m/C VHS. **IT** Anne Heywood, Jose Suarez, Pierre Brasseur; **D:** Carmine Gallone. NO

Cartier Affair 🎞 1984 A beautiful television actress unwittingly falls in love with the man who wants to steal her jewels. Collins designed her own wardrobe. Made for television. 120m/C VHS, Beta. Joan Collins, David Hasselhoff, Telly Savalas, Ed Lauter, Joe La Due; **D:** Rod Holcomb; **C:** Hanania Baer. ORI, WAR

Cartouche 🎞🎞🎞 Swords of Blood 1962 A swashbuckling action-comedy set in 18th-century France. Belmondo plays a charming thief who takes over a Paris gang, aided by the lovely Cardinale. When he is captured, she sacrifices her life to save him and Belmondo and his cohorts vow to have their revenge. Based on a French legend and a well-acted combination of tragedy, action, and farce. In French with English subtitles. 115m/C VHS. **FR IT** Jean-Paul Belmondo, Claudia Cardinale, Odile Versois, Philippe Lemaire; **D:** Philippe de Broca; **W:** Philippe de Broca; **M:** Georges Delerue. FCT, HTV

Carve Her Name with Pride 🎞🎞½ 1958 The true story of Violette Szabo who at age nineteen became a secret agent with the French Resistance in WWII. 119m/B VHS, Beta. Virginia McKenna, Paul Scofield. LCA

Casablanca 🎞🎞🎞🎞 1942 (PG) Can you see George Raft as Rick? Jack Warner did, but producer Hal Wallis wanted Bogart. Considered by many to be the best film ever made and one of the most quoted movies of all time, it rocketed Bogart from gangster roles to romantic leads as he and Bergman (who never looked lovelier) sizzle on screen. Bogart runs a gin joint in Morocco during the Nazi occupation, and meets up with Bergman, an old flame, but romance and politics do not mix, especially in Nazi-occupied French Morocco. Greenstreet, Lorre, and Rains all create memorable characters, as does Wilson, the piano player to whom Bergman says the oft-misquoted, "Play it, Sam." Without a doubt, the best closing scene ever written; it was scripted on the fly during the end of shooting, and actually shot several ways. Written from an unproduced play. See it in the original black and white. Laserdisc edition features restored imaging and sound and commentary by film historian Ronald Haver about the production, the play it was based on, and the famed evolution of the screenplay on audio track two. 50th Anniversary Edition contains a restored and remastered print, the original 1942 theatrical trailer, a film documentary narrated by Lauren Bacall, and a booklet. 102m/B VHS, Beta, LV, 8mm, Closed Caption. Humphrey Bogart, Ingrid Bergman, Paul Henreid, Claude Rains, Peter Lorre, Sydney Greenstreet, Conrad Veidt, S.Z. Sakall, Dooley Wilson, Marcel Dalio, John Qualen, Helmut Dantine; **D:** Michael Curtiz; **W:** Julius J. Epstein, Philip C. Epstein, Howard Koch; **M:** Max Steiner. Academy Awards '43: Best Director (Curtiz), Best Picture, Best Screenplay; National Board of Review Awards '45: 10 Best Films of the Year; Nominations: Academy Awards '43: Best Actor (Bogart), Best Black and White Cinematography, Best Film Editing, Best Supporting Actor (Rains), Original Dramatic/Comedy Score. MGM, FOX, TLF

Casablanca Express 🎞 1989 Nazi commandos hijack Churchill's train in this action-adventure drama. 90m/C VHS, Beta. Glenn Ford, Donald Pleasence, Jason Connery; **D:** Sergio Martino. NO

Casanova 🎞🎞 1987 (PG-13) A comedic romp through the bedrooms of 18th-century Europe with Chamberlain as the legendary lover. Lots of lovely ladies and hammy performances. Made for television. 122m/C VHS, Beta, LV, Closed Caption. Richard Chamberlain, Faye Dunaway, Sylvia Kristel, Ornella Muti, Hanna Schygulla, Sophie Ward, Frank Finlay, Kenneth Colley; **D:** Simon Langton; **W:** George MacDonald Fraser; **C:** Giuseppe Rotunno. TTC

Casanova Brown 🎞🎞½ 1944 Lighthearted comedy about a shy English professor (Cooper) who learns that his recent ex-wife (Wright) has had a baby (guess whose). When Cooper learns Wright has decided to give their daughter up for adoption he kidnaps the tyke and attempts fatherhood in a hotel room. When Wright finds out where he is, the twosome (who have really been in love all along) decide to remarry and be a family. Cooper, with baby and surrounded by diapers, makes a comedic sight. Based on the play "The Little Accident" by Floyd Dell and Thomas Mitchell. 94m/B VHS, Beta. Gary Cooper, Teresa Wright, Frank Morgan, Anita Louise, Patricia Collinge, Edmund Breon, Jill Esmond, Emory Parnell, Isobel Elsom, Mary Treen, Halliwell Hobbes; **D:** Sam Wood; **W:** Nunnally Johnson; **M:** Arthur Lange. Nominations: Academy Awards '44: Best Interior Decoration, Best Sound, Original Dramatic/Comedy Score. MGM, FCT

Casanova '70 🎞🎞½ 1965 Mastroianni plays a handsome soldier who has a knack for enticing liberated women in this comic rendition of the much-cinematized legendary yarn. Trouble is, he's in the mood only when he believes that he's in imminent danger. In Italian with English subtitles. 113m/C VHS. **IT** Marcello Mastroianni, Virna Lisi, Michele Mercier, Guido Alberti, Margaret Lee, Bernard Blier, Liana Orfei; **D:** Mario Monicelli; **W:** Tonino Guerra. Nominations: Academy Awards '65: Best Story & Screenplay. FOX

Casanova's Big Night 🎞🎞½ 1954 Classic slapstick comedy stars Hope masquerading as Casanova to test Fontaine's virtue before her marriage to a duke. The all-star cast provides one hilarious scene after another in this dated film. Price has a cameo as the "real" Casanova. Based on a story by Aubrey Wisberg. 85m/C VHS, LV. Bob Hope, Joan Fontaine, Audrey Dalton, Basil Rathbone, Hugh Marlowe, Vincent Price, John Carradine, Raymond Burr; **D:** Norman Z. McLeod; **W:** Hal Kanter, Edmund Hartmann; **C:** Lionel Lindon. PAR, CCB

A Case for Murder 🎞🎞½ 1993 (R) Jack Hammet has just become the youngest full partner ever at his Chicago law firm, with a knack for winning impossible cases. His next one's a beaut. Seems an envious colleague has gotten himself murdered and his estranged wife is the prime suspect. Jack decides to work with newly-arrived lawyer Kate Weldon but as the two become personally involved, Kate begins to question Jack's ethics. Seems the evidence is more than a little shady and Jack isn't telling all. 94m/C VHS, LV, Closed Caption. Peter Berg, Jennifer Grey, Belinda Bauer; **D:** Duncan Gibbins; **W:** Duncan Gibbins, Pablo F. Fenjves. USH

A Case of Deadly Force 🎞🎞🎞 1986 Based on the true story of a black man wrongfully killed by Boston's Tactical Police Force who mistook him for a robber. The police investigation calls it self-defense but the family and the attorney they hire fight to change the verdict. Excellent cast, great dramatic story. Originally made for television. 95m/C VHS, LV. Richard Crenna, John Shea, Lorraine Toussaint, Frank McCarthy, Tom Isbell; **D:** Michael Miller. CAF

A Case of Libel 🎞🎞½ 1983 A made for television dramatization based on attorney Louis Nizer's account of Quentin Reynolds' libel suit against columnist Westbrook Pegler. 90m/C VHS, Beta. Daniel J. Travanti, Ed Asner; **D:** Eric Till. LIV

Case of the Baby Sitter 🎞 1947 A private eye investigates jewel thieves posing as nobility. 40m/B VHS, Beta, LV. Tom Neal, Allen Jenkins, Pamela Blake. SNC

The Case of the Frightened Lady 🎞 The Frightened Lady 1939 A homicidal family does its collective best to keep its dark past a secret in order to collect some inheritance money. Watch, if you're still awake, for the surprise ending. 80m/B VHS, Beta. **GB** Marius Goring, Helen Haye, Penelope Dudley Ward, Felix Aylmer, Patrick Barr; **D:** George King. SNC

The Case of the Lucky Legs 🎞🎞½ 1935 Yes, there was a Perry Mason before Raymond Burr. Erle Stanley Gardner's sleuthing litigator's first appearance was 1934's "The Case of the Howling Dog," which initiated Warner Bros' "A"-grade (but soon-to-be "B"-grade) series. More akin to Nick Charles than to Gardner's character or to his later TV incarnation, the "Lucky Legs" Perry is a high-living, interminably hungover tippler who winces and wisecracks as he unravels the case of the corpse of a crooked con man. William, who left shortly after the series was downgraded to "B" status, plays the esquire; Tobin plays his smart-mouthed secretary, and Ellis is the tomato suspected of murder. **76m/B VHS, Beta.** Warren William, Genevieve Tobin, Patricia Ellis, Lyle Talbot, Allen Jenkins, Barton MacLane, Peggy Shannon, Porter Hall; **D:** Archie Mayo. *SNC, RXM*

The Case of the Missing Lady 🎬½ **1983** A famous Arctic explorer asks Tommy and Tuppence to find his missing fiancee. Based on the Christie story. **51m/C VHS, Beta.** *GB* Francesca Annis, James Warwick. *TPV*

The Case of the Mukkinese Battle Horn 🎬🎬 **1956** The cast of Britain's "The Goon Show" takes over in a zany, slapdash featurette-length mystery spoof. **27m/C VHS, Beta, 8mm.** *GB* Peter Sellers, Spike Milligan, Dick Emery; **M:** Edwin Astley. *VYY*

Casey at the Bat **1985** From Shelley Duvall's made for cable television "Tall Tales and Legends" series, in which the immortal poem is brought to life. Rousing comedy for the whole family. **52m/C VHS, Beta, Closed Caption.** Bill Macy, Hamilton Camp, Elliott Gould, Carol Kane, Howard Cosell; **D:** David Steinberg. *FOX*

Casey Jones and Fury (Brave Stallion) **1957** An episode from each of these early adventure series. **60m/B VHS, Beta.** Alan Hale Jr., Peter Graves. *NOS, DVT*

Casey's Shadow 🎬🎬 **1978 (PG)** The eight-year-old son of an impoverished horse trainer raises a quarter horse and enters it in the world's richest horse race. **116m/C VHS, Beta.** Walter Matthau, Alexis Smith, Robert Webber, Murray Hamilton; **D:** Martin Ritt; **C:** John A. Alonzo. *COL*

Cash McCall 🎬🎬½ **1960** McCall (Garner) is a corporate raider who just loves making money. But problems come in when he falls for the lovely daughter (Wood) of his latest takeover target, failing businessman Jagger. Based on the novel by Cameron Hawley. **116m/C VHS, Beta.** James Garner, Natalie Wood, Dean Jagger, Nina Foch, E.G. Marshall, Henry Jones, Otto Kruger, Roland Winters, Parley Baer, Dabbs Greer; **D:** Joseph Pevney; **W:** Lenore Coffee, Marion Hargrove; **M:** Max Steiner. *WAR*

Casino 🎬½ **1980** A made-for-television thriller about back-stabbings and ritzy romance aboard a high-priced gambling liner. **100m/C VHS, Beta.** Mike Connors, Lynda Day George, Bo Hopkins, Gary Burghoff, Joseph Cotten, Robert Reed, Barry Sullivan; **D:** Don Chaffey. *PSM*

Casino 🎬🎬🎬 **1995 (R)** Final part of the Scorsese underworld crime trilogy that began with "Mean Streets" and continued in "GoodFellas." Casino boss Sam "Ace" Rothstein (De Niro), his ex-hustler wife Ginger (Stone), and his loose-cannon enforcer pal Nicky (Pesci) are the principals in this lengthy, fictionalized account of how the mob lost Las Vegas in a haze of drugs, sex, coincidence and betrayal. Flashy, intricate, and unflinchingly violent account of mob-run '70s Vegas clicks when exploring the inner workings of a major casino and its hierarchy. Although Stone shines as a hedonistic money chaser, visuals are great and the soundtrack is a killer, story line suffers from deja vu. Pileggi again adapted the screenplay from his own book.**CW:** Brutal violence, pervasive strong language, drug use and some sexuality. **177m/C VHS, LV, Closed Caption.** Robert De Niro, Joe Pesci, Sharon Stone, James Woods, Don Rickles, Alan King, Kevin Pollak, L.Q. Jones, Dick Smothers, Jim Bloom; **Cameos:** Frankie Avalon, Steve Allen, Jayne Meadows, Jerry Vale; **D:** Martin Scorsese; **W:** Nicholas Pileggi, Martin Scorsese; **C:** Robert Richardson. Golden Globe Awards '96: Best Actress—Drama (Stone); Nominations: Academy Awards '95: Best Actress (Stone); Golden Globe Awards '96: Best Director (Scorsese); MTV Movie Awards '96: Best Female Performance (Stone), Best Villain (Pesci). *USH*

Casino Royale 🎬 **1967** The product of five directors, three writers and a mismatched cast of dozens, this virtually plotless spoof of James Bond films can stand as one of the low-water marks for 1960s comedy. And yet, there are some marvelous bits within, scenes of bizarre hilarity. Welles and Sellers literally couldn't stand the sight of one another, and their scenes together were filmed separately, with stand-ins. **130m/C VHS, Beta, LV.** David Niven, Woody Allen, Peter Sellers, Ursula Andress, Orson Welles, Jacqueline Bisset, Deborah Kerr, Peter O'Toole, Jean-Paul Belmondo, Charles Boyer, Joanna Pettet, John Huston, William Holden, George Raft; **D:** John Huston, Ken Hughes, Robert Parrish, Val Guest, Joseph McGrath; **C:** Jack Hildyard; **M:** Burt Bacharach. Nominations: Academy Awards '67: Best Song ("The Look of Love"). *MRV, COL*

Casper 🎬🎬🎬 **1995 (PG)** World's friendliest ghost appears on the big screen with outstanding visual trickery (from Industrial Light and Magic) and a lively, if hokey, story. Evilish Carrigan Crittenden (Moriarty) inherits ghost-infested Whiplash Manor and hires scatterbrained "ghost therapist" Dr. Harvey (Pullman) to get rid of its unwanted occupants. His daughter Kat (Ricci) is soon the object of Casper's friendly attention while the good doc must contend with Casper's mischievous uncles—Stinkie, Fatso, and Stretch. Exec producer Spielberg shows his influence with numerous topical gags and screen references that help amuse the adults while the ghosts work their magic on the kiddies. Silberling's directorial debut; based on the comic-book and television cartoon character created more than 30 years ago. **95m/C VHS, LV, Closed Caption.** Christina Ricci, Bill Pullman, Cathy Moriarty, Eric Idle, Amy Brenneman; **Cameos:** Don Novello, Rodney Dangerfield, Clint Eastwood, Mel Gibson, Dan Aykroyd; **D:** Brad Silberling; **W:** Sherri Stoner, Deanna Oliver; **C:** Dean Cundey; **M:** James Horner; **V:** Malachi Pearson, Joe Nipote, Joe Alaskey, Brad Garrett. *USH*

Casque d'Or 🎬🎬🎬 *Golden Marie* **1952** Crime passionnel in turn-of-the-century Paris as an honest carpenter (Reggiani) gets drawn into the netherworld of pimps and thieves. He's finally driven to murder—all for love of gangster's moll Marie (a very sultry Signoret). French with subtitles. **96m/B VHS.** *FR* Serge Reggiani, Simone Signoret, Claude Dauphin, Raymond Bussieres, Gaston Modot; **D:** Jacques Becker; **W:** Jacques Becker, Jacques Companeez; **C:** Robert Le Febvre; **M:** Georges Van Parys. *FCT*

Cass 🎬 **1978** Disenchanted filmmaker returns home to Australia to experiment with alternative lifestyles. **90m/C VHS, Beta.** Michelle Fawden, John Waters, Judy Morris, Peter Carroll. *NO*

Cass Timberlane 🎬🎬½ **1947** Scandalous story of a May-December romance set in a small Midwestern town. Tracy stars as Cass Timberlane, a widowed judge who falls for a voluptuous young girl from the wrong side of the tracks (Turner). They marry and experience problems when she is shunned by his snobbish friends. Good performances, especially from the supporting cast, dominate this fairly predictable film. Based on the novel by Sinclair Lewis. **119m/B VHS.** Spencer Tracy, Lana Turner, Zachary Scott, Tom Drake, Mary Astor, Albert Dekker, Margaret Lindsay, John Litel, Mona Barrie, Josephine Hutchinson, Rose Hobart, Selena Royle; **Cameos:** Walter Pidgeon; **D:** George Sidney; **W:** Donald Ogden Stewart. *MGM*

Cassandra 🎬 **1987 (R)** A fragile young woman has dreams that foretell the future—specifically, a series of grisly murders. **94m/C VHS, Beta, LV.** Shane Briant, Brionny Behets, Tessa Humphries, Kit Taylor, Lee James; **D:** Colin Eggleston. *VTR*

The Cassandra Crossing 🎬½ **1976 (R)** A terrorist with the plague causes havoc on a transcontinental luxury train. Turgid adventure filmed in France and Italy. **129m/C VHS, Beta.** *GB* Sophia Loren, Richard Harris, Ava Gardner, Burt Lancaster, Martin Sheen, Ingrid Thulin, Lee Strasberg, John Phillip Law, Lionel Stander, O.J. Simpson, Ann Turkel, Alida Valli; **D:** George P. Cosmatos; **W:** George P. Cosmatos, Tom Mankiewicz; **M:** Jerry Goldsmith. *FOX*

Cassie 🎬 **1987 (R)** Follows the rise of Cassie, a successful country and western singer, and documents all her trials along the way. **75m/C VHS, Beta.** Marilyn Chambers; **D:** Godfrey Daniels. *NO*

Cast a Dark Shadow 🎬🎬🎬 **1955** Bogarde is the charmer who decides to reap his reward by marrying and murdering elderly women for their fortunes. But Bogarde meets his match when he plots against his latest intended (Lockwood). Tidy thriller with effective performances. Based on the play "Murder Mistaken" by Janet Green. **82m/B VHS.** *GB* Dirk Bogarde, Margaret Lockwood, Mona Washbourne, Kay Walsh, Kathleen Harrison, Robert Flemyng, Walter Hudd; **D:** Lewis Gilbert; **W:** John Cresswell. *FCT*

Cast a Deadly Spell 🎬🎬🎬 **1991 (R)** A bubbly, flavorful witch's brew of private-eye and horror cliches, set in a fantasy version of 1948 Los Angeles where sorcery and voodoo abound, but gumshoe Harry P. Lovecraft uses street smarts instead of magic to track down a stolen Necronomicon—and if you know what that is you'll want to watch. Wild creatures and f/x wizardry complement this made-for-cable-TV trick and treat.**CW:** Some language and horror violence. **93m/C VHS, LV, Closed Caption.** Fred Ward, David Warner, Julianne Moore, Clancy Brown, Alexandra Powers; **D:** Martin Campbell; **W:** Joseph Dougherty, Dave Edison. *HBO, FCT*

Cast a Giant Shadow 🎬🎬 **1966** Follows the career of Col. David "Mickey" Marcus, an American Jew and WWII hero who helped turn Israel's army into a formidable fighting force during the 1947-48 struggle for independence. **142m/C VHS, Beta, Closed Caption.** Kirk Douglas, Senta Berger, Angie Dickinson, John Wayne, James Donald, Chaim Topol, Frank Sinatra, Yul Brynner; **D:** Melville Shavelson; **W:** Melville Shavelson; **M:** Elmer Bernstein. *MGM, FCT*

Cast the First Stone 🎬🎬 **1989** Made for TV soaper based on the true story of a former nun who becomes a small town schoolteacher. After being raped, Diane Martin discovers she's pregnant and when she decides to keep the baby the school board dismisses her. The plot centers around her fight to regain her job and dignity—while trying to convince everybody that she doesn't deserve to lose her job simply because she is an unwed mother. Eikenberry gives a strong performance, but it can't carry this lackluster film. **94m/C VHS, LV.** Jill Eikenberry, Richard Masur, Joe Spano, Lew Ayres, Holly Palance; **D:** John Korty; **M:** Ira Newborn. *COL*

Castaway 🎬🎬½ **1987 (R)** Based on the factual account by Lucy Irvine. The story of Michael Wilmington, who placed an ad for a young woman to spend a year on a Pacific atoll with him, and the battle of the sexes that followed. **118m/C VHS, Beta, Closed Caption.** Oliver Reed, Amanda Donohoe, Tony Rickards, Georgina Hale, Frances Barber, Todd Rippon; **D:** Nicolas Roeg; **W:** Allan Scott; **M:** Stanley Myers. *WAR*

The Castaway Cowboy 🎬🎬 **1974 (G)** A shanghaied cowboy becomes partners with a widow when she turns her Hawaiian potato farm into a cattle ranch. Good, clean "family fare." **91m/C VHS, Beta.** James Garner, Robert Culp, Vera Miles; **D:** Vincent McEveety; **M:** Robert F. Brunner. *DIS, OM*

The Castilian 🎬🎬½ *Valley of the Swords* **1963** Some very odd casting in this historical tale of heroism and swordplay about a Spanish nobleman who leads his followers against the invading Moors and their evil king (Crawford). Based on a 13th century poem. **128m/C VHS.** Cesar Romero, Broderick Crawford, Alida Valli, Frankie Avalon, Espartaco Santoni, Fernando Rey, Jorge Rigaud; **D:** Javier Seto; **W:** Sidney Pink. *WAR, FCT*

The Castle 🎬🎬🎬 *Das Schloss* **1968** A man is summoned by the seemingly invisible occupants of a castle to their village. All his efforts to meet with those inhabiting the castle are futile and the task gradually becomes his obsession. Both wonderfully acted and shot, this is a well-executed adaptation of Franz Kafka's novel. **90m/C VHS,**

Beta. *GE SI* Maximilian Schell, Cordula Trantow, Trudik Daniel, Helmut Qualtinger; **D:** Rudolf Noelte. *NO*

Castle Freak 🐾🐾 **1995 (R)** Italian countess leaves her creepy haunted castle to her American nephew and his family. They find an unwelcome surprise lurking in the cellar. **CW:** Some strong violence and gore, a scene of sexuality and some language. **90m/C VHS, LV.** Jeffrey Combs, Barbara Crampton, Jonathan Fuller, Jessica Dollarhide; **D:** Stuart Gordon; **W:** Dennis Paoli; **C:** Mario Vulpiani; **M:** Richard Band. *FLL*

Castle in the Desert 🐾🐾½ **1942** Charlie Chan investigates murder and other strange goings-on in a spooky old castle. One of the last in the series. **62m/B VHS, Closed Caption.** Sidney Toler, Arleen Whelan, Richard Derr, Douglass Dumbrille, Henry Daniell, Victor Sen Yung; **D:** Harry Lachman. *FOX*

Castle of Blood 🐾🐾 *Castle of Terror; Coffin of Terror; Danza Macabra* **1964** Staying overnight in a haunted castle, a poet is forced to deal with a number of creepy encounters. Cult favorite Steele enhances this atmospheric chiller. Dubbed in English. **85m/B VHS.** *IT FR* Barbara Steele, George Riviere, Margrete Robsahm, Henry Kruger, Montgomery Glenn, Sylvia Sorente; **D:** Anthony (Antonio Margheriti) Dawson. *SNC*

The Castle of Cagliostro 1980 An animated Japanese adventure tale featuring a hero named Wolf, who's a thief. Wolf infiltrates the suspicious country of Cagliostro, whose one industry is conterfeiting money, and winds up rescuing a princess. Lots of violence to go with the action. In Japanese with English subtitles. **100m/C VHS.** *JP STP*

Castle of Evil woof! **1966** Group of heirs gathers on a deserted isle to hear the reading of the will of your basic mad scientist. One by one, they fall victim to a humanoid created by the loony doc in his own image. Inspired moments of unintentional fun. **81m/C VHS.** Scott Brady, Virginia Mayo, Lisa Gaye, David Brian, Hugh Marlowe, William Thourlby, Shelly Morrison; **D:** Francis D. Lyon. *REP, FCT*

The Castle of Fu Manchu 🐾 *Assignment: Istanbul; Die Folterkammer des Dr. Fu Manchu* **1968 (PG)** The final chapter in a series starring Lee as the wicked doctor. This time, Lee has developed a gadget which will put the earth into a deep freeze, and at his mercy. To fine tune this contraption, he enlists the help of a gifted scientist by abducting him. However, the helper/hostage has a bad ticker, so Lee must abduct a heart surgeon to save his life, and thus, the freezer project. Most critics felt this was the weakest installment in the series. **92m/C VHS.** *GE SP IT GB* Christopher Lee, Richard Greene, H. Marion Crawford, Tsai Chin, Gunther Stoll, Rosalba (Sara Bay) Neri, Maria Perschy; **D:** Jess (Jesus) Franco. *MRV*

Castle of the Creeping Flesh woof! **1968** A surgeon's daughter is brutally murdered. Vowing to bring her back he begins ripping out the organs of innocent people and transplanting them into her body. Has the dubious honor of being one of the few movies to sport actual open heart surgery footage. So bad it's...just bad. **85m/C VHS, Beta.** Adrian Hoven, Janine Reynaud, Howard Vernon; **D:** Percy G. Parker. *NO*

Castle of the Living Dead 🐾🐾 *Il Castello de Morti Vivi* **1964** Evil Count Drago's hobbies include mummifying a traveling circus group visiting his castle. Lee is as evil as ever, but be sure to look for Sutherland's screen debut. In a dual role, he plays not only the bumbling inspector, but also a witch, in drag. **90m/B VHS.** *IT FR* Christopher Lee, Gaia Germani, Phillipe LeRoy, Jacques Stanislawsky, Donald Sutherland; **D:** Herbert Wise. *SNC, MRV*

Casual Sex? 🐾½ **1988 (R)** Two young women, looking for love and commitment, take a vacation at a posh resort where they are confronted by men with nothing on their minds but sex, be it casual or the more formal black-tie variety. Supposedly an examination of safe sex in a lightly comedic vein, though the comic is too light and the morality too limp. Adapted from the play

by Wendy Goldman and Judy Toll. **87m/C VHS, Beta, LV.** Lea Thompson, Victoria Jackson, Stephen Shellan, Jerry Levine, Mary Gross, Andrew Dice Clay; **D:** Genevieve Robert. *USH*

Casualties of Love: The "Long Island Lolita" Story 1993 (PG-13) Told from the Buttafuoco's point of view, Amy Fisher was nothing but a wacko fatally attracted teenager who misunderstood Joey's harmless flirtations and deliberately went after his wife with a gun. The Buttafuocos received $300,000 from CBS to tell their side of the story which features Milano, who resembles Amy not in the least, as the lead. One of three competing network television versions of the sordid story. See also: "The Amy Fisher Story" and "Lethal Lolita—Amy Fisher: My Story." **CW:** Violence and drug use and sexual subject matter. **94m/C VHS.** Jack Scalia, Alyssa Milano, Phyllis Lyons, Jack Kehler, Michael Bowen, J.E. Freeman, Nicky Corello, Lawrence Tierney, Peter Van Norden, Anne DeSalvo; **D:** John Herzfeld; **W:** John Herzfeld. *COL*

Casualties of War 🐾🐾🐾 **1989 (R)** A Vietnam war morality play about army private Fox in the bush who refuses to let his fellow soldiers and commanding sergeant (Penn) skirt responsibility for the rape and murder of a native woman. Fox achieves his dramatic breakthrough. Based on the true story by Daniel Lang. **120m/C VHS, Beta, LV, 8mm, Closed Caption.** Sean Penn, Michael J. Fox, Don Harvey, Thuy Thu Le, John Leguizamo, Sam Robards, John C. Reilly, Erik King; **D:** Brian DePalma; **W:** David Rabe; **C:** Stephen Burum; **M:** Ennio Morricone. *COL*

A Casualty of War 🐾🐾½ **1990 (R)** Made-for-TV adaptation of Frederick Forsyth's thriller about modern-day arms smuggling (Libya to Ireland) and espionage. Well-acted, with the exception of Hack. **96m/C VHS.** Shelley Hack, David Threlfall, Richard Hope, Alan Howard, Clarke Peters; **D:** Tom Clegg; **W:** Frederick Forsyth. *NO*

The Cat 1966 A boy and a tamed mountain lion become friends on the run from a murderous poacher. **95m/C VHS, Beta.** Peggy Ann Garner, Roger Perry, Barry Coe; **D:** Ellis Kadison. *COL, NLC*

Cat and Mouse 🐾🐾🐾½ **1978 (PG)** A very unorthodox police inspector is assigned to investigate a millionaire's mysterious death. Who done it? French dialogue with English subtitles. **107m/C VHS, Beta.** *FR* Michele Morgan, Serge Reggiani, Jean-Pierre Aumont, Philippe Labro, Philippe Leotard, Valerie Lagrange, Michel Perelon, Christine Laurent; **D:** Claude Lelouch; **W:** Claude Lelouch; **C:** Andre Perlstein; **M:** Francis Lai. *COL*

The Cat and the Canary 🐾🐾🐾 **1927** A great silent film about the ghost of a madman that wanders nightly through the corridors of an old house. Remade twice, once in 1939 and again in 1979. **70m/B VHS, Beta.** Laura La Plante, Creighton Hale, Tully Marshall, Gertrude Astor; **D:** Paul Leni. *NOS, MRV, VYY*

The Cat and the Canary 🐾🐾 **1979 (PG)** A stormy night, a gloomy mansion, and a mysterious will combine to create an atmosphere for murder. An entertaining remake of the 1927 silent film. **96m/C VHS, Beta.** *GB* Carol Lynley, Michael Callan, Wendy Hiller, Olivia Hussey, Daniel Massey, Honor Blackman, Edward Fox, Wilfrid Hyde-White; **D:** Radley Metzger. *COL, OM*

The Cat and the Fiddle 🐾🐾🐾 **1934** Lovely Jerome Kern-Oscar Hammerstein operetta in which Novarro plays a struggling composer who forces his affections on MacDonald. She sings in response to his romantic proposals. The final sequence is in color. ♫The Night Was Made for Love; She Didn't Say 'Yes'; A New Love is Old; Try to Forget; One Moment Alone; Don't Ask Us Not To Sing; I Watch the Love Parade; The Breeze Kissed Your Hair; Impressions in a Harlem Flat. **90m/B VHS.** Ramon Novarro, Jeanette MacDonald, Frank Morgan, Charles Butterworth. *MGM*

Cat Ballou 🐾🐾🐾½ **1965** At the turn of the century, a schoolmarm turns outlaw with the help of a drunken gunman. Marvin played Kid Shelleen and his silver-nosed evil twin Tim Strawn in this cheery spoof of westerns. Cole and Kaye sing the narration in a one of a kind Greek chorus. **96m/C VHS, Beta.** Jane Fonda, Lee Marvin, Michael Callan, Dwayne Hickman, Reginald Denny, Nat King Cole, Stubby Kaye; **D:** Elliot Silverstein; **W:** Frank Pierson. Academy Awards '65: Best Actor (Marvin); Berlin International Film Festival '65: Best Actor (Marvin); British Academy Awards '65: Best Actor (Marvin); Golden Globe Awards '66: Best Actor—Musical/Comedy (Marvin); National Board of Review Awards '65: 10 Best Films of the Year, Best Actor (Marvin); Nominations: Academy Awards '65: Best Adapted Score, Best Adapted Screenplay, Best Film Editing, Best Song ("The Ballad of Cat Ballou"). *COL, BTV*

Cat Chaser 🐾🐾 **1990** Weller walks listlessly through the role of an ex-soldier in Miami who has an affair with the wife of an exiled—but still lethal—military dictator. Surpisingly low-key, sometimes effective thriller that saves its energy for sex scenes, also available in a less steamy, 90-minute "R" rated version. Based on an Elmore Leonard novel. **97m/C VHS.** Kelly McGillis, Peter Weller, Charles Durning, Frederic Forrest, Tomas Milian, Juan Fernandez; **D:** Abel Ferrara; **W:** Elmore Leonard, Jim Borrelli; **M:** Chick Corea. *VES*

The Cat from Outer Space 🐾🐾 **1978 (G)** An extraterrestrial cat named Jake crashes his spaceship on Earth and leads a group of people on endless escapades. Enjoyable Disney fare. **103m/C VHS.** Ken Berry, Sandy Duncan, Harry (Henry) Morgan, Roddy McDowall, McLean Stevenson; **D:** Norman Tokar. *DIS, OM*

Cat Girl 🐾 **1957** A young bride on her honeymoon finds she has inherited the family curse—she has a psychic link to a ferocious leopard. Numerous murders ensue. Poor production value and a weak script, despite Shelley's fine acting, make this an unworthwhile film. **69m/B VHS.** Barbara Shelley, Robert Ayres, Kay Callard, Paddy Webster; **D:** Alfred Shaughnessy. *PAR, COL*

Cat in the Cage 🐾½ **1968** A young man finds many things have changed at home while he was in a mental institution. Dad has remarried, the housekeeper is practicing witchcraft, the chauffeur is after his mistress, and the cat is gone. So where'd that cat go? **96m/C VHS, Beta.** Colleen Camp, Sybil Danning, Mel Novak, Frank De Kova; **D:** Tony Zarin Dast. *GHV*

The Cat o' Nine Tails 🐾 **1971 (PG)** A blind detective and a newsman team up to find a sadistic killer. A gory murder mystery. **112m/C VHS, 8mm.** *GE FR IT* Karl Malden, James Franciscus, Catherine Spaak, Cinzia de Carolis, Carlo Alighiero; **D:** Dario Argento; **W:** Dario Argento; **M:** Ennio Morricone. *SIM*

Cat on a Hot Tin Roof 🐾🐾🐾½ **1958** Tennessee Williams' powerful play about greed and deception in a patriarchal Southern family. Big Daddy (Ives) is dying. Members of the family greedily attempt to capture his inheritance, tearing the family apart. Taylor is a sensual wonder as Maggie the Cat, though the more controversial elements of the play were toned down for the film version. Intense, believable performances from Ives and Newman. **108m/C VHS, Beta, LV.** Paul Newman, Burl Ives, Elizabeth Taylor, Jack Carson, Judith Anderson; **D:** Richard Brooks; **W:** Richard Brooks, James Poe; **C:** William H. Daniels. National Board of Review Awards '58: 10 Best Films of the Year; Nominations: Academy Awards '58: Best Actor (Newman), Best Actress (Taylor), Best Adapted Screenplay, Best Color Cinematography, Best Director (Brooks), Best Picture. *MGM, FCT, CCB*

Cat on a Hot Tin Roof 🐾🐾 **1984** In this adaptation of the Tennessee Williams play, fights over the family inheritance tear a family apart. **122m/C VHS, Beta, LV.** Jessica Lange, Tommy Lee Jones, Rip Torn, David Dukes; **D:** Jack Hofsiss. *MGM, LIV, VES*

Cat People 🐾🐾🐾 1942 A young dress designer is the victim of a curse that changes her into a deadly panther who must kill to survive. A classic among the horror genre with unrelenting terror from beginning to end. First horror film from producer Val Lewton. 73m/B VHS, Beta, LV. Jane Randolph, Elizabeth Russell, Jack Holt, Alan Napier, Simone Simon, Kent Smith, Tom Conway; D: Jacques Tourneur. MED, BTV, TTC

Cat People 🐾🐾½ 1982 (R) A beautiful young woman learns that she has inherited a strange family trait—she turns into a vicious panther when sexually aroused. The only person with whom she can safely mate is her brother, a victim of the same genetic heritage. Kinski is mesmerizing as the innocent, sensual woman. Remake of the 1942 film. 118m/C VHS, Beta, LV. Nastassia Kinski, Malcolm McDowell, John Heard, Annette O'Toole, Ruby Dee, Ed Begley Jr., John Larroquette; D: Paul Schrader; W: Alan Ormsby; C: John Bailey. USH, FCT

Cat Women of the Moon 🐾🐾 Rocket to the Moon 1953 Scientists land on the moon and encounter an Amazon-like force of skimpily attired female chauvinists. Remade as "Missile to the Moon." Featuring the Hollywood Cover Girls as various cat women. Available in its original 3-D format. 65m/C VHS, Beta. Sonny Tufts, Victor Jory, Marie Windsor, Bill Phipps, Douglas Fowley, Carol Brewster, Suzanne Alexander, Susan Morrow; D: Arthur Hilton; M: Elmer Bernstein. RHI, SNC, EEL

Cataclysm 🐾🐾½ 1981 (R) A swell flick about a sadistic demon who spends his time either finding people willing to join him or killing the people who won't. Also on video as "Satan's Supper." 94m/C VHS, Beta. Cameron Mitchell, Marc Lawrence, Faith Clift, Charles Moll; D: Tom McGowan, Greg Tallas, Philip Marshak. FOX, ACA

Catacombs 🐾 1989 (R) An investigative monk and a beautiful photographer stumble across a mysterious, centuries-old evil power. 112m/C VHS, Beta. Timothy Van Patten, Laura Schaefer, Ian Abercrombie, Jeremy West; D: David Schmoeller; W: C. Courtney Joyner; M: Pino Donaggio. TWE

The Catamount Killing 🐾½ 1974 (PG) The story of a small town bank manager and his lover. They decide to rob the bank and run for greener pastures only to find their escape befuddled at every turn. 82m/C VHS, Beta. GE Horst Buchholz, Ann Wedgeworth; D: Krzysztof Zanussi. NO

Catch as Catch Can 🐾 Lo Scatenato 1968 An Italian male model is comically besieged by animals of every type, making a mess of his life and career. Dubbed. 95m/C VHS, Beta. IT Vittorio Gassman, Martha Hyer, Gila Golan; D: Franco Indovina; M: Luis Bacalov. NLC

Catch Me a Spy 🐾½ To Catch a Spy 1971 A foreign agent attempts to lure an innocent man into becoming part of a swap for an imprisoned Russian spy. 94m/C VHS, Beta. GB FR Kirk Douglas, Tom Courtenay, Trevor Howard, Marlene Jobert, Bernard Blier, Patrick Mower, Bernadette LaFont; D: Dick Clement; W: Dick Clement, Ian LaFrenais; M: Claude Bolling. PSM

Catch Me...If You Can 🐾🐾 1989 (PG) High school class president Melissa doesn't want to see the school torn down. To raise fast cash, she teams up with a drag racer and the fun begins. 105m/C VHS, LV, Closed Caption. Matt Lattanzi, Loryn Locklin, M. Emmet Walsh, Geoffrey Lewis; D: Stephen Sommers. MCG

Catch the Heat 🐾 Feel the Heat 1987 (R) Alexandra is an undercover narcotics agent sent to infiltrate Steiger's South American drug operation. 90m/C VHS, Beta. Tiana Alexandra, David Dukes, Rod Steiger; D: Joel Silberg; W: Stirling Silliphant; M: Tom Chase, Steve Rucker. MED, VTR

Catch-22 🐾🐾🐾 1970 (R) Buck Henry's adaptation of Joseph Heller's black comedy about a group of fliers in the Mediterranean during WWII. A biting anti-war satire portraying the insanity of the situation in both a humorous and disturbing manner. Perhaps too literal to the book's masterfully chaotic structure, causing occasional problems in the "are you following along department?" Arkin heads a fine and colorful cast. 121m/C VHS, Beta, LV. Alan Arkin, Martin Balsam, Art Garfunkel, Jon Voight, Richard Benjamin, Buck Henry, Bob Newhart, Paula Prentiss, Martin Sheen, Charles Grodin, Anthony Perkins, Orson Welles, Jack Gilford; D: Mike Nichols; W: Buck Henry; C: David Watkin. PAR

The Catered Affair 🐾🐾🐾 Wedding Breakfast 1956 Davis, anti-typecast as a Bronx housewife, and Borgnine, as her taxi-driving husband, play the determined parents of soon-to-be-wed Reynolds set on giving her away in a style to which she is not accustomed. Based on Paddy Chayefsky's teleplay, the catered affair turns into a familial trial, sharing the true-to-life poignancy that marked "Marty," the Oscar-winning Chayefsky drama of the previous year. 92m/B VHS. Bette Davis, Ernest Borgnine, Debbie Reynolds, Barry Fitzgerald, Rod Taylor, Robert Simon; D: Richard Brooks; W: Gore Vidal; C: John Alton; M: Andre Previn. MGM, FCT, CCB

Catherine & Co. 🐾½ 1976 (R) Lonely, penniless girl arrives in Paris and "opens shop" on the streets of Paris. As business booms, she takes a cue from the big corporations and sells stock in herself. 91m/C VHS, Beta. FR IT Jane Birkin, Patrick Dewaere, Jean-Pierre Aumont, Jean-Claude Brialy; D: Michel Boisrond. NO

Catherine the Great 🐾🐾½ The Rise of Catherine the Great 1934 Slow but lavish and engrossing British dramatization of the tortured and doomed love affair between Catherine, Empress of Russia, and her irrational, drunken husband Peter. 88m/B VHS, Beta, LV. GB Douglas Fairbanks Jr., Elisabeth Bergner, Flora Robson; D: Paul Czinner; C: Georges Perinal. National Board of Review Awards '34: 5 Best Foreign Films of the Year. BAR, VYY, HEG

Catholic Hour 🐾🐾 1960 A dramatized version of the life story of Thomas Frederick Price who co-founded the Maryknoll Missionaries in the early 1900's. 30m/B VHS, Beta. Edward Cullen, Arthur Gary. VYY

Catholics 🐾🐾🐾 The Conflict 1973 A sensitive exploration of contemporary mores and changing attitudes within the Roman Catholic church. Sheen is sent by the Pope to Ireland to reform some priests. Based on Brian Moore's short novel and made for television. 86m/C VHS, Beta. Martin Sheen, Trevor Howard; D: Jack Gold; M: Carl Davis. NO

Cathy's Curse 🐾 Cauchemares 1977 The spirit of her aunt, who died as a child, possesses a young girl in this Canadian-French collaboration. Tries to capitalize on the popularity of "The Exorcist," but falls seriously short. 90m/C VHS, Beta. FR CA Alan Scarfe, Beverly Murray; D: Eddy Matalon. NO

Catlow 🐾🐾½ 1971 (PG-13) A comedic western with Brynner aiming to steal 2 million dollars in gold from under the nose of his friend, lawman Crenna. Based on the novel by Louis L'Amour. 103m/C VHS. Yul Brynner, Richard Crenna, Leonard Nimoy, JoAnn Pflug, Jeff Corey, Michael Delano, David Ladd, Bessie Love; D: Sam Wanamaker; W: Scot Finch, J.J. Griffith. MGM

Cats Don't Dance 🐾🐾 1997 (G) Animated musical/comedy finds Danny (Bakula) a hoofer wannabe trying to break into '30s Hollywood. Only problem is that he's a cat and can't understand why he only gets parts playing animals. He gets into trouble with bratty human star Darla Dimple (Peldon) and nearly sees his chance at a career vanish. Combines "Singin' in the Rain" and "Who Framed Roger Rabbit," with some showbiz cynicism from "The Player" to create a cartoon that will most likely sail over the heads of its target audience. Most of the time, as in the old Warner Bros. classics, that's a good thing. Not in this case, however. 77m/C VHS, LV, Closed Caption. D: Mark Dindal; W: Cliff Ruby, Roberts Gannaway, Elana Lesser, Theresa Pettengill; M: Steve Goldstein, Randy Newman; V: Scott Bakula, Jasmine Guy, Ashley Peldon, Kathy Najimy, John Rhys-Davies, George Kennedy, Rene Auberjonois, Hal Holbrook, Don Knotts, Frank Welker, David Johansen, Natalie Cole. WAR

Cat's Eye 🐾🐾 1985 (PG-13) An anthology of three Stephen King short stories connected by a stray cat who wanders through each tale. 94m/C VHS, Beta, LV, Closed Caption. Drew Barrymore, James Woods, Alan King, Robert Hays, Candy Clark, Kenneth McMillan, James Naughton, Charles S. Dutton; D: Lewis Teague; W: Stephen King; C: Jack Cardiff; M: Alan Silvestri. FOX, FCT

Cat's Play 🐾🐾 1974 A widowed music teacher makes a ceremonial occasion of a weekly dinner with an old flame. Then an old friend from her youth suddenly reappears and begins an affair with the gentleman, causing self-destructive passions to explode. In Hungarian with English subtitles. 115m/C VHS. HU Margit Dayka, Margit Makay, Elma Bulla; D: Karoly Makk. Nominations: Academy Awards '74: Best Foreign Language Film.CVC

Cattle Queen of Montana 🐾🐾½ 1954 Reagan stars as an undercover federal agent investigating livestock rustlings and Indian uprisings. 88m/C VHS, Beta, LV. Ronald Reagan, Barbara Stanwyck, Jack Elam, Gene Evans, Lance Fuller, Anthony Caruso; D: Allan Dwan; W: Robert Blees. NO

Caught 🐾 1949 A woman marries for wealth and security and is desperately unhappy. She runs away and takes a job with a struggling physician, and falls in love with him. Her husband finds her, forcing her to decide between a life of security or love. 90m/B VHS. James Mason, Barbara Bel Geddes, Robert Ryan, Curt Bois, Natalie Schafer, Art Smith; D: Max Ophuls; C: Lee Garmes. REP

Caught 🐾🐾 1996 (R) Homeless Irishman Nick (Verveen) winds up in the New Jersey fish shop run by Joe (Olmos) and his wife Betty (Alonso). Betty takes a liking to the good-looking young man and encourages Joe to offer him a job and even invites Nick to stay with them in departed son Danny's (Schub) old room. Soon, room and board isn't all the spicy Betty is offering and Nick's willing to please, especially since Joe turns a blind eye. Too bad the manic Danny, a failed comedian, returns home and immediately becomes jealous of the interloper. He's also too willing to drag secrets out into the open, whatever the cost. Based on Pomerantz's novel "Into It." CW: Strong sexuality and language, and for some violence and drug use. 109m/C VHS, LV, Closed Caption. Edward James Olmos, Maria Conchita Alonso, Arie Verveen, Steven Schub, Bitty Schram, Shawn Elliot; D: Robert M. Young; W: Edward Pomerantz; C: Michael Barrow; M: Chris Botti. Nominations: Independent Spirit Awards '97: Best Actress (Alonso), Best Director (Young), Debut Performance (Verveen). COL

Caught in the Act 🐾🐾½ 1993 (PG-13) Scott McNally (Harrison) is an out-of-work actor who teaches acting classes to make a buck. Into one of his classes walks the sultry Rachel (Hope) and they start a hot affair. Then Rachel calls Scott, claiming to be kidnapped, he suddenly finds 10 million dollars in his bank account, and his landlord is murdered. Scott finds himself the pawn in an embezzlement scheme and framed for murder. But this is one role Scott doesn't want and he intends to work with a new script of his own devise. Made for cable television. 93m/C VHS, LV, Closed Caption. Gregory Harrison, Leslie Hope, Patricia Clarkson, Kevin Tighe; D: Deborah Reinisch; W: Ken Hixon. USH

Caught in the Draft 🐾🐾🐾 1941 Hope's funniest role has him as a Hollywood star trying to evade the draft in WW II, but he ends up accidentally enlisting himself. Lamour plays the daughter of a colonel in the Army whom Hope plans to marry, thinking it will get him out of the service. Very funny military comedy and one of Hope's best. Based on a story by Harry Tugend. 82m/B VHS, Closed Caption. Bob Hope, Dorothy Lamour, Lynne Overman, Eddie Bracken, Clarence Kolb, Paul Hurst, Ferike Boros, Irving Bacon; D: David Butler; W: Harry Tugend. USH, BTV

Cauldron of Blood 🎬🎬½ *Blind Man's Bluff; El Coleccionista de Cadaveres* **1967 (PG)** Blind sculptor Karloff unwittingly uses human skeletons supplied by his crazed wife Lindfors as the framework of his art pieces. **95m/C VHS.** *SP* Boris Karloff, Viveca Lindfors, Jean-Pierre Aumont, Rosenda Monteros, Ruben Rojo, Dianik Zurakowska; *D:* Edward Mann; *W:* Edward Mann. *REP, VDC, FCT*

Cause for Alarm 🎬🎬½ **1951** A jealous husband recovering from a heart attack begins to lose his mind. He wrongly accuses his wife of having an affair and attempts to frame her for his own murder. A fast-paced thriller with a nifty surprise ending. **74m/B VHS.** Loretta Young, Barry Sullivan, Bruce Cowling, Margalo Gillmore, Irving Bacon, Carl "Alfalfa" Switzer; *D:* Tay Garnett; *M:* Andre Previn. *NOS, SNC, MGM*

Cause of Death 🎬½ **1990 (R)** After the accidental death of his brother, Colombian drug lord Manuel Ramirez is lured to L.A. to collect his millions in blood money. **90m/C VHS.** Michael Barak, Sydney Coale Phillips, Daniel Martine; *D:* Philip Jones. *VSE*

Cavalcade 🎬🎬🎬 **1933** Traces the lives of the British Marryot family from the death of Queen Victoria, through WWI, the Jazz Age, and the Depression. A wistful adaptation of the hit play by Noel Coward with its touching portrayal of one family trying to weather good times and bad together. **110m/B VHS.** Diana Wynyard, Clive Brook, Herbert Mundin, Una O'Connor, Ursula Jeans, Beryl Mercer, Merle Tottenham, Frank Lawton, John Warburton, Margaret Lindsay, Billy Bevan; *D:* Frank Lloyd; *C:* Ernest Palmer. Academy Awards '33: Best Director (Lloyd), Best Interior Decoration, Best Picture; Nominations: Academy Awards '33: Best Actress (Wynyard). *FXV, FCT*

Cavalcade of the West 🎬🎬 **1936** Typical western with two brothers, separated by a kidnapping, growing up on opposite sides of the law. Much later they meet, and the question is: will the outlaw be reformed and reunited with his happy family? **70m/B VHS, Beta.** Hoot Gibson, Rex Lease, Marion Shilling, Earl Dwire; *D:* Harry Fraser. *GPV, DVT, VCN*

The Cavalier 🎬 **198?** Chinese cavalier faces love, danger and intrigue while deploying martial arts skills. **90m/C VHS, Beta.** Tang Wei, Lung Fei, Yeh Yuen, Tseng Tsao. *UNI*

Cavalier of the West 🎬 **1931** An Army captain is the only negotiating force between the white man and a primitive Indian tribe. **66m/B VHS, Beta, LV.** Harry Carey Sr., Kane Richmond, George "Gabby" Hayes; *D:* John P. McCarthy. *NOS*

Cavalry 🎬½ **1936** A Union Army Lieutenant is reunited with his family after the Civil War, bringing them happiness and joy. **60m/B VHS, Beta.** Bob Steele, Frances Grant, Karl Hackett, Hal Price; *D:* Robert North Bradbury. *NOS, DVT*

Cavalry Charge 🎬🎬½ *The Last Outpost* **1951** Vance Britton (Reagan) is the captain of a brigade of Confederate troops wreaking havoc on Union outposts. His brother Jeb (Bennett) is a Union soldier sent to the western frontier to take care of the Confederate problem. Vance's former fiance Julie (Fleming) is also living in the territories with her new husband. All three converge when the Union fort, where Julie is living and Jeb is defending, is attacked by Apaches. Brother Vance rides to the rescue. Lots of action. **72m/C VHS.** Ronald Reagan, Bruce (Herman Brix) Bennett, Rhonda Fleming, Noah Beery Jr., Bill Williams, Peter Hanson, Hugh Beaumont, John Ridgely, Lloyd Corrigan, James Burke, Richard Crane, Ewing Mitchell; *D:* Lewis R. Foster; *W:* Geoffrey Homes, George Worthing Yates, Winston Miller; *C:* Loyal Griggs. *IVY*

Cavalry Command 🎬🎬½ *Cavalleria Commandos* **1963** Good will and integrity characterize the U.S. soldiers called into a small village to quiet a guerrilla rebellion. **77m/C VHS, Beta.** John Agar, Richard Arlen, Myron Healey, Alicia Vergel, William Phipps, Eddie Infante; *D:* Eddie Romero; *W:* Eddie Romero. *RHI*

Cave Girl WOOF! *Cavegirl* **1985 (R)** After falling through a time-warp during a high-school field trip, a social pariah makes a hit with a pre-historic honey. Sexist teen exploitation film, with few original ideas and a not-so-hot cast. **85m/C VHS, Beta, LV.** Daniel Roebuck, Cindy Ann Thompson, Saba Moor, Jeff Chayette; *D:* David Oliver; *W:* David Oliver. *COL*

Cave of the Living Dead WOOF! *Der Fluch Der Gruenen Augen* **1965** Mad professor with a past is up to something in a cave under castle. Villagers summon Inspector Doren of Interpol to solve a rash of nasty murders that they've blamed on green-eyed, cave-dwelling vampires. A challenge to watch till the end. Filmed in Sepiatone. **87m/B VHS, Beta.** *DE* YU Adrian Hoven, Erika Remberg, Carl Mohner, Wolfgang Preiss, Karin Field, John Kitzmiller, Akos Von Rathony; *D:* Akos Von Rathony. *MSP*

Caveman 🎬🎬 **1981 (PG)** Starr stars in this prehistoric spoof about a group of cavemen banished from different tribes who band together to form a tribe called "The Misfits." **92m/C VHS, Beta.** Ringo Starr, Barbara Bach, John Matuszak, Dennis Quaid, Jack Gilford, Shelley Long, Cork Hubbert; *D:* Carl Gottlieb; *W:* Carl Gottlieb, Rudy DeLuca; *M:* Lalo Schifrin. *MGM, FOX*

CB4: The Movie 🎬½ **1993 (R)** Falling somewhere between a serious attempt and parody, CB4 tries to do both and succeeds at neither. Written in the key of "Wayne's World" by "Saturday Night Live's" Rock, it starts out as a "rockumentary" (please refer to "This is Spinal Tap"), but quickly turns into a sitcom after two gangsta rap friends assume the identity of a local club owner when he is in jail. Hartman, also of SNL, appears as a right-wing city councilman. Chock full of violence, sexism, and profanity tucked into a wandering plot. *CW:* Strong language, drug content, and sexuality. **83m/C VHS, LV, Closed Caption.** Chris Rock, Allen Payne, Deezer D, Phil Hartman, Charlie Murphy, Khandi Alexander, Art Evans, Chris Elliott, Willard Pugh, Theresa Randle; *D:* Tamra Davis; *W:* Chris Rock, Nelson George, Robert Locash; *M:* John Barnes. *USH*

Cease Fire 🎬🎬 **1985 (R)** The story of a troubled Vietnam vet who finds solace in a veterans' therapy group. Adapted from the play by George Fernandez. **97m/C VHS, Beta.** Don Johnson, Robert F. Lyons, Lisa Blount; *D:* David Nutter; *M:* Gary Fry. *CNG*

Ceiling Zero 🎬🎬🎬 **1935** Cagney is an irrepressible pilot who does as he pleases and loves to aggravate his soft-hearted boss O'Brien. He falls for aviatrix Travis and neglects his duties to woo her, which leads to tragedy. Naturally, this sobers Cagney up and he volunteers for a dangerous test flight. Lots of fast-paced action and Cagney is at his swaggering best. Based on a play by Frank Wead, who also wrote the screenplay. Remade in 1941 as "International Squadron." **95m/B VHS.** James Cagney, Pat O'Brien, June Travis, Stuart Erwin, Henry Wadsworth, Isabel Jewell, Barton MacLane; *D:* Howard Hawks; *W:* Frank Wead. *MGM, FCT*

Celebrity 🎬½ **1985** In this television film, a tragic childhood secret must be confronted by three friends when one is charged with murder. Based on the Thomas Thompson novel. **313m/C VHS, Beta.** Michael Beck, Ben Masters, Joseph Bottoms; *D:* Paul Wendkos. *NO*

Celeste 🎬🎬🎬 **1981** Adlon (who later made the offbeat comedy "Sugarbaby") directed this longish but finely detailed and beautifully photographed biographical look at French writer Marcel (Remembrance of Things Past) Proust. Based on the memoirs of Proust's housekeeper, Celeste Albaret, an uneducated farmgirl, portraying the woman's devoted relationship ('til death did them part) with the middle-aged, homosexual author. It does so with wit, poignancy, and insight, but is not entirely successful in its attempt to render Proust's verbal literary style into a visual medium. In German with English subtitles. **107m/C VHS.** *GE* Eva Mattes, Jurgen Arndt, Norbert Wartha, Wolf Euba; *D:* Percy Adlon; *W:* Percy Adlon. *NYF, FCT, APD*

Celestial Clockwork 🎬🎬½ *Mecaniques Celestes* **1994** Runaway Venezuelan bride Ana (Gil), an aspiring opera singer, takes off for Paris clutching her Maria Callas poster. God must protect the innocent because she meets a friendly cabbie, immediately finds a place to live, and gets the perfect singing teacher, a cranky Russian emigre named Grigorief (Debrane). In fact, the only problem in this Cinderella's life is jealous would-be star Celeste (Dombasle), who wants the same lead theatrical role that Ana is also interested in. French with subtitles. **85m/C VHS.** *FR* Ariadna Gil, Arielle Dombasle, Evelyne Didi, Frederic Longbois, Lluis Homar, Michel Debrane; *D:* Fina Torres; *W:* Fina Torres; *C:* Ricardo Aronvich. *EVE*

Celia: Child Of Terror 🎬🎬 **1989** Set in the 1950s, this film deals with the awful results of a young girl's inability to handle disappointment. **110m/C VHS, Beta.** *AU* Rebecca Smart, Nicholas Eadie, Victoria Longley, Mary-Anne Fahey; *D:* Ann Turner. *NO*

Celine and Julie Go Boating 🎬🎬 **1974** Strange fantasy follows magician Celine (Berto) and her librarian friend, Julie (Labourier). Celine sometimes works as a governess for a little girl who lives with her widowed father in a possibly haunted house. Two women are in love with the father but he'd promised his wife never to remarry as long as their invalid daughter was still alive. Celine and Julie become worried for the little girl and decide to rescue her. An adaptation of the Henry James story "A Romance of Certain Old Clothes." French with subtitles. **193m/C VHS.** Juliet Berto, Dominique Labourier, Bulle Ogier, Marie-France Pisier, Barbet Schroeder, Philippe Clevenot, Nathalie Asnor; *D:* Jacques Rivette; *W:* Jacques Rivette, Eduardo Di Gregorio; *C:* Jacques Renard; *M:* Jean-Marie Senia. *NYF*

The Cellar 🎬½ **1990 (PG-13)** A young boy finds an ancient Comanche monster spirit in the basement of his home. His parents, as usual, don't believe him, so he must battle the monster alone. **90m/C VHS.** Patrick Kilpatrick, Suzanne Savoy, Chris Miller, Ford Rainey; *D:* Kevin S. Tenney. *HMD*

Cellar Dweller WOOF! **1987** A cartoonist moves into an old house and soon discovers it's haunted by a demonic cartoonist who killed himself thirty years earlier. What a coincidence. Low-budget scare-'em-upper filmed on one set and lit by a floodlamp. **78m/C VHS, Beta, LV.** Pamela Bellwood, Deborah Muldowney, Brian Robbins, Vince Edwards, Jeffrey Combs, Yvonne De Carlo; *D:* John Carl Buechler. *NWV*

Cellblock Sisters: Banished Behind Bars 🎬½ **1995 (R)** Biker babe Harris reunites with college girl sis Wood to off their disgusting stepfather who separately sold them to adoptive families after killing their junkie mom. Harris does the crime but Wood does the time—until her guilty sibling deliberately gets thrown behind bars in order to protect her. Has all the standard jail chicks elements. *CW:* Violence, sexuality, and language. **95m/C VHS.** Gail Harris, Annie Wood, Ace Ross; *D:* Henri Charr. *PMH*

The Celluloid Closet 🎬🎬🎬½ **1995 (R)** Terrific documentary on how Hollywood films have depicted homosexual characters, subliminally and otherwise. Working chronologically and in an historical context, beginning with silent films, there are clips from more than 100 films, along with interviews from writers and actors. (Notable is writer Gore Vidal's comments on the gay subtext in 1959's "Ben-Hur".) Based on Vito Russo's 1981 book. *CW:* Some graphic footage of sexuality and violence, and for language. **102m/C VHS, LV, Closed Caption.** *D:* Robert Epstein, Jeffrey Friedman; *W:* Armistead Maupin; *C:* Nancy Schreiber; *M:* Carter Burwell. *COL*

Celtic Pride 🎬🎬 **1996 (PG-13)** Mike O'Hara (Stern) and Jimmy Flaherty (Aykroyd) are the worst kind of crazy. They're sports nuts. They are so consumed with passion for their beloved Celtics that they kidnap foul-mouthed superstar Lewis Scott (Wayans) of the Utah Jazz before game seven of the NBA finals. If this sounds far fetched, well...it is, unless you have an ESPN junkie in your life. There's not as much court action as you would expect, since most of the story revolves around intermittent trash-talking and escape attempts. If you're a Celtic hater, stick around for the end, when the Boston Garden is demolished using special effects.*CW:* Language and an abundance of crude humor. 90m/C **VHS, LV, Closed Caption.** Damon Wayans, Daniel Stern, Dan Aykroyd, Gail O'Grady, Adam Hendershott, Paul Guilfoyle, Deion Sanders, Christopher McDonald, Gus Williams, Ted Rooney, Vladimir Cuk; *Cameos:* Bill Walton, Larry Bird; *D:* Tom DeCerchio; *W:* Judd Apatow; *C:* Oliver Wood; *M:* Basil Poledouris. **TOU**

The Cement Garden 🎾🎾 1993 Fatherless 15-year-old Jack (Robertson) and 16-year-old sister Julie (Gainsbourg) are afraid that they and their two younger siblings Sue (Coulthard) and Tom (Birkin) will be taken into foster care after their mother dies at home. So to keep their secret, they bury her in the basement and try to assume a normal family life. Not that this works for long—Jack and Julie give into an incestuous fascination and the household slowly sinks into chaotic squalor around them. Gainsbourg is the director's niece and the young Birkin is his son. Based on Ian McEwan's 1978 novel. 105m/C VHS. FR GE GB Charlotte Gainsbourg, Andrew Robertson, Alice Coulthard, Ned Birkin, Sinead Cusack, Hanns Zischler, Jochen Horst; *D:* Andrew Birkin; *W:* Andrew Birkin; *C:* Stephen Blackman; *M:* Ed Shearmur. **NYF**

The Cemetery Club 🎾🎾½ 1993 (PG-13) Story of three Jewish widows who make weekly visits to their husband's graves while attempting to cope with their lives. Doris (Dukakis) is loyal to the memory of her husband and acts as the moral conscience of the trio. Lucille (Ladd) is a merry widow who wears clothes more suitable for younger women, but she also harbors a painful secret. Esther (Burstyn) struggles with her loneliness until a widowed cab driver begins to woo her. Commendably, the characters are given more dimension than Hollywood usually grants women of a certain age. Based on the play "The Cemetary Club" by Menchell, who also wrote the screenplay.*CW:* Some language and sensuality. 114m/C **VHS, Beta, LV, Closed Caption.** Ellen Burstyn, Olympia Dukakis, Diane Ladd, Danny Aiello, Lainie Kazan, Christina Ricci, Bernie Casey, Alan Mason, Sam Schwartz, Jeff Howell, Robert Costanzo, Wallace Shawn, Louis Guss; *D:* Bill Duke; *W:* Ivan Menchell; *C:* Steven Poster; *M:* Elmer Bernstein. **TOU, BTV**

Cemetery High 🎾 1989 Beautiful high school girls decide to lure the local boys into a trap and kill them. 80m/C **VHS, Beta.** Debi Thibeault, Karen Nielsen, Lisa Schmidt, Ruth Collins, Simone, Tony Kruk, David Coughlin, Frank Stewart; *D:* Gorman Bechard; *W:* Gorman Bechard, Carmine Capobianco. **UNI, HHE**

Cemetery Man 🎾🎾 *Dellamorte Delamore; Of Death, Of Love* 1995 (R) Grotesque little saga about zombies and necrophilia set in a small Italian cemetery. Thanks to a weird post-death plague the corpses refuse to stay quietly in their graves, forcing watchman Francisco Dellamorte (Everett) and mute gravedigger Gnaghi (Hadji-Lazaro) to split their heads open. But when Francisco's dead sweetheart (Falchi) rises from her grave, he's a little slow to rebury the still-active corpse. Based on the Italian graphic novel "Dellamorte Dellamore," from the "Dylan Dog" series by Tiziano Sclavi.*CW:* Macabre violence and gore, strong sexuality, some language. 100m/C VHS, **Closed Caption.** *IT* Rupert Everett, Anna Falchi, Francois Hadji-Lazaro; *D:* Michele (Michael) Soavi; *W:* Gianni Romoli; *C:* Mauro Marchetti; *M:* Manuel De Sica. **FOX**

Center of the Web 🎾🎾 1992 (R) John Phillips is a victim of mistaken identity—someone thinks he's a professional hit man. After surviving an apparent mob attempt on his life, Phillips is persuaded by a CIA operative to go along with the deception in order to capture a potential political assassin. At least that's what Phillips is told, but

he soon realizes that the deeper he gets into his new role, the deadlier the plot becomes. Davi is one of the best bad guys around and the fast-paced stunts and plot twists make this watchable.*CW:* Language and violence. 88m/C VHS, LV. Ted Prior, Robert Davi, Tony Curtis, Charlene Tilton, Bo Hopkins, Charles Napier; *D:* David A. Prior. **AIP**

The Centerfold Girls WOOF! 1974 (R) Microscopic storyline involves a deranged man who is determined to kill all the voluptuous young women who have posed nude for a centerfold. 93m/C VHS, Beta. Andrew Prine, Tiffany Bolling, Aldo Ray, Jeremy Slate, Ray Danton, Francine York; *D:* John Peyser. **MED**

Century 🎾🎾 1994 (R) Ambitious young doctor Paul Reisner (Owen), the son of a prosperous Jewish father (Stephens), gets a position at a London research hospital headed by the charismatic Professor Mandry (Dance). Paul manages to disgrace himself by provoking Mandry and is dismissed but finds out some disturbing information and is determined to discredit his former mentor. Anti-Semitism lurks as does the change from Victorian mores to the challenging dawn of the 20th century. Complex performances are somewhat undermined by the static direction.*CW:* Some scenes of sexuality. 112m/C VHS. GB Clive Owen, Charles Dance, Miranda Richardson, Robert Stephens, Joan Hickson, Lena Headey, Neil Stuke; *D:* Stephen Poliakoff; *W:* Stephen Poliakoff; *C:* Witold Stok; *M:* Michael Gibbs. **PGV**

A Century of Women 1994 Three-part look at the lives and accomplishments of American women over the past 100 years, including the changing role of women in the workplace and the home. The documentary segments are interspersed with a fictional story spanning five generations of women who reunite for a weekend. On 3 cassettes. 360m/C VHS. Teresa Wright, Olympia Dukakis, Justine Bateman, Talia Shire, Madge Sinclair, Jasmine Guy, Brooke Smith. **TTC**

Certain Fury 🎾 1985 (R) Two timid women go on the lam when they are mistaken for escaped prostitutes who shot up a courthouse. The sooner they get caught, the better. 88m/C VHS, Beta, LV. Tatum O'Neal, Irene Cara, Peter Fonda, Nicholas Campbell, Moses Gunn; *D:* Stephen Gyllenhaal. **NWV, VTR**

Certain Sacrifice 🎾 1980 Nineteen-year-old Madonna expresses herself in her film debut. Seeking revenge on the man who raped her, she murders him in a strange ritualistic manner underneath the Brooklyn Bridge. Poor is the man whose pleasures depend on the permission of another?*CW:* Language and violence. 60m/C VHS, Beta, LV. Madonna, Jeremy Pattnosh, Charles Kurtz; *D:* Stephen Lewicki. **WOV, MVD**

Cesar 🎾🎾🎾🎾 1936 This is the third and most bittersweet part of Pagnol's famed trilogy based on his play depicting the lives and loves of the people of Provence, France. Marius returns after a 20-year absence to his beloved Fanny and his now-grown son, Cesariot. The first two parts of the trilogy are "Marius" and "Fanny" and were directed by Alexander Korda and Marc Allegret respectively. In French with English subtitles. 117m/B VHS, Beta, LV. FR Raimu, Pierre Fresnay, Orane Demazis, Charpin, Andre Fouche, Alida Rauffe; *D:* Marcel Pagnol; *W:* Marcel Pagnol; *M:* Vincent Scotto. **NOS, MRV, INT**

Cesar & Rosalie 🎾🎾🎾 1972 (PG) Acclaimed French comedy depicts the love triangle between a beautiful divorcee, her aging live-in companion and a younger man. Engaging portrait of how their relationship evolves over time. In French with English subtitles. 110m/C VHS, Beta, LV. FR Romy Schneider, Yves Montand, Sami Frey, Umberto Orsini; *D:* Claude Sautet. **TPV**

Cesare Borgia 🎾🎾 1923 Veidt stars in this bloodthirsty saga as the ruthless son of Pope Alexander VI who'll let nothing come between him and his desires. 83m/B VHS. GE Conrad Veidt; *D:* Richard Oswald. **FCT**

Chain Gang Killings 🎾 1985 Pair of shackled prisoners, one black, the other white, escape from a truck transporting them to prison. 99m/C VHS, Beta. Ian Yule, Ken Gampu. **NO**

Chain Gang Women WOOF! 1972 (R) Sordid violence. Two escaped convicts plunder, rob, and rape until a victim's husband comes looking for revenge. 85m/C VHS. Robert Lott, Barbara Mills, Michael Stearns, Linda York; *D:* Lee Frost. **NO**

Chain Lightning 🎾 1950 Bogart stars as a bomber pilot who falls in love with a Red Cross worker (Parker) while fighting in Europe in 1943. They lose touch after the war until Bogie goes to work as a test pilot for the same shady airplane manufacturer (Massey) where Parker works. He is given the chance to test a new plane, which has already cost the life of one of his friends. Bogart has more success, along with rekindling the flames of romance. Average script but the flying sequences are well-done. 94m/B VHS. Humphrey Bogart, Eleanor Parker, Raymond Massey, Richard Whorf; *D:* Stuart Heisler. **MGM**

Chain of Command 🎾🎾 1995 (R) Anti-terrorist agent Merrill Ross (Dudikoff) goes up against hired mercenaries trying to overthrow the government of the oil-rich republic of Qumir. Then Ross realizes he's been manipulated and it could be by any number of players.*CW:* Language, violence, brief nudity. 97m/C VHS. Michael Dudikoff, R. Lee Ermey. **AVE**

Chain of Desire 🎾🎾 1993 Nightclub inside Manhattan's Chrysler Building is the spot for numerous folk to have lot of meaningless sexual encounters and look at the emptiness of their lives. 107m/C VHS, Beta, LV. Linda Fiorentino, Elias Koteas, Malcolm McDowell, Grace Zabriskie, Tim Guinee, Assumpta Serna, Patrick Bauchau, Seymour Cassel, Kevin Conroy, Angel Aviles, Holly Marie Combs, Jamie Harold, Dewey Weber, Suzanne Douglas; *D:* Temistocles Lopez; *W:* Temistocles Lopez; *C:* Nancy Schreiber; *M:* Nathan Birnbaum. Nominations: Independent Spirit Awards '94: Best Cinematography. **PSM**

Chain Reaction 🎾½ *Nuclear Run* 1980 When a nuclear scientist is exposed to radiation after an accident at an atomic power plant, he must escape to warn the public of the danger. 87m/C VHS, Beta, LV. Steve Bisley, Ross Thompson; *D:* Ian Barry; *C:* Russell Boyd. **NO**

Chain Reaction 🎾🎾½ *Dead Drop* 1996 (PG-13) Government/scientific conspiracy chase story finds Chicago lab tech Eddie Kasalivich (Reeves) a member of a research team that's discovered the formula for cheap, pollution-free energy. This doesn't sit well with someone since the team's leader is murdered and the lab destroyed in an explosion. Eddie and scientist Lily Sinclair (Weisz) become prime suspects and are pursued by the feds as they try to find the real culprits. Old pro Freeman, as money man Paul Shannon, is the best reason to watch (as usual). Davis did "The Fugitive," so he knows his tension-filled chases but this is just more same old-same old.*CW:* Some intense action/violence. 107m/C VHS, LV, Closed Caption. Keanu Reeves, Morgan Freeman, Rachel Weisz, Fred Ward, Brian Cox, Kevin Dunn, Joanna Cassidy, Chelcie Ross, Tzi Ma, Nicholas Rudall; *D:* Andrew Davis; *W:* J.F. Lawton, Michael Bortman; *C:* Frank Tidy; *M:* Jerry Goldsmith. Nominations: Golden Raspberry Awards '96: Worst Actor (Reeves). **TCF**

Chained 🎾🎾½ 1934 Crawford and Gable star in this love triangle that somehow never sizzles. Crawford, in love with married businessman Kruger, takes a South American cruise to get away from it all, meets Gable, and of course falls in love. Seems simple enough, but wait! Crawford goes back to New York City and marries Kruger (his wife grants him a divorce) and is miserable. But then Gable shows up, further complicating matters. Choices, choices. Predictable script was not helped by half-hearted performances. 73m/B VHS, Beta. Joan Crawford, Clark Gable, Otto Kruger, Stuart Erwin, Una O'Connor; *D:* Clarence Brown. **MGM, CCB**

Chained for Life WOOF! 1951 Daisy and Violet Hilton, real life Siamese twins, star in this old-fashioned "freak" show. When a gigolo deserts one twin on their wedding night, the other twin shoots him dead. The twins go on trial and the judge asks the viewer to hand down the verdict. Exploitative and embarrassing to watch. **81m/B VHS, Beta.** Daisy Hilton, Violet Hilton; **D:** Harry Fraser. *SNC, NOS, RHI*

Chained Heat 🎬🎬 1983 (R) Seamy tale of the vicious reality of life for women behind bars. Naive Blair is imprisoned again (after another bad jailhouse gig in "Born Innocent") and has usual assortment of negative experiences with domineering prisoners, degenerative guards, and the creepy warden who maintains a prison bachelor pad equipped with hot tub. Needless to say, she grows up in a hurry. Trashifying, archetypal women-in-prison effort that aims to satisfy full range of low-quality audience demands. Sequel to 1982 "Concrete Jungle." **97m/C VHS, Beta, LV.** Linda Blair, Stella Stevens, Sybil Danning, Tamara Dobson, Henry Silva, John Vernon, Nita Talbot, Louisa Moritz; **D:** Paul Nicholas; **C:** Mac Ahlberg. *Golden Raspberry Awards '83: Worst Supporting Actress (Danning).VES*

Chained Heat 2 🎬½ 1992 (R) Another sordid tale of women behind bars. Nielsen stars as the psychotic stiletto-heeled warden of an infamous prison, complete with sadistic heroin-smuggling guards. This drug ring also deals in prostitution, which results in two imprisoned sisters (innocent, naturally) being separated from one another. One sister is determined to find true justice. **98m/C VHS, LV, Closed Caption.** Brigitte Nielsen, Paul Koslo, Kari Whitman, Kimberley Kates; **D:** Lloyd A. Simanol; **W:** Chris Hyde. *NLC*

Chains 🎬 1989 (R) A Chicago gangland feud entraps two couples in its web, and the innocents must take care of themselves when the situation goes from bad to worse. **93m/C VHS, LV.** Jimi Jourdan, Michael Dixon, John L. Eves; **D:** Roger J. Barski. *IMP*

Chains of Gold 🎬🎬 1992 (R) Kind social worker (Travolta) befriends teen who wants to get out of the crack-dealing gang in which he's involved. He infiltrates the gang and risks his life helping the boy get out. Originally aired on cable television. **95m/C VHS, Closed Caption.** John Travolta, Marilu Henner, Bernie Casey, Hector Elizondo, Joey Lawrence; **D:** Rod Holcomb; **M:** Trevor Jones. *ACA*

The Chair 🎬🎬 *Hot Seat* 1987 (R) The penitentiary where an evil superintendent was fried in his own electric chair during an inmate uprising is reopened after two decades. The new warden (Benedict), who used to be a subordinate to the dead man, believes in rigid control of the inmates and locks horns with the big-house shrink (Coco), who on the surface is an intelligent humanitarian, but may have a darker side. This acrimonious dispute takes a back seat, when it appears that the spirit of the late warden has come back to make the inmates pay for his untimely death.**CW:** Language and strong violence. **90m/C VHS, LV, Closed Caption.** James Coco, Paul Benedict, Stephen Geoffreys, Trini Alvarado, John Bentley; **D:** Waldemar Korzeniowsky. *IMP*

The Chalk Garden 🎬🎬🎬 1964 A woman with a mysterious past takes on the job of governess for an unruly 14-year-old girl, with unforeseen consequences. An excellent adaptation of the Enid Bagnold play although not as suspenseful as the stage production. **106m/C VHS, Beta.** *GB* Deborah Kerr, Hayley Mills, Edith Evans, John Mills, Elizabeth Sellars, Felix Aylmer; **D:** Ronald Neame; **W:** John Michael Hayes; **M:** Malcolm Arnold. *National Board of Review Awards '64: 10 Best Films of the Year, Best Supporting Actress (Evans); Nominations: Academy Awards '64: Best Supporting Actress (Evans). USH*

The Challenge 🎬🎬🎬 1938 Story of the courageous party of explorers who conquered the Matterhorn. Incredible avalanche scenes. **77m/B VHS, Beta.** Luis Trenker, Robert Douglas. *DVT, VYY*

Challenge WOOF! 1974 (PG) When his entire family is killed, dad decides to seek revenge with his shotgun. Very bloody and violent and very nearly plotless. **90m/C VHS.** Earl Owensby, William T. Hicks, Katheryn Thompson, Johnny Popwell; **D:** Martin Beck. *FOX*

The Challenge 🎬🎬½ 1982 (R) A contemporary action spectacle which combines modern swordplay with the mysticism and fantasy of ancient Samurai legends. **108m/C VHS, Beta.** Scott Glenn, Toshiro Mifune; **D:** John Frankenheimer; **W:** John Sayles, Richard Maxwell; **M:** Jerry Goldsmith. *FOX*

Challenge of a Lifetime 🎬🎬½ 1985 Marshall stars as a divorcee whose dream is to compete in the Hawaiian Ironman Triathlon. Cult favorite; Woronov has a substantial supporting role. **100m/C VHS.** Penny Marshall, Richard Gilliland, Jonathan Silverman, Mary Woronov, Paul Gleason, Mark Spitz, Cathy Rigby; **D:** Russ Mayberry. *TTC, MOV*

Challenge of McKenna 🎬🎬 1983 Run-of-the-prairie horse opera has drifter Ireland stumble upon danger and intrigue when he enters a mysterious town. **90m/C VHS.** John Ireland, Robert Woods. *PMH*

Challenge of the Masters 🎬 1989 A young Kung-Fu artist wins a new tutor in a contest. Soon he's fighting for a friend to protect his family's honor. **97m/C VHS.** Liu Chia Hui, Liu Chia-Hui, Chen Kuan-Tai, Chiang Yang; **D:** Lu Chia-Liang. *HMD*

Challenge the Ninja 🎬 1987 One talented fighter defends a town from high-kicking hordes. Lots of kung fu action for martial arts fans. **92m/C VHS, Beta.** Bruce Baron, Pierre Tremblay, Richard Berman, Eric Redner. *TWE*

Challenge To Be Free 🎬🎬 *Mad Trapper of the Yukon* 1976 (G) Action adventure geared toward a young audience depicting the struggles of a man being pursued by 12 men and 100 dogs across a thousand miles of frozen wilderness. The last film directed by Garnett, who has a cameo as Marshal McGee. Produced in 1972, the release wasn't until 1976. **90m/C VHS, Beta.** Mike Mazurki, Jimmy Kane; **Cameos:** Tay Garnett; **D:** Tay Garnett. *MED, VTR*

Challenge to Lassie 🎬🎬½ 1949 (G) When Lassie's Scottish master dies, the faithful pup remains at his grave. An unsympathetic policeman orders Lassie to leave the premises, inspiring a debate among the townsfolk as to the dog's fate. Based on a true story (although the original hero was a Skye Terrier); remade as "Greyfriar's Bobby." **76m/C VHS, Beta.** Edmund Gwenn, Donald Crisp, Geraldine Brooks, Reginald Owen, Alan Webb, Henry Stephenson, Alan Napier, Sara Allgood; **D:** Richard Thorpe; **M:** Andre Previn. *MGM, FCT*

Challenge to White Fang 🎬½ 1986 (PG) A courageous dog prevents a scheming businessman from taking over an old man's gold mine. **89m/C VHS, Beta.** Harry Carey Jr., Franco Nero; **D:** Lucio Fulci. *TWE*

The Challengers 🎬🎬½ 1993 Young Mackie wants to join local rock band The Challengers, only to discover their main rule is no girls. So Mackie disguises herself as her male cousin Mac—getting ever more confused as she tries to juggle her dual identities. Then she gets found out. **97m/C VHS.** Gema Zamprogna, Gwynyth Walsh, Eric Christmas, Eric Till; **W:** Clive Endersby. *TRI*

The Chamber 🎬🎬 1996 (R) Dull retelling of yet another John Grisham legal thriller fails to engross. White supremacist Sam Cahill (Hackman) is on Mississippi's death row for killing two Jewish boys in a 1967 bombing. Young Chicago lawyer Adam Hall (O'Donnell), seeking to find out more about his family's odious past, volunteers to work on his grandfather's case and win a stay of execution. Sam's an unrepentent racist but there's some question about whether he was the only culprit. Hackman and Dunaway (as his alcoholic daughter) are their usual professional selves while the charming O'Donnell seems out of his depth. Co-screenwriter Robinson used the pseud Chris Reese.**CW:** Violent images and some language. **113m/C VHS, LV, Closed Caption.** Gene Hackman, Chris O'Donnell, Faye Dunaway, Lela Rochon, Robert Prosky, Raymond J. Barry, Bo Jackson, David Marshall Grant, Millie Perkins; **D:** James Foley; **W:** Phil Alden Robinson, William Goldman; **C:** Ian Baker; **M:** Carter Burwell. *Nominations: Golden Raspberry Awards '96: Worst Supporting Actress (Dunaway). USH*

Chamber of Horrors 🎬🎬½ *The Door With Seven Locks* 1940 A family is brought together at an English castle to claim a fortune left by an aristocrat. However, there's a catch—seven keys may open the vault with the fortune, or leave the key turner dead. Based on the work by Edgar Wallace. **80m/B VHS, Beta.** *GB* Leslie Banks, Lilli Palmer; **D:** Norman Lee. *NOS, MRV, SNC*

Chameleon 1981 A freeform dramatic examination of a day in the life of a Los Angeles pusher. **90m/C VHS, Beta.** Bob Glaudini; **D:** Jon Jost. *FCT*

Chameleon 🎬🎬 1995 (R) Undercover agent, who's a master of disguise, has his family murdered by drug cartel head and he seeks revenge.**CW:** Some violence. **108m/C VHS.** Anthony LaPaglia, Kevin Pollak, Melora Hardin, Wayne Knight; **D:** Michael Pavone; **W:** Michael Pavone; **C:** Ross Berryman; **M:** John Debney. *AVE*

Chameleon Street 🎬🎬🎬 1989 (R) Entertaining fact-based account of William Douglas Street, a Detroit man who successfully impersonated, among others, a Time magazine reporter and a surgeon until he was caught and sent to prison. He escaped and went to Yale, faked his identity as a student, and then returned to Michigan to impersonate a lawyer for the Detroit Human Rights Commission. Harris wrote and directed this insightful look into the man who fooled many people, including the mayor of Detroit, Coleman A. Young, who appears briefly as himself.**CW:** Language and sexual dialogue. **95m/C VHS, LV.** Wendell B. Harris Jr., Angela Leslie, Amina Fakir, Paula McGee, Mano Breckenridge, David Kiley, Anthony Ennis; **Cameos:** Coleman A. Young; **D:** Wendell B. Harris Jr.; **W:** Wendell B. Harris Jr.; **C:** Daniel S. Noga; **M:** Peter S. Moore. *Sundance Film Festival '90: Grand Jury Prize. ACA, FCT*

The Champ 🎬🎬🎬 1932 A washed up boxer dreams of making a comeback and receives support from no one but his devoted son. Minor classic most notorious for jerking the tears and soiling the hankies, this was the first of three Beery/Cooper screen teamings. **87m/B VHS, Beta, LV.** Wallace Beery, Jackie Cooper, Irene Rich, Roscoe Ates, Edward Brophy, Hale Hamilton, Jesse Scott, Marcia Mae Jones; **D:** King Vidor; **W:** Frances Marion. *Academy Awards '32: Best Actor (Beery), Best Story; Nominations: Academy Awards '32: Best Director (Vidor), Best Picture. MGM, FCT, BTV*

The Champ 🎬½ 1979 (PG) An ex-fighter with a weakness for gambling and drinking is forced to return to the ring in an attempt to keep custody of his son. Excessive sentiment may cause cringing. Remake of the 1931 classic. **121m/C VHS, Beta, LV.** Jon Voight, Faye Dunaway, Rick Schroder, Jack Warden, Arthur Hill, Strother Martin, Joan Blondell, Elisha Cook Jr.; **D:** Franco Zeffirelli; **C:** Fred W. Koenekamp; **M:** Dave Grusin. *Nominations: Academy Awards '79: Best Original Score. MGM*

Champagne 🎬🎬 1928 A socialite's father fakes bankruptcy to teach his irresponsible daughter a lesson. Early, silent endeavor from Hitchcock is brilliantly photographed. **93m/B VHS.** *GB* Betty Balfour, Gordon Harker, Ferdinand von Alten, Clifford Heatherly, Jack Trevor; **D:** Alfred Hitchcock; **W:** Alfred Hitchcock. *GPV, MLB, VEC*

Champagne for Breakfast 🎬 1935 (R) Sex comedy follows the fun-filled adventures of "Champagne," a free-spirited beauty living life to the fullest. **69m/B VHS.** Mary Carlisle, Hardie Albright, Joan Marsh, Lila Lee, Sidney Toler, Bradley Page, Emerson Treacy; **D:** Melville Brown. *NO*

Champagne for Caesar ✓✓✓ 1950

The laughs keep coming in this comedy about a self-proclaimed genius-on-every-subject who goes on a television quiz show and proceeds to win everything in sight. The program's sponsor, in desperation, hires a femme fatale to distract the contestant before the final program. Wonderful spoof of the game-show industry. **90m/B VHS, Beta, LV.** Ronald Colman, Celeste Holm, Vincent Price, Art Linkletter, Barbara Britton; **D:** Richard Whorf. *VCI*

Champion ✓✓✓½ 1949

An ambitious prizefighter alienates the people around him as he desperately fights his way to the top. When he finally reaches his goal, he is forced to question the cost of his success. From a story by Ring Lardner. Certainly one of the best films ever made about boxing, with less sentiment than "Rocky" but concerned with sociological correctness. **99m/B VHS, Closed Caption.** Kirk Douglas, Arthur Kennedy, Marilyn Maxwell, Ruth Roman, Lola Albright, Paul Stewart; **D:** Mark Robson; **W:** Carl Foreman; **C:** Franz Planer; **M:** Dimitri Tiomkin. Academy Awards '49: Best Film Editing; Nominations: Academy Awards '49: Best Actor (Douglas), Best Black and White Cinematography, Best Screenplay, Best Supporting Actor (Kennedy), Original Dramatic/Comedy Score. *REP*

The Champion/His New Job ✓✓✓

Champion Charlie 1915 Two classic silent shorts by Chaplin, with music; the first is alternately entitled "Champion Charlie." **53m/B VHS, Beta, 8mm.** Charlie Chaplin, Edna Purviance, Ben Turpin, Gloria Swanson, Mack Swain, "Broncho" Billy Anderson; **D:** Charlie Chaplin. *VYY*

Champion Operation ✓ 1987

Hong Kong heavies pose as police officers. The action follows them from the slums to the red-light district. Lots of martial arts action. **100m/C VHS.** Tong Chun Chung, Yu Ka Hei, Tang Ho Kwong. *MGI*

Champions ✓✓ 1984

Moving but cliched story of Bob Champion, a leading jockey who overcame cancer to win England's Grand National Steeplechase. A true story, no less. **113m/C VHS, Beta, LV, Closed Caption.** *GB* John Hurt, Gregory Jones, Mick Dillon, Ann Bell, Jan Francis, Peter Barkworth, Edward Woodward, Ben Johnson, Kirstie Alley, Alison Steadman; **D:** John Irvin; **W:** Evan Jones; **M:** Carl Davis. *NLC*

Chan Is Missing ✓✓✓ 1982

Two cab drivers try to find the man who stole their life savings. Wry, low-budget comedy filmed in San Francisco's Chinatown was an art-house smash. The first full-length American film produced exclusively by an Asian-American cast and crew. **80m/B VHS.** Wood Moy, Marc Hayashi, Laureen Chew, Judy Mihei, Peter Wang, Presco Tabios, Frankie Allarcon, Virginia Cerenio, Roy Chan, George Woo, Emily Yamasaki, Ellen Yeung; **D:** Wayne Wang; **W:** Wayne Wang, Terrel Seltzer, Isaac Cronin; **C:** Michael G. Chin; **M:** Robert Kikuchi-Yngojo. *NYF*

Chance ✓½ 1989

With over a million dollars in diamonds missing, Haggerty and Jacobs throw out all the stops to recover them in this action thriller. **90m/C VHS.** Dan Haggerty, Lawrence-Hilton Jacobs, Addison Randall, Roger Rudd, Charles Gries, Pamela Dixon; **D:** Addison Randall, Charles Kanganis. *PMH*

Chances Are ✓✓✓ 1989 (PG)

After her loving husband dies in a chance accident, a pregnant woman remains unmarried, keeping her husband's best friend as her only close male companion. Years later, her now teenage daughter brings a friend home for dinner, but due to an error in heaven, the young man begins to realize that this may not be the first time he and this family have met. A wonderful love-story hampered only minimally by the unbelievable plot. **108m/C VHS, Beta, LV, 8mm, Closed Caption.** Cybill Shepherd, Robert Downey Jr., Ryan O'Neal, Mary Stuart Masterson, Josef Sommer, Christopher McDonald, Joe Grifasi, James Noble, Susan Ruttan, Fran Ryan; **D:** Emile Ardolino; **W:** Perry Howze, Randy Howze; **M:** Maurice Jarre. Nominations: Academy Awards '89: Best Song ("After All"). *COL, FCT*

Chandu on the Magic Island ✓✓ 1934

Chandu the Magician takes his powers of the occult to the mysterious lost island of Lemuri to battle the evil cult of Ubasti. Sequel to "Chandu the Magician" and just as campy. **67m/B VHS, Beta.** Bela Lugosi, Maria Alba, Clara Kimball Young. *NOS, SNC, VYY*

Chandu the Magician ✓✓ 1932

Bad guy searches desperately for the secret of a powerful death ray so he can (surprise!) destroy civilization. Not well received in its day, but makes for great high-camp fun now. One of Lugosi's most melodramatic performances. **70m/B VHS, Beta.** Edmund Lowe, Bela Lugosi, Irene Ware, Henry B. Walthall; **D:** William Cameron Menzies, Marcel Varnel; **C:** James Wong Howe. *MLB, RXM*

Chanel Solitaire ✓✓ 1981 (R)

Uninspiring biography follows the fabulous (simply fabulous) career of dress designer Gabrielle "Coco" Chanel. Ah, go sew something. **124m/C VHS, Beta.** Marie-France Pisier, Rutger Hauer, Timothy Dalton, Karen Black, Brigitte Fossey; **D:** George Kaczender. *MED, FCT*

Chang: A Drama of the Wilderness ✓✓✓½ 1927

A farmer and his family have settled a small patch of ground on the edge of the jungle and must struggle for survival against numerous wild animals. The climatic elephant stampede is still thrilling. Shot on location in Siam. **67m/B VHS.** **D:** Ernest B. Schoedsack; **W:** Merian C. Cooper, Ernest B. Schoedsack. *MIL*

Change of Habit ✓✓ 1969 (G)

Three novitiates undertake to learn about the world before becoming full-fledged nuns. While working at a ghetto clinic a young doctor forms a strong, affectionate relationship with one of them. Presley's last feature film. ♫Change of Habit; Let Us Pray; Rubberneckin'. **93m/C VHS, Beta.** Elvis Presley, Mary Tyler Moore, Barbara McNair, Ed Asner, Ruth McDevitt, Regis Toomey; **D:** William A. Graham; **C:** Russell Metty; **M:** Billy Goldenberg. *USH, GKK*

A Change of Seasons ✓✓ 1980 (R)

One of them so-called sophisticated comedies that look at the contemporary relationships and values of middle-class, middle-aged people who should know better. The wife of a college professor learns of her husband's affair with a seductive student and decides to have a fling with a younger man. The situation reaches absurdity when the couples decide to vacation together. **102m/C Beta.** Shirley MacLaine, Bo Derek, Anthony Hopkins, Michael Brandon, Mary Beth Hurt; **D:** Richard Lang; **W:** Erich Segal; **M:** Henry Mancini. *FOX*

The Changeling ✓✓½ 1980 (R)

A music teacher moves into an old house and discovers that a young boy's ghostly spirit is his housemate. The ghost wants revenge against the being that replaced him upon his death. Scary ghost story with some less than logical leaps of script. **114m/C VHS, Beta, LV.** *CA* George C. Scott, Trish Van Devere, John Russell, Melvyn Douglas, Jean Marsh; **D:** Peter Medak. Genie Awards '80: Best Film. *VES*

Changes ✓ 1969 (PG)

A young man leaves home and thumbs across the California coast in order to find himself. On the road again. **103m/C VHS, Beta.** Kent Lane, Michele Carey, Jack Albertson, Marcia Strassman; **D:** Hall Bartlett. *PSM*

Changing Habits ✓½ 1996 (R)

Starving artist Soosh (Kelly) moves into a nunnery, in exchange for doing chores, in order to save money. She's so broke, she's taken to stealing art supplies, but salesman Felix (Walsh) is more interested in romancing Soosh than turning her in. Dull, dull, dull, and a waste of a talented cast. **92m/C VHS, LV, Closed Caption.** Moira Kelly, Christopher Lloyd, Teri Garr, Shelley Duvall, Dylan Walsh, Marissa Ribisi, Francis Bay, Bob Gunton, Anne Haney, Eileen Brennan; **D:** Lynn Roth; **W:** Scott Davis Jones; **C:** Mike Mayers; **M:** David McHugh. *APX*

The Channeler ✓ 1989

The traditional dopey students probe an old Colorado mine and encounter black-robed, demon whazzits. A spunky cast and nice scenery didn't stop the

Hound from switching channels on this one. **90m/C VHS, Beta.** Dan Haggerty, Richard Harrison, Jay Richardson, David Homb, Oliver Darrow, Robin Sims, Charles Solomon; **D:** Grant Austin Waldman. *NO*

Chantilly Lace ✓✓½ 1993 (R)

Ensemble cast tries hard in this story of modern American women and friendship in the nineties. Val (Eilenberry) gathers a group of seven close friends at her new house in Sundance. Turns out trying to "have it all" is causing some emotional crises to surface, which are explored over the course of a year. Actresses improvised their dialogue from basic character information. Lots of weeping and bonding. Made for cable television. **CW:** Strong language and scene of sexuality. **102m/C VHS, Closed Caption.** Jill Eikenberry, Ally Sheedy, Helen Slater, Lindsay Crouse, JoBeth Williams, Martha Plimpton, Talia Shire; **D:** Linda Yellen; **W:** Linda Yellen, Rosanne Ehrlich; **M:** Patrick Seymour. *COL*

Chapayev ✓✓✓ 1934

Striking propagandist drama dealing with the exploits of a legendary Red Army commander during the 1919 battle with the White Russians. Stunning, and carefully choreographed, battle scenes. Adapted from a biographical novel by Dmitri Furmanov. In Russian with English subtitles. **101m/B VHS, Beta.** *RU* Boris Babochkin, Leonid Kmit; **D:** Sergei Vasiliev, Gregory Vasiliev. National Board of Review Awards '35: 5 Best Foreign Films of the Year. *VYY, AUD, IHF*

Chaplin ✓✓✓ 1992 (PG-13)

The life and career of "The Little Tramp" is chronicled by director Attenborough and brilliantly portrayed by Downey, Jr, as Chaplin. A flashback format traces his life from its poverty-stricken Dickensian origins in the London slums through his directing and acting career, to his honorary Oscar in 1972. Slow-moving at parts, but captures Chaplin's devotion to his art and also his penchant towards jailbait. In a clever casting choice, Chaplin's own daughter from his fourth marriage to Oona O'Neill, Geraldine Chaplin, plays her own grandmother who goes mad. **CW:** Language and nudity. **135m/C VHS, LV, Closed Caption.** *GB* Robert Downey Jr., Dan Aykroyd, Geraldine Chaplin, Kevin Dunn, Anthony Hopkins, Milla Jovovich, Moira Kelly, Kevin Kline, Diane Lane, Penelope Ann Miller, Paul Rhys, John Thaw, Marisa Tomei, Nancy Travis, James Woods, David Duchovny, Deborah Maria Moore, Bill Paterson, John Standing, Robert Stephens, Peter Crook; **D:** Richard Attenborough; **W:** Bryan Forbes, William Boyd, William Goldman; **C:** Sven Nykvist; **M:** John Barry. British Academy Awards '92: Best Actor (Downey); Nominations: Academy Awards '92: Best Actor (Downey), Best Art Direction/Set Decoration, Best Original Score. *LIV, MOV, FCT*

The Chaplin Revue ✓✓ 1958

The "Revue," put together by Chaplin in 1958, consists of three of his best shorts: "A Dog's Life" (1918), the WWI comedy "Shoulder Arms" (1918), and "The Pilgrim," in which a convict hides out in a clerical guise (1922). Chaplin added self-composed score, narration, and some documentary on-the-set material. **121m/B VHS, Beta.** Charlie Chaplin, Edna Purviance, Sydney Chaplin, Mack Swain; **D:** Charlie Chaplin. *FOX*

Chapter in Her Life ✓✓½ 1923

An early silent film by Lois Weber which examines the relationships between an orphaned child and the adults in her life. **87m/B VHS, Beta.** **D:** Lois Weber. *GVV*

Chapter Two ✓✓ 1979 (PG)

Loosely based on Neil Simon's marriage to Mason and his Broadway hit of the same name. A writer, grief-stricken over the death of his first wife, meets the woman who will become his second. Witty dialogue in first half deteriorates when guilt strikes. **124m/C VHS, Beta, LV, Closed Caption.** James Caan, Marsha Mason, Valerie Harper, Joseph Bologna; **D:** Robert Moore; **W:** Neil Simon. Nominations: Academy Awards '79: Best Actress (Mason). *COL*

Charade ✓✓ 1953

Mason and wife Pamela star in this trilogy of love and violence. "Portrait of a Murderer" has a young artist sketching the picture of the man who—unknown to her—has just murdered her girlfriend. "Duel at Dawn" concerns an 1880s Austrian officer who steals a woman from another officer and is then challenged to a duel. "The Midas Touch" revolves around a successful but dissatisfied man who abandons his riches to find the meaning of life. Mason himself had said he hoped "this curiosity" would disappear. **83m/B VHS.** James Mason, Pamela Mason, Scott Forbes, Paul Cavanagh, Bruce Lester, Sean McClory, Vince Barnett; **D:** Roy Kellino. *NOS*

Charade 🐾🐾🐾½ **1963** After her husband is murdered, a young woman finds herself on the run from crooks and double agents who want the $250,000 her husband stole during WWII. Hepburn and Grant are charming and sophisticated as usual in this stylish intrigue filmed in Paris. Based on the story "The Unsuspecting Wife" by Marc Behm and Peter Stone. **113m/C VHS, Beta.** Cary Grant, Audrey Hepburn, Walter Matthau, James Coburn, George Kennedy; **D:** Stanley Donen; **W:** Peter Stone; **C:** Charles B(ryant) Lang; **M:** Henry Mancini. British Academy Awards '64: Best Actress (Hepburn); Edgar Allan Poe Awards '63: Best Screenplay; Nominations: Academy Awards '63: Best Song ("Charade"). *CNG, MRV, USH*

The Charge of the Light Brigade 🐾🐾🐾 **1936 (PG-13)** A British army officer stationed in India deliberately starts the Balaclava charge to even an old score with Surat Khan, who's on the other side. Still an exciting film, though it's hardly historically accurate. De Havilland is along to provide the requisite romance with Flynn. Also available colorized. **CW:** Epic battle scenes. **115m/B VHS, Beta, LV, Closed Caption.** Olivia de Havilland, Errol Flynn, David Niven, Nigel Bruce, Patric Knowles, Donald Crisp, Sir C. Aubrey Smith, J. Carrol Naish, Henry Stephenson, E.E. Clive, Scotty Beckett; **D:** Michael Curtiz; **M:** Max Steiner. Nominations: Academy Awards '36: Best Sound, Best Original Score. *MGM, FCT, FOX*

The Charge of the Light Brigade 🐾🐾½ **1968 (PG-13)** Political indictment of imperialistic England in this revisionist retelling of the notorious British defeat by the Russians at Balaclava. Battle scenes are secondary to this look at the stupidity of war. Fine cast; notable animation sequences by Richard Williams. **130m/C VHS.** **GB** Trevor Howard, John Gielgud, David Hemmings, Vanessa Redgrave, Harry Andrews, Jill Bennett, Peter Bowles, Mark Burns, Alan Dobie, T.P. McKenna, Corin Redgrave, Norman Rossington, Rachel Kempson, Donald Wolfit; **D:** Tony Richardson; **W:** Charles Wood; **C:** David Watkin; **M:** John Addison. *MGM*

Charge of the Model T's 🐾½ **1976 (G)** Comedy about a WWI German spy who tries to infiltrate the U.S. army. **90m/C VHS, Beta.** Louis Nye, John David Carson, Herb Edelman, Carol Bagdasarian, Arte Johnson; **D:** Jim McCullough.

Chariots of Fire 🐾🐾🐾½ **1981 (PG)** A lush telling of the parallel stories of Harold Abraham and Eric Liddell, English runners who competed in the 1924 Paris Olympics. One was compelled by a hatred of anti-Semitism, the other by the love of God. Outstanding performances by the entire cast. **123m/C VHS, Beta, LV, DVD.** **GB** Ben Cross, Ian Charleson, Nigel Havers, Ian Holm, Alice Krige, Brad Davis, Dennis Christopher, Patrick Magee, Cheryl Campbell, John Gielgud, Lindsay Anderson, Nigel Davenport; **D:** Hugh Hudson; **W:** Colin Welland; **C:** David Watkin; **M:** Vangelis. Academy Awards '81: Best Costume Design, Best Original Screenplay, Best Picture, Best Original Score; British Academy Awards '81: Best Film, Best Supporting Actor (Holm); Golden Globe Awards '82: Best Foreign Film; New York Film Critics Awards '81: Best Cinematography; Nominations: Academy Awards '81: Best Director (Hudson), Best Film Editing, Best Supporting Actor (Holm). *WAR, FCT, BTV*

Charlemagne 🐾🐾½ **1995** British miniseries follows the life of the royal conqueror who civilized western Europe and ruled as emperor from 800-814. On 5 cassettes. **250m/C VHS.** **GB** Christian Brendel, Anna Dupery; **D:** Clive Donner. *TVC, ACN*

Charles & Diana: A Palace Divided 🐾🐾½ **1993** Trashy scandalous tale of the disintegration of the fairytale romance and marriage of Prince Charles and Princess Diana.

Oxenberg stars as Princess Di, a role she played a decade ago in "The Royal Romance of Charles and Diana," and Rees does a fine job playing the conservative Prince Charles. Although the film covers all of the couple's highly-publicized troubles, it's such a quick superficial treatment that it's often hard to follow. Nonetheless, it's a flashingly inviting look into the privileged House of Windsor. **92m/C VHS, Closed Caption.** Roger Rees, Catherine Oxenberg, Benedict Taylor, Tracy Brabin, Amanda Walker, David Quilter, Jane How; **D:** John Power. *TTC*

Charles et Lucie 🐾🐾🐾 **1979** A has-been couple are ripped off, pursued, persecuted, and saddled with very bad luck in the South of France. Essentially a character study; semi-acclaimed. In French with subtitles. **96m/C VHS, Beta.** **FR** Daniel Ceccaldi, Ginette Garcin, Jean-Marie Proslier, Samson Fainsilber; **D:** Nelly Kaplan. *FCT*

Charleston 🐾🐾🐾 **1926** Renoir's third film, a simple erotic dance fantasy that caused much controversy in its day. Silent, with jazz score and historical introduction. **30m/B VHS, Beta.** Catherine Hessling; **D:** Jean Renoir. *FCT*

Charley and the Angel 🐾🐾½ **1973 (G)** Touching story of a man who changes his cold ways with his family when informed by an angel that he hasn't much time to live. Amusing Disney movie set in the Great Depression. **93m/C VHS.** Fred MacMurray, Cloris Leachman, Harry (Henry) Morgan, Kurt Russell, Vincent Van Patten, Kathleen Cody; **D:** Vincent McEveety. *DIS, OM*

Charley Chase Festival, Vol. 1 🐾🐾 **1923** Six classic Charley Chase comedies: "At First Sight" (1923), "Fighting Fluid" (1924), "Young Oldfield" (1924), "Ten Minute Egg" (1924), "Stolen Goods" (1924), and "Long Fliv the King" (1926). **70m/B VHS, Beta.** Charley Chase. *VDM*

Charley Varrick 🐾🐾🐾 **1973 (PG)** Matthau, a small-town hood, robs a bank only to find out that one of its depositors is the Mob. Baker's the vicious hit-man assigned the job of getting the loot back. A well-paced, on-the-mark thriller. **111m/C VHS, Beta.** Walter Matthau, Joe Don Baker, Felicia Farr, John Vernon, Sheree North, Norman Fell, Andrew (Andy) Robinson; **D:** Donald Siegel; **M:** Lalo Schifrin. *USH*

Charley's Aunt 🐾🐾½ **1925** Amusing Victorian farce in which two young male students convince an older fellow student to dress up as their female chaperon so they can pitch woo to two local lovelies. Fun performances and well-paced direction by Sidney. Based on the Brandon Thomas farce, the movie was remade in 1930, starring Charles Ruggles, and again in 1941, with Jack Benny. **75m/B VHS, Beta.** Sydney Chaplin, Ethel Shannon, Lucien Littlefield, Alec B. Francis, Mary Akin, Priscilla Bonner, Jimmy Harrison, David James, Eulalie Jensen, James E. Page, Phillips Smalley; **D:** Scott Sidney; **W:** F. McGrew Willis, Joe Farnham; **C:** Gus Peterson, Paul Garnett. *GPV, FCT*

Charlie and the Great Balloon Chase 🐾🐾 **1982** When a grandfather takes his grandson on a cross-country balloon trip, they are hotly pursued by the boy's mother, her stuffy fiance (who wants the boy in military school), the FBI, a reporter, and the Mafia. Made for television. **98m/C VHS, Beta.** Jack Albertson, Adrienne Barbeau, Slim Pickens, Moosie Drier; **D:** Larry Elikann. *TLF*

Charlie Boy 🐾½ **1981** The new owner of an ancient African idol enters the world of the supernatural when he casts a death spell on six people. **60m/C VHS, Beta.** Leigh Lawson, Angela Bruce, Marius Goring; **D:** Robert M. Young. *LIV*

Charlie Bravo 🐾 **198?(R)** A commando group is commanded to rescue a captured nurse in Vietnam. Dubbed. **94m/C VHS, Beta.** **FR** Bruno Pradal, Karen Verlier, Jean-Francois Poron; **D:** Rene Demoulin. *GEM*

A Charlie Brown Celebration **1984** The Peanuts gang in an extended adventure in which Lucy courts Schroeder, Patty goes to obedience school, and Charlie Brown finally kicks the football. **49m/C VHS, Beta. D:** Bill Melendez. *BAR*

A Charlie Brown Christmas **1965** Disillusioned by the commercialization of the holiday season, Charlie Brown sets out to find the true meaning of Christmas. **30m/C VHS, Beta, Closed Caption. D:** Bill Melendez. *MED, SHL, FCT*

A Charlie Brown Thanksgiving **1981** The Peanuts gang learns that Thanksgiving is more than just turkey and stuffing in this family favorite. **25m/C VHS, Beta. D:** Bill Melendez, Phil Roman. *BAR, KAR*

Charlie Brown's All-Stars **1966** Charlie Brown and the whole Peanuts gang is here to delight young and old alike. **26m/C VHS, Closed Caption. D:** Bill Melendez. *MED*

Charlie Chan and the Curse of the Dragon Queen 🐾½ **1981 (PG)** The famed Oriental sleuth confronts his old enemy the Dragon Queen, and reveals the true identity of a killer. **97m/C VHS, Beta.** Peter Ustinov, Lee Grant, Angie Dickinson, Richard Hatch, Brian Keith, Roddy McDowall, Michelle Pfeiffer, Rachel Roberts; **D:** Clive Donner; **W:** David Axelrod, Stanley Burns. *MED*

Charlie Chan at the Opera 🐾🐾🐾 **1936** The great detective investigates an amnesiac opera star (Karloff) who may have committed murder. Considered one of the best of the series. Interesting even to those not familiar with Charlie Chan. **66m/B VHS, LV, Closed Caption.** Warner Oland, Boris Karloff, Keye Luke, Charlotte Henry, Thomas Beck, Nedda Harrigan, William Demarest; **D:** H. Bruce Humberstone. *FOX*

Charlie Chan at the Wax Museum 🐾½ **1940** Charlie and number one son must find a criminal hiding out in a wax museum. Chills abound when the fugitive heads for the chamber of horrors. **63m/B VHS, LV, Closed Caption.** Sidney Toler, Victor Sen Yung, C. Henry Gordon, Marc Lawrence, Joan Valerie, Marguerite Chapman, Ted Osborn, Michael Visaroff; **D:** Lynn Shores. *FOX*

Charlie Chan in Paris 🐾🐾½ **1935** Chan scours the city of lights to track down a trio of counterfeiters. Top-notch plot and plenty of suspense will please all. **72m/B VHS, LV, Closed Caption.** Warner Oland, Mary Brian, Thomas Beck, Erik Rhodes, John Miljan, Minor Watson, John Qualen, Keye Luke, Henry Kolker; **D:** Lewis Seiler. *FOX*

Charlie Chan in Rio 🐾🐾 **1941** Local police call on Chan to help solve a double murder. One of the series' weaker entries but with fine setting and music. **60m/B VHS, LV, Closed Caption.** Sidney Toler, Mary Beth Hughes, Cobina Wright Jr., Ted North, Victor Jory, Harold Huber, Victor Sen Yung; **D:** Harry Lachman. *FOX*

Charlie Chan in the Secret Service 🐾½ **1944** Toler's Chan is now a government agent who is assigned to find the killer of an inventor. Moreland joins up as Chan's taxi-driving, constantly terrified sidekick. The series moved from 20th-century Fox to low-budget Monogram Pictures with this entry, with an ensuing drop in production quality. **64m/B VHS.** Sidney Toler, Mantan Moreland, Gwen Kenyon, Arthur Loft, Marianne Quon, Lela Tyler, Benson Fong; **D:** Phil Rosen. *MGM*

Charlie Chan's Secret 🐾🐾 **1935** Chan must solve the murder of the heir to a huge fortune. A good, logical script with plenty of suspects to keep you guessing. **72m/B VHS, Closed Caption.** Warner Oland, Rosina Lawrence, Charles Quigley, Henrietta Crosman, Edward Trevor, Astrid Allwyn; **D:** Gordon Wiles. *FOX*

Charlie Chaplin: Night at the Show 🐾🐾🐾 **1915** Chaplin plays two different mugs, both out for a night on the town. Mr. Pest, a sharp-dressed upper-cruster, clings to his disgusting habits, and Mr. Rowdy is his working-class doppleganger. Both obnoxious Chaplins-indisguise collaborate to wreak havoc on a local theater. Contains original organ score. **?m/B VHS, Beta.** Charlie Chaplin, Edna Purviance; **D:** Charlie Chaplin; **W:** Charlie Chaplin. *VYY*

Charlie Chaplin: The Early Years, Vol. 1 1917 Package includes Chaplin's "The Immigrant," "The Count," and "Easy Street." Silent. **62m/B VHS, LV.** Charlie Chaplin, Edna Purviance, John Rand, Eric Campbell. *REP, FCT, KIV*

Charlie Chaplin: The Early Years, Vol. 2 1917 Package includes Chaplin's "The Pawnshop" (1916), "The Adventurer" (1917), and "One A.M." (1916). **61m/B VHS, LV.** Charlie Chaplin, Edna Purviance, Eric Campbell, Albert Austin, Henry Bergman, John Rand. *REP, FCT, KIV*

Charlie Chaplin: The Early Years, Vol. 3 1916 Package includes Chaplin's "The Cure" (1916), "The Floorwalker" (1916), and "The Vagabond." **64m/B VHS, LV.** Charlie Chaplin, Edna Purviance, Eric Campbell, Albert Austin. *REP, FCT, KIV*

Charlie Chaplin: The Early Years, Vol. 4 1916 Package includes Chaplin's "Behind the Screen," "The Pawnshop" (1916), and "The Rink" (1916). **63m/B VHS, Beta, LV.** Charlie Chaplin, Edna Purviance, Eric Campbell, Lloyd Bacon, Albert Austin. *REP, FCT, KIV*

Charlie Chaplin...Our Hero! 1915 Two shorts from 1915 written and directed by Chaplin, "Night at the Show" and "In the Park," as well as a 1914 film, "Hot Finish," in which Charlie plays the villain. **58m/B VHS, Beta, 8mm.** Charlie Chaplin, Edna Purviance, Lloyd Bacon, Mabel Normand, Chester Conklin, Mack Sennett; **D:** Charlie Chaplin. *VYY*

Charlie Chaplin's Keystone Comedies #1 1914 Six one-reelers which Chaplin filmed in 1914, his first movie-making year: "Making a Living," Chaplin's first, in which he plays a villain; "Kid Auto Races," in which Charlie now sports baggy pants, bowler hat and cane; "A Busy Day," featuring Charlie in drag; "Mabel's Married Life;" "Laughing Gas;" and "The New Janitor." Silent with musical score. **59m/B VHS, Beta.** Charlie Chaplin, Mabel Normand, Mack Swain. *VYY, KIV*

Charlie Chaplin's Keystone Comedies #2 1914 Three hilarious early Chaplin shorts, "His Trysting Place," "Getting Acquainted," and "The Fatal Mallet." Silent with musical score. **60m/B VHS, Beta.** Charlie Chaplin, Mabel Normand, Mack Swain, Mack Sennett. *VYY, KIV*

Charlie Chaplin's Keystone Comedies #3 1914 Three more vintage early Chaplin shorts: "Caught in a Cabaret," "The Masquerader," and "Between Showers." Silent, includes a musical score. **59m/B VHS, Beta.** Charlie Chaplin, Mack Swain, Mabel Normand, Chester Conklin; **D:** Charlie Chaplin. *VYY, KIV*

Charlie Chaplin's Keystone Comedies #4 1914 Four classic silent shorts featuring Chaplin in 1914, Including "Caught in the Rain (in the Park)," "His Million Dollar Job," "Mabel's Busy Day," and "The Face on the Bar Room Floor." With musical score. **54m/B VHS, Beta, 8mm.** Charlie Chaplin, Mack Swain, Alice Davenport, Fatty Arbuckle, Mabel Normand, Chester Conklin, Slim Summerville, Cecile Arnold, Alice Howell. *VYY, KIV*

Charlie Chaplin's Keystone Comedies #5 1914 Four classic silent features: "Mabel's Strange Predicament," "The Rounders," "Tango Tangles," and "The Star Border." **57m/B VHS, Beta.** Charlie Chaplin; **D:** Charlie Chaplin. *VYY, KIV*

Charlie Chase and Ben Turpin 1921 Three silent comedy classics, "All Wet," "Publicity Pays," and "A Clever Dummy." **67m/B VHS, Beta.** Ben Turpin, Charley Chase, Wallace Beery, Juanita Hansen. *VYY*

Charlie Grant's War ♫♫ 1980 The true story of a Canadian businessman who hears of Nazi brutality and determines to save European Jews from persecution during the Holocaust. Not

among the more distinguished works of its kind. **130m/C VHS, Beta.** GB Jan Rubes, R.H. Thomson. *MOV*

Charlie, the Lonesome Cougar ♫♫ 1967 (G) Life for a rugged logger will never be the same after he adopts an orphaned cougar. From the Disney factory. **75m/C VHS, Beta.** Linda Wallace, Jim Wilson, Ron Brown, Brian Russell, Clifford Peterson; **D:** Winston Hibler. *DIS*

Charlie's Ghost: The Secret of Coronado ♫♫½ *Charlie's Ghost Story* 1994 (PG) Kid who has trouble fitting in is befriended by the ghost of a Spanish conquistador. **92m/C VHS.** Richard "Cheech" Marin, Trenton Knight, Anthony Edwards, Linda Fiorentino, Daphne Zuniga. *PSM*

Charlotte Forten's Mission: Experiment in Freedom ♫♫♫ *Half Slave, Half Free 2* 1985 Fact-based story, set during the Civil War. A wealthy, educated black woman, determined to prove to President Lincoln that blacks are equal to whites, journeys to a remote island off the coast of Georgia. There she teaches freed slaves to read and write. Part of the "American Playhouse" series on PBS. Preceded by "Solomon Northrup's Odyssey." **120m/C VHS.** Melba Moore, Mary Alice, Ned Beatty, Carla Borelli, Micki Grant, Moses Gunn, Anna Maria Horsford, Bruce McGill, Glynn Turman, Roderick Wimberly; **D:** Barry Crane; **W:** Samm-Art Williams. *FCT, PTB, XVC*

Charlotte's Web ♫♫½ 1979 (G) E.B. White's classic story of a friendship between a spider and a pig is handled only adequately by Hanna-Barbera studios. Some okay songs. **94m/C VHS, Beta, LV.** **D:** Charles A. Nichols; **V:** Debbie Reynolds, Agnes Moorehead, Paul Lynde, Henry Gibson. *PAR, FCT, HMV*

Charly ♫♫♫ 1968 A retarded man becomes intelligent after brain surgery, then romances a kindly caseworker before slipping back into retardation. Moving account is well served by leads Robertson and Bloom. Adapted from the Daniel Keyes novel "Flowers for Algernon." **103m/C VHS, Beta, LV.** Cliff Robertson, Claire Bloom, Lilia Skala, Leon Janney, Dick Van Patten, William Dwyer; **D:** Ralph Nelson; **W:** Stirling Silliphant. Academy Awards '68: Best Actor (Robertson); Golden Globe Awards '69: Best Screenplay; National Board of Review Awards '68: 10 Best Films of the Year, Best Actor (Robertson). *FOX, BTV*

Charm of La Boheme ♫♫½ 1936 A vintage German musical based on the Puccini opera. With English subtitles. **90m/B VHS, Beta.** GE Jan Kiepura, Martha Eggerth, Paul Kemp; **D:** Geza von Bolvary. *NOS, DVT, APD*

The Charmer ♫♫½ 1989 Havers stars as Ralph Gorse, a charming but amoral con man who uses any means to get what he wants. This includes using the affection (and money) of an older woman, blackmail, and even murder. Set in the late 30s. Made for British television miniseries on 6 cassettes. **312m/C VHS.** GB Nigel Havers, Rosemary Leach, Bernard Hepton, Fiona Fullerton, Abigail McKern, George Baker, Judy Parfitt; **D:** Alan Gibson; **W:** Allan Prior. *SIG, VCO*

Charro! ♫♫ 1969 (G) Presley in a straight role as a reformed bandit hounded by former gang members. Western fails on nearly all accounts, with Presley hopelessly acting outside the bounds of his talent. Furthermore, he sings only one song. **98m/C VHS.** Elvis Presley, Ina Balin, Victor French, Lynn Kellogg, Barbara Werle, Paul Brinegar, James B. Sikking; **D:** Charles Marquis Warren; **W:** Charles Marquis Warren; **M:** Hugo Montenegro. *WAR*

The Chase ♫♫ 1946 Not realizing that his boss-to-be is a mobster, Cummings takes a job as a chauffeur. Naturally, he falls in love with the gangster's wife (Morgan), and the two plan to elope. Somewhat miffed, the cuckolded mafioso and his bodyguard (Lorre) pursue the elusive couple as they head for Havana. The performances are up to snuff, but the story's as unimaginative as the title, with intermittent bouts of suspense. **86m/B VHS, Beta, LV.** Robert Cummings, Michele Morgan, Peter Lorre, Steve Cochran, Lloyd Corrigan, Jack Holt, Don

Wilson; **D:** Arthur Ripley; **W:** Philip Yordan. *NOS, MRV, SNC*

The Chase ♫♫½ 1966 Southern community is undone when rumors circulate of a former member's prison escape and return home. Excellent cast only partially shines. Brando is outstanding as the beleaguered, honorable sheriff, and Duvall makes a splash in the more showy role of a cuckold who fears the escapee is returning home to avenge a childhood incident. Reliable Dickinson also makes the most of her role as Brando's loving wife. Fonda, however, was not yet capable of fashioning complex characterizations, and Redford is under-utilized as the escapee. Adapted from the play by Horton Foote. Notorious conflicts among producer, director, and writer kept it from being a winner. **135m/C VHS, Beta, LV.** Marlon Brando, Robert Redford, Angie Dickinson, E.G. Marshall, Jane Fonda, James Fox, Janice Rule, Robert Duvall, Miriam Hopkins, Martha Hyer; **D:** Arthur Penn; **W:** Lillian Hellman, Horton Foote; **M:** John Barry. *COL*

Chase ♫½ 1985 A big-city lawyer returns to her small hometown to defend a killer and ends up at odds with the town, including an ex-lover. Routine made for television drama. **104m/C VHS, Beta.** Jennifer O'Neill, Robert Woods, Richard Farnsworth, Michael Parks; **D:** Rod Holcomb; **M:** Charles Bernstein. *FOX*

The Chase ♫♫ 1991 (PG-13) Routine made for television actioner. An ex-con killer leads a ruthless cop and a TV news team on a wild chase. Loosely based on a true story. **93m/C VHS, LV, Closed Caption.** Casey Siemaszko, Ben Johnson, Gerry Bamman, Robert Beltran, Barry Corbin, Ricki Lake, Megan Follows. *THV*

The Chase ♫♫½ 1993 (PG-13) Heiress Natalie Voss (Swanson) is in the wrong place at the wrong time when she's carjacked by escaped con Jack Hammond (Sheen) who uses a Butterfinger for his weapon. Frantic chases ensues as it turns out that Daddy Voss is a media hungry millionaire and he's followed by not only the cops but the media as well. One-dimensional characters aren't helped by a one-dimensional script, but slick filmmaking and a little charm helps. Skewers the media hype that surrounds crime, taking on news programs that offer immediate coverage and reality based shows with glee. **CW:** Some language, violence, and scene of sensuality. **87m/C VHS, LV, Closed Caption.** Joao Fernandes, Kristy Swanson, Charlie Sheen, Josh Mostel, Ray Wise, Henry Rollins, Flea; **D:** Adam Rifkin; **W:** Adam Rifkin; **M:** Richard Gibbs. *FXV*

Chasers ♫♫ 1994 (R) Gruff Navy petty officer Rock Reilly (Berenger) and his conniving partner Eddie Devane (McNamara) are stuck escorting maximum security prisoner Toni Johnson (Eleniak) to a Charleston naval base. Imagine their surprise when Toni turns out to be a beautiful blonde whose one purpose is to escape her jailsentence for going AWOL. Considering how dumb her jailers are this shouldn't be too difficult. Lots of sneering, leering, and macho posturing. **CW:** Strong language and one scene of sexuality. **100m/C VHS, LV, Closed Caption.** Tom Berenger, William McNamara, Erika Eleniak; *Cameos:* Gary Busey, Crispin Glover, Dean Stockwell, Seymour Cassel, Frederic Forrest, Marilu Henner, Dennis Hopper; **D:** Dennis Hopper; **W:** Joe Batteer, John Rice, Dan Gilroy; **M:** Dwight Yoakam, Pete Anderson. *WAR*

Chasing Amy ♫♫½ 1997 (R) Holden (Affleck) and best friend Banky (Lee), New Jersey comic book artists, attend a convention in New York where Holden is immediately attracted to fellow artist Alyssa (Adams). His ego is quickly deflated when Alyssa lets him know she's a lesbian. They try for friendship, head into a rocky romance, and then Holden discovers Alyssa's had a wild (and heterosexual) past, which pushes all his emotional buttons. Writer/director Smith supplies his trademark sharp dialogue, and the leads all contribute fine performances. Jay (Mewes) and Silent Bob (Smith), from Smith's earlier pics, make another appearance and supply the story that gives the film its title. **CW:** Strong graphic sex-related dialogue, language, sexuality and drug content. 105m/C VHS. Ben Affleck, Joey Lauren Adams, Jason Lee, Dwight Ewell, Jason Mewes, Kevin Smith; **D:** Kevin Smith; **W:** Kevin Smith; **C:** David Klein; **M:** David Pirner. *NYR*

Chasing Butterflies 🐾🐾 *La Chasse aux Papillons* 1994 Society's decline is represented by a once-grand, now-decaying chateau, located in a small French village, and its equally decaying inhabitants. Marie-Agnes, confined to a wheelchair, is attended to by her cousin Solange and sullen maid Valerie. When Marie-Agnes suddenly dies, the greedy relatives descend, as well as untrustworthy antiques dealers, and Japanese businessmen interested in acquiring foreign real estate. The film is also an acquired taste. French with subtitles. 115m/C VHS. *FR* Thamar Tarassachvili, Narda Blanchet, Pierrette Pompom Bailhache, Alexandre Tcherkassoff; **D:** Otar Iosseliani; **W:** Otar Iosseliani. *NYF, FCT*

Chasing Dreams 🐾½ 1981 (PG) Sickly melodrama about a farmboy who finds fulfillment as a baseball player. Lame film promoted as Costner baseball vehicle, but the star of "Bull Durham" and "Field of Dreams" appears only briefly in a secondary role. 96m/C VHS, Beta. David G. Brown, John Fife, Jim Shane, Lisa Kingston, Matt Clark, Kevin Costner; **D:** Sean Roche, Therese Conte. *PSM*

Chasing the Deer 🐾🐾 1994 In 1745, Scotland's Bonnie Prince Charlie (Carrara) has returned from France intent on resurrecting the Jacobite cause and regaining the English throne. Reluctant Alistair Campbell (Zajac) joins the army only to protect his son Euan (Rae), who's supposedly being held prisoner for shooting a Highlander. Euan's actually fallen into the hands of a sympathetic Englishman, Major Elliot (Blessed), advisor to the government's troops. The Jacobites begin their march south until that fateful day on Culloden Moor, which will determine all their futures. 92m/C VHS. *GB* Brian Blessed, Matthew Zajac, Iain Cuthbertson, Lewis Rae, Dominique Carrara, Fish; **D:** Graham Holloway; **W:** Jerome Vincent, Bob Carruthers, Steve Gillham; **C:** Alan M. Trow; **D:** John Wetton. *VIF*

Chasing Those Depression Blues 1935 Four '30s comedy shorts: "Money on Your Life," "Dental Follies," "Any Day in Hollywood" and "Art in the Raw." 58m/B VHS, Beta. Danny Kaye, Pinky Lee, Edgar Kennedy, Ben Turpin. *VYY*

Chato's Land 🐾🐾½ 1971 (PG) An Indian is tracked by a posse eager to resolve a lawman's death. Conventional violent Bronson vehicle is bolstered by presence of masterful Palance. 100m/C VHS, Beta, Closed Caption. Charles Bronson, Jack Palance, Richard Basehart, James Whitmore, Simon Oakland, Richard Jordan, Ralph Waite, Victor French, Lee Patterson; **D:** Michael Winner. *MGM, GKK*

Chattahoochee 🐾🐾½ 1989 A man suffering from post-combat syndrome lands in a horrifying institution. Strong cast, with Oldman fine in the lead, and Hopper memorable in extended cameo. Fact-based film is, unfortunately, rather conventionally rendered. 97m/C VHS, LV. Gary Oldman, Dennis Hopper, Frances McDormand, Pamela Reed, Ned Beatty, M. Emmet Walsh, William De Acutis, Lee Wilkof, Matt Craven, Gary Klar; **D:** Mick Jackson; **W:** James Cresson. *HBO, IME, FCT*

Chattanooga Choo Choo 🐾🐾½ 1984 (PG) A football team owner must restore the Chattanooga Choo Choo and make a 24-hour run from Chattanooga to New York in order to collect one-million dollars left to him in a will. The train never leaves the station. 102m/C VHS, Beta. Barbara Eden, George Kennedy, Melissa Sue Anderson, Joe Namath, Bridget Hanley, Christopher McDonald, Clu Gulager, Tony Azito; **D:** Bruce Bilson. *HBO*

Chatterbox 🐾🐾 1976 A starlet's life and career are severely altered when her sex organs begin speaking. So why didn't they warn her about movies like this? Plenty of B-queen Rialson on view. Good double bill with "Me and Him."

73m/C VHS, Beta. Candice Rialson, Larry Gelman, Jean Kean, Perry Bullington; **D:** Tom De Simone. *LIV, VES*

The Cheap Detective 🐾🐾🐾 1978 (PG) Neil Simon's parody of the "Maltese Falcon" gloriously exploits the resourceful Falk in a Bogart-like role. Vast supporting cast—notable Brennan, DeLuise, and Kahn—equally game for fun in this consistently amusing venture. 92m/C VHS. Peter Falk, Ann-Margret, Eileen Brennan, Sid Caesar, Stockard Channing, James Coco, Dom DeLuise, Louise Fletcher, John Houseman, Madeline Kahn, Fernando Lamas, Marsha Mason, Phil Silvers, Vic Tayback, Abe Vigoda, Paul Williams, Nicol Williamson; **D:** Robert Moore; **W:** Neil Simon; **C:** John A. Alonzo. *CSM, COL*

Cheap Shots 🐾½ 1991 (PG-13) Cheap best describes this. Two guys running a sleazy New York State resort motel plot to videotape patrons having sex, but capture an apparent mob murder instead. More of a character study than sexploitation, but who needs these characters? Not a stellar writing/directing debut for Ureles and Stoeffhaas. 90m/C VHS. Louis Zorich, David Patrick Kelly, Mary Louise Wilson, Michael Twaine, Patience Moore; **D:** Jeff Ureles; **W:** Jeff Ureles, Jerry Stoeffhaas; **M:** Jeff Beal. *HMD*

Cheaper by the Dozen 🐾🐾🐾 1950 Turn-of-the-century family comedy based on the book by Frank B. Gilbreth, Jr. and Ernestine Gilbreth Carey, which chronicled life in the expansive Gilbreth household—12 children, efficiency expert father Frank (Webb) and psychologist mother Lillian (Loy). Stern dad likes to test his theories on the family (and have everything his own way) while nuturing mom easily manages him as well as their large household. There are various family crises (times twelve) but it's all very heartwarming. Followed by "Belles On Their Toes." 85m/C VHS. Clifton Webb, Myrna Loy, Jeanne Crain, Edgar Buchanan, Mildred Natwick, Sara Allgood, Betty Lynn, Barbara Bates, Norman Ollestad; **D:** Walter Lang; **W:** Lamar Trotti; **C:** Leon Shamroy; **M:** Cyril Mockridge. *FXV*

Cheaper to Keep Her woof! 1980 (R) Alleged comedy about a private detective hired to track likely alimony dodgers. Loathsome, repellent fare, with Davis hopeless in the lead. 92m/C VHS, Beta. Mac Davis, Tovah Feldshuh, Jack Gilford, Rose Marie; **D:** Ken Annakin; **W:** Herschel Weingrod, Timothy Harris. *MED*

The Cheat 🐾🐾🐾 1915 Ward plays a frivolous socialite heavily indebted to Hayakawa as the Japanese money lender. Hayakawa makes Ward pay with her honor and her flesh by branding her. A dark and captivating drama. Silent with piano score. 55m/B VHS, Beta. Fannie Ward, Sessue Hayakawa; **D:** Cecil B. DeMille. *GPV, KIV*

The Cheaters 🐾 1976 (R) A young gambler runs away with his boss's son's girlfriend, and is pursued therein. 91m/C VHS, Beta. *IT* Dayle Haddon, Luc Merenda, Lino Troisi, Enrico Maria Salerno; **D:** Sergio Martino. *PSM*

Cheaters 🐾½ 1984 Two middle class couples are having affairs with each other's spouses. Complications arise when their respective children decide to marry each other. 103m/C VHS, Beta. Peggy Cass, Jack Kruschen. *NO*

Cheatin' Hearts 🐾🐾½ 1993 (R) Kirkland is a woman beset by woe: she's about to lose her house, her philandering husband (Brolin) wanders back to town with his latest bimbo in tow, and her daughter's getting married. This should be a good thing, except hubby makes a fool of himself at the wedding and nearly ruins everything. Well, at least local rancher Kristofferson is around to lift a woman's spirits. And yes, there's a (predictably) happy ending. 88m/C VHS, LV, Closed Caption. Sally Kirkland, James Brolin, Kris Kristofferson, Pamela Gidley, Laura Johnson; **D:** Rod McCall. *THV*

Check & Double Check 🐾 1930 Radio's original Amos 'n' Andy (a couple of black-faced white guys) help solve a lover's triangle in this film version of the popular radio series. Interesting only as a novelty. Duke Ellington's band

plays "Old Man Blues" and "Three Little Words." 85m/B VHS, Beta, LV. Freeman Gosden, Charles Correll, Duke Ellington; **D:** Melville Brown; **M:** Max Steiner. *NOS, MRV, VYY*

Check Is in the Mail 🐾½ 1985 (R) Lame comedy about a financier determined to make his home entirely independent from the rat-race of capitalist society. Dependables Dennehy and Archer are wasted. 83m/C VHS, Beta. Brian Dennehy, Anne Archer, Dick Shawn; **D:** Joan Darling. *MED, VTR*

Check Your Guns 🐾🐾 1948 A crooked judge and a gang of outlaws team up to prey on law-abiding folk and cause headaches for the new sheriff, who's pushing an unsuccessful Old West version of gun control. Nothing really noteworthy here. 55m/B VHS. Eddie Dean, Roscoe Ates, Nancy Gates, George Chesebro, I. Stanford Jolley, Mikel Conrad, William "Bill" Fawcett; **D:** Ray Taylor. *NOS*

The Checkered Flag 🐾 1963 Lame auto-racing drama about an aging, millionaire race car driver with an alcoholic wife who would like nothing more than to see him dead. She talks a young rookie into helping her dispose of hubby. Plans go awry—with horrifying results. Racing scenes overshadow incredibly weak script and performances. 110m/C VHS. Joe Morrison, Evelyn King, Charles G. Martin, Peggy Vendig; **D:** William Grefe; **W:** William Grefe. *SNC*

Checking Out 🐾½ 1989 (R) Black comedy about a manic hypochondriac who is convinced that his demise soon occur. You'll pray that he's right. Daniels can't make it work, and supporters Mayron and Magnuson also have little chance in poorly conceived roles. 95m/C VHS, Beta, LV. Jeff Daniels, Melanie Mayron, Michael Tucker, Kathleen York, Ann Magnuson, Allen Havey, Jo Harvey Allen, Felton Perry, Alan Wolfe; **D:** David Leland; **W:** Joe Eszterhas; **M:** Carter Burwell. *NO*

Cheech and Chong: Still Smokin' 🐾½ *Still Smokin'* 1983 (R) Not really. More like still trying to make a buck. Veteran marijuana-dazed comedy duo travel to Amsterdam to raise funds for a bankrupt film festival group by hosting a dope-a-thon. Lots of concert footage used in an attempt to hold the slim plot together. Only for serious fans of the dopin' duo. 91m/C VHS, Beta, LV. Richard "Cheech" Marin, Thomas Chong; **D:** Thomas Chong; **W:** Richard "Cheech" Marin, Thomas Chong; **M:** George S. Clinton. *PAR*

Cheech and Chong: Things Are Tough All Over 🐾🐾 1982 (R) Stoner comedy team are hired by two rich Arab brothers (also played by Cheech and Chong in acting stretch) and unwittingly drive a car loaded with money from Chicago to Las Vegas. Tired fourth in the series. 87m/C VHS, Beta. Richard "Cheech" Marin, Thomas Chong, Shelby Fiddis, Rikki Marin, Evelyn Guerrero, Rip Taylor; **D:** Tom Avildsen; **W:** Richard "Cheech" Marin, Thomas Chong. *COL*

Cheech and Chong's Next Movie 🐾🐾 1980 (R) A pair of messed-up bumblers adventure into a welfare office, massage parlor, nightclub, and flying saucer, while always living in fear of the cops. Kinda funny, like. Sequel to "Up in Smoke." 95m/C VHS, Beta, LV. Richard "Cheech" Marin, Thomas Chong, Evelyn Guerrero, Edie McClurg, Paul (Pee Wee Herman) Reubens, Phil Hartman; **D:** Thomas Chong; **W:** Richard "Cheech" Marin, Thomas Chong. *USH*

Cheech and Chong's Nice Dreams 🐾🐾 1981 (R) The spaced-out duo are selling their own "specially mixed" ice cream to make cash and realize their dreams. Third in the series. 97m/C VHS, Beta, LV. Richard "Cheech" Marin, Thomas Chong, Evelyn Guerrero, Stacy Keach, Paul (Pee Wee Herman) Reubens; **D:** Thomas Chong, Timothy Leary; **W:** Richard "Cheech" Marin, Thomas Chong; **M:** Harry Betts. *COL*

Cheech and Chong's The Corsican Brothers woof! 1984 (PG) Wretched swashbuckler features the minimally talented duo in a variety of worthless roles. Dumas would vomit in his casket if he knew about this. Fifth in the series. 91m/C VHS, LV. Richard "Cheech" Marin, Thomas Chong, Roy Dotrice, Rae Dawn Chong, Shelby Fiddis, Rikki Marin, Edie McClurg; D: Thomas Chong; W: Richard "Cheech" Marin, Thomas Chong. LIV

Cheech and Chong's Up in Smoke 🐾🐾½ 1979 (R) A pair of free-spirited burn-outs team up for a tongue-in-cheek spoof of sex, drugs, and rock and roll. First and probably the best of the dopey duo's cinematic adventures. A box-office bonanza when released and still a cult favorite. 87m/C VHS, Beta, LV. Richard "Cheech" Marin, Thomas Chong, Stacy Keach, Tom Skerritt, Edie Adams, Strother Martin, Cheryl "Rainbeaux" Smith; D: Lou Adler; W: Richard "Cheech" Marin, Thomas Chong. PAR

The Cheerful Fraud 🐾🐾½ 1927 Denny, who appeared in some two hundred-odd films in his career, masquerades as a butler to be near the girl he loves. A fool for love is a cheerful fraud. A zanily romantic silent comedy. 64m/B VHS, Beta. Reginald Denny, Gertrude Olmsted, Emily Fitzroy, Gertrude Astor; D: William A. Seiter. GPV

Cheering Section woof! 1973 (R) High school football teams compete for the grand prize—the privilege of ravishing the losing school's cheerleaders. Rah, rah, rah. 84m/C VHS. Rhonda Foxx, Tom Leindecker, Gregg D'Jah, Patricia Michelle, Jeff Laine; D: Harry Kerwin. NO

Cheerleader Camp woof! Bloody Pom Poms 1988 (R) Nubile gals are stalked by a psychopath while they cavort semi-clad at summer camp. 89m/C VHS, Beta. Betsy Russell, Leif Garrett, Lucinda Dickey, Lorie Griffin, George Flower, Teri Weigel, Rebecca Ferratti; D: John Quinn. PSM, PAR

The Cheerleaders woof! 1972 (R) Dimwitted exploitation effort has the usual suspects—moronic jocks and lamebrained gals—cavorting exuberantly. Followed by "Revenge of the Cheerleaders." 84m/C VHS, Beta, LV. Stephanie Fondue, Denise Dillaway, Jovita Bush, Debbie Lowe, Sandy Evans; D: Paul Glickler. PSM, IME

Cheerleaders' Wild Weekend woof! 1985 (R) Group of cheerleaders are held captive by a disgruntled former football star. Pom poms wave. 87m/C VHS, Beta. Jason Williams, Kristine DeBell; D: Jeff Werner. LIV, VES

Cheers for Miss Bishop 🐾🐾½ 1941 The story of a woman who graduates from college then teaches at the same institution for the next 50 years. Somewhat moving. Based on Bess Streeter Aldrich's novel. 95m/B VHS, Beta. Martha Scott, William Gargan, Edmund Gwenn, Sterling Holloway, Rosemary DeCamp; D: Tay Garnett; W: Edward Ward. Nominations: Academy Awards '41: Original Dramatic/Comedy Score. NOS, MRV, VYY

Cheetah 🐾🐾 1989 (G) Two California kids visiting their parents in Kenya embark on the adventure of their lives when, with the help of a young Masai, they adopt and care for an orphaned cheetah. Usual Disney kids and animals story. 80m/C VHS, LV, Closed Caption. Keith Coogan, Lucy Deakins, Collin Mothupi; D: Jeff Blyth; W: John Cotter; C: Thomas Burstyn. DIS

A Chef in Love 🐾🐾 Les Mille et Une Recettes du Cuisinier Amoureux; The Cook in Love 1996 (PG-13) In 1920, Parisian Pascal Ishac (Richard) meets Georgian Princess Cecilia (Kirtadze) while travelling and decides to stay and open a French restaurant in the capital of Tbilisi. When the capital is invaded by the Red Army in 1921, communist leader Zigmund (Kahmhadze) forces Cecilia to marry him and shuts down Pascal's eatery. With his great love and his restaurant both gone, Pascal writes a master cookbook and memoir that is later discovered and translated by Cecilia's son (Gautier), who also discovers that Pascal is his father. French with subtitles.CW: Nudity, sexual situations and some images of violence. 100m/C VHS. FR Pierre Richard, Nino Kirtadze, Temur Kahmhadze, Jean-Yves Gautier, Vladimir Ilyine, Danielle Darrieux, Micheline Presle; D: Nana Dzhordzadze; W: Irakli Kvirikadze; C: Georgi Beridze; M: Goran Bregovic. Nominations: Academy Awards '96: Best Foreign Language Film. NYR

The Cherokee Kid 🐾🐾½ 1996 (PG-13) Cable western/comedy about a novice gunslinger (Sinbad) avenging his family. There's a corrupt banker (Coburn), a bounty hunter (Hines), a Mexican freedom fighter (Martinez), and a gang of bankrobbing nuns to keep things interesting while the Kid learns his outlaw ways.CW: Wild West violence, language and some sex-related material. ?m/C VHS. Sinbad, James Coburn, Burt Reynolds, Gregory Hines, A. Martinez, Ernie Hudson; D: Paris Barclay; W: Tim Kazurinsky, Denise DeClue; M: Stanley Clarke. HBO

Cherry Hill High woof! 1976 (R) Five teen girls compete for former-virgin status. Pass on this one. 92m/C VHS, Beta. Linda McInerney, Carrie Olsen, Nina Carson, Lynn Hastings, Gloria Upson, Stephanie Lawlor; D: Alex E. Goiten. USH

Cherry 2000 🐾🐾 1988 (PG-13) Futuristic flick concerns a man who short-circuits his sex-toy robots and embarks on a search for replacement parts across treacherous territory, only to meet a real female—Griffith. Offbeat, occasionally funny. 94m/C VHS, Beta, LV, Closed Caption. Melanie Griffith, David Andrews, Ben Johnson, Tim Thomerson, Michael C. Gwynne; D: Steve DeJarnatt; W: Michael Almereyda; M: Basil Poledouris. ORI

Chesty Anderson USN 🐾 Anderson's Angels 1976 Ultra-lame sexploitation about female naval recruits. Minimal nudity. 90m/C VHS, Beta. Shari Eubank, Dorri Thompson, Rosanne Katon, Marcie Barkin, Scatman Crothers, Frank Campanella, Fred Willard; D: Ed Forsyth. NO

Cheyenne Autumn 🐾🐾½ 1964 The newly restored version of the ambitious, ultimately hit-and-miss western epic about three hundred Cheyenne Indians who migrate from Oklahoma to their Wyoming homeland in 1878. The cavalry, for once, are not the good guys. Widmark is strong in the lead. Stewart is memorable in his comic cameo as Wyatt Earp. Last film from genre master Ford, capturing the usual rugged panoramas. Based on a true story as told in the Mari Sandoz novel. 156m/C VHS, Beta. Richard Widmark, Carroll Baker, Karl Malden, Dolores Del Rio, Sal Mineo, Edward G. Robinson, Ricardo Montalban, Gilbert Roland, Arthur Kennedy, John Carradine, Victor Jory, Mike Mazurki, George O'Brien, John Qualen; Cameos: James Stewart; D: John Ford; C: William Clothier; M: Alex North. Nominations: Academy Awards '64: Best Color Cinematography. WAR, FCT

Cheyenne Kid 🐾½ 1933 Determined bronco buster is up against a gang of bad guys. 40m/B VHS, Beta. Tom Keene, Mary Mason, Roscoe Ates; M: Max Steiner. NOS, DVT

Cheyenne Rides Again 🐾½ 1938 Cheyenne poses as an outlaw to hunt a gang of rustlers. 60m/B VHS, Beta. Tom Tyler, Lucille Browne, Lon Chaney Jr., Roger Williams, Charles "Slim" Whitaker; D: Robert F. "Bob" Hill. NOS, VYY, VCN

The Cheyenne Social Club 🐾🐾 1970 (PG) Stewart inherits a brothel and Fonda helps him operate it. Kelly directs, sort of. Some laughs, but this effort is beneath this trio. 103m/C VHS. Henry Fonda, James Stewart, Shirley Jones, Sue Ane Langdon, Elaine Devry; D: Gene Kelly; C: William Clothier. WAR

Cheyenne Takes Over 🐾 1947 Lash sniffs out the bad guy in the case of a murdered ranch heir. 56m/B VHS, Beta. Lash LaRue, Al "Fuzzy" St. John, George Chesebro; D: Ray Taylor. COL

Cheyenne Warrior 🐾🐾½ 1994 (PG) Pregnant young bride Rebecca heads west with a husband who soon winds up dead, leaving her stranded at an isolated trading post. She takes in a wounded Cheyenne warrior, nurses him back to health, and he tries to convince her to let his tribe care for her. Respectable performances if unexciting. 90m/C VHS, LV. Kelly Preston, Pato Hoffmann, Bo Hopkins, Dan Haggerty, Charles Powell, Rick Dean, Clint Howard; D: Mark Griffiths; W: Michael B. Druxman. NHO

Chicago Joe & the Showgirl 🐾🐾 1990 (R) A London-based GI befriends a loopy showgirl and helps her in various crimes during WWII. Appealing Lloyd overwhelms Sutherland, who shows only limited acting ability here. Kensit and Pigg are fine in smaller roles. 105m/C VHS, LV, Closed Caption. GB Emily Lloyd, Kiefer Sutherland, Patsy Kensit, Keith Allen, Liz Fraser, Alexandra Pigg, Ralph Nossek, Colin Bruce; D: Bernard Rose; M: Hans Zimmer. LIV, IME

The Chicken Chronicles 🐾 1977 (PG) An affluent high school dude longs to get horizontal with his dream girl. Set in the 1960s. First feature film appearance for Guttenberg. 94m/C VHS, Beta. Phil Silvers, Ed Lauter, Steve Guttenberg, Lisa Reeves, Meredith Baer; D: Francis Simon. COL

Chiefs 🐾🐾 1983 A police chief in a Southern town discovers a series of murders concealed by town big wigs. Made for TV film boasts a surprisingly strong cast, but provides otherwise conventional entertainment. 200m/C VHS, Beta. Charlton Heston, Paul Sorvino, Keith Carradine, Brad Davis, Billy Dee Williams, Wayne Rogers, Stephen Collins, Tess Harper, Victoria Tennant; D: Jerry London. VTR, NWV

Child Bride of Short Creek 🐾🐾½ 1981 A young Korean war veteran returns to his community where polygamy is allowed, to find that his father intends to marry again, this time to a 15-year-old. Conflict ensues. Made for television. Based on an actual event that occurred in the 1950s. 100m/C VHS, Beta. Diane Lane, Conrad Bain, Christopher Atkins, Kiel Martin, Helen Hunt; D: Robert Lewis. PSM

Child in the Night 🐾🐾 1990 (R) A shaken eight-year old boy is a witness to murder in his family, and a psychologist with plenty of her own problems must get him to testify. First film for Wood. Middling TV-movie suspense. 93m/C VHS, Beta. Tom Skerritt, JoBeth Williams, Darren McGavin, Season Hubley, Elijah Wood; D: Mike Robe. TRI

A Child is Waiting 🐾🐾🐾 1963 Poignant and provocative story of teachers in an institution for the mentally retarded. Fine performances include Lancaster as the institution's administrator and Garland as a teacher who cares too much for everyone's good. Cassavetes incorporates footage using handicapped children as extras—not entirely seamlessly—providing a sensitive and candid edge. 105m/B VHS, Beta. Burt Lancaster, Judy Garland, Gena Rowlands, Steven Hill, Bruce Ritchey; D: John Cassavetes; W: Abby Mann; M: Ernest Gold. MGM

Child of Darkness, Child of Light 🐾½ 1991 (PG-13) A priest is sent to investigate two virgin pregnancies and discovers that one child will be a savior and the other the Anti-Christ. Totally mindless brain candy resembling the "Omen" movies and "Rosemary's Baby." Made for cable television. Adapted from James Patterson's book "Virgin." 85m/C VHS, Beta, Closed Caption. Anthony John Denison, Brad Davis, Paxton Whitehead, Claudette Nevins, Sydney Penny, Kristin Datillo, Viveca Lindfors, Sela Ward, Alan Oppenheimer, Eric Christmas; D: Marina Sargenti; W: Brian Taggert. PAR

Child of Glass 🐾🐾 1978 (G) A young boy's family moves into a huge New Orleans mansion, and soon after encounters a young girl's ghost and lost treasure from the Civil War. A Disney made for TV movie. 93m/C VHS, Beta. Barbara Barrie, Biff McGuire, Anthony Zerbe, Nina Foch, Steve Shaw, Katy Kurtzman, Olivia Barash; D: John Erman. DIS

Child of the Prairie 🐾 1918 An early Mix film about a young cowboy and his city-loving wife down on their luck in a western town. Silent with music score. 63m/B VHS, Beta, 8mm. Tom Mix. VYY

The Children woof! 1980 (R) Familiar nuclear leak leads to monster mutants done to a novel (though extremely low-budget) turn: after a school bus passes through radioactive fog, the kiddies inside assume the ability to incinerate whoever they hug. They also assume a certain zombie-like demeanor and sport black fingernails. None of this is noted by their uncaring and less-than-observant parents, many of whom are enticed into a very warm hug. This may be intended as social satire. Not only are the little microwaves extremely dangerous, the only way to kill them is to chop off their hands, leading to a wild limbless finale. 89m/C VHS, Beta. Martin Shaker, Gale Garnett, Gil Rogers; **D:** Max Kalmanowicz. VES, FCT, RHI

The Children 🐾🐾½ 1990 Kingsley stars as a middle-aged engineer who finds himself caring for seven children in this touching love story from novelist Edith Wharton. Shot on location in Venice, the cinematography is excellent and the cast is superb, but the film lags in places. A remake of "The Marriage Playground." 90m/C VHS. GB GE Ben Kingsley, Kim Novak, Siri Neal, Geraldine Chaplin, Joe Don Baker, Britt Ekland, Donald Sinden, Karen Black, Robert Stephens, Rupert Graves, Rosemary Leach; **D:** Tony Palmer. HMD

The Children Are Watching Us 🐾🐾🐾 The Little Martyr; I Bambini Ci Guardano 1944 Sobering drama of a family dissolution as seen by a child. A four-year-old boy drifts unloved by his suicidal father and by his mother, who's only interested in her own love affair. Worthy example of Italian neo-realism marks the first collaboration between Zavattini and De Sica. In Italian with subtitles. 92m/B VHS. IT Luciano de Ambrosis, Isa Pola, Emilio Cigoli; **D:** Vittorio De Sica; **W:** Cesare Zavattini, Vittorio De Sica. FCT, HMV

Children in the Crossfire 🐾🐾½ 1984 When youngsters from war-torn Northern Ireland spend a summer in America with children from the Republic of Ireland, both sides find their nationalistic prejudices falling away. But a great challenge awaits them when they return home from their summer of fun. Nicely done drama made for television. 96m/C VHS, LV. Charles Haid, Karen Valentine, Julia Duffy, David Hoffman; **D:** George Schaefer; **M:** Brad Fiedel. LIV, VES

Children of a Lesser God 🐾🐾🐾½ 1986 (R) Based upon the play by Mark Medoff, this sensitive, intelligent film deals with an unorthodox speech teacher at a school for the deaf, who falls in love with a beautiful and rebellious ex-student. Inarguably romantic; the original stage production won the Best Play Tony in 1980. Hurt and Matlin reportedly continued their romance off-screen as well. 119m/C VHS, Beta, LV, 8mm, Closed Caption. William Hurt, Marlee Matlin, Piper Laurie, Philip Bosco, E. Katherine Kerr; **D:** Randa Haines; **W:** Hesper Anderson, Mark Medoff; **C:** John Seale; **M:** Michael Convertino. Academy Awards '86: Best Actress (Matlin); Golden Globe Awards '87: Best Actress—Drama (Matlin); Nominations: Academy Awards '86: Best Actor (Hurt), Best Adapted Screenplay, Best Picture, Best Supporting Actress (Laurie). PAR, BTV

The Children of An Lac 🐾🐾½ 1980 Three women attempt to rescue hundreds of Vietnamese orphans before Saigon falls to the communists. The film derives from actress Balin's actual wartime experience. Made for television. 100m/C VHS, Beta. Shirley Jones, Ina Balin, Beulah Quo, Alan Fudge, Ben Piazza, Lee Paul, Kieu Chinh, Vic Diaz. FRH

Children of Divorce 🐾½ 1980 Made-for-television drama shows divorce from the children's point of view. Standard fare. 96m/C VHS, Beta. Barbara Feldon, Lance Kerwin, Stacey Nelkin, Billy Dee Williams; **D:** Joanna Lee; **M:** Minette Alton. LIV

Children of Fury 🐾🐾 1994 (PG-13) Fact-based TV movie covers the death of self-proclaimed prophet, Utah polygamist Addam Swapp. His equally fanatical widow and son-in-law bomb a Morman church in retaliation, causing a 13-day

siege of his heavily armed home by the FBI. **CW:** Some violent content. 85m/C VHS. Ed Begley Jr., Tess Harper, Dennis Franz, Kyle Secor, Paul LeMat; **D:** Charles Haid; **W:** Rich Husky. NHO

Children of Nature 🐾🐾½ Born Natturunnar 1991 A 78-year-old man unwillingly enters a nursing home where he meets a long-ago sweetheart. The two fall in love again and decide to escape from the home and return to their childhood village. Sweet love story about late-blooming passions laced with fantasy and humor. Iceland's first Academy Award nomination. In Icelandic with English subtitles. 85m/C VHS. IC Gisli Halldorsson, Sigridur Hagalin, Bruno Ganz; **D:** Fridrik Thor Fridriksson; **W:** Fridrik Thor Fridriksson, Einar Mar Gudmundsson; **M:** Hilmar Orn Hilmarsson. Nominations: Academy Awards '92: Best Foreign Language Film. FXL, ING

The Children of Noisy Village 🐾🐾½ 1995 Noisy Village is a small town in the Swedish countryside consisting of three red frame houses. In the town, a group of adventurous children discover a multitude of fantasy lands right in their own backyard—their backyard being the beautiful pastures, ponds, and fields of Sweden. Based on the stories of Astrid "Pippi Longstocking" Lindgren. Dubbed. 88m/C VHS. SW Linda Bergstrom, Anna Sahlin, Ellem Demerus, Harsald Lonnbro; **D:** Lasse Hallstrom. FRF

Children of Paradise 🐾🐾🐾🐾 Les Enfants du Paradise 1944 Considered by many to be the greatest film ever made, certainly one of the most beautiful. In the Parisian theatre district of the 1800s an actor falls in love with a seemingly unattainable woman. Although circumstances keep them apart, their love never dies. Produced in France during WWII right under the noses of Nazi occupiers; many of the talent (including the writer, poet Jacques Prevert) were active resistance fighters. Laserdisc version features: interview with director Marcel Carne, production photos, analysis of influences of French painting on the film, and audio essay by film authority Brian Stonehill. In French with English subtitles. 188m/B VHS, LV. FR Jean-Louis Barrault, Arletty, Pierre Brasseur, Maria Casares, Albert Remy, Leon Larive, Marcel Herrand, Pierre Renoir, Jeanne Marken, Gaston Modot; **D:** Marcel Carne; **W:** Jacques Prevert; **C:** Roger Hubert; **M:** Maurice Thiriet, Joseph Kosma. Nominations: Academy Awards '46: Best Original Screenplay. HMV, CRC, FCT

Children of Rage 🐾🐾½ 1975 (PG) High-minded and long-winded drama dealing with the Israeli/Palestinian war and terrorism from the viewpoint of an Israeli doctor yearning for peace. 106m/C VHS, Beta. GB IS Simon Ward, Cyril Cusack, Helmut Griem, Olga Georges-Picot; **D:** Arthur Seidelman; **W:** Richard Alfieri. ACA

Children of Sanchez 🐾🐾 1979 (PG) Mexican man attempts to provide for his family with very little mutual faith and love. U.S./Mexican production based on Oscar Lewis' novel. 103m/C VHS, Beta. MX Anthony Quinn, Dolores Del Rio, Katy Jurado, Lupita Ferrer; **D:** Hall Bartlett; **W:** Hall Bartlett; **M:** Chuck Mangione. MON

Children of the Corn 🐾½ 1984 (R) Young couple lands in a small Iowa town where children appease a demon by murderously sacrificing adults. Time to move or dispense with some major spankings. Infrequently scary. Another feeble attempt to translate the horror of a Stephen King book to film. 93m/C VHS, Beta, LV. Peter Horton, Linda Hamilton, R.G. Armstrong, John Franklin, Courtney Gains, Robbie Kiger; **D:** Fritz Kiersch; **M:** Jonathan Elias. VTR

Children of the Corn 2: The Final Sacrifice 🐾½ 1992 (R) Reporter working for a tabloid paper gets more than he bargained for when he decides to do a story on the adults murdered in the town of Gatlin, Nebraska. Gatlin's surviving children, who killed their parents in the first film, are now living in a neighboring town and free to kill again. This youthful satanic cult does in authority figures in a number of sacrifical ways,

working ever more smartly to create the prime attraction—blood flow. Not based on anything written by Stephen King. **CW:** Language and horror violence. 93m/C VHS, Closed Caption. Terence Knox, Paul Scherrer, Rosalind Allen, Christie Clark, Ned Romero, Ryan Bollman, Ted Travelstead; **D:** David F. Price; **W:** Gilbert Adler, A.L. Katz. PAR

Children of the Corn 3: Urban Harvest 🐾🐾 1995 (R) Joshua (Melendez) and younger brother Eli (Cerny) are adopted by a wealthy couple and transplanted from Nebraska to Chicago's suburbia. But when Eli grows a corn patch that resurrects an evil force, only Joshua can stop his reign of terror. Contrived premise but lots of nifty special effects. **CW:** Horror violence and gore; language. 103m/C VHS, LV, Closed Caption. Daniel Cerney, Ron Melendez, Mari Morrow, Duke Stroud, Jim Metzler, Nancy Lee Grahn; **D:** James D.R. Hickox; **W:** Dode Levenson; **C:** Gerry Lively; **M:** Daniel Licht. TOU

Children of the Corn 4: The Gathering 🐾 1996 (R) Medical student Grace Rhodes (Watts) seeks to free the children of her Nebraska hometown from a mysterious plague and a shadowy figure. 85m/C VHS, LV, Closed Caption. Naomi Watts, Brent Jennings, Jaime Renee Smith, William Windom, Karen Black; **D:** Greg Spence; **W:** Stephen Berger, Greg Spence; **C:** Richard Clabaugh; **M:** David Williams. TOU

Children of the Damned 🐾🐾 1963 Six children, who are a sample of what man will evolve to in a million years, are born all around the world with genius IQs, ray-gun eyes, and murderous dispositions. Two investigators bring the children together, and while they are being examined by scientists they escape. The children hide out in a church, but they are doomed because their destiny is to be destroyed to teach a lesson to modern man. A sequel to "Village of the Damned" based loosely on the novel "The Midwich Cuckoos" by John Wyndham. 90m/B VHS, LV. GB Ian Hendry, Alan Badel, Barbara Ferris, Alfred Burke, Sheila Allen, Clive Powell, Frank Summerscales, Mahdu Mathen, Gerald Delsol, Roberta Rex, Franchesca Lee, Harold Goldblatt, Ralph Michael, Martin Miller, Lee Yoke-Moon; **D:** Anton Leader; **W:** John Briley. MGM

Children of the Full Moon 🐾 1984 A young couple find themselves lost in a forest that is the home of a family of werewolves. Earns praise only for brevity. Even bad movie aficionados will want to skip this howler. 60m/C VHS, Beta. GB Christopher Cazenove, Celia Gregory, Diana Dors, Jacof Witken, Robert Urquhart; **D:** Tom Clegg. LIV

Children of the Night 🐾½ 1992 (R) Allburg seems like a typically quiet small town far removed from any danger—until a vampire is released from an underground crypt and decides to make the town his bloodthirsty target. When a teacher, whose girlfriend is visiting Allburg, learns of the supernatural goings on he decides to investigate, which may be a deadly mistake. **CW:** Language and horror violence. 92m/C VHS. Peter DeLuise, Karen Black, Ami Dolenz; **D:** Tony Randel; **C:** Gil Hubbs. COL

Children of the Revolution 🐾🐾 1995 (R) Mockumentary covering 45 years of Australian history and politics, beginning in 1951 when the conservative Prime Minister attempts to ban the Australian Communist Party. Party member (and Stalin admirer) Joan Fraser (Davis) helps to prevent the ban, bringing her to the Russian leader's attention, and she's invited to Moscow. There, Joan winds up in bed with Stalin (Abraham) and comes home pregnant. Eventually, son Joe (Rush) makes an entry into the Australian political scene, resulting in chaos. There's almost too much more for the film to handle, although the actors don't seem to have any problems. **CW:** Some strong sexuality and language. 99m/C VHS. AU Judy Davis, Sam Neill, Richard Roxburgh, Rachel Griffiths, Geoffrey Rush, F. Murray Abraham; **D:** Peter Duncan; **W:** Peter Duncan; **C:** Martin Garth; **M:** Nigel Westlake. Australian Film Institute '96: Best Actress (Davis), Best Art

Direction/Set Decoration, Best Costume Design; Nominations: Australian Film Institute '96: Best Director (Duncan), Best Film.

Children of the Wild 🐾🐾½ *Killers of the Wild* **1937** Adventure story about a pack of dogs surviving in the Rocky Mountain wilderness. Splendid scenery and some interesting sequences. **65m/B VHS.** Patsy Moran. *VYY*

The Children of Theatre Street 1977 Absorbing documentary follows three children attending the renowned Kirov Ballet School. A show for all ages that may be especially enjoyed by kids who are interested in ballet. Kelly's last film appearance. **92m/C VHS, Beta.** *RU* Angelina Armeiskaya, Alec Timoushin, Lena Voronzova, Michaela Cerna, Galina Messenzeva, Konstantin Zaklinsky; *D:* Robert Dornhelm; *W:* Beth Gutcheon; *C:* Karl Kofler. Nominations: Academy Awards '77: Best Feature Documentary. *MVD, PBC, KUL*

The Children of Times Square 🐾🐾 **1986** A mother pursues her son who has fled home and joined a gang of drug dealers in New York City's seedy Times Square. Ordinary television film despite strong casting of Cassidy and Rollins. **95m/C VHS, Beta, Closed Caption.** Joanna Cassidy, Howard E. Rollins Jr., Brandon Douglas, David Ackroyd, Griffin O'Neal, Danny Nucci, Larry B. Scott; *D:* Curtis Hanson; *M:* Patrick Gleeson. *FRH*

Children Shouldn't Play with Dead Things 🐾🐾½ *Revenge of the Living Dead* **1972** A band of foolhardy hippie filmmakers on an island cemetary skimp on special effects by using witchcraft to revive the dead. The plan works. Soon the crew has an island full of hungry ghouls to contend with. Film strives for yucks, frequently succeeds. A late night fave, sporting some excellent dead rising from their grave scenes as well as a selection of groovy fashions. Screenwriter/star Ormsby went on to write the remake of "Cat People," while director Clark would eventually helm "Porky's." **85m/C VHS, Beta.** Alan Ormsby, Valerie Mamches, Jeff Gillen, Anya Ormsby, Paul Cronin, Jane Daly, Roy Engelman, Robert Philip, Bruce Solomon, Alecs Baird, Seth Sklarey; *D:* Bob (Benjamin) Clark; *W:* Alan Ormsby, Bob (Benjamin) Clark. *VCI, MPI*

The Children's Hour 🐾🐾 *The Loudest Whisper* **1961** The teaching careers of two women are ruined when girls begin circulating vicious rumors. Only an occasionally taut drama despite forceful handling of a lesbian theme. Updated version of Lillian Hellman's play (adapted by Hellman) is more explicit, but less suspenseful in spite of excellent performances from the talented cast. Remake of Wyler's own "These Three." **107m/C VHS, LV, Closed Caption.** Shirley MacLaine, Audrey Hepburn, James Garner, Miriam Hopkins, Veronica Cartwright, Fay Bainter; *D:* William Wyler; *W:* John Michael Hayes; *M:* Alex North. Nominations: Academy Awards '61: Best Art Direction/Set Decoration (B & W), Best Black and White Cinematography, Best Costume Design (B & W), Best Sound, Best Supporting Actress (Bainter). *MGM, BTV, FCT*

Child's Christmas in Wales 1988 A film of Dylan Thomas's Christmas story about an old, traditional Christmas in Wales circa 1910. **55m/C VHS, Beta.** Mathonwy Reeves; *D:* Don McBrearty. *LIV, VES, HMV*

Child's Play 🐾🐾½ **1988 (R)** A boy discovers that his new doll named Chucky is actually the embodiment of a deranged killer. His initially skeptical mom and a police officer come around after various killings. Exciting, if somewhat moronic, fare, with fine special effects. Followed by "Child's Play 2." **95m/C VHS, Beta, LV, Closed Caption.** Catherine Hicks, Alex Vincent, Chris Sarandon, Dinah Manoff, Brad Dourif, Tommy Swerdlow, Jack Colvin; *D:* Tom Holland; *W:* Don Mancini, John Lafia, Tom Holland; *C:* Bill Butler; *M:* Joe Renzetti. *MGM*

Child's Play 2 woof! **1990 (R)** Chuckie lives. Basic doll-on-a-rampage story, a metaphor for the Reagan years, lives on in the sequel (you remember: somehow guy-doll Chuckie made it past the quality control people with a highly inflammable temper). A little dotty from playing with

dolls, young Vincent finds himself fostered by two new parents, and plagued by an obnoxious and very animated doll that fosters ill will toward all. What's worse is the doll is transmigratory, craving the boy's body as his next address. Chef d'effects Kevin Yagher's new toy is bad, real bad, and so are the other part two FX. Little Chuckie's saga, however grows a tad tiresome. A bad example for small children. **84m/C VHS, Beta, LV, Closed Caption.** Alex Vincent, Jenny Agutter, Gerrit Graham, Christine Elise, Grace Zabriskie; *D:* John Lafia; *W:* Don Mancini; *M:* Graeme Revell; *V:* Brad Dourif. *USH*

Child's Play 3 🐾 **1991 (R)** Possessed doll Chucky returns to life again in search of a new child to control, and luckily finds his old pal (Whalin) at a military school filled with the usual stereotypes. Gory sequel in a mostly awful series. "Don't F— With the Chuck" was its catch phrase; that should indicate the level of this junk. *CW:* Language and horror violence. **89m/C VHS, Beta, LV, Closed Caption.** Justin Whalin, Perrey Reeves, Jeremy Sylvers, Peter Haskell, Dakin Matthews, Travis Fine, Dean Jacobson, Matthew Walker, Andrew (Andy) Robinson; *D:* Jack Bender; *W:* Don Mancini; *M:* Cory Lerios, John D'Andrea; *V:* Brad Dourif. *USH*

Chill Factor 🐾🐾 **1990 (R)** A television reporter for an investigative news show uncovers evidence of an international conspiracy. Plot twists abound. **?m/C VHS.** Paul Williams, Patrick Macnee, Andrew Prine, Carrie Snodgress, Patrick Wayne, Gary Crosby; *D:* David L. Stanton. *NO*

Chillers 🐾 **1988** Travellers waiting for a bus are besieged by carnivorous zombies and voracious vampires. How this is different from the standard bus trip is unclear. **90m/C VHS, Beta.** Jesse Emery, Marjorie Fitzsimmons, Laurie Pennington, Jim Wolfe, David Wohl; *D:* Daniel Boyd; *W:* Daniel Boyd. *PSM*

The Chilling woof! *Gamma 693* **1989 (R)** Corpses preserved in a deep freeze come alive and plague Kansas City as brain-chomping zombies. Utterly worthless film doesn't even provide convincing effects. *CW:* Horror violence and one sensual scene. **91m/C VHS.** Linda Blair, Dan Haggerty, Troy Donahue, Jack A. De Rieux, Ron Vincent; *D:* Deland Nuse, Jack A. Sunseri. *HMD*

Chilly Scenes of Winter 🐾🐾½ *Head Over Heels* **1979 (PG)** Quirky comedy with a cult following about a man obsessed with regaining the love of a former girlfriend who is now married. He must also deal with an insane mom and various other problems. Strong, subtle performances from Heard and Riegert. Hurt is somewhat less satisfying as the supposedly fascinating woman. Released with a different, inferior ending as "Head Over Heels." Adapted by Joan Micklin Silver from Ann Beattie's first novel. Watch for Beattie's cameo as a waitress. **96m/C VHS, Beta.** John Heard, Mary Beth Hurt, Peter Riegert, Kenneth McMillan, Gloria Grahame, Nora Heflin, Griffin Dunne; *Cameos:* Ann Beattie; *D:* Joan Micklin Silver; *W:* Joan Micklin Silver. *MGM*

Chimes at Midnight 🐾🐾🐾🐾 *Falstaff; Campanadas a Medianoche* **1967** Classic tragedy—derived by Welles from five Shakespeare plays—about a corpulent blowhard and his friendship with a prince. Crammed with classic sequences, including a battle that is both realistic and funny. The love scene between massive Welles and a nonetheless willing Moreau also manages to be both sad and amusing. Great performances all around, but Welles understandably dominates. The film's few flaws (due to budget problems) are inconsequential before considerable strengths. This one ranks among Welles', and thus the entire cinema's, very best. **115m/B VHS, Beta.** *SP SI* Orson Welles, Jeanne Moreau, Margaret Rutherford, John Gielgud, Marina Vlady, Keith Baxter, Fernando Rey, Norman Rodway; *D:* Orson Welles; *W:* Orson Welles; *M:* Angelo Francesco Lavagnino. *FCT*

China 🐾🐾½ **1943** David Jones (Ladd) is an unfeeling profiteer who's making money off the Japanese invading China (it's 1941). But he and buddy Johnny Sparrow (Bendix) have their truck

hijacked by a group of Chinese guerrillas, lead by China-born American teacher Carolyn Grant (Young), who need a group of schoolgirls driven to safety through enemy lines. Naturally, Jones has a change of heart (and sides) and battles the Japanese troops. Typically fervent propaganda film. Based on the play by Archibald Forbes. **79m/B VHS, Closed Caption.** Alan Ladd, Loretta Young, William Bendix, Philip Ahn, Victor Sen Yung, Marianne Quon, Richard Loo; *D:* John Farrow; *W:* Frank Butler; *C:* Leo Tover. *USH*

China Beach 🐾🐾🐾 **1988** TV movie/pilot launched the acclaimed series about American military women behind the lines during the chaos of the Vietnam War. Nurse McMurphy has only seven days left on her first tour of duty, and in spite of her hate of the brutality of the war, she has mixed feelings about leaving her friends and her work. A USO singer on a one week tour finds her search for men brings the war too close for comfort. Cherry, a new Red Cross volunteer, shows up at the Beach. Skillfully introduces the viewer to all the characters, their problems and joys, without melodrama or redundancy. **95m/C VHS, Beta, Closed Caption.** Dana Delany, Chloe Webb, Michael Picardo, Nan Woods, Michael Boatman, Marg Helgenberger, Tim Ryan, Concetta Tomei, Jeff Kober, Brian Wimmer; *D:* Rod Holcomb; *W:* John Sacret Young. *WAR*

China Cry 🐾🐾½ **1991 (PG-13)** Based on the true story of Sung Neng Yee who escaped from Communist China to the freedom of Hong Kong in the early '60s. Fine portrayal of the young woman from a privileged background who witnessed some of the atrocities of Mao's government policies. **103m/C VHS.** Julia Nickson-Soul, Russell Wong, James Shigeta, France Nuyen; *D:* James F. Collier. *IGP*

China Gate 🐾🐾🐾 **1957** A band of multi-national troops follows a French officer against a communist stronghold in Indochina. Conventional fare bolstered considerably by director Fuller's flair for action. Weak male leads, but Dickinson shines. **97m/B VHS.** Gene Barry, Angie Dickinson, Nat King Cole, Paul Dubov, Lee Van Cleef, George Givot, Marcel Dalio; *D:* Samuel Fuller; *W:* Samuel Fuller; *M:* Max Steiner. *REP*

China Girl 🐾🐾½ **1987 (R)** An Italian-American boy and a Chinese-American girl romance despite a war between gangs in their respective NYC communities. This often violent drama is enriched by director Ferrara's slick, high-energy approach. **90m/C VHS, Beta, LV.** Richard Panebianco, James Russo, Sari Chang, Russell Wong, David Caruso, Joey Chin; *D:* Abel Ferrara; *W:* Nicholas St. John; *C:* Bojan Bazelli; *M:* Joe Delia. *VES*

The China Lake Murders 🐾🐾½ **1990 (PG-13)** A made for cable crazy cop on the loose fable in which a serial killer disguised as a highway patrolman practices population control on the inhabitants of a small town in the Mojave desert. Meanwhile the local sheriff (Skerritt), unwittingly befriends the killer-patrolman. **100m/C VHS, Beta, Closed Caption.** Tom Skerritt, Michael Parks, Nancy Everhard, Lauren Tewes, Bill McKinney, Lonny Chapman; *D:* Alan Metzger; *W:* Nevin Schreiner. *USH*

China Moon 🐾🐾 **1991 (R)** Convoluted police thriller, set in Florida, about beautiful Rachel (Stowe), who's married to rich-but-abusive Rupert (Dance). Kyle (Harris) is the lonely homicide detective who's besotted with Rachel and conveniently helps her dispose of her murdered husband's body. Kyle's problems increase when his rookie partner (Del Toro) turns out to be smarter than anyone thinks. Good performances but the suspense is only average. *CW:* Language, violence, and sensuality. **99m/C VHS, LV, Closed Caption.** Ed Harris, Madeleine Stowe, Benicio Del Toro, Charles Dance; *D:* John Bailey; *W:* Roy Carlson; *M:* George Fenton. *ORI*

China, My Sorrow 🐾🐾½ **1989** Thirteen-year-old "Little Four Eyes" is sent to a Chinese re-education camp for the crime of playing a love song to a girl. There he befriends another enemy of the revolution and a Buddhist monk who help him maintain his familial traditions and identity. Tragi-comic look at how freedom's spirit survived the Cultural Revolution. In Mandarin and Shanghaiese with English subtitles. **86m/C VHS.** *CH* Guo Yiang Yi, Tieu Quan Nghieu, Vong Han Lai, Chi-Vy Sam, Chang Cheung Siang; *D:* Dai Sijie; *W:* Dai Sijie, Shan Yuan Zhu; *M:* Chen Qi Gang. *CVC, FCT*

China O'Brien *♂♂½* 1988 (R) Gorgeous police officer with martial arts expertise returns home for a little R & R, but finds she has to kick some major butt instead. Violent, dimwitted action drama proves only that cleavage can be macho too.*CW:* Martial arts violence. **90m/C VHS, Closed Caption.** Cynthia Rothrock, Richard Norton, Patrick Adamson, David Blackwell, Steven Kerby, Robert Tiller, Lainie Watts, Keith Cooke; *D:* Robert Clouse; *M:* Paul Antonelli. *IMP, BTV*

China O'Brien 2 *♂♂½* 1989 (R) The unbreakable China, now a sheriff, battles the standard-issue Vietnam-vet druglord who invades her little town. Made back-to-back with the first film (note that both pics' bad guys have the same gang of henchmen!), and in both films Rothrock is basically invincible, so there's no suspense.*CW:* Violence. **85m/C VHS, Closed Caption.** Cynthia Rothrock, Richard Norton, Keith Cooke; *D:* Robert Clouse. *IMP*

China Seas *♂♂♂* 1935 The captain of a commercial steamship on the China route has to fight off murderous Malay pirates, a spurned woman, and a raging typhoon to reach port safely. Fast-moving romantic action taken from Crosbie Garstin's novel. **89m/B VHS, Beta.** Clark Gable, Jean Harlow, Wallace Beery, Rosalind Russell, Lewis Stone, Sir C. Aubrey Smith, Dudley Digges, Robert Benchley; *D:* Tay Garnett. *MGM*

China Sky *♂♂* 1944 An American doctor fights alongside Chinese guerillas against the Japanese during WWII. Drama, to its credit, often opts for character conflict instead of warfare, but this makes it merely dull instead of cliched. Adapted from a Pearl S. Buck novel. **78m/B VHS, Beta, LV.** Randolph Scott, Ellen Drew, Ruth Warrick, Anthony Quinn, Carol Thurston, Richard Loo, Philip Ahn; *D:* Ray Enright. *TTC*

The China Syndrome *♂♂♂½* 1979 (PG) A somewhat unstable executive at a nuclear plant uncovers evidence of a concealed accident, takes drastic steps to publicize the incident. Lemmon is excellent as the anxious exec, while Fonda and Douglas are scarcely less distinguished as a sympathetic TV journalist and camera operator, respectively. Tense, prophetic thriller that ironically preceded the Three Mile Island accident by just a few months. Produced by Douglas. **123m/C VHS, Beta, LV, Closed Caption.** Jane Fonda, Jack Lemmon, Michael Douglas, Scott Brady, James Hampton, Peter Donat, Wilford Brimley, James Karen; *D:* James Bridges; *W:* Mike Gray, T.S. Cook, James Bridges. British Academy Awards '79: Best Actor (Lemmon), Best Actress (Fonda); Cannes Film Festival '79: Best Actor (Lemmon); National Board of Review Awards '79: 10 Best Films of the Year; Writers Guild of America '79: Best Original Screenplay; Nominations: Academy Awards '79: Best Actor (Lemmon), Best Actress (Fonda), Best Art Direction/Set Decoration, Best Original Screenplay. *COL*

China White 1991 (R) Violence erupts in the streets of Paris, Amsterdam and Bangkok, when international drug cartels battle over the ownership of China White - premium heroin, its sources and its outlets. Rousing, realistic action.*CW:* Language and strong violence and drug content. **?m/C VHS, Closed Caption.** Billy Drago, Russell Wong, Lisa Schrage, Steven Leigh; *D:* Ronny Yu. *IMP*

Chinatown *♂♂♂♂* 1974 (R) Private detective finds himself overwhelmed in a scandalous case involving the rich and powerful of Los Angeles. Gripping, atmospheric mystery excels in virtually every aspect, with strong narrative drive and outstanding performances from Nicholson, Dunaway, and Huston. Director Polanski also appears in a suitable unsettling cameo. Fabulous. A sneaky, snaking delight filled with seedy charac-

ters and plots-within-plots. Followed more than 15 years later by "The Two Jakes." **131m/C VHS, Beta, LV, 8mm, Closed Caption.** Jack Nicholson, Faye Dunaway, John Huston, Diane Ladd, John Hillerman, Burt Young, Perry Lopez, Darrell Zwerling; *Cameos:* Roman Polanski; *D:* Roman Polanski; *W:* Robert Towne; *C:* John A. Alonzo; *M:* Jerry Goldsmith. Academy Awards '74: Best Original Screenplay; British Academy Awards '74: Best Actor (Nicholson), Best Director (Polanski), Best Screenplay; Edgar Allan Poe Awards '74: Best Screenplay; Golden Globe Awards '75: Best Actor—Drama (Nicholson), Best Director (Polanski), Best Film—Drama, Best Screenplay; National Board of Review Awards '74: 10 Best Films of the Year; New York Film Critics Awards '74: Best Actor (Nicholson); National Society of Film Critics Awards '74: Best Actor (Nicholson); Writers Guild of America '74: Best Original Screenplay; Nominations: Academy Awards '74: Best Actor (Nicholson), Best Actress (Dunaway), Best Art Direction/Set Decoration, Best Cinematography, Best Costume Design, Best Director (Polanski), Best Film Editing, Best Picture, Best Sound, Original Dramatic/Comedy Score. *PAR*

Chinatown After Dark *♂* 1931 Ludicrous, inane melodrama about a white girl raised by the Chinese. **50m/B VHS.** Rex Lease, Barbara Kent, Carmel Myers; *D:* Stuart Paton. *SNC, NOS, DVT*

Chinatown Connection *♂* 1990 (R) For some inexplicable reason, local drug dealers start selling poisoned cocaine. Two renegade cops discover the super-secret organization doing the poisoning, arm themselves heavily, and kill lots of people while putting an end to the poisonings. Violent, foolish film with dull performances. **94m/C VHS.** Bruce Ly, Lee Majors, Pat McCormick, Art Camacho, Susan Frailey, Scott Richards; *D:* Jean-Paul Ouellette. *NO*

The Chinatown Kid *♂* 1978 Tan Tung escapes from Red China on a ship bound for San Francisco. There he becomes involved in a local extortion racket and he'll need all his martial arts skills to overcome the two gangs fighting for power. **115m/C VHS.** Alexander Fu Sheng, Sun Chein, Shirley Yu, Shaw Yin-Yin; *D:* Chen Chen. *HMD, FXL*

The Chinatown Murders: Man Against the Mob *♂♂* 1992 (R) A tough cop is up against the Chinese mafia and his own corrupt police force as he tries to stay alive and find some justice. **96m/C VHS, Closed Caption.** George Peppard, Charles Haid, Richard Bradford, Ursula Andress. *THV*

Chinese Boxes *♂♂½* 1984 An American man in Berlin is framed in a murder and becomes caught in an international web of crime and intrigue. Low budget but interesting thriller. **87m/C VHS, Beta.** *GE GB* Will Patton, Adelheid Arndt, Robbie Coltrane; *D:* Christopher Petit; *W:* L.M. Kit Carson. *LIV, VES*

The Chinese Cat *♂* 1944 Poorly scripted formula mystery has the younger Chan smitten with a girl who needs the elder Chan's detective skills in finding her father's killer. **65m/B VHS.** Sidney Toler, Benson Fong, Mantan Moreland, Weldon Heyburn, Joan Woodbury, Ian Keith, Sam Flint; *D:* Phil Rosen. *MGM*

Chinese Connection *♂♂½* Fist of Fury; The Iron Hand 1973 (R) A martial arts expert tracks sadistic brutes who slew his instructor. Wild action sequences provide a breathtaking view of Lee's skill. Dubbed. **90m/C VHS, Beta, LV.** *CH* Bruce Lee, James Tien, Robert Baker; *D:* Lo Wei. *FOX, MRV, REP*

Chinese Connection 2 *♂♂* 1984 A martial-arts expert learns that the school when he trained is now run by an unappealing master. Conflict ensues. Bruce Li is not Bruce Lee, but he is fairly good in action portions of this otherwise dull, sloppy venture. **96m/C VHS, Beta.** Bruce Li. *TWE*

Chinese Roulette *♂♂½* 1986 A host of unappealing characters convene at a country house for sexual shenanigans and a cruel game masterminded by a sadistic crippled girl. Cold effort from German master Fassbinder. In German with English subtitles. **96m/C VHS, Beta, LV.** *GE* Anna Karina, Margit Carstensen, Ulli Lommel, Brigitte Mira, Macha Meril, Andrea Schober, Volker Spengler; *D:* Rainer Werner Fassbinder; *W:* Rainer Werner Fassbinder; *C:* Michael Ballhaus. *CVC*

Chinese Web *♂* 1978 Spiderman adventure in which Spidey becomes entwined in international intrigue and corrupt officials. **95m/C VHS, Beta, Closed Caption.** Nicholas Hammond, Robert F. Simon, Rosalind Chao, Ted Danson; *D:* Donald McDougall. *FOX*

Chino *♂♂* Valdez the Half Breed; The Valdez Horses 1975 (PG) A half-Indian horse rancher struggles to maintain his livelihood in this spaghetti western. Not among Bronson's stronger—that is, more viscerally effective—films. Adapted from Lee Hoffman's novel. **97m/C VHS, Beta.** *IT* Charles Bronson, Jill Ireland, Vincent Van Patten; *D:* John Sturges. *MPI, MRV, VTR*

The Chipmunk Adventure *♂♂* 1987 The three animated chipmunks, Simon, Theodore and Alvin, get involved with a diamond smuggling ring. Original songs. In HiFi Stereo. **76m/C VHS, Beta, LV, Closed Caption.** *D:* Janice Karman; *W:* Janice Karman, Ross Bagdasarian; *M:* Randy Edelman. *ORI, WAR*

Chips, the War Dog *♂♂½* 1990 A WWII Army recruit, who's scared of dogs, is assigned to train a German shepherd for duty. Made for cable television. **90m/C VHS.** Brandon Douglas, Ned Vaughn, Paxton Whitehead, Ellie Cornell, William Devane; *D:* Ed Kaplan. *DIS*

The Chisholms *♂♂½* 1979 If you're into oaters, here's a high fiber six-hour serial: Chisolm (Preston) leads the family as they head west and find trouble with a capital "T" en route from Virginia to Californ-i-a. Originally a network miniseries, it's now a two-cassette rentable; adapted by Evan Hunter from his novel. **300m/C VHS, Beta.** Robert Preston, Rosemary Harris, Brian Keith, Ben Murphy, Charles Frank; *D:* Mel Stuart; *M:* Elmer Bernstein. *LIV*

Chisum *♂½* 1970 (G) Cattle baron faces various conflicts, including a confrontation with Billy the Kid. Lame Wayne vehicle contributes nothing to exhausted western genre. Laserdisc available in widescreen letterbox edition. **111m/C VHS, Beta, LV.** John Wayne, Forrest Tucker, Geoffrey Deuel, Christopher George, Ben Johnson, Bruce Cabot, Patric Knowles, Richard Jaeckel, Glenn Corbett; *D:* Andrew V. McLaglen; *W:* Andrew J. Fenady; *C:* William Clothier. *WAR, TLF*

Chitty Chitty Bang Bang *♂♂* 1968 (G) An eccentric inventor spruces up an old car and, in fantasy, takes his children to a land where the evil rulers have forbidden children. Poor special effects and forgettable score stall effort. Loosely adapted by Roald Dahl and Hughes from an Ian Fleming story. *♫* Chitty Chitty Bang Bang; Hushabye Mountain; Truly Scrumptious; You Two; Toot Sweet; Me Ol' Bam-Boo; Lovely Lonely Man; Posh; The Roses of Success. **142m/C VHS, Beta, LV, Closed Caption.** *GB* Dick Van Dyke, Sally Ann Howes, Lionel Jeffries, Gert Frobe, Anna Quayle, Benny Hill; *D:* Ken Hughes; *W:* Ken Hughes, Roald Dahl. Nominations: Academy Awards '68: Best Song ("Chitty Chitty Bang Bang"). *FOX, MGM, TLF*

Chloe in the Afternoon *♂♂♂* 1972 (R) A married man finds himself inexplicably drawn to an ungainly young woman. Sixth of the "Moral Tales" series is typical of director Rohmer's talky approach. Not for all tastes, but rewarding for those who are drawn to this sort of thing. In French with English subtitles. **97m/C VHS, Beta.** *FR* Bernard Verley, Zouzou, Francoise Verley, Daniel Ceccaldi, Malvina Penne, Babette Ferrier, Suze Randall, Marie-Christine Barrault; *D:* Eric Rohmer; *W:* Eric Rohmer; *C:* Nestor Almendros. National Board of Review Awards '72: 5 Best Foreign Films of the Year. *FCT*

Chocolat *♂♂♂½* 1988 (PG-13) A woman recalls her childhood spent in French West Africa and the unfulfilled sexual tension between her mother and black servant. Vivid film provides a host of intriguing characters and offers splendid panoramas of rugged desert landscapes. Profound, if somewhat personal filmmaking from novice director Denis. In French with English subtitles. **105m/C VHS, Beta, LV.** Mireille Perrier, Emmet Judson Williamson, Cecile Ducasse, Giulia Boschi, Francois Cluzet, Isaach de Bankole, Kenneth Cranham; *D:* Claire Denis; *W:* Claire Denis, Jean-Pol Fargeau. *ORI*

The Chocolate Soldier 🎭 1941 Dull musical in which an opera star tests his wife's fidelity. Lovers of the musical genre will find that this one has too much talking, not enough singing. Lovers of fine films will realize that more singing would hardly improve things. Based loosely on Molnar's play "The Guardsman." **102m/B VHS.** Nelson Eddy, Rise Stevens, Nigel Bruce, Florence Bates, Dorothy Gilmore, Nydia Westman; **D:** Roy Del Ruth; **C:** Karl Freund. Nominations: Academy Awards '41: Best Black and White Cinematography, Best Sound, Scoring of a Musical. *MGM*

The Chocolate War 🎭🎭🎭 1988 (R) An idealistic student and a hardline headmaster butt heads at a Catholic boys' school over an unofficial candy business in this tense, unsettling drama. Glover is notable in his familiar villain role, and Gordon is effective in his first effort as director. Based on the Robert Cormier novel. **95m/C VHS, Beta, LV, Closed Caption.** John Glover, Jenny Wright, Wally Ward, Bud Cort, Ilan Mitchell-Smith, Adam Baldwin; **D:** Keith Gordon; **W:** Keith Gordon. *MCG*

The Choice 🎭🎭 1981 A young woman must make the choice between aborting or keeping her baby in this fairly insipid television drama. **96m/C VHS, Beta.** Susan Clark, Jennifer Warren, Mitchell Ryan, Largo Woodruff; **D:** David Greene. *LIV*

Choice of Arms 🎭🎭½ 1983 A gangster's rural retirement is undone by a dimwitted criminal in this sometimes gripping drama. Montand and Deneuve are serviceable in undemanding roles of the gangster and his glamorous wife; Depardieu is more impressive as the trouble-making punk. In French with English subtitles. **FR** Gerard Depardieu, Catherine Deneuve, Yves Montand; Alain Corneau. *MED*

Choice of Weapons 🎭🎭 *A Dirty Knight's Work; Trial by Combat* 1976 Ex-cop trying to solve murders focuses on a curious group of 20th-century men who live within a 12th-century fantasy—jousting for sport and chivalrous honor. Offbeat lance thruster notable for incongruity and all-star cast. **88m/C VHS, Beta.** *GB* David Birney, Peter Cushing, Donald Pleasence, Barbara Hershey, John Mills, Margaret Leighton; **D:** Kevin Connor; **W:** Julian Bond. *NO*

Choices 🎭½ 1981 A hearing-impaired athlete suffers alienation when banned from the football squad. What? Controversial covergirl Moore is a supporting player in this, her first film. **90m/C VHS, Beta.** Paul Carafotes, Victor French, Lelia Goldoni, Val Avery, Dennis Patrick, Demi Moore; **D:** Rami Alon. *VHE, HHE, VTR*

Choices 🎭🎭½ 1986 Scott is a 62-year-old man with a lovely second wife (Bisset) and a rebellious grown daughter (Gilbert), who announces she's pregnant and is getting an abortion. Meanwhile, his wife also discovers she's pregnant and wants the child, although Scott is adamantly opposed to raising a second family at his age. Family strife carried by fine performances. Made for television. **95m/C VHS.** George C. Scott, Jacqueline Bisset, Melissa Gilbert; **D:** David Lowell Rich. *CAF*

The Choirboys 🎭 1977 (R) Thoroughly mediocre production about overbearing L.A. cops and their off-hours handling of job stress. Few of the strong cast emerge unscathed. Based on the Joseph Wambaugh novel. **120m/C VHS, Beta.** Charles Durning, Louis Gossett Jr., Perry King, Clyde Kusatsu, Stephen Macht, Tim McIntire, Randy Quaid, Chuck Sacci, Don Stroud, James Woods, Burt Young, Robert Webber, Barbara Rhoades, Vic Tayback, Blair Brown, Charles Haid, Jim Davis; **D:** Robert Aldrich; **C:** Joseph Biroc. *USH*

Choke Canyon 🎭🎭 1986 (PG) An environmentalist thwarts the henchmen of an industrialist eager to coverup a nuclear dump in a picturesque canyon. Good intentions do not necessarily make for a good movie. **95m/C VHS, Beta.** Stephen Collins, Bo Svenson, Lance Henriksen; **D:** Chuck Bail. *MED*

C.H.O.M.P.S. 🎭½ 1979 (PG) Comedy in which a youthful inventor and a popular robot guard dog become the target of a business takeover. Harmless but unfunny and unfun. **90m/C VHS, Beta.** Jim Backus, Valerie Bertinelli, Wesley Eure, Conrad Bain, Chuck McCann, Red Buttons; **D:** Don Chaffey. *NO*

Choose Me 🎭🎭🎭½ 1984 (R) Comedy-drama about sad, lonely, and often quirky characters linked to an unlikely L.A. radio sex therapist. Moody, memorable fare features especially strong playing from Bujold as a sexually inexperienced sex therapist and Warren as one of her regular listeners. Typically eccentric fare from director Rudolph. **106m/C VHS, Beta, LV.** Keith Carradine, Genevieve Bujold, Lesley Ann Warren, Rae Dawn Chong, John Larroquette, John Considine; **D:** Alan Rudolph; **W:** Alan Rudolph. *MED*

Chopper Chicks in Zombietown 🎭🎭 1991 (R) Tough but sexy Chopper Chicks show up in that American vacation mecca, Zombietown, for a little rest and relaxation. Little do they know that a mad mortician has designs on turning our hot heroines into mindless zombie slaves. Can the buxom biker babes thwart the evil embalmer before it's too late, or will they abandon their Harleys to shuffle about in search of human flesh? From the Troma Team. **86m/C VHS, LV, Closed Caption.** Jamie Rose, Catherine Carlen, Lycia Naff, Vicki Frederick, Kristina Loggia, Martha Quinn, Don Calfa; **D:** Dan Hoskins; **W:** Dan Hoskins. *COL, NLC*

The Choppers 🎭 1961 Naw, not a fable about false teeth. Teen punk Hall operates a car theft ring made up of fellow punksters. Rock'n'roll tunes by the Hall-meister include the much-overlooked "Monkey in my Hatband." **66m/B VHS, Beta.** Arch Hall Jr., Marianne Gaba, Robert Paget, Tom Brown, Rex Holman, Bruno Ve Sota; **D:** Leigh Jason. *SNC*

Chopping Mall 🎭½ *Killbots* 1986 (R) A freak electric storm unleashes killer security robots on a band of teens trapped inside the mall. Nobody shops. Premise undone by obscure humor, lack of flair, action, or horror. Updated imitation of the 1973 TV movie "Trapped." **77m/C VHS, Beta.** Paul Bartel, Mary Woronov, Kelli Maroney, Tony O'Dell, Dick Miller, Suzee Slater, Russell Todd, Karrie Emerson; **D:** Jim Wynorski; **W:** Jim Wynorski. *LIV*

A Chorus Line 🎭🎭 1985 (PG-13) A range of performers reveal their insecurities and aspirations while auditioning before a hardnosed director in this adaptation of the popular, overblown Broadway musical. Singing and dancing is rarely rousing. Director Attenborough probably wasn't the right choice for this one. ♫Dance 10, Looks 3; What I Did for Love; At the Ballet; I Can Do That; Let Me Dance For You; I Hope I Get It; Nothing; The Music and the Mirror; And. **118m/C VHS, Beta, LV, 8mm, Closed Caption.** Michael Douglas, Audrey Landers, Gregg Burge, Alyson Reed, Janet Jones, Michael Blevins, Terrence Mann, Cameron English, Vicki Frederick, Nicole Fosse, Michelle Johnson; **D:** Richard Attenborough; **W:** Arnold Schulman; **M:** Marvin Hamlisch, Ralph Burns. Nominations: Academy Awards '85: Best Film Editing, Best Song ("Surprise, Surprise"), Best Sound. *NLC*

A Chorus of Disapproval 🎭½ 1989 (PG) Adaptation of prolific Alan Ayckbourn's play about a withdrawn, somewhat dimwitted British widower who attempts social interaction by joining community theater, then finds himself embroiled in romantic shenanigans and theatrical intrigue. Irons is fine in the lead, but Hopkins sparkles in the more spectacular role of the musical production's demanding but beleaguered director. Seagrove is impressive as an amoral sexpot. Sharper focus from director Winner would have improved this one, but the film is fun even when it isn't particularly funny. **105m/C VHS, Beta.** Jeremy Irons, Anthony Hopkins, Jenny Seagrove, Lionel Jeffries, Patsy Kensit, Gareth Hunt, Prunella Scales, Sylvia Syms, Richard Briers, Barbara Ferris; **D:** Michael Winner; **W:** Michael Winner, Alan Ayckbourn; **M:** John Du Prez. *NO*

The Chosen woof! *Holocaust 2000* 1977 (R) Executive of a nuclear power facility located in the Sahara Desert realizes that his son is the Anti-Christ bent on the world's destruction. This truly horrible film provides nothing in terms of entertainment. It's rarely even laughably bad. **102m/C VHS, Beta.** Kirk Douglas, Simon Ward, Agostina Belli, Anthony Quayle, Virginia McKenna, Alexander Knox; **D:** Alberto De Martino; **M:** Ennio Morricone. *FOX, LIV, VES*

The Chosen 🎭🎭🎭 1981 Set in 1940's Brooklyn about the friendship between two teenagers—Benson, the Hassidic son of a rabbi and Miller, whose father is a Zionist professor. Based on the novel by Chaim Potok. **108m/C VHS.** Robby Benson, Barry Miller, Maximilian Schell, Rod Steiger, Hildy Brooks, Ron Rifkin, Val Avery; **D:** Jeremy Paul Kagan; **M:** Elmer Bernstein. *FXV*

Christ Stopped at Eboli 🎭🎭🎭🎭 *Eboli* 1979 Subdued work about an anti-Fascist writer exiled to rural Italy in the 1930s. Excellent performances from the lead Volonte and supporting players Papas and Cuny. Slow, contemplative film is probably director Rosi's masterpiece. Adapted from Carlo Levi's book. In Italian with English subtitles. **118m/C VHS, Beta.** *IT FR* Gian Marie Volonte, Irene Papas, Paolo Bonacelli, Francois Simon, Alain Cuny, Lea Massari; **D:** Francesco Rosi; **W:** Francesco Rosi; **C:** Pasquale De Santos. British Academy Awards '82: Best Foreign Film; National Board of Review Awards '80: 5 Best Foreign Films of the Year. *COL, APD*

Christabel 🎭🎭 1989 Condensed version of the BBC mini-series based on the true-life WWII exploits of Christabel Bielenberg, a British woman who battled to save her German husband from the horrors of the Ravensbruck concentration camp. **148m/C VHS, Beta, Closed Caption.** *GB* Elizabeth Hurley, Stephen Dillon, Nigel le Vaillant, Geoffrey Palmer; **W:** Dennis Potter. *FOX*

Christian the Lion 🎭🎭½ 1976 (G) The true story of Christian, a lion cub raised in a London zoo, who is transported to Africa to learn to live with other lions. With the principals from "Born Free." **87m/C VHS, Beta.** *GB* Virginia McKenna, Bill Travers, George Adamson, James Hill; **D:** Bill Travers. *UNI*

Christiane F. 🎭🎭🎭 1982 (R) Gripping, visually impressive story of a bored German girl's decline into drug use and prostitution. Based on a West German magazine article. Sobering and dismal look at a milieu in which innocence and youth have run amok. The film's impact is only somewhat undermined by poor dubbing. Bowie appears in a concert sequence. **120m/C VHS, Beta.** *GE* Natja Brunkhorst, Thomas Haustein, David Bowie; **D:** Uli Edel; **M:** David Bowie. *MED, GLV*

Christina 🎭🎭½ 1974 (PG) Gloomy suspense fare in which a beautiful woman pays a forlorn fellow $25,000 to marry her, then disappears as he begins to actually fall in love with her. His search takes him to various gothic settings. Intriguing, but not really fulfilling. Parkins, however, is appropriately mysterious in the lead. **95m/C VHS, Beta.** *CA* Barbara Parkins, Peter Haskell; **D:** Paul Krasny. *MPI*

Christine 🎭🎭½ 1984 (R) Unassuming teen gains possession of a classic auto equipped with a murderous will. The car more than returns the care and consideration its owner provides it. Are you listening GMC? Based on a novel by Stephen King. **110m/C VHS, Beta, LV, 8mm, Closed Caption.** Keith Gordon, John Stockwell, Alexandra Paul, Robert Prosky, Harry Dean Stanton, Kelly Preston; **D:** John Carpenter; **W:** Bill Phillips; **C:** Donald M. Morgan; **M:** John Carpenter, Alan Howarth. *COL*

A Christmas Carol 🎭🎭🎭 1938 An early version of Dickens' classic tale about miser Scrooge, who is instilled with the Christmas spirit after a grim evening with some ghosts. Good playing from Owen as Scrooge and Lockhart as the hapless Bob Cratchit. Scary graveyard sequence too. **70m/B VHS, Beta, LV.** Reginald Owen,

Gene Lockhart, Terence Kilburn, Leo G. Carroll, Lynne Carver, Ann Rutherford; **D:** Edwin L. Marin. *MGM*

A Christmas Carol 𝄞𝄞𝄞𝄞 *Scrooge* **1951** A fine retelling of the classic tale about a penny-pinching holiday hater who learns appreciation of Christmas following a frightful, revealing evening with supernatural visitors. Perhaps the best rendering of the Dickens classic. "And God bless Tiny Tim!" **86m/B VHS, Beta, LV.** *GB* Alastair Sim, Kathleen Harrison, Jack Warner, Michael Hordern, Patrick Macnee, Mervyn Johns, Hermione Baddeley, Clifford Mollison, George Cole, Carol Marsh, Miles Malleson, Ernest Thesiger, Hattie Jacques, Peter Bull, Hugh Dempster; **D:** Brian Desmond Hurst; **W:** Noel Langley; **M:** Richard Addinsell. *MLB, HMV*

A Christmas Carol 𝄞𝄞 **1954** Musical version of the Dickens' classic about a stingy old man who is visited by three ghosts on Christmas Eve. **54m/B VHS, Beta.** Fredric March, Basil Rathbone, Ray Middleton, Bob Sweeney, Christopher Cook. *CFV*

A Christmas Carol 𝄞𝄞𝄞 **1984 (PG)** Excellent TV adaptation of the Dickens Christmas classic features a memorable Scott as miserly misanthrope Ebenezer Scrooge, who gets a scary look at his life thanks to a Christmas Eve visit from the ghosts of Christmas Past, Present, and Future. Terrific supporting cast; filmed on location in Shrewsbury, England. **100m/C VHS, Closed Caption.** *TCF*

The Christmas Coal Mine Miracle 𝄞½ **1977** Syrupy made-for-television story about miners struggling for survival in a collapsed mine on Christmas Eve. Also titled "Christmas Miracle in Caulfield, U.S.A." **98m/C VHS, Beta, Closed Caption.** Mitchell Ryan, Kurt Russell, Andrew Prine, John Carradine, Barbara Babcock, Melissa Gilbert, Don Porter, Shelby Leverington; **D:** Jud Taylor. *FOX*

Christmas Comes to Willow Creek 𝄞𝄞 **1987** Mutually antagonistic brothers are enlisted to deliver Christmas gifts to an isolated Alaskan community. Can brotherly love be far off? Two leads played together in the rowdy TV series "Dukes of Hazzard." This is hardly an improvement. **96m/C VHS, Beta.** John Schneider, Tom Wopat, Hoyt Axton, Zachary Ansley, Kim Delaney; **D:** Richard Lang; **M:** Charles Fox. *LIV, FHE*

Christmas in Connecticut 𝄞𝄞𝄞 *Indiscretion* **1945** Lightweight comedy about a housekeeping magazine's successful columnist who isn't quite the expert homemaker she presents herself to be. When a war veteran is invited to her home as part of a publicity gimmick, she must master the ways of housekeeping or reveal her incompetence. Stanwyck is winning in the lead role. Also available in a colorized version. **101m/B VHS, Beta, LV.** Barbara Stanwyck, Reginald Gardiner, Sydney Greenstreet, Dennis (Stanley Morner) Morgan, S.Z. Sakall, Una O'Connor, Robert Shayne, Joyce Compton; **D:** Peter Godfrey. *MGM*

Christmas in Connecticut 𝄞𝄞 **1992** Cannon hosts a weekly television show as America's favorite homemaker/hostess. A local forest ranger (Kristofferson) becomes a hero by saving a little boy's life and her network stages a media event by inviting him to her home for a traditional Christmas dinner. There's only one problem: she can't cook. Schwarzenegger's directorial debut lacks challenge in this fluffy remake. See the original instead. Made for cable television. **93m/C VHS, Closed Caption.** Dyan Cannon, Kris Kristofferson, Tony Curtis, Kelly Cinnante, Gene Lithgow, Vivian Bonnell; **D:** Arnold Schwarzenegger; **W:** Janet Brownell. *TTC*

Christmas in July 𝄞𝄞𝄞½ **1940** A young man goes on a spending spree when he thinks he's won a sweepstakes. Things take a turn for the worse when he finds out that it was all a practical joke. Powell provides a winning performance in this second film from comic master Sturges. **67m/B VHS, Beta, LV.** Dick Powell, Ellen Drew, Raymond Walburn, William Demarest, Franklin Pangborn; **D:** Preston Sturges. *USH, FCT*

The Christmas Kid 𝄞½ **1968** A desperado struggles to determine his true identity while stopping in a frontier town. Gunplay ensues. Don't bother with this one. **87m/C VHS.** *SP* Jeffrey Hunter, Louis Hayward, Gustavo Rojo, Perla Cristal, Luis Prendes; **D:** Sidney Pink. *NO*

Christmas Lilies of the Field 𝄞𝄞½ **1984** This made-for-television sequel to "Lilies of the Field" follows an ex-soldier who returns to the church he helped build. This time he sets out to build an orphanage. **98m/C VHS, Beta.** Billy Dee Williams, Maria Schell, Fay Hauser, Judith Piquet; **D:** Ralph Nelson. *MPI*

A Christmas Story 𝄞𝄞𝄞 **1983 (PG)** Unlikely but winning comedy of a boy's single-minded obsession to acquire a Red Ryder BB-gun for Christmas. Particularly great sequence involving an impatient department-store Santa. Fun for everyone. Based on "In God We Trust, All Others Pay Cash," an autobiographical story by Shepherd. **95m/C VHS, Beta, LV.** Peter Billingsley, Darren McGavin, Melinda Dillon, Ian Petrella; **D:** Bob (Benjamin) Clark; **W:** Bob (Benjamin) Clark, Leigh Brown, Jean Shepherd. Genie Awards '84: Best Director (Clark). *MGM*

The Christmas That Almost Wasn't 𝄞½ *Il Natale Che Quasi Non Fu* **1966 (G)** Loathsome humbug decides to destroy Christmas forever by removing Santa Claus from the North Pole. Crude Italian-made children's film nonetheless remembered fondly by a generation of kids. ♫The Christmas That Almost Wasn't; Christmas is Coming; Hustle Bustle; I'm Bad; Kids Get All the Breaks; The Name of the Song is Prune; Nothing to do But Wait; Santa Claus; Time For Christmas. **95m/C VHS, Beta.** *IT* Rossano Brazzi, Paul Tripp, Lidia Brazzi, Sonny Fox, Mischa Auer; **D:** Rossano Brazzi. *HBO*

A Christmas to Remember 𝄞𝄞½ **1978 (G)** Depression-era Minnesota farmer who has lost his son in WWI brings his city-bred grandson to the farm for a holiday visit. Somber, occasionally poignant film buoyed by Robards presence, and Saint's as well. Made for television. **96m/C VHS, Beta.** Jason Robards Jr., Eva Marie Saint, Joanne Woodward; **D:** George Englund. *NO*

The Christmas Wife 𝄞𝄞½ **1988** A lonely man pays a woman to be his holiday companion at a mountain retreat. Sturdy performances by Robards and Harris manage to keep this one from going to the dogs. Based on a story by Helen Norris. Made for cable television. **73m/C VHS, Beta, Closed Caption.** Jason Robards Jr., Julie Harris, Don Francks, Patricia Hamilton, Deborah Grover, James Eckhouse; **D:** David Jones. *HBO*

A Christmas Without Snow 𝄞𝄞½ **1980** Made-for-television film about a lonely divorced woman finding communal happiness within a local church choir led by a crusty choir master. **96m/C VHS, Beta, Closed Caption.** Michael Learned, John Houseman, Ramon Bieri, James Cromwell, Valerie Curtin, Ruth Nelson, Beah Richards, Calvin Levels; **D:** John Korty; **M:** Ed Bogas. *FOX*

Christopher Columbus 𝄞𝄞½ **1949** Step-by-step biography of the fifteenth-century explorer, his discovery of America, the fame that first greeted him, and his last days. **103m/C VHS.** *GB* Fredric March, Florence Eldridge, Francis L. Sullivan; **D:** David MacDonald. *FCT, IGP, LCA*

Christopher Columbus 𝄞𝄞½ **1985** The man who explored the New World is shown in all his flawed complexity in this film that takes a contemporary approach to the discoveries and character of Christopher Columbus. Shot on location in Spain, Malta, and the Dominican Republic, the film features an exact replica of Columbus' flagship, the Santa Maria. Originally aired as a six-hour television miniseries. **128m/C VHS.** Gabriel Byrne, Faye Dunaway, Oliver Reed, Max von Sydow, Eli Wallach, Nicol Williamson, Jose Ferrer, Virna Lisi, Raf Vallone; **D:** Alberto Lattuada. *WAR*

Christopher Columbus: The Discovery 𝄞 **1992 (PG-13)** The 500th anniversary of Columbus' voyage brought this lame excursion in historical biography to the screen briefly. Columbus is portrayed as a swashbuckling adventurer who finally gets the Queen of Spain to agree to finance his voyage of discovery (which primarily consists of discovering a lot of bare-breasted native women). Story is secondary to the banality of the entire production, including the acting. Brando is briefly seen as Torquemada—another film in which he took his substantial paycheck and ran.*CW:* Nudity and action violence. **120m/C VHS, Beta, LV, Closed Caption.** Georges Corraface, Rachel Ward, Tom Selleck, Marlon Brando, Robert Davi, Oliver Cotton, Benicio Del Toro, Catherine Zeta Jones, Matthieu Carriere, Nigel Terry, Branscombe Richmond; **D:** John Glen; **W:** John Briley, Mario Puzo, Cary Bates; **M:** Cliff Eidelman. Golden Raspberry Awards '92: Worst Supporting Actor (Selleck). *WAR*

Christopher Strong 𝄞𝄞½ **1933** Interesting Hepburn turn as a daredevil aviatrix who falls in love with a married British statesman. **77m/B VHS, Beta, LV.** Katharine Hepburn, Billie Burke, Colin Clive, Helen Chandler; **D:** Dorothy Arzner; **M:** Max Steiner. *TTC*

Christy 1994 Pilot movie for the TV series finds 19-year-old Christy Huddleston (Martin) leaving her privileged Southern life to teach school in the Great Smoky Mountains. It's 1912 in Cutter Gap, Tennessee and her students are literally dirt poor, with ignorance and superstition the norm. Christy's inspiration in Miss Alice (Daly), a middle-aged Quaker who runs the mission school. And Christy needs encouragement as she struggles to cope with her new life and responsibilities. Based on the novel by Catherine Marshall, which is a fictional biography of her mother. **90m/C VHS.** Kellie Martin, Tyne Daly, Tess Harper, Randall Batinkoff, Annabelle Price, Stewart Finlay-McLennan; **D:** Michael Rhodes; **M:** Ron Ramin. *GKK*

Chrome and Hot Leather 𝄞½ **1971 (PG)** A Green Beret is out for revenge after vicious bikers kill his fiance. Conventional, tasteless genre fare notable only as Gaye's first film. **91m/C VHS, Closed Caption.** William Smith, Tony Young, Michael Haynes, Peter Brown, Marvin Gaye, Michael Stearns, Katherine Baumann, Wes Bishop, Herbert Jeffries; **D:** Lee Frost. *ORI*

Chrome Hearts 𝄞 *C.C. & Company* **1970 (R)** Rebel biker rescues a buxom gal from a fate worse than death, than vies for control of the gang. Laughable, with Namath hopeless in his film debut. Redeemed only by Ann-Margret in continual disarray. **91m/C VHS, Beta.** Joe Namath, Ann-Margret, William Smith, Jennifer Billingsley, Teda Bracci, Greg Mullavey, Sid Haig, Bruce Glover; **D:** Seymour Robbie. *COL, SIM*

Chrome Soldiers 𝄞𝄞 **1992** Five Vietnam veterans come together to avenge a friend's murder in a town controlled by drug dealers. Busey, as the murdered man's brother, leads the "Chrome Soldiers" in their battle to expose the killers and end local corruption. **92m/C VHS, Beta, Closed Caption.** Gary Busey, Ray Sharkey, William Atherton, Yaphet Kotto, Nicholas Guest, Kim Robillard, Norman Skaggs, D. David Morin; **D:** Thomas J. Wright; **W:** Nick Randall; **C:** Billy Dickson. *PAR*

The Chronicles of Narnia 1989 Exceptional BBC production of the C.S. Lewis fantasy about four brave children who battle evil in a mythical land where the animals talk and strange creatures roam the countryside. In three volumes; aired on PBS as part of the "Wonderworks" family movie series. **180m/C VHS, Closed Caption.** *GB* Barbara Kellerman, Jeffery Perry, Richard Dempsey, Sophie Cook, Jonathan Scott, Sophie Wilcox, David Thwaites, Tom Baker; **D:** Alex Kirby; **F:** PME, TVC

Chu Chu & the Philly Flash woof! **1981 (PG)** A has-been baseball player and a lame dance teacher meet while hustling the same corner; he sells hot watches, she's a one-woman band. A briefcase full of government secrets soon involves them with the feds, the mob, and a motley collection of back-alley bums. Insipid comedy is actually worse than its title, with Burnett and Arkin both trying too hard. Supporters Warden, Aiello, and Glover don't help either. **102m/C VHS, Beta.** Alan Arkin, Carol Burnett, Jack Warden, Danny Aiello, Ruth Buzzi, Danny Glover, Lou Jacobi; **D:** David Lowell Rich; **W:** Barbara Dana. *FOX*

Chuck Amuck: The Movie 1991 An indepth look at legendary animator/director Chuck Jones. **51m/C VHS.** Chuck Jones. *WAR, FCT*

Chuck Berry: Hail! Hail! Rock 'n' Roll 🐾🐾🐾½ 1987 (PG) Engaging, energetic portrait of one of rock's founding fathers, via interviews, behind-the-scenes footage and performance clips of Berry at 60. Songs featured: "Johnny B. Goode," "Roll Over Beethoven," "Maybelline," and more. Appearances by Eric Clapton, Etta James, John and Julian Lennon, Roy Orbison, Linda Ronstadt, Bo Diddley and Bruce Springsteen among others. **121m/C VHS, Beta.** Chuck Berry, Eric Clapton, Etta James, Robert Cray, Julian Lennon, Keith Richards, Linda Ronstadt, John Lennon, Roy Orbison, Bo Diddley, Jerry Lee Lewis, Bruce Springsteen, Kareem Abdul-Jabbar; **D:** Taylor Hackford. *USH, MVD, FCT*

C.H.U.D. woof! 1984 (R) Cannibalistic Humanoid Underground Dwellers are what it's about. Exposed to toxic wastes, a race of flesh-craving, sewer-dwelling monstrosities goes food shopping on the streets of New York. Don't be fooled by the presence of real actors, this one is inexcusable. Followed by a sequel. **90m/C VHS, Beta, LV.** John Heard, Daniel Stern, Christopher Curry, Kim Greist, John Goodman; **D:** Douglas Cheek; **W:** Shepard Abbott. *VTR, MRV*

C.H.U.D. 2: Bud the Chud woof! 1989 (R) Asinine teens steal a corpse that is actually a zombie cannibal capable of passing the trait to anyone it bites (but doesn't eat entirely). Graham excels as the kidnapped corpse, but this horror-comedy is consistently repellent. Contains one of Jagger's few film appearances, a situation of no despair. **84m/C VHS, Beta, LV.** Brian Robbins, Bill Calvert, Gerrit Graham, Tricia Leigh Fisher, Bianca Jagger, Robert Vaughn, Larry Cedar; **D:** David Irving. *LIV, VES, IME*

Chuka 🐾🐾½ 1967 A gunfighter tries to resolve a conflict between Indians and unlikeable troops while simultaneously romancing the fort's beautiful occupant. Pedestrian western keeps convincing playing from the always reliable Taylor. **105m/C VHS, Closed Caption.** Rod Taylor, Ernest Borgnine, John Mills, Luciana Paluzzi, James Whitmore, Angela Dorian, Louis Hayward, Michael Cole, Hugh Reilly; **D:** Gordon Douglas. *PAR, FCT*

A Chump at Oxford 🐾🐾½ 1940 Two street cleaners foil a bank robbery and receive an all-expenses-paid education at Oxford as their reward. This loopy Laurel and Hardy vehicle provides regular amusement in detailing the duo's exploits in Britain. **63m/B VHS, Beta, LV.** Stan Laurel, Oliver Hardy, James Finlayson, Wilfrid Lucas, Peter Cushing, Charlie Hall; **D:** Alfred Goulding. *MED, CCB, FCT*

Chungking Express 🐾🐾🐾 1995 (PG-13) Director Kar-wai presents two quirky tales of loneliness and love, loosely linked by a snack bar in the tourist section of Hong Kong. Cops and drugs are still a part of the storyline, but this is no chopsocky action movie. Both male protagonists are cops, identified only by their badge numbers, who have recently been dumped by their girlfriends. One has a fixation for canned pineapple and expiration dates, the other talks to the inanimate objects in his apartment. The women they eventually fall for are a blonde-wigged heroin dealer and a shy counter girl who bops to "California Dreaming" after breaking in and cleaning the cop's apartment without his knowledge. Shot cinemado-style in 23 days during the hiatus of Wong's "Ashes of Time" without permits or professional lighting. The high energy is reflected in the pacing and acting performances. Chosen by Quentin

Tarantino as the first release of his Miramax-backed Rolling Thunder imprint. **CW:** Some violence, sexuality and drug content. **102m/C VHS, LV, Closed Caption.** HK Bridget Lin, Takeshi Kaneshiro, Tony Leung, Faye Wang, Valerie Chow, Piggy Chan; **D:** Wong Kar-Wai; **W:** Wong Kar-Wai; **C:** Christopher Doyle, Lau Wai-Keung; **M:** Frankie Chan, Roel A. Garcia. Nominations: Independent Spirit Awards '97: Best Foreign Film. *MAX*

The Church 🐾🐾🐾 La Chiesa 1990 Italian thrill-meister Argento scripted and produced this ecclesiastical gorefest. A gargoyle-glutted gothic cathedral which happens to stand on the site of a gruesome mass murder is renovated, and the kirk-cleaning turns into a special-effects loaded demonic epiphany. It'll have you muttering your pater noster. Unrated, it's also available in an R-rated version. **110m/C VHS.** IT Tomas Arana, Hugh Quarshine, Feodor Chaliapin Jr; **D:** Michele (Michael) Soavi; **W:** Dario Argento; **M:** Keith Emerson. *NO*

Churchill and the Generals 🐾🐾 1981 The true story of how Winston Churchill led England away from the bleak Dunkirk battle and rallied the Allied generals to a D-Day victory. Based upon Churchill's memoirs. **180m/C VHS, Beta.** Timothy West, Joseph Cotten, Arthur Hill, Eric Porter, Richard Dysart. *PSM*

C.I.A.: Code Name Alexa 🐾½ 1992 (R) Alexa is the beautiful and deadly protege of Victor, who heads an international crime ring. A CIA agent decides the best way to stop Victor is to turn Alexa against her boss. Lots of action and violence. **CW:** Language, violence, and sexuality. **93m/C VHS, LV, Closed Caption.** Kathleen Kinmont, Lorenzo Lamas, Alex Cord, O.J. Simpson, Stephen Quadros, Pamela Dixon, Michael Smith; **D:** Joseph Merhi. *PMH*

C.I.A. 2: Target Alexa 🐾🐾 1994 When a nuclear guidance system is stolen from a government facility CIA agent Mark Graver (Lamas) reteams with former terrorist Alexa (Kinmont) to retrieve the system from international terrorist Franz Klug (Savage). Complicating things are ex-CIA agent Straker (Ryan), who now heads his own commando army and wants to sell the device to the highest bidder. **90m/C VHS, LV.** Lorenzo Lamas, Kathleen Kinmont, John Savage, John P. Ryan, Pamela Dixon, Larry Manetti; **D:** Lorenzo Lamas; **W:** Michael January. *PMH*

Ciao Federico! Fellini Directs Satyricon 1969 A documentary of Frederico Fellini's filming of Petronius' "Satyricon." Portrays the Italian filmmaker's larger-than-life directorial approach and relationship with his actors. In English and Italian, with English subtitles. **60m/C VHS, Beta.** Federico Fellini, Martin Potter, Hiram Keller, Roman Polanski, Sharon Tate; **D:** Gideon Bachmann. *MFV, TPV*

Ciao, Professore! 🐾🐾½ Io Speriamo Che Me La Cavo 1994 (R) Okay comedy about conventional teacher Marco Sperelli (Villaggio), from northern Italy, who is mistakenly sent to a ramshackle village school in Naples, populated by poor, wily, unruly students. Both, of course, manage to learn from each other. Humor derived from northern vs. southern Italian culture clash may bypass most viewers although the cast of amateur kid actors provide charm. Italian with subtitles. **91m/C VHS, LV.** IT Paolo Villaggio, Isa Danieli, Ciro Esposito; **D:** Lina Wertmuller; **W:** Leo Benvenuti, Piero De Bernardi, Alessandro Bencivenni, Domenico Saverni, Lina Wertmuller. *MAX*

The Cigarette Girl of Mosselprom 🐾🐾½ 1924 A lowly cigarette girl is thrust into the world of moviemaking in this sharp Russian satire. Silent with orchestral score. **78m/B VHS.** RU D: Yuri Zhelyabuzhsky. *KIV, FCT*

Cimarron 🐾🐾 1931 Hopelessly overblown saga of an American frontier family from 1890 to 1915. Hokey, cliched, with only sporadic liveliness. How did this one win an Oscar? An adaptation of Edna Ferber's novel, featuring Dunne in an early major role. Remade in 1960. **130m/B VHS, Beta.** Richard Dix, Irene Dunne, Estelle Taylor, Nance O'Neil, William Collier Jr., Roscoe Ates, George E. Stone,

Stanley Fields, Edna May Oliver, Dennis O'Keefe; **D:** Wesley Ruggles; **M:** Max Steiner. Academy Awards '31: Best Adapted Screenplay, Best Interior Decoration, Best Picture; National Board of Review Awards '31: 10 Best Films of the Year; Nominations: Academy Awards '31: Best Actor (Dix), Best Actress (Dunne), Best Cinematography, Best Director (Ruggles). *MGM, BTV*

Cimarron 🐾🐾½ 1960 Director Mann's remake of the 1931 Academy Award-winning film about frontier life in Oklahoma. This version features Ford as a carefree survivor of the Old West with an extreme case of wanderlust. Schell plays his civilizing wife. Based on Edna Ferber's novel. **140m/C VHS.** Glenn Ford, Maria Schell, Anne Baxter, Arthur O'Connell, Russ Tamblyn, Mercedes McCambridge, Vic Morrow, Robert Keith, Charles McGraw; **D:** Anthony Mann; **W:** Arnold Schulman; **M:** Franz Waxman. Nominations: Academy Awards '60: Best Art Direction/Set Decoration (Color), Best Sound. *MGM*

The Cincinnati Kid 🐾🐾½ 1965 Cardsharks gather for a major stakes poker game, with some romance on the side. Conventional fare helped along by serviceable performances and some stunning cinematography. Sam Peckinpah was dismissed as director from this one. Guess he took the script with him. **104m/C VHS, Beta, LV.** Steve McQueen, Edward G. Robinson, Ann-Margret, Tuesday Weld, Karl Malden, Joan Blondell, Rip Torn, Jack Weston, Cab Calloway; **D:** Norman Jewison; **W:** Ring Lardner Jr., Terry Southern; **M:** Lalo Schifrin. National Board of Review Awards '65: Best Supporting Actress (Blondell). *MGM*

The Cinder Path 🐾🐾½ 1994 Coming-of-age story begins in 1913 with unassuming Charlie MacFell (Owen) forced to take over the family farm. Charlie (who needs a spine transplant) also goes along with an arranged marriage to local lovely Victoria (Jones), a disaster since she's little more than a well-bred tart and it's her younger sister Nellie (Miles) who's really in love with Charlie anyway. As if Charlie didn't have enough to cope with, he's soon an army soldier as WWI begins and up against vindictive Ginger (Byrne), a former farmhand who resents the monied classes Charlie represents. Based on the novel by Catherine Cookson. **145m/C VHS.** GB Lloyd Owen, Catherine Zeta Jones, Maria Miles, Antony Byrne, Tom Bell; **D:** Simon Langton; **W:** Alan Seymour; **M:** Barrington Pheloung. *VCO*

Cinderella 🐾🐾🐾½ 1950 Classic Disney animated fairytale about the slighted beauty who outshines her evil stepsisters at a royal ball, then returns to her grim existence before the handsome prince finds her again. Engaging film, with a wicked stepmother, kindly fairy godmother, and singing mice. ♫Cinderella; Bibbidy-Bobbidi-Boo; So This Is Love; A Dream Is a Wish Your Heart Makes; The Work Song; Oh Sing, Sweet Nightingale. **76m/C VHS, Beta. D:** Wilfred Jackson; **V:** Ilene Woods, William Phipps, Verna Felton, James MacDonald. Venice Film Festival '50: Special Jury Prize; Nominations: Academy Awards '50: Best Song ("Bibbidy-Bobbidi-Boo"), Best Sound, Scoring of a Musical. *DIS*

Cinderella 🐾🐾 1964 A made-for-television rendition of the fairy tale as scored by Rodgers and Hammerstein. Songs include "The Loveliness of Evening", "Ten Minutes Ago" and "Do I Love You (Because You're Beautiful?)." **83m/C VHS, Beta, LV, Closed Caption.** Lesley Ann Warren, Ginger Rogers, Walter Pidgeon, Stuart Damon, Celeste Holm; **D:** Charles S. Dubin; **M:** Richard Rodgers, Oscar Hammerstein. *FOX, FCT*

Cinderella 1984 From the "Faerie Tale Theatre" comes the classic tale of a poor girl who goes to a ball to meet the man of her dreams, despite her nasty stepmother and stepsisters. **60m/C VHS, Beta, LV, Closed Caption.** Jennifer Beals, Jean Stapleton, Matthew Broderick, Eve Arden; **D:** Mark Cullingham. *FOX, FCT, HMV*

Cinderella Liberty 🐾🐾🐾 1973 (R) Bittersweet romance in which a kindly sailor falls for a brash hooker with a son. Sometimes funny, sometimes moving, with sometimes crude direction overcome by truly compelling performances from Caan and Mason. Story written by Darryl Ponicsan from his novel. **117m/C VHS, Beta.** James Caan, Marsha Mason, Eli Wallach, Kirk Calloway, Burt Young, Bruce Kirby, Dabney Coleman, Sally Kirkland; **D:** Mark Rydell; **W:** Darryl Ponicsan; **C:** Vilmos Zsigmond; **M:** John Williams. Golden Globe Awards '74: Best Actress— Drama (Mason); Nominations: Academy Awards '73: Best Actress (Mason), Best Song ("You're So Nice to Be Around"), Original Dramatic/Comedy Score.*FOX*

Cinderella 2000 🕮🕮 **1978 (R)** Soft-core musical version of the classic fairy tale. It's the year 2047 and sex is outlawed, except by computer. Strains of Sugarman's score, including "Doin' Without" and "We All Need Love," set the stage for Erhardt's Cinderella to meet her Prince Charming at that conventional single prince romance venue, a sex orgy. Trouble is, it wasn't a shoe Cinderella lost before she fled, and the charming one must interface, as it were, with the local pretenders to the throne in order to find his lost princess. Touching. **86m/C VHS.** Catharine Erhardt, Jay B. Larson, Vaughn Armstrong; **D:** Al Adamson; **M:** Sparky Sugarman. *NO*

Cinderfella 🕮🕮½ **1960** This twist on the classic children's fairy tale features Lewis as the hapless buffoon guided by his fairy godfather. Somewhat overdone, with extended talking sequences and gratuitous musical interludes. Lewis, though, mugs effectively. **88m/C VHS, Beta.** Jerry Lewis, Ed Wynn, Judith Anderson, Anna Maria Alberghetti, Henry Silva, Count Basie, Robert Hutton; **D:** Frank Tashlin; **W:** Frank Tashlin. *LIV*

Cinema Paradiso 🕮🕮🕮 *Nuovo Cinema Paradiso* **1988** Memoir of a boy's life working at a movie theatre in small-town Italy after WWII. Film aspires to both majestic sweep and stirring poignancy, but only occasionally hits its target. Still manages to move the viewer, and it features a suitably low-key performance by the masterful Noiret. Autobiographically inspired script written by Tornatore. The version shown in America is approximately a half-hour shorter than the original Italian torn. **123m/C VHS, LV, 8mm.** *IT* Philippe Noiret, Jacques Perrin, Salvatore Cascio, Marco Leonardi, Agnes Nano, Leopoldo Trieste; **D:** Giuseppe Tornatore; **W:** Giuseppe Tornatore; **M:** Ennio Morricone. Academy Awards '89: Best Foreign Language Film; British Academy Awards '90: Best Actor (Noiret), Best Foreign Film, Best Original Screenplay, Best Supporting Actor (Cascio); Cannes Film Festival '89: Grand Jury Prize; Golden Globe Awards '90: Best Foreign Film. *HBO, APD*

Circle Canyon 🕮 **1933** In a remote canyon two opposing outlaw gangs battle to the death. **48m/B VHS, Beta.** Buddy Roosevelt. *NO*

Circle Man 🕮 **1987** A made-for-video action drama about the underground sporting phenomenon, bare-knuckle fighting. **90m/C VHS, Beta.** William Sanderson. *ACA*

Circle of Death 🕮½ **1936** Average formula western about a white boy who is raised as an Indian. Later he falls in love with a white girl and leaves the tribe. **55m/B VHS, Beta.** Monte Montana, Yakima Canutt. *NOS, VDM*

Circle of Deceit 🕮🕮½ **1994** SAS officer John Neil (Waterman) is called back into service in Belfast two years after his wife and child were killed by terrorists. His assignment is to assume the identity of recently deceased IRA soldier Jackie O'Connell and learn about an arms shipment headed for Northern Ireland. But can his disguise hold against local IRA commander Liam McAuley (Vaughan)? Made for British TV. **103m/C VHS.** *GB* Dennis Waterman, Peter Vaughan, Derek Jacobi, Clare Higgins; **W:** Jean-Claude Carriere. *VCO*

Circle of Fear 🕮½ **1989 (R)** An ex-hitman who worked for the Mob upends the black market for sex and drugs in the Philippines while looking for his daughter who was sold into a sex slave ring. El cheapo exploiter. **90m/C VHS, Beta.** *PH* Patrick Dollaghan, Welsey Pfenning, Joey Aresco, Vernon Wells; **D:** Clark Henderson. *MGM*

Circle of Friends 🕮🕮½ **1994 (PG-13)** Nostalgic Irish coming-of-ager focuses on three friends and the trials and tribulations they face when hearts and hormones conflict with a strict Catholic upbringing. Small-town teenager Benny (Driver), overweight and slightly awkward, reunites with her friends at university in Dublin. Benny begins a romance with gentle, doe-eyed Jack Foley (O'Donnell) and endures the humorous but sometimes painful passage from adolescence to womanhood. Sentimental moments can be too sticky-sweet at times, but humor, disappointment, and small triumphs are convincingly portrayed, offering a universal appeal. Adapted from the Maeve Binchy novel.*CW:* Contains sexual situations. **96m/C VHS.** Chris O'Donnell, Minnie Driver, Geraldine O'Rawe, Saffron Burrows, Colin Firth, Alan Cumming, Aidan Gillen; **D:** Pat O'Connor; **W:** Andrew Davies; **M:** Michael Kamen. *HBO*

Circle of Iron 🕮🕮½ *The Silent Flute* **1978 (R)** Plenty of action and martial arts combat abound in this story of one man's eternal quest for truth. Originally co-written by and intended for Bruce Lee as a rib-crunching vehicle, until he died before production began and was replaced by Kung-Fu Carradine. A cut above most chop-socky actioners. Filmed in Israel. **102m/C VHS, Beta.** *GB* Jeff Cooper, David Carradine, Roddy McDowall, Eli Wallach, Christopher Lee; **D:** Richard Moore; **W:** Bruce Lee, James Coburn, Stirling Silliphant; **M:** Bruce Smeaton.

Circle of Love 🕮🕮 **1964** Episodic melodrama drifts from romance to romance in contemporary Paris. A somewhat pretentious remake of Ophuls classic "La Ronde," which was in turn adapted from Arthur Schnitzler's play. Credible performers are undone by Vadim's strained direction. **110m/C VHS, Beta.** *FR* Jane Fonda, Francine Berge, Marie DuBois, Jean-Claude Brialy, Catherine Spaak, Claude Giraud; **D:** Roger Vadim; **W:** Jean Anouilh. *JEF*

Circle of Power 🕮½ *Brainwash; The Naked Weekend; Mystique* **1983 (R)** Mimieux must cure various business men of their problems (homosexuality, alcoholism and the like) to help them become better executives. Intriguing and somewhat disturbing, supposedly based on a true story. **103m/C VHS.** *GB* Yvette Mimieux, John Considine, Terence Knox, Cindy Pickett, Christopher Allport; **D:** Bobby Roth; **W:** Stephen F. Bello; **C:** Alfonso Beato. *MED*

Circle of Two 🕮🕮 **1980 (PG)** A platonic friendship between an aging artist and a young girl is misunderstood by others. Well, of course they do meet in a porno theater. Pedestrian fare adapted from a story by Marie Therese Baird. **90m/C VHS, Beta.** *CA* Richard Burton, Tatum O'Neal, Kate Reid; **D:** Jules Dassin. *VES, VTR*

Circonstances Attenuantes 🕮🕮½ *Extenuating Circumstances* **1936** French classic about a retired judge who moves to the outskirts of Paris with his wife and attempts to convert the locals from disreputable to law-abiding citizens. Also available dubbed. **90m/B VHS.** *FR* Michel Simon, Arletty; **D:** Jean Boyer. *FRA, FCT*

Circuit Breaker 🕮🕮 **1996 (R)** Traveling repairman Foster Carver (Bernsen) and his wife encounter a broken-down spaceship with a lone survivor. Then they discover he's a cyborg trying to create a new breed of humans.*CW:* Strong sexuality, sci-fi violence and some language. **88m/C VHS.** Richard Grieco, Corbin Bernsen, Lara Harris. *NHO*

Circuitry Man 🕮🕮½ **1990 (R)** Post-apocalyptic saga of future American life as a woman tries to deliver a briefcase full of computer chips to the underground Big Apple. Along the way she runs into Plughead, a humanoid with electrical outlets that allow him to "plug in" to other people's fantasies. Intelligent retelling of a standard tale with an inspired soundtrack by Deborah Holland. Witty and original. **85m/C VHS, LV.** Jim Metzler, Dana Wheeler-Nicholson, Lu Leonard, Vernon Wells, Barbara Alyn Woods, Dennis Christopher; **D:** Steven Lovy; **W:** Steven Lovy; **M:** Deborah Holland. *COL*

Circumstances Unknown 🕮½ **1995 (R)** Paul Kinsey (Nelson) is a serial killer who drowns his victims, including a woman who happens to be the fiance of his friend Tim (Moses). Years later, Tim has married and Paul decides to stalk him and wife Deena (Glasser). Too many loose ends since you never know why Paul kills. Based on the novel by Jonellen Heckler.*CW:* Some violence/terror. **91m/C VHS, Beta, Closed Caption.** Judd Nelson, Isabel Glasser, William R. Moses; **D:** Robert Lewis; **W:** Thomas Hood, Emily Shoemaker; **C:** Bruce Worrall. *PAR*

Circumstantial Evidence 🕮🕮 **1935** Newspaper reporter (Chandler) goes to extremes for a story and nearly dies as a result. Chandler sets it up to look like he's murdered a colleague, and he's tried and convicted on, you guessed it, circumstantial evidence. The colleague's then supposed to come forward but there's a problem. **69m/B VHS.** Chick Chandler, Shirley Grey, Dorothy Revier, Arthur Vinton; **D:** Charles Lamont; **W:** Ewart Adamson. *SNC*

The Circus 🕮🕮🕮½ **1919** Classic comedy silent details the tramp's exploits as a member of a traveling circus, including a romance with the bareback rider. Hilarious, less sentimental than most of Chaplin's feature films. Chaplin won a special Academy Award for "versatility and genius in writing, acting, directing and producing" for this one. Outrageous final scenes. **105m/B VHS, Closed Caption.** Charlie Chaplin, Merna Kennedy; **D:** Charlie Chaplin. Nominations: Academy Awards '28: Best Actor (Chaplin), Best Director (Chaplin). *FOX*

Circus Angel 🕮🕮🕮 **1965** The renowned director of "The Red Balloon" creates a fantasy about a klutzy burglar transformed by a found nightgown into an angel. He begins to serve the dreams and actions of an odd lot of characters. Subtitled in English. **80m/B VHS, Beta.** *FR* Philippe Avron, Mirielle Negre; **D:** Albert Lamorisse. *NLC*

Circus of Fear 🕮½ *Psycho-Circus* **1967** A travelling troupe is stalked by a murderer. The unedited version is occasionally scary. **92m/C VHS, Beta.** *GB GE* Christopher Lee, Leo Genn, Anthony Newlands, Heinz Drache, Eddi Arent, Klaus Kinski, Margaret Lee, Suzy Kendall; **D:** John Llewellyn Moxey. *INC, SNC, NOS*

Circus of Horrors 🕮🕮½ **1960** Nip 'n tuck horror about a plastic surgeon who takes over a circus to escape a disfigured patient bent on revenge. The circus is staffed by former patients with new faces who, one by one, fall victim in fine circus style. A bloody one-ring extravaganza. **87m/C VHS, Beta.** *GB* Donald Pleasence, Anton Diffring, Erika Remberg, Yvonne Monlaur, Jane Hylton, Kenneth Griffith; **D:** Sidney Hayers; **W:** George L. Baxt. *REP*

Circus World 🕮🕮½ *The Magnificent Showman* **1964** A circus boss tries to navigate a reckless, romancing crew through a European tour while searching for aerialist who loved 15 years before and whose daughter he has reared. Too long and too familiar, but nonetheless well done with an excellent finale. **132m/C VHS, Beta, LV.** John Wayne, Rita Hayworth, Claudia Cardinale, Lloyd Nolan, Richard Conte; **D:** Henry Hathaway; **W:** Ben Hecht, James Edward Grant, Julian Zimet; **C:** Jack Hildyard. Golden Globe Awards '65: Best Song ("Circus World"). *NO*

The Cisco Kid **1950** Renaldo is the heroic Cisco, a do-gooder who, with his sidekick Pancho, championed the poor and downtrodden. The first TV series shown in color. Features two episodes: "Quarterhorse" and "The Postmaster". Additional episodes are available. **60m/C VHS.** Duncan Renaldo, Leo Carrillo. *HEG, MOV*

The Cisco Kid 🕮🕮½ **1994** The Cisco Kid and his sidekick Pancho went from O. Henry's short story, to silent movies, talkies, a '50s TV series, and now this made for TV movie. Benito Juarez is leading an uprising to overthrow the French-backed Emperor Maximilian in 1867 Mexico. Cisco's (Smits) supplying the rebels with guns while carrying on romantic escapades (watch for the tango). Meanwhile, true-believer Pancho tries to convince his friend to become a revolutionary. Light-hearted with pedestrian action shots. Filmed on location in Mexico. **96m/C VHS, LV, Closed Caption.** Jimmy Smits, Richard "Cheech" Marin, Sadie Frost, Tim Thomerson, Bruce Payne; **D:** Luis Valdez; **W:** Michael Kane, Luis Valdez. *TTC*

The Citadel ✷✷✷ 1938 From the A.J. Cronin novel, the intelligent and honest Hollywood drama about a young British doctor who is morally corrupted by his move from a poor mining village to a well-off practice treating wealthy hypochondriacs. Somewhat hokey but still consistently entertaining, with Donat fine in the lead. **114m/C VHS, Beta.** *GB* Robert Donat, Rosalind Russell, Rex Harrison, Ralph Richardson, Emlyn Williams, Penelope Dudley Ward; **D:** King Vidor; **W:** Harry Stradling. National Board of Review Awards '38: 10 Best Films of the Year; New York Film Critics Awards '38: Best Film; Nominations: Academy Awards '38: Best Actor (Donat), Best Director (Vidor), Best Picture, Best Screenplay. *MGM, HMV*

Citizen Cohn ✷✷ 1992 (R) An appallingly fascinating look at a human monster. Told in hallucinatory flashbacks, as he lays dying from AIDS, Roy Cohn is a lawyer and power broker, probably best-remembered as the malevolent sidekick to Communist-hunting Senator Joseph McCarthy. But his contempt also extended to antisemitism and gay-bashing (though Cohn was both homosexual and Jewish), and his past comes, literally, back to haunt him. Woods does an exceptional job in bringing this sociopathic heel to wretched life. Adapted from the biography by Nicholas Hoffman. Made for cable television.**CW:** Strong language. **112m/C VHS, LV, Closed Caption.** James Woods, Joe Don Baker, Joseph Bologna, Ed Flanders, Frederic Forrest, Lee Grant, Pat Hingle; **D:** Frank Pierson; **W:** David Franzoni; **C:** Paul Elliott. National Academy of Cable Programming ACE Awards '93: Best Movie/Miniseries, Best Director (Pierson), Best Writing (Franzoni). *HBO, BTV*

Citizen Kane ✷✷✷✷ 1941 Extraordinary film is an American tragedy of a newspaper tycoon (based loosely on William Randolph Hearst) from his humble beginnings to the solitude of his final years. One of the greatest films ever made—a stunning tour-de-force in virtually every aspect, from the fragmented narration to breathtaking, deep-focus cinematography; from a vivid soundtrack to fabulous ensemble acting. Welles was only 25 when he co-wrote, directed, and starred in this masterpiece. Three disc laser edition was reproduced from a superior negative and features liner notes and running commentary from film historian Robert J. Carringer. Watch for Ladd and O'Connell as reporters. **119m/B VHS, Beta, LV, 8mm, Closed Caption.** Orson Welles, Joseph Cotten, Everett Sloane, Dorothy Comingore, Ruth Warrick, George Coulouris, Ray Collins, William Alland, Paul Stewart, Erskine Sanford, Agnes Moorehead, Alan Ladd, Gus Schilling, Philip Van Zandt, Harry Shannon, Sonny Bupp, Arthur O'Connell; **D:** Orson Welles; **W:** Orson Welles, Herman J. Mankiewicz; **C:** Gregg Toland; **M:** Bernard Herrmann. Academy Awards '41: Best Original Screenplay; National Board of Review Awards '41: 10 Best Films of the Year; New York Film Critics Awards '41: Best Film; Nominations: Academy Awards '41: Best Actor (Welles), Best Black and White Cinematography, Best Director (Welles), Best Film Editing, Best Interior Decoration, Best Picture, Best Sound, Original Dramatic/Comedy Score. *CRC, FCT, TTC*

Citizen Ruth ✷✷½ *Precious; Meet Ruth Stoops* 1996 (R) Glue-sniffing, pregnant Ruth Stoops (Dern) has already borne four children and been declared an unfit mother. In trouble again, Ruth's quietly told it's in her best interests to get an abortion but a couple (Smith and Place) from the pro-life community bail her out and give her a place to stay, while the group uses her as a propaganda symbol. Added to the commotion is a smarmy televangelist (Reynolds) and tough pro-choice Diane (Kurtz), who manages to get Ruth to stay with her while Ruth ineffectually tries to get some control over her wayward life. Doesn't take sides—both the pro-choice and pro-life camps are tweaked, with neither willing to compromise.**CW:** Substance abuse, strong language and a sex

scene. **104m/C VHS, LV, Closed Caption.** Laura Dern, Swoosie Kurtz, Mary Kay Place, Kurtwood Smith, Kelly Preston, Burt Reynolds, M.C. Gainey, Kenneth Mars, Kathleen Noone, David Graf, Tippi Hedren, Alicia Witt, Diane Ladd; **D:** Alexander Payne; **W:** Alexander Payne, Jim Taylor; **C:** James Glennon; **M:** Rolfe Kent. Montreal World Film Festival '95: Best Actress (Dern). *TOU*

Citizen X ✷✷✷ 1995 (R) Based on the true story of '80's Russian serial killer Andrei Chikatilo (DeMunn) and his 52 victims. Viktor Burakov (Rea) is a beleagured rural forensics expert who is blatantly told by party officials that the Soviet state does not have serial killers—in spite of a rising body count. His only ally is Col. Fetisov (Sutherland), who's adept at political maneuvering, but it takes the duo eight frustrating years to bring the grisly killer to justice. Fine performances highlight a literate script from Robert Cullen's book "The Killer Department." Filmed on location in Budapest, Hungary. Made for cable television.**CW:** Strong, graphic violence and related language. **100m/C VHS.** Stephen Rea, Donald Sutherland, Jeffrey DeMunn, John Wood, Joss Ackland, Max von Sydow, Ralph Nossek, Imelda Staunton; **D:** Chris Gerolmo; **W:** Chris Gerolmo; **C:** Robert Fraisse; **M:** Randy Edelman. *HBO*

Citizens Band ✷✷✷ *Handle With Care* 1977 (PG) Episodic, low-key comedy about people united by their CB use in a midwestern community. Notable performance from Clark as a soft-voiced guide for truckers passing through. Demme's first comedy is characteristically idiosyncratic. **98m/C VHS, Beta.** Paul LeMat, Candy Clark, Ann Wedgeworth, Roberts Blossom, Charles Napier, Marcia Rodd, Bruce McGill, Ed Begley Jr., Alix Elias; **D:** Jonathan Demme; **W:** Paul Brickman; **C:** Jordan Cronenweth; **M:** Bill Conti. National Society of Film Critics Awards '77: Best Supporting Actress (Wedgeworth). *PAR*

The City ✷ 1976 Police desperately search for a psychotic determined to kill a country singer. He shouldn't be too hard to find. Made for television. **78m/C VHS, Beta.** Don Johnson, Robert Forster, Ward Costello, Jimmy Dean, Mark Hamill; **D:** Harvey Hart. *WOV*

The City and the Dogs ✷✷✷ *La Ciudad y los Perros* 1985 A brutal, cynical adaptation of Mario Vargas Llosa's novel. A young military recruit rebels against the authority establishments around him. In Spanish with English subtitles. **135m/C VHS, Beta.** *SP* **D:** Francisco J. Lombardi Pery. *FCT*

City Boy ✷✷✷ 1993 At the turn of the century the orphaned Nick makes his way from Chicago to the Pacific Northwest in search of his natural father. He takes a job guarding Limberlost, a valuable old-growth forest, from thieves and is torn between the ideals of two new friends. His mentor Tom sees the forest as timber that will build homes and provide jobs, while Angelica sees the forest as an irreplaceable sanctuary. Filmed on location in Vancouver, British Columbia. Adaptation of "Freckles" by Gene Stratton Porter. **120m/C VHS, Closed Caption.** *GB CA* Christian Campbell, James Brolin, Sarah Chalke, Wendel Meldrum, Christopher Bolton; **D:** John Kent Harrison; **W:** John Kent Harrison. *PME, BTV, HMV*

City for Conquest ✷✷✷ 1940 Two lovers go their separate ways to pursue individual careers. He attempts to become a boxing champ, but is blinded in the ring and ends up selling newspapers. She takes a shot at a dancing career but hooks up with an unscrupulous partner. Will the ill-fated pair find happiness again? **101m/B VHS, Beta.** James Cagney, Ann Sheridan, Frank Craven, Donald Crisp, Arthur Kennedy, Frank McHugh, George Tobias, Anthony Quinn, Blanche Yurka, Elia Kazan, Bob Steele; **D:** Anatole Litvak; **C:** James Wong Howe; **M:** Max Steiner. *MGM, CCB*

City Girl ✷✷½ *Our Daily Bread* 1930 Friedrich Murnau, who directed the silent vampire classic "Nosferatu," was removed from the director's chair before "City Girl" was completed and it shows. But so do the marks of his inimitable cam-

era direction. The story concerns a Minnesota grain grower who visits the Windy City and returns with a waitress as his wife. Frustratingly inconsistent, leading you to wonder what could have been had Murnau remained behind the camera (he died the following year). Silent. **90m/B VHS, Beta.** Charles Farrell, Mary Duncan; **D:** F.W. Murnau. *GPV, FCT*

City Hall ✷✷✷ 1995 (R) Investigating the deaths of a heroic cop, a drug dealer, and six-year old boy in a shoot-out, idealistic deputy mayor Cusack uncovers a web of corruption and deceit in the Big Apple. Pacino excels as charismatic mayor John Pappas by showing the crafty string-puller behind the glossy image of the modern politico. Supporting cast is also strong, including Aiello as a Rodgers and Hammerstein-loving Brooklyn boss, and Fonda as the police union lawyer and standard issue love interest. Screenplay was conceived by Ken Lipper, who was once deputy mayor under Ed Koch, but the involvement of three other scripters causes confusion over what type of picture it's aiming to be. Cash-strapped New York rented its actual city hall out for filming at a price of $50,000.**CW:** Language and some violence. **111m/C VHS, LV, Closed Caption.** Al Pacino, John Cusack, Bridget Fonda, Danny Aiello, David Paymer, Martin Landau, Anthony (Tony) Franciosa, Lindsay Duncan, Nestor Serrano, Mel Winkler, Richard Schiff; **D:** Harold Becker; **W:** Paul Schrader, Nicholas Pileggi, Bo Goldman, Ken Lipper; **C:** Michael Seresin; **M:** Jerry Goldsmith. *COL*

City Heat ✷✷½ 1984 (PG) A hardnosed cop and a plucky private eye berate each other while opposing the mob in this overdone comedy. Both Eastwood and Reynolds spoof their screen personas, but the results are only slightly satisfactory. Good back-up, though, from Alexander and Kahn as the dames. Screenplay written by Blake Edwards under the pseudonym Sam O. Brown. **98m/C VHS, Beta, LV, Closed Caption.** Clint Eastwood, Burt Reynolds, Jane Alexander, Irene Cara, Madeline Kahn, Richard Roundtree, Rip Torn, Tony LoBianco, William Sanderson; **D:** Richard Benjamin; **W:** Blake Edwards; **M:** Lennie Niehaus. *WAR*

City in Fear ✷✷✷ 1980 Stellar cast lights up a made-for-television drama about a tired newspaper columnist (Janssen) who communicates directly with a murdering psychotic (Rourke), as publisher Vaughn applauds and hypes. Rourke's first role. Janssen's last, and Smithee is actually Jud Taylor. **135m/C VHS, Beta.** David Janssen, Robert Vaughn, Mickey Rourke, William Daniels, Perry King, Susan Sullivan, William Prince; **D:** Alan Smithee. *LIV, HHE*

City in Panic ✷ 1986 A detective and radio talk show host try to catch a psychotic mass murderer busy offing homosexuals throughout the city. Violent with no redeeming social qualities. **85m/C VHS, Beta.** Dave Adamson, Ed Chester, Leeann Westegard; **D:** Robert Bouvier. *TWE*

City Killer ✷ 1987 A lunatic tries to blackmail the girl he loves into going out on a few dates by committing huge destructive acts of inner-city terrorism (flowers won't do). Made for television. **120m/C VHS, Beta.** Heather Locklear, Gerald McRaney, Terence Knox, Peter Mark Richman, John Harkins; **D:** Robert Lewis. *PSM*

City Lights ✷✷✷✷ 1931 Masterpiece that was Chaplin's last silent film. The "Little Tramp" falls in love with a blind flower seller. A series of lucky accidents permits him to get the money she needs for a sight-restoring surgery. One of the most eloquent movies ever filmed, due to Chaplin's keen balance between comedy and tragedy. **86m/B VHS, Beta, LV.** Charlie Chaplin, Virginia Cherrill, Florence Lee, Hank Mann, Harry Myers, Henry Bergman, Jean Harlow; **D:** Charlie Chaplin. National Board of Review Awards '31: 10 Best Films of the Year. *FOX*

City Limits ✷ 1985 (PG-13) In a post-apocalyptic city, gangs of young people on choppers clash. **85m/C VHS, Beta, LV.** John Stockwell, Kim Cattrall, Darrell Larson, Rae Dawn Chong, Robby Benson, James

Earl Jones, Jennifer Balgobin; **D:** Aaron Lipstadt. *VES, LIV, HHE*

City of Blood ♂♂½ 1988 (R)
A South African doctor is embroiled in mystery with racial overtones when prostitutes are being killed with a spiked club. Packaged as a horror film, this movie actually deals with the questions of South African racial tensions in a sophisticated, ultimately tragic manner. **96m/C VHS, Beta.** *SA* Joe Stewardson, Ian Yule, Susan Coetzer; **D:** Darrell Roodt. *NO*

City of Hope ♂♂♂ 1991 (R)
The picture that "Bonfire of the Vanities" wanted to be, an eventful few days in the fictional metropolis of Hudson: an ugly racial incident threatens to snowball, the corrupt mayor pushes a shady real-estate deal, and a botched robbery has profound implications. Some of the subplots resolve too easily, but this cynical, crazy-quilt of urban life is worthy of comparison with "American Graffiti" and "Nashville" as pure Americana.**CW:** Strong language and one sensual scene. **132m/C VHS, LV, 8mm, Closed Caption.** Vincent Spano, Tony LoBianco, Joe Morton, Todd Graff, David Strathairn, Anthony John Denison, Barbara Williams, Angela Bassett, Gloria Foster, Lawrence Tierney, John Sayles, Maggie Renzi, Kevin Tighe, Chris Cooper, Jace Alexander, Frankie Faison, Tom Wright, Michael Mantell, Josh Mostel, Joe Grifasi, Louis Zorich, Gina Gershon, Rose Gregorio, Bill Raymond, Maeve Kinkead, Ray Aranha; **D:** John Sayles; **W:** John Sayles; **C:** Robert Richardson; **M:** Mason Daring. Independent Spirit Awards '92: Best Supporting Actor (Strathairn). *COL*

City of Industry ♂♂ 1996 (R)
Efficient contemporary noir that doesn't always live up to its promise. Old pro thief Roy Egan (Keitel), now retired, is drawn into the final jewel heist of his younger brother, Lee (Hutton), who's also vowed to get out of the game. Unfortunately for him, Lee's picked one wrong partner in volatile wheelman Skip Kovich (Ulrich). When the violent Skip decides he doesn't want to share the goods it starts an elaborate cat-and-mouse hunt through the seedier sides of L.A.**CW:** Strong language, violence and some sexuality. **97m/C VHS.** Harvey Keitel, Stephen Dorff, Famke Janssen, Timothy Hutton, Michael Jai White, Wade Dominguez, Reno Wilson; **D:** John Irvin; **W:** Ken Solarz; **C:** Thomas Burstyn; **M:** Stephen Endelman. *NYR*

City of Joy ♂♂ 1992 (PG-13)
Disillusioned American heart surgeon Swayze flees to India after losing a patient. In Calcutta he is beaten by a street gang and loses his money and passport, but finds help from a farmer (Puri) who takes him to a nearby clinic in the City of Joy, one of Calcutta's poorest areas. Collins runs the clinic and recruits the reluctant doctor, who undergoes a life-changing transformation. The squalor of Calcutta is shown, but the city's portrayal as a magical place where problems miraculously disappear is unrealistic. Swayze lacks the emotional range for his part, but Collins and Puri are excellent in their roles. Adapted from the book by Dominique Lapierre. **134m/C VHS, LV.** *GB FR* Patrick Swayze, Pauline Collins, Om Puri, Shabana Azmi, Art Malik, Ayesha Dharker, Santu Chowdhury, Imran Badsah Khan, Shyamanand Jalan; *Cameos:* Sam Wanamaker; **D:** Roland Joffe; **W:** Mark Medoff; **C:** Peter Biziou; **M:** Ennio Morricone. *COL*

The City of Lost Children ♂♂♂
La Cite des Enfants Perdus 1995 (R) Weird not-for-the-kiddies fairytale finds crazed inventor Krank (Emilfork) getting his evil one-eyed minions, the appropriately-named Cyclops', to kidnap local children so that he can steal their dreams (because Krank himself is incapable of dreaming). The latest victim is young Denree (Lucien), the adopted brother of sideshow strongman One (Perlman), who single-mindedly pursues a way to get Denree back—aided by 9-year-old feral child Miette (Vittet) and a band of orphan thieves. Freaks galore with avant-garde designer Jean-Paul Gaultier in charge of costumes. French with subtitles or dubbed.**CW:** Disturbing and grotesque images of violence and menace. **114m/C VHS, LV, Closed Caption.** *FR* Ron Perlman, Daniel Emilfork, Joseph Lucien, Judith Vittet, Dominique Pinon, Jean Claude Dreyfus, Odile Mallet, Genevieve Brunet, Mireille Mosse; **D:** Jean-Marie Jeunet, Marc Caro; **W:** Jean-Marie Jeunet, Marc Caro, Gilles Adrien; **C:** Darius Khondji; **M:** Angelo Badalamenti; **V:** Jean-Louis Trintignant. Cesar Awards '96: Best Art Direction/Set Decoration; Nominations: Cesar Awards '96: Best Cinematography, Best Costume Design, Best Score; Independent Spirit Awards '96: Best Foreign Film. *COL*

City of Shadows ♂♂ 1986 (R)
Twins separated at birth are reunited by a criminal mind with evil intentions. Double trouble? **97m/C VHS, Beta.** John P. Ryan, Paul Coufos, Tony Rosato; **D:** David Mitchell; **M:** Tangerine Dream. *VTR, NWV*

City of the Walking Dead ♂
Nightmare City; Nightmare 1983 Eco-misery as a community must contend with prowling, radiation-zapped zombies who enjoy chewing through human flesh. **92m/C VHS.** *IT SP* Mel Ferrer, Hugo Stiglitz, Laura Trotter, Francesco Rabal; **D:** Umberto Lenzi. *NO*

City of Women ♂♂ 1981 (R)
Visually stunning, but otherwise thin fantasy/drama about a man smothered with women. A journalist wanders through a feminist theme park replete with a roller rink and screening room. Some worthwhile adventures are mixed in with rather dull stretches. Not among the best from either Mastroianni, who is under utilized, or Fellini, who here seems incapable of separating good ideas from bad. Plenty of buxom babes, but otherwise undistinguished. In Italian with English subtitles. **140m/C VHS, Beta.** *IT* Marcello Mastroianni, Ettore Manni, Anna Prucnall, Bernice Stegers; **D:** Federico Fellini; **W:** Federico Fellini; **C:** Giuseppe Rotunno; **M:** Luis Bacalov. *NYF, FCT*

City on Fire woof! 1978 (R)
An arsonist starts a fire that could engulf an entire city. Flaming bore. **101m/C VHS, Beta.** *CA* Barry Newman, Susan Clark, Shelley Winters, Leslie Nielsen, Henry Fonda, Ava Gardner; **D:** Alvin Rakoff.

City Slickers ♂♂♂ 1991 (PG-13)
Three men with mid-life crises leave New York City for a cattle-ranch vacation that turns into an arduous, character-building stint. Many funny moments supplied by leads Crystal, Stern, and Kirby, but Palance steals the film as a salty, wise cowpoke. Slater is fetching as the lone gal vacationer on the cattle drive. Box office winner notable for a realistic calf birthing scene, one of few in cinema history. From an idea by Crystal, who also produced. Palance stole the show from Oscar ceremonies host Crystal a second time when he accepted his award and suddenly started doing one-arm push-ups, startling the audience into laughter. **114m/C VHS, Beta, LV, 8mm, Closed Caption.** Billy Crystal, Daniel Stern, Bruno Kirby, Patricia Wettig, Helen Slater, Jack Palance, Noble Willingham, Tracey Walter, Josh Mostel, David Paymer, Bill Henderson, Jeffrey Tambor, Phill Lewis, Kyle Secor, Yeardley Smith, Jayne Meadows; **D:** Ron Underwood; **W:** Lowell Ganz, Babaloo Mandel; **C:** Dean Semler; **M:** Marc Shaiman. Academy Awards '91: Best Supporting Actor (Palance); Golden Globe Awards '92: Best Supporting Actor (Palance); MTV Movie Awards '92: Best Comedic Performance (Crystal); People's Choice Awards '92: Best Film—Musical/Comedy. *COL, NLC*

City Slickers 2: The Legend of Curly's Gold ♂♂½ 1994 (PG-13)
Mid-life crisis meets the wild west, part deux. Crystal and his fellow urban dudes discover a treasure map in the hat of departed trail boss Curly and decide to go a-huntin'. Palance is back as Curly's seafarin', equally cantankerous, twin brother. Lovitz occupies the screen as Crystal's ne'er-do-well brother, replacing sidekick Bruno Kirby. A bit of a rehash, formulaic and occasionally straining for a punchline, it's still pretty darn funny, especially when the boys start to improvise.**CW:** Off-color humor and comic sex scene. **116m/C VHS, LV, Closed Caption.** Billy Crystal, Daniel Stern, Jon Lovitz, Jack Palance, Patricia Wettig, Pruitt Taylor Vince, Bill McKinney, Lindsay Crystal, Noble Willingham, David Paymer, Josh Mostel; **D:** Paul Weiland; **W:** Billy Crystal, Lowell Ganz, Babaloo Mandel; **M:** Marc Shaiman. *COL*

City That Never Sleeps ♂♂½ 1953
A Chicago cop must decide whether or not to run off with an entertainer, or continue his life with his family. Decisions, decisions. Moody but dated melodrama that's finely acted and indecisively directed, with good use of dim city lights. Nothing new here. **90m/B VHS.** Gig Young, Mala Powers, Edward Arnold, Paula Raymond, Chill Wills, Marie Windsor; **D:** John H. Auer. *REP*

City Unplugged ♂♂ *Darkness in Tallinn.*
1995 Heist film with some twists. $970 million in gold, in Paris for safekeeping since WWII, has been returned to the treasury in the newly independent Republic of Estonia. The thieves, who belong to the Russian mob, plan to cut all electricity in the capital city of Tallinn, break into the bank, and move the gold to a nearby cigarette factory where it can be melted down and repackaged as cigarettes. The mob's use of local electrician Toivo proves to be their undoing in a comedy of errors. Estonian with subtitles. **99m/C VHS.** Peter Oja, Ivo Uukkivi, Milena Gulbe, Monika Mager; **D:** Ilkka Jarvilaturi; **W:** Paul Kolsby; **C:** Rein Kotov. *LEO*

City Without Men ♂½ 1943
Melodramatic story about a boarding house near a prison where the women tenants await the release of their imprisoned men. Little plot, no suspense. **75m/B VHS.** Linda Darnell, Sara Allgood, Michael Duane, Edgar Buchanan, Leslie Brooks, Glenda Farrell, Margaret Hamilton, Sheldon Leonard; **D:** Sidney Salkow. *RXM*

The City's Edge ♂½ 1983
A young man becomes involved with the mysterious residents of a boarding house on the edge of the ocean. **86m/C VHS, Beta.** *AU* Mark Lee; **D:** Ken Quinnell. *MGM*

Civil War Diary *Across Five Aprils* 1990
Too young to go to war, a young man struggles for the survival of his family amidst harsh winters, the devastation of the Civil War and his own personal nightmares. Winner of the International Heritage Award in 1990. Based on the Newberry Award winning young people's novel "Across Five Aprils." **82m/C VHS.** *RHI*

The Civil War, Episode 1: The Cause—1861 ♂♂♂♂ 1990
The blowout PBS hit mini-series, five years in the making by author and filmmaker Ken Burns, is a staggering historical achievement. Episode 1 focuses on the causes of the Civil War from the schism created by Lincoln's election, John Brown's assault on Harper's Ferry, and the firing on Fort Sumpter. Also available as a set for $179.95. **99m/C VHS, Closed Caption. D:** Ken Burns; **W:** Ken Burns. *WAR, SIG, PBS*

The Civil War, Episode 2: A Very Bloody Affair—1862 ♂♂♂♂ 1990
Second in the enormously popular PBS series looks at the unexpectedly extreme costs in human life of the War Between the States. **69m/C VHS, Closed Caption. D:** Ken Burns; **W:** Ken Burns. *WAR, SIG, PBS*

The Civil War, Episode 3: Forever Free—1862 ♂♂♂♂ 1990
Third volume in the PBS Emmy-nominated mini-series covers Antietam, Robert E. Lee and Stonewall Jackson planning Confederate strategy, and Lincoln's decision to free the slaves. **76m/C VHS, Closed Caption. D:** Ken Burns; **W:** Ken Burns. *WAR, SIG, PBS*

The Civil War, Episode 4: Simply Murder—1863 ♂♂♂♂ 1990
Union forces meet disaster at Fredericksburg, and Gen. Lee wins a victory but loses Stonewall Jackson in the fourth episode of the Emmy-nominated PBS mini-series. **62m/C VHS, Closed Caption. D:** Ken Burns; **W:** Ken Burns. *WAR, SIG, PBS*

The Civil War, Episode 5: The Universe of Battle—1863 ♂♂♂♂
1990 Gettysburg, the battleground which claimed 150,000 American lives, is examined in the 5th episode of the Emmy-nominated PBS mini-series. **95m/C VHS, Closed Caption. D:** Ken Burns; **W:** Ken Burns. *WAR, SIG, PBS*

The Civil War, Episode 6: Valley of the Shadow of Death—1864 🎬🎬🎬🎬 1990 Profiles of Grant and Lee are offered, plus Sherman's assault on Atlanta, in this volume from the Emmy-nominated PBS mini-series. 70m/C VHS, Closed Caption. *D:* Ken Burns; *W:* Ken Burns. WAR, SIG, PBS

The Civil War, Episode 7: Most Hallowed Ground—1864 1990 The nation re-elects Abraham Lincoln, and the North turns General Lee's mansion into Arlington National Cemetery in this episode of the Emmy-nominated PBS mini-series. 72m/C VHS, Closed Caption. *D:* Ken Burns; *W:* Ken Burns. WAR, SIG, PBS

The Civil War, Episode 8: War is All Hell—1865 🎬🎬🎬🎬 1990 Sherman marches to the sea and Lee surrenders to Grant in this episode from the Emmy-nominated PBS mini-series. 69m/C VHS, Closed Caption. *D:* Ken Burns; *W:* Ken Burns. WAR, SIG, PBS

The Civil War, Episode 9: The Better Angels of Our Nature—1865 🎬🎬🎬🎬 1990 In this final episode of the Emmy-nominated PBS mini-series, Lincoln's assasination is summarized, and the central characters of the war are summarized. 68m/C VHS, Closed Caption. *D:* Ken Burns; *W:* Ken Burns. WAR, SIG, PBS

Civilization 🎬🎬🎬 1916 A silent epic about the horrors and immorality of war as envisioned by the ground-breaking film pioneer Ince, who was later murdered. Famous scene involves Christ walking through body-ridden battlefields. 80m/B VHS, Beta. Howard Hickman, Enid Markey, Lola May; *D:* Thomas Ince, Reginald Barker, Raymond B. West. GPV, VYY, GVV

Claire of the Moon 🎬🎬 1992 Famous satirist Claire goes to a women writers retreat in the Pacific Northwest where she's assigned a room with Noel, a solemn sex therapist. Noel's recovering from a disastrous love affair while Claire is promiscuous and unwilling to commit. Inspite of their differences, the two women find themselves drawn together. Too many philosophical debates slow the story down but the gentle romance works well. 102m/C VHS. Trisha Todd, Karen Trumbo, Faith McDevitt, Damon Craig; *D:* Nicole Conn; *W:* Nicole Conn; *M:* Michael Allen Harrison. FXL, FXL, BTV

Claire's Knee 🎬🎬🎬½ 1971 A grown man about to be married goes on a holiday and develops a fixation on a young girl's knee. Another of Rohmer's Moral Tales exploring sexual and erotic obsessions. Lots of talk, little else. You'll either find it fascinating or fail to watch more than 10 minutes. Most, however, consider it a classic. Sophisticated dialogue, lovely visions of summer on Lake Geneva. In French with English subtitles. 105m/C VHS, Beta, LV. FR Jean-Claude Brialy, Aurora Cornu, Beatrice Romand; *D:* Eric Rohmer; *W:* Eric Rohmer; *C:* Nestor Almendros. National Board of Review Awards '71: 5 Best Foreign Films of the Year; National Society of Film Critics Awards '71: Best Film. MED, FCT, APD

Clambake 🎬 1967 Noxious Elvis vehicle about a rich man's son who wants success on his own terms, so he trades places with a water-skiing teacher. Inane, even in comparison to other Elvis ventures. ♫Clambake; The Girl I Never Loved; Hey, Hey, Hey; Confidence; Who Needs Money?; A House That Has Everything. 98m/C VHS, Beta. Elvis Presley, Shelley Fabares, Bill Bixby, James Gregory, Gary Merrill, Will Hutchins, Harold Peary; *D:* Arthur Nadel. MGM

The Clan of the Cave Bear 🎬½ 1986 (R) A scrawny cavegirl is taken in by Neanderthals after her own parents are killed. Hannah is lifeless as a primitive gamine, and the film is similarly DOA. Ponderous and only unintentionally funny. Based on the popular novel by Jean M. Auel. 100m/C VHS, Beta, LV, Closed Caption. Daryl Hannah, James Remar, Pamela Reed, John Doolittle, Thomas G. Waites; *D:* Michael Chapman; *W:* John Sayles;

C: Jan De Bont; *M:* Alan Silvestri. Nominations: Academy Awards '86: Best Makeup. FXV, FOX

Clara's Heart 🎬 1988 (PG-13) A Jamaican maid enriches the lives of her insufferable, bourgeois employers and their particularly repellent son. A kinder, gentler waste of film and Goldberg; sentimental clap-trap which occasionally lapses into comedy. 108m/C VHS, Beta, LV, Closed Caption. Whoopi Goldberg, Michael Ontkean, Kathleen Quinlan, Neil Patrick Harris, Spalding Gray, Beverly Todd, Hattie Winston; *D:* Robert Mulligan; *W:* Mark Medoff; *M:* Dave Grusin. WAR, FCT

Clarence 🎬🎬½ 1991 (G) Clarence, the benevolent angel from the classic "It's a Wonderful Life" is back, risking his wings for a beautiful young woman. Made for cable. 92m/C VHS, Closed Caption. Robert Carradine, Kate Trotter; *D:* Eric Till; *W:* Lorne Cameron. REP

Clarence Darrow 🎬🎬🎬 1978 Riveting one-man stage performance shot for television and based on Darrow's writings, adapted from the play by Irving Stone. 81m/C VHS, Beta, LV. Henry Fonda; *D:* John Rich. ALL, KAR, IME

Clarence, the Cross-eyed Lion 🎬🎬🎬 1965 Follows the many adventures of a cross-eyed lion and his human compatriots. Great family viewing from the creator of "Flipper." 98m/C VHS. Marshall Thompson, Betsy Drake, Richard Haydn, Cheryl Miller, Rockne Tarkington, Maurice Marsac; *D:* Andrew Marton; *W:* Alan Caillou. MGM, FCT

Clark & McCullough 🎬🎬½ 1933 The zany duo, a hit in burlesque and night clubs, transferred some of their crazy antics onto film. Their comedy shorts include "Fits in a Fiddle" (1933), "Love and Kisses" (1934), "Alibi Bye Bye" (1935), and a rehearsal of "Mademoiselle from New Rochelle" from "Strike Up the Band" (with George Gershwin on piano). 53m/B VHS, Beta. Bobby Clark, Paul McCullough, George Gershwin, James Finlayson. GVV, DVT, VYY

Clash by Night 🎬🎬🎬½ 1952 A wayward woman marries a fisherman, then beds his best friend. Seamy storyline is exploited to the hilt by master filmmaker Lang. An utterly unflinching melodrama. Early Monroe shines in a supporting role too. Based on the Clifford Odets play. 105m/B VHS. Barbara Stanwyck, Paul Douglas, Marilyn Monroe, Robert Ryan, J. Carrol Naish; *D:* Fritz Lang. TTC

Clash of the Ninja 🎬½ 1986 Evil Occidental ninja runs medical smuggling operation. Interpol ninja sets out to stop him. Wild ninja nonsense includes ninja with rotating head and exploding ninja. Dubbed poorly. 90m/C VHS, Beta. HK Paul Torcha, Louis Roth, Eric Neff, Bernie Junker, Joe Redner, Klaus Mutter, Eddie Chan, Max Kwan, Tom Allen, Stanley Tong; *D:* Wallace Chan; *W:* Kurt Spielberg. TWE

Clash of the Titans woof! 1981 (PG) Mind-numbing fantasy derived from Greek legends about heroic Perseus, who slays the snake-haired Medusa and rescues a semi-clad maiden from the monstrous Kraken. Wooden Hamlin plays Perseus and fares better than more accomplished Olivier and Smith, who seem in need of enemas as they lurch about Mt. Olympus. Only Bloom seems truly godlike in a supporting role. Some good, some wretched special effects from pioneer Harryhausen. 118m/C VHS, Beta, LV. GB Laurence Olivier, Maggie Smith, Claire Bloom, Ursula Andress, Burgess Meredith, Harry Hamlin, Sian Phillips, Judi Bowker; *D:* Desmond Davis; *W:* Beverley Cross; *C:* Ted Moore. MGM, MLB

Class 🎬🎬 1983 (R) A prep school student discovers that his mother is the lover whom his roommate has bragged about. Lowe is serviceable as the stunned son of sexy Bisset, who woos McCarthy, even in an elevator. Too ludicrous to be enjoyed, but you may watch just to see what happens next. 98m/C VHS, Beta, LV. Jacqueline Bisset, Rob Lowe, Andrew McCarthy, Cliff Robertson, John Cusack, Stuart Margolin, Casey Siemaszko; *D:* Lewis John Carlino; *M:* Elmer Bernstein. VES

Class Act 🎬🎬½ 1991 (PG-13) Rappers Kid 'N' Play team up once again in this role reversal comedy. A straight-laced brain and a partying, macho bully find their school records and identifications switched when they enroll in a new high school. This turns out to be good for the character of both young men, as the egghead learns to loosen up and the bully learns what it feels like to be respected for his ideas rather than a fierce reputation. Comedy is very uneven but the duo are energetic and likable. 98m/C VHS, LV. Christopher Reid, Christopher Martin, Meshach Taylor, Karyn Parsons, Doug E. Doug, Rick Ducommun, Lamont Jackson, Rhea Perlman; *D:* Randall Miller; *M:* Vassal Benford. WAR

Class Action 🎬🎬🎬 1991 (R) 1960s versus 1990s ethics clash when a father and daughter, both lawyers, wind up on opposing sides of a litigation against an auto manufacturer. Hackman and Mastrantonio give intense, exciting performances, almost surmounting the melodramatic script. 110m/C VHS, Beta, LV, Closed Caption. Mary Elizabeth Mastrantonio, Gene Hackman, Joanna Merlin, Colin Friels, Laurence "Larry" Fishburne, Donald Moffat, Jan Rubes, Matt Clark, Fred Dalton Thompson, Jonathan Silverman, Dan Hicks; *D:* Michael Apted; *W:* Samantha Shad, Christopher Ames; *M:* James Horner. FXV

Class of Fear 🎬½ 1991 (R) The new kid in school is having a particularly rough time. He's been framed for murdering a teacher and must prove his innocence before he winds up in prison. 105m/C VHS. Julianne McNamara, Noah Blake. MOV

Class of '44 🎬½ 1973 (PG) The sequel to "Summer of '42" finds insufferable boys becoming insufferable men at military school. Worse than its predecessor, and notable only in that it is Candy's film debut. 95m/C VHS, Beta. Gary Grimes, Jerry Houser, Oliver Conant, Deborah Winters, William Atherton, Sam Bottoms, John Candy; *D:* Paul Bogart; *M:* David Shire. WAR

The Class of Miss MacMichael 🎬🎬 1978 (R) A dedicated instructor inherits and ultimately inspires a class of high school misfits and malcontents. Derivative venture is beneath considerable talents of Jackson. Based on a novel by Sandy Hutson. 95m/C VHS, Beta, Closed Caption. GB Glenda Jackson, Oliver Reed, Michael Murphy, Rosalind Cash; *D:* Silvio Narizzano; *W:* Judd Bernard. FOX, MED

Class of 1984 woof! 1982 (R) Teacher King must face a motley crew of teenagers in the classroom. Ring leader and student psychopath Van Patten leads his groupies on a reign of terror through the high school halls, stopping to gang rape King's wife. Teacher attempts revenge. Bloody and thoughtless update of "Blackboard Jungle." Early Fox appearance. Followed by "Class of 1999." 93m/C VHS, Beta, LV. CA Perry King, Roddy McDowall, Timothy Van Patten, Michael J. Fox, Merrie Lynn Ross, Stefan Arngrim, Al Waxman; *D:* Mark L. Lester; *W:* Mark L. Lester, Tom Holland; *M:* Lalo Schifrin. VES

Class of 1999 🎬 1990 (R) Freewheeling sci-fi set in the near future where teen gangs terrorize seemingly the entire country. A high school principal determines to enforce law and order by installing human-like robots with rocket launchers for arms. Violent, crude entertainment. Class dismissed. Sequel to "Class of 1984" and available in an unrated version. 98m/C VHS, Beta. Bradley Gregg, Traci Lind, Malcolm McDowell, Stacy Keach, Patrick Kilpatrick, Pam Grier, John P. Ryan, Darren E. Burrows, Joshua Miller; *D:* Mark L. Lester; *W:* C. Courtney Joyner. VES, LIV

Class of 1999 2: The Substitute 🎬½ 1993 (R) High school in 1999 is filled with violent gangs who murder at random. Enter substitute teacher John Bolen, who has his own ideas of discipline—leading to an even higher body count. John just doesn't seem human and when a CIA agent starts investigating, school may never be the same. 90m/C VHS, LV, Closed Caption. Sasha Mitchell, Nick Cassavetes, Caitlin Dulany, Jack Knight, Gregory West, Rick Hill; *D:* Spiro Razatos; *W:* Mark Sevi. THV

Class of Nuke 'Em High ✗½ 1986 (R) Team Troma once again experiments with the chemicals, with violent results. Jersey high school becomes a hotbed of mutants and maniacs after a nuclear spill occurs. Good teens Chrissy and Warren succumb, the school blows, life goes on. High camp, low budget, heavy gore. Followed by "Class of Nuke 'Em High Part 2." **84m/C VHS, Beta.** Janelle Brady, Gilbert Brenton, Robert Prichard; **D:** Richard W. Haines, Lloyd (Samuel Weil) Kaufman. *MED*

Class of Nuke 'Em High 2: Subhumanoid Meltdown ✗ 1991 (R) The Troma team brings us back into the world of the strange. In this adventure, the evil Nukamama Corporation holds secret experiments at their "college" and create sub-humanoids as slave labor, swelling unemployment and wrecking the economy. This does not fare too well with the rest of society, including our heroes Roger the reporter, Professor Holt, and the scantily clad sub-humanoid Victoria. **CW:** Language, nudity, comic horror violence, and sexuality. **96m/C VHS, Beta, LV, Closed Caption.** Lisa Gaye, Brick Bronsky, Leesa Rowland; **D:** Eric Louzil. *VTR, MED, FXV*

Class of Nuke 'Em High 3: The Good, the Bad and the Subhumanoid woof! 1994 (R) Revisit Tromie the nuclear rodent and the other disaster-prone denizens of Tromaville, USA. Admire the classic good twin vs. evil subhumanoid twin plot as they battle against each other, aided by chicks with guns and tin undergarments. Supposedly inspired by Shakespeare's Comedy of Errors. Tip: stick to the BBC production for your senior thesis. **CW:** Gross presentation of sex, language, and gore. **95m/C VHS.** Brick Bronsky, Lisa Gaye; **D:** Eric Louzil; **W:** Lloyd (Samuel Weil) Kaufman. *TTV*

Class of '61 ✗✗½ 1992 1861, that is, as this class of West Point cadets prepares for the outbreak of war. Three close friends find themselves on opposing sides and with romantic entanglements, as well. Illustrated history, complete with voiceover passages from soldiers' letters, tend to slow the action, although the battles scenes are well done. Made for TV. **95m/C VHS, Closed Caption.** Dan Futterman, Clive Owen, Joshua Lucas, Sophie Ward, Laura Linney, Andre Braugher, Len Cariou, Dana Ivey, Scott Burkholder, Niall O'Brien, Christien Anholt, Paul Guilfoyle, Beverly Todd, Ed Wiley, Sue-Ann Leeds; **D:** Gregory Hoblit; **W:** Jonas McCord; **C:** Janusz Kaminski. *USH*

Class of '63 ✗✗ 1973 An unfulfilled woman finally discovers the lover she lost nearly ten years ago at her college reunion. Nearly average made for television drama. **74m/C VHS, Beta.** James Brolin, Joan Hackett, Cliff Gorman, Ed Lauter; **D:** John Korty. *ORI*

Class Reunion woof! 1987 (X) Sexual highjinks are the order of the day at a 10-year high school reunion. Insipid softcore effort. It's cheaper just to cut out heads from yearbooks and paste 'em to skin mags torsos. Not to be confused with "National Lampoon's Class Reunion," equally bad but nonetheless distinct. **90m/C VHS, Beta, LV.** Marsha Jordan, Renee Bond, Terry Johnson. *MED*

Class Reunion Massacre woof! 1977 (R) Typically lame-brained horror about the mysterious deaths of former school jerks who've reconvened for the 10-year reunion. Worthless flick stars someone named Finkbinder. Contains graphic violence that is not for the squeamish. Also titled "The Redeemer." **87m/C VHS, Beta.** T.K. Finkbinder, Damien Knight, Nick Carter. *NO*

Claudia ✗✗ 1985 (R) A wealthy woman who's part of London's high society falls for a lowly musician while trying to escape her dominating husband. Melodramatic meanderings not likely to move you. **CW:** Strong sexuality. **88m/C VHS.** Deborah Raffin, Nicholas Ball; **D:** Anwar Kawadri. *TTC*

The Claw 1927 A young British profligate goes to Africa to prove his manhood to the woman who rejected him. Silent. **?m/B VHS, Beta, 8mm.** Claire Windsor, Norman Kerry; **D:** Sidney Olcott. *GVV*

Claws ✗ 1977 (PG) A woodsman, a game commissioner and an Indian band together to stop a grizzly bear who is killing residents of a small Alaskan town. **100m/C VHS, Beta.** Leon Ames, Jason Evers, Anthony Caruso, Glenn Sipes, Carla Layton, Myron Healey; **D:** Richard Bansbach, R.E. Pierson. *GEM*

Claws woof! 1985 A lone farmboy is subjected to repeated attacks by feline mutants. Meow, baby. **84m/C VHS, Beta.** Jason Roberts, Brian O'Shaughnessy, Sandra Prinsloo. *NO*

The Clay Pigeon ✗✗½ 1949 Seaman comes to in the hospital after a long coma and discovers he's about to be court-martialed for treason and murder. Effective suspense as he goes after the man who incriminated him. **63m/B VHS, Beta.** Bill Williams, Barbara Hale, Richard Loo; **D:** Richard Fleischer. *NO*

Clayton County Line ✗ 198? Plucky buddies decide to end a cruel sheriff's reign of terror. Derivative and unredeeming. **80m/C VHS.** Kelly Bradish, Vince Csapos, Michael Heinz, Donald Kenney, Kathy Kenney, Gregg Schultz, Dan Quine, Steve Szilagyi, Dean Wilson; **D:** Dean Wilson. *NO*

Clean and Sober ✗✗✗½ 1988 (R) A drug addict hides out at a rehabilitation clinic and actually undergoes treatment. A serious, subtle, and realistic look at the physical/emotional detoxification of an obnoxious, substance-abusing real estate broker; unpredictable and powerful without moralizing. Keaton is fine in unsympathetic lead, with both Baker and Freeman excelling in lesser roles. Not for all tastes, but it's certainly a worthwhile work. Caron, creator of TV's "Moonlighting," debuts here as director. **124m/C VHS, Beta, LV, 8mm, Closed Caption.** Michael Keaton, Kathy Baker, Morgan Freeman, M. Emmet Walsh, Claudia Christian, Pat Quinn, Ben Piazza, Brian Benben, Luca Bercovici, Tate Donovan, Henry Judd Baker, Mary Catherine Martin; **D:** Glenn Gordon Caron; **W:** Tod Carroll; **C:** Jan Kiesser. National Society of Film Critics Awards '88: Best Actor (Keaton). *WAR, FCT*

Clean, Shaven ✗✗ 1993 Schizophrenic Peter Winter (Greene in a stunning performance) is searching bleak Miscou Island, off the New Brunswick coast, for the young daughter his mother put up for adoption after Peter was institutionalized and his wife died. Peter's being tailed by Detective McNally (Albert), who suspects him of a child's murder, and his tenuous hold on reality slowly disintegrates into torment and self-mutilation. Debut for director/writer Kerrigan. **80m/C VHS.** Peter Greene, Robert Albert, Jennifer MacDonald, Megan Owen, Molly Castelloe; **D:** Lodge Kerrigan; **W:** Lodge Kerrigan; **C:** Teodoro Maniaci; **M:** Hahn Rowe. Nominations: Independent Spirit Awards '95: Best First Feature. *ORI*

Clean Slate ✗✗ 1994 (PG-13) Private-eye Maurice Pogue (Carvey) sustains injuries that cause a rare type of amnesia making every day seem like the first day of his life. As the only witness to a crime, he bumbles through mix-ups with the mob and his job as a bodyguard. Lightweight comedy fare is good for a few yuks but doesn't work as well as the similar "Groundhog Day." Barkley the sight-impaired dog steals nearly every scene he's in. **CW:** Language. **106m/C VHS, Beta, LV, Closed Caption.** Dana Carvey, Valeria Golino, James Earl Jones, Kevin Pollak, Michael Murphy, Michael Gambon, Jayne Brook, Vyto Ruginis, Olivia D'Abo, Peter Crook; **D:** Mick Jackson; **W:** Robert King; **M:** Alan Silvestri. *MGM*

Clear and Present Danger ✗✗½ 1994 (PG-13) Ford returns for a second go at CIA agent Jack Ryan in the third installment of Tom Clancy's bestselling adventures. With the Cold War over, the U.S. government is the bad guy as Ryan discovers a link between a South American drug cartel and a Presidential advisor. Viewers will also finally get an answer to that nagging question at the end of "Patriot Games:" is it a boy or a girl? Archer's back as Ryan's annoying wife, and Birch and Jones also return. Keep alert for complex plot twists in lieu of tons of action, though there's enough to keep action fans happy. **CW:** Language and intense action; violence. **141m/C VHS, Beta, Closed Caption.** Harrison Ford, Anne Archer, James Earl Jones, Willem Dafoe, Thora Birch, Henry Czerny, Harris Yulin, Raymond Cruz, Joaquim de Almeida, Miguel Sandoval, Donald Moffat, Theodore (Ted) Raimi, Dean Jones; **D:** Phillip Noyce; **W:** Steven Zaillian, Donald Stewart, John Milius. Blockbuster Entertainment Awards '95: Action Actor, Theatrical (Ford); Blockbuster Entertainment Awards '96: Action Actor, Video (Ford); Nominations: Academy Awards '94: Best Sound; MTV Movie Awards '95: Best Action Sequence. *PAR*

Clearcut ✗✗½ 1992 (R) Progressive lawyer finds his liberalism and his survival skills tested among modern Canadian Indians, when a militant native resorts to kidnapping the businessman who threatens their land. Well-acted, brutal drama that asks tough questions; it includes what purports to be the first authentic sweat-lodge ceremony ever filmed. **CW:** Language and strong torture and violence. **98m/C VHS.** Graham Greene, Ron Lea, Michael Hogan, Floyd "Red Crow" Westerman, Rebecca Jenkins; **D:** Richard Bugajski. *ACA*

Clearing the Range ✗✗½ 1931 Hoot wants the bad guy who knocked off his brother so he poses as a cringing coward in the hopes of uncovering the villain. Eilers is the love interest as well as his real-life wife. **64m/B VHS, Beta.** Hoot Gibson, Sally Eilers, Hooper Atchley; **D:** Otto Brower. *NOS, VCN, DVT*

Cleo from 5 to 7 ✗✗✗½ Cleo de 5 a 7 1961 A singer strolls through Paris for 90 minutes, and reconsiders her life while awaiting the results of medical tests for cancer. Typical documentary-like effort from innovative filmmaker Varda, who constructed the film in real time. Look for a brief appearance of master director Jean-Luc Godard. In French with English subtitles. **90m/B VHS, Beta.** FR Corinne Marchand, Antoine Bourseiller, Dorothee Blanck, Michel Legrand, Jean-Claude Brialy, Jean-Luc Godard, Anna Karina, Eddie Constantine, Sami Frey; **D:** Agnes Varda; **W:** Agnes Varda. *FCT*

Cleo/Leo ✗ 1989 (R) Crude and sexist jerk Leo gets chased into the East River by a gun-toting feminist. Reincarnated, Leo returns as Cleo and endures the same Neanderthal remarks and attitudes that "he" used to dish out. Tasteless, exploitive comedy only cynically explores the sex reversal theme. **94m/C VHS.** Jane Hamilton, Scott Thompson Baker, Kevin Thomas, Alan Naggar, Ginger Lynn Allen; **D:** Chuck Vincent. *VTR, MED*

Cleopatra ✗✗ 1934 Early Hollywood DeMille version of the Egyptian temptress's lust for Marc Antony after Julius Caesar's death. Intermittently interesting extravaganza. Colbert seems to be enjoying herself in the lead role in this hokey, overdone epic. Includes the original theatrical trailer on laser-track 2. Remade in 1963. **100m/B VHS, Beta, LV, Closed Caption.** Claudette Colbert, Henry Wilcoxon, Warren William, Gertrude Michael, Joseph Schildkraut, Sir C. Aubrey Smith; **D:** Cecil B. DeMille; **C:** Victor Milner. Academy Awards '34: Best Cinematography; Nominations: Academy Awards '34: Best Film Editing, Best Picture, Best Sound. *USH*

Cleopatra ✗ 1963 And we thought DeMille's version was extravagant. After the death of Julius Caesar, Cleopatra, Queen of Egypt, becomes infatuated with Mark Antony. Costly four-hour epic functions like a blimp-sized, multi-colored sleeping tablet. Historical characters are utterly dwarfed by the film's massive scope, and audiences are benumbed by a spectacle of crowd scenes and opulent, grotesque interiors. Taylor looks and often acts like a sex bomb ruler, while Harrison has some notion of Caesar's majesty. Burton, however, is hopelessly wooden. Hard to believe this came from director Mankiewicz. **246m/C VHS, Beta, LV.** Elizabeth Taylor, Richard Burton, Rex Harrison, Roddy McDowall, Martin Landau, Pamela Brown, Michael Hordern, Kenneth Haigh, Andrew Keir, Hume Cronyn, Carroll O'Connor; **D:** Joseph L. Mankiewicz; **W:** Joseph L. Mankiewicz; **C:** Leon Shamroy; **M:** Alex North. Academy Awards '63: Best Art Direction/Set Decoration (Color), Best Color Cinematography (Color), Best Costume Design (Color), Best Visual Effects; National Board of Review Awards '63: Best Actor (Harrison); Nominations: Academy Awards '63: Best Actor (Harrison), Best Film Editing, Best Picture, Best Sound, Best Original Score. *FOX*

Cleopatra Jones ✍✍ 1973 (PG) Lean and lethal government agent with considerable martial arts prowess takes on loathsome drug lords. Dobson is fetching as the lead performer in this fast-paced, violent flick. Followed by "Cleopatra Jones and the Casino of Gold." **89m/C VHS, Beta.** Tamara Dobson, Shelley Winters, Bernie Casey, Brenda Sykes; **D:** Jack Starrett. *WAR*

Cleopatra Jones & the Casino of Gold ✍✍ 1975 (R) Dobson returns as the lethal, physically imposing federal agent to Hong Kong to take on a powerful druglord in this sequel to "Cleopatra Jones." Watch for sexy Stevens as the Dragon Lady. **96m/C VHS, Beta.** Tamara Dobson, Stella Stevens, Norman Fell; **D:** Chuck Bail. *WAR*

The Clergyman's Daughter ✍1/2 1984 A clergyman's daughter calls upon detectives Tommy and Tuppence to investigate some murders at the family's country house. Made for British television and based on the Agatha Christie story. **60m/C VHS, Beta.** *GB* James Warwick, Francesca Annis. *TPV*

Clerks ✍✍✍ 1994 (R) "What kind of convenience store do you run here?" Day in the life of a convenience store clerk is an often hilarious lesson in the profane from first time writer/director Smith (who has a cameo as Silent Bob). Twenty-two-year-old Dante Hicks (O'Halloran) is a disaffected New Jersey Quick Stop employee who spends most of his time bored and dealing with borderline crazies. The next-door video store is clerked by his best friend Randal (Anderson), who derives equal delight from tormenting his customers and debating absolutely anything (especially anything sexual). Nothing much actually happens but the very low-budget ($27,575) production has a decidedly scuzzy charm and a cult following. Based on the director's four years of clerking at the Quick Stop and shot on location. **CW:** Explicit sex-related dialogue. **89m/B VHS, LV, Closed Caption.** Brian O'Halloran, Jeff Anderson, Marilyn Ghigliotti, Lisa Spoonhauer, Jason Mewes; *Cameos:* Kevin Smith; **D:** Kevin Smith; **W:** Kevin Smith; **M:** Scott Angley. Sundance Film Festival '94: Filmmakers Trophy; Nominations: Independent Spirit Awards '95: Best First Feature, Debut Performance (Anderson), First Screenplay. *MAX*

The Client ✍✍1/2 1994 (PG-13) Another legal thriller from the Grisham factory. Reggie Love (Sarandon) is a troubled attorney hired by 11-year-old Mark (Renfro), who witnessed the suicide of a Mafia attorney and now knows more than he should. Ambitious federal prosecutor Foltrigg's (Jones) willing to risk the boy's life in exchange for career advancement. Lacks the mega-big Hollywood names of "The Firm" and "The Pelican Brief" but gains solid acting in return with Renfro a find in his film debut. No frills, near-faithful adaptation by Schumacher basically travels down the path of least resistance. Filmed on location in Memphis. **CW:** Brief language and child in jeopardy. **121m/C VHS, LV, 8mm, Closed Caption.** Susan Sarandon, Tommy Lee Jones, Brad Renfro, Mary-Louise Parker, Anthony LaPaglia, Bradley Whitford, Anthony Edwards, Ossie Davis, Walter Olkewicz, J.T. Walsh, Will Patton, Anthony Heald; **D:** Joel Schumacher; **W:** Robert Getchell, Akiva Goldsman. British Academy Awards '94: Best Actress (Sarandon); Nominations: Academy Awards '94: Best Actress (Sarandon); Screen Actors Guild Award '94: Best Actress (Sarandon). *WAR*

Cliffhanger ✍✍✍ 1993 (R) Action-packed thriller. Expert climber Gabe Walker (Stallone) faces his greatest challenge when criminal mastermind Lithgow and his henchman appear on the scene. Turner plays fellow climber and love interest. Lithgow makes a particularly convincing, if not downright chilling, murderous thief. Filmed in the Italian Alps with a budget of $70 million-plus; boasts stunning cinematography and breathtaking footage of the Dolomite mountain range. Harlin's expert pacing and direction combine to produce maximum thrills and suspense. The hit Stallone's been waiting for, placing eighth on the list of top 1993 box office grossers. **CW:** Language and violence. **113m/C VHS, Beta, LV, 8mm, Closed Caption.** Sylvester Stallone, John Lithgow, Michael Rooker, Janine Turner, Rex Linn, Caroline Goodall, Leon, Paul Winfield, Ralph Waite, Craig Fairbrass, Michelle Joyner, Max Perlich; **D:** Renny Harlin; **W:** Sylvester Stallone, Michael France; **C:** Alex Thomson; **M:** Trevor Jones. Nominations: Academy Awards '93: Best Sound, Best Sound Effects Editing, Best Visual Effects; MTV Movie Awards '94: Best Action Sequence. *COL, BTV, FCT*

Clifford WOOF! 1992 (PG) Short plays a 10-year-old in an effort delayed by Orion's financial crisis. Creepy little Clifford's uncle Martin (Grodin) rues the day he volunteered to babysit his nephew to prove to his girlfriend (Steenburgen) how much he likes kids. Clifford terrorizes Grodin in surprisingly nasty ways when their plans for visiting Dinosaurworld fall through, although Grodin sees to well-deserved revenge. Not just bad in the conventional sense, but bad in a bizarre sort of alien fashion that raises questions about who was controlling the bodies of the producers. To create the effect of Short really being short, other actors stood on boxes and sets were built slightly larger. **90m/C VHS, LV, Closed Caption.** Martin Short, Charles Grodin, Mary Steenburgen, Dabney Coleman, Sonia Jackson; **D:** Paul Flaherty; **W:** Bobby Von Hayes, Jay Dee Rock, Steven Kampmann, Will Aldis; **C:** John A. Alonzo; **M:** Richard Gibbs. *ORI*

A Climate for Killing ✍✍1/2 1991 (R) Arizona police are baffled when a woman murdered 16 years earlier is again found dead. Case open? Hunks Bauer and Beck are earnest in leads, and Ross and Sara are foxy. Passable entertainment. **CW:** Language, violence, and sensuality. **104m/C VHS, Beta, LV, Closed Caption.** Steven Bauer, John Beck, Katharine Ross, Mia Sara, John Diehl, Phil Brock, Dedee Pfeiffer, Lu Leonard, Jack Dodson, Eloy Casados; **D:** J.S. Cardone; **W:** J.S. Cardone; **M:** Robert Folk. *MED*

The Climax ✍✍1/2 1944 Technicolor highlights this horror saga of obsession. House physician for Vienna's Royal Theatre, Dr. Hohner (Karloff) kills opera singer Marcellina (Vincent) when she rejects him. Twenty years later, Hohner hears the beautiful voice of Angela (Foster), a near duplicate of Marcellina's, and hypnotizes her to prevent her singing. Now, it's up to Angela's composer friend Franz (Bey) to overcome the doctor's evil influence. Adapted from a play by Edward Locke. Waggner directed this "The Phantom of the Opera" clone using the same sets as the 1943 "Phantom" remake. **86m/C VHS, Closed Caption.** Boris Karloff, Susanna Foster, Turhan Bey, Gale Sondergaard, Thomas Gomez, June Vincent, Jane Farrar, Scotty Beckett; **D:** George Waggner; **C:** Curt Siodmak, Lynn Starling; **C:** Hal Mohr, William Howard Greene; **M:** Edward Ward. *USH*

The Climb ✍✍1/2 1987 (PG) German mountain climbers attempt to conquer the Himalayan Nanga Parbat, the world's fifth highest peak. Sometimes compelling film based on 1953 expedition in which only one member succeeded in reaching the summit. **90m/C VHS, Beta, LV.** Bruce Greenwood, James Hurdle, Kenneth Welsh; **D:** Donald Shebib; **W:** Donald Shebib; **M:** Peter Jermyn. *IME*

Clipped Wings ✍✍1/2 1953 The Bowery Boys are at their best as they inadvertantly join the army while visiting a friend and in the process of their usual bumblings, uncover a Nazi plot. **62m/B VHS.** Leo Gorcey, Huntz Hall, Bernard Gorcey, David Condon, Bennie Bartlett, June Vincent, Mary Treen, Philip Van Zandt, Elaine Riley, Jeanne Dean, Lyle Talbot; **D:** Edward L. Bernds. *WAR*

Cloak and Dagger ✍✍ 1946 An American physicist joins the secret service during WWII and infiltrates Nazi territory to release a kidnapped scientist who is being forced to build a nuclear bomb. Disappointing spy show with muted anti-nuclear tone. **106m/B VHS, LV.** Gary Cooper, Lilli Palmer, Robert Alda, James Flavin, Vladimir Sokoloff, J. Edward Bromberg, Marc Lawrence, Ludwig Stossel; **D:** Fritz Lang; **W:** Ring Lardner Jr., Albert Maltz; **M:** Max Steiner. *REP, FCT*

Cloak & Dagger ✍✍1/2 1984 (PG) A young boy, last seen befriending E.T., depends upon his imaginary super-friend to help him out when some real-life agents are after his video game. Coleman is particularly fun as both dad and fantasy hero in an interesting family adventure. **101m/C VHS, Beta, LV, Closed Caption.** Dabney Coleman, Henry Thomas, Michael Murphy, John McIntire, Jeanette Nolan; **D:** Richard Franklin; **W:** Tom Holland; **M:** Brian May. *USH*

The Clock ✍✍✍ Under the Clock 1945 Appealing romance about an office worker who meets and falls in love with a soldier on two-day leave in New York City. Likeable Walker and likeable Garland make a fine screen couple, and Wynn is memorable as the drunk. The original theatrical trailer is included on the laserdisc format. **91m/B VHS, LV.** Judy Garland, Robert Walker, James Gleason, Marshall Thompson, Keenan Wynn; **D:** Vincente Minnelli; **M:** George Bassman. *BTV, MGM, FCT*

Clockers ✍✍✍ 1995 (R) Strike (Phifer), leader of a group of bottom-feeding drug dealers ("clockers"), engages in a power struggle with his boss (Lindo), his do-the-right-thing brother Victor (Washington), and his own conscience. He's also suspected of murder by relentless narcotics cop Rocco Klein (Keitel). Supported by an excellent cast, first-timer Phifer surprises with a fierce and powerful performance. Lindo, in particular, stands out as the paternally evil Rodney. Aggressively edited, with Turturro's performance mostly lost on the cutting room floor. Critically lauded cinematography is marred by the occasional boom shot. Poignant and compelling street drama is based on the Richard Price novel. Lee took over after Scorsese and De Niro dropped out to make "Casino." **CW:** Strong graphic violence; strong language; drug content. **128m/C VHS, LV, Closed Caption.** Mekhi Phifer, Harvey Keitel, Delroy Lindo, Isaiah Washington, John Turturro, Keith David; **D:** Spike Lee; **W:** Richard Price, Spike Lee; **C:** Malik Hassan Sayeed; **M:** Terence Blanchard. *USH*

The Clockmaker ✍✍✍1/2 1976 Contemplative drama about a clockmaker whose life is shattered when his son is arrested as a political assassin. Tavernier regular Noiret excels in the lead. In French with English subtitles. **105m/C VHS, Beta, LV.** *FR* Philippe Noiret, Jean Rochefort, Jacques Denis, William Sabatier, Christine Pascal; **D:** Bertrand Tavernier. National Board of Review Awards '76: 5 Best Foreign Films of the Year. *FCT, LUM*

Clockwise ✍✍1/2 1986 (PG) Monty Python regular Cleese is a teacher preoccupied by punctuality. His neurosis proves his undoing when he falls victim to misadventure while traveling to deliver a speech. Cleese is acceptable, dialogue and story is less so, though sprinkled with a fair amount of humor. **96m/C VHS, LV, Closed Caption.** *GB* John Cleese, Penelope Wilton, Alison Steadman, Stephen Moore, Sharon Maiden; **D:** Christopher Morahan; **W:** Michael Frayn; **M:** George Fenton. *REP*

A Clockwork Orange ✍✍✍✍ 1971 (R) In the Britain of the near future, a sadistic punk leads a gang on nightly rape and murder sprees, then is captured and becomes the subject of a grim experiment to eradicate his violent tendencies in this extraordinary adaptation of Anthony Burgess's controversial novel. The film is an exhilarating experience, with an outstanding performance by McDowell as the funny, fierce psychopath. Many memorable, disturbing sequences, including a rape conducted while assailant McDowell belts "Singing in the Rain." Truly outstanding, provocative work from master filmmaker Kubrick. **137m/C VHS, Beta, LV, Closed Caption.** *GB* Malcolm McDowell, Patrick Magee, Adrienne Corri, Michael Bates, Warren Clarke, Aubrey Morris, James Marcus, Steven Berkoff, David Prowse; *D:* Stanley Kubrick; *W:* Stanley Kubrick. New York Film Critics Awards '71: Best Director (Kubrick), Best Film; Nominations: Academy Awards '71: Best Adapted Screenplay, Best Director (Kubrick), Best Film Editing, Best Picture. *WAR, FCT, FUS*

Clodhopper *🎬🎬* **1917** A farmboy decides to head out for New York where he achieves fame on Broadway for his dance number, the "Clophooper Glide." He stays true to his hometown girl, however, and returns to save his father's farm from financial ruin. **47m/B VHS, Beta.** Charles Ray, Margery Wilson; *D:* Victor Schertzinger. *GPV, CCB, DVT*

The Clones *🎬🎬* **1973 (PG)** A doctor discovers a government experiment engineered to murder him with a perfect clone. **90m/C VHS, Beta.** Michael Greene, Gregory Sierra; *D:* Paul Hunt, Lamar Card. *LIV, HHE*

Clones of Bruce Lee *🎬🎬* **1980 (R)** It's a martial arts free-for-all as bold masters from throughout the world duel for supremacy in the realm of self defense. If you like martial arts movies, you'll probably like this one. If you don't know if you like martial arts movies, find out with one of the actual Bruce Lee's flicks. **87m/C VHS, Beta.** Dragon Lee, Bruce Le, Bruce Lai, Bruce Thai; *D:* Joseph Kong. *MED*

The Clonus Horror *🎬½* Parts: The Clonus Horror **1979** A scientist discovers a government plot to clone the population by freezing bodies alive and using their parts in surgery. **90m/C VHS, Beta.** Tim Donnelly, Keenan Wynn, Peter Graves, Dick Sargent, Paulette Breen; *D:* Robert S. Fiveson. *LIV*

Close Encounters of the Third Kind *🎬🎬🎬🎬* **1977 (PG)** Middle-American strangers become involved in the attempts of benevolent aliens to contact earthlings. Despite the sometimes mundane nature of the characters, this Spielberg epic is a stirring achievement. Studded with classic sequences, the ending is an exhilarating experience of special effects and peace-on-earth feelings. Dreyfuss and Dillon excel as friends who are at once bewildered and obsessed by the alien presence, and French filmmaker Truffaut is also strong as the stern, ultimately kind scientist. Laserdisc includes formerly edited scenes, live interviews with Spielberg, special effects man Douglas Trumbull, and composer Williams, publicity materials, and over 1,000 production photos. **152m/C VHS, Beta, LV, Closed Caption.** Richard Dreyfuss, Teri Garr, Melinda Dillon, Francois Truffaut, Bob Balaban, Cary Guffey, J. Patrick McNamara; *D:* Steven Spielberg; *W:* Steven Spielberg; *C:* Vilmos Zsigmond; *M:* John Williams. Academy Awards '77: Best Cinematography, Best Sound Effects Editing; National Board of Review Awards '77: 10 Best Films of the Year; Nominations: Academy Awards '77: Best Art Direction/Set Decoration, Best Director (Spielberg), Best Film Editing, Best Sound, Best Supporting Actress (Dillon), Best Original Score. *COL, CRC, FUS*

Close My Eyes *🎬🎬* **1991 (R)** A hot, steamy summer arouses vibrant passions in a brother and sister, and neither marriage nor blood relation can halt the inevitable. *CW:* Language and strong sensuality. **105m/C VHS.** Alan Rickman, Clive Owen, Saskia Reeves; *D:* Stephen Poliakoff. *ACA*

Close to Eden *🎬🎬* Urga **1990 (PG)** A peasant couple living in inner Mongolia with their three children are prevented by strict Chinese law from having a fourth. The husband sets out from his village to obtain birth control from the nearby town. While on his way, the farmer (Bayaertu) saves a Russian truck driver (Gostukhin) after he drives into a lake. Sergei is introduced to another way of life when he's taken home by his rescuer to meet the family and becomes accustomed to the tranquility of farm life in the rural Mongolian steppe. Essentially a story about the changes modern civilization can bring to a rural way of life. Filmed in Mongolia. In Russian with English subti-

---

tles. **109m/C VHS, Beta.** *RU* Baoyinhexige, Badema, Nikita Mikhalkov; *D:* Nikita Mikhalkov; *W:* Rustam Ibragimbekov; *M:* Eduard Artemyev. Venice Film Festival '91: Best Film; Nominations: Academy Awards '92: Best Foreign Language Film. *PAR, FCT*

Close to Home *🎬🎬* **1986** A runaway fleeing a home life of abuse and neglect befriends a TV journalist doing a story on similar girls. She turns to him for support after she is arrested and returned home. Merely mediocre. **93m/C VHS, Beta.** *CA* Daniel Allman, Jillian Fargey, Anne Petrie; *D:* Rick Beairsto. *TWE*

Closely Watched Trains *🎬🎬🎬½* **1966** A novice train dispatcher attempts to gain sexual experience in German-occupied Czechoslovakia during WWII. Many funny scenes in this film regarded by some as a classic. Based upon the Czech novel by Bohumil Hrabal. In Czech with English subtitles. **89m/B VHS, Beta, LV.** *CZ* Vaclav Neckar, Jitka Bendova, Vladimir Valenta, Josef Somr; *D:* Jiri Menzel; *W:* Jiri Menzel. Academy Awards '67: Best Foreign Language Film. *FXL, COL*

The Closer *🎬🎬½* **1991 (R)** Aiello is "The Closer," a high-powered salesman whose world is falling apart. Somewhere between the money and the power, he's lost touch with his family and the truly important things in life. Is it too late to get them back? *CW:* Language. **87m/C VHS, LV.** Danny Aiello, Michael Pare, Joe Cortese, Justine Bateman, Diane Baker, James Karen, Rick Aiello, Michael Lerner; *D:* Dimitri Logothetis; *W:* Robert Keats, Louis LaRusso II; *M:* Al Kasha. *ACA*

Closet Land *🎬🎬½* **1990 (R)** Severe, stylized political allegory aims high but fails to convincingly distill totalitarian repression into just two characters—a government inquisitor and his captive, a woman subjected to hideous mental and physical torture. Child-molesting emerges as an ill-advised subtheme. A better video on the same subject: "Interrogation," from Poland. *CW:* Language and psychological torture. **95m/C VHS, Beta, LV, Closed Caption.** Madeleine Stowe, Alan Rickman; *D:* Radha Bharadwaj; *W:* Radha Bharadwaj; *M:* Richard Einhorn. *FXV, VTR*

Cloud Dancer *🎬🎬* **1980 (PG)** A self-absorbed acrobat uses and abuses those around him, including his girlfriend. Carradine and O'Neill fail to distinguish themselves in this mediocre film. **107m/C VHS, Beta.** David Carradine, Jennifer O'Neill, Joseph Bottoms, Colleen Camp; *D:* Barry Brown; *W:* William Goodhart. *PSM*

Cloud Waltzing *🎬🎬½* **1987** The screen version of a Harlequin romance about a journalist who arrives in France to interview a vintner and finds romance and danger. Melodrama bolstered by the presence of photogenic Beller. **103m/C VHS, Beta.** Kathleen Beller, Francois-Eric Gendron, Paul Maxwell, Therese Liotard, Claude Gensac, David Baxt; *D:* Gordon Flemyng. *PAR*

The Clouded Yellow *🎬🎬🎬* **1951** Young, lovely, and a little unstable, Sophie Malraux (Simmons) is accused of murdering the handyman who worked for her guardians (Jones and Dresdel). Ex-British Secret Service agent David Somers (Howard), who's in love with Sophie, helps her escape from jail and the two head for Liverpool and a ship to Mexico. But the police (hoping to find the real killer) are hot on their trail. Romantic suspense with good lead pairing. **95m/B VHS.** *GB* Jean Simmons, Trevor Howard, Sonia Dresdel, Barry Jones, Maxwell Reed, Kenneth More, Andre Morell, Geoffrey Keen; *D:* Ralph Thomas; *W:* Eric Ambler; *C:* Geoffrey Unsworth. *HMV*

Clouds Over Europe *🎬🎬🎬* Q Planes **1939** A test pilot and a man from Scotland Yard team up to find out why new bomber planes are disappearing. **82m/B VHS, Beta, LV.** Laurence Olivier, Valerie Hobson, Ralph Richardson, George Curzon, George Merritt, Gus McNaughton, David Tree, Sandra Storme, Hay Petrie, Frank Fox, Gordon McLeod, John Longden, Reginald Purdell, John Laurie, Pat Aherne; *D:* Tim Whelan; *W:* Ian Dalrymple; *C:* Harry Stradling.

Clown *🎬🎬½* **1953** A broken-down funny man with a worshipful son obtains one last career opportunity. This "Champ"-derived tearjerker features credible playing from Skelton and Considine as father and son, respectively. **91m/B VHS, Beta.** Red Skelton, Jane Greer, Tim Considine, Steve Forrest; *D:* Robert Z. Leonard; *C:* Paul Vogel. *MGM*

Clown House *🎬* **1988 (R)** Young brothers are stalked in their home by three demonic clowns. **95m/C VHS, Beta, LV, Closed Caption.** Nathan Forrest Winters, Brian McHugh, Sam Rockwell, Viletta Skillman, Timothy Enos, Tree; *D:* Victor Salva. *COL*

Clown Murders *🎬½* **1983** Posh Halloween party is undone when a cruel group fakes a kidnapping to ruin a too-prosperous pal's business deal. Awkward thriller boasts little suspense. Candy plays it straight, mostly, in this one. **94m/C VHS, Beta.** John Candy, Al Waxman, Susan Keller, Lawrence Dane; *D:* Martyn Burke. *TWE*

Clowning Around *🎬🎬½* **1992** Simon, who has lived in foster homes all his life, dreams of becoming a famous circus clown. When he's sent to a new home, his new foster parents think his idea is silly, so he runs away and joins the circus. There he meets Anatole, a European clown has-been who can no longer perform because of injuries. Simon believes Anatole can teach him about clowning, so he follows Anatole to Paris to help make his dream come true. Part of the "Wonderworks" series. **165m/C VHS.** *AU* Clayton Williamson, Jean-Michel Dagory, Ernie Dingo. *PME, HMV, BTV*

Clowning Around 2 *🎬🎬½* **1993** The continuing story of Sim, whose dream is to become a world-famous clown. Now a member of the Winter Circus in Paris, he is still training with his mentor Anatole. But Sim is dissatisfied and when he befriends Eve, another young clown, he learns an experimental style of clowning which gets them both fired. He first follows Eve to her home in Montreal but then returns to his own home in Australia where he has been left the co-owner of a less-than-successful circus by a former employer. Filmed on location in Paris, France and Perth, Australia. **120m/C VHS.** *AU* Clayton Williamson, Jean-Michel Dagory, Ernie Dingo, Frederique Fouche; *D:* George Whaley. *PME, BTV*

The Clowns *🎬🎬🎬½* **1971 (G)** An idiosyncratic documentary about circus clowns. Director Fellini has fashioned an homage that is sincere, entertaining, and personal. Contains some truly poignant sequences. Made for Italian television with English subtitles. **90m/C VHS, Beta.** *IT D:* Federico Fellini; *W:* Federico Fellini; *M:* Nino Rota. National Board of Review Awards '71: 5 Best Foreign Films of the Year. *HTV, NOS, MRV*

The Club *🎬🎬🎬* Players **1981 (PG)** A soccer coach tries to train and motivate a mediocre squad into one worth playing for—and perhaps even winning—the league cup. Conventional sports story is significantly improved by Thompson's rendering of the coach. **99m/C VHS, Beta.** *AU* Jack Thompson, Graham Kennedy, John Wood, John Howard, Alan Cassell; *D:* Bruce Beresford; *W:* David Williamson. *ACA*

The Club *🎬* **1994 (R)** Typical teens-in-peril flick finds the high school prom held in a mysterious old castle with ghouls out to get the unfortunate seniors. Visuals are decent but frights are tepid. **88m/C VHS, LV.** Kim Coates, Joel Wyner, Andrea Roth, Rino Romano, Zack Ward, Kelli Taylor, Matthew Ferguson; *D:* Benton Spencer; *W:* Robert Cooper; *M:* Paul Zaza. *IMP*

Club Extinction *🎬🎬½* Docteur M **1989 (R)** A near-future thriller in which Berlin is plagued by a wave of suicides. An investigator suspects a spa representative and a media tycoon of being involved. Features a fine international cast, but the film is a lesser venture from prolific master Chabrol. *CW:* Language, violence, and sensuality. **105m/C VHS, Beta.** *GE* Alan Bates, Andrew McCarthy, Jennifer Beals, Jan Niklas, Hanns Zischler, Benoit Regent,

Peter Fitz, Wolfgang Preiss, Isolde Barth; **D:** Claude Chabrol. *PSM, FCT*

Club Fed ♂½ 1990 (PG-13) A rigid prison warden's plot to impose greater discipline is undone by inmate highjinks. Crude laughs and one-dimensional play from a cast of recognizable names and faces. 93m/C VHS, Beta. Judy Landers, Sherman Hemsley, Karen Black, Burt Young, Rick Schmidt, Allen (Goorwitz) Garfield, Joseph Campanella, Lyle Alzado, Mary Woronov, Debbie Lee Carrington; **D:** Nathaniel Christian; **C:** Arledge Armenaki. *PSM*

Club Havana ♂½ 1946 A benevolent nightclub owner tries to save one of his singers from the depths of despair by reuniting her with her boyfriend. Minor musical with minor musical numbers. ♫Besame Mucho; Tico Tico. 62m/B VHS, Beta. Tom Neal, Margaret Lindsay, Don Douglas, Isabelita, Dorothy Morris, Ernest Truex; **D:** Edgar G. Ulmer. *SNC*

Club Life ♂ 1986 (R) A hardened biker finds sex, drugs, and violence on the Hollywood streets. What did he expect? Peace, love, and understanding? 93m/C VHS, Beta. Tony Curtis, Dee Wallace Stone, Tom Parsekian, Michael Parks, Jamie Barrett; **D:** Norman Thaddeus Vane. *PAR*

Club Med ♂ 1983 (PG) An insecure comedian and his goofy friend try to make the most of a ski vacation. Perhaps your only chance to see Thicke, Killy, and Coolidge together. 60m/C VHS, Beta. Alan Thicke, Jim Carrey, Jean-Claude Killy, Rita Coolidge, Ronnie Hawkins; **D:** David Mitchell, Bob Giraldi; **M:** Peter Bernstein. *AHV*

Club Paradise ♂♂½ 1986 (PG-13) A Chicago fireman flees the big city for a faltering tropical resort and tries to develop some night life. Somewhat disappointing with Williams largely playing the straight man. Most laughs provided by Martin, particularly when she is assaulted by a shower, and Moranis, who gets lost while windsurfing. 96m/C VHS, Beta, LV, Closed Caption. Robin Williams, Peter O'Toole, Rick Moranis, Andrea Martin, Jimmy Cliff, Brian Doyle-Murray, Twiggy, Eugene Levy, Adolph Caesar, Joanna Cassidy, Mary Gross, Carey Lowell, Robin Duke, Simon Jones; **D:** Harold Ramis; **W:** Harold Ramis, Brian Doyle-Murray; **M:** David Mansfield, Van Dyke Parks. *WAR*

Clubhouse Detectives ♂♂½ 1996 (PG) When Billy witnesses a crime at a neighbor's no one believes him—except his friends, so the clubhouse detectives decide to investigate. 85m/C VHS, LV. Michael Ballem, Michael Galeota, Jimmy Galeota, Suzanne Barnes; **D:** Eric Hendershot. *APX*

Clue ♂♂½ 1985 (PG) The popular boardgame's characters must unravel a night of murder at a spooky Victorian mansion. The entire cast seems to be subsisting on sugar, with wild eyes and frantic movements the order of the day. Butler Curry best survives the uneven script and direction. Warren is appealing too. The theatrical version played with three alternative endings, and the video version shows all three successively. 96m/C VHS, Beta, LV, Closed Caption. Lesley Ann Warren, Tim Curry, Martin Mull, Madeline Kahn, Michael McKean, Christopher Lloyd, Eileen Brennan, Howard Hesseman, Lee Ving, Jane Wiedlin, Colleen Camp, Bill Henderson; **D:** Jonathan Lynn; **W:** Jonathan Lynn, John Landis; **M:** John Morris. *PAR*

Clueless ♂♂♂ *I Was a Teenage Teenager; No Worries* 1995 (PG-13) Watch out "Beverly Hills 90210," here comes Cher. No, not the singer Cher, but ultra-filthy-rich brat Cher, who's out to make over her classmates and teachers, specifically flannel-shirted transfer student Tai (Murphy). Aerosmith vamp Silverstone stars as the teenage manipulator who knows all too well how to spend her trust fund. The only person who can match her wits is disapproving stepbrother Josh (Rudd). (Ah, love.) Loosely based on Jane Austen's "Emma," Heckerling of, "Fast Times at Ridgemont High" fame, knows this territory and directs a bright, surprisingly satirical romp. **CW:** Sex related dialogue; some teen use of alcohol and drugs. 113m/C VHS. Alicia Silverstone, Stacey Dash, Paul Rudd, Brittany Murphy, Donald A. Faison, Julie Brown, Jeremy

Sisto, Dan Hedaya, Wallace Shawn, Breckin Meyer, Elisa Donovan, Aida Linares; **W:** Amy Heckerling; **C:** Amy Heckerling; **C:** Bill Pope; **M:** David Kitay. MTV Movie Awards '96: Best Female Performance (Silverstone), Most Desirable Female (Silverstone); National Society of Film Critics Awards '95: Best Screenplay; Blockbuster Entertainment Awards '96: Female Newcomer, Theatrical (Silverstone); Nominations: MTV Movie Awards '96: Best Film, Best Comedic Performance (Silverstone); Writers Guild of America '95: Best Original Screenplay. *PAR*

The Clutching Hand ♂♂ 1936 The Clutching Hand seeks a formula that will turn metal into gold and detective Craig Kennedy is out to prevent him from doing so. A serial in 15 chapters on three cassettes. 268m/B VHS, Beta. Jack Mulhall, Rex Lease. *SNC, NOS, VDM*

Coach ♂♂½ 1978 (PG) Sexy woman is unintentionally hired to coach a high school basketball team and mold rookies into lusty young champions. Low-grade roundball fever. 100m/C VHS, Beta. Cathy Lee Crosby, Michael Biehn, Keenan Wynn, Sidney Wicks; **D:** Bud Townsend. *MED*

Coal Miner's Daughter ♂♂♂ 1980 (PG) A strong bio of country singer Loretta Lynn, who rose from Appalachian poverty to Nashville riches. Spacek is perfect in the lead, and she even provides acceptable rendering of Lynn's tunes. Band drummer Helm shines as Lynn's father, and Jones is strong as Lynn's downhome husband. Uneven melodrama toward the end, but the film is still a good one. ♫Coal Miner's Daughter; Sweet Dreams of You; I'm a Honky-Tonk Girl; You're Lookin' at Country; One's On the Way; You Ain't Woman Enough to Take My Man; Back in My Baby's Arms. 125m/C VHS, Beta, LV. Sissy Spacek, Tommy Lee Jones, Levon Helm, Beverly D'Angelo; **D:** Michael Apted; **C:** Ralf Bode. Academy Awards '80: Best Actress (Spacek); Golden Globe Awards '81: Best Actress—Musical/Comedy (Spacek), Best Film—Musical/Comedy; Los Angeles Film Critics Association Awards '80: Best Actress (Spacek); National Board of Review Awards '80: 10 Best Films of the Year, Best Actress (Spacek); New York Film Critics Awards '80: Best Actress (Spacek); National Society of Film Critics Awards '80: Best Actress (Spacek); Nominations: Academy Awards '80: Best Adapted Screenplay, Best Art Direction/Set Decoration, Best Cinematography, Best Film Editing, Best Picture, Best Sound. *USH, BTV*

The Coast Patrol ♂♂½ 1925 B. Reeves Eason, responsible for the chariot scene in the silent "Ben Hur" and the action scenes in "The Charge of the Light Brigade," directed Fay in one of her earliest parts, silent years before the role that prompted her to say "I didn't realize that King Kong and I were going to be together for the rest of our lives, and longer... " Much Eason-style high action when smugglers meet the coast patrol. 63m/B VHS, Beta. Kenneth McDonald, Claire De Lorez, Fay Wray; **D:** Bud Barsky. *NOS, GPV, FCT*

Coast to Coast ♂♂ 1980 (PG) A wacky woman escapes from a mental institution and teams with a pugnacious trucker for a cross-country spree. Ostensibly freewheeling comedy is only occasionally worthwhile despite appropriate playing from leads Cannon and Blake, who deserve better. 95m/C VHS, Beta, LV. Dyan Cannon, Robert (Bobby) Blake, Quinn Redeker, Michael Lerner, Maxine Stuart, William Lucking; **D:** Joseph Sargent; **M:** Charles Bernstein. *PAR*

Cobb ♂♂♂ 1994 (R) Biography of Ty Cobb (Jones), the universally acknowledged "most hated man in baseball" who, near the end of his life, realizes he doesn't want to be remembered in that way. So he hires sportswriter Al Stump (Wuhl) to ghostwrite (read: sugarcoat) his life story. As seen through Stump's eyes, Cobb is an unrelenting, petty, bigoted, hateful, paranoid, drunken, and yet compelling man. They form an uneasy bond as Stump duly records the fiction Cobb is feeding him, secretly deciding to write the truth after the legend's death. Jones is at his scene-chewing, antagonistic best, while Wuhl seems both overwhelmed and overshadowed as the embattled

Stump. Shelton has something to say about American hero worship and a celebrity's desire for posterity, but with the focus intent on portraying Cobb's meanness, it's hard to say what. Surprisingly little baseball action for a baseball bio. Based on Stump's "Cobb; A Biography." **CW:** Strong language; scenes of nudity and violent behavior. 128m/C VHS, LV, Closed Caption. Tommy Lee Jones, Robert Wuhl, Lolita Davidovich; **D:** Ron Shelton; **W:** Ron Shelton; **C:** Russell Boyd. *WAR*

Cobra ♂ 1925 To pay off the debts incurred by his profligate playaboyance, Valentino takes a job with an antique dealer, falls for the dealer's secretary and arranges an assignation with the dealer's wife, who is inconveniently killed at the designated rendezvous. Complications abound as Valentino finds himself Sheik out of luck. Lesser Valentino effort was released a year before the famous heartthrob's untimely death and enjoyed a rather acrid critical reception. Which isn't to say the public didn't flock to see the Italian stallion flare his nostrils. 70m/B VHS, Beta. Rudolph Valentino, Nita Naldi, Casson Ferguson, Gertrude Olmsted; **D:** Joseph Henabery. *VYY, FCT, GPV*

The Cobra ♂ *Il Cobra; El Cobra* 1968 A tight-lipped U.S. agent ogles a voluptuous siren when not fighting opium smugglers from the Middle East. A must for all admirers of Ekberg. 93m/C VHS. Dana Andrews, Anita Ekberg; **D:** Mario Sequi. *NO*

Cobra ♂♂½ *le Sant de l'Ange* 1971 A hired killer destroys most of a mob family and becomes the target of revenge for the lone survivor. Moody thriller boasts an international cast. 93m/C VHS, Beta. **FR IT** Sterling Hayden, Senta Berger, Jean Yanne; **D:** Yves Boisset. *UNI*

Cobra ♂ 1986 (R) A cold-blooded cop protects a model from a gang of deranged killers. Lowbrow, manipulative action fare void of feeling. Truly exploitive, with little expression from the leads. Highlight is the extended chase sequence. Based on the Paula Gosling novel "Fair Game," which was remade under the book's title (and in a more faithful adaptation) in 1995. 87m/C VHS, Beta, LV, Closed Caption. Sylvester Stallone, Reni Santoni, Brigitte Nielsen, Andrew (Andy) Robinson; **D:** George P. Cosmatos; **W:** Sylvester Stallone. *WAR*

Cobra Against Ninja ♂ 1987 Once again, two martial arts experts try to kill each other. Can't be many of these fellas left. 88m/C VHS. Jimmy Bosco, Paul Branney, Gary Carter, Alan Friss, Alfred Pears; **D:** Joseph Lai. *IMP*

The Cobra Strikes ♂½ 1948 Nosey thief gets more than he bargained for when he works his way through an inventor's studio. Low-budget and unexceptional. 62m/B VHS. Sheila Ryan, Richard Fraser, Leslie Brooks, Herbert Heyes; **D:** Charles F. Reisner. *NOS, MOV, RXM*

Cobra Woman ♂♂½ 1944 Technicolor adventure fantasy about the jungle queen (Montez) of a cobra-worshiping cult and her evil twin sister who wants the throne for herself. 70m/C VHS. Maria Montez, Jon Hall, Sabu, Edgar Barrier, Lois Collier, Lon Chaney Jr.; **D:** Robert Siodmak; **W:** Richard Brooks; **C:** William Howard Greene. *NO*

The Cobweb ♂♂ 1955 Shady goings on are uncovered at a psychiatric ward run by a bunch of neurotic administrators. A strong cast, director and producer do not add much to this dull outing. 125m/C LV. Lauren Bacall, Richard Widmark, Gloria Grahame, Charles Boyer, Lillian Gish, John Kerr, Susan Strasberg, Oscar Levant, Tommy Rettig, Paul Stewart, Adele Jergens, Bert Freed, Sandy Descher, Fay Wray, Virginia Christine; **D:** Vincente Minnelli. *MGM*

The Coca-Cola Kid ♂♂♂½ 1984 (R) A smug sales executive treks to Australia to improve regional sales and becomes embroiled in sexual and professional shenanigans. Roberts is strong in the difficult lead role, and Scacchi is compelling in an awkwardly constructed part. Ambitious satire is somewhat scattershot, with more storylines than it needs. Still, filmmaker Makavejev is usually capable of juggling the entire enterprise. **94m/C VHS, Beta, LV, Closed Caption.** *AU* Eric Roberts, Greta Scacchi, Bill Kerr; *D:* Dusan Makavejev. *LIV, VES, FCT*

Cocaine Cowboys 🎬½ 1979 (R) Lame rockers support themselves between gigs by peddling drugs then find out they've run afoul of the mob. Palance is the only worthwhile aspect of this rambling venture produced at Andy Warhol's home. **90m/C VHS, Beta.** Jack Palance, Andy Warhol, Tom Sullivan, Suzanna Love; *D:* Ulli Lommel. *MED, OM*

Cocaine Fiends 🎬🎬 *The Pace That Kills* 1936 Drug use leads siblings into a squalid life of addiction, crime, prostitution, and eventually suicide. Ostensibly straight morality tale functions better as loopy camp. Features memorable slang. **74m/B VHS, Beta.** Lois January, Noel Madison; *D:* William O'Connor. *SNC, NOS, MED*

Cocaine: One Man's Seduction 🎬🎬½ 1983 Made-for-television film documents one man's degeneration into drug addiction. Weaver snorts convincingly in lead. **97m/C VHS, Beta.** Dennis Weaver, Karen Grassle, Pamela Bellwood, David Ackroyd; *D:* Paul Wendkos; *M:* Brad Fiedel. *FRH*

Cocaine Wars 🎬 1986 (R) An undercover U.S. agent kills dozens while trying to rescue his kidnapped girlfriend from an evil South American drug tycoon. Violent, but otherwise unaffecting. **82m/C VHS, Beta.** John Schneider, Kathryn Witt, Royal Dano; *D:* Hector Olivera. *MED, VTR*

Cockeyed Cavaliers 🎬🎬 1934 Wheeler and Woolsey are stockaded for stealing the Duke's horses and carriage. To escape jail they swap clothes with some drunken royalty. **70m/B VHS, Beta.** Bert Wheeler, Robert Woolsey, Dorothy Lee, Thelma Todd; *D:* Mark Sandrich. *CCB*

Cockfighter 🎬🎬🎬 *Gamblin' Man; Born to Kill; Wild Drifters* 1974 (R) A unique, grim portrait of a cockfighting trainer. Oates, in the lead, provides voiceover narrations, but the film otherwise remains silent until the end. Strong support from Stanton. Interesting, violent fare. **84m/C VHS, Beta.** Warren Oates, Harry Dean Stanton, Richard B. Shull, Troy Donahue, Millie Perkins; *D:* Monte Hellman; *C:* Nestor Almendros; *M:* Michael Franks.

Cocktail 🎬🎬½ 1988 (R) A smug young man finds fame and fortune as a proficient, flashy bartender, charming the ladies with his bottle and glass juggling act. Slick, superficial film boasts a busy soundtrack and serviceable exchanges between male leads Cruise and Brown. There's less chemistry between Cruise and love interest Shue. Filmed in a high-tech rock video style. **103m/C VHS, Beta, LV, 8mm, Closed Caption.** Tom Cruise, Bryan Brown, Elisabeth Shue, Lisa Banes, Laurence Luckinbill, Kelly Lynch, Gina Gershon, Ron Dean, Paul Benedict; *D:* Roger Donaldson; *W:* Heywood Gould; *C:* Dean Semler; *M:* J. Peter Robinson. Golden Raspberry Awards '88: Worst Picture, Worst Screenplay. *TOU*

The Cocoanuts 🎬🎬½ 1929 In their film debut, the Marx Brothers create their trademark, indescribable mayhem. Stagey, technically crude comedy nonetheless delights with zany, free-for-all exchanges, antics. Includes famous "viaduct" exchange. **96m/B VHS, Beta, LV.** Groucho Marx, Chico Marx, Harpo Marx, Zeppo Marx, Margaret Dumont, Kay Francis, Oscar Shaw, Mary Eaton; *D:* Robert Florey, Joseph Santley; *W:* George S. Kaufman, Morrie Ryskind; *M:* Irving Berlin. *USH*

Cocoon 🎬🎬🎬 1985 (PG-13) Humanist fantasy in which senior citizens discover their fountain of youth is actually a breeding ground for aliens. Heartwarming, one-of-a kind drama showcases elderly greats Ameche, Brimley, Gilford, Cronyn, and Tandy. A commendable, recommendable venture. Based on David Saperstein's novel and followed by "Cocoon: The Return." **117m/C VHS, Beta, LV, Closed Caption.** Wilford Brimley, Brian Dennehy, Steve Guttenberg, Don Ameche, Tahnee Welch, Jack Gilford, Hume Cronyn, Jessica Tandy, Gwen Verdon, Maureen Stapleton, Tyrone Power Jr., Barret Oliver, Linda Harrison, Herta Ware, Clint Howard; *D:* Ron Howard; *W:* Tom Bene-

dek; *M:* James Horner. Academy Awards '85: Best Supporting Actor (Ameche), Best Visual Effects. *FOX, FCT, BTV*

Cocoon: The Return 🎬🎬 1988 (PG) Old timers who left with aliens in "Cocoon" return to earth and face grave problems. Less compelling sequel misses guiding hand of earlier film's director, Ron Howard. Still, most of cast from the original is on board here, and the film has its moments. **116m/C VHS, Beta, LV, Closed Caption.** Don Ameche, Wilford Brimley, Steve Guttenberg, Maureen Stapleton, Hume Cronyn, Jessica Tandy, Gwen Verdon, Jack Gilford, Tahnee Welch, Courteney Cox, Brian Dennehy, Barret Oliver; *D:* Daniel Petrie; *C:* Tak Fujimoto; *M:* James Horner. *FOX*

C.O.D. 🎬 1983 (PG) Bosom buddies must develop advertising campaign for brassiere producer or find their careers are bust. Premise milked for all its worth, so you may want to keep abreast of this one. On the other hand, you may not give a hoot. Oh well, tit for tat. **96m/C VHS, Beta.** Chris Lemmon, Olivia Pascal, Jennifer Richards, Corinne Alphen, Teresa Ganzel, Carole Davis; *D:* Chuck Vincent; *W:* R.J. Marx. *VES, LIV*

Code Name Alpha 🎬🎬 *Red Dragon; A-009 Missione Hong Kong* 1967 You don't have to have a federal case of intelligence to figure out where this FBI story's going and how it's going to get there. Someone's smuggling sophisticated electrical components to the communists, and a team of intelligence agents, including Granger and Schiaffino, hike over to Hong Kong to break up the party. Based on the story "Le Riviere des Trois Jonques" by Georges Godefroy. **89m/C VHS.** *IT GE* Stewart Granger, Rosanna Schiaffino, Harald Juhnke, Paul Klinger, Helga Sommerfeld, Horst Frank; *D:* Ernest Hofbauer. *SNC*

Code Name: Chaos 🎬🎬 *Spies, Lies, and Alibis* 1990 (R) A political spoof featuring a group of renegade spies trying to come up with a get-rich-quick scheme. It involves inventing a global crisis in a small Asian country but the plan comes under the scrutiny of a CIA agent who's not in on the scheme. **CW:** Language. **96m/C VHS.** Robert Loggia, Diane Ladd, David Warner, Alice Krige, Brian Kerwin; *D:* Antony Thomas. *LIV, MOV, LIV*

Code Name: Dancer 🎬 1987 A retired spy leaves her peaceful life, husband and family to take care of business in Cuba. Made for television. **93m/C VHS.** Kate Capshaw, Jeroen Krabbe, Gregory Sierra, Cliff DeYoung. *THV*

Code Name: Diamond Head 🎬 1977 In Hawaii, a secret agent is assigned to retrieve a deadly chemical that has been hidden by a master of disguises. Made for television. **78m/C VHS, Beta.** Roy Thinnes, France Nuyen, Zulu, Ian McShane; *D:* Jeannot Szwarc. *WOV*

Code Name: Emerald 🎬 1985 (PG) WWII drama in which an American agent must stop an enemy spy with knowledge of impending D-Day invasion. Conventional TV fare boasts a fine performance by von Sydow, but Stolz is hopelessly miscast as an adult. Perhaps the only film featuring both Buchholz and Berger. First feature film by NBC-TV network. **95m/C VHS, Beta, LV, Closed Caption.** Ed Harris, Max von Sydow, Eric Stoltz, Horst Buchholz, Helmut Berger, Cyrielle Claire, Patrick Stewart, Graham Crowden; *D:* Jonathan Sanger; *W:* Ronald Bass; *M:* John Addison. *FOX*

Code Name: Zebra 🎬½ 1984 The Zebra Force helps the cops put bad guys away. When the bad guys get out, they want revenge. The result: lots of violence and action. Wasn't released theatrically. **96m/C VHS, Beta.** Jim Mitchum, Mike Lane, Tim Brown, Joe Dante, Deana Jurgens, Frank Sinatra Jr.; *D:* Joe Tornatore. *TWE*

Code of Honor 🎬🎬½ *Sweet Revenge* 1984 A young woman vows revenge on the military commanders who caused her brother's demise. Neatly made psychological thriller is surprisingly good for a TV movie. **105m/C VHS.** Kevin Dobson, Wings Hauser, Alec Baldwin, Merritt Butrick, Kelly McGillis,

Alfre Woodard, Savannah Smith, Helen Hunt, Dana Elcar; *D:* David Green. *XVC, VTR*

Code of Honor 🎬 1988 Prominent businessman embarks on mission of revenge when police fail to apprehend his wife's rapist. No surprise here. You either enjoy this sort of thing or you lead a reasonably fulfilling life. **90m/C VHS.** Cameron Mitchell, Mark Sabin. *NO*

Code of Silence 🎬🎬 1985 (R) A police loner must contend with both a gang war and police department corruption. Hectic, violent action-drama with some wild stunts. **100m/C VHS, Beta, LV.** Chuck Norris, Henry Silva, Bert Remsen, Molly Hagan, Nathan Davis, Dennis Farina; *D:* Andrew Davis; *W:* Michael Butler, Mike Gray. *NO*

Code of the Fearless 🎬 1939 A cowboy wins the heart of a beautiful maiden while bringing evildoers to justice. **56m/B VHS.** Fred Scott, Claire Rochelle, John Merton, Harry Harvey, Walter McGrail, Roger Williams; *D:* Raymond K. Johnson. *NOS, DVT*

Codename: Foxfire 🎬🎬 *Slay It Again, Sam* 1985 An attractive secret agent is framed for wrongdoing and must clear her name by tracking the enemy spy lurking within the intelligence network. Always interesting Cassidy is an asset, but this by-the-numbers TV film is otherwise a misappropriation of the term "intelligence" in relation to espionage. **99m/C VHS, Beta.** Joanna Cassidy, John McCook, Sheryl Lee Ralph, Henry Jones, Luke Andreas; *D:* Corey Allen. *USH*

Codename: Icarus 🎬🎬 1985 A young mathematical genius, enrolled at a special school for accelerated study uncovers evil government plots to use the students for espionage. Made for British television. **106m/C VHS, Beta, Closed Caption.** *GB* Barry Angel, Jack Galloway; *D:* Marilyn Fox. *FOX, TVC, VCO*

Codename Kyril 🎬🎬½ 1991 (R) Woodward plays a British spy pitted against Soviet assassin Kyril (Charleson) who's been sent to England by the KGB to rout out a double agent. Turns out there's more to it than Kyril knows, and nobody loves an assassin. Based on John Trenhaile's "A Man Called Kyril," the script is slow from the gun, but eventually builds something akin to momentum. Made for cable TV. **115m/C VHS.** Edward Woodward, Ian Charleson, Denholm Elliott, Joss Ackland, Richard E. Grant, Sven-Bertil Taube, Catherine Nielson, John McEnery, Peter Vaughan, James Laurenson; *D:* Ian Sharp; *W:* John Hopkins. *TTC*

Codename: Terminate 🎬½ 1990 Title says it all in this tender exploration of the human condition. Jungle-trained mercenaries grab their guns and go after an American pilot shot down behind enemy lines. **84m/C VHS.** Robert Mason, Jim Gaines. *NO*

Codename: Vengeance 🎬 1987 (R) A macho fellow tries to stop a killer holding the shah's wife and son hostage. Dated. **97m/C VHS.** Robert Ginty, Cameron Mitchell, Shannon Tweed; *D:* David Winters. *VTR, MCG*

Codename: Wildgeese 🎬½ *Geheimecode Wildganse* 1984 (R) The big-name cast of this meandering mercenary macho-rama probably wish they'd been credited under code names; solid histrionics cannot a silly script save. A troop of commandos-for-hire are engaged by the Drug Enforcement Administration to obliterate an opium operation in Asia's infamous Golden Triangle, and much mindless agitation ensues. **101m/C VHS.** *IT GE* Lewis Collins, Lee Van Cleef, Ernest Borgnine, Klaus Kinski, Mimsy Farmer; *D:* Anthony (Antonio Margheriti) Dawson. *VTR, NWV*

Cody 🎬 1967 A former bronco buster wants his son to "take it like a man" when the boy's dog dies. Then a mystical goose arrives to mellow the old man. That's really the plot. **82m/C VHS, Beta.** Tony Becker, Terry Evans. *NO*

A Coeur Joie 🐾🐾 *Two Weeks in September* **1967** Sixties set piece about a gorgeous woman who must choose between her much older lover or her newfound stud. Bardot and U.K. scenery keep this one from sinking entirely. In French with English subtitles. 100m/C VHS, Beta. **FR** Brigitte Bardot, Laurent Terzieff; **D:** Serge Bourguignon. *BAR*

Coffy 🐾🐾 **1973 (R)** A beautiful woman feigns drug addiction to discover and destroy the evil dealers responsible for her sister's death. Grier is everything in this exploitative flick full of violence and nudity. 91m/C VHS, Beta, LV. Pam Grier, Booker Bradshaw, Robert DoQui, Allan Arbus; **D:** Jack Hill; **M:** Roy Ayers. *ORI, FCT*

Cohen and Tate 🐾🐾 **1988 (R)** Two antagonistic mob hitmen kidnap a 9-year-old who witnessed his parent's recent murder by the mob. In order to survive, the boy begins to play one psycho off the other. 113m/C VHS, Beta, LV, Closed Caption. Roy Scheider, Adam Baldwin, Harley Cross, Cooper Huckabee; **D:** Eric Red; **M:** Bill Conti. *NLC*

Cold Blood 🐾½ **197?(R)** A small dubbed Dutch film about a pair of kidnap victims who turn the tables on their captors. 90m/C VHS, Beta. **NL** Rutger Hauer. *SIM*

Cold Comfort 🐾🐾½ **1990 (R)** A father arranges his teen daughter's romance, but finds his plans going awry in this Canadian thriller. Nominated for several Canadian television awards, including Best Actress, Best Actor, Best Picture and Best Musical Score. 90m/C VHS. **CA** Margaret Langrick, Maury Chaykin; **D:** Vic Sarin. *REP*

Cold Comfort Farm 🐾🐾🐾 **1994 (PG)** Stella Gibbons classic 1932 comedic novel is brought to life in this TV adaptation, which finds orphaned London lass Flora Poste (Beckinsdale) trying to take charge of the lives of her very odd country cousins, the Starkadders. The rowdy family and their dilapidated farm are putty in practical Flora's hands as she works to make everybody happy (including herself). Terrific ensemble cast, with a fast pace and wicked humor. 104m/C VHS, LV, Closed Caption. **GB** Kate Beckinsale, Eileen Atkins, Ian McKellen, Sheila Burrell, Rufus Sewell, Maria Miles, Freddie Jones, Ivan Kaye, Miriam Margolyes, Joanna Lumley, Stephen Fry, Christopher Bowen; **D:** John Schlesinger; **W:** Malcolm Bradbury; **C:** Chris Seager; **M:** Robert Lockhart. *USH*

Cold Days 🐾🐾½ **1966** Four men await execution for their part in the WWII massacre of Jews and Serbs. Their reminiscences and justifications, if any, are examined. Stunning cinematography and unusual theme for 1960s Hungarian political climate. 102m/C VHS. **HU D:** Andras Kovacs. *FCT*

Cold Eyes of Fear 🐾 **197?** A man and his girlfriend are besieged by a raving convict whom his uncle, a judge, had put away years before. Shades of "Cape Fear" on a low budget. 88m/C VHS, Beta. Fernando Rey, Frank Wolfe, Karin Schubert; **D:** Enzo G. Castellari; **M:** Ennio Morricone. *TWE*

Cold Feet 🐾🐾½ **1984 (PG)** Light romantic comedy about a television director just recovering from a failed marriage and his fall for a lab researcher who just went through a break-up herself. 96m/C VHS, Beta, Closed Caption. Griffin Dunne, Marissa Chibas, Blanche Baker, Mark Cronogue; **D:** Bruce Van Dusen. *FOX*

Cold Feet 🐾🐾½ **1989 (R)** Modern-day western in which a trio of loopy desperados smuggle jewels inside a racehorse's stomach. Quirky comedy offers wild performances from Waits and sexbomb Kirkland, but could use a few more laughs. Filmed largely on McGuane's ranch. 94m/C VHS, Beta, LV. Keith Carradine, Tom Waits, Sally Kirkland, Rip Torn, Kathleen York, Bill Pullman, Vincent Schiavelli, Jeff Bridges; **D:** Robert Dornhelm; **W:** Thomas McGuane, Jim Harrison; **C:** Bryan Duggan; **M:** Tom Bahler. *LIV*

Cold Fever 🐾🐾 **1995** Japanese yuppie Atsushi Hirata (Nagase) is expecting to vacation in the tropical paradise of Hawaii not the frozen reaches of Iceland. But instead he must perform a memorial ritual on the remote Icelandic spot where his parents died some time before. He arrives in a blizzard and things just go downhill from there. Some quirky characters but the film loses focus. 85m/C VHS. **IC** Masatoshi Nagase, Gisli Halldorsson, Lili Taylor, Fisher Stevens; **D:** Fridrik Thor Fridriksson; **W:** Fridrik Thor Fridriksson, Jim Stark; **M:** Hilmar Orn Hilmarsson. *FXL*

Cold Front 🐾½ **1989 (R)** A hired assassin turned serial killer is hunted by two dedicated cops. 94m/C VHS, Beta, LV. **CA** Martin Sheen, Michael Ontkean, Beverly D'Angelo, Kim Coates; **D:** Allan Goldstein; **C:** Thomas Burstyn. *HBO*

Cold Heat 🐾🐾 **1990** When a custody battle rocks a crime boss' world, he pulls out all the stops in the war against his wife. 85m/C VHS, Beta. John Phillip Law, Britt Ekland, Robert Sacchi, Roy Summerset, Joanne Watkins, Chance Michael Corbitt; **D:** Ulli Lommel. *AIP*

Cold Heaven 🐾½ **1992 (R)** Alex and Marie Davenport are on vacation when an accident occurs and Alex dies—or does he? The next day his body disappears and his unfaithful wife begins to have paranoid delusions that he is returning to exact retribution for her affair. But these aren't her only visions, for during the past year Marie has also had religious visions she believes are part of a personal battle with God. Harmon does what he can with his role as the alleged corpse but Russell is uncharacteristically whiny and bland. Convoluted story of marriage, death, and spirituality; doesn't pan out on any accounts. Based on a novel by Brian Moore.**CW:** Language and sensuality. 103m/C VHS, LV, Closed Caption. Theresa Russell, Mark Harmon, James Russo, Talia Shire, Will Patton, Richard Bradford; **D:** Nicolas Roeg; **W:** Allan Scott. *HMD, FCT*

Cold Justice 🐾 **1989 (R)** An ex-prizefighter (Daltrey) and his friends welcome an English priest into their tough southside Chicago neighborhood. The good father seems too good to be true as he befriends the locals—even raising funds for the children's hospital. When the funds never make it to the hospital and the neighborhood begins to experience a number of violent tragedies, the residents decide to take their own revenge.**CW:** Language. 106m/C VHS, LV. Dennis Waterman, Roger Daltrey, Penelope Milford, Ron Dean, Bert Rosario; **D:** Terry Green; **W:** Terry Green. *COL*

Cold Light of Day 🐾🐾 **1995** Police officer Victor Marek (Grant) is hunting a serial killer of young children in the English countryside—and he'll do anything, including using a young girl as bait. Marek seduces single mother Milena (Baxter) to use her young daughter to set a trap for the killer but can he catch the madman before it's too late? 101m/C VHS. **GB** Richard E. Grant, Lynsey Baxter, Heathcote Williams; **D:** Rudolf Van Den Berg. *PGV*

Cold River 🐾🐾½ **1981 (PG)** An experienced guide takes his two children on an extended trip through the Adirondacks. For the children, it's a fantasy vacation until their father succumbs to a heart attack in the chilly mountains. "Cold River" is a journey of survival, and an exploration of human relationships. 94m/C VHS, Beta. Pat Petersen, Richard Jaeckel, Suzanne Weber; **D:** Fred G. Sullivan. *FOX*

Cold Room 🐾½ *The Prisoner* **1984** College student on vacation with her father in East Berlin discovers the horrors hidden in an antiquated hotel room next to hers. Made for cable television. From the novel by Jeffrey Caine. 95m/C VHS, Beta. George Segal, Renee Soutendijk, Amanda Pays, Warren Clarke, Anthony Higgins; **D:** James Dearden; **M:** Michael Nyman. *FOX*

Cold Sassy Tree 🐾🐾🐾½ **1989** Endearing romance of a scandalous May-December marriage as perceived by the younger woman's teenage son. Dunaway and Widmark shine, and small town pettiness is vividly rendered. Adapted from the books by Olive Ann Burns. A superior made-for-cable production. 95m/C VHS. Faye Dunaway, Richard Widmark, Neil Patrick Harris, Frances Fisher,

Lee Garlington, John M. Jackson; **D:** Joan Tewkesbury; **W:** Joan Tewkesbury; **M:** Brad Fiedel. *TTC*

Cold Steel 🐾½ **1987 (R)** Standard revenge drama about a hardnosed Los Angeles cop tracking his father's disfigured psycho-killer. Cast includes the always intense Davis, ex-pop star Ant, and screen scorchstress Stone. Still it's predictable, low-grade fare. 91m/C VHS, Beta. Brad Davis, Jonathan Banks, Adam Ant, Sharon Stone; **D:** Dorothy Ann Puzo. *COL*

Cold Steel for Tortuga 🐾 **1965** An Italian epic about a mercenary rescuing his woman and his gold from an evil governor. Dubbed. 95m/C VHS, Beta. **IT** Guy Madison, Rik Battaglia, Ingeborg Schoener; **D:** Luigi Capuano. *NO*

Cold Sweat 🐾🐾 *L'Uomo Dalle Due Ombre; De la Part des Copains* **1974 (PG)** A brutal drug trader takes his ultra-violent revenge after his wife is captured by a drug boss' moronic henchmen. Typical Bronson flick boasts superior supporting cast of Ullmann and Mason. Writing and direction, however, are mediocre. 94m/C VHS, Beta. **IT FR** Charles Bronson, Jill Ireland, Liv Ullmann, James Mason; **D:** Terence Young. *GEM, MRV*

Cold Sweat 🐾🐾 **1993 (R)** A professional hit man (Cross) is literally haunted by the ghost of his last victim (who happens to be female and usually appears naked), so he decides his next assignment will be his last. A ruthless businessman suspects his very sexy wife (Tweed) has been unfaithful but she has lots of other secrets to hide.**CW:** Language, violence, and strong sexuality. 93m/C VHS, Beta, Closed Caption. Ben Cross, Shannon Tweed, Adam Baldwin, Dave Thomas; **D:** Gail Harvey; **W:** Richard Beattie. *PAR, VTR*

Cold Turkey 🐾🐾🐾 **1971 (PG)** Often witty satire about what happens when an entire town tries to stop smoking for a contest. Van Dyke is fine as the anti-smoking minister; newscasters Bob and Ray are riotous; oldtimer Horton's swansong. Wholesome, somewhat tame fare. 99m/C VHS, Beta, LV. Dick Van Dyke, Pippa Scott, Tom Poston, Bob Newhart, Vincent Gardenia, Barnard Hughes, Jean Stapleton, Graham Jarvis, Edward Everett Horton; **D:** Norman Lear; **W:** Norman Lear; **M:** Randy Newman. *MGM*

Cold War Killers 🐾½ **1986 (PG)** Soviet and British agents vie for control of prized cargo plane recently retrieved from the sea floor. 85m/C VHS, Beta. **GB** Terence Stamp; **D:** William Brayne. *NO*

Coldblooded 🐾½ **1994 (R)** Minor mob flunky (and dim bulb) Cosmo (Priestley) is unwillingly promoted to the position of hit man by his mobster boss. He's tutored by the organization's primo professional (Riegert) and finds out he has a real knack for murder. More sophomoric than satiric and a waste of Riegert's talents; Williams is attractive as Priestley's clueless girlfriend. Directorial debut of Wolodarsky.**CW:** Some graphic violence, sexual dialogue and language. 92m/C VHS. Jason Priestley, Peter Riegert, Kimberly Williams, Robert Loggia, Janeane Garofalo, Josh Charles, David Anthony Higgins, Doris Grau; **Cameos:** Talia Balsam, Michael J. Fox; **D:** M. Wallace Wolodarsky; **W:** M. Wallace Wolodarsky; **C:** Robert Yeoman; **M:** Steve Bartek. *PGV*

Coldfire 🐾½ **1990** Two rookie cops work to undo the havoc unleashed on the streets of LA because of a deadly new drug sought for its powerful high. Not many surprises here. 90m/C VHS, LV. Wings Hauser, Kamar Reyes, Robert Viharo, Gary Swanson; **D:** Wings Hauser. *PMH*

The Colditz Story 🐾🐾½ **1955** Prisoners of war from the Allied countries join together in an attempt to escape from Colditz, an allegedly escape-proof castle-prison deep within the Third Reich. 93m/B VHS, Beta. John Mills, Eric Portman, Lionel Jeffries, Bryan Forbes, Ian Carmichael, Anton Diffring; **D:** Guy Hamilton. *REP, CNG*

Cole Justice 🐾🐾 **1989** An older man, haunted by the memory of his girlfriend's rape and murder thirty-five years earlier, takes to the streets to protect innocent citizens from lowlife criminals. Somewhat unusual revenge pic filmed in and around Tulsa, Oklahoma. **90m/C VHS, Beta.** Carl Bartholomew, Keith Andrews, Mike Wiles, Nick Zickefoose; **D:** Carl Bartholomew. **NO**

The Collector 🐾🐾🐾½ 1965 Compelling adaptation of the John Fowles novel about a withdrawn butterfly collector who decides to add to his collection by kidnapping a beautiful girl he admires. He locks her in his cellar hoping she will fall in love with him. Chilling, unsettling drama with Stamp unnerving, yet sympathetic in lead. **119m/C VHS, Beta, LV.** *GB* Terence Stamp, Samantha Eggar, Maurice Dallimore, Mona Washbourne; **D:** William Wyler; **C:** Robert Krasker, Robert L. Surtees; **M:** Maurice Jarre. Cannes Film Festival '65: Best Actor (Stamp), Best Actress (Eggar); Golden Globe Awards '66: Best Actress—Drama (Eggar); Nominations: Academy Awards '65: Best Actress (Eggar), Best Adapted Screenplay, Best Director (Wyler).*COL*

Collector's Item 🐾🐾🐾 1989 Two lovers reunite after 16 years and a flurry of memories temporarily rekindles their passion, which comes dangerously close to obsession. Casting of the physically bountiful Antonelli helps this effective erotic drama. **99m/C VHS, Beta.** *IT* Laura Antonelli, Florinda Bolkan; **D:** Giuseppe Patroni Griffi. *NO*

College 🐾🐾🐾½ 1927 A high school valedictorian tries out for every sport in college, hoping to win the girl. Vintage Keaton antics, including disaster as a soda jerk, an attempt to be a track star, and the pole vault through a window to rescue the damsel in distress. **60m/B VHS, Beta, LV.** Buster Keaton, Anne Cornwall, Harold Goodwin; **D:** James W. Horne; **M:** John Muri. *DVT, MRV, CCB*

College Swing 🐾½ *Swing, Teacher, Swing* 1938 Lightweight, lackluster musical about Allen inheriting a small town college which she turns into a hangout for her vaudeville pals. Top cast is basically wasted performing many forgettable songs and familiar routines. Based on an adaptation by Frederick Hazlitt Brennan from a story by Ted Lesser. ♫College Swing; What Did Romeo Say to Juliet?; I Fall In Love With You Every Day; You're a Natural; The Old School Bell; Moments Like This; How D'ja Like to Love Me?; What a Rumba Does to Romance. **86m/B VHS, Closed Caption.** George Burns, Gracie Allen, Martha Raye, Bob Hope, Edward Everett Horton, Ben Blue, Betty Grable, Jackie Coogan, John Payne; **D:** Raoul Walsh. *USH, BTV*

Collision Course 🐾 1989 (PG) A wisecracking cop from Detroit teams up with Japan's best detective to nail a ruthless gang leader. Release was delayed until 1992 due to a lawsuit, but it was resolved in time to coordinate the release with Leno's debut as the host of "The Tonight Show." Pretty marginal, but diehard fans of Leno may appreciate it. Filmed on location in Detroit. **99m/C VHS, Beta, LV, Closed Caption.** Noriyuki "Pat" Morita, Jay Leno, Chris Sarandon, Al Waxman; **D:** Lewis Teague. *HBO*

The Colombian Connection 🐾½ 1991 America's best undercover agent battles a powerful cocaine empire deep in the jungles of the Amazon, where slave labor and political corruption abound. **90m/C VHS, Beta.** Miles O'Keeffe, Henry Silva. *NO*

Colonel Chabert 🐾🐾 1994 In the 1807 Battle of Eylau, French officer Chabert (Depardieu) is thought dead and stripped of all he possesses. After 10 years of imprisonment, a man shows up in the office of Paris lawyer Derville (Luchini), claiming to be the dead Chabert. His remarried wife (Ardant), now the Countess Ferraud, has used his fortune to bolster the political aspirations of her second husband (Dussolier) and refuses to acknowledge this stranger's claims. Is Chabert a fraud? And what exactly are the motives of all the players? Based on the novel by Honore de Balzac. Directorial debut of Angelo. French with subtitles. **111m/C VHS.** *FR* Gerard Depardieu, Fanny Ardant, Fabrice Luchini, Andre Dussollier; **D:** Yves Angelo; **W:** Yves Angelo, Jean Cosmos, Veronique Lagrange; **C:** Bernard Lutic. Nominations: Cesar Awards '94: Best Actor (Depardieu). *REP*

Colonel Effingham's Raid 🐾🐾½ *Man of the Hour* 1945 A retired army colonel uses military tactics to keep an old historical courthouse open, while defeating some crooked politicians in the process. **70m/B VHS, Beta.** Joan Bennett, Charles Coburn, William Eythe, Donald Meek; **D:** Irving Pichel. *NOS, HEG*

Colonel Redl 🐾🐾🐾🐾 1984 (R) Absorbing, intricately rendered psychological study of an ambitious officer's rise and fall in pre-WWI Austria. Brandauer is excellent as the vain, insecure homosexual ultimately undone by his own ambition and his superior officer's smug loathing. Muller-Stahl and Landgrebe are particularly distinguished among the supporting players. The second in the Szabo/Brandauer trilogy, after "Mephisto" and before "Hanussen." In German with English subtitles. **114m/C VHS, Beta, LV.** *GE HU* Klaus Maria Brandauer, Armin Mueller-Stahl, Gudrun Landgrebe, Jan Niklas, Hans-Christian Blech, Laszlo Mensaros, Andras Balint; **D:** Laszlo Szabo; **C:** Lajos Koltai. British Academy Awards '85: Best Foreign Film; Cannes Film Festival '85: Special Jury Prize; Nominations: Academy Awards '85: Best Foreign Language Film. *FCT, GLV, TPV*

Colonel Wolodyjowski 🐾🐾½ 1969 An adaptation of the monumental novels by Henryk Sinkiewicz chronicling the attack on Poland's eastern border by the Turks in 1668. In Polish with English subtitles. **160m/C VHS.** *PL* Tadeusz Loniski, Magdalena Zawadzka, Daniel Olbrychski; **D:** Jerzy Hoffman. *FCT*

The Colony 🐾🐾½ 1995 (PG-13) "The Colony" is a luxurious and exclusive gated community owned by secretive billionaire developer Phillip Denning (Linden). Newest residents, security expert Rick Knowlton (Ritter), wife Leslie (Keller) and their two children, find out things are just too good to be true—and that trying to leave could be the very last thing they'll ever do. **CW:** Some violence. **93m/C VHS, Closed Caption.** John Ritter, Hal Linden, Mary Page Keller, Marshall Teague, Frank Bonner, Michelle Scarabelli, June Lockhart, Todd Jeffries, Alexandra Picatto, Cody Dorkin; **D:** Rob Hedden; **W:** Rob Hedden. *USH*

Color Me Blood Red woof! *Model Massacre* 1964 Artist decides that the red in his paintings is best rendered with human blood. He even manages to continue his art career—when not busy stabbing and mutilating the unsuspecting citizenry. Short and shoddy. Also known as "Model Massacre." **74m/C VHS, Beta.** Don Joseph, Sandi Conder; **D:** Herschell Gordon Lewis. *NO*

Color Me Dead 🐾½ 1969 (R) A victim of an extremely slow-acting poison frantically spends his final days trying to uncover his killer. Another inferior remake of B-thriller "D.O.A." Rent that one instead. **97m/C VHS.** *AU* Tom Tryon, Carolyn Jones, Rick Jason, Patricia Connolly, Tony Ward; **D:** Eddie Davis. *REP*

Color of a Brisk and Leaping Day 🐾🐾 1995 While living in L.A. at the end of WWII, Chinese-American John Lee (Alexander) learns that the Yosemite Valley Railroad is being scrapped and he becomes determined to save it—in part as a homage to his grandfather who emigrated to work as a railroad laborer. A romantic train fanatic himself, Lee arranges financing from wealthy businessman Pinchot (Diehl) but must make the railroad pay within a year—unlikely as the automobile rapidly takes over as preferred transportation. Well-captures a '40s atmosphere but pacing and dialogue are uneven. **87m/B VHS.** Peter Alexander, Jeri Arredondo, Henry Gibson, Michael Stipe, John Diehl, David Chung, Diana Larkin, Bok Yun Chon; **D:** Christopher Munch; **W:** Christopher Munch; **C:** Rob Sweeney. Sundance Film Festival '96: Best Cinematography; Nominations: Independent Spirit Awards '97: Best Cinematography. *NYR*

The Color of Evening 🐾🐾 1995 Aging painter Landau tries to regain his youth by pursuing his young model Skye, but it's the older Burstyn who really inspires his imagination. **?m/C VHS.** Martin Landau, Ellen Burstyn, Ione Skye. *YHV*

The Color of Money 🐾🐾🐾 1986 (R) Flashy, gripping drama about former pool hustler Fast Eddie Felsen (Newman) who, after years off the circuit, takes a brilliant but immature pool shark (Cruise) under his wing. Strong performances by Newman as the grizzled veteran, Cruise as the showboating youth, and Mastrantonio and Shaver as the men's worldly girlfriends. Worthy sequel to "The Hustler." **119m/C VHS, Beta, LV.** Paul Newman, Tom Cruise, Mary Elizabeth Mastrantonio, Helen Shaver, John Turturro, Forest Whitaker; **D:** Martin Scorsese; **W:** Richard Price; **C:** Michael Ballhaus. Academy Awards '86: Best Actor (Newman); National Board of Review Awards '86: Best Actor (Newman); Nominations: Academy Awards '86: Best Adapted Screenplay, Best Art Direction/Set Decoration, Best Supporting Actress (Mastrantonio). *TOU, BTV*

Color of Night 🐾½ 1994 (R) Psychologist Dr. Bill Capa (Willis) takes over a murdered colleague's therapy group hoping to find out the killer's identity. Then he meets temptress Rose (March) and gets involved in a hot affair, but she's not what she seems—nor is anyone else. Preposterous thriller fails to deliver necessary suspense although the eroticism could spark some interest, particularly in the director's cut, which puts the sex back in the sex scenes between Willis and March (and is 15 minutes longer than the theatrical release). **136m/C VHS.** Bruce Willis, Jane March, Scott Bakula, Ruben Blades, Lesley Ann Warren, Lance Henriksen, Kevin J. O'Connor, Andrew Lowery, Brad Dourif, Eriq La Salle, Jeff Corey, Shirley Knight, Kathleen Wilhoite; **D:** Richard Rush; **W:** Matthew Chapman, Billy Ray, Richard Rush; **M:** Dominic Frontiere. Golden Raspberry Awards '94: Worst Picture; Nominations: Golden Globe Awards '95: Best Song ("The Color of the Night"); Golden Raspberry Awards '94: Worst Actor (Willis). *HPH*

The Color of Pomegranates 🐾🐾🐾 *Sayat Nova; Tsvet Granata* 1969 Paradjanov's depiction of the life of Armenian poet Arutiun Sayadin, known as Sayat Nova, who rises from carpet weaver to court minstrel to archbishop. Eloquent imagery and symbols are derived from Armenian paintings, poetry and history. In Armenian with English subtitles. Also includes "Hagop Hovnatanian," a 12-minute short on the artist. **80m/C VHS.** *RU* Sofiko Chiaureli, M. Aleksanian, V. Galstian; **D:** Sergei Paradjanov; **W:** Sergei Paradjanov. *NYF, FCT*

The Color Purple 🐾🐾🐾½ 1985 (PG-13) Celie is a poor black girl who fights for her self-esteem when she is separated from her sister and forced into a brutal marriage. Spanning 1909 to 1947 in a small Georgia town, the movie chronicles the joys, pains, and people in her life. Adaptation of Alice Walker's acclaimed book features strong lead from Goldberg (her screen debut), Glover, Avery, and talk-show host Winfrey (also her film debut). It's hard to see director Spielberg as the most suited for this one, but he acquits himself nicely, avoiding the facileness that sometimes flaws his pics. Brilliant photography by Allen Daviau and musical score by Jones (who co-produced) compliment this strong film. **154m/C VHS, Beta, LV, Closed Caption, DVD.** Whoopi Goldberg, Danny Glover, Oprah Winfrey, Margaret Avery, Adolph Caesar, Rae Dawn Chong, Willard Pugh, Akosua Busia; **D:** Steven Spielberg; **C:** Allen Daviau; **M:** Chris Boardman, Quincy Jones. Directors Guild of America Awards '85: Best Director (Spielberg); Golden Globe Awards '86: Best Actress—Drama (Goldberg); National Board of Review Awards '85: 10 Best Films of the Year, Best Actress (Goldberg); Nominations: Academy Awards '85: Best Actress (Goldberg), Best Adapted Screenplay, Best Art Direction/Set Decoration, Best Cinematography, Best Costume Design, Best Makeup, Best Picture, Best Song ("Miss Celie's Blues (Sister)"), Best Supporting Actress (Avery, Winfrey), Best Original Score. *WAR, FCT*

Colorado 🐾½ 1940 Roy tries to find his brother, a Union deserter, during the Civil War. **54m/B VHS, Beta.** Roy Rogers, George "Gabby" Hayes, Milburn Stone; **D:** Joseph Kane. *NOS, MED, DVT*

Colorado Serenade 🐾🐾 1946 Standard oater has Dean, Sharpe and Ates trying to prevent a young outlaw from bullying the local citizenry. Sharpe shows off his athletic prowess, and King provides some laughs. Other than that, it's pretty routine stuff. **68m/C VHS.** Eddie Dean, David Sharpe, Roscoe Ates, Forrest Taylor, Dennis Moore, Warner Richmond, Bob Duncan, Charles "Blackie" King; **D:** Robert Emmett Tansey. *NOS, RXM, HEG*

Colorado Sundown 🐾 1952 A conniving brother and sister attempt to cheat a man out of his inheritance. **67m/B VHS.** Rex Allen, Mary Ellen Kay, Slim Pickens, June Vincent, Koko; **D:** William Witney. *NOS, DVT*

Colors 🐾🐾🐾½ 1988 (R) Vivid, realistic cop drama pairs sympathetic veteran Duvall and trigger-tempered rookie Penn on the gang-infested streets of East Los Angeles. Fine play from leads is one of the many assets in this controversial, unsettling depiction of deadly streetlife. Colorful, freewheeling direction from the underrated Hopper. Rattling rap soundtrack too. Additional footage has been added for video release. **120m/C VHS, Beta, LV, Closed Caption.** Sean Penn, Robert Duvall, Maria Conchita Alonso, Trinidad Silva, Randi Brooks, Grand Bush, Don Cheadle, Rudy Ramos; **D:** Dennis Hopper; **W:** Michael Schiffer; **C:** Haskell Wexler; **M:** Herbie Hancock. *ORI, FCT*

Colossus and the Amazon Queen 🐾½ 1964 Idle gladiators are unwillingly recruited for service to Amazons. Doesn't seem like the worst way to make a living. But lead actor Taylor—so notable in comedies, thrillers, and action flicks—is too good for this sort of thing. Dubbed. **94m/C VHS, Beta, 8mm.** *IT* Rod Taylor, Dorian Gray, Ed Fury. *VYY*

Colossus of the Arena 🐾🐾 1960 In 4th century Rome, Forest plays a mighty gladiator who uncovers a plot to imprison a beautiful princess. Through an incredible series of feats and combats, he exposes an evil duke as a traitor. **?m/C VHS.** Mark Forest, Scilla Gabel. *SNC*

Colossus: The Forbin Project 🐾🐾🐾 *The Forbin Project* 1970 A computer designed to manage U.S. defense systems teams instead with its Soviet equal and they attempt world domination. Wire-tight, suspenseful film seems at once dated yet timely. Based on the novel by D.F. Jones. **100m/C VHS, Beta.** Eric (Hans Gudegast) Braeden, Susan Clark, Gordon Pinsent, William Schallert, Georg Stanford Brown; **D:** Joseph Sargent; **W:** James Bridges; **C:** Gene Polito; **M:** Michel Colombier. *USH*

Colt Comrades 🐾🐾 1943 A bad guy's monopoly on water rights is jeopardized when Boyd and Clyde strike water while drilling for oil. Nothing really notable here, except for Bob (Robert) Mitchum and George ("Superman") Reeves in minor roles. **67m/B VHS.** William Boyd, Andy Clyde, Jay Kirby, George Reeves, Gayle Lord, Earle Hodgins, Victor Jory, Douglas Fowley, Herbert Rawlinson, Robert Mitchum; **D:** Lesley Selander. *NOS*

Columbo: Murder By the Book 🐾🐾½ 1971 The rumpled, cigar-smoking television detective investigates the killing of a mystery writer. Scripted by Bochco of "Hill Street Blues" and "L.A. Law" fame. **79m/C VHS, Beta.** Peter Falk, Jack Cassidy, Rosemary Forsyth, Martin Milner; **D:** Steven Spielberg; **W:** Steven Bochco. *USH*

Columbo: Prescription Murder 1967 Falk's debut as the raincoat-clad lieutenant who always has just one more question. In the TV series pilot he investigates the death of a psychiatrist's wife. Rich with subplots. Good mystery fare. **99m/C VHS, Beta.** Peter Falk, Gene Barry, Katherine Justice, William Windom, Nina Foch, Anthony James, Virginia Gregg; **D:** Richard Irving; **W:** Richard Levinson, William Link. *USH*

Coma 🐾🐾🐾 1978 (PG) A doctor discovers murder and corpse-nabbing at her Boston hospital, defies her male bosses, and determines to find out what's going on before more patients die. Exciting, suspenseful fare, with Bujold impressive in lead. Based on the novel by Robin Cook. **113m/C VHS, Beta, LV.** Genevieve Bujold, Michael Douglas, Elizabeth Ashley, Rip Torn, Richard Widmark, Lois Chiles, Hari Rhodes, Tom Selleck, Ed Harris; **D:** Michael Crichton; **W:** Michael Crichton; **M:** Jerry Goldsmith. *MGM*

Comanche Station 🐾🐾½ 1960 Loner Jefferson Cody (Scott) agrees to rescue Mrs. Lowe (Gates), a senator's wife who's been captured by the Comanches. After Cody achieves her rescue, they fall in with outlaw Ben Lane (Akins) and his two young proteges, who insist on accompanying them back to the Lowe homestead, saying that they'll need additional protection. But Cody soon realizes that Lane is after the reward money and is planning an ambush. **73m/C VHS.** Randolph Scott, Nancy Gates, Claude Akins, Skip Homeier, Richard Rust, Rand Brooks; **D:** Budd Boetticher; **W:** Burt Kennedy; **C:** Charles Lawton Jr. *COL*

Comanche Territory 🐾🐾🐾 1950 Western frontiersman Jim Bowie travels to Comanche country and helps the Indians save their land from settlers. Routine oater. Based on a story by Meltzer. **76m/C VHS, Closed Caption.** Maureen O'Hara, MacDonald Carey, Will Geer, Charles Drake; **D:** George Sherman; **W:** Oscar Brodney, Lewis Meltzer. *USH*

The Comancheros 🐾🐾🐾 1961 Texas Ranger Wayne and his prisoner fight with the Comancheros, an outlaw gang who is supplying guns and liquor to the dreaded Comanche Indians. Musical score adds flavor. Last film by Curtiz. **108m/C VHS, Beta, LV, Closed Caption.** John Wayne, Ina Balin, Stuart Whitman, Nehemiah Persoff, Lee Marvin, Bruce Cabot; **D:** Michael Curtiz; **C:** William Clothier; **M:** Elmer Bernstein. *FOX*

Combat! 1962 Morrow and Jason starred in this gritty series about an Army platoon in Europe during the final years of WWII. In "The Bridge at Chalons" Marvin guest stars as a demolitions expert. Additional episodes available. **50m/B VHS, Beta.** Vic Morrow, Rick Jason, Lee Marvin. *GKK, MOV*

Combat Academy 🐾 1986 Weak comedy about two goofballs sent to a military academy to straighten out, but instead turn the academy on its ear with their antics. Unremarkable. **96m/C VHS, LV.** Keith Gordon, Jamie Farr, Sherman Hemsley, John Ratzenberger, Bernie Kopell, Charles Moll; **D:** Neal Israel. *VTR, NWV*

Combat Killers 🐾🐾 1980 A WWII Army captain grabs for individual glory on the battlefield, and jeopardizes the lives of his platoon. **96m/C VHS, Beta.** Paul Edwards, Marlene Dauden, Claude Wilson; **D:** Ken Loring. *MED*

Combat Shock 🐾 *American Nightmares* 1984 (R) A Vietnam veteran returns home and can't cope with the stresses of modern life, including the lowlifes who have been taking over the streets. So he goes after some scum who have been trying to kill him, succeeds, but things don't end well. Familiar plot handled in a conventional manner. **85m/C VHS, Beta.** Ricky Giovinazzo, Nick Nasta, Veronica Stork; **D:** Buddy Giovinazzo. *PSM*

Combination Platter 🐾🐾½ 1993 Anxious young immigrant Robert (Lau), newly arrived from Hong Kong, becomes a waiter at the Szechuan Inn in Queens, New York, where he gets a crash course in American culture and romance (as well as tipping). Gentle comedy works best with little details that ring true: overheard customer conversations, staff banter, the kitchen scenes. Lau's earnest, but effort feels like a series of small vignettes rather than a complete story. Still, a worthy first effort for the then 24-year-old Chan, who directed on a $250,000 budget, using his parents restaurant after hours for a set. **84m/C VHS.** Jeff Lau, Colleen O'Brien, Lester Chan, Thomas S. Hsiung, David Chung, Colin Mitchell, Kenneth Lu, Eleonara Khilberg, James DuMont; **D:** Tony Chan; **W:** Tony Chan, Edwin Baker; **C:** Yoshifumi Hosoya; **M:** Brian Tibbs. Sundance Film Festival '93: Best Screenplay; Nominations: Independent Spirit Awards '94: Best First Feature, Best Screenplay, Best Supporting Actor (Chung). *AVI*

Come Along with Me 🐾🐾½ 1984 A made-for-television adaptation of Shirley Jackson's unfinished novel about a woman who sells all and leaves her hometown when her husband dies, determined to start a new career as a seer. **60m/C VHS, Beta.** Estelle Parsons, Barbara Baxley, Sylvia Sidney; **D:** Joanne Woodward. *MON, KAR*

Come and Get It 🐾🐾🐾 *Roaring Timber* 1936 A classic adaptation of the Edna Ferber novel about a lumber king battling against his son for the love of a woman. Farmer's most important Hollywood role. **99m/B VHS, Beta.** Frances Farmer, Edward Arnold, Joel McCrea, Walter Brennan, Andrea Leeds, Charles Halton; **D:** William Wyler, Howard Hawks. Academy Awards '36: Best Supporting Actor (Brennan); Nominations: Academy Awards '36: Best Film Editing. *HBO, BTV*

Come and See 🐾🐾🐾🐾 *Idi i Smotri; Go and See* 1985 Harrowing, unnerving epic which depicts the horrors of war as a boy soldier roams the Russian countryside during the Nazi invasion. Some overwhelming sequences, including tracer-bullets flashing across an open field. War has rarely been rendered in such a vivid, utterly grim manner. Outstanding achievement from Soviet director Klimov. In Russian with English subtitles. **142m/C VHS.** *RU* Alexei Kravchenko, Olga Mironova, Lubomiras Lauciavicus; **D:** Elem Klimov. *KIV, FCT, TPV*

Come Back, Little Sheba 🐾🐾🐾½ 1952 Unsettling, drama about a worn-out housewife, her abusive, alcoholic husband and a comely boarder who causes further marital tension. The title refers to the housewife's despairing search for her lost dog. Booth, Lancaster, and Moore are all excellent. Based on the play by William Inge, this film still packs an emotional wallop. **99m/B VHS, Beta, LV, Closed Caption.** Burt Lancaster, Shirley Booth, Terry Moore, Richard Jaeckel, Philip Ober, Lisa Golm, Walter Kelley; **D:** Daniel Mann; **C:** James Wong Howe. Academy Awards '52: Best Actress (Booth); Cannes Film Festival '53: Best Actress (Booth); Golden Globe Awards '53: Best Actress—Drama (Booth); New York Film Critics Awards '52: Best Actress (Booth); Nominations: Academy Awards '52: Best Film Editing, Best Supporting Actress (Moore). *PAR, FCT, BTV*

Come Back to the Five & Dime Jimmy Dean, Jimmy Dean 🐾🐾🐾 1982 (PG) Five women convene at a run-down Texas drugstore for a 20-year reunion of a local James Dean fan club. The women recall earlier times and make some stunning revelations. Altman's filming of Ed Graczyk's sometimes funny, sometimes wrenching play proves fine vehicle for the actresses. Cher is probably the most impressive, but Dennis and Black are also memorable. **109m/C VHS, Beta, LV.** Sandy Dennis, Cher, Karen Black, Kathy Bates, Sudie Bond, Marta Heflin; **D:** Robert Altman.

Come Blow Your Horn 🐾🐾🐾 1963 Neil Simon's first major Broadway success is a little less successful in its celluloid wrapper, suffering a bit from a familiar script. Sinatra's a playboy who blows his horn all over town, causing his close-knit New York Jewish family to warp a bit. Dad's not keen on his son's pledge of allegiance to the good life, and kid brother Bill would like to be his sibling's understudy in playboyhood. **115m/C VHS, Beta, Closed Caption.** Frank Sinatra, Lee J. Cobb, Tony Bill, Molly Picon, Barbara Rush, Jill St. John; **D:** Bud Yorkin; **W:** Norman Lear; **C:** William H. Daniels. Nominations: Academy Awards '63: Best Art Direction/Set Decoration (Color). *PAR*

Come On, Cowboys 🐾½ 1937 The Three Mesquiteers rescue an old circus friend from certain death. Part of "The Three Mesquiteers" series. **54m/B VHS, Beta.** Bob Livingston, Ray Corrigan. *MED, DVT*

Come On Danger! 🐾🐾½ 1932 Keene makes his "B" Western debut, out to avenge the death of his brother and battle an outlaw gang. Haydon is forced into a life of crime in order to save her ranch from villain Ellis and only Texas Ranger Keene can set her free. **60m/B VHS.** Tom Keene, Julie Haydon, Roscoe Ates, Robert Ellis, Wade Boteler; **D:** Robert F. "Bob" Hill; **W:** Bennett Cohen. *MOV*

Come On Rangers *♂* 1938 Also called "Come On Ranger." Rogers and his friends go to Texas to avenge the death of a comrade. 54m/B **VHS, Beta.** Roy Rogers, George "Gabby" Hayes. *NOS, DVT, RXM*

Come On Tarzan *♂*½ 1932 Maynard and his trusty horse Tarzan save wild horses from the bad guys who want to turn them into dog food. 60m/B **VHS, Beta.** Ken Maynard. *NOS, VDM, DVT*

Come See the Paradise *♂♂♂* 1990 (R) Jack McGurn (Quaid) takes a job at a movie theatre in Los Angeles' Little Tokyo and falls for owner's daughter Lily (Tomita). They marry, but after the bombing of Pearl Harbor all Japanese-Americans are interned. Told in flashback, the story offers a candid look at the racism implicit in the relocations and the hypocrisy that often lurks beneath the surface of the pursuit of liberty and justice for all. Sometimes melodramatic script indulges a bit too much in the obvious, but the subject is worthwhile, one that has not yet been cast into the vast bin of Hollywood cliches. The cast, apart from Quaid's misguided attempt at seriousness, is excellent. 135m/C **VHS, Beta, LV, Closed Caption.** Dennis Quaid, Tamlyn Tomita, Sab Shimono, Shizuko Hoshi, Stan Egi, Ronald Yamamoto, Akemi Nishino, Naomi Nakano, Brady Tsurutani, Pruitt Taylor Vince, Joe Lisi; *D:* Alan Parker; *W:* Alan Parker; *M:* Randy Edelman. *FOX, FCT, CCB*

Come September *♂♂*½ 1961 American business tycoon Robert Talbot (Hudson) maintains a holiday villa on the Italian Riviera. But the only time he uses the place is the month of September, so when Talbot arrives in July he discovers his enterprising major domo Maurice (Slezak) has been managing the place as a hotel the rest of the year. Talbot finds his home filled with tourists and, to make matters worse, discovers his Italian lover Lisa (Lollobrigida) about to get married. Darin and Dee are the film's romantic ingenues and wound up getting married after filming wrapped; his screen debut. 114m/C **VHS, Closed Caption.** Rock Hudson, Gina Lollobrigida, Sandra Dee, Bobby Darin, Walter Slezak, Joel Grey, Brenda de Banzie; *D:* Robert Mulligan; *W:* Stanley Shapiro, Maurice Richlin; *C:* William H. Daniels; *M:* Hans J. Salter. *USH*

Come to the Stable *♂♂♂* 1949 Warm, delightful story about two French nuns, Young and Holm, who arrive in New England and set about building a children's hospital. Although Catholic in intent, pic demonstrates that faith and tenacity can move mountains. (This film must have been Fox's response to Paramount's "Going My Way" and "The Bells of Saint Mary's.") Based on a story by Clare Boothe Luce. 94m/B **VHS.** Loretta Young, Celeste Holm, Hugh Marlowe, Elsa Lanchester, Regis Toomey, Mike Mazurki; *D:* Henry Koster; *W:* Oscar Millard, Sally Benson; *C:* Joseph LaShelle; *M:* Cyril Mockridge. Nominations: Academy Awards '49: Best Actress (Young), Best Art Direction/Set Decoration (B & W), Best Black and White Cinematography, Best Song ("Through a Long and Sleepless Night"), Best Story, Best Supporting Actress (Holm, Lanchester). *FXV*

The Comeback *♂* *The Day the Screaming Stopped* 1977 A singer attempting a comeback in England finds his wife murdered. 100m/C **VHS, Beta:** *GB* Jack Jones, Pamela Stephenson, David Doyle, Bill Owen, Sheila Keith, Richard Johnson; *D:* Pete Walker. *ORI*

Comeback *♂♂*½ 1983 The story of a disillusioned rock star, played by Eric Burdon (the lead singer of the Animals), who gives up his life in the fast lane and tries to go back to his roots. 105m/C **VHS, Beta.** Eric Burdon; *D:* Christel Bushmann; *M:* Eric Burdon. *MGM*

Comeback Kid *♂♂* 1980 An ex-big league baseball player is conned into coaching an urban team of smarmy street youths, and falls for their playground supervisor. Made for television. 97m/C **VHS, Beta.** John Ritter, Susan Dey; *D:* Peter Levin. *NLC*

The Comedians *♂♂*½ 1967 Disturbing and powerful drama of political intrigue set against the murderous dictatorship of "Papa Doc" Duvalier. Burton plays the cynical owner of a resort hotel with Taylor as his German mistress. Ustinov is great as he does his usual scene-stealing in his role as a South American ambassador married to Taylor. Excellent cast was somewhat held back by sluggish direction and an uninspired script. Based on the novel of the same name by Graham Greene. 148m/C **VHS.** Elizabeth Taylor, Richard Burton, Alec Guinness, Peter Ustinov, Paul Ford, Lillian Gish, Raymond St. Jacques, Zakes Mokae; *D:* Peter Glenville; *W:* Graham Greene. National Board of Review Awards '67: Best Supporting Actor (Ford). *MGM*

The Comedy of Terrors *♂♂♂* 1964 Comedy in which some deranged undertakers take a hands-on approach to insuring their continued employment. Much fun is supplied by the quartet of Price, Lorre, Karloff, and Rathbone, all veterans of the horror genre. 84m/C **VHS, LV.** Vincent Price, Peter Lorre, Boris Karloff, Basil Rathbone, Joe E. Brown, Joyce Jameson; *D:* Jacques Tourneur; *W:* Richard Matheson; *C:* Floyd Crosby; *M:* Les Baxter. *MOV*

Comes a Horseman *♂♂*½ 1978 (PG) Robards is a cattle baron, attempting to gobble up all the oil-rich land his neighbor owns. Neighbor Fonda has the courage to stand up to him, with the help of a WWII veteran and the local old timer Farnsworth, in this slow-moving but intriguing western drama. 119m/C **VHS, Beta.** James Caan, Jane Fonda, Jason Robards Jr., George Grizzard, Richard Farnsworth, Jim Davis, Mark Harmon; *D:* Alan J. Pakula; *W:* Dennis Lynton Clark; *C:* Gordon Willis. National Board of Review Awards '78: 10 Best Films of the Year, Best Supporting Actor (Farnsworth); National Society of Film Critics Awards '78: Best Supporting Actor (Farnsworth); Nominations: Academy Awards '78: Best Supporting Actor (Farnsworth). *MGM*

Comfort and Joy *♂♂*½ 1984 (PG) After his kleptomaniac girlfriend deserts him, a Scottish disc jockey is forced to reevaluate his life. He becomes involved in an underworld battle between two mob-owned local ice cream companies. Another odd comedy gem from Forsyth, who did "Gregory's Girl" and "Local Hero". Music by Dire Straits guitarist Knopfler. 93m/C **VHS, Beta.** *GB* Bill Paterson, Eleanor David, C.P. Grogan, Alex Norton, Patrick Malahide, Rikki Fulton, Roberto Berrardi; *D:* Bill Forsyth; *C:* Chris Menges; *M:* Mark Knopfler. National Society of Film Critics Awards '84: Best Cinematography. *USH*

The Comfort of Strangers *♂♂♂* 1991 (R) Atmospheric psychological thriller. Mary and Colin (Richardson and Everett), a handsome young British couple, take a Venetian holiday to rediscover the passion in their relationship. Lost in the city, they chance, it seems, upon Robert (Walken), a sort of Virgil in an Italian suit. He later reappears and, abetted by his wife Caroline (Mirren), gradually leads the couple on an eerie tour of urbane decadence that hints at danger. Psychologically tantalizing and horrifyingly erotic, the movie's based on Ian McEwan's novel. *CW:* Obsessive and perverse sexuality. 102m/C **VHS, Beta, Closed Caption.** Christopher Walken, Natasha Richardson, Rupert Everett, Helen Mirren; *D:* Paul Schrader; *W:* Harold Pinter; *C:* Dante Spinotti; *M:* Angelo Badalamenti. *PAR, FCT*

The Comic *♂♂♂* 1969 (PG) Van Dyke is terrific as a silent screen comedian (a composite of several real-life screen comics) whose ego destroys his career. Recreations of silent films, and the blend of comedy and pathos, are especially effective. 96m/C **VHS, Beta, LV.** Dick Van Dyke, Mickey Rooney, Michele Lee, Cornel Wilde, Nina Wayne, Pert Kelton, Jeannine Riley; *D:* Carl Reiner; *W:* Carl Reiner. *COL*

The Comic *♂* 1985 In a future police state, a young comedian kills the star and takes his place in the show. His future rises, but who cares? 90m/C **VHS, Beta.** Steve Munroe, Bernard Plant, Jeff Pirie; *D:* Richard Driscoll. *NO*

Comic Book Kids *♂*½ 1982 (G) Two youngsters enjoy visiting their friend's comic strip studio, since they have the power to project themselves into the cartoon stories. Viewers will be less impressed. 90m/C **VHS, Beta.** Joseph Campanella, Mike Darnell, Robyn Finn, Jim Engelhardt, Fay De Witt. *GEM*

Comic Cabby woof! 1987 A day in the life of an introvert cabby seems to last forever. From "New York City Cab Driver's Joke Book" by Jim Pietsch. 59m/C **VHS, Beta.** Bill McLaughlin, Al Lewis. *VES, LIV*

Comin' Round the Mountain *♂♂*½ 1951 The duo are caught in a Kentucky family feud while seeking a fortune in gold. Funniest bit has backwoods witch Hamilton squaring off with Costello when he refuses to pay for the love potion she's made him. 77m/B **VHS, Closed Caption.** Bud Abbott, Lou Costello, Dorothy Shay, Kirby Grant, Joseph Sawyer, Margaret Hamilton, Glenn Strange, Guy Wilkerson; *D:* Charles Lamont; *W:* John Grant, Robert Lees, Frederic Rinaldo. *USH*

Coming Home *♂♂♂*½ 1978 (R) Looks at the effect of the Vietnam War on home front. The wife of a gung-ho Marine officer volunteers as an aide in a Veteran's Hospital, befriends and eventually falls in love with a Vietnam vet, paralyzed from war injuries. His attitudes, pain, and firsthand knowledge of the war force her to re-examine her previously automatic responses. Honest look at the everyday life of disabled veterans, unusual vision of the possibilities of simple friendship between men and women. Fonda and Voight are great; Dern's character suffers from weak scriptwriting late in the film. Critically acclaimed. Compelling score from late '60s music. 130m/C **VHS, Beta, LV, Closed Caption.** Jane Fonda, Jon Voight, Bruce Dern, Penelope Milford, Robert Carradine, Robert Ginty; *D:* Hal Ashby; *W:* Robert C. Jones; *C:* Haskell Wexler. Academy Awards '78: Best Actor (Voight), Best Actress (Fonda); Cannes Film Festival '78: Best Actor (Voight); Golden Globe Awards '79: Best Actor—Drama (Voight), Best Actress—Drama (Fonda); Los Angeles Film Critics Association Awards '78: Best Actor (Voight), Best Actress (Fonda), Best Film; New York Film Critics Awards '78: Best Actor (Voight); Writers Guild of America '78: Best Original Screenplay; Nominations: Academy Awards '78: Best Director (Ashby), Best Film Editing, Best Picture, Best Supporting Actor (Dern), Best Supporting Actress (Milford). *MGM, FOX, FCT*

The Coming of Amos *♂♂♂* 1925 A wonderful send-up of all those Fairbanks-style melodramas, with La Rocque as an Aussie on vacation on the French Riviera falling for and eventually rescuing Goudal, as the Russian princess held captive by the lustful Beery. 60m/B **VHS, Beta.** Rod La Rocque, Jetta Goudal, Noah Beery Sr., Florence Vidor; *D:* Paul Sloane. *GVV*

Coming Out Alive *♂♂*½ 1984 Tense thriller about a woman and her hired mercenary who try to rescue her kidnapped son from her estranged father—a radical is involved in an assassination plot. Hylands is especially compelling. 73m/C **VHS, Beta.** Helen Shaver, Scott Hylands, Michael Ironside, Monica Parker. *TWE*

Coming Out of the Ice *♂♂♂* 1982 (PG) Engrossing true story of Victor Herman, an outstanding American athlete who worked in Russia in the 1930s. He was imprisoned in Siberia (for 38 years!) for refusing to renounce his American citizenship. Made for television. 100m/C **VHS, Beta, Closed Caption.** John Savage, Willie Nelson, Ben Cross, Francesca Annis, Peter Vaughan; *D:* Waris Hussein; *M:* Maurice Jarre. *FOX*

Coming Through *♂♂*½ 1985 Writer D.H. Lawrence meets the married Frieda von Richthofer and begins a scandalous affair which intertwines with his own writings, and the life of a young man in the present day. Made for British television production lacks passion. 78m/C **VHS.** *GB* Kenneth Branagh, Helen Mirren, Alison Steadman, Philip Martin Brown, Norman Rodway; *D:* Peter Barber-Fleming; *W:* Alan Plater. *TVC, VCO*

Coming to America ✍✍✍ 1988 (R) An African prince (Murphy) decides to come to America in search of a suitable bride. He lands in Queens, and quickly finds American women to be more confusing than he imagined. Sometimes overly-cute entertainment relieved by clever costume cameos by Murphy and Hall. Later lawsuit resulted in columnist Art Buchwald being given credit for story. **116m/C VHS, Beta, LV, 8mm, Closed Caption.** Eddie Murphy, Arsenio Hall, James Earl Jones, John Amos, Madge Sinclair, Shari Headley, Don Ameche, Louie Anderson, Paul Bates, Allison Dean, Eriq La Salle, Calvin Lockhart, Samuel L. Jackson, Cuba Gooding Jr., Vanessa Bell, Frankie Faison, Vondie Curtis-Hall; **D:** John Landis; **W:** David Sheffield, Barry W. Blaustein; **M:** Nile Rodgers. Nominations: Academy Awards '88: Best Costume Design. *PAR, FCT*

Coming Up Roses ✍✍½ *Rhosyn A Rhith* 1987 (PG) Pleasant comedy about the residents of a small mining village in the South of Wales who fight to keep their local movie house from being shut down. In Welsh with English subtitles. **95m/C VHS, Beta.** *GB* Dafydd Hywel, Iola Gregory, Olive Michael, Mari Emlyn, Bill Paterson; **D:** Stephen Bayly; **W:** Ruth Carter; **M:** Michael Storey. *FCT*

Command Decision ✍✍½ 1948 Upon realizing he must send his men on missions-of-no-return to destroy German jet production, Gable's WWII flight commander becomes tactically at odds with his political superior, Pidgeon (who's not keen to have his precision bombing plans placed in an unflattering light). Based on the stage hit by William Wister Haines, it's a late war pic by Wood, who earlier directed such diverse efforts as "A Night at the Opera," "The Devil and Miss Jones," and "Our Town." Vintage war-is-hell actioner. **112m/B VHS.** Clark Gable, Walter Pidgeon, Van Johnson, Brian Donlevy, Charles Bickford, John Hodiak; **D:** Sam Wood; **M:** Miklos Rozsa. *MGM, FCT*

Commandments ✍✍ 1996 (R) When Seth Warner (Quinn) loses his wife (Going), job, and even his dog, he finds no solace in faith and decides to test why God would make a good man suffer by breaking every one of the 10 commandments. Rachel (Cox), his wife's sister, persuades him to move in with her and her jerk husband Harry (LaPaglia), who can't really be bothered by Seth's problems. The three leads certainly have presence but given the ambivalence of the material, the movie doesn't hang together. **CW:** Language and sexuality. **86m/C VHS.** Aidan Quinn, Courteney Cox, Anthony LaPaglia, Louis Zorich, Pat McNamara, Tom Aldredge, Pamela Gray, Alice Drummond, Jack Gilpin; **Cameos:** Joanna Going; **D:** Daniel Taplitz; **W:** Daniel Taplitz; **C:** Slawomir Idziak; **M:** Joseph Vitarelli. *USH*

Commando ✍✍✍ 1985 (R) An ex-commando leader's daughter is kidnapped in a blackmail scheme to make him depose a South American president. He fights instead, and proceeds to rescue his daughter amid a torrential flow of falling bodies. Violent action spiced with throwaway comic lines. **90m/C VHS, Beta, LV, Closed Caption.** Arnold Schwarzenegger, Rae Dawn Chong, Dan Hedaya, Vernon Wells, James Olson, David Patrick Kelly, Alyssa Milano, Bill Duke; **D:** Mark L. Lester; **W:** Steven E. de Souza; **M:** James Horner. *FXV, TLF*

Commando Attack ✍½ 1967 A tough sergeant leads a group of misfit soldiers to blow up a German radio transmitter the day before D-Day. **90m/C VHS, Beta.** Michael Rennie, Monica Randall, Bob Sullivan. *UNI*

Commando Invasion ✍ 1987 When an army captain is accused of murder, he hunts down the man he knows is responsible for the crime. Jungle revenge mayhem is confusing. Set in Viet Nam. **90m/C VHS.** Jim Gaines, Michael James, Gordon Mitchell, Carol Roberts, Pat Vance, Ken Watanabe; **D:** John Gale. *NO*

Commando Squad ✍ 1976 (R) During WWII, soldiers go to battle to prevent the development of a device that re-animates human flesh. The script stays dead. **82m/C VHS, Beta.** Chuck Alford, Peter Owen, April Adams; **D:** Charles Nizet. *GHV*

Commando Squad ✍ 1987 (R) Story of drug agents undercover in Mexico, and a female agent who rescues her kidnapped lover. Firepower is wasted, but Shower is a former "Playboy" Playmate of the Year. **90m/C VHS, Beta.** Brian Thompson, William Smith, Kathy Shower, Sid Haig, Robert Quarry, Ross Hagen, Mel Welles, Marie Windsor, Russ Tamblyn; **D:** Fred Olen Ray. *TWE*

Commandos ✍½ 1973 (PG) Commando operation against Rommel's forces in North Africa during WWII. Too much said, not enough action. Also know as "Sullivan's Marauders." **100m/C VHS, Beta.** *GE IT* Lee Van Cleef, Jack Kelly; **D:** Armando Crispino. *GEM, MRV, PSM*

Commandos Strike at Dawn ✍✍½ 1943 Norwegian villagers, including Muni, fight the invading Nazis, and eventually help the British Navy battle them over an Arctic supply line. Okay script helped along by veteran actors Muni and Gish. Based on a C.S. Forester story. **100m/B VHS, Beta.** Paul Muni, Lillian Gish, Cedric Hardwicke, Anna Lee, Ray Collins, Robert Coote, Alexander Knox, Rosemary DeCamp; **D:** John Farrow; **W:** Irwin Shaw; **C:** William Mellor. Nominations: Academy Awards '43: Original Dramatic/Comedy Score. *COL*

Comment Ca Va? ✍✍ *How Is It Going?* 1976 The boss and workers in a Communist publishing house decide to make a simple film about how information is manufactured. But Odette, one of the workers, has some strange ideas about filmmaking. In French with English subtitles. **76m/C VHS.** *FR* Anne-Marie Mieville; **D:** Jean-Luc Godard. *FCT*

The Commies are Coming, the Commies are Coming ✍✍ 1957 Cult classic will leave viewers red from laughing in disbelief. Webb narrates this anti-communist movie about the Russians taking over the United States. Filmed in a documentary style, it captures the paranoia of the times. Re-released in 1984, just before the Evil Empire collapsed. **60m/B VHS, Beta.** Jack Webb, Andrew Duggan, Robert Conrad, Jack Kelly, Peter Brown; **D:** George Waggner. *RHI*

Commissar ✍✍✍✍ *Komissar* 1968 Before the Soviet Union ended up in the ashcan of history, this film was labeled as "treason" and shelved in Red Russia. Now, even Americans can view the story of a female Soviet soldier who becomes pregnant during the civil war of 1922. The Soviet military has no policy regarding pregnancy, so the woman is dumped on a family of outcast Jews to complete her pregnancy. This film makes the strong statement that women were just as discriminated against in the U.S.S.R. as were many races or creeds, especially Jews. In Russian with English subtitles. Released in the U.S. in 1988. **105m/B VHS.** *RU* Nonna Mordyukova, Rolan Bykov; **D:** Alexander Askoldov. *KIV*

The Commitments ✍✍✍ 1991 (R) Convinced that they can bring soul music to Dublin, a group of working-class youth form a band. High-energy production paints an interesting, unromanticized picture of modern Ireland and refuses to follow standard showbiz cliches, even though its lack of resolution hurts. Honest, whimsical dialog laced with poetic obscenities, delivered by a cast of mostly unknowns. Very successful soundtrack features the music of Wilson Pickett, James Brown, Otis Redding, Aretha Franklin, Percy Sledge, and others, and received a Grammy nomination. Based on the book "The Commitments" by Roddy Doyle, part of a trilogy which includes "The Snapper" and "The Van." **116m/C VHS, Beta, LV, Closed Caption.** *IR* Andrew Strong, Bronagh Gallagher, Glen Hansard, Michael Aberne, Dick Massey, Ken McCluskey, Robert Arkins, Dave Finnegan, Johnny Murphy, Angeline Ball, Felim Gormley, Maria Doyle, Colm Meaney; **D:** Alan Parker; **W:** Dick Clement, Roddy Doyle, Ian LaFrenais. British Academy Awards '91: Best Adapted Screenplay, Best Director (Parker), Best Film; Nominations: Academy Awards '91: Best Film Editing. *FXV, CCB, IME*

Committed ✍½ 1991 (R) Schlock-meister Levey's latest directorial effort is a step above his earlier "Slumber Party" and "Happy Hooker Goes to Washington," a statement ringing with the faintest of praise. Thinking she's applying for a job at an asylum, a nurse discovers she has committed herself. Try as she may, not even a committed nurse can snake her way out of the pit of madness they call "The Institute." **93m/C VHS, Closed Caption.** Jennifer O'Neill, William Windom, Robert Forster, Ron Palillo, Sydney Lassick; **D:** William A. Levey. *MED, VTR*

The Committee ✍✍ 1968 (PG) Comedy film of the seminal comedy troupe "The Committee," specialists in short, punchy satire. Dated, but of interest to comedy buffs. **88m/C VHS, Beta.** Wolfman Jack, Howard Hesseman, Barbara Bosson, Peter Bonerz, Garry Goodrow, Carl Gottlieb; **D:** Jack Del. *NO*

Common Bonds ✍✍½ 1991 (PG) After being put together in an experimental outreach program, two mismatched partners struggle to break free from a system that threatens to destroy them both. **109m/C VHS, Beta, Closed Caption.** Rae Dawn Chong, Michael Ironside, Brad Dourif; **D:** Allan Goldstein; **M:** Graeme Coleman. *ACA*

Common Law Wife ✍ 1963 (R) Made-for-the-drive-in flick about a man whose common law marriage is threatened by his niece, who wants his money. Murder and mayhem abound when the man's moonshine is poisoned. Cheap and exploitative. **81m/B VHS.** Lacy Kelly, Shugfoot Rainey, Annabelle Lee, Jody Works, Anne MacAdams, George Edgely; **D:** Eric Sayers. *SNC*

Common Threads: Stories from the Quilt 1989 The heavily awarded, made-for-cable-TV documentary about the Quilt: an immense 14-acre blanket created by the survivors of AIDS victims as a monument to their loved ones' premature deaths. All proceeds from the sale of this tape go to the NAMES Project Foundation in support of the Quilt and AIDS service providers. **79m/C VHS, Beta, LV, Closed Caption.** **D:** Robert Epstein, Jeffrey Friedman. Academy Awards '89: Best Feature Documentary. *WAR, HBO, IME*

Communion ✍✍ 1989 (R) A serious adaptation of the purportedly nonfictional bestseller by Whitley Strieber about his family's abduction by extraterrestrials. Spacey new age story is overlong and hard to swallow. **103m/C VHS, Beta, LV.** Christopher Walken, Lindsay Crouse, Frances Sternhagen, Joel Carlson, Andreas Katsulas, Basil Hoffman; **D:** Philippe Mora; **M:** Eric Clapton. *NO*

The Companion ✍✍ 1994 (R) In 2015 romance novelist Gillian Tanner (Harrold) decides to hide out at a remote mountain cabin to get over a broken love affair. For safety's sake, Gillian takes along custom-designed android companion Geoffrey (Greenwood). But then Gillian decides to tinker with Geoffrey's programming, turning him from domestic guardian to devoted lover. Unfortunately, Geoffrey doesn't understand the difference between fantasy and reality (especially since he's getting his ideas from Gillian's romance novels) and becomes lethally obsessed. **CW:** Some violence; sexuality. **94m/C VHS, LV, Closed Caption.** Kathryn Harrold, Bruce Greenwood, Talia Balsam, Brion James, Bryan Cranston, Joely Fisher; **D:** Gary Fleder; **W:** Ian Seeberg, Valerie Bennett; **C:** Rick Bota; **M:** David Shire. *USH*

Company Business ✍½ 1991 (PG-13) Sam Boyd is a retired CIA agent who's brought back to swap Pyiotr Grushenko (Baryshnikov), a Russian mole in the State Department, for a U-2 pilot being held in Moscow. The swap is to be made in Berlin and also involves two million dollars of what turns out to be Colombian drug money. When things inevitably go wrong (both intelligence agencies would like them out of the way permanently) the two men find they must depend on each other if they want to stay alive. An unimaginative plot wastes a stalwart cast in this old-fashioned spy drama. **104m/C VHS.** Gene Hackman,

Mikhail Baryshnikov, Kurtwood Smith, Terry O'Quinn; **D:** Nicholas Meyer; **W:** Nicholas Meyer. *MGM*

The Company of Wolves 🎬🎬🎬 1985
(R) A young girl on the threshold of womanhood listens to her grandmother tell fairy tales and dreams of a medieval fantasy world inhabited by wolves and dangerous men. An adult "Little Red Riding Hood" type comedy heavy on Freudian symbolism. Not really for kids. 95m/C VHS, Beta, LV, **Closed Caption.** Angela Lansbury, David Warner, Stephen Rea, Tusse Silberg, Sarah Patterson, Brian Glover, Danielle Dax, Graham Crowden, Micha Bergese; **D:** Neil Jordan; **W:** Neil Jordan, Angela Carter; **M:** George Fenton. *VES, LIV*

The Competition 🎬🎬🎬 1980 (PG)
Two virtuoso pianists meet at an international competition and fall in love. Will they stay together if one of them wins? Can they have a performance career and love too? Is he trying to distract her with sex, so he can win? Dreyfuss and Irving are fine (they practiced for four months to look like they were actually playing the pianos), and Remick's character has some interesting insights into the world of art. 125m/C VHS, Beta, LV. Richard Dreyfuss, Amy Irving, Lee Remick, Sam Wanamaker, Joseph Cali, Ty Henderson, Priscilla Pointer, James B. Sikking; **D:** Joel Oliansky; **M:** Lalo Schifrin. Nominations: Academy Awards '80: Best Film Editing, Best Song ("People Alone"). *COL, TVC*

The Compleat Beatles 🎬🎬🎬 1982
Music, interviews, film clips, animation and live performances make up this "rockumentary" on the Beatles. New interviews are featured, as well as vintage film clips and studio footage with narration by Malcolm McDowell. The first U.S. press conference, legendary Hamburg footage, and an in-depth interview with George Martin are highlights. 120m/C VHS, Beta, LV. John Lennon, Paul McCartney, Ringo Starr, George Harrison, George Martin, Brian Epstein, Billy Preston, Milt Oken, Bruce Johnston, Roger McGuinn, Mike McCartney, Mick Jagger; **D:** Patrick Montgomery. *MVD, MGM*

Complex World 🎬🎬½ 1992 (R)
The Heartbreak Hotel is a notorious rock club which may not be around much longer. It seems the young owner's father is an ex-CIA redneck who is running for President and his son's profession is a political liability. Meanwhile, the town's mayor wants to replace the club with a shopping mall. A bomb is planted in the club's basement, terrorists lurk, and a gang of bikers is spoiling for a fight but the crowd at the Heartbreak just rocks on.**CW:** Language and drug use. 81m/C VHS. Dan Welch, Bob Owczarek, Jay Charbonneau, Tilman Gandy Jr., David P.B. Stephens; **D:** James Wolpaw; **W:** James Wolpaw. *NO*

Compromising Positions 🎬🎬 1985 (R)
A philandering dentist is killed on Long Island, and a bored housewife begins to investigate, uncovering scandal after scandal. Black comedy mixed unevenly with mystery makes for unsatisfying brew. However, Ivey is a standout as Sarandon's best friend. Screenplay was written by Susan Isaacs, based on her novel of the same title. 99m/C VHS, Beta, LV, **Closed Caption.** Susan Sarandon, Raul Julia, Edward Herrmann, Judith Ivey, Mary Beth Hurt, Joe Mantegna, Josh Mostel, Anne DeSalvo; **D:** Frank Perry; **M:** Brad Fiedel. *PAR*

Compulsion 🎬🎬🎬½ 1959
Artie Strauss (Dillman) is a mother-dominated sadist who, along with submissive friend Judd Steiner (Stockwell), plan and execute a cold-blooded murder. Flamboyant lawyer Jonathan Wilk (brilliantly portrayed by Welles) knows he has no defense so he attacks the system and establishment, seeking to at least save his clients from death. A suspenseful shocker with taut direction and a tight script. Based on the notorious 1924 Leopold and Loeb murder trial, also filmed as "Rope" and "Swoon." 103m/B VHS. Orson Welles, Bradford Dillman, Dean Stockwell, Diane Varsi, E.G. Marshall, Martin Milner, Richard Anderson, Robert Simon, Edward Binns, Robert Burton, Wilton Graff, Gavin MacLeod; **D:** Richard Fleischer; **W:** Richard Murphy; **C:** William Mellor. *FXV*

Computer Beach Party 🎬 1988
A couple of surf-head college computer hackers foil their mayor's plans to develop their favorite beach. The title, at least, is original. 97m/C VHS, Beta. Hank Amigo, Stacey Nemour, Andre Chimene; **D:** Gary A. Troy. *VES, LIV*

Computer Wizard 🎬 1977 (G)
Boy genius builds a powerful electronic device. His intentions are good, but the invention disrupts the town and lands him in big trouble. Not the "Thomas Edison Story." 91m/C VHS, Beta. Henry Darrow, Kate Woodville, Guy Madison, Marc Gilpin; **D:** John Florea. *NO*

The Computer Wore Tennis Shoes 🎬½ 1969 (G)
Disney comedy (strictly for the kids) about a slow-witted college student who turns into a genius after a "shocking" encounter with the campus computer. His new brains give the local gangster headaches. Sequel: "Now You See Him, Now You Don't." 87m/C VHS, Beta. Kurt Russell, Cesar Romero, Joe Flynn, William Schallert, Alan Hewitt, Richard Bakalayan; **D:** Robert Butler; **M:** Robert F. Brunner. *DIS, OM*

Comrade X 🎬🎬½ 1940
Gable is an American correspondent in Moscow who is blackmailed into marrying die-hard Communist Lamarr in this comedic spinoff of "Ninotchka." The two stars failed to create any sparks as a love duo, although their previous film "Boom Town" was a hit. Based on a story by Walter Reisch. 87m/B VHS. Clark Gable, Hedy Lamarr, Oscar Homolka, Felix Bressart, Eve Arden, Sig Rumann, Natasha Lytess, Vladimir Sokoloff; **D:** King Vidor; **W:** Ben Hecht, Charles Lederer. Nominations: Academy Awards '40: Best Story. *MGM*

Comrades in Arms 🎬½ 1991 (R)
When an international drug cartel threatens to take over the world, the United States and Russia must set their differences aside and team up to stop them.**CW:** Language and strong action violence. 91m/C VHS, **Closed Caption.** Lyle Alzado, Rick Washburne, John Christian, Lance Henriksen; **D:** J. Christian Ingvordsen; **W:** J. Christian Ingvordsen. *REP*

The Comrades of Summer 🎬🎬½ 1992 (R)
Mantegna plays big-league baseball coach Sparky Smith, whose fiery temper gets him into big trouble. Out of a job, he discovers the only team willing to take a chance on him happens to be Russian. Sparky finds the players of the Russian National team need a lot of help—and not just with their English. Made for cable television.**CW:** Language. 90m/C VHS, LV, **Closed Caption.** Joe Mantegna, Natalia Negoda, Mark Rolston, John Fleck, Eric Allen Kramer, Michael Lerner, Ian Tracey; **D:** Tommy Lee Wallace; **W:** Robert Rodat; **M:** William Olvis. *HBO*

Con Air 🎬🎬🎬 1997 (R)
Producer Bruckheimer flies solo for the first time, and has a very successful flight. Cage re-ups as former Ranger Cameron Poe, jailed for manslaughter, who gets paroled just in time to catch a ride home aboard a plane filled with the worst of America's criminals. Led by Cyrus "The Virus" Grissom (Malkovich), the first-class psycho passengers take over the plane, and Cameron must save the day. Among the snappy one-liners, chases, shoot-outs, and stuff blowin' up real good, comes Federal Marshal Larkin (Cusack) to help Poe from the ground. Cusack can't shake his indie-film, quirky-kid image enough to really pass as an action hero, but he gives it his all. Flick supplies everything you'd expect from a summer blockbuster actioner, but it's best seen on a big-screen with surround sound to get the full effect.**CW:** Strong violence and language. 110m/C VHS. Nicolas Cage, John Malkovich, John Cusack, Mykel T. Williamson, Ving Rhames, Steve Buscemi, Colm Meaney, Rachel Ticotin, Dave Chappelle, M.C. Gainey, Danny Trejo, Nicholas Chinlund, Jesse Borrego, Angela Featherstone, Monica Potter, John Roselius, Renoly Landry Bilbeth, Jose Zuniga; **D:** Simon West; **W:** Scott Rosenberg; **C:** David Tattersall; **M:** Mark Mancina, Trevor Rabin. *NYR*

The Con Artists 🎬½ *The Con Man* 1980
After con man Quinn is sprung from prison, he and his protege set up a sting operation against the beautiful Capucine. Not clever or witty enough for the caper to capture interest. 86m/C VHS, Beta. *IT* Anthony Quinn, Adriano Celentano, Capucine, Corinne Clery; **D:** Sergio Corbucci. *HHE*

Con Man 🎬🎬 1992
Robin Mitchell is a small-time con man on the fringes of London's underworld. He witnesses a brutal mob hit, which means they want him dead, and his girlfriend has decided it's just too dangerous being a part of his life. But Mitchell is convinced his luck will change for the better as he puts together a million-dollar long-shot that could secure him for life—if he survives. 91m/C VHS. Ian McShane, Gayle Hunnicutt, Keith Barron, Alan Lake, Luan Peters; **D:** Francis Megahy. *NO*

Conagher 🎬🎬½ *Louis L'Amour's Conagher* 1991
A lyrical, if poorly plotted Western about a veteran cowboy who takes the whole movie to decide to end up in the arms of the pretty widow lady. Cable-TV adaptation of Louis L'Amour's novel doesn't have much intensity, though Elliott captures his character well. 94m/C VHS, Beta, **Closed Caption.** Sam Elliott, Katharine Ross, Barry Corbin, Buck Taylor, Dub Taylor, Daniel Quinn, Anndi McAfee, Billy Green Bush, Ken Curtis; **D:** Reynaldo Villalobos. *TTC*

Conan the Barbarian 🎬🎬🎬 1982 (R)
A fine sword and sorcery tale featuring brutality, excellent production values, and a rousing score. Conan's parents are killed and he's enslaved. But hardship makes him strong, so when he is set free he can avenge their murder and retrieve the sword bequeathed him by his father. Sandahl Bergman is great as The Queen of Thieves, and Schwarzenegger maintains an admirable sense of humor throughout. Jones is dandy, as always. Based on the character created by Robert E. Howard. Sequel: "Conan the Destroyer." 115m/C VHS, Beta, LV, **Closed Caption.** Arnold Schwarzenegger, James Earl Jones, Max von Sydow, Sandahl Bergman, Mako, Ben Davidson, Valerie Quennessen, Cassandra Gaviola, William Smith; **D:** John Milius; **W:** John Milius, Oliver Stone; **M:** Basil Poledouris. *USH*

Conan the Destroyer 🎬🎬½ 1984 (PG)
Conan is manipulated by Queen Tamaris into searching for a treasure. In return she'll bring Conan's love Valeria back to life. On his trip he meets Jones and Chamberlain, who later give him a hand. Excellent special effects, good humor, camp fun, somewhat silly finale. Sequel to the better "Conan the Barbarian." 101m/C VHS, Beta, LV, **Closed Caption.** Arnold Schwarzenegger, Grace Jones, Wilt Chamberlain, Sarah Douglas, Mako, Jeff Corey, Olivia D'Abo; **D:** Richard Fleischer; **C:** Jack Cardiff; **M:** Basil Poledouris. Golden Raspberry Awards '84: Worst New Star (D'Abo). *USH*

Concealed Weapon 🎬½ 1994 (R)
A struggling actor gets the part of a lifetime but then becomes the prime suspect in a brutal crime.**CW:** Violence; sexuality; language. 80m/C VHS. Daryl Haney, Suzanne Wouk, Monica Simpson, Mark Driscoll, Karen Stone; **D:** Dave Payne, Milan Zivkovich. *NHO*

The Concentratin' Kid 🎬🎬 1930
An unusual horse opera sans shootouts and fisticuffs. Hoot's fiancee is kidnapped and taken to the range so that the renegade cowpokes can, uh, benefit from a female perspective on home decorating. Despite being outnumbered, Hoot concentrates and sets the rescue in motion, taking on the gang of rustlers without firing a shot. 54m/B VHS, Beta. Hoot Gibson, Kathryn Crawford, Duke Lee, Robert E. Homans, James Mason; **D:** Arthur Rosson. *GPV*

The Concorde: Airport '79 🎬 *Airport '79* 1979 (PG)
A supersonic film in the "Airport" tradition has the Concorde chased by missiles and fighter aircraft before it crashes in the Alps. Incredibly far-fetched nonsense with an all-star cast doesn't fly. 103m/C VHS, Beta. Alain Delon, Susan Blakely, Robert Wagner, Sylvia Kristel, John Davidson, Charo, Sybil Danning, Jimmie Walker, Eddie Albert, Bibi Andersson, Monica Lewis, Andrea Marcovicci, Martha

Raye, Cicely Tyson, Mercedes McCambridge, George Kennedy, David Warner; **D:** David Lowell Rich; **W:** Eric Roth; **M:** Lalo Schifrin. *USH*

Concrete Angels ✶ **1987 (R)** A poignant glimpse at the influence of rock music in its infancy. A group of deprived teens in Toronto form a band and audition to open for the Beatles. Lack of nostalgia is refreshing, but too much of this is amateurish. **97m/C VHS, Beta. CA** Joseph Dimambro, Luke McKeehan, Omie Craden, Dean Bosacki. *ACA*

Concrete Beat ✶✶½ **1984** A newspaper reporter simultaneously searches for a murderer, tries to win his ex-wife back, and writes front page stories for his editor/ex-father-in-law. Tough assignment. Made for television. **74m/C VHS, Beta.** Kenneth McMillan, John Getz, Darlanne Fluegel, Rhoda Gemignani; **D:** Robert Butler. *PSM*

The Concrete Cowboys ✶✶½ *Ramblin' Man* **1979** Two bumbling cowboys from Montana come to the metropolis of Nashville and promptly turn detective to foil a blackmail scheme and locate a missing singer. Barbara Mandrell and Roy Acuff play themselves. Silly made-for-TV pilot of short-lived series. **100m/C VHS.** Jerry Reed, Tom Selleck, Morgan Fairchild, Claude Akins, Gene Evans, Roy Acuff, Barbara Mandrell; **D:** Burt Kennedy. *FOX, EDV, HHE*

The Concrete Jungle ✶✶ *The Criminal* **1982 (R)** After being set up by her no-good boyfriend, Bregman is sent to a correctional facility for drug smuggling. There she must learn to fend for herself (or else). Typical prison for gals fare with cute babes in revealing outfits, a topless riot, the bad warden, and a concerned social worker. Followed by "Chained Heat." **106m/C VHS, Beta.** Tracy Bregman, Jill St. John, Barbara Luna, Peter Brown, Aimee Eccles, Nita Talbot, Sondra Currie; **D:** Tom De Simone; **W:** Alan J. Adler. *COL*

Condemned to Hell woof! **198?** A tough-as-iron street punk gets thrown into a women's prison, where she must fight for her existence. Low-brow violence galore. **97m/C VHS, Beta. IT** Leonor Benedetto. *TWE*

Condemned to Live ✶✶ **1935** Mild-mannered doctor Ralph Morgan and his fiancee Maxine Doyle seem like your average early 20th Century Middle-European couple...but the doctor's hunchbacked servant Mischa Auer is a tipoff that this is a horror movie of some sort. Like many men, the doctor has suffered from a vampire curse all his life. And, like many men, he is unaware of his blood-sucking habit, thanks to the concealment efforts of his loyal (hunchback) servant. Doyle discovers that fiance's sanguine secret, but not before she finds out she really loves Gleason, anyway. Answers the question: just how do you jilt a vampire? **68m/B VHS.** Ralph Morgan, Maxine Doyle, Russell Gleason, Pedro de Cordoba, Mischa Auer, Lucy Beaumont, Carl Stockdale; **D:** Frank Strayer. *SNC, LSV*

Condition Red ✶✶ **1995 (R)** Philadelphia prison guard Russo's illicit involvement with inmate Williams turns deadly.**CW:** Violence, sexuality, language and drug use. **85m/C VHS.** James Russo, Cynda Williams, Paul Calderone; **D:** Mika Kaurismaki. *AVI*

Condorman ✶✶½ **1981 (PG)** Woody Wilkins, an inventive comic book writer, adopts the identity of his own character, Condorman, in order to help a beautiful Russian spy defect. A Disney film, strictly for the small fry. **90m/C VHS, Beta.** Michael Crawford, Oliver Reed, Barbara Carrera, James Hampton, Jean-Pierre Kalfon, Dana Elcar; **D:** Charles Jarrott; **W:** Glenn Gordon Caron; **M:** Henry Mancini. *DIS*

Conduct Unbecoming ✶✶½ **1975 (PG)** Late nineteenth century India is the setting for a trial involving the possible assault of a British officer's wife. Ambitious production based on a British stage play suffers from claustrophobic atmosphere but is greatly redeemed by the first rate cast. **107m/C VHS. GB** Michael York, Richard Attenborough, Trevor Howard, Stacy Keach, Christopher Plummer,

Susannah York, James Faulkner, Michael Culver, Persis Khambatta; **D:** Michael Anderson Sr. *CRV*

The Conductor ✶✶ *Dyrygent* **1980** A famous Polish-born conductor (Gielgud) returns to his birthplace after 50 years of living in the U.S. A dying man, he decides to work with a struggling provincial orchestra, much to the dismay of their own conductor. But the conductor finds himself being used in government schemes to take advantage of his return. In English and Polish with subtitles. **101m/C VHS. PL** John Gielgud, Krystyna Janda, Andrzej Seweryn, Jan Ciercierski, Tadeusz Czechowski; **D:** Andrzej Wajda; **W:** Andrzej Kijowski. *NYF, ING*

Coneheads ✶✶½ **1993 (PG)** Comedy inspired by once popular characters from "Saturday Night Live" coasts in on the coattails of "Wayne's World." Aykroyd and Curtin reprise their roles as Beldar and Prymaat, the couple from the planet Remulak who are just trying to fit in on Earth. Newman, who created the role of teenage daughter Connie, appears as Beldar's sister, while Burke takes over as Connie (toddler Connie is Aykroyd's daughter, in her film debut). One-joke premise is a decade late and a dime short, though cast of comedy all-stars provides a lift. **86m/C VHS, Beta, Closed Caption.** Dan Aykroyd, Jane Curtin, Laraine Newman, Jason Alexander, Michelle Burke, Chris Farley, Michael Richards, Lisa Jane Persky, Sinbad, Shishir Kurup, Michael McKean, Phil Hartman, David Spade, Dave Thomas, Jan Hooks, Chris Rock, Adam Sandler, Julia Sweeney, Danielle Aykroyd; **D:** Steven Barron; **W:** Dan Aykroyd, Tom Davis, Bonnie Turner, Terry Turner. *PAR, BTV*

Confessing to Laura ✶✶ *Confesion a Laura* **1990** Set in Colombia after the 1948 assassination of liberal leader Jorge Elieser Gaitain, which begets a violent civil war. Two people are trapped at Laura's house by the riots—setting up a night of volatile emotion. Spanish with subtitles. **90m/C VHS. CL D:** Jaime Osorio Gomez. *FCT*

The Confession ✶✶½ **1920** A priest hears a killer's confession and must protect the oath of confidentiality, even as his own brother is being convicted of the murder. **78m/B VHS.** Henry B. Walthall, Francis McDonald, William H. Clifford, Margaret McWade, Margaret Landis; **D:** Bertram Bracken. *GPV*

The Confessional ✶ *House of Mortal Sin* **1975 (R)** A mad priest unleashes a monster from his confessional to wreak havoc upon the world. Pray for your VCR. **108m/C VHS, Beta. GB** Anthony Sharp, Susan Penhaligon, Stephanie Beacham, Norman Eshley, Sheila Keith; **D:** Pete Walker. *PSM*

The Confessional ✶✶½ *Le Confessionnal* **1995** Ambiguous psychological drama that's, in part, a homage to Alfred Hitchcock's 1952 film "I Confess," which was filmed in the same Quebec City locations. Pierre (Bluteau) returns to Quebec in 1989 for his father's funeral and to reunite with his adoptive brother Marc (Goyette). Marc's mother Rachel (who committed suicide shortly after his birth) refused to name his father, thought to be a priest, perhaps at the church where Hitchcock filmed his movie. Flashbacks depict the rotund director (Burrage) and his assistant (Scott Thomas) and their production. Lots of intriguing visuals, thanks to director Lepage's innovative stage background. French with subtitles. **100m/C VHS. CA FR GB** Lothaire Bluteau, Patrick Goyette, Jean-Louis Millette, Kristin Scott Thomas, Ron Burrage, Richard Frechette, Francois Papineau, Marie Gignac; **D:** Robert Lepage; **W:** Robert Lepage; **C:** Alan Dostie; **M:** Sacha Puttnam. Genie Awards '95: Best Art Direction/Set Decoration, Best Director (Lepage), Best Film; Nominations: Genie Awards '95: Best Actor (Bluteau).*NYR*

Confessions of a Hit Man ✶✶ **1994 (R)** Nephew who stole millions from his mobster uncle must amend his sordid past.**CW:** Language. **93m/C VHS, LV.** James Remar, Michael Wright, Emily Longstreth; **D:** Larry Leahy; **W:** Tony Cinciripini, Larry Leahy; **M:** Billy Talbot. *HMD*

Confessions of a Police Captain ✶✶ **1972 (PG)** A dedicated police captain tries to wipe out the bureaucratic corruption that is infecting his city. Balsam gives a fine performance in a heavy-going tale. **104m/C VHS, Beta. IT** Martin Balsam, Franco Nero, Marilu Tolo; **D:** Damiano Damiani. *SNC*

Confessions of a Serial Killer ✶✶ **1987** True story based on the life of Henry Lee Lucas, one of the nation's most vicious killers. Burns plays Lucas in this grisly account of his most violent murders. Shocking realistic look inside the mind of a serial killer. **85m/C VHS, Closed Caption.** Robert Burns, Dennis Hill; **D:** Mark Blair. *NHO*

Confessions of a Vice Baron ✶ **1942** Vice Baron Lombardo makes it big as a drug dealer and flesh peddler, then loses it all when he falls in love. Sleazy exploitation. **70m/B VHS, Beta.** Willy Castello; **D:** John Melville. *SNC*

Confessions of Tom Harris ✶ *Tale of the Cock; Childish Things* **1972 (PG)** Somewhere between all the prize-fighting, leg-breaking for the mob, and jail terms for rape, Tom Harris finds time for a life-changing encounter with love. Based on true story. **90m/C VHS, Beta.** Don Murray, Linda Evans, David Brian, Gary Clarke, Logan Ramsey, Angelique Pettyjohn; **D:** John Derek, David Nelson; **W:** Don Murray. *NO*

Confidential ✶✶½ **1935** A G-man goes under cover to infiltrate a crime ring. Well made and full of action, fun array of character actors. Naish particularly good as nasty killer. **67m/B VHS.** Donald Cook, Evalyn Knapp, Warren Hymer, J. Carrol Naish, Herbert Rawlinson, Morgan Wallace, Kane Richmond, Theodore von Eltz, Reed Howes; **D:** Edward L. Cahn. *VYY*

Confidential woof! **1986 (R)** A '40s detective tries to solve a decades-old axe murder, only to disappear himself. Horrible fare from our friends north of the border. **95m/C VHS, Beta. CA** Neil Munro, August Schellenberg, Chapelle Jaffe, Tom Butler; **D:** Bruce Pittman. *NO*

Confidentially Yours ✶✶✶ *Vivement Dimanche!; Finally, Sunday* **1983 (PG)** Truffaut's homage to Hitchcock, based on Charles Williams' "The Long Saturday Night." A hapless small-town real estate agent is framed for a rash of murders and his secretary, who is secretly in love with him, tries to clear his name. Truffaut's last film is stylish and entertaining. In French with English subtitles. **110m/B VHS, Beta, LV. FR** Fanny Ardant, Jean-Louis Trintignant, Philippe Morier-Genoud, Philippe Laudenbach, Caroline Sihol; **D:** Francois Truffaut; **W:** Suzanne Schiffman; **C:** Nestor Almendros; **M:** Georges Delerue. *FOX, HMV*

Conflict ✶✶✶ **1945** Bogart falls for his sister-in-law and asks his wife for a divorce. She refuses, he plots her murder, and thinks up the alibi. When the police fail to notify him of her death, Bogart is forced to report his wife missing. But is she dead? Her guilty husband smells her perfume, sees her walking down the street, and discovers the body is missing from the scene of the crime. Suspenseful thriller also features Greenstreet as a psychologist/family friend who suspects Bogart knows more than he's telling. **86m/B VHS.** Humphrey Bogart, Alexis Smith, Sydney Greenstreet, Rose Hobart, Charles Drake, Grant Mitchell; **D:** Curtis Bernhardt. *MGM*

Conflict of Interest ✶½ **1992 (R)** Gideon (Nelson) is a thug who runs stolen cars, drugs, and women from his heavy-metal club on the wrong side of town. Mickey Flannery (McDonald) is the new cop determined to get Gideon behind bars, especially after Gideon kills Mickey's wife, sets up his son on a phony murder rap, and kidnaps his son's girlfriend. Now it's personal and Mickey will stop at nothing to get his revenge. Over-the-top performance by Nelson will have the viewer hoping he gets it soon and puts the film out of its misery.**CW:** Language, violence, and strong sexuality. **88m/C VHS.** Judd Nelson, Christopher McDonald, Alyssa Milano, Dey Young, Gregory Alan Harris; **D:** Gary Davis; **W:** Gregory Miller, Michael Angeli; **C:** Bryan England. *HBO*

The Conformist 🎬🎬🎬🎬 *Il Conformista* 1971 (R) Character study of young Italian fascist, plagued by homosexual feelings, who must prove his loyalty by killing his old professor. Decadent and engrossing story is brilliantly acted. Based on the novel by Alberto Moravia. **108m/C VHS, Beta, LV.** *IT FR GE* Jean-Louis Trintignant, Stefania Sandrelli, Dominique Sanda, Pierre Clementi, Gastone Moschin, Pasquale Fortunato; *D:* Bernardo Bertolucci; *W:* Bernardo Bertolucci; *C:* Vittorio Storaro; *M:* Georges Delerue. National Board of Review Awards '71: 5 Best Foreign Films of the Year; National Society of Film Critics Awards '71: Best Cinematography (Storaro), Best Director (Bertolucci); Nominations: Academy Awards '71: Best Adapted Screenplay. *PAR, APD*

Congo 🎬🎬 1995 (PG-13) Communications company supervisor jets off to the African jungle along with a primatologist to search for a lost city's priceless diamonds, and to return Amy, a gorilla who communicates with sign language to her natural habitat. Why she would want to return to volcanoes and bloodthirsty mutant gray gorillas is anybody's guess. This appropriately technology-laden adaptation of Michael Crichton's novel delivers all the cliches of the old B-movie jungle flicks, but none of the thrills or fun of other Crichton adaptations. *CW:* Jungle adventure terror and action; brief strong language. **109m/C VHS, Beta, Closed Caption.** Dylan Walsh, Laura Linney, Ernie Hudson, Tim Curry, Grant Heslov, Joe Don Baker; *D:* Frank Marshall; *W:* John Patrick Shanley; *C:* Allen Daviau; *M:* Jerry Goldsmith. Nominations: Golden Raspberry Awards '95: Worst Picture. *NYR*

Congress Dances 🎬🎬 *Der Kongress Tanzt* 1931 A rare German musical about a romance in old Vienna. Popular in its day, it was subsequently banned by the Nazis in 1937. In German with English subtitles. **92m/B VHS, Beta.** *GE* Lilian Harvey, Conrad Veidt, Willy Fritsch; *D:* Erik Charell. *NOS, HHT, GLV*

A Connecticut Yankee 🎬🎬🎬 1931 A charming, if somewhat dated, version of the popular Mark Twain story, "A Connecticut Yankee in King Arthur's Court." Rogers is a radio shop owner who dreams his way back to the Knights of the Round Table. Story rewritten to fit Rogers' amiable style and to make then-current wisecracks. Great cast overcomes weak points in the script. **96m/B VHS.** Will Rogers, Myrna Loy, Maureen O'Sullivan, William Farnum; *D:* David Butler. *FOX, FCT*

A Connecticut Yankee in King Arthur's Court 🎬🎬½ *A Yankee in King Arthur's Court* 1949 A pleasant version of the famous Mark Twain story about a 20th century man transported to Camelot and mistaken for a dangerous wizard. This was the third film version of the classic, which was later remade as "Unidentified Flying Oddball," a made for television movie and an animated feature. ♫Once and For Always; Busy Doin' Nothin'; If You Stub Your Toe on the Moon; When Is Sometime?; Twixt Myself and Me. **108m/C VHS, Beta, LV.** Bing Crosby, Rhonda Fleming, William Bendix, Cedric Hardwicke, Henry Wilcoxon, Murvyn Vye, Virginia Field; *D:* Tay Garnett; *C:* Ray Rennahan. *USH*

A Connecticut Yankee in King Arthur's Court 🎬🎬½ 1989 The Mark Twain classic has had a gender switch in this TV version, with Pulliam as the time-travelling heroine who winds up in the royal court. **100m/C VHS.** Keisha Knight Pulliam, Jean Marsh, Rene Auberjonois, Emma Samms, Whip Hubley, Michael Gross; *D:* Mel Damski. *FHE*

The Connection 🎬🎬🎬½ 1961 The Living Theatre's ground-breaking performance of Jack Gelber's play about heroin addicts waiting for their connection to arrive, while a documentary filmmaker hovers nearby with his camera. **105m/B VHS, Beta.** Warren Finnerty, Carl Lee, William Redfield, Roscoe Lee Browne, Garry Goodrow, James Anderson, Jackie McLean; *D:* Shirley Clarke. *MFV, FCT*

The Connection 🎬🎬½ 1973 Durning steps in to work a deal between hotel jewel thieves and the insurance company. Complex plot handled deftly by all concerned. Made for television. **74m/C VHS, Beta.** Charles Durning, Ronny Cox,

Dennis Cole, Zohra Lampert, Heather MacRae, Dana Wynter; *D:* Tom Gries. *THV*

The Conqueror woof! 1956 Wayne in pointed helmet and goatee is convincingly miscast as Genghis Khan in this woeful tale of the warlord's early life and involvement with the kidnapped daughter of a powerful enemy. Rife with stilted, unintentionally funny dialogue, Oriental western was very expensive to make (with backing by Howard Hughes), and is now listed in the "Fifty Worst Films of All Time." No matter; it's surreal enough to enable viewer to approximate an out-of-body experience. Even those on the set suffered; filming took place near a nuclear test site in Utah and many members of the cast and crew eventually developed cancer. **111m/C VHS, Beta.** John Wayne, Susan Hayward, William Conrad, Agnes Moorehead, Lee Van Cleef, Pedro Armendariz Sr., Thomas Gomez, John Hoyt; *D:* Dick Powell; *W:* Oscar Millard; *C:* Joseph LaShelle. *USH*

Conqueror & the Empress woof! 1964 Low-budget tale of English explorers who roust an island prince from his throne, motivating him to engage in inspired blood-letting. **89m/C VHS, Beta.** Guy Madison, Ray Danton, Mario Petri, Alberto Farnese. *NO*

The Conqueror Worm 🎬🎬🎬 *Witchfinder General; Edgar Allan Poe's Conqueror Worm* 1968 Price turns in a fine performance portraying the sinister Matthew Hopkins, a real-life 17th century witchhunter. No "ham" in this low-budget, underrated thriller. One of three films from director Reeves, who died from an accidental overdose in 1969. Also available with "Tomb of Ligeia" on LaserDisc. **95m/C VHS.** *GB* Vincent Price, Ian Ogilvy, Hilary Dwyer, Rupert Davies, Robert Russell, Patrick Wymark, Wilfrid Brambell; *D:* Michael Reeves. *HBO, FCT*

Conquest 🎬🎬🎬 *Marie Walewska* 1937 Garbo, as the Polish countess Marie Walewska, tries to persuade Napoleon (Boyer) to free her native Poland from the Russian Tsar. Garbo, Boyer, and Ouspenskaya are outstanding, while the beautiful costumes and lavish production help, but the script is occasionally weak. A box office flop in the U.S., which ended up costing MGM more than any movie it had made up until that time. **115m/B VHS, Beta.** Greta Garbo, Charles Boyer, Reginald Owen, Alan Marshal, Henry Stephenson, Leif Erickson, May Whitty, Maria Ouspenskaya, Vladimir Sokoloff, Scotty Beckett; *D:* Clarence Brown; *C:* Karl Freund. Nominations: Academy Awards '37: Best Actor (Boyer). *MGM, FCT*

Conquest 🎬½ 1983 (R) Sword and sorcery tale of two mighty warriors against an evil sorceress who seeks world domination. Excellent score. **92m/C VHS, Beta.** *IT SP MX* Jorge Rivero, Andrea Occhipinti, Violeta Cela, Sabrina Siani; *D:* Lucio Fulci; *M:* Claudio Simonetti. *MED*

Conquest of Cochise 🎬🎬 1953 Mediocre oater about a cavalry officer who must stop the war between the Apache and Comanche tribes and a group of Mexicans in the Southwest of the 1850s. **70m/C VHS, Beta.** John Hodiak, Robert Stack, Joy Page; *D:* William Castle. *GKK*

Conquest of Mycene 🎬½ *Ercole Contro Molock* 1963 Hercules battles an evil queen and this time he may actually lose! Muscleman mayhem will entertain the kids. **102m/C VHS.** *IT FR* Gordon Scott, Rosalba (Sara Bay) Neri, Jany Clair; *D:* Giorgio Ferroni. *SNC*

Conquest of Space 🎬½ 1955 A spaceship sets off to explore Mars in spite of the commander's attempts to sabotage the voyage. He believes the flight is an heretical attempt to reach God. An uneasy mixture of religion and space exploration detracts from the nifty special effects which are the only reason to watch. **81m/C VHS, Closed Caption.** Walter Brooke, Eric Fleming, Mickey Shaughnessy, Phil Foster, William Redfield, William Hopper, Benson Fong, Ross Martin; *D:* Byron Haskin; *C:* Lionel Lindon. *PAR*

Conquest of the Normans 🎬 1962 During the Norman invasion of England, Oliver is accused of kidnapping the King. To save his life, Oliver must find the true identity of the abductors. With so much plot, there should have been some suspense. **83m/C Beta.** Cameron Mitchell. *AIP*

Conquest of the Planet of the Apes 🎬🎬½ 1972 (PG) The apes turn the tables on the human Earth population when they lead a revolt against their cruel masters in the distant year of 1990. Sure, there's plenty of cliches—but the story drags you along. The 4th film in the series. Followed by "Battle for the Planet of the Apes." **87m/C VHS, Beta, LV, Closed Caption.** Roddy McDowall, Don Murray, Ricardo Montalban, Natalie Trundy, Severn Darden, Hari Rhodes; *D:* J. Lee Thompson; *C:* Bruce Surtees. *FOX*

Conrack 🎬🎬🎬 1974 (PG) The true story of Pat Conroy, who tried to teach a group of illiterate Black children in South Carolina by using common-sense teaching techniques to inspire their interest. Voight is convincing as the earnest teacher. Based on Conroy's novel "The Water Is Wide." **111m/C VHS, Beta, Closed Caption.** Jon Voight, Paul Winfield, Madge Sinclair, Hume Cronyn, Martin Ritt; *D:* Martin Ritt; *W:* Harriet Frank Jr., Irving Ravetch; *C:* John A. Alonzo; *M:* John Williams. *FOX*

Consenting Adult 🎬🎬½ 1985 Made for television movie about a distressed family coming to terms with a favorite son's homosexuality. Restrained exploration of the controversial subject. Based on Laura Z. Hobson's novel. **100m/C VHS.** Marlo Thomas, Martin Sheen, Barry Tubb, Talia Balsam, Ben Piazza, Corinne Michaels; *D:* Gilbert Cates; *W:* John McGreevey. *NO*

Consenting Adults 🎬🎬 1992 (R) Cookie-cutter thriller capitalizes on popular "psycho-destroys-your-normal-life" theme. Average yuppie couple (Kline and Mastrantonio) are startled and then seduced by the couple moving in next door (Spacey and Miller), who conduct a considerably less-restrained lifestyle. Wife-swapping leads to murder and an innocent man is framed. Plot and characters are underdeveloped yet manage to hold interest through decent performances. *CW:* Language, violence, and sexuality. **100m/C VHS, Beta, LV, Closed Caption.** Kevin Kline, Mary Elizabeth Mastrantonio, Kevin Spacey, Rebecca Miller, Forest Whitaker, E.G. Marshall, Billie Neal; *D:* Alan J. Pakula; *W:* Matthew Chapman. *HPH, IME*

Consolation Marriage 🎬🎬½ *Married in Haste* 1931 A couple meet and marry after being jilted by others, then must make a choice when their old flames return. Dunne and O'Brien make a charming couple in this early talkie. One of Dunne's early starring roles. **82m/B VHS, Beta.** Irene Dunne, Pat O'Brien, John Halliday, Matt Moore, Myrna Loy, Lester Vail; *D:* Paul Sloane. *TTC*

Conspiracy 🎬🎬 1989 (R) Defense Secretary William Baine is haunted by a past sexual encounter, and a top secret team moves in to avert any hint of what could become a "sex scandal." Based on a true story. **87m/C VHS, Beta.** James Wilby, Kate Hardie, Glyn Houston; *D:* Christopher Barnard. *ACA*

Conspiracy of Hearts 🎬🎬🎬 1960 A convent of nuns hide Jewish children in 1943 Italy despite threats to their personal safety. Suspenseful tale despite the familiar plot. **113m/B VHS, Beta.** *GB* Lilli Palmer, Yvonne Mitchell, Sylvia Syms, Ronald Lewis; *D:* Ralph Thomas; *W:* Robert Presnell. *LCA*

A Conspiracy of Love 🎬 1987 A made-for-television movie about three generations of a divorce-torn family trying to pull itself back together. Sugary domestic tale tries to be uplifting, succeeds in being cliche-ridden. **93m/C VHS.** Robert Young, Drew Barrymore, Glynnis O'Connor, Elizabeth Wilson, Michael Laurence, John Fujioka, Alan Fawcett; *D:* Noel Black. *VTR, NWV*

Conspiracy of Terror ♂♂ 1975 Married detectives investigate a series of murders and unearth a grisly cult in a quiet suburb. Standard fare with a few too cute lines concerning the leads' mixed-faith marriage. Made for television pilot. **78m/C VHS.** Michael Constantine, Barbara Rhoades, Mariclare Costello, Roger Perry, David Opatoshu, Logan Ramsey; **D:** John Llewellyn Moxey. *LIV*

Conspiracy: The Trial of the Chicago Eight ♂♂♂ 1987 Courtroom drama focuses on the rambunctious trial of the Chicago Eight radicals, charged with inciting a riot at the Democratic National Convention of 1968. Dramatized footage mixed with interviews with the defendants. Imaginative reconstruction of history. **118m/C VHS, Beta.** Peter Boyle, Elliott Gould, Robert Carradine, Martin Sheen, David Clennon, David Kagen, Michael Lembeck, Robert Loggia; **D:** Jeremy Paul Kagan. *NO*

Conspiracy Theory ♂♂♂ 1997 Whacked-out New York cabbie Jerry Fletcher (Gibson) writes a newsletter on conspiracy theories, which he finds in every possible place and situation. Naturally, he doesn't keep his thoughts to himself and exasperated Justice Department attorney Alice Sutton (Roberts) is stuck listening to the love-struck fool. But as the saying goes just because you're paranoid doesn't mean they're not out to get you. Sure enough, one of Jerry's conspiracies turns out to be true and suddenly he and Alice are being pursued by CIA shrink Dr. Jonas (Stewart), who's not what he seems to be either. Gibson's more geek than hero but appealing regardless, as is heroine Roberts. Another successful, enjoyable, and highly profitable, teaming of Donner, Gibson and producer Joel Silver. **?m/C VHS.** Mel Gibson, Julia Roberts, Patrick Stewart, Cylk Cozart; **D:** Richard Donner; **W:** Brian Helgeland. *NYR*

Conspirator ♂♂½ 1949 Somewhat engrossing drama about a beautiful young girl who discovers that her new husband, a British army officer, is working with the Communists. Elizabeth Taylor stars as the naive American wife and Robert Taylor plays her Russkie agent husband. Although madly in love with his wife, he is given orders to kill her. Picture falls apart at end due to weak script. Based on the novel by Humphrey Slater. **85m/B VHS.** *GB* Robert Taylor, Elizabeth Taylor, Robert Flemyng, Harold Warrender, Honor Blackman, Marjorie Fielding, Thora Hird; **D:** Victor Saville; **W:** Sally Benson, Gerard Fairlie; **C:** Frederick A. (Freddie) Young. *MGM*

Consuming Passions ♂♂½ 1988 (R) A ribald, food-obsessed English comedy about a young idiot who rises within the hierarchy of a chocolate company via murder. You'll never guess what the secret ingredient in his wonderful chocolate is. Based on a play by Michael Palin and Terry Jones (better known as part of the Monty Python troupe), the film is sometimes funny, more often gross, and takes a single joke far beyond its limit. **95m/C VHS, Beta, LV.** *GB* Vanessa Redgrave, Jonathan Pryce, Tyler Butterworth, Freddie Jones, Prunella Scales, Sammi Davis, Thora Hird; **D:** Giles Foster; **W:** Michael Palin, Andrew Davies. *NO*

Contact ♂♂½ 1997 (PG) Thought-provoking drama rather than sci-fi spectacular (though it has its fair share of special effects). Radio astronomer Dr. Ellie Arroway (Foster) discovers signals being transmitted from the distant star Vega. When they're deciphered, the signals turn out to be blueprints for a craft that will take its occupant into space and a first meeting with aliens. Ellie fights to become that first spokesperson for Earth's inhabitants. More philosophical than the usual sci-fi alien encounter epic, but the excellent cast, led by Foster, pulls it off nicely. Based on the novel by Carl Sagan. **?m/C VHS.** Jodie Foster, Matthew McConaughey, James Woods, Tom Skerritt, Angela Bassett, John Hurt, David Morse, Rob Lowe, Jake Busey; **D:** Robert Zemeckis; **W:** Michael Goldenberg; **M:** Alan Silvestri. *NYR*

Contagion ♂½ 1987 Innocent real estate agent meets a reclusive, eccentric millionaire who offers him unlimited wealth and beautiful women, but only if he kills someone. Interesting ethical premise loses its philosophic purity. **90m/C VHS, Beta.** *AU* John Doyle, Nicola Bartlett, Roy Barrett, Nathy Gaffney, Pamela Hawksford; **D:** Karl Zwicky. *NO*

Contempt ♂♂♂½ *Le Mepris; Il Disprezzo* 1964 A film about the filming of a new version of "The Odyssey," and the rival visions of how to tell the story. Amusing look at the film business features Fritz Lang playing himself, Godard as his assistant. Bardot is pleasant scenery. Adapted from Moravia's "A Ghost at Noon." **102m/C VHS, Beta, LV.** *IT FR* Brigitte Bardot, Jack Palance, Fritz Lang, Georgia Moll, Michel Piccoli; **D:** Jean-Luc Godard; **W:** Jean-Luc Godard; **M:** Georges Delerue. *COL*

Continental Divide ♂♂ 1981 (PG) A hard-nosed political columnist takes off for the Colorado Rockies on an "easy assignment"—interviewing a reclusive ornithologist, with whom he instantly falls in love. A city slicker, he first alienates her, but she eventually falls for him, too. But it's not exactly a match made in heaven. Story meanders to a conclusion of sorts. Probably the most normal Belushi ever was on screen. **103m/C VHS, Beta, LV.** John Belushi, Blair Brown, Allen (Goorwitz) Garfield, Carlin Glynn, Val Avery, Tony Ganios, Tim Kazurinsky; **D:** Michael Apted; **W:** Lawrence Kasdan; **C:** John Bailey. *USH*

Contraband ♂½ 1986 The leader of a smuggling gang escapes from an ambush in which his brother was murdered. He searches for a haven of safety while his cronies seek brutal revenge. Average crime yarn lacks much excitement. Dubbed into English. **95m/C VHS, Beta.** *IT* Fabio Testi, Ivana Monti; **D:** Lucio Fulci. *NO*

Control ♂½ 1987 Tedious tale of fifteen volunteers for a 20-day fallout shelter habitation experiment who become trapped when a real nuclear emergency occurs. Filmed in Rome. Made for cable TV. **83m/C VHS, Beta.** *IT* Burt Lancaster, Kate Nelligan, Ben Gazzara, Andrea Ferreol, Lavinia Segurini, Andrea Occhipinti, Cyrielle Claire, Jean Benguigui, Kate Reid, Erland Josephson, Ingrid Thulin; **D:** Guiliano Montaldo. *CNG, HBO*

The Convent ♂♂ 1995 Idiosyncratic saga of Paris-based American scholar Michael Padovic (Malkovich) and his French wife Helene (Deneuve) who travel to an ancient Portuguese monastery so Michael may do research at their library. The convent's guardian is the charming and sinister Baltar (Cintra), who flirts with neglected Helene, while playing Mephistopheles to Michael's Faust. Lots of mysticism and religious iconography. Portuguese, French, and English dialogue. **90m/C VHS.** *PT FR* John Malkovich, Catherine Deneuve, Luis Miguel Cintra, Leonor Silveira; **D:** Manoel de Oliveira; **W:** Manoel de Oliveira; **C:** Mario Barroso. *FXL*

The Conversation ♂♂♂½ 1974 (PG) Hackman plays a surveillance expert increasingly uneasy about his job as he begins to suspect he is an accomplice to murder. Powerful statement about privacy, responsibility and guilt. One of the best movies of the '70s. **113m/C VHS, Beta, LV.** Gene Hackman, John Cazale, Frederic Forrest, Allen (Goorwitz) Garfield, Cindy Williams, Robert Duvall, Teri Garr, Michael Higgins, Elizabeth McRae, Harrison Ford; **D:** Francis Ford Coppola; **W:** Francis Ford Coppola; **C:** Bill Butler; **M:** David Shire. Cannes Film Festival '74: Best Film; National Board of Review Awards '74: 10 Best Films of the Year, Best Actor (Hackman), Best Director (Coppola); National Society of Film Critics Awards '74: Best Director (Coppola); Nominations: Academy Awards '74: Best Original Screenplay, Best Picture, Best Sound. *PAR*

Conversation Piece ♂♂♂ *Violence et Passion; Gruppo di Famiglia in un Interno* 1975 (R) An aging art historian's life is turned upside down when a Countess and her daughters rent out the penthouse in his estate. Sometimes-talky examination of scholarly pretensions. **112m/C VHS, Beta.** *IT FR* Burt Lancaster, Silvana Mangano, Helmut Berger,

Claudia Cardinale; **D:** Luchino Visconti; **C:** Pasquale De Santos. *NO*

Convict Cowboy ♂♂½ 1995 (R) Hardbitten professional rodeo cowboy Ry Weston (Voight) killed a man and now works the Montana prison rodeo circuit. Newcomer greenhorn Clay Treyton (Chandler) wants to get out of kitchen duty and decides Ry is the perfect ridin' and ropin' teacher. Only Ry isn't interested in wasting his time (at first). It's a predictable bonding experience in a melodramatic cable movie. **CW:** Strong language; some violence. **106m/C VHS.** Jon Voight, Kyle Chandler, Ben Gazzara, Marcia Gay Harden, Glenn Plummer, Stephen McHattie; **D:** Rod Holcomb; **C:** James L. Carter. *MGM*

Convicted ♂♂½ 1932 Lean thriller about a woman cleared of a murder charge, but only when a second, identical murder occurs while she is jailed. **57m/B VHS, Beta, LV.** Aileen Pringle, Jameson Thomas, Harry Myers, Dorothy Christy, Richard Tucker; **D:** Christy Cabanne. *NOS*

Convicted ♂♂½ 1986 Solid story of innocent man imprisoned for rape, and his wife's determined efforts to free him. Larroquette does well in unexpected role. Based on a true story. Made for television. **94m/C VHS, Beta.** John Larroquette, Carroll O'Connor, Lindsay Wagner; **D:** David Lowell Rich; **M:** Stephen Dorff. *TTC*

Convicted: A Mother's Story ♂ 1987 Jillian embezzles cash from her employer, all for the sake of a bum of a boyfriend, and goes to jail. Odd casting hinders a ho-hum plot. Made for television. **95m/C VHS, Beta.** Ann Jillian, Kiel Martin, Fred Savage, Gloria Loring, Christa Denton; **D:** Richard T. Heffron; **M:** David Shire. *JTC*

Convicts at Large ♂ 1938 An escaped convict steals the clothes of a inept architect. Left with only prison duds, the architect stumbles into the bad side of town and gets involved with the mob. Inane. **58m/B VHS, Beta, LV.** Ralph Forbes, Paula Stone. *NO*

Convoy ♂♂½ 1940 Life aboard a convoy ship in the North Sea during WWII. The small cruiser is picked on by a German U-Boat. Will a rescuer appear? Noted for technical production values. **90m/B VHS.** Clive Brook, John Clements, Edward Chapman, Judy Campbell, Edward Rigby, Stewart Granger, Michael Wilding, George Benson; **D:** Pen Tennyson. *NOS*

Convoy ♂♂ 1978 (R) A defiant trucker leads an indestructible truck convoy to Mexico to protect high gasoline prices. Lightweight stuff was inspired by the song "Convoy" by C.W. McCall. **106m/C VHS, Beta.** Kris Kristofferson, Ali MacGraw, Ernest Borgnine, Burt Young, Madge Sinclair, Franklin Ajaye, Cassie Yates; **D:** Sam Peckinpah; **C:** Harry Stradling Jr. *NO*

Coogan's Bluff ♂♂♂ 1968 (R) An Arizona deputy sheriff (Eastwood) travels to New York in order to track down a killer on the loose. First Eastwood/Siegel teaming is tense actioner. The television series "McCloud" was based on this film. **100m/C VHS, Beta, LV.** Clint Eastwood, Lee J. Cobb, Tisha Sterling, Don Stroud, Betty Field, Susan Clark, Tom Tully; **D:** Donald Siegel; **M:** Lalo Schifrin. *USH*

The Cook, the Thief, His Wife & Her Lover ♂♂♂½ 1990 (R) An exclusive restaurant houses four disturbing characters. Greenaway's powerful vision of greed, love, and violence may be too strong for some tastes. Available in several different versions: the standard unrated theatrical release, the unrated version in a letterboxed format, an R-rated cut which runs half an hour shorter, and a Spanish-subtitled version. **CW:** Psychological intensity/violence. **123m/C VHS.** *GB* Richard Bohringer, Michael Gambon, Helen Mirren, Alan Howard, Tim Roth; **D:** Peter Greenaway; **W:** Peter Greenaway; **C:** Sacha Vierny; **M:** Michael Nyman. *THV*

Cookie ♂♂ 1989 (R) Light comedy about a Mafia don's daughter trying to smart mouth her way into the mob's good graces. A character-driven vehicle, this plot takes a backseat to casting. Wiest is superb as Falk's moll. **93m/C VHS, Beta, LV, 8mm, Closed Caption.** Emily Lloyd, Peter Falk, Dianne

Wiest, Jerry Lewis, Brenda Vaccaro, Ricki Lake, Lionel Stander, Michael V. Gazzo, Adrian Pasdar, Bob Gunton, Rockets Redglare, G. Anthony Sirico; **D:** Susan Seidelman; **W:** Alice Arlen, Nora Ephron; **M:** Thomas Newman. *WAR*

Cooking Up Trouble ♂♂ 1944 The crazy trio become foster dads in this "Stooge" type comedy. ?m/C VHS. Shemp Howard, Billy Gilbert, Maxie "Slapsie" Rosenbloom. *LOO*

Cool As Ice ♂ 1991 (PG) "Rapper" Vanilla Ice makes his feature film debut as a rebel with an eye for the ladies, who motors into a small, conservative town. Several so-so musical segments. For teenage girls only. 92m/C VHS, Beta, LV, **Closed Caption.** Vanilla Ice, Kristin Minter, Michael Gross, Sydney Lassick, Dody Goodman, Naomi Campbell, Candy Clark; **D:** David Kellogg; **C:** Janusz Kaminski; **M:** Stanley Clarke. Golden Raspberry Awards '91: Worst New Star (Vanilla Ice). *USH*

Cool Blue ♂1/2 1988 (R) An unsuccessful painter meets the woman of his dreams, has a brief affair, then tries to locate her in the greater Los Angeles metro area. Good luck. Watch for Penn's cameo. 93m/C VHS, Beta, LV, **Closed Caption.** Woody Harrelson, Hank Azaria, Ely Pouget, John Diehl; **Cameos:** Sean Penn; **D:** Mark Mullin, Richard Shepard. *COL*

Cool Hand Luke ♂♂♂1/2 1967 One of the last great men-in-chains films. A man (Newman) sentenced to sweat out a term on a prison farm refuses to compromise with authority. Martin shines in his supporting role as the oily warden, uttering that now-famous phrase, "What we have here is a failure to communicate." Kennedy's performance as leader of the chain gang won him an Oscar. Based on the novel by Donn Pearce. 126m/C VHS, Beta, LV, DVD. Paul Newman, George Kennedy, J.D. Cannon, Strother Martin, Dennis Hopper, Anthony Zerbe, Lou Antonio, Wayne Rogers, Harry Dean Stanton, Ralph Waite, Joe Don Baker, Richard Davalos, Jo Van Fleet; **D:** Stuart Rosenberg; **W:** Frank Pierson; **C:** Conrad Hall; **M:** Lalo Schifrin. Academy Awards '67: Best Supporting Actor (Kennedy); Nominations: Academy Awards '66: Best Adapted Screenplay, Best Original Score; Academy Awards '67: Best Actor (Newman). *WAR, BTV*

Cool Mikado ♂♂ 1963 A jazzy modernization of the Gilbert-Sullivan operetta, in which an American soldier is kidnapped by the gangster fiance of the Japanese girl he loves. 81m/C VHS, Beta. GB Stubby Kaye, Frankie Howerd, Dennis Price; **D:** Michael Winner. *JEF*

Cool Runnings ♂♂1/2 1993 (PG) Bright, slapstick comedy based on the true story of the Jamaican bobsled team's quest to enter the 1988 Winter Olympics in Calgary. Candy is recruited to coach four unlikely athletes who don't quite exemplify the spirit of the Games. He accepts the challenge not only because of its inherent difficulty but because he needs to reconcile himself to past failures as a former sledder. When our heroes leave their sunny training ground for Calgary, their mettle is tested by serious sledders from more frigid climes who pursue the competition with a stern sense of mission. An upbeat story which will appeal to children, its target audience. 98m/C VHS, LV, **Closed Caption.** Leon, Doug E. Doug, John Candy, Marco Brambilla, Malik Yoba, Rawle Lewis, Raymond J. Barry, Peter Outerbridge, Larry Gilman, Paul Coeur; **D:** Jon Turteltaub; **M:** Hans Zimmer. *DIS*

The Cool Surface ♂♂ 1992 (R) Sex and ambition, Hollywood style. Dani, a wannbe actress, and Jarvis, an aspiring screenwriter become lovers. Jarvis turns their hot affair into a sizzling novel and then a script. Dani may have inspired the lead role but that doesn't mean she'll get the part. But it won't be for lack of trying (anything). **CW:** Language, nudity, violence, and sexual situations. 88m/C VHS. Robert Patrick, Teri Hatcher, Matt McCoy, Cyril O'Reilly, Ian Buchanan; **D:** Erik Anjou; **W:** Erik Anjou; **M:** Dave Kopplin. *COL*

Cool World ♂♂ 1992 (PG-13) Underground cartoonist Jack Deebs enters his own adult cartoon "Cool World," lured by his sex-kitten character "Holli Would," who needs him to leave her animated world and become human. Holli's plan is opposed by the only other human to occupy Cool World, a slick detective whose main job is to prevent noids (humans) and doodles (cartoons) from having sex and destroying the balance between the two existences. A mixture of live-action and wild animation. Director Bakshi's creations are not intended for children but this is less explicit than usual, which may be one of the problems. Little humor and a flat script leave this film too uninvolving. 101m/C VHS, Beta, LV, **Closed Caption.** Gabriel Byrne, Kim Basinger, Brad Pitt, Michele Abrams, Deirdre O'Connell, Carrie Hamilton, Frank Sinatra Jr.; **D:** Ralph Bakshi; **C:** John A. Alonzo. *PAR, PMS*

Cooley High ♂♂♂ 1975 (PG) Black high school students in Chicago go through the rites of passage in their senior year during the '60s. Film is funny, smart and much acclaimed. Great soundtrack featuring Motown hits of the era is a highlight. Sequel to the TV series "What's Happening." 107m/C VHS, LV. Glynn Turman, Lawrence-Hilton Jacobs, Garrett Morris, Cynthia Davis; **D:** Michael A. Schultz; **W:** Eric Monte. *ORI, FCT, PTB*

Cooperstown ♂♂1/2 1993 Harry (Arkin) is a former major-league pitcher who now works as a baseball scout in Florida. He's been angry for 30 years over giving up a home-run pitch that kept his team (the ficitional Chicago Barons) out of the World Series. Harry's feels this error cost him his chance at induction into the Baseball Hall of Fame in Cooperstown, New York, and he's always blamed ex-friend and former catcher Raymond (Greene), who's just had the gall to be elected. Only Raymond's just died—but his ghostly figure visits Harry and urges him to take a road trip not only to the baseball shrine but into his past. Made for cable television. 100m/C VHS. Alan Arkin, Graham Greene, Hope Lange, Josh Charles, Ed Begley Jr., Maria Pitillo, Ann Wedgeworth, Paul Dooley, Joanna Miles, Charles Haid; **D:** Charles Haid; **W:** Lee Blessing. *NO*

Cop ♂♂1/2 1988 (R) Left by his wife and child, a ruthless and work-obsessed detective goes after a brutal serial killer. Woods' exceptional ability to play sympathetic weirdos is diluted by a script—based on James Ellroys's novel "Blood on the Moon"—that warps the feminist theme, is violent, and depends too heavily on coincidence. 110m/C VHS, Beta, LV, **Closed Caption.** James Woods, Lesley Ann Warren, Charles Durning, Charles Haid, Raymond J. Barry, Randi Brooks, Annie McEnroe, Victoria Wauchope; **D:** James B. Harris; **W:** James B. Harris; **M:** Michel Colombier. *PAR*

Cop and a Half ♂1/2 1993 (PG) Streetwise 8-year-old (Golden) accidentally witnesses a murder and then bullys police into letting him join the force (for a day) when he withholds key information. Enter his partner for the day—hard-edged detective Reynolds, who claims to hate kids, but who we know will learn to love them. Meanwhile, the outlaw (Sharkey) knows Devon saw him and is trying to silence him permanently. Predictable fantasy may appeal to kids, but will make most adults yawn. One of Sharkey's last roles. 87m/C VHS, LV, **Closed Caption.** Norman D. Golden II, Burt Reynolds, Ruby Dee, Ray Sharkey, Holland Taylor, Frank Sivero, Marc Macaulay, Rocky Giordani, Sammy Hernandez; **D:** Henry Winkler; **W:** Arne Olsen; **C:** Bill Butler; **M:** Alan Silvestri. Golden Raspberry Awards '93: Worst Actor (Reynolds). *USH*

The Cop & the Girl ♂ 1986 A cop falls for a teenage runaway, ends up on the lam. Confused story overpowered by camera work. Lots of violence and strong language. Dubbed. 94m/C VHS, Beta. GE Juergen Prochnow, Annette Von Klier; **D:** Peter Keglevic. *NO*

Cop in Blue Jeans ♂ 1978 Undercover cop goes after a mob kingpin in this violent, badly dubbed crime yarn. 92m/C VHS, Beta. Tomas Milian, Jack Palance, Maria Rosaria Omaggio, Guido Mannari; **D:** Bruno Corbucci. *THV*

Cop-Out ♂♂ 1991 A cop is framed. His brother is mad. Teamed up with a sexy lawyer, he exposes the filth that is corrupting the city. Okay melodrama. 102m/C VHS, Beta, LV. David Buff, Kathryn Luster, Dan Ranger, Reggie DeMorton, Lawrence L. Simeone; **D:** Lawrence L. Simeone; **W:** Lawrence L. Simeone. *AIP*

Copacabana ♂♂ 1947 A shady theatrical agent (Groucho) books a nightclub singer into two shows at the same time at New York's ritzy nightclub. Lots of energy spent trying to enliven a routine script. Also available colorized. ♫Tico Tico; Stranger Things Have Happened; Je Vous Amie; My Heart Was Doing a Bolero; Let's Do the Copacabana; I Haven't Got a Thing to Sell; We've Come to Copa. 91m/B VHS, LV. Groucho Marx, Carmen Miranda, Steve Cochran, Gloria Jean, Andy Russell, Earl Wilson; **D:** Alfred E. Green. *REP, FCT, MLB*

Copkillers WOOF! 1977 (R) Two men desperate for an easy way to make money embark on a murderous shooting spree. Mostly blanks. 93m/C VHS, Beta. Jason Williams, Bill Osco. *TWE*

Copland ♂ 1997 (R) Partially deaf sheriff (Stallone), whose small New Jersey town is home to a number of retired cops, has divided loyalties when a criminal investigation could implicate his department and the cops he idolizes. Stallone wanted to put "actor" back on his resume, and made the ultimate sacrifice of his physique for the role by gaining some 35 pounds and letting his muscles go. Writer-director Mangold, who grew up in an upstate New York town populated by NYC cops and firemen, pairs his earnest morality tale with a Western feel to provide the excellent, Method-Actors All-Star Team cast a chance to do what they do best. Welcome departure from the usual summer bombast. ?m/C VHS. Sylvester Stallone, Robert De Niro, Annabella Sciorra, Harvey Keitel, Peter Berg, Janeane Garofalo, Michael Rapaport, Ray Liotta, Cathy Moriarty; **D:** James Mangold; **W:** James Mangold. *NYR*

Copper Canyon ♂♂1/2 1950 Milland plays a Confederate Army officer who heads West after the Civil War, meets up with Lamarr, and sparks a romance. Good chemistry between the leads in this otherwise standard western. 84m/B VHS, **Closed Caption.** Ray Milland, Hedy Lamarr, MacDonald Carey, Mona Freeman, Harry Carey Jr., Frank Faylen, Taylor Holmes, Peggy Knudsen; **D:** John Farrow. *PAR, FCT*

Copperhead ♂ 1984 (R) A group of copperhead snakes attack a family who possess a stolen Incan gold necklace. This one bites. 90m/C VHS, Beta. Jack Renner, Gretta Ratliff, David Fritts, Cheryl Nickerson. *VCI*

Cops and Robbers ♂♂1/2 1973 (PG) Two cops use a Wall Street parade for returning astronauts as a cover for a multi-million dollar heist. Exceptional caper film thanks to the likable leads and genuine suspense. 89m/C VHS. Joseph Bologna, Dick Ward, Shepperd Strudwick, John P. Ryan, Ellen Holly, Dolph Sweet, Joe Spinell, Cliff Gorman; **D:** Aram Avakian; **W:** Donald E. Westlake. *MGM*

Cops and Robbersons ♂ 1994 (PG) Bored, dim-witted dad Chase, a TV cop-show junkie, wishes his life had a little more danger and excitement. How lucky for him when hard-nosed cop Palance sets up a command post in his house to stake out the mobster living next door (Davi). Predictable plot isn't funny and drags Chase's bumbling idiot persona on for too long; Wiest and Davi are two bright spots, but their talents are wasted, while Palance does little more than reincarnate his "City Slickers" character. Poor effort for otherwise notable director Ritchie. 93m/C VHS, LV, 8mm, **Closed Caption.** Chevy Chase, Jack Palance, Dianne Wiest, Robert Davi, Jason James Richter, Fay Masterson, Miko Hughes, Richard Romanus,

David Barry Gray; **D:** Michael Ritchie; **W:** Bernie Somers; **M:** William Ross. COL

Cops/One Week 1922 Two vintage Keaton shorts, with original organ score. **51m/B VHS, Beta, 8mm.** Buster Keaton; **D:** Buster Keaton, Eddie Cline. VYY

Copycat 🎬🎬 1995 (R) Crowded serial killer genre yields crooner Connick as southern psychopath stuck on murder. Soon he's in jail, advising the police in their hunt for another serial killer who imitates the murders of other infamous serial killers. Agoraphobic, boozing criminal psychologist Helen Hudson (Weaver), still suffering the after effects of an attack by sicko subject Darryl Lee Cullum (Connick), is enlisted to help detective M.J. Monahan (Hunter) catch the homage specialist. Weaver and Hunter bring sparks to the usually testosterone-laden formula, helping mask the preponderance of serial killer cliches and giant holes in the script. Connick's turn as a nut-job killer won't make you forget Anthony Hopkins, or even Frank Sinatra. Exploitative and imitative, and always faithful to the formula. **CW:** Violence, language. **124m/C VHS, Closed Caption.** Sigourney Weaver, Holly Hunter, Dermot Mulroney, Harry Connick Jr., William McNamara, Will Patton, John Rothman; **D:** Jon Amiel; **W:** Ann Biderman, David Madsen; **C:** Laszlo Kovacs; **M:** Christopher Young. WAR

Coquette 🎬🎬½ 1929 Pickford's first talkie portrays her as a flirtatious flapper from a well-to-do family who falls in love with a poor man her father despises. So much in fact that daddy kills the young man and then commits suicide, leaving his daughter to face the world alone. Pickford and Brown get to share a melodramatic death scene and audiences flocked to hear "America's Sweetheart" speak onscreen. Based on a play by George Abbott and Anne Preston. **75m/B VHS.** Mary Pickford, Johnny Mack Brown, Matt Moore, John St. Polis, Henry Kolker, George Irving, Louise Beavers, William Janney; **D:** Sam Taylor; **C:** Karl Struss. Academy Awards '29: Best Actress (Pickford). MGM

Cord & Dischords/Naughty Nurse 🎬🎬 1928 Two vintage silent shorts featuring some lesser known slapstick clowns cavorting in blackface. **50m/B VHS, Beta.** Fred Parker, Jack Cooper, Ella MacKenzie, Spencer Williams Jr. VYY

Coriolanus, Man without a Country 🎬 1964 When the Romans begin to abuse their rights, the Plebians call upon the brave and mighty Coriolanus to lead them into battle against their oppressors. Predictable muscle man outing. **?m/C VHS, Beta.** IT Gordon Scott, Alberto Lupo, Lilla Brignone. SNC

Corleone 🎬 1979 (R) Limp tale about two boyhood friends who grow up to fight the evil landowners who dominate Italy. To accomplish this, one becomes a mobster, the other a politician. **115m/C VHS, Beta.** IT Claudia Cardinale, Giuliano Gemma; **D:** Pasquale Squitieri. Montreal World Film Festival '79: Best Actor (Gemma). MGM

The Corn is Green 🎬🎬🎬 1945 Touching story of a school teacher in a poor Welsh village who eventually sends her pet student to Oxford. Davis makes a fine teacher, though a little young, while the on-site photography provides atmosphere. Based on the play by Emlyn Williams. Remade in 1979. **115m/B VHS, Beta.** Bette Davis, John Dall, Nigel Bruce, Joan Lorring, Arthur Shields, Mildred Dunnock, Rhys Williams, Rosalind Ivan; **D:** Irving Rapper; **M:** Max Steiner. Nominations: Academy Awards '45: Best Supporting Actor (Dall), Best Supporting Actress (Lorring). MGM, FCT

Cornbread, Earl & Me 🎬🎬 1975 (R) A high school basketball star from the ghetto is mistaken for a murderer by cops and shot, causing a subsequent furor of protest and racial hatred. Superficial melodrama. **95m/C VHS, Beta.** Moses Gunn, Rosalind Cash, Bernie Casey, Tierre Turner, Madge Sinclair, Keith Wilkes, Antonio Fargas; **D:** Joseph Manduke; **M:** Donald Byrd. NO

Cornered 🎬 1932 McCoy is a sheriff, chasing bad guys, whose life is saved by Welch. Basically boring. **62m/B VHS.** Tim McCoy, Niles Welch, Raymond Hatton, Noah Beery Sr., Shirley Grey, Walter Long; **D:** B. Reeves Eason. GPV

Cornered 🎬🎬🎬 1945 Tough Powell plays an airman released from a German prison camp who pursues a Nazi war criminal to avenge the death of his wife and child. **102m/B VHS, Beta, LV.** Dick Powell, Walter Slezak, Micheline Cheirel, Luther Adler; **D:** Edward Dmytryk. TTC

Coroner Creek 🎬🎬½ 1948 Chris Danning's (Scott) fiancee commits suicide after being held hostage during an Indian attack on her stagecoach and a payroll robbery. Danning sets out to trace the loot and exact his revenge. A superior production, notable for being one of the first westerns with an adult theme. **89m/B VHS.** Randolph Scott, Marguerite Chapman, George Macready, Sally Eilers, Edgar Buchanan, Wallace Ford, Forrest Tucker; **D:** Ray Enright. COL

Corporate Affairs 🎬🎬 1990 (R) A ruthless business woman climbing her way to the top literally seduces her boss to death. **92m/C VHS.** Peter Scolari, Mary Crosby, Chris Lemmon, Ken Kercheval; **D:** Terence H. Winkless; **W:** Terence H. Winkless, Geoffrey Baere. MGM

The Corporation 🎬½ Subliminal Seduction; Roger Corman Presents Subliminal Seduction 1996 (R) Darrin Danver (Ziering), the new exec at a computer game company, discovers the games are controlling their users with powerful, subliminal messages. So he tries to expose his employers' lethal manipulations before they can kill him. Standard-issue made-for-TV movie doesn't bring anything new to the "evil company" genre. Shot on location in L.A. and Las Vegas. **?m/C VHS.** Ian Ziering, Andrew Stevens, Katherine Kelly Lang, Dee Wallace Stone, Larry Manetti, Kim Morgan Greene, Kin Shriner, Stella Stevens; **D:** Andrew Stevens; **W:** Karen Kelly; **C:** Gary Graver; **M:** Terry Plumeri. NHO

The Corpse Grinders woof! 1971 (R) Low-budget bad movie classic in which a cardboard corpse-grinding machine makes nasty cat food that makes cats nasty. Sets are cheap, gore effects silly, and cat attacks ridiculous. **73m/C VHS, Beta.** Sean Kenney, Monika Kelly, Sandford Mitchell; **D:** Ted V. Mikels; **W:** Ted V. Mikels. NO

The Corpse Vanishes 🎬🎬½ 1942 Lugosi at his chilling best as a diabolical scientist who snatches young brides and drains their blood in an effort to keep his 70-year-old wife eternally youthful. Not for newlyweds! **64m/B VHS, Beta.** Bela Lugosi, Luana Walters, Tristram Coffin, Elizabeth Russell, Vince Barnett, Joan Barclay, Angelo Rossitto; **D:** Wallace Fox. NOS, MRV, SNC

Corregidor 🎬🎬 1943 A love triangle develops between doctors treating the wounded during the WWII battle. A poor propaganda piece which contains only shaky stock footage for its "action" sequences. **73m/B VHS.** Otto Kruger, Elissa Landi, Donald Woods, Rick Vallin, Frank Jenks, Wanda McKay, Ian Keith; **D:** William Nigh. NOS, MOV, HEG

The Corridor: Death 1989 Two Americans are involved in a car accident in Israel which triggers a debate on the Jewish perspective of death and the afterlife. Filmed on location at Hadassah Hospital on St. Scopus, Jerusalem. The final part of the trilogy preceded by "The Eighth Day: Circumcision" and "The Journey: Bar Mitzvah." **25m/C VHS, Beta.** ERG

Corridors of Blood 🎬🎬½ The Doctor from Seven Dials 1958 Karloff is a doctor, in search of a viable anesthetic, who accidently becomes addicted to drugs, then turns to grave robbers to support his habit. Karloff plays usual threatening doctor to perfection. **86m/B VHS, Beta.** GB Boris Karloff, Betta St. John, Finlay Currie, Christopher Lee, Francis Matthews, Adrienne Corri, Nigel Green; **D:** Robert Day. MPI

Corrina, Corrina 🎬🎬½ 1994 (PG) Newly-widowed jingle-writer Liotta needs someone to care for his withdrawn eight year-old daughter. Enter Whoopi, as housekeeper and eventual love interest. Sweet, nostalgic romance set in the 1950's. Goldberg also found off-screen romance (again), this time with the film's union organizer Lyle Trachtenberg. Last role for Ameche. **115m/C VHS, LV, Closed Caption.** Whoopi Goldberg, Ray Liotta, Don Ameche, Tina Majorino, Wendy Crewson, Jenifer Lewis, Larry Miller, Erica Yohn; **Cameos:** Anita Baker; **D:** Jessie Nelson; **W:** Jessie Nelson. NLC, TTC

Corrupt 🎬🎬🎬 Order of Death; Cop Killers 1984 (PG) Bad narcotics cop goes after murderer, but mysterious Lydon gets in the way. An acquired taste, best if you appreciate Lydon, better known as Johnny Rotten of the Sex Pistols. **99m/C VHS, Beta.** IT Harvey Keitel, John (Johnny Rotten) Lydon, Sylvia Sidney, Nicole Garcia, Leonard Mann; **D:** Roberto Faenza; **M:** Ennio Morricone. NO

The Corrupt Ones 🎬🎬½ Il Sigillo de Pechino; Die Holle von Macao; Les Corrompus; The Peking Medallion; Hell to Macao 1967 Everyone's after a photographer who has a medallion that will lead to buried treasure in China. Great characters hampered by pedestrian script. **87m/C VHS, Beta.** Robert Stack, Elke Sommer, Nancy Kwan, Christian Marquand, Werner Peters; **D:** James Hill; **W:** Brian Clemens. NLC

Corruption woof! 1989 (R) Mostly soft-porn. Alleged plot: The Mob is interested in having Shea work for them, and makes it worth his while. **80m/C VHS.** Mary McGee, Patrick Shea. NO

Corsair 🎬🎬 1931 Actioner about a gorgeous debutante and a handsome gangster who find themselves caught up with a gang of bootlegging pirates. Todd is always worth watching. **73m/B VHS, Beta.** Chester Morris, Thelma Todd, Frank McHugh, Ned Sparks, Mayo Methot; **D:** Roland West. GPV, RXM, HEG

The Corsican Brothers 🎬🎬½ 1942 Alexander Dumas' classic about twins who, although separated, remain spiritually tied throughout their various adventures. Fairbanks takes on dual roles in this entertaining swashbuckler. Remade for television in 1984. **111m/B VHS, Beta, LV.** Douglas Fairbanks Jr., Akim Tamiroff, Ruth Warrick, J. Carrol Naish, H.B. Warner, Henry Wilcoxon, Veda Ann Borg; **D:** Gregory Ratoff; **C:** Harry Stradling. Nominations: Academy Awards '42: Original Dramatic/Comedy Score. VTR, LIV

Corvette Summer 🎬 The Hot One 1978 (PG) After spending a semester restoring a Corvette in his high school shop class, an L.A. student must journey to Las Vegas to recover the car when it is stolen. There he meets a prostitute, falls in love, and steps into the "real world" for the first time. Potts intriguing as the low-life love interest, but she can't save this one. **104m/C VHS, Beta.** Mark Hamill, Annie Potts, Eugene Roche, Kim Milford, Richard McKenzie, William Bryant; **D:** Matthew Robbins; **W:** Matthew Robbins, Hal Barwood. MGM

Cosh Boy woof! The Slasher 1961 Vicious male youths stalk women on the streets of London in this low-budget Jack the Ripper rip-off. **90m/B VHS, Beta.** Joan Collins, James Kennedy. NO

Cosi 🎬🎬🎬 1995 (R) Amiable Lewis (Mendelsohn) is hired to help with drama therapy at the local Sydney mental institution. Pressured by long-term patient Roy (Otto), Lewis finds himself agreeing to stage a production of Mozart's opera "Cosi Fan Tutte" though none of the patients can speak Italian or sing. Rehearsals prove a challenge, there are numerous setbacks, and then it's show time. Fine ensemble cast delivers; adapted from Nowra's play. Friels stepped into the role of security guard Errol when Bruno Lawrence died before filming was completed; pic is dedicated to Lawrence. **CW:** Language. **100m/C VHS.** AU Ben Mendelsohn, Barry Otto, Aden Young, Toni Collette, Rachel Griffiths, Colin Friels, Paul Chubb, Pamela Rabe, Jacki Weaver, David Wenham, Colin Hay, Tony Llewellyn-Jones; **Cameos:** Greta Scacchi, Paul Mercurio; **D:** Mark Joffe; **W:** Louis Nowra; **C:** Ellery Ryan; **M:** Stephen Endelman. Australian Film Institute '96: Best Adapted Screenplay, Best

Supporting Actress (Collette); Nominations: Australian Film Institute '96: Best Supporting Actor (Otto).*NYR*

The Cosmic Eye 🎬🎬🎬 **1971** Animated tale of three musicians from outer space who come to earth to spread the message of world-wide peace and harmony. A variety of cultural perspectives about the origins and destiny of the Earth are offered. Rather moralizing but the animation is impressive. **71m/C VHS, Beta, LV.** *D:* Faith Hubley; *V:* Dizzy Gillespie, Maureen Stapleton, Benny Carter. *LTY, DIS, BTV*

The Cosmic Man 🎬½ **1959** An alien arrives on Earth with a message of peace and restraint. He is regarded with suspicion by us nasty Earthlings. Essentially "The Day the Earth Stood Still" without the budget, but interesting nonetheless. **72m/B VHS, Beta.** Bruce (Herman Brix) Bennett, John Carradine, Angela Greene, Paul Langton, Scotty Morrow; *D:* Herbert Greene. *SNC*

The Cosmic Monsters 🎬½ *The Strange World of Planet X* **1958** Scientist accidentally pops a hole in the ionosphere during a magnetism experiment. Then huge, mean insects arrive to plague mankind. Coincidence? You figure it out. **75m/B VHS, Beta.** Forrest Tucker, Gaby Andre, Alec Mango, Hugh Latimer, Martin Benson; *D:* Gilbert Gunn. *MRV, SNC, EEL*

Cosmic Slop 🎬🎬 **1994 (R)** Three-part anthology. "Space Traders," based on a story by Derrick Bell, finds a fleet of aliens offering to solve all of U.S. society's most pressing social ills if they can have the entire black population in return (for what purpose is never explained). "The First Commandment" features a Catholic priest in a Latino parish who comes up against his parishoners pagan beliefs in Santeria. "Tang," based on a story by Chester Himes, finds a poor, desperately unhappy married couple dreaming about what they'll do with the rifle mysteriously delivered in a flower carton to their door.*CW:* Some strong language. **87m/C VHS, Closed Caption.** Robert Guillaume, Jason Bernard, Nicholas Turturro, Richard Herd, Paula Jai Parker, Chi McBride; *D:* Reginald Hudlin, Warrington Hudlin, Kevin Sullivan; *W:* Warrington Hudlin, Trey Ellis, Kyle Baker; *C:* Peter Deming. *HBO*

Cosmo Jones, Crime Smasher 🎬🎬 **1943** Murder mystery based on a forties radio program. **?m/C VHS.** Mantan Moreland, Frank Graham. *SNC*

Cosmos: War of the Planets woof! *Cosmo 2000: Planet Without a Name; War of the Planets* **1980 (PG)** The ultimate battle for survival is fought in outer space, though not very well and on a small budget. Special effects especially laughable. **90m/C VHS, Beta.** *IT* Katia Christine, West Buchanan, John Richardson, Yanti Somer; *D:* Al Bradley. *NO*

Cottage to Let 🎬½ *Bombsight Stolen* **1941** Propaganda thriller about a Nazi plot to kidnap the inventor of a new bombsight. Focused cast struggles with lackluster script. **90m/B VHS, Beta.** *GB* Leslie Banks, Alastair Sim, John Mills, Jeanne de Casalis, Carla Lehmann, George Cole, Michael Wilding, Frank Cellier, Wally Patch, Catherine Lacey; *D:* Anthony Asquith. *SNC*

Cotter 🎬 **1972** A Native American rodeo clown feels responsible for a cowboy's death, returns home to reflect on his life. Fair story, best at the small town feeling. **94m/C VHS, Beta.** Don Murray, Carol Lynley, Rip Torn, Sherry Jackson; *D:* Paul Stanley. *XVC*

Cotton Candy 🎬🎬 **1982** Follows the faintly interesting trials and tribulations of a high school senior who tries to form a rock band. At first he meets failure, but is ultimately successful with the band and romance. Made for television. Joint script-writing venture by brothers Clint and Ron Howard. **97m/C VHS, Beta.** Charles Martin Smith, Clint Howard, Leslie King; *D:* Ron Howard; *W:* Clint Howard, Ron Howard. *TLF*

The Cotton Club 🎬🎬🎬 **1984 (R)** With $50 million in his pocket, Francis reaches for an epic and delivers: handsome production, lots of dance, bit of singing, confused plot, uneven performances, tad too long. A musician playing at

the Cotton Club falls in love with gangster Dutch Schultz's girlfriend. A black tap dancer falls in love with a member of the chorus line who can pass for white. These two love stories are told against a background of mob violence and music. Excellent performances by Hoskins and Gwynne. ♫ Minnie the Moocher; Ill Wind; The Mooch; Ring Dem Bells; Drop Me Off in Harlem; Cotton Club Stomp; Truckin; Mood Indigo; Copper Colored Gal. **121m/C VHS, Beta, LV, 8mm, Closed Caption.** Diane Lane, Richard Gere, Gregory Hines, Lonette McKee, Bob Hoskins, Fred Gwynne, James Remar, Nicolas Cage, Lisa Jane Persky, Allen (Goorwitz) Garfield, Gwen Verdon, Joe Dallesandro, Jennifer Grey, Tom Waits, Diane Venora; *D:* Francis Ford Coppola; *W:* Francis Ford Coppola, William Kennedy, Mario Puzo; *M:* John Barry. Nominations: Academy Awards '84: Best Art Direction/Set Decoration, Best Film Editing. *NLC*

Cotton Comes to Harlem 🎬🎬🎬 **1970 (R)** Cambridge and St. Jacques star as Harlem plainclothes detectives Grave Digger Jones and Coffin Ed Johnson in this successful mix of crime and comedy. They're investigating a suspicious preacher's back-to-Africa scheme which they suspect is a swindle. Directorial debut of Davis. Filmed on location in Harlem, New York. Based on the novel by Chester Himes. Followed by a weak sequel, "Come Back, Charleston Blue." **97m/C VHS.** Godfrey Cambridge, Raymond St. Jacques, Calvin Lockhart, Judy Pace, Redd Foxx, John Anderson, Emily Yancy, J.D. Cannon, Teddy Wilson, Eugene Roche, Cleavon Little, Lou Jacobi; *D:* Ossie Davis; *W:* Ossie Davis. *MGM*

Cotton Queen 🎬½ *Crying Out Loud* **1937** Romance and light intrigue plague the children of two rival textile mill owners. **80m/B VHS, Beta, 8mm.** Will Fyffe, Stanley Holloway; *D:* Bernard Vorhaus. *VYY, FCT*

A Couch in New York 🎬🎬 *Un Divan a New York* **1995 (R)** Limp romantic comedy features that old standby—opposites attracting. French dancer Beatrice (Binoche) responds to an ad for a temporary Paris-New York apartment switch placed by a stuffy psychoanalyst, Henry Harriston (Hurt). Henry's patients presume Beatrice is his replacement (he works at home) and the free-spirit begins giving them ad hoc advice. Meanwhile in Paris, Henry's plagued by all Beatrice's heartsick boyfriends and decides to come back early. When he arrives unannounced, she assumes he's a new patient and he's intrigued enough to go along. Lots of yakking, not too many sparks, and a strange artificiality make for a dull mix. **104m/C VHS.** *FR BE GE* William Hurt, Juliette Binoche, Paul Guilfoyle, Stephanie Buttle, Richard Jenkins, Kent Broadhurst, Henry Bean, Barbara Garrick; *D:* Chantal Akerman; *W:* Chantal Akerman, Jean-Louis Benoit; *C:* Dietrich Lohmann; *M:* Paolo Conte, Sonia Atherton. *BMG*

The Couch Trip 🎬½ **1987 (R)** Aykroyd is an escapee from a mental institution who passes himself off as a radio psychologist and becomes a media sensation. There are a few laughs and some funny characters but for the most part this one falls flat. **98m/C VHS, Beta, LV, Closed Caption.** Dan Aykroyd, Walter Matthau, Charles Grodin, Donna Dixon, Richard Romanus, Arye Gross, David Clennon, Mary Gross; *D:* Michael Ritchie; *W:* Will Aldis, Steven Kampmann; *M:* Michel Colombier. *ORI*

Could It Happen Here? 🎬 **198?** A lurid Italian spectacle about a metropolis thrown into a state of chaotic martial law by terrorism. Dubbed. **90m/C VHS, Beta.** *IT* Luc Merenda, Marcella Michelangeli; *D:* Massimo Pirri. *NO*

The Count 🎬🎬½ **1916** Chaplin pretends to be the secretary of his boss, who in turn is posing as a count. Silent with musical soundtrack added. **20m/B VHS, Beta.** Charlie Chaplin; *D:* Charlie Chaplin. *CAB*

Count/Adventurer 1917 Two Chaplin two-reelers: "The Count (The Phoney Nobleman)" (1916), in which Charlie impersonates a count at the home of Miss Moneybags, and "The Adventurer" (1917), Chaplin's final film for Mutual, in

which he plays an escaped convict with the law relentlessly on his trail. Silent with musical score. **52m/B VHS, Beta.** Charlie Chaplin, Eric Campbell, Edna Purviance, Frank Coleman; *D:* Charlie Chaplin. *VYY*

Count Dracula 🎬🎬½ **1971 (R)** Passable version of the Dracula legend (based on the novel by Bram Stoker) has Lee as the thirsty count on the prowl for fresh blood. **90m/C VHS.** *SP GE IT* Christopher Lee, Herbert Lom, Klaus Kinski, Frederick Williams, Maria Rohm, Soledad Miranda; *D:* Jess (Jesus) Franco. *REP, FCT*

Count Dracula's Great Love 🎬🎬 **1972** European horror superstar Naschy plays Dracula; stylishly done in the Hammer tradition. Considered by many to be Naschy's best horror film. **?m/C VHS.** Paul Naschy. *SNC, SMW*

The Count of Monte Cristo 🎬🎬½ **1912** One of the first full-length features starring popular stage stars of the day. The first truly American feature, it was based on the classic tale of revenge by Alexander Dumas. Silent. Remade many times. Lead actor O'Neill was the father of famed American playwright, Eugene O'Neill, who covered his father's success in this role in his own family drama "Long Day's Journey Into Night." **90m/B VHS, Beta.** James O'Neill; *D:* Edwin S. Porter. *NOS, VYY, DVT*

The Count of Monte Cristo 🎬🎬🎬 **1934** A true swashbuckling revenge tale about Edmond Dantes, who unjustly spends years in prison. After escaping, he gains ever so sweet and served quite cold revenge. Adaptation of the Alexandre Dumas classic. **114m/B VHS, Beta.** Robert Donat, Elissa Landi, Louis Calhern, Sidney Blackmer, Irene Hervey, Raymond Walburn, O.P. Heggie; *D:* Rowland V. Lee. *CCB, MED, MOV*

The Count of Monte Cristo 🎬🎬½ **1974** The Alexander Dumas classic about an innocent man (Chamberlain) who is imprisoned, escapes, and finds the treasure of Monte Cristo, which he uses to bring down those who wronged him. Good version of the historical costumer. Originally shown in theaters in Europe, but broadcast on television in the U.S. **104m/C VHS, Beta.** *GB* Richard Chamberlain, Kate Nelligan, Donald Pleasence, Alessio Orano, Tony Curtis, Louis Jourdan, Trevor Howard, Taryn Power; *D:* David Greene. *LIV, FUS*

The Count of the Old Town 🎬🎬 *Munkbrogreven* **1934** Feisty townsfolk settle the score after a gang of booze smugglers trick them out of their money. Bergman's film debut as a maid swept off her feet by a mysterious young stranger. Adapted from the play "Greven fran Gamla Sta'n" by Arthur and Sigfried Fischer. In Swedish with English subtitles. **90m/B VHS, Beta.** *SW* Edvin Adolphson, Ingrid Bergman, Sigurd Wallen, Valdemar Dahlquist; *D:* Edvin Adolphson, Sigurd Wallen; *W:* Gosta Stevens. *WAC*

Count Yorga, Vampire 🎬🎬½ **1970 (PG)** The vampire Count Yorga is practicing his trade in Los Angeles, setting up a coven and conducting seances. Good update of the traditional character, with Quarry suitably solemn and menacing. Followed by "The Return of Count Yorga." Also available with "Cry of the Banshee" on laserdisc. **90m/C VHS, Beta.** Robert Quarry, Roger Perry, Michael Murphy, Michael Macready, Donna Anders, Judith Lang; *D:* Bob Kelljan. *NO*

Countdown 🎬🎬½ **1968** Documentary-type fictional look at the first moon mission and its toll on the astronauts and their families. Timely because the U.S. was trying to send a man to the moon in 1968. Interesting as a look at the developing Altman style. **102m/C VHS, Beta.** James Caan, Robert Duvall, Michael Murphy, Ted Knight, Joanna Moore, Barbara Baxley, Charles Aidman, Steve Ihnat, Robert Altman; *D:* Robert Altman. *WAR*

Counter Attack 🎬½ **1984** Story of murder and insurance fraud takes place on the back lots of the Hong Kong film industry. As good as these get. **105m/C VHS, Beta.** Bruce Li, Dan Inosanto, John Ladalski, Young Kong; *D:* Bruce Li. *WVE*

Counter Measures 🗡 **198?** A helicopter pilot stumbles on to a bizarre chain of crimes and disasters. **98m/C VHS, Beta.** Monte Markham; **D:** Gerban Ceth. *NO*

Counter Punch 🗡🗡½ *Ripped Off; The Boxer; Uomo Dalla Pelle Dura* **1971 (R)** Blake is a boxer framed for the murder of his manager who sets out to clear his name by finding the killers. Fair rendition of a familiar plot. **72m/C VHS, Beta.** *IT* Robert (Bobby) Blake, Ernest Borgnine, Gabriele Ferzetti, Catherine Spaak, Tomas Milian; **D:** Franco Prosperi. *SIM, LIV*

Counterblast 🗡🗡 *The Devil's Plot* **1948** A Nazi spy assumes the role of a British scientist in order to gain classified information for the Fatherland. The trouble begins when he refuses to carry out an order to execute a pretty young assistant. Appealing performances distract from the somewhat confusing plot. **99m/B VHS, Beta.** *GB* Robert Beatty, Mervyn Johns, Nova Pilbeam, Margaretta Scott, Sybilla Binder, Marie Lohr, Karel Stepanek, Alan Wheatley; **D:** Paul Stein. *SNC, RXM*

The Counterfeit Traitor 🗡🗡🗡½ **1962** Suspense thriller with Holden playing a double agent in Europe during WWII. Based on the true adventures of Eric Erickson, the top Allied spy of WW II, who was captured by the Gestapo but escaped. **140m/C VHS, Beta, Closed Caption.** William Holden, Lilli Palmer, Hugh Griffith, Werner Peters, Eva Dahlbeck; **D:** George Seaton; **W:** George Seaton; **C:** Jean Bourgoin. *PAR*

Counterforce 🗡 **1987 (R)** A rough group of mercenaries is hired to guard a Mideastern leader being chased by his country's ruling despot. Mild action with predictable story. **98m/C VHS, Beta, LV.** George Rivero, George Kennedy, Andrew Stevens, Isaac Hayes, Louis Jourdan, Kevin Bernhardt, Hugo Stiglitz, Robert Foster, Susana Dosamantes; **D:** J. Anthony Loma. *LIV*

A Countess from Hong Kong 🗡 **1967 (G)** Very bad romantic comedy features impoverished Russian countess Natasha (would you believe Loren is Russian?) stowing away in the luxury liner suite of stuffy American diplomat Ogden Mears (equally miscast Brando). The ship is sailing from Hong Kong to Honolulu and Natasha has until then to persuade Ogden to assist her. Chaplin's final film. **108m/C VHS, Closed Caption.** Marlon Brando, Sophia Loren, Sydney Chaplin, Tippi Hedren, Patrick Cargill, Michael Medwin, Oliver Johnston, Margaret Rutherford; **D:** Charlie Chaplin; **W:** Charlie Chaplin; **C:** Arthur Ibbetson; **M:** Charlie Chaplin. *USH*

Country 🗡🗡🗡 **1984 (PG)** Strong story of a farm family in crisis when the government attempts to foreclose on their land. Good performances all around and an excellent portrayal of the wife by Lange. "The River" and "Places In the Heart," both released in 1984, also dramatized the plight of many American farm families in the early 1980s. **109m/C VHS, Beta, LV.** Jessica Lange, Sam Shepard, Wilford Brimley, Matt Clark, Therese Graham, Levi L. Knebel; **D:** Richard Pearce; **W:** William D. Wittliff. Nominations: Academy Awards '84: Best Actress (Lange). *TOU*

Country Gentlemen 🗡🗡 **1936** Vaudeville team, Olsen and Johnson, play fast-talking conmen who sell shares in a worthless oil field to a bunch of WWI veterans. What a surprise when oil is actually found there. Not one of the duo's better performances. **54m/B VHS, Beta.** Ole Olsen, Chic Johnson, Joyce Compton, Lila Lee, Ray Corrigan, Donald Kirke, Pierre Watkin; **D:** Ralph Staub. *NOS, MRV, VYY*

Country Girl 🗡🗡🗡½ **1954** In the role that completely de-glamorized her (and won her an Oscar), Kelly plays the wife of alcoholic singer Crosby who tries to make a comeback with the help of director Holden. One of Crosby's four dramatic parts, undoubtedly one of his best. Seaton won an Oscar for his adaptation of the Clifford Odets play. Remade in 1982. 🎵The Search Is Through; Dissertation on the State of Bliss; It's Mine, It's Yours; The Land Around Us. **104m/B VHS, Beta.** Bing Crosby, Grace Kelly, William Holden,

Gene Reynolds, Anthony Ross; **D:** George Seaton; **W:** George Seaton. Academy Awards '54: Best Actress (Kelly), Best Screenplay; Golden Globe Awards '55: Best Actress—Drama (Kelly); National Board of Review Awards '54: 10 Best Films of the Year, Best Actress (Kelly); New York Film Critics Awards '54: Best Actress (Kelly); Nominations: Academy Awards '54: Best Actor (Crosby), Best Art Direction/Set Decoration (B & W), Best Black and White Cinematography, Best Director (Seaton), Best Picture. *PAR, BTV*

Country Girl 🗡 **1982** Aging, alcoholic actor is desperate for a comeback. His director blames his fiercely loving wife for the downfall. Poor cable TV remake of 1954 version with Bing Crosby. **137m/C VHS, Beta.** Dick Van Dyke, Faye Dunaway, Ken Howard. *NO*

The Country Kid 🗡🗡🗡 **1923** A freckle-faced teenager and his two brothers are beset by a wicked uncle out to steal their inheritance. One of Barry's best-remembered films. **60m/B VHS, Beta.** Wesley Barry, "Spec" O'Donnell, Bruce Guerin, Kate Toncray, Helen Jerome Eddy, George Nicholls Jr.; **D:** William Beaudine. *NO*

Country Life 🗡🗡 **1995 (PG-13)** Down Under adaptation of Chekov's "Uncle Vanya," has Blakemore returning to Aussie farm roots after 22-year stint as unsuccessful London theater critic. His bored young wife (Scacchi) upsets the business-as-usual life of her husband's brother-in-law (Hargreaves) and abandoned daughter, Sally (Fox), who is also jealous of the attention paid the beautiful Deborah by both her uncle and longtime crush, Dr. Askey (Neill). Exchanges Chekov's emotional exploration for a light comedy of manners and a message of Australian independence from England. **CW:** Some sex-related scenes. **107m/C VHS, LV, Closed Caption.** *AU* Sam Neill, Greta Scacchi, Kerry Fox, John Hargreaves, Googie Withers, Patricia Kennedy, Michael Blakemore; **D:** Michael Blakemore; **W:** Michael Blakemore; **C:** Stephen Windon; **M:** Peter Best. *TOU*

Countryman 🗡🗡 **1983 (R)** A dope-smuggling woman crashes her plane in Jamaica and is rescued by Countryman, a rasta super hero. Not very good, but at least there's great music by Bob Marley and others. **103m/C VHS, Beta.** Hiram Keller, Kristine Sinclair; **D:** Dickie Jobson. *MVD, MED*

County Fair 🗡🗡 **1920** This early silent film is an adaptation of Neil Burgess' play about life in New England. **60m/B VHS, Beta.** Helen Jerome Eddy, David Butler. *NOS, DVT, HEG*

Coup de Grace 🗡🗡½ **1978** Engaging political satire about a wealthy aristocratic woman in Latvia during the 1919-1920 Civil War, and how she attempts to maintain her lifestyle as German soldiers are housed on her estate. Her unrequited love for a German officer adds to her troubles. In German with English subtitles. Co-written by von Trotta and based on the novel by Marguerite Yourcenar. **96m/B Beta.** *GE FR* Margarethe von Trotta, Matthias Habich, Rudiger Kirschstein, Matthieu Carriere; **D:** Volker Schlondorff; **W:** Margarethe von Trotta. *COL, APD, GLV*

Coup de Torchon 🗡🗡🗡 *Clean Slate* **1981** Set in 1938 French West Africa, Noiret plays corrupt police chief Lucien Cordier who is consistently harrassed by his community, particularly by the town pimp. He usually overlooks the pimp's crimes, but when Cordier catches him and a friend shooting at plague victims' bodies floating down the river he decides to murder them in cold blood. Based on the novel "POP 1280" by Jim Thompson. In French with English subtitles. **128m/C VHS.** *FR* Philippe Noiret, Isabelle Huppert, Guy Marchand, Stephane Audran, Eddy Mitchell, Jean-Pierre Marielle, Irene Skobline; **D:** Bertrand Tavernier; **W:** Bertrand Tavernier. Nominations: Academy Awards '82: Best Foreign Language Film. *HMV*

Coupe de Ville 🗡🗡½ **1990 (PG-13)** Three brothers are forced by their father to drive mom's birthday present from Detroit to Florida in the summer of '63. Period concerns and music keep it interesting. **98m/C VHS, Beta, LV, Closed Caption.** Patrick Dempsey, Daniel Stern, Arye Gross, Joseph Bologna,

Alan Arkin, Annabeth Gish, Rita Taggart, James Gammon; **D:** Joe Roth; **W:** Mike Binder; **M:** James Newton Howard. *USH*

Courage 🗡🗡🗡 **1986** Based on fact, a television movie about a Hispanic mother in New York City who, motivated by her drug-troubled children, goes undercover and exposes a multimillion-dollar drug ring. Loren is great in a decidedly non-glamorous role. **141m/C VHS, Beta, Closed Caption.** Sophia Loren, Billy Dee Williams, Hector Elizondo, Val Avery, Dan Hedaya, Ron Rifkin, Jose Perez; **D:** Jeremy Paul Kagan. *VTR, NWV*

Courage Mountain 🗡 **1989 (PG)** If you're looking for a good sequel to Johanna Spyri's classic "Heidi" this isn't it. Europe is on the brink of WWI when teenage Heidi leaves her beloved mountain for an exclusive boarding school in Italy. Not surprisingly in a war zone, the military takes over and the kids are sent to an orphanage run by nasties (see also "Oliver!"). The girls escape to the mountains and are saved by none other than Sheen as Heidi's pal Peter (who cast the twenty-something Sheen as a teenager? Bad mistake.) Ridiculous sequel to the classic tale will appeal to kids despite what the critics say. **92m/C VHS, Beta, LV, Closed Caption.** Juliette Caton, Joanna Clarke, Nicola Stapleton, Charlie Sheen, Jan Rubes, Leslie Caron, Jade Magri, Kathryn Ludlow, Yorgo Voyagis; **D:** Christopher Leitch; **W:** Weaver Webb; **M:** Sylvester Levay. *COL, FCT*

Courage of Black Beauty 🗡🗡½ **1957** Another version of the perennial heart warmer about a boy and his horse. **80m/C VHS, Beta.** Johnny Crawford, Mimi Gibson, John Bryant, Diane Brewster, J. Pat O'Malley; **D:** Harold Schuster. *LIV*

Courage of Lassie 🗡🗡½ *Blue Sierra* **1946 (G)** Fourteen-year-old Taylor is the heroine in this girl loves dog tale. In this case, the dog is actually called Bill, not Lassie, in spite of the film's title. Bill is found wounded by Taylor and she nurses him back to health. He proves to be loving, loyal, and useful, so much so that, through a complicated plotline, he winds up in the Army's K-9 division and returns home with the doggie version of shell-shock. Taylor's still there to nurse him back to his old kind self again. **93m/C VHS.** Elizabeth Taylor, Frank Morgan, Tom Drake, Selena Royle, Harry Davenport; **D:** Fred M. Wilcox. *MGM*

Courage of Rin Tin Tin 🗡🗡 **1983** Rusty and his faithful dog Rin Tin Tin help the cavalry soldiers of Fort Apache keep law and order in a small Arizona town. The perennial kid-pleasing German Shepherd comes through again. **90m/C VHS, Beta.** James Brown, Lee Aaker. *MON*

Courage of the North 🗡½ **1935** The Mounties break up a fur-stealing ring with the help of Captain Dog and Dynamite Horse. Bound to set your hair on end. **55m/B VHS, Beta.** John Preston, June Love, William Desmond, Tom London, Jimmy Aubrey. *NO*

Courage Under Fire 🗡🗡🗡 **1996 (R)** Army Lt. Col. Nat Serling (Washington) is unexpectedly assigned to review the candidacy of Capt. Karen Emma Walden (Ryan, seen only in flashbacks) to receive the posthumous Medal of Honor for bravery in combat. A Gulf War Medevac pilot, Walden would be the first woman awarded the honor if Serling can figure out the truth from her surviving crew's wildly conflicting reports. Ironically, Serling's dealing with a guilt complex since four members of his tank unit died in the war under friendly fire. Stellar performances, including a frightening one by Phillips. Based on the novel by Duncan, who also did the screenplay; Washington and director Zwick previously worked together on "Glory." **CW:** War violence and language. **120m/C VHS.** Denzel Washington, Meg Ryan, Matt Damon, Lou Diamond Phillips, Michael Moriarty, Scott Glenn, Bronson Pinchot, Seth Gilliam, Sean Astin, Regina Taylor, Tim Guinee, Ken Jenkins, Kathleen Widdoes; **D:** Edward Zwick; **W:** Patrick Sheane Duncan; **C:** Roger Deakins; **M:** James Horner. *TCF*

Courageous Avenger ⚉ 1935 A sheriff brings a treacherous ore mine foreman to justice. **59m/B VHS, Beta, LV.** Johnny Mack Brown. *MLB*

Courageous Dr. Christian ⚉⚉ 1940 Dr. Christian is faced with an epidemic of meningitis among the inhabitants of a shanty town. Typical entry in the "Dr. Christian" series. **66m/B VHS, Beta.** Jean Hersholt, Dorothy Lovett, Tom Neal, Robert Baldwin, Maude Eburne; **D:** Bernard Vorhaus; **C:** John Alton. *NOS, VYY, DVT*

The Courageous Mr. Penn ⚉⚉ *Penn of Pennsylvania* 1941 Slow-moving British film, outlining the achievements of William Penn, the Quaker founder of Pennsylvania. **79m/B VHS, Beta.** *GB* Clifford Evans, Deborah Kerr, Dennis Arundell, Aubrey Mallalieu, D.J. Williams, O.B. Clarence, Charles Carson, Henry Oscar, J.H. Roberts; **D:** Lance Comfort. *NOS, VYY, VEC*

The Courier ⚉⚉ 1988 (R) A former drug addict seeks revenge on the dealers who killed his friend. Only thing that saves it are the songs by U2, The Pogues, and Hothouse Flowers. Musical score by Elvis Costello. **85m/C VHS, Beta, LV.** *IR* Gabriel Byrne, Ian Bannen, Padraig O'Loingsigh, Cait O'Riordan, Patrick Bergin; **D:** Frank Deasy, Joe Lee; **M:** Elvis Costello. *VES, LIV*

Courier of Death ⚉ 1984 A courier is embroiled in a mob war/struggle over a locked briefcase with mysterious contents. **77m/C VHS, Beta.** Joey Johnson, Barbara Garrison; **D:** Tom Shaw. *VES, LIV*

Court Jester ⚉⚉⚉½ 1956 Swashbuckling comedy stars Danny Kaye as a former circus clown who teams up with a band of outlaws trying to dethrone a tyrant king. Kaye poses as the court jester so he can learn of the evil king's intentions. Filled with more color, more song, and more truly funny lines than any three comedies put together, this is Kaye's best performance. ♫They'll Never Outfox the Fox; Baby, Let Me Take You Dreaming; My Heart Knows a Lovely Song; The Maladjusted Jester. **101m/C VHS, Beta, LV.** Danny Kaye, Glynis Johns, Basil Rathbone, Angela Lansbury, Cecil Parker, John Carradine, Mildred Natwick, Robert Middleton; **D:** Norman Panama, Melvin Frank; **W:** Norman Panama. *PAR*

The Court Martial of Billy Mitchell ⚉⚉⚉ *One-Man Mutiny* 1955 Terrific courtroom drama depicts the secret trial of Billy Mitchell, head of the Army Air Service in the 1920s, who predicted the role of airpower in subsequent warfare and the danger of war with Japan. Mitchell incurred the wrath of the military by publicly faulting the lack of U.S. preparedness for invasion. Steiger is outstanding as the attorney; Cooper is great as Mitchell. Debut for Montgomery. **100m/C VHS, LV.** Gary Cooper, Charles Bickford, Ralph Bellamy, Rod Steiger, Elizabeth Montgomery, Fred Clark, James Daly, Jack Lord, Peter Graves, Darren McGavin, Robert Simon, Jack Perrin, Charles Dingle; **D:** Otto Preminger; **C:** Sam Leavitt. Nominations: Academy Awards '55: Best Story & Screenplay. *REP*

The Court Martial of Jackie Robinson ⚉⚉⚉½ 1990 (R) True story of a little known chapter in the life of the famous athlete. During his stint in the Army, Robinson refused to take a back seat on a bus and subsequently faced the possibility of court martial. Originally made for cable television. **94m/C VHS, Beta, Closed Caption.** Andre Braugher, Daniel Stern, Ruby Dee, Stan Shaw, Paul Dooley, Bruce Dern; **D:** Larry Peerce; **W:** Dennis Lynton Clark; **C:** Don Burgess. *TTC, FCT*

The Courtesans of Bombay 1985 Gritty docudrama, set in Pavanpul, the poverty-stricken brothel section of Bombay, looks at how the impoverished women support themselves through a combination of prostitution and performing. Made for British television. **74m/C VHS, Beta.** *GB* Kareem Samar, Zohra Segal, Saeed Jaffrey; **D:** Ismail Merchant, James Ivory, Ruth Prawer Jhabvala. *NLC*

Courtin' Wildcats ⚉½ 1929 Early Gibson programmer in which he plays a frail eastern college boy who was sent west by his father to toughen up. Once there, he meets Gilbert and ends up marrying her. **56m/B VHS.** Hoot Gibson, Eugenia Gilbert, Monte Montague; **D:** Jerome Storm. *GPV*

The Courtney Affair ⚉⚉½ *The Courtneys of Curzon Street* 1947 An aristocratic young Britisher causes a stir when he marries an Irish maid. As a result, the couple must face terrific social ostracism. Classy soap opera family saga was a big money maker in England. **112m/B VHS.** *GB* Anna Neagle, Michael Wilding, Gladys Young, Michael Medwin, Coral Browne, Jack Watling, Bernard Lee; **D:** Herbert Wilcox. *VYY*

Courtship ⚉⚉⚉ 1987 From renowned playwright Horton Foote comes this touching story about a sheltered, upper-crust young girl who shocks her family and friends by eloping with a traveling salesman. Made for television. **84m/C VHS, Beta.** Hallie Foote, William Converse-Roberts, Amanda Plummer, Rochelle Oliver, Michael Higgins; **D:** Howard Cummings. *ORI, WAR*

The Courtship of Eddie's Father ⚉⚉⚉ 1962 A clever nine-year-old boy plays matchmaker for his widowed dad in this rewarding family comedy-drama (the inspiration for the TV series). Some plot elements are outdated, but young Howard's performance is terrific; he would later excel at direction. Based on the novel by Mark Toby. **117m/C VHS.** Glenn Ford, Shirley Jones, Stella Stevens, Dina Merrill, Ron Howard, Jerry Van Dyke; **D:** Vincente Minnelli; **W:** John Gay; **C:** Milton Krasner. *MGM, FCT*

The Courtyard ⚉⚉ 1995 (R) Jonathan Hoffman (McCarthy) seems to have the perfect life—a great job, great girl, great California apartment. But then his apartment complex is bedeviled by a series of sinister crimes and Jonathan becomes the prime suspect. **CW:** Language, sexuality and some violence. **103m/C VHS, Closed Caption.** Andrew McCarthy, Madchen Amick, Richard "Cheech" Marin, Vincent Schiavelli; **D:** Fred Walton; **W:** Christopher Hawthorne. *REP*

Cousin, Cousine ⚉⚉⚉½ 1976 (R) Pleasant French comedy about distant cousins who meet at a round of family parties, funerals, and weddings and become friends, but their relationship soon becomes more than platonic. Remade in the U.S. in 1989 as "Cousins." In French with English subtitles. **95m/C VHS, Beta, LV.** *FR* Marie-Christine Barrault, Marie-France Pisier, Victor Lanoux, Guy Marchand, Ginette Garcin, Sybil Maas; **D:** Jean-Charles Tacchella; **W:** Jean-Charles Tacchella; **M:** Gerard Anfosso. Cesar Awards '76: Best Supporting Actress (Pisier); National Board of Review Awards '76: 5 Best Foreign Films of the Year; Nominations: Academy Awards '76: Best Actress (Barrault), Best Foreign Language Film, Best Original Screenplay. *TPV, IME, FOX*

The Cousins ⚉⚉⚉ *Les Cousins* 1959 Set against the backdrop of Parisian student life, two very different cousins (one twisted, the other saintly) vie for the hand of Mayniel. This country mouse, city mouse adult fable ultimately depicts the survival of the fittest. Chabrol's lovely but sad second directorial effort. **112m/B VHS.** *FR* Jean-Claude Brialy, Gerard Blain, Juliette Mayniel, Claude Cerval, Genevieve Cluny; **D:** Claude Chabrol; **W:** Claude Chabrol. *PAR*

Cousins ⚉⚉⚉½ 1989 (PG-13) An American remake of "Cousin, Cousine," in which two distant cousins-by-marriage meet at a wedding and, due to their respective spouses' infidelities, fall into each other's arms. A gentle love story with a humorous and biting look at the foibles of extended families. **110m/C VHS, Beta, LV, Closed Caption.** Isabella Rossellini, Sean Young, Ted Danson, William L. Petersen, Norma Aleandro, Lloyd Bridges, Keith Coogan; **D:** Joel Schumacher; **W:** Stephen Metcalfe; **C:** Ralf Bode; **M:** Angelo Badalamenti. *PAR, FCT, HMV*

Cover Girl ⚉⚉⚉ 1944 A vintage wartime musical about a girl who must decide between a nightclub career and a future as a cover model. Hayworth is beautiful, Kelly dances like a dream, and Silvers and Arden are hilarious. Cinematography by Rudolph Mate. ♫Cover Girl; Sure Thing; Make Way For Tomorrow; Put Me to the Test; Long Ago and Far Away; That's the Best of All; The Show Must Go On; Who's Complaining?; Poor John. **107m/C VHS, Beta, LV.** Rita Hayworth, Gene Kelly, Phil Silvers, Otto Kruger, Lee Bowman, Jinx Falkenberg, Eve Arden, Edward Brophy, Anita Colby; **D:** Charles Vidor; **M:** Ira Gershwin, Jerome Kern. Academy Awards '44: Original Dramatic/Comedy Score; Nominations: Academy Awards '44: Best Color Cinematography, Best Interior Decoration, Best Song ("Long Ago and Far Away"), Best Sound. *COL*

Cover Girl Models ⚉ 1975 An action-packed seventies adventure in which beautiful models are forced to fight for survival. **82m/C VHS, Beta.** Lindsay Bloom, Pat Anderson, John Kramer, Rhonda Leigh Hopkins, Mary Woronov; **D:** Cirio H. Santiago. *NO*

The Cover Girl Murders ⚉⚉½ 1993 (PG-13) Six beautiful models have been brought together on a remote island to shoot a magazine's popular swimsuit issue. Each one wants to be the cover model—but someone is willing to kill to get the job. **87m/C VHS, Beta, Closed Caption.** Lee Majors, Jennifer O'Neill, Adrian Paul, Beverly Johnson, Vanessa Angel; **D:** James A. Contner; **W:** Douglas Barr, Bernard Maybeck; **M:** Rick Marotta. *PAR*

Cover Me ⚉⚉ 1995 (R) When beautiful models turn up dead, L.A. detectives Bobby Colter (Rossovich) and J.J. Davis (Sorvino) discover they were all on the cover of L.A. Erotica magazine. So detective Holly Jacobsen, Colter's girlfriend, (Taylor) goes undercover at the magazine and learns more about the seamy sex underworld than the killer wants her to know. **CW:** Strong sexuality; language; violence. **94m/C VHS, Beta, Closed Caption.** Courtney Taylor, Rick Rossovich, Paul Sorvino, Elliott Gould, Corbin Bernsen; **D:** Michael Schroeder; **W:** Steve Johnson. *PAR*

Cover Story ⚉½ 1993 Journalist Matt McKendree falls in love with a mystery woman whose story he's investigating. Too bad she's dead—or is she. **93m/C VHS.** William Wallace, Tuesday Knight, Robert Forster, Christopher McDonald. *AVI*

Cover-Up ⚉½ 1991 (R) Terrorist attacks on U.S. military bases in Israel are just a smokescreen for a greater threat. The below-par actioner stands out only for the hokey religious symbolism in its Good Friday climax. **CW:** Language, strong violence, and sensuality. **89m/C VHS, LV, Closed Caption.** Dolph Lundgren, Louis Gossett Jr., John Finn; **D:** Manny Coto. *LIV, IME*

The Covered Wagon ⚉⚉½ 1923 Prototypical silent Western began the genre. Wagon train moves cross-country, battling weather and wild Indians. By today's standards, somewhat bucolic and uneventful, but the location photography holds up quite well. Big budget film in its day, and enormously popular. **98m/B VHS, LV.** Warren Kerigan, Lois Wilson, Alan Hale, Ernest Torrence; **D:** James Cruze. *PAR*

Covered Wagon Days ⚉⚉ 1940 The Three Mesquiteers set out after silver smugglers who have framed Rico's brother for murder. **54m/B VHS.** Bob Livingston, Raymond Hatton, Duncan Renaldo, John Merton, Reed Howes; **D:** George Sherman. *REP*

Covered Wagon Trails ⚉ 1940 Substandard Western has good guy Randall dealing with the shifty cattleman's association and making the West safe for the hardworking locals. Future Frankenstein monster Strange plays the hired muscle. **52m/B VHS.** Jack Randall, Sally Cairns, David Sharpe, Lafe McKee, Budd Buster, Glenn Strange; **D:** Raymond K. Johnson; **W:** Tom Gibson. *MOV*

Covergirl ⚉½ *Dreamworld* 1983 (R) Wealthy man decides to relieve his boredom by molding a young woman into a supermodel. She finds the glamorous life isn't always what it's cracked up to be. TV-type melodrama. **98m/C VHS, Beta, Closed Caption.** *CA* Jeff Conaway, Irena Ferris, Cathie Shirriff, Roberta Leighton, Deborah Wakeham; **D:** Jean-Claude Lord. *VTR*

Covert Action 🎬½ **1988** A drug kingpin who desires to protect his business tries to frame a captain for a crime he did not commit. **85m/C VHS, Beta.** Rick Washburne, John Christian, Stuart Garrison Day, Amanda Zinsser, Johnny Stumper; **D:** J. Christian Ingvordsen. *MCG*

Covert Assassin 🎬🎬 **1994 (R)** Anti-terrorist specialist is hired by wealthy widow to avenge her husband's murder. Adapted from the novel "Wild Justice" by Wilbur Smith. **CW:** Terrorist violence. **114m/C VHS.** Roy Scheider, Sam Wanamaker, Ted McGinley, Christopher Buchholz; **D:** Tony Wharmby. *THV*

Cow Town 🎬🎬 **1950** A range war results when ranchers begin fencing in their land to prevent cattle rustling. Autry's 72nd film has some good songs and a dependable cast. **70m/B VHS, Beta.** Gene Autry, Gail Davis, Jock Mahoney, Harry Shannon; **D:** John English. *CCB*

The Coward 🎬🎬 **1962** A schoolteacher and his wife are living in a remote Slovak village during the last days of WWII. The wife supports the anti-Nazi partisans while her husband collaborates with the Germans that occupy the village. Eventually, he finds the courage to save some innocent victims of the Nazi purge. Czech with subtitles. **113m/C VHS.** *CZ* **D:** Jiri Weiss. *FCT*

Coward of the County 🎬🎬½ **1981** A devout pacifist is put to the test when his girlfriend is raped. Good performances by all concerned. Based on the lyrics of Kenny Rogers' hit song of the same name. Made for television. **115m/C VHS, Beta.** Kenny Rogers, Frederic Lehne, Largo Woodruff, Mariclare Costello, Ana Alicia, Noble Willingham; **D:** Dick Lowry. *ORI, WAR*

Cowboy 🎬🎬🎬 **1958** Western roundup based on the memoirs of tenderfoot-turned-cowpoke Frank Harris. Harris (Lemmon) is a Chicago hotel clerk who meets cattle boss Tom Reece (Ford) who's in the city on business. Losing his money in a poker game, Reece reluctantly accepts a loan from Harris in exchange for a piece of his cattle business. So Harris and Reece hit the dusty trail on a cattle drive that takes them into Mexico where Harris falls in love with Maria (Kashfi), the daughter of a wealthy rancher, and gradually turns from city slicker into hardened trail boss. Good cast, no fuss. From the book "Reminiscences As a Cowboy" by Harris. **92m/C VHS.** Jack Lemmon, Glenn Ford, Anna Kashfi, Brian Donlevy, Dick York, Victor Manuel Mendoza, Richard Jaeckel, King Donovan; **D:** Delmer Daves; **W:** Edmund H. North; **C:** Charles Lawton Jr.; **M:** George Duning. Nominations: Academy Awards '58: Best Film Editing. *COL*

The Cowboy & the Ballerina 🎬🎬 **1984** A television movie about an aging rodeo star who falls in love with a petite ballerina defecting from a Russian Dance Company. Good cast makes it watchable. **96m/C VHS, Beta.** Lee Majors, Leslie Wing, Christopher Lloyd, Anjelica Huston, George de la Pena; **D:** Jerry Jameson; **M:** Bruce Broughton. *PSM*

Cowboy & the Bandit 🎬 **1935** A cowboy comes to the aid of a widow being victimized by outlaws. **58m/B VHS, Beta.** Rex Lease, Bobby Nelson, William Desmond; **D:** Al(bert) Herman. *NOS*

The Cowboy and the Lady 🎬🎬½ **1938** Oberon plays a madcap heiress who is deposited by her politician father on their Florida estate to keep her out of trouble while he seeks the Presidential nomination. She is bored and decides to go to a local rodeo where she meets cowboy Cooper. Both are instantly smitten and marry on impulse. Cooper doesn't know about her wealth and when her father finds out about the marriage he's appalled that his daughter has married beneath her. Since this is a comedy all comes out right in the end. Good cast, weak story. **91m/B VHS.** Gary Cooper, Merle Oberon, Patsy Kelly, Walter Brennan, Fuzzy Knight, Mabel Todd, Henry Kolker, Harry Davenport; **D:** H.C. Potter; **C:** Gregg Toland. Academy Awards '38: Best Sound; Nominations: Academy Awards '38: Best Song ("The Cowboy and the Lady"), Best Original Score. *FCT, HBO*

Cowboy & the Senorita 🎬🎬 **1944** A cowboy solves the mystery of a missing girl and wins her lovely cousin. The first film that paired Rogers and Evans, who went on to become a winning team, on and offscreen. **56m/B VHS, Beta.** Roy Rogers, John Hubbard, Dale Evans. *NOS, MRV, DVT*

Cowboy Commandos 🎬½ **1943** Improbable plot has cowboys riding out after Nazi spies, who want to steal valuable ore. **53m/B VHS.** Ray Corrigan, Dennis Moore, Max Terhune, Budd Buster, John Merton; **D:** S. Roy Luby. *DVT, RXM, HEG*

Cowboy Counselor 🎬 **1933** Cowboy Hoot Gibson helps an enchanting girl clear her innocent brother's name. **60m/B VHS, Beta.** Hoot Gibson. *VCI*

Cowboy Millionaire 🎬🎬½ **1935** An Englishwoman comes to an American dude ranch and falls in love with one of the ranch hands. Entertaining Western comedy. **65m/B VHS.** George O'Brien, Evalyn Bostock, Edgar Kennedy, Alden Chase; **D:** Eddie Cline. *NOS, DVT, RXM*

The Cowboy Way 🎬½ **1994 (PG-13)** A mess from start to finish made somewhat watchable by cowpoke charm of the leads and one good horse chase. Two rodeo stars (Harrelson and Sutherland) from New Mexico ride into New York City to avenge a buddy's death, with Hudson as a mounted NYC cop who always yearned to be a cowboy. Great premise is overcome by tasteless humor and a patched-up plot shot full of holes. Good for a gander is the 90-foot Times Square billboard of Harrelson's character as a Calvin Klein underwear model, which stopped traffic even in jaded New York. **CW:** Some language, violence, and comic sensuality. **106m/C VHS, LV, Closed Caption.** Woody Harrelson, Kiefer Sutherland, Dylan McDermott, Ernie Hudson, Cara Buono, Marg Helgenberger, Tomas Milian, Joaquin Martinez; **Cameos:** Travis Tritt; **D:** Gregg Champion; **W:** William D. Wittliff, Rob Thompson; **M:** David Newman. *USH*

The Cowboys 🎬🎬🎬 **1972 (PG)** Wayne stars as a cattle rancher who is forced to hire eleven schoolboys to help him drive his cattle 400 miles to market. Clever script makes this one of Wayne's better Westerns. Carradine's film debut. Inspired the television series. Laserdisc available in widescreen letterbox edition. **128m/C VHS, Beta, LV.** John Wayne, Roscoe Lee Browne, A. Martinez, Bruce Dern, Colleen Dewhurst, Slim Pickens, Robert Carradine, Clay O'Brien; **D:** Mark Rydell; **W:** Harriet Frank Jr., Irving Ravetch; **C:** Robert L. Surtees; **M:** John Williams. *WAR, TLF*

Cowboys Don't Cry 🎬🎬 **1988** When a modern cowboy's wife is killed in an automobile accident, he must change his immature ways and build a solid future with his teenage son or perish in loneliness. **96m/C VHS, Beta.** Rebecca Jenkins, Ron White, Janet-Laine Green. *USH*

Cowboys from Texas 🎬½ **1939** The Three Mesquiteers bring about a peaceful settlement to a fight between cattlemen and homesteaders. Part of "The Three Mesquiteers" series. **54m/B VHS, Beta.** Bob Livingston, Raymond Hatton, Duncan Renaldo, Carole Landis. *MED*

Cowboys of the Saturday Matinee **1984** The history of B-movie westerns is traced from the beginning of the sound era. **75m/B VHS, Beta.** Gene Autry, Tex Ritter, Roy Rogers. *ORI, FCT, WAR*

Coyote Trails 🎬½ **1935** Standard western adventure has cowboy Tyler helping a damsel in distress. **68m/B VHS, Beta.** Tom Tyler. *NOS, VCN, RXM*

Crack House 🎬🎬 **1989 (R)** A man seeks revenge for the murder of a relative by drug dealers. Average exploitation flick. **91m/C VHS, Beta, LV.** Jim Brown, Richard Roundtree, Anthony Geary, Angel Tompkins, Greg Gomez Thomsen, Clyde Jones, Cheryl Kay; **D:** Michael Fischa; **C:** Arledge Armenaki. *MGM, WAR*

Crack Shadow Boxers 🎬 **197?** Through a series of misadventures, Wu Lung and Chu San battle to protect the inhabitants of a small village from the onslaught of relentless ban-

dits. **91m/C VHS, Beta.** *HK* Ku Feng, Chou Li Lung, Han Guo Gai; **D:** Weng Yao Hai. *MGI*

Crack-Up 🎬🎬½ **1946** Largely ignored at the time of its release, this tense tale is now regarded as a minor classic of film noir. An art expert suffers a blackout while investigating a possible forgery and must piece together the missing hours to uncover a criminal conspiracy. **70m/B VHS, Beta, LV.** Pat O'Brien, Claire Trevor, Herbert Marshall, Ray Collins, Wallace Ford, Damian O'Flynn, Erskine Sanford; **D:** Irving Reis. *TTC*

The Cracker Factory 🎬🎬½ **1979** Wood is impressive as a woman committed to a mental institution who attempts to charm her way out of treatment. Made for television. **90m/C VHS, Beta.** Natalie Wood, Perry King, Shelley Long, Vivian Blaine, Juliet Mills, Peter Haskell; **D:** Burt Brinckerhoff; **M:** Billy Goldenberg. *NO*

Cracker: To Be a Somebody **1994** The murder of an Asian shopkeeper first prompts the Manchester police to look for their suspect in the violent world of skinheads. But when the professor helping to profile the killer is murdered, the cops are forced to call in irascible forensic psychologist "Fitz" Fitzgerald (Coltrane) to aid in their investigation. Made for TV. **150m/C VHS.** *GB* Robbie Coltrane, Robert Carlyle, Barbara Flynn, Christopher Eccleston, Geraldine Sommerville, Lorcan Cranitch; **D:** Tim Fywell; **W:** Jimmy McGovern. *AAE*

Crackerjack 🎬🎬 **1994 (R)** Chicago cop Jack Wild (Griffith) agrees to join his brother's family at a vacation resort in the Rocky Mountains. Coincidentally, a team of mercenaries are determined to hijack $50 million in diamonds from the resort and it's up to Jack to stop them. **96m/C VHS, LV, Closed Caption.** Thomas Ian Griffith, Nastassia Kinski, Christopher Plummer; **D:** Michael Mazo; **W:** Jonas Quastel, Michael Bafaro; **C:** Danny Nowak; **M:** Peter Allen. *REP*

Crackers 🎬🎬 **1984 (PG)** The offbeat story of two bumbling thieves who round up a gang of equally inept neighbors and go on the wildest crime spree you have ever seen. A would-be comic remake of "Big Deal on Madonna Street." **92m/C VHS, Beta, LV.** Donald Sutherland, Jack Warden, Sean Penn, Wallace Shawn, Larry Riley, Trinidad Silva, Christine Baranski, Charlaine Woodard, Tasia Valenza; **D:** Louis Malle. *USH*

Cracking Up 🎬½ *Smorgasbord* **1983 (PG)** Accident-prone misfit's mishaps on the road to recovery create chaos for everyone he meets. Lewis plays a dozen characters in this overboard comedy with few laughs. **91m/C VHS, Beta.** Jerry Lewis, Herb Edelman, Foster Brooks, Milton Berle, Sammy Davis Jr., Zane Buzby, Dick Butkus, Buddy Lester; **D:** Jerry Lewis. *WAR*

The Crackler 🎬🎬 **1984** During the '20s, a husband-and-wife private investigation team (Tommy and Tuppence) set out to find a gang of forgers operating in high society circles. Based on a story by Agatha Christie. Made for British television. **60m/C VHS, Beta.** *GB* James Warwick, Francesca Annis. *TPV*

The Cradle Will Fall woof! **1983** A made-for-television adaptation of the pulpy bestselling mystery by Mary Higgins Clark about a woman who cannot convince anyone she witnessed a murder. The cast of "The Guiding Light" appear. Poor script and poor direction do not a thriller make. **103m/C VHS, Beta.** Lauren Hutton, Ben Murphy, James Farentino, Charita Bauer, Peter Simon; **D:** John Llewellyn Moxey. *ORI, WAR*

The Craft 🎬🎬½ **1996 (R)** Call it "Heathers" with hexes. Troubled 17-year-old Sarah (Tunney) moves to L.A. and begins her senior year at St. Benedict's Academy. She takes up with three rebels—Nancy (Balk), Bonnie (Campbell), and Rochelle (True)—who like to dabble in witchcraft. Now, with the addition of would-be witch Sarah, these black magic women start slinging spells at their uppity classmates. Works best when concentrating on the girls and their problems, but degenerates into a special effects barrage toward the end. Alas, no one is turned into a newt. *CW:* Some terror and violence, and for brief language. **100m/C VHS, LV, 8mm, Closed Caption, DVD.** Robin Tunney, Fairuza Balk, Neve Campbell, Rachel True, Skeet Ulrich, Helen Shaver, Cliff DeYoung, Christine Taylor, Assumpta Serna; *D:* Andrew Fleming; *W:* Andrew Fleming, Peter Filardi; *C:* Alexander Grusynski; *M:* Graeme Revell. MTV Movie Awards '97: Best Fight (Fairuza Balk/Robin Tunney). COL

Craig's Wife 🎬🎬🎬 1936 A classic soap opera about a pitiful woman driven to total ruin by her desire for social acceptance and material wealth. Russell makes her surprisingly sympathetic. Based on a Pulitzer Prize-winning George Kelly play. Remake of a silent film, was also remade as "Harriet Craig." **75m/B VHS, Beta.** Rosalind Russell, John Boles, Alma Kruger, Jane Darwell, Billie Burke; *D:* Dorothy Arzner. NO

Crainquebille 🎬🎬🎬 1923 The classic satire based on the Anatole France story about a street merchant in Paris unfairly imprisoned and eventually surviving peacefully as a tramp. Silent. **50m/B VHS, Beta.** *FR* Maurice Feraudy; *D:* Jacques Feyder. FCT, GPV

The Cranes Are Flying 🎬🎬🎬½ *Letyat Zhuravit* 1957 When her lover goes off to fight during WWII, a girl is seduced by his cousin. Touching love story is free of politics. Filmed in Russia; English subtitles. **91m/B VHS, Beta, LV.** *RU* Tatyana Samoilova, Alexei Batalov, Vasily Merkuryev, A. Shvorin; *D:* Mikhail Kalatozov. Cannes Film Festival '58: Best Film. IHF, CVC

Crash 🎬🎬 1995 (NC-17) You can always expect surreal kinkiness from Cronenberg and this film, awarded a Special Jury Prize at Cannes for "daring, originality, and audacity," won't prove the exception. It's "auto" erotica taken to the max, with car crashes and bodily injury turned into fetishes. James (Spader) lands in the hospital after an accident, which injured Helen (Hunter), a passenger in the other car. Helen and James' shared experience soon leads to a sexual relationship, which doesn't bother James' wife, Catherine (Unger). Then there's Vaughan (Koteas) and his group, who like to reenact famous auto crashes (like those of James Dean and Jayne Mansfield). Oh yes, there's lots more sex (in various combinations). Based on J.G. Ballard's 1973 cult novel. An R-rated version clocks in at 90 minutes. *CW:* Numerous explicit sex scenes, accident gore, some graphic language. **98m/C VHS, Closed Caption.** *CA* James Spader, Holly Hunter, Elias Koteas, Deborah Unger, Rosanna Arquette, Peter MacNeill; *D:* David Cronenberg; *W:* David Cronenberg; *C:* Peter Suschitzsky; *M:* Howard Shore. Cannes Film Festival '96: Special Jury Prize; Genie Awards '96: Best Adapted Screenplay, Best Cinematography, Best Director (Cronenberg), Best Film Editing; Nominations: Genie Awards '96: Best Film, Best Sound. NLC

Crash and Burn 🎬½ 1990 (R) Rebels in a repressive future police state reactivate a huge, long-dormant robot to battle the establishment's army of powerful androids. Special effects by David Allen make the mayhem interesting. **85m/C VHS, Beta, LV, Closed Caption.** Ralph Waite, Paul Ganus, Eva LaRue, Bill Moseley, Jack McGee; *D:* Charles Band; *W:* J.S. Cardone; *M:* Richard Band. PAR

Crash Dive 🎬🎬½ 1943 WWII glory film provides comic relief in the form of romance. Second-in-command Power falls hopelessly in love with school teacher Baxter, only to find out later that she is Lt. Commander Andrews' fiance. Once this little tidbit of information is disclosed, the two officers embark on a mission to destroy a Nazi U-Boat responsible for laying mines in the North Atlantic. Fantastic special effects and sound. Based on the story by W.R. Burnett. **105m/B VHS.** Tyrone Power, Anne Baxter, Dana Andrews, James Gleason, May Whitty, Harry (Henry) Morgan, Ben Carter, Frank Conroy, Florence Lake, John Archer, Minor Watson, Kathleen Howard, Stanley Andrews, Thurston Hall, Trudy Marshall; *D:* Archie Mayo; *W:* Jo Swerling; *C:* Leon Shamroy; *M:* David

Buttolph. Academy Awards '44: Best Special Effects (Sersen). FXV

Crash Dive 🎬🎬 1996 (R) An atomic submarine is taken hostage by Richter (Schone) and his band of terrorists, who demand a billion dollars in gold or Washington D.C. will become a nuclear disaster. Naturally, there's one hero—sub designer James Carter (Dudikoff)—who manages to sneak aboard and plots to save the day. Fast pace and top special effects make this one watchable. *CW:* Violence, a scene of sexuality, and brief language. **90m/C VHS.** Michael Dudikoff, Reiner Schone, Frederic Forrest, Jay Acovone; *D:* Andrew Stevens; *W:* William Martell; *C:* Michael Slovis; *M:* Eric Wurst, David Wurst. CAF

The Crash of Flight 401 🎬🎬½ 1978 A plane, full of recognizable TV stars, crashes in the Florida Everglades. "Airport" for a smaller screen. Based on a real event. Made for televisiion. **97m/C VHS, Beta.** William Shatner, Adrienne Barbeau, Eddie Albert, Brooke Bundy, Christopher Connelly, Lorraine Gary, Ron Glass, Sharon Gless, Brett Halsey, George Maharis, Gerald S. O'Loughlin; *D:* Barry Shear. FRH

Crashout 🎬🎬½ 1955 Six men break out of prison in this entertaining melodrama. Bendix plays the gang's leader to nasty perfection. **82m/B VHS.** William Bendix, Gene Evans, Arthur Kennedy, Luther Adler, William Talman, Marshall Thompson, Beverly Michaels; *D:* Lewis R. Foster. REP

The Crater Lake Monster woof! 1977 (PG) The dormant egg of a prehistoric creature hatches after a meteor rudely awakens the dozing dino. He's understandably miffed and begins a revenge campaign. Prehistoric yawner. **85m/C VHS, Beta.** Richard Cardella, Glenn Roberts, Mark Siegel, Bob Hyman, Kacey Cobb; *D:* William R. Stromberg. VCI, MRV

The Craving 🎬 1980 (R) Naschy returns as El Hombre Lobo for the umpteenth time and once again battles a female vampire (see "Werewolf vs. the Vampire Woman"). Although continental Europe's biggest horror star, this film was such a box office disaster that Naschy went bankrupt. He was then forced to turn to Japan for financing (see "The Human Beasts"). Naschy also directed under a pseudonym. **93m/C VHS, Beta.** *MX* Paul Naschy, Julie Saly; *D:* Jack Molina. VES, LIV

The Crawlers 🎬 1993 (R) Illegal radioactive dumping has caused a living, lethal organism to invade in a small western town. Seems the local sheriff and the nuclear plant manager were partners in a toxic dumping scheme that went awry and two teenagers are the only ones willing to expose the truth. More to the point—scary monster attacks woman with artistically enhanced cleavage. **94m/C VHS, Closed Caption.** Jason Saucier, Mary Sellers; *D:* Martin Newlin; *W:* Dan Price, Martin Newlin. COL

The Crawling Eye 🎬🎬 *The Trollenberg Terror* 1958 Hidden in a radioactive fog on a mountaintop, the crawling eye decapitates its victims and returns these humans to Earth to threaten mankind. Average acting, but particularly awful special effects. Based on a British TV series. **87m/B VHS, Beta, LV.** *GB* Forrest Tucker, Laurence Payne, Janet Munro, Jennifer Jayne, Warren Mitchell; *D:* Quentin Lawrence; *W:* Jimmy Sangster; *M:* Stanley Black. SNC, MRV, MED

The Crawling Hand woof! 1963 An astronaut's hand takes off without him on an unearthly spree of stranglings. Silly stuff is a handsdown loser. **98m/B VHS, Beta, LV.** Alan Hale Jr., Rod Lauren, Richard Arlen, Peter Breck, Kent Taylor, Arline Judge, Allison Hayes; *D:* Herbert L. Strock. NOS, RHI, GEM

Crawlspace 🎬 1986 (R) Beautiful girls lease rooms from a murdering, perverted doctor who spies on them, then kills. You may find Kinski amusing but not terrifying. **86m/C VHS, Beta.** Klaus Kinski, Talia Balsam, Joyce Van Patten, Sally Brown, Barbara Whinnery; *D:* David Schmoeller; *W:* David Schmoeller; *M:* Pino Donaggio. VES, LIV

Craze 🎬🎬 *The Infernal Idol; Demon Master* 1974 (R) Toungue-in-cheek tale of a crazed antique dealer who slays a number of women as sacrifices to an African idol named Chuku. **96m/C VHS, Beta.** Jack Palance, Diana Dors, Julie Ege, Suzy Kendall, Michael Jayston, Edith Evans, Hugh Griffith, Trevor Howard; *D:* Freddie Francis. MRV

Crazed woof! 1982 Dull plodder about a psychopath who keeps a dead girl's body in his boarding house and kills all intruders to keep his secret. **88m/C VHS, Beta.** Laslo Papas, Belle Mitchell, Beverly Ross; *D:* Richard Cassidy. TWE

Crazed Cop 🎬 1988 A man's mind snaps when his wife is found raped and murdered, and nothing will stop him on his quest for revenge. Low budget and violent. **85m/C VHS, Beta.** Ivan Rogers, Sandy Brooke, Rich Sutherlin, Doug Irk, Abdulah the Great; *D:* Paul Kyriazi. UNI

The Crazies 🎬🎬 *Code Name: Trixie* 1973 (R) A poisoned water supply makes the residents of a small town go on a chaotic, murderous rampage. When the army is called into to quell the anarchy, a small war breaks out. Message film about the military is muddled and derivative. **103m/C Beta.** Lane Carroll, W.G. McMillan, Harold W. Jones, Lloyd Hollar, Lynn Lowry; *D:* George A. Romero; *W:* George A. Romero. NO

Crazy Fat Ethel II woof! 1985 A fat, hungry, homicidal female psychopath gets released from the asylum and goes on a cannabalistic rampage. Offensive junk. Sequel to "Criminally Insane." **90m/C VHS, Beta.** Priscilla Alden, Michael Flood, Jane Lambert, Robert Copple; *D:* Nick Phillips. NO

Crazy for Love 🎬🎬½ 1952 A village idiot stands to inherit the town inn if he can get a diploma within a year. With English subtitles. **80m/B VHS, Beta.** *FR* Brigitte Bardot, Bourvil, Jane Marken, Nadine Basile. DVT, GVV

Crazy from the Heart 🎬🎬🎬 1991 Sweet made-for-cable TV tale of a high school principal in a small south Texas town who discovers the romance of her life one weekend with a Mexican janitor. Strong, nuanced performances from Lahti and Blades make this chestnut of a story work beautifully, with able help from supporting actors. **104m/C VHS, Beta, LV, Closed Caption.** Christine Lahti, Ruben Blades, Mary Kay Place, Brent Spiner, William Russ, Louise Latham, Tommy Muntz, Robin Lively, Bibi Besch, Kamala Lopez; *D:* Thomas Schlamme. TTC

Crazy Horse 🎬🎬🎬 1996 TV bio of the Oglala Sioux warrior (Greyeyes) whose home in the Black Hills of South Dakota was threatened by western expansion and the constant breaking of government treaties. As war chief, Crazy Horse, along with Teton Sioux leader Sitting Bull (Schellenberg), lead the Cheyenne and Sioux against Custer (Horton) at the battle of Little Bighorn. They elude capture but constant harassment by troops lead to Crazy Horse's surrender and death in 1877, betrayed by both the whites and some of his own people. Gripping story with a fine cast. **120m/C VHS.** Michael Greyeyes, Jimmy Herman, Wes Studi, Irene Bedard, Peter Horton, John Finn, Steve Reevis, Gordon Tootoosis, August Schellenberg, Sheldon Peters Wolfchild, Ned Beatty; *D:* John Irvin; *W:* Robert Schenkkan; *C:* Thomas Burstyn; *M:* Lennie Niehaus. TTC

Crazy Horse and Custer: "The Untold Story" 🎬 1990 (R) Long before Little Big Horn, two legendary enemies find themselves trapped together in deadly Blackfoot territory. George Armstrong Custer and Crazy Horse are forced to form a volatile alliance in their life-or-death struggle against the murderous Blackfoot Tribe. History takes a back seat to Hollywood scriptwriting. **120m/C VHS.** Slim Pickens, Wayne Maunder, Mary Ann Mobley, Michael Dante. NO

Crazy in Love 🎬🎬 1992 Three generations of women live on an island in the home that has been in their family for years. Hunter is wildly in love with her husband, but misses (and doesn't quite trust) him when he is away on business.

Enter Sands, who showers her with affection and fills the void in her life. The supporting cast fleshes out the story nicely and illustrates the reasons behind Hunter's insecurity. Enjoyable romantic comedy doesn't throw out anything heavy. Adapted from the novel by Luanne Rice; made for television. **93m/C VHS, LV, Closed Caption.** Holly Hunter, Gena Rowlands, Bill Pullman, Julian Sands, Frances McDormand, Herta Ware, Joannne Baron; **D:** Martha Coolidge; **W:** Gerald Ayres. National Academy of Cable Programming ACE Awards '93: Best Supporting Actress (Ware). *TTC*

Crazy Mama 🦴🦴½ 1975 **(PG)** Three women go on a crime spree from California to Arkansas, picking up men and having a hoot. Crime and comedy in a campy romp. Set in the 1950s and loaded with period kitsch. **81m/C VHS, Beta.** Cloris Leachman, Stuart Whitman, Ann Sothern, Jim Backus, Linda Purl; **D:** Jonathan Demme.

Crazy Moon 🦴🦴½ *Huggers* 1987 **(PG-13)** A rich high school nerd falls in love with a deaf girl, and must struggle against his domineering father's and older brother's prejudices. The viewer must struggle against the romantic cliches and heavy-handed message to enjoy a basically tender tale of romance. **89m/C VHS, Beta, LV, Closed Caption.** Kiefer Sutherland, Vanessa Vaughan, Peter Spence, Ken Pogue, Eve Napier; **D:** Allan Eastman; **W:** Tom Berry, Stefan Wodoslawsky; **M:** Lou Forestieri. *NLC*

Crazy People 🦴½ 1990 **(R)** Advertising exec Emory Leeston (Moore) writes commercials that describe products with complete honesty, and is committed to a mental hospital as a result. He meets a variety of characters at the hospital, including Hannah, with whom he falls in love. Tepid box-office blunder sounds funnier than it is. We give half a bone for the ad slogans, the funniest part of the movie. Our favorite: "Most of our passengers arrive alive" for an airline. **91m/C VHS, Beta, LV, Closed Caption.** Dudley Moore, Daryl Hannah, Paul Reiser, Mercedes Ruehl, J.T. Walsh, Ben Hammer, Dick Cusack, Alan North, David Paymer, Danton Stone, Doug Yasuda, Bill Smitrovich, Paul Bates, Floyd Vivino; **D:** Tony Bill; **W:** Mitch Markowitz; **M:** Cliff Eidelman. *PAR*

The Crazy Ray 🦴🦴🦴 *Paris Qui Dort* 1922 The classic silent fantasy about a mad scientist who endeavors to put the whole population of Paris in a trance. Vintage Clair nonsense. **60m/B VHS, Beta.** *FR* Henri Rollan, Albert Prejean, Marcel Vallee, Madeleine Rodrigue; **D:** Rene Clair. *SNC, FCT, MRV*

The Crazysitter 🦴🦴½ 1994 **(PG-13)** Edie (D'Angelo), a petty thief recently released from jail, is hired as a sitter to the twins-from-hell. So, she decides to sell the little monsters.*CW:* Crude humor, thematic material. **92m/C VHS, LV.** Beverly D'Angelo, Ed Begley Jr., Carol Kane, Phil Hartman, Brady Bluhm, Rachel Duncan; *Cameos:* Nell Carter, Steve Landesburg; **D:** Michael James McDonald; **C:** Christopher Baffa. *NHO*

Creation of Adam 🦴🦴 1993 Weirdly mystical Russian drama finds Andrey's marriage in trouble because his wife thinks he's gay. She may be right because during a business meeting, Andrey is drawn to the charasmatic Philip, who, it turns out, is some sort of angelic messenger whose mission seems to be to give Andrey confidence in love. Good performances although the plot lacks coherence and is not helped by the poor subtitling. Russian with subtitles. **93m/C VHS.** *RU* Alexander Strizhenov, Anzhelika Nevolina, Saulus Balandis, Serghei Vinogradov, Irina Metlitshkaya; **D:** Yuri Pavlov. *WBF*

The Creation of the Humanoids woof! 1962 Set in the familiar post-holocaust future, this is a tale of humans outnumbered by androids and the resulting struggle for survival. Slow and silly low-budget sets. For some reason, Andy Warhol was reported to love this film. **84m/C VHS, Beta.** Don Megowan, Frances McCann, Erica Elliot, Don Doolittle, Dudley Manlove; **D:** Wesley E. Barry. *MRV, SNC*

Creator 🦴🦴 1985 **(R)** A Frankenstein-like scientist plans to clone a being based on his wife, who died thirty years ago. As his experiments begin to show positive results, his romantic attention turns towards his beautiful lab assistant. O'Toole as the deranged scientist almost saves this one. Based on a novel by Jeremy Leven. **108m/C VHS, Beta, LV.** Peter O'Toole, Mariel Hemingway, Vincent Spano, Virginia Madsen, David Ogden Stiers, John Dehner, Karen Kopins, Jeff Corey; **D:** Ivan Passer; **C:** Robbie Greenberg. *NO*

Creature 🦴 *Titan Find* 1985 **(R)** A two thousand-year-old alien life form is killing off astronauts exploring the planet Titan. "Alien" rip-off has its moments, but not enough of them. Kinski provides some laughs. **97m/C VHS, Beta, LV, Closed Caption.** Klaus Kinski, Stan Ivar, Wendy Schaal, Lyman Ward, Annette McCarthy, Diane Salinger; **D:** William Malone; **M:** Tom Chase, Steve Rucker. *MED*

Creature from Black Lake 🦴 1976 **(PG)** Two anthropology students from Chicago travel to the Louisiana swamps searching for the creature from Black Lake. Predictably, they find him. McClenny, incidentally, is Morgan Fairchild's sister. **95m/C VHS, Beta.** Jack Elam, Dub Taylor, Dennis Fimple, John David Carson, Bill Thurman, Catherine McClenny; **D:** Joy Houck Jr. *MRV, VES, LIV*

Creature from the Black Lagoon 🦴🦴🦴 1954 An anthropological expedition in the Amazon stumbles upon the Gill-Man, a prehistoric humanoid fish monster who takes a fancy to fetching Adams, a coed majoring in "science," but the humans will have none of it. Originally filmed in 3-D, this was one of the first movies to sport top-of-the-line underwater photography and remains one of the most enjoyable monster movies ever made. Gershenson's score became a "Creature Features" standard. Based on a story by Maurice Zimm. Sequels: "Revenge of the Creature" and "The Creature Walks Among Us." **79m/B VHS, Beta, LV.** Richard Carlson, Julie Adams, Richard Denning, Antonio Moreno, Whit Bissell, Nestor Paiva, Ricou Browning; **D:** Jack Arnold; **W:** Arthur Ross; **M:** Hans J. Salter. *USH, GKK*

Creature from the Haunted Sea 🦴🦴 1960 Monster movie satire set in Cuba shortly after the revolution and centering around an elaborate plan to loot the Treasury and put the blame on a strange sea monster. Corman comedy is predictably low budget but entertaining. "Wain" is really Robert Towne, winner of an Oscar for screenwriting. Remake of "Naked Paradise." **76m/B VHS, Beta.** Antony Carbone, Betsy Jones-Moreland, Beach Dickerson, Edward Wain, Edmundo Rivera Alvarez, Robert Bean; **D:** Roger Corman, Monte Hellman; **W:** Charles B. Griffith. *NOS, MRV, SNC*

Creature of Destruction 🦴 1967 A beautiful young woman is hypnotized and inadvertantly reverted to her past life as a hideous sea monster. Buchanan's remake of his own 1956 production, "The She Creature." **?m/B VHS.** Les Tremayne, Aron Kincaid, Pat Delaney, Neil Fletcher, Ann McAdams; **D:** Larry Buchanan. *NO*

Creature of the Walking Dead 🦴½ *La Marca del Muerto* 1960 Scientist brings his grandfather back to life with horrifying results for the cast and the audience. Made cheaply and quickly in Mexico in 1960, then released with added footage directed by Warren. **74m/B VHS.** *MX* Rock Madison, Ann Wells, George Todd, Willard Gross, Bruno Ve Sota; **D:** Frederic Corte, Jerry Warren. *NOS, MRV, SNC*

The Creature Walks Among Us 🦴½ 1956 Sequel to "Revenge of the Creature" has the Gill-Man once again being captured by scientists for studying purposes. Through an accidental lab fire, the creature's gills are burned off and he undergoes surgery in an attempt to live out of water. Final entry in the Creature series has little magic of the original. Also shot in 3-D. Available on laserdisc as part of a special Encore Edition Double Feature with "Revenge of the Creature." **79m/B VHS, LV, Closed Caption.** Jeff Morrow, Rex Reason, Leigh Snowden, Gregg Palmer; **D:** John Sherwood; **W:** Arthur Ross; **M:** Joseph Gershenson. *USH, FCT*

Creature with the Blue Hand 🦴🦴 1970 A German horror film based on a passable Edgar Wallace story about a man unjustly convicted of murders actually committed by a lunatic. Dubbed. **92m/C VHS, Beta.** *GE* Klaus Kinski, Harald Leopold, Hermann Leschau, Diana Kerner, Carl Lange, Ilse Page; **D:** Alfred Vohrer. *NO*

Creatures the World Forgot woof! 1970 A British-made bomb about two tribes of cavemen warring over power and a cavewoman. No special effects, dinosaurs, or dialogue. **96m/C VHS, Beta.** Julie Ege, Robert John, Tony Bonner, Rosalie Crutchley, Sue Wilson; **D:** Don Chaffey; **W:** Michael Carreras. *COL, MLB*

The Creeper 🦴🦴 1948 After experimenting with a variety of serums, a doctor turns into a murderous monster with feline paws. **65m/B VHS, Beta.** Eduardo Ciannelli, Onslow Stevens, June Vincent, Ralph Morgan; **D:** Jean Yarbrough. *MLB*

Creepers 🦴🦴½ *Phenomena* 1985 **(R)** A young girl talks to bugs and gets them to follow her instructions, which comes in handy when she battles the lunatic who is killing her school chums. Argento weirdness—and graphic gore—may not be for all tastes. **82m/C VHS, Beta.** *IT* Jennifer Connelly, Donald Pleasence, Daria Nicolodi, Elenora Giorgi, Dalia di Lazzaro, Patrick Bauchau, Fiore Argento; **D:** Dario Argento; **W:** Franco Ferrini, Dario Argento; **M:** Simon Boswell. *MED*

The Creeping Flesh 🦴🦴½ 1972 **(PG)** A scientist decides he can cure evil by injecting his patients with a serum derived from the blood of an ancient corpse. Some truly chilling moments will get your flesh creeping. **89m/C VHS, Beta, LV.** *GB* Peter Cushing, Christopher Lee, Lorna Heilbron, George Benson; **D:** Freddie Francis. *COL, IME, MLB*

Creeping Terror woof! *The Crawling Monster; Dangerous Charter* 1964 Gigantic alien carpet monster (look for the tennis shoes sticking out underneath) devours slow-moving teenagers. Partially narrated because some of the original soundtrack was lost, with lots of bad acting, a worse script, laughable sets, and a ridiculous monster. Beware of the thermometer scene. **81m/B VHS, Beta.** Vic Savage, Shannon O'Neal, William Thourlby, Louise Lawson, Robin James; **D:** John Sherwood. *NO*

Creepozoids 🦴 1987 In the near future, a monster at an abandoned science complex stalks army deserters hiding out there. Violent nonsense done better by others. **72m/C Beta, LV.** Linnea Quigley, Ken Abraham, Michael Aranda; **D:** David DeCoteau. *NO*

Creepshow 🦴🦴½ 1982 **(R)** Stephen King's tribute to E.C. Comics, those pulp horror comic books of the 1950s that delighted in grisly, grotesque, and morbid humor, the film tells five horror tales. Features King himself in one segment, as a none-too-bright farmer who unknowingly cultivates a strange, alien-origin moss. With despicable heroes and gory monsters, this is sure to delight all fans of the horror vein. Those easily repulsed by cockroaches beware! **120m/C VHS, Beta, LV, Closed Caption.** Hal Holbrook, Adrienne Barbeau, Viveca Lindfors, E.G. Marshall, Stephen King, Leslie Nielsen, Carrie Nye, Fritz Weaver, Ted Danson, Ed Harris; **D:** George A. Romero; **W:** Stephen King. *WAR*

Creepshow 2 🦴½ 1987 **(R)** Romero adapted three Stephen King stories for this horror anthology which presents gruesome looks at a hit-and-run driver, a wooden Indian, and a vacation gone wrong. Gory and childish stuff from two masters of the genre. Look for King as a truck driver. **92m/C VHS, Beta, LV, Closed Caption.** Lois Chiles, George Kennedy, Dorothy Lamour, Tom Savini, Domenick John, Frank S. Salsedo, Holt McCallany, David Holbrook, Page Hannah, Daniel Beer, Stephen King; **D:** Michael Gornick; **W:** George A. Romero. *VTR, NWV*

The Cremators woof! 1972 A meteorite carrying an alien lands at a seaside resort and everyone begins bursting into flames. Low budget effort from the scripter of "It Came from Outer

Space." **90m/C VHS, Beta.** Marvin Howard, Maria de Aragon; **D:** Harry Essex. *NO*

The Crew 🎬🎬 **1995 (R)** Sometimes it doesn't pay to be a good samaritan—as a boatload of pleasure cruisers discover when they rescue two psychopaths from a burning boat in the Bahamas.***CW:*** Strong language. **99m/C VHS, Closed Caption.** Viggo Mortensen, Jeremy Sisto, Pamela Gidley, Donal Logue, Laura Del Sol, Grace Zabriskie, John Philbin; **D:** Carl Colpaert; **W:** Carl Colpaert. *LIV*

Cria 🎬🎬🎬 *Cria Cuervos; Raise Ravens* **1976 (PG)** The award-winning story of a 9-year-old girl's struggle for maturity in a hostile adult world. In Spanish with English subtitles. **115m/C VHS, Beta, LV.** *SP* Geraldine Chaplin, Ana Torrent, Conchita Perez; **D:** Carlos Saura. Cannes Film Festival '76: Grand Jury Prize; National Board of Review Awards '77: 5 Best Foreign Films of the Year. *INT, TPV, APD*

Cricket on the Hearth 🎬🎬 **1923** An adaptation of Charles Dickens' short story about a mail carrier and his bride, who find the symbol of good luck, a cricket on the hearth, when they enter their new home. Silent with organ score. **68m/B VHS, Beta.** Paul Gerson, Virginia Brown Faire, Paul Moore, Joan Standing. *CCB*

Cries and Whispers 🎬🎬🎬 *Viskingar Och Rop* **1972 (R)** As a woman dies slowly of tuberculosis, three women care for her: her two sisters, one sexually repressed, the other promiscuous, and her servant. The sisters remember family love and closeness, but are too afraid to look death in the face to aid their sister. Only the servant can touch her in her dying and only the servant believes in God and his will. Beautiful imagery, focused through a nervous camera, which lingers on the meaningless and whisks away from the meaningful. Absolute mastery of cinematic art by Bergman. **91m/C VHS, Beta, LV.** *SW* Harriet Andersson, Ingrid Thulin, Liv Ullmann, Kary Sylway, Erland Josephson, Henning Moritzen; **D:** Ingmar Bergman; **C:** Sven Nykvist. Academy Awards '73: Best Cinematography; National Board of Review Awards '73: 5 Best Foreign Films of the Year, Best Director (Bergman); New York Film Critics Awards '72: Best Actress (Ullmann), Best Director (Bergman), Best Film, Best Screenplay; National Society of Film Critics Awards '72: Best Cinematography, Best Screenplay; Nominations: Academy Awards '73: Best Costume Design, Best Director (Bergman), Best Picture, Best Story & Screenplay. *HMV, WAR, BTV*

Crime & Passion 🎬½ **1975 (R)** Two scheming lovers plan to get rich by having the woman marry a multimillionaire and sue for a quick divorce. The multimillionaire is no patsy, however, and seeks a deadly revenge. Three scripts by six writers were combined to create this story. That explains the many problems. **92m/C VHS, Beta.** Omar Sharif, Karen Black, Joseph Bottoms, Bernhard Wicki; **D:** Ivan Passer. *VES, LIV*

Crime and Punishment 🎬🎬🎬 **1935** Pared down but well-executed version of the Dostoyevski novel. Lorre is superb as Raskolnikov, who robs and murders an elderly pawnbroker. Believing he has committed the perfect murder, he accepts the invitation of police inspector Porfiry (Arnold) to observe the investigation. Gradually Raskolnikov's conscience begins to overwhelm him as Porfiry slowly works to wring a confession from the killer. Von Sternberg's subdued directorial approach worked well to explore the psychological aspects of guilt, although the melodramatic French film version (released at the same time) scored better with the critics. **88m/B VHS.** Peter Lorre, Edward Arnold, Marian Marsh, Tala Birell, Elisabeth Risdon, Robert Allen, Douglass Dumbrille, Gene Lockhart; **D:** Josef von Sternberg; **W:** S.K. Lauren, Joseph Anthony. *COL*

Crime and Punishment 🎬🎬🎬🎬 *Crime et Chatiment* **1935** Original French production (preceding the American version by just one week) of Dostoyevski's novel, the tale of a young murderer, his crime, and ultimately, his confession. Generally considered better than the American version, the French throw out all that is not dramatic, keep-

ing the psychology and suspense. Remade in 1958. **110m/B VHS.** Harry Baur, Pierre Blanchar, Madeleine Ozeray, Marcelle Geniat, Lucienne Lemarchand; **D:** Pierre Chenal; **W:** Marcel Ayme, Chenal, Christian Stengel, Wladimir Strijewski; **M:** Arthur Honegger. *FCT*

Crime and Punishment 🎬🎬 **1970** Ponderous, excruciatingly long adaptation of the Dostoyevski classic involving a haunted murderer and the relentless policeman who seeks to prove him guilty. In Russian with English subtitles. **200m/B VHS.** *RU* Georgi Taratorkin, Victoria Fyodorova; **D:** Lev Kulijanov; **W:** Lev Kulijanov. *DVT, HEG, TPV*

Crime Broker 🎬🎬 **1994** A respected judge (Bisset) decides to experience life on the other side of the bench for a change. So she hooks up with a handsome partner to execute a series of high-profile robberies of bank vaults and museums. Implied sex so don't look for this under erotic thrillers. **93m/C VHS.** Jacqueline Bisset, Masaya Kato, Gary Day; **D:** Ian Barry; **W:** Tony Morphett; **C:** Dan Burstall; **M:** Roger Mason. *APX*

Crime Busters 🎬½ **1978 (PG)** Two guys attempt to pull off a bank heist but accidentally join the Miami police force instead. Hill and Spencer are enjoyable as usual but the film suffers from poor dubbing. Remake of "Two Supercops." **114m/C VHS, Beta.** *IT* Terence Hill, Bud Spencer, Laura Gemser, Luciana Catenacci, David Huddleston; **D:** E.B. Clucher. *WAR*

Crime Killer 🎬 **1985** Confusing shenanigans about an explosive ex-CIA agent enlisted by the FBI to battle a brutal crime syndicate shipping guns to nasty Arabs. **90m/C VHS, Beta.** George Pan-Andreas, Leo Morrell, Althan Karras; **D:** George Pan-Andreas; **C:** Arledge Armenaki. *VTR, NWV*

Crime Lords 🎬🎬 **1991 (R)** When a pair of cops are suspended from the force for committing a blunder, they travel to Hong Kong to continue their investigation. Little do they know their sleuthing has drawn then into a confrontation with one of largest crime syndicates in the world. Lots of action, beautiful women, and exotic locations keep this basic buddy plot moving well.***CW:*** Language, strong violence, and sensuality. **96m/C VHS.** Wayne Crawford, Martin Hewitt, Susan Byun, Mel Castelo, James Hong; **D:** Wayne Crawford. *ACA*

The Crime of Dr. Crespi 🎬🎬 **1935** A doctor takes his revenge on a man who is after his girlfriend by injecting him with suspended animation serum. Extremely campy performance from von Stroheim; Frye's biggest role in terms of screen time. **64m/B VHS, Beta.** Erich von Stroheim, Dwight Frye, Paul Guilfoyle, Harriett Russell, John Bohn; **D:** John H. Auer. *NOS, SNC, MLB*

Crime of Honor 🎬 **1985** A European executive goes public with his company's corruption, and his family suffers predictable ruin as a result. Based on a true story. **95m/C VHS, Beta.** Maria Schneider, David Suchet; **D:** John Goldschmidt. *ACA*

The Crime of Monsieur Lange 🎬🎬🎬 *Le Crime de Monsieur Lange* **1936** Charming French socialist fantasy where workers at a publishing company turn the business into a thriving cooperative while their evil boss is gone. When he returns, worker Lefevre plots to kill him. Rather talky, but humorous. In French with subtitles. French script booklet also available. **90m/B VHS, Beta.** *FR* Rene Lefevre, Jules Berry, Florelle, Sylvia Bataille, Jean Daste, Nadia Sibirskaia; **D:** Jean Renoir; **W:** Jacques Prevert. *FCT, INT, APD*

Crime of Passion 🎬🎬½ **1957** Stanwyck plays a femme fatale whose ambitions for detective hubby lead to murder. Good performances from Stanwyck, Hayden, and Burr make this an above-average, although outlandish, crime-drama. **85m/B VHS, Closed Caption.** Barbara Stanwyck, Sterling Hayden, Raymond Burr, Fay Wray, Royal Dano, Virginia Grey, Dennis Cross, Robert Griffin, Jay Adler, Malcolm Atterbury, S. John Launer, Brad Trumbull, Skipper McNally, Jean Howell, Peg La Centra, Nancy Reynolds, Marjorie Owens, Robert Quarry, Joe Conley, Stuart Whit-

man; **D:** Gerd Oswald; **W:** Jo Eisinger; **C:** Joseph LaShelle; **M:** Paul Dunlap. *MGM, FCT*

Crime of the Century 🎬🎬½ **1996 (PG-13)** Another look at the 1932 kidnapping and death of Charles Lindbergh's 18-month-old son. Based on the 1985 book "The Airman and the Carpenter" by Ludovic Kennedy, it's clear the author regards Bruno Richard Hauptmann (Rea), who was executed in 1936, as an innocent scapegoat essentially railroaded thanks to media and political pressures. Made for cable.***CW:*** Some intense thematic elements, including an execution scene. **116m/C VHS.** Stephen Rea, J.T. Walsh, David Paymer, John Harkins, Michael Moriarty, Isabella Rossellini, Bert Remsen, Allen (Goorwitz) Garfield, Don Harvey, Gerald S. O'Loughlin, Barry Primus; **D:** Mark Rydell; **W:** William Nicholson; **C:** Toyomichi Kurita; **M:** John Frizzell. *HBO*

Crime Story 🎬🎬 *Hard to Die* **1993 (R)** Police Inspector Eddie Chan (Chan) tries to crack a kidnapping case and discovers his partner, Detective Hung (Cheng), is not on the up-and-up. Usual arobatic stunts from Chan and company. Cantonese with subtitles. **104m/C VHS, LV, Closed Caption.** *HK* Jackie Chan, Kent Cheng, Law Hang Kang, Christine Ng; **D:** Kirk Wong; **C:** Arthur Wong, Ardy Lam. *TOU*

Crime Story: The Complete Saga
1986 All 42 episodes of the 1986-1988 NBC cops-versus-mobsters series set first in Chicago in 1963, and later in Las Vegas. The series was created by Michael Mann, the executive producer of "Miami Vice." Del Shannon updated the lyrics to his hit "Runaway" for the series theme. Available as a boxed set of ten tapes or individually. **?m/C VHS.** Dennis Farina, Anthony John Denison, Bill Smitrovich, Steve Ryan, Bill Campbell, Paul Butler, Stephen Lang, Darlanne Fluegel. *VTR, MOV*

Crime Zone 🎬🎬½ **1988 (R)** In a totalitarian, repressive, future society, two young lovers try to beat the system and make it on their own. A well-made, if occasionally muddled, low-budget film shot in Peru, of all places. **96m/C VHS.** David Carradine, Peter Nelson, Sherilyn Fenn, Orlando Sacha, Don Manor, Michael Shaner; **D:** Luis Llosa; **W:** Daryl Haney; **M:** Rick Conrad. *MGM*

Crimebusters 🎬½ **1979 (PG)** A man exacts revenge against a government conspiracy that kidnapped his loved ones. **90m/C VHS, Beta.** Henry Silva, Antonio Sabato; **D:** Michael Tarantini. *NO*

Crimes & Misdemeanors 🎬🎬🎬 **1989 (PG-13)** One of Allen's most mature films, exploring a whole range of moral ambiguities through the parallel and eventually interlocking stories of a nebbish filmmaker—who agrees to make a profile of a smug Hollywood television comic and then sabotages it—and an esteemed ophthalmologist who is being threatened with exposure by his neurotic mistress. Intriguing mix of drama and comedy few directors could pull off. Look for Daryl Hannah in an unbilled cameo. **104m/C VHS, Beta, LV, Closed Caption.** Martin Landau, Woody Allen, Alan Alda, Mia Farrow, Joanna Gleason, Anjelica Huston, Jerry Orbach, Sam Waterston, Claire Bloom, Jenny Nichols, Caroline Aaron; **Cameos:** Daryl Hannah, Nora Ephron, Jerry Zaks; **D:** Woody Allen; **W:** Woody Allen; **C:** Sven Nykvist. National Board of Review Awards '89: Best Supporting Actor (Alda); New York Film Critics Awards '89: Best Supporting Actor (Alda); Writers Guild of America '89: Best Original Screenplay; Nominations: Academy Awards '89: Best Director (Allen), Best Original Screenplay, Best Supporting Actor (Landau). *ORI*

Crimes at the Dark House 🎬🎬🎬 **1939** In this campy, melodramatic adaptation of Wilkie Collins's novel "The Woman in White," a man kills his rich wife and puts a disguised mental patient in her place. Later remade using the book's title. **69m/B VHS.** *GB* Tod Slaughter, Hilary Eaves, Sylvia Marriott, Hay Petrie, Geoffrey Wardwell; **D:** George King. *NOS, MRV, SNC*

Crimes of Dr. Mabuse ✶✶✶½ 1932
Supernatural horror classic about the evil Dr. Mabuse controlling an underworld empire while confined to an insane asylum. One of the best "mad doctor" movies ever made. Also known as "The Testament of Dr. Mabuse" or "The Last Will of Dr. Mabuse." **120m/B VHS. GE** Rudolf Klein-Rogge, Otto Wernicke, Gustav Diessl, Karl Meixner; **D:** Fritz Lang. SNC

Crimes of Passion ✶✶✶ 1984
Vintage whacked-out Russell, not intended for the kiddies. A business-like fashion designer becomes a kinky prostitute at night. A disturbed street preacher makes her the heroine of his erotic fantasies. A dark terrifying vision of the underground sex world and moral hypocrisy. Sexually explicit and violent, with an extremely black comedic center. Turner's portrayal is honest and believable, Perkins overacts until he nearly gets a nosebleed, but it's all for good effect. Cut for "R" rating to get it in the theatres; this version restores some excised footage. Also available in rated version. **101m/C VHS, Beta, LV, Closed Caption.** Kathleen Turner, Anthony Perkins, Annie Potts, John Laughlin, Bruce Davison, Norman Burton; **D:** Ken Russell; **W:** Barry Sandler; **M:** Rick Wakeman. Los Angeles Film Critics Association Awards '84: Best Actress (Turner). NWV, VTR

The Crimes of Stephen Hawke ✶✶
Strangler's Morgue 1936 The world knows Stephen Hawke as a big-hearted money lender. What they don't know is his favorite hobby is breaking peoples' spines. An entertaining thriller set in the 1800s. **65m/B VHS, Beta. GB** Tod Slaughter, Marjorie Taylor, D.J. Williams, Eric Portman, Ben Soutten; **D:** George King. SNC, MRV, HEG

Crimes of the Heart ✶✶½ 1986 (PG-13)
Based on Beth Henley's acclaimed play. A few days in the lives of three very strange Southern sisters, one of whom has just been arrested for calmly shooting her husband after he chased her black lover out of town. Spacek as the suicidal sister is a lark. A tart, black comedy that works better as a play than a film. **105m/C VHS, Beta, LV, Closed Caption.** Sissy Spacek, Diane Keaton, Jessica Lange, Sam Shepard, Tess Harper, Hurd Hatfield; **D:** Bruce Beresford; **W:** Beth Henley; **C:** Dante Spinotti; **M:** Georges Delerue. Golden Globe Awards '87: Best Actress—Musical/Comedy (Spacek); New York Film Critics Awards '86: Best Actress (Spacek); Nominations: Academy Awards '86: Best Actress (Spacek), Best Adapted Screenplay, Best Supporting Actress (Harper). ORI, WAR

Crimetime ✶½ 1996 (R)
Silly thriller has actor Bobby (Baldwin) finding unexpected success portraying a serial killer in a crime re-enactment TV show called "Crimetime." Meanwhile, Sydney (Postlethwaite), who's the real killer Bobby's character is based on, becomes seduced by the media frenzy surrounding the crimes and seeing them re-enacted on television. He goes on killing, so the show can literally go on. **CW:** Violence, sexuality, and language. **118m/C VHS, Closed Caption.** Stephen Baldwin, Pete Postlethwaite, Sadie Frost, Geraldine Chaplin, Karen Black, James Faulkner; **Cameos:** Marianne Faithfull; **D:** George Sluizer; **W:** Brendan Somers; **C:** Jules Van Den Steenhoven. THV

Crimewave ✶✶
The XYZ Murders; Broken Hearts and Noses 1985 (PG-13) Zany spoof about serial killers set in Detroit (director Raimi's hometown). A rhapsody to comic book style, short on plot and long on style. With such credentials you expect more. **83m/C VHS, Beta, Closed Caption.** Louise Lasser, Paul Smith, Brion James, Bruce Campbell, Reed Birney, Sheree J. Wilson, Edward R. Pressman, Julius W. Harris; **D:** Sam Raimi; **W:** Ethan Coen, Joel Coen, Sam Raimi. NLC

Criminal Act ✶½ 1988
A newspaper editor hits the street to prove she's still a tough reporter, but uncovers a dangerous scandal in the process. **94m/C VHS, Beta.** Catherine Bach, Charlene Dallas, Nicholas Guest, John Saxon, Vic Tayback; **D:** Mark Byers. PSM

Criminal Code ✶✶½ 1931
Aging melodrama about a young man who's jailed for killing in self-defense. His life worsens at the hands of a prison warden when the head guy's daughter falls for him. Remade as "Penitentiary" and "Convicted." **98m/B VHS, Beta.** Walter Huston, Phillips Holmes, Boris Karloff, Constance Cummings, Mary Doran, DeWitt Jennings, John Sheehan; **D:** Howard Hawks. Nominations: Academy Awards '31: Best Adapted Screenplay. COL, MLB

Criminal Court ✶✶ 1946
A man accused of murdering his blackmailer hires the real killer as his attorney. Hard to follow, with an interesting premise that turns flat. **63m/B VHS, Beta.** Tom Conway, Martha O'Driscoll, Robert Armstrong, Addison Richards, June Clayworth, Pat Gleason, Steve Brodie; **D:** Robert Wise. NO

Criminal Hearts ✶✶ 1995 (R)
Jilted young woman picks up a hitchhiker/thief who's stolen Mob money and goes on the run after being framed for murder. **CW:** Violence, sexuality, and language. **92m/C VHS.** Kevin Dillon, Amy Locane, Morgan Fairchild, M. Emmet Walsh; **D:** Dave Payne; **W:** Dave Payne. AVE

Criminal Justice ✶✶✶ 1990 (R)
A black man is accused of a crime by a woman with whom he was involved. Is it justice or revenge? Strong cast in important story. Made for cable TV. **92m/C VHS, Closed Caption.** Forest Whitaker, Jennifer Grey, Rosie Perez, Anthony LaPaglia, Tony Todd; **D:** Andy Wolk; **W:** Andy Wolk. HBO

Criminal Law ✶✶ 1989 (R)
An ambitious young Boston lawyer gets a man acquitted for murder, only to find out after the trial that the man is guilty and renewing his killing spree. Realizing he's the only one privy to the killer's trust, the lawyer decides to stop him himself. A white-knuckled thriller burdened by a weak script. **113m/C VHS, Beta, LV.** Kevin Bacon, Gary Oldman, Karen Young, Joe Don Baker, Tess Harper; **D:** Martin Campbell; **W:** Mark Kasden; **M:** Jerry Goldsmith. HBO, WAR

The Criminal Life of Archibaldo de la Cruz ✶✶✶
Ensayo de un Crimen; Rehearsal for a Crime 1955 Seeing the death of his governess has a lasting effect on a boy. He grows up to be a demented cretin whose failure with women leads him to conspire to kill every one he meets, a task at which he also fails. Hilarious, bitter Bunuelian diatribe. In Spanish with English subtitles. **95m/B VHS, Beta. MX SP** Ernesto Alonso, Ariadne Welter, Rita Macedo, Rodolfo Landa, Andrea Palma, Miroslava Stern; **D:** Luis Bunuel. FCT, WBF

The Criminal Mind ✶✶ 1993 (R)
L.A. District Attorney Nick August (Rossi) reunites with his long-lost brother (Cross), whom he discovers is very familiar with the other side of the law. Tied up with the mob, Cross forces his bro to watch a hit and then Rossi winds up the next target for a group of assassins and some corrupt cops. **93m/C VHS, Closed Caption.** Ben Cross, Frank Rossi, Tahnee Welch, Lance Henriksen, Joseph Ruskin, Lynn-Holly Johnson; **D:** Joseph Vittorie; **W:** Sam A. Scribner. COL

Criminally Insane ✶ 1975
Authorities release 250 pounds of cleaver-wielding maniacal fury from the loony bin. She seeks food and human blood. They should have known better. Followed by "Crazy Fat Ethel II." **97m/C VHS, Beta.** Priscilla Alden, Michael Flood; **D:** Nick Phillips. NO

Criminals Within ✶
Army Mystery 1941 A scientist working on a top secret formula is murdered and a detective tries to nail the spy ring responsible. Very confusing, poor usage of some fine female cast members. **67m/B VHS, Beta.** Eric Linden, Ann Doran, Constance Worth, Donald Curtis, Weldon Heyburn, Ben Alexander; **D:** Joseph H. Lewis. SNC

The Crimson Cult ✶
The Crimson Altar; Curse of the Crimson Altar 1968 (PG) Eden and his girlfriend are invited to a mysterious mansion. They discover that Lee is out to enact revenge as his ancestor was burned for witchcraft by Eden's. An all-star horror disaster. Karloff was eighty and confined to a wheelchair. Despite ads claiming this as his last film, he had four more in Mexico. Highlights include the scantily clad Steele in sado-masochistic sequences and a psychedelic party with strippers and body painters. **87m/C VHS. GB** Boris Karloff, Christopher Lee, Mark Eden, Barbara Steele, Virginia Wetherell, Michael Gough, Rupert Davies; **D:** Vernon Sewell. MOV

Crimson Pirate ✶✶✶½ 1952
An 18th-century buccaneer pits his wits and brawn against the might of a ruthless Spanish nobleman. Considered by many to be one of the best swashbucklers, laced with humor and enthusiastically paced. Showcase for Lancaster and Cravat's acrobatic talents. **104m/C VHS, Beta, LV. GB** Burt Lancaster, Eva Bartok, Torin Thatcher, Christopher Lee, Nick Cravat; **D:** Robert Siodmak. WAR

Crimson Romance ✶✶ 1934
Two unemployed American pilots in Europe decide to join the German airforce for want of anything better to do. Conflicts revolve around a warmongering Commandant and his pilot. **70m/B VHS, Beta, 8mm.** Ben Lyon, Sari Maritza, James Bush, Erich von Stroheim, Jason Robards Sr., Herman Bing, Vince Barnett; **D:** David Howard. NOS, VYY, RXM

Crimson Tide ✶✶✶ 1995 (R)
Mutiny erupts aboard the submarine USS Alabama as Captain Ramsey (Hackman) and his Executive Officer Hunter (Washington) clash over the validity of orders to launch the sub's missiles. Ramsey, who wants to fire the missiles, and Hunter, who refuses to comply until the message is verified, battle for control of the sub. Suspenseful and well-paced thriller lets Hackman and Washington show off their considerable screen presence, while Bruckheimer, Simpson, and Scott show that they haven't lost any of their trademark big-budget, testosterone-laden flash. Original screenplay went under the knife of a number of script doctors, most notably Quentin Tarantino. **CW:** Strong language. **116m/C VHS, LV, Closed Caption.** Gene Hackman, Denzel Washington, George Dzundza, Viggo Mortensen, James Gandolfini, Matt Craven, Lillo Brancato, Danny Nucci, Steve Zahn, Rick Schroder, Vanessa Bell Calloway, Rocky Carroll; **Cameos:** Jason Robards Jr.; **D:** Tony Scott; **W:** Michael Schiffer, Richard P. Henrick; **C:** Darius Wolski; **M:** Hans Zimmer. Nominations: Academy Awards '95: Best Film Editing, Best Sound; MTV Movie Awards '96: Best Male Performance (Washington). TOU

The Crimson Trail ✶✶½ 1935
Buck believes his uncle may be involved in cattle rustling. Lots of action, minimal plot. **56m/B VHS.** Buck Jones, Polly Ann Young, Carl Stockdale, Charles French, Ward Bond, Robert F. (Bob) Kortman, Bud Osborne, Charles Brinley, Robert Walker; **D:** Al Raboch; **W:** Jack Natteford. GPV

The Crippled Masters ✶✶ 1982 (R)
After Li Ho's (Shum) arms are cut off by an evil warlord, he wanders the countryside facing ridicule until he teams up with disfigured Dax Oh Jen (Conn). Helped by an elderly yoga master, the duo unite to seek revenge. Features kung-fu masters with real-life disabilities. **CW:** Violence. **90m/C VHS.** Frankie Shum, Jack Conn; **D:** Joe Law. NLC

Crisis at Central High ✶✶✶ 1980
A dramatic television recreation of the events leading up to the 1957 integration of Central High in Little Rock, Arkansas. Based on teacher Elizabeth Huckaby's journal. Emmy-nominated performance by Woodward as Huckaby. **120m/C VHS, Beta.** Joanne Woodward, Charles Durning, William Ross, Henderson Forsythe; **D:** Lamont Johnson; **M:** Billy Goldenberg. NO

Criss Cross ✶✶✶ 1948
A classic grade-B film noir, in which an armored car driver is suckered into a burglary by his ex-wife and her hoodlum husband. Multiple back-stabbings and double-crossings ensue. **98m/B VHS, Beta.** Burt Lancaster, Yvonne De Carlo, Dan Duryea, Stephen McNally, Richard Long, Tony Curtis; **D:** Robert Siodmak; **W:** Daniel Fuchs; **M:** Miklos Rozsa. USH

Crisscross ✶✶½
Alone Together 1992 (R) It's 1969 and Tracy Cross is a divorced mom whose ex-husband is a traumatized Vietnam vet who has left her alone to raise their 12 year-old son Chris during some hard times. She works two jobs, as a waitress and, unbeknownst to her son, as a stripper in a local club. When Chris sneaks into the club and sees her act he takes drastic measures

to help out—by selling drugs. Film is sluggish and relies too much on voice-overs to explain thoughts but Hawn gives a convincing and restrained performance as the mother.**CW:** Language, drug-related scenes, and one strong sensual scene. **107m/C VHS, Beta, LV, Closed Caption.** Goldie Hawn, David Arnott, Arliss Howard, James Gammon, Keith Carradine, J.C. Quinn, Steve Buscemi, Paul Calderone; **D:** Chris Menges; **M:** Trevor Jones. MGM

Critical Condition 🎬 1986 (R) During a blackout, a criminal masquerades as a doctor in a city hospital. Limp comedy embarrassing for Pryor. **99m/C VHS, Beta, LV, Closed Caption.** Richard Pryor, Rachel Ticotin, Ruben Blades, Joe Mantegna; **D:** Michael Apted; **C:** Ralf Bode; **M:** Alan Silvestri. PAR

Critters 🎬🎬½ 1986 (PG-13) A gang of furry, razor-toothed aliens escapes from its prison ship to Earth with their bounty hunters right behind them. They make it to a small town in Kansas where they begin to attack anything that moves. Not just a thrill-kill epic, but a sarcastic otherworldly thrill-kill epic. **86m/C VHS, Beta, LV.** Dee Wallace Stone, M. Emmet Walsh, Billy Green Bush, Scott Grimes, Nadine Van der Velde, Terrence Mann, Billy Zane, Don Opper, Terrence Mann; **D:** Stephen Herek; **W:** Stephen Herek; **M:** David Newman. COL

Critters 2: The Main Course 🎬🎬 1988 (PG-13) Sequel to the hit horror-comedy, wherein the voracious alien furballs return in full force to Grovers Bend, Kansas, from eggs planted two years before. Occasionally inspired "Gremlins" rip. **93m/C VHS, Beta, LV, Closed Caption.** Scott Grimes, Liane Curtis, Don Opper, Barry Corbin, Terrence Mann; **D:** Mick Garris; **W:** Mick Garris, David N. Twohy; **C:** Russell Carpenter. COL

Critters 3 🎬🎬 1991 (PG-13) The not-so-loveable critters are back, terrorizing the occupants of a tenement building. **86m/C VHS, Closed Caption.** Francis Bay, Aimee Brooks, Leonardo DiCaprio, Don Opper; **D:** Kristine Peterson; **W:** David J. Schow. COL, NLC

Critters 4 🎬🎬 1991 (PG-13) The ghoulish critters are back, and this time a strain of genetically engineered mutant critters (what's the difference?) wants to take over the universe. **94m/C VHS, LV, Closed Caption.** Don Opper, Paul Whitthorne, Angela Bassett, Brad Dourif, Terrence Mann; **D:** Rupert Harvey; **W:** David J. Schow. NLC, COL

Crocodile woof! 1981 (R) Giant crocodile attacks a beach town, killing and devouring dozens of people. The locals sit around trying to figure a way to stop the critter. Special effects include rear-projected croc. Lots of blood but lacking humor of "Alligator." Filmed in Thailand and Korea. **95m/C VHS, Beta.** Nat Puvanai, Tiny Tim; **D:** Herman Cohen. NO

Crocodile Dundee 🎬🎬🎬½ 1986 (PG-13) New York reporter Sue Charlton is assigned to the Outback to interview living legend Mike Dundee. When she finally locates the man, she is so taken with him that she brings him back to New York with her. There, the naive Aussie wanders about, amazed at the wonders of the city and unwittingly charming everyone he comes in contact with, from high-society transvestites to street hookers. One of the surprise hits of 1986. **98m/C VHS, Beta, LV, 8mm, Closed Caption.** AU Paul Hogan, Linda Kozlowski, John Meillon, David Gulpilil, Mark Blum; **D:** Peter Faiman; **W:** Paul Hogan, John Cornell; **C:** Russell Boyd; **M:** Peter Best. Golden Globe Awards '87: Best Actor—Musical/Comedy (Hogan); Nominations: Academy Awards '86: Best Original Screenplay. PAR

Crocodile Dundee 2 🎬🎬½ 1988 (PG) In this sequel Mike Dundee, the loveable rube, returns to his native Australia looking for new adventure, having "conquered" New York City. He inadvertently gets involved in stopping a gang of crooks active in Australia and New York. Lacks the charm and freshness of the first film. **110m/C VHS, Beta, LV, Closed Caption.** Paul Hogan, Linda Kozlowski, Kenneth Welsh, John Meillon, Ernie Dingo, Juan Fernandez, Charles S. Dutton; **D:** John Cornell; **W:** Paul Hogan; **C:** Russell Boyd; **M:** Peter Best. PAR

Crocodiles in Amsterdam 🎬🎬 Krokodillen in Amsterdam 1989 Lunatic girl-meets-girl movie about flighty Gino and would-be terrorist Nina who team up to rob Gino's rich uncle. Dutch with subtitles. **88m/C VHS.** NL Joan Nederlof, Yolanda Entius; **D:** Annette Apon. WBF

Cromwell 🎬🎬½ 1970 (G) A lavish British-made spectacle about the conflict between Oliver Cromwell and Charles I, and the British Civil War. History is twisted as Cromwell becomes the liberator of the oppressed. Harris gives a commanding performance and the battle scenes are stunners. **139m/C VHS, Beta, LV.** GB Richard Harris, Alec Guinness, Robert Morley, Frank Finlay, Patrick Magee, Timothy Dalton; **D:** Ken Hughes; **W:** Ken Hughes; **C:** Geoffrey Unsworth. Academy Awards '70: Best Costume Design; Nominations: Academy Awards '70: Best Original Score. COL, TVC

Cronos 🎬🎬 1994 (R) Stylish Mexican variation of the vampire tale. Aged antiques dealer Jesus Gris (Luppi) comes across the mysterious title object—a 14th century golden egg possessing magical powers to grant eternal life. But can its possessor stand the consequences, which include a developing taste for blood? Another problem is Gris isn't the only one to know about the device. First feature for writer/director del Toro. Spanish with subtitles.**CW:** Language; horror violence. **92m/C VHS, LV.** MX Federico Luppi, Ron Perlman, Claudio Brook, Tamara Shanath; **D:** Guillermo del Toro; **W:** Guillermo del Toro; **M:** Ian Deardon. THV

The Crooked Circle 🎬½ 1932 More comedy than mystery as slapstick policeman Gleason goes under cover as a swami. Not helped at all by a weak script and poor photography. **68m/B VHS.** Ben Lyon, ZaSu Pitts, James Gleason, C. Henry Gordon, Raymond Hatton, Roscoe Karns; **D:** H. Bruce Humberstone. SNC, NOS

Crooked Hearts 🎬🎬 1991 (R) Dysfunctional family drama means well but lays it on too thick, as a father/son rivalry threatens to sunder the tight-knit Warrens. Based on a novel by Robert Boswell.**CW:** Language and one sensual scene. **113m/C VHS, Beta, LV, Closed Caption.** Peter Coyote, Jennifer Jason Leigh, Peter Berg, Cindy Pickett, Vincent D'Onofrio; **D:** Michael Bortman; **W:** Michael Bortman. MGM

Crooked Trail 🎬 1936 A lawman and bad guy become friends. **58m/B VHS, Beta, LV.** Johnny Mack Brown. NO

Crooklyn 🎬🎬🎬 1994 (PG-13) Director Lee turns from the life of Malcolm X to the early lives of Generation X in this profile of an African-American middle class family growing up in 1970's Brooklyn. Lee's least politically charged film to date is a joint effort between him and sibs Joie and Cinque, and profiles the only girl in a family of five children coming of age. Tender and real performances from all, especially newcomer Harris, propel the sometimes messy, music-laden trip to nostalgia land.**CW:** Drug content. **112m/C VHS, LV, Closed Caption.** Alfre Woodard, Delroy Lindo, Zelda Harris, David Patrick Kelly, Carlton Williams, Sharif Rashed, Tse-March Washington, Christopher Knowings, Jose Zuniga, Isaiah Washington, Ivelka Reyes, N. Jeremi Duru, Frances Foster, Norman Matlock, Patriece Nelson, Joie Lee, Vondie Curtis-Hall, Tiasha Reyes, Spike Lee; **D:** Spike Lee; **W:** Joie Lee, Cinque Lee; **M:** Terence Blanchard. USH

Crooks & Coronets 🎬½ Sophie's Place 1969 (PG) Two-bit crooks plot to rob the country estate of an eccentric British dowager. **106m/C VHS, Beta.** GB Cesar Romero, Telly Savalas, Warren Oates, Edith Evans; **D:** James O'Connolly. WAR

The Cross & the Switchblade 🎬½ 1972 (PG) An idealistic priest tries to bring the message of religion to the members of a vicious street gang. They don't wanna listen. Spanish language version available. **105m/C VHS, Beta.** Pat Boone, Erik Estrada, Jackie Giroux, Jo-Ann Robinson; **D:** Don Murray. VBL

Cross Country 🎬½ 1983 (R) Action revolves around the brutal murder of a call girl, with initial suspicion falling on a television advertising director involved with the woman. The story twists and turns from the suspect to investigating detective Ironside without becoming particularly interesting. **95m/C VHS, Beta, LV.** CA Richard Beymer, Nina Axelrod, Michael Ironside; **D:** Paul Lynch; **W:** Logan N. Danforth. NLC

Cross Creek 🎬🎬½ 1983 (PG) Based on the life of Marjorie Kinnan Rawlings, author of "The Yearling," who, after 10 years as a frustrated reporter/writer, moves to the remote and untamed Everglades. There she meets colorful local characters and receives the inspiration to write numerous bestsellers. Well acted though overtly sentimental at times. **115m/C VHS, Beta.** Mary Steenburgen, Rip Torn, Peter Coyote, Dana Hill, Alfre Woodard, Malcolm McDowell; **D:** Martin Ritt; **C:** John A. Alonzo. Nominations: Academy Awards '83: Best Costume Design, Best Supporting Actor (Torn), Best Supporting Actress (Woodard), Best Original Score. REP

Cross Examination 🎬½ 1932 A boy is charged with his father's murder, and a defense attorney struggles to acquit him. **61m/B VHS, Beta, LV.** H.B. Warner, Sally Blane, Sarah Padden. NO

Cross Mission 🎬 1989 (R) Predictable actioner about a photographer and a soldier who are captured by the enemy. Packed with a bit of ninja, ammo, and occult. **90m/C VHS.** Richard Randall; **D:** Al Bradley. CAN

Cross My Heart 🎬🎬 1988 (R) Light comedy about two single people with complicated, post-divorce lives who go on a date and suffer accordingly. Will true love prevail? **91m/C VHS, Beta.** Martin Short, Annette O'Toole, Paul Reiser, Joanna Kerns; **D:** Armyan Bernstein; **W:** Armyan Bernstein; **M:** Bruce Broughton. USH

Cross My Heart 🎬🎬 1991 A group of school children conspire to hide the death of one of the group's mothers. This will prevent his placement in the state orphanage. Interesting premise is blandly treated by Fansten. Child actors don't seem realistic, photography is without flair. In French with English subtitles. **?m/C VHS, Beta.** FR Sylvain Copans; **D:** Jacques Fansten. FXL

Cross of Iron 🎬🎬½ 1976 (R) During WWII, two antagonistic German officers clash over personal ideals as well as strategy in combatting the relentless Russian attack. Followed by "Breakthrough." **120m/C VHS, Beta.** James Coburn, Maximilian Schell, James Mason, David Warner, Senta Berger; **D:** Sam Peckinpah; **W:** Julius J. Epstein; **M:** Ernest Gold. MED

Crossbar 🎬🎬 1979 Aaron Kornylo is determined to reach Olympic qualifications in the high jump despite having only one leg. Inspired by a true story, this program dramatically shows how far determination and work can take a person. **77m/C VHS, Beta.** John Ireland, Brent Carver, Kate Reid; **D:** John Trent. TWE, LCA

Crosscut 🎬🎬 1995 (R) Mob hitman Martin Niconi (Mandylor) makes a mistake that could cost him his life when a barroom brawl leads him to shooting the son of a Mafia don. He escapes to a small California logging town, changes his identity, and falls for single mom Anna (Gallagher) but the mob manages to track him down. Big shootout.**CW:** Strong violence and language, and for some drug use and brief nudity. **90m/C VHS, LV.** Costas Mandylor, Megan Gallagher, Casey Sander, Allen Cutler, Zack Norman, George Murdock; **D:** Paul Raimondi; **W:** Paul Raimondi, David Masiel, Scott Phillips; **C:** David Bridges; **M:** Christopher Tyng. APX

Crossfire 🎬🎬🎬½ 1947 A Jewish hotel guest is murdered and three soldiers just back from Europe are suspected of the crime. The first Hollywood film that explored racial bigotry. Due to the radical nature of its plot, the director and the producer were eventually black-listed for promoting "un-American" themes. Loosely based on Richard Brooks' "The Brick Foxhole." **86m/B VHS,**

Beta. Robert Young, Robert Mitchum, Robert Ryan, Gloria Grahame, Paul Kelly; **D:** Edward Dmytryk. Edgar Allan Poe Awards '47: Best Screenplay; National Board of Review Awards '47: 10 Best Films of the Year; Nominations: Academy Awards '47: Best Director (Dmytryk), Best Picture, Best Screenplay, Best Supporting Actor (Ryan), Best Supporting Actress (Grahame). *TTC*

Crossfire 🎬 *The Bandit* 1967 **(PG)** Two bandits are almost hung in the midst of the Mexican revolution. Released in the U.S. in 1979. **82m/C VHS, Beta.** MX Robert Conrad, Jan-Michael Vincent, Manuel Lopez Ochoa, Roy Jenson; **D:** Robert Conrad, Alfredo Zacharias. *ACA*

Crossfire 🎬🎬 1989 **(R)** A rescue team heads to Vietnam to pick up their MIA comrades. With no help from the government and the enemy at every turn, can they possibly succeed? **99m/C VHS, LV.** Richard Norton, Michael Meyer, Daniel Dietrich, Don Pemrick, Eric Hahn, Wren Brown, Steve Young; **D:** Anthony Maharaj; **W:** Noah Blough. *NO*

The Crossing 🎬🎬 1992 **(R)** Powerful coming-of-age tale in which Meg, a sheltered young woman, falls in love with an ambitious artist named Sam. When he decides to leave their small town to pursue his career, she turns to his best friend for comfort and companionship. However, when Sam unexpectedly returns, Meg is forced to make a choice that could drastically change all of their lives. **CW:** Language and sensuality. **92m/C VHS, LV, Closed Caption.** AU Russell Crowe, Danielle Spencer, Robert Mammone; **W:** Ranald Allan; **M:** Martin Armiger. *REP*

Crossing Delancey 🎬🎬🎬 1988 **(PG)** Jewish woman (Bozyk), in old world style, plays matchmaker for her independent thirtysomething granddaughter. Charming modern-day New York City fairy tale deftly manipulates cliches and stereotypes. Lovely performance from Irving as the woman whose heart surprises her. Riegert is swell playing the gentle but never wimpy suitor. Perfectly cast Bozyk was a star on the Yiddish vaudeville stage, this is her film debut. Appealing music by the Roches, with Suzzy Roche giving a credible performance as Irving's friend. Adapted for the big screen by Sandler from her play of the same name. **97m/C VHS, Beta, LV, 8mm, Closed Caption.** Amy Irving, Reizl Bozyk, Peter Riegert, Jeroen Krabbe, Sylvia Miles, Suzzy Roche, George Martin, John Bedford Lloyd, Rosemary Harris, Amy Wright, Claudia Silver; **D:** Joan Micklin Silver; **W:** Susan Sandler. *WAR, FCT, HMV*

The Crossing Guard 🎬🎬🎬 1994 **(R)** Nicholson headlines as Freddy Gale, a revenge-minded father who hunts down a drunk driver (Morse), who killed his daughter five years previous. Story focuses on dual emotions of the two men: Gale seeks an end to his grief and rage; Booth attempts to deal with guilt and regret. Writer Penn pairs one-time lovers Nicholson and Huston (playing ex-spouses here) in his sophomore directorial effort with explosive results. Focus is, accordingly, on emotional performances while narrative and directorial finesse take a back seat. **CW:** Sexuality and strong language. **111m/C VHS, LV, Closed Caption.** Jack Nicholson, Anjelica Huston, David Morse, Robin Wright, Robbie Robertson, Piper Laurie, Richard Bradford, John Savage, Priscilla Barnes, Kari Wuhrer, Jennifer Leigh Warren, Richard Sarafian, Jeff Morris, Joe Viterelli, Eileen Ryan, Ryo Ishibashi, Michael Ryan, Nicky Blair, Gene Kirkwood, Jason Kristofer, Hadda Brooks; **D:** Sean Penn; **W:** Sean Penn; **C:** Vilmos Zsigmond; **M:** Jack Nitzsche. Nominations: Golden Globe Awards '96: Best Supporting Actress (Huston); Independent Spirit Awards '96: Best Supporting Actor (Morse); Screen Actors Guild Award '95: Best Supporting Actress (Huston). *TOU*

Crossing the Bridge 🎬🎬 1992 **(R)** An after high-school tale of three buddies and their restless lives as they take their uncertain steps towards adulthood. It's 1975 in Detroit and Mort, Danny, and Tim cling to high-school memories as they pass time on petty jobs, drinking, and cruising across the Ambassador Bridge to check out

the Canadian strip joints. Their big moment—for better or worse—comes when they are offered the chance to make a lot of quick cash if they'll smuggle hash from Toronto to Detroit. Directorial debut of Binder. **CW:** Language and drug use. **105m/C VHS, Beta, LV, Closed Caption.** Josh Charles, Jason Gedrick, Stephen Baldwin, Cheryl Pollak, Jeffrey Tambor; **D:** Mike Binder; **W:** Mike Binder. *TOU*

Crossing the Line 🎬 1990 **(R)** Two motocross racers battle it out for the championship. **90m/C VHS, Beta, LV, Closed Caption.** Jon Stafford, Rick Hearst, Paul Smith, Cameron Mitchell, Vernon Wells, Colleen Morris, John Saxon; **D:** Gary Graver. *COL*

Crossover 🎬½ 1982 **(R)** A devoted male nurse works the graveyard shift in the psychiatric ward and neglects his personal life. **96m/C VHS, Beta.** James Coburn, Kate Nelligan; **D:** John Guillermin. *VES, LIV*

Crossover Dreams 🎬🎬½ 1985 Actor and musician Blades moves this old story along. Sure that he has at last made the international Big Time, a salsa artist becomes a self-important back-stabber after cutting an album. Great music. Blades's first film. 🎵Good For Baby; Liz's Theme; Sin Fe; Todos Vuelven; Elegua; Merecumbe; Judy, Part 2; Yiri Yiri Bon. **86m/C VHS, Beta.** Ruben Blades, Shawn Elliott, Elizabeth Pena, Virgilio Marti, Tom Signorelli, Frank Robles, Joel Diamond, Amanda Barber, John Hammil; **D:** Leon Ichaso; **W:** Ruben Blades, Leon Ichaso, Manuel Arce; **M:** Mauricio Smith. *CNG*

Crossroads 🎬🎬½ 1986 **(R)** A blues-loving young white man, classically trained at Juilliard, befriends an aging black blues-master. After helping the old man escape from the nursing home, the two hop trains to the South where it's literally a duel with the devil. Fine performances by Macchio, Gertz, and Morton, and a wonderful score. **100m/C VHS, Beta, LV, Closed Caption.** Ralph Macchio, Joe Seneca, Jami Gertz, Joe Morton, Robert Judd, Harry Carey Jr.; **D:** Walter Hill; **W:** John Fusco; **C:** John Bailey; **M:** Ry Cooder. *COL*

Crossworlds 🎬🎬 1996 **(PG-13)** All dimensions of the universe collide in the mystical valley of Crossworlds. When alien night riders attack Joe Talbolt (Charles), he escapes with girlfriend Laura (Roth) and they meet up with mercenary A.T. (Hauer). Turns out the crystal pendant Joe's father left him is one of the keys that unlock the boundaries between the worlds. Along with a scepter, they give the owner unlimited power. So the trio enter Crossworlds to fight a battle between good and evil. **CW:** Action violence and brief strong language. **91m/C VHS, LV, Closed Caption.** Rutger Hauer, Josh Charles, Andrea Roth, Stuart Wilson; **D:** Krishna Rao; **W:** Raman Rao, Krishna Rao; **M:** Christophe Beck. *THV*

The Crow 🎬🎬½ 1993 **(R)** Revenge-fantasy finds Eric Draven (Lee) resurrected on Devil's Night, a year after his death, in order to avenge his own murder and that of his girlfriend. 90% of the scenes are at night, in the rain, or both, and it's not easy to tell what's going on (a blessing considering the violence level). Very dark, but with good performances, particularly from Lee, in his last role before an unfortunate on set accident caused his death. That footage has been destroyed, but use of a stunt double and camera trickery allowed for the movie's completion. Film was dedicated to Lee and his fiance Eliza. Based on the comic strip by James O'Barr. The video release includes Brandon Lee's final interview. **100m/C VHS, LV, Closed Caption.** Brandon Lee, Ernie Hudson, Michael Wincott, David Patrick Kelly, Rochelle Davis, Angel David, Michael Massee, Bai Ling, Lawrence Mason, Bill Raymond, Marco Rodriguez, Anna Thomson, Sofia Shinas, Jon Polito, Tony Todd; **D:** Alex Proyas; **W:** David J. Schow, John Shirley; **C:** Darius Wolski; **M:** Graeme Revell. MTV Movie Awards '95: Best Song ("Big Empty"); Nominations: MTV Movie Awards '95: Best Film, Best Male Performance (Lee). *TOU*

The Crow 2: City of Angels 🎬🎬 1996 **(R)** James O'Barr's cult graphic-novel "hero" returns in a new incarnation. It's 8 years later (in film time) and the setting's changed from Detroit to L.A. but the horror remains. Ashe (Perez) and his young son witness a murder and are killed themselves by scumbags working for drug lord Judah (Brooks). So the Crow brings back Ashe to get revenge. Also involved is Sarah (Kirshner), who retains her role as story narrator but is now a grown-up tattoo artist who falls in love with Ashe. Lots of kink and flash—no substance—and confusing as well. The eerie sepia-toned look is created with sodium lighting. **CW:** Strong violence, drug content, language and sexuality. **93m/C VHS, LV, Closed Caption.** Vincent Perez, Mia Kirshner, Iggy Pop, Richard Brooks, Ian Dury, Thuy Trang, Thomas Jane, Vincent Castellanos, Tracey Ellis; **D:** Tim Pope; **W:** David S. Goyer; **C:** Jean-Yves Escoffier; **M:** Graeme Revell. *TOU*

Crow Hollow 🎬🎬 1952 A Victorian mansion inhabited by three whacko sisters is the site of a murder committed in an attempt to cash in on an inheritance. When a young woman investigates, eyebrows are raised. **69m/B VHS, Beta.** GB Donald Houston, Natasha Parry, Nora Nicholson, Esma Cannon, Melissa Stribling; **D:** Michael McCarthy. *SNC, RXM*

The Crowd 🎬🎬🎬🎬 1928 A look at the day-to-day trials of a working-class family set against the backdrop of wealthy society. True-to-life, it's peppered with some happy moments, too. One of the best silent films. Available on laserdisc as a double feature with another '20s classic, "The Wind." **104m/B VHS, Beta, LV.** Eleanor Boardman, James Murray, Bert Roach, Daniel G. Tomlinson, Dell Henderson, Lucy Beaumont; **D:** King Vidor. Nominations: Academy Awards '28: Best Director (Vidor). *MGM*

Crows and Sparrows 🎬🎬🎬 *Wuya Yu Maque* 1949 Poor tenants of a Shanghai boardinghouse are about to lose their home when their greedy landlord decides to sell and move to Taiwan. But the advancing Red Army causes a change in plans and they're saved! Sounds politically turgid but isn't, thanks to naturalistic acting and dialog. Completed just before the revolution, the film was censored by the Nationalist Kuomintang government but cuts were restored when the Communists came to power. Mandarin with subtitles. **108m/B VHS.** CH Zhao Dan, Wu Yin, Wei Heling, Sun Dao-Lin, Li Tianji, Ouyang Yunzhu; **D:** Zheng Junli; **W:** Zhao Dan, Zheng Junli; **C:** Miao Zhenhua, Hu Zhenhua; **M:** Wang Yunjie. *HTV, FCT*

The Crucible 🎬🎬🎬 *The Witches of Salem* 1957 Signoret is outstanding in this version of Arthur Miller's play about the Salem witch trials in 17th-century New England. Miller's depiction of witch hunts was written as a searing commentary on McCarthyism and the anti-communist panic that swept America in the 1950s. Film was made in France because Miller was blacklisted in America and blackballed by Hollywood at the time. In French with English subtitles. **108m/B VHS.** FR Simone Signoret, Yves Montand, Mylene Demongeot, Jean Debucourt; **D:** Raymond Rouleau; **W:** Jean-Paul Sartre. *HTV*

The Crucible 🎬🎬🎬 1996 **(PG-13)** Mass hysteria reigns in 17th century Salem, Mass., when a group of teenaged girls, caught performing heathen rituals in the woods, concoct an elaborate story to exonerate themselves by whipping the town into a witch-hunting frenzy. Chief liar is Abigail Williams (Ryder), who was cast aside by married farmer John Proctor (Day-Lewis), for whom she still lusts. The deranged lass puts her dubious talents into getting Proctor's wife (Allen) out of the picture. Director Hytner demanded authentic period reproduction, down to the finest detail. Impressive cast does justice to the story, especially Scofield's delightfully odious Judge Danforth. Based on Miller's 1953 play which, not so coincidentally, opened during the communist witch hunts of the early 1950s. Screenwriter Miller willingly slashed dialogue from his original work for cinematic purposes. Filmed at the remote wildlife sanctuary of Hog Island, Massachusetts. **CW:** Intense depiction of the Salem witch trials. 123m/C VHS, LV, Closed Caption. Daniel Day-Lewis, Winona Ryder, Paul Scofield, Joan Allen, Bruce Davison, Jeffrey Jones, Rob Campbell, Peter Vaughan, Karron Graves, Charlaine Woodard, Frances Conroy, Elizabeth Lawrence, George Gaynes; **D:** Nicholas Hytner; **M:** George Fenton. British Academy Awards '96: Best Supporting Actor (Scofield); Broadcast Film Critics Association Awards '96: Best Supporting Actress (Allen); Nominations: Academy Awards '96: Best Adapted Screenplay, Best Supporting Actress (Allen); British Academy Awards '96: Best Adapted Screenplay; Golden Globe Awards '97: Best Supporting Actor (Scofield), Best Supporting Actress (Allen). FXV

Crucible of Horror 🎬🎬 Velvet House; The Corpse 1969 Chilling story of a terrorized wife, who, along with her daughter, plots to murder her sadistic husband to end his abusive treatment of them. However, he isn't yet ready to die and comes back to drive them mad. 91m/C VHS, Beta. GB Michael Gough, Yvonne Mitchell, Sharon Gurney; **D:** Viktors Ritelis. MGM, FCT

Crucible of Terror woof! 1972 Mad sculptor covers beautiful models with hot wax, then imprisons them in a mold of bronze. 95m/C VHS, Beta. Mike Raven, Mary Maude, James Bolam. PSM, MRV, GEM

The Crucifer of Blood 🎬½ 1991 A disappointing Sherlock Holmes yarn, made for cable TV. Heston is adequate as the Baker Street sleuth, but the mystery—about two retired British soldiers who share an accursed secret and a vengeful comrade—unreels clumsily in the form of flashbacks that give away most of the puzzle from the start. Interesting only in that Dr. Watson has a love affair, more or less. Adapted from a play (and looking like it) by Paul Giovanni, inspired by Arthur Conan Doyle's "The Sign of Four." 105m/C VHS, Beta, Closed Caption. Charlton Heston, Richard Johnson, Susannah Harker, John Castle, Clive Wood, Simon Callow, Edward Fox; **D:** Fraser Heston. TTC

The Crucified Lovers 🎬🎬🎬½ Chikamatsu Monogatari 1954 A shy scrollmaker falls in love with his master's wife. Excellent Japanese tragedy with fine performances all around. 100m/B VHS. JP Kazuo Hasegawa, Kyoko Kagawa, Yoko Minamida, Eitaro Shindo, Sakae Ozawa; **D:** Kenji Mizoguchi. FCT

The Crude Oasis 🎬🎬½ 1995 (R) Shot in 14 days on a $25,000 budget, producer/writer/director Graves' debut is an aggressively moody suspenser. Karen (Taylor) is a neglected, suicidal Kansas housewife who is haunted by dreams of a mystery man. He turns up in the form of Shields, the pump jockey at a local gas station. Obsessed by the stranger, Karen begins following him, leading to situations paralleling her dream. Adept at setting up an atmosphere of small-town menace and constructing a plot with surprising twists and turns, Graves can't quite deliver the payoff required. **CW:** Language. 82m/C VHS, Beta, Closed Caption. Jennifer Taylor, Aaron Shields, Robert Peterson, Mussef Sibay, Lynn Bieler, Roberta Eaton; **D:** Alex Graves; **W:** Alex Graves; **C:** Steven Quale. PAR

Cruel Sea 🎬🎬🎬 1953 Well-made documentary-like account of a Royal Navy corvette on convoy duty in the Atlantic during WWII. 121m/B VHS, Beta. GB Jack Hawkins, Stanley Baker, Denholm Elliott, Virginia McKenna; **D:** Charles Frend. Nominations: Academy Awards '53: Best Screenplay. REP, BMV, HMV

The Cruel Story of Youth 🎬🎬🎬 Seishun Zanoku Monogatari; Naked Youth; A Story of the Cruelties of Youth 1960 A teenage girl and her criminal boyfriend use sex to get money out of rich, middle-aged men in this controversial look at the disillusionment of youth and the breaking of old values and traditions in Japan after WWII. In Japanese with English subtitles. 96m/C VHS. JP Yusuke Kawazu, Miyuki Kuwano, Yoshiko Kuga; **D:** Nagisa Oshima; **W:** Nagisa Oshima. NYF

Cruise into Terror woof! 1978 A sarcophagus brought aboard a pleasure cruise ship unleashes an evil force that slowly starts to kill off the ship's passengers, most of whom likely thought they were on the Love Boat. Made for television. 100m/C VHS, Beta. Ray Milland, Hugh O'Brian, John Forsythe, Christopher George, Dirk Benedict, Frank Converse, Lynda Day George, Stella Stevens; **D:** Bruce Kessler. PSM

Cruise Missile 🎬 1978 Unique task force is on a mission to keep the world from nuclear holocaust. 100m/C VHS, Beta. Peter Graves, Curt Jurgens, Michael Dante; **D:** Ted V. Mikels. NO

Cruisin' High 🎬 1975 (R) Two city street gangs battle it out. 109m/C VHS, Beta. David Kyle, Kelly Yaegermann, Rhodes Reason. VES, LIV

Cruising 🎬🎬 1980 (R) Rookie cop Pacino is deep undercover investigating the bizarre murders of homosexuals in New York's West Village. Sexually explicit but less than suspenseful mystery. Release was sensationalized, with many gay rights groups voicing loud disapproval of the sordid gay characterization, while others feared copy-cat crimes. Excellent NYC cinematography. 102m/C VHS, Beta. Al Pacino, Paul Sorvino, Karen Allen, Powers Boothe; **D:** William Friedkin; **W:** William Friedkin; **M:** Jack Nitzsche. WAR

Crumb 🎬🎬🎬½ 1994 (R) Countercultural documentary looking at the life of underground cartoonist Robert Crumb—sixties satirist and social misfit who created such drug and sex characters as Fritz the Cat and Mr. Natural. Crumb's extraordinarily dysfunctional family play a significant role, with his mother and two brothers, elder brother Charles and younger brother Max, also interviewed as well as Crumb's friends and current and former wives. The dead abusive father also plays a part. Director Zwigoff spent six years filming his material, and gained wider distribution for his work after taking the Grand Jury prize at Sundance. **CW:** Graphic sex-related cartoons; language. 119m/C VHS, LV, Closed Caption. **D:** Terry Zwigoff. National Society of Film Critics Awards '95: Best Feature Documentary; Sundance Film Festival '95: Best Cinematography, Grand Jury Prize. COL

The Crusades 🎬🎬½ 1935 Typical DeMille extravaganza, loosely based on the Third Crusade, which finds Richard the Lionheart (Wilcoxon) and the armies of Europe battling Saladin and the Mahommedan horde in order to reclaim Jerusalem. Meanwhile, Richard marries by proxy in order to gain supplies for his men—something that enrages his bride Berengaria (Young). Once he realizes how beautiful she is, Richard tries to win her love. Obviously, not historically accurate and it's all secondary to the battle scenes, anyway. Based on the Harold Lamb book "The Crusade: Iron Men and Saints." 126m/B VHS, Closed Caption. Henry Wilcoxon, Loretta Young, Sir C. Aubrey Smith, Ian Keith, Katherine DeMille, Joseph Schildkraut, Alan Hale, C. Henry Gordon, George Barbier, Lumsden Hare, William Farnum, Hobart Bosworth, Montagu Love, Pedro de Cordoba, Mischa Auer; **D:** Cecil B. DeMille; **W:** Waldemar Young, Dudley Nichols, Harold Lamb; **C:** Victor Milner; **M:** Rudolph Kopp. Nominations: Academy Awards '35: Best Cinematography. USH

The Crush 🎬½ 1993 (R) Wealthy 14-year-old temptress Silverstone (in her debut) develops an obsessive crush on handsome 28-year-old Elwes, who rents her family's guest house. In an attempt to win his heart, she rewrites his poorly composed magazine articles. This doesn't convince him they should mate for life, so she sabotages his apartment to vent her rage. Sound familiar? The plot's lifted right out of "Fatal Attraction" and Shapiro doesn't offer viewers anything inventively different. He does manage to substitute new methods for the spurned lover to snare her prey. Limp plot would have been exciting if we hadn't seen it so many times before. **CW:** Language and terror violence. 89m/C VHS, Beta, LV, Closed Caption. Cary Elwes, Alicia Silverstone, Jennifer Rubin, Kurtwood Smith, Gwynyth Walsh, Amber Benson; **D:**

Alan Shapiro; **W:** Alan Shapiro; **M:** Graeme Revell. MTV Movie Awards '94: Breakthrough Performance (Silverstone), Best Villain (Silverstone). WAR

Crush 1993 Christina is a local New Zealand literary critic on her way to interview Colin, a reclusive novelist. Along for the ride is her seductive American friend Lane who manages to crash the car but walk away with hardly a scratch. Christina appears to be dead and Lane abandons her, finding her way to the home Colin shares with his teenage daughter Angela. Lane promptly sets out to seduce Colin, making Angela jealous, (oh, and Christina's not dead after all). Poor script finds the characters actions baffling and why Lane is so wildly attractive is never apparent. 97m/C VHS. NZ Marcia Gay Harden, Donough Rees, William Zappa, Caitlin Bossley; **D:** Alison Maclean; **W:** Alison Maclean, Anne Kennedy. FXL, ORI

Crusoe 🎬🎬½ 1989 (PG-13) A lushly photographed version of the Daniel Defoe classic. Crusoe is an arrogant slave trader stranded on a desert island populated by unfriendly natives. Themes of prejudice, fear, and choice appear in this never-padded, thoughtful film. Quinn gives an excellent performance as the stranded slave-trader. 94m/C VHS, Beta, LV. Aidan Quinn, Ade Sapara, Jimmy Nail, Timothy Spall, Colin Bruce, Michael Higgins, Shane Rimmer, Hepburn Grahame; **D:** Caleb Deschanel; **W:** Walon Green, Christopher Logue; **M:** Michael Kamen. NO

Cry-Baby 🎬🎬🎬 1990 (PG-13) An homage and spoof of '50s teen-rock melodramas by the doyen of cinematic Bad Taste, involving a terminal bad-boy high schooler who goes with a square blond and starts an inter-class rumble. Musical numbers, throwaway gags and plenty of knee-bending to Elvis, with a weak story supported by offbeat celeb appearances. 85m/C VHS, Beta, LV, Closed Caption. Johnny Depp, Amy Locane, Polly Bergen, Traci Lords, Ricki Lake, Iggy Pop, Susan Tyrrell, Patty Hearst, Kim Mcguire, Darren E. Burrows, Troy Donahue, Willem Dafoe, David Nelson, Mink Stole, Joe Dallesandro, Joey Heatherton, Robert Walsh; **D:** John Waters; **W:** John Waters; **M:** Patrick Williams. USH

Cry Danger 🎬🎬🎬 1951 A falsely imprisoned man is released from jail, and he searches for those who framed him. 80m/B VHS. Dick Powell, Rhonda Fleming, William Conrad, Richard Erdman; **D:** Robert Parrish; **C:** Joseph Biroc. REP

A Cry for Love 🎬🎬 1980 An amphetamine addict and an alcoholic meet, fall in love, and help each other recover. Based on the best seller by Jill Schary Robinson, "Bedtime Story." 96m/C VHS, Beta. Susan Blakely, Powers Boothe, Gene Barry, Charles Siebert, Herb Edelman, Fern Fitzgerald, Lainie Kazan; **D:** Paul Wendkos. FRH

Cry Freedom 🎬🎬½ 1987 (PG) A romantic look at the short life of South African activist Steven Biko, and his friendship with the white news editor, Donald Woods. The film focuses on Woods' escape from Africa while struggling to bring Biko's message to the world. Based on a true story. 157m/C VHS, Beta, LV. Kevin Kline, Denzel Washington, Penelope Wilton, Kevin McNally, John Thaw, Timothy West, John Hargreaves, Alec McCowen, Zakes Mokae, Ian Richardson, Juanita Waterman; **D:** Richard Attenborough; **W:** John Briley; **M:** George Fenton, Jonas Gwangwa. Nominations: Academy Awards '87: Best Song ("Cry Freedom"), Best Supporting Actor (Washington), Best Original Score. USH, KUI, FCT

A Cry from the Mountain 🎬 1985 (PG) Heavily religious film about a father and son who go on a kayak trip through Alaska's wilderness so the father can break the news of his impending divorce. A series of events occurs that change their lives, and they meet a mysterious mountain man who relies on his faith in God to get by in the wilderness. Features an appearance by Rev. Billy Graham. 78m/C VHS, Beta, LV. James Cavan, Wes Parker, Rita Walter, Chris Kidd, Coleen Gray, Jerry Ballew, Allison Argo, Glen Alsworth, Myrna Kidd; **D:** James F. Collier. LIV

A Cry from the Streets 🎬🎬 1957
Drama about the plight of orphan children and dedicated social workers in England. 100m/C VHS. *GB* Max Bygraves, Barbara Murray, Kathleen Harrison, Colin Petersen; *D:* Lewis Gilbert; *M:* Larry Adler. *FCT*

A Cry in the Dark 🎬🎬🎬½ *Evil Angels* 1988 (PG-13) Tight film story of the infamous Australian murder trial of Lindy Chamberlain, who was accused of killing her own baby, mostly because of the intensely adverse public opinion, aroused by vicious press, that surrounded the case. Chamberlain blamed the death on a wild dingo dog. Near-documentary style, with Streep excellent as the religious, unknowable mother. Based on the book "Evil Angels" by John Bryson. This case was also detailed in the film "Who Killed Baby Azaria?" 120m/C VHS, Beta, LV, 8mm, Closed Caption. *AU* Meryl Streep, Sam Neill, Bruce Myles, Charles Tingwell, Nick Tate, Neil Fitzpatrick, Maurice Fields, Lewis Fitz-gerald; *D:* Fred Schepisi; *W:* Fred Schepisi, Robert Caswell; *C:* Ian Baker; *M:* Bruce Smeaton. Australian Film Institute '89: Best Actor (Neill), Best Actress (Streep), Best Film; Cannes Film Festival '89: Best Actress (Streep); New York Film Critics Awards '88: Best Actress (Streep); Nominations: Academy Awards '88: Best Actress (Streep). *WAR, FCT*

A Cry in the Night 🎬🎬½ 1993 (PG-13) After Jenny (Higgins Clark) marries an internationally-acclaimed artist, she thinks her life is complete. However, once she and her two daughters move into his country estate, her life takes a tragic turn as she's haunted by the mysterious deaths of her ex-husband and newborn child. King plays the new husband who turns out to have a few psychological quirks of his own. Based on the bestselling novel by Mary Higgins Clark. Actress Higgins Clark is the novelist's daughter. Made for television. *CW:* Violence. 99m/C VHS, Closed Caption. Perry King, Carol Higgins Clark; *D:* Robin Spry; *W:* Robin Spry. *REP*

A Cry in the Wild 🎬🎬🎬 1990 (PG) A 14 year old boy must find his way back to civilization when he's the lone survivor of an airplane crash. Strong acting from Rushton, excellent nature photography make this well-used story work again. 93m/C VHS, Closed Caption. Jared Rushton, Ned Beatty, Pamela Sue Martin, Stephen Meadows; *D:* Mark Griffiths; *W:* Catherine Cyran. *MGM*

Cry of a Prostitute: Love Kills 🎬 1972 (R) Former prostitute joins with a professional assassin in an effort to pacify rival gangsters in Italy. 86m/C VHS, Beta. Henry Silva, Barbara Bouchet; *D:* Andrew Bianchi. *PSM*

Cry of Battle 🎬🎬½ *To Be a Man* 1963 Anxious for the challenges of manhood, a well-heeled young man joins a guerrilla militia in the Philippines. 99m/B VHS, Beta. Van Heflin, Rita Moreno, James MacArthur; *D:* Irving Lerner. *PSM, MRV, FGF*

Cry of the Banshee 🎬🎬½ 1970 (PG) Witch-hunter Price and family are tormented by Satanic powers seeking revenge. Superior horror period piece. Also available with "Count Yorga, Vampire" on Laserdisc. 87m/C VHS, Beta. *GB* Vincent Price, Elisabeth Bergner, Essy Persson, Hugh Griffith, Hilary Dwyer, Sally Geeson, Patrick Mower; *D:* Gordon Hessler; *M:* Les Baxter. *HBO*

Cry of the Innocent 🎬🎬🎬 1980 An action-packed thriller about a Vietnam veteran who is out to find a group of Irish terrorists that killed his family. 93m/C VHS, Beta. Cyril Cusack, Alexander Knox, Rod Taylor, Joanna Pettet, Nigel Davenport; *D:* Michael O'Herlihy. *TTV*

The Cry of the Owl 🎬🎬 *Le Cri du Hibou* 1992 Robert (Malavoy) has divorced the dreadful Veronique (Thevenet) and struck up a friendship with Juliette (May). He admires the way her life seems so satisfied and orderly but Juliette decides she doesn't like this idea of herself and impulsively drops her swinish fiance Patrick (Penot) and pursues Robert instead. But Robert is only interested in friendship, leading to some very twisted revenge plots. Suspenseful look at what obsessions can drive people to do. Adapted from the novel by Patricia Highsmith. In French with English subtitles. 102m/C VHS. *FR IT* Christophe MaLavoy, Mathilda May, Virginie Thevenet, Jacques Penot, Jean-Pierre Kalfon, Patrice Kerbrat; *D:* Claude Chabrol; *W:* Claude Chabrol, Odile Barski; *M:* Matthieu Chabrol. *CVC*

Cry of the Penguins 🎬🎬½ *Mr. Forbush and the Penguins* 1971 Womanizing biologist Forbush (Hurt) heads off on an Antartic expedition to study penguins when his would-be romance with Tara (Mills) comes to naught. Beautiful photography, shallow story. Adapted from the novel "Mr. Forbush and the Penguins" by Graham Billing. Note the similarities with "Never Cry Wolf." 105m/C VHS. *GB* John Hurt, Hayley Mills, Dudley Sutton, Tony Britton, Thorley Walters, Judy Campbell, Joss Ackland, Nicholas Pennell; *D:* Albert T. Viola; *W:* Anthony Shaffer; *M:* John Addison. *TVC*

Cry of the Werewolf 🎬🎬 1944 A beautiful New Orleans gypsy protects her mother's mummified remains by periodically turning into a werewolf and killing people. 63m/B VHS. Nina Foch, Stephen Crane, Osa Massen, Blanche Yurka, Barton MacLane, Ivan Triesault, John Abbott, Fritz Leiber; *D:* Henry Levin; *W:* Charles "Blackie" O'Neal. *MOV*

Cry Panic 🎬🎬 1974 A man is thrown into a strange series of events after accidentally running down a man on a highway. Made for television. 74m/C VHS, Beta. John Forsythe, Anne Francis, Earl Holliman, Claudia McNeil, Ralph Meeker; *D:* James Goldstone. *PSM*

Cry Terror 🎬🎬 1974 Two escaped convicts take two beautiful women hostage trying to gain their own freedom. Only a quick-thinking undercover police officer can save the girls. Made for television. 71m/C VHS, Beta. *GB* Bob Hoskins, Susan Hampshire, Gabrielle Drake. *NO*

Cry, the Beloved Country 🎬🎬🎬½ *African Fury* 1951 A black country minister travels to Johannesberg to be with his son after the youth is accused of killing a white man. Through the events of the trial, the horror, oppression, and destruction of South Africa's apartheid system are exposed. Startling and moving, the first entertainment feature set against the backdrop of apartheid. Still trenchant; based on the novel by Alan Paton. 111m/B VHS. *GB* Canada Lee, Charles Carson, Sidney Poitier, Joyce Carey, Geoffrey Keen; *D:* Zoltan Korda; *C:* Robert Krasker. *MON, FCT*

Cry, the Beloved Country 🎬🎬🎬 1995 (PG-13) Alan Paton's classic South African novel (first filmed in 1951) depicts a Zulu Christian pastor and a wealthy white farmer finding common ground through personal loss—both of their sons were killed in regional violence. Rural black minister Stephen Kumalo (Jones), travels to Johannesburg only to discover his sister (Kente) is a prostitute, his younger brother John (Dutton) no longer believes in Christianity and his son is in prison for the murder of a white man. That man turns out to be the son of rich farmer James Jarvis (Harris), from Kumalo's own village. Both Jones and Harris turn in wonderfully understated performances in this hopeful tale of potential racial harmony. *CW:* Emotional thematic elements and brief language. 120m/C VHS, LV, Closed Caption. *SA* James Earl Jones, Richard Harris, Charles S. Dutton, Leleti Khumalo, Dambisa Kente, Vusi Kunene, Eric Miyeni, Ian Robers; *D:* Darrell Roodt; *W:* Ronald Atwood; *C:* Paul Gilpin; *M:* John Barry. Nominations: Screen Actors Guild Award '95: Best Actor (Jones). *TOU*

Cry Uncle 🎬½ 1971 (R) Comic account of a private eye who investigates a blackmailing case involving a film of orgies in which, much to his chagrin, he participated. 85m/C VHS. Allen (Goorwitz) Garfield, Paul Sorvino, Devin Goldenberg, Madeleine Le Roux; *D:* John G. Avildsen; *W:* David Odell; *C:* John G. Avildsen. *TTV*

Cry Vengeance 🎬🎬½ 1954 A falsely-imprisoned detective gets out of jail and searches for the people who framed him and killed his family. 83m/B VHS, Beta. Mark Stevens, Joan Vohs, Martha Hyer, Skip Homeier; *D:* Mark Stevens. *REP*

Cry Wolf 🎬🎬 1947 Weak mystery thriller places Stanwyck in creepy environs when she goes to claim her inheritance from her late husband's estate. Based on the novel by Marjorie Carleton. 83m/B VHS. Errol Flynn, Barbara Stanwyck, Richard Basehart, Geraldine Brooks, Jerome Cowan, John Ridgely, Patricia White; *D:* Peter Godfrey; *W:* Catherine Turney. *MGM*

The Crying Child 🎬½ 1996 (PG-13) Madeline Jeffreys (Hemingway) and her husband Ran (DelHoyo) retreat to their 19th-century island vacation cottage after the stillbirth of their first child. Madeline begins to hear a child crying in the house and sees a ghostly apparition—now she has to discover what the spirit wants (and convince everyone she's not just going crazy). TV movie based on the novel by Barbara Michaels. *CW:* Supernatural terror and thematic elements. 93m/C VHS, Closed Caption. Mariel Hemingway, George DelHoyo, Finola Hughes, Kin Shriner, Collin Wilcox Paxton; *D:* Robert Lewis; *W:* Rob Gilmer; *C:* Stephen Lighthill; *M:* Shirley Walker. *USH*

The Crying Game 🎬🎬🎬½ 1992 (R) PR lesson in how to launch a small movie into the hypersphere and ensure critical silence on salient characterization. Jordan's gritty drama is on par with his best, a complex blend of violence, love, betrayal, guilt, and redemption and is not about what it seems to be about much of the time. Wonderful performances by all, including Rea as the appealing, conscience-stricken Fergus; Richardson as the cold, violent IRA moll Jude; and Davidson, in a film debut, as the needy, charismatic Dil. Whitaker is terrific in his 15 minutes of intense screen time. Filled with definite surprises and unexpected pleasures. Title is taken from a top-5 British hit of 1964, three versions of which are heard. *CW:* Language, full frontal nudity, strong violence, and sexuality. 112m/C VHS, LV, Closed Caption. *IR* Stephen Rea, Jaye Davidson, Miranda Richardson, Forest Whitaker, Adrian Dunbar, Jim Broadbent, Ralph Brown, Breffini McKenna, Joe Savino, Birdie Sweeney, Andre Bernard; *D:* Neil Jordan; *W:* Neil Jordan; *C:* Ian Wilson; *M:* Anne Dudley. Academy Awards '92: Best Original Screenplay; Australian Film Institute '93: Best Foreign Film; Chicago Film Critics Awards '92: Best Foreign Film; Independent Spirit Awards '93: Best Foreign Film; Los Angeles Film Critics Association Awards '92: Best Foreign Film; New York Film Critics Awards '92: Best Screenplay, Best Supporting Actress (Richardson); National Society of Film Critics Awards '92: Best Actor (Rea); Writers Guild of America '92: Best Original Screenplay; Nominations: Academy Awards '92: Best Actor (Rea), Best Director (Jordan), Best Film Editing, Best Picture, Best Supporting Actor (Davidson). *LIV, MOV, BTV*

Crypt of Dark Secrets 🎬 1976 (R) Vietnam veteran recovering from wounds in the Louisiana swamps encounters a friendly Indian spirit who saves him from death. 100m/C VHS, Beta. Maureen Chan, Ronald Tanet, Wayne Mack, Herbert G. Jahncke; *D:* Jack Weis. *NO*

Crypt of the Living Dead woof! 1973 (PG) An undead woman from the 13th century makes life miserable for visitors on Vampire Island. 75m/C VHS, Beta. Andrew Prine, Mark Damon, Teresa Gimpera, Patty Shepard, Francisco (Frank) Brana; *D:* Ray Danton. *NO*

Crystal Heart 🎬 1987 (R) A medically isolated songwriter with an incurable disease falls in love with a lovely rock singer. 103m/C VHS, Beta. Lee Curreri, Tawny Kitaen, Lloyd Bochner; *D:* Gil Bettman; *M:* Joel Goldsmith. *VTR, NWV*

Crystalstone 🎬 1988 (PG) A wooden cross leads a pair of orphans on a dangerous search for the legendary Crystalstone. 103m/C VHS, Beta. Frank Grimes, Kamlesh Gupta, Laura Jane Goodwin, Sydney Bromley; *D:* Antonio Pelaez. *MCG*

Cthulhu Mansion woof! 1991 (R) The oldest-looking juvenile delinquents you've ever seen release evil spirits when they take over a magician's estate. Not very special effects and abominable dialogue; it claims to be based on H.P. Lovecraft stories, but that's a load of dung.*CW:* Language and horror violence/drug related scenes. 95m/C VHS, Closed Caption. Frank Finlay, Marcia Layton, Brad Fisher, Melanie Shatner, Luis Fernando Alves, Kaethe Cherney, Paul Birchard, Francisco (Frank) Brana; *D:* J. Piquer Simon; *W:* J. Piquer Simon. REP

Cuba ♂♂♂ 1979 (R) Cynical, satirical adventure/love story. Mercenary soldier rekindles an old affair during the Castro revolution. Charismatic cast and good direction make for an entertaining, if overlooked, Connery vehicle. 121m/C VHS, Beta. Sean Connery, Brooke Adams, Jack Weston, Hector Elizondo, Denholm Elliott, Chris Sarandon, Lonette McKee; *D:* Richard Lester; *W:* Charles Wood; *C:* David Watkin. MGM, FOX

Cujo ♂♂ 1983 (R) A rabid dog goes berserk and attacks a mother and her child who are trapped inside a broken-down Pinto. Frighteningly realistic film is based on Stephen King's bestseller. 94m/C VHS, Beta, LV. Dee Wallace Stone, Daniel Hugh-Kelly, Danny Pintauro, Ed Lauter, Christopher Stone; *D:* Lewis Teague; *C:* Jan De Bont; *M:* Charles Bernstein. WAR

Cul de Sac ♂♂♂ 1966 A macabre, psychological thriller set in a dreary castle on a small island off the British coast. Pleasence is an eccentric, middle-aged hermit living acrimoniously with his young, nympho wife (Dorleac) when their home is invaded by two wounded gangsters (Stander and MacGowran), who proceed to hold the couple hostage. MacGowran soon dies of his wounds, leaving Stander and Pleasence to fight it out, encouraged by the luscious Dorleac, who finds her fun where she can. A bleak, sinister film considered one of Polanski's best. 111m/C VHS. GB Donald Pleasence, Francoise Dorleac, Lionel Stander, Jack MacGowran, Jacqueline Bisset; *D:* Roman Polanski; *W:* Roman Polanski, Gerard Brach. FCT

Culpepper Cattle Co. ♂♂½ 1972 (PG) A young, starry-eyed yokel wants to be a cowboy and gets himself enlisted in a cattle drive, where he learns the harsh reality of the West. 92m/C VHS, Beta. Gary Grimes, Billy Green Bush, Bo Hopkins, Charles Martin Smith, Geoffrey Lewis; *D:* Dick Richards; *M:* Jerry Goldsmith. FOX

Cult of the Cobra ♂♂ 1955 Mysterious horror film that became minor camp classic. It seems ex-servicemen are being killed by exotic snake-lady Domergue. Cheesy film that can be fun. Based on a story by Jerry Davis. 75m/B VHS, Closed Caption. Faith Domergue, Richard Long, Marshall Thompson, William Reynolds, Jack Kelly, Kathleen Hughes; *D:* Francis D. Lyon; *W:* Jerry Davis. USH

Cult People ♂½ 1989 Interviews and film clips featuring a host of filmmaking's favorite cult personalities. 60m/C VHS. Patrick Macnee, Cameron Mitchell, James Karen, Russ Meyer, Curtis Harrington, Waris Hussein, Michael Sarne. FCT

Cup Final ♂♂ *G'mar Giviya* 1992 The similarities and contradictions in war and sports, where passions and competition run high, are depicted in this emotional drama. Set in 1982 during Israel's invasion of Lebanon. Cohen is an Israeli soldier passionately interested in the World Cup soccer tournament. When he is taken prisoner by the PLO he discovers his captor Ziad shares his interest in the Italian national team. This common interest brings the two antagonists reluctantly together. In Hebrew and Arabic with English subtitles. 107m/C VHS. IS Moshe Ivgi, Muhamad Bacri, Suheil Haddad; *D:* Eran Riklis; *W:* Eyal Halfon; *M:* Raviv Gazil. FRF, BTV

Cupid ♂½ 1996 (R) Eric (Galligan) develops a deadly obsession for beautiful Jennifer (Laurence), who discovers that Jack and his equally crazy sister Dana (Crosby) have a nasty habit of

killing the women that don't measure up to Jack's fantasies.*CW:* Language, violence, adult themes. 94m/C VHS, LV, Closed Caption. Zach Galligan, Ashley Laurence, Mary Crosby, Joseph Kell, Michael Bowen; *D:* Doug Campbell; *W:* David Benullo; *C:* M. David Mullen. LIV

Curdled ♂♂½ 1995 (R) And you thought your job sucked. Tarantino-funded dark comedy arouses interest with that tag line alone. Gore-obsessed Gabriela (Jones) gets her dream job cleaning up blood and guts with the Post-Forensic Cleaning Service and becomes obsessed with serial killer to the rich Paul (Baldwin), who is keeping her company hopping with one beheading after another. Cultishly violent pic culminates in a tango by the gruesome twosome around a murder scene. Tarantino spotted Jones, starring in Braddock's original student short, while touring with "Reservoir Dogs" and borrowed her for "Pulp Fiction," only to return the favor by exec producing this interesting feature debut. Soundtrack adds spice to the formaldehyde flavor.*CW:* Violence/ gore, brief language. 87m/C VHS, LV, Closed Caption. Angela Jones, William Baldwin, Mel Gorham, Barry Corbin, Bruce Ramsey, Daisy Fuentes, Lois Chiles, Carmen Lopez; *D:* Reb Braddock; *W:* John Maass, Reb Braddock; *C:* Steve Bernstein; *M:* Joseph Julian Gonzalez. TOU

The Cure 1917 Chaplin arrives at a spa to take a rest cure, accompanied by a trunk full of liquor that somehow gets dumped into the water at the resort. Silent with music track. 20m/B VHS, Beta. Charlie Chaplin, Edna Purviance, Eric Campbell, Albert Austin; *D:* Charlie Chaplin. VYY, GVV, CAB

The Cure ♂♂½ 1995 (PG-13) Erik (Renfro), the neighborhood bad kid, befriends Dexter (Mazzello), a boy with AIDS. As Dexter's health weakens, Erik decides they must go on a quest for a cure, Huck Finn style, by floating along the Mississippi River to New Orleans. Despite film's preposterous plot, the performances of the two young leads do inspire a level of sentiment.*CW:* Emotional thematic elements, language. 99m/C VHS, LV, Closed Caption. Brad Renfro, Joseph Mazzello, Annabella Sciorra, Diana Scarwid, Bruce Davison; *D:* Peter Horton; *W:* Robert Kuhn; *C:* Andrew Dintenfass; *M:* Dave Grusin. USH

Curfew ♂♂ 1988 (R) A young woman rushes home so she doesn't break her curfew, only to find two killers with time on their hands waiting for her. Violent. 86m/C VHS, Beta, LV. John Putch, Kyle Richards, William Wellman Jr., Bert Remsen; *D:* Gary Winick. VTR, NWV

The Curfew Breakers ♂ 1957 Dim teen-exploitation/message-movie finds a pair of community workers investigating the murder of a gas station attendent by a drug-crazed youth. 78m/B VHS. Regis Toomey, Paul Kelly, Cathy Downs, Marilyn Madison, Sheila Urban; *D:* Alex Wells. SNC, SMW, TPV

Curiosity Kills ♂½ 1990 (R) Young people find more than they bargained for when they begin to investigate the death of a fellow tenant. Tense made-for-cable thriller.*CW:* Violence. 86m/ C VHS. Rae Dawn Chong, C. Thomas Howell, Courteney Cox, Paul Guilfoyle, Jeff Fahey; *D:* Colin Bucksey; *W:* Joe Batteer, John Rice; *C:* Bojan Bazelli. USH

The Curious Dr. Humpp ♂ 1970 A mad scientist (Barbero) kidnaps exotic dancers and extracts their libidos to preserve his youth. Under the guise of research, he encourages his victims to engage in trysts so that their carnal energies will increase. Everything is hunky dory until a reporter (Bauleo) starts snooping around the laboratory, discovering Dr. Humpp observing multiple couplings via closed-circuit television. Boldly exploitative, the American distributor added about 10 minutes of raunchy hard-core footage of exotic dance routines. 87m/B VHS. AR Ricardo Bauleo, Aldo Barbero; *D:* Emilio Vieyra. SMW, TPV

Curley ♂♂ 1947 High-spirited youngsters play pranks on their schoolteacher. A part of the Hal Roach Comedy Carnival. 53m/C VHS, Beta. Larry Olsen, Frances Rafferty, Eilene Janssen, Walter Abel; *D:* Bernard Carr. DVT, NOS, HHT

Curly Sue ♂♂ 1991 (PG) Adorable, homeless waif Porter and her scheming, adoptive father Belushi plot to rip off single, career-minded female attorney Lynch in order to take in some extra cash. Trouble is, all three heartstrings are tugged, and the trio develop a warm, caring relationship. A throwback to the Depression era's Shirley Temple formula films met with mixed reviews. Undiscriminating younger audiences should have a good time, though. Available in widescreen format on laserdisc. 102m/C VHS, Beta, LV, 8mm, Closed Caption. James Belushi, Kelly Lynch, Alison Porter, John Getz, Fred Dalton Thompson; *D:* John Hughes; *W:* John Hughes; *M:* Georges Delerue. WAR, CCB

Curly Top ♂♂½ 1935 (G) Orphan Temple helps land a husband for her beautiful sister. Along the way, she sings "Animal Crackers in My Soup." Remake of the silent "Daddy Long Legs," which was remade again in 1955. 74m/B VHS, Beta, Closed Caption. Shirley Temple, John Boles, Rochelle Hudson, Jane Darwell, Esther Dale, Arthur Treacher, Rafaela Ottiano; *D:* Irving Cummings. FOX, MLT

The Curse ♂ *The Farm* 1987 (R) After a meteorite lands near a small farming community and contaminates the area, a young boy tries to prevent residents from turning into slime-oozing mutants. Remake of "Die, Monster, Die." 92m/C VHS, Beta, LV, Closed Caption. Wil Wheaton, Claude Akins, Malcolm Danare, Cooper Huckabee, John Schneider, David Keith, Amy Wheaton, David Chaskin; *D:* David Keith; *W:* David Chaskin. MED, IME

Curse 2: The Bite ♂ 1988 (R) Radiation affected snakes are transformed into deadly vipers whose bites change their unsuspecting victims into horrible creatures. 97m/C VHS, Beta. Jill Schoelen, J. Eddie Peck, Jamie Farr, Savina Gersak, Bo Svenson; *D:* Fred Goodwin. TWE

Curse 3: Blood Sacrifice *Panga* 1990 (R) An African sugar cane plantation becomes host to a horrible nightmare when a voodoo curse is placed on the owners. The monstrous God of the Sea is summoned to avenge the accidental death of a baby, and the hellish journey into insanity begins. 91m/C VHS, LV. Christopher Lee, Jenilee Harrison, Henry Cele; *D:* Sean Barton. COL

Curse 4: The Ultimate Sacrifice ♂½ *Catacombs* 1990 (R) Beneath the monastery at San Pietro lies buried the beast of the Apocalypse. For 400 years the secret has been kept and then an American priest and a lovely school teacher unwittingly break the seal and unleash the cursed beast upon an unsuspecting world. 84m/C VHS, LV, Closed Caption. Timothy Van Patten, Laura Schaefer, Jeremy West, Ian Abercrombie; *D:* David Schmoeller. COL

The Curse of Frankenstein ♂♂½ 1957 Young Victor Frankenstein reenacts his father's experiments with creating life from the dead resulting in a terrifying, hideous creature. The first in Hammer's Frankenstein series and followed by "Revenge of Frankenstein." From the Shelley story. Make-up by Jack Pierce, who also created the famous make-up for Universal's Frankenstein monster. 83m/C VHS, Beta. GB Peter Cushing, Christopher Lee, Hazel Court, Robert Urquhart, Valerie Gaunt; *D:* Terence Fisher; *W:* Jimmy Sangster; *M:* James Bernard. WAR, MLB

The Curse of King Tut's Tomb ♂½ 1980 Made-for-television movie is set in 1922 where archaeologists have just opened Tutankhamen's tomb. The curse of the boy king is unleashed as tragic events bring the adventurers uncommon gloom. Oh boy. 98m/C VHS, Beta. Robin Ellis, Harry Andrews, Eva Marie Saint, Raymond Burr, Wendy Hiller; *D:* Philip Leacock. GKK

The Curse of the Aztec Mummy woof! *La Maldicion de la Momia Azteca* 1959 A mad scientist schemes to rob a Mayan pyramid of its treasure but the resident mummy will have none of it. Sequel to "Robot vs. the Aztec Mummy" and followed by "Wrestling Women vs. the Aztec Mummy." 65m/B VHS. *MX* Ramon Gay, Rosita Arenas, Crox Alvarado; *D:* Rafael Portillo. *SNC*

Curse of the Aztec Mummy/Robot vs. the Aztec Mummy woof! 1959

Vengeful mummy of an Aztec warrior stalks those who attempt to steal a fabulous treasure. A mad criminal scientist wants the treasure and uses gangsters and a human robot to get what he wants. 130m/B VHS, Beta. Ramon Gay, Rosita Arenas, Crox Alvarado, Luis Aceves Cantaneda; *D:* Rafael Portillo. *HHT*

Curse of the Black Widow 𝒵𝒵 *Love Trap* 1977

An investigator follows a trail of brutal murders to the lair of a supernatural gigantic spider in the middle of Los Angeles. Made for television. 100m/C VHS, Beta. Patty Duke, Anthony (Tony) Franciosa, Donna Mills, June Lockhart, Sid Caesar, Vic Morrow, June Allyson, Roz Kelly, Jeff Corey; *D:* Dan Curtis. *NO*

Curse of the Blue Lights woof! 1988

(R) Mysterious lights begin appearing at the local romantic spot. Little do the young lovers know, it hails the monstrous arrival of a ghoul, intent on raising the dead. Also available in an unedited version. Unfortunately, nothing can resurrect this film. 93m/C VHS, Beta. Brent Ritter; *D:* John H. Johnson. *NO*

Curse of the Cat People 𝒵𝒵𝒵 1944

A young sensitive girl is guided by the vision of her dead mother. Sequel to "Cat People." Available in a colorized version. 70m/B VHS, Beta, LV. Simone Simon, Kent Smith, Jane Randolph, Elizabeth Russell, Ann Carter; *D:* Robert Wise, Gunther Von Fritsch. *MED, TTC*

The Curse of the Crying Woman 𝒵½ *La Maldicion de a Llorona; La Casa Embrujada* 1961

Unknowing descandant of a witch is lured to her aunt's home to perform the act that will revive the monstrous crying woman and renew a reign of evil. 74m/B VHS, Beta. *MX* Rosita Arenas, Abel Salazar, Rita Macedo. *SNC, HHT*

Curse of the Crystal Eye 𝒵𝒵 1993

(PG-13) A gunrunner tries to get the treasure of Ali Baba aided by the requisite lovely lady and opposed by your usual bad guys. *CW:* Depiction of a burning man. 90m/C VHS. Jameson Parker, Cynthia Rhodes, Mike Lane, David Sherwood, Andre Jacobs; *D:* Joe Tornatore. *NHO*

Curse of the Demon 𝒵𝒵𝒵½ *Night of the Demon* 1957

A famous psychologist investigates a colleague's mysterious death and enters a world of demonology and the occult, climaxing in a confrontation with a cult's patron demon. Superb thriller based upon the story "Casting the Runes" by M.R. James. 81m/B VHS, Beta. *GB* Dana Andrews, Peggy Cummins, Niall MacGinnis, Maurice Denham; *D:* Jacques Tourneur; *W:* Charles Bennett. *GKK, MLB*

Curse of the Devil 𝒵½ *El Retorno de la Walpurgis* 1973

(R) This time Naschy is turned into a werewolf by annoyed gypsies whose ancestors were slain by his. 73m/C VHS. *MX SP* Paul Naschy, Maria Silva, Patty Shepard, Fay Falcon; *D:* Carlos Aured; *W:* Paul Naschy. *SNC*

Curse of the Headless Horseman 1972

The headless horseman rides again, bringing terror to all who cross his path! 80m/C VHS. Don Carrara, Claudia Dean, B.G. Fisher, Margo Dean, Lee Byers, Joe Cody; *D:* John Kirkland. *NO*

Curse of the Living Corpse 𝒵 1964

A millionaire comes back to rotting life to kill his negligent relatives. Scheider's first film. 84m/C VHS, Beta. Candace Hilligoss, Roy Scheider, Helen Warren, Margot Hartman; *D:* Del Tenney. *PSM*

Curse of the Living Dead 𝒵 1989

Two siblings are forced to eat flesh for eternity after their witch-doctor mother puts a curse on them. 90m/C VHS, Beta. *D:* Lawrence Foldes. *ELV, HHE*

Curse of the Pink Panther 𝒵𝒵 1983

(PG) Clifton Sleigh, an inept New York City detective played by Wass, is assigned to find the missing Inspector Clouseau. His efforts are complicat-

ed by an assortment of gangsters and aristocrats who cross paths with the detective. So-so attempt to keep popular series going after Seller's death. Niven's last film. 110m/C VHS, Beta, Closed Caption. Ted Wass, David Niven, Robert Wagner, Herbert Lom, Joanna Lumley, Capucine, Robert Loggia, Harvey Korman, Leslie Ash, Denise Crosby; *D:* Blake Edwards; *W:* Blake Edwards; *M:* Henry Mancini. *MGM*

Curse of the Queerwolf 𝒵𝒵 1987

A man is bitten on the butt by gay werewolf and transforms into the title character. Filmed in Santa Barbara in 8mm; some funny moments. From the director of "A Polish Vampire in Burbank." 90m/C VHS. Michael Palazzolo, Kent Butler, Taylor Whitney; *D:* Mark Pirro. *HHE*

Curse of the Starving Class 𝒵𝒵 1994

(R) Ineffective adaptation of Sam Shepard's 1977 play exploring family disintegration. Weston (Woods) is the alcoholic, irresponsible patriarch of a decaying farm. His unhappy wife, Ella (Bates), wants to sell out to land speculator Taylor (Quaid) and move to Paris while rebellious teenager Emma (Fiorella) plans to run off to Mexico and sullen older brother Wesley (Thomas) desires to stay and make a go of things. One-dimensional characterizations don't translate well from stage to screen. *CW:* Language; scene of nudity. 102m/C VHS, LV, Closed Caption. James Woods, Kathy Bates, Henry Thomas, Kristin Fiorella, Randy Quaid, Louis Gossett Jr.; *D:* Michael McClary; *W:* Bruce Beresford; *C:* Dick Quinlan. *THV*

Curse of the Stone Hand woof! 1964

A pair of stone hands causes folks to do suicidal things. A mutation of a Mexican and a Chilean horror film, each purchased and monster-mashed into one by Warren. 72m/B VHS. *MX* John Carradine, Ernest Walch, Sheila Bon, Katherine Victor, Lloyd Nelson; *D:* Jerry Warren. *NOS, LOO*

Curse of the Swamp Creature 𝒵 1966

A mad scientist in the Everglades attempts to create half human/half alligator monsters. In turn, a geologic expeditionary force attempts to stop his experimentation. Low budget thrills courtesy of Larry Buchanan. 80m/C VHS. John Agar, Francine York, Shirley McLine, Bill Thurman, Jeff Alexander; *D:* Larry Buchanan. *MOV, VDM*

Curse of the Undead 𝒵½ 1959

Mediocre vampire western finds a small town suffering from the deaths of several young women—all with small wounds in the neck. Suspicions fall on gunslinger Drake Robey (Pate) and it's up to preacher Dan Young (Fleming) to take care of the bloodsucking miscreant. 89m/B VHS, Closed Caption. Eric Fleming, Michael Pate, Kathleen Crowley, John Hoyt, Bruce Gordon, Edward Binns, Jimmy Murphy, Jay Adler; *D:* Edward Dein; *W:* Edward Dein, Mildred Dein; *C:* Ellis W. Carter; *M:* Irving Gertz. *USH*

The Curse of the Werewolf 𝒵𝒵½ 1961

Horror film about a 19th-century European werewolf that is renowned for its ferocious departure from the stereotypical portrait of the beast. 91m/C VHS, Beta. *GB* Oliver Reed, Clifford Evans, Yvonne Romain, Catherine Feller, Anthony Dawson, Michael Ripper; *D:* Terence Fisher. *USH, TLF, MLB*

Curse of the Yellow Snake 𝒵𝒵 1963

Voluminous yarn features a running battle over an ancient Chinese artifact, with crazed Chinese cultists running through foggy London streets. 98m/C VHS, Beta. *GE* Joachim Berger, Werner Peters; *D:* Franz Gottlieb. *VYY*

The Cursed Mountain Mystery 𝒵½ 1993

(R) Two petty thieves steal a legendary precious gem rumored to cursed. The immortal warrior supposed to guard the gem lures the crooks to Sher Mountain, where he intends to eliminate them and return the stone to its keeper. 87m/C VHS. Phillip Avalon, Tom Richards, Joe Bugner; *D:* Vince Martin; *W:* Denis Whitburn. *COL*

Curtain Up 𝒵𝒵 1953

"Little theatre" dramatics and the exasperating temperaments of amateur theatricals are exposed in this adaptation of the play "On Monday Next," by Philip King.

82m/C VHS, Beta. *GB* Robert Morley, Margaret Rutherford, Olive Sloane; *D:* Ralph Smart; *W:* Jack Davies; *M:* Malcolm Arnold. *LCA*

Curtains woof! 1983

(R) Director has a clash of wills with a film star that spells "Curtains" for a group of aspiring actresses gathered together at a haunted house for an audition. Hamfest with no thrills, chills, gore, or gratuitous skin. No wonder why director Richard Ciupka hides behind pseudonym Stryker. 90m/C VHS, Beta. *CA* John Vernon, Samantha Eggar; *D:* Jonathan Stryker; *W:* Robert Guza Jr. *VES*

Curtis's Charm 𝒵½ 1996

Thanks to his drug paranoia, crack addict Curtis (Wint) believes his wife Cookie (Crawford) and mother-in-law (Barnes-Hopkins) have put a voodoo spell on him. His friend Jim (Callum Rennie), a former addict, tries to help Curtis by coming up with some magic of his own, intended to convince the addled druggie that it will protect him. Lots of narration does little to make the character's friendship convincing. Based on a short story by Jim Carroll. 74m/B VHS. *CA* Maurice Dean Wint, Keith Callum Rennie, Rachael Crawford, Barbara Barnes-Hopkins; *D:* John L'Ecuyer; *W:* John L'Ecuyer; *C:* Harald Bachmann; *M:* Mark Korven. Genie Awards '96: Best Score; Nominations: Genie Awards '96: Best Adapted Screenplay. *NYR*

Custer's Last Fight 𝒵½ 1912

Re-enactment of the American West period when the Sioux and Cheyenne Indian tribes bitterly opposed the white man. Silent. 50m/B VHS. *D:* Francis Ford. *NOS, DVT, CCP*

Custer's Last Stand 𝒵½ 1936

Feature-length version of the Mascot serial recounting the last days of the famous General. 70m/B VHS, Beta. Frank McGlynn, Rex Lease, Nancy Caseell, Lona Andre, William Farnum, Reed Howes, Jack Mulhall, Josef Swickard, Ruth Mix; *D:* Elmer Clifton. *VCN, GPV*

The Custodian 𝒵𝒵 1994

(R) Honest cop must battle corruption of Australian police precinct while dealing with numerous personal problems. Good cast goes a long way in routine story. *CW:* Language, violence, and sexuality. 110m/C VHS, LV. *AU* Anthony LaPaglia, Hugo Weaving, Barry Otto, Bill Hunter, Kelly Dingwall, Gosia Dobrowolska, Naomi Watts; *D:* John Dingwall. *ACA*

Cut and Run 𝒵 1985

(R) Two journalists follow a lead to the former South American home of Jim Jones, and are instantly captured by local guerrillas. 87m/C VHS, Beta. Michael Berryman, Willie Aames, Lisa Blount, Karen Black. *VTR, NWV*

The Cut Throats 𝒵 1989

(R) Americans stumble upon an isolated Nazi outpost stocked with gold and beautiful women. Exploitation at its worst. 80m/C VHS. Jay Scott, Joanne Douglas, Jeff Letham, Pat Michaels, Barbara Lane; *D:* John Hayes; *W:* John Hayes. *TPV*

Cutter's Way 𝒵𝒵½ *Cutter and Bone* 1981

(R) An embittered and alcoholic disabled Vietnam vet and his small-time crook/gigolo friend wrestle with justice and morality when the drifter uncovers a murder but declines to get involved. An unusually cynical mystery from the novel by Newton Thorburg. 105m/C VHS, Beta, LV. Jeff Bridges, John Heard, Lisa Eichhorn, Ann Dusenberry, Stephen Elliott, Nina Van Pallandt, George Dickerson; *D:* Ivan Passer; *C:* Jordan Cronenweth; *M:* Jack Nitzsche. Edgar Allan Poe Awards '81: Best Screenplay. *MGM*

Cutthroat Island 𝒵𝒵½ 1995

(PG-13) Big-budget swashbuckling adventure—long on action and short on plot and character. Female pirate captain Morgan Adams (Davis) is left part of a treasure map by her father and "persuades" educated slave/thief William Shaw (Modine), who has lots of charm and no morals, to assist her. Her scurvy Uncle Dawg (despically well-played by Langella) also has a portion of the map and is willing to let Morgan find the treasure—on Cutthroat Island—before taking it for himself. Director Harlin likes lots of big, noisy explosions (when he doesn't know what else to do) but Davis' exuberance for her pirate queen role is appealing. *CW:*

Some strong pirate action/violence and brief sensuality. **123m/C VHS, LV, Closed Caption, DVD.** Geena Davis, Matthew Modine, Frank Langella, Patrick Malahide, Stan Shaw, Maury Chaykin, Harris Yulin, George Murcell; **D:** Renny Harlin; **W:** Robert King, Marc Norman; **C:** Peter Levy; **M:** John Debney. LIV

Cutting Class 🐾🐾 **1989 (R)** Murders proliferate in a high school, where a student with a history of mental illness is number one on the suspect list. Tongue-in-cheek mayhem. **91m/C VHS, LV.** Jill Schoelen, Roddy McDowall, Donovan Leitch, Martin Mull, Brad Pitt; **D:** Rospo Pallenberg. REP

The Cutting Edge 🐾🐾½ **1992 (PG)** Spoiled figure skater's lifelong quest for Olympic gold is seriously hampered by her inability to be nice to her partners. In a final effort to snag the medal she teams up with a cocky guy who thinks the only sport on ice is hockey, but whose own dreams of NHL stardom were cut short by an injury. Saddled with a predictable and thin plot, it sometimes looks and feels like a TV movie. So why bother? Because the chemistry between photogenic leads Kelly and Sweeney is terrific. Add half a bone for the flying sparks and snappy dialogue, sit back, and enjoy. **101m/C VHS, LV, Closed Caption.** D.B. Sweeney, Moira Kelly, Roy Dotrice, Terry O'Quinn, Dwier Brown, Rachelle Ottley, Jo Jo Starbuck; **D:** Paul Michael Glaser; **W:** Tony Gilroy; **C:** Elliot Davis; **M:** Patrick Williams. MGM

Cyber Bandits 🐾½ **1994 (R)** In a future society, navigator Jack Morris (Kemp) has just sailed a pleasure craft to the island city of Pacifica. His passengers included wealthy Morgan Wells (Hays), whose scientists have developed a deadly virtual reality weapon, and Wells' mistress Rebecca (Paul). Rebecca steals the plans for the weapon and seduces Jack into having the data digitally transferred onto his back in the form of a tattoo. Then Rebecca disappears and Jack finds himself in big trouble. **86m/C VHS, LV, Closed Caption.** Martin Kemp, Alexandra Paul, Robert Hays, Adam Ant, Grace Jones; **D:** Erik Fleming; **W:** James Robinson, Winston Beard; **M:** Steve Hunter. COL

Cyber Ninja 🐾🐾½ **1994** Warrior princess Saki is captured by the Dark Overlord, who plans to sacrifice her. It's up to a mercenary to come to her rescue. Lightweight, action-oriented Japanese mix of samurais and science fiction. Dubbed. **80m/C VHS.** JP Hanbei Kawai, Hiroki Ida. FXL

Cyber-Tracker 🐾½ **1993 (R)** In the judicial system of the future androids hunt down vicious criminals and execute them immediately. When secret service agent Eric Phillips is framed for murder, he's also marked for death. His only chance is to link up with rebels fighting the mechanized monsters. **?m/C VHS, LV, Closed Caption.** Don "The Dragon" Wilson, Richard Norton, Joseph Ruskin, Abby Dalton, Jim Aprea; **D:** Richard Pepin. PMH

Cyber-Tracker 2 🐾½ **1995 (R)** An international weapons dealer has gotten control of the cybertracker technology and created cyborg lookalikes of secret agent Eric Phillips (Wilson) and his newscaster wife Connie (Foster). When the cyborgs commit murder on live TV, the human duo become fugitives who must expose the real killers. **CW:** Non-stop violence, and for language. **97m/C VHS, Closed Caption.** Don "The Dragon" Wilson, Stacie Foster, Stephen Burton. PMH

Cyberstalker 🐾½ **1996** Detective twosome must track down a serial killer who uses the Internet to select his victims. **96m/C VHS.** Blake Bahner, Jeffrey Combs, Annie Biggs, Schnele Wilson. SDE

Cyberzone 🐾½ **1995 (R)** Intergalactic investigator pursues four dangerous androids who are hiding on earth. **CW:** Nudity, a strong sex scene, and some violence. **95m/C VHS.** Marc Singer, Matthias Hues. NHO

Cyborg 🐾 **1989 (R)** In a deathly, dirty, post-holocaust urban world, an able cyborg battles a horde of evil mutant thugs. Poorly-made action flick. **85m/C VHS, Beta, LV.** Jean-Claude Van Damme,

Deborah Richter, Vincent Klyn, Dayle Haddon; **D:** Albert Pyun; **W:** Kitty Chalmers; **M:** Kevin Bassinson. MGM

Cyborg 2 🐾🐾 **1993 (R)** In the year 2074 cyborgs have replaced humans at all levels. A devious company which manufactures cyborgs decides to get rid of its chief competition by literally killing them off. They plan to inject cyborg Cash Reese (Jolie) with a liquid explosive that will detonate her and everything else in sight. Tech-master Mercy (Palance) clues Cash in and she escapes with the help of the human Colton (Koteas) but they've become prey to a group of ruthless hunters. **99m/C VHS, LV, Closed Caption.** Angelina Jolie, Elias Koteas, Jack Palance, Billy Drago. THV

Cyborg 3: The Recycler 🐾🐾 **1995 (R)** Female cyborg has been programmed to become a creator—essentially making mankind useless. **CW:** Non-stop violence, some nudity. **90m/C VHS.** Khrystyne Haje, Zach Galligan, Andrew Bryniarski, Richard Lynch, Malcolm McDowell; **D:** Michael Schroeder; **W:** Barry Victor, Troy Bolotnick. AVE

Cyborg Cop 🐾½ **1993 (R)** DEA agent Phillip (Jenson) is captured during a foreign drug raid and is turned into a half-man, half-machine by mad scientist Kessel (Rhys-Davies), who wants to sell his cyborgs as unstoppable hitmen. Phillip's brother Jack (Bradley) tries to come to his rescue. Lots of stunts and car chases and even a minor romantic subplot with Jack and a tough reporter (Shaw). **97m/C VHS, LV, Closed Caption.** David Bradley, John Rhys-Davies, Todd Jensen, Alonna Shaw; **W:** Glenn A. Bruce. THV

Cyborg Soldier 🐾🐾½ Cyborg Cop 2 **1994 (R)** Loose cannon cop Jack Ryan (Bradley) is up against psycho killer Starkraven (Hunter) who gets turned into a new-model cyborg by your basic suspicious government agency. But when the cyborg decides to go on an unplanned human killing spree, Ryan gets to break out the heavy artillery to mow him down. Also available in an unrated version. **96m/C VHS, LV, Closed Caption.** David Bradley, Morgan Hunter, Jill Pierce; **D:** Sam Firstenberg; **W:** Jon Stevens. NLC

Cycle Psycho woof! Numbered Days; Savage Abduction **1972 (R)** Serial killer blackmails the businessman whose wife he was contracted to kill into bringing him young girls to slaughter. The businessman hires out the job to sleazy motorcycle gang. **80m/C VHS, Beta.** Joe Turkel, Tom Drake, Stephen Oliver; **D:** John Lawrence; **W:** John Lawrence. ACA

Cycle Vixens woof! The Young Cycle Girls **1979 (R)** Three girls jump on their hogs and head from Colorado to California. Much leather, motor revving and other obligatory motorcycle-trash trimmings. **90m/C VHS.** Loraine Ferris, Daphne Lawrence, Deborah Marcus, Lonnie Pense, Kevin O'Neill, Bee Lechat, Billy Bullet; **D:** Peter Perry. SIM

Cyclone 🐾🐾 **1987 (R)** The girlfriend of a murdered scientist must deliver a secretly devised motorcycle into righteous government hands, much to the dismay of evil agents and corrupt officials. Good fun, sparked by a stellar "B" cast. **89m/C VHS, Beta, LV.** Heather Thomas, Jeffrey Combs, Ashley Ferrare, Dar Robinson, Martine Beswick, Robert Quarry, Martin Landau, Huntz Hall, Troy Donahue, Michael Reagan, Dawn Wildsmith, Bruce Fairbairn, Russ Tamblyn; **D:** Fred Olen Ray; **C:** Paul Elliott. COL

Cyclone Cavalier **1925** A dauntless hero travels through Central America on an adventurous spree. **58m/B VHS, Beta.** Reed Howes; **D:** Albert Rogell. GPV, GVV

Cyclone of the Saddle 🐾 **1935** Typical Western about a range war. **53m/B VHS, Beta.** Rex Lease, Bobby Nelson, William Desmond, Yakima Canutt; **D:** Elmer Clifton. NO

Cyclops 🐾🐾 **1956** When an expedition party searches throughout Mexico for a woman's long lost fiance, they are shocked when they find out that radiation has turned him into a one-eyed monster. **72m/B VHS, Beta.** Tom Drake, Gloria Talbot, Lon Chaney Jr., James Craig; **D:** Bert I. Gordon. LIV, MLB

Cyclotrode "X" The Crimson Ghost **1946** The Crimson Ghost attempts to kidnap the inventor of the title machine, which would enable him to rule the world. Moore (The Lone Ranger) plays a bad guy. Serial in 12 episodes. Also available in a 93-minute colorized edition. **100m/B VHS, Beta.** Charles Quigley, Linda Stirling, I. Stanford Jolley, Clayton Moore, Kenne Duncan; **D:** William Witney, Fred Brannon. VCN, REP, MLB

Cyrano de Bergerac 🐾🐾🐾 **1925** Silent version of Edmond Rostand's novel about romantic Cyrano who fears to reveal his love to Roxanne because he feels his enormous nose makes him unattractive. So, he serves as a surrogate lover by encouraging another man's attentions to her. Color-tinted. **114m/C VHS.** IT FR Pierre Magnier, Linda Moglia, Angelo Ferrari; **D:** Augusto Genina; **M:** Carlo Moser. KIV

Cyrano de Bergerac 🐾🐾🐾🐾 **1950** Edmund Rostand's famous story of a large nosed yet poetic cavalier, who finds himself too ugly to be loved. He bears the pain of his devotion to Roxanne from afar, and helps the handsome but tongue-tied Christian to romance her. Ferrer became famous for this role, which won him an Oscar. Based on Brian Hooke's translation of the play. Also available colorized. **112m/B VHS, LV.** Jose Ferrer, Mala Powers, William Prince, Elena Verdugo, Morris Carnovsky; **D:** Michael Gordon; **W:** Carl Foreman; **M:** Dimitri Tiomkin. Academy Awards '50: Best Actor (Ferrer); Golden Globe Awards '51: Best Actor—Drama (Ferrer); National Board of Review Awards '50: 10 Best Films of the Year. MON, MRV, NOS

Cyrano de Bergerac **1985** Edmond Rostand's gallant poet and swordsman, with the extraordinary nose, is well-portrayed by Jacobi in this Royal Shakespeare Company production. Translated and adapted by Anthony Burgess. **177m/C VHS.** GB Derek Jacobi, Sinead Cusack. TVC, TTC

Cyrano de Bergerac 🐾🐾🐾🐾 **1990 (PG)** Depardieu brings to exhilarating life Rostand's well-loved play about the brilliant but grotesque-looking swordsman/poet, afraid of nothing—except declaring his love to the beautiful Roxanne. One of France's costliest modern productions, a multi-award winner for its cast, costumes, music and sets. English subtitles (by Anthony Burgess) are designed to capture the intricate rhymes of the original French dialogue. **135m/C VHS, LV.** FR Gerard Depardieu, Jacques Weber, Anne Brochet, Vincent Perez, Roland Bertin, Josiane Stoleru, Phillipe Volter, Philippe Morier-Genoud, Pierre Maguelon; **D:** Jean-Paul Rappeneau; **W:** Jean-Claude Carriere, Jean-Paul Rappeneau. Academy Awards '90: Best Costume Design; Cannes Film Festival '90: Best Actor (Depardieu); Cesar Awards '91: Best Actor (Depardieu), Best Art Direction/Set Decoration, Best Cinematography, Best Costume Design, Best Director (Rappeneau), Best Film, Best Sound, Best Supporting Actor (Weber), Best Score; Golden Globe Awards '91: Best Foreign Film; Nominations: Academy Awards '90: Best Actor (Depardieu), Best Art Direction/Set Decoration, Best Foreign Language Film, Best Makeup. ORI, FCT, BTV

D-Day on Mars 🐾🐾 **1945** Alien invader the Purple Monster is bent on taking over Earth. Originally a 15-part Republic serial titled "The Purple Monster Strikes." **100m/B VHS.** Dennis Moore, Linda Stirling, Roy Barcroft, James Craven, Bud Geary, Mary Moore; **D:** Spencer Gordon Bennet, Fred Brannon. REP

D-Day, the Sixth of June 🐾🐾🐾 The Sixth of June **1956** An American soldier has an affair with a Englishwoman weeks before D-Day, where he unhappily finds himself fighting side by side with her husband. Based on the novel by Lionel Shapiro. **106m/C VHS, Beta.** Richard Todd, Dana Wynter, Robert Taylor, Edmond O'Brien, John Williams, Jerry Paris, Richard Stapley; **D:** Henry Koster; **C:** Lee Garmes. FXV

Da 🐾🐾½ **1988 (PG)** A middle-aged man returns to Ireland for his father's funeral. As he sorts out his father's belongings, his father returns as a ghostly presence to chat with him about life, death, and their own relationship. Based on the

Hugh Leonard play with Hughes recreating his Tony-award winning role. **102m/C VHS, Beta, LV, Closed Caption.** Barnard Hughes, Martin Sheen, William Hickey, Hugh O'Conor; *D:* Matt Clark; *W:* Hugh Leonard; *M:* Elmer Bernstein. *NO*

Dad 🎬🎬½ **1989 (PG)** Hoping to make up for lost time, a busy executive rushes home to take care of his father who has just had a heart attack. What could have easily become sappy is made bittersweet by the convincing performances of Lemmon and Danson. Based on the novel by William Wharton. **117m/C VHS, Beta, LV, Closed Caption.** Jack Lemmon, Ted Danson, Ethan Hawke, Olympia Dukakis, Kathy Baker, Zakes Mokae, J.T. Walsh, Kevin Spacey, Chris Lemmon; *D:* Gary David Goldberg; *W:* Gary David Goldberg; *M:* James Horner. National Media Owl Awards '90: First Prize; Nominations: Academy Awards '89: Best Makeup. *USH*

Daddy Long Legs 🎬🎬🎬 **1955** Far from the great musicals, but enjoyable. An eccentric millionaire glimpses a French orphan and becomes her anonymous benefactor. Her musing over his identity spawns some surreal (often inexplicable) dance numbers, but love conquers all, even lesser Johnny Mercer songs. From a story by Jean Webster, also done in 1919 with Mary Pickford, 1931 with Janet Gaynor and 1935 with Shirley Temple as "Curly Top." ♫Daddy Long Legs; Something's Got To Give; Sluefoot; Dream; History of the Beat; C-A-T Spells Cat; Welcome Egghead. **126m/C VHS, LV, Closed Caption.** Fred Astaire, Leslie Caron, Terry Moore, Thelma Ritter, Fred Clark, Charlotte Austin, Larry Keating; *D:* Jean Negulesco; *C:* Leon Shamroy; *M:* Alex North. Nominations: Academy Awards '55: Best Art Direction/Set Decoration (Color), Best Song ("Something's Gotta Give"), Scoring of a Musical. *FXV, FCT*

Daddy Nostalgia 🎬🎬🎬 *These Foolish Things* **1990** Birkin plays the estranged daughter of Bogarde, who rushes from her home in England to France to be with her seriously ill father. She must come to terms with her feelings for him just as Bogarde must deal with his own mortality. Wonderful performances, with Bogarde a charming and dominating presence. In French with English subtitles. **105m/C VHS.** *FR* Dirk Bogarde, Jane Birkin, Odette Laure; *D:* Bertrand Tavernier; *W:* Colo Tavernier O'Hagan; *M:* Antoine Duhamel. *FCT*

Daddy-O 🎬 *Out on Probation* **1959** Drag racer Daddy-O traps the killers of his best friend and lands the blonde bombshell Jana. It might seem bad since it's dated, but, hey, it may have been bad in 1959, too! **74m/B VHS.** Dick Contino, Sandra Giles; *D:* Lou Place; *W:* David Moessinger. *COL*

Daddy's Boys 🎬½ **1987 (R)** Since farming during the Depression is a rather low-paying endeavor, this family turns to thieving instead. But all-for-one and one-for-all is not the credo for one of the sons who decides to branch out on his own. Produced by Roger Corman. **90m/C VHS, Beta, LV.** Daryl Haney, Laura Burkett, Raymond J. Barry, Dan Shor; *D:* Joe Minion; *W:* Daryl Haney. *COL*

Daddy's Dyin'...Who's Got the Will? 🎬🎬½ **1990 (PG-13)** Based on the critically acclaimed play, this bittersweet comedy stars Bridges and D'Angelo as two members of the spiteful Turnover clan. When Daddy is on his deathbed, the entire family uses the opportunity to stab each other in the back. Non-stop humor and deep-hearted honesty carries this delightful adaptation quickly from beginning to end. **95m/C VHS, Beta, LV, Closed Caption.** Beau Bridges, Beverly D'Angelo, Tess Harper, Judge Reinhold, Amy Wright, Keith Carradine, Patrika Darbo, Molly McClure, Bert Remsen; *D:* Jack Fisk; *W:* Del Shores; *C:* Paul Elliott; *M:* David McHugh. *MGM*

Daddy's Girl 🎬½ **1996 (R)** When adopted Jody's new family is threatened she'll stop at nothing to protect herself and them.*CW:* For violence and menace perpetrated by a child. **95m/C VHS, LV, Closed Caption.** William Katt, Michelle Greene, Roxana Zal, Mimi Craven, Whip Hubley, Gabrielle Boni; *D:* Martin Kitrosser; *W:* Steve Pesce. *LIV*

Daddy's Gone A-Hunting 🎬🎬🎬 **1969 (PG)** It's an eye for an eye, a baby for a baby in this well-done psychological thriller. A happily married woman is stalked by her deranged ex-boyfriend, whose baby she aborted years before. Now he wants the life of her child as just compensation for the loss of his. **108m/C VHS.** Carol White, Paul Burke, Scott Hylands, Rachel Ames, Mala Powers, James B. Sikking; *D:* Mark Robson; *W:* Larry Cohen; *C:* Ernest Laszlo; *M:* John Williams. *WAR*

Daens 🎬🎬½ **1992** Looks at the disparity between rich and poor at the turn of the century. Daens, a priest, returns home to Flanders to find desperate poverty among the Flemish-speaking workers of the local textile mill. The French-speaking mill owners are supported by the local Catholic church while Daens believes in the rights of the workers. Decleir makes his priest a complex and troubled man, who must choose between his conscience and social reform and the dictates of his church. Marred by somewhat cardboard villains and a complex political/social situation that isn't adequately explained. Based on the novel by Louis Paul Boon. Flemish and French with English subtitles. **134m/C VHS.** *FR BE NL* Jan Decleir, Gerard Desarthe, Antje De Boeck, Michael Pas, Johan Leysen, Idwig Stephane, Linda Van Dijck, Wim Meuwissen; *D:* Stijn Coninx; *W:* Francois Chevallier, Stijn Coninx; *M:* Dirk Brosse. Nominations: Academy Awards '92: Best Foreign Language Film. *ORI*

Daffy Duck's Movie: Fantastic Island **1983 (G)** A compilation of classic Warner Brothers cartoons, starring Daffy Duck, Speedy Gonzales, Bugs Bunny, Porky Pig, Sylvester, Tweety, Pepe Le Pew, Pirate Sam, Granny, Foghorn Leghorn and the Tasmanian Devil. **78m/C VHS, Beta, LV.** *D:* Isadore "Friz" Freleng; *V:* Mel Blanc, June Foray, Les Tremayne. *WAR, FCT*

Daffy Duck's Quackbusters **1989 (G)** Daffy, with help from pals Bugs and Porky, sets up his own "ghostbusting" service. Good compilation of old classics such as "Night of the Living Duck," plus a new feature, "The Duxcorcist." Video is also available in Spanish. **79m/C VHS, Beta, LV, Closed Caption.** *D:* Greg Ford, Terry Lennon; *V:* Mel Blanc. *WAR, FCT, APD*

Dagger Eyes 🎬½ **198?** A political assassin at work is inadvertently captured on film by a photographer. The assassin's mob employers will go to any lengths to destroy the film. Say cheeeeeese! **84m/C VHS, Beta.** Carole Bouquet, Philip Coccioletti, John Steiner; *D:* Carlo Vanzina. *NO*

The Dagger of Kamui 🎬🎬½ **1985** Jiro is pursued by minions of the evil Tenkai as he races from Japan to the American Old West and back again. He's trying to avenge the murder of his father and Jiro's only weapon is the mysterious Dagger of Kamui, which holds the secret to a treasure and the future of Japan. In Japanese with English subtitles. **132m/C VHS, LV.** *JP ANI, CPM*

Dagora, the Space Monster woof! *Dagora; Space Monster Dagora; Uchudai Dogora; Uchu Daikaiju Dogora* **1965** Giant, slimy, pulsating mass from space lands on Earth and begins eating everything in sight. Scientists join together in a massive effort to destroy the creature. Believe it or not, it's sillier than most of the Japanese sci-fi genre. **80m/C VHS, Beta.** *JP* Yosuke Natsuki, Yoko Fujiyama, Akiko Wakabayashi, Hiroshi Koizumi; *D:* Inoshiro Honda; *W:* Shinichi Sekizawa; *C:* Hajime Koizumi. *VYY*

The Dain Curse 🎬🎬 *Dashiell Hammett's The Dain Curse* **1978** In 1928, private eye Hamilton Nash must recover stolen diamonds, solve a millionaire's suicide, avoid being murdered, and end a family curse. Based on the novel by Dashiell Hammett. Made-for-television as a 312-minute miniseries. **138m/C VHS, Beta.** James Coburn, Jason Miller, Jean Simmons, Beatrice Straight, Hector Elizondo, Nancy Addison; *D:* E.W. Swackhamer. *MTX*

Daisy Miller 🎬🎬½ **1974 (G)** Shepherd portrays the title character in this adaptation of the Henry James novella about a naive young American woman travelling through Europe and getting a taste of the Continent during the late 19th century. Though it is intelligently written and has a good supporting cast, the film seems strangely flat, due in large part to Shepherd's hollow performance. **93m/C VHS, Beta.** Cybill Shepherd, Eileen Brennan, Cloris Leachman, Mildred Natwick; *D:* Peter Bogdanovich; *W:* Frederic Raphael. National Board of Review Awards '74: 10 Best Films of the Year; Nominations: Academy Awards '74: Best Costume Design. *PAR*

Dakota 🎬🎬 **1945** Fine cast becomes embroiled in railroad land dispute. In the meantime, love strikes The Duke. Standard Wayne western saga never quite gets on track. **82m/B VHS, LV.** John Wayne, Vera Ralston, Walter Brennan, Ward Bond, Ona Munson; *D:* Joseph Kane. *REP*

Dakota 🎬🎬 **1988 (PG)** A troubled half-breed teenager works for a rancher, romances his daughter, and befriends his crippled 12-year-old son. A well-meaning, but predictable drama. **96m/C VHS, Beta, LV, Closed Caption.** Lou Diamond Phillips, Dee Dee Norton, Eli Cummins, Herta Ware; *D:* Fred Holmes. *HBO*

Dakota Incident 🎬🎬 **1956** Decent western about stagecoach passengers travelling through Dakota Territory who must defend themselves against an Indian attack. **88m/C VHS.** Dale Robertson, Ward Bond, Linda Darnell, John Lund; *D:* Lewis R. Foster. *REP*

Daleks—Invasion Earth 2150 A.D. 🎬🎬½ *Invasion Earth 2150 A.D* **1966** A sequel to "Dr. Who and the Daleks," wherein the popular British character endeavors to save the Earth from a robotic threat. **81m/C VHS, Beta.** *GB* Peter Cushing, Andrew Keir, Jill Curzon, Ray Brooks; *D:* Gordon Flemyng. *NO*

The Dallas Connection 🎬 **1994 (R)** Three of the four scientists working on a satellite weapons system are assassinated by a trio of sexy but lethal females. Now the remaining scientist is under federal protection in Dallas while he continues his work. Lots of T&A.*CW:* Nudity; sexual situations; violence; language. **90m/C VHS.** Julie Strain, Samantha Phillips, Julie K. Smith, Wendy Hamilton; *D:* Andy Sidaris. *MNC*

Dalva 🎬½ **1995** Dull TV movie finds restless Dalva Northridge (Fawcett) deciding to search for the son she was forced to give up for adoption some 20 years before. But she gets sidetracked juggling two love affairs—with Sam Creekmouth (Boothe), whose Indian heritage is tied to Dalva's family, and alcoholic university professor Michael (Coyote) who wants the Northridge family diaries for his research on the Great Plains. Based on the novel by Jim Harrison. **?m/C VHS.** Farrah Fawcett, Powers Boothe, Peter Coyote, Rod Steiger, Carroll Baker. *NYR*

Dam Busters 🎬🎬🎬½ **1955** Well-done and exciting film details the efforts of British scientists trying to devise a method of destroying a strategic dam in Nazi Germany during WWII. Definitely one of the better in the war movie genre. **119m/B VHS, Beta.** *GB* Michael Redgrave, Richard Todd, Ursula Jeans, Basil Sydney; *D:* Michael Anderson Sr. *HMV, CNG*

Damage 🎬🎬🎬 **1992 (R)** The elegant Irons portrays Stephen, a middle-aged, married British politican who has always been completely in control of his life, especially where his feelings are concerned. Then he meets Anna (Binoche), his son's less-than-innocent fiance, and immediately begins an obsessive, wildly sexual affair with her. Stephen should have listened to Anna's warning about herself "Damaged people are dangerous, they know they can survive," because their passion leads to betrayal and tragedy. Binoche is more icon than human being but the film still hypnotizes as an exploration of passion. Based on the novel by Josephine Hart. An unrated version is also available. **CW:** Language and strong sexuality. **111m/C VHS, LV, Closed Caption.** *GB FR* Jeremy Irons, Juliette Binoche, Rupert Graves, Miranda Richardson, Ian Bannen, Leslie Caron, Peter Stormare, Gemma Clark, Julian Fellowes; **D:** Louis Malle; **W:** David Hare; **C:** Peter Biziou; **M:** Zbigniew Preisner. British Academy Awards '92: Best Supporting Actress (Richardson); Los Angeles Film Critics Association Awards '92: Best Score; Nominations: Academy Awards '92: Best Supporting Actress (Richardson). *COL, IME, MOV*

Dames 🎬 1934 A millionaire with fanatically religious beliefs tries to stop the opening of a Broadway show. In the last of the grand budget-breaking spectacles before the "production code" came into being, distinguished choreographer Busby Berkeley took his imagination to the limit: watch for the dancing clothes on an ironing board and dancing girls with puzzle pieces on their backs which form the real Keeler. ♫Dames; I Only Have Eyes For You; When You Were a Smile on Your Mother's Lips and a Twinkle in Your Father's Eye; Try To See It My Way; The Girl at the Ironing Board. **95m/B VHS, Beta, LV.** Dick Powell, Joan Blondell, Ruby Keeler, ZaSu Pitts, Guy Kibbee, Busby Berkeley; **D:** Ray Enright; **W:** Delmer Daves; **C:** George Barnes. *MGM, FOX*

Dames Ahoy 🎬 1930 Three sailors on shore leave try to find the blonde who tricked one of them out of his pay. This is the original silent version with a piano score. **52m/B VHS.** Glenn Tryon, Otis Harlan, Eddie Gribbon, Helen Wright, Gertrude Astor; **D:** William James Craft. *GPV, FCT*

Damien: Omen 2 🎬🎬 1978 (R) Sequel to "The Omen" about Damien, a young boy possessed with mysterious demonic powers, who kills those people who anger him. Followed by "The Final Conflict." **110m/C VHS, Beta, LV.** William Holden, Lee Grant, Lew Ayres, Robert Foxworth, Sylvia Sidney, Lance Henriksen, Jonathan Scott-Taylor; **D:** Don Taylor; **W:** Mike Hodges; **C:** Bill Butler; **M:** Jerry Goldsmith. *FOX*

Damien: The Leper Priest 🎬🎬 *Father Damien: The Leper Priest* 1980 True story of a Roman Catholic priest who doomed himself by voluntarily serving on a leper colony one hundred years ago. Somewhat disappointing considering the dramatic material. Originally a vehicle for David Janssen, who died prior to filming. Made for television. **100m/C VHS, Beta.** Ken Howard, Mike Farrell, Wilfrid Hyde-White, William Daniels, David Ogden Stiers; **D:** Steven Gethers. *LIV*

Damn the Defiant 🎬🎬🎬 *HMS Defiant* 1962 Adventure abounds when Guinness, as captain of the HMS Defiant during the Napoleonic wars, finds himself up against not only the French but his cruel second-in-command (Bogarde) and a mutinous crew as well. In the end, both a fleet-wide mutiny and a French invasion of England are avoided. Much attention is paid to period detail in this well-crafted drama. **101m/C VHS, Beta, LV.** *GB* Alec Guinness, Dirk Bogarde, Maurice Denham, Anthony Quayle; **D:** Lewis Gilbert. *COL, FCT*

Damn Yankees 🎬🎬🎬 *What Lola Wants* 1958 Musical feature adapted from the Broadway hit. A baseball fan frustrated by his team's lack of success makes a pact with the devil to become the team's new star. Verdon is dynamite as the devil's accomplice. Great Bob Fosse choreography. ♫Whatever Lola Wants; (You Gotta Have) Heart; Shoeless Joe From Hannibal Mo; Goodbye, Old Girl; A Little Brains, A Little Talent; Who's Got the Pain; Two Lost Souls; There's Something About an Empty Chair; Those Were the Good Old Days. **110m/C VHS, Beta, LV, Closed Caption.** Gwen Verdon, Ray Walston, Tab Hunter, Jean Stapleton, Russ Brown; **D:** George Abbott, Stanley Donen. Nominations: Academy Awards '58: Scoring of a Musical. *WAR, FCT, HMV*

Damnation Alley 🎬½ 1977 (PG) A warrior, an artist, and a biker jump in tank and set off in search of civilization after Armageddon. They go to Albany instead. So-so attempt to revive the post-nuclear holocaust genre which was more successfully accomplished by the "Mad Max" se-

ries. Adapted from Roger Zelazny's novel. **87m/C VHS, Beta.** George Peppard, Jan-Michael Vincent, Paul Winfield, Dominique Sanda, Jackie Earle Haley; **D:** Jack Smight; **W:** Alan Sharp, Lukas Heller; **C:** Harry Stradling Jr.; **M:** Jerry Goldsmith. *FOX*

The Damned 🎬🎬½ 1969 (R) Depicts the Nazi takeover of a German industrialist family and their descent into greed, lust, and madness. Comes in dubbed or subtitled formats. **146m/C VHS, Beta.** *IT GE* Dirk Bogarde, Ingrid Thulin, Helmut Griem, Charlotte Rampling, Helmut Berger; **D:** Luchino Visconti; **M:** Maurice Jarre. National Board of Review Awards '69: 5 Best Foreign Films of the Year; Nominations: Academy Awards '69: Best Story & Screenplay. *WAR, APD*

Damned River 🎬½ 1989 (R) Four friends take a guided tour down Zimbabwe's Zambezi River, only to find midway down that their guide is a murderous psycho. Survival becomes a priority. **93m/C VHS, Beta, Closed Caption.** Stephen Shellan, Lisa Aliff, John Terlesky, Marc Poppel, Bradford Bancroft; **D:** Michael Schroeder; **W:** John Crowther. *FOX*

A Damsel in Distress 🎬🎬🎬 1937 Astaire falls for an upper-class British girl, whose family wants her to have nothing to do with him. Features memorable songs from the Gershwins. ♫A Foggy Day in Londontown; Nice Work If You Can Get It; Stiff Upper Lip; Put Me to the Test; I Can't Be Bothered Now; The Jolly Tar and the Milkmaid; Things Are Looking Up; Sing of Spring; Ah Che a Voi Perdoni Iddio. **101m/B VHS, Beta, LV.** Fred Astaire, Joan Fontaine, George Burns, Gracie Allen, Ray Noble, Montagu Love, Reginald Gardiner; **D:** George Stevens; **M:** George Gershwin, George Bassman, Ira Gershwin. Nominations: Academy Awards '37: Best Interior Decoration. *CCB, MED, TTC*

Dan Candy's Law 🎬½ *Alien Thunder* 1973 A Canadian mountie becomes a driven hunter, and then desperate prey, when he tries to track down the Indian who killed his partner. **90m/C VHS, Beta.** *CA* Donald Sutherland, Gordon Tootoosis, Chief Dan George, Kevin McCarthy; **D:** Claude Fournier; **M:** Georges Delerue. *PSM, SIM*

Dance 🎬½ 1990 Two ballet dancers struggle to find love amidst the backstage treacheries and demanding schedules of their profession. **90m/C VHS, Beta.** John Revall, Ellen Troy, Carlton Wilborn, Charlene Campbell; **D:** Robin Murray. *AIP*

Dance Fools Dance 🎬🎬🎬 1931 Fast-paced drama has Crawford and Bakewell as a pair of spoiled rich kids who are forced to face poverty when the stock market crashes. He meets up with Gable, who's producing liquor illegally, while she gets a job at a newspaper. When Gable arranges something akin to the St. Valentine's Day Massacre, Bakewell's investigative reporting of the situation produces fatal results. The Hays Office had a problem with Crawford and friends appearing in their underwear. Cast notes: Gable was just starting out at MGM, which is why he was billed sixth; the William Holden here is not THE William Holden, and Edwards went on to provide the voice of Jiminy Cricket in "Pinocchio." **82m/B VHS, Beta.** Joan Crawford, Lester Vail, Cliff Edwards, William "Billy" Bakewell, Clark Gable; **D:** Harry Beaumont; **C:** Charles Rosher. *MGM, FCT*

Dance, Girl, Dance 🎬🎬 1940 The private lives and romances of a wartime nightclub dance troupe. Standard Hollywood potpourri of dance, drama, comedy. ♫Mother, What Do I Do Now?; Jitterbug Bite; Morning Star. **88m/B VHS, Beta, LV.** Maureen O'Hara, Louis Hayward, Lucille Ball, Virginia Field, Ralph Bellamy, Maria Ouspenskaya, Mary Carlisle, Katherine Alexander, Edward Brophy; **D:** Dorothy Arzner. *TTC*

The Dance Goes On 🎬🎬 1992 After the death of an uncle, Keach and his estranged son Almond reunite at the old Quebec family farm left to them. The father is country-bred and appreciates the property but his Los Angeles-reared son wants to sell for a quick profit. Director Almond cast his own son in the starring role as well as ex-wife Bujold, who plays the ambitious show-biz mother. **104m/C VHS.** James Keach, Matt Almond,

Genevieve Bujold, Cary Lawrence; **D:** Paul Almond; **W:** Paul Almond. *MNC*

Dance Hall 🎬½ 1941 A Pennsylvania dance hall owner is propelled into romantic confusion with the introduction of a sultry blond dancer into his club. **73m/B VHS, Beta.** Cesar Romero, Carole Landis, William Henry, June Storey, Charles Halton; **D:** Irving Pichel. *NOS, BAR, HEG*

Dance Hall Racket 🎬🎬 1958 A sleazy, stilted expose of dance hall vice featuring a brief appearance by Bruce and his wife, Harlow. **60m/B VHS, Beta.** Lenny Bruce, Honey Harlow; **D:** Phil Tucker. *DVT, HEG*

Dance Macabre 🎬 1991 (R) Englund takes on a dual role as a man with a split personality—one of whom is deadly. Jessica, an American ballerina, enrolls in a Russian dance academy and meets mesmerizing choreographer, Anthony. Unfortunately for Jessica she happens to look exactly like Anthony's long-dead lover and he becomes obsessed with her. Also, her fellow dancers are being brutally murdered. Are the events connected? **CW:** Violence and sensuality. **97m/C VHS, LV.** Robert Englund, Michelle Zeitlin, Marianna Moen, Julene Renee, Alexander Sergeyev; **D:** Greydon Clark; **W:** Greydon Clark. *COL*

Dance Me Outside 🎬🎬½ 1995 (R) Native Canadian teens look for some excitement on their Northern Ontario reservation and find themselves cut off from their tradition-bound parents in this slice of life drama. Friends Silas and Blackie plot revenge against a white who murdered a native girl while Silas' sister Illiana comes to visit from Toronto, with her Yuppie lawyer husband, just as her ex-boyfriend returns from a prison stint. Based on the novel by W.P. Kinsella. **CW:** Language, brief violence. **91m/C VHS, LV.** *CA* Ryan Black, Adam Beach, Michael Greyeyes, Lisa Lacroix; **D:** Bruce McDonald; **W:** Bruce McDonald, Don McKellar, John Frizzell. Genie Awards '95: Best Film Editing. *APX*

Dance of Death *woof!* *House of Evil; Macabre Serenade* 1968 Just before his death, Karloff agreed to appear in footage for four Mexican cheapies that were practically thrown together (Karloff actually filmed his scenes in Los Angeles). If they had mixed the footage instead of matched it, the flicks couldn't be any worse. This one concerns a lunatic toy-maker whose toys kill and maim his heirs. **89m/C VHS, Beta.** *MX* Boris Karloff, Julissa, Andres Garcia, Jack Hill; **D:** Juan Ibanez. *SNC, MPI*

Dance of Death 🎬 1984 A girl learns kung fu and kills many warriors by kicking them in the ribs and head. **81m/C VHS, Beta.** Mao Ying, Shih Tien, Shiao Bou-Lo, Chien Pay, Chia Kai, Noh Tikki. *UNI*

Dance of Life 🎬🎬½ 1929 A look at the backstage goings-on at a burlesque theater. A successful entertainer's life goes down the tubes when he hits the bottle. His wife leaves him because of his philandering, but returns when she sees how much he really needs her. One scene of the Ziegfeld Follies uses two-tone Technicolor technology. This was re-made twice: as "Swing High, Swing Low" in 1937 and as "When My Baby Smiles at Me" in 1948. Carroll replaced the stage lead, who was said to have no "name recognition"—Barbara Stanwyck. ♫True Blue Lou; King of Jazzmania; Cuddlesome Baby; Flippity Flop; Ladies of the Dance; The Mightiest Matador; Sweet Rosie O'Grady; In the Gloaming; Sam, the Accordion Man. **115m/B VHS.** Nancy Carroll, Hal Skelly, Ralph Theadore, Charles D. Brown, Dorothy Revier, Al "Fuzzy" St. John, Oscar Levant; **D:** John Cromwell. *NOS, MLB*

Dance of the Damned 🎬🎬 1988 (R) A case where low-budget isn't synonymous with bomb. Fascinating noir-ish plot concerning a vampire who wants to learn more about the life of his next victim, a deep-thinking stripper, who has lost the will to live it. Surprisingly well-done and acted; above-par for this genre. **83m/C VHS, Beta, LV.** Cyril

O'Reilly, Starr Andreeff; **D:** Katt Shea Ruben; **W:** Katt Shea Ruben, Andy Ruben. *NO*

Dance or Die 🎥 1987 Just goes to show that in Las Vegas you can't have your dance and drugs too, because if the Mob doesn't get you, the Feds will. Made for video (though maybe it shouldn't have been made at all). In HiFi Stereo. **90m/C VHS, Beta.** Ray Kieffer, Rebecca Barrington; **D:** Richard W. Munchkin. *NO*

Dance with a Stranger 🎥🎥🎥½ 1985 (R) The engrossing and factual story of Ruth Ellis who gained notoriety as the last woman hanged in Great Britain. This emotional and sometimes violent film mirrors the sensationalism produced in the 1950s. The film follows Ellis's pre-trial life and her perpetual struggle to maintain her independence. Newcomer Richardson portrays the Marilyn Monroe look-alike barmaid. **101m/C VHS, Beta, LV, Closed Caption.** *GB* Miranda Richardson, Rupert Everett, Ian Holm, Joanne Whalley, Matthew Carroll, Tom Chadbon, Jane Bertish, David Trughton, Paul Mooney, Stratford Johns, Susan Kyd, Leslie Manville, Sallie-Anne Field, Martin Murphy, Michael Jenn, Daniel Massey; **D:** Mike Newell; **W:** Shelagh Delaney; **C:** Peter Hannam; **M:** Richard Hartley. Cannes Film Festival '85: Best Film. *VES, LIV*

Dance with Death 🎥 1991 (R) When strippers turn up brutally murdered, a young journalist goes undercover to solve the case. *CW:* Language, strong violence, and strong sensuality. **90m/C VHS, LV, Closed Caption.** Maxwell Caulfield, Barbara Alyn Jones, Martin Mull, Drew Snyder, Catya Sassoon; **D:** Charles Philip Moore. *HBO*

Dance with Me, Henry 🎥½ 1956 When Lou becomes involved with Bud's gambling debts and the local district attorney turns up dead, Lou's not only wanted by the law, but by the mafia as well. This was the great comedy duo's last picture together and it's clear the pair are not happy about working with each other, even on this mediocre effort. **90m/B VHS.** Bud Abbott, Lou Costello, Gigi Perreau, Rusty Hamer, Mary Wickes, Ted de Corsia; **D:** Charles T. Barton. *MGM*

Dancers 🎥½ 1987 (PG) During the filming of the ballet "Giselle" in Italy, a famous, almost-over-the-hill dancer (Baryshnikov, ten years after his role in "The Turning Point") coaches a young, inexperienced starlet. He hopes to revitalize his life and his dancing. Features dancers from the Baryshnikov-led American Ballet Theatre. **99m/C VHS, Beta, LV, Closed Caption.** Mikhail Baryshnikov, Leslie Browne, Julie Kent, Mariangela Melato, Alessandra Ferri, Lynn Seymour, Victor Barbee, Tommy Rall; **D:** Herbert Ross; **M:** Pino Donaggio. *CTH, WAR, FCT*

Dances with Wolves 🎥🎥🎥 1990 (PG-13) The story of a U.S. Army soldier, circa 1870, whose heroism in battle allows him his pick of posts. His choice, to see the West before it disappears, changes his life. He meets, understands and eventually becomes a member of a Lakota Sioux tribe in the Dakotas. Costner's first directorial attempt proves him a talent of vision and intelligence. This sometimes too objective movie lacks a sense of definitive character, undermining its gorgeous scenery and interesting perspective on the plight of Native Americans. Lovely music and epic proportions. Adapted by Blake from his novel. **181m/C VHS, Beta, LV, Closed Caption.** Kevin Costner, Mary McDonnell, Graham Greene, Rodney Grant, Floyd "Red Crow" Westerman, Tantoo Cardinal, Robert Pastorelli, Charles Rocket, Maury Chaykin, Jimmy Herman, Nathan Lee Chasing His Horse, Wes Studi; **D:** Kevin Costner; **W:** Michael Blake; **C:** Dean Semler; **M:** John Barry. Academy Awards '90: Best Adapted Screenplay, Best Cinematography, Best Director (Costner), Best Film Editing, Best Picture, Best Sound, Best Original Score; Directors Guild of America Awards '90: Best Director (Costner); Golden Globe Awards '91: Best Director (Costner), Best Film—Drama, Best Screenplay; National Board of Review Awards '90: 10 Best Films of the Year, Best Director (Costner); Writers Guild of America '90: Best Adapted Screenplay; Nominations: Academy Awards '90: Best Actor (Costner), Best Art Direction/Set Decoration, Best Costume Design, Best Supporting Actor (Greene), Best Supporting Actress (McDonnell). *ORI, FCT, IME*

Dancing in the Dark 🎥🎥½ 1986 (PG-13) An interesting but slow-moving Canadian film about the perfect housewife who learns that after 20 years of devotion to him, her spouse has been unfaithful. Realizing how her life has been wasted she murders her husband and, in the end, suffers a mental breakdown. **93m/C VHS, Beta.** *CA* Martha Henry, Neil Munro, Rosemary Dunsmore, Richard Monette; **D:** Leon Marr; **W:** Leon Marr; **M:** Erik Satie. Genie Awards '87: Best Actress (Henry). *VTR, NWV*

Dancing Lady 🎥🎥½ 1933 Rarely seen film is MGM's answer to "42nd Street," with Crawford as a small-time hoofer trying to break into Broadway. The screen debuts of Astaire and Eddy. 🎵Everything I Have Is Yours; Heigh-Ho! The Gang's All Here; Hold Your Man; That's the Rhythm of the Day; My Dancing Lady; Let's Go Bavarian; Hey Young Fella. **93m/B VHS, Beta.** Clark Gable, Joan Crawford, Fred Astaire, Franchot Tone, Nelson Eddy, Ted Healy, Moe Howard, Shemp Howard, Larry Fine; **D:** Robert Z. Leonard. *MGM, TTC, FCT*

Dancing Man 🎥½ 1933 A gigolo romances both mother and daughter and winds up implicated in murder as a result. Dismissable. **65m/B VHS, Beta, 8mm.** Judith Allen, Reginald Denny, Natalie Moorhead; **D:** Albert Ray. *VYY*

Dancing Mothers 🎥🎥½ 1926 A fast-living woman becomes involved with her mother's roguish boyfriend in this silent film with accompanying musical score. **85m/B VHS, Beta.** Clara Bow, Alice Joyce, Conway Tearle, Donald Keith; **D:** Herbert Brenon. *NOS, MRV, DVT*

Dancing Pirate 🎥🎥 1936 A Boston dance instructor is kidnapped by pirates and jumps ship in Mexico, where he romances a mayor's daughter. The silly story boasts some Rodgers and Hart tunes, plus the early use of Technicolor, exploited here for all it was worth and then some. 🎵Are You My Love?; When You're Dancing the Waltz. **83m/C VHS.** Charles Collins, Frank Morgan, Steffi Duna, Luis Alberni, Victor Varconi, Jack LaRue; **D:** Lloyd Corrigan. *NOS, LOO*

The Dancing Princesses 1984 When five naughty princesses wear the soles of their slippers out every night, their father the King must foot the bill. He soon tires of this expense and offers a reward to the person who can discover how this happens. A handsome prince becomes invisible to follow the lovely ladies and discover their secret. From the "Faerie Tale Theatre" series. Made for television. **60m/C VHS, Beta, Closed Caption.** Lesley Ann Warren, Peter Weller, Sachi Parker, Roy Dotrice; **D:** Peter Medak. *FOX, FCT*

Dancing with Danger 🎥🎥½ 1993 (PG-13) A private investigator is hired to find out why a taxi dancer's customers all end up dead. Soon the PI's employer is the next victim of a serial killer whose ultimate target is the dancer herself. **90m/C VHS, Beta, Closed Caption.** Cheryl Ladd, Ed Marinaro, Miguel Sandoval, Pat Skipper; **D:** Stuart Cooper; **W:** Elisa Bell. *PAR*

Dandelions 🎥 1974 German soft-core flick starring Hauer in an early role as a man jilted by his wife. To make himself feel better he decides to explore the sleazier side of life. Meaningless film evokes no sympathy but some may appreciate the titillation. Dubbed. **92m/C VHS, Beta.** *GE* Rutger Hauer, Dagmar Lassander; **D:** Adrian Hoven. *NO*

Dandy in Aspic 🎥½ 1968 (R) A double-agent is assigned to kill himself in this hard to follow British spy drama. The film is based on Derek Marlowe's novel. Mann died midway through shooting and Harvey finished direction. **107m/C VHS, Beta, LV.** *GB* Laurence Harvey, Tom Courtenay, Lionel Stander, Mia Farrow, Harry Andrews, Peter Cook, Per Oscarsson; **D:** Anthony Mann; **M:** Quincy Jones. *COL*

Danger Ahead 🎥 1940 Newill stars again as Renfrew of the Mounties—this time he tries to rid the north woods of the baddies who are trying to take over. **57m/B VHS.** James Newill, Dorothea Kent,

Guy Usher, Dave O'Brien, Bob Terry; **D:** Ralph Staub. *DVT, HEG*

Danger: Diabolik 🎥 *Diabolik* 1968 (PG-13) A superthief called Diabolik (Law) continuously evades the law while performing his criminal antics. **99m/C VHS, Closed Caption.** *IT* John Phillip Law, Marisa Mell, Michel Piccoli, Terry-Thomas; **D:** Mario Bava; **M:** Ennio Morricone. *PAR*

Danger in the Skies 🎥½ *The Pilot* 1979 (PG) An alcoholic airline pilot tries to straighten out his life when he nearly loses everything while drinking on the job. Made for cable television. **99m/C VHS, Beta.** Cliff Robertson, Diane Baker, Dana Andrews, Gordon MacRae, Milo O'Shea, Frank Converse, Edward Binns; **D:** Cliff Robertson; **C:** Walter Lassally. *HHE*

Danger Lights 🎥½ 1930 Depicts the railroads and the railroad men's dedication to each other and their trains. **73m/B VHS, Beta.** Jean Arthur, Louis Wolheim, Robert Armstrong; **D:** George B. Seitz. *PEN, MRV, NOS*

Danger Man 1961 British tv series starring McGoohan as NATO agent John Drake. Half-hour episodes were known as "Danger Man" in England, when the series went to 60 minutes the title was changed to "Secret Agent" with the premise remaining the same. Additional episodes available. **30m/B VHS.** *GB* Patrick McGoohan. *MPI, MOV*

Danger of Love 🎥½ 1995 (R) Married teacher Michael Carlin (Penny) has an affair with seductive colleague Carolyn Warmus (Robertson) but when he's about to end it, his wife is murdered. The detective (Bologna) thinks Michael is guilty but it's Carolyn who's hiding all the secrets. Based on a true story; made for TV. *CW:* Violence and some sexual material. **95m/C VHS.** Joe Penny, Jenny Robertson, Joseph Bologna, Richard Lewis, Fairuza Balk, Deborah Benson, Sydney Walsh; **D:** Joyce Chopra. *THV*

Danger on the Air 🎥🎥 1938 A radio program sponsor—a much-despised misogynist—is murdered, and the sound engineer attempts to solve the mystery. Features Cobb in one of his earliest roles; Garrett also directed "Lady in the Morgue" that year. **70m/B VHS, Beta.** Donald Woods, Nan Grey, Berton Churchill, Jed Prouty, William Lundigan, Richard "Skeets" Gallagher, Edward Van Sloan, George Meeker, Lee J. Cobb, Johnny Arthur, Linda Hayes, Louise Stanley; **D:** Otis Garrett. *SNC*

Danger Trails 🎥½ 1935 Rehashed western programmer. Features the hero who must save the rancher's honor as well as the ranch, while fighting detestable hombres with the traditional fare as an arsenal. **55m/B VHS, Beta.** Guinn "Big Boy" Williams, Marjorie Gordon, Wally Wales, John Elliott, Ace Cain, Edmund Cobb; **D:** Robert F. "Bob" Hill. *NOS, DVT, GPV*

Danger UXB 🎥🎥½ 1981 During the 1940 London blitz "Danger UXB" was scrawled wherever there was, or thought to be, an unexploded German bomb. This miniseries covers the exploits of the Royal Engineers whose job it was, with little training and lots of nerve, to defuse the bombs. Based on the memoirs of Major A.B. Hartley of the Royal Engineers. On five cassettes. Made for television. **660m/C VHS, Beta.** *GB* Anthony Andrews, Judy Geeson, Maurice Roeves, Kenneth Cranham, Jeremy Sinden, Iain Cuthbertson, George Innes, Norman Chappell, Kenneth Farrington, Gordon Kane, Ken Kitson, Robert Longden, Robert Pugh, Deborah Watling. *SIG, TVC, FUS*

Danger Zone 🎥🎥 1951 A man is hired to bid for a saxophone at an auction and then has the instrument stolen from him. He discovers it contained stolen jewelry and tries to recover it. **56m/B VHS, Beta, LV.** Hugh Beaumont, Tom Neal, Richard Travis, Virginia Dale. *NO*

Danger Zone woof! 1987 (R) A low-budget, low-brow flick about an all-female rock band whose bus breaks down in the middle of the desert, leaving the girls to defend themselves against a merciless motorcycle gang. You'll wish this one was a mirage. **90m/C VHS, Beta.** Robert Canada, Jason

Williams, Kriss Braxton, Dana Dowell, Jamie Ferreira; **D:** Henry Vernon. *NLC*

Danger Zone 🎬🎬 **1995 (R)** An American mining expert uncovers a worldwide nuclear plot when he's lured to East Africa to supposedly contain a toxic spill. Instead, he's being used to recover a load of plutonium.**CW:** Commando violence. **92m/C VHS, LV, Closed Caption.** Billy Zane, Ron Silver, Robert Downey Jr., Cary-Hiroyuki Tagawa; **D:** Allan Eastman; **W:** Jeff Albert; **C:** Yossi Wein. *LIV*

Danger Zone 2 🎬 **1989 (R)** A pernicious biker is released from prison on a technicality and decides to pay a social call to the undercover cop who set him up. **95m/C VHS.** Jason Williams, Robert Random; **D:** Geoffrey G. Bowers; **W:** Dulany Ross Clements. *MCG*

Danger Zone 3: Steel Horse War 🎬 **1990 (R)** The "Danger Zone" dude is back and this time he's taken on a bevy of biker-types in a most gruesome battle to make our deserts safe. **91m/C VHS, Beta.** Jason Williams, Robert Random, Barne Suboski, Juanita Ranney, Rusty Cooper, Giles Ashford; **D:** Douglas Bronco. *PMR*

Dangerous 🎬🎬½ **1935** Davis won her first Oscar for her rather overdone portrayal of a has-been alcoholic actress reformed by a smitten architect who recognizes her from her days as a star. **72m/B VHS, Beta, LV.** Bette Davis, Franchot Tone, Margaret Lindsay, Alison Skipworth, John Eldridge, Dick Foran; **D:** Alfred E. Green. Academy Awards '35: Best Actress (Davis). *MGM, BTV*

The Dangerous 🎬½ **1995 (R)** New Orleans' seamy underworld is the setting for a hot-headed cop (Pare), a mystery man (Davi), and the beauty (Barbieri) they're both interested in. Also available unrated.**CW:** Strong brutal violence, sexuality and language. **96m/C VHS, LV, Closed Caption.** Robert Davi, Michael Pare, Paula Barbieri, Elliott Gould, John Savage, Joel Grey; **D:** Maria Dante, Rod Hewitt; **W:** Rod Hewitt. *ORI*

A Dangerous Age 🎬½ **1957** A young girl, hoping to marry her lover, runs away from boarding school. **?m/C VHS.** Ben Piazza, Ann Pearson. *SNC*

Dangerous Appointment 🎬🎬 **1934** Story of an innocent store clerk accused of theft and attempted murder. **?m/C VHS.** Charles Starrett, Dorothy Wilson. *SNC*

Dangerous Charter 🎬½ **1962** A group of fishermen discover a deserted yacht and man its helm. But their good fortune takes a decided turn for the worst as they become caught in mob-propelled danger. **76m/C VHS, Beta.** Chris Warfield, Sally Fraser, Richard Foote, Peter Foster, Wright King; **D:** Robert Gottschalk. *NOS, ACA*

Dangerous Curves 🎬🎬½ **1988 (PG)** Two friends are assigned to deliver a new Porsche to a billionaire's daughter - one of them talks the other into taking a little detour, and the trouble begins. This one went straight to video. **93m/C VHS, Beta.** Robert Stack, Tate Donovan, Danielle von Zerneck, Robert Klein, Elizabeth Ashley, Leslie Nielsen; **D:** David Lewis. *VES, LIV*

Dangerous Game 🎬½ **1990 (R)** A computer hacker leads his friends through a department store's security system, only to find they can't get out until morning. They soon discover they are not alone when one of the group turns up dead. **102m/C VHS, Beta, LV, Closed Caption.** Miles Buchanan, Sandy Lillingston, Kathryn Walker, John Polson; **D:** Stephen Hopkins. *ACD*

Dangerous Game 🎬🎬 *Snake Eyes* **1993 (R)** Abrasive filmmaker Eddie Israel's (Keitel) new movie is about a couple's disintegrating marriage turning violent. Stars Sarah (Madonna) and Francis (Russo) find the on-camera violence spilling over into their tangled private lives while Eddie finds his personal traumas intruding more and more into the fictional material. Very raw movie within a movie features volatile Keitel (who also worked with Ferrera on "Bad Lieutenant") and suitably histrionic Russo; Madonna manages to

hold her own in the least showy role, a cinematic first. Eddie's betrayed and bewildered wife is sympathetically portrayed by Ferrara, director Abel's wife. Also available in an unrated version.**CW:** Language and sexuality. **107m/C VHS, LV, Closed Caption.** Harvey Keitel, James Russo, Madonna, Nancy Ferrara; **D:** Abel Ferrara; **W:** Nicholas St. John. *MGM*

Dangerous Ground 🎬🎬 **1996 (R)** Hackneyed thriller has expatriate South African Vusi (Cube) returning to his homeland to find his younger brother Steven, who has double-crossed the head of a drug cartel. Since Vusi's departure 12 years ago, apartheid's been replaced by gangs and drugs, and while combing the dangerous streets of Johannesburg, the graduate student implausibly turns into a gun-wielding hero. Rhames's sinister drug lord Muki is pic's best character. Lead Cube shows just how limited his acting ability is while Hurley displays the picture's clearly limited wardrobe budget. Interracial relationships are glossed over, while South Africa's sociological problems are used as plot devices and then ignored. Filmed on location in South Africa, this shoot-em-up's locale could easily be Anytown, USA.**CW:** Strong violence, drug use and language, and for some nudity. **92m/C VHS, LV, Closed Caption.** Ice Cube, Elizabeth Hurley, Ving Rhames, Eric Miyeni, Sechaba Morojele; **D:** Darrell Roodt; **W:** Darrell Roodt, Greg Latter; **C:** Paul Gilpin; **M:** Stanley Clarke. *NLC*

Dangerous Heart 🎬🎬 **1993 (R)** A crooked undercover cop steals a bundle from a drug dealer and gets himself killed for his troubles. Only the dealer doesn't know where the money is. So he decides to befriend the cop's widow, get romantically involved, and see what she knows. **93m/C VHS, LV, Closed Caption.** Timothy Daly, Lauren Holly, Jeffrey Nordling, Alice Carter, Joe Pantoliano; **D:** Michael Scott; **W:** Patrick Cirillo. *USH*

Dangerous Holiday 🎬🎬 **1937** A young violin prodigy would rather be just "one of the boys" than be forced to practice all the time. He decides to run away but has everyone in an uproar thinking he's been kidnapped. **54m/B VHS, Beta.** Hedda Hopper, Guinn "Big Boy" Williams, Jack LaRue, Franklin Pangborn, Grady Sutton. *VYY*

Dangerous Hours 🎬🎬 **1919** An anti-communist propaganda film with Hughes as the innocent young college boy who gets duped by the evil Marxists until he realizes the truth of his all-American upbringing. Silent with original organ score. **88m/B VHS, Beta, 8mm.** Lloyd Hughes; **D:** Fred Niblo; **C:** George Barnes. *VYY, FCT, GPV*

Dangerous Indiscretion 🎬🎬 **1994 (R)** Ad exec finds his girlfriend is actually a woman married to a very powerful man, who's not going to be happy to find out about their liaison.**CW:** Strong sexuality. **81m/C VHS, Closed Caption.** Joan Severance, C. Thomas Howell, Malcolm McDowell; **D:** Richard Kletter; **W:** Richard Kletter, Jack Tarpon; **M:** Richard Gibbs. *PAR*

Dangerous Liaisons 🎬🎬 *Les Liaisons Dangereuses; Dangerous Love Affairs* **1960** A couple take each other to the brink of destruction via their insatiable desire for extra-marital affairs. Vadim attempted to repeat his success with Brigitte Bardot by featuring wife Annette as a new sex goddess, but lightning didn't strike twice. **111m/B VHS, LV.** *FR* **IT** Gerard Philipe, Jeanne Moreau, Jeanne Valeri, Annette Vadim, Simone Renant, Jean-Louis Trintignant, Nikolas Vogel; **D:** Roger Vadim; **W:** Roger Vadim. *INT, APD, TPV*

Dangerous Liaisons 🎬🎬🎬 **1988 (R)** Stylish and absorbing, this adaptation of the Laclos novel and the Christopher Hampton play centers around the relationship of two decadent members of 18th-century French nobility. The two, Close and Malkovich, spend their time testing and manipulating the loves of others. They find love often has a will of its own. Possibly the best of the several versions available. Interesting to comparison-view with director Milos Forman's version of this story, 1989's "Valmont." **120m/C**

VHS, Beta, LV, 8mm, Closed Caption. John Malkovich, Glenn Close, Michelle Pfeiffer, Uma Thurman, Keanu Reeves, Swoosie Kurtz, Mildred Natwick, Peter Capaldi; **D:** Stephen Frears; **W:** Christopher Hampton; **C:** Philippe Rousselot; **M:** George Fenton. Academy Awards '88: Best Adapted Screenplay, Best Art Direction/Set Decoration, Best Costume Design; British Academy Awards '89: Best Adapted Screenplay, Best Supporting Actress (Pfeiffer); Cesar Awards '90: Best Foreign Film; Writers Guild of America '88: Best Adapted Screenplay; Nominations: Academy Awards '88: Best Actress (Close), Best Picture, Best Supporting Actress (Pfeiffer), Best Original Score.*WAR, FCT*

Dangerous Life 🎬🎬 **1989** Explosive drama brings to the screen the story of the Philippine uprising. It shows the horrible events that lead to the fall of Marcos and permitted the rise of Corazon Aquino. **163m/C VHS, Beta, LV.** Gary Busey; **W:** David Williamson. *NO*

Dangerous Love woof! **1987** Advice to the lovelorn: Avoid this one. Female members of a video dating service are being filmed in a death scene—their own. **87m/C VHS, Beta.** Lawrence Monoson, Brenda Bakke, Peter Marc, Elliott Gould, Anthony Geary; **D:** Marty Ollstein. *MED*

A Dangerous Man: Lawrence after Arabia 🎬🎬🎬 **1991** At the 1919 Paris Peace Conference, T.E. Lawrence serves as the liaison to the Hashemite delegation in an effort to have the Allies agree to Arab independence. He finds the diplomatic fields more treacherous than anything he encountered during WWI. Fiennes does well in the difficult role of the reluctant, ambivalent hero. Made for television. **104m/C VHS, Closed Caption.** *GB* Ralph Fiennes, Denis Quilley, Alexander Siddig, Nicholas Jones, Roger Hammond, Peter Copley, Paul Freeman, Polly Walker; **D:** Christopher Menaul; **W:** Tim Rose Price. *PBS*

Dangerous Minds 🎬🎬½ *My Posse Don't Do Homework* **1995 (R)** Based on the autobiography of LouAnne Johnson (Pfeiffer), a 10-year Marine turned inspirational inner-city high school English teacher. Naturally, Johnson has to take on the establishment educational system to fight for her kids. If you can buy Pfeiffer as an ex-jarhead, a tough teacher should be no problem. A subplot romance involving Pfeiffer and Andy Garcia was cut from the film to focus on the teacher/student byplay (which seems a real shame); Elaine May did a uncredited script rewrite. Kinda squishy and surprisingly successful.**CW:** Language. **99m/C VHS, LV, Closed Caption.** Michelle Pfeiffer, George Dzundza, Courtney B. Vance, Robin Bartlett, Renoly Santiago, Lorraine Toussaint; *Cameos:* John Neville; **D:** John N. Smith; **W:** Ronald Bass; **C:** Pierre Letarte. Blockbuster Entertainment Awards '96: Drama Actress, Theatrical (Pfeiffer); Nominations: MTV Movie Awards '96: Best Film, Best Female Performance (Pfeiffer), Most Desirable Female (Pfeiffer), Best Song ("Gangsta's Paradise"). *TOU*

Dangerous Mission 🎬½ **1954** A young woman witnesses a mob murder in New York and flees to the Midwest, pursued by killers and the police. Good cast couldn't do much with this one. **75m/B VHS, Beta.** Victor Mature, Piper Laurie, Vincent Price, William Bendix; **D:** Louis King; **W:** W.R. Burnett, Charles Bennett. *MED*

Dangerous Moonlight 🎬🎬🎬 *Suicide Squadron* **1941** Polish concert pianist becomes a bomber pilot for the British in WWII, though his wife wants him to stay at the piano. Great battle and music sequences; the piece "Warsaw Concerto" became a soundtrack hit. **97m/B VHS, Beta.** *GB* Anton Walbrook, Sally Gray, Derrick DeMarney, Cecil Parker, Percy Parsons, Keneth Kent, Guy Middleton, John Laurie, Frederick Valk; **D:** Brian Desmond Hurst. *TTC*

Dangerous Moves 🎬🎬🎬 *La Diagonale du Fou* **1984 (PG)** A drama built around the World Chess championship competition between a renowned Russian master and a young, rebellious dissident. The chess game serves as both metaphor and background for the social and political tensions it produces. With English subtitles. **96m/C VHS, Beta, LV.** *SI* Liv Ullmann, Michel Piccoli, Leslie Caron, Alexandre Arbatt; **D:** Richard Dembo; **W:** Richard Dembo;

C: Raoul Coutard. Academy Awards '84: Best Foreign Language Film. *ORI, IME*

Dangerous Obsession 🎭 *Divine Obsession; Mortal Sins* 1988 (R) A woman kidnaps the doctor she blames for her boyfriend's death and instead of exacting revenge, she makes him her personal sex slave. In the case of this flick, it's really a fate worse than death.*CW:* Language and strong sexuality. 81m/C VHS. *IT* Corinne Clery, Brett Halsey; *D:* Lucio Fulci; *M:* Simon Boswell. *AIP*

Dangerous Orphans 🎭½ 1986 (R) Not completely awful tale of three brothers, orphaned as boys when their father is murdered before their very eyes, and the vendetta they have against the killer. 90m/C VHS, Beta. *NZ* Peter Stevens, Peter Bland, Ian Mune, Ross Girven, Jennifer Ward-Lealand; *D:* John Laing. *ACA*

Dangerous Passage 🎭🎭 1944 A ne'er-do-well inherits 200 grand but gets in trouble before he can collect it. He ends up falling in with assorted misfits aboard a tramp steamer. 60m/B VHS, Beta, 8mm. Robert Lowery, Phyllis Brooks, Jack La-Rue, Victor Kilian; *D:* William (Lester Williams) Berke. *VYY*

Dangerous Passion 🎭 1995 Underworld figure gets a promotion from his lethal boss and finds himself in the unenviable position of becoming involved with the ruthless guy's beautiful wife. 94m/C VHS. Billy Dee Williams, Carl Weathers, Lonette McKee; *D:* Michael Miller. *LIV*

A Dangerous Place 🎭🎭½ 1994 (R) Teenaged Ethan (Roberts) joins a karate team to prove his older brother's death was not a suicide. But the Scorpion's leader (Feldman) has a definite mean streak.*CW:* Violence. 97m/C VHS, LV, Closed Caption. Ted Jan Roberts, Corey Feldman, Mako, Erin Gray, Dick Van Patten; *D:* Jerry P. Jacobs. *PMH*

Dangerous Prey 🎭½ 1995 (R) Young woman, looking for adventure while vacationing in Europe, gets more than she bargained for when she gets mixed up with a high-tech training school for female mercenaries.*CW:* Nudity, sexual situations, violence, language. 93m/C VHS. Shannon Whirry, Ciara Hunter; *D:* Lloyd A. Simanol. *MNC*

Dangerous Pursuit 🎭🎭 1989 A woman discovers that a man she slept with years ago is an assassin. Knowing too much, she finds herself next on his hit list. Decent psycho-thriller that was never released theatrically. 95m/C VHS, Beta, LV, Closed Caption. Gregory Harrison, Alexandra Powers, Scott Valentine, Brian Wimmer, Elena Stiteler; *D:* Sandor Stern. *PAR*

Dangerous Relations 🎭🎭½ *Father & Son: Dangerous Relations* 1993 (PG-13) Made for TV drama with Gossett as a tough convict at the end of 15-year prison sentence whose authority is challenged by young punk prisoner Underwood. Imagine his surprise when the old con realizes the punk is the son he hasn't seen since he started his time behind bars. Things don't improve (well, not at first) when they are paroled into each other's custody.*CW:* Language, urban violence, and scene of sensuality. 93m/C VHS. Louis Gossett Jr., Blair Underwood, Rae Dawn Chong, Clarence Williams III. *ACA*

Dangerous Summer 🎭🎭 *The Burning Man* 1982 In Australia, an American businessman building a resort is the victim of elaborate arson/murder insurance schemes. 100m/C VHS, Beta. *AU* Tom Skerritt, James Mason, Ian Gilmour, Wendy Hughes; *D:* Quentin Masters; *W:* David Ambrose. *NO*

Dangerous Touch 🎭½ 1994 (R) A very charming sociopath seduces a radio host/therapist into a willing, if kinky, sexual relationship. But everything she values is put at risk when he threatens to show an incriminating video tape if she doesn't continue to do as he demands. An unrated version is also available. 101m/C VHS, LV, Closed Caption. Lou Diamond Phillips, Kate Vernon; *D:* Lou Diamond Phillips. *THV*

Dangerous When Wet 🎭🎭 1953 A typical Williams water-musical. A farm girl dreams of fame by swimming the English Channel. One famous number pairs Williams with cartoon characters Tom & Jerry in an underwater frolic. 🎵 I Got Out of Bed on the Right Side; Ain't Nature Grand; I Like Men; Fifi; In My Wildest Dreams. 96m/C VHS, Beta, LV. Esther Williams, Fernando Lamas, Charlotte Greenwood, William Demarest, Jack Carson; *D:* Charles Walters; *M:* Arthur Schwartz, Johnny Mercer. *MGM*

A Dangerous Woman 🎭🎭 1993 (R) No, this isn't the femme fatale romance the word "dangerous" suggests. Instead, the eponymous character is a mildly retarded woman, Martha (Winger), whose simplistic view on life places her in ethically compromising positions. When a hunky Irish handyman (Byrne) comes on the scene and seduces both her and the aunt with whom she lives (Hershey), Martha awakens to feelings she has never experienced. Winger's performance is both sensitive and provocative, but is wasted in a film filled with two-dimensional characters, and really, not too much of a point. Adapted from a novel by Mary McGarry Morris. Screenplay by Foner, wife of director Gyllenhaal.*CW:* Sexuality. 101m/C VHS, LV, Closed Caption. Debra Winger, Barbara Hershey, Gabriel Byrne, David Strathairn, Chloe Webb, John Terry, Jan Hooks, Paul Dooley, Viveka Davis, Richard Riehle, Laurie Metcalf; *D:* Stephen Gyllenhaal; *W:* Naomi Foner; *C:* Robert Elswit; *M:* Carter Burwell. Golden Globe Awards '94: Best Actress—Drama (Winger). *USH*

Dangerous Youth 🎭 *These Dangerous Years* 1958 Would-be Liverpool rocker Vaughan is drafted into the army where he becomes a man. He gets into trouble, goes AWOL, but manages to set things right. The Brit version of the troubled-teen exploitation flick. 97m/B VHS. *GB* Frankie Vaughan, George Baker, Carole Lesley, Jackie Lane, Eddie Byrne, Thora Hird; *D:* Herbert Wilcox; *W:* Jack Trevor Story. *SNC*

Dangerously Close 🎭½ 1986 (R) A group of anti-crime high school students organize a hall monitoring gang that becomes a group of neo-fascist disciplinarian elite. 96m/C VHS, Beta, Closed Caption. John Stockwell, Carey Lowell, J. Eddie Peck; *D:* Albert Pyun; *C:* Walt Lloyd. *MED*

Daniel 🎭🎭½ 1983 (R) The children of a couple who were executed for espionage (patterned after the Rosenbergs) struggle with their past in the dissident 1960s. So-so adaptation of E.L. Doctorow's "The Book of Daniel." 130m/C VHS, Beta. Timothy Hutton, Amanda Plummer, Mandy Patinkin, Lindsay Crouse, Ed Asner, Ellen Barkin; *D:* Sidney Lumet; *C:* Andrzej Bartkowiak. *PAR*

Daniel and the Towers 199? Daniel and his friends enjoy making fun of Sam, the man who is building glass towers in Watts, California. But when Daniel must pay for the repairs of a shopkeeper's window, he turns to Sam for help. Sam agrees to fix the windows if Daniel helps him collect glass for the towers. In the process, Sam and Daniel become friends and Sam teaches Daniel valuable lessons about beauty and determination. Although this story is fictional, the glass towers, built by Sam Rodia, really stand in Watts. A viewers' guide is included. Part of the "Wonderworks" series. 58m/C VHS. Allan Arbus, Michael McKean, Carmen Zapata, Miguel Alamo; *D:* Paul Schneider. *PME, BTV*

Daniel Boone 🎭🎭½ 1934 Daniel Boone guides a party of settlers from North Carolina to the fertile valleys of Kentucky, facing Indians, food shortages and bad weather along the way. O'Brien turns in a fine performance as the early American frontier hero. 75m/B VHS, Beta. George O'Brien, Heather Angel, John Carradine; *D:* David Howard. *NOS, MRV, VCN*

Daniel Boone: Trail Blazer 🎭🎭½ 1956 Low-budget, though surprisingly well-acted rendition of the frontiersman's heroics, filmed in Mexico. 75m/B VHS. Bruce (Herman Brix) Bennett, Lon Chaney Jr., Faron Young, Damian O'Flynn, Fred Kohler Jr.,

Claudio Brook, Kem Dibbs; *D:* Ismael Rodriguez, Albert C. Gannaway; *W:* John Patrick, Tom Hubbard. *NOS, MRV, REP*

Danielle Steel's Changes 🎭🎭½ *Changes* 1991 Ladd is a successful, divorced New York television anchorwoman who turns her life upside-down when she marries an equally successful, widowed Los Angeles surgeon (Nouri). Can they overcome their bicoastal careers to make things work? What do you think. Made for television. 96m/C VHS, Closed Caption. Cheryl Ladd, Michael Nouri, Christopher Gartin, Randee Heller, Charles Frank, James Sloyan, Cynthia Bain; *D:* Charles Jarrott. *CMB, WOV*

Danielle Steel's "Daddy" 🎭🎭½ *Daddy* 1991 Ad exec Oliver Watson (Duffy) is happily married to Sarah (Mulgrew) and living the good life with their three kids—or so he thinks. Then Sarah announces she's leaving and Oliver's left to cope with family crisis as a single parent. A move to a new job in LA finds Oliver falling for an actress (Carter) and wondering if his family can ever be put back together again. Made for television. 95m/C VHS, Closed Caption. Patrick Duffy, Lynda Carter, Kate Mulgrew; *D:* Michael Miller. *CMB, WOV*

Danielle Steel's Heartbeat 🎭🎭½ *Heartbeat* 1993 Shameless soap opera with Draper as Adrian Townsend, an L.A. TV-news producer with a self-involved ad-exec hubby (Kilner) who never wants children because of his own lousy childhood. When Adrian gets preggers the louse dumps her and she's left to weep prettily. That is until lovable divorced dad Bill Grant (Ritter) comes along to dry her eyes. Predictable and glossy adaptation of the Steel best-seller. Made for television. 95m/C VHS. Polly Draper, John Ritter, Kevin Kilner, Michael Lembeck, Nancy Morgan, Victor Dimattia, Christian Cousins; *D:* Michael Miller; *W:* Jan Worthington. *CMB*

Danielle Steel's Kaleidoscope 🎭🎭½ *Kaleidoscope* 1990 Three sisters are separated in childhood, after the mysterious deaths of their parents. Then a detective is hired to reunite the adult siblings. But Hilary, the eldest, has secrets she doesn't want her sisters to share. Made for television. 96m/C VHS, Closed Caption. Jaclyn Smith, Perry King, Colleen Dewhurst, Donald Moffat; *D:* Jud Taylor. *CMB, WOV*

Danielle Steel's Palomino 🎭🎭½ *Palomino* 1991 Bittersweet romance with Frost as an ambitious photojournalist who gets involved with a headstrong cowboy (Horsley). Their differences drive them apart and tragedy strikes when Frost becomes a paraplegic after a horse-riding accident. This leads her to new goals and the eventual return of her old flame. Between the palomino's blond mane and the equally impressive blond locks of Frost, there's a lot of streaming in the wind hair shots. Horsley's merely tall, dark, and handsome. Made for television. 90m/C VHS. Lindsay Frost, Lee Horsley, Eva Marie Saint, Rod Taylor, Michelle Greene, Beau Gravitte. *CMB*

Danielle Steel's Star 🎭½ *Star* 1993 Garth is the country girl with big dreams of a singing career but an unhappy love life. She falls for an idealist lawyer (Bierko) but their romance is put on hold by career ambitions. She goes to Hollywood and gets discovered, becoming a singing/acting sensation who's under the thumb of her increasingly obsessed manager, Wass. Meanwhile, Bierko's trapped in a miserable marriage to the wealthy, influential Farrell. Do the true lovers get together? (Take a guess). Although the story spans 15 years and lots of tribulations the young Garth never ages a day. Made for television. 90m/C VHS. Jennie Garth, Craig Bierko, Ted Wass, Terry Farrell, Penny Fuller, Mitchell Ryan, Jim Haynie; *D:* Michael Miller; *W:* Claire Labine. *CMB*

Danny 🎭🎭½ 1979 (G) Charming story of a lonely young girl who receives an injured horse that was no longer fit for the spoiled daughter of the rich owners. 90m/C VHS, Beta. Rebecca Page, Janet Zarish, Barbara Jean Earhardt, Gloria Maddox, George Luce; *D:* Gene Feldman. MON, WOM, HHE

Danny Boy *♂½* **1946** Veteran dog, returning from the war, has difficulty adjusting to life back home. Things get worse for him and his young master when Danny Boy is assumed to be shell-shocked and dangerous. One of the few shell-shocked dog stories ever filmed. 67m/B VHS, Beta. VYY

Danny Boy *♂♂♂* **1984 (R)** Takes place in Ireland where a young saxaphonist witnesses a murder and, in an effort to understand it, sets out to find the killer. Thought-provoking film is meant to highlight the continuing struggles in Ireland. 92m/C VHS, Beta. *IR* Stephen Rea, Veronica Quilligan, Honor Heffernan, Marie Kean, Donal McCann, Ray McAnally; *D:* Neil Jordan; *W:* Neil Jordan. COL

Dante's Inferno *♂♂♂* **1924** Abandon all hope you who watch this film. A one-time friend sends his ruthless capitalist nemesis a copy of Dante's "Inferno," and the man reads the book and dreams he's gone to hell (would that be the dress circle?) A silent film that was controversial in its day: the body-stockinged actors were believed to be nude (which would have made it the first nudie Comedy). 54m/B VHS. Lawson Butt, Howard Gaye, Ralph Lewis, Pauline Starke, Josef Swickard; *D:* Henry Otto. CNM

Dante's Inferno: Life of Dante Gabriel Rossetti *♂♂* **1969** The flamboyant life of mid-19th century English Pre-Raphaelite artist/poet Dante Gabriel Rossetti is depicted with the usual Russell flair. The drunken, drug-taking, womanizing Rossetti was part of the leading intellectual group of his age, which included Swinburne, Morris, Ruskin, and Rossetti's sister, the poet Christina Rossetti. 90m/B VHS. *GB* Oliver Reed; *D:* Ken Russell. TPV

Dante's Peak *♂♂½* **1997 (PG-13)** Northwest volcano serves up a smorgasbord of molten disaster in the second most desirable town in the U.S.—the titular Dante's Peak. Brosnan is the intuitive scientist who comes to Washington to match wits with the conical adversary and joins forces with the town's tres femme mayor Wando (Hamilton). Ashes fall like snow in January, computer generated lava flows profusely, poisonous gases leak out and water turns to acid, all with desired nail-biting effect. Wando's two kids, dog and grandma lend folksy charm and the requisite loved-ones-in-grave-danger, but this heated disaster flick is not exactly for the whole family. Cliched and predictable, flick runs the Disaster Movie Playbook page by page as plot takes a backseat to nonstop action. *CW:* Disaster related peril and gore. 112m/C VHS, LV, Closed Caption. Pierce Brosnan, Linda Hamilton, Charles Hallahan, Grant Heslov, Elizabeth Hoffman, Jaime Renee Smith, Arabella Field, Tzi Ma, Jeremy Foley, Brian Reddy, Kirk Trutner; *D:* Roger Donaldson; *W:* Leslie Bohem; *C:* Andrzej Bartkowiak; *M:* John Frizzell. USH

Danton *♂♂♂♂* **1982 (PG)** A sweeping account of the reign of terror following the French Revolution. Focuses on the title character (wonderfully portrayed by Depardieu) and is directed with searching parallels to modern-day Poland by that country's premier filmmaker, Andrzej Wajda. Well-done period sets round out a memorable film. In French with English subtitles. 136m/C VHS, Beta, LV. *PL FR* Gerard Depardieu, Wojciech Pszoniak, Patrice Chereau, Angela Winkler, Boguslaw Linda; *D:* Andrzej Wajda; *W:* Jean-Claude Carriere, Agnieszka Holland, Boleslaw Michalek, Jacek Gasiorowski, Andrzej Wajda. British Academy Awards '83: Best Foreign Film; Cesar Awards '83: Best Director (Wajda); Montreal World Film Festival '83: Best Actor (Depardieu). COL

Danzon *♂♂♂½* **1991 (PG)** Julia (Rojo), a single, working-class mom escapes the drudgery of her simple existence by going to a Mexico City dance hall every Wednesday. There she loses herself to the movement of the danzon, a dance with Haitian roots, popular in Mexico for over 100

years. When her partner of six years, Carmelo (Rergis), doesn't show up one night, her life is turned upside down. So begins a search for Carmelo—and herself. Quiet and restrained, like the ballroom-style danzon at the center of the plot. Applauded at Cannes. In Spanish with English subtitles. 103m/C VHS. *SP* Maria Rojo, Carmen Salinas, Blanca Guerra, Tito Vasconcelos, Victor Carpinteiro, Victor Vasconcelos; *D:* Maria Novaro; *W:* Maria Novaro, Beatriz Novaro. COL, FCT

Darby O'Gill & the Little People *♂♂♂½* **1959 (G)** Set in Ireland, a roguish old story teller tumbles into a well and visits the land of leprechauns who give him three wishes in order to rearrange his life. When he tries to tell his friends what happened, they think that it is only another one of his stories. A wonderful Disney production (despite its disappointing box-office performance) with wit, charm and an ounce or two of terror. 93m/C VHS, Beta, LV. Albert Sharpe, Janet Munro, Sean Connery, Estelle Winwood; *D:* Robert Stevenson; *C:* Winton C. Hoch. DIS

Darby's Rangers *♂♂½* *Young Invaders* **1958** WWII pot-boiler with Garner as the leader of a commando team put together for covert operations in North Africa and Italy. Successful battle sequences combine with slow-paced romantic scenes as the soldiers chase women when not chasing the enemy. 122m/B VHS. James Garner, Jack Warden, Edd Byrnes, Peter Brown, Stuart Whitman, David Janssen, Etchika Choureau, Venetia Stevenson, Torin Thatcher, Joan Elan, Corey Allen, Murray Hamilton; *D:* William A. Wellman; *W:* Guy Trosper; *C:* William Clothier; *M:* Max Steiner. WAR

Daredevils of the Red Circle **1938** Three young men set out to free a man held prisoner by an escaped convict. A serial in twelve chapters. 195m/B VHS. Charles Quigley, Bruce (Herman Brix) Bennett, Carole Landis; *D:* John English, William Witney. REP, VCN, MLB

Daring Danger *♂½* **1932** McCoy is nearly killed in a fight with the villainous Alexander. When he recovers he finds Alexander has joined forces with a rustler (Ellis), so McCoy battles both of them—while his horse goes for help. 58m/B VHS. Tim McCoy, Richard Alexander, Robert Ellis, Alberta Vaughn, Wallace MacDonald, Murdock McQuarrie, Max Davidson; *D:* David Ross Lederman. GPV

Daring Dobermans *♂♂* **1973 (PG)** In this sequel to "The Doberman Gang," the barking bank-robbers have a new set of crime-planning masters. A young Indian boy who loves the dogs enters the picture and may thwart their perfect crime. 88m/C VHS, Beta, Closed Caption. Charles Robinson, Tim Considine, David Moses, Claudio Martinez, Joan Caulfield; *D:* Byron Ross Chudnow. FOX

Daring Game *♂♂* **1968** A group of scuba divers nicknamed the Flying Fish attempt to rescue a woman's husband and daughter from an island dictatorship. Failed series pilot by producer Ivan Tors, better known for "Sea Hunt" and "Flipper." 100m/C VHS, Beta. Lloyd Bridges, Brock Peters, Michael Ansara, Joan Blackman; *D:* Laslo Benedek; *M:* George Bruns. NO

Dario Argento's Trauma *♂♂* *Trauma* **1993 (R)** When a teenage girl's parents are decapitated, she and an artist friend start following the clues to a psychotic killer known as "The Headhunter." Trademark horror work for Italian cult director Argento with high suspense quotient and equally high gore. An unrated version is also available. *CW:* Nudity, extreme violence, and sexual situations. 106m/C VHS, Closed Caption. Christopher Rydell, Asia Argento, Laura Johnson, James Russo, Brad Dourif, Frederic Forrest, Piper Laurie; *D:* Dario Argento; *W:* Ted Klein, Dario Argento. REP, WOV

The Dark *♂½* *The Mutilator* **1979 (R)** A supernatural beast commits a string of gruesome murders. 92m/C VHS, Beta. William Devane, Cathy Lee Crosby, Richard Jaeckel, Keenan Wynn, Vivian Blaine; *D:* John Cardos. MED

The Dark *♂½* **1994 (R)** Cop and scientist seek a mysterious graveyard creature who holds both the power to heal and destroy. One man wants to kill it, one man wants to save it, and they race to be the first to find either. *CW:* Horror violence. 90m/C VHS, LV, Closed Caption. Brion James, Jaimz Woolvett, Cynthia Belliveau, Stephen McHattie; *D:* Craig Pryce; *W:* Robert Cooper. IMP

A Dark Adapted Eye *♂♂♂* **1993** Sinister TV mystery adapted from the psychological thriller by Ruth Rendell (writing as Barbara Vine). In 1951 Vera Hillyard (Imrie) is hung for murdering her younger sister Eden (Ward)—an act that has profound effects on the family, including young niece Faith (Bonham Carter). Long haunted by the "why" of the crime, Faith later begins an investigation into her family's past—and discovers very dark and disturbing secrets dating back to WWII. Title refers to a vision problem caused by remaining in darkness too long. 150m/C VHS. *GB* Helena Bonham Carter, Celia Imrie, Sophie Ward, Robin Ellis, Ciaran Hinds, Pip Torrens, William Gaminara, Polly Adams, Bernice Stegers, Steven Mackintosh, Jason Durr; *D:* Tim Fywell; *W:* Sandy Welch; *M:* David Ferguson. FOX

Dark Age *♂♂½* **1988 (R)** An Australian conservationist must track down a rampaging, giant, semi-mythical alligator before it is killed by bounty hunters. Based on the novel (and Aboriginal legend) "Numunwari." 90m/C VHS, Beta, LV. *AU* John Jarratt, David Gulpilil, Max Phipps, Ray Meagher, Nikki Coghill, Burnam Burnam; *D:* Arch Nicholson. NLC

The Dark Angel *♂♂♂* **1991** Maud is the young and innocent heiress to a fortune in this gothic mystery of creeping unease. She is intrigued by the romantic portrait of her youthful and unknown Uncle Silas. But her mysterious uncle is no longer the Byronic hero. What secret wickedness does his ravaged face hide? And what about Maud's drug-addicted governess and the brutish young man in the cemetary? Does Uncle Silas just want Maud's fortune or Maud herself? Excellent performances by O'Toole as the decadent uncle and Edney as the innocent-but-not-stupid Maud. Based on the novel "Uncle Silas" by J.S. Le Fanu. Made for British TV. 150m/C VHS. *GB* Peter O'Toole, Beatie Edney, Jane Lapotaire, Tim Woodward, Alan MacNaughton, Barbara Shelley, Guy Rolfe; *D:* Peter Hammond. FOX, VCO

Dark Angel: The Ascent *♂♂* **1994 (R)** She-devil gets tired of hell and decides to get a look at the world upstairs. She also decides to turn vigilante and dispatch some bad guy souls to her former home. *CW:* Language, horror violence, and sexuality. 80m/C VHS, Beta, Closed Caption. Charlotte Stewart, Daniel Markel, Michael C. Mahon, Nicholas Worth, Milton James; *D:* Linda Hassani; *W:* Matthew Bright; *M:* Fuzzbee Morse. PAR

Dark August *♂♂* **1976 (PG)** A New Yorker drops out and transplants to rural Vermont, where he accidentally kills a young girl and then suffers numerous horrors as a result of a curse put on him by the girl's grandfather. 87m/C VHS, Beta. J.J. Barry, Carole Shelyne, Kim Hunter, William Robertson; *D:* Martin Goldman. VES, LIV

The Dark Backward *♂♂½* **1991 (R)** A dark, subversive comedy about a garbage man who dreams of making it big in show biz as a stand-up comedian. He's terrible until a third arm starts growing out of his back and the sheer grotesqueness of his situation makes him a temporary star. Caan and Newton are interestingly cast, but young, first-time director Rifkin's foray into David Lynch territory was not well received by critics. *CW:* Bizarre comic sensuality. 97m/C VHS, LV. Judd Nelson, Bill Paxton, Wayne Newton, Lara Flynn Boyle, James Caan, Rob Lowe, Claudia Christian; *D:* Adam Rifkin; *W:* Adam Rifkin. COL

Dark Before Dawn *♂♂½* **1989 (R)** American farmers and Vietnam veterans team up against corrupt government officials and ruthless businessmen in this violent film about the plight of the underdog. 95m/C VHS, Beta, LV. Doug McClure,

Sonny Gibson, Ben Johnson, Billy Drago, Rance Howard, Morgan Woodward, Buck Henry, Jeffery Osterhage, Red Steagall, John Martin, Gary Cooper; **D:** Robert Totten. VES, LIV

Dark Breed ✍✍ 1996 (R) Ewww, yuck, it's sci-fi infestation time once again as Nick Saxon (Scalia) is assigned to find the bodies of six astronauts whose top secret space craft has mysteriously crashed. He discovers that the bodies are playing host to reptilian parasites with designs on world domination. 104m/C VHS. Jack Scalia, Jonathan Banks, Robin Curtis, Donna W. Scott; **D:** Richard Pepin. PMH

Dark Command ✍✍✍ 1940 The story of Quantrell's Raiders who terrorized the Kansas territory during the Civil War until one man came along to put a stop to it. Colorful and talented cast add depth to the script. Also available colorized. 95m/B VHS, Beta. John Wayne, Walter Pidgeon, Claire Trevor, Roy Rogers, Marjorie Main, George "Gabby" Hayes; **D:** Raoul Walsh. Nominations: Academy Awards '40: Best Interior Decoration, Best Original Score. REP, FCT

Dark Corner ✍✍✍ 1946 Gripping, intricate film noir about a detective, already framed once, who may go up the river yet again—this time for the murder of his ex-partner, the guy who framed him the first time. Loyal secretary Ball helps to extricate him from this tangled web. 99m/B VHS, Beta, Closed Caption. Lucille Ball, Mark Stevens, Clifton Webb, William Bendix, Cathy Downs, Reed Hadley, Constance Collier, Kurt Kreuger; **D:** Henry Hathaway. FOX

The Dark Crystal ✍✍✍ 1982 (PG) Jen and Kira, two of the last surviving Gelflings, attempt to return a crystal shard (discovered with the help of a sorceress) to the castle where the Dark Crystal lies, guarded by the cruel and evil Skeksis. Designed by Brian Froud. From the creators of the Muppets. 93m/C VHS, Beta, LV. **D:** Jim Henson, Frank Oz; **W:** David Odell; **C:** Oswald Morris; **M:** Trevor Jones; **V:** Jim Henson, Frank Oz, Kathryn Mullen, Dave Goelz. TOU

The Dark Dancer ✍½ 1995 (R) Psychology prof Maggie (Tweed), who authors books on feminine sexual behavior, gets her experience first-hand by working in a strip club. Now, she's also the target of a police investigation. Also available unrated.**CW:** Numerous strong sex scenes, language and brutal violence. ?m/C VHS. Shannon Tweed. TCE

The Dark Dealer ✍✍ 1995 Three terror tales find the Devil's assistant dealing a deadly game of blackjack to a trio in limbo, with the cards propelling each man into a horrific adventure. Provides some real scares along with effective (if low-budget) special effects. 85m/C VHS. Mark Fickert, Richard Hull, Vincent Gaskins, Rocky Patterson, Gordon Fox; **D:** Tom Alexander. SDE

Dark Eyes ✍✍✍½ Les Yeux Noirs; Oci Ciornie 1987 An acclaimed Italian film based on a several short stories by Anton Chekov. Mastroianni is a weak-willed Italian, trapped in a marriage of convenience, who falls in love with a mysterious, also married, Russian beauty he meets in a health spa. He embarks on a journey to find her and, perhaps, his lost ideals. Hailed as Mastroianni's consummate performance. In Italian with English subtitles. 118m/C VHS, Beta. IT Marcello Mastroianni, Silvana Mangano, Elena Sofonova, Marthe Keller; **D:** Nikita Mikhalkov; **C:** Franco Di Giacomo. Cannes Film Festival '87: Best Actor (Mastroianni); Nominations: Academy Awards '87: Best Actor (Mastroianni). GHV, FOX

Dark Forces ✍✍ Harlequin 1983 (PG) A faithhealer promises to help a senator's dying son and finds the politician's wife also desires his assistance. This Australian film is uneven and predictable. Though rated "PG," beware of two rather brief, but explicit, nudity scenes. 96m/C VHS, Beta. AU Robert Powell, David Hemmings, Broderick Crawford, Carmen Duncan; **D:** Simon Wincer. MED

Dark Habits ✍✍½ Entre Tinieblas 1984 An early Almodovar farce about already-demented nuns in a failing convent trying to raise funds with the help of a nightclub singer who is on the run. Although certainly irreverant, it doesn't quite have the zing of his later work. In Spanish with subtitles. 116m/C VHS, Beta, LV. SP Carmen Maura, Christina Pascual, Julieta Serrano, Marisa Paredes; **D:** Pedro Almodovar; **W:** Pedro Almodovar. CCN, TPV

The Dark Half ✍✍ 1991 (R) Flawed chiller based on a Stephen King novel. Thad Beaumont's serious novels have been failures, but writing as George Stark, he's had phenomenal success with grisly horror stories. In a publicity stunt Thad kills off and publicly buries George (who doesn't want to stay dead). Soon everyone who's crossed Thad is brutally murdered. Hutton acquits himself well in a change of pace dual role. Otherwise, the psychological thrills are few and the gore is plentiful. Pittsburgh serves as location double for King's usual New England territory. Film's release was delayed due to Orion's bankruptcy problems.**CW:** Language and violence. 122m/C VHS, Closed Caption. Timothy Hutton, Amy Madigan, Michael Rooker, Julie Harris, Robert Joy, Kent Broadhurst, Beth Grant, Rutanya Alda, Tom Mardirosian, Chelsea Field, Royal Dano; **D:** George A. Romero; **W:** George A. Romero; **M:** Christopher Young. ORI

Dark Horse ✍✍½ 1992 (PG) Meyers is a young woman distraught over the death of her mother. She gets into trouble and is assigned to do community service work at a horse farm where she finds herself caring for a prize-winning horse. 98m/C VHS. Ari Meyers, Mimi Rogers, Ed Begley Jr., Donovan Leitch, Samantha Eggar; **D:** David Hemmings. LIV, MOV, FCT

The Dark Hour ✍½ 1936 Two detectives team up to solve a murder in which multiple suspects are involved. Based on Sinclair Gluck's "The Last Trap." 72m/B VHS, Beta. Ray Walker, Irene Ware, Berton Churchill, Hedda Hopper, Hobart Bosworth, E.E. Clive; **D:** Charles Lamont. NOS, LOO, SNC

Dark Journey ✍✍✍ The Anxious Years 1937 WWI Stockholm is the setting for a love story between a double agent and the head of German Intelligence. Clever, sophisticated production; Leigh is stunning. 82m/B VHS, Beta. GB Vivien Leigh, Conrad Veidt, Joan Gardner, Anthony Bushell, Ursula Jeans; **D:** Victor Saville. NOS, MRV, CAB

Dark Justice ✍✍½ 1991 Judge by day, avenger by night in this actioner created from three episodes of the late-night television series. Judge Nicholas Marshall is disgusted by the criminals sprung on legal loopholes and backroom deals. So he decides to take justice into his own hands. 99m/C VHS. Ramy Zada, Dick O'Neill, Clayton Prince, Begona Plaza. WAR

Dark Mirror ✍✍✍ 1946 A psychologist and a detective struggle to determine which twin sister murdered a prominent physician. Good and evil siblings finely-acted by de Havilland. 85m/B VHS. Olivia de Havilland, Lew Ayres, Thomas Mitchell, Garry Owen; **D:** Robert Siodmak; **C:** Milton Krasner. Nominations: Academy Awards '46: Best Story. REP

Dark Mountain ✍½ 1944 A forest ranger rescues his gal from the clutches of a hardened criminal. 56m/B VHS. Robert Lowery, Ellen Drew, Regis Toomey, Eddie Quillan, Elisha Cook Jr.; **D:** William (Lester Williams) Berke, William C. Thomas. NOS, DVT

Dark Night of the Scarecrow ✍✍½ 1981 Thriller with a moral. Prejudiced townspeople execute a retarded man who was innocently befriended by a young girl. After his death unusual things begin to happen. Slow to start but effective. Made for television. 100m/C VHS, Beta, Closed Caption. Charles Durning, Tanya Crowe, Larry Drake; **D:** Frank de Felitta. FOX, HHE

Dark Obsession ✍✍ Diamond Skulls 1990 (R) Byrne portrays a husband who lives out his dark erotic fantasies with his wife (Donohoe), and is involved in a hit-and-run accident. Driven by guilt, madness slowly begins to take him. Ugly

and depressing. Based on a true scandal. Available in an "NC-17" rated version.**CW:** Language and strong sensuality. 97m/C VHS, Beta. Gabriel Byrne, Amanda Donohoe, Michael Hordern, Judy Parfitt, Douglas Hodge, Sadie Frost, Ian Carmichael; **D:** Nick Broomfield; **W:** Tim Rose Price; **C:** Michael Coulter; **M:** Hans Zimmer. PSM

Dark of the Night ✍✍½ Mr. Wrong 1985 A young woman, new to the city, purchases a used Jaguar and finds she must share it with the car's former owner—a woman murdered inside the Jag. Decent psycho-thriller with some suspenseful and amusing moments. 88m/C VHS, Beta. NZ Heather Bolton, David Letch, Gary Stalker, Michael Haigh, Danny Mulheron, Kate Harcourt; **D:** Gaylene Preston; **W:** Gaylene Preston, Geoff Murphy, Graham Tetley; **C:** Thomas Burstyn; **M:** Jonathan Crayford. LIV

Dark of the Sun ✍✍½ The Mercenaries 1968 (PG) Lots of action; routine plot. Taylor is a tough mercenary hired to retrieve a supply of uncut diamonds from a beseiged town in the Congo during the 1950's rebellion. Oh, and if he can help out the town's inhabitants that's okay too. Based on the novel by Wilbur A. Smith. 101m/C VHS. GB Rod Taylor, Jim Brown, Yvette Mimieux, Kenneth More, Peter Carsten, Calvin Lockhart, Andre Morell; **D:** Jack Cardiff; **W:** Quentin Werty, Adrian Spies; **M:** Jacques Loussier. MGM

Dark Passage ✍✍½ 1947 Bogart plays a convict who escapes from San Quentin to prove he was framed for the murder of his wife. He undergoes plastic surgery and is hidden and aided by Bacall as he tries to find the real killer. Stars can't quite compensate for a far-fetched script and so-so direction. 107m/B VHS, Beta, LV. Humphrey Bogart, Lauren Bacall, Agnes Moorehead, Bruce (Herman Brix) Bennett, Tom D'Andrea; **D:** Delmer Daves. MGM

The Dark Past ✍✍✍ 1949 A crazy, escaped convict holds a psychologist and his family hostage, and the two men engage in psychological cat-and-mouse combat. An underrated thriller with off-beat casting. 75m/B VHS, Beta. William Holden, Lee J. Cobb, Nina Foch, Adele Jergens; **D:** Rudolph Mate; **M:** George Duning. COL

Dark Places ✍✍ 1973 (PG) Masquerading as a hospital administrator, a former mental patient inherits the ruined mansion of a man who had killed his wife and children and died insane. As he lives in the house, the spirit of its former owner seems to overcome him with a need to repeat the crime. Meanwhile, Lee, Collins, and Lom think the nut is hiding money they would like to get their collective hands on. Low-budget but fairly effective. 91m/C VHS, Beta. GB Joan Collins, Christopher Lee, Robert Hardy; **D:** Don Sharp.

The Dark Power ✍ 1985 Ex-cowboy LaRue and his trusty whip provide this flick with its only excitement. As sheriff, he must deal with the dead Mexican warriors who rise to wreak havoc when a house is built on their burial ground. 87m/C VHS, Beta. Lash LaRue, Anna Lane Tatum; **D:** Phil Smoot. NO

The Dark Ride ✍½ 1984 Lunatic picks up women with the intention of raping and killing them. Ugly thriller based on the evil deeds of serial murderer Ted Bundy. 83m/C VHS, Beta. James Luisi, Susan Sullivan, Martin Speer; **D:** Jeremy Hoenack. MED

Dark Rider 1991 Dark Rider is a mysterious, motorcycle riding hero who comes to the rescue of a small town. Besieged by a gangster who buys up all their land, the townspeople must abandon their homes and indeed, their very dreams. That is until Dark Rider rolls into town to enact his own unique brand of vengeance. 94m/C VHS. Joe Estevez, Doug Shanklin, Alicia Kowalski, David Shark, Chuck Williams; **W:** Chuck Williams, Bob Ivy. AIP

Dark River: A Father's Revenge ✍ 1990 When his daughter is killed in a toxic waste dump accident, a man begins revenge on the company and its managers. Tense, with important message. 95m/C VHS. Helen Hunt, Mike Farrell, Tess Harper. TTC

Dark Sanity woof! *Straight Jacket 1982* Uninvolving attempt at horror has a recently de-institutionalized woman envisioning death and destruction (something you'll wish the film would do) while everyone else just thinks she's losing her marbles. Problem is we don't really care. 89m/C VHS, Beta. Aldo Ray, Kory Clark, Andy Gwyn, Bobby Holt; **D:** Martin Greene. *PSM*

The Dark Secret of Harvest Home 🐾🐾½ 1978 An urban couple confront a pagan cult in the New England town into which they've moved. Based upon the Thomas Tryon novel. Made for television. 118m/C VHS, Beta. Bette Davis, Rosanna Arquette, David Ackroyd, Rene Auberjonois, Michael O'Keefe; **D:** Leonard Penn. *USH*

Dark Secrets 🐾 1995 (R) Society gal goes slumming at underground club that caters to fulfilling sexual fantasies. The unrated version is 99 minutes. **CW:** Strong sexuality and graphic nudity, and for language. 90m/C VHS, Closed Caption. Monique Parent, Julie Strain, Justine Carroll. *APX*

Dark Shadows 1967 "Dark Shadows" had already been on television for about eight months when the character of Barnabas Collins was introduced. This volume serves to familiarize the viewer with characters and situations that were running on the series at that time. These are the first five episodes that feature Barnabas. Original air dates are April 17 to May 1, 1967. Contains both B&W and color episodes. Additional episodes available. 120m/B VHS. Joan Bennett, Kathryn Leigh Scott, John Karlen, Alexandra Moltke, Jonathan Frid, David Selby, Kate Jackson; **D:** John Sedwick. *MPI, MOV*

Dark Shadows: Episode 1 1991 The short-lived primetime remake of the 1960s camp television classic about eerie Collinwood mansion and the mysterious and tragic Collins family, including cousin Barnabas who happens to be a vampire. The revival featured more explicit sex and violence and a darker tone. In 12 parts. 105m/C VHS. Ben Cross, Jean Simmons, Roy Thinnes, Barbara Steele, Joanna Going, Lysette Anthony, Michael T. Weiss; **D:** Dan Curtis. *MPI, TPV*

Dark Side of Genius 🐾🐾 1994 (R) Jennifer Cole (Hughes), a reporter for an L.A. arts weekly, tries to get the story on artist Julian Jons (Fraser), who's just been paroled after being imprisoned for the murder of his model. Now his lurid new paintings of a sultry nude model hint at some obsessive behavior and Jennifer's reporter instincts may be the death of her. 86m/C VHS, Beta, Closed Caption. Finola Hughes, Brendan Fraser, Glenn Shadix, Moon Zappa, Patrick Richwood, Seymour Cassel; **D:** Phedon Papamichael; **W:** Fred Stroppel; **C:** Phedon Papamichael; **M:** Tom Hiel. *PAR*

The Dark Side of Love 🐾½ 1979 A young girl gets involved with the rougher side of New Orleans society, gets pregnant, and realizes how she's been degraded. 94m/C VHS, Beta. James Stacy, Glynnis O'Connor, Jan Sterling, Mickey Rooney. *GEM*

Dark Side of Midnight 🐾½ *The Creeper* 1986 (R) A super-detective tracks down a psychopathic killer. 108m/C VHS, Beta. James Moore, Wes Olsen, Sandy Schemmel, Dave Bowling. *PSM*

Dark Side of the Moon 🐾🐾 1990 (R) Members of a space ship sent on a routine mission to the far side of the moon, discover an unknown force that feeds on human emotion and consumes the soul. Lukewarm science fiction/horror. 96m/C VHS, LV. William Bledsoe, Alan Blumenfeld, John Diehl, Robert Sampson, Wendy MacDonald, Camilla More, Joe Turkel; **D:** D.J. Webster. *THV*

Dark Star 🐾🐾 1974 (G) John Carpenter's directorial debut is a low-budget, sci-fi satire which focuses on a group of scientists whose mission is to destroy unstable planets. During their journey, they battle their alien mascot (who closely resembles a walking beach ball), as well as a "sensitive" and intelligent bombing device which starts to question the meaning of its existence. Enjoyable early feature from John "Halloween"

Carpenter and Dan "Aliens" O'Bannon. Fun, weird, and unpredictable. 95m/C VHS, Beta, LV. Dan O'Bannon, Brian Narelle; **D:** John Carpenter; **W:** Dan O'Bannon, John Carpenter; **M:** John Carpenter. *HHT, IME, VCI*

Dark Tide 🐾🐾 1993 (R) Erotic action thriller about a pair of deep sea divers whose love life is disturbed when their boat captain becomes sexually fixated on the woman. Also available in an uncut, unrated version. 92m/C VHS, LV. Brigitte Bako, Richard Tyson, Chris Sarandon. *THV*

Dark Tower 🐾 1987 (R) Decent cast is wasted in yet another inept attempt at horror. An architect is dismayed to learn that an evil force is inhabiting her building and it might just be the ghost of her dearly departed husband. 91m/C VHS, Beta, LV. Michael Moriarty, Jenny Agutter, Theodore Bikel, Carol Lynley, Anne Lockhart, Kevin McCarthy; **D:** Ken Barnett; **W:** Robert J. Avrech, Kenneth G. Blackwell. *VTR, IME*

Dark Universe 🐾½ 1993 (R) An alien terror wants to conquer the Earth and make its inhabitants their new food source. 83m/C VHS, Beta. Blake Pickett, Cherie Scott, Bently Tittle, John Maynard, Paul Austin Saunders, Tom Ferguson, Steve Barkett, Joe Estevez, Patrick Moran; **D:** Steve Latshaw; **W:** Patrick Moran. *PSM*

Dark Victory 🐾🐾🐾½ 1939 A spoiled young heiress discovers she is dying from a brain tumor. She attempts to pack a lifetime of parties into a few months, but is rescued by her doctor, with whom she falls in love. Classic final scene with Davis at the top of her form. Bogart plays an Irish stable hand, but not especially well. Also available in a colorized version. 106m/B VHS, Beta, LV, Closed Caption. Bette Davis, George Brent, Geraldine Fitzgerald, Humphrey Bogart, Ronald Reagan, Henry Travers; **D:** Edmund Goulding; **M:** Max Steiner. Nominations: Academy Awards '39: Best Actress (Davis), Best Picture, Best Original Score. *MGM*

Dark Waters 🐾🐾 1944 The drowning death of her parents has left a young woman mentally unstable. She returns to her family home in the backwaters of Louisiana with her peculiar aunt and uncle to serve as guardians. It eventually becomes apparent that someone is trying to drive her insane. This one tends to be rather murky and it's not simply due to the plentiful scenes of misty swampland. 93m/B VHS, Beta, LV. Merle Oberon, Franchot Tone, Thomas Mitchell, Fay Bainter, Elisha Cook Jr., John Qualen, Rex Ingram; **D:** Andre de Toth; **M:** Miklos Rozsa. *VTR*

The Dark Wind 🐾½ 1991 (R) The first of Tony Hillerman's popular Native American mysteries comes to the screen in a lame adaptation. Phillips stars as the Navaho cop investigating a murder on a New Mexico Indian reservation. Since the Navaho believe a "dark wind" enters a man's soul when he does evil, expect some "spirited" goings-on as well. 111m/C VHS, LV, Closed Caption. Lou Diamond Phillips; **D:** Errol Morris; **W:** Eric Bergren. *LIV*

Darker than Amber 🐾🐾 1970 (R) John D. MacDonald's houseboat-dwelling detective Travis McGee (Taylor) rescues a girl (Kendall) he's fallen for, and soon discovers that the mugs who thugged her were part of a collection racket. A violent action melodrama upgraded from its original "R" rating. 96m/C VHS. Rod Taylor, Suzy Kendall, Theodore Bikel, Jane Russell, James Booth, Janet MacLachlan, William Smith, Ahna Capri, Chris Robinson; **D:** Robert Clouse. *NO*

Darkest Africa *Batmen of Africa; King of the Jungleland* 1936 Legendary animal trainer Beatty is the hero of this 15 episode cliffhanger serial as he vies with beasts—both animal and human. 270m/B LV. Clyde Beatty, Manuel King, Elaine Shepard; **D:** Joseph Kane, B. Reeves Eason. *REP, MOV*

Darkman 🐾🐾🐾 1990 (R) Raimi's disfigured-man-seeks-revenge suspenser is comicbook kitsch cross-pollinated with a strain of gothic horror. Neeson plays a scientist who's on the verge of discovering the key to cloning body parts; brutally attacked by the henchmen of a crooked poli-

tico, his lab is destroyed and he's left for dead. Turns out he's not dead—just horribly disfigured and a wee bit chafed—and he stalks his deserving victims from the shadows, using his lab know-how to disguise his rugged bad looks. Exquisitely violent. Montage by Pablo Ferro. 96m/C VHS, Beta, LV, Closed Caption. Liam Neeson, Frances McDormand, Larry Drake, Colin Friels, Nelson Mashita, Jenny Agutter, Rafael H. Robledo; **D:** Sam Raimi; **W:** Sam Raimi, Ivan Raimi; **M:** Danny Elfman. *USH, CCB*

Darkman 2: The Return of Durant 🐾🐾½ 1994 (R) The first in a series of direct-to-video adventures about disfigured scientist Peyton "Darkman" Westlake (now played by Vosloo), who's continuing his liquid skin research in the hopes of transforming his grotesque appearance. He finds an ally in scientist David Brinkman but Westlake's nemesis, crime boss Robert G. Durant (Drake), wants the property where Brinkman's lab is located. And what Durant wants, he takes. Sam Raimi, who directed the original film, is one of the series producers. **CW:** Language; brutal violence. 93m/C VHS, LV, Closed Caption. Arnold Vosloo, Larry Drake, Kim Delaney, Renee O'Connor, Rod Wilson; **D:** Bradford May; **W:** Steven McKay, Chuck Pfarrer; **C:** Bradford May; **M:** Randy Miller. *USH*

Darkman 3: Die Darkman Die 🐾🐾½ 1995 (R) The second direct-to-video Darkman saga finds Dr. Peyton Westlake (Vosloo) disrupting the drug-dealing activities of underworld boss Peter Rooker (Fahey). The obsessed Rooker is determined to figure out the secret to Darkman's enormous strength, employing the feminine wiles of his mistress, Dr. Bridget Thorne (Fluegel). Then Westlake/Darkman finds himself drawn to Rooker's neglected wife and young daughter. Our hero suffers a lot (as usual) and there's lots of action (as usual). **CW:** Violent action and some violence. 87m/C VHS, LV, Closed Caption. Arnold Vosloo, Jeff Fahey, Darlanne Fluegel, Nigel Bennett, Roxann Biggs-Dawson; **D:** Bradford May; **W:** Mike Werb; **M:** Randy Miller. *USH*

Darkroom 🐾½ 1990 An unstable young man devises a scheme to photograph his father in bed with his mistress, and then use the pics to blackmail dear ol' dad. 90m/C VHS. Jill Pierce, Jeffrey Allen Arbaugh, Sara Lee Wade, Aaron Teich; **D:** Terrence O'Hara. *NO*

The Darkside 🐾½ 1987 (R) In this frightening drama, a young prostitute and an innocent cabbie attempt to escape the clutches of a maniacal film producer with a secret he won't let them reveal. 95m/C VHS. Tony Galati, Cyndy Preston; **D:** Constantino Magnatta. *THV*

Darktown Strutters 🐾 *Get Down and Boogie* 1974 (PG) Effort to satirize racial stereotypes is humorless and ineffective. Black female motorcycle gang searches for the kidnapped mother of one of the members. 85m/C VHS, Beta. Trina Parks, Roger E. Mosley, Shirley Washington; **D:** William Witney. *NLC*

Darling 🐾🐾🐾½ 1965 Young amoral model tries to hold boredom at bay by having a number of love affairs. She joins the international jet set and manages to reach the top of European society by marrying a prince. She then learns what an empty life she has. Christie won an Oscar for her portrayal of the disillusioned, cynical young woman. 122m/B VHS, Beta, LV. *GB* Julie Christie, Dirk Bogarde, Laurence Harvey; **D:** John Schlesinger; **W:** Frederic Raphael. Academy Awards '65: Best Actress (Christie), Best Costume Design (B & W), Best Story & Screenplay; British Academy Awards '65: Best Actor (Bogarde), Best Actress (Christie), Best Screenplay; Golden Globe Awards '66: Best Foreign Film; National Board of Review Awards '65: 10 Best Films of the Year, Best Actress (Christie), Best Director (Schlesinger); New York Film Critics Awards '65: Best Actress (Christie), Best Director (Schlesinger), Best Film; Nominations: Academy Awards '65: Best Director (Schlesinger), Best Picture. *COL, BTV*

Darling Lili 🐾🐾½ 1970 Big-budget WWI spy comedy/musical with Andrews as a German agent posing as an English music hall performer, who falls in love with squadron leader Hudson and finds she can't betray him. A critical flop when first released, film has its charms though director Edwards did much better for Andrews in "Victor/Victoria." ♫Whistling Away the Dark; The Girl In No Man's Land; Smile Away Each Rainy Day; I'll Give You Three Guesses; Your Good Will Ambassador; Darling Lili; The Little Birds. **136m/C VHS.** Julie Andrews, Rock Hudson, Jeremy Kemp, Jacques Marin, Michael Witney, Vernon Dobtcheff; **D:** Blake Edwards; **W:** Blake Edwards, William Peter Blatty; **M:** Henry Mancini, Johnny Mercer. Golden Globe Awards '71: Best Song ("Whistling Away the Dark"); Nominations: Academy Awards '70: Best Costume Design, Best Song ("Whistling Away the Dark"), Original Song Score and/or Adaptation. *PAR*

D.A.R.Y.L. *♫♫* **1985 (PG)** The little boy found by the side of the road is too polite, too honest and too smart. His friend explains to him the necessity of imperfection (If you don't want the grown-ups to bother you too much) and he begins to become more like a real little boy. But the American military has a top-secret interest in this child, since he is in fact the combination of a cloned body and a computer brain. More interesting when it's involved with the human beings and less so when it focuses on science. **100m/C VHS, Beta, LV, Closed Caption.** Mary Beth Hurt, Michael McKean, Barret Oliver, Colleen Camp, Danny Corkill; **D:** Simon Wincer; **W:** David Ambrose, Allan Scott; **M:** Marvin Hamlisch. *PAR*

Das Boot *♫♫♫♫* *The Boat* **1981 (R)** Superb detailing of life in a German U-boat during WWII. Intense, claustrophobic atmosphere complemented by nail-biting action provides a realistic portrait of the stressful conditions that were endured on these submarines. Excellent performances, especially from Prochnow. In German with subtitles. From the novel by Lothar-Guenther Buccheim. Originally a 6-hour special made for German television. The director's cut is released at 209 minutes on 2 cassettes. **CW:** Some war violence and brief language. **210m/C VHS, Beta, LV. GE** Juergen Prochnow, Herbert Gronemeyer, Klaus Wennemann, Hubertus Bengsch, Martin Semmelrogge, Bernd Tauber, Erwin Leder, Martin May, Heinz Honig, U. A. Ochsen, Claude-Oliver Rudolph, Jan Fedder, Ralph Richer, Joachim Bernhard, Oliver Stritzel, Konrad Becker, Lutz Schnell, Martin Hemme; **D:** Wolfgang Petersen; **W:** Wolfgang Petersen; **M:** Klaus Doldinger. Nominations: Academy Awards '82: Best Adapted Screenplay, Best Cinematography, Best Director (Petersen), Best Film Editing, Best Sound. *COL, APD, GLV*

Das Testament des Dr. Mabuse *♫♫♫*½ *The Testament of Dr. Mabuse* **1933** The third, and only sound, Mabuse film by Lang. The infamous crime lord/megalomaniac plots the world's destruction from the confines of an asylum cell. In German, with English subtitles. Released as "The Last Will of Dr. Mabuse" in the U.S. in 1943. **122m/B VHS, Beta. GE** Rudolf Klein-Rogge, Otto Wernicke, Gustav Diesl, Karl Meixner; **D:** Fritz Lang. *SNC, GLV*

Date Bait *♫* **1960** When a teen couple decides—much to their parents' chagrin—to elope, they find themselves on a date with danger when their post-nuptials are plagued by pushers and assorted other bad guys. **71m/B VHS, Beta.** Gary Clarke, Marlo Ryan, Richard Gering, Danny Logan; **D:** O'Dale Ireland. *SNC*

Date with an Angel *♫*½ **1987 (PG)** When aspiring musician Knight fishes a beautiful angel out of the swimming pool, he is just trying to rescue her. But the beauty of the angel overwhelms him and he finds himself questioning his upcoming wedding to Cates, a cosmetic mogul's daughter. Sickeningly cute and way too sentimental, though Beart's beauty is other-worldly. **114m/C VHS, Beta, LV.** Emmanuelle Beart, Michael E. Knight, Phoebe Cates, David Dukes, Bibi Besch, Albert Macklin, David Hunt, Michael Goodwin; **D:** Tom McLoughlin. *NO*

A Date with Judy *♫♫* **1948** Standard post-war musical dealing with teenage mix-ups in and around a big high school dance. Choreography by Stanley Donen. ♫Cuanto La Gusto; Strictly on the Corny Side; It's a Most Unusual Day; Judaline; I've Got a Date with Judy; I'm Gonna Meet My Mary; Temptation; Mulligatawny. **114m/C VHS, Beta, LV, Closed Caption.** Jane Powell, Elizabeth Taylor, Carmen Miranda, Wallace Beery, Robert Stack, Xavier Cugat, Selena Royle, Leon Ames; **D:** Richard Thorpe; **C:** Robert L. Surtees. *MGM, MLB*

Daughter of Darkness *♫♫*½ **1989 (R)** A young woman goes to Hungary in search of her family tree, only to discover vampires nestled there. **CW:** Violence; sexuality. **93m/C VHS.** Mia Sara, Anthony Perkins, Robert Reynolds, Jack Coleman; **D:** Stuart Gordon. *THV*

Daughter of Death *♫* *Julie Darling* **1982 (R)** A little mentally off-center since she witnessed the gruesome rape and murder of her mother, a teenage girl doesn't bond well with her new mom when dad remarries. **100m/C VHS. CA GE** Anthony (Tony) Franciosa, Isabelle Mejias, Sybil Danning, Cindy Gurling, Paul Hubbard, Benjamin Schmoll; **D:** Paul Nicholas. *FCT*

The Daughter of Dr. Jekyll *♫*½ **1957** The doc's daughter believes she may have inherited her father's evil curse when several of the locals are found dead. **71m/B VHS, Beta.** John Agar, Arthur Shields, John Dierkes, Gloria Talbott; **D:** Edgar G. Ulmer. *FOX*

Daughter of Don Q *♫♫*½ **1946** Delores' father is very rich with a huge real estate empire and she is his only heir. Greedy cousin Carlos would like to change that—by killing Delores. Delores must dodge speeding cars, hurling harpoons, and more to escape Carlos' evil plot. Part of "The Cliffhanger Serials" series. **166m/B VHS.** Adrian Booth, Kirk Alyn, Leroy Mason. *REP, MOV*

Daughter of Horror *♫♫* *Dementia* **1955** A young woman finds herself involved with a porcine mobster who resembles her abusive father. Trouble is, Dad's dead, and daughter dearest abetted his departure. Obscure venture into expressionism that was initially banned by the New York State Board of Censors. Shot on a low budget (how low was it? So low that McMahon narrated because shooting with sound was too expensive). The 55 minutes tend to lag, although the film should be intriguing to genre enthusiasts and to fans of things pseudo-Freudian. **60m/B VHS.** Adrienne Barrett, Bruno Ve Sota, Ben Roseman; **D:** John Parker; **W:** John Parker. *NOS, SNC, MRV*

Daughter of the Dragon *♫♫* **1931** Fu Manchu is again on the prowl, this time sending his daughter to murder Fletcher to avenge the death of his wife and son during China's Boxer Rebellion. Based on a Sax Rohmer story. **70m/B VHS.** Anna May Wong, Warner Oland, Sessue Hayakawa, Bramwell Fletcher, Holmes Herbert; **D:** Lloyd Corrigan. *NOS*

Daughter of the Tong *♫* **1939** FBI agent gets tong twisted when he tries to put a lid on a smuggling ring headed by a woman (who's beautiful, of course). Something that resembles acting is wasted in a mess of a movie. **56m/B VHS, Beta.** Evelyn Brent, Grant Withers, Dorothy Short, Dave O'Brien; **D:** Raymond K. Johnson. *NOS, SNC*

Daughters of Darkness *♫♫♫* *Le Rouge aux Levres* **1971 (R)** Newlyweds on their way to England stop at a posh French hotel. There they meet a beautiful woman whom the hotel owner swears had been there forty years ago, even though she hasn't aged a bit. When she introduces herself as Countess of Bathory (the woman who bathed in the blood of virgins to stay young) folks begin to wonder. A really superb erotic vampire film charged with sensuality and a sense of dread. **87m/C VHS, Beta.** *BE GE IT FR* Delphine Seyrig, John Karlen, Daniele Ouimet, Andrea Rau, Paul Esser, Georges Jamin, Joris Collet, Fons Rademakers; **D:** Harry Kumel. *FCT*

Daughters of Satan *♫♫* **1972 (R)** Selleck, in an early role as a virile museum buyer, antagonizes a coven of witches when he purchases a painting. His wife, played by Grant, becomes a target of the witches' revenge and salacious shenanigans ensue. **96m/C VHS, Beta.** Tom Selleck, Barra Grant, Paraluman, Tani Phelps Guthrie; **D:** Hollingsworth Morse. *NO*

Daughters of the Dust *♫♫♫*½ **1991** Five women of a Gullah family living on the Sea Islands off the Georgia coast in 1902 contemplate moving to the mainland in this emotional tale of change. The Gullah are descendants of West African slaves and their isolation has kept their superstitions and native dialect (a mixture of Western African, Creole, and English) intact. Family bonds and memories are celebrated with a quiet narrative and beautiful cinematography in Dash's feature-film directorial debut. **113m/C VHS.** Cora Lee Day, Barbara O, Alva Rogers, Kaycee Moore, Cheryl Lynn Bruce, Adisa Anderson, Eartha D. Robinson, Bahni Turpin, Tommy Hicks, Malik Farrakhan, Cornell (Kofi) Royal, Vertamae Crosvenor, Umar Abdurrahman, Sherry Jackson, Rev. Ervin Green; **D:** Julie Dash; **W:** Julie Dash; **C:** A. Jafa Fielder; **M:** John Barnes. Sundance Film Festival '91: Best Cinematography. *KIV, FCT, PMS*

Dave *♫♫♫* **1993 (PG-13)** Regular guy Dave Kovic (Kline) is a dead ringer for the President, launching him into the White House after the prez suffers a stroke in embarrassing circumstances. Seamless comedy prompts lots of hearty laughs and the feel-good faith that despite the overwhelming odds, everything will turn out just fine. Political cameos abound: look for real-life Senators Alan Simpson, Paul Simon, Howard Metzenbaum, Tom Harkin, and Christopher Dodd as well as the commentators from TV's "The McLaughlin Group," and Stone, poking fun at himself on "Larry King Live," as he tries to convince the public there's a conspiracy going on. **CW:** Brief profanity and one sexual situation. **110m/C VHS, Beta, LV, Closed Caption.** Kevin Kline, Sigourney Weaver, Frank Langella, Kevin Dunn, Ving Rhames, Ben Kingsley, Charles Grodin, Faith Prince, Laura Linney, Bonnie Hunt, Parley Baer, Stefan Gierasch, Anna Deavere Smith, Bonnie Bartlett; **Cameos:** Oliver Stone, Arnold Schwarzenegger, Jay Leno, Larry King; **D:** Ivan Reitman; **W:** Gary Ross; **M:** James Newton Howard. Nominations: Academy Awards '93: Best Original Screenplay; Golden Globe Awards '94: Best Actor—Musical/Comedy (Kline), Best Film—Musical/Comedy; Writers Guild of America '93: Best Original Screenplay. *WAR, BTV, FCT*

David *♫♫♫*½ **1979** A haunting portrait of the survival of a Jewish teenager in Berlin during the Nazi reign of terror, based on the novel by Joel Koenig. Universally acclaimed, this was the first film about the Holocaust made in Germany by a German Jew. In German with English subtitles. **106m/C VHS, Beta. GE** Mario Fischel, Walter Taub, Irene Vrkijan, Torsten Hentes, Eva Mattes; **D:** Peter Lilienthal. Berlin International Film Festival '79: Golden Berlin Bear. *KIV, GLV*

David *♫♫*½ **1997** TNT's Old Testament biblical series continues with the story of shepherd boy David (Turner) who succeeds Saul (Pryce) to become king over the tribes of Israel. When King David (Parker) becomes smitten with the married Bathsheba (Lee), he sends her husband into battle, soon leaving her a comely widow (although not for long). And there's also subplots involving three of David's children: Absalom (Rowan), Amnon (Hall), and Tamar (Bellar). Lots of action. **?m/C VHS.** Nathaniel Parker, Sheryl Lee, Jonathan Pryce, Leonard Nimoy, Dominic Rowan, Edward Hall, Clara Bellar, Marco Leonardi, Franco Nero, Ben Daniels, Maurice Roeves, Gina Bellman, Gideon Turner; **D:** Robert Markowitz; **W:** Larry Gross; **C:** Raffaele Mertes; **M:** Carlo Siliotto. *TTC*

David and Bathsheba *♫♫♫* **1951** The Bible story comes alive in this lush and colorful Fox production. Peck and Hayward are great together and Peck is properly concerned about the wrath of God over his transgressions. Terrific costumes and special effects, lovely music and a fine supporting cast keep this a notch above other Biblical epics. **116m/C VHS, LV, Closed Caption.** Gregory Peck, Susan Hayward, Raymond Massey, Kieron Moore, James Robertson Justice, Jayne Meadows, John Sutton, Dennis Hoey, Francis X. Bushman, George Zucco; *D:* Henry King; *W:* Philip Dunne; *C:* Leon Shamroy. Nominations: Academy Awards '51: Best Art Direction/Set Decoration (Color), Best Color Cinematography (Color), Best Costume Design (Color), Best Story & Screenplay, Original Dramatic/Comedy Score. FXV, FOX

David and Lisa 🎞🎞🎞 1962 Director Perry was given an Oscar for this sensitive independently-produced film. Adapted from Theodore Isaac Rubin's true case history novel concerning a young man and woman who fall in love while institutionalized for mental illness. Dullea and Margolin are excellent in the title roles of this sleeper. **94m/B VHS, Beta, LV.** Keir Dullea, Janet Margolin, Howard da Silva, Neva Patterson, Clifton James; *D:* Frank Perry. Nominations: Academy Awards '62: Best Adapted Screenplay, Best Director (Perry). COL, MRV

David Copperfield 🎞🎞🎞🎞 1935 Superior adaptation of Charles Dickens' great novel. An orphan ascends to manhood in Victorian England with a wide variety of help and harm. Terrific acting by Bartholomew, Fields, Rathbone, and all the rest. Lavish production, lovingly filmed. **132m/B VHS, Beta, LV.** Lionel Barrymore, W.C. Fields, Freddie Bartholomew, Maureen O'Sullivan, Basil Rathbone, Lewis Stone, Frank Lawton, Madge Evans, Roland Young, Edna May Oliver, Lennox Pawle, Elsa Lanchester, Una O'Connor, Arthur Treacher; *D:* George Cukor; *W:* Howard Estabrook, Hugh Walpole; *M:* Herbert Stothart. National Board of Review Awards '35: 10 Best Films of the Year; Nominations: Academy Awards '35: Best Film Editing, Best Picture. MGM

David Copperfield 🎞🎞½ 1970 This British made-for-television production is more faithful to the Dickens classic than any of its predecessors. The added material, however, fails to highlight any one character as had the successful 1935 MGM version. Still, the exceptional (and largely stage-trained) cast do much to redeem the production. **118m/C VHS, Closed Caption.** Richard Attenborough, Cyril Cusack, Edith Evans, Pamela Franklin, Susan Hampshire, Wendy Hiller, Ron Moody, Laurence Olivier, Robin Phillips; *D:* Delbert Mann; *M:* Malcolm Arnold. FOX, TVC

David Holzman's Diary 🎞🎞🎞 1967 Director McBride helmed this fake underground movie, a legendary put-on focusing on film student pretensions. Holzman is a sincere geek who seeks the meaning of life by filming his own existence in oh-so-chic grainy black and white verite. He learns reality is more important than film. Drolly captures the state of the art in late '60's America. **71m/B VHS, LV.** L.M. Kit Carson; *D:* Jim McBride; *W:* L.M. Kit Carson, Jim McBride. FXL

DaVinci's War 🎞🎞 1992 (R) Frank DaVinci's sister is murdered and he wants revenge. So he hooks up with a professional killer and a bunch of Vietnam vets and gets the firepower he needs to blow the bad guys away. *CW:* Language, strong violence, and strong sexuality. **94m/C VHS.** Joey Travolta, Michael Nouri, Vanity, Richard Foronjy, Branscombe Richmond, Sam Jones, Jack Bannon; *Cameos:* Brian Robbins, James Russo; *D:* Raymond Martino; *W:* Raymond Martino; *M:* Jeff Lass. TRI

Davy Crockett and the River Pirates 🎞🎞½ 1956 (G) Another Disney splice and dice of two episodes from the television series, chronicling the further adventures of our frontier hero. Davy meets up with Mike Fink, the King of the Ohio River, and the two engage in a furious keelboat race, and then unite to track down a group of thieves masquerading as Indians and threatening the peace. **81m/C VHS, Beta, LV.** Fess Parker, Buddy Ebsen, Jeff York; *D:* Norman Foster; *M:* George Bruns. DIS

Davy Crockett, King of the Wild Frontier 🎞🎞🎞 1955 (PG) Three episodes of the popular Disney television series are blended together here to present the life and some of the adventures of Davy Crockett. These include his

days as an Indian fighter and his gallant stand in defense of the Alamo. Well-done by a splendid cast, the film helped to spread Davy-mania among the children of the 1950s. **93m/C VHS, Beta, Closed Caption.** Fess Parker, Buddy Ebsen, Hans Conried, Ray Whiteside, Pat Hogan, William "Billy" Bakewell, Basil Ruysdael, Kenneth Tobey; *D:* Norman Foster; *M:* George Bruns. DIS, BTV

Dawn! 🎞🎞 1983 True story of Dawn Fraser, an Olympic champion swimmer and an unfulfilled woman willing to fight for her happiness. **114m/C VHS, Beta.** Bronwyn MacKay-Payne, Tom Richards. NO

Dawn Express 🎞½ 1942 Nazi spies infiltrate the U.S. in search of a secret formula designed to enhance the power of gasoline. Another film made to contribute to the war effort that doesn't make much sense. **63m/B VHS, Beta.** Michael Whalen, Anne Nagel, William "Billy" Bakewell, Constance Worth, Hans von Twardowski, Jack Mulhall, George Pembroke, Kenneth Harlan, Robert Frazer; *D:* Al(bert) Herman. SNC

Dawn of the Dead 🎞🎞🎞½ 1978 Romero's gruesome sequel to his "Night of the Living Dead." A mysterious plague causes the recently dead to rise from their graves and scour the countryside for living flesh. Very violent, gory, graphic, and shocking, yet not without humor. Gives interesting consideration to the violence created by the living humans in their efforts to save themselves. **126m/C VHS, Beta, LV.** David Emge, Ken Foree, Gaylen Ross; *D:* George A. Romero; *W:* George A. Romero. REP, FCT

Dawn of the Mummy woof! 1982 Lousy plot and bad acting—not to mention gore galore—do this one in. A photographer and a bevy of young fashion models travel to Egypt for a special shoot. They unwittingly stumble upon an ancient tomb, teeming with vengeance-minded mummies. **93m/C VHS, Beta.** Brenda King, Barry Sattels, George Peck, Joan Levy; *D:* Frank Agrama. NO

Dawn on the Great Divide 🎞🎞½ 1942 Jones' last film before his tragic and untimely death trying to save people from a fire at the Coconut Grove in Boston. Wagon train has to battle not only Indians, but bad guys as well. Plot provides more depth than the usual western fare. **57m/B VHS, Beta.** Buck Jones, Tim McCoy, Raymond Hatton, Mona Barrie, Robert Lowery, Betty Blythe, Jan Wiley, Harry Woods, Roy Barcroft; *D:* Howard Bretherton. NOS, MRV, VCN

Dawn Patrol 🎞🎞🎞 1938 Flynn plays a flight commander whose nerves are shot in this story of the British Royal Flying Corps during WWI. The focus is on the effects that the pressures and deaths have on all those concerned. Fine performances from all in this well-done remake of the 1930 film. **103m/B VHS, Beta.** Errol Flynn, David Niven, Basil Rathbone, Donald Crisp, Barry Fitzgerald, Melville Cooper; *D:* Edmund Goulding; *C:* Gaetano Antonio "Tony" Gaudio; *M:* Max Steiner. FOX, MGM

Dawn Rider 🎞🎞 1935 Formula western has all the right ingredients: Wayne as a cowboy out to get revenge on the gang that murdered his father. Features stuntman Canutt in rare acting role. **60m/B VHS.** John Wayne, Marion Burns, Yakima Canutt; *D:* Robert North Bradbury. COL, REP, MRV

Dawn Rider/Frontier Horizon 1939 A double feature of two of Wayne's earliest western films. **114m/B VHS, Beta.** John Wayne, Jennifer Jones, Marion Burns; *D:* Robert North Bradbury, George Sherman. REP

The Dawning 🎞🎞½ 1988 An Irish revolutionary in the 1920's draws a young woman into his dangerous world of romance, intrigue and death. Howard's last film. Based on the novel "Old Jest" by Jennifer Johnston. **97m/C VHS, LV.** GB Anthony Hopkins, Jean Simmons, Trevor Howard, Rebecca Pidgeon, Hugh Grant, Tara MacGowran; *D:* Robert Knights. LIV, PMS

The Dawson Patrol 🎞½ 1978 Royal Canadian Mountie dog-sled race turns into a dramatic battle for survival. **75m/C VHS, Beta.** George R. Robinson, Tim Henry, Neil Dainaro, James B. Douglas; *D:* Peter Kelly. TWE

The Day After 🎞🎞🎞 1983 Powerful drama graphically depicts the nuclear bombing of a midwestern city and its after-effects on the survivors. Made for television, and very controversial when first shown, gathering huge ratings and vast media coverage. **122m/C VHS, Beta, LV.** Jason Robards Jr., JoBeth Williams, John Lithgow, Steve Guttenberg, John Cullum; *D:* Nicholas Meyer. PAR

The Day and the Hour 🎞🎞½ Today We Live; Le Jour et L'Heure; Il Giorno e L'Ora; Viviamo Oggi 1963 A woman becomes accidentally involved in the resistance movement during the Nazi occupation of France in WWII. **110m/C VHS, Beta.** FR JP Simone Signoret, Stuart Whitman, Genevieve Page, Michel Piccoli, Reggie Nalder, Pierre Dux, Billy Kearns; *D:* Rene Clement; *M:* Claude Bolling. NO

A Day at the Races 🎞🎞🎞½ 1937 Though it seems labored at times, the brilliance of the brothers Marx still comes through in this rather weak tale of a patient in a sanitorium who convinces horse doctor Groucho to take on running the place. 🎵A Message from the Man in the Moon; On Blue Venetian Waters; Tomorrow is Another Day; All God's Chillun Got Rhythm. **111m/B VHS, Beta, LV.** Groucho Marx, Harpo Marx, Chico Marx, Sig Rumann, Douglass Dumbrille, Margaret Dumont, Allan Jones, Maureen O'Sullivan; *D:* Sam Wood; *C:* Joseph Ruttenberg; *M:* George Bassman. MGM, CCB

Day for Night 🎞🎞🎞🎞 La Nuit Americaine 1973 (PG) A wryly affectionate look at the profession of moviemaking—its craft, character, and the personalities that interact against the performances commanded by the camera. In French with English subtitles. **116m/C VHS, Beta.** FR Jean-Pierre Leaud, Jacqueline Bisset, Jean-Pierre Aumont, Valentina Cortese, Alexandra Stewart, Dani, Nathalie Baye, Francois Truffaut; *D:* Francois Truffaut; *W:* Suzanne Schiffman, Jean-Louis Richard, Francois Truffaut; *M:* Georges Delerue. Academy Awards '73: Best Foreign Language Film; British Academy Awards '73: Best Director (Truffaut), Best Film, Best Supporting Actress (Cortese); New York Film Critics Awards '73: Best Director (Truffaut), Best Film, Best Supporting Actress (Cortese); National Society of Film Critics Awards '73: Best Director (Truffaut), Best Film, Best Supporting Actress (Cortese); Nominations: Academy Awards '74: Best Director (Truffaut), Best Original Screenplay, Best Supporting Actress (Cortese). WAR, APD

A Day for Thanks on Walton's Mountain 🎞🎞 1982 Many of the original television-show cast members returned for this sentimental Thanksgiving reunion on Walton's Mountain. Made for television. **97m/C VHS.** Ralph Waite, Ellen Corby, Judy Norton-Taylor, Eric Scott, Jon Walmsley, Robert Wightman, Mary McDonough, David W. Harper, Kami Cotler, Joe Conley, Ronnie Clair Edwards, Richard Gilliland, Melinda Naud; *D:* Harry Harris. WAR

A Day in October 🎞🎞½ 1992 (PG-13) 1943, Copenhagen, Denmark. There are signs the Jewish population is in danger from occupying Nazi officials and the resistance movement is active. Wounded resistance fighter Sweeney is rescued by the Jewish Sara (Wolf), and their relationship deepens as the realities of WWII change their lives. Based on historical fact, but there's little explanation of the politics or the fierce nationalism and intense loyalty most Danes felt towards their fellow countrymen, a loyalty that ultimately saved most of the Danish Jews from the Holocaust. Good performances, particularly Benzali as Sara's father, help overcome the script weaknesses. Filmed on location in Denmark. *CW:* Some violence. **96m/C VHS, Closed Caption.** D.B. Sweeney, Kelly Wolf, Tovah Feldshuh, Daniel Benzali, Ole Lemmeke, Kim Romer, Anders Peter Bro, Lars Oluf Larsen; *D:* Kenneth Madsen; *W:* Damian F. Slattery; *M:* Jens Lysdal. ACA, FOX

A Day in the Country 🎬🎬🎬½ *Une Partie de Campagne* **1946** The son of the famed painter gives us the moving tale of a young woman's sudden and intense love for a man she meets while on a picnic with her family. Beautifully adapted from a story by Guy de Maupassant. Renowned photographer Henri Cartier-Bresson contributed to the wonderful cinematography. In French with English subtitles. **40m/B VHS, Beta.** *FR* Sylvia Bataille, Georges Darnoux, Jane Marken, Paul Temps; **D:** Jean Renoir. *NOS, MRV, DVT*

A Day in the Death of Joe Egg 🎬🎬🎬 **1971 (R)** Based on the Peter Nichols play, an unlikely black comedy about a British couple trying to care for their retarded/autistic child, nearly destroying their marriage in the process. They begin to contemplate euthanasia as a solution. Well-acted, but potentially offensive to some. **106m/C VHS, Beta.** *GB* Alan Bates, Janet Suzman, Elizabeth Robillard, Peter Bowles, Joan Hickson, Sheila Gish; **D:** Peter Medak; **W:** David Deutsch. *COL*

The Day It Came to Earth woof! **1977 (PG)** Completely silly and unbelievable sci-fi flick has meteor crashing into the watery grave of a mobster. The decomposed corpse is revived by the radiation and plots to take revenge on those who fitted him with cement shoes. **89m/C VHS, Beta.** Roger Manning, Wink Roberts, Bob Ginnaven, Rita Wilson, Delight de Bruine; **D:** Harry Z. Thomason. *NO*

The Day My Parents Ran Away 🎬🎬½ **1993 (PG)** Rebellious 16-year-old gets a tough lesson in responsibility when his parents get tired of his antics and decide to leave home in search of a new life. He finds out things aren't so easy on your own. **95m/C VHS, LV, Closed Caption.** Matt Frewer, Bobby Jacoby, Brigid Conley Walsh, Blair Brown, Martin Mull; **D:** Martin Nicholson; **W:** Handel Glassberg; **M:** J. Peter Robinson. *COL, IME*

Day of Atonement 🎬🎬½ **1993 (R)** It's a war for power between rival druglords when Hanin is released from prison and finds out his son and cousin are battling over turf. Then Walken is dragged into the fracas. Beals is the government agent trying to regain some control of the dangerous situation. **CW:** Strong language and strong violence. **127m/C VHS, LV, Closed Caption.** Christopher Walken, Jennifer Beals, Jill Clayburgh, Roger Hanin, Richard Berry. *THV*

Day of Judgment 🎬½ **1981** A mysterious stranger arrives in a town to slaughter those people who violate the Ten Commandments. **101m/C VHS, Beta.** William T. Hicks, Harris Bloodworth, Brownlee Davis; **D:** C.D.H. Reynolds. *NO*

Day of the Animals 🎬 *Something is Out There* **1977 (PG)** Nature gone wild. It seems a depleted ozone layer has exposed the animals to the sun's radiation, turning Bambi and Bugs into brutal killers. A group of backpackers trek in the Sierras, unaware of the transformation. Farfetched and silly (we hope). **95m/C VHS.** Christopher George, Leslie Nielsen, Lynda Day George, Richard Jaeckel, Michael Ansara, Ruth Roman, Jon Cedar, Susan Backlinie, Andrew Stevens, Gil Lamb; **D:** William Girdler; **W:** William W. Norton Sr. *MED*

Day of the Assassin 🎬 **1981** A Mideast shah's yacht explodes, sending a huge fortune to the bottom of a murky bay. This sets off a rampage of treasure hunting by a variety of ruthless mercenaries. **94m/C VHS, Beta.** Glenn Ford, Chuck Connors, Richard Roundtree, Henry Silva, Jorge Rivero; **D:** Brian Trenchard-Smith. *PSM*

Day of the Cobra 🎬½ **1984** A corrupt narcotics bureau official hires an ex-cop to find a heroin kingpin on the back streets of Genoa, Italy. **95m/C VHS, Beta.** *IT* Franco Nero, Sybil Danning, Mario Maranzana, Licinia Lentini, William Berger; **D:** Enzo G. Castellari. *MED*

Day of the Dead 🎬½ **1985** The third in Romero's trilogy of films about flesh-eating zombies taking over the world. Romero hasn't thought up anything new for the ghouls to do, and the humans are too nasty to care about this time

around. For adult audiences. **91m/C VHS, Beta, LV.** Lori Cardillo, Terry Alexander, Joseph Pilato, Jarleth Conroy; **D:** George A. Romero; **W:** George A. Romero. *MED, IME, VTR*

The Day of the Dolphin 🎬🎬 **1973 (PG)** Research scientist, after successfully working out a means of teaching dolphins to talk, finds his animals kidnapped; espionage and assassination are involved. Dolphin voices by Henry, who also wrote the screenplay. **104m/C VHS, Beta, LV.** George C. Scott, Trish Van Devere, Paul Sorvino, Fritz Weaver, Jon Korkes, John Dehner, Edward Herrmann, Severn Darden; **D:** Mike Nichols; **W:** Buck Henry; **M:** Georges Delerue; **V:** Buck Henry. National Board of Review Awards '73: 10 Best Films of the Year; Nominations: Academy Awards '73: Best Sound, Original Dramatic/Comedy Score. *NLC*

The Day of the Jackal 🎬🎬🎬½ **1973 (PG)** Frederick Forsyth's best-selling novel of political intrigue is splendidly brought to the screen by Zinnemann. A brilliant and ruthless assassin hired to kill Charles de Gaulle skirts the international intelligence pool, while intuitive police work to stop him. Tense, suspenseful, beautiful location photography. Excellent acting by Fox, Cusack and Britton. **142m/C VHS, Beta, LV.** Edward Fox, Alan Badel, Tony Britton, Derek Jacobi, Cyril Cusack, Olga Georges-Picot; **D:** Fred Zinnemann; **M:** Georges Delerue. Nominations: Academy Awards '73: Best Film Editing. *USH*

The Day of the Locust 🎬🎬🎬½ **1975 (R)** Compelling adaptation of Nathaniel West's novel concerning the dark side of 1930s' Hollywood. A no-talent amoral actress's affair with a meek accountant leads to tragedy and destruction. Told from the view of a cynical art director wise to the ways of Hollywood. **140m/C VHS, Beta, LV.** Donald Sutherland, Karen Black, Burgess Meredith, William Atherton, Billy Barty, Bo Hopkins, Richard Dysart, Geraldine Page; **D:** John Schlesinger; **C:** Conrad Hall; **M:** John Barry. National Board of Review Awards '75: 10 Best Films of the Year; Nominations: Academy Awards '75: Best Cinematography, Best Supporting Actor (Meredith). *PAR*

Day of the Maniac 🎬½ **1977 (R)** Psychotic drug addict will stop at nothing to support his growing habit. **89m/C VHS, Beta.** George Hilton, Susan Scott; **D:** Sergio Martino. *REP*

Day of the Panther 🎬½ **1988** The Panthers—the world's most formidable martial artists—are mighty torqued when panther-Linda is pithed, and they're not known to turn the other cheek. Much chop-socky kicking and shrilling. **86m/C VHS, Beta.** John Stanton, Eddie Stazak; **D:** Brian Trenchard-Smith. *CEL*

Day of the Triffids 🎬🎬🎬 **1963** The majority of Earth's population is blinded by a meteor shower which also causes plant spores to mutate into giant carnivores. Well-done adaptation of John Wyndham's science fiction classic; Philip Yordan acknowledged "fronting" for blacklisted screenwriter Gordon, who finally received credit in 1996. **94m/C VHS, Beta, LV.** Howard Keel, Janet Scott, Nicole Maurey, Kieron Moore, Mervyn Johns, Alison Leggatt, Ewan Roberts, Janina Faye; **D:** Freddie Francis, Steve Sekely; **W:** Bernard Gordon. *MED, MRV, DME*

Day of the Warrior 🎬🎬 **1996 (R)** Babes who belong to a paramilitary law-and-order group infiltrate crime lord, the Warrior's, smuggling operations, strip joints and porn palaces. **96m/C VHS.** Julie Strain, Marcus Bagwell; **D:** Andy Sidaris. *MNC*

Day of Triumph **1954** A dynamic version of the life of Christ as seen through the eyes of the apostles Andrew and Zadok, the leaders of the Zealot underground. **110m/C VHS.** Lee J. Cobb, Robert Wilson, Ralph Freud; **D:** Irving Pichel. *REP*

Day of Wrath 🎬🎬🎬 *Vredens Dag* **1943** An involving psychological thriller based on records of witch trials from the early 1600s. An old woman, burned at the stake as a witch, puts a curse on the local parson and his family. Grim and unrelentingly pessimistic, moving from one horrific scene to another, director Dreyer creates a masterpiece of terror. Based on a play by Hans Wiers

Jenssen. In Danish with English subtitles. **110m/B VHS.** *DK* Thorkild Roose, Sigrid Neiiendam, Lisbeth Movin, Preben Lerdorff, Anna Svierker; **D:** Carl Theodor Dreyer; **W:** Carl Theodor Dreyer; **M:** Poul Schierbeck. National Board of Review Awards '48: 10 Best Films of the Year. *HTV, NOS, SNC*

Day One 🎬🎬🎬 **1989** Vivid recreation of one of the most turbulent periods of American history—the WWII race to build the atomic bomb. Chronicles the two year top-secret efforts of the Manhattan Project, with General Leslie Groves (Dennehy) having to supervise the project and contain the scientific rivalries. Outstanding cast, with Strathairn notable as physicist J. Robert Oppenheimer. Adapted from "Day One: Before Hiroshima and After" by Peter Wyden. Made for television. **141m/C VHS, Closed Caption.** Brian Dennehy, David Strathairn, Michael Tucker, Hume Cronyn, Richard Dysart, Barnard Hughes, Hal Holbrook, David Ogden Stiers, John McMartin; **D:** Joseph Sargent; **W:** David W. Rintels; **M:** Mason Daring. *WOV*

The Day That Shook the World 🎬🎬 **1978 (R)** Slow-moving but intriguing account of events surrounding the assassination of Archduke Ferdinand of Austria that triggered WWI. Garnered an R-rating due to some disturbing graphic scenes. **111m/C VHS.** Christopher Plummer, Florinda Bolkan, Maximilian Schell; **D:** Veljko Bulajic. *NO*

Day the Bookies Wept 🎬🎬 **1939** Decent yarn about cabbies tricked into buying a "racehorse." Turns out she's old as the hills and hooked on alcohol to boot, but they enter her in the big race anyway. **50m/B VHS, Beta.** Betty Grable, Joe Penner, Tom Kennedy, Richard Lane; **D:** Leslie Goodwins. *CCB*

The Day the Earth Caught Fire 🎬🎬🎬½ **1961** The earth is knocked out of orbit and sent hurtling toward the sun when nuclear testing is done simultaneously at both the North and South Poles. Realistic and suspenseful, this is one of the best of the sci-fi genre. **95m/B VHS, Beta.** Janet Munro, Edward Judd, Leo McKern; **D:** Val Guest; **W:** Val Guest, Wolf Mankowitz. British Academy Awards '61: Best Screenplay. *REP, KAR*

The Day the Earth Froze 🎬🎬 **1959** Witch steals the sun because she couldn't have a magical mill that produced grain, salt, and gold. Everything on Earth freezes. Based on a Finnish epic poem. **67m/B VHS.** *FI RU* Nina Anderson, Jon Powers, Ingrid Elhardt, Paul Sorenson; **D:** Gregg Sebelious. *SNC*

The Day the Earth Stood Still 🎬🎬🎬½ **1951** A gentle alien lands on Earth to deliver a message of peace and a warning about experimenting with nuclear power. He finds his views echoed by a majority of the population, but not the ones who are in control. In this account based loosely on the story of Christ, Rennie is the visitor backed by the mighty robot Gort. One of the greatest science fiction films of all time. **92m/B VHS, Beta, LV.** Michael Rennie, Patricia Neal, Hugh Marlowe, Sam Jaffe, Frances Bavier, Lock Martin, Billy Gray; **D:** Robert Wise; **W:** Edmund H. North; **C:** Leo Tover; **M:** Bernard Herrmann. *FOX, FCT, MLB*

The Day the Sky Exploded 🎬½ *Death From Outer Space; La Morte Viene Dalla Spazio; Le Danger Vient de l'Escape* **1957** Sci-fi disaster drama doesn't live up to the grandiose title, as a runaway rocket ship hits the sun, unleashing an asteroid shower that threatens Earth with tidal waves, earthquakes, heat waves and terrible dialogue. The highlight of this Franco-Italian effort is the cinematography by horror director Mario Bava. **80m/B VHS.** *FR IT* Paul Hubschmid, Madeleine Fischer, Fiorella Mari, Ivo Garrani, Dario Michaelis; **D:** Richard Benson. *NOS, FCT*

The Day the Sun Turned Cold 🎬🎬🎬 *Tianguo Niezi* **1994** In an apparent crisis of conscience a young man (Zhong Hua) enters a police station and tries to convince a weary captain (Hu) that his mother (Gowa) murdered his cruel father (Jingwu) 10 years before in order to marry another man. The detective eventually concludes he should investigate the supposed crime, which happened in a remote village, but Zhong Hua's accusations naturally stir up a great deal of resentment and anger. There's lots of questions about guilt, innocence, and motives—on everybody's part. Mandarin with subtitles. **99**m/C VHS. *HK* Siqin Gowa, Tuo Zhong Hua, Wai Zhi, Ma Jingwu, Li Hu; **D:** Yim Ho; **W:** Yim Ho; **C:** Hou Yong; **M:** Yoshihide Otomo. *KIV*

The Day the Women Got Even ♂½ **1980** Four suburban homemakers take up the life of vigilantes to save unsuspecting actresses from a talent agent's blackmail scheme. Made for television. **98**m/C VHS, Beta. JoAnn Pflug, Tina Louise, Georgia Engel, Barbara Rhoades, Julie Hagerty, Ed O'Neill; **D:** Burt Brinckerhoff; **M:** Brad Fiedel. *TLF*

Day the World Ended ♂ **1955** The first science fiction film of exploitation director Roger Corman. Five survivors of nuclear holocaust discover a desert ranch fortress owned by a survivalist (Birch) and his daughter (Nelson). With relatively abundant supplies, they fatuously wallow in false misery until a disfigured visitor, wasting away from radiation, stumbles into their paradise. His mutation into an alien being confronts them with the horror that lurks outside. **79**m/B VHS. Paul Birch, Lori Nelson, Adele Jergens, Raymond Hatton, Paul Dubov, Richard Denning, Mike Connors; **D:** Roger Corman; **W:** Lou Rusoff. *COL*

Day Time Ended ♂♂ *Vortex; Timewarp* **1980** A pair of glowing UFO's streaking across the sky and an alien mechanical device with long menacing appendages are only two of the bizarre phenomena witnessed from a lone house in the desert. Good special effects. Also released as "Time Warp" (1978). **80**m/C VHS, Beta, LV. Chris Mitchum, Jim Davis, Dorothy Malone; **D:** John Cardos; **W:** David Schmoeller, J. Larry Carroll; **M:** Richard Band. *MED, MRV*

The Day Will Dawn ♂♂♂ *The Avengers* **1942** Suspenseful British-made WWII thriller about a reporter and a young Norwegian girl who plot to sabotage a secret Nazi U-boat base near the girl's town. **100**m/B VHS, Beta, 8mm. *GB* Deborah Kerr, Hugh Williams, Griffith Jones, Ralph Richardson, Francis L. Sullivan, Roland Culver, Niall MacGinnis, Finlay Currie, Patricia Medina; **D:** Harold French; **W:** Terence Rattigan. *VYY*

Day with Conrad Green **1980** Set in 1927, this program presents a somewhat farcical look at a successful Broadway producer as he attempts to cope with a full schedule of personal and business problems on the day of the funeral of his longtime assistant. **60**m/C VHS, Beta. Fred Gwynne. *MTP*

Daybreak ♂♂½ **1993 (R)** In the near future America has been decimated by a nameless, sexually transmitted disease (read AIDS parable) and public policy is to quarantine the infected in concentration camp-like prisons. This leads to a quasi-official group of green-shirted thugs roaming the streets and imprisoning or killing anyone they suspect has the disease. A small resistance movement is lead by Torch (Gooding, Jr.), who happens to fall in love with Blue (Kelly), the sister of one of the fascist leaders. Based on Alan Bowne's play "Beirut, Daybreak." Made for cable television. **91**m/C VHS. Cuba Gooding Jr., Moira Kelly, Omar Epps, Martha Plimpton, Alice Drummond, David Eigenberg, John Savage; *Cameos:* Phil Hartman; **D:** Stephen Tolkin; **W:** Stephen Tolkin. *HBO*

The Daydreamer ♂♂½ *Absent-Minded; Le Distrait* **1975** Actor/director/writer Richard stars as a bumbling fool let loose in the French corporate world with comical results. In French with subtitles. **90**m/C VHS, Beta. *FR* Pierre Richard, Bernard Blier, Maria Pacome, Marie-Christine Barrault; **D:** Pierre Richard; **W:** Pierre Richard; **M:** Vladimir Cosma. *FCT*

Daylight ♂♂ **1996 (PG-13)** After a massive explosion seals both ends of New York's Holland Tunnel (The Tunneling Inferno?), a small band of stock disaster flick survivors are trapped under the waters of the Hudson River. Fortunately, a cab driver with a really square jaw who, conveniently, is an ex-emergency rescue worker AND who knows the entire layout of the tunnel happens to be driving toward the tunnel at the exact moment of the disaster. Coincidence? Nope, just Hollywood. Kit Latura (Stallone) leads the survivors through cave-ins, floods, fire, rats and poison gas (The Poison-Hiding Adventure!) only to discover to their dismay that they have emerged in New Jersey. Long on special effects but short on character development, this nod to the catastrophe movies of the 70's is still enjoyable for those who like to watch things go boom. *CW:* Disaster-related peril, death and destruction. **109**m/C VHS, LV, Closed Caption. Sylvester Stallone, Viggo Mortensen, Amy Brenneman, Stan Shaw, Claire Bloom, Renoly Santiago, Sage Stallone, Dan Hedaya, Jay O. Sanders, Karen Young, Vanessa Bell Calloway, Colin Fox, Danielle Harris, Jo Anderson, Mark Rolston, Rosemary Forsyth, Barry Newman; **D:** Rob Cohen; **W:** Leslie Bohem; **C:** David Eggby; **M:** Randy Edelman. Nominations: Academy Awards '96: Best Sound Effects Editing; Golden Raspberry Awards '96: Worst Actor (Stallone), Worst Song ("Whenever There is Love"). *USH*

Days and Nights in the Forest ♂♂½ **1970** Four men living in Calcutta decide to leave the city for a brief vacation. Each has a different emotional experience which will change him forever, including a brief love affair and finding true romance. In Bengali with English subtitles. **120**m/C VHS. *IN* **D:** Satyajit Ray. *FCT*

Days of Glory ♂♂½ **1943** Peck's screen debut finds him as a Russian peasant bravely fighting the Nazi blitzkrieg almost single-handedly. **86**m/B VHS, Beta. Tamara Toumanova, Gregory Peck, Alan Reed, Maria Palmer, Lowell Gilmore, Hugo Haas; **D:** Jacques Tourneur; **C:** Gaetano Antonio "Tony" Gaudio. *TTC*

Days of Heaven ♂♂♂½ **1978 (PG)** Drifter Gere, his younger sister, and a woman he claims is his sister become involved with a Texas sharecropper. Told through the eyes of the younger girl, this is a sweeping vision of the U.S. before WWI. Loss and loneliness, deception, frustration, and anger haunt these people as they struggle to make the land their own. Deservedly awarded an Oscar for breathtaking cinematography. **95**m/C VHS, Beta, LV. Richard Gere, Brooke Adams, Sam Shepard, Linda Manz, Stuart Margolin; **D:** Terence Malick; **W:** Terence Malick; **C:** Nestor Almendros; **M:** Ennio Morricone. Academy Awards '78: Best Cinematography; Cannes Film Festival '79: Best Director (Malick); Los Angeles Film Critics Association Awards '78: Best Cinematography; National Board of Review Awards '78: 10 Best Films of the Year; New York Film Critics Awards '78: Best Director (Malick); National Society of Film Critics Awards '78: Best Cinematography, Best Director (Malick), Best Film; Nominations: Academy Awards '78: Best Costume Design, Best Sound, Best Original Score. *PAR*

Days of Hell ♂ *I Giorni Dell'Inferno* **1984** Forgettable tale of four mercenaries who are hired to rescue a doctor and his daughter held captive by guerrillas somewhere in Afghanistan only to find out they're pawns in an even bigger scheme. **90**m/C VHS, Beta. Conrad Nichols, Richard Raymond, Stephen Elliott, Kinako Harada; **D:** Anthony Richmond. *NO*

Days of Thrills and Laughter ♂♂♂½ **1961** Delightful compilation of clips from the era of silent films, showcasing the talents of the great comics as well as daring stuntman. **93**m/B VHS, Beta. Buster Keaton, Charlie Chaplin, Harold Lloyd, Stan Laurel, Oliver Hardy, Douglas Fairbanks Sr.; **D:** Robert Youngson. *MPI*

Days of Thunder ♂♂ **1990 (PG-13)** "Top Gun" in race cars! Cruise follows the same formula he has followed for several years now (with the notable exception of "Born on the Fourth of July.") Cruise and Towne co-wrote the screenplay concerning a young kid bursting with talent and raw energy who must learn to deal with his mentor, his girlfriend, and eventually the bad guy. First film that featured cameras that were actually on the race cars. If you like Cruise or race cars then this is the movie for you. **108**m/C VHS, Beta, LV, Closed Caption. Tom Cruise, Robert Duvall, Randy Quaid, Nicole Kidman, Cary Elwes, Michael Rooker, Fred Dalton Thompson, John C. Reilly; **D:** Tony Scott; **W:** Tom Cruise, Robert Towne; **M:** Hans Zimmer. Nominations: Academy Awards '90: Best Sound. *PAR*

Days of Wine and Roses ♂♂½ **1958** The original "Playhouse 90" television version of J.P. Miller's story which was adapted for the big screen in 1962. An executive on the fast track and his young wife, initially only social drinkers, find themselves degenerating into alcoholism. A well-acted, stirring drama. **89**m/B VHS, Beta. Cliff Robertson, Piper Laurie; **D:** John Frankenheimer. *RHI, MGM, BTV*

Days of Wine and Roses ♂♂♂½ **1962** A harrowing tale of an alcoholic advertising man who gradually drags his wife down with him into a life of booze. Part of the "A Night at the Movies" series, this tape simulates a 1962 movie evening with a Bugs Bunny cartoon, "Martian Through Georgia," a newsreel, and coming attractions for "Gypsy" and "Rome Adventure." Big screen adaptation of the play originally shown on television. ♫Days of Wine and Roses. **138**m/B VHS, Beta, LV. Jack Lemmon, Lee Remick, Charles Bickford, Jack Klugman, Jack Albertson; **D:** Blake Edwards; **M:** Henry Mancini, Johnny Mercer. Academy Awards '62: Best Song ("Days of Wine and Roses"); Nominations: Academy Awards '62: Best Actor (Lemmon), Best Actress (Remick), Best Art Direction/Set Decoration (B & W), Best Costume Design (B & W). *WAR*

Dayton's Devils ♂♂ **1968** Nielsen is the leader of a motley crew of losers who plan to rob a military base bank in this action-packed heist flick. **107**m/C VHS, Beta. Rory Calhoun, Leslie Nielsen, Lainie Kazan, Eric (Hans Gudegast) Braeden, Georg Stanford Brown; **D:** Jack Shea. *NO*

The Daytrippers ♂♂½ **1996** Happily married Eliza D'Amico is living on Long Island while husband Louis (Tucci) goes to work in Manhattan. That is she's happy until she finds what appears to be a love letter addressed to her husband. Frantic, Eliza runs to aggressive mom Rita (Meara), who decides that her daughter should immediately confront her possibly-erring husband at his office. So Eliza, her mom and dad (McNamara), sarcastic younger sister Jo (Posey), and Jo's pretentious boyfriend Carl (Schreiber) all pile into the family station wagon and head into the city. Only Louis isn't at his office and they scour Manhattan to track him down. **88**m/C VHS. Hope Davis, Anne Meara, Parker Posey, Liev Schreiber, Pat McNamara, Stanley Tucci, Campbell Scott, Marcia Gay Harden, Andy Brown; **D:** Greg Mottola; **W:** Greg Mottola; **C:** John Inwood. *NYR*

Dazed and Confused ♂♂♂ **1993 (R)** A day in the life of a bunch of high schoolers should prove to be a trip back in time for those coming of age in the 70's. Eight seniors facing life after high school have one last year long hurrah, as they search for Aerosmith tickets and haze the incoming freshmen. Keen characterization by writer/director Linklater captures the spirit of a generation shaped by Watergate, the Vietnam War, feminism, and marijuana. Groovy soundtrack features Alice Cooper, Deep Purple, KISS, and Foghat. *CW:* Extremely vulgar language; sex talk and substance abuse. **97**m/C VHS, LV, Closed Caption. Jason London, Rory Cochrane, Sasha Jensen, Wiley Wiggins, Michelle Burke, Adam Goldberg, Anthony Rapp, Marissa Ribisi, Parker Posey, Joey Lauren Adams; **D:** Richard Linklater; **W:** Richard Linklater. *USH*

D.C. Cab ♂♂½ **1984 (R)** A rag-tag group of Washington, D.C. cabbies learn a lesson in self-respect in this endearing comedy. Though not without flaws, it's charming all the same. **100**m/C VHS, Beta, LV, Closed Caption. Mr. T, Leif Erickson, Adam Baldwin, Charlie Barnett, Irene Cara, Anne DeSalvo, Max Gail, Gloria Gifford, Gary Busey, Jill Schoelen, Marsha Warfield; **D:** Joel Schumacher; **W:** Joel Schumacher; **C:** Dean Cundey. *USH*

De Mayerling a Sarajevo 🎬🎬½ *Mayerling to Sarajevo; Sarajevo* 1940 Looks at the romance and marriage, as well as royal pomp and circumstance, of the Countess Sophie (Feuillere) and the Archduke Franz-Ferdinand (Lodge). The assassination of these innocuous rulers at Sarajevo would lead to the outbreak of WWI. French with subtitles. 89m/B VHS. *FR* Edwige Feuillere, John Lodge, Aime Clairmond, Gabrielle Dorziat; *D:* Max Ophuls; *W:* Kurt Alexander; *C:* Curt Courant, Otto Heller; *M:* Oscar Straus. *WBF*

The Dead 🎬🎬🎬½ 1987 (PG) The poignant final film by Huston, based on James Joyce's short story. At a Christmas dinner party in turn-of-the-century Dublin, a man discovers how little he knows about his wife when a song reminds her of a cherished lost love. Beautifully captures the spirit of the story while providing Huston an opportunity to create a last lament on the fickle nature of time and life. 82m/C VHS, Beta, LV, Closed Caption. *GB* Anjelica Huston, Donal McCann, Marie Kean, Donal Donnelly, Dan O'Herlihy, Helen Carroll, Frank Patterson; *D:* John Huston; *C:* Fred Murphy; *M:* Alex North. Independent Spirit Awards '88: Best Director (Huston), Best Supporting Actress (Huston); National Board of Review Awards '87: 10 Best Films of the Year; National Society of Film Critics Awards '87: Best Film; Nominations: Academy Awards '87: Best Adapted Screenplay, Best Costume Design. *LIV, VES, TVC*

Dead Again 🎬🎬🎬½ 1991 (R) Branagh's first film since his brilliant debut as the director/star of "Henry V" again proves him a visionary force on and off camera. As the smart L.A. detective hired to discover the identity of a beautiful, but mute woman, he's realistic, clever, tender and cynical. He finds that he's apparently trapped in a nightmarish cycle of murder begun years before. Literate, lovely to look at, suspenseful, with a sense of humor to match its high style. 107m/C VHS, LV, Closed Caption. Kenneth Branagh, Emma Thompson, Andy Garcia, Lois Hall, Richard Easton, Derek Jacobi, Hanna Schygulla, Campbell Scott, Wayne Knight, Christine Ebersole; *Cameos:* Robin Williams; *D:* Kenneth Branagh; *W:* Scott Frank; *M:* Patrick Doyle. National Board of Review Awards '91: 10 Best Films of the Year. *PAR, CCB*

Dead Ahead 🎬🎬 1996 (PG-13) Skilled archer Maura Loch (Zimbalist) is enjoying a camping trip with her family until four bankrobbers on the lam stumble across them and take Maura's son hostage. Armed with her bow, Maura tracks the criminals to save her child. Made for cable TV.*CW:* Violence, drug use. 92m/C VHS, Closed Caption. Stephanie Zimbalist, Sarah Chalke, Tom Butler, Brendan Fletcher, Peter Onorati, John Tench, Michael Tayles, Douglas Arthurs; *D:* Stuart Cooper; *W:* David Alexander. *PAR*

Dead Ahead: The Exxon Valdez Disaster 🎬🎬🎬 *Disaster at Valdez* 1992 (PG-13) Focuses on the first crucial days after the March 24, 1989 oil spill when the Exxon Valdez ran aground off Alaska in Prince William Sound. Portrays the inadequate precautions, incompetence, greed, and petty bureaucracy that made an appalling situation even worse. Lloyd stars as Exxon official Frank Iarossi, in charge of the actual cleanup, caught between onsite confusion and corporate bungling while Heard is outraged environmentalist Dan Lawn. News and home videotapes of the actual spill are used to enhance the dramatization. Filmed in Vancouver, British Columbia. Made for cable television.*CW:* Strong language used once. 90m/C VHS. Christopher Lloyd, John Heard, Rip Torn, Michael Murphy, Don S. Davies, Ken Walsh, Bob Gunton, Mark Metcalf, Paul Guilfoyle, David Morse, Jackson Davies; *D:* Paul Seed; *W:* Michael Baker; *M:* David Ferguson. *IMP*

Dead Aim woof! 1987 (R) A dud about Soviet spies who introduce even more drugs into New York City, ostensibly to bring about the downfall of the U.S. Obviously a completely farfetched plot. 91m/C VHS, LV. Ed Marinaro, Isaac Hayes, Corbin Bernsen; *D:* William Vanderkloot. *LIV, HHE*

Dead Air 🎬🎬 1994 (PG-13) Atmospheric murder mystery finds radio deejay Hines getting calls from a mystery woman who says she knows him well and has kidnapped his new girlfriend. Meanwhile, a woman claiming to be a reporter wants to interview him and things around the radio station start looking decidedly sinister.*CW:* Violence and views of murder victims. 91m/C VHS, LV, Closed Caption. Gregory Hines, Debrah Farentino, Gloria Reuben, Beau Starr, Laura Harrington, Michael Harris, W. Earl Brown, Veronica Cartwright; *D:* Fred Walton; *W:* David Amann; *M:* Dana Kaproff. *USH*

Dead Alive 🎬🎬 1993 (R) This outrageously over-the-top horror flick from New Zealand is a gore aficionado's delight (think "Evil Dead" movies for comparison). Set in 1957 and satirizing the bland times, the "plot" has the mom of a nerdy son getting bitten by an exotic monkey, which promptly turns her into a particularly nasty ghoul. This condition is apparently contagious (except for her son who tries to hide the fact mom is literally a monster) and calls for lots of spurting blood and body parts which take on lives of their own. For those with strong stomachs and senses of humor.*CW:* Outrageous gore. 97m/C VHS, LV, Closed Caption. *NZ* Timothy Balme, Elizabeth Moody, Diana Penalver, Ian Watkin; *D:* Peter Jackson; *W:* Peter Jackson. *THV, FCT*

Dead and Buried 🎬🎬½ 1981 (R) Farentino is the sheriff who can't understand why the victims of some pretty grisly murders seem to be coming back to life. Eerily suspenseful. 95m/C VHS, Beta. James Farentino, Jack Albertson, Melody Anderson, Lisa Blount, Bill Quinn, Michael Pataki; *D:* Gary Sherman; *W:* Dan O'Bannon. *VES*

Dead as a Doorman 🎬½ 1985 A young writer takes a part-time post as a doorman and becomes the target of a murderous lunatic. 83m/C VHS, Beta. Bradley Whitford, Sharon Schlarth, Bruce Taylor; *D:* Gary Youngman. *LIV, VES*

Dead Badge 🎬🎬½ 1994 (R) An honest cop is reassigned to a corrupt precinct and becomes targeted for death. 95m/C VHS, Closed Caption. Brian Wimmer, Olympia Dukakis, Yaphet Kotto, M. Emmet Walsh, James B. Sikking, Marta DuBois. *CAF*

Dead Bang 🎬🎬½ 1989 (R) A frustrated cop uncovers a murderous white supremacist conspiracy in L.A. Frankenheimer's deft directorial hand shapes a somewhat conventional cop plot into an effective vehicle for Johnson. 102m/C VHS, Beta, LV, 8mm. Don Johnson, Bob Balaban, William Forsythe, Penelope Ann Miller, Tim Reid, Frank Military, Michael Higgins, Michael Jeter, Evans Evans, Tate Donovan; *D:* John Frankenheimer; *W:* Robert Foster; *M:* Gary Chang, Michael Kamen. *WAR*

Dead Beat 🎬🎬½ 1994 (R) Teen love and lust—and murder—all set in Albuquerque, New Mexico, circa 1965. Womanizer Kit (Ramsey) will use any tale to score with his dates—and is happy to pass on tips to adoring disciple Rudy (Getty). When Kit meets up with rebellious rich girl Kirsten (Wagner), she demands proof of his love and he confides he once murdered a girl. Kirsten tries to tighten her stranglehold on Kit with this info and force Rudy from his life but Kit's dark side doesn't stay hidden either.*CW:* Language; sociopathic behavior, including violence and sexuality. 94m/C VHS, Closed Caption. Bruce Ramsay, Natasha Gregson Wagner, Balthazar Getty, Meredith Salenger, Sara Gilbert, Deborah Harry, Max Perlich, Alex Cox; *D:* Adam Dubov; *W:* Adam Dubov. *WEA, LIV*

Dead Boyz Can't Fly 🎬🎬 1993 (R) Disturbing look at urban violence. Dysfunctional punk leads his equally amoral cohorts on a looting spree in a near-empty highrise in revenge against a patronizing businessman. The unrated version contains 10 more minutes of violence. 92m/C VHS. Delia Sheppard, Sheila Kennedy, Ruth Collins, Mark McCulley, Brad Friedman; *D:* Howard Winters. *NO*

Dead Calm 🎬🎬🎬 1989 (R) A taut Australian thriller based on a novel by Charles Williams. A young married couple is yachting on the open seas when they happen upon the lone survivor of a sinking ship. They take him on board only to discover he's a homicidal maniac. Makes for some pretty suspenseful moments that somewhat make up for the weak ending. 97m/C VHS, Beta, LV, 8mm, Closed Caption. *AU* Sam Neill, Billy Zane, Nicole Kidman, Rod Mullinar; *D:* Phillip Noyce; *W:* Terry Hayes; *C:* Dean Semler; *M:* Graeme Revell. *WAR, FCT*

Dead Center 🎬🎬 *Crazy Joe* 1994 (R) Street punk gets trained as assassin by secret government agency that frames him for the murder of a U.S. senator. So now he has to stay alive long enough to prove his innocence. 90m/C VHS, LV, Closed Caption. Justin Lazard, Eb Lottimer, Rachel York; *D:* Steve Carver. *THV*

Dead Certain 🎬 1992 (R) A "Silence of the Lambs" rip-off. Dourif (again specializing in weirdos) is the jailed serial killer providing tantalizing clues to the identity of a new killer on the loose. 93m/C VHS. Brad Dourif, Francesco Quinn, Karen Russell, Joel Kaiser; *D:* Anders Palm; *W:* Anders Palm. *HMD*

Dead Cold 🎬🎬½ 1996 (R) Writer and his wife's second honeymoon at a remote cabin is disturbed by a sinister stranger. But then the writer discovers his wife is not what she seems. Decent thriller is slow to start but picks up speed in the second half.*CW:* Violence, sexuality, and language. 91m/C VHS, LV, Closed Caption. Lysette Anthony, Chris Mulkey, Peter Dobson, Alina Thompson, Michael Champion; *D:* Kurt Anderson; *W:* Richard Brandes. *LIV*

Dead Connection 🎬🎬 1994 (R) Beautiful reporter Bonet is in cahoots with cop Madsen to see justice brought the "phone sex killer" who is terrorizing Los Angeles. 93m/C VHS, Closed Caption. Michael Madsen, Lisa Bonet, Gary Stretch; *D:* Nigel Dick; *W:* Larry Grolin; *M:* Rolfe Kent. *PGV*

The Dead Don't Die 🎬 1975 Unbelievable plot set in the 1930s has Hamilton as a detective trying to prove his brother was wrongly executed for murder. He ultimately clashes with the madman who wants to rule the world with an army of zombies. Perhaps if they had cast Hamilton as Master of the Zombies. Made for television. 74m/C VHS, Beta. George Hamilton, Ray Milland, Linda Cristal, Ralph Meeker, Joan Blondell, James McEachin; *D:* Curtis Harrington. *WOV, GKK*

Dead Easy 🎬🎬 1982 Livin' ain't easy for a Sydney sleaze-club owner, his working-girl girlfriend, and a slandered cop when they're caught between machete-wielding enemy gangs (it seems somebody made the crime boss REALLY mad). The three fine in that quintessential escape vehicle—a two-ton truck—to qualify the effort as an Australian contender for greatest chase scene ever (heavy chassis category). 92m/C VHS, Beta. *AU* Scott Burgess, Rosemary Paul; *D:* Bert Deling. *MCG*

Dead End 🎬🎬🎬½ *Cradle of Crime* 1937 Sidney Kingsley play, adapted for the big screen by Lillian Hellman, traces the lives of various inhabitants of the slums on New York's Lower East Side as they try to overcome their surroundings. Gritty drama saved from melodrama being by some genuinely funny moments. Film launched the Dead End Kids. 92m/B VHS, Beta, LV. Sylvia Sidney, Joel McCrea, Humphrey Bogart, Wendy Barrie, Claire Trevor, Allen Jenkins, Marjorie Main, Leo Gorcey, Charles Halton; *D:* William Wyler; *C:* Gregg Toland. Nominations: Academy Awards '37: Best Cinematography, Best Interior Decoration, Best Picture, Best Supporting Actress (Trevor).*MGM, MLB*

Dead End City 🎬½ 1988 Street-wise resident of L.A. organizes fellow citizens into a vigilante force to fight the gangs for control of the city. 88m/C VHS, Beta. Dennis Cole, Greg Cummins, Christine Lunde, Robert Z'Dar, Darrell Nelson, Alena Downs; *D:* Peter Yuval; *W:* Michael Bogert. *AIP*

Dead End Drive-In 🐾🐾 1986 (R) In a surreal, grim future a man is trapped at a drive-in theater-cum-government-run concentration camp, where those considered to be less than desirable members of society are incarcerated. 92m/C VHS, **Beta, Closed Caption.** *AU* Ned Manning, Natalie McCurry, Peter Whitford; *D:* Brian Trenchard-Smith. *VTR, NWV*

Dead End Street 🐾½ 1983 Young prostitute attempts to change her self-destructive lifestyle. It's not easy. 86m/C VHS, Beta. *IS* Anat Atzman, Yehoram Gaon. *TWE*

Dead Eyes of London 🐾🐾½ *Dark Eyes of London; Die Toten Augen von London* 1961 Blind old German men are dying to lower their premiums in this geriatric thriller: someone (perhaps the director of the home for the blind?) is killing off the clientele for their insurance money, and a Scotland Yard inspector aims to expose the scam. Relatively early vintage Kinski, it's a remake of the eerie 1939 Lugosi vehicle, "The Human Monster" (originally titled "Dark Eyes of London"), adapted from Edgar Wallace's "The Testament of Gordon Stuart." 95m/B VHS. *GE* Joachim Fuchsberger, Karin Baal, Dieter Borsche, Ady Berber, Klaus Kinski, Eddi Arent, Wolfgang Lukschy; *D:* Alfred Vohrer. *SNC*

Dead for a Dollar 🐾½ 197? A Colonel, a con man, and a mysterious woman team up in the Old West to search for the two hundred thousand dollars they stole from a local bank. 92m/C VHS, **Beta.** John Ireland, George Hilton, Piero Vida, Sandra Milo. *UNI, MOV*

Dead Funny 🐾🐾 1994 (R) Vivian (Pena) returns to her Manhattan walk-up to find boyfriend Reggie (McCarthy) dead on her kitchen table, skewered by a Samurai sword. Instead of calling the police, Viv gets gal pal Louise (Turco) to come over to figure out who did Reg in. Instead, they get drunk and discuss Reggie's (who seen in flashbacks) immaturity and penchant for practical jokes. Good performances, twist ending, but situation runs out of steam.*CW:* Language, some sexuality. 91m/C VHS, LV. Elizabeth Pena, Andrew McCarthy, Paige Turco, Blanche Baker, Lisa Jane Persky, Michael Mantell; *D:* John Feldman; *W:* John Feldman; *M:* Sheila Silver. *APX*

Dead Girls 🐾 1990 (R) A rock group whose lyrics focus on suicide goes on vacation. The members find themselves stalked by a serial killer who decides to take matters out of the musicians' hands and into his own. Graphic violence. 105m/C VHS. Diana Karanikas, Angela Eads; *D:* Dennis Devine. *HHE*

Dead Heat 🐾½ 1988 (R) Some acting talent and a few funny moments unfortunately don't add up to a fine film, though they do save it from being a complete woofer. In this one even the cops are zombies when one of them is resurrected from the dead to help his partner solve his murder and rid the city of the rest of the undead. 86m/C VHS, **Beta, LV, Closed Caption.** Joe Piscopo, Treat Williams, Lindsay Frost, Darren McGavin, Vincent Price, Keye Luke, Clare Kirkconnell; *D:* Mark Goldblatt; *W:* Terry Black; *M:* Ernest Troost. *VTR, NWV*

Dead Heat on a Merry-Go-Round 🐾🐾🐾 1966 (R) Coburn turns in a great performance as the ex-con who masterminds the heist of an airport safe. Intricately woven plot provides suspense and surprises. The film is also notable for the debut of Ford in a bit part (he has one line as a hotel messenger). 108m/C VHS, **Beta.** James Coburn, Camilla Sparv, Aldo Ray, Nina Wayne, Robert Webber, Rose Marie, Todd Armstrong, Marian Moses, Severn Darden, Harrison Ford; *D:* Bernard Girard; *C:* Lionel Lindon. *COL*

Dead in the Water 🐾½ 1991 (PG-13) Brown is Charlie Deegan, a big-time lawyer with a rich wife that he'd rather see dead. Charlie and his mistress plot the perfect murder to dispose of his spouse and collect her money. When plans go awry, he ends up as a suspect for the wrong murder in this story of infidelity and greed. 90m/C VHS, **Beta, Closed Caption.** Bryan Brown, Teri Hatcher,

Anne DeSalvo, Veronica Cartwright; *D:* Bill Condon; *W:* Eleanor Gaver, Robert Seidenberg, Walter Klenhard. *USH*

Dead Lucky 🐾½ 1960 A novice tries gambling and wins a fortune, but his luck leads him into an entanglement with an assassin, a scam artist, and a beautiful woman. Based on the novel "Lake of Darkness." 91m/B VHS, Beta. *GB* Vincent Ball, Betty McDowall, John Le Mesurier, Alfred Burke, Michael Ripper; *D:* Montgomery Tully. *FCT, VCO*

Dead Man 🐾🐾 1995 (R) Depp wanders throughs the 19th-century American west as William Blake, an Ohio accountant who runs afoul of the law. Hooking up with a Native American named Nobody (Farmer), who envisions Blake as the famous English poet, the two try to stay one step ahead of the hired guns and lawmen out to get them. Action is sporadic and pace is all over the road in this offbeat and long-winded western, while Farmer's performance and Jarmusch's polished visuals are high points.*CW:* Moments of strong violence, a graphic sex scene and some language. 121m/B VHS, LV, **Closed Caption.** Johnny Depp, Gary Farmer, Lance Henriksen, Michael Wincott, Mili Avital, Crispin Glover, Gabriel Byrne, Iggy Pop, Billy Bob Thornton, Jared Harris, Jimmie Ray Weeks, Mark Bringleson, John Hurt, Alfred Molina, Robert Mitchum; *D:* Jim Jarmusch; *W:* Jim Jarmusch; *C:* Robby Muller; *M:* Neil Young. New York Film Critics Awards '96: Best Cinematography; National Society of Film Critics Awards '96: Best Cinematography; Nominations: Independent Spirit Awards '97: Best Cinematography, Best Film, Best Screenplay, Best Supporting Actor (Farmer). *TOU*

Dead Man on Campus 🐾🐾 1997 Failing college freshman Scott and Gosselaar learn that if your roomie commits suicide, you get a straight-A average for the year. So they decide to find a new roommate who's on the edge and make certain to push him over. Anyone who's ever done time in the dorms has heard this rumor, so it was only a matter of time before someone turned it into a screenplay. The wait wasn't long enough. One-joke premise can't sustain a whole movie, and Gosselaar goes a long way toward duplicating "Saved By the Bell" co-star Elizabeth Berkley's "Showgirls" um, success. ?m/C VHS. Tom Everett Scott, Mark Paul Gosselaar; *D:* Alan Cohn. *NYR*

Dead Man Out 🐾🐾🐾 1989 Both Glover and Blades turn in exceptional performances in this thought-provoking drama. A convict on Death Row (Blades) goes insane and therefore cannot be executed. The state calls in a psychiatrist (Glover) to review the case and determine whether he can be cured so that the sentence can be carried out. Powerful and riveting morality check. 87m/C VHS, Beta, LV. Danny Glover, Ruben Blades, Tom Atkins, Larry Block, Sam Jackson, Maria Ricossa; *D:* Richard Pearce; *M:* Cliff Eidelman. *HBO*

Dead Man Walking 🐾🐾 1988 (R) In a post-holocaust future, half the population has been stricken with a deadly plague. Hauser is a mercenary, dying from the disease, who is hired to rescue a young woman who was kidnapped and is being held in the plague zone. 90m/C VHS. Wings Hauser, Brion James, Pamela Ludwig, Sy Richardson, Leland Crooke, Jeffrey Combs; *D:* Gregory Brown; *W:* R.J. Marx. *REP*

Dead Man Walking 🐾🐾🐾½ 1995 (R) True story of a nun whose anti-death penalty beliefs put her in moral crisis with grieving victims when she becomes the spiritual advisor to a death-row murderer. Based on the book by Sister Helen Prejean, Sarandon stars as the nun who develops a relationship of understanding with inmate Poncelet (Penn), unwavering in her Christian beliefs even though Penn's character shows little or no remorse for the two young lovers he was accused of murdering. Penn offers one of the best performances (but worst hair-dos) of his career, while writer/director Robbins presents both sides of the death-penalty issue mingled with simple human compassion.*CW:* Depiction of a rape and murder. 122m/C VHS, LV, DVD. Susan Sarandon, Sean Penn, Robert Prosky, Raymond J. Barry, R. Lee Er-

mey, Celia Weston, Lois Smith, Scott Wilson, Roberta Maxwell, Margo Martindale, Barton Heyman, Larry Pine; *D:* Tim Robbins; *W:* Tim Robbins; *C:* Roger Deakins; *M:* David Robbins. Academy Awards '95: Best Actress (Sarandon); Independent Spirit Award '95: Best Actor (Penn); Screen Actors Guild Award '95: Best Actress (Sarandon); Nominations: Academy Awards '95: Best Actor (Penn), Best Director (Robbins), Best Song ("Dead Man Walking"); Australian Film Institute '96: Best Foreign Film; Golden Globe Awards '96: Best Actor—Drama (Penn), Best Actress—Drama (Sarandon), Best Screenplay; Independent Spirit Awards '96: Best Supporting Actress (Weston); MTV Movie Awards '96: Best Female Performance (Sarandon); Screen Actors Guild Award '95: Best Actor (Penn). *PGV*

Dead Man's Eyes/Pillow of Death 194? In 1944's "Dead Man's Eyes" artist Chaney is accidentally blinded but may get a second chance through an eye operation. His father-in-law offers his own eyes after he dies—and then he's murdered. In 1945's "Pillow of Death" attorney Chaney is accused of smothering various family members to death. Based on radio's "The Inner Sanctum Mysteries." ?m/C VHS. Lon Chaney Jr., Brenda Joyce, George Cleveland, Clara Blandick, Paul Kelly, Jean Parker, George Meeker. *USH*

Dead Man's Revenge 🐾🐾½ 1993 (PG-13) Ruthless railroad mogul Payton McCay (Dern) doesn't let anyone stand in his way—even if it means framing innocent homesteader Hatcher (Ironside) in order to get his land. Hatcher escapes from jail and goes after McCay, trailed by bounty hunter Bodeen (Couloris). But Bodeen's not what he seems and has his own plans on getting even with the villainous McCay. 92m/C VHS, LV, **Closed Caption.** Bruce Dern, Michael Ironside, Keith Coulouris, Randy Travis; *D:* Alan J. Levi; *W:* Jim Byrnes, David Chisholm. *USH*

Dead Mate 🐾 1988 A woman marries a mortician after a whirlwind romance only to discover that, to her husband, being an undertaker is not just a job, it's a way of life. 93m/C VHS, Beta. Elizabeth Mannino, David Gregory, Lawrence Bockus, Adam Wahl; *D:* Straw Weisman. *PSM*

Dead Men Can't Dance 🐾🐾 1997 (R) A military intelligence group's latest mission is to destroy a North Korean nuclear power plant. 97m/C VHS, LV, **Closed Caption.** Michael Biehn, Adrian Paul, Kathleen York; *D:* Stephen Anderson; *W:* Mark Sevi, Bill Kerby, Paul Sinor; *C:* Levie Isaacks; *M:* Rick Marvin. *LIV*

Dead Men Don't Die 🐾½ 1991 (PG-13) An anchorman is slain by criminals but resurrected as a shambling voodoo zombie. Few viewers notice the difference in this inoffensive but repetitious farce. The living-dead Gould appears to be having a lot of fun. 94m/C VHS. Elliott Gould, Melissa Anderson, Mark Moses, Philip Bruns, Jack Betts, Mabel King; *D:* Malcolm Marmorstein; *W:* Malcolm Marmorstein. *ACA*

Dead Men Don't Wear Plaid 🐾🐾½ 1982 (PG) Martin is hilarious as a private detective who encounters a bizarre assortment of suspects while trying to find out the truth about a scientist's death. Ingeniously interspliced with clips from old Warner Brothers films. Features Humphrey Bogart, Bette Davis, Alan Ladd, Burt Lancaster, Ava Gardner, Barbara Stanwyck, Ray Milland and others. Its only flaw is that the joke loses momentum by the end of the film. 89m/B VHS, Beta, LV. Steve Martin, Rachel Ward, Reni Santoni, George Gaynes, Frank McCarthy, Carl Reiner; *D:* Carl Reiner; *W:* Steve Martin, Carl Reiner; *C:* Michael Chapman; *M:* Miklos Rozsa. *USH, FCT, HMV*

Dead Men Walk 🐾🐾 1943 A decent, albeit low budget, chiller about twin brothers (Zucco in a dual role); one a nice, well-adjusted member of society, the other a vampire who wants to suck his bro's blood. Sibling rivalry with a bite. 65m/B VHS, Beta. George Zucco, Mary Carlisle, Dwight Frye, Nedrick Young, Al "Fuzzy" St. John; *D:* Sam Newfield. *NOS, MRV, SNC*

The Dead Next Door ✗ 1989 Eerily reminiscent of "Night of the Living Dead." A scientist manufactures a virus which inhabits corpses and multiplies while replacing the former cells with its own. But the newly living corpses need human flesh to survive. In response, the government creates "The Zombie Squad" who do heroic battle with the stiffs. When a bizarre cult whose goal is the eradication of the human race befriend the dead, the battle gets ugly. 84m/C VHS. Scott Spiegel, Peter Terry; **W:** J.R. Bookwalter. *TEM, MOV*

Dead of Night ✗✗✗ 1945 The template for episodic horror films, this suspense classic, set in a remote country house, follows the individual nightmares of five houseguests. Redgrave turns in a chillingly convincing performance as a ventriloquist terrorized by a demonic dummy. Not recommended for light-sleepers. Truly spine-tingling. 102m/B VHS, Beta. *GB* Michael Redgrave, Sally Ann Howes, Basil Radford, Naunton Wayne, Mervyn Johns, Roland Culver, Googie Withers, Frederick Valk, Antony Baird, Judy Kelly, Miles Malleson, Ralph Michael, Mary Merrall, Renee Gadd, Michael Allan, Robert Wyndham, Esme Percy, Peggy Bryan, Hartley Power, Elizabeth Welch, Magda Kun, Carry Marsh; **D:** Alberto Cavalcanti, Charles Crichton, Basil Dearden, Robert Hamer; **W:** T.E.B. Clarke, John Baines, Angus MacPhail; **C:** Jack Parker, H. Julius; **M:** Georges Auric. *REP, RXM, CNG*

Dead of Night ✗½ 1977 This trilogy features Richard Matheson's tales of the Supernatural: "Second Chance," "Bobby," and "No Such Thing As a Vampire," all served up by your hostess, Elvira. 76m/C VHS, Beta, LV. Joan Hackett, Ed Begley Jr., Patrick Macnee, Anjanette Comer; **D:** Dan Curtis. *LIV*

Dead of Winter ✗✗✗ 1987 (R) A young actress is suckered into a private screen test for a crippled old director, only to find she is actually being remodeled in the guise of a murdered woman. Edge-of-your-seat suspense as the plot twists. 100m/C VHS, Beta, LV, Closed Caption. Mary Steenburgen, Roddy McDowall, Jan Rubes, Ken Pogue, William Russ; **D:** Arthur Penn; **W:** Mark Shmuger, Mark Malone; **M:** Richard Einhorn. *MGM, FOX*

Dead On ✗½ 1993 (R) Illicit lovers want to get rid of their inconvenient spouses so they can be together always. But their perfect plan doesn't work out as expected. Also available in an unrated version. 87m/C VHS, LV, Closed Caption. Matt McCoy, Shari Shattuck, David Ackroyd, Thomas Wagner; **D:** Ralph Hemecker; **W:** April Wayne. *ORI*

Dead on Sight ✗✗½ 1994 (R) A college student dreams of a masked man, a knife, a bound woman, and other terrors. Too bad her nightmares match the actions of a serial killer. 96m/C VHS, Closed Caption. Jennifer Beals, Daniel Baldwin, Kurtwood Smith, William H. Macy; **D:** Ruben Preuss; **W:** Lewis Green; **M:** Harry Manfredini. *PAR*

Dead on the Money ✗✗½ 1991 Adequate made for TV suspenser about a woman who believes her lover plots a dire fate for her cousin. But nothing is what it seems here. Confusing, droopy in spots, but fun. 92m/C VHS, Beta, Closed Caption. Corbin Bernsen, Amanda Pays, John Glover, Eleanor Parker, Kevin McCarthy; **D:** Mark Cullingham; **W:** Gavin Lambert. *TTC*

Dead or Alive ✗½ 1941 Tex and the Texas Rangers pretend to be outlaws in order to join a gang terrorizing a town. 54m/B VHS, Beta. Tex Ritter, Dave O'Brien, Guy Wilkerson, Charles "Blackie" King, Bud Osborne, Reed Howes; **D:** Elmer Clifton. *GPV, RXM, VCN*

Dead Pigeon on Beethoven Street ✗✗½ 1972 (PG) Sandy (Corbett) is a detective whose partner gets murdered while investigating blackmailers who take compromising pictures of international big-wigs. So Sandy goes undercover and joins the gang. Cheeky paranoia from Fuller. 92m/C VHS. Glenn Corbett, Christa Lang, Anton Diffring, Alexander D'Arcy; **D:** Samuel Fuller; **W:** Samuel Fuller. *FCT*

Dead Pit woof! 1989 (R) Leave this one in the pit it crawled out of. Twenty years ago a mad scientist was killed as a result of horrible experiments he was conducting on mentally ill patients at an asylum. A young woman stumbles across his experiments, awakening him from the dead. 90m/C VHS, Beta. Jeremy Slate, Steffen Gregory Foster; **D:** Brett Leonard. *IMP*

Dead Poets Society ✗✗✗½ 1989 (PG) An idealistic English teacher inspires a group of boys in a 1950s' prep school to pursue individuality and creative endeavor, resulting in clashes with school and parental authorities. Williams shows he can master the serious roles as well as the comic with his portrayal of the unorthodox educator. Big box office hit occasionally scripted with a heavy hand in order to elevate the message. The ensemble cast is excellent. 128m/C VHS, Beta, LV, 8mm. Robin Williams, Ethan Hawke, Robert Sean Leonard, Josh Charles, Gale Hansen, Kurtwood Smith, James Waterson, Dylan Kussman, Lara Flynn Boyle, Melora Hardin; **D:** Peter Weir; **W:** Tom Schulman; **C:** John Seale; **M:** Maurice Jarre. Academy Awards '89: Best Original Screenplay; British Academy Awards '89: Best Film; Cesar Awards '91: Best Foreign Film; Nominations: Academy Awards '89: Best Actor (Williams), Best Director (Weir), Best Picture. *TOU*

The Dead Pool ✗✗½ 1988 (R) Dirty Harry Number Five features a new twist on the sports pool: a list of celebrities is distributed and bets are placed on who will be first to cross the finish line, literally. Unfortunately someone seems to be hedging their bet by offing the celebs themselves. When Harry's name appears on the list, he decides to throw the game. 92m/C VHS, Beta, LV, 8mm, Closed Caption. Clint Eastwood, Liam Neeson, Patricia Clarkson, Evan C. Kim, David Hunt, Michael Currie, Michael Goodwin; **D:** Buddy Van Horn; **M:** Lalo Schifrin. *WAR, TLF*

Dead Presidents ✗✗½ 1995 (R) Sophomore release for the Hughes brothers falls short of impact of "Menace II Society," but not for lack of ambition. Combination coming of age tale, war story, period piece and caper film follows Anthony ("Menace" veteran Tate) from his Bronx neighborhood in 1968 to Vietnam (for "Platoon" adventures in the wilds of Florida) and then back to the 'hood, where his life continues to spiral downward. Desperate to escape, he becomes involved in an armoured car heist to grab some cash (the "dead presidents"). Supported by hard-edged and effective acting, the Hughes continue to develop their control of cinematic imagery, displaying genius for staging violent, confrontational scenes. But the script, based on a story by the brothers, fails to live up to the vision, with characterization and dialogue lagging. Pounding period soundtrack with contributions by Curtis Mayfield, James Brown, and Marvin Gaye keeps things humming.**CW:** Strong graphic violence, language, a sex scene, some drug use. 120m/C VHS, LV, Closed Caption. Larenz Tate, Keith David, Chris Tucker, Freddy Rodriguez, N'Bushe Wright, Bokeem Woodbine, Rose Jackson, Clifton Powell; **D:** Albert Hughes, Allen Hughes; **W:** Michael Henry Brown; **C:** Lisa Rinzler; **M:** Danny Elfman. *TOU*

Dead Reckoning ✗✗✗ 1947 Bogart and Prince are two WWII veterans en route to Washington when Prince disappears. Bogart trails Prince to his Southern hometown and discovers he's been murdered. Blackmail and more murders follow as Bogie tries to uncover the truth. Suspenseful with good performances from all, especially Bogart. 100m/B VHS, Beta, LV, Closed Caption. Humphrey Bogart, Lizabeth Scott, Morris Carnovsky, Charles Cane, Wallace Ford, William Prince, Marvin Miller; **D:** John Cromwell. *CCB, COL*

Dead Reckoning ✗½ 1989 (R) A plastic surgeon and his lovely wife embark on a cruise aboard his new luxury yacht. The intrigue begins with a storm, an isolated island, and the discovery that the captain is the wife's former lover. 95m/C VHS, LV. Cliff Robertson, Susan Blakely, Rick Springfield; **D:** Robert Lewis. *USH*

Dead Right ✗✗½ *If He Hollers, Let Him Go* 1968 A black man is unjustly put into prison in the Deep South. He manages to escape in order to try and prove his innocence. 111m/C VHS, Beta. Raymond St. Jacques, Dana Wynter, Kevin McCarthy, Barbara McNair. *PSM*

Dead Ringers ✗✗✗ 1988 (R) A stunning, unsettling chiller, based loosely on a real case and the bestseller by Bari Wood and Jack Geasland. Irons, in an excellent dual role, is effectively disturbing as the twin gynecologists who descend into madness when they can no longer handle the fame, fortune, drugs, and women in their lives. Acutely upsetting film made all the more so due to its graphic images and basis in fact. 117m/C VHS, Beta, LV, 8mm. **CA** Jeremy Irons, Genevieve Bujold, Heidi von Palleske, Shirley Douglas, Stephen Lack; **D:** David Cronenberg; **W:** Norman Snider, David Cronenberg; **M:** Howard Shore. Genie Awards '89: Best Actor (Irons), Best Director (Cronenberg), Best Film; Los Angeles Film Critics Association Awards '88: Best Director (Cronenberg), Best Supporting Actress (Bujold); New York Film Critics Awards '88: Best Actor (Irons). *CCB, MED, VTR*

Dead Silence 1990 (R) Screenwriter Cliff Morgan has written a classic film noir screenplay... with the money, it seems all Cliff's problems are solved... or are they?**CW:** Language. 92m/C VHS, Closed Caption. Clete Keith, Doris Anne Soyka, Joseph Scott, Craig Fleming; **D:** Harrison Ellenshaw. *NO*

Dead Silence ✗✗½ 1996 (R) Three escaped convicts, including ruthless Ted Handy (Coates), have hijacked a busload of deaf children and their teacher (Matlin) and are holding them hostage in an abandoned slaughterhouse. Veteran FBI negotiator John Cooper (Garner) is called in but he not only has to deal with a tense and possibly tragic situation but with a grandstanding politician (Smith) who's criticizing his every action. Cable movie based on the novel "A Maiden's Grave" by Jeffery Deaver.**CW:** Strong violence and language. 105m/C VHS. James Garner, Kim Coates, Marlee Matlin, Charles Martin Smith, Lolita Davidovich, Kenneth Welsh; **D:** Dan Petrie Jr.; **W:** Donald Stewart; **M:** Jonathan Goldsmith. *HBO*

Dead Sleep ✗✗ 1991 (R) A nurse discovers that comatose patients at a private clinic have been used as guinea pigs by an overzealous doctor. This minor-league chiller from Down Under is said to have been inspired by an actual medical scandal.**CW:** Sensuality. 95m/C VHS. Linda Blair, Tony Bonner; **D:** Alec Mills. *VES*

Dead Solid Perfect ✗✗ 1988 Quaid stars as a golf pro whose life on the PGA tour is handicapped by his taste for scotch and his eye for the ladies. Based on the book by Dan Jenkins. 97m/C VHS, Beta. Randy Quaid, Kathryn Harrold, Jack Warden, Larry Riley, Brett Cullen, Corinne Bohrer; **D:** Bobby Roth; **W:** Dan Jenkins, Bobby Roth. *WAR, BTV*

Dead Space ✗ 1990 (R) Dead space lay between the ears of whoever thought we needed this remake of 1982's "Forbidden World." At a lab on a hostile planet an experimental vaccine mutates into a prickly puppet monster who menaces the medicos. Needed: a vaccine against cheapo "Alien" ripoffs.**CW:** Violence and sensuality. 72m/C VHS, LV. Marc Singer, Laura Tate, Bryan Cranston, Judith Chapman; **D:** Fred Gallo. *COL*

Dead Tides ✗✗ 1997 (R) Former Navy SEAL winds up a patsy while piloting the pleasure craft of a drug dealer's wife. 100m/C VHS, LV. Roddy Piper, Tawny Kitaen, Trevor Goddard, Miles O'Keeffe, Juan Fernandez; **D:** Serge Rodnunsky; **W:** Serge Rodnunsky. *LIV*

Dead to Rights ✗✗½ *Donato and Daughter* 1993 (R) TV movie finds veteran LAPD cop Donato (Bronson) on the trail of a serial killer along with his new partner—who's not only his daughter but his superior officer.**CW:** Some violence. 90m/C VHS. Charles Bronson, Dana Delany, Xander Berkeley, Bonnie Bartlett, Jenette Goldstein, Louis Giambalvo; **D:** Rod Holcomb. *THV*

Dead Weekend ♂♂ 1995 (R) Made for cable sci fier finds Lt. Weed (Baldwin) given the task of finding and destroying a seductively dangerous female alien. Turns out she has the ability to physically change into a number of different women—all of whom attract the willing-and-eager soldier.*CW:* Violence, language, nudity, sexual situations. 82m/C VHS, Closed Caption. Stephen Baldwin, David Rasche, Damian Jones; *D:* Amos Poe; *W:* Joel Rose. *PAR*

Dead Women in Lingerie woof! 1990 (R) When beautiful models are turning up dead, a detective is called in to solve the mystery. Perhaps they committed suicide to avoid being in this picture any longer than necessary. Title sounds like the next episode of "Geraldo." 87m/C VHS. June Lockhart, Lyle Waggoner, John Romo, Jerry Orbach, Maura Tierney; *D:* Erika Fox. *NO*

Dead Wrong ♂½ 1983 Undercover agent falls in love with the drug smuggler she's supposed to bring to justice. 93m/C VHS, Beta, Closed Caption. Britt Ekland, Winston Rekert, Jackson Davies. *MED*

Dead Zone ♂♂♂ 1983 (R) A man gains extraordinary psychic powers following a near-fatal accident. He is forced to decide between seeking absolute seclusion in order to escape his frightening visions, or using his "gift" to save mankind from impending evil. A good adaptation of the Stephen King thriller. 104m/C VHS, Beta, LV, Closed Caption. Christopher Walken, Brooke Adams, Tom Skerritt, Martin Sheen, Herbert Lom, Anthony Zerbe, Colleen Dewhurst; *D:* David Cronenberg; *W:* Jeffrey Boam; *M:* Michael Kamen. *PAR*

Deadbolt ♂♂ 1992 (R) Divorced med student Marty Hiller (Bateman) desperately needs a roommate and Alec Danz (Baldwin) seems perfect. Soon they're sharing more than the rent, until Danz kills her friends and imprisons her in the apartment (equipped of course with soundproof walls and bulletproof glass—one wonders why she doesn't bang on the floor to gain attention.) Predictable and silly would-be thriller attempts to capitalize on the roommate from hell theme that started with "Single White Female," but isn't nearly as effective. Went straight to video and showed up on network TV several months later.*CW:* Strong violence. 95m/C VHS, LV. Justine Bateman, Adam Baldwin, Michelle Scarabelli, Chris Mulkey, Cyndi Pass, Isabelle Truchon; *D:* Douglas Jackson. *NLC*

Deadfall ♂♂½ 1993 (R) Father/son grifters plan an elaborate scam that goes wrong when son Joe (Biehn) inadvertently kills dear old dad (Coburn). When Joe is going through his father's effects he finds out about an unknown twin uncle, who also turns out to be a racketeer. Along with Uncle Lou's mistrustful henchman Eddie (Cage), they plan another con but swindles and vendettas abound. 99m/C VHS, LV, Closed Caption. Michael Biehn, Sarah Trigger, Nicolas Cage, James Coburn, Charlie Sheen, Peter Fonda; *D:* Christopher Coppola; *W:* Christopher Coppola, David Peoples. *THV*

Deadline ♂½ 1981 Journalist must find out the truth behind a minor earthquake in Australia. 94m/C VHS, Beta. Barry Newman, Trisha Noble, Bill Kerr. *WOV*

Deadline ♂♂ 1982 Eerie tale of horror writer's life as it begins to reflect his latest story in this play on the "truth is stranger than fiction" adage. 85m/C VHS, Beta. Stephen Young, Sharon Masters, Cindy Hinds, Phillip Leonard; *D:* Mario Azzopardi. *NO*

Deadline ♂♂ 1987 (R) Walken is a cynical American journalist assigned to cover the warring factions in Beirut. He finds himself becoming more and more involved in the events he's supposed to report when he falls in love with a German nurse who is aiding the rebel forces. Tense, though sometimes murky drama. 110m/C VHS, Beta, LV. *GE* Christopher Walken, Hywel Bennett, Marita Marschall; *D:* Nathaniel Gutman. *VTR*

Deadline Assault ♂½ *Act of Violence* 1990 (R) Kate McSweeny is a beautiful young reporter who is brutally attacked and raped by a gang of savage youths. Kate must now face the unsettling facts; they're still on the streets and they may be stalking her again. 91m/C VHS. Elizabeth Montgomery, James Sloyan, Sean Frye, Biff McGuire, Michael Goodwin, Linden Chiles; *D:* Paul Wendkos. *ELV, HHE*

Deadline at Dawn ♂♂ 1946 Hayward is an aspiring actress who tries to help a sailor (Williams) prove that he is innocent of murder. Based on a novel by Cornell Woolrich. 82m/B VHS, Beta. Bill Williams, Susan Hayward, Lola Lane, Paul Lukas, Joseph Calleia; *D:* Harold Clurman; *W:* Clifford Odets. *MLB, TTC*

Deadline Auto Theft ♂ 1983 A fun lovin' guy drives fast cars and meets beautiful women. Nudge, nudge, wink, wink. 90m/C VHS, Beta. H.B. Halicki, Hoyt Axton, Marion Busia, George Cole, Judi Gibbs, Lang Jeffries Jr.; *D:* H.B. Halicki. *IMP*

Deadlock ♂♂½ 1991 (R) Hauer and Rogers star as inmates in a prison of the future. This prison has no walls, no fences and no guards - and no one EVER escapes. Each prisoner wears an explosive collar that is tuned to the same frequency as one of the other prisoner's. Should the two separate by more than 100 yards, the collars explode. When Rogers convinces Hauer that they are on the same frequency, the two escape. Trouble is, they are being pursued not only by the police, but by Hauer's former partners in crime as well. Can the two find the freedom they are looking for - without losing their heads? Originally made for cable television.*CW:* Language and strong violence. 103m/C VHS, Beta, LV, Closed Caption. Rutger Hauer, Mimi Rogers, Joan Chen, James Remar, Stephen Tobolowsky, Basil Wallace; *D:* Lewis Teague. *VTR, FXV, MED*

Deadlock 2 ♂♂ *Deadlocked: Escape from Zone 14* 1994 (R) Same basic plot as in the first TV movie. Tony Archer (Morales) and Allie Thompson (Peeples), two strangers who have been set up by the same corrupt businessman, are being held in a violent correctional facility. Inmates wear electronic collars programmed to explode if they venture too far apart. But Tony figures a way around this trap only to discover he and Allie are caught in another.*CW:* Strong sexuality, violence and language. 120m/C VHS. Esai Morales, Nia Peeples, Stephen McHattie, Jon Cuthbert; *D:* Graeme Campbell. *HMK*

Deadly Advice ♂♂ 1993 (R) Meek bookseller Jodie (Horrocks) and her sister are constantly humiliated by their overbearing mother (Fricker), who also objects to Jodie's romance with the local doctor (Pryce). As life becomes increasingly unbearable, Jodie discovers a book on infamous killers and is visited by their ghosts, including Jack the Ripper, who is happy to suggest ways to get rid of mom.*CW:* Some sexuality, violence and language. 91m/C VHS. Jane Horrocks, Imelda Staunton, Brenda Fricker, Jonathan Pryce; *D:* Mandie Fletcher. *HMK*

Deadly Alliance ♂ 1978 Two impecunious filmmakers (who happen to be hunks) and a babe (for good measure) poke their noses in where they're not wanted in the shady business of an international oil cartel. "Deadly Dull" would be a more appropriate moniker. 90m/C VHS, Beta. Kathleen Arc, Tony de Fonte, Michele Marsh, Walter Prince; *D:* Paul S. Parco. *NO*

The Deadly and the Beautiful ♂ *Wonder Women* 1973 (PG) Dr. Tsu sends her "deadly but beautiful" task force to kidnap the world's prime male athletes for use in her private business enterprise. 82m/C VHS, Beta. *PH* Nancy Kwan, Ross Hagen, Maria de Aragon, Roberta Collins, Tony Lorea, Sid Haig, Vic Diaz, Shirley Washington, Gale Hansen; *D:* Robert Vincent O'Neil. *MED*

Deadly Bet ♂½ 1991 (R) A made-for-video saga of a kickboxer who loses his money and his girl when he loses the big match. Lots of fight sequences as he works to regain his career.*CW:* Kickboxing violence. 93m/C VHS, LV. Jeff Wincott, Charlene Tilton, Steven Leigh; *D:* Richard W. Munchkin. *PMH*

Deadly Blessing ♂♂ 1981 (R) A young, recently widowed woman is visited in her rural Pennsylvania home by some friends from the city. Something's not quite right about this country life and they become especially suspicious after meeting their friend's very religious in-laws. 104m/C VHS, Beta. Maren Jensen, Susan Buckner, Sharon Stone, Ernest Borgnine, Karen Jensen, Jeff East, Lisa Hartman Black, Lois Nettleton; *D:* Wes Craven; *W:* Wes Craven, Glenn Benest, Matthew F. Barr; *M:* James Horner.

Deadly Breed ♂½ 1989 Beware your friendly neighborhood cop. A band of white supremacists has infiltrated the local police force, intent on causing violence, not keeping the peace. 90m/C VHS. William Smith, Addison Randall, Blake Bahner, Joe Vance; *D:* Charles Kanganis. *PMH*

Deadly Business ♂♂♂ 1986 The true story of a man who turned from crime to become a government informant. As a garbage man, he works to stop the illegal dumping of chemicals in New Jersey. An interesting made-for-televison drama. 100m/C VHS. Alan Arkin, Armand Assante, Michael Learned, Jon Polito, George Morfogen, James Rebhorn; *D:* John Korty. *REP*

Deadly Business ♂½ 19?? Hard-nosed collection man for a lethal loan shark finds he is the one with the debt to pay as he's stalked through the city street by hit men. 95m/C VHS, Beta. David Peterson, John Lazarus, Leo Gabrowski. *ACA*

Deadly Companions ♂♂½ 1961 Keith is an ex-gunslinger who agrees to escort O'Hara through Apache territory in order to make up for inadvertently killing her son. Director Peckinpah's first feature film. 90m/C VHS, Beta, LV. Maureen O'Hara, Brian Keith, Chill Wills, Steve Cochran; *D:* Sam Peckinpah; *C:* William Clothier. *VTR, NWV*

Deadly Conspiracy ♂♂ 1991 (R) Saxon plays a corrupt businessman who kills an employee about to blow the whistle on his shady dealings. Hauser is the good cop, with the bad personal life, who makes it his mission to bring Saxon to justice. The prolific Hauser brings some fast-paced action to this routine story.*CW:* Language, violence, and sexuality. 92m/C VHS, Closed Caption. Wings Hauser, John Saxon, Frances Fisher, Patti D'Arbanville, Margaux Hemingway, Greg Mullavey; *D:* Paul Leder. *MNC*

Deadly Currents ♂♂ 1993 (R) Scott plays a former sea captain who owns a bar on the island of Curacao and enjoys regaling his patrons with his sea-going tales. Petersen is the exiled CIA agent stuck as the security officer of the American consulate. The dangerous pasts of both men catch them up and find them caught in a web of international intrigue. Based on the novel "The Prince of Malta" by James David Buchanan. 93m/C VHS, Closed Caption. George C. Scott, William L. Petersen, Julie Carmen, Alexei Sayle, Trish Van Devere, Philip Anglim, Maria Ellingsen; *D:* Carl Schultz; *W:* James David Buchanan. *COL*

Deadly Dancer ♂♂½ 1990 It's up to a lone cop to find out who's been offing the hoofers in L.A. 88m/C VHS. Adolfo "Shabba Doo" Quinones, Smith Wordes, Walter W. Cox, Steve Jonson; *D:* Kimberly Casey; *W:* David A. Prior. *AIP*

Deadly Daphne's Revenge ♂♂½ 1993 Gory story of rape and revenge from the Troma Team. Hitchhiker Cindy is beaten and raped by Charlie Johnson. When she seeks justice via the local police, Johnson makes plans to have her snuffed out. Meantime, another of his victims escapes from the asylum she's been in and comes looking for him with murder on her mind. 98m/C VHS, LV. *AIP*

Deadly Darling woof! **1985** Muddled, completely awful tale centering on two different rapes with no discernible attempt made to link the two or establish a plot. **91m/C VHS, Beta.** Fonda Lynn, Warren Chan, Bernard Tsui, Cherry Kwok; **D:** Karen Young. *UNI*

Deadly Desire ✗✗ **1991 (R)** Seduced by the beautiful Harrold, security guard Scalia finds himself putting his life on the line when Harrold asks him to help cheat her husband out of millions in an insurance scam. Trouble ensues when they try to outsmart Harrold's powerful entrepreneurial husband.**CW:** Sensuality. **93m/C VHS, Closed Caption.** Jack Scalia, Kathryn Harrold, Will Patton, Joe Santos; **D:** Charles Correll. *PAR, HHE*

Deadly Diamonds ✗½ **1991** Cop is on the trail of diamond smugglers who leave a trail of death in their wake. **90m/C VHS, Beta.** Dan Haggerty, Troy Donahue, Eli Rich, Kathleen Kane, Kenna Grob, Nicholas Mercer; **D:** Thomas Atcheson; **W:** Ron Herbst. *DMP, GNS, HHT*

Deadly Dreams ✗✗ **1988 (R)** A young boy's parents are killed by a maniac who then commits suicide. Years later, he dreams that he is being stalked anew by the same killer. Nightmares turn into reality in this decent horror/suspense flick. **79m/C VHS, Beta, LV.** Mitchell Anderson, Xander Berkeley, Thom Babbes, Juliette Cummins; **D:** Kristine Peterson; **W:** Thom Babbes. *NO*

Deadly Embrace woof! **1988 (R)** Sordid tale of wealthy man (Vincent) who wants to get rid of his wife—permanantly. He enlists the aid of a beautiful young coed. Soft-core sleaze with nary a redeemable quality. **82m/C VHS, Beta.** Jan-Michael Vincent, Jack Carter, Ty Randolph, Linnea Quigley, Michelle (McClellan) Bauer, Ken Abraham; **D:** Ellen Cabot. *PSM*

Deadly Encounter ✗✗✗ **1972** Thrilling actioner in which Hagman portrays a helicopter pilot—a former war ace—who allows an old flame to talk him into helping her escape from the mobsters on her trail. Terrific edge-of-your-seat aerial action. **90m/C VHS, Beta.** Larry Hagman, Susan Anspach, Michael C. Goetz, James Gammon; **D:** William A. Graham. *NO*

Deadly Encounter woof! **1978 (R)** Lacking any redeemable qualities, this film shows just how low some people go. Merrill hosts a dinner to garner financial support for a budding playwright, but what we get is a look at the lifestyles of the rich and perverse. **90m/C VHS, Beta.** Dina Merrill, Carl Betz, Leon Ames, Vicki Powers, Mark Rasmussen, Susan Logan; **D:** R. John Hugh. *CNG*

Deadly Exposure ✗✗ **1993 (R)** Benson stars as a burned-out journalist doing his own investigation of the right-wing extremist group that killed his father. Aspiring reporter Johnson helps out and turns up a conspiracy between the extremists, the government, and a plot to assassinate a U.S. senator. Also available in an unrated version.**CW:** Strong sexuality and violence; brief language. **100m/C VHS, Closed Caption.** Robby Benson, Laura Johnson, Paul Hampton, Andrew Prine, Bentley Mitchum, Isaac Hayes; **D:** Lawrence Mortorff; **W:** Asher Brauner. *AVE*

Deadly Eyes ✗½ *The Rats* **1982 (R)** After eating grain laced with steroids a group of rats grows to mammoth proportions (dachshunds in rat drag were used). Their appetites grow accordingly—now they crave humans. Amid the nibbling by the giant rat-dogs, romance blooms. Silly adaptation of Charles Eglee of Frank Herbert's "The Rats." **93m/C VHS, Beta.** Sam Groom, Sara Botsford, Scatman Crothers, Lisa Langlois, Cec Linder; **D:** Robert Clouse. *WAR*

Deadly Fieldtrip ✗½ **1974** Four female students and their teacher are abducted by a biker gang and held hostage on a deserted farm. **91m/C VHS, Beta.** Zalman King, Brenda Fogarty, Robert Porter; **D:** Earl Barton. *NO*

Deadly Force ✗½ **1983 (R)** Ex-cop turned private detective stalks a killer in Los Angeles who has left an "X" carved in the forehead of each of his 17 victims. If he had just signed his name, things could have been tidied up much earlier. **95m/C VHS, Beta.** Wings Hauser, Joyce Ingalls, Paul Shenar, Al Ruscio, Arlen Dean Snyder, Lincoln Kilpatrick; **D:** Paul Aaron; **W:** Robert Vincent O'Neil, Barry Schneider. *NLC*

Deadly Friend ✗✗ **1986 (R)** A well-meaning horror flick? That's what Wes Craven has tried to provide for us. When the girlfriend of a lonely teenage genius is accidentally killed, he decides to insert his robot's "brain" in her body, though the results aren't entirely successful. The same can be said for the film which was based on Diana Henstell's more effective novel "Friend." **91m/C VHS, Beta, LV, Closed Caption.** Matthew Laborteaux, Kristy Swanson, Michael Sharrett, Anne Twomey, Richard Marcus, Anne Ramsey; **D:** Wes Craven; **W:** Bruce Joel Rubin; **M:** Charles Bernstein. *WAR*

Deadly Game ✗✗ **1982 (R)** A reunion at a remote hotel leads to an ordeal of psychological terror and murderous intrigue. **CW:** Strong action violence. **108m/C VHS, Beta.** George Segal, Robert Morley, Trevor Howard, Emlyn Williams, Alan Webb; **D:** George Schaefer.

Deadly Game ✗½ **1983** Much-maligned and preyed-upon witness is protected by a weary cop, who speaks with the use of English subtitles. **90m/C VHS, Beta.** **GE** Mel Ferrer, Helmut Berger, Barbara Sukowa; **D:** Karoly Makk, Dieter Geissler. *VCD, GLV*

The Deadly Game ✗✗ **198?** East-West intrigue prior to the fall of the Berlin Wall finds a Western operative returning from a dangerous mission, only to walk into a trap set by his own side. **104m/C VHS.** **GB** David Hemmings. *FCT*

Deadly Game ✗½ **1991 (R)** Horribly burned, a vengeful millionaire invites seven people he believes have wronged him to spend the weekend on his isolated island. He has promised them each a reward for their good deeds, but instead plans to have a big-game hunt with his "guests" as the prey. **93m/C VHS, Beta, Closed Caption.** Roddy McDowall, Jenny Seagrove, Marc Singer, Michael Beck; **D:** Tom Wright; **W:** Wes Claridge. *PAR*

Deadly Games ✗✗ **1980** Ineffective plot involving a series of murders in a small town is seemingly played out by the principal characters in a horror board game. Film is saved from being a complete waste by Groom's good performance as the local cop. **94m/C VHS, Beta.** Sam Groom, Jo Ann Harris, Steve Railsback, Dick Butkus, June Lockhart, Colleen Camp; **D:** Scott Mansfield. *MON*

Deadly Harvest ✗ **1972 (PG)** Scientists' worst fears have been realized—due to ecological abuse and over-development of the land, food has become extremely scarce. This in turn has caused people to become a bit savage. They are particularly nasty to a farmer and his family. Not a bad plot, but a poorly acted film. **86m/C VHS, Beta.** Clint Walker, Nehemiah Persoff, Kim Cattrall, David G. Brown, Gary Davies; **D:** Timothy Bond. *VTR, NWV*

Deadly Hero ✗✗✗ **1975 (R)** Gripping tale of a young woman who becomes the prey of a New York City cop after questioning the brutal methods he employed while saving her from being assaulted, ultimately killing her attacker. Williams makes film debut in this chilling suspenser. **102m/C VHS, Beta.** Don Murray, James Earl Jones, Diahn Williams, Lilia Skala, Conchata Ferrell, George S. Irving, Treat Williams, Josh Mostel; **D:** Ivan Nagy; **C:** Andrzej Bartkowiak; **M:** Brad Fiedel. *NO*

Deadly Heroes ✗✗ **1996 (R)** Terrorists highjack an American plane at Athens International Airport with the demand that their leader, Carlos (Drago), who's jailed in Miami, be delivered to them. CIA agent and ex-Navy SEAL, Captain Cody Grant (Vincent), is forced to take Carlos to Athens but having captured Carlos once, Grant is determined that the terrorist and his associates won't be free for long. **104m/C VHS, Closed Caption.** Jan-Michael Vincent, Billy Drago, Michael Pare, Claudette Mink; **D:** Menahem Golan; **W:** Damian Lee, Gregory Lee. *COL*

Deadly Illusion ✗✗ *Love You to Death* **1987 (R)** Williams is a private detective who manages to get himself tangled in a complex web of intrigue and winds up framed for murder. Decent outing for all. **95m/C VHS, Beta, LV, Closed Caption.** Billy Dee Williams, Morgan Fairchild, Vanity, John Beck, Joe Cortese; **D:** William Tannen, Larry Cohen; **W:** Larry Cohen; **M:** Patrick Gleeson. *COL*

Deadly Impact ✗½ **1984** Las Vegas casinos are targeted for rip-off by means of a computer. Svenson and Williamson give good performances, but that's not enough to save this one. **90m/C VHS, Beta.** **IT** Bo Svenson, Fred Williamson, Marcia Clingan, John Morghen, Vincent Conti; **D:** Larry Ludman. *LIV, VES*

Deadly Innocence ✗½ **1988 (R)** A shy, lonely girl works at an isolated gas station. After her father's death, she takes in a boarder—a mysterious woman being chased by her past. **90m/C VHS.** Mary Crosby, Andrew Stevens, Amanda Wyss; **D:** John D. Patterson, Hugh Parks. *NO*

Deadly Intent ✗½ **1988** The widow of a murdered archeologist becomes the target of fortune hunters when they try to get their hands on the priceless jewel her husband brought back from a dig. **83m/C VHS.** Lisa Eilbacher, Steve Railsback, Maud Adams, Lance Henriksen, Fred Williamson, Persis Khambatta; **D:** Nigel Dick. *FRH*

Deadly Intruder ✗½ **1984** Quiet vacation spot is being terrorized by an escapee from a mental institution. So much for a little R and R. **86m/C VHS, Beta.** Chris Holder, Molly Creek. *NO*

Deadly Lessons ✗✗ **1994** Misfit Ann gets shunned by the college "in" crowd but then a childhood friend comes to her aid and decides to take revenge on the nasty students. **90m/C VHS.** Andrea Gall, Mat McGinnis, Dana Wise; **D:** Leslie Delano. *SWI*

The Deadly Mantis ✗½ *The Incredible Praying Mantis* **1957** A gigantic praying mantis lies in a million-year-old sleep in the frozen reaches of the Arctic. Then a volcanic eruption releases the critter and the flying beastie does it's destructive best on Washington, DC and New York City until the military can gas it into oblivion. Typically silly fifties sci-fi with decent special effects. **79m/B VHS, Closed Caption.** Craig Stevens, William Hopper, Alix Talton, Pat Conway, Donald Randolph; **D:** Nathan (Hertz) Juran; **W:** Martin Berkeley. *USH*

Deadly Mission ✗½ **1978 (R)** Five soldiers in WWII France are convicted of crimes against the Army, only to escape from lock-up and become focal points in a decisive battle. **99m/C VHS, Beta.** Bo Svenson, Peter Hooten, Fred Williamson. *LIV*

Deadly Neighbor ✗✗ **1991** New neighbor moves in, dead neighborhood housewives move out. Another neighbor becomes suspicious and investigates. **90m/C VHS.** Don Leifert, George Stover, Lydia Laurans; **D:** Donald M. Dohler. *VCI*

Deadly Obsession ✗½ **1988 (R)** A disfigured lunatic stalks a young co-ed hoping to extort $1 million from the wealthy dean of the school. **93m/C VHS.** Jeffrey R. Iorio; **D:** Jeno Hodl; **W:** Brian Cox. *REP, FCT*

Deadly Outbreak ✗✗ **1996 (R)** A chemical weapons facility is taken over by a renegade colonel who threatens to unleash a deadly plague. Now it's up to one man (Speakman) to free the hostage scientist who knows the formula for the antidote.**CW:** Non-stop violence, language. **94m/C VHS, LV, Closed Caption.** Jeff Speakman, Ron Silver, Rochelle Swanson; **D:** Rick Avery. *LIV*

Deadly Passion ✗½ **1985 (R)** A James Cain-like thriller about a private eye getting carnally involved with a beautiful and treacherous woman who is manipulating her late husband's estate through murder and double-crossing. **100m/C VHS, Beta.** **SA** Brent Huff, Ingrid Boulting, Harrison Coburn, Lynn Maree; **D:** Larry Larson. *LIV*

Deadly Past ⚔️½ 1995 (R) Predictable story finds dumb ex-con bartender (Marquette) making the mistake of getting involved with a femme fatale (Alt) from his past. Also available in an unrated version.*CW:* Some strong sexuality; some violence and language. **90m/C VHS.** Ron Marquette, Carol Alt, Dedee Pfeiffer, Mark Dacascos. *AVE*

Deadly Possession ⚔️⚔️ 1988 A college student plays amateur detective when she tries to clear her ex-husband's name after he's accused of the horrible murder of a fellow student. **99m/C VHS, Beta, LV.** *AU* Penny Cook, Anna-Maria Winchester, Liddy Clark, Olivia Hamnett; **D:** Craig Lahiff. *LIV, VES*

Deadly Prey woof! 1987 (R) Prior is up against a fully outfitted army of bloodthirsty mercenaries who are using innocent people as "live targets" at their secret bootcamp. Plot lifted from "The Most Dangerous Game" has more than its share of gruesome violence. **87m/C VHS, Beta.** Cameron Mitchell, Troy Donahue, Ted Prior, Fritz Matthews; **D:** David A. Prior; **W:** David A. Prior. *NO*

Deadly Reactor ⚔️⚔️ 1989 Into a post-nuclear future a lone preacher turns into an armed vigilante to protect the people of a town being terrorized by a vicious motorcycle gang. **88m/C VHS, Beta.** David Heavener, Stuart Whitman, Darwyn Swalve, Allyson Davis; **D:** David Heavener. *AIP*

Deadly Recruits ⚔️½ 1986 The Russians did it! The Russians did it! Stamp is convinced that the downfall of several top students at Oxford, amid scandal and rumor, is due to a KGB conspiracy. **92m/C VHS, Beta.** *GB* Terence Stamp, Michael Culver, Carmen Du Sautoy, Robin Sachs; **D:** Roger Tucker. *NO*

Deadly Revenge ⚔️ 1983 (R) Action-adventure pic with not much adventure and even less action. Small-town reporter finds himself up against a mob boss when he takes over the nightclub business of a friend killed by the mobsters. Dubbed. **90m/C VHS, Beta.** *IT* Rodolfo Ranni, Julio de Grazia, Silvia Montanari, Fred Commoner; **D:** Juan Carlos Sesanzo. *UNI*

Deadly Rivals ⚔️⚔️ 1992 (R) Stevens plays a laser specialist in Miami for a top-secret weapons conference. A beauty takes an interest in him but then she's first accused of being a spy and then mistaken for a courier in the pay of a ruthless crime boss. Can Stevens find the truth?*CW:* Language, violence, and sexuality. **93m/C VHS, LV, Closed Caption.** Andrew Stevens, Cela Wise, Joseph Bologna, Margaux Hemingway, Richard Roundtree, Francesco Quinn, Randi Ingerman; **D:** James Dodson; **W:** Redge Mahaffey; **M:** Ashley Irwin. *USH*

Deadly Sanctuary woof! 1968 Censors stopped production of this film several times. The Marquis de Sade's writings provided the inspiration (though there's nothing inspired about it) for this tale of two recently orphaned young women who get caught up in prostitution, an S&M club, and murder. **92m/C VHS, Beta.** Jack Palance, Mercedes McCambridge, Sylva Koscina, Klaus Kinski, Akim Tamiroff, Romina Power; **D:** Jess (Jesus) Franco. *NO*

The Deadly Secret ⚔️⚔️ 1994 Randall Parks is a successful real estate agent with a past he has managed to hide for twenty years. When he is blackmailed, he decides to take matters into his own hands and track down his accusers. **98m/C VHS, Beta.** Joe Estevez, Tracy Spaulding, Reggie Cale, Douglas Stalgren; **D:** Jason Hammond; **W:** Douglas Stalgren; **M:** Erik Hansen. *AIP*

Deadly Sins ⚔️⚔️½ 1995 (R) Deputy sheriff Jack Gates (Keith) hooks up with P.I. Christina Herrera (Milano) to investigate a murder in a Catholic girls school. Christina poses as a student and uncovers sinister secrets.*CW:* Strong sexuality; violence; language. **98m/C VHS.** David Keith, Alyssa Milano, Terry David Mulligan, Corrie Clark; **D:** Michael Robison; **W:** John Langley, Malcolm Barbour. *AVE*

Deadly Spygames 1989 A special agent for the United States Special Operations Bureau finds himself in deep trouble. **?m/C VHS.** Troy Donahue, Tippi Hedren; **D:** Jack M. Sell; **W:** Jack M. Sell. *UNI*

Deadly Sting ⚔️½ 1982 Silva devises an intricate scheme to gain revenge on the men who cheated him out of his share of a gold bullion heist. **90m/C VHS, Beta.** *FR* Henry Silva, Philip Clay, Andre Pousse; **D:** Jean-Claude Roy. *NO*

Deadly Stranger ⚔️ *Border Heat* 1988 Fluegel's talents could have been put to much better use than as the selfish mistress of a plantation owner who is taking advantage of the migrant workers toiling on his land. Moore is a drifter and hired hand who rallies the workers to stand up to the owner. **93m/C VHS.** Darlanne Fluegel, Michael J. Moore, John Vernon, Ted White; **D:** Max Kleven. *MCG*

Deadly Strangers ⚔️⚔️ 1982 Two people meet up on the road and decide to share a ride. We discover that one of them is an insane killer who's escaped from a mental institution. Suspense builds nicely, but the ending is flawed. **89m/C VHS, Beta.** *GB* Hayley Mills, Simon Ward, Sterling Hayden, Ken Hutchison; **D:** Sidney Hayers. *NO*

Deadly Sunday ⚔️½ 1982 A family's weekly Sunday drive turns terrifying when desperate jewel thieves detour them and hold them hostage. **85m/C VHS, Beta.** Dennis Ely, Henry Sanders, Gylian Roland, Douglas Alexander; **D:** Donald M. Jones. *LIV*

Deadly Surveillance ⚔️⚔️ 1991 (R) Two tough policemen investigate a series of drug-related murders and stake out a possible suspect—a beautiful woman who's the lover of one of the lawmen. Tension in this Canadian-made cop opera evaporates in the third act for a standard buddy-buddy action finale. Made for television.*CW:* Language, violence, and sensuality. **92m/C VHS, Closed Caption.** Michael Ironside, Christopher Bondy, Susan Almgren, Vlasta Vrana, David Carradine; **D:** Paul Ziller. *REP*

Deadly Target ⚔️½ 1994 (R) Detective Charles Prince (Daniels) is sent to L.A. to return a notorious Chinese gangster to Hong Kong for trial. But Prince finds out his would-be prisoner's escaped and soon he's involved in martial arts mayhem. **90m/C VHS.** Gary Daniels, Kenneth McLeod, Max Gail, Susan Byun. *PMH*

Deadly Thief ⚔️⚔️ *Shalimar* 1978 A former jewel thief comes out of retirement to challenge those who are now tops in the profession to try and steal the world's most precious ruby from him. Of course all they have to lose is their lives. What could have been an exciting adventure is made curiously boring. **90m/C VHS, Beta.** *IN* Rex Harrison, John Saxon, Sylvia Miles, Dharmendra, Zenat Aman, Shammi Kapoor; **D:** Krishna Shah. *PSM*

The Deadly Trackers ⚔️ 1973 (PG) If gorey oaters are your thing, this one's definitely for you; if not, make tracks. Harris plays a spiteful sheriff who heads south of the border to get his pound of flesh from the outlaws who slew his family in a bank robbery. Overlong revenge-o-rama based on Samuel Fuller's short story, "Riata"; might have been bearable if Fuller hadn't been bumped from the director's chair (as it is, he and other contributors refused to be listed in the credits). **104m/C VHS, LV, Closed Caption.** Richard Harris, Rod Taylor, Al Lettieri, Neville Brand, William Smith, Paul Benjamin, Pedro Armendariz Jr.; **D:** Barry Shear. *WAR, FCT*

The Deadly Trap ⚔️ *Death Scream* 1971 (PG) Confusing thriller that couldn't. Dunaway is the mentally unstable wife of an ex-spy. His former employers have targeted him with plans to use her and her fragile state-of-mind to their advantage. **96m/C VHS.** *FR IT* Faye Dunaway, Frank Langella, Barbara Parkins, Maurice Ronet; **D:** Rene Clement. *FCT*

Deadly Twins woof! 1985 After being beaten and gang-raped, twin sister singers are out to get revenge. Nothing new here; don't waste your time. **87m/C VHS, Beta.** Audrey Landers, Judy Landers, Ellie Russell, Wayne Allison; **D:** Joe Oaks. *PSM*

Deadly Vengeance ⚔️ 1981 It's strictly low budget as the mob kills Jones's boyfriend, forcing her to mount a vengeful but inexpensive offensive against the crime syndicate's bigwigs. **84m/C VHS, Beta.** Grace Jones, Alan Marlowe, Arthur Roberts. *NO*

Deadly Voyage ⚔️⚔️½ 1996 (R) In 1992, nine Ghanaian dockworkers are discovered hiding aboard a Ukrainian freighter bound for New York. Since each stowaway would cost the shipping company a hefty fine, sadistic first officer Ion (Pertwee) orders them killed. Only one, Kingsley (Epps), manages to survive and reveal the truth. Made for cable.*CW:* Graphic violence, strong language and some nudity. **92m/C VHS.** Omar Epps, Sean Pertwee, Joss Ackland, David Suchet, Jean LaMarre, Andrew Divoff; **D:** John MacKenzie; **C:** Stuart Urban; **M:** John Scott. *HBO*

Deadly Weapon ⚔️ 1988 (PG-13) It's a bit of nerdish wish fulfillment when 15-year-old geek Eastman finds a secret anti-matter weapon conveniently lost by the military in an Arizona stream. You won't like the kid any more than you'll like the story of this low rent boy-gets-back-at-bullies sci fi fiasco. **89m/C VHS.** Rodney Eastman, Gary Frank, Michael Horse, Ed Nelson, Kim Walker; **D:** Michael Miner; **W:** Michael Miner; **C:** James L. Carter. *TWE, HHE*

Deadly Weapons ⚔️ 1970 (R) Chesty Morgan, she of the 73-inch bustline, takes on the mob using only her God-given abilities. One of Joe Bob Brigg's "Sleaziest Movies in the History of the World" series, and he is welcome to it. **90m/C VHS.** Chesty Morgan, Harry Reems; **D:** Doris Wishman. *NO*

Deadman's Curve ⚔️⚔️ 1978 Decent bio pic detailing the lives of Jan Berry and Dean Torrence who, as Jan and Dean, started the surf music wave only to wipe out after an almost-fatal car wreck. Shows how they deal with and recover from the tragedy. Made for television. **100m/C VHS.** Richard Hatch, Bruce Davison, Pamela Bellwood, Susan Sullivan, Dick Clark, Wolfman Jack; **D:** Richard Compton. *GEM*

Deadtime Stories ⚔️½ 1986 Mother Goose it's not. Fairy tales "Little Red Riding Hood" and "Goldilocks and the Three Bears," among others, are presented like you've never before seen them—as low-budget horror tales. **93m/C VHS, Beta, LV.** Michael Mesmer, Brian DePersia, Scott Valentine, Phyllis Craig, Melissa Leo, Nicole Picard; **D:** Jeffrey Delman. *NO*

Deadwood ⚔️½ 1965 In the untamed West, a young cowboy is mistaken for the notorious Billy the Kid. **100m/C VHS, Beta.** Arch Hall Jr., Jack Lester, Melissa Morgan, Robert Dix; **D:** James Landis; **C:** Vilmos Zsigmond. *RHI, FCT*

Deadwood Pass ⚔️ 1933 Below-standard fare has Tyler rescuing Monti more times than seems reasonable. Monti was once an all-around helper to W.C. Fields. **62m/B VHS.** Tom Tyler, Alice Dahl, Wally Wales, Buffalo Bill Jr., Lafe McKee, Bud Osborne, Charles "Slim" Whitaker, Charlotte (Carlotta) Monti; **D:** J.P. McGowan. *DVT, HEG, GPV*

Deal of the Century ⚔️⚔️ 1983 (PG) A first-rate hustler and his cohorts sell second-rate weapons to third-world nations; unfortunately, their latest deal threatens to blow up in their faces—literally. **99m/C VHS, Beta, LV.** Chevy Chase, Sigourney Weaver, Gregory Hines, Richard Libertini, Wallace Shawn; **D:** William Friedkin; **W:** Paul Brickman. *WAR*

Dealers ⚔️½ 1989 (R) Two money-hungry stock traders mix business and pleasure, then set their sights on one final all or nothing score. **92m/C VHS, Beta, LV.** *GB* Rebecca DeMornay, Paul McGann, Derrick O'Connor; **D:** Colin Bucksey. *ACA, IME*

Dear America: Letters Home from Vietnam ⚔️⚔️½ 1988 (PG) Acclaimed documentary featuring pictures and film of the war with voice-overs by dozens of Hollywood stars reading the words of American GIs. Initially made for cable television. **84m/C VHS, Beta, Closed Caption.** **D:** Bill Couturie; **W:** Bill Couturie; **M:** Todd Boekelheide. *HBO, AMB*

Dear Boys 🎞🎞 1980 A stylized film of sexual fantasies and romance between a moody writer and a carefree young man who relentlessly pursues excitement. Based on the novel by Gerald Reve. 90m/C VHS. *NL* Hugo Netsers, Hans Dagelet, Bill Van Dijk, Albert Mol; *D:* Paul de Lussanet. *FCT*

Dear Brigitte 🎞🎞 1965 A young American kid ("Lost in Space" tyke Mumy) writes a love letter to Brigitte Bardot and travels to Paris to meet her in person. Based on the novel "Erasmus with Freckles" by John Haase. 100m/C VHS, Beta, **Closed Caption.** James Stewart, Billy Mumy, Glynis Johns, Fabian, Cindy Carol, John Williams, Jack Kruschen, Brigitte Bardot, Ed Wynn, Alice Pearce; *D:* Henry Koster; *W:* Hal Kanter. *FOX*

Dear Dead Delilah 🎞½ 1972 Moorehead is Delilah, the matriarch of a southern family, who is on her deathbed. Her heirs are fighting to the bitter—and bloody—end to be the first to find Delilah's money, buried somewhere on her land. 90m/C VHS, Beta. Agnes Moorehead, Will Geer, Michael Ansara, Patricia Carmichael, Dennis Patrick; *D:* John Farris.

Dear Detective 🎞🎞 *Dear Inspector; Tendre Poulet* 1977 Comedy/thriller/romance finds female police inspector (Girardot) investigating a murder while romancing a somewhat pompous professor of Greek (Noiret). French with subtitles. 105m/C VHS. *FR* Annie Girardot, Philippe Noiret, Catherine Alric, Guy Marchand, Simone Renant; *D:* Philippe de Broca; *W:* Philippe de Broca, Michel Audiard; *M:* Georges Delerue. *FRA*

Dear Detective 🎞🎞 1978 Vaccaro is the head of the police homicide unit who is trying to track down the killer of several politicians. In the midst of her investigation, she falls for an old friend, a professor of Greek language. Made for television and based on a French television series. 90m/C VHS. Brenda Vaccaro, Arlen Dean Snyder, Michael MacRae, John Dennis Johnston, Jack Ging, Stephen McNally, M. Emmet Walsh, Constance Forslund, R.G. Armstrong; *D:* Dean Hargrove; *M:* Georges Delerue. *FCT*

Dear God 🎞 1996 (PG) TV vets Marshall (director) and Kinnear team up for a sappy and predictable "Miracle on Melrose," a little piece of Capra-corn that feels like it lodged in your tooth. Cynical con man Tom (Kinnear) goes to work for the post office and gets stuck with a group of misfits at the Dead Letter Office, sorting mail for the likes of Elvis, Santa, and God. Even though he's merely working the ultimate angle for easy cash, the oddball team of postal workers think he's on a mission from the Lord and joins him in aiding the needy. Most unbelievable is the premise that single mom and love interest Gloria (Pitillo) can give the hardened criminal an instant psychological makeover. Broadly characterized supporting cast, including Conway and Metcalf, suffer at the hands of script. Strictly a star vehicle for Kinnear's budding movie career, it won't help. It also won't do anything for Marshall's downward-spiraling reputation. Ironic cameo from Christopher Darden as a reporter outside the courtroom, and Marshall himself as Postmaster General. 112m/C VHS, Beta, **Closed Caption.** Greg Kinnear, Laurie Metcalf, Maria Pitillo, Hector Elizondo, Tim Conway, Roscoe Lee Browne, Jon Seda, Anna Maria Horsford, Donal Logue, Nancy Marchand, Larry Miller, Rue McClanahan, Toby Huss, Jack Klugman; *Cameos:* Garry Marshall; *D:* Garry Marshall; *W:* Ed Kaplan, Warren Leight; *C:* Charles Minsky. *PAR*

Dear Murderer 🎞🎞 1947 A husband suspects his wife of having an affair, and devises an ingenious, if complicated, trap for her both. Inspired performances from the leads, but the plot is grim and confusing. 94m/B VHS, Beta. *GB* Eric Portman, Greta Gynt, Dennis Price, Jack Warner, Maxwell Reed, Hazel Court, Andrew Crawford, Jane Hylton; *D:* Arthur Crabtree. *SNC*

Dear Wife 🎞🎞½ 1949 Comedy about those ties that bind. Even though her father is runnning for reelection to the State Senate, Freeman wants her brother-in-law (Holden) to run against him. Sequel to "Dear Ruth." 88m/B VHS, Beta. William Hol-

den, Joan Caulfield, Edward Arnold, Billy DeWolfe, Mona Freeman; *D:* Richard Haydn. *BAR*

Death and the Maiden 🎞🎞🎞 1994 (R) Former political prisoner and torture victim (Weaver) turns the tables on the man she believes was her tormentor 15 years before. Pressing her civil rights lawyer husband (Wilson) into duty as defense attorney, she becomes prosecutor, judge, and jury. The accused (Kingsley) learns the dangers of picking up stranded motorists, as he is bound, gagged, and roughed up by the now empowered and vengeful Paulina. Tense, claustrophobic political thriller features a talented ensemble both on screen and behind the scenes. From the Ariel Dorfman play.*CW:* Contains strong language, violence, and graphic descriptions of rape and torture. 103m/C VHS, LV, **Closed Caption.** Sigourney Weaver, Ben Kingsley, Stuart Wilson; *D:* Roman Polanski; *W:* Rafael Yglesias, Ariel Dorfman; *C:* Tonino Delli Colli; *M:* Wojciech Kilar. Nominations: Independent Spirit Awards '95: Best Director (Polanski). *TTC, NLC, IME*

The Death Artist 🎞½ 1995 (R) Struggling artist finds fame creating sculptures from dead bodies. Gruesome plot is a remake of Corman's 1960 "A Bucket of Blood" but the same premise was done much better with Vincent Price in 1953's "House of Wax." 79m/C VHS. Anthony Michael Hall, Darcy Demoss, Shadoe Stevens, Paul Bartel, Mink Stole; *D:* Michael James McDonald. *NHO*

Death at Love House 🎞½ 1975 A screen writer becomes obsessed when he is hired to write the life story of a long dead silent movie queen. Filmed at the Harold Lloyd estate. Made for television. 74m/C VHS, Beta. Robert Wagner, Kate Jackson, Sylvia Sidney, Joan Blondell, John Carradine; *D:* E.W. Swackhamer. *PSM*

Death Be Not Proud 🎞🎞🎞 1975 Based on the book by John Gunther detailing the valiant battle fought by his son against the brain tumor that took his life at the age of 17. Wonderfully acted by the three principals, especially Alexander, this film leaves us feeling hopeful despite its subject. Made for television. 74m/C VHS, Beta. Arthur Hill, Robby Benson, Jane Alexander, Linden Chiles, Wendy Phillips; *D:* Donald Wrye. *LCA*

Death Becomes Her 🎞🎞🎞 1992 (PG-13) Aging actress Streep will do anything to stay young and beautiful, especially when childhood rival Hawn shows up, 200 pounds lighter and out to revenge the loss of her fiance, Streep's henpecked hubby. Doing anything arrives in the form of a potion that stops the aging process (and keeps her alive forever). Watch for the hilarious party filled with dead celebrities who all look as good as the day they died. Great special effects and fun performances by Streep and Hawn playing their glamour-girl roles to the hilt add merit to this biting commentary on Hollywood's obsession with beauty and youth. 105m/C VHS, Beta, LV, **Closed Caption.** Meryl Streep, Bruce Willis, Goldie Hawn, Isabella Rossellini, Sydney Pollack, Michael Caine, Ian Ogilvy, Adam Storke, Nancy Fish, Alaina Reed Hall, Michelle Johnson, Mimi Kennedy, Jonathan Silverman; *Cameos:* Fabio Lanzoni; *D:* Robert Zemeckis; *W:* Martin Donovan, David Koepp; *C:* Dean Cundey; *M:* Alan Silvestri. Academy Awards '92: Best Visual Effects. *MGM, PMS*

Death Before Dishonor 🎞½ 1987 (R) Formula actioner stars Dryer as a tough Marine sergeant who battles ruthless Middle Eastern terrorists after they slaughter his men and kidnap his commanding officer (Keith). 95m/C VHS, Beta, LV, **Closed Caption.** Fred Dryer, Brian Keith, Joanna Pacula, Paul Winfield; *D:* Terry J. Leonard; *C:* Don Burgess. *NWV, VTR*

Death Benefit 🎞🎞½ 1996 (PG-13) Corporate attorney Steven Keeney (Horton) takes on the case of Lou Anne Wilkins (Ruscio), who's having trouble getting her insurance company to cover the funeral expenses for her teenaged daughter Melissa, who died in a fall. The more Steven investigates, the more suspicious Melissa's death becomes—and he discovers money is

the root of all evil. Based on the book "Death Benefit" by David Heilbroner. Made for cable.*CW:* Scene of sensuality and thematic elements. 89m/C VHS, **Closed Caption.** Peter Horton, Carrie Snodgress, Wendy Makkena, Elizabeth Ruscio, Belita Morena, Lee DeBroux; *D:* Mark Piznarski; *W:* Philip Rosenberg. *USH*

Death Blow 🎞½ 1987 (R) The victims of a violent rapist team together to stop the criminal after he repeatedly skirts conviction. 90m/C VHS, Beta. Martin Landau, Frank Stallone, Jerry Van Dyke, Terry Moore, Henry Darrow, Jack Carter, Peter Lapis, Don Swayze, Donna Denton; *D:* Raphael Nussbaum. *NO*

Death by Dialogue 🎞 1988 (R) Muddled story of some teenagers who discover an old film script from a project never produced because it was haunted by tragic accidents. 90m/C VHS, Beta. Laura Albert, Ken Sagoes; *D:* Tom Dewier. *NO*

Death by Prescription 🎞½ 198? After adjusting his patients' wills to benefit himself, an evil physician sees to their mysterious deaths. 75m/C VHS, Beta. Timothy West, Nigel Davenport. *ACA, MOV*

Death Challenge 🎞½ 1980 Gangs battle without weapons, motive or discretion in this kung fu extravaganza. 94m/C VHS, Beta. Steve Leving, Susan Wong. *UNI*

Death Chase 🎞½ 1987 An average Joe, just jogging down the street, is thrown into a desperate game of cat-and-mouse when a body lands at his feet. 86m/C VHS, Beta. William Zipp, Paul Smith, Jack Starrett, Bainbridge Scott; *D:* David A. Prior. *NO*

Death Collector 🎞½ 1989 (R) In the future when insurance companies run the world, if you don't pay your premium, you die.*CW:* Language, violence, and sensuality. 90m/C VHS, Beta. Daniel Chapman, Ruth Collins; *D:* Tom Gniazdowski. *VTR*

Death Cruise 🎞½ 1974 The six winners of a free cruise find that there is a fatal catch to the prize in this made-for-TV movie. 74m/C VHS, Beta. Kate Jackson, Celeste Holm, Tom Bosley, Edward Albert, Polly Bergen, Michael Constantine, Richard Long; *D:* Ralph Senensky. *AHV*

The Death Curse of Tartu woof! 1966 Another aspiring cult classic. (Read: A low-budget flick so bad it's funny). Students accidentally disturb the burial ground of an Indian medicine man who comes to zombie-like life with a deadly prescription. 84m/C VHS, Beta. Fred Pinero, Doug Hobart, William Grefe. *NO*

Death Dreams 🎞🎞 1992 Crista thinks she has a perfect life with her wealth, beautiful daughter Jennie, and handsome new husband George. Then Jennie tragically drowns. It appears to be an accident until Jennie contacts her mother from beyond the grave to tell what really happened. Is the tragedy turning Crista's mind or is there truly something sinister going on—something that involves George? Based on the novel by William Katz. Routine suspenser originally appeared on cable television. 94m/C VHS, LV. Marg Helgenberger, Christopher Reeve, Fionnula Flanagan; *D:* Martin Donovan; *W:* Robert Glass. *NLC*

Death Driver 🎞½ 1978 In order to make a comeback, a stuntman attempts to do a stunt that was responsible for ending his career ten years earlier. Obviously brave but none too smart. 93m/C VHS, Beta. Earl Owensby, Mike Allen, Patty Shaw, Mary Ann Hearn; *D:* Jimmy Huston. *NO*

Death Drug 🎞½ 1983 Cliched alarmist film about a talented musician ruining his career by becoming addicted to the drug angel dust. 73m/C VHS, Beta. Philip Michael Thomas, Vernee Watson-Johnson, Rosalind Cash; *D:* Oscar Williams. *ACA*

Death Feud 1989 A man tries to save the woman he loves from the man who would destroy her and her former pimp. 98m/C VHS, Beta. Karen Mayo Chandler, Chris Mitchum, Frank Stallone. *HMD*

Death Force ✰½ 1978 (R) When a Vietnam veteran comes to New York City, he becomes a hitman for the Mafia. 90m/C VHS, Beta. Jayne Kennedy, Leon Isaac Kennedy, James Iglehart, Carmen Argenziano; **D:** Cirio H. Santiago. **NO**

Death from a Distance ✰½ 1936 A reporter and a detective put the moves on a group of astronomers who may be responsible for a murder. 73m/B VHS, Beta. Russell Hopton, Lola Lane, George F. Marion Sr., John St. Polis, Lee Kohlmar, Lew Kelly, Wheeler Oakman, Robert Frazer, Cornelius Keefe; **D:** Frank Strayer. **SNC**

Death Games ✰½ 1982 Two young men shooting a documentary about an influential music promoter ask too many wrong questions, causing the powers-that-be to want them out of the picture for good. 78m/C VHS, Beta. Lou Brown, David Clendenning, Jennifer Cluff. **NO**

Death Goes to School ✰✰ 1953 A strangler is loose in a girl's school, and the music teacher has a hunch as to who it is. 65m/B VHS, Beta. **GB** Barbara Murray, Gordon Jackson, Pamela Allan, Jane Aird, Beatrice Varley; **D:** Stephen Clarkson. **SNC**

Death House ✰½ 1988 Derek Keillor is on Death Row at Townsend State Prison when he discovers a plot to use inmates for scientific experiments in biological warfare. He decides the best way to get out is to volunteer, which means convincing the man who put him in prison that they're now on the same side. 92m/C VHS. Dennis Cole, Anthony (Tony) Franciosa, Michael Pataki, John Saxon; **D:** John Saxon. **AIP**

Death Hunt ✰✰ 1981 (R) A man unjustly accused of murder pits his knowledge of the wilderness against the superior numbers of his pursuers. 98m/C VHS, Beta, LV. Charles Bronson, Lee Marvin, Ed Lauter, Andrew Stevens, Carl Weathers, Angie Dickinson; **D:** Peter Hunt; **W:** Mark Victor, Michael Grais. **FXV, FOX**

Death in Brunswick ✰✰ *Nothing to Lose* 1990 Carl Fitzgerald (Neill) seems to be one of life's born losers— his wife's left him, his mother nags him, his house is falling apart, and he's unemployed. At least until he gets a job as a chef in a sleazy rock 'n' roll club and finds Sophie (Carides), the lovely barmaid, who just happens to be engaged to the club's owner. Of course, with Carl's luck, things go from bad to downright dangerous. Based on the novel by Boyd Oxlade.**CW:** Language; some sexuality. 106m/C VHS. **AU** Sam Neill, Zoe Carides, Yvonne Lawley, Boris Brkic, John Clarke; **D:** John Ruane; **W:** John Ruane, Boyd Oxlade; **C:** Ellery Ryan. **COL**

Death in Deep Water ✰✰ 1974 A sensuous woman lures a man into a plot to kill her incredibly rich husband. 71m/C VHS, Beta. Bradford Dillman, Suzan Farmer. **LIV**

Death in the Garden ✰✰ *La Mort en Ce Jardin; Evil Eden* 1956 Surreal film, filled with symbolism, about a group of French people, living in a South American settlement, who must flee a riot between soldiers and striking miners. Local adventurer, Chark (Marchal), agrees to lead them to safety but their trek through the jungle is fraught with peril (and not just from the animal life). French with subtitles. 90m/C VHS. **MX FR** Georges Marchal, Simone Signoret, Charles Vanel, Michele Girardon, Michel Piccoli, Tito Junco; **D:** Luis Bunuel; **W:** Luis Bunuel, Luis Alcoriza, Raymond Queneau; **C:** Jorge Stahl Jr.; **M:** Paul Misraki. **INT**

Death in Venice ✰✰✰½ *Morte a Venezia* 1971 (PG) A lush, decadent adaptation of the Thomas Mann novella about an aging and jaded composer, here suggested to be Gustav Mahler, tragically obsessed with ideal beauty as personified in a young boy. 124m/C VHS, Beta, LV. **IT** Dirk Bogarde, Mark Burns, Bjorn Andresen, Marisa Berenson, Silvana Mangano; **D:** Luchino Visconti; **C:** Pasquale De Santos; **M:** Gustav Mahler. Nominations: Academy Awards '71: Best Costume Design.**WAR, PME**

Death Is Called Engelchen ✰✰✰½ *For We Too Do Not Forgive* 1963 An influential, important work of the Czech new wave. A survivor of WWII remembers his experiences with the SS leader Engelchen in a series of flashbacks. In Czech with subtitles. 111m/B VHS, Beta. **CZ D:** Jan Kadar, Elmar Klos. **FCT**

Death Journey ✰✰½ 1976 (R) Producer and director Williamson portrays private eye Jesse Crowder, hired by the New York D.A. to escort a key witness cross-country. A regular Williamsonfest. 90m/C VHS, Beta. Fred Williamson, D'Urville Martin, Bernie Kuby, Heidi Dobbs, Stephanie Faulkner; **D:** Fred Williamson. **UNI**

The Death Kiss ✰✰½ 1933 Creepy thriller about eerie doings at a major Hollywood film studio where a sinister killer does away with his victims while a cast-of-thousands movie spectacular is in production. 72m/B VHS, Beta, 8mm. Bela Lugosi, David Manners, Adrienne Ames, Edward Van Sloan, Vince Barnett; **D:** Edwin L. Marin. **NOS, SNC, CAB**

Death Kiss ✰½ 1977 (R) When a man hires a psychopath to murder his wife, his plan doesn't proceed exactly as expected. 90m/C VHS, Beta. Larry Daniels, Dorothy Moore. **PSM, LSV**

Death Machine ✰✰½ 1995 (R) New company exec Hayden Cale (Pouget) uncovers questionable scientific project at weapons technology company and scientist in charge Jack Dante (Dourif) decides to get even by testing his death machine, which works by sensing fear, in corporate headquarters.**CW:** Sci-fi terror and violence; language; brief sexuality. 99m/C VHS, LV, Closed Caption. Brad Dourif, Ely Pouget, William Hootkins; **D:** Stephen Norrington; **W:** Stephen Norrington; **C:** John de Borman. **THV**

Death Machines ✰½ 1976 (R) Young karate student must face the "Death Machines," a team of deadly assassins who are trained to kill on command. 93m/C VHS, Beta. Ron Marchini, Michael Chong, Joshua Johnson; **D:** Paul Kyriazi. **NO**

Death Magic ✰½ 1992 A group of five ceremonial magicians performs a spell to bring someone back from the dead, but the man they bring back, a soldier from the Civil War, decides to go on a vicious murdering spree to kill the descendants of the people who convicted him of murder in 1875. A suspenseful first entry from director Clinco. 93m/C VHS. Anne Coffrey, Keith DeGreen, Jack Dunlap, Danielle Frons, Norman Stone; **D:** Paul E. Clinco; **W:** Paul E. Clinco. **NO**

Death Mask of the Ninja ✰½ 198? Two princes, separated at birth, reunite and kick everyone in the head. Dubbed. 95m/C VHS, Beta. Joey Lee, Tiger Tung, Jon Chen. **MOV**

Death Match ✰ 1994 (R) John Larson gives up kickboxing after a tragedy but when his friend disappears, John is forced into a fighting bout with no rules and only one outcome.**CW:** Strong martial arts violence. 90m/C VHS. Matthias Hues, Martin Kove, Ian Jacklin, Nick Hill, Renee Ammann; **D:** Joe Coppoletta. **MNC**

The Death Merchant ✰ 1991 Foundering attempt at a nuclear thriller. A modern mad man hopes to sell a computer chip to third world countries but is thwarted by a secret agent. Confusing, illogical plot highlighted by mediocre performances. 90m/C VHS. Lawrence Tierney, Martina Castle, Melody Munyan, Monika Schnarre; **D:** James R. Winburn; **W:** Kari Holman. **AIP**

Death Nurse ✰✰ 1987 Fresh from "Crazy Fat Ethel II," aspiring Queen of Camp Alden takes up residence in a health care establishment, much to the dismay of the patients who give up their lives in exchange for their money. 80m/C VHS. Priscilla Alden, Michael Flood; **D:** Nick Phillips. **VCD**

Death of a Bureaucrat ✰✰✰ 1966 A Cuban hero dies, and in tribute, the Communist government buries him with his union card. His widow, however, needs the card in order to collect a pension, and she enlists her nephew's help to

retrieve it. The nephew soon finds himself buried in red tape, and digs himself in ever-deeper as he seeks to disinter his late uncle. A wry satire of the communist bureaucracy in Cuba, brimming with comedic tributes to Harold Lloyd, Buster Keaton and Laurel & Hardy. Alea's film was only briefly released in 1966 and was promptly banned, eventually finding its way to the U.S. in 1979. In Spanish with English subtitles. 87m/B VHS, Beta. **CU** Salvador Wood, Silvia Planas, Manuel Estanillo, Gaspar de Santelices, Carlos Ruiz de la Tejera, Omar Alfonso, Ricardo Suarez, Luis Romay, Elsa Montero; **D:** Tomas Gutierrez Alea. **NYF, FCT**

Death of a Centerfold ✰✰ 1981 Drama based on the life and tragic death of Playboy model and actress Dorothy Stratten. More effectively handled in Bob Fosse's "Star 80." 96m/C VHS, Beta. Jamie Lee Curtis, Bruce Weitz, Robert Reed, Mitchell Ryan, Bibi Besch; **D:** Gabrielle Beaumont. **MGM**

Death of a Gunfighter ✰✰ 1969 (PG) A western town courting eastern investors and bankers seeks a way to kill their ex-gunslinger sheriff. 94m/C VHS, Beta. Richard Widmark, Lena Horne, Carroll O'Connor, John Saxon, Larry Gates; **D:** Donald Siegel; **W:** Robert Totten. **USH**

Death of a Salesman ✰✰✰½ 1986 A powerful made-for-television adaptation of the famous Arthur Miller play. Hoffman won an Emmy (as did Malkovich) for his stirring portrayal of Willy Loman, the aging salesman who realizes he's past his prime and tries to come to grips with the life he's wasted and the family he's neglected. Reid also turns in a fine performance as his long-suffering wife. 135m/C VHS, Beta, LV, Closed Caption. Dustin Hoffman, John Malkovich, Charles Durning, Stephen Lang, Kate Reid, Louis Zorich; **D:** Volker Schlondorff; **C:** Michael Ballhaus; **M:** Alex North. **ORI, FCT, WAR**

Death of a Scoundrel ✰✰½ *Loves of a Scoundrel* 1956 A womanizing entrepreneur is murdered and the culprit could be any one of his many jealous romantic conquests. 119m/B VHS, Beta, LV. George Sanders, Zsa Zsa Gabor, Yvonne De Carlo, Victor Jory; **D:** Charles Martin; **M:** Max Steiner. **NO**

Death of a Soldier ✰✰ 1985 (R) During WWII, the uneasy U.S.-Australian alliance explodes when a psychotic American soldier murders three Melbourne women. The lawyer hired to defend him has to fight political as well as legal influences. Based on a true story. 93m/C VHS, Beta, Closed Caption. **AU** James Coburn, Reb Brown, Maurie Field, Belinda Darey; **D:** Philippe Mora. **FOX**

The Death of Adolf Hitler ✰✰½ 1984 British made-for-television film depicting Hitler's last ten days in an underground bunker. Drug-addled, suicidal, and Eva Braun-haunted, he receives the news of the fall of the Third Reich. While the film avoids cliche, it lacks emotional depth. 107m/C VHS, Beta. **GB** Frank Finlay, Caroline Mortimer; **D:** Rex Firlin. **ORI, TLF, WAR**

Death of an Angel ✰½ 1986 When her crippled daughter runs away to join a cult in Mexico, a recently ordained priest (Bedelia) follows her, only to become caught up herself with the leader of the group. 95m/C VHS, Beta, LV. Bonnie Bedelia, Nick Mancuso, Pamela Ludwig, Alex Colon; **D:** Petru Popescu; **M:** Jay Michael Ferguson. **NO**

The Death of Richie ✰✰ *Richie* 1976 Gazzara does a fine job as a father driven to kill his drug-addicted teenage son, portrayed by Benson. Occasionally lapses into melodrama, but all-in-all a decent adaptation of Thomas Thompson's book "Richie" which was based on a true story. Made for television. 97m/C VHS, Beta. Ben Gazzara, Robby Benson, Eileen Brennan, Clint Howard; **D:** Paul Wendkos. **PSM, LCA**

Death of the Incredible Hulk ✰½ 1990 Scientist David Banner's new job just may provide the clues for stopping his transformation into the monstrous Incredible Hulk. But first there are terrorists after the Hulk who need to be defeated and Banner's new romance to contend with. Made for television. 96m/C VHS. Bill Bixby, Lou

Ferrigno, Elizabeth Gracen, Philip Sterling; **D:** Bill Bixby. *RHI*

Death on the Nile 🎬🎬½ **1978 (PG)** Agatha Christie's fictional detective, Hercule Poirot, is called upon to interrupt his vacation to uncover who killed an heiress aboard a steamer cruising down the Nile. Ustinov's first stint as the Belgian sleuth. Anthony Powell's costume design won an Oscar. **135m/C VHS, Beta, LV.** *GB* Peter Ustinov, Jane Birkin, Lois Chiles, Bette Davis, Mia Farrow, David Niven, Olivia Hussey, Angela Lansbury, Jack Warden, Maggie Smith, George Kennedy, Simon MacCorkindale, Harry Andrews, Jon Finch; **D:** John Guillermin; **W:** Anthony Shaffer; **C:** Jack Cardiff; **M:** Nino Rota. Academy Awards '78: Best Costume Design; National Board of Review Awards '78: Best Supporting Actress (Lansbury). *REP*

Death Promise 🎬 **1978 (R)** Ho-hum excuse for a horror flick has murderous landlord trying to evict his tenants using whatever means are necessary. **90m/C VHS, Beta.** Charles Bonet. *NO*

Death Race 2000 🎬🎬½ **1975 (R)** In the 21st century, five racing car contenders challenge the national champion of a cross country race in which drivers score points by killing pedestrians. Gory fun. Based on the 1956 story by Ib Melchior, and followed by "Deathsport." Made for television. **80m/C VHS, Beta.** David Carradine, Simone Griffeth, Sylvester Stallone, Mary Woronov; **D:** Paul Bartel; **W:** Charles B. Griffith, Robert Thom. *NHO*

Death Rage 🎬½ **1977 (R)** A hitman comes out of retirement to handle the toughest assignment he has ever faced: search for and kill the man who murdered his brother. He finds out he's the victim of a Mafia doublecross. **92m/C VHS, Beta.** *IT* Yul Brynner, Martin Balsam, Barbara (Margheriti) Dawson. *NO*

Death Ray woof! **19??** It's a race to the finish as terrorists threaten to unleash the world's most powerful weapon. A very poor James Bond rip-off. **93m/C VHS, Beta.** Gordon Scott; **D:** Frank G. Carroll. *BFV, MRV*

Death Ray 2000 🎬½ *T.R. Sloane* **1981** Bondian superspy T.R. Sloane must search out the whereabouts of a stolen military device that could kill all life on Earth. TV pilot for the series "A Man Called Sloane." **100m/C VHS, Beta.** Robert F. Logan, Ann Turkel, Maggie Cooper, Dan O'Herlihy; **D:** Lee H. Katzin. *WOV, MOV*

Death Rides the Plains 🎬🎬 **1944** Western with a twist. A man lures prospective buyers to his ranch, kills them, and steals their money. It's up to our heroes to ride to the rescue. **53m/B VHS, Beta.** Bob Livingston, Al "Fuzzy" St. John, Nica Doret, Ray Bennett; **D:** Sam Newfield. *VYY, VDM*

Death Rides the Range 🎬½ **1940** Russian spies start a range war as a cover for an operation to pipe helium off a ranch and over the border. Maynard, an undercover FBI agent posing as a cowboy, is out to stop them. **58m/B VHS.** Ken Maynard, Fay McKenzie, Ralph Peters, Julian Rivero, Charles "Blackie" King, John Elliott, Bud Osborne; **D:** Sam Newfield. *GPV, NOS, DVT*

Death Ring 🎬 **1993 (R)** Basic action/martial arts tale about three men who must battle the bad guys to ensure their own survival. **CW:** Language, strong violence, and sexuality. **90m/C VHS, Beta.** Mike Norris, Chad McQueen, Don Swayze, Billy Drago, Isabel Glasser; **D:** Robert J. Kizer; **W:** George T. LeBrun. *COL, NLC*

Death Row Diner 🎬½ **1988** A movie mogul, executed for a crime he didn't commit, is brought back to life by a freak electrical storm. Nothing will stop him from exacting revenge. **90m/C VHS, Beta.** Jay Richardson, Michelle (McClellan) Bauer, John Content, Tom Schell, Dennis Mooney, Frank Sarcinello Sr., Dana Mason. *NO*

Death Scream 🎬🎬 *Street Kill* **1975** Drama based on the New York murder of Kitty Genovese, whose cries for help while being assaulted went ignored by her neighbors. Good casting but the pacing deteriorates. Made for television. **100m/C VHS.** Raul Julia, John P. Ryan, Lucie Arnaz, Ed

Asner, Art Carney, Diahann Carroll, Kate Jackson, Cloris Leachman, Tina Louise, Nancy Walker, Eric (Hans Gudegast) Braeden, Allyn Ann McLerie, Tony Dow, Sally Kirkland, Helen Hunt; **D:** Richard T. Heffron; **W:** Stirling Silliphant. *ACE*

Death Screams 🎬 **1983 (R)** Attractive college coeds have a party and get hacked to pieces for their troubles by a machete-wielding maniac. **88m/C VHS, Beta.** Susan Kiger, Jennifer Chase, Jody Kay, William T. Hicks, Martin Tucker. *GEM*

Death Sentence 🎬½ *Murder One* **1974** When a woman juror on a murder case finds out that the wrong man is on trial, she is stalked by the real killer. Made for television. **74m/C VHS, Beta.** Cloris Leachman, Laurence Luckinbill, Nick Nolte, William Schallert; **D:** E.W. Swackhamer. *PSM*

Death Ship 🎬 **1980 (R)** A luxury liner is destroyed by an ancient, mysterious freighter on open seas, leaving the survivors to confront the ghost ship's inherent evil in this slow-going horror flick. **91m/C VHS, Beta.** *GB CA* George Kennedy, Richard Crenna, Nick Mancuso, Sally Ann Howes, Saul Rubinek, Kate Reid; **D:** Alvin Rakoff. *NLC*

Death Shot 🎬 **1973** Two plainclothes detectives (who seem just as sleazy as the criminals they're trying to bust) try to break up a drug ring and find that, with a little coercion, their best sources of information are the pimps and junkies they want to stop. Senseless attempt to make an action pic. **90m/C VHS.** Richard C. Watt, Frank Himes; **D:** Mitch Brown. *NO*

Death Spa woof! **1987 (R)** A health club is possessed by the spirit of a vengeful woman. The fitness craze takes on a campy new twist. **87m/C VHS.** William Bumiller, Brenda Bakke, Merritt Butrick; **D:** Michael Fischa. *MPI*

Death Sport 🎬🎬 **1978 (R)** In this sequel to the cult hit "Death Race 2000," a group of humans play a game of death in the year 3000. The object is to race cars and kill as many competitors as possible. Not as good as the original, but still watchable. **83m/C VHS, Beta.** David Carradine, Claudia Jennings, Richard Lynch, Will Smithers, Will Walker, David McLean, Jesse Vint; **D:** Henry Suso, Allan Arkush. *WAR, OM*

The Death Squad 🎬½ **1973** A police commissioner hires an ex-cop to find a group of vigilante cops who are behind a series of gangland-style executions. Good cast, though that's about all this flick has got going for it. Made for television. **74m/C VHS, Beta.** Robert Forster, Melvyn Douglas, Michelle Phillips, Mark Goddard, Bert Remsen, Claude Akins; **D:** Harry Falk. *PSM*

Death Stalk 🎬½ **1974** Dream vacation turns nightmarish for two couples when the wives are taken hostage by several escaped convicts. Made for television. **90m/C VHS, Beta.** Vince Edwards, Vic Morrow, Anjanette Comer, Robert Webber, Carol Lynley, Neville Brand, Norman Fell; **D:** Robert Day. *CNG, GEM, HHE*

Death Target 🎬½ **1983** Three former mercenaries team up for one last mission that gets sidetracked when one of the soldiers-of-fortune falls for a worker with a habit. **72m/C VHS, Beta.** Jorge Montesi, Elaine Lakeman; **D:** Peter Hyams. *PSM*

Death Tide 🎬🎬 **1958** Hoodlums pirate a ship full of diamonds in this story of death and crime on the high seas. **?m/C VHS.** Frank Silvera. *SNC*

Death Train 🎬½ **1979** Dead man seems to have been struck by a train, but clueless investigator can't figure out where the train came from. **96m/C VHS, Beta.** Hugh Keays-Byrne, Ingrid Mason, Max Meldrum; **D:** Igor Auzins. *NO*

Death Valley 🎬½ **1946** Greed turns gold prospectors in Death Valley against each other. **70m/C VHS, Beta.** Robert Lowery, Helen Gilbert, Sterling Holloway; **D:** Lew (Louis Friedlander) Landers. *NO*

Death Valley 🎬½ **1981 (R)** Good cast, lousy plot. Youngster (Billingsley) gets caught up with a psycho cowpoke while visiting mom in Arizona. **90m/C VHS, Beta.** Paul LeMat, Catherine Hicks,

Peter Billingsley, Wilford Brimley, Edward Herrmann, Stephen McHattie; **D:** Dick Richards; **C:** Stephen Burum. *USH*

Death Valley Days: No Gun Behind His Badge **1965** Western anthology series which ran on television from 1952-1970 and was noted for its longtime sponsor, 20 Mule Team Borax, as well as its hosts, including Stanley Andrews, Ronald Reagan, Robert Taylor, and Dale Robertson. On this tape: the premiere episode plus "Halo for a Bad Man." Each additional tape contains two episodes. **55m/C VHS.** Robert Taylor, Ronald Reagan. *NO*

Death Valley Manhunt 🎬🎬 **1943** A marshal hired to protect a man's oil wells discovers that the company manager is keeping the profits for himself. **55m/B VHS, Beta.** Wild Bill Elliott, George "Gabby" Hayes, Anne Jeffreys; **D:** John English. *DVT*

Death Valley Rangers 🎬½ **1944** The hero pretends to be an outlaw to expose a gang robbing gold-laden stagecoaches. **59m/B VHS.** Ken Maynard, Hoot Gibson, Bob Steele, Linda Brent, Kenneth Harlan; **D:** Robert Emmett Tansey. *NOS, DVT*

Death Warmed Up 🎬½ **1985** A crazed brain surgeon turns ordinary people into bloodthirsty mutants, and a small group of young people travel to his secluded island to stop him. **83m/C VHS, Beta.** Michael Hurst, Margaret Umbers, David Letch; **D:** David Blyth. *LIV, VES*

Death Warrant 🎬🎬 **1990 (R)** Van Damme whams and bams a little less than usual in this cop-undercover-in-prison testosterone fest. As a Royal Canadian Mountie undercover in prison—where inmates are perishing under mysterious circumstances—the pectoral-perfect Muscles from Brussels is on the brink of adding two plus two when an inmate transferee threatens his cover. Contains the requisite gratuitous violence, prison bromide, and miscellaneous other Van Dammages. **111m/C VHS, LV, Closed Caption.** Jean-Claude Van Damme, Robert Guillaume, Cynthia Gibb, George Dickerson, Patrick Kilpatrick; **D:** Deran Sarafian; **C:** Russell Carpenter. *MGM*

Death Watch 🎬🎬 **1980 (R)** In the future, media abuse is taken to an all time high as a terminally ill woman's last days are secretly filmed by a man with a camera in his head. Intelligent, adult science fiction with an excellent cast. **128m/C VHS, LV.** *FR GE* Romy Schneider, Harvey Keitel, Harry Dean Stanton, Max von Sydow; **D:** Bertrand Tavernier; **W:** Bertrand Tavernier, David Rayfiel.

Death Weekend 🎬½ *House by the Lake* **1976** A woman is stalked by a trio of murderous, drunken hoodlums who seek to spoil her weekend. **89m/C VHS, Beta.** *CA* Brenda Vaccaro, Don Stroud, Chuck Shamata, Richard Ayres, Kyle Edwards; **D:** William Fruet. *LIV, VES*

Death Wish 🎬🎬½ **1974 (R)** A middle-aged businessman turns vigilante after his wife and daughter are violently attacked and raped by a gang of hoodlums (one is Goldblum in his film debut). He stalks the streets of New York seeking revenge on other muggers, pimps, and crooks, making the neighborhood safer for those less macho. **93m/C VHS, Beta, LV.** Charles Bronson, Vincent Gardenia, William Redfield, Hope Lange, Jeff Goldblum, Stuart Margolin, Olympia Dukakis; **D:** Michael Winner; **W:** Wendell Mayes; **M:** Herbie Hancock. *MGM, PAR*

Death Wish 2 woof! **1982 (R)** Bronson recreates the role of Paul Kersey, an architect who takes the law into his own hands when his family is victimized once again. Extremely violent sequel to the successful 1974 movie. Followed by "Death Wish 3" (1985) and 4 (1987) in which Bronson continues to torture the street scum and the viewers as well. **89m/C VHS, Beta, LV.** J.D. Cannon, Charles Bronson, Jill Ireland, Vincent Gardenia, Anthony (Tony) Franciosa; **D:** Michael Winner; **M:** Jimmy Page. *WAR, OM*

Death Wish 3 🎬½ **1985 (R)** Once again, Charles Bronson blows away the low lifes who have killed those who were dear to him and were spared in the first two films. **100m/C VHS, Beta, LV.**

Charles Bronson, Martin Balsam, Deborah Raffin, Ed Lauter, Alex Winter, Marina Sirtis; **D:** Michael Winner; **M:** Jimmy Page. *MGM*

Death Wish 4: The Crackdown 🎬

1987 (R) The four-times-weary urban vigilante hits crack dealers this time, hard. **100m/C VHS, Beta, LV, Closed Caption.** Charles Bronson, John P. Ryan, Kay Lenz; **D:** J. Lee Thompson. *MED, VTR*

Death Wish 5: The Face of Death woof!

1994 (R) Paul Kersey (Bronson) returns to vigilantism when his clothing manufacturer fiancee Olivia (Downs) has her business threatened by mobsters, one of whom turns out to be her sadistic ex (Parks). Bronson looks bored with the rehashed material. Lots of explicit and grisly violence. **CW:** Strong language, nudity, and extreme violence & cruelty. **95m/C VHS, LV, Closed Caption.** Charles Bronson, Lesley-Anne Down, Michael Parks, Kenneth Welsh; **D:** Allan Goldstein; **W:** Allan Goldstein; **M:** Terry Plumer. *THV*

Death Wish Club 🎬½ *Carnival of Fools*

1983 Young woman gets involved in a club with an unusual mission—suicide. **93m/C VHS, Beta.** Meridith Haze, Rick Barns, J. Martin Sellers, Ann Fairchild; **D:** John Carr. *NO*

Deathcheaters 🎬½

1976 (G) Australian Secret Service offers two stuntmen a top secret mission in the Philippines. **96m/C VHS, Beta.** John Hargreaves, Grant Page, Noel Ferrer; **D:** Brian Trenchard-Smith; **W:** Michael Cove. *VES*

Deathdream 🎬🎬½ *Dead of Night; Night Walk; The Veteran*

1972 In this reworking of the "Monkey's Paw" tale, a mother wishes her dead son would return from Vietnam. He does, but he's not quite the person he used to be. Gripping plot gives new meaning to the saying, "Be careful what you wish for—it might come true." **98m/C VHS, Beta.** *CA* John Marley, Richard Backus, Lynn Carlin; **D:** Bob (Benjamin) Clark; **W:** Alan Ormsby. *MPI*

Deathfight 🎬½

1993 (R) Let's face it, no one watches these movies because they have a plot. This is a fast-paced B-grade martial arts flick with numerous butts getting kicked. Oh, all right, if you insist on plot—Norton's evil half-brother (Guerrero) is trying to turn their legitimate family business into a criminal front by framing Norton for murder. **92m/C VHS, Closed Caption.** Richard Norton, Franco Guerrero, Karen Moncrieff, Chuck Jeffreys, Ron Vreeken, Tetchie Agbayani, Joe Mari Avellana; **D:** Anthony Maharaj; **W:** Tom Huckabee. *ACA*

Deathhead Virgin 🎬½

1974 (R) An evil virgin spirit is waiting to possess one of two men eager to find a sunken fortune. The fate of the fortunate one is only death! **94m/C VHS, Beta.** Jock Gaynor, Larry Ward, Diane McBain, Vic Diaz. *NO*

Deathmask 🎬🎬

1969 A four-year-old boy's corpse is found buried in a cardboard box, and a medical examiner—whose daughter met a similar fate—investigates the murder. Could've been done more tastefully. **102m/C VHS, Beta.** Farley Granger, Ruth Warrick, Danny Aiello; **D:** Richard S. Friedman. *PRD*

Deathmoon 🎬🎬½

1978 A businessman plagued by recurring werewolf nightmares goes on a Hawaiian vacation to try to forget his troubles. Made for television. **90m/C VHS, Beta.** Robert Foxworth, Joe Penny, Debralee Scott, Dolph Sweet, Charles Haid; **D:** Bruce Kessler. *NO*

Deathrow Gameshow 🎬½

1988 Condemned criminals can either win their freedom or die in front of millions on a new television show that doesn't win the host many friends. **78m/C VHS, Beta, LV.** John McCafferty, Robin Bluthe, Beano, Mark Lasky; **D:** Mark Pirro. *MED*

Deathstalker woof! *El Cazador de la Muerte*

1983 (R) Deathstalker sets his sights on seizing the evil wizard Munkar's magic amulet so he can take over Munkar's castle. The only excuse for making such an idiotic film seems to have been to fill it with half-naked women. Filmed in Argentina and followed by two sequels that were an improvement. **80m/C VHS, Beta, LV.** Richard Hill, Barbi Benton,

---

Richard Brooker, Victor Bo, Lana Clarkson; **D:** John Watson; **W:** Howard R. Cohen. *LIV, VES*

Deathstalker 2: Duel of the Titans 🎬🎬

1987 (R) Campy fantasy comically pits the lead character against an evil wizard. Sword-and-sorcery spoof doesn't take itself too seriously. **85m/C VHS, Beta, LV.** John Terlesky, Monique Gabrielle, John Lazar, Toni Naples, Maria Socas, Queen Kong; **D:** Jim Wynorski; **W:** Jim Wynorski. *LIV, VES*

Deathstalker 3 🎬🎬½ *Deathstalker 3: The Warriors From Hell*

1989 (R) Another humorous entry in the Deathstalker saga. This time there's action, romance, magic and the Warriors From Hell. **85m/C VHS, Beta, LV.** John Allen Nelson, Carla Herd, Terri Treas, Thom Christopher; **D:** Alfonso Corona; **W:** Howard R. Cohen. *LIV, VES, HHE*

Deathstalker 4: Match of Titans 🎬

1992 (R) The sword and sorcery epic continues, with our hero revealing yet more musculature in his efforts to defeat an evil queen and her legion of stone warriors. **CW:** Adventure violence and sensuality. **85m/C VHS.** Richard Hill, Maria Ford, Michelle Moffett, Brent Baxter Clark; **D:** Howard R. Cohen. *NHO*

Deathtrap 🎬🎬

1982 (PG) A creatively-blocked playwright, his ailing rich wife, and a former student who has written a surefire hit worth killing for, are the principals in this compelling comedy-mystery. Cross and double-cross are explored in this film based on the Broadway hit by Ira Levin. **118m/C VHS, Beta.** Henry Jones, Michael Caine, Christopher Reeve, Dyan Cannon, Irene Worth; **D:** Sidney Lumet; **W:** Jay Presson Allen; **C:** Andrzej Bartkowiak. *WAR*

The Decameron 🎬🎬🎬½

1970 (R) Pasolini's first epic pageant in his "Trilogy of Life" series. An acclaimed, sexually explicit adaptation of a handful of the Boccaccio tales. In Italian with English subtitles. **CW:** Some language and sensuality. **111m/C VHS, Beta, LV.** *FR IT GE* Franco Citti, Ninetto Davoli, Angela Luce, Patrizia Capparelli, Jovan Jovanovich, Silvana Mangano, Pier Paolo Pasolini; **D:** Pier Paolo Pasolini; **C:** Tonino Delli Colli; **M:** Ennio Morricone. Berlin International Film Festival '71: Silver Prize. *WBF, APD*

Decameron Nights 🎬🎬½

1953 Story of Boccaccio's pursuit of a recently-widowed young women is interwoven amongst the three of the fourteenth-century Italian writer's bawdy tales. **87m/C VHS, Beta.** *GB* Louis Jourdan, Joan Fontaine, Binnie Barnes, Joan Collins, Marjorie Rhodes; **D:** Hugo Fregonese. *NOS, MRV, QNE*

Deceit 🎬🎬

1993 (R) A sci-fi sex comedy with an environmental premise. Bailey and Brick are two aliens working for their planet's Environmental Protection Agency, whose idea of protection is to vaporize polluter planets. Guess which planet is next on their hit list. But before they get down to business, our two alien studs want to do the horizontal bop with two of the local lovelies, who decide that isn't how they want to spend their last moments on earth. It has a happy ending. **92m/C VHS.** Scott Paulin, Norbert Weisser, Samantha Phillips; **D:** Albert Pyun; **W:** Kitty Chalmers. *COL*

Deceived 🎬🎬 **1991 (PG-13)** A successful career woman with a passionate husband and a young daughter feels she has it all until her husband is apparently killed in a bizarre tragedy. But just how well did she know the man she married? Who was he really and what secrets are hidden in his past? As she struggles to solve these mysteries, her own life becomes endangered in this psychological thriller. **115m/C VHS, Beta, Closed Caption.** Goldie Hawn, John Heard, Ashley Peldon, Jan Rubes, Amy Wright, Maia Filar, Robin Bartlett, Tom Irwin, Beatrice Straight, Kate Reid; **D:** Damian Harris; **W:** Mary Agnes Donoghue, Derek Saunders; **C:** Jack N. Green; **M:** Thomas Newman. *TOU*

The Deceivers 🎬🎬 **1988 (PG-13)** Brosnan stars as a British officer sent on a dangerous undercover mission in 1820s India. He's to infiltrate the notorious Thuggee cult, known for robbing and murdering unwary travelers. Interesting premise falters due to slow pacing and Brosnan's

---

lack of believability. **112m/C VHS, Beta, LV, Closed Caption.** *IN GB* Pierce Brosnan, Saeed Jaffrey, Shashi Kapoor, Keith Michell; **D:** Nicholas Meyer; **C:** Walter Lassally. *WAR*

December 🎬🎬

1991 (PG) Four prep-school students in New Hampshire must confront the reality of war when the Japanese bomb Pearl Harbor. A touching story of courage and friendship that takes place in one night during the suprise-attack. **92m/C VHS, LV, Closed Caption.** Wil Wheaton, Chris Young, Brian Krause, Balthazar Getty, Jason London; **D:** Gabe Torres; **W:** Gabe Torres. *NO*

December Bride 🎬🎬½

1991 Determined young woman (Reeves) becomes the housekeeper to two taciturn Irish farmer/brothers (Hinds and McCann) and proceeds to bully them into prosperity in early 20th century rural Ireland. She also scandalizes the community by sleeping with both men and refusing to marry either—even after she becomes pregnant. Based on the novel by Sam Hanna Bell. **88m/C VHS.** *IR* Saskia Reeves, Ciaran Hinds, Donal McCann, Patrick Malahide, Brenda Bruce; **D:** Thaddeus O'Sullivan; **W:** David Rudkin; **C:** Bruno de Keyzer; **M:** Jurgen Knieper. *FXL*

December Flower 🎬🎬½

19?? A young woman arrives at her aunt's estate so she can nurse her back to health, but she finds her aunt a bit down in the mouth: seems someone is trying to kill her, and she could be next in line. **65m/C VHS.** Jean Simmons, Mona Washbourne, Bryan Forbes. *FCT, MOV*

December 7th: The Movie 🎬🎬½

1991 Banned for 50 years by the U.S. Government, this planned Hollywood explanation to wartime audiences of the Pearl Harbor debacle offers such "offensive" images as blacks fighting heroically alongside whites, loyal Japanese-Americans, and Uncle Sam asleep on the morning of the attack. The Chief of Naval Operations confiscated the original film, claiming it demeaned the Navy. The battle scenes were so realistic they fooled even documentarians. This isn't the most incisive video on the event—just an unforgettable snapshot. **82m/B VHS.** Walter Huston, Harry Davenport; **D:** John Ford. *KIT, CPM, FUS*

Deception 🎬🎬🎬

1946 Davis is a pianist torn between two loves: her intensely jealous sponsor (Rains) and her cellist boyfriend (Henreid). Plot in danger of going over the melodramatic edge is saved by the very effective performances of the stars. **112m/B VHS, Beta.** Bette Davis, Paul Henreid, Claude Rains, John Abbott, Benson Fong; **D:** Irving Rapper. *MGM*

Deception 🎬½ *Ruby Cairo*

1992 (PG-13) Talented cast is wasted in an old-fashioned mystery that lacks a coherent script. MacDowell is married to Mortensen, the owner of an aircraft salvage company. He's supposedly killed in a plane crash but she thinks he's just pulled a fast one and sets off to find him. Tracking her hubby's secret bank accounts takes her all over the world, and finally to Cairo, Egypt where she meets Neeson. Together they discover Mortensen's scam involves smuggling poison gas and the duo then try to outwit the hoods on their trail. Film was originally released at 110 minutes. **CW:** Brief language and a shooting. **90m/C VHS, LV, Closed Caption.** Andie MacDowell, Liam Neeson, Viggo Mortensen, Jack Thompson, Jeff Corey, Miriam Reed, Luis Cortes, Paco Mauri; **D:** Graeme Clifford; **W:** Robert Dillon, Michael Thomas; **M:** John Barry. *LIV*

Deceptions 🎬🎬

1990 (R) A risque, semi-erotic thriller about a wealthy society woman (Sheridan) who kills her husband. Sheridan claims that she acted in self-defense, but macho cop Hamlin has a different view. He interrogates her, grows increasingly attracted, and is drawn into her web of seduction. **105m/C VHS, LV, Closed Caption.** Harry Hamlin, Nicolette Sheridan. *REP*

The Decline of the American Empire 🎬🎬🎬½ *Le Declin De L'Empire Americain*

1986 (R) The critically acclaimed French-Canadian film about eight academic intellectuals who spend a weekend shedding their sophistication and engaging in intertwining sexual affairs. Examines the differing attitudes of men and women in regards to sex and sexuality. In French with English subtitles. **102m/C VHS, Beta.** *CA* Dominique Michel, Dorothee Berryman, Louise Portal, Genevieve Rioux; *D:* Denys Arcand; *W:* Denys Arcand. Genie Awards '87: Best Director (Arcand), Best Film, Best Supporting Actor (Arcand), Best Supporting Actress (Portal); New York Film Critics Awards '86: Best Foreign Film; Toronto-City Award '86: Best Canadian Feature Film; Nominations: Academy Awards '86: Best Foreign Language Film. *USH*

Decline of Western Civilization

1 🎬🎬🎬 **1981** The L.A. hard core punk scene. Music by X, Circle Jerks, Black Flag, Fear and more. **100m/C VHS, Beta, LV.** *D:* Penelope Spheeris. *MVD, MED*

Decline of Western Civilization 2: The Metal Years

1988 (R) Following Spheeris's first documentary about hardcore punk, she in turn delves into the world of heavy metal rock. We are given a look at some of the early rockers, as well as some of the smaller bands still playing L.A. clubs. Features appearances by Alice Cooper, Ozzy Osbourne, Poison, Gene Simmons and Megadeth. **90m/C VHS, Beta, Closed Caption.** Alice Cooper, Ozzy Osbourne, Gene Simmons, Lizzie Borden; *D:* Penelope Spheeris. *COL, MVD, FCT*

Deconstructing Sarah 🎬🎬 **1994 (R)**

Sarah Vincent (Ticotin) is a high-powered but bored ad exec who assumes an alter-ego, Ruth, when she heads for the wrong side of the tracks in her pursuit of casual sex. Her secret life is discovered when Sarah is murdered and best friend Elizabeth (Kelley) begins to turn up some likely suspects. Fast-paced whodunnit with good cast work. Made for TV. *CW:* Some sexuality. **120m/C VHS.** Rachel Ticotin, Sheila Kelley, A. Martinez, David Andrews, John Vickery, Jenifer Lewis, Dwier Brown, Peter Jason; *D:* Craig R. Baxley; *W:* Lee Rose; *C:* Joao Fernandes; *M:* Tom Scott. *USH*

Decoration Day 🎬🎬🎬 **1990 (PG)** Garner

plays a retired Southern judge who aids an angry childhood friend who has refused to accept his long-overdue Medal of Honor. Investigating the past leads to a decades-old mystery and a tragic secret that has repercussions for everyone involved. Based on the novel by John William Corrington. A Hallmark Hall of Fame presentation. **99m/C VHS, LV, Closed Caption.** James Garner, Bill Cobbs, Judith Ivey, Ruby Dee, Laurence "Larry" Fishburne, Jo Anderson; *D:* Robert Markowitz. *REP*

Decoy 🎬🎬 **1995 (R)** Two ex-government

operatives, Baxter (Weller) and Travis (Patrick), are hired by their former commanding officer, Wellington (Breck), to protect his daughter Diana (Vogel) from business rival Jensen (Hylands) who's got a grudge against dad. But then it turns out the job's a set up, and Wellington and Jensen have their own deadly agenda. *CW:* Strong violence; some language. **98m/C VHS, LV.** Peter Weller, Robert Patrick, Darlene Vogel, Charlotte Lewis, Peter Breck, Scott Hylands; *D:* Victor Rambaldi; *W:* Robert Sarno; *C:* Jon Kranhouse; *M:* Mark Adler. *TTC*

Dedee d'Anvers 🎬🎬½ *Dedee; Woman of Antwerp*

1949 A gritty dockside melodrama about a drunken prostitute abused by her pimp. A sailor and a local barkeep don't like it. In French with subtitles. **95m/B VHS, Beta.** Simone Signoret, Marcel Dalio, Bernard Blier, Marcel Pagliero, Jane Marken; *D:* Yves Allegret; *C:* Jean Bourgoin. *NOS, FCT*

A Dedicated Man **1986** A lonely woman

agrees to act as a wife for a businessman to lend him credibility. A British "Romance Theater" presentation. **60m/C VHS.** *GB* Alec McCowen, Joan Plowright; *D:* Robert Knights. *PSM*

The Deep 🎬🎬 **1977 (PG)** An innocent couple get involved in an underwater search for a shipwreck, and they quickly find themselves in over their heads. Gorgeous photography manages to keep this slow mover afloat. Famous for Bisset's wet T-shirt scene. Based on the novel by Peter Benchley. The laserdisc edition offers widescreen format. **123m/C VHS, Beta, LV.** Nick Nolte, Jacqueline Bisset, Robert Shaw, Louis Gossett Jr., Eli Wallach; *D:* Peter Yates; *W:* Peter Benchley, Tracy Keenan Wynn; *M:* John Barry. Nominations: Academy Awards '77: Best Sound. *GKK*

Deep Cover 🎬½ **1988 (R)** A man dares to go beyond the walls of a mysterious English manor in order to expose the secrets that lie within the manor. **81m/C VHS, Beta.** Tom Conti, Donald Pleasence, Denholm Elliott, Kika Markham, Phoebe Nicholls; *D:* Richard Loncraine. *PSM, PAR*

Deep Cover 🎬🎬½ **1992 (R)** Fishburne plays Russell Stevens Jr., a straight-arrow cop who goes undercover to infiltrate a Latin American cocaine cartel. While undercover, he becomes partners with drug dealer David Jason (Goldblum), and undergoes an inner transformation until he realizes he is betraying his cause. Confusing and commercial, yet marked with a moral rage. *CW:* Language, violence and drug use, and sensuality. **107m/C VHS, LV, Closed Caption.** Laurence "Larry" Fishburne, Jeff Goldblum, Victoria Dillard, Charles Martin Smith, Sydney Lassick, Clarence Williams III, Gregory Sierra, Roger Guenveur Smith, Cory Curtis, Glynn Turman, Def Jef; *D:* Bill Duke; *W:* Michael Tolkin, Henry Bean; *C:* Bojan Bazelli; *M:* Michel Colombier. *NLC*

Deep Down 🎬½ **1994 (R)** When young Andy (Young) moves into a new apartment, he discovers his neighbor (Roberts) is a gorgeous married woman just looking for a little fun on the side. Too bad her husband (Segal) is a violent psychopath, totally suspicious of his wife's fidelity. Just how far will everyone go to get what they want? Also available in an unrated version. *CW:* Strong sexuality; language; some violence. **86m/C VHS, Closed Caption.** Tanya Roberts, Chris Young, George Segal. *IMP*

Deep End 🎬🎬🎬 **1970** A 15-year-old boy working as an attendant in a bath house falls in love with a 20-year-old woman in this tragic tale of a young man obsessed. Good British cast and music by Cat Stevens. **88m/C VHS.** *GB GE* Jane Asher, John Moulder-Brown, Diana Dors, Karl Michael Vogler, Christopher Sandorf; *D:* Jerzy Skolimowski; *W:* Jerzy Skolimowski, Jerry Gruza, Boleslav Sulik; *C:* Charly Steinberger; *M:* Cat Stevens. *NO*

Deep in My Heart 🎬🎬½ **1954** A musical biography of the life and times of composer Sigmund Romberg, with guest appearances by many MGM stars. ♫Leg of Mutton; You Will Remember Vienna; Softly, as in a Morning Sunrise; Mr. & Mrs.; I Love to Go Swimmin' with Wimmin; The Road to Paradise; Will You Remember; It; Serenade. **132m/C VHS, Beta.** Jose Ferrer, Merle Oberon, Paul Henreid, Walter Pidgeon, Helen Traubel, Rosemary Clooney, Jane Powell, Howard Keel, Cyd Charisse, Gene Kelly, Ann Miller; *D:* Stanley Donen. *MGM*

Deep in the Heart 🎬🎬 *Handgun* **1983 (R)** When a young teacher is raped at gunpoint on a second date, she takes the law into her own hands. Just-off-the-target film tries to take a stand against the proliferation of guns in the U.S. Thought-provoking all the same. **99m/C VHS, Beta.** *GB* Karen Young, Clayton Day, Ben Jones, Suzie Humphreys; *D:* Tony Garnett; *W:* Tony Garnett. *NO*

Deep Red 🎬🎬 **1994 (R)** When a young girl has an encounter with an extra-terrestrial spacecraft her blood chemistry is mysteriously altered. Now the proteins her body manufactures can lead to immortality and ruthless scientist Newmeyer wants to take advantage of the fact—any way he can. *CW:* Violence. **85m/C VHS, LV, Closed Caption.** Michael Biehn, Joanna Pacula, John de Lancie; *D:* Craig R. Baxley; *W:* D. Brent Mote. *USH*

Deep Red: Hatchet Murders 🎬🎬½ *The Hatchet Murders; Profundo Rosso; Dripping Deep Red*

1975 A stylish but gruesome rock music-driven tale of a composer who reads a book on the occult which happens to relate to the sadistic, sangfroid murder of his neighbor. When he visits the book's author, he discovers that she has been horribly murdered as well. **100m/C VHS, Beta.** David Hemmings, Daria Nicolodi; *D:* Dario Argento. *QVD*

Deep Six 🎬🎬½ **1958** A WWII drama that examines the conflict between pacifism and loyalty. A staunch Quaker is called to active duty as a lieutenant in the U.S. Navy, where his beliefs put him into disfavor with shipmates. **110m/C VHS, Beta.** Alan Ladd, William Bendix, James Whitmore, Keenan Wynn, Efrem Zimbalist Jr., Joey Bishop; *D:* Rudolph Mate. *NO*

Deep Space 🎬½ **1987** A flesh-eating alien lands on earth and, after devouring a cop, is stalked by his partner. An "Alien" rip-off. Some humorous moments keep us from thinking too hard about how much the monster resembles our friend from "Alien." **90m/C VHS, Beta.** Charles Napier, Ann Turkel, Ron Glass, Bo Svenson, Julie Newmar; *D:* Fred Olen Ray. *TWE*

Deepstar Six 🎬½ **1989 (R)** When futuristic scientists try to set up an undersea research and missile lab, a group of subterranean monsters get in the way. **97m/C VHS, Beta, LV.** Taurean Blacque, Nancy Everhard, Greg Evigan, Miguel Ferrer, Matt McCoy, Nia Peeples, Cindy Pickett, Marius Weyers; *D:* Sean S. Cunningham; *W:* Lewis Abernathy. *NO*

The Deer Hunter 🎬🎬🎬🎬 **1978 (R)** A powerful and vivid portrait of Middle America with three steel-working friends who leave home to face the Vietnam War. Controversial, brutal sequences in Vietnam are among the most wrenching ever filmed; the rhythms and rituals of home are just as purely captured. Neither pro- nor anti-war, but rather the perfect evocation of how totally and forever altered these people are by the war. Emotionally shattering; not to be missed. **183m/C VHS, Beta, LV.** Robert De Niro, Christopher Walken, Meryl Streep, John Savage, George Dzundza, John Cazale, Chuck Aspegren, Rutanya Alda, Shirley Stoler, Amy Wright; *D:* Michael Cimino; *W:* Deric Washburn, Michael Cimino; *C:* Vilmos Zsigmond; *M:* John Williams. Academy Awards '78: Best Director (Cimino), Best Film Editing, Best Picture, Best Sound, Best Supporting Actor (Walken); Directors Guild of America Awards '78: Best Director (Cimino); Golden Globe Awards '79: Best Director (Cimino); Los Angeles Film Critics Association Awards '78: Best Director (Cimino); New York Film Critics Awards '78: Best Film, Best Supporting Actor (Walken); National Society of Film Critics Awards '78: Best Supporting Actress (Streep); Nominations: Academy Awards '78: Best Actor (De Niro), Best Cinematography, Best Original Screenplay, Best Supporting Actress (Streep). *USH, FCT, BTV*

The Deerslayer 🎬½ **1978** Low-budget snoozer based on the classic novel by James Fenimore Cooper. Frontiersman Hawkeye and his Indian companion Chingachgook set out to rescue a beautiful Indian maiden and must fight bands of hostile Indians and Frenchmen along the way. **98m/C VHS, Beta.** Steve Forrest, Ned Romero, John Anderson, Joan Prather; *D:* Richard Friedenberg; *M:* Andrew Belling. *NO*

Def by Temptation 🎬🎬 **1990 (R)** A potent horror fantasy about a young black theology student who travels to New York in search of an old friend. There he meets an evil woman who is determined to seduce him and force him to give in to temptation. Great soundtrack. **95m/C VHS, Beta, LV.** James Bond III, Kadeem Hardison, Bill Nunn, Samuel L. Jackson, Minnie Gentry, Rony Clanton; *D:* James Bond III; *W:* James Bond III. *SGE, IME*

Def-Con 4 🎬½ **1985 (R)** Three marooned space travelers return to a holocaust-shaken Earth to try to start again, but some heavy-duty slimeballs are in charge and they don't want to give it up. Good special effects bolster a weak script. **85m/C VHS, Beta.** Maury Chaykin, Kate Lynch, Tim Choate; *D:* Paul Donovan. *NWV, VTR*

The Defender 🎬🎬½ 1957 CBS "Studio One" presentation of a live courtroom drama. First shown in 1957. Made for television. 112m/B **VHS, Beta.** Steve McQueen, William Shatner, Ralph Bellamy, Martin Balsam. *FCT, RHI*

Defenders of the Law 🎬🎬 1931 Early action talkie concerned with gang warfare and law enforcement. 64m/B **VHS.** John Holland, Mae Busch, Alan Cooke, Joseph Girard, Edmund Breese, Catherine Dale Owen, Robert Gleckler; *D:* Joseph Levering. *GPV*

Defending Your Life 🎬🎬🎬 1991 (PG) Brooks' cock-eyed way of looking at the world travels to the afterlife in this uneven comedy/romance. In Judgement City, where everyone goes after death, past lives are examined and judged. If you were a good enough person you get to stay in heaven (where you wear funny robes and eat all you want without getting fat). If not, it's back to earth for another go-round. Brooks plays an L.A. advertising executive who crashes his new BMW and finds himself defending his life. When he meets and falls in love with Streep, his interest in staying in heaven multiplies. Occasionally charming, seldom out-right hilarious. 112m/C **VHS, LV, 8mm, Closed Caption.** Albert Brooks, Meryl Streep, Rip Torn, Lee Grant, Buck Henry, George Wallace, Lillian Lehman, Peter Schuck, Susan Walters; *D:* Albert Brooks; *W:* Albert Brooks; *C:* Allen Daviau; *M:* Michael Gore. *WAR*

The Defense Never Rests 🎬🎬 1990 Perry Mason, the lawyer who never loses a case, aids his friend and secretary, Della Street, in this made-for-television movie. 95m/C **VHS, Beta.** Raymond Burr, Barbara Hale, Al Freeman Jr., William Katt, Patrick O'Neal. *MCG*

Defense of the Realm 🎬🎬🎬½ 1985 (PG) A British politician is accused of selling secrets to the KGB through his mistress and only a pair of dedicated newspapermen believe he is innocent. In the course of finding the answers they discover a national cover-up conspiracy. An acclaimed, taut thriller. 96m/C **VHS, Beta, LV, Closed Caption.** *GB* Gabriel Byrne, Greta Scacchi, Denholm Elliott, Ian Bannen, Bill Paterson, Fulton Mackay, Robbie Coltrane; *D:* David Drury; *C:* Roger Deakins. British Academy Awards '85: Best Supporting Actor (Elliott). *COL*

Defense Play 🎬½ 1988 (PG) Two teenagers are unwittingly stuck in the middle of a Soviet plot to steal the plans that created a technologically advanced helicopter. 95m/C **VHS, Beta.** David Oliver, Susan Ursitti, Monte Markham, William Frankfather, Patch MacKenzie; *D:* Monte Markham. *TWE*

Defenseless 🎬🎬 1991 (R) Hershey tries hard in an unplayable part as a giddy attorney who finds herself trapped in a love-affair/legal case that turns murderous. Good cast and interesting twists contend with a sexist sub-text, which proves a woman can't "have it all." 106m/C **VHS, LV, Closed Caption.** Barbara Hershey, Sam Shepard, Mary Beth Hurt, J.T. Walsh, Sheree North; *D:* Martin Campbell; *W:* James Cresson; *M:* Trevor Jones. *LIV*

Defiance 🎬🎬 1979 (PG) A former merchant seaman moves into a tenement in a run-down area of New York City. When a local street gang begins terrorizing the neighborhood, he decides to take a stand. Familiar plotline handled well in this thoughtful film. 101m/C **VHS, Beta.** Jan-Michael Vincent, Art Carney, Theresa Saldana, Danny Aiello; *D:* John Flynn; *W:* Tom Donnelly; *M:* John Beal, Basil Poledouris. *ORI, LIV, VES*

Defiant 🎬½ *The Wild Pack; The Sandpit Generals* 1970 Two rival street gangs clash when one admits a young orphan girl. 93m/C **VHS, Beta.** Kent Lane, John Rubinstein, Tisha Sterling; *D:* Hall Bartlett. *LIV*

The Defiant Ones 🎬🎬🎬½ 1958 Thought-provoking story about racism revolves around two escaped prisoners (one black, one white) from a chain gang in the rural South. Their societal conditioning to hate each other dissolves as they face constant peril together. Critically acclaimed. 97m/B **VHS, Beta, Closed Caption.** Tony Curtis, Sidney Poitier, Theodore Bikel, Lon Chaney Jr., Charles McGraw, Cara Williams; *D:* Stanley Kramer; *W:* Nedrick

Young, Harold Jacob Smith; *C:* Sam Leavitt; *M:* Stephen Dorff. Academy Awards '58: Best Black and White Cinematography, Best Story & Screenplay; British Academy Awards '58: Best Actor (Poitier); Edgar Allan Poe Awards '58: Best Screenplay; Golden Globe Awards '58: Best Film—Drama; New York Film Critics Awards '58: Best Director (Kramer), Best Film, Best Screenplay; Nominations: Academy Awards '58: Best Actor (Curtis), Best Actor (Poitier), Best Director (Kramer), Best Film Editing, Best Picture, Best Supporting Actor (Bikel), Best Supporting Actress (Williams). *MGM*

The Defilers 🎬 1965 (R) Disturbing, low-budget J.D. movie in which two thugs imprison a young girl in a basement and force her to be their love slave. ?m/B **VHS.** Byron Mabe, Jerome Eden, Mae Johnson; *D:* David Friedman. *SNC, TPV*

Deja Vu 🎬 1984 (R) A lame romantic thriller about the tragic deaths of two lovers and their supposed reincarnation 50 years later. 95m/C **VHS, Beta, LV.** *GB* Jaclyn Smith, Nigel Terry, Claire Bloom, Shelley Winters; *D:* Anthony Richmond; *W:* Ezra D. Rappaport; *M:* Pino Donaggio. *MGM*

Deja Vu 🎬🎬 1989 Thriller set in 1925 and moving between Chicago and Odessa. A Chicago hitman is hired by the mob to kill a traitor who has fled to Odessa. Niczypur, the traitor, has been using the newly opened Chicago-Constantinople-Odessa shipping line for his own smuggling operation. Filled with shoot-outs, brawls, and chases. In English, Russian, and Polish with English subtitles. 108m/C **VHS.** *PL* Jerzy Stuhr, Galina Pietrowa, Nikolai Karaczencow, Wladimir Golowin; *D:* Juliusz Machulski. *FCT*

The Deliberate Stranger 🎬🎬🎬 1986 Harmon is engrossing as charismatic serial killer Ted Bundy, sentenced to death for several Florida murders and suspected in the killings of a least 35 women in several states. After eluding police for five years Bundy was finally arrested in Florida in 1979. His case became a cause celebre on capital punishment as it dragged on for nine years. Bundy was finally executed in 1989. Based on the book "Bundy: The Deliberate Stranger" by Richard W. Larsen. Made for television. 188m/C **VHS, Beta.** Mark Harmon, M. Emmet Walsh, Frederic Forrest, John Ashton, George Grizzard, Ben Masters, Glynnis O'Connor, Bonnie Bartlett, Billy Green Bush, Lawrence Pressman; *D:* Marvin J. Chomsky. *WAR, PMS*

The Delicate Delinquent 🎬🎬½ 1956 Lewis's first movie without Dean Martin finds him in the role of delinquent who manages to become a policeman with just the right amount of slapstick. 101m/B **VHS, Beta, LV, Closed Caption.** Jerry Lewis, Darren McGavin, Martha Hyer, Robert Ivers, Horace McMahon; *D:* Don McGuire; *W:* Don McGuire. *PAR*

Delicatessen 🎬🎬🎬 1992 (R) Set in 21st-century Paris, this hilarious debut from directors Jeunot and Caro focuses on the lives of the oddball tenants of an apartment building over a butcher shop. Although there is a famine, the butcher shop is always stocked with fresh meat—made from the building's tenants. Part comedy, part horror, part romance, this film merges a cacophony of sights and sounds with intriguing results. Watch for the scene involving a symphony of creaking bed springs, a squeaky bicycle pump, a cello, and clicking knitting needles. In French with English subtitles. 95m/C **VHS, Beta, LV, Closed Caption.** *FR* Marie-Laure Dougnac, Dominique Pinon, Karin Viard, Jean Claude Dreyfus, Ticky Holgado, Anne Marie Pisani, Edith Ker, Patrick Paroux, Jean-Luc Caron; *D:* Jean-Marie Jeunet, Marc Caro; *W:* Gilles Adrien; *M:* Carlos D'Alessi. Cesar Awards '92: Best Art Direction/Set Decoration, Best Writing. *PAR, BTV*

Delightfully Dangerous 🎬🎬 1945 Often Deadly Dull. A farfetched musical rooted in yesteryear about mismatched sisters, one a 15-year-old farm girl, the other a New York burlesque dancer, in competition on Broadway. ♫I'm Only Teasin'; In a Shower of Stars; Mynah Bird; Through Your Eyes to Your Heart; Delightfully Dangerous; Once Upon a Song. 92m/B **VHS.** Jane

Powell, Ralph Bellamy, Constance Moore, Arthur Treacher, Louise Beavers; *D:* Arthur Lubin. *DVT, NOS, VDM*

Delinquent Daughters 🎬½ 1944 Slow-paced drama about a high school girl who commits suicide and the cop and reporter who try to find out why so darn many kids are getting into trouble. 71m/B **VHS, Beta.** June Carlson, Fifi d'Orsay, Teala Loring; *D:* Al(bert) Herman. *SNC, VYY, DVT*

Delinquent Parents 🎬½ 1938 A wayward girl gives up her baby for adoption. She turns her life around and becomes a juvenile court judge. Years later, who should come up before her for misdeeds but her long-lost daughter. The Hound cannot improve on a contemporary critic who reviewed this "Delinquent Producers." 62m/B **VHS.** Doris Weston, Maurice Murphy, Helen MacKellar, Terry Walker, Richard Tucker, Morgan Wallace; *D:* Nick Grinde. *NOS, LOO*

Delinquent School Girls woof! *Bad Girls* 1984 (R) Three escapees from an asylum get more than they bargained for when they visit a Female Correctional Institute to fulfill their sexual fantasies. Buys into just about every conceivable stereotype. 89m/C **VHS, Beta.** Michael Pataki, Bob Minos, Stephen Stucker; *D:* Gregory Corarito. *LIV, VES*

Delirious 🎬½ 1991 (PG) A writer for a television soap opera wakes from a bash on the head to find himself inside the story where murder and mayhem are brewing. Can he write himself back to safety, and find romance along the way? Somehow Candy just isn't believeable as a romantic lead and the film has few laughs. 96m/C **VHS, Beta, LV, 8mm, Closed Caption.** John Candy, Mariel Hemingway, Emma Samms, Raymond Burr, David Rasche, Dylan Baker, Charles Rocket, Jerry Orbach, Renee Taylor, Robert Wagner; *D:* Tom Mankiewicz; *W:* Lawrence J. Cohen; *M:* Cliff Eidelman. *MGM*

Delirium woof! *Psycho Puppet* 1977 Homicidal maniac goes on a killing spree and has just one thing in mind—women. Angry group of citizens inadvertently includes the demonic villain in their vigilante club. Nothing redeeming here. 94m/C **VHS, Beta.** Turk Cekovsky, Debi Shanley, Terry Ten Broeck; *D:* Peter Maris. *NO*

Deliverance 🎬🎬🎬🎬 1972 (R) Terrifying exploration of the primal nature of man and his alienation from nature, based on the novel by James Dickey, which he adapted for the film (he also makes an appearance as a sheriff). Four urban professionals, hoping to get away from it all for the weekend, canoe down a southern river, encounter crazed backwoodsmen, and end up battling for survival. Excellent performances all around, especially by Voight. Debuts for Beatty and Cox. Watch for O'Neill as a sheriff, and director Boorman's son Charley as Voight's son. "Dueling Banjos" scene and tune are memorable as is scene where the backwoods boys promise to make the fellows squeal like pigs. 109m/C **VHS, Beta, LV.** Jon Voight, Burt Reynolds, Ronny Cox, Ned Beatty, James Dickey, Bill McKinney, Ed O'Neill, Charley Boorman; *D:* John Boorman; *W:* James Dickey; *C:* Vilmos Zsigmond; *M:* Eric Weissburg. National Board of Review Awards '72: 10 Best Films of the Year; Nominations: Academy Awards '72: Best Director (Boorman), Best Film Editing, Best Picture. *WAR, FCT*

Delivery Boys 🎬½ 1984 (R) The "Delivery Boys," three breakdancers aiming to win the $10,000 New York City Break-Off, find unusual perils that may keep them from competing. 94m/C **VHS, Beta.** Joss Marcano, Tom Sierchio, Jim Soriero, Mario Van Peebles, Samantha Fox; *D:* Ken Handley. *VTR, NWV*

Delos Adventure 🎬 1986 (R) A geological expedition in South America stumbles upon covert Russian activities and must battle to survive in this overly-violent actioner. 98m/C **VHS, Beta.** Roger Kern, Jenny Neumann, Kevin Brophy; *D:* Joseph Purcell. *TWE*

Delta Force 🎬🎬 1986 (R) Based on the true hijacking of a TWA plane in June 1985. Arab terrorists take over an airliner; the Delta Force, led by Lee Marvin and featuring Norris as its best fighter, rescue the passengers in ways that cater directly to our nationalistic revenge fantasies. Average thriller, exciting and tense at times, with fine work from Marvin, Norris, and Forster. 125m/C VHS, Beta, LV, Closed Caption. Lee Marvin, Chuck Norris, Shelley Winters, Martin Balsam, George Kennedy, Hanna Schygulla, Susan Strasberg, Bo Svenson, Joey Bishop, Lainie Kazan, Robert Forster, Robert Vaughn, Kim Delaney; D: Menahem Golan; W: James Bruner; M: Alan Silvestri. MED, VTR

Delta Force 2: Operation Stranglehold *🎬🎬½* 1990 (R) Delta Force is back with martial artist and military technician Norris at the helm. Action-packed and tense. 110m/C VHS, Beta, LV, Closed Caption. John P. Ryan, Chuck Norris, Billy Drago, Richard Jaeckel, Paul Perri; D: Aaron Norris; W: Lee Reynolds; C: Joao Fernandes. MED, BTV, VTR

Delta Force 3: The Killing Game *🎬½* Young Commandos 1991 (R) A terrorist mastermind plants an atomic bomb in an American city, and the President has only one choice...call in the Delta Force. The leading men in this lackluster thriller are the sons of some of Hollywood's biggest stars. CW: Language and war violence. 97m/C VHS, LV. Nick Cassavetes, Eric Douglas, Mike Norris, Matthew Penn, John P. Ryan, Sandy Ward; D: Sam Firstenberg; W: Boaz Davidson. CAN

Delta Force Commando *🎬½* 1987 (R) Two U.S. Fighter pilots fight against terrorism in the deadly Nicaraguan jungle. 90m/C VHS. Fred Williamson, Bo Svenson. RHI

Delta Force Commando 2 *🎬* Priority Red One 1990 (R) The celluloid was hardly dry on the first "Delta Force Commando" before the resourceful Italians began grinding out this follow-up, with the lead commando getting the Force entangled in a deadly international conspiracy. CW: Some language and strong violence. 100m/C VHS. IT Richard Hatch, Fred Williamson, Giannina Facio, Van Johnson; D: Frank Valenti. LIV

Delta Fox *🎬🎬* 1977 Delta Fox is carrying a million dollars for the mob, but the mob is carrying a grudge and the chase is on. 90m/C VHS, Beta. Priscilla Barnes, Richard Lynch, Stuart Whitman, John Ireland; D: Beverly Sebastian, Ferd Sebastian. NO

Delta Heat *🎬🎬* 1992 (R) A new designer drug hits L.A. and detective Mike Bishop (Edwards) follows his partner to the drug's source in Louisiana. When Bishop arrives he discovers his partner has been tortured and murdered in order to keep the drug lord's foes in line. Bishop must then save himself and find justice in the steamy streets of New Orleans. Routine lone guy vs. bad guys actioner. CW: Language and violence. 91m/C VHS, Closed Caption. Anthony Edwards, Lance Henriksen, Betsy Russell, Linda Dona, Rod Masterson, John McConnell, Clayton Landey; D: Michael Fischa. ACA

Delta of Venus *🎬½* 1995 (R) Paris, 1940—beautiful young American Elena (England), an aspiring author, falls for handsome Lawrence (Mandylor), a writer of dirty books. But she finds out Lawrence isn't faithful and winds up supporting herself as a nude model and writing her own erotic tales. Lots of sex scenes and an equal amount of pretensions. Based on the erotic novel "Delta of Venus" by Anais Nin. Prague substitutes for Paris as the film location. Also availble unrated; the theatrical version came out as NC-17. CW: Strong erotic content. 100m/C VHS, LV, Closed Caption. Audie England, Costas Mandylor, Erick Da Silva; D: Zalman King; W: Patricia Louisianna Knop, Elisa Rothstein; C: Eagle Egilsson; M: George S. Clinton. NLC

Deluge *🎬🎬* 1933 Tidal waves causd by earthquakes have destroyed most of New York (though some may think this is no great loss) in this early sci-fi pic. 72m/B VHS, Beta. Edward Van Sloan, Peggy Shannon, Sidney Blackmer, Fred Kohler Sr., Matt Moore, Samuel S. Hinds, Lane Chandler; D: Felix Feist. EEL

The Deluge *🎬🎬* Potop 1973 Romance woven around the Polish-Swedish war in the 17th century. Adapted from the 1886 novel by Nobel prize-winning author Henryk Sienkiewicz, and filmed largely on location in authentic castles of the era. Polish with subtitles. 185m/C VHS. PL Daniel Olbrychski, Malgorzata Braunek, Wladyslaw Hancza, Leszek Herdegen, Andrzej Lapicki; D: Jerzy Hoffman; C: Jerzy Wojcik; M: Kazimierz Serocki. Nominations: Academy Awards '73: Best Foreign Language Film. FCT

Delusion *🎬½* The House Where Death Lives 1984 (R) Gothic thriller in which invalid Cotten and family are harassed by a possibly supernatural killer as told by Cotten's nurse. Filmed in 1980. Ending is a let-down. 93m/C VHS, Beta. Patricia Pearcy, David Hayward, John Dukakis, Joseph Cotten, Simone Griffeth; D: Alan Beattie.

Delusion *🎬🎬½* 1991 (R) A yuppie with an embezzled fortune is held up in the Nevada desert by a psycho hood with a showgirl lover. But who's really in charge here? The snappy, hip, film-noir thriller takes a few unlikely twists and has an open Lady-or-the-Tiger finale that may infuriate. Available in a widescreen edition on laserdisc. CW: Language and sensuality. 100m/C VHS, LV. Jim Metzler, Jennifer Rubin, Kyle Secor, Robert Costanzo, Tracey Walter, Jerry Orbach; D: Carl Colpaert; W: Carl Colpaert, Kurt Voss; M: Barry Adamson. COL

Delusions of Grandeur *🎬🎬½* La Folle des Grandeurs 1976 A French comedy of court intrigue set in 17th-century Spain. In French with English subtitles. Based loosely on Victor Hugo's "Ruy Blas." 85m/C VHS, Beta. FR Yves Montand, Louis de Funes, Alice Sapritch, Karin Schubert, Gabriele Tinti; D: Gerard Oury. FCT

Demented *🎬* 1980 (R) Beautiful and talented woman is brutally gang-raped by four men, but her revenge is sweet and deadly as she entices each to bed and gives them a big dose of their own medicine. All-too-familiar plot offers nothing new. 92m/C VHS, Beta. Sallee Elyse, Bruce Gilchrist. MED

Dementia 13 *🎬🎬½* The Haunted and the Hunted 1963 This eerie thriller, set in a creepy castle, is an early Coppola film about the members of an Irish family who are being offed by an axe murderer one-by-one. 75m/B VHS, Beta. William Campbell, Luana Anders, Bart Patton, Patrick Magee; D: Francis Ford Coppola; W: Francis Ford Coppola. NOS, MRV, SNC

Demetrius and the Gladiators *🎬🎬½* 1954 A sequel to "The Robe," wherein the holy-robe-carrying slave is enlisted as one of Caligula's gladiators and mixes with the trampy empress Messalina. 101m/C VHS, Beta, LV, Closed Caption. Victor Mature, Susan Hayward, Michael Rennie, Debra Paget, Anne Bancroft, Jay Robinson, Barry Jones, Richard Egan, William Marshall, Ernest Borgnine; D: Delmer Daves; W: Philip Dunne; C: Milton Krasner. FOX

The Demi-Paradise *🎬🎬🎬* Adventure for Two 1943 Tongue-in-cheek look at people's perceptions of foreigners has Olivier as a Russian inventor (?!) who comes to England with some trepidation. Though the Brits are plenty quirky, he manages to find romance with Ward in this charming look at British life. 110m/B VHS, Beta. GB Laurence Olivier, Penelope Dudley Ward, Margaret Rutherford, Wilfrid Hyde-White; D: Anthony Asquith. NOS, VDM, DVT

Demolition *🎬½* 1977 Ex-international courier finds that the "simple" task he has consented to do for his old employers is deceptively hazardous. 90m/C VHS, Beta. John Waters, Belinda Giblin, Fred Steele, Vincent Ball; D: Kevin Dobson. NO

Demolition High *🎬🎬½* 1995 (R) Standard actioner finds New York kid Lenny (Haim) having problems adjusting to his new California high school, where he's labeled a troublemaker. But real trouble comes along when a group of terrorists, fleeing police after a robbery, take over the school and hold the teachers and students as hostages. Fortunately, Lenny is able to lead a se-

cret counterattack. CW: Violence and some language. 85m/C VHS, Closed Caption. Corey Haim, Alan Thicke, Jeff Kober, Dick Van Patten; D: Jim Wynorski; W: Steve Jankowski; C: Zoran Hochstatter; M: Kevin Kiner. CAF

Demolition Man *🎬🎬* 1993 (R) No-brain sci-fier rests on the action skills of Stallone and Snipes. Psychovillain Snipes (sporting a Dennis Rodman 'do) is pursued by equally violent cop Stallone in the late 1990s. Then they're cryogenically frozen, defrosted in 2032, and back to their old tricks. One problem. This is not a fun future: virtual reality sex is the only kind allowed and puritan ethics and political correctness are enforced to the max. Cop and bad guy get to show this highly orderly society some really violent times. Implausible plot and minimal acting, but lots of action and violence for fans. CW: Strong language, partial nudity, and non-stop action violence. 115m/C VHS, Beta, LV, 8mm, Closed Caption. Sylvester Stallone, Wesley Snipes, Sandra Bullock, Nigel Hawthorne, Benjamin Bratt, Bob Gunton, Glenn Shadix, Denis Leary; D: Marco Brambilla; W: Daniel Waters, Robert Reneau, Peter M. Lenkov; M: Elliot Goldenthal. Nominations: MTV Movie Awards '94: Best Villain (Snipes). WAR

The Demolitionist *🎬🎬* 1995 (R) Tough undercover cop Alyssa Lloyd (Eggert) is killed by a crimelord (Grieco) and then resurrected by a scientist (Abbott) as a hard-hitting futuristic superheroine who's out to save Metro City from evil. CW: Strong violence, some nudity and language. 100m/C VHS, LV. Nicole Eggert, Richard Grieco, Bruce Abbott, Susan Tyrrell; D: Robert Kurtzman. APX

The Demon *🎬½* 1981 (R) A small town may be doomed to extinction, courtesy of a monster's thirst for the blood of its inhabitants. 94m/C VHS, Beta. Cameron Mitchell, Jennifer Holmes. NO

Demon Barber of Fleet Street *🎬🎬½* Sweeney Todd: The Demon Barber of Fleet Street 1936 Loosely based on an actual event, this film inspired the 1978 smash play "Sweeney Todd." Slaughter stars as a mad barber who doesn't just cut his client's hair. He happens to have a deal cooked up with the baker to provide him with some nice 'juicy' filling for his meat pies. Manages to be creepy and funny at the same time. 68m/B VHS, Beta. GB Tod Slaughter, Eve Lister, Bruce Seton; D: George King. VYY, MRV, SNC

Demon City Shinjuku *🎬🎬½* 1993 In the near future the evil Levih Rah has created a Demon City in Shinjuku, located in the heart of Tokyo, where he commands his army of thugs and monsters. Sayama and the streetwise Kyoya venture into Shinjuku in search of Sayama's kidnapped father. They encounter the mystical Mephisto, who may be able to help them, but time is running out—Levih Rah is set to destroy the entire planet in three days! In Japanese with English subtitles. 82m/C VHS, LV. JP CPM

Demon for Trouble *🎬* 1934 Outlaws are murdering land buyers in this routine western. 58m/B VHS, Beta. Bob Steele. NOS, RXM

Demon Hunter *🎬½* 1988 Terror reigns while a deranged killer stalks his next victim. 90m/C VHS, Beta. George Ellis, Erin Fleming, Marrianne Gordon; D: Massey Cramer. NO

A Demon in My View *🎬🎬½* 1992 (R) In a role similar to his infamous Norman Bates in "Psycho," Perkins stars as a man who hides a terrible secret—he is a former serial killer. When a fellow tenant in his apartment house accidentally destroys his doll, Perkins' tenuous sanity is shaken and he begins killing again. A smart thriller. Perkins last big-screen role. CW: Violence and some sexuality. 98m/C VHS, LV, Closed Caption. Anthony Perkins, Sophie Ward, Stratford Johns; D: Petra Haffter. THV, MOV

The Demon Lover woof! 1977 (R) Leader of a satanic cult calls forth the devil when he doesn't get his way. Poorly acted and badly produced. Features comic book artists Val "Howard the Duck" Mayerick and Gunnar ."Leatherface"

Hansen. Also on video as "Devil Master" and "Master of Evil." 87m/C VHS, Beta. Christmas Robbins, Val Mayerick, Gunnar Hansen, Tom Hutton, David Howard; **D:** Donald G. Jackson, Jerry Younkins; **W:** Donald G. Jackson, Jerry Younkins. UNI, PMR

Demon Lust 📽 19?? A couple's lovely country vacation is turned into a nightmare when two drifters terrorize them. 76m/C VHS, Beta. **D:** Bernard Buys. GHV

Demon of Paradise woof! 1987 (R) Dynamite fishing off the coast of Hawaii unearths an ancient, man-eating lizard-man. Uneven, unexciting horror attempt. 84m/C VHS, Beta. Kathryn Witt, William Steis, Leslie Huntly, Laura Banks; **D:** Cirio H. Santiago. WAR

Demon Possessed 📽½ 1993 (R) When Tom is critically injured in a snowmobile race in a remote woods, he and his friends find shelter in a deserted children's camp. It turns out the camp was run by a secret religious cult that practiced occult murder and the demon that haunted the place has never left. When Tom dies this satanic spirit finds the perfect host to return to human form and continue its bloody work. 97m/C VHS, LV. Dawn Laurrie, Aaron Kjenaas, David Fields, Eve Montgomery; **D:** Christopher Webster; **W:** Julian Weaver; **M:** John Tatgenhorst. AIP

Demon Queen 📽 1980 A vampirish woman seduces, then murders, many men. 70m/C VHS, Beta. Mary Fanaro, Dennis Stewart, Cliff Dance; **D:** Donald Farmer. NO

Demon Rage 📽½ Satan's Mistress; Fury of the Succubus; Dark Eyes 1982 (R) Neglected housewife drifts under the spell of a phantom lover. 98m/C VHS, Beta. Britt Ekland, Lana Wood, Kabir Bedi, Don Galloway, John Carradine, Sherry Scott; **D:** James Polakof. HHE

Demon Seed 📽📽📽 1977 (R) When a scientist and his wife separate so he can work on his computer, the computer takes over the house and impregnates the wife. Bizarre and taut. 97m/C VHS, Beta, LV. Julie Christie, Fritz Weaver, Gerrit Graham, Berry Kroeger, Ron Hays; **D:** Donald Cammell; **C:** Bill Butler; **V:** Robert Vaughn. MGM

Demon Wind 📽½ 1990 (R) A gateway to Hell opens up on a secluded farm and various heroic types try to close it. Meanwhile, demons attempt to possess those humans in their midst. Zombies abound in this near-woof. 97m/C VHS, Beta, LV. Eric Larson, Francine Lapensee, Rufus Norris; **D:** Charles Philip Moore. PAR

Demon with a Glass Hand 📽½ 1964 In the vein of "The Terminator," a man goes back two hundred years in time to escape the evil race that rules the planet. 63m/B VHS, Beta. Robert Culp, Arlene Martel, Abraham Sofaer. MGM

Demonic Toys 📽½ 1990 (R) The possessed play-things attack a bunch of unfortunates in a warehouse, and pumped-up lady cop Scoggins deserves an award for keeping a straight face. Skimpily scripted gore from the horror assembly-line at Full Moon Productions. Far more entertaining are the multiple behind-the-scenes featurettes on the tape. **CW:** Language and fantasy/horror violence. 86m/C VHS, Beta, LV, Closed Caption. Tracy Scoggins, Bentley Mitchum, Michael Russo, Jeff Weston, Daniel Cerney, Pete Schrum; **D:** Peter Manoogian. PAR

Demonoid, Messenger of Death 📽 Macabra 1981 (R) Discovery of an ancient temple of Satan worship drastically changes the lives of a young couple when the husband becomes possessed by the Demonoid, which initially takes on the form of a severed hand. Poor script needs hand, producing a number of unintentionally laughable moments. 85m/C VHS, Beta. Samantha Eggar, Stuart Whitman, Roy Cameron Jenson; **D:** Alfredo Zacharias. MED

The Demons 📽 1974 (R) As she slips into death, a tortured woman curses her torturers. 90m/C VHS, Beta. Anne Libert, Britt Nichols, Doris Thomas. UNI

Demons 📽½ Demoni 1986 (R) A horror film in a Berlin theater is so involving that its viewers become the demons they are seeing. The new monsters turn on the other audience members. Virtually plotless, very explicit. Rock soundtrack by Accept, Go West, Motley Crue, and others. Revered in some circles, blasted in others. Followed by "Demons 2." 89m/C VHS, Beta, LV. IT Urbano Barberini, Natasha Hovey, Paolo Cozza, Karl Zinny, Fiore Argento, Fabiola Toledo, Nicoletta Elni; **D:** Lamberto Bava. NWV

Demons 2 📽½ 1987 Inferior sequel to "Demons." The son of horror-meister Mario Bava, Lamberto collaborated with Italian auteur Argento (who co-wrote and produced) to create an improbable sequel (storywise) which seems to have been edited by some kind of crazed cutting room slasher with equally hackneyed dubbing. Residents of a chi-chi high rise watching a documentary about the events of "Demons"—a sort of high-tech play-within-a-play ploy—when a demon emerges from the TV, spreads his creepy cooties, and causes the tenants to sprout fangs and claws and nasty tempers. Lots of blood drips from ceilings, plumbing fixtures, and various body parts. 88m/C VHS, LV. IT David Knight, Nancy Brill, Coralina Cataldi Tassoni, Bobby Rhodes, Asia Argento, Virginia Bryant; **D:** Lamberto Bava; **W:** Dario Argento, Lamberto Bava; **M:** Simon Boswell. IMP

Demons in the Garden 📽📽📽 Demonios En El Jardin 1982 (R) Centers on the disintegration of a family after the end of the Spanish Civil War, due to sibling rivalries and a variety of indiscretions. Problems mount as two brothers become involved with their stepsister. Story takes on poignancy in its narration by a young boy. Beautiful cinematography. In Spanish with English subtitles. 100m/C VHS. SP Angela Molina, Ana Belen, Encarna Paso, Imanol Arias; **D:** Manuel Gutierrez Aragon; **C:** Jose Luis Alcaine. CVC, TPV, FCT

Demons of Ludlow 📽 1975 Demons attend a small town's bicentennial celebration intent on raising a little hell of their own. 83m/C VHS, Beta. Paul von Hauser, Stephanie Cushna, James Robinson, Carol Perry; **D:** Steven Kuether. TWE

Demons of the Mind 📽📽 1972 (R) A sordid psychological horror film about a baron in 19th century Austria who imprisons his children, fearing that mental illness is a family trait. Also on video as "Blood Evil." 85m/C VHS, Beta. GB Michael Hordern, Patrick Magee, Yvonne Mitchell, Robert Hardy, Gillian Hills, Virginia Wetherell, Shane Briant, Paul Jones; **D:** Peter Sykes. REP, MLB

Demonstone 📽 Heartstone 1989 (R) A television reporter becomes possessed by a Filipino demon and carries out an ancient curse against the family of a corrupt government official. 90m/C VHS, Beta, LV. R. Lee Ermey, Jan-Michael Vincent, Nancy Everhard; **D:** Andrew Prowse. FRH

Demonstrator 📽📽½ 1971 A father and son are at odds when dad heads an Asian military coalition and junior protests. Notable for being one of the first major Australian films to use an entirely native cast. 82m/C VHS. AU Joe James, Irene Inescort, Gerard Maguire, Wendy Lingham, Harold Hopkins; **D:** Warwick Freeman. ACA

Demonwarp woof! 1987 A vengeance-minded hunter journeys into an evil, primeval forest to kill the monsters that abducted his daughter. 91m/C VHS, Beta. George Kennedy, Emmett Alston. THV

Dempsey 📽📽 1983 In this made for television film based on Jack Dempsey's autobiography, Williams plays the role of the famed world heavyweight champ. His rise through the boxing ranks as well as his personal life are chronicled. A bit slow-moving considering the pounding fists and action. 110m/C VHS, Beta. Treat Williams, Sam Waterston, Sally Kellerman, Victoria Tennant, Peter Mark Richman, Jesse Vint, Bonnie Bartlett, James Noble; **D:** Gus Trikonis; **M:** Billy Goldenberg. MED

Denial: The Dark Side of Passion 📽📽 1991 (R) A strong-willed woman tries to put a destructive love affair behind her—but if she succeeded there'd be no movie. Torrid stuff with a watchable cast. **CW:** Sensuality. 103m/C VHS, LV, Closed Caption. Robin Wright, Jason Patric, Barry Primus, Christina Harnos, Rae Dawn Chong; **D:** Eric Dignam; **W:** Eric Dignam. REP

Denise Calls Up 📽📽½ 1995 (PG-13) Comedy about futility and complications of urban relationships among overworked professionals. A group of six work-at-home city friends socialize, romance, and date entirely via phone, fax, and computer without ever meeting or leaving their homes, even for a close friend's funeral (who dies, oddly enough, while on the phone). Subplot involves title character, Denise (Ubach) tracking down sperm donor Martin (Gunther) and eventually giving birth, with the help of her cellular coaches. Funny premise is executed well, but doesn't hold up over a (barely) feature length film. **CW:** Sexual references and nudity. 79m/C VHS, LV, Closed Caption. Timothy Daly, Dana Wheeler-Nicholson, Caroleen Feeney, Liev Schreiber, Dan Gunther, Aida Turturro, Alanna Ubach, Sylvia Miles; **D:** Hal Salwen; **W:** Hal Salwen; **C:** Mike Mayers; **M:** Lynne Geller. COL

Dennis the Menace 📽📽½ 1993 (PG) Straight from the Hughes kiddie farm comes Kevin McAllister—oops!—Dennis Mitchell (newcomer Gamble), curious, crafty, and blond 5-year-old. He dreams and schemes, but everything he does manages to be a threat to the physical and mental well-being of hot-head neighbor Mr. Wilson (Matthau, perfectly cast as the grump). Lloyd is very nasty as protagonist Switchblade Sam; Plowright, Thompson, and Stanton round out the cast as Mrs. Wilson and the Mitchell parents, respectively. Sure to please young kids, but parents may be less enthralled with this adaptation of the popular '50s comic strip and subsequent TV series. 96m/C VHS, Beta, LV, 8mm, Closed Caption. Walter Matthau, Mason Gamble, Joan Plowright, Christopher Lloyd, Lea Thompson, Robert Stanton, Billie Bird, Paul Winfield, Amy Sakasitz, Kellen Hathaway, Arnold Stang; **D:** Nick Castle; **W:** John Hughes; **C:** Thomas Ackerman; **M:** Jerry Goldsmith. WAR

Dennis the Menace: Dinosaur Hunter 📽📽½ 1993 (G) Another version of Hank Ketchum's mischievous cartoon character brought to life to have adventures and disturb his neighbor Mr. Wilson. This time Dennis discovers a huge, primitive bone in his backyard and when an archaeologist declares it's a dinosaur bone, news crews, tourists, and scientists are suddenly everywhere. This badly disturbs Mr. Wilson's retirement and Dennis and his friends must save the day (and their neighborhood). 118m/C VHS, LV, Closed Caption. Victor Dimattia, William Windom, Pat Estrin, Jim Jansen, Patsy Garrett. THV

The Dentist 📽📽📽½ 1932 Fields treats several oddball patients in his office. After watching the infamous tooth-pulling scene, viewers will be sure to brush regularly. 22m/B VHS, Beta. W.C. Fields, Elise Cavanna, Babe Kane, Bud Jamison, Zedna Farley. CCB, GVV

The Dentist 📽½ 1996 (R) After seeing this movie, you may never want to sit in that dental chair again. When his marriage falls apart, L.A. dental specialist Dr. Alan Feinstone (Bernsen) takes to pill popping and psychotic behavior, including demonic drilling and particularly bloody oral surgery. **CW:** Graphic violence including scenes of dental torture, sexuality and some language. 93m/C VHS. Corbin Bernsen, Ken Foree, Linda Hoffman, Michael Stadvec; **D:** Brian Yuzna. THV

The Denver & Rio Grande 📽📽½ 1951 Action-packed western about two rival railroads competing to be the first to complete a line through the Royal Gorge. Plot is predictable, but the scene featuring two trains crashing into each other is worth it (Haskin used actual trains for this stunt). 89m/C VHS, Closed Caption. Edmond O'Brien,

Sterling Hayden, Dean Jagger, ZaSu Pitts, J. Carrol Naish; **D:** Byron Haskin. *PAR*

Department Store 🎬 *Bargain Basement* **1935** Confusing crime-drama involving a store manager who mistakes an ex-convict for his employer's heir. Based on a story by H. F. Maltby. **65m/B VHS.** *GB* Garry Marsh, Eve Gray, Sebastian Shaw, Geraldine Fitzgerald, Jack Melford; **D:** Leslie Hiscott. *DVT*

The Deputy Drummer 🎬½ **1935** Second-rate early British musical, notable as a later vehicle for silent-era star Lane. He plays a penniless composer who impersonates an aristocrat to attend a party, and catches jewel robbers in the act. **71m/B VHS.** *GB* Lupino Lane, Jean Denis, Kathleen Kelly, Wallace Lupino, Margaret Yarde, Syd Crossley. *NOS*

Deputy Marshall 🎬½ **1950** Hall trails a pair of bankrobbers, fights off landgrabbers, and finds romance as well. **75m/B VHS, Beta.** Jon Hall, Frances Langford, Dick Foran. *RXM*

Der Purimshpiler 🎬🎬½ *The Purim Player; The Jester; The Jewish Jester* **1937** A drifter embarks on a quest for happiness, which takes him to various small towns. In one, he meets and falls in love with a shoemaker's daughter. In Yiddish with English subtitles. **90m/B VHS.** *PL* Miriam Kressyn, Zygmund Turkow, Hymie Jacobsen; **D:** Joseph Green. *ERG*

Deranged 🎬🎬🎬 **1974 (R)** Of the numerous movies based on the cannibalistic exploits of Ed Gein ("Psycho," "Texas Chainsaw Massacre," etc.), this is the most accurate. A dead-on performance by Blossom and a twisted sense of humor help move things along nicely. The two directors, Gillen and Ormsby, previously worked together on the classic "Children Shouldn't Play with Dead Things." An added attraction is the early special effect work of gore wizard Tom Savini. **82m/C VHS.** *CA* Roberts Blossom, Cosette Lee, Robert Warner, Marcia Diamond, Brian Sneagle; **D:** Jeff Gillen, Alan Ormsby. *FRG, MRV*

Deranged 🎬½ **1987 (R)** A mentally unstable, pregnant woman is attacked in her apartment after her husband leaves town. She spends the rest of the movie engaged in psychotic encounters, real and imagined. Technically not bad, but extremely violent and grim. Not to be confused with 1974 movie of the same name. **85m/C VHS.** Jane Hamilton, Paul Siederman, Jennifer Delora, James Gillis, Jill Cumer, Gary Goldman; **D:** Chuck Vincent. *REP*

Derby 🎬🎬🎬 **1971 (R)** The documentary story of the rise to fame of roller-derby stars on the big rink. **91m/C VHS, Beta.** Charlie O'Connell, Lydia Gray, Janet Earp, Ann Colvello, Mike Snell; **D:** Robert Kaylor. *PSM, FAF*

Dersu Uzala 🎬🎬🎬½ **1975** An acclaimed, photographically breathtaking film about a Russian surveyor in Siberia who befriends a crusty, resourceful Mongolian. They begin to teach each other about their respective worlds. Produced in Russia; one of Kurosawa's stranger films. **124m/C VHS, Beta.** *JP RU* Yuri Solomin, Maxim Munzuk; **D:** Akira Kurosawa. Academy Awards '75: Best Foreign Language Film. *KIV*

Descending Angel 🎬🎬🎬 **1990 (R)** The premise is familiar: a swastika-friendly collaborator is forced out of the closet. But the cast and scripting make this made-for-cable there's-a-Nazi-in-the-woodwork suspenser better than average, despite its flawed finale. Scott plays a well-respected Romanian refugee—active in the community, in the church, and in Romanian-American activities—whose daughter's fiance (Roberts) suspects him of Nazi collusion. *CW:* Language and sensuality. **96m/C VHS, LV, Closed Caption.** George C. Scott, Diane Lane, Eric Roberts, Mark Margolis, Vyto Ruginis, Amy Aquino, Richard Jenkins, Jan Rubes; **D:** George C. Scott, Jeremy Paul Kagan; **W:** George C. Scott. *HBO*

Desert Bloom 🎬🎬🎬 **1986 (PG)** On the eve of a nearby nuclear bomb test, a beleaguered alcoholic veteran and his family struggle through tensions brought on by a promiscuous visiting aunt and the chaotic, rapidly changing world. Gish

shines as the teenage daughter through whose eyes the story unfolds. From a story by Corr and Linda Ramy. **103m/C VHS, Beta, LV.** Jon Voight, JoBeth Williams, Ellen Barkin, Annabeth Gish, Allen (Goorwitz) Garfield, Jay Underwood; **D:** Eugene Corr; **W:** Eugene Corr; **C:** Reynaldo Villalobos; **M:** Brad Fiedel. *NO*

Desert Commandos 🎬🎬 **196?** When the Allies appear to be winning WWII, the Nazis devise a plan to eliminate all of the opposing forces' leaders at once. **?m/C VHS.** Kenneth Clark, Horst Frank, Jeanne Valeri, Carlo Hinterman, Gianni Rizzo. *NO*

The Desert Fox 🎬🎬🎬 *Rommel—Desert Fox* **1951** Big-budgeted portrait of German Army Field Marshal Rommel, played by Mason, focuses on the soldier's defeat in Africa during WWII and his subsequent, disillusioned return to Hitler's Germany. Mason played Rommel again in 1953's "Desert Rats." **87m/B VHS, Beta, LV.** James Mason, Cedric Hardwicke, Jessica Tandy, Luther Adler; **D:** Henry Hathaway. *FOX, TLF*

Desert Gold 🎬½ **1936** A fierce Indian chief battles a horde of greedy white men over his tribe's gold mine. Based on a novel by Zane Grey. **58m/B VHS, Beta.** Buster Crabbe, Robert Cummings, Marsha Hunt, Tom Keene, Raymond Hatton, Monte Blue, Leif Erickson; **D:** Charles T. Barton. *NOS, DVT*

Desert Guns/Six-Shootin' Sheriff 🎬🎬 **1936** Double feature includes a rare Tearle "B" film and a Maynard oater from 1938. **?m/C VHS.** Conway Tearle, Ken Maynard. *RXM*

Desert Hearts 🎬🎬🎬 **1986 (R)** An upstanding professional woman travels to Reno, Nevada in 1959 to obtain a quick divorce, and slowly becomes involved in a lesbian relationship with a free-spirited casino waitress. **93m/C VHS, Beta, LV.** Helen Shaver, Audra Lindley, Patricia Charbonneau, Andra Akers, Dean Butler, Jeffrey Tambor, Denise Crosby, Gwen Welles; **D:** Donna Deitch; **W:** Natalie Cooper; **C:** Robert Elswit. *LIV, VES*

Desert Kickboxer 🎬🎬 **1992 (R)** A border guard takes on a cocaine dealer and his henchmen, fighting for gold and, of course, a beautiful woman. Lots of kickboxing action. *CW:* Violence and some sexuality. **86m/C VHS, LV, Closed Caption.** John Haymes Newton, Judie Aronson, Sam DeFrancisco, Paul Smith; **D:** Isaac Florentine. *HBO*

Desert of the Lost 🎬🎬½ **1927** Wales flees to Mexico after shooting a man in self-defense. He's aided by Montgomery and, in turn, helps save her from a forced marriage. **58m/B VHS.** Wally Wales, Peggy Montgomery, William J. Dyer, Edward Cecil, Richard Neill, Kelly Cafford, Ray Murro, George Magrill, Charles "Slim" Whitaker; **D:** Richard Thorpe. *GPV*

The Desert of the Tartars 🎬 *Le Desert des Tartares* **1976 (PG)** Story of a young soldier who dreams of war and discovers that the real battle for him is with time. **140m/C VHS, Beta.** Jacques Perrin; **M:** Ennio Morricone.

Desert Phantom 🎬½ **1936** Villains threaten to rob a woman of her ranch until a stranger rescues her. **66m/B VHS, Beta, LV.** Johnny Mack Brown, Sheila Mannors, Charles "Blackie" King, Ted Adams, Hal Price, Nelson McDowell; **D:** S. Roy Luby. *GPV*

The Desert Rats 🎬🎬🎬 **1953** A crusty British captain (Burton) takes charge of an Australian division during WWII. Thinking they are inferior to his own British troops, he is stiff and uncaring to the Aussies until a kind-hearted drunk and the courage of the division win him over. Crack direction by Wise and Newton's performance (as the wag) simply steal the movie. Mason reprises his role as Germany Army Field Marshal Rommel from "The Desert Fox." **88m/B VHS, Beta.** Richard Burton, Robert Newton, Robert Douglas, Torin Thatcher, Chips Rafferty, Charles Tingwell, James Mason; **D:** Robert Wise. Nominations: Academy Awards '53: Best Story & Screenplay. *FXV, FCT*

Desert Snow 🎬🎬 **1989 (R)** Here's a non-formulaic dope opera oater: cowboys 'n' drug runners battle it out for an out-of-the-way, underpopulated western town. About as clever as the title.

90m/C VHS, Beta. Frank Capizzi, Flint Carney, Shelley Hinkle, Sam Incorvia, Carolyn Jacobs; **D:** Paul de Cruccio. *NO*

The Desert Song 🎬🎬½ **1953** MacRae secretly leads a band of do-gooders against the evil forces of a dastardly sheik. Grayson is the general's daughter who falls in love with our disguised hero. Third filmed version of the Sigmund Romberg operetta creaks along with the talents of MacRae and Grayson rising about the hackneyed plot. 🎵 The Desert Song; Gay Parisienne; Long Live the Night; One Alone; One Flower; The Riff Song; Romance. **96m/C VHS.** Gordon MacRae, Kathryn Grayson, Raymond Massey, Steve Cochran, Dick Wesson, Allyn Ann McLerie, Ray Collins, William Conrad; **D:** H. Bruce Humberstone; **W:** Roland Kibbee; **C:** Robert Burks; **M:** Max Steiner. *FCT*

Desert Steel 🎬½ **1994 (PG)** Rival racers risk their lives in the big off-road race. **89m/C VHS.** David Naughton, Brian Skinner, Amanda Wyss, Russ Tamblyn; **D:** Glenn Gebhard. *MNC*

Desert Trail 🎬½ **1935** Wayne is a championship rodeo rider accused of bank robbery. **57m/B VHS, Beta.** John Wayne, Paul Fix, Mary Kornman; **D:** Robert North Bradbury. *COL, REP, MRV*

Desert Warrior 🎬 **1988 (PG-13)** Earth becomes a waste site after a nuclear war. Ferrigno stars as a post-nuke hero in this low-budget action film. Very bad acting. **89m/C VHS, Beta.** Lou Ferrigno, Shari Shattuck, Kenneth Peer, Anthony East; **D:** Jim Goldman; **W:** Frederick Bailey. *PSM*

The Deserters 🎬½ **198?** Sergeant Hawley, a Vietnam-era hawk, hunts deserters and draft-dodgers in Canada. There, he confronts issues of war and peace head-on. **110m/C VHS, Beta.** Alan Scarfe, Dermot Hennelly, Jon Bryden, Barbara March; **M:** Michael Conway Baker. *MOV*

The Designated Mourner 🎬½ **1997 (R)** Adapted from the play by Wallace Shawn, this pointy-headed inaction movie laments the passing of the class of people who "appreciate the poetry of John Donne" and other forms of high art. It's probably the same class that would like this movie. Set in an unnamed politically repressive country that resembles a large table, Nichols plays the eponymous mourner Jack, a journalist who once ran with a literary crowd but betrayed their ideals for survival. Richardson plays his wife Judy, the daughter of final talking head Howard (de Keyser), who is a humanist poet who doesn't like people. If you need a lecture on culture written by a man who was in "Mom and Dad Save the World" and played the geeky social studies teacher in "Clueless," then this is your movie. To quote Shawn: "Inconceivable!" *CW:* Some language. **94m/C VHS.** *GB* Mike Nichols, Miranda Richardson, David de Keyser; **D:** David Hare; **W:** Wallace Shawn; **C:** Oliver Stapleton; **M:** Richard Hartley. *NYR*

Designing Woman 🎬🎬🎬 **1957** Bacall and Peck star in this mismatched tale of romance. She's a chic high-fashion designer, he's a rumpled sports writer. The fun begins when they try to adjust to married life together. Neither likes the other's friends or lifestyle. Things get even crazier when Bacall has to work with her ex-lover Helmore on a fashion show and Peck's former love Gray shows up as well. And as if that weren't enough, Peck is being hunted by the mob because of a boxing story he's written. It's a fun, quick, witty tale that is all entertainment and no message. Bacall's performance is of note because Bogart was dying of cancer at the time. **118m/C VHS, Beta, LV.** Gregory Peck, Lauren Bacall, Dolores Gray, Sam Levene, Tom Helmore, Mickey Shaughnessy, Jesse White, Chuck Connors, Edward Platt, Alvy Moore, Jack Cole; **D:** Vincente Minnelli; **W:** George Wells; **C:** John Alton; **M:** Andre Previn. Academy Awards '57: Best Story & Screenplay. *MGM*

Desire 🎬🎬🎬 **1936** Jewel thief Madeleine (Dietrich) manages to involve innocent tourist Tom (Cooper) into carrying her ill-gotten goods across the Spanish border. Then she entices him into joining her at the country estate of her partner-in-crime. By this time Tom is in love—and so is Madeleine but she doesn't think she's good enough for him. Lots of lying until the twosome can figure out what to do. Cooper manages to hold his own with the sophisticated Dietrich in their second film together (after "Morocco"). **96m/ B VHS.** Marlene Dietrich, Gary Cooper, John Halliday, William Frawley, Ernest Cossart, Akim Tamiroff, Alan Mowbray; **D:** Frank Borzage; **W:** Edwin Justus Mayer, Waldemar Young; **M:** Friedrich Hollander. *USH, FCT*

Desire 🎬🎬 1993 (R) A free-spirited woman finds herself attracted to a local fisherman. Hardly her intellectual equal but then what she really wants is his body. **CW:** Strong language and sexuality. **108m/C VHS.** Greta Scacchi, Vincent D'Onofrio; **D:** Andrew Birkin. *ACA*

Desire 🎬🎬 1995 (R) Security consultant Lauren Allen (Hodge) is working for a perfume manufacturer whose fragrance, Desire, is the fave of a Beverly Hills serial killer who likes to douse his victims in the scent. The prime suspect is scent expert Gordon Lewis (Kemp) and naturally Lauren falls for him. Standard erotic thriller fare. **CW:** Sexuality, violence, and some language. **90m/C VHS.** Kate Hodge, Martin Kemp, Deborah Shelton, Robert Miranda. *MNC*

Desire and Hell at Sunset Motel 🎬½ 1992 (PG-13) Low-budget thriller takes place at the Sunset Motel in 1950s Anaheim. Fenn is the bombshell wife of a toy salesman who's in town for a sales meeting, while she just wants to visit Disneyland. She's soon fooling around with another guy and her husband hires a psychotic criminal to spy on her as her new lover plots to kill hubby. Very confusing plot isn't worth figuring out. Film's only redeeming quality is the imaginative and creative work used in the visuals. Castle's directorial debut. **90m/C VHS, Beta, LV, Closed Caption.** Sherilyn Fenn, Whip Hubley, David Hewlett, David Johansen, Paul Bartel; **D:** Alien Castle; **W:** Alien Castle. *FXV, VTR*

Desire Under the Elms 🎬🎬½ 1958 Ives, the patriarch of an 1840s New England farming family, takes a young wife (Loren) who promptly has an affair with her stepson. Loren's American film debut. Based on the play by Eugene O'Neill. **114m/B VHS, Beta, LV, Closed Caption.** Sophia Loren, Anthony Perkins, Burl Ives, Frank Overton; **D:** Delbert Mann; **C:** Daniel F. Fapp; **M:** Elmer Bernstein. Nominations: Academy Awards '58: Best Black and White Cinematography. *BAR, FCT, PAR*

Desiree 🎬🎬½ 1954 A romanticized historical epic about Napoleon and his 17-year-old mistress, Desiree. Based on the novel by Annemarie Selinko. Slightly better than average historical fiction piece. **110m/C Beta, LV, Closed Caption.** Marlon Brando, Jean Simmons, Merle Oberon, Michael Rennie, Cameron Mitchell, Elizabeth Sellars, Cathleen Nesbitt; **D:** Henry Koster; **W:** Daniel Taradash; **C:** Milton Krasner; **M:** Alex North. Nominations: Academy Awards '54: Best Art Direction/Set Decoration (Color), Best Costume Design (Color). *FOX, IME*

Desk Set 🎬🎬🎬 *His Other Woman* 1957 One of the later and less dynamic Tracy/Hepburn comedies, about an efficiency expert who installs a giant computer in an effort to update a television network's female-run reference department. Still, the duo sparkle as they bicker, battle, and give in to love. Based on William Marchant's play. **103m/C VHS, Beta, LV, Closed Caption.** Spencer Tracy, Katharine Hepburn, Joan Blondell, Gig Young, Dina Merrill, Neva Patterson; **D:** Walter Lang; **C:** Leon Shamroy. *FOX, FCT*

Desolation Angels 🎬🎬 1995 Nick Adams (Rodrick) returns to New York after a month spent unhappily visiting his mother and discovers his girlfriend Mary (Thomas) has been raped by his best friend Sid (Bassett). At least that's how Nick interprets the situation after an unwilling Mary admits they had sex. Nick goes after Sid, gets beaten up, hires a couple of thugs who botch a retaliation, and just gets increasingly enraged over his inability to settle the situation. The focus is on Nick and Rodrick is more than up

to the director McCann's demands. **90m/C VHS.** Michael Rodrick, Peter Bassett, Jennifer Thomas; **D:** Tim McCann; **W:** Tim McCann; **C:** Matt Howe. *FXL*

Despair 🎬🎬🎬 1978 A chilling and comic study of a victimized chocolate factory owner's descent into madness, set against the backdrop of the Nazi rise to power in the 1930s. Adapted from the Nabokov novel by Tom Stoppard. **120m/C VHS, Beta.** GE Dirk Bogarde, Andrea Ferreol, Volker Spengler, Klaus Lowitsch; **D:** Rainer Werner Fassbinder; **W:** Tom Stoppard; **C:** Michael Ballhaus; **M:** Peer Raben. *GLV*

Desperado 🎬🎬🎬 *El Mariachi 2* 1995 (R) Rodriguez's nameless guitar player-turned-gunman returns—this time in the persona of heartthrob Banderas. The director also has a studio budget to play with (a sizable increase over the $7000 for "El Mariachi"), so the action's on a bigger, more violent scale (you'll quickly lose count of flying bodies and bullets) as El Mariachi tracks infamous drug lord Bucho (de Almeida). Gringo Buscemi provides assistance, beautiful bookstore owner Carolina (Hayek) offers solace, and Tarantino meets his well-deserved cameo demise. You'll also find original Mariachi, Gallardo, in a cameo role as a musician/gunslinger amigo of the hero. Filmed in Mexico. **CW:** Strong bloody violence; strong sex sequence; language. **103m/C VHS, LV, 8mm, Closed Caption, DVD.** Antonio Banderas, Salma Hayek, Joaquim de Almeida, Steve Buscemi, Richard "Cheech" Marin, Carlos Gomez; **Cameos:** Quentin Tarantino, Carlos Gallardo; **D:** Robert Rodriguez; **W:** Robert Rodriguez; **C:** Guillermo Navarro. Nominations: MTV Movie Awards '96: Most Desirable Male (Banderas), Best Kiss (Antonio Banderas/Salma Hayek). *COL*

The Desperadoes 🎬🎬½ 1943 Sheriff Steve Upton (Scott) has a peaceful little Utah town but things change when his old friend, outlaw Cheyenne Rodgers (Ford), comes to visit. Claiming to have gone straight, Rodgers falls for the lovely Allison (Keyes) but is soon accused of robbing the local bank. However, Sheriff Upton believes in his old friend's innocence, helps him escape jail, and together they go after the real criminals. Based on a story by Max Brand. **85m/C VHS.** Randolph Scott, Glenn Ford, Evelyn Keyes, Claire Trevor, Edgar Buchanan, Raymond Walburn, Porter Hall, Guinn "Big Boy" Williams; **D:** Charles Vidor; **W:** Robert Carson. *COL*

Desperados 🎬🎬½ 1969 (PG) After the Civil War, a murderous renegade and two of his sons go on a looting rampage, eventually kidnapping the child of the third son who just wants to live in peace. Made in Spain. **90m/C VHS, Beta.** SP Jack Palance, Vince Edwards, Christian Roberts, George Maharis, Neville Brand, Sylvia Syms; **D:** Henry Levin; **W:** Walter Brough; **C:** Sam Leavitt. *COL*

The Desperados 🎬½ 198? When a young woman is raped by outlaws robbing her stagecoach, a bevy of western heroes band together to avenge her. **86m/C VHS.** Keenan Wynn, Henry Silva, Michele Carey, John Anderson, Joe Turkel; **D:** Ron Joy. *SIM, COL*

Desperate 🎬🎬½ 1947 An honest truck driver witnesses a mob crime and must escape with his wife in this minor film noir. Eventually, the law is on his tail, too. **73m/B VHS, Beta.** Steve Brodie, Audrey Long, Raymond Burr, Jason Robards Sr., Douglas Fowley, William Challee, Ilka Gruning, Nan Leslie; **D:** Anthony Mann. *TTC*

Desperate Cargo 🎬½ 1941 Two showgirls stranded in a Latin American town manage to get aboard a clipper ship with hoodlums who are trying to steal the vessel's cargo. **69m/B VHS, Beta.** Ralph Byrd, Carol Hughes, Jack Mulhall. *NOS, DVT, HEG*

Desperate Characters 🎬🎬🎬 1971 (R) A slice-of-city-life story about a middle-class couple living in a once-fashionable section of Brooklyn, New York, who watch their neighborhood disintegrate around them. Their marriage on remote control, the two find their lives a series of small disappointments, routine work, uncertain friendships, and pervasive violence. Excellent perfor-

mances, especially by MacLaine as the harried wife, but the film's depressing nature made it a complete box office flop. **87m/C VHS, Closed Caption.** Shirley MacLaine, Kenneth Mars, Gerald S. O'Loughlin, Sada Thompson, Michael Higgins, Rose Gregorio, Jack Somack, Chris Gampel, Mary Alan Hokanson, Patrick McVey, Carol Kane; **D:** Frank D. Gilroy; **W:** Frank D. Gilroy. *PAR*

Desperate Crimes 🎬🎬 1993 Two rival mobs battle over the prostitution and drug trade. When an innocent woman is murdered her brother looks for revenge with the help of a beautiful prostitute. **92m/C VHS.** Traci Lords, Denise Crosby, Franco Columbu, Van Quattro, Rena Niehaus, Nicoletta Boris, Elizabeth Kaitan, Randi Ingerman; **D:** Andreas Marfori. *AIP*

Desperate Hours 🎬🎬🎬 1955 A tough, gritty thriller about three escaped convicts taking over a suburban home and holding the family hostage. Plenty of suspense and fine acting. Based on the novel and play by Joseph Hayes. **112m/B VHS, Beta.** Humphrey Bogart, Fredric March, Martha Scott, Arthur Kennedy, Gig Young, Dewey Martin, Mary Murphy, Robert Middleton, Richard Eyer; **D:** William Wyler; **C:** Lee Garmes. Edgar Allan Poe Awards '55: Best Screenplay; National Board of Review Awards '55: Best Director (Wyler). *PAR*

Desperate Hours 🎬🎬 1990 (R) An escaped prisoner holes up in a suburban couple's home, waiting for his lawyer/accomplice to take him to Mexico. Tensions heighten between the separated couple and the increasingly nerve-wracked criminals. Terrific, if not downright horrifying, performance by Rourke in an overall tepid remake of the 1955 thriller. **105m/C VHS, Beta, LV, Closed Caption.** Mickey Rourke, Anthony Hopkins, Mimi Rogers, Kelly Lynch, Lindsay Crouse, Elias Koteas, David Morse, Shawnee Smith, Danny Gerard, Matt McGrath; **D:** Michael Cimino; **W:** Mark Rosenthal. *MGM, FHE*

Desperate Journey 🎬🎬½ 1942 Flynn and Reagan are two of five Allied fighters shot down over Nazi occupied Poland. They go through various tight squeezes such as stealing Goering's car in Berlin, and eliminating a few Nazis at a chemical factory to get back to the safety of England. All the while they are hunted by Massey as Nazi Major Otto Baumester, who of course bumbles and fumbles the whole affair. Strictly propaganda intended to keep up morale on the homefront. Flynn was not pleased about having Reagan as his co-star, seeing as he was usually paired with female leads. **108m/B VHS, Beta.** Errol Flynn, Ronald Reagan, Raymond Massey, Nancy Coleman, Alan Hale, Arthur Kennedy, Helmut Dantine; **D:** Raoul Walsh; **M:** Max Steiner. *MGM*

Desperate Lives 🎬🎬 1982 High school siblings come into contact with drugs and join their guidance counselor in the war against dope. Average made for TV fare. **100m/C VHS, Beta.** Diana Scarwid, Doug McKeon, Helen Hunt, William Windom, Art Hindle, Tom Atkins, Sam Bottoms, Diane Ladd, Dr. Joyce Brothers; **D:** Robert Lewis; **M:** Bruce Broughton. *LIV*

Desperate Living 🎬🎬½ 1977 Typical John Waters trash. A mental patient (Stole) is released and becomes paranoid that her family may be out to kill her. After aiding in the murder of her husband (the hefty maid, Hill, suffocates him by sitting on him), Stole and Hill escape to Mortville, a town populated by outcasts such as transsexuals, murderers, and the woefully disfigured. **90m/C VHS, Beta.** Jean Hill, Mink Stole, Edith Massey, Mary Vivian Pearce, Liz Renay, Susan Lowe; **D:** John Waters; **W:** John Waters. *NLC*

Desperate Measures 🎬🎬🎬 1997 (R) Police officer Frank Connor (Garcia) desperately searches for a bone marrow donor for his dying son. Turns out the perfect match is vicious murderer Pete McCabe (Keaton), a death row inmate who looks on his hospital stay as his chance to escape. Connor and a task force must now track McCabe, but Connor also must ensure his capture is harm-free. Surprisingly chilling performance by Keaton as a psycho killer highlights this otherwise predictable and implausible cat and mouse chase. **?m/C VHS.** Andy Garcia, Michael Keaton, Marcia Gay Harden, Brian Cox; **D:** Barbet Schroeder; **W:** Neal Jimenez, David Klass, Henry Bean; **M:** Trevor Jones. *NYR*

Desperate Motives 🐾🐾 *Distant Cousins* **1992 (R)** Keith and his fiancee Helgenberger are a charming couple who arrive to stay with Keith's distant cousin (Katt) and his family. Only what the family doesn't realize is that the duo have escaped from an asylum for the criminally insane and want to take over their lives. **CW:** Language and violence. **92m/C VHS, LV.** David Keith, Marg Helgenberger, William Katt, Mel Harris, Mary Crosby, Brian Bonsall, Cyndi Pass; **D:** Andrew Lane; **W:** C. Courtney Joyner. *NLC*

Desperate Moves 🐾🐾 **1986** An Oregon-transplanted geek in San Francisco sets out to make himself over in order to win his dream girl. Sometimes effective, often sappy treatment of his coming to terms with the big city. **90m/C VHS, Beta.** Isabel Sanford, Steve Tracy, Paul Benedict, Christopher Lee, Eddie Deezen; **D:** Oliver Hellman. *TWE*

Desperate Prey 🐾½ *Redheads* **1994 (R)** Lucy (Karvan) videotapes herself having sex with lawyer Brewster (Hembrow) and then accidentally films his murder. So she's stalked by the killer. **102m/C VHS, Closed Caption.** *AU* Claudia Karvan, Catherine McClements, Mark Hembrow; **D:** Danny Vendramini; **W:** Danny Vendramini. *APX*

Desperate Remedies 🐾🐾 **1993 (R)** Enjoyment will rest on the viewer's appreciation of campy melodrama. In a Victorian-era New Zealand town, regal shop owner Dorothea Brook (Ward-Lealand) is trying to find a husband for her difficult younger sister Rose (Mills)—who happens to be pregnant and a drug addict. She spots handsome sailor Lawrence (Smith) and decides he'll do but Lawrence is instantly smitten with Dorothea (who's also having heart palpitations over the hunk). Unfortunately, her current lover is Anne (Chappell) and Dorothea has also decided on a marriage of convenience with ambitious politician William (Hurst). It's all very operatic. **CW:** Some graphic sexuality. **92m/C VHS, Beta, Closed Caption.** *NZ* Jennifer Ward-Lealand, Kevin Smith, Lisa Chappell, Michael Hurst, Kiri Mills, Clifford Curtis; **D:** Stewart Main, Peter Wells; **W:** Stewart Main, Peter Wells; **C:** Leon Narbey; **M:** Peter Scholes. *PAR*

Desperate Scoundrel/The Pride of Pikeville 1922 Two classic comedy films back to back featuring the best of the early silent comics. **44m/B VHS, Beta.** Ford Sterling, Ben Turpin, The Keystone Cops. *CCB*

Desperate Target 🐾½ **1980** Courageous people fight against all odds to survive. **90m/C VHS, Beta.** Chris Mitchum. *NO*

Desperate Teenage Lovedolls 🐾 **1984** A trashy version of the formation of a tacky all-girl punk group. **60m/C VHS, Beta.** Jennifer Schwartz, Hilary Rubens, Steve McDonald, Tracy Lea; **D:** David Markey. *HHT*

The Desperate Trail 🐾🐾½ **1994 (R)** Prostitute, convicted of killing an abusive client, manages to escape from the marshal who's escorting her to her hanging. She teams up with a con man in a plot to rob a bank while the marshal enlists a posse to track her down. Strong performances augmented by blazing guns, hobbled by weak writing. Made for cable television. **CW:** Strong western violence; some nudity. **93m/C VHS.** Sam Elliott, Linda Fiorentino, Craig Sheffer, Frank Whaley; **D:** P.J. Pesce; **W:** P.J. Pesce, Tom Abrams; **C:** Michael Bonvillain; **M:** Stephen Endelman. *TTC*

Desperate Women 🐾½ **1978** Made for television western about three unjustly accused female convicts rescued en route to prison by an ex-hired gun. **98m/C VHS, Beta.** Susan St. James, Dan Haggerty, Ronee Blakley, Ann Dusenberry, Susan Myers; **D:** Earl Bellamy. *LIV*

Desperately Seeking Susan 🐾🐾 **1985 (PG-13)** A bored New Jersey housewife gets her kicks reading the personals. When she becomes obsessed with a relationship between two lovers who arrange their meetings through the columns, she decides to find out for herself who they are. But when she is involved in an accident the housewife loses her memory and thinks she is Susan, the free-spirited woman in the personals. Unfortunately, Susan is in a lot of trouble with all sorts of unsavory folk and our innocent housewife finds herself caught in the middle. Terrific characters, with special appeal generated by Arquette and Madonna. Quinn winningly plays the romantic interest. **104m/C VHS, Beta, LV.** Rosanna Arquette, Madonna, Aidan Quinn, Mark Blum, Robert Joy, Laurie Metcalf, Steven Wright, John Turturro, Richard Hell, Annie Golden, Ann Magnuson; **D:** Susan Seidelman; **W:** Leora Barish; **M:** Thomas Newman. British Academy Awards '85: Best Supporting Actress (Arquette); National Board of Review Awards '85: Best Supporting Actress (Arquette). *FCT*

Destination Moon 🐾🐾½ **1950** Story of man's first lunar voyage contains Chesley Bonstell's astronomical artwork and a famous Woody Woodpecker cartoon. Includes previews of coming attractions from classic science fiction films. **91m/C VHS, Beta, LV.** Warner Anderson, Tom Powers, Dick Wesson, Erin O'Brien Moore; **D:** Irving Pichel; **C:** Lionel Lindon. Academy Awards '50: Best Special Effects; Nominations: Academy Awards '50: Best Art Direction/Set Decoration (Color). *SNC, MED*

Destination Moonbase Alpha 🐾🐾 **1975** In the 21st century, an explosion has destroyed half the moon, causing it to break away from the Earth's orbit. The moon is cast far away, but the 311 people manning Alpha, a research station on the moon, must continue their search for other life forms in outer space. A thankless task. Pilot for the television series "Space: 1999." **93m/C VHS, Beta.** Martin Landau, Barbara Bain, Barry Morse. *FOX*

Destination Saturn 🐾🐾 *Buck Rogers* **1939** Buck Rogers awakens from suspended animation in the twenty-fifth century. **90m/B VHS, Beta.** Buster Crabbe, Constance Moore; **D:** Ford Beebe. *NOS, CAB, VYY*

Destination Tokyo 🐾🐾 **1943** A weathered WWII submarine actioner, dealing with the search-and-destroy mission of a U.S. sub sent into Tokyo harbor. Available in a colorized version. **135m/B VHS, Beta.** Cary Grant, John Garfield, Alan Hale, Dane Clark, John Ridgely, Warner Anderson, William Prince, Robert Hutton, Tom Tully, Peter Whitney, Faye Emerson, John Forsythe; **D:** Delmer Daves. Nominations: Academy Awards '43: Best Story. *MGM*

Destiny Turns on the Radio 🐾🐾 **1995 (R)** Mystic figure Johnny Destiny (Tarantino) dabbles in the lives of various stock characters in Las Vegas after emerging from a glowing swimming pool. Three years after this grand entrance, he enlists escaped con Julian and partner Thoreau (McDermott and Le Gros, respectively) to help him return to his place of origin. Julian has other plans, which involve getting his ex, Lucille (Travis), back from sleazy casino owner Tuerto (Belushi). Aggressively cheezy, dime novel dialogue and threadbare, convoluted plot wastes talents of interesting cast. Too much time and energy spent trying to be hip. Sadly, Tarantino's only participation was in front of the camera. **CW:** Language, brief nudity. **101m/C VHS, Closed Caption.** Dylan McDermott, Nancy Travis, James LeGros, Quentin Tarantino, Allen (Goorwitz) Garfield, James Belushi, Tracey Walter, Bob(cat) Goldthwait; **D:** Jack Baran; **W:** Robert Ramsey, Matthew Stone; **C:** James L. Carter; **M:** Steven Soles. *HBO*

Destroy All Monsters 🐾🐾½ *Kaiju Soshingeki* **1968 (G)** When alien babes take control of Godzilla and his monstrous colleagues, it looks like all is lost for Earth. Adding insult to injury, Ghidra is sent in to take care of the loose ends. Can the planet possibly survive this madness? Classic Toho monster slugfest also features

Mothra, Rodan, Son of Godzilla, Angila, Varan, Baragon, Spigas and others. **88m/C VHS.** *JP* Akira Kubo, Jun Tazaki, Yoshio Tsuchiya, Kyoko Ai, Yukiko Kobayashi, Kenji Sahara, Andrew Hughes; **D:** Inoshiro Honda. *FRG*

Destroy All Planets 🐾🐾 *Gamera Tai Viras; Gamera Tai Uchukaiju Bairasu; Gamera Vs. Viras; Gamera Vs. Outer Space Monster Viras* **1968** Aliens whose spaceships turn into giant flying squids are attacking Earth. It's up to Gammera, the flying, fire-breathing turtle to save the day. **?m/C VHS.** *JP* Peter Williams, Kojiro Hongo, Toru Takatsuka; **D:** Noriaki Yuasa. *SNC*

Destroyer 🐾🐾🐾 **1943** Trials and tribulations aboard a WWII destroyer result in tensions, but when the time comes for action, the men get the job done. **99m/B VHS, Beta.** Edward G. Robinson, Glenn Ford, Marguerite Chapman, Edgar Buchanan, Leo Gorcey, Regis Toomey, Edward Brophy, Larry Parks; **D:** William A. Seiter. *NO*

Destroyer 🐾 **1988 (R)** Small-budget film crew goes to an empty prison to shoot, and are stalked by the ghost/zombie remains of a huge serial killer given the electric chair 18 months before. **94m/C VHS, Beta, LV.** Anthony Perkins, Deborah Foreman, Lyle Alzado; **D:** Robert Kirk. *NO*

The Destructors 🐾🐾 *The Marseille Contract* **1974 (PG)** An American narcotics enforcement officer in Paris seeks the help of a hitman in order to catch a druglord. **89m/C VHS, Beta.** *GB* Anthony Quinn, Michael Caine, James Mason, Maureen Kerwin, Alexandra Stewart; **D:** Robert Parrish; **W:** Judd Bernard. *LIV, VES, HHE*

Destry Rides Again 🐾🐾🐾🐾 *Justice Rides Again* **1939** An uncontrollably lawless western town is whipped into shape by a peaceful, unarmed sheriff. A vintage Hollywood potpourri with Dietrich's finest post-Sternberg moment; standing on the bar singing "See What the Boys in the Back Room Will Have." The second of three versions of this Max Brand story. First was released in 1932; the third in 1954. **94m/B VHS, Beta, LV.** James Stewart, Marlene Dietrich, Brian Donlevy, Charles Winninger, Mischa Auer, Irene Hervey, Una Merkel, Billy Gilbert, Jack Carson, Samuel S. Hinds, Allen Jenkins; **D:** George Marshall; **W:** Gertrude Purcell, Felix Jackson, Henry Myers; **C:** Hal Mohr; **M:** Frank Skinner. *USH, FCT*

Details of a Duel: A Question of Honor 🐾🐾½ **1989** A butcher and a teacher collide in this comedy, and prodded by the church, militia and town officals, must duel before the entire town. In Spanish with English subtitles. **97m/C VHS.** *SP* **D:** Sergio Cabrera. *FRF, FCT*

The Detective 🐾🐾🐾 *Father Brown* **1954** Based on G.K. Chesterton's "Father Brown" detective stories, a slick, funny English mystery in which the famous priest tracks down a notorious, endlessly crafty antique thief. **91m/B VHS, Beta.** *GB* Alec Guinness, Peter Finch, Joan Greenwood, Cecil Parker, Bernard Lee; **D:** Robert Hamer; **M:** Jerry Goldsmith. *COL*

The Detective 🐾🐾🐾 **1968** A New York detective investigating the mutilation murder of a homosexual finds political and police department corruption. Fine, gritty performances prevail in this suspense thriller. Based on the novel by Roderick Thorpe. **114m/C VHS, Beta, LV.** Frank Sinatra, Lee Remick, Ralph Meeker, Jacqueline Bisset, William Windom, Robert Duvall, Tony Musante, Jack Klugman, Al Freeman Jr.; **D:** Gordon Douglas; **W:** Abby Mann; **C:** Joseph Biroc. *FOX*

Detective Sadie & Son 🐾 **1984** A television movie about an elderly detective and her young son cracking a case. **96m/C VHS, Beta.** Debbie Reynolds, Sam Wanamaker, Brian McNamara. *NO*

Detective School Dropouts 🐾🐾 *Dumb Dicks* **1985 (PG)** Since they couldn't pass detective school, are they smart enough to outwit a kidnapper? Find out and get a few laughs at the same time. **92m/C VHS, Beta.** Lorin Dreyfuss, David Landsberg, Christian de Sica, George Eastman; **D:** Filippo Ottoni. *MGM*

Detective Story 🎬🎬🎬½ 1951 Intense drama about a New York City police precinct with a wide array of characters led by a disillusioned and bitter detective (Douglas). Excellent casting is the strong point, as the film can be a bit dated. Based on Sydney Kingsley's Broadway play. **103m/B VHS.** Kirk Douglas, Eleanor Parker, Lee Grant, Horace McMahon, William Bendix, Craig Hill, Cathy O'Donnell, Bert Freed, George Macready, Joseph Wiseman, Gladys George, Frank Faylen, Warner Anderson, Gerald Mohr; **D:** William Wyler; **W:** Philip Yordan, Robert Wyler; **C:** Lee Garmes. Cannes Film Festival '52: Best Actress (Grant); Edgar Allan Poe Awards '51: Best Screenplay; Nominations: Academy Awards '51: Best Actress (Parker), Best Director (Wyler), Best Screenplay, Best Supporting Actress (Grant). PAR

Detonator 🎬🎬 Alistair MacLean's Death Train; Death Train 1993 (R) A renegade Russian general has stolen a nuclear bomb and is transporting it from Germany to Iraq on a hijacked train commandeered by his hired band of mercenaries. Stewart is the U.N. troubleshooter delegated to stop the plot, aided by a commando team featuring Brosnan and Paul. Based on the novel "Death Train" by Alistair MacLean. Made for cable television.**CW:** Some language and violence. **98m/C VHS, Closed Caption.** Pierce Brosnan, Patrick Stewart, Ted Levine, Alexandra Paul, Christopher Lee; **D:** David S. Jackson; **W:** David S. Jackson. NLC

Detonator 2: Night Watch 🎬🎬½ Alistair MacLean's Night Watch; Night Watch 1995 (R) Made-for-cable movie finds Brosnan and Paul returning as operatives for the secret United Nations Anti-Crime Organization (UNACO). Mike Graham and Sabrina Carver are teamed by their boss Nick Caldwell (Devane) when it's discovered that Rembrandt's "Night Watch" has been replaced by a forgery. This takes our intrepid duo to Hong Kong, and a suspicious satellite about to be launched by North Korea. Based on a story by Alistair MacLean.**CW:** Some violence. **99m/C VHS, LV, Closed Caption.** Pierce Brosnan, Alexandra Paul, William Devane, Michael J. Shannon, Lim Kay Siu, Irene Ng; **D:** David S. Jackson; **W:** David S. Jackson; **M:** John Scott. NLC

Detour 🎬🎬🎬 1946 Considered to be the creme de la creme of "B" movies, a largely unacknowledged but cult-followed noir downer. Well-designed, stylish, and compelling, if a bit contrived and sometimes annoyingly shrill. Shot in only six days with six indoor sets. Down-on-his-luck pianist Neal hitches cross-country to rejoin his fiancee. His first wrong turn involves the accidental death of the man who picked him up, then he's en route to Destiny with a capital "D" when he picks up fatal femme Savage, as vicious a vixen as ever ruined a good man. Told in flashback, it's also been called the most despairing of all "B"-pictures. As noir as they get. **67m/B VHS, Beta, LV.** Tom Neal, Ann Savage, Claudia Drake, Edmund MacDonald, Tim Ryan, Esther Howard; **D:** Edgar G. Ulmer; **W:** Martin Goldsmith; **M:** Erdody. BAR, MRV, SNC

Detour to Danger woof! 1945 Two young men set out on a fishing expedition and run into crooks and damsels in distress. Unintentionally hilarious "acting" by the no-name cast make this a grade-Z "B" movie. Of interest only because it was filmed in the three-color Kodachrome process used primarily in documentaries. **56m/C VHS, Beta, 8mm.** Britt Wood, John Day, Nancy Brinckman; **D:** Richard Talmadge. VYY

Detroit 9000 🎬½ 1973 (R) A pair of Detroit policemen investigate a robbery that occurred at a black congressman's fundraising banquet. Also on video as "Detroit Heat." **106m/C VHS, Beta.** Alex Rocco, Scatman Crothers, Hari Rhodes, Lonette McKee, Herbert Jefferson Jr.; **D:** Arthur Marks. NO

Deutschland im Jahre Null 🎬🎬🎬½ 1947 The acclaimed, unsettling vision of post-war Germany as seen through the eyes of a disturbed boy who eventually kills himself. Lyrical and grim, in German with subtitles. **75m/B VHS, Beta.** GE Franz Gruber; **D:** Roberto Rossellini. FCT, GLV

Devastator 🎬 Kings Ransom; The Destroyers 1985 (R) A Vietnam vet exacts violent revenge on the murderer of an old army buddy. **79m/C VHS, Beta.** Richard Hill, Katt Shea Ruben, Crofton Hardester; **D:** Cirio H. Santiago. MGM

Devi 🎬🎬🎬 1960 A minor film in the Ray canon, it is, nonetheless, a strange and compelling tale of religious superstition. An Indian farmer becomes convinced that his beautiful daughter-in-law is the reincarnation of the goddess Kali. The girl is then pressured into accepting a worship that eventually drives her mad. In Bengali with English subtitles. **96m/B VHS, Beta.** IN Chhabi Biswas, Sharmila Tagore, Soumitra Chatterjee; **D:** Satyajit Ray. WFV, DVT, TIM

Devices and Desires 🎬🎬🎬 P.D. James' Devices & Desires 1991 Typically complicated mystery adapted from the novel by P.D. James. Scotland Yard Commander Adam Dalgliesh (Marsden) is on holiday on the east coast of England where, of course, there's blackmail, murder, suicide, and trouble at a nearby nuclear power station for him to contend with. Made for TV; on six cassettes. **312m/C VHS, Beta.** GB Roy Marsden, Susannah York, Gemma Jones, James Faulkner, Tony Haygarth, Tom Georgeson, Tom Chadbon, Nicola Cowper, Suzan Crowley, Robert Hines, Harry Burton, Helena Michell; **D:** John Davies; **W:** Thomas Ellice. TVC, AAE

The Devil & Daniel Webster 🎬🎬🎬½ All That Money Can Buy; Here Is a Man; A Certain Mr. Scratch 1941 In 1840s New Hampshire, a young farmer, who sells his soul to the devil, is saved from a trip to Hell when Daniel Webster steps in to defend him. This classic fantasy is visually striking and contains wonderful performances. Adapted from the story by Stephen Vincent Benet who based it on Goethe's Faust. **106m/B VHS, Beta, LV.** James Craig, Edward Arnold, Walter Huston, Simone Simon, Gene Lockhart, Jane Darwell, Anne Shirley, John Qualen, H.B. Warner; **D:** William Dieterle; **M:** Bernard Herrmann. Academy Awards '41: Original Dramatic/Comedy Score; Nominations: Academy Awards '41: Best Actor (Huston). HMV, CRC, FCT

Devil & Leroy Basset 🎬 1973 (PG) Keema Gregwolf kills a deputy, breaks from jail with the Basset brothers, hijacks a church bus, kidnaps a family, and gets into other troublesome situations while on a posse-eluding cross-country adventure. **85m/C VHS, Beta.** Cody Bearpaw, John Goff, George Flower; **D:** Robert E. Pearso; **M:** Les Baxter. PSM

The Devil & Max Devlin 🎬½ 1981 (PG) Good cast wanders aimlessly in Disney family fantasy. The recently deceased Max Devlin strikes a bargain with the devil. He will be restored to life if he can convince three mortals to sell their souls. **95m/C VHS, Beta.** Elliott Gould, Bill Cosby, Susan Anspach, Adam Rich, Julie Budd; **D:** Steven Hilliard Stern; **W:** Jimmy Sangster; **M:** Marvin Hamlisch, Buddy Baker. DIS, OM

The Devil & Miss Jones 🎬🎬🎬½ 1941 Engaging romantic comedy finds a big business boss posing as an ordinary salesclerk to weed out union organizers. He doesn't expect to encounter the wicked management or his beautiful co-worker, however. **90m/B VHS.** Jean Arthur, Robert Cummings, Charles Coburn, Edmund Gwenn, Spring Byington, William Demarest, S.Z. Sakall; **D:** Sam Wood; **C:** Harry Stradling. Nominations: Academy Awards '41: Best Original Screenplay, Best Supporting Actor (Coburn). REP

The Devil at 4 O'Clock 🎬🎬½ 1961 An alcoholic missionary and three convicts work to save a colony of leper children from a South Seas volcano. Quality cast barely compensates for mediocre script. **126m/B VHS, Beta, LV.** Spencer Tracy, Frank Sinatra, Kerwin Mathews, Jean-Pierre Aumont; **D:** Mervyn LeRoy; **C:** Joseph Biroc; **M:** George Duning. GKK, IME

The Devil Bat 🎬🎬 Killer Bats 1941 Madman Lugosi trains a swarm of monstrous blood-sucking bats to attack whenever they smell perfume. Followed by the sequel "Devil Bat's Daughter." **67m/B VHS, Beta.** Bela Lugosi, Dave O'Brien, Suzanne

Kaaren, Yolande Donlan; **D:** Jean Yarbrough. NOS, SNC, PSM

The Devil Bat's Daughter 🎬½ 1946 A young woman, hoping to avoid becoming insane like her batty father, consults a psychiatrist when she starts to have violent nightmares. Unsuccessful sequel to "Devil Bats." **66m/B VHS, Beta.** Rosemary La Planche, Michael Hale, John James, Molly Lamont; **D:** Frank Wisbar. COL, MRV

Devil Diamond 🎬🎬 1937 Mystery-suspense yarn about two amateur detectives who find themselves facing danger after tracking down a gang of evil jewel thieves. **?m/C VHS.** Kane Richmond, Frankie Darro. SNC, VYY

Devil Dog: The Hound of Hell 🎬 1978 A family has trouble with man's best friend when they adopt a dog that is the son of the "Hound of Hell" in this made for television movie. **95m/C VHS, Beta.** Richard Crenna, Yvette Mimieux, Kim Richards, Victor Jory; **D:** Curtis Harrington. NO

Devil Dogs of the Air 🎬🎬½ 1935 Cagney and O'Brien team up in another air drama with Cagney once again the cocky pilot who, this time, joins the Marine Air Corp. O'Brien plays his flying idol (and later rival). Cagney finds all his wisecracking and luck are no match for knowledge and experience but he learns. Good stunt flying; shot on location at the San Diego naval air base. **85m/B VHS.** James Cagney, Pat O'Brien, Margaret Lindsay, Frank McHugh, Robert Barrat, Russell Hicks, Ward Bond; **D:** Lloyd Bacon. MGM, FCT

Devil Doll 🎬🎬🎬 1936 An escaped convict uses a mad scientist's human-shrinking formula to evil ends—he sends out miniature assassins in the guise of store-bought dolls. Rarely seen horror oldie. **80m/B VHS, Beta.** Lionel Barrymore, Maureen O'Sullivan, Frank Lawton; **D:** Tod Browning; **W:** Tod Browning, Erich von Stroheim. MGM, MLB

Devil Doll 🎬🎬 1964 Ventriloquist's dummy, which contains the soul of a former performer, eyes a beautiful victim in the crowd. Newspaper guy senses trouble. Cut above the usual talking, stalking dummy story. **80m/B VHS, Beta.** GB Bryant Holiday, William Sylvester; **D:** Lindsay Shonteff. NO

Devil Girl from Mars 🎬½ 1954 Sexy female from Mars and her very large robot arrive at a small Scottish inn to announce that a Martian feminist revolution has occurred. The distaff aliens then undertake a search of healthy Earth males for breeding purposes. Believe it or not, the humans don't want to go and therein lies the rub. A somewhat enjoyable space farce. **76m/B VHS, Beta.** GB Hugh McDermott, Hazel Court, Patricia Laffan, Peter Reynolds, Adrienne Corri, Joseph Tomelty, Sophie Stewart, John Laurie, Anthony Richmond; **D:** David MacDonald; **W:** John C. Mather, James Eastwood. NOS, MRV, SNC

Devil Horse 🎬🎬 1932 A boy's devotion to a wild horse marked for destruction as a killer leads him into trouble. A serial in twelve, thirteen-minute chapters. **156m/B VHS, Beta.** Frankie Darro, Harry Carey Sr., Noah Beery Jr.; **D:** Otto Brower, Richard Talmadge. GPV, VCN, DVT

Devil in a Blue Dress 🎬🎬🎬 1995 (R) Down-on-his-luck Easy Rawlins (Washington) is an out of work aircraft worker in 1948 LA. He's hired to find mystery woman Daphne (Beals) by a shady businessman (Sizemore). What he finds are the usual noir staples: government corruption backed by thugs who want him to mind his own business. Easy and Daphne's torrid romance featured in the Walter Mosley novel is missing but the racism and violence are intact. Realism and accuracy in period detail enhance solid performance by Washington, though the deliberate, literary pace is at times lulling. Cheadle takes over whenever he shows up as Mouse, Rawlins' loyal friend and muscle.**CW:** Violence; sexuality; language. **102m/C VHS, LV, Closed Caption.** Denzel Washington, Jennifer Beals, Don Cheadle, Tom Sizemore, Maury Chaykin, Terry Kinney, Mel Winkler, Albert Hall; **D:** Carl Franklin; **W:** Carl Franklin; **C:** Tak Fujimoto; **M:** Elmer Bernstein. Los Angeles Film Critics Association Awards '95: Best Supporting Actor (Cheadle); National Society of Film Critics Awards '95: Best Cinematography, Best Supporting Actor (Cheadle); Nominations: Screen Actors Guild Award '95: Best Supporting Actor (Cheadle).COL

The Devil in Silk 🎬🎬½ 1956 A composer marries a woman, not knowing that she is psychotically jealous. After she commits suicide, he must prove to the police that he did not kill her. Original dialogue in German. 102m/B VHS, Beta. *GE* Lilli Palmer, Curt Jurgens, Winnie Markus; *D:* Rolf Hansen. NOS, SNC

Devil in the Flesh 🎬🎬🎬 *Le Diable au Corps* 1946 Acclaimed drama about a French soldier's wife having a passionate affair with a high school student while her husband is away fighting in WWI. From the novel by Raymond Radiguet. Dubbed. Updated and remade in 1987. 112m/B VHS, Beta. *FR* Gerard Philipe, Micheline Presle, Denise Grey; *D:* Claude Autant-Lara. NOS, FCT, APD

Devil in the Flesh 🎬🎬 *Il Diavolo in Corpo* 1987 (R) An angst-ridden, semi-pretentious Italian drama about an obsessive older woman carrying on an affair with a schoolboy, despite her terrorist boyfriend and the objections of the lad's psychiatrist father, who had treated her. In Italian with subtitles. Famous for a graphic sex scene, available in the unrated version. Updated remake of the 1946 French film.*CW:* Strong language and strong sexuality. 110m/C VHS, Beta, LV. *IT* Maruschka Detmers, Federico Pitzalis; *D:* Marco Bellocchio; *W:* Marco Bellocchio. ORI

Devil Kiss 🎬 1977 Gothic horror including zombies, virgins, sorcery, and the inevitable living dead. 93m/C VHS, Beta. Oliver Mathews, Evelyn Scott. HMV

Devil Monster 🎬 1946 A world-weary traveler searches for a girl's fiance in the South Pacific, and is attacked by a large manta. 65m/B VHS, Beta, LV. Barry Norton, Blanche Mehaffey; *D:* S. Edwin Graham. SNC

Devil of the Desert Against the Son of Hercules 🎬🎬½ 1962 The grandson of Zeus ventures into the wasteland to take on a feisty foe. ?m/C VHS, Beta. *IT* Kirk Morris, Michele Girardon; *D:* Riccardo (Robert Hampton) Freda. SNC

Devil on Horseback 🎬🎬 1954 A miner's son journeys to London to become a jockey in this comedy/drama. As he tries to bully his way into the racing circuit, he succeeds, but not in the way he anticipated. 88m/B VHS, Beta, 8mm. *GB* Googie Withers, John McCallum, Jeremy Spenser, Liam Redmond; *D:* Cyril Frankel; *M:* Malcolm Arnold. VYY

The Devil on Wheels 🎬 1947 Inspired by his dad's reckless driving, a teenager becomes a hot rodder and causes a family tragedy. A rusty melodrama that can't be described as high-performance. 67m/B VHS. James B. Cardwell, Noreen Nash, Darryl Hickman, Jan Ford, Damian O'Flynn, Lenita Love. NOS, LOO

The Devil, Probably 🎬🎬 *Le Diable, Probablement* 1977 Ennui among Parisian youth, lost in their polluted, consumer society. Charles (Monnier) spins deeper into depression, despite the efforts of his friends, and finally makes a bargain with a junkie to shoot him in Pere Lachaise cemetery. French with subtitles. 95m/C VHS. *FR* Antoine Monnier, Tina Irissari, Henri De Maublanc; *D:* Robert Bresson; *W:* Robert Bresson; *C:* Pasquale De Santos; *M:* Philippe Sarde. NYF

Devil Rider 🎬🎬½ 1991 A monster from Hell, the Devil Rider, once rode the plains in search of human fodder. In the present day, a pleasure ranch is built on his old territory, and people begin dying in the most horrific manners. Could this mean the return of the Devil Rider? 90m/C VHS. NO

Devil Riders 🎬🎬½ 1944 Unspectacular horse opera has a crooked lawyer trying to get his grubby hands on some choice land. Enter Crabbe to set things straight. 56m/B VHS. Buster Crabbe, Al "Fuzzy" St. John, Patti McCarty, Charles "Blackie" King, John Merton, Kermit Maynard, Frank LaRue, Jack Ingram,

George Chesebro, Edward Cassidy; *D:* Sam Newfield. NOS, MRV

The Devil Thumbs a Ride 🎬🎬🎬 1947 A naive traveller picks up a hitchhiker, not knowing he's wanted for murder. Will history repeat itself in this interesting noir? 63m/B VHS, Beta. Ted North, Lawrence Tierney, Nan Leslie; *D:* Felix Feist. NO

The Devil Thumbs a Ride/Having Wonderful Crime 1947 A mystery double feature. In "Devil Thumbs a Ride," a ruthless killer-bank robber hitches a ride from an inebriated travelling salesman. In "Having Wonderful Crime," a criminal lawyer investigates the disappearance of a magician. 132m/B VHS, Beta. Lawrence Tierney, Pat O'Brien, George Murphy, Carole Landis, Nan Leslie, George Zucco; *D:* Felix Feist, Edward Sutherland. NO

Devil Times Five 🎬🎬½ *People Toys; The Horrible House on the Hill* 1974 (R) To take revenge for being incarcerated in a mental hospital, five children methodically murder the adults who befriend them. 87m/C VHS, Beta. Gene Evans, Sorrell Booke, Shelly Morrison; *D:* Sean McGregor. MED

Devil Wears White 🎬🎬 1986 (R) A student's vacation is disrupted when he becomes involved in a war with an insane arms dealer who wants to take over a Latin American Republic. 92m/C VHS, Beta. Robert Livesy, Jane Higginson, Guy Ecker, Anthony Cordova; *D:* Steven A. Hull. TWE

Devil Woman woof! 1976 (R) A Filipino Gorgon-woman seeks reptillian revenge on the farmers who killed her family. Bad news. 79m/C VHS. PH Rosemarie Gil; *D:* Albert Yu, Felix Vilars. SNC

Devilfish 🎬 1984 A small seaside community is ravaged by berserk manta rays in this soggy saga. 92m/C VHS, Beta. *IT D:* Lamberto Bava. THV

The Devils 🎬🎬🎬 1971 (R) In 1631 France, a priest is accused of commerce with the devil and sexual misconduct with nuns. Since he is also a political threat, the accusation is used to denounce and eventually execute him. Based on Aldous Huxley's "The Devils of Loudun," the movie features masturbating nuns and other excesses—shocking scenes typical of film director Russell. Supposedly this was Russell's attempt to wake the public to their desensitization of modern horrors of war. Controversial and flamboyant. 109m/C VHS, Beta. *GB* Vanessa Redgrave, Oliver Reed, Dudley Sutton, Max Adrian, Gemma Jones, Murray Melvin; *D:* Ken Russell; *W:* Ken Russell; *C:* David Watkin. National Board of Review Awards '71: Best Director (Russell). WAR

Devil's Angels 🎬 1967 A motorcycle gang clashes with a small-town sheriff. Cheap 'n' sleazy fare. 84m/C VHS. John Cassavetes, Beverly Adams, Mimsy Farmer, Salli Sachse, Nai Bonet, Leo Gordon; *D:* Daniel Haller; *W:* Charles B. Griffith. NO

The Devil's Brigade 🎬🎬 1968 "Dirty Dozen" style film with Holden as the leader of special commando brigade consisting of the usual misfits and oddballs. The team is trained to take on the Nazis in Scandanavia but has their assignment cancelled. Instead, they take them on in the Italian Alps, making for some perilous adventures. Non-acting notables include former football great Hornung and former boxing champ Gene Fullmer. 130m/C VHS, Beta. William Holden, Cliff Robertson, Vince Edwards, Michael Rennie, Dana Andrews, Gretchen Wyler, Andrew Prine, Claude Akins, Carroll O'Connor, Richard Jaeckel, Jack Watson, Paul Hornung, Jeremy Slate, Don Megowan, Patric Knowles, James Craig, Richard Dawson, Tom Stern, Luke Askew; *D:* Andrew V. McLaglen; *W:* William Roberts; *C:* William Clothier; *M:* Alex North. MGM

The Devil's Brother 🎬🎬 *Fra Diavolo; Bogus Bandits; The Virtuous Tramps* 1933 In one of their lesser efforts, Laurel and Hardy star as bumbling bandits in this comic operetta based on the 1830 opera by Daniel F. Auber. Also available with "Laurel & Hardy's Laughing 20's" on laserdisc. 88m/B VHS. Stan Laurel, Oliver Hardy, Dennis King, Thelma Todd, James Finlayson, Lucille Browne; *D:* Charles R. Rogers, Hal Roach. MGM, MLB, CCB

Devil's Canyon 🎬🎬 1953 An ex-lawman, serving time in an Arizona prison, is beset by a jailed killer seeking vengeance for his own incarceration. Filmed in 3-D. 92m/B VHS, Beta. Dale Robertson, Virginia Mayo, Stephen McNally, Arthur Hunnicutt, Robert Keith, Jay C. Flippen, Whit Bissell; *D:* Alfred Werker. TTC

The Devil's Cargo 🎬½ 1948 When a man is accused of killing a racetrack operator, he calls in the Falcon to clear his name. The master detective finds this to be a most difficult task however, especially when the accused is found poisoned in his cell. One of the final three "Falcon" films, in which Calvert replaced Tom Conway. 61m/B VHS, Beta. John Calvert, Rochelle Hudson, Roscoe Karns, Lyle Talbot, Tom Kennedy; *D:* John F. Link. SNC

The Devil's Commandment 🎬🎬 *I, Vampiri; Lust of the Vampires* 1956 A lurid melodrama about a Parisian newspaperman's journey into a network of crime and perversion. Cinematography by Mario Bava. 90m/B VHS, Beta, LV. *FR* Gianna Maria Canale, Dario Michaelis, Carlo D'Angelo, Wandisa Guida, Paul Muller, Renato Tontini; *D:* Riccardo (Robert Hampton) Freda. SNC

Devil's Crude 🎬 1971 Adventurous sailor and a young oil heir uncover a conspiracy within a giant corporation. 85m/C VHS, Beta. *IT* Franco Nero. TWE

The Devil's Daughter 🎬½ *Pocomania; Poncomania* 1939 A sister's hatred and voodoo ceremonies play an important part in this all-black drama. 60m/B VHS, Beta. Nina Mae McKinney, Jack Carter, Ida James, Hamtree Harrington. SNC, VYY, DVT

The Devil's Daughter 1991 (R) Satan, in a desperate bid to take over the planet, orders his minions to flood the earth with horrific evil. Only one woman can prevent the HellMaster from succeeding, and she may be too late!*CW:* Horror violence. 112m/C VHS, Closed Caption. *IT* Kelly Curtis, Herbert Lom, Maria Angela Giordano, Michel Hans Adatte, Carla Cassola, Angelika Maria Boeck, Tomas Arana; *D:* Michele (Michael) Soavi; *W:* Dario Argento; *M:* Pino Donaggio. REP

The Devil's Disciple 🎬🎬🎬 1959 Entertaining adaptation of George Bernard Shaw play set during the American Revolution. Standout performances by Douglas as a romantic rogue, Lancaster as a New England pastor, and Olivier as British General Burgoyne. Film suffers from choppy direction, but the excellent cast more than makes up for it. 82m/B VHS, Closed Caption. *GB* Burt Lancaster, Kirk Douglas, Laurence Olivier, Janet Scott, Eva LeGallienne, Harry Andrews, Basil Sydney, George Rose; *D:* Guy Hamilton; *C:* Jack Hildyard; *M:* Richard Rodney Bennett. MGM

The Devil's Eye 🎬🎬 *Djavulens Oga* 1960 The devil dispatches Don Juan to tempt and seduce a young virgin bride-to-be, a reverend's daughter, no less. Based on the Danish radio play "Don Juan Returns." 90m/B VHS, Beta. *SW* Bibi Andersson, Jarl Kulle; *D:* Ingmar Bergman; *W:* Ingmar Bergman. NLC

Devil's Gift woof! 1984 A young boy's toy is possessed by a demon and havoc ensues. 112m/C VHS, Beta. Bob Mendlesolin, Vicki Saputo, Steven Robertson; *D:* Kenneth Berton. LIV, VES

The Devil's Hand 🎬 *Devil's Doll; The Naked Goddess; Live to Love* 1961 When Alda finds a doll that represents his ideal woman in a curio shop, the shop's owner (Hamilton, aka Commissioner Gordon), tells him the dream girl who modeled for the doll lives nearby. Trouble is, she's part of a voodoo cult, and guess who's head voodoo-man. Big trouble for Alda; big snooze for you. 71m/B VHS. Linda Christian, Robert Alda, Neil Hamilton, Ariadne Welter; *D:* William Hole Jr. NOS, SNC, LOO

The Devil's Mistress 🎬½ 1968 A gang of criminals on a pillaging spree murder a man and rape his Indian wife, only to find out she's a she-demon who won't let bygones be bygones. Lame. 66m/C VHS. Joan Stapleton, Robert Gregory, Forrest Westmoreland, Douglas Warren, Oren Williams, Arthur Resley; **D:** Orville Wanzer; **W:** Orville Wanzer. *SNC*

The Devil's Nightmare 🐾½ *Succubus; The Devil Walks at Midnight* 1971 (R) A woman leads seven tourists (representing the seven deadly sins) on a tour of a medieval European castle. There they experience demonic tortures. Lots of creepy moments. Euro-horror/sex star Blanc is fantastic in this otherwise mediocre production. **88m/C VHS, Beta.** *BE IT* Erika Blanc, Jean Servais, Daniel Emilfork, Lucien Raimbourg, Jacques Monseau, Colette Emmanuelle, Ivana Novak, Shirley Corrigan, Frederique Hender; **D:** Jean Brismee. *APP*

The Devil's Own 🐾🐾🐾 1996 (R) Irish-American New York cop Tom O'Meara (Harrison) and wife Sheila (Colin) take charming Irish emigre Rory Devaney (Pitt) into their home and make him part of the family. But Rory, AKA Frankie McGuire, turns out to be an IRA terrorist who has hustled out of trouble in Belfast and now has a bloody purpose for coming to America. When Tom discovers just what it is, he tries to stop Rory before he destroys any more lives—including his own. More a low-key character study than a slam-bang actioner, with Pitt cooly charismatic as the troubled gunman while Ford does his usual professional work as a good cop caught up in a bad situation. **CW:** Strong brutal violence, and for language. **110m/C VHS.** Harrison Ford, Brad Pitt, Margaret Colin, Ruben Blades, Treat Williams, George Hearn, Natascha McElhone, Mitchell Ryan, Simon Jones, Paul Ronan; **D:** Alan J. Pakula; **W:** Kevin Jarre, David Aaron Cohen, Vincent Patrick; **C:** Gordon Willis; **M:** James Horner. *COL*

The Devil's Partner 🐾½ 1958 Yet another uninspired devil yarn in which an old-timer trades in his senior citizenship by dying and coming back in the form of his younger self. Young again, he takes a new wife and indulges in multiple ritual sacrifices. Noteworthy only by virtue of the cast's later TV notoriety—Buchanan and Foulger would later appear on "Petticoat Junction," Nelson played Dr. Rossi on "Peyton Place," and Crane beached a role on "Hawaiian Eye." **75m/B VHS.** Ed Nelson, Jean Allison, Edgar Buchanan, Richard Crane, Spencer Carlisle, Byron Foulger, Claire Carleton; **D:** Charles R. Rondeau. *SNC, MRV, CNM*

Devil's Party 🐾🐾 1938 A tenement boy's reunion party turns into a night of horror when one of the guests is killed. As a result, the childhood friends band together to uncover the murderer's identity. **65m/B VHS, Beta.** Victor McLaglen, Paul Kelly, William Gargan, Samuel S. Hinds, Scotty Beckett; **D:** Ray McCarey. *NOS, MRV, DVT*

The Devil's Playground 🐾🐾🐾 1976 Sexual tension rises in a Catholic seminary, distracting the boys from their theological studies. The attentions of the priests only further their sexual confusion. Winner of many Australian film awards. **107m/C Beta.** *AU* Arthur Dignam, Nick Tate, Simon Burke, Charles Frawley, Jonathon Hardy, Gerry Dugan, Thomas Keneally; **D:** Fred Schepisi; **W:** Fred Schepisi; **C:** Ian Baker; **M:** Bruce Smeaton. Australian Film Institute '76: Best Actor (Tate), Best Actor (Burke), Best Film. *ALL*

The Devil's Possessed 🐾½ 1974 A Middle Ages despot tortures and maims the peasants in his region until they rise up and enact an unspeakable revenge. **90m/C VHS, Beta.** *AR SP* Paul Naschy; **D:** Leon Klimovsky. *NO*

Devil's Rain 🐾½ 1975 (PG) The rituals and practices of devil worship, possession, and satanism are gruesomely related. Interesting cast. **85m/C VHS, Beta, LV.** Ernest Borgnine, Ida Lupino, William Shatner, Eddie Albert, Keenan Wynn, John Travolta, Tom Skerritt; **D:** Robert Fuest. *NO*

The Devil's Sleep 🐾 1951 When a crusading woman sets out to break up a teen narcotics ring, the threatened thugs attempt to draw her daughter into their sleazy affairs, thus assuring the mother's silence. **81m/B VHS, Beta.** Lita Grey Chaplin, Timothy Farrell, John Mitchum, William Thomason, Tracy Lynn; **D:** W. Merle Connell. *SNC*

Devil's Son-in-Law woof! 1977 (R) A black stand-up comic makes a deal with a devil. **95m/C VHS, Beta.** Rudy Ray Moore; **D:** Cliff Roguemore. *NO*

The Devil's Undead 🐾🐾½ 1975 (PG) When a Scottish orphanage is besieged by a rash of cold-blooded murders, the detectives Lee and Cushing are summoned to investigate. Interesting spin on that old possessed by demons theme. **90m/C VHS, Beta.** *GB* Christopher Lee, Peter Cushing; **D:** Peter Sasdy. *MLB*

Devil's Wanton 🐾🐾½ *Fangelse; Prison* 1949 A young girl tries to forget an unhappy relationship by beginning a new romance with an equally frustrated beau. Gloomy, but hopeful. **80m/B VHS, Beta.** *SW* Doris Svedlund, Eva Henning, Hasse Ekman; **D:** Ingmar Bergman; **W:** Ingmar Bergman. *VYY, MRV, DVT*

The Devil's Web 🐾½ 1974 (PG) A demonic nurse infiltrates, manipulates, and corrupts three beautiful sisters. **73m/C VHS, Beta.** Diana Dors, Andrea Marcovicci, Ed Bishop, Cec Linder, Michael Culver. *LIV*

Devil's Wedding Night woof! 1973 (R) An archaeologist and his twin brother fight over a ring that lures virgins into Count Dracula's Transylvanian castle. Vampire queen Bay seduces the dimwit twins and strips at every chance she gets. **85m/C VHS, Beta.** Mark Damon, Rosalba (Sara Bay) Neri, Frances Davis; **D:** Paul Solvay. *NO*

Devlin 🐾🐾 1992 (R) Devlin is a tough cop with an alcohol problem and a bad marriage. His father-in-law, Brennan, is a powerful local political boss. When Brennan's son is murdered, Devlin is the fall guy. Seeking to clear himself, he discovers a conspiracy going back thirty years. Made for cable television. **CW:** Language, violence and drug use, and sexuality. **110m/C VHS, Beta, LV.** Bryan Brown, Roma Downey, Lloyd Bridges; **D:** Rick Rosenthal; **M:** Minette Alton. *FXV, VTR*

The Devlin Connection 🐾🐾 1982 Retired private investigator helps his son learn the ropes as he embarks on a Los Angeles crime fighting career. Hudson's last starring television series, excluding his "Dynasty" role. All thirteen episodes are available separately. **50m/C VHS, Beta.** Rock Hudson, Jack Scalia, Louis Giambalvo, Leigh Taylor-Young, Jack Kruschen; **D:** Christian Nyby. *TWE*

Devonsville Terror 🐾🐾 1983 (R) Strange things begin to happen when a new school teacher arrives in Devonsville, a town that has a history of torture, murder, and witchcraft. The hysterical townspeople react by beginning a 20th-century witchhunt. **97m/C VHS, Beta.** Suzanna Love, Donald Pleasence, Deanna Haas, Mary Walden, Robert Walker Jr., Paul Wilson; **D:** Ulli Lommel; **W:** Ulli Lommel.

Devotion 🐾🐾½ 1931 A lovesick British miss disguises herself as a governess so she can be near the object of her affection, a London barrister. **80m/B VHS.** Ann Harding, Leslie Howard, Robert Williams, O.P. Heggie, Louise Closser Hale, Dudley Digges; **D:** Robert Milton. *TTC*

D.I. 🐾🐾 1957 A tough drill sergeant is faced with an unbreakable rebellious recruit, threatening his record and his platoon's status. Webb's film features performances by actual soldiers. **106m/B VHS, Beta.** Jack Webb, Don Dubbins, Jackie Loughery, Lin McCarthy, Virginia Gregg; **D:** Jack Webb. *WAR*

The Diabolical Dr. Z 🐾🐾 *Miss Muette; Dans les Griffes du Maniaque* 1965 When dad dies of cardiac arrest after the medical council won't let him make the world a kinder gentler place with his personality-altering technique, his dutiful daughter—convinced the council brought on dad's demise—is out to change some personalities in a big way. **86m/B VHS.** *SP FR* Mabel Karr, Fernando Montes, Estella Blain, Antonio J. Escribano, Howard Vernon; **D:** Jess (Jesus) Franco. *SNC*

Diabolically Yours 🐾🐾½ *Diaboliquement Votre* 1967 A French thriller about an amnesiac who struggles to discover his lost identity. Tensions mount when his pretty spouse and friends begin

to wonder if it's all a game. Dubbed. **94m/C VHS, Beta.** *FR* Alain Delon, Senta Berger; **D:** Julien Duvivier. *UNI*

Diabolique 🐾🐾🐾½ *Les Diabolique* 1955 The mistress and the wife of a sadistic schoolmaster conspire to murder the man, carry it out, and then begin to wonder if they have covered their tracks effectively. Plot twists and double-crosses abound. In French with English subtitles. Remade for television as "Reflections of Murder." **107m/B VHS, Beta, LV, 8mm.** *FR* Simone Signoret, Vera Clouzot, Paul Meurisse, Charles Vanel, Michel Serrault; **D:** Henri-Georges Clouzot. National Board of Review Awards '55: 5 Best Foreign Films of the Year; New York Film Critics Awards '55: Best Foreign Film. *VYY, NOS, SNC*

Diabolique 🐾½ 1996 (R) Remake of the 1955 French noir classic, updated for '90s sensibilities, finds timid teacher Mia (Adjani) married to overbearing school head Guy (Palminteri), who's having an affair with fellow teacher Nicole (Stone). The two women, who loathe Guy equally, plot to kill him. But when a P.I. (Bates) investigates, it seems possible that Guy isn't dead after all. If you're having trouble accessorizing with leopard skin, watch Stone. Otherwise, watch the far superior original. The usually publicity hungry Stone refused to have anything to do with this picture after its release due to a spat with director Chechik. **CW:** Violence/terror, sexuality and language. **105m/C VHS, LV.** Sharon Stone, Isabelle Adjani, Chazz Palminteri, Kathy Bates, Spalding Gray, Shirley Knight, Adam Hann-Byrd, Allen (Goorwitz) Garfield; **D:** Jeremiah S. Chechik; **W:** Don Roos; **C:** Peter James; **M:** Randy Edelman. *WAR*

Dial Help 🐾½ 1988 (R) A lame Italian-made suspenser about a model plagued by ghostly phone calls. **94m/C VHS, Beta.** *IT* Charlotte Lewis, Marcello Modugno, Mattia Sbragia, Victor Cavallo; **D:** Ruggero Deodato. *NO*

Dial "M" for Murder 🐾🐾🐾 1954 An unfaithful husband devises an elaborate plan to murder his wife for her money, but when she accidentally stabs the killer-to-be, with scissors no less, he alters his methods. Part of the "A Night at the Movies" series, this tape simulates a 1954 movie evening with a Daffy Duck cartoon, "My Little Duckaroo," a newsreel, and coming attractions for "Them" and "A Star Is Born." Filmed in 3-D. Based on the play by Frederick Knotts. **123m/C VHS, Beta, LV.** Ray Milland, Grace Kelly, Robert Cummings, John Williams, Anthony Dawson; **D:** Alfred Hitchcock; **C:** Robert Burks; **M:** Dimitri Tiomkin. *WAR, TLF*

Diamond Fleece 🐾🐾½ 1992 Rick (Cross) is a convicted diamond thief who's given a parole just so he can guard the world's largest uncut gemstone. But Inspector Outlaw (Dennehy) figures Rick will never be able to resist stealing the gem himself and the law can finally lock Rick away for good. Oh, and Holly, she thinks a maybe-ex-diamond thief will bring a little romance to her life. **93m/C VHS.** Ben Cross, Brian Dennehy, Kate Nelligan; **D:** Al Waxman; **W:** Michael Norell. *PSM*

Diamond Head 🐾🐾½ 1962 A Hawaiian landowner brings destruction and misery to his family via his stubbornness. Based on the Peter Gilman novel. **107m/C VHS, Beta, LV.** Charlton Heston, Yvette Mimieux, George Chakiris, France Nuyen, James Darren; **D:** Guy Green; **C:** Sam Leavitt; **M:** John Williams. *COL*

Diamond Run 🐾½ 1990 (R) A streetwise American expatriate frantically searches for his girlfriend after unwittingly involving her in an assassination plot. **89m/C VHS, Beta, LV.** William Bell Sullivan, Ava Lazar, Ayu Azhari, David Thornton, Peter Fox; **D:** Robert Chappell. *NO*

Diamond Trail 🐾½ 1933 East Coast jewel thieves bring their operation to the West, trailed by a New York reporter. **58m/B VHS, Beta.** Rex Bell, Frances Rich, Bud Osborne, Lloyd Whitlock, Norman Feusier; **D:** Harry Fraser. *NOS, DVT*

The Diamond Trap 🎬🎬 1991 (PG) A Manhatten detective finds himself in the middle of a diamond heist and involved with a con artist. Made for television. 93m/C VHS, LV, Closed Caption. Howard Hesseman, Brooke Shields, Ed Marinaro, Twiggy; *D:* Don Taylor; *W:* David Peckinpah. THV

Diamonds 🎬🎬 1972 (PG) A tense film in which the Israel Diamond Exchange is looted by a motley array of criminal heisters. Shaw plays a dual role as twin brothers. 108m/C VHS, Beta. IS Robert Shaw, Richard Roundtree, Barbara Hershey, Shelley Winters; *D:* Menahem Golan. NLC

Diamonds Are Forever 🎬🎬🎬½ 1971 (PG) 007 once again battles his nemesis Blofeld, this time in Las Vegas. Bond must prevent the implementation of a plot to destroy Washington through the use of a space-orbiting laser. Fabulous stunts include Bond's wild drive through the streets of Vegas in a '71 Mach 1. Connery returned to play Bond in this film after being offered the then record-setting salary of one million dollars. 120m/C VHS, Beta, LV, Closed Caption. GB Sean Connery, Jill St. John, Charles Gray, Bruce Cabot, Jimmy Dean, Lana Wood, Bruce Glover, Putter Smith, Norman Burton, Joseph Furst, Bernard Lee, Desmond Llewelyn, Laurence Naismith, Leonard Barr, Lois Maxwell, Margaret Lacey, Joe Robinson, Donna Garrat, Trina Parks; *D:* Guy Hamilton; *W:* Tom Mankiewicz; *C:* Ted Moore; *M:* John Barry. Nominations: Academy Awards '71: Best Sound. MGM, TLF

Diamond's Edge 🎬🎬 *Just Ask for Diamond* 1988 (PG) An adolescent private eye and his juvenescent brother snoop into the affairs of the Fat Man, and find out that the opera ain't over until they find out what's in the Fat Man's mysterious box of bon-bons. A genre-parodying kid mystery, written by Horowitz, based on his novel, "The Falcon's Malteser." 83m/C VHS, Beta, Closed Caption. Susannah York, Peter Eyre, Patricia Hodge, Nickolas Grace; *D:* Stephen Bayly; *W:* Anthony Horowitz; *M:* Trevor Jones. HBO

Diamonds of the Night 🎬🎬🎬🎬 *Demanty Noci* 1964 A breakthrough masterpiece of the Czech new wave, about two young men escaping from a transport train to Auschwitz and scrambling for survival in the countryside. Surreal, powerfully expressionistic film, one of the most important of its time. In Czech with English subtitles. Accompanied by Nemec's short "A Loaf of Bread." 71m/B VHS, Beta. CZ Ladislav Jansky, Antonin Kumbera, Ilse Bischofova; *D:* Jan Nemec; *W:* Arnost Lustig, Jan Nemec. FCT

Diana: Her True Story 🎬🎬½ 1993 Britain's royals are held up to scandalous review in this made for tv adaptaion of Andrew Morton's sympathetic bio of the Princess of Wales. Taking Diana from her lonely childhood to her "fairytale" nuptials and subsequent disillusionment with being a royal, including her bulimia and half-hearted suicide attempts. Charles is portrayed as an arrogant, emotional cold fish, only interested in farming and continuing his liaison with Camilla Parker-Bowles. Handsome production with appropriate inpersonations by the cast. 180m/C VHS, Closed Caption. Serena Scott Thomas, David Threlfall, Elizabeth Garvie, Jemma Redgrave, Tracy Hardwick, Anne Stallybrass, Jeffrey Harmer, Donald Douglas; *D:* Kevin Connor; *W:* Stephen Zito. NO

Diane 🎬🎬 1955 Overstuffed medieval drama featuring Turner as Diane de Poitier, the mistress of a sixteenth century French King. Moore plays the king in his Hollywood debut. Gorgeous sets and costumes couldn't boost this film at the box office, which had disappointing figures in spite of the expense bestowed upon it. Based on the novel "Diane de Poitier" by John Erskine. 110m/C VHS, LV. Lana Turner, Pedro Armendariz Sr., Roger Moore, Marisa Pavan, Cedric Hardwicke, Torin Thatcher, Taina Elg, John Lupton, Henry Daniell, Sean McClory, Michael Ansara; *D:* David Miller; *W:* Christopher Isherwood; *M:* Miklos Rozsa. MGM

Diary of a Chambermaid 🎬🎬🎬 1946 A chambermaid wants to marry a rich man and finds herself the object of desire of a poor servant willing to commit murder for her. Excellent comic drama, but very stylized in direction and set design. Produced during Renoir's years in Hollywood. Adapted from a story by Octave Mirbeau, later turned into a play. Remade in 1964 by Luis Bumel. 86m/B VHS. Paulette Goddard, Burgess Meredith, Hurd Hatfield, Francis Lederer, Judith Anderson, Florence Bates, Almira Sessions, Reginald Owen; *D:* Jean Renoir. REP, FCT

Diary of a Chambermaid 🎬🎬🎬½ *Le Journal d'une Femme de Chambre; Il Diario di una Cameriera* 1964 Vintage Bunuelian social satire about a young girl taking a servant's job in a provincial French family, and easing into an atmosphere of sexual hypocrisy and decadence. In French with English subtitles. Remake of the 1946 Jean Renoir film. 97m/C VHS, Beta, LV. FR Jeanne Moreau, Michel Piccoli, Georges Geret, Francoise Lugagne, Daniel Ivernel; *D:* Luis Bunuel; *W:* Luis Bunuel, Jean-Claude Carriere. APD, IME, XVC

Diary of a Country Priest 🎬🎬🎬½ *Le Journal d'un Cure de Campagne* 1950 With "Balthazar" and "Mouchette," this is one of Bresson's greatest, subtlest films, treating the story of an alienated, unrewarded young priest with his characteristic austerity and Catholic humanism. In French and English subtitles. 120m/B VHS, Beta. FR Claude Layou, Jean Riveyre, Nicole Ladmiral; *D:* Robert Bresson; *W:* Robert Bresson. DVT, APD, IGP

Diary of a Hitman 🎬🎬½ 1991 (R) A hitman is hired to knock off the wife and child of a commodities broker who claims his wife is a drug addict and the infant is a crack baby and not his. The hired killer wants out of the business, but needs to pull off one more job for a down payment on his apartment. Beset by doubts, he breaks conduct by conversing with the victim and discovers the broker lied. Based on the play "Insider's Price" by Pressman. *CW:* Language and sensuality. 90m/C VHS, LV, Closed Caption. Forest Whitaker, James Belushi, Sherilyn Fenn, Sharon Stone, Seymour Cassel, Lewis Smith, Lois Chiles, John Bedford-Lloyd; *D:* Roy London; *W:* Kenneth Pressman; *M:* Michel Colombier. COL

Diary of a Lost Girl 🎬🎬🎬½ 1929 The second Louise Brooks/G.W. Pabst collaboration (after "Pandora's Box") in which a frail but mesmerizing German girl plummets into a life of hopeless degradation. Dark and gloomy, the film chronicles the difficulties she faces, from rape to an unwanted pregnancy and prostitution. Based on the popular book by Margarete Boehme. Silent. Made after flapper Brooks left Hollywood to pursue greater opportunities and more challenging roles under Pabst's guidance. 99m/B VHS, Beta, LV. GE Louise Brooks, Fritz Rasp, Josef Rovensky, Sybille Schmitz; *D:* G.W. Pabst. GPV, MRV, VDM

Diary of a Mad Housewife 🎬🎬🎬 1970 (R) Despairing of her miserable family life, a housewife has an affair with a writer only to find him to be even more selfish and egotistical than her no-good husband. Snodgress plays her character perfectly, hearing the insensitive absurdity of her husband and her lover over and over again, enjoying her martyrdom even as it drives her crazy. 94m/C VHS, Beta. Carrie Snodgress, Richard Benjamin, Frank Langella; *D:* Frank Perry. Golden Globe Awards '71: Best Actress—Musical/Comedy (Snodgress); National Board of Review Awards '70: 10 Best Films of the Year, Best Supporting Actor (Langella); Nominations: Academy Awards '70: Best Actress (Snodgress). GKK

Diary of a Mad Old Man 🎬🎬 *Dagboek Van Een Oude Dwaas* 1988 (PG-13) A wistful drama about an old man who's lost everything except his desire for his daughter-in-law, which sends him into fits of nostalgia. 93m/C VHS, Beta. Derek De Lint, Ralph Michael, Beatie Edney. MED

Diary of a Madman 🎬🎬 1963 Price is once again possessed by an evil force in this gothic thriller. Fairly average Price vehicle, based on Guy de Maupassant's story. 96m/C VHS, Beta. Vincent Price, Nancy Kovack, Chris Warfield, Ian Wolfe, Nelson Olmstead; *D:* Reginald LeBorg. MGM, FCT

Diary of a Rebel 🎬 1984 A fictional account of the rise of Cuban rebel leader Che Guevara. 89m/C VHS, Beta. John Ireland, Francesco Rabal. NO

Diary of a Teenage Hitchhiker 🎬 1982 Teen girl ignores family restrictions and police warnings about a homicidal rapist stalking the area and continues to thumb rides to her job at a beach resort. One night she's picked up for ride she'll never forget. 96m/C VHS, Beta. Charlene Tilton, Dick Van Patten; *D:* Ted Post. NO

Diary of a Young Comic 🎬🎬 1979 New York comedian searches for the meaning of lunacy. He finds it after Improvisation in Los Angeles. 74m/C VHS, Beta. Stacy Keach, Dom DeLuise, Richard Lewis, Bill Macy, George Jessel, Gary Muledeer, Nina Van Pallandt; *D:* Gary Weis. NO

The Diary of Anne Frank 🎬🎬🎬½ 1959 In June 1945, a liberated Jewish refugee returns to the hidden third floor of an Amsterdam factory where he finds the diary kept by his youngest daughter, Anne. The document recounts their years in hiding from the Nazis. Based on the actual diary of 13-year-old Anne Frank, killed in a death camp during WWII. 150m/B VHS, Beta, LV, Closed Caption. Millie Perkins, Joseph Schildkraut, Shelley Winters, Richard Beymer, Gusti Huber, Ed Wynn, Lou Jacobi, Diane Baker; *D:* George Stevens; *C:* William Mellor. Academy Awards '59: Best Art Direction/Set Decoration (B & W), Best Black and White Cinematography, Best Supporting Actress (Winters); National Board of Review Awards '59: 10 Best Films of the Year; Nominations: Academy Awards '59: Best Costume Design (B & W), Best Director (Stevens), Best Picture, Best Supporting Actor (Wynn), Original Dramatic/Comedy Score. KUI, FOX, BTV

Diary of Forbidden Dreams 🎬🎬🎬 *What?; Che?* 1973 (R) A beautiful young girl finds herself drawn into bizarre incidents at an eccentric millionaire's mansion that cause her to go insane. Set on the Italian Riviera, it's the most offbeat rendition of "Alice in Wonderland" you're apt to find. Unfortunately, the convoluted plot lessens its appeal. Unedited version, under the original title "What!," released at 113 minutes, is also available. 94m/C VHS, Beta. IT Marcello Mastroianni, Hugh Griffith, Sydne Rome, Roman Polanski; *D:* Roman Polanski; *W:* Roman Polanski, Gerard Brach. VDM, TWE, FCT

Diary of the Dead 🎬 198? (PG) A newlywed kills his aggravating mother-in-law, only to have her repeatedly return from the grave. 93m/C Beta. Hector Elizondo, Geraldine Fitzgerald, Salome Jens; *D:* Arvin Brown. NO

Dick Barton, Special Agent 🎬 1948 Dick Barton is called in when a mad scientist threatens to attack London with germ-carrying bombs. The first film production for Hammer Studios, later to be known for its horror classics. 70m/B VHS, Beta. GB Don Stannard, Geoffrey Ford, Jack Shaw; *D:* Alfred Goulding. SNC, VYY

Dick Barton Strikes Back 🎬🎬½ 1948 "Mr. French" Cabot has a nuclear weapon and is willing to use it; that is, until Dick Barton arrives to put the Frenchman out of commission. Generally considered the best of the Dick Barton film series. 73m/B VHS, Beta. GB Don Stannard, Sebastian Cabot, Jean Lodge; *D:* Godfrey Grayson. SNC, VYY

Dick Tracy 1937 Serial, based on the comic-strip character, in fifteen chapters. Tracy tries to find his kidnapped brother as he faces the fiend "Spider." The first chapter is thirty minutes and each additional chapter is twenty minutes. 310m/B VHS, Beta, LV. Ralph Byrd, Smiley Burnette, Irving Pichel, Jennifer Jones; *D:* John English. SNC, VYY, VCI

Dick Tracy ✍✍✍½ 1990 (PG) Beatty wears the caps of producer, director, and star, performing admirably on all fronts. One minor complaint: his Tracy is somewhat flat in comparison to the outstanding performances and makeup of the unique villains, especially Pacino. Stylistically superior, shot in only 7 colors, the timeless sets capture the essence rather than the reality of the city, successfully bringing the comic strip to life. Madonna is fine as the seductive Breathless Mahoney, belting out Stephen Sondheim like she was born to do it. People expecting the gothic technology of "Batman" may be disappointed, but moviegoers searching for a memory made real will be thrilled. ♫Sooner or Later. 105m/C VHS, Beta, LV, Closed Caption. Warren Beatty, Madonna, Charlie Korsmo, Glenne Headly, Al Pacino, Dustin Hoffman, James Caan, Mandy Patinkin, Paul Sorvino, Charles Durning, Dick Van Dyke, R.G. Armstrong, Catherine O'Hara, Estelle Parsons, Seymour Cassel, Michael J. Pollard, William Forsythe, Kathy Bates, James Tolkan; **D:** Warren Beatty; **W:** Jim Cash, Jack Epps Jr.; **M:** Danny Elfman, Stephen Sondheim. Academy Awards '90: Best Art Direction/Set Decoration, Best Makeup, Best Song ("Sooner or Later"); Nominations: Academy Awards '90: Best Cinematography, Best Costume Design, Best Sound, Best Supporting Actor (Pacino). **TOU, FCT, IME**

Dick Tracy, Detective ✍✍ 1945 The first Dick Tracy feature film, in which Splitface is on the loose, a schoolteacher is murdered, the Mayor is threatened, and a nutty professor uses a crystal ball to give Tracy the clues needed to connect the crimes. 62m/B VHS, Beta. Morgan Conway, Anne Jeffreys, Mike Mazurki, Jane Greer, Lyle Latell; **D:** William (Lester Williams) Berke. **SNC, MED, VYY**

Dick Tracy, Detective/The Corpse Vanishes ✍✍½ 1942 On one tape, the first Dick Tracy feature film and Lugosi's minor epic about a mad scientist using virgin's blood to restore youth to an aging countess. 126m/B VHS, Beta. Bela Lugosi, Morgan Conway, Luana Walters, Tristram Coffin, Mike Mazurki, Jane Greer, Lyle Latell; **D:** William (Lester Williams) Berke. **AOV**

Dick Tracy Double Feature #1 1945 Mystery-adventure double feature presents Chester Gould's popular comic strip hero in live action. Includes "Dick Tracy, Detective" and "Dick Tracy's Dilemma." 122m/B VHS, Beta. Ralph Byrd, Lyle Latell, Morgan Conway, Anne Jeffreys. **VCI**

Dick Tracy Double Feature #2 ✍✍ 1947 Chester Gould's famous comic strip character is personified in "Dick Tracy Meets Gruesome" and "Dick Tracy vs. Cueball," a double-feature videocassette featuring Dick Tracy battling two of his arch-enemies. 127m/B VHS, Beta. Boris Karloff, Ralph Byrd, Morgan Conway, Anne Jeffreys. **VCI**

Dick Tracy Meets Gruesome ✍✍ *Dick Tracy's Amazing Adventure; Dick Tracy Meets Karloff* 1947 Gruesome and his partner in crime, Melody, stage a bank robbery using the secret formula of Dr. A. Tomic. Tracy has to solve the case before word gets out and people rush to withdraw their savings, destroying civilization as we know it. 66m/B VHS. Boris Karloff, Ralph Byrd, Lyle Latell; **D:** John Rawlins. **NOS, MRV, SNC**

Dick Tracy Returns 1938 15-chapter serial. Public Enemy Paw Stark and his gang set out on a wave of crime that brings them face to face with dapper Dick. 100m/B VHS, Beta, LV. Ralph Byrd, Charles Middleton; **D:** William Witney. **VCI, IME, MLB**

Dick Tracy: The Original Serial, Vol. 1 ✍✍✍ 1937 The first seven parts of the original popular serial. The comic strip character comes to life and tries to stop the spider, a dangerous criminal. 150m/B VHS, Beta. Ralph Byrd, Smiley Burnette, Kay Hughes, Francis X. Bushman, Lee Van Atta; **D:** Ray Taylor; **W:** Alan James. **GKK**

Dick Tracy: The Original Serial, Vol. 2 ✍✍✍ 1937 The last eight parts of the highly acclaimed serial. Tracy is still tracking down the Spider in this action-packed adventure.

160m/B VHS, Beta. Ralph Byrd, Smiley Burnette, Kay Hughes, Francis X. Bushman, Lee Van Atta; **D:** Ray Taylor; **W:** Alan James. **GKK**

Dick Tracy: The Spider Strikes 1937 Dick Tracy, his bumbling sidekick, and his beautiful, brainy assistant go up against the master criminal, The Spider. 60m/B VHS, Beta. Ralph Byrd, Francis X. Bushman. **KAR**

Dick Tracy vs. Crime Inc. 1941 Dick Tracy encounters many difficulties when he tries to track down a criminal who can make himself invisible. A serial in 15 chapters. 100m/B VHS, Beta, LV. Ralph Byrd, Ralph Morgan, Michael Owen; **D:** William Witney; **W:** John English. **VCI, IME, MLB**

Dick Tracy vs. Cueball ✍✍ 1946 Dick Tracy has his work cut out for him when the evil gangster Cueball appears on the scene. Based on Chester Gould's comic strip. 62m/B VHS, Beta. Morgan Conway, Anne Jeffreys; **D:** Gordon Douglas. **NOS, VCI, VYY**

Dick Tracy's Dilemma ✍✍ *Mark of the Claw* 1947 The renowned police detective Dick Tracy tries to solve a case involving the Claw. Based on the Chester Gould comic strip. 60m/B VHS, Beta. Ralph Byrd, Lyle Latell, Kay Christopher, Jack Lambert, Ian Keith, Jimmy Conlin; **D:** John Rawlins. **MRV, VCI, VYY**

Dick Turpin ✍✍½ 1925 In this rare film, Mix plays the famed English highwayman who seeks adventure in historical Britain. 60m/B VHS, Beta. Tom Mix, Alan Hale; **D:** John Blystone. **GB**

Didn't You Hear? ✍ 1983 (PG) An alien-ated college student discovers that dreams have a life of their own when he becomes immersed in his own fantasy world. 94m/C VHS, Beta. Dennis Christopher, Gary Busey, Cheryl Waters, John Kauffman. **PSM**

Die! Die! My Darling! ✍½ *Fanatic* 1965 A young widow visits her mad ex-mother-in-law in a remote English village, and is imprisoned by the mourning woman as revenge for her son's death. Bankhead's last role. 97m/C Beta. **GB** Tallulah Bankhead, Stefanie Powers, Peter Vaughan, Maurice Kaufman, Donald Sutherland, Gwendolyn Watts, Yootha Joyce, Winifred Dennis; **D:** Silvio Narizzano; **W:** Richard Matheson. **COL, MLB**

Die Grosse Freiheit Nr. 7 ✍½ 1945 A man tries to stop his niece's love affair with a sailor. Nazi propaganda minister Goebbels banned this film in Germany, since it showed German soldiers getting drunk and also had Hildebrand cast as a prostitute. After the war, however, it enjoyed great popularity throughout Germany. Albers sings the classic "Auf der Reeperbahn." In German with no English translation. 100m/C VHS, Beta. **GE** Hans Albers, Hilde Hildebrand. **IHF**

Die Hard ✍✍✍ 1988 (R) High-voltage action thriller pits a lone New York cop against a band of ruthless high-stakes terrorists who attack and hold hostage the employees of a large corporation as they celebrate Christmas in a new L.A. high rise. It's just as unbelievable as it sounds, but you'll love it anyway. Rickman, who later charmed audiences as the villain in "Robin Hood: Prince of Thieves," turns in a marvelous performance as the chief bad guy. Based on the novel "Nothing Lasts Forever" by Roderick Thorp. 114m/C VHS, Beta, LV, Closed Caption. Bruce Willis, Bonnie Bedelia, Alan Rickman, Alexander Godunov, Paul Gleason, William Atherton, Reginald Vel Johnson, Hart Bochner, James Shigeta, Mary Ellen Trainor, De'voreaux White, Robert Davi, Rick Ducommun; **D:** John McTiernan; **W:** Jeb Stuart, Steven E. de Souza; **C:** Jan De Bont; **M:** Michael Kamen. Nominations: Academy Awards '88: Best Film Editing, Best Sound. **FOX**

Die Hard 2: Die Harder ✍✍✍ 1990 (R) Fast, well-done sequel brings another impossible situation before the wise-cracking, tough-cookie cop. Our hero tangles with a group of terrorists at an airport under siege, while his wife remains in a plane circling above as its fuel dwindles. Obviously a repeat of the plot and action of the first "Die Hard," with references to the former

in the script. While the bad guys lack the fiendishness of their predecessors, this installment features energetic and finely acted performances. Fairly gory, especially the icicle-in-the-eyeball scene. Adapted from the novel "58 Minutes" by Walter Wager and characters created by Roderick Thorp. 124m/C VHS, LV, Closed Caption. Bruce Willis, William Atherton, Franco Nero, Bonnie Bedelia, John Amos, Reginald Vel Johnson, Dennis Franz, Art Evans, Fred Dalton Thompson, William Sadler, Sheila McCarthy, Robert Patrick, John Leguizamo, Robert Costanzo, Tom Verica; **D:** Renny Harlin; **W:** Doug Richardson, Steven E. de Souza; **M:** Michael Kamen. **FOX**

Die Hard: With a Vengeance ✍✍½ *Die Hard 3* 1995 (R) Third time is not a charm in the "Die Hard" series. McClane (Willis) is back home in the Big Apple and having another bad day. More Eurotrash terrorists, led by the brilliant and vengeful Simon (Irons), are out to blow things up, snag some gold, and make life miserable for McClane and his reluctant partner, Zeus Carver (Jackson). The claustrophobic settings of the first two outings have been replaced by the exhausting expanse of New York City, to good effect, but frenetic action scenes and good chemistry between Willis and Jackson don't quite compensate for a lackluster script and more cartoony feel. Jackson brings a fresh perspective and vitality to what will probably be the last ride of John McClane.**CW:** Strong violence; pervasive strong language. 131m/C VHS, LV, Closed Caption. Bruce Willis, Samuel L. Jackson, Jeremy Irons, Graham Greene, Colleen Camp, Larry Bryggman, Tony Peck, Nick Wyman, Sam Phillips; **D:** John McTiernan; **W:** Jonathan Hensleigh; **C:** Peter Menzies Jr.; **M:** Michael Kamen. Nominations: MTV Movie Awards '96: Best Action Sequence.**FXV**

Die Laughing woof! 1980 (PG) A cab driver unwittingly becomes involved in murder, intrigue, and the kidnapping of a monkey that has memorized a scientific formula that can destroy the world. Writer/actor/composer Benson might consider renaming it "Die from Embarassment." 108m/C VHS, Beta. Robby Benson, Charles Durning, Bud Cort, Elsa Lanchester, Peter Coyote; **D:** Jeff Werner; **W:** Robby Benson, Scott Parker; **M:** Robby Benson. **WAR**

Die, Monster, Die! ✍✍ *Monster of Terror* 1965 A reclusive scientist experiments with a radioactive meteorite and gains bizarre powers. Karloff is great in this adaptation of H.P. Lovecraft's "The Color Out of Space." 80m/C VHS, LV. **GB** Boris Karloff, Nick Adams, Suzan Farmer, Patrick Magee, Freda Jackson, Terence de Marney; **D:** Daniel Haller; **M:** Don Banks. **NO**

Die Screaming, Marianne ✍ *Die, Beautiful Marianne* 1973 A girl is on the run from her father, a crooked judge, who wants to kill her before her 21st birthday, when she will inherit evidence that will put him away for life. 81m/C VHS, Beta. **GB** Michael Rennie, Susan George, Karin Dor; **D:** Pete Walker. **UNI**

Die Sister, Die! ✍ 1974 Thriller about a gothic mansion with an eerie secret in the basement features a battle between a senile, reclusive sister and her husband, tormenting brother. 88m/C VHS, Beta. Jack Ging, Edith Atwater, Antoinette Bower, Kent Smith, Robert Emhardt; **D:** Randall Hood. **NO**

Die Watching ✍½ 1993 (R) Sleazy erotic thriller about a video director (Atkins) who not only likes to film some hot Hollywood babes but may also like to kill them as well. His latest discovery just could be the next victim. 92m/C VHS. Christopher Atkins, Vali Ashton, Tim Thomerson, Carlos Palomino, Mike Jacobs Jr.; **D:** Charles Davis; **W:** Kenneth J. Hall. **TRI**

Different for Girls ✍✍✍ 1996 (R) Boyish motorcycle dispatch rider Paul Prentice (Graves) nearly gets run over by a London taxi whose passenger Kim Foyle (Mackintosh) seems strangely familiar. Then Paul discovers Kim used to be his boyhood school chum Karl. After a shaky start, the duo discover a genuine attraction but when they get into an argument that leads to a police call and Paul gets thrown in jail, Kim's first instincts are to retreat to her sister's (Reeves) family and back into her quiet life. Director Spence refrains from camping up the situation and some fine performances, especially from the engaging Graves, make this quirky film well worth a watch.**CW:** Nudity, brief graphic sexuality and strong language. 92m/C VHS. *GB* Rupert Graves, Steven Mackintosh, Miriam Margolyes, Saskia Reeves, Neil Dudgeon, Charlotte Coleman; *D:* Richard Spence; *W:* Tony Merchant; *C:* Sean Van Hales; *M:* Stephen Warbeck. Montreal World Film Festival '95: Best Film. *NYR*

A Different Kind of Love *♂* 1985 A romantic novel on tape, in modern settings. Love, frustration, tragedy. 60m/C Beta. Joyce Redman. *PSM*

Different Story *♂♂½* 1978 **(PG)** Romance develops when a lesbian real estate agent offers a homosexual chauffeur a job with her firm. Resorts to stereotypes when the characters decide to marry. 107m/C VHS, Beta. Perry King, Meg Foster, Valerie Curtin, Peter Donat, Richard Bull; *D:* Paul Aaron. *NLC*

Digby, the Biggest Dog in the World *♂* 1973 **(G)** Poor comedy-fantasy about Digby, a sheepdog, who wanders around a scientific laboratory, drinks an experimental fluid, and grows and grows and grows. 88m/C VHS, Beta. *GB* Jim Dale, Angela Douglas, Spike Milligan, Dinsdale Landen; *D:* Joseph McGrath; *M:* Edwin Astley. *PSM*

Digger *♂♂½* 1994 **(PG)** Digger (Hann-Byrd) arrives at a Pacific Northwest island to stay with relatives, including his Grandma (Dukakis) who's being romanced by the fun-loving Arthur (Nielsen). He makes friends with another youth who turns out to have a terminal heart ailment. 92m/C VHS, Closed Caption. Adam Hann-Byrd, Olympia Dukakis, Leslie Nielsen, Joshua Jackson, Barbara Williams, Timothy Bottoms; *D:* Robert Turner; *W:* Rodney Gibbons; *M:* Todd Boekelheide. *PAR*

Digging Up Business woof! 1991 **(PG)** Johnson tries to save the family funeral home business from financial ruin with some unique interment services. This film needs a decent burial. 89m/C VHS. Lynn-Holly Johnson, Billy Barty, Ruth Buzzi, Murray Langston, Yvonne Craig, Gary Owens; *D:* Mark Byers. *NO*

Diggstown *♂♂½* 1992 **(R)** Lightweight, good-natured sports comedy about a boxing scam. Con man Gabriel Caine (Woods), fresh out of prison, heads for Diggstown and the unregulated boxing matches arranged by town boss, John Gillon (Dern). The bet is that Caine's one boxer can beat any 10 boxers, chosen by Gillon, in a 24-hour period. So Caine decides to hook up with an old friend, former prizefighter "Honey" Roy Palmer (Gosset Jr.), to run the scam of his life. Dern is sufficiently nasty and Woods his usual nervy self but it's Gossett Jr. who manages to hold everything together as the aging boxer. Based on the novel "The Diggstown Ringers" by Leonard Wise.**CW:** Language. 97m/C VHS, Beta, LV, Closed Caption. James Woods, Louis Gossett Jr., Bruce Dern, Oliver Platt, Heather Graham, Randall "Tex" Cobb, Thomas Wilson Brown, Duane Davis, Willie Green, George Wallace; *D:* Michael Ritchie; *W:* Steven McKay; *M:* James Newton Howard. *MGM*

Digital Man *♂*½ 1994 **(R)** High-tech military super-soldier prototype has his programming sabotaged and a team of human and robotic commandoes must prevent him from starting WWIII.**CW:** Futuristic military; some sexuality. 95m/C VHS, Closed Caption. Ken Olandt, Adam Baldwin, Ed Lauter, Matthias Hues, Kristen Dalton, Paul Gleason; *D:* Phillip J. Roth; *W:* Phillip J. Roth, Ronald Schmidt. *REP*

Dillinger *♂♂♂* 1945 John Dillinger's notorious career, from street punk to public enemy number one, receives a thrilling fast-paced treatment. Tierney turns in a fine performance in this interesting account of the criminal life. 70m/C VHS, Beta. Lawrence Tierney, Edmund Lowe, Anne Jeffreys, Elisha Cook Jr.; *D:* Max Nosseck; *W:* Philip Yordan. Nominations: Academy Awards '45: Best Original Screenplay. *FOX, FCT*

Dillinger *♂♂½* 1973 **(R)** The most colorful period of criminality in America is brought to life in this story of bank-robber John Dillinger, "Baby Face" Nelson, and the notorious "Lady in Red." 106m/C VHS, Beta, LV. Warren Oates, Michelle Phillips, Richard Dreyfuss, Cloris Leachman, Ben Johnson, Harry Dean Stanton; *D:* John Milius; *W:* John Milius. *LIV, VES*

Dillinger *♂♂½* The Last Days of John Dillinger 1991 Harmon stars as the Depression-era bank robber, who became public enemy number one, in this TV gangster story. Fenn's girlfriend Billy Frenchette, with Patton particularly beady-eyed as G-man Melvin Purvis. 95m/C VHS, Closed Caption. Mark Harmon, Sherilyn Fenn, Will Patton, Patricia Arquette, Vince Edwards, Bruce Abbott; *D:* Rupert Wainwright; *C:* Donald M. Morgan. *WAR*

Dillinger and Capone *♂♂½* 1995 **(R)** Supposedly the FBI has killed the wrong Dillinger and the gangster (Sheen) decides to make a new life. But his old friend Al Capone (Abraham), newly released from prison, is holding Dillinger's wife (Hicks) and son hostage as insurance that first he'll retrieve $15 million from a mob-owned Chicago bank.**CW:** Language, violence, brief nudity. 95m/C VHS, LV. Martin Sheen, F. Murray Abraham, Catherine Hicks, Stephen Davies, Don Stroud, Clint Howard; *D:* Jon Purdy; *W:* Michael B. Druxman. *NHO*

Dim Sum: A Little Bit of Heart *♂♂♂* 1985 **(PG)** The second independent film from the director of "Chan Is Missing." A Chinese-American mother and daughter living in San Francisco's Chinatown confront the conflict between traditional Eastern ways and modern American life. Gentle, fragile picture made with humor and care. In English and Chinese with subtitles. 88m/C VHS, Beta, LV. Laureen Chew, Kim Chew, Victor Wong, Ida F.O. Chong, Cora Miao, John Nishio, Joan Chen; *D:* Wayne Wang; *W:* Terrel Seltzer; *M:* Todd Boekelheide. *FCT, IME, TPV*

Dimples *♂♂½* 1936 **(PG)** When Shirley's pickpocket grandfather is caught red-handed, she steps in, takes the blame, and somehow ends up in show business. Re-issued version is rated. Also available colorized. ♪Hey, What Did the Bluebird Say?; He Was a Dandy; Picture Me Without You; Oh Mister Man Up in the Moon; Dixie-Anna; Get On Board; Swing Low Sweet Chariot. 78m/B VHS, Beta, Closed Caption. Shirley Temple, John Carradine, Frank Morgan, Helen Westley, Berton Churchill, Robert Kent, Delma Byron; *D:* William A. Seiter. *FOX*

Diner *♂♂♂½* 1982 **(R)** A group of old high school friends meet at "their" Baltimore diner to find that more has changed than the menu. A bittersweet look at the experiences of a group of Baltimore post-teenagers growing up, circa 1959. Particularly notable was Levinson's casting of "unknowns" who have since become household names. Features many humorous moments and fine performances. 110m/C VHS, Beta, LV. Steve Guttenberg, Daniel Stern, Mickey Rourke, Kevin Bacon, Ellen Barkin, Timothy Daly, Paul Reiser, Michael Tucker; *D:* Barry Levinson; *C:* Peter Sova. National Society of Film Critics Awards '82: Best Supporting Actor (Rourke); Nominations: Academy Awards '82: Best Original Screenplay.*MGM*

Dingaka *♂♂½* 1965 A controversial drama from the writer and director of "The Gods Must Be Crazy" about a South African tribesman who avenges his daughter's murder by tribal laws, and is then tried by white man's laws. A crusading white attorney struggles to acquit him. 96m/C VHS, Beta. Stanley Baker, Juliet Prowse, Ken Gampu; *D:* Jamie Uys. *COL, NLC, FCT*

Dingo *♂♂½* 1990 In Davis' only film appearance he's, what else, a famous jazz trumpeter. Paris-based Billy Cross (Davis) and his combo are on tour in 1969 and momentarily stuck at a remote Australian airstrip. They give an impromptu concert heard by John "Dingo" Anderson (Friels), who instantly decides that music is the life for him. Over the years Dingo keeps in touch with his idol as he works outback bars and secret-

ly saves to go to Paris and check out the scene—even if it means sacrificing his wife and family. 108m/C VHS. *FR AU* Colin Friels, Miles Davis, Helen Buday, Bernadette LaFont; *D:* Rolf de Heer; *W:* Marc Rosenberg; *C:* Denis Lenoir; *M:* Miles Davis, Michel Legrand. *GRE*

The Dining Room *♂♂½* 1986 Six performers play more than 50 roles in this adaptation of A.R. Gurney Jr.'s play set in a dining room, where people live out dramatic and comic moments in their lives. From the "American Playhouse" series. 90m/C VHS, Beta. Remak Ramsay, Pippa Perthree, John Shea, Frances Sternhagen; *D:* Allan Goldstein. *PBS, ACA*

Dinner at Eight *♂♂♂♂* 1933 A social-climbing woman and her husband throw a dinner party for various members of the New York elite. During the course of the evening, all of the guests reveal something about themselves. Special performances all around, especially Barrymore, Dressler, and Harlow. Superb comedic direction by Cukor. Adapted from the play by Edna Ferber and George Kaufman. 110m/C VHS, Beta, LV, 8mm. John Barrymore, Lionel Barrymore, Wallace Beery, Madge Evans, Jean Harlow, Billie Burke, Marie Dressler, Phillips Holmes, Jean Hersholt, Lee Tracy, Edmund Lowe, Karen Morley, May Robson; *D:* George Cukor; *W:* Herman J. Mankiewicz, Frances Marion, Donald Ogden Stewart; *C:* William H. Daniels. *MGM*

Dinner at Eight *♂♂* 1989 A social-climbing romance novelist throws an elegant dinner party. Made for television remake of the 1933 film does not compare well. 100m/C VHS, Beta. Lauren Bacall, Charles Durning, Ellen Greene, Harry Hamlin, John Mahoney, Marsha Mason, Tim Kazurinsky; *D:* Ron Lagomarsino. *TTC*

Dinner at the Ritz *♂♂½* 1937 Daughter of a murdered Parisian banker vows to find his killer with help from her fiance. 78m/B VHS, Beta. *GB* David Niven, Annabella, Paul Lukas, Patricia Medina; *D:* Harold Schuster. *NOS, MRV, VYY*

Dino *♂*½ 1957 Social worker joins a young woman in helping a seventeen-year-old delinquent re-enter society. 96m/B VHS, Beta. Sal Mineo, Brian Keith, Susan Kohner; *D:* Thomas Carr. *REP*

Dinosaur Island *♂* 1993 **(R)** Five military men survive a plane crash and discover an island where scantily-clad (leather bikinis being the fashion choice) lascivious ladies live. Will the awesome power of testosterone overcome the fierce dinosaurs which stand between the men and their objects of desire?**CW:** Abundant nudity and sexuality. 85m/C VHS. Ross Hagen, Richard Gabai, Antonia Dorian, Peter Spellos, Tom Shell, Griffin Drew, Steve Barkett, Toni Naples; *D:* Jim Wynorski, Fred Olen Ray; *W:* Bob Sheridan, Christopher Wooden. *NHO, HVL*

Dinosaurus! *♂* 1960 Large sadistic dinosaurs appear in the modern world. They eat, burn, and pillage their way through this film. Also includes a romance between a Neanderthal and a modern-age woman. 85m/C VHS, Beta. Ward Ramsey, Kristina Hanson, Paul Lukather; *D:* Irvin S. Yeaworth Jr. *NWV, SNC*

Diplomaniacs *♂♂½* 1933 Wheeler and Woolsey, official barbers on an Indian reservation, are sent to the Geneva peace conference to represent the interests of their tribe. Slim plot nevertheless provides quite a few laughs. Fun musical numbers. 62m/B VHS, Beta, LV. Bert Wheeler, Robert Woolsey, Marjorie White, Hugh Herbert; *D:* William A. Seiter; *W:* Joseph L. Mankiewicz, Henry Myers; *M:* Max Steiner. *CCB, IME, TTC*

Diplomatic Courier *♂♂♂* 1952 Cold-war espionage saga has secret agent Power attempting to re-steal sensitive documents from the hands of Soviet agents. Involved and exciting thriller. Michael Ansara, Charles Bronson and Lee Marvin made brief appearances. 97m/B VHS. Tyrone Power, Patricia Neal, Stephen McNally, Hildegarde Neff, Karl Malden; *D:* Henry Hathaway; *C:* Lucien Ballard. *TCF*

Diplomatic Immunity ♫½ 1991 (R) Vicious killer gets off scot-free due to his diplomatic immunity. That is, until the victim's ex-soldier father follows this low-life to the jungles of Paraguay to exact revenge. *CW:* Language, violence, and sensuality. 95m/C VHS, Beta, LV, Closed Caption. Bruce Boxleitner, Billy Drago, Meg Foster, Robert Forster; *D:* Peter Maris. FRH, IME

Direct Hit ♫♫½ 1993 (R) A CIA assassin discovers retiring is not an option. John Hatch (Forsythe) decides he wants out, particularly when his next kill, Savannah (Champa), turns out to be an innocent pawn. So Hatch turns protector and decides to beat the agency at its own deadly game. *CW:* Language, plentiful violence, and some sexuality. 91m/C VHS, LV, Closed Caption. William Forsythe, Richard Norton, Jo Champa, John Aprea, Juliet Landau, George Segal; *D:* Joseph Merhi; *W:* Jacobsen Hart. REP

Dirkham Detective Agency ♫½ 1983 Three children team up to form the Dirkham Detective Agency and are hired by a veterinarian to recover two dognapped poodles. 60m/C VHS, Beta. Sally Kellerman, Stan Shaw, John Quade, Gordon Jump, Randy Morton. NO

Dirt Bike Kid ♫½ 1986 (PG) A precocious brat is stuck with a used motorbike that has a mind of its own. Shenanigans follow in utterly predictable fashion as he battles bankers and bikers with his bad bike. 91m/C VHS, Beta, LV, 8mm, Closed Caption. Peter Billingsley, Anne Bloom, Stuart Pankin, Patrick Collins, Sage Parker, Chad Sheets; *D:* Hoite C. Caston; *W:* Lewis Colick, David Brandes. COL, NLC

Dirt Gang ♫ 1971 (R) A motorcycle gang terrorizes the members of a film crew on location in the desert. 89m/C VHS, Beta. Paul Carr, Michael Pataki, Michael Forest; *D:* Jerry Jameson. MPI

Dirty Dancing ♫♫♫ 1987 (PG-13) An innocent 17-year-old (Grey) is vacationing with her parents in the Catskills in 1963. Bored with the program at the hotel, she finds the real fun at the staff dances. Falling for the sexy dance instructor (Swayze), she discovers love, sex, and rock and roll dancing. An old story, with little to save it, but Grey and Swayze are appealing, the dance sequences fun, and the music great. Swayze, classically trained in ballet, also performs one of the soundtrack songs. ♫(I've Had) the Time of My Life; Be My Baby; Big Girls Don't Cry; Cry to Me; Do You Love Me?; Hey Baby; Hungry Eyes; In the Still of the Nite; Love is Strange. 97m/C VHS, Beta, LV, Closed Caption, DVD. Patrick Swayze, Jennifer Grey, Cynthia Rhodes, Jerry Orbach, Jack Weston, Jane Brucker, Kelly Bishop, Lonny Price, Charles "Honi" Coles, Bruce Morrow; *D:* Emile Ardolino; *W:* Eleanor Bergstein; *M:* John Morris. Academy Awards '87: Best Song ("(I've Had) the Time of My Life"); Golden Globe Awards '88: Best Song ("(I've Had) the Time of My Life"); Independent Spirit Awards '88: Best First Feature. LIV, VES

Dirty Dishes ♫♫♫ 1982 (R) A French film sardonically examining the fruitless life of the average housewife as she confronts a series of bizarre but pointless experiences during the day. Dubbed and subtitled versions available. The director is the American daughter-in-law of the late Luis Bunuel. 99m/C VHS, Beta. FR Carol Laurie, Pierre Santini; *D:* Joyce Bunuel.

The Dirty Dozen ♫♫♫ 1967 (PG) A tough Army major is assigned to train and command twelve hardened convicts offered absolution if they participate in a suicidal mission into Nazi Germany in 1944. Well-made movie is a standout in its genre. Rough and gruff Marvin is good as the group leader. Three made-for-television sequels followed in the '80s. 149m/C VHS, Beta, LV. Lee Marvin, Ernest Borgnine, Charles Bronson, Jim Brown, George Kennedy, John Cassavetes, Clint Walker, Donald Sutherland, Telly Savalas, Robert Ryan, Ralph Meeker, Richard Jaeckel, Trini Lopez; *D:* Robert Aldrich. Academy Awards '67: Best Sound Effects Editing; Nominations: Academy Awards '67: Best Film Editing, Best Sound, Best Supporting Actor (Cassavetes). MGM, TLF

The Dirty Dozen: The Deadly Mission ♫♫½ 1987 A second made-for-TV sequel to the '67 movie finds Borgnine ordering another suicide mission. Savalas (killed in the original, he's playing a new character) must pick 12 convicted army prisoners for an assault on a Nazi-held French monastery. Their mission is to rescue six scientists who are working on a deadly new nerve gas. Followed by "The Dirty Dozen: The Fatal Mission." 96m/C VHS. Ernest Borgnine, Telly Savalas, Vince Edwards, Gary Graham, James Van Patten, Vincent Van Patten, Bo Svenson; *D:* Lee H. Katzin. MGM

The Dirty Dozen: The Fatal Mission ♫♫½ 1988 This third TV sequel has Borgnine learning of a plan to bring a group of high-ranking Nazis to Instanbul via the Orient Express. Naturally, he assigns Savalas the task of getting his motley gang together to thwart the Nazi schemes. To add intrigue, a female has joined the ranks of the Dirty Dozen and a spy may also have infiltrated the group. 91m/C VHS. Ernest Borgnine, Telly Savalas, Hunt Block, Jeff Conaway, Erik Estrada, Ray "Boom Boom" Mancini, Heather Thomas, Alex Cord; *D:* Lee H. Katzin. MGM

The Dirty Dozen: The Next Mission ♫♫ 1985 Disappointing made for television sequel to the 1967 hit, with Marvin reprising his role as the leader of the motley pack. In this installment, the rag-tag toughs are sent on yet another suicide mission inside Nazi Germany, this time to thwart an assassination attempt of Hitler. Followed by two more sequels. 97m/C VHS, Beta, Closed Caption. Lee Marvin, Ernest Borgnine, Richard Jaeckel, Ken Wahl, Larry Wilcox, Sonny Landham, Ricco Ross; *D:* Andrew V. McLaglen. MGM

Dirty Games ♫½ 1993 Nicola Kendra is part of a team sent to Africa to inspect a nuclear waste site. Once there, the scientists discover terrorists are plotting to blow up the nuclear complex unless Nicola and her new allies can prevent it. 97m/C VHS. Jan-Michael Vincent, Valentina Vargas, Ronald France, Michael McGovern; *D:* Gray Hofmeyr. AIP

Dirty Gertie from Harlem U.S.A. ♫♫ 1946 All-black cast performs a variation of W. Somerset Maugham's "Rain." Gertie goes to Trinidad to hide out from her jilted boyfriend. 60m/B VHS, Beta. Gertie LaRue, Spencer Williams Jr., Francine Everett. VYY, DVT, VYY

Dirty Hands ♫♫ *Les Innocents aux Mains Sales* 1976 A woman and her lover conspire to murder her husband. A must for fans of the sexy Schneider. Cinematography provides moments that are both interesting and eerie. 102m/C VHS. FR Rod Steiger, Romy Schneider, Paul Giusti, Jean Rochefort, Hans-Christian Blech; *D:* Claude Chabrol. FCT

Dirty Harry ♫♫♫½ 1971 (R) Rock-hard cop Harry Callahan attempts to track down a psychopathic rooftop killer before a kidnapped girl dies. Harry abuses the murderer's civil rights, however, forcing the police to return the criminal to the streets, where he hijacks a school bus and Harry is called on once again. The only answer to stop this vicious killer seems to be death in cold blood, and Harry is just the man to do it. Taut, suspenseful direction by Siegel, who thoroughly understands Eastwood's on-screen character. Features Callahan's famous "Do you feel lucky?" line, the precursor to his "Go ahead, make my day." 103m/C VHS, Beta, LV, 8mm. Clint Eastwood, Harry Guardino, John Larch, Andrew (Andy) Robinson, Reni Santoni, John Vernon; *D:* Donald Siegel; *C:* Bruce Surtees; *M:* Lalo Schifrin. WAR, TLF

Dirty Heroes ♫♫ *Dalle Ardenne All'Inferno* 1971 (R) A band of escaped WWII POWs battle the Nazis for a precious treasure in the war's final days. 117m/C VHS, Beta. John Ireland, Curt Jurgens, Adolfo Celi, Daniela Bianchi, Michael Constantine; *D:* Alberto De Martino; *M:* Ennio Morricone. NO

Dirty Laundry woof! 1987 (PG-13) Insipid wreck of a comedy about a klutz who accidentally gets his laundry mixed up with $1 million dollars in drug money. Features Olympians Lewis and Louganis. Never released theatrically. 81m/C VHS, Beta. Leigh McCloskey, Jeanne O'Brien, Frankie Valli, Sonny Bono, Carl Lewis, Greg Louganis, Nicholas Worth; *D:* William Webb. NO

Dirty Mary Crazy Larry ♫♫♫ 1974 (PG) A racecar driver, his mechanic, and a sexy girl hightail it from the law after pulling off a heist. Great action, great fun, and an infamous surprise ending. 93m/C VHS, Beta, LV. Peter Fonda, Susan George, Adam Roarke, Vic Morrow, Roddy McDowall; *D:* John Hough; *W:* Leigh Chapman. FOX

Dirty Mind of Young Sally woof! 1972 (R) Sally's erotic radio program broadcasts from a mobile studio, which must stay one step ahead of the police. 84m/C VHS, Beta. Sharon Kelly. TPV

Dirty Rotten Scoundrels ♫♫♫ 1988 (PG) A remake of the 1964 "Bedtime Story," in which two confidence tricksters on the Riviera endeavor to rip off a suddenly rich American woman, and each other. Caine and Martin are terrific, Martin has some of his best physical comedy ever, and Headly is charming as the prey who's always one step ahead of them. Fine direction from Oz, the man who brought us the voice of Yoda in "The Empire Strikes Back." 112m/C VHS, Beta, LV, Closed Caption. Steve Martin, Michael Caine, Glenne Headly, Anton Rodgers, Barbara Harris, Dana Ivey; *D:* Frank Oz; *W:* Dale Launer, Stanley Shapiro; *C:* Michael Ballhaus; *M:* Miles Goodman. ORI

Dirty Tricks ♫½ 1981 (PG) History professor Gould fights with bad guys for a letter written by George Washington. Thoroughly forgettable comedy lacking in laughs. 91m/C VHS, Beta. CA Elliott Gould, Kate Jackson, Arthur Hill, Rich Little; *D:* Alvin Rakoff; *W:* William W. Norton Sr.; *M:* Hagood Hardy. COL

Dirty Work ♫♫ 1992 (R) A drug-dealing bail bondsman (Ashton) steals counterfeit money from the mob and then sets up his partner (Dobson) as the fall guy. Can Dobson survive long enough to set things straight? *CW:* Violence. 88m/C VHS, Beta, Closed Caption. John, Ashton, Kevin Dobson, Roxann Biggs-Dawson, Donnelly Rhodes, Jim Byrnes, Mitchell Ryan; *D:* John McPherson; *W:* Aaron Julien. PAR

Disappearance ♫♫ 1981 (R) A hired assassin discovers an ironic link between his new target and his missing wife. 80m/C VHS, Beta. CA Donald Sutherland, David Hemmings, John Hurt, Christopher Plummer, David Warner, Virginia McKenna; *D:* Stuart Cooper. VES, RHI

The Disappearance of Aimee ♫♫♫ 1976 Dramatic recreation of events surrounding the 1926 disappearance of evangelist Aimee Semple McPherson. She claimed she was abducted, but her mother insisted she ran away to have an affair. Excellent made for television movie with an exceptional cast. Originally to star Ann-Margret. 110m/C VHS, Beta. Faye Dunaway, Bette Davis, James Sloyan, James Woods, John Lehne, Lelia Goldoni, Barry Brown, Severn Darden; *W:* Anthony Harvey. LIV

The Disappearance of Christina ♫♫½ 1993 (PG-13) Successful entrepreneur Joe Seldon (Stamos) is married to heiress Christina (Yarlett) and they seem to be the perfect couple. But when Christina mysteriously vanishes during a sailing trip, was it really an accident? Detective Nora Davis (Pounder) doesn't think so and naturally, Joe is suspect numero uno. 93m/C VHS, LV, Closed Caption. John Stamos, Kim Delaney, Robert Carradine, Claire Yarlett, CCH Pounder; *D:* Karen Arthur; *W:* Camille Thomasson. USH

Disaster at Silo 7 ♫♫ 1988 When the engine of a Titan missile goes on the fritz, the Air Force tries to prevent a nuclear disaster. Based on an actual Titan II missile incident near Little Rock, Arkansas. Made for television. 92m/C VHS. Peter Boyle, Patricia Charbonneau, Perry King, Michael O'Keefe, Joe Spano, Dennis Weaver; *D:* Larry Elikann; *W:* Douglas Lloyd McIntosh; *C:* Roy Wagner. TRI

The Disciple 🎬½ 1915 Vintage silent western wherein Hart's unsmiling good-bad guy tries to clean up a lawless town and win back his wife, who has shamelessly fallen in with a corrupt saloon-keeper. **80m/B VHS, Beta, 8mm.** William S. Hart, Dorothy Dalton, Robert McKim, Jean Hersholt; **D:** William S. Hart; **W:** Thomas Ince. *VYY, GPV*

Disciple of Death 🎬 1972 (R) Raven plays "The Stranger," a ghoul who sacrifices virgins to the Devil. **82m/C VHS, Beta.** GB Mike Raven, Ronald Lacey, Stephen Bradley, Virginia Wetherell; **D:** Tom Parkinson. *UNI*

Disclosure 🎬🎬 1994 (R) Likable, responsible executive and family man (Douglas) finds himself sexually harassed by his ex-lover turned dragon-lady boss (Moore). But when he rejects her lusty come-on, she points the finger at him. One-dimensional characters and hollow material turn sexual harassment into a trivial issue. High-tech saga of corporate politics, while flashy, is nothing we haven't seen before. Douglas just can't pass up these "Regular Joe meets beautiful, horny babe, bad things happen" roles, can he? Based on the Michael Crichton novel.**CW:** Contains strong language, sexual references, and one sexual episode. **129m/C VHS, LV, Closed Caption.** Michael Douglas, Demi Moore, Donald Sutherland, Caroline Goodall, Dylan Baker, Dennis Miller, Rosemary Forsyth, Roma Maffia; **D:** Barry Levinson; **W:** Paul Attanasio; **M:** Ennio Morricone. Blockbuster Entertainment Awards '95: Drama Actress, Theatrical (Moore); Blockbuster Entertainment Awards '96: Drama Actress, Video (Moore); Nominations: MTV Movie Awards '95: Most Desirable Female (Moore), Best Villain (Moore). *WAR*

Disconnected 🎬½ 1987 "Sorry, Wrong Number" is updated, with more than ample doses of sex and violence. **81m/C VHS, Beta.** Mark Walker. *NO*

Discontent 🎬½ 1916 An early silent film by Lois Weber in which a cantankerous old vet goes to live with his wealthy nephew. The harmonious family life is disrupted by his meddling ways. **30m/B VHS, Beta. D:** Lois Weber. *GVV*

The Discovery Program 🎬🎬½ 1989 Four award-winning short films on one video: "Ray's Male Heterosexual Dance Hall," "Greasy Lake," "The Open Window," and "Hearts of Stone." The subjects range from humorous and offbeat to tragic and deadly serious. **106m/C VHS, Beta.** Academy Awards '87: Best Live Action Short Film ("Ray's Male Heterosexual Dance Hall"). *FCT*

The Discreet Charm of the Bourgeoisie 🎬🎬🎬 *Le Charme Discret de la Bourgeoisie* 1972 (R) Bunuel in top form, satirizing modern society. These six characters are forever sitting down to dinner, yet they never eat. Dreams and reality, actual or contrived, prevent their feast. **100m/C VHS, Beta, LV.** FR Fernando Rey, Delphine Seyrig, Jean-Pierre Cassel, Bulle Ogier, Michel Piccoli, Stephane Audran, Luis Bunuel; **D:** Luis Bunuel; **W:** Luis Bunuel, Jean-Claude Carriere. Academy Awards '72: Best Foreign Language Film; British Academy Awards '73: Best Actress (Seyrig), Best Screenplay; National Board of Review Awards '72: 5 Best Foreign Films of the Year; National Society of Film Critics Awards '72: Best Director (Bunuel), Best Film; Nominations: Academy Awards '72: Best Story & Screenplay. *MED, APD*

Discretion Assured 🎬🎬½ 1993 (R) Successful businessman Trevor McCabe (York) finds himself in a romantic quandry with three women, leading to his involvement in embezzlement and murder.**CW:** Language and sexuality. **97m/C VHS.** Michael York, Jennifer O'Neill, Dee Wallace Stone, Elizabeth Gracen; **D:** Odorico Mendes. *MNC*

Dishonored 🎬🎬½ 1931 Dated spy drama has Dietrich playing secret agent X-27 in WWI and masquerading on the side as a peasant girl. Although not one of the more famous Dietrich-Sternberg productions, its camp plot and Dietrich's lavish performance make it worth watching. Based on the infamous spy Mata Hari, who was shot by the French in 1917 for espionage. **91m/B VHS, Closed Caption.** Marlene Dietrich, Victor McLaglen,

Lew Cody, Gustav von Seyffertitz, Warner Oland, Barry Norton, Davison Clark, Wilfrid Lucas; **D:** Josef von Sternberg; **W:** Josef von Sternberg, Daniel N. Rubin; **C:** Lee Garmes. *USH, FCT*

Dishonored Lady 🎬½ 1947 After her ex-boyfriend is murdered, a female art director finds that she's the number one suspect. When put on trial for the dastardly deed, she takes the fifth in this mediocre melodrama. **85m/B VHS, Beta.** Hedy Lamarr, Dennis O'Keefe, William Lundigan, John Loder; **D:** Robert Stevenson. *SNC, NOS, CAB*

Disney's Storybook Classics 1982 A collection of classic children's fables, featuring "Little Toot" (1948, excerpted from "Melody Time"), the story of a little harbor tugboat; "Chicken Little" (1943); "The Grasshopper and the Ant" (1934, a "Silly Symphony"); and "Peter and the Wolf" (1946, excerpted from "Make Mine Music"), a Disneyized version of Prokofiev's famous concert piece. **121m/C VHS, Beta.** Sterling Holloway, The Andrews Sisters. *DIS*

Disorderlies 🎬 1987 (PG) Members of the popular rap group cavort as incompetent hospital orderlies assigned to care for a cranky millionaire. Fat jokes abound with performances by the Fat Boys. **86m/C VHS, Beta, LV, Closed Caption.** The Fat Boys, Ralph Bellamy; **D:** Michael A. Schultz; **M:** Anne Dudley. *WAR*

Disorderly Orderly 🎬½ 1964 When Jerry Lewis gets hired as a hospital orderly, nothing stands upright long with him around. Vintage slapstick Lewis running amuck in a nursing home. **90m/C VHS, Beta, LV.** Jerry Lewis, Glenda Farrell, Everett Sloane, Kathleen Freeman, Susan Oliver; **D:** Frank Tashlin. *PAR*

Disorganized Crime 🎬🎬 1989 (R) On the lam from the law, Bernsen attempts to organize a group of his ex-con buddies to pull off the perfect heist. Before the boys can organize, however, the cops are hot on Bernsen's trail, and he must vacate the meeting place. Good cast attempts to lift this movie beyond script. **101m/C VHS, Beta, LV, Closed Caption.** Lou Diamond Phillips, Fred Gwynne, Corbin Bernsen, Ruben Blades, Hoyt Axton, Ed O'Neill, Daniel Roebuck, William Russ; **D:** Jim Kouf; **M:** David Newman. *TOU*

Disraeli 🎬🎬🎬 1930 Arliss deservedly won the Best Actor Oscar for his title role as the famed British prime minister to Queen Victoria. This particular slice of the cunning statesman's life depicts his efforts to secure the Suez Canal for England against the Russians. Arliss' wife also played his screen spouse. One of Warner's earliest and best biographical films. Based on a play by Louis Napoleon Parker. **87m/B VHS.** George Arliss, Joan Bennett, Florence Arliss, Anthony Bushell, David Torrence, Doris Lloyd, Ivan Simpson, Gwendolyn Logan; **D:** Alfred E. Green; **C:** Lee Garmes. Academy Awards '30: Best Actor (Arliss); Nominations: Academy Awards '30: Best Picture, Best Writing. *MGM*

Distant Drums 🎬🎬 1951 A small band of adventurers tries to stop the Seminole War in the Florida Everglades. **101m/C VHS, Beta.** Gary Cooper, Mari Aldon, Robert Barrat, Richard Webb, Ray Teal, Arthur Hunnicutt; **D:** Raoul Walsh; **M:** Max Steiner. *REP, FCT*

Distant Justice 🎬½ 1992 (R) Tokyo police inspector Rio (Sugawara) is vacationing in Boston with his wife and daughter, where he can also visit old friend, Chief Bradfield (Kennedy). But Rio's wife is murdered and his daughter kidnapped by vicious drug dealer Roy Pennola (Carradine) and Bradfield assigns young officer Charlie Givens (Lutes) to see that Rio doesn't get himself killed as well.**CW:** Strong violence; a rape; sexuality; some language. **91m/C VHS.** Bunta Sugawara, George Kennedy, David Carradine, Eric Lutes; **D:** Toru Murakawa. *COL*

Distant Thunder 🎬🎬🎬½ 1973 A bitter, unrelenting portrait of a small Bengali neighborhood as the severe famines of 1942, brought about by the "distant thunder" of WWII, take their toll. A mature achievement from Ray; in Bengali

with English subtitles. **92m/C VHS, Beta.** IN Soumitra Chatterjee, Sandhya Roy, Babita, Gobinda Chakravarty, Romesh Mukerji; **D:** Satyajit Ray. Berlin International Film Festival '73: Golden Berlin Bear. *FCT*

Distant Thunder 🎬🎬 1988 (R) A scarred Vietnam vet, who has become a recluse, and his estranged son reunite in the Washington State wilderness, causing him to reflect on his isolation. Strong premise and cast watered down by weak script. **114m/C VHS, Beta, LV, Closed Caption.** CA John Lithgow, Ralph Macchio, Kerrie Keane, Janet Margolin, Rick Rosenthal; **D:** Rick Rosenberg; **C:** Ralf Bode; **M:** Maurice Jarre. *PAR*

Distant Voices, Still Lives 🎬🎬🎬 1988 A profoundly executed, disturbing film chronicling a British middle-class family through the maturation of the three children, under the dark shadow of their abusive, malevolent father. An evocative, heartbreaking portrait of British life from WWII on, and of the rhythms of dysfunctional families. A film festival favorite. **87m/C VHS, Beta, LV.** GB Freda Dowie, Pete Postlethwaite, Angela Walsh, Dean Williams, Lorraine Ashbourne; **D:** Terence Davies; **W:** Terence Davies. Los Angeles Film Critics Association Awards '89: Best Foreign Film. *LIV*

The Distinguished Gentleman 🎬🎬 1992 (R) A small-time con man (Murphy) manages to scam his way into a political career and winds up in Congress. The other characters serve mostly as foils for Murphy's comedic talent. Viewers will laugh despite the story's predictablity.**CW:** Language and one sexual scene. **122m/C VHS, LV, Closed Caption.** Eddie Murphy, Lane Smith, Sheryl Lee Ralph, Joe Don Baker, Victoria Rowell, Grant Shaud, Kevin McCarthy, Charles S. Dutton, James Garner; **D:** Jonathan Lynn; **W:** Marty Kaplan; **M:** Randy Edelman. *TOU*

Distortions 🎬🎬 1987 (PG) Hussey is a widow whose evil aunt (Laurie) is holding her hostage. What the film lacks in suspense throughout most of the movie is made up for in the end. **90m/C VHS, Beta.** Piper Laurie, Steve Railsback, Olivia Hussey, Edward Albert, Rita Gam, Terence Knox; **D:** Armand Mastroianni. *ACA*

Disturbance 🎬½ 1989 The two personas of a young schizophrenic get him entangled in a mysterious string of murders. **81m/C VHS, Beta.** Timothy Greeson, Lisa Geoffreion; **D:** Cliff Guest. *NO*

Disturbed 🎬 1990 (R) Lusty mental hospital director McDowell meets sex starved and suicidal Gidley in this less-than-stellar erotic creeper. Redeemed only by McDowell's performance and more evidence that the droog's career hasn't been just peachy since "Clockwork Orange." **96m/C VHS, LV.** Malcolm McDowell, Geoffrey Lewis, Priscilla Pointer, Pamela Gidley, Clint Howard; **D:** Charles Winkler; **W:** Emerson Bixby, Charles Winkler. *LIV*

Diva 🎬🎬🎬½ 1982 (R) While at a concert given by his favorite star, a young French courier secretly tapes a soprano who has refused to record. The film follows the young man through Paris as he flees from two Japanese recording pirates, and a couple of crooked undercover police who are trying to cover-up for the chief who not only has a mistress, but runs a prostitution ring. Brilliant and dazzling photography compliment the eclectic soundtrack. **123m/C VHS, Beta, LV.** FR Frederic Andrei, Roland Bertin, Richard Bohringer, Gerard Darmon, Jacques Fabbri, Wilhelmenia Wiggins Fernandez, Dominique Pinon; **D:** Jean-Jacques Beineix; **W:** Jean-Jacques Beineix; **C:** Philippe Rousselot; **M:** Vladimir Cosma. Cesar Awards '82: Best Cinematography, Best Sound, Best Score; National Society of Film Critics Awards '82: Best Cinematography. *MGM, APD*

The Dive 🎬🎬 1989 (PG-13) Two North Sea oil-rig workers are trapped far below the waves when the lifeline to their diving bell snaps in rough seas. **90m/C VHS, Beta, LV, Closed Caption.** Bjorn Sundquist, Frank Grimes, Einride Eidsvold, Michael Kitchen; **D:** Tristan De Vere Cole. *NO*

Dive Bomber 🎬🎬 1941 Exciting aviation film that focuses on medical problems related to flying. Flynn stars as an aviator-doctor who conducts experiments to eliminate pilot-blackout.

MacMurray, Toomey, and Heydt perform well as three flyboys stationed in Hawaii. Great flying sequences filmed at San Diego's naval base with extra scenes shot at Pensacola. Warner Bros. released this film just months before the Japanese attacked Pearl Harbor. Based on the story "Beyond the Blue Sky" by Frank Wead. **130m/B VHS, Closed Caption.** Errol Flynn, Fred MacMurray, Ralph Bellamy, Alexis Smith, Regis Toomey, Robert Armstrong, Allen Jenkins, Craig Stevens; **D:** Michael Curtiz; **W:** Frank Wead, Robert Buckner; **M:** Max Steiner. Nominations: Academy Awards '41: Best Color Cinematography. *MGM*

Divided by Hate 🐾🐾 1996 **(PG-13)** In 1984, struggling farmer Louis Gibbs (Walsh) and his wife Carol (Roth), and their children fall under the spell of charismatic preacher Steve Riordan (Skerritt) whose anti-government sentiments lead to the forming of a local militia. Naturally, the FBI gets involved and there's a struggle between the feds and the militia, with the family caught in the middle. If it sounds familiar that's because it's based on the 1995 Branch Davidian incident. **CW:** Thematic elements and some violence. **92m/C VHS, Closed Caption.** Dylan Walsh, Andrea Roth, Tom Skerritt; **D:** Tom Skerritt. *USH*

Divine 🐾🐾½ 1990 Two Divine flicks from Waters. First, Divine plays a naughty girl who, not surprisingly, since this one is titled "The Diane Linkletter Story," ends up a successful suicide. "The Neon Woman" is a rare live performance, with Divine a woman who owns a strip joint and has a slew of problems you won't read about in Dear Abbey. **110m/C VHS.** Divine; **D:** John Waters. *FCT*

The Divine Enforcer 🐾½ 1991 A monsignor in a crime-ridden L.A. neighborhood reaches his wit's end in trying to stave off perpetrators of injustice. Fortunately, help arrives in the form of a mysterious priest who is equally handy with his fists, nunchakus, and guns. From then on it's no more mister nice guy, and the criminals haven't a prayer. **90m/C VHS, Beta.** Jan-Michael Vincent, Erik Estrada, Jim Brown, Judy Landers, Don Stroud, Robert Z'Dar, Michael Foley, Carrie Chambers, Hiroko; **D:** Robert Rundle. *PSM*

Divine Nymph 🐾½ 1971 **(R)** Charts the erotic adventures of the beautiful and young Manuela, who is dangerously pursued by two cousins. **100m/C VHS, Beta.** IT Laura Antonelli, Marcello Mastroianni, Terence Stamp; **D:** Giuseppe Patroni Griffi; **M:** Ennio Morricone. *MPI*

Diving In 🐾🐾 1990 **(PG-13)** Have you heard the one about the acrophobic diver? It seems a paralyzing fear of heights is the only thing between a young diver and Olympic gold. Much splashing about and heartstring-tugging. **92m/C VHS, Beta, Closed Caption.** Burt Young, Matt Adler, Kristy Swanson, Matt Lattanzi, Richard Johnson, Carey Scott, Yolanda Jilot; **D:** Strathford Hamilton; **C:** Hanania Baer; **M:** Guy Moon, Paul Buckmaster. *PAR, FCT*

Divorce American Style 🐾🐾½ 1967 Dated but still amusing look at love, marriage, and the big D. Richard (Van Dyke) and Barbara (Reynolds) Harmon find their longtime marriage in a tailspin as they spend all their time arguing. They split but find single life and the dating game have their own pitfalls. **103m/C VHS.** Dick Van Dyke, Debbie Reynolds, Jason Robards Jr., Jean Simmons, Van Johnson, Lee Grant, Joe Flynn, Shelley Berman, Martin Gabel, Tom Bosley, Dick Gautier, Eileen Brennan; **D:** Bud Yorkin; **W:** Norman Lear; **C:** Conrad Hall; **M:** Dave Grusin. Nominations: Academy Awards '67: Best Story & Screenplay. *COL*

Divorce His, Divorce Hers 🐾🐾 1972 The first half of this drama shows the crumbling of a marriage through the husband's eyes. The second half offers the wife's perspective. Made for television. **144m/C VHS, Beta.** Richard Burton, Elizabeth Taylor; **D:** Waris Hussein. *NO*

Divorce—Italian Style 🐾🐾🐾½ *Divorzio All'Italiana* 1962 A middle-aged baron bored with his wife begins directing his amorous attentions to a teenage cousin. Since divorce in Italy is impossi-

ble, the only way out of his marriage is murder—and the baron finds a little-known law that excuses a man from murdering his wife if she is having an affair (since he would merely be defending his honor). A hilarious comedy with a twist ending. Available in Italian with English subtitles or dubbed in English. **104m/B VHS.** IT Marcello Mastroianni, Daniela Rocca, Leopoldo Trieste; **D:** Pietro Germi; **W:** Pietro Germi, Ennio de Concini, Alfredo Giannetti. Academy Awards '62: Best Story & Screenplay; British Academy Awards '63: Best Actor (Mastroianni); Golden Globe Awards '63: Best Actor—Musical/Comedy (Mastroianni), Best Foreign Film; Nominations: Academy Awards '62: Best Actor (Mastroianni), Best Director (Germi). *HTV*

The Divorce of Lady X 🐾🐾½ 1938 A spoiled British debutante, in the guise of "Lady X," makes a woman-hating divorce lawyer eat his words through romance and marriage. Based on the play by Gilbert Wakefield. **92m/C VHS, Beta, LV.** GB Merle Oberon, Laurence Olivier, Ralph Richardson, Binnie Barnes; **D:** Tim Whelan; **C:** Harry Stradling; **M:** Miklos Rozsa. *NOS, MRV, UNI*

The Divorcee 🐾🐾½ 1930 Early Leonard film (he'd later direct "The Great Ziegfeld" and "Pride and Prejudice") casts Shearer as a woman out to beat her husband at philandering. Married to a journalist, she cavorts with her husband's best friend and a discarded old flame as only a pre-production code gal could. Shearer—who Lillian Hellman described as having "a face unclouded by thought"—grabbed an Oscar. Based on the novel "Ex-Wife" by Ursula Parrott. **83m/B VHS.** Norma Shearer, Chester Morris, Conrad Nagel, Robert Montgomery, Mary Doran, Tyler Brooke, George Irving, Helen Johnson; **D:** Robert Z. Leonard. Academy Awards '30: Best Actress (Shearer); Nominations: Academy Awards '30: Best Director (Leonard), Best Picture, Best Writing. *MGM, FCT, BTV*

Dixiana 🐾½ 1930 A Southern millionaire falls for a circus performer shortly before the start of the Civil War. Part color. ♫Dixiana; Here's to the Old Days; A Tear, a Kiss, a Smile; My One Ambition is You; A Lady Loved a Soldier; Mr. & Mrs. Sippi; Guiding Star. **99m/B VHS, Beta.** Bebe Daniels, Bert Wheeler, Robert Woolsey, Dorothy Lamour, Bill Robinson; **D:** Luther Reed; **M:** Max Steiner. *NOS, DVT*

Dixie: Changing Habits 🐾🐾🐾 1985 A New Orleans madam and a Mother Superior go head to head in this amusing made-for-television movie. In the end all benefit as the nuns discover business sense and pay off a debt, while the former bordello owner cleans up her act. Above-average scripting and directing for the medium. **100m/C VHS.** Suzanne Pleshette, Cloris Leachman, Kenneth McMillan, John Considine, Geraldine Fitzgerald, Judith Ivey; **D:** George Englund. *LIV*

Dixie Dynamite 🐾 1976 **(PG)** The two daughters of a Georgia moonshiner set out to avenge the murder of their father. The music is performed by Duane Eddy and Dorsey Burnette. **88m/C VHS, Beta.** Warren Oates, Christopher George, Jane Anne Johnstone, Kathy McHaley, R.G. Armstrong, Wes Bishop; **D:** Lee Frost. *VCI*

Dixie Jamboree 🐾 1944 Low-budget musical has gangster on the lam using an unusual method to escape from St. Louis—the last Mississippi Showboat. ♫Dixie Showboat; No, No, No; If It's a Dream; You Ain't Right with the Lord; Big Stuff. **69m/B VHS, Beta.** Guy Kibbee, Frances Langford, Louise Beavers, Charles Butterworth; **D:** Christy Cabanne. *NOS, VYY, DVT*

Dixie Lanes 🐾 1988 A relentlessly nostalgic comedy set in a small town at the end of WWII. A woman, troubled by her nephew's restless antics, puts him to work. Unfortunately she adds to his plight, as his business involves the Black Market. **92m/C VHS, Beta.** Hoyt Axton, Karen Black, Art Hindle, John Vernon, Ruth Buzzi, Tina Louise, Pamela Springsteen, Nina Foch; **D:** Don Cato. *CEL*

Django 🐾½ 1968 **(PG)** Django is a stranger who arrives in a Mexican-border town to settle a dispute between a small band of Americans and Mexicans. **90m/C VHS, Beta.** Franco Nero, Loredana Nusciak, Angel Alvarez; **D:** Sergio Corbucci. *NO*

Django Shoots First 🐾½ 1974 Spaghetti western with usual amount of action and plot twists. **96m/C VHS, Beta.** Glen Saxson, Evelyn Stewart, Alberto Lupo. *VYY*

Do or Die 🐾½ 1991 **(R)** Former "Playboy" centerfolds Speir and Vasquez team up as a couple of federal agent babes who take on international crime boss Morita. But the crimelord is ready for our scantily clad heroines with a sick game of revenge—and the stakes are their very lives! **CW:** Nudity and sensuality. **97m/C VHS, LV.** Erik Estrada, Dona Speir, Roberta Vasquez, Noriyuki "Pat" Morita, Bruce Penhall, Carolyn Liu, Stephanie Schick; **D:** Andy Sidaris; **W:** Andy Sidaris. *COL*

Do the Right Thing 🐾🐾🐾½ 1989 **(R)** An uncompromising, brutal comedy about the racial tensions surrounding a white-owned pizzeria in the Bed-Stuy section of Brooklyn on the hottest day of the summer, and the violence that eventually erupts. Ambivalent and, for the most part, hilarious; Lee's coming-of-age. **120m/C VHS, Beta, LV, Closed Caption.** Spike Lee, Danny Aiello, Richard Edson, Ruby Dee, Ossie Davis, Giancarlo Esposito, Bill Nunn, John Turturro, John Savage, Rosie Perez, Frankie Faison; **D:** Spike Lee; **W:** Spike Lee. Los Angeles Film Critics Association Awards '89: Best Director (Lee), Best Film, Best Supporting Actor (Aiello); New York Film Critics Awards '89: Best Cinematography; Nominations: Academy Awards '89: Best Original Screenplay, Best Supporting Actor (Aiello). *USH, FCT*

D.O.A. 🐾🐾🐾½ 1949 A man is given a lethal, slow-acting poison. As his time runs out, he frantically seeks to learn who is responsible and why he was targeted for death. Dark film noir remade in 1969 as "Color Me Dead" and in 1988 with Dennis Quaid and Meg Ryan. Also available colorized. **83m/B VHS, Beta.** Edmond O'Brien, Pamela Britton, Luther Adler, Neville Brand, Beverly Garland, Lynne Baggett, William Ching, Henry Hart, Laurette Luez, Virginia Lee, Jess Kirkland, Cay Forrester, Michael Ross; **D:** Rudolph Mate; **W:** Russel Rouse, Clarence Green; **C:** Ernest Laszlo; **M:** Dimitri Tiomkin. *SNC, NOS, VYY*

D.O.A. 🐾🐾½ 1988 **(R)** Well-done remake of the 1949 thriller with Quaid portraying a college professor who is poisoned and has only 24 hours to identify his killer. His search for the suspect is further complicated by the fact that he is being sought by the police on phony charges of murder. Directed by the same people who brought "Max Headroom" to television screens. **98m/C VHS, Beta, LV, Closed Caption.** Dennis Quaid, Meg Ryan, Charlotte Rampling, Daniel Stern, Jane Kaczmarek, Christopher Neame, Jay Patterson; **D:** Rocky Morton, Annabel Jankel; **W:** Charles Edward Pogue; **M:** Chaz Jankel. *TOU*

The Doberman Gang 🐾🐾 1972 **(PG)** Clever thieves train a gang of Dobermans in the fine art of bank robbery. Sequelled by "The Daring Dobermans." **85m/C VHS, Beta, Closed Caption.** Byron Mabe, Hal Reed, Julie Parrish, Simmy Bow, JoJo D'Amore; **D:** Byron Ross Chudnow; **W:** Frank Ray Perilli. *FOX*

Doc Hollywood 🐾🐾½ 1991 **(PG-13)** A hotshot young physician on his way to a lucrative California practice gets stranded in a small Southern town. Will the wacky woodsy inhabitants persuade the city doctor to stay? There aren't many surprises in this fish-out-of-water comedy, but the cast injects it with considerable charm. Adapted from Neil B. Shulman's book "What?...Dead Again?" **104m/C VHS, Beta, LV, 8mm, Closed Caption.** Michael J. Fox, Julie Warner, Woody Harrelson, Barnard Hughes, David Ogden Stiers, Frances Sternhagen, Bridget Fonda, George Hamilton, Roberts Blossom, Helen Martin, Macon McCalman, Barry Sobel; **D:** Michael Caton-Jones; **W:** Daniel Pyne, Jeffrey Price, Peter S. Seaman; **C:** Michael Chapman; **M:** Carter Burwell. *WAR*

Doc Savage 🎭🎭½ 1975 (PG) Doc and "The Amazing Five" fight a murderous villain who plans to take over the world. Based on the novels of Kenneth Robeson. 100m/C VHS, Beta. Ron Ely, Pamela Hensley, Paul Gleason, Paul Wexler, William Lucking; D: Michael Anderson Sr.; W: George Pal, Joe Morhaim; C: Fred W. Koenekamp. WAR

Docks of New York 🎭🎭🎭 1928 Von Sternberg made his mark in Hollywood with this silent drama about two dockside losers finding love amid the squalor. A rarely seen, early masterpiece. 60m/B VHS, Beta. George Bancroft, Betty Compson, Olga Baclanova; D: Josef von Sternberg; M: Gaylord Carter. PAR

The Doctor 🎭🎭½ 1991 (PG-13) A hotshot doctor develops throat cancer and gets treated at his own hospital, an ordeal that teaches him a respect and compassion for patients that he formerly lacked. Potential melodrama is saved by fine acting and strong direction. Based on the autobiographical book "A Taste of My Own Medicine" by Dr. Edward Rosenbaum. 125m/C VHS, Beta, LV, Closed Caption. William Hurt, Elizabeth Perkins, Christine Lahti, Mandy Patinkin, Wendy Crewson, Charlie Korsmo, Adam Arkin, Bill Macy; D: Randa Haines; W: Robert Caswell; C: John Seale; M: Michael Convertino. TOU

Dr. Alien 🎭 1988 (R) Alien poses as beautiful scientist and turns a college freshman into a sex-addicted satyr. Likewise, the cast turns this flick into a dog. 90m/C VHS, Beta, LV, Closed Caption. Billy Jacoby, Olivia Barash, Stuart Fratkin, Troy Donahue, Arlene Golonka, Judy Landers; D: David DeCoteau. PAR

The Doctor and the Devils 🎭🎭½ 1985 (R) Based on an old screenplay by Dylan Thomas, this is a semi-Gothic tale about two criminals who supply a physician with corpses to study, either digging them up or killing them fresh. 93m/C VHS, Beta. GB Timothy Dalton, Julian Sands, Jonathan Pryce, Twiggy, Stephen Rea, Beryl Reid, Sian Phillips, Patrick Stewart, Phyllis Logan, T.P. McKenna; D: Freddie Francis; W: Ronald Harwood; M: John Morris. FOX

Doctor at Large 🎭🎭½ 1957 A fledgling doctor seeks to become a surgeon at a hospital for the rich. Humorous antics follow. The third of the "Doctor" series. 98m/C VHS, Beta. GB Dirk Bogarde, Muriel Pavlow, James Robertson Justice, Shirley Eaton, Donald Sinden, Anne Heywood; D: Ralph Thomas. NO

Doctor at Sea 🎭🎭½ 1956 To escape a troublesome romantic entanglement and the stresses of his career, a London physician signs on a cargo boat as a ship's doctor and becomes involved with French bombshell Bardot. The second of the "Doctor" series. 93m/C VHS, Beta. GB James Robertson Justice, Dirk Bogarde, Brigitte Bardot; D: Ralph Thomas; W: Jack Davies. FCT

Dr. Bethune 🎭🎭🎭 Bethune, The Making of a Hero 1990 Canadian surgeon Norman Bethune was a larger-than-life hero with equally great flaws. A crusader for socialized medicine and an outspoken opponent of Fascism (as well as an alcoholic womanizer), he worked for the Loyalist forces in the Spanish Civil War and was instrumental in developing mobile medical units for treating battlefield wounded. He's also credited with bringing modern medical care to China, where he attended to Mao's revolutionary forces. Sutherland's strong performance shows the intensity and vision of a complicated man; he previously played the doctor in 1977's "Bethune." Awkward jumps in time and place rob the story of narrative drive. 115m/C VHS. CA FR Donald Sutherland, Helen Mirren, Helen Shaver, Colm Feore, Anouk Aimee, Ronald Pickup, Harrison Liu; D: Phillip Borsos; W: Ted Allan; C: Raoul Coutard; M: Alan Reeves. FXL, ING

Dr. Black, Mr. Hyde 🎭 Dr. Black and Mr. White; The Watts Monster 1976 (R) Not-so-horrifying tale of a black Jekyll who metamorphoses into a white monster with the help of the special potion. Unintended laughs lessen suspense. 88m/C VHS, Beta. Rosalind Cash, Stu Gilliam, Bernie Casey, Marie O'Henry; D: William Crain. VCI

Doctor Blood's Coffin 🎭🎭½ 1962 The aptly named doctor performs hideous experiments on the unsuspecting denizens of a lonely village. Good cast in this effective chiller. 92m/C VHS. GB Kieron Moore, Hazel Court, Ian Hunter; D: Sidney J. Furie. SNC

Doctor Butcher M.D. woof! Queen of the Cannibals 1980 (R) Mad doctor's deranged dream of creating "perfect people" by taking parts of one person and interchanging them with another backfires as his monstrosities develop strange side effects. The M.D., by the way, stands for "Medical Deviate." Dubbed. 81m/C VHS, Beta. IT Ian McCulloch, Alexandra Cole, Peter O'Neal, Donald O'Brien; D: Frank Martin. NO

Dr. Caligari 🎭🎭 1989 (R) The granddaughter of the original Dr. Caligari promotes "better living through chemistry" in her insane asylum while using her patients as guinea pigs in her bizarre sexual experiments. Nothing outstanding here in terms of story or performance, but "Dick Tracy" has nothing on the visually compelling set designs and make-up. 80m/C VHS, LV. Madeleine Reynal, Fox Harris, Laura Albert, Jennifer Balgobin, John Durbin, Gene Zerna, David Parry, Barry Phillips; D: Stephen Sayadian. FCT

Dr. Christian Meets the Women 🎭½ 1940 This entry in the "Dr. Christian" series of films has the small-town physician once again exposing a con man trying to filch the townspeople. 63m/B VHS, Beta, 8mm. Jean Hersholt, Edgar Kennedy, Rod La Rocque, Dorothy Lovett, Veda Ann Borg; D: William McGann. VYY

Dr. Cyclops 🎭🎭½ 1940 The famous early Technicolor fantasia about a mad scientist miniaturizing a group of explorers who happen upon his jungle lab. Landmark F/X and a slow-moving story. 76m/C VHS, Beta, LV. Albert Dekker, Janice Logan, Victor Kilian, Thomas Coley, Charles Halton, Frank Yaconelli; D: Ernest B. Schoedsack; W: Tom Kilpatrick; C: Winton C. Hoch, Henry Sharp. USH, FCT, MLB

Dr. Death, Seeker of Souls 🎭 1973 (R) Evil doctor discovers a process for transmigrating his soul into the bodies of people he murdered 1000 years ago. Now he seeks to revive his wife. Final role for 77-year-old "Stooge" Moe Howard. 93m/C VHS, Beta. John Considine, Barry Coe, Cheryl Miller, Stewart Moss, Leon Askin, Jo Morrow, Florence Marly, Sivi Aberg, Athena Lorde, Moe Howard; D: Eddie Saeta. PSM

Doctor Detroit 🎭🎭 1983 (R) Aykroyd is funny in thin film, portraying a meek college professor who gets involved with prostitutes and the mob, under the alias "Dr. Detroit." Aykroyd later married actress Donna Dixon, whom he worked with on this film. Features music by Devo, James Brown, and Pattie Brooks. 91m/C VHS, Beta, LV. Dan Aykroyd, Howard Hesseman, Donna Dixon, T.K. Carter, Lynn Whitfield, Lydia Lei, Fran Drescher, Kate Murtagh, George Furth, Andrew Duggan, James Brown, Glenne Headly; D: Michael Pressman; W: Carl Gottlieb, Robert Boris; M: Lalo Schifrin. USH

Doctor Dolittle 🎭🎭 1967 An adventure about a 19th century English doctor who dreams of teaching animals to speak to him. Realistic premise suffers from poor script. Based on Hugh Lofting's acclaimed stories. ♫Doctor Dolittle; My Friend the Doctor; Talk to the Animals; I've Never Seen Anything Like It; Beautiful Things; When I Look in Your Eyes; After Today; Fabulous Places; Where Are the Words?. 144m/C VHS, Beta, LV, Closed Caption. Rex Harrison, Samantha Eggar, Anthony Newley, Richard Attenborough, Geoffrey Holder, Peter Bull; D: Richard Fleischer; W: Leslie Bricusse; C: Robert L. Surtees; M: Leslie Bricusse. Academy Awards '67: Best Song ("Talk to the Animals"), Best Visual Effects; Golden Globe Awards '68: Best Supporting Actor (Attenborough); National Board of Review Awards '67: 10 Best Films of the Year; Nominations: Academy Awards '67: Best Art Direction/Set Decoration, Best Cinematography, Best Film Editing, Best Picture, Best Sound, Best Original Score. FOX, FCT, MLT

Doctor Faustus 🎭½ 1968 A stilted, stagy, but well-meaning adaptation of the Christopher Marlowe classic about Faust, who sold his soul to the devil for youth and the love of Helen of Troy. 93m/C VHS, Beta. Richard Burton, Andreas Teuber, Elizabeth Taylor, Ian Marter; D: Richard Burton, Nevill Coghill. COL

Dr. Frankenstein's Castle of Freaks 🎭 1974 (PG) Dr. Frankenstein and his dwarf assistant reanimate a few Neanderthals that are terrorizing a nearby Rumanian village. 87m/C VHS, Beta. IT Rossano Brazzi, Michael Dunn, Edmund Purdom, Christiane Royce; D: Robert Oliver. SNC

Dr. Giggles 🎭 1992 (R) Drake plays the psycho-genius Dr. Giggles, an escaped mental patient who sets out to avenge the death of his psycho-genius father (dementia runs in the family). He returns to his family home to procure the necessary medical instruments, most notably a hypodermic needle, and starts killing people—on screen with the tools and in the audience with remarkably stupid one-liners. Opening scenes are especially mired in gore. CW: Language and horror violence and gore. 96m/C VHS, Beta, LV, Closed Caption. Larry Drake, Holly Marie Combs, Glenn Quinn, Keith Diamond, Cliff DeYoung; D: Manny Coto; W: Graeme Whifler, Manny Coto; M: Brian May. USH

Dr. Goldfoot and the Bikini Machine 🎭🎭 1966 A mad scientist employs gorgeous female robots to seduce the wealthy and powerful, thereby allowing him to take over the world. Title song by the Supremes. 90m/C VHS. Vincent Price, Frankie Avalon, Dwayne Hickman, Annette Funicello, Susan Hart, Kay Elkhardt, Fred Clark, Deanna Lund, Deborah Walley; D: Norman Taurog; M: Les Baxter. AIP

Dr. Hackenstein 🎭½ 1988 (R) A doctor tries to revive his wife by "borrowing" parts from unexpected (and unsuspecting) guests. 88m/C VHS, Beta. Travis Crivey, Catherine Davis Cox, Dyanne DiRosario, Anne Ramsey, Logan Ramsey; D: Richard Clark. MCG

Dr. Heckyl and Mr. Hype 🎭🎭 1980 (R) A naughty, comical version of the Jekyll and Hyde story. Exuberantly wicked performances from Reed and Coogan; stellar cast of "B" veterans. 100m/C VHS, Beta. Oliver Reed, Sunny Johnson, Maia Danzinger, Mel Welles, Virgil Frye, Kedrick Wolfe, Jackie Coogan, Corinne Calvet, Dick Miller, Lucretia Love; D: Charles B. Griffith; W: Charles B. Griffith; M: Richard Band. NO

Doctor in Distress 🎭🎭½ 1963 Aging chief surgeon falls in love for the first time. His assistant tries to further the romance as well as his own love life. Comedic fourth in the six-film "Doctor" series. 102m/C VHS, Beta. GB Dirk Bogarde, James Robertson Justice, Leo McKern, Samantha Eggar; D: Ralph Thomas. NO

Doctor in the House 🎭🎭🎭½ 1953 Four medical student/roommates seek only to examine lovely women and make lots of cash. In the process, they are also tempted by the evils of drink, but rally to make their grades. A riotous British comedy with marvelous performances all around. Led to six sequels and a television series. 92m/C VHS. GB Dirk Bogarde, Muriel Pavlow, Kenneth More, Donald Sinden, Kay Kendall, James Robertson Justice, Donald Houston, Geoffrey Keen, George Coulouris, Shirley Eaton, Joan Hickson, Richard Wattis; D: Ralph Thomas. British Academy Awards '54: Best Actor (More). PAR, HMV

Dr. Jack/For Heaven's Sake 1926 In "Dr. Jack" (1922) and "For Heaven's Sake" (1926) Lloyd acts respectively as an unorthodox doctor and as a debonair millionaire who falls in love with a poor girl. Silent comedy shorts from Lloyd. 88m/B VHS, Beta. Harold Lloyd, Jobyna Ralston; D: Sam Taylor. TLF

Dr. Jekyll and Ms. Hyde 🎭🎭½ 1995 (PG-13) Chemist Richard Jacks (Daly) stumbles across the secret formula of great-grandad Dr. Jekyll and, after trying to improve the potion, he finds himself transformed into wicked woman Helen Hyde (Young). Cheap cross-gender gags abound.*CW:* Crude sex-related scenes and humor, nudity and brief strong language. **89m/C VHS.** Timothy Daly, Sean Young, Lysette Anthony, Stephen Tobolowsky, Harvey Fierstein, Polly Bergen, Stephen Shellan; *D:* David F. Price; *W:* William Davies, William Osborne, Tim John, Oliver Butcher; *C:* Tom Priestley; *M:* Mark McKenzie. *HBO*

Dr. Jekyll and Mr. Hyde 🎩🎩🎩 1920
The first American film version of Robert Louis Stevenson's horror tale about a doctor's experiments that lead to his developing good and evil sides to his personality. Silent. Kino Video's edition also contains the rarely seen 1911 version of the film, as well as scenes from a different 1920 version. **96m/B VHS, LV.** John Barrymore, Martha Mansfield, Brandon Hurst, Charles Lane, J. Malcolm Dunn, Nita Naldi; *D:* John S. Robertson. *SNC, REP, MRV*

Dr. Jekyll and Mr. Hyde 🎩🎩🎩 1932
The hallucinatory, feverish classic version of the Robert Louis Stevenson story, in which the good doctor becomes addicted to the formula that turns him into a sadistic beast. Possibly Mamoulian's and March's best work, and a masterpiece of subversive, pseudo-Freudian creepiness. Eighteen minutes from the original version, lost until recently, have been restored, including the infamous whipping scene. **96m/B VHS, Beta, LV.** Fredric March, Miriam Hopkins, Halliwell Hobbes, Rose Hobart, Holmes Herbert, Edgar Norton; *D:* Rouben Mamoulian; *C:* Karl Struss. Academy Awards '32: Best Actor (March); Venice Film Festival '31: Best Actor (March); Nominations: Academy Awards '32: Best Adapted Screenplay, Best Cinematography.*MGM, BTV*

Dr. Jekyll and Mr. Hyde 🎩🎩🎩 1941
Strangely cast adaptation of the Robert Louis Stevenson story about a doctor's experiment on himself to separate good and evil. **113m/B VHS, Beta, LV.** Spencer Tracy, Ingrid Bergman, Lana Turner, Donald Crisp; *D:* Victor Fleming; *C:* Joseph Ruttenberg. Nominations: Academy Awards '41: Best Black and White Cinematography, Best Film Editing, Original Dramatic/Comedy Score. *MGM*

Dr. Jekyll and Mr. Hyde 1968 Yet another production of Robert Louis Stevenson's classic story of a split-personality. **90m/C VHS, Beta.** Jack Palance. *LIV*

Dr. Jekyll and Mr. Hyde 🎩🎩 1973 Dr. Jekyll discovers a potion that turns him into the sinister Mr. Hyde. Based on the classic story by Robert Louis Stevenson. **90m/C VHS, Beta, LV.** Kirk Douglas, Michael Redgrave, Susan George, Donald Pleasence; *D:* David Winters. *IME*

Dr. Jekyll and Sister Hyde 🎩🎩½
1971 (R) A tongue-in-cheek variation on the split-personality theme, which has the good doctor transforming himself into a sultry, knife-wielding woman who kills prostitutes. **94m/C VHS, Beta.** *GB* Ralph Bates, Martine Beswick, Gerald Sim; *D:* Roy Ward Baker; *W:* Brian Clemens. *MLB*

Dr. Jekyll and the Wolfman 🎩 Dr. Jekyll y el Hombre Lobo 1971 (R) Naschy's sixth stint as El Hombre Lobo. This time he visits a mysterious doctor in search of a cure but ends up turning into Mr. Hyde, a man who likes to torture women. **85m/C VHS.** *SP* Paul Naschy, Shirley Corrigan, Jack Taylor; *D:* Leon Klimovsky. *SNC*

Dr. Jekyll vs. the Werewolf 🎩½
1971 A man afflicted with the characteristics of a wolf seeks a cure from Dr. Jekyll's grandson. **?m/C VHS.** Paul Naschy, Jack Taylor. *SNC*

Dr. Jekyll's Dungeon of Death 🎩
1982 (R) Dr. Jekyll and his lobotomized sister, Hilda, scour the streets of San Francisco looking for human blood to recreate his great-grandfather's secret serum. Also on video as "Dr. Jekyll's Dungeon of Darkness." **90m/C VHS, Beta.** James Mathers, Dawn Carver Kelly, John Kearney, Jake Pearson; *D:* James Wood. *GHV*

Dr. Kildare's Strange Case 🎩🎩 1940
Dr. Kildare administers a daring treatment to a man suffering from a mental disorder of a dangerous nature. One in the film series. **76m/B VHS, Beta.** Lew Ayres, Lionel Barrymore, Laraine Day; *D:* Harold Bucquet. *NOS, HHT, DVT*

Dr. Mabuse, Parts 1 & 2 🎩🎩🎩½
Doktor Mabuse der Spieler 1922 The massive, two-part crime melodrama, introducing the raving mastermind/extortionist/villain to the world. The film follows Dr. Mabuse through his life of crime until he finally goes mad. Highly influential and inventive. Lang meant this to be a criticism of morally bankrupt post-WWI Germany. Followed some time later by "Testament of Doctor Mabuse" and "The Thousand Eyes of Doctor Mabuse." Silent. **242m/B VHS, Beta.** *GE* Rudolf Klein-Rogge, Aud Egede Nissen, Alfred Abel, Gertrude Welcker, Lil Dagover, Paul Richter; *D:* Fritz Lang. *SNC, MRV, NOS*

Dr. Mabuse vs. Scotland Yard 🎩🎩½ 1964 A sequel to the Fritz Lang classics, this film features the arch-criminal attempting to take over the world with a mind-controlling camera. **90m/B VHS, Beta.** *GE* Sabine Bethmann, Peter Van Eyck; *D:* Paul May. *VYY, SNC, GLV*

Doctor Mordrid: Master of the Unknown 🎩🎩 1990 (R) Two immensely powerful sorcerers from the 4th dimension cross over into present time with two very different missions—one wants to destroy the Earth, one wants to save it.*CW:* Language and one sexual scene. **102m/C VHS, Beta, Closed Caption.** Jeffrey Combs, Yvette Nipar, Jay Acovone, Brian Thompson; *D:* Albert Band, Charles Band; *M:* Richard Band. *PAR*

Dr. No 🎩🎩🎩 1962 (PG) The world is introduced to British secret agent 007, James Bond, when it is discovered that a mad scientist is sabotaging rocket launchings from his hideout in Jamaica. The first 007 film is far less glitzy than any of its successors but boasts the sexiest "Bond girl" of them all in Andress, and promptly made stars of her and Connery. On laserdisc, the film is in wide-screen transfer and includes movie bills, publicity photos, location pictures, and the British and American trailers. The sound effects and musical score can be separated from the dialogue. Audio interviews with the director, writer, and editor are included as part of the disc. **111m/C VHS, Beta, LV, Closed Caption.** *GB* Sean Connery, Ursula Andress, Joseph Wiseman, Jack Lord, Zena Marshall, Eunice Gayson, Margaret LeWars, John Kitzmiller, Lois Maxwell, Bernard Lee, Anthony Dawson; *D:* Terence Young; *C:* Ted Moore; *M:* John Barry. *MGM, CRC, TLF*

Dr. Orloff's Invisible Horror 🎩½
1972 In this horror film, Dr. Orloff creates an invisible ape-monster that escapes and goes on a rampage. **?m/C VHS.** Howard Vernon. *SNC*

Dr. Orloff's Monster woof! 1964 As if "The Awful Dr. Orloff" wasn't awful enough, the doctor is back, this time eliminating his enemies with his trusty killer robot. Awful awful. **88m/B VHS.** *SP* Jose Rubio, Agnes Spaak; *D:* Jess (Jesus) Franco. *SNC, VYY*

Dr. Otto & the Riddle of the Gloom Beam 🎩½ 1986 (PG) Ernest is in your face again. Fresh from the TV commercials featuring "Ernest" comes Varney playing a villain out to wreck the global economy. He also plays all the other characters, too. Way bizarre, "Know whut I mean?" **92m/C VHS, Beta.** Jim Varney; *D:* John R. Cherry III. *GKK*

Dr. Petiot 🎩🎩 Le Docteur Petiot 1990 Based on the true life story of a French WWII doctor who promised to smuggle Jews to freedom but instead killed them for their money and possessions. He was executed in 1946—accused of 60 murders and convicted of 27. The gruesome details are left to the imagination rather than shown. In French with subtitles. **102m/C VHS.** *FR* Michel Serrault, Berangere Bonvoisin; *W:* Christian de Chalonge, Dominique Garnier; *C:* Patrick Blossier. *WAC, FCT*

Doctor Phibes Rises Again 🎩🎩½
1972 (PG) The despicable doctor contines his quest to revive his beloved wife. Fun, superior sequel to "The Abominable Dr. Phibes." **89m/C VHS, Beta.** *GB* Vincent Price, Robert Quarry, Peter Cushing, Beryl Reid, Hugh Griffith, Terry-Thomas; *D:* Robert Fuest; *W:* Robert Blees. *LIV, VES, ORI*

Doctor Quinn, Medicine Woman 🎩🎩½ 1992 The small western town of Colorado Springs has advertised for a doctor and is pleased to hire Dr. "Mike" Quinn from Boston. Only to the town's surprise, and dismay, who should arrive but Dr. Michaela Quinn. This eastern lady has her work cut out for her just trying to convince the townsfolk that a woman can practice medicine. But she's determined and with the aid of the brooding, handsome Sully she opens her practice. Made for television. **?m/C VHS.** Jane Seymour, Diane Ladd, Joe Lando. *FXV*

Doctor Satan's Robot 🎩🎩½ 1940 Indestructible robot is battled by insane Dr. Satan in reedited serial, "Mysterious Dr. Satan." **100m/B VHS.** Eduardo Ciannelli, Robert Wilcox, William Newell, Ella Neal; *D:* William Witney, John English. *VCN*

Dr. Strange 🎩½ 1978 A made-for-television pilot based upon the Marvel Comics character who, with the help of a sorcerer, practices witchcraft in order to fight evil. **94m/C VHS, Beta.** Peter Hooten, Clyde Kusatsu, Jessica Walter, Eddie Benton, John Mills; *D:* Philip DeGuere. *USH*

Dr. Strangelove, or: How I Learned to Stop Worrying and Love the Bomb 🎩🎩🎩🎩 1964 Sellers plays a tour-de-force triple role in Kubrick's classic black anti-war comedy. While a U.S. President (Sellers) deals with the Russian situation, a crazed general (Hayden) implements a plan to drop the A-bomb on the Soviets. Famous for Pickens' wild ride on the bomb, Hayden's character's "purity of essence" philosophy, Scott's gumchewing militarist, a soft-drink vending machine dispute, and countless other scenes. Based on the novel "Red Alert" by Peter George. **93m/B VHS, Beta, LV, 8mm.** *GB* Peter Sellers, George C. Scott, Sterling Hayden, Keenan Wynn, Slim Pickens, James Earl Jones, Peter Bull; *D:* Stanley Kubrick; *W:* Terry Southern, Peter George, Stanley Kubrick; *M:* Laurie Johnson. British Academy Awards '64: Best Film; New York Film Critics Awards '64: Best Director (Kubrick); Nominations: Academy Awards '64: Best Actor (Sellers), Best Adapted Screenplay, Best Director (Kubrick), Best Picture. *COL, HMV*

Dr. Syn 🎩🎩 1937 The story of a seemingly respectable vicar of Dymchurch who is really a former pirate. The last film of George Arliss. **90m/B VHS, Beta.** *GB* George Arliss, Margaret Lockwood, John Loder; *D:* Roy William Neill. *NOS, MRV, CAB*

Dr. Syn, Alias the Scarecrow 🎩🎩½
1964 (G) A mild-mannered minister is, in reality, a smuggler and pirate avenging King George III's injustices upon the English people. Originally broadcast in three parts on the Disney television show. **129m/C VHS, Beta.** Patrick McGoohan, George Cole, Tony Britton, Michael Hordern, Geoffrey Keen, Kay Cole; *D:* James Neilson. *DIS*

Doctor Takes a Wife 🎩🎩🎩 1940 A fast, fun screwball comedy wherein two ill-matched career people are forced via a publicity mix-up to fake being married. **89m/B VHS, Beta.** Ray Milland, Loretta Young, Reginald Gardiner, Gail Patrick, Edmund Gwenn, George Metaxa, Charles Halton; *D:* Alexander Hall; *W:* George Seaton. *COL*

Dr. Tarr's Torture Dungeon woof!
1975 (R) A mysterious man is sent to the forest to investigate the bizarre behavior of Dr. Tarr who runs a torture asylum. **90m/C VHS, Beta.** Claudio Brook, Ellen Sherman, Robert Dumont. *NO*

Dr. Terror's House of Horrors 🎩🎩½ The Blood Suckers 1965 On a train, six traveling companions have their fortunes told by a mysterious doctor. Little do they realize that their final destination has changed. Creepy and suspenseful, especially the severed-hand

chase sequence. **92m/C VHS.** *GB* Christopher Lee, Peter Cushing, Donald Sutherland; *D:* Freddie Francis. *REP, MLB*

Doctor Who ♂♂½ 1996 The late British sci-fi series, which ended in 1989, has been resurrected in this TV movie. The TARDIS is forced down in 1999 San Francisco and renegade Time Lord The Master's sluglike remains escape from the Doctor (McCoy) and into a temporary host body (Roberts). Meanwhile, the Doctor's been hospitalized and a botched operation by Dr. Grace Holloway (Ashbrook) leaves him clinically dead—until he manages to regenerate once again (as McGann). With Grace's help, the Doctor tries to stop his enemy from destroying the world on New Year's Eve in a plot that will also give the Master the Doctor's body as his new home. Production design and special effects are lavish (particularly in relation to the cheesiness of the series). **?m/C VHS.** *GB CA* Paul McGann, Eric Roberts, Daphne Ashbrook, Yee Jee Tso, Sylvester McCoy; *D:* Geoffrey Sax; *W:* Matthew Jacobs; *C:* Glen MacPherson; *M:* John Debney. *NYR*

Doctor Who: An Unearthly Child 1963 In the long-running British series' first episode, Doctor Who and his granddaughter travel to prehistoric times to witness the discovery of fire. Additional episodes are available. **98m/B VHS.** *GB* William Hartnell; *D:* Waris Hussein. *FXV, MOV*

Doctor Who and the Daleks 1965 The Time Lord and his two grandchildren accidentally transport themselves to a futuristic planet inhabited by the Daleks, who capture the travelers and hold them captive. A feature film version of the long-running British television show. **78m/C VHS, Beta, Closed Caption.** *GB* Peter Cushing, Roy Castle; *D:* Gordon Flemyng. *REP*

Doctor X ♂♂½ 1932 An armless mad scientist uses a formula for "synthetic flesh" to grow temporary limbs and commit murder. A classic, rarely seen horror oldie, famous for its very early use of two-color Technicolor. **77m/C VHS, Beta, LV.** Lionel Atwill, Fay Wray, Lee Tracy, Preston Foster; *D:* Michael Curtiz. *MGM, MLB*

Doctor Zhivago ♂♂♂ 1965 (PG-13) Sweeping adaptation of the Nobel Prize-winning Boris Pasternak novel. An innocent Russian poet-intellectual is caught in the furor and chaos of the Bolshevik Revolution. Essentially a poignant love story filmed as a historical epic. Panoramic film popularized the song "Lara's Theme." Lean was more successful in "Lawrence of Arabia," where there was less need for ensemble acting.*CW:* Mature themes. **197m/C VHS, Beta, LV, Closed Caption.** Omar Sharif, Julie Christie, Geraldine Chaplin, Rod Steiger, Alec Guinness, Klaus Kinski, Ralph Richardson, Rita Tushingham, Siobhan McKenna, Tom Courtenay; *D:* David Lean; *W:* Robert Bolt; *C:* Frederick A. (Freddie) Young; *M:* Maurice Jarre. Academy Awards '65: Best Adapted Screenplay, Best Art Direction/Set Decoration (Color), Best Color Cinematography, Best Costume Design (Color), Best Original Score; Golden Globe Awards '66: Best Actor—Drama (Sharif), Best Director (Lean), Best Film—Drama, Best Screenplay, Best Score; National Board of Review Awards '65: 10 Best Films of the Year, Best Actress (Christie); Nominations: Academy Awards '65: Best Director (Lean), Best Film Editing, Best Picture, Best Sound, Best Supporting Actor (Courtenay). *MGM, RDG, HMV*

Doctors and Nurses ♂♂ 1982 A children's satire of soap operas wherein the adults play the children and vice-versa. **90m/C VHS, Beta.** Rebecca Rigg, Drew Forsythe, Graeme Blundell; *D:* Maurice Murphy. *NO*

Doctors' Wives ♂½ 1970 (R) An adaptation of the Frank Slaughter potboiler about a large city hospital's doctors, nurses, and their respective spouses, with plenty of affairs, medical traumas, and betrayals. **102m/C VHS, Beta.** Dyan Cannon, Richard Crenna, Gene Hackman, Carroll O'Connor, Rachel Roberts, Janice Rule, Diana Sands, Ralph Bellamy, John

Colicos; *D:* George Schaefer; *W:* Daniel Taradash; *C:* Charles B(ryant) Lang; *M:* Elmer Bernstein. *COL*

Dodes 'ka-den ♂♂♂½ *Clickety Clack* 1970 In this departure from his samurai-genre films, Kurosawa depicts a throng of fringe-dwelling Tokyo slum inhabitants in a semi-surreal manner. Fascinating presentation and content. **140m/C VHS, Beta.** *JP* Yoshitaka Zushi, Junzaburo Ban, Kiyoko Tange; *D:* Akira Kurosawa. Nominations: Academy Awards '71: Best Foreign Language Film. *NO*

Dodge City ♂♂♂ 1939 Flynn stars as Wade Hutton, a roving cattleman who becomes the sheriff of Dodge City. His job: to run a ruthless outlaw and his gang out of town. De Havilland serves as Flynn's love interest, as she did in many previous films. A broad and colorful shoot-em-up! **104m/C VHS, Beta, LV, Closed Caption.** Errol Flynn, Olivia de Havilland, Bruce Cabot, Ann Sheridan, Alan Hale, Frank McHugh, Victor Jory, Henry Travers, Charles Halton; *D:* Michael Curtiz; *M:* Max Steiner. *MGM, FOX, FCT*

Dodsworth ♂♂♂½ 1936 The lives of a self-made American tycoon and his wife are drastically changed when they take a tour of Europe. The success of their marriage seems questionable as they re-evaluate their lives. Huston excels as does the rest of the cast in this film, based upon the Sinclair Lewis novel. **101m/B VHS, Beta, LV.** Walter Huston, David Niven, Paul Lukas, John Payne, Mary Astor, Ruth Chatterton, Maria Ouspenskaya, Charles Halton; *D:* William Wyler. Academy Awards '36: Best Interior Decoration; New York Film Critics Awards '36: Best Actor (Huston); Nominations: Academy Awards '36: Best Actor (Huston), Best Director (Wyler), Best Picture, Best Screenplay, Best Sound, Best Supporting Actress (Ouspenskaya). *HBO*

Does This Mean We're Married? ♂♂ 1990 (PG-13) A stand-up comedian is trying to find success in the comedy clubs of Paris but without her green card she may soon be deported. She finds a sleazy marriage broker who fixes her up with a womanizing songwriter who needs money. As usual, immigration officials suspect that the marriage is a fake and the mismatched couple must live together to prove them wrong. **93m/C VHS, LV.** Patsy Kensit, Stephane Freiss; *D:* Carol Wiseman. *COL, NLC*

Dog Day ♂♂½ *Canicule* 1983 An American traitor, who is on the lam from the government, and his cronies, takes refuge on a small farm. A surprise awaits him when the farmers come up with an unusual plan to bargain for his life. **101m/C VHS, Beta.** *FR* Lee Marvin, Miou-Miou, Victor Lanoux; *D:* Yves Boisset. *LIV*

Dog Day Afternoon ♂♂♂½ 1975 (R) Based on a true story, this taut, yet fantastic thriller centers on a bi-sexual and his slow-witted buddy who rob a bank to obtain money to fund a sex change operation for the ringleader's lover. Pacino is breathtaking in his role as the frustrated robber, caught in a trap of his own devising. Very controversial for its language and subject matter when released, it nevertheless became a huge success. Director Lumet keeps up the pace, fills the screen with pathos without gross sentiment. **124m/C VHS, Beta, LV, Closed Caption.** Al Pacino, John Cazale, Charles Durning, James Broderick, Chris Sarandon, Carol Kane, Lance Henriksen, Dick Williams; *D:* Sidney Lumet; *W:* Frank Pierson. Academy Awards '75: Best Original Screenplay; British Academy Awards '75: Best Actor (Pacino); National Board of Review Awards '75: 10 Best Films of the Year, Best Supporting Actor (Durning); Writers Guild of America '75: Best Original Screenplay; Nominations: Academy Awards '75: Best Actor (Pacino), Best Director (Lumet), Best Film Editing, Best Picture, Best Supporting Actor (Sarandon).*WAR*

Dog Eat Dog ♂ *Einer Frisst den Anderen; La Morte Vestita di Dollar* 1964 Centering on a heist scheme by Mitchell, this one has nothing to offer except Mansfield's attributes. **86m/B VHS, Beta, 8mm.** Cameron Mitchell, Jayne Mansfield, Isa Miranda; *D:* Ray Nazarro. *VYY, HEG*

A Dog of Flanders ♂♂½ 1959 A young Dutch boy and his grandfather find a severely beaten dog and restore it to health. **96m/C VHS, Beta.** David Ladd, Donald Crisp, Theodore Bikel, Max Croiset, Monique Ahrens; *D:* James B. Clark. *PAR*

Dog Pound Shuffle ♂♂♂ *Spot* 1975 (PG) Two drifters form a new song-and-dance act in order to raise the funds necessary to win their dog's freedom from the pound. Charming Canadian production. **98m/C VHS, Beta, Closed Caption.** *CA* Ron Moody, David Soul; *D:* Jeffrey Bloom; *W:* Jeffrey Bloom. *FOX*

Dog Star Man ♂♂♂ 1964 The silent epic by the dean of experimental American film depicts man's spiritual and physical conflicts through Brakhage's characteristically freeform collage techniques. **78m/C VHS, Beta.** *D:* Stan Brakhage. *MFV, FCT, TPV*

The Dog Who Stopped the War ♂♂ 1984 (G) A Canadian children's film about a dog who puts a halt to an escalating snowball fight between rival gangs. **90m/C VHS, Beta.** *CA* Andre Melancon. *NO*

Dogfight ♂♂♂ 1991 (R) It's 1963 and a baby-faced Marine and his buddies are spending their last night in San Francisco before leaving the U.S. for a tour of duty in Vietnam. They agree to throw a "dogfight," a competition to see who can bring the ugliest date to a party. Birdlace (Phoenix) chooses Taylor, a shy, average-looking waitress who dreams of becoming a folk singer and realizes too late that she doesn't deserve the treatment he's about to subject her to. This quiet film didn't see a wide release, but is worth renting due to an above average script which is held up by the splendid performances of Phoenix and Taylor.*CW:* Pervasive strong language and one sexual scene. **94m/C VHS, Beta, LV, 8mm.** River Phoenix, Lili Taylor, Richard Panebianco, Anthony Clark, Mitchell Whitfield, E.G. Daily, Holly Near, Brendan Fraser, Peg Phillips; *D:* Nancy Savoca; *W:* Bob Comfort. *WAR*

The Dogfighters ♂♂ 1995 (R) Ex-Air Force pilot Rowdy Wells (Davi) is blackmailed into trying to destroy a plutonium plant in an eastern European country. That is, if Rowdy can survive an air battle with nemisis Lothar Krasna (Godunov). Small budget is reflected in the mediocre aerial sequences.*CW:* Language, nudity, violence. **96m/C VHS, LV, Closed Caption.** Robert Davi, Alexander Godunov, Ben Gazzara, Lara Harris; *D:* Barry Zetlin; *W:* Sean Smith, Anthony Stark; *M:* Jimmie Haskell. *LIV*

Dogs in Space ♂♂ 1987 A low-budget Australian film about a clique of aimless Melbourne rock kids in 1978, caught somewhere between post-hippiedom and punk, free love and heroin addiction. Acclaimed. Includes music by Hutchence, Brian Eno, Iggy Pop, and others. **109m/C VHS, Beta.** *AU* Michael Hutchence, Saskia Post, Nique Needles, Tony Helou, Deanna Bond; *D:* Richard Lowenstein; *W:* Richard Lowenstein. *FOX*

Dogs of Hell ♂½ 1983 (R) The sheriff of an idyllic resort community must stop a pack of killer dogs from terrorizing the residents. **90m/C VHS, Beta.** Earl Owensby, Bill Gribble, Jerry Rushing; *D:* Worth Keeter. *MED*

The Dogs of War ♂♂½ 1981 (R) A graphic depiction of a group of professional mercenaries, driven by nothing but their quest for wealth and power, hired to overthrow the dictator of a new West African nation. Has some weak moments which break up the continuity of the movie. Based on the novel by Frederick Forsyth. **102m/C VHS, Beta, LV.** *GB* Christopher Walken, Tom Berenger, Colin Blakely, Paul Freeman, Hugh Millais, Victoria Tennant, JoBeth Williams; *D:* John Irvin; *W:* Gary De Vore; *C:* Jack Cardiff; *M:* Geoffrey Burgon. *MGM*

Doin' Time ♂ 1985 (R) At the John Dillinger Memorial Penitentiary, the inmates take over the prison under the supervision of warden "Mongo." Silliness prevails. **80m/C VHS, Beta.** Jeff Altman, Dey Young, Richard Mulligan, John Vernon, Colleen Camp, Melanie Chartoff, Graham Jarvis, Pat McCormick, Eddie Velez, Jimmie Walker, Judy Landers, Nicholas Worth, Mike Mazurki, Muhammad Ali, Melinda Fee, Francesca "Kitten" Natividad, Ron Palillo; **D:** George Mendeluk; **W:** Dee Caruso; **M:** Charles Fox. *WAR*

Doin' Time on Planet Earth 🎬🎬½
1988 (PG-13) A young boy feels out of place with his family and is convinced by two strange people (aliens themselves?) that he is really an extraterrestrial. Amusing, aimless fun directed by the son of Walter Matthau. **83m/C VHS, Beta, Closed Caption.** Adam West, Candice Azzara, Hugh O'Brian, Matt Adler, Timothy Patrick Murphy, Roddy McDowall, Maureen Stapleton, Andrea Thompson; **D:** Charles Matthau. *WAR*

Dolemite 🎬½
1975 (R) An ex-con attempts to settle the score with some of his former inmates. He forms a band of kung-fu savvy ladies. Strange combination of action and comedy. **88m/C VHS.** Rudy Ray Moore, Jerry Jones; **D:** D'Urville Martin. *XVC*

Dolemite 2: Human Tornado 🎬½
The Human Tornado **1976 (R)** Nobody ever said Moore was for everybody's taste. But, hey, when blaxploitation movies were the rage, Rudy the standup comic was out there rapping through a series of trashy movies that, when viewed today, have survived the test of time. This one's just as vile, violent, and sexist as the day it was released. When Rudy is surprised in bed with a white sheriff's wife, he flees and meets up with a madam and a house of kung-fu-skilled girls who are embroiled in a fight with a local mobster. **98m/C VHS.** Rudy Ray Moore, Lady Reed. *XVC*

The Doll 🎬🎬
La Poupee; He, She or It **1962** A lonely night watchman happens upon two burglars and, in the chase, the thieves knock over a mannequin. The watchman reports the mannequin stolen, brings it home and begins to have conversations with it. Soon, the doll's needs cause him to steal jewelry and clothes, until his brutish neighbor discovers his secrets. In Swedish with English subtitles. **96m/B VHS.** SW Per Oscarsson, Gio Petre, Tor Isedal, Elsa Prawitz; **D:** Arne Mattson. *FCT, DVT, AUD*

Doll Face 🎬🎬½
Come Back to Me **1946** Story of a stripper who wants to go legit and make it on Broadway. Film was adapted from the play "The Naked Genius" by tease queen Gypsy Rose Lee. 🎵Dig You Later; Here Comes Heaven Again; Chico-Chico; Somebody's Walkin' In My Dreams; Red Hot and Beautiful. **80m/B VHS, Beta, LV.** Vivian Blaine, Dennis O'Keefe, Perry Como, Carmen Miranda, Martha Stewart, Reed Hadley; **D:** Lewis Seiler. *NOS, HHT, DVT*

The Doll Squad 🎬
Hustler Squad **1973 (PG)** Three voluptuous special agents fight an ex-CIA agent out to rule the world. **93m/C VHS, Beta.** Michael Ansara, Francine York, Anthony Eisley, Tura Satana; **D:** Ted V. Mikels. *GHV, MRV*

Dollar 🎬🎬
1938 The actress wife of an industrialist, convinced that he is having an affair, follows him to a ski lodge in attempt to catch him in the act. In Swedish with English subtitles. **74m/B VHS, Beta, LV.** SW Georg Rydeberg, Ingrid Bergman, Kotti Chave, Tutta Rolf, Hakan Westergren, Elsa Burnett, Edvin Adolphson, Gosta Cederlund, Eric Rosen; **D:** Gustaf Molander. *WAC*

Dollars 🎬🎬🎬
The Heist **1971 (R)** A bank employee and his dizzy call-girl assistant plan to steal the German facility's assets while installing its new security system. Lighthearted fun. **119m/C VHS, Beta, LV.** Warren Beatty, Goldie Hawn, Gert Frobe, Scott Brady, Robert Webber; **D:** Richard Brooks; **W:** Richard Brooks; **M:** Quincy Jones. *GKK*

The Dollmaker 🎬🎬½
1984 Excellent made for television adaptation of Harriette Arnow's novel. A strong-willed Kentucky mother of five helps move her family to Detroit in the 1940s. Petrie's direction moves the story along and creates a lovely period vision. **140m/C VHS, Beta, Closed Caption.** Jane Fonda, Levon Helm, Geraldine Page, Amanda Plummer, Susan Kingsley; **D:** Daniel Petrie. *FOX*

Dollman 🎬½
1990 (R) An ultra-tough cop from an Earth-like planet (even swear words are the same) crashes in the South Bronx—and on this world he's only 13 inches tall. The filmmakers squander a great premise and cast with bloody shootouts and a sequel-ready non-ending.**CW:** Language and sci-fi violence. **86m/C VHS, LV, Closed Caption.** Tim Thomerson, Jackie Earle Haley, Kamala Lopez, Humberto Ortiz, Nicholas Guest, Michael Halsey, Eugene Glazer, Judd Omen, Frank Collison, Vincent Klyn; **D:** Albert Pyun. *PAR*

Dollman vs Demonic Toys 🎬🎬
1993 (R) Let's combine elements from three separate films and make one disgusting sequel: "Dollman," the 13-inch cop from the planet Arturus; his new girlfriend, Dollchick, who was shrunk to a diminutive 10 inches in "Bad Channels;" and tough cop Judith Grey, who's once again battling those loathsome playthings from "Demonic Toys." If you feel the need for a plot—Dollchick is kidnapped by Baby Doll and needs to be rescued.**CW:** Language, violence and sexuality. **84m/C VHS, Beta, Closed Caption.** Tim Thomerson, Tracy Scoggins, Melissa Behr, Phil Brock, Phil Fondacaro; **D:** Charles Band; **W:** Craig Hamann; **M:** Richard Band. *PAR*

The Dolls woof!
1983 A tropically located photographer recruits an area beauty into the fashion world with his winning smile and macho charm, only to learn native traditions forbid her to follow him. **96m/C VHS, Beta, LV.** Tetchie Agbayani, Max Thayer, Carina Schally, Richard Seward; **D:** Hubert Frank. *LIV, VES*

Dolls 🎬🎬½
1987 (R) A group of people is stranded during a storm in an old, creepy mansion. As the night wears on, they are attacked by hundreds of antique dolls. Tongue-in-cheek. **77m/C VHS, Beta.** Ian Patrick Williams, Carolyn Purdy-Gordon, Carrie Lorraine, Stephen Lee, Guy Rolfe, Bunty Bailey, Cassie Stuart, Hilary Mason; **D:** Stuart Gordon; **W:** Ed Naha; **M:** Richard Band. *LIV, VES*

A Doll's House 🎬🎬½
1959 An all-star cast is featured in this original television production of Henrik Ibsen's classic play about an independent woman's quest for freedom in nineteenth-century Norway. **89m/B VHS, Beta.** Julie Harris, Christopher Plummer, Jason Robards Jr., Hume Cronyn, Eileen Heckart, Richard Thomas. *MGM, FCT*

A Doll's House 🎬🎬
1973 (G) Fonda plays Nora, a subjugated 19th-century housewife who breaks free to establish herself as an individual. Based on Henrik Ibsen's classic play; some controversy regarding Fonda's interpretation of her role. **98m/C VHS, Beta.** Jane Fonda, Edward Fox, Trevor Howard, David Warner, Delphine Seyrig; **D:** Joseph Losey; **W:** Christopher Hampton; **M:** John Barry. *PSM*

A Doll's House 🎬🎬🎬
1989 (G) A Canadian production of the Henrik Ibsen play about a Norwegian woman's search for independence. **96m/C VHS, Beta, LV.** CA Claire Bloom, Anthony Hopkins, Ralph Richardson, Denholm Elliott, Anna Massey, Edith Evans; **D:** Patrick Garland. *HMD*

Dolly Dearest 🎬½
1992 (R) Strange things start happening after an American family takes over a run-down Mexican doll factory. They create a new doll called "Dolly Dearest" with deadly results. In the same tradition as the "Chucky" series.**CW:** Horror violence. **94m/C VHS, LV, Closed Caption.** Rip Torn, Sam Bottoms, Denise Crosby; **D:** Maria Lease. *THV*

The Dolly Sisters 🎬🎬½
1946 Competent musical about sisters Jenny (Grable) and Rosie (Haver), who become turn-of-the-century vaudeville stars and also find romance. Good songs, extravagant costuming, fine support work, and the charms of the two leading actresses provide simple enjoyment. 🎵I Can't Begin to Tell You; I'm Always Chasing Rainbows; Powder, Lipstick and Rouge; Give Me the Moonlight; On the Mississippi; We Have Been Around; Carolina In the Morning; Arrah Go On, I'm Gonna Go Back to Oregon; The Darktown Strutter's Ball. **114m/C VHS, Closed Caption.** Betty Grable, June Haver, John

Payne, Frank Latimore, S.Z. Sakall, Reginald Gardiner, Gene Sheldon, Sig Rumann; **D:** Irving Cummings; **W:** Marian Spitzer, John Larkin; **C:** Ernest Palmer. Nominations: Academy Awards '46: Best Song ("I Can't Begin to Tell You"). *FXV*

Dolores Claiborne 🎬🎬🎬
1994 (R) Stephen King gets the Hollywood treatment again (the check cleared, King approved), with better results than previous outings (remember "Needful Things"?). Successful but neurotic New York journalist Selena (Leigh) confronts her troubled past when coarse, hard-talking mom Dolores (Bates) is accused of murdering her wealthy employer (Parfitt). Plummer is vengeful detective John Mackey who, like everyone else on the fictitious Maine island, believes Dolores murdered her husband 15 years before. Top-notch performances by Bates and Leigh highlight this sometimes manipulative tale. Straithairn is wonderfully despicable as the stereotypically deadbeat dad.**CW:** Language; domestic abuse; nudity. **132m/C VHS, LV, Closed Caption.** Kathy Bates, Jennifer Jason Leigh, Christopher Plummer, Judy Parfitt, David Strathairn, John C. Reilly; **D:** Taylor Hackford; **W:** Tony Gilroy; **M:** Danny Elfman. *COL*

The Dolphin 🎬🎬½
1987 A dolphin visits a Brazilian fishing village each full moon, turns himself into a man, and casts a spell of seduction over the women. Villagers are both enchanted and angered by the dolphin-man, since his presence creates desire in local women but scares fish from the waters. In Portuguese with English subtitles. **95m/C VHS.** BR Carlos Alberto Riccelli, Cassia Kiss, Ney Latorraca; **D:** Walter Lima Jr.; **W:** Walter Lima Jr. *FXL, FCT*

Dominick & Eugene 🎬🎬🎬
1988 (PG-13) Dominick is a little slow, but he makes a fair living as a garbageman—good enough to put his brother through medical school. Both men struggle with the other's faults and weaknesses, as they learn the meaning of family and friendship. Well-acted, especially by Hulce, never melodramatic or weak. **96m/C VHS, Beta, LV, Closed Caption.** Ray Liotta, Tom Hulce, Jamie Lee Curtis, Todd Graff, Bill Cobbs, David Strathairn; **D:** Robert M. Young; **W:** Alvin Sargent, Corey Blechman; **M:** Trevor Jones. *ORI, FCT*

Dominion 🎬🎬½
1994 (R) Six buddies take off for a weekend hunting trip that turns deadly when a murderous hunter believes they've trespassed on his territory and begins stalking them.**CW:** Strong violence; language. **98m/C VHS, Closed Caption.** Brad Johnson, Brion James, Tim Thomerson, Woody Brown, Glen Morshower, Richard Riehle, Geoffrey Blake; **D:** Michael Kehoe; **W:** Woody Brown, Michael Kehoe. *TTC*

Dominique Is Dead 🎬🎬
1979 (PG) A woman is driven to suicide by her greedy husband; now someone is trying to drive him mad. A.K.A. "Dominique" and "Avenging Spirit." **95m/C VHS, Beta.** Cliff Robertson, Jean Simmons, Jenny Agutter, Simon Ward, Ron Moody; **D:** Michael Anderson Sr. *PSM*

Domino 🎬
1988 (R) A beautiful woman and a mysterious guy link up for sex, murder and double-crosses. Dubbed. Tries to be arty and avant-garde, but only succeeds in being a piece of softcore fluff. **95m/C VHS, Beta, LV.** IT Brigitte Nielsen, Tomas Arana, Daniela Alzone; **D:** Ivana Massetti. *LIV*

The Domino Principle 🎬½
The Domino Killings **1977 (R)** It's got nothing to do with pizza. Viet vet Hackman is a doltish convict sprung from the joint by a government organization to do some dirty work: working as a political assassin. Heavy-handed direction and lack of suspense make it less than it should be. **97m/C VHS, Beta.** Gene Hackman, Candice Bergen, Richard Widmark, Mickey Rooney, Edward Albert, Eli Wallach; **D:** Stanley Kramer; **C:** Fred W. Koenekamp; **M:** Billy Goldenberg. *CCB, FOX*

Don Amigo/Stage to Chino 194?
A western double feature: The Cisco Kid and Pancho ride together again in "Don Amigo," and in "Stage to Chino," a postal inspector investigates a gang who robs rival stage lines. **122m/B VHS,**

Beta. Duncan Renaldo, Leo Carrillo, George O'Brien, Roy Barcroft; **D:** Edward Killy. TTC

Don Daredevil Rides Again 🎞 1951
A greedy political boss tries to take over homesteaders' claims for their mineral rights. One settler adopts the identity of an ancestor (Don Daredevil), and a black mask, and becomes a frontier avenger. A 12-episode serial. 180m/B VHS, Beta. Ken Curtis, Aline Towne, Roy Barcroft. REP, MLB, MED

The Don Is Dead 🎞½ *Beautiful But Deadly*
1973 (R) A violent Mafia saga wherein a love triangle interferes with Family business, resulting in gang wars. 96m/C VHS, Beta. Anthony Quinn, Frederic Forrest, Robert Forster, Al Lettieri, Ina Balin, Angel Tompkins, Charles Cioffi; **D:** Richard Fleischer; **W:** Michael Butler; **M:** Jerry Goldsmith. USH

Don Juan 🎞🎞½ 1926 Barrymore stars as the swashbuckling Italian duke with Spanish blood who seduces a castleful of women in the 1500s. Many exciting action sequences, including classic sword fights in which Barrymore eschewed a stunt double. Great attention is also paid to the detail of the costumes and settings of the Spanish-Moor period. Noted for employing fledgling movie sound effects and music-dubbing technology, which, ironically, were responsible for eclipsing the movie's reputation. Watch for Loy as an Asian vamp and Oland as a pre-Charlie Chan Cesare Borgia. 90m/B VHS, LV. John Barrymore, Mary Astor, Willard Louis, Estelle Taylor, Helene Costello, Myrna Loy, June Marlowe, Warner Oland, Montagu Love, Hedda Hopper, Gustav von Seyffertitz; **D:** Alan Crosland. MGM, FCT

Don Juan DeMarco 🎞🎞½ 1994 (PG-13)
Burned-out clinical psychiatrist Dr. Jack Meckler (Brando) is romantically inspired by a cape-wearing, suicidal man-child from Queens (Depp), who thinks he's legendary lover Don Juan. Delusional Depp recounts, in a convincing Castilian accent, thousands of conquests as the sympathetic shrink decides it's time to bring some spice to his own ho-hum life and marriage (to Dunaway). Depp turns in a sincere, engaging performance that avoids the huge potential for melodrama and compensates for inconsistent pacing. Brando and Dunaway make a charmingly quirky couple. Watch for slain Tejano queen Selena in a musical interlude.**CW:** Sexual content; brief nudity; suggestive dialogue. 92m/C VHS, LV, Closed Caption. Marlon Brando, Johnny Depp, Faye Dunaway, Geraldine Pailhas, Rachel Ticotin, Bob Dishy, Talisa Soto; **D:** Jeremy Leven; **W:** Jeremy Leven; **C:** Ralf Bode. Nominations: Academy Awards '95: Best Song ("Have You Ever Really Loved a Woman?"); Golden Globe Awards '96: Best Song ("Have You Ever Really Loved a Woman?"), Best Score. TTC, NLC

Don Juan, My Love 🎞🎞🎞 *Don Juan, Mi Querido Fantasma* 1990 Sexy comedy finds the ghost of Don Juan given a chance, after 450 years in Purgatory, to perform a good deed and free his soul. In Spanish with English subtitles. 96m/C VHS, LV. SP Juan Luis Galiardo, Rossy de Palma, Maria Barranco, Loles Leon; **D:** Antonio Mercero; **M:** Bernardo Bonazzi. FXL, FCT

Don Q., Son of Zorro 🎞🎞 1925 Zorro's son takes up his father's fight against evil and injustice. Silent sequel to the 1920 classic. 111m/B VHS, Beta, LV. Douglas Fairbanks Sr., Mary Astor. NOS, WFV, CCB

Don Quixote 🎞🎞🎞🎞 1935 Miguel de Cervantes' tale of the romantic who would rather be a knight in shining armor than shining armor at night. Chaliapin stars as the knight-errant on his nightly errands, tilting at windmills and charging flocks of sheep. Certain scenes were adapted to fit the pre-WWII atmosphere, as it was filmed during the same time that the Nazis were burning books. 73m/B VHS. Feodor Chaliapin, George Robey, Sidney Fox, Miles Mander, Oscar Asche, Emily Fitzroy, Wally Patch; **D:** G.W. Pabst; **W:** Paul Morand, Alexandre Arnoux; **M:** Jacques Ibert. NOS, MLB, VEC

Don Quixote 🎞🎞🎞½ 1957 The lauded, visually ravishing adaptation of the Cervantes classic, with a formal integrity inherited from Eisenstein and Dovshenko. In Russian with English subtitles. 110m/B VHS, Beta. SP RU Nikolai Cherkassov, Yuri Tobubeyev; **D:** Grigori Kosintsev. FCT

Don Segundo Sombra 🎞🎞½ 1969 An interesting film seen through the eyes of an old gaucho, who is the mentor of a young boy growing to manhood. Based on the novel by Ricardo Guiraldes. In Spanish with English subtitles. 110m/C VHS, Beta. SP Juan Carballido, Juan Carlos Gene, Soledad Silveyra, Alejandra Boero; **D:** Manuel Antin. MED

Don Winslow of the Coast Guard 1943 Serial in 13 episodes features comic-strip character Winslow as he strives to keep the waters of America safe for democracy. 234m/B VHS, Beta. Don Terry, Elyse Knox; **D:** Ford Beebe, Ray Taylor. NOS, MED, VDM

Don Winslow of the Navy 1943 Thirteen episodes centered around the evil Scorpion, who plots to attack the Pacific Coast, but is thwarted by comic-strip hero Winslow. 234m/B VHS, Beta. Don Terry, Walter Sande, Anne Nagel; **D:** Ford Beebe, Ray Taylor. VYY, MED, MLB

Dona Flor and Her Two Husbands 🎞🎞🎞 *Dona Flor e Seus Dois Maridos* 1978 A woman becomes a widow when her philandering husband finally expires from drink, gambling, and ladies. She remarries, but her new husband is so boring and proper that she begins fantasizing spouse number one's return. But is he only in her imagination? Based on the novel by Jorge Amado. In Portuguese with English subtitles. Remade as "Kiss Me Goodbye." 106m/C VHS, Beta, LV. BR Sonia Braga, Jose Wilker, Mauro Mendonca; **D:** Bruno Barreto; **W:** Bruno Barreto; **M:** Chico Buarque. FXL, IME, TPV

Dona Herlinda & Her Son 🎞🎞 *Dona Herlinda y Su Hijo* 1986 A Mexican sex comedy about a mother who manipulates her bisexual son's two lovers (one male, one female), until all four fit together into a seamless unit. In Spanish with English subtitles. Slow, but amusing. 90m/C VHS, Beta, LV. MX Guadalupe Del Toro, Arturo Meza, Marco Antonio Trevino, Leticia Lupersio; **D:** Jaime Humberto Hermosillo. TPV, CCN

Donkey Skin 🎞🎞🎞 *Peau d'Ane* 1970 A charming, all-star version of the medieval French fairy tale about a king searching for a suitable wife in a magical realm after his queen dies. In his quest for the most beautiful spouse, he learns that his daughter is that woman. She prefers Prince Charming, however. In French with English subtitles. 89m/C VHS, Beta. FR Catherine Deneuve, Jean Marais, Delphine Seyrig, Jacques Perrin; **D:** Jacques Demy; **C:** Ghislan Cloquet. NO

Donner Pass: The Road to Survival 🎞🎞 1984 Tame retelling of the western wagon-train pioneers who were forced to resort to cannibalism during a brutal snowstorm in the Rockies. The tragedy is lightly implied, keeping the film suitable for family viewing. 98m/C VHS, Beta. Robert Fuller, Diane McBain, Andrew Prine, John Anderson, Michael Callan; **D:** James L. Conway. VTR, HHE

Donnie Brasco 🎞🎞🎞 1996 (R) Excellent look at the unglamourous working end of the mob and an undercover operation. In the late '70s, FBI agent Joe Pistone (Depp) infiltrates the New York Bonanno crime family, under the alias of Donnie Brasco, where he's mentored by aging low-level hood Lefty (Pacino). As Joe/Donnie gets deeper into the wiseguy life, Lefty takes a fatherly pride in his protege and the agent also becomes ensnared by his new identity—to the possible detriment of both feds and friend. Terrific lead performances. Based on a true story and adapted from the book by Pistone and Richard Woodley.**CW:** Some strong graphic violence, pervasive strong language and brief nudity and sexuality. 126m/C VHS, LV, Closed Caption. Johnny Depp, Al Pacino, Anne Heche, Michael Madsen, Bruno Kirby, James Russo, Zeljko

Ivanek, Gerry Becker, Zach Grenier, Robert Miano; **D:** Mike Newell; **W:** Paul Attanasio; **C:** Peter Sova; **M:** Patrick Doyle. COL

The Donor 🎞½ 1994 (R) Cartel stalks victims and kills them for a human organ black market.**CW:** Sexuality and some language. 94m/C VHS. Jeff Wincott, Michelle Johnson, Gordon Thomson; **D:** Damian Lee; **W:** Neal Dobrofsky, Tippi Dobrofsky. AVE

Donor Unknown 🎞🎞 1995 (R) Driven businessman Nicholas Stillman (Onorati) has always put work before his family—and both wife Alice (Krige) and teenaged daughter Danielle (Herbst) have suffered from his attitude. When Nick is hit by a massive heart attack and gets a transplant, he insists on knowing everything about the donor. What he uncovers is a black market in organ procurement and Nash Creed (Brown), who'll do anything to stop Nick from exposing his lucrative business. Based on the novel "Corazon" by William H. Mooney.**CW:** Violence and a scene of sexuality. 93m/C VHS, Closed Caption. Peter Onorati, Alice Krige, Clancy Brown, Becky Herbst, Sam Robards, Richard Portnow, T.J. Castranovo, Leo Garcia, John Dorman; **D:** John Harrison; **W:** John Harrison. USH

Donovan's Brain 🎞🎞🎞 1953 A scientist maintains the still-living brain of a dead millionaire and begins to be controlled by its powerful force. Based on Curt Siodmak's novel. 85m/B VHS, Beta, LV. Lew Ayres, Gene Evans, Nancy Davis, Steve Brodie; **D:** Felix Feist; **C:** Joseph Biroc. MGM, IME, MLB

Donovan's Reef 🎞🎞🎞 1963 Two WWII buddies meet every year on a Pacific atoll to engage in a perpetual bar-brawl, until a stuck-up Bostonian maiden appears to find her dad, a man who has fathered a brood of lovable half-casts. A rollicking, good-natured film from Ford. 109m/C VHS, Beta, LV. John Wayne, Lee Marvin, Jack Warden, Elizabeth Allen, Dorothy Lamour, Mike Mazurki, Cesar Romero; **D:** John Ford; **C:** William Clothier. PAR, TLF

Don's Party 🎞🎞🎞 1976 A rather dark comedy focusing on Australian Yuppie-types who decide to watch the election results on television as a group. A lot more goes on at this party, however, than talk of the returns. Sexual themes surface. Cast members turn fine performances, aided by top-notch script and direction. 90m/C VHS, Beta. AU Pat Bishop, Graham Kennedy, Candy Raymond, Veronica Lang, John Hargreaves, Ray Barrett, Claire Binney, Graeme Blundell, Jeanie Drynan; **D:** Bruce Beresford; **W:** David Williamson; **C:** Donald McAlpine. Australian Film Institute '77: Best Actress (Bishop). FCT

Don't Answer the Phone 🎞 *The Hollywood Strangler* 1980 (R) Deeply troubled photographer stalks and attacks the patients of a beautiful psychologist talk-show hostess. 94m/C VHS, Beta. James Westmoreland, Flo Gerrish, Ben Frank; **D:** Robert Hammer; **M:** Byron Allred. MED

Don't Be a Menace to South Central While Drinking Your Juice in the Hood 🎞🎞 1995 (R) Parody of "life in the hood" movies pokes fun at the attitudes and characters that are quickly becoming cliches in the genre. Shawn Wayans plays G-next-door Ashtray, sent by his mother to discover "what it is to be a man" from his father in South Central L.A. He hooks up with his homey Loc Dog (Marlon Wayans), a gun-crazed beer-swilling gangsta who packs a nuclear warhead. As the title implies, almost every major black film in recent memory is given the Wayans' drive-by treatment, with a majority of the plot lifted from "Boyz in the Hood." Fans of the T.V. series "In Living Color" will love this twisted look at ghetto life, but others may be offended.**CW:** Strong language, sexuality, some drug content and violence. 88m/C VHS, LV, Closed Caption. Shawn Wayans, Marlon Wayans, Tracey Cherelle Jones, Chris Spencer, Suli McCullough, Darrell Heath, Helen Martin, Isaiah Barnes, Lahmard Tate; *Cameos:* Keenen Ivory Wayans; **D:** Paris Barclay; **W:** Shawn Wayans, Marlon Wayans, Phil Beauman; **C:** Russ Brandt; **M:** John Barnes. TOU

Don't Be Afraid of the Dark 🐾🐾½
1973 A young couple move into their dream house only to find that demonic little critters are residing in their basement and they want more than shelter. Made for TV with creepy scenes and eerie makeup for the monsters. 74m/C VHS, Beta. Kim Darby, Jim Hutton, Barbara Anderson, William Demarest, Pedro Armendariz Jr.; **D:** John Newland. LIV

Don't Bother to Knock 🐾🐾½ 1952 As a mentally unstable hotel babysitter, Monroe meets a pilot (Widmark) and has a brief rendezvous with him. When the little girl she is babysitting interrupts, Monroe is furious, and later tries to murder the girl. This is one of Monroe's best dramatic roles. Bancroft's film debut as the Widmark's girlfriend. 76m/B VHS. Richard Widmark, Marilyn Monroe, Anne Bancroft, Elisha Cook Jr., Jim Backus, Lurene Tuttle, Jeanne Cagney, Donna Corcoran; **D:** Roy Ward Baker; **W:** Daniel Taradash. FXV

Don't Change My World 🐾½ 1983 (G)
To preserve the natural beauty of the north woods, a wildlife photographer must fight a villainous land developer and a reckless poacher. Eco-correct. 89m/C VHS, Beta. Roy Tatum, Ben Jones, Edie Kramer, George Macrenais, Paul Newmark, David Eidson; **D:** Robert Rector. LIV

Don't Cry, It's Only Thunder 🐾🐾½
1982 (PG) A young army medic who works in a mortuary in Saigon becomes involved with a group of Vietnamese orphans and a dedicated army doctor. Based on a true story. 108m/C VHS, Beta. Dennis Christopher, Susan St. James, Roger Brown, Li Lu, Thu Thuy, James Whitmore; **D:** Peter Werner; **M:** Maurice Jarre. COL

Don't Do It 🐾🐾½ 1994 (PG-13) Three twentysomething couples, attempting to find love, all wind up in the same cafe and try to tell the truth about how they feel and whom they desire. **CW:** Language, mild sexual situations. 90m/C VHS. James Marshall, James LeGros, Sheryl Lee, Esai Morales, Alexis Arquette, Balthazar Getty, Sarah Trigger, Heather Graham; **D:** Eugene Hess; **W:** Eugene Hess. TRI

Don't Drink the Water 🐾🐾½ 1969 (G)
Based on Woody Allen's hit play, this film plays an average Newark, New Jersey, family behind the Iron Curtain, where their vacation photo-taking gets them accused of spying. 100m/C VHS, Beta. Jackie Gleason, Estelle Parsons, Joan Delaney, Ted Bessell, Michael Constantine; **D:** Howard Morris. COL

Don't Go in the House 🐾 1980 (R)
Long-dormant psychosis is brought to life by the death of a young man's mother. 90m/C VHS, Beta. Dan Grimaldi, Robert Osth, Ruth Dardick; **D:** Joseph Ellison; **M:** Richard Einhorn. MED

Don't Go in the Woods woof! 1981
(R) Routine exercise in "don't do that" terror genre (includes warnings about going into houses, answering phones, looking into basements, opening windows, etc.). This time, four young campers are stalked by a crazed killer armed with prerequisite ax. 88m/C VHS, Beta. VES

Don't Go Near the Water 🐾🐾 1957
Somewhat amusing comedy about the happenings at a Naval installation on a South Pacific tropical paradise. Clark outshines the others in his role as a frustrated officer. Based on the novel by William Brinkley. 107m/C VHS. Glenn Ford, Gia Scala, Earl Holliman, Anne Francis, Keenan Wynn, Fred Clark, Eva Gabor, Russ Tamblyn; **D:** Charles Walters; **W:** Dorothy Kingsley; George Wells. MGM

Don't Go to Sleep 🐾🐾 1982 After a fatal car crash, a young girl misses mom and dad so much she returns from the grave to take them where they can be one big happy family again. Better than most made-for-TV junk-food frightfests, written by Keenan Wynn's son, Ned. 93m/C VHS. Dennis Weaver, Valerie Harper, Robin Ignico, Kristin Cummings, Ruth Gordon, Robert Webber; **D:** Richard Lang; **W:** Ned Wynn. UNI

Don't Hang Up 🐾🐾½ 1990 Handicapped New York actress Sarah (Arquette) wants to do a production of agoraphobic London writer Joe's (Suchet) play. So she calls him up to get his permission and the two begin a phone relationship that develops from business to romance. 84m/C VHS. GB Rosanna Arquette, David Suchet. WBF

Don't Let Your Meat Loaf 🐾½ 1995
Three struggling comedians take their act on the road, including subway stations and street corners, in order to get the money to open their own comedy club. 82m/C VHS. Leander Sales, Dana S. Hubbard, Brad Albright; **D:** Leander Sales. SDE

Don't Look Back 🐾🐾🐾 1996 (R) Musician and heroin addict Jesse Parish (Stoltz) stumbles across a suitcase full of cash after witnessing a drug deal gone bad. He heads back to family and friends in Texas so he can kick his habit, but is marked for death by the dealers who want their money back. Strong script and performances; made for cable TV. **CW:** Strong violence, language and drug content. 91m/C VHS, Closed Caption. Eric Stoltz, John Corbett, Josh Hamilton, Annabeth Gish, Dwight Yoakam, Amanda Plummer; **D:** Geoff Murphy; **W:** Billy Bob Thornton, Tom Epperson. HBO

Don't Look Back: The Story of Leroy "Satchel" Paige 🐾🐾½ 1981
Drama of the legendary baseball pitcher who helped break down racial barriers, based on his autobiography. Made-for-TV fare. Gossett hits a home run in the lead, but the overall effort is a ground-rule triple. 98m/C VHS, Beta. Louis Gossett Jr., Beverly Todd, Cleavon Little, Clifton Davis, John Beradino, Jim Davis, Ossie Davis, Hal Williams; **D:** George C. Scott; Richard A. Colla. ABC

Don't Look in the Attic woof! 1981 A couple finds a haunted house with cows in the attic. 90m/C VHS, Beta. Beba Loncar, Jean-Pierre Aumont; **D:** Carl Ausino. NO

Don't Look in the Basement 🐾½
1973 (R) Things get out of hand at an isolated asylum and a pretty young nurse is caught in the middle. Straight-jacketed by a low budget. 95m/C VHS, Beta. Rosie Holotik, Anne MacAdams, William Bill McGhee, Rhea MacAdams, Gene Ross, Betty Chandler, Camilla Carr, Robert Dracup, Jessie Kirby, Hugh Feagin, Harryete Warren, Jessie Lee Fulton, Michael Harvey; **D:** S.F. Brownrigg. MPI

Don't Look Now 🐾🐾🐾 1973 (R) A psychological thriller about a couple's trip to Venice after their child drowns. Notable for a steamy love scene and a chilling climax. Based on the novel by Daphne Du Maurier. 110m/C VHS, Beta, LV. Donald Sutherland, Julie Christie, Hilary Mason; **D:** Nicolas Roeg; **W:** Chris Bryant, Allan Scott; **M:** Pino Donaggio. PAR

Don't Mess with My Sister! 🐾🐾½
1985 A married, New York junkyard worker falls in love with a belly dancer he meets at a party. The affair leads to murder and subsequently, revenge. An interesting, offbeat film from the director of "I Spit on Your Grave." 90m/C VHS, Beta, LV. Joe Perce, Jeannine Lemay, Jack Gurci, Peter Sapienza, Laura Lanfranchi; **D:** Mier Zarchi. NO

Don't Open the Door! woof! 1974 (PG)
A young woman is terrorized by a killer located inside her house. 90m/C VHS, Beta. Susan Bracken, Gene Ross, Jim Harrell; **D:** S.F. Brownrigg. GEM

Don't Open Till Christmas woof!
1984 A weirdo murders various Santa Clauses in assorted gory ways. Best to take this one back to the department store. 86m/C VHS, Beta. GB Edmund Purdom, Caroline Munro, Alan Lake, Belinda Mayne, Gerry Sundquist, Mark Jones; **D:** Edmund Purdom. LIV, VES

Don't Raise the Bridge, Lower the River 🐾🐾 1968 (G) After his wife leaves him, an American with crazy, get-rich-quick schemes turns his wife's ancestral English home into a Chinese discotheque. Domestic farce that comes and goes; if mad for Lewis, rent "The Nutty Professor." 99m/C VHS, Beta. Jerry Lewis, Terry-Thomas, Jacqueline Pearce; **D:** Jerry Paris. COL

Don't Shove/Two Gun Gussie 1919
Two early Harold Lloyd shorts feature the comedian's embryonic comic style as a young fellow impressing his date at a skating rink ("Don't Shove") and a city slicker out West ("Two Gun Gussie"). Silent with piano scores. 27m/B VHS, Beta. Harold Lloyd, Bebe Daniels, Noah Young, Snub Pollard. CCB

Don't Talk to Strangers 🐾🐾½ 1994
(R) Formula thriller has Brosnan marrying divorcee Reed and becoming instant father to her 9-year-old son. But someone appears to be a whacko—is it the kid's real dad (Quinn) or is Brosnan just too good to be true? **CW:** Some terror and violence. 94m/C VHS, LV, Closed Caption. Pierce Brosnan, Shanna Reed, Terry O'Quinn; **D:** Robert Lewis; **W:** Neill D. Hicks, Jon George, Nevin Schreiner. USH

Don't Tell Her It's Me 🐾 The Boyfriend School 1990 (PG-13) Guttenberg is determined to win the heart of an attractive writer. With the assistance of his sister, he works to become a dream man. Clever premise, promising cast, lame comedy. From the novel by Sarah Bird. 101m/C VHS, Beta, LV, Closed Caption. Steve Guttenberg, Jami Gertz, Shelley Long, Kyle MacLachlan, Madchen Amick; **D:** Malcolm Mowbray; **W:** Sarah Bird; **M:** Michael Gore. HBO

Don't Tell Mom the Babysitter's Dead 🐾½ 1991 (PG-13) Their mother traveling abroad, the title situation leaves a houseful of teenagers with the whole summer to themselves. Eldest daughter Applegate cons her way into the high-powered business world while the metalhead son parties hardy. Many tepid comic situations, not adding up to very much. 105m/C VHS, Beta, LV, 8mm, Closed Caption. Christina Applegate, Keith Coogan, Joanna Cassidy, John Getz, Josh Charles, Concetta Tomei, Eda Reiss Merin; **D:** Stephen Herek. HBO

The Doolins of Oklahoma 🐾🐾½ The Great Manhunt 1949 Scott is the leader of the last of the southwestern desert outlaw gangs, pursued by lawmen and changing times with the onset of the modern age. Fast-paced and intelligent. 90m/B VHS, Beta. Randolph Scott, George Macready, Louise Allbritton, John Ireland, Virginia Huston, Charles Kemper, Noah Beery Jr.; **D:** Gordon Douglas; **M:** George Duning. GKK

Doom Asylum woof! 1988 (R) Several sex kittens wander into a deserted sanatorium and meet up with the grisly beast wielding autopsy instruments. The people involved with this spoof should have been (more) committed. 77m/C VHS, Beta. Patty Mullen, Ruth Collins, Kristen Davis, William Hay, Kenny L. Price, Harrison White, Dawn Alvan, Michael Rogan; **D:** Richard S. Friedman. ACA

The Doom Generation 🐾🐾🐾 1995 (R)
Alienated trio on the road trip to hell (doubling as L.A.). Beautiful 17-year-old druggie Amy Blue (McGowan), her sweetly dim boyfriend Jordan White (Duval), and hot-tempered stud/drifter Xavier Red (Schaech) flee after Red kills a store clerk. They're basically from nowhere, going nowhere, and finding sex and (lots of gruesomely depicted) violence along the way. The subtitle, "A Heterosexual Movie by Gregg Araki," may be technically accurate but the homoerotic subtext is very clear. Terrific performances. Second film in Araki's teen trilogy, following "Totally F***ked Up," and preceding "Nowhere." An unrated version is also available. **CW:** Violence, language, nudity, sexual situations. 84m/C VHS. Rose McGowan, James Duval, Johnathon Schaech; **Cameos:** Parker Posey, Lauren Tewes, Christopher Knight, Margaret Cho, Skinny Puppy; **D:** Gregg Araki; **W:** Gregg Araki; **C:** Jim Fealy. Nominations: Independent Spirit Awards '96: Debut Performance (McGowan). THV

Doomed at Sundown 🐾🐾½ 1937 Decent Steele vehicle has the tough cowpoke as a sheriff's son known for playing practical jokes. When his father gets knifed, it's no laughing matter and he takes off after the killers. Based on a story by Fred Myton. 55m/B VHS. Bob Steele, Laraine Day, Warner Richmond, Harold Daniels, David Sharpe; **D:** Sam Newfield; **W:** George Plympton. GPV, DVT

Doomed Caravan 🏆🏆🏆 1941 Hoppy and his pals lend a hand when some villains try to monopolize the wagon train business. Location shooting was done in the valleys of central California. **60m/B VHS.** William Boyd, Russell Hayden, Andy Clyde, Minna Gombell, Morris Ankrum, Georgia Hawkins, Trevor Bardette, Pat O'Brien; **D:** Lesley Selander. *NOS*

Doomed Love 🏆🏆½ 1983 Love is hell, especially when the object of your affection happens to be deceased. A professor of literature in the throes of unrequited love decides to reunite himself with his lost love. Won awards when released in Berlin. **75m/C VHS.** Bill Rice; **D:** Andrew Horn. *MWF, FCT*

Doomed to Die 🏆🏆 1940 Cargo of stolen bonds leads to a tong war and the murder of a shipping millionaire. Part of Mr. Wong series. Worth a look if only for Karloff's performance. **67m/B VHS, Beta.** Boris Karloff, Marjorie Reynolds, Grant Withers; **D:** William Nigh. *NOS, MRV, SNC*

Doomsday 🏆🏆½ 1928 Vidor marries for wealth instead of love and, in classic fashion, finds that money doesn't buy happiness. **73m/B VHS.** Florence Vidor, Gary Cooper, Lawrence Grant; **D:** Rowland V. Lee. *GPV*

The Doomsday Flight 🏆🏆 1966 Uneven made-for-television thriller. O'Brien plants an altitude-triggered bomb on a jet in an effort to blackmail the airline. Search for the bomb provides some suspenseful and well-acted moments. **100m/C VHS, Beta.** Jack Lord, Edmond O'Brien, Van Johnson, John Saxon, Katherine Crawford, Michael Sarrazin, Ed Asner, Greg Morris, Richard Carlson, Don Stewart; **D:** William A. Graham; **W:** Rod Serling. *USH*

Doomsday Gun 🏆🏆½ 1994 Fact-based thriller about arms manufacturer Gerald Bull (Langella), who dreams of building the world's biggest gun—a behemoth with a range of 1000 miles. Only problem is Bull's willingness to sell the weapon to the highest bidder, who happens to be Saddam Hussein. This doesn't sit well with Israeli Mossad agent Yossi (Arkin). Made for cable TV. **110m/C VHS.** Frank Langella, Alan Arkin, Kevin Spacey, Tony Goldwyn, James Fox, Michael Kitchen, Francesca Annis, Marianne Denicourt; **D:** Robert M. Young; **W:** Lionel Chetwynd, Walter Bernstein; **C:** Ian Wilson. *HBO*

Doomwatch 🏆🏆½ 1972 A scientist discovers a chemical company is dumping poison into local waters, deforming the inhabitants of an isolated island when they eat the catch of the day. Unsurprising. **89m/C VHS, Beta.** *GB* Ian Bannen, Judy Geeson, John Paul, Simon Oates, George Sanders; **D:** Peter Sasdy. *MON*

Door to Door 🏆🏆 1984 A made-for-cable comedy about two door-to-door salesmen who race to stay one step ahead of the law and their own company. Fairly lightweight, but it has its moments. **93m/C VHS, Beta.** Ron Leibman, Jane Kaczmarek, Arliss Howard, Alan Austin; **D:** Patrick Bailey. *MED*

Door to Door Maniac 🏆½ *Five Minutes to Live* 1961 Criminals hold a bank president's wife hostage, unaware that the husband was looking to get rid of her in favor of another woman. Cash's screen debut. Aside from the strange cast ensemble, not particularly worth seeing. **80m/B VHS, Beta.** Johnny Cash, Ron Howard, Vic Tayback, Donald Woods, Cay Forrester, Pamela Mason; **D:** Bill Karn. *VDM, AOV*

Door with the Seven Locks 🏆🏆½ 1962 Bizarre Edgar Wallace story of man who leaves seven keys to a treasure vault in his will. Remake of "Chamber of Horrors." **96m/C VHS.** *GE* Eddi Arent, Heinz Drache, Klaus Kinski, Ady Berber; **D:** Alfred Vohrer. *SNC*

The Doors 🏆🏆½ 1991 (R) Stone approached Jim Morrison with an early incarnation of this docudrama, but it's hard to believe even the Lizard King could play himself with any more convincing abandon than Kilmer, in a great performance. Trouble is, the story—one of drugs, abuse, and abject self-indulgence—grows tiresome, and the audience, with the exception of die-hard fans, may lose sight of any sympathy they might have had. Ryan is forgettable as Morrison's hippie-chick wife, MacLachlan sports a funny wig and dabbles on the keyboards as Ray Manszarek, and Quinlan is atypically cast as a sado-masochistic journalist paramour. Based on "Riders on the Storm" by John Densmore.**CW:** Strong language, heavy drug content, and strong sexuality. **138m/C VHS, LV, 8mm, Closed Caption, DVD.** Val Kilmer, Meg Ryan, Kevin Dillon, Kyle MacLachlan, Frank Whaley, Michael Madsen, Kathleen Quinlan, Crispin Glover, Josh Evans, John Densmore, William Jordan, Mimi Rogers, Paul Williams, Bill Graham, Billy Vera, William Kunstler, Wes Studi, Costas Mandylor, Billy Idol, Michael Wincott, Dennis Burkley; **D:** Oliver Stone; **W:** Oliver Stone, Ralph Thomas, Randy Johnson, J. Randall Johnson; **C:** Robert Richardson. *COL, FCT, VES*

The Doors: Soft Parade, a Retrospective 1969 The Doors' final TV appearance in 1969 forms the centerpiece of this concert-video tie-in to the Oliver Stone film. Fans should a-Door previously unreleased backstage interviews and a notable version of "The Unknown Soldier." **50m/C VHS, LV, Closed Caption. D:** Ray Manzarek. *USH*

Doppelganger: The Evil Within 🏆🏆 1990 (R) Holly Gooding (Barrymore) seems like such a nice girl—until the police suspect her of the brutal murder of her mother. Her new friend Patrick (Newbern) begins to see another side to the vulnerable Holly—a seductress capable of doing anything to get what she wants.**CW:** Language, strong violence, and sexuality. **105m/C VHS, LV, Closed Caption.** Drew Barrymore, George Newbern, Dennis Christopher, Sally Kellerman, Leslie Hope; **D:** Avi Nesher; **W:** Avi Nesher. *FXV*

Dorian Gray 🏆½ *The Secret of Dorian Gray; Il Dio Chiamato a Dorian; Das Bildness des Dorian Gray* 1970 (R) Modern-day version of the famous tale by Oscar Wilde about an ageless young man whose portrait reflects the ravages of time and a life of debauchery. More sex, less acting with Berger in lead. Not nearly as good as the original version, "The Picture of Dorian Gray." **92m/C VHS.** *IT* Richard Todd, Helmut Berger, Herbert Lom; **D:** Massimo Dallamano. *REP, FCT*

Dorm That Dripped Blood woof! 1982 (R) Five college students volunteer to close the dorm during their Christmas vacation. A series of grisly and barbaric incidents eliminates the youngsters one by one. As the terror mounts, the remaining students slowly realize that they are up against a terrifyingly real psychopathic killer. Merry Christmas. **84m/C VHS, Beta.** Laura Lopinski, Stephen Sachs, Pamela Holland; **D:** Stephen Carpenter, Jeffrey Obrow; **W:** Stephen Carpenter. *MED*

Dos Cruces en Danger Pass 🏆🏆🏆 1971 Charming fairy tale about a widowed king in search of a beautiful wife. Gorgeous color production. Also known as "Peau D'Ane." In French with English subtitles. **0090m/C VHS, Beta.** *FR* Catherine Deneuve, Jacques Perrin, Jéan Marais, Delphine Seyrig; **D:** Jacques Demy.

Double Agents 🏆 *La Nuit Des Espions; Night Encounter* 1959 Two double agents are sent on a rendezvous to exchange vital government secrets. Dubbed in English. **81m/B VHS, Beta.** *FR* Marina Vlady, Robert Hossein. *VYY*

Double Cross 🏆🏆 1992 (R) Tank Polling (Connery), a British journalist, uses the secrets of an ex-hooker (Donohoe) to get back at a corrupt politician who ruined Polling's life five years earlier. Lots of action and a few graphic murders in this thriller.**CW:** Strong language, strong violence, and strong sexuality. **96m/C VHS.** Amanda Donohoe, Peter Wyngarde, Jason Connery; **D:** James Marcus. *VTR*

Double Cross 🏆🏆 1994 (R) Man has what seems to be a chance erotic encounter with a beautiful blonde. But this wouldn't be if it ended there, so there's blackmail and murder to contend with as well. **95m/C VHS, Closed Caption.** Patrick Bergin, Jennifer Tilly, Kelly Preston, Matt Craven, Kevin Tighe. *PAR*

Double-Crossed 🏆🏆½ 1991 In 1984 Barry Seal agrees to inform on Colombia's Medellin Cartel and its links to the Sandanista government of Nicaragua in exchange for leniency on drug-smuggling charges. Little does he know that the personal consequences will turn deadly when his cover is blown and the government double-crosses him. Hopper's hyped-up performance as drug smuggler turned DEA informant Seal showcases this true-crime tale. **111m/C VHS, LV, Closed Caption.** Dennis Hopper, Robert Carradine, G.W. Bailey, Adrienne Barbeau; **C:** Donald M. Morgan; **M:** Richard Bellis. *WAR*

Double Deal 🏆🏆 1939 An honest man and a gangster are rivals in love. The gangster robs a jewelry store and tries to pin the crime on the good guy. This is a movie with a moral so don't expect him to get away with it. **60m/C VHS.** Monte Hawley, Jeni Le Gon, Edward Thompson, Florence O'Brien; **D:** Arthur Dreifuss. *FCT*

Double Deal 🏆½ 1950 Murder, mayhem, and industrial espionage come into play as parties fight over an oil field. **65m/B VHS, Beta.** Marie Windsor, Richard Denning, Taylor Holmes; **D:** Abby Berlin. *DVT*

Double Deal 🏆½ 1984 Unfaithful woman and her lover plot to steal priceless opal from hubby. Lifeless and silly. **90m/C VHS, Beta.** Louis Jourdan, Angela Punch McGregor; **D:** Brian Kavanagh. *NO*

Double Double Toil and Trouble 🏆🏆½ 1994 The twins come to the financial rescue of their family when Dad's business gets into trouble and their home is threatened. But first they need to get a magic moonstone from their wicked Aunt Agatha (Leachman) and rescue kind Aunt Sophia, all before midnight on Halloween. Made for TV. **93m/C VHS, Closed Caption.** Ashley Olsen, Mary-Kate Olsen, Cloris Leachman, Meshach Taylor; **D:** Jeff Franklin; **W:** Jeff Franklin. *WAR*

Double Dragon 🏆🏆½ 1994 (PG-13) Generally harmless brain candy, based on the videogame, finds orphaned brothers Jimmy (Dacascos) and Billy (Wolf) living in the rubble of post earthquake L.A., circa 2007. They have half of a mystical dragon amulet and obsessed mogul Koga Shuko (Patrick), who possesses the other half, after them. Seems he needs the entire amulet in order to control its vast power. Non-stop action should keep the kiddies amused.**CW:** Martial arts violence. **96m/C VHS, LV, Closed Caption.** Scott Wolf, Mark Dacascos, Robert Patrick, Alyssa Milano, Kristina Malandro Wagner, Julia Nickson-Soul; **D:** Jim Yukich; **W:** Michael Paul Davis, Peter Gould; **M:** Jay Michael Ferguson. *USH*

Double Dynamite 🏆½ *It's Only Money* 1951 A bank teller is at a loss when his racetrack winnings are confused with the cash lifted from his bank during a robbery. Forgettable, forgotten shambles. Originally filmed in 1948. **80m/B VHS, Beta.** Frank Sinatra, Jane Russell, Groucho Marx, Don McGuire, Howard Freeman, Harry Hayden, Nestor Paiva, Lou Nova, Joe Devlin; **D:** Irving Cummings; **W:** Melville Shavelson. *TTC*

Double Edge 🏆🏆 1992 (PG-13) The Palestinian-Israeli conflict is the focus of this drama about an ambitious reporter (Dunaway). On her first foreign assignment, New Yorker Faye Milano finds herself way out of her depth when she covers a colleague's beat in Jerusalem. Unable to remain a detached observer, Faye instead becomes an active participant, alternating between her affair with an Israeli reserves officer and her friendship with a family of Palestinian intifada leaders. Dunaway and Kollek are unfortunately stiff in their performances but the location (Israel and the West Bank) is interesting and the story surprisingly balanced.**CW:** One violent scene. **85m/C VHS, Beta.** *IS* Faye Dunaway, Amos Kollek, Muhamad Bakri, Shmuel Shilo, Makram Khouri, Michael Schneider, Anat Atzman, Ann Belkin; **D:** Amos Kollek; **W:** Amos Kollek. *WAR*

Double Exposure 🎬🎬 1982 (R) A young photographer's violent nightmares become the next day's headlines. Unsurprising vision. 95m/C VHS, Beta. Michael Callan, James Stacy, Joanna Pettet, Cleavon Little, Pamela Hensley, Seymour Cassel; D: William B. Hillman. VES

Double Exposure 🎬½ 1993 (R) A possessive husband discovers his wife's infidelity and decides to get revenge, only his plan doesn't work out as he intends. CW: Language, rape scene, and strong sexuality. 93m/C VHS, LV. Ron Perlman, Ian Buchanan, Jennifer Gatti, William R. Moses, James McEachin, Dedee Pfeiffer; D: Claudia Hoover; W: Christine Colfer, Bridget Hoffman, Claudia Hoover. PSM

Double Exposure: The Story of Margaret Bourke-White 🎬🎬½ Margaret Bourke-White 1989 Beautifully shot but slow biography of a woman who became a well-known professional photographer for "Life" magazine during the 1930s and 1940s, as well as the first official female photojournalist of WWII. Made for cable television. 105m/C VHS, LV. Farrah Fawcett, Frederic Forrest, Mitchell Ryan, David Huddleston, Jay Patterson, Ken Marshall; D: Lawrence Schiller; C: Robert Elswit. TTC

Double Face 🎬½ 1970 A wealthy industrialist kills his lesbian wife with a car bomb, but she seems to haunt him through pornographic films. 84m/C VHS, Beta. Klaus Kinski, Annabella Incontrera. UNI

Double Happiness 🎬🎬🎬 1994 (PG-13) Slice of life comedy-drama finds twentysomething Chinese-Canadian Jade Li (Oh) struggling to balance her would-be acting career and new world romance with her family's traditional values. Jade wants to please her old world father (Chang) so she endures her arranged dates and puts on a pleasant demeanor for family friends. But Jade must decide who she wants to be when she gets involved with non-Asian college student Mark (Rennie). Fine performances and assured direction from Shum in her feature film debut. CW: One scene of sexuality; brief strong sexuality. 87m/C VHS, LV, Closed Caption. CA Sandra Oh, Stephen Chang, Alannah Ong, Frances You, Johnny Mah, Keith Callum Rennie; D: Mina Shum; W: Mina Shum; C: Peter Wunstorf. Genie Awards '94: Best Actress (Oh), Best Film Editing; Nominations: Genie Awards '94: Best Director (Shum), Best Film. TTC, NLC

Double Identity 🎬🎬½ 1989 (PG-13) Former college professor turned criminal Mancuso moves to a corn patch called New Hope in hopes of returning to the straight and narrow. He finds a good woman to stand by him, but, alas, crime, like smoking, is easier to start than to quit. Much intrigue and deceit. 95m/C VHS. CA FR Nick Mancuso, Leah K. Pinsent, Patrick Bauchau, Anne LeTourneau, Jacques Godin; D: Yves Boisset. NO

Double Impact 🎬½ 1991 (R) Van Damme plays twins re-united in Hong Kong to avenge their parents' murder by local bad guys, but this lunkhead kick-em-up doesn't even take advantage of that gimmick; the basic story would have been exactly the same with just one Jean-Claude. Lots of profane dialogue and some gratuitous nudity for the kiddies. CW: Strong violence, strong sensuality, and strong language. 107m/C VHS, Beta, LV, 8mm, Closed Caption. Jean-Claude Van Damme, Cory Everson, Geoffrey Lewis; D: Sheldon Lettich; W: Jean-Claude Van Damme, Sheldon Lettich. COL, CCB

Double Indemnity 🎬🎬🎬🎬 1944 The classic seedy story of an insurance agent seduced by a deadly woman into killing her husband so they can collect together from his company. Terrific, influential film noir, the best of its kind. Based on the James M. Cain novel. 107m/B VHS, Beta, LV. Fred MacMurray, Barbara Stanwyck, Edward G. Robinson, Tom Powers, Porter Hall, Jean Heather, Byron Barr, Fortunio Bonanova; D: Billy Wilder; W: Raymond Chandler, Billy Wilder; M: Miklos Rozsa. Nominations: Academy Awards '44: Best Actress (Stanwyck), Best Black and White Cinematography, Best Director (Wilder), Best Picture, Best Screenplay, Best Sound, Original Dramatic/Comedy Score. USH, FCT

Double Jeopardy 🎬🎬 1992 (R) Boxleitner stars as a married man who risks his family and life when his sexy ex-lover returns to town. She easily involves him in deception—and murder. A cake-walk for Ward as the femme fatale. Made for cable television. 101m/C VHS, Beta, LV. Bruce Boxleitner, Rachel Ward, Sela Ward, Sally Kirkland; D: Lawrence Schiller; M: Eduard Artemyev. FXV, PMS

A Double Life 🎬🎬🎬 1947 Colman plays a Shakespearean actor in trouble when the characters he plays begin to seep into his personal life and take over. Things begin to look really bad when he is cast in the role of the cursed Othello. Colman won an Oscar for this difficult role, and the moody musical score garnered another for Rosza. 107m/B VHS, Closed Caption. Ronald Colman, Shelley Winters, Signe Hasso, Edmond O'Brien, Ray Collins, Millard Mitchell; D: George Cukor; W: Ruth Gordon, Garson Kanin; C: Milton Krasner; M: Miklos Rozsa. Academy Awards '47: Best Actor (Colman), Original Dramatic/Comedy Score; Golden Globe Awards '48: Best Actor—Drama (Colman); Nominations: Academy Awards '47: Best Director (Cukor), Best Original Screenplay. REP, FCT, BTV

The Double Life of Veronique 🎬🎬 La Double Vie de Veronique 1991 (R) They say everyone has a twin, but this is ridiculous. Two women—Polish Veronika and French Veronique—are born on the same day in different countries, share a singing talent, a cardiac ailment, and, although the two never meet, a strange awareness of each other. Jacob is unforgettable as the two women, and director Krzysztof creates some spellbinding scenes but the viewer has to be willing to forgo plot for atmosphere. CW: Sexuality. 96m/C VHS, Beta, LV, Closed Caption. FR PL Irene Jacob, Phillipe Volter, Sandrine Dumas, Aleksander Bardini, Louis Ducreux, Claude Duneton, Halina Gryglaszewska, Kalina Jedrusik; D: Krzysztof Kieslowski; W: Krzysztof Kieslowski, Krzysztof Piesiewicz; C: Slawomir Idziak. Cannes Film Festival '91: Best Actress (Jacob); National Society of Film Critics Awards '91: Best Foreign Film. PAR

The Double McGuffin 🎬🎬 1979 (PG) A plot of international intrigue is uncovered by teenagers—a la the Hardy Boys—when a prime minister and her security guard pay a visit to a small Virginia community. They're not believed, though. Action-packed from the makers of Benji. Dogs do not figure prominently here. 100m/C VHS, Beta. Ernest Borgnine, George Kennedy, Elke Sommer, Ed "Too Tall" Jones, Lisa Whelchel, Vincent Spano; D: Joe Camp; M: Euel Box; V: Orson Welles. VES

The Double Negative 🎬½ Deadly Companion 1980 A photojournalist pursues his wife's killer in a confusing story. Based on Ross MacDonald's "The Three Roads." 96m/C VHS, Beta. CA Michael Sarrazin, Susan Clark, Anthony Perkins, Howard Duff, Kate Reid, Al Waxman, Elizabeth Shepherd, John Candy; D: George Bloomfield; W: Janis Allen. BFV

The Double O Kid 🎬🎬½ 1992 (PG-13) Lance is a 17-year-old video game master who's interning at the Agency, a covert spy organization. Ordered to push a package to Los Angeles, Lance discovers that a madman computer virus designer and his henchwoman desperately want what he's carrying. Aided by the prerequisite pretty girl, Lance must avoid all the hazards sent his way. CW: Some language and some violence. 95m/C VHS, Beta, Closed Caption. Corey Haim, Wallace Shawn, Brigitte Nielsen, Nicole Eggert, John Rhys-Davies, Basil Hoffman, Karen Black; Cameos: Anne Francis; D: Duncan McLachlan; W: Andrea Buck, Duncan McLachlan. PSM

Double Obsession 🎬½ 1993 (R) College roommates Heather (Hemingway) and Claire (d'Abo) are inseparable friends—until Claire falls in love. Heather becomes possessive and, though the years pass, her obsession with Claire only grows. When Heather's affections turn deadly, can Claire stop her? 88m/C VHS. Margaux Hemingway, Maryam d'Abo, Frederic Forrest, Scott Valentine; D: Eduardo Montes; W: Jeffrey Delman, R.J. Marx, Eduardo Montes. COL

Double Play 🎬🎬½ 1996 (PG) Updated version of "The Prince and the Pauper" finds teen-aged computer genius Rudy (Jackson) inheriting his dad's successful computer company. But his evil Uncle Mike (Shatner), who's not the boy's guardian, wants the company for himself and hires some thugs to kidnap the kid and force him to sign over control of the business. But Rudy just happens to have a double—a high school baseball star who's in town for the championship game—and confusion rules when he takes his place. Jackson's brother, Richard Lee Jackson, plays his cousin in the movie. 101m/C VHS. Jonathan Jackson, William Shatner, Richard Lee Jackson. HMK

Double Revenge 🎬🎬 1989 Two men feel they have a score to settle after a bank heist gone sour leaves two people dead. 90m/C VHS. Joe Dallesandro, Nancy Everhard, Leigh McCloskey, Richard Rust, Theresa Saldana; D: Armand Mastroianni. REP

Double Standard 🎬½ 1988 You'll be less concerned with the plot—a community discovers that a prominent judge has maintained two marriages for nearly twenty years—than with the possibility that such dim-witted myopes might actually have existed in the real world. This made-for-TV slice of bigamy is for fans of the oops-I-forgot-I'm-married genre only. 95m/C VHS. Robert Foxworth, Michelle Greene, Pamela Bellwood, James Kee; D: Louis Rudolph. FRH

Double Suicide 🎬🎬🎬 Shinju Ten No Amijima 1969 From a play by Monzarmon Chikamatsu, a tragic drama about a poor salesman in 18th century Japan who falls in love with a geisha and ruins his family and himself trying to requite the hopeless passion. Stylish with Iwashita turning in a wonderful dual performance. In Japanese with subtitles. 105m/B VHS, Beta. JP Kichiemon Nakamura, Shima Iwashita, Yusuke Takita, Hosei Komatsu; D: Masahiro Shinoda. NO

Double Team 🎬🎬 1997 (R) Counter-terrorist expert Jack Quinn (Van Damme) teams with weapons specialist Yaz (Rodman, in his film debut) to take down international terrorist Stavros (Roarke). After Jack kills Stavros's son, he is sent to a high-security superspy retirement village. When his wife and newborn son are kidnapped, Jack escapes, with Yaz's help, to finish the job and try to save his family. Van Damme teams with his third famous Hong Kong action director, Tsui Hark (the other two are John Woo and Ringo Lam) to create yet another disappointment. He's slightly more charismatic than usual (not saying much), but Rodman easily steals the flick as he gets most of the good lines, and delivers them with relish. CW: Non-stop action violence. 91m/C VHS. Jean-Claude Van Damme, Dennis Rodman, Mickey Rourke, Natasha Lindinger, Paul Freeman, Valeria Cavalli, Jay Benedict; D: Tsui Hark; W: Paul Mones, Don Jakoby; C: Peter Pau; M: Gary Chang. NYR

Double Threat 🎬🎬 1992 (R) An aging sex star makes her return to the screen opposite a younger actor with whom she is having an affair. When the director wants to include nude sex scenes in the film she agrees to use a younger body-double. Then the actress discovers her lover is involved in off-screen action with the double as well. This does not please her and she decides to take a deadly revenge. An unrated version is also available. CW: Language and strong sexuality. 94m/C VHS. Sally Kirkland, Andrew Stevens, Lisa Shane, Richard Lynch, Anthony (Tony) Franciosa, Sherrie Rose, Chick Vennera; D: David A. Prior. AIP

Double Trouble 🎬🎬 1967 When rock star Presley falls in love with an English heiress, he winds up involved in an attempted murder. The king belts out "Long Legged Girl" while evading cops, criminals, and crying women. A B-side. Based on a story by Marc Brandell. 92m/C VHS, Beta. Elvis Presley, Annette Day, John Williams, Yvonne Romain, Michael Murphy, Chips Rafferty; D: Norman Taurog; W: Jo Heims. MGM

Double Trouble 🎬 1991 (R) Twin brothers—one a cop, one a jewel thief—team up to crack the case of an international jewel smuggling ring headed by a wealthy and politically well-connected businessman and his righthand man. **CW:** Language and violence. 87m/C VHS, LV. David Paul, Peter Paul, James Doohan, Roddy McDowall, Steve Kanaly, A.J. Johnson, David Carradine; **D:** John Paragon. COL

Double Vision 🎬🎬 1992 (PG-13) Suspense thriller starring Cattrall as Caroline, a medical student who goes to London to check out the strange disappearance of her twin sister, Lisa. Assuming her identity, Caroline gets deeply involved in a kinky lifestyle that may result in murder. Based on a short story by Mary Higgins Clark. **CW:** Some language, some violence, and some sex-related situations. 92m/C VHS, Closed Caption. Kim Cattrall, Gale Hansen, Christopher Lee; **D:** Robert Knights. REP

Double Wedding 🎬🎬🎬 1937 Madcap comedy starring Powell as a wacky painter who doesn't believe in working and Loy as a workaholic dress designer. Loy has chosen a fiance for her younger sister, Irene, to marry, but Irene has plans of her own. When Irene and her beau meet bohemian Powell, the fun really begins. Script suffers slightly from too much slapstick and not enough wit, although the stars (in their seventh outing as a duo) play it well. Based on the play "Great Love" by Ferenc Molnar. 86m/B VHS. William Powell, Myrna Loy, Florence Rice, John Beal, Jessie Ralph, Edgar Kennedy, Sidney Toler, Mary Gordon; **D:** Richard Thorpe; **W:** Jo Swerling. MGM

Doubting Thomas 🎬🎬½ 1935 Rogers' last film, which was in theatres when he was killed in a plane crash. Silly story of a husband and his doubts about his wife and her amateur-acting career. The show goes on in spite of his doubts, her forgotten lines, and wardrobe goofs. Remake of 1922's silent film "The Torch Bearers." 78m/B VHS. Will Rogers, Billie Burke, Alison Skipworth, Sterling Holloway; **D:** David Butler. FOX, FCT

Doughboys 🎬🎬½ Forward March 1930 Keaton's second talkie is a so-so comedy about a rich man who mistakenly enlists in the Army during WWI. He manages to bumble his way through basic training and win the heart of a pretty girl. There are a few bright moments, particularly a musical number between Keaton and "Ukulele Ike" Edwards. 80m/B VHS. Buster Keaton, Cliff Edwards, Edward Brophy, Sally Eilers, Victor Potel, Arnold Korff, Frank Mayo; **D:** Edward Sedgwick. MGM

Doughnuts & Society 🎬½ 1936 Two elderly ladies who run a coffee shop suddenly strike it rich and find that life among the bluebloods is not all it's cracked up to be. No sprinkles. 70m/B VHS, Beta. Louise Fazenda, Maude Eburne, Eddie Nugent, Ann Rutherford, Hedda Hopper, Franklin Pangborn. VYY

The Dove 🎬🎬½ 1974 (PG-13) The true story of a 16-year-old's adventures as he sails around the world in a 23-foot sloop. The trip took him five years and along the way he falls in love with a girl who follows him to exotic locales. Photography and scenery are magnificent. 105m/C VHS, Beta, Closed Caption. Joseph Bottoms, Deborah Raffin, Dabney Coleman, Peter Gwynne; **D:** Charles Jarrott; **W:** Peter S. Beagle; **C:** Sven Nykvist. PAR, BMV

Down Among the Z Men 🎬🎬 1952 Enlisted man helps a girl save an atomic formula from spies. Funny in spots but weighed down by musical numbers from a female entourage. From the pre-Monty Python comedy troupe "The Goons." 71m/B VHS, Beta, LV. GB Peter Sellers, Spike Milligan, Harry Secombe, Michael Bentine, Carole Carr; **D:** Maclean Rogers. NO

Down & Dirty 🎬🎬🎬 Brutti, Sporchi, e Cattivi 1976 A scathing Italian satire about a modern Roman family steeped in petty crime, incest, murder, adultery, drugs, and arson. In Italian with English subtitles. 115m/C VHS, Beta, Closed Caption. IT Nino Manfredi, Francesco Anniballi, Maria Bosco; **D:** Ettore Sco-

la; **W:** Ettore Scola. Cannes Film Festival '76: Best Director (Scola). MED

Down and Out in Beverly Hills 🎬🎬½ 1986 (R) A modern retelling of Jean Renoir's classic "Boudu Sauve des Eaux" with some nice star turns. A spoiled wealthy couple rescue a suicidal bum from their swimming pool. He, in turn, beds the wife, the maid and the daughter, solves the dog's identity crisis, rescues the man and his son from frustration and finds he doesn't like being a bum. A box-office hit. 103m/C VHS, Beta, LV. Nick Nolte, Bette Midler, Richard Dreyfuss, Little Richard, Tracy Nelson, Elizabeth Pena, Evan Richards, Valerie Curtin, Barry Primus, Dorothy Tristan, Alexis Arquette; **D:** Paul Mazursky; **W:** Paul Mazursky, Leon Capetanos; **M:** Andy Summers. TOU

Down Argentine Way 🎬🎬🎬 1940 A lovely young woman falls in love with a suave Argentinian horse breeder. First-rate Fox musical made a star of Grable and was Miranda's first American film. 🎵South American Way; Down Argentina Way; Two Dreams Met; Mama Yo Quiero; Sing to Your Senorita. 90m/C VHS, Beta, LV, Closed Caption. Don Ameche, Betty Grable, Carmen Miranda, Charlotte Greenwood, J. Carrol Naish, Henry Stephenson, Leonid Kinskey; **D:** Irving Cummings; **C:** Leon Shamroy. Nominations: Academy Awards '40: Best Color Cinematography, Best Interior Decoration, Best Song ("Down Argentine Way"). FOX, MLB

Down by Law 🎬🎬🎬 1986 (R) In Jarmusch's follow-up to his successful "Stranger than Paradise," he introduces us to three men: a pimp, an out-of-work disc jockey, and an Italian tourist. When the three break out of prison, they wander through the Louisiana swampland with some regrets about their new-found freedom. Slow-moving at times, beautifully shot throughout. Poignant and hilarious, the film is true to Jarmusch form: some will love the film's offbeat flair, and others will find it bothersome. 107m/C VHS, Beta, Closed Caption. John Lurie, Tom Waits, Roberto Benigni, Ellen Barkin, Billie Neal, Rockets Redglare, Vernel Bagneris, Nicoletta Braschi; **D:** Jim Jarmusch; **W:** Jim Jarmusch; **M:** John Lurie, Tom Waits. FOX

Down Came a Blackbird 🎬🎬½ 1994 (R) Anna Lenka (Redgrave), a Holocaust survivor, runs a clinic for healing both the physical and psychological wounds of torture victims. Journalist Helen McNulty (Dern), herself a survivor, decides to write about the clinic but Anna believes Helen's covering up the pain she's never dealt with. Also at the clinic is Tomas Ramirez (Julia), a former college professor with a terrible secret, with whom Helen discovers a special rapport. Conventional script with some fine performances; Julia died shortly after principal photography was completed on the TV film, which is dedicated to his memory. **CW:** Depictions of torture, and some sexuality. 112m/C VHS, LV, Closed Caption. Vanessa Redgrave, Laura Dern, Raul Julia, O. Sanders, Cliff Gorman, Sarita Choudhury, L. Scott Caldwell, Jeffrey DeMunn; **D:** Jonathan Sanger; **W:** Kevin Droney; **C:** Kees Van Oostrum; **M:** Graeme Revell. REP

Down Dakota Way 🎬½ 1949 Strange coincidence between a recent murder and a fatal cow epidemic. Rogers helps some locals bring the link to light. 67m/C VHS. Roy Rogers, Dale Evans, Pat Brady, Monte Montana, Elisabeth Risdon, Byron Barr, James B. Cardwell, Roy Barcroft, Emmett Vogan; **D:** William Witney. REP

Down Mexico Way 🎬🎬 1941 Two cowboys come to the aid of a Mexican town whose residents have been hoodwinked by a phony movie company. Very exciting chase on horseback, motorcycle, and in automobiles. 78m/B VHS, Beta. Gene Autry, Smiley Burnette, Fay McKenzie, Duncan Renaldo; **D:** Joseph Santley. CCB

Down, Out and Dangerous 🎬🎬 1995 (R) Expectant couple find out the charming homeless man they've befriended is really a psycho killer. **CW:** Scenes of violence and terror. 90m/C VHS, Beta, Closed Caption. Richard Thomas, Bruce

Davison; **D:** Noel Nosseck; **W:** Carey Hayes, Chad Hayes. PAR

Down Periscope 🎬🎬½ 1996 (PG-13) Tom Dodge (Grammer) dreams of commanding a nuclear sub, but gets stuck with an out-of-mothballs, rusting WWII vintage tub with the usual goof-off crew. In order for Dodge to get his dream assignment, he and his losers must beat the nuclear subs of generic mean authority figure Admiral Graham (Dern), in a war game. Predictable comedy is kept afloat by amusing cast, especially Schneider as the weaselly Executive Officer Pascal. Many jokes revolve around Dodge's tattoo, which is on a body part that is normally private first-class. Denied cooperation from the U.S. Navy, the shipyard scenes were filmed on three barges tied together in the San Francisco Bay area, with empty discarded frigates and destroyers belonging to the U.S. Department of Transportation playing the fleet. **CW:** Some crude language. 92m/C VHS, Closed Caption. Kelsey Grammer, Lauren Holly, Bruce Dern, Rob Schneider, Rip Torn, Harry Dean Stanton, William H. Macy, Ken Campbell, Toby Huss, Duane Martin, Jonathan Penner, Bradford Tatum, Hal Williams; **D:** David S. Ward; **W:** Hugh Wilson, Andrew Kurtzman, Eliot Wald; **C:** Victor Hammer; **M:** Randy Edelman. FXV

Down Texas Way 🎬🎬 1942 One of the "Rough Riders" series. When one of the boys is accused of murdering his best friend, his two companions search for the real killer. 57m/B VHS, Beta. Buck Jones, Tim McCoy, Raymond Hatton; **D:** Howard Bretherton. NOS, VCN, TIM

Down the Drain 🎬🎬 1989 (R) A broad-as-a-city-block farce about an unscrupulous criminal lawyer and his assortment of crazy clients. A fine first half but someone pulls the plug in the middle of the bath. 90m/C VHS, Beta, LV. Andrew Stevens, John Matuszak, Teri Copley, Joseph Campanella, Don Stroud, Stella Stevens, Jerry Mathers, Benny "The Jet" Urquidez; **D:** Robert C. Hughes. COL

Down the Wyoming Trail 🎬 1939 Western hero Ritter battles some rustlers who are terrorizing farmers during the winter, while still managing to find time to warble some tunes. 52m/B VHS. Tex Ritter, Horace Murphy, Mary Brodel, Bobby Lawson, Charles "Blackie" King, Bob Terry; **D:** Al(bert) Herman; **W:** Peter Dixon, Roger Merton. MOV

Down to Earth 🎬🎬🎬 1917 Ever-gallant lover Fairbanks overruns a mental hospital to save his sweetheart. Once inside, he's determined to show the patients that their illness is illusion, and reality's the cure. A quixotic gem from Fairbanks' pre-swashbuckling social comic days. Director Emerson's wife was the scenarist, and Victor Fleming, who went on to direct "The Wizard of Oz" and "Gone with the Wind" (to name a few), was the man behind the camera. 68m/B VHS, Beta. Douglas Fairbanks Sr., Eileen Percy, Gustav von Seyffertitz, Charles P. McHugh, Charles Gerrard, William H. Keith, Ruth Allen, Fred Goodwine; **D:** John Emerson. GPV, FCT

Down to Earth 🎬🎬 1947 A lackluster musical and box office flop with an impressive cast. Hayworth is the Greek goddess of dance sent to Earth on a mission to straighten out Broadway producer Parks and his play that ridicules the Greek gods. Anita Ellis dubs the singing of Hayworth. A parody of "Here Comes Mr. Jordan," remade in 1980 as "Xanadu." 101m/C VHS, LV. Rita Hayworth, Larry Parks, Marc Platt, Roland Culver, James Gleason, Edward Everett Horton, Adele Jergens, George Macready, William Frawley, James Burke, Fred F. Sears, Lynn Merrick, Myron Healey; **D:** Alexander Hall; **W:** Edwin Blum; **M:** George Duning. COL, COB

Down to the Sea in Ships 🎬🎬½ The Last Adventurers 1922 Bow made her movie debut in this drama about the whalers of the 19th-century Massachusetts. Highlighted by exciting action scenes of an actual whale hunt. Silent with music score and original tinted footage. 83m/B VHS, Beta. Marguerite Courtot, Raymond McKee, Clara Bow; **D:** Elmer Clifton. NOS, CCB, GPV

Down Twisted 🎬 1989 (R) A young woman gets involved with a thief on the run in Mexico in this "Romancing the Stone" derivative. The muddled plot deserves such a confusing title. 89m/C VHS, Beta, Closed Caption. Carey Lowell, Charles Rocket, Trudi Dochtermann, Thom Mathews, Linda Kerridge, Courteney Cox; **D:** Albert Pyun; **W:** Albert Pyun; **C:** Walt Lloyd; **M:** Eric Allaman. MED

Down Under 🎬 1986 Two gold-hungry beach boys go to Australia looking for riches, and document their adventures on film. Essentially a crudely shot, tongue-in-cheek travelogue narrated by Patrick Macnee. 90m/C VHS, Beta. Don Atkinson, Donn Dunlop, Patrick Macnee. NO

Downdraft 🎬🎬 1996 (R) A special forces unit has six hours to penetrate a subterranean bunker, which protects a supercomputer that's about to launch a nuclear attack. Assaulted by a variety of sophisticated weapons, the unit must also outwit the computer's android defender. **CW:** Violence, adult language. 101m/C VHS, Closed Caption. Vincent Spano, Kate Vernon, Paul Koslo. REP

Downhill Racer 🎬🎬½ 1969 (PG) An undisciplined American skier locks ski-tips with his coach and his new-found love while on his way to becoming an Olympic superstar. Character study on film. Beautiful ski and mountain photography keep it from sliding downhill. 102m/C VHS, Beta, LV. Robert Redford, Camilla Sparv, Gene Hackman, Dabney Coleman; **D:** Michael Ritchie. PAR

Downhill Willie 🎬½ 1996 (PG) Willie (Coogan) isn't the brightest guy around—except on skies. Now he wants to enter the Kamikaze Run, which takes place on an extreme race course, and win the half-million top prize as well as the prettiest snow bunny (Keanan) on the slopes. 90m/C VHS. Keith Coogan, Staci Keanan, Lochlan Munroe, Estelle Harris, Fred Stoller, Lee Reherman; **D:** David Mitchell; **W:** Stephanie Cedar; **C:** David Pelletier; **M:** Norman Orenstein. BMG

Downtown 🎬½ 1989 (R) Urban comedy about a naive white suburban cop who gets demoted to the roughest precinct in Philadelphia, and gains a streetwise black partner. Runs a routine beat. 96m/C VHS, Beta, LV, Closed Caption. Anthony Edwards, Forest Whitaker, Joe Pantoliano, Penelope Ann Miller; **D:** Richard Benjamin; **M:** Alan Silvestri. FOX

D.P. 1985 A black orphan attaches to the only other black in post-WWII Germany. From a story by Kurt Vonnegut, Jr. Made for television. 60m/C VHS. Stan Shaw, Rosemary Leach, Julius Gordon. MON, KAR

Drachenfutter 🎬🎬🎬 *Dragon's Food; Dragon Chow* 1987 Powerful story dealing with a Pakistani immigrant's attempts to enter the Western world. Themes of alienation and helplessness are emphasized. Dialogues occur in 12 languages, predominantly German and Mandarin Chinese; subtitled in English. 75m/B VHS, Beta. GE SI Bhasker, Ric Young, Buddy Uzzaman; **D:** Jan Schütte; **W:** Thomas Strittmatter; **M:** Claus Bantzer. NYF

Dracula 🎬🎬🎬 1931 Lugosi, in his most famous role, plays a vampire who terrorizes the countryside in his search for human blood. From Bram Stoker's novel. Although short of a masterpiece due to slow second half, deservedly rated a film classic. What would Halloween be like without this movie? Sequelled by "Dracula's Daughter." 75m/B VHS, Beta, LV. Bela Lugosi, David Manners, Dwight Frye, Helen Chandler, Edward Van Sloan; **D:** Tod Browning; **C:** Karl Freund. USH, TLF, HMV

Dracula 🎬🎬½ 1973 Count on squinty-eyed Palance to shine as the Transylvanian vampire who must quench his thirst for human blood. A made-for-television adaptation of the Bram Stoker novel that really flies. 105m/C VHS, Beta, LV. Jack Palance, Simon Ward, Fiona Lewis, Nigel Davenport; **D:** Dan Curtis. LIV

Dracula 🎬🎬½ 1979 (R) Langella recreates his Broadway role as the count who needs human blood for nourishment. Notable for its portrayal of Dracula as a romantic and tragic figure in history.

Overlooked since the vampire spoof "Love at First Bite" came out at the same time. 109m/C VHS, Beta, LV. Frank Langella, Laurence Olivier, Kate Nelligan, Donald Pleasence; **D:** John Badham; **W:** W.D. Richter; **M:** John Williams. USH

Dracula & Son 🎬 *Dracula Pere et Fils* 1976 (PG) Dracula spoof in which the count fathers a son who prefers girls and football to blood. Poor English dubbing and choppy ending drive a stake through the heart. 88m/C VHS, Beta. FR Christopher Lee, Bernard Menez, Marie Breillat; **D:** Edouard Molinaro; **M:** Vladimir Cosma. GKK

Dracula Blows His Cool 🎬 1982 (R) Three voluptuous models and their photographer restore an ancient castle and open a disco in it. The vampire lurking about the castle welcomes the party with his fangs. 91m/C VHS, Beta, LV, Closed Caption. John Garco, Betty Verges; **D:** Carlo Ombra; **W:** Carlo Ombra. MED

Dracula: Dead and Loving It woof! 1995 (PG-13) King of the spoofs Nielsen takes on the title role as the ever-loving, if clumsy, Count who still enjoys necking—particularly with luscious damsels in distress, Lucy (Anthony) and Mina (Yasbeck). And he's still got his bug-eating minion Renfield (MacNichol) and egomaniacal vampire-hunter Van Helsing (Brooks) around. As usual, Brooks throws everything possible on the screen, hoping some schtick will stick (not very much does). **CW:** Comedic sensuality and gore. 90m/C VHS, LV, Closed Caption. Leslie Nielsen, Mel Brooks, Peter MacNicol, Lysette Anthony, Amy Yasbeck, Steven Weber, Harvey Korman, Anne Bancroft; **D:** Mel Brooks; **W:** Mel Brooks, Rudy DeLuca, Steve Haberman; **C:** Michael D. O'Shea; **M:** Hummie Mann. COL

Dracula/Garden of Eden 🎬🎬 1928 The abridged version of the chilling vampire film "Nosferatu" is coupled with "The Garden of Eden," in which Tini Le Brun meets her Prince Charming while vacationing with her Baroness friend. Silent. 52m/B VHS, Beta. Max Schreck, Alexander Granach, Corine Griffith, Charles Ray, Louise Dresser. CCB

Dracula Has Risen from the Grave 🎬🎬½ 1968 (G) Lee's Dracula is foiled by the local priest before he can drain the blood from innocent villagers. Effectively gory. One of the Hammer series of Dracula films followed by "Taste the Blood of Dracula." 92m/C VHS, Beta. GB Christopher Lee, Rupert Davies, Veronica Carlson, Barbara Ewing, Barry Andrews, Michael Ripper; **D:** Freddie Francis; **M:** James Bernard. WAR

Dracula, Prince of Darkness 🎬🎬 1966 Sequel to 1958's "Horror of Dracula" finds the Count (Lee) extending his hospitality at Castle Dracula to four unwary tourists, one of whom is immediately killed for his blood. Then Dracula takes the dead man's wife (Shelley) and turns her into a vampire and the gruesome twosome go after the remaining couple. Standard Hammer horror. 90m/C VHS. GB Christopher Lee, Barbara Shelley, Andrew Keir, Francis Matthews, Suzan Farmer, Charles Tingwell, Thorley Walters; **D:** Terence Fisher; **W:** John Sansom; **C:** Michael Reed; **M:** James Bernard. VTR

Dracula Rising 🎬🎬½ 1993 (R) A modern-day art historian (Travis) turns out to have been a witch, burned at the stake, in a past life. She was also the blood-drinking Count's lost love. Now Dracula's a monk and when he sees this reincarnated beauty is he going to be able to keep his hands—er, fangs—off her? **CW:** Vampire violence and sexuality. ?m/C VHS. Christopher Atkins, Stacy Travis; **D:** Fred Gallo. UAV

Dracula (Spanish Version) 🎬🎬½ 1931 Filmed at the same time as the Bela Lugosi version of "Dracula," using the same sets and the same scripts, only in Spanish. Thought to be more visually appealing and more terrifying than the English-language counterpart. The only thing it's missing is a presence like Lugosi. Based on the novel by Bram Stoker. 104m/B VHS. Carlos Villarias, Lupita Tovar, Eduardo Arozamena, Pablo Alvarez Ru-

bio, Barry Norton, Carmen Guerrero; **D:** George Melford; **W:** Garrett Fort. USH

Dracula Sucks 🎬 1979 (R) A soft-core edit of a hardcore sex parody about Dracula snacking on the usual bevy of screaming quasi-virgins. 90m/C VHS, Beta. James Gillis, Reggie Nalder, Annette Haven, Kay Parker, Serena, Seka, John Leslie; **D:** Philip Marshak. UNI, OM

Dracula: Up in Harlem woof! 1983 When the Prince of Darkness gets together with the people of the night, the Pentagon rolls out the heavy metal. This may suck your brain out. 90m/C VHS, Beta. NO

Dracula vs. Frankenstein 🎬 1969 An alien reanimates Earth's most infamous monsters in a bid to take over the planet. Rennie's last role. Also on video as, "Assignment: Terror." 91m/C VHS. IT GE SP Michael Rennie, Paul Naschy, Karin Dor, Patty Shepard; **D:** Hugo Fregonese, Tulio Demicheli; **W:** Paul Naschy. UAV

Dracula vs. Frankenstein woof! *Blood of Frankenstein; They're Coming to Get You; Dracula Contra Frankenstein; The Revenge of Dracula; Satan's Bloody Freaks* 1971 (R) The Count makes a deal with a shady doctor to keep him in blood. Vampire spoof that's very bad but fun. Last film for both Chaney and Naish. Features a cameo by genre maven Forrest J. Ackerman. 90m/C VHS. SP J. Carrol Naish, Lon Chaney Jr., Regina Carrol, Russ Tamblyn, Jim Davis, Anthony Eisley, Zandor Vorkov, John Bloom, Angelo Rossitto; **Cameos:** Forrest J. Ackerman; **D:** Al Adamson. NO

Dracula's Daughter 🎬🎬🎬 1936 Count Dracula's daughter, Countess Marya Zaleska, heads to London supposedly to find the cure to a mysterious illness. Instead she finds she has a taste for human blood, especially female blood. She also finds a man, falls in love, and tries to keep him by casting a spell on him. A good script and cast keep this sequel to Bela Lugosi's "Dracula" entertaining. 71m/B VHS, Closed Caption. Gloria Holden, Otto Kruger, Marguerite Churchill, Irving Pichel, Edward Van Sloan, Nan Grey, Hedda Hopper; **D:** Lambert Hillyer. USH

Dracula's Great Love woof! *Gran Amore del Conde Dracula; Count Dracula's Great Love; Dracula's Virgin Lovers* 1972 (R) Four travellers end up in Dracula's castle for the night, where the horny Count takes a liking to one of the women. Left out in the sun too long. 96m/C VHS, Beta. SP Paul Naschy, Charo Soriano; **D:** Javier Aguirre. SNC, MPI

Dracula's Last Rites woof! *Last Rites* 1979 (R) Blood-curdling tale of a sheriff and a mortician in a small town who are up to no good. Technically inept: film equipment can be spotted throughout. Don't stick your neck out for this one. 86m/C VHS, Beta. Patricia Lee Hammond, Gerald Fielding, Victor Jorge; **D:** Domonic Paris. MGM, CAN, FCT

Dracula's Widow 🎬🎬 1988 (R) Countess Dracula, missing her hubby and desperately in need of a substitute, picks innocent Raymond as her victim. His girlfriend and a cynical cop fight to save his soul from the Countess' damnation. Directed by the nephew of Frances Ford Coppola. 85m/C VHS, Beta, Closed Caption. Sylvia Kristel, Josef Sommer, Lenny Von Dohlen, George Stover; **D:** Christopher Coppola. HBO

Dragnet 🎬🎬½ 1954 Sgt. Joe Friday and Officer Frank Smith try to solve a mob slaying but have a rough time. Alexander plays the sidekick in "Dragnet" pre-Morgan days. Just the facts: feature version of the TV show that's suspenseful and well-acted. 88m/C VHS, Beta. Jack Webb, Ben Alexander, Richard Boone, Ann Robinson; **D:** Jack Webb. USH

Dragnet 🎬🎬½ 195? Detectives Joe Friday and Frank Smith make the streets of Los Angeles safe in this police series which ran from 1951-1959. Two episodes per tape. 55m/C VHS. Jack Webb, Ben Alexander. MOV, MRV

Dragnet 🦴🦴 1987 (PG-13) Semi-parody of the vintage '60s television cop show. Sgt. Joe Friday's straight-laced nephew and his sloppy partner take on the seamy crime life of Los Angeles. Neither Aykroyd nor Hanks can save this big-budget but lackluster spoof that's full of holes. 106m/C **VHS, Beta, LV, Closed Caption.** Dan Aykroyd, Tom Hanks, Christopher Plummer, Harry (Henry) Morgan, Elizabeth Ashley, Dabney Coleman; **D:** Tom Mankiewicz; **W:** Dan Aykroyd, Tom Mankiewicz, Alan Zweibel; **M:** Ira Newborn. USH

Dragon Force 🦴½ 1982 Korean martial artists fend off Japanese invaders in the 1930s. 101m/C VHS, Beta. Kanjoe Lee; **D:** Key-Nam Nam. CNG

Dragon Fury 🦴½ 1995 Evil dictator tries to conquer what remains of America in the year 2099—a world peopled by barbarians and victims of a deadly plague. Naturally, there's a martial arts hero around to stop him. 80m/C VHS. Robert Chapin, Richard Lynch, Chona Jason, Deborah Stamble; **D:** David Heavener. MNC

Dragon Fury 2 🦴½ 1996 Futuristic action finds a heroic female struggling alone against a violent gang who want to rule the world (with the help of a computer chip). But a scientist unthaws an ancient warrior to help her out. Of course, things don't go exactly as expected. 90m/C VHS. Mike Norris, Robert Chapin, Cathleen Ann Gardner, Cole Andersen, Walter O'Neill, Kayla Murphy; **D:** Bryan Michael Stoller; **W:** Parker Bostwick. SLI

Dragon Lord 🦴 1982 Young kung-fu hero (Chan) defends his village against greedy outlaws. Comic interludes tend to slow the action. 90m/C VHS. Jackie Chan. TAI

Dragon Princess 🦴 197? When the king of karate and his dragon princess confront the blind master of the bloody blades, sparks fly. 90m/C VHS, Beta. Sonny Chiba, Sue Shiomi. NO

Dragon Seed 🦴🦴 1944 The lives of the residents of a small Chinese village are turned upside down when the Japanese invade it. Based on the Pearl S. Buck novel. Lengthy and occasionally tedious, though generally well-made with heart-felt attempts to create Oriental characters, without having Asians in the cast. 145m/B VHS, Beta. Katharine Hepburn, Walter Huston, Agnes Moorehead, Akim Tamiroff, Hurd Hatfield, J. Carrol Naish, Henry Travers, Turhan Bey, Aline MacMahon; **D:** Jack Conway. Nominations: Academy Awards '44: Best Black and White Cinematography, Best Supporting Actress (MacMahon). MGM, FCT

Dragon: The Bruce Lee Story 🦴🦴🦴 1993 (PG-13) Entertaining, inspiring account of the life of Chinese-American martial-arts legend Bruce Lee. Jason Scott Lee (no relation) is great as the talented artist, exuding his joy of life and gentle spirit, before his mysterious brain disorder death at the age of 32. Ironically, this release coincided with son Brandon's accidental death on a movie set. The martial arts sequences in "Dragon" are extraordinary, but there's also romance as Lee meets and marries his wife (Holly, who acquits herself well). Based on the book "Bruce Lee: The Man Only I Knew" by his widow, Linda Lee Caldwell. **CW:** Martial arts violence and sensuality. 121m/C VHS, LV, Closed Caption. Jason Scott Lee, Lauren Holly, Robert Wagner, Michael Learned, Nancy Kwan, Kay Tong Lim, Sterling Macer, Ric Young, Sven Ole-Thorsen; **D:** Rob Cohen; **W:** Edward Khmara, John Raffo, Rob Cohen; **C:** David Eggby; **M:** Randy Edelman. Nominations: MTV Movie Awards '94: Breakthrough Performance (Lee). USH, BTV, FCT

Dragon vs. Needles of Death 🦴 1982 It's a battle to the finish against the unstoppable deadly needles in this Kung-Fu adventure. 86m/C VHS, Beta. Don Chien, Wong Ting. FOX

Dragonard 🦴½ 1988 (R) Slaves on a West Indies island rebel against their cruel masters. 93m/C VHS, Beta, Closed Caption. Eartha Kitt, Oliver Reed, Annabel Schofield, Patrick Warburton; **D:** Gerard Kikoine; **W:** R.J. Marx. WAR

Dragonfight 🦴½ 1992 (R) Corporations rule the world and vie for supremacy through gladiator combat in this action-adventure saga set in the near future. Fights are to the death and when the current champ refuses a new challenger the corporate honchos decide to provoke him into battle by having the challenger mow down innocent bystanders. Several execs also decide the slaughter has to stop but they may be the next targets. **CW:** Violence. 84m/C VHS, Beta. Robert Z'Dar, Michael Pare, Paul Coufos, Charles Napier, James Hong, Alexa Hamilton, Fawna MacLaren. WAR

Dragonfly Squadron 🦴🦴 1954 Korean war drama about pilots and their romantic problems. Never gets off the ground. 82m/C VHS. John Hodiak, Barbara Britton, Bruce (Herman Brix) Bennett, Jess Barker; **D:** Lesley Selander. NO

Dragonheart 🦴🦴🦴 1996 (PG-13) Okay, get past the fact that Connery's Scottish burr is coming out of the teeth-filled mouth of an 18 ft. tall, 43 ft. long dragon and you'll be well on your way to enjoying this 10th-century fantasy. Knightly Bowen (Quaid) is the one-time mentor of evil-hearted King Einon (Thewlis) and it's up to him, Draco the dragon, feisty Kara (Meyer), and some fearful peasants to band together and free themselves from the king's tyranny. There's some slow spots but Bowen and Draco make for an amusing pairing and the dragon does seem, well, real. Work on Draco took more than a year of Industrial Light & Magic's expertise. **CW:** Action/violence. 103m/C VHS, LV, Closed Caption. Dennis Quaid, David Thewlis, Pete Postlethwaite, Dina Meyer, Julie Christie, Jason Isaacs, Brian Thompson, Wolf Christian, Terry O'Neill; **D:** Rob Cohen; **W:** Charles Edward Pogue; **C:** David Eggby; **M:** Randy Edelman; **V:** Sean Connery, John Gielgud. Nominations: Academy Awards '96: Best Visual Effects. USH

Dragon's Claw 🦴 198? A young man's parents are murdered, and he trains in shaolin skills in order to exact revenge. 90m/C VHS, Beta. Jimmy Liu, Hwang Cheng Li; **D:** Joseph Kuo. GEM

Dragons Forever 🦴½ 1988 A big time lawyer is persuaded to work against a chemical plant who wants to take over a site used by local fisherman. Complications arise when he falls for the beautiful cousin of the fishery's owner. A comic king-fu battle between Chan, Hung, and Biao is the rousing finale. In Cantonese with English subtitles. 88m/C VHS. **CH** Jackie Chan, Yuen Biao, Samo Hung; **D:** Samo Hung. TAI, FCT

The Dragon's Showdown 🦴 1983 After witnessing the brutal decapitations of his parents, a young man learns Kung-Fu to avenge their deaths. 90m/C VHS, Beta. Dragon Lee; **D:** Godfrey Ho. GEM

Dragonslayer 🦴🦴🦴 1981 (PG) A sorcerer's apprentice suddenly finds himself the only person who can save the kingdom from a horrible, fire-breathing dragon. Extreme violence but wonderful special effects, smart writing, and a funny performance by Richardson. 110m/C VHS, Beta, LV. Peter MacNicol, Caitlin Clarke, Ralph Richardson, John Hallam, Albert Salmi, Chloe Salaman; **D:** Matthew Robbins; **W:** Matthew Robbins, Hal Barwood; **M:** Alex North. Nominations: Academy Awards '81: Best Original Score. PAR, COL

Dragonworld 🦴🦴½ 1994 (PG) Five-year-old Johnny McGowan is sent to Scotland to live with his grandfather. A wish for a friend has Johnny mysteriously awakening a baby dragon he names Yowler. Years later, the financially strapped adult Johnny agrees to loan Yowler to an amusement park only to find out the park's owner never intends to give Yowler back. Both baby dragon and young Johnny are unbearably cute. 86m/C VHS, Beta, Closed Caption. Sam Mackenzie, Courtland Mead, Brittney Powell, John Calvin, Andrew Keir, Lila Kaye, John Woodvine; **D:** Ted Nicolaou; **W:** Ted Nicolaou, Suzanne Glazener Naha; **M:** Richard Band. PAR

Dragstrip Girl 🦴🦴 1957 An 18-year-old girl comes of age while burning rubber at the dragstrip—the world of boys, hot rods, and horsepower. A definite "B" movie that may seem dated. 70m/B VHS. Fay Spain, Steven Terrell, John Ashley, Frank Gorshin; **D:** Edward L. Cahn. COL

The Drake Case 🦴 1929 A slight courtroom drama made during the waning days of the silent era. You'll probably recognize Brit Lloyd from her later career. 56m/B VHS, Beta. Robert Frazer, Doris Lloyd, Gladys Brockwell. GPV, FCT

The Draughtsman's Contract 🦴🦴🦴 1982 (R) A beguiling mystery begins when a wealthy woman hires an artist to make drawings of her home. Their contract is quite unusual, as is their relationship. Everything is going along at an even pace until murder is suspected, and things spiral down to darker levels. A simple story turned into a bizarre puzzle. Intense enough for any thriller fan. 103m/C VHS. GB Anthony Higgins, Janet Suzman, Anne Louise Lambert, Hugh Fraser; **D:** Peter Greenaway; **W:** Peter Greenaway; **C:** Sacha Vierny; **M:** Michael Nyman. MGM, FCT

Draw! 🦴🦴 1981 Two has-been outlaws warm up their pistols again in this old-fashioned Western. Star power and some smart moments make it worthwhile. Made for TV. 98m/C VHS, Beta. Kirk Douglas, James Coburn, Alexandra Bastedo, Graham Jarvis; **D:** Steven Hilliard Stern. med

Dreadnaught Rivals 🦴 198? A student is taught by his drunken servant how to avenge himself on the culprits who kidnapped his girlfriend. Dubbed. 90m/C VHS, Beta. Sinon Lin, Kent Ko, Louisa Monk. MOV

Dream a Little Dream 🦴🦴 1989 (PG-13) Strange teen transformation drama about an old man and his wife trying mystically to regain their youth. When they collide bikes with the teenagers down the street, their minds are exchanged and the older couple with the now young minds are transported to a permanent dream-like state. Same old switcheroo made bearable by cast. 114m/C VHS, Beta, LV, Closed Caption. Corey Feldman, Corey Haim, Meredith Salenger, Jason Robards Jr., Piper Laurie, Harry Dean Stanton, Victoria Jackson, Alex Rocco, Billy McNamara; **D:** Marc Rocco; **W:** Marc Rocco. LIV, VES, HHE

Dream a Little Dream 2 🦴½ 1994 (PG-13) Friends Dinger Holefield (Haim) and Bobby Keller (Feldman) receive a mysterious package containing two pairs of sunglasses, which they discover have magic powers. The wearer of one pair is driven to do the bidding of the wearer of the second pair of specs—whether for good or evil. Naturally, there are evildoers who want the glasses as well. 91m/C VHS, Closed Caption. Corey Haim, Corey Feldman, Stacie Randall, Michael Nicolosi; **D:** James Lemmo; **W:** David Weissman, Susan Forman. COL

Dream Chasers 🦴 1984 (PG) A bankrupt old codger and an 11-year-old boy stricken with cancer run away together during the Great Depression. 97m/C VHS, Beta, Closed Caption. Harold Gould, Justin Dana. FOX

Dream Date 🦴🦴½ 1993 (PG-13) Lovely teenager is wooed by hip, playful suitor until trouble ensues when goofball sidekick enters the picture. Family entertainment. **CW:** Elements of sensuality. 96m/C VHS. Tempestt Bledsoe, Clifton Davis, Kadeem Hardison, Anne-Marie Johnson, Pauly Shore, Richard Moll; **D:** Anson Williams. TRI, PMS

Dream Demon 🦴 1988 The appearance of Wilhoite, a visiting American, disrupts the status quo at a spooky British manor where the charming Redgrave debates her impending marriage to wealthy rogue Greenstreet. Aside from a terrific opening dream sequence, most of the scary bits have been done before. 89m/C VHS. GB Jemma Redgrave, Kathleen Wilhoite, Timothy Spall, Jimmy Nail, Mark Greenstreet; **D:** Harley Cokliss. WAR

A Dream for Christmas 🦴🦴🦴 1973 Earl Hamner, Jr. (best known for writing the "The Waltons") wrote this moving story of a black minister whose church in Los Angeles is scheduled to be demolished. Made for television. 100m/C VHS. Hari Rhodes, Beah Richards, George Spell, Juanita Moore,

Joel Fluellen, Robert DoQui, Clarence Muse; **D:** Ralph Senensky. *LIV, WAR*

Dream Lover 🏆🏆 **1985 (R)** Terrifying nightmares after an assault lead McNichol to dream therapy. Treatment causes her tortured unconscious desires to take over her waking behavior, and she becomes a violent schizophrenic. Slow, heavy, and not very thrilling. **105m/C VHS, Beta.** Kristy McNichol, Ben Masters, Paul Shenar, Justin Deas, Joseph Culp, Gayle Hunnicutt, John McMartin; **D:** Alan J. Pakula; **W:** Jon Boorstin; **C:** Sven Nykvist. *MGM*

Dream Lover 🏆🏆 **1993 (R)** Divorced architect Ray (Spader) meets and marries Lena (Amick), beautiful and seemingly perfect, who nonetheless warns him that she's just your average mixed-up gal. Suspense is supposed to come into play as Ray suspects Lena's been lying to him about her past. Visually appealing (considerably helped by the attractive leads) but good looks don't make up for the lack of substance and the minimal number of surprises expected in a thriller. Directorial debut of Kazan. Also available in an unrated version. **103m/C VHS, LV.** James Spader, Madchen Amick, Frederic Lehne, Bess Armstrong, Larry Miller, Kathleen York, Blair Tefkin, Scott Coffey, William Shockley, Clyde Kusatsu; **D:** Nicholas Kazan; **W:** Nicholas Kazan; **M:** Christopher Young. *PGV*

Dream Machine 🏆½ **1991 (PG)** A childish teen comedy, based on that old urban legend of the lucky kid given a free Porshe by the vengeful wife of a wealthy philanderer. The gimmick is that the husband's body is in the trunk; the murderer is in pursuit. The tape includes an anti-drug commerical—but nothing against reckless driving, which the picture glorifies. **88m/C VHS, LV.** Corey Haim, Evan Richards, Jeremy Slate, Randall England, Tracy Fraim, Brittney Lewis, Susan Seaforth Hayes; **D:** Lyman Dayton. *LIV*

Dream Man 🏆🏆½ **1994 (R)** Kris Anderson (Kensit) is a Seattle cop with the clairvoyant ability to see crimes as they're committed. But that doesn't stop her from getting involved with the handsome murder suspect (McCarthy) she's supposed to be investigating.**CW:** Violence, sexuality, language. **94m/C VHS, LV, Closed Caption.** Patsy Kensit, Andrew McCarthy, Bruce Greenwood; **D:** Rene Bonniere; **W:** Michael Alexander Miller; **M:** Graeme Coleman. *REP*

Dream No Evil 🏆½ **1975** A mentally disturbed woman is forced to commit bizarre murders to protect her warped fantasy world. **93m/C VHS, Beta.** Edmond O'Brien, Brooke Mills, Marc Lawrence, Arthur Franz; **D:** John Hayes. *AHV*

A Dream of Kings 🏆🏆🏆 **1969 (R)** Quinn is exceptional in this Petrakis story of an immigrant working to get his dying son home to Greece. Last film appearance for Stevens before committing suicide at age 36. **107m/C VHS.** Anthony Quinn, Irene Papas, Inger Stevens, Sam Levene, Val Avery; **D:** Daniel Mann; **M:** Alex North. *WAR*

A Dream of Passion 🏆½ **1978 (R)** A woman imprisoned in Greece for murdering her children becomes the object of a publicity stunt for a production of "Medea," and she and the lead actress begin to exchange personalities. Artificial gobbledygook. **105m/C VHS, Beta.** *GR SI* Ellen Burstyn, Melina Mercouri, Andreas Voutsinas; **D:** Jules Dassin; **W:** Jules Dassin. *NLC*

Dream Street 🏆🏆 **1921** A weak morality tale of London's lower classes. Two brothers, both in love with the same dancing girl, woo her in their own way, while a Chinese gambler plans to take her by force. Silent with music score. Based on Thomas Burke's "Limehouse Nights." **138m/B VHS, Beta.** Tyrone Power Sr., Carol Dempster, Ralph Graves, Charles Mack; **D:** D.W. Griffith. *VYY*

The Dream Team 🏆🏆½ **1989 (PG-13)** On their way to a ball game, four patients from a mental hospital find themselves lost in New York City after their doctor is knocked out by murderers. Some fine moments from a cast of dependable comics. Watch for numerous nods to "One

Flew Over the Cuckoo's Nest," another Lloyd feature. Keaton fans won't want to miss this one. **113m/C VHS, Beta, LV, Closed Caption.** Michael Keaton, Christopher Lloyd, Peter Boyle, Stephen Furst, Lorraine Bracco, Milo O'Shea, Dennis Boutsikaris, Philip Bosco, James Remar, Cynthia Belliveau; **D:** Howard Zieff; **W:** Jon Connolly, David Loucka; **M:** David McHugh. *USH*

Dream to Believe 🏆🏆 **1985** Slice of the life of your typical high school coed—mom's dying, stepdad's from hell, sports injury hurts, and, oh yeah, championship gymnastic competitions loom. Designed to make you feel oh-so-good in that MTV kind of way. Reeves is most excellent as the girl's blushing beau. **96m/C VHS, Beta.** Rita Tushingham, Keanu Reeves, Olivia D'Abo; **D:** Paul Lynch. *HHE*

Dream Trap 🏆½ **1990** A young man is obsessed with a girl in his dreams. When he meets a girl who really exists, fantasy louses up every opportunity for the real thing. **90m/C VHS.** Kristy Swanson, Sasha Jensen, Jeanie Moore; **D:** Tom Logan, Hugh Parks; **W:** Tom Logan. *NO*

Dreamchild 🏆🏆🏆 **1985 (PG)** A poignant story of the autumn years of Alice Hargreaves, the model for Lewis Carroll's "Alice in Wonderland." Film follows her on a visit to New York in the 1930s, with fantasy sequences including Wonderland characters created by Jim Henson's Creature Shop invoking the obsessive Reverend Dodgson (a.k.a. Carroll). **94m/C VHS, Beta.** *GB* Coral Browne, Ian Holm, Peter Gallagher, Jane Asher, Nicola Cowper, Amelia Shankley, Caris Corfman, Shane Rimmer, James Wilby; **D:** Gavin Millar; **W:** Dennis Potter; **C:** Billy Williams; **M:** Max Harris, Stanley Myers. *MGM*

Dreamer 🏆🏆 **1979 (PG)** The excitement of bowling is exploited for all it's worth in this "strike or die" extravaganza. One of a kind. **86m/C VHS.** Tim Matheson, Susan Blakely, Jack Warden, Richard B. Shull; **D:** Noel Nosseck; **W:** Larry J. Bischof; **M:** Bill Conti. *FOX*

Dreaming Lips 🏆🏆½ **1937** An orchestra conductor's wife falls in love with her husband's violinist friend. Tragedy befalls the couple. Bergner outstanding in a familiar script. **70m/B VHS, Beta.** *GB* Raymond Massey, Elisabeth Bergner, Romney Brent, Joyce Bland, Charles Carson, Felix Aylmer; **D:** Paul Czinner, Lee Garmes; **C:** Lee Garmes. *VYY, CCB*

Dreaming of Rita 🏆🏆 **1994** Bob (Oscarsson) named his daughter Rita after long-lost love Sabine's resemblance to Hollywood goddess, Rita Hayworth. Now an elderly widower, Bob suddenly decides to try and find Sabine, taking off across the Swedish countryside. The unhappily married Rita (Lagercrantz), leaving husband and children behind, goes after him—and meets sympathetic hitchhiker Erik (Ersgard), who's happy to offer a little romance. Swedish with subtitles. **108m/C VHS.** *SW* Per Oscarsson, Marika Lagercrantz, Patrick Ersgard, Philip Zanden; **D:** Jon Lindstrom; **W:** Jon Lindstrom, Rita Holst; **C:** Kjell Lagerros. *FCT, FRF*

Dreaming Out Loud 🏆🏆 **1940** Screen debut of popular radio team Lum 'n Abner. The boys get involved in several capers to bring progress to their small Arkansas town. Rural wisecracks make for pleasant outing. First in film series for the duo. **65m/B VHS, Beta.** Frances Langford, Phil Harris, Clara Blandick, Robert Wilcox, Chester Lauck, Norris Goff, Frank Craven, Bobs Watson, Irving Bacon; **D:** Harold Young. *NOS, DVT, VYY*

Dreams 🏆🏆 *Kvinn odrom; Journey into Autumn* **1955** Unfocused film about the lives and loves of two successful women. Subtitled. **86m/B VHS, Beta, LV.** *SW* Harriet Andersson, Gunnar Bjornstrand, Eva Dahlbeck, Ulf Palme; **D:** Ingmar Bergman; **W:** Ingmar Bergman. *HMV, NLC*

Dreams Come True 🏆 **1984 (R)** Silly young comedy-romance about two young lovers who discover the trick of out-of-body travel, and have various forms of spiritual contact while their bodies are sleeping. **95m/C VHS, Beta.** Michael Sanville, Stephanie Shuford; **D:** Max Kalmanowicz. *MED*

Dreams Lost, Dreams Found 🏆½ **1987** A young widow journeys from the U.S. to Scotland in search of her heritage. The third "Harlequin Romance Movie," made for cable television. **102m/C VHS.** Kathleen Quinlan, Betsy Brantley, Charles Gray; **D:** Willi Patterson. *PAR*

Dreamscape 🏆🏆½ **1984 (PG-13)** When a doctor teaches a young psychic how to enter into other people's dreams in order to end their nightmares, somebody else wants to use this psychic for evil purposes. The special effects are far more convincing than the one man-saves-the-country-with-his-psychic-powers plot. **99m/C VHS, Beta, LV.** Dennis Quaid, Max von Sydow, Christopher Plummer, Eddie Albert, Kate Capshaw, David Patrick Kelly, George Wendt, Jana Taylor; **D:** Joseph Ruben; **W:** Chuck Russell; **C:** Brian Tufano; **M:** Maurice Jarre. *IME*

Dress Gray 🏆🏆🏆 **1986** Fine, exciting adaptation of the Lucian K. Truscott IV novel about a coverup at an Eastern military academy. Baldwin is cadet Slaight, an upperclassman who finds more secrets than he can handle when a younger cadet (Cassidy), with whom he had an adversarial relationship, is murdered. He's torn between investigating the death or keeping quiet—for the sake of his career if not his life. Originally a television miniseries. **192m/C VHS, Beta.** Alec Baldwin, Hal Holbrook, Eddie Albert, Lloyd Bridges, Susan Hess, Timothy Van Patten, Patrick Cassidy, Alexis Smith, James B. Sikking, Lane Smith; **D:** Glenn Jordan; **W:** Gore Vidal; **M:** Billy Goldenberg. *WAR*

Dressed for Death 🏆½ *Straight on Till Morning; Til Dawn Do Us Part* **1974 (R)** A tale of true love gone bad as a woman is chased and murdered in her castle by the psychopath she loves. **121m/C VHS, Beta.** *GB* Rita Tushingham, Shane Briant, Tom Bell, Annie Ross, Katya Wyeth, James Bolam, Claire Kelly; **D:** Peter Collinson. *ACA*

Dressed to Kill 🏆🏆½ **1946** Sherlock Holmes finds that a series of music boxes holds the key to plates stolen from the Bank of England. The plot's a bit thin, but Rathbone/Bruce, in their final Holmes adventure, are always a delight. **72m/B VHS, LV, Closed Caption.** Basil Rathbone, Nigel Bruce, Patricia Morison, Edmund Breon, Tom Dillon; **D:** Roy William Neill. *CNG, MRV, REP*

Dressed to Kill 🏆🏆½ **1980 (R)** Contemporary thriller merges bombastic DePalma with a tense Hitchcockian flare. Sexually unsatisfied Dickinson ends up in bed with a man who catches her eye in a museum. Then she's found brutally murdered. Her son teams up with a prostitute to track and lure the killer into their trap. Suspenseful and fast paced. Dickinson's museum scene is wonderfully photographed and edited. DePalma was repeatedly criticized for using a stand-in during the Dickinson shower scene; he titled his next film "Body Double" as a rebuttal. **105m/C VHS, Beta, LV.** Angie Dickinson, Michael Caine, Nancy Allen, Keith Gordon, Dennis Franz, David Margulies, Brandon Maggart; **D:** Brian DePalma; **W:** Brian DePalma; **C:** Ralf Bode; **M:** Pino Donaggio. *WAR, OM*

The Dresser 🏆🏆🏆½ **1983 (PG)** Film adaptation of Harwood's play (he also wrote the screen version) about an aging English actor/manager (Finney), his dresser (Courtenay), and their theater company touring England during WWII. Marvelous showbiz tale is lovingly told, superbly acted. **119m/C VHS, Beta, LV, Closed Caption.** Albert Finney, Tom Courtenay, Edward Fox, Michael Gough, Zena Walker, Eileen Atkins, Cathryn Harrison; **D:** Peter Yates; **W:** Ronald Harwood; **M:** James Horner. Golden Globe Awards '84: Best Actor—Drama (Courtenay); Nominations: Academy Awards '83: Best Actor (Courtenay), Best Actor (Finney), Best Adapted Screenplay, Best Director (Yates), Best Picture. *COL*

Dressmaker 🏆🏆½ **1956** French comedian Fernandel stars as a man's tailor who designs dresses in secret so as not to compete with his dressmaker wife. Lightweight but entertaining. English subtitled. **95m/B VHS, Beta, LV.** *FR* Fernandel, Francoise Fabian; **D:** Jean Boyer. *NOS, GVV, DVT*

The Dressmaker ♫♫½ 1989 Two sisters in WWII Liverpool must deal with their young niece's romantic involvement with an American soldier. Plowright and Whitelaw turn in fine performances as the two siblings with very different outlooks on life. **90m/C VHS.** *GB* Joan Plowright, Billie Whitelaw, Pete Postlethwaite, Jane Horrocks, Tim Ransom; **D:** Jim O'Brien; **C:** Michael Coulter; **M:** George Fenton. *CTL*

Drift Fence ♫♫½ *Texas Desperadoes* 1936 Good early oater about a Texas ranger who goes in search of the man responsible for the murder of his buddy. Routine story saved by high quality production. Based on the story "Nevada" by Zane Grey. **57m/B VHS.** Buster Crabbe, Katherine DeMille, Tom Keene, Benny Baker; **D:** Otho Lovering; **W:** Stuart Anthony, Robert Yost. *DVT, GPV*

The Drifter ♫♫ 1932 A lumberjack makes sacrifices for the love between his brother and the lumbermill owner's daughter. **56m/B VHS, Beta, LV.** William Farnum, Noah Beery Sr., Phyliss Barrington. *NOS, VYY, HEG*

The Drifter ♫♫½ 1988 (R) It's psychos, psychos everywhere as a beautiful young woman learns to regret a one-night stand. A good, low-budget version of "Fatal Attraction." Director Brand plays the cop. **90m/C VHS.** Kim Delaney, Timothy Bottoms, Miles O'Keeffe, Al Shannon, Thomas Wagner, Larry Brand; **D:** Larry Brand; **W:** Larry Brand; **M:** Rick Conrad. *MGM*

The Driftin' Kid ♫ 1941 Poorly produced western has Keene posing as a rancher in order to nab a bunch of cattle rusters. So bad that even the sound of the punches are seconds off from the blows. **57m/B VHS.** Tom Keene, Betty Miles, Frank Yaconelli, Slim Andrews, Stanley Price, Glenn Strange; **D:** Robert Emmett Tansey; **W:** Robert Emmett Tansey, Frances Kavanaugh. *MOV*

Driftin' River ♫♫½ 1946 A shipment of horses bound for the Army is hijacked and the soldiers sent to investigate the theft are murdered. Investigators Deans and Ates are sent to take care of the culprits. Routine oater. **57m/B VHS.** Eddie Dean, Roscoe Ates, Shirley Patterson, William "Bill" Fawcett, Dennis Moore, Bob Callahan, Lottie Harrison, Forrest Taylor; **D:** Robert Emmett Tansey; **W:** Frances Kavanaugh. *GPV*

Drifting ♫♫½ *Nagooa* 1982 A controversial Israeli film about a homosexual filmmaker surviving in modern-day Jerusalem. First such movie to be made in Israel. In Hebrew with English titles. **103m/C VHS, Beta.** *IS* Jonathan Sagalle, Ami Traub, Ben Levine, Dita Arel; **D:** Amos Guttman. *FCT*

Drifting Souls ♫♫ 1932 In order to save her father's life, a beautiful young woman marries for money instead of love. **65m/C VHS, Beta.** Lois Wilson, Theodore von Eltz, Shirley Grey, Raymond Hatton, Gene Gowing, Bryant Washburn; **D:** Louis King. *GPV*

Drifting Weeds ♫♫♫½ *Floating Weeds; The Duckweed Story; Ukigusa* 1959 A remake by Ozu of his 1934 silent film about a troupe of traveling actors whose leader visits his illegitimate son and his lover after years of separation. Classic Ozu in his first color film. In Japanese with English subtitles. **128m/B VHS, Beta, LV.** *JP* Ganjiro Nakamura, Machiko Kyo, Haruko Sugimura, Ayako Wakao; **D:** Yasujiro Ozu. *HMV, MRV, FCT*

Driller Killer woof! 1974 (R) Frustrated artist goes insane and begins to kill off Manhattan residents with a carpenter's drill. Likewise, the plot is full of holes. **78m/C VHS, Beta.** Jimmy Laine, Carolyn Marz, Bob DeFrank; **D:** Abel Ferrara; **W:** Joe Delia. *NO*

Drive-In woof! 1976 (PG) A low-budget bomb showing a night in the life of teenage yahoos at a Texas drive-in. **96m/C VHS, Beta.** Lisa Lemole, Glen Morshower, Gary Cavagnaro; **D:** Rod Amateau. *COL*

Drive-In Massacre woof! 1974 (R) Two police detectives investigate a bizarre series of slasher murders at the local drive-in. Honk the horn at this one. **78m/C VHS, Beta, LV.** Jake Barnes, Adam Lawrence. *NO*

Driven to Kill ♫♫ 1990 No-name cast assemble in low-rent suspenser portraying the ugly side of love: bent on revenge, a man is out to obliterate the thugs who made his life a horrible experience highlighted by misery and boredom. **?m/C VHS.** Jake Jacobs, Chip Campbell, Michele McNeil. *PMH*

The Driver ♫♫½ 1978 (PG) A police detective will stop at nothing to catch "The Driver," a man who has the reputation of driving the fastest getaway car around. Chase scenes win out over plot. **131m/C VHS, Beta, Closed Caption.** Ryan O'Neal, Bruce Dern, Isabelle Adjani, Ronee Blakley, Matt Clark; **D:** Walter Hill; **W:** Walter Hill. *FOX*

Driver's Seat woof! *Psychotic; Identikit* 1973 (R) Extremely bizarre film with a cult following that was adapted from the novel by Muriel Spark. Liz stars as a deranged woman trying to keep a rendezvous with her strange lover in Rome. In the meantime she wears tacky clothes and delivers stupid lines. **101m/C VHS, Beta.** *IT* Elizabeth Taylor, Ian Bannen, Mona Washbourne, Andy Warhol; **D:** Giuseppe Patroni Griffi.

Driving Force ♫ 1988 (R) In an effort to capitalize on the popularity of the "Road Warrior" movies, features a lone trucker battling a gang of roadhogs in another post-holocaust desert. Ultimately, runs off the road. **90m/C VHS, Beta, LV.** Sam Jones, Catherine Bach, Don Swayze; **D:** A.J. Prowse; **W:** Patrick Edgeworth. *ACA*

Driving Me Crazy ♫♫½ 1991 (PG-13) When an East German car inventor comes to America, it's laughs in the fast lane in this all-star comedy. **88m/C VHS, LV.** Billy Dee Williams, Thomas Gottschalk, Dom DeLuise, Milton Berle, Steve Kanaly, Michelle Johnson, Richard Moll, Morton Downey Jr., George Kennedy; **D:** Jon Turteltaub. *NO*

Driving Miss Daisy ♫♫♫½ 1989 (PG) Tender and sincere portrayal of a 25-year friendship between an aging Jewish woman and the black chauffeur forced upon her by her son. Humorous and thought-provoking, skillfully acted and directed, it subtly explores the effects of prejudice in the South. The development of Aykroyd as a top-notch character actor is further evidenced here. Part of the fun is watching the changes in fashion and auto design. Adapted from the play by Alfred Uhry. **99m/C VHS, Beta, LV, 8mm, Closed Caption.** Jessica Tandy, Morgan Freeman, Dan Aykroyd, Esther Rolle, Patti LuPone; **D:** Bruce Beresford; **W:** Alfred Uhry; **M:** Hans Zimmer. Academy Awards '89: Best Actress (Tandy), Best Adapted Screenplay, Best Makeup, Best Picture; British Academy Awards '90: Best Actress (Tandy); Golden Globe Awards '90: Best Actor—Musical/Comedy (Freeman), Best Actress—Musical/Comedy (Tandy), Best Film—Musical/Comedy; National Board of Review Awards '89: 10 Best Films of the Year, Best Actor (Freeman); National Media Owl Awards '90: Second Prize; Writers Guild of America '89: Best Adapted Screenplay; Nominations: Academy Awards '89: Best Actor (Freeman), Best Art Direction/Set Decoration, Best Costume Design, Best Film Editing, Best Supporting Actor (Aykroyd). *WAR, FCT, BTV*

Drop Dead Fred woof! 1991 (PG-13) As a little girl, Lizzie Cronin had a manic, imaginary friend named Fred, who protected her from her domineering mother. When her husband dumps her twenty years later, Fred returns to "help" as only he can. Although the cast is fine, incompetent writing and direction make this a truly dismal affair. Plus, gutter humor and mean-spirited pranks throw the whole "heart-warming" premise out the window. Filmed in Minneapolis. **103m/C VHS, LV, Closed Caption.** Phoebe Cates, Rik Mayall, Tim Matheson, Marsha Mason, Carrie Fisher, Daniel Gerroll, Ron Eldard; **D:** Ate De Jong; **W:** Carlos Davis, Anthony Fingleton; **M:** Randy Edelman. *LIV*

Drop-Out Mother ♫♫ 1988 A woman gives up her executive position to become a housewife and full-time mom; expected domestic turmoil follows. Standard made for television fare and sort of a sequel to "Drop-Out Father," shown in 1982. **100m/C VHS.** Valerie Harper, Wayne Rogers,

Carol Kane, Kim Hunter, Danny Gerard; **D:** Charles S. Dubin. *FRH*

DROP Squad ♫♫ 1994 (R) Not quite on target social satire revolving around buppie Burford Jackson, Jr. (La Salle), a token minority ad exec who's job is to push questionable products, using gross stereotypes to the black community. His family's appalled and Buford becomes a prime target of D.R.O.P. (Deprogramming and Restoration of Pride), a vigilante organization that kidnaps erring black bretheren and leads them back to their cultural heritage. Frequently intense performances but the script raises some serious issues it doesn't deliver on. Based on the short story "The Deprogrammer" by David Taylor. **88m/C VHS, LV, Closed Caption.** Eriq La Salle, Vondie Curtis-Hall, Ving Rhames, Kasi Lemmons, Vanessa Williams, Nicole Powell, Afemo Omilami; **Cameos:** Spike Lee; **D:** David Johnson; **W:** David Johnson, Butch Robinson, David Taylor; **M:** Michael Bearden. *USH*

Drop Zone ♫♫ 1994 (R) Routine action-thriller finds U.S. marshal Pete Nessip (Snipes) and his brother Terry (Warner) assigned to protect drug cartel snitch Earl Leedy (Jeter). The plane they're on is skyjacked by criminal Moncrief (Busey) who parachutes off with Leedy, Terry's killed, and while Pete's on suspension he decides to go undercover into the world of sky-diving with the aid of ex-con cutie Jessie (Butler). Plot holes are big enough to pilot a plane through but the stunts are good and Snipes is never less than professional. **CW:** Some strong language and scenes of extreme violence. **101m/C VHS, Beta, Closed Caption.** Wesley Snipes, Gary Busey, Yancy Butler, Michael Jeter, Corin "Corky" Nemec, Kyle Secor, Luca Bercovici, Malcolm Jamal Warner, Rex Linn, Grace Zabriskie, Sam Hennings, Claire Stansfield, Mickey Jones, Andy Romano; **D:** John Badham; **W:** John Bishop, Peter Barsocchini; **M:** Hans Zimmer. *PAR*

The Dropkick ♫♫♫ 1927 Erstwhile D.W. Griffith leading man Barthelmess stars in this pigskin whodunnit: a coach's suicide looks like murder, and the prime suspect is the team's most valuable player. Cast includes ten bona fide university football players and Hedda "nobody's interested in sweetness and light" Hopper, while The Duke makes cameo. Webb later went on to direct a musical with Eddie Cantor and Rudy Vallee ("Glorifying the American Girl"). Silent. Based on the story "Glitter" by Katherine Brush. **62m/B VHS, Beta.** Richard Barthelmess, Barbara Kent, Dorothy Revier, Eugene Strong, Alberta Vaughn, Brooks Benedict, Hedda Hopper; **Cameos:** John Wayne; **D:** Millard Webb; **W:** Winifred Dunn. *GPV, FCT*

Drowning by Numbers ♫♫♫½ 1987 (R) Three generations of women, each named Cissie Colpitts, solve their marital problems by drowning their husbands and making deals with a bizarre coroner. Further strange visions from director Greenaway, complemented by stunning cinematography courtesy of Sacha Vierny. A treat for those who appreciate Greenaway's uniquely curious cinematic statements. **CW:** Language, nudity, and sensuality. **121m/C VHS, LV.** *GB* Bernard Hill, Joan Plowright, Juliet Stevenson, Joely Richardson; **D:** Peter Greenaway; **W:** Peter Greenaway; **C:** Sacha Vierny; **M:** Michael Nyman. *LIV*

The Drowning Pool ♫♫ 1975 (PG) Newman returns as detective Lew Harper (of "Harper" by Ross MacDonald) to solve a blackmail case. Uneventful script and stodgy direction, but excellent character work from all the cast members keep this watchable. Title is taken from a trap set for Newman, from which he must escape using most of his female companion's clothing. Adapted from a character created by Ross MacDonald. **109m/C VHS, Beta.** Paul Newman, Joanne Woodward, Anthony (Tony) Franciosa, Murray Hamilton, Melanie Griffith, Richard Jaeckel; **D:** Stuart Rosenberg; **W:** Tracy Keenan Wynn, Walter Hill; **C:** Gordon Willis; **M:** Charles Fox. *WAR*

Drug Wars 2: The Cocaine Cartel 🎞️🎞️ 1992 Muddled drama featuring crazy unpredictable DEA agents executing the downfall of Colombia's Medellin drug kingpins. Average sequel to the award-winning miniseries "Drug Wars." **200m/C VHS.** Alex McArthur, Dennis Farina, Julie Carmen, John Glover, Karen Young, Michele Placido, Gustav Vintas, Geno Silva; **D:** Paul Krasny. USH

Drugstore Cowboy 🎞️🎞️🎞️½ 1989 (R) A gritty, uncompromising depiction of a pack of early 1970s drugstore-robbing junkies as they travel around looking to score. Brushes with the law and tragedy encourage them to examine other lifestyles, but the trap seems impossible to leave. A perfectly crafted piece that reflects the "me generation" era, though it tends to glamorize addiction. Dillon's best work to date. Based on a novel by prison inmate James Fogle. **100m/C VHS, Beta, LV.** Matt Dillon, Kelly Lynch, James Remar, James LeGros, Heather Graham, William S. Burroughs, Beah Richards, Grace Zabriskie, Max Perlich; **D:** Gus Van Sant; **W:** Gus Van Sant, Daniel Yost; **M:** Elliot Goldenthal. Independent Spirit Awards '90: Best Actor (Dillon), Best Cinematography, Best Screenplay, Best Supporting Actor (Perlich); Los Angeles Film Critics Association Awards '89: Best Screenplay; New York Film Critics Awards '89: Best Screenplay; National Society of Film Critics Awards '89: Best Director (Van Sant), Best Film, Best Screenplay. LIV, FCT

Drum woof! 1976 (R) This steamy sequel to "Mandingo" deals with the sordid interracial sexual shenanigans at a Southern plantation. Bad taste at its best. **101m/C VHS, Beta.** Ken Norton, Warren Oates, Pam Grier, Yaphet Kotto, Fiona Lewis, Isela Vega, Cheryl "Rainbeaux" Smith; **D:** Steve Carver; **C:** Lucien Ballard. LIV, VES, WAR

Drum Beat 🎞️🎞️ 1954 An unarmed Indian fighter sets out to negotiate a peace treaty with a renegade Indian leader. Bronson is especially believable as chief. Based on historical incident. **111m/C VHS, Beta.** Alan Ladd, Charles Bronson, Marisa Pavan, Robert Keith, Rodolfo Acosta, Warner Anderson, Elisha Cook Jr., Anthony Caruso; **D:** Delmer Daves. NO

Drum Taps 🎞️🎞️ 1933 Maynard saves the day for a young girl who is being pushed off her land by a group of speculators. **55m/B VHS, Beta.** Ken Maynard, Dorothy Dix, Frank "Junior" Coghlan, Kermit Maynard; **D:** J.P. McGowan. NOS, VDM, VYY

Drums 🎞️🎞️½ The Drum 1938 A native prince helps to save the British army in India from being annihilated by a tyrant. Rich melodrama with interesting characterizations and locale. **96m/B VHS, Beta, LV.** GB Sabu, Raymond Massey, Valerie Hobson, Roger Livesey, David Tree; **D:** Zoltan Korda.

Drums Along the Mohawk 🎞️🎞️🎞️½ 1939 Grand, action-filled saga about pre-Revolutionary America, detailing the trials of a colonial newlywed couple as their village in Mohawk Valley is besieged by Indians. Based on the Walter Edmonds novel, and vintage Ford. **104m/C VHS, Beta, LV, Closed Caption.** Henry Fonda, Claudette Colbert, Edna May Oliver, Eddie Collins, John Carradine, Dorris Bowdon, Arthur Shields, Ward Bond, Jessie Ralph, Robert Lowery; **D:** John Ford; **C:** Ray Rennahan. Nominations: Academy Awards '39: Best Color Cinematography, Best Supporting Actress (Oliver). FOX

Drums in the Deep South 🎞️🎞️ 1951 A rivalry turns ugly as two former West Point roommates wind up on opposite sides when the Civil War breaks out. Historical drama hampered by familiar premise. **87m/C VHS, Beta.** James Craig, Guy Madison, Craig Stevens, Barbara Payton, Barton MacLane; **D:** William Cameron Menzies; **W:** Philip Yordan. NOS, MRV, VGR

Drums of Fu Manchu 🎞️🎞️🎞️ 1940 Fu Manchu searches for the scepter of Genghis Khan, an artifact that would give him domination over the East. Brandon smoothly evil as the Devil Doctor. Originally a serial in 15 chapters. **150m/B VHS, Beta.** Henry Brandon, Robert Kellard, George Cleveland, Dwight Frye, Gloria Franklin, Tom Chatterton; **D:** William Witney, John English. VCN, MLB

Drums of Jeopardy 🎞️ Mark of Terror 1931 A father wanders through czarist Russia and the U.S. to seek revenge on his daughter's killer. Cheap copy of "Dr. Fu Manchu." **65m/B VHS.** Warner Oland, June Collyer, Lloyd Hughes, George Fawcett, Mischa Auer; **D:** George B. Seitz. NOS, SNC, DVT

Drums O'Voodoo woof! She Devil 1934 A voodoo princess fights to eliminate the town bad guy in this all-black feature that is greatly hampered by shoddy production values. **70m/B VHS, Beta.** Laura Bowman, J. Augustus Smith, Edna Barr; **D:** Arthur Hoerl. SNC

Drunken Angel 🎞️🎞️🎞️ 1948 Alcoholic doctor gets mixed up with local gangster. Kurosawa's first major film aided by strong performances. With English subtitles. **108m/B VHS, Beta.** JP Toshiro Mifune, Takashi Shimura, Choko Iida; **D:** Akira Kurosawa. DVT, MRV

Drunks 🎞️🎞️ 1996 (R) Ensemble story set in a church basement in Manhattan where a diverse group of people go to their Alcoholics Anonymous meetings. Recovering alcoholic Jim (Lewis) has gone on a bender after his wife's death; Rachel's (Wiest) an overworked doctor with drug and alcohol dependencies; alcoholic Becky's (Dunaway) a divorcee with problem kids; Brenda's (Hamilton) an ex-heroin addict who's HIV positive; Joseph's (Rollins) still haunted by his son's death, which he caused while driving drunk. There's more and everyone gets their chance at the spotlight. Adapted from Lennon's play "Blackout." **88m/C VHS.** Richard Lewis, Faye Dunaway, Dianne Wiest, Lisa Gay Hamilton, Howard E. Rollins Jr., Parker Posey, Spalding Gray, Amanda Plummer, Calista Flockhart, George Martin, Anna Thomson; **D:** Peter Cohn; **W:** Gary Lennon; **C:** Peter Hawkins; **M:** Joe Delia. BMG

A Dry White Season 🎞️🎞️🎞️ 1989 (R) A white Afrikaner living resignedly with apartheid confronts the system when his black gardener, an old friend, is persecuted and murdered. A well-meaning expose that, like many others, focuses on white people. **105m/C VHS, Beta, LV, Closed Caption.** Donald Sutherland, Marlon Brando, Susan Sarandon, Zakes Mokae, Janet Suzman, Juergen Prochnow, Winston Ntshona, Susannah Harker, Thoko Ntshinga, Rowan Elmes; **D:** Euzhan Palcy; **W:** Colin Welland, Euzhan Palcy; **M:** Dave Grusin. Nominations: Academy Awards '89: Best Supporting Actor (Brando). FOX, FCT

Drying Up the Streets 🎞️ 1976 Tepid message tale of a police drug squad out to terminate the pattern that has young women turning to a life of prostitution and drugs. **90m/C VHS, Beta.** CA Len Cariou, Don Francks, Sarah Torgov, Calvin Butler; **D:** Robin Spry. LIV, VES

D3: The Mighty Ducks 🎞️🎞️ 1996 (PG) Estevez proves that he'll quack for a dollar in the latest redux of the Disney franchise. This time the members of the rag-tag team are drafted by an exclusive prep school where, once again, they don't fit in. Go figure! Although billed as the star, Estevez only appears briefly at the beginning and end of the movie, leaving team captain Charlie (Jackson) as the focus of the story. Facing off against the new coach and the snooty elitist varsity team, the players learn lessons about maturity, responsibility and whacking people with sticks. In all probability, Disney will not be happy with just the hat trick, so don't be surprised if you see "D4: Mighty Old to Still Be Playing Kids" in a theater near you soon. Cameo from professional Mighty Duck and fellow Disney employee Paul Kariya. **104m/C VHS.** Emilio Estevez, Jeffrey Nordling, Joshua Jackson, David Selby, Heidi Kling, Joss Ackland, Elden Ratliff, Shaun Weiss, Matt Doherty, Michael Cudlitz, Vincent A. Larusso, Matt Doherty, Colombe Jacobsen, Aaron Lohr, Christopher Orr; **D:** Robert Lieberman; **W:** Steven Brill, Jim Burnstein; **C:** David Hennings; **M:** J.A.C. Redford. TOU

D2: The Mighty Ducks 🎞️🎞️ The Mighty Ducks 2 1994 (PG) When an injury forces Gordon (Estevez) out of the minor leagues, he is tapped by promotor Tibbles (Tucker) to coach Team U.S.A. in the Junior Goodwill Games. Upon arriving in LA, the coach's head is turned by the mon-

ey to be made in endorsements, and he soon gets a lesson in character-building (hey, it's Disney). The duck redux premise is lame, but kids will want ice time to see more of the hockey action that made the first a hit. **107m/C VHS, LV, Closed Caption.** Emilio Estevez, Michael Tucker, Jan Rubes, Kathryn Erbe, Shaun Weiss, Kenan Thompson, Ty O'Neal; **Cameos:** Kristi Yamaguchi, Kareem Abdul-Jabbar, Wayne Gretzky; **D:** Sam Weisman; **W:** Steven Brill; **M:** J.A.C. Redford. DIS

Dual Alibi 🎞️🎞️ 1947 Identical twin trapeze artists murder a colleague for a winning lottery ticket. Lom plays the brothers in a dual role. **87m/B VHS, Beta.** GB Herbert Lom, Terence de Marney, Phyllis Dixey, Ronald Frankau, Abraham Sofaer, Harold Berens, Sebastian Cabot; **D:** Alfred Travers. NOS, SNC

Dual Flying Kicks 🎞️ 1982 Chinese provincial mayor allies himself to a group of bandits amid much high kicking. **95m/C VHS, Beta.** Chen Hsing, Tan Tao Liang. WVE

Dubarry 🎞️🎞️½ 1930 Early sound version of the romantic experiences of Madame Dubarry, the alluring French heroine of David Belasco's "DuBarry." Talmadge's last film. **81m/B VHS, Beta.** Norma Talmadge, Conrad Nagel, William Farnum, Hobart Bosworth, Alison Skipworth; **D:** Sam Taylor. NOS, DVT, HEG

DuBarry Was a Lady 🎞️🎞️½ 1943 Skelton is a washroom attendant who daydreams that he is King Louis XV of France. Dorsey's band gets to dress in period wigs and costumes. 🎵DuBarry Was a Lady; Do I Love You, Do I?; Friendship; Well, Did You Evah; Taliostro's Dance; Katie Went to Haiti; Madame, I Love Your Crepes Suzettes; Thinking of You; A Cigarette, Sweet Music and You. **112m/C VHS, Beta.** Lucille Ball, Gene Kelly, Red Skelton, Virginia O'Brien, Zero Mostel, Dick Haymes, Rags Ragland, Donald Meek, George Givot, Louise Beavers; **D:** Roy Del Ruth; **W:** Irving Brecher; **C:** Karl Freund. MGM, CCB

Dubeat-E-O 🎞️½ 1984 A filmmaker races against time to finish making a documentary about the Los Angeles underground hardcore punk scene, and becomes immersed in the subculture. Somewhat of a haphazard exercise in filmmaking that is best appreciated by rock fans. **84m/C VHS, Beta.** Ray Sharkey, Joan Jett, Derf Scratch, Len Lesser, Nora Gaye; **D:** Alan Sacks. MVD, MED

The Duchess and the Dirtwater Fox 🎞️½ 1976 (PG) Period western strung together with many failed attempts at humor, all about a music-hall hooker who meets a bumbling card shark on the make. **105m/C VHS, Beta, LV.** George Segal, Goldie Hawn, Conrad Janis, Thayer David; **D:** Melvin Frank; **W:** Barry Sandler; **C:** Joseph Biroc; **M:** Charles Fox. FOX

The Duchess of Duke Street 🎞️🎞️🎞️ 1978 Cockney Rosa Lewis (Jones), a clockmaker's daughter born in 1869, goes into service with the ambition to become the best cook in London. She learns from a society household's French chef, where she was a kitchen maid, and eventually won success by an unexpected opportunity to cook for Edward, the Prince of Wales. A marriage-of-convenience and a mysterious legacy allows Rosa to buy the rundown Bentinck Hotel (actually the Cavendish) and cater fashionable dinners. By unceasing hard work, Rosa turns her establishment into an exclusive and discreet haunt for aristocrats, the wealthy, and various celebrities. British series on 7 cassettes. **880m/C VHS.** GB Gemma Jones, Christopher Cazenove, John Welsh, George Pravda, June Brown, Victoria Plucknett, Richard Vernon, Doreen Mantle, Elizabeth Bennett, Donald Burton, John Cater, Holly DeJong, John Rapley; **D:** Cyril Coke, Gerry Mill, Simon Langton, Bill Bain, Raymond Menmuir; **W:** Julian Bond, Julia Jones, Rosemary Anne Sisson, Maggie Wadey, Jeremy Paul, Jack Rosenthal, Bill Craig, John Hawkesworth. SIG

The Duchess of Idaho 🎞️🎞️½ 1950 Williams tries to help her roommate patch up a romance gone bad, but ends up falling in love herself. MGM guest stars liven up an otherwise routine production. 🎵Baby Come Out of the

Clouds; You Can't Do Wrong Doin' Right; Let's Choo Choo to Idaho; Of All Things; Or Was It Spring; Warm Hands, Cold Heart; Singlefoot Serenade; You Won't Forget Me. **98m/C VHS.** Esther Williams, Van Johnson, John Lund, Paula Raymond, Amanda Blake, Eleanor Powell, Lena Horne; **D:** Robert Z. Leonard. *MGM*

Duck Soup 🎬🎬🎬🎬 **1933** The Marx Brothers satiric masterpiece (which failed at the box office). Groucho becomes the dictator of Freedonia, and hires Chico and Harpo as spies. Jampacked with the classic anarchic and irreverent Marx shtick; watch for the mirror scene. Zeppo plays a love-sick tenor, in this, his last film with the brothers. **70m/B VHS, Beta, LV.** Groucho Marx, Chico Marx, Harpo Marx, Zeppo Marx, Louis Calhern, Margaret Dumont, Edgar Kennedy, Raquel Torres, Leonid Kinskey, Charles Middleton; **D:** Leo McCarey; **W:** Harry Ruby, Nat Perrin, Bert Kalmar, Arthur Sheekman; **M:** Harry Ruby, Bert Kalmar. *USH, FCT*

DuckTales the Movie: Treasure of the Lost Lamp 🎬🎬½ **1990 (G)** Uncle Scrooge and company embark on a lost-ark quest, ala Harrison Ford, for misplaced treasure (a lamp that can make the sky rain ice cream). Based on the daily Disney cartoon of the same name, it's more like an extended-version Saturday morning sugar smacks'n'milk 'toon. See it with someone young. **74m/C VHS, Beta, LV, Closed Caption. D:** Bob Hathcock; **W:** Alan Burnett; **M:** David Newman; **V:** Alan Young, Christopher Lloyd, Rip Taylor, June Foray, Chuck McCann, Richard Libertini, Russi Taylor, Joan Gerber, Terence McGovern. *DIS*

Dude Bandit 🎬 **1932** An unscrupulous money-lender tries to gain control of a ranch but Gibson comes to the rescue. Gibson actually plays three roles: the rancher's best friend, an aw-shucks cowpoke disguise in order to find out what's going on, and the title character used to bedevil the crooks. **68m/B VHS, Beta.** Hoot Gibson, Gloria Shea. *VYY, VCI, VCN*

Dude Ranger 🎬🎬½ **1934** Well-acted Zane Grey story about an easterner who gets caught up in a range war and cattle rustling when he takes possession of some property out west. **58m/B VHS, Beta.** Smiley Burnette, George O'Brien, Irene Hervey; **D:** Eddie Cline. *VDM*

Dudes 🎬 **1987 (R)** Three city kids head for the desert and run afoul of some rednecks. Tired grade-6 revenge story. **90m/C VHS, Beta, LV.** Jon Cryer, Catherine Mary Stewart, Daniel Roebuck, Flea, Lee Ving, Calvin Bartlett, Pete Willcox, Glenn Withrow; **D:** Penelope Spheeris; **M:** Charles Bernstein. *NO*

Duel 🎬🎬🎬 **1971 (PG)** Spielberg's first notable film, a made-for-television exercise in paranoia. A docile traveling salesman is repeatedly attacked and threatened by a huge, malevolent tractor-trailer on an open desert highway. Released theatrically in Europe. **90m/C VHS, Beta.** Dennis Weaver, Lucille Benson, Eddie Firestone, Cary Loftin; **D:** Steven Spielberg; **W:** Richard Matheson; **M:** Billy Goldenberg. *USH*

Duel at Diablo 🎬🎬🎬 **1966** An exceptionally violent film that deals with racism in the Old West. Good casting; western fans will enjoy the action. **103m/C VHS, Closed Caption.** James Garner, Sidney Poitier, Bibi Andersson, Dennis Weaver, Bill Travers; **D:** Ralph Nelson. *MGM*

Duel at Silver Creek 🎬🎬½ **1952** A group of claim jumpers murder anyone who gets in their way, including the family of the Silver Kid (Murphy), who's deputized by Sheriff Lightning (McNally) to help him get the varmints. **76m/B VHS.** Audie Murphy, Faith Domergue, Stephen McNally, Susan Cabot, Gerald Mohr, Eugene Iglesias, Kyle James, Lee Marvin; **D:** Donald Siegel; **W:** Gerald Drayson Adams; **C:** Irving Glassberg; **M:** Hans J. Salter. *USH*

Duel in the Sun 🎬🎬🎬 **1946** A lavish, lusty David O. Selznick production of a minor western novel about a vivacious half-breed Indian girl, living on a powerful dynastic ranch, who incites two brothers to conflict. Selznick's last effort at outdoing his epic success with "Gone With the

Wind." **130m/C VHS, Beta.** Gregory Peck, Jennifer Jones, Joseph Cotten, Lionel Barrymore, Lillian Gish, Butterfly McQueen, Harry Carey Sr., Walter Huston, Charles Bickford, Herbert Marshall; **D:** King Vidor; **C:** Ray Rennahan. Nominations: Academy Awards '46: Best Actress (Jones), Best Supporting Actress (Gish). *FOX*

Duel of Champions 🎬 *Orazi e Curiazi* **1961** It's ancient Rome, and the prodigal gladiator has come home. Now the family must have a duel to decide who will rule. **90m/C VHS, Beta.** *IT SP* Alan Ladd, Francesca Bett; **D:** Ferdinando Baldi. *NO*

Duel of Fists 🎬 **1989** When the owner of a boxing institute dies, he instructs his son in his will to go searching for his long-lost brother in Thailand. All he can go on is an old photograph and the knowledge that his brother is a Thai boxer. **111m/C VHS, Beta.** David Chiang, Chen Hsing, Ti Lung, Tang Ti. *HMD, MOV*

Duel of Hearts 🎬🎬 **1992 (PG-13)** Beautiful Caroline falls in love with wealthy Lord Vane Brecon, who unfortunately is accused of murder. When Caroline tries to help him clear his name she discovers he's hiding a number of secrets. Based on the romance novel "Duel of Love" by Barbara Cartland. Nothing too inspiring here, although regency romance fans will appreciate the attention to detail. Originally made for cable television. **95m/C VHS, Beta, LV, Closed Caption.** *GB* Alison Doody, Michael York, Geraldine Chaplin, Benedict Taylor, Billie Whitelaw, Virginia McKenna, Richard Johnson, Jeremy Kemp, Beryl Reid, Suzanna Hamilton, Jolyon Baker, Julie Kate; **D:** John Hough. *TTC*

Duel of the Iron Fist 🎬 **1972 (R)** Master of the martial arts must do battle with a brutal gang to save his own group from extinction. **98m/C VHS, Beta.** David Chiang, Ti Lung, Wang Ping, Yu Hui. *HHT*

Duel of the Seven Tigers 🎬🎬 **1980** Nine of the world's greatest Kung Fu and Karate exponents team up in this martial arts spectacular. **80m/C VHS, Beta.** Cliff Lok, Ka Sa Fa, Chio Chi Ling, Lam Men Wei, Yang Pan Pan, Charlie Chan. *TWE*

The Duellists 🎬🎬🎬 **1977 (PG)** A beautifully photographed picture about the long-running feud between two French officers during the Napoleonic wars. Based on "The Duel" by Joseph Conrad. **101m/C VHS, Beta.** *GB* Keith Carradine, Harvey Keitel, Albert Finney, Edward Fox, Tom Conti, Christina Raines, Diana Quick; **D:** Ridley Scott. *PAR*

Duet for One 🎬🎬 **1986 (R)** A famous concert violinist learns she is suffering from multiple sclerosis and is slowly losing her ability to play. Convinced that her life is meaningless without music, she self-destructively drifts into bitter isolation. From the play by Tom Kempinski. **108m/C VHS, Beta.** Julie Andrews, Max von Sydow, Alan Bates, Liam Neeson; **D:** Andrei Konchalovsky. *MGM*

The Duke is Tops 🎬🎬½ **1938** In Horne's earliest existing film appearance, she's off to attempt the "big-time," while her boyfriend joins a traveling medicine show. 🎵I Know You Remember. **80m/C VHS, Beta.** Ralph Cooper, Lena Horne, Marie Bryant. *NOS, MRV, VCN*

Duke of the Derby 🎬🎬 *Le Gentleman D'epsom* **1962** A scheming racehorse handicapper bets over his head and ruins his higher-than-means lifestyle. In French with English subtitles. **83m/C VHS, Beta.** *FR* Jean Gabin; **D:** Gilles Grangier. *FCT, DVT, HEG*

Dumb & Dumber 🎬🎬½ **1994 (PG-13)** Moronic limo driver Lloyd Christmas (Carrey) and equally dense dog groomer Harry Dunne (Daniels) travel (in the hilarious "sheep dog" van) from Rhode Island to Colorado—at one point going east!—to return a briefcase full of cash to a beautiful socialite (Holly). Engaging in all sorts of gross-out bathroom, bodily function, and slapstick humor, this one will certainly not appeal to the stuffy critic or arthouse snob. It will provide plenty of laughs, however embarrassingly rendered, for everyone else. Daniels proves a convincing dimwit sidekick, while Carrey mugs shamelessly. Oc-

casional "Seinfeld" writer Farrelly makes his directorial debut. **CW:** Off-color humor. **110m/C VHS, LV, Closed Caption, DVD.** Jim Carrey, Jeff Daniels, Lauren Holly, Teri Garr, Karen Duffy, Mike Starr, Charles Rocket, Victoria Rowell, Felton Perry; **D:** Peter Farrelly; **W:** Bennett Yellin, Bobby Farrelly, Peter Farrelly; **M:** Todd Rundgren. MTV Movie Awards '95: Best Comedic Performance (Carrey), Best Kiss (Jim Carrey/Lauren Holly); Blockbuster Entertainment Awards '96: Comedy Actor, Video (Carrey); Nominations: MTV Movie Awards '95: Best On-Screen Duo (Jim Carrey/Jeff Daniels). *TTC, NLC*

Dumb Waiter **1987** A mini-play by Harold Pinter about two hitmen awaiting instructions for a job in an empty boardinghouse, and getting comically mixed messages. Made for television. **60m/C VHS, Beta.** John Travolta, Tom Conti; **D:** Robert Altman; **W:** Harold Pinter. *PSM*

Dumbo 🎬🎬🎬🎬 **1941** Animated Disney classic about a baby elephant growing up in the circus who is ridiculed for his large ears, until he discovers he can fly. The little elephant who could fly then becomes a circus star. Expressively and imaginatively animated, highlighted by the hallucinatory dancing pink elephants sequence. Endearing songs by Frank Churchill, Oliver Wallace, and Ned Washington, including "Baby Mine," "Pink Elephants on Parade," and "I See an Elephant Fly." **63m/C VHS, Beta, LV, Closed Caption. D:** Ben Sharpsteen; **W:** Joe Grant, Dick Huemer; **M:** Frank Churchill, Oliver Wallace; **V:** Sterling Holloway, Edward Brophy, Verna Felton, Herman Bing, Cliff Edwards. Academy Awards '41: Scoring of a Musical; National Board of Review Awards '41: 10 Best Films of the Year; Nominations: Academy Awards '41: Best Song ("Baby Mine"). *DIS, APD, SCH*

The Dummy Talks 🎬🎬 **1943** When a ventriloquist is murdered, a midget goes undercover as a dummy to find the killer. Watch closely and you might see his lips move. **85m/B VHS, Beta.** *GB* Jack Warner, Claude Hulbert, Beryl Orde, Derna-Hazell, Ivy Benson, Manning Whiley; **D:** Oswald Mitchell. *SNC*

Dune 🎬🎬 **1984 (PG-13)** Lynch sci-fi opus based on the Frank Herbert novel boasting great set design, muddled scripting, and a good cast. The story: controlling the spice drug of Arrakis permits control of the universe in the year 10991. Paul, the heir of the Atreides family, leads the Freemen in a revolt against the evil Harkhonens who have violently seized control of Arrakis, also known as Dune, the desert planet. That's as clear as it ever gets. **137m/C VHS, Beta, LV, Closed Caption.** Kyle MacLachlan, Francesca Annis, Jose Ferrer, Sting, Max von Sydow, Juergen Prochnow, Linda Hunt, Freddie Jones, Dean Stockwell, Virginia Madsen, Brad Dourif, Kenneth McMillan, Silvana Mangano, Jack Nance, Sian Phillips, Paul Smith, Richard Jordan, Everett McGill, Sean Young; **D:** David Lynch; **W:** David Lynch; **M:** Brian Eno. Nominations: Academy Awards '84: Best Sound. *USH, FCT*

Dune Warriors 🎬½ **1991 (R)** Earth is a parched planet in the year 2040. Renegade bands cruise the desert, making short shrift of civilized people who band together in remote villages. When peaceful farmer Carradine's family falls prey to the pillagers, surely he and the most evil warlord of all must clash. Good action and stunts, but the dummy plot doesn't get you first. **CW:** Some language, graphic violence, and sensuality. **77m/C VHS, LV.** David Carradine, Richard Hill, Luke Askew, Jillian McWhirter, Blake Boyd; **D:** Cirio H. Santiago. *COL*

The Dunera Boys 🎬🎬🎬 **1985 (R)** Hoskins shines in this story about Viennese Jews who, at the onset of WWII, escape to England where they are suspected as German spies. Subsequently, the British shipped them all to an Australian prison camp, where they recreated in peace their Viennese lifestyle. **150m/C VHS, Beta, LV.** *AU* Bob Hoskins, Joe Spano, Warren Mitchell, Joseph Furst, Moshe Kedem, Dita Cobb, John Meillon, Mary-Anne Fahey, Simon Chilvers, Steven Vidler; **D:** Sam Lewin. *PSM*

Dungeon of Harrow 🎬 1964 Unbelievably cheap tale of shipwrecked comrades who encounter a maniacal family on an otherwise deserted island. Not your stranded-on-a-desert-island fantasy come true. Filmed in San Antonio; a harrowing bore. **74m/B VHS.** Russ Harvey, Helen Hogan, Bill McNulty, Pat Boyette; **D:** Pat Boyette. *SNC*

Dungeonmaster 🎬½ *Ragewar* 1983 (PG-13) A warlord forces a computer wiz to participate in a bizarre "Dungeons and Dragons" styled game in order to save a girl held captive. Consists of seven segments, each by a different director. Save yourself the trouble. **80m/C VHS, Beta, LV.** Jeffrey Byron, Richard Moll, Leslie Wing, Danny Dick; **D:** John Carl Buechler, Charles Band, David Allen, Stephen Ford, Peter Manoogian, Ted Nicolaou, Rosemarie Turko; **W:** Allen Actor; **M:** Richard Band. *LIV*

Dunston Checks In 🎬🎬½ 1995 (PG) This just in: Hollywood thinks monkeys are funny. But, as far as "stupid people learn important life lessons from a monkey who wears clothes" movies go, this one's not bad. Robert Grant (Alexander) is the manager of a five-star hotel. His Leona Helmsley-esque boss (Dunaway) is convinced that aristocratic guest Lord Rutledge (Everett) is a travel guide critic who is there to bestow an elusive sixth star on the hotel. Actually he's a jewel thief, and Dunston the orangutan is his accomplice. When Dunston flees from his abusive owner, he's adopted by Grant's two children. Together, Dunston and the kids are left to straighten out the whole mess. **88m/C VHS, LV, Closed Caption.** Jason Alexander, Faye Dunaway, Eric Lloyd, Rupert Everett, Graham Sack, Paul (Pee Wee Herman) Reubens, Glenn Shadix, Nathan Davis, Jennifer Bassey; **Cameos:** Paul (Pee Wee Herman) Reubens; **W:** Bruce Graham, John Hopkins; **C:** Peter Collister; **M:** Miles Goodman. Nominations: Golden Raspberry Awards '96: Worst Supporting Actress (Dunaway). *FXV*

The Dunwich Horror 🎬🎬 1970 Young warlock acquires a banned book of evil spells, starts trouble on the astral plane. Stockwell hammy. Loosely based on H. P. Lovecraft story. **90m/C VHS, Beta.** Sandra Dee, Dean Stockwell, Lloyd Bochner, Ed Begley Sr., Sam Jaffe, Joanna Moore; **D:** Daniel Haller; **W:** Curtis Hanson; **M:** Les Baxter.

Duplicates 🎬🎬 1992 (PG-13) Harrison and Greist are a married couple whose young son has disappeared. When the boy is found he has no memory of his former life or parents. The couple discover he's the victim of secret experiments which transfer human memories into computer banks. Will they become the next targets? **CW:** Violence. **92m/C VHS, Beta, Closed Caption.** Gregory Harrison, Kim Greist, Cicely Tyson, Lane Smith, William Lucking, Kevin McCarthy; **D:** Sandor Stern. *PAR, PMS*

Dupont Lajoie 🎬🎬 *Rape of Innocence* 1974 At a tourist campground Lajoie (Carmet) accidentally kills his son's girlfriend when she resists his sexual advances. To save his life he accuses Arabs of committing the crime and begins a racist campaign of vengeance. French with subtitles. **103m/C VHS.** *FR* Jean Carmet; **D:** Yves Boisset. *FCT*

Durango Valley Raiders 🎬½ 1938 Sheriff is the leader of the outlaws, and a young cowboy finds out. **55m/B VHS, Beta.** Bob Steele; **D:** Sam Newfield. *VCN, DVT*

Dust 🎬🎬🎬 1985 A white woman in South Africa murders her father when he shows affection for a young black servant. Controversial and intense. **87m/C VHS, Beta.** *FR BE* Jane Birkin, Trevor Howard, John Matshikiza, Nadine Uwampa, Lourdes Christina Sayo, Rene Diaz; **D:** Marion Hansel; **W:** Marion Hansel; **M:** Martin St. Pierre. *TPV*

Dust Devil 🎬🎬 1993 (R) Three travelers find themselves in Namibia's vast desert: a policeman, a woman on the run, and her abusive husband. They all have the misfortune of meeting up with a supernatural being known as the "Dust Devil," who kills humans in order to steal their souls and increase his other worldly powers. **87m/C VHS, Beta, Closed Caption.** Robert John Burke, Chelsea Field, Zakes Mokae, Rufus Swart, John Matshikiza, William Hootkins, Marianne Saegebrecht; **D:** Richard Stanley; **W:** Richard Stanley; **M:** Simon Boswell. *PAR*

Dust to Dust 1985 A short mystery made for British television about an aging gentleman who answers a request for correspondence and discovers ulterior, and evil, motives. **60m/C VHS, Beta.** *GB* Patricia Hodge, Michael Jayston, Judy Campbell. *PSM*

Dusty 🎬🎬 1985 Touching story of a wild dingo dog raised by an Australian rancher and trained to herd sheep. Filmed in the Australian bush and based on the children's book by Frank Dalby Davison. **89m/C VHS, Beta.** *AU* Bill Kerr, Noel Trevarthen, Carol Burns, Nicholas Holland, John Stanton; **D:** John Richardson. *MED, FCT, FHE*

Dutch 🎬½ 1991 (PG-13) Working class boob attempts to pick up his girlfriend's son from boarding school. Their trip together gives them an unexpected chance to connect, if they don't kill each other first. Silly premise from the Hughes factory has little innovation and uses type-casting instead of acting. **107m/C VHS, Closed Caption.** Ed O'Neill, Ethan Randall, JoBeth Williams; **D:** Peter Faiman; **W:** John Hughes. *FXV, IME*

Dutch Girls woof! 1987 Muddled mayhem as a horny high school field hockey team travels through Holland, cavorts about, and discovers the meaning of life. **83m/C VHS, Beta.** *GB* Bill Paterson, Colin Firth, Timothy Spall; **D:** Giles Foster. *ACA*

Dutch Treat 🎬 1986 (R) Two nerds con a sultry, all-girl rock band into thinking they're powerful record company execs. Nobody's buying. **95m/C VHS, Beta.** Lorin Dreyfuss, David Landsberg; **D:** Boaz Davidson. *MGM*

Dutchman 🎬🎬🎬 1967 Film presentation of Amiri Baraka's one act play depicting the claustrophobic reality of the black man's situation in America. Black man shares subway conversation with a white woman who questions his race and middle class aspirations. Enraged, one takes the other's life. **55m/C VHS.** *GB* Al Freeman Jr., Shirley Knight; **D:** Anthony Harvey; **M:** John Barry. Cannes Film Festival '67: Best Film. *CAL*

D.W. Griffith Triple Feature 🎬🎬½ 1913 A collection of three short D.W. Griffith films including "The Battle of Elderbush Gulch," "Iola's Promise," and "The Goddess of Sagebrush Gulch." **50m/B VHS, Beta.** Mae Marsh, Lillian Gish, Mary Pickford, Blanche Sweet, Charles West; **D:** D.W. Griffith. *BAR, FCT*

The Dwelling Place 🎬🎬½ 199? Sixteen-year-old girl struggles to hold her family together after the death of their parents. But her situation turns tragic when she's raped and left pregnant by a drunken young aristocrat. Based on a novel by Catherine Cookson. **145m/C VHS.** *GB GB* Tracy Whitwell, James Fox, Edward Rawle-Hicks; **D:** *VCO, FCT*

The Dybbuk 🎬🎬🎬½ 1937 A man's bride is possessed by a restless spirit. Set in the Polish-Jewish community before WWI and based on the play by Sholom Anski. Considered a classic for its portrayal of Jewish religious and cultural mores. In Yiddish with English subtitles. **123m/B VHS, Beta.** *PL* Abraham Morewski, Isaac Samberg, Moshe Lipman, Lili Liliana, Dina Halpern; **D:** Michal Waszynski. *IHF, FCT, NCJ*

Dying Game 🎬🎬 1994 Sorority girls are being stalked and murdered and the detective investigating the crimes falls for the sorority's president. Now, he has to find the killer before his girlfriend becomes the next victim. **85m/C VHS.** Michael Hughes, Mathea Webb, D.J. Boozer; **D:** Kris Hughes. *SWI*

Dying Room Only 🎬🎬½ 1973 Travelling through the desert, a woman's husband suddenly disappears after they stop at a secluded roadside diner. Made for television flick is a real spooker. **74m/C VHS.** Cloris Leachman, Ross Martin, Ned Beatty, Louise Latham, Dana Elcar, Dabney Coleman; **D:** Philip Leacock; **W:** Richard Matheson; **M:** Charles Fox. *LIV*

Dying to Remember 🎬½ 1993 (PG-13) A fashion designer (Gilbert) regresses to a past life during hypnotherapy and discovers she was murdered in 1963. She flies to San Francisco to discover more about her past but finds that somemome wants to keep things secret—and is willing to kill again. Tedious and predictable. **87m/C VHS, Beta, Closed Caption.** Melissa Gilbert, Ted Shackleford, Scott Plank, Christopher Stone, Jay Robinson; **D:** Arthur Seidelman; **W:** George Schenck, Frank Cardea, Brian Ross. *PAR*

The Dying Truth 🎬🎬 1991 A wrongfully accused prisoner lies dying in his cell. Trouble is, he can't die in peace until he solves the murder they say he committed. Interesting mix of the supernatural and mystery, although perhaps not one of Carradine's more memorable roles. **80m/C VHS.** David Carradine, Stephanie Beacham, Stephen Greif, Stephan Chase, Larry Carby, Lesley Dunlop; **D:** John Hough. *NO*

Dying Young 🎬½ 1991 (R) Muted romance has a wealthy leukemia victim hire a spirited, unschooled beauty as his nurse. They fall in love, but the film is either too timid or too unimaginative to mine emotions denoted by the title. Nobody dies, in fact, a grim ending (faithful to the Marti Leimbach novel on which this was based) got scrapped after testing poorly with audiences. The actors try their best, photography is lovely, and Kenny G's mellow music fills the soundtrack, but this is basically overmelodramatic drivel. Scott is the late Dewhurst's son. **CW:** Language. **111m/C VHS, Closed Caption.** Julia Roberts, Campbell Scott, Vincent D'Onofrio, Colleen Dewhurst, Ellen Burstyn, David Selby; **D:** Joel Schumacher; **W:** Richard Friedenberg; **C:** Juan Ruiz-Anchia. *FXV*

Dynamite 🎬 1949 Romance explodes as two young demolitions experts vie for the same girl. Stand back. **68m/B VHS, Beta.** William Gargan, Virginia Welles, Richard Crane, Irving Bacon; **D:** William H. Pine. *NOS, DVT, HEG*

Dynamite and Gold 🎬🎬 *Where the Hell's the Gold?* 1988 (PG) Nelson and crew embark on a search for lost gold, battling hostile Indians, the Mexican army and assorted bandits along the way. A mediocre television movie. **91m/C VHS, LV.** Willie Nelson, Delta Burke, Jack Elam, Alfonso Arau, Gregory Sierra, Michael Wren, Gerald McRaney; **D:** Burt Kennedy; **W:** Burt Kennedy. *ACA*

The Dynamite Brothers 🎬 1974 (R) Two tough guys, one a Hong Kong immigrant with martial arts skills, the other a brother from the streets of the ghetto, team up to rid Los Angeles of a Chinese crimelord. **90m/C VHS.** James Hong, Aldo Ray, Alan Tang, Timothy Brown, Carolyn Ann Speed, Don Oliver; **D:** Al Adamson; **M:** Charles Earland. *RHI*

Dynamite Canyon 🎬🎬 1941 Average oater has villain Price committing murder in order to keep secret the location of a lode of copper. Standard western fare. **58m/B VHS.** Tom Keene, Evelyn Finley, Sugar Dawn, Stanley Price, Kenne Duncan; **D:** Robert Emmett Tansey; **W:** Robert Emmett Tansey, Frances Kavanaugh. *DVT*

Dynamite Chicken 🎬🎬 1970 (R) Melange of skits, songs, and hippie satire is dated. Includes performances by Joan Baez, Lenny Bruce, B.B. King, and others. **75m/C VHS, Beta.** Joan Baez, Richard Pryor, Lenny Bruce, Jimi Hendrix; **D:** Ernie Pintoff. *NO*

Dynamite Dan 🎬½ 1924 A man knocks out the heavyweight boxing champion after he flirts with his girlfriend and decides to give up his day job to become a championship boxer. He is a success, and in the end he has to face the champion again. Will he win? **62m/B VHS, Beta.** Kenneth McDonald, Frank Rice, Boris Karloff, Eddie Harris, Diana Alden, Harry Woods, Jack Richardson; **D:** Bruce Mitchell. *GPV, LSV*

Dynamite Pass 🎬🎬 1950 Offbeat oater about disgruntled ranchers attempting to stop the construction of a new road. **61m/B VHS.** Tim Holt, Richard Martin, Regis Toomey, Lynn (Mary Hart) Roberts, Denver Pyle; **D:** Lew (Louis Friedlander) Landers. *MED*

Dynamite Ranch ✂ 1932 Ranchers fight tooth and nail to keep their rights and property in this Maynard oater. 60m/B VHS, Beta. Ken Maynard. *NOS, VCI, DVT*

Dynasty ✂✂ 1977 A leader of the Ming Dynasty is killed by evil Imperial Court eunuch and his son the monk sets out to avenge him. In 3-D. Run-of-the-mill kung-fu stunts. 94m/C VHS, Beta. Bobby Ming, Lin Tashing, Pai Ying, Tang Wei, Jin Gang; **D:** Zhang Meijun. *BFV*

Dynasty ✂✂ 1982 Pulitzer Prize-winning author James Michener creates the usual sweeping saga of a family torn by jealousy, deception, and rivalry in love and business as husband, wife, and brother-in-law seek their fortune in the Ohio frontier of the 1820s. 90m/C VHS, Beta. Sarah Miles, Harris Yulin, Stacy Keach. *TLF*

Dynasty of Fear ✂½ *Fear in the Night; Honeymoon of Fear* 1972 (PG) Matters get rather sticky at a British boys' school when the headmaster's wife seduces her husband's assistant. Together they conspire to murder her husband and share his fortune. 93m/C VHS, Beta. *GB* Peter Cushing, Joan Collins, Ralph Bates, Judy Geeson, James Cossins; **D:** Jimmy Sangster; **W:** Jimmy Sangster. *REP, ACA*

E. Nick: A Legend in His Own Mind 1984 Satire of videos and magazines designed for adults. 75m/C VHS, Beta. Don Calfa, Cleavon Little, Andra Akers, Pat McCormick; **D:** Robert Hegyes. *LIV*

Each Dawn I Die ✂✂½ 1939 Cagney stars as a reporter who is a fervent critic of the political system. Framed for murder and imprisoned, he is subsequently befriended by fellow inmate, Raft, a gangster. Once hardened by prison life, Cagney shuns his friend and becomes wary of the system. Despite its farfetched second half and mediocre script, the film makes interesting viewing thanks to a stellar performance from Cagney. 92m/B VHS, Beta. James Cagney, George Raft, George Bancroft, Jane Bryan, Maxie "Slapsie" Rosenbloom, Alan Baxter, Thurston Hall, Stanley Ridges, Victor Jory; **D:** William Keighley. *MGM*

The Eagle ✂✂✂ 1925 In this tale of a young Cossack "Robin Hood," Valentino assumes the persona of the Eagle to avenge his father's murder. The romantic rogue encounters trouble when he falls for the beautiful Banky much to the chagrin of the scorned Czarina Dresser. Fine performances from Valentino and Dresser. Silent, based on a Alexander Pushkin story. Released on video with a new score by Davis. 77m/B VHS, Beta, LV. Rudolph Valentino, Vilma Banky, Louise Dresser, George Nicholls Jr., James Marcus; **D:** Clarence Brown; **C:** George Barnes; **M:** Carl Davis. *NOS, HBO, VYY*

The Eagle and the Hawk ✂✂✂ 1933 Americans Jerry Young (March), Henry Crocker (Grant), and Mike Richards (Oakie) volunteer for flying duty with the British Army in 1918. Jerry is a heroic pilot but becomes depressed by the horrors of war, while gung ho Henry, who's serving as his observer/gunner, also becomes his rival. On leave, Jerry briefly finds solace with a society babe (Lombard) only to discover on his return that Henry's cockiness has gotten their buddy Mike killed. He denounces the war but Henry manages to ensure Jerry's status as a hero despite his actions. 73m/B VHS, Closed Caption. Fredric March, Cary Grant, Jack Oakie, Carole Lombard, Guy Standing, Forrester Harvey, Kenneth Howell, Leyland Hodgson; **D:** Stuart Walker; **W:** Seton I. Miller, Bogart Rogers; **C:** Harry Fishbeck. *USH*

The Eagle Has Landed ✂✂✂ 1977 (PG) Duvall, portraying a Nazi colonel in this WWII spy film, commissions Sutherland's Irish, English-hating character to aid him in his mission to kill Prime Minister Winston Churchill. Adapted from the bestselling novel by Jack Higgins. A restored version is available at 134 minutes. 123m/C VHS, Beta. Michael Caine, Donald Sutherland, Robert Duvall,

Larry Hagman, Jenny Agutter, Donald Pleasence, Treat Williams, Anthony Quayle; **D:** John Sturges; **W:** Tom Mankiewicz; **M:** Lalo Schifrin. *FOX, FCT*

The Eagle Has Two Heads ✂✂✂ *L'Aigle a Deux Tetes; The Eagle with Two Heads* 1948 Set during the 19th century, poet/anarchist Marais sets out to assassinate the queen, but when he sees the beautiful monarch, it's love at first sight. Adapted from Cocteau's hugely successful play. In French with English subtitles. 93m/B VHS. *FR* Edwige Feuillere, Jean Marais; **D:** Jean Cocteau; **W:** Jean Cocteau. *WBF*

Eagles Attack at Dawn ✂½ 1974 (PG) After escaping from an Arab prison, an Israeli soldier vows to return with a small commando force to kill the sadistic warden. 96m/C VHS, Beta. *IS* Rick Jason, Peter Brown, Joseph Shiloal. *NO*

Eagle's Shadow ✂ 1984 After a poor orphan boy rescues an aged beggar, the grateful old man tutors the lad in Snake-Fist techniques. 101m/C VHS, Beta. Jackie Chan, Juan Jan Lee, Simon Yuen, Roy Horan; **D:** Yuen Woo Ping. *WVE*

Eagle's Wing ✂½ 1979 John Briley, screenwriter of the award-winning epic "Gandhi," attempts to weave the threads of allegory smoothly in this white man vs. red man Western from England. The mediocre story finds Native American Waterston dueling white trapper Sheen in a quest to capture an elusive, exotic white stallion. 111m/C VHS, Beta. *GB* Martin Sheen, Sam Waterston, Harvey Keitel, Stephane Audran, Caroline Langrishe; **D:** Anthony Harvey; **W:** John Briley; **C:** Billy Williams. *MED*

Early Cinema Vol. 1 1919 A compendium of early silent shorts, mostly predating 1920, which includes: Melies' "Conquest of the North Pole"; Linder's "Man and the Statue" and "Max's Mother In Law"; Drew's "Auntie's Portrait"; Normand's "Mabel's Dramatic Career"; Mix's "An Angelic Attitude" Sennett and Swain's "Cowboy Ambrose"; Lloyd's "Just Neighbors" and Parrott's "Take the Air." 118m/B VHS, Beta. Mabel Normand, Harold Lloyd, Sidney Drew, Max Linder, Paul Parrott, Tom Mix, Mack Swain; **D:** Mabel Normand, Harold Lloyd, Max Linder, Georges Melies, Mack Sennett. *FCT*

Early Days ✂✂ 1981 A cantankerous, salty, once-powerful politician awaits death. 67m/C VHS, Beta. Ralph Richardson. *FOX*

Early Frost ✂½ 1984 Near suspenseful whodunit centering around a simple divorce investigation that leads to the discovery of a corpse. 95m/C VHS, Beta, LV. Diana McLean, Jon Blake, Janet Kingsbury, David Franklin; **D:** Terry O'Connor. *NO*

An Early Frost ✂✂✂½ 1985 Highly praised, surprisingly intelligent made-for-television drama following the anguish of a successful lawyer who tells his closed-minded family that he is gay and dying of AIDS. Sensitive performance by Quinn in one of the first TV films to focus on the devastating effects of HIV. Rowlands adeptly displays her acting talents as the despairing mother. 97m/C VHS, Beta, LV. Aidan Quinn, Gena Rowlands, Ben Gazzara, John Glover, D.W. Moffett, Sylvia Sidney; **D:** John Erman. *FCT, COL*

Early Summer ✂✂✂ *Bakushu* 1951 A classic from renowned Japanese director Ozu, this film chronicles family tensions in post-WWII Japan caused by newly-independent women rebelling against the social conventions they are expected to fulfill. Perhaps the best example of this director's work. Winner of Japan's Film of the Year Award. In Japanese with English subtitles. 150m/B VHS, Beta. *JP* Ichiro Sugai, Chishu Ryu, Setsuko Hara, Chikage Awashima, Chieko Higashiyama, Haruko Sugimura, Kuniko Miyake, Kan Nihon-yanagi, Shuji Sano, Toyoko Takahashi, Seiji Miyaguchi; **D:** Yasujiro Ozu. *FCT*

The Earrings of Madame De... ✂✂✂✂ *Diamond Earrings; Madame De* 1954 A simple story about a society woman who sells a pair of diamond earrings that her husband gave her, then lies about it. Transformed by Ophuls into his most opulent, overwrought masterpiece, the film displays a triumph of form over content. In

French with English subtitles. 105m/C VHS, Beta. *FR* Charles Boyer, Danielle Darrieux, Vittorio De Sica, Lea di Lea, Jean Debucourt; **D:** Max Ophuls. Nominations: Academy Awards '54: Best Costume Design (B & W). *FCT, MRV, CVC*

Earth ✂✂✂✂ *Zemlya; Soul* 1930 Classic Russian silent film with English subtitles. Problems begin in a Ukrainian village when a collective farm landowner resists handing over his land. Outstanding camera work. Kino release runs 70 minutes. 57m/B VHS, Beta. *RU* Semyon Svashenko, Mikola Nademsy, Stephan Shkurat, Yelena Maximova; **D:** Alexander Dovzhenko. *VYY, CCB, IHF*

Earth Entranced ✂✂ *Terra em Transe* 1966 A complex political lamentation from Rocha, the premiere director of Brazil's own new wave cinema. Here a writer switches his allegiance from one politician to another, only to find that he (and the masses) lose either way. In Portuguese with English subtitles. 105m/C VHS. *BR* Jose Lewgoy, Paulo Gracindo, Jardel Filho, Glauce Rocha; **D:** Glauce Rocha; **W:** Glauce Rocha. *FCT*

Earth Girls Are Easy ✂✂½ 1989 (PG) Valley girl Valerie is having a bad week: first she catches her fiancee with another woman, then she breaks a nail, then furry aliens land in her swimming pool. What more could go wrong? When the aliens are temporarily stranded, she decides to make amends by giving them a head-to-toe makeover. Devoid of their excessive hairiness, the handsome trio of fun-loving extraterrestrials set out to experience the Southern California lifestyle. Sometimes hilarious sci-fi/musical, featuring bouncy shtick and a gleeful dismantling of modern culture. 100m/C VHS, Beta, LV, Closed Caption. Geena Davis, Jeff Goldblum, Charles Rocket, Julie Brown, Jim Carrey, Damon Wayans, Michael McKean, Angelyne, Larry Linville, Rick Overton; **D:** Julien Temple; **W:** Julie Brown, Charlie Coffey, Terrance McNally; **M:** Nile Rodgers. *LIV, VES*

Earth vs. the Flying Saucers ✂✂½ *Invasion of the Flying Saucers* 1956 Extraterrestrials land on Earth and issue an ultimatum to humans concerning their constant use of bombs and missiles. Peace is threatened when the military disregards the extraterrestrials' simple warning. Superb special effects by Ray Harryhausen. 83m/B VHS, Beta, LV. Hugh Marlowe, Joan Taylor, Donald Curtis, Morris Ankrum; **D:** Fred F. Sears; **W:** George Worthing Yates, Bernard Gordon. *COL, MLB*

Earth vs. the Spider ✂ *The Spider* 1958 Man-eating giant mutant (teenage ninja?) tarantula makes life miserable for a small town in general and high school partyers in particular. Silly old drive-in fare is agony for many, camp treasure for a precious few. 72m/B VHS. Edward Kemmer, June Kennedy, Gene Persson, Gene Roth, Hal Torey, Mickey Finn; **D:** Bert I. Gordon; **W:** Laszlo Gorog, George Worthing Yates; **C:** Jack Marta. *COL, MLB*

Earthling ✂✂½ 1980 (PG) A terminally ill Holden helps a young Schroder survive in the Australian wilderness after the boy's parents are killed in a tragic accident. Lessons of life and the power of the human heart are passed on in this panoramic, yet mildly sentimental film. 102m/C VHS, Beta. *AU* William Holden, Rick Schroder, Jack Thompson, Olivia Hamnett, Alwyn Kurts; **D:** Peter Collinson; **W:** Lanny Cotler. *LIV, VES*

Earthquake ✂✂ 1974 (PG) Less-than mediocre drama centers on a major earthquake in Los Angeles and its effect on the lives of an engineer, his spoiled wife, his mistress, his father-in-law, and a suspended policeman. Filmed in much-hyped Sensurround—a technique intended to shake up the theater a bit, but which will have no effect on your television set. Good special effects, but not enough to compensate for lackluster script. 123m/C VHS, Beta, LV. Charlton Heston, Ava Gardner, George Kennedy, Lorne Greene, Genevieve Bujold, Richard Roundtree, Marjoe Gortner, Barry Sullivan, Victoria Principal, Lloyd Nolan, Walter Matthau, Scott Hylands; **D:** Mark Robson; **W:** Mario Puzo; **M:** John Williams. Academy Awards '74: Best Sound, Best Visual Effects;

Nominations: Academy Awards '74: Best Art Direction/Set Decoration, Best Cinematography, Best Film Editing. *USH*

Earthworm Tractors ♡♡½ **1936** Ambitious tractor salesman Alexander Botts will do anything to make a sale. Brown excels as the fast-talking lead. Comedy is strengthened by its supporting cast. Based on characters first appearing in the "Saturday Evening Post." *63m/B VHS.* Joe E. Brown, June Travis, Guy Kibbee, Dick Foran, Carol Hughes, Gene Lockhart, Olin Howlin; *D:* Ray Enright. *NOS, RXM, HEG*

East and West ♡♡♡ **1924** Morris Brown, a worldly New York Jew, returns home to Galicia with his daughter Mollie for a traditional family wedding. She teaches the young villagers how to dance and box but meets her romantic match in a young yeshiva scholar who forsakes tradition to win her heart. Picon shines as the exuberant flapper. With English and Yiddish intertitles. *85m/B VHS. AU* Molly Picon, Jacob Kalish, Sidney Goldin; *D:* Ivan Abramson, Sidney Goldin. *NCJ*

East L.A. Warriors ♡½ **1989** A mobster, Hilton-Jacobs, manipulates Los Angeles gangs in this non-stop action adventure. *90m/C VHS, Beta.* Tony Bravo, Lawrence-Hilton Jacobs, Kamar Reyes, William Smith; *D:* Addison Randall. *PAR*

East of Borneo ♡½ **1931** Tropical adventure involving a "lost" physician whose worried wife sets out to find him in the jungle. She locates her love only to discover he has a prestigious new job tending to royalty and didn't want to be found. *76m/B VHS, Beta.* Charles Bickford, Rose Hobart, Georges Renavent; *D:* George Melford. *SNC, DVT, CAB*

East of Eden ♡♡♡♡ **1954** Steinbeck's contemporary retelling of the biblical Cain and Abel story receives superior treatment from Kazan and his excellent cast. Dean, in his first starring role, gives a reading of a young man's search for love and acceptance that defines adolescent pain. Though filmed in the 1950s, this story still rivets today's viewers with its emotional message. *115m/C VHS, Beta, LV, Closed Caption.* James Dean, Julie Harris, Richard Davalos, Raymond Massey, Jo Van Fleet, Burl Ives, Albert Dekker; *D:* Elia Kazan; *M:* Leonard Rosenman. Academy Awards '55: Best Supporting Actress (Van Fleet); Golden Globe Awards '56: Best Film—Drama; National Board of Review Awards '55: 10 Best Films of the Year; Nominations: Academy Awards '55: Best Actor (Dean), Best Director (Kazan), Best Screenplay. *WAR, BTV, HMV*

East of Eden ♡♡½ **1980** Remade into a television mini series, this Steinbeck classic tells the tale of two brothers who vie for their father's affection and the woman who comes between them. Seymour is notable as the self-serving mother who abandons her babies to lead a disreputable life. Rife with biblical symbolism and allusions. *375m/C VHS, Beta, LV.* Jane Seymour, Bruce Boxleitner, Warren Oates, Lloyd Bridges, Anne Baxter, Timothy Bottoms, Soon-Teck Oh, Karen Allen, Hart Bochner, Sam Bottoms, Howard Duff, Richard Masur, Wendell Burton, Nicholas Pryor, Grace Zabriskie, M. Emmet Walsh, Matthew "Stymie" Beard; *D:* Harvey Hart. *VTR, LIV*

East of Elephant Rock ♡½ **1976** In 1948, a young first secretary of the British Embassy returns from leave in England to a tense atmosphere in a colony in southeast Asia. Beautiful scenery can't make up for weak plot. *93m/C VHS, Beta. GB* John Hurt, Jeremy Kemp, Judi Bowker, Christopher Cazenove; *D:* Don Boyd; *W:* Don Boyd.

East of Kilimanjaro ♡♡ **1957** A freelance photographer and a doctor search frantically to find the carrier of a fatal disease near the slopes of the majestic Mt. Kilimanjaro. Routine killer virus flick filmed in Africa. Also know as "The Big Search." *75m/C VHS.* Marshall Thompson, Gaby Andre, Fausto Tozzi; *D:* Arnold Belgard.

East Side Kids ♡♡ **1940** Early East Side kids. A hoodlum wants to prevent his brother from beginning a similar life of crime. *60m/B VHS, Beta.* Leon Ames, Harris Berger, Dennis Moore, Joyce Bryant; *D:* Robert F. "Bob" Hill. *NOS, MRV, DVT*

East Side Kids/The Lost City **1935** The first East Side Kids film introduces some soon-familiar faces. "The Lost City" is a composite of all twelve episodes of the serial; edited for brevity. *135m/B VHS, Beta.* Dennis Moore, Vince Barnett, William "Stage" Boyd, Kane Richmond. *AOV*

East Side, West Side ♡♡ **1949** Stanwyck and Mason try hard to make this simple-minded soaper work, with mixed results. A wealthy couple experiences marital woes, aggravated by a ambitious young woman and a soft-hearted man suffering from unrequited love. Based on the popular novel by Marcia Davenport. *110m/B VHS.* Barbara Stanwyck, James Mason, Ava Gardner, Van Heflin, Gale Sondergaard, William Frawley, Nancy Davis; *D:* Mervyn LeRoy; *C:* Charles Rosher; *M:* Miklos Rozsa. *MGM*

Easter Parade ♡♡♡½ **1948** A big musical star (Astaire) splits with his partner (Miller) claiming he could mold any girl to replace her in the act. He tries and finally succeeds after much difficulty. Astaire and Garland in peak form, aided by a classic Irving Berlin score. ♫Happy Easter; Drum Crazy; It Only Happens When I Dance With You; Everybody's Doin' It; I Want to Go Back to Michigan; Beautiful Faces Need Beautiful Clothes; A Fella With an Umbrella; I Love a Piano; Snookey Ookums. *103m/C VHS, Beta, LV.* Fred Astaire, Judy Garland, Peter Lawford, Ann Miller, Jules Munshin, Joi Lansing; *D:* Charles Walters; *W:* Sidney Sheldon; *C:* Harry Stradling; *M:* Irving Berlin. Academy Awards '48: Scoring of a Musical. *MGM, HMV*

Easy Come, Easy Go ♡♡ **1967** Elvis, as a Navy frogman, gets excited when he accidentally discovers what he believes is a vast sunken treasure. Music is his only solace when he finds his treasure to be worthless copper coins. ♫Easy Come, Easy Go; The Love Machine; Yoga is as Yoga Goes; Sing, You Children; You Gotta Stop; I'll Take Love. *96m/C VHS, Beta.* Elvis Presley, Dodie Marshall, Pat Priest, Elsa Lanchester, Frank McHugh, Pat Harrington; *D:* John Rich. *PAR*

Easy Kill ♡½ **1989** A man takes the law into his own hands to exact revenge on drug lords. *100m/C VHS, Beta.* Jane Badler, Cameron Mitchell, Frank Stallone; *D:* Josh Spencer. *NO*

The Easy Life ♡♡♡ **1963** Haunting film about a hedonistic man from a small Italian village who takes a mild-mannered student pleasure-seeking. The ride turns sour and the playboy is ultimately destroyed by his own brutality. *105m/B VHS. IT* Vittorio Gassman, Catherine Spaak, Jean-Louis Trintignant, Luciana Angiolillo; *D:* Dino Risi. *FST*

Easy Living ♡♡½ **1949** Compromised melodrama about an over-the-hill football player who must cope with his failing marriage and looming retirement. Based on an Irwin Shaw story. *77m/B VHS, Beta, LV.* Victor Mature, Lucille Ball, Jack Paar, Lizabeth Scott, Sonny Tufts, Lloyd Nolan, Paul Stewart; *D:* Jacques Tourneur. *MED, TTC*

Easy Money ♡♡ **1983 (R)** A basic slob has the chance to inherit $10 million if he can give up his loves: smoking, drinking, and gambling among others. Dangerfield is surprisingly restrained in this harmless, though not altogether unpleasing comedy. *95m/C VHS, Beta, LV.* Rodney Dangerfield, Joe Pesci, Geraldine Fitzgerald, Jennifer Jason Leigh, Tom Ewell, Candice Azzara, Taylor Negron; *D:* James Signorelli; *W:* Rodney Dangerfield, Dennis Blair. *VES*

Easy Rider ♡♡♡½ **1969 (R)** Slim-budget, generation-defining movie. Two young men in late 1960s undertake a motorcycle trek throughout the Southwest in search of the real essence of America. Along the way they encounter hippies, rednecks, prostitutes, drugs, Nicholson, and tragedy. One of the highest-grossing pictures of the decade, undoubtedly an influence on two generations of "youth-oriented dramas," which all tried unsuccessfully to duplicate the original accomplishment. Psychedelic scenes and a great role for Nicholson are added bonuses. Look for the graveyard dancing scene in New Orleans. Features

one of the best '60s rock scores around, including "Mean Streets" and "The Wanderers." *94m/C VHS, Beta, LV, 8mm.* Peter Fonda, Dennis Hopper, Jack Nicholson, Karen Black, Toni Basil, Robert Walker Jr., Luana Anders, Luke Askew, Toni Basil, Warren Finnerty, Mac Mashorian, Antonio Mendoza, Sabrina Scharf, Phil Spector; *D:* Dennis Hopper; *W:* Terry Southern, Peter Fonda, Dennis Hopper; *C:* Laszlo Kovacs. New York Film Critics Awards '69: Best Supporting Actor (Nicholson); National Society of Film Critics Awards '69: Best Supporting Actor (Nicholson); Nominations: Academy Awards '69: Best Story & Screenplay, Best Supporting Actor (Nicholson). *COL, CCB*

Easy Street ♡♡♡ **1916** Chaplin portrays a derelict who, using some hilarious methods, reforms the residents of Easy Street. Chaplin's row with the town bully is particularly amusing. Silent with musical soundtrack added. *20m/B VHS, Beta.* Charlie Chaplin; *D:* Charlie Chaplin. *CAB*

Easy to Love ♡♡½ **1953** Williams is in love with her boss, but he pays her no attention until a handsome singer vies for her affections. Set at Florida's Cypress Gardens, this aquatic musical features spectacular water ballet productions choreographed by Busby Berkeley, and the title song penned by Cole Porter. ♫Easy to Love; Coquette; Beautiful Spring; That's What Rainy Day is For; Look Out! I'm Romantic; Didja Ever. *96m/C VHS.* Esther Williams, Van Johnson, Tony Martin, John Bromfield, King Donovan, Carroll Baker; *D:* Charles Walters; *W:* William Roberts. *MGM*

Easy Virtue ♡♡½ **1927** Hitchcock directs this adaptation of a Noel Coward play as a social melodrama. Larita is an unhappily married socialite with a lover. When her husband discovers her infideltiy they divorce and she is marked as a woman of loose morals. Her reputation is not enhanced by her marriage to a younger man whose family diapproves. *79m/B VHS, Beta. GB* Isabel Jeans, Ian Hunter, Frank Dyall, Eric Bransby Williams, Robin Irvine, Violet Farebrother; *D:* Alfred Hitchcock. *GPV, MRV, NOS*

Easy Wheels ♡♡½ **1989** Like most decent biker movies, "Wheels" is propelled by bad taste and a healthy dose of existentialistic nihilism. But there's an unusual plot twist in this parody. A biker named She-Wolf and her gang kidnap female babies and let wolves rear the children. Their elaborate plan is to create a race of super women who will subdue the troublesome male population. But can this "noble" plan succeed? *94m/C VHS, Beta, LV.* Paul LeMat, Eileen Davidson, Marjorie Bransfield, Jon Menick, Mark Holton, Karen Russell, Jami Richards, Roberta Vasquez, Barry Livingston, George Plimpton; *D:* David O'Malley; *W:* Ivan Raimi, Celia Abrams, David O'Malley; *M:* John Ross. *FRH*

Eat a Bowl of Tea ♡♡♡ **1989 (PG-13)** Endearing light drama-comedy concerning a multi-generational Chinese family. They must learn to deal with the problems of life in America and in particular, marriage, when Chinese women are finally allowed to immigrate with their husbands to the United States following WWII. Adaptation of Louis Chu's story, directed by the man who brought us "Dim Sum." A PBS "American Playhouse" presentation. *102m/C VHS, Beta, LV, Closed Caption.* Cora Miao, Russell Wong, Lau Siu Ming, Eric Tsiang Chi Wai, Victor Wong, Jessica Harper, Lee Sau Kee; *D:* Wayne Wang; *W:* Judith Rascoe; *M:* Mark Adler. *COL*

Eat and Run ♡ **1986 (R)** A bloody comedy about a 400-pound alien with a taste for Italian (people, that is). *85m/C VHS, Beta.* Ron Silver, R.L. Ryan, Sharon Schlarth; *D:* Christopher Hart. *VTR, NWV*

Eat Drink Man Woman ♡♡♡½ **1994 (R)** In Taipei, widowed master chef serves weekly feast of elaborate food and familial guilt to his three grown daughters, all of whom still live at home. They spend their time sorting out professional and romantic difficulties, searching for independence, and fulfilling traditional family obligations. Each character has a lot going on, but no one's story gets lost in the mix. Lee uses irony to great effect, introducing us to the culinary artist who has lost his sense of taste and has a daughter who works at a Wendy's. Food preparation scenes (more than 100 recipes are served up) illustrate a careful attention to detail (and are guaranteed to make you hungry). Lee's follow-up to "The Wedding Banquet" is a finely observed, comic tale of generational drift, the richness of tradition, and the power of love to redeem or improve. In Chinese with subtitles or dubbed. **123m/C VHS, LV.** *TW* Sihung Lung, Kuei-Mei Yang, Yu-Wen Wang, Chien-Lien Wu, Sylvia Chang, Winston Chao, Ah-Leh Gua, Lester Chen; *D:* Ang Lee; *W:* Ang Lee, James Schamus, Hui-Ling Wang; *C:* Jong Lin; *M:* Mader. National Board of Review Awards '94: Best Foreign Film; Nominations: Academy Awards '94: Best Foreign Language Film; Golden Globe Awards '95: Best Foreign Film; Independent Spirit Awards '95: Best Actor (Lung), Best Actress (Wu), Best Cinematography, Best Director (Lee), Best Film, Best Screenplay. *HMK*

Eat My Dust 🐾🐾 **1976 (PG)** Teenage son of a California sheriff steals the best stock cars from a race track to take the town's heartthrob for a joy ride. Subsequently he leads the town on a wild car chase. Brainless but fast-paced. **89m/C VHS, Beta.** Ron Howard, Christopher Norris, Warren Kemmerling, Rance Howard, Clint Howard, Corbin Bernsen; *D:* Charles B. Griffith.

Eat the Peach 🐾🐾½ **1986** An idiosyncratic Irish comedy about two young unemployed rebels who attempt to break free from their tiny coast town by becoming motorcycle champs after seeing the Elvis Presley film "Roustabout." Together they create the "wall of death,"—a large wooden barrel in which they can perform various biker feats. **90m/C VHS, Beta, Closed Caption.** *IR* Stephen Brennan, Eamon Morrissey, Catherine Byrne, Niall Toibin, Tony Doyle, Joe Lynch; *D:* Peter Ormrod; *W:* Peter Ormrod, John Kelleher; *M:* Donal Lunny. *FOX*

Eat the Rich 🐾🐾 **1987 (R)** A British farce about a group of terrorists who take over the popular London restaurant, Bastard's. Led by a former, disgruntled transvestite employee, they turn diners into menu offerings. Music by Motorhead. **89m/C VHS, Beta.** *GB* Nosher Powell, Lanah Pellay, Fiona Richmond, Ronald Allen, Sandra Dorne, Angie Bowie, Sandie Shaw; *Cameos:* Paul McCartney, Linda McCartney, Bill Wyman, Koo Stark, Miranda Richardson; *D:* Peter Richardson. *COL*

Eaten Alive 🐾🐾 *Death Trap; Starlight Slaughter; Legend of the Bayou; Horror Hotel Massacre* **1976 (R)** A Southerner takes an unsuspecting group of tourists into a crocodile death trap. Director Tobe Hooper's follow-up to "The Texas Chainsaw Massacre." Englund is more recognizable with razor fingernails as Freddy Krueger of the "Nightmare on Elm Street" films. **96m/C VHS, Beta.** Neville Brand, Mel Ferrer, Carolyn Jones, Marilyn Burns, Stuart Whitman, Robert Englund; *D:* Tobe Hooper; *M:* Wayne Bell. *PSM*

Eating 🐾🐾½ **1990 (R)** Set in Southern California, women gather to celebrate birthdays for three of their friends who are turning 30, 40 and 50. As the party commences, women from two generations discuss their attitudes towards food and men...and discover hilarious parallels.*CW:* Language. **110m/C VHS, Beta, LV, Closed Caption.** Nelly Alard, Frances Bergen, Mary Crosby, Lisa Richards, Gwen Welles, Daphna Kastner, Elizabeth Kemp, Marlena Giovi, Marina Gregory, Toni Basil; *D:* Henry Jaglom; *W:* Henry Jaglom; *C:* Hanania Baer. *PAR*

Eating Raoul 🐾🐾🐾½ **1982 (R)** The Blands are a happily married couple who share many interests: good food and wine, entrepreneurial dreams, and an aversion to sex. The problem is, they're flat broke. So, when the tasty swinger from upstairs makes a pass at Mary and Paul accidentally kills him, they discover he's got loads of money; Raoul takes a cut in the deal by disposing of—or rather recycling—the body. This may just be the way to finance that restaurant they've been wanting to open. Wonderful, offbeat, hilariously dark comedy. **83m/C VHS, Beta.** Mary Woronov, Paul Bartel, Robert Beltran, Buck Henry, Ed Begley Jr., Edie McClurg, John Paragon, Richard Blackburn, Hamilton Camp, Bill Curtis, Susan Saiger; *D:* Mary Woronov, Paul Bartel; *W:* Paul Bartel, Richard Blackburn. *FOX*

Ebbtide 🐾🐾½ **1994 (R)** Lawyer Jeff Warren (Hamlin) takes on the case of a mother who says her son's died from chemicals dumped by the Poseidon Pacific Co. Jeff got the case when the previous lawyer died mysteriously but this doesn't stop him checking out the chemical company or its beautiful president. **90m/C VHS, Closed Caption.** Harry Hamlin, Judy McIntosh, Susan Lyons, John Gregg, Frankie J. Holden; *D:* Craig Lahiff; *W:* Robert Ellis, Peter Goldsworthy. *PAR*

Ebony Dreams **1980** WWII documentary focuses on the experience of female factory workers during and after the war. Five contemporary women relate their personal endeavors and struggles to retain their jobs once the war ended. Excellent use of newsreel footage and interesting interviews with the women. **85m/C VHS.** Philomena Nowlin; *D:* Bill Brame. *NO*

Ebony Tower 🐾🐾½ **1986** Based on the John Fowles novel about a crusty old artist who lives in a French chateau with two young female companions. They are visited by a handsome young man, thereby initiating sexual tension and recognizably Fowlesian plot puzzles. Made for British television. Features some partial nudity. **80m/C Beta.** *GB* Laurence Olivier, Roger Rees, Greta Scacchi, Toyah Wilcox; *D:* Robert Knights; *M:* Richard Rodney Bennett. *NO*

Echo Murders 🐾½ **1945** A Sexton Blake mystery wherein he investigates a mine owner's mysterious death, opening up a veritable can of murdering, power-hungry worms. **75m/B VHS, Beta.** David Farrar, Dennis Price. *NOS, VYY*

Echo Park 🐾🐾½ **1986 (R)** An unsung sleeper comedy about three roommates living in Los Angeles' Echo Park: a body builder, a single-mother waitress, and an itinerant songwriter. Charts their struggles as they aim for careers in showbiz. Offbeat ensemble effort. **93m/C VHS, Beta, LV.** *AU* Tom Hulce, Susan Dey, Michael Bowen, Richard "Cheech" Marin, Christopher Walker, Shirley Jo Finney, Cassandra Peterson, Yana Nirvana, Timothy Carey; *D:* Robert Dornhelm; *W:* Michael Ventura; *M:* David Rickets. *BAR*

Echoes 🐾🐾 **1983 (R)** A young painter's life slowly comes apart as he is tormented by nightmares that his stillborn twin brother is attempting to murder him. **90m/C VHS, Beta.** Gale Sondergaard, Mercedes McCambridge, Richard Alfieri, Ruth Roman, John Spencer, Nathalie Nell; *D:* Arthur Seidelman; *W:* Richard Alfieri, Richard J. Anthony; *C:* Hanania Baer. *NO*

Echoes in the Darkness 🐾🐾½ **1987** Television mini series based on the true-life Joseph Wambaugh bestseller about the "Main Line" murder investigation in Pennsylvania in 1979. Police are baffled when a teacher is murdered and her children vanish. Suspicion falls on a charismatic coworker and the school's principal. On two tapes. **234m/C VHS.** Peter Coyote, Robert Loggia, Stockard Channing, Peter Boyle, Cindy Pickett, Gary Cole, Zeljko Ivanek, Alex Hyde-White, Treat Williams; *D:* Glenn Jordan. *NWV*

Echoes of Conflict 🐾🐾 **1989** The turbulent Middle East and Arab-Israeli tensions are spotlighted in three new wave films from Israel. Includes "The Cage," "The Movie," and "Don't Get Involved." In Hebrew with English subtitles. In color and black and white. **91m/C VHS.** *IS* FCT, KIV

Echoes of Paradise 🐾½ *Shadows of the Peacock* **1986 (R)** After a series of earth-shattering events, a depressed woman journeys to an island where she falls for a Balinese dancer. Soon she must choose between returning home or beginning life anew in paradise. **90m/C VHS, Beta, LV.** *AU* Wendy Hughes, John Lone, Rod Mullinar, Peta Toppano, Steve Jacobs, Gillian Jones; *D:* Phillip Noyce. *ACA*

The Eclipse 🐾🐾🐾½ *L'eclisse* **1966** The last of Antonioni's trilogy (after "L'Avventura" and "La Notte"), wherein another fashionable and alienated Italian woman passes from one lover to another searching unsuccessfully for truth and love. Highly acclaimed. In Italian with subtitles. **123m/B**

VHS, Beta. *IT* Monica Vitti, Alain Delon, Francesco Rabal, Louis Seigner; *D:* Michelangelo Antonioni; *W:* Michelangelo Antonioni; *C:* Carlo DiPalma. *TPV, MRV, FCT*

Eclipse 🐾½ **1994** Sexual roundelay set in Toronto shortly before a total solar eclipse, which is apparently affecting all the generally listless characters in such a way that they meet and mate in joyless abandon. First feature for Podeswa. **96m/C VHS.** *CA GE* Von Flores, John Gilbert, Pascale Montpetit, Manuel Aranguiz, Maria Del Mar, Matthew Ferguson, Earl Pastko, Greg Ellwand, Daniel Maclvor, Kirsten Johnson; *D:* Jeremy Podeswa; *W:* Jeremy Podeswa; *C:* Miroslaw Baszak; *M:* Ernie Tollar. *FCT*

Ecstasy 🐾🐾½ *Extase; Ekstase; Symphony of Love* **1933** A romantic, erotic story about a young woman married to an older man, who takes a lover. Features Lamarr, then Hedy Kiesler, before her discovery in Hollywood. Film subsequently gained notoriety for Lamarr's nude scenes. In Czech with English subtitles. **90m/B VHS, Beta, 8mm.** *CZ* Hedy Lamarr, Jaromir Rogoz; *D:* Gustav Machaty. *VYY, NOS, MRV*

Ecstasy woof! **1984 (R)** Soft core fluff about a film director's wife's erotic adventures. **82m/C VHS, Beta.** Tiffany Bolling, Franc Luz, Jack Carter, Britt Ekland, Julie Newmar. *MGM*

Ed woof! **1996 (PG)** A must see for all fans of flatulent animatronic chimpanzees who play third base. Everyone else should stay away. LeBlanc (who should've been tipped off when they couldn't even get a real chimp to appear) plays Coop, a phenom pitcher stuck on a losing team in the minor leagues. After Ed the chimpanzee is bequeathed to the team by the late Mickey Mantle, (forgive them Mick, they know not what they do) he starts playing the hot corner like Brooks Robinson. Surprise! Ed becomes a national sensation, the team goes on a winning streak and sets up the showdown game climax. Most of the humor is derived from Ed tearing things up and passing gas, while LeBlanc yells in pop-eyed exasperation. Cameo from Tommy Lasorda playing a fat major league manager. **94m/C VHS, LV, Closed Caption.** Matthew LeBlanc, Jayne Brook, Bill Cobbs, Jack Warden, Doren Fein, Patrick Kerr, Charlie Schlatter, Carl Anthony Payne II, Curt Kaplan, Zack Ward, Mike McGlone, James Caviezel, Valente Rodriguez; *D:* Bill Couturie; *W:* David Mickey Evans; *C:* Alan Caso; *M:* Stephen Endelman. Nominations: Golden Raspberry Awards '96: Worst Picture, Worst Screenplay. *USH*

Ed and His Dead Mother 🐾🐾 **1993 (PG-13)** Ed's just an average guy who happens to really love his mother. So much so that when she dies Ed tries to bring her back from the dead—and succeeds. Only death has made a few changes in Mom's personality. Now she's a bug-eating, chainsaw-wielding fiend. Just what's a good son supposed to do? **93m/C VHS, LV, Closed Caption.** Ned Beatty, Steve Buscemi, John Glover, Miriam Margolyes; *D:* Jonathan Wacks; *W:* Chuck Hughes. *FXV*

Ed Wood 🐾🐾🐾½ **1994 (R)** Leave it to Burton to bring to the screen the story of a director many consider to be the worst of all time (he's at least in the top three) and who now occupies a lofty position as a cult icon. In this hilarious and touching tribute to a Hollywood maverick with grade-Z vision, detailed homage is paid to Wood's single-mindedness and optimism in the face of repeated failure and lack of financing, even down to the black and white photography. Depp is convincing (and engaging) as Ed Wood, Jr., the cross-dressing, angora-sweater-wearing, low-budget auteur of such notoriously "bad" cult films as "Glen or Glenda" and "Plan 9 From Outer Space." Depp is supported by terrific portrayals of the motley Wood crew, led by Landau's morphine-addicted, down-on-his-luck Bela Lugosi. Burton focuses on Wood's relationship with Lugosi, whose career is over by the time Wood befriends him. Based on Rudolph Grey's book, "Nightmare of Ecstasy: The Life and Art of Edward D. Wood, Jr." **127m/B VHS, LV, Closed Caption.** Johnny Depp, Sarah Jessica Parker, Martin Landau, Bill

Murray, Jim Myers, Patricia Arquette, Jeffrey Jones, Lisa Marie, Vincent D'Onofrio; **D:** Tim Burton; **W:** Scott Alexander, Larry Karaszewski; **C:** Stefan Czapsky. Academy Awards '94: Best Makeup, Best Supporting Actor (Landau); Chicago Film Critics Awards '94: Best Cinematography, Best Supporting Actor (Landau); Golden Globe Awards '95: Best Supporting Actor (Landau); Los Angeles Film Critics Association Awards '94: Best Cinematography, Best Supporting Actor (Landau), Best Original Score; New York Film Critics Awards '94: Best Cinematography, Best Supporting Actor (Landau); National Society of Film Critics Awards '94: Best Cinematography, Best Supporting Actor (Landau); Screen Actors Guild Award '94: Best Supporting Actor (Landau); Nominations: British Academy Awards '95: Best Supporting Actor (Landau); Golden Globe Awards '95: Best Actor—Musical/Comedy (Depp), Best Film—Musical/Comedy; Writers Guild of America '94: Best Original Screenplay. *TOU*

Ed Wood: Look Back in Angora
1994 Biography of the eccentric low-budget filmmaker frequently considered the worst director in Hollywood and now a cult fave. Wood was responsible for "Plan 9 from Outer Space," among other movie disasters but his private peculiarities (including an angora fetish) rivaled his professional ones. Director Tim Burton brings Wood's life to the big screen with the theatrical release of "Ed Wood." **51m/C VHS. D:** Ted Newsom; **W:** Ted Newsom. *AVE*

Eddie ⅃⅃ 1996 (PG-13)
Basketball nut Edwina (Goldberg) wins a chance to be honorary coach for her beloved Knicks in a free throw contest. When some of her courtside advice works, and the other fans seem to respond to her, the publicity-seeking maverick owner (Langella) gives her the job full-time. Predictable comedy with the usual "new team member leads underdogs to contention" characters won't suprise, or particularly thrill, anyone. Goldberg's lively performance somewhat redeems standard script but reduces everyone around her, including an All-Star roster of NBA players, to window dressing. Basically the hoops version of "Little Big League."**CW:** Some language and brief sexuality. **100m/C VHS, LV, Closed Caption.** Whoopi Goldberg, Frank Langella, Dennis Farina, Richard Jenkins, Lisa Ann Walter, John Benjamin Hickey, John Salley; **D:** Steve Rash; **W:** Jon Connolly, David Loucka, Eric Champnella, Keith Mitchell, Steve Zacharias, Jeff Buhai; **C:** Victor Kemper; **M:** Stanley Clarke. Nominations: Golden Raspberry Awards '96: Worst Actress (Goldberg). *TOU*

Eddie and the Cruisers ⅃⅃ 1983 (PG)
In the early 1960s, rockers Eddie and the Cruisers score with one hit album. Amid their success, lead singer Pare dies mysteriously in a car accident. Years later, a reporter decides to write a feature on the defunct group, prompting a former band member to begin a search for missing tapes of the Cruisers' unreleased second album. Questions posed at the end of the movie are answered in the sequel. Enjoyable soundtrack by John Cafferty and the Beaver Brown Band. **90m/C VHS, Beta, LV, 8mm, Closed Caption.** Tom Berenger, Michael Pare, Ellen Barkin, Joe Pantoliano, Matthew Laurance, Helen Schneider, David Wilson, Michael "Tunes" Antunes, Joe Cates, John Stockwell, Barry Sand, Howard Johnson, Robin Karfo, Rufus Harley, Bruce Brown, Louis D'Esposito, Michael Toland, Bob Garrett, Joanne Collins; **D:** Martin Davidson; **W:** Martin Davidson, Arlene Davidson; **C:** Fred Murphy; **M:** John Cafferty. *MVD, NLC*

Eddie and the Cruisers 2: Eddie Lives! ⅃½ 1989 (PG-13)
A sequel to the minor cult favorite, in which a rock star believed to be dead emerges under a new name in Montreal to lead a new band. The Beaver Brown Band again provides the music. **106m/C VHS, Beta, LV.** *CA* Michael Pare, Marina Orsini, Matthew Laurance, Bernie Coulson, Anthony Sherwood; **D:** Jean-Claude Lord; **W:** Charles Zev Cohen; **M:** Leon Aronson. *CCB, IME*

Eddie Macon's Run ⅃⅃ 1983 (PG)
Based on a true story; Eddie Macon has been unjustly jailed in Texas and plans an escape to run to Mexico. He is followed by a tough cop who is determined to catch the fugitive. Film debut of Goodman. **95m/C VHS, Beta, LV.** Kirk Douglas, John

---

Schneider, Lee Purcell, John Goodman, Leah Ayres; **D:** Jeff Kanew; **M:** Wendy Blackstone. *USH*

Eddie Murphy: Raw ⅃⅃ 1987 (R)
Murphy's second stand-up performance film, featuring many of his woman-bashing observations on life. **90m/C VHS, Beta, LV, 8mm, Closed Caption.** Eddie Murphy; **D:** Robert Townsend. *PAR*

The Eddy Duchin Story ⅃⅃ 1956
Glossy tearjerker that profiles the tragic life of Eddy Duchin, the famous pianist/bandleader of the 30s and 40s. Features almost 30 songs, including classics by Cole Porter, George and Ira Gershwin, Hammerstein, Chopin, and several others. **123m/C VHS, LV, Closed Caption.** Tyrone Power, Kim Novak, Victoria Shaw, James Whitmore, Rex Thompson; **D:** George Sidney; **C:** Harry Stradling; **M:** George Duning. Nominations: Academy Awards '56: Best Color Cinematography, Best Sound, Best Story, Scoring of a Musical. *COL, MVD, TVC*

Eden ⅃⅃ 1992
Eden is a luxury resort designed to cater to personal fantasies and filled with numerous intrigues. Part-owner Eve Sinclair faces a number of professional and personal complications, including the tragic death of her husband, a brother-in-law who's interested in more than business, and an old friend with uncertain motives. Lots of sex in beautiful settings. Made for cable television. **?m/C VHS.** Barbara Alyn Woods, Jack Armstrong, Steve Chase, Darcy Demoss, Jeff Griggs; **D:** Victor Lobl; **W:** Stephen Black, Henry Stern. *UND*

Eden 2 ⅃⅃ 1993 (R)
The continuing saga of the luxury resort Eden. Owner Eve is still having erotic dreams of late husband Grant while fending off the very real advances of his brother Josh and becoming attracted to Paul, her late husband's best friend. The guests are equally caught up in erotic dilemmas involving sexual blackmail. Made for cable television.**CW:** Language and numerous sex-related scenes. **102m/C VHS.** Barbara Alyn Woods, Jack Armstrong, Steve Chase, Darcy Demoss, Jeff Griggs; **D:** Kristine Peterson; **W:** Stephen Black, Henry Stern. *UND*

Eden 3 ⅃⅃ 1993 (R)
Yet another chapter in this sexy made for cable saga. Eve Sinclair risks losing her share of the tropical resort unless she remarries, which she doesn't want to do, although fitness trainer Randi would be delighted to pick up the option. Meanwhile, an heiress discovers her new bridegroom has murderous intentions.**CW:** Language and sex-related scenes. **?m/C VHS.** Barbara Alyn Woods, Jack Armstrong, Steve Chase, Darcy Demoss, Jeff Griggs, Dean Scofield; **D:** Victor Lobl. *UND*

Eden 4 ⅃⅃ 1993 (R)
Further adventures in the cable series. Eve, Eden's co-owner, must cope with both Josh's jealous rage and Randi's continuing scheming as she tries to keep her guests happy at the posh resort. One of the guests, a beautiful author, gets too caught up in her sexual fantasies and may find herself in danger.**CW:** Sex-related scenes. **?m/C VHS.** Barbara Alyn Woods, Jack Armstrong, Steve Chase, Darcy Demoss, Jeff Griggs, Dean Scofield; **D:** Kristine Peterson. *UND*

Eden Valley ⅃⅃⅃ 1994
A low-key intensity marks this northeast England drama that's produced, written, and directed by an eight-member film cooperative, the Amber Production Team. Troubled Newcastle teenager Billy (Bell) is put on probation for drug and theft charges and in a last-ditch chance at turning his life around goes to live with his estranged father, Hoggy (Hogg). They haven't seen each other in 10 years and Hoggy lives on a farm in County Durham where he raises and trains horses for harness racing. Naturally, their relationship is strained and there aren't any easy solutions (kinda like in real life). **95m/C VHS.** *GB* Darren Bell, Brian Hogg, Mike Elliott, Jimmy Killeen. *HTV*

Edge of Darkness ⅃⅃⅃½ 1943
Compelling war-drama about the underground movement in Norway during Nazi takeover of WWII. Flynn plays a Norwegian fisherman who leads the local underground movement and Sheridan is his

---

loyal fiancee. Although several problems occurred throughout filming, this picture earned high marks for its superb performances and excellent camerawork. Based on the novel by William Woods. **120m/B VHS, Closed Caption.** Errol Flynn, Ann Sheridan, Walter Huston, Nancy Coleman, Helmut Dantine, Judith Anderson, Ruth Gordon, John Beal; **D:** Lewis Milestone; **W:** Robert Rossen. *MGM*

Edge of Darkness ⅃⅃ 1986
Originally produced as a mini series for British television, this mystery involves a police detective who investigates his daughter's murder and uncovers a web of espionage and intrigue. **307m/C VHS, Beta, Closed Caption.** *GB* Bob Peck, Joe Don Baker, Jack Woodson, John Woodvine, Joanne Whalley; **D:** Martin Campbell; **M:** Eric Clapton, Michael Kamen. *FOX, TVC, VCO*

Edge of Honor ⅃½ 1991 (R)
Young Eagle Scouts camping in the Pacific Northwest discover a woodland weapons cache and wage guerilla war against killer lumberjacks out to silence them. A boneheaded, politically correct action bloodbath; you don't have to like the logging industry to disapprove of the broad slurs against its men shown here.**CW:** Language and strong violence. **92m/C VHS.** Corey Feldman, Meredith Salenger, Scott Reeves, Ken Jenkins, Christopher Neame, Don Swayze; **D:** Michael Spence; **W:** David O'Malley. *ACA*

Edge of Sanity ⅃½ 1989 (R)
An overdone Jekyll-Hyde reprise, with cocaine serving as the villainous substance. The coke-created Hyde is posited as a prototype for Jack the Ripper. Not for the easily queazy. Available in a 90 minute, unrated version. **85m/C VHS, Beta, LV, Closed Caption.** *GB* Anthony Perkins, Glynis Barber, David Lodge, Sarah Maur-Thorp; **D:** Gerard Kikoine. *NO*

Edge of the Axe 1989
A small town is held in the grip of terror by a demented slasher. **91m/C VHS, Beta.** Barton Faulks, Christina Marie Lane, Page Moseley, Fred Hollyday; **D:** Joseph Braunstein. *MCG*

Edge of the World ⅃⅃⅃ 1937
Moody, stark British drama of a mini-society in its death throes, expertly photographed on a six-square-mile island in the Shetlands. A dwindling fishing community of fewer than 100 souls agonize over whether to migrate to the mainland; meanwhile the romance of a local girl with an off-islander takes a tragic course. Choral effects were provided by the Glasgow Orpheus Choir. **80m/B VHS.** *GB* Finlay Currie, Niall MacGinnis, Grant Sutherland, John Laurie, Michael Powell; **D:** Michael Powell; **W:** Michael Powell. *NOS*

Edie & Pen ⅃⅃½ 1995 (PG-13)
Tilly seems to be making a career of playing the ditz who's smarter than she seems as she shows here as Edie, who meets Pen (Channing) in Reno where both are looking for quickie divorces. They hit a bar to celebrate and hook up with soft-hearted Harry (Glenn), who's been dumped by his wife. Some drunken life discussions follow and then Edie finds out that her fiance is Pen's cold-hearted, newly-ex hubby (Wilson). Slight script, charming performances.**CW:** Mature themes, sexual situations, language. **97m/C VHS.** Jennifer Tilly, Stockard Channing, Scott Glenn, Stuart Wilson; **Cameos:** Beverly D'Angelo, Louise Fletcher, Joanna Gleason, Michael McKean, Martin Mull, Michael O'Keefe, Chris Sarandon, Randy Travis, Jean Smart, Victoria Tennant; **D:** Matthew Irmas; **W:** Victoria Tennant; **C:** Alicia Weber; **M:** Shawn Colvin. *PGV*

Edie in Ciao! Manhattan ⅃⅃ *Ciao! Manhattan* 1972 (R)
Real-life story of Edie Sedgwick, Warhol superstar and international fashion model, whose life in the fast lane led to ruin. **84m/C VHS, Beta.** Edie Sedgwick, Baby Jane Holzer, Roger Vadim, Paul America, Viva. *FCT, PBS*

Edison the Man ⅃⅃½ 1940
Story of Tommy Edison's early years of experimentation in the basement. The young genious eventually invents light bulbs, motion pictures, and a sound recording device. Well played by Tracy. **108m/C VHS, Beta.** Spencer Tracy, Rita Johnson, Lynne Overman, Charles Coburn, Gene Lockhart, Henry Travers, Felix Bres-

sart; **D:** Clarence Brown. Nominations: Academy Awards '40: Best Story. *MGM*

Edith & Marcel 🎬½ 1983 A fictionalization of the love affair between chanteuse Edith Piaf and boxer Marcel Cerdan (played by his son, Marcel Cerdan, Jr.). In French, with English subtitles. 104m/C VHS, Beta. **FR** Evelyne Bouix, Marcel Cerdan Jr., Charles Aznavour, Jacques Villeret; **D:** Claude Lelouch. *MED*

Ed's Next Move 🎬🎬½ 1996 (R) Genial indie NYC comedy with a Woody Allen feel is littered with whimsical one-liners. Title character Ed (Ross) moves from small-town Wisconsin to New York after a break-up with his girlfriend. Being that he's a rice geneticist, it's not a big leap to conclude that Ed's a bit uptight, so it's imperative that Ed's big city roommate, the suave Ray (Carroll), hip him up to better meet the ladies. Soon, Ed falls for boho Lee (Thorne) leader of a band called "Ed's Redeeming Qualities." Fun fantasy sequence involving Ed, his old girlfriend and two translators is a highlight. Low-budgeter, with a first time writer/director (Walsh), and it shows, but in a good-natured way. Though more could be asked visually, it does boast good performers and well-drawn characters.**CW:** Scene of sexuality and some language. 88m/C VHS. Matt Ross, Calliope Thorne, Kevin Carroll, Ramsey Faragallah, Nina Shevaleva, Jimmy Cummings; **D:** John Walsh; **W:** John Walsh; **C:** Peter Nelson. *ORI*

Educating Rita 🎬🎬🎬½ 1983 (PG) Walters and Caine team beautifully in this adaptation of the successful Willy Russell play which finds an uneducated hairdresser determined to improve her knowledge of literature. In so doing, she enlists the aid of a tutor: a disillusioned alcoholic, adeptly played by Caine. Together, the two find inspiration in one another's differences and experiences. Ultimately, the teacher receives a lesson in how to really appreciate his work and the classics as he observes his pupil's unique approach to her studies. Some deem this a "Pygmalion" for the '80s. 110m/C VHS, Beta, LV, 8mm, Closed Caption. **GB** Michael Caine, Julie Walters, Michael Williams, Maureen Lipman; **D:** Lewis Gilbert; **W:** Willy Russell. British Academy Awards '83: Best Actor (Caine), Best Actress (Walters), Best Film; Golden Globe Awards '84: Best Actor—Musical/Comedy (Caine), Best Actress—Musical/Comedy (Walters); Nominations: Academy Awards '83: Best Actor (Caine), Best Actress (Walters), Best Adapted Screenplay. *COL*

The Education of Sonny Carson 🎬🎬½ 1974 (R) Chilling look at the tribulations of a black youth living in a Brooklyn ghetto amid drugs, prostitution, crime, and other forms of vice. Based on Sonny Carson's autobiography. Still pertinent some twenty years after its theatrical release. 104m/C VHS, Beta. Rony Clanton, Don Gordon, Paul Benjamin; **D:** Michael Campus. *MED*

Edvard Munch 🎬🎬 1974 Biographical portrait of the Norwegian Expressionist painter and his tormented life in the stuffy society of 19th-century Oslo. Concentrates mainly on his early years, including the deaths of his mother and younger sister, his brother's suicide, Munch's affair with a married woman, and his struggle to maintain his sanity. Based on Munch's memoirs. In German and Norwegian with English subtitles. 167m/C VHS. **NO** Geir Westby, Gro Fraas, Eli Ryg; **D:** Peter Watkins; **W:** Peter Watkins. *FCT, NYF*

Edward and Mrs. Simpson 🎬🎬 1980 Made-for-television dramatic reconstruction of the years leading to the abdication of King Edward VIII, who forfeited the British throne in 1936 so that·he could marry American divorcee Wallis Simpson. Originally aired on PBS. 270m/C VHS, Beta. Edward Fox, Cynthia Harris; **D:** Waris Hussein. *HBO, TVC, VIF*

Edward Scissorhands 🎬🎬🎬 1990 (PG-13) Depp's a young man created by loony scientist Price, who dies before he can attach hands to his boy-creature. Then the boy is rescued from his lonely existence outside of suburbia by an ingratiating Avon lady. With scissors in place of hands, he has more trouble fitting into suburbia than would most new kids on the block, and he struggles with being different and lonely in a cardboard-cutout world. Visually captivating fairy tale full of splash and color, however predictable the Hollywood-prefab denouement. 100m/C VHS, Beta, LV, Closed Caption. Johnny Depp, Winona Ryder, Dianne Wiest, Vincent Price, Anthony Michael Hall, Alan Arkin, Kathy Baker, Conchata Ferrell, Caroline Aaron, Dick Anthony Williams, Robert Oliveri, John Davidson; **D:** Tim Burton; **W:** Caroline Thompson, Tim Burton; **C:** Stefan Czapsky; **M:** Danny Elfman. Nominations: Academy Awards '90: Best Makeup. *FOX, FCT*

Edward II 🎬🎬½ 1992 (R) Jarman's controversial adaptation of Christopher Marlowe's play "The Troublesome Reign of Edward II" portrays the weak-willed monarch as neglecting his kingdom for love. Unfortunately, it's not for his queen but for his commoner male lover. His neglect of both queen and country lead to a swift and brutal downfall. Jarman's use of contemporary anachronisms, stream of conscienceness approach, and heavy symbolism may leave more than one viewer wondering what's going on.**CW:** Some language, strong violence, and strong sensuality. 91m/C VHS, LV. **GB** Steven Waddington, Kevin Collins, Andrew Tiernan, John Lynch, Dudley Sutton, Tilda Swinton, Jerome Flynn, Jody Graber, Nigel Terry, Annie Lennox; **D:** Derek Jarman; **W:** Derek Jarman; **M:** Simon Fisher Turner. Venice Film Festival '92: Best Actress (Swinton). *COL*

Eegah! woof! 1962 Another Arch Hall (Merriwether) epic in which an anachronistic Neanderthal falls in love in '60s California. Reputed to be one of the worst films of all time. 93m/C VHS, Beta. Marilyn Manning, Richard Kiel, Arch Hall Jr., William Waters; **D:** Ray Dennis Steckler. *RHI, FCT*

The Eel 🎬🎬🎬 *Unagi* 1996 Yamashita (Yakusho) has just been paroled after spending eight years in prison for killing his adulterous wife in a jealous rage. While there, he found and cared for an eel, which became his only confidante, and which accompanies him to his new life as a barber in a small town outside Tokyo. The newcomer is soon befriended by the locals but Yamashita's life changes most when he saves the suicidal Keiko (Shimizu) from drowning. She comes to work in his shop and would obviously like a more intimate relationship but some secrets in her past and some strange incidents in the town may jeopordize Yamashita's hopes for a normal life. Based on the novel "Glimmering in the Dark" by Akira Yoshimura. Japanese with subtitles. 117m/C VHS. **JP** Koji Yakusho, Misa Shimizu, Mitsuko Baisho, Shou Aikawa, Fujio Tsuneta, Akira Emoto, Etsuko Ichihara, Tomoroh Taguchi, Ken Kobayashi, Sabu Kawara; **D:** Shohei Imamura; **W:** Shohei Imamura, Motofumi Tomikawa, Daisuke Tengan; **C:** Shigeru Komatsubara; **M:** Shinichiro Ikebe. Cannes Film Festival '97: Best Film. *NYR*

The Effect of Gamma Rays on Man-in-the-Moon Marigolds 🎬🎬🎬 1973 (PG) A wonderful drama based on the Pulitzer Prize winning play by Paul Zindel. The story centers around eccentric young Matilda and her depressed family. Matilda is preparing her experiment for the school science fair, determined to beat her competition. Her exhibit shows how radiation sometimes kills the helpless marigolds, but sometimes causes them to grow into even more beautiful mutations. This mirrors Matilda, who flowers even amidst the drunkenness of her mother and the dullness of her sister. 100m/C VHS. Joanne Woodward, Nell Potts, Roberta Wallach, Judith Lowry, Richard Venture; **D:** Paul Newman. Cannes Film Festival '73: Best Actress (Woodward). *NO*

Effi Briest 🎬🎬🎬½ *Fontane Effi Briest* 1974 A 19th-century tragedy well-played by Schygulla and empowered with Fassbinder's directorial skills. Effi (Schygulla) is a 17 year-old beauty, unhappily married to a much older man. She drifts into a brief affair, which is not discovered for several years. When her husband does discover her past infidelity, the Prussian legal code permits him a chilling revenge. Based on a popular 19th-century novel by Theodor Fontane. In German with English subtitles. 135m/B VHS. **GE** Hanna Schygulla, Wolfgang Schenck, Lilo Pempeit, Ulli Lommel; **D:** Rainer Werner Fassbinder; **W:** Rainer Werner Fassbinder. *NYF, PMS*

The Efficiency Expert 🎬🎬½ *Spotswood* 1992 (PG) Lighthearted Australian comedy about a dingy moccasin factory where a rigid efficiency consultant is invited to save the eccentric family-run company from bankruptcy. Predictable ending contains a nevertheless timely message about the importance of the bottom line. 97m/C VHS, Beta, Closed Caption. **AU** Anthony Hopkins, Ben Mendelsohn, Alwyn Kurts, Bruno Lawrence, Angela Punch McGregor, Russell Crowe, Rebecca Rigg, Toni Collette; **D:** Mark Joffe; **W:** Andrew Knight, Max Dann; **M:** Ricky Fataar. *PAR, BTV*

Egg 🎬🎬½ 1988 Striking film from Holland chronicles the life of a quiet, middle-aged baker who answers a personal ad from a schoolteacher. After much correspondence, the teacher visits the baker in his village, and the townspeople take great interest in what happens next. In Dutch with English subtitles. 58m/C VHS, LV. **NL** Johan Leysen, Marijke Vengelers; **D:** Danniel Danniel. *KIV, LUM*

Egg and I 🎬🎬🎬 1947 Based on the true-life adventures of best-selling humorist Betty MacDonald. A young urban bride agrees to help her new husband realize his life-long dream of owning a chicken farm. A dilapidated house, temperamental stove, and suicidal chickens test the bride's perseverance, as do the zany antics of her country-bumpkin neighbors, Ma and Pa Kettle, who make their screen debut. Plenty of old-fashioned laughs. 104m/B VHS, Beta, LV. Claudette Colbert, Fred MacMurray, Marjorie Main, Percy Kilbride, Louise Allbritton, Richard Long, Billy House, Donald MacBride; **D:** Chester Erskine; **C:** Milton Krasner. Nominations: Academy Awards '47: Best Supporting Actress (Main). *USH*

The Egyptian 🎬🎬½ 1954 Based on the sword-and-sandal novel by Mika Waltari, this is a ponderous big-budget epic about a young Egyptian in Akhnaton's epoch who becomes physician to the Pharaoh. 140m/C VHS, Beta, LV, Closed Caption. Edmund Purdom, Victor Mature, Peter Ustinov, Bella Darvi, Gene Tierney, Henry Daniell, Jean Simmons, Michael Wilding, Judith Evelyn, John Carradine, Carl Benton Reid; **D:** Michael Curtiz; **W:** Philip Dunne, Casey Robinson; **C:** Leon Shamroy. Nominations: Academy Awards '54: Best Color Cinematography. *FOX, IME*

The Eiger Sanction 🎬🎬 1975 (R) An art teacher returns to the CII (a fictionalized version of the CIA) as an exterminator hired to assassinate the killers of an American agent. In the process, he finds himself climbing the Eiger. Beautiful Swiss Alps scenery fails to totally compensate for several dreary lapses. Based on the novel by Trevanian. 125m/C VHS, Beta, LV. Clint Eastwood, George Kennedy, Vonetta McGee, Jack Cassidy, Thayer David; **D:** Clint Eastwood; **M:** John Williams. *USH, TLF*

8-A 🎬🎬 *Ochoa* 1992 Reconstructs the 1989 trial and execution of Cuban general Arnaldo Ochoa Sanchez, a hero of the revolution who, along with other government officials, advocated the resignation of Fidel Castro as the solution to the country's economic and political crises. At the trial Ochoa and four other officials were convicted of illegal drug trafficking and shot by a firing squad. Spanish with subtitles. 84m/C VHS. **CU** Orlando Jiminez-Leal. *NYF*

8 1/2 🎬🎬🎬🎬 *Otto E Mezzo; Federico Fellini's 8 1/2* 1963 The acclaimed Fellini self-portrait of a revered Italian film director struggling with a fated film project wanders through his intermixed life, childhood memories, and hallucinatory fantasies. Subtitled in English. 135m/B VHS, Beta, LV. **IT** Marcello Mastroianni, Claudia Cardinale, Anouk Aimee, Sandra Milo, Barbara Steele, Rossella Falk, Eddra Gale, Mark Herron, Madeleine LeBeau, Caterina Boratto; **D:** Federico Fellini; **W:** Tullio Pinelli, Ennio Flaiano, Brunello Rondi, Federico Fellini; **M:** Nino Rota. Academy Awards '63: Best Costume Design (B & W), Best Foreign Language Film; National

Board of Review Awards '63: 5 Best Foreign Films of the Year; New York Film Critics Awards '63: Best Foreign Film; Nominations: Academy Awards '63: Best Art Direction/Set Decoration (B & W), Best Director (Fellini), Best Story & Screenplay. *VES, MRV, MPI*

8 Heads in a Duffel Bag ♂♂ 1996 (R) Mob bag man Tommy (Pesci, in a real stretch) loses his heads, the evidence of a successful hit, to med student Charlie Pritchett (Comeau), who's headed for a Mexican vacation with his fiance's (Swanson) uptight family. Desperate, Tommy "persuades" Charlie's roommates (Spade and Louiso) to help him find some replacement noggins. Excellent premise is almost done in by a timid script that relies a little too much on slapstick. Schulman's uneven directorial debut does little to mask the problem. Newcomer Comeau tries for a "Bachelor Party" era Tom Hanks thing, but doesn't quite get there. Pesci and Spade save flick from disaster, and get most of the good lines, pitted in a generational "battle of the smart-asses," but neither one strays from their previous screen personas. Louiso hilariously makes the most of his role as the naive roommate. *CW:* Language. 95m/C VHS. Joe Pesci, David Spade, Andy Comeau, Kristy Swanson, George Hamilton, Dyan Cannon, Todd Louiso, Frank Roman, Anthony Mangano, Joe Basile, Ernestine Mercer, Howard George; *D:* Tom Schulman; *W:* Tom Schulman; *C:* Adam Holender; *M:* Andrew Gross. *NYR*

800 Leagues Down the Amazon ♂♂½ 1993 (PG-13) A 19th-century journey down the Amazon on a raft with a planter, his daughter, and various complications. Based on a novel by Jules Verne. 100m/C VHS. Daphne Zuniga, Barry Bostwick, Adam Baldwin, Tom Verica, E.E. Bell; *D:* Luis Llosa; *W:* Laura Schiff, Jackson Barr. *NHO*

Eight Men Out ♂♂♂½ 1988 (PG) Taken from Eliot Asinof's book, a moving, full-blooded account of the infamous 1919 "Black Sox" scandal, in which members of the Chicago White Sox teamed to throw the World Series for $80,000. A dirge of lost innocence, this is among Sayles' best films. Provides an interesting look at the "conspiracy" that ended "Shoeless" Joe Jackson's major-league career. The actual baseball scenes are first-rate, and Straithairn, Sweeney, and Cusack give exceptional performances. Sayles makes an appearance as Ring Lardner. Enjoyable viewing for even the non-sports fan. 121m/C VHS, Beta, LV, Closed Caption. John Cusack, D.B. Sweeney, Perry Lang, Jace Alexander, Bill Irwin, Clifton James, Michael Rooker, Michael Lerner, Christopher Lloyd, Studs Terkel, David Strathairn, Charlie Sheen, Kevin Tighe, John Mahoney, John Sayles, Gordon Clapp, Richard Edson, James Read, Don Harvey, John Anderson, Maggie Renzi; *D:* John Sayles; *W:* John Sayles; *C:* Robert Richardson; *M:* Mason Daring. *ORI, FCT*

8 Million Ways to Die ♂♂ 1985 (R) An ex-cop hires himself out to rescue a pimp-bound hooker, and gets knee-deep in a mess of million-dollar drug deals, murder, and prostitution. Slow-moving but satisfying. Based on the book by Lawrence Block. 115m/C VHS, Beta, LV, Closed Caption. Jeff Bridges, Rosanna Arquette, Andy Garcia, Alexandra Paul; *D:* Hal Ashby; *W:* Oliver Stone; *C:* Stephen Burum; *M:* James Newton Howard. *FOX*

Eight on the Lam ♂ 1967 (PG) Unfunny comedy features widower Henry Dimsdale (Hope) taking off with his kids and family maid Golda (Diller) when he's accused of embezzling bank funds. Jasper Lynch (Winters) is on their trail until Henry can prove who the real culprit is. 103m/C VHS, Closed Caption. Bob Hope, Phyllis Diller, Jonathan Winters, Jill St. John, Shirley Eaton; *D:* George Marshall; *W:* Albert Lewin, Arthur Marx, Bob Fisher, Burt Styler; *C:* Alan Stenvold; *M:* George Romanis. *MGM*

8 Seconds ♂♂½ *The Lane Frost Story* 1994 (PG-13) Love, not sports, dominates the true-life story of rodeo star Lane Frost (Perry), a world champion bull rider killed in the ring at the age of 25 in 1990. A decent guy, he finds quick success on the rodeo circuit, marries (to Geary), and finds his career getting in the way of his happiness.

Bull-riding sequences are genuinely stomach churning, the performances low-key. Title refers to the amount of time a rider must stay aboard his animal. *CW:* Strong language and violence. 104m/C VHS, LV, Closed Caption. Luke Perry, Cynthia Geary, Stephen Baldwin, James Rebhorn, Carrie Snodgress, Red Mitchell, Ronnie Clair Edwards; *D:* John G. Avildsen; *W:* Monte Merrick; *M:* Bill Conti. *NLC*

Eight Witnesses ♂♂ 1954 Suspense thriller about a man being murdered in front of eight blind witnesses. ?m/C VHS. Peggy Ann Garner. *LOO*

18 Again! ♂♂½ 1988 (PG) After a bump on the head, an 81-year-old man and his 18-year-old grandson mentally switch places, giving each a new look at his life. Lightweight romp with Burns in especially good form, but not good enough to justify redoing this tired theme. 100m/C VHS, Beta, LV, Closed Caption. George Burns, Charlie Schlatter, Anita Morris, Jennifer Runyon, Tony Roberts, Red Buttons, Miriam Flynn, George DiCenzo; *D:* Paul Flaherty; *W:* Jonathan Prince, Josh Goldstein; *M:* Billy Goldenberg. *VTR, NWV*

Eighteen Jade Arhats ♂ 1984 A kung fu epic with a blind heroine who nevertheless kicks other people in the eyes. 95m/C VHS, Beta. Chia Ling, Ou-Yang Ksiek, Sun Chia-Lin, Otae Mofo. *UNI*

1860 ♂♂ 1933 During the Battle of Calatafimi in May of 1860, Sicilian peasants revolted against the King of Naples' army. The story focuses on four people caught up in the fighting: the spouse of a revolutionary, a foppish intellectual, a rebel priest, and the young shepherd who is sent with a message to Genoa asking for assistance. Blasetti made great use of location filming and natural light. In Italian with English subtitles. 72m/C VHS. IT *D:* Alessandro Blasetti. *FCT, WBF*

The Eighth Day ♂♂½ *Le Huitieme Jour* 1995 Sugary story about workaholic businessman Harry (Auteuil), whose wife Julie (Miou-Miou) has just left him, taking their daughters. Driving home, Harry finds Georges (Duquenne) by the side of the road. Georges, who has Downs syndrome, has left the institution he's been living in and, though Harry tries to take him to the nearest police station, Georges refuses to leave him. Naturally, the emotionally deprived Harry begins to loosen up and, when Georges is finally returned to his group home, all his friends decide to help with Harry's attempts to win back his family. Thick with whimsy but the lead performances are excellent. French with subtitles. 108m/C VHS, LV. FR BE Daniel Auteuil, Pascal Duquenne, Miou-Miou, Henri Garcin, Fabienne Loriaux, Isabelle Sadoyan, Helene Roussel, Michele Maes; *D:* Jaco Van Dormael; *W:* Jaco Van Dormael; *C:* Walther Vanden Ende; *M:* Pierre Van Dormael. Cannes Film Festival '96: Best Actor (Auteuil), Best Actor (Duquenne); Nominations: Cesar Awards '97: Best Actor (Auteuil); Golden Globe Awards '97: Best Foreign Film. *PGV*

The Eighties ♂♂½ 1983 A comic, pseudo-documentary romp through the making of a musical. Not just another dime-a-dozen song-and-dance flick, but plays with the genre with humor and intelligence, treating us to an insider's view of a performance arranged at a shopping plaza, from the rigorous auditions to the tedium of the production of songs and routines. Treated in a light-hearted, sensitive, just on the verge of laughable manner, it concludes with 30 minutes of song and dance. In French with English subtitles. 86m/C VHS. FR Aurore Clement, Lio, Magali Noel, Pascale Salkin; *D:* Chantal Akerman; *W:* Chantal Akerman, Jean Gruault. *WAC, FCT*

84 Charing Cross Road ♂♂♂ 1986 (PG) A lonely woman in New York and a bookseller in London begin corresponding for business reasons. Over a twenty-year period, their relationship grows into a friendship, and then a romance, though they communicate only by mail. Based on a true story. 100m/C VHS, Beta, LV. Anne Bancroft, Anthony Hopkins, Judi Dench, Jean De Baer, Maurice Denham, Eleanor David, Mercedes Ruehl, Daniel Gerroll, Hugh Whitemore; *D:* David Jones; *M:* George Fenton. British

Academy Awards '87: Best Actress (Bancroft). *COL, TVC, HMV*

84 Charlie Mopic ♂♂♂ 1989 (R) A widely acclaimed drama about the horrors of Vietnam seen through the eyes of a cameraman assigned to a special front-line unit. Filled with a cast of unknowns, this is an unsettling film that sheds new light on the subject of the Vietnam war. Powerful and energetic; music by Donovan. 89m/C VHS, Beta, LV. Richard Brooks, Christopher Burgard, Nicholas Cascone, Jonathon Emerson, Glen Morshower, Jason Tomlins, Byron Thames; *D:* Patrick Duncan; *W:* Patrick Duncan; *C:* Alan Caso; *M:* Donovan. *COL*

Eijanaika ♂♂♂½ *Why Not?* 1981 A gripping story of a poor Japanese man who returns to his country after a visit to America in the 1860s. Memorable performances make this an above-average film. In Japanese with English subtitles. 151m/C VHS, LV. JP Ken Ogata, Shigeru Izumiya; *D:* Shohei Imamura. *KIV, FCT*

El ♂♂ *This Strange Passion* 1952 Bizarre black-comedy finds virginal middle-aged Francisco (De Cordova) marrying a beautiful young woman (Garces) and becoming jealously paranoid when he believes she's been unfaithful. He's eventually driven to insanity and attempted murder. Spanish with subtitles. 88m/B VHS. MX Arturo de Cordova, Delia Garces, Luis Beristain, Aurora Walker; *D:* Luis Bunuel; *W:* Luis Bunuel, Luis Alcoriza; *C:* Gabriel Figueroa; *M:* Luis Hernandez Breton. *HTV*

El Amor Brujo ♂♂♂ *Love, the Magician* 1986 An adaptation of the work of Miguel de Falla, in which flamenco dancers enact the story of a tragic romance. 100m/C VHS, Beta, LV. Antonio Gades, Christina Hoyos, Laura Del Sol; *D:* Carlos Saura. *CTH, FCT, APD*

El Barbaro ♂ 1984 In the beginning of civilization, when evil powers rule, a barbarian has two ambitions in life: to seek revenge for his friend's death and to rescue the world from a sorcerer's power. 88m/C VHS, Beta. SP Andrea Occhipinti, Maria Scola, Violeta Cela, Sabrina Sellers. *MED*

El Bruto ♂♂½ *The Brute* 1952 A mid-Mexican-period Bunuel drama, about a brainless thug who is used as a bullying pawn in a struggle between a brutal landlord and discontented tenants. In Spanish with English titles. 83m/B VHS, Beta. MX Pedro Armendariz Sr., Katy Jurado, Andres Soler, Rosita Arenas; *D:* Luis Bunuel. *FCT, APD*

El Cid ♂♂♂ 1961 Charts the life of Rodrigo Diaz de Bivar, known as El Cid, who was the legendary eleventh-century Christian hero who freed Spain from Moorish invaders. Noted for its insanely lavish budget, this epic tale is true to its setting and elaborate battle scenes. 184m/C VHS, Beta, LV. Charlton Heston, Sophia Loren, Raf Vallone, Hurd Hatfield, Genevieve Page; *D:* Anthony Mann; *W:* Philip Yordan; *C:* Robert Krasker; *M:* Miklos Rozsa. Nominations: Academy Awards '61: Best Art Direction/Set Decoration (Color), Best Song ("Love Theme (The Falcon and the Dove)"), Original Dramatic/Comedy Score. *BFV, FCT, KAR*

El Cochecito ♂♂♂ *The Wheelchair* 1960 Great Spanish actor Isbert stars as the head of a large family whose closest friends are all joined together in a kind of fraternity defined by the fact that they each use a wheelchair. He feels excluded because he does not have or need one, so he goes to great lengths to gain acceptance in this "brotherhood." In Spanish with English subtitles. 90m/B VHS, Beta. SP Jose Isbert; *D:* Marco Ferreri. *FCT*

El Condor ♂½ 1970 (R) Two drifters search for gold buried in a Mexican fort. 102m/C VHS. SP Jim Brown, Lee Van Cleef, Patrick O'Neal, Marianna Hill, Iron Eyes Cody, Elisha Cook Jr.; *D:* John Guillermin; *W:* Larry Cohen, Steven W. Carabatsos; *M:* Maurice Jarre. *WAR*

El Diablo ♂♂½ 1990 (PG-13) A young man finds the West more wild than he expected. He finds "help" in the shape of Gossett as he tries to free a young girl who's being held by the notorious El Diablo. Made for television. Better than average. **107m/C VHS, Closed Caption.** Louis Gossett Jr., Anthony Edwards, John Glover, Robert Beltran, M.C. Gainey, Miguel Sandoval, Sarah Trigger, Joe Pantoliano; **D:** Peter Markle; **W:** John Carpenter, Bill Phillips. *WAR, HBO*

El Diablo Rides ⏃½ 1939 A fierce feud between cattlemen and sheepmen develops, with touches of comedy in between. **57m/B VHS, Beta.** Bob Steele, Carleton Young, Kit Guard. *VDM, VCN, VYY*

El Diputado ⏃⏃⏃ *The Deputy* 1978 A famous politician jeopardizes his career when he has an affair with a young man. In Spanish with English subtitles. **111m/C VHS.** *SP* Jose Sacristan, Maria Luisa San Jose, Jose Alonso; **D:** Eloy De La Iglesia. *FCT*

El Dorado ⏃⏃⏃ 1967 A gunfighter rides into the frontier town of El Dorado to aid a reckless cattle baron in his war with farmers over land rights. Once in town, the hired gun meets up with an old friend—the sheriff—who also happens to be the town drunkard. Switching allegiances, the gunslinger helps the lawman sober up and defend the farmers. This Hawks western displays a number of similarities to the director's earlier "Rio Bravo" (1959), staring Wayne, Dean Martin, and Ricky Nelson—who charms viewers as the young sidekick "Colorado" much like Caan does as "Mississippi" in El Dorado. **126m/C VHS, Beta, LV.** John Wayne, Robert Mitchum, James Caan, Charlene Holt, Ed Asner, Arthur Hunnicutt, Christopher George, R.G. Armstrong, Jim Davis, Paul Fix, Johnny Crawford, Michele Carey; **D:** Howard Hawks. *PAR, TLF*

El Mariachi ⏃⏃⏃ 1993 (R) Extremely low-budget but clever mixture of humor and violence in a tale of mistaken identity set in a small Mexican border town. 24-year-old director Rodriguez makes his feature film debut with this $7000 feature, originally intended only for the Spanish-language market. Film festival awards and critical attention brought the work to wider release. In Spanish with English subtitles or dubbed. The laserdisc version includes director's commentary and Rodriguez's 8 minute film "Bedhead."**CW:** Strong violence. **81m/C VHS, Beta, LV, 8mm.** *MX* Carlos Gallardo, Consuelo Gomez, Peter Marquardt, Jaime de Hoyos, Reinol Martinez, Ramiro Gomez; **D:** Robert Rodriguez; **W:** Robert Rodriguez, Carlos Gallardo; **C:** Robert Rodriguez. Independent Spirit Awards '94: Best First Feature; Sundance Film Festival '93: Audience Award; Nominations: Independent Spirit Awards '94: Best Director (Rodriguez). *COL, FCT, BTV*

El Muerto ⏃½ 1975 In 19th-century Buenos Aires, a young man flees his home after killing an enemy. Arriving in Montevideo, he becomes a member of a smuggling ring. In Spanish with English subtitles. **103m/C VHS, Beta.** *SP* Thelma Biral, Juan Jose Camero, Francesco Rabal; **D:** Hector Olivera. *MED*

El Norte ⏃⏃⏃⏃ 1983 (R) Gripping account of a Guatemalan brother and sister, persecuted in their homeland, who make an arduous journey north ("El Norte") to America. Their difficult saga continues as they struggle against overwhelming odds in an attempt to realize their dreams. Passionate, sobering, and powerful. In English and Spanish with English subtitles. Produced in association with the "American Playhouse" series for PBS. Produced by Anna Thomas who also cowrote the story with Nava. **139m/C VHS, Beta.** *SP* David Villalpando, Zaide Silvia Gutierrez, Ernesto Cruz, Eraacio Zepeda, Stella Quan, Alicia del Lugo, Lupe Ontiveros; **D:** Gregory Nava; **W:** Anna Thomas, Gregory Nava. Nominations: Academy Awards '84: Best Original Screenplay. *FOX, APD*

El Paso Stampede ⏃½ 1953 Cowboy investigates raids on cattle herds used to feed Americans fighting in the Spanish-American War. **50m/B VHS, Beta.** Allan "Rocky" Lane, Eddy Waller, Phyllis Coates; **D:** Harry Keller. *VCN*

El Super ⏃⏃⏃ 1979 A Cuban refugee, still homesick after many years, struggles to make a life for himself in Manhattan as an apartment superintendent. In Spanish with English subtitles; an American production shot on location in New York City. **90m/C VHS.** *SP* Raymundo Hidalgo-Gato, Orlando Jiminez-Leal, Zully Montero, Raynaldo Medina, Juan Granda, Hilda Lee, Elizabeth Pena; **D:** Leon Ichaso; **W:** Leon Ichaso, Manuel Arce. *APD, NYF*

El: This Strange Passion ⏃⏃⏃ 1952 Disturbing drama in which a man, convinced he is cuckolded, slowly descends into madness. Bunuel's surreal, almost Freudian look at the Spanish male's obsession with female fidelity. In Spanish with English subtitles. **82m/B VHS.** *SP* Arturo de Cordova, Delia Garces, Luis Beristain, Aurora Walker; **D:** Luis Bunuel. *HTV, FCT*

Ele, My Friend ⏃⏃½ 1993 The British Raj still rules India in the 1920s, when 10-year-old Charles comes across a herd of wild elephants living in the jungle. Charles befriends a baby elephant he names Ele but what can he do when hunters also discover the animals? Filmed on location in south India. **104m/C VHS.** Jacob Paul Guzman, Gazan Khan, R.S. Shivaji, Amjad Khan, Prabhu; **D:** Dharan Mandrayar; **W:** Dharan Mandrayar; **M:** Barry Phillips. *VCI, BTV*

Eleanor & Franklin ⏃⏃⏃½ 1976 An exceptional television dramatization of the personal lives of President Franklin D. Roosevelt and his wife Eleanor. Based on Joseph Lash's book, this Emmy award-winning film features stunning performances by Alexander and Herrmann in the title roles. **208m/C VHS, Beta.** Jane Alexander, Edward Herrmann, Ed Flanders, Rosemary Murphy, MacKenzie Phillips, Pamela Franklin, Anna Lee, Linda Purl, Linda Kelsey, Lindsay Crouse; **D:** Daniel Petrie; **M:** John Barry. *SIG, TLF*

Eleanor: First Lady of the World ⏃⏃½ 1982 (G) Stapleton plays the former first lady after her husband's death as she goes on to work at the United Nations and emerges as even more of an influential public figure. Made for television. **96m/C VHS.** Jean Stapleton, E.G. Marshall, Coral Browne, Joyce Van Patten, Gail Strickland, Kenneth Kimmins; **D:** John Erman; **M:** John Addison. *COL*

Electra ⏃⏃ 1995 Sex-bomb Lorna (Tweed) does her oedipal best with stepson Billy (Tab), who was implanted with the secret of physical regeneration by his late scientist dad. Cybervillian Roach (Erik) wants the info, which can only be obtained through intimate contact, and Lorna's the right woman for the job. Funny how Billy's just so uncooperative. Very over-the-top. **85m/C VHS.** Shannon Tweed, Joe Tab, Sten Eirik; **D:** Julian Grant. *NHO*

Electra Glide in Blue ⏃⏃ 1973 (R) An Arizona motorcycle cop uses his head in a world that's coming apart at the seams. Good action scenes; lots of violence. **113m/C VHS, LV.** Robert (Bobby) Blake, Billy Green Bush, Mitchell Ryan, Jeannine Riley, Elisha Cook Jr., Royal Dano; **D:** James W. Guercio; **W:** Robert Boris; **C:** Conrad Hall. *MGM*

Electric Dreams ⏃⏃½ 1984 (PG) A young man buys a computer that yearns to do more than sit on a desk. First it takes over his apartment, then it sets its sights on the man's cello-playing neighbor—the same woman his owner is courting. To win her affections, the over-eager computer tries to dazzle her with a variety of musical compositions from his unique keyboard. Cort supplies the voice of Edgar the computer in this film that integrates a rock-music video format. **95m/C VHS, Beta, LV.** Lenny Von Dohlen, Virginia Madsen, Maxwell Caulfield, Bud Cort, Koo Stark; **D:** Steven Barron. *MGM*

The Electric Horseman ⏃⏃½ 1979 (PG) Journalist Fonda sets out to discover the reason behind the kidnapping of a prized horse by an ex-rodeo star. The alcoholic cowboy has taken the horse to return it to its native environment, away from the clutches of corporate greed. As Fonda investigates the story she falls in love with rebel Redford. Excellent Las Vegas and remote western settings. **120m/C VHS, Beta, LV.** Robert Redford, Jane Fonda, John Saxon, Willie Nelson, Valerie Perrine, Wilford Brimley, Nicolas Coster, James B. Sikking; **D:**

Sydney Pollack; **M:** Dave Grusin. Nominations: Academy Awards '79: Best Sound.*USH*

The Electronic Monster ⏃⏃ *Escapement; The Electric Monster* 1957 Insurance claims investigator Cameron looks into the death of a Hollywood starlet and discovers an exclusive therapy center dedicated to hypnotism. At the facility, people vacation for weeks in morgue-like body drawers, while evil Dr. Illing uses an electronic device to control the sleeper's dreams and actions. Eerie. Intriguingly, it is one of the first films to explore the possibilities of brainwashing and mind control. **72m/B VHS.** *GB* Rod Cameron, Mary Murphy, Meredith Edwards, Peter Illing; **D:** Montgomery Tully. *SNC*

The Elegant Criminal ⏃⏃½ 1992 Based on the true story of France's most infamous killer, Pierre Lacenaire. The film begins with Lacenaire in prison, writing his memoirs, receiving his admirers, and awaiting his execution (in 1836). A series of flashbacks detail his life and the supposed social clime which hindered his better instincts and turned him to the criminal life. However, Auteuil has such a wonderful time playing the charming bad guy that any blame to society fails to convince. In French with English subtitles. **120m/C VHS.** *FR* Daniel Auteuil, Jean Poiret, Jacques Weber, Marie-Armelle DeGuy, Maiwenn Le Besco, Patrick Pineau; **D:** Francois Girod; **W:** George Conchon, Francois Girod. *ORI, BTV, FCT*

The Element of Crime ⏃⏃½ *Forbrydelsens Element* 1984 In a monochromatic, post-holocaust future, a detective tracks down a serial killer of young girls. Made in Denmark, this minor festival favorite features an impressive directional debut and awaits cult status. Filmed in Sepiatone. **104m/C VHS, Beta.** *DK* Michael Elphick, Esmond Knight, Jerold Wells, Meme Lei, Astrid Henning-Jensen, Preben Leerdorff-Rye, Gotha Andersen; **D:** Lars von Trier. *UNI, TPV*

The Elementary School ⏃⏃ *Obecna Skola* 1991 Screenwriter Sverak's memories of his childhood are the basis for this child's eye view of the mysteries surrounding the adult world. In 1945, 10-year-old Eda (Jakoubek) is living in a village outside Prague. His school class is so wild that the teacher quits and is replaced by the strict Igor Hnizdo (Triska), who turns out to have a weakness for young women. Czech with subtitles. **100m/C VHS.** *CZ* Jan Triska, Vaclav Jakoubek, Zdenek Sverak, Radoslav Budas, Libuse Safrankova, Rudolf Hrusinsky, Petr Cepek; **D:** Jan Sverak; **W:** Zdenek Sverak; *F.A. Brabec.* Nominations: Academy Awards '91: Best Foreign Language Film. *NYF*

Elena and Her Men ⏃⏃⏃ *Paris Does Strange Things; Elena et les Hommes* 1956 The romantic entanglements and intrigues of a poor Polish princess are explored in this enjoyable French film. Beautiful cinematography by Claude Renoir. In French with subtitles. **98m/C VHS, Beta, LV.** *FR* Ingrid Bergman, Jean Marais, Mel Ferrer, Jean Richard, Magali Noel, Pierre Bertin, Juliette Greco; **D:** Jean Renoir. *INT, FCT, TPV*

Eleni ⏃⏃ 1985 (PG) The true story of "New York Times" reporter Nicholas Gage and his journey to Athens to discover the truth about his mother's execution by Communists during the Greek rebellion after WWII. Adapted by Steve Tesich from Gage's bestselling book. **117m/C VHS, Beta, LV, 8mm, Closed Caption.** John Malkovich, Kate Nelligan, Linda Hunt, Oliver Cotton, Ronald Pickup, Dimitra Arliss, Rosalie Crutchley; **D:** Peter Yates; **W:** Steve Tesich; **C:** Billy Williams; **M:** Bruce Smeaton. *COL, IGP, NLC*

Elephant Boy ⏃⏃⏃ 1937 An Indian boy helps government conservationists locate a herd of elephants in the jungle. Sabu's first film. Available in digitally remastered stereo. **80m/B VHS, Beta, LV.** *GB* Sabu, Walter Hudd, W.E. Holloway; **D:** Robert Flaherty, Zoltan Korda. Venice Film Festival '37: Best Director (Flaherty). *HBO, WAR*

The Elephant Man 🐾🐾🐾🐾 1980 (PG) A biography of John Merrick, a severely deformed man who, with the help of a sympathetic doctor, moved from freak shows into posh London society. Lynch's first mainstream film, shot in black and white, it presents a startlingly vivid picture of the hypocrisies evident in the social moves of the Victorian era. Moving performance from Hurt in title role. **125m/B VHS, Beta, LV.** *SP* Anthony Hopkins, John Hurt, Anne Bancroft, John Gielgud, Wendy Hiller, Freddie Jones, Kenny Baker; *D:* David Lynch; *W:* Eric Bergren, Christopher DeVore, David Lynch; *M:* John Morris, Samuel Barber. British Academy Awards '80: Best Actor (Hurt), Best Film; Cesar Awards '82: Best Foreign Film; National Board of Review Awards '80: 10 Best Films of the Year; Nominations: Academy Awards '80: Best Actor (Hurt), Best Adapted Screenplay, Best Art Direction/Set Decoration, Best Costume Design, Best Director (Lynch), Best Film Editing, Best Picture, Best Original Score. *PAR*

Elephant Walk 🐾🐾½ 1954 Sri Lanka's balmy jungles provide the backdrop for a torrid love triangle in this post-prime Dieterle effort. Taylor, ignored by her wealthy drunkard hubby, finds solace in the arms of her spouse's sexy right-hand man. As if keeping the affair secret weren't a big enough task, she also braves a cholera epidemic and a pack of vengeful elephants who take an unscheduled tour of her humble home. Lethargic lead performances make this more of a sleep walk, but Sofaer and Biberman's supporting roles are worth the price of rental. Taylor replaced Vivian Leigh early in the filming after she fell ill, but footage of Leigh in faraway shots is included. **103m/C VHS, Closed Caption.** Elizabeth Taylor, Dana Andrews, Peter Finch, Abraham Sofaer, Abner Biberman; *D:* William Dieterle; *C:* Loyal Griggs. *PAR, FCT*

11 Harrowhouse 🐾🐾🐾 *Anything for Love; Fast Fortune* 1974 (PG) The Consolidated Selling System at 11 Harrowhouse, London, controls much of the world's diamond trade. Four adventurous thieves plot a daring heist relying on a very clever cockroach. A rather successful stab at spoofing detailed "heist" films. **95m/C VHS, Beta, Closed Caption.** *GB* Charles Grodin, Candice Bergen, James Mason, Trevor Howard, John Gielgud; *D:* Aram Avakian; *W:* Jeffrey Bloom. *FOX*

Eli Eli 🐾🐾½ 1940 An American Yiddish film about a family forced to live apart because of their farm's failure. Lighthearted and fun. In Yiddish with English titles. **85m/B VHS, Beta.** Esther Feild, Lazar Fried, Muni Serebroff; *D:* Joseph Seiden; *M:* Sholom Secunda. *VYY, AUD, FCT*

The Eliminators 🐾 1986 (PG) A cyborgian creature endeavors to avenge himself on his evil scientist creator with help from a kung fu expert and a Mexican. The group uses time travel and other devices to achieve their mission. **95m/C VHS, Beta, Closed Caption.** Roy Dotrice, Patrick Reynolds, Denise Crosby, Andrew Prine, Conan Lee; *D:* Peter Manoogian; *W:* Danny Bilson, Paul DeMeo; *M:* Richard Band. *FOX*

Elisa 🐾🐾 1994 Teenaged sexpot Marie (Paradis) has grown up in a reform school, thanks to her mother Elisa's suicide. Along with friends Solange (Courau) and Ahmed (Sall), Marie spends her time on the Paris streets shoplifting and flirting. Obsessed with finding her long-gone father, Marie discovers that Lebovitch (Depardieu), the writer of the popular song "Elisa," is daddy dearest. He's now a drunk, living on a fishing island, and Marie sets out to right the wrongs she believes drove her mother to suicide. Based on the song by Serge Gainsbourg. French with subtitles. **111m/C VHS.** *FR* Vanessa Paradis, Gerard Depardieu, Clothilde Courau, Sekkou Sall, Florence Thomassin; *D:* Jean Becker; *W:* Jean Becker, Fabrice Carazo; *C:* Etienne Becker; *M:* Zbigniew Preisner. Cesar Awards '95: Best Supporting Actress (Courau), Best Score. *NYR*

Elisa, Vida Mia 🐾🐾 *Elisa, My Love; Elisa, My Life* 1977 A long-estranged father and daughter are reunited when he falls ill. She stays to help him write his biography and gradually begins to see things through his perspective. The shifting narrative can confuse but worth seeing are Rey and

Chaplin's subtle performances. Spanish with subtitles. **125m/C VHS.** *SP* Fernando Rey, Geraldine Chaplin, Norman Brisky, Isabel Mestres, Joaquin Hinojosa; *D:* Carlos Saura; *W:* Carlos Saura; *M:* Erik Satie. Cannes Film Festival '77: Best Actor (Rey). *FCT*

Elizabeth of Ladymead 🐾🐾🐾 1948 Four generations of a British family live through their experiences in the Crimean War, Boer War, WWI, and WWII. Neagle, playing the wives in all four generations, aptly explores the woman's side of war. Enjoyable performances from husband and wife team Neagle and Wilcox. **97m/C VHS, Beta.** Anna Neagle, Hugh Williams, Bernard Lee, Michael Lawrence, Nicholas Phipps, Isabel Jeans; *D:* Herbert Wilcox. *DVT, VEC*

Elizabeth R 🐾🐾🐾 1972 Jackson is outstanding in the title role of this TV drama focusing on the life of Elizabeth I, from 17 to 70. Constantly besieged by court intrigue and political machinations, the Virgin Queen managed to restore England to glory and power amidst private and public turmoil. Six 90-minute cassettes. **540m/C VHS.** *GB* Glenda Jackson, Rosalie Crutchley, Robin Ellis, Robert Hardy, Peter Jeffrey, Stephen Murray, Vivian Pickles, Sarah Frampton, Ronald Hines; *D:* Claude Whatham, Herbert Wise, Roderick Graham, Richard Martin, Donald Whatham; *W:* Hugh Whitemore, John Hale, Julian Mitchell, John Prebble, Ian Rodger, Rosemary Anne Sisson. *FOX, VIF*

Elizabeth, the Queen 🐾🐾 *The Private Lives of Elizabeth and Essex* 1968 Historical drama recreates the struggle for power by Robert Devereaux, Earl of Essex, whom the aging Queen Elizabeth I both loved and feared, and whose downfall she finally invoked. Part of "George Schaefer's Showcase Theatre." **76m/C VHS, Beta.** Judith Anderson, Charlton Heston; *D:* George Schaefer. *FHS*

Eliza's Horoscope 🐾🐾½ 1970 A frail Canadian woman uses astrology in her search for love in Montreal, and experiences bizarre and surreal events. An acclaimed Canadian film. **120m/C VHS, Beta.** *CA* Tommy Lee Jones, Elizabeth Moorman; *D:* Gordon Sheppard. *AHV*

Elke 🐾½ *Friend of the Family* 1995 While backpacking across the U.S., Elke (O'Brien) is invited to stay in Malibu with the Stillman family— husband Jeff, wife Linda, and their twenty-something children, Josh and Montana. Naturally, the sexy Elke becomes very involved with the family. **98m/C VHS.** Shauna O'Brien, C.T. Miller, Griffin Drew, Lisa Boyle. *TRI*

Ella Cinders 🐾🐾🐾 1926 The American mania for breaking into the movies is satirized in this look at a girl who wins a trip to Hollywood in a small-town beauty contest. Silent with original organ score. **60m/B VHS, Beta.** Colleen Moore, Harry Langdon, Lloyd Hughes, Jed Prouty, Vera Lewis; *D:* Alfred E. Green. *NOS, GPV, VYY*

Ellie 🐾½ 1984 (R) A murderous widow's stepdaughter tries to save her father from being added to the woman's extensive list of dearly departed husbands. **90m/C VHS, Beta.** Shelley Winters, Sheila Kennedy, Pat Paulsen, George Gobel, Edward Albert; *D:* Peter Wittman. *LIV, VES*

Elmer 🐾½ 1976 (G) Follows the adventures of a temporarily blinded youth and a lovable hound dog who meet in the wilderness and together set off in search of civilization. **82m/C VHS, Beta.** Elmer Swanson, Phillip Swanson; *D:* Christopher Cain. *LIV*

Elmer Gantry 🐾🐾🐾½ 1960 The classic multi-Oscar-winning adaptation of the Sinclair Lewis novel written to expose and denounce the flamboyant, small-town evangelists spreading through America at the time. In the film, Lancaster is the amoral Southern preacher who exacts wealth and power from his congregation, and takes a nun as a mistress. Jones stars as his ex-girlfriend who resorts to a life of prostitution. **146m/C VHS, Beta, LV.** Burt Lancaster, Shirley Jones, Jean Simmons, Dean Jagger, Arthur Kennedy, Patti Page, Edward Andrews, John McIntire, Hugh Marlowe, Rex Ingram; *D:* Richard Brooks; *W:* Richard Brooks; *C:* John Alton; *M:* Andre Previn. Academy Awards '60: Best Actor (Lancaster),

Best Adapted Screenplay, Best Supporting Actress (Jones); Golden Globe Awards '61: Best Actor—Drama (Lancaster); National Board of Review Awards '60: 10 Best Films of the Year, Best Supporting Actress (Jones); New York Film Critics Awards '60: Best Actor (Lancaster); Nominations: Academy Awards '60: Best Picture, Original Dramatic/Comedy Score. *FOX, MGM, FCT*

Elsa, Elsa 1985 Satire of moviemaking life finds a scriptwriter-director distracted by the loss of his girlfriend and unable to concentrate on writing a memoir of his career as a child actor. He creates a subplot dealing with his romantic problems, and puts the film in jeopardy. Fine acting and witty dialogue. In French with English subtitles. **85m/C VHS.** *FR* Didier Haudepin. *FCT*

The Elusive Corporal 🐾🐾🐾½ *Le Caporal Epingle* 1962 Set in a P.O.W. camp on the day France surrendered to Germany, this is the story of the French and Germans, complete with memories of a France that is no more. **108m/B VHS, Beta, LV.** Jean-Pierre Cassel, Claude Brasseur, O.E. Hasse, Claude Rich; *D:* Jean Renoir. *VYY, INT, APD*

The Elusive Pimpernel 🐾🐾½ *The Fighting Pimpernel* 1950 Niven sparkles in this otherwise undistinguished adaptation of Baroness Orczy's "The Scarlet Pimpernel." **109m/C VHS, Beta.** *GB* David Niven, Margaret Leighton, Jack Hawkins, Cyril Cusack, Robert Coote, Edmund Audran, Danielle Godet, Patrick Macnee; *D:* Michael Powell; *W:* Michael Powell, Emeric Pressburger. *HMV, FCT*

Elves 🐾 1989 (PG-13) A group of possessed, neo-Nazi elves performs serious human harm at Christmas time in this tongue-in-check thriller. **95m/C VHS, Beta.** Dan Haggerty, Deanna Lund, Julie Austin, Borah Silver; *D:* Jeffrey Mandel. *AIP*

Elvira Madigan 🐾🐾🐾 1967 (PG) Chronicles the 19th-century Swedish romance between a young officer and a beautiful circus tight-rope walker. Based on a true incident. Exceptional direction and photography. In Swedish with English subtitles. **90m/C VHS, Beta, LV.** *SW* Pia Degermark, Thommy Berggren, Lennart Malmer, Nina Widerberg, Cleo Jensen; *D:* Bo Widerberg; *W:* Bo Widerberg. Cannes Film Festival '67: Best Actress (Degermark); National Board of Review Awards '67: 5 Best Foreign Films of the Year. *WAC, FCT, TPV*

Elvira, Mistress of the Dark 🐾🐾 1988 (PG-13) A manic comedy based on Peterson's infamous B-movie horror-hostess character. The mega-busted terror-queen inherits a house in a conservative Massachusetts town and causes double-entendre chaos when she attempts to sell it. **96m/C VHS, Beta, LV, Closed Caption.** Cassandra Peterson, Jeff Conaway, Susan Kellerman, Edie McClurg, Daniel Greene, W. Morgan Shepherd; *D:* James Signorelli; *C:* Hanania Baer. *VTR, NWV*

Elvis and Me 🐾½ 1988 A TV mini series based on Priscilla Beaulieu Presley's autobiography about her life with the Pelvis. Features many of Presley's biggest hits, sung by country star Ronnie McDowell. Film may aggravate Elvis fans, however, as the King is often depicted negatively from his ex-wife's point of view. **187m/C VHS, Beta, Closed Caption.** Dale Midkiff, Susan Walters, Billy Green Bush, Linda Miller, Jon Cypher; *D:* Larry Peerce. *VTR, NWV*

Elvis in Hollywood 🐾🐾🐾 1993 A tribute highlighting Presley's first four films, "Love Me Tender," "Loving You," "Jailhouse Rock," and "King Creole," completed prior to his reporting for active duty in the army. Features his 1956 screen test at Paramount Studios; photos from the movie sets; interviews with co-stars, directors, writers, business associates, songwriters, and friends; and home movies as well as out-take footage from "Jailhouse Rock." **65m/C VHS, LV.** *D:* Frank Martin. *BMG, BTV*

Elvis: The Movie 🐾🐾½ 1979 A made-for-television biography of the legendary singer, from his high school days to his Las Vegas comeback. Russell gives a convincing performance and lip syncs effectively to the voice of the King (provided by country singer Ronnie McDowell).

Also available in 150-minute version. **117m/C VHS, Beta.** Kurt Russell, Season Hubley, Shelley Winters, Ed Begley Jr., Dennis Christopher, Pat Hingle, Bing Russell, Joe Mantegna; **D:** John Carpenter. LIV, VES

Emanon 🎞½ **1986 (PG-13)** A coming-of-age tale about a young kid and the Christ-like vagabond, named Emanon (or "no name" if spelled in reverse), he befriends. **101m/C VHS, Beta.** Stuart Paul, Cheryl Lynn, Jeremy Miller; **D:** Stuart Paul. NLC

Embassy 🎞🎞 *Target: Embassy* **1972** In this mediocre espionage thriller, von Sydow is a Soviet defector under asylum at the U.S. embassy in Beirut. Colonel Connors, a Russian spy, penetrates embassy security and wounds von Sydow. He is caught, escapes, is captured, escapes, and is caught again. Great cast, but script is often too wordy and contrived. **90m/C VHS.** GB Richard Roundtree, Chuck Connors, Max von Sydow, Ray Milland, Broderick Crawford, Marie-Jose Nat; **D:** Gordon Hessler. WVE

Embassy 🎞🎞 **1985** A made-for-television movie about an American family in Rome that unknowingly possesses a secret computer chip, and thus is pursued by ruthless agents. **104m/C VHS, Beta.** Nick Mancuso, Blanche Baker, Eli Wallach, Sam Wanamaker, Richard Gilliland, Mimi Rogers, George Grizzard, Richard Masur, Kim Darby; **D:** Robert Lewis. NO

Embrace of the Vampire 🎞🎞 **1995 (R)** Innocent young Charlotte (Milano) must make a choice between her college boyfriend Chris (Pruett) and a new nighttime lover (Kemp) with some decidedly different habits. Seems Charlotte looks exactly like a love lost hundreds of years ago and he's not going to take no for an answer. Also available in an unrated version. **CW:** Strong sexuality; nudity; graphic violence; language. **90m/ C VHS, LV, Closed Caption.** Alyssa Milano, Martin Kemp, Harrison Pruett, Charlotte Lewis, Jordan Ladd, Rachel True; **Cameos:** Jennifer Tilly; **D:** Anne Goursaud; **W:** Halle Eaton, Nicole Coady, Rick Bitzelberger; **M:** Joseph Williams. TTC, IME

Embryo 🎞🎞 *Created to Kill* **1976 (PG)** An average sci-fi drama about a scientist who uses raw genetic material to artificially produce a beautiful woman, with ghastly results. **108m/C VHS, Beta.** Rock Hudson, Barbara Carrera, Diane Ladd, Roddy McDowall, Ann Schedeen, John Elerick, Dr. Joyce Brothers; **D:** Ralph Nelson; **C:** Fred W. Koenekamp. LIV

The Emerald Forest 🎞🎞🎞 **1985 (R)** Captivating adventure about a young boy who is kidnapped by a primitive tribe of Amazons while his family is traveling through the Brazilian jungle. Boothe is the father who searches 10 years for him. An engrossing look at tribal life in the vanishing jungle. Beautifully photographed and based upon a true story. Features the director's son as the kidnapped youth. **113m/C VHS, Beta, LV, 8mm, Closed Caption.** Powers Boothe, Meg Foster, Charley Boorman, Dira Pass, Rui Polonah; **D:** John Boorman; **W:** Rospo Pallenberg; **C:** Philippe Rousselot. NLC

Emerald Jungle 🎞½ *Eaten Alive by Cannibals* **1980** While searching for her missing sister in the jungle, Agren encounters cannibal tribes and a colony of brainwashed cult followers. Originally titled "Eaten Alive by Cannibals," this Italian feature was cut for its U.S. release. **92m/C VHS, Beta.** IT Robert Kerman, Janet Agren, Mel Ferrer, Luciano Martino, Mino Loy; **D:** Umberto Lenzi. NO

Emerald of Artama 🎞 **1967** Anyone viewing the most precious and sought after stone in the history of man does not live to tell about it. **93m/C VHS.** Rory Calhoun. NO

The Emigrants 🎞🎞🎞 *Utvandrarna* **1972 (PG)** Farmer von Sydow decides to gather his wife (Ullmann) and family together and leave 19th-century Sweden for the promise of a new life in America. Film is divided into their leaving, the voyage over, and the journey to a settlement in Minnesota. Pacing is somewhat slow; notable cinematography (by director Troell). Adapted from the novels by Vilhelm Moberg. Dubbed into English. Followed by "The New Land." Also edited with the sequel for TV as "The Emigrant Saga."

151m/C VHS. SW Max von Sydow, Liv Ullmann, Allan Edwall, Eddie Axberg, Svenolof Bern, Aina Alfredsson, Monica Zetterlund, Pierre Lindstedt; **D:** Jan Troell; **W:** Jan Troell, Bengt Forslund; **M:** Erik Nordgren. New York Film Critics Awards '72: Best Actress (Ullmann); Nominations: Academy Awards '72: Best Actress (Ullmann), Best Adapted Screenplay, Best Director (Troell), Best Picture. WAR, MOV

Emil and the Detectives 🎞🎞½ *Emil Und Die Detektive* **1964** A German ten-year-old is robbed of his grandmother's money by gangsters, and subsequently enlists the help of pre-adolescent detectives to retrieve it. Good Disney dramatization of the Erich Kastner children's novel. Remake of the 1931 German film starring Rolf Wenkhaus. **99m/C VHS, Beta.** Bryan Russell, Walter Slezak, Roger Mobley; **D:** Peter Tewkesbury; **W:** A.J. Carothers. DIS

Emily WOOF! **1977** Returning from her exclusive Swiss finishing school, licentious young Emily discovers mama is a prostitute and deals with the scalding news by delving into a series of erotic encounters at the hands of her willing "instructors." Stark's first venture into the realm of soft porn. **87m/C VHS, Beta.** Koo Stark; **D:** Henry Herbert; **C:** Jack Hildyard. MGM

Eminent Domain 🎞🎞½ **1991 (PG-13)** A communist party member wakes up to find himself stripped of power in a Kafkaesque purge, not knowing what he is accused of—or why. A potent premise, indifferently handled despite filming on location in Poland. Based on actual events that befell the family of scriptwriter Androej Krakowski. **102m/C VHS.** Donald Sutherland, Anne Archer, Paul Freeman, Bernard Hepton, Francoise Michaud, Jodhi May; **D:** John Irvin; **W:** Andrzej Krakowski, Richard Greggson; **M:** Zbigniew Preisner. IME

Emissary 🎞🎞 **1989 (R)** An American politician and his wife are blackmailed in Africa by the Russians into revealing state secrets that could spark WWIII. **98m/C VHS, Beta, LV.** SA Robert Vaughn, Ted Leplat, Terry Norton, Andre Jacobs; **D:** Jan Scholtz. NO

Emma 🎞🎞½ **197?** BBC TV version of the Jane Austen saga with young Emma trying her matchmaking skills on all her friends and neighbors—with disastrous results. Mr. Knightly tries to provide both a voice of reason and romance, if only Emma could realize it. **257m/C VHS.** GB Doran Goodwin, Vivienne Moore, John Carson, Donald Eccles, Debbie Bowen. VCO

Emma 🎞🎞🎞 *Jane Austen's Emma* **1997** British TV adaptation of the Jane Austen novel featuring young, matchmaking Emma (Beckinsale) wrecking havoc amongst her friends and neighbors with her would-be romantic alliances. Screenplay is truer to the book, with slightly less likable personalities than the 1996 big-screen version. Excellent cast, and beautiful locations and costumes make this one worth seeing. A&E Network offered "Emma" after the overwhelming success of their miniseries "Pride and Prejudice," also adapted from Austen. **107m/C VHS, Closed Caption.** GB Kate Beckinsale, Mark Strong, Samantha Bond, Prunella Scales, Bernard Hepton, Raymond Coulthard, Dominic Rowan, James Hazeldine, Samantha Morton, Lucy Robinson, Olivia Williams; **D:** Diarmuid Lawrence; **W:** Andrew Davis. AAE, WMI, VIF

Emma 🎞🎞🎞 **1996 (PG)** Jane Austen's 1816 novel about wealthy, 21-year-old Emma Woodhouse (Paltrow) who makes it her goal to "fix" the lives of all her friends, while ignoring her own problems (the modern adaptation was "Clueless"). Emma focuses much of her attention on Harriet Smith (Collete), a simple young woman who Emma believes is in need of the perfect mate. Meanwhile, Emma neglects to notice the attractive, and exasperated, Mr. Knightley (Northam). McGrath's screenplay makes Emma and Knightley more likable than in the book, but otherwise stays true. After the success of "Sense and Sensibility," Austen's name is making it in the movies in the footsteps of the likes of John Grisham. **120m/C VHS, LV, Closed Caption.** Gwyneth Paltrow, Jeremy Northam, Greta Scacchi, Toni Collette, Alan

Cumming, Juliet Stevenson, Polly Walker, Ewan McGregor, James Cosmo, Sophie Thompson, Phyllida Law; **D:** Douglas McGrath; **W:** Douglas McGrath; **C:** Ian Wilson; **M:** Rachel Portman. Academy Awards '96: Best Original Score; Nominations: Academy Awards '96: Best Costume Design; Writers Guild of America '96: Best Adapted Screenplay. TOU

Emmanuelle 🎞🎞½ **1974** Filmed in Bangkok, a young, beautiful woman is introduced by her husband to an uninhibited world of sensuality. Above-average soft-core skin film, made with sophistication and style. Kristel maintains a vulnerability and awareness, never becoming a mannequin. **92m/C VHS, Beta.** FR Sylvia Kristel, Alain Cuny, Marika Green, Daniel Sarky; **D:** Just Jaeckin; **C:** Richard Suzuki; **M:** Pierre Bachelet. COL

Emmanuelle 4 🎞 **1984 (R)** Emmanuelle flees a bad relationship and undergoes plastic surgery to mask her identity. Ultimately, she becomes a beautiful young model in the form of a different actress, of course. **95m/C VHS, Beta.** FR Sylvia Kristel, Mia Nygren, Patrick Bauchau; **D:** Francis Giacobetti. MGM

Emmanuelle 5 🎞½ **1987 (R)** This time around sexy Emmanuelle flees aboard a convenient yacht when she's chased by adoring fans at the Cannes Film Festival. But she winds up being forced to join an Arab sheik's harem of slaves. A good example of a series that should have quit while it was ahead. **78m/C VHS.** FR Monique Gabrielle, Charles Foster; **D:** Steve Barnett, Walerian Borowczyk; **M:** Pierre Bachelet. NHO

Emmanuelle 6 🎞 **1992 (R)** The saga of the sexy beauty continues. This time Emmanuelle and a group of models head for the paradise of an Amazon jungle where they promptly become the prized captives of a drug lord. **CW:** Language and strong sensuality. **80m/C VHS.** NHO

Emmanuelle & Joanna 🎞 **1986** A mistreated newlywed bride goes to her sister's whorehouse and stumbles across lots of soft-core antics. **90m/C VHS, Beta.** FR Sherry Buchanan, Danielle Dublino. MED

Emmanuelle in the Country 🎞 **1978** Emmanuelle becomes a nurse in an attempt to bring comfort and other pleasures to those in need. **90m/C VHS, Beta, LV.** FR Laura Gemser. IME

Emmanuelle on Taboo Island 🎞½ **1976 (R)** Marooned young man discovers a beautiful woman on his island. This delights him. **95m/C VHS, Beta.** FR Laura Gemser, Paul Giusti, Arthur Kennedy. NO

Emmanuelle, the Joys of a Woman 🎞 **1976** The amorous exploits of a sensuous, liberated couple take them and their erotic companions to exotic Hong Kong, Bangkok, and Bali. **92m/C VHS, Beta, LV, 8mm.** FR Sylvia Kristel, Umberto Orsini, Catherine Rivet, Frederic Lagache; **D:** Francis Giacobetti. PAR

Emmanuelle, the Queen 🎞 **1975** Seeking revenge, Emmanuelle plots the murder of her sadistic husband. The lecherous assassin she hires tries to blackmail her, and she challenges him at his own game of deadly seduction. **90m/C VHS, Beta.** Laura Gemser. NO

Emmanuelle's Daughter 🎞 **1979** A Greek-made thriller in which a vapidly sensuous heroine cavorts amid episodes of murder, blackmail, and rape. **91m/C Beta.** GR Laura Gemser, Gabriele Tinti, Livia Russa, Vagelis Varton, Nadia Neri. NO

Emma's Shadow 🎞🎞🎞 *Skyggen af Emma* **1988** In the 1930s, a young girl fakes her own kidnapping to get away from her inattentive family and comes to befriend an ex-convict sewer worker. In Danish with English subtitles. Winner of the Prix de la Jeunesse at Cannes, it was voted 1988's Best Danish Film. **93m/C VHS.** DK Bjorje Ahistedt, Line Kruse; **D:** Soeren Kragh-Jacobsen. ORI, FCT, FXL

Emperor Jones 🎬🎬½ 1933 Loosely based on Eugene O'Neill's play, film portrays the rise and fall of a railroad porter whose exploits take him from a life sentence on a chain gang to emperor of Haiti. Robeson recreates his stage role in his first screen appearance. **72m/B VHS, Beta, LV.** Paul Robeson, Dudley Digges, Frank Wilson, Fredi Washington, Ruby Elzy; **D:** Dudley Murphy. *SNC, NOS, HHT*

Emperor Jones/Paul Robeson: Tribute to an Artist 1933 A classic, rarely viewed version of the Eugene O'Neill play about a criminal who schemes his way into becoming the king of a Caribbean island. Robeson's only true dramatic film appearance. The film is accompanied by a documentary profile of Robeson, made in 1979. **102m/B VHS, Beta.** Paul Robeson, Dudley Digges, Frank Wilson; **D:** Dudley Murphy. *COL, HMV*

Emperor of the Bronx 🎬 1989 A look at crime, sleaze, violence, and the actions of bad guys in the inner-city. **90m/C VHS, Beta.** William Smith. *HHE*

Emperor Waltz 🎬🎬½ 1948 Typical Hollywood musical finds phonograph salesman Crosby travelling to Vienna, hoping to sell his goods to the Austrian royal family of Emperor Franz Joseph. He meets up with the Emperor's snobby niece (Fontaine) and attempts to charm her into an audience with her royal uncle. Naturally the two fall in love and everything ends in a happy fade-out. ♫The Emperor's Waltz; Friendly Mountains; Get Yourself a Phonograph; The Kiss in Your Eyes; I Kiss Your Hand, Madame; The Whistler and His Dog. **106m/C VHS, Closed Caption.** Bing Crosby, Joan Fontaine, Roland Culver, Richard Haydn, Lucile Watson, Sig Rumann, Harold Vermilyea; **D:** Billy Wilder; **W:** Billy Wilder, Charles Brackett; **C:** George Barnes; **M:** Victor Young. Nominations: Academy Awards '48: Scoring of a Musical. *USH*

The Emperor's New Clothes 1984 The story of an emperor and the unusual outfit he gets from his tailor. A "Faerie Tale Theatre" presentation. **60m/C VHS, Beta, Closed Caption.** Art Carney, Alan Arkin, Dick Shawn; **D:** Peter Medak. *KUI, FOX, FCT*

The Empire of Passion 🎬🎬🎬 1976 A peasant woman and her low-life lover kill the woman's husband, but find the future they planned with each other is not to be. The husband's ghost returns to haunt them, and destroy the passionate bond which led to the murder. Oshima's follow-up to "In the Realm of the Senses." In Japanese with English subtitles. **110m/C VHS.** *JP* Nagisa Oshima, Kazuko Yoshiyuki, Tatsuya Fuji, Takahiro Tamura, Takuzo Kawatani; **D:** Nagisa Oshima. Cannes Film Festival '78: Best Director (Oshima). *FCT*

Empire of the Ants 🎬½ 1977 (PG) A group of enormous, nuclear, unfriendly ants stalk a real estate dealer and prospective buyers of undeveloped oceanfront property. Story originated by master science-fiction storyteller H. G. Wells. **90m/C VHS, Beta.** Joan Collins, Robert Lansing, John David Carson, Albert Salmi, Jacqueline Scott, Robert Pine; **D:** Bert I. Gordon; **W:** Bert I. Gordon; **C:** Reginald Morris.

Empire of the Dragon 🎬 198? Riproaring martial arts adventure featuring standard number of wide-ranging kicks. **90m/C VHS, Beta.** Chen Tien Tse, Chia Kai, Chang Shan. *NO*

Empire of the Sun 🎬🎬🎬 1987 (PG) Spielberg's mature, extraordinarily vivid return to real filmmaking, from the best-selling J.G. Ballard novel. Yearns to be a great film, but occasional flat spots keep it slightly out of contention. Young, wealthy British Bale lives in Shanghai, but is thrust into a life of poverty and discomfort when China is invaded by Japan at the onset of WWII and he's separated from his family and interred in a prison camp. A mysterious, breathtaking work, in which Spielberg's heightened juvenile romanticism has a real, heartbreaking context. Two other

1987 releases explore the WWII memories of young boys: "Au Revoir Les Enfants" and "Hope and Glory." **153m/C VHS, Beta, LV, 8mm, Closed Caption.** Christian Bale, John Malkovich, Miranda Richardson, Nigel Havers, Joe Pantoliano, Leslie Phillips, Rupert Frazer, Ben Stiller, Robert Stephens, Burt Kwouk, Masato Ibu, Emily Richard; **Cameos:** J.G. Ballard; **D:** Steven Spielberg; **W:** Tom Stoppard; **C:** Allen Daviau; **M:** John Williams. National Board of Review Awards '87: 10 Best Films of the Year, Best Director (Spielberg); Nominations: Academy Awards '87: Best Art Direction/Set Decoration, Best Cinematography, Best Costume Design, Best Film Editing, Best Sound, Best Original Score. *WAR*

Empire Records 🎬🎬 1995 (PG-13) Well, the soundtrack's good and that's about all this frantic movie has going for it (besides a photogenic cast). Joe's (LaPaglia) the manager of an independent record store about to be taken over by a faceless conglomerate unless he and his young-and-crisis-prone staff can come up with the cash to buy the place within 24 hours. **CW:** Sexual situations, language, a drug issue. **91m/C VHS, Closed Caption.** Anthony LaPaglia, Rory Cochrane, Liv Tyler, Renee Zellweger, Johnny Whitworth, Robin Tunney, Ethan Randall, Maxwell Caulfield, Debi Mazar; **D:** Allan Moyle; **W:** Carol Heikkinen; **C:** Walt Lloyd. *WAR*

Empire State 🎬 1987 (R) When his friend disappears from a posh London nightclub, a young man searches for him and finds more action and intrigue than he can handle. Even so, this movie's still pretty bland. **102m/C VHS, Beta.** *GB* Cathryn Harrison, Martin Landau, Ray McAnally; **D:** Ron Peck. *THV*

The Empire Strikes Back 🎬🎬🎬🎬 1980 (PG) Second film in the epic "Star Wars" trilogy finds young Luke Skywalker and the Rebel Alliance plotting new strategies as they prepare to battle the evil Darth Vader and the forces of the Dark Side. Luke learns the ways of a Jedi knight from master Yoda, while Han and Leia find time for romance and a few adventures of their own. Introduces the charismatic Lando Calrissian, vulgar and drooling Jabba the Hut, and a mind-numbing secret from Vadar. Offers the same superb special effects and hearty plot as set by 1977's excellent "Star Wars." Followed by "Return of the Jedi" in 1983. Also available on Laserdisc with "The Making of 'Star Wars'." **124m/C VHS, Beta, LV, Closed Caption.** Mark Hamill, Carrie Fisher, Harrison Ford, Billy Dee Williams, Alec Guinness, David Prowse, Kenny Baker, Frank Oz, Anthony Daniels, Peter Mayhew, Clive Revill, Julian Glover, John Ratzenberger; **D:** Irvin Kershner; **W:** Leigh Brackett, Lawrence Kasdan; **C:** Peter Suschitzky; **M:** John Williams; **V:** James Earl Jones. Academy Awards '80: Best Sound, Best Visual Effects; People's Choice Awards '81: Best Film; Nominations: Academy Awards '80: Best Art Direction/Set Decoration, Best Original Score. *FOX, FCT, RDG*

Employees' Entrance 🎬🎬🎬 1933 William stars as a ruthless department store manager in this story about commerce and compromise during the Depression. Young gives an excellent performance as the wife of one of his employees. Outrageous, and racy, this pre-Code film was expertly-directed by veteran craftsman Del Ruth. Based on a play by David Boehm. **74m/B VHS, Closed Caption.** Warren William, Loretta Young, Wallace Ford, Alice White, Allen Jenkins; **D:** Roy Del Ruth; **W:** Robert Presnell. *MGM*

The Empty Beach 🎬½ 1985 A tough private detective investigates the disappearance of a wealthy business tycoon. **87m/C VHS, Beta.** *AU* Bryan Brown, Anna Maria Monticelli; **D:** Chris Thomson. *LIV*

An Empty Bed 🎬🎬🎬 1990 Award-winning independent production depicting Bill Frayne, an older homosexual, and the challenges of his everyday life. Told mostly in flashbacks as Bill encounters people and places during the course of one day, this is a delicate drama with important statements about homosexuality, aging and honesty. **60m/C VHS.** John Wylie, Mark Clifford Smith, Conan McCarty, Dorothy Stinnette, Kevin Kelly, Thomas Hill, Harriet Bass; **D:** Mark Gasper; **W:** Mark Gasper. *FRF, FCT, YOC*

Empty Canvas 🎬½ *La Noia; L'Ennui Et Sa Diversion, L'Erotisme* 1964 A spiritually-bankrupt artist becomes obsessively jealous of his mistress who refuses to marry him in the hope that someone better will come along. Based on the Alberto Moravia novel. **118m/B VHS, Beta.** *FR IT* Horst Buchholz, Catherine Spaak, Bette Davis; **D:** Damiano Damiani; **M:** Luis Bacalov. *MLB*

Enchanted April 🎬🎬½ 1992 (PG) Two women, tired of their overbearing husbands, rent a villa in Portofino, Italy for a month with two other very different women—a beautiful but bored socialite, and a crusty old woman with an impeccable literary pedigree. The effects of the charming villa, with plenty of wisteria and sunshine, do wonders for the women. A charming and romantic period piece. Based on the 1922 novel by Elizabeth von Arnim. **93m/C VHS, Beta, LV, Closed Caption.** *GB* Miranda Richardson, Joan Plowright, Josie Lawrence, Polly Walker, Alfred Molina, Jim Broadbent, Michael Kitchen, Adriana Fachetti; **D:** Mike Newell; **W:** Peter Barnes; **M:** Richard Rodney Bennett. Golden Globe Awards '93: Best Actress—Musical/Comedy (Richardson), Best Supporting Actress (Plowright); Nominations: Academy Awards '92: Best Adapted Screenplay, Best Costume Design, Best Supporting Actress (Plowright). *PAR, MOV, WAR*

The Enchanted Cottage 🎬🎬½ 1945 Represents Hollywood's "love conquers all" fantasy hokum, as a disfigured war vet and a homely girl retreat from the horrors of the world into a secluded cottage, where they both regain youth and beauty. A four-tissue heart-tugger. Adopted from the Arthur Pinero play. **91m/B VHS, Beta, LV.** Dorothy McGuire, Robert Young, Herbert Marshall, Mildred Natwick, Spring Byington, Hillary Brooke, Richard Gaines, Robert Clarke; **D:** John Cromwell. Nominations: Academy Awards '45: Original Dramatic/Comedy Score. *NOS, TTC*

The Enchanted Forest 🎬🎬½ 1945 An elderly man teaches a boy about life and the beauty of nature when the boy gets lost in a forest. **78m/C VHS, Beta, LV.** *AR* Harry Davenport, Edmund Lowe, Brenda Joyce; **D:** Lew (Louis Friedlander) Landers. *NOS, NWV, HEG*

Enchanted Island 🎬½ 1958 Sailor stops on an island to find provisions and ends up falling in love with a cannibal princess. Thinly based upon Herman Melville's "Typee." **94m/C VHS, Beta.** Jane Powell, Dana Andrews, Arthur Shields; **D:** Allan Dwan. *NO*

The Enchantress 🎬½ *I Skiachtra* 1985 A daring boy experiences his first true loves and passions when he journeys through a mystical land in order to find a beautiful fairy. In Greek with subtitles. **93m/C VHS, Beta, Closed Caption.** *GR* Alkis Kourkoulos, Sofia Aliberti, Lily Kokodi, Antogone Amanitou, Vicky Koulianou, Nicols Papaconstantinou, Stratos Pachis; **D:** Manoussos Manoussakis. *FCT*

Encino Man 🎬🎬 *California Man* 1992 (PG) Two, like, totally uncool Valley dudes dig up a 10,000-year old caveman in the backyard. After giving him a makeover and teaching him the necessities like the four basic food groups (Milk Duds in the dairy group, Sweet Tarts in the fruit group), they use the gnarly caveman as their ticket to popularity and dates to the prom. Juvenile humor appealing to teens; strictly brain candy. **88m/C VHS, Beta, Closed Caption.** Sean Astin, Brendan Fraser, Pauly Shore, Megan Ward, Robin Tunney, Rick Ducommun, Mariette Hartley, Richard Masur, Michael DeLuise; **D:** Les Mayfield; **W:** Shawn Schepps; **C:** Robert Brinkmann. Golden Raspberry Awards '92: Worst New Star (Shore). *HPH*

Encore 🎬🎬🎬 1952 The third W. Somerset Maugham omnibus (following "Quartet" and "Trio") which includes: "Winter Cruise," "The Ant and the Grasshopper," and "Gigolo and Gigolette." **85m/B VHS, Beta.** *GB* Nigel Patrick, Kay Walsh, Roland Culver, John Laurie, Glynis Johns, Ronald Squire, Noel Purcell, Peter Graves; **D:** Pat Jackson, Anthony Pelissier, Harold French. *NO*

Encounter at Raven's Gate 🎬½
1988 (R) Punk rockers and extraterrestrials meet amid hard rock and gallons of gore. **85m/C VHS, Beta, LV, Closed Caption.** Eddie Cleary, Steven Vidler; *D:* Rolf de Heer. *IME*

Encounter with the Unknown 🎬🎬½
1975 Relates three fully documented supernatural events including a death prophesy and a ghost. **90m/C VHS, Beta.** Rosie Holotik, Gene Ross; *D:* Harry Z. Thomason. *VCI*

The End 🎬🎬🎬 **1978 (R)** Reynolds plays a young man who discovers he is terminally ill. He decides not to prolonging his suffering and attempts various tried-and-true methods for committing suicide, receiving riotous help from the crazed DeLuise. **100m/C VHS, Beta, LV.** Burt Reynolds, Sally Field, Dom DeLuise, Carl Reiner, Joanne Woodward, Robby Benson, Kristy McNichol, Norman Fell, Pat O'Brien, Myrna Loy, David Steinberg; *D:* Burt Reynolds; *W:* Jerry Belson; *M:* Paul Williams. *MGM, FOX*

End of August 🎬🎬 **1982 (PG)** A spinster of New Orleans Creole aristocracy, circa 1900, breaks out of her sheltered life and experiences new sexual and romantic awareness. Adapted from "The Awakening" by Kate Chopin. **104m/C VHS, Beta.** Sally Sharp, David Marshall Grant, Paul Roebling; *D:* Bob Graham; *W:* Anna Thomas, Gregory Nava; *C:* Robert Elswit. *NLC*

End of Desire 🎬🎬 **1962** Schell discovers that her husband, Marquand, has married her for her money and is having an affair with the maid in this melodrama based on De Maupassant's story, "Une Vie." A period piece that is a little on the slow side. In French with English subtitles. **86m/C VHS.** *FR* Maria Schell, Christian Marquand, Pascale Petit, Ivan Desny; *D:* Alexandre Astruc. *NO*

The End of Innocence 🎬🎬 **1990 (R)** In her attempts to please everyone in her life, a woman experiences a nervous breakdown. Released two years after Schaeffer's murder. **102m/C VHS, Beta, Closed Caption.** Dyan Cannon, John Heard, George Coe, Lola Mason, Rebecca Schaeffer, Stephen Meadows, Billie Bird, Michael Madsen, Madge Sinclair, Renee Taylor, Viveka Davis; *D:* Dyan Cannon; *W:* Dyan Cannon; *M:* Michael Convertino. *PAR, FCT*

The End of St. Petersburg 🎬🎬🎬½
1927 A Russian peasant becomes a scab during a workers' strike in 1914. He is then forced to enlist in the army prior to the 1917 October Revolution. Fascinating, although propagandistic film commissioned by the then-new Soviet government. Silent. **75m/B VHS, Beta.** Ivan Chuvelov; *D:* Vsevolod Pudovkin. *NOS, MRV, WFV*

End of the Line 🎬🎬½ **1988 (PG)** Two old-time railroad workers steal a locomotive for a cross-country jaunt to protest the closing of the local railroad company. Produced by Steenburgen. **103m/C VHS, Beta, LV, Closed Caption.** Wilford Brimley, Levon Helm, Mary Steenburgen, Kevin Bacon, Holly Hunter, Barbara Barrie, Bob Balaban, Howard Morris, Bruce McGill, Clint Howard, Trey Wilson, Rita Jenrette; *D:* Jay Russell; *W:* John Wohlbruck; *M:* Andy Summers. *BAR, WAR*

End of the Road 🎬🎬½ **1970 (X)** Keach is a troubled college professor whose bizarre treatment by his psychologist (Jones) produces tragic results. He eventually enters into an affair with the wife of a co-worker. Fascinating, if uneven script adapted from John Barth's story. Rated X upon release for adult story and nudity. **110m/C VHS, Beta, Closed Caption.** Stacy Keach, James Earl Jones, James Coco, Harris Yulin, Dorothy Tristan; *D:* Aram Avakian; *W:* Terry Southern; *C:* Gordon Willis. *FOX*

End of the World woof! **1976 (PG)** A coffee machine explodes, sending a man through a window and into a neon sign, where he is electrocuted. A priest witnesses this and retreats to a convent where he meets his alien double and heads for more trouble with outer space invaders. Interesting premise. **88m/C VHS, Beta.** Christopher Lee, Sue Lyon, Lew Ayres, MacDonald Carey, Dean Jagger, Kirk Scott; *D:* John Hayes; *M:* Andrew Belling. *MED*

Endangered 🎬½ **1994** Environmentalists battle bad guys for survival in the wilderness. **91m/C VHS.** Rick Aiello, Martin Kove, Sandra Hess, Tim Quill, Richard Hench, Dale Dye, Craig Alan, Kent MacLachlan, Renee Estevez; *D:* Nick Kellis; *W:* Nick Kellis. *ACA*

Endangered Species 🎬🎬½ **1982 (R)** Offbeat thriller with sci-fi leanings about a retired New York cop on vacation in America's West who is drawn into a female sheriff's investigation of a mysterious series of cattle killings. Could it be UFOs? Based on a true story. **97m/C VHS, Beta.** Robert Urich, JoBeth Williams, Paul Dooley, Hoyt Axton, Peter Coyote, Harry Carey Jr., Dan Hedaya, John Considine; *D:* Alan Rudolph; *W:* Alan Rudolph, John Binder. *MGM*

Endgame 🎬 **1985** Grotesquely deformed survivors of WWIII fight their way out of radioactive New York City to seek a better life. **98m/C VHS, Beta.** Al Oliver, Moira Chen, Jack Davis, Bobby Rhodes, Jill Elliot; *D:* Steve Benson. *MED*

Endless Descent woof! *La Grieta* **1990 (R)** At least it seems endless. A group of scientist-types set out in search of a sunken sub, but somehow take a wrong turn into the rift, the deepest chasm at the bottom of the sea. There, they discover unimaginable horrors—that is, if you've never seen "Alien," or just about any other icky-monster flick. A Spanish film, shot in English, by director Simon, whose other works of art include "Pieces" and "Slugs". **79m/C VHS, Beta, LV.** *SP* Jack Scalia, R. Lee Ermey, Ray Wise, Deborah Adair, Ely Pouget; *D:* J. Piquer Simon; *W:* David Coleman. *LIV*

The Endless Game 🎬🎬 **1989 (PG-13)** Cold War suspenser has British secret-agent-man Finney attempting to solve the murder of his erstwhile fellow agent-lover, much to the dismay of the government. Written by director Forbes, this made-for-cable would-be thriller is a decidedly mediocre waste of a talented cast. Also of note, it was actor-director Sir Anthony Quayle's final appearance. **123m/C VHS, Closed Caption.** *GB* Albert Finney, George Segal, Derek De Lint, Monica Guerritore, Ian Holm, John Standing, Anthony Quayle, Kristin Scott Thomas; *M:* Ennio Morricone. *PSM, FCT*

Endless Love 🎬🎬 **1981 (R)** Although only 17, David and Jade are in love. Her parents think they are too serious and demand that the two spend time apart. David attempts to win her parents' affection and approval, goes mad in the process, and commits a foolish act (he burns the house down) that threatens their love forever. Based on the novel by Scott Spencer. Of interest only to those with time on their hands or smitten by a love so bad that this movie will seem grand in comparison. Features Cruise's first film appearance. **115m/C VHS, Beta, LV.** Brooke Shields, Martin Hewitt, Don Murray, Shirley Knight, Beatrice Straight, Richard Kiley, Tom Cruise, James Spader, Robert Moore, Jami Gertz; *D:* Franco Zeffirelli; *W:* Judith Rascoe; *C:* David Watkin. Nominations: Academy Awards '81: Best Song ("Endless Love"). *LIV, VES*

Endless Night 🎬🎬 *Agatha Christie's Endless Night* **1971** An adaptation of an Agatha Christie tale. Focuses on a young chauffeur who wants to build a dream house, and his chance meeting with an American heiress. **95m/C VHS, Beta, LV.** *GB* Hayley Mills, Hywel Bennett, Britt Ekland, George Sanders, Per Oscarsson, Peter Bowles; *D:* Sidney Gilliat. *REP*

The Endless Summer 🎬🎬🎬 **1966** Classic surfing documentary about the freedom and sense of adventure that surfing symbolizes. Director Brown follows two young surfers around the world in search of the perfect wave. (They finally find it at a then-unknown break off Cape Saint Francis in South America.) Besides the excellent surfing photography, Big Kahuna Brown provides the amusing tongue-in-cheek narrative. Considered by many to be the best surf movie ever. **90m/C VHS, Beta, LV.** Mike Hynson, Robert August; *D:* Bruce Brown; *W:* Bruce Brown. *FCT, HMV, PBS*

The Endless Summer 2 🎬🎬🎬 *Bruce Brown's The Endless Summer 2* **1994 (PG)** You don't have to personally hang ten to get stoked about this long-awaited sequel that once again follows two surfer dudes in their quest for the perfect wave. This time out pro surfers O'Connell and Weaver circle the globe seeking adventure and the world's best waves. Traces the evolution of surfing from the lazy, golden days of the '60s to the worldwide phenomenon it is today, complete with its own pro tour circuit. Breathtaking scenery and spectacular surfing sequences highlight this look at a unique subculture. Thirty years later and it's still a great ride, though the travelogue wears thin and the sub-culture's now fairly well exploited. **107m/C VHS, LV, Closed Caption.** Robert "Wingnut" Weaver, Pat O'Connell, Robert August; *D:* Bruce Brown; *W:* Bruce Brown, Dana Brown. *NLC*

Endplay 🎬🎬½ **1975** An Australian-made crime/horror drama in which two brothers cover for each other in a series of murders involving blonde hitchhikers. Based on a novel by Russell Braddon. **110m/C VHS.** *AU* George Mallaby, John Waters, Ken Goodlet, Delvene Delaney, Charles Tingwell, Robert Hewett, Kevin Miles; *D:* Tim Burstall. *ACA*

Enemies, a Love Story 🎬🎬🎬½ **1989 (R)** A wonderfully resonant, subtle tragedy based on the novel by Isaac Bashevis Singer. A post-Holocaust Jew, living in Coney Island, can't choose between three women—his current wife (who hid him during the war), his tempestuous lover, and his reappearing pre-war wife he presumed dead. A hilarious, confident tale told with grace and patience. **119m/C VHS, Beta, LV, Closed Caption.** Ron Silver, Lena Olin, Anjelica Huston, Margaret Sophie Stein, Paul Mazursky, Alan King, Judith Malina, Rita Karin, Phil Leeds, Elya Baskin, Marie-Adele Lemieux; *D:* Paul Mazursky; *W:* Paul Mazursky; *C:* Fred Murphy; *M:* Maurice Jarre. New York Film Critics Awards '89: Best Director (Mazursky), Best Supporting Actress (Olin); National Society of Film Critics Awards '89: Best Supporting Actress (Huston); Nominations: Academy Awards '89: Best Adapted Screenplay, Best Supporting Actress (Huston, Olin). *MED, VTR*

Enemy Below 🎬🎬🎬 **1957** Suspenseful WWII sea epic, in which an American destroyer and a German U-Boat chase one another and square off in the South Atlantic. **98m/C VHS, Beta.** Robert Mitchum, Curt Jurgens, David Hedison, Theodore Bikel, Doug McClure, Russell Collins; *D:* Dick Powell. Academy Awards '57: Best Special Effects; National Board of Review Awards '57: 10 Best Films of the Year. *FOX, FCT*

Enemy Gold 🎬½ **1993 (R)** A crime czar and a beautiful killer without a conscience go after federal agents who have stumbled across a cache of Confederate gold. Basically, a babes-with-guns blowout. *CW:* Nudity, violence, and sexuality. **92m/C VHS, Beta, LV.** Bruce Penhall, Rodrigo Obregon, Mark Barriere, Suzi Simpson, Tai Collins, Julie Strain; *D:* Drew Sidaris; *W:* Wess Rahn, Christian Sidaris. *PSM*

Enemy Mine 🎬🎬 **1985 (PG-13)** A space fantasy in which two pilots from warring planets, one an Earthling, the other an asexual reptilian Drac, crash land on a barren planet and are forced to work together to survive. **108m/C VHS, Beta, LV, Closed Caption.** Dennis Quaid, Louis Gossett Jr., Brion James, Richard Marcus, Lance Kerwin, Carolyn McCormick; *D:* Wolfgang Petersen; *W:* Edward Khmara; *M:* Maurice Jarre. *FOX*

Enemy of the Law 🎬🎬½ **1945** Texas rangers battle evil in an old frontier town. **59m/B VHS, Beta.** Tex Ritter, Dave O'Brien; *D:* Harry Fraser. *NOS, VCN, DVT*

Enemy of Women 🎬½ *The Private Life of Paul Joseph Goebbels* **1944** Chronicles the life and loves of Nazi propagandist Dr. Joseph Goebbels. **90m/B VHS, Beta.** Claudia Drake, Paul Andor, Donald Woods, H.B. Warner, Sigrid Gurie, Ralph Morgan, Gloria Stuart, Charles Halton; *D:* Alfred Zeisler; *W:* Alfred Zeisler. *NOS, DVT, GLV*

Enemy Territory 🐾🐾 1987 (R) A handful of citizens trapped in a New York City housing project after dark are stalked by a violent, murderous street gang. 89m/C VHS, Beta, Closed Caption. Ray Parker Jr., Jan-Michael Vincent, Gary Frank, Frances Foster; **D:** Peter Manoogian. *FOX*

Enemy Unseen 🐾 1991 (R) A bickering squad of mercenaries slog through the African jungle to find a girl abducted by crocodile-worshipping natives. Dull Jungle-Jim-style adventure, notable for the hilariously phony crocs that occasionally clamp onto the characters. 90m/C VHS. Vernon Wells, Stack Pierce, Ken Gampu, Michael McCabe, Angela O'Neill; **D:** Elmo De Witt. *AIP*

The Enemy Within 🐾🐾½ 1994 Cable TV remake of the 1964 political thriller "Seven Days in May." Set in the late 1990's, President William Foster's (Waterston) approval rating is at an all-time low and his heavy defense cuts have certain government officials plotting a coup. Hero of the tale is Joint Chief of Staffs officer, Col. Mac Casey (Whitaker), whose military career is warring with his sense of ethics. The updating is fairly clunky; for true suspense stick with the original. 86m/C VHS. Forest Whitaker, Sam Waterston, Josef Sommer, Jason Robards Jr., Dana Delany, George Dzundza; **D:** Jonathan Darby; **W:** Darryl Ponicsan, Ronald Bass; **C:** Kees Van Oostrum. *HBO*

The Enforcer 🐾🐾½ *Murder, Inc* 1951 A district attorney goes after an organized gang of killers in this film noir treatment of the real-life "Murder, Inc." case. 87m/B VHS, LV. Humphrey Bogart, Zero Mostel, Ted de Corsia, Everett Sloane, Roy Roberts, Lawrence Tolan, King Donovan, Bob Steele, Adelaide Klein, Don Beddoe, Tito Vuolo, John Kellogg; **D:** Bretaigne Windust, Raoul Walsh; **W:** Martin Rackin; **C:** Robert Burks. *REP*

The Enforcer 🐾🐾½ 1976 (R) Dirty Harry takes on a female partner and a vicious terrorist group that is threatening the city of San Francisco. See how many "punks" feel lucky enough to test the hand of the tough cop. 96m/C VHS, Beta, LV. Clint Eastwood, Tyne Daly, Harry Guardino, Bradford Dillman, John Mitchum; **D:** James Fargo; **W:** Stirling Silliphant. *WAR*

Enforcer from Death Row 🐾 1978 An ex-con is recruited by a secret international peacekeeping organization to track down and eliminate a band of murderous spies. 87m/C VHS, Beta. Cameron Mitchell, Leo Fong, Darnell Garcia, Booker T. Anderson, John Hammond, Mariwin Roberts. *LIV, GHV*

The English Patient 🐾🐾🐾🐾 1996 (R) Filled with flashbacks and moral ambiguities, this adult romance is a complicated WWII saga that finds fragile French-Canadian nurse Hana (Binoche) caring for Almasy (Fiennes), an enigmatic, dying burn patient, in an abandoned monastery in Tuscany. Hana's joined by thief-turned-spy Caravaggio (Defoe), who has a private score to settle with Almasy, and two British bomb disposal experts, Kip (Andrews), a Sikh who falls in love with Hana, and Sgt. Hardy (Whately). Almasy spends his days recalling his illicit love affair with Katharine Clifton (Scott Thomas), the wife of fellow cartographer, Geoffrey (Firth), as they map the North African desert. Exquisitely photographed in a golden glow by Seale with wonderful performances by the entire cast. Based on the novel by Michael Ondaatje.**CW:** Sexuality, some violence and language. 162m/C VHS. Ralph Fiennes, Kristin Scott Thomas, Juliette Binoche, Willem Dafoe, Naveen Andrews, Colin Firth, Julian Wadham, Juergen Prochnow, Kevin Whately, Clive Merrison, Nino Castelnuovo; **D:** Anthony Minghella; **W:** Anthony Minghella; **C:** John Seale; **M:** Gabriel Yared. Academy Awards '96: Best Art Direction/Set Decoration, Best Cinematography, Best Costume Design, Best Director (Minghella), Best Film Editing, Best Picture, Best Sound, Best Supporting Actress (Binoche), Original Dramatic/Comedy Score; British Academy Awards '96: Best Adapted Screenplay, Best Cinematography, Best Film, Best Supporting Actress (Binoche), Best Score; Directors Guild of America Awards '96: Best Director (Minghella); Golden Globe Awards '97: Best Film—Drama, Best Original Score; Los Angeles Film Critics Association Awards '96: Best Cine-matography; National Board of Review Awards '96: Best Supporting Actress (Binoche), Best Supporting Actress (Scott Thomas); Broadcast Film Critics Association Awards '96: Best Director (Minghella), Best Screenplay; Nominations: Academy Awards '96: Best Actor (Fiennes), Best Actress (Scott Thomas), Best Adapted Screenplay, Best Sound Effects Editing; British Academy Awards '96: Best Actor (Fiennes), Best Actress (Scott Thomas), Best Director (Minghella); Golden Globe Awards '97: Best Actor—Drama (Fiennes), Best Actress—Drama (Scott Thomas), Best Director (Minghella), Best Screenplay, Best Supporting Actress (Binoche); Screen Actors Guild Award '96: Best Actor (Fiennes), Best Actress (Scott Thomas), Best Supporting Actress (Binoche), Cast; Writers Guild of America '96: Best Adapted Screenplay. *MAX*

An Englishman Abroad 🐾🐾🐾 1983 During the Cold War, a British actress visits Moscow and chances to meet a notorious English defector. Behind their gossip and small talk is a tragicomic portrait of the exiled traitor/spy. He was the infamous Guy Burgess; the actress was Coral Browne, here playing herself in a pointed recreation. Made for British TV; nuances may be lost on yank viewers. Winner of several British awards. 63m/C VHS. *GB* Alan Bates, Coral Browne, Charles Gray; **D:** John Schlesinger; **W:** Alan Bennett; **M:** George Fenton. *FOX, FCT, PRV*

The Englishman Who Went Up a Hill But Came Down a Mountain 🐾🐾🐾 1995 (PG) Charming if slight tale of town pride based on writer/director Monger's family stories. In 1917 two English cartographers—pompous George (McNeice) and naive Reginald (Grant)—travel into Wales to measure the height of Ffynnon Garw (a running gag has the surveyors struggling with the Welsh language). To the proud locals it is the first mountain in Wales, and without that designation they might as well redraw the maps and be part of England—God forbid. But in order to be designated a mountain Ffynnon Garw must be 1000 feet high, and she measures only 984. Grant stammers boyishly as the Englishman who is not only captivated by the village, but by spirited local lass Betty (Fitzgerald, with whom he starred in "Sirens"). Meaney slyly shines as innkeeper Morgan the Goat, leading the townful of color characters. Wales is shown to great advantage by cinematographer Layton. 96m/C VHS, LV, Closed Caption. *GB* Hugh Grant, Tara Fitzgerald, Colm Meaney, Ian McNeice, Ian Hart, Kenneth Griffith; **D:** Christopher Monger; **W:** Christopher Monger; **C:** Vernon Layton; **M:** Stephen Endelman. *TOU*

Enid Is Sleeping 🐾🐾 *Over Her Dead Body* 1990 (R) Well-done comedy noir in the now-popular there's-a-corpse-in-the-closet subgenre. A woman in a mythical New Mexican town tries to hide the body of her sister Enid, who she's accidentally killed. Enid, it turns out, wasn't thrilled to discover her sister sleeping with her police-officer husband. Phillips and Perkins restored the film to its original state after it was ruthlessly gutted by the studio.**CW:** Language and sensuality. 105m/C VHS. Elizabeth Perkins, Judge Reinhold, Rhea Perlman; **D:** Maurice Phillips; **W:** Maurice Phillips; **C:** Alfonso Beato. *VES, LIV*

Enigma 🐾🐾 1982 (PG) Trapped behind the Iron Curtain, a double agent tries to find the key to five pending murders by locating a Russian coded microprocessor holding information that would unravel the assassination scheme. 101m/C VHS, Beta, LV. *FR GB* Martin Sheen, Brigitte Fossey, Sam Neill, Derek Jacobi, Frank Finlay, Michael Lonsdale, Warren Clarke; **D:** Jeannot Szwarc; **W:** John Briley.

Enigma Secret 🐾🐾 1979 Three Polish mathematicians use their noggins to break the Nazi secret code machine during WWII. Based on a true story; in Polish with English subtitles. 158m/C VHS. *PL* Tadeusz Borowski, Piotr Fronczewski, Piotr Garlicki. *FCT*

Enjo 🐾🐾 *Conflagration; The Flame of Torment* 1958 True story of a tormented young monk, studying at the Golden Pavilion in Kyoto, who becomes disillusioned by the pervasive corruption of the temple. In desperation, he sets fire to the national shrine in an attempt to preserve the monument from further contamination. Very disturbing yet beautiful to watch. Adapted from Mishima's novel "Temple of the Golden Pavilion." Japanese with subtitles. 98m/B VHS. *JP* Raizo Ichikawa, Ganjiro Nakamura, Tatsuya Nakadai; **D:** Kon Ichikawa; **W:** Natto Wada, Keiji Hasebe, Toshiro Mayazumi. *NYF*

Enola Gay: The Men, the Mission, the Atomic Bomb 🐾🐾 1980 Based on the bestselling book by Gordon Thomas and Max Gordon Witts, this made for television drama tells the story of the airmen aboard the B-29 that dropped the first atomic bomb. Details the events during WWII leading up to the decision to bomb Hiroshima and the concerns of the crew assigned the task. 150m/C VHS, Beta. Patrick Duffy, Billy Crystal, Kim Darby, Gary Frank, Gregory Harrison, Ed Nelson, Robert Walden, Stephen Macht, Robert Pine, James Shigeta, Henry Wilcoxon; **D:** David Lowell Rich; **M:** Maurice Jarre. *PSM*

Enormous Changes 🐾🐾🐾 *Enormous Changes at the Last Minute* 1983 Three stories about New York City women and their personal relationships. Based on the stories of Grace Paley. 115m/C VHS, Beta, LV. Ellen Barkin, David Strathairn, Ron McLarty, Maria Tucci, Lynn Milgrim, Kevin Bacon; **D:** Mirra Bank; **W:** John Sayles. *THV*

Enrapture 🐾½ 1990 (R) A chauffeur is the prime suspect when a promiscuous passenger is murdered in his limousine. The driver did it? 87m/C VHS, LV. Ona Simms, Harvey Siegel, Richard Parnes; **D:** Chuck Vincent. *ATL*

Ensign Pulver 🐾🐾 1964 A continuation of the further adventures of the crew of the U.S.S. Reluctant from "Mister Roberts," which was adapted from the Broadway play. 104m/C VHS, Beta. Walter Matthau, Robert Walker Jr., Larry Hagman, Jack Nicholson, Millie Perkins, James Coco, James Farentino, Burl Ives, Gerald S. O'Loughlin, Al Freeman Jr.; **D:** Joshua Logan. *WAR*

Entangled 🐾🐾 1993 (R) David Mirkin (Nelson) is a struggling writer living in Paris with his beautiful girlfriend Annabelle (Treil). As she becomes ever more successful as a fashion model, David becomes ever more jealous and mistrustful. So he hires a detective (Brosnan) to spy on her. And then there's the small matter of a murder. Adapted from the novel "Les Veufs" by Boileau Narcejac. 98m/C VHS, LV, Closed Caption. Judd Nelson, Pierce Brosnan, Laurence Treil, Roy Dupuis; **D:** Max Fischer. *COL*

Enter Laughing 🐾🐾 1967 Based on Reiner's semi-autobiographical novel and play, depicts the botched efforts of a Bronx-born schlump to become an actor. Worthwhile, but doesn't live up to the original. 112m/C VHS, Beta. Reni Santoni, Jose Ferrer, Elaine May, Shelley Winters, Jack Gilford, Don Rickles, Michael J. Pollard, Janet Margolin, Rob Reiner; **D:** Carl Reiner; **W:** Carl Reiner; **C:** Joseph Biroc; **M:** Quincy Jones. *NO*

Enter the Dragon 🐾🐾🐾 *The Deadly Three* 1973 (R) The American film that broke Bruce Lee worldwide combines Oriental conventions with 007 thrills. Spectacular fighting sequences including Karate, Judo, Tae Kwon Do, and Tai Chi Chuan are featured as Lee is recruited by the British to search for opium smugglers in Hong Kong. 98m/C VHS, Beta, LV, Closed Caption. Bruce Lee, John Saxon, Jim Kelly; **D:** Robert Clouse; **C:** Gil Hubbs; **M:** Lalo Schifrin. *WAR*

Enter the Ninja 🐾🐾 1981 (R) First and most serious of the Cannon canon of relatively well-done ninja epics (faint praise) that created original box-office stir for genre (mostly among adolescents needing outlet). Ninja Nero visits old friend in Philippines who's being pressured by ruthless evil guy George to give up the farm. Nero dispatches numerous thugs before indulging in ninja slugfest using Kosugi. **99m/C VHS, Beta.** Franco Nero, Susan George, Sho Kosugi, Christopher George, Alex Courtney; **D:** Menahem Golan; **W:** Judd Bernard. *MGM*

Enter the Panther 🎬 1979 Amidst, and regardless of, a double-crossing plot featuring a treacherous family and a sought-after gold mine, a young man kicks heads and punches his way to fame. **91m/C VHS, Beta.** Bruce Li, Tsai Chin, Tse Lan. *GEM*

Enter Three Dragons 🎬 1981 (R) Kung Fu artistry abounds in this head-kicking action-adventure film. **90m/C VHS.** Dragon Lee, Bruce Lea, Yang Tsze, Samuel Walls, Chang Li, Bruce Li, Jackie Chin. *SUN*

The Entertainer 🎬🎬🎬½ 1960 Splendid drama of a down and out vaudevillian who tries vainly to gain the fame his dying father once possessed. His blatant disregard for his alcoholic wife and his superficial sons brings his world crashing down around him, and he discovers how self-destructive his life has been. Remade in 1975 for television. Adapted from the play by John Osborne. **97m/B VHS.** *GB* Laurence Olivier, Brenda de Banzie, Roger Livesey, Joan Plowright, Daniel Massey, Alan Bates, Shirley Anne Field, Albert Finney, Thora Hird; **D:** Tony Richardson; **W:** Nigel Kneale, John Osborne; **C:** Oswald Morris; **M:** John Addison. Nominations: Academy Awards '60: Best Actor (Olivier). *TPV*

Entertaining Mr. Sloane 🎬🎬½ 1970 Playwright Joe Orton's masterpiece of black comedy concerning a handsome criminal who becomes the guest and love interest of a widow and her brother. **90m/C VHS, Beta.** Beryl Reid, Harry Andrews, Peter McEnery, Alan Webb; **D:** Douglas Hickox. *NO*

The Entity 🎬🎬 1983 (R) Supposedly based on a true story about an unseen entity that repeatedly rapes a woman. Hershey's the victim whom nobody believes. She eventually ends up at a university for talks with parapsychologist Silver. Pseudo-science to the rescue as the over-sexed creature is frozen dead in its tracks. Exploitative violence, gore, and nudity aplenty, balanced to a degree by Hershey's strong performance. **115m/C VHS, Beta.** Barbara Hershey, Ron Silver, Alex Rocco; **D:** Sidney J. Furie; **W:** Frank de Felitta; **C:** Stephen Burum; **M:** Charles Bernstein. *FOX*

Entr'acte 1924 Clair's famous dada-surrealist classic short, reflecting his sense of humor, as various eccentric characters become involved in a crazy chase. Silent. **21m/B VHS, Beta.** *FR* **D:** Rene Clair. *MRV, GVV*

Entre-Nous 🎬🎬🎬½ *Between Us; Coup de Foudre* 1983 (PG) Two attractive, young French mothers find in each other the fulfillment their husbands cannot provide. One of the women was confined in a concentration camp during WWII; the other is a disaffected artist. In French with English subtitles. **112m/C VHS, Beta.** *FR* Isabelle Huppert, Miou-Miou, Guy Marchand; **D:** Diane Kurys; **W:** Diane Kurys; **M:** Luis Bacalov. Nominations: Academy Awards '83: Best Foreign Language Film. *MGM*

Epitaph 🎬 1987 An average American family's life is disrupted by the mother's habitual axe-murdering. **90m/C VHS, Beta.** **D:** Joseph Merhi. *NO*

The Equalizer: Memories of Manon 🎬🎬½ 1988 Feature-length episode of the popular television crime thriller about an ex-agent who uses guns and espionage tactics to help people who are being persecuted by ruthless villians on the streets of New York City. In this installment, McCall, the Equalizer, learns that he has a daughter and that her life is in peril. **96m/C VHS, Beta.** Edward Woodward, Melissa Sue Anderson, Anthony Zerbe, George DiCenzo, Jon Polito, Robert Lansing, Keith Szarabajka; **D:** Tony Wharmby. *USH*

Equalizer 2000 🎬 1986 (R) A warrior in a post-holocaust future plots to overthrow a dictatorship by using a high-powered gun. **85m/C VHS, Beta.** Richard Norton, Corinne Wahl, William Steis; **D:** Cirio H. Santiago. *MGM*

Equinox 🎬🎬🎬 1971 (PG) Young archaeologists uncover horror in a state forest. The ranger, questing for a book of spells that the scientists have found, threatens them with wonderful special effects, including winged beasts, huge apes, and Satan. Though originally an amateur film, it is deemed a minor classic in its genre. **80m/C VHS.** Edward Connell, Barbara Hewitt, Frank Bonner, Robin Christopher, Jack Woods; **D:** Jack Woods. *NO*

Equinox 🎬🎬 1993 (R) Modine gets to try his hand (and does well) at a dual role, with his portrayal of identical twins, separated at birth and raised in completely different environs. Garage worker Henry lives in a tenement while slick brother Freddie is a gangster's chauffeur married to the materialistic Sharon (Singer). Fate brings the brothers together when a janitor discovers a letter that reveals their parentage and the fact that a fortune has been left to them. Set in the near future, in the surreal and decaying city of Empire, this is typical Rudolph with its moody stylized appearance and convoluted plot. **110m/C VHS, LV, Closed Caption.** Matthew Modine, Lara Flynn Boyle, Lori Singer, Marisa Tomei, Fred Ward, M. Emmet Walsh, Tyra Ferrell, Tate Donovan, Kevin J. O'Connor, Gailard Sartain; **D:** Alan Rudolph; **W:** Alan Rudolph; **C:** Elliot Davis. Nominations: Independent Spirit Awards '94: Best Actor (Modine), Best Cinematography, Best Film, Best Supporting Actress (Boyle). *COL, FCT*

Equinox Flower 🎬🎬 1958 Ozu's first color film tells the sensitive story of two teenage girls who make a pact to protect each other from the traditional prearranged marriages their parents have set up. Lovely film that focuses on the generation gap between young and old in the Japanese family. In Japanese with English subtitles. **118m/C VHS, Closed Caption.** *JP* Shin Saburi, Kinuyo Tanaka, Ineko Arima, Miyuki Kuwano, Chishu Ryu; **D:** Yasujiro Ozu. *NYF, FCT, ING*

Equus 🎬🎬½ 1977 (R) A psychiatrist undertakes the most challenging case of his career when he tries to figure out why a stable-boy blinded horses. Based upon the successful play by Peter Shaffer, but not well transferred to film. **138m/C VHS, Beta, LV.** Richard Burton, Peter Firth, Jenny Agutter, Joan Plowright, Colin Blakely, Harry Andrews; **D:** Sidney Lumet; **W:** Peter Shaffer; **C:** Oswald Morris; **M:** Richard Rodney Bennett. British Academy Awards '77: Best Supporting Actress (Agutter); Golden Globe Awards '78: Best Actor—Drama (Burton), Best Supporting Actor (Firth); National Board of Review Awards '77: 10 Best Films of the Year; Nominations: Academy Awards '77: Best Actor (Burton), Best Adapted Screenplay, Best Supporting Actor (Firth). *MGM*

ER 🎬🎬🎬 1994 TV pilot for the hit medical series about the trials and traumas of the Chicago emergency room of an urban teaching hospital. Edwards is Dr. Mark Greene, the standards-setting team leader trying to juggle professional and personal resonsibilities, Douglas Ross (Clooney) is a womanizing pediatric resident, Susan Lewis (Stringfield) a workaholic second-year resident, Peter Benton (La Salle) is the perfectionist surgical resident with no people skills, which disconcerts third year medical student John Carter (Wyle) who falls under Benton's stern gaze. Fast-paced action is enough to make you dizzy. **88m/C VHS, Closed Caption.** Anthony Edwards, George Clooney, Eriq La Salle, Noah Wyle, Sherry Stringfield, Julianna Margulies, Christina Harnos, William H. Macy. *WAR*

Era Notte a Roma 🎬🎬🎬 1960 An American, Russian, and British soldier each escape from a concentration camp in the waning days of WWII and find refuge in the home of a young woman. **145m/C VHS.** *IT* **D:** Roberto Rossellini; **W:** Roberto Rossellini. *NO*

Eraser 🎬🎬½ 1996 (R) Arnold returns to familiar big-budget action territory and looks right at home. He plays elite U.S. Marshal John Kruger, who protects federal witnesses by "erasing" their previous identities. When a beautiful witness uncovers a high-level conspiracy, the two go on the run to stay alive long enough to expose the truth.

Fans of the big bang Schwarzenegger of yore will not be disappointed. Rumors of production delays and budget overruns, not to mention difficulties between director Russell and producer Kopelson, brought up the spectre of "Waterworld," but the final result is more reminiscent of the success of "True Lies." **CW:** Violent action throughout and some language. **115m/C VHS, LV, Closed Caption, DVD.** Arnold Schwarzenegger, Vanessa Williams, James Caan, James Coburn, Robert Pastorelli, Andy Romano, James Cromwell, Danny Nucci, Nicholas Chinlund, Mark Rolston, Gerry Becker; **D:** Chuck Russell; **W:** Walon Green, Tony Puryear; **C:** Adam Greenberg; **M:** Alan Silvestri. Nominations: MTV Movie Awards '97: Best Action Sequence. *WAR*

Eraserhead 🎬🎬🎬 1978 The infamous cult classic about a numb-brained everyman wandering through what amounts to a sick, ironic parody of the modern urban landscape, innocently impregnating his girlfriend and fathering a pestilent embryonic mutant. Surreal and bizarre, the film has an inner, completely unpredictable logic all its own. Lynch's first feature-length film stars Nance, who later achieved fame in Lynch's "Twin Peaks" as Pete the Logger. **90m/B VHS, Beta, LV.** Jack Nance, Charlotte Stewart, Jack Fisk, Jeanne Bates; **D:** David Lynch; **W:** David Lynch; **C:** Frederick Elmes. *COL, OM*

Erendira 🎬🎬½ 1983 Based on Gabriel Garcia-Marquez's story about a teenage girl prostituting herself to support her witch-like grandmother after accidentally torching the elder's house. The film follows the two as they travel across the desert trying out new and inventive ways to survive. Unusual ending tops off a creative, if not eclectic, movie. In Spanish with English subtitles. **103m/C VHS, Beta.** *FR MX GE* Irene Papas, Claudia Ohana, Michael Lonsdale, Rufus, Jorge Fegan; **D:** Ruy Guerra. *XVC, MED, APD*

Eric 🎬🎬🎬 1975 Made-for-television tear-jerker about a young athlete who fights for his life after he's diagnosed with leukemia. Based on the true-life account written by Eric's mother Doris Lund. **100m/C VHS, Beta.** Patricia Neal, John Savage, Claude Akins, Sian Barbara Allen, Mark Hamill, Nehemiah Persoff, Tom Clancy; **D:** James Goldstone; **M:** Dave Grusin. *LIV*

Erik 🎬🎬 1990 An ex-government agent working in Central America finds his loyalties divided when he is approached by a female activist and his old CIA friends. They want him to help expose his current boss as a drug smuggler. **90m/C VHS, Beta.** Stephen McHattie, Deborah Van Valkenburgh. *NO*

Erik, the Viking 🎬🎬 1972 The Norse Warrior discovers not only the New World but traitorous subordinates among his crew, calling for drastic measures. **95m/C VHS, Beta.** Giuliano Gemma, Gordon Mitchell. *UNI*

Erik the Viking 🎬½ 1989 (PG-13) A mediocre Monty Pythonesque farce about a Viking who grows dissatisfied with his barbaric way of life and decides to set out to find the mythical Asgaard, where Norse gods dwell. Great cast of character actors is wasted. **104m/C VHS, Beta, LV, Closed Caption.** *GB* Tim Robbins, Terry Jones, Mickey Rooney, John Cleese, Imogen Stubbs, Anthony Sher, Gordon John Sinclair, Freddie Jones, Eartha Kitt; **D:** Terry Jones; **W:** Terry Jones. *ORI*

Ermo 🎬🎬🎬 1994 Hard-working noodle-maker Ermo (Alia) supports her slothful husband, Chief (Zhijun), and their son in their northern China village. Her smitten truck-driver neighbor Blindman (Peiqi) has an equally unpleasant wife, Fat Woman (Haiyan), with whom Ermo has an ongoing rivalry. They own a color TV (the only one in the village) and Ermo becomes determined to get a bigger and better set by selling her noodles in a nearby town and compulsively saving her money. Of course, her entrepreneurial has some unexpected consequences. Mandarin Chinese with subtitles. **93m/C VHS.** *CH* Alia, Liu Peiqi, Ge Zhijun, Zhang Haiyan; **D:** Zhou Xiaowen; **C:** Lu Gengxin; **M:** Zhou Xiaowen. *EVE*

Ernest Goes to Camp *ℐℐ½* 1987 (PG) A screwball, slapstick summer camp farce starring the character Ernest P. Worrell as an inept camp counselor. When progress threatens the camp, Ernest leads the boys on a turtle-bombing, slop-shooting attack on the construction company. Followed by "Ernest Saves Christmas" and "Ernest Goes to Jail." 92m/C VHS, Beta. Jim Varney, Victoria Racimo, John Vernon, Iron Eyes Cody, Lyle Alzado, Gailard Sartain, Daniel Butler, Hakeem Abdul-Samad; **D:** John R. Cherry III; **W:** John R. Cherry III. *TOU*

Ernest Goes to Jail *ℐℐ* 1990 (PG) The infamous loon Ernest P. Worrell winds up in the jury box and the courtroom will never be the same again. Jury duty suddenly becomes hard-time in the slammer for poor Ernest when he is mistaken for a big-wig organized crime boss. Sequel to "Ernest Goes to Camp" and "Ernest Saves Christmas." 81m/C VHS, LV, Closed Caption. Jim Varney, Gailard Sartain, Randall "Tex" Cobb, Bill Byrge, Barry Scott, Charles Napier; **D:** John R. Cherry III; **W:** Charlie Cohen; **M:** Bruce Arntson. *TOU*

Ernest Goes to School *ℐℐ½* 1994 (PG) Ernest must finish high school if he wants to keep his job as school janitor. He's "aided" by two crazy science teachers who give him an experimental IQ booster. 89m/C VHS, Closed Caption. Jim Varney, Linda Kash, Bill Byrge; **D:** Coke Sams. *MNC*

The Ernest Green Story *ℐℐ½* 1993 Made-for-cable drama based on the integration of Central High in Little Rock, Arkansas by nine black students in 1957. Green was the only senior in the group and the movie follows a year of verbal and physical abuse, vandalism, and unfair academic treatment, as he struggles to withstand every difficulty in order to graduate. 92m/C VHS, Closed Caption. Morris Chestnut, CCH Pounder, Gary Grubbs, Tina Lifford, Avery Brooks, Ruby Dee, Ossie Davis; **D:** Eric Laneuville. *DIS*

Ernest Rides Again *ℐℐ½* 1993 (PG) Ernest P. "Knowwhutimean?" Worrell (Varney) is back, aiding a college professor friend who has a cockamamie theory that the British crown jewels were hidden in a Revolutionary War cannon. Naturally he's right and Ernest must battle British spies and a greedy antiquities collector to get the gems back. Goofy slapstick sticks to the formula of the other films. 93m/C VHS. Jim Varney, Ron James, Duke Ernsberger, Jeffrey Pillars, Linda Kash, Tom Butler; **D:** John R. Cherry III; **W:** John R. Cherry III, William M. Akers; **M:** Bruce Arntson, Kirby Shelstad. *MNC*

Ernest Saves Christmas *ℐℐ½* 1988 (PG) Ernest P. Worrell is back. When Santa decides that it's time to retire, Ernest must help him recruit a has-been children's show host who is a bit reluctant. For Ernest fans only, and only the most dedicated of those. Second in the series featuring the nimble-faced Varney, the first of which was "Ernest Goes to Camp," followed by "Ernest Goes to Jail." 91m/C VHS, Beta, LV. Jim Varney, Douglas Seale, Oliver Clark, Noelle Parker, Billie Bird; **D:** John R. Cherry III. *TOU*

Ernest Scared Stupid *ℐℐ½* 1991 (PG) Pea-brained Ernest P. Worrell returns yet again in this silly comedy. When he accidentally releases a demon from a sacred tomb a 200-year-old curse threatens to destroy his hometown, unless Ernest can come to the rescue. Would you want your love depending on Ernest's heroics? Who would have thought that the annoying Ernest P. Worrell could appear in one movie, let alone four? 93m/C VHS, Beta, Closed Caption. Jim Varney, Eartha Kitt, Austin Nagler, Jonas Moscartolo, Shay Astar; **D:** John R. Cherry III; **W:** John R. Cherry III; **C:** Hanania Baer; **M:** Bruce Arntson. *TOU*

Ernesto *ℐℐ½* 1979 A lushly erotic Italian film depicting the troubled relationship between a young, devil-may-care gay youth and his older, coolly seducing lover. In Italian with subtitles. 98m/C VHS, Beta. *IT* Martin Halm, Michele Placido; **D:** Salvatore Samperi. *FCT*

Ernie Kovacs: Between the Laughter *ℐℐ* 1984 A made for television version of the television comic's life and career, ending with his tragic death in a car accident in 1962. Shows the brand of humor that made Kovacs famous as well as the devastation that he suffered after the tragic kidnapping of his children by his first wife during divorce proceedings. Kovac's second wife, Edie Adams, makes a brief appearance. 95m/C VHS, Beta. Jeff Goldblum, Cloris Leachman, Melody Anderson, Madolyn Smith, John Glover; **Cameos:** Edie Adams; **D:** Lamont Johnson; **M:** Ralph Burns. *NO*

Erotic Escape *ℐ* 1986 Soft-core fun about party girls taking over a small French town. Originally in French, but dubbed in English. Check your brain at the door. 86m/C VHS, Beta. *FR* Marie-Claire Davy, Pauline Larrieu. *MED*

Erotic Images woof! 1985 (R) A beautiful psychology teacher publishes her doctoral thesis on sex and becomes a best-selling author, which threatens her marriage. 93m/C VHS, Beta. Britt Ekland, Edd Byrnes, John McCann; **D:** Declan Langan. *LIV, VES*

Erotic Touch of Hot Skin *ℐ* 1965 Sex, murder, false identities, car crashes, and striptease in the Riviera. 78m/B VHS, Beta. Fabienne Dali, Sophie Hardy, Jean Valmont, Francois Dryek; **D:** Max Pecas. *VDM*

Erotique *ℐℐ* 1994 Sex quartet from female filmmakers. "Let's Talk About Sex" finds struggling Latina actress Rosie (Lopez-Dawson) supporting herself by working at a phone sex agency where a caller (Cranston) wants to know about her sexual fantasies. "Taboo Parlor" finds lesbian lovers Claire (Barnes) and Julia (Soeberg) picking up boy toy Victor (Carr) and planning some s/m fun. "Wonton Soup" has Australian-born Chinese Adrian (Lounibos) reuniting with his lover Ann (Man) in Hong Kong and deciding to hold her interest by practicing some ancient Chinese sexual techniques. And in "Final Call," a school teacher (Ohana) tries a sexual adventure with a stranger. 120m/C VHS. Kamala Lopez-Dawson, Bryan Cranston, Priscilla Barnes, Camilla Soeberg, Michael Carr, Tim Lounibos, Hayley Man, Claudia Ohana; **D:** Lizzie Borden, Monika Treut, Clara Law, Ana Maria Magalhaes; **W:** Lizzie Borden, Monika Treut, Susie Bright, Eddie L.C. Fong; **C:** Larry Banks, Elfi Mikesch, Arthur Wong. *FXL, FCT*

The Errand Boy *ℐℐ½* 1961 Jerry Lewis' patented babbling schnook hits Hollywood in search of a job. When he lands a position as an errand boy, Hollywood may never be the same again in this prototypical comedy; a must for Lewis fans only. 92m/B VHS, Beta, LV. Jerry Lewis, Brian Donlevy, Dick Wesson, Howard McNear, Felicia Atkins, Fritz Feld, Sig Rumann, Renee Taylor, Doodles Weaver, Mike Mazurki, Lorne Greene, Michael Landon, Dan Blocker, Pernell Roberts, Snub Pollard, Kathleen Freeman; **D:** Jerry Lewis; **W:** Jerry Lewis. *LIV*

The Errors of Youth *ℐℐ* Wild Oats 1978 Dimitri (Zhdanko), a construction worker in Siberia, is disillusioned over a failed love affair and moves to Leningrad where he falls in with black marketeers and a marriage of convenience. Because of political problems, director Frumin left the film unfinished when he emigrated to the U.S. and it wasn't until 1989 that he returned to Leningrad to complete the project. Russian with subtitles. 87m/C VHS. *RU* Stanislav Zhdanko, Marina Neyelova, Natalia Varley, Mikhail Vaskov; **D:** Boris Frumin. *FCT*

Escapade *ℐℐℐ* 1955 Sons thinking their parents are en route to divorce court create a scheme to achieve peace worldwide. The pacifist father's reaction juxtaposes idealistic youth with the cynicism of adulthood. Adapted from a play by Roger MacDougall. 87m/B VHS. *GB* John Mills, Yvonne Mitchell, Alastair Sim, Jeremy Spenser, Andrew Ray, Marie Lohr, Peter Asher; **D:** Philip Leacock. *VYY, MOV*

Escapade in Florence *ℐℐ* 1962 As two students in Florence paint their way to immortality, an elaborate art-forging ring preys upon their talents. 81m/C VHS, Beta. Tommy Kirk, Ivan Desny; **D:** Steve Previn. *DIS*

Escapade in Japan *ℐℐ* 1957 A Japanese youth helps an American boy frantically search the city of Tokyo for his parents. Shot in Japan. 93m/C VHS, Beta. Cameron Mitchell, Teresa Wright, Jon Provost, Roger Nakagawa, Philip Ober, Clint Eastwood; **D:** Arthur Lubin; **M:** Max Steiner. *NO*

Escape *ℐℐ* 1940 (PG) A fun-loving, care-free Irish officer is sent to oversee the toughest POW prison in Scotland. There, he becomes consumed with keeping the facility secure despite the intricate escape plans laid out by a group of rioters. 90m/C VHS. Brian Keith, Helmut Griem; **D:** Lamont Johnson. *NO*

Escape *ℐℐ½* 1990 (R) A woman attempts to track down her brother's killer and finds an entire town mysteriously controlled by a sadistic and powerful man. Features General Hospital's bad-boy Shriner. 100m/C VHS. Elizabeth Jeager, Kim Richards, Kin Shriner; **D:** Richard Styles. *HHE*

The Escape Artist *ℐℐ½* 1982 (PG) Award-winning cinematographer Deschanel's first directorial effort is this quirky film about a teenage escape artist who sets out to uncover the identity of his father's killers. 96m/C VHS, Beta, LV. Griffin O'Neal, Raul Julia, Teri Garr, Joan Hackett, Desi Arnaz Sr., Gabriel Dell, Huntz Hall, Jackie Coogan; **D:** Caleb Deschanel; **W:** Melissa Mathison; **C:** Stephen Burum; **M:** Georges Delerue. *LIV, VES*

Escape Clause *ℐℐ* 1996 (R) Insurance exec Richard Ramsay (McCarthy) gets a call from a hitman informing him that his wife Sarah (McNeil) has hired him to kill Richard. The hitman says if Richard will pay him, the contract's off. Instead Richard tries to figure out what's going on, with some help from police detective Ferrand (Sorvino), who discovers Richard has been treated for paranoid delusions. Fast-paced cable mystery with a few too many twists. **CW:** Violence, sexuality and language. 131m/C VHS, Closed Caption. Andrew McCarthy, Paul Sorvino, Kate McNeil, Peter Donaldson, Kenneth Welsh, Connie Britton, Stan Egi, John Evans; **D:** Brian Trenchard-Smith; **W:** Danilo Bach; **M:** Ken Thorne, Rick Marvin. *MGM*

Escape from Alcatraz *ℐℐℐ* 1979 (PG) A fascinating account of the one and only successful escape from the maximum security prison at Alcatraz in 1962. The three men were never heard from again. 112m/C VHS, Beta, LV. Clint Eastwood, Patrick McGoohan, Roberts Blossom, Fred Ward, Danny Glover; **D:** Donald Siegel; **C:** Bruce Surtees. *PAR*

Escape from Cell Block 3 *ℐ* 1978 Five escaped female convicts take it on the lam for Mexico and freedom. 82m/C VHS, Beta. Carolyn Judd, Teri Guzman, Bonita Kalem. *PSM*

Escape from Death Row *ℐ* 1976 (R) Convicted criminal mastermind, sentenced to die, devises a brilliant and daring plan of escape on the eve of his execution. 85m/C VHS, Beta. Lee Van Cleef, James Lane, Barbara Moore, Alice Belios. *NO*

Escape from DS-3 *ℐℐ* 198? Bostwick and "Police Academy" alumnus Smith team up in a familiar story: framed for a serious crime, a man attempts to escape from a maximum security satellite prison. About as good as you'd expect. 88m/C VHS. Jackson Bostwick, Bubba Smith. *MOV*

Escape from El Diablo *ℐ* 1983 (PG) Two juvenile delinquents harass guards at a Mexican prison. Being from California, they use frisbees and skateboards to help their escape. 92m/C VHS, Beta. *SP GB* Jimmy McNichol, Timothy Van Patten, John Ethan Wayne; **D:** Gordon Hessler. *MED*

Escape from Fort Bravo *ℐℐ½* 1953 A Civil War era western set in an Arizona stockade. Holden is the hard-bitten Union cavalry officer who ruthlessly guards his Confederate prisoners, who are led by Forsythe. Parker is a southern spy whose job is to break the rebels out of jail by seducing Holden from his duty, which she does. When Holden discovers what's happened, he recaptures his prisoners only to be beset by hostile Mescalero Indians while trying to get everyone back to the fort. It's an old story but well-executed with lots of action. **98m/C VHS, Beta, Closed Caption.** William Holden, Eleanor Parker, John Forsythe, William Demarest, William Campbell, Polly Bergen, Richard Anderson, Carl Benton Reid, John Lupton, Howard McNear, Alex Montoya, Forrest Lewis, Fred Graham, William Newell; *D:* John Sturges; *W:* Frank Fenton; *C:* Robert L. Surtees. MGM, FCT

Escape from Galaxy Three 🎞 1976
(G) A pair of space travelers fight off a bevy of evil aliens. **90m/C VHS, Beta.** James Milton, Cheryl Buchanan. PSM

Escape from Hell woof! *Hellfire on Ice, Part 2: Escape from Hell* 1989
Two scantily clad women escape from a jungle prison and are pursued by their sadistic warden. **?m/C VHS.** Anthony Steffen, Ajita Wilson; *D:* Edward Muller. HHE

Escape from L.A. 🎞🎞½ 1976
John Carpenter's Escape from L.A. 1996 (R) Well, Snake Plissken is back (Russell once again) and so's Carpenter, who did the original "Escape from New York" saga, and technology's advanced a lot in 15 years, so sit back and enjoy the action. In 2013, L.A.'s been turned into a gang-infested island, thanks to a 9.6 earthquake, where Snake is forced to find a doomsday weapon in just 10 hours. Seems he's been injected with a virus that will kill him unless he can complete his job and escape to get the antidote. Naturally, there's lots of bad guys who'll try to stop him. Russell not only reprises his old role but found Snake's original leathers, which still fit, and wore the outfit in some scenes of the sequel. *CW:* Violence and some language. **101m/C VHS, Beta, Closed Caption.** Kurt Russell, Georges Corraface, Stacy Keach, Peter Fonda, Steve Buscemi, Pam Grier, Valeria Golino, Cliff Robertson, Michelle Forbes, Bruce Campbell, A.J. Langer; *D:* John Carpenter; *W:* Kurt Russell, John Carpenter, Debra Hill; *C:* Gary B. Kibbe; *M:* John Carpenter, Shirley Walker. PAR

Escape from New York 🎞🎞½ 1981 (R)
The ultimate urban nightmare: a ruined, future Manhattan is an anarchic prison for America's worst felons. When convicts hold the President hostage, a disgraced war hero unwillingly attempts an impossible rescue mission. Cynical but largely unexceptional sci-fi action, putting a good cast through tight-lipped peril. **99m/C VHS, Beta, LV.** Kurt Russell, Lee Van Cleef, Ernest Borgnine, Donald Pleasence, Isaac Hayes, Adrienne Barbeau, Harry Dean Stanton, Season Hubley; *D:* John Carpenter; *W:* John Carpenter, Nick Castle; *C:* Dean Cundey; *M:* John Carpenter. NLC, FUS

Escape from Planet Earth 🎞 *The Doomsday Machine* 1967
A spaceship is damaged deep in space and only a few of the crew can make it back to Earth. But who will decide who lives or dies? (Unfortunately, the Earth has been totally destroyed so who cares anyway.) Lousy special effects. **91m/B VHS, Closed Caption.** Grant Williams, Bobby Van, Ruta Lee, Henry Wilcoxon, Mala Powers, Casey Kasem, Mike Farrell, Harry Hope; *D:* Lee Sholem. ACA

Escape from Safehaven woof! 1988
(R) Brutal slimeballs rule a mad, sadistic world in the post-apocalyptic future, and a family tries to escape them. In very poor taste. **87m/C VHS, Beta.** Rick Gianisi, Mollie O'Mara, John Wittenbauer, Roy MacArthur, William Beckwith; *D:* Brian Thomas Jones, James McCalmont. NO

Escape from Sobibor 🎞🎞🎞 1987
(PG-13) Nail-biting, true account of the largest successful escape from a Nazi prison camp, adapted from Richard Rashke's book. Made for TV. **120m/C VHS.** Alan Arkin, Joanna Pacula, Rutger Hauer, Hartmut Becker, Jack Shepherd; *D:* Jack Gold; *M:* Georges Delerue. LIV

Escape from the Bronx 🎞 1985 (R)
Invading death squads seek to level the Bronx. Local street gangs cry foul and ally to defeat the uncultured barbarians. Sequel to "1990: The Bronx Warriors." **82m/C VHS, Beta.** Mark Gregory, Henry Silva, Valeria D'Obici, Timothy Brent, Andrea Coppola; *D:* Enzo G. Castellari. MED

Escape from the KGB woof! 1987
A CIA agent escapes from a Soviet prison, taking plans for a new space installation with him. **99m/C VHS, Beta.** Thomas Hunter, Ivan Desny, Marie Versini, Walter Barns; *D:* Harald Phillipe. NO

Escape from the Planet of the Apes 🎞🎞🎞 1971 (G)
Reprising their roles as intelligent, English-speaking apes, McDowall and Hunter flee their world before it's destroyed, and travel back in time to present-day America. In L.A. they become the subjects of a relentless search by the fearful population, much like humans Charlton Heston and James Franciscus were targeted for experimentation and destruction in similan society in the earlier "Planet of the Apes" and "Beneath the Planet of the Apes." Sequelled by "Conquest of the Planet of the Apes" and a television series. **98m/C VHS, Beta, LV, Closed Caption.** Roddy McDowall, Kim Hunter, Sal Mineo, Ricardo Montalban, William Windom, Bradford Dillman, Natalie Trundy, Eric (Hans Gudegast) Braeden; *D:* Don Taylor; *C:* Joseph Biroc; *M:* Jerry Goldsmith. FOX, FUS

Escape Me Never 🎞½ 1947
Flynn plays a struggling composer in this sappy period piece about poverty-stricken artists in Italy at the turn of the century. Flynn falls for his brother's wealthy fiancee (Parker), although he is married to the faithful Lupino. Atypical role for Flynn and definitely not one of his best. Based on the novel "The Fool of the Family," by Margaret Kennedy and the play "Escape Me Never" by Kennedy. **101m/B VHS, Closed Caption.** Errol Flynn, Ida Lupino, Eleanor Parker, Gig Young, Reginald Denny, Isobel Elsom; *D:* Peter Godfrey; *W:* Thomas Williamson. MGM

Escape to Athena 🎞🎞½ 1979 (PG)
A motley group is stuck in a German P.O.W. camp on a Greek island during WWII. **102m/C VHS, Beta.** GB Roger Moore, Telly Savalas, David Niven, Claudia Cardinale, Richard Roundtree, Stefanie Powers, Sonny Bono, Elliott Gould, William Holden; *D:* George P. Cosmatos; *W:* Edward Anhalt; *M:* Lalo Schifrin. FOX

Escape to Burma 🎞½ 1955
A man on the run for a murder he did not commit finds refuge and romance in an isolated jungle home. **86m/C VHS, Beta.** Barbara Stanwyck, Robert Ryan, Reginald Denny; *D:* Allan Dwan. DIS, TOU

Escape to Love 🎞½ 1982
Beautiful student helps a famous dissident escape from Poland, only to lose him to another heroic venture. **105m/C Beta.** Clara Perryman, Louis Jourdan; *D:* Herbert Stein. PSM

Escape to Paradise 🎞½ 1939
The last of Breen's films for RKO has him as a South American motorcycle-taxi driver acting as a guide for tourist Taylor. When Breen sets Taylor up with Shelton, trouble ensues. 🎵Tra-La-La; Rhythm of the Rio; Ay, Ay, Ay. **60m/B VHS.** Bobby Breen, Kent Taylor, Marla Shelton, Joyce Compton, Rosina Galli, Frank Yaconelli; *D:* Erle C. Kenton. NOS, RXM

Escape to the Sun 🎞½ *Habricha el Hashemesh* 1972 (PG)
Pair of Russian university students plan to flee their homeland so they can be allowed to live and love free from oppression. **94m/C VHS, Beta.** IS Laurence Harvey, Josephine Chaplin, John Ireland, Jack Hawkins, Lila Kedrova, Clive Revill; *D:* Menahem Golan. NO

Escape to Witch Mountain 🎞🎞🎞 1975 (G)
Two young orphans with supernatural powers find themselves on the run from a greedy millionaire who wants to exploit their amazing gift. Adapted from a novel by Alexander Key. **97m/C VHS, Beta, LV.** Kim Richards, Ike Eisenmann, Eddie Albert, Ray Milland, Donald Pleasence; *D:* John Hough. DIS, BTV

Escape 2000 woof! *Turkey Shoot* 1981 (R)
In a future society where individuality is considered a crime, those who refuse to conform are punished by being hunted down in a jungle. Gross, twisted takeoff of Richard Connell's "The Most Dangerous Game." **80m/C VHS, Beta.** AU Steve Railsback, Olivia Hussey, Michael Craig; *D:* Brian Trenchard-Smith; *W:* George Schenck; *M:* Brian May. VTR

Escapes 🎞🎞 1986
In the tradition of "The Twilight Zone," Vincent Price introduces five short thrillers featuring time travel, aliens, and telepathy. Produced with computer assistance for sharper, more contrasted images. **72m/C VHS, Beta.** Vincent Price, Jerry Grisham, Lee Canfield, John Mitchum, Gil Reade; *D:* David Steensland. PSM

Escapist woof! 1983
A professional escape artist becomes involved in a perverted corporate plot and must escape to save his life and livelihood. **87m/C VHS, Beta.** Bill Shirk, Peter Lupus; *D:* Eddie Beverly Jr. LIV, VES

E.S.P. 1983
A young man is given the amazing power of extra-sensory perception. **96m/C VHS, Beta.** Jim Stafford, George Deaton. BFV

Estate of Insanity 🎞 1970
An English lord and his second wife become involved in a web of death when a maniac stalks their ancient estate. **90m/C VHS, Beta.** John Turner, Heather Sears, Ann Lynn; *D:* Robert Hartford-Davis. NO

Esther and the King 🎞½ 1960
Biblical costumer with Egan as Persian king and Collins as the Judean maiden he wants in place of the murdered queen. Long, rambling, and torturous. **109m/C VHS, Beta.** IT Joan Collins, Richard Egan, Denis O'Dea, Sergio Fantoni; *D:* Raoul Walsh; *W:* Raoul Walsh, Michael Elkins; *M:* Angelo Francesco Lavagnino. FXV

Et La Tenoresse?...Bordel! 🎞🎞 1984
A French comedy about a color-blind painter and his kinky fashion photographer roommate living in Paris. In French with subtitles. **100m/C VHS, Beta.** FR D: Patrick Schulmann. FCT

E.T.: The Extra-Terrestrial 🎞🎞🎞🎞 1982 (PG)
Spielberg's famous fantasy, one of the most popular films in history, portrays a limpid-eyed alien stranded on earth and his special bonding relationship with a young boy. A modern fairy tale providing warmth, humor and sheer wonder. Held the first place spot as the highest grossing movie of all time for years until a new Spielberg hit replaced it—"Jurassic Park." Debra Winger contributed to the voice of E.T. **115m/C VHS, Beta, LV, Closed Caption.** Henry Thomas, Dee Wallace Stone, Drew Barrymore, Robert MacNaughton, Peter Coyote, C. Thomas Howell, Sean Frye, K.C. Martel; *D:* Steven Spielberg; *W:* Melissa Mathison; *C:* Allen Daviau; *M:* John Williams. Academy Awards '82: Best Visual Effects, Best Original Score; Golden Globe Awards '83: Best Film—Drama, Best Score; Los Angeles Film Critics Association Awards '82: Best Director (Spielberg), Best Film; National Society of Film Critics Awards '82: Best Director (Spielberg); People's Choice Awards '83: Best Film; Writers Guild of America '82: Best Original Screenplay; Nominations: Academy Awards '82: Best Cinematography, Best Director (Spielberg), Best Film Editing, Best Original Screenplay, Best Picture, Best Sound. USH, APD, RDG

Eternal Evil 🎞 1987 (R)
A bored television director is taught how to have out-of-body experiences by his devil-worshipping girlfriend. He eventually realizes that when he leaves his body, it runs around killing people. **85m/C VHS, Beta, LV.** Karen Black, Winston Rekert, Lois Maxwell; *D:* George Mihalka. LIV

Eternal Return 🎞🎞½ *L'Eternel Retour; Love Eternal* 1943
A lush modern retelling of the Tristan/ Isolde legend. Patrice (Marais) brings the beautiful Nathalie (Sologne) to his family's castle, as his uncle's (Murat) intended bride. But thanks to a love potion, it's Nathalie and Patrice who fall in love—with tragic results. In French with English subtitles. **111m/B VHS, Beta.** FR Jean Marais, Madeleine Sologne, Jean Murat; *D:* Jean Delannoy; *W:* Jean Cocteau. WBF, NLC, FCT

The Eternal Waltz 🐾🐾 *Ewiger Walzer* **1954** Overly sentimental chronicle of the life of composer Johann Strauss. Only director Verhoeven's touch holds the viewer's interest, though the production values are excellent. **97m/C VHS.** Bernhard Wicki, Hilde Krahl, Annemarie Duerringer, Friedl Loor, Eduard Strauss Jr., Gert Frobe, Arnulf Schroeder; **D:** Paul Verhoeven. *NOS*

Eternally Yours 🐾🐾½ **1939** A witty magician's career threatens to break up his marriage. **95m/B VHS, Beta.** David Niven, Loretta Young, Hugh Herbert, Broderick Crawford, Sir C. Aubrey Smith, Billie Burke, Eve Arden, ZaSu Pitts; **D:** Tay Garnett. Nominations: Academy Awards '39: Best Original Score. *NOS, MRV, HHT*

Eternity 🐾 **1990 (R)** While trying to uncover corrupt corporate America a television reporter falls in love with a model who works for a media king and puts his credibility on the line. He believes he and the woman shared romance in a past life. **122m/C VHS.** Jon Voight, Armand Assante, Wilford Brimley, Eileen Davidson, Kaye Ballard, Lainie Kazan, Joey Villa, Steven Keats, Eugene Roche, Frankie Valli, John P. Ryan; **D:** Steven Paul. *ACA*

Ethan 🐾½ **1971** A missionary in the Philippines falls in love with a woman and exiles himself for his fall from grace. **97m/C VHS, Beta.** Robert Sampson, Rosa Rosal, Eddie Infante; **D:** Michael DuPont. *GHV*

Ethan Frome 🐾🐾½ **1992 (PG)** Neeson stars as the lonely, poverty-stricken 19th-century New England farmer who has long and faithfully cared for his bitter, invalid wife. When his wife's distant young cousin comes to take over as housekeeper they both succumb to their forbidden passion with tragic results. The performers carry the burden of the film's sluggish pacing, where the bleak setting of Massachusetts in winter tends to overwhelm the events. Based on the novel by Edith Wharton. **107m/C VHS, Beta, LV, Closed Caption.** Liam Neeson, Patricia Arquette, Joan Allen, Tate Donovan, Katharine Houghton, Stephen Mendillo; **D:** John Madden; **W:** Richard Nelson; **C:** Bobby Bukowski. *TOU, FCT*

Eubie! **1982** The popular Broadway musical revue based on the life and songs of Eubie Blake is presented in a video transfer. Some of Eubie's best known songs, performed here by members of the original cast, include "I'm Just Wild About Harry," "Memories of You," "In Honeysuckle Time" and "The Charleston Rag." **100m/C VHS, Beta.** Gregory Hines, Maurice Hines, Leslie Dockery, Alaina Reed, Lynnie Godfrey, Mel Johnson Jr., Jeffrey V. Thompson; **D:** Julianne Boyd. *WAR, OM*

Eureka! 🐾🐾½ **1981 (R)** A bizarre, wildly symbolic slab of Roegian artifice that deals with the dream-spliced life of a rich, bored gold tycoon who becomes tortured over his daughter's marriage and his own useless wealth. Eventually he is bothered by the Mafia and led to the courtroom by business competitors. From the book by Paul Mayersberg. **130m/C VHS, Beta.** *GB* Gene Hackman, Theresa Russell, Joe Pesci, Rutger Hauer, Mickey Rourke, Ed Lauter, Jane Lapotaire; **D:** Nicolas Roeg. *MGM*

Eureka Stockade 🐾🐾 *Massacre Hill* **1949** Four early Australian gold prospectors join forces to fight their governor and the police for the rights to dig on the continent. **103m/B VHS, Beta.** *AU* Chips Rafferty, Peter Finch, Jane Barrett, Peter Illing; **D:** Harry Watt. *NOS, DVT, HEG*

Europa, Europa 🐾🐾🐾½ **1991 (R)** The incredible, harrowing and borderline-absurdist true story of Solomon Perel, a young Jew who escaped the Holocaust by passing for German at an elite, Nazi-run academy. Such a sharp evocation of the era that the modern German establishment wouldn't submit it for the Academy Awards. In German and Russian with English subtitles. **CW:** Mature subject matter. **115m/C VHS.** *GE* Marco Hofschneider, Klaus Abramowsky, Michele Gleizer, Rene Hofschneider, Nathalie Schmidt, Delphine Forest, Julie Delpy; **D:** Agnieszka Holland; **W:** Agnieszka Holland. Golden Globe Awards '92: Best Foreign Film; National Board of Review Awards '91: Best Foreign Film; New York Film Critics

Awards '91: Best Foreign Film; Nominations: Academy Awards '91: Best Adapted Screenplay. *ORI, BTV*

Europa '51 🐾🐾½ *The Greatest Love* **1952** The despairing portrait of post-war malaise, as an American woman, whose son committed suicide, lives in Rome searching for some semblance of meaning, and ends up in an asylum. One of Bergman & Rossellini's least-loved films. In Italian with subtitles. **110m/B VHS, Beta.** Ingrid Bergman, Alexander Knox, Ettore Giannini, Giulietta Masina; **D:** Roberto Rossellini. *FCT*

The Europeans 🐾🐾🐾 **1979** Fine adaptation of Henry James's satiric novel. British brother and sister visit their staid American cousins in 19th-century New England in an effort to improve their prospects through fortuitous marriages. **90m/C VHS, Beta.** Lee Remick, Lisa Eichhorn, Robin Ellis, Wesley Addy, Tim Woodward; **D:** James Ivory; **W:** Ruth Prawer Jhabvala. National Board of Review Awards '79: 10 Best Films of the Year; Nominations: Academy Awards '79: Best Costume Design. *CVC, LUM*

Evangeline 🐾🐾½ **1929** Based on the Henry Wadsworth Longfellow poem about the struggles of Evangeline and the tragedy of lost love. **79m/B VHS.** Dolores Del Rio, Roland Drew, Alec B. Francis, George F. Marion Sr.; **D:** Edwin Carewe. *FCT*

Eve of Destruction woof! **1990 (R)** Hell knows no fury like a cutting-edge android-girl on the warpath. Modeled after her creator, Dr. Eve Simmons, Eve VII has android-babe good looks and a raging nuclear capability. Wouldn't you know, something goes haywire during her trial run, and debutante Eve turns into a PMS nightmare machine, blasting all the good Doctor's previous beaux. That's where military agent Hines comes in, though you wonder why. Dutch actress Soutendijk plays dual Eves in her first American film. **CW:** Strong language and strong violence. **101m/C VHS, Beta, LV, Closed Caption.** Gregory Hines, Renee Soutendijk, Kevin McCarthy, Ross Malinger, Eugene Glazer; **D:** Duncan Gibbins; **W:** Duncan Gibbins. *COL, NLC*

Evel Knievel 🐾🐾 **1972 (PG)** The life of motorcycle stuntman Evel Knievel is depicted in this movie, as portrayed by George Hamilton. Stunts will be appreciated by Evel Knievel fans. **90m/C VHS, Beta.** George Hamilton, Bert Freed, Rod Cameron, Sue Lyon; **D:** Marvin J. Chomsky; **W:** John Milius. *NO*

Evelyn Prentice 🐾🐾½ **1934** Powell and Loy again team up as a married couple (after their "The Thin Man" success) but this time things aren't so rosy. He is an attorney with a wandering eye who has an affair with Russell (in her film debut). Loy finds out and turns for sympathy to Stephens but then she decides to stay with her husband after all. Only she's written some steamy letters to Stephens and he tries blackmailing her—and winds up dead. Dramatic courtroom scene straightens things out. Adapted from the novel by W.E. Woodward. Film was remade as "Stronger Than Desire" in 1939. **78m/B VHS.** Myrna Loy, William Powell, Harvey Stephens, Isabel Jewell, Una Merkel, Rosalind Russell, Henry Wadsworth, Edward Brophy, Cora Sue Collins, Jessie Ralph, Sam Flint, Pat O'Malley; **D:** William K. Howard; **W:** Lenore Coffee. *MGM*

Even Angels Fall 🐾🐾 **1990** One of heartthrob singer Humperdinck's scattered dramatic projects, a mystery thriller about a romance novelist moving into a New York brownstone whose previous inhabitant committed suicide—or was it murder? **?m/C VHS.** Morgan Fairchild, Engelbert Humperdinck; **D:** Thomas Calabrese. *NO*

Even Cowgirls Get the Blues 🐾½ **1994 (R)** '70s counterculture loses its ill-defined charm in a meandering adaptation of cult author Tom Robbins' 1976 novel. An interesting failure, but likely to alienate both Van Sant and Robbins fans. Sissy Hackshaw (Thurman) possesses enormous thumbs which she hopes will make her the greatest hitchhiker in the world. But first they take her to a NYC modeling career for The Countess (Hurt in a high camp performance), who sends her to the Rubber Rose ranch, recently lib-

erated by female cowhands, who are happy to welcome her. Theatrical release was delayed numerous times as Van Sant recut but it doesn't matter—the only successful feature is the soundtrack. **106m/C VHS, LV.** Uma Thurman, John Hurt, Rain Phoenix, Lorraine Bracco, Noriyuki "Pat" Morita, Angie Dickinson, Keanu Reeves; **Cameos:** Sean Young, Crispin Glover, Roseanne, Ed Begley Jr.; **D:** Gus Van Sant; **W:** Gus Van Sant; **C:** Eric Alan Edwards, John Campbell; **M:** k.d. lang, Ben Mink. Nominations: Golden Raspberry Awards '94: Worst Actress (Thurman). *COL*

The Evening Star 🐾🐾½ **1996 (PG-13)** Sequel to 1983's "Terms of Endearment" starts in 1988 and finds the overbearing Aurora (MacLaine) now wreaking havoc on the lives of her three grown grandchildren (and vice versa). And Aurora's lovelife is as active as ever—old beau Hector Scott (Moffat) is hanging around, young psychiatrist Jerry Bruckner (Paxton) becomes her lover, and former astronaut flame Garrett Breedlove (Nicholson) also makes a brief appearance to cock an eyebrow at the shenanigans. Last screen role for Johnson as neighbor Arthur Cotten. Based on the novel by Larry McMurtry. Bring a hankie for the tears. **CW:** Some sexual situations and brief strong language. **128m/C VHS, Beta, Closed Caption.** Shirley MacLaine, Juliette Lewis, George Newbern, MacKenzie Astin, Bill Paxton, Miranda Richardson, Marion Ross, Ben Johnson, Donald Moffat, Scott Wolf, China Kantner; **Cameos:** Jack Nicholson; **D:** Robert Harling; **W:** Robert Harling; **C:** Don Burgess; **M:** William Ross. Nominations: Golden Globe Awards '97: Best Supporting Actress (Ross). *PAR*

Event Horizon 🐾🐾½ **1997 (R)** Cross between "Alien" and "The Shining" has Fishburne heading an ensemble cast out to rescue a prototype spaceship that's been missing for seven years. Their own ship is sabotaged by their own demons and certain extraterrestrial ones, too, that cause much mayhem on their once peaceful mission. **?m/C VHS.** Laurence "Larry" Fishburne, Sam Neill, Kathleen Quinlan, Joely Richardson, Richard T. Jones; **D:** Paul Anderson; **W:** Philip Eisner; **C:** Adrian Biddle. *NYR*

Evergreen 🐾🐾 **1934** The daughter of a retired British music hall star is mistaken for her mother and it is thought that she has discovered the secret of eternal youth. Daddy Wouldn't Buy Me a Bow-Wow; When You've Got a Little Springtime in Your Heart; If I Give in to You; Tinkle, Tinkle, Tinkle; Dear, Dear; Dancing on the Ceiling; Just by Your Example; Over My Shoulder. **91m/B VHS, Beta, LV.** *GB* Jessie Matthews, Sonnie Hale, Betty Balfour, Barry Mackay, Ivor McLaren, Hartley Power, Patrick Ludlow, Marjorie Gaffney; **D:** Victor Saville; **W:** Emlyn Williams; **M:** Richard Rodgers, Harry Woods, Lorenz Hart, Harry Woods. *VYY, HMV, THV*

The Everlasting Secret Family 🐾🐾 **1988** Politics and family life make strange bedfellows. A top political figure joins a secret homosexual organization in his search for power. **93m/C VHS.** *AU* Arthur Dignam, Mark Lee, Dennis Miller, Heather Mitchell; **D:** Michael Thornhill. *FCT, CCN, TPV*

Eversmile New Jersey 🐾½ **1989 (PG)** A dentist travels through Patagonia, offering dental care and advice to anyone in need, and a young woman, taken with the dental knight, dumps her boyfriend and stows away with him. When he discovers his admirer, he is less than ecstatic, but a chance tooth extraction on the road reveals the young woman's natural dental talents, and the two bond. From the director of "The Official Story." **88m/C VHS, Beta, LV.** *AR* Daniel Day-Lewis, Mirjana Jokovic; **D:** Carlos Sorin; **W:** Jorge Goldenberg, Roberto Scheuer, Carlos Sorin. *FXV, MED*

Every Breath 🐾🐾 **1993 (R)** A kinky couple's games can be deadly and now they have someone new to play with. Jimmy couldn't resist the wife's seductive allure and if he wants to survive, he'll have to beat them at their own game. **CW:** Language, some scenes of victims buried alive, and sexuality. **88m/C VHS, Closed Caption.** Judd Nelson, Joanna Pacula, Patrick Bauchau; **D:**

Steve Bing; **W:** Judd Nelson, Andrew Fleming, Steve Bing; **M:** Nils Lofgren. COL

Every Day's a Holiday 🎬🎬½ 1938 In
the 1890s, West stars as confidence woman Peaches O'Day, who sells the Brooklyn Bridge and is run out of New York City. But she comes back, in disguise as a French singer, to expose some crooked cops. The Hays office again came down heavily on Mae's suggestive behavior, which left her with little to rely on. West's last film for Paramount. 79m/B VHS. Mae West, Edmund Lowe, Charles Butterworth, Charles Winninger, Walter Catlett, Lloyd Nolan, Herman Bing; **D:** Edward Sutherland; **W:** Mae West. USH, BTV

Every Girl Should Be
Married 🎬🎬½ 1948 A shopgirl sets her sights on an eligible bachelor doctor. 84m/B VHS, Beta, LV. Cary Grant, Betsy Drake, Diana Lynn, Franchot Tone; **D:** Don Hartman. TTC

Every Girl Should Have One 🎬½
1978 A rambunctious comedy about a chase following a million-dollar diamond theft. 90m/C VHS, Beta. Zsa Zsa Gabor, Robert Alda, Alice Faye, Sandra Vacey, John Lazar. GEM

Every Man for Himself & God
Against All 🎬🎬🎬🎬 The Mystery of Kaspar Hauser; Jeder fur Sich und Gott Gegen Alle; The Enigma of Kaspar Hauser 1975 Kaspar Hauser is a young man who mysteriously appears in the town square of Nuremberg, early in the 19th century. He cannot speak or stand upright and is found to have been kept in a dungeon for the first 18 years of his life. He becomes an attraction in society with his alternate vision of the world and attempts to reconcile with reality. A lovely, though demanding film which is based on a true story. In German with English subtitles. 110m/C VHS, Beta. GE Bruno S, Brigitte Mira, Walter Laderigast, Hans Musaus, Willy Semmelrogge, Michael Kroecher, Henry van Lyck; **D:** Werner Herzog; **W:** Werner Herzog; **M:** Albinoni Pachelbel, Orlando Di Lasso. NYF, APD, GLV

Every Man's Law 🎬½ 1935 A cowboy
who poses as a hired gunman is almost lynched by ranchers who think he is a murderer. 60m/B VHS, Beta. Johnny Mack Brown. VCN

Every Other Weekend 🎬🎬🎬 Un Week-
end sur Deux 1991 Camille Valmont (Baye) is an actress who has sacrificed everything for her now-fading career. She's divorced loving husband Adrian (Manojlovic) and given him custody of their two young children—often ignoring her every other weekend visitation rights. In financial straits, Camille takes a job out of town and decides to take the kids with her, without telling Adrian. Self-centered and easily distracted, Camille tries to get close but manages to destroy what little rapport she has with her children. Camille isn't likable but Baye is such a gifted actress that you'll still feel pity. Director Garcia's debut; French with subtitles. 100m/C VHS. FR Nathalie Baye, Miki Manojlovic, Joachim Serreau, Felicie Pasotti; **D:** Nicole Garcia; **W:** Nicole Garcia, Jacques Fieschi; **C:** William Lubtchansky; **M:** Oswald D'Andrea. NYF

Every Time We Say
Goodbye 🎬🎬½ 1986 (PG-13) In 1942, Jerusalem, an American flyboy falls in love with a young Sephardic Jewish girl, whose family resists the match. 97m/C VHS, Beta, LV. Tom Hanks, Christina Marsillach, Benedict Taylor, Anat Atzman, Gila Almagor; **D:** Moshe Mizrahi; **W:** Moshe Mizrahi, Leah Appet; **M:** Philippe Sarde. LIV

Every Which Way But Loose 🎬🎬
1978 (R) Fairly pointless Eastwood foray featuring Clint as a beer-guzzling, country-music loving truck driver earning a living as a barroom brawler. He and his orangutan travel to Colorado in pursuit of the woman he loves. Behind him are a motorcycle gang and an L.A. cop. All have been victims of his fists. Sequel is "Any Which Way You Can." 119m/C VHS. Clint Eastwood, Sondra Locke, Geoffrey Lewis, Beverly D'Angelo, Ruth Gordon; **D:** James Fargo; **M:** Stephen Dorff. WAR

Everybody Sing 🎬🎬 1938 A down-on-
their-luck theatrical family, including Garland (who is kicked out of boarding school for singing Mendelssohn with a swing beat) decides to put on a show in hopes of making a comeback. Dumb plot and boring songs make this one for die-hard Garland fans only. ♫Swing, Mr. Mendelssohn, Swing; The One I Love; Down on Melody Farms; The Show Must Go On; I Wanna Swing; Never Was There Such a Perfect Day; Quainty Dainty Me; Why? Because; Snooks. 80m/B VHS. Allan Jones, Fanny Brice, Judy Garland, Reginald Owen, Billie Burke, Reginald Gardiner, Lynne Carver, Monty Woolley; **D:** Edwin L. Marin; **M:** George Bassman. MGM, MVD

Everybody Wins 🎬🎬 1990 (R) A mystery-
romance about a befuddled private eye trying to solve a murder and getting caught up with the bizarre prostitute who hired him. Arthur Miller based this screenplay on his stage drama "Some Kind of Love Story." Confused and, given its pedigree, disappointing mystery. 110m/C VHS, Beta, LV, Closed Caption. Nick Nolte, Debra Winger, Will Patton, Jack Warden, Kathleen Wilhoite, Frank Converse, Frank Military, Judith Ivey; **D:** Karel Reisz; **W:** Arthur Miller; **C:** Ian Baker. ORI

Everybody's All American 🎬🎬 1988
(R) Shallow, sentimental melodrama about a college football star and his cheerleader wife whose lives, subsequent to their youthful glories, is a string of disappointments and tragedies. Decently acted and based on Frank Deford's novel. 127m/C VHS, Beta, LV, 8mm, Closed Caption. Jessica Lange, Dennis Quaid, Timothy Hutton, John Goodman, Carl Lumbly, Ray Baker, Savannah Smith; **D:** Taylor Hackford; **M:** James Newton Howard. WAR

Everybody's Dancin' 🎬½ 1950 A ball-
room proprietor's business is marred by random killings in her establishment as the bands play on. ♫Foolish Tears; Oblivious; Deep Freeze Dinah; I Shook; Rhumba Boogie. 66m/B VHS, Beta, LV. Spade Cooley, Dick Lane, Hal Derwin, The Pioneers, Roddy McDowall; **D:** Will Jason. NO

Everybody's Fine 🎬🎬½ Stanno Tutti Bene
1990 (PG-13) Mastroianni stars in this bittersweet story of a father on a mission to reunite his five grown children. His journey takes him all over Italy as he tries to bring them together in this touching film about enduring family love. In Italian with English subtitles. 115m/C VHS, LV, Closed Caption. IT Marcello Mastroianni, Salvatore Cascio, Valeria Cavalli, Norma Martelli, Marino Cenna, Roberto Nobile, Michele Morgan, Fabio Iellini; **D:** Giuseppe Tornatore; **W:** Giuseppe Tornatore, Tonino Guerra; **M:** Ennio Morricone. COL

Everyone Says I Love You 🎬🎬🎬
1996 (R) Woody sings! Granted, he doesn't sing very well, but who else could twist a story of love among the neurotic rich with lavish production numbers from the golden age of movie musicals? The excellent cast (who weren't told that they were in a musical until after they signed) prove that as singers, they're pretty good actors. The plot centers around the wandering love lives of Steffi (Hawn), her husband Bob (Alda), her ex-husband Joe (Allen) and their assorted children; especially the preppy Skylar (Barrymore) and her fiance Holden (Norton). Some of the musical productions are shaky (Allen's duet with Julia Roberts is straight out of Tin Ear Alley), but the feeling behind them is genuine; Besides, where else are you going to hear Groucho's "Hooray for Captain Spaulding" sung in French or a chorus of pregnant women sing "Makin' Whoopee"? **CW:** Use of strong language. 97m/C VHS. Woody Allen, Alan Alda, Drew Barrymore, Goldie Hawn, Gaby Hoffman, Edward Norton, Natalie Portman, Julia Roberts, Tim Roth, Natasha Lyonne, Lukas Haas, David Ogden Stiers; **D:** Woody Allen; **W:** Woody Allen; **C:** Carlo Di Palma; **M:** Dick Hyman. Los Angeles Film Critics Association Awards '96: Best Supporting Actor (Norton); National Board of Review Awards '96: Best Supporting Actor (Norton); Nominations: Golden Globe Awards '97: Best Film—Musical/Comedy. TOU

Everything Happens at Night 🎬🎬🎬
1939 Rival reporters Milland and Cummings are torn between the woman they love and the story of a lifetime. One of Henie's best romantic skating vehicles due to the strong performances by the leading men. Henie does take to the ice for a couple of numbers, but this film was largely designed to expand her image as a serious actress. Although it failed to do that, it's good entertainment nonetheless. 76m/B VHS. Sonja Henie, Ray Milland, Robert Cummings, Maurice Moscovich, Leonid Kinskey, Alan Dinehart, Fritz Feld; **D:** Irving Cummings; **W:** Art Arthur, Robert Harari. FXV

Everything You Always Wanted to
Know about Sex (But Were Afraid to Ask) 🎬🎬🎬 1972 (R) Satiric comical sketches about sex includes a timid sperm cell, an oversexed court jester, a sheep folly, and a giant disembodied breast. Quite entertaining in its own jolly way. Based on the book by Dr. David Reuben. 88m/C VHS, Beta, LV. Woody Allen, John Carradine, Lou Jacobi, Louise Lasser, Anthony Quayle, Geoffrey Holder, Lynn Redgrave, Tony Randall, Burt Reynolds, Gene Wilder, Robert Walden, Jay Robinson; **D:** Woody Allen; **W:** Woody Allen. MGM, FOX, FCT

The Evictors woof! 1979 (PG) Young cou-
ple moves into an abandoned, haunted farmhouse in a small Louisiana town. Unfortunately, they don't know anything about its horrible bloody history. And the real estate agent acts kinda funny. AIP Amityville scare-a-thon. 92m/C VHS, Beta. Vic Morrow, Michael Parks, Jessica Harper, Sue Ane Langdon, Dennis Fimple; **D:** Charles B. Pierce; **W:** Charles B. Pierce. LIV, VES

The Evil 🎬🎬 1978 (R) A psychologist must
destroy an evil force that is killing off the members of his research team residing at an old mansion. 80m/C VHS, Beta. Richard Crenna, Joanna Pettet, Andrew Prine, Victor Buono, Cassie Yates; **D:** Gus Trikonis.

Evil Altar 🎬 1989 (R) A man controls a small
town, but only so long as he offers sacrifices to the devil! 90m/C VHS. William Smith, Robert Z'Dar, Pepper Martin, Theresa Cooney, Ryan Rao; **D:** James R. Winburn. HMD

The Evil Below 🎬 1987 A couple hits the
high seas in search of the lost treasure ship "El Diablo," resting on the ocean floor. In the process they trigger an evil curse and then must attempt to thwart it. 90m/C VHS, Beta. SA June Chadwick, Wayne Crawford; **D:** Jean-Claude Dubois. NO

Evil Clutch 🎬½ 1989 (R) A young couple
vacationing in the Alps encounter several creepy locals when they find themselves in the midst of a haunted forest. The cinematography is extremely amateurish in this Italian gorefest and the English dubbing is atrocious. However, the special makeup effects are outstanding and the musical score adds a touch of class to this otherwise inept horror film. 88m/C VHS, LV, Closed Caption. IT Coralina Cataldi Tassoni, Diego Riba, Elena Cantarone, Luciano Crovato, Stefano Molinari; **D:** Andreas Marfori; **W:** Andreas Marfori. UND, RHI

Evil Dead 🎬🎬½ 1983 (NC-17) Five vacation-
ing college students unwittingly resurrect demons which transform the students into evil monsters. Exuberantly gory low-budgeter followed by two sequels. 126m/C VHS, Beta, LV. Bruce Campbell, Ellen Sandweiss, Betsy Baker, Hal Delrich; **D:** Sam Raimi; **W:** Sam Raimi. IME

Evil Dead 2: Dead by Dawn 🎬🎬½
1987 (R) A gory, tongue-in-cheek sequel/remake of the original festival of gag and gore, in which an ancient book of magic invokes a crowd of flesh-snacking, joke-tossing ghouls. Followed by yet a third bloodfest. 84m/C VHS, Beta, LV. Bruce Campbell, Sarah Berry, Dan Hicks, Kassie Wesley, Theodore (Ted) Raimi, Denise Bixler, Richard Domeier; **D:** Sam Raimi; **W:** Sam Raimi, Scott Spiegel; **M:** Joseph Lo Duca. LIV, VES

Evil Ed 🎬½ 1996 (R) Formerly mild-man-
nered film editor Ed (Ruebeck) becomes obsessed with the horror series he's working on, goes off the deep end, and begins a series of

killings that mimic the ones from the films. Lots of splatter.*CW:* Saidstic violence and gore, language and some sexuality in a horror comedy. **90m/C VHS.** *SW* Johan Ruebeck, Olof Rhodin, Pete Lofbergh; *D:* Anders Jacobsson. *APX*

Evil Has a Face 🎬🎬½ **1996 (R)** Chicago police sketch artist Gwen McGarrell (Young) travels to rural Minnesota to help investigator Tom Sawyer (Moses) locate a child molester. But the face she draws turns out to be that of her abusive stepfather (Ross), who's been presumed dead. Made for cable.*CW:* Some violence and terror. **92m/C VHS, Closed Caption.** Sean Young, William R. Moses, Joe Guzaldo, Chelcie Ross, Brighton Hertford, Dick Cusack; *D:* Robert M. Fresco; *W:* Robert M. Fresco. *USH*

Evil Judgement 🎬½ **1985** A young girl investigates a series of murders and finds the culprit is a psychopathic judge. **93m/C VHS, Beta.** Pamela Collyer, Jack Langedijk, Nanette Workman; *D:* Claude Castravelli. *MED*

Evil Laugh woof! **1986 (R)** Medical students and their girlfriends party at an abandoned orphanage, until a serial killer decides to join them. **90m/C VHS.** Tony Griffin, Kim McKamy, Jody Gibson, Dominick Brascia; *D:* Dominick Brascia. *CEL*

The Evil Mind 🎬🎬½ *The Clairvoyant* **1934** A fraudulent mind reader predicts many disasters that start coming true. **80m/B VHS, Beta.** *GB* Claude Rains, Fay Wray, Jane Baxter, Felix Aylmer; *D:* Maurice Elvey; *W:* Charles Bennett. *SNC, FCT, BAR*

Evil Obsession 🎬 **1996** Disturbed young man becomes obsessed with a supermodel and later becomes a suspect in the murders of 12 other models. **93m/C VHS.** Corey Feldman, Kimberly Stevens, Mark Derwin, Brion James; *D:* Richard W. Munchkin. *PRE*

The Evil of Frankenstein 🎬🎬 **1964** The third of the Hammer Frankenstein films, with the mad doctor once again finding his creature preserved in ice and thawing him out. Preceded by "The Revenge of Frankenstein" and followed by "Frankenstein Created Woman." **84m/C VHS, Beta.** *GB* Peter Cushing, Duncan Lamont, Peter Woodthorpe, Sandor Eles, Kiwi Kingston, Katy Wild; *D:* Freddie Francis; *M:* Don Banks. *USH, MLB*

Evil Spawn 🎬 *Deadly Sting; Alive by Night; Alien Within* **1987** A fading movie queen takes an experimental drug to restore her youthful beauty, but it only turns her into a giant silverfish. Releases under several alternate titles, and with varying running times. **70m/C VHS, Beta.** Bobbie Bresee, John Carradine, Drew Godderis, John Terrance, Dawn Wildsmith; *D:* Kenneth J. Hall. *NO*

Evil Spirits 🎬½ **1991 (R)** Boardinghouse tenants are murdered while the crazy landlady cashes their social security checks. This seedy horror cheapie doesn't take itself seriously, and like-minded genre buffs may enjoy the cult-film cast.*CW:* Graphic violence and one sensual scene. **95m/C VHS, Beta, LV.** Karen Black, Arte Johnson, Virginia Mayo, Michael Berryman, Martine Beswick, Bert Remsen, Yvette Vickers, Robert Quarry, Mikel Angel, Debra Lamb; *D:* Gary Graver; *W:* Mikel Angel. *PSM*

The Evil That Men Do 🎬🎬 **1984 (R)** A hitman comes out of retirement to break up a Central American government's political torture ring and, in the process, brings a friend's killer to justice. Based on the novel by R. Lance Hill. **90m/C VHS, Beta, LV, 8mm, Closed Caption.** Charles Bronson, Theresa Saldana, Joseph Maher, Jose Ferrer, Rene Enriquez, John Glover, Raymond St. Jacques, Antoinette Bower, Enrique Lucero, Jorge Luke; *D:* J. Lee Thompson; *W:* John Crowther. *COL*

Evil Toons 🎬½ **1990 (R)** A quartet of lovely coeds on a cleaning job venture into a deserted mansion. There they accidentally release a vulgar, lustful, animated demon who proceeds to cause their clothes to fall off. Can the girls escape the haunted mansion with their sanity, virtue and wardrobes intact?*CW:* Some language, nudity, and comic sex-related violence. **86m/C VHS, Beta.** David Carradine, Dick Miller, Monique Gabrielle, Suzanne

Ager, Stacy Nix, Madison Stone, Don Dowe, Arte Johnson, Michelle (McClellan) Bauer; *D:* Fred Olen Ray. *PSM*

Evil Town 🎬 **1987 (R)** In this poorly made film, a wandering guy discovers a town overrun with zombies created by a mad doctor. **88m/C VHS, Beta.** Dean Jagger, James Keach, Robert Walker Jr., Doria Cook, Michele Marsh; *D:* Edward Collins. *TWE, HHE*

Evil under the Sun 🎬🎬 **1982 (PG)** An opulent beach resort is the setting as Hercule Poirot attempts to unravel a murder mystery. Based on the Agatha Christie novel. **112m/C VHS, Beta, LV.** *GB* Peter Ustinov, Jane Birkin, Maggie Smith, Colin Blakely, Roddy McDowall, Diana Rigg, Sylvia Miles, James Mason, Nicholas Clay; *D:* Guy Hamilton; *W:* Anthony Shaffer. *REP*

The Evil Within woof! *Baby Blood* **1994 (R)** Parasitic beast, with an unquenchable thirst for blood, slithers from the center of the earth into the convenient womb of a young woman. She takes to murdering everyone within reach while preparing to give birth. As disgusting as it sounds. **88m/C VHS.** Emmanuelle Escourrou, Jean-Francois Guillotte; *D:* Alain Robak; *W:* Alain Robak, Serge Cukier. *APX*

Evil's Commandment 🎬🎬½ **1956** Original vampire film which started the classic Italian horror cycle. A gorgeous Countess needs blood to stay young, otherwise she reverts to a 200-year-old vampire. **?m/B VHS.** *IT* Gianna Maria Canale; *D:* Riccardo (Robert Hampton) Freda. *SMW*

Evils of the Night 🎬 **1985** Teenage campers are abducted by sex-crazed alien vampires. Bloody naked mayhem follows. **85m/C VHS, Beta.** John Carradine, Julie Newmar, Tina Louise, Neville Brand, Aldo Ray, Karrie Emerson, Bridget Hollman; *D:* Marti Rustam; *W:* Phillip D. Connors. *LIV*

Evilspeak woof! **1982 (R)** Bumbling misfit enrolled at a military school is mistreated by the other cadets. With the help of his computer, he retaliates with satanic power. Bits, bytes, and gore. **89m/C VHS, Beta.** Clint Howard, Don Stark, Lou Gravance, Lauren Lester, R.G. Armstrong, Joe Cortese, Claude Earl Jones, Haywood Nelson; *D:* Eric Weston. *FOX*

Evita 🎬🎬½ **1996 (PG)** Webber/Rice rock opera about the life and death of Eva Peron finally comes to the big screen with all its extravaganza intact. Madonna's in the title role (in fine voice, lavishly costumed but unflatteringly lit) about an ambitious poor girl willing to do anything to make her mark—in this version by sleeping her way up the ladder of power to Argentine strongman Juan Peron (Pryce, as wax dummy). Evita becomes a would-be champion of the people, even as the government ruthlessly suppresses their freedoms. The surprisingly strong-voiced Banderas (perhaps his emphatic enunciation is to make his English as clear as possible) is everyman narrator Che (changed from the stage version's revolutionary Che Guevara). The highlight is still Madonna's balcony scene, singing "Don't Cry for Me, Argentina," but some of the other songs are drowned by loud orchestration. Director Parker has a cameo as a frustrated film director trying to work with Evita. **133m/C VHS.** Madonna, Antonio Banderas, Jonathan Pryce, Jimmy Nail, Victoria Sus, Julian Littman, Olga Meediz, Laura Pallas, Julia Worsley; *Cameos:* Alan Parker; *D:* Alan Parker; *W:* Oliver Stone, Alan Parker; *C:* Darius Khondji; *M:* Andrew Lloyd Webber, Tim Rice. Academy Awards '96: Best Song ("You Must Love Me"); Golden Globe Awards '97: Best Actress—Musical/Comedy (Madonna), Best Film—Musical/Comedy, Best Song ("You Must Love Me"); Nominations: Academy Awards '96: Best Art Direction/Set Decoration, Best Cinematography, Best Film Editing, Best Sound; British Academy Awards '96: Best Adapted Screenplay; Golden Globe Awards '97: Best Actor—Musical/Comedy (Banderas), Best Director (Parker); MTV Movie Awards '97: Best Female Performance (Madonna), Best Song ("Don't Cry for Me Argentina"). *TOU*

Evolver 🎬½ **1994 (R)** Teenager Kyle Baxter (Randall) wins a robot patterned after a video arcade game but the robot has a secret military weapon's program built into its brain, causing it to evolve into a killing machine.*CW:* Violence; language; some nudity. **90m/C VHS, LV, Closed Caption.** Ethan Randall, John de Lancie, Cassidy Rae, Cindy Pickett,

Paul Dooley; *D:* Mark Rosman; *W:* Mark Rosman; *C:* Jacques Haitkin; *V:* William H. Macy. *THV*

The Ewok Adventure 🎬🎬½ **1984 (G)** Those adorable, friendly and funny characters from "Return of the Jedi" make the jump from film to television in a new adventure from George Lucas. In this installment, the Ewoks save a miraculous child from harm with the help of a young human. This fun-filled adventure has Lucas's thumbprint all over it and great special effects. Followed by "Ewoks: The Battle for Endor." **96m/C VHS, Beta, LV, Closed Caption.** Warwick Davis, Eric Walker, Aubree Miller, Fionnula Flanagan; *D:* John Korty; *M:* Elmer Bernstein, Peter Bernstein. *MGM, FCT*

The Ewoks: Battle for Endor 🎬🎬½ **1985** A television movie based on the furry creatures from "Return of the Jedi," detailing their battle against an evil queen to retain their forest home. Preceded by "The Ewok Adventure." **98m/C VHS, Beta, LV, Closed Caption.** Wilford Brimley, Warwick Davis, Aubree Miller, Sian Phillips, Paul Gleason, Eric Walker, Carel Struycken, Niki Botholo; *D:* Jim Wheat, Ken Wheat; *M:* Peter Bernstein. *MGM, FCT*

The Ex 🎬🎬½ **1996 (R)** Architect David Kenyon (Mancuso) has a new life, with a sweet second wife (Amis) and a five-year-old son. Then the ex, Deirdre (Butler), comes sauntering back and it seems she and David had a very kinky relationship. Now Deirdre decides it's time to get revenge. Familiar plotline is given a high gloss and some chills.*CW:* Sex, violence, nudity. **87m/C VHS, LV.** Yancy Butler, Nick Mancuso, Suzy Amis; *D:* Mark L. Lester; *W:* John Lutz; *C:* Richard Letterman; *M:* Paul Zaza. *LIV*

Ex-Cop 🎬🎬 **1993** Pete Danberg is a cop with a drinking problem. He's fired from the force but not before he puts away the "Las Vegas Slasher." Unfortunately for Pete the Slasher makes parole and is out for revenge—using Pete's kidnapped daughter as bait. **97m/C VHS.** Rick Savage, Sandy Hackett, Joan Chamberlain, Douglas Terry, Angi Davidson, Richard Cornell, Jim Williams; *D:* Patrick Kerby; *W:* Daniel S. Sample. *AIP*

Ex-Lady 🎬🎬 **1933** Davis stars as a liberated woman who loves advertising writer Raymond, but doesn't want to marry him. However, she believes living together is the most suitable arrangement. The two open up an ad agency and complications ensue. Remake of "Illicit," which was filmed only two years earlier with Barbara Stanwyck in the lead role. **65m/B VHS, Closed Caption.** Bette Davis, Gene Raymond, Frank McHugh, Claire Dodd, Monroe Owsley, Ferdinand Gottschalk; *D:* Robert Florey. *MGM*

Ex-Mrs. Bradford 🎬🎬🎬 **1936** Amateur sleuth Dr. Bradford teams up with his ex-wife to solve a series of murders at the race track. Sophisticated comedy-mystery; witty dialogue. **80m/B VHS, Beta, LV.** William Powell, Jean Arthur, James Gleason, Eric Blore, Robert Armstrong; *D:* Stephen Roberts. *NOS, MED*

Excalibur 🎬🎬🎬½ **1981 (R)** A sweeping, visionary retelling of the life of King Arthur, from his conception, to the sword in the stone, to the search for the Holy Grail and the final battle with Mordred. An imperfect, sensationalized version, but still the best yet filmed. **140m/C VHS, Beta, LV.** Nigel Terry, Nicol Williamson, Nicholas Clay, Helen Mirren, Cherie Lunghi, Paul Geoffrey, Gabriel Byrne, Liam Neeson, Patrick Stewart, Charley Boorman, Corin Redgrave; *D:* John Boorman; *W:* John Boorman, Rospo Pallenberg; *M:* Trevor Jones. Nominations: Academy Awards '81: Best Cinematography. *WAR, TVC*

Excess Baggage 🎬🎬½ **1996** Attention-seeking rich girl Emily (Silverstone), fakes her own kidnapping to get back at dear old dad, involving car thief Vincent Roche (del Toro) in the crime. Things get out of control when her creepy "Uncle" Ray (Walken), who's an ex-CIA assassin, is hired by Emily's father to get her back. First picture in Silverstone's pricey production deal with Columbia went through the rumor mill (for supposed clashes between Silverstone and director

Brambilla) and was originally scheduled for release in the fall of '96. **?m/C VHS.** Alicia Silverstone, Benicio Del Toro, Christopher Walken, Harry Connick Jr., Jack Thompson, Nicholas Turturro, Michael Bowen, Leland Orser; **D:** Marco Brambilla; **W:** Mikhaila Max Adams, Dick Clement, Ian LaFrenais. NYR

Excessive Force ⚔️½ 1993 (R) Routine actioner lives up to its title by offering lots of violence, but little else. Gang leader Young seeks revenge on the cops he believes ruined a $3 million drug deal. Loner cop Griffith is the only one to survive the grudge killings and goes after Young himself. Talented cast underachieves. Limited theatrical release sent this one almost straight to video. **CW:** Strong language, strong violence and drug use, and sexuality. **87m/C VHS, LV, Closed Caption.** Thomas Ian Griffith, Lance Henriksen, James Earl Jones, Charlotte Lewis, Tony Todd, Burt Young, W. Earl Brown; **D:** Jon Hess; **W:** Thomas Ian Griffith; **C:** Donald M. Morgan; **M:** Charles Bernstein. NLC, IME

Excessive Force 2: Force on Force ⚔️½ 1995 (R) Special agent Harly Cordell (Randall) volunteers to hunt down an assassination squad that is turning L.A. into murder central. Seems her former lover Francis Lydell (Gauthier) is head killer and Harly's got a score to settle. Lots of action and nifty weapons. **88m/C VHS, LV, Closed Caption.** Stacie Randall, Dan Gauthier, Jay Patterson, John Mese; **D:** Jonathan Winfrey; **W:** Mark Sevi; **C:** Russ Brandt; **M:** Kevin Kiner. NLC, IME

The Execution ⚔️½ 1985 A made-for-television film about five female friends who discover that the Nazi doctor who brutalized them in a concentration camp during WWII is now living a normal life in California. Together they plot his undoing. **92m/C VHS, Beta.** Loretta Swit, Valerie Harper, Sandy Dennis, Jessica Walter, Rip Torn, Barbara Barrie, Robert Hooks, Michael Lerner; **D:** Paul Wendkos; **M:** Georges Delerue. PSM

The Execution of Private Slovik ⚔️⚔️½ 1974 This quiet powerhouse of a TV movie recounts in straightforward terms the case of Eddie Slovik, a WWII misfit who became the only American soldier executed for desertion since the Civil War. The Levinson/Link screenplay (based on the book by William Bradford Huie) ends up deifying Slovik, which some might find hard to take. But there's no arguing the impact of the drama, or of Sheen's unaffected lead performance. **122m/C VHS.** Martin Sheen, Mariclare Costello, Ned Beatty, Gary Busey, Matt Clark, Ben Hammer, Warren Kemmerling; **D:** Lamont Johnson; **W:** Richard Levinson, William Link; **C:** Bill Butler. USH

Execution of Raymond Graham ⚔️⚔️½ 1985 The lawyers and family of Raymond Graham struggle to keep him from being executed for murder. Based on a true story; made for television. **104m/C VHS, Beta.** Morgan Freeman, Jeff Fahey, Kate Reid, Laurie Metcalf, Josef Sommer; **D:** Daniel Petrie. NO

The Executioner ⚔️⚔️ 1970 (PG) A thriller wherein a British spy must prove that his former colleague is a double agent. Elements of backstabbing, betrayal, and espionage abound. **107m/C VHS, Beta.** GB Judy Geeson, Oscar Homolka, Charles Gray, Nigel Patrick, George Peppard, Joan Collins, Keith Michell; **D:** Sam Wanamaker. COL, GKK

The Executioner ⚔️ Like Father, Like Son; Massacre Mafia Style 1978 (R) A very cheap, very "Godfather"-like story of a mafia family gone awry. Also known as "Like Father, Like Son" and "Massacre Mafia Style." **84m/C VHS, Beta.** Duke Mitchell, Vic Caesar, Dominic Micelli, John Strong, Jim Williams, Lorenzo Dodo; **D:** Duke Mitchell; **W:** Duke Mitchell. GEM, MRV

Executioner of Venice ⚔️ 1963 Marauding pirates with time on hands swarm in from the Adriatic Sea and attempt to rob the Venetians blind. The Doge and his godson come to the rescue. **90m/C VHS, Beta.** Guy Madison, Lex Barker, Alessandra Panaro; **D:** Louis Capauno. NO

The Executioner, Part 2: Frozen Scream ⚔️ 1984 (R) Brutal feud rocks the Mafia, and a crime kingpin's passionate son seeks revenge on his father's slayers. Not a sequel to any other films bearing similar titles. Strange thing is, no "Executioner, Part I" was ever made. Pretty laughable. **150m/C VHS, Beta.** Chris Mitchum, Aldo Ray, Antoine John Mottet, Renee Harmon; **D:** James Bryant. GEM

The Executioners ⚔️⚔️½ 1993 When a nuclear explosion contaminates most of the city's drinking water, the remainder falls under the harsh control of the Black Knight. Now, it's up to the Heroic Trio to defeat their nemesis. Sequel to "The Executioners;" Chinese with subtitles. **100m/C VHS, LV.** HK Anita Mui, Michelle Yeoh, Maggie Cheung; **D:** Ching Siu Tung. TAI

The Executioner's Song ⚔️⚔️½ 1982 European version of the television movie based on Norman Mailer's Pulitzer Prize-winner, recounting the life and death of convicted murderer Gary Gilmore. Features adult-minded footage not seen in the U.S. version. **157m/C VHS, Beta.** Tommy Lee Jones, Rosanna Arquette, Eli Wallach, Christine Lahti, Jenny Wright, Jordan Clark, Steven Keats; **D:** Lawrence Schiller. LIV

Executive Action ⚔️⚔️½ 1973 (PG) Political thriller providing a different look at the events leading to the assassination of JFK. In this speculation, a millionaire pays a professional spy to organize a secret conspiracy to kill President Kennedy. Ryan's final film. Adapted by Dalton Trumbo from Mark Lane's "Rush to Judgement." **91m/C VHS, Beta, LV.** Burt Lancaster, Robert Ryan, Will Geer, Gilbert Green, John Anderson; **D:** David Miller; **C:** Robert Steadman; **M:** Randy Edelman. WAR

Executive Decision ⚔️⚔️ 1996 (R) Those wacky terrorists are at it again. You would think that after getting their butts kicked in almost every action picture since 1980 that they would learn. But here they are, hijacking a 747, cutting off communications, and affixing a nerve gas bomb to the plane. This time a group of high tech commandos, led by Russell and (briefly) Seagal, must sneak onto the plane and generally mess up the bad guys' plans. Brave stewardess Berry helps tango with the central casting mad dog terrorists. The title refers to the President's decision on whether or not to blow the plane up in order to avert disaster. Or maybe "Die Hard: Ad Nauseum" wasn't available. **CW:** Violence and brief language. **132m/C VHS, LV, Closed Caption.** Kurt Russell, Halle Berry, Oliver Platt, John Leguizamo, Steven Seagal, Joe Morton, David Suchet, B.D. Wong, Len Cariou, Whip Hubley, J.T. Walsh; **D:** Stuart Baird; **W:** Jim Thomas, John Thomas; **C:** Alex Thomson; **M:** Jerry Goldsmith. Nominations: Golden Raspberry Awards '96: Worst Supporting Actor (Seagal). WAR

Executive Suite ⚔️⚔️⚔️ 1954 One of the first dog-eat-dog dramas about high finance and big business. The plot centers on the question of a replacement for the freshly buried owner of a gigantic furniture company. **104m/B VHS, Beta, Closed Caption.** William Holden, June Allyson, Barbara Stanwyck, Fredric March, Walter Pidgeon, Louis Calhern, Shelley Winters, Paul Douglas, Nina Foch, Dean Jagger; **D:** Robert Wise; **W:** Ernest Lehman. Nominations: Academy Awards '54: Best Art Direction/Set Decoration (B & W), Best Black and White Cinematography, Best Costume Design (B & W), Best Supporting Actress (Foch). MGM

Exiled in America ⚔️⚔️ 1990 A Central American freedom fighter (Albert) flees his country for the United States, settling in a small town with his wife. She gets a waitressing job at a local diner, telling the owner her husband died in an accident, and the owner's son winds up falling in love with her. Things get complicated when the death squad, led by a corrupt CIA agent, follows Albert to his hiding place, and the local sheriff threatens to blow his cover. **84m/C VHS.** Maxwell Caulfield, Edward Albert, Viveca Lindfors, Kamala Lopez, Stella Stevens, Wings Hauser; **D:** Paul Leder; **W:** Paul Leder. PSM

Exiled to Shanghai ⚔️⚔️½ 1937 A couple of newsreel men invent a television device that revolutionizes the business. **65m/B VHS.** Wallace Ford, June Travis, Dean Jagger, William "Billy" Bakewell, Arthur Lake, Jonathan Hale, William Harrigan, Sarah Padden; **D:** Nick Grinde. NOS, DVT, HEG

Exit ⚔️ 1995 (R) Gang of criminals, lead by pscho Charles (Bradley), take a strip club's dancers as hostages when their robbery attempt goes bad. Exotic dancer Diane (Whirry) manages to escape and hook up with ex-ATF agent Alex (Bucci) to stop the creeps. Lame action, silly dialogue, very attractive Whirry. **CW:** Violence, language and some strong sexuality. **90m/C VHS, Closed Caption.** Shannon Whirry, David Bradley, Larry Manetti, Joe Bucci; **D:** Ric Roman Waugh; **W:** Joe Augustyn, Brent Friedman, David Robinson; **C:** David B. Nowell; **M:** Kevin Kiner. REP

Exit to Eden ⚔️½ 1994 (R) Anne Rampling's (aka Anne Rice) novel focused on fulfilling S&M sexual fantasies, but director Marshall goes for laughs with a buddy cops-out-of-water sitcom subplot, as undercover cops Aykroyd and O'Donnell track a suspected jewel thief to the fantasy resort of Eden, run by dominatrix Delany. (What was the pitch for this one? Think "Another Stakeout" meets "Tie Me Up, Tie Me Down." It'll be great. Really.) Neither plot works, resulting in a kinky movie with no kink, and a comedy with few laughs. O'Donnell holds up her end, providing what few yuks there are. Everyone else, especially Aykroyd and Delany, seem to be sleepwalking. Lucky for them. **CW:** Nudity and sex-related scenes. **113m/C VHS, Closed Caption.** Dan Aykroyd, Rosie O'Donnell, Dana Delany, Paul Mercurio, Hector Elizondo, Stuart Wilson, Iman, Sandi Korn; **D:** Garry Marshall; **W:** Deborah Amelon, Bob Brunner; **M:** Patrick Doyle. Golden Raspberry Awards '94: Worst Supporting Actress (O'Donnell). HBO

Exodus ⚔️⚔️⚔️ 1960 Chronicles the postWWII partition of Palestine into a homeland for Jews; the anguish of refugees from Nazi concentration camps held on ships in the Mediterranean; the struggle of the tiny nation with forces dividing it from within and destroying it from the outside; and the heroic men and women who saw a job to be done and did it. Based on the novel by Leon Uris; filmed in Cyprus and Israel. Preminger battled the Israeli government, the studio, and the novel's author to complete this epic. Cost more than $4 million, a phenomenal amount at the time. **208m/C VHS, Beta, LV, Closed Caption.** Paul Newman, Eva Marie Saint, Lee J. Cobb, Sal Mineo, Ralph Richardson, Hugh Griffith, Gregory Ratoff, Felix Aylmer, Peter Lawford, Jill Haworth, John Derek, David Opatoshu, Marius Goring, Alexandra Stewart, Michael Wager, Martin Benson, Paul Stevens, George Maharis; **D:** Otto Preminger; **W:** Dalton Trumbo; **M:** Ernest Gold. Academy Awards '60: Original Dramatic/Comedy Score; Golden Globe Awards '61: Best Supporting Actor (Mineo); Nominations: Academy Awards '60: Best Color Cinematography, Best Supporting Actor (Mineo). FOX, SWC

Exorcism ⚔️½ 1974 A satanic cult in a small English village commits a series of gruesome crimes that have the authorities baffled. **90m/C VHS, Beta.** Paul Naschy, Maria Perschy; **D:** Juan Bosch. HHE

Exorcism's Daughter ⚔️ House of Insane Women 1974 (R) While running an insane asylum, a man discovers that a woman has lost her mind because as a child, she witnessed her mother's death during an exorcism. Pretty grim but interesting for genre fans. A natural double feature with "House of Psychotic Women." **93m/C VHS.** SP Amelia Gade, Francesco Rabal, Espartaco Santoni; **D:** Rafael Morena Alba. SNC

The Exorcist ⚔️⚔️⚔️½ 1973 (R) Truly terrifying story of a young girl who is possessed by a malevolent spirit. Brilliantly directed by Friedkin, with underlying themes of the workings and nature of fate. Impeccable casting and unforgettable, thought-provoking performances. A rare film that remains startling and engrossing with every viewing, it spawned countless imitations and changed the way horror films were made. Based on the bestseller by Blatty, who also wrote the screenplay. Not for the squeamish. When first released, the film created mass hysteria in theaters, with people fainting and paramedics on the scene. **120m/C VHS, Beta, LV, DVD.** Ellen Burstyn, Linda Blair, Jason Miller, Max von Sydow, Jack MacGowran, Lee J. Cobb, Kitty Winn; **D:** William Friedkin; **W:** William Peter Blatty; **C:** Owen Roizman; **M:** Jack Nitzsche. Academy Awards '73: Best Adapted Screenplay, Best Sound; Golden Globe Awards '74: Best Director (Friedkin), Best Film—Drama, Best Screenplay, Best Supporting Actress (Blair); Nominations: Academy Awards '73: Best Actress (Burstyn), Best Art Direction/Set Decoration, Best Cinematography, Best Director (Friedkin), Best Film Editing, Best Picture, Best Supporting Actor (Miller), Best Supporting Actress (Blair). *WAR*

The Exorcist 2: The Heretic
1977 (R) Unnecessary sequel to the 1973 hit "The Exorcist" which featured extensive recutting by Boorman. After four years, Blair is still under psychiatric care, suffering from the effects of being possessed by the devil. Meanwhile, a priest investigates the first exorcist's work as he tries to help the head-spinning lass. Decent special effects. **118m/C VHS, Beta.** Richard Burton, Linda Blair, Louise Fletcher, Kitty Winn, James Earl Jones, Ned Beatty, Max von Sydow; **D:** John Boorman; **M:** Ennio Morricone. *WAR*

Exorcist 3: Legion *√√* 1990 (R)
Apparently subscribing to the two wrongs make a right school of sequels, this time novelist Blatty is the director. The result is slightly better than the first sequel, but still a far cry from the original. Fifteen years after later, Detective Kinderman (Scott) is faced with a series of really gross murders bearing the mark of a serial killer who was flambeed in the electric chair on the same night as the exorcism of the pea-soup expectorating devil of the original. With the aid of priests Flanders and Dourif, the detective stalks the transmigratory terror—without the help of Linda Blair, who was at the time spoofing "The Exorcist" in "Repossessed." **105m/C VHS, Beta, LV, Closed Caption.** George C. Scott, Ed Flanders, Jason Miller, Nicol Williamson, Scott Wilson, Brad Dourif, Nancy Fish, George DiCenzo, Viveca Lindfors; **D:** William Peter Blatty; **W:** William Peter Blatty. *FOX, CCB*

Exotica *√√√* 1994 (R)
Daunting look at eroticism, secrecy, and despair. Christina (Kirshner) is at the center of some complicated relationships. She dresses as a schoolgirl while working at the Exotica strip club in Toronto, where her former lover Eric (Koteas) is the creepily suggestive DJ. Christina's also the obsession of seemingly mild-mannered tax man Francis (Greenwood), who has turned her table dancing into a strange private ritual. Lest this seem to make sense be assured that director Egoyan has much, much more going on—not all of it clear and most of it disturbing. **CW:** Some sexuality and language. **104m/C VHS, LV, Closed Caption.** CA Mia Kirshner, Elias Koteas, Bruce Greenwood, Don McKellar, Victor Garber, Arsinee Khanjian, Sarah Polley, Calvin Green, David Hemblen; **D:** Atom Egoyan; **W:** Atom Egoyan; **C:** Paul Sarossy; **M:** Mychael Danna. Genie Awards '94: Best Art Direction/Set Decoration, Best Cinematography, Best Costume Design, Best Director (Egoyan), Best Film, Best Screenplay, Best Supporting Actor (McKellar), Best Original Score; Toronto-City Award '94: Best Canadian Feature Film; Nominations: Genie Awards '94: Best Actor (Greenwood), Best Actor (Koteas); Independent Spirit Awards '96: Best Foreign Film. *MAX*

Expect No Mercy *√* 1995 (R)
Government agent must rescue a fellow agent being held in a virtual reality center that trains assassins to commit murder. **CW:** Martial arts violence and shootings. **91m/C VHS.** Billy Blanks, Jalal Merhi. *AVE*

The Expendables *√½* 1989 (R)
A rugged captain turns a platoon of criminals and misfits into a tough fighting unit for a particularly dangerous mission from which they might not return. See the "Dirty Dozen" instead. **89m/C VHS, Beta, LV.** An-

thony Finetti, Peter Nelson, Loren Haynes, Kevin Duffis; **D:** Cirio H. Santiago; **W:** Phillip Alderton. *MED*

Experience Preferred... But Not Essential *√√½* 1983 (PG)
An English schoolgirl gets her first job at a resort where she learns about life. Made for British television. **77m/C VHS, Beta.** GB Elizabeth Edmonds, Sue Wallace, Geraldine Griffith, Karen Meagher, Ron Bain, Alun Lewis, Robert Blythe; **D:** Peter Duffell; **W:** June Roberts; **C:** Phil Meheux. *MGM*

Experiment in Terror *√√√* 1962
A psychopath kidnaps a girl in order to blackmail her sister, a bank teller, into embezzling $100,000. **123m/B VHS, Beta, LV.** Lee Remick, Glenn Ford, Stefanie Powers, Ross Martin; **D:** Blake Edwards; **M:** Henry Mancini. *COL, IME*

Experiment Perilous *√√√* 1945
A psychologist and a recently widowed woman band together to find her husband's murderer. An atmospheric vintage mystery. **91m/B VHS, Beta.** Hedy Lamarr, Paul Lukas, George Brent, Albert Dekker; **D:** Jacques Tourneur. Nominations: Academy Awards '45: Best Interior Decoration. *MED*

The Expert *√√* 1995 (R)
Special operations expert John Lomax (Speakman) helps catch the creep who murdered his sister. But the killer gets a slap-on-the-wrist sentence, ticking Lomax off mightily. Now, the duo prepare for a deadly last confrontation. **CW:** Brutal violence; some language. **92m/C VHS, Closed Caption.** Jeff Speakman, James Brolin, Michael Shaner, Alex Datcher, Wolfgang Bodison, Elizabeth Gracen, Red West, Jim Varney; **D:** Rick Avery; **W:** Max Allan Collins; **C:** Levie Isaacks; **M:** Ashley Irwin. *ORI*

The Experts *√√* 1989 (PG-13)
When the KGB needs real Americans for their spies to study, they kidnap two out-of-work New Yorkers who mistakenly believe that they have been hired to open a nightclub in Nebraska. Shot on location in Canada. Sometimes funny and directed by former Second City TV MacKenzie Brother, Dave Thomas. **94m/C VHS, Beta, LV, 8mm, Closed Caption.** John Travolta, Arye Gross, Charles Martin Smith, Kelly Preston, James Keach, Deborah Foreman, Brian Doyle-Murray; **D:** Dave Thomas; **W:** Nick Thiel, Eric Alter; **M:** Marvin Hamlisch. *PAR*

Explorers *√√½* 1985 (PG)
Intelligent family fare involving three young boys who use a contraption from their makeshift laboratory to travel to outer space. From the director of "Gremlins," displaying Dante's characteristic surreal wit and sense of irony. **107m/C VHS, Beta, LV, Closed Caption.** Ethan Hawke, River Phoenix, Jason Presson, Amanda Peterson, Mary Kay Place, Dick Miller, Robert Picardo, Dana Ivey, Meshach Taylor, Brooke Bundy; **D:** Joe Dante; **W:** Eric Luke; **M:** Jerry Goldsmith. *PAR*

Explosion *√½* 1969 (R)
Distraught and disturbed young man evades the draft after losing a brother in Vietnam. Arriving in Canada, he meets another draft-dodger with whom he embarks on a murderous rampage. **96m/C VHS, Beta.** Don Stroud, Gordon Thomson, Michele Chicione, Richard Conte; **D:** Jules Bricken. *TWE*

Exposed *√√* 1983 (R)
High fashion model Kinski falls in with a terrorist gang through a connection with violinist Nureyev. Weak plotting undermines the end of this political thriller. However, Kinski is brilliant, stripping the barrier between performance and audience. **100m/C VHS, Beta.** Nastassia Kinski, Rudolf Nureyev, Harvey Keitel, Ian McShane, Bibi Andersson; **D:** James Toback; **W:** James Toback; **C:** Henri Decae; **M:** Georges Delerue. *MGM*

Exposure *√* 1991 (R)
A rugged American photographer (Coyote) on assignment in Rio turns vigilante to locate the vicious killer of a young prostitute. Coyote and his girlfriend (Pays) get caught up in the deadly underworld of international arms trading and drug running as they search for the murderer. **CW:** Language, strong graphic violence, and sensuality. **99m/C VHS, Closed Caption.** Peter Coyote, Amanda Pays, Tcheky Karyo; **M:** Todd Boekelheide. *HBO*

Express to Terror *√½* 1979
Passengers aboard an atomic-powered train en route to Los Angeles attempt to kill a sleazy theatrical agent. Pilot for the "Supertrain" series. **120m/C VHS, Beta.** Steve Lawrence, George Hamilton, Vic Morrow, Broderick Crawford, Robert Alda, Don Stroud, Fred Williamson, Stella Stevens, Don Meredith; **D:** Dan Curtis. *PSM*

Exquisite Corpses *√½* 1988
An Oklahoma hayseed charges to New York with a new, slick image. He meets the wife of a wealthy man, and together they organize a murderous operation. **95m/C VHS, LV.** Zoe Tamerlane Lund, Gary Knox, Daniel Chapman, Ruth Collins; **D:** Temistocles Lopez. *NO*

The Exterminating Angel *√√√½*
1962 A fierce, funny surreal nightmare, wherein dinner guests find they cannot, for any definable reason, leave the dining room; full of dream imagery and characteristically scatological satire. One of Bunuel's best, in Spanish with English subtitles. **95m/B VHS, Beta.** MX SP Silvia Pinal, Enrique Rambal, Jacqueline Andere, Jose Baviera, Augusto Benedico, Luis Beristain; **D:** Luis Bunuel. *HTV, FCT, APD*

Exterminator *√* 1980 (R)
Vietnam veteran hunts down the gang that assaulted his friend and becomes the target of the police, the CIA and the underworld in this bloody banal tale of murder and intrigue. Followed by creatively titled "Exterminator II." **101m/C VHS, Beta, LV.** Christopher George, Samantha Eggar, Robert Ginty; **D:** James Glickenhaus. *NLC*

Exterminator 2 *√* 1984 (R)
The Exterminator battles the denizens of New York's underworld after his girlfriend is crippled, then murdered by the ruthless Mr. X. Violence galore. **88m/C VHS, Beta.** Robert Ginty, Mario Van Peebles, Deborah Geffner, Frankie Faison; **D:** Mark Buntzman; **W:** Mark Buntzman. *MGM*

Exterminators in the Year 3000 WOOF! 1983 (R)
The Exterminator and his mercenary girlfriend battle with nuclear mutants over the last remaining tanks of purified water on Earth. Low-budget Road Warrior rip-off. **91m/C VHS.** IT SP Robert Jannucci, Alicia Moro, Alan Collins, Fred Harris; **D:** Jules Harrison. *NLC*

Extra Girl *√√* 1923
A silent melodrama/farce about a farm girl, brilliantly played by Normand, who travels to Hollywood to be a star. Once in the glamour capital, she gets used and abused for her trouble. **87m/B VHS, Beta, LV, 8mm.** Mabel Normand, Ralph Graves, Vernon Dent; **D:** F. Richard Jones; **W:** Mack Sennett. *VYY, GPV*

Extramuros *√√* 1985
A nun (Maura), living in a convent during the Spanish Inquisition, tries to repress her lesbian desires while the convent vies for fame and money through faked visions. Spanish with subtitles. **120m/C VHS.** SP Carmen Maura; **D:** Miguel Picazo. *FCT*

The Extraordinary Adventures of Mr. West in the Land of the Bolsheviks *√√* 1924
The first achievement from the Kuleshov workshop, a wacky satire on American insularity depicting a naive and prejudiced American visiting Russia and being taken advantage of. Silent. **55m/B VHS, Beta.** Vsevolod Pudovkin, Boris Barnet; **D:** Lev Kuleshov. *FCT*

Extreme Justice *√√½* 1993 (R)
A violent expose of the Special Investigations Section of the Los Angeles Police Department, an elite, undercover squad which specialized in catching violent repeat offenders. But their tactics left something to be desired. They were accused of stalking their prey until they committed a crime and then dealing with the criminal by shooting them in the act. Lots of gunplay. Originally a theatrical film that was pulled for release in the wake of the Rodney King verdict. **96m/C VHS, LV, Closed Caption.** Lou Diamond Phillips, Scott Glenn, Yaphet Kotto, Ed Lauter, Chelsea Field; **W:** Robert Boris. *THV*

Extreme Measures *√√½* 1996 (R)
Dr. Grant, Action Guy! Cast against type, Grant takes on action-suspense in this urbane medical thriller, and it works. Plot is pretty standard for the

genre—doctor Luthan (Grant) suspects foul play when homeless people are turning up with mysterious symptoms before expiring in his ward. Seeking to expose what he believes is a medical conspiracy, his "darn meddling" gets him in all kinds of trouble. Enter Dr. Lawrence Myrick (Hackman), a genius neurologist who reeks of suspicion. Luthan must get by him to uncover the dangerous human experimentation that's been going on. Producer and real-life love Hurley may have had something to do with the fact that Grant pulls off a mostly convincing turn, where his normally comic persona is used to humanize an otherwise cardboard hero. Adapted from a book by Michael Palmer.*CW:* Violence, language, some nudity and graphic ER activity. **111m/C VHS, LV, Closed Caption.** Hugh Grant, Gene Hackman, Sarah Jessica Parker, David Cronenberg, Bill Nunn, Debra Monk, John Toles-Bey, Paul Guilfoyle, Andre De Shields, Shaun Austin-Olsen, Peter Appel; *D:* Michael Apted; *W:* Tony Gilroy; *C:* John Bailey; *M:* Danny Elfman. *COL*

Extreme Prejudice ♂♂ 1987 (R) A redneck Texas Ranger fights a powerful drug kingpin along the U.S.-Mexican border. Once best friends, they now fight for justice and the heart of the woman they both love. **104m/C VHS, Beta, LV.** Nick Nolte, Powers Boothe, Maria Conchita Alonso, Michael Ironside, Rip Torn; *D:* Walter Hill; *W:* Deric Washburn; *M:* Jerry Goldsmith. *LIV*

Extreme Vengeance ♂♂ 1993 Police officer David puts mafia crime boss Mario Blanco away for ten years, then exposes police corruption and goes into hiding. When Blanco gets out, he seeks revenge on David's family, forcing David out of hiding to protect what is his. Available in Spanish subtitles. **97m/C VHS, LV.** *NHO*

Extremities ♂♂ 1986 (R) An adaptation of the topical William Mastrosimone play about an intended rape victim who turns on her attacker, captures him, and plots to kill him. Violent and exploitive. **83m/C VHS, Beta, LV, 8mm, Closed Caption.** Farrah Fawcett, Diana Scarwid, James Russo, Alfre Woodard; *D:* Robert M. Young; *W:* William Mastrosimone. *PAR*

The Eye Creatures ♂ 1965 Alien creatures in the form of eyeballs are fought off by a teenager and his girlfriend. A low-budget, gory, science fiction feature. **80m/B VHS.** John Ashley, Cynthia Hull, Warren Hammack, Chet Davis, Bill Peck; *D:* Larry Buchanan. *NOS, SNC*

An Eye for an Eye ♂♂ 1981 (R) A story of pursuit and revenge with Norris as an undercover cop pitted against San Francisco's underworld and high society. **106m/C VHS, Beta.** Chuck Norris, Christopher Lee, Richard Roundtree, Matt Clark, Mako, Maggie Cooper; *D:* Steve Carver; *W:* James Bruner; *M:* William Goldstein. *NLC*

An Eye for an Eye ♂ 1995 (R) A made-for-TV script that ended up on the feature film pile (and we do mean pile). Manipulative story has Karen McCann (Field) listening on the phone as her daughter is raped and killed by a scuzzball drifter (Sutherland). He's caught, but released on a technicality, driving Mom to join a vigilante group and plot revenge. Not a great career move for the director or surprisingly distinguished cast, who are given nothing but cardboard characters and push-button emotional cliches to work with. Shamelessly plays on middle class fears of crime and doubts about the judicial system. Based on the novel by Erika Holzer.*CW:* Language and disturbing violence, which includes rape. **102m/C VHS, Beta, Closed Caption.** Sally Field, Ed Harris, Kiefer Sutherland, Beverly D'Angelo, Joe Mantegna, Keith David; *D:* John Schlesinger; *W:* Amanda Silver, Rick Jaffa; *C:* Amir M. Mokri; *M:* James Newton Howard. *PAR*

Eye of the Demon ♂ 1987 A couple moves to a small town in Massachusetts and discovers that the area had once been a haven for witchcraft. To their horror, they soon find that old habits die hard, and the spellcasting continues in a nearby graveyard. Made for cable television. **92m/C VHS.** Tim Matheson, Pamela Sue Martin, Woody

Harrelson, Barbara Billingsley, Susan Ruttan; *D:* Carl Schenkel. *THV*

Eye of the Eagle ♂½ 1987 (R) A special task force is given a dangerous assignment during the Vietnam war. **84m/C VHS, Beta.** Brett Clark, Ed Crick, Robert Patrick, William Steis, Cec Verrell; *D:* Cirio H. Santiago. *MGM*

Eye of the Eagle 2 ♂ 1989 (R) When his platoon is betrayed and killed in Vietnam, a surviving soldier joins with a beautiful girl and seeks revenge. **79m/C VHS, Beta.** Todd Field, Andy Wood, Ken Jacobson, Ronald Lawrence; *D:* Carl Franklin. *MGM*

Eye of the Eagle 3 ♂½ 1991 (R) Filipino-made Vietnam-War shoot-em-up, rack-em-up, shoot-em-up again, with U.S. forces pinned down against seemingly overwhelming odds. Violent. **90m/C VHS.** Steve Kanaly, Ken Wright, Peter Nelson, Carl Franklin; *D:* Cirio H. Santiago; *W:* Carl Franklin. *NHO*

Eye of the Needle ♂♂½ 1981 (R) Based on Ken Follett's novel about a German spy posing as a shipwrecked sailor on a deserted English island during WWII. Lonely, sad, yet capable of terrible violence, he is stranded on an isolated island while en route to report to his Nazi commander. He becomes involved with an English woman living on the island, and begins to contemplate his role in the war. **112m/C VHS, Beta.** Donald Sutherland, Kate Nelligan, Ian Bannen, Christopher Cazenove, Philip Brown, Stephen MacKenna, Faith Brook, Colin Rix, Alex McCrindle, John Bennett, Sam Kydd, Rik Mayall, Bill Fraser; *D:* Richard Marquand; *W:* Stanley Mann; *M:* Miklos Rozsa. *MGM, FOX*

Eye of the Storm ♂♂½ 1991 (R) At the highway gas station/motel/diner where they live, two young brothers witness their parent's murder. Their younger brother is blinded in the same incident. Ten years later both brothers are still there and the tragedy may have turned one of them psychotic. When the abusive Gladstone and his young and sexy wife are stranded at the gas station it brings out the worst in everyone, with a violent climax during an equally violent thunderstorm.*CW:* Language and strong violence. **98m/C VHS.** Craig Sheffer, Bradley Gregg, Lara Flynn Boyle, Dennis Hopper, Leon Rippy; *D:* Yuri Zeltser. *NLC*

Eye of the Stranger ♂½ 1993 (R) Suspenser about a nameless stranger who sets out to solve the mystery of a small western town and its corrupt mayor.*CW:* Brutal violence and scene of strong sexuality. **96m/C VHS.** David Heavener, Sally Kirkland, Martin Landau, Don Swayze, Stella Stevens, John Pleshette, Joe Estevez, Thomas F. Duffy; *D:* David Heavener; *W:* David Heavener; *M:* Robert Garrett. *MNC*

Eye of the Tiger ♂♂ 1986 (R) A righteous ex-con battles a crazed, crack-dealing motorcycle gang that terrorized and murdered his wife, and is moving on to infest his town. **90m/C VHS, Beta.** Gary Busey, Yaphet Kotto, Seymour Cassel, Bert Remsen, William Smith; *D:* Richard Sarafian; *C:* Peter Collister. *LIV*

Eye of the Wolf ♂♂½ 1995 (PG-13) Zoologist (Fahey) brings a wild wolf into civilization and then must fight to save the animal from execution. Kazan (a wolf-dog mix) is the true star—and rightly so.*CW:* Elements of violence. **96m/C VHS.** Jeff Fahey, Sophie Duez. *THV*

Eye on the Sparrow ♂♂½ 1991 (PG) A couple (Winningham and Carradine) desperately want to raise a child of their own, but the system classifies them as unfit parents since they are both blind. Together they successfully fight the system in this inspiring made for television movie that was based on a true story. **94m/C VHS, Closed Caption.** Mare Winningham, Keith Carradine, Conchata Ferrell, Sandy McPeak, Karen Lee, Bianca Rose; *D:* John Korty. *REP*

Eye Witness ♂♂½ *Your Witness* 1949 An American attorney goes abroad to free a friend from the British legal system. A book of poems becomes the necessary device in deducing the whereabouts of the witness testifying to his

friend's alibi. **104m/B VHS.** *GB* Robert Montgomery, Felix Aylmer, Leslie Banks, Michael Ripper, Patricia Wayne; *D:* Robert Montgomery; *M:* Malcolm Arnold. *NOS, SNC, RXM*

Eyeball woof! *Gatto Rossi In Un Labirinto Do Vetro* 1978 (R) An intrepid policeman is stumped by a madman who is removing eyeballs from his victims. At least they won't have to watch this movie. **87m/C VHS, Beta.** *IT* John Richardson, Martine Brochard; *D:* Umberto Lenzi. *PSM*

Eyes Behind the Stars ♂ 1972 A news photographer accidentally gets a few pictures of invading aliens, but nobody takes him seriously, particularly the government. **95m/C VHS, Beta.** *IT* Martin Balsam, Robert Hoffman, Nathalie Delon, Sherry Buchanan; *D:* Roy Garrett. *NO*

Eyes of a Stranger woof! 1981 (R) Terrifying maniac stalks his female prey by watching their every move. Tewes is cast as a journalist, the stronger of the two sisters in this exploitative slasher. **85m/C VHS, Beta.** Lauren Tewes, John Disanti, Jennifer Jason Leigh; *D:* Ken Wiederhorn; *W:* Eric L. Bloom; *M:* Richard Einhorn. *WAR*

Eyes of a Witness ♂♂½ 1994 American businessman Roy Baxter (Travanti) travels to Kenya to rescue his daughter (Grey) from danger in the African bush. But Roy is falsely charged with murdering a government official and must take on the police to prove his innocence. **90m/C VHS, LV.** Daniel J. Travanti, Jennifer Grey, Carl Lumbly. *NLC, IME*

Eyes of an Angel ♂♂½ 1991 (PG-13) A widower (Travolta), who's heavily involved in gambling, is forced to go on the run with his young daughter (Raab) when a deal goes sour. She must abandon the family dog, who manages to follow them from Chicago to California anyway. Talk about loyalty!*CW:* Mature themes. **91m/C VHS, LV, Closed Caption.** John Travolta, Elie Raab, Jeffrey DeMunn; *D:* Robert Harmon. *LIV*

Eyes of Fire ♂♂ 1984 (R) In early rural America, a group of pioneers set up camp in the wilderness and are besieged during the night by Indian witchcraft. **86m/C VHS, Beta.** *W:* Dennis Lipscomb, Rebecca Stanley, Fran Ryan, Rob Paulsen, Guy Boyd, Karlene Crockett; *D:* Avery Crounse; *W:* Avery Crounse; *M:* Brad Fiedel. *VES*

Eyes of Julia Deep ♂♂ 1918 Rare silent film featuring the ill-fated Minter as Julia, a woman who prevents Terry (Forrest) from killing himself. Piano scored. **54m/B VHS, Closed Caption.** Mary Miles Minter, Alan Forrest, Alice Wilson, George Periolat; *D:* Lloyd Ingraham. *GPV*

Eyes of Laura Mars ♂♂½ 1978 (R) A photographer exhibits strange powers—she can foresee a murder before it happens through her snapshots. In time she realizes that the person responsible for a series of killings is tracking her. Title song performed by Barbra Streisand. **104m/C VHS, Beta, LV, Closed Caption.** Faye Dunaway, Tommy Lee Jones, Brad Dourif, Rene Auberjonois, Raul Julia, Darlanne Fluegel, Michael Tucker; *D:* Irvin Kershner; *W:* John Carpenter, David Zelag Goodman. *GKK*

Eyes of Texas ♂½ 1948 Bryant, a lawyer who uses a pack of killer dogs to get the land she wants, is pursued by a U.S Marshal played decently by Rogers. **54m/B VHS, Beta.** Roy Rogers, Lynn (Mary Hart) Roberts, Andy Devine, Nana Bryant, Roy Barcroft; *D:* William Witney. *NOS, VCN, TIM*

The Eyes of the Amaryllis ♂½ 1982 (R) A young girl becomes involved in a mysterious game when she arrives in Nantucket to care for her insane, invalid grandmother. Based on the story by Natalie Babbitt and filmed on location on Nantucket Island. **94m/C VHS, Beta.** Martha Byrne, Ruth Ford, Guy Boyd, Jonathan Bolt, Katharine Houghton; *D:* Frederick King Keller. *LIV, VES*

Eyes of the Beholder ♂♂ 1992 (R) Janice is a psychopathic serial killer who suffered brain damage from a botched surgical attempt to reverse his insanity. Now he's escaped from the state mental institution, heading straight for the secluded home of the doctor who made him crazier than ever. During a raging storm, Janice stalks the doctor, his wife, and their two hapless dinner guests in a sadistic game of cat-and-mouse.**CW:** Violence and sexuality. 89m/C VHS, LV, **Closed Caption.** Lenny Von Dohlen, Joanna Pacula, Matt McCoy, George Lazenby, Kylie Travis, Charles Napier; **D:** Lawrence L. Simeone; **W:** Lawrence L. Simeone; **M:** Greg Turner. COL

Eyes of the Panther 1990 One of Shelley Duvall's "Nightmare Classics" series, this adaptation of an Ambrose Bierce story concerns a pioneer girl haunted for years by the animal urges of a wild cat. 60m/C VHS, Beta, LV. Daphne Zuniga, C. Thomas Howell, John Stockwell; **D:** Noel Black. NO

Eyes of Turpin Are Upon You! 🎬🎬 1921 Two early Turpin silent comedies: "Idle Eyes" and "A Small Town Idol." 56m/B VHS, Beta. Ben Turpin, Ramon Novarro, Marie Prevost, James Finlayson. VYY

The Eyes of Youth 🎬🎬 1919 A young woman searches her soul for answers: to marry or not to marry is the question. A little foresight, in the form of a glimpse into the hypothetical future, helps her make the right choice. Very early Valentino fare in which the sheik plays a cad. 78m/B VHS, Beta. Clara Kimball Young, Edmund Lowe, Rudolph Valentino. VYY, FCT, VYY

Eyes Right! 🎬🎬 1926 Based on a story by Ernest Grayman, this portrayal of life in a military prep school has its main character experience struggle, recognition, love, jealousy, and triumph. Silent. 46m/B VHS, Beta. Francis X. Bushman. VYY, GPV

The Eyes, the Mouth 🎬🎬 1983 (R) A young man has an affair with his dead twin brother's fiancee. Happiness eludes them as they are haunted by the deceased's memory and the family's grief. In Italian with English subtitles. 100m/C VHS, Beta. FR IT Lou Castel, Angela Molina; **D:** Marco Bellocchio; **W:** Marco Bellocchio. COL

Eyewitness 🎬🎬½ The Janitor 1981 (R) When a murder occurs in the office building of a starstruck janitor, he fabricates a tale in order to initiate a relationship with the television reporter covering the story. Unfortunately the killers think he's telling the truth, which plunges the janitor and reporter into a dangerous and complicated position, pursued by both police and foreign agents. Somewhat contrived, but Hurt and Weaver are always interesting. Woods turns in a wonderful performance as Hurt's somewhat-psychotic best friend. 102m/C VHS, Beta, LV. William Hurt, Sigourney Weaver, Christopher Plummer, James Woods, Kenneth McMillan, Pamela Reed, Irene Worth, Steven Hill, Morgan Freeman; **D:** Peter Yates; **W:** Steve Tesich. FXV, FOX

Eyewitness to Murder 🎬½ 1993 Stevens plays a cop who is assigned to protect beautiful artist Wolter. They both have their tragic flaws: he is a grieving widower, she has been blinded by an unknown attacker. Their flaws may draw them together. Somewhat more engaging than a television police action drama. 75m/C VHS. Andrew Stevens, Adrian Zmed, Sherilyn Wolter, Carl Strano, Robin Drue; **D:** Jag Mundhra. NHO

F. Scott Fitzgerald in Hollywood 🎬🎬 1976 Dramatization begins in the late 1930s when Fitzgerald was lured to Hollywood to work in the burgeoning film industry. It covers the period when, with his wife in a mental institution, he lived with Sheila Graham and struggled against alcoholism. Interesting story made dull and depressing by Miller's uninspired performance, but it's almost saved by Weld's portrayal of Zelda. Made for television. 98m/C VHS, Beta. Jason Miller, Tuesday Weld, Julia Foster, Dolores Sutton, Michael Lerner, James Woods; **D:** Anthony Page. NO

F/X 🎬🎬🎬 1986 (R) A Hollywood special effects expert is contracted by the government to fake an assassination to protect a mob informer. After completing the assignment, he learns that he's become involved in a real crime and is forced to reach into his bag of F/X tricks to survive.

Twists and turns abound in this fast-paced story that was the sleeper hit of the year. Followed by a sequel. 109m/C VHS, Beta, LV, **Closed Caption.** Bryan Brown, Cliff DeYoung, Diane Venora, Brian Dennehy, Jerry Orbach, Mason Adams, Joe Grifasi, Martha Gehman; **D:** Robert Mandel; **W:** Robert T. Megginson, Gregory Fleeman; **M:** Bill Conti. FCT

F/X 2: The Deadly Art of Illusion 🎬🎬 1991 (PG-13) Weak follow-up finds the special-effects specialist set to pull off just one more illusion for the police. Once again, corrupt cops use him as a chump for their scheme, an over-complicated business involving a stolen Vatican treasure. 107m/C VHS, LV, Closed Caption. Bryan Brown, Brian Dennehy, Rachel Ticotin, Philip Bosco, Joanna Gleason; **D:** Richard Franklin; **W:** Bill Condon; **M:** Michael Boddicker, Lalo Schifrin. ORI, IME

Fabiola 🎬🎬🎬 1948 The first of the big Italian spectacle movies, this one opened the door for a flood of low-budget imitators. Fabiola, the daughter of a Roman senator, becomes a Christian when her father's Christian servants are accused of murdering him. In the meantime, the Emperor Constantine speeds toward Rome to convert it to Christian status. You can bet plenty of Christians will lose their heads, be thrown to the lions and generally burn at the stake before he does. 96m/C VHS. IT Michel Simon, Henri Vidal, Gino Cervi; **D:** Alessandro Blasetti. SNC, FCT

The Fable of the Beautiful Pigeon Fancier 🎬🎬½ Fabula de la Bella Palomera 1988 A powerful man who has always gotten what he wanted spies a beautiful young married woman and sets out to make her his own. Based on the Gabriel Gracia Marquez novel "Love in the Time of Cholera." In Spanish with English subtitles. 73m/C VHS, LV. SP Ney Latorraca, Claudia Ohana, Tonia Carrero, Dina Stat, Chico Diaz; **D:** Ruy Guerra. FXL, FCT

Fabulous Adventures of Baron Munchausen 🎬🎬 1961 The legendary Baron Munchausen, known for his tall tales, relates the story of his trek to the strange and beautiful land of Trukesban in a mixture of live action and animation. Wonderful special effects but a boring storyline. In German with English subtitles. 84m/C VHS, Beta. GE Milos Kopecky, Jana Brejchova, Rudolph Jelinek, Jan Werich; **D:** Karel Zeman. LIV, VES, TPV

The Fabulous Baker Boys 🎬🎬🎬 1989 (R) Two brothers have been performing a tired act as nightclub pianists for fifteen years. When they hire a sultry vocalist to revitalize the routine, she inadvertently triggers long-suppressed hostility between the "boys." The story may be a bit uneven, but fine performances by the three leading actors, the steamy 1940s atmosphere, and Pfeiffer's classic rendition of "Makin' Whoopee," are worth the price of the rental. 116m/C VHS, Beta, LV, 8mm. Michelle Pfeiffer, Jeff Bridges, Beau Bridges, Elie Raab, Jennifer Tilly; **D:** Steven Kloves; **W:** Steven Kloves; **C:** Michael Ballhaus; **M:** Dave Grusin. Golden Globe Awards '90: Best Actress—Drama (Pfeiffer); Los Angeles Film Critics Association Awards '89: Best Actress (Pfeiffer), Best Cinematography; National Board of Review Awards '89: Best Actress (Pfeiffer); New York Film Critics Awards '89: Best Actress (Pfeiffer); National Society of Film Critics Awards '89: Best Actress (Pfeiffer), Best Cinematography, Best Supporting Actor (Bridges); Nominations: Academy Awards '89: Best Actress (Pfeiffer), Best Cinematography, Best Film Editing, Best Original Score. LIV, FCT

The Fabulous Dorseys 🎬🎬 1947 The musical lives of big band leaders Tommy and Jimmy Dorsey are portrayed in this less than fabulous biography that's strong on song but weak on plot. Guest stars include Art Tatum, Charlie Barnet, Ziggy Elman, Bob Eberly and Helen O'Connell. Highlights are the tunes. 🎵At Sundown; I'll Never Say Never Again; To Me; Green Eyes; Dorsey Concerto; Art's Blues; Everybody's Doin' It; The Object of My Affection; Runnin' Wild. 91m/B VHS, LV. Tommy Dorsey, Jimmy Dorsey, Janet Blair, Paul Whiteman, Sara Allgood, Arthur Shields; **D:** Alfred E. Green. NOS, MRV, HHT

Fabulous Joe 🎬🎬 1947 A talking dog named Joe gets involved in the life of a henpecked husband. 54m/C VHS, Beta. Walter Abel, Donald Meek, Margot Grahame, Marie Wilson; **D:** Harve Foster. NOS

The Face at the Window 🎬🎬 1939 Melodramatic crime story of a pair of ne'er-do-well brothers who terrorize Paris to conceal their bank robberies. 65m/B VHS. Tod Slaughter, Marjorie Taylor, John Warwick, Robert Adair, Harry Terry; **D:** George King. NOS, MRV, HEG

A Face in the Crowd 🎬🎬🎬½ 1957 Journalist (Neal) discovers a down-home philosopher (Griffith) and puts him on her television show. His aw-shucks personality soon wins him a large following and increasing influence—even political clout. Off the air he reveals his true nature to be insulting, vengeful, and power-hungry—all of which Neal decides to expose. Marks Griffith's spectacular film debut as a thoroughly despicable character and debut of Remick as the pretty cheerleader in whom he takes an interest. Schulburg wrote the screenplay from his short story "The Arkansas Traveler." He and director Kazan collaborated equally well in "On the Waterfront." 126m/B VHS, Beta. Andy Griffith, Patricia Neal, Lee Remick, Walter Matthau, Anthony (Tony) Franciosa; **D:** Elia Kazan; **W:** Budd Schulberg; **C:** Harry Stradling. WAR, FCT

A Face in the Fog 🎬🎬 1936 Two newspaper reporters set out to solve a number of murders that have plagued the cast of a play. Also interested in the playwright. Good low-budget thriller. 66m/B VHS, Beta. June Collyer, Lloyd Hughes, Lawrence Gray, Al "Fuzzy" St. John, Jack Mulhall, Jack Cowell, John Elliott, Sam Flint, Forrest Taylor, Edward Cassidy; **D:** Robert F. "Bob" Hill. NOS, SNC

Face of Another 🎬🎬 1966 A severely burned man gets a second chance when a plastic surgeon makes a mask to hide the disfigurement. Unfortunately this face leads him to alienation, rape, infidelity, and murder. In Japanese with English subtitles. 124m/B VHS, Beta. JP Tatsuya Nakadai, Machiko Kyo; **D:** Hiroshi Teshigahara. NO

Face of the Screaming Werewolf 🎬½ La Casa Del Terror; House of Terror 1959 Originally a Mexican horror/comedy that was bought for U.S. distribution by Jerry Warren, who earned his spot in the horror hall of fame with "The Incredible Petrified World" and "Teenage Zombies." A scientist brings a mummy back to life, but when he removes the bandages (gasp), the subject turns out to be of the canine persuasion. Suffers from comic evisceration; not much to scream about. 60m/B VHS. MX Lon Chaney Jr., Landa Varle, Raymond Gaylord; **D:** Gilberto Martinez Solares, Jerry Warren. SNC, MRV

Face/Off 🎬🎬🎬½ 1997 (R) Woo returns to his blood-soaked, violence-as-poetry-in-motion roots with the story of a fed who assumes the identity of the presumed-dead terrorist who killed his son. When the master criminal wakes up, he "steals" the cop's identity. Travolta's back for another wild ride, eating up the scenery when he takes on the bad-guy role. Cage, fresh from action hits in "The Rock" and "Con Air" gets to study the nature of good and evil (another Woo specialty) while he learns the nuances of the "leap across the room with two pistols blazing" move. Woo's Hong Kong efforts have always explored the blurry line between the good guys and the bad guys, and with Cage and Travolta, he has the perfect actors to display his findings. Woo cultists will welcome the return to the old style, while those only familiar with his stateside work will understand what all the fuss is about. 140m/C VHS. John Travolta, Nicolas Cage, Joan Allen, Alessandro Nivola, Gina Gershon, Nick Cassavetes, Dominique Swain, Harve Presnell, Margaret Cho, CCH Pounder, Colm Feore, John Carroll Lynch, Matt Ross; **D:** John Woo; **W:** Mike Werb, Michael Colleary; **C:** Oliver Wood; **M:** John Powell. NYR

Face the Music 🐾½ 1992 (PG-13) Ringwald and Dempsey were once stormily married and pursuing successful, collaborative careers as singer/songwriters for the movies. But they've abandoned the work, along with the marriage, until a movie producer makes them a very lucrative offer for a new song. Only Dempsey's new girlfriend has some voracious objections. **CW:** Drug-related content and sensuality. **93m/C VHS.** LIV Patrick Dempsey, Molly Ringwald, Lysette Anthony. LIV

Face to Face 🐾🐾½ 1952 Dramatic adaptation of two short stories, "The Secret Sharer," by Joseph Conrad, and Stephen Crane's "The Bride Comes to Yellow Sky." The Conrad story features Mason as a sea captain who discovers a fugitive stowaway aboard his ships. The Crane story features Preston as a sheriff threatened by an old-time gunfighter. **92m/B VHS.** Bretaigne Windust, James Mason, Michael Pate, Robert Preston, Marjorie Steele, Gene Lockhart, Minor Watson; **D:** John Brahm. NO

Face to Face 🐾🐾🐾 Ansikte mot Ansikte 1976 Bergman's harrowing tale of a mental breakdown. Ullmann has a bravura role as a psychiatrist deciding to vacation at her grandparent's house in the country. Once there she begins to experience depression and hallucinations tied to her past with both her mother and grandmother. Her deeply repressed feelings eventually lead to a suicide attempt, which brings some much needed help. Originally a four-hour series made for Swedish television. In Swedish with English subtitles. **136m/C VHS.** SW Liv Ullmann, Erland Josephson, Gunnar Bjornstrand, Aino Taube-Henrikson, Sven Lindberg, Kary Sylway, Sif Ruud; **D:** Ingmar Bergman; **W:** Ingmar Bergman; **C:** Sven Nykvist. Golden Globe Awards '77: Best Foreign Film; Los Angeles Film Critics Association Awards '76: Best Actress (Ullmann), Best Foreign Film; National Board of Review Awards '76: Best Actress (Ullmann); New York Film Critics Awards '76: Best Actress (Ullmann); Nominations: Academy Awards '76: Best Actress (Ullmann), Best Director (Bergman). PAR

Faces 🐾🐾🐾½ 1968 (R) Cassavetes' first independent film to find mainstream success portrays the breakup of the 14-year marriage of middle-aged Richard (Marley) and Maria (Carlin) Forst. Both seek at least momentary comfort with others—Richard with prostitute Jeannie (Rowlands) and Maria with aging hippie Chet (Cassel). The director's usual improvisational and documentary style can either be viewed as compelling or tedious but the performances are first-rate. **CW:** Adult themes. **129m/B VHS.** John Marley, Lynn Carlin, Gena Rowlands, Seymour Cassel, Val Avery, Dorothy Gulliver, Joanne Moore Jordan, Fred Draper, Darlene Conley; **D:** John Cassavetes; **W:** Al Ruban; **M:** Jack Ackerman. National Society of Film Critics Awards '68: Best Screenplay, Best Supporting Actor (Cassel); Nominations: Academy Awards '68: Best Story & Screenplay, Best Supporting Actor (Cassel), Best Supporting Actress (Carlin). FXL

Faces of Women 🐾🐾 1985 Two stories about women in contemporary Africa. In the first, an unhappy young woman is married to a very jealous man. When her brother-in-law visits, she decides to give her husband something to worry about. The second story finds a businesswoman running into problems when she tries to open a restaurant—problems that her daughter helps to solve. French and indigenous languages with English subtitles. **103m/C VHS.** Eugenie Cisse Roland, Sidiki Bakaba, Albertine N'Guessan; **D:** Desire Ecare. NYF

The Facts of Life 🐾🐾½ 1960 (PG-13) Risque bedroom comedy finds Larry Gilbert (Hope) and Kitty Weaver (Ball) running off from boredom in suburbia and their respective spouses (Hussey and DeFore) to have a little interlude together. **103m/B VHS, Closed Caption.** Bob Hope, Lucille Ball, Ruth Hussey, Don DeFore, Louis Nye, Philip Ober; **D:** Melvin Frank; **W:** Melvin Frank, Norman Panama; **C:** Charles Lang Jr.; **M:** Leigh Harline. Academy Awards '60: Best Costume Design (B & W); Nominations: Academy Awards '60: Best Art Direction/Set Decoration (B & W), Best

Black and White Cinematography, Best Song ("The Facts of Life"), Best Story & Screenplay. MGM

Fade to Black woof! 1980 (R) Young man obsessed with movies loses his grip on reality and adopts the personalities of cinematic characters (Hopalong Cassidy and Dracula among them) to seek revenge on people who have wronged him. Thoroughly unpleasant, highlighted by clips from old flicks. **100m/C VHS, Beta.** Dennis Christopher, Tim Thomerson, Linda Kerridge, Mickey Rourke, Melinda Fee; **D:** Vernon Zimmerman. MED, MLB

Fade to Black 🐾🐾 1993 (R) Busfield stars as a college professor with voyeuristic tendencies and a handy camcorder. After viewing his latest tape, he realizes he's filmed his neighbor's murder and that he can recognize the killer. Before he can warn the killer's girlfriend, she disappears and our nosy prof is framed for the death. **CW:** Violence. **84m/C VHS, Beta, Closed Caption.** Timothy Busfield, Heather Locklear, Michael Beck, Louis Giambalvo, Cloris Leachman, David Byron; **D:** John McPherson; **W:** Douglas Barr. PAR

Fahrenheit 451 🐾🐾🐾 1966 Chilling adaptation of the Ray Bradbury novel about a futuristic society that has banned all reading material and the firemen whose job it is to keep the fires at 451 degrees: the temperature at which paper burns. Werner is a fireman who begins to question the rightness of his actions when he meets the book-loving Christie—who also plays the dual role of Werner's TV-absorbed wife. Truffaut's first color and English-language film. **112m/C VHS, Beta, LV.** FR Oskar Werner, Julie Christie, Cyril Cusack, Anton Diffring; **D:** Francois Truffaut. USH, MLB

Fail-Safe 🐾🐾🐾½ 1964 A nail-biting nuclear age nightmare, in which American planes have been erroneously sent to bomb the USSR, with no way to recall them. An all-star cast impels this bitterly serious thriller, the straight-faced flipside of "Dr. Strangelove." **111m/B VHS, Beta, LV, Closed Caption.** Henry Fonda, Dan O'Herlihy, Walter Matthau, Larry Hagman, Fritz Weaver, Dom DeLuise; **D:** Sidney Lumet; **W:** Walter Bernstein. COL

Fair Game woof! 1982 (R) Three young women decide to ditch their private school for a weekend of fun but find out the resort town they've chosen is run by sociopaths who get their kicks by stalking our chicks. **90m/C VHS, Beta.** AU Kim Trengove, Kerry Mack, Marie O'Loughlina, Karen West; **D:** Christopher Fitchett. IMP

Fair Game woof! 1985 In the Australian outback, three loathesome excuses for human beings come across a beautiful woman alone on a remote farm. Naturally, they try to do despicable things but she fights back. **83m/C VHS.** AU Cassandra Delaney, Peter Ford, David Sandford, Gary Who; **D:** Mario Andreacchio. ORI

Fair Game woof! 1989 (R) A psychotic but imaginative ex-boyfriend locks his former girlfriend in her apartment with a lethal giant Mamba snake. Understandably uninterested in its serpentine attention, the young woman must trespass against the Hollywood code and keep her wits in the face of danger. Guaranteed not to charm you. **81m/C VHS, LV.** Greg Henry, Trudie Styler, Bill Moseley; **D:** Mario Orfini. THV

Fair Game 🐾🐾½ 1995 (R) Miami police detective Max (Baldwin) defies orders so he can protect family attorney Kate (Crawford, in her big-screen debut) from high-tech assassins. Nice work if you can get it. Generic action plot provides Crawford and first-time director Sipes with relatively safe proving ground. Cindy wears the "Die Hard" dirty white tank top look fetchingly enough (and showers when the action slackens), while Baldwin is no slouch in the babe department (male division) either. Based on Paula Gosling's 1978 novel "Fair Game," which was previously filmed as 1986's "Cobra." **CW:** Intermittent strong violence, language, and a scene of sexuality. **91m/C VHS, LV, Closed Caption.** William Baldwin, Cindy Crawford, Miguel Sandoval, Christopher McDonald, Johann Car-

lo, Salma Hayek, John Bedford Lloyd, Jenette Goldstein; **D:** Andrew Sipes; **W:** Charlie Fletcher; **C:** Richard Bowen; **M:** Mark Mancina. Nominations: Golden Raspberry Awards '95: Worst New Star (Crawford). WAR

Fairy Tales 🐾🐾 Fairytales 1976 (R) A ribald musical fantasy follows the equally risque "Cinderella." In order to save the kingdom, the prince must produce an heir. The problem is that only the girl in the painting of "Princess Beauty" can "interest" the prince and she must be found. Good-natured smut. **83m/C VHS, Beta.** Don Sparks, Prof. Irwin Corey, Brenda Fogarty, Sy Richardson, Nai Bonet, Martha Reeves; **D:** Harry Tampa. MED

Faith 🐾 1992 (R) When young dancer Faith's parents are killed in an accident she winds up in a frightening foster home. Running away, she meets a gentlemanly mobster who helps her attain her dance dreams. Laughably implausible. **CW:** Language and violence. **104m/C VHS, LV, Closed Caption.** Sylvia Seidel, Ami Dolenz, Richard Maldone. THV

Faithful 🐾🐾½ 1995 (R) Black comedy about depressed, rich housewife Margaret (Cher) who is rudely interrupted by Tony the hitman (Palminteri) while trying to commit suicide on her 20th wedding anniversary. Unfaithful hubby Jack (O'Neal), who has put the contract out on Margaret, is conveniently away on business. As Margaret sits tied to a chair and Tony waits for a call to confirm the hit, the two connect and decide to turn the tables. Director Mazursky succeeds in bringing Palminteri's three-character play to the screen, even if it does suffer at times from too much stage talk and not enough action. First film for Cher since 1990's "Mermaids" and the first for O'Neal since 1989's "Chances Are." Big rift between Mazursky and the film's producers over final cut led him to threaten to pull his name from the credits. Mazursky cameos as the hitman's therapist. **CW:** Language and sex-related dialogue. **91m/C VHS, LV, Closed Caption.** Cher, Ryan O'Neal, Chazz Palminteri; **Cameos:** Paul Mazursky; **D:** Paul Mazursky; **W:** Chazz Palminteri; **C:** Fred Murphy. NLC

Fake Out 🐾 Nevada Heat 1982 Nightclub singer is caught between the mob and the police who want her to testify against her gangland lover. Typical vanity outing for Zadora. **89m/C VHS, Beta.** Pia Zadora, Telly Savalas, Desi Arnaz Jr.; **D:** Matt Cimber. CNG

Falcon 🐾 1974 Brave knight battles for the honor of a beautiful maiden; with or without the Falcon's help. **105m/C VHS, Beta.** Franco Nero. TWE

The Falcon and the Snowman 🐾🐾🐾 1985 (R) True story of Daulton Lee and Christopher Boyce, two childhood friends who, almost accidentally, sell American intelligence secrets to the KGB in 1977. Hutton and Penn are excellent, creating a relationship we care about and strong characterizations. **110m/C VHS, Beta, LV, Closed Caption.** Sean Penn, Timothy Hutton, Lori Singer, Pat Hingle, Dorian Harewood, Richard Dysart, David Suchet, Jennifer Runyon, Priscilla Pointer, Nicholas Pryor, Joyce Van Patten, Mady Kaplan, Michael Ironside; **D:** John Schlesinger; **W:** Steven Zaillian; **C:** Allen Daviau; **M:** Lyle Mays, Pat Metheny. LIV, VES

The Falcon in Hollywood 🐾🐾½ 1944 The falcon gets caught up with the murder of an actor who was part of a Tinseltown love triangle. The film takes place on RKO's back lot for a behind-the-scenes view of Hollywood. Part of the popular "Falcon" series from the 1940s. **67m/B VHS.** Tom Conway, Barbara Hale, Veda Ann Borg, Sheldon Leonard, Frank Jenks, Rita (Paula) Corday, John Abbott; **D:** Gordon Douglas. MED

The Falcon in Mexico 🐾½ 1944 When paintings from a supposedly dead artist turn up for sale in New York City, the Falcon and the artist's daughter wind up journeying to Mexico to solve the mystery. Part of "The Falcon" series. **70m/B VHS, Beta.** Tom Conway, Mona Maris, Nestor Paiva; **D:** William (Lester Williams) Berke. MED

The Falcon Takes Over/Strange Bargain 🐾🐾 1949 A mystery double feature. In "The Falcon Takes Over," The Falcon becomes involved in a series of murder and an ex-con's last love, and in "Strange Bargain," an underpaid bookkeeper gets in on an insurance swindle. 131m/B VHS, Beta. George Sanders, Ward Bond, Allen Jenkins, Martha Scott, Harry (Henry) Morgan, James Gleason, Anne Revere, Hans Conried, Turhan Bey; *D:* Irving Reis. TTC

The Falcon's Adventure/Armored Car Robbery 🐾🐾½ 1950 A mystery double feature: The Falcon uncovers a vicious plot to steal a formula for synthetic diamonds in "The Falcon's Adventure," and four participants in an armored car robbery flee after slaying a policeman in "Armored Car Robbery." 122m/B VHS, Beta. Tom Conway, Madge Meredith, William Talman, Charles McGraw, Adele Jergens; *D:* William (Lester Williams) Berke. TTC

The Falcon's Brother 🐾🐾 1942 Enemy agents intent on killing a South American diplomat are foiled by the Falcon's brothers at a steep personal cost. The plot enabled Sanders' real-life brother Conway to take over the title role in "The Falcon" mystery series, a role which he played nine more times. 64m/B VHS, Beta. Tom Conway, George Sanders, Keye Luke, Jane Randolph; *D:* Stanley Logan. MED

Fall and Rise of Reginald Perrin 1 🐾🐾🐾 1978 Starring Leonard Rossiter, this BBC show has Reginald getting out of the rat race. 107m/C VHS. *GB* Leonard Rossiter. VCO, HMV, FUS

Fall and Rise of Reginald Perrin 2 🐾🐾🐾 1978 After part one's escape from the rat race, this time Reginald is back in suburbia. 120m/C VHS. *GB* Leonard Rossiter. VCO, HMV, FUS

Fall from Grace 🐾🐾½ 1994 American and British intelligence officers take deadly risks in 1943 Europe in an effort to convince Hitler to end the war. 180m/C VHS. *GB* James Fox, Michael York, Patsy Kensit, Gary Cole; *D:* Waris Hussein. AVE, FCT

Fall from Innocence 🐾🐾½ 1988 A girl is driven to a life of prostitution and drugs by the sexual abuse inflicted upon her by her father. 81m/C VHS. Isabelle Mejias, Thom Haverstock, Amanda Smith, Rob McEwan; *D:* Carey Connor. NO

The Fall of the House of Usher 🐾 1949 Lord Roderick Usher is haunted by his sister's ghost in this poor adaptation of the Poe classic. 70m/B VHS. *GB* Kay Tendeter, Gwen Watford, Irving Steen, Lucy Pavey; *D:* Ivan Barnett. SNC, FCT

The Fall of the House of Usher 🐾🐾🐾 *House of Usher* 1960 The moody Roger Corman/Vincent Price interpretation, the first of their eight Poe adaptations, depicting the collapse of the famous estate due to madness and revenge. Terrific sets and solid direction as well as Price's inimitable presence. 85m/C VHS, Beta. Vincent Price, Myrna Fahey, Mark Damon; *D:* Roger Corman; *W:* Richard Matheson; *C:* Floyd Crosby; *M:* Les Baxter. NO

The Fall of the House of Usher 🐾½ 1980 (PG) Another version of Edgar Allan Poe's classic tale of a family doomed to destruction. Stray to the Roger Corman/Vincent Price version to see how it should have been done. 101m/C VHS, Beta. Martin Landau, Robert Hays, Charlene Tilton, Ray Walston; *D:* James L. Conway. NO

The Fall of the Roman Empire 🐾🐾🐾 1964 An all-star, big budget extravaganza set in ancient Rome praised for its action sequences. The licentious son of Marcus Aurelius arranges for his father's murder and takes over as emperor while Barbarians gather at the gate. Great sets, fine acting, and thundering battle scenes. 187m/C VHS, Beta, LV. Sophia Loren, Alec Guinness, James Mason, Stephen Boyd, Christopher Plummer, John Ireland, Anthony Quayle, Eric Porter, Mel Ferrer, Omar Sharif; *D:* Anthony Mann; *W:* Philip Yordan; *C:* Robert Krasker. Golden Globe Awards '65: Best Score;

Nominations: Academy Awards '64: Best Original Score. BFV, KAR, FCT

Fall Time 🐾🐾 *Falltime* 1994 (R) Crime drama set in small-town Minnesota, circa 1957. Three high schoolers set in motion a prank that turns bad when they pull up in front of the local bank. David (Arquette), Joe (Blechman), and Tim (London) intend to stage a mock robbery—too bad a real robbery is going down and the teens wind up the terrified hostages of creepy criminals Florence (Rourke) and Leon (Baldwin). Promising premise derailed by narrative inadequacies. *CW:* Scenes of brutality and violence; strong language; scene of sexuality. 88m/C VHS, LV, Closed Caption. Mickey Rourke, Stephen Baldwin, Jason London, David Arquette, Jonah Blechman, Sheryl Lee; *D:* Paul Warner; *W:* Steve Alden, Paul Skemp; *C:* Mark J. Gordon. LIV

Fallen Angel 🐾🐾½ 1981 Television movie about a child pornographer and a particular young girl he finds easily exploitable because of her unbalanced home situation. Fine cast, solid direction. 100m/C Beta. Dana Hill, Richard Masur, Melinda Dillon, Ronny Cox; *D:* Robert Lewis; *M:* Richard Bellis. COL

Fallen Angels 1 🐾🐾🐾 1993 Trilogy of hard-boiled, film noirish tales set in Los Angeles. "The Frightening Frammis" concerns a grifter (Gallagher) who meets his match in a mystery woman (Rossellini) in this adaptation of a Jim Thompson story. Cruise's directorial debut. "Murder, Obliquely" finds a plain Jane (Dern) falling for a heel (Rickman) who may have murdered his previous girl in a Cornell Woolrich tale. "Since I Don't Have You" has Buzz Meeks (Busey) hired to find a dame sought by both Howard Hughes (Matheson) and gangster Mickey Cohen (Woods). From a story by James Elroy. Made for cable television. 90m/C VHS, Closed Caption. Peter Gallagher, Isabella Rossellini, Nancy Travis, John C. Reilly, Bill Erwin, Laura Dern, Alan Rickman, Diane Lane, Robin Bartlett, Gary Busey, Tim Matheson, James Woods, Aimee Graham, Dick Miller, Ken Lerner; *D:* Tom Cruise, Alfonso Cuaron, Jonathan Kaplan; *W:* Jon Robin Baitz, Howard A. Rodman, Amanda Silver, Steven Katz; *M:* Elmer Bernstein. PGV

Fallen Angels 2 🐾🐾🐾 1993 Three more film noir stories set in L.A. "Dead End for Delia" finds a police detective (Oldman) arriving at a murder scene to find his estranged wife (Anwar) the victim. Based on a short story by William Campbell Gault. "I'll Be Waiting" has Kirby as a hapless hotel detective who falls for a beautiful guest (Helgenberger) and winds up a mob pawn. Adaptation of a Raymond Chandler tale. "The Quiet Room" has Bedelia and Mantegna as a pair of corrupt cops who find their shakedown schemes going very wrong. From a story by Jonathan Craig. Made for cable television. 90m/C VHS, Closed Caption. Gary Oldman, Gabrielle Anwar, Meg Tilly, Patrick Masset, Vondie Curtis-Hall, Paul Guilfoyle, Dan Hedaya, John Putch, Wayne Knight, Bruno Kirby, Marg Helgenberger, Jon Polito, Peter Scolari, Dick Miller, Joe Mantegna, Bonnie Bedelia, Vinessa Shaw, J.E. Freeman, Peter Gallagher, Patrick Breen, Genia Michaela, Wayne Grace; *Cameos:* Tom Hanks; *D:* Phil Joanou, Tom Hanks, Steven Soderbergh; *W:* Scott Frank, C. Gaby Mitchell, Howard A. Rodman. PGV

Fallen Champ: The Untold Story of Mike Tyson 🐾🐾🐾 1993 Director Kopple's provocative documentary on the boxing champ, from his roots in a Brooklyn ghetto to his conviction for rape in 1991. Tyson is shown as pathetic, vulnerable, and violent—psychologically unprepared for both acclaim and responsibility, as well as easily manipulated by promoters and opportunists. A mixture of ring footage and interviews with sportswriters, promoters, trainers, and others as well as media coverage of Tyson. Made for television. 93m/C VHS, Closed Caption. *D:* Barbara Kopple. COL, BTV

The Fallen Idol 🐾🐾🐾 *The Lost Illusion* 1949 A young boy wrongly believes that a servant he admires is guilty of murdering his wife. Unwittingly, the child influences the police investigation of the crime so that the servant becomes the prime

suspect. Richardson as the accused and Henrey as the boy are notable. Screenplay adapted by Greene from his short story, "The Basement Room." 92m/B VHS, Beta, LV. *GB* Ralph Richardson, Bobby Henrey, Michele Morgan, Sonia Dresdel, Jack Hawkins, Bernard Lee, Denis O'Dea, Dora Bryan, Walter Fitzgerald, Karel Stepanek, Geoffrey Keen, James Hayter, Dandy Nichols, George Woodbridge, John Ruddock, Joan Young, Gerard Heinz; *D:* Carol Reed; *W:* Graham Greene, Lesley Storm, William Templeton; *C:* Georges Perinal. British Academy Awards '48: Best Film; National Board of Review Awards '49: 10 Best Films of the Year, Best Actor (Richardson); New York Film Critics Awards '49: Best Director (Reed); Nominations: Academy Awards '49: Best Director (Reed), Best Screenplay. NOS, MRV, PSM

The Fallen Sparrow 🐾🐾🐾 1943 Garfield is superb as a half-mad veteran of the Spanish Civil War. Captured and brutalized, he never revealed the whereabouts of a valuable possession. His return to the U.S. continues his torture as Nazi agent Slezak uses the woman Garfield loves to set a trap and finish the job. Solid performances and good plot are highlights. 94m/B VHS, Beta. John Garfield, Maureen O'Hara, Walter Slezak, Patricia Morison, Martha O'Driscoll, Bruce Edwards, John Miljan, John Banner, Hugh Beaumont; *D:* Richard Wallace. Nominations: Academy Awards '43: Original Dramatic/Comedy Score. MED, IME

Falling Down 🐾🐾 1993 (R) Douglas is "D-FENS" (taken from his license plate), a normally law-abiding white-collar geek who snaps while stuck in a traffic jam on a hot day in LA. Like Charles Bronson in "Death Wish," he decides to take matters into his own hands. Unlike Bronson, he is not avenging an attack by a specific criminal, but raging against whomever gets in his way. Duvall is a detective on his last day before retirement, Hershey has the thankless role of Douglas' ex. Essentially a revenge fantasy that was vilified by some for catering to the baser emotions. *CW:* Strong language and violence. 112m/C VHS, LV, Closed Caption. Michael Douglas, Robert Duvall, Barbara Hershey, Rachel Ticotin, Tuesday Weld, Frederic Forrest, Lois Smith, D.W. Moffett, Dedee Pfeiffer, Vondie Curtis-Hall, Michael Paul Chan, Raymond J. Barry, Jack Kehoe, John Diehl; *D:* Joel Schumacher; *W:* Ebbe Roe Smith; *C:* Andrzej Bartkowiak; *M:* James Newton Howard. WAR, FCT

Falling from Grace 🐾🐾½ 1992 (PG-13) Bud Parks (Mellencamp) is a successful country singer who, accompanied by his wife and daughter, returns to his small Indiana hometown to celebrate his grandfather's 80th birthday. He's tired of both his career and his marriage and finds himself taking up once again with an old girlfriend (Lenz), who is not only married to Bud's brother but is also having an affair with his father. Bud believes he's better off staying in his old hometown but the problems caused by his return may change his mind. Surprisingly sedate, although literate, family drama with good ensemble performances. Actor-director debut for Mellencamp. 100m/C VHS, LV, Closed Caption. John Cougar Mellencamp, Mariel Hemingway, Kay Lenz, Claude Akins, Dub Taylor, Brent Huff, Deirdre O'Connell, Larry Crane; *D:* John Cougar Mellencamp; *W:* Larry McMurtry. COL, FCT

Falling in Love 🐾🐾½ 1984 (PG-13) Two married New Yorkers unexpectedly fall in love after a coincidental meeting at the Rizzoli Book Store. Weak but gracefully performed reworking of "Brief Encounter," where no one seems to ever complete a sentence. An unfortunate re-teaming for Streep and De Niro after their wonderful work in "The Deer Hunter." 106m/C VHS, Beta, LV, Closed Caption. Robert De Niro, Meryl Streep, Harvey Keitel, Dianne Wiest, George Martin, Jane Kaczmarek, David Clennon; *D:* Ulu Grosbard; *W:* Michael Cristofer; *M:* Dave Grusin. PAR

Falling in Love Again 🐾½ *In Love* 1980 (PG) Romantic comedy about middle-aged dreamer Gould and realistic wife York. They travel from Los Angeles to their hometown of New York for his high school reunion, where Gould is suddenly attacked by nostalgia vibes for his youth, seen in countless flashbacks, and prominently featuring

Pfeiffer, notable in her film debut. Like watching a home movie about people you don't care about. **103m/C VHS, LV.** Elliott Gould, Susannah York, Michelle Pfeiffer; **D:** Steven Paul; **W:** Ted Allan. *APX*

False Arrest 𝄞𝄞½ **1992** A woman is falsely accused of killing her husband's business partner and winds up in prison where she continues to fight to prove her innocence. Mills does well in this less-than-glamorous role. Based on a true story. Made for television. **102m/C VHS, Beta, Closed Caption.** Donna Mills, Steven Bauer, James Handy, Lane Smith, Lewis Van Bergen, Dennis Christopher, Robert Wagner; **D:** Bill W.L. Norton. *TTC, PMS*

False Colors 𝄞 **1943** Hopalong Cassidy unmasks a crook posing as a ranch heir. This was the 49th Hopalong Cassidy feature. **54m/B VHS, Beta.** William Boyd, Robert Mitchum, Andy Clyde, Jimmy Rogers; **D:** George Archainbaud. *NOS, MRV, VYY*

False Faces 𝄞 **1918** Secret agent known as The Lone Wolf is working in France for the Allies when he learns a German master spy is headed for the U.S. to cause trouble. So he heads for New York to stop him. Lots of thrills. **65m/B VHS.** Henry B. Walthall, Lon Chaney Sr., Mary Anderson, Milton Ross; **D:** Irvin Willat. *FCT*

False Faces 𝄞½ **1932** A ruthless, money-hungry quack is hounded by the law and the victims of his unscrupulous plastic surgery. **80m/B VHS, Beta.** Lowell Sherman, Peggy Shannon, Lila Lee, Joyce Compton, Berton Churchill, David Landau, Eddie Anderson, Ken Maynard, Veda Ann Borg; **D:** Lowell Sherman. *VYY*

False Identity 𝄞½ **1990 (PG-13)** A radio psychologist buys a Purple Heart medal at a garage sale and then tries to find out about the original recipient. But her questions are making a number of folks uneasy, including a potentially dangerous stranger. **97m/C VHS, Beta, LV.** Genevieve Bujold, Stacy Keach, Veronica Cartwright, Tobin Bell, Mimi Maynard; **D:** James Keach; **W:** Sandra K. Bailey. *PAR*

False Witness 𝄞𝄞½ **1989** A New Orleans district attorney and her lover, a private investigator, find themselves working the same rape-murder case. When their methods disagree both land themselves in danger. Adapted from a novel by Dorothy Uhnak. Made for television. **96m/C VHS.** Phylicia Rashad, Philip Michael Thomas, Terri Austin, George Grizzard; **D:** Arthur Seidelman; **M:** Charles Fox. *VTR*

Fame 𝄞𝄞𝄞 **1980 (R)** Follows eight talented teenagers from their freshmen year through graduation from New York's High School of Performing Arts. Insightful and absorbing, director Parker allows the kids to mature on screen, revealing the pressures of constantly trying to prove themselves. A faultless parallel is drawn between these "special" kids and the pressures felt by high schoolers everywhere. Great dance and music sequences. The basis for the television series. ♫Fame; Red Light; I Sing the Body Electric; Dogs in the Yard; Hot Lunch Jam; Out Here On My Own; Is It OK If I Call You Mine?. **133m/C VHS, Beta, LV.** Irene Cara, Barry Miller, Paul McCrane, Anne Meara, Joanna Merlin, Richard Belzer, Maureen Teefy; **D:** Alan Parker; **M:** Michael Gore. Academy Awards '80: Best Song ("Fame"), Best Original Score; Golden Globe Awards '81: Best Song ("Fame"); Nominations: Academy Awards '80: Best Film Editing, Best Original Screenplay, Best Song ("Out Here on My Own"), Best Sound. *MGM, FCT*

Fame Is the Spur 𝄞𝄞½ **1947** A lengthy but interesting look at the way power corrupts, plus an insight into the Conservative versus Labor dynamics of British government. Redgrave is a poor, idealistic worker who decides to help his fellow workers by running for Parliament. There, he falls prey to the trappings of office with surprising consequences. Look hard for Tomlinson, who went on to star in "Mary Poppins" and "Bedknobs and Broomsticks" for Disney. **116m/B VHS.** GB Michael Redgrave, Rosamund John, Bernard Miles, Hugh Burden, Guy Verney, Carla Lehmann, Seymour Hicks, David Tomlinson; **D:** Roy Boulting. *NOS, VEC*

The Family 𝄞½ **1973** As a New Orleans hit-man who resists joining the mob, Bronson initiates an all-out war on the syndicate and its boss, played by Savalas. A poorly dubbed Italian action film. **94m/C VHS, Beta.** IT Charles Bronson, Jill Ireland, Telly Savalas; **D:** Sergio Sollima. *MPI*

The Family 𝄞𝄞𝄞 **La Famiglia 1987** An 80-year-old patriarch prepares for his birthday celebration reminiscing about his family's past triumphs, tragedies and enduring love. The charming flashbacks, convincingly played, all take place in the family's grand old Roman apartment. In Italian with English subtitles or dubbed. **128m/C VHS, Beta, LV.** IT Vittorio Gassman, Fanny Ardant, Philippe Noiret, Stefania Sandrelli, Andrea Occhipinti, Jo Ciampa; **D:** Ettore Scola; **W:** Ettore Scola, Ruggero Maccari, Furio Scarpelli; **M:** Armando Trovajoli. Nominations: Academy Awards '87: Best Foreign Language Film. *LIV, VES, TPV*

Family Business 𝄞𝄞½ **1989 (R)** A bright Ivy Leaguer, impressed by the exploits and vitality of his criminal grandfather, recruits him and his ex-con dad to pull off a high-tech robbery, which goes awry. Caper film, with its interest in family relationships and being true to one's nature. Casting Connery, Hoffman, and Broderick as the three leaves a big believability problem in the family department. **114m/C VHS, Beta, LV, 8mm, Closed Caption.** Sean Connery, Dustin Hoffman, Matthew Broderick, Rosana De Soto, Janet Carroll, Victoria Jackson, Bill McCutcheon, Deborah Rush, Marilyn Cooper, Salem Ludwig, Rex Everhart, James Tolkan; **D:** Sidney Lumet; **W:** Vincent Patrick; **C:** Andrzej Bartkowiak; **M:** Cy Coleman. *COL, FCT*

Family Dog: Complete Series 1992 Ten episodes from the animated television series executive produced by Tim Burton and Steven Spielberg. This put-upon pup is property of the Binfords family and succeeds in getting himself involved in all sorts of unhappy situations. **235m/C VHS, LV, Closed Caption. D:** Chris Buck; **W:** Dennis Klein; **V:** Daniel Mann, Martin Mull, Molly Cheek, Zak Huxtable Epstein, Cassie Cole. *USH*

Family Enforcer 𝄞 **Death Collector 1976 (R)** A small-time hoodlum is bent on becoming the best enforcer in an underworld society. **82m/C VHS, Beta.** Joe Cortese, Lou Criscuola, Joe Pesci, Anne Johns, Keith Davis; **D:** Ralph De Vito. *VCI, VTR*

The Family Game 𝄞𝄞𝄞 **1983** An obsessive satire about a poor, belligerent college student hired by a wealthy contemporary Japanese family to tutor their spoiled teenage son. Provides an all-out cultural assault on the Japanese bourgeoisie. From an original story by Yohei Honma. In Japanese with English subtitles. **107m/C VHS, Beta.** JP Junichi Tsujita, Yusaku Matsuda, Juzo Itami, Saori Yuki, Ichirota Miyagawa; **D:** Yoshimitsu Morita; **W:** Yoshimitsu Morita. *FCT*

Family Jewels 𝄞𝄞 **1965** A spoiled child-heiress has to choose among her six uncles to decide which should be her new father. If you like Jerry Lewis, you can't miss this! In addition to playing all six uncles, Lewis plays the chauffeur, as well as serving as producer, director, and coauthor of the script. **100m/C VHS.** Jerry Lewis, Donna Butterworth, Sebastian Cabot, Robert Strauss; **D:** Jerry Lewis; **W:** Jerry Lewis. *PAR*

Family Life 𝄞𝄞½ **Wednesday's Child 1971** A portrait of a 19-year-old girl battling her parents to establish her own identity. She is subjected to increasingly vigorous psychological interventions in this documentary-style effort originally made for British television. **108m/C VHS, Beta.** GB Sandy Ratcliff, Bill Dean, Grace Cave; **D:** Ken Loach. *COL*

Family Life 𝄞𝄞 **Zycie Rodzinne 1971** Melancholy mood piece finds an engineer reluctantly returning to his family's delapidated country mansion after six years in Warsaw. He must confront his own life as well as his alcoholic father and slightly mad sister. Polish with subtitles. **93m/C VHS.** PL Daniel Olbrychski, Jan Nowicki, Jan Kreczmar, Maja Komorowska, Halina Mikolajska; **D:** Krzysztof Zanussi; **W:** Krzysztof Zanussi; **M:** Wojciech Kilar. *FCT*

The Family Man 𝄞𝄞 **1979** A brief encounter-between a married Manhattanite (Asner) and a much younger single woman (Baxter Birney) is sensitively handled in this film which explores their passionate affair. Made-for-television. **98m/C VHS, Beta.** Ed Asner, Meredith Baxter, Paul Clemens, Mary Joan Negro, Anne Jackson, Martin Short, Michael Ironside; **D:** Glenn Jordan; **M:** Billy Goldenberg. *TLF*

A Family Matter 𝄞𝄞 **Vendetta: Secrets of a Mafia Bride 1991 (R)** A Mafia chieftain adopts a child whose father was killed by hit men. She grows into a beautiful woman bent on revenge. Melodramatic Italian-American co-production, made for TV. **CW:** Gangster violence and sensuality. **100m/C VHS, LV.** Eric Roberts, Carol Alt, Eli Wallach, Burt Young. *THV*

Family of Cops 𝄞𝄞½ **1995 (PG-13)** Trouble comes calling on Inspector Paul Fein's (Bronson) close-knit Milwaukee family when his party girl daughter Jackie (Featherstone) comes home to visit. She's soon accused of murdering a wealthy businessman she picked up in a drunken stupor and her cop family gets deeply involved in the investigation. Made for TV. **CW:** Violence and some sexuality. **90m/C VHS.** Charles Bronson, Daniel Baldwin, Angela Featherstone, Sebastian Spence, Lesley-Anne Down, Barbara Williams, Simon MacCorkindale; **D:** Ted Kotcheff; **W:** Joel Basberg. *THV*

Family Pictures 𝄞𝄞𝄞 **1993** A photographer remembers growing up in the 50's with her autistic brother, the mother who lavished her attention on him almost to the exclusion of her five other children, and the father who blamed his wife for their son's deficiencies. Interesting portrait of a typical American family, which eventually cracks under pressure and splits up. Adapted from the novel by Sue Miller (no relation to screenwriter Jennifer). **240m/C VHS.** Anjelica Huston, Sam Neill, Kyra Sedgwick, Dermot Mulroney, Gemma Barry, Tara Charendoff, Torri Higginson, Jamie Harold; **D:** Philip Saville; **W:** Jennifer Miller. *NYR*

Family Plot 𝄞𝄞½ **1976 (PG)** Alfred Hitchcock's last film focuses on the search for a missing heir which is undertaken by a phony psychic and her private-eye boyfriend, with all becoming involved in a diamond theft. Campy, lightweight mystery that stales with time and doesn't fit well into Hitchcock's genre. **120m/C VHS, Beta, LV.** Karen Black, Bruce Dern, Barbara Harris, William Devane, Ed Lauter, Katherine Helmond; **D:** Alfred Hitchcock; **W:** Ernest Lehman; **M:** John Williams. Edgar Allan Poe Awards '76: Best Screenplay; National Board of Review Awards '76: 10 Best Films of the Year. *USH*

Family Prayers 𝄞𝄞½ **1991 (PG)** Coming-of-age drama, set in 1969 Los Angeles, about 13-year-old Andrew and his family troubles. His father Martin (Mantegna) is a compulsive gambler which causes wife Rita (Archer) untold anxiety and constant friction between the two. Tension is heightened by Nan (LuPone), Rita's opinionated older sister who has bailed the family out of their money problems more than once. Meanwhile, Andrew tries to look out for his younger sister and prepare for his bar-mitzvah. A little too much of a nostalgic golden glow surrounds what is essentially a family tragedy. **109m/C VHS.** Tzvi Ratner-Stauber, Joe Mantegna, Anne Archer, Patti LuPone, Paul Reiser, Allen (Goorwitz) Garfield, Conchata Ferrell, David Margulies; **D:** Scott Rosenfelt; **W:** Steven Ginsburg. *COL*

Family Reunion 𝄞½ **1988** A young man brings a pretty hitchhiker to his family reunion where they mistake her for his fiancee (who recently dumped him). **97m/C VHS, Beta.** David Eisner, Rebecca Jenkins, Henry Beckman, Linda Sorensen; **D:** Dick Sarin. *NO*

Family Secrets 𝄞𝄞½ **1984** A made-for-television drama about a daughter, mother, and grandmother overprotecting and manipulating each other during a weekend together. **96m/C Beta.** Maureen Stapleton, Stefanie Powers, Melissa Gilbert, James Spader; **D:** Jack Hofsiss. *NO*

Family Sins 🎟🎟 **1987** A television movie about a domineering father who dotes on his sports-oriented son while willfully neglecting the other. Eventually this leads to calamity. **93m/C VHS.** James Farentino, Jill Eikenberry, Andrew Bendarski, Mimi Kuzyk, Brent Spiner, Michael Durrell, Tom Bower; **D:** Jerrold Freedman. **REP**

A Family Thing 🎟🎟🎟 **1996 (PG-13)** Racial issues are addressed in this character-driven story of two brothers. Southerner Earl Pilcher (Duvall) learns his biological mother was black and that she died during his birth. In a letter written by the recently deceased woman who raised him, Earl discovers he also has a half brother, Ray (Jones), who is black and living in Chicago. He drives to Chicago, and seeks out Ray, who is not exactly thrilled about the family ties, either. As the two brothers, expertly played by Duvall and Jones, slowly find common ground, Hall steals the show as the irascible Aunt T.**CW:** Some strong language, brief violence and a childbirth scene. **109m/C VHS, LV, Closed Caption.** Robert Duvall, James Earl Jones, Irma P. Hall, Michael Beach, Grace Zabriskie, Regina Taylor, Mary Jackson, Paula Marshall, Jim Harrell; **D:** Richard Pearce; **W:** Billy Bob Thornton, Tom Epperson; **C:** Fred Murphy. **MGM**

Family Upside Down 🎟🎟🎟 **1978** An aging couple fight their separation after the husband has a heart attack and is put into a nursing home. The fine cast received several Emmy nominations, with Astaire the winner. Made-for-television. **100m/C VHS, Beta.** Helen Hayes, Fred Astaire, Efrem Zimbalist Jr., Patty Duke; **D:** David Lowell Rich; **M:** Henry Mancini. **COL**

Family Viewing 🎟🎟🎟 **1987** Surrealistic depiction of a family—obsessed with television and video—whose existence is a textbook model of home sweet dysfunctional home. An early, experimental film from Canada's Egoyan, it won considerable praise for its social commentary. **92m/C VHS, LV.** *CA* David Hemblen, Aidan Tierney, Gabrielle Rose, Arsinee Khanjian; **D:** Atom Egoyan; **W:** Atom Egoyan; **M:** Mychael Danna. Toronto-City Award '87: Best Canadian Feature Film. **FXL, FCT**

Famous Five Get into Trouble 🎟🎟 **1987** Four precocious youngsters and a dog get involved with a criminal plot and cutely wind their way out of it. Scandinavian; dubbed in English. **90m/C VHS, Beta.** Astrid Villaume, Ove Sprogoe, Lily Broberg; **D:** Trine Hedman. **TWE**

The Fan 🎟🎟 **1981 (R)** A Broadway star is threatened and her immediate circle cut down when a lovestruck fan feels he has been rejected by his idol. The stellar cast makes this bloody and familiar tale seem better than it is. **95m/C VHS, Beta, LV.** Lauren Bacall, Maureen Stapleton, James Garner, Hector Elizondo, Michael Biehn, Griffin Dunne; **D:** Edward Bianchi; **W:** Priscilla Chapman; **M:** Pino Donaggio. **PAR**

The Fan 🎟🎟½ **1996 (R)** Obsessed baseball fan Gil Renard (De Niro, who owns the copyright on playing deranged) stalks favorite player Bobby Rayburn (Snipes) who just signed a big contract with the hometown team. When Rayburn goes into a slump, Renard figures he can help his idol—by any means necessary. As an added bonus, Gil's a knife salesman. De Niro does the psycho thing with his usual aplomb, while Snipes successfully returns to the diamond. Scott keeps the familiar storyline from becoming tedious. Based on the book by Peter Abrahams.**CW:** Strong language throughout and some intense violence. **117m/C VHS, LV, 8mm, Closed Caption.** Robert De Niro, Wesley Snipes, Ellen Barkin, John Leguizamo, Benicio Del Toro, Patti D'Arbanville; **D:** Tony Scott; **W:** Phoef Sutton; **C:** Darius Wolski; **M:** Hans Zimmer. Nominations: MTV Movie Awards '97: Best Villain (De Niro). **COL**

Fanci's Persuasion 🎟½ **1995** San Francisco-set gay farce features lesbian Fanci (Patton) 24 hours away from marrying lover Loretta (Boa) and in panic mode. Her parents refuse to come to the ceremony and there are numerous and inexplicable complications to deal with. Deliberately over-the-top performances and contrived dialogue and situations can't really take the strain despite the pic's good looks. **78m/C VHS.** Jessica Patton, Boa, Justin Bond, Robert Coffman, Charles Herman-Wurmfeld; **D:** Charles Herman-Wurmfeld; **W:** Charles Herman-Wurmfeld; **C:** David Rush Morrison. **WBF**

Fancy Pants 🎟🎟½ **1950** Remake of "Ruggles of Red Gap" features Hope, a British actor posing as a butler. Also featuring Ball, an amusing contrast. Fine performances all around. ♫Fancy Pants; Home Cookin'. **92m/C VHS, Beta, LV, Closed Caption.** Bob Hope, Lucille Ball, Bruce Cabot, Jack Kirkwood, Lea Penman, Eric Blore, John Alexander, Norma Varden; **D:** George Marshall; **C:** Charles B(ryant) Lang. **PAR**

Fandango 🎟🎟½ **1985 (PG)** Five college friends take a wild weekend drive across the Texas Badlands for one last fling before graduation and the prospect of military service. Expanded by Reynolds with assistance from Steven Spielberg, from his student film. Provides a look at college and life during the '60s Vietnam crisis. **91m/C VHS, Beta.** Judd Nelson, Kevin Costner, Sam Robards, Chuck Bush, Brian Cesak, Elizabeth Daily, Suzy Amis, Glenne Headly, Pepe Serna, Marvin J. McIntyre; **D:** Kevin Reynolds; **W:** Kevin Reynolds; **M:** Alan Silvestri. **WAR**

Fanfan la Tulipe 🎟🎟🎟 *Fanfan the Tulip; Fearless Little Soldier* **1951** Fanfan (Philipe) escapes an unwanted marriage by joining the army of Louis XV (Herrand), after being promised an illustrious career and a royal marriage. And after many heroics, it all comes true. Amusing satire of swashbucklers and historical romance movies. French with subtitles. **98m/B VHS.** *FR* Gerard Philipe, Gina Lollobrigida, Marcel Herrand, Sylvia Pelayo, Genevieve Page, Noel Roquevort; **D:** Christian-Jaque; **W:** Rene Wheeler, Jean Fallet, Christian-Jaque; **C:** Christian Matras; **M:** Georges Van Parys, Maurice Thiriet. Cannes Film Festival '52: Best Director. **FCT**

Fangs 🎟½ **1975 (R)** Unfriendly reptile-stomping villagers take the life of Mr. Snakey's favorite serpent. He sends his slithering pets on a vengeful and poisonous spree. **90m/C VHS, Beta.** Les Tremayne, Janet Wood, Bebe Kelly, Marvin Kaplan, Alice Nunn; **D:** Vittorio Schiraldi. **GEM, MRV**

Fangs of Fate 🎟½ **1925** A gang of bad guys battles the town's new marshal. **67m/B VHS, Beta, 8mm.** Bill Patton, Dorothy Donald. **GPV, VYY**

Fangs of the Living Dead 🎟½ *Malenka, the Vampire; La Nipote del Vampiro; The Niece of the Vampire; The Vampire's Niece* **1968** When a young woman inherits a castle, her uncle, who happens to be a vampire, tries to persuade her to remain among the undead. **80m/C VHS.** *SP IT* Anita Ekberg, Rossana Yanni, Diana Lorys, Fernando Bilbao, Paul Muller, Julian Ugarte, Adriana Ambesi; **D:** Armando de Ossorio; **W:** Armando de Ossorio. **SNC**

Fangs of the Wild 🎟🎟 *Follow the Hunter* **1954** When a young boy witnesses a murder at his father's hunting lodge, no one but the killer believes him. When the killer decides to get rid of the boy, Buck the Wonder Dog gets involved. **72m/B VHS.** Charles Chaplin Jr., Onslow Stevens, Margia Dean, Freddy Ridgeway, Phil Tead, Robert Stevenson; **D:** William Claxton. **NOS, DVT, HEG**

Fanny 🎟🎟🎟 **1932** Second part of Marcel Pagnol's trilogy depicting the lives of the people of Provence, France. The poignant tale of Fanny, a young woman who marries an older man when Marius, her young lover, leaves her pregnant when he goes to sea. Remade several times but the original holds its own very well. "Marius" was first in the trilogy; "Cesar" was third. **128m/B VHS, Beta, LV.** *FR* Raimu, Charpin, Orane Demazis, Pierre Fresnay, Alida Rauffe; **D:** Marc Allegret; **W:** Marcel Pagnol; **C:** Vincent Scotto. **INT, MRV, HHT**

Fanny 🎟🎟🎟 **1961** Young girl falls in love with an adventurous sailor, and finds herself pregnant after he returns to the sea. With the help of the sailor's parents, she finds, marries, and eventually grows to love a much older man, who in turn cares for her and adores her son as if he were his own. When the sailor returns, all involved must confront their pasts and define their futures. Beautifully made, with fine performances and a plot which defies age or nationality. Part of the "A Night at the Movies" series, this tape simulates a 1961 movie evening, with a Tweety Pie cartoon, a newsreel and coming attractions for "Splendor in the Grass" and "The Roman Spring of Mrs. Stone." **148m/C VHS, Beta.** *FR* Leslie Caron, Maurice Chevalier, Charles Boyer, Horst Buchholz, Lionel Jeffries; **D:** Joshua Logan; **W:** Julius J. Epstein, Philip C. Epstein; **C:** Jack Cardiff. National Board of Review Awards '61: 10 Best Films of the Year; Nominations: Academy Awards '61: Best Actor (Boyer), Best Color Cinematography, Best Film Editing, Best Picture, Original Dramatic/Comedy Score. **NOS, WAR**

Fanny and Alexander 🎟🎟🎟🎟 *Fanny Och Alexander* **1983 (R)** The culmination of Bergman's career, this autobiographical film is set in a rural Swedish town in 1907. It tells the story of one year in the lives of the Ekdahl family, as seen by the young children, Fanny and Alexander. Magic and religion, love and death, reconciliation and estrangement are skillfully captured in this carefully detailed, lovingly photographed film. In Swedish with English subtitles or dubbed. **197m/C VHS, Beta, LV, Closed Caption.** *SW* Pernilla Allwin, Bertil Guve, Gunn Walgren, Allan Edwall, Ewa Froling, Erland Josephson, Harriet Andersson, Jarl Kulle, Jan Malmsjo; **D:** Ingmar Bergman; **W:** Ingmar Bergman; **C:** Sven Nykvist; **M:** Daniel Bell. Academy Awards '83: Best Art Direction/Set Decoration, Best Cinematography, Best Costume Design, Best Foreign Language Film; Cesar Awards '84: Best Foreign Film; Golden Globe Awards '84: Best Foreign Film; Los Angeles Film Critics Association Awards '83: Best Cinematography, Best Foreign Film; New York Film Critics Awards '83: Best Director (Bergman), Best Foreign Film; Nominations: Academy Awards '83: Best Director (Bergman), Best Original Screenplay. **COL, NLC**

Fanny Hill 🎟🎟 **1983 (R)** A softcore adaptation of the racy Victorian classic. **80m/C VHS, Beta.** *GB* Lisa Raines, Shelley Winters, Wilfrid Hyde-White, Oliver Reed. **WAR**

Fanny Hill: Memoirs of a Woman of Pleasure woof! **1964** Sexual exploits of an innocent in bawdy 18th-century London, as directed by notorious "Super Vixen" Meyer (though by Meyer standards, proceedings are fairly innocuous, if inept). Based on the novel. **105m/B VHS, Beta.** Miriam Hopkins, Walter Giller, Alexander D'Arcy, Leticia Roman; **D:** Russ Meyer. **NO**

Fantasia 🎟🎟🎟🎟 **1940** Disney's most personal animation feature first bombed at the box office and irked purists who couldn't take the plotless, experimental mix of classical music and cartoons. It became a cult movie, embraced by more liberal generations of moviegoers. Reissue of the original version, painstakingly restored, ceased because of a planned remake. ♫Toccata & Fugue in D; The Nutcracker Suite; The Sorcerer's Apprentice; The Rite of Spring; Pastoral Symphony; Dance of the Hours; Night on Bald Mountain; Ave Maria; The Cossack Dance. **116m/C VHS, LV, Closed Caption.** **DIS, FCT, RDG**

Fantasies woof! *And Once Upon a Love* **1973 (R)** Teenage lovers Derek and Hooten return to their Greek island home and decide to improve their village by turning it into a tourist haven. First collaboration of the Dereks is a loser, lacking plot, direction, and decent acting. Bo shows no talent but the obvious one and is actually credited as Kathleen Collins. **81m/C VHS, Beta.** Bo Derek, Peter Hooten, Anna Alexiades; **D:** John Derek. **FOX**

The Fantasist 🎟 **1989 (R)** Sex crime thriller features a deranged killer who makes obscene, yet seductive phone calls to young ladies before murdering them. **98m/C VHS.** Timothy Bottoms, Christopher Cazenove; **D:** Robin Hardy. **REP**

Fantastic Balloon Voyage 🎟 **198? (G)** Three men embark on a journey across the equator in a balloon, experiencing myriad adventures along the way. Much hot air. **100m/C VHS, Beta.** Hugo Stiglitz, Jeff Cooper. **GEM**

Fantastic Planet ✔✔✔ *La Planete Sauvage* **1973 (PG)** A critically acclaimed French, animated, sci-fi epic based on the drawings of Roland Topor. A race of small humanoids are enslaved and exploited by a race of giants on a savage planet, until one of the small creatures manages to unite his people and fight for equality. **68m/C VHS, Beta.** *FR D:* Rene Laloux; *W:* Rene Laloux; *V:* Barry Bostwick. *VYY, MRV, SNC*

Fantastic Seven ✔½ **1982** The Fantastic Seven is a daredevil team sent to rescue a Hollywood sex symbol who has been kidnapped and held for ransom while shooting on location off the coast of Miami. **96m/C VHS, Beta.** Elke Sommer, Christopher Connelly. *TLF*

Fantastic Voyage ✔✔✔ *Microscopia; Strange Journey* **1966** An important scientist, rescued from behind the Iron Curtain, is so severely wounded by enemy agents that traditional surgery is impossible. After being shrunk to microscopic size, a medical team journeys inside his body where they find themselves threatened by the patient's natural defenses. Great action, award-winning special effects. **100m/C VHS, Beta, LV.** Stephen Boyd, Edmond O'Brien, Raquel Welch, Arthur Kennedy, Donald Pleasence, Arthur O'Connell, William Redfield, James Brolin; *D:* Richard Fleischer; *C:* Ernest Laszlo. Academy Awards '66: Best Art Direction/Set Decoration (Color), Best Visual Effects; Nominations: Academy Awards '66: Best Color Cinematography, Best Film Editing. *FOX, CCB*

The Fantastic World of D.C. Collins ✔✔ **1984** Gary Coleman plays a daydreaming teenager who thinks he is being pursued by mysterious strangers seeking a videotape that was unknowingly slipped to him. Made for television. **100m/C VHS.** Gary Coleman, Bernie Casey, Shelley Smith, Fred Dryer, Marilyn McCoo, Philip Abbott, George Gobel, Michael Ansara; *D:* Leslie Martinson. *VTR, NWV*

Fantasy Island ✔ **1976** Three people fly ("De plane, boss!") to an island paradise and get to live out their fantasies for a price. Made for television; the basis for the TV series. **100m/C VHS, Beta.** Ricardo Montalban, Bill Bixby, Sandra Dee, Peter Lawford, Carol Lynley, Hugh O'Brian, Eleanor Parker, Dick Sargent, Victoria Principal; *D:* Richard Lang. *PSM*

Fantasy Man ✔½ **1984** A restless middle-aged man tries to relieve his mid-life crisis with the help of three women. **100m/C VHS, Beta.** *AU* Harold Hopkins, Jeanie Drynan, Kerry Mack, Kate Fitzpatrick; *D:* John Meagher; *W:* John Meagher. *VCD*

Far and Away ✔✔½ **1992 (PG-13)** Meandering old-fashioned epic about immigrants, romance, and settling the American West. In the 1890s, Joseph Donelly (Cruise) is forced to flee his Irish homeland after threatening the life of his landlord, and emigrates to America in the company of the landlord's daughter, feisty Shannon Christie (Kidman). Particularly brutal scenes of Cruise earning his living as a bare-knuckled boxer contrast with the expansiveness of the land rush ending. Slow, spotty, and a little too slick for its own good, though real-life couple Cruise and Kidman are an attractive pair. Filmed in 70-mm Panavision on location in Ireland and Montana. Also available in a letter boxed version. **140m/C VHS, Beta, LV, Closed Caption.** Tom Cruise, Nicole Kidman, Thomas Gibson, Robert Prosky, Barbara Babcock, Colm Meaney, Eileen Pollock, Michelle Johnson, Cyril Cusack, Clint Howard, Rance Howard; *D:* Ron Howard; *W:* Bob Dolman; *C:* Mikael Salomon; *M:* John Williams. *USH*

Far Away and Long Ago ✔✔½ **1974** Based on the autobiographical novel by Guillermo Hudson which details the memories which haunted his childhood—the Argentinian pampas, its gauchos, witchcraft, and women. In Spanish with English subtitles. **91m/C VHS.** *AR* Juan Jose Camero, Leonor Manso; *D:* Manuel Antin. *FCT*

Far Country ✔✔✔ **1955** Cattlemen must battle the elements and frontier lawlessness in this classic. Stewart leads his herd to the Yukon in hopes of large profits, but ends up having to kidnap it back from the crooked sheriff and avenging the deaths of his friends. Entertaining and the Yukon setting takes it out of the usual Western arena. **97m/C VHS, Beta.** James Stewart, Ruth Roman, Walter Brennan, Harry (Henry) Morgan, Corinne Calvet, Jay C. Flippen, John McIntire; *D:* Anthony Mann; *C:* William H. Daniels; *M:* Henry Mancini. *BAR*

Far Cry from Home ✔ **197?** A battered wife attempts to escape from her domineering husband before it's too late. **87m/C VHS, Beta.** Mary Ann McDonald, Richard Monette. *TWE*

Far East ✔½ **1985** Two ex-lovers meet in Southeast Asia and join forces to find the woman's missing husband, a reporter. **105m/C VHS, Beta.** Bryan Brown, Helen Morse; *D:* John Duigan. *ORI, VTR*

Far from Home ✔✔ **1989 (R)** Drew Barrymore is the seductive teen being scoped by a psychotic killer while on vacation with her father. Lots of over-the-top performances by the familiar cast. **86m/C VHS, LV.** Matt Frewer, Drew Barrymore, Richard Masur, Karen Austin, Susan Tyrrell, Anthony Rapp, Jennifer Tilly, Andras Jones, Dick Miller; *D:* Meiert Avis; *C:* Paul Elliott; *M:* Jonathan Elias. *LIV, VES*

Far from Home: The Adventures of Yellow Dog ✔✔ **1994 (PG)** Stalwart lad Angus (Bradford) and his faithful pooch Yellow (Dakotah) battle the elements, wild animals and fatigue as they try to get back home after being shipwrecked on a remote island in British Columbia. Good thing Dad (Davidson) gave them all those cool survival tips before they left, or else they never would've known that you can eat bugs. (Okay, the dog probably knew that already.) Mom (Rogers) does her bit by making sure the search mission stays focused. You usually can't go wrong with a kid and his dog lost in the wilderness, but this one is really short—on time and drama. Nice scenery, though. **81m/C VHS, LV, Closed Caption.** Jesse Bradford, Bruce Davison, Mimi Rogers, Tom Bower; *D:* Phillip Borsos; *W:* Phillip Borsos. *FXV*

Far from the Madding Crowd ✔✔✔ **1967 (PG)** A lavish, long adaptation of Thomas Hardy's nineteenth century classic about the beautiful Bathsheba and the three very different men who love her. Her first love is a handsome and wayward soldier (Stamp), her second the local noble lord (Finch) and her third the ever-loving and long-patient farmer (Bates). Christie is well cast as the much-desired beauty. Gorgeous cinematography by Nicolas Roeg. **165m/C VHS, Beta, LV.** *GB* Julie Christie, Terence Stamp, Peter Finch, Alan Bates, Prunella Ransome; *D:* John Schlesinger; *W:* Frederic Raphael; *M:* Richard Rodney Bennett. National Board of Review Awards '67: 10 Best Films of the Year, Best Actor (Finch); Nominations: Academy Awards '67: Best Original Score. *MGM*

Far Frontier ✔✔ **1948** Roy Rogers saves the day by thwarting a band of outlaws who are being smuggled across the border in soybean oil cans. Includes magical numbers and horse tricks. **60m/B VHS.** Roy Rogers, Andy Devine, Clayton Moore. *NOS, TIM, REP*

Far North ✔✔½ **1988 (PG-13)** Quirky comedy about a woman who returns to her rural family homestead after her father is seriously injured by a horse, and tries to deal with her eccentric family's travails. Fine cast never reaches its potential. Shepard's directing debut. **96m/C VHS, Beta, LV, 8mm, Closed Caption.** Jessica Lange, Charles Durning, Tess Harper, Donald Moffat, Ann Wedgeworth, Patricia Arquette, Nina Draxton; *D:* Sam Shepard; *W:* Sam Shepard; *C:* Robbie Greenberg. *NLC*

A Far Off Place ✔✔ **1993 (PG-13)** Adolescent boy, adolescent girl, adolescent bushperson, and mature dog set out across the African desert to escape elephant poachers who want to kill them. The boy and girl find romance in the sand, bushperson finds water by listening, and dog gets very nice walk. Strong performances by the youthful leads lend charm to this Disney/Amblin flick, particularly Bok as the bushperson. Unusually violent film for studios involved (animals and people bite sand), though care is taken to edit actual blood shed on screen. Filmed in Zimbabwe and Namibia and based on the books "A Story Like the Wind" and "A Far Off Place" by Laurens van der Post. **CW:** Mild language and violence. **107m/C VHS, Beta, LV, Closed Caption.** Reese Witherspoon, Ethan Randall, Sarel Bok, Jack Thompson, Maximilian Schell, Robert John Burke, Patricia Kalember, Daniel Gerroll, Miles Anderson; *D:* Mikael Salomon; *W:* Robert Caswell, Jonathan Hensleigh, Sally Robinson; *C:* Juan Ruiz-Anchia; *M:* James Horner. *DIS*

Far Out Man woof! **1989 (R)** An unalterable middle-aged hippie is sent by his worried family and his psychiatrist on a cross-country journey to rediscover himself. The script makes no sense and has very few laughs. **105m/C VHS, Beta, LV.** Thomas Chong, Rae Dawn Chong, C. Thomas Howell, Shelby Chong, Martin Mull, Paris Chong, Paul Bartel, Judd Nelson, Michael Winslow, Richard "Cheech" Marin; *D:* Thomas Chong; *W:* Thomas Chong. *COL*

The Far Pavilions ✔✔½ *Blade of Steel* **1984** A British officer falls in love with an Indian princess during the second Afghan War. Cross is appropriately noble and stiff-upper-lipped but Irving is miscast as his mistress. Based on the romantic bestseller by M.M. Kaye, this lavish production was made for cable television. **108m/C VHS, Beta.** Ben Cross, Amy Irving, Omar Sharif, Benedict Taylor, Rossano Brazzi, Christopher Lee; *D:* Peter Duffell; *C:* Jack Cardiff; *M:* Carl Davis. *KAR*

Faraway, So Close! ✔✔ *In Weiter Ferne, So Nah!* **1993 (PG-13)** Wenders' erratic follow-up to his magnificent "Wings of Desire." Cassiel (Sander), the angel left behind when Damiel (Ganz) chose to become human, once again surveys Berlin, noticing the changes (not necessarily for the better). Angelic companion Raphaela (Kinski) watches events passively, including an old man's (Ruahmnn) reflections on life and the philosophical musings of Emit Flesti (Dafoe, Time Itself, get it?), even as Cassiel impulsively chooses humanity over his heavenly world. Falk makes a return appearance to little effect. Overlong and underdeveloped. **CW:** Language. **146m/C VHS, LV, Closed Caption.** *GE* Otto Sander, Peter Falk, Horst Buchholz, Nastassia Kinski, Heinz Ruhmann, Bruno Ganz, Solveig Dommartin, Ruediger Vogler, Willem Dafoe, Lou Reed; *D:* Wim Wenders; *W:* Ulrich Zieger, Richard Reitinger, Wim Wenders; *M:* Laurent Petitgrand. Cannes Film Festival '93: Grand Jury Prize; Nominations: Golden Globe Awards '94: Best Song ("Stay"). *COL*

Farewell My Concubine ✔✔ *Bawang Bie Ji* **1993 (R)** Exotic film covers 50 years of sexual, social, and political Chinese history wrapped around the story of two male Peking Opera stars. Deposited as boys at the Opera's training school Douzi and Shitou become fast friends in their hermetically sealed world, but their friendship is tested during the chaos of Communism and the cultural revolution. Sumptuous and well-acted, but the sheer length and emotional detachment prove to be drawbacks. Adapted from a novel by Lee, who based the work on a 2000-year-old Chinese opera about an imperial concubine. Filmed on location in Beijing. In Mandarin Chinese with subtitles. **CW:** Language/strong thematic material. **157m/C VHS, LV.** *HK* Leslie Cheung, Zhang Fengyi, Gong Li, Lu Qi, Ying Da, Ge You; *D:* Chen Kaige; *W:* Lilian Lee, Lu Wei; *C:* Gu Changwei; *M:* Zhao Jiping. British Academy Awards '93: Best Foreign Film; Cannes Film Festival '93: Best Film; Golden Globe Awards '94: Best Foreign Film; Los Angeles Film Critics Association Awards '93: Best Foreign Film; National Board of Review Awards '93: Best Foreign Film; New York Film Critics Awards '93: Best Foreign Film, Best Supporting Actress (Li); Nominations: Academy Awards '93: Best Cinematography, Best Foreign Language Film. *TOU*

Farewell, My Lovely ✔✔✔ **1975 (R)** A remake of the 1944 Raymond Chandler mystery, "Murder, My Sweet," featuring private eye Phillip Marlowe hunting for an ex-convict's lost sweetheart in 1941 Los Angeles. Perhaps the most accurate of Chandler adaptations, but far from the best, this film offers a nicely detailed production. Mitchum is a bit too world-weary as the seen-it-all detective. **95m/C VHS, Beta.** *GB* Robert Mitchum, Charlotte Rampling, Sylvia Miles, John Ireland, Anthony Zerbe, Jack O'Halloran, Harry Dean Stanton, Sylvester Stallone, Cheryl "Rainbeaux" Smith; *D:* Dick Richards; *W:* David Zelag Goodman; *C:* John A. Alonzo; *M:* David Shire. National Board of Review Awards '75: 10 Best Films of the Year; Nominations: Academy Awards '75: Best Supporting Actress (Miles).

A Farewell to Arms 🐾🐾🐾 1932 The original film version of Ernest Hemingway's novel about the tragic love affair between an American ambulance driver and an English nurse during the Italian campaign of WWI. The novelist disavowed the ambiguous ending, but the public loved the film. Fine performances and cinematography. **85m/B VHS, Beta, LV.** Helen Hayes, Gary Cooper, Adolphe Menjou, Mary Philips, Jack LaRue, Blanche Frederici; *D:* Frank Borzage; *C:* Charles B(ryant) Lang. Academy Awards '33: Best Cinematography, Best Sound; National Board of Review Awards '32: 10 Best Films of the Year; Nominations: Academy Awards '33: Best Interior Decoration, Best Picture. *CNG, MRV, NOS*

Farewell to the King 🐾🐾½ 1989 (PG-13) During WWII, a ship-wrecked American deserter becomes the chief of a tribe of Borneo headhunters until his jungle kingdom is caught between the forces of the U.S. and Japanese. With the help of a British officer he helps them defend themselves when the Japanese invade. An old-fashioned war epic with a beautiful location and solid if uninspired-performances by the leads. Based on Pierre Schoendoerffer's novel "L'Adieu Au Roi." **114m/C VHS, Beta, LV, Closed Caption.** Nick Nolte, Nigel Havers, Marius Weyers, Frank McRae, Marilyn Tokuda, Elan Oberon, William Wise, James Fox, Aki Aleong; *D:* John Milius; *W:* John Milius; *C:* Dean Semler; *M:* Basil Poledouris. *ORI*

Fargo 🐾🐾🐾 1996 (R) Another malicious, extra-dark comedy from the Coen brothers. Car salesman Jerry Lundegaard (Macy) hires a couple of losers to kidnap his wife so he can swindle the ransom money out of his father-in-law. Naturally, the scheme begins to unravel and the very pregnant police chief Marge Gunderson (McDormand) treks through the frozen tundra of Minnesota to put the pieces of the puzzle together. McDormand's performance as the chatty competent chief is first rate. Needling the flat-accented Midwesterners of their youth, the Coens have also returned to their filmmaking roots after the disappointing big-budget "Hudsucker Proxy." Because Minneapolis was having its warmest, driest winter in 100 years, the Coens were forced to shoot most of the exteriors in wintery North Dakota.*CW:* Strong violence, language and sexuality. **97m/C VHS, LV, Closed Caption, DVD.** William H. Macy, Frances McDormand, Steve Buscemi, Peter Stormare, Harve Presnell, Steve Reevis, John Carroll Lynch, Kristin Rudrud, Steve Park; *Cameos:* Jose Feliciano; *D:* Joel Coen; *W:* Ethan Coen, Joel Coen; *C:* Roger Deakins; *M:* Carter Burwell. Academy Awards '96: Best Actress (McDormand), Best Original Screenplay; Australian Film Institute '96: Best Foreign Film; British Academy Awards '96: Best Director (Coen); Cannes Film Festival '96: Best Director (Coen); Independent Spirit Awards '97: Best Actor (Macy), Best Actress (McDormand), Best Cinematography, Best Director (Coen), Best Film, Best Screenplay; National Board of Review Awards '96: Best Actress (McDormand), Best Director (Coen); New York Film Critics Awards '96: Best Film; Screen Actors Guild Award '96: Best Actress (McDormand); Writers Guild of America '96: Best Original Screenplay; Broadcast Film Critics Association Awards '96: Best Actress (McDormand), Best Film; Nominations: Academy Awards '96: Best Cinematography, Best Director (Coen), Best Film Editing, Best Picture, Best Supporting Actor (Macy); British Academy Awards '96: Best Actress (McDormand), Best Film, Best Original Screenplay; Cesar Awards '97: Best Foreign Film; Directors Guild of America Awards '96: Best Director (Coen); Golden Globe Awards '97: Best Actress—Musical/Comedy (McDormand), Best Director (Coen), Best Film—Musical/Comedy, Best Screenplay; MTV Movie Awards '97: Best On-Screen Duo (Peter Stor-

mare/Steve Buscemi); Screen Actors Guild Award '96: Best Supporting Actor (Macy). *PGV*

Fargo Express 🐾½ 1932 When the kid brother of Maynard's true love is falsely accused of robbing a stagecoach, Maynard works to clear his name. Routine stuff. **60m/B VHS, Beta.** Ken Maynard, Helen Mack, Paul Fix; *D:* Alan James. *NOS, VCN, DVT*

Farinelli 🐾🐾 *Farinelli the Castrato; Farinelli Il Castrato* 1994 (R) A movie to make men cringe. Floridly depicts the complex professional and personal ties of 18th-century opera composer Riccardo Broschi (Lo Verso) and his younger brother Carlo (Dionisi), a celebrated castrato singer under the stage name "Farinelli." In part, because of an early church prohibition against women singing in public, boys were castrated before puberty to preserve their pure soprano voices while vocal power and agility grew as they became men. Castrati were the rock stars of their day and Farinelli lived a flamboyant life before retiring to the Spanish court of Philip V. The castrato voice heard in the movie is an electronic mixture of counter-tenor Derek Lee Ragin and soprano Ewa Mallas Godlewska. French and Italian with subtitles.*CW:* Depiction of adult themes and sexuality. **110m/C VHS, LV.** *FR IT BE* Stefano Dionisi, Enrico Lo Verso, Jeroen Krabbe, Elsa Zylberstein, Caroline Cellier, Omero Antonutti, Jacques Boudet; *D:* Gerard Corbiau; *W:* Gerard Corbiau, Andree Corbiau, Marcel Beaulieu; *C:* Walther Vanden Ende; *M:* Christopher Rousset. Cesar Awards '95: Best Art Direction/Set Decoration, Best Sound; Golden Globe Awards '95: Best Foreign Film; Nominations: Academy Awards '94: Best Foreign Language Film. *COL*

Farmer & Chase 🐾🐾 1996 (R) It's always nice to see an old pro like Gazzara but it's a shame it couldn't have been in something less predictable. Farmer's (Gazzara) a hold-up man who's been working with partner Ollie (Jones) for 20 years. But when Ollie's killed, Farmer, who wants to pull one last job before retiring, makes the mistake of teaming up with his pacifist son Chase (Field). And then Chase involves his new gal pal Hillary (Boyle) in on the scheme. Dumb move, dumb movie.*CW:* Violence, a scene of sexuality and pervasive strong language. **97m/C VHS.** Ben Gazzara, Todd Field, Lara Flynn Boyle, Steven Anthony Jones, Ron Kaell, David Booth; *D:* Michael Seitzman; *W:* Michael Seitzman; *C:* Michael Maley; *M:* Tony Saunders. *AVI*

The Farmer Takes a Wife 🐾🐾½ 1935 Henry Fonda's first film, recreating his stage role, as a mid-nineteenth century farmer at odds with the woman he loves. Remade as a musical in 1953. **91m/B VHS.** Janet Gaynor, Henry Fonda, Charles Bickford, Slim Summerville, Jane Withers; *D:* Victor Fleming. *TCF*

The Farmer Takes a Wife 🐾🐾 1953 Poor musical remake of the 1935 drama, about the trials of a struggling 1850s farmer and the Erie canal boat cook he loves. Contains no memorable music and Robertson can't compete with Henry Fonda's original role as the farmer. ♫We're in Business; On the Erie Canal; We're Doing it for the Natives in Jamaica; When I Close My Door; Today I Love Everybody; Somethin' Real Special; With The Sun Warm Upon Me; Can You Spell Schenectady? **81m/C VHS, Beta, LV, Closed Caption.** Betty Grable, Dale Robertson, Thelma Ritter, John Carroll, Eddie Foy Jr.; *D:* Henry Levin. *FOX*

The Farmer's Daughter 🐾🐾🐾 1947 Young portrays Katrin Holmstrom, a Swedish farm girl who becomes a maid to Congressman Cotten and winds up running for office herself (not neglecting to find romance as well). The outspoken and multi-talented character charmed audiences and was the basis of a television series in the 1960s. **97m/B VHS, Beta.** Loretta Young, Joseph Cotten, Ethel Barrymore, Charles Bickford, Harry Davenport, Lex Barker, James Arness, Rose Hobart; *D:* H.C. Potter; *C:* Milton Krasner. Academy Awards '47: Best Actress

(Young); Nominations: Academy Awards '47: Best Supporting Actor (Bickford). *FOX, BTV*

The Farmer's Other Daughter 🐾🐾 *Farm Girl* 1965 A rural comedy about Farmer Brown whose lovely daughter is eyed by all the farmhands. He also has to contend with dastardly Mr. Barksnapper who wants to take his farm away from him until one of his daughter's beaus comes to the rescue. **84m/C VHS.** Ernest Ashworth, Judy Pennebaker, Bill Michael; *D:* John Patrick Hayes. *COL*

The Farmer's Wife 🐾🐾½ 1928 Silent British comedy about a recently widowed farmer searching for a new wife. Meanwhile, his lovely housekeeper would be the perfect candidate. Based on Eden Philpott's play. **97m/B VHS.** *GB* Jameson Thomas, Lillian Hall-Davis, Gordon Harker; *D:* Alfred Hitchcock; *W:* Alfred Hitchcock. *REP, SNC, MLB*

Fashions of 1934 🐾🐾 *Fashions* 1934 A typical, lightweight thirties musical with impressive choreography by Busby Berkeley. Powell plays a disreputable clothing designer who goes to Paris to steal the latest fashion designs and winds up costuming a musical and falls in love. ♫Spin a Little Web of Dreams; Broken Melody. **78m/B VHS, Beta.** Bette Davis, William Powell, Frank McHugh, Hugh Herbert, Reginald Owen, Busby Berkeley; *D:* William Dieterle. *VDM*

Fass Black 🐾🐾 1977 (R) Yet another man against the mob flick straight out of Bartlett's familiar plot lines. Amidst gratuitous music and violence, a disco owner locks horns with the syndicate after they try to take over his place. There's a good reason disco is dead. **105m/C VHS.** John Poole, Jeanne Bell, Cal Wilson, Harold Nicholas, Nicholas Lewis; *D:* D'Urville Martin. *XVC*

The Fast and the Furious 🐾🐾 1954 On the lam after being falsely charged with murder, Ireland picks up a fast car and a loose woman (or is it a loose car and a fast woman?) and makes a run for the border by entering the Pebble Beach race. **73m/B VHS.** John Ireland, Dorothy Malone, Bruce Carlisle, Iris Adrian; *D:* John Ireland, Edwards Sampson. *NOS*

Fast Break 🐾½ 1979 (PG) New York deli clerk who is a compulsive basketball fan talks his way into a college coaching job. He takes a team of street players with him, with predictable results on and off the court. Kaplan's screen debut. **107m/C VHS, Beta.** Gabe Kaplan, Harold Sylvester, Randee Heller; *D:* Jack Smight; *M:* David Shire. *GKK*

Fast Bullets 🐾½ 1944 Texas Rangers fight a gang of smugglers and rescue a kidnap victim in this typical western. **52m/B VHS, Beta.** Tom Tyler, Rex Lease. *NOS, VCN, DVT*

Fast Company 🐾🐾 1978 The life story of champion race car driver Lonnie Johnson including women, money, and the drag racing sponsors. **90m/C VHS, Beta.** William Smith, John Saxon, Claudia Jennings, Nicholas Campbell, Don Francks; *D:* David Cronenberg; *W:* David Cronenberg. *AOV*

Fast Food 🐾 1989 A super-cheap, strangulated attempt at low comedy, wherein an entrepreneurial hamburger peddler invents a secret aphrodisiac sauce. Look for former porn-star Traci Lords. **90m/C VHS, Beta, LV.** Clark Brandon, Tracy Griffith, Randal Patrick, Traci Lords, Kevin McCarthy, Michael J. Pollard, Jim Varney; *D:* Michael A. Simpson; *W:* Clark Brandon. *FRH*

Fast Forward 🐾½ 1984 (PG) A group of eight teenagers from Ohio learn how to deal with success and failure when they enter a national dance contest in New York City. A break-dancing variation on the old show business chestnut. ♫Fast Forward; How Do You Do; As Long As We Believe; Pretty Girl; Mystery; Curves; Showdown; Do You Want It Right Now?; Hardrock. **110m/C VHS, Beta, LV, Closed Caption.** John Scott Clough, Don Franklin, Tracy Silver, Cindy McGee; *D:* Sidney Poitier; *W:* Richard Wesley; *M:* Tom Bahler. *COL*

Fast Getaway *dd* 1991 (PG) Chases scenes proliferate when a teen criminal mastermind plots bank heists for his outlaw father. Relatively painless adolescent action-comedy, cleverly acted, quickly forgotten. 91m/C VHS, LV, 8mm. Corey Haim, Cynthia Rothrock, Leo Rossi, Ken Lerner, Marcia Strassman; *D:* Spiro Razatos. COL

Fast Getaway 2 *dd½* 1994 (PG-13) Ex-bank robber Nelson (Haim) has given up a life of crime to open a business with gal pal Patrice (Buxton) while waiting for his partner/dad Sam (Rossi) to get out of jail. Then Nelson gets set up by Lily (Rothrock) and finds himself trying to convince an FBI agent of his innocence. Innocuous. 90m/C VHS. Corey Haim, Sarah Buxton, Leo Rossi, Cynthia Rothrock, Peter Paul Liapis; *D:* Oley Sassone; *W:* Mark Sevi; *M:* David Robbins. LIV

Fast Gun *d½* 1993 (R) Weapons-loving ex-CIA spook decides to take over a town—with your basic one lone hero to stop him. 90m/C VHS. Richard Hill, Kaz Garas, Robert Dryer, Brenda Bakke, Cirio H. Santiago. NHO

Fast Kill *d* 1973 A terrorist plot begins to fall apart when the conspirators fight among themselves. 94m/C VHS. Tom Adams, Susie Hampton, Michael Culver, Peter Halliday; *D:* Lindsay Shonteff. GEM

Fast Money *d½* 1983 Three pals can't resist the temptation of big bucks from flying drugs in from Mexico, but they find danger along the way. 92m/C VHS, Beta. Sammy Allred, Sonny Carl Davis; *D:* Doug Holloway. LIV

Fast Money *d* 1996 (R) Car thief Francesca Marsh (Butler) and journalist Jack Martin (McCoy) go on the lam from the mob (and everyone else) with a briefcase containing $2.7 million. *CW:* Violence and language. 93m/C VHS. Yancy Butler, Matt McCoy, John Ashton, Trevor Goddard, Andy Romano, Carole Cook, Patrika Darbo; *D:* Alexander Wright; *W:* Alexander Wright; *C:* Thomas Jewett. ORI

Fast Talking *dd* 1986 The story of a quick-talking, incorrigible, fifteen-year-old Australian boy's humorous though tragic criminal schemes. The young protagonist slides his way through a life marked by a degenerate home life, a brother who forces him to sell drugs, and a future that holds no promise. 93m/C VHS, Beta. AU Steve Bisley, Tracey Mann, Peter Hehir, Dennis Moore, Rod Zuanic, Toni Allaylis, Chris Truswell; *D:* Ken Cameron; *W:* Ken Cameron. NLC

Fast Times at Ridgemont High *ddd* 1982 (R) Teens at a Southern California high school revel in sex, drugs, and rock 'n' roll. A full complement of student types meet at the Mall—that great suburban microcosm percolating with angst-ridden teen trials—to contemplate losing their virginity, plot skipping homeroom, and move inexorably closer to the end of their adolescence. The talented young cast became household names: Sean Penn is most excellent as the California surfer dude who antagonizes teacher, Walston, aka "Aloha Mr. Hand." Based on the best-selling book by Cameron Crowe, it's one of the best of this genre. 91m/C VHS, Beta, LV. Sean Penn, Jennifer Jason Leigh, Judge Reinhold, Robert Romanus, Brian Backer, Phoebe Cates, Ray Walston, Scott Thomson, Vincent Schiavelli, Amanda Wyss, Forest Whitaker, Kelli Maroney, Eric Stoltz, Pamela Springsteen, James Russo, Martin Brest, Anthony Edwards; *D:* Amy Heckerling; *W:* Cameron Crowe. USH

Fast Walking *dd* 1982 (R) A prison guard is offered fifty-thousand dollars to help a militant black leader escape from jail, the same man his cousin has contracted to kill. 116m/C VHS, Beta. James Woods, Kay Lenz, M. Emmet Walsh, Robert Hooks, Tim McIntire, Timothy Carey, Susan Tyrrell; *D:* James B. Harris. FOX, HHE

Faster Pussycat! Kill! Kill! *dd* 1966 It doesn't get any better than this! Three sexy go-go dancers get their after-work kicks by hot-rodding in the California desert. They soon find themselves enveloped in murder, kidnapping, lust and robbery after a particular race gets out of hand.

Easily the most watchable, fun and funny production to spring from the mind of Russ Meyer. Those who haven't seen this cannot truly be called "cool." 83m/B VHS. Tura Satana, Haji, Lori Williams, Susan Bernard, Stuart Lancaster, Paul Trinka, Dennis Busch, Ray Barlow, Mickey Foxx; *D:* Russ Meyer; *W:* Jack Moran, Russ Meyer. RMF, FCT, TPV

Fastest Guitar Alive *d½* 1968 Debut of the legendary Orbison is strictly for inveterate fans only. Rebel operative/crooner during the Civil War, whose rhythm is good but timing is bad, steals a Union gold supply, but the war ends before he makes it back to the land of Dixie. Seems that makes him a common thief. 88m/C VHS, Beta. Roy Orbison, Sammy Jackson, Margaret Pierce, Joan Freeman; *D:* Michael Moore; *M:* Fred Karger. MGM, MVD

Fastest Gun Alive *ddd* 1956 Suspenseful western with ex-gunfighter Ford challenged to a showdown by Crawford. 89m/C VHS, Closed Caption. Glenn Ford, Jeanne Crain, Broderick Crawford, Russ Tamblyn, Allyn Joslyn, Leif Erickson, John Dehner, Noah Beery Jr., J.M. Kerrigan, Rhys Williams; *D:* Russel Rouse; *W:* Russel Rouse, Frank D. Gilroy; *M:* Andre Previn. MGM

Fat and the Lean *ddd* 1961 An early short film from Roman Polanski that satirizes government tyranny and absurdity. 16m/C VHS, Beta. *D:* Roman Polanski. IHF, FLI, GVV

Fat City *ddd½* 1972 (PG) One of Huston's later triumphs, a seedy, street-level drama based on the Leonard Gardner novel about an aging alcoholic boxer trying to make a comeback and his young worshipful protege. Highly acclaimed. Tyrrell earned an Oscar nomination as the boxer's world-weary lover. 93m/C VHS, Beta. Stacy Keach, Jeff Bridges, Susan Tyrrell, Candy Clark, Nicholas Colasanto; *D:* John Huston; *C:* Conrad Hall; *M:* Marvin Hamlisch. Nominations: Academy Awards '72: Best Supporting Actress (Tyrrell). COL

Fat Guy Goes Nutzoid woof! Zeisters 1986 A crude farce about an obese mental patient who escapes from the mental hospital and joins two teenagers on a wild trip to New York City. 85m/C VHS, Beta. Tibor Feldman, Peter Linari, John MacKay, Joan Allen; *D:* John Golden. TTV, PSM

Fat Man and Little Boy *dd½* 1989 (PG-13) A lavish, semi-fictional account of the creation of the first atomic bomb, and the tensions between J. Robert Oppenheimer and his military employer, Gen. Leslie Groves. Overlong but interesting. Cusack, whose character never existed, is especially worthwhile as an idealistic scientist. 127m/C VHS, Beta, LV, 8mm, Closed Caption. Paul Newman, Dwight Schultz, Bonnie Bedelia, John Cusack, Laura Dern, John C. McGinley, Natasha Richardson, Ron Frazier; *D:* Roland Joffe; *W:* Bruce Robinson, Tony Garnett, Roland Joffe; *M:* Ennio Morricone. PAR, FCT, HMV

Fatal Attraction *dd* Head On 1980 (R) Couple meet after an auto accident. They begin an affair which turns dark and bizarre. Fine cast doesn't get far with this peculiar premise, although every one tries hard. 90m/C VHS, Beta. CA Sally Kellerman, Stephen Lack, John Huston, Lawrence Dane; *D:* Michael Grant. VES

Fatal Attraction *ddd* 1987 (R) When a very married New York lawyer is seduced by a beautiful blonde associate, the one-night stand leads to terror as she continues to pursue the relationship. She begins to threaten his family and home with possessive, violent acts. An expertly made, manipulative thriller; one of the most hotly discussed films of the 1980s. A successful change of role for Close as the sexy, scorned, and deadly other woman. Also available in a special "director's series" edition, featuring Lyne's original, controversial ending. 120m/C VHS, Beta, LV, 8mm, Closed Caption. Michael Douglas, Glenn Close, Anne Archer, Stuart Pankin, Ellen Hamilton-Latzen, Ellen Foley, Fred Gwynne, Meg Mundy, J.J. Johnston; *D:* Adrian Lyne; *W:* James Dearden; *C:* Howard Atherton; *M:* Maurice Jarre. People's Choice Awards '88: Best Film—Drama; Nominations: Academy Awards '87: Best Actress (Close), Best Adapted Screenplay, Best Director (Lyne), Best Film

Editing, Best Picture, Best Supporting Actress (Archer). PAR, FCT, CCB

Fatal Beauty *dd½* 1987 (R) A female undercover cop in Los Angeles tracks down a drug dealer selling cocaine (from which the title is taken). Elliott is the mob bodyguard who helps her out. Violent and sensational, the film tries to capitalize on the success of "Beverly Hills Cop" and fails miserably. Goldberg is wasted in this effort and the picture tiptoes around the interracial romance aspects that are implied. 104m/C VHS, Beta, LV, Closed Caption. Whoopi Goldberg, Sam Elliott, Ruben Blades, Harris Yulin, Richard "Cheech" Marin, Brad Dourif; *D:* Tom Holland; *M:* Harold Faltermeyer. MGM

Fatal Bond *d½* 1991 (R) Blair plays a small-town hairdresser caught in an obsessive love affair with a drifter. When she suspects her boyfriend is committing a string of rape-murders, will she turn him in or protect him? Or is she next? *CW:* Language, violence, and sexuality. 89m/C VHS. Linda Blair, Jerome Elhers, Stephen Leeder, Donal Gibson, Caz Lederman, Tao Gerbert, Penny Pederson, Joe Bugner; *D:* Vincent Monton; *W:* Phillip Avalon. COL

Fatal Charm *dd* 1992 (R) There's a serial killer at work in a small town. So far six women have been raped and murdered. But cute-teen Valerie can't believe it when the townspeople accuse that sweet guy Adam, especially since he's the one boy Valerie is so very attracted to. *CW:* Violence and sexuality. 90m/C VHS, Closed Caption. Christopher Atkins, Amanda Peterson, Mary Frann, James Remar, Andrew (Andy) Robinson, Peggy Lipton; *D:* Alan Smithee; *W:* Nicholas Niciphor. ACA

Fatal Chase *dd* Nowhere to Hide 1977 Van Cleef is a U.S. Marshal assigned to protect ex-hitman Musante from his vengeful former employers. And you thought you didn't get along with your boss. Typical made-for-TV fodder written by Anhalt, who usually manages to be a trifle more entertaining. 78m/C VHS. Lee Van Cleef, Tony Musante, Charles Robinson, Lelia Goldoni, Noel Fournier, Russell Johnson, Edward Anhalt; *D:* Jack Starrett; *W:* Edward Anhalt. SIM

Fatal Combat *d½* 1996 (R) Reclusive billionaire Houston Armstrong (Fitzpatrick) privately broadcasts a program called "No Exit" that features combat-to-the-death. (Live on TV!) But Armstrong tends to run out of combatants so when he hears about John Stoneman (Wincott), a master martial artist, he has his minions kidnap him along with Stoneman's pupil, Jason (Demambro). Now, it's fight or die. 93m/C VHS, Closed Caption. Jeff Wincott, Richard Fitzpatrick, Joe Demambro, Sven-Ole Thorsen; *D:* Damian Lee; *W:* Damian Lee, John Howard Lawson. COL

Fatal Confinement *dd½* 1964 Wrenching drama finds Crawford, having lived 15 years in seclusion with her young daughter, forced to sell her land to a giant corporation bent on expansion. Interesting also for the similarities to Crawford's real-life "Mommie Dearest" lifestyle. 70m/C VHS. GB Joan Crawford, Paul Burke, Charles Bickford; *D:* Robert Guest. FCT, MOV, TPV

Fatal Error *d½* Outsider in Amsterdam; The Outsider; Grijpstra and de Gier 1983 Dutch police thriller about the investigation of a cop killing. Based on the mystery series by Janwillem van de Wetering. Dubbed. 85m/C VHS, Beta. NL Rutger Hauer, Rijk de Gooyer, Willeke Van Ammelrooy, Donald M. Jones; *D:* Wim Verstappen; *M:* Ennio Morricone. NO

Fatal Exposure *dd* 1990 The insatiably sanguinary Jack the Ripper lives on in the form of his great grandson, who avails himself of modern technology to capture those magic moments on videotape. Just goes to show home movies don't have to be bland. ?m/C VHS. Blake Bahner, Ena Henderson, Julie Austin, Dan Schmale, Renee Cline, Gary Wise, Joy Ovington. HHE

Fatal Exposure 🎬🎬 1991 (PG-13) A divorcee on vacation with her young sons accidentally picks up the wrong snapshots at the developers'. It turns out she has her hands on some incriminating photos, and the subject will resort to anything, even murder, to keep her quiet. Originally made for television. 89m/C VHS, Beta, LV, **Closed Caption.** Mare Winningham, Nick Mancuso, Christopher McDonald, Geoffrey Blake, Christopher Pettiet; **D:** Alan Metzger. PAR

Fatal Fix 🎬½ 198? A French film expose of urban heroin addiction. Music by the Pretenders. 90m/C VHS, Beta. FR Helmut Berger, Corinne Clery; **D:** Massimo Pirri. NO

Fatal Games 🎬½ 1984 Young female athletes are mysteriously disappearing at the Falcon Academy of Athletics and a crazed killer is responsible. 88m/C VHS, Beta. Sally Kirkland, Lynn Banashek, Sean Masterson. MED

The Fatal Glass of Beer 1933 Fields' son returns to his home in the north woods after serving a jail term in this slapstick comedy short. 18m/B VHS, Beta. W.C. Fields, Rosemary Theby, George Chandler, Richard Cramer. CCB, GVV

The Fatal Hour 🎬½ 1940 Karloff is enlisted to aid police in solving the murder of a detective. As Karloff is rounding up suspects, three more murders take place. Feeble. 68m/B VHS, Beta, 8mm. Boris Karloff, Marjorie Reynolds, Grant Withers, Charles Trowbridge, John Hamilton, Frank Puglia, Jason Robards Sr.; **D:** William Nigh. VYY, SNC

The Fatal Image 🎬🎬½ 1990 A mother and daughter on vacation in Paris inadvertently videotape an international mob hit, making them the target of ruthless assassins. Filmed on location in Paris. Made for television. 96m/C VHS. Michele Lee, Justine Bateman, Francois Dunoyer, Jean-Pierre Cassel, Sonia Petrovna; **D:** Thomas J. Wright. WOV

Fatal Images 🎬 1982 A camera mysteriously causes all the models who pose for it to die, prompting the photographer to investigate. 90m/C VHS, Beta. Lane Coyle; **D:** Dennis Devine. AHV

Fatal Instinct 🎬½ 1992 (R) A tough-guy cop trying to solve a murder instead finds himself a victim of sexual obsession in this erotic thriller. Also available in an unrated version. Not to be confused with (but doesn't everything sound familiar) "Basic Instinct." 93m/C VHS. Michael Madsen, Laura Johnson, Tony Hamilton; **D:** Carl Hamilton. NLC, COL

Fatal Instinct 🎬🎬 1993 (PG-13) Spoof on erotic thrillers such as "Fatal Attraction" and "Basic Instinct." Suave Assante plays a guy with dual careers—he's both cop and attorney, defending the criminals he's arrested. Young plays a lovelorn psycho who's lost her panties. Plot is worth mentioning only in passing, since the point is to mercilessly skewer the entire film noir tradition. The gags occasionally hit deep-chuckle level, though for every good joke there's at least three that misfire. Clemmons of "E Street Band" fame wanders around with sax for background music purposes, typical of the acute self-consciousness of the film.**CW:** Language, violence, and sexuality. 90m/C VHS, LV, **Closed Caption.** Armand Assante, Sean Young, Sherilyn Fenn, Kate Nelligan, Christopher McDonald, James Remar, Tony Randall; **Cameos:** Clarence Clemmons, Doc Severinsen; **D:** Carl Reiner; **W:** David O'Malley; **M:** Richard Gibbs. MGM

A Fatal Inversion 🎬🎬½ 1992 When 19-year-old Hodge inherits a remote English estate from his great-uncle, he invites best friend Northam to spend a carefree summer, after both have told their parents they're vacationing in Greece. The boys are soon joined by Todd, Ford, and Warnecke in an informal commune but several disasters cause them to break off all contact for 12 years—until the remains of two bodies are discovered on the grounds and a police investigation is started. Made for British TV; based on the psychological thriller by Ruth Rendell (writing as Barbara Vine). 150m/C VHS. GB Douglas Hodge, Jeremy Northam, Saira Todd, Julia Ford, Gordon Warnecke, Nicholas Woodeson, Peter Attard, Rachel Joyce, Nicholas Le

Prevost, Ben Chaplin; **D:** Tim Fywell; **W:** Sandy Welch; **C:** Barry McCann; **M:** David Ferguson. FOX

Fatal Justice 🎬 199? Mars is a topnotch assassin who's been in the business too long and knows too much so the agency he works for decides to kill him off. They send young and beautiful professional Diana to do the job but will she be able to when she discovers Mars is actually her father? 90m/C VHS. Joe Estevez. AIP

Fatal Mission 🎬 1989 (R) A Vietnam soldier captures a female Chinese guerilla and uses her as his hostage and guide through the jungle. 84m/C VHS, Beta, LV, **Closed Caption.** Peter Fonda, Mako, Tia Carrere, Ted Markland, Jim Mitchum; **D:** George Rowe; **C:** Phil Parmet. MED, VTR

Fatal Passion 🎬 1994 Two sisters escape from the city after an accidental murder but run straight into the middle of a sacrificial backwoods cult. 90m/C VHS. Lisa Hayland, Joseph Pilato. SWI

Fatal Past 🎬🎬 1994 (R) Bodyguard gets up close and personal with his client—who happens to be a mobster's mistress. As if this weren't trouble enough their pasts provide doom and gloom as well.**CW:** Language, violence, and strong sexuality. 85m/C VHS, **Closed Caption.** Costas Mandylor, Kaisa Figura; **D:** Clive Fleury; **W:** Richard Ryan. PAR

Fatal Pulse WOOF! 1988 Sorority girls are being killed off in grisly ways. Basic slasher/gore. 90m/C VHS, Beta. Michelle McCormick, Ken Roberts, Joe Phelan, Alex Courtney. CEL

Fatal Skies 🎬 1990 An evil schemer plots to dump toxic waste in a small town's water supply until a group of teens comes to the rescue. 88m/C VHS, Beta. Timothy Leary. AIP

Fatal Vision 🎬🎬½ 1984 The television film version of Joe McGinniss' controversial book about the murder trial of Dr. Jeffrey MacDonald, the former Green Berets physician accused of murdering his whole family and blaming the killings on crazed hippies. McGinniss first believed MacDonald may have been innocent but his subsequent investigation, and his book, proved otherwise. The starring debut for Cole. MacDonald still protests his innocence. 192m/C VHS, Beta, LV. Gary Cole, Karl Malden, Eva Marie Saint, Andy Griffith, Barry Newman; **D:** David Greene. COL

Fatally Yours 🎬🎬 1995 Real-estate agent Danny (Rossovich) decides to restore a long-vacant house where a mob massacre occurred in 1928. While in the house, he's "contacted" by the ghostly Sara (MacDonnell), whose husband and gangster father were among the dead. Sara tells him about a hidden treasure of jewels, which leads some present-day gangsters to take an interest in Danny's new property. 90m/C VHS. Rick Rossovich, George Lazenby, Roddy McDowall, Sage Stallone, Sarah MacDonnell; **D:** Tim Everitt. MNC

Fate 🎬🎬½ 1990 (PG-13) Sweet comedy. A young man plans his love-affair carefully, but his biggest problem is meeting the girl of his dreams. Cheerful acting from Lynn and Paul. Stylish and charming. 115m/C VHS. Cheryl Lynn, Stuart Paul, Kaye Ballard, Susannah York; **D:** Stuart Paul. ACA

Father 🎬🎬🎬 1967 After WWII, a Hungarian youth makes up stories about his dead father's heroism that enhance his own position. Eventually he becomes obsessed with the facts surrounding his father's death at the hands of the enemy and, learning the truth, lays the past to rest. In Hungarian with English subtitles. 89m/B VHS, Beta, LV. HU Andras Balint, Miklos Gabor; **D:** Istvan Szabo; **W:** Istvan Szabo. VYY, DVT, HEG

Father 🎬🎬 1990 (PG-13) A woman receives an anonymous telephone call telling her to watch a television news program and learn the truth about her beloved father. What she sees is her father's face superimposed over that of a young Nazi soldier and an aging, unstable woman accusing her father of war crimes. The daughter fiercely believes her father to be a victim of mis-

taken identity but questions keep nagging at her. Very similiar in plot to "Music Box" and just as pedestrian in spite of some good performances.**CW:** Some language and thematic elements. 106m/C VHS. AU Max von Sydow, Carol Drinkwater, Julia Blake, Steve Jacobs; **D:** John Power. Australian Film Institute '90: Best Actor (von Sydow), Best Actress (Blake). MNC

Father and Scout 🎬🎬½ 1994 (PG) Would-be Eagle Scout Michael (Bonsall) has a problem when he takes his city-bred, whiny, basically incompetent, dad Spenser (Saget) on a camping trip. Made for TV. 92m/C VHS, LV, **Closed Caption.** Bob Saget, Brian Bonsall, Heidi Swedberg, Stuart Pankin, David Graf, Troy Evans; **D:** Richard Michaels; **M:** David Kitay. TTC

The Father Clements Story 🎬🎬½ 1987 The true story of a black priest in Chicago who battled the Roman Catholic hierarchy in order to adopt a troubled teenager. Made for television. 100m/C VHS. Louis Gossett Jr., Malcolm Jamal Warner, Carroll O'Connor, Leon Robinson, Rosetta LeNoire, Ron McClarty; **D:** Edwin Sherin. LIV

Father Figure 🎬½ 1980 When a divorced man attends his ex-wife's funeral, he discovers that he must take care of his estranged sons. Based on young adult writer Richard Peck's novel; a well-done made-for-television movie. 94m/C VHS, Beta. Hal Linden, Timothy Hutton, Cassie Yates, Martha Scott, Jeremy Licht; **D:** Jerry London; **M:** Billy Goldenberg. NO

Father Goose 🎬🎬½ 1964 During WWII, a liquor-loving plane-spotter stationed on a remote Pacific isle finds himself stuck with a group of French refugee schoolgirls and their teacher. Some predictable gags, romance, and heroism fill out the running time pleasantly. Scriptwriters Stone and Tarloff, who were competitors, not collaborators on the project, shared an Oscar. 116m/C VHS, **Closed Caption.** Cary Grant, Leslie Caron, Trevor Howard; **D:** Ralph Nelson; **W:** Peter Stone, Frank Tarloff; **C:** Charles B(ryant) Lang; **M:** Cy Coleman. Academy Awards '64: Best Story & Screenplay; Nominations: Academy Awards '64: Best Film Editing, Best Sound. REP

Father Hood 🎬 1993 (PG-13) Family drama has Swayze playing a small-time criminal whose daughter tracks him down after leaving the foster-care shelter where she and her brother are being abused. The family takes to the road, running from both the police and a journalist (Berry) who wants to expose the corrupt foster-care system. The children are obnoxious, Swayze is miscast, and the entire film is a misfire.**CW:** Thematic material/threatened kids. 94m/C VHS, LV, **Closed Caption.** Patrick Swayze, Halle Berry, Sabrina Lloyd, Brian Bonsall, Diane Ladd, Michael Ironside, Bob Gunton; **D:** Darell Roodt; **W:** Scott Spencer. TOU

Father of the Bride 🎬🎬🎬½ 1950 A classic, quietly hilarious comedy about the tribulations of a father preparing for his only daughter's wedding. Tracy is suitably overwhelmed as the loving father and Taylor radiant as the bride. A warm vision of American family life, accompanied by the 1940 MGM short "Wedding Bells." Also available in a colorized version. Followed by "Father's Little Dividend" and later a television series. Remade in 1991. 106m/C VHS, Beta, LV, **Closed Caption.** Spencer Tracy, Elizabeth Taylor, Joan Bennett, Billie Burke, Leo G. Carroll, Russ Tamblyn, Don Taylor, Moroni Olsen; **D:** Vincente Minnelli; **W:** Frances Goodrich, Albert Hackett; **C:** John Alton. Nominations: Academy Awards '50: Best Actor (Tracy), Best Picture, Best Screenplay. MGM

Father of the Bride 🎬🎬½ 1991 (PG) Remake of the 1950 comedy classic portrays one of the most overextravagant weddings in recent film history, but falls short of the original. Predictable plot and characters don't hide any surprises, but nothing detracts from the purpose of the film: to be a nice, charming movie. Martin is fine as the reluctant dad but Keaton is little more than window dressing as the bride's mom; Short is annoying as a pretentious wedding coordinator. Williams pulls off a nice film debut—and was almost immediately cast in a TV ad as a young-bride-to-be calling her dad long distance to tell him she's engaged. Adapted from a novel by Edward Streeter. **105m/C VHS, Beta, LV, Closed Caption.** Steve Martin, Diane Keaton, Kimberly Williams, Kieran Culkin, George Newbern, Martin Short, B.D. Wong, Peter Michael Goetz, Kate McGregor Stewart, Martha Gehman; *Cameos:* Eugene Levy; *D:* Charles Shyer; *W:* Charles Shyer, Nancy Meyers; *C:* John Lindley; *M:* Alan Silvestri. TOU

Father of the Bride Part II 🎬🎬½

1995 (PG) Sweetly sentimental update of the 1951 film "Father's Little Dividend" finds George Banks (Martin) once again thrown for a loop—first by his beloved daughter Annie's (Williams) pregnancy and then by wife Nina's (the radiant Keaton) announcement that they are about to become parents themselves. George doesn't deal very well with either situation but, aided by fey party planner Franck (Short), he manages to get through the predictable chaos. Martin's physical expressiveness and sly charm are a big plus. **106m/C VHS, LV, Closed Caption.** Steve Martin, Diane Keaton, Kimberly Williams, Martin Short, George Newbern, Kieran Culkin, Peter Michael Goetz, Kate McGregor Stewart, Eugene Levy, B.D. Wong, Jane Adams; *D:* Charles Shyer; *W:* Nancy Meyers, Charles Shyer; *C:* William A. Fraker; *M:* Alan Silvestri. Nominations: Golden Globe Awards '96: Best Actor—Musical/Comedy (Martin). TOU

Father Was a Fullback 🎬🎬½ 1949

College football coach (MacMurray) has a losing team, problems with the administration and alumni, and two daughters with growing pains at home. Wife O'Hara supplies the sympathetic shoulder. **99m/B VHS.** Fred MacMurray, Maureen O'Hara, Betty Lynn, Rudy Vallee, Thelma Ritter, Natalie Wood, Jim Backus; *D:* John M. Stahl. FCT

Fatherland 🎬🎬½ 1994

It's 1964 and 20 years earlier Hitler has won WWII in this what-if TV movie. The Nazi leader is about to sign a historic alliance with the U.S. President in Berlin when a series of murders of high-ranking Third Reich officers begins. SS detective Xavier March (Hauer) investigates, along with visiting American journalist Charlie Maguire (Richardson), leading the two to the Gestapo coverup of the Holocaust. If the secret gets out it could ruin the summit, so guess who's in big danger? Intriguing premise but the thriller fails to sustain tension. Based on the novel by Robert Harris. Filmed in Prague, Czech Republic. **106m/C VHS, Closed Caption.** Rutger Hauer, Miranda Richardson, Peter Vaughan, Jean Marsh, Michael Kitchen, John Woodvine, John Shrapnel, Clare Higgins; *D:* Christopher Menaul; *W:* Stanley Weiser, Ron Hutchinson; *C:* Peter Sova; *M:* Gary Chang. WAR

Fathers and Sons 🎬½ 1992 (R)

Max is a brooding, former bad-boy movie director living on the Jersey Shore. His wife's death causes him to rethink his life and deal with his drinking problem. He also tries to get to know his equally brooding teenage son, Ed. Turns out addiction may run in the family as Ed experiments with drugs. Ill-fitting subplot deals a serial killer stalking the community. Goldblum brings an uneasy gentleness to the father's role in an otherwise slow, talky, and obviously symbolic flick. *CW:* Language, some violence and drug content, and sensuality. **100m/C VHS, LV.** Jeff Goldblum, Rory Cochrane, Mitchell Marchand, Famke Janssen, Natasha Gregson Wagner, Ellen Greene, Samuel L. Jackson, Joie Lee, Rosanna Arquette, Michael Disend; *D:* Paul Mones; *W:* Paul Mones; *C:* Ron Fortunato; *M:* Mason Daring. COL

Father's Day 🎬🎬½ 1996 (PG-13)

The comedy team of Williams and Crystal makes its feature film debut in this affable take on fatherhood. Freelance writer Putley (Williams) unites with attorney Lawrence (Crystal) to help their mutual ex-girlfriend Kinski search for her runaway son (she's led each man to believe he's the boy's father). Their quest leads to some inevitable sticky situations, but the erratic, adolescent Williams is wonderfully balanced by the calm, upstanding Crystal. Who needs a son when you have to deal with

Williams? Together, they're fun to watch and almost make you forget the contrived plot. Almost. Remake of the 1984 French film "Les Comperes." *CW:* Some sex-related humor and drug references. **98m/C VHS.** Robin Williams, Billy Crystal, Nastassia Kinski, Julia Louis-Dreyfus, Charlie Hofheimer, Bruce Greenwood, Jared Harris; *D:* Ivan Reitman; *W:* Lowell Ganz, Babaloo Mandel; *C:* Stephen Burum; *M:* James Newton Howard. NYR

Father's Little Dividend 🎬🎬🎬 1951

Tracy expects a little peace and quiet now that he's successfully married off Taylor in this charming sequel to "Father of the Bride." However, he's quickly disillusioned by the news he'll soon be a grandfather - a prospect that causes nothing but dismay. Reunited the stars, director, writers, and producer from the successfull first film. **82m/B VHS, Beta, LV.** Spencer Tracy, Joan Bennett, Elizabeth Taylor, Don Taylor, Billie Burke, Russ Tamblyn, Moroni Olsen; *D:* Vincente Minnelli; *W:* Frances Goodrich, Albert Hackett. CNG, MRV, NOS

A Father's Revenge 🎬🎬½ 1988 (R)

Dennehy is the only reason to bother with this average hostage drama. He's the father of a stewardess who's one of a group being held by terrorists. They're scheduled to die in 72 hours unless Dennehy can find a way to rescue them. Made for television. *CW:* Terrorist violence. **93m/C VHS, LV.** Brian Dennehy, Joanna Cassidy, Ron Silver; *D:* John Herzfeld; *M:* Klaus Doldinger. THV

Fatso 🎬½ 1980 (PG)

After the shocking death of his obese cousin, an obsessive overeater struggles to overcome his neurosis with the aid of his sister and a self-help group called "Chubby Checkers." Bancroft's first work as both writer and director. **93m/C VHS, Beta, Closed Caption.** Dom DeLuise, Anne Bancroft, Ron Carey, Candice Azzara; *D:* Anne Bancroft; *W:* Anne Bancroft. FOX

Fatty and Mabel Adrift/Mabel, Fatty and the Law 1916

Fatty and Mabel have problems enjoying their wedded bliss in these two silent shorts, which have a newly recorded orchestral score on the soundtrack. **40m/B VHS, Beta.** Fatty Arbuckle, Mabel Normand, Al "Fuzzy" St. John, Minta Durfee. CCB, GVV

Fatty Finn 🎬½ 1984

A children's gagfest about young kids and bullies during the Depression, based on Syd Nicholls' comic strip. **91m/C VHS, Beta.** AU Ben Oxenbould, Bart Newton; *D:* Maurice Murphy. NO

Faust 🎬🎬🎬½ 1926

The classic German silent based upon the legend of Faust, who sells his soul to the devil in exchange for youth. Based on Goethe's poem, and directed by Murnau as a classic example of Germanic expressionism. Remade as "All That Money Can Buy" in 1941. **117m/B VHS, Beta.** GE Emil Jannings, Warner Fuetterer, Gosta Ekman, Camilla Horn; *D:* F.W. Murnau. GPV, MRV, NOS

The Favor 🎬🎬½ 1992 (R)

Lighthearted romance rife with comic confusion, vivid fantasies, secrets, and the all-important favor. Kathy (Kozak) seeks to relieve the boredom of her marriage through best friend Emily's (McGovern) tryst with Kathy's old beau, Tom. Or so she thinks, until Em spills all the juicy details. In a change of pace, the males take a back seat to the women. Good comic performances from Kozak and McGovern and witty dialogue help overcome the plot's sheer silliness. Damian Elwes (actor Cary's brother) provided Pitt's paintings. Theatrical release was delayed three years due to financial crisis at Orion Pictures. *CW:* Adult situations. **97m/C VHS, LV, Closed Caption.** Harley Jane Kozak, Elizabeth McGovern, Bill Pullman, Brad Pitt, Ken Wahl, Larry Miller, Holland Taylor; *D:* Donald Petrie; *W:* Josann McGibbon, Sara Parriott; *M:* Thomas Newman. NYR

The Favor, the Watch, & the Very Big Fish 🎬🎬 1992 (R)

Set in a fairytale version of Paris. Hoskins is a photographer of religious subjects searching for a man to pose as Jesus. He discovers his subject in the hirsute

Goldblum, a mad bar pianist who actually thinks he's the savior. Richardson plays the object of Hoskin's shy affections, an actress who does dubbing work by providing the moaning and groaning for porno flicks. Messy attempt at screwball-comedy with some brief humorous moments. *CW:* Language and sensuality. **89m/C VHS, LV, Closed Caption.** GB FR Bob Hoskins, Jeff Goldblum, Natasha Richardson, Michel Blanc, Jacques Villeret, Angela Pleasence, Jean-Pierre Cassel, Bruce Altman; *D:* Ben Lewin; *W:* Ben Lewin; *M:* Vladimir Cosma. THV, FCT

The Favorite Son 🎬🎬🎬 Le Fils Prefere

1994 Troubled family history is examined between three adult French brothers and their Italian immigrant father. A dutiful son, hotel manager Jean-Paul (Lanvin) regularly visits elderly father Raphael (Herlitzka). But Jean-Paul has problems. Desperate for cash to pay his loan shark, he approaches estranged younger brother Philippe (Barr), a wealthy lawyer, who is loath to help, while older schoolteacher brother Francis (Giraudeau) has little spare cash. Jean-Paul decides to take out a life insurance policy on dad—who promptly disappears—leaving the brothers to reluctantly come to terms in order to find him. French with subtitles. **100m/C VHS.** FR Gerard Lanvin, Jean-Marc Barr, Bernard Giraudeau, Roberto Herlitzka, Margherita Buy; *D:* Nicole Garcia; *W:* Nicole Garcia; *C:* Eric Gautier; *M:* Philippe Sarde. Cesar Awards '95: Best Actor (Lanvin); Nominations: Cesar Awards '95: Best Director (Garcia), Best Film. NYR

Fawlty Towers 1977

Cleese stars as the most obnoxious and inept hotel proprietor on earth in these three comedy episodes from the BBC series: "A Touch of Class," "Hotel Inspectors," and "The Germans," (which features Cleese's extraordinary goose-stepping). Additional episodes available. **90m/C VHS, Closed Caption.** GB John Cleese, Prunella Scales, Connie Booth, Andrew Sachs; *W:* John Cleese, Connie Booth. FOX, MOV, SIG

FBI Girl 🎬🎬 1952

An FBI clerk is used as bait to trap a murderer and break up a gang. Burr, pre-Perry Mason, plays a bad guy. **74m/B VHS, Beta, LV.** Cesar Romero, George Brent, Audrey Totter, Raymond Burr, Tom Drake; *D:* William (Lester Williams) Berke. RXM

The FBI Story 🎬🎬🎬 1959

Mr. Stewart goes to Washington in this anatomy of the Federal Bureau of Investigation. If you're a fan of the gangster genre (LeRoy earlier directed "Little Caesar"), and not especially persnickety about fidelity to the facts, this actioner offers a pseudo-factual (read fictional) glimpse—based on actual cases from the 1920s through the 1950s—into the life of a fictitious agent-family man. **149m/C VHS, LV, Closed Caption.** James Stewart, Vera Miles, Nick Adams, Murray Hamilton, Larry Pennell; *D:* Mervyn LeRoy; *C:* Joseph Biroc; *M:* Max Steiner. WAR, FCT, CCB

Fear 🎬🎬 1946

An impoverished medical student murders the professor he believes is tormenting him and his life suddenly gets better. He falls in love and gets a scholarship but the police are closing in on his crime. Except...did any of it really happen? Or is he suffering from hallucinations. Low-budget psycho-drama with some good paranoid moments. **68m/B VHS.** Peter Cookson, Warren William, Anne Gwynne, James B. Cardwell, Nestor Paiva; *D:* Alfred Zeisler. VES

Fear 🎬 1988 (R)

A vacationing family is plagued by a murderous Vietnam vet and other psychotic cons. **96m/C VHS, Beta, LV.** Frank Stallone, Cliff DeYoung, Kay Lenz, Robert Factor; *D:* Robert A. Ferretti. NO

Fear 🎬🎬½ 1990 (R)

A young psychic (Sheedy) delves into the minds of serial killers and writes novels about her experiences. But what happens when the next killer is also a psychic and decides to play mind-games with her? Above average suspense sustains this made-for-cable thriller. **98m/C VHS.** Ally Sheedy, Lauren Hutton, Michael O'Keefe, Stan Shaw, Dina Merrill, John Agar, Marta DuBois; *D:* Rockne S. O'Bannon; *M:* Henry Mancini. VES

The Fear 🎬½ **1994 (R)** Student psychologist (Bowz) takes a group to a remote cabin to explore their fears as part of his research project. Then, they begin to die horribly and gradually figure out that the cabin's wooden mascot, Morty (Weiss), is coming to life and doing them in.*CW:* Strong sexuality and language; some terror and violence. **98m/C VHS.** Eddie Bowz, Darin Heames, Anna Karin, Leland Hayward, Monique Mannen, Heather Medway, Antonio Todd, Erick Weiss, Vince Edwards, Ann Turkel; *Cameos:* Wes Craven; *D:* Vincent Robert; *W:* Ron Ford; *C:* Bernd Heinl; *M:* Robert O. Ragland. *APX*

Fear 🎬½ *No Fear* **1996 (R)** Wahlberg (the former Marky Mark) is a parents' worse nightmare: the violent, obsessed boyfriend of a sixteen-year old girl (Witherspoon) as "Fatal Attraction" goes to the prom. Some cleverness, but ultimately follows a familiar, cliched path littered with one-dimensional characters and predictable plot twists. Gory, unconvincing climax kills any credibility that was left. The one standout is Petersen as the girl's protective father.*CW:* Profanity, violence and sexual situations. **96m/C VHS, LV, Closed Caption.** Reese Witherspoon, Mark Wahlberg, William L. Petersen, Amy Brenneman, Alyssa Milano, Tracy Fraim, Christopher Gray, Todd Caldecott; *D:* James Foley; *W:* Christopher Crowe; *C:* Thomas Kloss; *M:* Carter Burwell. MTV Movie Awards '97: Best Song ("Machinehead"); Nominations: MTV Movie Awards '97: Best Villain (Wahlberg). *USH*

Fear, Anxiety and Depression 🎬½ **1989 (R)** A neurotic aspiring playwright in New York has various problems with his love life. Sub-Woody Allen comedy attempt, with a few bright spots. The dregs of New York, with all the violence and degradation, are brought to the screen here. **84m/C VHS, Beta, Closed Caption.** Todd Solondz, Stanley Tucci; *D:* Todd Solondz; *W:* Todd Solondz. *NO*

The Fear Chamber woof! *Torture Zone; Chamber of Fear; La Camara Del Terror* **1968** Hardly a Karloff vehicle. Boris shot the footage for this and three other Mexican "horror" films in LA, an unfortunate swan song to his career, though he was fortunate to be quickly written out of this story. The near plot concerns a mutant rock that thrives on human fear. Doctor Karloff and his assistants make sure the rock is rolling in sacrificial victims (women, of course). A prodigious devaluation of the "B"-grade horror flick, it's so bad it's just bad. **88m/C VHS.** *MX* Boris Karloff, Yerye Beirut, Julissa, Carlos East; *D:* Juan Ibanez, Jack Hill. *SNC, MPI*

Fear City 🎬½ **1985 (R)** Two partners who own a talent agency are after the psychopath who is killing off their prized strippers with the aid of a local cop. Sleazy look at Manhattan low life. **93m/C VHS, Beta, LV.** Billy Dee Williams, Tom Berenger, Jack Scalia, Melanie Griffith, Rae Dawn Chong, Joe Santos, Maria Conchita Alonso, Rossano Brazzi; *D:* Abel Ferrara; *W:* Nicholas St. John. *NO*

Fear in the City 🎬 **1981** The Sicilian Mafia and a black crime gang battle for control of the streets. **90m/C VHS, Beta.** *IT* Michael Constantine, Fred Williamson, Gianni Manera; *D:* Gianni Manera. *NO*

Fear in the Night 🎬🎬🎬 **1947** Suspenseful tale of a murder committed by a man under hypnosis. Fearing his nightmares are real Kelley talks his detective friend into investigating his "crime", which leads them to a mansion, a mirrored room, and a plot that takes some clever and unexpected twists. Remade in 1956 as "Nightmare." **72m/B VHS.** Paul Kelly, DeForest Kelley, Ann Doran, Kay Scott, Robert Emmett Keane; *D:* Maxwell Shane. *SNC*

The Fear Inside 🎬🎬½ **1992 (R)** Lahti plays a woman suffering from agoraphobia who, because of her fear, has not left her home in more than a year. To help out, Lahti invites a seemingly charming college student to live with her. When the young woman's equally charming "brother" comes to visit, Lahti discovers the two aren't so charming after all. A standard woman-in-terror film with a better-than-average cast. Made for cable television.*CW:* Language, violence, and sexuality. **100m/C VHS, Beta, LV, Closed Caption.** Christine Lahti, Jennifer Rubin, Dylan McDermott, David Ackroyd, Thomas Ian Nicholas, Paul Linke, Leon Ichaso; *D:* Leon Ichaso; *W:* David Birke; *C:* Bojan Bazelli. *FXV, VTR*

Fear No Evil 🎬🎬 **1980 (R)** A teenager who is the human embodiment of the demon Lucifer commits acts of demonic murder and destruction. His powers are challenged by an 18-year-old girl, who is the embodiment of the archangel Gabriel. First feature from La Loggia is better than it sounds. **90m/C VHS, Beta.** Stefan Arngrim, Kathleen Rowe McAllen, Elizabeth Hoffman; *D:* Frank Laloggia; *W:* Frank Laloggia. *COL*

Fear of a Black Hat 🎬🎬 **1994 (R)** Think "Spinal Tap" as gangsta rap and you've the plot of this good-natured imitator. The dim-witted Ice Cold (Cundilieff), Tone-Def (Lawrence), and Tasty-Taste (Scott), the trio known as NWH (Niggaz With Hats), are touring in support of their album and trying to convince filmmaker Nina Blackburn (Lemmons) of their street credibility. Like Taps metalheads, the more they explain themselves, the less sense they make.*CW:* Considerable profanity; comic violence; nudity. **87m/C VHS, Closed Caption.** Larry B. Scott, Mark Christopher Lawrence, Kasi Lemmons, Rusty Cundieff; *D:* Rusty Cundieff; *W:* Rusty Cundieff; *C:* John L. Demps Jr. *FXV*

Fear Strikes Out 🎬🎬🎬 **1957** Perkins plays Jimmy Piersall, star outfielder for the Boston Red Sox, and Malden, his demanding father, in the true story of the baseball star's battle for sanity. One of Perkins' best screen performances. **100m/B VHS, Beta, LV, Closed Caption.** Anthony Perkins, Karl Malden, Norma Moore, Adam Williams, Perry Wilson; *D:* Robert Mulligan; *W:* Raphael David Blau; *M:* Elmer Bernstein. *PAR*

Fearless 🎬 **1978** An Italian detective has found a Viennese banker's daughter, but continues to pursue the unanswered questions of the case, embroiling himself in a web of intrigue and plotting. **89m/C VHS, Beta.** Joan Collins, Maurizio Merli, Franz Antel. *NWV*

Fearless 🎬🎬🎬 **1993 (R)** Two plane crash survivors reach out to each other as they try and cope with everday life. Bridges is riveting as the transformed Max, and Perez compelling as the sorrowful Carla. Hulce provides dead-on amusement as a casualty lawyer who knows he's slime but can't help himself. Opening sequences of smoke in the corn fields are haunting as are flashbacks of the crash itself. Weir provides an engrossing look at facing death, both psychological and spiritual, but the ending is something of a letdown in its sappiness. Based on the novel by Yglesias.*CW:* Language and airplane crash realism. **122m/C VHS, Beta, LV, Closed Caption.** Jeff Bridges, Isabella Rossellini, Rosie Perez, Tom Hulce, John Turturro, Benicio Del Toro, Deirdre O'Connell, John de Lancie; *D:* Peter Weir; *W:* Rafael Yglesias; *C:* Allen Daviau; *M:* Maurice Jarre. Los Angeles Film Critics Association Awards '93: Best Supporting Actress (Perez); Nominations: Academy Awards '93: Best Supporting Actress (Perez); Golden Globe Awards '94: Best Supporting Actress (Perez). *WAR*

Fearless Tiger 🎬½ **1994 (R)** Martial arts action flick includes the usual combination of fierce swordplay, hand-to-hand showdowns, and the intrigue of exotic locations.*CW:* Language and martial arts violence; drug content. **?m/C VHS, LV, Closed Caption.** Bolo Yeung, Monika Schnarre, Jamie Farr, Jalal Merhi; *D:* Ron Hulme; *W:* Ron Hulme; *M:* Varouje. *IMP*

The Fearless Vampire Killers 🎬🎬🎬 *Pardon Me, Your Teeth are in My Neck; Dance of the Vampires* **1967** Underrated, off-off-beat, and deliberately campy spoof of vampire films in which Tate is kidnapped by some fangy villains. Vampire trackers MacGowran and Polanski pursue the villains to the haunted castle and attempt the rescue. Only vampire movie with a Jewish bloodsucker ("Boy, have you got the wrong vampire," he proclaims to a maiden thrusting a crucifix at him). Inside the castle, Polanski is chased by the count's gay vampire son. Highlight is the vampire ball with a wonderful mirror scene. Many other amusing moments. **98m/C VHS, Beta, LV.** *GB* Jack MacGowran, Roman Polanski, Alfie Bass, Jessie Robbins, Sharon Tate, Ferdinand "Ferdy" Mayne, Iain Quarrier; *D:* Roman Polanski; *W:* Roman Polanski, Gerard Brach. *MGM*

Fearmaker *House of Fear; Violent Rage* **1989 (PG)** After the mysterious death of her father, the heiress to his fortune is tangled in a web of treachery created by other potential inheritors. **90m/C VHS, Beta.** *MX* Katy Jurado, Paul Picerni, Sonia Amelio, Carlos East; *D:* Anthony Carras. *PSM*

Feast for the Devil 🎬½ **197?** A woman searches for her missing sister in a mysterious coastal village, only to fall under the occult spell of a mad doctor. **90m/C VHS, Beta.** Krista Nell, Teresa Gimpera. *NO*

Feast of July 🎬🎬 **1995 (R)** Victorian-era drama, adapted from an H. E. Bates novel, has young Bella (Davidtz) pregnant and abandoned by super-cad Arch (Wise) whom she sets out to find. After a miscarriage, she is taken in by the Wainwright family where she becomes the object of the affections of the three grown sons. Predictably, she falls for and weds the troubled loafer, Con (Chaplin). Naturally (this being Victorian England) tragedy results. Well-crafted, a given considering the producers, but ultimately a familiar telling of an average story. Feature film debut for director Menaul, after an award-winning career in British television.*CW:* Brief violence and sexuality; childbirth scene. **116m/C VHS, LV, Closed Caption.** Embeth Davidtz, Ben Chaplin, Tom Bell, Gemma Jones, James Purefoy, Kenneth Anderson, Greg Wise; *D:* Christopher Menaul; *W:* Christopher Neame; *C:* Peter Sova; *M:* Zbigniew Preisner. *TOU*

Federal Agent 🎬🎬 **1936** Lots of cliches fill this crime film about a federal agent chasing foreign spys who are looking for a new explosive. **53m/B VHS, Beta.** William Boyd, Charles A. Browne, Irene Ware, George Cooper, Lentia Lace, Dan Alvarado; *D:* Sam Newfield. *GPV*

Federal Agents vs. Underworld, Inc. *Golden Hands of Kurigal* **1949** Super G-Man Dave Worth goes up against Nila, a greedy villainess bent on finding the golden hands of Kurigal so she may rule the world. A 12-episode serial edited onto two cassettes. **167m/B VHS.** Kirk Alyn, Rosemary La Planche, Roy Barcroft, Carol Forman, James Dale, Bruce Edwards; *D:* Fred Brannon. *REP, MLB*

Federal Hill 🎬🎬 **1994 (R)** Familiar plot and characters are still well-handled by cast and first time writer/director Corrente. Federal Hill is a working-class, Little Italy section of Providence, Rhode Island. Five buddies, mostly losers, hang out together at a weekly card game. Nicky's (De Sando) a small-time dealer who meets his uptown Brown University sweetie, Wendy (Langdon), when he sells her cocaine. His friends try to warn him, especially short-fused burglar Ralphie (Turturro). And, of course, things go very wrong for practically everyone. The video is available colorized or in the director's version in B&W.*CW:* Strong language; some sexuality and drug content. **100m/B VHS, LV, Closed Caption.** Anthony De Sando, Nicholas Turturro, Libby Langdon, Michael Raynor, Jason Andrews, Frank Vincent, Robert Turano, Michael Corrente; *D:* Michael Corrente; *W:* Michael Corrente; *C:* Richard Crudo; *M:* Bob Held, David Bravo. Nominations: Independent Spirit Awards '95: Best Supporting Actor (Turturro). *THV*

Federal Operator 99 🎬🎬½ **1945** A fortune in stolen jewels, a chemical plant, and a priceless violin all figure in this 12 chapter serial. And it's up to Jerry Blake, Federal Operator 99, to save the day. Part of "The Cliffhanger Serials" series. **169m/B VHS.** Marten Lamont, Helen Talbot, George Lewis. *REP, MOV*

Feds 🎬½ **1988 (PG-13)** Two women enter the FBI Academy and take on the system's inherent sexism with feebly comic results. **82m/C VHS, Beta, LV, Closed Caption.** Rebecca DeMornay, Mary Gross, Ken

Marshall, Fred Dalton Thompson, Larry Cedar, James Luisi, Raymond Singer; **D:** Dan Goldberg; **W:** Dan Goldberg, Len Blum; **M:** Randy Edelman. WAR

Feel My Pulse 🎬🎬 1928 Silent comedy about a rich fanatic who leaves everything in his will to his young niece on the stipulation that she lead a germ-free life; when she reaches 21, she moves into the sanitarium she's inherited, not knowing it has become a base for prohibition-era rum runners. **86m/B VHS, Beta.** Bebe Daniels, Richard Arlen, William Powell; **D:** Gregory La Cava. VYY

Feel the Motion 🎬 1986 A female auto-mechanic wants to make it big in the music biz. She sees her chance when she slips her demo tape onto a hit TV-music show. **98m/C VHS, Beta.** Sissy Kelling, Frank Meyer-Brockman, Ingold Locke, Falco, Meat Loaf. THV

Feelin' Screwy 🎬 1990 A couple of misfit dweebs attempt to rid their town of the local drug dealer in order to impress a couple of babes in this limp coming-of-ager. **90m/C VHS.** Quincy Reynolds, Larry Gamal, Darin McBride, Hassan Jamal, Marsha Carter, Brooks Morales, Anna Fuentes; **D:** Riffat A. Khan; **W:** Riffat A. Khan. NO

Feelin' Up woof! 1976 (R) A young man sells all his possessions to come to New York in search of erotic adventures. **84m/C VHS, Beta.** Malcolm Groome, Kathleen Seward, Rhonda Hansome, Tony Collado, Charles Douglass; **D:** David Secter. LIV, VES

Feeling Minnesota 🎬 1996 (R) A truly stupid movie about truly stupid, mostly nasty people. Petty criminal Jjaks (Reeves) shows up at sleazy older brother Sam's (D'Onofrio) wedding and promptly falls for beautiful-but-unhappy bride Freddie (Diaz), who's being forced into the marriage by local crime boss Red (Lindo). Manipulative Freddie easily convinces Jjaks to run away to Vegas with her but Sam isn't willing to let his bride go so easily. The only character who comes off with any dignity is the diner waitress played by Love. A very lame first effort from Baigelman. Title's from a Soundgarden song about "looking California and feeling Minnesota." **CW:** Violence, sexuality and language. **96m/C VHS, LV, Closed Caption.** Keanu Reeves, Cameron Diaz, Vincent D'Onofrio, Delroy Lindo, Dan Aykroyd, Courtney Love, Tuesday Weld, Levon Helm; **D:** Steven Baigelman; **C:** Walt Lloyd. NLC

Feet First 🎬🎬½ 1930 A shoe salesman puts on "upper crust" airs as he begins a shipboard romance with a girl who thinks he's wealthy. Lloyd's second sound film shows him grappling with technique and has scenes that recall highlights of his silent hits. **85m/B VHS, Beta.** Harold Lloyd, Barbara Kent, Robert McWade; **D:** Clyde Bruckman. TLF

Feet Foremost 🎬½ 1985 A made-for-British-television horror story about an industrialist haunted by the spirit of a teenage girl. **60m/C VHS, Beta.** GB Jeremy Kemp. PSM

Felix the Cat: The Movie 🎬½ 1991 Classic cartoon creation Felix returns in a trite feature. The feline and his bag of tricks enter a dimension filled with He-Man/Mutant Ninja Turtles leftovers; new-age princess, comic reptiles, robots and a Darth Vader clone who's defeated with ridiculous ease. Strictly for undemanding kids. **83m/C VHS, Beta, Closed Caption. D:** Tibor Hernadi; **V:** Chris Phillips, Alice Playten, Maureen O'Connell. TOU, FCT

Fellini Satyricon 🎬🎬🎬 Satyricon 1969 (R) Fellini's famous, garish, indulgent pastiche vision of ancient Rome, based on the novel "Satyricon" by Petronius, follows the adventures of two young men through the decadences of Nero's reign. Actually an exposition on the excesses of the 1960s, with the actors having little to do other than look good and react to any number of sexual situations. Crammed with excesses of every variety. In Italian with English subtitles. Also available on laserdisc with additional footage and letterboxing. **129m/C VHS, Beta, LV.** IT Martin Potter, Capucine, Hiram Keller, Salvo Randone, Max Born; **D:** Federico Fellini; **W:** Federico Fellini; **C:** Giuseppe Rotunno; **M:** Nino Rota. Nomi-

nations: Academy Awards '70: Best Director (Fellini). MGM, FCT, TVC

Fellini's Roma 🎬🎬½ Roma 1972 (R) Fellini reviews his youth in this stream-of-consciousness homage to Rome and Italy. Best left for fervent Fellini fans. **128m/C VHS, Beta, LV.** FR IT Peter Gonzales, Britta Barnes, Pia de Doses, Fiona Florence, Marne Maitland, Renato Giovannoli; **D:** Federico Fellini; **W:** Federico Fellini; **M:** Nino Rota; **V:** Federico Fellini. MGM, FCT, APD

Fellow Traveler 🎬🎬🎬 1989 Two old friends, an actor and a screenwriter, both successful, get blacklisted for reputed Communist leanings in 1950s Hollywood. Good performances and a literate script. Made for cable television. **97m/C VHS, Beta.** Ron Silver, Hart Bochner, Daniel J. Travanti, Imogen Stubbs, Katherine Borowitz, Jonathan Hyde; **D:** Philip Saville; **W:** Colin Towns. PAR

Felony 🎬½ 1995 (R) Police seek revenge when 12 cops are murdered. Turns out the culprit is a rogue CIA agent, whose spree was captured on video by a tabloid-show cameraman. **CW:** Violence and some sexuality. **90m/C VHS, Closed Caption.** Lance Henriksen, Leo Rossi, Joe Don Baker, Charles Napier, Ashley Laurence, Cory Everson; **D:** David A. Prior; **W:** David A. Prior. NLC

Female 🎬🎬½ 1933 Feminist look at life in the 30's stars Chatterton as the wealthy president of an auto factory who wines and dines the office men and then gives them the strictly business line the next day. However, she finally meets her match when Brent walks through the door. (The two stars were a real-life married couple at the time.) Funny, role-reversal story directed by Curtiz of "Casablanca" fame. Based on a story by Donald Henderson Clark. **60m/B VHS, Closed Caption.** Ruth Chatterton, George Brent, Philip Reed, Ruth Donnelly, Johnny Mack Brown, Lois Wilson, Gavin Gordon, Ferdinand Gottschalk; **D:** Michael Curtiz, William Dieterle; **W:** Gene Markey, Kathryn Scola. MGM

The Female Bunch woof! 1969 (R) The man-free world of an all-woman settlement is shattered by the arrival of a handsome stranger. Some of this garbage was filmed on location at the notorious Charles Manson ranch, and that's the least of its flaws. **86m/C VHS.** Jennifer Bishop, Russ Tamblyn, Lon Chaney Jr., Nesa Renet, Geoffrey Land, Regina Carrol; **D:** Al Adamson, John Cardos. SNC

The Female Jungle 🎬 The Hangover 1956 Below-average whocares whodunnit directed by Roger Corman stock-company actor Ve Sota. Police sergeant Tierney is caught between a rock and a hard place. The prime suspect in a murder case, Tierney discovers a series of clues that implicate his friend Carradine. Interesting only for the screen debut of the nympho-typecast Miss Jayne—of whom Bette Davis said "Dramatic art in her opinion is knowing how to fill a sweater." **56m/B VHS.** Lawrence Tierney, John Carradine, Jayne Mansfield, Burt Kaiser, Kathleen Crowley, James Kodl, Rex Thorson, Jack Hill; **D:** Bruno Ve Sota. COL, FCT

Female Trouble 🎬🎬½ 1974 (R) Divine leads a troublesome existence in this $25,000 picture. She turns to a life of crime and decadence, seeking to live out her philosophy: "Crime is beauty." Look closely at the Divine rape scene where she plays both rapist and victim. Climax of her deviant ways comes with her unusual night club act, for which the law shows no mercy. Trashy, campy; for die-hard Waters fans. **95m/C VHS, Beta.** Divine, David Lochary, Mary Vivian Pearce, Mink Stole, Edith Massey, Danny Mills, Cookie Mueller, Susan Walsh; **D:** John Waters; **W:** John Waters. NO

Femalien 🎬 1996 (R) Advanced alien beings, composed of pure light energy, travel to earth to assume corporal form so they can once again experience sexual pleasure. **CW:** Sexuality and nudity. **90m/C VHS, LV.** Vanessa Taylor, Jacqueline Lovell, Matt Schue; **D:** Cybil Richards. AFE

Femme Fatale 🎬🎬½ Fatal Woman 1990 (R) When a man's new bride disappears he teams up with an artist pal to track her down. Their search reveals her secret double life and takes them to L.A.'s avant-garde art scene—and deeper into deception and mystery. Billy Zane (Elijah) and Lisa Zane are brother and sister. **CW:** Language, violence, and sensuality. **96m/C VHS, LV, Closed Caption.** Colin Firth, Lisa Zane, Billy Zane, Scott Wilson, Lisa Blount; **D:** Andre Guttfreund; **W:** John Brancato. REP

Femme Fontaine: Killer Babe for the C.I.A. woof! 1995 (R) Beautiful assassin Drew "Killer Babe" Fontaine (Hope) gets help from CIA-agent-turned-monk Master Sun (Hong) in order to avenge her father's death. Fishnet-clad women with big guns are always a Troma treat. **CW:** Sexuality, violence, and language. **93m/C VHS.** Margot Hope, James Hong, Arthur Roberts, Catherine Dao, David Shark, Kevin Fry, Harry Mok; **D:** Margot Hope; **W:** Margot Hope; **C:** Gary Graver; **M:** Gardner Cole. TTV

Femmes de Paris 🎬🎬 1953 A funny and risque French musical comedy about the comings and goings of the cast of a naughty nightclub shows. In French with English subtitles. **79m/C VHS, Beta.** FR Robert Dhery, Collette Brosset, Louis de Funes. VDM, TPV

The Fence 🎬🎬½ 1994 Interesting presentation of standard bad boy grows up, attempts to go straight. Terry Griff (Wirth) has been bounced from juvenile detention to prison since he was 15. On the streets for the first time in 14 years, Terry wants to lead a clean life with potential girlfriend Jackie (Gimp). But when Terry gets on the wrong side of his dishonest parole officer, the harsh world of the streets pulls him back. Bleak urban drama with sincere performances. **90m/C VHS.** Billy Wirth, Erica Gimpel, Marc Alaimo, Paul Benjamin, Lorenzo Clemons; **D:** Peter Pistor; **W:** Peter Fedorenko; **M:** Jeff Beal. TRI

Fer-De-Lance 🎬½ Operation Serpent 1974 A stricken submarine is trapped at the bottom of the sea, with a nest of deadly snakes crawling through the ship. Made for television. **120m/C VHS, Beta.** David Janssen, Hope Lange, Ivan Dixon, Jason Evers; **D:** Russ Mayberry. WOV

Fergie & Andrew: Behind Palace Doors 🎬🎬 1993 More soap-opera from the British royals in this tale of feisty redhead, Sarah Ferguson, and the neglectful Prince Andrew. He's away a lot, she's bored by all the palace propriety and causes too many scandals, and their marriage falls apart. Made for television. **92m/C VHS, Beta, Closed Caption.** Pippa Hinchley, Sam Miller, Peter Cellier, Harold Innocent, Edita Brychta; **D:** Michael Switzer. TTC

Fernandel the Dressmaker 🎬🎬½ 1957 Fernandel dreams of designing exquisite dresses, but when the opportunity arises, he finds his cheating partners get in the way. In French with English subtitles. **95m/B VHS, Beta, 8mm.** FR Fernandel, Suzy Delair, Francoise Fabian, Georges Chamarat; **D:** Jean Boyer. VYY, FCT

Ferngully: The Last Rain Forest 🎬🎬½ 1992 (G) Animated eco-musical follows the adventures of independent-minded flying sprite Crysta, who lives in a rain forest beset by pollution. She discovers the outside world and becomes smitten with the human Zak, who is helping to cut down the forest. Crysta decides to reduce him to her size and show him the error of his ways. She's aided by fellow sprite, Pips, and a crazy bat (Batty Koda with a voice provided by the lively Williams). So-so script with politically pristine environmental message may grow tiresome for both adults and children, though decent animation and brilliant coloring enlivens the tale. **72m/C VHS, LV. D:** Bill Kroyer; **W:** Jim Cox; **M:** Alan Silvestri; **V:** Samantha Mathis, Christian Slater, Robin Williams, Tim Curry, Jonathan Ward, Grace Zabriskie, Richard "Cheech" Marin, Thomas Chong, Tone Loc, Jim Cox. FXV, MLT

Ferocious Female Freedom Fighters 🎬 1988 A typical foreign-made action flick with female wrestlers is spoofed by the L.A. Connection comedy troupe which did the totally ridiculous dubbed dialog. 90m/C VHS, Beta, LV. Eva Arnaz, Barry Prima. MED, IME

Ferris Bueller's Day Off 🎬🎬🎬 1986 (PG-13) It's almost graduation and if Ferris can get away with just one more sick day—it had better be a good one. He sweet talks his best friend into borrowing his dad's antique Ferrari and sneaks his girlfriend out of school to spend a day in Chicago. Their escapades lead to fun, adventure, and almost getting caught. Broderick is charismatic as the notorious Bueller with Grey amusing as his tattle-tale sister doing everything she can to see him get caught. Early Sheen appearance as a juvenile delinquent who pesters Grey. Led to TV series. One of Hughes' more solid efforts. 103m/C VHS, Beta, LV, 8mm, Closed Caption. Matthew Broderick, Mia Sara, Alan Ruck, Jeffrey Jones, Cindy Pickett, Edie McClurg, Charlie Sheen, Del Close, Virginia Capers, Max Perlich, Louis Anderson; D: John Hughes; W: John Hughes; C: Tak Fujimoto; M: Ira Newborn. PAR, TLF

Ferry to Hong Kong 🎬½ 1959 World-weary, heavy drinking traveler comes aboard the "Fat Annie," a ship skippered by the pompous Captain Hart. The two men clash, until an act of heroism brings them together. Embarrassingly hammy performance by Welles as the ferry skipper. 103m/C VHS, Beta. Curt Jurgens, Orson Welles, Sylvia Syms; D: Lewis Gilbert.

The Feud 🎬🎬 1990 (R) A wacky comedy about the ultimate "family feud." The Bullards of Millville and the Bealers of Hornbeck engage in a battle of the witless, and no one in either town is safe. A silly, irreverent comedy of the slapstick variety. Based on a novel by Thomas Berger. 87m/C VHS. Rene Auberjonois, Ron McLarty, Joe Grifasi, David Strathairn, Gale Mayron; D: Bill D'Elia; W: Bill D'Elia. THV

Feud Maker 🎬½ 1938 Steele rides to the rescue in this range war between the bad guys and the cowmen. Hackett plays a schemer who falsely befriends both sides, plotting to buy up cheap land when the participants have killed each other off. Based on a story by Harry F. Olmsted. 55m/B VHS. Bob Steele, Marion Weldon, Karl Hackett, Frank Ball, Budd Buster, Lew Meehan, Roger Williams; D: Sam Newfield; W: George Plympton. MOV

Feud of the Trail 🎬 1937 A cowboy saves a range family's gold and falls in love with their daughter in the process. Tyler plays both the hero and the villain here. 56m/B VHS. Tom Tyler, Harlin Wood, Guinn "Big Boy" Williams; D: Robert F. "Bob" Hill. NOS, DVT

Feud of the West 🎬½ 1935 Old West disagreements settled with guns in this outing for cowboy star Gibson, here portraying a rodeo performer. 60m/B VHS. Hoot Gibson, Buzz Barton, Robert F. (Bob) Kortman, Edward Cassidy, Joan Barclay, Nelson McDowell, Reed Howes, Lew Meehan; D: Harry Fraser. NOS, VCI, VCN

Fever 🎬🎬🎬 1981 Controversial Polish film based on Andrzej Strug's novel "The Story of One Bomb." Focusing on a period in Polish history marked by anarchy, violence, resistance, and revolution, it was banned before it won eventual acclaim at the Gdansk Film Festival. In Polish with English subtitles. 115m/C VHS. PL D: Agnieszka Holland. FCT

Fever 🎬 1988 (R) A once-honest cop trades his good life in for a shot at dealing drugs. Meanwhile, his wife's lover wants to murder him. 83m/C VHS, Beta, LV. Bill Hunter, Gary Sweet, Mary Regan, Jim Holt; D: Craig Lahiff. ACA

Fever 🎬 1991 (R) An ex-con and a high-powered lawyer join forces to rescue the woman both of them love from a vicious killer. Made for cable television. Available in Spanish. CW: Language, violence and drug content, and sensuality. 99m/C VHS, Closed Caption. Armand Assante, Sam Neill,

Marcia Gay Harden, Joe Spano; D: Larry Elikann; W: Larry Brothers. HBO

Fever Mounts at El Pao 🎬🎬½ Los Ambiciosos 1959 A minor effort from director Bunuel about the regime of a dictator in an imaginary South American country. In Spanish with English subtitles. 97m/B VHS, Beta. MX Gerard Philipe, Jean Servais; D: Luis Bunuel. NOS, FCT, FST

Fever Pitch woof! 1985 (R) Sordid story of a sports writer (O'Neal) who becomes addicted to gambling. Very poor script. 95m/C VHS, Beta, Closed Caption. Ryan O'Neal, Catherine Hicks, Giancarlo Giannini, Bridgette Anderson, Chad Everett, John Saxon, William Smith, Patrick Cassidy, Chad McQueen; D: Richard Brooks; W: Richard Brooks; M: Thomas Dolby. FOX

A Few Good Men 🎬🎬🎬½ 1992 (R) Strong performances by Cruise and Nicholson carry this story of a peacetime military coverup. Cruise is a smart aleck Navy lawyer sleepwalking through his comfortable career in DC. He's ready to write off two soldiers pinned for the murder of their cohort until he interviews their commanding officer, Nicholson. Cruise smells a rat, but Nicholson practically dares him to prove it. Moore is another military lawyer assigned to the case, though her function seems to be holding Kaffee's hand (there's no actual romance between the two). Incredible fireworks between Cruise and Nicholson in the courtroom. Based on the play by Sorkin, who also wrote the screenplay. CW: Language. 138m/C VHS, Beta, LV, 8mm, Closed Caption. Tom Cruise, Jack Nicholson, Demi Moore, Kevin Bacon, Kevin Pollak, Kiefer Sutherland, James Marshall, J.T. Walsh, Christopher Guest, J.A. Preston, Matt Craven, Wolfgang Bodison, Xander Berkeley, Cuba Gooding Jr.; D: Rob Reiner; W: Aaron Sorkin; C: Robert Richardson; M: Marc Shaiman. Chicago Film Critics Awards '93: Best Supporting Actor (Nicholson); MTV Movie Awards '93: Best Film; National Board of Review Awards '92: Best Supporting Actor (Nicholson); People's Choice Awards '93: Best Film, Best Film—Drama; Nominations: Academy Awards '92: Best Film Editing, Best Picture, Best Sound, Best Supporting Actor (Nicholson). COL, CRC, MOV

A Few Moments with Buster Keaton and Laurel and Hardy 🎬🎬🎬 1963 Three short appearances: "The Tree in a Test Tube," a government film with Stan & Ollie about wood's role in the war effort; an episode of "The Ed Sullivan Show," with the duo, and a commercial for Simon Pure Beer featuring Keaton. 17m/B VHS, Beta, 8mm. Stan Laurel, Oliver Hardy, Buster Keaton, Ed Sullivan, Pete Smith. VYY

ffolkes 🎬🎬 Assault Force; North Sea Hijack 1980 (PG) Rufus Excalibur Ffolkes is an eccentric underwater expert who is called upon to stop a madman (Perkins, indulging himself) from blowing up an oil rig in the North Sea. Entertaining farce with Moore playing the opposite of his usual suave James Bond character. 99m/C VHS, Beta. Roger Moore, James Mason, Anthony Perkins, David Hedison, Michael Parks; D: Andrew V. McLaglen. USH

Fiances 🎬🎬 The Engagement; I Fidanzati 1963 Young man from Milan takes a welding job in Sicily that will separate him from his fiancee for 18 months. He thinks the separation will be good for them but loneliness and the strange environment makes him long for her. Non-professional leads provide strength. Italian with subtitles. 84m/B VHS. IT Carlo Carbrini, Anna Canzi; D: Ermanno Olmi; W: Ermanno Olmi; C: Lamberto Caimi; M: Gianni Ferrio. FCT

Fiction Makers 🎬🎬 1967 Roger Moore stars as Simon Templar, also known as "The Saint," a sophisticated detective who is hired to help Amos Klein. Klein turns out to be an alias for a beautiful novelist who is being threatened by the underworld crime ring. Based on the Leslie Chateris' character. 102m/C VHS, Beta. Roger Moore, Sylvia Syms. FOX

Fictitious Marriage 1988 Eldad Ilan, a high school teacher experiencing a mid-life crisis, travels to Israel to get away from his family in order to consider his life's direction. In Hebrew with En-

glish subtitles. 90m/C VHS. Shlomo Bar-Aba, Irit Sheleg, Ofra Veingarten; D: Haim Bouzaglo. ERG

Fiddler on the Roof 🎬🎬🎬½ 1971 (G) Based on the long-running Broadway musical. The poignant story of Tevye, a poor Jewish milkman at the turn of the century in a small Ukrainian village, and his five dowry-less daughters, his lame horse, his wife, and his companionable relationship with God. Topol, an Israeli who played the role in London, is charming, if not quite as wonderful as Zero Mostel, the Broadway star. Finely detailed set decoration and choreography, strong performances from the entire cast create a sense of intimacy in spite of near epic proportions of the production. Play was based on the Yiddish stories of Tevye the Dairyman, written by Sholem Aleichem. ♬ Tradition; Matchmaker, Matchmaker; If I Were a Rich Man; Sabbath Prayer; To Life; Miracle of Miracles; Tevye's Dream; Sunrise, Sunset; Wedding Celebration. 184m/C VHS, Beta, LV, Closed Caption. Chaim Topol, Norma Crane, Leonard Frey, Molly Picon; D: Norman Jewison; C: Oswald Morris; M: John Williams. Academy Awards '71: Best Cinematography, Best Sound, Original Song Score and/or Adaptation; Golden Globe Awards '72: Best Actor—Musical/Comedy (Topol), Best Film—Musical/Comedy; Nominations: Academy Awards '71: Best Actor (Topol), Best Art Direction/Set Decoration, Best Director (Jewison), Best Picture, Best Supporting Actor (Frey). FOX, MGM, TLF

The Fiddlin' Buckaroo 🎬½ 1933 Maynard plays a government agent who disguises himself as a musical ventriloquist to capture Kohler and his band of outlaws. Everybody sings a lot. 63m/B VHS. Ken Maynard, Gloria Shea, Fred Kohler Sr., Frank Rice, Jack Mower, Charles "Slim" Whitaker, Robert F. (Bob) Kortman, Hank Bell, Jack Rockwell; D: Ken Maynard; W: Nate Gatzert. GPV

The Field 🎬🎬🎬½ 1990 (PG-13) After an absence from the big screen, intense and nearly over the top Harris won acclaim as an iron-willed peasant fighting to retain a patch of Irish land he's tended all his life, now offered for sale to a wealthy American. His uncompromising stand divides the community in this glowing adaptation of John B. Keane's classic play, an allegory of Ireland's internal conflicts. 113m/C VHS, LV. GB Richard Harris, Tom Berenger, John Hurt, Sean Bean, Brenda Fricker, Frances Tomelty, Sean McGinley, Jenny Conroy; D: Jim Sheridan; W: Jim Sheridan. Nominations: Academy Awards '90: Best Actor (Harris). LIV, TVC

Field of Dreams 🎬🎬🎬½ 1989 (PG) Uplifting mythic fantasy based on W.P. Kinsella's novel "Shoeless Joe." Iowa corn farmer heeds a mysterious voice that instructs "If you build it, he will come" and cuts a baseball diamond in his corn field. Soon the ball field is inhabited by the spirit of Joe Jackson and others who were disgraced in the notorious 1919 "Black Sox" baseball scandal. Jones, as a character based on reclusive author J.D. Salinger, is reluctantly pulled into the mystery. It's all about chasing a dream, maintaining innocence, finding redemption, reconciling the child with the adult, and celebrating the mythic lure of baseball. Costner and Madigan are strong, believable characters. 106m/C VHS, Beta, LV, Closed Caption. Kevin Costner, Amy Madigan, James Earl Jones, Burt Lancaster, Ray Liotta, Timothy Busfield, Frank Whaley, Gaby Hoffman; D: Phil Alden Robinson; W: Phil Alden Robinson; M: James Horner. Nominations: Academy Awards '89: Best Adapted Screenplay, Best Picture, Best Original Score. USH, FCT, HMV

Field of Fire 🎬🎬 1992 (R) One of America's top military experts has been taken hostage and it's up to a top general to rescue him. But the rescue doesn't come off as planned and all must fight their way through the Cambodian jungle to safety. CW: Language, nudity, and war violence. 96m/C VHS, LV, Closed Caption. David Carradine; D: Cirio H. Santiago; W: Thomas McKelvey Cleaver. HBO

Field of Honor ♂♂½ **1986** (R) A look at the harrowing experience of jungle combat through the eyes of a Dutch infantryman in Korea. 93m/C VHS, Beta, LV. Everett McGill, Ron Bradsteder, Hey Young Lee; **D:** Hans Scheepmaker. MGM

Field of Honor ♂♂½ Champ d'Honneur **1987** (PG) A quiet French anti-war drama set during the Franco-Prussian war in 1869 in which a peasant boy volunteers to fight in place of a rich man's son. He is befriended behind enemy lines by a young boy and both try to avoid capture. In French with English subtitles. 87m/C VHS, Beta. FR Cris Campion, Eric Wapler, Pascale Rocard, Frederic Mayer; **D:** Jean-Pierre Denis. Cesar Awards '88: Best Score.ORI

The Fiend ♂ **1971** (R) A religious cultist, already unbalanced, grabs a knife and starts hacking away Jack-the-Ripper style. 87m/C VHS, Beta. GB Ann Todd, Patrick Magee, Tony Beckley, Madeline Hinde, Suzanna Leigh, Percy Herbert; **D:** Robert Hartford-Davis. NO

Fiend woof! **1983** Glowing supernatural thing flits around graveyard before animating dead guy who needs to kill in order to go on living. Murderous dead guy becomes a small-town music teacher feeding parasitically on his students to satisfy his supernatural hunger. His neighbor suspects some discord. Low-budget time waster. 93m/C VHS, Beta. Don Leifert, Richard Nelson, Elaine White, George Stover; **D:** Donald M. Dohler. PSM

Fiend Without a Face ♂♂ **1958** An isolated air base in Canada is the site for a scientist using atomic power in an experiment to make a person's thoughts materialize. Only his thoughts are evil and reveal themselves as flying brains with spinal cords that suck human brains right out of the skull. Tons of fun for fifties SF fans and anyone who appreciates the sheer silliness of it all. 77m/B VHS, LV. Marshall Thompson, Kim Parker, Terence Kilburn, Michael Balfour, Gil Winfield, Shane Cordell; **D:** Arthur Crabtree. CCB, REP, MLB

The Fiendish Plot of Dr. Fu Manchu woof! **1980** (PG) A sad farewell from Sellers, who in his last film portrays Dr. Fu in his desperate quest for the necessary ingredients for his secret life-preserving formula. Sellers portrays both Dr. Fu and the Scotland Yard detective on his trail, but it's not enough to save this picture, flawed by poor script and lack of direction. 100m/C VHS, Beta, LV. GB Peter Sellers, David Tomlinson, Sid Caesar, Helen Mirren; **D:** Piers Haggard. WAR, FCT

Fierce Creatures ♂♂ **1996** (PG-13) This not-really-a-sequel features the same cast as "A Fish Called Wanda" and was jokingly known as "Death Fish II" until a more appropriate title was thought of. A failing London zoo gets a new lease on life, and officious new manager Rollo Lee (Cleese) by stocking only man-eating predators. This plan has kindly, insect house manager Bugsy (Palin) tongue-tied at the thought of destroying the zoo's cuddly current occupants. Kline is again in fine form with his dastardly dual role of zoo's Aussie owner Rod McCain and his idiot son, Vince. Curtis displays her obvious talents as Willa Weston, Vince's more sympathetic partner. Despite inspired moments, flick's not as tightly told or as wickedly funny as "Fish," (an admittedly tough act to follow). A family-friendlier attitude has effectively declawed this "Creature." Many scenes were reshot after unfavorable advance screenings, necessitating a new director and the recall of the actors from far and wide.CW: Sexual innuendo and language. 93m/C VHS, LV, Closed Caption. John Cleese, Jamie Lee Curtis, Kevin Kline, Michael Palin, Ronnie Corbett, Robert Lindsay, Carey Lowell, Bille Brown, Derek Griffiths, Cynthia Cleese; **D:** Robert M. Young, Fred Schepisi; **W:** John Cleese, Iain Johnstone; **C:** Adrian Biddle, Ian Baker; **M:** Jerry Goldsmith. USH

Fiesta ♂♂ **1947** A girl comes from Mexico City to her father's hacienda where her old boyfriend awaits her return with a proposal of marriage. Full of authentic Mexican dances and music. ♫Fantasia Mexican; La Bamba; La Luna Enamorada; Miriano; Romeria Vasca. 44m/C VHS, Beta. Ann Ayars, George Negrete, Armida; **D:** Richard Thorpe; **C:** Charles Rosher. Nominations: Academy Awards '47: Original Dramatic/Comedy Score. VYY, DVT

The Fifteen Streets ♂♂½ **1990** Kind-hearted dock worker John O'Brien (Teale) is the quiet one in a boozing, brawling Irish family living in near poverty in late-Victorian England. He meets well-bred schoolteacher Mary Llewellyn (Holman) and the two fall in love but bigotry, scandal, and tragedy challenge their chances at happiness. Based on a novel by Catherine Cookson. 108m/C VHS. GB Owen Teale, Clare Holman, Sean Bean, Billie Whitelaw, Ian Bannen, Jane Horrocks, Anny Tobin, Leslie Schofield; **D:** David Wheatley; **W:** Rob Bettinson. VCO

Fifth Avenue Girl ♂½ **1939** An unhappy millionaire brings home a poor young woman to pose as his mistress to make his family realize how they've neglected her. As this below-par social comedy drones toward its romantic conclusion, the rich folks see the error of their ways and love conquers all. 83m/B VHS, Beta, LV. Ginger Rogers, Walter Connolly, Tim Holt, James Ellison, Franklin Pangborn; **D:** Gregory La Cava. IME, TTC

Fifth Day of Peace ♂♂ **1972** (PG) In the aftermath of the WWI armistice, two German soldiers are tried and executed for desertion by their commander, even though the Allies forbade German military trials. An interesting plot that is marred by too obvious plot twists. Based on a true story. 95m/C VHS, Beta. IT Richard Johnson, Franco Nero, Larry Aubrey, Helmut Schneider; **D:** Guiliano Montaldo. PSM

The Fifth Element ♂♂½ **1997** (PG-13) Besson's view of the future is colorful, loud and fashionable. Dressed in costumes by Jean Paul Gaultier, Willis (in a blonde dye job) is New York City cab driver turned unwilling hero Korban Dallas, who must save earth from destruction at the hands of evil arms dealer Zorg (Oldman). Bruce is up to the old heroics that made him a household name, and takes time to romance orange-haired nymph Jovovich, who holds the key to all the madness going on. Oldman is over-the-top as the icy villain with a distinct southern accent, which makes him more of a bad gag than a bad guy. Jumbled story fortunately takes a backseat to weird aliens and stunning visuals which makes this an eye-catching (albeit confusing) sci-fi trip.CW: Intense sci-fi violence, some sexuality and brief nudity. 125m/C VHS. Bruce Willis, Gary Oldman, Ian Holm, Milla Jovovich, Luke Perry, Lee Evans, Chris Tucker; **D:** Luc Besson; **W:** Luc Besson; **C:** Thierry Arbogast; **M:** Eric Serra. NYR

The Fifth Floor woof! **1980** (R) College disco dancer overdoses on drugs and winds up in an insane asylum, complete with menacing attendant Hopkins and apathetic doctor Ferrer. Pathetic, exploitative trash. 90m/C VHS, Beta. Bo Hopkins, Dianne Hull, Patti D'Arbanville, Mel Ferrer; **D:** Howard (Hikmet) Avedis; **W:** Howard (Hikmet) Avedis. MED

The Fifth Monkey ♂½ **1990** (PG-13) A man embarks on a journey to sell four monkeys in order to fill a dowry for his bride, but along the way he encounters all sorts of obstacles and adventures. Filmed on location in Brazil 93m/C VHS, LV. Ben Kingsley; **D:** Eric Rochant; **W:** Eric Rochant. COL, FCT

The Fifth Musketeer ♂♂ Behind the Iron Mask **1979** (PG) A campy adaptation of Dumas's "The Man in the Iron Mask," wherein a monarch's evil twin impersonates him while imprisoning the true king. A good cast and rich production shot in Austria make for a fine entertaining swashbuckler. 90m/C Beta. GB Beau Bridges, Sylvia Kristel, Ursula Andress, Cornel Wilde, Ian McShane, Alan Hale Jr., Helmut Dantine, Olivia de Havilland, Jose Ferrer, Rex Harrison, Helmut Dantine; **D:** Ken Annakin; **W:** David Ambrose; **C:** Jack Cardiff. COL

The Fifth Seal ♂♂ **1976** A group of friends are arrested when one makes a casual remark that offends a commandant. This leads to a series of tasks that test their commitment to their moral ideals. Set at the close of WWII in Hungary. In Hungarian with English subtitles. 116m/C VHS. HU D: Zoltan Fabri. FCT

Fifty/Fifty ♂♂ **1993** (R) Jake and Frenchie are a couple of mercenaries forced by the CIA not only to work together but with a bunch of incompetent guerillas to overthrow a Southeast Asian dictator. Weller handles the violence, Hays handles the comedy, and both get chased a lot.CW: Language and violence. 101m/C VHS, LV, Closed Caption. Robert Hays, Peter Weller, Ramona Rahman, Charles Martin Smith; **D:** Charles Martin Smith; **W:** Dennis Shryack, Michael Butler; **C:** David Connell; **M:** Peter Bernstein. WAR, CAN

$50,000 Reward ♂½ **1925** Maynard's first western finds him being victimized by an unscrupulous banker who wants Maynard's land deeds for property on which a new dam is being built. 49m/B VHS, Beta. Ken Maynard, Esther Ralston. GPV, CCB, HEG

52 Pick-Up ♂♂½ **1986** (R) After a fling, a wealthy industrialist is blackmailed by a trio of repulsive criminals and determines to save himself. First he becomes deeply caught in their web of murder. Based on an Elmore Leonard novel with lots of gruesome violence and good performances. 111m/C VHS, Beta, LV, Closed Caption. Roy Scheider, Ann-Margret, Vanity, John Glover, Doug McClure, Clarence Williams III, Kelly Preston, Robert Trebor, Lonny Chapman; **D:** John Frankenheimer; **W:** John Steppling, Elmore Leonard; **M:** Gary Chang. MED, VTR

55 Days at Peking ♂♂♂ **1963** A costume epic depicting the Chinese Boxer Rebellion and the fate of military Britishers caught in the midst of the chaos. Standard fare superbly handled by director Ray and an all-star cast. 150m/C VHS, Beta, LV. Charlton Heston, Ava Gardner, David Niven, John Ireland, Flora Robson, Paul Lukas, Jacques Sernas; **D:** Nicholas Ray; **W:** Philip Yordan; **C:** Jack Hildyard. Nominations: Academy Awards '63: Best Song ("So Little Time"), Best Original Score. BFV, KAR

The Fig Tree **1987** After her mother passes away, Miranda becomes tormented by the fear of death. Now her aunt must help her cope with this difficult part of life. Adapted from the short story by Katherine Anne Porter. Aired on PBS as part of the "Wonderworks" family movie series. 58m/C VHS, Closed Caption. Olivia Cole, William Converse-Roberts, Doris Roberts, Teresa Wright, Karron Graves; **D:** Calvin Skaggs. PME, FCT, BTV

Fight for Gold ♂ **1986** In the frozen wastes of the North, a man becomes embroiled in a violent quest for gold. 107m/C VHS. GE Doug McClure, Harald Leipnitz, Heinz Reni, Roberto Bianco, Angelica Ott, Kristina Nel; **D:** Harald Reinl. ACA

A Fight for Jenny ♂♂ **1990** (PG) Miami Viceroy Thomas and Warren play an interracial couple who fight for custody of the wife's child from a previous marriage. Standard made-for-TV meaningful drama (bite-sized issues served with a modicum of melodrama). 95m/C VHS. Philip Michael Thomas, Lesley Ann Warren, Jean Smart, Lynne Moody, William Atherton; **D:** Gilbert Moses. PSM

Fight for Survival ♂½ **1977** (R) Young female aspirant of kung fu must recover sacred books that were stolen by disguised kung fu masters. 101m/C VHS, Beta. Shangkuan Ling-Feng. FOX

Fight for the Title ♂ **1957** Benny Leonard's reign as the lightweight boxing champ has just begun when WWII is declared. Against his manager's wishes, Benny decides to enlist. 30m/C VHS. Michael Landon, George Brenlin; **D:** Eric Kenton. FCT, RHI

Fight for Us ♂½ L'Insoumis **1989** (R) A social activist, recently released from prison, takes on the death squads terrorizing the countryside in post-Marcos Philippines. In Spanish with English subtitles. **92m/C VHS, Beta, LV.** Phillip Salvador, Dina Bonnevie, Gina Alajar, Benbol Roco. *NO*

Fight for Your Life *🎞* **1979** Three escaped convicts—a white bigot, an Asian, and a Chicano—take a black minister's family hostage. After suffering all manner of vicious torture, the family exacts an equally brutal revenge. Shades of "The Desperate Hours" and "Extremities," but with much more graphic violence and a racial twist. **89m/C VHS, Beta.** *CA* William Sanderson, Robert Judd, Lela Small. *NO*

Fight to the Death *🎞* **1983** An evil businessman hires a group of deadly assassins to assist with the Japanese invasion of China at the start of WWII. Includes self-defense tips segment. **100m/C VHS.** Chang Li, Ron Van Cliff. *NO*

The Fighter *🎞🎞🎞* *The First Time* **1952** A Mexican patriot, involved in a struggle to overthrow a dictator, falls for a co-revolutionist. Flashbacks show the destruction of his family and village, and his pugilistic expertise, which he uses to fight for a huge purse to help the cause. Adapted from Jack London's "The Mexican." **78m/B VHS.** Richard Conte, Vanessa Brown, Lee J. Cobb, Frank Silvera, Roberta Haynes, Hugh Sanders, Claire Carleton, Martin Garralaga; *D:* Herbert Kline. *DVT, HEG*

The Fighter *🎞½* **1995 (R)** French soldier Charlemont (Gruner) gets involved with desperate farmers opposing a greedy landlord (Ermey) and is forced to compete against former rival Ziegfield (Singer). Strange western/kickboxing hybrid that does have lots of action.*CW:* Martial arts and western violence. **91m/C VHS.** Olivier Gruner, Marc Singer, R. Lee Ermey, Ian Ziering, James Brolin, Ashley Laurence; *D:* Isaac Florentine. *APX*

Fighter Attack *🎞🎞* **1953** Story of a WWII pilot, based in Corsica, who is shot down during a mission to destroy a Nazi supply station. He meets with a woman of the Italian underground, and succeeds in destroying his target with her help. **80m/C VHS.** Sterling Hayden, J. Carrol Naish, Joy Page; *D:* Lesley Selander. *REP*

Fightin' Ranch *🎞🎞* **1930** A famous lawman saves his reputation, previously tainted. A Maynard classic. **60m/B VHS, Beta.** Ken Maynard. *NO*

The Fighting American *🎞* **1924** A frat boy proposes to a girl on a brotherly dare, and, unflattered by the fraternal proposal, the girl flees to the Far East to return to the bosom of her family. But it turns out the boy really does love the girl, by golly, and he's got just enough of that fighting American spirit to prove it. Predates Oland's Charlie Chan career by seven years. **65m/B VHS, Beta.** Pat O'Malley, Mary Astor, Raymond Hatton, Warner Oland; *D:* Tom Forman. *GPV, FCT*

Fighting Back *🎞* *Death Vengeance* **1982 (R)** Reactionary tale of an angry resident in a crime-ridden Philadelphia neighborhood who organizes a patrol of armed civilian vigilantes. The police attempt to head off a racial confrontation in this effective drama graced with fine performances. **96m/C VHS, Beta.** Tom Skerritt, Patti LuPone, Michael Sarrazin, Yaphet Kotto; *D:* Lewis Teague; *W:* David Zelag Goodman; *C:* Franco Di Giacomo. *PAR*

Fighting Black Kings *🎞* **1976 (PG)** Martial arts and karate masters appear in this tale of action. **90m/C VHS, Beta.** William Oliver, Charles Martin, Willie Williams, Mas Oyama. *WAR, OM*

Fighting Caballero *🎞* **1935** Lease and his pals easily handle a gang of mine-harassing outlaws. **60m/B VHS, Beta.** Rex Lease; *D:* Elmer Clifton. *NO*

Fighting Caravans *🎞🎞* *Blazing Arrows* **1931** In this early big-budget western, based on a story by Zane Grey, a wagon train sets out west from Missouri. Cooper emerges as the hero after warding off an Indian attack that takes the lives of the original leaders. **80m/B VHS, Beta.** Gary Cooper, Ernest Torrence, Tully Marshall, Fred Kohler Sr., Lili Damita; *D:* Otto Brower, David Burton. *NOS, MRV, VYY*

Fighting Champ *🎞* **1933** Cowpunching gives way to boxing as Steele steps into the ring and takes on all comers. Poor combination of riding and boxing makes for a disappointing Western. **57m/B VHS.** Bob Steele, Arletta Duncan, George "Gabby" Hayes, Charles "Blackie" King, Lafe McKee, Kit Guard, George Chesebro; *D:* John P. McCarthy; *W:* Wellyn Totman. *MOV*

Fighting Cowboy *🎞* **1933** Bill settles a tungsten mine dispute with a greedy miner and some outlaws. **50m/B VHS, Beta, LV.** Buffalo Bill Jr.; *D:* Victor Adamson. *NO*

Fighting Devil Dogs *🎞* **1938** Two Marine lieutenants are assigned the task of obtaining a deadly secret weapon controlled by crooks. A serial in twelve chapters. **195m/B VHS.** Lee Powell, Bruce (Herman Brix) Bennett; *D:* John English, William Witney. *REP, VCN, MLB*

Fighting Father Dunne *🎞🎞* **1948** Mega-hokey Hollywood steamroller about a tough priest caring for St. Louis newsboys in the early 1900s. Based on a true story. **92m/B VHS.** Pat O'Brien, Darryl Hickman, Charles Kemper, Una O'Connor, Arthur Shields, Harry Shannon, Joseph Sawyer, Anna Q. Nilsson, Donn Gift, Myrna Dell; *D:* Ted Tetzlaff. *TTC*

Fighting Fists of Shanghai Joe *🎞* **1965** Fearsome fighting man from the Far East engages a vile American land baron in a battle of honor. **94m/C VHS, Beta.** Klaus Kinski, Gordon Mitchell, Carla Romanelli, Robert Hundar, Chen Lee; *D:* Mario Ciano. *TWE*

Fighting Fool *🎞* **1932** Average oater has McCoy as a sheriff constantly in pursuit of an outlaw named "The Shadow." Of course, romance blossoms between McCoy and Day, too. The real identity of "The Shadow" turns out to be quite a surprise for McCoy. **57m/B VHS.** Tim McCoy, Marceline Day, Robert Ellis, Arthur Rankin, Dorothy Granger; *D:* Lambert Hillyer. *MOV*

Fighting Jack *🎞🎞* **1926** After he saves a girl from a watery death, a man is accused of horse stealing and trespassing. **52m/B VHS, Beta.** Bill Bailey, Hazel Deane, Frona Hale, John Byron, Sailor Sharkey, Herma Cordova; *D:* Louis Chaudet. *GPV*

The Fighting Kentuckian *🎞🎞½* **1949** Homeward bound from the Battle of New Orleans in 1814, a Kentucky rifleman lingers in a French settlement in Alabama. His romance with the daughter of a French general is blocked by the father until the American saves the community from an assault by land grabbers. Hardy as a frontiersman is well worth the view. An action-packed, well-photographed hit. **100m/B VHS, Closed Caption.** John Wayne, Oliver Hardy, Vera Ralston, Marie Windsor, Philip Dorn, John Howard, Hugo Haas, Grant Withers; *D:* George Waggner. *REP*

The Fighting Legion *🎞🎞* **1930** Maynard shows his foresight here, making this one of the first westerns to fully exploit sound by adding music and singing. Standard plot has Maynard going after the villain who murdered his brother. **69m/B VHS.** Ken Maynard, Dorothy Dwan, Ernie Adams, Stanley Blystone, Frank Rice; *D:* Harry Joe Brown. *GPV, DVT, HEG*

Fighting Mad *🎞½* **1939** A singing Mountie tangles with border-crossing robbers and saves the reputation of a woman they exploit. One of the "Renfrew of the Mounties" series. **57m/B VHS, Beta.** James Newill, Milburn Stone, Sally Blane; *D:* Sam Newfield. *VDM*

Fighting Mad *🎞🎞½* **1976 (R)** A peaceful land owner is driven to violence when he discovers that the business men who want his property are planning to murder two of his family members in order to get it. The local sheriff's apathy forces the man to take the law into his own hands. Unlike other Fonda films of the time which consist of chaotic violence and car crashes, this story is a well performed character study. **90m/C VHS.** Peter Fonda, Lynn Lowry, John Doucette, Phil Carey, Scott Glenn, Kathleen Miller; *D:* Jonathan Demme; *W:* Jonathan Demme. *NO*

Fighting Mad *🎞½* *Fierce* **1977 (R)** Soldiers leave their buddy for dead in wartime Vietnam. He is alive, but captured by Japanese soldiers who believe they are still fighting in WWII. **96m/C VHS.** James Iglehart, Jayne Kennedy, Leon Isaac Kennedy; *D:* Cirio H. Santiago. *NO*

Fighting Marines *🎞½* **1936** U.S. Marines are trying to establish an air base on Halfway Island in the Pacific, but are thwarted by the "Tiger Shark," a modern-day pirate. First appeared as a serial. **69m/B VHS, Beta.** Jason Robards Sr., Grant Withers, Ann Rutherford, Pat O'Malley; *D:* Joseph Kane, B. Reeves Eason. *VYY, VCN, VDM*

The Fighting Marshal *🎞🎞* **1932** After serving time for a crime he didn't commit, McCoy assumes the identity of a dead sheriff and tries to find the felons who done him wrong. **58m/B VHS.** Tim McCoy, Dorothy Gulliver, Mary Carr, Matthew Betz, Pat O'Malley; *D:* David Ross Lederman. *MOV*

Fighting Parson *🎞* **1935** In order to infiltrate a lawless town Gibson, a gunsliging cowboy, dresses as a revivalist preacher. **65m/B VHS, Beta.** Hoot Gibson, Marceline Day, Robert Frazer, Stanley Blystone, Skeeter Bill Robbins, Charles "Blackie" King; *D:* Harry Fraser. *VCI, GPV*

Fighting Pilot **1935** Talmadge is a real fighter in this classic talkie. His assignment is to rescue the plans for a secret aircraft from ill fate. **62m/B VHS, Beta.** Richard Talmadge, Victor Mace, Gertrude Messinger, Eddie Davis, Robert Frazer, J: Noel Mason Smith. *NOS, DVT, GPV*

The Fighting Prince of Donegal *🎞🎞½* **1966** An Irish prince battles the invading British in 16th Century Ireland. Escaping their clutches, he leads his clan in rescuing his mother and his beloved in this Disney swashbuckler. Based on the novel "Red Hugh, Prince of Donegal" by Robert T. Reilly. **110m/C VHS, Beta.** Peter McEnery, Susan Hampshire, Tom Adams, Gordon Jackson, Andrew Keir; *D:* Michael O'Herlihy; *M:* George Bruns. *DIS*

The Fighting Redhead *🎞🎞* **1950** Final entry in the "Red Ryder" series has Hart as a cattle rustling murderer and Bannon as the hero, Red Ryder. Based on the comic strip, "Red Ryder." **55m/C VHS.** Jim Bannon, Don Reynolds, Emmett Lynn, Marin Sais, Peggy Stewart, John Hart, Lane Bradford; *D:* Lewis D. Collins; *W:* Paul Franklin, Jerry Thomas. *MOV*

Fighting Renegade *🎞½* **1939** The search for an Indian burial ground in Mexico prompts two murders and McCoy, disguised as a notorious bandit part of the time, is wrongly accused. Justice triumphs in the end. **60m/B VHS, Beta.** Tim McCoy; *D:* Sam Newfield. *NOS, VCN, DVT*

The Fighting Rookie *🎞½* **1934** LaRue, better known for playing hoods, is a rookie cop set up and disgraced by the mob. But he fights back to regain his honor and bring the gang to justice. **65m/B VHS, Beta, 8mm.** Jack LaRue; *D:* Spencer Gordon Bennet. *VYY*

Fighting Seabees *🎞🎞½* **1944** As a hot-tempered construction foreman who battles Navy regulations as well as the Japanese, Wayne emerges as a larger-than-life hero in this action-packed saga of the Pacific theater of WWII. Extremely popular patriotic drama depicts the founding of the Seabees, the naval construction corps, amidst the action and the would-be romance with a woman reporter. Also available colorized. **100m/B VHS, Closed Caption.** John Wayne, Susan Hayward, Dennis O'Keefe, William Frawley; *D:* Edward Ludwig. Nominations: Academy Awards '44: Original Dramatic/Comedy Score. *REP*

Fighting Shadows *🎞½* **1935** McCoy plays a tough lawman who rids his town of an unscrupulous bandit gang guilty of harassing the locals. Highlighted by some excellent trick riding—for which Western star McCoy was known. **58m/B VHS.** Tim McCoy, Robert Allen, Geneva Mitchell, Ward Bond, Si Jenks; *D:* David Selman; *W:* Ford Beebe. *MOV*

The Fighting Sheriff ☞ 1931 Routine oater mixes action and romance when a sheriff is thrown together with a society debutante. 65m/B VHS. Buck Jones, Loretta Sayers, Robert Ellis, Harlan E. Knight, Paul Fix, Lilian Worth; **D:** Louis King; **W:** Stuart Anthony. *MOV*

The Fighting 69th ☞☞☞ 1940 Cornball but entertaining WWI drama with lots of action. Cagney is a Brooklyn street tough who joins the all-Irish 69th New York regiment but could care less about its famed military history. He promptly defies his superiors and barely scrapes through his training. Sent to France the swaggering Cagney turns coward when confronted with the horrors of war but eventually redeems himself. O'Brien is the famed regimental chaplain Father Duffy, while Brent is commander "Wild Bill" Donovan, who would later found the OSS in WWII. Lots of heart-tugging emotion backed with a fine supporting cast. 90m/B VHS. James Cagney, Pat O'Brien, George Brent, Jeffrey Lynn, Alan Hale, Frank McHugh, Dennis (Stanley Morner) Morgan, William Lundigan, Dick Foran, Guinn "Big Boy" Williams, Henry O'Neill, John Litel, George Reeves; **D:** William Keighley; **W:** Fred Niblo, Norman Reilly Raine, Dean Franklin; **C:** Gaetano Antonio "Tony" Gaudio. *MGM, FCT*

The Fighting Stallion ☞☞☞ 1926 Canutt stars as a drifter hired by a rancher who's determined to capture a beautiful wild stallion (played by Boy the Wonder Horse). Silent with original organ score. 76m/B VHS, Beta, 8mm. Yakima Canutt, Neva Gerber, Bud Osborne. *GPV, VYY*

The Fighting Sullivans ☞☞☞½ *The Sullivans* 1942 The true story of five brothers killed on the Battleship Juneau at Guadalcanal during WWII. The tale tells of the fury felt by the siblings after Pearl Harbor, their enlistment to fight for their country, and their tragic fate in the heat of battle. Truly a stirring tribute to all lives lost in combat. 110m/B VHS. Anne Baxter, Thomas Mitchell, Selena Royle, Eddie Ryan, Trudy Marshall, James B. Cardwell, Roy Roberts, Ward Bond, Mary McCarty, Bobby Driscoll, Addison Richards, Selmer Jackson, Mae Marsh, Harry Strang, Barbara Brown; **D:** Lloyd Bacon. *IVY*

Fighting Texans ☞ 1933 An entire town invests in an oil well, on the advice of young salesman Bell, that the bankers are sure is a dud. Imagine their surprise when it turns out to be a gusler. 60m/B VHS. Rex Bell, Luana Walters, Betty Mack, Gordon DeMain; **D:** Armand Schaefer. *NOS, DVT*

Fighting Thru ☞ *California in 1878* 1930 Maynard fights off the bad guys and wins the girl after some nifty riding in his first all-talkie western. 60m/B VHS, Beta. Ken Maynard, Jeanette Loff; **D:** William Nigh. *NOS, DVT*

The Fighting Trooper ☞½ 1934 Based on the James Oliver Curwood story, "Footprints," this frontier tale presents a Mountie who goes undercover as a trapper in the Northwest. He is out to catch a murderer. 57m/B VHS, Beta. Kermit Maynard. *NOS, VDM, DVT*

Fighting Valley ☞☞ 1943 Texas Rangers O'Brien, Newill, and Wilkerson ride off to break up an outlaw gang that is trying to monopolize the ore smelting business. O'Brien later went on to directing for TV and also wrote for Red Skelton. 60m/B VHS. Dave O'Brien, James Newill, Guy Wilkerson, Patti McCarty, John Merton, Curly Dresden; **D:** Oliver Drake; **W:** Oliver Drake. *DVT, HEG*

Fighting Vigilantes ☞☞ 1947 A villainous food distributor is terrorizing his rivals until LaRue whips him. Holt and her father put together a committee called "The Vigilantes" to help out. Holt is the daughter of movie good guy Jack Holt. 61m/B VHS. Lash LaRue, Al "Fuzzy" St. John, Jennifer Holt, George Chesebro, Lee Morgan, Russell Arms, Steve Clark; **D:** Ray Taylor. *NOS*

The Fighting Westerner ☞½ *Rocky Mountain Mystery* 1935 Scott stars as a mining engineer who becomes entangled in mysterious murders. Mrs. Leslie Carter stars in a rare screen role. 54m/B VHS, Beta, 8mm. Randolph Scott, Chic Sale, Ann Sheridan, Charles T. Barton. *VYY, MRV*

Fighting with Kit Carson 1933 Famous guide and Indian fighter lead bands of settlers westward. Action-packed. Twelve chapters. 230m/B VHS, Beta. Johnny Mack Brown, Noah Beery Sr., Noah Beery Jr., Betsy King Ross; **D:** Armand Schaefer, Colbert Clark. *VYY, VCN, VDM*

Film House Fever ☞ 1986 A compilation of clips from sleazy, cult-type movies, including "Blood Feast" and "Hot Night at the Go Go Lounge." 58m/C VHS. Jamie Lee Curtis, James Keach, Lon Chaney Jr., Harvey Korman. *LIV, VES*

The Final Alliance ☞ 1989 (R) A tough loner takes on a vicious motorcycle gang that's terrorizing a small town, and realizes that they're also responsible for his family's death. 90m/C VHS, Beta, LV, Closed Caption. David Hasselhoff, John Saxon, Bo Hopkins, Jeanie Moore; **D:** Mario Di Leo. *COL*

Final Analysis ☞☞½ 1992 (R) Glossy thriller starring Gere as a San Francisco psychiatrist who falls for the glamorous sister of one of his patients. Basinger plays the femme fatale and Thurman is Gere's sexually neurotic patient. Although heavily influenced by "Vertigo," this film never comes close to attaining the depth of Hitchcock's cinematic masterpiece. Roberts gives the most gripping performance in this slick suspense movie as Basinger's sleazy gangster husband. **CW:** Language, violence, and one scene of strong sensuality. 125m/C VHS, LV, Closed Caption. Richard Gere, Kim Basinger, Uma Thurman, Eric Roberts, Paul Guilfoyle, Keith David, Robert Harper, Jolyon Baker, Harris Yulin, Agustin Rodriguez; **D:** Phil Joanou; **W:** Wesley Strick, Robert Berger; **C:** Jordan Cronenweth; **M:** George Fenton. *WAR*

Final Appeal ☞☞½ 1993 (PG-13) Christine Biondi (Williams) is an abused wife, living in terror of her drug-addicted doctor husband, Ed. When Christine walks in on Ed and his mistress, she's forced to kill him in self-defense. But Ed's mistress swears it was murder and Christine's on trial. Now her only chance is her hard-drinking lawyer brother Perry (Dennehy)—who doesn't believe her story. Fact-based made for TV fare. **CW:** Thematic material concerning substance abuse and domestic violence. 94m/C VHS, Closed Caption. JoBeth Williams, Brian Dennehy, Lindsay Crouse, Tom Mason, Eddie Jones, Ashley Crow, Betsy Brantley, Michael Beach; **M:** Charles Bernstein. *REP*

Final Approach ☞☞ 1991 (R) Test pilot Jason Halsey (Sikking) crashes in the desert and awakens in the office of psychiatrist Dio Gottlieb (Elizondo). Halsey can't remember anything about his past, or his own name for that matter, but through word association games and psychological tests, he begins to remember as Gottlieb tries to pry information from his brain. Showy computer effects are excellent, but they only serve to fill holes in a story that has an unsatisfying ending. Notable as first film mde with digital sound. Also available in a letterboxed version. **CW:** Language. 100m/C VHS, LV, Closed Caption. James B. Sikking, Hector Elizondo, Madolyn Smith, Kevin McCarthy, Cameo Kneuer, Wayne Duvall; **D:** Eric Steven Stahl. *THV*

Final Assignment ☞ 1980 A Canadian television reporter agrees to smuggle a dissident Soviet scientist's ill granddaughter out of Russia for treatment along with a videotape documenting tragic experiments on children with steroids. She manages to evade the KGB while carrying on with a Russian press officer, and enlists the support of a Jewish fur trader. Location shooting in Canada instead of Russia is just one pitfall of this production. Also on video as, "The Moscow Chronicle." 101m/C VHS, Beta. *CA* Genevieve Bujold, Michael York, Burgess Meredith, Colleen Dewhurst; **D:** Paul Almond. *LIV, VES*

Final Comedown ☞ 1972 (R) A black revolutionary attempts to get white radicals behind his war against racism. He fails and starts a racial bloodbath. 84m/C VHS, Beta. Billy Dee Williams, D'Urville Martin, Celia Kaye, Raymond St. Jacques, Pamela Jones, R.G. Armstrong; **D:** Oscar Williams. *NLC, SIM*

The Final Conflict ☞☞½ *The Omen 3* 1981 (R) Unwelcomed third installment in the "Omen" series, concerning Satan's son Damien. Now 32, and the head of an international conglomerate, he is poised for world domination but fears another savior is born. Several monks and many babies meet gruesome deaths before he gets his comeuppance. The last theatrical release was then followed by a made-for-television movie called "Omen 4: The Awakening" (1991). 108m/C VHS, Beta, LV. Sam Neill, Lisa Harrow, Barnaby Holm, Rossano Brazzi; **D:** Graham Baker; **W:** Andrew Birkin; **C:** Phil Meheux; **M:** Jerry Goldsmith. *FOX*

The Final Countdown ☞☞☞ 1980 (PG) A U.S. nuclear-powered aircraft carrier, caught in a time warp, is transported back to 1941, just hours before the bombing of Pearl Harbor. The commanders face the ultimate decision—leave history intact or stop the incident and thus avoid WWII. Excellent photography and a surprise ending. 92m/C VHS, Beta, LV. Kirk Douglas, Martin Sheen, Katharine Ross, James Farentino, Charles Durning; **D:** Don Taylor; **W:** Thomas Hunter, David Ambrose. *VES*

Final Cut ☞½ 1988 While filming in a secluded swampland, a crew stumbles on a local sheriff's crooked scheme and one by one, the crew members disappear. 92m/C VHS, Beta. Carla De Lane, T.J. Kennedy, Joe Rainer, Brett Rice, Jordan Williams; **D:** Larry G. Brown. *THV*

The Final Cut ☞☞☞ 1995 Follows "House of Cards" and "To Play the King" in portraying the political adventures of Francis Urquardt (Richardson), Prime Minister. At 65, Urquardt has two goals: he wants to beat Margaret Thatcher's 11-year reign and he wants to establish a secret retirement fund (the plot involves Cyprus and could—finally—leads to Urquardt's downfall). Author Michael Dobbs objected to the adaptation and insisted his name be removed from the script. On 2 cassettes. 200m/C VHS. *GB* Ian Richardson, Diane Fletcher, Paul Freeman, Isla Blair, Nick Brimble, Erika Hoffman, Nickolas Grace, Julian Fellowes; **D:** Mike Vardy; **W:** Andrew Davies; **C:** Ian Punter; **M:** Jim Parker. *FOX, FCT*

The Final Cut ☞☞ 1996 (R) John Pierce (Elliott) is a retired bomb squad specialist who's unwillingly called back to active duty to stop a bomber who's targeting Seattle. Along with ambitious officer Kathleen Hardy (Ramsay), Pierce tries to discover the bomber's next move—only to have suspicion fall upon himself. 99m/C VHS, LV, Closed Caption. Sam Elliott, Charles Martin Smith, Anne Elizabeth Ramsay, Matt Craven, Ray Baker, John Hannah, Amanda Plummer; **D:** Roger Christian; **W:** Raul Inglis; **C:** Mike Southon; **M:** Ross Vannelli. *REP*

The Final Days ☞☞½ 1989 (PG) TV drama follows the presidency of Richard Nixon (Smith) from Watergate through his resignation. Based on the Pulitzer Prize-winning book by Bob Woodward and Carl Bernstein. 150m/C VHS, Closed Caption. Lane Smith, Richard Kiley, David Ogden Stiers, Ed Flanders, Theodore Bikel; **D:** Richard Pearce. *REP*

Final Embrace ☞½ 1992 (R) When Laurel's famous sister is murdered she decides to do a little investigating on her own. She's aided by a young cop who just happened to be obsessed with the murdered woman. **CW:** Language, violence, and sensuality. ?m/C VHS, LV. Robert Rusler, Nancy Valen, Dick Van Patten, Linda Dona; **D:** Oley Sassone; **W:** R.J. Robertson, Jim Wynorski; **M:** Daniel Licht. *NHO*

Final Equinox ☞½ 1995 Mysterious alien artifact, which has the power to spontaneously create new life, is stolen and both the government and the mob try to be the first to find—and control—it. Cop Kove opposes them both. **90m/C VHS.** Martin Kove, Joe Lara, David Warner. *MNC*

Final Exam woof! 1981 (R) Psychotic killer stalks college students during exam week. This one's too boring to be scary. You root for the psycho to off everyone just to have the movie over. **90m/C VHS, Beta.** Cecile Bagdadi, Joel Rice; *D:* Jimmy Huston. *COL*

The Final Executioner 🎞 *The Last Warrior* 1983 A valiant man finds a way to stop the slaughter of innocent people in a post-nuclear world. **95m/C VHS, Beta.** William Mang, Marina Costa, Harrison Muller, Woody Strode; *D:* Romolo Guerrieri. *MGM*

Final Extra 🎞🎞 1927 Ambitious reporter's career gets a boost when he's assigned to investigate the murder of a rival. Silent with music score. **60m/B VHS, Beta, 8mm.** Grant Withers, Marguerite de la Motte. *NOS, VYY, DVT*

Final Impact 🎞½ 1991 (R) Nick Taylor seeks vengeance on reigning kickboxing champ Jake Gerard through his prodigy, Danny Davis. Will sweet revenge for the wicked beating, suffered at the hands of Gerard years earlier, be his?*CW:* Language and kickboxing violence. **99m/C VHS.** Lorenzo Lamas, Kathleen Kinmont, Mimi Lessoes, Kathrin Lautner, Jeff Langton, Mike Worth; *D:* Joseph Merhi, Stephen Smoke; *M:* John Gonzalez. *PMH*

Final Judgement 🎞🎞 1992 (R) Daniel Tyrone (Dourif) is a former gang member, now a troubled priest, who's the prime suspect in the Los Angeles murder of a beautiful stripper. Determined to find the killer Father Tyrone heads into L.A.'s underground sex industry to search for clues, which brings him face to face with evil and his own desires. **90m/C VHS.** Brad Dourif, Isaac Hayes, Maria Ford, Karen Black, Orson Bean, David Ledingham; *D:* Louis Morneau; *W:* Kirk Honeycutt, Louis Morneau. *COL*

Final Justice 🎞 1984 (R) A small-town Texan sheriff wages a war against crime and corruption that carries him to Italy and the haunts of Mafia hitmen. **90m/C VHS, Beta.** Joe Don Baker, Rossano Brazzi, Patrizia Pellegrino; *D:* Greydon Clark; *M:* David Bell. *VES*

Final Mission 🎞 1984 Vengeful one-man army follows the professional hit man who slaughtered his family from L.A. to Laos. His pursuit leads to a jungle showdown. Gee, sounds like "Rambo, First Blood," though obviously less grand and glorious. **97m/C VHS, Beta.** Richard Young, John Dresden, Kaz Garas, Christine Tudor; *D:* Cirio H. Santiago. *REP*

Final Mission 🎞🎞 1993 (R) Virtual reality becomes a weapon in a military conspiracy when pilots start dying. Air Force jets are supposed to be unstoppable thanks to the new technology and a general is only too willing to blame the deaths on pilot error but one fly boy is out to find the truth. **91m/C VHS, LV, Closed Caption.** Billy Wirth, Corbin Bernsen, Elizabeth Gracen, Steve Railsback. *THV*

Final Notice 🎞 1989 A detective tracking a serial killer has as his only evidence a trail of shredded photos of nude women. Not released theatrically. **91m/C VHS, Beta, LV, Closed Caption.** Gil Gerard, Steve Landesburg, Jackie Burroughs, Melody Anderson, Louise Fletcher, David Ogden Stiers, Kevin Hicks; *D:* Steven Hilliard Stern; *W:* John Gay; *M:* Tom Scott. *PAR*

The Final Option 🎞 *Who Dares Wins* 1982 (R) An agent of England's Special Air Services team goes undercover as one of a band of anti-nuclear terrorists that take over the U.S. Embassy in London. Violent, but unconvincing. **125m/C VHS, Beta.** *GB* Lewis Collins, Judy Davis, Richard Widmark, Robert Webber, Edward Woodward, Ingrid Pitt, Kenneth Griffith, Tony Doyle, John Duttine; *D:* Ian Sharp; *W:* Reginald Rose; *C:* Phil Meheux. *MGM*

The Final Programme 🎞🎞½ *The Last Days of Man on Earth* 1973 In this futuristic story, a man must rescue his sister—and the world—from their brother, who holds a microfilmed plan for global domination. Meanwhile, he must shield himself from the advances of a bisexual computer programmer who wants to make him father to a

new, all-purpose human being. Based on the Michael Moorcock "Jerry Cornelius" stories, the film has gained a cult following. **85m/C VHS, Beta.** *GB* Hugh Griffith, Harry Andrews, Jon Finch, Jenny Runacre, Sterling Hayden, Patrick Magee, Sarah Douglas; *D:* Robert Fuest.

Final Round 🎞½ 1993 (R) A kickboxer and his girlfriend are kidnapped by a millionaire who stages hunt the humans games for the pleasure of his gambling syndicate. Stiff but with a few good action sequences.*CW:* Language, violence, and sexuality. **90m/C VHS, Closed Caption.** Lorenzo Lamas, Anthony de Longis, Kathleen Kinmont, Clark Johnson, Isabelle Jamieson; *D:* George Erschbamer; *W:* Arne Olsen; *M:* Graeme Coleman. *WOV*

Final Sanction 🎞🎞½ 1989 After a nuclear holocaust exhausts their military resources, the U.S. and the Soviets each send one-man armies to battle each other for final control of the world. **90m/C VHS, Beta.** Robert Z'Dar, Ted Prior; *D:* David A. Prior; *W:* David A. Prior. *AIP, HHE*

Final Shot: The Hank Gathers Story 🎞🎞½ 1992 Inspirational story of Gathers, who rose from the ghetto to become one of America's top college basketball stars at Loyola Marymount, until tragedy strikes during a game. **92m/C VHS, Beta.** Victor Love, Duane Davis, Nell Carter, George Kennedy. *PSM*

The Final Terror 🎞🎞 *Campsite Massacre; Bump in the Night; The Forest Primeval* 1983 (R) Group of young campers is stalked by a mad killer in a desolate, backwoods area. Better-than-average stalked-teens entry is notable for the presence of some soon-to-be stars. **90m/C VHS, Beta, LV.** John Friedrich, Rachel Ward, Adrian Zmed, Daryl Hannah, Joe Pantoliano, Ernest Harden, Mark Metcalf, Lewis Smith, Cindy Harrel, Akosua Busia; *D:* Andrew Davis. *LIV, VES*

Final Verdict 🎞🎞½ 1991 A trial lawyer defends a man he knows is guilty, throwing his life and his family into turmoil. Made for cable television. **93m/C VHS, Beta, Closed Caption.** Treat Williams, Glenn Ford, Amy Wright, Olivia Burnette; *D:* Jack Fisk; *C:* Paul Elliott. *TTC*

Final Warning 🎞🎞½ *Chernobyl: The Final Warning* 1990 A dramatization of actual events surrounding the 1986 melt-down of the nuclear power plant at Chernobyl. Made for television. **94m/C VHS, Closed Caption.** Jon Voight, Jason Robards Jr., Sammi Davis; *D:* Anthony Page. *TTC*

Find the Lady 🎞½ *Call the Cops; Kopek and Broom* 1975 (R) Candy assumes a supporting role as a bumbling cop who is part of an incompetent police team trying to rescue a kidnapped socialite. **100m/C VHS, Beta.** *CA* John Candy, Peter Cook, Mickey Rooney, Lawrence Dane, Alexandra Bastedo; *D:* John Trent. *NO*

Finders Keepers 🎞🎞 1984 (R) A wild assortment of characters on board a train en route from California to Nebraska search for five million dollars hidden in the baggage car. **96m/C VHS, Beta, Closed Caption.** Michael O'Keefe, Beverly D'Angelo, Ed Lauter, Louis Gossett Jr., Pamela Stephenson, Jim Carrey, David Wayne, Brian Dennehy, John Schuck; *D:* Richard Lester; *W:* Ronny Graham. *FOX*

Fine Gold 🎞🎞 1988 A false charge of embezzlement leaves a man without home and family, so he decides to turn the tables on those who betrayed him. **91m/C VHS, Beta.** Andrew Stevens, Ray Walston, Ted Wass, Stewart Granger, Lloyd Bochner, Jane Badler; *D:* J. Anthony Loma. *MCG*

A Fine Madness 🎞🎞🎞 1966 A near-classic comedy about a lusty, rebellious poet thrashing against the pressures of the modern world, and fending off a bevy of lobotomy-happy psychiatrists. Shot on location in New York City, based on Elliot Baker's novel. **104m/C VHS, Beta.** Sean Connery, Joanne Woodward, Jean Seberg, Patrick O'Neal, Colleen Dewhurst, Clive Revill, John Fiedler; *D:* Irvin Kershner; *M:* John Addison. *WAR*

A Fine Mess 🎞½ 1986 (PG) Two buffoons cash in when one overhears a plan to dope a racehorse, but they are soon fleeing the plotters' slapstick pursuit. The plot is further complicated by the romantic interest of a gangster's wife. The television popularity of the two stars did not translate to the big screen; perhaps it's Edwards' fault. **100m/C VHS, Beta, LV, Closed Caption.** Ted Danson, Howie Mandel, Richard Mulligan, Stuart Margolin, Maria Conchita Alonso, Paul Sorvino; *D:* Blake Edwards; *W:* Blake Edwards; *C:* Harry Stradling Jr.; *M:* Henry Mancini. *COL*

A Fine Romance 🎞🎞 1992 (PG-13) An improbable romance set in Paris features Andrews and Mastroianni as abandoned spouses falling in love. Andrews is the prim English Pamela who has been abandoned by her docter husband. Mastroianni is the irrepressible Cesareo, whose wife has just happened to run off with the aforementioned doctor. They meet to plan how to get their spouses back and wind up with opposites attracting. Not much story and the charm is spread thin. Based on the play "Tchin, Tchin" by Francois Billetdoux.*CW:* Nudity. **83m/C VHS.** Julie Andrews, Marcello Mastroianni, Ian Fitzgibbon, Jean-Pierre Castaldi, Jean-Jacques Dulon, Maria Machado, Jean-Michel Cannone, Catherine Jarrett, Gene Saks; *W:* Ronald Harwood; *M:* Pino Donaggio. *ACA*

Fine Things 🎞🎞½ *Danielle Steel's Fine Things* 1990 Bernie Fine thinks everything will be dandy now that he has a beautiful new bride and a cute stepdaughter. Then his wife dies and his stepdaughter's unreliable father wants sole custody. What's a nice guy to do? Based on the novel by Danielle Steel. Made for television. **145m/C VHS, Closed Caption.** D.W. Moffett, Tracy Pollan, Judith Hoag, Cloris Leachman, Noley Thornton; *D:* Tom Moore; *W:* Peter Lefcourt. *CMB, WOV*

Finessing the King 🎞🎞½ 1984 Private eyes Tommy and Tuppence follow a mysterious newspaper notice to a masked ball where a murder is about to occur. Based on the Agatha Christie story. Made for British television. **60m/C VHS, Beta.** *GB* James Warwick, Francesca Annis. *TPV*

The Finest Hour 🎞½ 1991 (R) Two Navy buddies have a falling out when they both fall for the same woman. But they must put aside their differences when their next mission sends them to Iraq to deal with the deadly threat of biological warfare.*CW:* Language and war violence. **105m/C VHS, LV, Closed Caption.** Rob Lowe, Gale Hansen, Tracy Griffith, Eb Lottimer; *D:* Shimon Dotan; *W:* Shimon Dotan. *COL*

The Finger Man 🎞🎞½ 1955 An ex-con cooperates with the feds rather than return to jail. The deal is that he gets the dirt on an underworld crime boss. Solid performances. **82m/B VHS.** Frank Lovejoy, Forrest Tucker, Peggy Castle, Timothy Carey, Glenn Gordon; *D:* Harold Schuster. *REP*

Finger on the Trigger 🎞🎞 *El Dedo En El Gatillo* 1965 Veterans from both sides of the Civil War are after a hidden supply of gold, but find that they must band together to fend off an Indian attack. Routine. **89m/C VHS, Beta.** Rory Calhoun, James Philbrook, Todd Martin, Silvia Solar, Brad Talbot; *D:* Sidney Pink. *NO*

Fingerprints Don't Lie 🎞 1951 A fingerprint expert pins the murder of the town mayor on an innocent guy, then suspects a frame-up. **56m/B VHS, Beta, LV.** Richard Travis, Sheila Ryan, Tom Neal; *D:* Sam Newfield. *NO*

Fingers 🎞🎞🎞 1978 (R) Keitel is Johnny Fingers, a mobster's son, reluctantly working as a mob debt-collector, all the while dreaming of his ambitions to be a concert pianist. The divisions between his dreams and reality cause him to crack. Toback's first film generates psychological tension and excellent performances. **89m/C VHS, Beta.** Harvey Keitel, Tisa Farrow, Jim Brown, Danny Aiello, Tanya Roberts, Marian Seldes, Michael V. Gazzo, James Toback; *D:* James Toback; *W:* James Toback; *C:* Michael Chapman; *M:* George Barrie. *TTC*

Finian's Rainbow 🎬🎬🎬 1968 (G) A leprechaun comes to America to steal back a pot of gold taken by an Irishman and his daughter in this fanciful musical comedy based on a 1947 Broadway hit. Both the sprite and the girl find romance; the share-cropping locals are saved by the cash; a bigot learns the error of his ways; and Finian (Astaire) dances off to new adventures. The fine production and talented cast are not used to their best advantage by the director who proved much better suited for "The Godfather." Entertaining, nonetheless. 🎵How Are Things in Glocca Morra?; Look To the Rainbow; That Old Devil Moon; If This Isn't Love; Something Sort of Grandish; The Be-Gat; This Time of Year; The Great Come and Get It Day; When I'm Not Near the Girl I Love. **141m/C VHS, Beta, LV.** Fred Astaire, Petula Clark, Tommy Steele, Keenan Wynn, Al Freeman Jr., Don Francks, Susan Hancock, Dolph Sweet; **D:** Francis Ford Coppola. Nominations: Academy Awards '68: Best Sound, Scoring of a Musical. *WAR, MVD*

Finish Line 🎬🎬½ 1989 A high school track star turns to steroids to enhance his performance after being pushed by an overzealous father. The father-and-son Brolins play the pair. Made for cable. **100m/C VHS.** James Brolin, Josh Brolin, Mariska Hargitay, Kristoff St. John, John Finnegan, Billy Vera, Stephen Lang; **D:** John Nicolella. *TTC*

Finishing School 🎬½ 1933 Girls' school roommates Rogers and Dee experience heartaches and loves lost while enduring disinterested parents and snobbish peers. Box office bomb when released, despite a strong cast. **73m/B VHS, Beta.** Ginger Rogers, Frances Dee, George Nicholls Jr., Beulah Bondi, Bruce Cabot, Billie Burke, John Halliday, Sara Haden, Jack Norton, Joan Barclay, Jane Darwell; **D:** George Nicholls Jr.; **M:** Max Steiner. *TTC*

The Finishing Touch 🎬🎬 1992 (R) Someone is stalking L.A.'s most gorgeous women and Detective Sam Stone (Nader) is assigned to the case. Stone discovers his prime suspect is a video artist with a taste for pornography. When Stone's investigation is cut short, his ex-wife, Detective Hannah Stone (Hack) is brought in to take over the case. Unfortunately, she finds herself falling for the suspect in this erotic thriller. **CW:** Language, violence, and sensuality. **82m/C VHS, Closed Caption.** Michael Nader, Shelley Hack, Arnold Vosloo, Art Evans, Clark Johnson, Theodore (Ted) Raimi; **D:** Fred Gallo. *COL*

Finnegan Begin Again 🎬🎬 1984 A middle-aged schoolteacher and a grouchy, 65-year-old newspaper editor find romance despite their other obligations. Winning performances add charm to this cable TV movie. **112m/C VHS, Beta.** Mary Tyler Moore, Robert Preston, Sam Waterston, Sylvia Sidney, David Huddleston; **D:** Joan Micklin Silver. *CNG, KAR*

Finnegan's Wake Passages from "Finnegans Wake"; Passages from James Joyce's "Finnegans Wake" 1963 Portions of the filmed adaptation of James Joyce's novel are shown in this program along with an interview with producer/director Mary Ellen Bute. **92m/B VHS, Beta.** *CMR, NVW*

Fiorile 🎬🎬🎬 Wild Flower 1993 (PG-13) Covers several generations of a Tuscan clan living under a family curse which dates back to Napoleon's invasion of Italy. At that time Jean, a handsome French lieutenant, falls in love with Tuscan peasant girl Elisabetta, nicknamed Fiorile. When Jean is executed for a theft committed by her brother, the pregnant Fiorile vows revenge. Throughout sucessive generations, haunted by the past, the family's personal bad luck persists. Several of the actors play their character's ancestors, lending continuity. Attractive cast does well with the Taviani brothers' visual style and romantic narrative. In Italian with English subtitles. **CW:** Nudity and violence. **118m/C VHS, LV.** *IT* Michael Vartan, Galatea Ranzi, Claudio Bigagli, Lino Capolicchio, Constanze Engelbrecht, Athina Cenci, Giovanni Guidelli, Chiara Caselli; **D:** Paolo Taviani, Vittorio Taviani; **W:** Paolo Taviani, Vittorio Taviani, Sandro Petraglia; **M:** Nicola Piovani. *NLC*

Fire 🎬½ 1977 A fire started by an escaped convict rages through Oregon timberland in this suspenseful made-for-television Irwin Allen disaster drama. **98m/C VHS, Beta.** Ernest Borgnine, Vera Miles, Patty Duke, Alex Cord, Donna Mills; **D:** Earl Bellamy. *WAR*

Fire Alarm 🎬 1938 A change of scene for Western star Brown as he portrays a fireman who, in-between his work, romances a career girl. **67m/B VHS, Beta, LV.** Johnny Mack Brown, Noel Francis; **D:** Karl Brown. *NOS, VYY, HEG*

Fire and Ice 🎬🎬½ 1983 (PG) An animated adventure film that culminates in a tense battle between good and evil, surrounded by the mystical elements of the ancient past. Designed by Frank Frazetta. **81m/C VHS, Beta, LV.** Randy Norton, Cynthia Leake; **D:** Ralph Bakshi; **W:** Ralph Bakshi, Willy Bogner, Gerry Conway; **V:** Susan Tyrrell, William Ostrander. *COL*

Fire and Ice 🎬 1987 (PG) A tale of love on the slopes. Two skiers realize that their feelings for each other are perhaps even stronger than their feelings about skiing. You won't care though, except for some fine ski footage. **83m/C VHS, Beta, LV, Closed Caption.** Suzy Chaffee, John Eaves; **D:** Willy Bogner; **W:** George Schlatter; **M:** Harold Faltermeyer.

Fire and Rain 🎬🎬 1989 Based on the real-life crash of a Delta Airlines plane in Dallas and the rescue efforts made following the disaster. Familiar cast-members turn in decent performance. Made for television. **89m/C VHS, Beta, LV, Closed Caption.** Angie Dickinson, Charles Haid, Tom Bosley, David Hasselhoff, Robert Guillaume, Susan Ruttan, John Beck, Patti LaBelle, Dean Jones, Lawrence Pressman, Penny Fuller; **D:** Jerry Jameson; **W:** Gary Sherman. *PAR*

Fire and Sword 🎬 1982 A Cornish knight must choose between loyalty for king and country and the love of an Irish woman in this medieval drama. A not very inspired retelling of the Tristan and Isolde legend. **84m/C VHS, Beta.** *GB* Peter Firth, Leigh Lawson, Antonia Preser, Christopher Waitz; **D:** Veith von Furstenberg. *LIV*

Fire Birds 🎬 Wings of the Apache 1990 (PG-13) Army attack helicopters and the people who fly them are used in the war on drugs in South America. Failed to match either the exciting flight sequences, the romantic interest or the box office of "Top Gun." **85m/C VHS, Beta, LV, Closed Caption.** Nicolas Cage, Tommy Lee Jones, Sean Young, Bryan Kestner, Dale Dye, Mary Ellen Trainor, J.A. Preston, Peter Onorati; **D:** David Green; **W:** Nick Thiel, Paul F. Edwards; **M:** David Newman. *TOU*

Fire Down Below 🎬½ 1957 Hayworth is the been-around-the-block beauty who persuades Mitchum and Lemmon, two small-time smugglers, to take her to a safe haven, no questions asked. Both men fall for her obvious charms, causing them to have a falling out until a life or death situation puts their friendship to the test. An unoriginal melodrama indifferently acted by everyone but Lemmon. Good location work in Trinidad and Tobago. **116m/C VHS, Beta, LV.** *GB* Robert Mitchum, Jack Lemmon, Rita Hayworth, Herbert Lom, Anthony Newley; **D:** Robert Parrish. *COL, COL, CCB*

Fire, Ice and Dynamite 🎬½ 1991 (PG) Moore is onscreen only briefly as an eccentric tycoon who fakes suicide to watch several teams of challengers scramble in a madcap winter-sports contest for his millions. A German-made avalanche of crazy stunts, bad jokes, and product plugs for countless European companies, commencing with a literal parade of guests, from astronaut Buzz Aldrin to soul man Isaac Hayes. Numbing; must be seen to be believed. **105m/C VHS.** Roger Moore, Shari Belafonte, Simon Shepherd, Uwe Ochsenknecht, Marjoe Gortner; **D:** Willy Bogner. *VES, LIV*

Fire in the Night 🎬½ 1985 In a small Southern town, a beautiful and sure-footed woman battles the limitless resources of the town's predominant dynastic family. **89m/C VHS, Beta.** Graciela Casillas, John Martin. *VTR, NWV*

Fire in the Sky 🎬🎬 1993 (PG-13) Mysterious disappearance of Sweeney sparks a criminal investigation, until he returns, claiming he was abducted by aliens. Though everybody doubts his story, viewers won't, since the alleged aliens have already made an appearance, shifting the focus to Sweeney as he tries to convince skeptics that his trauma is genuine. Perhaps this mirrors what director Lieberman went through while trying to convince backers the film should be made. He could have benefitted by understanding the difference between what he was telling viewers and what he was showing them. Captivating special effects are one of the few bright spots. Based on a story that might be true. **CW:** Strong language, some strong violence, and some strong sensuality. **98m/C VHS, Beta, LV, Closed Caption.** D.B. Sweeney, Robert Patrick, Craig Sheffer, Peter Berg, James Garner, Henry Thomas; **D:** Robert Liebmann; **W:** Tracy Torme; **M:** Mark Isham. *PAR*

The Fire in the Stone 🎬🎬 1985 A young boy discovers an opal mine and dreams of using the treasure to reunite his family. However, when the jewels are stolen from him, he enlists his friends to help get them back. Based on the novel by Colin Thiele. **97m/C VHS, Beta.** *AU* Paul Smith, Linda Hartley, Theo Pertsindis. *WAR*

Fire Maidens from Outer Space 🎬 1956 Fire maidens prove to be true to the space opera code that dictates that all alien women be in desperate need of male company. Astronauts on an expedition to Jupiter's thirteenth moon discover the lost civilization of Atlantis, which, as luck would have it, is inhabited by women only. Possibly an idea before its time, it might've been better had it been made in the sixties, when space-exploitation came into its own. **80m/B VHS.** *GB* Anthony Dexter, Susan Shaw, Paul Carpenter, Harry Fowler, Jacqueline Curtiss, Sydney Tafler, Maya Koumani, Jan Holden, Kim Parker, Rodney Diak, Owen Berry; **D:** Cy Roth; **W:** Cy Roth. *CNM, MLB*

Fire Monsters Against the Son of Hercules 🎬🎬 1962 The son of the muscular one does battle with a hydra-headed monster in this average sword and sandal adventure. **?m/C VHS.** Reg Lewis. *SNC*

The Fire Next Time 🎬🎬½ 1993 In the year 2017, the United States is being ravaged by an ecological holocaust caused by a deadly combination of pollution and global warming. Nelson, Bedelia and their children are forced from their Louisiana home by a natural disaster and decide to head for better times in Canada. Their travels aren't easy. Made for television. **195m/C VHS, Closed Caption.** Craig T. Nelson, Bonnie Bedelia, Juergen Prochnow, Richard Farnsworth, Justin Whalin, Charles Haid, Sal Lopez, Shawn Toovey, Ashley Jones; **Cameos:** Odetta; **D:** Tom McLoughlin; **W:** James Henerson. *CAF*

Fire Over England 🎬🎬🎬 1937 Young naval officer volunteers to spy at the Spanish court to learn the plans for the invasion of his native England and to identify the traitors among the English nobility. He arouses the romantic interest of his queen, Elizabeth I, one of her ladies, and a Spanish noblewoman who helps with his missions, and later leads the fleet to victory over the huge Spanish Armada. The first on-screen pairing of Olivier and Leigh is just one of the many virtues of this entertaining drama. **81m/B VHS, Beta.** *GB* Flora Robson, Raymond Massey, Laurence Olivier, Vivien Leigh, Leslie Banks, James Mason; **D:** William K. Howard; **C:** James Wong Howe. *NOS, MRV, VYY*

Fire with Fire 🎬🎬 1986 (PG-13) A boy at a juvenile detention center and a Catholic school girl fall in love. However, they find themselves on the run from the law when he escapes to be with her. Sheffer and Madsen are appealing in this otherwise unspectacular film. **103m/C VHS.** Craig Sheffer, Virginia Madsen, Jon Polito, Kate Reid, Jean Smart, D.B. Sweeney; **D:** Duncan Gibbins; **W:** Bill Phillips, Paul Boorstin, Sharon Boorstin; **M:** Howard Shore. *PAR*

The Fire Within 🐾🐾🐾 *Le Feu Follet; Fuoco Fatuo* 1964 Ronet plays an alcoholic writer recently released from a sanitorium after a breakdown. Believing his life will only continue its downward spiral, he pays a final visit to friends and calmly plots his suicide. Malle clearly and pitilessly describes a man beyond despair. Based on a novel by Pierre Drieu La Rochelle, which itself fictionalized the suicide of writer Jacques Rigaut. In French with English subtitles. 104m/B VHS. **FR** Maurice Ronet, Lena Skerla, Yvonne Clech, Hubert Deschamps, Jean-Paul Moulinot; **D:** Louis Malle; **W:** Louis Malle; **C:** Ghislan Cloquet. *NYF, PMS*

Fireback 🐾½ 1978 A Vietnam vet's wife is kidnapped by the mob, causing him to take up arms and spill blood yet again. 90m/C VHS, Beta. Bruce Baron, Richard Harrison. *LIV*

Fireball Forward 🐾🐾 1972 (PG) A battalion fighting in France during WWII is having a bad time until Gazzara takes over and turns them into a crack fighting team. Uses some battle footage from the movie "Patton." Made for television. 100m/C VHS. Ben Gazzara, Eddie Albert, Ricardo Montalban, Dana Elcar, L.Q. Jones, Anne Francis; **D:** Marvin J. Chomsky. *QVD*

Fireballs 🐾½ 1990 Sexploitaton pic set at a firehouse, where a batch of female recruits turn up the heat for three stud hose-bearers. The title should give you some idea of the intellectual level. 89m/C VHS. Mike Shapiro, Goren Kalezik; **D:** Mike Shapiro. *ATL*

Firebird 2015 A.D. 🐾 1981 (PG) Dreary action adventure set in a 21st century society where automobile use is banned because of an extreme oil shortage. Private cars are hunted down for destruction by the Department of Vehicular Control. One over-zealous enforcer decides to make it a package deal and throws in the owners as well. Everyone connected with effort should have been cited for running stop sign. 97m/C VHS, Beta. Darren McGavin, George Touliatos, Doug McClure; **D:** David Robertson.

Firecracker 🐾 1971 Female martial arts expert retaliates against the crooks who murdered her sister. 83m/C VHS, Beta. Jillian Kesner, Darby Hinton; **D:** Cirio H. Santiago. *NO*

Firecreek 🐾🐾 1968 Fonda and his thugs terrorize a small town protected by part-time sheriff Stewart. Beautiful photography and competent cast, but meandering and long. 104m/C VHS. Henry Fonda, James Stewart, Inger Stevens, Gary Lockwood, Dean Jagger, Ed Begley Sr., Jay C. Flippen, Jack Elam, Barbara Luna; **D:** Vincent McEveety; **C:** William Clothier. *WAR, VTR, MTX*

Firefall 🐾🐾 *Freefall* 1994 Wildlife photog Katy Mazur (Gidley) has a brief affair with sportsman Grant Orion (Roberts) while on assignment in Africa. When they meet again, Orion tells Katy he's actually an Interpol agent who's assigned to protect her—although she has no idea why. Katy's fiance (Fahey) thinks this is strange. 95m/C VHS, LV, Closed Caption. Pamela Gidley, Eric Roberts, Jeff Fahey; **D:** John Irvin. *THV*

Firefight 🐾 1987 After a nuclear holocaust, convicted criminals endeavor to rule the wasteland. 100m/C VHS, Beta. James Pfeiffer, Janice Carraher, Jack Tucker; **D:** Scott Pfeiffer. *TWE*

The Firefly 🐾🐾½ 1937 Although slow-paced and long, this adaptation of the 1912 Rudolf Friml operetta was one of MacDonald's most popular films. Co-star Jones gets to sing the best song in the film, "Donkey Serenade," while MacDonald sings most of the others. ♫Love Is Like a Firefly; English March; A Woman's Kiss; He Who Loves and Runs Away; When a Maid Comes Knocking at Your Heart; When the Wine Is Full of Fire; The Donkey Serenade; Giannina Mia; Sympathy. 140m/B VHS, Closed Caption. Jeanette MacDonald, Allan Jones, Warren William, Billy Gilbert, Henry Daniell, Douglass Dumbrille, George Zucco; **D:** Robert Z. Leonard. *MGM*

Firefox 🐾🐾½ 1982 (PG) A retired pilot sneaks into the Soviet Union for the Pentagon to steal a top-secret, ultra-sophisticated warplane and fly it out of the country. Best for the low-altitude flight and aerial battle sequences, but too slow on character and much too slow getting started. 136m/C VHS, Beta, LV. Clint Eastwood, Freddie Jones, David Huffman, Warren Clarke, Ronald Lacey, Kenneth Colley, Nigel Hawthorne, Kai Wulff; **D:** Clint Eastwood; **C:** Bruce Surtees; **M:** Maurice Jarre. *WAR*

Firehawk 🐾🐾 1992 (R) Several American soldiers survive the crash of their helicopter into the jungles of Vietnam. They think their only enemy is the Vietcong but when they discover the copter has been sabotaged the hunt is on for the traitor among them. **CW:** Strong language and war violence. 92m/C VHS, LV. Martin Kove, Matt Salinger, Vic Trevino; **D:** Cirio H. Santiago; **W:** Jeff Yonis. *LIV*

Firehead 🐾🐾½ 1990 (R) A pyrokinetic Soviet defector begins using his powers to destroy American munitions in the name of peace. When a clandestine pro-war organization hears of this, they attempt to capture the man and use him for their own evil purposes. 88m/C VHS, Beta, LV. Christopher Plummer, Chris Lemmon, Martin Landau, Gretchen Becker, Brett Porter; **D:** Peter Yuval. *AIP*

Firehouse 🐾🐾 1972 Tempers ignite in a lily-white firehouse when a black rookie replaces an expired veteran. March—of "Paper Lion" renown—directed this made-for-TV emergency clone, which ran ever-so-briefly as an adventure series on TV in 1974 (with a largely different cast). 73m/C VHS. Richard Roundtree, Vince Edwards, Andrew Duggan, Richard Jaeckel, Sheila Frazier, Val Avery, Paul LeMat, Michael Lerner; **D:** Alex March. *XVC*

Firehouse 🐾 1987 (R) In the style of "Police Academy," three beautiful and sex-starved fire-fighting recruits klutz up an urban firehouse. A softcore frolic. 91m/C VHS, Beta. Barrett Hopkins, Shannon Murphy, Violet Brown, John Anderson; **D:** J. Christian Ingvordsen. *ACA*

The Fireman 🐾🐾½ 1916 Chaplin portrays a fireman who becomes a hero. Silent with musical soundtrack added. 20m/B VHS, Beta. Eric Campbell, Edna Purviance, Charlie Chaplin; **D:** Charlie Chaplin. *CAB, GVV, VYY*

The Firemen's Ball 🐾🐾🐾 1968 A critically acclaimed comedy about a small-town ball held for a retiring fire chief. Plans go amusingly awry as beauty contestants refuse to show themselves, raffle prizes and other items—including the gift for the guest of honor—are stolen, and the firemen are unable to prevent an old man's house from burning down. Forman's second film is sometimes interpreted as political allegory; Czech with subtitles. 73m/C VHS, Beta. **CZ** Vaclav Stockel, Josef Svet; **D:** Milos Forman. Nominations: Academy Awards '68: Best Foreign Language Film. *HMV, COL, BTV*

Firepower 🐾🐾½ 1979 (R) Loren blames her chemist husband's death on a rich industrialist and hires hitman Coburn to take care of the matter. Less than compelling. 104m/C VHS, Beta. Sophia Loren, James Coburn, O.J. Simpson, Christopher F. Bean; **D:** Michael Winner; **W:** Michael Winner; **M:** Gato Barbieri. *FOX*

Firepower 🐾½ 1993 (R) Two cops chase "The Swordsman" into a federally sanctioned area of legalized gambling, prostitution and crime (Las Vegas?), risking life and limb in the treacherous "Caged Ring of Death." ?m/C VHS, LV, Closed Caption. Chad McQueen, Gary Daniels, Jim Hellwig, Joseph Ruskin, George Murdock. *PMH*

Fires on the Plain 🐾🐾🐾 *Nobi* 1959 A grueling Japanese antiwar film about an unhinged private in the Philippines during WWII who roams the war-torn countryside encountering all manner of horror and devastation. In Japanese with English subtitles. 105m/B VHS, Beta. **JP** Eiji Funakoshi, Osamu Takizawa, Mickey Custis, Asao Suno; **D:** Kon Ichikawa. *MRV, HHT, NLC*

Fires Within 🐾🐾 1991 (R) A curiously flat romance with political overtones. After eight years as a political prisoner in Cuba, Nestor (Smits) is released and goes to Miami to be reunited with his wife and daughter. Once there he finds his wife has fallen in love with another man. Now Nestor must choose between his politics and the chance to win back his family. Secondary plot lines fizzle out and a talented cast is largely wasted. Scacchi is beautiful but hardly believable as the Cuban wife. **CW:** Language and sensuality. 90m/C VHS, Beta. Jimmy Smits, Greta Scacchi, Vincent D'Onofrio; **D:** Gillian Armstrong; **W:** Cynthia Cidre. *MGM*

Firestarter 🐾🐾 1984 (R) A C.I.A.-like organization is after a little girl who has the ability to set anything on fire in this filmed adaptation of Stephen King's bestseller. Good special effects help a silly plot. 115m/C VHS, Beta, LV, Closed Caption. David Keith, Drew Barrymore, Freddie Jones, Martin Sheen, George C. Scott, Heather Locklear, Louise Fletcher, Moses Gunn, Art Carney, Antonio Fargas, Drew Snyder; **D:** Mark L. Lester; **M:** Tangerine Dream. *USH*

Firestorm: 72 Hours in Oakland 🐾🐾½ 1993 Residents of an Oakland community face the threat of a big brush fire. 94m/C VHS. LeVar Burton, Jill Clayburgh, Michael Gross; **D:** Michael Tuchner. *ABC*

Firewalker 🐾 1986 (PG) An "Indiana Jones" clone about three mercenaries endeavoring to capture a fortune in hidden gold. Paper-mache sets and a villain with an eye patch that consistently changes eyes are just some of the gaffes that make this one of the worst edited movies in history. 106m/C VHS, Beta, LV, Closed Caption. Chuck Norris, Louis Gossett Jr., Melody Anderson; **D:** J. Lee Thompson; **W:** Norman Aladjem; **M:** Gary Chang. *MED, VTR*

The Firing Line 🐾🐾 1991 The Central American government hires a mercenary rebel-buster to squash insurgents. Everything's great until he finds out he agrees with the rebel cause, and he trains them to fight the government. Below average renegade-with-a-hidden-heart warpic. 93m/C VHS, LV. Reb Brown, Shannon Tweed; **D:** John Gale. *AIP*

The Firm 🐾🐾🐾 1993 (R) Top-flight cast promises a good time—the script based on the top-selling 1991 novel by John Grisham nearly guarantees it. Ambitious, idealistic Ivy League law school grad Cruise accepts a great offer from a small but wealthy Memphis law firm. As with anything that seems too good to be true, he discovers too late that nothing in life is free. Good performances by nearly everyone involved makes up for predictability. Sorvino has an uncredited cameo as a mob boss. Book fans beware: the script is fairly faithful until the end. The movie rights were snapped up before the book was published. Placed third in the 1993 race for top box office gross. **CW:** Language and some violence. 154m/C VHS, Beta, LV, CD-I, Closed Caption. Tom Cruise, Jeanne Tripplehorn, Gene Hackman, Hal Holbrook, Terry Kinney, Wilford Brimley, Ed Harris, Holly Hunter, David Strathairn, Gary Busey, Steven Hill, Tobin Bell, Barbara Garrick, Jerry Hardin, Karina Lombard, John Beal; **Cameos:** Paul Sorvino; **D:** Sydney Pollack; **W:** Robert Towne, David Rayfiel; **C:** John Seale; **M:** Dave Grusin. Nominations: Academy Awards '93: Best Supporting Actress (Hunter), Best Original Score; British Academy Awards '93: Best Supporting Actress (Hunter); MTV Movie Awards '94: Best Actor (Cruise), Most Desirable Male (Cruise). *PAR, BTV, FCT*

First Affair 1983 A made-for-television film about a young innocent girl undergoing the pressures of freshman life at college, including her first love affair, which is with the husband of a female professor. 95m/C VHS, Beta. Loretta Swit, Melissa Sue Anderson, Joel Higgins; **D:** Gus Trikonis. *FOX*

First & Ten 🐾🐾 1985 A failing football team emphasizes sexual, rather than athletic conquests, under the guidance of their female owner. Made for cable TV and followed by "First & Ten: The Team Scores Again." 88m/C VHS, Beta. Delta

Burke, Geoffrey Scott, Reid Shelton, Ruta Lee, Fran Tarkenton; *D:* Donald Kushner. *LIV, VES*

First & Ten: The Team Scores Again 🎬 1985 A sequel to the made-for-cable-television comedy "First and Ten" about a football team's relationship with their female owner. 101m/C VHS, Beta. Delta Burke, Geoffrey Scott, Ruta Lee, Reid Shelton, Clayton Landey, Fran Tarkenton. *LIV, VES*

First Blood 🎬🎬 1982 (R) Stallone is a former Green Beret survivor of Vietnam whose nightmares of wartime horrors are triggered by a wrongful arrest in a small town. He escapes into the mountains of the Northwest and leads his pursuers to all manner of bloody ends. Finally, the Army is summoned to crush him. Extremely violent and frequently confused, fueled on the revenge fantasy and not much concerned with the rules of plot realism. Screen debut of Caruso. Based on David Morrell's novel. A box-office hit that launched the "Rambo" series. Followed by "Rambo: First Blood, Part 2." 96m/C VHS, Beta, LV. Sylvester Stallone, Richard Crenna, Brian Dennehy, Jack Starrett, David Caruso; *D:* Ted Kotcheff; *W:* Sylvester Stallone; *M:* Jerry Goldsmith. *LIV, TLF*

First Born 🎬🎬½ 1984 (PG-13) In search of romance, divorced mother Garr finds an intriguing man, Weller. Trouble erupts when her son learns Weller is a cocaine dealer. Talented cast makes most of story. 100m/C VHS, Beta, LV, Closed Caption. Teri Garr, Peter Weller, Christopher Collet, Corey Haim, Sarah Jessica Parker, Robert Downey Jr.; *D:* Michael Apted; *C:* Ralf Bode. *NO*

The First Deadly Sin 🎬½ 1980 (R) Police lieutenant Sinatra tracks down a homicidal killer in spite of wife Dunaway's illness and his impending retirement. Read Lawrence Sanders' bestselling novel; it's a lot more exciting than this. 112m/C VHS, Beta, LV. Frank Sinatra, Faye Dunaway, David Dukes, Brenda Vaccaro, James Whitmore; *D:* Brian G. Hutton; *C:* Jack Priestley. *WAR*

First Degree 🎬½ 1995 (R) New York City homicide detective Rick Mallory (Lowe) goes up against the mob while investigating the murder of a rich man and falling for the widow. Made for cable.*CW:* Language, violence, and some sexuality. 98m/C VHS. CA Rob Lowe, Leslie Hope, Tom McCamus, Nadia Capone, Brett Halsey; *D:* Jeff Woolnough; *W:* Ron Base; *C:* Glen MacPherson. *PGV*

First Family 🎬½ 1980 (R) Flat satire of life in the White House. The humor is weak and silly at best, despite the excellent comedy cast. Henry's first directorial effort. 100m/C VHS, Beta. Bob Newhart, Madeline Kahn, Gilda Radner, Richard Benjamin; *D:* Buck Henry; *W:* Buck Henry; *M:* Ralph Burns. *WAR*

First Kid 🎬🎬 1996 (PG) Formulaic "Home Alone Guarding Tess" does have its moments, but if you're over 14, probably not enough of them. Latest in a bevy of films to be inaugurated into the white hot "White House" genre-of-the-moment. Innocuous family comedy casts Sinbad as Sam Simms, an offbeat Secret Service agent who is given the menial job of guarding Prez's bratty son Luke (Pierce). Simms sees that Luke is merely a misunderstood misfit like himself, and helps the lad have more fun than a Presidential son is allowed. Flick's clean, inoffensive humor makes it hard to dislike. Watch for cameo from Sonny Bono. 101m/C VHS, LV, Closed Caption. Sinbad, Brock Pierce, James Naughton, Blake Boyd, Timothy Busfield, Art LaFleur, Robert Guillaume, Lisa Eichhorn, Zachery Ty Bryan, Bill Cobbs; *D:* David Mickey Evans; *W:* Tim Kelleher; *C:* Anthony B. Richmond; *M:* Richard Gibbs. *TOU*

First Knight 🎬½ 1995 (PG-13) King Arthur/Camelot legend comes to life again, but isn't worth the time it takes to watch. Wandering swordsman Lancelot (Gere) saves beautiful Guinevere (Ormond), soon to be Arthur's (Connery) queen, from evil renegade knight Malagant. They yearn, they gaze, they kiss—you gag. Written like a Harlequin romance, the dialogue (especially

when uttered by Gere) is unintentionally funny, and the plot will cause much eye-rolling. Connery's regal (he knows his costume epics) and Ormond's lovely, but Gere is badly miscast. He offers a contemporary take on the flawed hero complete with American accent, an amazing feat in the 13th century. Big-scale battles, betrayals, passion, even Disneyland-like Camelot sets—the pieces for a tremendous epic are all here, it just doesn't work.*CW:* Some brutal medieval battles. 134m/C VHS, LV, 8mm, Closed Caption, DVD. Sean Connery, Richard Gere, Julia Ormond, Ben Cross, John Gielgud, Liam Cunningham, Christopher Villiers, Valentine Pelka; *D:* Jerry Zucker; *W:* William Nicholson; *C:* Adam Greenberg; *M:* Jerry Goldsmith. *COL*

First Legion 🎬🎬½ 1951 Boyer and Addy are seminarians struggling with their faith when they are confronted with a supposed miracle. Low-key examination of religion and conflict within a religious community. 77m/B VHS, Beta. Charles Boyer, Barbara Rush, William Demarest, Leo G. Carroll; *D:* Douglas Sirk. *LIV*

First Love 🎬🎬½ 1939 Best known for Durbin's first screen kiss, this lightweight romance finds orphaned Connie Harding moving to New York to live with her wealthy Uncle James Clinton (Pallette) and his family. Connie meets handsome rich boy Ted Drake (Stack's screen debut) but her snobby debutante cousin Barbara (Parrish) already has Ted in her sights. Barbara tries to prevent Connie from going to the Drakes fancy dance but, in Cinderella fashion, the Clinton family servants help her become the belle of the ball. Durbin also does some singing. ♫One Fine Day; Amapola; Sympathy; A Change of Heart; Deserted; Spring In My Heart; Home Sweet Home. 85m/B VHS, Closed Caption. Deanna Durbin, Robert Stack, Eugene Pallette, Helen Parrish, Leatrice Joy, June Storey, Frank Jenks, Kathleen Howard, Charles Coleman, Mary Treen; *D:* Henry Koster; *W:* Bruce Manning, Lionel Houser; *C:* Joseph Valentine; *M:* Frank Skinner. Nominations: Academy Awards '39: Best Black and White Cinematography, Best Score. *USH*

First Love 🎬🎬½ 1970 (R) A sixteen year old lad falls in love with a slightly older woman only to have his feelings rejected and to discover that she's his father's mistress. Actor Schell's directorial debut. 90m/C VHS, Beta. GE SI John Moulder-Brown, Dominique Sanda, Maximilian Schell, Valentina Cortese; *D:* Maximilian Schell; *C:* Sven Nykvist. Nominations: Academy Awards '70: Best Foreign Language Film. *CNG*

First Love 🎬🎬½ 1977 (R) A story of an idealistic college student who takes love (and especially making love) more seriously than the rest of his peers, including his girlfriend. Based on Harold Brodkey's story "Sentimental Education." Darling's directorial debut. 92m/C VHS, Beta. William Katt, Susan Dey, John Heard, Beverly D'Angelo, Robert Loggia; *D:* Joan Darling; *M:* John Barry. *PAR*

First Man into Space 🎬🎬 *Satellite of Blood* 1959 An astronaut returns to Earth covered with strange space dust and with an organism feeding inside him (shades of "Alien"). The alien needs human blood to survive and starts killing in order to get it. 78m/B VHS, Beta. Marshall Thompson, Marla Landi, Bill Edwards; *D:* Robert Day. *DVT, RHI, HEG*

First Men in the Moon 🎬🎬 1964 A fun, special effects-laden adaptation of the H. G. Wells novel about an Edwardian civilian spacecraft visiting the moon and the creature found there. Visual effects by Ray Harryhausen. Finch makes a brief appearance. 103m/C VHS, Beta, LV. GB Martha Hyer, Edward Judd, Lionel Jeffries, Erik Chitty, Peter Finch; *D:* Nathan (Hertz) Juran; *W:* Nigel Kneale, Jan Read. *COL, MLB*

First Monday in October 🎬🎬½ 1981 (R) A comedy concerning the first woman appointed to the Supreme Court, a conservative, and her colleague, a crusty but benign liberal judge. Though based on a Broadway hit, it ended up seeming to foreshadow the real-life appointment of Sandra Day O'Connor, which occurred at about

the time the film was released. The title refers to the date the court begins its sessions. 99m/C VHS, Beta, LV. Walter Matthau, Jill Clayburgh, Barnard Hughes, James Stephens, Jan Sterling; *D:* Ronald Neame; *C:* Fred W. Koenekamp. *PAR*

The First Movie Cowboy 1913 Three shorts featuring the very first movie cowboy, Bronco Billy. 47m/B VHS, Beta, 8mm. "Broncho" Billy Anderson; *D:* "Broncho" Billy Anderson. *VYY*

First Name: Carmen 🎬🎬🎬 *Prenom: Carmen* 1983 Carmen, although posing as an aspiring filmmaker, really is a bank robber and terrorist. She is also such a femme fatale that during a bank robbery one of the guards decides to run away with her. Godard cast himself as Carmen's uncle. Amusing late Godard. 95m/C VHS, Beta, LV. FR Maruschka Detmers, Jacques Bonaffe, Jean-Luc Godard, Myriem Roussel, Christophe Odent; *D:* Jean-Luc Godard; *W:* Anne-Marie Mieville; *C:* Raoul Coutard. *CVC, TPV*

The First Nudie Musical 🎬🎬 1975 (R) A producer tries to save his studio by staging a 1930s style musical, but with a naked cast and risque lyrics. Has attained semi-cult/trash status. ♫The First Nudie Musical; The Lights and the Smiles; Orgasm; Lesbian Butch Dyke; Dancing Dildos; Perversion; Honey, What Ya Doin' Tonight; Let 'Em Eat Cake; I Don't Have to Hide Anymore. 93m/C VHS, Beta. Cindy Williams, Stephen Nathan, Diana Canova, Bruce Kimmel; *D:* Mark Haggard. *MED, HHT*

The First Olympics: Athens 1896 🎬🎬½ 1984 Recounts the organization and drama surrounding the first modern-day Olympic games when the inexperienced American team shocked the games with their success. Made for television. 260m/C VHS, Beta. Louis Jourdan, Angela Lansbury, David Ogden Stiers, Virginia McKenna, Jason Connery, Alex Hyde-White, Honor Blackman, Bill Travers; *D:* Alvin Rakoff; *M:* Bruce Broughton. *COL*

The First Power 🎬½ 1989 A detective and psychic join forces to track down a serial killer who, after being executed, uses his satanic powers to kill again. 90m/C VHS, Beta, LV, 8mm, Closed Caption. Lou Diamond Phillips, Tracy Griffith, Jeff Kober, Mykel T. Williamson, Elizabeth Arlen; *D:* Robert Resnikoff; *W:* Robert Resnikoff; *M:* Stewart Copeland. *COL, NLC*

First Spaceship on Venus 🎬🎬🎬 *Der Schweigende Stern; Milczaca Gwiazda* 1960 Eight scientists from various countries set out for Venus and find the remains of a civilization far in advance of Earth's that perished because of nuclear weapons. A sometimes compelling anti-nuclear sci-fi effort made with German and Polish backing. Originally released at 130 minutes. 78m/C VHS, Beta. GE PL Yoko Tani, Oldrich Lukes, Ignacy Machowski, Julius Ongewe, Michal Postnikow, Kurt Rackelmann, Gunther Simon, Tang-Hua-Ta, Lucyna Winnicka; *D:* Kurt Maetzig. *NOS, MRV, SNC*

First Strike 🎬 1985 The United States and the USSR engage in nuclear submarine warfare when the Soviets hijack a U.S. sub and aims its weapons at Arab oil fields. 90m/C VHS, Beta. Stuart Whitman, Persis Khambatta. *VCD*

The First Time 🎬½ *You Don't Need Pajamas at Rosie's; The Beginners Three; The Beginners; They Don't Wear Pajamas at Rosie's; Doin' It* 1969 (R) It's pre-Porky's zaniness as a vacationing youth understandably wants to spend his "first time" with Bisset. Other than her presence, this film has little to offer. 90m/C VHS. Jacqueline Bisset, Wes Stern, Rick Kelman, Wink Roberts; *D:* James Neilson. *NO*

First Time 🎬🎬½ *Doin' It* 1982 (R) A comedy about a college student who can't quite succeed with women, despite coaching from his roommate and counseling from a psychology professor whose assistance is part of a research project. 96m/C VHS, Beta. Tim Choate, Krista Errickson, Marshall Efron, Wallace Shawn, Wendie Jo Sperber, Cathryn Damon; *D:* Charles Loventhal. *NO*

First Turn On 🎬 1983 (R) Not to be confused with "The Thomas Edison Story," this sex-comedy follows the adventures of several young campers who decide to die happy when an avalanche leaves them trapped in a cave. A longer unrated version is available. 84m/C VHS, Beta. Georgia Harrell, Michael Sanville, Googy Gress, Jenny Johnson, Heide Basset, Vincent D'Onofrio, Sheila Kennedy; **D:** Michael Herz, Lloyd (Samuel Weil) Kaufman. *LIV*

The First Wives Club 🎬🎬½ 1996 (PG) As the first Mrs. Trump, who makes a most appropriate cameo, so wisely puts it, "Don't get mad, get everything." But to the three rich, middle-aged friends who are dumped by their husbands so the guys can marry younger "trophy" wives, there's just nothing like revenge. Comedy begins in 1969 with the young and idealistic Annie (Keaton), Brenda (Midler), Elise (Hawn) and Cynthia graduating college, then moves to the present with the wronged Cynthia (Channing) ledge-diving from her swanky Manhattan apartment because her husband left her. The remaining mistreated trio goes into action, using their exes' own money, businesses, power, and various mistresses against them. This film's appeal and success had Hollywood tongues wagging, predicting the dawn of new roles for older actresses. Based on the book by Olivia Goldsmith. 104m/C VHS, Beta, Closed Caption. Goldie Hawn, Diane Keaton, Bette Midler, Sarah Jessica Parker, Heather Locklear, Marcia Gay Harden, Elizabeth Berkley, Victor Garber, Dan Hedaya, Stephen Collins, Maggie Smith, Stockard Channing, Jennie Dundas, Eileen Heckart, Philip Bosco, Rob Reiner, James Naughton; **D:** Hugh Wilson, Hugh Wilson; **W:** Robert Harling; **C:** Donald E. Thorin; **M:** Marc Shaiman. Nominations: Academy Awards '96: Best Original Score. *PAR*

First Yank into Tokyo 🎬🎬 *Mask of Fury* 1945 An American army pilot who grew up in Japan undergoes plastic surgery in order to infiltrate Japanese lines and get information from an American scientist. Some last minute editing to capitalize on current events made this the first American film to deal with the atomic bomb. 83m/B VHS, Beta. Tom Neal, Richard Loo, Barbara Hale, Marc Cramer; **D:** Gordon Douglas. *TTC*

A Fish Called Wanda 🎬🎬🎬 1988 (R) Absurd, high-speed farce about four criminals trying to retrieve $20 million they've stolen from a safety deposit box—and each other. Meanwhile, barrister Cleese falls in love with the female thief (Curtis). Some sick, but tastelessly funny, humor involves Palin's problem with stuttering and some very dead doggies. Written by Monty Python alum Cleese and director Crichton, who understand that silence is sometimes funnier than speech, and that timing is everything. Wickedly funny. 98m/C VHS, Beta, LV, Closed Caption. John Cleese, Kevin Kline, Jamie Lee Curtis, Michael Palin, Tom Georgeson, Maria Aitken, Patricia Hayes, Geoffrey Palmer; **D:** Charles Crichton; **W:** John Cleese, Charles Crichton; **M:** John Du Prez. Academy Awards '88: Best Supporting Actor (Kline); British Academy Awards '88: Best Actor (Cleese), Best Supporting Actor (Palin); Nominations: Academy Awards '88: Best Director (Crichton), Best Original Screenplay. *MGM, BTV, FOX*

Fish Hawk 🎬½ 1979 (G) When an alcoholic Indian, Fish Hawk, meets a young boy in the forest, they strike up a friendship and he attempts to clean up his act. Attempts to be heartwarming. 95m/C VHS, Beta. CA Will Sampson, Charlie Fields; **D:** Donald Shebib. *MED, VTR*

The Fish that Saved Pittsburgh 🎬🎬 1979 (PG) A floundering basketball team hires an astrologer to try and change their luck. She makes sure all the team members' signs are compatible with their star's Pisces sign (the fish). Produced a disco soundtrack with several Motown groups who also performed in the movie. 104m/C VHS, Beta. Jonathan Winters, Stockard Channing, Flip Wilson, Julius Erving, Margaret Avery, Meadowlark Lemon, Nicholas Pryor, James Bond III, Kareem Abdul-Jabbar, Jack Kehoe, Debbie Allen; **D:** Gilbert Moses; **M:** Thom Bell. *ORI, WAR*

The Fisher King 🎬🎬🎬 1991 (R) In derelict-infested Manhattan a down-and-out radio deejay meets a crazed vagabond (Williams) obsessed with medieval history and in search of the Holy Grail. At first the whimsical mix of Arthurian myth and modern urban hell seems amazingly wrongheaded. In retrospect it still does. But while this picture runs it weaves a spell that pulls you in, especially in its quiet moments. Your reaction to the silly ending depends entirely on how well you're bamboozled by a script that equates madness with enlightment and the homeless with holy fools. Filmed on the streets of New York, with many street people playing themselves. **CW:** Language and violence. 138m/C VHS, Beta, LV, 8mm, Closed Caption. Robin Williams, Jeff Bridges, Amanda Plummer, Mercedes Ruehl, Michael Jeter, Harry Shearer, John de Lancie, Kathy Najimy, David Hyde Pierce; **D:** Terry Gilliam; **W:** Richard LaGravenese. Academy Awards '91: Best Supporting Actress (Ruehl); Chicago Film Critics Awards '91: Best Supporting Actress (Ruehl); Golden Globe Awards '92: Best Actor—Musical/Comedy (Williams), Best Supporting Actress (Ruehl); Los Angeles Film Critics Association Awards '91: Best Actress (Ruehl); Nominations: Academy Awards '91: Best Actor (Williams), Best Art Direction/Set Decoration, Best Original Screenplay, Best Original Score. *COL, CCB*

Fisherman's Wharf 🎬½ 1939 Breen stars as an orphan adopted by a San Francisco fisherman who runs away when his aunt and bratty cousin come to live with them. 72m/B VHS. Bobby Breen, Leo Carrillo, Henry Armetta, Lee Patrick, Rosina Galli, Leon Belasco; **D:** Bernard Vorhaus. *NOS*

F.I.S.T. 🎬🎬½ 1978 (R) A young truck driver turns union organizer for idealistic reasons, but finds himself teaming with gangsters to boost his cause. His rise to the top of the union comes at the cost of his integrity, as Stallone does a character resembling Jimmy Hoffa. 145m/C VHS, Beta, LV. Sylvester Stallone, Rod Steiger, Peter Boyle, David Huffman, Melinda Dillon, Tony LoBianco, Kevin Conway, Peter Donat, Cassie Yates, Brian Dennehy; **D:** Norman Jewison; **W:** Sylvester Stallone; **M:** Bill Conti. *MGM, FCT*

Fist 🎬 1979 (R) Street fighter battles his way through the urban jungle seeking personal freedom and revenge. 84m/C VHS, Beta. Richard Lawson, Annazette Chase, Dabney Coleman. *NO*

Fist Fighter 🎬½ 1988 (R) The ups and downs of a professional bare-knuckle fighter as he avenges a friend's murder. 99m/C VHS, Beta, LV. George Rivero, Edward Albert, Brenda Bakke, Mike Connors, Simon Andrew, Matthias Hues; **D:** Frank Zuniga; **W:** Max Bloom. *NO*

Fist of Fear, Touch of Death 🎬 1977 (R) Madison Square Garden is the scene for a high stakes martial arts face-off. Standard kung-fu film highlighted by short clips of the late Bruce Lee. 90m/C VHS, Beta. Fred Williamson, Ron Van Cliff, Adolph Caesar, Aaron Banks, Bill Louie; **D:** Matthew Mallinson. *LIV*

Fist of Glory 🎬½ 1995 (R) In the waning days of the Vietnam War, a commando searches for the comrade who saved his life. He discovers his pal is a drug-addicted POW who's forced to fight in order to survive. 93m/C VHS. Dale "Apollo" Cook, Maurice Smith, Robert Marius, Eric Hahn; **D:** Joe Mari Avellana. *THV*

Fist of Honor 🎬 1992 (R) A young boxer seeks to avenge his fiance's death, a beautiful girl squares off against a bad-cop, and two mobster leaders try to take control of the same city. When a member of one family breaks a truce and begins killing rival family members, the violence escalates and old scores will be settled. **CW:** Language, violence, and sexuality. 90m/C VHS, Closed Caption. Sam Jones, Joey House, Harry Guardino, Nicholas Worth, Frank Stivero, Abe Vigoda, Bubba Smith; **D:** Richard Pepin; **W:** Charles Kanganis. *PMH*

Fist of Steel 🎬½ 1993 In this futuristic martial arts film, modern day gladiators fight to the death in tournaments run by a vicious syndicate. When top gladiator Amp makes an escape bid he's hunted by henchman Mainframe, who plans to meet Amp in a fixed fight in order to become the new champion. 97m/C VHS, LV. Dale "Apollo" Cook, Greg Douglass, Cynthia Khan, Don Nakaya Nielsen, Jim Gaines, Ned Hourani, Nick Nicholson, Kris Aguilar; **D:** Irvin Johnson; **W:** Anthony Jesu. *AIP*

Fist of the North Star 🎬🎬 1995 (R) Legendary warrior Kenshiro (Daniels) returns from the grave to avenge the death of his father (McDowell) and restore his North Star clan. He must battle evil Lord Shin (Mandylor) and his henchmen in a post-apocalyptic future. Based on the Japanese comic book series, which is also available in anime form. 90m/C VHS. Gary Daniels, Costas Mandylor, Christopher Penn, Julie Brown, Malcolm McDowell, Melvin Van Peebles, Isako Washio; **D:** Tony Randel; **W:** Tony Randel; **C:** Jacques Haitkin. *BMG*

The Fist, the Kicks, and the Evils 1980 A young man who's father is murdered learns kung fu and sets out for revenge. 90m/C VHS, Beta. Kao Fei, Bruce Liang. *MGI*

Fistful of Death 🎬 1967 Kinski portrays a vengefully violent and desperate cowpoke in the days of the old West. 84m/C VHS, Beta. Klaus Kinski. *TWE*

A Fistful of Dollars 🎬🎬🎬 1964 (R) The epitome of the "spaghetti western" pits Eastwood as "the man with no name" against two families who are feuding over land. A remake of Kurosawa's "Yojimbo," and followed by Leone's "For a Few Dollars More", and "The Good, The Bad, and The Ugly." **CW:** Violence. 101m/C VHS, Beta, LV, Closed Caption. IT Clint Eastwood, Gian Marie Volonte, Marianne Koch; **D:** Sergio Leone; **M:** Ennio Morricone. *MGM, FCT, TLF*

A Fistful of Dynamite 🎬🎬🎬 *Duck, You Sucker; Giu la Testa* 1972 (PG) A spaghetti western, with Leone's trademark humor and a striking score by Morricone. An Irish demolitions expert and a Mexican peasant team up to rob a bank during a revolution in Mexico. 138m/C VHS, Beta, LV. IT James Coburn, Rod Steiger, Romolo Valli; **D:** Sergio Leone; **M:** Ennio Morricone. *MGM*

Fists of Blood 🎬½ 1987 A martial arts expert seeks revenge on the drug baron who murdered his friend and kidnapped his girl. 90m/C VHS, Beta. AU Eddie Stazak; **D:** Brian Trenchard-Smith. *CEL*

Fists of Dragons 🎬 1969 Vengeful, sacrificial bloodshed abounds in this Chinese boxing extravaganza. 92m/C VHS, Beta. Huang I Lung, Ou Ti; **D:** Yeh Yung Chu. *TWE*

Fists of Fury 🎬🎬🎬 *The Big Boss* 1973 (R) Bruce Lee stars in this violent but charming Kung Fu action adventure in which he must break a solemn vow to avoid fighting in order to avenge the murder of his teacher by drug smugglers. 102m/C VHS, Beta. Bruce Lee, Maria Yi; **D:** Lo Wei. *FOX*

Fists of Fury 2 🎬½ 1980 (R) Chen Shan must survive the Organizations' onslaughts to kill him. He escapes their perilous plots only to return to battle against them after they kill his mother for her inability to disclose Chen's hiding place. Finally Chen defeats the Evil Organization himself. 90m/C VHS, Beta. Bruce Li, Ho Chung Do, Shum Shim Po. *GEM*

Fists of Iron 🎬½ 1994 (R) Tough guy, skilled in martial arts, seeks revenge on the fighter and promoter who caused the death of his best friend. **CW:** Strong martial arts violence and some sexuality. 94m/C VHS, LV, Closed Caption. Mike Worth, Matthias Hues, Sam Jones, Marshall Teague, Jenilee Harrison. *WEA*

Fit for a King 🎬🎬 1937 A reporter becomes a princess' knight in shining armor when he foils an assassination plot in this screwball romance. 73m/B VHS, Beta. Joe E. Brown, Leo Carrillo, Helen Mack, Paul Kelly, Harry Davenport; **D:** Edward Sedgwick; **C:** Paul Vogel. *NOS, DVT*

Fit to Kill 🎬½ 1993 (R) Once again special agents Donna Hamilton and Nicole Justine (former Playboy centerfolds Speir and Vasquez) re-team for an adventure that matches them with an old enemy, double agents, diamonds, and revenge. Filmed on location in Hawaii. **94m/C VHS.** Dona Speir, Roberta Vasquez, R.J. Moore, Bruce Penhall, Julie Strain, Rodrigo Obregon, Cynthia Brimhall, Tony Peck; **D:** Andy Sidaris; **W:** Andy Sidaris. **COL**

Fitzcarraldo 🐾🐾🐾🐾 **1982 (PG)** Although he failed to build a railroad across South America, Fitzcarraldo is determined to build an opera house in the middle of the Amazon jungles and have Enrico Caruso sing there. Based on a true story of a charismatic Irishman's impossible quest at the turn of the century. Of note: No special effects were used in this movie—everything you see actually occurred during filming, including hauling a large boat over a mountain. **157m/C VHS, Beta. GE** Klaus Kinski, Claudia Cardinale, Jose Lewgoy, Miguel Angel Fuentes, Paul Hittscher; **D:** Werner Herzog; **W:** Werner Herzog; **M:** Popul Vuh. Cannes Film Festival '82: Best Director (Herzog). **WAR, APD**

Five Came Back 🐾🐾 **1939** When a plane with twelve passengers crashes in the South American jungle, only five can ride in the patched-up wreck. Since the remainder will be left to face head hunters, intense arguments ensue. Same director remade this as "Back from Eternity" in 1956. **93m/B VHS, Beta, LV.** Lucille Ball, Chester Morris, John Carradine, Wendy Barrie, Kent Taylor, Joseph Calleia, Sir C. Aubrey Smith, Patric Knowles; **D:** John Farrow. **TTC**

Five Card Stud 🐾½ **1968 (PG)** Five members of a lynching party are being killed one by one, and a professional gambler, who tried to prevent the lynching, attempts to ensnare the killer with the aid of a preacher with a gun. The poor script was based on a novel by Ray Gaulden. **103m/C VHS, Beta.** Robert Mitchum, Dean Martin, Inger Stevens, Roddy McDowall, Yaphet Kotto, John Anderson, Katherine Justice; **D:** Henry Hathaway; **M:** Maurice Jarre. **PAR**

Five Corners 🐾🐾🐾 **1988 (R)** A quixotic, dramatic comedy about the inhabitants of the 5 Corners section of the Bronx in 1964, centering around a girl being wooed by a psychotic rapist, her crippled boyfriend, and the hero-turned-racial-pacifist who cannot rescue her out of principle. **92m/C VHS, Beta.** Jodie Foster, John Turturro, Todd Graff, Tim Robbins, Elizabeth Berridge, Rose Gregorio, Gregory Rozakis, Rodney Harvey, John Seitz; **D:** John Patrick Shanley; **C:** Fred Murphy; **M:** James Newton Howard. Independent Spirit Awards '89: Best Actress (Foster). **MGM**

5 Dark Souls 🐾½ **1996** Three high-schoolers, anxious to be part of the "in" crowd, are sent by five members of the most popular clique on a sinister woodland adventure as stars in a snuff film. **90m/C VHS.** Tina Ona Paukstelis, Mick Wynhoff, Matthew Winkler, Christopher D. Harder, Karen Dilloo, Sy Stevens, William Krekling; **D:** Jason Paul Collum. **MRV**

Five Days One Summer 🐾🐾 **1982 (PG)** Set in 1932, the story of a haunting and obsessive love affair between a married Scottish doctor and a young woman who happens to be his niece. While on vacation in the Swiss Alps, the doctor must vie for her love with their handsome young mountain climbing guide. Based on a story by Kay Boyle. **108m/C VHS, Beta.** Sean Connery, Betsy Brantley, Lambert Wilson; **D:** Fred Zinnemann; **W:** Michael Austin; **M:** Elmer Bernstein. **WAR**

Five Easy Pieces 🐾🐾🐾🐾 **1970 (R)** Nicholson's superb acting brings to life this character study of a talented musician who has given up a promising career and now works on the oil rigs. After twenty years he returns home to attempt one last communication with his dying father and perhaps, reconcile himself with his fear of failure and desire for greatness. Black, Anspach, and Bush create especially memorable characters. Nicholson ordering toast via a chicken salad sandwich is a classic. **98m/C VHS, Beta, LV, 8mm.** Jack Nicholson, Karen Black, Susan Anspach, Lois Smith, Billy Green Bush, Fannie Flagg, Ralph Waite, Sally Struthers, Helena Kallianiotes; **D:** Bob Rafelson; **W:** John (Carole Eastman) Joyce, Bob Rafelson. Golden Globe Awards '71: Best Supporting Actress (Black); National

Board of Review Awards '70: Best Supporting Actress (Black); New York Film Critics Awards '70: Best Supporting Actress (Black), Best Director (Rafelson), Best Film, Best Supporting Actress (Black); National Society of Film Critics Awards '70: Best Supporting Actress (Smith); Nominations: Academy Awards '70: Best Actor (Nicholson), Best Picture, Best Story & Screenplay, Best Supporting Actress (Black). **COL, WME**

Five Fighters from Shaolin 🐾 **197?** Five high-kicking fighters endeavor to recapture their temple from an evil duke. **88m/C VHS, Beta.** Chang Shen, Lung Kwan, Dhiu Min Shien; **D:** Ko Shu-How. **MPI, MOV**

Five Fingers 🐾🐾🐾½ *Operation Cicero* **1952** Under the alias "Cicero," Albanian valet Mason joins the espionage ring, selling highly confidential British war papers to the Germans during WWII. True story with odd real-life ending—unconvinced of document authenticity, the Nazis never acted on the information, even when they had the time and the clue of the European invasion! Fast-paced and absorbing. Adapted from the book "Operation Cicero" by L.C. Moyzisch. **108m/B VHS.** James Mason, Danielle Darrieux, Michael Rennie, Walter Hampden, Oscar Karlweis, Herbert Berghof, John Wengraf, Michael Pate, Ivan Triesault, Hanne Axman, David Wolfe, Nestor Paiva, Richard Loo, Keith McConnell; **D:** Joseph L. Mankiewicz; **W:** Michael Wilson; **M:** Bernard Herrmann. Golden Globe Awards '53: Best Screenplay; Nominations: Academy Awards '52: Best Director (Mankiewicz), Best Screenplay. **FXV**

Five for Hell 🐾 **1967** The army picks five of its meanest men for a suicide mission during WWII. They must go behind German lines and find the plans for the enemy offensive. **88m/C VHS, Beta. IT** Klaus Kinski, Gianni "John" Garko, Nick Jordan, Margaret Lee; **D:** Frank Kramer. **TWE, CNG**

Five Giants from Texas 🐾 *I Cinque Della Vendetta* **1966** El cheapo spaghetti western features Madison, television's former Wild Bill Hickock, as a rancher fighting off displaced Mexican peasants and outlaws. **103m/C VHS, Beta.** Guy Madison, Monica Randall; **D:** Aldo Florio. **TWE**

Five Golden Dragons 🐾 **1967** A typical action film about an American running afoul of ruthless gold trafficking in Hong Kong. Even this stellar cast can't help the script. **92m/C VHS, Beta. GB** Robert Cummings, Christopher Lee, Brian Donlevy, Klaus Kinski, George Raft, Dan Duryea, Margaret Lee; **D:** Jeremy Summers. **NO**

Five Graves to Cairo 🐾🐾🐾 **1943** Tense WWII thriller finds British soldier John Bramble (Tone) stranded in a small desert town after the defeat of the British garrison by General Rommel's (Von Stroheim) Afrika Korps. Arab hotel owner Farid (Tamiroff) agrees to let Bramble assume the identity of a dead hotel waiter, much to the dismay of French maid Moush (Baxter), whose only interest is in getting her brother out of a German POW camp. The real waiter turns out to have been a secret Nazi spy, fortunately known to Rommel only by name, so Bramble attempts to learn where the German supply depots have been hidden (the "five graves" of the title)—that is, unless Moush decides to betray him to win her brother's release. Based on the play "Hotel Imperial" by Lajos Biro. **97m/B VHS, Closed Caption.** Franchot Tone, Anne Baxter, Erich von Stroheim, Akim Tamiroff, Peter Van Eyck, Fortunio Bonanova, Miles Mander, Konstantin Shayne; **D:** Billy Wilder; **W:** Billy Wilder, Charles Brackett; **C:** John Seitz; **M:** Miklos Rozsa. Nominations: Academy Awards '43: Best Black and White Cinematography, Best Film Editing. **USH**

The Five Heartbeats 🐾🐾🐾 **1991 (R)** Well told story of five black singers in the 1960s, their successes and failures as a group and as individuals. Although every horror story of the music business is included, the story remains fresh and the acting excellent. Music is fine, but secondary to the people. Well written characters with few cliches. Skillfully directed by Townsend (of "Hollywood Shuffle") who did research by talking to the Dells. Less than memorable showing at the box office but fun and entertaining. **CW:** Lan-

guage. **122m/C VHS, Beta, LV, Closed Caption.** Robert Townsend, Tressa Thomas, Michael Wright, Harry J. Lennix, Diahann Carroll, Leon, Hawthorne James, Chuck Patterson, Roy Fegan, Tico Wells, John Canada Terrell, Harold Nicholas, Paul Benjamin, Norma Donaldson, Eugene Glazer; **D:** Robert Townsend; **W:** Robert Townsend, Keenen Ivory Wayans; **M:** Stanley Clarke. **FXV**

Five Miles to Midnight 🐾 **1980** Brett and Danny have to depend on a photographer (Collins) for help to smuggle a gangster out of Italy. From the British "Persuaders" adventure series. Made for television. **52m/C VHS.** GB Roger Moore, Tony Curtis, Joan Collins. **NO**

Five Minutes to Love 🐾 *The Rotten Apple; It Only Take Five Minutes* **1963** McClanahan (one of TV's "Golden Girls") plays a young, sleazy hussy named "Poochie, the girl from the shack." This exploitation schlocker appears to be McClanahan's first film. **85m/B VHS.** Rue McClanahan, Paul Leder, King Moody; **D:** John Hayes. **SNC, TPV**

The Five of Me 🐾🐾½ **1981** A man with five personalities finds that livin' ain't easy and seeks professional help. Made for television, based on the autobiography of Henry Hawksworth. **100m/C VHS.** David Birney, Dee Wallace Stone, Mitchell Ryan, John McLiam, James Whitmore Jr., Ben Piazza; **D:** Paul Wendkos. **LIV**

The Five Pennies 🐾🐾½ **1959** Sentimental biography starring Kaye as famed jazzman Red Nichols features performances by legendary musicians Bob Crosby, Bobby Troup, Ray Anthony and Louis Armstrong. This movie marked Weld's film debut. 🎵 Good Night Sleep Tight; The Five Pennies; Battle Hymn of the Republic; When the Saints Go Marching In; The Music Goes 'Round and Around; Jingle Bells; Carnival of Venice; Paradise. **117m/C VHS, Beta, Closed Caption.** Danny Kaye, Louis Armstrong, Barbara Bel Geddes, Tuesday Weld, Harry Guardino; **D:** Melville Shavelson; **W:** Melville Shavelson, Jack Rose; **C:** Daniel F. Fapp. Nominations: Academy Awards '59: Best Color Cinematography, Best Costume Design (Color), Best Song ("The Five Pennies"), Scoring of a Musical. **PAR**

The 5000 Fingers of Dr. T 🐾🐾🐾 **1953 (G)** In Dr. Seuss' only non-animated movie, a boy tries to evade piano lessons and runs right into the castle of the evil Dr. Terwilliger, where hundreds of boys are held captive for piano lessons. Worse yet, they're forced to wear silly beanies with "happy fingers" waving on top. Luckily, the trusted family plumber is on hand to save the day through means of an atomic bomb. Wonderful satire, horrible music, mesmerizing Seussian sets. The skating brothers (who are joined at their beards) are a treat. **88m/C VHS, Beta, LV.** Peter Lind Hayes, Mary Healy, Tommy Rettig, Hans Conried; **D:** Roy Rowland; **W:** Theodore "Dr. Seuss" Geisel, Allan Scott. Nominations: Academy Awards '53: Scoring of a Musical. **COL, XVC, FCT**

Five Weeks in a Balloon 🐾🐾 **1962 (PG)** This adaptation of the Jules Verne novel follows the often-comic exploits of a 19th-century British expedition that encounters many adventures on a balloon trek across Africa. Pleasant fluff with a good cast. **101m/C VHS, Beta, LV.** Fabian, Peter Lorre, Red Buttons, Cedric Hardwicke, Barbara Eden; **D:** Irwin Allen; **W:** Charles Bennett, Irwin Allen; **C:** Winton C. Hoch. **FXV, FCT**

The $5.20 an Hour Dream 🐾🐾 **1980** Lavin is a divorced mother and factory worker burdened with debt and determined to get and keep a job on the higher-paying, traditionally all-male assembly line. Lesser feminist drama on the heels of "Norma Rae." Made for television. **96m/C VHS, Beta.** Linda Lavin, Richard Jaeckel, Nicholas Pryor, Pamela McMyler, Mayf Nutter, Taurean Blacque, Robert Davi, Dennis Fimple, Dana Hill, Ernie Hudson; **D:** Russ Mayberry. **TLF**

The Fix 🐾 *The Agitators* **1984** A group of cocaine smugglers get their just desserts as the federal government catches them in a sting operation. **95m/C VHS, Beta.** Vince Edwards, Richard Jaeckel,

Julie Hill, Charles Dierkop, Byron Cherry, Robert Tessier; **D:** Will Zens. *NO*

The Fixer ✶✶✶ 1968 (PG-13) Based on the true story of a Jewish handyman (Bates) in 1911 Tsarist Russia who's accused of murdering a gentile boy. Wrongly imprisoned he's tortured to confess to the crime, which he refuses to do. Bogarde is the lawyer who tries to help him. Strong direction and acting in an unrelenting drama. Adapted from Bernard Malamud's Pulitzer Prizewinning novel. 132m/C VHS. Alan Bates, Dirk Bogarde, Georgia Brown, Hugh Griffith, Elizabeth Hartman, Ian Holm, David Opatoshu, David Warner, Carol White, Murray Melvin, Peter Jeffrey, William Hutt; **D:** John Frankenheimer; **W:** Dalton Trumbo; **M:** Maurice Jarre. Nominations: Academy Awards '68: Best Actor (Bates). *MGM*

Flambards ✶✶½ 19?? In the early 1900's teenaged orphan Christine is sent to live with her tyrannical Uncle Russell and his two sons in their crumbling English estate, Flambards. Bitter rivalries and jealousies abound between arrogant, tradition bound Mark and younger brother William, who's obsessed with the new-fangled airplane. Quarrels intensify as both young men fall in love with Christine and WWI begins, leading to sacrifice and tragedy. Based on the trilogy by K.M. Peyton. Made for British television; 12 episodes on 6 cassettes. 676m/C VHS. *GB* Christine McKenna, Stephen Grives, Alan Parnaby, Edward Judd, Sebastian Abineri, Peter Settelen, Carol Leader, Frank Mills. *TVC, VCO*

The Flame & the Arrow ✶✶✶ 1950 Dardo the Arrow, a Robin Hood-like outlaw in medieval Italy, leads his band of mountain fighters against a mercenary warlord who has seduced his wife and kidnapped his son. Spectacular acrobatics, with Lancaster performing his own stunts, add interest to the usual swashbuckling. 88m/C VHS, Beta, LV. Burt Lancaster, Virginia Mayo, Aline MacMahon, Nick Cravat, Robert Douglas, Frank Allenby; **D:** Jacques Tourneur; **M:** Max Steiner. Nominations: Academy Awards '50: Best Color Cinematography, Original Dramatic/Comedy Score. *WAR*

The Flame Is Love ✶✶½ 1979 A made-for-television adaptation of one of Barbara Cartland's romantic novels. An American heiress falls tragically in love with a Parisian journalist despite her engagement to an Englishman. Takes place at the turn of the century. 98m/C VHS, Beta. Linda Purl, Timothy Dalton, Shane Briant; **D:** Michael O'Herlihy. *LIV*

Flame of Araby ✶✶½ 1951 When Princess Tanya's (O'Hara) father is murdered, she's threatened with an unwanted marriage and loss of the throne. But if she can win a horse race, Tanya has a chance for freedom. Now, if she can only convince handsome Bedouin chief Tamerlane (Chandler), who has the fastest black stallion in the desert, to come to her aid. 78m/C VHS. Maureen O'Hara, Jeff Chandler, Lon Chaney Jr., Buddy Baer, Maxwell Reed, Susan Cabot, Royal Dano, Richard Egan; **D:** Charles Lamont; **W:** Gerald Drayson Adams; **C:** Russell Metty. *USH*

Flame of the Barbary Coast ✶✶½ 1945 A rancher from Montana vies with a gambling czar for a beautiful dance hall queen and control of the Barbary Coast district of San Francisco. The great earthquake of 1906 provides the plot with a climax. Also available colorized. 91m/B VHS. John Wayne, Ann Dvorak, Joseph Schildkraut, William Frawley; **D:** Joseph Kane. Nominations: Academy Awards '45: Best Sound, Original Dramatic/Comedy Score. *MED, REP*

Flame of the Islands ✶✶ 1955 De Carlo plays a smoldering, passionate chanteuse who struggles with love and gangsters for possession of a Bahamian casino in this tropical heat wave. 92m/C VHS, Beta. Yvonne De Carlo, Howard Duff, Zachary Scott, James Arness, Kurt Kasznar, Barbara O'Neil; **D:** Edward Ludwig. *NO*

Flame Over India ✶✶✶ *Northwest Frontier* 1960 When Moslems lay siege to a British fortress in India, Governess Wyatt (Bacall) and Captain Scott (More) save the Maharaja's son and escape by commandeering a train. Along the way they find treason, adventure and love. 130m/C VHS. *GB* Kenneth More, Lauren Bacall, Herbert Lom, Wilfrid Hyde-White, I.S. Johar, Ursula Jeans, Ian Hunter, Eugene Deckers, Jack Gwillim, Govind Raja Ross, Frank Olegario; **D:** J. Lee Thompson; **C:** Geoffrey Unsworth. *HEG, DVT*

Flame to the Phoenix ✶✶½ 1985 A WWII drama about the Polish cavalry forces' decimation to German Panzer tanks. 80m/C VHS, Beta. *GB* Paul Geoffrey, Ann Firbank, Frederick Treves; **D:** William Brayne. *NO*

The Flame Trees of Thika ✶✶✶ 1981 In 1913, a British family travels to East Africa to start a coffee plantation. Seen through the eyes of the young daughter, her childhood consists of the local Masai and Kikuyu tribes, the eccentric and sometimes unhappy English neighbors, and the wild animals that roam the plains. Based on the memoirs of writer Elspeth Huxley. 4 cassettes; shown on PBS "Masterpiece Theatre." 366m/C VHS. *GB* Hayley Mills, Holly Aird, David Robb, Ben Cross. *SIG, TVC, VIF*

Flaming Bullets ✶✶ 1945 Last of the Texas Rangers series has solid action scenes, but little else. Ritter leads the Texas Rangers in breaking up a gang with a devious scheme: breaking men out of jail, then killing them for the cash reward. 55m/B VHS. *MOV*

Flaming Frontiers 1938 A frontier scout matches wits against gold mine thieves. In fifteen episodes. 300m/B VHS, Beta. Johnny Mack Brown, Eleanor Hanson, Ralph Bowman; **D:** Ray Taylor. *VYY, VCN, NOS*

Flaming Lead ✶½ 1939 A hard-drinkin' ranch owner hires a nightclub cowboy to help him get an Army horse contract. 57m/B VHS. Ken Maynard, Eleanor Stewart, Walter Long, Tom London; **D:** Sam Newfield. *NOS, DVT, HEG*

Flaming Signal ✶½ 1933 Featuring Flash the Wonder Labrador, this action-packed film deals with a pilot who crash-lands near a Pacific island, just as the natives, provoked by an exploitative German trader, are rising up against the whites. Both Flash and his master manage to rescue the missionary's pretty daughter. 64m/B VHS, Beta, LV. Noah Beery Sr., Marceline Day, Carmelita Geraghty, Mischa Auer, Henry B. Walthall. *SNC, LSV, RXM*

Flaming Star ✶✶✶ 1960 In 1870s Texas, a family with a white father and an Indian mother is caught in the midst of an Indian uprising. The mixed-blood youth, excellently played by Presley, must choose a side with tragic results for all. A stirring, well-written drama of frontier prejudice and one of Presley's best films. 101m/C VHS, Beta. Elvis Presley, Dolores Del Rio, Barbara Eden, Steve Forrest, John McIntire, Richard Jaeckel, L.Q. Jones; **D:** Donald Siegel. *FOX, MVD*

The Flaming Teen-Age ✶ 1956 Schlocky pseudo-documentary demonstrating the evils of drugs and alcohol. Exploitative, and the teenagers look really old. Cheaply made, and it shows. 67m/B VHS. Noel Reyburn, Ethel Barrett, Jerry Frank, Shirley Holmes; **D:** Irvin S. Yeaworth Jr., Charles Edwards. *SNC*

The Flaming Urge 1953 A small town is plagued by mysterious fires. Could a pyromaniac be on the loose? 67m/B VHS, Beta. Harold Lloyd Jr., Cathy Downs. *SNC*

The Flamingo Kid ✶✶✶ 1984 (PG-13) Brooklyn teen Dillon gets a summer job at a fancy beach club on Long Island. His father, a plumber, remembers how to dream but is also aware of how rough the world is on dreamers. Suddenly making lots of money at a mostly easy job, the kid's attracted to the high style of the local sports car dealer, and finds his father's solid life a bore. By the end of the summer, he's learned the true value of both men, and the kind of man he wants

to be. Excellent performances all around, nice ensemble acting among the young men who play Dillon's buddies. Great sound track. Film debut of Jones, who seems a little old for her part as a California college sophomore. 100m/C VHS, Beta, LV, Closed Caption. Matt Dillon, Hector Elizondo, Molly McCarthy, Martha Gehman, Richard Crenna, Jessica Walter, Carole Davis, Janet Jones, Fisher Stevens, Bronson Pinchot; **D:** Garry Marshall. *PAR, VES, LIV*

Flamingo Road ✶✶✶ 1949 A scandalously entertaining melodrama in which Crawford portrays a carnival dancer who intrigues Scott and Brian in a small Southern town where the carnival stops. Crawford shines in a role that demands her to be both tough and sensitive in a corrupt world full of political backstabbing and sleazy characters. Remade as a TV movie and television soap-opera series in 1980. 94m/B VHS, LV, Closed Caption. Joan Crawford, Zachary Scott, David Brian, Sydney Greenstreet, Gertrude Michael, Gladys George, Virginia Huston, Fred Clark, Alice White; **D:** Michael Curtiz; **W:** Edmund H. North, Robert Wilder; **M:** Max Steiner. *MGM*

The Flash ✶✶ 1990 When police scientist Barry Allen is accidentally doused by chemicals and then struck by lightening the combination makes him into a new superhero. His super quickness help his quest in fighting crime in Central City where he's aided by fellow scientist Tina McGee (the only other person to know his secret). In this adventure, the Flash seeks out the violent and mesmerizing leader of a biker gang who caused the death of Barry's brother. Based on the DC comic book character, this is the pilot episode for the short-lived television series. The look is dark and stylized and not played for camp. 94m/C VHS, Beta, LV, Closed Caption. John Wesley Shipp, Amanda Pays, Michael Nader; **M:** Danny Elfman. *WAR*

The Flash 2: Revenge of the Trickster ✶✶½ 1991 Every good superhero needs his nemesis—and this time around the Flash (Shipp) has that murderous mischiefmaker the Trickster (Hamill) who, along with his femme fatale sidekick Prank, is determined to outwit our hero. Can super speed and strength be enough to keep Central City safe? Based on the DC comic book character and taken from two episodes of the television series. 92m/C VHS, Beta, Closed Caption. John Wesley Shipp, Amanda Pays, Mark Hamill, Richard Belzer. *WAR*

Flash & Firecat ✶ 1975 (PG) A beautiful blonde and a crazy thief steal and race their way across the country in a dune buggy with the police hot on their trail. 90m/C VHS, Beta. Roger Davis, Tricia Sembera, Dub Taylor, Richard Kiel; **D:** Ferd Sebastian. *NO*

Flash Gordon ✶✶ 1980 (PG) Camp version of the adventures of Flash Gordon in outer space. This time, Flash and Dale Arden are forced by Dr. Zarkov to accompany him on a mission to far-off Mongo, where Ming the Merciless is threatening the destruction of Earth. Music by Queen. 111m/C VHS, Beta, LV. Sam Jones, Melody Anderson, Chaim Topol, Max von Sydow, Ornella Muti, Timothy Dalton, Brian Blessed; **D:** Mike Hodges; **M:** Howard Blake. *USH*

Flash Gordon Conquers the Universe *Purple Death from Outer Space* 1940 Ravaging plague strikes the earth and Flash Gordon undertakes to stop it. A serial in twelve chapters. 240m/B VHS, Beta. Buster Crabbe, Carol Hughes, Charles Middleton, Frank Shannon. *VYY, MRV, SNC*

Flash Gordon: Mars Attacks the World *The Deadly Rays From Mars; Flash Gordon's Trip to Mars* 1938 The earth is plagued by the evil Ming, but Flash Gordon steps in. From the serial. 87m/B VHS, Beta. Buster Crabbe, Jean Rogers, Charles Middleton; **D:** Robert F. "Bob" Hill, Ford Beebe. *CAB*

Flash Gordon: Rocketship ✶✶½ *Spaceship to the Unknown; Perils from Planet Mongo; Space Soldiers; Atomic Rocketship* 1936 Re-edited from the original Flash Gordon serial in which Flash and company must prevent the planet Mongo from colliding with Earth. Good character acting and good clean fun. **97m/B VHS, Beta.** Buster Crabbe, Jean Rogers, Frank Shannon, Charles Middleton, Priscilla Lawson, Jack Lipson; *D:* Frederick Stephani. VYY, PSM, CAB

Flash Gordon: Vol. 1 1953 Join Flash Gordon and Dale Arden as they struggle to maintain peace in the galaxy in this pair of episodes from the series. Additional volumes available. **60m/B VHS, Beta.** Steve Holland, Irene Champlin. DVT

A Flash of Green 🎷🎷 1985 A crooked politician is helping a construction firm exploit valuable waterfront property. He enlists the influence of a hesitant local journalist, who then falls for the woman leading the homeowner's conservation drive against the development plan. Made for American Playhouse and produced by costar Jordon. Based on the work of John D. MacDonald. **122m/C VHS, Beta.** Ed Harris, Blair Brown, Richard Jordan, George Coe; *D:* Victor Nunez; *W:* Victor Nunez; *M:* Charles Engstrom. MED

Flashback 🎷🎷🎷 1989 (R) FBI agent Sutherland's assignment sounds easy: escort aging 1960s radical Hopper to prison. But Hopper is cunning and decides not to go without a fight. He uses his brain to outwit the young Sutherland and to turn him against himself. Good moments between the two leads and with Kane, as a woman who never left the sixties behind. **108m/C VHS, Beta, LV, Closed Caption.** Dennis Hopper, Kiefer Sutherland, Carol Kane, Cliff DeYoung, Paul Dooley, Michael McKean, Richard Masur; *D:* Franco Amurri; *M:* Barry Goldberg. PAR

Flashdance 🎷🎷 1983 (R) 18-year-old Alex wants to dance. She works all day as a welder (and has a hot affair going with her boss), dances at a local bar at night, and hopes someday to get enough courage to audition for a spot at the School of Ballet. Glossy music video redeemed somewhat by exciting choreography with Marine Jahan doing the dancing for Beals. Oscar-winning title song sung by Irene Cara. Inspired the torn-sweatshirt trend in fashion of the period. ♫Flashdance...What a Feeling; I Love Rock 'n Roll; Manhunt; Gloria; Lady, Lady, Lady; Seduce Me Tonight. **95m/C VHS, Beta, LV, 8mm, Closed Caption.** Jennifer Beals, Michael Nouri, Belinda Bauer, Lilia Skala, Cynthia Rhodes, Sunny Johnson, Lee Ving, Kyle T. Heffner, Ron Karabatsos, Robert Wuhl, Elizabeth Sagal; *D:* Franca Pasut. Academy Awards '83: Best Song ("Flashdance...What a Feeling"); Golden Globe Awards '84: Best Song ("Flashdance...What a Feeling"), Best Score; Nominations: Academy Awards '83: Best Cinematography, Best Film Editing, Best Song ("Maniac"). PAR

Flashfire 🎷🎷½ 1994 (R) The torching of an apartment building and the murder of a cop seem unrelated until troubled detective Jack Flinder (Zane) becomes involved. Soon, he and murder witness Lisa (Minter) are on the run from the arsonists and crooked police.*CW:* Language, nudity, violence. **88m/C VHS.** Billy Zane, Kristin Minter, Louis Gossett Jr.; *D:* Elliot Silverstein; *W:* John Warren, Dan York; *M:* Sylvester Levay. THV

Flashpoint 🎷🎷 1984 (R) A pair of Texas border patrolmen discover an abandoned jeep that contains a fortune in cash, apparently from the 1960s. As they try to figure out how it got there, they become prey to those who want to keep the secret. With this cast, flick ought to be better. **95m/C VHS, Beta, LV, Closed Caption.** Treat Williams, Kris Kristofferson, Tess Harper, Rip Torn, Miguel Ferrer, Roberts Blossom; *D:* William Tannen; *W:* Michael Butler. NO

Flashpoint Africa 🎷½ 1984 When a news team follows a terrorist group's activities it winds up in a power struggle with terrifying consequences. **99m/C VHS, Beta.** Trevor Howard, Gayle Hunnicutt, James Faulkner. NO

Flat Top 🎷🎷½ 1952 The training of Navy fighter pilots aboard "flat top" aircraft carriers during WWII provides the drama here. A strict commander is appreciated only after the war when the pilots realize his role in their survival. The film makes good use of actual combat footage; fast-paced and effective. **85m/C VHS, Beta, LV.** Sterling Hayden, Richard Carlson, Keith Larsen, John Bromfield; *D:* Lesley Selander. Nominations: Academy Awards '52: Best Film Editing. REP, FCT

Flatbed Annie and Sweetiepie: Lady Truckers 🎷🎷½ *Flatbed Annie* 1979 A couple of good ol' gals hit the road and encounter a variety of bad guys out to steal their truck. Made for television. **100m/C VHS, Beta.** Annie Potts, Kim Darby, Harry Dean Stanton, Arthur Godfrey, Rory Calhoun, Bill Carter; *D:* Robert Greenwald. HBO, CNG

Flatfoot 🎷🎷 *The Knock-Out Cop* 1978 (PG) Tough police officer will let nothing stop him from finding and arresting drug smugglers. Good for laughs as well as lots of action. **113m/C VHS, Beta.** IT GE Bodo, Werner Pochat, Bud Spencer, Enzo Cannavale, Dagmar Lassander, Joe Stewardson; *D:* Steno. NO

Flatliners 🎷🎷 1990 (R) A group of medical students begin after-hours experimentation with death and out-of-body experiences. Some standard horror film images but Roberts and Sutherland create an energy that makes it worth watching. **111m/C VHS, Beta, LV, 8mm, Closed Caption.** Kiefer Sutherland, Julia Roberts, William Baldwin, Oliver Platt, Kevin Bacon, Kimberly Scott, Joshua Rudoy; *D:* Joel Schumacher; *C:* Jan De Bont; *M:* James Newton Howard. COL

Fled 🎷🎷 1996 (R) Charles Piper (Fishburne) and Luke Dodge (Baldwin) are combative prison escapees who need to find a stash of cash and a computer disk that could save them from both the Cuban mob and the cops. Bombshell Cora (Hayek) decides to help the duo and tries to get steamy with Piper. Lots of chases, lots of violence, not much sense. The climatic battle (the film was shot around Atlanta) takes place in a sightseeing gondola at Georgia's Stone Mountain.*CW:* Strong violence and language and for some nudity. **98m/C VHS, LV, Closed Caption.** Laurence "Larry" Fishburne, Stephen Baldwin, Salma Hayek, Will Patton, Robert John Burke; *D:* Kevin Hooks; *W:* Preston A. Whitmore II; *C:* Matthew F. Leonetti; *M:* Graeme Revell. MGM

Flesh 🎷🎷🎷 1968 An Andy Warhol-produced seedy urban farce about a bisexual street hustler who meets a variety of drug-addicted, deformed, and sexually deviant people. Dallesandro fans will enjoy his extensive exposure (literally). **90m/C VHS, Beta.** Joe Dallesandro, Geraldine Smith, Patti D'Arbanville; *D:* Paul Morrissey. TPV, PAR, FCT

Flesh and Blood 🎷🎷 1922 An unjustly convicted lawyer is released from prison to find out his wife has died. He vows revenge on those who falsely imprisoned him and assumes the disguise of a crippled beggar to begin his plot. Silent with musical score. **75m/B VHS, Beta, 8mm.** Lon Chaney Sr.; *D:* Irving Cummings. SNC, VYY, GVV

Flesh and Blood 🎷🎷½ *The Rose and the Sword* 1985 (R) A rowdy group of 16th Century hellions makes off with a princess who is already spoken for and pillage and plunder their way to revenge. Hauer leads the motley group through sword fights, raids, and the like. Dutch director Verhoeven's first English language film. Not for children; with rape scenes, nudity, and graphic sex. **126m/C VHS, Beta, LV.** Rutger Hauer, Jennifer Jason Leigh, Tom Burlinson, Susan Tyrrell, Jack Thompson, Ronald Lacey, Brion James, Bruno Kirby; *D:* Paul Verhoeven; *W:* Paul Verhoeven, Gerard Soeteman; *C:* Jan De Bont; *M:* Basil Poledouris. LIV, VES

Flesh and Blood Show 🎷 *Asylum of the Insane* 1973 (R) Rehearsal turns into an execution ritual for a group of actors at a mysterious seaside theatre. Truth in titling: features blood, gore, and some sex. Shot in part in 3-D. **93m/C VHS, Beta.** GB Robin Askwith, Candace Glendenning, Tristan Rogers, Ray Brooks, Jenny Hanley, Luan Peters, Patrick Barr; *D:* Pete Walker. NO

Flesh and Bone 🎷🎷🎷 1993 (R) Quaid is exact as a vending machine distributor with a desolate rural Texas circuit, haunted by the memory of a decades-old murder committed by his father (Caan) during a botched farm-house robbery. Alcoholic Ryan (Quaid's real-life wife) emerges from a bad marriage and helps Quaid rebuild his life, never suspecting that they may have met before. Challenging but successful role for Ryan, better known for her girlish, romantic-comedy appeal. Paltrow's unforgettable as a heartless casket robber and Caan's partner/girlfriend. Director Kloves extracts moments of earthy beauty from the bleak, humble West Texas setting. **127m/C VHS, Beta, LV, Closed Caption.** Dennis Quaid, Meg Ryan, James Caan, Gwyneth Paltrow, Scott Wilson, Christopher Rydell; *D:* Steven Kloves; *W:* Steven Kloves; *M:* Thomas Newman. PAR

The Flesh and the Devil 🎷🎷🎷½ 1927 Classic Garbo at her seductive best as a woman who causes a feud between two friends. Gilbert is an Austrian officer, falls for the married Garbo and winds up killing her husband in a duel. Banished to the African Corps he asks his best friend (Hanson) to look after his lady love. But Hanson takes his job too seriously, falling for the lady himself. Great silent movie with surprise ending to match. The first Gilbert and Garbo pairing. **112m/B VHS, Beta.** John Gilbert, Greta Garbo, Lars Hanson, Barbara Kent, George Fawcett, Eugenie Besserer; *D:* Clarence Brown; *C:* William H. Daniels. MGM

Flesh and the Spur 🎷½ 1957 A cowboy tracks the killer of his brother. Future Mannix Mike Connors (nicknamed 'Touch' at the time) joins the search. Unedifying western with oddball touches, notably a theme song by Chipmunks creator Ross Bagdasarian. **78m/C VHS.** John Agar, Marla English, Mike Connors, Raymond Hatton, Maria Monay, Joyce Meadows, Kenne Duncan; *D:* Edward L. Cahn. NOS, LOO

The Flesh Eaters 🎷½ 1964 A claustrophobic low-budget thriller about a film queen and her secretary who crash-land on an island inhabited by your basic mad scientist. His latest experiment is with tiny flesh-eating sea creatures. Shock ending. **87m/C VHS, Beta.** Martin Kosleck, Rita Morley, Byron Sanders, Barbara Wilkin, Ray Tudor; *D:* Jack Curtis. SNC

Flesh Eating Mothers 🎷 1989 Housewives are transformed into cannibals after a mystery virus hits their town. Their kids must stop the moms from eating any more people. **90m/C VHS, Beta.** Robert Lee Oliver, Donatella Hecht, Valorie Hubbard, Neal Rosen, Terry Hayes; *D:* James Aviles Martin. ACA

Flesh Feast woof! 1969 Classically horrendous anti-Nazi bosh, in which a mad female plastic surgeon (Lake) rejuvenates Hitler and then tortures him to death with maggots to avenge her mother's suffering. Lake's last film, and the sorriest sign-off any actress ever had. **72m/C VHS, Beta.** Veronica Lake, Phil Philbin, Heather Hughes, Martha Mischon, Yanka Mann, Dian Wilhite, Chris Martell; *D:* Brad F. Ginter. NO

Flesh Gordon 🎷 1972 Soft-core spoof of the "Flash Gordon" series. Flesh takes it upon himself to save Earth from the evil Wang's sex ray; Wang, of course, being the leader of the planet Porno. Lackluster special effects and below par story dull an already ridiculous movie. Look for cameo by real-life porn starlet Candy Samples. The restored (90-minute) version also includes the theatrical trailer; a 72-minute R-rated version is also available. **90m/C VHS, LV.** Jason Williams, Suzanne Fields, Joseph Hudgins, John Hoyt, Howard Ziehf, Michael Benveniste; *Cameos:* Candy Samples; *D:* Mike Light; *V:* Craig T. Nelson. HTV, IME, MED

Flesh Gordon 2: Flesh Gordon Meets the Cosmic Cheerleaders 🎷 1990 Emperor Wang (Hunt) threatens the Universe with his powerful Impotence ray. Flesh (Murdocco), along with Dale (Kelly) and Dr. Flexi Jerkoff (Travis), do battle with a belt of farting asteroids and other weirdos. Director Ziehm delivers this one on a shoestring of under $1 million, even improving technically on the original. The sex scenes are, however, more watered down in an apparent attempt to gain a wider audience. Scatological jokes are the basis for much of the humor. **98m/C VHS.** *CA* Vince Murdocco, Tony Travis, William Dennis Hunt, Robyn Kelly; *D:* Howard Ziehm. *NHO*

Fleshburn *Ω* **1984 (R)** An Indian Vietnam War veteran escapes from a mental institution to get revenge on the four psychiatrists who committed him. **91m/C VHS, Beta.** Steve Kanaly, Karen Carlson, Sonny Landham, Macon McCalman; *D:* George Gage. *MED*

Fleshpot on 42nd Street *Ω* **1971** Stark, realistic look at the streetwalking profession. Dusty leaves her blue collar boyfriend to move in with a transvestite and then she meets a dashing young Staten Island native (like the director). Their romance blooms until he is run over by a car, sending Dusty into a tailspin which lands her back on 42nd Street. Along the way, various rustic hookers and venerable old floozies liven up director Mulligan's version of New York. Less emphasis on the sleaze than the grittiness. **78m/C VHS.** Diana Lewis, Lynn Flanagan, Bob Walters; *D:* Andy Milligan. *SMW, TPV*

Fleshtone *ΩΩ* **1994 (R)** Artist Matthew Greco's (Kemp) work is not for the faint-hearted since he paints grisly suicides and murders. No wonder he's lonely—so lonely that he answers a phone-sex ad and is hooked up with Edna (Cutter), who becomes an obsession. Matthew even depicts her murder in one of his paintings and then she's found dead—only it turns out not to be Edna, who doesn't exist. Just what has Matthew gotten himself into? Provocative but ending is a letdown. An unrated version is also available. *CW:* Language, violence, and strong sexuality. **89m/C VHS, LV.** Martin Kemp, Lise Cutter, Tim Thomerson; *D:* Harry Hurwitz; *W:* Harry Hurwitz. *PSM*

Fletch *ΩΩ* **1985 (PG)** Somewhat charming comedy. When newspaper journalist Fletch goes undercover to get the scoop on the local drug scene, a wealthy young businessman enlists his help in dying. Something's rotten in Denmark when the man's doctor knows nothing of the illness and Fletch comes closer to the drug scene than he realizes. Throughout the entire film, Chevy Chase assumes a multitude of flippant comic characters to discover the truth. Based on Gregory McDonald's novel. **98m/C VHS, Beta, LV, Closed Caption.** Chevy Chase, Tim Matheson, Joe Don Baker, Dana Wheeler-Nicholson, M. Emmet Walsh, Kenneth Mars, Geena Davis, Richard Libertini, George Wendt, Kareem Abdul-Jabbar, Alison La Placa; *D:* Michael Ritchie; *W:* Andrew Bergman; *M:* Harold Faltermeyer. *USH*

Fletch Lives *ΩΩ* **1989 (PG)** In this sequel to "Fletch," Chase is back again as the super-reporter. When Fletch learns of his inheritance of a Southern estate he is eager to claim it. During his down-home trip he becomes involved in a murder and must use his disguise skills to solve it before he becomes the next victim. Based on the novels of Gregory MacDonald. **95m/C VHS, Beta, LV, Closed Caption.** Chevy Chase, Hal Holbrook, Julianne Phillips, Richard Libertini, R. Lee Ermey, Cleavon Little; *D:* Michael Ritchie; *W:* Leon Capetanos; *M:* Harold Faltermeyer. *USH*

Flicks *Hollyweird; Loose Joints* **1985 (R)** A compilation of skits parodying the tradition of Saturday afternoon matinees, including coming attractions and a cartoon. Never released theatrically. **79m/C VHS, Beta.** Martin Mull, Joan Hackett, Pamela Sue Martin, Betty Kennedy, Richard Belzer; *D:* Peter Winograd. *MED*

The Flight *ΩΩ* **1989** A non-narrative view of glider planes as they soar over the countryside and rivers of the Laurentians and Canadian Rockies. Useful in language arts classes. **96m/C VHS, Beta, LV.** Eli Danker, Sandy McPeak, Lindsay Wagner; *D:* Paul Wendkos. *VES, IME*

Flight from Glory *ΩΩ½* **1937** A group of pilots fly supplies over the Andes from their isolated base camp to even more isolated mines. Morris is their leader who watches as, one by one, the men are killed on their dangerous flights. To make a bad situation worse, Heflin arrives as a new recruit—along with his pretty wife. **66m/B VHS, Beta.** Chester Morris, Onslow Stevens, Whitney Bourne, Van Heflin; *D:* Lew (Louis Friedlander) Landers. *NO*

Flight from Singapore *Ω½* **1962** Transporting desperately needed blood to Malaysia, a flight crew is forced to crash land in the jungle. Nicely done if trite. **74m/B VHS, Beta.** *GB* Patrick Allen, Patrick Holt, William Abney, Harry Fowler; *D:* Dudley Birch; *W:* Dudley Birch. *SNC*

Flight from Vienna *ΩΩ* **1958** A high-ranking Hungarian security officer, disenchanted with communism, stages a daring escape from his country. In Vienna, he asks the British for political asylum, but is sent back to Hungary to help a scientist escape in order to prove his loyalty. Cold war drama hangs together on strength of Bikel's performance. **54m/B VHS, Beta.** Theodore Bikel, John Bentley, Donald Gray. *VYY*

Flight of Black Angel *ΩΩ½* **1991 (R)** Wacked-out F-16 pilot fancies himself an angel of death, and, after annihilating a number of trainees, sets out to make Las Vegas a nuked-out ghost town. Squadron commander Strauss, however, is not pleased with his pilot's initiative. Made for cable TV script runs out of gas and heads into a nosedive. **102m/C VHS.** Peter Strauss, William O'Leary, James O'Sullivan, Michael Keys Hall; *D:* Jonathan Mostow; *W:* Henry Dominick. *THV*

Flight of Dragons *ΩΩ½* **1982** Animated tale takes place between the Age of Magic and the Age of Science, in a century when dragons ruled the skies. **98m/C VHS, Beta.** *D:* Arthur Rankin Jr., Jules Bass; *V:* John Ritter, Victor Buono, James Earl Jones, Don Messick, Larry Storch. *WAR*

A Flight of Rainbirds *ΩΩ* **1981** In a dual role, Krabbe plays a biologist who dreams he must lose his virginity within a week or die and his alter ego who joins him in the search for the perfect woman. In Dutch with English subtitles. **94m/C VHS, LV.** *NL* Jeroen Krabbe; *D:* Ate De Jong. *NO*

Flight of the Eagle *ΩΩ* **1982** Based on the actual ill-fated expedition of Salomon Andree who, with two friends, attempted to fly from Sweden to the North Pole in a hydrogen balloon in 1897. The last half of the film drags somewhat after their balloon crashes. Beautifully photographed adventure. In Swedish with English subtitles. **115m/C VHS, Beta, LV.** *SW* Max von Sydow, Goran Stangertz, Clement Harari, Sverre Anker; *D:* Jan Troell. Nominations: Academy Awards '82: Best Foreign Language Film. *AHV*

Flight of the Grey Wolf *Ω½* **1976** A tame, innocent wolf is mistaken for a killer and must run for his life with the help of his boy-owner. **82m/C VHS, Beta.** Bill Williams, Barbara Hale, Jeff East. *DIS*

Flight of the Innocent *ΩΩ½* **1993 (R)** The innocent 10-year-old Vito comes from a family who make their living as kidnappers. He is the only witness (and the only survivor) when his family is massacred by a rival gang. Vito flees the carnage and sets off to find his cousin who lives in Rome. But his journey truly ends when he is taken in by a wealthy industrialist family whose own son has been kidnapped. Directorial debut of Carlei who tends to rely on striking visuals rather than his characters. In Italian with English subtitles. *CW:* Violence. **105m/C VHS, LV.** *IT* Manuel Colao, Francesca Neri, Jacques Perrin, Frederico Pacifici, Sal Borgese; *D:* Carlo Carlei; *W:* Carlo Carlei, Gualtiero Rosella. Nominations: Golden Globe Awards '94: Best Foreign Film. *MGM*

Flight of the Intruder *Ω½* **1990 (PG-13)** Vietnam naval pilots aboard an aircraft carrier don't like the way the war is being handled, so they go rogue and decide to go on a mission to bomb an enemy air base in Hanoi. Loads of male bonding. **115m/C VHS, Beta, LV, Closed Caption.** Danny Glover, Willem Dafoe, Brad Johnson, Rosanna Arquette, Tom Sizemore; *D:* John Milius; *W:* Robert Dillon; *C:* Fred W. Koenekamp; *M:* Basil Poledouris. *PAR*

Flight of the Navigator *ΩΩ½* **1986 (PG)** A boy boards an alien spacecraft and embarks on a series of time-travel adventures with a crew of wisecracking extraterrestrial creatures. When he returns home eight years later, a NASA investigation ensues. Paul Reubens, better known as Pee Wee Herman, provides the voice of the robot. **90m/C VHS, Beta, LV.** Joey Cramer, Veronica Cartwright, Cliff DeYoung, Sarah Jessica Parker, Matt Adler, Howard Hesseman; *D:* Randal Kleiser; *W:* Michael Burton, Matt MacManus; *M:* Alan Silvestri; *V:* Paul (Pee Wee Herman) Reubens. *DIS*

The Flight of the Phoenix *ΩΩΩ* **1965** A group of men stranded in the Arabian desert after a plane crash attempt to rebuild their plane in order to escape before succumbing to the elements. Big budget, all-star survival drama based on the novel by Elleston Trevor. **147m/C VHS, Beta, LV, Closed Caption.** James Stewart, Richard Attenborough, Peter Finch, Hardy Kruger, Dan Duryea, George Kennedy, Ernest Borgnine, Ian Bannen; *D:* Robert Aldrich; *C:* Joseph Biroc. Nominations: Academy Awards '65: Best Film Editing, Best Supporting Actor (Bannen). *FOX*

Flight to Fury *Ω½* **1966** A cheap independent adventure film, featuring the novice Hellman-Nicholson team, about a few assorted mercenaries searching for a horde of diamonds when their plane crashes in the wilderness of the Philippines. Based on a story by director/producer Hellman. **73m/B VHS, Beta.** Jack Nicholson, Dewey Martin, Fay Spain, Vic Diaz, Jacqueline Hellman; *D:* Monte Hellman; *W:* Jack Nicholson. *NO*

Flight to Mars *ΩΩ* **1952** An expedition crash lands on the red planet and discovers an advanced underground society that wants to invade earth using the U.S. spacecraft. Includes previews of coming attractions from classic science fiction films. First movie of this genre to be shot in color. **72m/C VHS, Beta, LV.** Cameron Mitchell, Marguerite Chapman, Arthur Franz; *D:* Lesley Selander. *MED, IME*

Flight to Nowhere woof! **1946** An FBI agent tracks down a stolen map of atomic bomb source material with the help of a charter pilot and a dizzy blonde. Muddled plot and no discernable acting. **74m/B VHS, Beta, LV.** Alan Curtis, Evelyn Ankers, Jack Holt; *D:* William Rowland. *SNC, VYY*

Flim-Flam Man *ΩΩ* *One Born Every Minute* **1967** A con man teams up with an army deserter to teach him the fine art of flim-flamming as they travel through small southern towns. Love may lead the young man back to the straight and narrow, but not his reprobate mentor. Scott is wonderful; and the slapstick episodes move at a good pace. **104m/C VHS, Beta, Closed Caption.** George C. Scott, Michael Sarrazin, Slim Pickens, Sue Lyon, Jack Albertson, Harry (Henry) Morgan; *D:* Irvin Kershner; *C:* Charles B(ryant) Lang; *M:* Jerry Goldsmith. *FOX*

Flinch *ΩΩ* **1994 (R)** Two models, who work as live mannequins, witness a murder and wonder if they'll be the next victims. *CW:* Rated R for some nudity and violence. **90m/C VHS, Closed Caption.** Judd Nelson, Nick Mancuso, Gina Gershon; *D:* George Erschbamer. *PAR*

The Flintstones **1960** The foibles of the two Stone Age families, the Flintstones and the Rubbles, are chronicled in these two animated episodes of the classic series. **50m/C VHS, Beta.** *V:* Alan Reed, Mel Blanc, Jean Vander Pyl, Bea Benadaret. *TTC*

The Flintstones *ΩΩ½* **1994 (PG)** Preceded by massive hype, popular '60s cartoon comes to life thanks to a huge budget and creative sets and props. Freds being set up by evil corporate types MacLachlan and Barry to take the fall for their embezzling scheme. Soon he gives up dining at RocDonald's for Cavern on the Green and cans best buddy Barney (Moranis). Forget the lame plot (32 writers took a shot at it) and sit back and enjoy the spectacle. Goodman's an amazingly true-to-type Fred, O'Donnell has Betty's giggle down pat, and Perkins looks a lot like Wilma. Wilma's original voice, VanderPyl, has a cameo; listen for Korman's voice as the Dictabird. Add half a bone if you're under 12. **92m/C VHS, LV, Closed Caption.** John Goodman, Rick Moranis, Elizabeth Perkins, Rosie O'Donnell, Elizabeth Taylor, Kyle MacLachlan, Halle Berry, Jonathan Winters, Richard Moll, Irwin Keyes, Dann Florek; *Cameos:* Laraine Newman, Jean VanDerPyl, Jay Leno; *D:* Tom S. Parker, Jim Jennewein, Steven E. de Souza; *C:* Dean Cundey; *M:* David Newman; *V:* Harvey Korman. Golden Raspberry Awards '94: Worst Supporting Actress (O'Donnell), Worst Screenplay; Nominations: MTV Movie Awards '95: Most Desirable Female (Berry); Golden Raspberry Awards '94: Worst Remake/Sequel, Worst Supporting Actress (Taylor). *USH*

Flipper 🎬🎬🎬 1963 A fisherman's son befriends an injured dolphin, is persuaded to return him to the wild, and earns the animal's gratitude. Prime kids' fare, as its sequels and television series attest. **87m/C VHS, Beta, Closed Caption.** Chuck Connors, Luke Halpin, Kathleen Maguire, Connie Scott; *D:* James B. Clark. *MVD, MGM*

Flipper 1964 Widower Porter Ricks (Kelly) is the chief ranger at Coral Key Park, Florida, who lives with sons, 15-year-old Sandy (Halpin) and 10-year-old Bud (Norden), and their pet dolphin Flipper. Adventures usually involved Flipper rescuing his trouble-prone charges from assorted aquatic dangers. The series ran from 1964-1968; two episodes are included per tape. Oh yes, Flipper was played by a girl dolphin named Suzy. **60m/C VHS, Closed Caption.** Brian Kelly, Luke Halpin, Tommy Norden. *HMK*

Flipper 🎬🎬🎬 1996 (PG) They still call him Flipper! Flipper, who in some scenes is played by a robot dolphin, reappears in a feature film for the first time since 1966. Sullen 14-year-old city boy Sandy Ricks (Wood) must spend the summer with crusty bachelor uncle Porter (Hogan), who would rather fish than look after his troublesome nephew. The duo witness the heartless killing of Flipper's family and are adopted by him. In addition to causing their seafood bill to skyrocket, the dolphin helps them uncover an illegal toxic waste dumper, who happens to be the same guy who made Flipper's mama sleep with the fishes. Updated along with the story is the soundtrack, which features a version of the famous theme song by Matthew Sweet. **97m/C VHS, LV, Closed Caption.** Elijah Wood, Paul Hogan, Chelsea Field, Isaac Hayes, Jonathan Banks, Luke Halpin; *D:* Alan Shapiro; *W:* Alan Shapiro; *C:* Bill Butler; *M:* Joel McNeely. *USH*

Flipper's New Adventure 🎬🎬🎬 *Flipper and the Pirates* 1964 Believing they are to be separated, Flipper and Sandy travel to a remote island. Little do they know, a British family is being held for ransom on the island they have chosen. It's up to the duo to save the day. An enjoyable, nicely done family adventure. **103m/C VHS, Beta.** Luke Halpin, Pamela Franklin, Tom Helmore, Francesca Annis, Brian Kelly, Joe Higgins, Ricou Browning; *D:* Leon Benson. *MGM, FCT*

Flipper's Odyssey 🎬🎬 1966 Flipper has disappeared and his adopted family goes looking for him, but when one of the boys gets trapped in a cave, Flipper is his only hope. **77m/C VHS, Beta.** Luke Halpin, Brian Kelly, Tommy Norden; *D:* Paul Landres. *CNG, PSM*

Flipping 🎬🎬 1996 (R) Quartet of none-too-bright wiseguy wannabes serve as debt collectors for gangster Leo Richards (David). Turns out gay undercover cop Billy (Proval) has infiltrated the gang—only to fall for ambitious hoodlum Michael (Amos)—and violent double-crosses abound. Debut for writer/director Mitchell.*CW:* Strong violence and language. **102m/C VHS, Closed Caption.** David Amos, David Proval, Gene Mitchell, Keith David, Shant Benjamin, Barry Primus, Mike Starr, Tony Burton, Paul Klar; *D:* Gene Mitchell; *W:* Gene Mitchell; *C:* Phil Parmet. *PAR*

Flirt 🎬🎬½ 1995 (R) Three variations on the same theme: love, jealousy, and the problems of committing are what comprise this interesting portrait of modern romance in three countries. One character in each of the three stories is faced with an ultimatum to commit and is given a 90-minute deadline. Each are already involved in various other romantic entanglements. The best scenes show the confused flirts receiving very amusing advice from strangers. First episode is the best, as the pace subsequently slows.*CW:* Language and nudity. **84m/C VHS, Closed Caption.** *GE JP* William Sage, Parker Posey, Martin Donovan, Dwight Ewell, Dominik Bender, Geno Lechner, Miho Nikaido, Toshizo Fujisawa; *D:* Hal Hartley; *W:* Hal Hartley; *C:* Michael Spiller; *M:* Ned Rifle. *COL*

Flirtation Walk 🎬🎬½ 1934 West point musical that has cadet Powell falling in love with the general's daughter (Keeler), who is already engaged to lieutenant Eldredge. Some fairly good numbers, including "Mr. and Mrs. Is The Name," and "Flirtation Walk." In an attempt to change her image, Keeler hardly dances at all, which is too bad for the viewer. Based on a story by Lou Edelman and Delmer Daves. **98m/B VHS.** Dick Powell, Ruby Keeler, Pat O'Brien, Ross Alexander; *D:* Frank Borzage; *W:* Delmer Daves. Nominations: Academy Awards '34: Best Picture. *MGM*

Flirting 🎬🎬🎬 1989 (R) Set in an Australian boarding school in 1965, a charming story following the misadventures of the adolescent Danny Embling, who has the misfortune to be both bright and sensitive, putting him seriously at odds with his masculine peers. He finds love with an outcast at the neighboring girls boarding school, the daughter of a diplomat from Uganda. Kidman has a supporting role as a snobbish older boarding school girl, not quite as bad as she seems. Tender and amusing. The second of director Duigan's coming-of-age trilogy, preceded by "The Year My Voice Broke" (the third film isn't yet completed).*CW:* Teen sexuality. **100m/C VHS, LV, Closed Caption.** *AU* Noah Taylor, Thandie Newton, Nicole Kidman, Bartholomew Rose, Felix Nobis, Josh Picker, Kiri Paramore, Marc Gray, Joshua Marshall, David Wieland, Craig Black, Leslie Hill; *D:* John Duigan; *W:* John Duigan. Australian Film Institute '90: Best Film. *THV, BTV*

Flirting with Disaster 🎬🎬🎬 1995 (R) Mel Coplin (Stiller) is your average neurotic New York entomologist searching for his birth parents so he can finally name his 4-month-old child and make love to his wife. Tagging along on his bumpy ride are his wife Nancy (Arquette), a beautiful quirky adoption agency shrink (Leoni), and a pair of bisexual FBI agents. The excellent cast also features Moore as Mel's bra baring adoptive mother, Segal as his weirdly paranoid adoptive father, and Alda and Tomlin as hilarious send-ups of ex-hippie mentality. As events spin madly out of control, every type of relationship is satired, and every character is left in their underwear. This is director Russell's first big budget movie, and is as close to a vintage screwball comedy as you'll see in the 90s.*CW:* Language, sexuality, and a comic drug scene. **92m/C VHS, LV, Closed Caption.** Ben Stiller, Patricia Arquette, Tea Leoni, Alan Alda, Mary Tyler Moore, George Segal, Lily Tomlin, Josh Brolin, Richard Jenkins, Celia Weston, Glenn Fitzgerald, Beth Ostrosky, Cynthia Lamontagne, David Patrick Kelly, John Ford Noonan, Charles Oberly; *D:* David O. Russell; *W:* David O. Russell; *C:* Eric Alan Edwards; *M:* Stephen Endelman. Nominations: Independent Spirit Awards '97: Best Director (Russell), Best Screenplay, Best Supporting Actor (Jenkins), Best Supporting Actress (Tomlin). *TOU*

Flirting with Fate 🎬🎬🎬 1916 Early Fairbanks-cum-acrobat vehicle. Having hired a hitman to rub himself out, a young man decides he doesn't want to die, after all. Seems there's a girl involved... **51m/B VHS, Beta.** Douglas Fairbanks Sr., Jewel Carmen, Howard Gaye, William E. Lawrence, George Beranger, Dorothy Hadel, Lillian Langdon; *D:* Christy Cabanne. *NOS, GPV, FCT*

Floating Life 🎬🎬 1995 The Chans have decided to emigrate from Hong Kong before the mainland China takeover and join daughter Bing (Yip) and her family in Sydney. High-strung Bing's determined to assimilate as much as possible into Australian society and bullies her newly-arrived family, who are naturally disoriented. The arrival of laggard son Gar Ming (Wong) and easy-going daughter Yen (Shun-Wah), who's been living in Germany, only provide further complications for a family completely adrift in their new world. Cantonese, German, and English dialogue. **95m/C VHS.** *AU* Annie Yip, Annette Shun-Wah, Anthony Wong, Edwin Pang, Cecilia Fong Sing Lee, Toby Wong, Toby Chan, Bruce Poon; *D:* Clara Law; *W:* Clara Law; *C:* Dion Beebe; *M:* Davood A. Tabrizi. Nominations: Australian Film Institute '96: Best Director (Law), Best Supporting Actress (Shun-Wah). *NYR*

Flood! 🎬🎬 1976 Irwin Allen's first made-for-television disaster film. A dam bursts and devastates a small town, so a helicopter pilot must save the day. Good cast is swept along in a current of disaster-genre cliches. **98m/C VHS, Beta.** Robert Culp, Martin Milner, Barbara Hershey, Richard Basehart, Carol Lynley, Roddy McDowall, Cameron Mitchell, Teresa Wright, Francine York; *D:* Earl Bellamy. *WAR*

The Floorwalker 🎬🎬🎬 1917 Chaplin becomes involved with a dishonest floorwalker in a department store. Silent. **20m/B VHS, Beta.** Charlie Chaplin; *D:* Charlie Chaplin. *CAB*

The Floorwalker/By the Sea 🎬🎬🎬 1915 Two early Chaplin short comedies, featuring a hilarious scene on an escalator in the first film. Silent. **51m/B VHS, Beta, 8mm.** Charlie Chaplin, Edna Purviance, Eric Campbell; *D:* Charlie Chaplin. *VYY*

Flor Silvestre 🎬 *Wild Flower* 1958 The son of a rich rancher romances a young woman against the background of the Mexican Revolution. **90m/B VHS, Beta.** *MX* Dolores Del Rio, Pedro Armendariz Sr.; *D:* Emilio Fernandez. *MAD*

The Florida Connection 🎬 1974 An action thriller set in the Florida Swamps with a collection of villains and a vague plot about smuggling. **90m/C VHS, Beta.** Dan Pastorini, June Wilkinson. *UNI*

Florida Straits 🎬🎬 1987 (PG-13) A recently released Cuban prisoner hires a few losers and their boat to return to the island, supposedly to find the girl he loves. The real quest is for gold buried during the Bay-of-Pigs invasion in this none-too-original made-for-cable movie that at least offers a good cast. **98m/C VHS, Beta, LV, Closed Caption.** Raul Julia, Fred Ward, Daniel H. Jenkins, Antonio Fargas; *D:* Mike Hodges; *W:* Stephen Metcalfe; *M:* Michel Colombier. *ORI*

Floundering 🎬½ 1994 (R) Misguided satire uses the 1992 L.A. riots as a backdrop to tell the saga of unemployed James Boyz (LeGros), whose life is a walking disaster. He owes the IRS, his unemployment compensation has run out, his brother (Hawke) has fled from a drug rehab clinic, and he finds his girlfriend (Zane) in bed with another man. John drags himself among the city's downtrodden as he fantasizes about life. Drag pretty much sums up the film despite good performances by LeGros and Hawke.*CW:* Strong language, sexuality and drug use and for some violence. **97m/C VHS.** James LeGros, Ethan Hawke, Steve Buscemi, John Cusack, Lisa Zane, Sy Richardson; *D:* Peter McCarthy; *W:* Peter McCarthy. *APX*

Flower Drum Song 🎬🎬 1961 The Rodgers and Hammerstein musical played better on Broadway than in this overblown adaptation of life in San Francisco's Chinatown. Umeki plays the young girl who arrives from Hong Kong for an arranged marriage. Her intended (Soo) is a fast-living nightclub owner already enjoying the love of singer Kwan. Meanwhile Umeki falls for the handsome Shigeta. Naturally, everything comes together in a happy ending. 🎵I Enjoy Being A Girl; Don't Marry Me; Grant Avenue; You Are Beautiful; A Hundred Million Miracles; Fan Tan Fanny; Chop Suey; The Other Generation; I Am Going to Like It Here. **133m/C VHS, Beta, LV.** Nancy Kwan, Jack Soo, James Shigeta, Miyoshi Umeki, Juanita Hall; *D:* Henry Koster; *C:* Russell Metty; *M:* Richard Rodgers, Oscar Hammerstein. Nominations: Academy Awards '61: Best Art Direction/Set Decoration (Color), Best Color Cinematography,

Best Costume Design (Color), Best Sound, Scoring of a Musical. *USH, FCT*

The Flower of My Secret 🐶🐶🐶 *La Flor de My Secreto* 1995 (R)
Emotional yet restrained story about middle-aged Leo (Paredes), whose longtime marriage is fast ending (and it's not her idea). Leo writes hugely popular romance novels under a pseudonym but her current work is so bleak it's unpublishable. So, Leo gets a job at a newspaper where editor Angel (Echanove) immediately falls for her, and indeed, lives up to his name as her guardian. Willfully myopic about her own life, Leo undergoes further trials until she slowly realizes the mess she's in and becomes willing to change. Surprisingly subdued given Almodovar's usual flamboyance but it's a welcome change of pace. Spanish with subtitles. *CW:* Language and brief sexuality. **107m/C VHS, LV, Closed Caption.** *SP FR* Marisa Paredes, Juan Echanove, Imanol Arias, Carmen Elias, Rossy de Palma, Chus Lampreave, Joaquin Cortes, Manuela Vargas; *D:* Pedro Almodovar; *W:* Pedro Almodovar; *C:* Alfonso Beato; *M:* Alberto Inglesias. *COL*

Flowers in the Attic 🐶½ 1987 (PG-13)
Based on the V.C. Andrews bestseller, a would-be thriller about four young siblings locked for years in their family's old mansion by their grandmother with their mother's selfish acquiescence. A chicken-hearted, clumsy flop that skimps on the novel's trashier themes. **93m/C VHS, Beta, LV, Closed Caption.** Victoria Tennant, Kristy Swanson, Louise Fletcher, Jeb Stuart Adams; *D:* Jeffrey Bloom; *W:* Jeffrey Bloom; *C:* Gil Hubbs. *NWV, VTR*

Flowers of Reverie 🐶🐶 1984
A former soldier is imprisoned for his work in the resistance during the Hungarian Revolution (1848-9), leading to tragedy. In Hungarian with English subtitles. **106m/C VHS.** *HU D:* Laszlo Lugossy. *FCT*

The Flowers of St. Francis 🐶🐶🐶 1950
Rossellini's presentation of St. Francis and his friars' attainment of spiritual harmony. In Italian with English subtitles. This is the British release version, 10-15 minutes longer than the U.S. version. **75m/B VHS, Beta.** *IT* Federico Fellini; *D:* Roberto Rossellini. *FCT*

Fluke 🐶🐶🐶 1995 (PG)
"Ghost" meets "Oh, Heavenly Dog" as Tom (Modine) dies in a suspicious car accident and is reincarnated as a dog who remembers his past life. He returns to his former family (Travis and Pomeranc) to protect them from his former business partner (Stoltz), battling such puppy perils as cosmetic testing labs and dogcatchers along the way. While there's plenty of squishy sentimentality to go around, some of the scenes involving animal abuse may be a little much for the target audience of pre-teen kids. Jackson and Stoltz trade "Pulp Fiction" for pup fiction, but this dog won't hunt. Based on the novel by James Herbert. **96m/C VHS, LV, Closed Caption.** Matthew Modine, Nancy Travis, Eric Stoltz, Max Pomeranc, Ron Perlman, Jon Polito, Bill Cobbs, Frederico Pacifici, Collin Wilcox Paxton; *D:* Carlo Carlei; *W:* James Carrington, Carlo Carlei; *C:* Raffaele Mertes; *M:* Samuel L. Jackson. *MGM*

Flush 🐶🐶 1981
Unorthodox comedy involving funny noises. **90m/C VHS.** William Calloway, William Bronder, Jeannie Linero; *D:* Andrew J. Kuehn. *NO*

The Flustered Comedy of Leon Errol 🐶🐶 1939
The popular Depression-era comedian Errol is showcased in three shorts: "Crime Rave," "Man-I-Cured," and "A Panic in the Parlor." **56m/B VHS, Beta, 8mm.** Leon Errol, Vivian Tobin, Dorothy Granger, Frank Faylen, Virginia Vale.

The Fly 🐶🐶🐶 1958
The historic, chillingly original '50s sci-fi tale about a hapless scientist experimenting with teleportation who accidentally gets anatomically confused with a housefly. Campy required viewing; two sequels followed, and a 1986 remake which itself has spawned one sequel. **94m/C VHS, Beta, LV.** Vincent Price, David Hedison, Herbert Marshall, Patricia Owens; *D:* Kurt Neumann; *W:* James Clavell; *C:* Karl Struss. *FOX*

The Fly 🐶🐶🐶 1986 (R)
A sensitive, humanistic remake of the 1958 horror film about a scientist whose flesh is genetically intermixed with a housefly via his experimental transportation device. A thoughtful, shocking horror film, with fine performances from Goldblum and Davis and a brutally emotional conclusion. Followed by "The Fly II" in 1989. **96m/C VHS, Beta, LV, Closed Caption.** Jeff Goldblum, Geena Davis, John Getz, Joy Boushel; *D:* David Cronenberg; *W:* David Cronenberg, Charles Edward Pogue; *M:* Howard Shore. Academy Awards '86: Best Makeup. *FOX*

The Fly 2 🐶½ 1989 (R)
Inferior sequel to Cronenberg's opus, in which the offspring of Seth Brundle achieves full genius maturity in three years, falls in love, and discovers the evil truth behind his father's teleportation device and the corporate auspices that backed it. **105m/C VHS, Beta, LV.** Eric Stoltz, Daphne Zuniga, Lee Richardson, John Getz, Harley Cross; *D:* Chris Walas; *W:* Mick Garris, Jim Wheat, Ken Wheat, Frank Darabont. *FOX, CCB*

Fly Away Home 🐶🐶🐶 *Father Goose; Flying Wild* 1996 (PG)
Does for geese what "Babe" did for pigs. Young Amy (Paquin) withdraws when she loses her mother in a car crash and is forced to live with her estranged father, Thomas (Daniels), a scruffy sculptor/inventor, in rural Ontario. Still dealing with her own mother's death, Amy suddenly becomes a mother herself to a tiny gaggle of goslings when she happens upon a nest of uprooted eggs. Extraordinary technical achievements make up for some unnecessary melodrama in the second half as the geese head South, led by Amy, in a glider built by her father. Touching but unsentimental, mostly well scripted and acted, and extraordinarily shot. Based on the true story of inventor Bill Lishman, who led domesticated geese on a winter migration from Toronto, Canada to North Carolina, leading the formation in his motor-powered glider. **107m/C VHS, LV, Closed Caption, DVD.** Jeff Daniels, Anna Paquin, Dana Delany, Terry Kinney, Jeremy Ratchford; *D:* Carroll Ballard; *W:* Robert Rodat, Vince McKewin; *C:* Caleb Deschanel; *M:* Mark Isham. Nominations: Academy Awards '96: Best Cinematography. *COL*

Fly by Night 🐶🐶 1993 (PG-13)
Mismatched New York rappers Rich and I join forces to make it big as hard-core gangstas. When they're propelled to the top of the charts, forces both personal and professional work to tear them apart. **93m/C VHS, Closed Caption.** Jeffrey D. Sams, Ron Brice, Darryl (Chill) Mitchell, Todd Graff, Leo Burmester, Soulfood Jed, Lawrence Gilliard, Omar Carter, Maura Tierney, Yul Vazquez, M.C. Lyte, Christopher-Michael Gerrard, Ebony Jo-Ann; *D:* Steve Gomer; *W:* Todd Graff; *C:* Larry Banks; *M:* Kris Parker, Sidney Mills, Dwayne Sumal. Sundance Film Festival '93: Filmmakers Trophy. *COL*

Fly with the Hawk 🐶🐶 19??
A troubled teenager gets lost in the wilderness for a year, and learns some important things from nature to take back to civilization. **90m/C VHS.** Peter Ferri, Peter Snook, Shelley Lynne Speigel; *D:* Robert Tanos. *NO*

Flying Blind 🐶½ 1941
Foreign agents are thwarted in their attempt to steal a vital air defense secret. Unconvincing espionage plot cobbled into a story about a Los Angeles-Las Vegas puddle jumper. **69m/B VHS, Beta.** Richard Arlen, Jean Parker, Marie Wilson. *NOS, DVT*

The Flying Deuces 🐶🐶🐶 *Flying Aces* 1939
Ollie's broken heart lands Laurel and Hardy in the Foreign Legion. The comic pair escape a firing squad only to suffer a plane crash that results in Hardy's reincarnation as a horse. A musical interlude with a Laurel soft shoe while Hardy sings "Shine On, Harvest Moon" is one of the film's highlights. **65m/B VHS, Beta, LV.** Stan Laurel, Oliver Hardy, Jean Parker, Reginald Gardiner, James Finlayson; *D:* Edward Sutherland. *CNG, MRV, NOS*

Flying Down to Rio 🐶🐶½ 1933
The first Astaire-Rogers musical, although they are relegated to supporting status behind Del Rio and Raymond. Still, it was enough to make them stars and a team that epitomizes the height of American musical films. The slim story revolves around singer Del Rio's two suitors and receives a splendid, art deco production. Showgirls dancing on plane wings in flight provide another memorable moment. ♪Music Makes Me; The Carioca; Orchids in the Moonlight; Flying Down to Rio. **89m/B VHS, Beta.** Fred Astaire, Ginger Rogers, Dolores Del Rio, Eric Blore, Gene Raymond, Franklin Pangborn; *D:* Thornton Freeland; *M:* Vincent Youmans, Max Steiner. Nominations: Academy Awards '34: Best Song ("Carioca"). *TTC, MED*

The Flying Fool 🐶🐶 1929
Ace pilot Bill returns from the war to find his younger brother has fallen for a singer. When Bill meets the lady, he also notices her charms and the two brothers have a duel in the skies to see who'll get the girl. **75m/B VHS, Beta.** William Boyd, Marie Prevost, Russell Gleason; *D:* Tay Garnett; *W:* James Gleason. *VYY, RXM, GPV*

Flying from the Hawk 🐶½ 1986
A 12-year-old boy sees something he shouldn't and soon finds that his friends and relatives are mysteriously vanishing. **110m/C VHS, Beta.** John Ireland, Diane McBain. *NO*

Flying Leathernecks 🐶🐶🐶 1951
Tough squadron leader Wayne fights with his fellow officer Ryan in Guadalcanal when their leadership styles clash. But when the real fighting begins all is forgotten as Wayne leads his men into victorious battle, winning the admiration and devotion of his fliers. Memorable WWII film deals with war in human terms. **102m/C VHS, Beta, LV.** John Wayne, Robert Ryan, Janis Carter; *D:* Nicholas Ray. *TLF, TTC*

The Flying Saucer 🐶½ 1950
U.S. and Russian scientists clash over their search for a huge flying saucer that is hidden under a glacier. The first movie to deal with flying saucers. The cassette includes animated opening and closing sequences plus previews of coming attractions. **120m/B VHS, Beta.** Mikel Conrad, Pat Garrison, Hanz von Teuffen; *D:* Mikel Conrad. *EEL, SNC*

Flying Saucers Over Hollywood: The Plan 9 Companion 1993
This documentary looks at what many consider to be the worst film of all time, "Plan 9 from Outer Space," released in 1959. The cult classic, directed by the equally bizarre Edward D. Wood, Jr., is revealed in all its absurdity, including interviews with cast, crew, and fans. **111m/C VHS.** *W:* Mark Patrick Carducci. *ATM*

The Flying Scotsman 🐶½ 1929
A fired railroad worker tries to wreck an express train on the engineer's last journey. The daughter of the intended victim saves the day. Silent, with sound added. **60m/B VHS, Beta.** Ray Milland, Pauline Johnson, Moore Marriott; *D:* Castleton Knight. *NOS, DVT, HEG*

Flying Tigers 🐶🐶½ 1942
Salutes the All-American Volunteer Group which flew for China under General Claire Chennault against the Japanese before the U.S. entered WWII. A squadron leader and a brash new recruit both vie for the affections of a pretty nurse in-between their flying missions. Romance and a few comic touches take a back seat to graphic scenes of aerial battles and dramatization of heroic sacrifice in this rousing war film. **101m/B VHS, LV, Closed Caption.** John Wayne, John Carroll, Anna Lee, Mae Clarke, Gordon Jones; *D:* David Miller. Nominations: Academy Awards '42: Best Sound, Original Dramatic/Comedy Score. *REP*

Flying Wild 🐶½ 1941
A gang of saboteurs is out to steal top-secret airplane blueprints. Who else but the Bowery Boys could conceivably stop them? **62m/B VHS.** Leo Gorcey, Bobby Jordan, Donald Haines, Joan Barclay, David Gorcey, Bobby Stone, Sammy Morrison; *D:* William West. *NOS, LOO*

FM 🐶🐶 *Citizen's Band* 1978 (PG-13)
The disc jockeys at an L.A. radio station rebel in the name of rock'n'roll. Despite the promising cast and setting (Mull makes his movie debut as a memorable space case), this is just disjointed and surprisingly unhip; one producer took his name off it due to

creative difficulties. The decent soundtrack includes concert footage of Jimmy Buffet and Linda Ronstadt. ♫FM; Do It Again; FM Reprise; Livingston Saturday Night; The Key To My Kingdom; Green Grass and High Tides; Life In The Fast Lane; Bad Man; Poor, Poor, Pitiful Me. **104m/C VHS, LV.** Eileen Brennan, Alex Karras, Cleavon Little, Martin Mull, Cassie Yates, Linda Ronstadt, Jimmy Buffett; **D:** Lamont Johnson. *USH*

The Fog 🎭🎭 1978 (R) John Carpenter's blustery follow-up to his success with "Halloween." An evil fog containing murderous, vengeful ghosts envelops a sleepy seaside town and subjects the residents to terror and mayhem. **91m/C VHS, Beta, LV, 8mm.** Hal Holbrook, Adrienne Barbeau, Jamie Lee Curtis, Janet Leigh, John Houseman; **D:** John Carpenter; **W:** John Carpenter; **C:** Dean Cundey; **M:** John Carpenter. *COL*

Fog Island 🎭½ 1945 Murder and terror lurk after a greedy inventor, who was framed for fraud by his business partner, is released from prison. He plots revenge by inviting his foes to his island home. **72m/B VHS.** George Zucco, Lionel Atwill, Terry Morse, Jerome Cowan, Veda Ann Borg; **D:** Terry Morse. *NOS, SNC, VCN*

Folks! 🎭 1992 (PG-13) Selleck is a Chicago stockbroker whose wife and kids have left him, the FBI is after him, and, worst of all, his parents have moved in with him. His parents don't want to be a burden, so Selleck decides that the best way to solve his financial woes is to help his parents commit suicide so he can collect on their insurance policies. Tasteless comedy that makes fun of aging and Alzheimer's Disease. Selleck is too sweet and cuddly for his role, but Ameche is good as the senile father, and Ebersole is great as Selleck's unpleasant sister. **109m/C VHS, Closed Caption.** Tom Selleck, Don Ameche, Anne Jackson, Christine Ebersole, Wendy Crewson, Robert Pastorelli, Michael Murphy, Kevin Timothy Chevalia, Margaret Murphy; **D:** Ted Kotcheff; **M:** Michel Colombier. *FXV*

Follies Girl 🎭🎭 1943 There's folly in expecting that this wartime tuner would hold up today. An army private romances a dress designer and a musical show somehow results. ♫Keep the Flag A-Flying; No Man In The House; Someone to Love; I Told A Lie; Shall We Gather at the Rhythm?; Fascination; I Knew Your Father's Son; Thoity Poiple Boids. **74m/B VHS.** Wendy Barrie, Doris Nolan, Gordon Oliver, Anne Barrett, Arthur Pierson; **D:** William Rowland. *NOS, LOO*

Follies in Concert 1985 A filmed record of the famed Stephen Sondheim musical play, performed at Lincoln Center in New York with an all-star cast. Songs include "I'm Still Here," "Losing My Mind," "Broadway Baby" and "The Ladies Who Lunch." **90m/C VHS, Beta, LV.** Carol Burnett, Lee Remick, Betty Comden, Andre Gregory, Adolph Green, Mandy Patinkin, Phyllis Newman, Elaine Stritch, Jim Walton, Licia Albanese. *MVD, FRH*

Follow Me 🎭🎭 1969 (G) Round-the-world odyssey of three moon doggies searching for adventure—and the perfect wave. Spectacular surfing scenes are complemented by songs performed by Dino, Desi, and Billy. **90m/C VHS.** Claude Codgen, Mary Lou McGinnis, Bob Purvey; **D:** Gene McCabe. *NO*

Follow Me, Boys! 🎭🎭🎭 1966 A Disney film about a simple man who decides to put down roots and enjoy the quiet life, after one year too many on the road with a ramshackle jazz band. That life is soon interrupted when he volunteers to lead a high-spirited boy scout troop. **120m/C VHS, Beta.** Fred MacMurray, Vera Miles, Lillian Gish, Charlie Ruggles, Elliott Reid, Kurt Russell, Luana Patten, Ken Murray; **D:** Norman Tokar; **M:** George Bruns. *DIS*

Follow Me Quietly 🎭🎭🎭 1949 Serial strangler who only kills in the rain is stalked by Lundigan. Very good little thriller which packs a punch in less than an hour. **59m/B VHS, Beta.** William Lundigan, Dorothy Patrick, Jeff Corey, Nestor Paiva, Charles D. Brown, Paul Guilfoyle; **D:** Richard Fleischer. *TTC, MLB, RXM*

Follow That Camel 🎭½ *Carry On Follow That Camel* 1967 Foreign Legion sergeant who invents acts of heroism finally gets a chance to really help out a friend in need. Part of the "Carry On" series. **95m/C VHS, Beta.** *GB* Phil Silvers, Kenneth Williams, Anita Harris, Jim Dale; **D:** Gerald Thomas. *NO*

Follow That Car 🎭 1980 (PG) Three southern kids become FBI agents and begin a thigh-slappin', rip-snortin' down-home escapade. **96m/C VHS, Beta.** Dirk Benedict, Tanya Tucker, Teri Nunn; **D:** Daniel Haller. *NLC*

Follow That Dream 🎭🎭 1961 (G) Elvis plays a musical hillbilly whose family is trying to homestead on government land along the sunny Florida coast. Based on Richard C. Powell's novel "Pioneer Go Home." The songs-the only reason to see this movie—include "Angel", and "What a Wonderful Life", and the title track. **111m/C VHS, Beta, LV.** Elvis Presley, Arthur O'Connell, Anne Helm, Simon Oakland, Jack Kruschen, Joanna Moore, Howard McNear; **D:** Gordon Douglas. *MGM*

Follow That Rainbow 🎭 1966 Believing that her long-lost father is a popular touring singer, a young lass pursues him from Switzerland to South Africa. **90m/C VHS, Beta.** Joe Stewardson, Memory Jane, Joan Bickhill. *NO*

Follow the Boys 🎭🎭🎭 1944 Vaudeville performer Tony West (Raft) heads out to California to try his luck and gets a double break when he's noticed by leading lady Gloria Vance (Zorina). Not only does he become a star but he marries Gloria as well. When WWII breaks out Tony's turned down for military service, so he organizes camp shows for the soldiers. They're a big success but misunderstandings have put his marriage in jeopardy. Plot's merely an excuse to have haute Hollywood (including Marlene Dietrich, Orson Welles, Jeanette MacDonald, and W.C. Fields) sing, dance, and tell jokes. ♫Beyond the Blue Horizon; I'll See You In My Dreams; The Bigger the Army and the Navy; Some of These Days; I'll Get By; I'll Walk Alone; Mad About Him Blues; The House I Live In. **111m/B VHS.** George Raft, Vera Zorina, Grace McDonald, Charles Butterworth, Martha O'Driscoll, Charley Grapewin, Elizabeth Patterson; **D:** Edward Sutherland; **W:** Lou Breslow, Gertrude Purcell. Nominations: Academy Awards '44: Best Song ("I'll Walk Alone"). *USH*

Follow the Fleet 🎭🎭🎭 1936 A song-and-dance man joins the Navy and meets two sisters in need of help in this Rogers/Astaire bon-bon featuring a classic Berlin score. Look for Betty Grable, Lucille Ball, and Tony Martin in minor roles. Hilliard went on to be best known as the wife of Ozzie Nelson in TV's "The Adventures of Ozzie and Harriet." ♫Let's Face the Music and Dance; We Saw the Sea; I'm Putting All My Eggs In One Basket; Get Thee Behind Me, Satan; But Where Are You?; I'd Rather Lead a Band; Let Yourself Go. **110m/B VHS, Beta, LV.** Fred Astaire, Ginger Rogers, Randolph Scott, Harriet Hilliard Nelson, Betty Grable, Lucille Ball; **D:** Mark Sandrich; **M:** Irving Berlin, Max Steiner. *MED, TTC, IME*

Follow the Leader 🎭🎭 *East of the Bowery* 1944 On leave from the Army, Hall and Gorcey discover that one of the gang has been jailed on a trumped-up charge and set about finding the real culprit. ♫Now and Then; All I Want to Do Play the Drums. **65m/B VHS.** Leo Gorcey, Huntz Hall, Gabriel Dell, Jack LaRue, Joan Marsh, Billy Benedict, Sammy Morrison; **D:** William Beaudine; **M:** Gene Austin. *NOS*

Follow the River 🎭🎭½ 1995 (PG) It's 1775 and Mary Ingles (Lee) is living with her husband and family on a frontier farm in the Blue Ridge Mountains. The community is raided by the Shawnee, lead by Wildcat (Schweig), who takes Mary and several other settlers miles away to their home camp. Once there, Mary befriends another captive, the older Gretl (Burstyn), proves her courage to the smitten Wildcat, and plots to escape and find her way home. Based on the 1981 novel by James Alexander Thom; filmed in North Carolina. **93m/C VHS.** Sheryl Lee, Eric Schweig, Ellen Burstyn, Tim Guinee, Renee O'Connor; **D:** Martin Davidson. *HMK*

Food of the Gods woof! 1976 (PG) On a secluded island giant rats, chickens, and other creatures crave human flesh, blood, bones, etc. This cheap, updated version of the H. G. Wells novel suffers from lousy performances and a lack of imagination. **88m/C VHS, Beta.** Marjoe Gortner, Pamela Franklin, Ralph Meeker, Ida Lupino, Jon Cypher; **D:** Bert I. Gordon. *LIV, VES*

Food of the Gods: Part 2 woof! *Gnaw: Food of the Gods 2* 1988 (R) The killer beasts and animals of the first film (and of H.G. Wells' classic novel) strike again; gigantic rats maim young girls. Easily as bad as the original. **93m/C VHS, Beta, LV.** Paul Coufos, Lisa Schrage; **D:** Damian Lee; **W:** E. Kim Brewster. *NO*

A Fool and His Money 🎭🎭½ 1988 (R) Adman Morris Codman (Penner) decides to market a shady new religion based on greed but, naturally, finds the true road. Bullock is skeptical girlfriend Debby. **84m/C VHS.** Jonathan Penner, Sandra Bullock, Gerald Orange, George Plimpton; **D:** Daniel Adams; **W:** Daniel Adams. *THV*

Fool for Love 🎭🎭 1986 (R) Explores the mysterious relationship between a modern-day drifter and his long-time lover, who may or may not be his half-sister, as they confront each other in a seedy New Mexico motel. Adapted by Shepard from his play. **108m/C VHS, Beta.** Sam Shepard, Kim Basinger, Randy Quaid, Harry Dean Stanton; **D:** Robert Altman; **W:** Sam Shepard; **M:** George Burt. *MGM*

The Fool Killer 🎭🎭½ *Violent Journey* 1965 In the post-Civil War south, a 12-year-old boy learns that a terrifying legend about an axe-murderer may be all too real. Offbeat film with striking visuals and photography. Debut film for Albert and another choice psycho role for Perkins. **100m/B VHS.** Anthony Perkins, Edward Albert, Dana Elcar, Henry Hull, Salome Jens, Arnold Moss; **D:** Servando Gonzalez. *REP*

A Fool There Was 🎭🎭½ 1914 The rocket that blasted Theda Bara to stardom and launched the vamp film genre. One of the few extant Bara films, it tells the now familiar story of a good man whom crumbles from the heights of moral rectitude thanks to the inescapable influence of an unredeemable vamp. Bette Davis described Bara as "divinely, hysterically, insanely malevolent." Much heavy emoting; subtitled (notoriously) "Kiss Me, My Fool!" Based on Rudyard Kipling's "The Vampire." **70m/B VHS, Beta.** Theda Bara, Edward Jose, Runa Hodges, Clifford Bruce; **D:** Frank Powell. *VYY, FCT, GVV*

Foolin' Around 🎭🎭½ 1980 (PG) An innocent Oklahoma farm boy arrives at college and falls in love with a beautiful heiress. He will stop at nothing to win her over, including crashing her lavish wedding ceremony. **101m/C VHS, Beta.** Gary Busey, Annette O'Toole, Eddie Albert, Tony Randall, Cloris Leachman; **D:** Richard T. Heffron; **W:** Michael Kane; **M:** Charles Bernstein.

Foolish Wives 🎭🎭🎭½ 1922 A remake of Von Stroheim's classic depicting the confused milieu of post-war Europe as reflected through the actions of a bogus count and his seductive, corrupt ways. Comes as close as possible to the original film. **107m/B VHS, Beta, LV.** Erich von Stroheim, Mae Busch, Maude George, Cesare Gravina, Harrison Ford; **D:** Erich von Stroheim. *KIV, CCB, HHT*

Fools 🎭 1970 (PG) Two lonely people—he an aging horror film actor and she a young woman estranged from her husband—start a warm romance when they meet in San Francisco. The husband reacts violently. Good cast seems lost. **93m/C VHS, Beta.** Jason Robards Jr., Katharine Ross, Scott Hylands; **D:** Tom Gries. *PSM*

Fools of Fortune ✂✂½ 1990 (PG-13) Adaptation of William Trevor's novel depicting Willie Clinton's childhood and adult experiences of family dramatics played against the backdrop of post-WWI Ireland. During the Irish war for independence, a family is attacked by British soldiers, creating emotional havoc for the survivors. Though well-acted and poignant, it's a rather disjointed and straying shamrock opera. 104m/C VHS, LV. *GB* Mary Elizabeth Mastrantonio, Iain Glen, Julie Christie, Michael Kitchen, Sean McClory, Frankie McCafferty; *D:* Pat O'Connor; *W:* Michael Hirst; *M:* Hans Zimmer. COL, FCT

Fools Rush In ✂✂ 1997 (PG-13) Uptight eastern yuppie Alex Whitman (Perry) meets cute in Vegas with beautiful Latina casino worker Isabel Fuentes (Hayek) and the duo spend the night together. Three months later, Isabel shows up at Alex's New York door to announce her pregnancy and say she's keeping the baby. Movie cliches collide with movie stereotypes when they decide to marry but find the relationship suffers over their vast ethnic and cultural differences. At least the leads are attractive. Perry's real-life dad plays his character's father.*CW:* Sensuality and brief language. 110m/C VHS, LV, Closed Caption. Matthew Perry, Salma Hayek, Jon Tenney, Carlos Gomez, Tomas Milian, John Bennett Perry, Jill Clayburgh, Stanley DeSantis, Anne Betancourt; *D:* Andy Tennant; *W:* Katherine Reback; *C:* Robbie Greenberg; *M:* Alan Silvestri. COL

Footlight Frenzy ✂✂ 1984 The Law Moan Spectacular comedy troupe are at it again as they perform a benefit play where everything goes wrong. 110m/C VHS, Beta. *GB* Alan Shearman, Diz White, Ron House, Frances Tomelty, Michael Aldridge, Ron Pember. NO

Footlight Parade ✂✂✂ 1933 Broadway producer Cagney is out of work. Sound films have scared off his backers until his idea for staging live musical numbers before the cinema features lures them back. Lots of authentic backstage action precedes three spectacular Busby Berkeley-choreographed numbers that climax the film, including the giant water ballet featuring more than 100 performers. ♫ Ah, the Moon is Here; Sittin' on a Backyard Fence; Honeymoon Hotel; By A Waterfall; Shanghai Lil. 104m/B Beta, LV. James Cagney, Joan Blondell, Dick Powell, Ruby Keeler, Guy Kibbee, Ruth Donnelly; *D:* Lloyd Bacon; *C:* George Barnes. MGM, FOX

Footlight Serenade ✂✂½ 1942 A boxer falls for a beautiful dancer with whom he's costarring in a Broadway play. Unfortunately, she's secretly married to another of the actors and her husband is becoming jealous of the boxer's intentions. Light, fun musical. One of a series of Grable movies made to boost morale during WWII. ♫ Are You Kidding?; I'm Still Crazy About You; I Hear the Birdies Sing; Living High; I'll Be Marching to a Love Song; Land On Your Feet; I'm Stepping Out With a Memory Tonight. 80m/B VHS, Beta, Closed Caption. Betty Grable, Victor Mature, John Payne, Jane Wyman, Phil Silvers, James Gleason, Mantan Moreland; *D:* Gregory Ratoff; *C:* Lee Garmes. FOX

Footloose ✂✂½ 1984 (PG) When a city boy moves to a small Midwestern town, he discovers some disappointing news: rock music and dancing have been forbidden by the local government. Determined to bring some '80s-style life into the town, he sets about changing the rules and eventually enlists the help of the daughter of the man responsible for the law. Rousing music, talented young cast, and plenty of trouble make this an entertaining musical-drama. ♫ Footloose; Let's Hear it for the Boy; The Girl Gets Around; Dancing in the Sheets; Somebody's Eyes; Almost Paradise; I'm Free; Never; Holding Out for a Hero. 107m/C VHS, Beta, LV, 8mm, Closed Caption. Kevin Bacon, Lori Singer, Christopher Penn, John Lithgow, Dianne Wiest, John Laughlin, Sarah Jessica Parker; *D:* Herbert Ross; *M:* Miles Goodman. Nominations: Academy Awards '84: Best Song ("Footloose"), Best Song ("Let's Hear It for the Boy"). PAR

Footsteps in the Dark ✂✂½ 1941 Fairly amusing comedy-mystery with investment counselor Flynn doubling as detective. Based on the play "Blondie White" by Ladislaus Fodor, Bernard Merivale, and Jeffrey Dell. 96m/B VHS. Errol Flynn, Brenda Marshall, Ralph Bellamy, Alan Hale, Lee Patrick, Allen Jenkins, Lucile Watson, William Frawley, Roscoe Karns, Grant Mitchell, Maris Wrixon, Noel Madison, Jack LaRue, Turhan Bey; *D:* Lloyd Bacon, Hugh MacMullen; *W:* Lester Cole, John Wexley. MGM

For a Few Dollars More ✂✂½ 1965 (PG) The Man With No Name returns as a bounty hunter who teams up with a gunslinger/rival to track down the sadistic leader of a gang of bandits. Violent. Sequel to "A Fistful of Dollars" (1964) and followed by "The Good, The Bad, and The Ugly". Letterboxed laserdisc edition features the original movie trailer. 127m/C VHS, Beta, LV, Closed Caption. *IT* Clint Eastwood, Lee Van Cleef, Klaus Kinski, Gian Marie Volonte; *D:* Sergio Leone; *M:* Ennio Morricone. FOX, MGM, FCT

For a Lost Soldier ✂✂ 1993 Middle-aged Dutch choreorapher Jeroen (Krabbe), working on a piece about the Allied liberation, recalls his relationship with a Canadian soldier more than 40 years before. During WWII, the 13-year-old Jeroen (Smit) is sent from Amsterdam to live in the country with a foster family. With the first twinges of puberty and sexuality he longs for a special friend, whom he finds in Walt (Kelley), a young gay Canadian soldier who is part of the Allied liberation forces. Very provocative subject, delicately handled, without any implication of child abuse. In English and Dutch with subtitles. 92m/C VHS. *NL* Marten Smit, Andrew Kelley, Jeroen Krabbe, Feark Smink, Elsje de Wijn, Derk-Jan Kroon; *D:* Roeland Kerbosch; *W:* Roeland Kerbosch; *M:* Joop Stokkermans. FXL, ORI

For Auld Lang Syne: The Marx Brothers 1932 Four classic comedy shorts: "Monkey Business Special," "Gai Dimanche," "Hooks and Jabs," and "For Auld Lang Syne." 46m/B VHS, Beta. Chico Marx, Groucho Marx, Alan Marx, Harpo Marx. VYY

For Better and For Worse ✂✂½ 1992 (PG) A nice young couple is planning to have your average nice wedding when one of their friends gets hold of an invitation and decides to jokingly invite the Pope to attend. But the joke is on them when the Pope accepts. Talk about upstaging the bride! 94m/C VHS, LV. Patrick Dempsey, Kelly Lynch. LIV

For Better or Worse ✂✂ 1995 (PG-13) Pathetic loser Michael Makeshift (Alexander, also making his directorial debut) falls in love with his new sister-in-law Valerie (Davidovich) even as he gets entangled in his brother Reggie's (Woods) business scams. Made for cable TV.*CW:* Language; some crude humor. 95m/C VHS. Jason Alexander, Lolita Davidovich, James Woods, Joe Mantegna, Jay Mohr, Beatrice Arthur, Robert Costanzo, John Amos, Eda Reiss Merin; *Cameos:* Rob Reiner, Rip Torn; *D:* Jason Alexander; *W:* Jeff Nathanson; *C:* Wayne Keenan; *M:* Miles Goodman. TTC

For Heaven's Sake ✂✂✂ 1926 Lloyd's first film for Paramount has him making an accidental donation to a skid row mission, then marrying the preacher's daughter and converting all the neighborhood tough guys. 60m/B VHS. Harold Lloyd, Jobyna Ralston, Noah Young, James Mason, Paul Weigel; *D:* Sam Taylor. NO

For Heaven's Sake ✂½ 1979 A bumbling basketball team is lent some heavenly assistance in the form of a meddling angel. But can he hit the jumper? Made for television. 90m/C VHS. Ray Bolger, Kent McCord. LIV

For Keeps ✂½ 1988 (PG-13) Two high school sweethearts on the verge of graduating get married after the girl becomes pregnant, and suffer all the trials of teenage parenthood. Tends toward the unrealistic and trite. 98m/C VHS, Beta, LV. Molly Ringwald, Randall Batinkoff, Kenneth Mars; *D:*

John G. Avildsen; *W:* Tim Kazurinsky, Denise DeClue; *M:* Bill Conti. COL

For Ladies Only ✂✂ 1981 A struggling actor takes a job as a male stripper to pay the rent. Among the leering ladies is Davis, daughter of former President Reagan. Made for television. 100m/C VHS, Beta. Gregory Harrison, Patricia Davis, Dinah Manoff, Louise Lasser, Lee Grant, Marc Singer, Viveca Lindfors, Steven Keats; *D:* Mel Damski. NO

For Love Alone ✂✂ 1986 A young Australian college co-ed in the 1930s falls in love with a handsome, controversial teacher and follows him to London, only to discover he's not her Mr. Right after all. 102m/C VHS, Beta. *AU* Helen Buday, Sam Neill, Hugo Weaving; *D:* Stephen Wallace. LIV

For Love of Ivy ✂✂ 1968 (PG) Poitier is a trucking executive who has a gambling operation on the side. Ivy is the Black maid of a rich white family who is about to leave her job to look for romance. The two are brought together but the road to true love doesn't run smooth. Based on a story by Poitier. 102m/C VHS, Beta. Sidney Poitier, Abbey Lincoln, Beau Bridges, Carroll O'Connor, Nan Martin; *D:* Daniel Mann; *M:* Quincy Jones. Nominations: Academy Awards '68: Best Song ("For Love of Ivy"). FOX

For Love or Money ✂✂ 1963 A super-rich hotel owner wants her lawyer to find her three beautiful daughters. However, she doesn't trust him enough not to meddle in the search. Lavish production and a good cast can't overcome the mediocrity of the script and direction. 108m/C VHS. Kirk Douglas, Mitzi Gaynor, Thelma Ritter, William Bendix, Julie Newmar, Gig Young, Leslie Parrish, William Windom, Dick Sargent; *D:* Michael Gordon. NO

For Love or Money ✂½ 1984 Made-for-television fare about game-show contestants finding money and romance. 91m/C VHS, Beta. Jamie Farr, Suzanne Pleshette, Gil Gerard, Ray Walston, Lawrence Pressman, Mary Kay Place; *D:* Terry Hughes; *M:* Billy Goldenberg. IME

For Love or Money ✂✂ 1988 (PG) A real estate man with Career on the mind has to choose between the woman in his life and the condo development that stands firmly between them and happily-ever-afterdom. ?m/C VHS. Timothy Daly, Haviland Morris, Kevin McCarthy. NO

For Love or Money ✂✂½ 1993 (PG) Struggling hotel concierge with a heart of gold finds himself doing little "favors" for a slimy entrepreneur who holds the key to his dreams—the cash to open an elegant hotel of his own. Romantic comedy is reminiscent of the classic screwball comedies of the '30s and '40s, but lacks the trademark tight writing and impeccable timing. Fox is appealing and likable as the wheeling and dealing concierge, a role undermined by a mediocre script offering too few laughs. 89m/C VHS, LV, Closed Caption. Michael J. Fox, Gabrielle Anwar, Isaac Mizrahi, Anthony Higgins, Michael Tucker, Bobby Short, Dan Hedaya, Bob Balaban, Udo Kier, Patrick Breen, Paula Laurence; *D:* Barry Sonnenfeld; *W:* Mark Rosenthal, Larry Konner; *M:* Bruce Broughton. USH

For Me and My Gal ✂✂½ 1942 In his film debut, Kelly plays an opportunistic song-and-dance man who lures a young vaudevillian (Garland) away from her current partners. WWI interrupts both their career and romance, but you can count on them being reunited. Loaded with vintage tunes. ♫ For Me and My Gal; They Go Wild, Simply Wild Over Me; The Doll Shop; Oh, Johnny, Oh; Oh, You Beautiful Doll; When You Wore A Tulip; Don't Leave Me Daddy; Do I Love You; By The Beautiful Sea. 104m/B VHS, Beta, LV, Closed Caption. Gene Kelly, Judy Garland, George Murphy, Martha Eggerth, Ben Blue, Richard Quine, Keenan Wynn, Stephen McNally; *D:* Busby Berkeley; *M:* George Bassman. Nominations: Academy Awards '42: Scoring of a Musical. MGM

For Pete's Sake ✂✂ *July Pork Bellies* 1974 (PG) Topsy-turvy comedy about a woman whose efforts to get together enough money to put her husband through school involve her with loan sharks, a madame, and even cattle rustling in New York City. Not one of Streisand's best. **90m/C VHS, Beta.** Barbra Streisand, Michael Sarrazin, Estelle Parsons, William Redfield, Molly Picon; **D:** Peter Yates; **M:** Artie Butler. *COL*

For Richer, For Poorer 🎬½ *Father, Son and the Mistress* **1992 (PG)** A very rich, successful businessman notices his son is happy just to sit back and let dad earn all the dough while he waits for his share. In order to teach his son a lesson, Dad decides to give all his money away. But the plan backfires when both realize that earning a second fortune may not be as easy as they assumed. Below average made for cable fare. **90m/C VHS, Closed Caption.** Jack Lemmon, Talia Shire, Joanna Gleason, Jonathan Silverman, Madeline Kahn, George Wyner; **D:** Jay Sandrich; **W:** Stan Daniels. *HBO*

For the Boys 🎬🎬 **1991 (R)** Midler stars as Dixie Leonard, a gutsy singer-comedian who hooks up with Eddie Sparks (Caan) to become one of America's favorite USO singing, dancing, and comedy teams. The movie spans 50 years and three wars—including Korea and Vietnam—and raises such issues as the blacklist and the role of politics in showbiz. Glitzy Hollywood entertainment falters despite Midler's strong performance. 🎵Billy-A-Dick; Come Rain or Come Shine; In My Life; Stuff Like That There.**CW:** Language. **120m/C VHS, Closed Caption.** Bette Midler, James Caan, George Segal, Patrick O'Neal, Christopher Rydell, Arye Gross, Norman Fell, Rosemary Murphy, Dori Brenner, Bud Yorkin, Jack Sheldon, Melissa Manchester, Brandon Call; **Cameos:** Arliss Howard; **D:** Mark Rydell; **W:** Marshall Brickman, Neal Jimenez, Lindy Laub; **M:** Dave Grusin. Golden Globe Awards '92: Best Actress—Musical/Comedy (Midler); Nominations: Academy Awards '91: Best Actress (Midler). *FXV*

For the First Time 🎬🎬½ **1959** In his last film, Lanza plays an opera singer who tours European cities to raise money for his deaf girlfriend's medical treatment. 🎵Oh Mon Amour; Bavarian Drinking Song; Ave Maria; Vesti La Giubba; La Donna e Mobile; Niun Mi Tema; Grand March; O Solo Mio; Ich Liebe Dich. **97m/C VHS, Closed Caption.** Mario Lanza, Zsa Zsa Gabor, Johanna von Koczian, Kurt Kasznar, Hans Sohnker, Peter Capell, Renzo Cesana, Sandro Giglio; **D:** Rudolph Mate; **W:** Andrew Solt. *MGM*

For the Love of Angela 🎬½ **1986** Pretty and young shop clerk involves herself with both the shopkeeper and his son. **90m/C Beta.** Louis Jourdan. *PSM*

For the Love of Benji 🎬🎬 **1977 (G)** In this second "Benji" film, the adorable little dog accompanies his human family on a Greek vacation. He is kidnapped to be used as a messenger for a secret code, but escapes, to have a series of comic adventures in this entertaining family fare. **85m/C VHS, Beta.** Benji, Patsy Garrett, Cynthia Smith, Allen Finzat, Ed Nelson; **D:** Joe Camp; **W:** Joe Camp; **M:** Euel Box. *FCT, APD, BFV*

For the Love of It 🎬½ **1980** Television stars galore try to hold together this farce about car chases in California, stolen secret documents, and (of course) true love. Outstandingly mediocre. Made for television. **100m/C VHS, Beta.** Deborah Raffin, Jeff Conaway, Tom Bosley, Norman Fell, Don Rickles, Henry Gibson, Noriyuki "Pat" Morita, William Christopher, Lawrence-Hilton Jacobs, Adrian Zmed, Barbi Benton, Adam West; **D:** Hal Kanter. *FRH*

For the Moment 🎬🎬½ **1994 (PG-13)** Aussie aviator Lachlan (Crowe) has joined the British Commonwealth Training Plan in 1942, a crash course for fighter pilots that drew men from several countries to bases across Canada. Stationed with best buddy Johnny (Outerbridge) in Manitoba, Lachlan falls for the married Lill (Hirt), sister of Johnny's honey Kate (McMillan), whose husband is away fighting. The emotional stakes are high for all concerned since they know the fliers will soon be sent off to combat. Old-fashioned (and sometimes slow-moving) romance with excellent performances and some gorgeous scenery.**CW:**

Sexual situations, language and a poignant death. **120m/C VHS, Closed Caption.** CA Russell Crowe, Christianne Hirt, Peter Outerbridge, Sara McMillan, Wanda Cannon, Scott Kraft; **D:** Aaron Kim Johnston; **W:** Aaron Kim Johnston; **C:** Ian Elkin; **M:** Victor Davies. *TCF*

For Those About to Rock: Monsters in Moscow 🎬🎬½ **1991 (R)** A tribute to the young people who defended Russia's new freedom during 1991's attempted coup. The first open-air festival-style concert ever to take place in Russia features the music of AC/DC, Metallica, The Black Crowes, Pantera, and Russia's Electro Shock Therapy.**CW:** Language. **84m/C VHS, Beta, LV. D:** Wayne Isham. *WAR, MVD, PMS*

For Us, the Living 🎬🎬🎬 **1988** The life and assassination of civil rights activist Medgar Evers are dramatically presented in this production of "American Playhouse" for PBS. Provides insight into Evers' character, not just a recording of the events surrounding his life. Adapted from the biography written by Evers' widow. **84m/C VHS, Beta.** Howard E. Rollins Jr., Rocky Aoki, Paul Winfield, Irene Cara, Margaret Avery, Roscoe Lee Browne, Laurence "Larry" Fishburne, Janet MacLachlan, Dick Anthony Williams; **D:** Michael A. Schultz. *MED, FCT*

For Whom the Bell Tolls 🎬🎬🎬½ **1943** Hemingway novel, gorgeously translated to the big screen, features a star-crossed romantic tale of derring-do. American schoolteacher Robert Jordan (Cooper) decides to aid the Spanish Civil War and fight the fascists. He's ordered to rendezvous with peasant guerillas, to aid in blowing up a bridge, and in the rebel camp Jordan meets the beautiful Maria (Bergman). Lots of heroics (and some romance under the stars). Both leads were personally selected by the author. Originally released at 170 minutes. **130m/C VHS.** Gary Cooper, Ingrid Bergman, Akim Tamiroff, Katina Paxinou, Arturo de Cordova, Vladimir Sokoloff, Mikhail Rasumny, Fortunio Bonanova, Victor Varconi; **D:** Sam Wood; **W:** Dudley Nichols; **C:** Ray Rennahan; **M:** Victor Young. Academy Awards '43: Best Supporting Actress (Paxinou); Nominations: Academy Awards '43: Best Actor (Cooper), Best Actress (Bergman), Best Color Cinematography, Best Film Editing, Best Interior Decoration, Best Picture, Best Supporting Actor (Tamiroff), Best Original Score. *USH*

For Your Eyes Only 🎬🎬🎬 **1981 (PG)** In this James Bond adventure, 007 must keep the Soviets from getting hold of a valuable instrument aboard a sunken British spy ship. Sheds the gadgetry of its more recent predecessors in the series in favor of some spectacular stunt work and the usual beautiful girl and exotic locale. Glen's first outing as director, though he handled second units on previous Bond films. Sheena Easton sang the hit title tune. **136m/C VHS, Beta, LV, Closed Caption.** GB Roger Moore, Carole Bouquet, Chaim Topol, Lynn-Holly Johnson, Julian Glover, Cassandra Harris, Jill Bennett, Michael Gothard, John Wyman, Jack Hedley, Lois Maxwell, Desmond Llewelyn, Geoffrey Keen, Walter Gotell, Charles Dance; **D:** John Glen; **W:** Michael G. Wilson; **M:** Bill Conti. Nominations: Academy Awards '81: Best Song ("For Your Eyes Only"). *MGM, FOX, TLF*

For Your Love Only 🎬🎬 **1979** A beautiful young student falls in love with her teacher and is blackmailed, leading her to murder her tormentor. Soap opera made for German television. Dubbed in English. **90m/C VHS, Beta.** GE Nastassia Kinski, Christian Quadflieg, Judy Winter, Klaus Schwarzkopf; **D:** Wolfgang Petersen. *GLV*

Forbidden 🎬🎬½ **1985** In Nazi Germany, a German countess has an affair with a Jewish intellectual, and she winds up hiding him from the S.S. Based on the novel "The Last Jews of Berlin" by Leonard Gross. Slow made-for-cable movie. **116m/C VHS, Beta, Closed Caption.** Jacqueline Bisset, Juergen Prochnow, Irene Worth, Peter Vaughan, Amanda Cannings, Avis Bunnage; **D:** Anthony Page; **W:** Leonard Gross. *SWC*

Forbidden Choices 🎬🎬 *The Beans of Egypt, Maine* **1994 (R)** Problems and attractions of the white trash Bean family as observed by enthralled neighbor girl Earlene (Plimpton). Hot-tem-

pered Reuben Bean (Hauer) has just landed a long prison term, leaving his brood of nine in the care of lover Roberta (Lynch), who's also involved with Bean nephew Beal (McGaw). Downtrodden Earlene is only too eager to give in to handsome Beal's charms, leading to more heartbreak. Based on Carolyn Chute's novel "The Beans of Egypt, Maine." Directorial debut of Warren.**CW:** Language; nudity; strong sexuality. **109m/C VHS, LV, Closed Caption.** Martha Plimpton, Kelly Lynch, Rutger Hauer, Patrick McGaw, Richard Sanders; **D:** Jennifer Warren; **W:** Bill Phillips; **C:** Stevan Larner; **M:** Peter Manning Rob. Nominations: Independent Spirit Awards '95: Best Cinematography, Best Supporting Actress (Lynch). *WEA*

The Forbidden Christ 🎬🎬 *Il Cristo Proibito* **1950** Bruno (Vallone) returns from the war to his Tuscan village after years as a POW, only to learn his younger brother, a Resistance fighter, was killed by the Nazis after being betrayed by someone in the town. Bruno wants revenge but when no one will help him find the truth, his rage leads him to kill the wrong man. The only film made by writer Malaparte, which was inspired by actual events, was a boxoffice disaster and caused him to abandon future film plans. Italian with subtitles. **98m/B VHS.** IT Raf Vallone, Gino Cervi, Alain Cuny, Elena Varzi; **D:** Curzio Malaparte; **W:** Curzio Malaparte; **C:** Gabor Pogany; **M:** Curzio Malaparte. *HTV*

The Forbidden City 🎬🎬 **1918** San San is a young Chinese maiden who has the misfortune to fall in love with a Western diplomat. After he is sent away on business San San keeps secret the fact she has born her lover a child but her actions are unforgiven by her father, a deposed mandarin. **72m/B VHS, Beta.** Norma Talmadge, Thomas Meighan; **D:** Sidney Franklin. *VYY, GVV, GPV*

The Forbidden Dance woof! **1990 (PG-13)** The first of several quickies released in 1990 applying hackneyed plots to the short-lived Lambada dance craze. The nonsensible plot has a Brazilian princess coming to the U.S. in order to stop further destruction of the rain forest. Instead, she winds up falling for a guy, teaching him to Lambada, and going on TV for a dance contest. Features an appearance by Kid Creole and the Coconuts. **90m/C VHS, Beta, LV, Closed Caption.** Laura Herring, Jeff James, Sid Haig, Richard Lynch; **D:** Greydon Clark. *COL*

Forbidden Fruit 🎬🎬🎬 *Le Fruit Defendu* **1952** Widowed country doctor (Fernandel), who lives with his domineering mother (Sylvie), marries an equally demanding woman (Nollier) and then finds himself involved with a compliant young prostitute (Arnoul). Comic Fernandel does very well with his change of pace role as a man whose illusions of middle-class respectibility are destroyed. Based on "Letter a Mon Juge" by Georges Simenon. French with subtitles. **103m/B VHS.** FR Fernandel, Francoise Arnoul, Claude Nollier, Sylvie, Jacques Castelot; **D:** Henri Verneuil; **W:** Jacques Companeez, Jean Manse, Henri Verneuil; **C:** Henri Alekan; **M:** Paul Durand. *FCT*

Forbidden Games 🎬🎬🎬🎬 *Les Jeux Interdits* **1952** Famous anti-war drama about two French children play-acting the dramas of war amid the carnage of WWII. Young refugee Fossey sees her parents and dog killed. She meets a slightly older boy whose family takes the girl in. The children decide to bury the animals they have seen killed in the same way that people are buried—even stealing crosses from the cemetery to use over the animal graves. Eventually they are discovered and Fossey is again separated from her newfound home. Acclaimed; available in both dubbed and English-subtitled versions. **90m/B VHS, Beta, LV.** FR Brigitte Fossey, Georges Poujouly, Amedee, Louis Herbert, Suzanne Courtal, Jacques Marin, Laurence Badie, Andre Wasley, Louis Sainteve; **D:** Rene Clement; **W:** Rene Clement, Jean Aurenche, Pierre Bost, Francois Boyer; **M:** Narciso Yepes. Academy Awards '52: Best Foreign Language Film; British Academy Awards '53: Best Film; National Board of Review Awards '52: 5 Best Foreign Films of the Year; New York Film Critics Awards '52: Best Foreign Film;

Venice Film Festival '52: Best Film; Nominations: Academy Awards '54: Best Story. *NOS, APD, NLC*

Forbidden Love ♂ 1982 A man in his early 20's falls in love with a woman twice his age, much to the chagrin of her daughters. Made for television. 96m/C VHS, Beta. Andrew Stevens, Yvette Mimieux, Dana Elcar, Lisa Lucas, Jerry Hauser, Randi Brooks, Lynn Carlin, Hildy Brooks, John Considine; *D:* Steven Hilliard Stern. *CNG*

Forbidden Passion: The Oscar Wilde Movie ♂♂½ 1987 A British-made look at Wilde's later years, emphasizing his homosexuality and the Victorian repression that accompanied it. 120m/C VHS, Beta. *GB* Michael Gambon, Robin Lermitte. *THV*

Forbidden Planet ♂♂♂½ 1956 In 2200 A.D., a space cruiser visits the planet Altair-4 to uncover the fate of a previous mission of space colonists. They are greeted by Robby the Robot and discover the only survivors of the Earth colony which has been preyed upon by a terrible space monster. A classic science fiction version of the Shakespearean classic "The Tempest." Laserdisc features formerly "cut" scenes, production and publicity photos, the original screen treatment, and special effects outtakes. 98m/C VHS, Beta, LV, DVD. Walter Pidgeon, Anne Francis, Leslie Nielsen, Warren Stevens, Jack Kelly, Richard Anderson, Earl Holliman, George Wallace; *D:* Fred M. Wilcox; *M:* Bebe Barron, Louis Barron. *MGM, CRC*

The Forbidden Quest ♂♂ 1993 In 1941, a journalist (Ward) tracks down the only survivor of the Hollandia's 1905 expedition to Antarctica, ship's carpenter Sullivan (O'Conor), to find out about the tragic journey. Director Delpeut mixes archival footage of actual turn-of-the-century voyages to reveal the Hollandia's murderous secrets. 75m/C VHS. *NL* Joseph O'Conor, Roy Ward; *D:* Peter Delpeut; *W:* Peter Delpeut. *KIV*

Forbidden Sun ♂ 1989 (R) An Olympic gymnastics coach and her dozen beautiful students go to Crete to train. When one of them is brutally raped, vengeance is meted out by the girls. 88m/C VHS, Beta, LV. Lauren Hutton, Cliff DeYoung, Renee Estevez; *D:* Zelda Barron. *ACA*

Forbidden Trails ♂½ 1941 Rough Riders adventure has Silver the horse saving his owner from the vengeance of two outlaws. Two more heroes go under cover to bring the bad guys to justice. 60m/B VHS, Beta. Buck Jones, Tim McCoy, Raymond Hatton; *D:* Robert North Bradbury. *NOS, VCN, DVT*

Forbidden World woof! *Mutant* 1982 (R) Lives of a genetic research team become threatened by the very life form they helped to create: a man-eating organism capable of changing its genetic structure as it grows and matures. Corman-produced quickie follow-up to "Galaxy of Terror" is a graphically violent rip-off of "Alien." 82m/C VHS, Beta, LV. Jesse Vint, Dawn Dunlap, June Chadwick, Linden Chiles; *D:* Allan Holzman; *W:* Jim Wynorski, R.J. Robertson, Tim Curnen. *ACA*

Forbidden Zone ♂½ 1980 (R) A sixth dimension kingdom is ruled by the midget, King Fausto, and inhabited by dancing frogs, bikini-clad tootsies, robot boxers, and degraded beings of all kinds. Original music by Oingo Boingo, and directed by founding member Elfman. 75m/B VHS, Beta. Herve Villechaize, Susan Tyrrell, Viva; *D:* Richard Elfman; *W:* Matthew Bright, Richard Elfman; *M:* Danny Elfman. *MED*

Forbidden Zone: Alien Abduction ♂ 1996 (R) Three babes sharing a sauna also share sexual confidences and discover they've each had an encounter with the same unusual man. Then one of the girls figures out they've had an alien encounter of the very close kind. *CW:* Sexual situations, nudity, and language. 90m/C VHS. Darcy Demoss, Pia Reyes, Dumitri Bogmaz, Carmen Lacatus, Alina Chivulescu, Florin Chiriac, Meredyth Holmes; *D:* Lucian S. Diamonde; *W:* Vernon Lumley; *C:* Adolfo Bartoli; *M:* Reg Powell. *AFE*

The Force ♂♂ 1994 (R) Rookie LAPD cop Cal Warner (Gedrick) crosses paths with maverick homicide detective Des Flynn (Hudson), who's on the trail of a brutal killer. But when Flynn dies mysteriously, it's Cal who's haunted by bizarre dreams—and finding the truth could be equally deadly. 94m/C VHS, LV, Closed Caption. Jason Gedrick, Gary Hudson, Cyndi Pass, Kim Delaney. *REP*

Force Five ♂ 1975 A group of ex-cons form an anti-crime undercover force turning their skills toward justice. Nothing new in this made for television film. 78m/C VHS, Beta. Gerald Gordon, Nicholas Pryor, James Hampton, David Spielberg, Leif Erickson, Bradford Dillman; *D:* Walter Grauman. *MED*

Force: Five ♂ 1981 (R) Mercenary gathers a group of like-minded action groupies together to rescue the daughter of a powerful man from a religious cult. All action and no brains. 95m/C VHS, Beta. Joe Lewis, Pam Huntington, Master Bong Soo Han; *D:* Robert Clouse; *W:* Robert Clouse; *M:* William Goldstein. *MED*

Force of Evil ♂♂♂ 1949 A cynical attorney who works for a mob boss and for Wall Street tries to save his brother from the gangster's takeover of the numbers operation. The honorable, though criminal, brother refuses the help of the amoral lawyer, and he is finally forced to confront his conscience. Garfield's sizzling performance and the atmospheric photography have made this a film noir classic. 82m/B VHS, LV, Closed Caption. John Garfield, Thomas Gomez, Marie Windsor, Sheldon Leonard, Roy Roberts; *D:* Abraham Polonsky; *W:* Abraham Polonsky; *C:* George Barnes. *REP*

Force of Evil ♂ 1977 A paroled murderer returns to his hometown to brutalize the family that refused to fabricate an alibi for him. Made for television. 100m/C VHS, Beta, LV. Lloyd Bridges, Eve Plumb, William Watson, Pat Crowley; *D:* Richard Lang. *WOV, GKK*

Force of Impulse ♂♂ 1960 J.D. schlocker featuring an impressive cast involved with everything from hot rods to robbery to parental problems. ?m/C VHS. J. Carrol Naish, Robert Alda, Tony Anthony, Christina Crawford, Jody McCrea, Lionel Hampton. *SNC*

Force of One ♂♂ 1979 (PG) A team of undercover narcotics agents is being eliminated mysteriously, and karate expert Norris saves the day in this sequel to "Good Guys Wear Black." 91m/C VHS, Beta. Chuck Norris, Bill Wallace, Jennifer O'Neill, Clu Gulager; *D:* Paul Aaron. *MED*

Force on Thunder Mountain ♂ 1977 A father and son go camping and encounter ancient Indian lore and flying saucers. 93m/C VHS, Beta. Christopher Cain, Todd Dutson. *VCI*

Force 10 from Navarone ♂♂ 1978 (PG) So-so sequel to Alistair MacLean's "The Guns of Navarone," follows a group of saboteurs whose aim is to blow up a bridge vital to the Nazi's in Yugoslavia. Keep an eye out for Ford, Nero, and Bach. Lots of double-crosses and action sequences, but doesn't quite hang together. 118m/C VHS, Beta, LV. Robert Shaw, Harrison Ford, Barbara Bach, Edward Fox, Carl Weathers, Richard Kiel, Franco Nero; *D:* Guy Hamilton; *W:* Robin Chapman. *WAR, OM*

Forced Entry ♂ *The Last Victim* 1975 (R) Psychopathic killer-rapist hesitates over one of his victims, and she murders him instead. 92m/C VHS, Beta. Tanya Roberts, Ron Max, Nancy Allen; *D:* Jim Sotos. *NO*

Forced March ♂♂½ 1990 On location in Hungary, an actor portrays a poet who fought in WWII and became a victim of the Holocaust. However, the deeper he gets into his role, the thinner the line between illusion and reality becomes. Flat drama. 104m/C VHS, Beta, LV. Chris Sarandon, Renee Soutendijk, Josef Sommer, John Seitz; *D:* Rick King. *SGE, MOV, IME*

Forced to Kill ♂½ 1993 (R) A repo man is on his way to deliver a Jaguar when he's captured by a bizarre family and forced to fight in an illegal bare-fist tournament run by the local lunatic sher-

iff. Professional stuntman Eubanks has his work cut out for him in this actioner. *CW:* Language, strong violence, and sexuality. 91m/C VHS, LV. Corey Michael Eubanks, Michael Ironside, Rance Howard, Don Swayze, Clint Howard, Brian Avery, Kari Whitman, Mickey Jones, Carl Ciarfalio, Cynthia J. Blessington, Alan Gelfant; *D:* Russell Solberg; *W:* Corey Michael Eubanks; *M:* Martin D. Bolin. *PMH*

Forced Vengeance ♂♂ 1982 (R) Vietnam vet pits himself against the underworld in Hong Kong. With Norris in the lead, you can take it for granted there will be plenty of martial arts action. 103m/C VHS, Beta. Chuck Norris, Mary Louise Weller; *D:* James Fargo; *M:* William Goldstein. *MGM*

Ford: The Man & the Machine ♂½ 1987 Episodic biography of ruthless auto magnate Henry Ford I from the building of his empire to his personal tragedies. The cast lacks spark and Robertson (Ford) is positively gloomy. The only one appearing to have any fun is Thomas (Ford's mistress). Based on the biography by Robert Lacey. 200m/C VHS. Cliff Robertson, Hope Lange, Heather Thomas, Michael Ironside, Chris Wiggins, R.H. Thomson; *D:* Allan Eastman; *C:* Thomas Burstyn. *CAF*

Foreign Affairs ♂♂♂ 1993 Vinnie Miller (Woodward) is a prim New England college teacher off to London on a research sabbatical. On the flight Vinnie's seatmate is boisterous good-ole-boy Chuck Mumpson (Dennehy), with whom she appears to have nothing in common. Naturally the two middle-aged romantics find a funny, though bittersweet, love together. A rather distracting subplot find's Vinnie's young colleague Fred (Stolz) involved in an affair with an older, eccentric British actress (Beacham). Based on the novel by Alison Lurie. Made for cable television. 100m/C VHS, LV. Joanne Woodward, Brian Dennehy, Eric Stoltz, Stephanie Beacham, Ian Richardson, Robert Hands; *D:* Jim O'Brien; *W:* Chris Bryant; *C:* Michael Coulter. National Academy of Cable Programming ACE Awards '93: Best Actor (Dennehy). *TTC*

Foreign Body ♂♂½ 1986 (PG-13) An Indian (played by "Passage to India" star, Banerjee) visiting London pretends to be a doctor and finds women flocking to him. Excellent overlooked British comedy. Based on the novel by Roderick Mann. 108m/C VHS. *GB* Victor Banerjee, Warren Mitchell, Trevor Howard, Geraldine James, Amanda Donohoe, Denis Quilley, Eve Ferret, Anna Massey; *D:* Ronald Neame; *W:* Celine La Freniere; *M:* Ken Howard. *HBO*

Foreign Correspondent ♂♂♂♂ 1940 A classic Hitchcock tale of espionage and derring-do. A reporter is sent to Europe during WWII to cover a pacifist conference in London, where he becomes romantically involved with the daughter of the group's founder and befriends an elderly diplomat. When the diplomat is kidnapped, the reporter uncovers a Nazi spy-ring headed by his future father-in-law. 120m/B VHS, Beta, LV, Closed Caption. Joel McCrea, Laraine Day, Herbert Marshall, George Sanders, Robert Benchley, Albert Basserman, Edmund Gwenn, Eduardo Ciannelli, Harry Davenport, Martin Kosleck, Charles Halton; *D:* Alfred Hitchcock; *W:* Robert Benchley, Charles Bennett, Joan Harrison, James Hilton; *M:* Alfred Newman. National Board of Review Awards '40: 10 Best Films of the Year; Nominations: Academy Awards '40: Best Black and White Cinematography, Best Interior Decoration, Best Original Screenplay, Best Picture, Best Supporting Actor (Basserman). *WAR*

A Foreign Field ♂♂½ 1993 Comedy/drama focuses on several WW2 veterans returning to the Normandy beaches in honor of the 50th anniversary of the invasion. Blustery British Cyril (McKern) and equally demanding Yank Waldo (Randolph) also must deal with their 50-year rivalry over their wartime love, the cheerfully vulgar Angelique (Moreau). Veteran performers get the chance to show their stuff but film descends into pathos. 90m/C VHS, Closed Caption. *GB* Leo McKern, John Randolph, Jeanne Moreau, Lauren Bacall, Alec Guinness, Edward Herrmann, Geraldine Chaplin; *D:* Charles Sturridge; *W:* Roy Clarke; *M:* Geoffrey Burgon. *FOX*

Foreign Student �⅛ 1994 (R) In 1956 Philippe (Hofschneider) is a French exchange student at a tradition-bound Virginia college. At a professor's home he meets part-time housekeeper April (Givens), who wants to practice her schoolbook French (among other things). They begin a romance but, since April is black, there's trouble. Hofschneider is charming though Givens appears too glamorous and self-aware. Dutton and Battle are notable in their small roles as blues musicians Howlin' Wolf and Sonny Boy Williamson. Directorial debut for Sereny. Based on the novel "The Foreign Student" by Philippe Labro.**CW:** Rough language; brief nudity; sex scene. **96m/C VHS.** Marco Hofschneider, Robin Givens, Jack Coleman, Edward Herrmann, Rick Johnson, Charlotte Ross, Charles S. Dutton, Hinton Battle; **D:** Eva Sereny; **W:** Menno Meyjes; **C:** Franco Di Giacomo; **M:** Jean-Claude Petit. USH

The Foreigner ⅛ 1978 Secret agent who comes to New York City to meet his contact becomes entrapped in a series of mysterious events revolving around the underground club scene. **90m/B VHS, Beta.** Eric Mitchell, Patti Astor, Deborah Harry; **D:** Amos Poe; **W:** Amos Poe. FCT

The Foreman Went to France ⅛½ *Somewhere in France* 1942 Industrial engineer travels to France during WWII to help prevent secret machinery from falling into the hands of the Nazis and their allies. **88m/B VHS, Beta.** GB Clifford Evans, Constance Cummings, Robert Morley; **D:** Charles Frend. NOS, MRV, DVT

Foreplay woof! *The President's Women* 1975 Inane trilogy of comedy segments involving characters with White House connections. Stories are introduced by former President Mostel discussing his downfall in a television interview. Lame rather than risque, wasting talents of all involved. Each segment was scripted and directed by a different team. **100m/C VHS, Beta.** Pat Paulsen, Jerry Orbach, Estelle Parsons, Zero Mostel; **D:** Bruce Malmuth, John G. Avildsen; **C:** Ralf Bode. LIV, VES

The Forest ⅛ 1983 Spooks and a cannibalistic killer terrorize a group of campers. Nothing that hasn't been done countless times before. **90m/C VHS, Beta.** **D:** Donald M. Jones. PSM

Forest of Little Bear ⅛⅛ 1979 A man returns to his impoverished family in 1928 and decides to seek the reward put on the head of a one-eared man-eating bear. He kills the bear but faces a dilemma when he sees the bear left a helpless cub behind. In Japanese with English subtitles. **124m/C VHS.** JP **D:** Toshio Goto. FCT

Forest Warrior ⅛⅛ 1995 (PG) Children fight to save the local forests of Tanglewood Mountain from greedy developer Kiser with the help of ghostly mountain man John McKenna (Norris), who was murdered in the same woods a century before. Mild adventure with good ecology theme. **98m/C VHS.** Chuck Norris, Terry Kiser, Max Gail; **D:** Aaron Norris; **W:** Ron Swanson. TTC

Forever ⅛⅛½ 1978 A teenage girl experiences true love for the first time and struggles with its meaning. Made for television adaptation of Judy Blume's novel. **100m/C VHS.** Stephanie Zimbalist, Dean Butler, John Friedrich, Beth Raines, Diana Scarwid; **D:** John Korty. GEM

Forever: A Ghost of a Love Story ⅛⅛½ 1992 (R) Coogan is a hot-shot music video director who moves into a haunted house and soon meets the resident ghost, who just happens to be a beautiful woman. He falls for the ghostly presence but his all-too-real female agent is also making her moves.**CW:** Sexuality. **93m/C VHS, Beta.** Keith Coogan, Sean Young, Diane Ladd, Sally Kirkland, Terence Knox, Nicholas Guest, Renee Taylor, Steve Railsback; **D:** Thomas Palmer Jr.; **W:** Thomas Palmer Jr. PSM

Forever Amber ⅛⅛½ 1947 Seventeenth century rags to riches story features Darnell as the poverty stricken girl who uses sex to gain wealth and status. She makes it to the bed of King Charles II, only to lose the one man she ever really loved (Wilde). The censorship of the 1940s hindered the film's erotic potential. Adapted from the best-selling novel by Kathleen Winsor. **140m/C VHS, Closed Caption.** Linda Darnell, Cornel Wilde, Richard Greene, George Sanders, Jessica Tandy, Anne Revere, John Russell, Leo G. Carroll, Robert Coote, Margaret Wycherly, Alan Napier, Edmund Breon, Alan Napier, Bill Ward, Richard Bailey, Skelton Knaggs, Norma Varden, Edith Evanson, Ellen Corby; **D:** Otto Preminger; **W:** Philip Dunne, Ring Lardner Jr.; **C:** Leon Shamroy; **M:** David Raksin. Nominations: Academy Awards '47: Original Dramatic/Comedy Score. FXV

Forever and a Day ⅛⅛⅛⅛ 1943 Tremendous salute to British history centers around a London manor originally built by an English admiral during the Napoleonic era and the exploits of succeeding generations. The house even manages to survive the blitz of WWII showing English courage during wartime. Once-in-a-lifetime casting and directing. **104m/B VHS.** Brian Aherne, Robert Cummings, Ida Lupino, Charles Laughton, Herbert Marshall, Ray Milland, Anna Neagle, Merle Oberon, Claude Rains, Victor McLaglen, Buster Keaton, Jessie Matthews, Roland Young, Sir C. Aubrey Smith, Edward Everett Horton, Elsa Lanchester, Edmund Gwenn; **D:** Rene Clair, Edmund Goulding, Cedric Hardwicke, Frank Lloyd, Victor Saville, Robert Stevenson, Herbert Wilcox, Kent Smith; **W:** Charles Bennett, Michael Hogan, Peter Godfrey, Christopher Isherwood, Gene Lockhart, Donald Ogden Stewart. HTV, MLB, TPV

Forever Darling ⅛⅛ 1956 Mixed effort from the reliable comedy duo sees Desi playing a dedicated chemist who neglects his wife while pursuing the next great pesticide. Lucy calls on her guardian angel (Mason) to help her rekindle her marriage. He advises her to go with Desi when he tests his new bug killer, and a series of hilarious, woodsy calamities occur. Lucy and Desi are always fun to watch, but '60s TV sitcom fans will enjoy the fact that Mrs. Howell (Schaefer) and Jane Hathaway (Kulp) appear in the same picture. **91m/C VHS, Beta.** Lucille Ball, Desi Arnaz Sr., James Mason, Louis Calhern, John Emery, John Hoyt, Natalie Schafer, Nancy Kulp; **D:** Alexander Hall. MGM, CCB

Forever Emmanuelle ⅛ 1982 (R) Sensual young woman finds love and the ultimate erotic experience in the wilds of the South Pacific in this sequel to the porn-with-production-values "Emmanuelle." **89m/C VHS, Beta, LV.** Annie Belle, Emmanuelle Arsan, Al Cliver. LIV, VES

Forever Evil ⅛ 1987 The vacationing denizens of a secluded cabin are almost killed off by the cult followers of a mythic god. **107m/C VHS, Beta.** Red Mitchell, Tracey Huffman, Charles Trotter, Howard Jacobsen, Kent Johnson. VCI

Forever Female ⅛⅛⅛ 1953 Bright comedy about show business, egos, and love. Holden is a young playwright whose first play is accepted by stage producer Douglas on the condition that the lead role, featuring a 19-year-old heroine, be rewritten for his ex-wife Rogers. She's an aging leading lady smitten by Holden's charms—as is the ingenue Crowley, who would be perfect for the role as written. Complications and manipulations abound as the play makes its way to production. Adaptation of the Sir James Barrie play "Rosalind." **93m/B VHS, Closed Caption.** Ginger Rogers, William Holden, Paul Douglas, Pat Crowley, James Gleason, Jesse White, George Reeves, Marjorie Rambeau, King Donovan, Vic Perrin, Marion Ross; **D:** Irving Rapper; **W:** Julius J. Epstein, Philip C. Epstein. PAR

Forever James Dean 1988 A profile of the legendary actor/cult hero, examining his life, short career and remaining legacy. Also includes the original previews of his three feature films. A must for serious Dean fans. **69m/C VHS, Beta, Closed Caption.** James Dean, Julie Harris, William Bast, Kenneth Kendall; **D:** Ara Chekmayan. WAR, FCT

Forever, Lulu ⅛ *Crazy Streets* 1987 (R) A down-on-her-luck novelist winds up involved with the mob and a gangster's girlfriend. Completely laughless comedy with amateurish direction. **86m/**C VHS, Beta, LV.** Hanna Schygulla, Deborah Harry, Alec Baldwin, Annie Golden, Paul Gleason, Dr. Ruth Westheimer; **D:** Amos Kollek. COL

Forever Mary ⅛⅛⅛ *Mery per Sempre* 1989 A teacher tries to better the lives of the boys sentenced to a reformatory in Palermo, Sicily, when a teenage transvestite prostitute (the title character) is admitted to the school. In Italian with English subtitles. **100m/C VHS.** IT Michele Placido, Alesandro Di-Sanzo, Francesco Benigno; **D:** Marco Risi; **W:** Sandro Petraglia. CCN

Forever Young ⅛⅛ 1985 A young boy immerses himself in Catholicism. Admiring a priest, he is unaware that the priest's friend is involved with his mother. Tangled, but delicate handling of the coming-of-age story. Made originally for British television. **85m/C VHS, Beta.** GB James Aubrey, Nicholas Gecks, Alec McCowen; **D:** David Drury; **W:** Ray Connelly. MGM

Forever Young ⅛⅛½ 1992 (PG) When test pilot Gibson's girlfriend is hit by a car and goes into a coma, he volunteers to be cryogenically frozen for one year. Oops!—he's left frozen for fifty years, until he is accidentally thawed out by a couple of kids. Predictable, designed to be a tear jerker, though it serves mostly as a star vehicle for Gibson who bumbles with 90s technology, finds his true love, and escapes from government heavies, adorable as ever. Through all the schmaltz, the relationship Gibson develops with the young Wood turns out to be the most authentic and endearing love in the film. **102m/C VHS, LV, 8mm, Closed Caption.** Mel Gibson, Jamie Lee Curtis, Elijah Wood, Isabel Glasser, George Wendt, Joe Morton, Nicolas Surovy, David Marshall Grant, Art LaFleur; **D:** Steve Miner; **W:** Jeffrey Abrams; **C:** Russell Boyd; **M:** Jerry Goldsmith. WAR, BTV

Forger of London ⅛⅛ 1961 Edgar Wallace tale in which Scotland Yard investigates a counterfeit ring connected to a prime suspect, an amnesiac playboy. **91m/C VHS.** GE Eddi Arent, Karin Dor, Viktor de Kowa, Hellmut Lange, Robert Graf; **D:** Harald Reinl. SNC

Forget Mozart ⅛⅛ *Zabudnite na Mozarta* 1985 On the day of Mozart's death, the head of the secret police gathers a group together for questioning. They include the composer's wife, his lyricist, the head of a Masonic lodge, and Salieri, Mozart's rival. Each has a different story to tell to the investigator about the composer's life and death. The film makes use of a number of sets and costumes from "Amadeus" and was also filmed on location in Prague. In German with English subtitles. **93m/C VHS.** GE Armin Mueller-Stahl, Catarina Raacke; **D:** Salvo Luther. WBF

Forget Paris ⅛⅛½ 1995 (PG-13) Pro basketball referee Mickey (Crystal) and airline executive Ellen (Winger) meet in Paris, fall in love and get married. But once the honeymoon is over, the marital bliss unravels due to conflicting work schedules and the lack of romantic scenery. This look at yuppie love and courtship finds Crystal in pre-"City Slickers 2" form, launching three-point one-liners and "When Harry Met Sally" sentiment. Bland direction and an obligation to be cute intensify the "been-there-seen-that" feeling. Winger's presence may hint of miscasting, but she has one of the films funniest scenes involving a stray pet and a pigeon.**CW:** Language, including fertility clinic scene. **101m/C VHS, LV, Closed Caption.** Billy Crystal, Debra Winger, Joe Mantegna, Cynthia Stevenson, Richard Masur, Julie Kavner, William Hickey, Cathy Moriarty, John Spencer; **D:** Billy Crystal; **W:** Billy Crystal, Lowell Ganz, Babaloo Mandel; **C:** Don Burgess; **M:** Marc Shaiman. COL

The Forgotten ⅛⅛ 1989 After 17 years as POWs, six Green Berets are freed, only to face a treacherous government conspiracy aimed at eliminating them. Made for television. **96m/C VHS, Beta, LV, Closed Caption.** Keith Carradine, Steve Railsback, Stacy Keach, Pepe Serna, Don Opper, Richard Lawson; **D:** James Keach; **W:** Keith Carradine, Steve Railsback, James Keach. PAR

The Forgotten One 🎬½ **1989 (R)** An uninspired author and a female reporter become mixed up in a century-old murder and the restless ghost it spawned. **89m/C VHS, Beta, LV.** Kristy McNichol, Terry O'Quinn, Blair Parker, Elisabeth Brooks; **D:** Phillip Badger. *ACA*

Forgotten Prisoners 🎬🎬 *Forgotten Prisoners: The Amnesty Files* **1990 (R)** Celluloid proof that conviction and true grit do not always entertainment make. Greenwald—whose credits range from "Xanadu" to "The Burning Bed"—directed this righteous but stationary drama about an Amnesty International official (Silver) who's assigned to look into the incarceration and egregious mistreatment of Turkish citizens. Made for cable TV. **92m/C VHS, Beta, Closed Caption.** Ron Silver, Roger Daltrey, Hector Elizondo; **D:** Robert Greenwald; **M:** Brad Fiedel. *TTC, FCT*

A Forgotten Tune for the Flute 🎬🎬🎬 **1988** A delightful, Glasnost-era romantic comedy. A bureaucrat caught up in a dull, stuffy existence has a heart attack and winds up falling in love with his nurse. He then must decide between his comfortable, cared-for life or the love which beckons him. In Russian with English subtitles. **131m/C VHS, Beta, LV.** *RU* Leonid Filatov, Tatiana Dogileva, Irina Kupchenko; **D:** Edgar Ryazanov. *FRH*

Forgotten Warrior 🎬½ **1986 (R)** Vengeance is the name of the game as a Vietnam vet tracks down the fellow officer who tried to kill him and shot his commander. **76m/C VHS, Beta.** Quincy Frazer, Sam T. Lapuzz, Ron Marchini, Joe Meyer; **D:** Nick Cacas, Charlie Ordonez. *NO*

Forlorn River 🎬½ **1937** Nevada and Weary, two law-abiding men, seek to return their hometown to peace by eliminating a gang of outlaws. Based on a novel by Zane Grey. **62m/B VHS.** Buster Crabbe, June Martel, John D. Patterson, Harvey Stephens, Chester Conklin, Lew Kelly, Syd Saylor; **D:** Charles T. Barton. *NOS, DVT, RXM*

The Formula 🎬½ **1980 (R)** Convoluted story about a secret formula for synthetic fuel that meanders it's way from the end of WWII to the present. A U.S. soldier waylays, and then joins forces with, a German general entrusted with the formula. Years later, after the American is murdered, his friend, a hard-nosed L.A. cop, starts investigating, meeting up with spies and a reclusive oil billionaire. Scott and Brando have one good confrontation scene but the rest of the movie is just hot air. From the novel by Steve Shagan. **117m/C VHS, Beta.** Marlon Brando, George C. Scott, Marthe Keller, G.D. Spradlin, Beatrice Straight, John Gielgud, Richard Lynch; **D:** John G. Avildsen; **M:** Bill Conti. Nominations: Academy Awards '80: Best Cinematography. *MGM*

Formula for a Murder 🎬 **1985** A very rich but paralyzed woman marries a scheming con artist who plots to kill her and inherit everything. **89m/C VHS, Beta.** Christina Nagy, David Warbeck, Rossano Brazzi. *LIV*

Forrest Gump 🎬🎬🎬🎬 **1994 (PG-13)** Grandly ambitious and slightly flawed, amounting to a wonderful bit of movie magic. As the intelligence-impaired Gump with a heart of gold and more than enough character and dignity, Hanks supplies another career highlight. Field contributes a nice turn as his dedicated mama (they were last together in "Punchline"), while Sinise is particularly effective as a handicapped Vietnam veteran with a bad attitude. Incredible special effects put Gump in the middle of historic events over a four decade period, but the real story is the life-affirming, non-judgmental power of Gump to transform the lives of those around him. From the novel by Winston Groom. **142m/C VHS, Beta, Closed Caption.** Tom Hanks, Robin Wright, Sally Field, Gary Sinise, Mykel T. Williamson; **D:** Robert Zemeckis; **W:** Eric Roth; **C:** Don Burgess. Academy Awards '94: Best Actor (Hanks), Best Adapted Screenplay, Best Director (Zemeckis), Best Film Editing, Best Picture, Best Visual Effects; Chicago Film Critics Awards '94: Best Actor (Hanks); Directors Guild of

America Awards '94: Best Director (Zemeckis); Golden Globe Awards '95: Best Actor—Drama (Hanks), Best Director (Zemeckis), Best Film—Drama; National Board of Review Awards '94: Best Actor (Hanks), Best Film, Best Supporting Actor (Sinise); Screen Actors Guild Award '94: Best Actor (Hanks); Writers Guild of America '94: Best Adapted Screenplay; Blockbuster Entertainment Awards '95: Movie, Theatrical, Drama Actor, Theatrical (Hanks); Blockbuster Entertainment Awards '96: Drama Actor, Video (Hanks); Nominations: Academy Awards '94: Best Art Direction/Set Decoration, Best Cinematography, Best Makeup, Best Sound, Best Supporting Actor (Sinise), Best Original Score; Golden Globe Awards '95: Best Screenplay, Best Supporting Actor (Sinise), Best Supporting Actress (Wright), Best Original Score; MTV Movie Awards '95: Best Film, Best Male Performance (Hanks), Breakthrough Performance (Williamson); Screen Actors Guild Award '94: Best Supporting Actor (Sinise), Best Supporting Actress (Field, Wright). *PAR*

Forsaking All Others 🎬🎬½ **1935** Screwball comedy featuring several MGM superstars. Friends since childhood, Gable has been in love with Crawford for 20 years, but she never realizes it and plans to marry Montgomery. Crawford is very funny in this delightful story of a wacky romantic triangle. **84m/B VHS, Closed Caption.** Joan Crawford, Clark Gable, Robert Montgomery, Charles Butterworth, Billie Burke, Rosalind Russell, Frances Drake; **D:** Woodbridge S. Van Dyke; **W:** Joseph L. Mankiewicz. *MGM*

Fort Apache 🎬🎬🎬½ **1948** The first of director Ford's celebrated cavalry trilogy, in which a fanatical colonel (Fonda) leads his reluctant men to an eventual slaughter, recalling George Custer at Little Big Horn. In residence: Ford hallmarks of spectacular landscapes and stirring action, as well as many vignettes of life at a remote outpost. Don't forget to catch "She Wore a Yellow Ribbon" and "Rio Grande," the next films in the series. Also available in a colorized version. **125m/B VHS, Beta, LV.** John Wayne, Henry Fonda, Shirley Temple, John Agar, Pedro Armendariz Sr., Victor McLaglen, Ward Bond, Anna Lee; **D:** John Ford; **C:** Archie Stout. *TTC, TLF*

Fort Apache, the Bronx 🎬🎬🎬 **1981 (R)** A police drama set in the beleaguered South Bronx of New York City, based on the real-life experiences of two former New York cops who served there. Newman is a decent cop who goes against every kind of criminal and crazy and against his superiors in trying to bring law and justice to a downtrodden community. **123m/C VHS, Beta, LV.** Paul Newman, Ed Asner, Ken Wahl, Danny Aiello, Rachel Ticotin, Pam Grier, Kathleen Beller; **D:** Daniel Petrie; **W:** Heywood Gould. *WAR, VES, CCB*

Fort Saganne 🎬🎬 **1984** Charles Saganne (Depardieu), a soldier from a peasant background, is posted to the French Sahara, where he becomes a natural leader. He gains fame and fortune, marries, and then WWI begins. Good, if cliched, adventure saga. Based on the novel by Louis Gardel. French with subtitles. **180m/C VHS.** *FR* Gerard Depardieu, Catherine Deneuve, Philippe Noiret, Sophie Marceau, Michael Duchaussoy; **D:** Alain Corneau; **W:** Alain Corneau, Louis Gardel; **M:** Philippe Sarde. *CVC*

Fortress 🎬 **1985 (R)** A teacher and her class are kidnapped from their one-room schoolhouse in the Australian outback. They must use their ingenuity and wits to save their lives in this violent made-for-cable-television suspense drama. **CW:** Strong language, strong violence, and sexuality. **90m/C VHS, Beta.** *AU* Rachel Ward, Sean Garlick, Rebecca Rigg; **D:** Arch Nicholson; **M:** Danny Beckerman. *CNG, HBO*

Fortress 🎬🎬 **1993 (R)** How come the future is never a place you'd want to be? Thanks to overpopulation a woman is only allowed one pregnancy. When John and Karen Brennick are caught trying to have a second child they are shipped to the Fortress, an underground prison in the middle of the desert. Discipline is enforced with numerous sadistic toys, including the intestinator, so-called because it's implanted in the stomach of each prisoner and infractions result in excruciating laser-activated pain. Lambert does well with his action hero but it's character actor

Smith as the warden, a techno-human with some sick fantasies, who has the real fun in this horrific depiction of the future. **CW:** Torture and bloody violence. **91m/C VHS, LV, Closed Caption.** Christopher Lambert, Kurtwood Smith, Loryn Locklin, Lincoln Kilpatrick; **D:** Stuart Gordon; **W:** Steve Feinberg, Troy Neighbors, Terry Curtis Fox; **C:** David Eggby. *LIV*

Fortress of Amerikka 🎬½ **1989** In the not-too-distant future, mercenaries get their hands on a secret weapon that could allow them to take over the USA. **?m/C VHS.** Gene Le Brock, Kellee Bradley. *IMP*

Fortune and Men's Eyes 🎬🎬 **1971 (R)** Exploitative and depressing film about life in a Canadian prison. A naive young man is sent to prison for marijuana possession and has to make a difficult choice—be regularly sodomized by a man who will protect him or be raped by everyone else. Based on the play by John Herbert. **102m/C VHS.** Wendell Burton, Michael Greer, Zooey Hall, Danny Freedman; **D:** Harvey Hart; **W:** John Herbert. *MGM*

The Fortune Cookie 🎬🎬🎬 *Meet Whiplash Willie* **1966** After receiving a minor injury during a football game, a TV cameraman is convinced by his seedy lawyer brother-in-law to exaggerate his injury and start an expensive lawsuit. A classic, biting comedy by Wilder. First of several Lemmon-Matthau comedies. The letterbox laserdisc version contains the original theatrical trailer. **125m/B VHS, Beta, LV.** Jack Lemmon, Walter Matthau, Ron Rich, Cliff Osmond, Judi West, Lurene Tuttle; **D:** Billy Wilder; **W:** Billy Wilder, I.A.L. Diamond; **C:** Joseph LaShelle; **M:** Andre Previn. Academy Awards '66: Best Supporting Actor (Matthau); Nominations: Academy Awards '66: Best Art Direction/Set Decoration (B & W), Best Black and White Cinematography, Best Story & Screenplay. *FOX, MGM, FCT*

Fortune Dane 🎬½ **1986 (PG)** Police detective Fortune Dane goes undercover to clear his name after he is framed for murder. **83m/C VHS, Beta.** Carl Weathers, Adolph Caesar; **D:** Nicholas Sgarro; **W:** Charles Correll. *THV*

Fortune's Fool 🎬🎬 **1921** A beef king and profiteer marries a younger woman and soon discovers the problems that ambition can cause. Silent. **60m/B VHS, Beta.** *GE* Emil Jannings, Daguey Servaes, Reinhold Schunzel; **D:** Reinhold Schunzel. *NOS, MRV, VYY*

Fortunes of War 🎬🎬🎬 **1987** British professor Guy Pringle arrives with his bride, Harriet, to take up a teaching post in the Balkans in 1939. The idealistic Guy soon becomes enmeshed in anti-fascist politics and involved with the local members of the British embassy. When threatened by war they travel to Athens and then Cairo, where Guy's increasing involvement in the political situation, and his neglect of Harriet, causes a crisis in their marriage. Slow-moving drama with some self-centered characters is redeemed by the acting skills of those involved. Based on the autobiographical novels of Olivia Manning. Originally shown on "Masterpiece Theater" on PBS. **160m/C VHS.** *GB* Kenneth Branagh, Emma Thompson, Rupert Graves, Ronald Pickup, Robert Stephens, Charles Kay, James Villiers, Harry Burton, Ciaran Madden, Diana Hardcastle, Greg Hicks, Alan Bennett, Jeremy Brundell, Jeremy Sinden; **D:** James Cellan Jones; **W:** Alan Plater. *FOX, FCT, TVC*

Fortunes of War 🎬🎬 **1994 (R)** Peter Kernan (Salinger) is a burned-out relief worker in Thailand. Desperate for money, he agrees to smuggle a rare medicine across the Cambodian border to a rural war lord. Travelling with refugee Khoy Thoun (Ngor) and French Red Cross worker, Johanna (Jenkins), Peter begins to realize his need to do the right thing, even if the cost is high. Filmed on location in Manila. **CW:** Language; violence; drug use. **107m/C VHS, LV, Closed Caption.** Matt Salinger, Michael Ironside, Haing S. Ngor, Sam Jenkins, Martin Sheen, Michael Nouri; **D:** Thierry Notz; **W:** Mark Lee. *COL*

Forty Carats �З✗½ 1973 (PG) Ullmann plays the just-turned forty divorcee who has a brief fling with the half-her-age Albert while on vacation in Greece. She figures she'll never see him again but, back in New York, he turns up on the arm of her beautiful daughter (Rafflin). Except he's still interested in mom. The rest of the movie is spent trying to convince Ullmann that love can conquer all. Ullmann's very attractive but not well-suited for the part; Raffins's screen debut. Based on the Broadway hit. 110m/C VHS, Beta. Liv Ullmann, Edward Albert, Gene Kelly, Binnie Barnes, Deborah Raffin, Nancy Walker; D: Milton Katselas; W: Jay Presson Allen; C: Charles B(ryant) Lang. COL

Forty Days of Musa Dagh ✗✗ 1985 Based on the true story of Armenia's fight for freedom against Turkey in the 1914 uprising and the dreadful cost. From the novel by Franz Werfel. 120m/C VHS, Beta. Michael Constantine, David Opatoshu. VCD

The Forty-Niners ✗ 1932 A forgettable oater about the hysteria surrounding the finding of gold in California. 59m/B VHS. Tom Tyler, Betty Mack, Alan Bridge, Fern Emmett, Gordon Wood, Frank Ball; D: John P. McCarthy. DVT, HEG, GPV

The Forty-Ninth Parallel ✗✗✗ The Invaders 1941 Six Nazi servicemen, seeking to reach neutral American land, are trapped and their U-boat sunk by Royal Canadian Air Force bombers, forcing them into Canada on foot, where they run into an array of stalwart patriots. Dated wartime propaganda made prior to the U.S. entering the war; riddled with entertaining star turns. 90m/B VHS, Beta, LV. GB Laurence Olivier, Leslie Howard, Eric Portman, Raymond Massey, Glynis Johns, Finlay Currie, Anton Walbrook; D: Michael Powell; W: Emeric Pressburger, Rodney Ackland. Academy Awards '42: Best Story; Nominations: Academy Awards '42: Best Screenplay. NO

40 Pounds of Trouble ✗✗½ 1962 Lake Tahoe casino/hotel manager Steve McCluskey (Curtis) likes to avoid complications in his life. But first he's charmed by his boss' niece Chris (Pleshette), the hotel's new headliner, and then he becomes a surrogate father to five-year-old Penny (Wilcox), abandoned by her debt-ridden dad. So what does Steve decide to do? Why take them to Disneyland, of course! Director Jewison's feature film debut. 106m/C VHS, Closed Caption. Tony Curtis, Suzanne Pleshette, Claire Wilcox, Phil Silvers, Larry Storch, Howard Morris, Stubby Kaye, Edward Andrews, Mary Murphy, Kevin McCarthy, Sharon Farrell; D: Norman Jewison; W: Marion Hargrove; M: Mort Lindsay. USH

Forty Thousand Horsemen ✗✗½ 1941 The story of the ANZACS of Australia, created to fight Germany in the Middle East during WWII. This Australian war drama is full of cavalry charges, brave young lads, and "Waltzing Matilda." 86m/B VHS, Beta. AU Chips Rafferty, Grant Taylor, Betty Bryant, Pat Twohill. VYY, FCT

42nd Street ✗✗✗ 1933 A Broadway musical producer faces numerous problems in his efforts to reach a successful opening night. Choreography by Busby Berkeley. A colorized version of the film is also available. ♪ You're Getting to Be a Habit With Me; Shuffle Off to Buffalo; Young and Healthy; Forty-Second Street; It Must Be June. 89m/B VHS, Beta, LV. Warner Baxter, Ruby Keeler, Bebe Daniels, George Brent, Dick Powell, Guy Kibbee, Ginger Rogers, Una Merkel, Busby Berkeley, Ned Sparks, George E. Stone; D: Lloyd Bacon; W: Rian James, James Seymour; M: Harry Warren, Al Dubin. Nominations: Academy Awards '33: Best Picture, Best Sound. MGM, FOX, HMV

47 Ronin, Part 1 ✗✗✗ The Loyal 47 Ronin; 47 Samurai 1942 Turn of the 18th-century epic chronicling the samurai legend. The warriors of Lord Asano set out to avenge their leader, tricked into committing a forced seppuku, or hara-kiri. The photography is generously laden with views of 18th century gardens as well as panoramic vistas. This is the largest and most popular film of the Kabuki version of the story by Seika Mayama.

In Japanese with English subtitles. 111m/C VHS. JP D: Kenji Mizoguchi. FCT

47 Ronin, Part 2 ✗✗✗ 1942 Second half of the film in which the famous Japanese folklore tale of Lord Asano and his warriors is told. The film follows Asano's samurai as they commit themselves to avenging their leader in 1703. In Japanese with English subtitles. 108m/C VHS. JP D: Kenji Mizoguchi. FCT

48 Hrs. ✗✗✗ 1982 (R) An experienced San Francisco cop (Nolte) springs a convict (Murphy) from jail for 48 hours to find a vicious murdering escaped con. Murphy's film debut is great and Nolte is perfect as his gruff foil. 97m/C VHS, Beta, LV, Closed Caption. Nick Nolte, Eddie Murphy, James Remar, Annette O'Toole, David Patrick Kelly, Sonny Landham, Brion James, Denise Crosby; D: Walter Hill; W: Walter Hill, Larry Gross, Steven E. de Souza, Roger Spottiswoode; M: James Horner. PAR

48 Hours to Live ✗ Man in the Middle 1960 A reporter travels to a nuclear scientist's secluded island only to find the scientist held hostage by nuclear weapon-seeking terrorists. 86m/B VHS, Beta. Anthony Steel, Ingemar Johannson, Marlies Behrens. NO

Foul Play ✗✗ 1976 Bearing no similarity to the Goldie Hawn vehicle of the same name, this Polish crimer is based on a true story, and stars two of Poland's Olympic boxers. A young man, accused of theft, is coerced by the Warsaw police to go undercover in return for having the charges against him dropped. With English subtitles. 98m/C VHS. PL Marek Powoski, Jan Szcepanski, Jerzy Kulej. FCT

Foul Play ✗✗✗ 1978 (PG) Hawn is a librarian who picks up a hitchhiker which leads to nothing but trouble. She becomes involved with San Francisco detective Chase in an effort to expose a plot to kill the Pope during his visit to the city. Also involved is Moore as an English orchestra conductor with some kinky sexual leanings. Chase is charming (no mugging here) and Hawn both bubbly and brave. A big winner at the box office; features Barry Manilow's hit tune "Ready to Take a Chance Again." 116m/C VHS, Beta, LV, 8mm. Goldie Hawn, Chevy Chase, Dudley Moore, Burgess Meredith, Billy Barty, Rachel Roberts, Eugene Roche, Brian Dennehy, Chuck McCann, Bruce Solomon; D: Colin Higgins; M: Charles Fox. Nominations: Academy Awards '78: Best Song ("Ready to Take a Chance Again"). PAR

Found Alive ✗ 1934 After a painful divorce, a woman kidnaps her son and steals away into the Mexican jungle, with only the help of her faithful butler. 65m/B VHS. Barbara Bedford, Maurice Murphy, Robert Frazer, Edwin Cross; D: Charles Hutchinson. SNC

The Fountainhead ✗✗✗ 1949 Cooper is an idealistic, uncompromising architect who refuses to change his designs. When he finds out his plans for a public housing project have been radically altered he blows up the building and winds up in court defending his actions. Neal is the sub-plot love interest. Based on the novel by Ayn Rand. 113m/C VHS, Beta. Gary Cooper, Patricia Neal, Raymond Massey, Ray Collins, Henry Hull; D: King Vidor; C: Robert Burks; M: Max Steiner. MGM, FOX

Four Adventures of Reinette and Mirabelle ✗✗✗ 1989 Small but touching Rohmer tale of the friendship between two women—one a naive country girl (Miquel, as Reinette), the other a sophisticated Parisian (Forde, as Mirabelle)—who share an apartment and a number of experiences, but who have a very different manner of inhabiting those experiences. A thoroughly French human comedy, one of Rohmer's better studies. In French with English subtitles. 95m/C VHS. FR Joelle Miquel, Jessica Forde, Philippe Laudenbach, Marie Riviere, Beatrice Romand, Yasmine Haury; D: Eric Rohmer; W: Eric Rohmer. NYF, FCT

Four Bags Full ✗✗½ 1956 A bitter comedy about two smugglers during WWII who try to get a slaughtered pig to the black market under the Nazis' noses. In French with English subtitles. 82m/C VHS, Beta. FR Jean Gabin, Louis de Funes, Bourvil, Jeanette Batti; D: Claude Autant-Lara. VDM, FCT

Four Daughters ✗✗✗ 1938 Classic, three-hankie outing in which four talented daughters of music professor Rains fall in love and marry. Garfield shines, in a role tailor-made for him, as the world-weary suitor driven to extremes in the name of love. Great performances from all. Based on the novel "Sister Act" by Fannie Hurst. 90m/B VHS. Claude Rains, John Garfield, May Robson, Priscilla Lane, Lola Lane, Rosemary Lane, Gale Page, Dick Foran, Jeffrey Lynn; D: Michael Curtiz; M: Max Steiner. Nominations: Academy Awards '38: Best Director (Curtiz), Best Picture, Best Screenplay, Best Sound, Best Supporting Actor (Garfield). MGM, CCB

Four Days in July ✗✗ 1985 Two couples from Belfast, one Catholic and one Protestant, find they have something in common when they meet in the maternity ward as both couples become first-time parents. Script and dialog were mainly improvised, which provides both dull stretches and the film's charm. Made for British television. 99m/C VHS. GB Des McAleer, Brid Brennan, Charles Lawson, Paula Hamilton, Shane Connaughton, Eileen Pollock, Stephen Rea; D: Mike Leigh. WBF, BTV

Four Deuces ✗✗½ 1975 Gang war is underway between the Chico Hamilton mob and Vic Morano and the Four Deuces during the Depression. Comedy and action combine with elements of strong language, strong sex, and strong violence. 87m/C VHS, Beta. Jack Palance, Carol Lynley, Warren Berlinger, Adam Roarke; D: William H. Bushnell Jr. VTR

Four Eyes and Six Guns ✗✗½ 1993 In 1882 a New York optometrist, who's a fan of the popular dime-store western novels, moves to Tombstone, Arizona in search of adventure. He's just in time to because Sheriff Wyatt Earp is trying to rid the town of those pesky Doom Brothers but is having a problem with his eyesight (causing his gunshots to go astray). Now if the greenhorn can just get Earp to wear his new glasses. Silly but harmless fluff. Made for cable television. 92m/C VHS, Beta, Closed Caption. Judge Reinhold, Patricia Clarkson, Dan Hedaya, M. Emmet Walsh, Austin Pendleton, Fred Ward; D: Piers Haggard; W: Leon Prochnik. TTC

Four Faces West ✗✗½ They Passed This Way 1948 McCrea is an honest rancher who nevertheless robs the local bank in order to save his father's ranch from foreclosure. His humanity in helping a diphtheria-ridden family leads to his capture, but the sheriff promises a light sentence, since he is not a typical bad guy. Fine performances strengthen this low-key western. 90m/B VHS. Joel McCrea, Frances Dee, Charles Bickford; D: Alfred E. Green. REP

The Four Feathers ✗✗✗✗ 1939 A grand adventure from a story by A.E.W. Mason. After resigning from the British Army a young man is branded a coward and given four white feathers as symbols by three of his friends and his lady love. Determined to prove them wrong he joins the Sudan campaign of 1898 and rescues each of the men from certain death. They then take back their feathers as does his girl upon learning of his true courage. Excellent performances by Smith and Richardson. 99m/C VHS, Beta, LV. GB John Clements, Ralph Richardson, Sir C. Aubrey Smith, June Duprez, Donald Gray, Jack Allen, Clive Baker, Allan Jeayes; D: Zoltan Korda; W: R.C. Sherriff; C: Georges Perinal; M: Miklos Rozsa. Nominations: Academy Awards '39: Best Color Cinematography. FCT, HMV

The Four Feathers ✗✗ 1978 Determined to return the symbols of cowardice, four feathers, to his friends and fiancee, a man courageously saves his friends' lives during the British Sudan campaign and regains the love of his lady. Made-for-television movie is the fifth remake. 95m/C VHS, Beta. Beau Bridges, Jane Seymour, Simon Ward,

Harry Andrews, Richard Johnson, Robert Powell; *D:* Don Sharp. *REP*

Four for Texas ♪ 1963 Perhaps Aldrich's later success with "The Dirty Dozen" can be attributed, in part, to this exercise in how not to make a comic western; poorly made, over long, and far too dependant on the feminine charisma of Ekberg and Andress. Slow-moving Sinatra-Martin vehicle tells the tale of con men in the Old West who battle bandits and bad bankers for a stash of loot. **124m/C VHS, Beta, LV, Closed Caption.** Frank Sinatra, Dean Martin, Anita Ekberg, Ursula Andress, Charles Bronson, Victor Buono, Jack Elam; *D:* Robert Aldrich; *C:* Ernest Laszlo. *WAR, FCT*

Four Friends ♪♪♪ *Georgia's Friends* 1981 (R) The magical good and bad dream of the 1960s is remembered in this story of four friends. A young woman and the three men in love with her first come together in high school and then separate, learning from college, war and drug abuse, and each other in this ambitious movie from Steve Tesich, the writer of "Breaking Away." Good performances by all. **114m/C VHS, Beta.** James Leo Herlihy, Craig Wasson, Jodi Thelen, Michael Huddleston, Jim Metzler, Reed Birney; *D:* Arthur Penn; *W:* Steve Tesich; *C:* Ghislan Cloquet. *WAR, OM*

The Four Horsemen of the Apocalypse ♪♪♪½ 1921 Silent classic and star maker for Valentino concerning an Argentine family torn apart by the outbreak of WWI. Valentino is a painter who moves from his native Argentina to France and is persuaded to enlist by a recruiter who invokes the image of the Biblical riders. His excellence as a soldier, however, proves to be his undoing. The 1962 remake can't hold a candle to original, adapted from a novel by Vicente Blasco-Ibanez. **110m/B VHS.** Rudolph Valentino, Alice Terry, Pomeroy Cannon, Josef Swickard, Alan Hale, Mabel van Buren, Yvette de Brulier, Bowditch Turner, Wallace Beery; *D:* Rex Ingram. *NO*

The Four Horsemen of the Apocalypse ♪♪½ 1962 The members of a German family find themselves fighting on opposite sides during WWII. This remake of the vintage Valentino silent failed at the box office, with complaints about its length, disjointed script, and uninspired performances. The title refers to the horrors of conquest, pestilence, war, and death. Adapted from the book by Vincente Blasco-Ibanez. **153m/C VHS, Beta.** Glenn Ford, Charles Boyer, Lee J. Cobb, Paul Henreid, Yvette Mimieux; *D:* Vincente Minnelli; *W:* John Gay; *C:* Milton Krasner; *M:* Andre Previn. *MGM*

The 400 Blows ♪♪♪♪ *Les Quartre Cents Coups* 1959 The classic, ground-breaking semi-autobiography that initiated Truffaut's career and catapulted him to international acclaim, about the trials and rebellions of a 12-year-old French schoolboy. One of the greatest and most influential of films, and the first of Truffaut's career-long Antoine Doinel series. With English subtitles. **97m/B VHS, Beta, LV.** *FR* Francois Truffaut, Jean-Pierre Leaud, Claire Maurier, Albert Remy, Guy Decomble, Georges Flament, Patrick Auffay, Jeanne Moreau, Jean-Claude Brialy, Jacques Demy, Robert Beauvais; *D:* Francois Truffaut; *W:* Francois Truffaut, Marcel Moussey; *C:* Henri Descae; *M:* Jean Constantin. Cannes Film Festival '59: Best Director (Truffaut); New York Film Critics Awards '59: Best Foreign Film; Nominations: Academy Awards '59: Best Story & Screenplay. *HMV, MRV, APD*

Four in a Jeep ♪♪½ 1951 In Vienna in 1945, soldiers from different countries are serving as an international military police force. They clash as a result of political demands and their love for the same woman. Shot on location in Austria. **83m/B VHS, Beta.** Ralph Meeker, Viveca Lindfors, Joseph Yadin, Michael Medwin; *D:* Leopold Lindtberg. *NOS*

Four Jacks and a Jill ♪♪ 1941 Four musicians are left in the lurch when their band singer leaves them for her gangster boyfriend and they must frantically search for a replacement. Not completely uninteresting, but rather bland and old now. Earlier versions of the story were re-

leased as "Street Girl" and "That Girl from Paris." ♫ I'm in Good Shape For the Shape I'm In; You Go Your Way and I'll Go Crazy; I Haven't A Thing to Wear; Wherever You Are; Boogie Woogie Conga. **68m/B VHS, Beta.** Anne Shirley, Ray Bolger, Desi Arnaz Sr., Jack Durant, June Havoc, Eddie Foy Jr., Fritz Feld; *D:* Jack Hively. *TTC*

The Four Minute Mile ♪♪ 1992 Four athletes become determined to break the record of running the mile in under four minutes. **186m/C VHS.** *GB* Richard Huw, Nique Needles, John Philbin, Lewis Fitz-gerald, Michael York. *WOV*

The Four Musketeers ♪♪♪ *The Revenge of Milady* 1975 (PG) A fun-loving continuation of "The Three Musketeers," reportedly filmed simultaneously. Lavish swashbuckler jaunts between France, England, and Italy, in following the adventures of D'Artagnan and his cohorts. Pictures give an amusing depiction of Lester-interpreted seventeenth-century Europe, with fine performances especially by Dunaway as an evil countess seeking revenge on our heroes and Welch as the scatterbrained object of York's affections. Followed, in 1989, by "The Return of the Musketeers." **108m/C VHS, Beta.** Michael York, Oliver Reed, Richard Chamberlain, Frank Finlay, Raquel Welch, Christopher Lee, Faye Dunaway, Jean-Pierre Cassel, Geraldine Chaplin, Simon Ward, Charlton Heston, Roy Kinnear, Nicole Calfan; *D:* Richard Lester; *M:* Lalo Schifrin. Nominations: Academy Awards '75: Best Costume Design. *LIV, OM*

Four Robbers ♪ 197? The ruthless Ma initiates his series of crimes throughout the Far East, somehow staying ahead of the cops. When the final showdown occurs, it's an all out kung fu massacre. **90m/C VHS, Beta.** Lau Chun, Shek Hon, Kong Seng, Lee Wing Shan. *MGI*

Four Rode Out ♪ 1969 A Mexican outlaw is pursued by his girlfriend, one-time partner, and the law. Brutal, inferior western. **99m/C VHS.** Pernell Roberts, Sue Lyon, Leslie Nielsen, Julian Mateos; *D:* John Peyser. *NO*

Four Rooms ♪♪ 1995 (R) Four stories by four hot indie filmers set in the same L.A. hotel on New Year's Eve are tied together by bellboy Roth, stumbling around in a Jerry/Carrey-like stupor. Leading off is Anders's roomful of witches trying to resurrect spirit of '50s stripper DeCadenet. After this disappointing start is Rockwell's bland look at infidelity, with wife Beals tied and gagged by her husband (Proval) over an alleged fling with Roth. Bandaras heads the best seg as a mobster who leaves his demonic children in Roth's hands. Tarantino is the anchor man with his take on Hitchcock, dealing with a macabre bet involving the removal of body parts. Altogether disjointed and uninspired. *CW:* Pervasive strong language, sexuality, and some drug use. **98m/C VHS, LV, Closed Caption.** Tim Roth, Antonio Banderas, Jennifer Beals, Paul Calderone, Sammi Davis, Valeria Golino, Madonna, Ione Skye, Marisa Tomei, Tamlyn Tomita, Bruce Willis, David Proval, Lili Taylor, Alicia Witt, Amanda DeCadenet, Danny Verduzco, Lana McKissack, Quentin Tarantino; *Cameos:* Salma Hayek; *D:* Quentin Tarantino, Alexandre Rockwell, Robert Rodriguez, Allison Anders; *W:* Quentin Tarantino, Alexandre Rockwell, Robert Rodriguez, Allison Anders; *C:* Phil Parmet, Guillermo Navarro, Andrzej Sekula, Rodrigo Garcia; *M:* Combustible Edison, Esquivel. Golden Raspberry Awards '95: Worst Supporting Actress (Madonna). *TOU*

The Four Seasons ♪♪½ 1981 (PG) Three upper-middle-class New York couples share their vacations together, as well as their friendship, their frustrations and their jealousies. Alda's first outing as a film director is pleasant and easy on the eyes. **108m/C VHS, Beta, LV.** Alan Alda, Carol Burnett, Sandy Dennis, Len Cariou, Jack Weston, Rita Moreno, Bess Armstrong; *D:* Alan Alda; *W:* Alan Alda. *USH*

Four Sided Triangle ♪ 1953 Two mad scientists find their friendship threatened when they discover that they are both in love with the same woman. So they do what anyone would do in this situation—they invent a machine and dupli-

cate her. **81m/B VHS.** *GB* James Hayter, Barbara Payton, Stephen Murray, John Van Eyssen, Percy Marmont; *D:* Terence Fisher; *M:* Malcolm Arnold. *NOS, SNC, MLB*

Four Ways Out ♪♪½ 1957 Four average guys are fed up by their lot in life and stage a box-office robbery of their local soccer stadium. They don't get to enjoy their ill-gotten gains. In Italian with subtitles or dubbed. **77m/B VHS.** *IT* Gina Lollobrigida, Renalto Baldini, Paul Muller; *D:* Pietro Germi. *SNC, VYY*

Four Weddings and a Funeral ♪♪♪ 1994 (R) Refreshing, intelligent adult comedy brimming with stiff upper-lip wit and sophistication. Thirtyish Brit bachelor Charles (Grant) spends his time attending the weddings of his friends, but manages to avoid taking the plunge himself. Then he falls for Carrie (MacDowell), who's about to wed another. Great beginning offers loads of laughs as the first two weddings unfold, then becomes decidedly bittersweet. While Grant makes this a star turn as the romantic bumbler, MacDowell charms without seeming particularly needed. Supporting characters are superb, especially Coleman as the "flirty" Scarlett and Atkinson as a new minister. Surprising box office hit found a broad audience. *CW:* Profanity, brief nudity, and sexual situations. **118m/C VHS, LV, DVD.** *GB* Hugh Grant, Andie MacDowell, Simon Callow, Kristin Scott Thomas, James Fleet, John Hannah, Charlotte Coleman, David Bower, Corin Redgrave, Rowan Atkinson, Rosalie Crutchley, Kenneth Griffith, Jeremy Kemp, Sophie Thompson; *D:* Mike Newell; *W:* Richard Curtis; *C:* Michael Coulter; *M:* Richard Rodney Bennett. Australian Film Institute '94: Best Foreign Film; British Academy Awards '94: Best Actor (Grant), Best Director (Newell), Best Film, Best Supporting Actress (Scott Thomas); Chicago Film Critics Awards '94: Most Promising Actor (Grant); Golden Globe Awards '95: Best Actor—Musical/Comedy (Grant); Writers Guild of America '94: Best Original Screenplay; Nominations: Academy Awards '94: Best Original Screenplay, Best Picture; Directors Guild of America Awards '94: Best Director (Newell); Golden Globe Awards '95: Best Actress—Musical/Comedy (MacDowell), Best Film—Musical/Comedy, Best Screenplay; MTV Movie Awards '95: Breakthrough Performance (Grant). *PGV*

The 4D Man ♪♪½ 1959 A physicist makes two fateful discoveries while working on a special project that gets out of control, leaving him able to pass through matter and see around corners. He also finds that his touch brings instant death. Cheap but effective sci-fier. Young Duke has a small part. **85m/C VHS, Beta, LV.** Robert Lansing, Lee Meriwether, James Congdon, Guy Raymond, Robert Strauss, Patty Duke; *D:* Irvin S. Yeaworth Jr. *NWV, MLB*

1492: Conquest of Paradise ♪♪½ 1992 (PG-13) Large-scale Hollywood production striving for political correctness is a drawn-out account of Columbus's (Depardieu) discovery and subsequent exploitation of the "New World." Skillful directing by Ridley Scott and impressive scenery add interest, yet don't make up for a script which chronicles events but tends towards trite dialogue and characterization. Available in both pan-and-scan and letterbox formats. *CW:* Historical violence and brutality. **142m/C VHS, Beta, LV, Closed Caption.** Gerard Depardieu, Sigourney Weaver, Armand Assante, Frank Langella, Loren Dean, Angela Molina, Fernando Rey, Michael Wincott, Steven Waddington, Tcheky Karyo, Kario Salem; *D:* Ridley Scott; *W:* Roselyne Bosch; *M:* Vangelis. *PAR, BTV*

The 4th Man ♪♪♪½ *Blunt* 1979 Steeped in saturated colors and jet black comedy, with an atmospheric score, Verhoeven's nouveau noir mystery enjoyed considerable art-house success but was not released in the US until 1984. The story is decidedly non-linear, the look stylish and symbolic. Krabbe is an alcoholic bisexual Catholic writer who inadvertently becomes the hypotenuse of a love triangle involving Herman, a young man he encounters at a railway station, and his lover Christine, who owns the Sphinx beauty parlor and whose three husbands died mysteriously. In Dutch with English subtitles. **104m/C VHS, Beta, LV.** *NL* Jeroen Krabbe, Renee Soutendijk, Thom Hoffman, Jon DeVries, Geert De Jong; **D:** Paul Verhoeven; **C:** Jan De Bont; **M:** Loek Dikker. Los Angeles Film Critics Association Awards '84: Best Foreign Film. XVC, MED

The Fourth Protocol 🎬🎬🎬 1987 (R)
Well-made thriller based on the Frederick Forsyth bestseller about a British secret agent trying to stop a young KGB agent from destroying NATO and putting the world in nuclear jeopardy. Brosnan, as the totally dedicated Russkie, gives his best performance to date while Caine, as usual, is totally believable as he goes about the business of tracking down the bad guys. 119m/C VHS, Beta, LV. **GB** Michael Caine, Pierce Brosnan, Ned Beatty, Joanna Cassidy, Julian Glover, Ray McAnally, Michael Gough, Ian Richardson, Betsy Brantley, Matt Frewer, Peter Cartwright, David Conville; **D:** John MacKenzie; **W:** Frederick Forsyth, Richard Burridge, George Axelrod; **C:** Phil Meheux; **M:** Lalo Schifrin, Francis Shaw. ORI, WAR

Fourth Story 🎬🎬🎬 1990 (PG-13)
A misfit detective is hired by a beautiful woman to find her missing husband. The investigation reveals some unseemly facts about the gentleman. Characterizations and plot twists keep this made-for-cable mystery interesting. 91m/C VHS, Beta, LV. Mark Harmon, Mimi Rogers, Cliff DeYoung, Paul Gleason, M. Emmet Walsh; **D:** Ivan Passer; **W:** Andrew Guerdat. MED, IME, VTR

The Fourth War 🎬🎬 1990 (R)
Scheider and Prochnow are American and Russian colonels, respectively, assigned to guard the West German-Czechoslovakian border against each other. With the end of the cold war looming, these two frustrated warriors begin to taunt each other with sallies into the other's territory, threatening to touch off a major superpower conflict. 109m/C VHS, Beta, LV, Closed Caption. Roy Scheider, Juergen Prochnow, Tim Reid, Lara Harris, Harry Dean Stanton; **D:** John Frankenheimer; **M:** Bill Conti. HBO

Fourth Wise Man 🎬🎬 1985
A Biblical Easter story about a rich physician searching for Christ in Persia. 72m/C VHS, Beta. Martin Sheen, Lance Kerwin, Alan Arkin, Harold Gould, Eileen Brennan, Ralph Bellamy, Adam Arkin, Richard Libertini. LIV, VES, IGP

Fourth Wish 🎬🎬 1975
When a single father learns his son is dying, he vows to make his son's last months as fulfilling as possible. Bring lots of hankies. 107m/C VHS, Beta. John Meillon, Robert Bettles, Robyn Nevin; **D:** Don Chaffey; **C:** Geoff Burton. Australian Film Institute '75: Best Actor (Meillon). NO

Fowl Play woof! 1983
An unlikely threesome encounter various hardships and mishaps on their way to the first cock-fighting Olympics. Let's hope it's the last cock-fighting Olympics. 90m/C VHS, Beta. Nancy Kwan. NO

Fox and His Friends 🎬🎬🎬½ Faustrecht der Freiheit; Fist Right of Freedom 1975
Fassbinder's breakthrough tragi-drama, about a lowly gay carnival barker who wins the lottery, thus attracting a devious, exploiting lover, who takes him for everything he has. In German with English subtitles. 123m/C VHS, Beta. **GE** Rainer Werner Fassbinder, Peter Chatel, Karl-Heinz Boehm, Adrian Hoven, Harry Baer, Ulla Jacobsson, Kurt Raab; **D:** Rainer Werner Fassbinder; **C:** Michael Ballhaus. FCT, NYF

The Fox and the Hound 🎬🎬🎬 1981 (G)
Sweet story of the friendship shared by a fox and hound. Young and naive, the animals become friends and swear their allegiance to one another when they are separated for a season. Upon return, the hound has become his master's best hunting dog and warns his friend the fox to stay clear of their hunting grounds, for the master is determined to catch the docile fox. Saddened, the fox retreats but soon finds himself boldly standing his ground against a bear that attacks the hound, and the hound inevitably protects the fox from the mean-spirited hunter. Very good animation, but not in the same class as other Disney favorites like "Beauty and the Beast." 83m/C VHS, Beta, Closed Caption. **D:** Art Stevens, Ted Berman, Richard Rich; **W:** Art Stevens, Peter Young, Steve Hulett, Earl Kress, Vance Gerry, Laury Clemmons, Dave Michener, Bur-

ny Mattinson; **M:** Buddy Baker; **V:** Mickey Rooney, Kurt Russell, Pearl Bailey, Jack Albertson, Sandy Duncan, Jeanette Nolan, Pat Buttram, John Fiedler, John McIntire, Richard Bakalayan, Paul Winchell, Keith Mitchell, Corey Feldman. DIS, OM

Foxes 🎬🎬 1980 (R)
Four young California girls grow up with little supervision from parents still trying to grow up themselves. They rely on each other in a world where they have to make adult choices, yet are not considered grown-up. They look for no more than a good time and no tragic mistakes. 106m/C VHS, Beta, Closed Caption. Jodie Foster, Cherie Currie, Marilyn Kagan, Scott Baio, Sally Kellerman, Randy Quaid, Laura Dern; **D:** Adrian Lyne; **W:** Gerald Ayres. MGM, FOX

Foxfire 🎬🎬🎬 1987 (PG)
In the role that won her Tony and Emmy awards, Tandy stars as Annie Nations, a woman who has lived her entire life in the Blue Ridge Mountains. Widowed, all she has left are the memories of her beloved husband, with whom she regularly communes. Her son tries to convince her to move, and it becomes a clash of the wills as Annie tries to decide to stay in her past or change her future. Made for television. 118m/C VHS, Closed Caption. Jessica Tandy, Hume Cronyn, John Denver, Gary Grubbs, Harriet Hall; **D:** Jud Taylor; **C:** Thomas Burstyn. National Media Owl Awards '88: Second Prize. REP

Foxfire 🎬🎬 1996 (R)
Not much more than "The Craft" without the hocus-pocus. Lusty Legs Sadovsky (Jolie) is a liberated drifter who empowers a quartet of abused teens to take action against their molester, who happens to be their biology teacher. Based on the book by Joyce Carol Oates originally written in the 1950s, modern adaptation suffers from time warp, most notably when the girls expose their teacher's behavior to their principal and he promptly suspends them without further ado. After some bonding and tattooing in an abandoned house, flick descends into the more masculine and mundane territory of car chases, kidnapping and gunplay. Filmmakers rather timidly back off of leather-clad Legs' obvious lesbianism and her relationship with the adoring Maddy (Burress). Decent acting by most would've benefitted from a more cohesive screenplay.**CW:** Teen nudity, drug use, strong language and some violent situations. 102m/C VHS, LV, Closed Caption. Angelina Jolie, John Diehl, Jenny Lewis, Cathy Moriarty, Richard Beymer, Hedy Burress, Jenny Shimizu, Sarah Rosenberg, Peter Facinelli; **D:** Annette Haywood-Carter; **W:** Elizabeth White; **C:** Newton Thomas Sigel; **M:** Michel Colombier. COL

Foxfire Light 🎬 1982 (PG)
A young woman vacationing in the Ozarks is drawn into a romance with a cowboy. But her mother's social ambitions and her own indecision may tear them apart. 102m/C VHS, Beta. Tippi Hedren, Lara Parker, Leslie Nielsen, Barry Van Dyke; **D:** Allen Baron; **C:** Thomas Ackerman. PSM

Foxstyle 🎬½ 1973
A wealthy nightclub owner struggles with his country roots and his city sophistication. 84m/C VHS, Beta. Juanita Moore, Richard Lawson, John Taylor, Jovita Bush; **D:** Clyde Houston. MOV

Foxtrap 🎬 1985
An L.A. courier is hired to find a runaway girl and, upon finding her in Europe, discovers he's been led into a trap. A low budget Italian co-production. 89m/C VHS, Beta. IT Fred Williamson, Christopher Connelly, Arlene Golonka; **D:** Fred Williamson. FCT, VES

Foxtrot 🎬🎬 The Other Side of Paradise 1976 (R)
A wealthy count isolates himself, his wife, and their two servants, on an island but cannot escape his past or the horrors of WWII. Even the good cast can't save the pretentious script and inadequate production. 91m/C VHS, Beta. SI MX Peter O'Toole, Charlotte Rampling, Max von Sydow, Jorge Luke; **D:** Arturo Ripstein. NLC

Foxy Brown 🎬 1974 (R)
A bitter woman poses as a prostitute to avenge the mob-backed deaths of her drug dealer brother and undercover cop boyfriend. Extremely violent black exploitation flick. 92m/C VHS, Beta. Pam Grier, Terry Carter, Antonio Fargas, Kathryn Loder; **D:** Jack Hill. ORI, FCT

F.P. 1 🎬🎬 1933
An artifical island (Floating Platform 1) in the Atlantic is threatened by treason. This slow-moving 1930s technothriller is the English-language version of the German "F.P. 1 Antwortet Nicht" ("F.P. 1 Doesn't Answer"). Both were directed at the same time by Hartl, using different casts. 74m/B VHS. **GE** Leslie Fenton, Conrad Veidt, Jill Esmond. NOS

F.P. 1 Doesn't Answer 🎬🎬 F.P. 1 Antwortet Nicht 1933
A mid-Atlantic refueling station (Floating Platform 1) is threatened by treason and a pilot sets out to put things right. Features pre-Hollywood vintage Lorre; Albers was Germany's number one box office draw at the time. In German. 74m/B VHS. **GE** Hans Albers, Sybille Schmitz, Paul Hartmann, Peter Lorre, Hermann Speelmanns; **D:** Karl Hartl. SNC, LSV

Frame by Frame 🎬🎬½ 1995 (R)
Cop partners Ekberg (Helgenberger) and Stash (Biehn), who share a passion on and off the job, become implicated in the mob-style murder of Stash's wife. Cable thriller.**CW:** Violence, some strong sexuality and language. 97m/C VHS, Closed Caption. Michael Biehn, Marg Helgenberger; **D:** Douglas Barr; **W:** Douglas Barr; **C:** Rodney Charters; **M:** Mark Snow. REP

Frame Up 🎬🎬 1991 (R)
A small town sheriff is trying to investigate a murder tied to a fraternity's initiation. However, he runs into opposition from the most powerful man in town.**CW:** Strong language, violence, and sensuality. 90m/C VHS, LV, Closed Caption. Wings Hauser, Bobby DiCicco, Frances Fisher, Dick Sargent, Robert Picardo; **D:** Paul Leder. REP

Framed 🎬🎬 1975 (R)
A nightclub owner is framed for murder, which understandably irks him. He's determined to get paroled and then seek revenge on the crooked cops responsible for his incarceration. This action melodrama features the writer, director and star of "Walking Tall." 106m/C VHS, Beta. Joe Don Baker, Gabriel Dell, Brock Peters, Conny Van Dyke, John Marley; **D:** Phil Karlson; **W:** Mort Briskin. PAR

Framed 🎬🎬 1990
An art forger gets tripped up by a beautiful con artist. However, when they meet again he is willingly drawn into her latest swindle. 87m/C VHS, Closed Caption. Jeff Goldblum, Kristin Scott Thomas, Todd Graff; **D:** Dean Parisot. HBO

Fran 🎬🎬 1985
A young woman is torn between her desperate need for a male companion and the care of her children. Well made, albeit depressing, Australian production. 92m/C VHS, Beta. **AU** Noni Hazlehurst, Annie Byron, Alan Fletcher; **D:** Glenda Hambly. Australian Film Institute '85: Best Actress (Hazlehurst). NO

France/Tour/Detour/Deux/Enfants 🎬🎬
A twelve-part television series made for French television in which Godard and Mieville chronicle, in their characteristically reflexive fashion, the lives of two French schoolchildren and how their everyday growth is informed by television and the media. In French with English subtitles. 26m/C VHS, Beta. FR **D:** Jean-Luc Godard, Anne-Marie Mieville. EAI

Frances 🎬🎬🎬 1982
The tragic story of Frances Farmer, the beautiful and talented screen actress of the 30's and early 40's, who was driven to a mental breakdown by bad luck, drug and alcohol abuse, a neurotic, domineering mother, despicable mental health care, and her own stubbornness. After being in and out of mental hospitals, she is finally reduced to a shadow by a lobotomy. Not nearly as bleak as it sounds, this film works because Lange understands this character from the inside out, and never lets her become melodramatic or weak. 134m/C VHS, Beta, LV. Jessica Lange, Kim Stanley, Sam Shepard; **D:** Graeme Clif-

ford; **W:** Christopher DeVore, Nicholas Kazan, Eric Bergren; **M:** John Barry. Nominations: Academy Awards '82: Best Actress (Lange), Best Supporting Actress (Stanley). *REP*

Francesco 🎬🎬 1993 (PG-13)
Set in 13th-century Italy and depicting the life of St. Francis of Assisi. Follows the pleasure-loving son of a wealthy merchant through his religious awakening, and the founding of the Franciscan order of monks. Rourke, in a definite change-of-pace role, is actually believable, while Bonham Carter offers fine support as a devoted disciple.**CW:** Nudity. 119m/C VHS, LV. Mickey Rourke, Helena Bonham Carter, Paolo Bonacelli, Andrea Ferreol, Hanns Zischler, Peter Berling; **D:** Liliana Cavani; **W:** Liliana Cavani. *HMD*

The Franchise Affair 🎬🎬 1952
A teenage girl in need of an alibi accuses two reclusive women of kidnapping and abusing her. It's up to a lawyer to sort out the truth. Based on the novel by Josephine Tey. 149m/C VHS. *GB* Michael Denison, Dulcie Gray, Anthony Nicholls, Marjorie Fielding, Athene Seyler, Ann Stephens, Patrick Troughton; **D:** Lawrence Huntington. *CF*

The Franchise Affair 🎬🎬½ 19??
A scandal is about to overtake the sleepy village of Milford in 1947. An elderly lady and her daughter, the owners of a forbidding country house, are accused of kidnapping and beating a teenaged girl until she agreed to work as their servant. A British TV production based on the novel by Josephine Tey and previously filmed for the big screen in 1952. 155m/C VHS. *GB* Patrick Malahide, Rosalie Crutchley, Joanna McCallum. *VCO*

Francis Covers the Big Town 🎬🎬½ 1953
The fourth in the series finds Peter Stirling (O'Connor) trying to become an ace reporter with a New York newspaper. Thanks to Francis he gets some big scoops but then runs afoul of the mob and is accused of murder. And it's up to his smarter pal to come to the rescue. 86m/B VHS, Closed Caption. Donald O'Connor, Yvette Dugay, Gene Lockhart, Nancy Guild, Larry Gates, Gale Gordon; **D:** Arthur Lubin; **W:** Oscar Brodney; **C:** Carl Guthrie; **M:** Joseph Gershenson; **V:** Chill Wills. *USH*

Francis Gary Powers: The True Story of the U-2 Spy 🎬🎬½ 1976
A television dramatization of the true experiences of Gary Powers, a CIA spy pilot whose plane was shot down over the Soviet Union in 1960. His capture, trial, and conviction are all portrayed in detail, taken from Power's own reminiscences. 120m/C VHS, Beta. Lee Majors, Noah Beery Jr., Nehemiah Persoff, Lew Ayres, Brooke Bundy; **D:** Delbert Mann. *WOV*

Francis Goes to the Races 🎬🎬½ 1951
The second in the talking-mule series finds O'Connor and Francis taking up residence on Kellaway's failing horse ranch. When mobsters seize control of the property to pay off a debt, Francis decides to check with the horses at the Santa Anita race track and find a sure winner to bet on. 88m/B VHS. Donald O'Connor, Piper Laurie, Cecil Kellaway, Jesse White, Barry Kelley, Hayden Rorke, Vaughn Taylor, Larry Keating; **D:** Arthur Lubin; **W:** Oscar Brodney; **M:** Frank Skinner; **V:** Chill Wills. *USH*

Francis Goes to West Point 🎬🎬½ 1952
Peter (O'Connor) and Francis get into West Point where the unfortunate freshman winds up last in his class. But thanks to Francis, Peter makes it past school hazing, grades, and other campus hijinks. Look for Leonard Nimoy in the bit role of a football player. Third in the series. 81m/B VHS, Closed Caption. Donald O'Connor, Lori Nelson, William Reynolds, Gregg Palmer, Alice Kelley, Les Tremayne, David Janssen, Paul Burke; **D:** Arthur Lubin; **W:** Oscar Brodney; **C:** Carl Guthrie; **M:** Joseph Gershenson; **V:** Chill Wills. *USH*

Francis in the Haunted House 🎬½ 1956
The sixth and last entry in the series finds star Donald O'Connor, director Arthur Lubin, and even Chill Wills (the voice of Francis) all abandoning the sinking series. So, its left to Rooney (as hapless David Prescott) to get himself into trouble (trapped in a haunted house with thieves) and for

Francis to get him out. Ho-hum. 80m/B VHS, Closed Caption. Mickey Rooney, Virginia Welles, James Flavin, Paul Cavanagh, David Janssen, Richard Deacon; **D:** Charles Lamont; **W:** Herbert Margolis, William Raynor; **C:** George Robinson; **M:** Joseph Gershenson; **V:** Paul Frees. *USH*

Francis in the Navy 🎬🎬 1955
The precocious talking mule, Francis, is drafted, and his buddy, played by O'Connor, comes to the rescue. The loquacious beast proves he has the superior grey matter however, and ends up doing all the thinking. Look for Clint Eastwood in his second minor role. 80m/B VHS. Donald O'Connor, Martha Hyer, Jim Backus, Paul Burke, David Janssen, Clint Eastwood, Martin Milner; **D:** Arthur Lubin. *USH*

Francis Joins the WACs 🎬🎬½ 1954
The fifth entry in the series finds O'Connor working as a bank clerk when he is mistakenly drafted back into the military—and sent to a WAC base. Francis tries to keep him out of trouble with the ladies. Wills, the voice of Francis, also turns up as a general. 94m/B VHS. Donald O'Connor, Julie Adams, Chill Wills, Mamie Van Doren, Lynn Bari, ZaSu Pitts, Joan Shawlee, Mara Corday, Allison Hayes; **D:** Arthur Lubin; **V:** Chill Wills. *USH*

Francis the Talking Mule 🎬🎬🎬 1949
The first of the silly but funny series about, what else, a talking mule. Peter Stirling (O'Connor) is the dim-bulb G.I. who hooks up with Francis while fighting in Burma. Francis helps Peter become a war hero but of course everyone thinks he's crazy when Peter insists the mule can talk. The joke is that Francis is smarter than any of the humans. O'Connor starred in six of the films, with Mickey Rooney taking over the final adventure. Director Lubin went on to create the television series "Mr. Ed", about a talking horse. Watch for Tony Curtis in a small role. 91m/B VHS, LV. Donald O'Connor, Patricia Medina, ZaSu Pitts, Ray Collins, John McIntire, Eduard Franz, Howland Chamberlin, Frank Faylen, Tony Curtis; **D:** Arthur Lubin; **M:** Frank Skinner; **V:** Chill Wills. *USH*

Frank and Jesse 🎬🎬½ 1994 (R)
Another revisionist western finds outlaw Jesse James (Lowe) brooding about his violent existence while brother Frank (Paxton) keeps the gang together and they all try to avoid capture by a vengeful Alan Pinkerton (Atherton) and his detective agency. 106m/C VHS, LV, Closed Caption. Rob Lowe, Bill Paxton, Randy Travis, William Atherton, Alexis Arquette; **D:** Robert Boris; **W:** Robert Boris; **C:** Walt Lloyd; **M:** Mark McKenzie. *THV*

Frank and Ollie 🎬🎬🎬 1995 (PG)
If you have children, chances are you have a collection of Disney classics, including "Cinderella", "Snow White and the Seven Dwarfs", or "Bambi". Look closely at any of the opening credits and you'll see that two of those names, part of Disney's famed "Nine Old Men", are 80-something animators Frank Thomas and Ollie Johnston. Documentary, from Thomas's son Theodore, highlights the 60-plus year friendship and storied careers of these two pioneers, who are still well-known thanks to the recent animation craze. Seven years from conception to release, the film has many great pencil drawings and scenes from the movies, but focuses as much on the men's longtime friendship. 89m/C VHS. **D:** Theodore Thomas; **W:** Theodore Thomas; **C:** Erik Daarstad; **M:** James Stemple. *NYR*

Frankenhooker 🎬½ 1990 (R)
Jeffrey Franken is a nice guy; he didn't mean to mow his fiancee down on the front lawn. But sometimes bad things just happen to good people. Luckily Jeff thought to save her head and decides to pair it up with the body of some sexy streetwalkers. Voila! You have Frankenhooker: the girlfriend with more than a heart. The posters say it best, "A Terrifying Tale of Sluts and Bolts."**CW:** Language, gore and drugs, and sensuality. 90m/C VHS, LV, Closed Caption. James Lorinz, Patty Mullen, Charlotte J. Helmkamp, Louise Lasser, Shirley Stoler; **D:** Frank Henenlotter. *SGE, FCT*

Frankenstein 🎬🎬🎬🎬 1931
The definitive expressionistic Gothic horror classic that set the mold. Adapted from the Mary Shelley novel about Dr. Henry Frankenstein, the scientist who creates a terrifying, yet strangely sympathetic monster. Great performance by Karloff as the creation, which made him a monster star. Several powerful scenes, excised from the original version, have been restored. Side two of the laser disc version contains the original theatrical trailer, plus a collection of photos and scenes replayed for study purposes. 71m/B VHS, Beta, LV. Boris Karloff, Colin Clive, Mae Clarke, John Boles, Dwight Frye, Edward Van Sloan, Frederick Kerr, Lionel Belman; **D:** James Whale; **W:** Francis Edwards Faragoh, Garrett Fort, John Balderston, Robert Florey; **M:** David Broeckman. *USH, TLF, HMV*

Frankenstein 🎬🎬½ 1973
A brilliant scientist plays God, unleashing a living monster from the remains of the dead. A TV movie version of the legendary horror story. Good atmosphere provided by producer Dan "Dark Shadows" Curtis. 130m/C VHS, Beta. Robert Foxworth, Bo Svenson, Willie Aames, Susan Strasberg; **D:** Glenn Jordan. *MPI*

Frankenstein 🎬🎬½ 1982
A remake of the horror classic, closely following the original story, wherein the creature speaks (and waxes philosophical), the doctor sees him as his dark subconscious, and the two die in an arctic confrontation. 81m/C VHS, Beta. Robert Powell, Carrie Fisher, David Warner, John Gielgud; **D:** James Ormerod. *LIV*

Frankenstein 🎬🎬½ 1993
Yet another remake of Mary Shelley's 1818 novel. Bergin stars as Dr. Victor Frankenstein, fanatically believing in the power of science to solve all mankind's ills. This leads him to prove his theories on the "secret of life" with his creation of the monster (Quaid), which Frankenstein finds he cannot ultimately control. Slow-moving story but while the monster isn't really terrifying, he's vengeful and intelligent enough to be a good enemy. Made for cable television. 117m/C VHS, Closed Caption. Patrick Bergin, Randy Quaid, John Mills, Lambert Wilson, Fiona Gilles, Jacinta Mulcahy, Timothy Stark; **D:** David Wickes; **W:** David Wickes. *TTC, BTV*

Frankenstein: A Cinematic Scrapbook 1991
A behind the scenes look at the world's most infamous monster, featuring interviews with Boris Karloff, Bela Lugosi and Lon Chaney, Jr. Also included are original movie trailers. In color and B&W. 60m/C VHS, Beta. **D:** Ted Newsom; **W:** Ted Newsom. *RHI, FCT*

Frankenstein and Me 🎬🎬½ 1996 (PG)
Monster-mad 12-year-old Earl Williams (Boulanger) lives in a small Mojave desert town and dreams about bringing Frankenstein's creature back to life. On Halloween, Earl and his friends visit a traveling carnival that claims to have the "authentic" monster, which happens to fall off the truck when the show leaves. Earl finds the dummy and makes numerous attempts to bring the creature back to life. Lots of fantasy sequences and the picture's fun without being too scary. 91m/C VHS. **CA** Jamieson Boulanger, Ricky Mabse, Louise Fletcher, Burt Reynolds, Miriam Cyr; **D:** Robert Tinnell; **W:** David Sherman, Richard Goudreau; **C:** Roxanne Di Santo; **M:** Normand Corbeil. *THV*

Frankenstein and the Monster from Hell 🎬🎬 1974 (R)
A young doctor is discovered conducting experiments with human bodies and thrown into a mental asylum run by none other than Dr. Frankenstein himself. They continue their gruesome work together, creating a monster who develops a taste for human flesh. This really lame film was the last of the Hammer Frankenstein series. 93m/C VHS, Closed Caption. Peter Cushing, Shane Briant, Madeleine Smith, David Prowse, John Stratton; **D:** Terence Fisher; **M:** James Bernard. *PAR*

Frankenstein '80 WOOF! 1979
Guy named Frankenstein pieces together a monster who goes on a killing spree. Bottom of the barrel Italian production with funky music and lots of gore. 88m/C VHS, Beta. *IT GE* John Richardson, Gordon Mitchell,

Leila Parker, Dada Galloti, Marisa Travers; **D:** Mario Mancini. *NO*

Frankenstein General Hospital WOOF! 1988
A completely laughless horror spoof wherein the twelfth grandson of the infamous scientist duplicates his experiments in the basement of a modern hospital. A must see for Frankenstein fans; considered by some the worst Frankenstein movie ever made. **90m/C VHS, Beta, LV.** Mark Blankfield, Kathy Shower, Leslie Jordan, Irwin Keyes; **D:** Deborah Roberts. *NO*

Frankenstein Island WOOF! 1981 (PG)
Four balloonists get pulled down in a storm and end up on a mysterious island. They are greeted by one Sheila Frankenstein and encounter monsters, amazons, and other obstacles. Completely inept; Carradine "appears" in a visionary sequence wearing his pajamas. **97m/C VHS, Beta.** Cameron Mitchell, Andrew Duggan, John Carradine; **D:** Jerry Warren. *NO*

Frankenstein Meets the Space Monster WOOF! 1965
Mars Invades Puerto Rico; Frankenstein Meets the Spacemen; Duel of the Space Monsters A classic grade-Z epic about a space robot gone berserk among Puerto Rican disco dancers. **80m/B VHS, Beta.** James Karen, Nancy Marshall, Marilyn Hanold, David Kerman, Robert Reilly, Lou Cutell; **D:** Robert Gaffney; **W:** George Garret; **C:** Saul Midwall. *PSM*

Frankenstein Meets the Wolfman 🐾🐾🐾 1942
The two famous Universal monsters meet and battle it out in this typical grade-B entry, the fifth from the series. The Werewolf wants Dr. Frankenstein to cure him, but only his monster (played by Lugosi) remains. **73m/C VHS, Beta, LV.** Lon Chaney Jr., Bela Lugosi, Patric Knowles, Lionel Atwill, Maria Ouspenskaya; **D:** Roy William Neill. *USH, MLB*

Frankenstein Sings...The Movie 🐾🐾½ 1995 (PG)
Musical horror spoof finds young couple seeking shelter in a creepy mansion that happens to belong to Dr. Frankenstein. Also visiting (it just happens to be Halloween) are Mr. and Mrs. Dracula, the Wolfman and his mother, and the mummified remains of Elvis and his agent. Some amusing one-liners and mediocre music; adapted from a stage musical. **83m/C VHS, LV.** Candace Cameron, Ian Bohen, Jimmie Walker, Anthony Crivello; **D:** Joel Cohen, Alec Sokolow. *TTC*

Frankenstein Unbound 🐾🐾🐾 1990 (R)
Roger Corman's Frankenstein Unbound Corman returns after nearly 20 years with a better than ever B movie. Hurt plays a nuclear physicist time traveler who goes back to the 1800s and runs into Lord Byron, Percy and Mary Shelley and their neighbor Dr. Frankenstein and his monster. Great acting, fun special effects, intelligent and subtle message, with a little sex to keep things going. **86m/C VHS, Beta, LV, Closed Caption.** John Hurt, Raul Julia, Bridget Fonda, Jason Patric, Michael Hutchence, Catherine Rabett, Nick Brimble, Catherine Corman, Mickey Knox; **D:** Roger Corman; **W:** Roger Corman, F.X. Feeney; **M:** Carl Davis; **V:** Terri Treas. *FOX*

Frankenstein's Daughter 🐾 1958
She Monster of the Night Demented descendant of Dr. Frankenstein sets a den of gruesome monsters loose, including the corpse of a teenaged girl he revitalizes, as he continues the mad experiments of his forefathers. **85m/B VHS, Beta.** John Ashley, Sandra Knight; **D:** Richard Cunha. *NOS, MRV, RHI*

Frankenstein's Great Aunt Tillie WOOF! 1983
An excruciatingly bad send up of the Frankenstein saga with the good doctor about to be evicted from his estate because of back taxes. Gabor appears for a few seconds in a flashback. **99m/C VHS, Beta.** Donald Pleasence, Yvonne Furneaux, Aldo Ray, June Wilkinson, Zsa Zsa Gabor; **D:** Myron G. Gold; **W:** Myron G. Gold. *VCD*

Frankenweenie 🐾🐾½ 1984 (PG)
"Frankenweenie" is the tale of a lovable spunky dog named Sparky and his owner, Victor Frankenstein. When Sparky is hit by a car, Victor brings him back to life through the use of electric shock.

This affectionate parody of "Frankenstein" launched renowned director Burton's career. **27m/B VHS, Beta, Closed Caption.** Shelley Duvall, Daniel Stern, Barret Oliver, Paul Bartel; **D:** Tim Burton; **W:** Tim Burton; **C:** Thomas Ackerman. *TOU*

Frankie and Johnny 🐾 1936
Based on the song of the same name, famed torch singer Morgan portrays a singer in a bordello who shoots her unfaithful lover. Release was delayed two years by the Hays Office's intervention in how a house of prostitution could be portrayed on screen. Too bad they reached an agreement. Not even Morgan's rendition of the title song redeems this. **68m/B VHS, Beta.** Helen Morgan, Chester Morris; **D:** Chester Erskine. *CCB*

Frankie and Johnny 🐾🐾½ 1965
Elvis is a riverboat gambler/singer with lousy luck until Kovack changes the odds. This upsets his girlfriend Douglas who shoots him (but not fatally). Elvis wears period costumes, but this is otherwise similar to his contemporary films. 🎵When the Saints Go Marching In; Look Out Broadway; Shout It Out; Frankie and Johnny; Chesay; Come Along; Petunia; The Gardner's Daughter; Beginner's Luck. **88m/C VHS, Beta.** Elvis Presley, Donna Douglas, Harry (Henry) Morgan, Audrey Christie, Anthony Eisley, Sue Ane Langdon, Robert Strauss, Nancy Kovack; **D:** Fred de Cordova. *MGM*

Frankie and Johnny 🐾🐾🐾 1991 (R)
Ex-con gets a job as a short-order cook and falls for a world-weary waitress. She doesn't believe in romance, but finally gives into his pleas for a chance and finds out he may not be such a bad guy after all. Nothing can make Pfeiffer dowdy enough for this role, but she and Pacino are charming together. In a change of pace role, Nelligan has fun as a fellow waitress who loves men. Based on the play "Frankie and Johnny in the Clair de Lune" by McNally who also wrote the screenplay. **CW:** Language and sensuality. **117m/C VHS, LV, Closed Caption.** Al Pacino, Michelle Pfeiffer, Hector Elizondo, Nathan Lane, Kate Nelligan, Jane Morris, Greg Lewis, Al Fann, K. Callan, Phil Leeds, Tracy Reiner, Dey Young; **D:** Garry Marshall; **W:** Terrance McNally; **C:** Dante Spinotti; **M:** Marvin Hamlisch. British Academy Awards '91: Best Supporting Actress (Nelligan); National Board of Review Awards '91: 10 Best Films of the Year, Best Supporting Actress (Nelligan). *PAR, CCB*

Frankie Starlight 🐾🐾½ 1995 (R)
Bernadette (Parillaud) leaves France after WWII, smuggled aboard an American troop ship. By the time the ship reaches Ireland, she's pregnant and gives birth to her dwarf son, Frankie, in Dublin. She's taken in by the family of customs officer Jack Kelly (Byrne), who instills in the boy a lifelong love of the stars. The adult Frankie (Walker) becomes a celebrity when he writes a novel combining his obsession with the cosmos and his mother's erotic history. Raymo adapts from his 1993 novel "The Dork of Cork." Great performances by both Pentony and Walker as the child and adult Frankies. **CW:** Language and some sexuality. **100m/C VHS, LV, Closed Caption.** IR Corban Walker, Alan Pentony, Gabriel Byrne, Anne Parillaud, Matt Dillon, Georgina Cates, Darbnia Molloy, Niall Toibin, Rudi Davies; **D:** Michael Lindsay-Hogg; **W:** Chet Raymo, Ronan O'Leary; **C:** Paul Laufer; **M:** Elmer Bernstein. *NLC*

Frantic 🐾🐾🐾
Elevator to the Gallows; Ascenseur Pour L'Echafaud 1958 From Louis Malle comes one of the first French New Wave film noir dramas. A man kills his boss with the connivance of the employer's wife, his lover, and makes it look like suicide. Meanwhile, teenagers have used his car and gun in the murder of a tourist couple and he is indicted for that crime. Their perfectly planned murder begins to unravel into a panic-stricken nightmare. A suspenseful and captivating drama. Director Malle's first feature film. Musical score by jazz legend Miles Davis. **92m/B VHS, Beta, 8mm.** FR Maurice Ronet, Jeanne Moreau, Georges Poujouly; **D:** Louis Malle; **M:** Miles Davis. *SNC, NOS, VYY*

Frantic 🐾🐾🐾 1988 (R)
While in Paris, an American surgeon's wife is kidnapped when she inadvertently picks up the wrong suitcase. Her kidnappers want their hidden treasure returned, which forces the husband into the criminal underground and into unexpected heroism when he seeks to rescue her. Contrived ending weakens on the whole, but Polanski is still master of the dark film thriller. **120m/C VHS, Beta, LV, Closed Caption.** Harrison Ford, Betty Buckley, John Mahoney, Emmanuelle Seigner, Jimmie Ray Weeks, Yorgo Voyagis, David Huddleston, Gerard Klein; **D:** Roman Polanski; **W:** Gerard Brach, Roman Polanski; **M:** Ennio Morricone. *WAR, FCT*

Franz 🐾 1972
A French mercenary and an insecure woman struggle with a doomed love affair. In French with English subtitles. **90m/C VHS, Beta.** FR Jacques Brel; **D:** Jacques Brel. *BAR*

Frasier the Sensuous Lion 🐾🐾 1973 (PG)
Frasier the Lovable Lion A zoology professor is able to converse with Frasier, a lion known for his sexual stamina and whose potency is coveted by a billionaire (shadow of monkey glands rejuvenation therapy). A fairly typical, if slightly risque, talking critter film. **97m/C VHS, Beta.** Michael Callan, Katherine Justice, Frank De Kova, Malachi Throne, Victor Jory, Peter Lorre Jr., Marc Lawrence; **D:** Pat Shields. *PSM*

Fraternity Vacation 🐾 1985 (R)
Two college fraternity men show a nerd the greatest time of his life while he's on vacation in Palm Springs. **95m/C VHS, Beta, LV, Closed Caption.** Stephen Geoffreys, Sheree J. Wilson, Cameron Dye, Leigh McCloskey, Tim Robbins, Matt McCoy, Amanda Bearse, John Vernon, Nita Talbot, Barbara Crampton, Jane Morris, Max Wright, Julie Payne, Franklin Ajaye, Charles Rocket, Britt Ekland; **D:** James Frawley; **M:** Brad Fiedel. *NWV, VTR*

Frauds 🐾½ 1993 (R)
Collins is an immoral insurance investigator who takes his victims for everything he can. Then he meets a couple who are out to beat him at his own game. **CW:** Terror/violence. **94m/C VHS, LV.** Phil Collins, Hugo Weaving, Josephine Byrnes. *LIV*

Freaked 🐾🐾 1993 (PG-13)
Bizarre little black comedy throws everything at the screen, hoping some of the gross-out humor will prove amusing (and some does). Greedy TV star Ricky Coogin (Winter) agrees to be the spokesman for E.E.S. Corporation, which markets a toxic green slime fertilizer to the third world. He's sent to South America to promote the product and is captured by the mad scientist proprietor (Quaid) of a mysterious sideshow, who douses him with the fertilizer. Before you know it he's an oozing half-man, half-beast, perfect to join other freaks as the latest attraction. Lots of yucky makeup. Reeves has an uncredited cameo as the Dog Boy. **80m/C VHS, LV.** Alex Winter, Randy Quaid, Megan Ward, Michael Stoyanov, Brooke Shields, William Sadler, Derek McGrath, Alex Zuckerman, Karyn Malchus, Mr. T, Morgan Fairchild; **Cameos:** Keanu Reeves, Tom Stern; **D:** Alex Winter, Tom Stern; **W:** Alex Winter, Tom Stern, Tim Burns; **M:** Kevin Kiner; **V:** Bob(cat) Goldthwait. *FXV*

The Freakmaker 🐾🐾
Mutations; The Mutation 1973 (R) Mad professor attempts to breed plants with humans in his lab and has the usual bizarre results. Experiments that fail go to Dunn, a dwarf who runs a freak show. Shamelessly includes real freaks as if plot was not strange enough. **90m/C VHS, Beta.** GB Donald Pleasence, Tom Baker, Brad Harris, Julie Ege, Michael Dunn, Jill Haworth; **D:** Jack Cardiff. *VDC*

Freaks 🐾🐾🐾½
Nature's Mistakes; Forbidden Love; The Monster Show 1932 The infamous, controversial, cult-horror classic about a band of circus freaks that exact revenge upon a beautiful aerialist and her strongman lover after enduring humiliation and exploitation. Based on Ted Robbins story "Spurs." It was meant to out-horror "Frankenstein" but was so successful that it was repeatedly banned. Browning's film may be a shocker but it is never intended to be exploitative since the "Freaks" are the only compassionate, loyal, and

loving people around. **66m/B VHS, Beta, LV.** Wallace Ford, Olga Baclanova, Leila Hyams, Roscoe Ates, Harry Earles; *D:* Tod Browning. *MGM*

Freakshow 🎞️ 1995 (R) Two teens wander into the sideshow at a local carnival and meet the Freakmaster (Hansen), whose grisly exhibits have equally grisly stories to tell. Campy horror with routine special effects.*CW:* Horror violence and gore, language and some sexuality. **102m/C VHS.** Gunnar Hansen, Veronica Carlson, Brian D. Kelly, Shannon Michelle Parsons; *D:* William Cooke, Paul Talbot. *AVI*

Freaky Friday 🎞️½ 1976 (G) A housewife and her teenage daughter inadvertently switch bodies and each then tries to carry on the other's normal routine. Mary Rodgers' popular book is brought to the screen with great charm in this above average Disney film. **95m/C VHS, Beta, Closed Caption.** Barbara Harris, Jodie Foster, Patsy Kelly, Dick Van Patten, Ruth Buzzi; *D:* Gary Nelson. *DIS*

Freddie the Frog 🎞️½ *Freddie as F.R.O.7* 1992 (G) Prince Frederick's life is shattered when his father is killed by his evil Aunt Messina, who wants to rule the kingdom. She even changes Frederick into a frog—but he manages to escape her with the help of friendly sea monster Nessie. But Freddie discovers that he has also been given super-frog powers, just in time to save Britain's landmarks, which are disappearing thanks to Aunt Messina's spells. **72m/C VHS, Closed Caption.** *GB D:* Jon Acevski; *W:* Jon Acevski, David Ashton; *V:* Ben Kingsley, Nigel Hawthorne, Jenny Agutter, John Sessions, Brian Blessed, Billie Whitelaw, Jonathan Pryce, Phyllis Logan, Michael Hordern. *USH*

Freddy's Dead: The Final Nightmare 🎞️ *Nightmare on Elm Street 6: Freddy's Dead* 1991 (R) Freddy's daughter journeys to Springwood, Ohio to put a stop to her father's evil ways. Will she be able to destroy this maniac, or is a new reign of terror just beginning? The sixth, and supposedly last, film in the "Nightmare" series.*CW:* Language and horror violence and drug content. **96m/C VHS, LV, Closed Caption.** Robert Englund, Lisa Zane, Shon Greenblatt, Leslie Deane, Ricky Dean Logan, Breckin Majer, Yaphet Kotto, Elinor Donahue, Roseanne, Johnny Depp, Alice Cooper; *D:* Rachel Talalay; *W:* Michael De Luca. *COL, NLC*

Free Amerika Broadcasting 1989 A drama about an alternate reality in which Richard Nixon was assassinated, leaving Spiro Agnew president. As a result, the country turns to violent revolution. **80m/C VHS.** Brian Kincaid; *D:* Dean Wilson. *NO*

Free and Easy 🎞️½ *Easy Go* 1930 Keaton plays the incompetent manager of a beauty contest winner (Page) from Gopher City, Kansas. Page and her overbearing mother, accompanied by Keaton, go to Hollywood to make the girl a star. They gate-crash the MGM studio where all cause havoc and it turns out Keaton is the one who lands in front of the cameras (Page has to settle for romancing Montgomery). Provides a behind-the-scenes look at the MGM studio, with a number of MGM stars making cameo appearances. **92m/B VHS.** Buster Keaton, Anita Page, Robert Montgomery, Trixie Friganza, Fred Niblo; *Cameos:* Cecil B. DeMille, Jackie Coogan, Lionel Barrymore, William Haines; *D:* Edward Sedgwick. *MGM*

Free Grass 🎞️ *Scream Free!* 1969 A gang of thoughtless hippie drug smugglers and abusers escape from the police, drink acid-spiked wine, shoot each other, and have love-ins. **82m/C VHS, Beta, LV.** Russ Tamblyn, Richard Beymer, Casey Kasem, Lana Wood, Warren Finnerty. *NO*

Free Ride 🎞️ 1986 (R) A kooky kid steals a sportscar to impress a girl, and gets involved with local hoods. They chase each other around. **92m/C VHS, Beta, LV.** Gary Hershberger, Reed Rudy, Dawn Schneider, Peter DeLuise, Brian MacGregor; *W:* Robert Bell. *LIV*

A Free Soul 🎞️½ 1931 Tippling litigator Barrymore helps low-life mobster Gable beat a murder rap, only to discover the hood has stolen his daughter's heart. Bargaining with his ditzy daughter, he vows to eschew the bottle if she'll stay away from good-for-nothing Gable. Directed by Brown, best known for his work with Garbo, and based on the memoirs of Adela Rogers St. John. The final courtroom scene—a cloak-and-gavel classic—cinched Barrymore's Oscar. Remade with Liz Taylor as "The Girl Who Had Everything" (although, ironically, the earlier version is the racier of the two). **94m/B VHS.** Norma Shearer, Leslie Howard, Lionel Barrymore, Clark Gable, James Gleason, Lucy Beaumont; *D:* Clarence Brown; *C:* William H. Daniels. Academy Awards '31: Best Actor (Barrymore); Nominations: Academy Awards '31: Best Actress (Shearer), Best Director (Brown). *MGM, FCT, BTV*

Free to Love 🎞️ 1925 Screen idol Bow plays a young woman, fresh out of prison, who is taken in by a kindly, affluent patron. But, as the silent drama axiom would have it, there's no escaping the past, and she's forced to defend her former life when her guardian is murdered. **61m/B VHS, Beta.** Clara Bow, Donald Keith, Raymond McKee; *D:* Frank O'Connor. *GPV, FCT*

Free, White, and 21 🎞️ 1962 A black motel owner is accused of raping a white civil rights worker. Produced in a "pseudo-documentary" form which sometimes drags. **104m/B VHS.** Frederick O'Neal, Annalena Lund, George Edgely, John Hicks, Hugh Crenshaw, George Russell; *D:* Larry Buchanan. *NO*

Free Willy 🎞️½ 1993 (PG) Sentimental story about a 12-year-old runaway (Richter) who befriends a whale. Should appeal to children for its heartwarming story and delightful sea acrobatics. An electronically operated stand-in whale was used for far-off shots; a domesticated performing whale named Keiko for the close-ups. Director Wincer was known to grumble about the temperamental Keiko during shooting. Suggested viewing for students of animal behavior. Proof that family films can make money, "Free Willy" placed tenth for total box office receipts in 1993. **112m/C VHS, LV, 8mm, Closed Caption.** Jason James Richter, Lori Petty, Jayne Atkinson, August Schellenberg, Michael Madsen; *D:* Simon Wincer; *W:* Keith A. Walker, Corey Blechman; *C:* Robbie Greenberg; *M:* Basil Poledouris. MTV Movie Awards '94: Best Song ("Will You Be There"); Nominations: MTV Movie Awards '94: Breakthrough Performance (Richter), Best Kiss (Jason James Richter/Willy). *WAR, BTV*

Free Willy 2: The Adventure Home 🎞️½ 1995 (PG) While camping in the Pacific Northwest, Jesse is reunited with his orca-pal Willy, who has found a new home along with his whale siblings. But an offshore oil spill separates Willy from his family and threatens their lives, so his human friends must once again come to the rescue. All the principal characters are back, except for Willy (real name Keiko), who is recuperating from a skin virus in Mexico. Animatronics and Gump-like digital effects were used to replicate the real Willy. **98m/C VHS, LV, Closed Caption.** Jason James Richter, Michael Madsen, Jayne Atkinson, August Schellenberg, Jon Tenney, Elizabeth Pena; *D:* Dwight Little; *W:* Corey Blechman, John Mattson; *C:* Laszlo Kovacs; *M:* Basil Poledouris. *WAR*

Free Willy 3: The Adventure 🎞️½ 1997 (PG) Isn't this poor whale ever going to be left in peace? This time around an illegal whaling operation threatens Willie and his orca pod. But 17-year-old Jesse (Richter), who has a summer job as a whale tracker on a research vessel, is determined to rescue his friend, aided by 10-year-old Max (Berry), who's horrified to discover his commercial fisherman father (Kilpatrick) is one of the whalers. **?m/C VHS.** Jason James Richter, Vincent Berry, August Schellenberg, Annie Corley, Patrick Kilpatrick; *D:* Sam Pillsbury; *W:* John Mattson. *NYR*

Freebie & the Bean 🎞️ 1974 (R) Two San Francisco cops nearly ruin the city in their pursuit of a numbers-running mobster. Top-flight car chases and low-level, bigoted humor combine. Watch for Valerie Harper's appearance as Arkin's wife. Followed by a flash-in-the-pan television series. **113m/C VHS, Beta, LV.** Alan Arkin, James Caan, Loretta Swit, Valerie Harper, Jack Kruschen, Mike Kellin; *D:* Richard Rush. *WAR*

Freedom 🎞️ 1981 A young man finds the price of freedom to be very high when he tries to escape from Australian society in a silver Porsche. **102m/C VHS, Beta.** Jon Blake, Candy Raymond, Jad Capelja, Reg Lye, John Clayton. *NO*

Freedom Is Paradise 🎞️ 1989 With his mother dead and his father missing, thirteen-year-old Sasha is growing up in a bleak reform school. Every time he runs away he is caught and severely beaten upon his return. When Sasha learns of his father's whereabouts he sets out on a 1,000 mile journey to the gulag-style prison where is father is being held. Bodrov's directorial debut. In Russian with English subtitles. **75m/C VHS.** *RU D:* Sergei Bodrov. Montreal World Film Festival '89: Best Film. *FCT*

Freedom Road 🎞️ 1979 A made for television drama about a Reconstruction Era ex-slave, portrayed by heavyweight champion Ali, who is elected to the U.S. Senate and subsequently killed while trying to obtain total freedom for his race. Based on a novel by Howard Fast. **186m/C VHS, Beta.** Ron O'Neal, Edward Herrmann, John McLiam, Ernest Dixon, Alfre Woodard, Kris Kristofferson, Muhammad Ali; *D:* Jan Kadar. *WOV, FCT*

Freejack 🎞️½ 1992 (R) Futuristic thriller set in the year 2009, where pollution, the hole in the ozone layer, and the financial gap between the social classes have grown to such horrific proportions that the rich must pillage the past to find young bodies to replace their own. Estevez is a young race car driver whose sudden death makes him an ideal candidate for this bizarre type of surgery. Once transported to the future, he becomes a "Freejack" who must run for his life. Good cast including Jagger and Hopkins brings this one up slightly. Adapted from the novel "Immortality Inc." by Robert Sheckley.*CW:* Language and violence. **110m/C VHS, Beta, LV.** Emilio Estevez, Mick Jagger, Rene Russo, Anthony Hopkins, Jonathan Banks, David Johansen, Amanda Plummer, Grand Bush, Frankie Faison, Esai Morales, John Shea; *D:* Geoff Murphy; *W:* Dan Gilroy, Ronald Shusett, Steven Pressfield; *M:* Trevor Jones, Michael Boddicker. *WAR*

Freeway 🎞️½ 1988 (R) A nurse attempts to find the obsessive killer who shot her husband. The murderer phones a radio psychiatrist from his car, using Biblical quotes, while cruising for new victims. Okay thriller, based on the L.A. freeway shootings. **91m/C VHS, Beta, LV, Closed Caption.** Darlanne Fluegel, James Russo, Billy Drago, Richard Belzer, Michael Callan, Steve Franken, Kenneth Tobey, Clint Howard; *D:* Francis Delia; *W:* Larry Ketron, Darrell Fetty, Francis Delia; *M:* Joe Delia. *NWV, VTR*

Freeway 🎞️½ 1995 (R) Grubby modern retelling of "Little Red Riding Hood" finds surly 16-year-old Vanessa (Witherspoon) escaping from her parole officer to avoid foster care when the cops arrest her mom and stepdad. She takes the family car and heads off to grandma's but car trouble on the freeway leads to a ride from the big bad wolf—Bob Wolverton (Sutherland)—a serial killer preying on young women. Lots of lurid unpleasantness.*CW:* Explicit sexual dialogue, some lurid violence, some sexual situations, drug content. **102m/C VHS, Closed Caption.** Reese Witherspoon, Kiefer Sutherland, Brooke Shields, Wolfgang Bodison, Dan Hedaya, Amanda Plummer, Bokeem Woodbine, Brittany Murphy; *D:* Matthew Bright; *W:* Matthew Bright; *C:* John Thomas; *M:* Danny Elfman. *REP*

The Freeway Maniac 🎬 1988 (R) A low budget thriller about an escaped convict who ends up on a movie set where he continues his former career: murder. Music by former "Doors" guitarist Robby Krieger. 94m/C VHS, Beta. Loren Winters, James Courtney, Shepard Sanders, Donald Hotton; **D:** Paul Winters; **M:** Robby Krieger. *MED*

Freeze-Die-Come to Life 🎬🎬🎬½ *Zamri Oumi Voskresni* 1990 First feature film from Kanevski, who spent 8 years in a labor camp before glasnost. The story of two children who overcome the crushing poverty and bleakness of life in a remote mining community with friendship and humor. Beautifully filmed images, fine acting, touching but never overly sentimental story. The title comes from a children's game of tag. In Russian with English subtitles. 105m/B VHS. RU Pavel Nazarov, Dinara Drukarova; **D:** Vitaly Kanevski. *FXL, BST, ING*

Freeze Frame 🎬🎬½ 1992 Doherty is a high school TV reporter who's determined to capture a biotech conspiracy on video in this funny, fast-paced action flick. Nothing objectionable here. 78m/C VHS, LV, Closed Caption. Shannen Doherty, Charles Haid, Robyn Douglass, Seth Michaels; **D:** William Bindley; **W:** William Bindley. *COL, NLC*

French Can-Can 🎬🎬🎬 *Only the French Can!* 1955 Dramatically sparse but visually stunning depiction of the can-can's revival in Parisian nightclubs. Gabin plays the theater impressario who discovers laundress Arnoul and decides to turn her into the dancing star of his new revue at the Moulin Rouge. In French with English subtitles. 93m/C VHS, Beta, LV. FR Jean Gabin, Francoise Arnoul, Maria Felix, Jean-Roger Caussimon, Edith Piaf, Patachou; **D:** Jean Renoir. *INT, APD*

The French Connection 🎬🎬🎬½ 1971 (R) Two NY hard-nosed narcotics detectives stumble onto what turns out to be one of the biggest narcotics rings of all time. Cat-and-mouse thriller will keep you on the edge of your seat; contains one of the most exciting chase scenes ever filmed. Hackman's portrayal of Popeye Doyle is exact and the teamwork with Scheider special. Won multiple awards. Based on a true story from the book by Robin Moore. Followed in 1975 by "French Connection 2." 102m/C VHS, Beta, LV. Gene Hackman, Roy Scheider, Fernando Rey, Tony LoBianco, Eddie Egan, Sonny Grosso, Marcel Bozzuffi; **D:** William Friedkin; **C:** Owen Roizman. Academy Awards '71: Best Actor (Hackman), Best Adapted Screenplay, Best Director (Friedkin), Best Film Editing, Best Picture; British Academy Awards '72: Best Actor (Hackman); Directors Guild of America Awards '71: Best Director (Friedkin); Edgar Allan Poe Awards '71: Best Screenplay; Golden Globe Awards '72: Best Actor—Drama (Hackman), Best Director (Friedkin), Best Film—Drama; National Board of Review Awards '71: 10 Best Films of the Year, Best Actor (Hackman); New York Film Critics Awards '71: Best Actor (Hackman); Writers Guild of America '71: Best Adapted Screenplay; Nominations: Academy Awards '71: Best Cinematography, Best Sound, Best Supporting Actor (Scheider). *FOX*

French Connection 2 🎬🎬🎬 1975 (R) New York policeman "Popeye" Doyle goes to Marseilles to crack a heroin ring headed by his arch nemesis, Frog One, who he failed to stop in the United States. Dour, super-gritty sequel to the 1971 blockbuster, and featuring one of Hackman's most uncompromising performances. 118m/C VHS, Beta, LV, Closed Caption. Gene Hackman, Fernando Rey, Bernard Fresson; **D:** John Frankenheimer; **W:** Robert Dillon. *FOX*

The French Detective 🎬🎬🎬 1975 Two detectives, one an old-time tough guy and the other a young cynic, are after a ruthless politician and his pet hood. Grim but entertaining. 90m/C VHS, Beta. FR Lino Ventura, Patrick Dewaere, Victor Lanoux; **D:** Pierre Granier-Deferre. *COL*

French Fried Vacation 1979 Zany antics erupt when a group of unattached and consenting adults vacation in Africa. French with English subtitles. 90m/C VHS. Josiane Balasko, Michel Blanc, Mariann Chazel; **D:** Patrice Leconte. *FRA*

French Intrigue 🎬🎬 19?? (R) International agents track drug lords from the U.S. to France in a so-so spy thriller. 90m/C VHS, Beta. Jane Birkin, Curt Jurgens. *BFV*

French Kiss 🎬🎬½ 1995 (PG-13) Ultra cute Kate (Ryan) has a fear of flying but she's more afraid of losing her fiance (Hutton) to a newly met French babe. She jets off to Paris and on the way meets a dashing, but disheveled, French rogue (Kline). What happens next is predictable, but amusing just the same. Plot drags a bit in the middle, but the scenery and banter between Ryan and Kline are a pleasant enough diversion. Kline is at his charming best, while Ryan is typically perky. Watch for Spielvogel's stereotypically rude French hotel concierge. He's a hoot.**CW:** Some sexuality, language, and drug references. 111m/C VHS, LV, Closed Caption. Meg Ryan, Kevin Kline, Timothy Hutton, Jean Reno, Francois Cluzet, Renee Humphrey, Michael Riley, Susan Anbeh, Laurent Spielvogel; **D:** Lawrence Kasdan; **W:** Adam Brooks; **C:** Owen Roizman; **M:** James Newton Howard. *FXV*

The French Lesson 🎬🎬½ *The Frog Prince* 1986 (PG) A romantic British farce from a screenplay by cartoonist Simmonds, dealing with an English girl who goes to school in Paris and finds love. 90m/C VHS, Beta, Closed Caption. GB Alexandre Sterling, Jane Snowdon; **D:** Brian Gilbert; **W:** Posy S. Simmonds. *WAR*

The French Lieutenant's Woman 🎬🎬🎬½ 1981 (R) Romantic love and tragedy in the form of two parallel stories, that of an 19th-century woman who keeps her mysterious past from the scientist who loves her, and the lead actor and actress in the film of the same story managing an illicit affair on the set. Extraordinary performances and beautifully shot. Based on the John Fowles novel. 124m/C VHS, Beta, LV. Meryl Streep, Jeremy Irons, Leo McKern, Lynsey Baxter; **D:** Karel Reisz; **W:** Harold Pinter; **M:** Carl Davis. British Academy Awards '81: Best Actress (Streep); Golden Globe Awards '82: Best Actress—Drama (Streep); Los Angeles Film Critics Association Awards '81: Best Actress (Streep); Nominations: Academy Awards '81: Best Actress (Streep), Best Adapted Screenplay, Best Art Direction/Set Decoration, Best Costume Design, Best Film Editing. *MGM, FOX*

The French Line 🎬🎬 1954 A millionairess beauty travels incognito while trying to sort out which men are after her money, and which ones aren't. The 3-D presentation of Russell's physique in skimpy costumes earned this the condemnation of the Catholic Legion of Decency, which pumped the box office even higher. Lacks the charm of "Gentlemen Prefer Blonds," which it imitates. ♫Comment Allez-Vous; Well, I'll Be Switched; Any Gal From Texas; What Is This That I Feel?; With A Kiss; By Madame Fuelle; Wait Till You See Paris; Poor Andre; The French Line. 102m/C VHS, Beta. Jane Russell, Gilbert Roland, Craig Stevens, Kim Novak, Arthur Hunnicutt, Joi Lansing; **D:** Lloyd Bacon. *CCB, TTC*

French Postcards 🎬🎬 1979 (PG) Three American students study all aspects of French culture while they spend their junior year of college at the Institute of French Studies in Paris. By the same writers who penned "American Graffiti" a few years earlier. 95m/C VHS, Beta. Miles Chapin, Blanche Baker, Valerie Quennessen, Debra Winger, Mandy Patinkin, Marie-France Pisier; **D:** Willard Huyck; **W:** Gloria Katz, Willard Huyck. *PAR*

French Quarter 🎬🎬½ 1978 (R) A dual story about a young girl in the modern-day French Quarter of New Orleans who is also the reincarnation of a turn-of-the-century prostitute. Everyone gets to play two roles but this film is more curiosity than anything else. 101m/C VHS, Beta. Bruce Davison, Virginia Mayo, Lindsay Bloom, Alisha Fontaine, Lance LeGault, Anne Michelle; **D:** Dennis Kane. *NO*

French Quarter Undercover 🎬 1985 (R) Two undercover cops in New Orleans thwart a terrorist plot aimed at the World's Fair. 84m/C VHS, Beta. Michael Parks, Bill Holiday; **D:** Joe Catalanotto. *LIV*

French Silk 🎬🎬½ 1994 (PG-13) Homicide detective (Horsley) falls for a lingerie designer (Lucci) who's a murder suspect. Filmed on location in New Orleans. Made for TV production with additional footage. "R" rating is for nudity (not Lucci's). Based on the novel by Sandra Brown.**CW:** Some sensuality. 90m/C VHS, LV. Susan Lucci, Lee Horsley, Shari Belafonte, R. Lee Ermey, Sarah Marshall, Bobby Hosea, Jim Metzler, Joe Warfield, Paul Rosenberg; **D:** Noel Nosseck. *APX*

The French Touch 🎬🎬½ 1954 Fernandel stars in this French farce about a shepherd who decides to open his own clip joint as a hairdresser and finds himself a hit among the Parisiennes. Fair to middling comedy. 84m/B VHS. FR Fernandel, Renee Devillers, Georges Chamarat; **D:** Jean Boyer. *NOS*

French Twist 🎬🎬½ *Bushwhacked; Gazon Maudit* 1995 (R) Romantic comedy about housewife Loli (Abril), tiredly coping with her realtor/husband Laurent (Chabat) and their two sons. Then Loli meets appealing stranger Marijo (Balasko), a very matter-of-fact lesbian, and when she discovers her hubby is a chronic philanderer, Loli gets revenge by inviting Marijo to move in with them. Laurent realizes he loves his wife but she's having too much fun and there's finally an interesting showdown between Laurent and Marijo over Loli. The French title, which translates literally to "Cursed Lawn," is an old slang term for lesbian. French with subtitles.**CW:** Sexuality, nudity and language. 100m/C VHS, LV, Closed Caption. FR Victoria Abril, Alain Chabat, Josiane Balasko, Ticky Holgado; **D:** Josiane Balasko; **W:** Josiane Balasko, Telsche Boorman; **C:** Gerard de Battista; **M:** Manuel Malou. Cesar Awards '96: Best Screenplay; Nominations: Cesar Awards '96: Best Actor (Chabat), Best Director (Balasko), Best Film, Best Supporting Actor (Holgado); Golden Globe Awards '96: Best Foreign Film. *TOU*

The French Way 🎬🎬½ 1940 One of the legendary Baker's few films, in which she portrays a Parisian nightclub owner playing matchmaker for a young couple. In French with English subtitles. 72m/B VHS, Beta. FR Josephine Baker, Micheline Presle, Georges Marchal; **D:** Jacques de Baroncelli. *VDM, FCT*

The French Woman 🎬 1979 (R) Softcore story of blackmail, murder, and sex involving French cabinet ministers mixing passion and politics. From the director of "Emmanuelle." 97m/C VHS, Beta. Francoise Fabian, Klaus Kinski; **D:** Just Jaeckin; **M:** Serge Gainsbourg. *NO*

Frenchman's Farm 🎬½ 1987 (R) A young woman witnesses a killing at a deserted farmhouse. When she tells the police, they tell her that the murder happened forty years before. Average thriller that probably won't keep you on the edge of your seat. 90m/C VHS, Beta. AU Tracey Tanish, David Reyne, John Meillon, Norman Kaye, Tui Bow; **D:** Ron Way. *NO*

Frenzy 🎬🎬½ *Latin Quarter* 1946 A sculptor, pushed over the brink of sanity when he discovers that his wife is having an affair, turns to his art for solace...and seals his wife's corpse in a statue. Creepy. 75m/B VHS. GB Derrick DeMarney, Frederick Valk, Joan Greenwood, Joan Seton, Valentine Dyall, Martin Miller; **D:** Vernon Sewell; **W:** Vernon Sewell. *SNC*

Frenzy 🎬🎬 1972 (R) The only film in which Hitchcock was allowed to totally vent the violence and perverse sexuality of his distinctive vision, in a story about a strangler stalking London women in the late '60s. Finch plays the convicted killer—only he's innocent and must escape prison to find the real killer. McGowen is wonderful as the put-upon police inspector. A bit dated, but still ferociously hostile and cunningly executed. 116m/C VHS, Beta, LV. GB Jon Finch, Barry Foster, Barbara Leigh-Hunt, Anna Massey, Alec McCowen, Vivien Merchant, Billie Whitelaw, Jean Marsh; **D:** Alfred Hitchcock; **W:** Anthony Shaffer. National Board of Review Awards '72: 10 Best Films of the Year. *USH*

Fresh 🐾🐾½ **1994 (R)** Intelligent 12-year-old boy runs heroin in the morning and sells crack after school in a tough Brooklyn neighborhood. Enterprising young man draws life lessons from chess-hustler father Jackson and heroin-dealing mentor Esposito, so he looks for a way out of the dead-end business. First time director Yakin plays it straight, foregoing the usual Hollywood-style rap and automatic weapons approach to convey the message that circumstances can kill innocence just as effectively as a bullet. Startling but subdued atmosphere allows the plot and characters to become more complicated than first suspected. Excellent performance by newcomer Nelson as the kid. 114m/C VHS, Beta, LV, Closed Caption. **FR** Samuel L. Jackson, Giancarlo Esposito, Sean Nelson, N'Bushe Wright, Ron Brice, Jean LaMarre, Luis Lantigua, Yul Vazquez, Cheryl Freeman; **D:** Boaz Yakin; **W:** Boaz Yakin; **C:** Adam Holender. Independent Spirit Awards '95: Debut Performance (Nelson); Sundance Film Festival '94: Special Jury Prize, Filmmakers Trophy; Nominations: Independent Spirit Awards '95: Best Supporting Actor (Esposito). *MAX*

Fresh Horses 🐾🐾 **1988 (PG-13)** A wrong-side-of-the-tracks Depression-era romance. McCarthy is the engaged college boy who falls for backwoods girl Ringwald, who turns out to have a destructive secret. 92m/C VHS, Beta, LV, Closed Caption. Molly Ringwald, Andrew McCarthy, Patti D'Arbanville, Ben Stiller; **D:** David Anspaugh; **M:** David Foster. *COL*

Fresh Kill 🐾 **1987** A young guy from Chicago goes to Hollywood, and gets mixed up in drugs and murder. Made for video. 90m/C VHS, Beta. Flint Keller, Patricia Parks; **D:** Joseph Merhi. *NO*

The Freshman 🐾🐾🐾🐾 **1925** Country boy Lloyd goes to college and, after many comic tribulations, saves the day with the winning touchdown at the big game and wins the girl of his dreams. This was one of the comedian's most popular films. 75m/B VHS, Beta. Harold Lloyd, Jobyna Ralston, Brooks Benedict, James Anderson, Hazel Keener; **D:** Fred Newmeyer, Sam Taylor; **W:** Sam Taylor. *TLF*

The Freshman 🐾🐾½ **1990 (PG)** Brando, in an incredible parody of his Don Corleone character, makes this work. Broderick is a college student in need of fast cash, and innocent enough to believe that any work is honest. A good supporting cast and a twisty plot keep things interesting. Sometimes heavy handed with its sight gags, but Broderick and Brando push the movie to hilarious conclusion. Don't miss Burt Parks' musical extravaganza. 102m/C VHS, Beta, LV, 8mm, Closed Caption. Marlon Brando, Matthew Broderick, Penelope Ann Miller, Maximilian Schell, Bruno Kirby, Frank Whaley, Jon Polito, Paul Benedict, Richard Gant, B.D. Wong, Bert Parks; **D:** Andrew Bergman; **W:** Andrew Bergman; **M:** David Newman. *COL, FCT*

Freud Leaving Home 🐾🐾 **1991** Freud (Roor) is the nickname of 25-year-old Angelique, who lives with her Jewish family in Stockholm. Problems erupt when her sister and brother return home for their mother's 60th birthday and all learn of her fatal illness. The siblings are forced to confront themselves and their relationships with each other and their mother. Swedish with subtitles. 100m/C VHS. **SW** Gunilla Roor, Ghita Norby, Philip Zanden, Jessica Zanden; **D:** Suzanne Bier. *FRF*

Frida 🐾🐾½ **1984** The life of controversial Mexican painter Frido Kahlo is told via deathbed flashbacks using the artist's paintings to set the scenes. In Spanish with English subtitles. 108m/C VHS, Beta, LV. **SP** Ofelia Medina, Juan Jose Gurrola, Max Kerlow; **D:** Paul Leduc. *CVC, IME, APD*

Friday 🐾🐾½ **1995 (R)** It's "Boyz N' the Hood" meets "Good Times". Ice Cube wrote and stars as Craig in this humorous look into life in the 'hood. Craig's just lost his job and spends his time sitting on the porch with his pot smoking sidekick Smokey (Tucker), with the two getting mixed up in a variety of crazy antics involving their kooky neighbors. The laughs come at the expense of overworn cliches and stereotypical characters, but

there's originality in the movie's energy and boldness (i.e. the local dope dealer is also the neighborhood ice cream man). To some, this "Friday" could be something to look forward to. **CW:** Pervasive strong language and drug use, and for a brutal fight. 91m/C VHS, LV, Closed Caption. Ice Cube, Chris Tucker, Bernie Mac, John Witherspoon, Regina King, Nia Long, Tiny Lister; **D:** F. Gary Gray; **W:** Ice Cube, DJ Pooh; **C:** Gerry Lively; **M:** Frank Fitzpatrick. Nominations: MTV Movie Awards '96: Breakthrough Performance (Tucker), Best On-Screen Duo (Chris Tucker/Ice Cube), Best Comedic Performance (Tucker). *NLC, TTC*

Friday Foster 🐾½ **1975 (R)** A beautiful, young photographer investigates an assassination attempt and uncovers a conspiracy against black politicians. Based on the Chicago Tribune comic strip. 90m/C VHS, Beta. Pam Grier, Yaphet Kotto, Thalmus Rasulala, Carl Weathers, Godfrey Cambridge; **D:** Arthur Marks. *ORI, FCT*

Friday the 13th 🐾🐾 **1980 (R)** Notable as among the first in a very long series of slasher flicks, with effects by Tom Savini. A New Jersey camp reopens after it's been closed for 20 years after a history of "accidental" deaths. And the horror begins again. Six would-be counselors arrive to get the place ready. Each is progressively murdered: knifed, speared, and axed. Followed by numerous, equally gory sequels. 95m/C VHS, Beta, LV, Closed Caption. Betsy Palmer, Adrienne King, Harry Crosby, Laurie Bartrarr, Mark Nelsor, Kevin Bacon; **D:** Sean S. Cunningham. *PAR*

Friday the 13th, Part 2 woof! **1981 (R)** New group of teen camp counselors are gruesomely executed by the still undead Jason. Equally as graphic as the first installment; followed by several more gorefests. 87m/C VHS, LV, Closed Caption. Amy Steel, John Furey, Adrienne King, Betsy Palmer; **D:** Steve Miner. *PAR*

Friday the 13th, Part 3 woof! **1982 (R)** Yet another group of naive counselors at Camp Crystal Lake fall victim to the maniacal Jason. The 3-D effects actually helped lessen the gory effects, but this is still awful. Followed by more disgusting sequels. 96m/C VHS, Beta, LV. Dana Kimmell, Paul Krata, Richard Brooker; **D:** Steve Miner. *PAR*

Friday the 13th, Part 4: The Final Chapter woof! **1984 (R)** Jason escapes from the morgue to once again slaughter and annihilate teenagers at a lakeside cottage. Preceded by three earlier "Friday the 13th" films, equally as graphic. The title's also a lie since there's several more sequels to look forward to. 90m/C VHS, Beta, LV, Closed Caption. Erich Anderson, Judie Aronson, Kimberly Beck, Peter Barton, Tom Everett, Corey Feldman, Crispin Glover; **D:** Joseph Zito; **W:** Barney Cohen; **C:** Joao Fernandes. *PAR*

Friday the 13th, Part 5: A New Beginning woof! **1985 (R)** Jason rises from the dead to slice up the residents of a secluded halfway house. The sequels, and the sameness, never stop. See Part 6... 92m/C VHS, Beta, LV, Closed Caption. John Shepherd, Melanie Kinnaman, Shavar Ross, Richard Young, Juliette Cummins, Corey Feldman; **D:** Danny Steinmann; **W:** David M. Cohen. *PAR*

Friday the 13th, Part 6: Jason Lives woof! **1986 (R)** One of the few youths not butchered by Jason digs him up and discovers he's not (and never will be) dead. Carnage ensues...and the sequels continue. 87m/C VHS, Beta, LV, Closed Caption. Thom Mathews, Jennifer Cooke, David Kagen; **D:** Tom McLoughlin. *PAR*

Friday the 13th, Part 7: The New Blood woof! **1988 (R)** A young camper with telekinetic powers accidentally unchains Jason from his underwater lair with the now-familiar results. There's still another bloody sequel to go. 90m/C VHS, Beta, LV, Closed Caption. Lar Park Lincoln, Kevin Blair, Susan Blu; **D:** John Carl Buechler; **W:** Daryl Haney; **C:** Paul Elliott. *PAR*

Friday the 13th, Part 8: Jason Takes Manhattan 🐾 **1989 (R)** Yet another sequel, with the ski-masked walking slaughterhouse transported to New York. Most of the previous action in the movie takes place on a cruise ship. This one is less gruesome than others in the series. Followed by "Jason Goes to Hell: The Final Friday." 96m/C VHS, Beta, LV, Closed Caption. Jensen Daggett, Scott Reeves, Peter Mark Richman, Barbara Bingham; **D:** Rob Hedden; **W:** Rob Hedden; **C:** Bryan England. *PAR*

Fridays of Eternity 🐾🐾 **1981** A romantic comedy about loyalty, fidelity, love, and lovers all with a tinge of the supernatural. In Spanish with English subtitles. 89m/C VHS. **AR** Thelma Biral, Hector Alterio; **D:** Hector Olivera. *NO*

Fried Green Tomatoes 🐾🐾🐾 **1991 (PG-13)** Two stories about four women, love, friendship, Southern charm, and eccentricity are untidily held together by wonderful performances. Unhappy, middle-aged Evelyn (Bates), meets the talkative 83-year-old Ninny Threadgoode (Tandy). Ninny reminisces about her Depression-era life in the town of Whistle Stop, Alabama and the two women, Idgie (Masterson) and Ruth (Parker), who ran the local cafe. Back-and-forth narrative as it tracks multiple storylines is occasionally confusing, though strong character development holds interest. Surprising box office hit adapted by Fannie Flagg from her novel "Fried Green Tomatoes at the Whistle Stop Cafe." 130m/C VHS, Beta, LV, Closed Caption. Kathy Bates, Jessica Tandy, Mary Stuart Masterson, Mary-Louise Parker, Cicely Tyson, Chris O'Donnell, Stan Shaw, Gailard Sartain, Timothy Scott, Gary Basaraba, Lois Smith, Grace Zabriskie; **D:** Jon Avnet; **W:** Fannie Flagg, Carol Sobieski; **M:** Thomas Newman. National Media Owl Awards '92: First Prize; Nominations: Academy Awards '91: Best Adapted Screenplay, Best Supporting Actress (Tandy). *USH*

Frieda 🐾🐾½ **1947** An RAF officer brings his German wife home after the war and she is naturally distrusted by his family and neighbors. An interesting look at post-war bigotry. 97m/B VHS. **GB** David Farrar, Glynis Johns, Mai Zetterling, Flora Robson, Albert Lieven; **D:** Basil Dearden. *NOS, VYY, VEC*

Friend of the Family 2 🐾 **1996 (R)** Disturbed young woman decides to get revenge on the man who used and abandoned her by becoming his family's nanny. Also available in an unrated version. 90m/C VHS, LV. Shauna O'Brien, Paul Michael Robinson. *TRI, ORI*

Friendly Fire 🐾🐾🐾 **1979** Based on a true story of an American family in 1970 whose soldier son is killed by "friendly fire" in Vietnam, and their efforts to uncover the circumstances of the tragedy. Touching and powerful, with an excellent dramatic performance by Burnett. Made for television. 146m/C VHS, Beta, Closed Caption. Carol Burnett, Ned Beatty, Sam Waterston, Timothy Hutton; **D:** David Greene. *FOX*

Friendly Persuasion 🐾🐾🐾 *Except For Me and Thee* **1956** Earnest, solidly acted tale about a peaceful Quaker family struggling to remain true to its ideals in spite of the Civil War which touches their farm life in southern Indiana. Cooper and McGuire are excellent as the parents with Perkins fine as the son worried he's using his religion to hide his cowardice. Based on a novel by Jessamyn West. 140m/C VHS, Beta, LV, Closed Caption. Gary Cooper, Dorothy McGuire, Anthony Perkins, Marjorie Main, Charles Halton; **D:** William Wyler; **W:** Michael Wilson; **C:** Ellsworth Fredericks; **M:** Dimitri Tiomkin. Cannes Film Festival '57: Best Film; Nominations: Academy Awards '56: Best Adapted Screenplay, Best Director (Wyler), Best Picture, Best Song ("Friendly Persuasion (Thee I Love)"), Best Sound, Best Supporting Actor (Perkins). *FOX*

Friends 🐾 **1971 (R)** Ho-hum drama about an orphaned French girl and an unloved English boy who meet, become friends, and decide to run away together, setting up house in a deserted beach cottage. They even have a baby before they're discovered. Provides no insight into the teenagers dilemmas. Followed by "Paul and Michelle." 101m/C VHS, Closed Caption. GB Sean Bury, Anicee Alvina, Pascale Roberts, Sady Rebbot, Ronald Lewis; D: Lewis Gilbert; M: Elton John. PAR

Friends 🎬🎬 1995 Story of three South African women sharing an apartment in Johannesburg. Fox is a white political activist, Burgers, an Afrikaner archaeologist, and Kente, a black teacher. When Fox plants a bomb that takes two innocent lives, their loyalties are tested. Debut for director Proctor. 109m/C VHS. Kerry Fox, Michele Burgers, Dambisa Kente; D: Elaine Proctor; W: Elaine Proctor. FRF

Friends Forever 🎬🎬🎬 1986 Conformity, sexuality, and friendship are explored in this coming-of-age drama. Kristian is a shy, conformist sixteen-year-old, starting off at a new school. He finds himself drawn to two different young men who equally dominate his class. Henrik's androgynous sexual charm is equaled by his independence while the moody Patrick is the leader of a band of troublemakers. Kristian gains in self-confidence by their friendship but is tested when he learns Patrick is gay. 95m/C VHS. DK D: Stefan Christian Henszelman. FCT

Friends, Lovers & Lunatics 🎬½ Crazy Horse; She Drives Me Crazy 1989 A weekend turns into a romantic nightmare/laugh-fest when a man visits his ex-girlfriend and her new "friend", and winds up in a new romance himself. 87m/C VHS, Beta, LV. CA Daniel Stern, Deborah Foreman, Sheila McCarthy, Page Fletcher, Elias Koteas; D: Stephen Withrow. FRH, IME

A Friendship in Vienna 🎬🎬½ 1988 The friendship of two young teenage girls, one Jewish, and the other the daughter of a Nazi collaborator, is tested as WWII looms over Europe and the Nazis begin their persecution of Austrian Jews. Adapted from the book "Devil in Vienna" by Doris Orgel. Made for cable television. 100m/C VHS, Closed Caption. Jenny Lewis, Ed Asner, Jane Alexander, Stephen Macht, Rosemary Forsyth, Ferdinand "Ferdy" Mayne, Kamie Harper; D: Arthur Seidelman; W: Richard Alfieri. DIS

Fright 🎬 Spell of the Hypnotist 1956 A woman—convinced that she died in 1889 as part of a suicide pact with Prince Rudolph of Austria—seeks help from a psychiatrist who promptly falls in love with her (didn't Freud say it was supposed to be the other way around?). ?m/B VHS. Nancy Malone, Eric Fleming, Frank Marth, Humphrey Davis, Ned Glass, Norman Burton; D: W. Lee Wilder. SNC

Fright 🎬🎬 Night Legs 1971 (PG) A baby-sitter is menaced by a mental hospital escapee. He turns out to be the father of the boy she is watching. Tense but violent thriller. 84m/C VHS. GB Susan George, Honor Blackman, Ian Bannen, John Gregson, George Cole, Dennis Waterman, Tara Collinson, Maurice Kaufman, Michael Brennan, Roger Lloyd Pack; D: Peter Collinson; W: Tutor Gates; C: Ian Wilson; M: Harry Robinson. REP, MOV

Fright House 🎬 1989 (R) Two stories of terror. "Fright House" features witches preparing an old mansion for a visit from the Devil. "Abandon" explains the prolonged youth of a teacher to her young student. 110m/C VHS, Beta. Al Lewis, Duane Jones; D: Len Anthony. NO

Fright Night 🎬🎬½ 1985 (R) It's Dracula-versus-the-teens time when Charley suspects that his new neighbor descends from Count Vlad's line. He calls in the host of "Fright Night," the local, late-night, horror-flick series, to help deghoul the neighborhood. But they have a problem when the vampire discovers their plans (and nobody belives them anyway). Sarandon is properly seductive as the bloodsucker. Followed by sequel. 106m/C VHS, Beta, LV, Closed Caption. William Ragsdale, Chris Sarandon, Amanda Bearse, Roddy McDowall, Stephen Geoffreys, Jonathan Stark, Dorothy Fielding; D: Tom Holland; W: Tom Holland; M: Brad Fiedel. COL

Fright Night 2 🎬🎬 1988 (R) The sequel to the 1985 release "Fright Night," in which the harassed guy from the original film learns slowly that the vampire's sister and her entourage have come to roost around his college. Not quite as good as the original but the special effects are worth a look. 108m/C VHS, Beta, LV. Roddy McDowall, William Ragsdale, Traci Lind, Julie Carmen; D: Tommy Lee Wallace; W: Tommy Lee Wallace, Tim Metcalfe; M: Brad Fiedel. LIV

The Frightened City 🎬🎬½ 1961 Waldo Zhernikov (Lom) decides to unite all six of London's crime syndicates into one conglomerate that would control the city. But when he gets power-mad, rival gangster Harry Foulcher (Marks) breaks away and forms his own organization. Naturally, there's a war between the factions. Paddy Damion (Connery in an early role), one of Waldo's gunsels, is sent to get rid of Foulcher. 91m/B VHS, Closed Caption. GB Herbert Lom, Alfred Marks, Sean Connery, John Gregson, Yvonne Romain, Kenneth Griffith; D: John Lemont; W: Leigh Vance; C: Desmond Dickinson; M: Norrie Paramor. REP, FCT

The Frighteners 🎬🎬½ 1996 (R) Con man Frank Bannister (Fox) has a unique scam—he works with a group of ghosts who haunt a home until Frank comes along to drive them out, for the right price. But the small town of Fairwater is plagued by a serial killer's evil spirit and Frank and his spiritual cronies face the challenge of getting rid of the ghost before the police decide to get rid of Frank. Interesting horror-comedy takes a lot of twists and turns to get where its going, but the payoff in gore and humor is worth it for fans of the genre. New Zealand helmer Jackson makes his American directorial debut. CW: Terror/violence. 106m/C VHS, LV, Closed Caption. Michael J. Fox, Trini Alvarado, Peter Dobson, Dee Wallace Stone, John Astin, Jeffrey Combs, Troy Evans, Chi McBride, Jake Busey, R. Lee Ermey; D: Peter Jackson; W: Peter Jackson, Frances Walsh; C: Alun Bollinger, John Blick; M: Danny Elfman. USH

Frightmare 🎬🎬½ Frightmare 2 1974 (R) A seemingly quiet British couple do indulge in one strange habit—they're cannibals. Released on video as "Frightmare 2" to avoid confusion with the 1981 film. 86m/C VHS, Beta. GB Deborah Fairfax, Kim Butcher, Rupert Davies, Sheila Keith; D: Pete Walker. PSM

Frightmare 🎬 1981 (R) Great horror star dies, but he refuses to give up his need for adoration and revenge. 84m/C VHS, Beta. Ferdinand "Ferdy" Mayne, Luca Bercovici, Nita Talbot, Peter Kastner; D: Norman Thaddeus Vane. VES

The Fringe Dwellers 🎬🎬½ 1986 (PG) An Aborigine family leave their shantytown and move to the white, middle-class suburbs of Australia, encountering prejudice and other difficulties. Well acted and interesting but the ending's a letdown. 98m/C VHS, Beta. AU Kristina Nehm, Justine Saunders, Bob Maza, Kylie Belling, Denis Walker, Ernie Dingo; D: Bruce Beresford; W: Bruce Beresford, Rhoisin Beresford; M: George Dreyfus. NO

The Frisco Kid 🎬🎬 No Knife 1979 (R) An innocent orthodox rabbi (Wilder) from Poland is sent to the wilds of San Francisco during the 1850s gold rush to lead a new congregation. He lands in Philadelphia, joins a wagon train and is promptly robbed and abandoned. He eventually meets up with a not-too-bright robber (Ford) who finds himself unexpectly befriending the man and undergoing numerous tribulations in order to get them both safely to their destination. This isn't a laugh riot and some scenes fall distinctly flat but Wilder is sweetness personified and lends the movie its charm. 119m/C VHS, Beta. Gene Wilder, Harrison Ford, Ramon Bieri, Val Bisoglio, George DiCenzo, Penny Peyser, William Smith; D: Robert Aldrich; W: Michael Elias; C: Robert B. Hauser. WAR

Frisk 🎬🎬 1995 Disturbing depictions of sex/murder fantasies come courtesy of letters written by Dennis (Gunther), a part of the L.A. S&M scene, to his former boyfriend, Julian (Laplante).

Just exactly how far Dennis has gone with some of his like-minded sexual partners is the question. Has he become the killer he claims to be? Adapted from Dennis Cooper's 1991 novel. 87m/C VHS. Michael Gunther, Jaie Laplante, Craig Chester, Parker Posey, James Lyons, Alexis Arquette, Raoul O'Connell, Michael Stock; D: Todd Verow; W: Todd Verow, Jim Dwyer, George LaVoo; C: Greg Watkins. FCT

Fritz the Cat 🎬🎬🎬 1972 Ralph Bakshi's animated tale for adults about a cat's adventures as he gets into group sex, college radicalism, and other hazards of life in the '60s. Loosely based on the underground comics character by Robert Crumb. Originally X-rated. 77m/C VHS, Beta. D: Ralph Bakshi; W: Ralph Bakshi; M: Ed Bogas. WAR, OM

Frog 1989 A boy adds a frog to his reptile collection but gets the surprise of his life when he finds it's really an enchanted Prince! Followed by "Frogs!" Part of the "Wonderworks" series. 55m/C VHS, Beta, LV, Closed Caption. Paul Williams, Scott Grimes, Shelley Duvall, Elliott Gould, David Grossman. ORI, IME

Frogs 🎬🎬½ 1972 (PG) An environmental photographer working on a small island in Florida interrupts the birthday celebration of a patriarch. He and the folks at the party soon realize that various amphibians animals in the surrounding area are going berserk and attacking humans. One of the first environmentally-motivated animal-vengeance films, and one of the best to come out of the '70s. 91m/C VHS, Beta. Ray Milland, Sam Elliott, Joan Van Ark, Adam Roarke, Judy Pace, Lynn Borden, Mae Mercer, David Gilliam, George Skaff; D: George McCowan; W: Robert Blees; M: Les Baxter. WAR, OM

Frogs! 199? Arlo is almost the most popular boy in school and is hoping to be crowned the king of his school's Spring Fling dance—until he and his friend Gus are turned into frogs by a witch. When Arlo and Gus discover their frog pond is being poisoned, they turn to the geeky Hannah for help. A sequel to "Frog." A viewers' guide is included. Part of the "Wonderworks" series. 55m/C VHS. Shelley Duvall, Elliott Gould, Paul Williams, Scott Grimes, Judith Ivey. PME, HMV, BTV

Frolics on Ice 🎬🎬 1940 Pleasant comedy-musical about a family man saving to buy the barber shop he works at. Irene Dare is featured in several ice skating production numbers. 65m/B VHS, Beta. Roscoe Karns, Lynn (Mary Hart) Roberts, Irene Dare, Edgar Kennedy. VYY

From Beyond 🎬🎬🎬 1986 (R) A gruesome, tongue-in-cheek adaptation of the ghoulish H.P. Lovecraft story. Scientists discover another dimension through experiments with the pineal gland. From the makers of "Re-Animator," and just as funny. 90m/C VHS, Beta, LV, Closed Caption. Jeffrey Combs, Barbara Crampton, Ted Sorel, Ken Foree, Carolyn Purdy-Gordon, Bunny Summers, Bruce McGuire; D: Stuart Gordon; W: Dennis Paoli, Brian Yuzna; M: Richard Band. LIV, VES

From Beyond the Grave 🎬🎬 Creatures 1973 (PG) This horror compendium revolves around a mysterious antique shop whose customers experience various supernatural phenomena, especially when they try to cheat the shop's equally mysterious owner. 98m/C VHS, Beta. GB Peter Cushing, David Warner, Ian Bannen, Donald Pleasence, Margaret Leighton, Lesley-Anne Down, Diana Dors, Ian Ogilvy; D: Kevin Connor. WAR

From Dusk Till Dawn 🎬🎬½ 1995 (R) Escaped cons Seth and Richie Gecko (Clooney and Tarantino) pick up an ex-preacher (Keitel) and his two kids (Lewis and Liu) as hostages en route to their Mexican rendezvous spot, a raunchy biker joint run (unbenownst to them) by vampires. Feels like two movies in one, as Rodriguez's and Tarantino's styles don't necessarily mesh as much as they coexist. The first half features Tarantino's gift for snappy dialogue and somewhat sympathetic scumbags while the barroom finale shows off Rodriguez's mastery of the go-for-broke action set piece. Clooney proves the jump from

TV to movies can be made successfully. Penned by Tarantino in 1990 during his video store days, he used the fee to get "Reservoir Dogs" off the ground. **CW:** Strong violence and gore, language and nudity. **108m/C VHS, LV, Closed Caption.** George Clooney, Quentin Tarantino, Harvey Keitel, Juliette Lewis, Fred Williamson, Richard "Cheech" Marin, Salma Hayek, Michael Parks, Tom Savini, Ernest Liu, Kelly Preston, John Saxon, Danny Trejo; **D:** Robert Rodriguez; **W:** Quentin Tarantino; **C:** Guillermo Navarro; **M:** Graeme Revell. MTV Movie Awards '96: Breakthrough Performance (Clooney); Nominations: Golden Raspberry Awards '96: Worst Supporting Actor (Tarantino). TOU

From Hell to Borneo 🐾½ 1964 (PG) A mercenary must defend his secluded island from pirates and gangsters. **90m/C VHS, Beta.** George Montgomery, Torin Thatcher, Julie Gregg, Lisa Moreno; **D:** George Montgomery. NO

From Hell to Victory 🐾🐾 1979 (PG) Group of friends of different nationalities vow to meet each year in Paris on the same date but WWII interrupts their lives and friendships. Director Lenzi used the alias Hank Milestone. Good battle scenes but nothing special. **100m/C VHS, Beta. SP FR** George Peppard, George Hamilton, Horst Buchholz, Jean-Pierre Cassel, Capucine, Sam Wanamaker, Anny Duperey, Ray Lovelock; **D:** Umberto Lenzi. MED, HHE, VTR

From Here to Eternity 🐾🐾🐾🐾 1953 Complex, hard-hitting look at the on and off-duty life of soldiers at the Army base in Honolulu in the days before the Pearl Harbor attack. There's sensitive Pvt. Pruitt (Clift), his always in trouble best friend Maggio (Sinatra), and their good-guy top sergeant (Lancaster) who just happens to be having a torrid affair with the commander's wife (Kerr). Pruitt, meanwhile, is introduced to a club "hostess" (Reed) who is a lot more vulnerable than she's willing to admit. A movie filled with great performances. Still has the best waves-on-the-beach love scene in filmdom. Based on the novel by James Jones, which was toned down by the censors. **118m/B VHS, Beta, LV, 8mm.** Burt Lancaster, Montgomery Clift, Frank Sinatra, Deborah Kerr, Donna Reed, Ernest Borgnine, Philip Ober, Jack Warden, Mickey Shaughnessy, George Reeves, Claude Akins; **D:** Fred Zinnemann; **W:** Daniel Taradash; **C:** Burnett Guffey; **M:** George Duning. Academy Awards '53: Best Black and White Cinematography, Best Director (Zinnemann), Best Film Editing, Best Picture, Best Screenplay, Best Sound, Best Supporting Actor (Sinatra), Best Supporting Actress (Reed); Directors Guild of America Awards '53: Best Director (Zinnemann); Golden Globe Awards '54: Best Supporting Actor (Sinatra); National Board of Review Awards '53: 10 Best Films of the Year; New York Film Critics Awards '53: Best Actor (Lancaster), Best Director (Zinnemann), Best Film; Nominations: Academy Awards '53: Best Actor (Clift), Best Actor (Lancaster), Best Actress (Kerr), Best Costume Design (B & W), Original Dramatic/Comedy Score; Golden Globe Awards '54: Best Director (Zinnemann). COL, BTV

From Here to Eternity 🐾🐾½ 1979 (PG-13) From here to eternity...and back on the silver screen. Remake of the 1953 classic is based on James Jones' novel about life on a Hawaiian military base just before WWII. Decent actioner, but no Oscar-winner this time around. Made for television. **110m/C VHS, Beta, LV.** Natalie Wood, Kim Basinger, William Devane, Steve Railsback, Peter Boyle, Will Sampson, Andy Griffith, Roy Thinnes, Barbara Hershey; **D:** Buzz Kulik. THV, FCT

From Here to Maternity 🐾🐾½ 1985 A made-for-television soap opera-based spoof about modern maternity. Three women want to be pregnant but their significant others aren't interested in paternity. **40m/C VHS, Beta.** Carrie Fisher, Arleen Sorkin, Lauren Hutton, Griffin Dunne, Paul Reiser. LIV, VES

From Hollywood to Deadwood 🐾🐾 1989 (R) A beautiful starlet is kidnapped and the private eye searching for her discovers blackmail and danger. **90m/C VHS, Beta, LV, Closed Caption.** Scott Paulin, Jim Haynie, Barbara Schock; **W:** Rex Pickett. MED, FCT, IME

From Noon Till Three 🐾🐾½ 1976 (PG) A change of pace role for Bronson as a two-bit gunfighter in a spoof of western legends. Bronson has a brief romance with Ireland who, believing him dead, fictionalizes their relationship in a series of books and builds the mediocre Dorsey into a western hero. When he turns up alive no one, including Ireland, believes that he is the real Dorsey and he's gradually driven crazy. Good script, weak direction but Bronson is likeable. **99m/C VHS.** Charles Bronson, Jill Ireland, Douglas Fowley, Stan Haze, Damon Douglas; **D:** Frank D. Gilroy; **W:** Frank D. Gilroy; **C:** Lucien Ballard; **M:** Elmer Bernstein. MGM

From Russia with Love 🐾🐾🐾½ 1963 (PG) Bond is back and on the loose in exotic Istanbul looking for a super-secret coding machine. He's involved with a beautiful Russian spy and has the SPECTRE organization after him, including villainess Rosa Klebb (she of the killer shoe). Lots of exciting escapes but not an over-reliance on the gadgetry of the later films. The second Bond feature, thought by many to be the best. The laserdisc edition includes interviews with director Terence Young and others on the creative staff. The musical score and special effects can be separated from the actors' dialogue. Also features publicity shots, American and British trailers, on-location photos, and movie posters. **125m/C VHS, Beta, LV, Closed Caption. GB** Sean Connery, Daniela Bianchi, Pedro Armendariz Sr., Lotte Lenya, Robert Shaw, Eunice Gayson, Walter Gotell, Lois Maxwell, Bernard Lee, Desmond Llewelyn, Nadja Regin, Alizia Gur, Martine Beswick, Leila; **D:** Terence Young; **C:** Ted Moore; **M:** John Barry. MGM, CRC, TLF

From "Star Wars" to "Jedi": The Making of a Saga 1983 Using copious amounts of actual footage from the films, this movie follows the production of all three "Star Wars" sagas, concentrating on the special effects involved. **65m/C VHS, Beta, Closed Caption.** David Prowse, Harrison Ford, Carrie Fisher, Billy Dee Williams, Alec Guinness; **D:** George Lucas. FOX, FLI

From the Dead of Night 🐾🐾🐾 1989 A spooky chiller about a near-death experience. Fashion designer Wagner narrowly escapes death but gets close enough to the other side that six of the dead feel cheated that she didn't join them. They decide to rectify the mistake and Wagner is pursued by the shadowy figures. Based on the novel "Walkers" by Gary Bradner. Made for television. **192m/C VHS.** Lindsay Wagner, Bruce Boxleitner, Diahann Carroll, Robert Prosky, Robin Thomas, Merritt Butrick, Joanne Linville; **D:** Paul Wendkos. AIP

From the Earth to the Moon 🐾🐾 1958 A mad scientist invents a new energy source and builds a rocket which takes him, his daughter, and two other men for some adventures on the moon. Based on the novel by Jules Verne. **100m/C VHS, Beta, LV.** George Sanders, Joseph Cotten, Debra Paget, Don Dubbins; **D:** Byron Haskin; **W:** Robert Blees. NO

From the Hip 🐾🐾 1986 (PG) A young lawyer (Nelson) gets the chance of a lifetime when his office assigns a murder case to him. The only problem is that he suspects his client is very guilty indeed and must discover the truth without breaking his code of ethics. Nelson's courtroom theatrics are a bit out of hand, as he flares his nostrils at every opportunity. The movie is encumbered by a weak script and plot as well as a mid-story switch from comedy to drama. **112m/C VHS, Beta, LV, Closed Caption.** Judd Nelson, Elizabeth Perkins, John Hurt, Ray Walston; **D:** Bob (Benjamin) Clark; **W:** Bob (Benjamin) Clark, David Kelly. ORI, WAR

From the Journals of Jean Seberg 🐾🐾 1995 An imaginary look at the life of the ill-fated actress, who began her career as a 17-year-old, miscast in Otto Preminger's "Saint Joan," achieved fame in Godard's "Breathless," and became a suicide at age 40 in 1979. Seberg (Hurt) dispassionately narrates her life story as she views film clips, from small-town Iowa teenager to would-be star, through abusive relationships, drugs and drinking, political activism, and FBI harassment. **97m/C VHS. D:** Mark Rappaport; **W:** Mark Rappaport; **C:** Mark Daniels. WBF, PPI

From the Life of the Marionettes 🐾🐾🐾 1980 (R) A repressed man in a crumbling marriage rapes and kills a young prostitute. Another look at the powers behind individual motivations from Bergman, who uses black and white and color to relate details of the incident. **104m/C VHS, Beta, LV. SW** Robert Atzorn, Christine Buchegger, Martin Benrath, Rita Russek, Lola Muethel, Walter Schmidinger, Heinz Bennent; **D:** Ingmar Bergman; **W:** Ingmar Bergman; **C:** Sven Nykvist. HMV

From the Manger to the Cross 🐾🐾 1915 This version of the Passion play was the first film to be done on location in Palestine. Reenacts the Nativity, the flight into Egypt, and the crucifixion. Color-tinted. **71m/C VHS.** R. Henderson-Bland, Alice Hollister, Gene Gauthier; **D:** Sidney Olcott; **W:** Gene Gauthier, Sidney Olcott. KIV

From the Mixed-Up Files of Mrs. Basil E. Frankweiler 🐾🐾½ 1995 (PG) Runaway siblings (Barnwell and Lee) secretly hide out in a New York art museum. They get caught up in trying to determine the authenticity of a sculpture (could it be the work of Michelangelo?) and turn to the statue's last owner, elusive art patron Mrs. Basil E. Frankweiler (Bacall). Based on the Newbery Award-winning novel by E.L. Konigsburg. Made for TV. **92m/C VHS.** Lauren Bacall, Jean Marie Barnwell, Jesse Lee; **D:** Marcus Cole. HMK

From the Terrace 🐾🐾½ 1960 Newman is a wealthy Pennsylvania boy who goes to New York and marries into even more money and social position when he weds Woodward. He gets a job with her family's investment company and neglects his wife for business. She turns to another man and when he goes home for a visit he also finds a new romance which leads to some emotional soul searching. The explicitness of O'Hara's very long novel was diluted by the censors and Newman's performance is a stilted disappointment. Loy, as Newman's alcoholic mother, earned the best reviews. **144m/C VHS, Beta, LV.** Paul Newman, Joanne Woodward, Myrna Loy, Ina Balin, Felix Aylmer, Leon Ames, George Grizzard, Patrick O'Neal, Barbara Eden, Mae Marsh; **D:** Mark Robson; **W:** Ernest Lehman; **M:** Elmer Bernstein. FOX

The Front 🐾🐾🐾 1976 (PG) Woody is the bookmaker who becomes a "front" for blacklisted writers during the communist witch hunts of the 1950s in this satire comedy. The scriptwriter and several of the performers suffered blacklisting themselves during the Cold War. Based more or less on a true story. **95m/C VHS, Beta, LV.** Woody Allen, Zero Mostel, Herschel Bernardi, Michael Murphy, Danny Aiello, Andrea Marcovicci; **D:** Martin Ritt; **W:** Walter Bernstein; **C:** Michael Chapman; **M:** Dave Grusin. National Board of Review Awards '76: 10 Best Films of the Year; Nominations: Academy Awards '76: Best Original Screenplay. COL

The Front Page 🐾🐾🐾½ 1931 The original screen version of the Hecht-MacArthur play about the shenanigans of a battling newspaper reporter and his editor in Chicago. O'Brien's film debut here is one of several hilarious performances in this breathless pursuit of an exclusive with an escaped death row inmate. **101m/B VHS, Beta.** Adolphe Menjou, Pat O'Brien, Edward Everett Horton, Mae Clarke, Walter Catlett; **D:** Lewis Milestone; **C:** Hal Mohr. National Board of Review Awards '31: 10 Best Films of the Year; Nominations: Academy Awards '31: Best Actor (Menjou), Best Director (Milestone), Best Picture. NOS, MRV, HHT

The Front Page 🐾🐾½ 1974 (PG) A remake of the Hecht-MacArthur play about the managing editor of a 1920s Chicago newspaper who finds out his ace reporter wants to quit the business and get married. But first an escaped convicted killer offers the reporter an exclusive interview. **105m/C VHS, LV.** Jack Lemmon, Walter Matthau, Carol Burnett, Austin Pendleton, Vincent Gardenia, Charles

Durning, Susan Sarandon; **D:** Billy Wilder; **W:** Billy Wilder, I.AL. Diamond; **C:** Jordan Cronenweth. USH

Frontier Days ♪½ **1934** Cody goes undercover to capture the leader of a gang of stagecoach robbers. He also manages to capture a killer along the way. **60m/B VHS, Beta.** Bill Cody, Ada Ince, Wheeler Oakman; **D:** Sam Newfield. NOS, DVT

Frontier Fugitives ♪½ **1945** When a trapper is murdered—allegedly by Indians—the Texas Rangers ride in to investigate. **58m/B VHS.** Tex Ritter, Dave O'Brien, Guy Wilkerson, Lorraine Miller, I. Stanford Jolley, Jack Ingram; **D:** Harry Fraser. NOS

Frontier Horizon ♪♪ **1939** Wayne and the Three Mesquiteers help out ranchers whose land is being bought up by crooked speculators. **55m/B VHS, Beta.** John Wayne, Jennifer Jones, Ray Corrigan, Raymond Hatton; **D:** George Sherman. REP, CAB

Frontier Justice ♪♪ **1935** Gibson is the foolish son of a cattle owner who has been forced into an insane asylum because of a battle over water rights. Naturally, he must take on responsibility and rescue his father. **56m/B VHS, Beta.** Hoot Gibson, Richard Cramer; **D:** Robert McGowan. NOS, VCN, DVT

Frontier Law ♪½ **1943** Hayden and the boys ride into town to clean out the bad guys and clear a friend wrongly accused of murder. **55m/B VHS.** Russell Hayden, Jennifer Holt, Dennis Moore, Fuzzy Knight, Jack Ingram, Hal Taliaferro; **D:** Elmer Clifton; **W:** Elmer Clifton. MOV

Frontier Outlaws ♪♪ **1944** A gang of villains is selling stolen cattle, and Crabbe poses as an interested buyer to catch them in the act. Laughs are provided by Lynn as a judge, and "Fuzzy" St. John as Crabbe's sidekick. **58m/B VHS.** Buster Crabbe, Al "Fuzzy" St. John, Frances Gladwin, Marin Sais, Charles "Blackie" King, Jack Ingram, Kermit Maynard, Edward Cassidy, Emmett Lynn, Budd Buster; **D:** Sam Newfield. GPV, MRV, NOS

Frontier Pony Express ♪♪ **1939** Roy and Trigger do their best to help the Pony Express riders who are being attacked by marauding gangs in California during the time of the Civil War. Plenty of action here. **54m/B VHS, Beta.** Roy Rogers; **D:** Joseph Kane. NOS, MED, DVT

Frontier Scout ♪♪ **1938** Action-packed western has Wild Bill Hickock, portrayed by former opera singer Houston, forcing Lee's surrender in the Civil War before pursuing cattle rustlers out West. **60m/B VHS, Beta.** George Houston, Mantan Moreland; **D:** Sam Newfield. NOS, DVT, RXM

Frontier Uprising ♪½ **1961** Stunning cinematography makes up for weak narrative in this otherwise routine oater. Davis stars as a frontier scout battling hordes of Mexicans and Indians while trying to gain control of California for the U.S. Based on the short story "Kit Carson" by George Bruce. **68m/B VHS.** Jim Davis, Nancy Hadley, Ken Mayer, Nestor Paiva, Don O'Kelly; **D:** Edward L. Cahn; **W:** Owen Harris. DVT

Frontier Vengeance ♪½ **1940** Barry is falsely accused of murder and works to clear his name while at the same time romancing a stagecoach driver who's trying to win a race with a rival stagecoach line. **54m/B VHS, Beta.** Donald (Don "Red") Barry, Nate Watt. MED, RXM

The Frontiersmen ♪♪ **1938** Things plod along at the little red schoolhouse until Hoppy and the guys have to take off after some rustlers. Features the members of the St. Brendan Boys Choir as the schoolboys. Unusual for its lack of gunplay until near the end. **71m/B VHS.** William Boyd, George "Gabby" Hayes, Russell Hayden, Evelyn Venable, Clara Kimball Young, Charles Hughes, Dick Jones, Roy Barcroft, Emily Fitzroy; **D:** Lesley Selander. NOS

Frostbiter: Wrath of the Wendigo ♪ **1994 (R)** Disappointing Troma entry takes itself a bit too seriously. It wants to be an "Evil Dead on Ice" (we even see a movie poster for same in the flick); the plot involves hunters trapped in the frozen woods of Northern Michigan

by the evil spirit "Wendigo." It's short on original horror and the laff-factor is not up to usual Troma standards (although the killer chili was a nice touch). The only saving grace is the quirky soundtrack, including said chili's theme song by Randall and Allan Lynch, "March of the Undead" by the 3-D Invisibles, and "I'm a Hellbilly" by Elvis Hitler. Based on the comic book character of the same name.**CW:** Horror violence and gore, and for some brief nudity and language. **90m/C VHS.** Ron Asheton, Lori Baker, Patrick Butler, Devlin Burton; **D:** Tom Chaney; **W:** Tom Chaney; **C:** Tom Chaney. TTV

Frozen Alive ♪ **1964** A scientist experiments with suspended animation but, wouldn't you know, someone murders his wife while he's on ice. Apparently being frozen stiff does not an alibi make, and he becomes the prime suspect. Much unanimated suspense. **80m/B VHS.** GB GE Mark Stevens, Marianne Koch, Delphi Lawrence, Joachim Hansen, Walter Rilla, Wolfgang Lukschy; **D:** Bernard Knowles. MOV

Frozen Assets ♪ **1992 (PG-13)** Pathetic attempt at comedy from Long and Bernsen. He's an ambitious executive who finds the "bank" of his corporation's latest acquisition deals in sperm and not cash. Still, he expects this acquisition to be a success and comes up with a number of tacky ways, much to the horror of the facility's administrator, to make that profit margin grow.**CW:** Sex-related elements. **93m/C VHS, Closed Caption.** Corbin Bernsen, Shelley Long, Larry Miller, Dody Goodman, Gerrit Graham, Paul Sand, Teri Copley, Matt Clark; **D:** George Miller; **W:** Don Klein, Tom Kartozian. FXV

Frozen Terror ♪ **1980 (R)** A madman resembling both Jack Frost and Jack the Ripper claims victims at random. **93m/C VHS, Beta.** Bernice Stegers; **D:** Lamberto Bava. LIV, VES

Fu Manchu **1956** Villainous arch-criminal Fu Manchu plots to enslave the world in "The Golden God" and "The Master Plan," two episodes from the television series. **60m/B VHS, Beta.** Glenn Gordon, Laurette Luez, Clark Howat, Lee Matthews. DVT

The Fugitive ♪♪♪♪ **1948** Fonda is a priest devoted to God and the peasants under his care when he finds himself on the run after religion is outlawed in this nameless South-of-the-border dictatorship. Despite the danger of capture, he continues to minister to his flock. His eventual martyrdom unites the villagers in prayer. Considered Fonda's best performance; Ford's favorite film. Shot on location in Mexico. Excellent supporting performances. Based on the Graham Greene novel "The Power and the Glory" although considerably cleaned up for the big screen—Greene's priest had lost virtually all of his faith and moral code. Here the priest is a genuine Ford hero. A gem. **99m/B VHS, Beta, LV, Closed Caption.** Henry Fonda, Dolores Del Rio, Pedro Armendariz Sr., J. Carrol Naish, Leo Carrillo, Ward Bond, Robert Armstrong, John Qualen; **D:** John Ford; **W:** Dudley Nichols. TTC

The Fugitive ♪♪♪½ **1993 (PG-13)** Exciting big-screen version of the '60s TV series with the same basic storyline: Dr. Richard Kimble's wife is murdered and he's implicated, so he goes on the lam to find the real killer, the mysterious one-armed man. Lots of mystery and action, particularly a spectacular train/bus crash sequence, keeps the tension high. Due to illness, Richard Jordan was replaced by Krabbe after production had begun. Alec Baldwin was originally slated to star as Kimble, but backed out and Ford was cast. Sound familiar? Ford also replaced Baldwin as Jack Ryan in "Patriot Games." The second highest grossing movie of 1993. **127m/C VHS, LV, Closed Caption, DVD.** Harrison Ford, Tommy Lee Jones, Jeroen Krabbe, Julianne Moore, Sela Ward, Joe Pantoliano, Andreas Katsulas, Daniel Roebuck; **D:** Andrew Davis; **W:** David N. Twohy, Jeb Stuart; **C:** Michael Chapman; **M:** James Newton Howard. Academy Awards '93: Best Supporting Actor (Jones); Golden Globe Awards '94: Best Supporting Actor (Jones); Los Angeles Film Critics Association Awards '93: Best Supporting Actor (Jones); MTV Movie Awards '94: Best On-Screen Duo (Harrison Ford/Tommy Lee Jones),

Best Action Sequence; Blockbuster Entertainment Awards '95: Action Actor, Video (Ford); Nominations: Academy Awards '93: Best Cinematography, Best Film Editing, Best Picture, Best Sound, Best Sound Effects Editing, Best Original Score; British Academy Awards '93: Best Supporting Actor (Jones); Directors Guild of America Awards '93: Best Director (Davis); Golden Globe Awards '94: Best Actor—Drama (Ford), Best Director (Davis); MTV Movie Awards '94: Best Actor (Ford), Best Film; Writers Guild of America '93: Best Adapted Screenplay. WAR

Fugitive Among Us ♪♪ **1992** Dedicated cop is determined to return an escaped rapist to a life behind bars and he's aided by a victim who would really rather forget the whole thing. Made for TV. **97m/C VHS, Closed Caption.** Peter Strauss, Eric Roberts, Elizabeth Pena, Lauren Holly. ABC, PAR

The Fugitive Kind ♪♪½ **1960** A young drifter walks into a sleepy Mississippi town and attracts the attention of three of its women with tragic results. Based upon the Tennessee Williams' play "Orpheus Descending." good performances but the writing never hangs well-enough together for coherence. **122m/B VHS, Beta.** Marlon Brando, Anna Magnani, Joanne Woodward, Victor Jory, R.G. Armstrong, Maureen Stapleton; **D:** Sidney Lumet; **C:** Boris Kaufman. MGM, FOX

The Fugitive: Premiere Episode **1963** In this introductory episode to the television series, Janssen plays Dr. Richard Kimble, who's wrongly convicted of murdering his wife. After a train taking him to prison derails, he makes his escape and begins his search for the real culprit, the mysterious one-armed man. But Kimble's pursued by the relentless Lt. Gerard. Additional episodes available. **45m/B VHS.** David Janssen, Barry Morse, Vera Miles, Brian Keith. MOV, GKK

Fugitive Rage ♪♪ **1996 (R)** Tara McCormick (Schumacher) winds up behind bars when she shoots the mobster who was acquitted for murdering her sister. She teams up with her cellmate (O'Brien) to fight back against the mob who's put a bounty on her head and a covert government agency also out to use her. Prerequisite prison shower sequences, tough babes, and lots of action.**CW:** Strong sexuality, some violence and brief language. **90m/C VHS.** Wendy Schumacher, Shauna O'Brien, Jay Richardson; **D:** Fred Olen Ray. APX

Fugitive Road ♪♪ **1934** The great von Stroheim stars as a crusty but soft-hearted border guard who arbitrarily detains people at the crossing. **69m/B VHS.** Erich von Stroheim, Wera Engels, Leslie Fenton, Harry Holman; **D:** Frank Strayer. NOS

The Fugitive: Taking of Luke McVane ♪♪ **1915** An early silent western in which Hart upholds the cowboy code of honor. **28m/B VHS, Beta.** William S. Hart, Enid Markey. VYY

The Fugitive: The Final Episode **1967** The final episode of the acclaimed series, aired on August 29, 1967, in which Dr. Richard Kimble meets up with the one-armed man who murdered his wife and tries to bring him to justice before Lt. Gerard can bring Kimble in. Episode was the most watched television program up to that time. **78m/C VHS.** David Janssen, Barry Morse, Bill Raisch, Diane Baker, Joseph Campanella, Michael Constantine. MOV

Fugitive Valley ♪½ **1941** Muddled plot has villains-turned-heroes on the trail of some outlaws and stolen money. Terhune shows off some of his vaudeville skills, and King sings some songs. **61m/B VHS.** Ray Corrigan, John "Dusty" King, Max Terhune, Julie Duncan, Glenn Strange, Robert F. (Bob) Kortman, Tom London, Reed Howes; **D:** S. Roy Luby. NOS, HEG

Fugitive X ♪½ **1996** Advertising exec gets to be the prey for a group of thrill-seeking hunters. He's got a handgun, a small head start, and the slime taking bets on how long he'll last. You've seen this before. **97m/C VHS.** David Heavener, Richard Norton, Lynn-Holly Johnson, William Windom, Chris Mitchum, Robert Z'Dar; **D:** David Heavener; **W:** David Heavener. SLI

Fulfillment ♂♂½ *The Fulfillment of Mary Gray* **1989 (PG-13)** Ladd stars as Mary Gray, a turn-of-the-century woman comfortably married to good but unexciting farmer, Jonathan (Levine). He's unable to give his wife the child they both desperately want and when his younger brother, Aaron (Smith), visits, the hope is Aaron can be persuaded to help out. The naturally volatile situation is heightened by the fact Mary is very drawn to the handsome Aaron anyway, and the feeling is mutual. Based on the novel "The Fulfillment" by LaVyrle Spencer. Made for television. **CW:** Mature subject matter. **96m/C VHS, Closed Caption.** Cheryl Ladd, Ted Levine, Lewis Smith; **D:** Piers Haggard. REP

Full Body Massage ♂♂ **1995 (R)** Wealthy art gallery owner Nina (Rogers) spends much of her time alone at her California dream home—except for a weekly appointment with young masseur Douglas (Burgard). But one week, the older Fitch (Brown) comes instead and begins discussing life and personal spirituality while he massages away the self-indulgent cares of the world-weary Nina. Good work by the leads in a chatty cable movie. **CW:** Nudity and some sexuality. **93m/C VHS, Closed Caption.** Mimi Rogers, Bryan Brown, Christopher Burgard, Elizabeth Barondes; **D:** Nicolas Roeg; **W:** Dan Gurskis; **C:** Anthony B. Richmond; **M:** Harry Griegson-Williams. PAR

Full Circle ♂♂ *The Haunting of Julia* **1977 (R)** Peter Straub wrote this eerie tale about a grief-stricken young woman whose child has recently died. To overcome her loss, she moves into a new house—which is haunted by the ghost of a long-dead child. **96m/C VHS, Beta. CA GB** Mia Farrow, Keir Dullea, Tom Conti, Jill Bennett, Robin Gammell; **D:** Richard Loncraine; **M:** Colin Towns. MED

Full Contact ♂♂ **1992** Nightclub bouncer Jeff helps his friend Sam escape from a loan shark. But Sam has doublecrossed him and now thinks that Jeff is dead in an arranged explosion. But Jeff's survived and plans to seek a suitable revenge. Cantonese with subtitles. **99m/C VHS.** HK Chow Yung Fat, Anthony Wong; **D:** Ringo Lam. TAI, FCT

Full Contact ♂♂ **1993 (R)** Farmhand Luke Powers heads for the decadence of Los Angeles to find his older brother. When three thugs make the mistake of trying to rob him, Luke shows off his martial arts skills. When Luke finds out his brother has been murdered by gamblers involved in an illegal back alley kickboxing circuit, he vows to get revenge. **97m/C VHS.** Jerry Trimble, Howard Jackson, Alvin Prouder, Gerry Blanck, Denise Buick; **D:** Rick Jacobson; **W:** Beverly Gray. COL

Full Eclipse ♂♂ **1993 (R)** Max Dire (Van Peebles) is seduced by the fetching Casey (Kensit) into joining a fierce elite group of underground cops whose mission is to wipe out crime. However, Max soon learns that the secret of their power is a serum which turns them into werewolves. Max is now faced with a decision: join forces with them, or expose them. Either way, blood will flow. Interesting special effects. Unrated version also available. **CW:** Language, brief nudity, and strong violence. **97m/C VHS, LV.** Mario Van Peebles, Patsy Kensit, Bruce Payne, Anthony John Denison; **D:** Anthony Hickox. HBO

Full Exposure: The Sex Tape Scandals ♂½ **1989 (R)** Sleazy drama about a murdered call girl who was blackmailing her clients with sex videos. A cop and his inexperienced female partner are assigned to catch the killer. Made for television. **95m/C VHS, Closed Caption.** Jennifer O'Neill, Lisa Hartman Black, Vanessa Williams, Anthony John Denison, Peter Jurasik; **D:** Noel Nosseck; **W:** Stephen Zito; **M:** Dana Kaproff. WOV

Full Fathom Five ♂½ **1990 (PG)** Central American militants, angered by America's invasion of Panama, hijack a submarine and threaten a nuclear assault on Houston. Boring and dumb. **81m/C VHS, Beta.** Michael Moriarty, Maria Rangel, Michael

Cavanaugh, John Lafayette, Todd Field, Daniel Faraldo; **D:** Carl Franklin; **W:** Bart Davis. MGM

Full Hearts & Empty Pockets ♂½ **1963** Follows the happy-go-lucky adventures of a young, handsome, impoverished gentleman on the loose in Rome. Dubbed in English. **88m/B VHS, Beta.** IT GE Linda Christian, Gino Cervi, Senta Berger; **D:** Camillo Mastrocinque. VYY

Full Metal Jacket ♂♂♂½ **1987 (R)** A three-act Vietnam War epic, about a single Everyman impetuously passing through basic training then working in the field as an Army photojournalist and fighting at the onset of the Tet offensive. First half of the film is the most realistic bootcamp sequence ever done. Unfocused but powerful. Based on the novel by Hasford, who also co-scripted. **116m/C VHS, Beta, LV, 8mm, Closed Caption.** Matthew Modine, R. Lee Ermey, Vincent D'Onofrio, Adam Baldwin, Dorian Harewood, Arliss Howard, Kevyn Major Howard, Ed O'Ross; **D:** Stanley Kubrick; **W:** Gustav Hasford, Stanley Kubrick, Michael Herr. Nominations: Academy Awards '87: Best Adapted Screenplay. WAR, FCT

Full Metal Ninja ♂ **1989** When his family is kidnapped, a trained martial artist trails their abductors and swears revenge. **90m/C VHS, Beta.** Patrick Allen, Pierre Kirby, Sean Odell, Jean Paul, Renato Sala; **D:** Charles Lee. IMP

The Full Monty ♂♂♂ **1996 (R)** A group of laid off Yorkshire mill workers come up with a unique way to earn some money in this amusing Britcom. When exuberant Gaz (Carlyle) notices the local women lining up to see the Chippendale dancers, he persuades his mates to launch a striptease act (to Donna Summer's "Hot Stuff") themselves. But these guys are hardly cover boy material—they're variously overweight, middle-aged, depressed, and shy. Nevertheless, they turn out to be an unexpected success despite numerous mishaps and misunderstandings. Title refers to the fact that they strip down to their birthday suits. **CW:** Language and some nudity. **90m/C VHS. GB** Robert Carlyle, Tom Wilkinson, Mark Addy, Steve Huison, William Snape; **D:** Peter Cattaneo; **W:** Simon Beaufoy; **C:** John de Borman. NYR

Full Moon in Blue Water ♂♂½ **1988 (R)** His wife's been dead a year, he owes back taxes on his bar, his father has Alzheimer's, and his only form of entertainment is watching old home movies of his wife. Floyd has problems. Enter Louise, a lonely spinster who feels that it is her personal duty to change his life. If she doesn't do it, the bizarre things that happen after her arrival will. **96m/C VHS, Beta, LV.** Gene Hackman, Teri Garr, Burgess Meredith, Elias Koteas, Kevin Cooney, David Doty; **D:** Peter Masterson; **W:** Bill Bozzone; **M:** Phil Marshall. MED, VTR

Full Moon in Paris ♂♂½ *Les Nuits De La Pleine* **1984 (R)** A young woman in Paris moves out on her architect lover in order to experience freedom. Through a couple of random relationships, she soon finds that what she hoped for is not what she really wanted. **101m/C VHS, Beta.** FR Pascale Ogier, Tcheky Karyo, Fabrice Luchini; **D:** Eric Rohmer; **W:** Eric Rohmer; **C:** Renato Berta. Venice Film Festival '84: Best Actress (Ogier). XVC, MED

Full of Life ♂♂½ **1956** Holliday stars in this domestic comedy about a non-religious young woman who had married, in a civil ceremony, into a strict, Italian-Catholic family. Although she is now eight months pregnant the family still wants the couple to have a church wedding. Holliday is a winning personality and the humor is lightly handled. **91m/C VHS.** Judy Holliday, Richard Conte, Salvatore Baccaloni, Esther Minciotti; **D:** Richard Quine. FCT

The Fuller Brush Girl ♂♂½ **1950** Lots of slapstick with Ball as a door-to-door saleswoman unexpectedly involved in a murder. She and dim-bulb boyfriend Albert are chased by cops, murderers, and smugglers in this frantic farce. Sequel to Red Skelton's (who has a cameo) 1948 film "The Fuller Brush Man." **84m/B VHS.** Lucille Ball,

Eddie Albert, Carl Benton Reid, Gale Robbins, Jeff Donnell, John Litel, Fred Graham, Lee Patrick; **Cameos:** Red Skelton; **D:** Lloyd Bacon; **W:** Frank Tashlin. COL

The Fuller Brush Man ♂♂½ *That Man Mr. Jones* **1948** A newly hired Fuller Brush man becomes involved in murder and romance as he tries to win the heart of his girlfriend. A slapstick delight for Skelton fans. **93m/B VHS, Beta, LV.** Red Skelton, Janet Blair, Don McGuire, Adele Jergens; **D:** Frank Tashlin. COL

Fun ♂♂ **1994** Another in the thrill kill genre. 14-year-old Bonnie (Witt) and 15-year-old Hillary (Humphrey) are best friends (and possibly lovers) who have stabbed to death an old woman—seemingly for kicks and to cement their loyalty to each other. (Can you say Leopold and Loeb?) Convicted and in a reformatory, they're documenting their actions, separately (in black & white sequences), to counselor Jane (Hope) and tabloid journalist John (Moses). Bleak dysfunction adapted by Bosley from his play. **95m/C VHS.** Alicia Witt, Renee Humphrey, Leslie Hope, William R. Moses, Ania Suli; **D:** Rafael Zelinski; **W:** James Bosley; **C:** Jens Sturup; **M:** Marc Tschantz. Nominations: Independent Spirit Awards '95: Debut Performance (Witt), First Screenplay. GRE, SPC

Fun & Fancy Free ♂♂♂ **1947 (G)** Part-animated, part-live-action Disney feature is split into two segments: "Bongo" with Dinah Shore narrating the story of a happy-go-lucky circus bear looking for love; and "Mickey and the Beanstalk"—a "new" version of an old fairy tale. Disney's last performance as the voice of Mickey and the only film to star Mickey, Donald Duck, Jiminy Cricket and Goofy. **73m/C VHS. V:** Walt Disney. DIS

Fun Down There woof! **1988** This small-town boy-comes-to-the-big city is so bad, it's...bad. A naive—and unsympathetic—gay man from upstate New York moves to Greenwich Village and has fun down there (and they don't mean Australia). **110m/C VHS.** Michael Waite, Nickolas Nagurney, Gretchen Somerville, Martin Goldin, Kevin Och; **D:** Roger Stigliano; **W:** Michael Waite, Roger Stigliano. WBF, FCT

Fun in Acapulco ♂♂ **1963** Former trapeze artist Elvis romances two beauties and acts as a part-time lifeguard and night club entertainer. He must conquer his fear of heights for a climactic dive from the Acapulco cliffs. Features ten musical numbers. ♪Fun in Acapulco; Vino, Dinero y Amor; Mexico; The Bullfighter Was A Lady; El Toro; Marguerita; (There's) No Room To Rhumba (In A Sports Car); I Think I'm Going To Like It Here; You Can't Say No In Acapulco. **97m/C VHS, Beta.** Elvis Presley, Ursula Andress, Elsa Cardenas, Paul Lukas, Alejandro Rey, Larry Domasin, Howard McNear; **D:** Richard Thorpe; **C:** Daniel F. Fapp. FOX, MVD

Fun with Dick and Jane ♂♂ **1977 (PG)** An upper-middle class couple turn to armed robbery to support themselves when the husband is fired from his job. Though it has good performances, the film never develops its intended bite. **104m/C VHS, Beta.** George Segal, Jane Fonda, Ed McMahon; **D:** Ted Kotcheff; **W:** Jerry Belson, David Giler, Mordecai Richler; **C:** Fred W. Koenekamp; **M:** Ernest Gold. COL

The Funeral ♂♂♂ **1984** A sharp satire of the clash of modern Japanese culture with the old. The hypocrisies, rivalries and corruption in an average family are displayed at the funeral of its patriarch who also happened to own a house of ill repute. Itami's breakthrough film; Japanese with subtitles. **112m/C VHS.** JP Tsutomu Yamazaki, Nobuko Miyamoto, Kin Sugai, Ichiro Zaitsu, Nekohachi Edoya, Shoji Otake; **D:** Juzo Itami. REP, FCT

The Funeral ♂♂♂ **1996 (R)** Ferrara fuels fantastic performances from his famous thesps in this fatalistic tale of a family of gangsters in 1930's New York. Flashbacks from the opening funeral scene show a complex and troubled family of Italian brothers (Walken, Penn, and Gallo), from their formative years through their quest for justice after youngest brother Johnny is murdered. Not just another mob movie; characters are multi-dimensional with interesting quirks and Penn, especially, sprints into his role. More subtle than "Bad Lieutenant" and less pretentious than "The Addiction," this Ferrara flick is the one to see. **CW:** Strong crude sex scenes, strong violence and language. **96m/C VHS.** Christopher Walken, Benicio Del Toro, Vincent Gallo, Christopher Penn, Isabella Rossellini, Annabella Sciorra, John Ventimiglia, Paul Hipp, Gretchen Mol; **D:** Abel Ferrara; **W:** Nicholas St. John; **C:** Ken Kelsch; **M:** Joe Delia. Nominations: Independent Spirit Awards '97: Best Actor (Penn), Best Cinematography, Best Director (Ferrara), Best Film, Best Screenplay. *HMK*

Funeral for an Assassin ♂½ 1977 **(PG)** A professional assassin seeks revenge for his imprisonment by the government of South Africa, a former client. Planning to kill all of the country's leading politicians, he masquerades as a black man, a cover which is designed to fool the apartheid establishment. **92m/C VHS, Beta.** Vic Morrow, Peter Van Dissel; **D:** Ivan Hall. *GEM, MRV, VTR*

Funeral Home ♂½ *2 Cries in the Night* 1982 Terrified teen spends her summer vacation at her grandmother's tourist home, a former funeral parlor. Rip-off of "Psycho." **90m/C VHS, Beta.** Lesleh Donaldson, Kay Hawtry; **D:** William Fruet. *NO*

Funeral in Berlin ♂♂♂ 1966 Second of the Caine/Harry Palmer espionage films (following up "Ipcress File"), in which the deadpan British secret serviceman arranges the questionable defection of a Russian colonel. Good look at the spy biz and postwar Berlin. "Billion Dollar Brain" continues the series. **102m/C VHS, Beta, LV.** Michael Caine, Eva Renzi, Oscar Homolka; **D:** Guy Hamilton; **W:** Evan Jones. *PAR*

The Funhouse ♂½ 1981 **(R)** Four teenagers spend the night at a carnival funhouse, witness a murder, and become next on the list of victims. From the director of cult favorite "Texas Chainsaw Massacre," but nothing that hasn't been seen before. **96m/C VHS, Beta, LV.** Elizabeth Berridge, Shawn Carson, Cooper Huckabee, Largo Woodruff, Sylvia Miles; **D:** Tobe Hooper; **W:** Larry Block; **M:** John Beal. *USH*

Funland ♂ 1989 **(PG-13)** In the world's weirdest amusement park a clown goes nuts over the new corporate owners' plans for the place and decides to seek revenge. **86m/C VHS, LV.** David Lander, William Windom, Bruce Mahler, Michael McManus; **D:** Michael A. Simpson. *LIV, IME, VES*

Funny About Love ♂½ 1990 **(PG-13)** Fairly absurd tale with dashes of inappropriate black humor about a fellow with a ticking biological clock. Nimoy sheds his Spock ears to direct a star-studded cast in this lame tale of middle-aged cartoonist Wilder who strays from wife Lahti after having problems on the conception end into the welcoming arms of fertile college co-ed Masterson in his quest to contribute to the population count. **107m/C VHS, Beta, LV, 8mm, Closed Caption.** Gene Wilder, Christine Lahti, Mary Stuart Masterson, Robert Prosky, Stephen Tobolowsky, Anne Jackson, Susan Ruttan, David Margulies; **D:** Leonard Nimoy; **W:** Norman Steinberg, David Frankel. *PAR*

Funny Bones ♂♂♂ 1994 **(R)** Struggling comedian Tommy Fawkes (Platt) bombs in Vegas big-time while his Mr. Showbiz father George (Lewis) easily overshadows him at every turn. So Tommy decides to head back to his childhood home in Blackpool, England and figure out his life. What he discovers are the Parkers, a family of British vaudevillians, and the fact that his father stole their routines and, briefly, Mrs. Parker (Caron), resulting in half-brother Jack (Evans) who has all the natural talent Tommy can only dream about. Serious, funny, and hostile with notable performances from Platt and Evans. **CW:** Some language; scene of tragic violence. **128m/C VHS, LV, Closed Caption.** Oliver Platt, Lee Evans, Leslie Caron, Jerry Lewis, Oliver Reed, Ian McNeice, Ruta Lee, Richard Griffith, George Carl, Freddie Davies; **D:** Peter Chelsom; **W:** Peter Chelsom, Peter Flannery; **C:** Eduardo Serra; **M:** John Altman. *TOU*

Funny, Dirty Little War ♂♂½ *No Hambra mas Penas ni Olvido; Funny Little Dirty War* 1983 An Argentinian farce about the petty rivalries in a small village erupting into a violent, mini-civil war. Based on the novel by Osvaldo Soriano. In Spanish with English subtitles. **80m/C VHS. AR** Federico Luppi, Julio de Grazia, Miguel Angel Sola; **D:** Hector Olivera. *NYF, MED, XVC*

Funny Face ♂♂♂ 1957 A musical satire on beatniks and the fashion scene also features the May-December romance between Astaire and the ever-lovely Hepburn. He is a high-fashion photographer (based on Richard Avedon); she is a Greenwich Village bookseller fond of shapeless, drab clothing. He decides to take her to Paris and show her what modeling's all about. The elegant musical score features classic Gershwin. The laserdisc includes the original theatrical trailer and is available in widescreen. ♫Let's Kiss and Make Up; He Loves and She Loves; Funny Face; How Long Has This Been Going On?; Clap Yo' Hands; S'Wonderful; Bonjour Paris; On How To Be Lovely; Marche Funebre. **103m/C VHS, Beta, LV, 8mm.** Fred Astaire, Audrey Hepburn, Kay Thompson, Suzy Parker; **D:** Stanley Donen; **M:** George Gershwin, Ira Gershwin. Nominations: Academy Awards '57: Best Art Direction/Set Decoration, Best Cinematography, Best Costume Design, Best Story & Screenplay. *PAR, FCT*

The Funny Farm ♂½ 1982 Comedy about a group of ambitious young comics striving to make it in the crazy world of comedy at Los Angeles' famous comedy club, The Funny Farm. **90m/C VHS, Beta, Closed Caption.** CA Miles Chapin, Eileen Brennan, Peter Aykroyd; **D:** Ron Clark; **W:** Ron Clark. *VTR*

Funny Farm ♂♂ 1988 **(PG)** Chevy Chase as a New York sportswriter finds that life in the country is not quite what he envisioned. The comedy is uneven throughout, with the best scenes coming at the end. **101m/C VHS, LV, Closed Caption.** Chevy Chase, Madolyn Smith, Joseph Maher, Jack Gilpin, Brad Sullivan, MacIntyre Dixon; **D:** George Roy Hill; **W:** Jeffrey Boam; **M:** Elmer Bernstein. *WAR*

Funny Girl ♂♂♂ 1968 **(G)** Follows the early career of comedian Fanny Brice, her rise to stardom with the Ziegfeld Follies and her stormy romance with gambler Nick Arnstein in a fun and funny look at back stage music hall life in the early 1900s. Streisand's film debut followed her auspicious performance of the role on Broadway. Score was augmented by several tunes sung by Brice during her performances. Excellent performances from everyone, captured beautifully by Wyler in his musical film debut. Followed by "Funny Lady." ♫My Man; Second Hand Rose; I'd Rather Be Blue Over You; People; Don't Rain On My Parade; I'm The Greatest Star; Sadie, Sadie; His Love Makes Me Beautiful; You Are Woman, I Am Man. **151m/C VHS, Beta, LV.** Barbra Streisand, Omar Sharif, Walter Pidgeon, Kay Medford, Anne Francis; **D:** William Wyler; **C:** Harry Stradling. Academy Awards '68: Best Actress (Streisand); Golden Globe Awards '69: Best Actress—Musical/Comedy (Streisand); Nominations: Academy Awards '68: Best Cinematography, Best Film Editing, Best Picture, Best Song ("Funny Girl"), Best Sound, Best Supporting Actress (Medford), Scoring of a Musical. *COL, BTV*

Funny Lady ♂♂½ 1975 **(PG)** A continuation of "Funny Girl," recounting Fanny Brice's tumultuous marriage to showman Billy Rose in the 1930s and her lingering affection for first husband Nick Arnstein. One of the rare sequels which are just as good, or at least almost, as the original. ♫How Lucky Can You Get?; Great Day; More Than You Know; Blind Date; So Long, Honey Lamb; Isn't This Better; Let's Hear It For Me; I Like Him/I Like Her; It's Only a Paper Moon. **137m/C VHS, Beta, LV.** Barbra Streisand, Omar Sharif, James Caan, Roddy McDowall, Ben Vereen, Carole Wells, Larry Gates, Heidi O'Rourke; **D:** Herbert Ross; **W:** Jay Presson Allen, Arnold Schulman; **C:** James Wong Howe. Nominations: Academy Awards '75: Best Cinematography, Best Costume Design, Best Song ("How Lucky Can You Get"),

Best Sound, Original Song Score and/or Adaptation. *COL, FCT*

Funny Money ♂ 1982 Pointed, satirical look at the British habit of financing life with the almighty credit card. Sometimes uneven comedy. **92m/C VHS, Beta. GB** Greg Henry, Elizabeth Daily, Gareth Hunt, Derren Nesbitt, Annie Ross; **D:** James Kenelm Clarke. *LIV*

A Funny Thing Happened on the Way to the Forum ♂♂♂ 1966 A bawdy Broadway farce set in ancient Rome where a conniving, slave plots his way to freedom by aiding in the romantic escapades of his master's inept son. Terrific performances by Mostel and Gilford. Keaton's second-to-last film role. The Oscar-winning score includes such highlights as "Comedy Tonight," "Lovely," and "Everybody Ought to Have a Maid." **100m/C VHS, Beta, LV.** Zero Mostel, Phil Silvers, Jack Gilford, Buster Keaton, Michael Hordern, Michael Crawford, Annette Andre; **D:** Richard Lester; **M:** Ken Thorne. Academy Awards '66: Best Adapted Score. *FOX, FCT*

Funnyman ♂♂ 1994 **(R)** Cartoon splatter courtesy of a demon dressed in classic British jester regalia. Rock 'n' roll mogul Young obtains Lee's creepy ancestral home in a card game but when he visits with his family, everyone but Young is killed by the Funnyman, who uses his victims own weaknesses to dispatch them. A second set of likely candidates arrive when Young's brother Devitt shows up with a motley collection of hangers-on, including psychic Black, who's the only one to realize something's seriously off. **CW:** Horror violence, language and drug content. **89m/C VHS. GB** Tim James, Benny Young, Matthew Devitt, Pauline Black, Ingrid Lacey; *Cameos:* Christopher Lee; **D:** Simon Sprackling; **W:** Simon Sprackling. *AVI*

Furious ♂ 1983 **(PG)** The sister of a young martial arts apprentice is killed by the master, with a great deal of action and special effects. **85m/C VHS, Beta.** Simon Rhee, Howard Jackson, Arlene Montano. *VHE*

The Furious Avenger ♂ 1976 A released convict, on his way to avenging his family's murder, stops a rape and takes on one opponent after another in this rousing kickfest. Dubbed. **84m/C VHS, Beta.** Hsiung Fei, Fan Ling, Chen Pei Ling, Tien Yeh, Wang Mo Chou. *UNI*

The Further Adventures of Tennessee Buck ♂ 1988 **(R)** Mercenary adventurer travels through tropical jungles acting as a guide to a dizzy couple. Along the way, they encounter cannibals, headhunters, and other bizarre jungle things in this lame take on "Indiana Jones." Shot on location in Sri Lanka. **90m/C VHS, Beta, LV.** David Keith, Kathy Shower, Brant Van Hoffman; **D:** David Keith; **M:** John Debney. *MED, VTR*

Further Adventures of the Wilderness Family, Part 2 ♂♂½ *Wilderness Family, Part 2* 1977 **(G)** Depicts the Robinson family who left civilization for the freedom of the Colorado wild. Predictable retread, but more good family adventure drama from the makers of "Adventures of the Wilderness Family." **104m/C VHS, Beta.** Heather Rattray, Ham Larsen, George Flower, Robert F. Logan, Susan Damante Shaw; **D:** Frank Zuniga. *MED, VTR*

Fury ♂♂♂½ 1936 Tracy gives an excellent performance as an innocent young man framed for kidnapping and then nearly murdered by a lynch mob. His plans for revenge are thwarted by his girlfriend, who fears that he will turn into the murderer he has been accused of being. Powerful anti-violence message is well-made, with strong ensemble acting. Lang's favorite of his American-made films. **96m/B VHS, Beta.** Spencer Tracy, Sylvia Sidney, Walter Abel, Bruce Cabot, Edward Ellis, Walter Brennan, Frank Albertson; **D:** Fritz Lang; **C:** Joseph Ruttenberg. Nominations: Academy Awards '36: Best Story. *MGM*

The Fury 🎬🎬 **1978 (R)** The head of a government institute for psychic research finds that his own son is snatched by supposed terrorists who wish to use his lethal powers. The father tries to use another a young woman with psychic power to locate him, with bloody results. A real chiller. **117m/C VHS, Beta.** Kirk Douglas, John Cassavetes, Carrie Snodgress, Andrew Stevens, Amy Irving, Charles Durning, Daryl Hannah; *D:* Brian DePalma; *M:* John Williams. *FOX*

Fury 🎬 **198?** A man and woman meet in the Amazonian jungle and the sparks begin to fly. **75m/C VHS, Beta.** Stuart Whitman, Laura Gemser. *NO*

Fury is a Woman 🎬🎬🎬½ **1961** A Polish version of Shakespeare's Macbeth which ranks with the greatest film translations of his work. In Czarist Russia the passionate wife of a plantation owner begins an affair with a farm hand, and poisons her father-in-law when he finds them out. As her madness grows, she plots the murder of the husband. Letterbox format. In Serbian with English subtitles. **93m/B VHS.** *RU* Olivera Markovic, Ljuba Tadic, Kapitalina Eric; *D:* Andrzej Wajda. *HTV*

The Fury of Hercules 🎬½ *La Furia Di Ercole; Fury of Samson* **1961** It's up to the mighty son of Zeus to free an enslaved group of people from an oppressive, evil ruler. Surely all who stand in his way will be destroyed. Another Italian muscleman film. **95m/C VHS.** *IT* Brad Harris, Brigitte Corey, Mara Berni, Carlo Tamberlani, Serge Gainsbourg, Elke Arendt, Alan Steel; *D:* Gianfranco Parolini. *GKK, SNC*

The Fury of the Wolfman 🎬 **1970** A murdering werewolf is captured by a female scientist who tries to cure his lycanthropy with drugs and brain implants. Pretty slow going, but hang in there for the wolfman versus werewolf climax. **80m/C VHS, Beta.** SP Paul Naschy, Perla Cristal; *D:* Jose Maria Zabalza; *W:* Paul Naschy. *LOO, LOO*

Fury on Wheels 🎬 **1971 (PG)** Tale of men who race cars and wreak havoc and vice versa. **89m/C VHS, Beta.** Judd Hirsch, Tom Ligon, Paul Sorvino, Logan Ramsey, Collin Wilcox-Horne. *NO*

Fury to Freedom: The Life Story of Raul Ries 🎬🎬 **1985** A young man raised in the volatile world of abusive and alcoholic parents grows into an abusive and violent adult. One night, however, he meets something he can't beat up, and it changes his life. **78m/C VHS.** Gil Gerard, John Quade, Tom Silardi. *VCI*

Future Cop 🎬🎬 *Trancers* **1976** A hard-nosed, old-fashioned cop is forced to team with the ultimate partner—a robot. Silly made-for-TV movie, but likable leads. **78m/C VHS, Closed Caption.** Ernest Borgnine, Michael J. Shannon, John Amos, John Larch, Herbert Nelson, Ronnie Clair Edwards; *D:* Jud Taylor; *W:* Danny Bilson, Paul DeMeo. *PAR*

Future Force 🎬 **1989 (R)** In the crime-filled future cops can't maintain order. They rely on a group of civilian mercenaries to clean up the streets. **90m/C VHS, Beta.** David Carradine, Robert Tessier, Anna Rapagna, William Zipp. *AIP*

Future Hunters 🎬 **1988** In the holocaust-blitzed future, a young couple searches for a religious artifact that may decide the future of the planet. **96m/C VHS, Beta, LV.** Robert Patrick, Linda Carol, Ed Crick, Bob Schott; *D:* Cirio H. Santiago. *LIV, VES*

Future Kill 🎬 **1985 (R)** Anti-nuclear activists battle fraternity brothers in this grim futuristic world. Shaky political alliances form between revenge-seeking factions on both sides. **83m/C VHS, Beta, LV.** Edwin Neal, Marilyn Burns, Doug Davis; *D:* Ronald W. Moore; *W:* Ronald W. Moore. *LIV, VES*

Future Shock 🎬🎬 **1993 (PG-13)** Dr. Russell Langdon is a psychiatrist who has been experimenting with virtual reality technology. Unbeknownst to three of his patients he decides to use them as guinea pigs in his work. But confronting their deepest fears only leads to new terrors. Also available in an unrated version.*CW:* Violence and threat. **93m/C VHS.** Bill Paxton, Vivian Schilling, Brion

James, Martin Kove; *D:* Eric Parkinson, Matt Reeves, Oley Sassone. *HMD*

Future Zone 🎬🎬 **1990 (R)** In an attempt to save his father from being murdered, a young man travels backwards in time. **88m/C VHS, LV.** David Carradine, Charles Napier, Ted Prior; *D:* David A. Prior. *AIP*

Futurekick 🎬½ **1991 (R)** In the not so distant future, a kickboxer with an attitude and cyborg capabilities must use every ounce of strength in a battle against evil. **80m/C VHS.** Don "The Dragon" Wilson, Meg Foster, Christopher Penn, Eb Lottimer; *D:* Damian Klaus; *W:* Damian Klaus. *NHO*

Futureworld 🎬🎬 **1976 (PG)** In the sequel to "Westworld," two reporters junket to the new "Futureworld" theme park, where they first support a scheme to clone and control world leaders. Includes footage shot at NASA locations. **107m/C VHS, Beta, LV.** Peter Fonda, Blythe Danner, Arthur Hill, Yul Brynner, Stuart Margolin; *D:* Richard T. Heffron; *W:* George Schenck. *WAR, OM*

Futz 🎬½ **1969** Story from off-Broadway is of a man who loves his pig and the world that can't understand the attraction. Better in original stage production. **90m/C VHS, Beta.** John Pakos, Victor Lipari, Sally Kirkland; *D:* Tom O'Horgan. *NO*

Fuzz 🎬🎬½ **1972 (PG)** Reynolds in the Boston cop on the track of a bomber killing policemen, punks setting winos on fire, and some amorous fellow officers. Combines fast action and some sharp-edged humor. **92m/C VHS, Beta.** Burt Reynolds, Tom Skerritt, Yul Brynner, Raquel Welch, Jack Weston, Charles Martin Smith; *D:* Richard A. Colla; *M:* Dave Grusin. *MGM, FOX*

Fyre 🎬½ **1978 (R)** Young beautiful girl moves from the Midwest to Los Angeles and becomes a prostitute. **90m/C VHS, Beta.** Allen (Goorwitz) Garfield, Lynn Theel, Tom Baker, Cal Haynes, Donna Wilkes, Bruce Kirby; *D:* Richard Grand. *MED*

"G" Men 🎬🎬🎬½ **1935** Powerful story based loosely on actual events that occurred during FBI operations in the early 1930s, with Cagney on the right side of the law, though still given to unreasonable fits of anger. Raised and educated by a well-known crime kingpin, a young man becomes an attorney. When his friend the FBI agent is killed in the line of duty, he joins the FBI to seek vengeance on the mob. But his mob history haunts him, forcing him to constantly prove to his superiors that he is not under its influence. Tense and thrilling classic. **86m/B VHS, Beta.** James Cagney, Barton MacLane, Ann Dvorak, Margaret Lindsay, Robert Armstrong, Lloyd Nolan, William Harrigan, Regis Toomey; *D:* William Keighley. *MGM, CCB*

G-Men Never Forget *Code 645* **1948** Moore, former stunt-man and future Lone Ranger, stars in this 12-part serial about FBI agents battling the bad guys. Lots of action. On two cassettes. **167m/B VHS.** Clayton Moore, Roy Barcroft, Ramsay Ames, Drew Allen, Tommy Steele, Eddie Acuff; *D:* Fred Brannon, Yakima Canutt. *REP, MLB*

G-Men vs. the Black Dragon 1943 Reedited serial of "Black Dragon of Manzanar" stars Cameron as Fed who battles Asian Axis agents during WWII. Action-packed. **244m/B VHS, LV.** Rod Cameron, Roland Got, Constance Worth, Nino Pipitone, Noel Cravat; *D:* William Witney. *REP, MED, MLB*

G. Whilliker! 🎬🎬 **1993** Brothers have decided a guy named Gus Whilliker is the perfect match for their older sister/guardian. Too bad she's already dating someone. **93m/C VHS.** Dan Brook, Robin Brooks, Matthew Tompkins, Jay Michael Ferguson, William Ryan Tilk, Chris Lloyd, Jody Miller; *D:* David McClendon; *W:* Brenda Brown-Canary, Michael Helderman; *M:* Drew F. Barlow. *FFC*

Gabriel Over the White House 🎬🎬🎬 **1933** Part political satire, part fantasy, and completely fascinating. Huston is a venal politician, completely in thrall to his crooked cohorts, who manages to get elected President. While recuperating from an auto accident Huston thinks he's sees a vision of the Archangel Gabriel,

who essentially tells him to change his crooked ways. From bought man Huston changes to righteous do-gooder, much to the dismay of his criminal companions, who'll stop at nothing to get rid of the man they think has simply gone insane. Huston gives a powerful performance in this decidedly oddball film. **86m/B VHS.** Walter Huston, Karen Morley, Arthur Byron, Franchot Tone, Dickie Moore, C. Henry Gordon, David Landau, Samuel S. Hinds, Jean Parker; *D:* Gregory La Cava. *MGM, MOV, BTV*

Gabriela 🎬🎬 **1984 (R)** A sultry romance develops between a Brazilian tavern keeper and the new cook he's just hired. Derived from Jorge Amado's novel. In Portuguese with English subtitles. **102m/C VHS, Beta.** BR Sonia Braga, Marcello Mastroianni, Nelson Xavier, Antonio Cantafora; *D:* Bruno Barreto; *W:* Bruno Barreto; *C:* Carlo DiPalma; *M:* Antonio Carlos. *MGM*

Gaby: A True Story 🎬🎬🎬 **1987 (R)** The story of a woman with congenital cerebral palsy who triumphs over her condition with the help of family and loved ones, and ends up a college graduate and acclaimed author. Based on a true story. **115m/C VHS, Beta, LV.** Rachel Levin, Liv Ullmann, Norma Aleandro, Robert Loggia, Lawrence Monoson, Robert Beltran, Tony Goldwyn; *D:* Luis Mandoki; *W:* Martin Salinas, Michael James Love; *C:* Lajos Koltai; *M:* Maurice Jarre. Nominations: Academy Awards '87: Best Supporting Actress (Aleandro). *COL*

Gal Young 'Un 🎬🎬🎬 **1979** Set during the Prohibition era, a rich, middle-aged woman living on her property in the Florida backwoods finds herself courted by a much younger man. She discovers she is being used to help him set up a moonshining business. Unsentimental story of a strong woman. Based on a Marjorie Kinnan Rawlings story. **105m/C VHS, Beta.** Dana Preu, David Peck, J. Smith; *D:* Victor Nunez. Sundance Film Festival '81: Grand Jury Prize. *ACA, ICA*

Galactic Gigolo woof! **1987 (R)** An alien broccoli (yes, the vegetable) descends to earth on vacation, and discovers he's irresistible to Connecticut women. Must be something in the water. Amateurish effort intended as science-fiction satire, but there's more sleaze than humor. **80m/C Beta.** Carmine Capobianco, Debi Thibeault, Ruth Collins, Angela Nicholas, Frank Stewart; *D:* Gorman Bechard. *AFE*

Galaxies Are Colliding 🎬🎬½ *Planet of Love* **1992 (R)** Adam (Brown) is so afraid of tying the knot that he abandons his bride at the altar and takes off on a journey of enlightenment, accompanied by best friend Peter (Grammer). They naturally meet any number of eccentrics along the way.*CW:* Language. **97m/C VHS.** Dwier Brown, Kelsey Grammer, Susan Walters, Karen Medak; *D:* John Ryman; *W:* John Ryman; *C:* Philip Lee; *M:* Stephen Barber. *PAR*

Galaxina 🎬½ **1980 (R)** In the 31st century, a beautiful robot woman capable of human feelings is created. Stumbling parody of superspace fantasies features murdered Playmate Stratten in one of few film appearances. **95m/C VHS, Beta, LV.** Dorothy Stratten, Avery Schreiber, Stephen Macht; *D:* William Sachs; *C:* Dean Cundey. *USH*

Galaxis 🎬½ **1995 (R)** The physically impressive Nielsen stars as space- and time-traveling freedom fighter Landera, who beams down to Earth to battle your basic evil, intergalatic villain Kyla (Moll) who has the power source that could save her civilization. **91m/C VHS.** Brigitte Nielsen, Richard Moll, Craig Fairbrass; *D:* William Mesa. *TTC*

Galaxy Invader 🎬 **1985 (PG)** Chaos erupts when an alien explorer crash lands his spacecraft in a backwoods area of the United States. **90m/C VHS, Beta.** Richard Ruxton, Faye Tilles, Don Leifert. *NO*

Galaxy of Terror 🎬½ *Mindwarp: An Infinity of Terror; Planet of Horrors* **1981 (R)** Astronauts sent to rescue a stranded spaceship get killed by vicious aliens. Big first: Moran (Joanie on "Happy Days") explodes. Inferior Corman-produced "Alien" imitation still manages to shock and displays generous gore. Followed by "Forbidden World." **85m/C VHS, Beta, LV.** Erin Moran, Edward Albert, Ray Walston,

Grace Zabriskie, Zalman King; **D:** B.D. Clark; **W:** Mark Siegler, B.D. Clark. ♫

Galgameth ♫♫ ½ *The Adventures of Galgameth* **1996 (PG)** Old-fashioned tale of a boy-hero and a friendly monster. 14-year-old Prince Davin (Oatway) accidentally injures his father during a joust and blames himself when the king suddenly dies. But his majesty's actually been poisoned by knight El El (Macht), who declares himself regent and terrorizes the kingdom. Davin's only hope to restore peace is a magical statue called Galgameth that the prince is able to bring to life. Romanian location provides proper storybook castles and medieval villages. **99m/C VHS.** Devin Oatway, Stephen Macht, Sean McNamara, Johna Stewart, Tom Dugan; **D:** Sean McNamara; **W:** James Angeli; **C:** Christian Sebaldt; **M:** Rick Marvin. THV

Gallagher's Travels ♫ **1987** A screwball male/female reporting team chase an animal smuggling ring through the wilds of Australia. **94m/ C VHS, Beta.** *AU* Ivar Kants, Joanne Samuel, Stuart Campbell, Jennifer Hagan; **D:** Michael Caulfield. TWE

The Gallant Fool ♫ ½ **1933** A man is wrongly accused of murder and tries to clear his name while eluding the law. **57m/B VHS.** Bob Steele, Arletta Duncan, George "Gabby" Hayes, John Elliott; **D:** Robert North Bradbury; **W:** Robert North Bradbury. GPV

The Gallant Hours ♫♫♫ **1960** Biography of Admiral "Bull" Halsey (Cagney) covers five weeks, October 18 through December 1, 1942, in the WWII battle of Guadalcanal in the South Pacific. Director Montgomery forgoes battle scenes to focus on the human elements in a war and what makes a great leader. Fine performance by Cagney. **115m/B VHS.** James Cagney, Dennis Weaver, Ward Costello, Richard Jaeckel, Les Tremayne, Robert Burton, Raymond Bailey, Karl Swenson, Harry Landers, James T. Goto; **D:** Robert Montgomery; **W:** Frank D. Gilroy. MGM

Gallipoli ♫♫♫♫ **1981 (PG)** History blends with the destiny of two friends as they become part of the legendary WWI confrontation between Australia and the German-allied Turks. A superbly filmed, gripping commentary on the wastes of war. Haunting score; excellent performances by Lee and a then-unknown Gibson. Remake of a lesser 1931 effort "Battle of Gallipoli." **111m/C VHS, Beta, LV.** *AU* Mel Gibson, Mark Lee, Bill Kerr, Bill Hunter, Robert Grubb; **D:** Peter Weir; **W:** David Williamson, Peter Weir; **C:** Russell Boyd. Australian Film Institute '81: Best Actor (Gibson), Best Film. PAR

Galloping Dynamite ♫ ½ **1937** Early western based on a James Oliver Curwood story. A ranger avenges the death of his brother killed for gold. **58m/B VHS, Beta.** Kermit Maynard; **D:** Harry Fraser. VDM

The Galloping Ghost ♫♫ ½ **1931** A 12-chapter serial starring football great "Red" Grange about big games, gambling, and underworld gangs. Grange is ousted from football when he's accused of throwing a game and he sets out to prove his innocence. **226m/B VHS, Beta.** Harold "Red" Grange, Dorothy Gulliver, Walter Miller, Tom Dugan; **D:** B. Reeves Eason. VYY, VDM, NOS

Galloping Romeo ♫ ½ **1933** Steele stars as a heartthrob on horseback in this romantic Western. Steele had a hard time pulling off the light comedy he was asked to do, so clips from his previous films were used to pad the movie. **59m/B VHS.** Bob Steele, Doris Hill, George "Gabby" Hayes, Frank Ball, Ernie Adams; **D:** Robert North Bradbury; **W:** Harry Fraser. GPV, MOV

Gallowglass ♫♫♫ **1995** A "gallowglass" is an ancient Gaelic term for a servant willing to sacrifice his life for his master. In this moody TV mystery that is dim Joe (Sheen), whose life was saved by manipulative, handsome Sandor (Rhys), who now demands his absolute loyalty. Sandor needs his help in kidnapping Nina (Whitely), an unhappy ex-model who was the victim of a kidnapping years before in Italy and now lives with her husband in wealthy seclusion in the country. There, Nina is under the protection of bodyguard/chauf-

feur Paul (McArdle), and their mutual attraction leads to unexpected complications. Based on the thriller by Ruth Rendell (writing as Barbara Vine). **150m/C VHS.** *GB* Paul Rhys, Michael Sheen, Arkie Whiteley, John McArdle, Claire Hackett, Gary Waldhorn; **D:** Tim Fywell. FOX

Galyon ♫ **1977 (PG)** Soldier of fortune is recruited by an oil tycoon to find his daughter and son-in-law who have been kidnapped by terrorists in South America. **92m/C VHS, Beta.** Stan Brock, Lloyd Nolan, Ina Balin. NO

Gambit ♫♫ ½ **1966** Caine's first Hollywood film casts him as a burglar who develops a "Topkapi"-style scheme to steal a valuable statue with MacLaine as the lure and Lom as the equally devious owner. Once Caine's careful plan is put into operation, however, everything begins to unravel. **109m/C VHS, Beta.** Shirley MacLaine, Michael Caine, Herbert Lom, Roger C. Carmel; **D:** Ronald Neame; **W:** Alvin Sargent, Jack Davies; **M:** Maurice Jarre. Nominations: Academy Awards '66: Best Art Direction/Set Decoration (Color), Best Costume Design (Color), Best Sound. USH

The Gamble ♫♫ **1988 (R)** A young man (Modine) seeks to rescue his father from gambling debts by wagering himself against a lustful countess (Dunaway). When he loses the bet, however, he flees and joins up with a runaway (Beals) with the countess and her henchmen in close pursuit. **108m/C VHS, Beta, LV, Closed Caption.** Matthew Modine, Jennifer Beals, Faye Dunaway; **D:** Carlo Vanzina. PSM

Gamble on Love ♫ **1986** Woman returns to her father's Las Vegas casino and falls for the man who manages the gaming room. **90m/C Beta.** Beverly Garland; **D:** Jim Balden. PSM

The Gambler ♫♫♫ **1974 (R)** College professor Axel Freed has a gambling problem so vast that it nearly gets him killed by his bookies. He goes to Las Vegas to recoup his losses and wins big, only to blow the money on stupid sports bets that get him deeper into trouble. Excellent character study of a compulsive loser on a downward spiral. **111m/C VHS, Beta, LV.** James Caan, Lauren Hutton, Paul Sorvino, Burt Young, James Woods; **D:** Karel Reisz; **W:** James Toback. PAR

The Gambler & the Lady ♫ ½ **1952** A successful London-based gambler and casino owner endeavors to climb the social ladder by having an affair with a member of the British aristocracy. He not only has to contend with his jilted nightclub singer girlfriend but also with the gangsters who would like to take over his clubs. Dull direction and a mediocre script. **72m/B VHS, Beta, LV.** *GB* Dane Clark, Naomi Chance, Kathleen Byron; **D:** Patrick Jenkins. NO

The Gambler Returns: The Luck of the Draw ♫♫ ½ **1993** You'll see lots of familiar western television stars as Rogers returns yet again as debonair gambler Brady Hawkes. This time he's on a cross country trip to San Francisco and the biggest card game around—only some varmints are out to stop him playing that first hand. **180m/C VHS, Closed Caption.** Kenny Rogers, Reba McEntire, Rick Rossovich, Chuck Connors, Patrick Macnee, Linda Evans, James Drury, Mickey Rooney, Jere Burns, Clint Walker, Claude Akins, Gene Barry, Doug McClure, Hugh O'Brian, Brian Keith, Park Overall, Jack Kelly, David Carradine, Johnny Crawford, Marianne Rogers; **D:** Dick Lowry. CAF

Gambler's Choice ♫♫ **1944** A police lieutenant and his boyhood friend find themselves on opposite sides of the law in this crime drama. Even though both men are romantically involved with the same woman, their friendship remains intact. **66m/B VHS.** Chester Morris, Nancy Kelly, Russell Hayden, Sheldon Leonard, Lee Patrick, Lloyd Corrigan, Tom Dugan, Lyle Talbot, Charles Arnt; **D:** Frank McDonald. NOS

The Gambling Man ♫♫ ½ **19??** Rent collector Rory O'Connor is ambitious to escape his humble past and his talent at gambling leads him to winning a fortune. But a lie and a tragedy

return to haunt him. Based on a book by Catherine Cookson. **150m/C VHS.** *GB* Robson Green, Sylvestria Le Touzel, Bernard Hill, Stephanie Putson, Anne Kent. VCO

The Gambling Samurai ♫♫ *Kunisada Chuji* **1960** A samurai returns to his village to find it besieged by a ruthless government. Instead of attacking, he bides his time and works to undermine the government—finally achieving his revenge. In Japanese with English subtitles. **101m/C VHS, Beta.** *JP* Toshiro Mifune, Michiyo Aratama; **D:** Senkichi Taniguhi. VDA

The Gambling Terror ♫♫ **1937** A cowboy goes after a mobster selling protection to hapless ranchers. **53m/B VHS, Beta.** Johnny Mack Brown, Charles "Blackie" King; **D:** Sam Newfield. NOS, VCN, HEG

The Game ♫♫ **1989** Three friends arrange a puzzle-murder-mystery for a selected group of guilty people, with $1 million as the prize—and death for the losers. **91m/C VHS, LV.** Tom Blair, Debbie Martin; **D:** Curtis Brown; **W:** Curtis Brown. TWE

Game for Vultures ♫ ½ **1986 (R)** Racial unrest in Rhodesia is the backdrop for this tale of a black revolutionary who fights racist sanctions. The noble topic suffers from stereotypes and oversimplification. **113m/C VHS, Beta.** *GB* Richard Harris, Richard Roundtree, Joan Collins, Ray Milland; **D:** James Fargo. TWE

The Game is Over ♫♫ ½ **1966 (R)** A wealthy neglected wife falls in love with her grown stepson, causing her to divorce her husband and shatter her life. A good performance by Fonda, then Vadim's wife. Modern version of Zola's "La Curee." **96m/C VHS, Beta.** *FR* Jane Fonda, Peter McEnery, Michel Piccoli; **D:** Roger Vadim; **M:** Jean Bouchety. MED

A Game of Crime ♫♫ **1960** Intriguing murder story with strong horror overtones. **?m/C VHS.** John Blythe Barrymore Jr., Luisa Rivelli. LOO

Game of Death ♫♫ *Goodbye Bruce Lee: His Last Game of Death; Bruce Lee's Game of Death* **1979 (R)** Bruce Lee's final kung fu thriller about a young martial arts movie star who gets involved with the syndicate. Lee died halfway through the filming of this movie and it was finished with out-takes and a double. **100m/C VHS, Beta, LV.** Bruce Lee, Dean Jagger, Kareem Abdul-Jabbar, Colleen Camp, Chuck Norris; **D:** Robert Clouse; **M:** John Barry. FOX

The Game of Love ♫♫ **1990 (PG)** Olin presides over Henry's bar, the lost and found of lonely hearts and lust, where people go to quench that deep thirst for love. **94m/C VHS, LV.** Ed Marinaro, Belinda Bauer, Ken Olin, Robert Rusler, Tracy Nelson, Max Gail, Janet Margolin, Brynn Thayer; **D:** Bobby Roth. ACA

Game of Seduction ♫ **1986** A murdering, womanizing playboy pursues a married woman and gets caught up in a treacherous cat-and-mouse game. Dubbed. **81m/C VHS, Beta.** Sylvia Kristel, Jon Finch, Nathalie Delon; **D:** Roger Vadim. NO

Game of Survival ♫ **1989** A young rebel warrior from another planet is sent to earth to battle six of the galaxy's most brutal warriors. **85m/C VHS, Beta.** Nikki Hill, Cindy Coatman, Roosevelt Miller Jr.; **D:** Armand Gazarian. NO

Gamera, the Invincible ♫ ½ *Gamera; Gammera; Daikaiju Gamera* **1966** This Japanese monster flick features the ultimate nuclear super-turtle who flies around destroying cities and causing panic. First in the series of notoriously bad films, this one is cool in black and white and has some impressive special effects. Dubbed in English. **86m/B VHS, LV.** *JP* Brian Donlevy, Albert Dekker, Diane Findlay, John Baragrey, Dick O'Neill, Eiji Funakoshi; **D:** Noriaki Yuasa. JFK, SNC

Gamera vs. Barugon ♫ ½ *Gamera Tai Barugon; Gambara vs. Barugon; The War of the Monsters* **1966** The monstrous turtle returns to Earth from his outer space prison, now equipped with his famous leg-jets. He soon wishes he had stayed airborne, however, when he is forced to do battle with 130-foot lizard Barugon and his rainbow-melting ray. Tokyo and Osaka get melted in the process. **101m/C VHS, Beta.** *JP* Kojiro Hongo, Kyoko Enami; *D:* Shigeo Tanaka. *JFK*

Gamera vs. Gaos ⚔️½ *The Return of the Giant Monsters; Gamera vs. Gyaos; Boyichi and the Supermonster; Gamera Tai Gaos* **1967** Now fully the good guy, Gamera slugs it out with a bat-like critter named Gaos. Suspense rules the day when Gaos tries to put out the super turtle's jets with his built-in fire extinguisher but luckily for Earth, Gamera has a few tricks of his own up his shell. **87m/C VHS, Beta, LV.** *JP* Kojiro Hongo, Kichijiro Ueda, Naoyuki Abe; *D:* Noriaki Yuasa. *JFK*

Gamera vs. Guiron ⚔️ *Attack of the Monsters; Gamera Tai Guiron* **1969** Gamera risks it all to take on an evil, spear-headed monster on a distant planet. Highlight is the sexy, leotard clad aliens who want to eat the little Earth kids' brains. **88m/C VHS, Beta.** *JP* Nobuhiro Kashima, Christopher Murphy, Miyuki Akiyama, Yuko Hamada, Eiji Funakoshi; *D:* Noriaki Yuasa. *JFK*

Gamera vs. Zigra ⚔️ *Gamera Tai Shinkai Kaiju Jigara; Gamera vs. the Deep Sea Monster Zigra* **1971** Gamera the flying turtle chose an ecological theme for this, his final movie. It seems that the alien Zigrans have come to Earth to wrest the planet from the hands of the pollutive humans who have nearly destroyed it. The aliens kill the staunch turtle, but the love and prayers of children revive him that he may defend Earth once more. **91m/C VHS, Beta, LV.** *JP* Reiko Kasahara, Mikiko Tsubouchi, Koji Fujiyama, Arlene Zoellner, Gloria Zoellner; *D:* Noriaki Yuasa. *JFK*

Games Girls Play ⚔️½ *The Bunny Caper; Sex Play* **1975** The daughter of an American diplomat organizes a contest at a British boarding school to see which of her classmates can seduce important dignitaries. **90m/C VHS, Beta.** Christina Hart, Jane Anthony, Jill Damas, Drina Pavlovic; *D:* Jack Arnold. *NO*

The Gamma People woof! **1956** A journalist discovers a Balkan doctor shooting children with gamma rays, creating an army of brainless zombies. Cult-renowned grade-Z tripe. **83m/B VHS, Beta.** *GB* Walter Rilla, Paul Douglas, Eva Bartok; *D:* John Gilling; *C:* Ted Moore. *NO*

Gandhi ⚔️⚔️⚔️½ **1982 (PG)** The biography of Mahatma Gandhi from the prejudice he encounters as a young attorney in South Africa, to his role as spiritual leader to the people of India and his use of passive resistance against the country's British rulers, and his eventual assassination. Kingsley is a marvel in his Academy Award-winning role and the picture is a generally riveting epic worthy of its eight Oscars. **188m/C VHS, Beta, LV.** *GB* Ben Kingsley, Candice Bergen, Edward Fox, John Gielgud, John Mills, Saeed Jaffrey, Trevor Howard, Ian Charleson, Roshan Seth, Athol Fugard, Martin Sheen, Daniel Day-Lewis, Rohini Hattangady; *D:* Richard Attenborough; *W:* John Briley; *C:* Billy Williams; *M:* George Fenton. Academy Awards '82: Best Actor (Kingsley), Best Art Direction/Set Decoration, Best Cinematography, Best Costume Design, Best Director (Attenborough), Best Film Editing, Best Original Screenplay, Best Picture, Best Sound; British Academy Awards '82: Best Actor (Kingsley), Best Director (Attenborough), Best Film, Best Supporting Actress (Hattangady); Directors Guild of America Awards '82: Best Director (Attenborough); Golden Globe Awards '83: Best Actor—Drama (Kingsley), Best Director (Attenborough), Best Foreign Film, Best Screenplay; Los Angeles Film Critics Association Awards '82: Best Actor (Kingsley); National Board of Review Awards '82: Best Actor (Kingsley); New York Film Critics Awards '82: Best Actor (Kingsley), Best Film; Nominations: Academy Awards '82: Best Makeup, Best Original Score. *COL, BTV, HMV*

Gang Bullets ⚔️ **1938** Mobster tries to continue his dirty systems in a new town, but finds the legal force incorruptible. **62m/B VHS, Beta.** Anne Nagel, Robert Kent, Charles Trowbridge, Morgan Wallace, J. Farrell MacDonald, Arthur Loft, John Merton; *D:* Lambert Hillyer. *SNC*

Gang Busters ⚔️½ **1955** Prisoners plan a breakout. Slow and uninteresting adaptation of the successful radio series. Filmed in Oregon. **78m/B VHS.** Myron Healey, Sam Edwards, Frank Gerstle; *D:* Bill Karn. *NOS, SNC*

Gang in Blue ⚔️⚔️½ **1996 (R)** Black officer Michael Rhoades (Van Peebles) is secretly investigating a white supremacist group of cops, called the Phantoms, within the LAPD. Marine Corp vet and police rookie Keith DeBruler (Brolin) becomes Rhoades' new partner and his racial comments make him a likely initiate for the Phantoms. So can he be trusted to be Rhoades' inside man and help Michael expose the corruption within the ranks? Made for cable. **CW:** Strong violence and language, and for some sexuality. **99m/C VHS.** Mario Van Peebles, Josh Brolin, Melvin Van Peebles, J.T. Walsh, Cynda Williams, Stephen Lang, Sean McCann; *D:* Mario Van Peebles, Melvin Van Peebles; *W:* David Fuller, Rick Natkin; *C:* Rhett Morita; *M:* Larry Brown. *HMK*

Gang Justice ⚔️ **1994** Low-budget melodrama finds sensitive Asian student Paul (Kim) battling racists at school and his crippled alcoholic father at home. Some martial arts fight scenes but this is amateur time. **92m/C VHS, LV.** Joon Kim, Jonathan Gorman, Erik Estrada, Angel Dashek; *D:* Richard W. Park. *AIP*

Gang War ⚔️ **1940** Low-budget gangster film with an all-black cast about two gangs fighting for control of the city's jukebox business. **60m/B VHS.** Ralph Cooper, Gladys Snyder, Reggie Fenderson, Lawrence Criner, Monte Hawley, Jesse C. Brooks, Maceo B. Sheffield; *D:* Leo Popkin. *NOS, RXM*

Gang Wars ⚔️ *Devil's Express* **1975 (R)** There's a riot going on as Puerto Rican, Black, and Chinese gangs fight it out for control of the city. **82m/C VHS.** Warhawk Tanzania, Larry Fleishman, Sam DeFazio, Wilfred Roldan, Elsie Roman, Sarah Nyrick; *D:* Barry Rosen. *SUN*

Gangbusters ⚔️⚔️ **1938** Men battle crime in the city in this serial in thirteen episodes based on the popular radio series of the same name. **253m/B VHS, Beta.** Kent Taylor, Irene Hervey, Robert Armstrong. *NOS, CAB, VCN*

The Gang's All Here ⚔️½ **1940** Darro joins a trucking firm whose rigs are being run off the road and hijacked by a competitor. Features "Charlie Chan" regulars Luke and Moreland. **63m/B VHS.** Frankie Darro, Marcia Mae Jones, Jackie Moran, Mantan Moreland, Keye Luke; *D:* Jean Yarbrough. *NOS, RXM, MOV*

Gangs, Inc. ⚔️⚔️ *Crimes, Inc.; Paper Bullets* **1941** A woman is sent to prison for a hit-and-run accident, actually the fault of a wealthy playboy. When she learns his identity she vows revenge and turns to crime to achieve her evil ends. Okay thriller suffers from plot problems. Ladd has a minor role filmed before he became a star. **72m/B VHS, Beta.** Joan Woodbury, Lash LaRue, Linda Ware, John Archer, Vince Barnett, Alan Ladd; *D:* Phil Rosen. *NOS, MRV, DVT*

The Gangster ⚔️⚔️½ **1947** Sullivan plays a small-time slum-bred hood who climbs to the top of the underworld, only to lose his gang because he allows his fears to get the better of him. (There's nothing to fear except when someone knows you're afeared.) Noir crimer with an interesting psychological perspective, though a bit sluggish at times. **84m/B VHS.** Barry Sullivan, Joan Lorring, Akim Tamiroff, Harry (Henry) Morgan, John Ireland, Fifi d'Orsay, Shelley Winters; *D:* Gordon Wiles. *FOX, FCT*

Gangster Wars ⚔️⚔️ **1981** A specially edited-for-video version of the television mini-series "The Gangster Chronicles." Based on fact, it deals with the growth of organized crime in America from the early days of this century, through the eyes of three ghetto kids who grow up to become powerful mobsters. **121m/C VHS, Beta.** Michael Nouri, Joe Penny, Brian Benben, Kathleen Lloyd, Madeleine Stowe, Robert Davi; *D:* Richard Sarafian. *USH*

Gangsters ⚔️ **1979** City is ruled by the mob and nothing can stop their bloody grip except "The Special Squad." **90m/C VHS, Beta.** *IT* Michael V. Gazzo, Tony Page, Vicki Sue Robinson, Nai Bonet; *D:* Mac Ahlberg. *VCD, HHE, MTX*

Gangster's Den ⚔️ **1945** A gang of renegades scare a woman out of buying a gold-laden piece of land and Billy the Kid comes to her rescue. **56m/B VHS, Beta.** Buster Crabbe, Kermit Maynard, Al "Fuzzy" St. John, Charles "Blackie" King; *D:* Sam Newfield. *VDM*

Gangster's Law woof! **1986** A look at a seedy gangster's downfall. Filmed on location in Italy. Dubbed. **89m/C VHS, Beta.** Klaus Kinski, Maurice Poli, Susy Anderson, Max Delys; *D:* Siro Marcellini. *TWE*

Gangsters of the Frontier ⚔️ **1944** The people of Red Rock are forced to work in the town mines by two prison escapees until Ritter and his friends ride to the rescue. Part of the "Texas Ranger" series. **56m/B VHS, Beta.** Tex Ritter, Dave O'Brien; *D:* Elmer Clifton; *W:* Elmer Clifton. *NOS, DVT, RXM*

Gangway ⚔️⚔️½ **1937** Pat Wayne (Matthews), a London newspaper reporter, is mistaken for a jewel thief and kidnapped by gangsters aboard a New York-bound ocean liner. In the meantime, the real thief is aboard posing as a Hollywood actress (Blakeney), and it's up to Scotland Yard inspector Bob Deering (Mackay) to solve the crime. Matthews was considered by many to be the English equivalent of America's Eleanor Powell. Based on an original story by Dwight Taylor. **90m/B VHS.** *GB* Jessie Matthews, Barry Mackay, Olive Blakeney, Liane Ordeyne, Patrick Ludlow, Nat Pendleton, Noel Madison, Alastair Sim, Doris Rogers, Laurence Anderson, Bennie Dorn; *D:* Sonnie Hale; *W:* Sonnie Hale, Lesser Samuels. *HEG*

Ganjasaurus Rex ⚔️ **1987 (R)** Monster spoof about a giant green dinosaur emerging from the pot-laden hills of California. Maybe it's all in your head, man. **100m/C VHS, Beta.** Paul Bassis, Dave Fresh, Rosie Jones; *D:* Ursi Reynolds. *RHI*

Gappa the Trifibian Monster ⚔️½ *Daikyoju Gappa; Monster from a Prehistoric Planet* **1967 (PG)** Researchers visiting a tropical island find a giant egg and take it back to Tokyo with them, dismaying the egg's giant monster parents. Dubbed. **90m/C VHS, Beta.** *JP* ORI

The Garbage Pail Kids Movie woof! **1987 (PG)** The disgusting youngsters, stars of bubblegum cards, make their first and last film appearance in this live action dud. The garbage is where it should be thrown. **100m/C VHS, Beta, LV.** Anthony Newley, MacKenzie Astin, Katie Barberi; *D:* Rod Amateau; *W:* Rod Amateau. *PAR, BAR, IME*

Garbo Talks ⚔️⚔️ **1984 (PG-13)** A dying eccentric's last request is to meet the reclusive screen legend Greta Garbo. Bancroft amusingly plays the dying woman whose son goes to extreme lengths in order to fulfill his mother's last wish. **104m/C VHS, Beta, Closed Caption.** Anne Bancroft, Ron Silver, Carrie Fisher, Catherine Hicks, Steven Hill, Howard da Silva, Dorothy Loudon, Harvey Fierstein, Hermione Gingold; *D:* Sidney Lumet; *C:* Andrzej Bartkowiak; *M:* Cy Coleman. *MGM, FOX*

The Garden ⚔️⚔️ **1990** Eternally provocative director Jarman does another take on sex and religion. He examines the role of the Church in the persecution of homosexuality by recreating the story of the Passion and replacing the figure of Christ in some sequences with two male lovers, who are arrested, humiliated, and tortured. **90m/C VHS.** *GB* Tilda Swinton, Johnny Mills, Philip MacDonald, Roger Cook, Kevin Collins, Pete Lee-Wilson, Spencer Lee, Jody Graber; *D:* Derek Jarman; *W:* Derek Jarman; *M:* Simon Fisher Turner. *FXL, FCT*

The Garden of Allah ⚔️⚔️⚔️ **1936** Dietrich finds hyper-romantic encounters in the Algerian desert with Boyer, but his terrible secret may doom them both. This early Technicolor production, though flawed, is an absolute must for Dietrich fans. Yuma, Arizona substituted for the exotic locale. **85m/C VHS, LV.** Marlene Dietrich, Charles Boyer, Basil Rathbone, Sir C. Aubrey Smith, Tilly Losch, Joseph Schildkraut, Henry Kleinbach (Brandon), John Carradine; **D:** Richard Boleslawski; **C:** William Howard Greene; **M:** Max Steiner. Nominations: Academy Awards '36: Best Original Score. *FOX*

The Garden of Delights 🐾🐾🐾 1970
A wicked black comedy about a millionaire, paralyzed and suffering from amnesia after a car accident. His horrendously greedy family tries to get him to remember and reveal his Swiss bank account number. Acclaimed; in Spanish with English subtitles. **95m/C VHS, Beta.** *SP* Jose Luis Lopez Vasquez, Lina Canelajas, Luchy Soto, Francisco Pierra, Charo Soriano; **D:** Carlos Saura. *HMV, CVC, FCT*

The Garden of Eden 🐾🐾🐾 1928
Milestone—whose "Two Arabian Nights" had won an Academy Award the previous year, and who went on to direct "All Quiet on the Western Front" and "Of Mice and Men"—directed this sophisticated ersatz Lubitsch sex comedy. Griffith, the so-called "Orchid Lady," is a young girl who dreams of diva-dom but falls deep into the underbelly of the seedy side of Budapest. With the aid of a fake baroness, however, she finds her way to Monte Carlo and has her turn in the limelight. A handsome production designed by William Cameron Menzies, art director for "Gone With the Wind." **115m/B VHS, Beta, 8mm.** Corine Griffith, Louise Dresser, Charles Ray, Lowell Sherman; **D:** Lewis Milestone. *NOS, VYY*

The Garden of the Finzi-Continis 🐾🐾🐾🐾 1971 (R)
Acclaimed film by De Sica about an aristocratic Jewish family living in Italy under increasing Fascist oppression on the eve of WWII. The garden wall symbolizes the distance between the Finzi-Continis and the Nazi reality about to engulf them. Flawless acting and well-defined direction. Based on the novel by Giorgio Bassani, who collaborated on the script but later repudiated the film. Music by De Sica's son, Manuel. In Italian with English subtitles or dubbed. **90m/C VHS, LV.** *IT* Dominique Sanda, Helmut Berger, Lino Capolicchio, Fabio Testi, Romolo Valli; **D:** Vittorio De Sica; **W:** Cesare Zavattini; **M:** Manuel De Sica. Academy Awards '71: Best Foreign Language Film; Berlin International Film Festival '71: Golden Bear; National Board of Review Awards '71: 5 Best Foreign Films of the Year; Nominations: Academy Awards '71: Best Adapted Screenplay. *VLL, IME, APD*

Gardens of Stone 🐾🐾 1987 (R)
A zealous young cadet during the Vietnam War is assigned to the Old Guard patrol at Arlington Cemetery, and clashes with the patrol's older officers and various pacifist civilians. Falls short of the mark, although Jones turns in an excellent performance. **112m/C VHS, Beta, LV, Closed Caption.** James Caan, James Earl Jones, D.B. Sweeney, Anjelica Huston, Dean Stockwell, Lonette McKee, Mary Stuart Masterson, Bill Graham, Sam Bottoms, Casey Siemaszko, Laurence "Larry" Fishburne; **D:** Francis Ford Coppola; **W:** Ronald Bass; **C:** Jordan Cronenweth; **M:** Carmine Coppola. *FOX*

Gargoyles, The Movie: The Heroes Awaken 🐾🐾½ 1994 (G)
Mythical crimefighting creatures, trapped in stone by day thanks to a sorcerer's spell but released to live at night, are displaced in time from their medieval Scottish home, winding up in modern-day New York City. But they discover they still have old enemies to fight. First aired as a five-episode part of the animated TV series. **80m/C VHS, Closed Caption.** **V:** Ed Asner, Keith David, Jonathon Frakes, Marina Sirtis, Bill Fagerbakke, Salli Richardson, Frank Welker, Thom Adcox, Jeff Bennett. *TOU*

Garringo 🐾🐾 1969
Lawmen attempt to bring to justice a man who is intent on killing the soldiers responsible for his father's death. **95m/C VHS, Beta.** *IT* *SP* Anthony Steffen, Peter Lee Lawrence, Jose Bodalo; **D:** Rafael Romero Marchent. *MAD*

Gas WOOF! 1981 (R)
This dog has tycoon Hayden buying up all the gas stations in town to create a crisis that will make him richer. Everyone in the cast wastes their time, especially Sutherland as a hip DJ reporting on the gas shortage. **94m/C VHS, Beta.** *CA* Donald Sutherland, Susan Anspach, Sterling Hayden; Peter Aykroyd, Howie Mandel, Helen Shaver; **D:** Les Rose; **W:** Dick Wolf. *PAR*

Gas Food Lodging 🐾🐾🐾 1992 (R)
Saga casts Adams as Nora, a weary waitress in Laramie, New Mexico, trying her best to raise two teenaged daughters on her own. The daughters, Skye and Balk, are disillusioned about love and family. Balk's special friend is Darius, an eccentric window dresser, played by Leitch, Skye's brother. Nothing works out quite as intended but multi-dimensional characters, poignant situtations, and enormous emotional appeal highlight the directorial debut of Anders. Based on the Richard Peck novel "Don't Look and It Won't Hurt." **CW:** Language and sensuality. **100m/C VHS, LV, Closed Caption.** Brooke Adams, Ione Skye, Fairuza Balk, James Brolin, Rob Knepper, Donovan Leitch, David Lansbury, Jacob Vargas, Chris Mulkey, Tiffany Anders; **D:** Allison Anders; **W:** Allison Anders; **C:** Dean Lent; **M:** J. Mascis, Barry Adamson. Independent Spirit Awards '93: Best Actress (Balk). *COL*

Gas Pump Girls 🐾½ 1979 (R)
Comedy about five lovely ladies who manage a gas station and use their feminine wiles to win the battle against a shady oil sheik. **102m/C VHS, Beta, LV.** Kirsten Baker, Dennis Bowen, Huntz Hall, Steve Bond, Leslie King, Linda Lawrence; **D:** Joel Bender. *VES*

Gas-s-s-s! 🐾🐾½
Gas-s-s-s... or, It May Become Necessary to Destroy the World in Order to Save It 1970 (PG) A gas main leak in an Alaskan defense plant kills everyone beyond thirtysomething and the post-apocalyptic pre-boomer survivors are left to muddle their way through the brume. Trouble is, AIP edited the heck out of the movie, much to Corman's chagrin, and the result is a truncated comedy; Corman was so displeased, in fact, he left to create New World studios. **79m/C VHS, Beta.** Robert Corff, Elaine Giftos, Pat Patterson, George Armitage, Alex Wilson, Ben Vereen, Cindy Williams, Bud Cort, Talia Shire; **D:** Roger Corman; **W:** George Armitage. *NO*

Gaslight 🐾 Angel Street 1940
A forgotten British classic that fell victim to the American production of the same title and theme that was filmed only five years later. Set in late Victorian London, Wynyard is the rich innocent married to the calculating Walbrook, who slowly tries driving his bride insane in order to discover some hidden family jewels. She comes under the protection of a Scotland Yard detective (Pettingell) who suspects Walbrook has already murdered once. An outstandingly eerie psychological thriller. Based on the play "Angel Street" by Patrick Hamilton. **88m/C VHS.** *GB* Anton Walbrook, Diana Wynyard, Frank Pettingell, Cathleen Cordell, Robert Newton, Jimmy Hanley, Minnie Rayner, Mary Hinton, Marie Wright, Jack Barty, Moyna MacGill, Darmora Ballet; **D:** Thorold Dickinson; **W:** A.H. Rawlinson, Bridget Boland; **C:** Bernard Knowles; **M:** Richard Addinsell. *FCT*

Gaslight 🐾🐾🐾½ The Murder in Thorton Square 1944
Lavish remake of the 1939 film, based on the Patrick Hamilton play "Angel Street." A man tries to drive his beautiful wife insane while searching for priceless jewels. Her only clue to his evil acts is the frequent dimming of their gaslights. A suspenseful Victorian era mystery. Lansbury's film debut, as the tarty maid. **114m/B VHS, Beta, LV.** Charles Boyer, Ingrid Bergman, Joseph Cotten, Angela Lansbury, Terry Moore, May Whitty, Barbara Everest, Emil Rameau, Edmund Breon, Halliwell Hobbes, Tom Stevenson; **D:** George Cukor; **C:** Joseph Ruttenberg. Academy Awards '44: Best Actress (Bergman), Best Interior Decoration; Golden Globe Awards '45: Best Actress—Drama (Bergman); Nominations: Academy Awards '44: Best Actor (Boyer), Best Black and White Cinematography, Best Picture, Best Screenplay, Best Supporting Actress (Lansbury). *MGM, BTV, VEC*

The Gate 🐾🐾 1987 (PG-13)
Kids generally like to explore and Dorff and Tripp are no exception. When a large hole is exposed in their backyard, it would be a childhood sin not to see what's in it, right? What they don't know is that this hole is actually a gateway to and from Hell. The terror they unleash includes more than just run-of-the-mill demons. Good special effects. Followed by "Gate 2." **85m/C VHS, Beta, LV.** Christa Denton, Stephen Dorff, Louis Tripp; **D:** Tibor Takacs. *LIV, VES*

Gate 2 🐾½ 1992 (R)
Tripp returns in his role as Terry, a young student of demonology in this lame sequel to "The Gate." Terry and a few of his teen buddies call up a group of demons that have been confined behind a gate for billions of years. The demons are used to grant modest wishes, but the wishes end up having very evil effects. Incredibly weak plot saved only by the special monster effects, which include live action and puppetry. **C:** Drug use. **90m/C VHS, LV, Closed Caption.** Louis Tripp, Simon Reynolds, Pamela Segall, James Villemaire, Neil Munro, James Kidnie, Andrea Ladanyi; **D:** Tibor Takacs; **W:** Michael Nankin; **C:** Bryan England; **M:** George Blondheim. *COL*

Gate of Hell 🐾🐾🐾½ Jigokumen 1954
Set in 12th-century Japan. A warlord desires a beautiful married woman and seeks to kill her husband to have her. However, he accidentally kills her instead. Filled with shame and remorse, the warlord abandons his life to seek solace as a monk. Heavily awarded and critically acclaimed; the first Japanese film to use color photography. In Japanese with English subtitles. **89m/C VHS, Beta, 8mm.** *JP* Kazuo Hasegawa, Machiko Kyo; **D:** Teinosuke Kinugasa. Academy Awards '54: Best Costume Design (Color), Best Foreign Language Film; Cannes Film Festival '54: Best Film; National Board of Review Awards '54: 10 Best Films of the Year. *VYY, DVT, VDM*

Gates of Hell WOOF! Paura Nella Citta Dei Morti Viventi; City of the Living Dead; The Fear; Twilight of the Dead; Fear in the City of the Living Dead 1983
Salem, Massachusetts, must battle the risen dead in this gorefest that tried to disguise itself under many other titles. **90m/C VHS, Beta.** Christopher George, Janet Agren, Katherine MacColl, Robert Sampson; **D:** Lucio Fulci. *IGP*

Gates of Hell 2: Dead Awakening 🐾 1996
Occultists performing an initiation rite reopen the portal to hell and a creature from its depths reawakens to cause the usual unholy terror. **87m/C VHS.** Tom Campitelli, Tamara Hext, Randy Strickland; **D:** G.D. Marcum. *TPV*

The Gathering 🐾🐾½ 1977
A dying man seeks out the wife and family he has alienated for a final Christmas gathering. James Poe authored this well-acted holiday tearjerker that won the 1977-78 Emmy for outstanding TV drama special. **94m/C VHS, Beta.** Ed Asner, Maureen Stapleton, Lawrence Pressman, Stephanie Zimbalist, Bruce Davison, Gregory Harrison, Veronica Hamel, Gail Strickland; **D:** Randal Kleiser; **M:** John Barry. *WOV*

A Gathering of Eagles 🐾🐾½ 1963
Hudson portrays a hard-nosed Air Force colonel during peacetime whose British wife must adjust to being a military spouse. **115m/C VHS.** Rock Hudson, Rod Taylor, Mary Peach, Barry Sullivan, Kevin McCarthy, Henry Silva, Leif Erickson; **D:** Delbert Mann; **M:** Jerry Goldsmith. *MGM*

The Gathering: Part 2 🐾🐾 1979
Sequel in which a widow has a Christmas reunion with her family, but conflict arises when she introduces a new man in her life. Not as effective as the original, also made for TV. **98m/C VHS.** Maureen Stapleton, Efrem Zimbalist Jr., Jameson Parker, Bruce Davison, Lawrence Pressman, Gail Strickland, Veronica Hamel; **D:** Charles S. Dubin. *TTC*

The Gathering Storm 🐾🐾 1974
Based on the first book of memoirs from Sir Winston Churchill, this drama examines the pre-WWII years. **72m/C Beta.** Richard Burton, Virginia McKenna, Ian Bannen; **D:** Herbert Wise. *PSM*

The Gatling Gun 🐾½ King Gun 1972 (PG)
Poor tale of the Cavalry, Apache Indians, and renegades all after the title weapon. **93m/C VHS.** Guy Stockwell, Woody Strode, Patrick Wayne, Robert Fuller, Barbara Luna, John Carradine, Pat Buttram, Phil Harris; **D:** Robert Gordon. *HHE*

Gator 🐾🐾 **1976 (PG)** Sequel to "White Lightning" (1973) follows the adventures of Gator (Reynolds), who is recruited to gather evidence to convict a corrupt political boss who also happens to be his friend. Reynolds in his good ole' boy role with lots of chase scenes. Talk show host Michael Douglas made his film debut in the role of the governor. First film Reynolds directed. **116m/C VHS, Beta.** Burt Reynolds, Jerry Reed, Lauren Hutton, Jack Weston, Alice Ghostley, Dub Taylor; *D:* Burt Reynolds; *W:* William W. Norton Sr.; *M:* Charles Bernstein. *MGM, FOX*

Gator Bait 🐾½ **1973 (R)** The Louisiana swamp is home to the beautiful Desiree, and woe be unto any man who threatens her family. Aims to please fans of the raunchy and violent. Followed by an equally vile sequel. **91m/C VHS, Beta, LV.** Claudia Jennings, Clyde Ventura, Bill Thurman, Janet Baldwin; *D:* Ferd Sebastian, Beverly Sebastian; *W:* Ferd Sebastian, Beverly Sebastian. *PAR*

Gator Bait 2: Cajun Justice 🐾 **1988 (R)** A city girl comes to the Louisiana swamp and turns violent in an effort to exact revenge on the men who have been tormenting her. **94m/C VHS, Beta, LV, Closed Caption.** Jan MacKenzie, Tray Loren, Paul Muzzcat, Brad Kepnick, Jerry Armstrong, Ben Sebastian; *D:* Ferd Sebastian, Beverly Sebastian; *W:* Ferd Sebastian, Beverly Sebastian. *PAR*

The Gaucho 🐾🐾🐾 **1927** Fairbanks stars as the title character, an immoral swashbuckler who lusts after a virginal religious (Greear) before undergoing a change of heart (but not before dancing a red-hot tango with the less-than-virginal Velez). **?m/B VHS.** Douglas Fairbanks Sr., Lupe Velez, Geraine Greear, Gustav von Seyffertitz; *D:* F. Richard Jones; *W:* Lotta Woods; *C:* Gaetano Antonio "Tony" Gaudio. *KIV*

The Gauntlet 🐾🐾 **1977 (R)** A cop is ordered to Las Vegas to bring back a key witness for an important trial—but the witness turns out to be a beautiful prostitute being hunted by killers. Violence-packed action. **111m/C VHS, Beta, LV, Closed Caption.** Clint Eastwood, Sondra Locke, Pat Hingle, Bill McKinney; *D:* Clint Eastwood; *W:* Michael Butler. *WAR, TLF*

The Gay Divorcee 🐾🐾🐾 *The Gay Divorce* **1934** Astaire pursues Rogers to an English seaside resort, where she mistakes him for the hired correspondent in her divorce case. Based on the musical play "The Gay Divorce" by Dwight Taylor and Cole Porter. The title was slightly changed for the movie because of protests from the Hays Office. ♫ Let It Bother You; A Needle in a Haystack; Let's K-nock K-nees; Night and Day; The Continental. **107m/B VHS, Beta, LV.** Fred Astaire, Ginger Rogers, Edward Everett Horton, Eric Blore, Alice Brady, Erik Rhodes, Betty Grable; *D:* Mark Sandrich; *M:* Max Steiner. Academy Awards '34: Best Song ("The Continental"); Nominations: Academy Awards '34: Best Interior Decoration, Best Picture, Best Sound, Best Score. *MED, TTC*

The Gay Lady 🐾🐾½ *Trottie True* **1949** Light romantic comedy set in the 1890s about an actress who climbs to stardom in London theater and winds up marrying into the aristocracy. Look for Christopher Lee and Roger Moore in early bit parts. **95m/C VHS.** GB Jean Kent, James Donald, Hugh Sinclair, Lana Morris, Bill Owen, Michael Medwin, Andrew Crawford; *D:* Brian Desmond Hurst. *MOV, UNI*

Gay Purr-ee 🐾🐾 **1962** Delightful tale of feline romance in the City of Lights. For all ages. **85m/C VHS, LV, Closed Caption.** *V:* Chuck Jones; *M:* Harold Arlen; *V:* Judy Garland, Robert Goulet, Red Buttons, Hermione Gingold, Mel Blanc. *WAR, FCT*

The Gay Ranchero 🐾🐾 **1942** Rogers, without Dale Evans, in an average tale of old west meets new crooks. Rogers is the sheriff who foils gangsters trying to take over an airport. The action doesn't stop him from singing a duet with leading lady Frazee on "Wait'll I Get My Sunshine in the Moonlight." **55m/B VHS, Beta.** Roy Rogers, Andy Devine, Tito Guizar, Jane Frazee, Estelita Rodriguez; *D:* William Witney. *NOS, VCN, CAB*

The Gazebo 🐾🐾🐾 **1959** Wacky comedy about a TV writer who is being blackmailed by someone who has nude photos of his Broadway star wife. He decides murder is the only solution to this problem. Reynolds sings "Something Called Love." Based on a play by Alec Coppel from a story by Myra and Alec Coppel. **102m/B VHS.** Glenn Ford, Debbie Reynolds, Carl Reiner, John McGiver, Doro Merande, Bert Freed, Martin Landau; *D:* George Marshall; *W:* George Wells. Nominations: Academy Awards '59: Best Black and White Cinematography. *MGM*

Geek Maggot Bingo 🐾 *The Freak From Suckweasel Mountain* **1983** It's too bad director Zed waited until mid-"Bingo" to post a sign warning "Leave Now, It Isn't Going Get Any Better!" Conceived by the New York underground's don of the "Cinema of Transgression" to be an off-the-rack cult classic, this horror spoof is too long on in-jokes and short on substance to earn its number in the cult hall of fame. It does, however, boast Death as Scumbalina the vampire queen and Hell as a punk cowboy crooner (before alternative country hit the airwaves). TV horror-meister Zacherle narrates. **70m/C VHS.** Richard Hell, Donna Death, John Zacherle; *D:* Nick Zedd. *MWF, MOV*

Geheimakte WB1 🐾🐾 *Secret Paper WB1* **1942** Historical drama centering on the invention of the U-boat by Sergeant Wilhelm Bauer during Denmark's WWII blockade of the ports of Schleswig-Holstein. In German with no subtitles. **91m/B VHS, Beta.** *GE* Alexander Golling; *D:* Herbert Selpin. *IHF*

A Geisha 🐾🐾🐾 *Gion Bayashi; Gion Festival Music* **1953** Miyoharu (Kogure) is a passive elderly geisha who agrees to train the naive young Eiko (Wakao) in her new role. But Eiko discovers that romantic notions of the geisha life are far from it's modern reality. Poignant look at the changing status of the geisha in Japan after WWII and the country's social upheavals. In Japanese with English subtitles. **86m/B VHS.** *JP* Michiyo Kogure, Ayako Wakao, Seizaburo Kawazu, Chieko Naniwa, Eitaro Shindo; *D:* Kenji Mizoguchi; *W:* Yoshikata Yoda; *M:* Ichiro Saito. *NYF, FCT, BTV*

The Geisha Boy 🐾🐾 **1958** Jerry is a floundering magician who joins the USO and tours the Far East. His slapstick confrontations with the troupe leader and an officer who dreams of attending his own funeral provide hearty laughs, plus Lewis finds romance with a Japanese widow after her son claims him as a father. Pleshette's film debut, with an appearance by the Los Angeles Dodgers. **98m/C VHS, Closed Caption.** Jerry Lewis, Marie McDonald, Sessue Hayakawa, Barton MacLane, Suzanne Pleshette, Nobu McCarthy; *D:* Frank Tashlin. *PAR*

Geisha Girl 🐾½ **1952** Forgotten sci-fi film about a mad scientist and his Japanese cohorts who develop small explosive pills that are more powerful than nuclear bombs. Their plans of world conquest are thwarted when the pills inadvertently fall into the hands of two American G.I.s. **67m/B VHS.** Martha Hyer, William Andrews, Archer MacDonald, Kekao Yokoo, Teddy Nakamura; *D:* George Breakston, C. Ray Stahl; *W:* C. Ray Stahl. *SNC*

Gemini Affair 🐾 **198?** Two women go to Hollywood to become rich and famous but end up being very disappointed. **88m/C VHS, Beta.** Marta Kristen, Kathy Kersh, Anne Seymour. *UNI*

Gene Autry Matinee Double Feature #1 **1953** Includes "Blue Canadian Rockies" (1952), where Autry must investigate a series of murders, and "Last of the Pony Riders" (1953), in which the final days of the pony express yield a sinister conspiracy. **117m/C VHS.** Gene Autry; *D:* George Archainbaud. *NO*

Gene Autry Matinee Double Feature #2 **1953** An exciting western double feature: A cowboy goes after the man who stole his rodeo winnings in "Melody Trail," and a territorial ranger investigates a series of Indian raids in "Winning of the West." **117m/C VHS, Beta.** Gene Autry, Smiley Burnette, Alan Bridge; *D:* George Archainbaud, Joseph Kane. *NO*

Gene Autry Matinee Double Feature #3 **1953** Gene stars in "Prairie Moon," in which he teaches some tough kids a lesson about life, and "On Top of Old Smokey," which sees a young woman trying to save her small town. **113m/B VHS, Beta.** Gene Autry, Smiley Burnette; *D:* George Archainbaud, Ralph Staub. *NO*

The Gene Krupa Story 🐾🐾½ **1959** The story of the famous jazz drummer and his career plunge after a drug conviction. Krupa recorded the soundtrack, mimed by Mineo, who was too young for a convincing portrayal. Gavin McLeod (of "Love Boat" fame) has a small part as Mineo's dad. **101m/B VHS, Beta.** Sal Mineo, James Darren, Susan Kohner, Susan Oliver, Anita O'Day, Red Nichols; *D:* Don Weis. *COL, FCT*

The General 🐾🐾🐾🐾 **1927** Keaton's masterpiece and arguably the most formally perfect and funniest of silent comedies. Concerns a plucky Confederate soldier who single-handedly retrieves a pivotal train from Northern territory. Full of eloquent man-vs-machinery images and outrageous sight gags. Remade as "The Great Locomotive Chase" in 1956 with Fess Parker. **78m/B VHS, Beta, LV, 8mm.** Buster Keaton, Marion Mack, Glen Cavender, Jim Farley, Joe Keaton; *D:* Buster Keaton, Clyde Bruckman. *VYY, HHT, NOS*

The General Died at Dawn 🐾🐾🐾 **1936** A clever, atmospheric suspense film about an American mercenary in Shanghai falling in love with a beautiful spy as he battles a fierce Chinese warlord who wants to take over the country. Playwright-to-be Odets' first screenplay; he, O'Hara and '30s gossip hound Skolsky have cameos as reporters. **93m/B VHS, Beta.** Gary Cooper, Madeleine Carroll, Akim Tamiroff, Dudley Digges, Porter Hall, William Frawley, Philip Ahn; *Cameos:* John O'Hara, Clifford Odets, Sidney Skolsky; *D:* Lewis Milestone; *W:* Clifford Odets; *C:* Victor Milner. Nominations: Academy Awards '36: Best Cinematography, Best Supporting Actor (Tamiroff), Best Original Score. *USH*

The General Line 🐾🐾🐾🐾 *The Old and the New* **1929** Eisenstein's classic pro-Soviet semi-documentary about a poor farm woman who persuades her village to form a cooperative. Transgresses its party-line instructional purpose by vivid filmmaking. The director's last silent film. **90m/B VHS, Beta.** *RU* Marfa Lapkina; *D:* Sergei Eisenstein. National Board of Review Awards '30: 5 Best Foreign Films of the Year. *NOS, MRV, DVT*

General Spanky 🐾🐾 **1936** The only feature "Our Gang" comedy goofed by transplanting them to a Civil War milieu popular at the time. Confederate kids Spanky and Alfalfa play soldier, ultimately outsmarting Union troops. The rascals are still funny sometimes, but Buckwheat's role as an eager slave is disturbing today. **73m/B VHS, LV.** George "Spanky" McFarland, Phillips Holmes, Ralph Morgan, Irving Pichel, Rosina Lawrence, Billie "Buckwheat" Thomas, Carl "Alfalfa" Switzer, Louise Beavers; *D:* Fred Newmeyer. Nominations: Academy Awards '36: Best Sound. *MGM, FCT*

Generale Della Rovere 🐾🐾🐾½ *Il Generale Della-Rovere* **1960** A WWII black marketeer is forced by the Nazis to go undercover in a local prison. To find out who the resistance leaders are, he poses as a general. But when prisoners begin to look to him for guidance, he finds the line between his assumed role and real identity diminished, leading to a tragic conclusion. Acclaimed film featuring a bravura lead performance by veteran director De Sica. In Italian with English subtitles. **139m/B VHS, Beta.** *IT* Vittorio De Sica, Otto Messmer, Sandra Milo; *D:* Roberto Rossellini. *NOS, CVC, HHT*

A Generation 🐾🐾🐾 **1954** During WWII, a young man escapes from the Warsaw Ghetto and finds his way to the Polish Resistance. He falls in love with the leader of the local group and finds the courage to fight for his freedom. Strong directorial debut from Wajda. Part 1 of his "War Trilogy," followed by "Kanal" and "Ashes and Diamonds." Scripted by Czeszko from his novel "Pokolenie." Polish with subtitles. **90m/B VHS.** *PL* Tadeusz Lomnicki, Ursula Modrzynska, Zbigniew Cybulski, Roman Polanski; **D:** Andrzej Wajda; **W:** Bohdan Czeszko. *FCT, HMV, PME*

Generation
🎞️🎞️ A Time For Caring 1969 A very pregnant bride informs everyone she'll give birth at home without doctors, and creates a panic. Based on the Broadway play by William Goodhart. **109m/C VHS, Beta.** David Janssen, Kim Darby, Carl Reiner, Andrew Prine, James Coco, Sam Waterston; **D:** George Schaefer; **W:** William Goodhart; **C:** Lionel Lindon; **M:** Dave Grusin.

Generations: Mind Control-From the Future
🎞️ 1980 Max Lang has lost all self-control and is being driven by evil forces beyond time, forced to kill while fleeing total extinction. **54m/C VHS, Beta.** *NO*

Genevieve
🎞️🎞️🎞️ 1953 A 1904 Darracq roadster is the title star of this picture which spoofs "classic car" owners and their annual rally from London to Brighton. Two married couples challenge each other to a friendly race which becomes increasingly intense as they near the finish line. **86m/C VHS, Beta.** *GB* John Gregson, Dinah Sheridan, Kenneth More, Kay Kendall, Geoffrey Keen, Reginald Beckwith, Arthur Wontner, Joyce Grenfell, Leslie Mitchell, Michael Medwin, Michael Balfour, Edie Martin, Harold Siddons; **D:** Henry Cornelius; **W:** William Rose; **M:** Larry Adler. British Academy Awards '53: Best Film; Golden Globe Awards '55: Best Foreign Film; Nominations: Academy Awards '54: Best Story & Screenplay, Original Dramatic/Comedy Score. *LCA*

Genghis Cohn
🎞️🎞️½ 1993 Black comedy follows the misadventures of a former Nazi concentration camp commander (Lindsay) who has settled in a small Bavarian town and taken on the position of police chief. But his quiet life is rocked by a series of murders, an affair with a kinky Baroness (Rigg), and by the ghost of Jewish comedian Genghis Cohn (Sher), a victim of the camps whose haunting presence exacts a particularly appropriate revenge. Adapted from Romain Gary's novel "The Dance of Genghis Cohn." Made for British TV. **100m/C VHS.** *GB* Robert Lindsay, Diana Rigg, Anthony Sher; **D:** Elijah Moshinsky; **W:** Stanley Price. *AAE*

Genie of Darkness
🎞️ 1960 The ashes of Nostradamus himself are retrieved in a bid to destroy his vampiric descendent. Edited from a Mexican serial; if you were able to sit through this one, look for "Curse of Nostradamus" and "The Monster Demolisher." **?m/B VHS.** *MX* German Robles; **D:** Frederick Curiel. *SNC, NOS, LOO*

Gentle Giant
🎞️🎞️ 1967 An orphaned bear is taken in by a boy and his family and grows to be a 750 pound giant who must be returned to the wild. "Gentle Ben" TV series was derived from this feature. **93m/C VHS.** Dennis Weaver, Vera Miles, Ralph Meeker, Clint Howard, Huntz Hall; **D:** James Neilson. *REP*

Gentle Savage
🎞️🎞️½ Camper John 1973 (R) When an Indian is wrongly accused of raping and beating a white woman, the white community seeks revenge. The vengeful mob, led by the victim's step-father, is unaware that it's really their ringleader who is responsible for the crime. When the accused's brother is slain, the Indian community retaliates. Violent but well-crafted. **85m/C VHS.** William Smith, Gene Evans, Barbara Luna, Joe Flynn; **D:** Sean McGregor. *LIV*

A Gentle Woman
🎞️🎞️ A Gentle Creature; Une Femme Douce 1969 Adaptation of Dostoevsky's short story about a young married woman who kills herself. Sanda marries pawnbroker Frangin, is miserable in her marriage, toys with killing her husband, and commits suicide instead, leaving the bewildered Frangin to try to figure out why. Several theories are offered but nothing is ever made clear. Debut of Sanda; Bressons' first film in color. French with subtitles. **89m/C VHS.** *FR* Domi-

nique Sanda, Guy Frangin, Jane Lobre; **D:** Robert Bresson; **W:** Robert Bresson; **C:** Ghislan Cloquet; **M:** Jean Wiener. *NYF, FCT*

Gentleman Bandit
🎞️🎞️ 1981 So-so drama about Father Bernard Pagano, a Boston priest mistakenly arrested as a stickup artist. Based on a true story. Made for television. **96m/C VHS, Beta.** Ralph Waite, Julie Bovasso, Jerry Zaks, Joe Grifasi, Estelle Parsons, Tom Aldredge; **D:** Jonathan Kaplan. *MTI*

The Gentleman from California
🎞️ The Californian 1937 The dashing son of a Mexican landowner returns home and finds his people's land stolen from them by greedy tax collectors. **56m/B VHS, Beta, 8mm.** Ricardo Cortez, Marjorie Weaver, Katherine DeMille; **D:** Gus Meins. *VYY*

Gentleman from Dixie
🎞️🎞️ 1941 After LaRue is released from prison, he looks to change his life by joining his brother on a farm and seeking revenge on the man who put him in the pokey. **61m/B VHS.** Jack LaRue, Marian Marsh, Clarence Muse, Mary Ruth, Robert Kellard, John Holland, Herbert Rawlinson; **D:** Al(bert) Herman. *MOV*

Gentleman from Texas
🎞️ 1946 Ropin', ridin', and romance figure in this less than dramatic oater. **55m/B VHS.** Johnny Mack Brown, Raymond Hatton, Claudia Drake, Reno Blair, Christine McIntyre; **D:** Lambert Hillyer. *NOS, DVT*

Gentleman Jim
🎞️🎞️🎞️½ 1942 A colorful version of the life of old-time heavyweight boxing great Jim Corbett, transformed from a typical Warner Bros. bio-pic by director Walsh into a fun-loving, anything-for-laughs donnybrook. Climaxes with Corbett's fight for the championship against the great John L. Sullivan. One of Flynn's most riotous performances. **104m/B VHS, Beta, LV, Closed Caption.** Errol Flynn, Alan Hale, Alexis Smith, Jack Carson, Ward Bond, Arthur Shields, William Frawley; **D:** Raoul Walsh. *MGM, FOX*

The Gentleman Killer
🎞️ 1978 A man-with-no-name clears a ravaged border town of murdering bandits. **95m/C VHS, Beta.** Anthony Steffen, Silvia Solar. *UNI*

Gentleman's Agreement
🎞️🎞️🎞️ 1947 A magazine writer (Peck) looks for a new angle for an article on anti-Semitism by pretending to be Jewish. His new identity pervades his life in unexpected ways, almost destroys his relationships, but contributes to the success of his magazine series. This movie was Hollywood's first major attack on anti-Semitism. Controversial in its day, yet still timely. **118m/B VHS, LV.** Gregory Peck, Dorothy McGuire, John Garfield, Celeste Holm, Anne Revere, June Havoc, Albert Dekker, Jane Wyatt, Dean Stockwell, Nicholas Joy; **D:** Elia Kazan; **W:** Moss Hart; **C:** Arthur C. Miller. Academy Awards '47: Best Director (Kazan), Best Picture, Best Supporting Actress (Holm); Golden Globe Awards '48: Best Director (Kazan), Best Film—Drama, Best Supporting Actress (Holm); New York Film Critics Awards '47: Best Director (Kazan), Best Film; Nominations: Academy Awards '47: Best Actor (Peck), Best Actress (McGuire), Best Film Editing, Best Screenplay, Best Supporting Actress (Revere). *FXV, BTV*

Gentlemen Prefer Blondes
🎞️🎞️🎞️ 1953 Amusing satire involving two show-business girls from Little Rock trying to make it big in Paris. Seeking rich husbands or diamonds, their capers land them in police court. Monroe plays Lorelei Lee, Russell is her sidekick. Despite an occasionally slow plot, the music, comedy, and performances are great fun. Film version of a Broadway adaption of a story by Anita Loos. Followed by (but without Monroe) "Gentlemen Marry Brunettes." ♫A (Two) Little Girl(s) From Little Rock; Bye, Bye Baby; Ain't There Anyone Here For Love?; When Love Goes Wrong; Diamonds Are A Girl's Best Friend. **91m/C VHS, Beta, LV.** Marilyn Monroe, Jane Russell, Charles Coburn, Elliott Reid, Tommy Noonan, George Winslow; **D:** Howard Hawks. *FOX*

Genuine Risk
🎞️½ 1989 (R) Gorgeous young woman turns off her crime boss boyfriend bigtime when she seduces his bodyguard. Genuine tripe. **89m/C VHS, LV.** Terence Stamp, Michelle John-

son, Peter Berg, M.K. Harris; **D:** Kurt Voss; **W:** Kurt Voss. *COL*

George!
🎞️½ 1970 (G) A carefree bachelor takes his girlfriend and his 250-pound St. Bernard on a trip to the Swiss Alps where he proves that a dog is not always man's best friend. **87m/C VHS, Beta.** Marshall Thompson, Jack Mullaney, Inge Schoner; **D:** Wallace C. Bennett; **W:** Wallace C. Bennett. *VCI*

George Balanchine's The Nutcracker
🎞️🎞️½ The Nutcracker 1993 (G) Pas de deux redeux. Tchaikovsky's classic ballet about the magic of Christmas and a little girl (Cohen) who dreams on Christmas Eve that she is in an enchanted kingdom. Culkin lamely grins through his wooden performance as the Nutcracker Prince, but the talent of the Sugarplum Fairy (Kistler) and the other dancers is such that conventional camera techniques sometimes fail to keep up with their exacting moves. Adapted from the 1816 book by E.T.A. Hoffmann. **93m/C VHS, LV, 8mm, Closed Caption.** Macaulay Culkin, Jessica Lynn Cohen, Bart Robinson Cook, Darci Kistler, Damian Woetzel, Kyra Nichols, Wendy Whelan, Gen Horiuchi, Margaret Tracey; **D:** Emile Ardolino; **W:** Susan Cooper; **C:** Ralf Bode. *WAR*

The George McKenna Story
🎞️🎞️½ 1986 Washington stars as the newly appointed principal of George Washington High in Los Angeles. The school is located in South Central, a gang and drug-infested war zone where the students are armed for their own protection. The situation appears hopeless but McKenna refuses to give up. Based on a true story. Made for television. **95m/C VHS.** Denzel Washington, Lynn Whitfield, Akosua Busia, Richard Masur; **D:** Eric Laneuville; **W:** Charles Eric Johnson; **M:** Herbie Hancock. *PSM*

George of the Jungle
🎞️🎞️½ 1997 (PG) The '60s cartoon hero goes big screen and live-action with Fraser starring as the clumsy jungle hero. While on safari, socialite Ursula (Mann) falls in love with George and takes him back to San Francisco, much to the chagrin of her fiance (Church). When poachers endanger his "family" back home George returns, aided by his brother, Ape (voiced by Cleese), and an elephant that thinks it's a dog. Fraser is an appealing lead, and the script retains creator Ward's smart, subversive edge. The stunts are more impressive than you'd usually expect from a cartoon adaptation. Hollywood's recycling project is still in overdrive, but this one actually works. **?m/C VHS.** Brendan Fraser, Leslie Mann, Thomas Haden Church, Holland Taylor, Richard Roundtree, Greg Cruttwell, Abraham Benrubi; **D:** Sam Weisman; **W:** Dana Olsen, Audrey Wells; **C:** Thomas Ackerman; **V:** John Cleese. *NYR*

George Washington
🎞️🎞️½ 1984 Bostwick stars as the father of our country in this made for television adaptation of James Thomas Flexner's biography. The destitute young Washington develops a close friendship with the wealthy Will Fairfax (Dukes), who provides him with the support to pursue his dreams, even though Washington has secretly fallen in love with Sally (Smith), Will's flirtatious wife. George himself has married the widowed Martha (Duke) and begins his military career, leading the American colonies against the Brits in the Revolutionary War. On three cassettes. **398m/C VHS, Beta, Closed Caption.** Barry Bostwick, David Dukes, Jaclyn Smith, Patty Duke, Hal Holbrook, Lloyd Bridges, Jose Ferrer, Trevor Howard, Richard Kiley, James Mason, Clive Revill, Robert Stack; **W:** Richard Fielder. *WAR*

George Washington Slept Here
🎞️🎞️🎞️ 1942 Hilarious side-splitter about a couple who moves from their Manhattan apartment to an old, broken-down country home in Connecticut. It's one catastrophe after another as the couple tries to renovate their home and deal with a greedy neighbor. Based on the play by George S. Kaufman and Moss Hart. **93m/B VHS.** Jack Benny, Ann Sheridan, Charles Coburn, Percy Kilbride, Hattie McDaniel, William Tracy; **D:** William Keighley. Nomi-

nations: Academy Awards '42: Best Interior Decoration. *MGM*

George Washington: The Forging of a Nation 🐾🐾½ **1986** Sequel to the "George Washington" miniseries finds Bostwick and Duke reprising their roles as George and Martha. Unfortunately, the later part of Washington's life isn't nearly as exciting. **208m/C VHS, Closed Caption.** Barry Bostwick, Patty Duke, Penny Fuller, Jeffrey Jones, Richard Bekins; **D:** William A. Graham; **M:** Bruce Broughton.

George White's Scandals 🐾🐾 **1945** A lightweight musical comedy look at the show biz world and why the show must go on. Based on White's Broadway extravaganzas. Jazz numbers by Gene Krupa and his band. Preceded by "George White's Scandals" of 1934 and 1935. ♫Bolero in the Jungle; E.H.S.; Leave Us Leap; I Want to be a Drummer in the Band; How Did You Get Out of My Dreams?; I Wake Up in the Morning; Who Killed Vaudeville?; Scandals; Liza. **95m/B VHS, Beta.** Joan Davis, Jack Haley, Jane Greer, Phillip Terry, Margaret Hamilton, Martha Holliday; **D:** Felix Feist. *CCB*

George's Island 🐾🐾🐾 **1991 (PG)** When young George is placed with the worst foster parents in the world, his eccentric grandfather helps him escape. They wind up on Oak's Island, where, legend has it, Captain Kidd's ghost and buried treasure reside. They soon find out the legends are real! **89m/C VHS, LV.** Ian Bannen, Sheila McCarthy, Maury Chaykin, Nathaniel Moreau, Vicki Ridler, Brian Downey, Gary Reineke; **D:** Paul Donovan; **W:** J. William Ritchie; **M:** Marty Simon. *COL, NLC*

Georgia 🐾🐾 **1987** Tough lawyer Nina Bailey (Davis) explores her past when she begins a search for information on her biological mother, Georgia White, a photographer who drowned herself years before. Only Nina has no idea about the Pandora's box of secrets she's about to unleash. Frequent flashbacks to Georgia's mysterious life and death (Davis well plays both roles). **90m/C VHS.** **AU** Judy Davis, Julia Blake, John Bach; **D:** Ben Lewin. *ORI, FXL*

Georgia 🐾🐾🐾 **1995 (R)** Character study about sibling rivalry, self-destruction, and the Seattle music scene. Struggling rock singer Sadie (Leigh), who relies on booze, drugs, and men to help her make it through the night, returns to Seattle to crash with big-sister Georgia (Winningham). Settled, with loving husband and kids, the much more talented Georgia is also a popular folk icon and has the type of personal/career success angry and ambitious Sadie can only dream about. Fine performances—particularly from the chameonlike Leigh; both leads do their own singing. Screenwriter Turner is Leigh's mother.**CW:** Substance abuse, language, and a sex scene. **117m/C VHS, LV, Closed Caption.** Jennifer Jason Leigh, Mare Winningham, Ted Levine, Max Perlich, John Doe, John C. Reilly, Jimmy Witherspoon; **D:** Ulu Grosbard; **W:** Barbara Turner; **C:** Jan Kiesser. Independent Spirit Awards '96: Best Supporting Actress (Winningham); Montreal World Film Festival '95: Best Actress (Leigh), Best Film; New York Film Critics Awards '95: Best Actress (Leigh); Nominations: Academy Awards '95: Best Supporting Actress (Winningham); Independent Spirit Awards '96: Best Actress (Leigh), Best Director (Grosbard), Best Supporting Actor (Perlich); Screen Actors Guild Award '95: Best Supporting Actress (Winningham). *TOU*

Georgia, Georgia 🐾½ **1972 (R)** Sands is a black entertainer on tour in Sweden who falls for a white photographer. Her traveling companion, who hates whites, takes drastic action to separate the lovers. Poor acting, script, and direction. Based on a book by Maya Angelou. **91m/C VHS, Beta.** Diana Sands, Dirk Benedict, Minnie Gentry; **D:** Stig Bjorkman; **W:** Maya Angelou. *PSM*

Georgy Girl 🐾🐾🐾 **1966** Redgrave finely plays the overweight ugly-duckling Georgy who shares a flat with the beautiful and promiscuous Meredith (Rampling). Georgy is, however, desired by the wealthy and aging Mason and soon by

Meredith's lover (Bates) who recognizes her good heart. When Meredith becomes pregnant, Georgy persuades her to let her raise the baby, leaving Georgy with the dilemma of marrying the irresponsible Bates (the baby's father) or the settled Mason. The film and title song (sung by the Seekers) were both huge hits. Based on the novel by Margaret Foster who also co-wrote the screenplay. **100m/B VHS, Beta, LV.** **GB** Lynn Redgrave, James Mason, Charlotte Rampling, Alan Bates, Bill Owen, Claire Kelly, Rachel Kempson; **D:** Silvio Narizzano. Golden Globe Awards '67: Best Actress—Musical/Comedy (Redgrave); National Board of Review Awards '66: 10 Best Films of the Year; New York Film Critics Awards '66: Best Actress (Redgrave); Nominations: Academy Awards '66: Best Actress (Redgrave), Best Black and White Cinematography, Best Song ("Georgy Girl"), Best Supporting Actor (Mason).*FCT, COL*

Germany in Autumn 🐾🐾 *Deutschland im Herbst* **1978** Twelve West German filmmakers offer political statements and artistic commentary on the political situation in their country after the kidnapping and murder of industrialist Hans Martin Schleyer. In German with English subtitles. **124m/C VHS.** **GE** **D:** Volker Schlondorff, Rainer Werner Fassbinder, Alf Brustellin, Alexander Kluge, Maximiliane Mainka, Edgar Reitz, Katja Rupe, Hans Peter Cloos, Bernhard Sinkel, Beate Mainka-Jellinghaus, Peter Schubert, Heinrich Boll; **W:** Heinrich Boll. *WAC, FCT*

Germicide 🐾 **1974** Scientist tries to warn the world of the threat posed by a horrifying bacterial weapon. Terrorists and his mistress hatch plots against him. **90m/C Beta.** Rod Taylor, Bibi Andersson. *PSM*

Germinal 🐾🐾🐾 **1993 (R)** Recounts the struggle of working-class coal miners in France, led by Depardieu and wife Miou-Miou, to stave off poverty. While greedy investors debate how far they should lower miners' wages, the Maheu family, spurred on by newly arrived Marxist and off-camera French pop star Renaud, lead a strike. Minor themes revolving around management's adulterous adventures provide some momentary relief to relieve short attention spans. Seems so self-consciously an epic drama, however, that the overall effect is ponderous. Adaptation of the 19th century novel by Zola. In French with English subtitles.*CW:* Violence; language; brief nudity. **158m/C VHS, LV.** **FR** Gerard Depardieu, Miou-Miou, Bernard Fresson, Jean Carmet, Laurent Terzieff, Anny Duperey, Renaud, Jacques Dacqmine; **D:** Claude Berri; **W:** Claude Berri, Arlette Langmann; **C:** Yves Angelo; **M:** Jean-Louis Roques. Cesar Awards '94: Best Cinematography, Best Costume Design. *COL*

Geronimo 🐾🐾½ **1962** In typical Hollywood casting Connors stars as the Indian leader on the warpath against the cavalry over broken treaties. Lots of action and the Indians are actually the good guys. **101m/C VHS, LV.** Chuck Connors, Ross Martin, Pat Conway, Kamala Devi, Adam West, Lawrence Dobkin, Denver Pyle, Enid Jaynes, Armando Silvestre, John Anderson; **D:** Arnold Laven. *MGM*

Geronimo 🐾🐾🐾 **1993** Not to be confused with the big screen version, this made for cable television drama uses three actors to portray the legendary Apache warrior (1829-1909) at various stages of his life. The intrepid teenager who leads attacks on Mexican troops, the adult fighting the duplicitous bluecoats, and the aged man witnessing the destruction of his way of life. The true story is told from the point of view of Native American culture and historical records. Somewhat overly earnest. **120m/C VHS.** Joseph Runningfox, Jimmy Herman, Ryan Black, Nick Ramus, Michelle St. John, Michael Greyeyes, Tailinh Forest Flower, Kimberly Norris, August Schellenberg, Geno Silva, Harrison Lowe; **D:** Roger Young; **W:** J.T. Allen; **M:** Patrick Williams. *TTC*

Geronimo: An American Legend 🐾🐾½ **1993 (PG-13)** Well-intentioned bio-actioner about the legendary Apache leader who fought the U.S. Army over forcing Native Americans onto reservations. Narrator is young Army officer Gatewood (Patric), whose division is

to round up the renegades led by Geronimo (Studi), whom he naturally comes to admire. Hackman and Duvall (as a General and a scout respectively) steal any scene they're in although the leads manage to hold their own. Too noble for its own good and somewhat plodding. Great location filming around Moab, Utah. **115m/C VHS, LV, 8mm, Closed Caption.** Wes Studi, Jason Patric, Robert Duvall, Gene Hackman, Matt Damon, Rodney Grant, Kevin Tighe, Carlos Palomino, Stephen McHattie; **D:** Walter Hill; **W:** John Milius, Larry Gross; **C:** Lloyd Ahern; **M:** Ry Cooder. Nominations: Academy Awards '93: Best Sound. *COL*

Geronimo's Revenge 🐾½ **1960** When Geronimo starts a battle with the settlers, a rancher he has befriended finds himself caught in the middle. The fourth soggy Disney TV oater from the "Tales of Texas John Slaughter" series. **77m/C VHS, Beta.** Tom Tryon, Darryl Hickman; **D:** Harry Keller. *NO*

Gertrud 🐾🐾🐾½ **1964** The simple story of an independent Danish woman rejecting her husband and lovers in favor of isolation. Cold, dry, minimalistic techniques make up Dreyer's final film. In Danish with subtitles. **116m/B VHS, Beta.** **DK** Nina Pens Rode, Bendt Rothe, Ebbe Rode; **D:** Carl Theodor Dreyer; **W:** Carl Theodor Dreyer. National Board of Review Awards '65: 5 Best Foreign Films of the Year. *FCT, DVT, HEG*

Gervaise 🐾🐾🐾 **1956** The best of several films of Emile Zola's "L'Assommoir." A 19th-century middle-class family is destroyed by the father's plunge into alcoholism despite a mother's attempts to save them. Well acted but overwhelmingly depressing. In French with English subtitles. **89m/B VHS, Beta.** **FR** Maria Schell, Francois Perier, Suzy Delair, Armand Mestral; **D:** Rene Clement; **M:** Georges Auric. British Academy Awards '56: Best Actor (Perier), Best Film; National Board of Review Awards '57: 5 Best Foreign Films of the Year; New York Film Critics Awards '57: Best Foreign Film; Venice Film Festival '56: Best Actress (Schell); Nominations: Academy Awards '56: Best Foreign Language Film. *DVT, FST, WFV*

Get Christie Love! 🐾🐾 **1974** Vintage blaxploitation from the genre's halcyon days, when going undercover meant a carte blanche for skimpy outfits. Based on Dorothy Uhnak's detective novel, the eponymous policewoman goes undercover to bring a thriving drug empire to it knees. The outcome: a TV series. Graves previously appeared on television as one of the "Laugh-In" party girls. **95m/C VHS.** Teresa Graves, Harry Guardino, Louise Sorel, Paul Stevens, Andy Romano, Debbie Dozier; **D:** William A. Graham. *XVC*

Get Crazy 🐾🐾 **1983** The owner of the Saturn Theatre is attempting to stage the biggest rock-and-roll concert of all time on New Year's Eve 1983, and everything is going wrong in this hilarious, off-beat film. **90m/C VHS, Beta, LV.** Malcolm McDowell, Allen (Goorwitz) Garfield, Daniel Stern, Gail Edwards, Ed Begley Jr., Lou Reed, Bill Henderson; **D:** Allan Arkush; **M:** Michael Boddicker. *NLC*

Get On the Bus 🐾🐾🐾 **1996 (R)** Lee looks at the personal side of the Million Man March through a fictional group of men who board a bus in south central L.A. and head for Washington, D.C. Practically ignoring the event itself, Lee and writer Bythewood focus on the the men who participated, their reasons, and their interaction with each other. Standouts in the melting pot of characters include Dutton as the attentive bus driver, a brash young actor (Braugher), a likable old man (Davis), an absentee father (Byrd) and his potentially delinquent son (Bonds), and a cop (Smith). Despite low budget (2.4 mil) and tight shooting schedule (21 days), Lee manages to drive the story home with fine dialogue and characterization that (for the most part) avoids stereotypes.*CW:* Language. **122m/C VHS, LV, Closed Caption.** Andre Braugher, Ossie Davis, Charles S. Dutton, De'Aundre Bonds, Gabriel Casseus, Albert Hall, Hill Harper, Harry J. Lennix, Bernie Mac, Wendell Pierce, Roger Guenveur Smith, Isaiah Washington, Steve White, Thomas Jefferson Byrd, Richard Belzer, Randy Quaid; **D:** Spike Lee; **W:**

Reggie Rock Bythewood; *C:* Elliot Davis; *M:* Terence Blanchard. *COL*

Get Out Your Handkerchiefs 🎬🎬🎬½ *Preparez Vous Mouchoirs* **1978 (R)** Unconventional comedy about a husband desperately attempting to make his sexually frustrated wife happy. Determined to go to any lengths, he asks a Mozart-loving teacher to become her lover. She is now, however, bored by both men. Only when she meets a 13-year-old genius at the summer camp where the three adults are counselors does she come out of her funk and find her sexual happiness. Laure is a beautiful character, but Depardieu and Dewaere are wonderful as the bewildered would-be lovers. Academy Award winner for best foreign film. In French with English subtitles. **109m/C VHS, Beta, LV.** *FR* Gerard Depardieu, Patrick Dewaere, Carole Laure; *D:* Bertrand Blier; *W:* Bertrand Blier; *M:* Georges Delerue. Academy Awards '78: Best Foreign Language Film; Cesar Awards '79: Best Score; National Society of Film Critics Awards '78: Best Film. *WAR, INT*

Get Rita 🎬🎬 *Gun Moll; Poopsie; Oopsie Poopsie; La Puppa del Gangster* **1975** Italian prostitute sets up her gangster boyfriend for a murder she committed and she winds up as mob boss. **90m/C VHS, Beta.** Sophia Loren, Marcello Mastroianni; *D:* Tom Rowe. *CTC*

Get Shorty 🎬🎬🎬 **1995 (R)** Low-level Miami loan shark and film buff Chili Palmer (Travolta) heads to Hollywood via Las Vegas, looking for a deadbeat drycleaner (Paymer) and a grade-Z movie producer (Hackman) who owes Vegas $150,000. Aided by B-movie scream-queen (Russo), Palmer is pitted against a variety of shady Hollywood-types, including egomaniacal star (DeVito) while trying to get into showbiz himself. Snappy scripting and performances finally do screen justice to an Elmore Leonard novel. DeVito, with the smaller title role, was originally cast as Chili Palmer, a role Travolta twice turned down until the ubiquitous Quentin Tarantino advised him to take it. *CW:* Language and some violence. **105m/C VHS, LV, Closed Caption, DVD.** John Travolta, Gene Hackman, Danny DeVito, Rene Russo, Dennis Farina, Delroy Lindo, David Paymer, James Gandolfini; *Cameos:* Bette Midler, Harvey Keitel, Penny Marshall; *D:* Barry Sonnenfeld; *W:* Scott Frank; *C:* Don Peterman; *M:* John Lurie. Golden Globe Awards '96: Best Actor—Musical/Comedy (Travolta); Nominations: Golden Globe Awards '96: Best Film—Musical/Comedy, Best Screenplay; Screen Actors Guild Award '95: Cast; Writers Guild of America '95: Best Adapted Screenplay. *MGM*

Get Smart, Again! 🎬🎬½ **1989** Would you believe Maxwell Smart is back again as CONTROL's most incompetent agent? How about Agent 99 as his sidekick? Hymie the robot and those no-good-niks at KAOS? Well, it's all true. This second reunion movie (following "The Nude Bomb") from the '60s TV show highlights all the wacky gadgetry, including the shoe phone, but fails to find the show's original outlandishness. Made for television. **93m/C VHS, Closed Caption.** Don Adams, Barbara Feldon, Dick Gautier, Bernie Kopell, Kenneth Mars, Harold Gould, Roger Price, Fritz Feld, Robert Karvelas, King Moody; *D:* Gary Nelson. *WOV*

Get That Girl 🎬 **1932** Minor western action pic marred by former silent-screen player Talmadge's heavy German accent which soon lead to him giving up acting for a directing career. **54m/B VHS.** Richard Talmadge, Shirley Grey, Carl Stockdale; *D:* George Crone. *GPV*

Get That Man 🎬🎬 **1935** When a cabby is mistaken for the murdered heir to a vast fortune, his life suddenly becomes complex. **57m/B VHS, Beta, LV.** Wallace Ford, Leon Ames, Lillian Miles, E. Alyn Warren; *D:* Spencer Gordon Bennet. *NOS*

The Getaway 🎬🎬 **1972 (PG)** McQueen plays a thief released on a parole arranged by his wife (McGraw) only to find out a corrupt politician wants him to rob a bank. After the successful holdup, McQueen finds out his cohorts are in the politician's pocket and trying to doublecross him.

McQueen and McGraw are forced into a feverish chase across Texas to the Mexican border, pursued by the politician's henchmen and the state police. Completely amoral depiction of crime and violence with McQueen taciturn as always and McGraw again showing a complete lack of acting skills. Based on a novel by Jim Thompson. McQueen and McGraw had a romance during filming and later married. Remade in 1993. **123m/C VHS, Beta.** Steve McQueen, Ali MacGraw, Ben Johnson, Sally Struthers, Al Lettieri, Slim Pickens, Jack Dodson, Dub Taylor, Bo Hopkins; *D:* Sam Peckinpah; *W:* Walter Hill; *C:* Lucien Ballard; *M:* Quincy Jones. *FCT*

The Getaway 🎬½ **1993 (R)** It was a bad movie in 1972 and the remake hasn't improved the situation. Doc and Carol are husband and wife crooks (played by marrieds Basinger and Baldwin). Doc gets double-crossed and winds up in a Mexican jail; Carol gets a well-connected crook (Woods) to spring her hubby—by sleeping with him and promising Doc will pull off another heist. The robbery's botched, there are double-crosses galore, and the couple go on the run. The stars are pretty but everything's predictable. An unrated version is also available. *CW:* Language, violence, and sexuality. **110m/C VHS, LV, Closed Caption.** Alec Baldwin, Kim Basinger, James Woods, Michael Madsen, Jennifer Tilly, David Morse; *D:* Roger Donaldson; *W:* Walter Hill, Amy Holden Jones; *C:* Peter Menzies Jr.; *M:* Mark Isham. Nominations: MTV Movie Awards '94: Most Desirable Female (Basinger). *USH*

Getting Away With Murder woof! **1996 (R)** An utterly distasteful bomb that proves the Holocaust just isn't as funny as it used to be. College professor Aykroyd takes matters into his own hands when he learns that his kindly neighbor (Lemmon) is a Nazi war criminal. After finding out he may have been a wee bit hasty, he marries the coot's daughter as penance. Writer-director Miller tries to squeeze gags out of such topics as Nazi death camps and Holocaust denial. Definitely career lows for everyone involved. (What were they thinking?) One of the last films released (with no advance warning and no advance screenings) by Savoy pictures. *CW:* Some sexual situations. **92m/C VHS.** Dan Aykroyd, Lily Tomlin, Jack Lemmon, Bonnie Hunt, Brian Kerwin; *D:* Harvey Miller; *W:* Harvey Miller; *C:* Frank Tidy; *M:* John Debney. *HBO*

Getting Even 🎬½ *Hostage: Dallas* **1986 (R)** A maniac threatens to poison the entire population of Texas with a deadly gas unless he gets $50 million. An adventurous businessman sets out to stop him. **90m/C VHS, Beta.** Edward Albert, Joe Don Baker, Audrey Landers; *D:* Dwight Little; *C:* Peter Collister. *LIV, VES*

Getting Even 🎬🎬 **1992 (R)** Dundee and Evans served together in Vietnam. Fifteen years later they're reunited by the FBI to track a former Marine, who once betrayed Evans to the enemy. Seems he's now a drug trafficker and arms dealer who also gets his sadistic pleasures by killing women. The two ex-Marines find they have one last battle to fight. *CW:* Language, violence, and sexuality. **93m/C VHS.** Richard Roundtree, Michael J. Aronin; *D:* Leandro Lucchetti. *GOL*

Getting Even with Dad 🎬½ **1994 (PG)** Crook Danson can't find the money he stole in his last heist. Why? because his precocious son has hidden it with the intention of blackmailing dear old dad into going straight and acting like a real father. Title is unintentionally funny in light of Mac's domineering dad Kit, who makes everybody in Hollywood want to go hide when he appears. Fairly bland family film squanders charm of Danson and Culkin, running formulaic plot into ground. Headly is likewise wasted as district attorney who prosecutes and then falls for Pops. And hey, Macaulay's precocious days are down to a precious few. **108m/C VHS, LV, Closed Caption.** Macaulay Culkin, Ted Danson, Glenne Headly, Hector Elizondo, Saul Rubinek, Gailard Sartain, Kathleen Wilhoite, Sam McMurray; *D:* Howard Deutch; *W:* Tom S. Parker, Jim Jen-

newein. Nominations: Golden Raspberry Awards '94: Worst Actor (Culkin). *MGM*

Getting Gotti 🎬🎬½ **1994 (R)** Story of the seven year investigation and six-month trial by U.S. Attorney's Office prosecutor Diane Giacalone (Bracco) against reputed mobster "Teflon Don" John Gotti. (She lost.) Made for television. *CW:* Violence. **93m/C VHS.** Lorraine Bracco, Anthony John Denison, Kathleen Lasky, August Schellenberg, Kenneth Welsh, Ellen Burstyn, Lawrence Bayne; *D:* Roger Young; *W:* James Henerson; *M:* Patrick Williams. *ACA*

Getting In 🎬½ *Student Body* **1994 (R)** Pressured by the family tradition of attending Johns Hopkins Medical School, Gabriel Higgs (Mailer) decides to bribe the rivals ahead of him on the waiting list. But one of them (McCarthy) decides the easiest thing to do is murder the other candidates and frame Gabe. *CW:* Mild violence; brief nudity; language. **94m/C VHS, LV, Closed Caption.** Steven Mailer, Kristy Swanson, Andrew McCarthy, Dave Chappelle; *D:* Doug Liman; *W:* P.J. Posner, Joel Posner, Jonathan Lewin. *THV*

Getting It On 🎬 **1983 (R)** High school student uses his new-found video equipment for voyeuristic activity. **100m/C VHS, Beta.** Martin Yost, Heather Kennedy, Jeff Edmond, Kathy Rockmeier, Mark Alan Ferri; *D:* William Olsen. *LIV, VES*

Getting It Right 🎬🎬½ **1989 (R)** A sweet-natured British comedy about an inexperienced, shy adult male who is quite suddenly pursued by a middle-aged socialite, a pregnant, unstable rich girl, and a modest single mother. Novel and screenplay by Elizabeth Jane Howard. **101m/C VHS, Beta, LV.** *GB* Jesse Birdsall, Helena Bonham Carter, Lynn Redgrave, Peter Cook, John Gielgud, Jane Horrocks, Richard Huw, Shirley Anne Field, Pat Haywood, Judy Parfitt, Bryan Pringle; *D:* Randal Kleiser; *W:* Elizabeth Jane Howard; *M:* Colin Towns, Steve Tyrell. *VTR*

The Getting of Wisdom 🎬🎬½ **1977** A 13-year-old girl from the Australian outback tries to establish her identity, and her individuality, within the restricting confines of a Victorian girl's boarding school. Based on the novel by Henry Handel Richardson. **100m/C VHS, Beta.** *AU* Susannah Fowle, Hilary Ryan, Alix Longman, Sheila Helpmann, Patricia Kennedy, Barry Humphries, John Waters; *D:* Bruce Beresford. *FCT, FOX*

Getting Out 🎬🎬½ **1994** Arlie (DeMornay) is an ex-con on her way home to Georgia after an eight year prison stint and what she hopes will be a reunion with the son she bore in jail. She thinks he's in a foster home but instead her mother (Burstyn) had the child adopted and if she interferes, Arlie's parole will be revoked. Arlie's trying desperately to rehabilitate herself but the system and old contacts are close to dragging her back down. TV movie adapted from Marsha Norman's 1977 play. **92m/C VHS, LV, Closed Caption.** Rebecca DeMornay, Ellen Burstyn, Rob Knepper, Richard Jenkins, Carol Mitchell-Leon, Tandy Cronyn, Norman Skaggs; *D:* John Korty; *W:* Eugene Corr, Ruth Shapiro; *M:* Mason Daring. *HMK*

Getting Over 🎬 **1981** A black promoter is hired as a figurehead by a bigoted record company president and proceeds to try to run the company his own way. He develops an all-girl group called "The Love Machine" and gets involved in a singer's kidnapping and a record company run by gangsters. Filled with cliches and stereotypes. **108m/C VHS, Beta.** John Daniels, Gwen Brisco, Mary Hopkins, John Goff, Andrew "Buzz" Cooper; *D:* Bernie Rollins; *W:* Bernie Rollins. *UNI*

Getting Physical 🎬½ **1984** After being mugged, a secretary decides to get in shape and enters the world of female body building. Crammed with workout scenes and disco music. Made for television. **95m/C VHS, Beta, Closed Caption.** Alexandra Paul, Sandahl Bergman, David Naughton; *D:* Steven Hilliard Stern; *M:* William Goldstein. *FOX*

Getting Straight 🎭🎭 **1970 (R)** A returning Vietnam soldier (Gould) goes back to his alma mater to secure a teaching degree and gets involved in the lives of his fellow students and the turbulence of the end of the '60s, including campus riots. A now-dated "youth" picture somewhat watchable for Gould's performance. **124m/C VHS, Beta.** Elliott Gould, Candice Bergen, Jeff Corey, Cecil Kellaway, Jeannie Berlin, Harrison Ford, John Rubinstein, Robert F. Lyons, Max Julien; **D:** Richard Rush. *COL*

Getting Up and Going Home 🎭🎭½ **1992** Jack (Skerritt) is a married man with a midlife crisis. So what does he do? Get involved with not one, but two, other women. Is he asking for trouble or what? Adapted from the book by Robert Anderson. **93m/C VHS, Beta, Closed Caption.** Tom Skerritt, Blythe Danner, Roma Downey, Julianne Phillips, Bruce Kirby, Gary Frank, Dorian Harewood, Paul Sand; **D:** Steven Schachter; **W:** Peter Nelson. *PSM*

Getting Wasted 🎭½ **1980 (PG)** Set in 1969 at a military academy for troublesome young men, chaos ensues when the cadets meet hippies. **98m/C VHS, Beta.** Brian Kerwin, Stephen Furst, Cooper Huckabee. *NO*

Gettysburg 🎭🎭🎭½ **1993 (PG)** Civil War buff Ted Turner (who has a cameo as a Confederate soldier) originally intended Michael Shaara's Pulitzer Prize-winning novel "The Killer Angels" to be adapted as a three-part miniseries for his "TNT" network, but the lure of the big screen prevailed, marking the first time the battle has been committed to film and the first time a film crew has been allowed to film battle scenes on the Gettysburg National Military Park battlefield. The greatest battle of the war and the bloodiest in U.S. history is realistically staged by more than 5,000 Civil War re-enactors. The all-male cast concentrates on presenting the human cost of the war, with Daniels particularly noteworthy as the scholarly Colonel Chamberlain, determined to hold Little Big Top for the Union. Last film role for Jordan, to whom the movie is co-dedicated. The full scale recreation of Pickett's Charge is believed to be the largest period scale motion-picture sequence filmed in North America since D.W. Griffith's "Birth of a Nation." **254m/C VHS, Closed Caption.** Jeff Daniels, Martin Sheen, Tom Berenger, Sam Elliott, Richard Jordan, Stephen Lang, Kevin Conway, C. Thomas Howell, Maxwell Caulfield, Andrew Prine, James Lancaster, Royce D. Applegate, Brian Mallon; **Cameos:** Ken Burns, Ted Turner; **D:** Ronald F. Maxwell; **W:** Ronald F. Maxwell; **M:** Randy Edelman. *TTC*

The Ghastly Ones woof! **1968** Three couples must stay in a haunted mansion to inherit an estate, but they're soon being violently killed off. No budget and no talent. Remade as "Legacy of Blood." **81m/C VHS, Beta.** Don Williams, Maggie Rogers, Hal Belsoe, Veronica Redburn; **D:** Andy Milligan. *NO*

Ghetto Blaster 🎭 **1989 (R)** A Vietnam vet takes on out-of-control street gangs to make his neighborhood safe. **86m/C VHS, Beta.** R.G. Armstrong, Richard Hatch, Richard Jaeckel, Harry Caesar, Rose Marie; **D:** Alan L. Stewart. *PSM*

Ghetto Revenge **19??** An embittered Vietnam vet gets caught between white supremacists and black radical activists in this coming home story. He returns and tries to build a life but succumbs to the desire for vengeance and things are never the same. **?m/C VHS.** Mike Sims. *NO*

Ghidrah the Three Headed Monster 🎭🎭½ *Ghidorah Sandai Kaiju Chikyu Saidai No Kessan; Ghidora, The Three-Headed Monster; Ghidrah; The Greatest Battle on Earth; The Biggest Right on Earth; Monster of Monsters* **1965** When a three-headed monster from outer-space threatens the world, humans, having nowhere else to turn, appeal to the friendly Mothra, Rodan, and Godzilla. Rock'em, sock 'em giant thrashing about as Tokyo once again gets trampled. Dependable afternoon monster fare complete with usual dubious dubbing. **85m/C VHS, Beta.** *JP* Yosuke Natsuki, Yuriko Hoshi; **D:** Inoshiro Honda. *HHT, VCN, VHE*

The Ghost 🎭½ *Lo Spettro* **1963** A woman is driven mad by her supposedly dead husband and their evil housekeeper. Sequel to "The Horrible Dr. Hichcock." **96m/C VHS, Beta.** *IT* Barbara Steele, Peter Baldwin, Leonard Eliott, Harriet White; **D:** Riccardo (Robert Hampton) Freda. *SNC*

Ghost 🎭🎭🎭 **1990 (PG-13)** Zucker, known for overboard comedies like "Airplane!" and "Ruthless People," changed tack and directed this undemanding romantic thriller, which was the surprising top grosser of 1990. Swayze is a murdered investment consultant attempting (from somewhere near the hereafter) to protect his lover, Moore, from imminent danger when he learns he was the victim of a hit gone afoul. Goldberg is the medium who suddenly discovers that the powers she's been faking are real. A winning blend of action, special effects (from Industrial Light and Magic) and romance. **127m/C VHS, Beta, LV, 8mm, Closed Caption.** Patrick Swayze, Demi Moore, Whoopi Goldberg, Tony Goldwyn, Rick Aviles, Vincent Schiavelli, Gail Boggs, Armelia McQueen, Phil Leeds; **D:** Jerry Zucker; **W:** Bruce Joel Rubin; **M:** Maurice Jarre. Academy Awards '90: Best Original Screenplay, Best Supporting Actress (Goldberg); British Academy Awards '90: Best Supporting Actress (Goldberg); Golden Globe Awards '91: Best Supporting Actress (Goldberg); People's Choice Awards '91: Best Film—Drama; Nominations: Academy Awards '90: Best Film Editing, Best Picture, Best Original Score. *PAR, FCT, BTV*

The Ghost and Mrs. Muir 🎭🎭🎭 **1947** A charming, beautifully orchestrated fantasy about a feisty widow who, with her young daughter, buys a seaside house and refuses to be intimidated by the crabby ghost of its former sea captain owner. When the widow falls into debt, the captain dictates his sea adventures, which she adapts into a successful novel. The ghost also falls in love with the beautiful lady. Tierney is exquisite and Harrison is sharp-tongued and manly. Based on R. A. Dick's novel. **104m/B VHS, Beta, LV, Closed Caption.** Gene Tierney, Rex Harrison, George Sanders, Edna Best, Anna Lee, Vanessa Brown, Robert Coote, Natalie Wood, Isobel Elsom; **D:** Joseph L. Mankiewicz; **W:** Philip Dunne; **C:** Charles B(ryant) Lang; **M:** Bernard Herrmann. Nominations: Academy Awards '47: Best Black and White Cinematography. *FOX, HMV*

The Ghost and Mr. Chicken 🎭🎭½ **1966** Fraidy cat Luther Heggs (Knotts) works for a small town newspaper and longs to be a hot-shot reporter. One night he thinks he sees a woman's corpse at the vacant Simmons mansion but of course there's no body when the cops come. The house is considered haunted and there is a 20-year-old murder scandal, so Luther is very reluctantly persuaded to spend the night and solve the sinister goings-on. **90m/C VHS, Closed Caption.** Don Knotts, Joan Staley, Dick Sargent, Liam Redmond, Skip Homeier, Reta Shaw, Lurene Tuttle, Philip Ober; **D:** Alan Rafkin; **W:** James Fritzell; **C:** William Margulies; **M:** Vic Mizzy. *USH*

The Ghost and the Darkness 🎭🎭½ **1996 (R)** Based on the true story of two man-eating lions who killed 130 people and nearly derailed the building of the East African railroad in 1896. Engineer John Patterson (Kilmer) is sent to build a bridge over the Tsavo river, but as African liaison Samuel (Kani) informs him, Tsavo prophetically means place of slaughter. The workers become convinced the lions, nicknamed "The Ghost" and "The Darkness" are actually demons and, try as he might, Patterson has little luck killing the beasts. Then, legendary big game hunter Remington (Douglas) is called in—but the lions still seem to have the advantage. Lots of crunching bones, slurping blood, and quick cut editing is used to depict the lions' attacks. *CW:* Some violence and gore involving animal attacks. **110m/C VHS, Beta, Closed Caption.** Val Kilmer, Michael Douglas, John Kani, Bernard Hill, Om Puri, Brian McCardie, Tom Wilkinson, Emily Mortimer, Henry Cele; **D:** Stephen Hopkins; **W:** William Goldman; **C:** Vilmos Zsigmond; **M:** Jerry Goldsmith. Academy Awards '96: Best Sound Effects Edit-

ing; Nominations: Golden Raspberry Awards '96: Worst Supporting Actor (Kilmer). *PAR*

The Ghost and the Guest 🎭🎭½ **1943** Newlyweds spend their honeymoon in a house in the country only to find that gangsters are using the place as a hideout. Chases involving secret passages ensue. **59m/B VHS, Beta.** James Dunn, Florence Rice, Mabel Todd; **D:** William Nigh; **W:** Morey Amsterdam. *SNC, VYY*

The Ghost Breakers 🎭🎭🎭 **1940** As a follow-up to the Hope/Goddard 1939 comedy thriller "The Cat and the Canary," this spooky comedy was even better. Lots of laughs and real chills as Hope and Goddard investigate a haunted mansion that she's inherited in Cuba. Effective horror scenes are expertly handled by director Marshall. Remade in 1953 as "Scared Stiff" with Dean Martin and Jerry Lewis. Based on the play by Paul Dickey and Charles Goddard. **83m/B VHS, LV, Closed Caption.** Bob Hope, Paulette Goddard, Richard Carlson, Paul Lukas, Willie Best, Pedro de Cordoba, Noble Johnson, Anthony Quinn; **D:** George Marshall; **C:** Charles B(ryant) Lang. *USH, BTV*

The Ghost Brigade 🎭🎭½ *The Killing Box* **1993 (R)** Civil War ghost story finds a Union general (Sheen) trying to discover who's slaughtering both Confederate and Union soldiers on the battlefield. So he sends Captain Harling (Pasdar) to investigate, with the help of rebel prisoner Strayn (Bernsen) and a slave (Williams). What they find is an evil brigade of soldiers—who already happen to be dead—and are eager for new recruits. **80m/C VHS, Closed Caption.** Adrian Pasdar, Corbin Bernsen, Martin Sheen, Cynda Williams, Ray Wise, Roger Wilson; **D:** George Hickenlooper; **W:** Matt Greenberg; **C:** Kent Wakeford. *TTC*

The Ghost Camera 🎭🎭½ **1933** Slight story of a man falsely accused of murder. A photograph taken at the murder scene can prove his innocence if only the missing camera can be discovered. **68m/B VHS.** *GB* Henry Kendall, Ida Lupino, John Mills; **D:** Bernard Vorhaus. *HCV*

Ghost Chase 🎭½ **1988 (PG-13)** A young filmmaker desperate for funds inherits his dead relative's clock, from which issues the ghost of the deceased's butler. The ghostly retainer aids in a search for the departed's secret fortune. Neither scary nor funny. **89m/C VHS, Beta, LV.** Jason Lively, Jill Whitlow, Tim McDaniel, Paul Gleason, Chuck "Porky" Mitchell; **D:** Roland Emmerich. *NO*

Ghost Chasers 🎭🎭½ **1951** The Bowery Boys become mixed up in supernatural hijinks when a seance leads to the appearance of a ghost that only Sach can see. **70m/B VHS.** Leo Gorcey, Huntz Hall, Billy Benedict, David Gorcey, Buddy Gorman, Bernard Gorcey, Jan Kayne, Philip Van Zandt, Lloyd Corrigan; **D:** William Beaudine. *WAR*

Ghost City 🎭 **1932** Our hero must deal with a masked gang that is "haunting" a town. **60m/B VHS.** Bill Cody, Helen Foster, Ann Rutherford, John Shelton, Reginald Owen; **D:** Harry Fraser. *NOS, DVT, HEG*

Ghost Crazy 🎭🎭 **1944** Three wild comedians and a gorilla create mayhem in a haunted house. **?m/C VHS.** Shemp Howard, Billy Gilbert, Maxie "Slapsie" Rosenbloom. *LOO*

Ghost Dad 🎭 **1990 (PG)** A widowed workaholic dad is prematurely killed and returns from the dead to help his children prepare for the future. Cosby walks through doors, walls, and other solid objects for the sake of comedy—only none of it is funny. **84m/C VHS, Beta, LV, Closed Caption.** Bill Cosby, Denise Nicholas, Ian Bannen, Christine Ebersole, Dana Ashbrook, Arnold Stang; **D:** Sidney Poitier; **W:** S.S. Wilson, Brent Maddock; **M:** Henry Mancini. *USH*

Ghost Dance 🎭 **1983** Sacred Indian burial ground is violated, with grim results. **93m/C VHS, Beta.** Sherman Hemsley, Henry Ball, Julie Amato; **D:** Peter Bufa. *TWE*

Ghost Fever woof! **1987 (PG)** Two bumbling cops try to evict the inhabitants of a haunted house and get nowhere. A bad rip-off of "Ghostbusters." Alan Smithee is a pseudonym used when a director does not want his or her name on a film—no wonder. **86m/C VHS, Beta, LV.** Sherman Hemsley, Luis Avalos; **D:** Alan Smithee; **W:** Oscar Brodney. *NLC*

The Ghost Goes West ✍✍✍ 1936 A brash American family buys a Scottish castle and transports the pieces to the United States along with the Scottish family ghost (Donat). Also along is the ghost's modern-day descendant (also played by Donat) who is the new castle caretaker and in love with the new owner's daughter. It turns out to be up to the ghost to get the two lovers together and find his own eternal rest. A rather lovable fantasy. Rene Clair's first English film. Available in digitally remastered stereo with original movie trailer. **90m/B VHS, Beta.** *GB* Robert Donat, Jean Parker, Eugene Pallette, Elsa Lanchester, Ralph Bunker, Patricia Hilliard, Everley Gregg, Mortan Selten, Chili Bouchier, Mark Daly, Herbert Lomas, Elliot Mason, Jack Lambert, Hay Petrie; **D:** Rene Clair; **W:** Robert Sherwood, Geoffrey Kerr; **C:** Harold Rosson. *HBO*

Ghost in the Machine ✍½ 1993 (R) Serial killer dies while undergoing an X-ray scan and somehow, because of a lightning storm and a power outage, his soul manages to infiltrate the hospital's computer and go on to terrorize more victims via their home computers and appliances. (You expect this to make sense?) Outlandish, predictable flick hovers between high-tech horror and satiric comedy and wastes some pretty decent talent. Horror buffs may get a kick out of it but be forewarned: You may never view your microwave, dishwasher, or electrical outlets in quite the same way again. **CW:** High-tech horror violence. **104m/C VHS, LV, Closed Caption.** Karen Allen, Chris Mulkey, Ted Marcoux, Jessica Walter, Rick Ducommun, Wil Horneff, Nancy Fish, Brandon Adams; **D:** Rachel Talalay; **W:** William Davies, William Osborne; **M:** Graeme Revell. *FXV*

Ghost in the Noonday Sun woof! 1974 Crew of a treasure-seeking pirate ship sets sail for high sea silliness in this slapstick adventure film. Not a theatrical release for one obvious reason—it's terrible. **90m/C VHS, Beta.** *GB* Peter Sellers, Spike Milligan, Anthony (Tony) Franciosa, Clive Revill, Rosemary Leach, Peter Boyle; **D:** Peter Medak. *NO*

Ghost in the Shell ✍✍ 1995 Animated cyber thriller set in 2029 finds neighborhoods replaced by virtual environments and humans struggling to coexist with sentient cyborgs, known as "shells." A virtual spy, known as the Puppet Master, has caused political and economic havoc through data manipulation and now has left its database world for a physical existence. The Puppet Master is tracked by a shell team that seeks the truth while learning about "ghost" or false memories planted within their circuitry that give the illusion of a past life. Based on a series of comic books by Masamune Shirow. Dubbed. **81m/C VHS, DVD.** *JP* **D:** Mamoru Oshii. *CPM*

Ghost Keeper ✍ 1980 Three girls are trapped in a mansion with an old hag and various supernatural apparitions. **87m/C VHS, Beta.** Riva Spier, Murray Ord, Georgie Collins; **D:** Vernon Sewell. *NWV*

The Ghost of Fletcher Ridge 198? Two friends on a hunting trip run into some backwoodsmen and uncover their moonshining operation. When one of the men is killed, the other flees to the forest in a desperate bid for survival. **90m/C VHS.** Campbell Scott, Bernie White, Virginia Lantry, Len Lesser; **D:** Michael Bordon. *NO*

The Ghost of Frankenstein ✍✍½ 1942 Fourth Frankenstein film in the Universal Studios series with Chaney filling in for Karloff as the monster. Not as good as its predecessors, but the cast is enjoyable, especially Lugosi as the monster's deformed sidekick, Ygor. Based on a story by Eric Taylor. **68m/B VHS, Closed Caption.** Cedric Hardwicke, Lon Chaney Jr., Lionel Atwill, Ralph Bellamy, Bela Lugosi, Evelyn Ankers, Dwight Frye; **D:** Erle C. Kenton; **W:** W. Scott Darling; **C:** Milton Krasner. *USH, FCT*

The Ghost of Rashmon Hall ✍ *Night Comes Too Soon* 1947 Doctor tries to rid his home of the ghosts of a sailor, his wife and her lover. **52m/B VHS, Beta.** Valentine Dyall, Anne Howard, Alex Flavorsham, Howard Douglas, Beatrice Marsden, Arthur Brander. *SNC, EEL*

The Ghost of Yatsuya ✍½ 1958 Based on the Japanese legend of a man who must betray his wife to get the power he seeks. When he does, however, what follows is a horrifying revenge. In Japanese with English subtitles. **100m/C VHS, Beta.** *JP* Shigeru Amachi. *VDA, TPV*

Ghost on the Loose 1943 The Bowery Boys take on Nazi spies. **65m/C VHS.** Leo Gorcey, Huntz Hall, Bela Lugosi; **D:** William Beaudine. *GPV*

Ghost Patrol ✍½ 1936 A cowboy duo kidnaps the inventor of a ray gun in order to hijack mail planes, but they're stopped by G-Man McCoy and friends. An odd hybrid of science fiction and western, to say the least. **57m/B VHS, Beta.** Tim McCoy, Walter Miller, Wheeler Oakman; **D:** Sam Newfield. *GPV, VCI, VCN*

Ghost Rider ✍ 1935 A lawman is aided in his outlaw-nabbing efforts by the ghost of a gunfighter. **56m/B VHS, Beta.** Rex Lease, Bobby Nelson, Franklyn Farnum, Lloyd Ingraham, Ed Parker, Lafe McKee; **D:** Jack Levine. *NOS, GPV*

Ghost Rider ✍✍ 1943 Former footballer Brown rides the range once again, this time with an element of the supernatural nipping at his heels. **58m/B VHS.** Johnny Mack Brown, Raymond Hatton, Tim Seidel, Beverly Boyd, Milburn Morante; **D:** Wallace Fox. *GPV*

Ghost Ship ✍½ 1953 Young couple is tortured by ghostly apparitions when they move into an old yacht with a dubious past. Grade "b" haunting featuring the murdered wife of the ship's former owner as the poltergeist. **69m/B VHS, Beta.** *GB* Dermot Walsh, Hazel Court, Hugh Burden, John Robinson; **D:** Vernon Sewell. *NOS, SNC*

Ghost Stories: Graveyard Thriller 1986 A compilation of stories with ghosts, vampires and other creatures of the night. **56m/C VHS, Beta. D:** Lynn Silver. *LIV, VES*

Ghost Story ✍✍ 1981 (R) Four elderly men, members of an informal social club called the Chowder Society, share a terrible secret buried deep in their pasts—a secret that comes back to haunt them to death. Has moments where it's chilling, but unfortunately they're few. Based on the best-selling novel by Peter Straub. **110m/C VHS, Beta, LV.** Fred Astaire, Melvyn Douglas, Douglas Fairbanks Jr., John Houseman, Craig Wasson, Alice Krige, Patricia Neal; **D:** John Irvin; **W:** Lawrence D. Cohen; **C:** Jack Cardiff. *USH*

Ghost Town ✍ 1937 Good guy Carey saves a mine from claim jumpers, but not before he is mistakenly incarcerated as his friend's murderer, and then proved innocent. **65m/B VHS, Beta, LV.** Harry Carey Sr.; **D:** Harry Fraser. *VDM*

Ghost Town ✍✍½ 1988 (R) Fine sleeper about a modern sheriff who follows a gal through a supernatural sandstorm and discovers a literal ghost town of bad guys. **85m/C VHS, LV.** Franc Luz, Catherine Hickland, Jimmie F. Skaggs, Penelope Windust, Bruce Glover, Blake Conway, Laura Schaefer; **D:** Richard Governor; **W:** Duke Sandefur; **M:** Harvey R. Cohen. *NWV*

Ghost Town Gold ✍ 1936 The Three Mesquiteers series continues as the trio outwits bank robbers who have hidden their loot in a ghost town. **53m/B VHS, Beta.** Bob Livingston, Ray Corrigan, Max Terhune; **D:** Joseph Kane. *NOS, DVT*

Ghost Town Law ✍½ 1942 The Rough Riders step in to save the day when a group of outlaws defend their hideout by murdering anyone who approaches. **62m/B VHS, Beta.** Buck Jones, Tim McCoy, Raymond Hatton; **D:** Howard Bretherton. *NOS, VCN, CAB*

Ghost Town Renegades ✍ 1947 A pair of government agents prevent a crook from gaining control of a mining town. **57m/B VHS, Beta.** Lash LaRue, Al "Fuzzy" St. John, Jennifer Holt; **D:** Ray Taylor. *COL*

Ghost Town Riders ✍½ 1938 An outlaw gang is holed up in an abandoned town, threatening to steal Shannon's gold mine, until Baker comes to the rescue. **55m/B VHS.** Bob Baker, Fay Shannon, George Cleveland, Glenn Strange, Forrest Taylor, Hank Worden, Murdock McQuarrie; **D:** George Waggner. *GPV*

The Ghost Train ✍✍ 1941 Passengers stranded at a train station are told tales of a haunted train. Forced to stay at the station overnight, they encounter a number of comically spooky situations. **85m/B VHS, Beta.** *GB* Arthur Askey, Richard Murdock, Kathleen Harrison; **D:** Walter Forde. *NOS, SNC*

Ghost Valley ✍✍½ 1932 When Keene and Kennedy inherit land rich in unmined ore, the administrator (Harris) attempts to scare them off. To foil his plan, Keene conceals his identity and takes a job as the administrator's assistant. Based on a story by Adele Buffington. **54m/B VHS.** Tom Keene, Merna Kennedy, Mitchell Harris, Billy Franey, Harry Bowen, Kate Campbell, Ted Adams, Buck Moulton, Harry Semels, Al Taylor, Charles "Slim" Whitaker; **D:** Fred Allen. *HEG*

The Ghost Walks ✍✍ 1934 A playwright has his new masterpiece acted out in front of an unsuspecting producer, who thinks that a real murder has taken place. But when the cast really does start disappearing, who's to blame? **69m/B VHS.** John Miljan, June Collyer, Richard Carle, Spencer Charters, Johnny Arthur, Henry Kolker; **D:** Frank Strayer. *SNC, NOS, DVT*

Ghost Writer ✍ 1989 (PG) A writer discovers the ghost of a movie star haunting her beach house, and together they solve the dead vamp's murder. **94m/C VHS, Beta.** Audrey Landers, Judy Landers, Jeff Conaway, David Doyle, Anthony (Tony) Franciosa, Joey Travolta, John Matuszak, David Paul, Peter Paul; **D:** Kenneth J. Hall. *PSM*

Ghostbusters ✍✍✍ 1984 (PG) After losing their scholastic funding, a group of "para-normal" investigators decide to go into business for themselves, aiding New York citizens in the removal of ghosts, goblins and other annoying spirits. This comedy-thriller about Manhattan being overrun by ghosts, contains great special effects, zany characters, and some of the best laughs of the decade. Also available in a laserdisc version with letterboxing, analysis of all special effects, complete screenplay, and original trailer. Followed by a sequel. **103m/C VHS, Beta, LV, 8mm, Closed Caption.** Bill Murray, Dan Aykroyd, Harold Ramis, Rick Moranis, Sigourney Weaver, Annie Potts, Ernie Hudson, William Atherton; **D:** Ivan Reitman; **W:** Dan Aykroyd, Harold Ramis; **M:** Elmer Bernstein. Nominations: Academy Awards '84: Best Song ("Ghostbusters"). *COL, APD, CRC*

Ghostbusters 2 ✍✍½ 1989 (PG) After being sued by the city for the damages they did in the original "Ghostbusters," the boys in khaki are doing kiddie shows at birthday parties. When a river of slime that is actually the physical version of evil is discovered running beneath the city, the Ghostbusters are back in action. They must do battle with a wicked spirit in a painting or the entire world will fall pray to its ravaging whims. **102m/C VHS, Beta, LV, 8mm, Closed Caption.** Bill Murray, Dan Aykroyd, Sigourney Weaver, Harold Ramis, Rick Moranis, Ernie Hudson, Peter MacNicol, David Margulies, Wilhelm von Homburg, Harris Yulin, Annie Potts; **D:** Ivan Reitman; **W:** Dan Aykroyd, Harold Ramis; **C:** Michael Chapman; **M:** Randy Edelman. *COL*

Ghosthouse ✍ 1988 It looks like an average suburban house, but it's haunted by the ghost of a little girl—and when she comes, evil is sure to follow. **91m/C VHS, Beta.** Lara Wendell, Gregg Scott; **D:** Humphrey Humbert. *IMP*

Ghostriders 🎬 1987 One hundred years after their hanging, a band of ghostly outlaws take revenge on the townfolk's descendents. 85m/C VHS, Beta. Bill Shaw, Jim Peters, Ricky Long, Cari Powell, Mike Ammons, Arland Bishop; *D:* Alan L. Stewart. PSM

Ghosts Can Do It 🎬½ 1990 The Hound doesn't like jumping to conclusions, but is it possible this obscurity was titled to be reminiscent of the more publicized Bo Derek vehicle "Ghosts Can't Do It" comedy about a man who returns to his sexy wife despite her efforts at killing him. 88m/C VHS. Garry McDonald, Pamela Stephenson. ATL, HHE

Ghosts Can't Do It 🎬 1990 (R) Another wet-shirted, Bo-dacious softcore epic, involving a young woman who would like to have the spirit of her virile, but unfortunately dead, husband return to inhabit a living body. 91m/C VHS, Beta, LV, Closed Caption. Bo Derek, Anthony Quinn, Don Murray, Leo Damian; *D:* John Derek. Golden Raspberry Awards '90: Worst Picture, Worst Actress (Derek), Worst Director (Derek). COL, TTC

Ghosts of Berkeley Square 🎬🎬½ 1947 The ghosts of two retired soldiers of the early 18th century are doomed to haunt their former home, and only a visit from a reigning monarch can free them. 85m/B VHS, Beta. Wilfrid Hyde-White, Robert Morley, Felix Aylmer; *D:* Vernon Sewell. VYY

The Ghosts of Hanley House 🎬½ 1968 No-budget spooker with no-brain plot. Several unlucky guests spend an evening in a creepy mansion...sound familiar? Shot in Texas. 80m/C VHS, Beta. Barbara Chase, Wilkie De Martel, Elsie Baker, Cliff Scott. SNC

Ghosts of Mississippi 🎬🎬 *Ghosts from the Past* 1996 (PG-13) Director Reiner attempts to tell the story of civil rights leader Medgar Evers, murdered in 1963, and the three trials of Byron De La Beckwith (Woods), who was finally convicted (after two hung juries) in 1994. Unfortunately, he filters the story through the eyes of white assistant D.A. Bobby De Laughter (Baldwin) while ignoring Evers' accomplishments almost completely. Woods chews up the scenery as the wily old racist, bringing perhaps a little too much glee into a portrait of true evil. Goldberg sleepwalks through her role as Evers' widow, Myrlie; Evers' sons, Darrell and Van, play themselves; daughter Reena plays a juror while her character is played by Yolanda King, the daughter of slain civil rights leader Martin Luther King, Jr. Filmed on location in Jackson, Mississippi. *CW:* Strong scene of violence and for racial dialogue. 123m/C VHS, LV, Closed Caption. Alec Baldwin, Whoopi Goldberg, James Woods, Craig T. Nelson, Wayne Rogers, William H. Macy, Michael O'Keefe, Yolanda King, Susanna Thompson, Lucas Black, James Pickens Jr., Virginia Madsen, Bill Cobbs; *D:* Rob Reiner; *W:* Lewis Colick; *C:* John Seale; *M:* Marc Shaiman. Nominations: Academy Awards '96: Best Makeup, Best Supporting Actor (Woods); Golden Globe Awards '97: Best Supporting Actor (Woods). COL

Ghosts That Still Walk 🎬 1977 Spooky phenomena occur. The demons possessing a young lad's soul may be responsible. 92m/C VHS, Beta. Ann Nelson, Matt Boston, Jerry Jenson, Caroline Howe, Rita Crafts; *D:* James T. Flocker. VCI, MRV

Ghostwarrior 🎬 *Swordkill* 1986 (R) A 16th century samurai warrior's ice-packed body is revived and runs amuck in the streets of modern-day Los Angeles. 86m/C VHS, Beta. Hiroshi Fujioka, Janet Julian, Andy Wood, John Calvin; *D:* Larry Carroll; *W:* Tim Curnen; *C:* Mac Ahlberg. VES

Ghostwriter 🎬🎬 1984 Based on Philip Roth's best-selling novel, the story is of a writer coming to terms with his past. Roth co-wrote the screenplay. First seen on PBS. 90m/C VHS, Beta. Sam Wanamaker, Claire Bloom, Rose Arrick, MacIntyre Dixon, Cecile Mann, Joseph Wiseman, Mark Linn-Baker, Paulette Smit; *D:* Tristam Powell; *W:* Phillip J. Roth. PBS

The Ghoul 🎬🎬½ 1934 An eccentric English Egyptologist desires a sacred jewel to be buried with him and vows to come back from the grave if the gem is stolen. When that happens, he makes good on his ghostly promise. A minor horror piece with Karloff only appearing at the beginning and end of the film. This leaves the middle very dull. 73m/B VHS. GB Boris Karloff, Cedric Hardwicke, Ernest Thesiger, Dorothy Hyson, Ralph Richardson, Anthony Bushell; *D:* T. Hayes Hunter. VYY, SNC, DVT

The Ghoul 🎬🎬 1975 (R) A defrocked clergyman has a cannibal son to contend with—especially after the drivers in a local auto race begin to disappear. Hurt is the lunatic family gardener. 88m/C VHS, Beta. GB Peter Cushing, John Hurt, Alexandra Bastedo, Don Henderson, Stewart Bevan; *D:* Freddie Francis. MED

Ghoul School 🎬 1990 (R) A spoof of horror films and college flicks, with lots of scantily clad women and bloody creatures in dark hallways. 90m/C VHS. Joe Franklin, Nancy Siriani, William Friedman. HHE

Ghoulies 🎬 1984 (PG-13) A young man gets more than he bargained for when he conjures up a batch of evil creatures when dabbling in the occult. Ridiculous but successful. Followed by two sequels. 81m/C VHS, Beta. Lisa Pelikan, Jack Nance, Scott Thomson, Tamara DeTreaux, Mariska Hargitay, Bobbie Bresee; *D:* Luca Bercovici; *W:* Luca Bercovici; *C:* Mac Ahlberg; *M:* Richard Band. LIV, VES, HHE

Ghoulies 2 🎬 1987 (R) Inept sequel to "Ghoulies" (1985), wherein the little demons haunt a failing carnival horror house, whose revenues begin to soar. Followed by a second sequel. 89m/C VHS, Beta, LV. Damon Martin, Royal Dano, Phil Fondacaro, J. Downing, Kerry Remsen; *D:* Albert Band. LIV, VES

Ghoulies 3: Ghoulies Go to College woof! 1991 (R) Third in the series has the best special effects and the worst storyline. Not satisfied with ripping off "Gremlins," this one imposes Three Stooges personae upon a trio of demons at large on a beer- and babe-soaked campus. 94m/C VHS. Kevin McCarthy, Griffin O'Neal, Evan Mackenzie; *D:* John Carl Buechler. VES, LIV

Ghoulies 4 🎬½ 1993 (R) Dopey series continues with the satanic creatures roaming the streets of Los Angeles, searching for a way to return to their netherworld home. They get their chance when they meet a Satan-worshiping dominatrix out on a killing spree. 84m/C VHS. Barbara Alyn Woods, Peter Paul Liapis; *D:* Jim Wynorski; *W:* Mark Sevi. COL

G.I. Blues 🎬🎬 1960 Three G.I.'s form a musical combo while stationed in Germany. Prowse is the nightclub singer Presley falls for. Presley's first film after his military service. ♫Shopping Around; Tonight Is So Right For Love; What's She Really Like?; Frankfurt Special; Didya Ever; Big Boots; Pocketful of Rainbows; Doin' the Best I Can; Blue Suede Shoes. 104m/C VHS, Beta, LV. Elvis Presley, Juliet Prowse, Robert Ivers, Leticia Roman, Ludwig Stossel, James Douglas, Jeremy Slate; *D:* Norman Taurog; *C:* Loyal Griggs. FOX, MVD

G.I. Executioner 🎬 *Wit's End; Dragon Lady* 1971 (R) An adventure set in Singapore featuring a Vietnam veteran turned executioner. 86m/C VHS, Beta. Tom Kenna, Victoria Racimo, Angelique Pettyjohn, Janet Wood, Walter Hill; *D:* Joel M. Reed. VES

G.I. Jane 🎬 1951 A television producer faints when he gets his draft notice and dreams his company is stranded at a desert post with a company of WACs. 62m/B VHS, Beta, LV. Jean Porter, Tom Neal, Iris Adrian, Jimmy Lloyd, Mara Lynn, Michael Whalen; *D:* Reginald LeBorg. NO

Giant 🎬🎬🎬½ 1956 Based on the Edna Ferber novel, this epic saga covers two generations of a wealthy Texas cattle baron (Hudson) who marries a strong-willed Virginia woman (Taylor) and takes her to live on his vast ranch. It explores the problems they have adjusting to life together, as well as the politics and prejudice of the time. Dean plays the resentful ranch hand (who secretly loves Taylor) who winds up striking oil and beginning a fortune to rival that of his former boss. Dean's last movie—he died in a car crash shortly before filming was completed. 201m/C VHS, Beta, LV, Closed Caption. Elizabeth Taylor, Rock Hudson, James Dean, Carroll Baker, Chill Wills, Dennis Hopper, Rod Taylor, Earl Holliman, Jane Withers, Sal Mineo, Mercedes McCambridge; *D:* George Stevens; *C:* William Mellor. Academy Awards '56: Best Director (Stevens); Directors Guild of America Awards '56: Best Director (Stevens); Nominations: Academy Awards '56: Best Actor (Dean), Best Actor (Hudson), Best Adapted Screenplay, Best Art Direction/Set Decoration (Color), Best Costume Design (Color), Best Film Editing, Best Picture, Best Supporting Actress (McCambridge), Original Dramatic/Comedy Score. WAR, BTV

The Giant Claw 🎬½ 1957 Giant, winged (and stringed) bird attacks from outer space and scientists Morrow, Corday and Ankrum attempt to pluck it. Good bad movie; Corday was Playboy's Miss October, 1958. 76m/B VHS. Jeff Morrow, Mara Corday, Morris Ankrum, Louis D. Merrill, Edgar Barrier, Robert Shayne, Morgan Jones, Clark Howat; *D:* Fred F. Sears. MOV

Giant from the Unknown woof! 1958 Giant conquistador is revived after being struck by lightning and goes on a murderous rampage. Unbelievably bad. 80m/B VHS, Beta. Edward Kemmer, Buddy Baer, Bob Steele, Sally Fraser; *D:* Richard Cunha. NOS, SNC, EEL

The Giant Gila Monster 🎬½ 1959 A giant lizard has the nerve to disrupt a local record hop, foolishly bringing upon it the wrath of the local teens. Rear-projection monster isn't particularly effective, but the film provides many unintentional laughs. 74m/B VHS. Don Sullivan, Lisa Simone, Shug Fisher, Jerry Cortwright, Beverly Thurman, Don Flourney, Pat Simmons; *D:* Ray Kellogg. NOS, RHI, SNC

The Giant of Marathon 🎬🎬 1960 Reeves shrugs off the role of Hercules to play Philippides, a marathoner (who uses a horse) trying to save Greece from invading Persian hordes. Lots of muscle on display, but not much talent. Cinematography by Mario Bava. 90m/C VHS. IT Steve Reeves, Mylene Demongeot, Daniela Rocca, Ivo Garrani, Alberto Lupo, Sergio Fantoni; *D:* Jacques Tourneur. SNC, MLB

The Giant of Metropolis 🎬🎬 *Il Gigante Di Metropolis* 1961 Muscle-bound hero goes shirtless to take on the evil, sadistic ruler of Atlantis (still above water) in 10,000 B.C. Ordinary Italian adventure, but includes interesting sets and bizarre torture scenes. 92m/C VHS. IT Gordon Mitchell, Roldano Lupi, Bella Cortez, Liana Orfei; *D:* Umberto Scarpelli. SNC

The Giant Spider Invasion 🎬 1975 (PG) A meteorite carrying spider eggs crashes to Earth and soon the alien arachnids are growing to humongous proportions. Notoriously bad special effects, but the veteran "B" cast have a good time. 76m/C VHS. Steve Brodie, Barbara Hale, Leslie Parrish, Robert Easton, Alan Hale Jr., Dianne Lee Hart, Bill Williams, Christianne Schmidtmer; *D:* Bill Rebane. MOV

Giant Steps 🎬🎬 19?? Williams plays Slate Hopson, a moody jazz legend idolized by a talented young trumpet player. When the two meet Hopson clues the boy into some of life's lessons and rediscovers his own joy at making music. 94m/C VHS. Billy Dee Williams, Michael Mahonen; *M:* Eric Leeds. MNC

Giants of Rome woof! 1963 Rome is in peril at the hands of a mysterious secret weapon that turns out to be a giant catapult. Ludicrous all around. 87m/C VHS, Beta, Closed Caption. IT Richard Harrison, Ettore Manni. SNC

The Giants of Thessaly 🎬🎬 1960 Jason and Orpheus search for the Golden Fleece, encountering and defeating monsters, wizards, and a scheming witch. 86m/C VHS. IT Roland Carey, Ziva Rodann, Massimo Girotti, Alberto Farnese; *D:* Riccardo (Robert Hampton) Freda. SNC

Gideon's Trumpet 🎬🎬½ 1980 True story of Clarence Earl Gideon, a Florida convict whose case was decided by the Supreme Court and set the precedent that everyone is entitled to defense by a lawyer, whether or not they can pay for it. Based on the book by Anthony Lewis. Made for television. **104m/C VHS, Beta.** Henry Fonda, Jose Ferrer, John Houseman, Dean Jagger, Sam Jaffe, Fay Wray; **D:** Robert Collins. *WOV*

Gidget ♪♪ 1959 A plucky, boy-crazy teen-age girl (whose nickname means girl midget) discovers romance and wisdom on the beaches of Malibu when she becomes involved with a group of college-aged surfers. First in a series of Gidget/surfer films. Based on a novel by Frederick Kohner about his daughter. **95m/C VHS, Beta, LV.** Sandra Dee, James Darren, Cliff Robertson, Mary Laroche, Arthur O'Connell, Joby Baker; **D:** Paul Wendkos; **C:** Burnett Guffey. *COL*

Gidget Goes Hawaiian ♪♪ 1961 Gidget is off to Hawaii with her parents and is enjoying the beach (and the boys) when she is surprised by a visit from boyfriend "Moondoggie." Sequel to "Gidget" and followed by "Gidget Goes to Rome." **102m/C VHS, Beta.** Deborah Walley, James Darren, Carl Reiner, Peggy Cass, Michael Callan, Eddie Foy Jr.; **D:** Paul Wendkos. *COL*

Gidget Goes to Rome ♪♪½ 1963 Darren returns in his third outing as boyfriend "Moondoggie" to yet another actress playing "Gidget" as the two vacation in Rome and find themselves tempted by other romances. Second sequel to "Gidget." **104m/C VHS, Beta.** Cindy Carol, James Darren, Jeff Donnell, Cesare Danova, Peter Brooks, Jessie Royce Landis; **D:** Paul Wendkos; **M:** John Williams. *COL*

The Gift ♪♪½ 1982 **(R)** Story of a 55-year-old man who chooses early retirement in the hopes of changing his dull and boring life. Unbeknownst to him, his co-workers arrange the ultimate retirement gift - a woman. Silly French sexual farce. Dubbed. **105m/C VHS, Beta.** *FR* Pierre Mondy, Claudia Cardinale, Clio Goldsmith, Jacques Francois, Cecile Magnet, Remy Laurent; **D:** Michael Lang. *FCT*

The Gift Horse ♪♪ *Glory at Sea* 1952 A WWII British naval officer dispatches his duties with an iron hand in an attempt to overturn the legacy of a court-martial eight years earlier. Angry rumblings from his crew threaten to upset the ship's stability. Against this foreboding backdrop, the Nazis give battle. Not historically accurate, but exciting. Based on a story by Ivan Goff and Ben Roberts. **99m/B VHS, Beta.** *GB* Trevor Howard, Richard Attenborough, Sonny Tufts, Bernard Lee; **D:** Compton Bennett. *DVT*

The Gift of Love ♪½ 1990 Saccharine, made-for-television adaption of O. Henry's Christmas romance "The Gift of the Magi." **96m/C VHS, Closed Caption.** James Woods, Marie Osmond, Timothy Bottoms, June Lockhart, David Wayne; **D:** Don Chaffey. *MON, KAR*

The Gig ♪♪½ 1985 In this small, independently-made film, a band of middle-aged amateur jazz musicians give up their stable occupations for a once-in-a-lifetime shot at a two-week gig in the Catskills. Film succeeds on the strength of it's well fleshed-out characters. **95m/C VHS, Beta, LV, Closed Caption.** Wayne Rogers, Cleavon Little, Warren Vache, Joe Silver, Daniel Nalbach, Andrew Duncan, Jay Thomas, Jerry Matz; **D:** Frank D. Gilroy; **W:** Frank D. Gilroy. *ORI, WAR*

Gigi ♪♪♪♪ 1958 Based on Colette's story of a young Parisian girl (Caron) trained to become a courtesan to the wealthy Gaston (Jourdan). But he finds out he prefers her to be his wife rather than his mistress. Chevalier is Gaston's roguish uncle, who casts an always admiring eye on the ladies. Gingold is Gigi's grandmother and former Chevalier flame, and Gabor amuses as Gaston's current, and vapid, mistress. One of the first MGM movies to be shot on location, this extravaganza features some of the best tributes to the French lifestyle ever filmed. Score includes memorable classics. ♪Gigi; Ah Yes, I Remember It Well; Thank Heaven For Little Girls; The Night They Invented Champagne; She's Not Thinking of Me; It's a Bore; Gossip; I'm Glad I'm Not Young Anymore; The Parisians. **119m/C VHS, Beta, LV, 8mm.** Leslie Caron, Louis Jourdan, Maurice Chevalier, Hermione

Gingold, Eva Gabor, Isabel Jeans, Jacques Bergerac; **D:** Vincente Minnelli; **W:** Alan Jay Lerner; **C:** Joseph Ruttenberg; **M:** Frederick Loewe. Academy Awards '58: Best Adapted Screenplay, Best Art Direction/Set Decoration, Best Color Cinematography, Best Costume Design, Best Director (Minnelli), Best Film Editing, Best Picture, Best Song ("Gigi"), Scoring of a Musical; Directors Guild of America Awards '58: Best Director (Minnelli); Golden Globe Awards '59: Best Director (Minnelli), Best Film—Musical/Comedy, Best Supporting Actress (Gingold); National Board of Review Awards '58: 10 Best Films of the Year. *MGM, BTV*

Gilda ♪♪♪½ 1946 An evil South American gambling casino owner hires young American Ford as his trusted aide, unaware that Ford and his sultry wife Hayworth have engaged in a steamy affair. Hayworth does a striptease to "Put the Blame on Mame" in this prominently sexual film. This is the film that made Hayworth into a Hollywood sex goddess. **110m/B VHS, Beta, LV, Closed Caption.** Rita Hayworth, Glenn Ford, George Macready, Joseph Calleia, Steve Geray; **D:** Charles Vidor. *COL*

The Gilded Cage ♪♪ 1954 Two brothers are falsely accused of art theft and must find the real crooks in order to clear their names. **77m/B VHS, Beta.** *GB* Alex Nicol, Veronica Hurst, Clifford Evans, Ursula Howells, Elwyn Brook-Jones, John Stuart; **D:** John Gilling. *SNC*

Gilligan's Island: Meet the Crew 1964 Join Gilligan and the Skipper of the S.S. Minnow and their unfortunate passengers—Ginger, Mary Ann, the Professor, and Mr. and Mrs. Thurston Howell III—as they try to survive life (and each other) on an uncharted desert isle. Three episodes per cassette from the slapstick television series. Additional episodes available. **?m/B VHS.** Bob Denver, Alan Hale Jr., Jim Backus, Natalie Schafer, Tina Louise, Russell Johnson, Dawn Wells. *CMB*

Gimme an F woof! *T & A Academy 2* 1985 **(R)** The handsome cheerleading instructor at Camp Beaver View ruffles a few pom-poms when he discovers that the camp's owner is about to enter into a shady deal with some foreigners. The film certainly deserves an "F" for foolishness if nothing else. **100m/C VHS, Beta.** Stephen Shellan, Mark Keyloun, John Karlen, Jennifer Cooke; **D:** Paul Justman. *FOX*

Gimme Shelter 1970 The sixties ended as violence occurred at a December 1969 free Rolling Stones concert attended by 300,000 people in Altamont, California. This "Woodstock West" became a bitter remembrance in rock history, as Hell's Angels (hired for security) do some ultimate damage to the spectators. A provocative look at an out-of-control situation. **91m/C VHS, Beta, LV.** Mick Jagger, Keith Richards, Charlie Watts, Bill Wyman, Mick Taylor; **D:** David Maysles; **C:** Haskell Wexler. *COL, MVD*

Gin Game ♪♪♪ 1984 Taped London performance of the Broadway play about an aging couple who find romance in an old age home. Two-character performance won awards; touching and insightful. **82m/C VHS, Beta.** Jessica Tandy, Hume Cronyn; **D:** Mike Nichols. *TTC*

Ginger ♪ 1972 Fabulous super-sleuth Ginger faces the sordid world of prostitution, blackmail and drugs. Prequel to "The Abductors" and followed eventually by "Girls Are for Loving." **90m/C VHS, Beta.** Cheri Caffaro, William Grannell; **D:** Don Schain. *MON*

Ginger Ale Afternoon ♪ 1989 A smutty comedy revolving around a triangle formed by a married couple and their sexy next-door neighbor. The film tries for fizz but only comes up flat. **88m/C VHS, Beta, LV.** Dana Anderson, John M. Jackson, Yeardley Smith; **D:** Rafal Zielinski; **W:** Gina Wendkos; **M:** Willie Dixon. *ACA, IME*

Ginger & Fred ♪♪♪ 1986 **(PG-13)** An acclaimed story of Fellini-esque poignancy about an aging dance team. Years before they had gained success by reverently impersonating the famous dancing duo of Astaire and Rogers. Now, after thirty years, they reunite under the gaudy lights of

a high-tech television special. Wonderful performances by the aging Mastroianni and the still sweet Masina. In Italian with English subtitles. **126m/C VHS, Beta.** *IT* Marcello Mastroianni, Giulietta Masina, Franco Fabrizi, Frederick Von Ledenberg, Martin Blau, Toto Mignone; **D:** Federico Fellini; **W:** Federico Fellini, Tonino Guerra, Tullio Pinelli; **C:** Tonino Delli Colli; **M:** Nicola Piovani. *MGM, FCT, APD*

Ginger in the Morning ♪♪ 1973 A salesman is enamored of a young hitchhiker whom he picks up on the road. This is the same year Spacek played the innocent-gone-twisted in "Badlands." **90m/C VHS, Beta.** Sissy Spacek, Slim Pickens, Monte Markham, Susan Oliver, Mark Miller; **D:** Gordon Wiles. *NO*

The Girl ♪♪♪ 1968 The first of Meszaros' trilogy, dealing with a young girl who leaves an orphanage to be reunited with her mother, a traditional country peasant. In Hungarian with English subtitles. Meszaros' first film. Followed by "Riddance" (1973) and "Adoption" (1975). **86m/B VHS, Beta.** *HU* **D:** Marta Meszaros. *KIV*

The Girl ♪½ 1986 **(R)** Nero is a wealthy attorney who agrees to pay Powney 300 crowns to have his way with her. Although somewhat ambivalent because of her scandalous age, he takes her anyway. Soon he informs his wife he needs to go on a long business trip, which fits in with her own adulterous plans. A snooping reporter (Brennan) out for some dirt upsets the apple cart, eventually leading to murder. **104m/C VHS, Beta.** Franco Nero, Christopher Lee, Bernice Stegers, Clare Powney, Frank Brennan; **D:** Arne Mattson. *VTR, NWV*

A Girl, a Guy and a Gob ♪♪ *The Navy Steps Out* 1941 A shy rich boy falls in love with a girl who has her sights on another. Silly but enjoyable cast. **91m/B VHS, Beta.** Lucille Ball, Edmond O'Brien, George Murphy, Franklin Pangborn, Henry Travers, Lloyd Corrigan; **D:** Richard Wallace. *TTC*

The Girl Can't Help It ♪♪½ 1956 Satiric rock and roll musical comedy about a retired mobster who hires a hungry talent agent to promote his girlfriend, a wannabe no-talent singer. Mansfield's first starring role. Classic performances by some of the early greats including Eddie Cochran, Gene Vincent, The Platters, Little Richard and Fats Domino. **99m/B VHS, Beta, LV.** Jayne Mansfield, Tom Ewell, Edmond O'Brien, Julie London, Ray Anthony; **D:** Frank Tashlin. *FOX*

Girl Crazy ♪♪♪ *When the Girls Meet the Boys* 1943 A wealthy young playboy is sent to an all-boy school in Arizona to get his mind off girls. Once there, he still manages to fall for a local girl who can't stand the sight of him. The eighth film pairing for Rooney and Garland. ♪Sam and Delilah; Embraceable You; I Got Rhythm; Fascinating Rhythm; Treat Me Rough; Bronco Busters; Bidin' My Time; But Not For Me; Do. **99m/B VHS, Beta, LV.** Mickey Rooney, Judy Garland, Nancy Walker, June Allyson; **D:** Norman Taurog; **C:** William H. Daniels; **M:** George Gershwin, Ira Gershwin. *MGM, TTC, FCT*

Girl from Calgary ♪ 1932 A female rodeo champ ropes her boyfriends much like she ropes her cows, but not without a knock-down, drag-out fight between the two which forces our cowgirl to make the choice she seems to know is fated. Stock rodeo footage is intercut with the heroine riding an obviously mechanical bucking bronc. **66m/B VHS, Beta, LV.** Fifi d'Orsay, Paul Kelly; **D:** Philip H. Whitman. *VYY*

Girl from Chicago ♪♪ 1932 In this crime melodrama a secret service agent falls in love while on assignment in Mississippi. When he's back in New York he finds a good friend of his girl's in serious trouble with the numbers racket. **69m/C VHS, Beta.** Starr Calloway, Grace Smith, Eugene Brooks, Frank Wilson; **D:** Oscar Micheaux. *FCT, BTV*

Girl from Hunan ♪♪♪ 1986 Turn-of-the-century China, a 12-year-old girl is married to a 2-year-old boy in a typical arranged marriage. She grows into womanhood treating her toddler husband with sibling affection, but conducts a secret love affair with a farmer. Intolerant village laws against adultry place her life in jeopardy. In Mandarin with English subtitles. **99m/C VHS.** Na Renhua, Deng Xiaotuang, Yu Zhang; *D:* Xie Fei. *NYF*

The Girl from Missouri 🎞🎞🎞 One Hundred Percent Pure **1934** Cute comedy in which Harlow tries to snag a millionaire without sacrificing her virtues. Lots of laughs and hilarious action, especially the scene where Harlow arrives at the yacht in Florida. Kelly is great as Harlow's wise-cracking girlfriend. Witty dialogue by Emerson and Loos, who also wrote "Gentleman Prefer Blondes." **75m/B VHS, Closed Caption.** Jean Harlow, Lionel Barrymore, Franchot Tone, Lewis Stone, Patsy Kelly, Alan Mowbray, Clara Blandick, Russell Hopton; *D:* Jack Conway; *W:* Anita Loos, John Emerson. *MGM*

The Girl from Petrovka 🎞🎞½ **1974 (PG)** A high-spirited Russian ballerina falls in love with an American newspaper correspondent. Their romance is complicated by the suspicious KGB. Bittersweet with a bleak ending. **103m/C VHS, Beta.** Goldie Hawn, Hal Holbrook, Anthony Hopkins; *D:* Robert Ellis Miller; *W:* Chris Bryant, Allan Scott; *M:* Henry Mancini. *USH*

The Girl from Tobacco Row 🎞 **1966** A Southern slut involved with a cache of stolen cash fools with both a convict and the sheriff. **90m/C VHS, Beta.** Tex Ritter, Rachel Romen, Earl Richards, Tim Ormond, Rita Faye, Ralph Emery; *D:* Ron Ormond. *NO*

Girl Happy 🎞🎞 **1965** The King's fans will find him in Fort Lauderdale, Florida this time as the leader of a rock 'n' roll group. His mission: to chaperone the daughter of a Chicago mobster who naturally falls for him. Why not? 🎵Girl Happy; Cross My Heart and Hope to Die; Do Not Disturb; Spring Fever; Wolf Call; Do the Clam; Fort Lauderdale Chamber of Commerce; Puppet On a String; I've Got to Find About My Baby. **96m/C VHS, Beta.** Elvis Presley, Harold J. Stone, Shelley Fabares, Gary Crosby, Nita Talbot, Mary Ann Mobley, Jackie Coogan; *D:* Boris Sagal; *W:* Harvey Bulloch. *MGM*

Girl Hunters 🎞🎞½ **1963** That intrepid private eye, Mike Hammer (played by his creator, Spillane), is caught up with communist spies, wicked women, and a missing secretary. Hammer is his usual judge-and-jury character but the action is fast-paced. **103m/B VHS, Beta.** Mickey Spillane, Lloyd Nolan, Shirley Eaton, Hy Gardner, Scott Peters; *D:* Roy Rowland. *SNC, NOS, DVT*

A Girl in a Million 🎞🎞 **1946** Williams dumps his verbose wife and seeks peace and quiet in a men-only War Department office. All is well until the arrival of a colonel and his daughter, mute from trauma. Finding her silence appealing, he marries her, but another trauma restores her speech. Sexist comedy may have played better in its day. **90m/B VHS.** *GB* Hugh Williams, Joan Greenwood, Naunton Wayne, Wylie Watson, Garry Marsh; *D:* Francis Searle. *NOS*

The Girl in a Swing 🎞½ **1989 (R)** An Englishman impulsively marries a beautiful German girl and both are subsequently haunted by phantoms from her past - are they caused by her psychic powers? Cliche-ridden silliness. Based on the Richard Adams novel. **119m/C VHS, Beta, LV.** Meg Tilly, Rupert Frazer, Elspet Gray, Lynsey Baxter, Nicholas Le Prevost, Jean Both; *D:* Gordon Hessler. *HBO*

Girl in Black 🎞🎞 **1956** The shy daughter of a once wealthy household gets the chance to escape her genteel poverty when she falls in love with the young man boarding with her family. He is attracted to her but a shocking tragedy changes everything. In Greek with English subtitles. **100m/C VHS, Beta.** Elli Lambetti; *D:* Michael Cacoyannis. *FCT*

Girl in Black Stockings 🎞🎞 **1957** Beautiful women are mysteriously murdered at a remote, Utah hotel. Interesting, little known thriller similar to Hitchcock's "Psycho," but pre-dating it by three years. **75m/B VHS.** Lex Barker, Anne Bancroft, Mamie Van Doren, Ron Randell, Marie Windsor, John Dehner, John Holland, Diana Van Der Vlis; *D:* Howard W. Koch; *M:* Les Baxter. *FRG*

The Girl in Blue 🎞🎞 **1974 (R)** A lawyer, ill at ease with his current romance, suddenly decides to search for a beautiful woman he saw once, and instantly fell in love with, years before. **103m/C VHS, Beta.** *CA* Maud Adams, David Selby, Gay Rowan, William Osler, Diane Dewey, Michael Kirby; *D:* George Kaczender. *PSM*

A Girl in Every Port 🎞🎞½ **1952** Navy buddies acquire an ailing racehorse and try to conceal it aboard ship along with a healthy horse they plan to switch it with in an upcoming race. Groucho flies without his brothers in this zany film. **86m/B VHS, Beta, LV.** Groucho Marx, William Bendix, Marie Wilson, Don DeFore, Gene Lockhart; *D:* Chester Erskine. *CCB*

Girl in Gold Boots 🎞 **1969** Aspiring starlet meets up with a draft evader and a biker on her way to Hollywood where she gets a job as a go-go dancer in a sleazy club. But things don't go smoothly when a murder and a drug theft are revealed. 🎵Do You Want to Laugh or Cry?; For You; Hello, Michelle; One Good Time, One Good Place; Lonesome Man; You Gotta Come Down; Everything I Touch Turns to Gold; Cowboy Santa; Wheels of Love. **94m/C VHS, Beta.** Jody Daniels, Leslie McRae, Tom Pace, Mark Herron; *D:* Ted V. Mikels. *NO*

Girl in His Pocket 🎞🎞 Amour de Poche; Nude in His Pocket **1957** Mad scientist creates a potion that turns things into three-inch statues. He uses it mostly to have trysts with his lab assistant so his fiancee won't find out. Based on "The Diminishing Draft" by Waldemar Kaempfert. **82m/C VHS.** *FR* Jean Marais, Genevieve Page, Agnes Laurent; *D:* Pierre Kast; *C:* Ghislan Cloquet. *SNC*

The Girl in Lover's Lane 🎞🎞 **1960** A drifter falls in love with a small town girl but becomes a murder suspect when she turns up dead. Interesting mainly for Elam's uncharacteristic portrayal of a village idiot. **78m/B VHS, Beta.** Brett Halsey, Joyce Meadows, Lowell Brown, Jack Elam; *D:* Charles R. Rondeau. *SNC*

The Girl in Room 2A woof! **1976 (R)** A young woman is trapped in a mansion with the elderly owner and her demented son. Routine horrorfest. **90m/C VHS, Beta.** Raf Vallone, Daniela Giordano. *PSM*

Girl in the Cadillac 🎞🎞½ **1994 (R)** Modern-day B-movie wannabe loosely adapted from the James M. Cain novella "The Enchanted Isle." 17-year-old freespirited Amanda (Eleniak) wants to get out of stifling small town Texas. She buys a bus ticket to find her long-gone daddy and winds up with not-too-smart cowpoke Rick (McNamara) instead. A bank robbery gone bad finds the twosome on the loose with $75 thou, a cherry red El Dorado convertible, and Rick's partners after them. Appealing lead performers can't overcome the cliches.*CW:* Language; some violence. **89m/C VHS.** Erika Eleniak, William McNamara, Michael Lerner, Bud Cort, Valerie Perrine, Ed Lauter, William Shockley; *D:* Lucas Platt; *W:* John Warren; *C:* Nancy Schreiber; *M:* Anton Sanko. *TTC*

The Girl in the Picture 🎞🎞½ **1986 (PG-13)** Sinclair stars in this light comedy as an unlucky photo clerk who discovers only too late that his ex-girlfriend may be the woman of his dreams. Typical understated but entertaining effort. **89m/C VHS, Beta.** *GB* John Gordon-Sinclair, Irina Brook, David McKay, Catherine Guthrie, Paul Young, Gregory Fisher; *D:* Cary Parker. *VES*

The Girl Most Likely 🎞🎞½ **1957** Light musical comedy about a romance-minded girl who dreams of marrying a wealthy, handsome man. She runs into a problem when she finds three prospects. Remake of 1941's "Tom, Dick and Harry" with Ginger Rogers. Choreography by great Gower Champion. 🎵The Girl Most Likely; All the Colors of the Rainbow; I Don't Know What I Want; Balboa; We Gotta Keep Up With the Joneses; Crazy Horse. **98m/C VHS, Beta, LV.** Jane Powell, Cliff Robertson, Tommy Noonan, Kaye Ballard, Una Merkel; *D:* Mitchell Leisen. *NO*

Girl of the Golden West 🎞🎞 **1938** A musical version of the David Belasco chestnut about a Canadian frontier girl loving a rogue. One of Eddy and MacDonald's lesser efforts but features Ebsen's song and dance talents. 🎵Camptown Races; Shadows on the Moon; Soldiers of Fortune; Soldiers of Fortune Reprise; Shadows on the Moon Reprise; The Wind in the Trees; Liebestraum; Ave Maria; Senorita. **120m/B VHS, Beta.** Jeanette MacDonald, Nelson Eddy, Walter Pidgeon, Leo Carrillo, Buddy Ebsen, Leonard Penn, Priscilla Lawson, Bob Murphy, Olin Howlin, Cliff Edwards, Billy Bevan; *D:* Robert Z. Leonard. *MGM*

A Girl of the Limberlost 🎞 **1990** A young Indiana farmgirl fights to bring her estranged parents back together, in spite of a meddling aunt and the unexplained phenomena that haunt her. Fine acting and beautiful scenery. Originally broadcast on public television as part of the "Wonderworks" family movie series, it's best appreciated by young teens. Adapted from Gene Stratton Porter's much-filmed novel. **120m/C VHS.** Annette O'Toole, Joanna Cassidy, Heather Fairfield. *PME, HMV, FCT*

Girl on a Chain Gang woof! **1965** A girl on the run gets caught by police and does her time on a chain gang—an otherwise all-male chain gang. Predictable. **96m/B VHS, Beta.** William Watson, Julie Ange, R.K. Charles; *D:* Jerry Gross; *W:* Jerry Gross. *SNC*

The Girl on a Motorcycle 🎞🎞 Naked Under Leather; La Motocyclette **1968 (R)** Singer Faithull is a bored housewife who dons black leather and hops on her motorcycle to meet up with her lover (Delon), all the while remembering their other erotic encounters. **92m/C VHS, Beta.** *GB* Alain Delon, Marianne Faithull, Roger Mutton; *D:* Jack Cardiff. *MLB*

A Girl on Her Own 🎞🎞 **1976** A young actress embarking on her first big role in Paris must also deal with family and political considerations in this drama set during the political upheaval of 1935. **112m/C VHS.** *FR* Sophie Chemineau, Bruno La Brasca; *D:* Philippe Nahoun. *FCT*

Girl Rush 🎞 **1944** Two bad vaudeville comics are stuck in California during the gold rush and are promised sacks of gold if they can persuade some women to come to a rowdy mining town. 🎵Annabella's Bustle; Rainbow Valley; If Mother Could Only See Us Now; Walking Arm in Arm With Jim. **65m/B VHS, Beta.** Wally Brown, Alan Carney, Frances Langford, Vera Vague, Robert Mitchum, Paul Hurst, Patti Brill, Sarah Padden, Cy Kendall; *D:* Gordon Douglas. *TTC*

The Girl Said No 🎞½ With Words and Music **1937** A sleazy bookie poses as a theatrical producer in order to get even with a dance hall floozy who once stiffed him. **72m/B VHS, Beta.** Robert Armstrong, Irene Hervey, William Haines; *D:* Andrew L. Stone; *W:* Andrew L. Stone. Nominations: Academy Awards '37: Best Sound. *NOS, DVT, VYY*

Girl Shy 🎞🎞🎞 **1924** Harold is a shy tailor's apprentice who is trying to get a collection of his romantic fantasies published. Finale features Lloyd chasing wildly after girl of his dreams. **65m/B VHS, Beta.** Harold Lloyd, Jobyna Ralston, Richard Daniels; *D:* Fred Newmeyer; *W:* Sam Taylor. *TLF*

Girl 6 🎞🎞½ **1996 (R)** Aspiring actress (Randle) takes job as a phone sex operator in order to make ends meet. After finally finding stardom in the world of titillating telecommunications, she starts to take her work home. Bound to be compared, unfairly and probably unfavorably, to Lee's debut "She's Gotta Have It." Terrific performance by Randle is hampered by the lack of a strong story and too many unresolved subplots. Features the obligatory Lee cameo, while Tarantino shows up as a young hotshot director. Prince provides old and new tunes (as well as his previous moniker, apparently) to the proceedings.*CW:* Explicit dialogue and nudity. **107m/C VHS.** Theresa Randle, Isaiah Washington, Ron Silver, John Turturro, Naomi Campbell, Halle Berry, Madonna, Quentin Tarantino, Debi

Mazar, Peter Berg, Richard Belzer, Spike Lee, Jenifer Lewis, Michael Imperioli, Kristen Wilson, Dina Pearlman, Maggie Rush, Desi Moreno, Susan Batson; **D:** Spike Lee; **W:** Suzan-Lori Parks; **C:** Malik Hassan Sayeed; **M:** Prince. *FXV*

The Girl, the Body and the Pill *♪*
1967 Sexploitation pic from director Lewis has a high school instructor getting fired for her sex education lectures—so she continues them in the privacy of her own home. Meanwhile, her students take up playing musical beds and learn about "the pill." **?m/C VHS.** Bill Rogers, Nancy Lee Noble; **D:** Herschell Gordon Lewis. *MOV*

A Girl to Kill For *♪♪½* **1990 (R)** A temptress lures a randy college guy into a plot of murder and betrayal. **85m/C VHS, Beta, LV.** Sasha Jensen, Karen Austin, Alex Cord, Rod McCary, Karen Medak; **D:** Richard Oliver. *COL*

Girl Under the Sheet *♪* **196?** A conman/archaeologist moves into an ancient castle and begins romancing a beautiful resident ghost. **89m/C VHS, Beta.** Chelo Alonso, Walter Chiari. *NO*

The Girl Who Had Everything *♪♪½* **1953** Good melodrama with top cast, intelligent script and smooth direction. Taylor plays the spoiled daughter of a criminal lawyer (Powell) who falls for her father's client (Lamas), a suave, underground syndicate boss. Remake of the 1931 film "A Free Soul," which starred Norma Shearer, Clark Gable, and Lionel Barrymore. Based on the novel of the same name by Adela Rogers St. John. **69m/B VHS.** Elizabeth Taylor, Fernando Lamas, William Powell, Gig Young, James Whitmore, Robert Burton; **D:** Richard Thorpe; **M:** Andre Previn. *MGM*

The Girl Who Spelled Freedom *♪♪♪* **1986** A young Cambodian girl, speaking little English, strives to adjust to life in Chattanooga, Tennessee. She faces her challenges by becoming a champion in the national spelling bee. Based on a true story. Made-for-television. **90m/C VHS, Beta, Closed Caption.** Wayne Rogers, Mary Kay Place, Jade Chinn, Kieu Chinh, Kathleen Sisk; **D:** Simon Wincer. *DIS*

The Girl with a Suitcase *♪♪* *La Ragazza con la Valgia* **1960** Young nightclub singer Aida (Cardinale) falls for rich cad Marcello (Pani) and leaves her job to follow him to his family home in Parma. He was just stringing her along and instructs his 16-year-old brother Lorenzo (Perrin) to get rid of Aida. But instead Lorenzo decides to become her protector and the unlikely duo fall in love. Italian with subtitles; the original release was 135 minutes. **111m/B VHS.** *IT* Claudia Cardinale, Jacques Perrin, Corrado Pani, Luciana Angelillo, Romolo Valli, Gian Marie Volonte; **D:** Valerio Zurlini; **W:** Valerio Zurlini; **C:** Tito Santoni; **M:** Mario Nascimbene. *IVY, FCT*

The Girl with the Hat Box *♪♪* **1927** Early Russian production about a poor working girl who's paid with a lottery ticket rather than rubles (an ironic pre-communist theme?). When she strikes it rich in the lottery, her boss gives chase and silent antics ensue. Silent with orchestral score. **67m/B VHS.** *RU* Anna Sten, Vladimar Fogel, Serafina Birman, Ivan Koval-Samborsky; **D:** Boris Barnet. *KIV, FCT*

The Girl with the Hungry Eyes *♪♪* **1994 (R)** In 1937, top fashion model and hotel owner Louise (Fulton) kills herself over a cheating fiancee. Except Louise doesn't die, instead she becomes a vampire and, in the present-day, decides to return to her now-derelict haunts. Louise is determined to restore her hotel to its former glory and get her revenge on men in general. Filmed in Miami's South Beach. Adapted from a short story by Fritz Leiber. **84m/C VHS.** Christina Fulton, Isaac Turner, Leon Herbert, Bret Carr, Susan Rhodes; **D:** Jon Jacobs; **W:** Jon Jacobs; **M:** Paul Inder. *COL*

Girlfriend from Hell *♪* **1989 (R)** The Devil inhabits the body of a teenage wallflower and turns her into an uncontrollable vamp. **95m/C VHS, Beta, LV.** Liane Curtis, Dana Ashbrook, Leslie Deane,

James Daughton, Anthony Barrie, James Karen; **D:** Daniel M. Peterson; **W:** Daniel M. Peterson. *LIV*

Girlfriends *♪♪♪* **1978 (PG)** Bittersweet story of a young Jewish photographer learning to make it on her own. Directorial debut of Weill reflects her background in documentaries as the true-to-life episodes unfold. **87m/C VHS, Beta.** Melanie Mayron, Anita Skinner, Eli Wallach, Christopher Guest, Amy Wright, Viveca Lindfors, Bob Balaban, Kathryn Walker, Kristopher Tabori, Mike Kellin, Kenneth McMillan; **D:** Claudia Weill; **W:** Vicki Polon. Sundance Film Festival '78: Grand Jury Prize. *WAR, FRF*

Girls Are for Loving *♪* **1973** Undercover agent Ginger faces real adventure when she battles it out with her counterpart, a seductive enemy agent. Her third adventure following "Ginger" (1970) and "The Abductors" (1971). **90m/C VHS, Beta.** Cheri Caffaro, Timothy Brown; **D:** Don Schain. *MON*

A Girl's Folly *♪♪½* **1917** A country girl falls in love with the leading man of a film shooting on location. She wants to become a rich actress, but fails miserably. The actor offers her all the luxuries she wants if she'll become his mistress. When she finally agrees, her mother shows up. What will our country maid do now? **66m/B VHS, Beta, 8mm.** Robert Warwick, Doris Kenyon, June Elvidge, Johnny Hines; **D:** Maurice Tourneur. *VYY, GPV*

Girls! Girls! Girls! *♪♪* **1962** Poor tuna boat fisherman Elvis moonlights as a nightclub singer to get his father's boat out of hock. He falls for a rich girl pretending to be poor; and after some romantic trials, there's the usual happy ending. ♪The Nearness of You; Never Let Me Go; Girls, Girls, Girls; Return to Sender; We're Coming in Loaded; A Boy Like Me, A Girl Like You; Song of the Shrimp; Earth Boy; The Walls Have Ears. **106m/C VHS.** Elvis Presley, Stella Stevens, Laurel Goodwin, Jeremy Slate, Benson Fong, Robert Strauss, Ginny Tiu, Guy Lee, Beulah Quo; **D:** Norman Taurog; **W:** Edward Anhalt; **C:** Loyal Griggs. *FOX, MVD*

Girls in Chains *♪½* **1943** Girls in a reformatory, a teacher, a corrupt school official, and the detective trying to nail him. There's also a murder with the killer revealed at the beginning of the film. **72m/B VHS, Beta.** Arline Judge, Roger Clark, Robin Raymond, Barbara Pepper, Dorothy Burgess, Clancy Cooper, Sid Melton, Betty Blythe, Peggy Stewart, Francis Ford; **D:** Edgar G. Ulmer; **W:** Albert Beich; **C:** Ira Morgan; **M:** Erdody. *NOS, SNC, DVT*

Girls in Prison *♪½* **1956** Anne Carson is sent to prison for a bank robbery she didn't commit, and although the prison chaplain believes her story, the other prisoners think she knows where the money is hidden. They plan a prison break, forcing Carson to go with them and get the money, but they soon run across the real robber, also searching for the loot. A below-average "B" prison movie, lacking the camp aspects of so many of these films. **87m/B VHS.** Richard Denning, Joan Taylor, Adele Jergens, Helen Gilbert, Lance Fuller, Jane Darwell, Raymond Hatton; **D:** Edward L. Cahn. *COL*

Girls Just Want to Have Fun *♪½* **1985 (PG)** An army brat and her friends pull out all the stops and defy their parents for a chance to dance on a national television program. Based loosely upon Cyndi Lauper's song of the same name. **90m/C VHS, Beta, LV, Closed Caption.** Sarah Jessica Parker, Helen Hunt, Ed Lauter, Holly Gagnier, Morgan Woodward, Lee Montgomery, Shannen Doherty, Biff Yeager; **D:** Alan Metter; **C:** Thomas Ackerman; **M:** Thomas Newman. *NWV, VTR*

Girls Next Door *♪* **1979 (R)** A bevy of boisterous beauties cavort and cause havoc in buffoon-cluttered suburbia. **85m/C VHS, Beta, LV.** Kirsten Baker, Perry Lang, Leslie Cederquist, Richard Singer; **D:** James Hong. *NO*

Girls Night Out *♪* *The Scaremaker* **1983 (R)** Ex-cop must stop a killer who is murdering participants in a sorority house scavenger hunt and leaving cryptic clues on the local radio station.

96m/C VHS, Beta. Hal Holbrook, Rutanya Alda, Julia Montgomery, James Carroll; **D:** Robert Deubel. *NO*

The Girls of Huntington House *♪♪* **1973** A teacher in a school for unwed mothers finds herself becoming increasingly absorbed in her students' lives. Made for television. **73m/C VHS.** Shirley Jones, Mercedes McCambridge, Sissy Spacek, William Windom, Pamela Sue Martin, Darrell Larson; **D:** Alf Kjellin. *LIV*

Girls of the White Orchid *♪* *Death Ride to Osaka* **1985** A naive American girl thinks she's getting a job singing in a Japanese nightclub, but it turns out to be a front for a prostitution ring run by the Japanese Yakuza. A made-for-television movie based on real stories, though the producers concentrate on the seamy side. **96m/C VHS, Beta.** Ann Jillian, Jennifer Jason Leigh; **D:** Jonathan Kaplan; **M:** Brad Fiedel. *ORI*

Girls on the Road *♪♪½* **1973 (PG)** Two girls are just out for fun cruising the California coast. But that handsome hitchhiker turns out to be a deadly mistake. **91m/C VHS, Beta.** *CA* Kathleen Cody, Michael Ontkean, Dianne Hull, Ralph Waite; **D:** Thomas J. Schmidt. *UNI*

Girls Riot *♪* **1988** Young, female juvenile delinquents have had enough! They decide to give their warden-like headmistress a taste of her own violence. **100m/C VHS, Beta.** Jocelyne Boisseau, Cornelia Calwer, Angelica Domrose, Ute Freight; **D:** Manfred Purzer. *ACN*

Girls School Screamers *♪* **1986 (R)** Six young women and a nun are assigned to spend the weekend checking the contents for sale in a scary mansion bequeathed to their school. Unfortunately, the psychotic killer inhabiting the place doesn't think that's a good idea. **85m/C VHS, Beta.** Mollie O'Mara, Sharon Christopher, Vera Gallagher; **D:** John P. Finegan. *TTV, LIV*

Girls' Town *♪* *The Innocent and the Damned* **1959** Typical bad girls and drag racing fifties flick has Van Doren sent to a correctional institute, run by nuns. This tough girl sees the error of her wicked ways and turns into a goody-two-shoes. **90m/B VHS.** Mamie Van Doren, Mel Torme, Paul Anka, Ray Anthony, Maggie Hayes, Cathy Crosby, Elinor Donahue, Gigi Perreau, Jim Mitchum, Gloria Talbott, Harold Lloyd Jr., Charles Chaplin Jr.; **D:** Charles Haas; **W:** Robert Smith; **M:** Van Alexander. *REP*

Girls Town *♪♪* **1995 (R)** Tough look at the lives of three working-class high school seniors who are shattered by the suicide of Nikki (Ellis), the fourth member of their group, who killed herself from guilt over an undisclosed rape. Single mom Patti (Taylor), ambitious Emma (Grace), and strong-willed Angela (Harris) argue, commiserate, battle their foes (Patti's abusive boyfriend, Nikki's rapist), and lean on each other as they struggle to figure out themselves and their ambiguous futures. Lots of time's spent in the girls' bathroom at school (how realistic can you get?) **CW:** Pervasive strong language and for drug use. **90m/C VHS.** Lili Taylor, Anna Grace, Bruklin Harris, Aunjanue Ellis, Guillermo Diaz, John Ventimiglia; **D:** Denise Casano; **W:** Denise Casano, Jim McKay, Lili Taylor, Anna Grace, Bruklin Harris, Aunjanue Ellis; **C:** Russell Fine. Sundance Film Festival '96: Filmmakers Trophy; Nominations: Independent Spirit Awards '97: Best Supporting Actress (Taylor). *HMK*

Girly *♪* *Mumsy, Nanny, Sonny, and Girly* **1970 (R)** An English gothic about an excessively weird family that lives in a crumbling mansion and indulges in murder, mental aberration, and sexual compulsion. **101m/C VHS, Beta.** *GB* Michael Bryant, Ursula Howells, Pat Heywood, Howard Trevor, Vanessa Howard, Michael Ripper; **D:** Freddie Francis. *PSM*

Git! *♪½* **1965** A young runaway and his faithful dog are taken in by a wealthy dog-breeder and trained by him into a crack hunting team. **90m/C VHS, Beta.** Jack Chaplain, Richard Webb, Heather North; **D:** Ellis Kadison. *COL, NLC*

Git Along Little Dogies *⅟₂* 1937 It's cattle ranchers versus oil men with Autry caught in the middle of the petro/cow war. But Gene still finds a little time to romance the town banker's pretty daughter. 60m/B VHS, Beta. Gene Autry, Judith Allen, Smiley Burnette, William Farnum; **D:** Joseph Kane. *NOS, VVY, DVT*

Give a Girl a Break *⅟₂* 1953 Three talented but unknown babes vie for the lead in a stage production headed for Broadway after the incumbent prima donna quits. After befriending one of the various men associated with the production, each starlet thinks she's a shoe-in for the part. Entertaining but undistinguished musical with appealing dance routines of Fosse and the Champions. Ira Gershwin, collaborating for the first and only time with Burton Lane, wrote the lyrics to two of the songs. ♫Give the Girl a Break; In Our United State; It Happens Every Time; Nothing is Impossible; Applause, Applause; Challenge Dance. 84m/C VHS. Marge Champion, Gower Champion, Debbie Reynolds, Helen Wood, Bob Fosse, Kurt Kasznar, Richard Anderson, William Ching, Larry Keating, Donna Martell; **D:** Stanley Donen; **M:** Andre Previn. *MGM, TTC, FCT*

Give 'Em Hell, Harry! 1975 James Whitmore's one-man show as Harry S. Truman filmed in performance on stage; Whitmore was nominated for a Tony. 103m/C VHS, Beta. James Whitmore; **D:** Steve Binder. Nominations: Academy Awards '75: Best Actor (Whitmore). *WOV*

Give Me a Sailor *⅟₂* 1938 Hope and Whiting play brothers, and fellow Naval officers, who meet sisters Grable and Raye on shore leave. Naturally, there's comic romantic complications until a double wedding ends the farce. Not much of a musical score from Ralph Rainger and Leo Robin but the movie's fun. Based on a play by Anne Nichols. ♫What Goes Here in My Heart?; A Little Kiss at Twilight; Give Me a Sailor; The US and You; It Don't Make Sense. 71m/B VHS. Bob Hope, Martha Raye, Betty Grable, Jack Whiting, Clarence Kolb, Nana Bryant, Emerson Treacy; **D:** Elliott Nugent; **W:** Frank Butler, Doris Anderson. *USH*

Give My Regards to Broad Street *⅟⅟* 1984 (PG) McCartney film made for McCartney fans. Film features many fine versions of the ex-Beatle's songs that accompany his otherwise lackluster portrayal of a rock star in search of his stolen master recordings. ♫Eleanor Rigby; Ballroom Dancing; Good Day, Sunshine; Silly Love Songs; No Values; No More Lonely Nights; Yesterday; Not Such a Bad Boy; The Long and Winding Road. 109m/C VHS, Beta, LV, Closed Caption. **GB** Paul McCartney, Bryan Brown, Ringo Starr, Barbara Bach, Tracey Ullman, Ralph Richardson, Linda McCartney; **D:** Peter Webb. *MVD, FOX*

The Gladiator *⅟⅟⅟½* 1938 Brown stars as a mild-mannered collegiate who accidently ingests a serum which turns him into a real he-man. Things take a turn for the funniest when the effects wear off, just as he is to wrestle Man Mountain Dean. Chock-full of Brown's trademark physical humor. 70m/B VHS. Joe E. Brown, Man Mountain Dean, June Travis, Dickie Moore, Lucien Littlefield, Robert Kent, Ethel Wales; **D:** Edward Sedgwick. *NOS*

The Gladiator *⅟½* 1986 An angry Los Angeles citizen turns vigilante against drunk drivers after his brother is one of their victims. Made for television. 94m/C VHS, Beta, LV, Closed Caption. Ken Wahl, Nancy Allen, Robert Culp, Stan Shaw, Rosemary Forsyth; **D:** Abel Ferrara. *VTR, NWV, HHE*

Gladiator *⅟½* 1992 (R) When suburban Golden Gloves boxing champion Tommy Riley (Marshall) is forced to move to the inner city because of his father's gambling debts, he becomes involved with an evil boxing promotor who thrives on pitting different ethnic races against each other in illegal boxing matches. Eventually Riley is forced to fight his black friend Lincoln (Gooding), even though Lincoln has been warned that another blow to the head could mean his life. Although

this film tries to serve some moral purpose, it falls flat on the mat. **CW:** Language and violence. 98m/C VHS, LV, Closed Caption. Cuba Gooding Jr., James Marshall, Robert Loggia, Ossie Davis, Brian Dennehy, Cara Buono, John Heard, Jon Seda, Lance Slaughter; **D:** Rowdy Herrington. *COL*

Gladiator Cop: The Swordsman 2 *⅟½* 1995 (R) A legendary sword, believed to have magic powers, is stolen and an ex-detective winds up fighting modern-day gladiators and a man who believes himself to be a reincarnation of Alexander the Great. **CW:** Strong violence, and for language and sexuality. 92m/C VHS. Lorenzo Lamas. *MNC*

Gladiator of Rome *⅟* *Il Gladiatore Di Roma* 1963 A gladiator flexes his pecs to save a young girl from death at the hands of evil rulers. 105m/C VHS. **IT** Gordon Scott, Wandisa Guida, Roberto Risso, Ombretta Colli, Alberto Farnese; **D:** Mario Costa. *SNC*

The Gladiators *⅟* *The Peace Game; Gladiator-erna* 1970 Televised gladiatorial bouts are designed to subdue man's violent tendencies in a futuristic society until a computer makes a fatal error. 90m/C VHS, Beta. Arthur Pentelow, Frederick Danner; **D:** Peter Watkins. *NO*

Gladiators 7 *⅟½* 1962 Sparta must be freed from the tyrannical rule of the Romans. In lieu of samurai or cowboys, who better than the Gladiators 7 to do the deed? Plenty of sword-to-sword action and scantily clad Italian babes. 92m/C VHS, Beta. **SP IT** Richard Harrison, Loredana Nusciak, Livio Lorenzon, Gerard Tichy, Edoardo Toniolo, Joseph Marco, Barta Barry; **D:** Pedro Lazaga. *SNC*

Glass *⅟½* 1990 A normally complacent man is driven to the brink of savagery when a killer begins stalking his employees. 92m/C VHS. Alan Lovell, Lisa Peers, Adam Stone, Natalie McCurry. *ATL*

The Glass Bottom Boat *⅟½* 1966 A bubbly but transparent Doris Day comedy, in which she falls in love with her boss at an aerospace lab. Their scheme to spend time together get her mistaken for a spy. Made about the time they stopped making them like this anymore, it's innocuous slapstick romance with a remarkable 1960's cast, including a Robert Vaughn cameo as the Man From U.N.C.L.E. Doris sings "Que Sera, Sera" and a few other numbers. 110m/C VHS, Beta, LV. Doris Day, Rod Taylor, Arthur Godfrey, Paul Lynde, Eric Fleming, Alice Pearce, Ellen Corby, John McGiver, Dom DeLuise, Dick Martin, Edward Andrews; **Cameos:** Robert Vaughn; **D:** Frank Tashlin; **W:** Everett Freeman; **C:** Leon Shamroy. *MGM*

The Glass Cage *⅟⅟* 1996 (R) Ex-CIA agent Paul Yeager (Tyson) takes a bartending job in New Orleans' French Quarter in order to get back his exotic dancer girlfriend but the bar's jealous owner and a dirty cop (Roberts) have other plans in mind for the duo. **CW:** Gangster violence, strong sexuality, and some language. 96m/C VHS. Charlotte Lewis, Richard Tyson, Eric Roberts, Stephen Nichols, Joseph Campanella, Richard Moll, Maria Ford, Lisa Marie Scott; **D:** Michael Schroeder. *ORI*

The Glass House *⅟⅟⅟* *Truman Capote's The Glass House* 1972 Alda stars as a middle-aged college professor, convicted on a manslaughter charge, who is sent to a maximum security prison and must learn to deal with life inside. Filmed at Utah State Prison, real-life prisoners as supporting cast add to the drama. Still has the power to chill, with Morrow particularly effective as one of the inmate leaders. Adapted from a Truman Capote story. Made for television. 92m/C VHS, Beta. Alan Alda, Vic Morrow, Clu Gulager, Billy Dee Williams, Dean Jagger, Kristopher Tabori; **D:** Tom Gries; **M:** Billy Goldenberg. *MOV, HHT*

The Glass Jungle 1988 Will a cab driver save Los Angeles? When armed terrorists and the FBI battle it out in the sunny California city an innocent cabby seems to hold the solution to survival. 94m/C VHS, Beta. Lee Canalito, Joe Filbeck, Diana Frank, Mark High, Frank Scala; **D:** Joseph Merhi. *HHE*

The Glass Key *⅟⅟⅟* 1942 The second version of Dashiell Hammet's novel, a vintage mystery movie concerning a nominally corrupt politician (Donlevy) being framed for murder, and his assistant sleuthing out the real culprit. One of Ladd's first starring vehicles; Lake is the mystery woman who loves him, and Bendix a particularly vicious thug. 85m/B VHS, Beta, LV. Alan Ladd, Veronica Lake, Brian Donlevy, William Bendix, Bonita Granville, Richard Denning, Joseph Calleia, Moroni Olsen, Dane Clark; **D:** Stuart Heisler. *USH*

The Glass Menagerie *⅟⅟⅟* 1987 (PG) An aging Southern belle deals with her crippled daughter Laura, whose one great love is her collection of glass animals. The third film adaptation of the Tennessee Williams classic, which preserves the performances of the Broadway revival cast, is a solid-but-not-stellar adaptation of the play. All-star acting ensemble. 134m/C VHS, Beta, LV. Joanne Woodward, Karen Allen, John Malkovich, James Naughton; **D:** Paul Newman; **W:** Tennessee Williams; **C:** Michael Ballhaus; **M:** Henry Mancini, Max Steiner. *USH*

The Glass Shield *⅟⅟½* 1995 (PG-13) Timely look at racism and corruption in the Los Angeles sheriff's department as seen through the eyes of African American rookie J.J. Johnson (Boatman). His dream of being a police officer turns to disillusionment when he slowly realizes his own department is framing a black man (Ice Cube) for a murder he did not commit. First half grabs your attention, but the momentum is lost in murky plot twists and a rushed ending. Made on a shoestring, but has an interesting cast, including the reliably slimy Ironside as (what else) one of the bad cops and an almost unrecognizable Petty, who becomes Johnson's only ally on the force. 109m/C VHS, LV, Closed Caption. Michael Boatman, Lori Petty, Michael Ironside, M. Emmet Walsh, Ice Cube, Richard Anderson, Elliott Gould; **D:** Charles Burnett; **W:** Charles Burnett; **C:** Elliot Davis; **M:** Stephen James Taylor. *TOU*

The Glass Slipper *⅟⅟* 1955 In this version of the "Cinderella" saga, Caron plays an unglamorous girl gradually transformed into the expected beauty. Winwood is the fairy godmother who inspires the girl to find happiness, rather then simply providing it for her magically. The film is highlighted by the stunning dance numbers, choreographed by Roland Petit and featuring the Paris ballet. 93m/C VHS, Beta. Leslie Caron, Michael Wilding, Keenan Wynn, Estelle Winwood, Elsa Lanchester, Barry Jones, Amanda Blake, Lurene Tuttle; **D:** Charles Walters. *MGM, FCT*

Glass Tomb *⅟⅟* *The Glass Cage* 1955 At a circus, a man performs the world's longest fast inside a glass cage, and becomes the raison d'etre for murder. 59m/B VHS, Beta, LV. John Ireland, Honor Blackman, Eric Pohlmann, Tonia Bern, Sidney James; **D:** Montgomery Tully. *NO*

The Glass Virgin *⅟⅟½* 199? In 1859, young Annabella Lagrange (Mortimer) discovers that her spendthrift father, Edmund (Haver), has been hiding the secrets surrounding her birth. These revelations force Annabella to find her own way in a new life. Based on a novel by Catherine Cookson. 150m/C VHS. **GB** Emily Mortimer, Nigel Havers, Brendan Coyle, Christine Kavanagh, Sylvia Syms, Samantha Glenn, Jan Graveson. *VCO*

Gleaming the Cube *⅟½* 1989 (PG-13) A skateboarding teen investigates his brother's murder. Film impresses with its stunt footage only. For those with adolescent interests. 102m/C VHS, Beta, LV, Closed Caption. Christian Slater, Steven Bauer, Min Luong, Art Chudabala, Le Tuan; **D:** Graeme Clifford; **W:** Michael Tolkin; **M:** Jay Michael Ferguson. *LIV, VES*

Glen and Randa *⅟⅟½* 1971 (R) Two young people experience the world after it has been destroyed by nuclear war. Early McBride, before the hired-gun success of "The Big Easy." 94m/C VHS, Beta, LV. Steven Curry, Shelley Plimpton; **D:** Jim McBride; **W:** Rudy Wurlitzer, Jim McBride. *VCI, IME*

Glen or Glenda: Confessions of Ed Wood woof!

He or She; I Changed My Sex; I Led Two Lives; The Transvestite **1953** An appalling, quasi-docudrama about transvestism, interspersed with meaningless stock footage, inept dream sequences and Lugosi sitting in a chair spouting incoherent prattle at the camera. Directorial debut of Wood, who, using a pseudonym, played the lead; one of the phenomenally bad films of this century. An integral part of the famous anti-auteur's canon. **70m/B VHS, Beta.** Bela Lugosi, Edward D. Wood Jr., Lyle Talbot, Donald Woods; *D:* Edward D. Wood Jr. *NOS, MRV, SNC*

Glengarry Glen Ross ♂♂♂ 1992 (R)

A seven-character study chronicling 48-hours in the lives of some sleazy real estate men in danger of getting the ax from their hard-driving bosses. A standout cast includes Pacino as the glad-handing sales leader, Lemmon as the hustler fallen on dim prospects, and Baldwin, briefly venomous, as the company hatchet-man. Brutal and hard-edged with very strong language. Mamet scripted from his Tony-award winning Broadway play. *CW:* Language. **100m/C VHS, LV, Closed Caption.** Al Pacino, Jack Lemmon, Ed Harris, Alec Baldwin, Alan Arkin, Kevin Spacey, Jonathan Pryce, Bruce Altman, Jude Ciccolella; *D:* James Foley; *W:* David Mamet; *C:* Juan Ruiz-Anchia; *M:* James Newton Howard. National Board of Review Awards '92: Best Actor (Lemmon); Venice Film Festival '93: Best Actor (Lemmon); Nominations: Academy Awards '92: Best Supporting Actor (Pacino). *LIV, MOV, BTV*

The Glenn Miller Story ♂♂ 1954 (G)

The music of the Big Band Era lives again in this warm biography of the legendary Glenn Miller, following his life from the late '20s to his untimely death in a WWII plane crash. Stewart's likably convincing and even fakes the trombone playing well. ♫Moonlight Serenade; In the Mood; Tuxedo Junction; Little Brown Jug; Adios; String of Pearls; Pennsylvania 6-5000; Stairway to the Stars; American Patrol. **113m/C VHS, Beta, LV.** James Stewart, June Allyson, Harry (Henry) Morgan, Gene Krupa, Louis Armstrong, Ben Pollack; *D:* Anthony Mann; *W:* Oscar Brodney; *C:* William H. Daniels; *M:* Henry Mancini. Academy Awards '54: Best Sound; Nominations: Academy Awards '54: Best Story & Screenplay, Scoring of a Musical. *USH, RDG*

The Glimmer Man ♂½ 1996 (R)

When a vicious LA serial killer starts dispatching whole families, NY detective Jack Cole (Seagal) is teamed with local homicide detective Jim Campbell (Wayans). Since, however, this is a Seagal movie, things have to be a little different. Cole, for example, is an ex-CIA operative who has been convinced by a Buddhist monk to stop killing people and start wearing goofy Nehru jackets and prayer beads. Campbell is a couch potato who cries over old movies (or perhaps he was watching the dailies from this one). After Cole's ex-wife is killed, he's implicated; and then somehow the Russian Mafia and the CIA are brought into the mix. Cole uses his unique brand of non-violence to slash, chop and impale his way to justice. Predictable when it's not being unbelievable, this could have been called "Hard to Watch." *CW:* Strong violence, language and some nudity. **92m/C VHS, LV, Closed Caption, DVD.** Steven Seagal, Keenen Ivory Wayans, Michelle Johnson, Brian Cox, Bob Gunton, Stephen Tobolowsky, John Strong, Ryan Cutrona; *D:* John Gray; *W:* Kevin Brodbin; *C:* Rick Bota; *M:* Trevor Rabin. *WAR*

Glitch! ♂½ 1988 (R)

A throng of beautiful Hollywood hopefuls draw two youngsters unconnected with the film into posing as the film's director and producer in the hopes of conducting personal interviews on the casting couch. Straight to video. **88m/C VHS, Beta, LV.** Julia Nickson-Soul, Will Egan, Steve Donmyer, Dan Speaker, Dallas Cole, Ji Tu Cumbuka, Dick Gautier, Ted Lange, Teri Weigel, Fernando Carzon, John Kreng, Lindsay Carr; *D:* Nico Mastorakis; *W:* Nico Mastorakis. *ACA*

The Glitter Dome ♂½ 1984

Two policemen discover the sleazier side of Hollywood when they investigate the murder of a pornographer. Based upon the novel by Joseph Wambaugh. Made for television. **90m/C VHS, Closed Caption.** Stuart Margolin, John Marley, James Garner, John Lithgow, Margot Kidder, Colleen Dewhurst; *D:* Stuart Margolin. *REP*

Glitz ♂♂½ 1988

A Miami cop and an Atlantic City lounge singer team up to investigate a callgirl's death and wind up too close to a drug ring. Based on the novel by Elmore Leonard. Made for television. **96m/C VHS, Beta.** Jimmy Smits, John Diehl, Markie Post, Ken Foree, Madison Mason, Robin Strasser; *D:* Sandor Stern. *WAR*

A Global Affair ♂½ 1963

Hope is a department head in the United Nations who finds an abandoned baby in the building. The inept bachelor is wooed by a number of international beauties seeking to adopt the child for their various countries but he becomes increasingly attached to the little tyke. **84m/B VHS, Beta.** Bob Hope, Lilo (Liselotte) Pulver, Michele Mercier, Yvonne De Carlo, Miiko Taka, Robert Sterling, Nehemiah Persoff, John McGiver, Mickey Shaughnessy; *D:* Jack Arnold; *W:* Charles Lederer, Arthur Marx, Bob Fisher; *C:* Joseph Ruttenberg. *MGM, FCT*

Gloria ♂♂½ 1980 (PG)

She used to be a Mafia moll, now she's outrunning the Mob after taking in the son of a slain neighbor. He's got a book that they want, and they're willing to kill to get it. Trademark Cassavetes effort in which he has actors plumb their souls to discomfiting levels. **123m/C VHS, Beta, LV.** Gena Rowlands, John Adams, Buck Henry, Julie Carmen; *D:* John Cassavetes; *M:* Bill Conti. Venice Film Festival '80: Best Film; Golden Raspberry Awards '80: Worst Supporting Actor (Adams); Nominations: Academy Awards '80: Best Actress (Rowlands). *COL*

Glorifying the American Girl ♂♂ 1930

Eaton's a chorus girl performing in the Ziegfeld Follies, which lends itself to numerous production numbers. The only film Ziegfeld ever produced. ♫What I Wouldn't Do For That Man; Blue Skies; I'm Just a Vagabond Lover; Baby Face; At Sundown; Beautiful Changes; Sam the Old Accordian Man; There Must Be Someone Waiting For Me. **96m/B VHS, Beta.** Mary Eaton, Dan Healey, Eddie Cantor, Rudy Vallee; *D:* Millard Webb. *NOS, HHT, DVT*

Glory ♂♂ 1956

O'Brien's a racehorse owner who tussles with her grandmother over how to keep the family farm open on a shoestring budget. Brennan enters the picture as the financial guru who lands them back on track, with enough left over to enter their prize filly in the Kentucky Derby. Lupton plays O'Brien's love interest. No surprises here. **100m/C VHS, Beta.** Margaret O'Brien, Walter Brennan, Charlotte Greenwood; *D:* David Butler. *NO*

Glory ♂♂♂½ 1989 (R)

A rich, historical spectacle chronicling the 54th Massachusetts, the first black volunteer infantry unit in the Civil War. The film manages to artfully focus on both the 54th and their white commander, Robert Gould Shaw. Based on Shaw's letters, the film uses thousands of accurately costumed "living historians" (re-enactors) as extras in this panoramic production. A haunting, bittersweet musical score pervades what finally becomes an anti-war statement. Stunning performances throughout, with exceptional work from Freeman and Washington. **122m/C VHS, Beta, LV, 8mm, Closed Caption.** Matthew Broderick, Morgan Freeman, Denzel Washington, Cary Elwes, Jihmi Kennedy, Andre Braugher, John Finn, Donovan Leitch, John Cullum, Bob Gunton, Jane Alexander, Raymond St. Jacques, Cliff DeYoung; *D:* Edward Zwick; *W:* Kevin Jarre; *C:* Freddie Francis; *M:* James Horner. Academy Awards '89: Best Cinematography, Best Sound, Best Supporting Actor (Washington); Golden Globe Awards '90: Best Supporting Actor (Washington); Nominations: Academy Awards '89: Best Art Direction/Set Decoration, Best Film Editing. *COL, FCT, BTV*

The Glory Boys ♂½ 1984

A secret agent is hired to protect an Israeli scientist who is marked for assassination by the PLO and IRA. **78m/C VHS, Beta.** Rod Steiger, Anthony Perkins, Gary Brown, Aaron Harris; *D:* Michael Ferguson. *VCO, VTR, PSM*

Glory Enough for All: The Discovery of Insulin ♂♂½ 1992

The drama behind the discovery of insulin in the 1920s focuses on the research of four men, sometimes not-so-friendly rivals, searching for a treatment for diabetes mellitus. Dr. Frederick Banting and science student Charles Best are granted permission by James Macleod, a Professor of Physiology at the University of Toronto, to conduct experiments on the pancreas. Macleod then assigns biochemist James Collip to assist them on developing a viable serum, an extract named insulin. Banting and Macleod were awarded the Nobel prize in 1923 for their discovery (though Banting felt Macleod was undeserving). Adapted from "The Discovery of Insulin" by Michael Bliss. Made for Canadian television. **196m/C VHS.** CA R.H. Thomson, Robert Wisden, John Woodvine, Michael Zelniker, Martha Henry, Heather Hess; *D:* Eric Till; *W:* Grahame Woods. *CCC*

Glory! Glory! ♂♂♂ 1990 (R)

Slashing satire about TV evangelism. Thomas as the meek son of founder of Church of the Champions of Christ brings in lewd female rock singer to save the money-machine ministry from financial ruin. Rock music, sex, and MTV-like camera work make it worth seeing. Whitmore is a treat. **152m/C VHS, Beta, LV.** Ellen Greene, Richard Thomas, Barry Morse, James Whitmore, Winston Reckert; *D:* Lindsay Anderson; *W:* Stan Daniels. *ORI, IME*

The Glory Stompers woof! 1967

Hopper prepares for his Easy Rider role as the leader of a motorcycle gang who battles with a rival leader over a woman. Very bad, atrocious dialogue, and a "love-in" scene that will be best appreciated by insomniacs. **85m/C VHS.** Dennis Hopper, Jody McCrea, Chris Noel, Jock Mahoney, Lindsay Crosby, Robert Tessier, Casey Kasem; *D:* Anthony M. Lanza. *NO*

The Glory Trail ♂½

Glorious Sacrifice **1936** A group of railroad workers and soldiers are constantly harassed by Indian attacks. **63m/B VHS.** Tom Keene, Joan Barclay, James Bush, Frank Melton, Walter Long; *D:* Lynn Shores. *GPV*

Glory Years ♂ 1987

Three old friends find themselves in charge of the scholarship fund at their 20th high school reunion. Unfortunately, they decide to increase the fund by gambling in Las Vegas and lose it all on a fixed fight! **150m/C VHS, Beta, Closed Caption.** George Dzundza, Archie Hahn, Tim Thomerson, Tawny Kitaen, Donna Pescow, Donna Denton; *D:* Arthur Seidelman. *HBO*

The Glove ♂½

The Glove: Lethal Terminator; Blood Mad **1978 (R)** Ex-cop turned bounty hunter has his toughest assignment ever. It's his job to bring in a six-and-a-half foot, 250-pound ex-con who's been wreaking havoc with an unusual glove—it's made of leather and steel. **93m/C VHS, Beta.** John Saxon, Roosevelt Grier, Joanna Cassidy, Joan Blondell, Jack Carter, Aldo Ray; *D:* Ross Hagen. *MED*

The Gnome-Mobile ♂♂ 1967

A lumber baron and his two grandchildren attempt to reunite a pair of forest gnomes with a lost gnome colony. Brennan has a dual role as both a human and a gnome grandfather. Wynn's last film. Based on a children's novel by Upton Sinclair. **84m/C VHS, Beta.** Walter Brennan, Richard Deacon, Ed Wynn, Karen Dotrice, Matthew Garber; *D:* Robert Stevenson; *C:* Edward Colman; *M:* Buddy Baker. *DIS, OM*

The Go-Between ♂♂♂½ 1971 (PG)

Wonderful tale of hidden love. Young boy Guard acts as a messenger between the aristocratic Christie and her former lover Bates. But tragedy befalls them all when the lovers are discovered. The story is told as the elderly messenger (now played by Redgrave) recalls his younger days as the go-between and builds to a climax when he is once again asked to be a messenger for the lady he loved long ago. Based on a story by L.P. Hartley. **116m/C VHS.** GB Julie Christie, Alan Bates, Dominic Guard, Margaret Leighton, Michael Redgrave, Michael

Gough, Edward Fox; **D:** Joseph Losey; **W:** Harold Pinter. British Academy Awards '71: Best Screenplay, Best Supporting Actor (Fox), Best Supporting Actress (Leighton); Cannes Film Festival '71: Best Film; Nominations: Academy Awards '71: Best Supporting Actress (Leighton). COL

Go Down Death 🎬½ 1941 In this early all-black film, a minister is caught in a moral dilemma literally between Heaven and Hell. Scenes of the afterlife are taken from early silent films. 63m/B VHS, Beta. Myra D. Hemmings, Samuel H. James, Eddy L. Houston, Spencer Williams Jr., Amos Droughan; **D:** Spencer Williams Jr. VYY, DVT, TIM

Go Fish 🎬🎬🎬 1994 (R) Low-budget girl-meets-girl romantic comedy finds Kia (McMillan) playing matchmaker for her roommate, energetic Max (Turner), by setting her up with shy Ely (Brodie). The opposites do, eventually, attract, with their friends eager for every detail. Good-natured and candid, with a welcome lack of melodrama. **CW:** Adult themes, blunt language, discreet nudity and sexuality. 87m/B VHS. Guinevere Turner, V.S. Brodie, T. Wendy McMillan, Anastasia Sharp, Migdalia Melendez; **D:** Rose Troche; **W:** Guinevere Turner, Rose Troche; **A:** Ann T. Rossetti; **M:** Brendan Dolan, Jennifer Sharpe. Nominations: Independent Spirit Awards '95: Best Supporting Actress (Brodie). HMK, FCT

Go for Broke! 🎬🎬½ 1951 Inexperienced officer Johnson heads a special WWII attack force which is made up of Japanese Americans. Sent to fight in Europe, they prove their bravery and loyalty to all. Good, offbeat story. 92m/B VHS, Beta. Van Johnson, Gianna Maria Canale, Warner Anderson, Lane Nakano, George Miki; **D:** Robert Pirosh; **C:** Paul Vogel. Nominations: Academy Awards '51: Best Story & Screenplay. NOS, MRV, VYY

Go for It 🎬🎬 1983 (PG) Oddball supercops go after a mad scientist—who has created a deadly "K"-bomb—and they encounter killer whales, karate busboys and malevolent Shirley Temple clones along the way. 109m/C VHS, Beta. IT Bud Spencer, Terence Hill, David Huddleston; **D:** E.B. Clucher. WAR

Go for the Gold 🎬 1984 A young marathon runner risks his girlfriend's love when he decides to pursue fame and fortune. 98m/C VHS, Beta. James Ryan, Cameron Mitchell, Sandra Horne. LIV

Go-Get-'Em-Haines 1935 Newsman Boyd follows a fleeing bankrupt utilities tycoon onto an ocean liner for an interview only to end up trying to solve the tycoon's murder. 61m/C VHS. William Boyd, Sheila Terry, Eleanor Hunt, Leroy Mason, Lloyd Ingraham, Jimmy Aubrey, Clarence Geldert, Louis Natheaux, Lee Shumway; **D:** Sam Newfield. GPV

The Go-Getter 🎬🎬 1954 Wild slapstick fun in the world of business. ?m/C VHS. Hank McCune, Beverly Garland. LOO

Go, Johnny Go! 🎬 1959 Rock promoter Alan Freed molds a young orphan into rock sensation "Johnny Melody." Musical performances include Ritchie Valens (his only film appearance), Eddie Cochran, Jackie Wilson. 75m/B VHS, Beta, LV. Alan Freed, Sandy Stewart, Chuck Berry, Jimmy Clanton, Eddie Cochran, Jackie Wilson, Ritchie Valens; **D:** Paul Landres. MED, AOV, VTR

Go Kill and Come Back 🎬 1968 (PG) A bounty hunter tracks down a notoriously dangerous train robber. 95m/C VHS, Beta. Gilbert Roland, George Helton, Ed Byrnes; **D:** Enzo G. Castellari. MON

The Go-Masters 🎬🎬🎬 Mikan No Taikyoku 1982 Historic co-production between Japan and China, centering on the ancient strategy board game "Go." A young competitor becomes obsessed with winning at any price. Episodic tale of the relationships between a Japanese and Chinese family spans 30 years and was critically acclaimed in both China and Japan. In Japanese and Chinese with English subtitles. 134m/C VHS, Beta. JP CH Huang Zong-Ying, Du Peng, Yu Shao-Kang, Lui Xin, Yoshiko Mita, Keiko Matsuzaka, Mayumi Ogawa, Rentaro Mikuni, Sun Dao-Lin, Shen Guan-Chu, Misako Honno; **D:** Junya Sato, Duan Jishun. Montreal World Film Festival '83: Best Film. FCT

Go Tell It On the Mountain 🎬🎬½ 1984 Young black boy tries to gain the approval of his stern stepfather in this fine adaptation of James Baldwin's semiautobiographical novel. Set in the 1930s; originally a PBS "American Playhouse" presentation. 100m/C VHS. Paul Winfield, Olivia Cole, Ruby Dee, Alfre Woodard, James Bond III, Rosalind Cash, Linda Hopkins; **D:** Stan Lathan. MON

Go Tell the Spartans 🎬🎬🎬 1978 (R) In Vietnam, 1964, a hard-boiled major is ordered to establish a garrison at Muc Wa with a platoon of burned out Americans and Vietnamese mercenaries. Blundering but politically interesting war epic pre-dating the flood of 1980s American-Vietnam apologetics. Based on Daniel Ford's novel. 114m/C VHS, Beta, LV. Burt Lancaster, Craig Wasson, David Clennon, Marc Singer; **D:** Ted Post; **W:** Wendell Mayes; **C:** Harry Stradling Jr. VES

Go West 🎬🎬½ 1940 The brothers Marx help in the making and un-making of the Old West. Weak, late Marx Bros., but always good for a few yucks. 80m/B VHS, Beta, LV. Groucho Marx, Chico Marx, Harpo Marx, John Carroll, Diana Lewis; **D:** Edward Buzzell; **M:** George Bassman. MGM, CCB

Go West, Young Man 🎬🎬½ 1936 West is a movie star whose latest film is premiering in a small town, where she's naturally a sensation. Scott is the muscular farm boy who catches her eye and she decides to hang around in order to catch the rest of him as well. The censors again cut West's most overt sexual and satiric barbs. 80m/B VHS. Mae West, Randolph Scott, Warren William, Alice Brady, Elizabeth Patterson, Lyle Talbot, Isabel Jewell; **D:** Henry Hathaway; **W:** Mae West; **C:** Karl Struss. USH, BTV

The Goalie's Anxiety at the Penalty Kick 🎬🎬🎬½ 1971 A chilling landmark film that established Wenders as one of the chief film voices to emerge from post-war Germany. The story deals with a soccer player who wanders around Vienna after being suspended, commits a random murder, and slowly passes over the brink of sanity and morality. A suspenseful, existential adaptation of the Peter Handke novel. In German with English subtitles. 101m/C VHS, Beta. GE Arthur Brauss, Erika Pluhar, Kai Fischer; **D:** Wim Wenders. FCT, GLV

Goblin woof! 1993 Newlywed couple regret the purchase of their new home when the devilish creature once brought to life by the previous homeowner, a witchcraft performing farmer, is raised from the depths of hell to rip to pieces anyone in its view. Any movie whose promo says "You won't believe your eyes...until he rips them from their sockets" is sure to be a crowd pleaser. Enjoy. 75m/C VHS. Bobby Westrick, Jenny Admire. TEM

God Bless the Child 🎬🎬🎬 1988 A young single mother loses her home and she and her seven-year-old daughter are forced to live on the streets. Harrowing made for television drama providing no easy answers to the plight of the homeless. 93m/C VHS, Closed Caption. Mare Winningham, Dorian Harewood, Grace Johnston, Charlaine Woodard, Obba Babatunde, L. Scott Caldwell; **D:** Larry Elikann; **W:** Dennis Nemec; **M:** David Shire. WOV

God, Man and Devil 🎬🎬½ 1949 A wager between God and Satan begins this allegory of money versus the spirit. A poor Torah scribe, Hershele Dubrovner, has a life that glorifies God until Satan, disguised as a business partner, turns him greedy and dishonest. Dubrovner's success destroys both his religion and his community leaving only betrayal and abandonment. In Yiddish with English subtitles. 100m/B VHS. Mikhal Mikhalesko, Gustav Berger; **D:** Joseph Seiden. NCJ

God Told Me To 🎬🎬½ Demon 1976 (R) A religious New York cop is embroiled in occult mysteries while investigating a series of grisly murders. He investigates a religious cult that turns out to be composed of half-human, half-alien beings. A cult-fave Larry Cohen epic. 89m/C VHS, Beta, LV.

Tony LoBianco, Deborah Raffin, Sylvia Sidney, Sandy Dennis, Richard Lynch; **D:** Larry Cohen; **W:** Larry Cohen. NLC

Godard/Truffaut Shorts 1958 A pair of early shorts directed by two French "new wave" masters: Jean-Luc Godard's "All the Boys Are Called Patrick" from 1957 and Francois Truffaut's "Les Mistons" from 1958. 39m/B VHS, Beta. FR D: Francois Truffaut, Jean-Luc Godard. DVT, MRV, HEG

The Goddess 🎬🎬🎬 1958 Sordid story of a girl who rises to fame as a celluloid star by making her body available to anyone who can help her career. When the spotlight dims, she keeps going with drugs and alcohol to a bitter end. 105m/B VHS, Beta, LV. Kim Stanley, Lloyd Bridges, Patty Duke; **D:** John Cromwell; **W:** Paddy Chayefsky. Nominations: Academy Awards '58: Best Story & Screenplay. NO

The Godfather 🎬🎬🎬🎬 1972 (R) Coppola's award-winning adaptation of Mario Puzo's novel about a fictional Mafia family in the late 1940s. Revenge, envy, and parent-child conflict mix with the rituals of Italian mob life in America. Minutely detailed, with excellent performances by Pacino, Brando, and Caan as the violence-prone Sonny. Film debut of Coppola's daughter Sophia, the infant in the baptism scene, who returns in "Godfather III." The horrific horse scene is an instant chiller. Indisputably an instant piece of American culture. Followed by two sequels. 171m/C VHS, Beta, LV, 8mm. Marlon Brando, Al Pacino, Robert Duvall, James Caan, Diane Keaton, John Cazale, Talia Shire, Richard Conte, Richard Castellano, Abe Vigoda, Alex Rocco, Sterling Hayden, John Marley, Al Lettieri, Sofia Coppola, Al Martino, Morgana King; **D:** Francis Ford Coppola; **W:** Mario Puzo, Francis Ford Coppola; **C:** Gordon Willis; **M:** Nino Rota. Academy Awards '72: Best Actor (Brando), Best Adapted Screenplay, Best Picture; Directors Guild of America Awards '72: Best Director (Coppola); Golden Globe Awards '73: Best Actor—Drama (Brando), Best Director (Coppola), Best Film—Drama, Best Screenplay, Best Score; National Board of Review Awards '72: 10 Best Films of the Year, Best Supporting Actor (Pacino); New York Film Critics Awards '72: Best Supporting Actor (Duvall); National Society of Film Critics Awards '72: Best Actor (Pacino); Writers Guild of America '72: Best Adapted Screenplay; Nominations: Academy Awards '72: Best Costume Design, Best Director (Coppola), Best Film Editing, Best Sound, Best Supporting Actor (Caan, Duvall, Pacino). PAR, BTV

The Godfather 1902-1959: The Complete Epic 🎬🎬🎬🎬 1981 Coppola's epic work concerning the lives of a New York crime family. Comprises the first two "Godfather" films, reedited into a chronological framework of the Corleone family history, with much previously discarded footage restored. 386m/C VHS, Beta, Closed Caption. Marlon Brando, Al Pacino, Robert Duvall, James Caan, Richard Castellano, Diane Keaton, Robert De Niro, John Cazale, Lee Strasberg, Talia Shire, Michael V. Gazzo, Troy Donahue, Joe Spinell, Abe Vigoda, Alex Rocco, Sterling Hayden, John Marley, Richard Conte, G.D. Spradlin, Bruno Kirby, Harry Dean Stanton, Roger Corman, Al Lettieri; **D:** Francis Ford Coppola; **W:** Mario Puzo, Francis Ford Coppola; **M:** Nino Rota. PAR, FCT

The Godfather, Part 2 🎬🎬🎬🎬 1974 (R) A continuation and retracing of the first film, interpolating the maintenance of the Corleone family by the aging Michael, and its founding by the young Vito (De Niro, in a terrific performance) 60 years before in New York City's Little Italy. Often considered the second half of one film, the two films stand as one of American film's greatest efforts, and as a 1970s high-water mark. Combined into one work for television presentation. Followed by a sequel. 200m/C VHS, Beta, LV, 8mm. Al Pacino, Robert De Niro, Diane Keaton, Robert Duvall, James Caan, Danny Aiello, John Cazale, Lee Strasberg, Talia Shire, Michael V. Gazzo, Troy Donahue, Joe Spinell, Abe Vigoda, Marianna Hill, Fay Spain, G.D. Spradlin, Bruno Kirby, Harry Dean Stanton, Roger Corman, Kathleen Beller, John Aprea, Morgana King; **D:** Francis Ford Coppola; **W:** Mario Puzo, Francis Ford Coppola; **C:** Gordon Willis; **M:** Nino Rota, Carmine Coppola. Academy Awards '74: Best Adapted Screenplay, Best Art Direction/Set Decoration, Best Director (Coppola), Best Picture, Best Supporting Actor (De Niro), Original Dramatic/Comedy Score; Directors Guild of America Awards '74: Best Director (Coppola); National Society of Film Critics Awards '74: Best Director (Coppola); Writers Guild of America '74: Best Adapted Screenplay; Nominations: Academy Awards '74: Best Actor (Pacino), Best Costume Design, Best Supporting Actor (Gazzo, Strasberg), Best Supporting Actress (Shire); National Society of Film Critics Awards '74: Best Cinematography. *PAR, BTV*

The Godfather, Part 3 ✓✓✓ 1990 (R)

Don Corleone (Pacino), now aging and guilt-ridden, determines to buy his salvation by investing in the Catholic Church, which he finds to be a more corrupt brotherhood than his own. Meanwhile, back on the homefront, his young daughter discovers her sexuality as she falls in love with her first cousin. Weakest entry of the trilogy is still a stunning and inevitable conclusion to the story; Pacino adds exquisite finishing touches to his time-worn character. Beautifully photographed in Italy by Gordon Willis. Video release contains the final director's cut featuring nine minutes of footage not included in the theatrical release. *CW:* Language and violence. **170m/C VHS, Beta, LV, 8mm, Closed Caption.** Al Pacino, Diane Keaton, Andy Garcia, Joe Mantegna, George Hamilton, Talia Shire, Sofia Coppola, Eli Wallach, Don Novello, Bridget Fonda, John Savage, Al Martino, Raf Vallone, Franc D'Ambrosio, Donal Donnelly, Richard Bright, Helmut Berger; **D:** Francis Ford Coppola; **W:** Mario Puzo, Francis Ford Coppola; **C:** Gordon Willis; **M:** Nino Rota, Carmine Coppola. Golden Raspberry Awards '90: Worst Supporting Actress (Coppola), Worst New Star (Coppola); Nominations: Academy Awards '90: Best Art Direction/Set Decoration, Best Cinematography, Best Director (Coppola), Best Film Editing, Best Picture, Best Song ("Promise Me You'll Remember"), Best Supporting Actor (Garcia). *PAR, FCT*

God's Bloody Acre woof! 1975 (R)

Three backwoods mountain-dwelling brothers kill construction workers in order to defend their land, and then begin preying on vacationers. **90m/C VHS, Beta.** Scott Lawrence, Jennifer Gregory, Sam Moree, Shiang Hwa Chyang; **D:** Harry Kerwin. *TWE*

God's Country ✓✓ 1946 A loner kills a

man in self-defense and escapes the pursuing law by disappearing into California Redwood country with his dog. **62m/C VHS, Beta, LV.** Robert Lowery, Helen Gilbert, William Farnum, Buster Keaton; **D:** Robert Emmett Tansey. *NO*

God's Country and the Man ✓✓

1937 Typical western adventurer about a cowboy out to nab a gunman who's been threatening the life of a dance hall girl. Plenty of two-fisted action when law-abiding Keene shows up. **56m/B VHS.** Tom Keene, Betty Compson, Charlotte Henry, Charles "Blackie" King, Billy Bletcher, Ed Parker; **D:** Robert North Bradbury; **W:** Robert Emmett. *MOV*

God's Gun ✓ A Bullet from God 1975 (R)

Preacher who was once a gunfighter seeks revenge on the men who tried to kill him. **93m/C VHS, Beta.** Richard Boone, Lee Van Cleef, Jack Palance, Sybil Danning; **D:** Frank Kramer. *CCB*

God's Little Acre ✓✓✓ 1958 Delves

into the unexpectedly passionate lives of Georgia farmers. One man, convinced there's buried treasure on his land, nearly brings himself and his family to ruin trying to find it. Based on the novel by Erskine Caldwell. **110m/B VHS, Beta.** Robert Ryan, Tina Louise, Michael Landon, Buddy Hackett, Vic Morrow, Jack Lord, Aldo Ray, Fay Spain; **D:** Anthony Mann; **W:** Philip Yordan; **M:** Elmer Bernstein. *PSM, VEC*

The Gods Must Be Crazy ✓✓✓½

1984 (PG) An innocent and charming film. A peaceful Bushman travels into the civilized world to return a Coke bottle "to the gods." Along the way he meets a transplanted schoolteacher, an oafishly clumsy microbiologist and a gang of fanatical terrorists. A very popular film, disarmingly crammed with slapstick and broad humor of every sort. Followed by a weak sequel. **109m/C VHS, Beta, LV, Closed Caption.** N!xau, Marius Weyers, Sandra Prinsloo, Louw Verwey, Jamie Uys, Michael Thys, Nic de Jager; **D:** Jamie Uys; **M:** Johnny Bishop, John Boshoff. *FOX, FCT, TVC*

The Gods Must Be Crazy 2 ✓✓½

1989 (PG) A slapdash sequel to the original 1981 African chortler, featuring more ridiculous shenanigans in the bush. This time the bushman's children find themselves in civilization and N!xau must use his unique ingenuity to secure their safe return. **90m/C VHS, Beta, LV, Closed Caption.** N!xau, Lena Farugia, Hans Strydom, Eiros Nadies, Eric Bowen; **D:** Jamie Uys; **M:** Charles Fox. *COL, TTC, FCT*

Gods of the Plague ✓✓✓ Gotter der

Pest 1969 Fassbinder goes noir—or grey with lots of sharp lighting—in this gangster-auteur tale of robbery gone awry. The requisite trappings of the crime genre (guys and dolls and cops and robbers) provide a vague backdrop (and a vague plot) for a moody story full of teutonic angst and alienation, and that certain Fassbinder feeling (which, need we say, isn't to everyone's taste). An early effort by the director, who remade the story later the same year as "The American Soldier" (Fassbinder acts in both). In German with (difficult-to-read) English subtitles. **92m/C VHS.** GE Hanna Schygulla, Harry Bear; **D:** Rainer Werner Fassbinder. *TPV*

The Godsend ✓ 1979 (R) "Omen" rip-off

about a little girl who is thrust upon a couple. After adopting her, they lose their natural family to her evil ways. **93m/C VHS, Beta.** CA Cyd Hayman, Malcolm Stoddard, Angela Pleasence, Patrick Barr; **D:** Gabrielle Beaumont. *VES*

Godson ✓✓✓ 1972 Emotionless assassin

lives a barren life under the surveillance of Paris police who suspect him in a recent killing. He suddenly discovers that his boss has a contract out on his life. Delon's performance raises this to an above-average crime drama. **103m/C VHS.** FR Alain Delon, Nathalie Delon, Francois Perier; **D:** Jean-Pierre Melville. *PSV*

Godzilla, King of the Monsters ✓✓✓½ Gojira 1956 An underwater

prehistoric reptile emerges from the depths to terrorize Tokyo after he has been awakened by atomic testing. Burr's scenes are intercut in the American version, where he serves as a narrator telling the monster's tale in flashbacks. Ridiculously primitive special effects even in its own day. One of the first post-WWII Japanese films to break through commercially in the U.S. **80m/B VHS, Beta, LV.** JP Raymond Burr, Takashi Shimura; **D:** Terry Morse. *PAR, VES*

Godzilla 1985 ✓½ 1985 (PG) Godzilla is

awakened from underwater slumber by trolling nuclear submarines belonging to the superpowers near Japan. The giant monster's newly acquired appetite for nuclear energy inadvertently precipitates an international incident. Burr is called in (as the only living American witness to Godzilla's destructive 1955 outburst) to help mediate the conflict. Film released to coincide with the 30th anniversary of the original. **91m/C VHS, Beta, LV.** JP Raymond Burr, Keiju Kobayashi, Ken Tanaka, Yasuka Sawaguchi; **D:** Kohji Hashimoto, Robert J. Kizer. *NWV, VTR*

Godzilla on Monster Island ✓✓

Godzilla vs. Gigan 1972 Even Godzilla himself cannot hope to take on both Ghidra and Gigan alone and hope to succeed. Therefore he summons his pal Angillus for help. Together, they offer Earth its only hope of survival. Though the terror may repel you, the movie is a must for Godzilla fans; it's his first speaking part. **89m/C VHS.** JP Hiroshi Ichikawa, Tomoko Umeda, Yuriko Hishimi, Minoru Takashima, Zan Fujita; **D:** Jun Fukuda. *SNC, MRV, NWV*

Godzilla Raids Again ✓✓ Gigantis, the

Fire Monster; Godzilla's Counter Attack 1959 Warner Bros. had a problem securing rights to Godzilla's name. Yearning for a change of pace, the King of Monsters opts to destroy Osaka instead of Tokyo, but the spiny Angorous is out to dethrone our hero. Citizens flee in terror when the battle royale begins. The first Godzilla sequel. **78m/B VHS.** JP Hugo Grimaldi, Makayama, Minoru Chiaki. *VTR*

Godzilla vs. Biollante ✓✓ 1989 (PG)

Doctor Surigama's secret plant formula could free the industrialized world from oil dependency. He also runs his pet Godzilla experiment from the same laboratory. When terrorist thieves attempt to steal the plant formula, a petri dish mixup unleashes the abominable fury of Biollante. The return of the real Godzilla is the world's only hope, but not before another Japanese city is crushed in the reptilian rumble. **104m/C VHS, Closed Caption.** JP **D:** Kazuki Ohmori; **W:** Kazuki Ohmori. *NO*

Godzilla vs. Megalon ✓½ Gojira Tai Megaro 1976 (G) Godzilla's creators show their gratitude to misguided but faithful American audiences by transforming the giant monster into a good guy. This time, the world is threatened by Megalon, the giant cockroach, and Gigan, a flying metal creature, simultaneously. Forchneately, the slippery hero's robot pal Jet Jaguar is on hand to slug it out side by side with Tokyo's ultimate defender. **80m/C VHS.** JP Katsuhiko Sasakai, Hiroyuki Kawase, Yutaka Hayashi, Robert Dunham; **D:** Jun Fukuda. *NOS, MRV, NWV*

Godzilla vs. Monster Zero ✓✓ Monster Zero; Battle of the Astros; Invasion of the Astro-Monsters; Invasion of the Astros; Invasion of Planet X; Kaiju Daisenso 1968 (G) Novel Godzilla adventure with the big guy and Rodan in outer space. Suspicious denizens of Planet X require the help of Godzilla and Rodan to rid themselves of the menacing Ghidra, whom they refer to as Monster Zero. Will they, in return, help Earth as promised, or is this just one big, fat double cross? **93m/C VHS, Beta.** JP Nick Adams; **D:** Inoshiro Honda. *PAR, FUS*

Godzilla vs. Mothra ✓✓ Godzilla vs. the Thing; Godzilla vs. the Giant Moth; Godzilla Fights the Giant Moth; Mothra vs. Godzilla; Mosura Tai Goira 1964 Mighty Mothra is called in to save the populace from Godzilla, who is on a rampage; and he's aided by two junior Mothras who hatch in the nick of time. The hesitant moth avoids the fire-breathing behemoth until succumbing to the pleadings of the Peanut Sisters to save humanity. Hilarious special effects inspire more laughter from derision than anything else. **88m/C VHS, Beta.** JP Akira Takarada, Yuriko Hoshi, Hiroshi Koizumi; **D:** Inoshiro Honda. *PAR, FUS*

Godzilla vs. the Cosmic Monster ✓✓ Godzilla Versus the Bionic Monster; Godzilla vs. Mechagodzilla; Gojira Tai Meka-Gojira 1974 (G) Godzilla's worst nightmares become a reality as he is forced to take on the one foe he cannot defeat - a metal clone of himself! To make matters worse, Earth is in dire peril at the hands of cosmic apes. We all need friends, and Godzilla is never more happy to see his buddy King Seeser, who gladly lends a claw. **80m/C VHS.** JP Masaki Daimon, Kazuya Aoyama, Reiko Tajima, Barbara Lynn, Akihiko Hirata; **D:** Jun Fukuda. *NWV, MRV, VYY*

Godzilla vs. the Sea Monster woof!

Nankai No Kai Ketto; Ebirah, Terror of the Deep; Big Duel in the North 1966 Godzilla makes friends with former rival Mothra (a giant moth) and together they bash on Ebirah, an enormous lobster backed by an evil cadre of (human) totalitarians. The unrepentant crusteacean turns the tables on our heroes, however, by growing a new tentacle everytime one is ripped off. Meanwhile, a frenzied batch of helpless humans are trapped on an island about to explode, if they aren't drowned first in a shower of reptilian backwash. **80m/C VHS, Beta.** JP **D:** Jun Fukuda. *DVT, MRV, HHT*

Godzilla vs. the Smog Monster ✓

Gojira Tai Hedora; Godzilla vs. Hedora 1972 (G) Godzilla battles a creature borne of pollution, a 400-pound sludge blob named Hedora. Early 1970's period piece conveys interesting attitude towards pollution; it's treated as a sinister force that people are powerless to stop. Japanese teenagers marshal their dancing talents to combat the threat amid the hypnotic swirl of disco lighting. Great opening song: "Save the Earth." Dubbed in English. **87m/C**

VHS, Beta. JP Akira Yamauchi, Hiroyuki Kawase, Toshio Shibaki; D: Yoshimitu Banno. ORI

Godzilla's Revenge *⊘* *Oru Kaiju Daishin-geki* 1969 A young boy who is having problems dreams of going to Monster Island to learn from Minya, Godzilla's son. Using the lessons in real life, the boy captures some bandits and outwits a bully. Uses footage from "Godzilla vs. the Sea Monster" and "Son of Godzilla" for battle scenes. One of the silliest Godzilla movies around. 70m/C VHS. JP Kenji Sahara, Tomonori Yazaki, Machiko Naka, Sachio Sakai, Chotaro Togin, Yoshibumi Tajima; D: Inoshiro Honda. NO

Goin' Coconuts *⊘* 1978 (PG) Donny and Marie are miscast as Donny and Marie in this smarmy story of crooks and jewels. Seems someone covets the chanteuse's necklace, and only gratuitous crooning can spare the twosome from certain swindling. Big bore on the big island. 93m/C VHS. Donny Osmond, Marie Osmond, Herb Edelman, Kenneth Mars, Ted Cassidy, Marc Lawrence, Harold Sakata; D: Howard Morris. NO

Goin' South *⊘⊘⊘* 1978 (PG) An outlaw is saved from being hanged by a young woman who agrees to marry him in exchange for his help working a secret gold mine. They try to get the loot before his old gang gets wind of it. A tongue-in-cheek western that served as Nicholson's second directorial effort. Movie debuts of Steenburgen and Belushi. 109m/C VHS, Beta, LV. Jack Nicholson, Mary Steenburgen, John Belushi, Christopher Lloyd, Veronica Cartwright, Richard Bradford, Danny DeVito, Luana Anders, Ed Begley Jr., Anne Ramsey; D: Jack Nicholson; W: Charles Shyer; C: Nestor Almendros; M: Perry Botkin. PAR

Goin' to Town *⊘⊘½* 1935 Complicated yarn with West as a woman who inherits an oil field and becomes the wealthiest woman in the state. She falls for British engineer Cavanagh and decides to become a "lady" in order to get his attention. There's a subplot about Buenos Aires and a crooked horse race, an in-name-only marriage to a high society type, and a murder before Mae finally gets her man. 71m/B VHS. Mae West, Paul Cavanagh, Gilbert Emery, Ivan Lebedeff, Marjorie Gateson, Tito Coral, Monroe Owsley; D: Alexander Hall; W: Mae West; C: Karl Struss. USH, BTV

Going Ape! *⊘⊘* 1981 (PG) Danza inherits a bunch of orangutans. If the apes are treated well, a legacy of $5 million will follow. This is all you need to know. 87m/C VHS, Beta. Tony Danza, Jessica Walter, Danny DeVito, Art Metrano, Rick Hurst; D: Jeremy Joe Kronsberg; M: Elmer Bernstein. PAR

Going Back *⊘½* 1983 Four friends reunite after college to relive a memorable summer they spent together after graduating from high school. 85m/C VHS, Beta. Bruce Campbell, Christopher Howe, Perry Mallette, Susan W. Yamasaki; D: Ron Teachworth. LIV, VES

Going Bananas *⊘⊘* 1988 (PG) Wacky adventure about a chimp who is being chased by a sinister circus owner. The monkey runs through Africa dragging along a boy, his caretaker, and a guide. The cast says it all. 95m/C VHS, Beta, Closed Caption. Dom DeLuise, Jimmie Walker, David Mendenhall, Herbert Lom; D: Boaz Davidson. MED, VTR

Going Berserk *⊘½* 1983 (R) The members of SCTV's television comedy troupe are featured in this comedy which lampoons everything from religious cults to kung fu movies to "Father Knows Best." Should have been more fun. 85m/C VHS, Beta, LV. CA John Candy, Joe Flaherty, Eugene Levy, Paul Dooley, Pat Hingle, Richard Libertini, Ernie Hudson; D: David Steinberg. USH

Going for the Gold: The Bill Johnson Story *⊘⊘* 1985 Biographical tale of the American downhill skier who went from hard-luck punk to Olympic champion in the 1984 games at Sarajevo, Yugoslavia. 100m/C VHS. Anthony Edwards, Dennis Weaver, Sarah Jessica Parker, Deborah Van Valkenburgh, Wayne Northrop; D: Don Taylor. COL

Going Hollywood *⊘⊘⊘* 1933 Amusing musical/romantic fluff about a French teacher (Davies) who falls in love with a radio crooner (Crosby in his first MGM film). He's got the movie bug and heads for Hollywood, where he becomes an overnight sensation with a sultry costar (D'Orsay). Davies follows and proceeds to get Crosby out of D'Orsay's clutches and winds up replacing her rival in the film, promptly becoming a star herself. The underrated Davies was a fine light comedienne and supplied glamour to the production as well. Kelly, in her film debut, supplied the slapstick. The last Hearst-Cosmopolitan production made with MGM. ♫Temptation; We'll Make Hay While the Sun Shines; Going Hollywood; Our Big Love Scene; After Sundown; Cinderella's Fella; Beautiful Girl; Just an Echo in the Valley. 78m/B VHS. Marion Davies, Bing Crosby, Fifi d'Orsay, Stuart Erwin, Patsy Kelly, Ned Sparks; D: Raoul Walsh; W: Donald Ogden Stewart. MGM

Going Home *⊘⊘½* 1986 During WWI, Canadian soldiers held in British camps awaiting transport back home stage a riot over the endless delays and intolerable conditions. A fact-based story of the events leading up to this tragedy. 100m/C VHS. Nicholas Campbell, Paul Maxwell, Eugene Lipinski. NO

Going in Style *⊘⊘⊘½* 1979 (PG) Three elderly gentlemen, tired of doing nothing, decide to liven up their lives by pulling a daylight bank stick-up. They don't care about the consequences because anything is better than sitting on a park bench all day long. The real fun begins when they get away with the robbery. Great cast makes this a winner. 91m/C VHS, Beta. George Burns, Art Carney, Lee Strasberg; D: Martin Brest; W: Martin Brest. WAR

Going My Way *⊘⊘⊘½* 1944 A musical-comedy about a progressive young priest assigned to a downtrodden parish who works to get the parish out of debt, but clashes with his elderly curate, who's set in his ways. Followed by "The Bells of St. Mary's." Fitzgerald's Oscar-winning Supporting Actor performance was also nominated in the Best Actor category. ♫The Day After Forever; Swinging on a Star; Too-ra-loo-ra-loo-ra; Going My Way; Silent Night; Habanera; Ave Maria. 126m/B VHS, Beta, LV. Bing Crosby, Barry Fitzgerald, Rise Stevens, Frank McHugh, Gene Lockhart, Porter Hall; D: Leo McCarey; W: Frank Butler, Frank Cavett, Leo McCarey; C: Lionel Lindon. Academy Awards '44: Best Actor (Crosby), Best Director (McCarey), Best Picture, Best Screenplay, Best Song ("Swinging on a Star"), Best Story, Best Supporting Actor (Fitzgerald); Golden Globe Awards '45: Best Director (McCarey), Best Film—Drama, Best Supporting Actor (Fitzgerald); National Board of Review Awards '44: 10 Best Films of the Year; New York Film Critics Awards '44: Best Actor (Fitzgerald), Best Director (McCarey), Best Film; Nominations: Academy Awards '44: Best Actor (Fitzgerald), Best Black and White Cinematography, Best Film Editing. USH, IGP, BTV

Going Overboard *⊘* *Babes Ahoy* 1989 (R) Cruise ship waiter dreams of becoming a comedian and gets his big break when the ship's comic disappears. 99m/C VHS. Adam Sandler, Burt Young, Billy Zane, Peter Berg; D: Valerie Breiman. THV

Going Places *⊘⊘⊘* *Les Valseuses; Making It* 1974 (R) A cynical, brutal satire about two young thugs traversing the French countryside raping, looting and cavorting as they please. Moreau has a brief role as an ex-con trying to go straight. An amoral, controversial comedy that established both its director and two stars. In French with English subtitles or dubbed. 122m/C VHS, Beta, LV. FR Gerard Depardieu, Patrick Dewaere, Miou-Miou, Isabelle Huppert, Jeanne Moreau, Brigitte Fossey; D: Bertrand Blier; W: Bertrand Blier. COL, INT

Going to Congress/Don't Park There 1924 Two typical silent Rogers shorts. With original organ score. 57m/B VHS, Beta, 8mm. Will Rogers. VYY

Going to Town *⊘* 1944 Radio team Lum and Abner in one of their last films, as two conmen who scheme to make money from a phony oil well. 77m/B VHS, Beta. Barbara Hale, Grady Sutton, Florence Lake. GVV

Going Under *⊘* 1991 (PG) Subsurface military satire about the U.S.S. Sub Standard, the worst nuclear vessel in the Navy. It's so poorly constructed that the brass would rather sink than inspect it - if only they could. Interesting cast sinks with script headed for dry dock. 81m/C VHS, Beta, Closed Caption. Bill Pullman, Wendy Schaal, Ned Beatty, Robert Vaughn, Bud Cort, Michael Winslow. WAR

Going Undercover *⊘* 1988 (PG-13) A bumbling private investigator is hired to protect a rich, beautiful, and spoiled young woman on her European vacation. Poor excuse for a comedy. 90m/C VHS, Beta, LV. Lea Thompson, Jean Simmons, Chris Lemmon; D: James Kenelm Clarke. THV

The Gold & Glory *⊘* 1988 (PG-13) Two brothers, one a musician, the other an athlete, vie for the affections of the same girl by competing in a footrace for a golden purse. 102m/C VHS, Beta, LV. Colin Friels, Josephine Smulders, Grant Kenny. LIV

Gold Diggers of 1933 *⊘⊘⊘½* 1933 In this famous period musical, showgirls help a songwriter save his Busby Berkeley-choreographed show. Followed by two sequels. ♫We're in the Money; Shadow Waltz; I've Got to Sing a Torch Song; Pettin' in the Park; Remember My Forgotten Man. 96m/B VHS, Beta, LV. Joan Blondell, Ruby Keeler, Aline MacMahon, Dick Powell, Guy Kibbee, Warren William, Ned Sparks, Ginger Rogers; D: Mervyn LeRoy. Nominations: Academy Awards '33: Best Sound. MGM, FOX

Gold Diggers of 1935 *⊘⊘⊘* 1935 The second Gold Diggers film, having something to do with a New England resort, romance, and a charity show put on at the hotel. Plenty of Berkeleian large-scale drama, especially the bizarre, mock-tragic "Lullaby on Broadway" number, which details the last days of a Broadway baby. ♫I'm Going Shopping With You; The Words Are in My Heart; Lullaby of Broadway. 95m/B VHS, Beta, LV. Dick Powell, Adolphe Menjou, Gloria Stuart, Alice Brady, Frank McHugh, Glenda Farrell, Grant Mitchell, Hugh Herbert, Wini Shaw; D: Busby Berkeley; C: George Barnes. Academy Awards '35: Best Song ("Lullaby of Broadway"). MGM, MLB

Gold Diggers: The Secret of Bear Mountain *⊘⊘½* 1995 (PG) Thirteen-year-old Beth (Ricci) moves to the small town of Wheaton, Washington and forms an unlikely friendship with rebellious tomboy Jody (Chlumsky). Together, the girls set out on a treasure hunt that takes them into a dangerous trek through sea-coast mountain terrain. The grownups are dumb (and the story's fairly boring) but the two heroines have real appeal. 94m/C VHS, LV, Closed Caption. Christina Ricci, Anna Chlumsky, Polly Draper, Brian Kerwin, Diana Scarwid, David Keith; D: Kevin J. Dobson; W: Barry Glasser; C: Ross Berryman; M: Joel McNeely. USH

The Gold of Naples *⊘⊘⊘* *L'Oro Di Napoli* 1954 A four-part omnibus film about life in Naples, filled with romance and family tragedies, by turns poignant, funny and pensive. Originally six tales; two were trimmed for U.S. release. In Italian with subtitles. 107m/B VHS, Beta. IT Vittorio De Sica, Eduardo de Filippo, Paolo Stoppa, Sophia Loren, Silvana Mangano; D: Vittorio De Sica. NOS, FCT, APD

Gold of the Amazon Women *⊘* *Amazon Women* 1979 When two explorers set out to find gold, they stumble onto a society of man-hungry women who follow them into the urban jungle of Manhattan. Made for television. There is also a European "R" rated version. 94m/C VHS, Beta. Bo Svenson, Anita Ekberg, Bond Gideon, Donald Pleasence; D: Mark L. Lester.

Gold Raiders *⊘* 1951 Larry, Moe, and Shemp team up with an insurance agent to take on the bad guys in the wild west. The Stooges are long past their prime. 56m/B VHS. George O'Brien,

Moe Howard, Moe Howard, Shemp Howard, Larry Fine, Sheila Ryan, Clem Bevans, Lyle Talbot; **D:** Edward L. Bernds. *MED*

Gold Raiders ♫½ 1984 Team of secret agents are sent to the Jungles of Laos to find a plane carrying $200 million worth of gold, and nothing will get in their way. 106m/C VHS, Beta. Robert Ginty, Sarah Langenfeld, William Steven. *MED*

The Gold Rush ♫♫♫♫ 1925 Chaplin's most critically acclaimed film. The best definition of his simple approach to film form; adept maneuvering of visual pathos. The "Little Tramp" searches for gold and romance in the Klondike in the mid-1800s. Includes the dance of the rolls, pantomime sequence of eating the shoe, and Chaplin's lovely music. 85m/B VHS, Beta, LV, 8mm. Charlie Chaplin, Mack Swain, Tom Murray, Georgia Hale; **D:** Charlie Chaplin. *CNG, NOS, CAB*

Gold Rush/Payday 1925 Chaplin drifts along the Arctic tundra, searching for gold and love in "The Gold Rush." In "Payday," he goes out drinking with his buddies. 92m/B VHS, Beta. Charlie Chaplin, Georgia Hale, Mack Swain; **D:** Charlie Chaplin. *FOX*

Golden Age of Comedy 1958 The great comedians of silent cinema are seen in clips from some of their funniest films. 78m/B VHS, Beta, LV. Ben Turpin, Harry Langdon, Will Rogers, Jean Harlow, Carole Lombard, Stan Laurel, Oliver Hardy, The Keystone Cops. *MLB*

Golden Boy ♫♫♫ 1939 Holden plays a young and gifted violinist who earns money for his musical education by working as a part-time prizefighter. Fight promoter Menjou has Stanwyck cozy up to the impressionable young man to convince him to make the fight game his prime concern. She's successful but it leads to tragedy. Holden's screen debut, with Cobb as his immigrant father and Stanwyck successfully slinky as the corrupting love interest. Classic pugilistic drama with well-staged fight scenes. Based on Clifford Odets' play with toned down finale. 99m/B VHS, Beta, LV. William Holden, Adolphe Menjou, Barbara Stanwyck, Lee J. Cobb, Joseph Calleia, Sam Levene, Don Beddoe, Charles Halton; **D:** Rouben Mamoulian; **W:** Daniel Taradash, Victor Heerman, Sarah Y. Mason. Nominations: Academy Awards '39: Best Original Score. *GKK*

The Golden Child ♫♫ 1986 (PG-13) When a Tibetan child with magic powers is kidnapped and transported to Los Angeles, Chandler, a professional "finder of lost children" must come to the rescue. The search takes him through Chinatown in a hunt that cliches every Oriental swashbuckler ever made. Good fun. 94m/C VHS, Beta, LV, 8mm, Closed Caption. Eddie Murphy, Charlotte Lewis, Charles Dance, Victor Wong, Randall "Tex" Cobb, James Hong; **D:** Michael Ritchie; **M:** Michel Colombier. *PAR*

The Golden Coach ♫♫♫ *Le Carrosse D'Or* 1952 Based on a play by Prosper Merimee, the tale of an 18th-century actress in Spanish South America who takes on all comers, including the local viceroy who creates a scandal by presenting her with his official coach. Rare cinematography by Claude Renoir. 101m/C VHS, Beta, LV. *FR* Anna Magnani, Odoardo Spadaro, Nada Fiorelli, Dante Rino, Duncan Lamont; **D:** Jean Renoir. *FCT, CRC, INT*

Golden Demon ♫♫½ *Konjiki Yasha* 1953 An acclaimed Japanese epic, from the novel by Koyo Ozaki, about the destructive powers of wealth on the lives of two star-crossed lovers in medieval Japan. In Japanese with English subtitles. 95m/C VHS, Beta. *JP* Jun Negami, Fujiko Yamamoto; **D:** Koji Shima. *NLC*

Golden Earrings ♫♫½ 1947 Enjoyable, yet incredulous story about British agent Milland joining up with gypsy Dietrich for espionage work. Absurd film was so bad it became a camp classic overnight. Although Dietrich and Milland couldn't stand each other and battled constantly during production, the movie did quite well at the box office. Based on a novel by Yolanda Foldes. 95m/

B VHS, Closed Caption. Ray Milland, Marlene Dietrich, Bruce Lester, Dennis Hoey, Quentin Reynolds, Reinhold Schunzel, Ivan Triesault, Mitchell Leisen; **W:** Abraham Polonsky, Frank Butler, Helen Deutsch; **C:** Daniel F. Fapp. *USH, FCT*

Golden Exterminators ♫ 197? Two brothers battle the forces of evil who have killed their martial arts master with the heels of their formidable feet. 86m/C VHS, Beta. Raymond Chan. *UNI*

Golden Gate ♫♫ 1993 (R) Young Fed Dillon is thrown into the hysteria of the communist witch hunt in 1952 San Francisco. He snares Song, a Chinese labor activist, on some very dubious charges. Ten years later he finds himself getting involved with Song's daughter Marilyn (Chen), who knows nothing about her lover's involvement with her family. Then she finds out. Everchanging moods, sometimes film noir, sometimes a love story, sometimes a nostalgic look back, are confusing. Promising storyline meanders and fades as Director Madden tries to do too much in a short time. Beware of broad stereotypes in every character. 95m/C VHS, LV, Closed Caption. Matt Dillon, Joan Chen, Bruno Kirby, Teri Polo, Tzi Ma, Stan Egi, Peter Murnik, Jack Shearer, George Giudall; **D:** John Madden; **W:** David Henry Hwang; **C:** Bobby Bukowski; **M:** Elliot Goldenthal. *TOU*

Golden Lady ♫½ 1979 Beautiful woman leads her female gang in a deadly game of international intrigue. 90m/C VHS, Beta. Christina World, Suzanne Danielle, June Chadwick; **D:** Joseph Larraz. *NO*

Golden Rendezvous ♫♫ *Nuclear Terror* 1977 A tale of treachery aboard a "gambler's paradise" luxury liner which is hijacked and held for ransom. Based on Alistair MacLean's novel. 103m/C VHS, Beta. Richard Harris, David Janssen, John Carradine, Burgess Meredith, Ann Turkel, John Vernon; **D:** Ashley Lazarus. *VES*

The Golden Salamander ♫♫ 1951 Howard shines in otherwise lackluster adventure about archaeologist searching for ancient ruins in Tunisia who must deal with gun runners and their evil leader, while torridly romancing a beautiful Tunisian girl. Filmed on location in Tunis. Based on the novel by Victor Canning. 96m/B VHS. *GB* Trevor Howard, Anouk Aimee, Herbert Lom, Miles Malleson, Walter Rilla, Jacques Sernas, Wilfrid Hyde-White, Peter Copely, Eugene Deckers, Henry Edwards, Marcel Poncin, Percy Walsh, Sybilla Binder, Kathleen Boutall, Valentine Dyall; **D:** Ronald Neame; **C:** Oswald Morris. *FCT*

The Golden Seal ♫♫½ 1983 (PG) Tale of a small boy's innocence put in direct conflict, because of his love of a rare wild golden seal and her pup, with the failed dreams, pride and ordinary greed of adults. 94m/C VHS, Beta, LV, 8mm. Steve Railsback, Michael Beck, Penelope Milford, Torquil Campbell; **D:** Frank Zuniga; **M:** John Barry.

The Golden Stallion ♫½ 1949 Trigger falls in love with a stunning mare. He sees her villainous owners abusing her and kills them. Roy takes the blame for his equine pal, but true love triumphs to save the day. 67m/B VHS. Roy Rogers, Dale Evans, Estelita Rodriguez, Pat Brady, Douglas Evans, Frank Fenton; **D:** William Witney. *REP*

Golden Sun ♫ 198? Young Kung Fu student decides to investigate the death of his hero, Bruce Lee, and comes up against a sinister conspiracy. 90m/C VHS, Beta. Lei Hsiao Lung, Chen Pei Ling, Ou-Yang Chung. *UNI*

The Golden Triangle ♫½ 1980 (PG) Big battle of the drug pushers set in the mountainous region surrounded by Laos, Thailand, and Burma. Rival gangs fight for control of the world's opium crop. 90m/C VHS, Beta. Lo Lieh, Sambat Metanen, Tien Ner. *MGI*

Golden Voyage of Sinbad ♫♫½ 1973 (G) In the mysterious ancient land of Lemuria, Sinbad and his crew encounter magical and mystical creatures. A statue of Nirvana comes to life and engages in a sword fight with Sinbad. He later meets up with a one-eyed centaur and a griffin. Ray Harryhausen can once again claim

credit for the unusual and wonderful mythical creatures springing to life. 105m/C VHS, Beta, LV, Closed Caption. John Phillip Law, Caroline Munro, Tom Baker, Douglas Wilmer, Martin Shaw, John David Garfield, Gregoire Aslan; **D:** Gordon Hessler; **W:** Brian Clemens; **C:** Ted Moore; **M:** Miklos Rozsa. *COL, MLB*

Goldeneye ♫♫♫ 1995 (PG-13) Bond is back, in the long-awaited (eight years) debut of Brosnan as legendary Brit agent 007. Since we're through the Cold War, Bond has to make do with the villainy of the Russian Mafia, who are planning to sabotage global financial markets utilizing the "Goldeneye" satellite weapon. There's a spectacularly impossible stunt to start things out in familiar territory and lots more noisy (if prolonged) action pieces. Brosnan (who looks great in a tux) is slyly self-aware that his character is more myth than man and Janssen does a suitably over-the-top job as bad Bond girl Xenia Onatopp. Tina Turner sings the dreary title track. **CW:** Action/violence and some sexuality. 130m/C VHS, LV, Closed Caption, DVD. Pierce Brosnan, Famke Janssen, Sean Bean, Izabela Scorupco, Joe Don Baker, Robbie Coltrane, Judi Dench, Tcheky Karyo, Gottfried John, Alan Cumming, Desmond Llewelyn, Michael Kitchen, Serena Gordon, Samantha Bond; **Cameos:** Minnie Driver; **D:** Martin Campbell; **W:** Michael France, Jeffrey Caine; **C:** Phil Meheux; **M:** Eric Serra. Blockbuster Entertainment Awards '96: Action Actor, Theatrical (Brosnan). *MGM*

Goldengirl ♫ 1979 (PG) A neo-Nazi doctor tries to make a superwoman of his daughter who has been specially fed, exercised, and emotionally conditioned since childhood to run in the Olympics. Anton's starring debut. 107m/C VHS, Beta. Susan Anton, James Coburn, Curt Jurgens, Robert Culp, Leslie Caron, Harry Guardino, Jessica Walter; **D:** Joseph Sargent; **M:** Bill Conti. *COL*

Goldenrod ♫½ 1977 A successful rodeo champion is forced to reevaluate his life when he sustains a crippling accident in the ring. Made for television. 100m/C VHS, Beta. *CA* Tony LoBianco, Gloria Carlin, Donald Pleasence, Donnelly Rhodes; **D:** Harvey Hart. *PSM*

Goldfinger ♫♫♫ 1964 (PG) Ian Fleming's James Bond, Agent 007, attempts to prevent international gold smuggler Goldfinger and his pilot Pussy Galore from robbing Fort Knox. Features villainous assistant Oddjob and his deadly bowler hat. The third in the series is perhaps the most popular. Shirley Bassey sings the theme song. The laserdisc edition includes audio interviews with the director, the writer, the editor, and the production designer; music and sound effects/ dialogue separation; publicity stills, movie posters, trailers, and on-location photos. A treat for Bond fans. 117m/C VHS, Beta, LV, Closed Caption. *GB* Sean Connery, Honor Blackman, Gert Frobe, Shirley Eaton, Tania Mallet, Harold Sakata, Cec Linder, Bernard Lee, Lois Maxwell, Desmond Llewelyn, Nadja Regin; **D:** Guy Hamilton; **C:** Ted Moore; **M:** John Barry. Academy Awards '64: Best Sound Effects Editing. *MGM, CRC, TLF*

Goldilocks & the Three Bears 1983 Entry from "Faerie Tale Theatre" tells the story of Goldilocks, who wanders through the woods and finds the home of three bears—only in this version Goldilocks is a nasty child, and it's the bears who'll get your sympathy. 60m/C VHS, Beta, LV, Closed Caption. Tatum O'Neal, Alex Karras, Brandis Kemp, Donovan Scott, Hoyt Axton, John Lithgow, Carole King; **D:** Gilbert Cates. *KUI, FOX, FCT*

The Goldwyn Follies ♫♫ 1938 Lavish disjointed musical comedy about Hollywood. A movie producer chooses a naive girl to give him advice on his movies. George Gershwin died during the filming. ♫Romeo and Juliet; Water Nymph; Here, Pussy, Pussy; Serenade To a Fish; Love Walked In; Love is Here to Stay; Spring Again; I Was Doing Alright; La Serenata. 115m/C VHS, Beta, LV. Adolphe Menjou, Vera Zorina, The Ritz Brothers, Helen Jepson, Phil Baker, Bobby Clark, Ella Logan, Andrea Leeds, Edgar Bergen; **D:** George Marshall; **C:** Gregg Toland; **M:** George Gershwin, Ira Gershwin. Nominations: Academy Awards '38: Best Interior Decoration, Best Score. HBO

Goldy: The Last of the Golden Bears ♂♂½ 1984
Orphaned child and a lonely prospector risk their lives to save a Golden Bear from a circus owner. Followed by "Goldy 2: The Saga of the Golden Bear." **91m/C VHS, Beta.** LIV, VES

Goldy 2: The Saga of the Golden Bear ♂♂ 1985
Continues the adventures in the High Sierras of an orphan girl and her friend, the Golden Bear. **96m/C VHS, Beta.** LIV, VES

The Golem ♂♂♂½ 1920
A huge clay figure is given life by a rabbi in hopes of saving the Jews in the ghetto of medieval Prague. Rarely seen Wegener expressionist myth-opus that heavily influenced the "Frankenstein" films of the sound era. **80m/B VHS, Beta.** GE Paul Wegener, Albert Steinruck, Ernst Deutsch, Syda Salmonava; **D:** Paul Wegener. SNC, NOS, MRV

Goliath Against the Giants ♂♂½
Goliath Contro I Giganti; Goliat Contra Los Gigantes; Goliath and the Giants 1963 Goliath takes on Bokan, who has stolen his throne. Goliath must fight Amazons, storms, and sea monsters to save the lovely Elea. Goliath conquers all. **95m/C VHS, Beta.** IT SP Brad Harris, Gloria Milland, Fernando Rey, Barbara Carroll; **D:** Guido Malatesta. SNC

Goliath and the Barbarians ♂♂
Il Terror Dei Baraberi 1960 Goliath and his men go after the barbarians who are terrorizing and ravaging the Northern Italian countryside during the fall of the Roman Empire. A basic Reeves muscleman epic. **86m/C VHS, Beta.** IT Steve Reeves, Bruce Cabot; **D:** Carlo Campogalliani; **M:** Les Baxter. MGM

Goliath and the Dragon woof!
La Vendetta De Ercole 1961 Even Goliath must have doubts as he is challenged by the evil and powerful King Eurystheus. A must for fans of ridiculous movies with ridiculous monsters. **90m/C VHS, Beta.** IT FR Bruce Cabot, Mark Forest, Broderick Crawford, Gaby Andre, Leonora Ruffo; **D:** Vittorio Cottafavi; **M:** Les Baxter. SNC

Goliath and the Sins of Babylon ♂♂
Maciste, L'Eroe Piu Grande Del Mondo 1964 Well-sculpted Forest plays yet another mesomorph to the rescue in this poorly dubbed spaghetti legend. Goliath must spare twenty-four virgins whom the evil Crisa would submit as human sacrifice. Forest—who played the mythic Maciste in a number of films—was randomly assigned the identity of Goliath, Hercules or Samson for US viewing; go figure. **80m/C VHS.** IT Mark Forest, Eleanora Bianchi, Jose Greco, Giuliano Gemma, Paul Muller; **D:** Michele Lupo. SNC

Goliath Awaits ♂♂ 1981
Harmon plays an oceanographer who discovers a ship that was sunk by German U-boats during WWI. Nothing much new there, except that the survivors still reside on board the vessel, some 40 years after the oceanliner was torpedoed. And get this: they're living a quasi-Utopian existence. Kind of hard to swallow. Made for TV, it originally aired in two parts. **110m/C VHS, LV.** Mark Harmon, Robert Forster, Christopher Lee, Eddie Albert, John Carradine, Alex Cord, Emma Samms, Jean Marsh; **D:** Kevin Connor; **M:** George Duning. THV

Goliathon woof!
The Mighty Peking Man 1979 A ten-story-tall gorilla resides in the jungle and is sought by a group of Hong Kong businessman who want to display the creature. Johnny, the hunter hired to find the beast, discovers both the gorilla and a beautiful jungle goddess. Incredibly campy, with badly dubbed and hilariously awful dialogue. **81m/C VHS.** HK Lee Hassen, Evelyn Kraft. VYY

Gone are the Days ♂♂½
The Man From C.O.T.T.O.N.; Purlie Victorious 1963 Shaky adaptation of the play, "Purlie Victorious." A black preacher wants to cause the ruin of a white plantation owner. Alda's screen debut. **97m/B VHS, Beta.** Ossie Davis, Ruby Dee, Sorrell Booke, Godfrey Cambridge, Alan Alda, Beah Richards; **D:** Nicholas Webster; **W:** Ossie Davis; **C:** Boris Kaufman. DIS

Gone are the Days ♂♂ 1984
Government agent (Korman) is assigned to protect a family who witnessed an underworld shooting, but the family would like to get away from both the mob and the police. Made-for-cable Disney comedy is well-acted but done in by cliches. **90m/C VHS, Beta.** Harvey Korman, Susan Anspach, Robert Hogan; **D:** Gabrielle Beaumont. DIS

Gone Fishin' woof! 1997 (PG)
Long delayed comedy (thanks to some on-set disasters and well-founded doubts about quality) finds best friends and bassmasters of disaster Gus (Glover) and Joe (Pesci) thinking they're going on a peaceful fishing trip. Instead they meet two women (Arquette and Whitfield) who are on the trail of a dangerous British con artist (Brimble). Pesci and Glover have reeled in one stinky old shoe of a movie here. Granted, it's not entirely their fault, but they should've known better. There are no surprises (or laughs) as every joke and set piece is tipped way ahead of time, just so you won't miss it. Less fun than a fish hook in the eye. **94m/C VHS.** Danny Glover, Joe Pesci, Rosanna Arquette, Lynn Whitfield, Willie Nelson, Nick Brimble, Gary Grubbs, Carol Kane, Edythe Davis; **D:** Christopher Cain; **W:** Jeffrey Abrams, Jill Mazursky Cody; **C:** Dean Semler; **M:** Randy Edelman. NYR

Gone in 60 Seconds ♂½ 1974
Car thief working for an insurance adjustment firm gets double-crossed by his boss and chased by the police. Forty minutes are consumed by a chase scene which destroyed more than 90 vehicles. **105m/C VHS, Beta.** H.B. Halicki, Marion Busia, George Cole, James McIntyre, Jerry Daugirda; **D:** H.B. Halicki. MED

Gone to Ground ♂ 1976
Mad killer terrorizes a group of vacationers who are trapped in an isolated beach house. **74m/C VHS, Beta.** Charles Tingwell, Elaine Lee, Eric Oldfield, Marion Johns, Robyn Gibbes, Judy Lynne, Dennis Grosvenor, Alan Penney, Marcus Hale. NO

Gone with the West ♂½ 1972
Little Moon and Jud McGraw seek revenge upon the man who stole their cattle. **92m/C VHS, Beta.** James Caan, Stefanie Powers, Sammy Davis Jr., Aldo Ray, Michael Conrad, Michael Walker Jr.; **D:** Bernard Giraudeau. UNI

Gone with the Wind ♂♂♂♂ 1939
Epic Civil War drama focuses on the life of petulant southern belle Scarlett O'Hara. Starting with her idyllic lifestyle on a sprawling plantation, the film traces her survival through the tragic history of the South during the Civil War and Reconstruction, and her tangled love affairs with Ashley Wilkes and Rhett Butler. Classic Hollywood doesn't get any better than this; one great scene after another, equally effective in intimate drama and sweeping spectacle. The train depot scene, one of the more cinematically adroit shots in movie history, involved hundreds of extras and dummies, and much of the MGM lot was razed to simulate the burning of Atlanta. Based on Margaret Mitchell's novel, screenwriter Howard was assisted by producer Selznick and novelist F. Scott Fitzgerald. For its 50th anniversary, a 231-minute restored version was released that included the trailer for "The Making of a Legend: GWTW." The laserdisc is available in a limited, numbered edition, fully restored to Technicolor from the original negative, with an enhanced soundtrack and seven minutes of rare footage, including the original trailer. **231m/C VHS, Beta, LV, Closed Caption.** Clark Gable, Vivien Leigh, Olivia de Havilland, Leslie Howard, Thomas Mitchell, Hattie McDaniel, Butterfly McQueen, Evelyn Keyes, Harry Davenport, Jane Darwell, Ona Munson, Barbara O'Neil, William "Billy" Bakewell, Rand Brooks, Ward Bond, Laura Hope Crews, Yakima Canutt, George Reeves, Marjorie Reynolds, Ann Rutherford, Victor Jory, Carroll Nye, Paul Hurst, Isabel Jewell, Cliff Edwards, Eddie Anderson, Oscar Polk, Eric Linden, Violet Kemble-Cooper; **D:** Victor Fleming; **W:** Sidney Howard; **C:** Ray Rennahan;

M: Max Steiner. Academy Awards '39: Best Actress (Leigh), Best Color Cinematography, Best Director (Fleming), Best Film Editing, Best Interior Decoration, Best Picture, Best Screenplay, Best Supporting Actress (McDaniel); National Board of Review Awards '40: 10 Best Films of the Year; New York Film Critics Awards '39: Best Actress (Leigh); Nominations: Academy Awards '39: Best Actor (Gable), Best Sound, Best Special Effects, Best Supporting Actress (de Havilland), Best Original Score. MGM, FUS, BTV

Gonza the Spearman ♂♂½ 1986
A gifted samurai lancer is accused of having an affair with the wife of the lord of his province. The lancer must leave to save the woman's honor, because to stay would mean death to them both. In Japanese with English subtitles. **126m/C VHS, LV.** JP Hiromi Goh, Shima Iwashita; **D:** Masahiro Shinoda. KIV

Good Day for a Hanging ♂♂½ 1958
Marshal Ben Cutler (MacMurray) finds unexpectedly opposition from the townspeople when he captures killer Eddie Campbell (Vaughn). The charismatic outlaw gains their sympathy and Cutler is going to have trouble when Campbell is sentenced to hang. **85m/C VHS.** Fred MacMurray, Robert Vaughn, Joan Blackman, Maggie Hayes, James Drury, Wendell Holmes, Emile Meyer, Bing Russell; **D:** Nathan (Hertz) Juran; **W:** Daniel Ullman, Maurice Zimm; **C:** Henry Freulich. COL

A Good Day to Die ♂♂½
Children of the Dust 1995 (R) Western made-for-TV saga, set during the 1880s land rush of the Oklahoma Territory, and adapted from the novel by Clancy Carlile. Half-black, half-Cherokee gunslinger Gypsy Smith (Poitier) reluctantly agrees to lead a wagontrain of freed slaves west to found their own community. Naturally, there's trouble with the Klan and Gypsy isn't the only one involved—young Cherokee brave White Wolf (Wirth), who has been raised among whites, has a forbidden romance with his foster sister, Rachel (Going), leading to lots of heartbreak. Fawcett has a brief role as the young Rachel's high-strung mother. Filmed in Alberta, Canada. **CW:** Areas of violence and some sexuality. **120m/C VHS.** Sidney Poitier, Michael Moriarty, Joanna Going, Billy Wirth, Regina Taylor, Hart Bochner, Shirley Knight, Robert Guillaume, Farrah Fawcett; **D:** David Greene; **W:** Joyce Eliason; **C:** Ronald Orieux; **M:** Mark Snow. THV

The Good Earth ♂♂♂½ 1937
Pearl S. Buck's classic recreation of the story of a simple Chinese farm couple beset by greed and poverty. Outstanding special effects. MGM's last film produced by master Irving Thalberg and dedicated to his memory. Rainer won the second of her back-to-back Best Actress Oscars for her portrayal of the self-sacrificing O-Lan. **138m/B VHS, Beta.** Paul Muni, Luise Rainer, Charley Grapewin, Keye Luke, Walter Connolly; **D:** Sidney Franklin; **C:** Karl Freund. Academy Awards '37: Best Actress (Rainer), Best Cinematography; Nominations: Academy Awards '37: Best Director (Franklin), Best Film Editing, Best Picture. MGM, BTV, CCB

Good Evening, Mr. Wallenberg ♂♂½ 1993
Raoul Wallenberg was an upper-class Swede who imported luxury goods from Hungary. He was also responsible for saving thousands of Hungarian Jews from extermination by the Nazis. Using phony documents he first had small groups of Jews smuggled to safety but when he learns that the 65,0000 Jews of the Budapest ghetto are to be killed he uses a bluff to prevent the deaths. Later taken prisoner by the Soviet Army, Wallenberg's fate has never been determined. Characters are dwarfed by the immensity of the events and Wallenberg remains an enigma. In Swedish, German, and Hungarian with English subtitles. **115m/C VHS.** SW Stellan Skarsgard, Erland Josephson, Katharina Thalbach; **D:** Kjell Grede; **W:** Kjell Grede. ORI, FCT

The Good Father ♂♂♂ 1987 (R)
An acclaimed British TV movie about a bitter divorced man trying to come to terms with his son, his ex-wife, and his own fury by supporting the courtroom divorce battle of a friend. **90m/C VHS, Beta,**

Closed Caption. *GB* Anthony Hopkins, Jim Broadbent, Harriet Walter, Frances Viner, Joanne Whalley, Simon Callow, Michael Byrne; *D:* Mike Newell; *W:* Christopher Hampton; *C:* Michael Coulter; *M:* Richard Hartley. *MED, FOX*

The Good Fight 🎬🎬½ 1992
Grace Cragin (Lahti) is a lawyer at a small firm who's asked by her son's best friend to represent him in a tough case against a powerful corporation. The young man is dying of mouth cancer and he wants to sue the tobacco company that makes the chewing tobacco he blames for his illness. Grace is wary of the high-powered litigation necessary but with the increasingly personal aid of her prominent lawyer ex-husband (O'Quinn), she is ready to battle the odds. Another fine performance by Lahti in this made for cable television drama. 91m/C VHS, Beta. Christine Lahti, Terry O'Quinn, Kenneth Welsh, Lawrence Dane, Adam Trese, Tony Rosato, Andrea Roth, Jonathan Crombie; *D:* John David Coles; *W:* Beth Gutcheon; *M:* W.G. Snuffy Walden. *PSM*

Good Girls Don't 🎬½ 1995
Jeannie (Estevez) and Bettina (Parton) are framed for murder and take it on the lam in a red convertible with a half million in cash. It's a comedy. 85m/C VHS. Renee Estevez, Julia Parton, Mary Woronov, Christopher Knight; *D:* Rick Sloane; *W:* Rick Sloane. *LEO*

Good Grief, Charlie Brown 1983
That lovably misunderstood Charlie Brown is featured again in this Peanuts production. 30m/C VHS. *D:* Bill Melendez, Sam Jaimes, Phil Roman. *BAR*

The Good Guys and the Bad Guys 🎬🎬½ 1969 (PG)
When Kennedy is abandoned by his gang of outlaws for being too old to keep up, he finds himself being hunted by lifelong marshall nemesis Mitchum. 91m/C VHS. Robert Mitchum, George Kennedy, David Carradine, Tina Louise, Douglas Fowley, Lois Nettleton, Martin Balsam, John Carradine; *D:* Burt Kennedy; *W:* Ronald M. Cohen; *C:* Harry Stradling Jr. *WAR*

Good Guys Wear Black 🎬🎬 1978 (PG)
A mild-mannered professor keeps his former life as leader of a Vietnam commando unit under wraps until he discovers that he's number one on the CIA hit list. Sequel is "A Force of One." 96m/C VHS, Beta, LV. Chuck Norris, Anne Archer, James Franciscus; *D:* Ted Post; *W:* Mark Medoff. *WAR, HBO, VES*

Good Luck 🎬🎬½ 1996 (R)
Inspirational buddy movie that manages to avoid the worst of sentimental excess. Tony Olezniak (D'Onofrio) is a football player left blind because of a game injury. He's on a downward spiral and winds up in jail, which is where paraplegic Bernard Lemley (Hines), once Tony's tutor, finds him. Bernard wants to enter a rigorous whitewater raft race held on Oregon's Rogue River and he needs Tony's strength to help him do it. The emotional payoff comes as the two bicker and bond instead of from the challenge of the raft race, which in itself is a change of pace. *CW:* Lots of charm. Partial nudity, adult language, adult situations. 95m/C VHS. Vincent D'Onofrio, Gregory Hines, Max Gail, James Earl Jones; *D:* Richard LaBrie; *W:* Bob Comfort; *C:* Maximo Munzi; *M:* Tim Truman. *APX*

A Good Man in Africa 🎬🎬 1994 (R)
Bumbling low-level British diplomat gets caught up in the high-level political turmoil of a newly independent African state. Confusing plot has borderline incompetent blackmailed by corrupt politician into bribing respected doctor for local land rights. Wow, corrupt officials, ineffectual bureaucrats—go figure! Does to the British diplomatic corps what "A Fish Called Wanda" did to England's legal community, without the humor. Performances by Connery, Gossett and Lithgow almost make up for shortcomings in key areas such as writing and direction. Adapted from the novel by William Boyd. 95m/C VHS. Colin Friels, Sean Connery, Louis Gossett Jr., John Lithgow, Joanne Whalley, Diana Rigg; *D:* Bruce Beresford; *W:* William Boyd; *C:* Andrzej Bartkowiak. *USH*

Good Morning, Babylon 🎬🎬🎬 *Good Morning Babilonia* 1987 (PG-13)
The Taviani brothers' first American film. Two young Italian brothers skilled in cathedral restoration come to America and find success building the sets to D.W. Griffith's "Intolerance." Eventually, their fortune is shattered by the onslaught of WWI. 113m/C VHS, Beta, LV. Vincent Spano, Joaquim de Almeida, Greta Scacchi, Charles Dance, Desiree Becker, Omero Antonutti, David Brandon; *D:* Paolo Taviani, Vittorio Taviani; *W:* Paolo Taviani, Vittorio Taviani, Tonino Guerra; *M:* Nicola Piovani. *LIV, VES*

Good Morning, Vietnam 🎬🎬🎬 1987 (R)
Based on the story of Saigon DJ Adrian Cronauer, although Williams' portrayal is reportedly a bit more extroverted than the personality of Cronauer. Williams spins great comic moments that may have been scripted but likely were not as a man with no history and for whom everything is manic radio material. The character ad-libs, swoops, and swerves, finally accepting adult responsibility. Engaging all the way with an outstanding period soundtrack. 121m/C VHS, Beta, LV, 8mm, Closed Caption. Robin Williams, Forest Whitaker, Bruno Kirby, Richard Edson, Robert Wuhl, J.T. Walsh, Noble Willingham, Floyd Vivino, Tung Thanh Tran, Chintara Sukapatana; *D:* Barry Levinson; *W:* Mitch Markowitz; *C:* Peter Sova; *M:* Alex North. Golden Globe Awards '88: Best Actor—Musical/Comedy (Williams); Nominations: Academy Awards '87: Best Actor (Williams). *TOU*

The Good Mother 🎬🎬½ 1988 (R)
A divorced mother works at creating a fulfilling life for herself and her daughter, with an honest education for her daughter about every subject, including sex. But her ex-husband, unsure of how far this education is being taken, fights her for custody of their 8-year old daughter after allegations of sexual misconduct against the mother's new lover. Based on Sue Miller's bestselling novel. Well acted, weakly edited and scripted. 104m/C VHS, Beta, LV, Closed Caption. Diane Keaton, Liam Neeson, Jason Robards Jr., Ralph Bellamy, James Naughton, Teresa Wright, Asia Vieira, Joe Morton, Katey Sagal, Tracy Griffith, Charles Kimbrough; *D:* Leonard Nimoy; *W:* Michael Bortman; *C:* David Watkin; *M:* Elmer Bernstein. *TOU*

Good Neighbor Sam 🎬🎬🎬 1964
A married advertising executive (Lemmon) agrees to pose as a friend's husband in order for her to collect a multimillion-dollar inheritance. Complications ensue when his biggest client mistakes the friend for his actual wife and decides they're the perfect couple to promote his wholesome product—milk. 130m/C VHS, Beta. Jack Lemmon, Romy Schneider, Dorothy Provine, Mike Connors, Edward G. Robinson, Joyce Jameson; *D:* David Swift. *GKK*

Good News 🎬🎬½ 1947
A vintage Comden-Green musical about the love problems of a college football star, who will flunk out if he doesn't pass his French exams. Revamping of the 1927 Broadway smash features the unlikely sight of Lawford in a song-and-dance role. ♫Varsity Drag; He's a Lady's Man; Good News; Tait Song; Students Are We; Just Imagine; If You're Not Kissing Me; Football; I Feel Pessimistic. 92m/C VHS, Beta, LV. June Allyson, Peter Lawford, Joan McCracken, Mel Torme; *D:* Charles Walters; *W:* Betty Comden. Nominations: Academy Awards '47: Best Song ("Pass That Peace Pipe"). *MGM, FCT*

The Good Old Boys 🎬🎬½ 1995
Debuting as both director and co-writer, Jones also stars as aging cowpoke Hewey Calloway. The n'er-do-well Hewey makes a surprise visit to the hardscrabble 1906 Texas farm of brother Walter (Kinney), whose wife Eve (McDormand) is none too happy to see the wanderer. But Walter needs help, the local banker (Brimley) is about to foreclose, and Hewey is also taken with spirited schoolmarm Spring Renfro (Spacek, who also starred with Jones in "Coal-Miner's Daughter"). And even Hewey realizes that the twentieth century is going to change his way of life forever. Easy-going drama with a fine cast. 118m/C VHS. Tommy Lee Jones, Sissy Spacek, Terry Kinney, Frances

McDormand, Wilford Brimley, Sam Shepard, Walter Olkewicz, Matt Damon, Bruce McGill, Park Overall; *D:* Tommy Lee Jones; *W:* Tommy Lee Jones, J.T. Allen; *C:* Alan Caso; *M:* John McEuen. *TTC*

Good Sam 🎬🎬 1948
An incurable "Good Samaritan" finds himself in one jam after another as he tries too hard to help people. Lots of missed opportunities for laughs with McCrarey's mediocre direction. 116m/B VHS. Gary Cooper, Ann Sheridan, Ray Collins, Edmund Lowe, Joan Lorring, Ruth Roman; *D:* Leo McCarey. *REP*

The Good Son 🎬🎬 1993 (R)
In a grand departure from cute, Culkin tackles evil as a 13-year-old obsessed with death and other unseemly hobbies. During a stay with his uncle, Mark (Wood) watches as his cousin (Culkin) gets creepier and creepier, and tries to alert the family. But will they listen? Nooo—they choose to ignore the little warning signs like the doll hanging by a noose in Culkin's room. And then there's the untimely death of a sibling. Hmmm. Culkin isn't as bad as expected, but doesn't quite get all the way down to bone-chilling terror either. Original star Jesse Bradford was dropped when Papa Culkin threatened to pull Mac off "Home Alone 2" if he wasn't cast in the lead. *CW:* Violence/terror involving children. 87m/C VHS, LV, Closed Caption. Macaulay Culkin, Elijah Wood, Wendy Crewson, David Morse, Daniel Hugh-Kelly, Quinn Culkin; *D:* Joseph Ruben; *W:* Ian McEwan; *C:* John Lindley; *M:* Elmer Bernstein. Nominations: MTV Movie Awards '94: Best Villain (Culkin). *FXV*

The Good, the Bad, and Huckleberry Hound 1988
Journeying out West to begin a ranch, Huckleberry Hound winds up becoming a sheriff in the small town of Two-Bit. Huckleberry stands up against a group of bully brothers who have been terrorizing the town. 94m/C VHS, Beta. *D:* Ray Patterson; *V:* Daws Butler. *TTC, IME*

The Good, the Bad and the Ugly 🎬🎬🎬½ 1967
Leone's grandiloquent, shambling tribute to the American Western. Set during the Civil War, it follows the seemingly endless adventures of three dirtbags in search of a cache of Confederate gold buried in a nameless grave. Violent, exaggerated, beautifully crafted, it is the final and finest installment of the "Dollars" trilogy: a spaghetti Western chef d'oeuvre. 161m/C VHS, Beta, LV. *IT* Clint Eastwood, Eli Wallach, Lee Van Cleef, Chelo Alonso, Luigi Pistilli; *D:* Sergio Leone; *W:* Sergio Leone; *C:* Tonino Delli Colli; *M:* Ennio Morricone. *FOX, MGM, FCT*

The Good Wife 🎬🎬½ *The Umbrella Woman* 1986 (R)
A bored and sexually frustrated wife scandalizes her small Australian town by taking up with the new hotel barman. There's no denying Ward's sexuality, but overall the movie is too predictable. 97m/C VHS, Beta, LV. *AU* Rachel Ward, Bryan Brown, Sam Neill, Steven Vidler, Bruce Barry, Jennifer Claire; *D:* Ken Cameron; *M:* Cameron Allan. *BAR, IME*

Goodbye Again 🎬🎬½ *Aimez-Vous Brahms* 1961
A romantic drama based on the novel by Francoise Sagan. Bergman is a middle-aged interior decorator whose lover, Montand, has a roaming eye. She finds herself drawn to the son (Perkins) of a client and begins an affair—flattered by the young man's attentions. Montand is outraged and vows to change his ways and marry Bergman if she will give up the young man. A bit soapy, but a must for Bergman fans. 120m/B VHS. Jessie Royce Landis, Ingrid Bergman, Anthony Perkins, Yves Montand, Diahann Carroll; *D:* Anatole Litvak. Cannes Film Festival '61: Best Actor (Perkins). *MGM, FCT*

The Goodbye Bird 🎬🎬½ 1993 (G)
Frank is accused by his school principal of stealing her prized talking parrot. With the aid of a kindly veterinarian Frank tries to discover who the thief really is. 91m/C VHS, Closed Caption. Cindy Pickett, Concetta Tomei, Wayne Rogers, Christopher Pettiet; *D:* William Clark. *WOV*

Goodbye Columbus ✠✠✠ 1969 (PG)
Philip Roth's novel about a young Jewish librarian who has an affair with the spoiled daughter of a nouveau riche family is brought to late-'60s life, and vindicated by superb performances all around. Benjamin and McGraw's first starring roles. 105m/C VHS, Beta, LV. Richard Benjamin, Ali MacGraw, Jack Klugman, Nan Martin, Jaclyn Smith; **D:** Larry Peerce. Writers Guild of America '68: Best Adapted Screenplay; Nominations: Academy Awards '69: Best Adapted Screenplay. *PAR*

Goodbye Cruel World ✠½ 1982 (R)
Black comedy about a suicidal television anchorman who decides to spend his last day filming the relatives who drove him to the brink. 90m/C VHS, Beta. Dick Shawn, Cynthia Sikes, Chuck "Porky" Mitchell; **D:** David Irving. *LIV*

Goodbye Emmanuelle ✠½ 1979 (R)
Follows the further adventures of Emmanuelle in her quest for sexual freedom and the excitement of forbidden pleasures. The second sequel to "Emmanuelle." 92m/C VHS, Beta. Sylvia Kristel. *NO*

The Goodbye Girl ✠✠✠ 1977 (PG) Neil Simon's story of a former actress, her precocious nine-year-old daughter and the aspiring actor who moves in with them. The daughter serves as catalyst for the other two to fall in love. While Mason's character is fairly unsympathetic, Dreyfuss is great and Simon's dialogue witty. 110m/C VHS, Beta, LV. Richard Dreyfuss, Marsha Mason, Quinn Cummings, Barbara Rhoades, Marilyn Sokol; **D:** Herbert Ross; **W:** Neil Simon; **M:** Dave Grusin. Academy Awards '77: Best Actor (Dreyfuss); British Academy Awards '78: Best Actor (Dreyfuss); Golden Globe Awards '78: Best Actor—Musical/Comedy (Dreyfuss), Best Actress—Musical/Comedy (Mason), Best Film—Musical/Comedy, Best Screenplay; Los Angeles Film Critics Association Awards '77: Best Actor (Dreyfuss); Nominations: Academy Awards '77: Best Actress (Mason), Best Original Screenplay, Best Picture, Best Supporting Actress (Cummings). *MGM, BTV*

Goodbye Love ✠½ 1934 Dull comedy about a group of ex-husbands who refuse to pay alimony and end up in jail. 65m/B VHS. Charlie Ruggles, Verree Teasdale, Sidney Blackmer, Mayo Methot, Phyllis Barry, Ray Walker, John Kelly, Hale Grace, Luis Alberni; **D:** Herbert Ross. *FCT*

Goodbye, Miss 4th of July ✠✠½ 1988 Inspired by the true story of the teenage daughter of Greek immigrants living in pre-WWI West Virginia, the prejudice they encounter, the relationship that begins between the family and an aging African-American ex-boxer, and the girl's efforts in the influenza epidemic. Based on the 1985 book by her brother. 89m/C VHS, Closed Caption. Roxana Zal, Louis Gossett Jr., Chris Sarandon, Chantal Contouri, Chynna Phillips, Mitchell Anderson, Conchata Ferrell, Ed Lauter; **D:** George Miller. *DIS*

Goodbye, Mr. Chips ✠✠✠½ 1939 An MGM classic, the sentimental rendering of the James Hilton novel about a shy Latin professor in an English school who marries the vivacious Garson only to tragically lose her. He spends the rest of his life devoting himself to his students and becoming a school legend. Multi award-winning soaper featuring Garson's first screen appearance, which was Oscar nominated. Special two-tape letterboxed laserdisc edition includes the original trailer and an extra-special production featurette. Remade in 1969 as a fairly awful musical starring Peter O'Toole. 115m/B VHS, Beta, LV, Closed Caption. Robert Donat, Greer Garson, Paul Henreid, John Mills; **D:** Sam Wood; **C:** Frederick A. (Freddie) Young. Academy Awards '39: Best Actor (Donat); National Board of Review Awards '39: 10 Best Films of the Year; Nominations: Academy Awards '39: Best Actress (Garson), Best Director (Wood), Best Film Editing, Best Picture, Best Screenplay, Best Sound. *MGM, BTV, HMV*

Goodbye, Mr. Chips ✠✠ 1969 Ross debuted as director with this big-budget (but inferior musical re-make) of the classic James Hilton novel about a gentle teacher at an English all-boys private school and the woman who helps him demonstrate his compassion and overcome his shyness. O'Toole, although excellent, is categorically a non-singer, while Clark, a popular singer at the time ("Downtown"), musters very little talent in front of the camera. The plot is altered unnecessarily and updated to the WWII era for little reason; the music is thoroughly forgettable. ♫Fill The World With Love; Where Did My Childhood Go; London is London; And the Sky Smiled; When I Am Older; Walk Through the World; What Shall I Do with Today?; What a Lot of Flowers; Schooldays. 151m/C VHS. Peter O'Toole, Petula Clark, Michael Redgrave, George Baker, Sian Phillips, Michael Bryant, Jack Hedley, Herbert Ross; **D:** Herbert Ross; **C:** Oswald Morris; **M:** Leslie Bricusse, John Williams. Golden Globe Awards '70: Best Actor—Musical/Comedy (O'Toole); National Board of Review Awards '69: Best Actor (O'Toole); National Society of Film Critics Awards '69: Best Supporting Actress (Phillips); Nominations: Academy Awards '69: Best Actor (O'Toole), Scoring of a Musical. *MGM*

Goodbye, My Lady ✠✠ 1956 Based on the novel by James Street, this is a tear-jerking film about a young Mississippi farmboy who finds and cares for a special dog that he comes to love but eventually must give up. 95m/B VHS, Beta, LV. Brandon de Wilde, Walter Brennan, Sidney Poitier, Phil Harris, Louise Beavers; **D:** William A. Wellman. *WAR, FCT*

Goodbye, New York ✠✠ 1985 (R) A New York yuppie on a vacation finds herself penniless and stranded in Israel. She makes the best of the situation by joining a kibbutz and falling for a part-time soldier. Well, of course. 90m/C VHS, Beta, LV. Julie Hagerty, Amos Kollek, Shmuel Shilo; **D:** Amos Kollek; **M:** Michael Abene. *VES*

Goodbye, Norma Jean ✠ 1975 (R) Detailed and sleazy recreation of Marilyn Monroe's early years in Hollywood. Followed by "Goodnight, Sweet Marilyn." 95m/C VHS, Beta. Misty Rowe, Terrence Locke, Patch MacKenzie; **D:** Larry Buchanan; **M:** Joe Beck. *NO*

The Goodbye People ✠✠½ 1983 Balsam is an elderly man who decides to reopen his Coney Island hot dog stand that folded 22 years earlier. Hirsch and Reed help him realize his impossible dream in this sweetly sentimental film. 104m/C VHS, Beta, LV, Closed Caption. Judd Hirsch, Martin Balsam, Pamela Reed, Ron Silver; **D:** Herb Gardner; **W:** Herb Gardner. *COL*

Goodbye Pork Pie ✠½ 1981 (R) With the police on their trail, two young men speed on a 1000-mile journey in a small, brand-new, yellow stolen car. Remember: journey of thousand miles always begin in stolen car. 105m/C VHS, Beta. NZ Tony Barry, Kelly Johnson; **D:** Geoff Murphy; **C:** Alun Bollinger.

Goodfellas ✠✠✠✠ 1990 (R) Quintessential picture about "wiseguys," at turns both violent and funny. A young man grows up in the mob, works hard to advance himself through the ranks, and enjoys the life of the rich and violent, oblivious to the horror of which he is a part. Cocaine addiction and many wiseguy missteps ultimately unravel his climb to the top. Excellent performances (particularly Liotta and Pesci, with De Niro pitching in around the corners), with visionary cinematography and careful pacing. Watch for Scorsese's mom as Pesci's mom. Based on the life of Henry Hill, ex-mobster now in the Witness Protection Program. Adapted from the book by Nicholas Pileggi. 146m/C VHS, Beta, LV, Closed Caption, DVD. Robert De Niro, Ray Liotta, Joe Pesci, Paul Sorvino, Lorraine Bracco, Frank Sivero, Mike Starr, Frank Vincent, Samuel L. Jackson, Tony Darrow, Chuck Low, Frank DiLeo, Christopher Serrone, Illeana Douglas, Debi Mazar; *Cameos:* Henny Youngman, Jerry Vale; **D:** Martin Scorsese; **W:** Nicholas Pileggi, Martin Scorsese; **C:** Michael Ballhaus. Academy Awards '90: Best Supporting Actor (Pesci); British Academy Awards '90: Best Adapted Screenplay, Best Director (Scorsese), Best Film; Los Angeles Film Critics Association Awards '90: Best Cinematography, Best Director (Scorsese), Best Film, Best Supporting Actor (Pesci), Best Supporting Actress (Bracco); National Board of Review Awards '90: Best Supporting Actor (Pesci); New York Film Critics Awards '90: Best Actor (De Niro), Best

Director (Scorsese), Best Film; National Society of Film Critics Awards '90: Best Director (Scorsese), Best Film; Nominations: Academy Awards '90: Best Adapted Screenplay, Best Director (Scorsese), Best Film Editing, Best Picture, Best Supporting Actress (Bracco); Golden Globe Awards '90: Best Director (Scorsese), Best Film—Drama, Best Screenplay, Best Supporting Actor (Pesci), Best Supporting Actress (Bracco). *WAR, FCT, BTV*

Goodnight, Michelangelo ✠✠½ 1989 (R) Funny, engaging and somewhat confusing story of the life of an Italian immigrant family as seen through the eyes of its youngest member, eight-year-old Michelangelo. Winner of the 1990 Best Comedy Award at the Greater Fort Lauderdale Film Festival.**CW:** Language and sexual situations. 91m/C VHS. *IT* Lina Sastri, Kim Cattrall, Giancarlo Giannini, Daniel Desanto; **D:** Carlo Liconti; **W:** Carlo Liconti. *NO*

Goodnight, Sweet Marilyn ✠ 1989 (R) Supposed "never-before-told" story of Marilyn Monroe's tragic death. According to this, her death was the result of pre-arranged "mercy-killing." Follow-up to director Buchanan's "Goodbye, Norma Jean" (1977) with Lane as the 1960s Marilyn intercut with scenes of Rowe from the first film as young Marilyn. You'd be better off leaving "Sweet Marilyn" to rest in peace. 100m/C VHS, Beta. Paula Lane, Jeremy Slate, Misty Rowe; **D:** Larry Buchanan. *NO*

Goof Balls WOOF! 1987 (R) The tourist denizens of a island golf resort putt and cavort about, and golf isn't all that's on their minds. 87m/C VHS, Beta. Ben Gordon, Laura Robinson. *ACA*

A Goofy Movie ✠✠½ 1994 (G) The dog finally gets his day. After 63 years of supporting roles, Disney's Goofy stars in his own movie along with his teenage son Max. When it comes to Goofy's attention that his rock music obsessed son is goofing off in school, Goofy decides to spend some quality time with Max via a road trip through the country. Their journey is plagued with mishaps, but through the obstacles, father and son bridge their generational gap and bond in the true Disney sense. A modest animated treat with six new songs that may induce some finger snapping and toe tapping. 78m/C VHS, Closed Caption. **D:** Kevin Lima; **W:** Jymn Magon, Brian Pimental, Chris Matheson; **V:** Bill Farmer, Jason Marsden, Jim Cummings, Kellie Martin, Rob Paulsen, Wallace Shawn, Florence Stanley, Jo Anne Worley. *DIS*

Goon Movie ✠✠ Stand Easy 1953 The cast of "The Goon Show," Britain's popular radio comedy series, perform some of their best routines in this, their only film appearance. 75m/B VHS, Beta. Peter Sellers, Spike Milligan, Harry Secombe. *VDM*

The Goonies ✠✠½ 1985 (PG) Two brothers who are about to lose their house conveniently find a treasure map. They pick up a couple of friends and head for the "X." If they can recover the treasure without getting caught by the bad guys, then all will be saved. Steven Spielberg produced this high-energy action fantasy for kids of all ages. The laserdisc edition comes in a widescreen format. 114m/C VHS, Beta, LV, Closed Caption. Sean Astin, Josh Brolin, Jeff B. Cohen, Corey Feldman, Martha Plimpton, John Matuszak, Robert Davi, Anne Ramsey, Mary Ellen Trainor, Jonathan Ke Quan, Kerri Green, Joe Pantoliano; **D:** Richard Donner; **W:** Chris Columbus, Steven Spielberg; **M:** Dave Grusin. *WAR*

Gor ✠½ 1988 (PG) Sword and sorcery: a magic ring sends a meek college professor to "Gor," a faraway world in which survival goes to the fittest and the most brutal. Followed by "Outlaw of Gor." 95m/C VHS, Beta, Closed Caption. Urbano Barberini, Rebecca Ferratti, Jack Palance, Paul Smith, Oliver Reed; **D:** Fritz Kiersch; **W:** R.J. Marx. *WAR*

Gorath ✠✠ Yosei Gorasu 1964 The world's top scientists are racing to stop a giant meteor from destroying the Earth. 77m/C VHS, Beta. JP **D:** Inoshiro Honda. *GEM, PSM*

Gordon's War *♂♂* 1973 (R) When a Vietnam vet returns to his Harlem home, he finds his wife overdosing on the drugs that have infiltrated his neighborhood. He leads a vigilante group in an attempt to clean up the area, which makes for a lot of action; however, there's also an excessive amount of violence. 89m/C VHS, Beta, Closed Caption. Paul Winfield, Carl Lee, David Downing, Tony King, Grace Jones; D: Ossie Davis; M: Angelo Badalamenti. FOX

Gordy *♂*½ 1995 (G) Perky talking porker Gordy manages to escape his fate as future bacon and find a couple of equally perky kids—motherless country-song-singing Jinnie Sue (Young) and lonely rich boy Hanky (Roescher), whom the pig manages to save from drowning. Plot scarcely matters and all the 25 piggies who performed as Gordy generally manage to outshine the humans, though country singer Stone (in his film debut) displays an easy charm. 90m/C VHS, Closed Caption. Doug Stone, Michael Roescher, Kristy Young, James Donadio, Deborah Hobart, Tom Lester, Ted Manson; D: Mark Lewis; C: Richard Michalak; M: Tom Bahler; V: Justin Garms. TOU

The Gore-Gore Girls *♂* 1972 Splatter horror director Lewis' final film follows a detective's search for a madman who's been mutilating and killing beautiful young bar dancers. 84m/C VHS. D: Herschell Gordon Lewis. MOV

Gore-Met Zombie Chef From Hell woof! 1987 A demon/vampire opens up a seafood restaurant and slaughters his customers. Deliberately campy and extremely graphic. 90m/C VHS, Beta. Theo Depuay, Kelley Kunicki, C.W. Casey, Alan Marx, Michael O'Neill; D: Don Swan. NO

Gore Vidal's Billy the Kid *♂♂*½ 1989 An unusual treatment of the William Bonney legend in which the Kid is merely a misunderstood teenager caught up in the midst of the brutal range wars. Made for cable television. 100m/C VHS. Val Kilmer, Duncan Regehr, Wilford Brimley, Julie Carmen, Michael Parks, Rene Auberjonois, Albert Salmi; D: William A. Graham. TTC

Gore Vidal's Lincoln *♂♂*½ Lincoln 1988 Waterston is a low-key but sympathetic Lincoln, with Moore as his high-strung wife Mary, in this made for television adaptation of the Vidal bestseller. Follows the couple from their first day in Washington, through the Civil War, family tragedies, up to the day of the President's burial. 190m/C VHS. Sam Waterston, Mary Tyler Moore, John Houseman, Richard Mulligan, John McMartin, Ruby Dee, Cleavon Little, Jeffrey DeMunn, James Gammon, Deborah Adair, Robin Gammell; D: Lamont Johnson; W: Ernest Kinoy; M: Ernest Gold. AVE

The Gorgeous Hussy *♂* 1936 Crawford stars in this fictionalized biography of Peggy Eaton, Andrew Jackson's notorious belle, who disgraces herself and those around her. A star-studded cast complete with beautiful costumes isn't enough to save this overly long and dull picture. 102m/B VHS, Closed Caption. Joan Crawford, Robert Taylor, Lionel Barrymore, Melvyn Douglas, James Stewart, Franchot Tone, Louis Calhern; D: Clarence Brown. Nominations: Academy Awards '36: Best Cinematography, Best Supporting Actress (Bondi). MGM

Gorgo *♂♂*½ 1961 An undersea explosion off the coast of Ireland brings to the surface a prehistoric sea monster, which is captured and brought to a London circus. Its irate mother appears looking for her baby, creating havoc in her wake. 76m/C VHS, Beta, LV. GB Bill Travers, William Sylvester, Vincent Winter, Bruce Seton, Christopher Rhodes; D: Eugene Lourie; C: Frederick A. (Freddie) Young. NOS, MRV, VCI

The Gorgon *♂♂* 1964 In pre-WWI Germany, the lovely assistant to a mad brain surgeon moonlights as a snake-haired gorgon, turning men to stone. A professor arrives in the village to investigate, only to become another victim. 83m/C VHS, Beta, LV. GB Peter Cushing, Christopher Lee, Richard Pasco, Barbara Shelley, Michael Goodliffe, Patrick Troughton; D: Terence Fisher; M: James Bernard. GKK, MLB

The Gorilla *♂♂* 1939 Bumbling Ritzes are hired to protect a country gentleman receiving threats from a killer. Lugosi portrays the menacing butler. Derived from the play by Ralph Spence. 67m/B VHS, Beta, LV. The Ritz Brothers, Anita Louise, Patsy Kelly, Lionel Atwill, Bela Lugosi; D: Allan Dwan. NOS, SNC, MRV

Gorilla *♂♂* 1956 A rampaging gorilla is sought by the local game warden and a journalist researching the natives. Filmed on location in the Belgian Congo. 79m/B VHS, Beta. SW Gio Petre, Georges Galley; D: Sven Nykvist, Lar Henrik Ottoson. FCT, VYY

Gorillas in the Mist *♂♂♂* 1988 (PG-13) The life of Dian Fossey, animal rights activist and world-renowned expert on the African gorilla, from her pioneering contact with mountain gorillas to her murder at the hands of poachers. Weaver is totally appropriate as the increasingly obsessed Fossey, but the character moves away from us, just as we need to see and understand more about her. Excellent special effects. 117m/C VHS, Beta, LV. Sigourney Weaver, Bryan Brown, Julie Harris, Iain Cuthbertson, John Omirah Miluwi, Constantin Alexandrov, Waigwa Wachira; D: Michael Apted; W: Anna Hamilton Phelan; C: John Seale; M: Maurice Jarre. Golden Globe Awards '88: Best Actress—Drama (Weaver); Golden Globe Awards '89: Best Score; Nominations: Academy Awards '88: Best Actress (Weaver), Best Adapted Screenplay, Best Film Editing, Best Sound, Best Original Score. USH, HMV

Gorky Park *♂♂♂* 1983 (R) Adaptation of Martin Cruz Smith's bestseller. Three strange, faceless corpses are found in Moscow's Gorky Park. There are no clues for the Russian police captain investigating the incident. He makes the solution to this crime his personal crusade, and finds himself caught in a web of political intrigue. Excellent police procedure yarn. 127m/C VHS, Beta, LV. William Hurt, Lee Marvin, Brian Dennehy, Joanna Pacula; D: Michael Apted; W: Dennis Potter; C: Ralf Bode; M: James Horner. Edgar Allan Poe Awards '83: Best Screenplay. VES

Gorp woof! 1980 (R) Sex, fun, and lewd, sophomoric humor reign at a summer camp. For the bored and witless or those who aspire. 90m/C VHS, Beta. Dennis Quaid, Rosanna Arquette, Michael Lembeck, Philip Casnoff, Frank Drescher; D: Joseph Ruben. HBO

Gospa *♂♂*½ 1994 (PG) Based on the true story of Father Jozo Zovko (Sheen), who was put on trial for treason by the communist government in Yugoslavia in 1981 when he protected six Coatian children who repeatedly claimed that they saw visions of the Virgin Mary. Somewhat ponderous but well-meaning story that also suffers from a plethora of accents. "Gospa" means "Our Lady" in Croatian. 121m/C VHS. Martin Sheen, Michael York, Morgan Fairchild, Frank Finlay; D: Jakov Sedlar; W: Ivan Aralica, Paul Gronseth; C: Vjekoslav Vrdoljak; M: Nona Hendryx. NYR

The Gospel According to St. Matthew *♂♂♂♂* Il Vangelo Secondo Matteo; L'Evangile Selon Saint-Matthieu 1964 Perhaps Pasolini's greatest film, retelling the story of Christ in gritty, neo-realistic tones and portraying the man less as a divine presence than as a political revolutionary. The yardstick by which all Jesus-films are to be measured. In Italian with English subtitles or dubbed. 142m/B VHS, Beta, LV, 8mm. IT Enrique Irazoqui, Susanna Pasolini, Margherita Caruso, Marcello Morante, Mario Socrate; D: Pier Paolo Pasolini; W: Pier Paolo Pasolini; C: Tonino Delli Colli; M: Luis Bacalov. National Board of Review Awards '66: 5 Best Foreign Films of the Year; Nominations: Academy Awards '66: Best Adapted Score, Best Art Direction/Set Decoration (B & W), Best Costume Design (B & W). NOS, MRV, WBF

The Gospel According to Vic *♂♂* Heavenly Pursuits 1987 (PG-13) A Scottish comedy about a skeptical teacher at a remedial school, who, having survived miraculously from a fall, is taken for proof of the sainthood of the school's patron namesake. 92m/C VHS, Beta, Closed Caption. GB Tom Conti, Helen Mirren; D: Charles Gormley; C: Michael Coulter. FOX

Gotcha! *♂♂*½ 1985 (PG-13) The mock assassination game "Gotcha!" abounds on the college campus and sophomore Edwards is one of the best. What he doesn't know is that his "assassination" skills are about to take on new meaning when he meets up with a female Czech graduate student who is really an international spy. 97m/C VHS, Beta, LV, Closed Caption. Anthony Edwards, Linda Fiorentino, Alex Rocco, Nick Corri, Marla Adams, Klaus Loewitsch, Christopher Rydell; D: Jeff Kanew; W: Dan Gordon; M: Bill Conti. USH

Gotham *♂♂♂* 1988 A wealthy financier hires private-eye Jones to track down beautiful wife Madsen. It seems that she keeps dunning her husband for money. Sounds easy enough to Jones until he learns that she has been dead for some time. Mystery ventures into the afterlife and back as it twists its way to its surprise ending. Intriguing throwback to '40s detective flicks. Made for television. 100m/C VHS, LV. Tommy Lee Jones, Virginia Madsen, Colin Bruce, Kevin Jarre, Denise Stephenson, Frederic Forrest; D: Lloyd Fonvielle; C: Michael Chapman; M: George S. Clinton. CAN

Gothic *♂♂♂* 1987 (R) Mary Shelley, Lord Byron, Percy Bysshe Shelley, and John Polidori spend the night in a Swiss villa telling each other ghost stories and experimenting with laudanum and sexual partner combinations. The dreams and realizations of the night will color their lives ever after. Interesting premise, well-carried out, although burdened by director Russell's typical excesses. Soundtrack by Thomas Dolby. 87m/C VHS, Beta, LV. Julian Sands, Gabriel Byrne, Timothy Spall, Natasha Richardson, Miriam Cyr; D: Ken Russell; W: Stephen Volk; M: Thomas Dolby. LIV, VES

Gotta Dance, Gotta Sing 1984 Compilation of memorable dance routines from great Hollywood films. 53m/C VHS, Beta. Fred Astaire, Ginger Rogers, Shirley Temple, Carmen Miranda, Betty Grable. NO

Gotti *♂♂*½ 1996 (R) Follows the career of the New York mobster known as the "Teflon Don." Gotti's (Assante) mentor is Neil Dellacroce (Quinn), underboss to the aging head of the Gambino crime family. When Gambino (Lawrence) dies, Gotti is incensed that Paul Castellano (Sarafian) is named as family successor and eventually has him killed. He then grabs power (and lots of tabloid headlines), manages to beat his first federal racketeering rap, but is brought down with the aid of his own underboss, Sammy the Bull (Forsythe), whom the feds get into court. Made for cable. CW: Graphic violence, strong language and some drug content. 118m/C VHS. Armand Assante, William Forsythe, Anthony Quinn, Richard Sarafian, Vinny Pastore, Robert Miranda, Frank Vincent, Marc Lawrence, Al Waxman, Alberta Watson, Silvio Oliviero, Nigel Bennett; D: Robert Harmon; W: Steve Shagan; C: Alan Kivilo; M: Mark Isham. HBO

Government Agents vs. Phantom Legion 1951 Agent Hal Duncan must stop an evil group who is stealing uranium shipments from under the government's nose. Edited from 12 episodes of the original serial on two cassettes. 167m/B VHS, Beta. Walter Reed, Mary Ellen Kay, Dick Curtis, John Pickard. REP, MLB

The Grace Kelly Story *♂♂*½ 1983 Ladd stars as the beautiful Philadelphia society girl who became an Oscar-winning actress and a seemingly fairy tale princess when she leaves Hollywood behind to marry Prince Rainier of Monaco. Standard TV bio but Ladd does look the part. 104m/C VHS, Closed Caption. Cheryl Ladd, Diane Ladd, Lloyd Bridges, Ian McShane, Alejandro Rey, William Schallert, Marta DuBois, Salome Jens, Edith Fellows; D: Anthony Page; W: Cynthia Mandelberg. COL

Grace of My Heart *♂♂*½ 1996 (R) Edna Buxton (Douglas), from a rich Philadelphia family, wins a song contest and winds up in New York at Manhattan's Brill Building, pop music's '60s song factory, where she's transformed into Denise Waverly and told to write the music—not sing it. She pens a lot of hits, winds up in hippie Malibu, and finally gets the courage to record her own concept album (think Carole King's "Tapestry"). Along the way there's a succession of wrong men and heartbreak before her independent triumph. Douglas does a fine job (her singing's dubbed by Kristen Vigard) but last minute melodrama turns this into typical showbiz kitsch. **CW:** Language, and for some sexuality and drug content. 116m/C VHS, LV, Closed Caption. Illeana Douglas, John Turturro, Matt Dillon, Eric Stoltz, Bruce Davison, Patsy Kensit, Bridget Fonda, Jennifer Leigh Warren, Chris Isaak; **D:** Allison Anders; **W:** Allison Anders; **C:** Jean-Yves Escoffier; **M:** Larry Klein; **V:** Peter Fonda. *USH*

Grace Quigley 🐾½ *The Ultimate Solution of Grace Quigley* 1984 (PG) An elderly woman, tired of life, hires a hitman to kill her. Instead they go into business together, bumping off other elderly folk who decide they'd rather be dead. Notoriously inept black comedy noted for being the career embarrassment for both of its stars. 87m/C VHS, Beta. Katharine Hepburn, Nick Nolte, Walter Abel, Chip Zien, Elizabeth Wilson, Kit Le Fever, William Duell, Jill Eikenberry; **D:** Anthony Harvey; **M:** John Addison. *MGM*

Grad Night 🐾 1981 (R) The anticipation for graduation in a small town high school brings surprises no one could have predicted, unless they've seen all the other typical adolescent films. 85m/C VHS, Beta. Joey Johnson, Suzanna Fagan, Barry Stolze, Sam Whipple, Caroline Bates; **D:** John Tenorio; **C:** Arledge Armenaki. *NO*

The Graduate 🐾🐾🐾 1967 (PG) Famous, influential slice of comic Americana stars Hoffman as Benjamin Braddock, a shy, aimless college graduate who, without any idea of responsibility or ambition, wanders from a sexual liaison with a married woman (the infamous Mrs. Robinson) to pursuit of her engaged daughter. His pursuit of Elaine right to her wedding has become a film classic. Extremely popular and almost solely responsible for establishing both Hoffman and director Nichols. The career advice given to Benjamin, "plastics," became a catchword for the era. Watch for Dreyfuss in the Berkeley rooming house, Farrell in the hotel lobby, and screenwriter Henry as the desk clerk. Based on the novel by Charles Webb. Laserdisc edition includes screen tests, promotional stills, and a look at the creative process involved in making a novel into a movie. A 25th Anniversary Limited Edition is also available, presented in a wide-screen format and including the original movie trailer and interviews with the cast and crew. 106m/C VHS, Beta, LV, 8mm, Closed Caption. Dustin Hoffman, Anne Bancroft, Katharine Ross, Murray Hamilton, Brian Avery, Marion Lorne, Alice Ghostley, William Daniels, Elizabeth Wilson, Norman Fell, Buck Henry, Richard Dreyfuss, Mike Nichols; **D:** Mike Nichols; **W:** Buck Henry, Calder Willingham; **C:** Robert L. Surtees; **M:** Paul Simon, Art Garfunkel, Dave Grusin. Academy Awards '67: Best Director (Nichols); British Academy Awards '68: Best Director (Nichols), Best Film, Best Screenplay; Directors Guild of America Awards '67: Best Director (Nichols); Golden Globe Awards '68: Best Actress—Musical/Comedy (Bancroft), Best Director (Nichols), Best Film—Musical/Comedy; National Board of Review Awards '67: 10 Best Films of the Year; New York Film Critics Awards '67: Best Director (Nichols); Nominations: Academy Awards '67: Best Actor (Hoffman), Best Actress (Bancroft), Best Adapted Screenplay, Best Cinematography, Best Picture, Best Supporting Actress (Ross). *NLC, CRC, BTV*

Graduation Day 🐾 1981 (R) Another teen slasher about the systematic murder of members of a high school track team. Notable mainly for brief appearance by Vanna White. 85m/C VHS, Beta. Christopher George, Patch MacKenzie, E. Danny Murphy, Vanna White; **D:** Herb Freed. *COL*

Graffiti Bridge 🐾½ 1990 (PG-13) Prince preaches love instead of sex and the result is boring. The Lavender One is a Minneapolis nightclub owner who battles with Day over the love of a beautiful woman. Chauvinistic attitudes toward women abound, but the females in the film don't seem to mind. Which must mean they were "acting." Visually interesting, although not as experimental as "Purple Rain." Music made Top

Ten. 90m/C VHS, Beta, LV, Closed Caption. Prince, Morris Day, Jerome Benton, Jill Jones, Mavis Staples, George Clinton, Ingrid Chavez; **D:** Prince; **W:** Prince; **C:** Bill Butler. *MVD, WAR*

Grain of Sand 🐾🐾🐾 1984 Based on a true story, an understated French drama about a troubled woman searching her past, and her home town in Corsica, for the man of her dreams. Directorial debut of Meffre. In French with English subtitles. 90m/C VHS, Beta. **FR** Delphine Seyrig, Genevieve Fontanel, Coralie Seyrig, Michel Aumont; **D:** Pomme Meffre. *FCT*

Grambling's White Tiger 🐾🐾½ 1981 The true story of Jim Gregory, the first white man to play on Grambling College's all-black football team. Jenner's is a little too old, but Belafonte, in his TV acting debut, is fine as legendary coach Eddie Robinson. Based on book by Bruce Behrenberg. Made for television. 98m/C VHS, Beta. Bruce Jenner, Harry Belafonte, LeVar Burton, Ray Vitte, Byron Stewart; **D:** Georg Stanford Brown; **M:** John D'Andrea. *USH*

Grand Canyon 🐾🐾🐾 1991 (R) Diverse group of characters is thrown together through chance encounters while coping with urban chaos in L.A. The main focus is the growing friendship between an immigration lawyer (Kline) and a tow-truck driver (Glover) who meet when Kline's car breaks down in a crime-ridden neighborhood. First-rate performances by the cast make up for numerous moral messages thrown at viewers with the subtlety of a brick. Sometimes funny, sometimes preachy became more relevant in light of the violence that exploded in L.A. during the summer of '92. **CW:** Language. 134m/C VHS, Closed Caption. Danny Glover, Kevin Kline, Steve Martin, Mary McDonnell, Mary-Louise Parker, Alfre Woodard, Jeremy Sisto, Tina Lifford, Patrick Malone, Mary Ellen Trainor; **D:** Lawrence Kasdan; **W:** Lawrence Kasdan, Meg Kasdan; **C:** Owen Roizman; **M:** James Newton Howard. National Board of Review Awards '91: 10 Best Films of the Year; Nominations: Academy Awards '91: Best Original Screenplay. *FXV*

Grand Canyon Trail 🐾½ 1948 Our hero is the owner of a played-out silver mine who is the target of an unscrupulous engineer who thinks there's silver to be found if you know where to look. The first appearance of the Riders of the Purple Sage, who replaced the Sons of the Pioneers. 68m/B VHS, Beta. Roy Rogers, Andy Devine, Charles Coleman, Jane Frazee, Robert Livingston; **D:** William Witney. *NOS, MED, DVT*

The Grand Duchess and the Waiter 🐾🐾🐾 1926 Menjou is a French millionaire who disguises himself as a waiter in order to enter the service of a grand duchess with whom he has fallen in love. 70m/B VHS, Beta. Adolphe Menjou, Florence Vidor, Lawrence Grant; **D:** Malcolm St. Clair. *GVV*

The Grand Duel 🐾🐾 1973 More spaghetti thrills as Lee plays a mysterious gunman who also acts as protector of a young ruffian falsely accused of murder. ?m/C VHS. **IT** Lee Van Cleef, Peter O'Brien, Jess Hahn, Horst Frank. *SNC, VTR*

Grand Hotel 🐾🐾🐾½ 1932 A star-filled cast is brought together by unusual circumstances at Berlin's Grand Hotel and their lives become hopelessly intertwined over a 24 hour period. Adapted (and given the red-carpet treatment) from a Vicki Baum novel; notable mostly for Garbo's world-weary ballerina. Time has taken its toll on the concept and treatment, but still an interesting star vehicle. 112m/B VHS, Beta, LV, Closed Caption. Greta Garbo, John Barrymore, Joan Crawford, Lewis Stone, Wallace Beery, Jean Hersholt, Lionel Barrymore; **D:** Edmund Goulding; **C:** William H. Daniels. Academy Awards '32: Best Picture. *MGM, FCT, BTV*

Grand Illusion 🐾🐾🐾🐾 1937 Unshakably classic anti-war film by Renoir, in which French prisoners of war attempt to escape from their German captors during WWI. An indictment of the way Old World, aristocratic nobility was brought to modern bloodshed in the Great War. Renoir's optimism remains relentless, but was easier to believe in before WWII. In French, with English subtitles. The laserdisc version includes an audio essay by Peter Crowe. 111m/B VHS, Beta, LV, 8mm. **FR** Jean Gabin, Erich von Stroheim, Pierre Fresnay, Marcel Dalio, Julien Carette, Gaston Modot, Jean Daste, Dita Parlo; **D:** Jean Renoir. National Board of Review Awards '38: 5 Best Foreign Films of the Year; New York Film Critics Awards '38: Best Foreign Film; Nominations: Academy Awards '38: Best Picture. *VYY, MRV, FOX*

Grand Isle 🐾🐾½ 1992 At the turn of the century Grand Isle is the place Louisiana gentry leisurely spend their summers. This is where Edna Pontellier (McGillis), the wife of a rich stockbroker, meets sensitive Creole artist Robert Le-Brun (Pasdar). Robert gives Edna all the attention sorely lacking in her marriage and they fall in love. However, Edna's attempts to liberate herself from the strictures of society lead her to tragedy. Based on "The Awakening" by Kate Chopin. Made for cable television. 94m/C VHS, LV, Closed Caption. Kelly McGillis, Adrian Pasdar, Julian Sands, Jon DeVries, Glenne Headly, Anthony De Sando, Ellen Burstyn; **D:** Mary Lambert; **W:** Hesper Anderson. *TTC*

Grand Larceny 🐾🐾 1992 The daughter of a millionaire/thief has to prove that she can take over the family "business." Lots of action and stunts. 95m/C VHS. Marilu Henner, Omar Sharif, Ian McShane, Louis Jourdan; **D:** Jeannot Szwarc. *CAF*

Grand Prix 🐾🐾 1966 A big-budget look at the world of Grand Prix auto racing, as four top competitors circle the world's most famous racing circuits. Strictly for those who like cars racing round and round; nothing much happens off the track. Letterboxed screen is featured in the laserdisc format. 161m/C VHS, Beta, LV, Closed Caption. James Garner, Eva Marie Saint, Yves Montand, Toshiro Mifune, Brian Bedford; **D:** John Frankenheimer; **C:** Lionel Lindon; **M:** Maurice Jarre. Academy Awards '66: Best Film Editing, Best Sound, Best Sound Effects Editing. *MGM, FCT*

Grand Theft Auto 🐾🐾 1977 (PG) In Howard's initial directorial effort, a young couple elopes to Las Vegas in a Rolls Royce owned by the bride's father. The father, totally against the marriage and angered by the stolen Rolls, offers a reward for their safe return and a cross-country race ensues. 84m/C VHS, Beta. Ron Howard, Nancy Morgan, Marion Ross, Barry Cahill, Clint Howard; **D:** Ron Howard; **W:** Ron Howard. *NHO*

Grand Tour: Disaster in Time 🐾🐾 1992 (PG-13) Greenglen is a quiet, small Midwestern town, until it is visited by a sinister group of time traveling aliens. Daniels plays a widowed innkeeper who must save the town from destruction and save his daughter from being kidnapped by the fiends. Made for cable television. 98m/C VHS, LV, Closed Caption. Jeff Daniels, Ariana Richards, Emilia Crow, Jim Haynie, Nicholas Guest, Marilyn Lightstone, George Murdock; **D:** David N. Twohy; **W:** David N. Twohy. *ACA*

Grandes Amigos 🐾 *Great Friends* 197? A young boy finds out the meaning of having a true friend in this comedy-drama in Spanish. 105m/C VHS, Beta. **SP** Nino Del Arco. *MAD*

Grandma's House 🐾 1988 (R) A brother and sister discover that the house in which they live with their grandmother is chock-full of secrets and strange happenings, including madness, incest, and murder. 90m/C VHS, Beta, LV. Eric Foster, Kim Valentine, Brinke Stevens, Ida Lee; **D:** Peter Rader. *ACA*

Grandview U.S.A. 🐾🐾½ 1984 (R) A low-key look at low-rent middle America, centering on a foxy local speedway owner and the derby-obsessed boys she attracts. Pre-"Dirty Dancing" choreography from Patrick Swayze and wife Lisa Niemi. 97m/C VHS, Beta, Closed Caption. Jamie Lee Curtis, Patrick Swayze, C. Thomas Howell, M. Emmet Walsh, Troy Donahue, William Windom, Jennifer Jason Leigh, Ramon Bieri, John Cusack, Joan Cusack, Jason Court; **D:** Randal Kleiser; **M:** Thomas Newman. *FOX*

The Granny 🎬½ **1994 (R)** Evil Granny Gargoli (Stevens) is so mean that just before she dies she swallows an ancient potion, enabling her to haunt her survivors. When Kelly (Whirry), the only one to really care for Granny, is cheated out of her inheritance, the rest of the family is in for some nasty shocks from the zombiefied oldster. Can't decide whether to be camp or horrific. **CW:** Violence and gore; crude sexuality; language. 85m/C VHS. Shannon Whirry, Stella Stevens; **D:** Luca Bercovici; **W:** Luca Bercovici. *AVE*

The Grapes of Wrath 🎬🎬🎬½ **1940** John Steinbeck's classic American novel about the Great Depression. We follow the impoverished Joad family as they migrate from the dust bowl of Oklahoma to find work in the orchards of California and as they struggle to maintain at least a little of their dignity and pride. A sentimental but dignified, uncharacteristic Hollywood epic. 129m/B VHS, Beta, LV, Closed Caption. Henry Fonda, Jane Darwell, John Carradine, Charley Grapewin, Zeffie Tilbury, Dorris Bowdon, Russell Simpson, John Qualen, Eddie Quillan, O.Z. Whitehead, Grant Mitchell; **D:** John Ford; **W:** Nunnally Johnson; **C:** Gregg Toland. Academy Awards '40: Best Director (Ford), Best Supporting Actress (Darwell); National Board of Review Awards '40: 10 Best Films of the Year; New York Film Critics Awards '40: Best Director (Ford), Best Film; Nominations: Academy Awards '40: Best Actor (Fonda), Best Film Editing, Best Picture, Best Screenplay, Best Sound, Best Original Score. *FXV, BTV, HMV*

The Grass Harp 🎬🎬½ **1995 (PG)** Rather dull retelling (with an excellent cast) of the Truman Capote novella covering the eccentricities of small town Southern life in the '30s and '40s. Teenaged Collin Fenwick (Furlong) is sent to live with his maiden aunts, artistic, impractical Dolly (Laurie) and shrewd, hard businesswoman Verena (Spacek). Charlie Cool's (Matthau) the retired judge who's sweet on Dolly, Morris Ritz (Lemmon) is a shady Chicago entrepreneur with plans for Verena's money, and there are various opinionated townspeople with stories to tell as well. Screen nostalgia directed by Matthau's son Charles. 107m/C VHS, LV, Closed Caption. Sissy Spacek, Piper Laurie, Edward Furlong, Walter Matthau, Nell Carter, Jack Lemmon, Mary Steenburgen, Roddy McDowall, Joe Don Baker, Charles Durning, Sean Patrick Flanery, Mia Kirshner; **D:** Charles Matthau; **W:** Stirling Silliphant; **C:** John A. Alonzo; **M:** Patrick Williams. *NLC*

The Grass is Always Greener Over the Septic Tank 🎬🎬 **1978** Based on Erma Bombeck's best-seller. A city family's flight to the supposed peace of the suburbs turns out to be a comic change of complications. Made for television. 98m/C VHS, Beta. Carol Burnett, Charles Grodin, Linda Gray, Alex Rocco, Robert Sampson, Vicki Belmonte, Craig Richard Nelson, Anrae Walterhouse, Eric Stoltz; **D:** Robert Day. *NO*

The Grass is Greener 🎬🎬½ **1961** An American millionaire invades part of an impoverished Earl's mansion and falls in love with the lady of the house. The Earl, who wants to keep his wife, enlists the aid of an old girlfriend in a feeble attempt to make her jealous. The two couples pair off properly in the end. 105m/C VHS, LV. Cary Grant, Deborah Kerr, Jean Simmons, Robert Mitchum; **D:** Stanley Donen. *REP*

The Grave 🎬🎬½ **1995 (R)** Rednecks King (Scheffer) and Tyn (Charles) escape from a North Carolina prison farm after learning about a possible fortune buried in a grave. Unfortunately, they can't keep their mouths shut and soon every other lowlife around them is hunting as well. **CW:** Violence, a sex scene and strong language. 90m/C VHS. Craig Sheffer, Josh Charles, Gabrielle Anwar, Donal Logue, John Diehl, Anthony Michael Hall, Eric Roberts; **D:** Jonas Pate; **W:** Jonas Pate; **C:** Frank Prinzi. *REP*

Grave Indiscretions 🎬🎬 *The Grotesque; Gentlemen Don't Eat Poets* **1996 (R)** Eccentric aristocrat, and amateur paleontologist, Sir Hugo Coal (Bates) is much more interested in the dinosaur skeleton he's attempting to assemble than in his crumbling estate or unsatisfied wife Harriet (Rus-

sell). Although he does take a dislike to the married servants his wife hires—sly butler Fledge (Sting) and his dipso cook/wife Doris (Styler). And then there's daughter Cleo (Headey) who's about to marry useles poet Sidney (Mackintosh) until he suddenly disappears. Which raises all sorts of questions, including just what the pigs have been eating recently. Based on McGrath's 1989 novel, "The Grotesque." **CW:** Nudity, sex and some gore. 97m/C VHS. *GB* Sting, Alan Bates, Theresa Russell, Trudie Styler, Lena Headey, Steven Mackintosh, Anna Massey, Jim Carter, Maria Aitken; **D:** John-Paul Davidson; **W:** Patrick McGrath; **C:** Andrew Dunn; **M:** Anne Dudlem. *LIV*

Grave of the Fireflies 🎬🎬🎬 **1988** In post-war Japan, in the city of Kobe's train station, a young boy lies dying. A janitor finds a metal canister lying next to the boy and when he opens it ashes fall out. As fireflies gather around, ghostly figures of the boy and his little sister appear, as the story flashes back to the orphaned, homeless Seita and his sister. The two youngsters struggle in the Japanese countryside but find they cannot escape the hardships of war and have no chance for survival. Stunning animated testimony to the human spirit. Based on the novel by Akiyuki Nosaka. In Japanese with English subtitles. 88m/C VHS, LV. *JP* **D:** Isao Takahata; **W:** Isao Takahata. *CPM*

Grave of the Vampire 🎬 *Seed of Terror* **1972 (R)** A vampire rapes and impregnates a modern-day girl. Twenty years later, their son, who grows up to be a bitter bloodsucker, sets out to find his father and kill him. 95m/C VHS, Beta. William Smith, Michael Pataki, Lyn Peters, Diane Holden, Jay Adler, Kitty Vallacher, Jay Scott, Lieux Dressler; **D:** John Hayes. *UNI*

Grave Secrets 🎬½ **1989 (R)** A professor of psychic phenomena teams up with a medium to find out who—or what—is controlling the life of a young woman. 90m/C VHS, LV. Paul LeMat, Renee Soutendijk, David Warner, Olivia Barash, Lee Ving; **D:** Donald P. Borchers. *SGE*

Grave Secrets: The Legacy of Hilltop Drive 🎬🎬 **1992** The Williams family finds out their dream house is built on the site of an old graveyard. The spirits are not only restless, they're deadly. Based on a true story. 94m/C VHS, Closed Caption. Jonelle Allen, Patty Duke, David Selby, David Soul, Blake Clark; **D:** John D. Patterson. *WOV, PMS*

The Graveyard 🎬🎬 *Persecution; Terror of Sheba; Sheba* **1974** A mommy spends many years torturing her little boy, David. In one blood-filled day, the fellow seeks his revenge. 90m/C VHS, Beta. Lana Turner, Trevor Howard, Ralph Bates, Olga Georges-Picot, Suzan Farmer; **D:** Don Chaffey. *ELV*

Graveyard of Horror 🎬 **1971** His wife and baby dead, a man seeking revenge discovers a horrible secret: his brother, a doctor, is stealing the heads from corpses. Dubbed. 105m/C VHS, Beta. *SP* Bill Curran, Francisco (Frank) Brana, Beatriz Lacy; **D:** Miguel Madrid. *NO*

Graveyard Shift 🎬½ **1987 (R)** A New York cabby on the night shift is actually a powerful vampire who uses his fares to build an army of vampires. Not to be confused with the 1990 Stephen King scripted film. Followed by "Understudy: Graveyard Shift II." 89m/C VHS, Beta. *IT* Silvio Oliviero, Helen Papas, Cliff Stoker; **D:** Gerard Ciccoritti. *VTR*

Graveyard Shift 🎬 *Stephen King's Graveyard Shift* **1990 (R)** Just because Stephen King wrote the original story doesn't mean its celluloid incarnation is guaranteed to stand your hair on end; unless that's your response to abject boredom. When a man takes over the night shift at a recently reopened textile mill, he starts to find remnants...and they aren't fabric. Seems there's a graveyard in the neighborhood. 89m/C VHS, Beta, LV, Closed Caption. David Andrews, Kelly Wolf, Stephen Macht, Brad Dourif; **D:** Ralph S. Singleton; **W:** Stephen King, John Esposito; **M:** Brian Banks. *PAR, FCT*

Gray Lady Down 🎬🎬 **1977 (PG)** A nuclear submarine sinks off the coast of Cape Cod and with their oxygen running out, a risky escape in an experimental diving craft seems to be their only hope. Dull, all-semi-star suspenser. 111m/C VHS, Beta. Charlton Heston, David Carradine, Stacy Keach, Ned Beatty, Ronny Cox, Christopher Reeve, Michael O'Keefe, Rosemary Forsyth; **D:** David Greene. *USH*

Grayeagle 🎬🎬 **1977 (PG)** When a frontier trapper's daughter is kidnapped by Cheyenne Indians, he launches a search for her recovery. More style than pace in this Western, but worth a look for fans of Johnson. 104m/C VHS, Beta. Ben Johnson, Iron Eyes Cody, Lana Wood, Alex Cord, Jack Elam, Paul Fix, Cindy Butler, Charles B. Pierce; **D:** Charles B. Pierce; **W:** Charles B. Pierce. *WAR, OM*

Grazuole 🎬🎬 **1969** A nine-year-old girl is mockingly made "Beauty Queen" by her malicious playmates. 71m/B VHS, Beta. **D:** Arunas Zhebrunas. *IHF*

Grease 🎬🎬🎬 **1978 (PG)** Film version of the hit Broadway musical about summer love. Set in the 1950s this spirited musical follows a group of high-schoolers throughout their senior year. The story offers a responsible moral: act like a tart and you'll get your guy; but, hey, it's all in fun anyway. Followed by a weak sequel. ♫ Grease; Summer Nights; Hopelessly Devoted To You; You're the One That I Want; Sandy; Beauty School Dropout; Look at Me, I'm Sandra Dee; Greased Lightnin'; It's Raining on Prom Night. 110m/C VHS, Beta, LV. John Travolta, Olivia Newton-John, Jeff Conaway, Stockard Channing, Eve Arden, Frankie Avalon, Sid Caesar; **D:** Randal Kleiser; **C:** Bill Butler. People's Choice Awards '79: Best Film; Nominations: Academy Awards '78: Best Song ("Hopelessly Devoted to You"). *PAR, FCT*

Grease 2 🎬🎬 **1982 (PG)** Continuing saga of the T-Birds, the Pink Ladies, and young love at Rydell High. Newton-John and Travolta have graduated, leaving Pfeiffer to lead on love-struck book-neb Caulfield. Some okay tunes, though lame story lacks good-humor flair of the original. 115m/C VHS, Beta, LV. Maxwell Caulfield, Michelle Pfeiffer, Adrian Zmed, Lorna Luft, Didi Conn, Eve Arden, Sid Caesar, Tab Hunter; **D:** Patricia Birch; **M:** Artie Butler. *PAR*

Greased Lightning 🎬🎬½ **1977 (PG)** The story of the first black auto racing champion, Wendell Scott, who had to overcome racial prejudice to achieve his success. Slightly-better-than-average Pryor comedy vehicle. 95m/C VHS, Beta, Closed Caption. Richard Pryor, Pam Grier, Beau Bridges, Cleavon Little, Vincent Gardenia; **D:** Michael A. Schultz; **W:** Leon Capetanos, Melvin Van Peebles. *WAR*

Greaser's Palace 🎬🎬½ **1972** Seaweed-head Greaser, owner of the town's saloon, faces his arch-nemesis in this wide-ranging satiric Christ allegory from the director of "Putney Swope." 91m/C VHS, Beta. Albert Henderson, Allan Arbus; **D:** Robert Downey; **M:** Jack Nitzsche. *COL, OM*

The Great Adventure 🎬🎬🎬½ *Det Stora Aventyret* **1953** Two farm boys capture and attempt to train a wild otter. Unfortunately, the otter longs to once again join his kind despite the boys' efforts. Arne Sucksdorff won an Oscar for his arresting view of animal life. 73m/B VHS, Beta. *SW* Anders Norberg, Kjell Sucksdorff, Arne Sucksdorff; **D:** Arne Sucksdorff; **W:** Arne Sucksdorff. *MED*

Great Adventure 🎬🎬 **1975 (PG)** In the severe environment of the gold rush days on the rugged Yukon territory, a touching tale unfolds of a young orphan boy and his eternal bond of friendship with a great northern dog. Based on a Jack London story. Paul Elliots is a pseudonym for Gianfranco Baldanello and Fred Romer is actually Fernando Romero. 90m/C VHS, Beta. *IT SP* Jack Palance, Joan Collins, Fred Romer, Elisabetta Virgili, Remo de Angelis, Manuel de Blas; **D:** Paul Elliotts. *MED, VTR*

The Great Alligator 🎬 *Il Fiume Del Grande Caimano* **1981** As if you couldn't guess, this one's about a huge alligator who does what other huge alligators do...terrorizes the people at a resort.

89m/C VHS, Beta. Barbara Bach, Mel Ferrer, Richard Johnson; **D:** Sergio Martino. *MPI*

The Great American Broadcast 🐾🐾🐾 1941 Two WWI vets want more than anything to strike it rich. After many failed endeavors, the two try that new-fangled thing called radio. The station takes off, as does the plot. The girlfriend of one vet falls for his partner and numerous other misunderstandings and complications ensue. Charming and crazy musical with an energetic cast. ♫I've Got a Bone To Pick With You; It's All In a Lifetime; I Take to You; Long Ago Last Night; Where You Are; The Great American Broadcast; Albany Bound; Give My Regards to Broadway; If I Didn't Care. **92m/B VHS.** Alice Faye, John Payne, Jack Oakie, Cesar Romero, James Newill, Mary Beth Hughes; **D:** Archie Mayo; **C:** Leon Shamroy. *MLB*

The Great American Sex Scandal 🐾🐾½ *Jury Duty* 1994 (PG-13) Sanford Lagelfust (Pinchot) is an meek accountant on trial for embezzlement, but when the prosecution's main witness turns out to be his sexy girlfriend Hope (Scoggins) the case turns into a courtroom sex scandal. Silly Canadian TV production. **94m/C VHS.** CA Bronson Pinchot, Tracy Scoggins, Heather Locklear, Stephen Baldwin, Lynn Redgrave, Alan Thicke, Madchen Amick, Barbara Bosson, Ilene Graff, Mark Blankfield, Danny Pintauro, Reginald Veljohnson, Jacklyn Zeman; **D:** Michael A. Schultz. *APX*

Great American Traffic Jam 🐾½ *Gridlock* 1980 (PG) A made-for-television farce about the humorous variety of characters interacting on the interstate during a massive California traffic jam. **97m/C VHS, Beta, Closed Caption.** Ed McMahon, Vic Tayback, Howard Hesseman, Abe Vigoda, Noah Beery Jr., Desi Arnaz Jr., John Beck, Shelley Fabares, James Gregory; **D:** James Frawley. *FOX*

The Great American Western Collection: Roy Rogers 194? Series of three great Roy Rogers classics. "West of the Badlands" is an adaptation of Zane Grey's novel "Border Legion." Rogers plays an outlaw who sacrifices himself to save a pair of lovers. In "Jesse James at Bay," Rogers plays a romanticized version of James, stealing from the rich and powerful railroad to help the poor settlers keep their land. Rogers and Dale Evans star together in the singing western classic, Yellow Rose of Texas. **180m/B VHS.** Roy Rogers, George "Gabby" Hayes, Dale Evans. *BPG*

The Great Armored Car Swindle 🐾🐾 1964 An anonymous English businessman becomes involved in international intrigue when he becomes a pawn in a plan to transfer money to a Middle Eastern government under communist rule. But thanks to his wife things don't go off as planned. **58m/B VHS, Beta.** Peter Reynolds, Dermot Walsh, Joanna Dunham, Lisa Gastoni, Brian Cobby; **D:** Lance Comfort. *SNC*

Great Balls of Fire 🐾🐾½ 1989 (PG-13) A florid, comic-book film of the glory days of Jerry Lee Lewis, from his first band to stardom. Most of the drama is derived from his marriage to his 13-year-old cousin. Somewhat overacted but full of energy. The soundtrack features many of the "Killer's" greatest hits re-recorded by Jerry Lee Lewis for the film. **108m/C VHS, Beta, LV, Closed Caption.** Dennis Quaid, Winona Ryder, Alec Baldwin, Trey Wilson, John Doe, Lisa Blount, Steve Allen, Stephen Tobolowsky, Lisa Jane Persky, Michael St. Gerard, Peter Cook; **D:** Jim McBride; **W:** Jack Baran, Jim McBride; **C:** Alfonso Beato; **M:** Jack Baran, Jim McBride. *ORI*

Great Bank Hoax 🐾🐾½ *The Great Georgia Bank Hoax; Shenanigans* 1978 (PG) Three bank managers decide to rob their own bank to cover up the fact that all the assets have been embezzled. **89m/C VHS, Beta, Closed Caption.** Richard Basehart, Ned Beatty, Burgess Meredith, Michael Murphy, Paul Sand, Arthur Godfrey; **D:** Joseph Jacoby; **C:** Walter Lassally. *WAR*

Great Bikini Off-Road Adventure 🐾½ 1994 (R) Duke Abbey is about to lose his jeep tour company because business is so slow that he can't pay the rent. Then Duke's niece Lori decides to get her bikini-clad friends to hire on as drivers, showing lots of sights on their desert tours. **90m/C VHS, LV, Closed Caption.** Avalon Anders, Lauren Hays, Floyd Irons, Laura Hudspeth, Dan Frank; **D:** Gary Orona. *IMP, IME*

The Great Caruso 🐾🐾½ 1951 The story of opera legend Enrico Caruso's rise to fame, from his childhood in Naples, Italy, to his collapse on the stage of the Metropolitan Opera House. Lanza is superb as the singer, and there are 27 musical numbers to satisfy the opera lover. ♫The Loveliest Night of the Year; Over the Waves; Vesti la Giubba; M'Appari; Celeste Aida; Numi, Pieta; La Fatal Pietra; Sextet from Lucia di Lammermoor; La Donne a Mobile. **113m/C VHS, Beta, LV.** Mario Lanza, Ann Blyth, Dorothy Kirsten; **D:** Richard Thorpe; **C:** Joseph Ruttenberg. Academy Awards '51: Best Sound; Nominations: Academy Awards '51: Best Costume Design (Color), Scoring of a Musical.*MGM*

Great Chase 🐾🐾½ 1963 A historical anthology of the funniest and most suspenseful classic movie chases, especially "The General." **79m/B VHS, Beta.** Buster Keaton, Lillian Gish, Pearl White, Noah Beery Jr.; **M:** Larry Adler. *NLC*

The Great Commandment 🐾 1941 Young man throws himself into a revolution against the overbearing Roman Empire in 30 A.D. His brother joins him but is killed. The man, who has become influenced by the teachings of Christ, decides to give up his revolution and go off with his brother's widow. (He always loved her anyway.) **78m/B VHS.** John Beal, Maurice Moscovich, Albert Dekker, Marjorie Cooley, Warren McCollum; **D:** Irving Pichel. *REP*

Great Dan Patch 🐾½ 1949 The story of the great Dan Patch, the horse that went on to become the highest-earning harness racer in history. **92m/B VHS, Beta.** Dennis O'Keefe, Gail Russell, Ruth Warrick; **D:** Joseph M. Newman. *VEC*

Great Day 🐾½ 1946 A soap opera set around the wartime visit of first lady Eleanor Roosevelt to a small British town. It focuses mainly on the wife and daughter of a bitter, alcoholic WWI vet. **62m/B VHS, Beta.** Eric Portman, Flora Robson, Sheila Sim, Isabel Jeans, Walter Fitzgerald, Philip Friend, Marjorie Rhodes, Maire O'Neill, Beatrice Varley; **D:** Lance Comfort. *TTC*

Great Day in the Morning 🐾🐾½ 1956 A rebel sympathizer and a Northern spy are both after Colorado gold to help finance the Civil War. But our Southern gentlemen soon find themselves equally interested in the local ladies. **92m/C VHS, Beta.** Robert Stack, Ruth Roman, Raymond Burr, Virginia Mayo, Alex Nicol, Regis Toomey; **D:** Jacques Tourneur. *NO*

The Great Dictator 🐾🐾🐾🐾 1940 Chaplin's first all-dialogue film, a searing satire on Nazism in which he has dual roles as a Jewish barber with amnesia who is mistaken for a Hitlerian dictator, Adenoid Hynkel. A classic scene involves Hynkel playing with a gigantic balloon of the world. Hitler banned the film's release to the German public due to its highly offensive portrait of him. The film also marked Chaplin's last wearing of the Little Tramp's (and Hitler's equally little) mustache. **126m/B VHS, Beta, LV.** Charlie Chaplin, Paulette Goddard, Jack Oakie, Billy Gilbert, Reginald Gardiner, Henry Daniell, Maurice Moscovich; **D:** Charlie Chaplin; **W:** Charlie Chaplin; **C:** Karl Struss. National Board of Review Awards '40: 10 Best Films of the Year; New York Film Critics Awards '40: Best Actor (Chaplin); Nominations: Academy Awards '40: Best Actor (Chaplin), Best Original Screenplay, Best Picture, Best Supporting Actor (Oakie), Best Original Score. *FOX, HMV, GLV*

The Great Elephant Escape 🐾🐾½ 1995 Vacationing American teen Gordon-Levitt teams up with Kenyan M'Cormac, who works at an animal orphanage, to save a baby elephant from an unscrupulous businessman and his poacher friends. Made for TV. **90m/C VHS, Closed Caption.** Joseph Gordon-Levitt, Frederick M'Cormac, Stephanie Zimbalist, Leo Burmester, Julian Sands; **D:** George Miller; **W:** John Sweet, Christopher Canaan. *CAF*

The Great Escape 🐾🐾🐾½ 1963 During WWII, troublesome allied POW's are thrown by the Nazis into an escape-proof camp, where they join forces in a single mass break for freedom. One of the great war movies, with a superb ensemble cast and lots of excitement. The story was true, based on the novel by Paul Brickhill. McQueen performed most of the stunts himself, against the wishes of director Sturges. Laserdisc features an analysis of the true story that inspired the movie, actual photos of the camp, prisoners, and guards, commentary by director Sturges, composer Bernstein, and stuntman Bud Ekins, excerpts from the script by novelist/screenwriter Clavell, over 250 production photos, and the original movie trailer. Followed by a made for TV movie 25 years later. **170m/C VHS, Beta, LV, Closed Caption.** Steve McQueen, James Garner, Richard Attenborough, Charles Bronson, James Coburn, Donald Pleasence, David McCallum, James Donald, Gordon Jackson; **D:** John Sturges; **W:** James Clavell, W.R. Burnett; **C:** Daniel F. Fapp; **M:** Elmer Bernstein. National Board of Review Awards '63: 10 Best Films of the Year; Nominations: Academy Awards '63: Best Film Editing. *MGM, FOX, CRC*

The Great Escape 2: The Untold Story 🐾🐾 1988 Bland actioner can't decide whether it's a remake of the original or a sequel; it pretends to be a sequel yet spends a lot of time retelling—poorly—the first great escape. Once it gets around to the sequel part, it dispenses with protocol: Pleasance, an escapee in the original, is a Nazi bad guy in this go-round. Poor casting, especially Reeves, unconvincing as a German-speaking British officer who rallies the surviving escapees in revenge against their WWII captors. Made for television and originally shown in two parts, but mercifully shortened for video. **93m/C VHS.** Christopher Reeve, Judd Hirsch, Ian McShane, Donald Pleasence, Anthony John Denison, Jud Taylor, Charles Haid; **D:** Michael Nader, Paul Wendkos. *THV, TLF*

Great Expectations 🐾🐾🐾🐾 1946 Lean's magisterial adaptation of the Dickens tome, in which a young English orphan is graced by a mysterious benefactor and becomes a well-heeled gentleman. Hailed and revered over the years; possibly the best Dickens on film. Well-acted by all, but especially notable is Hunt's slightly mad and pathetic Miss Havisham. Remake of the 1934 film. **118m/B VHS, Beta, LV.** GB John Mills, Valerie Hobson, Anthony Wager, Alec Guinness, Finlay Currie, Jean Simmons, Bernard Miles, Francis L. Sullivan, Martita Hunt, Freda Jackson, Torin Thatcher, Hay Petrie, Eileen Erskine, George "Gabby" Hayes, Everley Gregg, O.B. Clarence; **D:** David Lean; **W:** David Lean, Ronald Neame; **C:** Guy Green. Academy Awards '47: Best Art Direction/Set Decoration (B & W), Best Black and White Cinematography; National Board of Review Awards '47: 10 Best Films of the Year; Nominations: Academy Awards '47: Best Director (Lean), Best Picture, Best Screenplay. *PAR, LCA, HMV*

Great Expectations 🐾🐾 1981 A British television mini-series adaptation of the Dickens epic about Pip and his mysterious benefactor in Victorian London. On two tapes. **300m/C VHS, Beta, Closed Caption.** GB Gerry Sundquist, Stratford Johns, Joan Hickson. *NO*

Great Expectations 🐾🐾🐾 1989 Dickens classic retold on 3 cassettes. A mysterious benefactor turns a poor orphan boy into a gentleman of means. **325m/C VHS, Beta, Closed Caption.** GB Jean Simmons, Anthony Hopkins, John Rhys-Davies; **D:** Kevin Connor. *DIS*

Great Expectations: The Untold Story 🐾🐾½ 1987 Magwitch is an escaped convict, hiding out in the Victorian English countryside, who is aided by the young orphan, Pip. Captured and sent to the penal colonies in Australia, Magwitch serves his time and then discovers a fortune in gold, which he decides to use to make Pip into a gentleman. But Magwitch's enemies would like to get Pip's inheritance for themselves. Based on the Dickens classic, this three-tape miniseries is also available in a 102-minute feature length version. **287m/C VHS.** John Stanton, Sigrid Thornton, Robert Coleby, Todd Boyce, Anne Louise Lambert, Ron Haddrick, Noel Ferrier; **D:** Tim Burstall. *FCT*

Great Flamarion ♂♂½ 1945 A woman-hating trick-shot artist is nevertheless duped into murdering the husband of his femme fatale assistant after he comes to believe she loves him. He's wrong. **78m/B VHS, Beta.** Dan Duryea, Erich von Stroheim, Mary Beth Hughes; **D:** Anthony Mann. *SNC, NOS, DVT*

The Great Gabbo ♂♂ 1929 A ventriloquist can express himself only through his dummy, losing his own identity and going mad at the end. Von Stroheim's first talkie. May quite possibly be the first mentally-twisted-ventriloquist story ever put on film. Von Stroheim hated the movie, believing it to be analogous to his own life. When he tried to buy the rights to the film, presumably to destroy the prints, he found that the property had been already purchased by real-life ventriloquist, Edgar Bergen. Based on a story by Ben Hecht. ♫The New Step; I'm Laughing Ickey; I'm in Love With You; The Ga-Ga Bird; The Web of Love; Every Now and Then. **82m/B VHS, Beta.** Erich von Stroheim, Betty Compson, Don Douglas, Marjorie Kane; **D:** James Cruze. *SNC, NOS, DVT*

The Great Gatsby ♂♂½ 1974 (PG) Adaptation of F. Scott Fitzgerald's novel of the idle rich in the 1920s. A mysterious millionaire crashes Long Island society, and finds his heart captured by an impetuous and emotionally impoverished girl. Skillful acting and directing captures the look and feel of this era, but the movie doesn't have the power of the book. **144m/C VHS, Beta, LV, Closed Caption.** Robert Redford, Mia Farrow, Bruce Dern, Karen Black, Patsy Kensit, Sam Waterston, Howard da Silva, Edward Herrmann; **D:** Jack Clayton; **W:** Francis Ford Coppola; **M:** Nelson Riddle. Academy Awards '74: Best Costume Design, Original Song Score and/or Adaptation; Golden Globe Awards '75: Best Supporting Actress (Black). *PAR, FCT*

The Great Gildersleeve ♂♂ 1943 Throckmorton P. Gildersleeve adds another problem to his list; the sister of a local judge wants to marry him. His niece and nephew won't allow it and his attempts to juggle everyone's desires make for fine fun. Peary was also the voice for the popular radio series of the same name. **62m/B VHS.** Harold Peary, Jane Darwell, Nancy Gates, Charles Arnt, Thurston Hall; **D:** Gordon Douglas. *MED*

Great Gold Swindle 1984 A dramatization of the 1982 swindling of the Perth Mint in Australia of over $650,000 worth of gold. **101m/C VHS, Beta.** Robert C. Hughes, Tony Rickards, Barbara Llewellyn. *LIV*

The Great Gundown ♂½ 1975 A violent tale set in the Old West. The peace of frontier New Mexico erupts when a half-breed Indian leads a brutal assault on an outlaw stronghold. **98m/C VHS, Beta.** Robert Padilla, Richard Rust, Milila St. Duval; **D:** Paul Hunt. *HHT*

Great Guns ♂♂ 1941 Stan and Ollie enlist in the army to protect a spoiled millionaire's son but wind up being targets at target practice instead. Not one of their better efforts. **74m/B VHS, Beta.** Stan Laurel, Oliver Hardy, Sheila Ryan, Dick Nelson; **D:** Montague Banks. *FOX, MLB*

Great Guy ♂½ *Pluck of the Irish* 1936 One of Cagney's lesser roles as an ex-boxer turned food inspector who wipes out graft in his town. **50m/B VHS, Beta.** James Cagney, Mae Clarke, Edward Brophy; **D:** John Blystone. *NOS, MRV, PSM*

The Great Hunter ♂ 1975 A village militia captain and his girlfriend seek to destroy the men who killed the girl's father. **91m/C VHS, Beta.** Chia Ling, Wang Yu, Hsu Feng. *UNI*

The Great Impostor ♂♂½ 1961 The true story of Ferdinand Waldo Demara, Jr., who during the 1950s, hoodwinked people by impersonating a surgeon, a college professor, a monk, a prison warden and a schoolteacher, with the FBI always one step behind him. **112m/C VHS, Beta.** Tony Curtis, Edmond O'Brien, Arthur O'Connell, Gary Merrill, Raymond Massey, Karl Malden, Mike Kellin, Frank Gorshin; **D:** Robert Mulligan; **C:** Robert Burks; **M:** Henry Mancini. *USH*

Great Jesse James Raid ♂½ 1949 Jesse James comes out of retirement to carry out a mine theft. Routine. **73m/C VHS, Beta.** Willard Parker, Barbara Payton, Tom Neal, Wallace Ford; **D:** Reginald LeBorg. *RXM, MRV*

Great K & A Train Robbery ♂♂½ 1926 A railroad detective is hired to find and stop the bandits who have been preying on the K & A Railroad. Silent. **55m/B VHS, Beta.** Tom Mix, Dorothy Dwan, William Walling, Harry Grippe, Carl Miller; **D:** Lewis Seiler. *GPV, GVV*

The Great Land of Small ♂♂ 1986 (G) Two children enter a fantasy world and try to save it from Evil. For kids. **94m/C VHS, Beta.** Karen Elkin, Michael Blouin, Michael Anderson Jr., Ken Roberts; **D:** Vojtech Jasny. *VTR, NWV, HHE*

Great Leaders of the Bibles 197? The inspiring stories of two Old Testament heroes, Gideon and Samson, are dramatized in this beautifully constructed film. **105m/C VHS, Beta.** Ivo Garrani, Fernando Rey, Giorgio Ceridni. *VCI*

The Great Lie ♂♂♂ 1941 A great soaper with Davis and Astor as rivals for the affections of Brent, an irresponsible flyer. Astor is the concert pianist who marries Brent and then finds out she's pregnant after he's presumed dead in a crash. The wealthy Davis offers to raise the baby so Astor can continue her career. But when Brent does return, who will it be to? Sparkling, catty fun. Astor's very short, mannish haircut became a popular trend. **107m/B VHS, Beta, LV.** Bette Davis, Mary Astor, George Brent, Lucile Watson, Hattie McDaniel, Grant Mitchell, Jerome Cowan; **D:** Edmund Goulding; **C:** Gaetano Antonio "Tony" Gaudio; **M:** Max Steiner. Academy Awards '41: Best Supporting Actress (Astor). *MGM, BTV*

The Great Locomotive Chase ♂♂½ *Andrews' Raiders* 1956 During the Civil War, Parker and his fellow soldiers head into Confederate territory to disrupt railroad supply lines. They take over a locomotive, but are pursued by Confederate Hunter, the conductor of another train; and soon a pursuit is underway. Based on the true story of Andrew's Raiders. **85m/C VHS, Beta.** Fess Parker, Jeffrey Hunter, Kenneth Tobey; **D:** Francis D. Lyon. *DIS*

The Great Los Angeles Earthquake ♂½ 1991 Made-for-TV disaster movie is the same old story; multiple soap-opera plotlines are spun around terrifying special effects, as L.A. is devastated by three major earth tremors and attendant disasters. Condensed from a two-part miniseries, also known as "The Big One: The Great Los Angeles Earthquake." **106m/C VHS, Closed Caption.** Ed Begley Jr., Joanna Kerns; **D:** Larry Elikann. *THV*

Great Love Experiment ♂ 1984 Everyone in a high school learns a valuable lesson about beauty and friendship when four popular students try to change the personality of an awkward classmate. **52m/C VHS, Beta.** Tracy Pollan, Esai Morales, Kelly Wolf, Scott Benderer. *NO*

The Great Lover ♂♂½ 1949 Aboard an ocean liner, a bumbler chaperoning school kids gets involved with a gambler, a duchess and a murder. Vintage Bob Hope. **80m/B VHS, Beta.** Bob Hope, Rhonda Fleming, Roland Young, Roland Culver, George Reeves, Jim Backus; **D:** Alexander Hall. *COL, FCT*

The Great Madcap ♂♂ A wealthy man believes in lavishly indulging himself which drives his excessively conservative family crazy. Bunuel satirizes behavioral extremes, Christianity, advertising, sex, and a number of other popular absurdities. In Spanish with English subtitles. **90m/B VHS.** MX Fernando Soler, Rosario Granados, Ruben Rogo; **D:** Luis Bunuel. *WBF*

The Great Man Votes ♂♂♂ 1938 Alcoholic college professor Barrymore falls into a deep depression after his wife's death. His children then plan to create a situation wherein his vote will decide the fate of the new town mayor, thus instilling in him a newly found sense of importance for himself and his children. Satiric and funny. **72m/B VHS, Beta.** John Barrymore, Peter Holden, Virginia Weidler, Katherine Alexander, Donald MacBride, Elisabeth Risdon, Granville Bates, Luis Alberni, J.M. Kerrigan, William Demarest, Roy Gordon; **D:** Garson Kanin; **C:** Russell Metty. *TTC*

The Great Man's Lady ♂♂½ 1942 Stanwyck stars in a "stand by your man" story in which she supported and was responsible for the good deeds of a now past town hero. Told in flashback sequence, Stanwyck's character, 109-year-old Hanna Sampler, reveals to a young biographer the trials and tribulations of her life with Ethan Hoyt, founder of Hoyt City, who is being honored with the dedication of a statue in the opening of the film. The picture reveals their secrets and the truth about the woman behind the man. Based on the story "The Human Side" by Vina Delmar. **89m/B VHS, Closed Caption.** Barbara Stanwyck, Joel McCrea, Brian Donlevy; **D:** William A. Wellman; **W:** Seena Owen, W.L. Rivers, Adela Rogers St. John; **C:** William Mellor; **M:** Victor Young. *USH*

The Great McGinty ♂♂♂½ *Down Went McGinty* 1940 Sturges' directorial debut, about the rise and fall of a small-time, bribe-happy politician is an acerbic, ultra-cynical indictment of modern politics that stands, like much of his other work, as bracingly courageous as anything that's ever snuck past the Hollywood censors. Political party boss Tamiroff chews the scenery with gusto while Donlevy, in his first starring role, is more than his equal as the not-so-dumb political hack. **82m/B VHS, Beta, LV.** Brian Donlevy, Muriel Angelus, Akim Tamiroff, Louis Jean Heydt, Arthur Hoyt, William Demarest; **D:** Preston Sturges; **W:** Preston Sturges; **C:** William Mellor. Academy Awards '40: Best Original Screenplay. *USH*

Great McGonagall ♂½ 1975 Tale of an unemployed Scot trying to become Britain's poet laureate. Sellers adds a semi-bright spot with his portrayal of Queen Victoria! **95m/C VHS, Beta.** GB Peter Sellers, Spike Milligan, Julia Foster; **D:** Joseph McGrath. *MOV, VTR*

The Great Mike ♂♂½ 1944 Unlikely but moving story of a young boy who convinces track management that his work horse has a chance against the touted thoroughbred. Sentimental, with little innovation, but generally well-acted. **72m/B VHS.** Stuart Erwin, Robert "Buzzy" Henry, Pierre Watkin, Gene Kenyon, Carl "Alfalfa" Switzer, Edythe Elliott, Marion Martin; **D:** Wallace Fox. *NOS*

Great Missouri Raid ♂♂ 1951 Follows the famous adventures of the James/Younger gang and their eventual demise. **81m/C VHS, Beta.** Wendell Corey, MacDonald Carey, Ellen Drew, Ward Bond; **D:** Gordon Douglas; **C:** Ray Rennahan. *BAR*

The Great Moment ♂♂ 1944 Story of the Boston dentist who discovered ether's use as an anesthetic in 1845. Confusing at times, changing from comedy to drama and containing flashbacks that add little to the story. Surprisingly bland result from ordinarily solid cast and director. **87m/B VHS, Beta, Closed Caption.** Joel McCrea, Betty Field, Harry Carey Sr., William Demarest, Franklin Pangborn, Porter Hall; **D:** Preston Sturges; **C:** Victor Milner. *USH*

The Great Mouse Detective ♂♂♂ *The Adventures of the Great Mouse Detective* 1986 (G) Animated version of the book "Basil of Baker Street" by Eve Titus. Fun adventure about Sherlock-of-the-mouse-world. Not as good as some of the other Disney animated features, but kids will enjoy it nonetheless. In 1992 it was rereleased. **74m/C VHS, Beta, LV, Closed Caption. D:** John Musker, Ron Clements, Dave Michener, Burny Mattinson; **W:** Ron Clements, Dave Michener; **M:** Henry Mancini; **V:** Vincent

Price, Barrie Ingham, Val Bettin, Susanne Pollatschek, Candido Candido, Eve Brenner, Alan Young, Melissa Manchester. *DIS, OM*

Great Movie Stunts & the Making of Raiders of the Lost Ark 1981 Two television specials: "Movie Stunts" demonstrates how major action sequences were designed and executed, and "Making of Raiders" captures the cast and crew as they tackle the many problems created in filming the spectacular scenes. 107m/C VHS, Beta, LV. Harrison Ford. *PAR*

The Great Muppet Caper 🐾🐾🐾 1981
(G) A group of hapless reporters (Kermit, Fozzie Bear, and Gonzo) travel to London to follow up on a major jewel robbery. 95m/C VHS, Beta, LV. Jim Henson's Muppets, Charles Grodin, Diana Rigg; *Cameos:* John Cleese, Robert Morley, Peter Ustinov, Peter Falk, Jack Warden; *D:* Jim Henson; *W:* Jack Rose; *C:* Oswald Morris; *V:* Frank Oz. Nominations: Academy Awards '81: Best Song ("The First Time It Happens"). *JHV, FOX*

The Great Northfield Minnesota Raid 🐾🐾½ 1972 (PG)
The Younger/James gang decides to rob the biggest bank west of the Mississippi, but everything goes wrong. Uneven, offbeat western, but Duvall's portrayal of the psychotic Jesse James and Robertson's cunning Cole Younger are notable. 91m/C VHS, Beta. Cliff Robertson, Robert Duvall, Elisha Cook Jr., Luke Askew, R.G. Armstrong, Donald Moffat, Matt Clark; *D:* Philip Kaufman; *W:* Philip Kaufman; *C:* Bruce Surtees; *M:* Dave Grusin. *USH*

The Great Outdoors 🐾🐾 1988 (PG)
Good cast is mostly wasted in another John Hughes' tale of vacation gone bad. A family's peaceful summer by the lake is disturbed by their uninvited, trouble-making relatives. Aykroyd and Candy are two funny guys done in by a lame script that awkwardly examines friendship and coming of age and throws in a giant bear when things get unbearably slow. May be fun for small fry. 91m/C VHS, Beta, LV, Closed Caption. Dan Aykroyd, John Candy, Stephanie Faracy, Annette Bening, Chris Young, Lucy Deakins; *D:* Howard Deutch; *W:* John Hughes; *M:* Thomas Newman. *USH*

The Great Race 🐾🐾½ 1965 A dastardly villain, a noble hero and a spirited suffragette are among the competitors in an uproarious New York-to-Paris auto race circa 1908, complete with pie fights, saloon brawls, and a confrontation with a feisty polar bear. Overly long and only sporadically funny. 160m/C VHS, Closed Caption. Jack Lemmon, Tony Curtis, Natalie Wood, Peter Falk, Keenan Wynn, George Macready; *D:* Blake Edwards; *M:* Henry Mancini. Academy Awards '65: Best Sound Effects Editing; Nominations: Academy Awards '65: Best Color Cinematography, Best Film Editing, Best Song ("The Sweetheart Tree"), Best Sound. *WAR, FCT*

Great Ride 🐾 1978 State police are after two dirt bikers who are riding through areas where bike riding is illegal. 90m/C VHS, Beta. Perry Lang, Michael MacRae, Michael Sullivan; *D:* Don Hulette. *NO*

The Great Riviera Bank Robbery 🐾🐾½ 1979 A genius executes a bank robbery on the French Riviera netting fifteen million dollars. Based on a true story, the film chronicles the unfolding of the heist. 98m/C VHS, Beta. Ian McShane, Warren Clarke, Stephen Greif, Christopher Malcolm; *D:* Francis Megahy. *MPI*

The Great Rupert 🐾🐾🐾 1950 Durante and family are befriended by a helpful squirrel (a puppet) in obtaining a huge fortune. Good fun; Durante shines. 86m/B VHS, Beta. Jimmy Durante, Terry Moore, Tom Drake, Frank Orth, Sara Haden, Queenie Smith; *D:* Irving Pichel. *DVT, HEG, VYY*

The Great St. Louis Bank Robbery 🐾🐾½ 1959 Three career criminals (Denton, Clarke, Dukas) and young turk McQueen are brought together for a bank heist. They don't trust each other, which proves fatal when the heist goes bad. Based on a true story and filmed in semi-documentary style. Nineteen-year-old McQueen's follow-up to "The Blob." 86m/

B VHS. Graham Denton, David Clarke, James Dukas, Steve McQueen, Molly McCarthy; *D:* Charles Guggenheim. *IVY*

The Great St. Trinian's Train Robbery 🐾🐾 1966 Train robbers hide their considerable loot in an empty country mansion only to discover, upon returning years later, it has been converted into a girls' boarding school. When they try to recover the money, the thieves run up against a band of pestiferous adolescent girls, with hilarious results. Based on the cartoon by Ronald Searle. Sequel to "The Pure Hell of St. Trinian's." 90m/C VHS, Beta. GB Dora Bryan, Frankie Howerd, Reg Varney, Desmond Walter Ellis; *D:* Sidney Gilliat, Frank Launder; *M:* Malcolm Arnold. *NO*

The Great Santini 🐾🐾🐾 Ace 1980 (PG)
Lt. Col. Bull Meechum, the "Great Santini," a Marine pilot stationed stateside, fights a war involving his frustrated career goals, repressed emotions, and family. His family becomes his company of marines, as he abuses them in the name of discipline, because he doesn't allow himself any other way to show his affection. With a standout performance by Duvall, the film successfully blends warm humor and tenderness with the harsh cruelties inherent with dysfunctional families and racism. Based on Pat Conroy's autobiographical novel, the movie was virtually undistributed when first released, but re-released due to critical acclaim. 118m/C VHS, Beta, 8mm. Robert Duvall, Blythe Danner, Michael O'Keefe, Julie Ann Haddock, Lisa Jane Persky, David Keith; *D:* Lewis John Carlino; *W:* Lewis John Carlino; *M:* Elmer Bernstein. Montreal World Film Festival '80: Best Actor (Duvall); National Board of Review Awards '80: 10 Best Films of the Year; Nominations: Academy Awards '80: Best Actor (Duvall), Best Supporting Actor (O'Keefe). *WAR*

Great Scout & Cathouse Thursday 🐾½ Wildcat 1976 (PG) Marvin and Reed vow to take revenge on their third partner, Culp, who made off with all their profits from a gold mine. The title refers to Marvin's May-December romance with prostitute Lenz. Already forgotten, unfunny, all-star comedy with cutesy title. 96m/C VHS, Beta. Lee Marvin, Oliver Reed, Robert Culp, Elizabeth Ashley, Kay Lenz; *D:* Don Taylor. *LIV, VES*

The Great Skycopter Rescue 🐾 1982 Ruthless businessmen hire a motorcycle gang to terrorize and scare away the inhabitants of an oil-rich town. A local teenage flying enthusiast organizes his friends into an attack force to fight back. 96m/C VHS, Beta. William Marshall, Aldo Ray, Russell Johnson, Terry Michos, Terry Taylor; *D:* Lawrence Foldes. *MGM*

Great Smokey Roadblock 🐾🐾 Last of the Cowboys 1976 (PG) While in the hospital, a sixty-year-old truck driver's rig is repossessed by the finance company. Deciding that it's time to make one last perfect cross country run, he escapes from the hospital, steals his truck, picks up six prostitutes, heads off into the night with the police on his tail, and becomes a folk hero. 84m/C VHS, Beta. Henry Fonda, Eileen Brennan, Susan Sarandon, John Byner; *D:* John Leone. *MED*

The Great Texas Dynamite Chase 🐾½ Dynamite Women 1976 (R) Two sexy young women drive across Texas with a carload of dynamite. They leave a trail of empty banks with the cops constantly on their trail. 90m/C VHS, Beta. Claudia Jennings, Jocelyn Jones, Johnny Crawford, Chris Pennock, Tara Strohmeier, Miles Watkins, Bart Braverman; *D:* Michael Pressman. *WAR, OM*

The Great Train Robbery 🐾🐾🐾 The First Great Train Robbery 1979 (PG) A dapper thief arranges to heist the Folkstone bullion express in 1855, the first moving train robbery. Well-designed, fast-moving costume piece based on Crichton's best-selling novel. 111m/C VHS, Beta, LV. GB Sean Connery, Donald Sutherland, Lesley-Anne Down, Alan Webb; *D:* Michael Crichton; *W:* Michael Crichton; *C:* Geoffrey Unsworth; *M:* Jerry Goldsmith. *MGM, FCT, HMV*

The Great Train Robbery: Cinema Begins 1903 Three pioneering film shorts: "Billy Whiskers," a collection of Lumiere footage from their most famous films, and the title short. 42m/B VHS, Beta, 8mm. "Broncho" Billy Anderson; *D:* Edwin S. Porter, Auguste Lumiere, Hans A. Spanuth. *VYY*

Great Treasure Hunt 🐾 197? Four Western rogues help a blind man steal a wealthy crook's gold. 90m/C VHS, Beta. Mark Damon, Stan Cooper, Luis Marin; *D:* Tonino Ricci. *TWE*

The Great Waldo Pepper 🐾🐾🐾 1975
(PG) Low key and (for Hill) less commercial film about a WWI pilot-turned-barnstormer who gets hired as a stuntman for the movies. Features spectacular vintage aircraft flying sequences. 107m/C VHS, Beta, LV. Robert Redford, Susan Sarandon, Margot Kidder, Bo Svenson, Scott Newman, Geoffrey Lewis, Edward Herrmann; *D:* George Roy Hill; *W:* William Goldman; *C:* Robert L. Surtees; *M:* Henry Mancini. *USH*

A Great Wall 🐾🐾🐾 The Great Wall Is a Great Wall 1986 (PG) A Chinese-American family travels to mainland China to discover the country of their ancestry and to visit relatives. They experience radical culture shock. Wang's first independent feature. In English and Chinese with subtitles. 103m/C VHS, Beta, LV. Peter Wang, Sharon Iwai, Kelvin Han Yee, Lin Qinqin, Hy Xiaoguang; *D:* Peter Wang; *W:* Peter Wang, Shirley Sun; *M:* David Liang, Ge Ganru. *FCT, IME, APD*

The Great Wallendas 🐾🐾 1978 The true story of the tragedies and triumphs of the Wallendas, a seven-person acrobatic family, who were noted for creating a pyramid on the high wire without nets below them. Made for television. 96m/C VHS, Beta. Lloyd Bridges, Britt Ekland, Cathy Rigby; *D:* Larry Elikann. *NO*

The Great Waltz 🐾🐾🐾 1938 The first of two musical biographies on the life of Johann Strauss sees the musician quit his banking job to pursue his dream of becoming a successful composer. A fine, overlooked production rich with wonderful music and romantic comedy. 🎵Tales of Vienna Woods; There'll Come A Time; One Day When We Were Young; Voices of Spring; Du und Du; The Bat; I'm In Love With Vienna; Revolutionary March. 102m/B VHS, LV. Luise Rainer, Fernand Gravet, Milza Korjus, Hugh Herbert, Lionel Atwill, Curt Bois, Leonid Kinskey, Al Shear, Minna Gombell, George Houston, Bert Roach, Herman Bing, Alma Kruger, Sig Rumann; *D:* Julien Duvivier; *C:* Joseph Ruttenberg. Academy Awards '38: Best Cinematography; Nominations: Academy Awards '38: Best Film Editing, Best Supporting Actress (Korjus). *MGM, FOX, FCT*

The Great War 🐾🐾 La Grande Guerre 1959 Two Italian soldiers find themselves in the midst of WWI, much against their will. They try a number of schemes to get out of fighting and working, but their circumstance dictates otherwise. Slightly muddled, but generally good acting. 118m/B VHS. FR IT Vittorio Gassman, Alberto Sordi, Silvana Mangano, Folco Lulli; *D:* Mario Monicelli; *M:* Nino Rota. Nominations: Academy Awards '59: Best Foreign Language Film. *FCT*

The Great White Hope 🐾🐾½ 1970
(PG) A semi-fictionalized biography of boxer Jack Johnson, played by Jones, who became the first black heavyweight world champion in 1910. Alexander makes her film debut as the boxer's white lover, as both battle the racism of the times. Two Oscar-nominated performances in what is essentially an "opened-out" version of the Broadway play. 103m/C VHS, Beta, Closed Caption. James Earl Jones, Jane Alexander, Lou Gilbert, Joel Fluellen, Chester Morris, Robert Webber, Hal Holbrook, R.G. Armstrong, Moses Gunn, Scatman Crothers; *D:* Martin Ritt; *C:* Burnett Guffey. Nominations: Academy Awards '70: Best Actor (Jones), Best Actress (Alexander). *FOX, FCT*

The Great White Hype 🐾🐾½ 1996 (R)
Screenwriter Shelton, who penned "Bull Durham" and "White Men Can't Jump," returns to the sports arena with this satire of the sleazy world of boxing. Jackson's the Don King-esque promoter and manager of heavyweight champ Wayans. Noticing that pay-per-view revenues are slipping,

he searches for a white boxer to generate interest and dollars and finds boxer-turned-musician Berg, who beat the champ in their Golden Glove days, and the publicity machine is cranked up for a veritable Lollapalooka. Jackson's performance as the flamboyant Rev. Fred Sultan fuels the entire movie. Concentrating on the shady wheeling and dealing, the boxing action is kept to a minimum. *CW:* Language and brief sexuality. 95m/C VHS, Closed Caption. Samuel L. Jackson, Damon Wayans, Peter Berg, Jeff Goldblum, Jon Lovitz, Corbin Bernsen, Richard "Cheech" Marin, John Rhys-Davies, Salli Richardson, Rocky Carroll, Jamie Foxx, Michael Jace; *D:* Reginald Hudlin; *W:* Ron Shelton, Tony Hendra; *C:* Ron Garcia; *M:* Marcus Miller. TCF

The Great Ziegfeld 🎞🎞🎞½ 1936

Big bio-pic of the famous showman; acclaimed in its time as the best musical biography ever done, still considered the textbook for how to make a musical. Look for cameo roles by many famous stars, as well as a walk-on role by future First Lady Pat Nixon. The movie would have stood up as a first-rate biography of Ziegfeld, even without the drop-dead wonderful songs. ♫Won't You Come Play With Me?; It's Delightful to be Married; If You Knew Susie; Shine On Harvest Moon; A Pretty Girl is Like a Melody; You Gotta Pull Strings; She's a Follies Girl; You; You Never Looked So Beautiful. 179m/B VHS, Beta, LV. William Powell, Luise Rainer, Myrna Loy, Frank Morgan, Reginald Owen, Nat Pendleton, Ray Bolger, Virginia Bruce, Harriet Hocter, Ernest Cossart, Robert Greig, Gilda Gray, Leon Errol, Dennis (Stanley Morner) Morgan, Mickey Daniels, William Demarest; *Cameos:* Fanny Brice; *D:* Robert Z. Leonard; *W:* William Anthony McGuire. Academy Awards '36: Best Actress (Rainer), Best Picture; New York Film Critics Awards '36: Best Actress (Rainer), Best Actress (Rainer); Nominations: Academy Awards '36: Best Director (Leonard), Best Film Editing, Best Interior Decoration, Best Story. MGM, BTV

The Greatest 🎞½ 1977 (PG)

Autobiography of Cassius Clay, the fighter who could float like a butterfly and sting like a bee. Ali plays himself, and George Benson's hit "The Greatest Love of All" is introduced. 100m/C VHS, Beta. Muhammad Ali, Robert Duvall, Ernest Borgnine, James Earl Jones, John Marley, Roger E. Mosley, Dina Merrill, Paul Winfield; *D:* Tom Gries; *W:* Ring Lardner Jr.; *C:* Harry Stradling Jr. COL

The Greatest Question 🎞🎞½ 1919

Gish is a girl menaced by a married couple whom she saw commit a murder years before. A rush job by Griffith to fulfill his studio obligations but Gish's performance is fine. 80m/B VHS. Lillian Gish, Robert "Bobbie" Harron, Ralph Graves, Eugenie Besserer, George Fawcett, George Nicholls Jr., Josephine Crowell, Carl Stockdale; *D:* D.W. Griffith. GPV

The Greatest Show on Earth 🎞🎞🎞 1952

DeMille is in all his epic glory here in a tale of a traveling circus wrought with glamour, romance, mysterious clowns, a tough ringmaster, and a train wreck. 149m/C VHS, Beta, LV. Betty Hutton, Cornel Wilde, James Stewart, Charlton Heston, Dorothy Lamour, Lawrence Tierney; *D:* Cecil B. DeMille. Academy Awards '52: Best Picture, Best Story; Golden Globe Awards '53: Best Director (DeMille), Best Film—Drama; Nominations: Academy Awards '52: Best Costume Design (Color), Best Director (DeMille), Best Film Editing. PAR, BTV

The Greatest Story Ever Told 🎞🎞 1965

Christ's journey from Galilee to Golgotha is portrayed here in true international-all-star-epic treatment by director Stevens. A lackluster version of Christ's life, remarkable only for Heston's out-of-control John the Baptist. 196m/C VHS, Beta, LV, Closed Caption. Max von Sydow, Charlton Heston, Sidney Poitier, Claude Rains, Jose Ferrer, Telly Savalas, Angela Lansbury, Dorothy McGuire, John Wayne, Donald Pleasence, Carroll Baker, Van Heflin, Robert Loggia, Shelley Winters, Ed Wynn, Roddy McDowall; *D:* George Stevens; *C:* William Mellor, Loyal Griggs. National Board of Review Awards '65: 10 Best Films of the Year; Nominations: Academy Awards '65: Best Art Direction/Set Decoration (Color), Best Color Cinematography, Best Costume Design (Color), Best Original Score. MGM, RDG, TVC

Greed 🎞🎞🎞🎞 1924

A wife's obsession with money drives her husband to murder. Although the original version's length (eight hours) was trimmed to 140 minutes, it remains one of the greatest and most highly acclaimed silent films ever made. Effective use of Death Valley locations. Adapted from the Frank Norris novel, "McTeague." 140m/B VHS, LV. Dale Fuller, Gibson Gowland, ZaSu Pitts, Jean Hersholt, Chester Conklin; *D:* Erich von Stroheim. MGM

The Greed of William Hart 🎞🎞 1948

Horror Maniacs Reworking of the Burke and Hare legend has grave robbers providing Edinburgh medical students with the requisite cadavers. 78m/B VHS. GB Tod Slaughter, Henry Oscar, Jenny Lynn, Winifred Melville; *D:* Oswald Mitchell. SNC

Greedy 🎞½ 1994 (PG-13)

Money-grubbing family suck up to elderly millionaire uncle (Douglas) when they fear he'll leave his money to the sexy, young former pizza delivery girl (d'Abo) he's hired as his nurse. Fox is the long-lost nephew who comes to the rescue. Wicked comedy from veterans Ganz and Mandel should zing, but instead falls flat thanks to a descent into the maudlin. Fox bares his backside and Douglas has fun as the mean old miser, but check out Hartman, a riot as a snarky relative. *CW:* Profanity, very brief nudity, and sexual suggestiveness. 109m/C VHS, LV, Closed Caption. Kirk Douglas, Michael J. Fox, Olivia D'Abo, Phil Hartman, Nancy Travis, Ed Begley Jr., Bob Balaban, Colleen Camp, Jere Burns, Khandi Alexander; *Cameos:* Jonathan Lynn; *D:* Jonathan Lynn; *W:* Lowell Ganz, Babaloo Mandel; *M:* Randy Edelman. USH

Greedy Terror 🎞 1978

A cross-country motorcycle trip becomes a real nightmare when two young men realize they're being stalked by a maniac with a thirst for blood. 90m/C VHS, Beta. Michael MacRae, Perry Lang. NO

Greek Street 🎞🎞 Latin Love 1930

The owner of small cafe in London discovers a poor girl singing in the street for food. He takes her in and spotlights her songs in his cafe. 51m/B VHS, Beta. GB Sari Maritza, Arthur Ahmbling, Martin Lewis; *D:* Sinclair Hill. VYY, DVT, HEG

The Greek Tycoon 🎞½ 1978 (R)

Old familiar story about widow of an American president who marries a billionaire shipping magnate and finds that money cannot buy happiness. A transparent depiction of the Onassis/Kennedy marriage, done to a turn. 106m/C VHS, Beta. Anthony Quinn, Jacqueline Bisset, James Franciscus, Raf Vallone, Edward Albert; *D:* J. Lee Thompson. USH

Green Archer 1940

Fifteen episodes of the famed serial, featuring a spooked castle complete with secret passages and tunnels, trapdoors, and the mysterious masked figure, the Green Archer. 283m/B VHS, Beta. Victor Jory, Iris Meredith, James Craven, Robert Fiske; *D:* James W. Horne. VYY, NOS, VCN

The Green Berets woof! 1968 (G)

Cliched wartime heroics co-directed by Wayne and based on Robin Moore's novel. The Duke stars as a Special Forces colonel, leading his troops against the Viet Cong. Painfully insipid pro-war propaganda, notable as the only American film to come out in support of U.S. involvement in Vietnam. Truly embarrassing but did spawn the hit single "Ballad of the Green Beret" by Barry Sadler. 135m/C VHS, Beta, LV, Closed Caption. John Wayne, David Janssen, Jim Hutton, Aldo Ray, George Takei, Raymond St. Jacques; *D:* John Wayne; *C:* Winton C. Hoch; *M:* Miklos Rozsa. WAR, TLF

Green Card 🎞🎞½ 1990 (PG-13)

Some marry for love, some for money, others for an apartment in the Big Apple. Refined, single MacDowell covets a rent-controlled apartment in Manhattan, but the lease stipulates that the apartment be let to a married couple. Enter brusque and burly Depardieu, who covets the elusive green card. The counterpoint between MacDowell, as a stuffy horticulturist, and Depardieu, as a French composer works well, and the two adroitly play a couple whose relationship covers the romantic contin-

uum. Director Weir wrote the screenplay with Depardieu in mind. Depardieu's English-language debut. 108m/C VHS, Beta, LV, Closed Caption. Gerard Depardieu, Andie MacDowell, Bebe Neuwirth, Gregg Edelman, Robert Prosky, Jessie Keosian, Ann Wedgeworth, Ethan Phillips, Mary Louise Wilson, Lois Smith, Simon Jones; *D:* Peter Weir; *W:* Peter Weir; *M:* Hans Zimmer. Golden Globe Awards '91: Best Actor—Musical/Comedy (Depardieu), Best Film—Musical/Comedy; Nominations: Academy Awards '90: Best Original Screenplay; Golden Globe Awards '91: Best Actress—Musical/Comedy (MacDowell). TOU

Green Dolphin Street 🎞🎞½ 1947

Flimsy romantic epic set in 19th century New Zealand. A young girl marries the beau she and her sister are battling over in this Oscar-winning special effects show which features one big earthquake. Based on the Elizabeth Goudge novel, this was one of MGM's biggest hits in 1947. 161m/B VHS, Beta. Lana Turner, Van Heflin, Donna Reed, Edmund Gwenn; *D:* Victor Saville. Academy Awards '47: Best Special Effects; Nominations: Academy Awards '47: Best Black and White Cinematography, Best Film Editing, Best Sound. MGM

Green Dragon Inn 🎞 1982

When trying to escort an accused murderer to trial, a Ming court emissary finds himself battling against Kung Fu masters. 94m/C VHS, Beta. Yue Hwa, Lo Lei, Shangkuan Ling-Feng. WVE

Green Eyes 🎞½ 1934

A costume party in a country mansion sets the scene for a routine murder mystery when the guests find their host stabbed to death in a closet. Based on the novel "The Murder of Stephen Kester" by H. Ashbrook. 68m/B VHS. Shirley Grey, Charles Starrett, Claude Gillingwater, John Wray, Dorothy Revier; *D:* Richard Thorpe; *W:* Melville Shyer. SNC

Green Eyes 🎞🎞🎞½ 1976

Winfield, an ex-GI, returns to postwar Vietnam to search for his illegitimate son who he believes will have green eyes. A highly acclaimed, made-for-television drama featuring moving performances from Winfield and Jonathan Lippe. 100m/C VHS, Beta. Paul Winfield, Rita Tushingham, Jonathon Lippe, Victoria Racimo, Royce Wallace, Claudia Bryar; *D:* John Erman. LIV

Green Fields 🎞🎞½ Grine Felder; Gruner Felder 1937

A quiet romance based on Peretz Hirschbein's legendary tale of a young scholar of the Talmud who leaves the shelter of the synagogue in order to learn about people in the real world. The search takes him to the countryside where he finds himself in the middle of a battle between two families who both want him as a tutor and a suitor for their daughters. In Yiddish with English subtitles. 95m/B VHS, Beta. Michael Goldstein, Herschel Bernardi, Helen Beverly; *D:* Jacob Ben-Ami. ERG, NCJ

Green Fire 🎞🎞½ 1955

The screen sizzles when emerald miner Granger meets plantation-owner Kelly in the exotic jungles of South America. Usual plot complications muddle the story, but who cares when the stars are this attractive? 100m/C VHS, Beta. Stewart Granger, Grace Kelly, Paul Douglas, John Ericson, Murvyn Vye, Jose Torvay, Robert Tafur, Nacho Galindo; *D:* Andrew Marton; *W:* Ivan Goff, Ben Roberts; *M:* Miklos Rozsa. MGM

Green for Danger 🎞🎞 1947

A detective stages a chilling mock operation to find a mad killer stalking the corridors of a British hospital during WWII. Sim's first great claim to fame (pre-"A Christmas Carol"). 91m/B VHS, Beta, LV. GB Trevor Howard, Alastair Sim, Leo Genn; *D:* Sidney Gilliat. HMV, RXM

The Green Glove 🎞🎞½ 1952

A jewel thief steals a beautiful relic from a tiny church. WWII makes it impossible for him to fence it and the church finds a relentless ally to track the thief. Excellent action sequences lift this standard plot slightly above the ordinary. 88m/B VHS. Glenn Ford, Geraldine Brooks, Cedric Hardwicke, George Macready, Gaby Andre, Roger Treville, Juliette Greco, Jean Bretonniere; *D:* Rudolph Mate; *W:* Charles Bennett. NOS, FCT, HEG

Green Grow the Rushes 🎬🎬 *Brandy Ashore* 1951 The English government tries to put a stop to brandy smuggling on the coast, but the townspeople drink up the evidence. A young Burton highlights this watered-down comedy. Based on a novel by co-scripter Harold Clewes. **77m/B VHS.** GB Roger Livesey, Honor Blackman, Richard Burton, Frederick Leister; **D:** Derek Twist. *HMV, NOS, VYY*

Green Horizon 🎬½ *Afurika Monogatari; A Tale of Africa* 1983 A bucolic old codger faces a dilemma when he must choose between his granddaughter's future and his disaster-prone natural environment. **80m/C VHS, Beta.** James Stewart, Philip Sayer, Elenora Vallone. *FHE*

The Green Hornet 1939 The feature version of the original serial, in which the Green Hornet and Kato have a series of crime-fighting adventures. **100m/B VHS, Beta.** Gordon Jones, Keye Luke, Anne Nagel, Wade Boteler, Walter McGrail, Douglas Evans, Cy Kendall. *NOS, GKK, MLB*

The Green House 🎬🎬 *The Greenhouse; Le Jardin des Plantes* 1996 Fernand Bonard (Rich) is the aged caretaker of the Paris zoo's botanical gardens during the waning days of WWII. His son Armand (Labarthe) is a collaborator who arrives at his father's home with 8-year-old daughter, Philippine (Stevenin), to celebrate her birthday. When Armand is suddenly killed by the Gestapo, Fernand begins an elaborate deception for his granddaughter, portraying her father as a hero of the French Resistance but his illusions take an unexpected turn. French with subtitles. **93m/C VHS.** FR Claude Rich, Salomee Stevenin, Samuel Labarthe, Catherine Jacob, Rose Thiery; **D:** Philippe de Broca; **W:** Philippe de Broca, Alexandre Jardin; **C:** Janos Kende; **M:** Charles Court. *FRF*

Green Ice 🎬½ 1981 An American electronics expert gets involved with a brutal South American government dealing with emeralds and plans a heist with his girlfriend and other cohorts. A little bit of romance, a little bit of action, a lot of nothing much. **109m/C VHS, Beta, LV, Closed Caption.** GB Ryan O'Neal, Anne Archer, Omar Sharif, John Larroquette; **D:** Ernest Day; **W:** Edward Anhalt, Robert De Laurentis. *NO*

Green Inferno 🎬 198? A wealthy eccentric who lives deep in the South American jungle incites the natives to rebel. Mercenary agents are then hired to kill him. **90m/C VHS, Beta.** Richard Yesteran, Didi Sherman, Caesar Burner. *NO*

The Green Man 🎬🎬🎬 1991 Maurice Allington (Finney), the alcoholic and randy owner of the Green Man Inn in rural England, jokes about the spirits that supposedly haunt the inn. It's not too funny, however, when he discovers the spirits are real and he has to figure out who the spirit of a 17th-century murderer is inhabiting before he kills again. A classy ghost story based on the novel by Kingsley Amis. **150m/C VHS.** GB Albert Finney, Sarah Berger, Linda Marlowe, Michael Hordern, Nickolas Grace, Michael Culver; **D:** Elijah Moshinsky; **W:** Malcolm Bradbury. *AAE, BTV, BST*

Green Mansions 🎬🎬 1959 Screen adaptation of W. H. Hudson's novel suffers due to miscasting of Hepburn as Rima the Bird Girl, who is not permitted to leave her sanctuary. Perkins is good as the male lead who fled to the jungle in search of wealth and instead finds a powerful love. Hepburn was married to director Ferrer at the time. **104m/C VHS.** Audrey Hepburn, Anthony Perkins, Lee J. Cobb, Sessue Hayakawa, Henry Silva, Nehemiah Persoff, Michael Pate; **D:** Mel Ferrer; **W:** Dorothy Kingsley; **C:** Joseph Ruttenberg. *MGM*

Green Pastures 🎬🎬🎬 1936 An adaptation of Marc Connelly's 1930 Pulitzer Prize-winning play which attempts to retell Biblical stories in Black English Vernacular of the '30s. Southern theater owners boycotted the controversial film which had an all-Black cast. **93m/C VHS, Beta.** Rex Ingram, Oscar Polk, Eddie Anderson, George Reed, Abraham Graves, Myrtle Anderson, Frank Wilson; **D:** William Keighley, Marc Connelly; **C:** Hal Mohr. National Board of Review Awards '36: 10 Best Films of the Year. *MGM, MOV, FOX*

The Green Promise 🎬🎬 *Raging Waters* 1949 A well-meaning but domineering farmer and his four motherless children face disaster as a result of the father's obstinacy. But when he is laid up, the eldest daughter takes over, tries modern methods and equipment, and makes the farm a success. **90m/B VHS, Beta.** Walter Brennan, Marguerite Chapman, Robert Paige, Natalie Wood; **D:** William D. Russell. *NOS, DVT, HEG*

The Green Room 🎬🎬 *La Chambre Verte* 1978 (PG) Truffaut's haunting tale of a man who, valuing death over life, erects a shrine to all the dead he has known. Offered a chance at love, he cannot overcome his obsessions to take the risk. Based on the Henry James story "Altar of the Dead." In French with subtitles. **95m/C VHS, Beta.** FR Francois Truffaut, Nathalie Baye, Jean Daste; **D:** Francois Truffaut; **C:** Nestor Almendros. *MGM*

The Green Slime woof! *Gamma Sango Uchu Daisakusen; Battle Beyond the Stars; Death and the Green Slime* 1968 (G) Danger and romance highlight the journey of a space ship assigned to intercept an oncoming asteroid. Little do the astronauts realize, but they have brought aboard the ship the malevolent alien creatures known as green slime (and we ain't talking jello here). Cheap, U.S./Japanese co-production will leave you feeling lousy in the morning. The title song is legendary among genre aficionados. **90m/C VHS, Beta.** JP Robert Horton, Richard Jaeckel, Luciana Paluzzi, Bud Widom, Ted Gunther, Robert Dunham; **D:** Kinji Fukasaku. *MGM*

Green Snake 🎬🎬 1993 Combo of mysticism and action based on a Chinese fable. Green Snake (Cheung) and Son Ching (Wong) are actual reptiles who have been practicing taking human form. When self-righteous Buddhist monk Fa-Hai discovers them, he thinks it's a sin to tamper with the natural order. The snakes don't appreciate his lack of compassion and plot destruction. Cantonese with subtitles. **102m/C VHS.** HK Maggie Cheung, Joey Wong; **D:** Tsui Hark. *FCT*

The Green Wall 🎬🎬🎬 1970 A city-dwelling young man attempts to homestead with his family in the Amazon. A lovely and tragic film with stunning photography of the Peruvian forests. First Peruvian feature to be shown in the U.S. In Spanish with English subtitles. **110m/C VHS.** SP Julio Aleman, Sandra Riva; **D:** Armando Robles Godoy; **W:** Armando Robles Godoy. *FCT, DVT, HEG*

Greenstone 🎬🎬 1985 (G) The green stone is a glowing rock in the forbidden forest that conveys a young boy into an exciting new world. **48m/C VHS, Beta.** Joseph Corey, John Riley, Kathleen Irvine, Jack Mauck; **D:** Kevin Irvine. *AHV*

Greetings 🎬🎬🎬 1968 (R) De Niro stars in this wild and crazy comedy about a man who tries to help his friend flunk his draft physical. One of DePalma's first films, and a pleasantly anarchic view of the late '60s, wrought with a light, intelligent tone. Followed by the sequel "Hi, Mom." **88m/C VHS, Beta, LV.** Robert De Niro, Gerrit Graham, Allen (Goorwitz) Garfield; **D:** Brian DePalma; **W:** Brian DePalma. *THV*

Gregory's Girl 🎬🎬🎬½ 1980 Sweet, disarming comedy established Forsyth. An awkward young Scottish schoolboy falls in love with the female goalie of his soccer team. He turns to his 10-year-old sister for advice, but she's more interested in ice cream than love. His best friend is no help, either, since he has yet to fall in love. Perfect mirror of teenagers and their instantaneous, raw, and all-consuming loves. Very sweet scene with Gregory and his girl lying on their backs in an open space illustrates the simultaneous simplicity and complexity of young love. **91m/C VHS, Beta.** GB Gordon John Sinclair, Dee Hepburn, Jake D'Arcy, Chic Murray, Alex Norton, John Bett, Clare Grogan; **D:** Bill Forsyth; **W:** Bill Forsyth; **C:** Michael Coulter. British Academy Awards '81: Best Screenplay. *TVC*

Gremlins 🎬🎬🎬 1984 (PG) Comedy horror with deft satiric edge. Produced by Spielberg. Fumbling gadget salesman Rand Peltzer is looking for something really special to get his son Billy. He finds it in a small store in Chinatown. The wise shopkeeper is reluctant to sell him the adorable "mogwai" but relents after fully warning him "Don't expose him to bright light, don't ever get him wet, and don't ever, ever feed him after midnight." Naturally, this all happens and the result is a gang of nasty gremlins who decide to tear up the town on Christmas Eve. Followed by "Gremlins 2, the New Batch" which is less black comedy, more parody, and perhaps more inventive. **106m/C VHS, Beta, LV, 8mm, Closed Caption.** Zach Galligan, Phoebe Cates, Hoyt Axton, Polly Holliday, Frances Lee McCain, Keye Luke, Dick Miller, Corey Feldman, Judge Reinhold; **D:** Joe Dante; **W:** Chris Columbus; **M:** Jerry Goldsmith. *WAR, TLF*

Gremlins 2: The New Batch 🎬🎬🎬½ 1990 (PG-13) The sequel to "Gremlins" is superior to the original, which was quite good. Set in a futuristic skyscraper in the Big Apple, director Dante presents a less violent but far more campy vision, paying myriad surreal tributes to scores of movies, including "The Wizard of Oz" and musical extravaganzas of the past. Also incorporates a Donald Trump parody, takes on television news, and body slams modern urban living. Great fun. **107m/C VHS, Beta, LV, 8mm, Closed Caption.** Phoebe Cates, Christopher Lee, John Glover, Zach Galligan; **Cameos:** Jerry Goldsmith; **D:** Joe Dante; **M:** Jerry Goldsmith. *WAR, HHE*

Grendel, Grendel, Grendel 🎬🎬 1982 An utterly urbane dragon wants to be friends, but for some reason people are just terrified of Grendel. It's true, he bites a head off once in a while, but nobody's perfect! An ingenious, animated retelling of Beowulf. **90m/C VHS, Beta.** AU D: Alexander Stitt; **M:** Bruce Smeaton; **V:** Peter Ustinov, Arthur Dignam, Julie McKenna, Keith Michell. *FHE*

Greta 🎬🎬🎬 1986 During WWII, a young Polish boy escapes from a detention camp. Now on the run, several bizarre twists of fate place him in the care of Greta, a young girl whose father is an officer in the S.S. In Polish with English subtitles. **60m/C VHS, Beta.** PL Janusz Grabowski, Agnieszka Kruszewska, Eva Borowik, Tomasz Grochoczki, Andrzej Precig; **D:** Krzysztof Gruber. *EVD*

The Grey Fox 🎬🎬🎬½ 1983 (PG) A gentlemanly old stagecoach robber tries to pick up his life after thirty years in prison. Unable to resist another heist, he tries train robbery, and winds up hiding out in British Columbia where he meets an attractive photographer, come to document the changing West. Farnsworth is perfect as the man who suddenly finds himself in the 20th century trying to work at the only craft he knows. Based on the true story of Canada's most colorful and celebrated outlaw, Bill Miner. **92m/C VHS, Beta, LV.** CA Richard Farnsworth, Jackie Burroughs, Wayne Robson, Timothy Webber, Ken Pogue; **D:** Phillip Borsos; **M:** Michael Conway Baker. Genie Awards '83: Best Director (Borsos), Best Film, Best Supporting Actress (Burroughs). *MED*

Greyfriars Bobby 🎬🎬½ 1961 A true story of a Skye terrier named Bobby who, after his master dies, refuses to leave the grave. Even after being coaxed by the local children into town, he still returns to the cemetery each evening. Word of his loyalty spreads, and Bobby becomes the pet of 19th century Edinburgh. Nicely told, with fine location photography and good acting. Great for children and animal lovers. **91m/C VHS.** Donald Crisp, Laurence Naismith, Kay Walsh; **D:** Don Chaffey. *DIS*

Greystoke: The Legend of Tarzan, Lord of the Apes 🎬🎬 1984 (PG) The seventh Earl of Greystoke becomes a shipwrecked orphan and is raised by apes. Ruling the ape-clan in the vine-swinging persona of Tarzan, he is discovered by an anthropologist and returned to his ancestral home in Scotland, where he is immediately recognized by his grandfather. The contrast between the behavior of man and ape is interesting, and Tarzan's introduction to society is fun, but there's no melodrama or cliff-hanging action, as we've come to expect of the Tarzan genre. Due to her heavy southern accent, Andie MacDowell (as Jane) had her voice dubbed by Glenn Close. **130m/C VHS, Beta, LV, Closed Caption.** Christopher Lambert, Ralph Richardson, Ian Holm, James Fox, Andie MacDowell, Ian Charleson, Cheryl Campbell, Nigel Davenport; **D:** Hugh Hudson; **W:** Michael Austin. New York Film Critics Awards '84: Best Supporting Actor (Richardson); Nominations: Academy Awards '84: Best Adapted Screenplay, Best Makeup, Best Supporting Actor (Richardson). *WAR*

Gridlock'd 🐾🐾🐾 1996 (R) Junkies and sometime-musicians Spoon (Shakur) and Stretch (Roth) decide to kick the habit after their singer Cookie (Newton) overdoses and slips into a coma. The hapless pair are thrown into the switches of social services programs and government offices where they shuffle endlessly but nothing happens. Think "Waiting for Godot" meets "Waiting for the Man." Meanwhile, their dealer is murdered and they're the prime suspects, pursued by the cops and the actual killers, who believe that they've stolen said dealer's stash. Shakur shows flashes of the brilliance that might have been as the more sensitive and sane of the pair, while Roth complements him perfectly as his bug-crazy short-sighted partner. Fellow actor Curtis-Hall's directorial debut. **CW:** Graphic drug use, pervasive strong language, some violence and brief nudity. **91m/C VHS, LV, Closed Caption.** Tim Roth, Tupac Shakur, Thandie Newton, Charles Fleischer, Howard Hesseman, James Pickens Jr., John Sayles, Tom Wright, Eric Payne, Tom Towles; **Cameos:** Vondie Curtis-Hall; **D:** Vondie Curtis-Hall; **W:** Vondie Curtis-Hall; **C:** Bill Pope; **M:** Stewart Copeland. *PGV*

Grief 🐾🐾 1994 Mark (Chester) is a writer on the syndicated daytime TV show "The Love Judge." Still numb from his lover's death from AIDS the previous year, Mark begins to take an interest in fellow writer Bill (Arquette), while writer Paula (Gutteridge) desires to become the show's new producer and secretary Leslie (Douglas) wants to take her place as the new writer. Present producer Jo (Beat) tries to keep her office family in line while sorting out her personal life. Writer-director Glatzer knows his territory since he spent five years writing for "Divorce Court." **86m/C VHS.** Craig Chester, Alexis Arquette, Lucy Gutteridge, Illeana Douglas, Jackie Beat, Carlton Wilborn; **D:** Richard Glatzer; **W:** Richard Glatzer. *ACA, SHV*

Grievous Bodily Harm 🐾🐾 1989 (R) Morris Martin's wife Claudine is missing. When he finds a videotape of Claudine in very compromising positions, he becomes murderously determined to find out where she has gone. **136m/C VHS, Beta.** John Waters, Colin Friels, Bruno Lawrence; **D:** Mark Joffe. *FRH*

Griffin and Phoenix: A Love Story 🐾🐾½ 1976 A sentimental film about the mortality of two vital people. Falk deserts his family when he learns he has terminal cancer. Clayburgh, also terminally ill, meets him for a short but meaningful affair. Good performances help overcome the tear-jerker aspects of the story. Made for television. **110m/C VHS.** Peter Falk, Jill Clayburgh, Dorothy Tristan, John Lehne; **D:** Daryl Duke. *FOX*

Griffith Biograph Program 1909 Some of the best Biograph shorts are featured: "The Lonely Villa," "The Lonedale Operator," "The New York Hat," "Friends," and "The Unseen Enemy," all produced between 1909 and 1912. **50m/B VHS, Beta, LV.** Mary Pickford, Blanche Sweet, Lillian Gish, Dorothy Gish; **D:** D.W. Griffith. *GVV*

The Grifters 🐾🐾🐾½ 1990 (R) Evocative rendering of a terrifying sub-culture. Huston, Cusak, and Bening are con artists, struggling to stay on top in a world where violence, money, and lust are the prizes. Bening and Huston fight for Cu-

sak's soul, while he's determined to decide for himself. Seamless performances and dazzling atmosphere, along with superb pacing, make for a provocative film. Based on a novel by Jim Thompson. **114m/C VHS, Beta, LV, Closed Caption.** Anjelica Huston, John Cusack, Annette Bening, Pat Hingle, J.T. Walsh, Charles Napier, Henry Jones, Gailard Sartain, Jeremy Piven; **D:** Stephen Frears; **W:** Donald E. Westlake; **M:** Elmer Bernstein. Independent Spirit Awards '91: Best Actress (Huston), Best Film; Los Angeles Film Critics Association Awards '90: Best Actress (Huston); National Society of Film Critics Awards '90: Best Actress (Huston), Best Supporting Actress (Bening); Nominations: Academy Awards '90: Best Actress (Huston), Best Adapted Screenplay, Best Director (Frears), Best Supporting Actress (Bening). *USH, HBO, FCT*

Grim 🐾 1995 (R) Lives up to its title as an extremely icky and evil subterranean creature is awakened from a long sleep by miners. Apparently not long enough, since he proceeds to rip apart anyone he comes in contact with. **CW:** Horror violence and gore, and for language. **86m/C VHS, LV.** Emmanuel Xuereb, Tres Handley, Peter Tregloan; **D:** Paul Matthews. *APX*

Grim Prairie Tales 🐾🐾 1989 (R) A city slicker and a crazed mountain man meet by a campfire in the high plains one night and pass the time sharing four tales of Western horror. Dourif and Jones are fun, the stories scary, making for an interesting twist on both the horror and the Western genres. **90m/C VHS, LV.** Brad Dourif, James Earl Jones, Marc McClure, William Atherton, Scott Paulin, Lisa Eichhorn; **D:** Wayne Coe; **W:** Wayne Coe; **C:** Janusz Kaminski. *ACA, FCT*

The Grim Reaper 🐾🐾🐾 *La Commare Secca* 1962 22-year-old Bertolucci directed his first feature with this grim and brutal treatment of the investigation of the murder of a prostitute, told via flashbacks and from the disparate perspectives of three people who knew the woman. A commercial bust, the critics were no kinder than the public at the time; not until two years later, with "Before the Revolution," did Bertolucci earn his directorial spurs. The script was written by Pasolini, with whom the erstwhile poet had collaborated on "Accattone" the previous year (as assistant). In Italian with English subtitles. **100m/B VHS, LV.** *IT* Francesco Rulu, Giancarlo de Rosa; **D:** Bernardo Bertolucci; **W:** Pier Paolo Pasolini. *CVC, FCT*

Grim Reaper 🐾½ 1981 (R) Mia Farrow's sister is one of a group of American students vacationing on a Greek island. Farrow learns of the twisted cannibalistic murderer who methodically tries to avenge the tragic deaths of his family. **81m/C VHS, Beta.** *IT* Tisa Farrow, George Eastman; **D:** Joe D'Amato. *NO*

Grisbi 🐾🐾 *Hands Off the Loot; Honour Among Thieves; Touchez Pas Au Grisbi* 1953 King of the French underworld, Gabin finds there's no honor among thieves when a gold heist goes wrong and the loot comes up missing. Moreau is the quintessential moll. Dubbed. **94m/C VHS.** *FR* Jean Gabin, Jeanne Moreau, Lino Ventura, Daniel Cauchy, Gaby Basset; **D:** Jacques Becker; **W:** Jacques Becker, Maurice Griffe; **M:** Jean Wiener. Venice Film Festival '54: Best Actor (Gabin). *FCT*

The Grissom Gang 🐾🐾🐾 1971 (R) Remake of the 1948 British film "No Orchids for Miss Blandish." Darby is a wealthy heiress kidnapped by a family of grotesques, led by a sadistic mother. The ransom gets lost in a series of bizarre events, and the heiress appears to be falling for one of her moronic captors. Director Robert Aldrich skillfully blends extreme violence with dark humor. Superb camera work, editing, and 1920s period sets. **127m/C VHS.** Kim Darby, Scott Wilson, Tony Musante, Ralph Waite, Connie Stevens, Robert Lansing, Wesley Addy; **D:** Robert Aldrich; **C:** Joseph Biroc. *FOX*

Grit of the Girl Telegrapher/In the Switch Tower 1915 A pair of silent railroad dramas, which feature thrilling chase sequences, nefarious schemers and virginal heroines. Silent with piano scores. **47m/B VHS, Beta.** Anna Q. Nilsson,

Hal Clements, Walter Edwards, Frank Borzage; **M:** Jon Mirsalis. *CCB, PEN, GVV*

Grizzly 🐾 *Killer Grizzly* 1976 (PG) Giant, killer grizzly terrorizes a state park in this blatant "Jaws" rip-off. From the same folks who produced "Abby," a blatant "Exorcist" rip-off. Filmed in Georgia. **92m/C VHS, Beta.** Christopher George, Richard Jaeckel, Andrew Prine, Victoria (Vicki) Johnson, Charles Kissinger; **D:** William Girdler. *MED*

Grizzly Adams: The Legend Continues 🐾½ 1990 A small town is saved from three desperados by Grizzly and his huge grizzly bear pet, Martha. **90m/C VHS.** Gene Edwards, Link Wyler, Red West, Tony Caruso, Acquanetta, L.Q. Jones; **D:** Ken Kennedy. *NO*

The Groove Tube 🐾🐾½ 1972 (R) A television series called "The Groove Tube" is the context for these skits that spoof everything on television from commercials to newscasts. Chevy Chase's movie debut. **75m/C VHS, Beta.** Lane Sarasohn, Chevy Chase, Richard Belzer, Marcy Mendham, Bill Kemmill; **D:** Ken Shapiro. *MED*

Gross Anatomy 🐾🐾½ 1989 (PG-13) Lightweight comedy/drama centers on the trials and tribulations of medical students. Modine is the very bright, but somewhat lazy, future doctor determined not to buy into the bitter competition among his fellow students. His lack of desire inflames Lahti, a professor dying of a fatal disease who nevertheless believes in modern medicine. She pushes and inspires him to focus on his potential, and his desire to help people. Interesting cast of up-and-comers. **107m/C VHS, Beta, LV, Closed Caption.** Matthew Modine, Daphne Zuniga, Christine Lahti, John Scott Clough, Alice Carter, Robert Desiderio, Zakes Mokae, Todd Field; **D:** Thom Eberhardt; **W:** Ron Nyswaner; **M:** David Newman. *TOU*

Gross Misconduct 🐾🐾 1993 (R) Charismatic university professor Justin Thorne (Smits) makes the nearly fatal mistake of getting involved with his student, Jennifer (Watts). Seems she's one of those obsessive types and when Thorne wants to break off the affair for the sake of his marriage, Jennifer goes over the edge. Thorne's charged with rape and unless Jennifer changes her story his life is over. Based on a true story that happened in the '50s but this version is set in the '90s. **CW:** Strong sexuality, a violent episode, and some language. **97m/C VHS, Closed Caption.** *AU* Jimmy Smits, Naomi Watts, Sarah Chadwick, Adrian Wright, Alan Fletcher; **D:** George Miller; **W:** Lance Peters, Gerard Maguire; **C:** David Connell. *AEE*

Grosse Fatigue 🐾🐾🐾 *Dead Tired* 1994 (R) Diminutive comic everyman Blanc successfully takes up the challenge of a dual role of mistaken identity (as well as directing and writing chores). He first plays himself, bewildered by accusations of lechery and other escapades, who learns he has a psychopath double who's stolen his celebrity. So it's up to Michel and pal Carole (the gorgeous Bouquet) to track down the mischief-maker before Blanc's reputation is in complete tatters. French with subtitles. **CW:** Language, nudity. **85m/C VHS, LV.** *FR* Michel Blanc, Carole Bouquet, Philippe Noiret, Josiane Balasko; **Cameos:** Charlotte Gainsbourg, Mathilda May, Thierry Lhermitte, Roman Polanski; **D:** Michel Blanc; **W:** Michel Blanc; **C:** Eduardo Serra; **M:** Rene Marc Bini. *TOU*

Grosse Pointe Blank 🐾🐾🐾 1997 (R) Stressed-out Martin Q. Blank (Cusack) debates with his nervous shrink (Arkin) about whether to attend his 10-year high school reunion. He doesn't want to deal with the Debi (Driver), the girl he ditched on prom night, the incessant small talk, or the prospect of telling his classmates that he's a professional hit man. Then there's the matter of rival pro Grocer (Aykroyd), who wants to start an assassins union. Dark comedy with excellent writing, a charmingly off-center lead by Cusack, who attended his own reunion as research, and a surprising amount of action. Pasadena fills in for most of Grosse Pointe, but the Detroit shots are real.*CW:* Strong violence, language and some drug content. **107m/C VHS.** John Cusack, Minnie Driver, Dan Aykroyd, Alan Arkin, Joan Cusack, Jeremy Piven, Mitchell Ryan, Hank Azaria, Michael Cudlitz, Benny "The Jet" Urquidez, Barbara Harris, Ann Cusack; *D:* George Armitage; *W:* Tom Jankiewicz, D.V. DeVincentis, Steve Pink, John Cusack; *C:* Jamie Anderson; *M:* Joe Strummer. *NYR*

Grotesque woof! **1987 (R)** After slaughtering a young woman's family as they vacationed in a remote mountain cabin, a gang of bloodthirsty punks are attacked by the family secret, the deformed son. The title says it all. **79m/C VHS, Beta, LV.** Linda Blair, Tab Hunter, Guy Stockwell, Donna Wilkes, Nels Van Patten; *D:* Joe Tornatore. *MED*

Ground Zero *&&&* **1988 (R)** Political thriller, set in the Australian outback in the fifties, in which a man searches for the reasons for his father's murder in the films of the British nuclear tests. **109m/C VHS, Beta, LV.** *AU* Colin Friels, Jack Thompson, Donald Pleasence, Natalie Bate, Simon Chilvers, Neil Fitzpatrick, Bob Maza, Peter Cummins; *D:* Bruce Myles, Michael Pattinson. *LIV*

Ground Zero *&&½* **1988 (R)** Ground Zero is the term used to describe the site of a nuclear explosion. San Francisco is threatened with just such a name in this story of nuclear blackmail. Someone plants an atomic bomb on the Golden Gate Bridge. It must be defused and the culprit caught. **90m/C VHS, Beta.** Ron Casteel, Melvin Belli, Yvonne D'Angiers; *D:* James T. Flocker. *GHV, VTR*

Groundhog Day *&&&* **1993 (PG)** Phil (Murray), an obnoxious weatherman, is in Punxatawney, PA to cover the annual emergence of the famous rodent from its hole. After he's caught in a blizzard that he didn't predict, he finds himself trapped in a time warp, doomed to relive the same day over and over again until he gets it right. Lighthearted romantic comedy takes a funny premise and manages to carry it through to the end. Murray has fun with the role, although he did get bitten by the groundhog during the scene when they're driving. Elliott, who has been missed since his days as the man under the seats on "Late Night with David Letterman" is perfectly cast as a smart-mouthed cameraman. **103m/C VHS, LV, Closed Caption.** Bill Murray, Andie MacDowell, Chris Elliott, Stephen Tobolowsky, Brian Doyle-Murray, Marita Geraghty, Angela Paton; *D:* Harold Ramis; *W:* Harold Ramis, Daniel F. Rubin; *C:* John Bailey; *M:* George Fenton. British Academy Awards '93: Best Original Screenplay. *COL, FCT, BTV*

The Groundstar Conspiracy *&&&* **1972 (PG)** Spy thriller brings to life L.P. Davies' novel, "The Alien." After an explosion kills all but one space project scientist, Peppard is sent to investigate suspicions of a cover-up. Meanwhile, the surviving scientist (Sarrazin) suffers from disfigurement and amnesia. He pursues his identity while Peppard accuses him of being a spy. Splendid direction by Lamont Johnson. Sarrazin's best role. **96m/C VHS.** *CA* George Peppard, Michael Sarrazin, Christine Belford, Cliff Potts, James Olson, Tim O'Connor, James McEachin, Alan Oppenheimer; *D:* Lamont Johnson. *USH*

The Group *&&½* **1966** Based upon the novel by Mary McCarthy, the well-acted story deals with a group of graduates from a Vassar-like college as they try to adapt to life during the Great Depression. Has some provocative subject matter, including lesbianism, adultery, and mental breakdowns. Soapy, but a good cast with film debuts of Bergen, Hackett, Pettet, Widdoes, and Holbrook. **150m/C VHS, Beta.** Candice Bergen, Joanna Pettet, Shirley Knight, Joan Hackett, Elizabeth Hartman, Jessica Walter, Larry Hagman, James Broderick, Kathleen Widdoes, Hal Holbrook, Mary-Robin Redd, Richard Mulligan, Carrie Nye; *D:* Sidney Lumet; *C:* Boris Kaufman. *FOX*

Group Marriage *&&½* **1972 (R)** Six young professionals fall into a marriage of communal convenience and rapidly discover the many advantages and drawbacks of their thoroughly modern arrangement. **90m/C VHS, Beta.** Victoria Vetri, Ai-

mee Eccles, Zack Taylor, Jeff Pomerantz, Claudia Jennings, Jayne Kennedy, Milt Kamen; *D:* Stephanie Rothman. *NO*

Growing Pains *&½* **1982** A young couple discover that their newly adopted son possesses extraordinary powers. **60m/C VHS, Beta.** Gary Bond, Barbara Keilermann, Norman Beaton. *LIV*

Grown Ups *&&* **1980** A newly married couple move into their first home only to discover that the wife's ditzy sister expects to live with them and that their next door neighbor was their former high school teacher. Made for British television. **95m/C VHS.** *GB* Philip Davis, Leslie Manville, Sam Kelly, Lindsay Duncan, Brenda Blethyn, Janine Duvitsky; *D:* Mike Leigh; *W:* Mike Leigh. *WBF, BTV, FCT*

Grown Ups *&&* **1986** A journalist watches his family slowly disintegrating around him in this adaptation of Jules Feiffer's play. **106m/C VHS, Beta.** Jean Stapleton, Martin Balsam, Charles Grodin, Marilu Henner, Kerry Segal; *D:* John Madden. *ORI, WAR*

Gruesome Twosome *&* **1967** Another guts/cannibalism/mutilation fun-fest by Lewis, about someone who's marketing the hair of some very recently deceased college coeds. **75m/C VHS, Beta.** Elizabeth Davis, Chris Martell; *D:* Herschell Gordon Lewis. *NO*

Grumpier Old Men *&&* **1995 (PG-13)** Max (Matthau) and John (Lemmon) are back at each other's throats, but with John happily married to Ariel (Ann-Margret), he's not much of a adversary. Enter Maria (Loren), who wants to turn the boys' favorite bait shop into an Italian restaurant. In a twist that should surprise no one, Max soon falls for the beautiful Maria, and she with him. Jokes are similar but more adolescent than in the first, and subplots involving John and Max's kids' wedding and Grandpa's (Meredith) romantic interests are forced. Suffers the standard sequel fate of not measuring up to the original.*CW:* Salty language and innuendos. **101m/C VHS, LV, Closed Caption.** Jack Lemmon, Walter Matthau, Ann-Margret, Sophia Loren, Kevin Pollak, Burgess Meredith, Daryl Hannah, Ann Guilbert; *D:* Howard Deutch; *W:* Mark Steven Johnson; *C:* Tak Fujimoto; *M:* Alan Silvestri. *WAR*

Grumpy Old Men *&&&* **1993 (PG-13)** Lemmon and Matthau team for their seventh movie, in parts that seem written just for them. Boyhood friends and retired neighbors, they have been feuding for so long that neither of them can remember why. Doesn't matter much, when it provides a reason for them to spout off at each other every morning and play nasty practical jokes every night. This, and ice-fishing, is life as they know it, until feisty younger woman Ann-Margret moves into the neighborhood and lights some long-dormant fires. 83-year-old Meredith is a special treat playing Lemmon's 90-something father. Filmed in Wabasha, Minnesota, and grumpy, in the most pleasant way.*CW:* Language. **104m/C VHS, LV, 8mm, Closed Caption, DVD.** Jack Lemmon, Walter Matthau, Ann-Margret, Burgess Meredith, Daryl Hannah, Kevin Pollak, Ossie Davis, Buck Henry, Christopher McDonald; *D:* Donald Petrie; *W:* Mark Steven Johnson; *M:* Alan Silvestri. *WAR*

Grunt! The Wrestling Movie woof! **1985 (R)** A spoof of documentaries about the behind-the-scenes world of wrestling. For fans only. **91m/C VHS, Beta.** Wally Greene, Steven Cepello, Dick Murdoch, John Tolos; *D:* Allan Holzman. *VTR, NWV*

Gryphon **1988** Ricky's new teacher can do all sorts of magical things. Hidden among her tricks are lessons about creativity, beauty, and imagination. Adapted from the short story by Charles Baxter. Aired on PBS as part of the "Wonderworks" family movie series. **58m/C VHS, Closed Caption.** Amanda Plummer, Sully Diaz, Alexis Cruz; *D:* Mark Cullingham. *PME, FCT, BTV*

Guadalcanal Diary *&&½* **1943** A vintage wartime flag-waver, with a typical crew of Marines battling the "Yellow Menace" over an important base on the famous Pacific atoll. Based on Richard Tregaskis' first-hand account. **93m/B VHS, Beta,**

LV. Preston Foster, Lloyd Nolan, William Bendix, Richard Conte, Anthony Quinn, Richard Jaeckel, Roy Roberts, Minor Watson, Miles Mander, Ralph Byrd, Lionel Stander, Reed Hadley; *D:* Lewis Seiler. *FOX, IME*

The Guardian *&&½* **1984 (R)** Residents of a chic New York apartment building hire a security expert/ex-military man to aid them in combatting their crime problem. But one of the liberal tenants thinks their guard's methods may come at too high a cost. Made for cable television. **102m/C VHS, Beta, LV, Closed Caption.** Martin Sheen, Louis Gossett Jr., Arthur Hill; *D:* David Greene. *LIV, VES*

The Guardian *&* **1990 (R)** A young couple unwittingly hires a human sacrificing druid witch as a babysitter for their child. Based on the book "The Nanny" by Dan Greenburg. **92m/C VHS, Beta, LV, Closed Caption.** Jenny Seagrove, Dwier Brown, Carey Lowell; *D:* William Friedkin; *W:* William Friedkin; *C:* John A. Alonzo. *USH*

Guardian Angel *&&½* *Beyond Justice* **1994 (R)** Detective Christy McKay (Rothrock) quits the force after her partner/lover is killed by icy seductress Nina (Denier), who manages to escape from jail. When McKay is hired to protect playboy Lawton Hobbs (McVicar), she finds that the threat comes from a psycho ex-girlfriend. Guess who. **97m/C VHS, Closed Caption.** Cynthia Rothrock, Lydie Denier, Daniel McVicar, Kenneth McLeod, Marshall Teague, John O'Leary, Dale Jacoby; *D:* Richard W. Munchkin. *PMH*

Guardian of the Abyss *&* **1982** A young couple who buy an antique mirror get more than they bargained for when they discover that it is the threshold to Hell and the devil wants to come through. **60m/C VHS, Beta.** Ray Lonnen, Rosalyn Landor, Paul Darrow, Barbara Ewing; *D:* Don Sharp. *LIV*

Guarding Tess *&&* **1994 (PG-13)** Long-suffering Secret Service agent Cage is nearing the end of his three year assignment to crotchety widowed First Lady MacLaine when the Prez extends his tour of duty. Feels like a TV movie, not surprising since writers Torokvei and Wilson have several sitcoms to their credit, including "WKRP in Cinncinnati." Nice chemistry between Cage and MacLaine results in a few funny moments, but there are too many formulaic plot twists. End result: a pleasant, if somewhat slow buddy comedy.*CW:* Some profanity and slight violence. **98m/C VHS, LV, 8mm, Closed Caption.** Shirley MacLaine, Nicolas Cage, Austin Pendleton, Edward Albert, Richard Griffiths; *D:* Hugh Wilson; *W:* Peter Torokvei, Hugh Wilson; *C:* Brian Reynolds; *M:* Michael Convertino. Nominations: Golden Globe Awards '95: Best Actress—Musical/Comedy (MacLaine). *COL*

The Guardsman *&&&* **1931** Broadway's illustrious couple Lunt and Fontanne shine in this adaptation of the clever marital comedy by French playwright Molnar in which they also starred. This sophisticated comedy was their only starring film, although they were offered large sums of money to appear in other movies—they just couldn't tear themselves away from the stage. Remade as "The Chocolate Soldier" and "Lily in Love." **89m/B VHS, Closed Caption.** Alfred Lunt, Lynn Fontanne, Roland Young, ZaSu Pitts, Maude Eburne, Herman Bing, Ann Dvorak; *D:* Sidney Franklin. Nominations: Academy Awards '32: Best Actor (Lunt), Best Actress (Fontanne). *MGM*

Guerilla Brigade *&&½* *Riders* **1939** A rarely seen Ukrainian epic about Russian/Ukrainian solidarity during the Civil War. In Russian with English subtitles. **90m/B VHS, Beta.** *RU D:* Igor Savchenko. *FCT*

Guess What We Learned in School Today? woof! **1970 (R)** Parents in a conservative suburban community protest sex education in the schools. Intended as a satire, but it only reinforces stereotypes. **85m/C VHS, Beta.** Richard Carballo, Devin Goldenberg; *D:* John G. Avildsen. *NO*

Guess Who's Coming to Dinner *&&&* **1967** Controversial in its time. A young white woman brings her black fiance home to meet her parents. The situation truly tests their open-mindedness and understanding. Hepburn and Tracy (in his last film appearance) are wonderful and serve as the anchors in what would otherwise have been a rather sugary film. Houghton, who portrays the independent daughter, is the real-life niece of Hepburn. **108m/C VHS, Beta, LV, Closed Caption.** Katharine Hepburn, Spencer Tracy, Sidney Poitier, Katharine Houghton, Cecil Kellaway; *D:* Stanley Kramer; *W:* William Rose; *C:* Sam Leavitt. Academy Awards '67: Best Actress (Hepburn), Best Story & Screenplay; British Academy Awards '68: Best Actor (Tracy), Best Actress (Hepburn); Nominations: Academy Awards '67: Best Actor (Tracy), Best Adapted Score, Best Art Direction/Set Decoration, Best Director (Kramer), Best Film Editing, Best Picture, Best Supporting Actor (Kellaway), Best Supporting Actress (Richards). **COL, FCT, COL**

Guest in the House 🐾🐾½ 1945 A seemingly friendly young female patient is invited to stay in the family home of her doctor. She skillfully attempts to dissect the family's harmony in the process. **121m/B VHS, Beta.** Anne Baxter, Ralph Bellamy, Ruth Warrick, Marie McDonald, Margaret Hamilton; *D:* John Brahm; *C:* Lee Garmes. Nominations: Academy Awards '45: Original Dramatic/Comedy Score. **NOS, CAB, VYY**

Guest Wife 🐾🐾½ 1945 Determined to impress his sentimental boss, a quick-thinking bachelor talks his best friend's wife into posing as his own wife, but the hoax gets a bit out of hand and nearly ruins the real couple's marriage. **90m/B VHS.** Claudette Colbert, Don Ameche, Dick Foran, Charles Dingle, Wilma Francis; *D:* Sam Wood; *C:* Joseph Valentine. Nominations: Academy Awards '45: Original Dramatic/Comedy Score. **REP**

A Guide for the Married Man 🐾🐾🐾 1967 One suburban husband instructs another in adultery, with a cast of dozens enacting various slapstick cameos. Based on Frank Tarloff's novel of the same name. Followed by "A Guide for the Married Woman." **91m/C VHS, Beta.** Walter Matthau, Robert Morse, Inger Stevens, Sue Ane Langdon, Claire Kelly, Elaine Devry; *Cameos:* Lucille Ball, Sid Caesar, Jack Benny, Wally Cox, Jayne Mansfield, Louis Nye, Carl Reiner, Phil Silvers, Terry-Thomas, Sam Jaffe, Jeffrey Hunter, Polly Bergen; *D:* Gene Kelly; *W:* Frank Tarloff; *M:* John Williams. **FOX**

A Guide for the Married Woman 🐾½ 1978 A bored housewife tries to take the romantic advice of a girlfriend to add a little spice to her life. A poor made-for-television follow-up to "A Guide for the Married Man." **96m/C VHS, Beta.** Cybill Shepherd, Barbara Feldon, Eve Arden, Chuck Woolery, Peter Marshall, Charles Frank; *D:* Hy Averback. **FOX**

Guilty as Charged 🐾½ 1992 (R) A butcher rigs his own private electric chair and captures and executes paroled killers in his personal quest for justice. But when a politician frames an innocent man for murder how far will this vigilante go? *CW:* Language and violence. **95m/C VHS, LV, Closed Caption.** Rod Steiger, Lauren Hutton, Heather Graham, Isaac Hayes; *D:* Sam Irvin; *M:* Steve Bartek. **COL**

Guilty as Sin 🐾🐾 1993 (R) Johnson is a ruthless Casanova accused of murdering his very wealthy wife and decides lawyer DeMornay is just the woman to defend him. Question is, who'll defend DeMornay from him? Johnson has fun as the menacing smoothie but DeMornay's supposedly hotshot criminal attorney is just plain dumb. It sounds like "Jagged Edge" but there's no sexual involvement between client and lawyer and no thrill in this thriller. *CW:* Language, violence, and some sexuality. **120m/C VHS, Beta, LV, Closed Caption.** Don Johnson, Rebecca DeMornay, Jack Warden, Stephen Lang, Dana Ivey, Ron White, Sean McCann, Luis Guzman; *D:* Sidney Lumet; *W:* Larry Cohen; *C:* Andrzej Bartkowiak. **HPH, BTV, TOU**

Guilty by Suspicion 🐾🐾½ 1991 (PG-13) Examination of the 1950's McCarthy investigations by the House Un-American Activities Committee comes off like a bland history lesson. De Niro plays a director who attended a Communist party meeting in the '30s but who otherwise

doesn't have any red connections. He takes the moral high ground and refuses to incriminate his buddy (Wendt) to get off the hook and finds himself blacklisted. Characterized by average performances (excepting Wettig who goes overboard) and a lightweight script. "The Front" (1976) does a better job on this topic. Directorial debut for producer Winkler. Available in widescreen on laserdisc. **105m/C VHS, LV, 8mm, Closed Caption.** Robert De Niro, Annette Bening, George Wendt, Patricia Wettig, Sam Wanamaker, Chris Cooper, Ben Piazza, Martin Scorsese, Barry Primus, Gailard Sartain, Stuart Margolin, Barry Tubb, Roxann Biggs-Dawson, Robin Gammell, Brad Sullivan, Luke Edwards, Adam Baldwin; *D:* Irwin Winkler; *W:* Irwin Winkler; *C:* Michael Ballhaus; *M:* James Newton Howard. **WAR**

Guilty of Innocence 🐾🐾 1987 (PG) A young African-American man finds he's guilty until proven innocent when he runs into the law in Texas. A bold lawyer joins his fight for justice. Based on a true story and made for television. **95m/C VHS, Closed Caption.** Dorian Harewood, Dabney Coleman, Hoyt Axton, Paul Winfield, Dennis Lipscomb, Debbi Morgan, Marshall Colt, Victor Love; *D:* Richard T. Heffron. **THV**

Guilty of Treason 🐾🐾½ 1950 A documentary on the life and times of Joszef Cardinal Mindszenty of Hungary, who was imprisoned by the communists as an enemy of the state for speaking out against the totalitarian regime. At the trial, it was revealed that the Cardinal's confession was obtained only by the use of drugs, hypnosis, and torture. A realistic look at the dark side of Communism. **86m/B VHS.** Charles Bickford, Paul Kelly, Bonita Granville, Richard Derr, Berry Kroeger, Elisabeth Risdon, Roland Winters, John Banner; *D:* Felix Feist. **NOS, MRV**

The Guinea Pig 🐾🐾½ *The Outsider* 1948 Jack Read (Attenborough), the son of a tobacconist, is sent to a posh public school as an experiment but finds problems between his simple upbringing and the reactions of teachers and other students. **97m/B VHS.** *GB* Richard Attenborough, Joan Hickson, Bernard Miles, Sheila Sim, Robert Flemyng, Timothy Bateson; *D:* Roy Boulting; *W:* Bernard Miles, Roy Boulting. **FCT**

Guitarman 🐾 1995 Modern version of "The Pied Piper of Hamlin" finds a mysterious musician saving a farming community's crops from a plague of locusts. But when the mayor reneges on paying the piper (so to speak), he takes the town's children instead. **92m/C VHS.** Nicholas Campbell, Donnelly Rhodes, Andrea Martin, Shawn Ashmore, Jack Semple; *D:* Will Dixon. **SDE**

Gulag 🐾🐾½ 1985 An American sportscaster is wrongly sentenced to ten years of hard labor in a Soviet prison, and plans his escape from the cruel guards. Good suspense. Made for television. **130m/C VHS, Beta.** *GB* David Keith, Malcolm McDowell, David Suchet, Warren Clarke, John McEnery; *D:* Roger Young; *M:* Elmer Bernstein. **PSM**

Gulliver's Travels 🐾🐾½ 1939 The Fleischer Studio's animated version of Jonathan Swift's classic about the adventures of Gulliver, an English sailor who is washed ashore in the land of Lilliput, where everyone is about two inches tall. **74m/C VHS.** *D:* Dave Fleischer; *V:* Lanny Ross, Jessica Dragonette. Nominations: Academy Awards '39: Best Song ("Faithful Forever"), Best Original Score. **CAF, MRV, NOS**

Gulliver's Travels 🐾🐾 1977 (G) In this partially animated adventure the entire land of Lilliput has been constructed in miniature. Cartoon and real life mix in a 3-dimensional story of Dr. Lemuel Gulliver and his discovery of the small people in the East Indies. From the classic by Jonathan Swift. **80m/C VHS, Beta.** *GB* Richard Harris, Catherine Schell; *D:* Peter Hunt. **VTR, HHE, RDG**

Gulliver's Travels 🐾🐾½ 1995 (PG) Faithful TV version of Jonathan Swift's 1726 satiric novel. Lemuel Gulliver (Danson) is confined to Bedlam, an English insane asylum, after having

been lost at sea for eight years. While in the asylum he relates his very odd adventures—in the tiny land of Lilliput, among the giants of Brobdingnag, with the silly and impractical intellectuals of Laputa, and finally amidst the brutish human Yahoos, who are ruled by rational talking horses, the Houyhnhnms. Meanwhile, Gulliver's wife Mary (Steenburgen) and son Tom (Sturridge) struggle to prove his sanity and win his release. On two cassettes. **187m/C VHS, LV, Closed Caption.** Ted Danson, Mary Steenburgen, Edward Fox, Thomas Sturridge, Edward Woodward, Nicholas Lyndhurst, Peter O'Toole, Phoebe Nicholls, Ned Beatty, Kate Maberly, Alfre Woodard, Geraldine Chaplin, John Gielgud, Kristin Scott Thomas, Omar Sharif, John Standing, Warwick Davis, Robert Hardy, Shashi Kapoor, Karyn Parsons, Edward Petherbridge; *D:* Charles Sturridge; *W:* Simon Moore; *C:* Howard Atherton; *M:* Trevor Jones. **HMK**

Gumball Rally 🐾🐾 1976 (PG) An unusual assortment of people converge upon New York for a cross country car race to Long Beach, California where breaking the rules is part of the game. **107m/C VHS, Beta.** Michael Sarrazin, Gary Busey, Raul Julia, Nicholas Pryor, Tim McIntire, Susan Flannery; *D:* Chuck Bail; *W:* Leon Capetanos. **WAR**

Gumby: The Movie 🐾🐾½ 1995 (G) Gumby and his musical group, the Clayboys, seek to save their neighbors' farms from foreclosure by putting on a benefit concert. And yes, pal Pokey is along to help out. But 90 minutes of our gentle clay hero stretches the patience of even the most enthusiastic fan. **90m/C VHS.** *D:* Art Clokey; *W:* Art Clokey. **KID**

Gumshoe 🐾🐾½ 1972 (G) An homage to American hard-boiled detectives. Finney plays a small-time worker in a Liverpool nightclub who decides to become a detective like his movie heroes. He bumbles through a number of interconnecting cases, but finds his way in the end. Good satire of film noir detectives. **85m/C VHS, Beta.** *GB* Albert Finney, Billie Whitelaw, Frank Finlay, Janice Rule, Carolyn Seymour; *D:* Stephen Frears; *C:* Chris Menges; *M:* Andrew Lloyd Webber. **NO**

The Gumshoe Kid 🐾 *The Detective Kid* 1989 (R) A college-bound kid enters the family detective business to prevent his mother from being evicted. He gets in over his head though, trying to track the fiancee of a wealthy mobster. **98m/C VHS, Beta, LV.** Jay Underwood, Tracy Scoggins, Vince Edwards, Arlene Golonka, Pamela Springsteen; *D:* Joseph Manduke. **ACA**

Gun Cargo 🐾 1949 Muddled story about a conniving shipowner who fires his crew for demanding shore leave. He replaces them with assorted low-lifes, resulting in the usual hijinks. A terrible performance by an otherwise great cast. **49m/C VHS, Beta, 8mm.** Rex Lease, Smith Ballew, William Farnum, Gibson Gowland. **VYY**

Gun Code 🐾½ 1940 The white-hatted cowboy-hero puts a stop to small-town racketeering. **52m/B VHS, Beta.** Tim McCoy, Ina Guest; *D:* Sam Newfield. **VDM**

Gun Crazy 🐾🐾🐾 *Deadly Is the Female* 1949 Annie Laurie Starr—Annie Oakley in a Wild West show—meets gun-lovin' Bart Tare, who says a gun makes him feel good inside, "like I'm somebody." Sparks fly, and the two get married and live happily ever after—until the money runs out and fatal femme Laurie's craving for excitement and violence starts to flare up. The two become lovebirds-on-the-lam. Now a cult fave, it's based on a MacKinlay Kantor story. Ex-stuntman Russell Harlan's photography is daring; the realism of the impressive robbery scenes is owed in part to the technical consultation of former train robber Al Jennings. And watch for a young Tamblyn as the 14-year-old Bart. **87m/B VHS.** Peggy Cummins, John Dall, Berry Kroeger, Morris Carnovsky, Anabel Shaw, Nedrick Young, Trevor Bardette, Russ Tamblyn, Harry Lewis, Mickey Little, Paul Frison, Dave Bair, Stanley Prager, Virginia Farmer, Anne O'Neal, Frances Irwin, Don Beddoe, Robert Osterloh, Shimen Ruskin, Harry Hayden; *D:* Joseph H.

Lewis; **W:** Dalton Trumbo; **C:** Russell Harlan; **M:** Victor Young. *FOX, FCT*

Gun Crazy ♂♂½ *A Talent for Loving* **1969** A gambler becomes enmeshed in an arranged marriage with a cursed Mexican family. Lightweight comedy, good cast. **110m/C VHS.** Richard Widmark, Chaim Topol, Cesar Romero, Genevieve Page, Judd Hamilton, Caroline Munro; **D:** Richard Quine. *SIM*

Gun Fight at Red Sands ♂♂ *Gringo; Duello Nel Texas* **1963** Landmark western in the history of Italian cinema. Long before Leone's Eastwood trilogy, this film introduced the theme of an avenging stranger to the genre. Harrison stars as the dark, brooding hero who is out for revenge after learning that his family has been attacked by a gang of bandits. **?m/C VHS.** *IT* Richard Harrison, Giacomo "Jack" Rossi-Stuart, Sara Lezana; **M:** Ennio Morricone. *SNC*

Gun Fury ♂♂½ **1953** A panoramic western about a Civil War veteran pursuing the bandits who kidnapped his beautiful bride-to-be. First screened as a 3-D movie. **83m/C VHS, Beta, LV.** Rock Hudson, Donna Reed, Phil Carey, Lee Marvin; **D:** Raoul Walsh. *COL*

Gun Girls ♂ **1956** Campy exploitation flick about a gun-toting gang of girls who rob anything or anyone. The guy who fences their goods ends up getting one of them pregnant. **?m/C VHS.** Timothy Farrell, Jean Ferguson, Jacquelyn Park, Jean Ann Lewis; **D:** Robert Deltano. *SNC*

Gun Glory ♂♂½ **1957** Granger plays Tom Early, a gunslinger who returns home after three years to find the town would rather not have him. He regains the town's respect when he stops a murderer from invading the town with his cattle herd. Based on the novel "Man of the West" by Philip Yordan. **88m/C VHS, Closed Caption.** Stewart Granger, Rhonda Fleming, Chill Wills, Steve Rowland, James Gregory, Jacques Aubuchon, Arch Johnson, William "Bill" Fawcett, Lane Bradford, Michael Dugan, Bud Osborne, May McAvoy, Charles Herbert, Carl Pitti; **D:** Roy Rowland; **W:** William Ludwig; **M:** Jeff Alexander. *MGM*

Gun Grit ♂½ **1936** An FBI agent is sent west to break up a protection racket. **51m/B VHS.** Jack Perrin, Ethel Beck, David Sharpe, Roger Williams, Budd Buster; **D:** William (Lester Williams) Berke. *GPV*

The Gun in Betty Lou's Handbag ♂♂ **1992 (PG-13)** Shy, small town librarian with a dull marriage is looking for excitement when she stumbles across a gun used in a murder. She decides excitement will follow her (false) confession to the crime leaving her husband thunderstruck, the police confused, and the gossip line humming. She also intrigues the real bad guy, who comes looking for her. Lame silliness is redeemed somewhat by Miller, but there's some surprisingly nasty violence given the comedy label. **99m/C VHS, Beta, LV, Closed Caption.** Penelope Ann Miller, Eric Thal, Alfre Woodard, Cathy Moriarty, William Forsythe, Julianne Moore, Xander Berkeley, Michael O'Neill, Christopher John Fields; **D:** Allan Moyle; **W:** Grace Cary Bickley; **M:** Richard Gibbs. *TOU*

A Gun in the House ♂ **1981** While being attacked in her own home, a woman shoots one of her assailants. The police find no conclusive evidence of attack and arrest the woman for murder. Exploitive drama on gun control. Made-for-television. **100m/C VHS, Beta.** Sally Struthers, David Ackroyd, Joel Bailey, Jeffrey Tambor; **D:** Ivan Nagy. *VHE, HHE*

Gun Law ♂½ **1933** The hero tackles the Sonora Kid, an outlaw terrorizing Arizona folk. One of the few sound westerns with Hoxie, a silent-era star who hung up his spurs when his voice proved non-photogenic. **59m/B VHS, Beta.** Jack Hoxie, Paul Fix, Mary Carr, Edmund Cobb, Robert Burns; **D:** Lewis D. Collins. *GPV*

Gun Lords of Stirrup Basin ♂♂ **1937** A cattleman and the daughter of a homesteader are in love in the Old West, but a seedy lawyer wants to douse their flame. Bullets and fists fly as a result. **55m/B VHS.** Bob Steele, Louise

Stanley, Karl Hackett, Ernie Adams, Frank LaRue, Frank Ball, Steve Clark; **D:** Sam Newfield. *NOS, DVT*

Gun Packer ♂♂ **1938** When an outlaw gang robs stagecoaches of their gold and uses the booty to salt barren mine shafts so the unsuspecting can be swindled out of their money on worthless gold mine certificates, hard-riding Randall is called in to save the day. **51m/B VHS.** Jack Randall, Louise Stanley, Charles "Blackie" King, Glenn Strange; **D:** Wallace Fox; **W:** Robert Emmett. *MOV*

Gun Play ♂♂ *Lucky Boots* **1936** Brother and sister venture west to run their father's ranch. Mexican bandits believe the ranch's property houses a revolutionary fortune, and set about recovering it. The duo defends his father's ranch along with a sidekick, who sweeps the sister off her feet. **59m/B VHS.** Guinn "Big Boy" Williams, Frank Yaconelli, Marion Shilling, Wally Wales, Charles French; **D:** Al(bert) Herman. *NOS, DVT, GPV*

The Gun Ranger ♂½ **1934** Our hero plays a Texas Ranger who becomes fed up with soft judges and shady prosecutors and decides to take the law into his own hands. **56m/B VHS, Beta.** Bob Steele, Eleanor Stewart, John Merton, Ernie Adams, Budd Buster; **D:** Robert North Bradbury. *NOS, DVT, GPV*

Gun Riders ♂½ *Five Bloody Graves; Five Bloody Days to Tombstone; Lonely Man* **1969** Gunman must seek out and stop a murderer of innocent people. **98m/C VHS, Beta.** Scott Brady, Jim Davis, John Carradine; **D:** Al Adamson. *CCB*

Gun Smugglers/Hot Lead ♂ **1951** A western double feature: Tim Holt and his sidekick Chito must recover a shipment of stolen guns in "Gun Smugglers," and the duo gallop into action against a gang of train robbers in "Hot Lead." **120m/B VHS, Beta.** Tim Holt, Richard Martin, Martha Hyer. *TTC*

Gunblast ♂ **197?** A convict is released from San Quentin and wastes no time in getting involved with mob-powered drug smuggling. **70m/C VHS, Beta.** Lloyd Allan, Christine Cardan, James Cunningham. *NO*

Guncrazy ♂♂ **1992 (R)** Girl from the wrong side of the tracks, abused her entire life, finds her freedom in a gun. She winds up killing the man who raped her, takes up with an equally lost ex-con, and the two armed misfits go on the run from the law. Barrymore's convincing and the movie is another well-made variation on the lovers-on-the-run theme. Film was inspired by, but is not a remake of, the 1949 movie "Gun Crazy." **CW:** Language, strong violence, and strong sensuality. **97m/C VHS, Beta, LV, Closed Caption.** Drew Barrymore, James LeGros, Billy Drago, Rodney Harvey, Ione Skye, Joe Dallesandro, Michael Ironside; **D:** Tamra Davis; **W:** Matthew Bright. *ACA, PMS*

A Gunfight ♂♂ **1971 (PG)** When Cash is stranded in a small Western town, he meets up with fellow old-time gunfighter Douglas. The two strike up a friendship, but discover the town folk expect a gun battle. Needing money, the two arrange a gunfight for paid admission — winner take all. Cash makes his screen debut. **90m/C Beta.** Kirk Douglas, Johnny Cash, Jane Alexander, Karen Black, Dana Elcar, Keith Carradine, Raf Vallone; **D:** Lamont Johnson; **W:** Harold Jack Bloom. *ALL, MTX*

Gunfight at Sandoval ♂♂½ **1959** A Texas Ranger investigates the headquarters of a criminal gang while hunting for the bandits who killed his partner. Adapted from the "Texas John Slaughter" episodes of the Disney television series. **72m/C VHS, Beta.** Tom Tryon, Beverly Garland, Dan Duryea. *DIS*

Gunfight at the O.K. Corral ♂♂♂ **1957** The story of Wyatt Earp and Doc Holliday joining forces in Dodge City to rid the town of the criminal Clanton gang. Filmed in typical Hollywood style, but redeemed by its great stars. **122m/C VHS, Beta, LV.** Burt Lancaster, Kirk Douglas, Rhonda Fleming, Jo Van Fleet, John Ireland, Kenneth Tobey, Lee Van Cleef, Frank Faylen, DeForest Kelley, Earl Holliman; **D:** John Sturges; **W:** Leon Uris; **C:** Charles B(ryant) Lang.

Nominations: Academy Awards '57: Best Film Editing, Best Sound. *PAR, FCT*

The Gunfighter ♂♂♂½ **1950** A mature, serious, Hollywood-western character study about an aging gunfighter searching for peace and quiet but unable to avoid his reputation and the duel-challenges it invites. One of King's best films. **85m/B VHS, Beta, LV.** Gregory Peck, Helen Westcott, Millard Mitchell, Jean Parker, Karl Malden, Skip Homeier, Mae Marsh; **D:** Henry King; **C:** Arthur C. Miller. Nominations: Academy Awards '50: Best Story. *FOX*

The Gunfighters ♂½ **1987** Lackluster pilot of a proposed Canadian series pits three individualistic relatives against a powerful empire-builder. **100m/C VHS, LV.** *CA* Art Hindle, Reiner Schoene, Tony Addabbo, George Kennedy, Michael Kane, Lori Hallier; **D:** Clay Borris. *THV*

Gunfighter's Moon ♂♂½ **1996 (PG-13)** Legendary gunslinger Frank Morgan (Henriksen) is called on by former lover, Linda (Lenz), to help her sheriff husband prevent a jailbreak. Frank's tired of his constant challengers but can't seem to make another life for himself. **CW:** Gunfighting. **95m/C VHS, Closed Caption.** Lance Henriksen, Kay Lenz, David McIlwraith; **D:** Larry Ferguson; **W:** Larry Ferguson; **C:** James L. Carter; **M:** Lee Holdridge. *CAF*

Gunfire ♂½ **1950** A Frank James look-alike cavorts, robs and loots the countryside until the real James decides to set things straight. **59m/B VHS, Beta, LV.** Donald (Don "Red") Barry, Robert Lowery, Pamela Blake, Wally Vernon; **D:** William (Lester Williams) Berke. *HHE*

Gunfire ♂♂ *China 9, Liberty 37* **1978** A gunfighter is rescued from the hangman's noose by railroad tycoons who want him to kill a farmer. He doesn't kill the man, but runs off with his wife instead, and the incensed railway honchos send assassins after the double-crossing gunman. Peckinpah's part is pretty puny in this leisurely horse opera. **94m/C VHS.** *IT* Fabio Testi, Warren Oates, Jenny Agutter, Sam Peckinpah; **D:** Monte Hellman; **M:** Pino Donaggio. *SIM*

Gung Ho! ♂♂ **1943** Carlson's Raiders are a specially trained group of Marine jungle fighters determined to retake the Pacific island of Makin during WWII. **88m/B VHS, Beta.** Robert Mitchum, Randolph Scott, Noah Beery Jr., Alan Curtis, Grace McDonald; **D:** Ray Enright; **C:** Milton Krasner. *REP, MRV, CNG*

Gung Ho ♂♂½ **1985 (PG-13)** A Japanese firm takes over a small-town U.S. auto factory and causes major cultural collisions. Keaton plays the go-between for employees and management while trying to keep both groups from killing each other. From the director of "Splash" and "Night Shift." Made into a short-lived television series. **111m/C VHS, Beta, LV, 8mm, Closed Caption.** Michael Keaton, Gedde Watanabe, George Wendt, Mimi Rogers, John Turturro, Clint Howard, Michelle Johnson, So Yamamura, Sab Shimono; **D:** Ron Howard; **W:** Babaloo Mandel, Lowell Ganz; **M:** Thomas Newman. *PAR*

Gunga Din ♂♂♂♂ **1939** The prototypical "buddy" film. Three veteran British sergeants in India try to suppress a native uprising, but it's their water boy, the intrepid Gunga Din, who saves the day. Friendship, loyalty, and some of the best action scenes ever filmed. Based loosely on Rudyard Kipling's famous poem, the story is credited to Ben Hecht, Charles MacArthur and William Faulkner (who is uncredited). Also available colorized. **117m/B VHS, Beta, LV.** Cary Grant, Victor McLaglen, Douglas Fairbanks Jr., Sam Jaffe, Eduardo Ciannelli, Montagu Love, Joan Fontaine, Abner Biberman, Robert Coote, Lumsden Hare, Cecil Kellaway; **D:** George Stevens; **W:** Fred Guiol, Joel Sayre; **M:** Alfred Newman. Nominations: Academy Awards '39: Best Black and White Cinematography. *TTC, MLB*

Gunman from Bodie ♂½ *Gun Man from Bodie* **1941** Second of the Rough Rider series. Jones, McCoy, and Hatton rescue a baby orphaned by rustlers and then go after the bad guys. **62m/B VHS, Beta.** Tim McCoy, Buck Jones, Raymond Hatton; **D:** Spencer Gordon Bennet. *NOS, MRV, VCN*

Gunman's Walk ✹✹½ 1958 Rancher Lee Hackett (Heflin) gained his power through his gunslinging skill but wants his two sons to be respectable citizens. However, hot-tempered eldest son Ed (Hunter) wants to best the old man's reputation while younger son Davy (Darren) has his own problems when he falls for Sioux half-breed Clee (Grant), whose brother was murdered by Ed. As Ed gets more ruthless, his father must decide how far he's willing to go to protect him. 95m/C VHS. Van Heflin, Tab Hunter, James Darren, Kathryn Grant, Mickey Shaughnessy, Robert F. Simon, Edward Platt, Bert Convy; **D:** Phil Karlson; **W:** Frank Nugent; **C:** Charles Lawton Jr. COL

Gunmen ✹✹ 1993 (R) A reluctant buddy team face down some bad guys. DEA agent Cole (Van Peebles) teams up with smuggler Dani (Lambert) to find stolen drug money also wanted by wheelchair-bound villain Loomis (Stewart) and his violence-loving henchman (Leary). Adds comedy to the mix as well as shameless action rip-offs from spaghetti westerns.**CW:** Language, violence, and sexuality. 90m/C VHS, LV. Christopher Lambert, Mario Van Peebles, Denis Leary, Patrick Stewart, Kadeem Hardison, Sally Kirkland; **Cameos:** Big Daddy Kane, Ed Lover, Eric B. Rakim, Dr. Dre; **D:** Deran Sarafian; **W:** Stephen Sommers; **M:** John Debney. LIV

Gunners & Guns ✹ 1934 Vintage western starring King. 51m/B VHS, Beta. Black King, Edmund Cobb, Edna Asetin, Eddie Davis; **D:** Robert Hoyt. VCN

Gunplay ✹½ 1951 Two cowboys befriend a boy whose father has been killed and search for the murderer. 61m/B VHS, Beta. Tim Holt, Joan Dixon, Richard Martin. MED

Gunpowder ✹ 1984 Two Interpol agents endeavor to stop a crime lord from causing the collapse of the world economy. 85m/C VHS, Beta. David Gilliam, Martin Potter, Gordon Jackson, Anthony Schaeffer. LIV, VES

The Gunrunner ✹½ 1984 (R) Costner plays a Canadian mobster, involved in liquor smuggling, who aids a Chinese rebellion in this 1920s drama. Interesting concept. Received more attention after Costner gained notoriety in later films. 92m/C VHS, LV. CA Kevin Costner, Sara Botsford, Paul Soles; **D:** Nardo Castillo. VTR, HHE

Guns ✹✹ 1990 (R) An international gunrunner puts the moves on buxom women between hair-raising adventures. 95m/C VHS, LV. Erik Estrada, Dona Speir; **D:** Andy Sidaris; **W:** Andy Sidaris. COL

The Guns and the Fury ✹½ 1983 Two American oil riggers in the Middle East, circa 1908, are forced to fight off an attack by a vicious Arab sheik and his tribe. 90m/C VHS, Beta. Peter Graves, Cameron Mitchell, Michael Ansara, Albert Salmi; **D:** Tony Zarindast. NO

Guns at Batasi ✹✹½ 1964 Attenborough plays a tough British Sergeant Major stationed in Africa during the anti-colonial 1960s. Ultimately the regiment is threatened by rebel Africans. Fine performances make this rather predictable film watchable. 103m/B VHS. GB Richard Attenborough, Jack Hawkins, Mia Farrow, Flora Robson, John Leyton; **D:** John Guillermin; **M:** John Addison. TCF, RXM

Guns Don't Argue ✹ 1957 Entertaining schlocker about the rise and fall of famous criminal Dillinger. Non-stop action also features Bonnie and Clyde, Pretty Boy Floyd and Baby Face Nelson. ?m/C VHS. Myron Healey, Jim Davis, Richard Crane. SNC

Guns for Dollars ✹✹ *They Call Me Hallelujah* 1973 Mex-Western has four men, including a secret agent and a cossack, tangled up in the Mexican Revolution as they search for a fortune in smuggled jewels. 94m/C VHS. MX George Hilton, Charles Southwood, Agata Flory, Roberto Camardiel, Paolo Gozlino, Rick Boyd; **D:** Anthony Ascot. ACA

Guns in the Dark ✹ 1937 A cowboy vows never to use a gun again when he believes that he accidentally shot his best friend. 60m/C VHS, Beta. Johnny Mack Brown, Claire Rochelle; **D:** Sam Newfield. NOS, DVT, RXM

Guns of Diablo ✹✹ 1964 Wagon train master Bronson has to fight a gang that controls the supply depot, all the while showing his young helper (beardless boy Russell) the fascinating tricks of the trade. 91m/C VHS. Charles Bronson, Kurt Russell, Susan Oliver; **D:** Boris Sagal. ACE, MTX, VTR

Guns of Fury ✹½ 1945 Cisco and Pancho solve the troubles of a small boy in this standard oater. 60m/B VHS, Beta. Duncan Renaldo. NOS, VCI, VCN

Guns of Justice ✹ *Colorado Ranger* 1950 Undercover Colorado rangers stop a swindler from forcing homesteaders off their land. 60m/B VHS, Beta, LV. James Ellison, Russell Hayden, Tom Tyler, Raymond Hatton; **D:** Thomas Carr. NO

The Guns of Navarone ✹✹✹½ 1961 During WWII, British Intelligence in the Middle East sends six men to the Aegean island of Navarone to destroy guns manned by the Germans. Consistently interesting war epic based on the Alistair MacLean novel, with a vivid cast. 159m/C VHS, Beta, LV. Gregory Peck, David Niven, Anthony Quinn, Richard Harris, Stanley Baker, Anthony Quayle, James Darren, Irene Papas; **D:** J. Lee Thompson; **C:** Oswald Morris. Academy Awards '61: Best Special Effects; Golden Globe Awards '62: Best Film—Drama, Best Score; Nominations: Academy Awards '61: Best Adapted Screenplay, Best Director (Thompson), Best Film Editing, Best Picture, Best Sound, Original Dramatic/Comedy Score. COL

Guns of the Law ✹½ 1944 The Texas Rangers try to stop a shifty lawyer who attempts to swindle a family out of a potential fortune in property. 56m/B VHS. Dave O'Brien, James Newill, Guy Wilkerson, Jack Ingram, Robert F. (Bob) Kortman, Bob Barron; **D:** Elmer Clifton; **W:** Elmer Clifton. MOV

Guns of the Magnificent Seven ✹✹½ 1969 (G) The third remake of "The Seven Samurai." Action-packed western in which the seven free political prisoners and train them to kill. The war party then heads out to rescue a Mexican revolutionary being held in an impregnable fortress. 106m/C VHS. George Kennedy, Monte Markham, James Whitmore, Reni Santoni, Bernie Casey, Joe Don Baker, Scott Thomas, Michael Ansara, Fernando Rey; **D:** Paul Wendkos; **M:** Elmer Bernstein. MGM

The Gunslinger ✹½ 1956 A woman marshall struggles to keep law and order in a town overrun by outlaws. Unique western with a surprise ending. 83m/C VHS. John Ireland, Beverly Garland, Allison Hayes, Jonathan Haze, Dick Miller, Bruno Ve Sota; **D:** Roger Corman; **W:** Charles B. Griffith. MLB, TIM, SNC

Gunslinger ✹½ 197? Armed to the teeth with weaponry, Sartana shows a mining town's heavies how to sling a gun or two. 90m/C VHS, Beta. Gianni "John" Garko, Antonio Vilar; **D:** Anthony Ascot. VDC

Gunsmoke: Return to Dodge ✹✹½ 1987 The first of the made-for-television movies which reunited most of the cast of the classic television western. Matt Dillon returns to Dodge and Miss Kitty after 12 years only to be trailed by a ruthless adversary. 100m/C VHS. James Arness, Amanda Blake, Buck Taylor, Fran Ryan, Earl Holliman, Steve Forrest; **D:** Vincent McEveety. FXV

Gunsmoke Trail ✹½ 1938 Cowpoke Randall saves an heiress from losing her estate to a phony uncle in low-budget Western. Also features the prolific "Fuzzy" St. John in his cowboy's sidekick stage (interestingly, St. John, a nephew of Fatty Arbuckle, later co-starred in the "Lone Rider" series with Randall's brother, Robert Livingston). 59m/C VHS. Jack Randall, Al "Fuzzy" St. John. NOS, MRV, MOV

Gus ✹✹½ 1976 (G) A Disney film about the California Atoms, a football team that has the worst record in the league until they begin winning games with the help of their field goal kicking mule of a mascot, Gus. The competition then plots a donkey-napping. Enjoyable comedy for the whole family. 96m/C VHS, Beta, LV. Ed Asner, Tim Conway, Dick Van Patten, Ronnie Schell, Bob Crane, Tom Bosley; **D:** Vincent McEveety; **W:** Arthur Alsberg; **M:** Robert F. Brunner. COL, DIS

GUY: Awakening of the Devil ✹✹ 1993 Guy and Raina, two despicable intergalactic soldiers of fortune, embark on a continuous skyraid adventure. Available in general release and uncut versions. Japanese with English subtitles. ?m/C VHS. JP CPM

The Guy from Harlem ✹✹ 1977 He's mad, he's from Harlem, and he's not going to take it any more. 86m/C VHS. Loye Hawkins, Cathy Davis, Patricia Fulton, Wanda Starr; **D:** Rene Martinez Jr. XVC

A Guy Named Joe ✹✹✹½ 1944 A sentimental, patriotic Hollywood fantasy about the angel of a dead WWII pilot guiding another young pilot through battle and also helping him to romance his girl, who's still too devoted to his memory. Remade in 1989 as "Always." 121m/B VHS, Beta. Spencer Tracy, Irene Dunne, Van Johnson, Ward Bond, James Gleason, Lionel Barrymore, Esther Williams; **D:** Victor Fleming; **W:** Dalton Trumbo; **C:** Karl Freund. Nominations: Academy Awards '44: Best Story.MGM

The Guyana Tragedy: The Story of Jim Jones ✹✹ 1980 Dramatization traces the story of the Reverend Jim Jones and the People's Temple from its beginnings in 1953 to the November 1978 mass suicide of more than 900 people. Boothe is appropriately hypnotic as the Reverend. Made for television. 240m/C VHS, Beta. Powers Boothe, Ned Beatty, Randy Quaid, Brad Dourif, Brenda Vaccaro, LeVar Burton, Colleen Dewhurst, James Earl Jones; **D:** William A. Graham; **C:** Gil Hubbs; **M:** Elmer Bernstein. VHE, HHE

Guys and Dolls ✹✹✹ 1955 New York gambler Sky Masterson takes a bet that he can romance a Salvation Army lady. Based on the stories of Damon Runyon with Blaine, Kaye, Pully, and Silver recreating their roles from the Broadway hit. Brando's not-always-convincing musical debut. ♫More I Cannot Wish You; My Time of Day; Guys and Dolls; Fugue for Tinhorns; Follow the Fold; Sue Me; Take Back Your Mink; If I Were a Bell; Luck Be a Lady. 150m/C VHS, Beta, LV, Closed Caption. Marlon Brando, Jean Simmons, Frank Sinatra, Vivian Blaine, Stubby Kaye, Sheldon Leonard, Veda Ann Borg; **D:** Joseph L. Mankiewicz; **W:** Joseph L. Mankiewicz; **C:** Harry Stradling; **M:** Frank Loesser. Golden Globe Awards '56: Best Actress—Musical/Comedy (Simmons), Best Film—Musical/Comedy; Nominations: Academy Awards '55: Best Art Direction/Set Decoration (Color), Best Color Cinematography, Best Costume Design (Color), Scoring of a Musical.HMK, FCT, FOX

The Guyver ✹½ 1991 A young college student is transformed into a super-human fighting machine thanks to his discovery of an alien device, "The Guyver." A CIA agent (Hamill) must keep the secret device from falling into the hands of human mutants, the Zoanoids. Based on a Japanese comic book. 92m/C VHS. Mark Hamill, Vivian Wu, David Gale, Jeffrey Combs, Michael Berryman; **D:** Steve Wang. COL, NLC

Guyver 2: Dark Hero ✹½ 1994 (R) The Guyver discovers an alien ship filled with weapons capable of destroying the planet. Naturally, he must battle the evil mutant Zoanoids in order to save the world. Adapted from a Japanese comic book.**CW:** Sci-fi violence and gore; language. 127m/C VHS, LV, Closed Caption. David Hayter, Kathy Christopherson, Christopher Michael; **D:** Steve Wang; **W:** Nathan Long. COL

Gymkata ✹ 1985 (R) A gymnast (Olympian Thomas) must use his martial arts skills to conquer and secure a military state in a hostile European country. 89m/C VHS, Beta. Kurt Thomas, Tetchie Agbayani, Richard Norton, Conan Lee; **D:** Robert Clouse; **W:** Charles Robert Carner. MGM

Gypsy 🎔🎔🎔 1962 The life story of America's most famous striptease queen, Gypsy Rose Lee. Russell gives a memorable performance as the infamous Mama Rose, Gypsy's stage mother. Based on both Gypsy Rose Lee's memoirs and the hit Broadway play by Arthur Laurents. ♫Small World; All I Need is the Girl; You'll Never Get Away From Me; Let Me Entertain You; Some People; Everything's Coming Up Roses; You Gotta Have a Gimmick; Baby Jane and the Newsboys; Mr. Goldstone, I Love You. **144m/C VHS, Beta, LV.** Rosalind Russell, Natalie Wood, Karl Malden, Ann Jillian, Parley Baer, Paul Wallace, Betty Bruce; **D:** Mervyn LeRoy; **C:** Harry Stradling. Golden Globe Awards '63: Best Actress—Musical/Comedy (Russell); Nominations: Academy Awards '62: Best Adapted Score, Best Color Cinematography, Best Costume Design (Color). *WAR*

Gypsy 🎔🎔 1975 A modern day gypsy-blooded Robin Hood cavorts between heists and romantic trysts. Dubbed. **90m/C VHS, Beta.** Alain Delon, Annie Girardot, Paul Meurisse; **D:** Jose Giovanni. *FCT*

Gypsy 🎔🎔½ 1993 If you like Bette brassy and larger than life, as only she can be, than this is the production for you. This television recreation of the 1959 Broadway musical stars Midler as notorious stage mother Mama Rose, who tries to realize all her frustrated ambitions by pushing her two young daughters, June and Louise, into vaudeville show biz. Her wish eventually comes true, in an unexpected fashion, when an adult Louise (Gibb) transforms herself into stripper Gypsy Rose Lee. ♫Everything's Coming Up Roses; You've Gotta Have a Gimmick; All I Need Is the Girl; Rose's Turn; Some People; Mr. Goldstone, I Love You; You'll Never Get Away From Me; Together, Wherever We Go. **150m/C VHS, LV, Closed Caption.** Bette Midler, Peter Riegert, Cynthia Gibb, Ed Asner, Christine Ebersole, Michael Jeter, Andrea Martin, Jennifer Beck, Linda Hart, Rachel Sweet; **D:** Emile Ardolino; **W:** Arthur Laurents; **C:** Ralf Bode; **M:** Jule Styne, Stephen Sondheim. *CAF*

Gypsy Angels 🎔 1994 (R) A daredevil stunt pilot has a terrifying accident and develops amnesia. With the help of a stripper (who is in love with him), he tries to rebuild his life, this time with her in it. White's no actress and unless you like stunt flying (and there's a lot of it), fly by this one. (You'll note the director won't admit to this, since Smithee is a pseudonym.)**CW:** Profanity. **92m/C VHS, Closed Caption.** Vanna White, Richard Roundtree, Gene Bicknell; **D:** Alan Smithee. *THV*

Gypsy Blood 🎔🎔 1918 One of the first screen versions of "Carmen," closer to Prosper Merrimee's story than to the opera, depicting the fated love between a dancing girl and a matador. Lubitsch's first notable film. Silent. **104m/B VHS, Beta.** Pola Negri; **D:** Ernst Lubitsch. *FCT, GPV*

Gypsy Colt 🎔🎔½ 1954 (G) Gypsy is the horse beloved by the young Corcoran. But a drought forces her family to sell the animal to a racing stable 500 miles from their home. Gypsy is having none of this, escapes the stables, and returns home to be with Corcoran. Both horse and child actress are naturally appealing. **72m/C VHS.** Donna Corcoran, Ward Bond, Frances Dee, Lee Van Cleef, Larry Keating; **D:** Andrew Marton. *MGM, FCT*

The Gypsy Warriors 🎔🎔½ 1978 Two Army captains during WWII infiltrate Nazi-occupied France in order to prevent the distribution of a deadly toxin and are aided by a band of Gypsies. Made for television. **77m/C VHS, Beta.** Tom Selleck, James Whitmore Jr., Joseph Ruskin, Lina Raymond; **D:** Lou Antonio. *USH*

H 🎔🎔 1990 Two junkies try to kick their heroin addiction and face the difficult withdrawal period. Includes glimpses into their past that shed light on the reasons they turned to drugs. Contains explicit footage. **93m/C VHS.** *CA* Martin Neufeld, Pascale Montpetit; **D:** Darrell Wasyk. Genie Awards '91: Best Actress (Montpetit); Toronto-City Award '90: Best Canadian Feature Film. *NYR*

H-Bomb woof! 1971 Mitchum stars as a CIA agent who is sent to Bangkok to retrieve two stolen nuclear warheads from a terrorist. It just so happens that his ex-girlfriend's father is the terrorist he must contend with in this stupid movie. **98m/C VHS, Beta.** Olivia Hussey, Chris Mitchum, Krung Savilai; **D:** P. Chalong. *NO*

H-Man woof! *Bijo to Ekitainigen* 1959 A Japanese sci-fi woofer about a radioactive mass of slime festering under Tokyo. Extremely lame special effects get quite a few unintentional laughs. Dubbed. **79m/C VHS, Beta.** *JP* Koreya Senda, Kenji Sahara, Yumi Shirakawa, Akihiko Hirata; **D:** Inoshiro Honda. *COL*

The Habitation of Dragons 🎔½ 1991 Family fueds and melodrama in 1930s West Texas. Wandering lawyer George Tolliver (Davis) argues with successful businessman brother Leonard (Forrest) while matriarch Leonora (Stapleton) presides and family skeletons rattle. Confusing hodgepodge. **94m/C VHS.** Jean Stapleton, Frederic Forrest, Brad Davis, Pat Hingle, Hallie Foote, Maureen O'Sullivan; **D:** Michael Lindsay-Hogg; **W:** Horton Foote; **M:** David Shire. *TTC*

Hack O'Lantern 🎔 1987 Granddad worships Satan, and gets his grandson involved: the result is much bloodshed, violence and evil. **90m/C VHS, Beta. D:** Jag Mundhra. *NO*

Hackers 🎔🎔 1995 (PG-13) Group of teenaged computer cyber-geeks surf the 'net and become the prime suspects in an industrial conspiracy when hacker Dade (Miller) breaks into the computer at Ellingson Oil Company. It's really an inside job but just try getting anyone (read "adult") to believe him. So the techno whiz kids band together, with cops and security all wanting to shut them down. Jolie (hacker Acid Burn) is the daughter of actor Jon Voight.**CW:** Some sexuality; brief strong language. **105m/C VHS, LV, Closed Caption.** Jonny Lee Miller, Angelina Jolie, Fisher Stevens, Lorraine Bracco, Jesse Bradford, Wendell Pierce, Alberta Watson, Laurence Mason, Renoly Santiago, Matthew Lillard, Penn Jillette; **D:** Iain Softley; **W:** Rafael Moreu; **C:** Andrzej Sekula; **M:** Simon Boswell. *MGM*

Hadley's Rebellion 🎔🎔½ 1984 (PG) A Georgia farm boy adjusts to relocation at an elitist California boarding school by flaunting his wrestling abilities. **96m/C VHS, Beta, Closed Caption.** Griffin O'Neal, Charles Durning, William Devane, Adam Baldwin, Dennis Hage, Lisa Lucas; **D:** Fred Walton; **W:** Fred Walton. *FOX*

Hail 🎔🎔 *Hail to the Chief; Washington, B.C* 1973 (PG) A biting satire of what-might-have-been if certain key cabinet members had their way. **85m/C VHS, Beta.** Richard B. Shull, Dick O'Neill, Phil Foster, Joseph Sirola, Dan Resin, Willard Waterman, Gary Sandy; **D:** Fred Levinson. *NO*

Hail Caesar 🎔🎔½ 1994 (PG) His job at an eraser factory is the only thing standing between Julius Caesar MacGruder (Hall) and fame and fortune as a rock 'n roll singer. **93m/C VHS, Beta, LV.** Anthony Michael Hall, Robert Downey Jr., Frank Gorshin, Samuel L. Jackson, Judd Nelson, Nicholas Pryor, Leslie Danon, Bobbie Philips; **D:** Anthony Michael Hall; **W:** Robert Mittenthal; **M:** Roger Tallman. *PSM*

Hail, Hero! 🎔½ 1969 (PG) A dated Vietnam War era drama about a confused hippie rebelling against his parents and the draft. First film for both Douglas and Strauss. Adapted from the novel by John Weston. Includes music by Gordon Lightfoot. **97m/C VHS, Beta.** Michael Douglas, Arthur Kennedy, Teresa Wright, John Larch, Charles Drake, Deborah Winters, Peter Strauss; **D:** David Miller; **C:** Robert B. Hauser. *FOX*

Hail Mary 🎔🎔½ *Je Vous Salue Marie* 1985 (R) A modern-day virgin named Mary inexplicably becomes pregnant in this controversial film that discards notions of divinity in favor of the celebration of a lively, intellectual humanism. Godard rejects orthodox narrative structure and bourgeois prejudices. Very controversial, but not up to his breathless beginning work. In French with English subtitles. **107m/C VHS, Beta, LV.** *FR SI GB* Myriem Roussel, Thierry Rode, Philippe Lacoste, Manon Anderson, Juliette Binoche, Johan Leysen; **D:** Jean-Luc Godard; **W:** Jean-Luc Godard. *LIV, VES*

Hail the Conquering Hero 🎔🎔🎔½ 1944 A slight young man is rejected by the Army. Upon returning home, he is surprised to find out they think he's a hero. Biting satire with Demarest's performance stealing the show. **101m/B VHS, Closed Caption.** Eddie Bracken, Ella Raines, William Demarest, Franklin Pangborn, Raymond Walburn; **D:** Preston Sturges. Nominations: Academy Awards '44: Best Original Screenplay. *USH*

Hair 🎔🎔🎔½ 1979 (PG) Film version of the explosive 1960s Broadway musical about the carefree life of the flower children and the shadow of the Vietnam War that hangs over them. Great music, as well as wonderful choreography by Twyla Tharp help portray the surprisingly sensitive evocation of the period so long after the fact. Forman has an uncanny knack for understanding the textures of American life. Watch for a thinner Nell Carter. **122m/C VHS, Beta, LV, Closed Caption.** Treat Williams, John Savage, Beverly D'Angelo, Annie Golden, Nicholas Ray; **D:** Milos Forman; **W:** Michael Weller. *MGM*

The Hairdresser's Husband 🎔🎔 1992 (R) Antoine (Rochefort) has had an odd obsession since boyhood—hairdressers—and in middle age he finds love with Mathilde (Galiena), a hairdresser he meets and proposes to as she cuts his hair. She accepts, and the two live their quiet lives in her barber shop as she cuts hair and he watches, occasionally breaking out in Arabian dances. A dark and odd yet refreshing film with fine performances by Rochefort and Galiena in this story about fetishism, obsession, and hair. In French with English subtitles. **84m/C VHS, LV, Closed Caption.** *FR* Jean Rochefort, Anna Galiena, Roland Bertin, Maurice Chevit, Philippe Clevenot, Jacques Mathou, Claude Aufaure; **D:** Patrice Leconte; **W:** Patrice Leconte; **M:** Michael Nyman. *PAR, BTV*

Hairspray 🎔🎔🎔 1988 (PG) Waters' first truly mainstream film, if that's even possible, and his funniest. Details the struggle among teenagers in 1962 Baltimore for the top spot in a local TV dance show. Deals with racism and stereotypes, as well as typical "teen" problems (hair-do's and don'ts). Filled with refreshingly tasteful, subtle social satire (although not without typical Waters touches that will please die-hard fans). Lake is lovable and appealing as Divine's daughter; Divine, in his last film, is likeable as an iron-toting mom. Look for Waters in a cameo and Divine as a man. Great '60s music, which Waters refers to as "the only known remedy to today's Hit Parade of Hell." **94m/C VHS, Beta, LV, Closed Caption.** Ricki Lake, Divine, Jerry Stiller, Colleen Fitzpatrick, Sonny Bono, Deborah Harry, Ruth Brown, Pia Zadora, Ric Ocasek, Michael St. Gerard, Leslie Ann Powers, Shawn Thompson; **Cameos:** John Waters; **D:** John Waters; **W:** John Waters. *NLC, FCT*

The Hairy Ape 🎔🎔 1944 Screen adaptation of the Eugene O'Neill play. A beast-like coal stoker becomes obsessed with a cool and distant passenger aboard an ocean liner. **90m/B VHS.** William Bendix, Susan Hayward, John Loder, Dorothy Comingore, Roman Bohnen, Alan Napier; **D:** Alfred Santell. Nominations: Academy Awards '44: Original Dramatic/Comedy Score. *NOS, MRV, FCT*

Half a Lifetime 1986 The stakes are too high for four friends playing a game of poker. **85m/C VHS, Beta.** Keith Carradine, Gary Busey, Nick Mancuso, Saul Rubinek. *HBO*

Half a Loaf of Kung Fu 🎔 1985 The worthy bodyguards of Sern Chuan are called upon to deliver a valuable jade statue. Thwarted again and again by ruthless robbers, they falter. Only Chan carries on, meeting the enemy alone. Fast action, good story. **98m/C VHS, Beta.** Jackie Chan. *NO*

Half a Sixpence 🎬🎬 1967 Former musician Sidney, who earlier directed "Showboat" and "Kiss Me Kate," shows a bit less verve in this production. Based on H.G. Wells' 1905 novel, "Kipps," it sports much of the original cast from its Broadway incarnation. Edwardian orphan Steele, a cloth-dealer-in-training, comes into a large sum of money and proceeds to lose it with great dispatch. Somewhere along the way he loses his girlfriend, too, but she takes him back because musicals end happily. ♫Half a Sixpence; Flash, Bang, Wallop!; All In The Cause Of Economy; I'm Not Talking To You; Money To Burn; The Race Is On; I Don't Believe A Word Of It; A Proper Gentleman; She's Too Far Above Me. **148m/C VHS, Closed Caption.** Tommy Steele, Julia Foster, Penelope Horner, Cyril Ritchard, Grover Dale; **D:** George Sidney; **W:** Beverley Cross; **C:** Geoffrey Unsworth. *PAR, FCT*

Half a Soldier 🎬🎬 1940 A spoiled girl gets a big surprise when she steals a car and discovers the body of a gangster in the trunk. **59m/B VHS, Beta.** Heather Angel, John "Dusty" King. *NOS, DVT, HEG*

The Half-Breed 🎬🎬 1951 Routine oater with settlers and Apaches fighting, and the obligatory half-breed stuck in the middle. **81m/B VHS, Beta.** Robert Young, Jack Buetel, Janis Carter, Barton MacLane, Reed Hadley, Porter Hall, Connie Gilchrist; **D:** Stuart Gilmore. *TTC*

Half Human 🎬½ 1958 Dull Japanese monster movie about an ape-human who terrorizes Northern Japan. When released in the U.S., Carradine and Morris were added. Without subtitles, just Carradine's narration. Director Honda made better movies before and after, with Godzilla and Rodan. **78m/B VHS.** JP John Carradine, Akira Takarada, Morris Ankrum; **D:** Inoshiro Honda. *SNC, MLB*

Half Moon Street 🎬🎬 *Escort Girl* 1986 (R) A brilliant woman scientist supplements her paltry fellowship salary by becoming a hired escort and prostitute, which leads her into various incidents of international intrigue. Adapted from a story by Paul Theroux, "Dr. Slaughter." **90m/C VHS, Beta, LV, 8mm, Closed Caption.** Sigourney Weaver, Michael Caine, Keith Buckley, Ian MacInnes; **D:** Bob Swaim. *NLC*

Half of Heaven 🎬🎬🎬 *La Mitad del Cielo* 1986 A critically popular film about a young Spanish woman who begins to share certain telepathic powers with her wizened grandmother. In Spanish with English subtitles. **95m/C VHS, Beta.** SP Angela Molina, Margarita Lozano; **D:** Manuel Gutierrez Aragon. *PBS, FCT, APD*

Half-Shot at Sunrise 🎬🎬 1930 Madcap vaudeville comedians play AWOL soldiers loose in 1918 Paris. Continuous one-liners, sight gags, and slapstick nonsense. First film appearance of comedy team Wheeler and Woolsey. **78m/B VHS, Beta.** Bert Wheeler, Robert Woolsey, Dorothy Lee, Robert Rutherford, Edna May Oliver; **D:** Paul Sloane; **M:** Max Steiner. *VYY, CAB, DVT*

Half Slave, Half Free 🎬🎬½ *Solomon Northrup's Odyssey* 1985 The true story of a free black man in the 1840s who is kidnapped and forced into slavery for 12 years. Made for television as part of the "American Playhouse" series on PBS. Followed by "Charlotte Forten's Mission: Experiment in Freedom." **113m/C VHS, Beta.** Avery Brooks, Mason Adams, Petronia Paley, John Saxon, Joe Seneca, Michael Tolan, Lee Bryant, Rhetta Greene, Janet League; **D:** Gordon Parks. *XVC, KAR, KUI*

The Halfback of Notre Dame 🎬🎬½ 1996 (G) Star football player (and coach's son) Craig Modeau (Hogan) is a lumbering misfit, ripe for high school teasing, anywhere but on the gridiron. But French exchange student Esmeralda (Vaugier) thinks he's sweet—much to the dismay of current boyfriend, obnoxious quarterback Archie (Cutler). Then Craig decides to quit the team right before the big game when dad says no fraternizing and it's up to his French flame to get the jock to change his mind. Made for TV reworking of Victor Hugo's "The Hunchback of Notre Dame."

97m/C VHS, LV, Closed Caption. Gabriel Hogan, Emmanuelle Vaugier, Scott Hylands, Sandra Nelson, Allen Cutler; **D:** Rene Bonniere; **W:** Richard Clark, Mark Trafficante; **C:** Maris Jansons; **M:** George Blondheim. *HMK*

Halfmoon 🎬🎬 *Paul Bowles: Halbmond* 1995 Trilogy of stories by Paul Bowles. "Merkala Beach" looks at the friendship of two young Moroccan men who are both seduced by the same mysterious woman. "Call at Corazon" finds the honeymoon journey of a mismatched British couple turning into a nightmare as they sail up the Amazon on a crowded cargo boat. "Allal" is a Moroccan boy who's an outcast in his village because of his illegitimacy. He befriends an old snake dealer and steals one of his cobras in order to charm the reptile. Then Allal winds up in a magical transformation with the creature. English and Arabic with subtitles. **90m/C VHS.** GE GE Samir Guesmi, Khalid Ksouri, Sondos Belhassan, Veronica Quilligan, Sam Cox, Said Zakir, Mohammed Belfquih; **D:** Irene von Alberti, Frieder Schlaich; **W:** Irene von Alberti, Frieder Schlaich; **C:** Volker Tittel; **M:** Roman Bunka. *FRF*

Hallelujah! 🎬🎬🎬½ 1929 Haynes plays an innocent young man who turns to religion and becomes a charismatic preacher after a family tragedy. He retains all his human weaknesses, however, including falling for the lovely but deceitful McKinney. Great music included traditional spirituals and songs by Berlin, such as "At the End of the Road" and "Swanee Shuffle." Shot on location in Tennessee. The first all-black feature film and the first talkie for director Vidor was given the go-ahead by MGM production chief Irving Thalberg, though he knew the film would be both controversial and get minimal release in the deep South. **90m/B VHS.** Daniel L. Haynes, Nina Mae McKinney, William Fontaine, Harry Gray, Fannie Belle DeKnight, Everett McGarrity; **D:** King Vidor; **M:** Irving Berlin. Nominations: Academy Awards '30: Best Director (Vidor). *MGM, MOV, BTV*

Hallelujah, I'm a Bum 🎬🎬½ *Hallelujah, I'm a Tramp; The Heart of New York; Happy Go Lucky; Lazy Bones* 1933 A happy-go-lucky hobo reforms and begins a new life for the sake of a woman. Bizarre Depression-era musical with a Rodgers and Hart score and continuously rhyming dialogue. The British version, due to the slang meaning of "bum," was retitled, substituting "tramp." ♫You Are Too Beautiful; I'll Do It Again; I've Got To Get Back To New York; What Do You Want With Money?; Hallelujah, I'm A Bum; My Pal Bumper; Dear June; Bumper Found a Grand. **83m/B VHS, Beta.** Al Jolson, Madge Evans, Frank Morgan, Chester Conklin; **D:** Lewis Milestone; **W:** Ben Hecht, S.N. Behrman; **M:** Richard Rodgers, Lorenz Hart. *LCA, MLB*

The Hallelujah Trail 🎬🎬 1965 Denver mining town in the late 1800s is about to batten down the hatches for a long winter, and there's not a drop of whiskey to be had. The U.S. Cavalry sends a shipment to the miners, but temperance leader Cora Templeton Massingale (Remick) and her bevy of ladies against liquor stand between the shipment and the would-be whistle whetters. Limp Western satire directed by Preston Sturges' brother, who fared much better when he kept a straight face (he also directed "The Great Escape"). Based on Bill Gulick's novel, "The Hallelujah Train." Two-laserdisc set includes additional footage (though it's already overlong), the original trailer, and a letterboxing. **166m/C VHS, LV.** Burt Lancaster, Lee Remick, Jim Hutton, Pamela Tiffin, Donald Pleasence, Brian Keith, Martin Landau; **D:** John Sturges; **W:** John Gay; **C:** Robert L. Surtees; **M:** Elmer Bernstein. *MGM, FCT*

Halloween 🎬🎬🎬½ 1978 (R) John Carpenter's horror classic has been acclaimed "the most successful independent motion picture of all time." A deranged youth returns to his hometown with murderous intent after fifteen years in an asylum. Very, very scary—you feel this movie more than see it. **90m/C VHS, Beta, LV.** Jamie Lee Curtis, Donald Pleasence, Nancy Loomis, P.J. Soles; **D:** John Car-

penter; **W:** John Carpenter, Debra Hill; **C:** Dean Cundey; **M:** John Carpenter. *MED, VTR*

Halloween 2: The Nightmare Isn't Over! 🎬½ 1981 (R) Trying to pick up where "Halloween" left off, the sequel begins with the escape of vicious killer Michael, who continues to murder and terrorize the community of Haddonfield, Illinois. Lacking the innovative intentions of its predecessor, it relies on old-fashioned buckets of blood. No chills, just trauma. Co-scripted by Carpenter, director of the original. **92m/C VHS, Beta, LV.** Jamie Lee Curtis, Donald Pleasence, Jeffrey Kramer, Charles Cyphers, Lance Guest; **D:** Rick Rosenthal; **W:** John Carpenter, Debra Hill; **C:** Dean Cundey; **M:** John Carpenter. *USH*

Halloween 3: Season of the Witch 🎬🎬 1982 (R) Modern druid plans to kill 50 million children with his specially made Halloween masks. Produced by John Carpenter, this second sequel to the 1978 horror classic is not based on the events or characters of its predecessors or successors. Followed by "Halloween 4," and "Halloween 5: The Revenge of Michael Myers" (1989). **98m/C VHS, Beta, LV.** Tom Atkins, Stacey Nelkin, Dan O'Herlihy, Ralph Strait; **D:** Tommy Lee Wallace; **C:** Dean Cundey; **M:** John Carpenter. *USH*

Halloween 4: The Return of Michael Myers 🎬🎬 1988 (R) The third sequel, wherein the lunatic that won't die returns home to kill his niece. **88m/C VHS, Beta, LV, Closed Caption.** Donald Pleasence, Ellie Cornell, Danielle Harris, Michael Pataki; **D:** Dwight Little; **C:** Peter Collister. *FOX*

Halloween 5: The Revenge of Michael Myers 🎬½ 1989 (R) Fifth in the series, this Halloween is an improvement over 2, 3, and 4, thanks to a few well-directed scare scenes. Unfortunately, the plot remains the same: a psycho behemoth chases down and kills more teens. An open ending promises yet another installment. **96m/C VHS, Beta, LV, Closed Caption.** Donald Pleasence, Ellie Cornell, Danielle Harris, Don Shanks, Betty Carvalho; **D:** Dominique Othenin-Girard; **W:** Shem Bitterman. *FOX*

Halloween 6: The Curse of Michael Myers 🎬 1995 (R) First the return. Then his revenge. And now, his curse, aimed square at the viewer. Lame series entry connects Michael Myers to an ancient Celtic ritual that drives him to murder whole families in his old stompin' grounds of Haddonfield. Before he finishes his reign of terror, Myers has to contend with Dr. Loomis (Pleasence), the man who knows his true evil. Though still a profit-making monster (the entire franchise had a combined budget of $20 million and grossed over $200 million), Michael should probably join Freddy and Jason at the old slashers' retirement home. Film marks the final screen appearance of Pleasence, who died shortly after its completion. **CW:** Strong horror violence, and some sexuality. **88m/C VHS, LV, Closed Caption.** Donald Pleasence, Mitchell Ryan, Marianne Hagan, Leo Geter, George P. Wilbur; **D:** Joe Chappelle; **W:** Daniel Farrands; **C:** Billy Dickson; **M:** Alan Howarth. *TOU*

Halloween Night 🎬🎬 1990 (R) Ancient evil rises up to destroy the perfect small town. **90m/C VHS.** Hy Pyke, Katrina Garner; **D:** Emilio P. Miraglio. *ATL*

Halloween with the Addams Family woof! 1979 A really pathetic production spawned during the "reunion" craze of the late '70s, sparked only by the lively performance of Coogan's Uncle Fester and the always lovable Lurch. Made for television. **87m/C VHS, Beta.** John Astin, Carolyn Jones, Jackie Coogan, Ted Cassidy. *GKK*

The Halls of Montezuma 🎬🎬½ 1950 Large, bombastic WWII combat epic. Depicts the Marines fighting the Japanese in the Pacific. **113m/C VHS, Beta.** Richard Widmark, Jack Palance, Reginald Gardiner, Robert Wagner, Karl Malden, Richard Boone, Richard Hylton, Skip Homeier, Jack Webb, Neville Brand, Martin Milner, Bert Freed; **D:** Lewis Milestone. *FOX*

Hallucination woof! *Hallucination Generation* **1967** Early flower-power exploiter about expatriate acid heads who murder an antique dealer under the influence of LSD and then attempt to hide at a monastery. Depicts LSD as the catalyst in bringing out the group's criminal behavior. In sepia while everyone's cool, breaking into color during the head trips. **90m/C VHS, Beta.** George Montgomery, Danny Stone; **D:** Edward Mann. *VDC*

Hallucinations of a Deranged Mind *Delirios de Um Anormal* **1970** A compilation of all the magic moments ever censored by the Brazilian military dictatorship. Includes scenes banned from over 10 different Mojica Marins films, including his "Coffin Joe" character. In Portuguese with English subtitles. **?m/C VHS.** BR Jose Mojica Marins; **D:** Jose Mojica Marins. *SMW, FCT*

Hambone & Hillie **1984 (PG)** An elderly woman makes a 3000-mile trek across the United States to search for the dog she lost in an airport. **97m/C VHS, Beta.** Lillian Gish, Timothy Bottoms, Candy Clark, O.J. Simpson, Robert Walker Jr., Jack Carter, Alan Hale Jr., Anne Lockhart; **D:** Roy Watts; **W:** Sandra K. Bailey. *VTR*

Hamburger Hill **1987 (R)** Popular war epic depicting the famous battle between Americans and Viet Cong over a useless hill in Vietnam. Made in the heyday of 1980s Vietnam backlash, and possibly the most realistic and bloodiest of the lot. **104m/C VHS, Beta, LV.** Michael Dolan, Daniel O'Shea, Dylan McDermott, Tommy Swerdlow, Courtney B. Vance, Anthony Barille, Michael Boatman, Don Cheadle, Tim Quill, Don James, Michael A. Nickles; **D:** John Irvin; **W:** Jim Carabatsos; **M:** Philip Glass. *LIV, VES, FCT*

Hamburger...The Motion Picture **1986 (R)** The life and times of students at Busterburger U., the only college devoted to hamburger franchise management. **90m/C VHS, Beta, LV, Closed Caption.** Leigh McCloskey, Dick Butkus, Randi Brooks, Sandy Hackett; **D:** Mike Marvin; **M:** Elmer Bernstein. *MED*

Hamlet **1948** Splendid adaptation of Shakespeare's dramatic play. Hamlet vows vengeance on the murderer of his father in this tight version of the four hour stage play. Some scenes were cut out, including all of Rosencrantz and Guildenstern. Beautifully photographed in Denmark. An Olivier triumph. Remade several times. **153m/B VHS.** GB Laurence Olivier, Basil Sydney, Felix Aylmer, Jean Simmons, Stanley Holloway, Peter Cushing, Christopher Lee, Eileen Herlie, John Laurie, Esmond Knight, Anthony Quayle; **D:** Laurence Olivier; **W:** Alan Dent; **M:** William Walton; **V:** John Gielgud. Academy Awards '48: Best Actor (Olivier), Best Art Direction/Set Decoration (B & W), Best Costume Design (B & W), Best Picture; British Academy Awards '48: Best Film; Golden Globe Awards '49: Best Actor—Drama (Olivier); New York Film Critics Awards '48: Best Actor (Olivier); Nominations: Academy Awards '48: Best Director (Olivier), Best Supporting Actress (Simmons), Original Dramatic/Comedy Score. *PAR, BTV, HMV*

Hamlet **1969 (G)** Williamson brings to the screen his stage performance as the classic Shakespeare character. Something is lost in the process, although there are some redeeming moments including those with Faithfull as Ophelia. **114m/C VHS, Beta.** GB Nicol Williamson, Anthony Hopkins, Marianne Faithfull, Gordon Jackson, Judy Parfitt, Mark Dingham, Anjelica Huston; **D:** Tony Richardson. *COL*

Hamlet **1990 (PG)** Zeffirelli—in his fourth attempt at Shakespeare—creates a surprisingly energetic and accessible interpretation of the Bard's moody play. Gibson brings charm, humor and a carefully calculated sense of violence, not to mention a good deal of solid flesh, to the eponymous role, and handles the language skillfully (although if you seek a poetic Dane, stick with Olivier). Exceptional work from Scofield and Bates; Close seems a tad hysterical (not to mention too young to play Gibson's mother), but brings insight and nuance to her role. Purists beware: this isn't a completely faithful adaptation. Beautifully costumed; shot on location in Northern Scotland. **135m/C VHS, Beta, LV, 8mm, Closed Caption.** Mel Gibson, Glenn Close, Alan Bates, Paul Scofield, Ian Holm, Elaine Bonham Carter, Nathaniel Parker, Pete Postlethwaite; **D:** Franco Zeffirelli; **W:** Franco Zeffirelli, Christopher DeVore; **C:** David Watkin. Nominations: Academy Awards '90: Best Art Direction/Set Decoration, Best Costume Design. *WAR, BTV, FCT*

Hamlet **1996 (PG-13)** Branagh tackles Shakespeare once again with the uncut, four-hour long story of the melancholy Dane (played by you-know-who). Branagh's decision to use the complete text, and move the action ahead 600 years to the 19th century adds an interesting external political dimension to the palace intrigue and gives this sixth screen adaptation the stature of Olivier's 1948 masterpiece. Jacobi and Christie stand out among a very large and brilliant cast. Lemmon and Crystal, however, should stick to American comedy. A two and a half hour version was also prepared for those with shorter attention spans, but the uncut version is well worth the time invested. **CW:** Some violent images and sexuality. **242m/C VHS, LV, Closed Caption.** GB Kenneth Branagh, Kate Winslet, Julie Christie, Derek Jacobi, Richard Briers, Brian Blessed, Michael Maloney, Timothy Spall, Reece Dinsdale, Jack Lemmon, Nicholas Farrell, Charlton Heston, Rosemary Harris, Gerard Depardieu, Robin Williams, Billy Crystal, Simon Russell Beale, Michael Bryant, John Gielgud, Richard Attenborough, Rufus Sewell, Judi Dench, Ian McElhinney, John Mills; **D:** Kenneth Branagh; **W:** Kenneth Branagh; **C:** Alex Thomson; **M:** Patrick Doyle. Nominations: Academy Awards '96: Best Adapted Screenplay, Best Art Direction/Set Decoration, Best Costume Design, Original Dramatic/Comedy Score. *COL*

Hammersmith is Out **1972 (R)** A violent lunatic cons an orderly into letting him escape. Chases, romance and craziness follow. **108m/C VHS, Beta.** Richard Burton, Elizabeth Taylor, Peter Ustinov, Beau Bridges, John Schuck; **D:** Peter Ustinov. *PSM*

Hammett **1982 (PG)** After many directors and script rewrites, Wenders was assigned to this arch neo-noir what-if scenario. Depicts Dashiell Hammett solving a complex crime himself, an experience he uses in his novels. Interesting, but ultimately botched studio exercise, like many from executive producer Francis Coppola, who is said to have reshot much of the film. **98m/C VHS, Beta.** Frederic Forrest, Peter Boyle, Sylvia Sidney, Elisha Cook Jr., Marilu Henner; **D:** Wim Wenders; **C:** Joseph Biroc; **M:** John Barry. *WAR*

Hamsin **1983** A Jewish landowner and an Arab worker encounter difficulties in their relationship when the government announces plans to confiscate Arab land. In Hebrew with English subtitles. **90m/C VHS, Beta.** Shlomo Tarshish, Yasin Shawap, Hemda Levy, Ruth Geler; **D:** Daniel Wachsmann. *ERG*

The Hand **1960** During WWII, three British POWs are tortured by the Japanese. Refusing to give information, two of them have their right hands cut off. The third opts to talk, thereby keeping his hand. After the war, a series of murders occur in London where the victims have their hands amputated. Could there be a connection? **61m/B VHS, Beta.** GB Derek Bond, Ronald Lee Hunt, Reed de Rouen, Ray Cooney, Brian Coleman; **D:** Henry Cass. *SNC*

The Hand **1981 (R)** A gifted cartoonist's hand is severed in a car accident. Soon, the hand is on the loose with a mind of its own, seeking out victims with an obsessive vengeance. Stone's sophomore directorial outing is a unique, surreal psycho-horror pastiche consistently underrated by most critics. **105m/C VHS, Beta.** GB Michael Caine, Andrea Marcovicci, Annie McEnroe, Bruce McGill, Viveca Lindfors; **D:** Oliver Stone; **W:** Oliver Stone; **M:** James Horner. *WAR*

Hand Gun **1993 (R)** Jack McCallister (Cassel) is wounded in a shoot-out with police but still manages to get away with half-a-million from a robbery. When word gets out, everybody begins looking for Jack, including his two sons—gun happy George (Williams) and small time con artist Michael (Schulze). **CW:** Rated R for shootings and beatings, strong language and some sexuality. **90m/C VHS, LV.** Seymour Cassel, Treat Williams, Paul Schulzie, Michael Rapaport; **D:** Whitney Ransick; **W:** Whitney Ransick. *TRI*

The Hand that Rocks the Cradle **1992 (R)** DeMornay is Peyton Flanders, the nanny from hell, in an otherwise predictable thriller. Sciorra's role is a thankless one as pregnant and unbelievably naive Claire Bartel, who unwittingly starts a horrific chain of events when she levels charges of molestation against her obstetrician. Transparent plot preys on the worst fears of viewers, and doesn't offer anything innovative or new. See this one for DeMornay's Jekyll and Hyde performance. **CW:** Language, terror and violence, and sexual molestation. **110m/C VHS, Beta, Closed Caption.** Annabella Sciorra, Rebecca DeMornay, Matt McCoy, Ernie Hudson, Julianne Moore, Madeline Zima, John de Lancie, Mitchell Laurance; **D:** Curtis Hanson; **W:** Amanda Silver; **C:** Robert Elswit; **M:** Graeme Revell. MTV Movie Awards '92: Best Villain (DeMornay). *HPH*

A Handful of Dust **1988 (PG)** A dry, stately adaptation of the bitter Evelyn Waugh novel about a stuffy young aristocrat's wife's careless infidelity and how it sends her innocent husband to a tragic downfall. A well-meaning version that captures Waugh's cynical satire almost in spite of itself. Set in post-WWI England. **114m/C VHS, Beta.** GB James Wilby, Kristin Scott Thomas, Rupert Graves, Alec Guinness, Anjelica Huston, Judi Dench, Cathryn Harrison, Pip Torrens, John Junkin; **D:** Charles Sturridge; **W:** Charles Sturridge, Tim Sullivan, Derek Granger; **M:** George Fenton. British Academy Awards '88: Best Supporting Actress (Dench); Nominations: Academy Awards '88: Best Costume Design. *COL, TVC*

The Handmaid's Tale **1990 (R)** A cool, shallow but nonetheless chilling nightmare based on Margaret Atwood's bestselling novel, about a woman caught in the machinations of a near-future society so sterile it enslaves the few fertile women and forces them into being childbearing "handmaids." **109m/C VHS, Beta, LV, Closed Caption.** Natasha Richardson, Robert Duvall, Faye Dunaway, Aidan Quinn, Elizabeth McGovern, Victoria Tennant, Blanche Baker, Traci Lind; **D:** Volker Schlondorff; **W:** Harold Pinter. *HBO, FCT, IME*

Hands Across the Border **1943** A musical western in which Roy helps a woman find the men who killed her father. **72m/B VHS.** Roy Rogers, Ruth Terry, Guinn "Big Boy" Williams, Onslow Stevens, Mary Treen, Joseph Crehan; **D:** Joseph Kane. *NOS, DVT, TIM*

Hands Across the Table **1935** Regi Allen (Lombard) is a fortune-hunting manicurist in a swanky hotel barber shop. Has-been millionaire playboy Theodore Drew, III (MacMurray) falls for her but he's about to marry money (Allwyn) and Regi's got a wheelchair-bound rich man (Bellamy) just waiting for her to say "I do." Snappy dialogue and light-hearted performances. Based on the story "Bracelets" by Vina Delmar. **80m/B VHS, Closed Caption.** Carole Lombard, Fred MacMurray, Ralph Bellamy, Astrid Allwyn, Ruth Donnelly, Marie Prevost, William Demarest, Edward Gargan; **D:** Mitchell Leisen; **W:** Norman Krasna, Vincent Lawrence, Herbert Fields; **C:** Ted Tetzlaff. *USH*

Hands of a Murderer *Sherlock Holmes and the Prince of Crime* **1990** Sherlock Holmes (Woodward) and the faithful Dr. Watson (Hillerman) are in pursuit of the great detective's most evil nemisis—the nefarious Moriarty (Andrews). This time, the fiend has escaped the gallows and stolen government secrets from the safe of Holmes' brother Mycroft. TV movie. **100m/C VHS.** Edward Woodward, John Hillerman, Anthony Andrews, Kim Thomson, Peter Jeffrey, Warren Clarke; **D:** Stuart Orme; **W:** Charles Edward Pogue. *TVC*

Hands of a Stranger 🎬🎬 1962 Another undistinguished entry in the long line of remakes of "The Hands of Orlac." A pianist who loses his hands in an accident is given the hands of a murderer, and his new hands want to do more than tickle the ivories. Kellerman has a very small role as does former "Sheena" McCalla. **95m/B VHS.** Paul Lukather, Joan Harvey, James Stapleton, Sally Kellerman, Irish McCalla; **D:** Newton Arnold. *SNC*

Hands of a Stranger 🎬🎬 1987 Policeman's wife is raped during an adulterous tryst. As the painful truth dawns on the cop, he himself dallies with a compassionate lady D.A. while hunting the attacker. About as sordid as a network TV-movie gets without toppling into sleaze; strong acting and a sober script pull it through. But the plot, from Robert Daly's novel, doesn't justify miniseries treatment; the two-cassette package is excessively long. **179m/C VHS.** Armand Assante, Beverly D'Angelo, Blair Brown, Michael Lerner, Philip Casnoff, Arliss Howard; **D:** Larry Elikann; **W:** Arthur Kopit. *WOV*

Hands of Death 🎬 1988 Thieves use their Ninja skills to stop any one in their path to evil. Action-packed, somewhat contrived. **90m/C VHS, Beta.** Richard Harrison, Mike Abbott; **D:** Godfrey Ho. *IMP*

The Hands of Orlac 🎬🎬 1925 Classic silent film about a pianist whose hands are mutilated in an accident. His hands are replaced by those of a murderer, and his urge to kill becomes overwhelming. Contains restored footage. **92m/B VHS.** *AT* Conrad Veidt, Fritz Kortner, Carmen Cartellieri, Paul Adkonas, Alexandra Sorina; **D:** Robert Wiene; **W:** Ludwig Nerz. *LSV*

The Hands of Orlac 🎬🎬 1960 *Hands of the Stranger* Third remake of Maurice Renard's classic tale. When a concert pianist's hands are mutilated in an accident, he receives a graft of a murderer's hands. Obsession sweeps the musician, as he believes his new hands are incapable of music, only violence. Bland adaptation of the original story. **95m/B VHS.** *GB FR* Mel Ferrer, Christopher Lee, Felix Aylmer, Basil Sydney, Donald Wolfit, Donald Pleasence; **D:** Edmond T. Greville; **M:** Claude Bolling. *SNC*

Hands of Steel woof! 1986 (R) A ruthless cyborg carries out a mission to find and kill an important scientist. Terrible acting, and lousy writing: an all-around woofer! **94m/C VHS, Beta.** Daniel Greene, John Saxon, Janet Agren, Claudio Cassinelli, George Eastman; **D:** Martin Dolman. *LIV*

Hands of the Ripper 🎬🎬½ 1971 (R) Jack the Ripper's daughter returns to London where she works as a medium by day and stalks the streets at night. Classy Hammer horror variation on the perennial theme. **85m/C VHS, Beta.** *GB* Eric Porter, Angharad Rees, Jane Merrow, Keith Bell; **D:** Peter Sasdy; **M:** Christopher Gunning. *MLB*

Hands Up 🎬🎬½ 1926 Jaunty Confederate spy (played by much-overlooked American comedian Griffith) attempts, amidst much comic nonsense, to thwart Yankee gold mining during the Civil War. Silent. **50m/B VHS, Beta.** Raymond Griffith, Mack Swain, Marion Nixon, Montagu Love; **D:** Clarence Badger. *GPV*

Hands Up 🎬🎬🎬 *Rece do Gory* 1981 Famed Polish film finished in 1967 but not released until 1981 for political reasons (prologue shot in '81 included). Doctors at a medical school reunion reflect upon the effect of Stalinist rule on their education and lives. In Polish with English subtitles. **78m/C VHS, Beta.** *PL* **D:** Jerzy Skolimowski. *FCT*

Hang 'Em High 🎬🎬½ 1967 (PG-13) A cowboy is saved from a lynching and vows to hunt down the gang that nearly killed him in this American-made spaghetti western. Eastwood's first major vehicle made outside of Europe.**CW:** Western action/violence. **114m/C VHS, Beta, LV.** Clint Eastwood, Inger Stevens, Ed Begley Sr., Pat Hingle, James MacArthur; **D:** Ted Post. *MGM, TLF*

Hangar 18 🎬½ *Invasion Force* 1980 (PG) Silly sci-fi drama about two astronauts who collide with a UFO during a shuttle flight. Later they learn that the government is hiding it in a hangar and they try to prove its existence. Shown on TV as "Invasion Force" with an entirely new ending. **97m/C VHS, Beta.** Darren McGavin, Robert Vaughn, Gary Collins, James Hampton, Philip Abbott, Pamela Bellwood, Tom Hallick, Cliff Osmond, Joseph Campanella; **D:** James L. Conway; **W:** David O'Malley. *WOV*

The Hanged Man 🎬🎬 1974 Tale of a gunslinger in the Old West who mystically escapes death by hanging. Reborn, he re-evaluates the meaning of justice. Made for television. **78m/C VHS.** Steve Forrest, Cameron Mitchell, Sharon Acker, Dean Jagger, Will Geer, Barbara Luna, Rafael Campos; **D:** Michael Caffey. *NO*

Hangfire 🎬🎬 1991 (R) When a New Mexican prison is evacuated thanks to a nasty chemical explosion, several prisoners decide it's time for a furlough, and they elect the local sheriff's wife as a traveling companion. Another mediocre actioner from director Maris, it gets an extra bone for stunts kids shouldn't try at home.**CW:** Language and violence. **91m/C VHS, LV.** Brad Davis, Yaphet Kotto, Lee DeBroux, Jan-Michael Vincent, George Kennedy, Kim Delaney; **D:** Peter Maris; **W:** Brian D. Jeffries. *COL*

Hangin' with the Homeboys 🎬🎬🎬 1991 (R) One night in the lives of four young men. Although the Bronx doesn't offer much for any of them, they have little interest in escaping its confines, and they are more than willing to complain. Characters are insightfully written and well portrayed, with strongest work from Serrano as a Puerto Rican who is trying to pass himself off as Italian. Lack of plot may frustrate some viewers.**CW:** Strong language and one strong sex scene. **89m/C VHS, LV, Closed Caption.** Mario Joyner, Doug E. Doug, John Leguizamo, Nestor Serrano, Kimberly Russell, Mary B. Ward; **D:** Joseph B. Vasquez; **W:** Joseph B. Vasquez. Sundance Film Festival '91: Best Screenplay.*NLC, FCT*

Hanging on a Star 🎬 1978 (PG) A small rock band encounters many comic adventures as it climbs its way up the charts. Raffin stars as the band's persistent and competent road agent. **92m/C VHS, Beta.** Deborah Raffin, Lane Caudell, Wolfman Jack, Jason Parker, Danil Torppe; **D:** Mike MacFarland. *MGM*

The Hanging Tree 🎬🎬 1959 Cooper plays a frontier doctor who rescues a thief (Piazza) from a lynch mob and nurses a temporarily blind girl (Schell). Malden is the bad guy who tries to attack Schell and Cooper shoots him. The townspeople take Cooper out to "The Hanging Tree" but this time it's Schell and Piazza who come to his rescue. Slow-paced western with good performances. Scott's screen debut. **108m/B VHS.** Gary Cooper, Maria Schell, Ben Piazza, Karl Malden, George C. Scott, Karl Swenson, Virginia Gregg, King Donovan; **D:** Delmer Daves; **W:** Wendell Mayes, Halsted Welles; **M:** Max Steiner. Nominations: Academy Awards '59: Best Song ("The Hanging Tree"). *WAR*

The Hanging Woman 🎬🎬½ *Return of the Zombies; Beyond the Living Dead* 1972 (R) A man is summoned to the reading of a relative's will, and discovers the corpse of a young woman hanging in a cemetery. As he investigates the mystery, he uncovers a local doctor's plans to zombify the entire world. Not bad at all and quite creepy once the zombies are out in force. Euro-horror star Naschy plays the necrophiliac grave digger, Igor. **91m/C VHS, Beta.** *SP IT* Stan Cooper, Vickie Nesbitt, Marcella Wright, Catherine Gilbert, Gerard Tichy, Paul Naschy; **D:** John Davidson. *NO*

Hangman's Knot 🎬🎬½ 1952 Members of the Confederate Cavalry rob a Union train, not knowing that the war is over. Now facing criminal charges, they are forced to take refuge in a stagecoach stop. Well-done horse opera with a wry sense of humor. **80m/C VHS.** Randolph Scott, Donna Reed, Claude Jarman Jr., Frank Faylen, Glenn Langan, Richard Denning, Lee Marvin, Jeanette Nolan; **D:** Roy Huggins. *COL*

Hangmen woof! 1987 (R) Ex-CIA agents battle it out on the East side of New York. If you're into very violent, very badly-acted films, then this one's for you. **88m/C VHS, Beta.** Jake La Motta, Rick Washburne, Doug Thomas; **D:** J. Christian Ingvordsen. *ACA*

Hank Aaron: Chasing the Dream 🎬🎬🎬 1995 Docudrama combines archival footage, interviews, and reenactments to tell the story of the life and career of Henry Aaron. Follows Aaron's development as a Hall of Fame outfielder for the Milwaukee and Atlanta Braves and as a leader in the civil rights movement. Emphasis on personal and societal issues, as well as on-the-field accomplishments, raises this one above most sports biography documentaries. **120m/C VHS.** *TTC*

Hanky Panky 🎬½ 1982 (PG) Insipid comic thriller in which Wilder and Radner become involved in a search for top-secret plans. **107m/C VHS, Beta, LV, Closed Caption.** Gene Wilder, Gilda Radner, Richard Widmark, Kathleen Quinlan; **D:** Sidney Poitier. *COL*

Hanna K. 🎬🎬 1983 (R) Story of divided passions set in the tumultuous state of Israel. American lawyer Clayburgh tries to settle her personal and political affairs with various Middle-Eastern men. Mediocre Disappointing. Release generated controversy over pro-Palestine stance. **111m/C VHS, Beta.** *FR* Jill Clayburgh, Gabriel Byrne, Jean Yanne, Muhamad Bakri, David Clennon, Oded Kotler; **D:** Constantin Costa-Gavras. *USH*

Hannah and Her Sisters 🎬🎬🎬½ 1986 (PG) Allen's grand epic about a New York showbiz family, its three adult sisters and their various complex romantic entanglements. Excellent performances by the entire cast, especially Caine and Hershey. Classic Allen themes of life, love, death, and desire are explored in an assured and sensitive manner. Witty, ironic, and heartwarming. **103m/C VHS, Beta, LV, Closed Caption.** Mia Farrow, Barbara Hershey, Dianne Wiest, Michael Caine, Woody Allen, Maureen O'Sullivan, Lloyd Nolan, Sam Waterston, Carrie Fisher, Max von Sydow, Julie Kavner, Daniel Stern, Tony Roberts, John Turturro; **D:** Woody Allen; **W:** Woody Allen; **C:** Carlo DiPalma. Academy Awards '86: Best Original Screenplay, Best Supporting Actor (Caine), Best Supporting Actress (Wiest); British Academy Awards '86: Best Director (Allen), Best Original Screenplay; Golden Globe Awards '87: Best Film—Musical/Comedy; Los Angeles Film Critics Association Awards '86: Best Film, Best Screenplay, Best Supporting Actress (Wiest); National Board of Review Awards '86: Best Director (Allen), Best Supporting Actress (Wiest); New York Film Critics Awards '86: Best Director (Allen), Best Film, Best Supporting Actress (Wiest); National Society of Film Critics Awards '86: Best Supporting Actress (Wiest); Writers Guild of America '86: Best Original Screenplay; Nominations: Academy Awards '86: Best Art Direction/Set Decoration, Best Director (Allen), Best Film Editing, Best Picture. *BTV*

Hanna's War 🎬🎬½ 1988 (PG-13) A moving film about Hanna Senesh, a young Hungarian Jew living in Palestine, who volunteered for a suicide mission behind Nazi lines during WWII. After her capture by the Germans, she was killed, and is now considered by many to have been a martyr. Detmers is very believable as Hanna and Burstyn puts in a good performance as her mother. **148m/C VHS, Beta, LV.** Ellen Burstyn, Maruschka Detmers, Anthony Andrews, Donald Pleasence, David Warner, Denholm Elliott, Vincenzo Ricotta, Ingrid Pitt; **D:** Menahem Golan; **W:** Menahem Golan; **M:** Dov Seltzer. *CCB, MED, SWC*

Hannie Caulder 🎬🎬 1972 (R) A woman hires a bounty hunter to avenge her husband's murder and her own rape at the hands of three bandits. Excellent casting but uneven direction. Boyd is uncredited as the preacher. **87m/C VHS, Closed Caption.** Raquel Welch, Robert Culp, Ernest Borgnine, Strother Martin, Jack Elam, Christopher Lee, Diana Dors, Stephen Boyd; **D:** Burt Kennedy; **W:** Burt Kennedy. *PAR, FCT, VTR*

Hanoi Hilton 🎬½ 1987 (R) A brutal drama about the sufferings of American POWs in Vietnamese prison camps. Non-stop torture, filth, and degradation. 126m/C VHS, Beta, LV, Closed Caption. Michael Moriarty, Paul LeMat, Jeffrey Jones, Lawrence Pressman, Stephen Davies, David Soul, Rick Fitts, Aki Aleong, Gloria Carlin; **D:** Lionel Chetwynd; **W:** Lionel Chetwynd. *WAR*

Hanover Street 🎬🎬 1979 (PG) An American bomber pilot and a married British nurse fall in love in war-torn Europe. Eventually the pilot must work with the husband of the woman he loves on a secret mission. A sappy, romantic tearjerker. 109m/C VHS, Beta, LV. Harrison Ford, Lesley-Anne Down, Christopher Plummer, Alec McCowen; **D:** Peter Hyams; **W:** Peter Hyams; **C:** David Watkin; **M:** John Barry. *COL*

Hans Brinker 🎬🎬½ 1969 Young Hans Brinker and his sister participate in an ice skating race, hoping to win a pair of silver skates. A musical version of the classic tale. 103m/C VHS, Beta. Robin Askwith, Eleanor Parker, Richard Basehart, Cyril Ritchard, John Gregson; **D:** Robert Scheerer. *WAR, OM*

Hans Christian Andersen 🎬🎬 1952 Sentimental musical story of Hans Christian Andersen, a young cobbler who has a great gift for storytelling. Digitally remastered editions available with stereo sound and original trailer. 🎵The King's New Clothes; I'm Hans Christian Andersen; Wonderful Copenhagen; Thumbelina; The Ugly Duckling; Anywhere I Wander; The Inch Worm; No Two People. 112m/C VHS, Beta, LV. Danny Kaye, Farley Granger, Zizi Jeanmaire, Joey Walsh; **D:** Charles Vidor; **W:** Moss Hart; **M:** Frank Loesser. Nominations: Academy Awards '52: Best Art Direction/Set Decoration (Color), Best Color Cinematography, Best Costume Design (Color), Best Song ("Thumbelina"), Best Sound, Scoring of a Musical. *HBO, FCT*

Hansel and Gretel 1982 From Shelly Duvall's "Faerie Tale Theatre" comes the story of two young children who get more than they bargained for when they eat a gingerbread house. 51m/C VHS, Beta, LV, Closed Caption. Rick Schroder, Joan Collins, Paul Dooley, Bridgette Anderson; **D:** James Frawley. *KUI, FCT, FCT*

Hanussen 🎬🎬🎬½ 1988 (R) The third of Szabo and Brandauer's price-of-power trilogy (after "Mephisto" and "Colonel Redl"), in which a talented German magician and clairvoyant (based on a true life figure) collaborates with the Nazis during their rise to power in the 1930s, although he can foresee the outcome of their reign. In German with English subtitles. 110m/C VHS, Beta, LV. *GE HU* Klaus Maria Brandauer, Erland Josephson, Walter Schmidinger; **D:** Istvan Szabo; **C:** Lajos Koltai. Nominations: Academy Awards '88: Best Foreign Language Film. *COL*

The Happiest Days of Your Life 🎬🎬🎬 1950 During the London Blitz, a girls academy is evacuated to the country and mistakeningly billeted with a boys school. The headmaster and headmistress clash and the bewildered students all try to get along. Good cast, lots of laughs. Adapted from a play by John Dighton. 81m/B VHS. *GB* Alastair Sim, Margaret Rutherford, Joyce Grenfell, Edward Rigby, Guy Middleton, John Bentley, Bernadette O'Farrell, Richard Wattis, Muriel Aked, Patricia Owens, John Turnbull, Arthur Howard; **D:** Frank Launder; **W:** Frank Launder, John Dighton; **M:** Mischa Spoliansky. *HMV, ING*

The Happiest Millionaire 🎬🎬 1967 A Disney film about a newly immigrated lad who finds a job as butler in the home of an eccentric millionaire. Based on the book "My Philadelphia Father," by Kyle Chrichton. 🎵What's Wrong With That?; Watch Your Footwork; Valentine Candy; Strengthen the Dwelling; I'll Always Be Irish; Bye-Yum Pum Pum; I Believe in This Country; Detroit; There Are Those. 118m/C VHS, Beta. Fred MacMurray, Tommy Steele, Greer Garson, Geraldine Page, Lesley Ann Warren, John Davidson; **D:** Norman Tokar; **W:** A.J. Carothers; **C:** Edward Colman. Nominations: Academy Awards '67: Best Costume Design.*DIS, OM*

Happily Ever After 🎬🎬 1982 Las Vegas star-maker recruits and manipulates two green performers. Show business life in Vegas is given a truthful treatment in made-for-television drama. 95m/C VHS, Beta. Suzanne Somers, John Rubinstein, Eric (Hans Gudegast) Braeden; **D:** Robert Scheerer. *TLF*

Happily Ever After 🎬🎬 *Alem Da Paixao* 1986 A Brazilian housewife meets a bisexual transvestite and has a passionate affair, bringing her into the depths of the criminal underworld. In Portuguese with English subtitles. Contains nudity. 106m/C VHS. *BR* Regina Duarte, Paul Castelli; **D:** Bruno Barreto; **C:** Alfonso Beato. *CTL, FCT, TPV*

Happily Ever After 🎬½ 1993 (G) Sequel to "Snow White" begins where the original ends, but isn't connected to the Walt Disney classic. Snow White and her Prince prepare for their wedding when the Wicked Queen is found dead by her brother, who vows revenge. So it's up to Snow and the Dwarfelles (Disney said no to using the Dwarfs), female cousins of the original Dwarfs, to rescue him. Interesting choices from the casting department: Diller is Mother Nature and Asner provides the voice of a rapping owl. Poorly animated drivel designed to ride in on Disney's coattails. While the kids might enjoy it, save your money for the original, finally slated for a video release. 74m/C VHS, Closed Caption. **D:** John Howley; **W:** Martha Moran, Robby London; **V:** Dom DeLuise, Phyllis Diller, Zsa Zsa Gabor, Ed Asner, Sally Kellerman, Irene Cara, Carol Channing, Tracey Ullman. *REP, WOV*

Happiness 🎬🎬 1934 Another zany comedy from the land of the hammer and sickle. Banned in Russia for 40 years, it was deemed to be risque and a bit too biting with the social satire. Silent with orchestral score. 69m/B VHS. *RU* **D:** Alexander Medvedkin. *KIV, FCT*

Happy Anniversary 007: 25 Years of James Bond 1987 Film clip retrospective of the dashing British spy created by Ian Fleming. Hosted by Roger Moore. 59m/C VHS, Beta, Closed Caption. Sean Connery, Roger Moore, George Lazenby, Timothy Dalton; **D:** Mel Stuart. *FOX*

Happy Birthday, Gemini 🎬½ 1980 (R) A coming-of-age comedy about a young man on his 21st birthday worrying about his sexual identity. Based on the play "Gemini" by Albert Innaurato. The closeness of the characters on stage did not translate to the screen. 107m/C VHS. Robert Viharo, Madeline Kahn, Rita Moreno, Alan Rosenberg, Sarah Holcomb, David Marshall Grant, David McIlwraith; **D:** Richard Benner; **W:** Richard Benner. *MGM*

Happy Birthday to Me 🎬½ 1981 (R) Several elite seniors at an exclusive private school are mysteriously killed by a deranged killer who has a fetish for cutlery. 108m/C VHS, Beta, LV. *CA* Melissa Sue Anderson, Glenn Ford, Tracy Bregman, Jack Blum, Matt Craven; **D:** J. Lee Thompson; **W:** Timothy Bond. *COL*

The Happy Ending 🎬🎬½ 1969 (PG) Woman struggles with a modern definition of herself and her marriage, causing pain and confusion for her family. Simmons is solid as the wife and mother seeking herself. Michel LeGrand's theme song "What Are You Doing With the Rest of Your Life?" was a big hit. 112m/C VHS. Jean Simmons, John Forsythe, Lloyd Bridges, Shirley Jones, Teresa Wright, Dick Shawn, Nanette Fabray, Bobby Darin, Tina Louise; **D:** Richard Brooks; **W:** Richard Brooks; **C:** Conrad Hall. Nominations: Academy Awards '69: Best Actress (Simmons), Best Song ("What Are You Doing the Rest of Your Life?"). *NO*

Happy Gilmore woof! 1996 (PG-13) Skating-impaired hockey player Gilmore (Sandler) translates his slap shot into a 400-foot tee shot and joins the pro golf tour. His unique style brings a new, less refined breed of fan to the game and upsets the reigning tour hotshot (McDonald). Sandler improves on "Billy Madison," which isn't saying much, but there's still plenty of ammo for his many detractors. Replacing bathroom humor with abusive behavior, he swears at or beats up about

90% of the supporting cast, including Bob Barker in a charity pro-am. Unfortunately, it won't make anyone forget "Caddyshack II."**CW:** Language and some comic sexuality. 92m/C VHS, Closed Caption. Adam Sandler, Christopher McDonald, Carl Weathers, Julie Bowen, Francis Bay, Ben Stiller, Richard Kiel, Joe Flaherty, Kevin Nealon, Alan Covert, Robert Smigel, Bob Barker, Dennis Dugan; **D:** Dennis Dugan; **W:** Adam Sandler, Tim Herlihy; **C:** Arthur Albert; **M:** Mark Mothersbaugh. MTV Movie Awards '96: Best Fight (Adam Sandler/Bob Barker); Nominations: MTV Movie Awards '96: Best Comedic Performance (Sandler); Golden Raspberry Awards '96: Worst Actor (Sandler).*USH*

Happy Go Lovely 🎬🎬 1951 An unscrupulous theatrical producer casts a chorus girl in a leading role in order to get closer to her boyfriend's fortune. Tired plot, but good performances in this lightweight musical. 🎵One-Two-Three; Would You, Could You; London Town. 95m/C VHS, Beta. Vera-Ellen, David Niven, Cesar Romero, Bobby Howes; **D:** H. Bruce Humberstone. *NOS, MRV, DVT*

The Happy Hooker 🎬🎬½ 1975 (R) Xaviera Hollander's cheeky (and bestselling) memoir of her transition from office girl to "working girl" has been brought to the screen with a sprightly (though sanitary) air of naughtiness, with Redgrave enjoyable in title role. Followed by "The Happy Hooker Goes to Washington" and "The Happy Hooker Goes Hollywood." 96m/C VHS, Beta, LV. Lynn Redgrave, Jean-Pierre Aumont, Nicholas Pryor; **D:** Nicholas Sgarro. *CAN, VES*

The Happy Hooker Goes Hollywood 🎬 1980 (R) Third film inspired by the title of Xaviera Hollander's memoirs, in which the fun-loving Xaviera comes to Hollywood with the intention of making a movie based on her book, but soon meets up with a series of scheming, would-be producers. 86m/C VHS, Beta, LV. Martine Beswick, Chris Lemmon, Adam West, Phil Silvers; **D:** Alan Roberts. *CAN, USH*

The Happy Hooker Goes to Washington 🎬½ 1977 (R) Further adventures of the world's most famous madam. Heatherton (not Redgrave) is Xaviera Hollander this time, testifying before the U.S. Senate in defense of sex. Fairly stupid attempt to milk box office of original. Second in the holy trilogy of Happy Hooker pictures, which also include "The Happy Hooker" and "The Happy Hooker Goes Hollywood." 89m/C VHS, Beta. Joey Heatherton, George Hamilton, Ray Walston, Jack Carter; **D:** William A. Levey. *CAN, VES*

Happy Hour 🎬½ 1987 (R) A young brewing scientist discovers a secret formula for beer, and everyone tries to take it from him. Little turns in a good performance as a superspy. 88m/C VHS, Beta, LV. Richard Gilliland, Jamie Farr, Tawny Kitaen, Ty Henderson, Rich Little; **D:** John DeBello; **W:** John DeBello. *LIV*

Happy Landing 🎬🎬½ 1938 Predictable, yet entertaining Henie vehicle about a plane that makes a forced landing in Norway near Henie's home. Romance follows with bandleader Romero and manager Ameche. 🎵Hot and Happy; Yonny and his Oompah; You Are The Music to the Words in my Heart; A Gypsy Told Me; You Appeal to Me. 102m/B VHS. Sonja Henie, Don Ameche, Jean Hersholt, Ethel Merman, Cesar Romero, Billy Gilbert, Wally Vernon, El Brendel; **D:** Roy Del Ruth; **W:** Milton Sperling, Boris Ingster. *FXV*

Happy New Year 🎬🎬🎬 *The Happy New Year Caper* 1974 Charming romantic comedy in which two thieves plan a robbery but get sidetracked by the distracting woman who works next door to the jewelry store. Available in both subtitled and dubbed versions. Remade in 1987. 114m/C VHS, Beta. *FR IT* Francoise Fabian, Lino Ventura, Andre Falcon; **D:** Claude Lelouch; **W:** Claude Lelouch.

A Happy New Year! 🎬🎬 1979 Two men and a woman, all engineers in a chemical plant, try to fight off a hangover as they deal with the comings and goings of friends throughout the day and night. In Hungarian with English subtitles. 84m/C VHS. *HU* Istvan Bujtor, Erika Bodnar, Cecilia Esztergalyos, Andras Balint; **D:** Reszo Szoreny; **W:** Peter Modos, Reszo Szoreny. *FCT*

Happy New Year 🎭🎭½ **1987 (PG)** Two sophisticated thieves plan and execute an elaborate jewel heist that goes completely awry. Remake of the 1974 French film of the same name. **86m/C VHS, Beta.** Peter Falk, Wendy Hughes, Tom Courtenay, Charles Durning, Joan Copeland; **D:** John G. Avildsen; **W:** Warren Lane; **M:** Bill Conti. Nominations: Academy Awards '87: Best Makeup. *COL*

Happy New Year, Charlie Brown **1982** Strife upsets the Peanuts gang as the New Year's Eve gala becomes a source of tension. **25m/C VHS, Beta. D:** Bill Melendez, Sam Jaimes. *BAR, KAR*

Happy Since I Met You 🎭🎭🎭 **1989** Comedy-drama about a scatterbrained drama teacher and a struggling young actor who become romantically involved. **55m/C VHS, Beta.** *GB* Julie Walters, Duncan Preston; **Cameos:** Tracey Ullman, Jim Bowen; **D:** Baz Taylor; **W:** Victoria Wood. *BIJ, WOM*

Happy Together 🎭 **1989 (PG-13)** An eager freshman accidentally gets a beautiful, impulsive girl as his roommate. Together they meet the challenges of secondary education. **102m/C VHS, Beta, LV.** Helen Slater, Patrick Dempsey, Dan Schneider, Marius Weyers, Barbara Babcock; **D:** Mel Damski; **M:** Robert Folk. *LIV*

Happy Together 🎭🎭 *Cheun Gwong Tsa Sit* **1996** Lovers Lai Yiu-Fai (Leung) and Ho Po-Wing (Cheung) travel to Argentina from Hong Kong looking for adventure but soon go their separate ways. Lai is working as a doorman at a tango bar when a badly beaten Ho unexpectedly re-enters his life. Lai looks after the self-destructive Ho but his restlessness causes him to desert Lai once again, even as Lai befriends young Taiwanese Chang (Chen). After Chang returns to Taipei, Lai begins to suffer from depression and serious homesickness, as well as still worrying about Ho. Edgy visuals and playful performances bely a serious nature. Chinese and Spanish with subtitles. **93m/C VHS.** *HK* Leslie Cheung, Tony Leung, Chang Chen; **D:** Wong Kar-Wai; **C:** Christopher Doyle. Cannes Film Festival '97: Best Director (Kar-Wai). *NYR*

Hard-Boiled 🎭🎭½ *Lashou Shentan* **1992** Police Inspector Yuen (Woo regular Yun-fat) is investigating, with his usual excessive force, the Triads organized crime syndicate and a group of gun smugglers who killed his partner. He joins forces with Tony, an undercover cop who's working as a gangster hitman. There's lots of gunplay and betrayals among all the participants. Usual Woo way with violence and action sequences although the plot is more contrived. In Mandarin and Chinese with English subtitles. **126m/C VHS.** *HK* Chow Yun-Fat, Tony Leung, Philip Chan, Anthony Wong, Teresa Mo; **D:** John Woo; **W:** Barry Wong; **M:** Michael Gibbs. *ORI, FCT*

Hard-Boiled Mahoney 🎭🎭½ **1947** Slip, Sach, and the rest of the Bowery Boys try to solve a mystery involving mysterious women and missing men. The last film in the series for Bobby Jordan, whose career was ended when he was injured in an accident involving a falling elevator. **64m/B VHS.** Leo Gorcey, Huntz Hall, Bobby Jordan, Billy Benedict, David Gorcey, Gabriel Dell, Teala Loring, Dan Seymour, Bernard Gorcey, Patti Brill, Betty Compson; **D:** William Beaudine. *WAR*

Hard Bounty 🎭🎭½ **1994 (R)** After five years of chasing desperadoes, bounty hunter Martin B. Kanning hangs up his guns to open a saloon—complete with frontier prostitutes. When one of his ladies is murdered, the other gals decide to chase after the killer. Naturally, Kanning can't let them go alone.**CW:** Violence, nudity, sexual situations. **90m/C VHS.** Matt McCoy, Kelly Le Brock, Rochelle Swanson, Felicity Waterman, Kimberly Kelley; **D:** Jim Wynorski. *TRI*

Hard Choices 🎭🎭🎭 **1984** A 15-year-old Tennessee boy is unjustly charged as an accessory to murder, until a female social worker decides to help him. From then on, nothing is predictable. Excellent work by Klenck, McCleery, and Seitz. Don't miss Sayles as an unusual drug dealer. Intelligent, surprising, and powerful. Based on a true story, this is a low profile film that deserves to be discovered. **90m/C VHS, Beta.** Margaret Klenck, Gary McCleery, John Seitz, John Sayles, Liane Curtis, J.T. Walsh, Spalding Gray; **D:** Rick King; **W:** Rick King. *BAR, ORI, WAR*

Hard Core Logo 🎭🎭 **1996** Mockumentary about a group of Canadian veteran punk rock musicians who, at thirty-something, have reunited for one last benefit concert. The semi-legendary Vancouver band are so pleased by how well the concert goes that they decide to head back on the road (in a decrepit van) for one last shot at glory, trailed by a documentary film crew (led by director McDonald). The documentary inserts reveal the band's ups and downs and the ego trips that ultimately drove them apart. Adapted from a novel by Michael Turner. McDonald describes "Hard Core Logo" as the last of his rock 'n' roll road trilogy, following "Roadkill" and "Highway 61." **96m/C VHS.** *CA* Hugh Dillon, Keith Callum Rennie, John Pyper-Ferguson, Bernie Coulson; **D:** Bruce McDonald; **W:** Noel S. Baker; **C:** Danny Nowak; **M:** Shaun Tozer. Genie Awards '96: Best Song ("Swamp Baby, Who the Hell Do You Think You Are?"); Nominations: Genie Awards '96: Best Adapted Screenplay, Best Director (McDonald), Best Film, Best Film Editing, Best Sound. *NYR*

Hard Country 🎭🎭½ **1981 (PG)** Caught between her best friend's success as a country singer and the old values of a woman's place, a small town girl questions her love and her life style. A warm and intelligent rural drama. Basinger's debut. **104m/C VHS, LV.** Jan-Michael Vincent, Kim Basinger, Michael Parks, Gailard Sartain, Tanya Tucker, Ted Neeley, Daryl Hannah, Richard Moll; **D:** David Greene; **W:** Michael Kane; **M:** Michael Martin Murphy. *NO*

A Hard Day's Night 🎭🎭🎭½ **1964** The Beatles' first film is a joyous romp through an average "day in the life" of the Fab Four, shot in a pseudo-documentary style with great flair by Lester and noted as the first music video. Laser version includes original trailer and an interview with Lester. 🎵A Hard Day's Night; Tell Me Why; I Should Have Known Better; She Loves You; I'm Happy Just To Dance With You; If I Fell; And I Love Her; This Boy; Can't Buy Me Love. **90m/B VHS, Beta, LV, CD-I.** *GB* John Lennon, Paul McCartney, George Harrison, Ringo Starr, Wilfrid Brambell, Norman Rossington, John Junkin, Victor Spinetti, Anna Quayle, Deryck Guyler, Richard Vernon, Lionel Blair, Eddie Malin, Robin Ray, Alison Seebohm, David Saxon; **D:** Richard Lester; **W:** Alun Owen. Nominations: Academy Awards '64: Best Adapted Score, Best Story & Screenplay (Owen). *MVD, MPI, CRC*

Hard Drive 🎭½ **1994** A high tech, interactive network offers shared fantasies to Will and Delilah. Then they become obsessed with making their dreams a reality. **92m/C VHS, LV.** Matt McCoy, Christina Fulton, Edward Albert, Leo Damian, Stella Stevens; **D:** James Merendino; **W:** James Merendino. *TRI*

Hard Drivin' 🎭 **1960** Rowdy action featuring Southern stock car drivers with well shot race scenes from the Southern 500. **90m/C VHS, Beta.** Rory Calhoun, John Gentry, Alan Hale Jr.; **D:** Paul Helmick. *NO*

Hard Eight 🎭🎭🎭 **1996 (R)** Performances are the highlight of this low-key story set in Reno, Nevada. Sydney (Hall) is a professional gambler who decides to take under his wing the destitute John (Reilly) and teach him the trade. John falls for waitress/hooker Clementine (Paltrow) but there has to be some snake in this gambler's would-be paradise and it shows up in the malevolent form of the scary Jimmy (Jackson), who the dim John befriends despite Sydney's warnings. Debut for writer/director Anderson. **101m/C VHS.** Philip Baker Hall, John C. Reilly, Gwyneth Paltrow, Samuel L. Jackson; **D:** Paul Thomas Anderson; **W:** Paul Thomas Anderson; **C:** Robert Elswit; **M:** Michael Penn, Jon Brion. *NYR*

Hard Evidence 🎭🎭½ **1994 (R)** Trent Turner (Harrison) winds up with major regrets when he joins his mistress (Timmins) on a business trip. Seems her "business" involves drug smuggling and he's forced to shoot a DEA agent to protect them. Some protection—now Turner and his wife (Severance) are caught up in murder, drugs, and blackmail.**CW:** Strong sexuality; some violence and language. **100m/C VHS.** Gregory Harrison, Joan Severance, Cali Timmins, Airlie, Nathaniel De-Veaux; **D:** Michael Kennedy; **W:** William Martell; **C:** Bruce Worrall; **M:** Barron Abramovitch. *AVE*

Hard Frame 🎭½ *Hunters Are For Killing* **1970** An ex-con returns home hoping all will turn to sweetness and light when he attempts to make nice-nice with his stepdad, who wouldn't stick by him during his trial. Reynolds' debut into TV moviedom; could be the hirsute actor was thinking of this one when he said his movies were the kind they show in prisons and airplanes because nobody can leave. **100m/C VHS.** Burt Reynolds, Melvyn Douglas, Suzanne Pleshette, Larry Storch, Martin Balsam, Peter Brown, Jill Banner, Donald (Don "Red") Barry, Angus Duncan, Ivor Francis; **D:** Bernard Girard. *SIM*

Hard Hombre 🎭 **1931** Gibson rides and shoots across the screen in one of his best western adventures. **60m/B VHS, Beta.** Hoot Gibson, Lena Basquette, Skeeter Bill Robbins, Jack Byron, Glenn Strange; **D:** Otto Brower. *GPV, VCN, VCI*

Hard Hunted 🎭½ **1992 (R)** Three macho undercover agents try to avoid death at the hands of high-tech guerillas trying to steal nuclear weapons. No-brain actioner, heavy on the display of feminine charms.**CW:** Language, nudity, and sexuality. **97m/C VHS, Closed Caption.** Dona Speir, Roberta Vasquez, Cynthia Brimhall, Bruce Penhall, R.J. Moore, Tony Peck, Rodrigo Obregon, Al Leong, Michael J. Shane; **D:** Andy Sidaris; **W:** Andy Sidaris. *COL*

Hard Justice 🎭🎭 **1995 (R)** Bureau of Alcohol, Tobacco & Firearms agent Nick Adams (Bradley) goes undercover in prison to find his partner's killer and discovers that Warden Pike (Napier) is running an illegal gun operation. Now, who's he gonna trust? Lots of action thrills in a routine story.**CW:** Non-stop brutal violence, language. **95m/C VHS, LV, Closed Caption.** David Bradley, Charles Napier, Yuji Okumoto, Vernon Wells; **D:** Greg Yaitanes; **W:** Nicholas Amendolare, Chris Bold; **C:** Moshe Levin; **M:** Don Peake. *TTC*

Hard Knocks 🎭🎭½ **1980** An ex-con goes from one tragic situation to another, and is eventually stalked by shotgun-wielding rednecks in this grim, powerful drama. Excellent performance by Mann holds this picture together. **85m/C Beta.** *AU* Tracey Mann, John Arnold, Bill Hunter, Max Cullen, Tony Barry; **D:** Don McLennan. Australian Film Institute '80: Best Actress (Mann). *NO*

Hard Knocks 🎭 **19??** A young man on the run is tormented by an aging actress and her husband. His attempt to leave a past of violence and pain creates even more havoc. **90m/C VHS, Beta.** Michael Christian, John Crawford, Donna Wilkes, Keenan Wynn. *NO*

Hard Knox 🎭 **1983** A hard-nosed Marine pilot is dumped from the service and takes up command at a military school filled with undisciplined punks. A made-for-television movie. **96m/C VHS, Beta.** Robert Conrad, Frank Howard, Alan Ruck, Red West, Bill Erwin, Dean Hill, Joan Sweeney; **D:** Peter Werner. *BAR, ORI*

Hard Labour 🎭🎭 **1973** Middle-aged housekeeper is humiliated at home by her children and tyrannical daughter-in-law. Made for British television. **70m/C VHS.** *GB* Alison Steadman, Ben Kingsley, Clifford Kershaw; **D:** Mike Leigh. *WBF, FCT*

Hard Part Begins 🎭 **198?** A naive country singer gets sucked into the pratfalls of show business. **87m/C VHS, Beta.** Donnelly Rhodes, Nancy Belle Fuller, Paul Bradley. *TWE*

Hard Promises 🎬🎬 **1992 (PG)** Absence doesn't necessarily make the heart fonder, as Joey finds out when he's accidentally invited to his wife's wedding. He's been away from home for so long he doesn't even realize he's been divorced and hightails it home to win his sweetheart back. Average performances and script round out this innocuous domestic comedy-drama. Originally made for cable television. **95m/C VHS, LV, 8mm, Closed Caption.** Sissy Spacek, William L. Petersen, Brian Kerwin, Mare Winningham, Peter MacNicol, Ann Wedgeworth, Amy Wright, Lois Smith, Rip Torn; **D:** Martin Davidson; **M:** George S. Clinton. COL

Hard Rain-The Tet 1968 1989 An American platoon stationed in Saigon must mobilize in the wake of the North Vietnamese Army's Tet offensive. An episode of television's "Tour of Duty." Other episodes are also available on tape. **89m/C VHS.** Terence Knox, Stephen Caffrey; **D:** Bill W.L. Norton. NWV

The Hard Ride 🎬🎬½ **1971 (PG)** Above average biker movie about a Vietnam vet who brings the body of a black buddy back home, then tries to persuade the dead man's white girlfriend and the leader of his motorcycle gang to attend the funeral. **93m/C VHS.** Robert Fuller, Sherry Bain, Tony Russell, Marshall Reed, Biff Elliot, William Bonner, R.L. Armstrong; **D:** Burt Topper; **W:** Burt Topper. ORI

Hard Rock Zombies 🎬½ **1985 (R)** Four heavy metal band members die horribly on the road and are brought back from the dead as zombies. This horror/heavy metal spoof is somewhat amusing in a goofy way. **90m/C VHS, Beta.** E.J. Curcio, Sam Mann; **D:** Krishna Shah; **W:** David Ball. LIV, VES

Hard Target 🎬🎬½ **1993 (R)** Van Damme continues his action-hero ways as Chance Boudreaux, a Cajun (which explains the accent) merchant seaman, who comes to the rescue of Natasha (Butler), albeit with lots of violence. Brimley provides the humor as Chance's bayou uncle. It's another variation of "The Most Dangerous Game" story but it moves. American directorial debut of over-the-top Hong Kong action director Woo who had to tone down his usual stylistic effects and repeatedly cut some of the more violent scenes to earn an "R" rating. **97m/C VHS, LV, Closed Caption.** Jean-Claude Van Damme, Lance Henriksen, Yancy Butler, Arnold Vosloo, Wilford Brimley, Kasi Lemmons; **D:** John Woo; **W:** Chuck Pfarrer; **C:** Russell Carpenter; **M:** Graeme Revell. Nominations: MTV Movie Awards '94: Most Desirable Male (Van Damme), Best Action Sequence. USH, BTV

Hard Ticket to Hawaii 🎬 **1987 (R)** A shot-on-video spy thriller about an agent trying to rescue a comrade in Hawaii from a smuggling syndicate. Supporting cast includes many Playboy Playmates. **96m/C VHS, Beta.** Ron Moss, Dona Speir, Hope Marie Carlton, Cynthia Brimhall; **D:** Andy Sidaris. BAR, ORI, WAR

Hard Times 🎬🎬🎬 **1975 (PG)** A Depression-era drifter becomes a bare knuckle street fighter, and a gambler decides to promote him for big stakes. One of grade-B meister Hill's first genre films. A quiet, evocative drama. **92m/C VHS, Beta, LV.** Charles Bronson, James Coburn, Jill Ireland, Strother Martin; **D:** Walter Hill; **W:** Walter Hill. GKK

Hard to Die 🎬 Tower of Terror **1990** Director Wynorski's comic homage to Carol Frank's "Sorority House Massacre." Five beauties (former Playboy Playmates Harris, Taylor, Dare, Moore, and Carney) find employment moving boxes in a deserted lingerie factory. The film takes off from there as they uncover a mysterious spirit called the Sorority House Killer in an ancient "Soul Box." Desperate to extinguish the evil threat, they focus their efforts in an armed struggle involving high-powered weaponry against the building maintenance man, whom they fear is possessed by the spirit. Accompanied by a lovely, touching group shower scene. **77m/C VHS.** Robin Harris, Melissa Moore, Debra Dare, Lindsay Taylor, Bridget Carney, Forrest J. Ackerman, Orville Ketchum; **D:** Jim Wynorski. NHO

Hard to Hold 🎬½ **1984 (PG)** Rockin' Rick's lukewarm film debut where he falls in love with a children's counselor after an automobile accident. Springfield sings "Love Somebody" with music by Peter Gabriel. **93m/C VHS, Beta, LV, Closed Caption.** Rick Springfield, Janet Eilber, Patti Hansen, Albert Salmi, Monique Gabrielle; **D:** Larry Peerce. USH

Hard to Kill 🎬🎬 **1989 (R)** Policeman Seagal is shot and left for dead in his bedroom, but survives against the odds, though his wife does not. After seven years, he is well enough to consider evening the score with his assailants. He hides while training in martial arts for the final battle. Strong outing from Seagal, with good supporting cast. **96m/C VHS, Beta, LV, 8mm, Closed Caption.** Steven Seagal, Kelly Le Brock, William Sadler, Frederick Coffin, Bonnie Burroughs, Zachary Rosencrantz, Dean Norris; **D:** Bruce Malmuth; **M:** Charles Fox. WAR

Hard Traveling 🎬🎬 **1985 (PG)** An unemployed Depression-era farmworker is accused of murder. He must fight a hostile court system to maintain his dignity and salvage the love and respect of his wife. Based on a novel by Alvah Bessie. **99m/C VHS, Beta.** J.E. Freeman, Ellen Geer, Barry Corbin, James Gammon, Jim Haynie; **D:** Dan Bessie; **W:** Dan Bessie. VTR, NWV

The Hard Truth 🎬🎬½ **1994 (R)** By-the-book actioner finds cop Jonah (Rooker) suspended for having an itchy trigger finger. His gal Lisa (Anthony) knows her sleazy boss has lots of mob money handy and proposes they grab it. But then Lisa gets a look at Chandler (Roberts), the electronic whiz blackmailed to assist in the heist, and the triangle leads to trouble. **CW:** Language; violence; nudity; sexual situations. **100m/C VHS.** Michael Rooker, Eric Roberts, Lysette Anthony, Ray Baker, Don Yesso; **D:** Kristine Peterson; **W:** Jonathan Tydor; **C:** Ross Berryman. LIV

Hard Vice 🎬½ **1994 (R)** Vice cops Joe Owens (Jones) and Andrea Thompson (Tweed) have their work cut out for them on their Las Vegas beat. When the bodies start piling up, the prime suspects turn out to be a group of high-priced hookers. **CW:** Language, violence, and strong sexuality. **86m/C VHS, LV.** Shannon Tweed, Sam Jones, James Gammon, Rebecca Ferratti; **D:** Joey Travolta; **W:** Joey Travolta. APX

Hard Way 🎬🎬 **1980** A world-weary assassin is pressured by his boss to perform one last assignment. A surprise awaits him if he accepts. **88m/C VHS, Beta.** Patrick McGoohan, Lee Van Cleef, Donal McCann, Edna O'Brien; **D:** Mihael Dryhurst. TWE

The Hard Way 🎬🎬🎬 **1991 (R)** Hollywood superstar Fox is assigned to hardened NYC cop Woods to learn the ropes as he trains for a role. Nothing special in the way of script or direction, but Woods and Fox bring such intensity and good humor to their roles that the package works. Fox pokes fun at the LA lifestyle as the annoying, self-absorbed actor, and Marshall has an entertaining appearance as his agent. Woods is on familiar over-the-edge turf as the brittle but dedicated detective. Silly finale almost destroys the film, but other small vignettes are terrific. **CW:** Strong language and some violence. **91m/C VHS, Beta, LV, Closed Caption.** James Woods, Michael J. Fox, Annabella Sciorra, Stephen Lang, LL Cool J, John Capodice, Christina Ricci, Karen Gorney, Luis Guzman; **Cameos:** Penny Marshall; **D:** John Badham; **W:** Daniel Pyne, Lem Dobbs; **C:** Robert Primes; **M:** Arthur B. Rubinstein. USH

Hardbodies 🎬 **1984 (R)** Three middle-aged men hit the beaches of Southern California in search of luscious young girls. They find them. Mid-life crisis done stupidly. Followed by a sequel. **88m/C VHS, Beta, LV, Closed Caption.** Grant Cramer, Teal Roberts, Gary Wood, Michael Rapport, Sorrels Pickard, Roberta Collins, Cindy Silver, Courtney Gains, Kristi Somers, Crystal Shaw, Kathleen Kinmont, Joyce Jameson; **D:** Mark Griffiths; **W:** Eric Alter. COL

Hardbodies 2 WOOF! **1986 (R)** A sequel to the original comedy hit, dealing with film crew in Greece that is distracted by hordes of nude natives. Sophomoric humor dependent on nudity and profanity for laughs. **89m/C VHS, Beta, LV.** Brad Zutaut, Brenda Bakke, Fabiana Udenio, James Karen; **D:** Mark Griffiths; **W:** Eric Alter; **M:** Eddie Arkin. COL

Hardcase and Fist 🎬🎬 **1989 (R)** A framed cop leaves prison with his mind on revenge. The godfather who used him is just his first target. **92m/C VHS, Beta.** Maureen Lavette, Ted Prior; **D:** Tony Zarindast. MCG

Hardcore 🎬🎬½ The Hardcore Life **1979 (R)** A Midwestern businessman who is raising a strict Christian family learns of his daughter's disappearance while she is on a church trip. After hiring a streetwise investigator, he learns that his daughter has become an actress in pornographic films out in California. Strong performance by Scott and glimpse into the hardcore pornography industry prove to be convincing points of this film, though it exploits what it condemns. **106m/C VHS, Beta, LV.** George C. Scott, Season Hubley, Peter Boyle, Dick Sargent; **D:** Paul Schrader; **W:** Paul Schrader; **C:** Michael Chapman; **M:** Jack Nitzsche. COL

The Harder They Come 🎬🎬½ **1972 (R)** A poor Jamaican youth becomes a success with a hit reggae record after he has turned to a life of crime out of desperation. Songs, which are blended nicely into the framework of the film, include "You Can Get It If You Really Want it" and "Sitting In Limbo." **93m/C VHS, Beta, LV.** Jimmy Cliff, Janet Barkley, Carl Bradshaw; **D:** Perry Henzell. CRC, FCT

The Harder They Fall 🎬🎬🎬 **1956** A cold-eyed appraisal of the scum-infested boxing world. An unemployed reporter (Bogart in his last role) promotes a fighter for the syndicate, while doing an expose on the fight racket. Bogart became increasingly debilitated during filming and died soon afterward. Based on Budd Schulberg's novel. **109m/B VHS, Beta.** Humphrey Bogart, Rod Steiger, Jan Sterling, Mike Lane, Max Baer Sr.; **D:** Mark Robson; **W:** Philip Yordan; **C:** Burnett Guffey. Nominations: Academy Awards '56: Best Black and White Cinematography. CCB, COL

Hardhat & Legs 🎬🎬 **1980** Comic complications arise when a New York construction worker falls in love with the woman who's teaching the modern sexuality course in which he's enrolled. Made for television. **96m/C VHS, Beta.** Sharon Gless, Kevin Dobson, Raymond Serra, Elva Josephson, Bobby Short, Jacqueline Brookes, W.T. Martin; **D:** Lee Philips; **W:** Ruth Gordon; **M:** Brad Fiedel. NO

Hardly Working 🎬 **1981 (PG)** A circus clown finds it difficult to adjust to real life as he fumbles about from one job to another. Lewis's last attempt at resuscitating his directorial career. His fans will love it, but others need not bother. **90m/C VHS, Beta.** Jerry Lewis, Susan Oliver, Roger C. Carmel, Gary Lewis, Deanna Lund; **D:** Jerry Lewis; **W:** Jerry Lewis. FOX

Hardware 🎬½ **1990 (R)** Rag-tag ripoff in which McDermott is a post-apocalyptic garbage picker who gives girlfriend Travis some robot remains he collected (ours is not to ask why), oblivious to the fact that the tidy android was a government-spawned population controller programmed to destroy warm bodies. Seems old habits die hard, and that spells danger, danger, Will Robinson. Much violence excised to avoid x-rating. **94m/C VHS, Beta, LV, Closed Caption.** Dylan McDermott, Stacy Travis, John Lynch, Iggy Pop; **D:** Richard Stanley; **M:** Simon Boswell. HBO, WAR

Hardware Wars & Other Film Farces 1981 (G) A collection of four award-winning spoofs of big-budget film epics, featuring "Hardware Wars," "Porklips Now," "Bambi Meets Godzilla," and "Closet Cases of the Nerd Kind." Some black-and-white segments. **48m/C VHS, Beta.** WAR, OM

Harem 🎞 1985 A beautiful stockbroker gets kidnapped by a wealthy OPEC oil minister and becomes part of his harem. Kingsley stars as the lonely sheik who longs for the love of a modern woman. 107m/C VHS, Beta, LV. *FR* Ben Kingsley, Nastassia Kinski; *D:* Arthur Joffe. *LIV, VES*

Harem 🎞🎞 1986 In the early 1900s, a dastardly Turkish sultan kidnaps an American beauty to add to his harem—mightily displeasing his jealous first wife. Lots of overwrought romance and drama until she is finally rescued. Made for television. 200m/C VHS. Omar Sharif, Nancy Travis, Ava Gardner, Julian Sands, Art Malik, Sarah Miles, Yaphet Kotto, Cherie Lunghi; *D:* Billy Hale. *VTR*

Harlan County, U.S.A. 1976 (PG) The emotions of 180 coal mining families are seen up close in this classic documentary about their struggle to win a United Mine Workers contract in Kentucky. Award-winning documentary. 103m/C VHS, Beta. *D:* Barbara Kopple; *C:* Phil Parmet. Academy Awards '76: Best Feature Documentary; National Board of Review Awards '77: 10 Best Films of the Year. *COL, FRF*

Harlem Nights 🎞🎞 1989 (R) Two Harlem nightclub owners in the 1930s battle comically against efforts by the Mob and crooked cops to take over their territory. High-grossing, although somewhat disappointing effort from Murphy, who directed, wrote, produced, and starred in this film. 118m/C VHS, Beta, LV, Closed Caption. Eddie Murphy, Richard Pryor, Redd Foxx, Danny Aiello, Jasmine Guy, Michael Lerner, Arsenio Hall, Della Reese, Eugene Glazer; *D:* Eddie Murphy; *M:* Herbie Hancock. Golden Raspberry Awards '89: Worst Screenplay; Nominations: Academy Awards '89: Best Costume Design. *PAR*

Harlem on the Prairie 🎞 *Bad Man of Harlem* 1938 This first-ever western with an all-black cast has Jeffries helping a young lady find hidden gold and foiling a villain. Even though the technical standards and acting are below par, this is worth watching for the singing and a comedy routine done by a well-known contemporary black team. 🎵Harlem On The Prairie; Romance In The Rain. 54m/B VHS. Herbert Jeffries, Mantan Moreland, F.E. Miller, Connie Harris, Maceo B. Sheffield, William Spencer Jr.; *D:* Sam Newfield. *NOS*

Harlem Rides the Range 🎞½ 1939 Jeffries must outsmart villainous Brooks, who means to swindle a radium mine away from its rightful owner. Early oater of interest only because of its atypical all-black cast and crew. 58m/B VHS. Herbert Jeffries, Lucius Brooks, Artie Young, F.E. Miller, Spencer Williams Jr., Clarence Brooks, Tom Southern, Wade Dumas, Leonard Christmas; *D:* Richard C. Kahn; *W:* F.E. Miller, Spencer Williams Jr. *NOS, MRV, TPV*

Harley 🎞🎞 1990 (PG) Diamond is Harley, an L.A. thug-on-a-hog, who's on his way to an extended stay at one of the state's luxury institutions when he's sent to a Texas rehabilitation community. There, he bonds with an ex-biker, and may just find his way back down the straight and narrow. And the usual longhorn rednecks applaud his efforts...not. 80m/C VHS. Lou Diamond Phillips, Eli Cummins, DeWitt Jan, Valentine Kim; *D:* Fred Holmes; *W:* Frank Kuntz, Sandy Kuntz. *THV*

Harley Davidson and the Marlboro Man 🎞 1991 (R) An awful rehash of "Butch Cassidy and the Sundance Kid" with blatant vulgarity and pointless sci-fi touches. The title duo are near-future outlaws who rob a bank to save their favorite bar, then find they've stolen mob money. Some action, but it's mostly talk: lewd, meant-to-be-whimsical soul-probing chats between H.D. and M.M. that would bore even the biker crowd—and did. *CW:* Language, violence, and sensuality. 98m/C VHS, Beta, LV, 8mm, Closed Caption. Mickey Rourke, Don Johnson, Chelsea Field, Tom Sizemore, Vanessa Williams, Robert Ginty, Daniel Baldwin; *D:* Simon Wincer; *C:* David Eggby. *MGM*

Harlow 🎞🎞½ 1965 The more lavish of the two Harlow biographies made in 1965, both with the same title. A sensationalized "scandal sheet" version of Jean Harlow's rise to fame that bears little resemblance to the facts of her life. 125m/C VHS, Beta. Carroll Baker, Martin Balsam, Red Buttons, Mike Connors, Angela Lansbury, Peter Lawford, Raf Vallone, Leslie Nielsen; *D:* Gordon Douglas; *W:* John Michael Hayes; *C:* Joseph Ruttenberg. *PAR*

Harmagedon 🎞 1983 When Princess Luna's jetliner explodes she is thrown into a psychic plane where she must battle Genma, an eternal being who has destroyed half the universe. Luna gathers together the heroic Psyonic Warriors and the cyborg Vega to aid in her battle. Animated; in Japanese with English subtitles. 131m/C VHS, LV. *JP CPM*

Harmon of Michigan 🎞🎞½ 1941 College football hero Harmon starred in this loosely adapted story of his life in and out of the pros and his career at Michigan. 65m/B VHS. Tom Harmon, Anita Louise, Forest Evashevski, Oscar O'Shea, Warren Ashe, Stanley Crown, Ken Christy, Tim Ryan, Lloyd Bridges, William Hall, Chester Conklin, Larry Parks; *D:* Charles T. Barton; *W:* Howard J. Green. *GPV*

Harmony Lane 🎞🎞 1935 Highly romanticised rendition of the life of American composer, Stephen Collins Foster (1826-1864). Montgomery, as Foster, manages to lend a hint of credibility to the syrupy, melodramatic script. Very little attention is given to historical fact and almost every scene is orchestrated to showcase the composer's songs. The music steals the show. 🎵Beautiful Dreamer; Old Folks at Home; Swanee River; Oh! Susanna; De Camptown Races. 84m/B VHS. Douglass Montgomery, Evelyn Venable, Adrienne Ames, Joseph Cawthorn, William Frawley, Florence Roberts, Smiley Burnette, Hattie McDaniel; *D:* Joseph Santley. *DVT, NOS, VYY*

Harmony Trail 🎞½ 1944 Maynard stars in another rip-roaring western adventure. 60m/B VHS, Beta. Ken Maynard. *NOS, VCN, DVT*

Harnessing Peacocks 🎞🎞½ 1992 Hebe (Scott Thomas) has a one-night stand with a mystery man during carnival time in Venice, gets pregnant, and winds up living a very independent life with her son in a British seaside community. She supports herself as both a chef and as an expensive mistress, with a very select group of admirers, but always dreams of reuniting with her son's father. Based on the novel by Mary Wesley. 108m/C VHS. *GB* Serena Scott Thomas, Peter Davison, Renee Asherson. *VTR, CCB*

Harold and Maude 🎞🎞🎞🎞 1971 (PG) Cult classic pairs Cort as a dead-pan disillusioned 20-year-old obsessed with suicide (his staged attempts are a highlight) and a loveable Gordon as a fun-loving 80-year-old eccentric. They meet at a funeral (a mutual hobby), and develop a taboo romantic relationship, in which they explore the tired theme of the meaning of life with a fresh perspective. The script was originally the 20-minute long graduate thesis of UCLA student Higgins, who showed it to his landlady, wife of film producer Lewis. Features music by the pre-Islamic Cat Stevens. 92m/C VHS, Beta, LV, 8mm. Ruth Gordon, Bud Cort, Cyril Cusack, Vivian Pickles, Charles Tyner, Ellen Geer; *D:* Hal Ashby; *W:* Colin Higgins; *C:* John A. Alonzo; *M:* Cat Stevens. *PAR*

Harper 🎞🎞🎞 *The Moving Target* 1966 A tight, fast-moving genre piece about cynical LA private eye Newman investigating the disappearance of Bacall's wealthy husband. From a Ross McDonald novel, adapted by William Golding. Later sequelled in "The Drowning Pool." 121m/C VHS, Beta, LV. Paul Newman, Shelley Winters, Lauren Bacall, Julie Harris, Robert Wagner, Janet Leigh, Arthur Hill; *D:* Jack Smight; *C:* Conrad Hall. Edgar Allan Poe Awards '66: Best Screenplay. *WAR*

Harper Valley P.T.A. 🎞🎞 1978 (PG) Eden raises hell in Harper Valley after the PTA questions her parental capabilities. Brain candy was adapted from a hit song; TV series followed. 93m/C VHS, Beta. Barbara Eden, Nanette Fabray, Louis Nye, Pat Paulsen, Ronny Cox, Ron Masak, Audrey Christie, John Fiedler, Bob Hastings; *D:* Richard Bennett; *W:* Barry Schneider. *VES*

Harrad Experiment 🎞½ 1973 (R) Adaptation of Robert Rimmer's love-power bestseller in which an experiment-minded college establishes a campus policy of sexual freedom. Famous for the Hedren/Johnson relationship, shortly before Johnson married Hedren's real-life daughter Melanie Griffith. Followed by "The Harrad Summer." 98m/C VHS, Beta. James Whitmore, Tippi Hedren, Don Johnson, Bruno Kirby, Laurie Walters, Victoria Thompson, Elliot Street, Sharon Taggart, Robert Middleton, Billy Sands, Melanie Griffith; *D:* Ted Post; *M:* Artie Butler. *VES*

Harrad Summer 🎞🎞 1974 (R) Sequel to "The Harrad Experiment." College coeds take their sex-education to the bedroom where they can apply their knowledge by more intensive means. 103m/C VHS. Richard Doran, Victoria Thompson, Laurie Walters, Robert Reiser, Bill Dana, Marty Allen; *D:* Steven Hilliard Stern. *NO*

Harriet Craig 🎞🎞🎞 1950 Tailor-made Crawford role finds her as seemingly perfect wife Harriet Craig. In reality, she's a domineering shrew, who's also a bully and a clean freak. Harriet squelches husband Walter's (Corey) promotion because it means he'll be travelling abroad, ruins his relationship with best friend Billy (Joslyn), and manages to sabotage her young cousin Clare's (Stevens) romance before anybody stands up to her. Third film adaptation of George Kelly's 1925 play "Craig's Wife." 94m/B VHS. Joan Crawford, Wendell Corey, Allyn Joslyn, William Bishop, K.T. Stevens, Lucile Watson, Raymond Greenleaf, Ellen Corby; *D:* Vincent Sherman; *W:* James Gunn; *C:* Joseph Walker; *M:* George Duning. *COL*

Harriet the Spy 🎞🎞½ 1996 (PG) Sixth-grade, 11-year-old tomboy Harriet M. Welsch (Trachtenberg) spies on everyone around her and, encouraged by her nanny Ole Golly (O'Donnell), writes down everything going on in her secret notebook, because she's determined to become a great writer. Unfortunately, Harriet's imagination sometimes gets the best of her and when her notebook is found, her friends and family are not too happy about its contents. Based on the award-winning novel by Louise Fitzhugh. Lovers of the book may not be enthusiastic about some of the changes but generally it's enjoyable fare. 102m/C VHS, Closed Caption. Michelle Trachtenberg, Rosie O'Donnell, Vanessa Lee Chester, Gregory Edward Smith, Robert Joy, Eartha Kitt, J. Smith-Cameron; *D:* Bronwen Hughes; *W:* Douglas Petrie, Theresa Rebeck; *C:* Francis Kenny; *M:* Jamshield Sharifi. *PAR*

Harry & Son 🎞🎞 1984 (PG) A widowed construction worker faces the problems of raising his son. Newman is miscast as the old man and we've all seen Benson play the young role too many times. 117m/C VHS, Beta, LV. Paul Newman, Robby Benson, Ellen Barkin, Wilford Brimley, Judith Ivey, Ossie Davis, Morgan Freeman, Joanne Woodward; *D:* Paul Newman; *M:* Henry Mancini. *VES*

Harry and the Hendersons 🎞🎞½ 1987 (PG) Ordinary American family vacationing in the Northwest has a collision with Bigfoot. Thinking that the big guy is dead, they throw him on top of the car and head home. Lo and behold, he revives and starts wrecking the furniture and in the process, endears himself to the at-first frightened family. Nice little tale efficiently told, with Lithgow fine as the frustrated dad trying to hold his Bigfoot-invaded home together. Basis for the television series. 111m/C VHS, Beta, LV, Closed Caption. John Lithgow, Melinda Dillon, Don Ameche, David Suchet, Margaret Langrick, Joshua Rudoy, Kevin Peter Hall, Lainie Kazan, M. Emmet Walsh; *D:* William Dear; *W:* William Dear, William E. Martin, Ezra D. Rappaport; *C:* Allen Daviau; *M:* Bruce Broughton. Academy Awards '87: Best Makeup. *USH, APD*

Harry and Tonto 🎞🎞🎞 1974 A gentle comedy about an energetic septuagenarian who takes a cross-country trip with his cat, Tonto. Never in a hurry, still capable of feeling surprise and joy, he makes new friends and visits old lovers. Carney deserved his Oscar. Mazursky has seldom been better. 115m/C VHS, Beta, Closed Caption.

Art Carney, Ellen Burstyn, Larry Hagman, Geraldine Fitzgerald, Chief Dan George, Arthur Hunnicutt, Josh Mostel; *D:* Paul Mazursky; *W:* Paul Mazursky; *M:* Bill Conti. Academy Awards '74: Best Actor (Carney); Golden Globe Awards '75: Best Actor—Musical/Comedy (Carney); National Board of Review Awards '74: 10 Best Films of the Year; Nominations: Academy Awards '74: Best Original Screenplay. *FOX, FCT, BTV*

Harry & Walter Go to New York
🐾🐾 **1976 (PG)** At the turn of the century, two vaudeville performers are hired by a crooked British entrepreneur for a wild crime scheme. The cast and crew try their hardest, but it's not enough to save this boring comedy. The vaudeville team of Caan and Gould perhaps served as a model for Beatty and Hoffman in "Ishtar." 111m/C VHS, Beta, LV. James Caan, Elliott Gould, Michael Caine, Diane Keaton, Burt Young, Jack Gilford, Charles Durning, Lesley Ann Warren, Carol Kane; *D:* Mark Rydell; *W:* John Byrum; *M:* David Shire. *COL*

Harry Black and the Tiger
🐾🐾 *Harry Black* **1958** Jungle adventure involving a one-legged hunter and a man-eating tiger. The hunter initially teams up with the old war buddy who cost him his leg. The motivation grows with each failure to catch the beast and to make matters worse, the friend's wife and son are lost somewhere in the perilous jungle. Filmed in India. 107m/C VHS. *GB* Stewart Granger, Barbara Rush, Anthony Steel; *D:* Hugo Fregonese. *TCF*

Harry Tracy
🐾🐾½ *Harry Tracy—Desperado* **1983 (PG)** Whimsical tale of the legendary outlaw whose escapades made him both a wanted criminal and an exalted folk hero. 111m/C VHS, Beta. *CA* Bruce Dern, Gordon Lightfoot, Helen Shaver, Michael C. Gwynne; *D:* William A. Graham; *C:* Allen Daviau. *VES*

Harry's War
🐾🐾 **1984 (PG)** A middle-class, middle-aged American declares military war on the IRS in this overdone comedy. 98m/C VHS, Beta. Edward Herrmann, Geraldine Page, Karen Grassle, David Ogden Stiers; *D:* Keith Merrill. *TPI*

Harum Scarum
🐾🐾 *Harem Holiday* **1965** Elvis tune-fest time! When a movie star (Presley) travels through the Middle East, he becomes involved in an attempted assassination of the king and falls in love with his daughter. He also sings at the drop of a veil: "Shake That Tambourine," "Harem Holiday," and seven others. 95m/C VHS, Beta. Elvis Presley, Mary Ann Mobley, Fran Jeffries, Michael Ansara, Billy Barty, Theo Marcuse, Jay Novello; *D:* Gene Nelson. *MGM*

Harvest
🐾🐾🐾🐾 **1937** A classically Pagnolian rural pageant-of-life melodrama, wherein a pair of loners link up together in an abandoned French town and completely revitalize it and the land around it. From the novel by Jean Giono. In French with English subtitles. 128m/B VHS, Beta. *FR* Fernandel, Gabriel Gabrio, Orane Demazis, Edouard Delmont, Henri Poupon; *D:* Marcel Pagnol; *W:* Marcel Pagnol; *M:* Arthur Honegger. National Board of Review Awards '39: 5 Best Foreign Films of the Year; New York Film Critics Awards '39: Best Foreign Film. *INT, MRV, FCT*

The Harvest
🐾🐾½ **1992 (R)** Sultry temptress Leilani sends Miguel's internal thermometer into convulsions with her preference for ice during lovemaking. However, their tryst turns sour (for him) when she takes Miguel to the beach where mystery thugs beat him unconscious and swipe his kidney. Bizarre story sure to ignite a small cult following.*CW:* Language, violence, and strong sexuality. 97m/C VHS, LV, Closed Caption. Miguel Ferrer, Leilani Sarelle Ferrer, Harvey Fierstein, Anthony John Denison, Tim Thomerson, Matt Clark, Henry Silva; *D:* David Marconi; *W:* David Marconi; *M:* Dave Allen, Rick Boston. *COL*

Harvest Melody
🐾🐾 **1943** Singing star Gilda Parker travels to farm country for a mere publicity stunt but decides to stay. Corny in more ways than one. ♫You Could Have Knocked Me Over With A Feather; Put It In Reverse; Let's Drive Out To The Drive-In; Tenderly. 70m/B VHS. Rosemary Lane, Johnny Downs, Sheldon Leonard, Char-

---

lotte Wynters, Luis Alberni, Claire Rochelle, Syd Saylor; *D:* Sam Newfield. *NOS, LOO*

Harvest of Fire
🐾🐾½ **1995 (PG)** A close-knit Amish farming community in Iowa has been the target of a series of barn burnings, which come under the investigation of FBI agent Sally Russell (Davidovich). But the community doesn't want an outsider around and Sally needs some help, which she finds with Amish widow Annie Beiler (Duke). And gradually the disparate duo find some common ground. A Hallmark Hall of Frame presentation. 90m/C VHS, Closed Caption. Patty Duke, Lolita Davidovich, J.A. Preston, Jean Louisa Kelly, Tom Aldredge, James Read, Craig Wasson; *D:* Arthur Allan Seidelman; *W:* Richard Alfieri; *C:* Neil Roach; *M:* Lee Holdridge. *HMK*

Harvey
🐾🐾🐾½ **1950** Straightforward version of the Mary Chase play about a friendly drunk with an imaginary 6-foot rabbit friend named Harvey, and a sister who tries to have him committed. A fondly remembered, charming comedy. Hull is a standout, well deserving her Oscar. 104m/B VHS, Beta, LV. James Stewart, Josephine Hull, Victoria Horne, Peggy Dow, Cecil Kellaway, Charles Drake, Jesse White, Wallace Ford, Nana Bryant; *D:* Henry Koster; *W:* Oscar Brodney; *C:* William H. Daniels. Academy Awards '50: Best Supporting Actress (Hull); Golden Globe Awards '51: Best Supporting Actress (Hull); Nominations: Academy Awards '50: Best Actor (Stewart). *USH, BTV, RDG*

The Harvey Girls
🐾🐾🐾 **1946** Lightweight musical about a restaurant chain that sends its waitresses to work in the Old West. ♫In the Valley Where the Evening Sun Goes Down; Wait and See; On the Atchison, Topeka and Santa Fe; It's a Great Big World; The Wild Wild West. 102m/C VHS, Beta, LV. Judy Garland, Ray Bolger, John Hodiak, Preston Foster, Angela Lansbury, Virginia O'Brien, Marjorie Main, Chill Wills, Kenny L. Baker, Selena Royle, Cyd Charisse; *D:* George Sidney; *M:* Harry Warren, Johnny Mercer. Academy Awards '46: Best Song ("On the Atchison, Topeka and Santa Fe"); Nominations: Academy Awards '46: Scoring of a Musical. *MGM, FCT*

A Hash House Fraud/The Sultan's Wife
1915 "A Hash House Fraud" (1915) features a frenetic Keystone chase. "The Sultan's Wife" (1917) concerns a woman who attracts the unwanted attention of a sultan. 33m/B VHS, Beta. Louise Fazenda, Hugh Fay, Chester Conklin, Gloria Swanson, Bobby Vernon. *CCB*

The Hasty Heart
🐾🐾 **1986** A rowdy, terminally ill Scotsman brings problems and friendships to a makeshift war-time hospital built in the jungles of Burma. Remake of 1949 flick with Richard Todd and Ronald Reagan in leading roles. 100m/C VHS, Beta. Gregory Harrison, Cheryl Ladd, Perry King; *D:* Martin Speer. *BAR, ORI, WAR*

Hat Box Mystery
🐾 **1947** A detective's secretary is tricked into shooting a woman and private eye Neal is determined to save her from prison. Although not outstanding, it's worth seeing as perhaps the shortest detective film (a mere 44 min.) to ever make it as a feature. 44m/B VHS, Beta, LV. Tom Neal, Pamela Blake, Allen Jenkins; *D:* Lambert Hillyer. *SNC, VYY*

Hatari!
🐾🐾🐾 **1962** An adventure-loving team of professional big game hunters ventures to East Africa to round up animals for zoos around the world. Led by Wayne, they get into a couple of scuffs along the way, including one with lady photographer Martinelli who is doing a story on the expedition. Extraordinary footage of Africa and the animals brought to life by a fantastic musical score. 158m/C VHS, Beta, LV. John Wayne, Elsa Martinelli, Red Buttons, Hardy Kruger, Gerard Blain, Bruce Cabot; *D:* Howard Hawks; *M:* Henry Mancini. Nominations: Academy Awards '62: Best Color Cinematography. *PAR*

Hatchet for the Honeymoon
🐾 *Blood Brides; Una Hacha Para la Luna de Miel; Il Roso Segno Della Pollias* **1970** A rather disturbed young man goes around hacking young brides to death as he tries to find out who murdered his wife. Typical sick Bava horror flick; confusing plot, but strong on vivid imagery. 90m/C VHS, Beta. *SP IT* Stephen

---

Forsythe, Dagmar Lassander, Laura Betti, Gerard Tichy; *D:* Mario Bava. *MED, HEG, FCT*

Hate
🐾🐾🐾 *La Haine; Hatred* **1995** Twenty-hours in the lives of young, disenfranchised Said (Taghmaoui), Vinz (Cassel), and Hubert (Kounde), who are living in a housing project outside Paris. A riot breaks out, thanks to police brutality of an Arab resident, and Vinz finds a gun the cops lost. A Paris sojourn leads to a police interrogation of Hubert and Said, a fight with some skinheads, a return to their home turf, and an unexpected conclusion. Intelligent look at the idiocy engendered by societal oppression and a buildup of hatred. French with subtitles. 95m/B VHS. *FR* Vincent Cassel, Hubert Kounde, Said Taghmaoui, Francois Levantal; *D:* Mathieu Kassovitz; *W:* Mathieu Kassovitz; *C:* Pierre Aim, Georges Diane. Cannes Film Festival '95: Best Director (Kassovitz); Cesar Awards '96: Best Film, Best Film Editing; Nominations: Cesar Awards '96: Best Actor (Cassel), Best Cinematography, Best Director (Kassovitz), Best Screenplay, Best Sound.*PGV*

The Hatfields & the McCoys
🐾🐾 **1975** A made-for-television re-telling of the most famous feud in American history—the legendary mountain war between the Hatfields and the McCoys. 90m/C VHS, Beta. Jack Palance, Steve Forrest, Richard Hatch, Karen Lamm; *D:* Clyde Ware. *WOV*

Hats Off
🐾 **1937** Clarke and Payne star as opposing press agents in this tedious musical. The only bright spot is the finale, which features white-robed girls on a cloud-covered carousel. ♫Where Have You Been All My Life?; Little Old Rhythm; Twinkle, Twinkle, Little Star; Let's Have Another; Zilch's Hats; Hats Off. 65m/B VHS. Mae Clarke, John Payne, Helen Lynd, Luis Alberni, Richard "Skeets" Gallagher, Franklin Pangborn; *D:* Boris L. Petroff. *NOS, MLB*

The Haunted
🐾 **1979** The ancient curse of an Indian woman haunts a present day family by possessing the body of a beautiful girl. Through the girl, a horrible vengeance is carried out. 81m/C VHS, Beta. Aldo Ray, Virginia Mayo, Anne Michelle, Jim Negele; *D:* Michael de Gaetano. *VHE, HHE*

Haunted
🐾🐾½ **1995 (R)** At their Sussex home, David Ash watches helplessly as his younger sister Juliet drowns. Flash-forward to 1925 and the grownup David (Quinn) returns to teach a university course debunking the supernatural. Still, he's drawn to a supposedly haunted mansion, inhabited by artist Robert Mariell (Andrews), his sister Christina (Beckinsale), brother Simon (Lowe), and their elderly nanny (Massey). David starts experiencing visions of his dead sister, while mysterious fires and other unexplained manifestations occur—all of which seem tied to the unholy Mariell trio. Based on a novel by James Herbert.*CW:* Sexuality and nudity. 108m/C VHS, Closed Caption. *GB* Aidan Quinn, Kate Beckinsale, Anthony Andrews, Alex Lowe, Anna Massey, Geraldine Somerville, Victoria Shalet; *Cameos:* John Gielgud; *D:* Lewis Gilbert; *W:* Lewis Gilbert, Bob Kellett, Tim Prager; *C:* Tony Pierce-Roberts; *M:* Debbie Wiseman. *HMK*

The Haunted Castle
🐾🐾🐾 *Schloss Vogelod* **1921** One of Murnau's first films, and a vintage, if crusty, example of German expressionism. A nobleman entertains guests at his country mansion when strange things start to occur. Silent, with English titles. 56m/B VHS, Beta. Arnold Korff, Lulu Keyser-Korff; *D:* F.W. Murnau. *SNC, NOS, VYY*

Haunted Gold
🐾🐾 **1932** A young Wayne, in his first Western for Warners, battles gold-hungry desperadoes and a mysterious cloaked phantom. Remake of "The Phantom City." 57m/B VHS, Closed Caption. John Wayne, Sheila Terry, Harry Woods; *D:* Mack V. Wright; *W:* Adele Buffington. *MGM, GPV*

Haunted Harbor
🐾🐾½ *Pirate's Harbor* **1944** A high-seas financier has been murdered by a crooked crony and Captain Jim Marsden's alibi is all wet. He's got to find the gold, the girl, and avoid the goons. Part of "The Cliffhanger Serials" series. 243m/B VHS. Kane Richmond, Kay Aldridge, Roy Barcroft. *REP, MOV*

Haunted Honeymoon ♂ 1986 (PG) Arthritic comedy about a haunted house and a couple trapped there. Sad times for the Mel Brooks alumni participating in this lame horror spoof. **82m/C VHS, Beta, LV.** Gene Wilder, Gilda Radner, Dom DeLuise, Jonathan Pryce, Paul Smith, Peter Vaughan, Bryan Pringle, Roger Ashton-Griffiths, Jim Carter; **D:** Gene Wilder; **W:** Gene Wilder. NO

The Haunted Palace ♂♂½ 1963 Price plays both a 17th-century warlock burned at the stake and a descendant who returns to the family dungeon and gets possessed by the mutant-breeding forebearer. The movie has its own identity crisis, with title and ambience from Poe but story from H.P. Lovecraft's "The Case of Charles Dexter Ward." Respectable but rootless chills, also available with the quasi-Lovecraft "Curse of the Crimson Altar" on laser disc. **87m/C VHS, Beta, LV.** Vincent Price, Debra Paget, Lon Chaney Jr., Frank Maxwell, Leo Gordon, Elisha Cook Jr., John Dierkes; **D:** Roger Corman. HBO, MLB

Haunted Ranch ♂½ 1943 Reno Red has been murdered and a shipment of gold bullion is missing. A gang on the lookout for the gold tries to convince people that Red's ranch is haunted by his ghost. **56m/B VHS, Beta.** John "Dusty" King, David Sharpe, Max Terhune, Rex Lease, Julie Duncan; **D:** Robert Emmett Tansey. NOS, DVT, VYY

The Haunted Strangler ♂♂½ The Grip of the Strangler 1958 Boris Karloff is a writer investigating a 20-year old murder who begins copying some of the killer's acts. **78m/B VHS, Beta.** GB Boris Karloff, Anthony Dawson, Elizabeth Allan; **D:** Robert Day. MED, MPI

Haunted Summer ♂♂ 1988 (R) Soft-focus, sex-and-drugs period piece of the bacchanalian summer of 1816 spent by free spirits Lord Byron, Percy Shelley, Mary Shelley, and John Polidori and others that led Mary Shelley to write "Frankenstein." Based on the novel of the same name by Anne Edwards. **106m/C VHS, Beta, LV.** Alice Krige, Eric Stoltz, Philip Anglim, Laura Dern, Alex Winter; **D:** Ivan Passer; **W:** Lewis John Carlino. MED

Haunted Symphony ♂ Blood Song 1994 (R) In the 18th century, a deranged composer (Wert) is discovered creating a symphony for the devil and killed by a mob. Years later, his niece Gabrielle (Burns) discovers the unfinished symphony hidden in an old piano and hires choir master Marius (Cross) to complete the score. But when he tries, demonic things begin to occur. **CW:** Nudity; sexual situations. **85m/C VHS.** Jennifer Burns, Ben Cross, Doug Wert, Beverly Garland; **D:** David Tausik. NHO

Haunted: The Ferryman ♂♂ 1974 Adapted by Julian Bond from a Kingsley Amis story, the film deals with a novelist who is mysteriously confronted with various events and macabre set-pieces from his own novel, including a dead ferryman rising from the grave. **50m/C VHS, Beta.** GB Jeremy Brett, Nastasha Parry, Lesley Dunlop; **D:** John Irvin. PSM

HauntedWeen ♂½ 1991 All trick, no treat, as a guy nailed by a frat house prank twenty years ago comes-back-for-revenge. **?m/C VHS.** Brien Blakely, Blake Pickett, Brad Hanks, Bart White, Leslee Lacey, Ethan Adler; **D:** Doug Robertson. CVD

The Haunting ♂♂♂½ 1963 A subtle, bloodless horror film about a weekend spent in a monstrously haunted mansion by a parapsychologist, the mansion's skeptic heir, and two mediums. A chilling adaptation of Shirley Jackson's "The Haunting of Hill House," in which the psychology of the heroine is forever in question. **113m/B VHS, Beta, LV.** Julie Harris, Claire Bloom, Russ Tamblyn, Richard Johnson; **D:** Robert Wise. MGM, FCT

Haunting Fear ♂ 1991 Poe's "The Premature Burial" inspired this pale cheapie about a wife with a fear of early interment. After lengthy nightmares and graphic sex, her greedy husband uses her phobia in a murder plot. **88m/C VHS.** Jan-

Michael Vincent, Karen Black, Brinke Stevens, Michael Berryman; **D:** Fred Olen Ray; **W:** Sherman Scott. RHI

The Haunting of Barney Palmer 199? Barney Palmer is sure he has inherited the family magic powers because he is haunted by the ghost of his great uncle. To destroy the curse, he must conquer his fears. Based on the book "The Haunting" by Margaret Mahy. Includes a viewers' guide. Part of the "Wonderworks" series. **58m/C VHS.** Ned Beatty, Alexis Banas, Eleanor Gibson. PME, FCT, BTV

Haunting of Harrington House ♂ 1982 A tame teenage haunted house film originally produced for television. **50m/C VHS, Beta.** Dominique Dunne, Roscoe Lee Browne, Edie Adams, Phil Leeds; **D:** Murray Golden. GEM

The Haunting of Morella ♂ 1991 (R) Poe-inspired cheapjack exploitation about a an executed witch living again in the nubile body of her teen daughter. Ritual murders result, in-between lesbian baths and nude swims. Producer Roger Corman did the same story with more class and less skin in his earlier anthology "Tales of Terror." **82m/C VHS, LV.** David McCallum, Nicole Eggert, Maria Ford, Lana Clarkson; **D:** Jim Wynorski; **W:** Jim Wynorski, R.J. Robertson. NHO

Haunting of Sarah Hardy ♂♂ 1989 Ward, as a recently wed heiress, returns to the scene of her unhappy childhood home. In a standard plot, Ward is torn between an apparent haunting and the question of her own sanity. Made for TV film is redeemed by the creditable acting. **92m/C VHS, Beta, LV, Closed Caption.** Sela Ward, Michael Woods, Roscoe Born, Polly Bergen, Morgan Fairchild; **D:** Jerry London. PAR

The Haunting of Seacliff Inn ♂♂½ 1994 (PG-13) Susan and Mark Enright struggle to start a bed-and-breakfast in their newly acquired Mendocino Victorian manse. But psychic Susie senses something—seems the former owner died violently, and, a hundred years ago, an owner was accused of murdering his wife in the house. Not-too-frightening ghost story but good cast work. Made for cable TV. **CW:** Ghostly terror and sensuality. **94m/C VHS, LV, Closed Caption.** Ally Sheedy, William R. Moses, Louise Fletcher, Lucinda Weist, Maxine Stuart, Tom McCleister, James Horan; **D:** Walter Klenhard; **W:** Walter Klenhard, Tom Walla. USH

The Haunting Passion ♂♂½ 1983 Newlywed Seymour moves into a haunted house only to be seduced by the ghost of the former occupant's dead lover. Effective and erotic presentation. Made for Television. **100m/C VHS, Beta.** Jane Seymour, Gerald McRaney, Millie Perkins, Ruth Nelson, Paul Rossilli, Ivan Bonar; **D:** John Korty. LIV

Haunts ♂½ The Veil 1977 (PG) Tormented woman has difficulty distinguishing between fantasy and reality after a series of brutal slayings lead police to the stunning conclusion that dead people have been committing the crimes. **97m/C VHS, Beta.** Cameron Mitchell, Aldo Ray, May Britt, William Gray Espy, Susan Nohr; **D:** Herb Freed; **M:** Pino Donaggio. MED

Haunts of the Very Rich ♂♂½ 1972 A loose remake of "Outward Bound" in which a group of spoiled people on a vacation find themselves spiritually dead. Made for TV. **72m/C VHS, Beta.** Lloyd Bridges, Anne Francis, Donna Mills, Tony Bill, Robert Reed, Moses Gunn, Cloris Leachman, Ed Asner; **D:** Paul Wendkos. THV

Havana ♂♂½ 1990 (R) During the waning days of the Batista regime, a gambler travels to Havana in search of big winnings. Instead, he meets the beautiful wife of a communist revolutionary. Unable to resist their mutual physical attraction, the lovers become drawn into a destiny which is far greater than themselves. Reminiscent of "Casablanca." **CW:** Strong language and sensuality. **145m/C VHS, Beta, LV, Closed Caption.** Robert Redford, Lena Olin, Alan Arkin, Raul Julia, Tomas Milian, Tony Plana, Betsy Brantley, Lise Cutter, Richard Farnsworth, Mark Rydell, Daniel Davis; **D:** Sydney Pollack; **W:**

Judith Rascoe, David Rayfiel; **C:** Owen Roizman; **M:** Dave Grusin. Nominations: Academy Awards '90: Best Original Score. USH, FCT, MOV

Have Rocket Will Travel ♂♂½ 1959 Three janitors (guess who) help a scientist who is about to lose her job if she can't send a rocket to Venus. They accidentally initiate the launch while still on board and introduce their brand of slapstick to a whole new planet. First of the late 50's-early 60's feature films to capitalize on the renewed popularity of the Three Stooges. **76m/B VHS.** Moe Howard, Larry Fine, Joe DeRita, Anna-Lisa, Jerome Cowan, Bob Colbert; **D:** David Lowell Rich; **W:** Raphael Hayes. COL

Having It All ♂♂ 1982 A wry television comedy about a love triangle. Dyan Cannon stars as a successful business woman with a husband on each coast, who finds dividing her time is more than she bargained for. **100m/C VHS, Beta, LV.** Dyan Cannon, Barry Newman, Hart Bochner, Melanie Chartoff, Sylvia Sidney; **D:** Edward Zwick; **M:** Miles Goodman. LIV

Having Wonderful Crime ♂♂½ 1945 Madcap comedy-thriller about a newly married couple who combine sleuthing with a honeymoon. With their criminal lawyer friend along, the trio winds up searching for a magician who has vanished. Fast-paced action and quick dialogue. **70m/B VHS, LV.** Pat O'Brien, George Murphy, Carole Landis, Lenore Aubert, George Zucco; **D:** Edward Sutherland. TTC, FCT, IME

Having Wonderful Time ♂♂½ 1938 A young girl tries to find culture and romance on her summer vacation at a resort in the Catskills. Film debut of comic Red Skelton, who wasn't always as old as the hills. Based on a Broadway hit by Arthur Kober. **71m/B VHS, Beta.** Ginger Rogers, Lucille Ball, Eve Arden, Red Skelton, Douglas Fairbanks Jr.; **D:** Alfred Santell. NO

Having Wonderful Time/Carnival Boat ♂♂½ 1938 A Ginger Rogers double feature: "Having Wonderful Time" (1938)-fun and frolic at an adult summer camp in the Catskills; and "Carnival Boat" (1932)-the lives and loves of rugged loggers in the Pacific Northwest. **134m/B VHS, Beta.** Ginger Rogers, Douglas Fairbanks Jr., Lucille Ball, Ann Miller, Red Skelton, William Boyd. TTC

Hawaii ♂♂♂ 1966 James Michener's novel about a New England farm boy who decides in 1820 that the Lord has commanded him to the island of Hawaii for the purpose of "Christianizing" the natives. Filmed on location. Also available in a 181 minute version with restored footage. Available in director's cut version with an additional 20 minutes. **161m/C VHS, Beta, LV.** Max von Sydow, Julie Andrews, Richard Harris, Carroll O'Connor, Bette Midler, Gene Hackman, Jocelyn Lagarde; **D:** George Roy Hill; **W:** Daniel Taradash, Dalton Trumbo; **M:** Elmer Bernstein. Golden Globe Awards '67: Best Supporting Actress (Lagarde), Best Score; Nominations: Academy Awards '66: Best Color Cinematography, Best Costume Design (Color), Best Song ("My Wishing Doll"), Best Sound, Best Supporting Actress (Lagarde), Best Original Score. FOX

Hawaii Calls ♂♂ 1938 Two young stowaways on a cruise ship are allowed to stay on after one of them (Breen) struts his stuff as a singer. The two then turn sleuth to catch a gang of spies. More ham than a can of Spam, but still enjoyable. ♫That's The Hawaiian In Me; Hawaii Calls; Down Where The Trade Winds Blow; Macushia; Aloha Oe. **72m/B VHS.** Bobby Breen, Ned Sparks, Irvin S. Cobb, Warren Hull, Gloria Holden, Pua Lani, Raymond Paige, Philip Ahn, Ward Bond; **D:** Eddie Cline. DVT, NOS, HEG

Hawaiian Buckaroo ♂ 1938 A couple of cowboys fight to save their pineapple plantation from a sneaky foreman. **62m/B VHS.** Smith Ballew, Evelyn Knapp, Benny Burt, Harry Woods, Pat O'Brien; **D:** Ray Taylor. NOS, DVT, GPV

The Hawk ♂♂½ 1993 (R) Okay thriller about suburban housewife Annie (Mirren) who suspects that her husband Stephen (Costigan) is a serial killer known as the Hawk. Since Annie has a history of depression and her husband is a known louse, her suspicions are dismissed as delusional. Some surprise twists help the weak story along. Contains some graphic views of corpses. Based on the novel by Ransley. **CW:** Language and terror. **84m/C VHS.** GB Helen Mirren, George Costigan, Owen Teale, Rosemary Leach; **D:** David Hayman; **W:** Peter Ransley; **M:** Nick Bicat. ACA

Hawk and Castle 19?? Bandits murder, pillage, and terrorize the nobility in Medieval Europe until the Hawk comes onto the scene. **95m/C VHS, Beta.** Tom Griffith, Jerry Cobb, Nurla Forway, Mari Real. NO

The Hawk of Powder River 🐾 1948 Cheapie western has Dean getting involved with a beautiful outlaw gang leader with a murderous streak. A large part of this film was lifted from earlier Dean oaters, as are all the tunes. **54m/B VHS.** Eddie Dean, Roscoe Ates, Jennifer Holt, June Carlson, Terry Frost, Lane Bradford; **D:** Ray Taylor. MOV

Hawk of the Wilderness Lost Island of Kioga 1938 A man, shipwrecked as an infant and reared on a remote island by native Indians, battles modern day pirates after an explorer finds a cache of treasure. Serial in 12 episodes. **213m/B VHS.** Bruce (Herman Brix) Bennett, Mala, William Boyle; **D:** William Witney. REP, MLB, VCN

Hawk the Slayer 🐾½ 1981 A comic book fantasy. A good warrior struggles against his villainous brother to possess a magical sword that bestows upon its holder great powers of destruction. Violent battle scenes; Palance makes a great villain. **93m/C VHS, Beta, LV.** Jack Palance, John Terry, Harry Andrews, Roy Kinnear, Ferdinand "Ferdy" Mayne; **D:** Terry Marcel. LIV

Hawken's Breed 🐾🐾 1987 (R) Drifter meets American Indian beauty and hears her tale of woe; the two fall for each other and set out together to avenge the murder of the woman's husband and son. Nothing much to crow about. **93m/C VHS, Beta, LV.** Peter Fonda, Serene Hedin, Jack Elam; **D:** Charles B. Pierce. THV, IME

Hawkeye 🐾½ 1988 After his best friend is murdered by gangsters in a seedy drug deal, Hawkeye, a rough and tumble Texas cop, and his slick new partner hit the streets of Las Vegas with a vengeance. **90m/C VHS, Beta.** Troy Donahue, Chuck Jeffreys, George Chung, Stan Wertlieb; **D:** Leo Fong. NO

Hawkeye: Premiere Episode 1995 Frontier scout Hawkeye (Horsley) and best friend Chingachgook (Grant) come to the aid of Elizabeth Shields (Carter), whose trading post owner husband has been captured during the French and Indian war. **82m/C VHS.** Lee Horsley, Rodney Grant, Lynda Carter. MOV

Hawks 🐾½ 1989 (R) Somewhere on the road to black-comedy this film gets waylaid by triviality. Two terminally ill men break out of the hospital, determined to make their way to Amsterdam for some last-minute fun. Mediocre at best. **105m/C VHS, Beta, LV, 8mm, Closed Caption.** GB Anthony Edwards, Timothy Dalton, Janet McTeer, Jill Bennett, Sheila Hancock, Connie Booth, Camille Coduri; **D:** Robert Ellis Miller; **W:** Roy Clarke. PAR

The Hawks & the Sparrows 🐾🐾 Uccellacci e Uccellini 1967 Shortly after "Mr. Ed" came Pasolini's garrulous crow, which follows a father and son's travels through Italy spouting pithy bits of politics. A comic Pasolinian allegory-fest full of then-topical political allusions, the story comes off a bit wooden. Worth watching to see Toto, the Italian comic, in his element. **91m/B VHS, LV.** IT Toto, Ninetto Davoli, Femi Benussi; **D:** Pier Paolo Pasolini; **W:** Pier Paolo Pasolini; **M:** Ennio Morricone. WBF

Hawmps! woof! 1976 (G) Idiotic comedy about a Civil War lieutenant who trains his men to use camels. When the soldiers and animals begin to grow fond of each other, Congress orders the camels to be set free. Hard to believe this was based on a real life incident. **98m/C VHS, Beta.** James Hampton, Christopher Connelly, Slim Pickens, Den-

ver Pyle; **D:** Joe Camp; **W:** William Bickley; **M:** Euel Box. VES

Hawthorne of the USA 🐾🐾½ 1919 Reid stars as Anthony Hamilton Hawthorne, American extraordinaire. After gambling a fortune away in Monte Carlo, Hawthorne heads to mainland Europe for rest and revelry. Instead, he finds the love of a princess and a Communist coup in the making. Silent with orchestral score. **55m/B VHS, Beta.** Wallace Reid, Harrison Ford, Lila Lee, Tully Marshall; **D:** James Cruze. GPV

Hazel's People 🐾½ 1975 (G) Bitter and hostile college student attends his friend's funeral in Mennonite country. He discovers not only a way of life he never knew existed, but a personal faith in a living Christ. From the Merle Good novel, "Happy as the Grass Was Green." **105m/C VHS, Beta.** Geraldine Page, Pat Hingle, Graham Beckel, Charles Davis. VCI

He is My Brother 🐾½ 1975 (G) Two boys survive a shipwreck, landing on an island that houses a leper colony. **90m/C VHS, Beta.** Keenan Wynn, Bobby Sherman, Robbie Rist; **D:** Edward Dmytryk. NO

He Kills Night After Night After Night 🐾½ 1970 British police are baffled as they seek the man who has been killing women in the style of Jack the Ripper. And he keeps doing it. **88m/C VHS, Beta.** Jack May, Linda Marlowe, Justine Lord. NO

He Knows You're Alone 🐾 1980 (R) Lame horror flick that focuses on a psychotic killer terrorizing a bride-to-be and her bridal party in his search for a suitable bride of his own. **94m/C VHS, Beta.** Don Scardino, Elizabeth Kemp, Tom Rolfing, Paul Gleason, Caitlin O'Heaney, Tom Hanks, Patsy Pease; **D:** Armand Mastroianni; **W:** Scott Parker. MGM

He Lives: The Search for the Evil One 🐾 1988 A man who was imprisoned by Nazis as a child attempts to keep Hitler, now living in Buenos Aires, from starting a 4th Reich. **90m/C VHS, Beta.** Lee Patterson. NO

He Said, She Said 🐾🐾½ 1991 (R) Romance is the topic, but this isn't a typical dating film, instead a couple's relationship unfolds from differing points of view: first, the guy's (by Kwapis) and then the girl's (by Silver). Bacon and Perkins, Baltimore journalists and professional rivals, tell how their romance wound up on the rocks, and why (or so they say). The end result is overlong and lacks the zing of other war between the sexes movies, but real-life couple Silver and Kwapis do humorously highlight the fact that men and women often view the same incidents very differently. Bacon overacts, Perkins overreacts, and Stone shines as Bacon's ex-girl. **115m/C VHS, LV, Closed Caption.** Elizabeth Perkins, Kevin Bacon, Sharon Stone, Nathan Lane, Anthony LaPaglia, Stanley Anderson, Charlaine Woodard, Danton Stone, Phil Leeds, Rita Karin; **D:** Marisa Silver, Ken Kwapis; **W:** Brian Hohlfield; **C:** Stephen Burum; **M:** Miles Goodman. PAR, CCB

He Walked by Night 🐾🐾🐾½ 1948 Los Angeles homicide investigators track down cop killer Ray Morgan (Basehart) in this excellent drama. The final confrontation takes place in the L.A. County Flood Control System, consisting of some 700 miles of underground tunnels. Based on a true story from the files of the Los Angeles police, this first rate production reportedly inspired Webb to create "Dragnet." **80m/B VHS.** Richard Basehart, Scott Brady, Roy Roberts, Jack Webb, Whit Bissell; **D:** Alfred Werker, Anthony Mann; **C:** John Alton. KIV, NOS, BAR

He Who Gets Slapped 🐾🐾🐾 1924 Chaney portrays a brilliant scientist whose personal and professional humiliations cause him to join a travelling French circus as a masochistic clown (hence the title). There he falls in love with a beautiful circus performer and plans a spectacular revenge. Brilliant use of lighting and Expressionist devices by director Sjostrom (who used the Americanized version of his name-Seastrom-in the credits). Adapted from the Russian play

"He, The One Who Gets Slapped" by Leonid Andreyev. **85m/B VHS.** Lon Chaney Sr., Norma Shearer, John Gilbert, Tully Marshall, Ford Sterling, Marc McDermott; **D:** Victor Sjostrom; **W:** Carey Wilson, Victor Sjostrom. FCT

He Who Walks Alone 1978 Made-for-television film documents the life of Thomas E. Gilmore, who became the South's first elected black sheriff in the 1960s. **74m/C VHS, Beta.** Louis Gossett Jr., Clu Gulager, Mary Alice, James McEachin, Barton Heyman, Barry Brown, Lonny Chapman; **D:** Jerrold Freedman. NO

The Head 🐾🐾 1959 A scientist comes up with a serum that can keep the severed head of a dog alive. Before too long, he tries the stuff out on a woman, transferring the head from her own hunchbacked body to that of a beautiful stripper. Weird German epic sports poor special effects and unintentional laughs, but is interesting nonetheless. **92m/B VHS.** GE Horst Frank, Michel Simon, Paul Dahlke, Karin Kernke, Helmut Schmidt; **D:** Victor Trivas; **W:** Victor Trivas. SNC

Head 🐾🐾🐾 1968 (G) Infamously plotless musical comedy starring the television fab four of the '60s, the Monkees, in their only film appearance. A number of guest stars appear and a collection of old movie clips are also included. ♫ Circle Sky; Can You Dig It; Long Title: Do I Have To Do This All Over Again; Daddy's Song; As We Go Along; The Porpoise Song. **86m/C VHS, Beta, LV.** Peter Tork, Mickey Dolenz, Davy Jones, Michael Nesmith, Frank Zappa, Annette Funicello, Teri Garr; **D:** Bob Rafelson; **W:** Jack Nicholson, Bob Rafelson. RHI, COL, MVD

Head of the Family 🐾🐾½ 1971 (PG) After a woman sacrifices her political ideals and career goals for her role as a family matriarch, she eventually falls apart. **105m/C VHS, Beta.** IT FR Nino Manfredi, Leslie Caron, Ugo Tognazzi, Claudine Auger; **D:** Nanni Loy; **W:** Nanni Loy. GEM

Head of the Family 🐾½ 1996 (R) Lance (Bailey) moves to Nob Hollow and discovers the Stackpool family's dreadful secrets—they're telepathic quadruplets under the control of brother Myron (Perra), who just happens to be a giant head that gets around in a wheelchair. Lance decides to use the whacko family to get rid of babe girlfriend Loretta's (Lovell) inconvenient husband. **CW:** Language, nudity, violence, sexual situations. **82m/C VHS.** Blake Bailey, Jacqueline Lovell, Bob Schott, J.W. Perra; **D:** Robert Talbot. AFE

Head Office 🐾🐾 1986 (PG-13) A light comedy revolving around the competition between corporate management and the lower echelon for the available position of chairman. **90m/C VHS, Beta.** Danny DeVito, Eddie Albert, Judge Reinhold, Rick Moranis, Jane Seymour; **D:** Ken Finkleman; **M:** James Newton Howard. NO

Head Over Heels 🐾🐾🐾 1967 A model married to an older man has an affair with a younger one and cannot decide between them. In French with subtitles. **89m/C VHS, Beta.** FR Brigitte Bardot, Laurent Terzieff, Michael Sarne; **D:** Serge Bourguignon. FCT

Head Winds 🐾🐾 1925 Silent romance in which Mr. Right spares helpless girl against her will from marrying Mr. Wrong. **52m/B VHS, Beta.** House Peters Sr., Patsy Ruth Miller. GPV

Headhunter 🐾½ 1989 Voodoo-esque killers are leaving headless bodies all around Miami. Plenty of prosthetic make-up. **92m/C VHS, Beta, LV.** Kay Lenz, Wayne Crawford, John Fatooh, Steve Kanaly, June Chadwick, Sam Williams; **D:** Francis Schaeffer. ACA, IME

Headin' for the Rio Grande 🐾 1936 A cowboy and his sheriff brother drive off cattle-rustlers in this Western saga. Ritter's film debut. Songs include "Campfire Love Song," "Jailhouse Lament," and "Night Herding Song." **60m/B VHS, Beta.** Tex Ritter, Eleanor Stewart, Syd Saylor, Warner Richmond, Charles "Blackie" King; **D:** Robert North Bradbury. NOS, DVT

Heading for Heaven ⚔⚔ 1947 A mistaken medical report leaves a frazzled realtor believing he has only three months to live, and when he disappears the family suspects the worst. A minor comedy based on a play by Charles Webb. **65m/B VHS.** Stuart Erwin, Glenda Farrell, Russ Vincent, Irene Ryan, Milburn Stone, George O'Hanlon; **D:** Lewis D. Collins. *NOS*

Heading Home ⚔⚔½ 1924 A very early version of the Babe Ruth story—starring none other than the Babe himself. A fair print, this film is orchestra scored. **56m/B VHS, Beta.** Babe Ruth. *GPV*

Headless Body in Topless Bar ⚔⚔½ 1996 Based on a famous New York Post headline and the crime that inspired it, this black comedy contains more than its lurid title lets on. Except for street footage at the opening and closing, the entire movie is set in a seedy strip club. After shooting the bartender in a robbery attempt, a crazed ex-con holds the patrons and employees hostage. He forces them to play a mind game called "Nazi truth," revealing the distasteful truth about the captives. Director Bruce and screenwriter Koper first worked together filming re-creations for "America's Most Wanted." The cast worked for "hostage scale," meaning if those playing captives stole the gun from the robber (a plot point), they got his pay for the day. If not, then he got their wages. **105m/C VHS.** Raymond J. Barry, Jennifer MacDonald, David Selby, Taylor Nichols, Paul Williams, Biff Yeager, Rustam Branaman, April Grace; **D:** James Bruce; **W:** Peter Koper; **C:** Kevin Morrisey; **M:** Charles P. Barnett. *NYR*

Headless Eyes ⚔½ 1983 Gory entry into the psycho-artist category. An artist is miffed when mistaken by a woman as a burglar he loses an eye. Not one to forgive and forget, he becomes quite the eyeball fetishist, culling donations from unsuspecting women. An eye for an eye ad finitum. **78m/C VHS.** Bo Brundin, Gordon Raman, Mary Jane Early; **D:** Kent Bateman; **W:** Kent Bateman. *NO*

Headline Woman ⚔⚔ 1935 An ongoing feud between a police commissioner and a newspaper's city editor causes a reporter to make a deal with a policeman in exchange for news. A good cast makes this otherwise tired story tolerable. **75m/B VHS, Beta.** Heather Angel, Roger Pryor, Jack LaRue, Ford Sterling, Conway Tearle; **D:** William Nigh. *NOS, DVT, HEG*

Heads ⚔⚔½ 1993 (R) Unassuming copyreader Guy Franklin (Cryer) gets promoted to reporter and his first assignment is a doozy. He's to cover a series of decapitation murders in a small town. Can he do the job without become the next victim—or being accused of the crimes? Made for cable TV; filmed in Manitoba, Canada. **102m/C VHS, Closed Caption.** CA Jon Cryer, Jennifer Tilly, Ed Asner, Roddy McDowall; **D:** Paul Shapiro; **W:** Adam Brooks. *REP*

Healer ⚔½ *Little Pal* 1936 A doctor forgets his pledge to help the lame and becomes a fashionable physician. A young crippled lad helps him eventually remember his original purpose was to serve others. **80m/B VHS, Beta.** Mickey Rooney, Ralph Bellamy, Karen Morley, Judith Allen, Robert McWade; **D:** Reginald Barker. *DVT*

Hear My Song ⚔⚔⚔½ 1991 (R) Mickey O'Neill (Dunbar) is an unscrupulous club promoter, who books singers with names like Franc Cinatra, while trying to revive his failing nightclub in this charming, hilarious comedy. He hires the mysterious Mr. X, who claims he is really the legendary exiled singer Josef Locke, only to find out he is an imposter. To redeem himself with his fiancee and her mother, he goes to Ireland to find the real Locke (Beatty) and bring him to Liverpool to sing. Dunbar is appealing in his role, and Beatty is magnificent as the legendary Locke—so much so that he was nominated for a Golden Globe for Best Supporting Actor. **CW:** Language and one sensual scene. **104m/C VHS, Beta, Closed**

Caption. *GB* Ned Beatty, Adrian Dunbar, Shirley Anne Field, Tara Fitzgerald, William Hootkins, David McCallum; **D:** Peter Chelsom; **W:** Peter Chelsom; **M:** John Altman. *PAR*

Hear No Evil ⚔½ 1993 (R) Below average thriller with a deaf victim (Matlin) involved in a game of cat-and-mouse with a corrupt cop (Sheen) who's looking for a valuable coin. Weak script plays up the woman in jeopardy theme but lacks the crucial element of suspense. A waste of an otherwise talented cast. **CW:** Profanity, brief nudity, violence, and sex. **98m/C VHS, LV, Closed Caption.** Marlee Matlin, D.B. Sweeney, Martin Sheen, John C. McGinley, Christina Carlisi, Greg Elam, Charley Lang; **D:** Robert Greenwald; **W:** Randall Badat, Kathleen Rowell; **M:** Graeme Revell. *FXV*

Hearing Voices ⚔½ 1990 Joyless Erica is a commercial model who suffers from a form of scoliosis. If she capitalized on her infirmity by advertising medical aids, she could make a lot of money but she firmly refuses her lover's pleas to do this. When her doctor suggests reconstructive surgery, she storms out of his office but not before attracting the attention of Lee, his gay lover. Erica and Lee begin a complex emotional relationship, upsetting to everyone around them. Uninvolving characters, inert direction, and amateurish acting work against Greytak's feature film debut. **87m/C VHS.** Erika Nagy, Stephen Gatta, Tim Ahearn, Michael Davenport; **D:** Sharon Greytak; **W:** Sharon Greytak. *WAC, FCT*

The Hearse WOOF! 1980 (PG) Incredibly boring horror film in which a young school teacher moves into a mansion left to her by her late aunt and finds her life threatened by a sinister black hearse. **97m/C VHS, Beta.** Trish Van Devere, Joseph Cotten; **D:** George Bowers; **W:** William Bleich. *MED*

The Hearst and Davies Affair ⚔⚔½ 1985 Married, middle-aged newspaper tycoon William Randolph Hearst falls for teenage Ziegfeld girl Marion Davies and tries to turn her into a Hollywood star. Davies was generally thought to be talented as a comedienne but Hearst insisted on choosing ill-suited dramatic roles for the blonde and her career was problematic. Their lavish lifestyle was enhanced when Hearst built San Simeon for Davies and their scandalous affair lasted 35 years. Made for television. **97m/C VHS.** Robert Mitchum, Virginia Madsen, Fritz Weaver; **D:** David Lowell Rich. *ABC, PSM*

Heart ⚔½ 1987 (R) A down-and-out small-time boxer is given a chance to make a comeback, and makes the Rocky-like most of it. **93m/C VHS, Beta.** Brad Davis, Jesse Doran, Sam Gray, Steve Buscemi, Frances Fisher; **D:** James Lemmo. *VTR, NWV*

Heart and Souls ⚔⚔½ 1993 (PG-13) Reincarnation comedy casts Downey, Jr. as a mortal whose body is inhabited by four lost souls who died on the night he was born. Now an adult, he must finish what they could not, no matter how outrageous it may be. Talented cast wears plot that's old hat. Downey Jr. must be looking to do a trilogy of tired reincarnated soul roles—this is his second, "Chances Are" was his first. **CW:** Sensuality. **104m/C VHS, LV, Closed Caption.** Robert Downey Jr., Charles Grodin, Tom Sizemore, Alfre Woodard, Kyra Sedgwick, Elisabeth Shue, David Paymer; **D:** Ron Underwood; **W:** Brent Maddock, S.S. Wilson, Gregory Hansen, Erik Hansen; **M:** Marc Shaiman. *USH, BTV*

Heart Beat ⚔⚔½ 1980 (R) The fictionalized story of Jack Kerouac (author of "On the Road"), his friend and inspiration Neal Cassady, and the woman they shared, Carolyn Cassady. Based on Carolyn Cassady's memoirs. Strong performances, with Nolte as Cassady and Spacek as his wife, overcome the sometimes shaky narrative. **105m/C VHS, Beta.** Nick Nolte, John Heard, Sissy Spacek, Ann Dusenberry, Ray Sharkey, Tony Bill, Steve Allen, John Larroquette; **D:** John Byrum; **W:** John Byrum; **M:** Jack Nitzsche. *WAR*

Heart Condition ⚔⚔½ 1990 (R) A deceased black lawyer's heart is donated to a bigoted Los Angeles cop who was stalking the lawyer when he was alive. Soon afterwards the lawyer's ghost returns to haunt the police officer, hoping the officer will help to avenge his murder. Both Hoskins and Washington display fine performances given the unlikely script. **95m/C VHS, LV.** Bob Hoskins, Denzel Washington, Chloe Webb, Ray Baker, Ja'net DuBois, Alan Rachins, Roger E. Mosley, Jeffrey Meek; **D:** James D. Parriott; **C:** Arthur Albert. *NLC*

The Heart is a Lonely Hunter ⚔⚔⚔ 1968 (G) Set in the South, Carson McCuller's tale of angst and ignorance, loneliness and beauty comes to the screen with the film debuts of Keach and Locke. Arkin gives an instinctive, gentle performance as the deaf mute; Locke's screen debut. **124m/C VHS, Beta, Closed Caption.** Alan Arkin, Cicely Tyson, Sondra Locke, Stacy Keach, Chuck McCann, Laurinda Barrett; **D:** Robert Ellis Miller; **C:** James Wong Howe; **M:** Dave Grusin. New York Film Critics Awards '68: Best Actor (Arkin); Nominations: Academy Awards '68: Best Actor (Arkin), Best Supporting Actress (Locke). *WAR*

Heart Like a Wheel ⚔⚔½ 1983 (PG) The story of Shirley Muldowney, who rose from the daughter of a country-western singer to the leading lady in drag racing. The film follows her battles of sexism and choosing whether to have a career or a family. Bedelia's perfomance is outstanding. Fine showings from Bridges and Axton in supporting roles. **113m/C VHS, Beta, LV, Closed Caption.** Bonnie Bedelia, Beau Bridges, Bill McKinney, Leo Rossi, Hoyt Axton, Dick Miller, Anthony Edwards; **D:** Jonathan Kaplan; **W:** Ken Friedman. Nominations: Academy Awards '83: Best Costume Design. *FOX*

Heart of a Champion: The Ray Mancini Story ⚔⚔ 1985 Made-for-TV movie based on the life of Ray "Boom Boom" Mancini, former lightweight boxing champion. Inspired by the career his father never had due to WWII, Mancini fought his way to the top. Sylvester Stallone staged the fight sequences. **94m/C VHS, Beta.** Robert (Bobby) Blake, Doug McKeon, Mariclare Costello; **D:** Richard Michaels. *FOX*

Heart of a Nation ⚔ *Untel Pere et Fils* 1943 Saga of the Montmarte family and their life during three wars, beginning with the Franco-Prussian War and ending with the Nazi occupation in France. Although ordered to be destroyed by the Nazis, this film was saved, along with many others, by the French "Cinema Resistance." In French with English subtitles. **111m/B VHS.** *FR* Louis Jouvet, Raimu, Suzy Prim, Michele Morgan, Renee Devillers; **D:** Julien Duvivier. *NOS, DVT, HEG*

Heart of Darkness ⚔⚔ 1993 Joseph Conrad's 1902 menacing novella set in the Belgian Congo is told through flashbacks by Marlow (Roth), whose employers, a Belgian trading company, hire him to find Kurtz (Malkovich), head of a remote trading station, who is rumored to be hoarding a huge cache of ivory. Marlow's journey up the river is beset by obstacles and Kurtz is rumored to be either insane or a prophet in his jungle kingdom. Filmed in Belize; made for television. Francis Ford Coppola's updated adaptation became "Apocalyse Now." **120m/C VHS, LV, Closed Caption.** Tim Roth, John Malkovich, James Fox, Isaach de Bankole, Patrick Ryecart, Geoffrey Hutchings, Peter Vaughan, Phoebe Nicholls, Allan Corduner, Alan Scarfe, Iman, Timothy Bateson; **D:** Nicolas Roeg; **W:** Benedict Fitzgerald; **M:** Stanley Myers. *TTC*

The Heart of Dixie ⚔⚔ 1989 (PG) Three college co-eds at a southern university in the 1950s see their lives and values change with the influence of the civil rights movement. College newspaper reporter Sheedy takes up the cause of a black man victimized by racial violence. Lightweight social-conscience fare. **96m/C VHS, Beta, LV, Closed Caption.** Virginia Madsen, Ally Sheedy, Phoebe Cates, Treat Williams, Kyle Secor, Francesca Roberts, Barbara Babcock, Don Michael Paul, Kurtwood Smith, Richard Bradford; **D:** Martin Davidson; **C:** Robert Elswit. *ORI*

Heart of Dragon 🎬🎬 1985 Police officer Chan takes care of his mentally challenged brother Hung, who gets mistaken for a robbery suspect. So Chan has to track down the real crooks. Features a 20-minute fight finale. Chinese with subtitles or dubbed. **85m/C VHS, LV.** *HK* Jackie Chan, Samo Hung, Emily Chu; *D:* Samo Hung. **TAI**

Heart of Glass 🎬🎬🎬 1974 A pre-industrial Bavarian village becomes deeply troubled when their glassblower dies without imparting the secret of making his unique Ruby glass. The townspeople go to extremes, from madness to murder to magic, to discover the ingredients. From German director Herzog (who hypnotized his cast daily), this somewhat apocalyptic tale is based on legend. The colors are incredible in their intensity. In German with English subtitles. **93m/C VHS.** *GE* Josef Bierbichler, Stefan Autter, Scheitz Clemens, Volker Prechtel, Sonia Skiba; *D:* Werner Herzog. **NYF, FCT**

Heart of Humanity 1918 An intense drama of love, patriotism, and sacrifice just before the war in a small Canadian village. A traveler who is really a Prussian army lieutenant finds his way to the house of a young man who is about to wed. He ends up falling in love with his fiancee and war is declared just before the wedding. A silent film with music score. **133m/B VHS, Beta, 8mm.** Dorothy Phillips, Erich von Stroheim; *D:* Allen Holubar. **GPV, VYY, GVV**

Heart of Midnight 🎬🎬½ 1989 (R) An emotionally unstable young woman inherits a seedy massage parlor. She works hard to turn it, and herself, into something better. Nice performance by Leigh. **93m/C VHS, Beta, LV.** Jennifer Jason Leigh, Brenda Vaccaro, Frank Stallone, Peter Coyote, Gale Mayron, Sam Schacht, Denise Dumont; *D:* Matthew Chapman; *W:* Matthew Chapman; *M:* Yanni. **NO**

Heart of Texas Ryan 🎬½ 1916 Flamboyant cowboy star fights with kidnappers and wins in this silent film. **50m/B VHS, Beta.** Tom Mix. **GPV, NOS, DVT**

Heart of the Golden West 🎬🎬 1942 Roy protects ranchers of Cherokee City from unjust shipping charges. **65m/B VHS, Beta.** Roy Rogers, Smiley Burnette, George "Gabby" Hayes, Bob Nolan, Ruth Terry; *D:* Joseph Kane. **NOS, VYY, VCN**

Heart of the Rio Grande 🎬½ 1942 Spoiled young rich girl tries to trick her father into coming to her "rescue" at a western dude ranch. **70m/B VHS, Beta.** Gene Autry, Smiley Burnette, Fay McKenzie, Edith Fellows, Joseph Stauch Jr.; *D:* William M. Morgan. **CCB, VCN**

Heart of the Rockies 🎬½ 1937 The Three Mesquiteers stop a mountain family's rustling and illegal game trappers. **54m/B VHS, Beta.** Bob Livingston, Ray Corrigan, Max Terhune, Lynn (Mary Hart) Roberts, Yakima Canutt, J.P. McGowan; *D:* Joseph Kane. **NOS, VCN, MED**

Heart of the Rockies 🎬½ 1951 Roy, along with his trusty horse and dog, takes care of a highway construction project. **67m/B VHS.** Roy Rogers, Penny Edwards, Gordon Jones, Ralph Morgan, Fred Graham, Mira McKinney; *D:* William Witney. **NOS, DVT, TIM**

Heart of the Stag 🎬🎬½ 1984 (R) On an isolated sheep ranch in the New Zealand outback, a father and daughter suffer the repercussions of an incestuous relationship when she becomes enamored with a hired hand. **94m/C VHS, Beta, LV.** *NZ* Bruno Lawrence, Mary Regan, Terence Cooper; *D:* Michael Firth. **VTR, NWV**

Heartaches 🎬🎬 1947 A reporter tries to track down a murderer who has killed twice. **71m/B VHS, Beta.** Chill Wills, Sheila Ryan, Edward Norris, James Seay. **NOS, DVT, HEG**

Heartaches 🎬🎬🎬 1982 A young pregnant woman (Potts) meets up with a crazy girlfriend (Kidder) in this touching film about love and friendship. Although a study in contrasts, the two end up sharing an apartment together in Toronto. Fine performances from Potts and Kidder give life to this romantic comedy. **90m/C VHS, Beta, LV.** *CA* Margot Kidder, Annie Potts, Robert Carradine, Winston Rekert; *D:* Donald Shebib. Genie Awards '82: Best Actress (Kidder). *LIV, VES*

Heartbeat 🎬🎬½ 1946 If you thought pointless Hollywood remakes of French films were a new phenomenon (see "Pure Luck," for example), then note this lighthearted remake of a 1940 Gallic farce. Rogers becomes the best student in a Parisian school for pickpockets, but when she tries out her skills on a dashing diplomat they fall in love instead. **100m/B VHS.** Ginger Rogers, Jean-Pierre Aumont, Adolphe Menjou, Basil Rathbone, Melville Cooper, Mona Maris, Henry Stephenson, Eduardo Ciannelli; *D:* Sam Wood; *C:* Joseph Valentine. *NOS, HEG*

Heartbeeps 🎬🎬 1981 (PG) In 1995, two domestic robot servants fall in love and run off together. On a beach they encounter the Energizer Bunny. No, that's not right. Young kids may enjoy the romantic robotic duo of Kaufman and Peters. **79m/C VHS, Beta.** Andy Kaufman, Bernadette Peters, Randy Quaid, Kenneth McMillan, Christopher Guest, Melanie Mayron, Jack Carter; *D:* Allan Arkush; *M:* John Williams. Nominations: Academy Awards '81: Best Makeup. *USH*

Heartbreak Hotel 🎬🎬½ 1988 (PG-13) Johnny Wolfe kidnaps Elvis Presley from his show in Cleveland and drives him home to his mother, a die-hard Elvis fan. Completely unbelievable, utterly ridiculous, and still a lot of fun. **101m/C VHS, Beta, LV, Closed Caption.** David Keith, Tuesday Weld, Charlie Schlatter, Angela Goethals, Jacque Lynn Colton, Chris Mulkey, Karen Landry, Tudor Sherrard, Paul Harkins; *D:* Chris Columbus; *W:* Chris Columbus; *M:* Georges Delerue. *TOU*

Heartbreak House 🎬🎬½ 1986 A production of George Bernard Shaw's classic play about a captain and his daughter who invite an odd assortment of people into their home for a few days. In the course of their visit, each person shares his ambitions, hopes, and fears. From the "American Playhouse" television series. **118m/C VHS, Beta.** Rex Harrison, Rosemary Harris, Amy Irving; *D:* Anthony Page. *ACA, PBS*

The Heartbreak Kid 🎬🎬🎬 1972 (PG) Director May's comic examination of love and hypocrisy. Grodin embroils himself in a triangle with his new bride and a woman he can't have, an absolutely gorgeous and totally unloving woman he shouldn't want. Walks the fence between tragedy and comedy, with an exceptional performance from Berlin. Based on Bruce Jay Friedman's story. **106m/C VHS, Beta, LV.** Charles Grodin, Cybill Shepherd, Eddie Albert, Jeannie Berlin, Art Metrano; *D:* Elaine May; *W:* Neil Simon; *C:* Owen Roizman. New York Film Critics Awards '72: Best Supporting Actress (Berlin); National Society of Film Critics Awards '72: Best Supporting Actor (Albert), Best Supporting Actress (Berlin); Nominations: Academy Awards '72: Best Supporting Actor (Albert), Best Supporting Actress (Berlin). *MED, VTR*

Heartbreak Ridge 🎬🎬🎬 1986 (R) An aging Marine recon sergeant is put in command of a young platoon to whip them into shape to prepare for combat in the invasion of Grenada. Eastwood whips this old story into shape too, with a fine performance of a man who's given everything to the Marines. The invasion of Grenada, though, is not epic material. (Also available in English with Spanish subtitles.) **130m/C VHS, Beta, 8mm, Closed Caption.** Clint Eastwood, Marsha Mason, Everett McGill, Arlen Dean Snyder, Bo Svenson, Moses Gunn, Eileen Heckart, Boyd Gaines, Mario Van Peebles; *D:* Clint Eastwood; *W:* Jim Carabatsos; *C:* Jack N. Green; *M:* Lennie Niehaus. Nominations: Academy Awards '86: Best Sound. *WAR, TLF*

Heartbreaker 🎬½ 1983 (R) Eastern Los Angeles explodes with vicious turf wars when Beto and Hector battle for the affection of Kim, the neighborhood's newest heartbreaker. **90m/C VHS, Beta, LV.** Fernando Allende, Dawn Dunlap, Michael D. Roberts, Robert Dryer, Apollonia; *D:* Frank Zuniga. *MED*

Heartbreakers 🎬🎬🎬 1984 (R) Two male best friends find themselves in the throes of drastic changes in their careers and romantic encounters. On target acting makes this old story new, with a fine performance by Wayne, in her last film before her death. **98m/C VHS, Beta.** Peter Coyote, Nick Mancuso, Carole Laure, Max Gail, James Laurenson, Carol Wayne, Jamie Rose, Kathryn Harrold; *D:* Bobby Roth; *W:* Bobby Roth; *C:* Michael Ballhaus; *M:* Tangerine Dream. *VES*

Heartburn 🎬🎬🎬 1986 (R) Based on Nora Ephron's own semi-autobiographical novel about her marital travails with writer Carl Bernstein, this is a tepid, bitter modern romance between writers already shell-shocked from previous marriages. **109m/C VHS, Beta, LV, 8mm, Closed Caption.** Meryl Streep, Jack Nicholson, Steven Hill, Richard Masur, Stockard Channing, Jeff Daniels, Milos Forman, Catherine O'Hara, Maureen Stapleton, Karen Akers, Joanna Gleason, Mercedes Ruehl, Caroline Aaron, Yakov Smirnoff, Anna Maria Horsford, Wilfrid Hyde-White; *D:* Mike Nichols; *W:* Nora Ephron; *C:* Nestor Almendros; *M:* Carly Simon. *PAR*

Heartland 🎬🎬🎬½ 1981 (PG) Set in 1910, this film chronicles the story of one woman's life on the Wyoming Frontier, the hazards she faces, and her courage and spirit. Stunningly realistic and without cliche. Based on the diaries of Elinore Randall Stewart. **95m/C VHS, Beta.** Conchata Ferrell, Rip Torn, Barry Primus, Lilia Skala, Megan Folson; *D:* Richard Pearce. Sundance Film Festival '81: Grand Jury Prize. *NO*

Hearts & Armour 🎬🎬 1983 A holy war between Christians and Moors erupts when a Moorish princess is kidnapped. Based on Ludovico Ariosto's "Orlando Furioso." **101m/C VHS, Beta.** *IT* Tanya Roberts, Leigh McCloskey, Ron Moss, Rick Edwards, Giovanni Visentin; *D:* Giacomo Battiato. *WAR*

Heart's Desire 🎬½ 1937 Opera great Tauber stars in this musical of an unknown Viennese singer who falls in love with an English girl. **79m/B VHS, Beta.** *GB* Richard Tauber, Lenora Corbett, Kathleen Kelly, Paul Graetz; *D:* Paul Stein. *NO*

Heart's Haven 🎬🎬½ 1922 An insensitive wife (Adams), who doesn't appreciate how wonderful her husband is, winds up running away with another man. **61m/B VHS, Beta.** Claire Adams, Robert McKim, Carl Gantvoort, Jean Hersholt; *D:* Benjamin B. Hampton. *GPV, FCT*

Hearts of Darkness: A Filmmaker's Apocalypse 🎬🎬🎬 1991 (R) This riveting, critically acclaimed documentary about the making of Francis Ford Coppola's masterpiece "Apocalypse Now" is based largely on original footage shot and directed by his wife Eleanor. Also included are recent interviews with cast and crew members including Coppola, Martin Sheen, Robert Duvall, Frederic Forrest and Dennis Hopper. *CW:* Language. **96m/C VHS, Beta, Closed Caption.** Sam Bottoms, Eleanor Coppola, Francis Ford Coppola, Robert Duvall, Laurence "Larry" Fishburne, Frederic Forrest, Albert Hall, Dennis Hopper, George Lucas, John Milius, Martin Sheen; *D:* Fax Bahr, George Hickenlooper; *W:* Fax Bahr, George Hickenlooper; *M:* Todd Boekelheide. National Board of Review Awards '91: Best Feature Documentary. *PAR*

Hearts of Fire 🎬 1987 A trio of successful rock 'n roll stars work out their confused romantic entanglements. Barely released and then, not even in the U.S. Sad outing for the cast, especially legendary Dylan. **90m/C VHS, Beta, LV, Closed Caption.** Bob Dylan, Fiona, Rupert Everett, Julian Glover; *D:* Richard Marquand; *W:* Joe Eszterhas; *M:* John Barry. *ORI, WAR*

Hearts of Humanity 🎬🎬 1932 Mawkish melodrama concerning a Jewish antique dealer and his relationship with the son of an Irish cop. An early "Chico and the Man" variant. **56m/B VHS.** Jean Hersholt, Jackie Searl, J. Farrell MacDonald, Claudia Dell, Charles Delaney, Lucille LaVerne, George Humbert; *D:* Christy Cabanne. *NOS, HEG*

Hearts of the West 🎬🎬🎬½ *Hollywood Cowboy* **1975 (PG)** A fantasy-filled farm boy travels to Hollywood in the 1930s and seeks a writing career. Instead, he finds himself an ill-suited western movie star in this small offbeat comedy-drama that's sure to charm. **103m/C VHS, Beta.** Jeff Bridges, Andy Griffith, Donald Pleasence, Alan Arkin, Blythe Danner; *D:* Howard Zieff; *W:* Rob Thompson. National Board of Review Awards '75: 10 Best Films of the Year; New York Film Critics Awards '75: Best Supporting Actor (Arkin). MGM

Hearts of the World 🎬🎬🎬 **1918** A vintage Griffith epic about a young boy who goes off to WWI and the tribulations endured by both him and his family on the homefront. Overly sentimental but powerfully made melodrama, from Griffith's waning years. Silent with music score. **152m/B VHS, Beta, LV, 8mm.** Lillian Gish, Robert "Bobbie" Harron, Dorothy Gish, Erich von Stroheim, Ben Alexander, Josephine Crowell, Noel Coward, Mary Gish; *D:* D.W. Griffith. GPV, REP, GVV

Heartstopper 🎬 **1992** Benjamin Latham, an innocent physician in Pittsburgh, was accused of being a vampire in colonial times and hung. 200 years later, he emerges from the grave, unscathed. While trying to figure out what has happened, he falls in love with a photojournalist, who helps him find his own descendent, Matthew Latham. Unfortunately, his deep freeze has left him with the compulsion to kill, but only evil members of society. **96m/B VHS.** Moon Zappa, Tom Savini, Kevin Kindlan. TEM, MOV

Heartstrings 🎬🎬 **1995** Melissa wants everything in her life to be perfect, including having the perfect man, which she thinks is New York gallery owner Peter. But will Melissa's heart compromise her ambitions? **94m/C VHS.** Michelle Little, Phyllis Diller. SWI

Heat 🎬🎬🎬 **1972** Another Andy Warhol-produced journey into drug-addled urban seediness. Features a former child actor/junkie and a has-been movie star barely surviving in a run-down motel. This is one of Warhol's better film productions; even non-fans may enjoy it. **102m/C VHS, Beta.** Joe Dallesandro, Sylvia Miles, Pat Ast; *D:* Paul Morrissey. TPV, PAR, FCT

Heat 🎬½ **1987 (R)** A Las Vegas bodyguard avenges the beating of an old flame by a mobster's son, and incites mob retaliation. Based on the William Goldman novel. **103m/C VHS, Beta, LV, Closed Caption.** Burt Reynolds, Karen Young, Peter MacNicol, Howard Hesseman; *D:* R.M. Richards; *W:* William Goldman; *M:* Michael Gibbs. PAR

Heat 🎬🎬🎬½ **1995 (R)** Pacino and De Niro in the same scene. Together. Finally. Obsessive master thief McCauley (De Niro) leads a crack crew on various military-style heists across L.A. while equally obsessive detective Hanna (Pacino) tracks him. Each man recognizes and respects the other's ability and dedication, even as they express the willingness to kill each other, if necessary. Excellent script with all the fireworks you'd expect, as well as a surprising look into emotional and personal sacrifice. Beautiful cinematography shows industrial landscape to great effect. Writer-director Mann held onto the screenplay for twelve years. *CW:* Violence and language. **171m/C VHS, LV, Closed Caption.** Robert De Niro, Al Pacino, Val Kilmer, Jon Voight, Diane Venora, Ashley Judd, Wes Studi, Tom Sizemore, Mykel T. Williamson, Amy Brenneman, Ted Levine, Dennis Haysbert, William Fichtner, Natalie Portman, Hank Azaria, Henry Rollins, Kevin Gage; *Cameos:* Tone Loc, Bud Cort, Jeremy Piven; *D:* Michael Mann; *W:* Michael Mann; *C:* Dante Spinotti; *M:* Elliot Goldenthal. WAR

Heat and Dust 🎬🎬🎬 **1982 (R)** A young bride joins her husband at his post in India and is inexorably drawn to the country and its prince of state. Years later her great niece journeys to modern day India in search of the truth about her scandalous and mysterious relative. More than the story of two romances, this is the tale of women rebelling against an unseen caste system which keeps them second-class citizens. Ruth Jhabvala wrote the novel and screenplay. **130m/C VHS, Beta.** GB Julie Christie, Greta Scacchi, Shashi Kapoor, Christopher Cazenove, Nickolas Grace, Julian Glover, Susan Fleetwood, Patrick Godfrey, Jennifer Kendal, Madhur Jaffrey, Barry Foster, Amanda Walker, Sudha Chopra, Sajid Khan, Zakir Hussain, Ratna Pathak, Charles McCaughan, Parveen Paul; *D:* James Ivory; *W:* Ruth Prawer Jhabvala, Saeed Jaffrey, Harish Khare; *C:* Walter Lassally; *M:* Richard Robbins. British Academy Awards '83: Best Adapted Screenplay. USH

Heat and Sunlight 🎬½ **1987** A photographer becomes obsessively jealous of his lover as their relationship comes to an end. Director Nilsson again used a unique improvisational, video-to-film technique, as he did with his previous film, "Signal 7." **98m/B VHS, Beta, LV.** Rob Nilsson, Consuelo Faust, Bill Bailey, Don Bajema, Ernie Fosselius; *D:* Rob Nilsson; *W:* Rob Nilsson; *M:* Mark Adler. Sundance Film Festival '88: Grand Jury Prize. CVC

Heat of Desire 🎬🎬 *Plein Sud* **1984 (R)** A philosophy professor abandons everything (including his wife) for a woman he barely knows and is conned by her "relatives." With English subtitles. **90m/C VHS, Beta, LV.** FR Clio Goldsmith, Patrick Dewaere, Jeanne Moreau, Guy Marchand; *D:* Luc Beraud. COL

The Heat of the Day 🎬🎬½ **1991** A British officer is accused of treason. As he attempts to find those who framed him, he meets a lovely woman all too willing to help. But whose side is she really on? Set in WWII. Tense and well-acted; made for TV. **120m/C VHS, Closed Caption.** Michael York, Patricia Hodge, Peggy Ashcroft, Anna Carteret, Michael Gambon; *W:* Harold Pinter. VTR, PBS, FCT

Heat of the Flame 🎬 **1982** A vicious woodsman captures and rapes a beautiful girl. Psychological games, eroticism and exploitive nudity ensue. **88m/C VHS, Beta.** Tony Ferrandis, Ellie MacLure, Raymond Young, Anthony Mayans. VCD

Heat Street 🎬 **1987** Two thugs exact revenge on street gangs for the murders of loved ones. Made for video. **90m/C VHS, Beta.** Quincy Adams, Deborah Gibson, Wendy MacDonald, Del Zamora; *D:* Joseph Merhi. HHE

Heat Wave 🎬½ **1954** A writer gets involved with a "femme fatale" who kills her wealthy husband for the love of a young pianist. **60m/B VHS, Beta, LV.** GB Alex Nicol, Hillary Brooke, Sidney James, Susan Stephen, Paul Carpenter; *D:* Ken Hughes; *W:* Ken Hughes. NO

Heat Wave 🎬🎬🎬 **1990 (R)** The Watts ghetto uprising of 1965 is a proving ground for a young black journalist. Excellent cast and fine script portrays the anger and frustration of blacks in Los Angeles and the U.S. in the 1960s and the fear of change felt by blacks and whites when civil rights reform began. Strong drama with minimal emotionalism. Made for cable TV. **92m/C VHS, Beta, Closed Caption.** Blair Underwood, Cicely Tyson, James Earl Jones, Sally Kirkland, Margaret Avery, David Strathairn, Robert Hooks, Adam Arkin, Paris Vaughan, Charlie Korsmo. TTC

Heated Vengeance 🎬 **1987 (R)** A Vietnam vet returns to the jungle to find the woman he left behind, and runs into some old enemies. **91m/C VHS, Beta.** Richard Hatch, Michael J. Pollard, Mills Watson, Cameron Dye; *D:* Edward Murphy. MED

Heathers 🎬🎬🎬½ **1989 (R)** Clique of stuck-up girls named Heather rule the high school social scene until the newest member (not a Heather) decides that enough is enough. She and her outlaw boyfriend embark (accidentally on her part, intentionally on his) on a murder spree disguised as a rash of teen suicides. Dense, take-no-prisoners black comedy with buckets of potent slang, satire and unforgiving hostility. Humor this dark is rare; sharply observed and acted, though the end is out of place. Slater does his best Nicholson impression. **102m/C VHS, Beta, LV, Closed Caption.** Winona Ryder, Christian Slater, Kim Walker, Shannen Doherty, Lisanne Falk, Penelope Milford, Glenn Shadix, Lance Fenton, Patrick Laborteaux; *D:* Michael Lehmann; *W:* Daniel Waters; *M:* David Newman. Edgar Allan Poe Awards '89: Best Screenplay; Independent Spirit Awards '90: Best First Feature. VTR, NWV, FCT

The Heat's On 🎬 *Tropicana* **1943** Gaxton is a broadway producer with a failing musical and an unhappy star in West. He cranks up the publicity machine and gets the show declared immoral by the Legion of Purity which results in its closing (not what he expected). Gaxton then runs a scam to become the producer of West's new show, which just happens to be financed by some Legion members. Very uneven plot and performances with thrown-in musical numbers. West wrote her own dialogue but unlike her early films she had little control over the production and it showed. West didn't make another movie for 27 years (the appalling "Myra Breckenridge"). ♫ Just a Stranger in Town; Hello, Mi Amigo; The White Keys and the Black Keys; There Goes That Guitar; Antonio; The Caissons Go Rolling Along; There Goes My Heart. **79m/B VHS.** Mae West, William Gaxton, Victor Moore, Almira Sessions, Lester Allen, Mary Roche, Alan Dinehart, Lloyd Bridges; *D:* Gregory Ratoff; *W:* Fitzroy Davis, George S. George, Fred Schiller. FCT

Heatseeker 🎬🎬 **1995 (R)** Corporations use mechanical fighters to participate in brutal kick-boxing contests in 2019 New America. Human Chance (Cooke) must battle cyborg opponent Xao if he wants to save his kidnapped trainer. Lots of action and even some intentional humor. *CW:* Martial arts violence; some sexuality and language. **91m/C VHS.** Keith Cooke, Gary Daniels, Norbert Weisser, Thom Mathews; *D:* Albert Pyun. THV

Heatwave 🎬🎬 **1983 (R)** Local residents oppose a multi-million dollar residential complex in Australia. Davis portrays a liberal activist, who wages war with the developers, and, in return, becomes involved with a possible murder case. **92m/C VHS, Beta.** AU Judy Davis, Richard Moir, Chris Haywood, Bill Hunter, John Gregg, Anna Jemison; *D:* Phillip Noyce. NO

Heaven 🎬🎬 **1987 (PG-13)** An exploration of "heaven" including the idea, the place, and people's views about it. Questions such as "How do you get there?" and "What goes on up there?" are discussed. Offbeat interviews mixed with a collage of celestial images. **80m/C VHS, Beta, LV.** *D:* Diane Keaton; *M:* Howard Shore. LTY, FCT

Heaven & Earth 🎬🎬🎬 **1990 (PG-13)** A samurai epic covering the battle for the future of Japan between two feuding warlords. The overwhelming battle scenes were actually filmed on location in Canada. In Japanese with English subtitles. **104m/C VHS, LV.** JP Masahiko Tsugawa, Takaai Enoki, Atsuko Asano, Tsunehiko Watase, Naomi Zaizen, Binpachi Ito. LIV

Heaven and Earth 🎬🎬 **1993 (R)** Conclusion of Stone's Vietnam trilogy (after "Platoon" and "Born on the Fourth of July") focuses on Vietnamese woman (film debut of Le) and her life under the French and American occupations. Jones is the American soldier who marries her and eventually brings her to the U.S. Not one for subtleties, Stone chases melodramatic excess with finesse of lumberjack, sawing away at guilt and remorse from a "woman's point of view." Cranky Tommy Lee shows up too late to save flick and is saddled with a perplexing I.D. to boot. Flawed, ambitious, and interesting if a student of Stone. Based on the two autobiographies of Le Ly Haslip, "When Heaven and Earth Changed Places" and "Child of War, Woman of Peace." Filmed on location in Thailand. *CW:* Language, violence, and sexuality. **142m/C VHS, LV, Closed Caption.** Hiep Thi Le, Tommy Lee Jones, Joan Chen, Haing S. Ngor, Debbie Reynolds, Conchata Ferrell, Dustin Nguyen, Liem Whatley, Dale Dye; *D:* Oliver Stone; *W:* Oliver Stone; *C:* Robert Richardson; *M:* Kitaro. Golden Globe Awards '94: Best Score. WAR

Heaven Can Wait 🐾🐾🐾 1943 Social satire in which a rogue tries to convince the Devil to admit him into Hell by relating the story of his philandering life and discovers that he was a more valuable human being than he thought. A witty Lubitsch treat based on the play "Birthdays." 112m/C VHS, Beta, LV, Closed Caption. Don Ameche, Gene Tierney, Laird Cregar, Charles Coburn, Marjorie Main, Eugene Pallette, Allyn Joslyn, Spring Byington, Signe Hasso, Louis Calhern, Dickie Moore, Florence Bates, Scotty Beckett, Charles Halton; *D:* Ernst Lubitsch. Nominations: Academy Awards '43: Best Color Cinematography, Best Director (Lubitsch), Best Picture. *FOX, FCT*

Heaven Can Wait 🐾🐾🐾 1978 (PG) A remake of 1941's "Here Comes Mr. Jordan," about a football player who is mistakenly summoned to heaven before his time. When the mistake is realized, he is returned to Earth in the body of a corrupt executive about to be murdered by his wife. Not to be confused with the 1943 film of the same name. 101m/C VHS, Beta, LV. Warren Beatty, Julie Christie, Charles Grodin, Dyan Cannon, James Mason, Jack Warden; *D:* Buck Henry; *W:* Warren Beatty, Elaine May; *C:* William A. Fraker; *M:* Dave Grusin. Academy Awards '78: Best Art Direction/Set Decoration; Golden Globe Awards '79: Best Actor—Musical/Comedy (Beatty), Best Film—Musical/Comedy, Best Supporting Actress (Cannon); Writers Guild of America '78: Best Adapted Screenplay; Nominations: Academy Awards '78: Best Actor (Beatty), Best Adapted Screenplay, Best Cinematography, Best Director (Beatty, Henry), Best Picture, Best Supporting Actor (Warden), Best Supporting Actress (Cannon), Best Original Score. *PAR, FOX, HMV*

Heaven Help Us 🐾🐾½ *Catholic Boys* 1985 (R) Three mischievous boys find themselves continually in trouble with the priests running their Brooklyn Catholic high school during the mid-1960s. Realistic and humorous look at adolescent life. 102m/C VHS, Beta, LV. Andrew McCarthy, Mary Stuart Masterson, Kevin Dillon, Malcolm Danare, Jennie Dundas, Kate Reid, Wallace Shawn, Jay Patterson, John Heard, Donald Sutherland, Yeardley Smith, Sherry Steiner, Calvert Deforest, Philip Bosco, Patrick Dempsey, Christopher Durang; *D:* Michael Dinner; *W:* Charles Purpura; *M:* James Horner. *NO*

Heaven is a Playground 🐾🐾½ 1991 (R) On Chicago's South Side an inner city basketball coach and an idealistic young lawyer are determined to change the fate of a group of high school boys. The men use the incentive of athletic scholarships to keep their team in school and away from drugs and gangs. *CW:* Language and drug content. 104m/C VHS, LV, Closed Caption. D.B. Sweeney, Michael Warren, Richard Jordan, Victor Love; *D:* Randall Fried; *W:* Randall Fried. *COL*

Heaven Knows, Mr. Allison 🐾🐾🐾 1957 Terrific two-character WWII drama finds tough (but tender-hearted) Marine sergeant Allison (Mitchum) stranded with Irish nun, Sister Angela (Kerr), on a Pacific island overrun by Japanese troops. The duo hide out during the day and forage for food by night, gradually revealing their pasts to each other. He falls hard while she resists his advances and they struggle to stay alive until U.S. forces invade the island. Lots of action and good performances. Based on the novel by Charles Shaw. 106m/C VHS, Closed Caption. Robert Mitchum, Deborah Kerr; *D:* John Huston; *W:* John Huston, John Lee Mahin; *C:* Oswald Morris; *M:* Georges Auric. Nominations: Academy Awards '57: Best Actress (Kerr), Best Adapted Screenplay. *TCF*

Heaven on Earth 🐾🐾½ 1989 The story of two orphaned British children who, along with thousands of orphans shipped from England to Canada between 1867 and 1914, try to make new lives in the Canadian wilderness. 101m/C VHS, Beta. *CA* R.H. Thomson, Sian Leisa Davies, Torquil Campbell, Fiona Reid; *D:* Allen Kroeker; *W:* Margaret Atwood. *NO*

Heaven Tonight 🐾🐾½ 1993 (R) Ex-rock star dad copes with midlife crisis by trying for his big comeback, this time with his son. *CW:* Language and violence. 97m/C VHS. *AU* John Waters, Rebecca Gilling, Guy Pearce, Kim Gyngell; *D:* Pino Amenta; *C:* David Connell. *ACA*

Heavenly Bodies woof! 1984 (R) A young woman who dreams of owning a health club will stop at nothing to accomplish her goals. When a rival tries to put her out of business, a "dancedown" takes place in this lame low-budget aerobics musical. 99m/C VHS, Beta. CA Cynthia Dale, Richard Rebrere, Laura Henry, Stuart Stone, Walter George Alton, Cec Linder; *D:* Lawrence Dane; *W:* Lawrence Dane, Ron Base; *C:* Thomas Burstyn. *FOX*

Heavenly Creatures 🐾🐾🐾½ 1994 (R) Haunting and surreal drama chronicles the true-life case of two young schoolgirls, Pauline and Juliet, who were charged with clubbing to death Pauline's mother in Christchurch, New Zealand in 1954. Opens two years before the murder, and follows the friendship as the two teens become obsessed with each other, retreating into a rich fantasy life. They create an elaborate, medieval kingdom where they escape to their dream lovers and romantic alter egos. Elaborate morphing and animation effects vividly express the shared inner fantasy world, while innovative camerawork creates the sensations of hysteria and excitement that the girls experience as their infatuation becomes uncontrollable. Leads Lynsky and Winslet are convincing as the awkward, quiet Pauline and the pretty, intelligent, upper class Juliet. Bizarre crime story is stylish and eerily compelling, and made more so by real life events: after the film was released, mystery writer Anne Perry was revealed as Juliet Hulme. *CW:* Chilling murder; brief sexual situations. 110m/C VHS, LV, Closed Caption. *NZ* Melanie Lynskey, Kate Winslet, Sarah Pierse, Diana Kent, Clive Merrison, Simon O'Connor; *D:* Peter Jackson; *W:* Peter Jackson, Frances Walsh; *C:* Alun Bollinger. Nominations: Academy Awards '94: Best Original Screenplay; Australian Film Institute '95: Best Foreign Film; Writers Guild of America '94: Best Original Screenplay. *TOU*

The Heavenly Kid 🐾🐾 1985 (PG-13) Leather-jacketed "cool" guy who died in a sixties hot rod crash finally receives an offer to exit limbo and enter heaven. The deal requires that he educate his dull earthly son on more hip and worldly ways. A big problem is that the soundtrack and wardrobe are 1955, whereas the cocky cool greaser supposedly died seventeen years ago in 1968. Mildly humorous. 92m/C VHS, Beta. Lewis Smith, Jane Kaczmarek, Jason Gedrick, Richard Mulligan; *D:* Cary Medoway; *W:* Cary Medoway, Martin Copeland. *NO*

Heaven's a Drag 🐾🐾½ *To Die For* 1994 Low-budget British cross between a tearjerker and a supernatural comedy. HIV-positive London drag performer Mark (Williams) lives with Simon (Arklie), a TV repairman who keeps his sexuality a secret from his co-workers and his emotional distance from his stricken lover. When Mark dies, Simon is quick to get on with his life—too quick for Mark, who's ghostly presence puts a damper on Simon's dating possibilities and brings up some old resentments. 96m/C VHS. *GB* Thomas Arklie, Ian Williams, Dilly Keane, Tony Slattery, Jean Boht, John Altman; *D:* Peter MacKenzie Litten; *W:* Johnny Byrne; *C:* John Ward. *FRF*

Heavens Above 🐾🐾🐾 1963 A sharp, biting satire on cleric life in England. Sellers stars as the quiet, down-to-earth reverend who is appointed to a new post in space. 113m/B VHS, Beta. *GB* Peter Sellers, Cecil Parker, Isabel Jeans, Eric Sykes, Ian Carmichael; *D:* John Boulting, Roy Boulting; *M:* Richard Rodney Bennett. *FCT*

Heaven's Gate 🐾🐾 1981 (R) The uncut version of Cimino's notorious folly. A fascinating, plotless, and exaggerated account of the Johnson County cattle war of the 1880s. Ravishingly photographed, the film's production almost singlehandedly put United Artists out of business. 220m/C VHS, Beta, LV. Kris Kristofferson, Christopher Walken, Isabelle Huppert, John Hurt, Richard Masur, Mickey Rourke, Brad Dourif, Joseph Cotten, Jeff Bridges, Sam Waterston, Terry O'Quinn, Geoffrey Lewis; *D:* Michael Cimino; *W:* Michael Cimino; *C:* Vilmos Zsigmond. Golden Raspberry Awards '81: Worst Director (Cimino); Nominations: Acade-

my Awards '81: Best Art Direction/Set Decoration. *MGM, FCT*

Heaven's Heroes 1987 Dennis Hill, a dedicated policeman, was killed in the line of duty on August 27, 1977. This film recalls his life and deep faith in Jesus. 72m/C VHS, Beta. David Ralphe, Heidi Vaughn, James O'Hagen; *D:* Donald W. Thompson.

Heaven's Prisoners 🐾🐾½ 1995 (R) Dave Robicheaux (Baldwin) is an ex-New Orleans homicide detective and recovering alcoholic, living a quiet life on a bayou with patient wife Annie (Lynch). They witness a plane crash and Dave rescues the only survivor, a young Salvadoran girl, whom they adopt. But the crash wasn't an accident and Dave's snooping around involves him with drug runners and local crime bosses, including old high school buddy, Bubba Rocque (Roberts), and his sirenish wife, Claudette (Hatcher). Convoluted plot with some moody touches but Baldwin scores as the flawed hero. Based on the mystery series by James Lee Burke. *CW:* Strong violence and language; some nudity. 135m/C VHS, LV, Closed Caption. Alec Baldwin, Kelly Lynch, Mary Stuart Masterson, Eric Roberts, Teri Hatcher, Vondie Curtis-Hall, Badja Djola, Joe Viterelli, Hawthorne James; *D:* Phil Joanou; *W:* Scott Frank, Harley Peyton; *C:* Harris Savides; *M:* George Fenton. Nominations: Golden Raspberry Awards '96: Worst Supporting Actress (Hatcher). *NLC*

Heavy 🐾🐾 1994 (R) Leisurely-paced character study with good performances. Victor (Vince) is an obese, socially withdrawn, 30-ish cook, living with his domineering mother (a subdued Winters) and helping her run their roadside diner, along with veteran waitress Delores (Harry). Then beautiful teenager Callie (Tyler) is hired and Victor begins to dream of a new life. Mom lands in the hospital, Delores puts the moves on him, Callie's life takes some unexpected turns, and Victor manages a few small steps into society. 104m/C VHS, Closed Caption. Pruitt Taylor Vince, Shelley Winters, Liv Tyler, Deborah Harry, Evan Dando, Joe Grifasi; *D:* James Mangold; *W:* James Mangold; *C:* Michael Barrow; *M:* Thurston Moore. Sundance Film Festival '95: Special Jury Prize. *COL*

Heavy Metal 🐾🐾🐾 1981 (R) Yes, the animated cult flick is now legally available on video, its copyright disputes finally resolved. A collection of science fiction and fantasy stories, inspired by the same-titled magazine and offered in a variety of graphic styles, that all encompass the theme of good versus evil. And don't always bet on the good. Features a soundtrack complied from the work of many top metal artists of the time as well as Bernstein's score with the London Philharmonic Orchestra. A three-minute transitional segment, called "Neverwhere Land," that was cut from the original version has been restored as an epilogue. 90m/C VHS, LV. *CA D:* Gerald Potterton; *W:* Dan Goldberg, Len Blum; *M:* Elmer Bernstein; *V:* John Candy, Joe Flaherty, Don Francks, Eugene Levy. *COL*

Heavy Petting 🐾🐾½ 1989 A hilarious compilation of "love scene" footage from feature films of the silent era to the sixties, newsreels, news reports, educational films, old TV shows, and home movies. 75m/C VHS, Beta, LV. David Byrne, Josh Mostel, Sandra Bernhard, Allen Ginsberg, Ann Magnuson, Spalding Gray, Laurie Anderson, John Oates, Abbie Hoffman, Jacki Ochs; *D:* Obie Benz. *ACA*

Heavy Traffic 🐾🐾🐾 1973 Ralph Bakshi's animated fantasy portrait of the hard-edged underside of city life. A young cartoonist draws the people, places, and paranoia of his environment. 76m/C VHS, Beta. *D:* Ralph Bakshi; *W:* Ralph Bakshi; *M:* Ed Bogas. *WAR, OM*

Heavyweights 🐾 1994 (PG) A product of Disney's sometimes assembly line approach to family entertainment (think "Mighty Ducks"). Nothing new saga of overweight youngsters sent to a fat camp run by tyrannical fitness guru Tony Perkis (Stiller). His methods cause the kids to band together and overthrow him and his "evil" tactics. Oh, by the way, there's a baseball competition with the more athletic camp kids on the other side of the lake. Guess who wins. Stiller as the fame obsessed fitness fanatic, sporting a David Copperfield make-over, is the only highlight in this exercise of excess fluff. Directorial debut of Brill. **98m/C VHS, LV, Closed Caption.** Jeffrey Tambor, Ben Stiller, Jerry Stiller, Anne Meara, Shaun Weiss, Kenan Thompson; **D:** Steven Brill; **W:** Judd Apatow, Steven Brill; **C:** Victor Hammer; **M:** J.A.C. Redford. *DIS*

Heck's Way Home 🐾🐾½ 1995 Heck is the Neufeld family dog and best friend of 11-year-old Luke (Krowchuk). The family is moving from Winnipeg to Australia and have a three-day layover in Vancouver. Heck is supposed to come along but instead, unbeknownst to the family, he gets captured by the local dogcatcher (Arkin) and the family are forced to leave without him. Naturally, Heck escapes and starts off on a 2000-mile journey to find his family before they fly away forever. Made for cable. **92m/C VHS.** Chad Krowchuk, Alan Arkin, Michael Riley, Shannon Lawson; **D:** Michael Scott. *HMK*

Hector's Bunyip 1986 What's a bunyip? People think it's just Hector's scaly imaginary friend. It therefore comes as quite a surprise when Hector gets kidnapped—by his supposed imaginary friend! Aired on PBS as part of the "Wonderworks" series. **58m/C VHS, Closed Caption.** Scott Bartle, Robert Coleby, Barbara Stephens, Tushka Hose; **D:** Mark Callan. *PME, FCT, BTV*

Hedd Wyn 🐾🐾 1992 True story of talented young poet Ellis Evans (Garmon), writing under the pseudonym Hedd Wyn, who dreams of winning a coveted literary prize. His hopes are put on hold when he's forced to fight in WWI, although he submits his antiwar poem "The Hero" to the competition. Welsh with subtitles. **123m/C VHS.** *GB* Huw Garmon, Catrin Fychan, Ceri Cunnington, Llio Silyn; **D:** Paul Turner; **W:** Alan Llwyd; **C:** Ray Orton; **M:** John E.R. Hardy. Nominations: Academy Awards '93: Best Foreign Language Film. *FXL*

Hedda 🐾🐾½ 1975 A dramatization of the Henrik Ibsen play, "Hedda Gabler," about a middle-class pregnant woman. The story finds her frustrated with her life and manipulating those around her with tragic results. **102m/C VHS, Beta.** *GB* Glenda Jackson, Peter Eyre, Timothy West, Jennie Linden, Patrick Stewart; **D:** Trevor Nunn. Nominations: Academy Awards '75: Best Actress (Jackson). *MED*

Hedda Hopper's Hollywood 1942 Newsreel version of the gossip-hound's column, featuring scoops on Ball, Cooper, Minelli and many more. **58m/B VHS.** Hedda Hopper, Gary Cooper, Lucille Ball, Gloria Swanson, Liza Minnelli. *REP*

Heidi 🐾🐾½ 1937 Johanna Spyri's classic tale puts Shirley Temple in the hands of a mean governess and the loving arms of her Swiss grandfather. Also available colorized. Remade in 1967. Also available with "Poor Little Rich Girl" on Laser Disc. **88m/B VHS, Beta, Closed Caption.** Shirley Temple, Jean Hersholt, Helen Westley, Arthur Treacher; **D:** Allan Dwan; **C:** Arthur C. Miller. *FXV, HMV, MLT*

Heidi 🐾🐾½ 1952 The Swiss do their own version of the children's classic by Johanna Spyri. A precocious little girl enjoys life in the Swiss Alps with her grandfather, until her stern aunt takes her away to live in the village in the valley. **98m/B VHS.** *SI* Elsbeth Sigmund, Heinrich Gretler, Thomas Klameth, Elsie Attenoff; **D:** Luigi Comencini. *CNG, MRV, KAR*

Heidi 🐾🐾🐾 1965 The classic story from Johanna Spyri's novel is filmed beautifully in the Swiss Alps in Eastmancolor. Heidi is kidnapped by her mean aunt and forced to work as a slave for a rich family. Her kindly old grandfather comes to her rescue. Family entertainment for all, dubbed in English. **95m/C VHS.** *AT GE* Eva Maria Singhammer, Gustav Knuth, Lotte Ledl; **D:** Werner Jacobs. *NO*

Heidi 🐾🐾 1967 The second American adaptation of the classic Johanna Spyri novel tells the story of an orphaned girl who goes to the Swiss Alps to live with her grandfather. Made for television. **100m/C VHS, Beta.** Maximilian Schell, Jennifer Ed-

wards, Michael Redgrave, Jean Simmons; **D:** Delbert Mann; **M:** John Williams. *LIV, VES, GLV*

Heidi 🐾🐾🐾 1993 (G) Yet another version of the children's classic, from German writer Johanna Spyri's 1881 novel. Thornton is charming as the orphan shuttled from relative to relative until she happily ends up with her crotchety grandfather (Robards) in his mountain cabin. Then her cousin comes along and whisks her off to the city to be a companion to the invalid Klara (Randall). Seymour is the snobbish, scowling governess. This "Heidi" is spunky enough to keep the sugar level tolerable. Filmed on location in Austria. Made for television. **167m/C VHS, LV, Closed Caption.** Noley Thornton, Jason Robards Jr., Jane Seymour, Lexi Randall, Sian Phillips, Patricia Neal, Benjamin Brazier, Michael Simkins, Andrew Bicknell, Jane Hazlegrove; **D:** Michael Rhodes; **W:** Jeanne Rosenberg; **M:** Lee Holdridge. *DIS*

The Heidi Chronicles 🐾🐾½ 1995 Some 25 years of boomer angst and friendship are covered in this cable adaptation of Wasserstein's 1988 Pulitzer Prize-winning play. Heidi Holland (Curtis) goes from prep school to Vassar to an art history career while searching for self-fulfillment, feminist ideals, and some romance along the way. The romance is on-and-off, thanks to caddish journalist Scoop (Friedman), but Heidi can always depend on soul mate, gay pediatrician Peter (Hulce), and Susan (Cattrall), her follow-the-fads confidante. Heidi's sometimes too morose for her own good but you won't mind spending a couple of hours in her company. **94m/C VHS.** Jamie Lee Curtis, Tom Hulce, Kim Cattrall, Peter Friedman, Eve Gordon, Shari Belafonte, Sharon Lawrence, Julie White, Debra Eisenstadt, Roma Maffia; **D:** Paul Bogart; **W:** Wendy Wasserstein; **C:** Isidore Mankofsky; **M:** David Shire. *TTC*

Heimat 1 1984 Sixteen-hour series follows the lives, loves, and tragedies of the German Simon family from the end of WWI to 1982. Based on Reitz's own family and his childhood. Shot over two years, the series has 28 lead performances and more than 140 speaking roles. German with subtitles; boxed 9-tape set. **924m/C VHS.** *GE* **D:** Edgar Reitz. *FCT*

Heimat 2 198? The continuation of the saga is composed of 25 half-hour segments and follows Hermann Simon's life in Munich from 1960 to 1970. A modernist musician and composer, Hermann falls in with a group of students, artists, and rebels. German with subtitles. **750m/C VHS.** *GE* **D:** Edgar Reitz. *FCT*

The Heiress 🐾🐾🐾½ 1949 Based on the Henry James novel "Washington Square," about a wealthy plain Jane, her tyrannical father, and the handsome fortune-seeking scoundrel who seeks to marry her. **115m/B VHS, Beta, LV.** Olivia de Havilland, Montgomery Clift, Ralph Richardson, Miriam Hopkins; **D:** William Wyler; **M:** Aaron Copland. Academy Awards '49: Best Actress (de Havilland), Best Art Direction/Set Decoration (B & W), Best Costume Design (B & W), Original Dramatic/Comedy Score; Golden Globe Awards '50: Best Actress—Drama (de Havilland); National Board of Review Awards '49: 10 Best Films of the Year, Best Actor (Richardson); New York Film Critics Awards '49: Best Actress (de Havilland); Nominations: Academy Awards '49: Best Black and White Cinematography, Best Director (Wyler), Best Picture, Best Supporting Actor (Richardson). *USH, MLB, BTV*

The Heist 🐾🐾 1988 (R) An explosive crime thriller... **93m/C VHS.** Lee Van Cleef, Karen Black, Edward Albert, Lionel Stander, Robert Alda. *NO*

The Heist 🐾🐾 1989 A made-for-cable-television film about an ex-con who, upon regaining his freedom, sets out to rip off the crook who framed him. Entertaining enough story with a first-rate cast. **97m/C VHS, Beta.** Pierce Brosnan, Tom Skerritt, Wendy Hughes; **D:** Stuart Orme. *HBO, HHE*

Helas Pour Moi 🐾🐾 Oh Woe is Me 1994 Perplexing, contemplative film on faith and love—and maybe a miracle. Told in flashback, publisher Alexander Klimt (Verley) travels to a Swiss lake-

side town where it's rumored that the beautiful Rachel Donnadieu (Masliah) has been "visited" by God, who wishes to experience the pleasures of love, in the form of her own husband, simple fisherman Simon (Depardieu). Story is derived from the Greek myth concerning Zeus, who seduced Alcmene in the shape of her husband Amphitryon. French with subtitles. **84m/C VHS.** *FR SI* Gerard Depardieu, Laurence Masliah, Bernard Verley; **D:** Jean-Luc Godard; **W:** Jean-Luc Godard; **C:** Caroline Champtier. *FCT*

Held for Murder 🐾 Her Mad Night 1932 When a vacationing daughter is accused of murder, her mom lovingly takes the blame. Will the daughter come back to clear her mom, or will she let her fry in the electric chair? **67m/B VHS, Beta.** Irene Rich, Conway Tearle, Mary Carlisle, Kenneth Thomson, William B. Davidson; **D:** E. Mason Hopper. *SNC*

Held Hostage 🐾🐾 1991 The true story of Jerry Levin, a reporter kidnapped by terrorists while on assignment in Beirut, and his wife, Sis, who struggled with the State Department for his release. Made for television. **95m/C VHS.** Marlo Thomas, David Dukes, G.W. Bailey, Ed Winter, Robert Harper, William Schallert; **D:** Roger Young. *SDE*

Helen of Troy 🐾½ 1956 Mythological fantasy finds Helen (Podesta), the beautiful daughter of Zeus, falling in love with Trojan prince Paris (Sernas)—an event that leads to the siege of Troy. Ignores script for lavish effects. Video includes behind-the-scenes footage. **135m/C VHS, LV, Closed Caption.** Rossana Podesta, Jacques Sernas, Cedric Hardwicke, Stanley Baker, Niall MacGinnis, Nora Swinburne, Robert Douglas, Torin Thatcher, Harry Andrews, Janette Scott, Ronald Lewis, Brigitte Bardot; **D:** Robert Wise; **W:** John Twist, N. Richard Nash; **C:** Harry Stradling; **M:** Max Steiner. *WAR, MOV*

Hell Comes to Frogtown 🐾 1988 (R) In a post-nuclear holocaust land run by giant frogs, a renegade who is one of the few non-sterile men left on earth must rescue some fertile women and impregnate them. Sci-fi spoof is extremely low-budget, but fun. Stars "Rowdy" Roddy Piper of wrestling fame. **88m/C VHS, Beta, LV.** Roddy Piper, Sandahl Bergman, Rory Calhoun, Donald G. Jackson; **D:** Robert J. Kizer. *VTR, NWV*

Hell Commandos 🐾½ 1969 Soldiers in WWII struggle to prevent the Nazis from releasing a deadly bacteria that will kill millions. Dubbed. **92m/C VHS, Beta.** *IT* Guy Madison, Stan Cooper; **D:** J.L. Merino. *NO*

Hell Fire Austin 🐾½ 1932 Maynard finds himself mixed up with outlaws in the Old West. **60m/B VHS, Beta.** Ken Maynard, Nat Pendleton, Jack Perrin; **D:** Forrest Sheldon. *NOS, VCN, DVT*

Hell Harbor 🐾🐾 1930 Caribbean love, murder and greed combine to make this early talkie. Exterior shots were filmed on the west coast of Florida and the beauty of the Tampa area in the 1930s is definitely something to see. **65m/B VHS, Beta.** Lupe Velez, Gibson Gowland, Jean Hersholt, John Holland; **D:** Henry King. *GVV*

Hell High 🐾 1986 (R) Four high schoolers plan a night of torture and humiliation for an annoying teacher, only to find she has some deadly secrets of her own. Dumber than it sounds. **84m/C VHS, Beta.** Christopher Stryker, Christopher Cousins, Millie Prezioso, Jason Brill; **D:** Douglas Grossman. *PSM*

Hell Hounds of Alaska 🐾 1973 (G) The Yukon, Yugoslav-style. European co-production goes back to the Gold Rush days for an adventure about a frontiersman tracking down a stolen shipment of the precious ore while trying to save the life of an injured boy. **90m/C VHS, Beta.** Doug McClure, Harald Leipnitz, Angelica Ott; **D:** Harald Reinl. *NO*

Hell Hunters 🐾 1987 Nazi-hunters foil the plot of an old German doctor to poison the population of L.A. Meanwhile, a daughter avenges the death of her mother by blowing up the doctor's jungle compound. **90m/C VHS, Beta.** Stewart Granger, Maud Adams, George Lazenby, Candice Daly, Romulo Arantes, William Berger. *NO*

Hell in the Pacific ♦♦♦ 1969 (PG) A marvelously photographed (by Conrad Hall) psycho/macho allegory, about an American and a Japanese soldier stranded together on a tiny island and the mini-war they fight all by themselves. Overly obvious anti-war statement done with style. 101m/C VHS, Beta, LV. Lee Marvin, Toshiro Mifune; **D:** John Boorman; **C:** Conrad Hall; **M:** Lalo Schifrin. *FOX*

Hell is for Heroes ♦♦♦½ 1962 McQueen stars as the bitter leader of a small infantry squad outmanned by the Germans in this tight WWII drama. A strong cast and riveting climax make this a must for action fans. 90m/B VHS, Beta, LV, Closed Caption. Steve McQueen, Bobby Darin, Fess Parker, Harry Guardino, James Coburn, Mike Kellin, Nick Adams, Bob Newhart; **D:** Donald Siegel; **W:** Robert Pirosh, Richard Carr. *PAR*

Hell Night woof! 1981 (R) Several young people must spend the night in a mysterious mansion as part of their initiation into Alpha Sigma Rho fraternity in this extremely dull low-budget horror flick. 100m/C VHS, Beta. Linda Blair, Vincent Van Patten, Kevin Brophy, Peter Barton, Jenny Neumann; **D:** Tom De Simone; **W:** Randy Feldman; **C:** Mac Ahlberg. *MED*

Hell on Frisco Bay ♦♦½ 1955 An ex-waterfront cop, falsely imprisoned for manslaughter, sets out to clear his name. His quest finds him taking on the Mob, in this thirties-style gangster film. Good performances all around, especially Robinson, who steals every scene he's in. 93m/C VHS, Beta. Alan Ladd, Edward G. Robinson, Joanne Dru, Fay Wray, William Demarest, Jayne Mansfield; **D:** Frank Tuttle; **M:** Max Steiner. *NO*

Hell on the Battleground ♦½ 1988 (R) Group of inexperienced recruits are led into combat by two battle-hardened veterans. Their only hope for survival is a counterattack by U.S. tanks. 91m/C VHS, Beta. William Smith, Ted Prior, Fritz Matthews; **D:** David A. Prior; **W:** David A. Prior. *AIP*

Hell on Wheels ♦♦ 1967 Two successful brothers in the racing industry are torn apart by the same girl. Brotherly love diminishes into a hatred so deep that murder becomes the sole purpose of both. 96m/C VHS, Beta. Marty Robbins, Jennifer Ashley, John Ashley, Gigi Perreau, Robert Dornan, Connie Smith, Frank Gerstle; **D:** Will Zens. *ACA*

Hell Raiders ♦½ 1968 A force invades a supposedly defenseless Pacific island, and finds itself fiercely attacked. 90m/C VHS, Beta. John Agar, Richard Webb, Joan Huntington; **D:** Larry Buchanan. *JEF*

Hell River ♦♦ 1975 (PG) In 1941 Yugoslavia, Yugoslav partisans and Nazis battle it out at a place called Hell River. 100m/C VHS, Beta. Rod Taylor, Adam West; **D:** Stole Jankovic. *VCD*

Hell-Ship Morgan ♦♦½ 1936 Bancroft is a womanizing tuna boat captain who falls for and marries Sothern. When they set up married life on the boat, she starts eyeing first mate Jory. And Bancroft finds out. 65m/B VHS. George Bancroft, Ann Sothern, Victor Jory, George Regas, Howard Hickman, Ralph Byrd; **D:** David Ross Lederman. *GPV*

Hell Ship Mutiny ♦½ 1957 Man comes to the aid of a lovely island princess, whose people have been forced to hand over their pearls to a pair of ruthless smugglers. Excellent cast in an unfortunately tepid production. 66m/B VHS, Beta. Jon Hall, John Carradine, Peter Lorre, Roberta Haynes, Mike Mazurki, Stanley Adams; **D:** Lee Sholem, Elmo Williams. *SNC, HEG*

Hell Squad ♦½ 1958 Lost in North Africa during WWII, five American GIs wander through the desert. They find numerous pitfalls and unexpected help. Overall, dismal and disappointing. 64m/B VHS. Wally Campo, Brandon Carroll; **D:** Burt Topper. *NOS*

Hell Squad ♦ 1985 (R) Unable to release his son from the Middle Eastern terrorists who kidnapped him, a U.S. ambassador turns to the services of nine Las Vegas showgirls. These gals moonlight as vicious commandos in this low-budget action film with skin. 88m/C VHS, Beta. Bainbridge

Scott, Glen Hartford, Tina Lederman; **D:** Kenneth Hartford; **W:** Kenneth Hartford; **M:** Charles P. Barnett. *MGM, GHV*

Hell to Eternity ♦♦½ 1960 The true story of how WWII hero Guy Gabaldon persuaded 2,000 Japanese soldiers to surrender. Features several spectacular scenes. 132m/B VHS, Beta. Jeffrey Hunter, Sessue Hayakawa, David Janssen, Vic Damone, Patricia Owens; **D:** Phil Karlson. *FOX*

Hell Up in Harlem woof! 1973 (R) A black crime lord recuperates from an assassination attempt and tries to regain his power. Poor sequel to the decent film "Black Caesar." 98m/C VHS, Beta. Fred Williamson, Julius W. Harris, Margaret Avery, Gerald Gordon, Gloria Hendry; **D:** Larry Cohen; **W:** Larry Cohen. *ORI*

Hellbenders ♦½ *Il Crudeli; Los Despiadados* 1967 (PG) A confederate veteran robs a Union train and must fight through acres of Civil War adversity. Dubbed. Poorly directed and acted. 92m/C VHS, Beta. *IT SP* Joseph Cotten, Norman Bengell, Julian Mateos; **D:** Sergio Corbucci; **W:** Ennio Morricone. *COL*

Hellbent 1990 A crazed musician and a revenge-obsessed housewife embark on an unusual adventure that challenges their very sanity. 90m/C VHS, Beta. Phil Ward, Lynn Levand, Cheryl Slean, David Marciano; **D:** Richard Casey; **W:** Richard Casey. *NO*

Hellbound ♦♦½ 1994 (R) Prosatanos (Neame), a powerful 12th-century wizard, is imprisoned and the source of his power (a scepter) is supposedly destroyed. Fast-forward several hundred years when Prosatanos manages to free himself and seek out the pieces of his scepter. Which happens to lead him to Chicago and a couple of unsuspecting cops (Norris, Levels). **CW:** Violence, language, gore. 95m/C VHS, Closed Caption. Chuck Norris, Christopher Neame, Calvin Levels, Sheree J. Wilson; **D:** Aaron Norris. *WAR*

Hellbound: Hellraiser 2 ♦♦ *Hellraiser 2* 1988 (R) In this, the first sequel to Clive Barker's inter-dimensional nightmare, the traumatized daughter from the first film is pulled into the Cenobites' universe. Gore and weird imagery abound. An uncut, unrated version is also available. 96m/C VHS, Beta, LV, Closed Caption. GB Ashley Laurence, Clare Higgins, Kenneth Cranham, Imogen Boorman, William Hope, Kenneth Cranham, Sean Chapman, Doug Bradley; **D:** Tony Randel; **W:** Peter Atkins. *VTR, NWV*

Hellcats woof! 1968 (R) A mob of sleazy, leather-clad female bikers terrorize small Midwestern towns in this violent girl-gang thriller. Even biker movie fans might find this one unworthy. 90m/C VHS, Beta. Ross Hagen, Dee Duffy, Sharyn Kinzie, Sonny West, Bob Slatzer; **D:** Bob Slatzer. *ACA*

Hellcats of the Navy ♦½ 1957 Soggy true saga of the WWII mission to sever the vital link between mainland Asia and Japan. The only film that Ronald and Nancy Davis Reagan starred in together and the beginning of their grand romance. 82m/B VHS, Beta. Ronald Reagan, Nancy Davis, Arthur Franz, Robert Arthur; **D:** Nathan (Hertz) Juran; **W:** Bernard Gordon, David Lang. *GKK*

Helldorado ♦♦ *Heldorado* 1946 A lively western starring the singing cowboy, Roy Rogers. 54m/B VHS, Beta. Roy Rogers, George "Gabby" Hayes, Dale Evans, Paul Harvey; **D:** William Witney. *NOS, VCN, CAB*

Heller in Pink Tights ♦♦ 1960 The Louis L'Amour story follows the adventures of a colorful theatrical troupe that visits the 1880s West. Performing amid Indians, bill collectors, and thieves, they are often just one step ahead of the law themselves in this offbeat western. 100m/C VHS, Beta, Closed Caption. Sophia Loren, Anthony Quinn, Margaret O'Brien, Steve Forrest, Edmund Lowe, Ramon Novarro; **D:** George Cukor; **W:** Walter Bernstein. *BAR, PAR, FCT*

Hellfighters ♦♦ 1968 (G) Texas oil well fire fighters experience trouble between themselves and the women they love. 121m/C VHS, Beta, LV. John Wayne, Katharine Ross, Jim Hutton, Vera Miles, Bruce Cabot, Jay C. Flippen; **D:** Andrew V. McLaglen; **C:** William Clothier. *USH*

Hellfire ♦♦ 1948 A gambler promises to build a church and follow the precepts of the Bible after a minister sacrifices his life for him. 90m/B VHS. William Elliott, Marie Windsor, Forrest Tucker, Jim Davis; **D:** R.G. Springsteen. *REP*

The Hellfire Club ♦♦ 1961 In 18th century Britain, a young man reaches adulthood and attempts to claim the estate of his father. No ordinary dad, his led the infamous Hellfire Club, an organization specializing in debauchery and depravity. His cousin challenges his claim and kidnaps his fiancee. Historical hokum, complete with swordplay. 88m/C VHS. GB Keith Michell, Kai Fischer, Adrienne Corri, Peter Arne, David Lodge, Bill Owen, Peter Cushing, Francis Matthews, Desmond Walter Ellis; **D:** Robert S. Baker, Monty Berman; **W:** Jimmy Sangster. *SNC*

Hellgate woof! 1989 (R) A woman hitchhiking turns out to be one of the living dead. Her benefactor lives to regret picking her up. 96m/C VHS, LV. Abigail Wolcott, Ron Palillo; **D:** William A. Levey. *THV*

Hellhole ♦ 1985 (R) A young woman who witnesses her mother's murder is sent to a sanitarium where the doctors are perfecting chemical lobotomies. Extremely weak script and poor acting make this a suspenseless thriller. 93m/C VHS, Beta, LV, Closed Caption. Judy Landers, Ray Sharkey, Mary Woronov, Marjoe Gortner, Edy Williams, Terry Moore, Dyanne Thorne; **D:** Pierre De Moro. *COL*

Hellmaster ♦ 1992 Your basic sicko mad scientist experiments on some unsuspecting college students by injecting them with an addictive drug. The drug also causes some horrifying mutations and makes its victims superhuman (but also super-ugly). Lots of gore. Creative special effects and make-up will appeal to fans of horror. 92m/C VHS. John Saxon, David Emge, Amy Raasch; **D:** Douglas Schulze; **W:** Douglas Schulze. *AIP*

Hello Again ♦♦ 1987 (PG) The wife of a successful plastic surgeon chokes to death on a piece of chicken. A year later she returns to life, with comical consequences, but soon discovers that life won't be the same. 96m/C VHS, Beta, LV, Closed Caption. Shelley Long, Corbin Bernsen, Judith Ivey, Gabriel Byrne, Sela Ward, Austin Pendleton, Carrie Nye, Robert Lewis, Madeleine Potter; **D:** Frank Perry; **M:** William Goldstein. *TOU*

Hello, Dolly! ♦♦ 1969 (G) Widow Dolly Levi, while matchmaking her friends, finds a match for herself. Based on the hugely successful Broadway musical adapted from Thornton Wilder's play "Matchmaker." Lightweight story needs better actors with stronger characterizations. Original Broadway score helps. ♫ Hello Dolly; Just Leave Everything to Me; Love is Only Love; Dancing; Walter's Gavotte; It Only Takes a Moment; Ribbons Down My Back; Elegance; It Takes a Woman. 146m/C VHS, Beta, LV, Closed Caption. Barbra Streisand, Walter Matthau, Michael Crawford, Louis Armstrong, E.J. Peaker, Marianne McAndrew, Tommy Tune; **D:** Gene Kelly; **W:** Ernest Lehman; **C:** Harry Stradling; **M:** Jerry Herman. Academy Awards '69: Best Art Direction/Set Decoration, Best Sound, Scoring of a Musical; Nominations: Academy Awards '69: Best Cinematography, Best Costume Design, Best Film Editing, Best Picture. *FOX, FCT*

Hello, Frisco, Hello ♦♦½ 1943 San Francisco's wild Barbary Coast is the setting for this romantic musical. Smoothie Payne opens up a saloon that features Faye, who's in love with him, as the star singing attraction. Unfortunately, Payne is involved with a society snob and Faye heads off to European success. When she returns, it's to a sadder and wiser man. ♫ Hello, Frisco, Hello; You'll Never Know; San Francisco; Ragtime Cowboy Joe; Sweet Cider Time; Has Anybody Here Seen Kelly; King Chanticleer; When You Wore a Tulip; Strike Up the Band; Here Comes a Sailor. 98m/C VHS. Alice Faye, John Payne, Jack Oakie, Lynn Bari, Laird Cregar, June Havoc, Ward Bond, Aubrey Mather, John Archer; **D:** H. Bruce Humberstone; **W:** Robert Ellis, Helen Logan. Academy Awards

'43: Best Song ("You'll Never Know"); Nominations: Academy Awards '43: Best Color Cinematography. *FXV*

Hello Mary Lou: Prom Night 2 🎬½
The Haunting of Hamilton High; Prom Night 2 1987 (R) A sequel to the successful slasher flick, wherein a dead-for-30-years prom queen relegates the current queen to purgatory and comes back to life in order to avenge herself. Wild special effects. **97m/C VHS, Beta, LV, Closed Caption.** Michael Ironside, Wendy Lyon, Justin Louis, Lisa Schrage, Richard Monette; **D:** Bruce Pittman; **W:** Ron Oliver. *NO*

Hello Trouble 1932 A Texas Ranger accidentally kills his friend, who was a former Ranger turned bandit, causing him to hang up his pistols. **63m/C VHS.** Buck Jones, Lena Basquette, Wallace MacDonald, "Spec" O'Donnell, Ward Bond, Frank Rice, Ruth Warren; **D:** Lambert Hillyer. *GPV*

Hellraiser 🎬🎬½ 1987 (R) A graphic, horror fantasy about a woman who is manipulated by the monstrous spirit of her husband's dead brother. In order for the man who was also her lover to be brought back to life, she must lure and kill human prey for his sustenance. Grisly and inventive scenes keep the action fast-paced; not for the faint-hearted. **94m/C Beta, LV, Closed Caption.** *GB* Andrew (Andy) Robinson, Clare Higgins, Ashley Laurence, Sean Chapman, Oliver Smith, Robert Hines; **D:** Clive Barker; **W:** Clive Barker; **M:** Christopher Young. *VTR, NWV*

Hellraiser 3: Hell on Earth 🎬🎬 1992 (R) Pinhead is back in this film based on characters created by horrormeister Clive Barker. A strange black box holds the key to sending Pinhead back to Hell and is sought by the heroine, a TV newswoman (Farrell). But Pinhead's human henchman, a nasty nightclub owner, isn't going to make things easy. Imaginative special effects and Bradley's commanding presence as Pinhead aid this shocker, which becomes unfortunately mired in excessive gore. An unrated version at 97 minutes is also available. **CW:** Language, strong violence, and strong sexuality. **91m/C VHS, LV, Closed Caption.** Doug Bradley, Terry Farrell, Kevin Bernhardt, Paula Marshall, Ken Carpenter, Peter Boynton, Ashley Laurence; **D:** Anthony Hickox; **W:** Peter Atkins. *PAR*

Hellraiser 4: Bloodline 🎬 1995 (R) You can't keep a bad Pinhead in Hell, as this unfortunate sequel demonstrates. Bradley reprises his role as the big bad S&M pincushion in the latest and supposedly last installment of Clive Barker's blood drenched series. Tracing the origin of the infernal Rubik's Cube that releases Pinhead, the plot jumps between 18th century France, present day New York and a 22nd century space station. Along the way, the Pointy One gets to flay, skewer, and impale to his evil heart's content. Special f/x guru Kevin Yeagher was so embarrassed by this outing that he took his director's credit off of the picture. Bad acting, bad plot, bad complexion. **CW:** Strong horror violence and gore, and for some sexuality and language. **81m/C VHS, LV, Closed Caption.** Bruce Ramsey, Valentina Vargas, Doug Bradley, Kim Myers, Christina Harnos, Charlotte Chatton, Paul Perri, Mickey Cottrell; **D:** Alan Smithee; **W:** Peter Atkins; **C:** Gerry Lively; **M:** Daniel Licht. *PAR*

Hellriders woof! 1984 (R) A motorcycle gang rides into a small town and subjects its residents to a reign of terror. **90m/C VHS, Beta.** Adam West, Tina Louise. *TWE*

Hell's Angels 🎬🎬🎬 1930 Classic WWI aviation movie is sappy and a bit lumbering, but still an extravagant spectacle with awesome air scenes. Studio owner Hughes fired directors Howard Hawks and Luther Reed, spent an unprecedented $3.8 million, and was ultimately credited as director (although Whale also spent some time in the director's chair). Three years in the making, the venture cost three pilots their lives and lost a bundle. Harlow replaced Swedish Greta Nissen when sound was added and was catapulted into blond bombshelldom as a two-timing dame. And the tinted and two-color scenes—restored in 1989—came well before Ted Turner ever wielded a crayola. **135m/B VHS.** Jean Harlow, Ben Lyon, James Hall, John Darrow, Lucien Prival; **D:** Howard Hughes; **W:** Harry Behn, Howard Estabrook, Joseph Moncure March. Nominations: Academy Awards '30: Best Cinematography. *USH, MRV*

Hell's Angels Forever 1983 (R) A revealing ride into the world of honor, violence, and undying passion for motorcycles on the road. Documentary was filmed with cooperation of the Angels. Features appearances by Willie Nelson, Jerry Garcia, Bo Diddley, Kevin Keating and Johnny Paycheck. **93m/C VHS, Beta.** Willie Nelson, Jerry Garcia, Johnny Paycheck, Bo Diddley; **D:** Richard Chase. *MED*

Hell's Angels on Wheels 🎬🎬½ 1967 Low-budget, two-wheeled Nicholson vehicle that casts him as a gas station attendant who joins up with the Angels for a cross country trip. Laszlo Kovacs is responsible for the photography. One of the better 1960s biker films. **95m/C VHS, Beta.** Jack Nicholson, Adam Roarke, Sabrina Scharf, Jana Taylor, John Garwood; **D:** Richard Rush. *THV*

Hell's Angels '69 🎬🎬 1969 (PG) Figuring on robbing Caesar's Palace for the thrill, two wealthy brothers plot a deadly game by infiltrating the ranks of the Hell's Angels. Upon figuring out that they've been duped, the Angels seek revenge. Average biker epic filmed in Nevada features Hell's Angels Oakland chapter. **97m/C VHS, Beta.** Tom Stern, Jeremy Slate, Conny Van Dyke; **D:** Lee Madden; **W:** Tom Stern, Jeremy Slate. *MED*

Hell's Belles 🎬½ *Girl in the Leather Suit* 1969 Biker has his ride stolen by a rival, who leaves a chick as payment. The two team up to get revenge, chasing the gang across the Arizona desert and picking them off one by one. **95m/C VHS.** Jeremy Slate, Adam Roarke, Jocelyn Lane, Angelique Pettyjohn, Michael Walker, William Lucking; **D:** Maury Dexter; **W:** James Gordon White, Robert McMullen; **M:** Les Baxter. *ORI*

Hell's Belles woof! 1995 (R) The Devil's bored so he leaves hell for some mortal fun but in order to stay he and his henchmen must sacrifice five ladies. **90m/C VHS.** Terence Cooper, Nadine Kalmes, K.C. Kelly, Eric Liddy, Martin Howeller, Robert Mansbridge, Jeffrey Richardson; **D:** Ed Hansen; **W:** Ed Hansen, Buck Flower, Simon Hartwell; **C:** Rick Lamb. *EPE*

Hell's Brigade: The Final Assault woof! 1980 (PG) Low-budget, poorly acted film in which a small band of American commandos is ordered on the most dangerous and important mission of WWII. **99m/C VHS, Beta.** Jack Palance, John Douglas, Carlos Estrada; **D:** Henry Mankiewirk. *MPI*

Hell's Headquarters 🎬 1932 A startling tale of murder and greed involving a hunt for a fortune in African ivory. **59m/B VHS.** Jack Mulhall, Barbara Weeks, Frank Mayo; **D:** Andrew L. Stone. *SNC, NOS, DVT*

Hell's Hinges 🎬½ 1916 The next to last Hart western, typifying his good/bad cowboy character. Perhaps Hart's best film. **65m/B VHS, Beta.** William S. Hart, Clara Williams, Jack Standing, Robert McKim; **D:** William S. Hart. *GPV, VYY, GVV*

Hell's House 🎬🎬 1932 After his mother dies, young lad Durkin goes to the city to live with relatives, gets mixed up with moll Davis and her bootlegger boyfriend O'Brien, and is sent to a brutal reform school. Interesting primarily for early appearances by Davis and O'Brien (before he was typecast as the indefatigable good-guy). **80m/B VHS, Beta.** Junior Durkin, Pat O'Brien, Bette Davis, Frank "Junior" Coghlan, Charley Grapewin, Emma Dunn; **D:** Howard Higgin. *NOS, MRV, CNG*

Hell's Wind Staff 🎬 1982 Two boys uncover a plot to sell their townsmen as slaves to other South East Asian countries. **95m/C VHS, Beta.** Hwang Jang Lee, Mang Yuen Man, Mang Hai. *WVE*

The Hellstrom Chronicle 🎬🎬🎬 1971 (G) A powerful quasi-documentary about insects, their formidable capacity for survival, and the conjectured battle man will have with them in the future. **90m/C VHS, Beta.** Lawrence Pressman; **D:** Walon Green; **W:** David Seltzer. Academy Awards '71: Best Feature Documentary. *COL, OM*

Helltown 🎬½ 1938 A western programmer based on Zane Grey's novel in which Wayne tracks down a cattle rustler. **60m/B VHS, Beta.** John Wayne; **D:** Charles T. Barton. *NOS, DVT, VCN*

Help! 🎬🎬🎬 1965 (G) Ringo's ruby ring is the object of a search by an Arab cult who chase the Fab Four all over the globe in order to acquire the bauble. The laserdisc version includes a wealth of Beatles memorabilia, rare footage behind the scenes and at the film's premiere, and extensive publicity material. ♫Help!; You're Gonna Lose That Girl; You've Got To Hide Your Love Away; The Night Before; Another Girl; Ticket To Ride; I Need You. **90m/C VHS, Beta, LV.** John Lennon, Paul McCartney, Ringo Starr, George Harrison, Leo McKern, Eleanor Bron; **D:** Richard Lester; **W:** Charles Wood, Marc Behm; **C:** David Watkin. *MPI, MVD, CRC*

Help Wanted Female 🎬 1968 Jo Jo, a prostitute with kung fu skills who likes to rob traveling salesmen, is in a quandary over her lesbian roommate's acid dropping friends, including Mr. Gregory, who has a penchant for murder. After recounting a previous trip in which he murdered an acquaintance, he succeeds in alienating his current companions, who must fight for their life to escape him. **71m/B VHS.** Sebastian Gregory, Inga Olsen; **D:** Harold Perkins. *SMW, TPV*

Help Wanted: Male 🎬½ 1982 When a magazine publisher discovers that her fiance cannot have children, she looks for someone else who can do the job right. Made for television. **97m/C VHS, Beta.** Suzanne Pleshette, Gil Gerard, Bert Convy, Dana Elcar, Harold Gould, Caren Kaye; **D:** William Wiard. *WOV*

Helter Skelter 🎬🎬½ 1976 The harrowing story of the murder of actress Sharon Tate and four others at the hands of Charles Manson and his psychotic "family." Based on the book by prosecutor Vincent Bugliosi, adapted by J.P. Miller. Features an outstanding performance by Railsback as Manson. A TV mini-series. **194m/C VHS, Beta, Closed Caption.** Steve Railsback, Nancy Wolfe, George DiCenzo, Marilyn Burns; **D:** Tom Gries; **M:** Billy Goldenberg. *FOX*

The Henderson Monster 🎬🎬½ 1980 Experiments of a genetic scientist are questioned by a community and its mayor. A potentially controversial television drama turns into typical romantic fluff. **105m/C VHS, Beta.** Jason Miller, Christine Lahti, Stephen Collins, David Spielberg, Nehemiah Persoff, Larry Gates; **D:** Waris Hussein. *LIV*

Hennessy 🎬🎬½ 1975 (PG) An IRA man plots revenge on the Royal family and Parliament after his family is violently killed. Tense political drama, but slightly far-fetched. **103m/C VHS.** *GB* Rod Steiger, Lee Remick, Richard Johnson, Trevor Howard, Peter Egan, Eric Porter; **D:** Don Sharp; **W:** John Gay. *NO*

Henry IV 🎬🎬½ 1985 The adaptation of the Luigi Pirandello farce about a modern-day recluse who shields himself from the horrors of the real world by pretending to be mad and acting out the fantasy of being the medieval German emperor Henry IV. In Italian with English subtitles. **94m/C VHS, Beta.** *IT* Marcello Mastroianni, Claudia Cardinale, Leopoldo Trieste, Paolo Bonacelli, Luciano Bartoli, Latou Chardons; **D:** Marco Bellocchio; **W:** Tonino Guerra, Marco Bellocchio, Astor Piazzolla. *MED, APD*

Henry V 🎬🎬🎬🎬 1944 Classic, epic adaptation of the Shakespeare play, and Olivier's first and most successful directorial effort, dealing with the medieval British monarch that defeated the French at Agincourt. Distinguished by Olivier's brilliant formal experiment of beginning the drama as a 16th Century performance of the play in the Globe Theatre, and having the stage eventually transform into realistic historical settings of storybook color. Filmed at the height of WWII suffering in Britain (and meant as a parallel to the British fighting the Nazis), the film was not released in the U.S. until 1946. **136m/C VHS, Beta.** *GB* Laurence

Olivier, Robert Newton, Leslie Banks, Esmond Knight, Renee Asherson, Leo Genn, George Robey, Ernest Thesiger, Felix Aylmer, Ralph Truman; *D:* Laurence Olivier; *W:* Laurence Olivier, Alan Dent; *C:* Robert Krasker; *M:* William Walton. National Board of Review Awards '46: 10 Best Films of the Year, Best Actor (Olivier); New York Film Critics Awards '46: Best Actor (Olivier); Nominations: Academy Awards '46: Best Actor (Olivier), Best Interior Decoration, Best Picture, Original Dramatic/Comedy Score. *PAR, HMV*

Henry V 🎬🎬🎬🎬 1989 Stirring, expansive retelling of Shakespeare's drama about the warrior-king of England. Branagh stars as Henry, leading his troops and uniting his kingdom against France. Very impressive production rivals Olivier's 1945 rendering but differs by stressing the high cost of war—showing the ego-mania, doubts, and subterfuge that underlie conflicts. Marvelous film-directorial debut for Branagh (who also adapted the screenplay). Wonderful supporting cast includes some of Britain's finest actors. 138m/C VHS, LV, Closed Caption. *GB* Kenneth Branagh, Derek Jacobi, Brian Blessed, Alec McCowen, Ian Holm, Richard Briers, Robert Stephens, Robbie Coltrane, Christian Bale, Judi Dench, Paul Scofield, Michael Maloney, Emma Thompson; *D:* Kenneth Branagh; *W:* Kenneth Branagh; *M:* Patrick Doyle. Academy Awards '89: Best Costume Design; British Academy Awards '89: Best Director (Branagh); National Board of Review Awards '89: Best Director (Branagh); Nominations: Academy Awards '89: Best Actor (Branagh), Best Director (Branagh). *FOX, SIG, TVC*

Henry & June 🎬🎬🎬½ 1990 (NC-17) Based on the diaries of writer Anais Nin which chronicled her triangular relationship with author Henry Miller and his wife June, a relationship that provided the erotic backdrop to Miller's "Tropic of Capricorn." Set in Paris in the early '30s, the setting moves between the impecunious expatriate's cheap room on the Left bank—filled with artists, circus performers, prostitutes, and gypsies—to the conservative, well-appointed home of Nin and her husband. Captures the heady atmosphere of Miller's gay Paris; no one plays an American better than Ward (who replaced Alec Baldwin). Notable for having prompted the creation of an NC-17 rating because of its adult theme. 136m/C VHS, LV, Closed Caption. Fred Ward, Uma Thurman, Maria De Medeiros, Richard E. Grant, Kevin Spacey; *D:* Philip Kaufman; *W:* Philip Kaufman; *C:* Philippe Rousselot. Nominations: Academy Awards '90: Best Cinematography. *USH, FCT*

Henry & Verlin 🎬🎬 1994 Verlin (Macintosh) is a 9-year-old who doesn't talk. He lives in rural Ontario (during the Depression) with his overprotective mother Minnie (Beatty) and indifferent father Ferris (Joy), as well as Ferris' childlike brother Henry (Farmer) who befriends Verlin. The misfit duo develop a strong bond that includes disabled retired prostitute Mabel (Kidder)—much to the resentment of some of the less-enlightened townsfolk. There's some melodramatic events but the performances skirt maudlin excess. 87m/C VHS. *CA* Gary Farmer, Keegan Macintosh, Nancy Beatty, Robert Joy, Margot Kidder, Eric Peterson; *Cameos:* David Cronenberg; *D:* Gary Ledbetter; *W:* Gary Ledbetter. Nominations: Genie Awards '94: Best Actor (Farmer), Best Actress (Beatty). *NYR*

Henry: Portrait of a Serial Killer 🎬🎬🎬🎬 1990 (X) Based on the horrific life and times of serial killer Henry Lee Lucas, this film has received wide praise for its straight-forward and uncompromising look into the minds of madmen. The film follows Henry and his roommate Otis as they set out on mindless murder sprees (one of which they videotape). Extremely disturbing and graphic film. Unwary viewers should be aware of the grisly scenes and use their own discretion when viewing this otherwise genuinely moving film. 90m/C VHS, Beta, LV. Michael Rooker, Tom Towles, Tracy Arnold; *D:* John McNaughton; *W:* Richard Fire, John McNaughton. *MPI*

Henry: Portrait of a Serial Killer 2: Mask of Sanity 🎬 1996 (R) Michael Rooker gave a chilling performance as serial killer Henry in part 1 but Giuntoli is merely dull. A sullen

drifter, Henry manages to get a job and fellow worker Kai (Komenich) invites him to crash at his place. Turns out Kai is a part-time arsonist for hire and Henry helps him out—also introducing Kai to the pleasures of casual murder. The gore is actually limited to a few bloody scenes (usually more is heard than shown) but the whole project is boring.*CW:* Strong grisly murders and violence, sex, language and some drug use. 84m/C VHS. Neil Giuntoli, Rich Komenich, Katherine Walsh, Carri Levinson, Penelope Milford; *D:* Chuck Parello; *W:* Chuck Parello; *C:* Michael Kohnhurst; *M:* Robert F. McNaughton. *NYR*

Her Alibi 🎬🎬 1988 (PG) When successful murder-mystery novelist Phil Blackwood runs out of ideas for good books, he seeks inspiration in the criminal courtroom. There he discovers a beautiful Romanian immigrant named Nina who is accused of murder. He goes to see her in jail and offers to provide her with an alibi. Narrated by Blackwood in the tone of one of his thriller novels. Uneven comedy, with appealing cast and arbitrary plot. 95m/C VHS, Beta, LV, 8mm, Closed Caption. Tom Selleck, Paulina Porizkova, William Daniels, James Farentino, Hurd Hatfield, Patrick Wayne, Tess Harper, Joan Copeland; *D:* Bruce Beresford; *W:* Charlie Peters; *M:* Georges Delerue. *WAR*

Her First Romance 🎬🎬½ *The Right Man* 1940 Mixed-up romance with Fellows and Wells as sisters, Linden their cousin, and Ladd her fiance. The sisters fall for Evans and use Ladd in their schemes, causing him to believe Evans is actually after Linden. Eventually, everyone pairs up properly. 77m/B VHS. Edith Fellows, Jacqueline Wells, Alan Ladd, Judith Linden, Wilbur Evans, Roger Daniel; *D:* Edward Dmytryk; *W:* Adele Comandini. *FCT*

Her Husband's Affairs 🎬 1947 Tone is an advertising wonder and Ball is his loving wife who always gets credit for his work. Tone does the advertising for an inventor who is searching for the perfect embalming fluid in this rather lifeless comedy. 83m/B VHS. Lucille Ball, Franchot Tone, Edward Everett Horton, Gene Lockhart, Larry Parks; *D:* Sylvan Simon; *M:* George Duning. *GKK*

Her Life as a Man 🎬½ 1983 A female reporter is refused a job as a sportswriter because of her gender. She makes herself up as a man, gets the job, and creates havoc when she has to deal with lustful women on the job. A made-for-television movie. 93m/C VHS, Beta. Robyn Douglass, Joan Collins, Robert Culp, Marc Singer, Laraine Newman; *D:* Robert Ellis Miller. *ORI*

Her Silent Sacrifice 🎬½ 1918 A silent melodrama about a French girl torn between material wealth and true love. 42m/B VHS, Beta. Alice Brady, Henry Clive. *VYY*

Herbie Goes Bananas 🎬½ 1980 (G) While Herbie the VW is racing in Rio de Janeiro, he is bothered by the syndicate, a pickpocket, and a raging bull. The fourth and final entry in the Disney "Love Bug" movies, but Herbie later made his way to a television series. 93m/C VHS, Beta. Cloris Leachman, Charles Martin Smith, Harvey Korman, John Vernon, Alex Rocco, Richard Jaeckel, Fritz Feld; *D:* Vincent McEveety. *DIS*

Herbie Goes to Monte Carlo 🎬🎬 1977 (G) While participating in a Paris-to-Monte-Carlo race, Herbie the VW takes a detour and falls in love with a Lancia. Third in the Disney "Love Bug" series. 104m/C VHS, Beta. Dean Jones, Don Knotts, Julie Sommars, Roy Kinnear; *D:* Vincent McEveety; *W:* Arthur Alsberg. *DIS*

Herbie Rides Again 🎬🎬½ 1974 (G) In this "Love Bug" sequel, Herbie comes to the aid of an elderly woman who is trying to stop a ruthless tycoon from raising a skyscraper on her property. Humorous Disney fare. Two other sequels followed. 88m/C VHS, Beta, LV. Helen Hayes, Ken Berry, Stefanie Powers, John McIntire, Keenan Wynn; *D:* Robert Stevenson; *M:* George Bruns. *DIS*

Hercules 🎬🎬½ *La Tatiche de Ercole* 1958 The one that started it all. Reeves is perfect as the mythical hero Hercules who encounters many dangerous situations while trying to win over his true love. Dubbed in English. Cinematography by Mario Bava. 107m/C VHS, Beta, LV. *IT* Steve Reeves, Sylva Koscina, Fabrizio Mioni, Gianna Maria Canale, Arturo Dominici; *D:* Pietro Francisci. *MRV, IME, VDM*

Hercules 🎬 1983 (PG) Lackluster remake of 1957 original finds legendary muscle guy Hercules in the person of Ferrigno's Hulkster fighting against the evil King Minos for his own survival and the love of Cassiopeia, a rival king's daughter. 100m/C VHS, Beta, LV, Closed Caption. *IT* Lou Ferrigno, Sybil Danning, William Berger, Brad Harris, Ingrid Anderson; *D:* Lewis (Luigi Cozzi) Coates; *W:* Lewis (Luigi Cozzi) Coates; *M:* Pino Donaggio. Golden Raspberry Awards '83: Worst Supporting Actress (Danning), Worst New Star (Ferrigno). *MGM, IME*

Hercules 🎬🎬🎬½ 1997 (G) After a couple of animated downers, Disney's latest adventure goes for a happy heroic tone by taking on Greek myths. Baby Herc is the son of Zeus, who rules on Mt. Olympus. Hades, Lord of the Underworld, plans a takeover and learns that only Hercules' strength will stand in his way. Hades manages to kidnap the tyke and turn him mortal but when the teenaged Herc learns his true origins, he also discovers that if he proves himself to be a hero he can regain his immortality and return to Mt. Olympus. He's aided by his flying horse Pegasus, satyr-like trainer Phil, and smart gal Meg, while Hades has his less-than-bright minions Pain and Panic. Lots of fun and lots of merchandising (even the movie makes fun of the inevitable tie-ins). ♫The Gospel Truth; Go the Distance; One Last Hope; I Won't Say; Zero to Hero. 92m/C VHS. *D:* John Musker, Ron Clements; *W:* John Musker, Ron Clements, Bob Shaw, Donald McEnery, Irene Mecchi; *M:* Alan Menken, David Zippel; *V:* Tate Donovan, James Woods, Danny DeVito, Matt Frewer, Bob(cat) Goldthwait, Susan Egan, Rip Torn, Samantha Eggar, Paul Shaffer, Barbara Barrie, Hal Holbrook, Amanda Plummer, Carol Shelley. *NYR*

Hercules 2 🎬 *The Adventures of Hercules* 1985 (PG) The muscle-bound demi-god returns to do battle with more evil foes amidst the same stunningly cheap special effects. 90m/C VHS. *IT* Lou Ferrigno, Claudio Cassinelli, Milly Carlucci, Sonia Viviani, William Berger, Carlotta Green; *D:* Lewis (Luigi Cozzi) Coates; *M:* Pino Donaggio. *MGM*

Hercules Against the Moon Men 🎬 *Maciste la Regina di Samar* 1964 It's no holds barred for the mighty son of Zeus when evil moon men start killing off humans in a desperate bid to revive their dead queen. 88m/C VHS, Beta. *IT FR* Alan Steel, Jany Clair, Anna Maria Polani; *D:* Giacomo Gentilomo. *SNC, MRV*

Hercules and the Captive Women 🎬🎬 *Hercules and the Haunted Women; Hercules and the Conquest of Atlantis; Ercole Alla Conquista di Atlantide* 1963 Hercules' son is kidnapped by the Queen of Atlantis, and the bare-chested warrior goes on an all-out rampage to save the boy. Directed by sometimes-lauded Cottafavi. 93m/C VHS, Beta. *IT* Reg Park, Fay Spain, Ettore Manni; *D:* Vittorio Cottafavi. *RHI, MRV, CCB*

Hercules and the Princess of Troy 🎬🎬½ 1965 Hercules is up to his pecs in trouble as he battles a hungry sea monster in order to save a beautiful maiden. Originally a pilot for a prospective television series, and shot in English, not Italian, with Hercules played by erstwhile Tarzan Scott. Highlights are special effects and color cinematography. ?m/C VHS, Beta. *IT* Gordon Scott, Diana Hyland, Paul Stevens, Everett Sloane. *SNC, MLB*

Hercules in New York 🎬½ *Hercules: The Movie; Hercules Goes Bananas* 1970 (G) Motion picture debut of Schwarzenegger (his voice is dubbed) as a Herculean mass of muscle sent by dad Zeus to Manhattan, where he behaves like a geek out of water and eventually becomes a professional wrestling superstar. 250 pounds of stupid, lighthearted fun. **93m/C VHS, Beta.** Arnold Schwarzenegger, Arnold Stang, Deborah Loomis, James Karen, Ernest Graves; **D:** Arthur Seidelman. *MPI*

Hercules in the Haunted World 🎬🎬½ *Ercole al Centro Della Terra* 1964

Long before the days of 24-hour pharmacies, Hercules—played yet again by Reeves-clone Park—must journey to the depths of Hell in order to find a plant that will cure a poisoned princess. Better than most muscle operas, thanks to Bava. **91m/C VHS, Beta.** *IT* Reg Park, Leonora Ruffo, Christopher Lee, George Ardisson; **D:** Mario Bava. *CCB, RHI, MRV*

Hercules, Prisoner of Evil 🎬 1964

Spaghetti myth-opera in which Hercules battles a witch who is turning men into werewolves. Made for Italian television by director Dawson (the nom-de-cinema of Antonio Margheriti). **?m/C VHS.** *IT* Reg Park; **D:** Anthony (Antonio Margheriti) Dawson. *SNC*

Hercules the Legendary Journeys, Vol. 1: And the Amazon Women 🎬🎬½ 1994

Half-man, half-god Hercules (Sorbo) and his friend Ioleus (Hurst) are summoned to a village to kill the beasts stealing livestock. Turns out those responsible are the village's women, who are mad at their husbands and have formed a band of Amazons, lead by Hippolyta (Downey), who happens to be working for Hercules' immortal enemy, the goddess Hera. Now it's up to Herc to convince Hippolyta that men and women can work together and outsmart Hera at the same time. **91m/C VHS, Closed Caption.** Kevin Sorbo, Michael Hurst, Roma Downey, Anthony Quinn, Lucy Lawless; **D:** Bill W.L. Norton; **M:** Joseph Lo Duca. *USH*

Hercules the Legendary Journeys, Vol. 2: The Lost Kingdom 🎬🎬½ 1994

Hera has hidden the kingdom of Troy and only a magic compass can point Hercules (Sorbo) in the right direction. He rescues a sacrificial virgin (O'Connor) and the duo manage to find the compass and get into Troy where she learns her father was once its king. Turns out dad sent his daughter away so he wouldn't have to sacrifice her to Hera and lost his kingdom instead. Now she wants her kingdom back and Hera still wants her sacrifice—especially if it's Hercules. **91m/C VHS, Closed Caption.** Kevin Sorbo, Michael Hurst, Anthony Quinn, Renee O'Connor, Robert Trebor; **D:** Harley Cokliss; **M:** Joseph Lo Duca. *USH*

Hercules the Legendary Journeys, Vol. 3: The Circle of Fire 🎬🎬½ 1994

Hera's stolen fire from mankind, which is slowly freezing to death, keeping one eternal torch for herself. A villager named Deianeira (Kitaen) enlists Hercules (Sorbo) to search for Prometheus (Ferguson), the god of fire, but Hera's stolen his flame as well. When Herc finds the torch it's encircled in a ring of fire, which Hera knows can destroy Hercules' immortality. **92m/C VHS, Closed Caption.** Kevin Sorbo, Michael Hurst, Anthony Quinn, Tawny Kitaen, Mark Ferguson; **D:** Doug Lefler; **M:** Joseph Lo Duca. *USH*

Hercules the Legendary Journeys, Vol. 4: In the Underworld 🎬🎬½ 1994

Having married Deianeira (Kitaen), Herc's a pretty happy guy until a mysterious maiden, Iole, comes to him for help. Seems a deadly crack has opened up in the earth and is swallowing villagers. But Iole has actually been sent by Hera to destroy Hercules and when Deianeira discovers her treachery she goes to warn her husband. Only Hera manages to trick her into walking off a cliff and falling to her death. Hercules must go into the underworld to save the world from Hera but when he learns Deianeira's fate, he accepts an impossible challenge from Hades (Ferguson) to bring his wife back to life. **91m/C VHS, Closed Caption.** Kevin Sorbo, Michael Hurst, Anthony Quinn, Tawny Kitaen, Mark Ferguson; **D:** Bill W.L. Norton; **M:** Joseph Lo Duca. *USH*

Hercules Unchained 🎬🎬 *Ercole e la Regina de Lidia* 1959

Sequel to "Hercules" finds superhero Reeves must use all his strength to save the city of Thebes and the woman he loves from the giant Antaeus. **101m/C VHS, Beta, LV.** *IT* Steve Reeves, Sylva Koscina, Silvia Lopel, Primo Carnera; **D:** Pietro Francisci. *VDM, MRV, SNC*

Here and Elsewhere *Ici et Ailleurs* 197? Godard, Gorin, and Mieville contrast the story of a French family with a look at the Palestine revolution as seen through the media of television, books, and pictures. The film was originally titled "Until Victory" and commissioned by the Palestinians to examine life in the Palestinian camps. After the defeat of the Palestinian army in the Six Day War, Godard and his cohorts transformed the film with their French family ("Here") and their impressions of Palestine ("Elsewhere"). In French with English subtitles. **?m/C VHS.** *FR* Anne-Marie Mieville; **D:** Jean-Pierre Gorin, Jean-Luc Godard. *FCT*

Here Come the Co-Eds 🎬🎬½ 1945

Bud & Lou are the caretakers of an all-girl college which is about to go bankrupt unless the boys can find a way to pay off the mortgage. And come to the rescue they do, including Bud getting into the wrestling ring with the "Masked Marvel" (Chaney, Jr. as the villain). There's also a classic silent scene with Lou served a bowl of oyster stew containing a live oyster, which promptly grabs his tie, bites his fingers, and squirts in his face. **90m/B VHS.** Bud Abbott, Lou Costello, Lon Chaney Jr., Peggy Ryan, Martha O'Driscoll, June Vincent, Donald Cook, Charles Dingle; **D:** Jean Yarbrough; **W:** Arthur T. Horman, John Grant. *USH, FCT*

Here Come the Girls 🎬½ 1953

An unfunny musical-comedy about a chorus boy (Hope) fired for incompetence and then rehired to set a trap when the new singer (Martin) is stalked by a killer. Weak script, weak songs. ♫ Girls Are Here To Stay; Never So Beautiful; You Got Class; Desire; When You Love Someone; Ali Baba Be My Baby; Heavenly Days; See the Circus; Peace. **100m/C VHS, Closed Caption.** Bob Hope, Tony Martin, Arlene Dahl, Rosemary Clooney, Millard Mitchell, William Demarest, Fred Clark, Robert Strauss; **D:** Claude Binyon; **W:** Hal Kanter. *PAR*

Here Come the Littles: The Movie 🎬½ 1985

A twelve-year-old boy finds many new adventures when he meets The Littles—tiny folks who reside within the walls of people's houses. Adapted from the books and TV series. **76m/C VHS, Beta, Closed Caption.** **D:** Bernard Deyries. *FOX*

Here Come the Marines 🎬🎬 *Tell It To the Marines* 1952

The Bowery Boys accidentally join the marines and wind up breaking up a gambling ring. **66m/B VHS.** Leo Gorcey, Huntz Hall, Tim Ryan; **D:** William Beaudine. *NOS*

Here Come the Waves 🎬🎬🎬 1945

Easy-going wartime musical finds Der Bingle as a singing idol drafted into the Navy, assigned to direct WAVE shows. The crooner meets identical twins (both played by Hutton) and falls hard. Only problem is he can't tell the gals apart—and one twin can't stand him. Amusing romantic complications mix well with some spoofing of a star's life. ♫ Ac-cent-tchu-ate the Positive; I Promise You; Let's Take the Long Way Home; That Old Black Magic; There's a Fellow Waiting in Poughkeepsie; Here Come the Waves; My Mama Thinks I'm a Star; Join the Navy. **99m/B VHS, Closed Caption.** Bing Crosby, Betty Hutton, Sonny Tufts, Ann Doran, Noel Neill, Mae Clarke, Gwen Crawford, Catherine Craig; **D:** Mark Sandrich; **W:** Zion Myers. Nominations: Academy Awards '45: Best Song ("Accentuate the Positive"). *USH*

Here Comes Cookie 🎬🎬½ 1935

Amusing farce finds Gracie (Allen) the daughter of wealthy Harrison Allen (Barbier), who's afraid of the fortune hunters eyeing other daughter Phyllis (Furness). So he temporarily turns over the family fortune to Gracie, who promptly turns their Park Avenue mansion into a home for down-on-their-luck vaudevillians. Lots of specialty acts and Burns is around as straight man. **65m/B VHS, Closed Caption.** Gracie Allen, George Burns, George Barbier, Betty Furness; **D:** Norman Z. McLeod; **W:** Don Hartman, Sam Mintz; **C:** Gilbert Warrenton. *USH*

Here Comes Kelly 🎬½ 1943

Controlling his temper and hanging on to his job is more than our hero can handle. **63m/C VHS, Beta.** Eddie Quillan, Joan Woodbury, Maxie "Slapsie" Rosenbloom; **D:** William Beaudine. *GPV*

Here Comes Mr. Jordan 🎬🎬🎬🎬 1941

Montgomery is the young prizefighter killed in a plane crash because of a mix-up in heaven. He returns to life in the body of a soon-to-be murdered millionaire. Rains is the indulgent and advising guardian angel. A lovely fantasy/romance remade in 1978 as "Heaven Can Wait." Laserdisc edition includes actress Elizabeth Montgomery talking about her father Robert Montgomery as well as her television show "Bewitched." **94m/B VHS, Beta, LV.** Robert Montgomery, Claude Rains, James Gleason, Evelyn Keyes, Edward Everett Horton, Rita Johnson, John Emery; **D:** Alexander Hall; **W:** Sidney Buchman, Seton I. Miller; **M:** Friedrich Hollander. Academy Awards '41: Best Screenplay, Best Story; National Board of Review Awards '41: 10 Best Films of the Year; Nominations: Academy Awards '41: Best Actor (Montgomery), Best Black and White Cinematography, Best Director (Hall), Best Picture, Best Supporting Actor (Gleason). *COL, CRC, FCT*

Here Comes Santa Claus 🎬½ 1984

A young boy and girl travel to the North Pole to deliver a very special wish to Santa Claus. **78m/C VHS, Beta.** Karen Cheryl, Armand Meffre; **D:** Christian Gion. *NWV, VTR*

Here Comes the Groom 🎬🎬 1951

Late, stale Capra-corn, involving a rogue journalist who tries to keep his girlfriend from marrying a millionaire by becoming a charity worker. Includes a number of cameos. ♫ In the Cool, Cool, Cool of the Evening; Bonne Nuit, Good Night; Misto Cristofo Columbo; Your Own Little House. **114m/B VHS, Beta, LV, Closed Caption.** Bing Crosby, Jane Wyman, Franchot Tone, Alexis Smith, James Barton, Connie Gilchrist, Robert Keith, Anna Maria Alberghetti, Charles Halton; **Cameos:** Dorothy Lamour, Phil Harris, Louis Armstrong; **D:** Frank Capra. Academy Awards '51: Best Song ("In the Cool, Cool, Cool of the Evening"); Nominations: Academy Awards '51: Best Story. *PAR*

Here We Go Again! 🎬🎬 1942

Fibber McGee and Molly are planning a cross-country trip for their 20th anniversary celebration, but complications abound. Based on the popular NBC radio series. **76m/B VHS, Beta.** Marian Jordan, Jim Jordan, Harold Peary, Gale Gordon, Edgar Bergen, Ray Noble; **D:** Allan Dwan. *CCB*

Here's Looking at You, Warner Bros. 🎬🎬🎬 1993

The 90-year history of Warner Bros. studios is profiled from the silent-era to its current success. Highlights cover the creation of Warners' gangster films, Busby Berkeley musicals, and "Looney Tunes" as well as bloopers and early screen tests by Marlo Brando, Paul Newman, Lana Turner, and Orson Welles. Includes interviews with stars, directors, and producers and numerous film clips. **108m/C VHS, LV. D:** Robert Guenette; **W:** Robert Guenette. *WAR*

Heritage of the Desert 🎬½ 1933

One of the earlier westerns made by the rugged Scott. **62m/B VHS, Beta.** Randolph Scott, Sally Blane, Guinn "Big Boy" Williams; **D:** Henry Hathaway. *DVT, TIM*

The Hero 🎬½ *Bloomfield* 1971 (PG)

A popular soccer player agrees to throw a game for big cash, and then worries about losing the respect of a young boy who idolizes him. Nothing new in this overly sentimental sports drama. **97m/C VHS, Beta.** Richard Harris, Romy Schneider, Kim Burfield, Maurice Kaufman; **D:** Richard Harris.

Hero 🎬🎬🎬 1992 (PG-13)

Interesting twist on Cinderella fable and modern media satire has television reporter Davis looking for the man who saved her life, expecting a genuine hero, and accepting without question the one who fits her vision. Critically considered disappointing, but wait—Garcia and Hoffman make a great team, and Davis is fetching as the vulnerable media person. Strong language and dark edges may keep away some of the kids, but otherwise this is a fine fable. **CW:** Strong language. 116m/C VHS, LV, 8mm, **Closed Caption.** Geena Davis, Dustin Hoffman, Andy Garcia, Joan Cusack, Kevin J. O'Connor, Chevy Chase, Maury Chaykin, Stephen Tobolowsky, Christian Clemenson, Tom Arnold, Warren Berlinger, Susie Cusack, James Madio, Richard Riehle, Don Yesso, Darrell Larson; **D:** Stephen Frears; **W:** David Peoples; **M:** George Fenton. COL

A Hero Ain't Nothin' But a Sandwich 🎬🎬½ 1978 (PG) A young urban black teenager gets involved in drugs and is eventually saved from ruin. Slow-moving, over-directed and talky. However, Scott turns in a fine performance. Based on Alice Childress' novel. 107m/C VHS, Beta, **Closed Caption.** Cicely Tyson, Paul Winfield, Larry B. Scott, Helen Martin, Glynn Turman, David Groh; **D:** Ralph Nelson. PAR, FCT

Hero and the Terror 🎬½ 1988 (R) Perennial karate guy Norris plays a sensitive policeman who conquers his fear of a not-so-sensitive maniac who's trying to kill him. Plenty of action and a cheesy subplot to boot. 96m/C VHS, Beta, LV, **Closed Caption.** Chuck Norris, Brynn Thayer, Steve James, Jack O'Halloran, Ron O'Neal, Billy Drago; **D:** William Tannen; **W:** Michael Blodgett. MED, VTR

Hero at Large 🎬🎬½ 1980 (PG) An unemployed actor foils a robbery while dressed in a promotional "Captain Avenger" suit, and instant celebrity follows. Lightweight, yet enjoyable. 98m/C VHS, Beta. John Ritter, Anne Archer, Bert Convy, Kevin McCarthy, Kevin Bacon; **D:** Martin Davidson; **W:** A.J. Carothers. MGM

Hero Bunker 🎬🎬 1971 Hero bunk about a platoon of heroic Greek soldiers who attempt, at the expense of their personal longevity, to defend an important bunker from enemy invasion. 93m/C VHS, Beta. John Miller, Maria Xenia; **D:** George Andrews. LIV

Hero of Rome 1963 Rome has many who could be called "hero," but one stands biceps and pecs above the rest. ?m/C VHS, Beta. IT Gordon Scott, Gabriella Pallotti. SNC

Hero of the Year 🎬🎬 1985 The characters from Falk's "Top Dog" return in this story of a Polish television personality who loses his job and is forced to face unemployment and job-seeking. 115m/C VHS. PL **D:** Feliks Falk. FCT

Herod the Great 1960 Biblical epic of the downfall of Herod, the ruler of ancient Judea. Scantily clad women abound. Dubbed. 93m/C VHS, IT Edmund Purdom, Sandra Milo, Alberto Lupo; **D:** Arnaldo Genoino. SNC

Heroes 🎬🎬 1977 (PG) An institutionalized Vietnam vet (Winkler) escapes, hoping to establish a worm farm which will support all his crazy buddies. On the way to the home of a friend he hopes will help him, he encounters Field. Funny situations don't always mix with serious underlying themes of mental illness and post-war adjustment. 97m/C VHS, Beta. Henry Winkler, Sally Field, Harrison Ford; **D:** Jeremy Paul Kagan; **W:** Jim Carabatsos; **M:** Jack Nitzsche. USH

Heroes Die Young 🎬½ 1960 A cheap independent feature depicting an American command mission with orders to sabotage German oil fields during WWII. 76m/B VHS, Beta. Krika Peters, Scott Borland, Robert Getz, James Strother. FOX, FCT

Heroes for Sale 🎬🎬🎬 1933 Fascinating melodrama about a WWI veteran who returns home and manages to survive one disaster after another. Barthelmess is great in his performance as an American Everyman who must deal with everything from morphine addiction to finding work during the Depression. Fast-paced, patriotic film is helped by ambitious script and the expert direction of Wellman. 72m/B VHS, **Closed Caption.** Richard Barthelmess, Loretta Young, Aline MacMahon, Robert Barrat, Grant Mitchell, Douglass Dumbrille, Charley

Grapewin, Ward Bond; **D:** William A. Wellman; **W:** Robert Lord, Wilson Mizner. MGM

Heroes in Blue 🎬🎬 1939 Two brothers join the police force, but one goes astray and hooks up with gangsters. Plenty of action distracts from the cliched story. 60m/B VHS, Beta. Dick Purcell, Charles Quigley, Bernadene Hayes, Edward Keane; **D:** William Watson. MGM

Heroes in Hell 🎬½ 1967 Two escaped WWII POWs join the Allied underground in an espionage conspiracy against the Third Reich. 90m/C VHS, Beta. Klaus Kinski, Ettore Manni. NO

The Heroes of Desert Storm 🎬🎬 1991 The human spirit of the people who fought in the high-tech Persian Gulf War is captured in this film that also features real war footage from ABC News. 93m/C VHS, Beta. Daniel Baldwin, Angela Bassett, Marshall Bell, Michael Alan Brooks, William Bumiller, Michael Champion, Maria Diaz; **D:** Don Ohlmeyer; **W:** Lionel Chetwynd. PSM

The Heroes of Telemark 🎬🎬½ 1965 In 1942, Norway is under Nazi occupation and Nazi scientists are dangerously close to producing an essential element for making an atomic bomb in a secret factory. Underground leader Knut Straud (Harris) enlists the help of Norwegian scientist Rolf Pedersen (Douglas) and a group of saboteurs to destroy the factory. But their raid only provides a short delay and our heroes must now prevent shipment of the component from ever reaching Germany. Filmed on location in Norway, with former members of the underground serving as technical advisors for director Mann. 130m/C VHS. GB Richard Harris, Kirk Douglas, Michael Redgrave, Ulla Jacobsson, David Weston, Sebastian Breaks, Alan Howard, Roy Dotrice, Patrick Jordan, Anton Diffring, Eric Porter, Ralph Michael; **D:** Anthony Mann; **W:** Ben Barzman; **C:** Robert Krasker; **M:** Malcolm Arnold. COL

Heroes of the Alamo 🎬½ 1937 Remember the Alamo...but forget this movie. Dull, threadbare dramatization of the battle that was scorned even back in '37. 75m/B VHS, Beta. Rex Lease, Lane Chandler, Roger Williams, Earle Hodgins, Julian Rivero; **D:** Harry Fraser. GPV

Heroes of the Heart 🎬🎬½ 1994 Residents of a West Virginia trailer park are devastated when their homes are destroyed in a flood. But then Basquette claims she was visited by God, who's directed here to bring the poor community together so that each can be granted their most secret wish. Nicely eccentric characters, serious theme with some whimsical touches, and a country-music soundtrack. 102m/C VHS. Lena Basquette, Larry Groce, Dusty Rhodes, Webb Wilder, John McIntire, Jennifer Gurney, Johnny Paycheck; **D:** Daniel Boyd; **W:** Daniel Boyd; **C:** Larry Kopelman; **M:** Michael Lipton. SLI

Heroes of the Hills 🎬🎬½ 1938 The Three Mesquiteers back up a plan that would allow trusted prisoners to work for neighboring ranchers. Part of "The Three Mesquiteers" series. 54m/B VHS, Beta. Bob Livingston, Ray Corrigan, Max Terhune. MED

Heroes of the West 🎬½ 1932 Early sound action western serial. 70m/B VHS, Beta. Noah Beery Jr. VCN, MLB

Heroes Stand Alone 🎬 1989 (R) When a U.S. spy plane is downed in Central America, a special force is sent in to rescue the crew. Another "Rambo" rip-off. 84m/C VHS, Beta. Bradford Dillman, Chad Everett, Wayne Grace, Rick Dean; **D:** Mark Griffiths; **W:** Thomas McKelvey Cleaver. MGM

Heroes Three 🎬🎬 1984 When his crewmate is murdered while on leave in the Far East, a Navy officer enlists the aid of a Chinese detective to track down the killer. 90m/C VHS, Beta. Rowena Cortes, Mike Kelly, Laurens C. Postma, Lawrence Tan; **D:** S.H. Lau. IMP

The Heroic Trio 🎬🎬½ 1993 Three superheroines battle the Lord of the Underground to prevent him from stealing any more human babies. Lots of martial arts and supernatural action. Chinese with subtitles or dubbed. 87m/C VHS, LV.

HK Michelle Yeoh, Maggie Cheung, Anita Mui, Anthony Wong; **D:** Ching Siu Tung, Johnny To. TAI

He's My Girl 🎬½ 1987 (PG-13) When a rock singer wins a trip for two to Hollywood, he convinces his agent to dress up as a woman so they can use the free tickets. 104m/C VHS, Beta. David Hallyday, T.K. Carter, Misha McK, Jennifer Tilly; **D:** Gabrielle Beaumont; **W:** Terence H. Winkless, Taylor Ames, Charles F. Bohl; **C:** Peter Collister. LIV

He's Your Dog, Charlie Brown! 1968 An animated Peanuts adventure wherein Charlie Brown decides to send Snoopy back to the Daisy Hill Puppy Farm for obedience lessons. 30m/C VHS, Beta, **Closed Caption.** MED

Hester Street 🎬🎬🎬 1975 Set at the turn of the century, the film tells the story of a young Jewish immigrant who ventures to New York City to be with her husband. As she re-acquaints herself with her husband, she finds that he has abandoned his Old World ideals. The film speaks not only to preserving the heritage of the Jews, but to cherishing all heritages and cultures. Highly regarded upon release, unfortunately forgotten today. 92m/B VHS, Beta. Carol Kane, Doris Roberts, Steven Keats, Mel Howard, Dorrie Kavanaugh, Stephen Strimpell; **D:** Joan Micklin Silver; **M:** William Bolcom. Nominations: Academy Awards '75: Best Actress (Kane). FRF, VES

Hexed 🎬½ 1993 (R) Walter Mitty lives in the person of bellboy Matthew Welsh, who enjoys masquerading as a debonair bon vivant. He finagles his way into the life of Hexina, a beautiful psychotic model who has checked into the hotel where Matthew works in order to murder her blackmailer. She tries to kill Matthew, apparently getting in a little practice, but he'll still follow her anywhere. Inane, charmless comedy that intends to satirize "Fatal Attraction" and similar films. **CW:** Language and sexuality. 93m/C VHS, LV, **Closed Caption.** Arye Gross, Claudia Christian, Adrienne Shelly, R. Lee Ermey, Norman Fell, Michael E. Knight; **D:** Alan Spencer; **W:** Alan Spencer. COL

Hey, Babu Riba 🎬🎬½ 1988 (R) A popular Yugoslavian fit of nostalgia about four men convening at the funeral of a young girl they all loved years before, and their happy, Americana-bathed memories therein. In Serbo-Croatian with English subtitles. 109m/C VHS, Beta, LV. YU Gala Videnovic, Nebojsa Bakocevic, Dragan Bjelogrlic, Marko Todorovic, Goran Radakovic, Relja Basic, Milos Zutic; **D:** Jovan Acin; **W:** Jovan Acin. ORI

Hey Good Lookin' 1982 Ralph Bakshi's irreverent look at growing up in the 1950s bears the trademark qualities that distinguish his other adult animated features, "Fritz the Cat" and "Heavy Traffic." 87m/C VHS, Beta. **D:** Ralph Bakshi; **W:** Ralph Bakshi. WAR

Hey There, It's Yogi Bear 🎬🎬 1964 When Yogi Bear comes out of winter hibernation to search for food, he travels to the Chizzling Brothers Circus. The first feature-length cartoon to come from the H-B Studios. 98m/C VHS, Beta, LV, **Closed Caption. D:** William Hanna; **V:** Daws Butler, James Darren, Mel Blanc, J. Pat O'Malley, Julie Bennett. WOV, IME

Hi-De-Ho 🎬🎬½ 1935 The great Cab Calloway and his red hot jazz are featured in this film, which has the band caught between rival gangsters. The plot is incidental to the music, anyway. ♫ Hi-De-Ho; I Got A Gal Named Nettie; Little Old Lady From Baltimore; A Rainy Sunday. 60m/B VHS, Beta. Cab Calloway, Ida James; **D:** Josh Binney. MVD, NOS, DVT

Hi-Di-Hi 1988 A British television comedy about the shenanigans that inevitably follow when a stuffy Cambridge professor becomes the entertainment manager for a holiday camp. 91m/C VHS, Beta. GB Simon Cadell, Ruth Madoc, Paul Shane, Jeffrey Holland, Leslie Dwyer. FOX

Hi Diddle Diddle 🎬🎬½ Diamonds and Crime; Try and Find It 1943 Topsy-turvy comedy features young lovers who long for conventional happiness. Instead they are cursed with con-artist parents who delight in crossing that law-abiding line. **72m/B VHS, Beta.** Adolphe Menjou, Martha Scott, Dennis O'Keefe, Pola Negri; **D:** Andrew L. Stone. Nominations: Academy Awards '43: Original Dramatic/Comedy Score. *NOS, DVT, HEG*

Hi-Jacked ⊘ 1950 When a parolee trucker's cargo is stolen, he inevitably becomes a suspect and must set out to find the true culprits. **66m/B VHS, Beta, LV.** Jim Davis, Paul Cavanagh, Marsha Jones. *RXM*

Hi, Mom! ⊘⊘⊘ *Confessions of A Peeping John; Blue Manhattan* 1970 **(R)** DePalma's follow-up to "Greetings" finds amateur pornographer/movie maker De Niro being advised by a professional in the field (Garfield) of sleazy filmmaking. De Niro films the residents of his apartment building and eventually marries one of his starlets. One of De Palma's earlier and better efforts with De Niro playing a crazy as only he can. **87m/C VHS.** Robert De Niro, Charles Durnham, Allen (Goorwitz) Garfield, Lara Parker, Jennifer Salt, Gerrit Graham; **D:** Brian DePalma; **W:** Brian DePalma. *FCT, HHE*

Hi-Riders ⊘ 1977 **(R)** A revenge-based tale about large, mag-wheeled trucks and their drivers. **90m/C VHS, Beta.** Mel Ferrer, Stephen McNally, Neville Brand, Ralph Meeker; **D:** Greydon Clark. *VCI*

The Hidden ⊘⊘⊘ 1987 **(R)** A seasoned cop (Nouri) and a benign alien posing as an FBI agent (MacLachlan) team up to track down and destroy a hyper-violent alien who survives by invading the bodies of humans, causing them to go on murderous rampages. Much acclaimed, high velocity action film with state-of-the-art special effects. **98m/C VHS, Beta, LV, Closed Caption.** Kyle MacLachlan, Michael Nouri, Clu Gulager, Ed O'Ross, Claudia Christian, Clarence Felder, Richard Brooks, William Boyett; **D:** Jack Sholder; **W:** Bob Hunt; **M:** Michael Convertino. *MED, CDV, VTR*

The Hidden 2 ⊘⊘½ 1994 **(R)** The hyper-violent alien of the 1987 movie returns. With its love of fast cars, high-caliber weapons, and heavy metal music, this body-possessing creature appears to be unstoppable. **91m/C VHS, LV, Closed Caption.** Raphael Sbarge, Kate Hodge, Michael Nouri; **D:** Seth Pinsker; **W:** Seth Pinsker; **M:** David McHugh. *NLC, IME*

Hidden Agenda ⊘⊘½ 1990 **(R)** A human rights activist and an American lawyer uncover brutality and corruption among the British forces in Northern Ireland. Slow-paced but strong performances. The Northern Irish dialect is sometimes difficult to understand as are the machinations on the British police system. Generally worthwhile. **108m/C VHS, LV, Closed Caption.** Frances McDormand, Brian Cox, Brad Dourif, Mai Zetterling, John Benfield, Des McAleer, Jim Norton, Maurice Roeves; **D:** Ken Loach; **W:** Jim Allen; **M:** Stewart Copeland. Cannes Film Festival '90: Special Jury Prize. *HBO, FCT*

Hidden Assassin ⊘ *The Shooter* 1994 **(R)** French hit woman Simone (Detmers) supposedly shoots the Cuban ambassador to the U.N. and escapes back to her home base in Prague, followed by Czech-born U.S. Marshal Mickey Dane (Lundgren). Mickey starts to doubt that Simone is the killer (she claims she's long retired and is being set up) and the duo try to find the truth amid lots of double-crosses. Doesn't make much sense in any case. **CW:** Strong violence, language and brief nudity. **89m/C VHS, LV, Closed Caption.** Dolph Lundgren, Maruschka Detmers, Assumpta Serna, Gavan O'Herlihy, John Ashton, Simon Andreu; **D:** Ted Kotcheff; **W:** Meg Thayer, Billy Ray, Yves Andre Martin; **C:** Fernando Arguelles; **M:** Stewart Mainetti. *TOU*

Hidden City ⊘⊘ 1987 A film archivist and a statistician become drawn into a conspiracy when a piece of revealing film is spliced onto the end of an innocuous government tape. **108m/C VHS, Beta.** Charles Dance, Cassie Stuart, Alex Norton, Tusse Silberg, Bill Paterson; **D:** Stephen Poliakoff. *NO*

Hidden Enemy ⊘½ 1940 During WWII, a scientist develops a new metal alloy that is stronger than steel yet lighter than aluminum. His nephew must protect his scientist/uncle from spies who would steal the formula to use against the Allies. **63m/B VHS, Beta.** Warren Hull, Kay Linaker, William von Brinken, George Cleveland; **D:** Howard Bretherton. *SNC, RXM*

Hidden Fears ⊘⊘½ 1993 Maureen Dietz (Foster) carries the gruesome memories of her husband's murder with her. Years later she goes to the police with new evidence to reopen her husband's case. Only the killers find out and return to finish off the eyewitnesses, and she's next! Based on the novel "Exercise in Terror" by Kaminsky, who also wrote the screenplay. **90m/C VHS, Beta.** Meg Foster, Frederic Forrest, Wally Taylor, Bever-Leigh Banfield, Marc Macaulay, Patrick Cherry, Scott Hayes; **D:** Jean Bodon; **W:** Stuart Kaminsky. *PSM*

The Hidden Fortress ⊘⊘⊘½ *Kakushi Toride No San Akunin; Three Rascals in the Hidden Fortress; Three Bad Men in the Hidden Fortress* 1958 Kurosawa's tale of a warrior who protects a princess from warring feudal lords. An inspiration for George Lucas' "Star Wars" series and deserving of its excellent reputation. In Japanese with English subtitles. The laserdisc edition is letterboxed to retain the film's original integrity. **139m/B VHS, Beta, LV.** *JP* Toshiro Mifune, Misa Vehara, Minoru Chiaki; **D:** Akira Kurosawa. Berlin International Film Festival '59: Best Director (Kurosawa). *HMV, FCT, CRC*

Hidden Gold ⊘½ 1933 Routine western for Mix, which has him going undercover to win the confidence of three outlaws and discover where they have hidden their loot. **57m/B VHS, Beta.** Tom Mix, Judith Barrie, Raymond Hatton; **D:** Arthur Rosson. *GPV, VCN, DVT*

Hidden Guns ⊘⊘⊘ 1956 Above-average tale of father-and-son lawmen out to reform a town and put the bad guys away. When dad is killed, son goes up against the villain alone. A Greek chorus adds an interesting twist to the action. Erich von Stroheim, Jr. is listed as assistant director. **66m/B VHS.** Bruce (Herman Brix) Bennett, Richard Arlen, John Carradine, Faron Young, Angie Dickinson, Guinn "Big Boy" Williams; **D:** Albert C. Gannaway. *NOS*

Hidden In America ⊘⊘½ 1996 **(PG-13)** Bill Januson (Bridges) has lost his auto-plant job because of downsizing and his wife to cancer. His savings exhausted and his prospects bleak, Januson struggles to put food on the table for his two kids. Cable movie produced in conjunction with the End Hunger Network, whose co-founder, Jeff Bridges, has a cameo. **CW:** Disturbing plot material. **100m/C VHS.** Beau Bridges, Bruce Davison, Jena Malone, Shelton Dane, Alice Krige, Josef Sommer, Frances McDormand; **Cameos:** Jeff Bridges; **D:** Martin Bell; **W:** Peter Silverman, Michael deGuzman; **C:** James R. Bagdonas; **M:** Mason Daring. *EVE*

Hidden Obsession ⊘½ 1992 **(R)** Newscaster Ellen is taking a much needed vacation at an isolated cabin when she learns that a serial killer has escaped from a nearby prison. Luckily, she has a hunky police officer neighbor for protection. But though the escaped killer is captured, the killings go on—with Ellen as the next target. **92m/C VHS, LV, Closed Caption.** Heather Thomas, Jan-Michael Vincent, Nicholas Celozzi; **D:** John Stewart; **W:** David Reskin. *USH*

The Hidden Room ⊘⊘⊘ *Obsession* 1949 A doctor finds out about his wife's affair and decides to get revenge on her lover. He kidnaps him, imprisons him in a cellar, and decides to kill him—slowly. Tense melodrama. **98m/B VHS, Beta.** *GB* Robert Newton, Sally Gray, Naunton Wayne, Phil Brown, Olga Lindo, Russell Waters, James Harcourt, Allan Jeayes, Stanley Baker; **D:** Edward Dmytryk; **W:** Alec Coppel; **M:** Nino Rota. *NOS, SNC, RXM*

Hidden Valley ⊘⊘ 1932 Early Steele western in which everyone is fighting over a map that leads to hidden treasure in the valley. **60m/B VHS.** Bob Steele, Gertrude Messinger, Francis McDonald; **D:** Robert North Bradbury. *GPV*

Hide and Go Shriek ⊘ 1987 **(R)** Several high school seniors are murdered one by one during a graduation party. Also available in an unrated, gorier version. **90m/C VHS, Beta, LV.** Annette Sinclair, Brittain Frye, Rebunkah Jones; **D:** Skip Schoolnik. *NO*

Hide and Seek ⊘ 1977 When a high school hacker converts his computer into a nuclear weapon, he finds that it has developed a mind of its own. **60m/C VHS, Beta.** Bob Martin, Ingrid Veninger, David Patrick. *ORI*

Hide and Seek ⊘ 1980 A study of children living in the land that would soon become Israel. Although they play as normal children, life is particularly difficult. This adversity will lay the foundation for their Israeli citizenry. In Hebrew with English subtitles. **90m/C VHS, Beta.** Gila Almagor, Doron Tavori, Chaim Hadaya; **D:** Dan Wolman. *ERG, TPV*

Hide in Plain Sight ⊘⊘⊘ 1980 **(PG)** A distraught blue-collar worker searches for his children who disappeared when his ex-wife and her mobster husband are given new identities by federal agents. Caan's fine directorial debut is based on a true story. **96m/C VHS, Beta.** James Caan, Jill Eikenberry, Robert Viharo, Kenneth McMillan, Josef Sommer, Danny Aiello; **D:** James Caan. *MGM*

Hide-Out ⊘⊘½ 1934 A man running from the law winds up at a small farm, falls in love, and becomes reformed by the good family that takes him in. Good supporting cast includes a very young Rooney. **83m/B VHS.** Robert Montgomery, Maureen O'Sullivan, Edward Arnold, Elizabeth Patterson, Mickey Rooney, Edward Brophy; **D:** Woodbridge S. Van Dyke. Nominations: Academy Awards '34: Best Story. *MGM*

Hideaway ⊘⊘ 1994 **(R)** Hodge podge movie finds Hatch Harrison (Goldblum) brought back from the other side after suffering injuries from a near-fatal car accident. He returns with the ability to psychically connect with Vassago (Sisto), a sadistic serial killer of young girls. Coincidentally, Harrison has a teenage daughter, Regina (Silverstone), and Vassago has her lined up as his next victim. The visual effects of spirits floating down a cosmic vortex are entertaining, but plot originality must have been hidden away to make room for the nifty special effects. Based on a novel by Dean R. Koontz. **CW:** Terror violence; language; scene of sexuality. **103m/C VHS, LV, Closed Caption.** Jeff Goldblum, Christine Lahti, Alicia Silverstone, Jeremy Sisto, Rae Dawn Chong; **D:** Brett Leonard; **W:** Andrew Kevin Walker, Neal Jimenez; **C:** Gale Tattersall; **M:** Trevor Jones. *COL*

The Hideaways ⊘⊘½ *From the Mixed-Up Files of Mrs. Basil E. Frankweiler* 1973 **(G)** A 12-year-old girl and her younger brother run away and hide in the Metropolitan Museum of Art. The girl becomes enamored of a piece of sculpture and sets out to discover its creator. Based on the children's novel by E.L. Konigsburg. **105m/C VHS, Beta.** Richard Mulligan, George Rose, Ingrid Bergman, Sally Prager, Johnny Doran, Madeline Kahn; **D:** Fielder Cook. *WAR, VHE, FCT*

Hideous Sun Demon ⊘⊘½ *Blood On His Lips; Terror From the Sun; The Sun Demon* 1959 A physicist exposed to radiation must stay out of sunlight or he will turn into a scaly, lizard-like creature. Includes previews of coming attractions from classic sci-fi films. **75m/B VHS, Beta.** Robert Clarke, Patricia Manning, Nan Peterson; **D:** Robert Clarke. *NOS, MRV, RHI*

Hider in the House ⊘⊘½ 1990 **(R)** In a peaceful neighborhood a family is about to spend an evening of terror when they discover a psychopath is hiding in the attic of their home. **109m/C VHS, Beta, LV.** Michael McKean, Gary Busey, Mimi Rogers, Kurt Christopher Kinder, Candy Hutson, Elizabeth Ruscio, Bruce Glover; **D:** Michael Patrick. *VES, LIV*

Hiding Out 🎬🎬 1987 (PG-13) A young stockbroker testifies against the Mafia and must find a place to hide in order to avoid being killed. He winds up at his cousin's high school in Delaware, but can he really go through all these teenage troubles once again? 99m/C VHS, Beta, Closed Caption. Jon Cryer, Keith Coogan, Gretchen Cryer, Annabeth Gish, Tim Quill; D: Bob Giraldi; M: Anne Dudley. HBO

The Hiding Place 🎬🎬 1975 True story of two Dutch Christian sisters sent to a concentration camp for hiding Jews during WWII. Film is uneven but good cast pulls it through. Based on the Corrie Ten Boom book and produced by Billy Graham's Evangelistic Association. 145m/C VHS. Julie Harris, Eileen Heckart, Arthur O'Connell, Jeanette Clift; D: James F. Collier. VBL, REP

High & Low 🎬🎬🎬½ Tengoku To Jigoku 1962 (R) Fine Japanese film noir about a wealthy businessman who is being blackmailed by kidnappers who claim to have his son. When he discovers that they have mistakenly taken his chauffeur's son he must decide whether to face financial ruin or risk the life of a young boy. Based on an Ed McBain novel. In Japanese with English subtitles. 143m/B VHS, Beta, LV. JP Toshiro Mifune, Tatsuya Mihashi, Tatsuya Nakadai; D: Akira Kurosawa. IME, TPV

High Anxiety 🎬🎬 1977 (PG) Brooks tries hard to please in this low-brow parody of Hitchcock films employing dozens of references to films like "Psycho," "Spellbound," "The Birds," and "Vertigo." Tells the tale of a height-fearing psychiatrist caught up in a murder mystery. The title song performed a la Sinatra by Brooks is one of the film's high moments. Brooks also has a lot of fun with Hitchcockian camera movements. Uneven (What? Brooks?) but amusing tribute. 92m/C VHS, Beta, LV, Closed Caption. Mel Brooks, Madeline Kahn, Cloris Leachman, Harvey Korman, Ron Carey, Howard Morris, Dick Van Patten; D: Mel Brooks; W: Mel Brooks, Ron Clark, Barry Levinson, Rudy DeLuca. FOX

High Ballin' 🎬🎬 1978 (PG) Truckers Fonda and Reed team up with lady trucker Shaver to take on the gang trying to crush the independent drivers. 100m/C VHS, Beta. CA Peter Fonda, Jerry Reed, Helen Shaver; D: Peter Carter; W: Paul F. Edwards. LIV, VES

High Command 🎬🎬½ 1937 To save his daughter from an ugly scandal, the British general of an isolated Colonial African outpost traps a blackmailer's killer. 84m/B VHS, Beta. GB Lionel Atwill, Lucie Mannheim, James Mason; D: Thorold Dickinson. NOS, MRV, VYY

High Country 🎬🎬½ The First Hello 1981 (PG) Two misfits, one handicapped, the other an ex-con, on the run from society learn mutual trust as they travel through the Canadian Rockies. 101m/C VHS, Beta. CA Timothy Bottoms, Linda Purl, George Sims, Jim Lawrence, Bill Berry; D: Harvey Hart. VES

High Crime 🎬🎬 1973 A "French Connection"-style suspense story about the heroin trade. Features high-speed chases and a police commissioner obsessed with capturing the criminals. 91m/C VHS, Beta. James Whitmore, Franco Nero, Fernando Rey; D: Enzo G. Castellari. MED

High Desert Kill 🎬🎬 1990 (PG) A science-fiction tale will keep you guessing. Aliens landing in the New Mexican desert want something totally unexpected, and a trio of friends will be the first to find out what it is. Written for cable by Cook ("The China Syndrome"). 93m/C VHS, Beta. Chuck Connors, Marc Singer, Anthony Geary, Micah Grant; D: Harry Falk; W: T.S. Cook. USH

High Frequency 🎬🎬 1988 Two young men monitoring a satellite relay station witness the murder of a woman. Believing they know who the killer's next victim will be, they set out to warn her. Lack of development mars what could have been a tidy little thriller. 105m/C VHS, LV. IT Oliver Benny, Vincent Spano, Isabelle Pasco, Anne Canovos; D: Faliero Rosati. MCG

High Gear 🎬 1933 Heartstring-tugger about a race car driver, his girlfriend and the orphan son of a driver killed in a crash. Try to guess the outcome. 65m/B VHS. James Murray, Joan Marsh, Jackie Searl, Theodore von Eltz, Lee Moran, Gordon DeMain; D: Leigh Jason. NOS, RXM

High Heels 🎬🎬 Docteur Popaul; Scoundrel in White 1972 A black comedy about a doctor who believes beauty is only skin deep and marries a plain woman. However, when he meets her beautiful sister, he begins to wonder. In French with English subtitles. FR Laura Antonelli, Jean-Paul Belmondo, Mia Farrow, Daniel Ivernel; D: Claude Chabrol. NO

High Heels 🎬🎬🎬 Tacones Lejanos 1991 (R) An outrageous combination murder-melodrama-comedy from Almodovar. Rebecca is a TV anchorwoman in Madrid whose flamboyant singer/actress mother has returned to the city for a concert. Rebecca happens to be married to one of her mother's not-so-ex-flames. When her husband winds up dead, Rebecca confesses to his murder during her newscast—but is she telling the truth or just covering up for mom? Mix in a drag queen/judge, a dancing chorus of women prison inmates, and a peculiar police detective, and see if the plot convolutions make sense. In Spanish with English subtitles. CW: Language and strong sensuality. 113m/C VHS, Beta, Closed Caption. SP Victoria Abril, Marisa Paredes, Miguel Bose, Feodor Atkine, Bibi Andersen, Rocio Munoz; D: Pedro Almodovar; W: Pedro Almodovar; M: Ryuichi Sakamoto. Cesar Awards '93: Best Foreign Film. PAR

High Hopes 🎬🎬🎬 1988 A moving yet nasty satiric comedy about a pair of ex-hippies maintaining their counterculture lifestyle in Margaret Thatcher's England, as they watch the signs of conservative "progress" overtake them and their geriatric, embittered Mum. Hilarious and mature. 110m/C VHS, Beta. GB Philip Davis, Ruth Sheen, Edna Dore, Philip Jackson, Heather Tobias, Leslie Manville, David Bamber; D: Mike Leigh; W: Mike Leigh; M: Andrew Dixon. ACA

High Ice 🎬½ 1980 Forest ranger and a lieutenant colonel are involved in a clash of wills over a rescue mission high in the snow-capped Washington state peaks. 97m/C VHS, Beta. David Janssen, Tony Musante; D: Eugene S. Jones. VES

High Lonesome 🎬🎬½ 1950 Barrymore is a drifter in Big Bend country, suspected in a series of mysterious murders. While he is being held captive, the real killers - thought dead - return to exact revenge on those they hold responsible for the range war in which they were wounded. This was LeMay's only stint as a director. 80m/C VHS. John Blythe Barrymore Jr., Chill Wills, John Archer, Lois Butler, Kristine Miller, Basil Ruysdael, Jack Elam; D: Alan LeMay; W: Alan LeMay. NOS

High Noon 🎬🎬🎬🎬 1952 Landmark Western about Hadleyville town marshal Will Kane (Cooper) who faces four professional killers alone, after being abandoned to his fate by the gutless townspeople who profess to admire him. Cooper is the ultimate hero figure, his sheer presence overwhelming. Note the continuing use of the ballad written by Dimitri Tiomkin, "Do Not Forsake Me, Oh My Darlin'" (sung by Tex Ritter) to heighten the tension and action. Laserdisc includes the original trailer, an essay by Howard Suber on audio 2, a photo essay of production stills, Carl Foreman's original notes of the film and the complete text of "The Tin Star," the story on which the film is based. ♫High Noon (Do Not Forsake Me, Oh My Darlin'). 85m/B VHS, LV, Closed Caption. Gary Cooper, Grace Kelly, Lloyd Bridges, Lon Chaney Jr., Thomas Mitchell, Otto Kruger, Katy Jurado, Lee Van Cleef, Harry (Henry) Morgan, Robert J. Wilke, Sheb Wooley; D: Fred Zinnemann; W: Carl Foreman; C: Floyd Crosby; M: Dimitri Tiomkin. Academy Awards '52: Best Actor (Cooper), Best Film Editing, Best Song ("High Noon (Do Not Forsake Me, Oh My Darlin')"), Original Dramatic/Comedy Score; Golden Globe Awards '53: Best Actor—Drama (Cooper), Best Supporting Actress (Jurado), Best Score;

National Board of Review Awards '52: 10 Best Films of the Year; New York Film Critics Awards '52: Best Director (Zinnemann), Best Film; Nominations: Academy Awards '52: Best Director (Zinnemann), Best Picture, Best Screenplay. REP, TLF, BTV

High Noon: Part 2 🎬 1980 Majors attempts to fill Gary Cooper's shoes, as Marshal Kane returns a year after the events of the original "High Noon" to remove the corrupt marshal who replaced him. Subtitled "The Return of Will Kane." Made for television. 96m/C VHS, Beta. Lee Majors, David Carradine, Pernell Roberts, Kathy Cannon; D: Jerry Jameson. FRH, VTR

High Plains Drifter 🎬🎬½ 1973 (R) A surreal, violent western focusing on a drifter who defends a town from gunmen intent on meting out death. One of Eastwood's most stylistic directorial efforts, indebted to his "Man with No Name" days with Sergio Leone. Laser format is letterboxed and includes chapter stops and the original theatrical trailer. 105m/C VHS, Beta, LV. Verna Bloom, Mitchell Ryan, Marianna Hill, Clint Eastwood; D: Clint Eastwood; M: Dee Barton. USH, TLF

High Risk 🎬½ 1976 (R) Improbable action-adventure of four unemployed Americans who battle foreign armies, unscrupulous gunrunners, and jungle bandits in a harrowing attempt to steal five million dollars from an expatriate American drug dealer living in the peaceful splendor of his Columbian villa. Interesting in its own run-on way. 94m/C VHS, Beta. James Brolin, Anthony Quinn, Lindsay Wagner, James Coburn, Ernest Borgnine, Bruce Davison, Cleavon Little; D: Stewart Raffill. VTR

High Road to China 🎬🎬 1983 (PG) A hard-drinking former WWI air ace is recruited by a young heiress who must find her father before his ex-partner takes over his business. Post-"Raiders of the Lost Ark" thrills and romance, but without that tale's panache. 105m/C VHS, Beta, LV. Bess Armstrong, Tom Selleck, Jack Weston, Robert Morley, Wilford Brimley, Brian Blessed; D: Brian G. Hutton; M: John Barry. WAR

High Rolling in a Hot Corvette 🎬 High Rolling 1977 (PG) Two carnival workers leave their jobs and hit the road in search of adventure and excitement, eventually turning to crime. 82m/C VHS, Beta. AU Joseph Bottoms, Greg Taylor, Judy Davis, Wendy Hughes; D: Igor Auzins. VES

High School Caesar 🎬 1956 A seedy teenage exploitation flick about a rich teenager, with no parental supervision, who starts his own gang to run his high school. 75m/B VHS, Beta. John Ashley; D: O'Dale Ireland. RHI, SNC

High School Confidential 🎬🎬 Young Hellions 1958 Teen punk Tamblyn transfers to Santo Bello high school from Chicago and causes havoc among the locals. He soon involves himself in the school drug scene and looks to be the top dog in dealing, but what no one knows is that he's really a narc! A must for midnight movie fans thanks to high camp values, "hep cat" dialogue and the gorgeous Van Doren as Tamblyn's sex-crazed "aunt." 85m/B VHS, Beta. Russ Tamblyn, Jan Sterling, John Blythe Barrymore Jr., Mamie Van Doren, Diane Jergens, Jerry Lee Lewis, Ray Anthony, Jackie Coogan, Charles Chaplin Jr., Burt Douglas, Michael Landon, Jody Fair, Phillipa Fallon, Robin Raymond, James Todd, Lyle Talbot, William Wellman Jr.; D: Jack Arnold. REP

High School High 🎬🎬½ 1996 (PG-13) Idealistic teacher Richard Clark (Lovitz) leaves the private school world for notorious inner city Marion Barry High. This school is so bad it has its own cemetery (it's a parody, folks), but Clark is determined to get through to the kids. "Clockers" star Phifer shows up as a helpful student. Penned by David Zucker of "Airplane!" fame, so don't expect a "Mr. Holland's Opus." CW: Crude sexual humor, partial nudity and some drug references. 86m/C VHS, LV, Closed Caption. Jon Lovitz, Tia Carrere, Mekhi Phifer, Louise Fletcher, Malinda Williams; D: Hart Bochner; W: David Zucker, Robert Locash, Pat Proft. COL

High School USA 🎬½ 1984 A high school class clown confronts the king of the prep-jock-bullies. Antics ensue in this made-for-television flick which features many stars from fifties and sixties sitcoms. 96m/C VHS, Beta. Michael J. Fox, Nancy McKeon, Bob Denver, Angela Cartwright, Elinor Donahue, Dwayne Hickman, Lauri Hendler, Dana Plato, Tony Dow, David Nelson; **D:** Rod Amateau; **M:** Miles Goodman. ORI, WAR

High Season 🎬🎬½ 1988 (R) A satire about a beautiful English photographer (Bisset) stranded on an idyllic Greek island with neither money nor inspiration, and the motley assembly of characters who surround her during the tourist season. 95m/C VHS, Beta, LV, 8mm. 🎬 Jacqueline Bisset, James Fox, Irene Papas, Sebastian Shaw, Kenneth Branagh, Robert Stephens, Leslie Manville; **D:** Clare Peploe; **W:** Mark Peploe, Clare Peploe; **C:** Chris Menges; **M:** Jason Osborn. FCT, NLC

High Sierra 🎬🎬🎬 1941 Bogart is Roy "Mad Dog" Earle, an aging gangster whose last job backfires, so he's hiding out from the police in the High Sierras. Bogart's first starring role. Based on the novel by W.R. Burnett. Remade in 1955 as "I Died A Thousand Times." Also available colorized. 96m/B VHS, Beta, LV. Humphrey Bogart, Ida Lupino, Arthur Kennedy, Joan Leslie, Cornel Wilde, Henry Travers, Henry Hull; **D:** Raoul Walsh; **W:** John Huston, W.R. Burnett; **C:** Gaetano Antonio "Tony" Gaudio. National Board of Review Awards '41: 10 Best Films of the Year. FOX

High Society 🎬🎬🎬 1956 A wealthy man attempts to win back his ex-wife who's about to be remarried in this enjoyable remake of "The Philadelphia Story." Letterboxed laserdisc format also includes the original movie trailer. 🎵High Society Calypso; Little One; Who Wants to Be a Millionaire?; True Love; You're Sensational; I Love You, Samantha; Now You Has Jazz; Well, Did You Evah?; Mind if I Make Love to You?. 107m/C VHS, Beta, LV, 8mm. Frank Sinatra, Bing Crosby, Grace Kelly, Louis Armstrong, Celeste Holm, Sidney Blackmer, Louis Calhern; **D:** Charles Walters; **C:** Paul Vogel; **M:** Cole Porter. Nominations: Academy Awards '56: Best Song ("True Love"), Best Story, Scoring of a Musical. MGM

High Spirits 🎬🎬 1988 (PG-13) An American inherits an Irish castle and a sexy 200-year-old ghost. A painful, clumsy comedy by the fine British director that was apparently butchered by the studio before its release. 99m/C VHS, Beta, LV, Closed Caption. Daryl Hannah, Peter O'Toole, Steve Guttenberg, Beverly D'Angelo, Liam Neeson, Martin Ferrero, Peter Gallagher, Jennifer Tilly; **D:** Neil Jordan; **W:** Neil Jordan; **M:** George Fenton. MED, VTR

High Stakes 🎬🎬 1989 (R) Kirkland stars as a prostitute who's battling the Mob and falling in love. Limited release in theaters but another fine performance from Kirkland. Also released as "Melanie Rose." 102m/C VHS, LV. Sally Kirkland, Robert LuPone, Richard Lynch, Sarah Gellar, Kathy Bates, W.T. Martin; **D:** Amos Kollek. THV

High Strung 🎬½ 1991 (PG) Writer Thane Furrows (Oedekerk) thinks his life can't get any worse since he's plagued by a nagging mom, pressuring boss, and an insurance salesman. Then mysterious voices and images (played by Carrey) tell him he'll die that night. Naturally, Thane tries to think of a way out of his predicament. You'll hope he dies sooner since the movie is so lame. Beware, Carrey has very little screen time in spite of the advertising. 96m/C VHS, Closed Caption. Steve Oedekerk, Thomas F. Wilson, Fred Willard, Jim Carrey. PAR

High Tide 🎬🎬🎬 1987 (PG-13) A strong and strange drama once again coupling the star and director of "My Brilliant Career." A small-time rock 'n' roll singer who is stranded in a small, beach town fortuitously meets up with her previously-abandoned teenage daughter. Acclaimed. 120m/C VHS, Beta, LV, 8mm. AU Judy Davis, Jan Adele, Claudia Karvan, Colin Friels, John Clayton, Mark Hembrow, Frankie J. Holden, Monica Trapaga; **D:** Gillian Armstrong; **W:** Laura Jones; **C:** Russell Boyd; **M:** Peter Best, Ricky Fataar, Mark

Moffiatt. Australian Film Institute '87: Best Actress (Davis); National Society of Film Critics Awards '88: Best Actress (Davis). FCT, NLC

High Velocity 🎬½ 1976 (PG) Lame adventure about two mercenaries involved in the challenge of a lifetime—rescuing a kidnapped executive from Asian terrorists. Filmed in Manila. 105m/C VHS, Beta. Ben Gazzara, Paul Winfield, Britt Ekland, Keenan Wynn; **D:** Remi Kramer; **M:** Jerry Goldsmith. MED

High Voltage 🎬🎬 1929 A fast-moving comedy adventure set in the High Sierras. 62m/B VHS, Beta. Carole Lombard, William Boyd, Gwen Moore, Billy Bevan; **D:** Howard Higgin. NOS, MRV, BAR

Higher and Higher 🎬🎬 1944 Bankrupt aristocrat conspires with servants to regain his fortune, and tries to marry his daughter into money. Sinatra's first big-screen role. 🎵You Belong in a Love Song; A Most Important Affair; The Music Stopped; Today I'm A Debutante; A Lovely Way To Spend An Evening; I Couldn't Sleep a Wink Last Night; You're On Your Own; I Saw You First; Disgustingly Rich. 90m/B VHS, Beta, LV. Frank Sinatra, Leon Errol, Michele Morgan, Jack Haley, Mary McGuire; **D:** Tim Whelan. Nominations: Academy Awards '44: Best Song ("I Couldn't Sleep A Wink Last Night"), Original Dramatic/Comedy Score. CCB, IME, TTC

Higher Education 🎬🎬 1988 (R) Andy leaves his small town for a big city college and falls head over heels for a student and a teacher. He didn't know college could be so much fun. 83m/C VHS. Kevin Hicks, Isabelle Mejias, Lori Hallier, Maury Chaykin, Richard Monette; **D:** John Sheppard. VTR

Higher Learning 🎬🎬 1994 (R) Racism, idealism, and the struggle for identity converge in this stylistically shot but rarely enlightening commentary on campus life and strife, focusing on three very different freshmen at fictional Columbus University—a bright track star (Ebbs) who questions the exploitation of black student athletes; a sheltered, sexually confused beauty from the 'burbs (Swanson); and a goony, paranoid loner who falls in with a group of skinheads (Rapaport). Singleton's honorable intention—to make a movie that makes a difference—is marred by cardboard supporting characters, a penchant for in-your-face irony, and a predictable, simplistic conclusion.**CW:** Scenes of violence and sexuality; strong language. 127m/C VHS, LV, Closed Caption. Omar Epps, Kristy Swanson, Michael Rapaport, Laurence "Larry" Fishburne, Jennifer Connelly, Ice Cube, Tyra Banks, Jason Wiles, Cole Hauser, Regina King; **D:** John Singleton; **W:** John Singleton; **C:** Peter Collister. COL

The Highest Honor 🎬🎬½ 1984 (R) True story set during WWII of a friendship between an Australian army officer, captured while attempting to infiltrate Singapore, and a Japanese security officer. Too long, but gripping. 99m/C VHS, Beta, LV. AU John Howard, Atsuo Nakamura, Stuart Wilson, Michael Aitkens, Steve Bisley; **D:** Peter Maxwell. VTR

Highlander 🎬🎬🎬 1986 (R) A strange tale about an immortal 16th-century Scottish warrior who has had to battle his evil immortal enemy through the centuries. The feud comes to blows in modern-day Manhattan. Connery makes a memorable appearance as the good warrior's mentor. Spectacular battle and death scenes. A cult favorite which spawned a weak sequel and a television series. Based on a story by Gregory Widen. 110m/C VHS, Beta, LV, Closed Caption. Christopher Lambert, Sean Connery, Clancy Brown, Roxanne Hart, Beatie Edney, Alan North, Sheila Gish, Jon Polito; **D:** Russell Mulcahy; **W:** Gregory Widen, Peter Bellwood, Larry Ferguson; **M:** Michael Kamen. REP

Highlander 2: The Quickening 🎬½
Highlander 2: Renegade Version 1991 (R) The saga of Connor MacLeod and Juan Villa-Lobos continues in this sequel set in the year 2024. An energy shield designed to block out the sun's harmful ultraviolet rays has left planet Earth in perpetual darkness, but there is evidence that the ozone layer has repaired itself. An environmental terrorist and her group begin a sabotage effort and are

joined by MacLeod and Villa-Lobos in their quest to save Earth. Stunning visual effects don't make up for the lack of substance. The Renegade version is a director's cut, which has been reedited and contains some 19 additional minutes of footage.**CW:** Some language and strong violence. 90m/C VHS, LV, 8mm, Closed Caption. Christopher Lambert, Sean Connery, Virginia Madsen, Michael Ironside, John C. McGinley; **D:** Russell Mulcahy; **W:** Peter Bellwood; **C:** Phil Meheux; **M:** Stewart Copeland. REP

Highlander: The Final Dimension 🎬½ Highlander 3: The Magician; Highlander 3: The Sorcerer 1994 (R) Immortal Conner MacLeod (Lambert) battles master illusionist Kane (Van Peebles), who seeks to rule the world. Aiding MacLeod is Alex Smith (Unger), a research scientist who discovers Kane was once buried beneath a mystical mountain along with three other immortal warriors some 300 years before. MacLeod returns to his old Scottish stomping grounds to prepare for battle. Lots of action and special effects, really dumb storyline and overacting—even for a fantasy film. Original theatrical release was PG-13 and 94 minutes; the director's cut has been re-edited and footage added.**CW:** Strong adventure violence; language; some strong sexuality. 99m/C VHS, LV, Closed Caption. Christopher Lambert, Mario Van Peebles, Deborah Unger, Mako; **D:** Andrew Morahan; **W:** Paul Ohl; **M:** J. Peter Robinson. TOU

Highlander: The Gathering 🎬🎬½ 1993 (PG-13) Re-edited episodes from the syndicated TV series finds good immortals Connor MacLeod (Lambert) and distant relative Duncan (Paul) battling against an evil immortal (Moll as a particularly nasty villain) and a misguided human (Vanity). Lots of sword-play and a little bit of romance (courtesy of Vandernoot).**CW:** Swordfight violence and sex scene. 98m/C VHS. Christopher Lambert, Adrian Paul, Richard Moll, Vanity, Alexandra Vandernoot, Stan Kirsh; **D:** Thomas J. Wright, Ray Austin; **W:** Lorain Despres, Dan Gordon. HMD

Highpoint 🎬 1980 (PG) When an unemployed man becomes the chauffeur of a wealthy family, he finds himself in the middle of a mysterious murder and part of an international CIA plot. Hard to figure what's happening in this one. 91m/C VHS, Beta, LV. CA Richard Harris, Christopher Plummer, Beverly D'Angelo, Kate Reid, Saul Rubinek; **D:** Peter Carter. VTR

Highway Patrolman 🎬🎬 El Patrullero 1991 Young Pedro Rojas (Sosa) has just graduated from the National Highway Patrol Academy and he and best friend Anibal (Bichir) have been assigned to the isolated roads of northern Durango. He quickly learns that most of the people he stops for minor violations are too poor to pay for licenses and fines. What Pedro does get is a wife, Griselda (Gutierrez), who's soon complaining about Pedro's meager wages. Pedro's resistance to bribery begins to weaken and he becomes more depressed as his ideals are destroyed and his rage increases. Spanish with subtitles. 104m/C VHS. MX Roberto Sosa, Zaide Silvia Gutierrez, Bruno Bichir, Vanessa Bauche; **D:** Alex Cox; **W:** Lorenzo O'Brien; **C:** Miguel Garzon; **M:** Zander Schloss. NYF

Highway 61 🎬🎬 1991 (R) Shy barber Pokey Jones lives in the small Canadian town of Pickerel Falls and becomes a celebrity when he discovers the frozen corpse of an unknown young man in his backyard. Jackie Bangs, a rock roadie who's stolen her band's stash of drugs, finds herself stranded in the same small town. So begins a wild road trip. Lackluster direction undercuts much of the first-rate acting and amusing story quirks.**CW:** Language and one sensual scene. 110m/C VHS. Valerie Buhagiar, Don McKellar, Earl Pastko, Peter Breck, Art Bergmann; **D:** Bruce McDonald; **W:** Don McKellar. PAR, FCT

Highway 13 🎬½ 1948 When a trucker witnesses an "accidental" death at the loading warehouse, he falls under suspicion. He then sets out to clear his name. 60m/B VHS, Beta, LV. Robert Lowery, Pamela Blake, Lyle Talbot, Michael Whalen, Maris Wrixon, Clem Bevans; **D:** William (Lester Williams) Berke. *NO*

Highway to Hell 🎬🎬 1992 (R) Bergen plays the devil in a horror-comedy about going to hell—even if you're not dead yet. Lowe and Swanson are newlyweds on their way to Las Vegas when they're stopped by a "hellcop," who kidnaps the bride and takes her to the netherworld to be the devil's new plaything. Her human hubby doesn't take kindly to this and goes to hell to rescue his bride. Campy flick is played for laughs and has some good special effects. **CW:** Nudity and bizarre fantasy violence. 93m/C VHS, **Closed Caption.** Patrick Bergin, Adam Storke, Chad Lowe, Kristy Swanson, Richard Farnsworth, C.J. Graham, Lita Ford, Kevin Peter Hall, Pamela Gidley, Brian Helgeland; **Cameos:** Gilbert Gottfried; **D:** Ate De Jong. *HBO*

Hijazo de Mi Vidaza 🎬 *Son of My Life* 197? The history of a family as told by a mother to her son. In Spanish. 90m/C VHS, Beta. Enrique Cuenca, Eduardo Manzano, Maria Fernanda, Fernando Casanova. *MAD*

Hill Number One 1951 A dramatization of the story of Easter, featuring Dean in one of his first major roles as John the Baptist. Made for television. 57m/B VHS, Beta. James Dean, Michael Ansara, Leif Erickson, Ruth Hussey, Roddy McDowall. *RHI, FCT, HEG*

Hill Street Blues, Vol. 1: Hill Street Station 1981 Landmark police drama which effectively combined a large cast of characters with plots filled with humor and tragedy. Set in an urban ghetto of a large (unnamed) American city, the precinct was run by Capt. Frank Furillo (Travanti) and staffed with "let's be careful out there!" Sgt. Phil Esterhaus (Conrad), as well as a host of offbeat detectives and beat cops. The pilot episode introduced the characters and the characteristic mayhem. Additional episodes available. 50m/C VHS. Daniel J. Travanti, Veronica Hamel, Michael Conrad, Bruce Weitz, James B. Sikking, Joe Spano, Taurean Blacque, Kiel Martin, Rene Enriquez, Michael Warren, Charles Haid, Betty Thomas, Ed Marinaro, Barbara Babcock. *MOV, MTM*

Hill 24 Doesn't Answer 🎬🎬🎬 1955 Four Zionist soldiers defend a strategic entrance to Jerusalem. While at their posts, they reflect on their lives and devotion to the cause. Made in Israel, in English. The first Israeli feature film. 101m/B VHS, Beta. *IS* Edward Mulhare, Haya Harareet, Michael Wager; **D:** Thorold Dickinson. *ERG*

Hillbillies in a Haunted House woof! 1967 Two country and western singers en route to the Nashville jamboree encounter a group of foreign spies "haunting" a house. Features Rathbone's last film performance. Sequel to "Las Vegas Hillbillies" (1966). Giant step down for everyone involved. 88m/C VHS, Beta. Ferlin Husky, Joi Lansing, Don Bowman, John Carradine, Lon Chaney Jr., Basil Rathbone; **D:** Jean Yarbrough. *VCI, AOV*

Hillbilly Blitzkrieg 🎬 *Enemy Round-Up* 1942 Two soldiers are sent to the boonies to guard a top-secret missile site from enemy agents. Come-to-life comic strip characters Snuffy Smith, Barney Google and Spark Plug join in the antics. 63m/B VHS. Bud Duncan, Cliff Nazarro, Edgar Kennedy, Doris Linden, Lucien Littlefield, Alan Baldwin; **D:** Roy Mack. *NOS, RXM*

The Hills Have Eyes woof! 1977 (R) Desperate family battles for survival and vengeance against a brutal band of inbred hillbilly cannibals. Craven gore-fest followed by Hills II. 83m/C VHS, Beta, LV. Susan Lanier, Robert Houston, Martin Speer, Dee Wallace Stone, Russ Grieve, John Steadman, James Whitworth, Michael Berryman; **D:** Wes Craven; **W:** Wes Craven. *NO*

The Hills Have Eyes, Part 2 🎬 1984 Craven reprises Hills with Eyes number one to ill effect. Ignorant teens disregard warnings of a "Hills Have Eyes" refugee, and go stomping into the grim reaper's proving grounds. Predictably bad things happen. 86m/C VHS, Beta. Michael Berryman, Kevin Blair, John Bloom, Janus Blythe, John Laughlin, Tamara Stafford; **D:** Wes Craven; **W:** Wes Craven. *REP*

The Hills of Home 🎬🎬🎬 *Master of Lassie* 1948 (G) Warm sentimental tale about a Scottish doctor and his beloved pet collie. One of the better films in the "Lassie" series. 97m/C VHS. Edmund Gwenn, Donald Crisp, Tom Drake, Janet Leigh; **D:** Fred M. Wilcox; **W:** William Ludwig. *MGM, FCT*

Hills of Oklahoma 🎬🎬 1950 Allen stars as the leader of a cattlemen's association who decides not to deal with dishonest meatpacker Keane, so he drives his herd across the desert to a slaughterhouse run by an honest businesswoman. Based on an original story by Cooper. 67m/B VHS. Rex Allen, Elisabeth Fraser, Elisabeth Risdon, Fuzzy Knight, Roscoe Ates, Robert Emmett Keane, Trevor Bardette; **D:** R.G. Springsteen; **W:** Olive Cooper, Victor Arthur. *MOV*

Hills of Utah 🎬½ 1951 Autry finds himself in the middle of a feud between the local mine operator and a group of cattlemen, while searching for his father's murderer. 70m/B VHS, Beta. Gene Autry, Pat Buttram, Denver Pyle; **D:** John English. *CCB*

The Hillside Strangler 🎬½ *The Case of the Hillside Stranglers* 1989 Made-for-television, crime-of-the-week drama about the investigation to apprehend the serial killer responsible for 10 deaths in 1977-78. 91m/C VHS, Beta. Richard Crenna, Dennis Farina, Billy Zane, Tony Plana, James Tolkan, Tasia Valenza; **D:** Steven Gethers. *FRH*

Himatsuri 🎬🎬🎬 *Fire Festival* 1985 An acclaimed film detailing the conflicts between man and nature, as a lumberjack in a Japanese forest believes he's the protector of the mountains through his divine relationship with the ancient gods. Outraged by the destruction, pollution, and commercial exploitation of the land he turns to violence. In Japanese with English subtitles. 120m/C VHS, Beta. *JP* Kinya Kitaoji, Kwako Taichi, Ryota Nakamoto, Norihei Miki; **D:** Mitsuo Yanagimachi; **W:** Kenji Nakagami; **M:** Toru Takemitsu. *ORI, WAR, AUD*

The Hindenburg 🎬🎬 1975 (PG) A dramatization of what might have happened on the fateful night the Hindenburg exploded. Scott plays an investigator who is aware that something is up, and has numerous suspects to interrogate. The laser edition features wide-screen format, digital Stereo Surround, the original trailer and chapter stops. 126m/C VHS, Beta, LV, Closed Caption. George C. Scott, Anne Bancroft, William Atherton, Roy Thinnes, Gig Young, Burgess Meredith, Charles Durning, Richard Dysart; **D:** Robert Wise; **C:** Robert L. Surtees; **M:** David Shire. Academy Awards '75: Best Sound Effects Editing, Best Visual Effects; Nominations: Academy Awards '75: Best Art Direction/Set Decoration, Best Cinematography, Best Sound. *USH*

Hips, Hips, Hooray 🎬🎬½ 1934 Two supposed "hot shot" salesmen are hired by a cosmetic company to sell flavored lipstick. This lavish musical comedy is one of Wheeler and Woolsey's best vehicles. ♪Tired of It All; Keep Romance Alive; Keep On Doin' What You're Doin'. 68m/B VHS, Beta, LV. Robert Woolsey, Bert Wheeler, Ruth Etting, Thelma Todd, Dorothy Lee; **D:** Mark Sandrich. *CCB*

Hired Hand 🎬🎬½ 1971 Two drifters settle on a farm belonging to one of their wives, only to leave again seeking to avenge the murder of a friend. TV prints include Larry Hagman in a cameo role. 93m/C VHS, Beta. Peter Fonda, Warren Oates, Verna Bloom, Severn Darden, Robert Pratt; **Cameos:** Larry Hagman; **D:** Peter Fonda. *BAR*

Hired to Kill 🎬½ *The Italian Connection* 1973 (R) A pair of Mafia hoods plot against each other over a $6 million drug shipment. 90m/C Beta. Henry Silva, Woody Strode, Adolfo Celi, Mario Adorf. *NO*

Hired to Kill 🎬½ 1991 (R) The granite-hewn Thompson plays a male-chauvinist commando grudgingly leading a squad of beautiful mercenary-ettes on an international rescue mission. Not as bad as it sounds (mainly because the ladies aren't complete bimbos), but between senseless plotting, gratuitous catfights, and a love scene indistinguishable from rape, the Hound found plenty to dislike. 91m/C VHS, Beta, Closed Caption. Brian Thompson, George Kennedy, Jose Ferrer, Oliver Reed, Penelope Reed, Michelle Moffett, Barbara Lee Alexander, Jordanna Capra; **D:** Nico Mastorakis, Peter Rader; **W:** Nico Mastorakis. *PAR*

Hiroshima 🎬🎬🎬 1995 (PG) Haunting depiction recreates the circumstances surrounding the dropping of the first atomic bomb in 1945. Juxtaposes scenes between the U.S., Japan, and their leaders—President Truman (Welsh) and Emperor Hirohito (Umewaka)—with the development of the Manhattan Project, the bombing itself, and its consequences. Filmed primarily in B&W, with newsreel and contemporary witness interviews in color; Japanese sequences are subtitled in English. Filmed on location in Montreal, PQ, and Tokyo, Japan; made for cable TV. 180m/C VHS. *JP CA* Kenneth Welsh, Naohiko Umewaka, Wesley Addy, Richard Masur, Hisashi Igawa, Ken Jenkins, Jeffrey DeMunn, Leon Pownall, Saul Rubinek, Timothy West, Koji Takahashi, Kazuo Kato; **D:** Roger Spottiswoode, Koreyoshi Kurahara; **W:** John Hopkins, Toshiro Ishido; **C:** Pierre Mignot, Shohei Ando. *HMK*

Hiroshima Maiden 1988 An American family gains new perspective when they meet a young survivor of the atomic bomb. Based on true stories of Japanese women who stayed with Americans while undergoing surgery to minimize their scars. Originally aired on PBS as part of the "Wonderworks" family movie series. 58m/C VHS. Susan Blakely, Richard Masur, Tamlyn Tomita; **D:** Joan Darling. *PME, WNE, HMV*

Hiroshima, Mon Amour 🎬🎬🎬🎬 1959 A profoundly moving drama exploring the shadow of history over the personal lives of a lonely French actress living in Tokyo and a Japanese architect with whom she's having an affair. Presented in a complex network of flashbacks. Highly influential; adapted by Marguerite Duras from her book. In Japanese with English subtitles. 88m/B VHS, Beta, 8mm. *JP FR* Emmanuelle Riva, Eiji Okada, Bernard Fresson, Stella Dassas, Pierre Barbaud; **D:** Alain Resnais; **W:** Marguerite Duras; **C:** Sacha Vierny; **M:** Georges Delerue, Giovanni Fusco. National Board of Review Awards '60: 5 Best Foreign Films of the Year; New York Film Critics Awards '60: Best Foreign Film; Nominations: Academy Awards '60: Best Story & Screenplay. *VYY, MRV, HHT*

Hiroshima: Out of the Ashes 🎬🎬🎬 1990 (PG) The terrible aftermath of the bombing of Hiroshima, August, 1945, as seen through the eyes of American and Japanese soldiers, the Japanese people, and a priest. Carefully detailed and realistic, creates an amazing emotional response. Don't miss the scene in which Nelson and his buddy find themselves surrounded by Japanese—the enemy—only to realize that their "captors" have been blinded by the blast. Created as an homage for the 45th anniversary of the bombing. 98m/C VHS. Max von Sydow, Judd Nelson, Mako, Tamlyn Tomita, Stan Egi, Sab Shimono, Noriyuki "Pat" Morita, Kim Miyori; **D:** Peter Werner. *THV*

His Brother's Ghost 🎬🎬 1945 When Fuzzy is rubbed out by bandits, Billy Carson (no longer called Billy the Kid thanks to mothers' protestations) convinces his twin brother to impersonate him in order to make the bandits believe they are the victims of hocus pocus from the otherworld. Crabbe—who dressed noir before it was chic—made this during his post sci-fi western period, when he slugged it through some fifty lowrent oaters (usually under the direction of Newfield at PRC studios). 54m/C VHS. Buster Crabbe, Al "Fuzzy" St. John, Charles "Blackie" King, Bud Osborne,

Karl Hackett, Archie Hall; **D:** Sam Newfield. *NOS, MRV, HEG*

His Butler's Sister ✓✓ **1944** Bachelor composer Charles Gerard (Tone) lives a sybarite's life in his Manhattan penthouse, which is run by his butler Martin Murphy (O'Brien). When Murphy's stepsister Ann Carter (Durbin) arrives unexpectedly, she's delighted to hear who Murphy works for because she's a singer and wants an audition—an absolute taboo in Gerard's household. So she fools him into thinking she's the new maid until she can get her big break. Nothing new but Durbin does get to work her pretty pipes. ♫Nessun Dorma; In the Spirit of the Moment; When You're Away; Is It True What They Say About Dixie?. **87m/B VHS, Closed Caption.** Deanna Durbin, Franchot Tone, Pat O'Brien, Evelyn Ankers, Akim Tamiroff, Alan Mowbray, Frank Jenks, Walter Catlett, Hans Conried, Florence Bates, Roscoe Karns, Franklin Pangborn; **D:** Frank Borzage; **W:** Samuel Hoffenstein, Bety Reinhardt; **C:** Woody Bredell; **M:** Hans J. Salter. Nominations: Academy Awards '44: Best Sound. *USH*

His Double Life ✓✓½ **1933** When a shy gentleman's valet dies, his master assumes the dead man's identity and has a grand time. From the play "Buried Alive" by Arnold Bennett. Remade in 1943 as "Holy Matrimony." **67m/B VHS, Beta.** Roland Young, Lillian Gish, Montagu Love; **D:** Arthur Hopkins. *NOS, MRV, BAR*

His Fighting Blood ✓½ **1935** Northwest Mounties in action. Based on a James Oliver Curwood story. **63m/B VHS, Beta.** Kermit Maynard. *VDM*

His First Command ✓½ **1929** An early talkie wherein a playboy falls in love with the daughter of a cavalry officer, and enlists in order to win her affections. **60m/B VHS, Beta, 8mm.** William Boyd, Dorothy Sebastian, Gavin Gordon; **D:** Gregory La Cava. *VYY*

His First Flame ✓✓✓ **1926** A classic Langdon silent romantic comedy. **62m/B VHS, Beta.** Harry Langdon, Vernon Dent, Natalie Kingston; **W:** Frank Capra. *NOS, VYY, GPV*

His Girl Friday ✓✓✓✓ **1940** Classic, unrelentingly hilarious war-between-the-sexes comedy in which a reporter and her ex-husband editor help a condemned man escape the law—while at the same time furthering their own ends as they try to get the big scoop on political corruption in the town. One of Hawks's most furious and inventive screen combats in which women are given uniquely equal (for Hollywood) footing, with staccato dialogue and wonderful performances. Based on the Hecht-MacArthur play "The Front Page," which was originally filmed in 1931. Remade again in 1974 as "The Front Page," and in 1988 as "Switching Channels." Also available colorized. **92m/B VHS, Beta.** Cary Grant, Rosalind Russell, Ralph Bellamy, Gene Lockhart, John Qualen, Porter Hall, Roscoe Karns, Abner Biberman, Cliff Edwards, Billy Gilbert, Helen Mack, Ernest Truex, Clarence Kolb, Frank Jenks; **D:** Howard Hawks; **W:** Charles Lederer; **M:** Morris Stoloff. *CNG, MRV, NOS*

His Kind of Woman ✓✓✓ **1951** A fall guy, being used to bring a racketeer back to the U.S. from Mexico, discovers the plan and tries to halt it. **120m/B VHS, Beta.** Robert Mitchum, Jane Russell, Vincent Price, Tim Holt, Charles McGraw, Raymond Burr, Jim Backus; **D:** John Farrow. *NO*

His Majesty O'Keefe ✓✓½ **1953** Lancaster stars as a South Seas swashbuckler dealing in the lucrative coconut-oil trade of the mid-1800s. The natives see him as a god and allow him to marry a beautiful maiden. When his reign is threatened by unscrupulous traders, Lancaster springs into action to safeguard his kingdom. Based on a real-life American adventurer, this was the first movie ever filmed in the Fiji Islands. **92m/C VHS, Beta, LV.** Burt Lancaster, Joan Rice, Benson Fong, Philip Ahn; Grant Taylor; **D:** Byron Haskin. *WAR*

His Majesty, the American ✓✓½ **1919** William Brooks (Fairbanks) is a young man whose heritage is unknown to him. It turns out he's an heir to a small European kingdom. When Brooks arrives in Alaine he discovers the war minister is trying to overthrow the present king. With his usual dash, our hero saves the day and also wins the hand of a beautiful princess. First picture released by United Artists studios, formed by Fairbanks, Mary Pickford, Charles Chaplin, and D.W. Griffith. **100m/B VHS.** Douglas Fairbanks Sr., Marjorie Daw, Lillian Langdon, Frank Campeau; **D:** Joseph Henabery. *GPV, GVV*

His Majesty, the Scarecrow of Oz/ The Magic Cloak of Oz ✓✓½ **1914** The creator of the Oz stories, L. Frank Baum, wrote, produced and directed these two stories himself, with all the characters from his best-selling children's books. **80m/B VHS, Beta.** **D:** L. Frank Baum. *GVV*

His Name was King woof! **1985** A man goes after the gang who murdered his brother and raped his young wife in the old West. **90m/C VHS, Beta.** *IT* Richard Harrison, Klaus Kinski, Anne Puskin; **D:** Don Reynolds. *NO*

His Picture in the Papers ✓✓ **1916** An early silent comedy wherein the robust, red-meat-eating son of a health food tycoon must get his father's permission to marry by getting his picture favorably in the paper for advertising's sake. **68m/B VHS, Beta, 8mm.** Douglas Fairbanks Sr., Clarence Handysides, Rene Boucicault, Jean Temple, Charles Butler, Homer Hunt, Loretta Blake, Helena Ruppert; **D:** John Emerson; **W:** John Emerson, Anita Loos. *NOS, VYY, GPV*

His Prehistoric Past/The Bank **1915** Two of Chaplin's classic early shorts. **54m/B VHS, Beta.** Charlie Chaplin, Mack Swain, Edna Purviance; **D:** Charlie Chaplin. *VYY, GVV*

His Private Secretary ✓½ **1933** Wayne plays the jet-setting son of a wealthy businessman who wants his boy to settle down. And he does - after he meets the minister's beautiful daughter. **68m/B VHS, Beta.** John Wayne, Evalyn Knapp, Alec B. Francis, Reginald Barlow, Natalie Kingston, Arthur Hoyt, Al "Fuzzy" St. John; **D:** Philip H. Whitman. *DVT, HEG*

His Royal Slyness/Haunted Spooks **1920** Two Harold Lloyd shorts. "His Royal Slyness" (1919) offers Harold impersonating the king of a small kingdom, while in "Haunted Spooks" (1920), Harold gets suckered into living in a haunted mansion. Both films include music score. **52m/B VHS, Beta.** Harold Lloyd; **D:** Harold Lloyd. *VYY, CCB, GVV*

His Wife's Lover ✓✓✓ *Zayn Vaybs Lubovnik* **1931** An actor disguised as an old man wins the heart of a lovely young woman. He decides to test her fidelity by reverting to his handsome young self and attempting to seduce her. An enchanting comedy in Yiddish with English subtitles. **77m/B VHS, Beta.** Ludwig Satz, Michael Rosenberg, Isadore Cashier, Lucy Levine; **D:** Sidney Goldin. *ERG, FCT*

History is Made at Night ✓✓✓ **1937** A wife seeks a divorce from a jealous husband while on an Atlantic cruise; she ends up finding both true love and heartbreak in this story of a love triangle at sea. **98m/B VHS, Beta, LV.** Charles Boyer, Jean Arthur, Leo Carrillo, Colin Clive; **D:** Frank Borzage; **C:** Gregg Toland. *WAR, FCT*

History of the World: Part 1 ✓✓ **1981 (R)** More misses than hits in this Brooks' parody of historic epics. A bluntly satiric vision of human evolution, from the Dawn of Man to the French Revolution told in an episodic fashion. Good for a few laughs. **90m/C VHS, Beta, LV, Closed Caption.** Mel Brooks, Dom DeLuise, Madeline Kahn, Harvey Korman, Cloris Leachman, Gregory Hines, Pamela Stephenson, Paul Mazursky, Beatrice Arthur, Fritz Feld, John Hurt, Jack Carter, John Hillerman, John Gavin, Barry Levinson, Ron Carey, Howard Morris, Sid Caesar, Jackie Mason; **D:** Mel Brooks; **W:** Mel Brooks. *FOX*

The History of White People in America **1985** A pseudo-documentary look at the complicated life of a white midwestern family. Succeeds in making hilarious fun of many traditional prejudices. Originally made for cable television. **48m/C VHS, Beta.** Martin Mull, Fred Willard, Mary Kay Place, Teri Garr, Bob Eubanks; **D:** Harry Shearer. *USH*

The History of White People in America: Vol. 2 **1985** Martin Mull's television-special comedy satirizing WASP society in America. **40m/C VHS, Beta.** Martin Mull; **D:** Harry Shearer. *USH*

Hit! ✓✓ **1973 (R)** When the 15-year-old daughter of a government agent dies of a drug overdose, he deals his revenge to top French heroin traffickers. **135m/C VHS, Closed Caption.** Billy Dee Williams, Richard Pryor, Gwen Welles, Paul Hampton, Warren Kemmerling, Sid Melton; **D:** Sidney J. Furie; **W:** Alan R. Trustman, David M. Wolf; **M:** Lalo Schifrin. *PAR*

The Hit ✓✓½ **1985 (R)** A feisty young hooker gets mixed-up with two strong-armed hired killers as they escort an unusual stool-pigeon from his exile in Spain to their angry mob bosses. Minor cult-noir from the director of "My Beautiful Launderette" and "Dangerous Liaisons." **105m/C VHS, Beta, LV.** *GB* Terence Stamp, John Hurt, Laura Del Sol, Tim Roth, Fernando Rey, Bill Hunter; **D:** Stephen Frears; **W:** Peter Prince; **C:** John A. Alonzo; **M:** Eric Clapton. *NLC*

Hit & Run ✓ *Revenge Squad* **1982** David Marks, a Manhattan cab driver, is haunted by recurring flashbacks of a freak hit-and-run accident in which his wife was struck down on a city street. **96m/C VHS, Beta.** Paul Perri, Claudia Cron; **D:** Charles Braverman; **M:** Brad Fiedel. *NO*

Hit Lady ✓✓ **1974** An elegant cultured woman becomes a hit lady for the syndicate in this predictable, yet slick gangster movie. Made for television. **74m/C VHS, Beta.** Yvette Mimieux, Dack Rambo, Clu Gulager, Keenan Wynn; **D:** Tracy Keenan Wynn. *PSM*

The Hit List ✓✓ **1988 (R)** A regular guy fights back brutally when his wife and child are mistakenly kidnapped by the Mafia. Fast-paced action makes up for thin plot. **87m/C VHS, Beta, LV.** Jan-Michael Vincent, Leo Rossi, Lance Henriksen, Charles Napier, Rip Torn; **D:** William Lustig; **W:** Peter Brosnan. *COL*

The Hit List ✓✓½ **1993 (R)** Charles Pike (Fahey) is a professional hitman working for attorney Peter Mayhew (Coburn) to wipe out drug lords. Then Mayhew gives Pike a new assignment. He introduces him to sexy widow Jordan Henning (Butler), who wants Pike to kill the man who murdered her husband. Pike finds himself mixing business with pleasure in a deadly combination that sees him dodging crooked cops and trained assassins. **97m/C VHS, LV, Closed Caption.** Jeff Fahey, Yancy Butler, James Coburn; **D:** William Webb; **W:** Reed Steiner. *COL*

The Hit Man ✓✓ *Il Sicario* **1961** A crime drama that profiles the crisis of a man unfit to commit murder but who does for a price. **100m/B VHS, Beta.** *CIG*

Hit Men ✓½ **1973** Double crosses and gun battles highlight this tale of inner-city crime. **90m/C VHS, Beta.** Henry Silva, Mario Adorf, Woody Strode, Adolfo Celi. *VDC*

Hit the Deck ✓½ **1955** Second-rate studio musical about sailors on leave and looking for romance. Based on the 1927 Broadway musical. ♫Sometimes I'm Happy; Hallelujah; Why, Oh Why; Keeping Myself For You; More Than You Know; I Know That You Know; Lucky Bird. **112m/C VHS, Beta, LV.** Jane Powell, Tony Martin, Debbie Reynolds, Walter Pidgeon, Vic Damone, Gene Raymond, Ann Miller, Russ Tamblyn, J. Carrol Naish, Kay Armen, Richard Anderson; **D:** Roy Rowland; **M:** Vincent Youmans. *MGM*

Hit the Dutchman ✓ **1992 (R)** Routine gangster flick about Dutch Schultz trying to rise to the top of the New York crime community—with or without the help of underworld pals Legs Diamond and Lucky Luciano. An unrated version is also available. **CW:** Language, gangster violence, and sexuality. **116m/C VHS, Closed Caption.** Bruce Nozick, Sally Kirkland, Will Kempe; **D:** Menahem Golan. *THV*

Hit the Ice 🎬🎬 1943 Newspaper photographers Bud and Lou are mistaken as gangsters in Chicago and the usual complications ensue. Includes an appearance by Johnny Long & His Orchestra. ♫I'm Like A Fish Out Of Water; Happiness Bound; I'd Like to Set You to Music; Slap Polka. **89m/C VHS, Beta.** Bud Abbott, Lou Costello, Patric Knowles, Elyse Knox, Ginny Simms; **D:** Charles Lamont. *USH*

Hit the Saddle 🎬🎬 1937 The Three Mesquiteers track down a gang involved in capturing wild horses in protected areas although one of three is more interested in the charms of a dance hall girl (played by starlet Rita Cansino who would soon become Rita Hayworth). **54m/B VHS, Beta.** Bob Livingston, Ray Corrigan, Max Terhune, J.P. McGowan, Yakima Canutt, Rita Hayworth; **D:** Mack V. Wright. *NOS, VCN, REP*

Hit Woman: The Double Edge 🎬🎬½ 1993 (R) Lucci plays a dual role as an FBI agent and the look-alike killer-for-hire that she's tracking. Originally made for television, the video version contains additional footage that earned the "R" rating. **92m/C VHS.** Susan Lucci, Robert Urich, Michael Woods, Robert Prosky. *APX*

The Hitch-Hiker 🎬🎬🎬 1953 Two young men off on the vacation of their dreams pick up a psychopathic hitchhiker with a right eye that never closes, even when he sleeps. Taut suspense makes this flick worth seeing. **71m/B VHS.** Edmond O'Brien, Frank Lovejoy, William Talman, Jose Torvay; **D:** Ida Lupino. *SNC*

The Hitcher 🎬🎬½ 1986 (R) A young man picks up a hitchhiker on a deserted stretch of California highway only to be tormented by the man's repeated appearances: is he real or a figment of his imagination? Ferociously funny, sadomasochistic comedy with graphic violence. **98m/C VHS, Beta, LV, Closed Caption.** Rutger Hauer, C. Thomas Howell, Jennifer Jason Leigh, Jeffrey DeMunn, John M. Jackson; **D:** Robert Harmon; **W:** Eric Red; **M:** Mark Isham. *NO*

The Hitchhiker 1985 HBO's chilling horror anthology series contains a trio of terrifying tales. Additional episodes are available. In this first collection, Hamlin stars in "The Curse," about Yuppie occult vengeance; "W.G.O.D.," finds Busey and Page caught up in radio religion; and "Hired Help," finds Black with a less than human handyman. **90m/C VHS, Beta, LV.** Harry Hamlin, Gary Busey, Geraldine Page, Karen Black. *WAR, MOV*

Hitchhiker 2 1985 Three more episodes from HBO's horror series: "Dead Man's Curve," "Nightshift," and "Last Scene." **90m/C VHS, Beta, LV.** Peter Coyote, Margot Kidder, Darren McGavin, Susan Anspach. *WAR*

Hitchhiker 3 1987 Three episodes from the anthology mystery series: "Ghost Writer," "And If We Dream," and "True Believer." Made-for-cable television. **90m/C VHS, Beta, LV.** Ornella Muti, Willem Dafoe, Barry Bostwick, Dayle Haddon, Stephen Collins, Robert Weiss, Tom Skerritt. *ORI, WAR*

Hitchhiker 4 1987 Three episodes of the cable-television suspense series: "Man's Best Friend," about a lonely man whose pet dog tears his enemies to bits. "Face to Face," about the revenge exacted upon a drug-abusing cosmetic surgeon after he mucks up an operation; and "Videodate," about a guy being lured into a sinister video performance piece via his use of video dating services. **90m/C VHS, Beta, LV.** Michael O'Keefe, Sybil Danning, Sonja Smits, Robert Vaughn, Shannon Tweed, Greg Henry. *ORI, WAR*

Hitchhikers woof! 1972 (R) Trash film about a bunch of scantily clad female hitchhikers who rob the motorists who stop to pick them up. Keep right on going when you spot this roadkill. **90m/C VHS, Beta.** Misty Rowe, Norman Klar, Linda Avery; **D:** Ferd Sebastian. *NO*

The Hitchhiker's Guide to the Galaxy 1981 The six episode BBC television adaptation of Douglas Adams' hilarious science-fiction books. Features the intergalactic Ford Prefect, sent to Earth to update its planetary listing in the Hitchhiker's Guide; hapless hero Arthur Dent, a typical Englishman caught up in space mayhem; and an odd assortment of aliens, including Marvin the Paranoid Android. The show's sheer cheesiness is part of the charm. Available in both single-cassette and double-cassette versions, the latter includes a copy of the book and a dedication from Adams. **194m/C VHS, LV.** *GB* Simon Jones, David Dixon, Sandra Dickinson, Mark Wing-Davey; **D:** Alan Bell. *FOX, MOV, FUS*

Hitler 🎬🎬½ *Women of Nazi Germany* 1962 The true story of the infamous Nazi dictator's rise to power and his historic downfall. **103m/B VHS, Beta.** Richard Basehart, Maria Emo, Cordula Trantow; **D:** Stuart Heisler. *FOX*

Hitler: Dead or Alive 🎬🎬 1943 Three ex-cons devise a scheme to gain a million-dollar reward for capturing Adolf Hitler in this low-budget production. **64m/B VHS, Beta.** Ward Bond, Dorothy Tree, Bruce Edwards, Warren Hymer, Paul Fix, Russell Hicks, Bobby Watson; **D:** Nick Grinde. *NOS, MRV, DVT*

Hitler: The Last Ten Days 🎬🎬 1973 (PG) Based on an eyewitness account, the story of Hitler's last days in an underground bunker gives insight to his madness. **106m/C VHS, Beta.** Alec Guinness, Simon Ward, Adolfo Celi; **D:** Ennio de Concini. *PAR, GLV*

Hitler's Children 🎬🎬🎬 1943 Two young people, a German boy and an American girl, are caught in the horror of Nazi Germany. He's attracted to Hitler's rant, she's repelled. Exploitative yet engrossing. **83m/B VHS, Beta.** Tim Holt, Bonita Granville, Otto Kruger, H.B. Warner, Irving Reis, Hans Conried, Lloyd Corrigan; **D:** Edward Dmytryk. *MED, IHF*

Hitler's Daughter 🎬 1990 (R) Made for TV movie following the trials and tribulations of the illegitimate daughter of Adolf Hitler. She's all grown up now...and wants to rule the United States. She secures a position of power during an election and now Nazi-hunters must figure out her identity before she takes over the world! **88m/C VHS, Beta, Closed Caption.** Kay Lenz, Veronica Cartwright, Melody Anderson, Patrick Cassidy, Carolyn Dunn, Lindsay Merrithew, George R. Robertson; **D:** James A. Contner. *PAR*

The Hitman 🎬🎬 1991 (R) Norris plays a cop undercover as a syndicate hit man in Seattle, where he cleans up crime by triggering a three-way mob bloodbath between beastly Italian mafiosi, snooty French-Canadian hoods, and fanatical Iranian scum. But he teaches a black kid martial arts, so you know he's politically correct. Action addicts will give this a passing grade; all others need not apply.**CW:** Language and strong gangster violence. **95m/C VHS, LV, 8mm, Closed Caption.** Chuck Norris, Michael Parks, Al Waxman, Alberta Watson, Salim Grant, Ken Pogue, Marcel Sabourin, Bruno Gerussi, Frank Ferrucci; **D:** Aaron Norris; **C:** Joao Fernandes. *CAN, WAR*

The Hitter 🎬🎬 1979 (R) A former prizefighter, his girlfriend, and a washed-up promoter are all on the run in this adventure tale. **94m/C VHS.** Ron O'Neal, Adolph Caesar, Sheila Frazier; **D:** Christopher Leitch. *NO*

Hittin' the Trail 🎬 1937 The Good Cowboy is mistaken for a murdering varmint, and must prove his innocence. **57m/B VHS, Beta.** Tex Ritter, Charles "Blackie" King, Ray Whitley, The Range Ramblers; **D:** Robert North Bradbury. *NOS, VDM*

Hitz 🎬½ 1992 (R) In a Los Angeles barrio, Musico, a Loco gang member, kills two rival gang members. Arrested and convicted when a young boy named Pepe is coerced into testifying against him, Musico is killed in the courtroom. But the violence doesn't stop. The judge, who wants to reform the juvenile court system, tries to protect Pepe, and both are targeted for death by the Loco

gang. **90m/C VHS, Closed Caption.** Elliott Gould, Emilia Crow, Karen Black, Cuba Gooding Jr. *THV*

The Hobbit 🎬🎬🎬 1978 An animated interpretation of J.R.R. Tolkien's novel of the same name. The story follows Bilbo Baggins and his journeys in Middle Earth and encounters with the creatures who inhabit it. He joins comrades to battle against evil beings and creatures. Made for television. **76m/C VHS, Beta, 8mm. D:** Arthur Rankin Jr., Jules Bass; **V:** Orson Bean, John Huston, Otto Preminger, Richard Boone. *WAR, CHI, FCT*

Hobgoblins 🎬 1987 Little creatures escape from a studio vault and wreak havoc. **92m/C VHS, Beta.** Jeffrey Culver, Tom Bartlett; **D:** Rick Sloane. *TWE*

The Hoboken Chicken Emergency 1984 Arthur's supposed to pick up a turkey for the family Thanksgiving dinner. Instead he returns with a 266-pound live chicken named Henrietta. Originally aired on PBS as part of the "Wonderworks" series. **55m/C VHS.** Dick Van Patten, Peter Billingsley, Gabe Kaplan, Arlene Golonka; **D:** Peter Baldwin. *PME, FCT, BTV*

Hobo's Christmas 🎬🎬 1987 A man who left his family to become a hobo comes home for Christmas 25 years later. Hughes turns in a delightful performance as the hobo in this made for television special. **94m/C VHS, Beta.** Barnard Hughes, William Hickey, Gerald McRaney, Wendy Crewson; **D:** Will MacKenzie. *NO*

Hobson's Choice 🎬🎬🎬 1953 A prosperous businessman in the 1890s tries to keep his daughter from marrying, but the strong-willed daughter has other ideas. Remade for television in 1983. **107m/B VHS, Beta, LV.** *GB* Charles Laughton, John Mills, Brenda de Banzie; **D:** David Lean; **C:** Jack Hildyard; **M:** Malcolm Arnold. British Academy Awards '54: Best Film. *ING, NLC, HMV*

Hobson's Choice 🎬🎬 1983 Made-for-television remake of the old family comedy about a crusty, penny-pinching businessman whose headstrong daughter proves to him she'll not become an old maid. Instead she marries one of his employees. Not bad, but not as good as the original. **95m/C VHS, Beta, Closed Caption.** Jack Warden, Sharon Gless, Richard Thomas, Lillian Gish; **D:** Gilbert Cates. *FOX*

Hockey Night 🎬🎬½ 1984 A movie for pre-and early teens in which a girl goalie makes the boys' hockey team. **77m/C VHS, Beta.** *CA* Megan Follows, Rick Moranis, Gail Youngs, Martin Harburg, Henry Ramer; **D:** Paul Shapiro. *FHE*

Hocus Pocus 🎬🎬½ 1993 (PG) The divine Miss M is back, but this time she's not so sweet. Midler, Najimy, and Parker are 17th century witches accidentally conjured up in the 20th century, appropriately enough on Halloween in Salem, Massachusetts. Seems they were hung 300 years back and they take their revenge in some surprisingly gruesome ways, given the Disney label. They rant, they rave, they sing (only once), they fly. See this one for the three stars who make up for the lack of substance with their comedic talents. **95m/C VHS, Beta, LV, Closed Caption.** Bette Midler, Kathy Najimy, Sarah Jessica Parker, Thora Birch, Doug Jones, Omri Katz, Vinessa Shaw, Stephanie Faracy, Charles Rocket; **Cameos:** Penny Marshall, Garry Marshall; **D:** Kenny Ortega; **W:** Neil Cuthbert, Mick Garris; **M:** John Debney. *DIS, BTV*

Hoffa 🎬🎬🎬 1992 (R) The story of union organizer James R. Hoffa who oversaw the rise of the Teamsters, a labor union composed mostly of truck drivers, from its fledgling infancy during the Great Depression to a membership of 2 million by the 1970's. Powerful performances by Nicholson in the title role and DeVito, who plays a union aide, a fictitious composite of several men who actually served Hoffa. This almost affectionate biographical treatment stands out in contrast from a career bristling with tension and violence. Proceeds through a series of flashbacks from the day Hoffa disappeared, July 30, 1975.**CW:** Strong language and violence. **140m/C VHS, LV, Closed**

Caption. Jack Nicholson, Danny DeVito, Armand Assante, J.T. Walsh, Frank Whaley, Kevin Anderson, John P. Ryan, Robert Prosky, Natalija Nogulich, Nicholas Pryor, John C. Reilly, Karen Young, Cliff Gorman; **D:** Danny DeVito; **W:** David Mamet; **C:** Stephen Burum; **M:** David Newman. Nominations: Academy Awards '92: Best Cinematography, Best Makeup. *FXV*

Hog Wild 🐾½ **1980 (PG)** A clique of high school nerds exact revenge on bullies from the local mean motorcycle gang, and a girl is torn between the two factions. **97m/C VHS, Beta.** *CA* Patti D'Arbanville, Tony Rosato, Michael Biehn; **D:** Les Rose. *NLC*

The Holcroft Covenant 🐾🐾 **1985 (R)** Based upon the complex Robert Ludlum novel. Details the efforts of a man trying to release a secret fund that his Nazi father humanistically set up to relieve the future sufferings of Holocaust survivors. Confusing, and slow, but interesting, nonetheless. **112m/C VHS, Beta, LV, Closed Caption.** *GB* Michael Caine, Victoria Tennant, Anthony Andrews, Lilli Palmer, Mario Adorf, Michael Lonsdale; **D:** John Frankenheimer; **W:** Edward Anhalt, John Hopkins, George Axelrod. *MGM*

Hold 'Em Jail 🐾🐾½ **1932** Some good laughs with Wheeler and Woolsey starting a competitive football team at Kennedy's Bidemore Prison. **65m/B VHS, Beta.** Bert Wheeler, Robert Woolsey, Edgar Kennedy, Betty Grable, Edna May Oliver; **D:** Norman Taurog. *CCB*

Hold Me, Thrill Me, Kiss Me 🐾🐾½ **1993 (R)** "Offbeat" barely begins to describe this comedy about a hapless loser who finds true love. Eli (Parrish) has escaped marriage to a rich girl named Twinkle (Young), unfortunately it took a little shooting to do it and now Eli's hiding out in a tacky pink trailer park where Sabra (Naschak), an insatiable stripper with a fondness for sex toys, immediately goes after Eli's bod. But he falls for her naive (and virginal) sister, Dannie (Shelly). Hershman manages to keep all the free-wheeling goings on under control. Film debut of former model Parrish. Directorial debut feature of Hershman. **CW:** Strong language and strong sexuality. **92m/C VHS.** Max Parrish, Adrienne Shelly, Andrea Naschak, Sean Young, Diane Ladd, Bela Lehoczky, Ania Suli; **Cameos:** Timothy Leary; **D:** Joel Hershman; **W:** Joel Hershman. *LIV*

Hold That Ghost 🐾🐾🐾 *Oh, Charlie* **1941** Abbott and Costello inherit an abandoned roadhouse where the illicit loot of its former owner, a "rubbed out" mobster, is supposedly hidden. **86m/B VHS, Beta.** Bud Abbott, Lou Costello, Joan Davis, Richard Carlson, Mischa Auer, The Andrews Sisters; **D:** Arthur Lubin. *USH*

Hold the Dream 🐾 **1985** A made-for-television mini-series sequel to Barbara Taylor Bradford's "A Woman of Substance". **195m/C VHS, Beta.** Jenny Seagrove, Stephen Collins, Deborah Kerr, James Brolin; **D:** Don Sharp. *NO*

Hold Your Man 🐾🐾🐾 **1933** Great star vehicle that turns from comedy to drama with Harlow falling for hustler Gable. Harlow and Gable are at their best in this unlikely story of a crooked couple. Direction drags at times, but snappy dialogue and the stars' personalities more than make up for it. **86m/B VHS, Closed Caption.** Jean Harlow, Clark Gable, Stuart Erwin, Dorothy Burgess, Garry Owen, Paul Hurst, Elizabeth Patterson, Laura La Plante; **D:** Sam Wood; **W:** Anita Loos, Howard Emmett Rogers. *MGM*

A Hole in the Head 🐾🐾½ **1959** A comedy-drama about a shiftless but charming lout who tries to raise money to save his hotel from foreclosure and learn to be responsible for his young son. Notable for the introduction of the song "High Hopes." 🎵 High Hopes; All My Tomorrows. **120m/C VHS, Beta, LV.** Frank Sinatra, Edward G. Robinson, Thelma Ritter, Carolyn Jones, Eleanor Parker, Eddie Hodges, Keenan Wynn, Joi Lansing; **D:** Frank Capra; **W:** Arnold Schulman; **C:** William H. Daniels. Academy Awards '59: Best Song ("High Hopes"). *MGM*

Hole in the Sky 🐾🐾½ *The Ranger, the Cook and a Hole in the Sky* **1995 (PG)** Teenaged Mac (O'Connell) is working for the Montana forestry service in the summer of 1919 under the tutelage of taciturn legend Bill Bell (a mustache-less Elliott). Mac learns some lessons about growing up, first love, card-playing—and never to rile the camp cook. Based on an autobiographical story by Norman MacLean. Made for TV; filmed on location in British Columbia. **94m/C VHS.** Sam Elliott, Jerry O'Connell, Ricky Jay, Molly Parker; **D:** John Kent Harrison; **W:** Robert W. Lenski. *HMK*

The Holes 🐾🐾½ *Les Gaspards* **1972 (PG)** A Parisian book shop owner's daughter vanishes along with other local citizens and American tourists, and he decides to investigate when the police won't. In French with subtitles. **92m/C VHS, Beta.** *FR* Philippe Noiret, Charles Denner, Michael Serrault, Gerard Depardieu. *FHE, FCT*

Holiday 🐾🐾🐾½ *Free to Live; Unconventional Linda* **1938** The classically genteel screwball comedy about a rich girl who steals her sister's fiance. A yardstick in years to come for sophisticated, urbane Hollywood romanticism. Based on the play by Philip Barry who later wrote "The Philadelphia Story." **93m/B VHS, Beta, LV.** Cary Grant, Katharine Hepburn, Doris Nolan, Edward Everett Horton, Ruth Donnelly, Lew Ayres, Binnie Barnes; **D:** George Cukor; **W:** Donald Ogden Stewart, Sidney Buchman. Nominations: Academy Awards '36: Best Interior Decoration. *COL*

Holiday Affair 🐾🐾½ **1949** Hollywood yuletide charmer about a pretty widow being courted by two very different men. **86m/B VHS, Beta, LV.** Robert Mitchum, Janet Leigh, Griff Barnett, Wendell Corey, Esther Dale, Henry O'Neill, Harry (Henry) Morgan, Larry J. Blake; **D:** Don Hartman. *TTC*

Holiday Hotel 🐾🐾 **1977 (R)** A group of wild French vacationers let loose at their favorite little resort hotel along the Brittany coast. Available in French with English subtitles or dubbed into English. **109m/C VHS, Beta.** *FR* Sophie Barjae, Daniel Ceccaldi; **D:** Michael Lang.

Holiday in Havana 🐾🐾 **1949** Desi Arnaz is back in Cuba winning hearts and dance contests. Watch only for Desi's presence. 🎵 Holiday in Havana; The Arnaz Jam; Straw Hat Song; Rhumba Rumbero; Copacobana; Made For Each Other; I'll Take Romance. **73m/B VHS.** Desi Arnaz Sr., Lolita Valdez, Mary Hatcher, Ann Doran; **D:** Jean Yarbrough. *GKK*

Holiday in Mexico 🐾🐾½ **1946** Pidgeon plays the U.S. ambassador to Mexico whose teenage daughter (Powell) tries to run his life along with his household. He falls for a singer while she develops a crush on an older, respected pianist (Iturbi playing himself). Lots of lively production numbers featuring Xavier Cugat and his orchestra. 🎵 I Think Of You; Walter Winchell Rhumba; Yo Te Amo Mucho—And That's That; And Dreams Remain; Holiday in Mexico; Ave Maria; Les Filles de Cadiz; Italian Street Song; Polonaise in A Flat Major. **127m/C VHS.** Walter Pidgeon, Jane Powell, Ilona Massey, Jose Iturbi, Roddy McDowall, Xavier Cugat, Hugo Haas; **D:** George Sidney; **W:** Isobel Lennart; **C:** Harry Stradling; **M:** Georgie Stoll. *MGM*

Holiday Inn 🐾🐾🐾 **1942** Fred Astaire and Bing Crosby are rival song-and-dance men who decide to work together to turn a Connecticut farm into an inn, open only on holidays. Remade in 1954 as "White Christmas." 🎵 White Christmas; Be Careful, It's My Heart; Plenty to Be Thankful For; Abraham, Abraham; Let's Say It With Firecrackers; I Gotta Say I Love You Cause I Can't Tell A Lie; Let's Start the New Year Right; Happy Holidays; Song of Freedom. **101m/B VHS, Beta, LV.** Bing Crosby, Fred Astaire, Marjorie Reynolds, Walter Abel, Virginia Dale; **D:** Mark Sandrich. Academy Awards '42: Best Song ("White Christmas"); Nominations: Academy Awards '42: Best Story, Scoring of a Musical. *USH*

Holiday Rhythm 🐾½ **1950** A television promoter is knocked out and dreams of a world-wide trip full of entertainment, comedy, and insanity. **61m/B VHS, Beta, LV.** Mary Beth Hughes, Tex Ritter, David Street, Donald MacBride. *NO*

Hollow Gate **1988** Trick or Treat?? Four kids find out when they run into a guy with hungry dogs. **90m/C VHS, Beta.** Addison Randall. *NO*

Hollow Point 🐾🐾 **1995 (R)** After an FBI agent and a DEA agent get in each other's way, they reluctantly team up to hunt the head of an international crime syndicate. **CW:** Violence and language. **103m/C VHS.** Thomas Ian Griffith, Tia Carrere, John Lithgow, Donald Sutherland; **D:** Sidney J. Furie. *THV*

Hollow Reed 🐾🐾🐾 *Believe Me* **1995** Heart-wrenching, though not maudlin, drama revolves around 9-year-old Oliver Wyatt (Bould). His parents, Martyn (Donovan) and Hannah (Richardson), have bitterly divorced after Martyn finally acknowledges his homosexuality and moves in with his lover, Tom (Hart). Hannah's new live-in boyfriend Frank (Flemyng) turns out to be abusive towards Oliver, who's reluctant to say anything to destroy his mother's new happiness. But when Martyn discovers what's happening, he instigates a custody battle for his son that has everyone at each other's throats, with the terrified Oliver caught in the crossfire. Compelling performances. **106m/C VHS.** *GB* Martin Donovan, Joely Richardson, Ian Hart, Jason Flemyng, Sam Bould; **D:** Angela Pope; **W:** Paula Milne; **C:** Remi Adefarasin; **M:** Anne Dudley. *NYR*

Hollywood After Dark 🐾 **1965** McClanahan plays a young starlet trying to make it big in Hollywood. Pure exploitation schlock. Not released theatrically until 1968. **?m/C VHS.** Rue McClanahan. *SNC, TPV*

Hollywood Bloopers 🐾🐾½ **195?** Hilarious outtakes from some of Hollywood's finest movies, featuring stars such as Bette Davis, James Cagney, Humphrey Bogart, Rosalind Russell, Errol Flynn, Kirk Douglas, and many more. **85m/B VHS, Beta.** Lauren Bacall, Ronald Reagan, James Stewart, Joan Blondell, Rosalind Russell, Errol Flynn, Kirk Douglas, Barbara Stanwyck. *VDM*

Hollywood Boulevard 🐾🐾½ **1976 (R)** Behind-the-scenes glimpse of shoestring-budget movie making offers comical sex, violence, sight gags, one-liners, comedy bits, and mock-documentary footage. Commander Cody and His Lost Planet Airmen are featured. **93m/C VHS, Beta.** Candice Rialson, Mary Woronov, Rita George, Jonathan Kaplan, Jeffrey Kramer, Dick Miller, Paul Bartel; **D:** Joe Dante, Allan Arkush; **C:** Jamie Anderson. *WAR, OM*

Hollywood Boulevard 2 🐾🐾 **1989 (R)** A "B" movie studio finds its top actresses being killed off and terror reigns supreme as the mystery grows more intense. Could that psycho-bimbo from outer space have something to do with it? **82m/C VHS, Beta, Closed Caption.** Ginger Lynn Allen, Kelly Monteith, Eddie Deezen, Ken Wright, Steve Vinovich; **D:** Steve Barnett. *MGM*

Hollywood Canteen 🐾🐾🐾 **1944** Star-studded extravaganza with just about every Warner Bros. lot actor in this tribute to love and nationalism. Lovesick G.I. Hutton falls for Leslie, wins a date with her in a phony raffle set up at the Hollywood Canteen, and the sparks fly right away. But he thinks she tricked him as he boards his train and she's not there to see him off. Lame story is redeemed by the talented cast and wonderful musical numbers which make this picture fly with charm and style. Before production began there were arguments over "unpatriotic" actors—labeled as such due to their lack of participation in this, and other similar movies produced at the time. 🎵 Don't Fence Me In; Sweet Dreams, Sweetheart; You Can Always Tell A Yank; We're Having a Baby; What Are You Doin' the Rest of Your Life; The General Jumped At Dawn; Gettin' Corns For My Country; Voodoo Moon; Tumblin' Tumbleweeds. **124m/B VHS.** Robert Hutton, Dane Clark, Janis Paige, Jonathan Hale, Barbara Brown, James

Flavin, Eddie Marr, Ray Teal, Bette Davis, Joan Leslie, Jack Benny, Jimmy Dorsey, Joan Crawford, John Garfield, Barbara Stanwyck, Ida Lupino, Eddie Cantor, Jack Carson, Eleanor Parker, Alexis Smith, S.Z. Sakall, Peter Lorre, Sydney Greenstreet, Helmut Dantine; **D:** Delmer Daves; **W:** Delmer Daves. Nominations: Academy Awards '44: Best Song ("Sweet Dreams Sweetheart"), Best Sound, Scoring of a Musical.*FOX, FCT*

Hollywood Chainsaw Hookers 🎬🎬
1988 (R) A campy, sexy, very bloody parody about attractive prostitutes who dismember their unsuspecting customers. 90m/C VHS, Beta. Linnea Quigley, Gunnar Hansen, Jay Richardson, Michelle (McClellan) Bauer; **D:** Fred Olen Ray. *NO*

Hollywood Chaos 🎬½ **1989** Director Ballantine's stars quit his production before it even starts, so he gets the next best thing - star lookalikes. However, his problems are just beginning. One of his new "stars" is kidnapped, and his reclusive stage manager is hunted as the object of desire for a female motorcycle gang. 90m/C VHS. Carl Ballantine, Tricia Leigh Fisher, Kathleen Freeman; **D:** Sean McNamara. *WLA*

Hollywood Cop 🎬½ **1987** (R) A tough cop in Hollywood goes up against the mob for the sake of a kidnapped boy. 101m/C VHS, Beta. Jim Mitchum, David Goss, Cameron Mitchell, Troy Donahue, Aldo Ray; **D:** Amir Shervan. *CEL*

The Hollywood Detective 🎬🎬 **1989** (PG) An average TV movie that spoofs "Kojak." A TV detective tries it out for real, and gets into troubles for which he can't pause "for a message from our sponsor." 88m/C VHS, Beta. Telly Savalas, Helene Udy, George Coe, Joe Dallesandro, Tom Reese; **D:** Kevin Connor. *USH*

Hollywood Dreams 🎬½ **1994** (R) Starlet on the Hollywood casting couch saga of a midwestern gal that comes to California with dreams of making it big.**CW:** Strong sexuality. 90m/C VHS. Kelly Cook, Danny Smith, Debra Beatty; **D:** Ralph Portillo. *CEL*

Hollywood Goes to War **1954** Five shorts produced for the entertainment of G.I.'s overseas or for home front bond drives: "The All-Star Bond Rally" features Hope, Crosby, Harry James and His Orchestra, Sinatra, Grable, Marx, and the Talking Pin-Ups; "Hollywood Canteen Overseas Special" features Shore, Cantor, Durante, and Skelton; "Mail Call (Strictly G.I.)" is a filmed "Mail Call" radio program; "G.I. Movie Weekly-Sing with the Stars" features Miranda and her fruit-basket hat and a Portuguese follow-the-bouncing-ball sing-along; and "Invaders in Greasepaint," the story of the North African USO tour of the "Four Jills in a Jeep." Also includes the Jill's memorable rendition of the wartime classic "Snafu," banned from the airwaves for its racy lyrics. 41m/B VHS, Beta. Bob Hope, Bing Crosby, Frank Sinatra, Betty Grable, Harpo Marx, Jimmy Durante, Eddie Cantor, Red Skelton, Bud Abbott, Lou Costello, Dinah Shore, Dorothy Lamour, Carmen Miranda. *NO*

Hollywood Harry 🎬 *Harry's Machine* **1986** (PG-13) A private-eye mystery/parody, about an inept detective who searches for a missing porn actress. 99m/C VHS, Beta. Robert Forster, Kathrine Forster, Joe Spinell, Shannon Wilcox; **D:** Robert Forster; **W:** Curt Allen. *MED*

Hollywood Heartbreak 🎬🎬 **1989** It's heartbreak in tinseltown for a young writer who's trying to pitch his movie script but winds up defending himself from slimy agents and persistent starlets. Another entry for Bartlett's familiar plotlines. 90m/C VHS. Mark Moses, Carol Mayo Jenkins, Ron Karabatsos, Richard Romanus, James LeGros; **D:** Lance Dickson. *VTR*

Hollywood High 🎬 **1977** (R) Four attractive teen couples converge on the mansion of an eccentric aging silent-film star for an unusual vacation experience in this teenage skin flick. Followed by a sequel. 81m/C VHS, Beta. Marcy Albrecht, Sherry Hardin, Rae Sperling, Susanne Kevin Mead; **D:** Patrick Wright. *LIV, VES*

Hollywood High, Part 2 🎬 **1981** (R) Ignored by their boyfriends for the lure of sun and surf, three comely high school students try their best to regain their interest. 86m/C VHS, Beta. April May, Donna Lynn, Camille Warner, Lee Thornburg; **D:** Caruth C. Byrd. *LIV, VES*

Hollywood Hot Tubs 🎬 **1984** (R) Teen sex romp has adolescent picking up some extra cash and a lot of fun repairing the hot tubs of the rich and famous. 103m/C VHS, Beta. Donna McDaniel, Michael Andrew, Katt Shea Ruben, Paul Gunning, Edy Williams, Jewel Shepard; **D:** Chuck Vincent. *LIV, VES, VTR*

Hollywood Hot Tubs 2: Educating Crystal 🎬 **1989** (R) A softcore comedy about a well-tanned ingenue learning about business in Hollywood during numerous hot tub trysts. 103m/C VHS, Beta, LV. Jewel Shepard, Patrick Day, Remy O'Neill, David Tiefen, Bart Braverman; **D:** Ken Raich. *CCB*

Hollywood in Trouble 🎬 **1987** A bumbling middle-aged fool decides to break into the wacky movie-making business. 90m/C VHS, Beta. Vic Vallard, Jean Levine, Jerry Tiffe, Pamela Dixon, Jerry Cleary. *NO*

Hollywood Man 🎬🎬 **1976** (R) A Hollywood actor wants to make his own film but when his financial support comes from the mob there's trouble ahead. 90m/C VHS, Beta. William Smith, Don Stroud, Jennifer Billingsley, Mary Woronov; **D:** Jack Starrett. *NO*

Hollywood Mystery 🎬½ *Hollywood Hoodlum* **1934** A publicity agent stops at nothing to promote his would-be starlet girlfriend. 53m/B VHS. June Clyde, Frank Albertson, Joe Crespo; **D:** B. Reeves Eason. *NOS, LOO*

Hollywood or Bust 🎬🎬½ **1956** The zany duo take their act on the road as they head for Tinsel Town in order to meet Lewis' dream girl Ekberg. This was the last film for the Martin & Lewis team and it's not the swan song their fans would have hoped for. 95m/C VHS, Beta. Dean Martin, Jerry Lewis, Anita Ekberg, Pat Crowley, Maxie "Slapsie" Rosenbloom, Willard Waterman; **D:** Frank Tashlin. *PAR, CCB*

Hollywood Outtakes & Rare Footage **1983** A collection of rare and unusual film clips and excerpts that feature dozens of Hollywood stars in screen tests, promotional shorts, home movies, outtakes, television appearances and WWII propaganda shorts. Some segments in black and white. 85m/C VHS, Beta, LV. Marilyn Monroe, James Dean, Joan Crawford, Judy Garland, Humphrey Bogart, Ronald Reagan, Bette Davis, Vivien Leigh, Carole Lombard. *COL, RXM*

Hollywood Party 🎬🎬½ **1934** Durante plays a film star who decides to throw a Hollywood bash. Any plot is incidental as it is mainly an excuse to have numerous stars of the day appear in brief comic bits or musical numbers. Mickey Mouse and the Big Bad Wolf of Disney fame also appear in color animated footage combined with live action. Numerous MGM directors worked on parts of the film but Dwan was given the task of trying to pull the various scenes together (he is uncredited onscreen). ♫Hollywood Party; Hello; Reincarnation; I've Had My Moments; Feeling High; Hot Chocolate Soldiers. 72m/B VHS. Jimmy Durante, Stan Laurel, Oliver Hardy, Lupe Velez, Ted Healy, Moe Howard, Curly Howard, Larry Fine, Robert Young, Charles Butterworth, Polly Moran, George Givot, Tom Kennedy; **D:** Allan Dwan; **V:** Walt Disney, Billy Bletcher. *MGM*

Hollywood Scandals and Tragedies **1988** A look at the skeletons-in-the-closet surrounding the deaths and private turmoils of James Dean, Rock Hudson, Vivien Leigh, Frances Farmer, Sal Mineo, Sharon Tate, Jayne Mansfield, and others. 90m/C VHS, Beta. *MPI*

Hollywood Shuffle 🎬🎬½ **1987** (R) Townsend's autobiographical comedy about a struggling black actor in Hollywood trying to find work and getting nothing but stereotypical roles. Written, directed, financed by Townsend, who created this often clever and appealing film on a $100,000 budget. 81m/C VHS, Beta, LV. Robert Townsend, Anne-

Marie Johnson, Starletta DuPois, Helen Martin, Keenen Ivory Wayans, Damon Wayans, Craigus R. Johnson, Eugene Glazer; **D:** Robert Townsend; **W:** Robert Townsend, Keenen Ivory Wayans; **M:** Patrice Rushen, Udi Harpaz. *NO*

Hollywood Stadium Mystery 🎬🎬
1938 A boxer turns up dead before a big match and a D.A. investigates. Performances hold this one up, especially by Hamilton who later played Commissioner Gordon on TV's "Batman." 66m/B VHS, Beta. Neil Hamilton, Evelyn Venable, Jimmy Wallington, Barbara Pepper, Lucien Littlefield, Lynn (Mary Hart) Roberts, Charles Williams, James Spottswood, Reed Hadley, Smiley Burnette; **D:** David Howard. *SNC*

The Hollywood Strangler Meets the Skid Row Slasher woof! *The Model Killer* **1979** (R) Voiced-over narration, canned music and an unfathomable plot are but a few of this would-be fright fest's finer points. Uninhibited by any narrative connection, two terrors strike fear in the heart of Tinseltown. While a psycho photographer cruises L.A. taking pictures of models he subsequently strangles, a woman working in a barebums magazine store takes a stab (with a knife) at lowering the city's derelict population. There's a word for this sort of dribble, and it isn't versimilitude. Steckler used an alias (as he usually does for this one—Wolfgang Schmidt. 72m/C VHS. Pierre Agostino, Carolyn Brandt, Forrest Duke, Chuck Alford; **D:** Ray Dennis Steckler. *NO*

Hollywood Uncensored **1987** A history of Hollywood censorship, including long-suppressed scenes from "King Kong," "The Outlaw," "Carnal Knowledge," "Baby Doll," "Easy Rider," "Woodstock," and more. 75m/C VHS, Beta. *LIV, FCT*

Hollywood Vice Sqaud 🎬 **1986** (R) Explores the lives of Hollywood police officers and the crimes they investigate. Contains three different story lines involving prostitution, child pornography, and organized crime. The film can't decide to be a comedy send-up of crime stories or a drama and is also crippled by a poor script. Written by the real-life chief of the Hollywood Vice Squad. 100m/C VHS, LV. Trish Van Devere, Ronny Cox, Frank Gorshin, Leon Isaac Kennedy, Carrie Fisher, Ben Frank, Robin Wright; **D:** Penelope Spheeris; **M:** Michael Convertino. *VTR, HHE, MTX*

Hollywood Zap woof! **1986** (R) Two losers, one a Southern orphan, the other a video game nut, hit Hollywood and engage in antics that are meant to be funny, but are actually tasteless.**CW:** Language and sexuality. 85m/C VHS, Beta. Ben Frank, Ivan E. Roth, De Waldron, Annie Gaybis, Chuck "Porky" Mitchell; **D:** David M. Cohen; **W:** David M. Cohen. *PSM*

Hollywood's New Blood 🎬 **1988** Young actors making a movie are haunted by a film crew from hell. 90m/C VHS, Beta. Bobby Johnson, Francine Lapensee; **D:** James Shyman. *VTR*

Holocaust 🎬🎬🎬½ **1978** The war years of 1935 to 1945 are relived in this account of the Nazi atrocities, focusing on the Jewish Weiss family, destroyed by the monstrous crimes, and the Dorf family, Germans who thrived under the Nazi regime. Highly acclaimed riveting made-for-television mini-series with an exceptional cast. Won eight Emmys. 475m/C VHS, Beta. Michael Moriarty, Fritz Weaver, Meryl Streep, James Woods, Joseph Bottoms, Tovah Feldshuh, David Warner, Ian Holm, Michael Beck, Marius Goring; **D:** Marvin J. Chomsky. *REP, SWC, WOV*

Holocaust Survivors...Remembrance of Love 🎬🎬 *Remembrance of Love* **1983** A concentration camp survivor and his daughter attend the 1981 World Gathering of Holocaust Survivors in Tel-Aviv and both find romance. Made for television. 100m/C VHS, Beta. Kirk Douglas, Pam Dawber, Chana Eden, Yoram Gal, Robert Clary; **D:** Jack Smight; **M:** William Goldstein. *THV*

Hologram Man 🎜🎜 **1995 (R)** Futuristic thriller finds psycho/terrorist Slash Gallagher (Lurie) captured by rookie cop Kurt Decoda (Lara). His prison term is to be served in Holographic Stasis, which means his mind is stored on a computer. Slash's gang manges to break his mind out of the computer but since his body is destroyed, Slash roams as a powerful electro-magnetic hologram. And it's up to cop Decoda to get Slash back.**CW:** Violence; nudity; language. **96m/C VHS, LV, Closed Caption.** Joe Lara, Evan Lurie, William Sanderson, Tiny Lister, Michael Nouri, John Amos; **D:** Richard Pepin; **W:** Evan Lurie; **M:** John Gonzalez. **PMH**

Holt of the Secret Service 1942 Secret service agent runs afoul of saboteurs and fifth-columnists in this 15-episode serial. **290m/B VHS.** Jack Holt, Evelyn Brent, Montague Shaw, Tristram Coffin, John Ward, George Chesebro; **D:** James W. Horne. **VYY, MED, DVT**

The Holy Innocents 🎜🎜🎜 *Los Santos Inocentes* **1984 (PG)** A peasant family is torn asunder by their feudal obligations to their patrons. Set in the 1960s in Franco's Spain. In Spanish with English subtitles. **108m/C VHS, Beta.** **SP** Alfredo Landa, Francesco Rabal; **D:** Mario Camus. Cannes Film Festival '84: Best Actor (Landa), Best Actor (Rabal). **ORI, APD**

Holy Matrimony 🎜🎜½ **1994 (PG-13)** Mild-mannered and pleasant comedy in spite of its potentially salacious plot. Thieves Peter (Donovan) and Havana (Arquette) take off to Canada to hide out in the Hutterite religious community where Peter grew up and where he's welcomed as the prodigal son. Peter hides their stolen loot but neglects to pass the word on before he's killed in an accident. Wanting to stay and search for the money, Havana uses the colony's reliance on biblical law to marry Peter's brother, Zeke (Gordon-Levitt). Only problem is Zeke is 12 and doesn't even like girls. Strictly brother-sister affection develops between the two. Amusing performances by both. **93m/C VHS, LV, Closed Caption.** Patricia Arquette, Joseph Gordon-Levitt, Armin Mueller-Stahl, Tate Donovan, John Schuck, Lois Smith, Courtney B. Vance, Jeffrey Nordling, Richard Riehle; **D:** Leonard Nimoy; **W:** David Weisberg, Douglas S. Cook; **C:** Bobby Bukowski; **M:** Bruce Broughton. **TOU**

Holy Terror 🎜🎜 **1965** The story of Florence Nightingale, who shocked Victorian society by organizing a nursing staff to aid British soldiers in the Crimean War, is told in this presentation from "George Schaefer's Showcase Theatre." **76m/C VHS, Beta.** Julie Harris, Denholm Elliott, Torin Thatcher, Kate Reid; **D:** George Schaefer. **FHS**

Homage 🎜🎜 **1995 (R)** Archie's (Whaley) an emotionally disturbed mathematical nerd who needs a break from academia and persuades widowed ex-teacher Katherine Samuel (Danner) to hire him as caretaker for her New Mexico ranch. The duo achieve a strange serenity that shatters when Katherine's TV star daughter, self-absorbed Lucy (Lee), arrives seeking shelter because of her drug and drinking problems. A nasty triangle ensues as Lucy makes the mistake of sexually enticing, then rejecting, the needy Archie. In fact, the mistake's fatal. Based on Medoff's play "The Homage That Follows."**CW:** Brief strong sexuality, language and an act of violence. **100m/C VHS.** Frank Whaley, Blythe Danner, Sheryl Lee, Bruce Davison, Danny Nucci; **D:** Ross Kagen Marks; **W:** Mark Medoff; **C:** Tom Richmond; **M:** W.G. Snuffy Walden. **AVI**

Hombre 🎜🎜🎜 **1967** A white man in the 1880s, raised by a band of Arizona Apaches, is forced into a showdown. In helping a stagecoach full of settlers across treacherous country, he not only faces traditional bad guys, but prejudice as well. Based on a story by Elmore Leonard. **111m/C VHS, Beta, LV.** Paul Newman, Fredric March, Richard Boone, Diane Cilento, Cameron Mitchell, Barbara Rush, Martin Balsam; **D:** Martin Ritt; **W:** Harriet Frank Jr., Irving Ravetch; **C:** James Wong Howe. **FOX**

Home Alone 🎜🎜🎜 **1990 (PG)** 8-year-old Kevin is accidentally left behind when his entire (and large) family makes a frantic rush for the airport. That's the plausible part. Alone and besieged by burglars, Culkin turns into a pint-sized Rambo defending his suburban castle with the wile and resources of a boy genius with perfect timing and unlimited wherewithal. That's the implausible part. Pesci and Stern, the targets of Macauley's wrath, enact painful slapstick with considerable vigor, while Candy has a small but funny part as the leader of a polka band traveling cross-country with mom O'Hara. The highest-grossing picture of 1990, surpassing "Ghost" and "Jaws." **105m/C VHS, Beta, LV, Closed Caption.** Macaulay Culkin, Catherine O'Hara, Joe Pesci, Daniel Stern, John Heard, Roberts Blossom, John Candy, Catherine O'Hara, Billie Bird, Angela Goethals, Devin Ratray, Kieran Culkin; **D:** Chris Columbus; **W:** John Hughes; **M:** John Williams. Nominations: Academy Awards '90: Best Song ("Somewhere in My Memory"), Best Original Score. **FXV, IME, RDG**

Home Alone 2: Lost in New York 🎜🎜½ **1992 (PG)** In an almost exact duplication of the original blockbuster, the harebrained McCallister family leaves Kevin behind in the shuffle to start their Florida vacation. Boarding the wrong plane, Kevin lands in NYC, where wonder of wonders, he meets crooks Pesci and Stern, prison escapees who somehow survived the torture meted out in the first film. And they want revenge. Loaded with cartoon violence and shameless gag replicas from HA1, mega-hit still produces genuine laughs and manages to incorporate fresh material. Culkin is as adorable as ever, with supporting cast all delivering fine performances. Filmed in New York City. **120m/C VHS, LV, Closed Caption.** Macaulay Culkin, Joe Pesci, Daniel Stern, Catherine O'Hara, John Heard, Tim Curry, Brenda Fricker, Devin Ratray, Hillary Wolf, Eddie Bracken, Dana Ivey, Rob Schneider, Kieran Culkin, Gerry Bamman; **Cameos:** Donald Trump; **D:** Chris Columbus; **W:** John Hughes; **M:** John Williams. People's Choice Awards '93: Best Film—Musical/Comedy. **FXV, BTV**

The Home and the World 🎜🎜🎜½ *Ghare Baire* **1984** Another masterpiece from India's Ray, this film deals with a sheltered Indian woman who falls in love with her husband's friend and becomes politically committed in the turmoil of 1907-1908. Based on Rabindranath Tagore's novel. In Bengali with English subtitles. **130m/C VHS, Beta.** **IN** Victor Banerjee, Soumitra Chatterjee; **D:** Satyajit Ray. **COL**

Home at Last 1988 An orphan in turn of the century New York finds himself shipped to Nebraska on an orphan train. There he works on the farm of his adopted family, whose own son has died. The boy finds that he must adjust to a new lifestyle as well as strive to be accepted as someone other than a replacement for the couple's son. From the "Wonderworks" series. **58m/C VHS.** Adrien Brody, Frank Converse, Caroline Lagerfelt, Sascha Radetsky. **PME, HMV, FCT**

Home Before Midnight 🎜½ **1984** A young songwriter falls in love with a 14-year-old, is discovered, and is subsequently charged with statutory rape. **115m/C VHS, Beta.** James Aubrey, Alison Elliott; **D:** Pete Walker. **ORI, WAR**

Home for Christmas 🎜🎜½ **1990** An elderly homeless man, with the love of a young girl, teaches a wealthy family the spirit of Christmas. **96m/C VHS.** Mickey Rooney, Joel Kaiser; **D:** Peter McCubbin. **RHI**

Home for the Holidays 🎜🎜 *Deadly Desires* **1972** Four daughters are called home on Christmas by their father who is convinced that his second wife is trying to poison him. Made for television. **74m/C VHS, Beta.** Eleanor Parker, Walter Brennan, Sally Field, Jessica Walter, Julie Harris; **D:** John Llewellyn Moxey. **THV**

Home for the Holidays 🎜🎜½ **1995 (PG-13)** Frantic dysfunctional family saga finds eldest daughter Claudia Larson (Hunter) on her way to Baltimore to spend Thanksgiving with her family. Frazzled Claudia must deal with badly bewigged mom Adele (Bancroft), genial dad Henry (Durning), and her siblings—frenzied gay brother Tommy (Downey, Jr.) and self-righteous sister Joanne (Stevenson), as well as screwy Aunt Glady (Chaplin) and Tommy's handsome friend Leo Fish (McDermott). Yes, there are moments of deja vu about your very own family holidays but the film seems badly paced and ultimately irritating. Adapted from a short story by Chris Radant.**CW:** Thematic material, language and brief drug use. **103m/C VHS, LV, Closed Caption.** Holly Hunter, Anne Bancroft, Charles Durning, Robert Downey Jr., Dylan McDermott, Cynthia Stevenson, Geraldine Chaplin, Steve Guttenberg, Claire Danes; **Cameos:** David Strathairn, Austin Pendleton; **D:** Jodie Foster; **W:** W.D. Richter; **C:** Lajos Koltai; **M:** Mark Isham. **PGV**

Home Free All 🎜🎜½ **1984** A Vietnam vet turned revolutionary, turned writer, tries to reacquaint himself with childhood friends only to find one has joined the mob and another is settled in suburbia and none of them are dealing well with adulthood. **89m/C VHS, Beta.** Allan Nicholls, Roland Caccavo, Maura Ellyn, Shelley Wyant, Lucille Rivim; **D:** Stuart Bird. **LIV, VES**

Home from the Hill 🎜🎜🎜 **1960** A solemn, brooding drama about a southern landowner and his troubled sons, one of whom is illegitimate. This one triumphs because of casting. Cinematography by Milton Krasner. **150m/C VHS, Beta, LV.** Robert Mitchum, George Peppard, George Hamilton, Eleanor Parker, Everett Sloane, Luana Parker, Constance Ford; **D:** Vincente Minnelli; **W:** Harriet Frank Jr., Irving Ravetch; **C:** Milton Krasner. National Board of Review Awards '60: Best Actor (Mitchum). **MGM**

Home in Oklahoma 🎜🎜 **1947** A boy will be swindled out of his inheritance and a killer will escape justice until Roy comes to the rescue. Standard series fare. **72m/B VHS, Beta.** Roy Rogers, Dale Evans, George "Gabby" Hayes, Carol Hughes; **D:** William Witney. **NOS, TIM, CAB**

Home Is Where the Hart Is 🎜🎜 **1988 (PG-13)** A rich 103-year-old is kidnapped by a nurse wanting to marry him and become heir to his estate. It's up to his sons, all in their 70s, to rescue him. **94m/C VHS, Beta, LV.** Martin Mull, Leslie Nielsen, Valri Bromfield, Stephen E. Miller, Eric Christmas, Ted Stidder; **D:** Rex Bromfield; **W:** Rex Bromfield. **PAR, IME**

Home Movies 🎜½ **1979 (PG)** Brian DePalma and his film students at Sarah Lawrence College devised this loose, sloppy comedy which hearkens back to DePalma's early films. Tells the story of a nebbish who seeks therapy to gain control of his absurdly chaotic life. **89m/C VHS, Beta, LV.** Kirk Douglas, Nancy Allen, Keith Gordon, Gerrit Graham, Vincent Gardenia, Mary Davenport; **D:** Brian DePalma; **W:** Brian DePalma; **C:** James L. Carter; **M:** Pino Donaggio. **LIV, VES, IME**

Home of Angels 🎜🎜½ **1994** Billy sneaks his granddad out of his nursing home in Philadelphia and together the twosome begin a perilous journey back to Billy's home in Long Island, New York so they can have a family Christmas. They're aided by a homeless man when they run into trouble with a street gang. **90m/C VHS.** Lance Robinson, Abe Vigoda, Sherman Hemsley, Joe Frazier; **D:** Nick Stagliano. **SDE**

A Home of Our Own 1975 An American priest sets up a home in Mexico for orphan boys and changes their lives for the better. A true story of Father William Wasson. **100m/C VHS, Beta.** Jason Miller. **WOV**

A Home of Our Own 🎜🎜½ **1993 (PG-13)** Semi-autobiographical tearjerker based on screenwriter Duncan's childhood. Widowed and poor mother of six (Bates) is fired from her job at a Los Angeles potato chip factory, packs up the tribe and heads for a better life and a home to call their own. They end up in Idaho, in a ramshackle house owned by lonely Mr. Moon (Oh) and what follows is a winter of discontent. Bates provides an intense performance as a poor but proud woman with a tough exterior. Furlong provides the story's narration as the eldest son. A story of spiritual triumph, this one is sure to make your heart weep. *CW:* Mild language and mild violence. 104m/C VHS, LV, **Closed Caption.** Kathy Bates, Edward Furlong, Soon-Teck Oh, Amy Sakasitz, Tony Campisi; *D:* Tony Bill; *W:* Patrick Duncan. PGV

Home of the Brave 🐾🐾🐾 1949 A black soldier is sent on a top secret mission in the South Pacific, but finds that he must battle with his white comrades as he is subjected to subordinate treatment and constant racial slurs. Hollywood's first outstanding statement against racial prejudice. 86m/B VHS, Beta, LV. Lloyd Bridges, James Edwards, Frank Lovejoy, Jeff Corey; *D:* Mark Robson. National Board of Review Awards '49: 10 Best Films of the Year. REP, FCT

Home Remedy 🐾🐾 1988 An introverted New Jersey bachelor's isolated lifestyle is invaded by a flirtatious housewife and her jealous husband. 92m/C VHS, Beta. Seth Barrish, Maxine Albert; *D:* Maggie Greenwald. NO

Home Sweet Home 🐾🐾½ 1914 Suggested by the life of John Howard Payne (actor, poet, dramatist, critic, and world-wanderer) who wrote the title song amid the bitterness of his sad life. Silent with musical score. 62m/B VHS, Beta. Lillian Gish, Dorothy Gish, Henry B. Walthall, Mae Marsh, Blanche Sweet, Donald Crisp, Robert "Bobbie" Harron; *D:* D.W. Griffith. VYY, KIV, GPV

Home Sweet Home 🐾½ 1980 *Slasher in the House* A murdering psychopath escapes from the local asylum, and rampages through a family's Thanksgiving dinner. 84m/C VHS, Beta. Jake Steinfeld, Sallee Elyse, Peter de Paula; *D:* Nettie Pena. MED

Home Sweet Home 🐾🐾 1982 Postman Stan fancies himself a ladies man, but his wife has left him. So Stan decides to assuage his loneliness by seducing his co-workers wives. Black comedy look at British social classism. Made for British television. 90m/C VHS. GB Eric Richard, Timothy Spall, Tim Barker, Su Elliot, Frances Barber, Kay Stonham; *D:* Mike Leigh; *W:* Mike Leigh. WBF, FCT

Home to Stay 🐾🐾 1979 A farmer who has suffered a stroke is fighting off repeated lapses into senility. His son and daughter have conflicting interests as to whether he should be committed to a nursing home. Made for television. 74m/C VHS, Beta. Henry Fonda, Frances Hyland, Michael McGuire; *D:* Delbert Mann; *M:* Hagood Hardy. TLF

Home Town Story 🐾🐾 1951 A politician is convinced big business is behind his election loss. Fair drama. Watch for Monroe in a bit part. 61m/B VHS. Jeffrey Lynn, Donald Crisp, Marjorie Reynolds, Alan Hale Jr., Marilyn Monroe, Barbara Brown, Melinda Plowman; *D:* Arthur Pierson. NOS, TPV

Homebodies 🐾🐾 1974 (PG) Six senior citizens, disgusted when they learn that they will be callously tossed out of their home, become violent murderers in their shocking attempt to solve their problem. An odd little film made in Cincinnati. 96m/C VHS, Beta. Ruth McDevitt, Linda Marsh, William Hansen, Peter Brocco, Frances Fuller; *D:* Larry Yust.

Homeboy 🐾🐾 1988 (R) A small-time club boxer who dreams of becoming middleweight champ is offered his big break, but the opportunity is jeopardized by his dishonest manager's dealings. Never released theatrically. 118m/C VHS, Beta, LV. Mickey Rourke, Christopher Walken, Debra Feuer, Kevin Conway, Antony Alda, Ruben Blades; *D:* Michael Seresin; *M:* Eric Clapton, Michael Kamen. NO

Homeboy 🐾½ 198? A Black boxer owes his career to the mob. When he tries to break free his wife is murdered - and he seeks revenge. 93m/C VHS. Dabney Coleman, Philip Michael Thomas. NO

Homeboys 🐾 1992 Two East L.A. brothers find themselves on opposite sides of the law in this quickie designed to cash in on gang violence and ghetto dramas. 91m/C VHS, LV. Todd Bridges, David Garrison, Ron Odriozola, Ken Michaels; *D:* Lindsay Norgard. AIP

Homecoming 🐾🐾🐾 1928 Two German prisoners of war escape from a Siberian lead mine. One reaches home first and has an affair with his comrade's wife. Silent. 74m/B VHS, Beta. GE Dita Parlo, Lars Hanson, Gustav Froehlich; *D:* Joe May. GLV

Homecoming 🐾🐾 1948 Average soap opera starring Gable and Turner set amidst the trenches of WW II. Gable plays a selfish doctor who leaves behind his wife and colleague to enlist in the Medical Corps as a major. Turner is the battlefield nurse who forever changes his life. Film is hindered by a story which is far below the talents of the excellent cast. Although voted by the New York Critics as one of the ten worst movies of 1948, the public loved it. Based on the story "The Homecoming of Ulysses" by Sidney Kingsley. 113m/B VHS. Clark Gable, Lana Turner, Anne Baxter, John Hodiak, Ray Collins, Gladys Cooper, Cameron Mitchell, Art Baker, Lurene Tuttle; *D:* Mervyn LeRoy; *W:* Paul Osborn, Jan Lustig. MGM

Homecoming 🐾🐾½ 1996 (PG) Mentally ill mother abandons her four children at a Connecticut shopping mall in the care of 13-year-old eldest daughter (Peterson). The children slowly make their way to a relative's (Bedelia) home in Bridgeport, but when she proves equally uncaring Dicey decides to continue the family trek to their maternal grandmother Ab's (Bancroft) house in Chrisfield, Maryland. No surprise when crazy grandma doesn't want them either but this time Dicey is determined to make them all a home. Based on the Newbéry Medal-winning children's novel by Cynthia Voight. Made for cable TV. ?m/C VHS. Anne Bancroft, Kimberlee Peterson, Bonnie Bedelia, Trever O'Brien, Hanna Hall, William Greenblatt. HMK

Homecoming: A Christmas Story 🐾🐾½ 1971 Made-for-television heart-tugger that inspired the television series "The Waltons." A depression-era Virginia mountain family struggles to celebrate Christmas although the whereabouts and safety of their father are unknown. Adapted from the autobiographical novel by Earl Hamner, Jr. 98m/C VHS, Beta, **Closed Caption.** Richard Thomas, Patricia Neal, Edgar Bergen, Cleavon Little, Ellen Corby; *D:* Fielder Cook. FOX

Homer and Eddie 🐾 1989 (R) A witless road comedy with Goldberg as a dying sociopath and a mentally retarded Belushi. They take off cross-country to make a little trouble, learn a little about life, and create a less than entertaining movie. 100m/C VHS, Beta, LV. Whoopi Goldberg, James Belushi, Karen Black; *D:* Andrei Konchalovsky; *W:* Patrick Cirillo; *C:* Lajos Koltai; *M:* Eduard Artemyev. HBO

Homer Comes Home 🐾🐾 1920 A homely and diligent inventor finds nothing but failure, but sticks it out in hopes of turning his luck around. Silent comedy starring down-home Ray. 55m/B VHS, Beta. Charles Ray. GPV

Homesteaders of Paradise Valley 🐾½ 1947 The Hume brothers oppose Red Ryder and a group of settlers building a dam in Paradise Valley. 54m/B VHS, Beta. Allan "Rocky" Lane, Robert (Bobby) Blake. NOS, VCN, CAB

Hometown Boy Makes Good 🐾🐾½ 1993 (R) Smalltown boy Boyd Geary moved to the big city to attend medical school. But what he never told his proud mom was that he dropped out and doesn't have the successful psychiatry practice she thinks he has, instead he's a barely surviving waiter. But when Boyd travels back home to confess to mom, the local mayor makes him an offer to set up his own practice and won't take no for an answer. *CW:* Language. 88m/C VHS, LV, **Closed Caption.** Anthony Edwards, Grace Zabriskie, Cyn-

thia Bain; *D:* David Burton Morris; *W:* Allen Rucker; *M:* Barry Goldberg. IMP, IME

Hometown U.S.A. woof! 1979 (R) Set in Los Angeles in the late 50s' this teenage cruising movie is the brainchild of director Baer who is better known as Jethro from that madcap television series "The Beverly Hillbillies." 97m/C VHS, Beta. Brian Kerwin, Gary Springer, David Wilson, Cindy Fisher, Sally Kirkland; *D:* Max Baer Jr. LIV, VES

Homeward Bound 🐾 1980 (G) A dying teenager tries to reunite his long-estranged father and grandfather. Made for television. 96m/C VHS, Beta. David Soul, Moosie Drier, Barnard Hughes; *D:* Richard Michaels. HMV

Homeward Bound 2: Lost in San Francisco 🐾🐾½ 1996 (G) House pets Chance, the feisty bulldog (Fox), Sassy the sophisticated feline (Field), and Shadow the sage golden retriever (Waite) find themselves on the loose again, this time in the tough streets of San Francisco. The animals escape from the airport as the family departs for a Canadian holiday, and on their way back home, encounter some tough mutts—a gang of streetwise dogs, (most notably comedian Sinbad as Riley) and, of course, some dog nappers. Chance even finds romance along the way with Delilah (Gugino). Not too scary for the little ones, flick carries the same charm of the first adventure. 88m/C VHS, **Closed Caption.** Robert Hays, Kim Greist, Veronica Lauren, Kevin Timothy Chevalia, Michael Rispoli, Max Perlich; *D:* David R. Ellis; *W:* Julie Hickson, Chris Hauty; *C:* Jack Conroy; *V:* Michael J. Fox, Sally Field, Ralph Waite, Al Michaels, Tommy Lasorda, Bob Uecker, Jon Polito, Adam Goldberg, Sinbad, Carla Gugino. TOU

Homeward Bound: The Incredible Journey 🐾🐾🐾 1993 (G) Successful remake of the 1963 Disney release "The Incredible Journey." Two dogs and a cat once again try to find their way home after their family relocates, armed with greater depth of character than the original. Hard not to shed a tear for the brave animal trio who develop a trusting bond through assorted misadventures. Based on the novel by Sheila Burnford. Superior family fare. 85m/C VHS, LV. Robert Hays, Kim Greist, Jean Smart, Benj Thall, Veronica Lauren, Kevin Timothy Chevalia; *D:* Duwayne Dunham; *W:* Linda Woolverton, Carolyn Thompson; *M:* Bruce Broughton; *V:* Don Ameche, Michael J. Fox, Sally Field. DIS, BTV

Homework 🐾 1982 (R) Young man's after-school lessons with a teacher are definitely not part of the curriculum. Yawning sexploitation. 90m/C VHS, Beta, LV. Joan Collins, Michael Morgan, Betty Thomas, Shell Kepler, Wings Hauser, Lee Purcell; *D:* James Beshears. USH

Homewrecker 🐾🐾 1992 (PG-13) Benson stars as a scientist who invents a computer, with a female voice, as the ultimate domestic worker. Only the computer turns possessive and against Benson's estranged wife. *CW:* Elements of terror and violence. 88m/C VHS, Beta, **Closed Caption.** Robby Benson, Sydney Walsh, Sarah Rose Karr; *D:* Fred Walton; *W:* Eric Harlacher; *V:* Kate Jackson. PAR

Homicidal Impulse 🐾½ 1992 (R) When Assistant D.A. Tim Casey has an affair with his boss' ambitious niece he doesn't realize the danger he's in. His lover decides to kill her uncle so boyfriend Tim will get his job. Some women will do anything for love. Also available in an unrated version. 84m/C VHS. Scott Valentine, Vanessa Angel. LIV

Homicide 🐾🐾🐾½ 1991 (R) Terrific police thriller with as much thought as action; a driven detective faces his submerged Jewish identity while probing an anti-Semitic murder and a secret society. Playwright/filmmaker Mamet creates nail-biting suspense and shattering epiphanies without resorting to Hollywood glitz. Rich (often profane) dialogue includes a classic soliloquy mystically comparing a lawman's badge with a Star of David. *CW:* Language and violence. 100m/C VHS, LV, 8mm, **Closed Caption.** Joe Mantegna, William H. Macy, Natalija Nogulich, Ving Rhames, Rebecca Pidgeon; *D:* David Mamet; **W:** David Mamet; **C:** Roger Deakins. National Board of Review Awards '91: 10 Best Films of the Year. COL, BTV

Homo Eroticus/Man of the Year &

1971 Handsome servant finds it difficult to satisfy the desires of Bergamo, Italy's socialite. **93m/C VHS, Beta.** *IT* Lando Buzzanca, Rossana Podesta. NO

Hondo &&&

1953 In 1874, whites have broken their treaty with the Apache nation who are now preparing for war. Calvary dispatch rider Hondo Lane (Wayne) encounters Angie (Page) and her young son at an isolated ranch and warns her of the danger but she refuses to leave. After various Indian attacks, Hondo persuades Angie (they've fallen in love) to leave for California with him. Based on the story "The Gift of Cochise" by Louis L'Amour. **84m/C VHS.** John Wayne, Geraldine Page, Ward Bond, Michael Pate, James Arness, Rodolfo Acosta, Leo Gordon, Lee Aaker, Paul Fix; **D:** John Farrow; **W:** James Edward Grant; **C:** Robert Burks, Archie Stout. Nominations: Academy Awards '53: Best Story. MPI

Honey &½

1981 Attractive writer pays an unusual visit to the home of a distinguished publisher. Brandishing a pistol, she demands that he read aloud from her manuscript. As he reads, a unique fantasy unfolds, a dreamlike erotic tale that may be the writer's own sexual awakening. Or maybe not. **89m/C VHS, Beta.** *IT SP* Clio Goldsmith, Fernando Rey, Catherine Spaak; **D:** Gianfranco Angelucci. VES

Honey, I Blew Up the Kid &&½

1992 (PG) Screwball suburban inventor Moranis reverses his shrinking process and this time manages to enlarge his two-year-old into a 112-foot giant who gets bigger every time he comes in contact with electricity. Yikes! Loaded with great special effects, this is a charming and funny film that's fit for the whole family. Sequel to "Honey I Shrunk the Kids." **89m/C VHS, Beta, LV, Closed Caption.** Rick Moranis, Marcia Strassman, Robert Oliveri, Daniel Shalikar, Joshua Shalikar, Lloyd Bridges, John Shea, Keri Russell, Gregory Sierra, Julia Sweeney, Kenneth Tobey, Peter Elbling; **D:** Randal Kleiser; **W:** Thom Eberhardt, Garry Goodrow; **M:** Bruce Broughton. DIS

Honey, I Shrunk the Kids &&½

1989 (G) The popular Disney fantasy about a suburban inventor. His shrinking device accidentally reduces his kids to 1/4 inch tall, and he subsequently throws them out with the garbage. Now they must journey back to the house through the jungle that was once the back lawn. Accompanied by "Tummy Trouble," the first of a projected series of Roger Rabbit Maroon Cartoons. Followed by "Honey, I Blew Up the Kids." **101m/C VHS, Beta, LV, Closed Caption.** Rick Moranis, Matt Frewer, Marcia Strassman, Kristine Sutherland, Thomas Wilson Brown, Jared Rushton, Amy O'Neill, Robert Oliveri; **D:** Joe Johnston, Rob Minkoff; **W:** Ed Naha, Tom Schulman, Stuart Gordon; **M:** James Horner; **V:** Charles Fleischer, Kathleen Turner, Lou Hirsch, April Winchell. DIS, MOV, RDG

The Honey Pot &&½

It Comes Up Murder; Anyone for Venice?; Mr. Fox of Venice **1967** A millionaire feigns death to see the reaction of three of his former lovers. Amusing black comedy with fine performances from all. Based on Moliere's "Volpone." **131m/C VHS.** Rex Harrison, Susan Hayward, Cliff Robertson, Capucine, Edie Adams, Maggie Smith, Adolfo Celi; **D:** Joseph L. Mankiewicz; **W:** Joseph L. Mankiewicz; **M:** John Addison. MGM

Honey, We Shrunk Ourselves &&½

1997 (PG) Scientist Wayne Szalinsky (Moranis) manages to shrink himself, his wife, his brother, and his sister-in-law. The kids just think their parents are out of town for the weekend (so they go nuts). The third in the "Honey" series, this one was released directly to video. Though adults may find it dull, it was made with the kids in mind. **76m/C VHS, Closed Caption.** Rick Moranis, Stuart Pankin, Robin Bartlett, Eve Gordon, Bug Hall; **D:** Dean Cundey; **W:** Karey Kirkpatrick, Nell Scovell, Joel Hodgson; **C:** Raymond N. Stella. TOU

Honeybaby &&

1974 (PG) A smooth international soldier of fortune and a bright, sexy American interpreter are entangled in Middle-Eastern turbulence when they must rescue a politician kidnapped by terrorists. **94m/C VHS.** Calvin Lockhart, Diana Sands; **D:** Michael A. Schultz. GEM, MRV, CNG

Honeyboy &&½

1982 Estrada tries to win fame, fortune, and a ticket out of the barrio as an up-and-coming boxer. Outstanding fight scenes, but little else in this made for television drama of the boxing scene. **100m/C VHS, Beta.** Erik Estrada, Morgan Fairchild, James McEachin, Robert Costanzo, Yvonne Wilder; **D:** John Berry. LIV

Honeymoon &&

1987 A young French woman visiting New York learns she will be deported when her boyfriend is arrested for drug-smuggling. To stay, she is set up in a marriage of convenience and told her new husband will never see or bother her. But hubby has other plans! **96m/C VHS, Beta.** John Shea, Nathalie Baye, Richard Berry, Peter Donat; **D:** Patrick Jamain; **W:** Phillip Setbon. ORI, WAR

Honeymoon Academy &&

For Better or For Worse **1990 (PG-13)** Newly married man has lots to learn in this comic outing. His new wife never told him about her unusual line of business—as an undercover agent! **94m/C VHS, LV, Closed Caption.** Robert Hays, Kim Cattrall, Leigh Taylor-Young; **D:** Gene Quintano; **W:** Gene Quintano; **M:** Robert Folk. HBO, IME

Honeymoon Horror &

197? Stranded on an island, three honeymooning couples soon realize their romantic retreat is a nightmare. A crazy man with an axe is tracking them down. Minimally effective. **90m/C VHS, Beta.** Cheryl Black, William F. Pecchi, Bob Wagner. NO

Honeymoon in Vegas &&½

1992 (PG-13) Romantic comedy turns frantic after Cage loses his fiancee to Caan in a high stakes Vegas poker game. Cage displays lots of talent for manic comedy as the distraught young groom-to-be who encounters numerous obstacles on his way to the altar. Lightweight and funny, featuring a bevy of Elvis impersonators in every size, shape, and color and new versions of favorite Elvis tunes. Look for former Las Vegas U basketball coach Jerry Tarkanian as one of Caan's gambling buddies. **95m/C VHS, LV, Closed Caption.** James Caan, Nicolas Cage, Sarah Jessica Parker, Noriyuki "Pat" Morita, John Capodice, Robert Costanzo, Anne Bancroft, Peter Boyle, Seymour Cassel, Tony Shalhoub; **D:** Andrew Bergman; **W:** Andrew Bergman; **M:** David Newman. COL, NLC, IME

Honeymoon Killers &&&

The Lonely Hearts Killers **1970 (R)** A grim, creepy filmization of a true multiple-murder case wherein an overweight woman and slimy gigolo living on Long Island seduce and murder one lonely woman after another. Independently made and frankly despairing. **103m/ C VHS, Beta, LV.** Tony LoBianco, Shirley Stoler, Mary Jane Higby, Dortha Duckworth, Doris Roberts, Marilyn Chris, Kip McArdle, Mary Breen, Barbara Cason, Ann Harris, Guy Sorel; **D:** Leonard Kastle. LIV, VES

The Honeymoon Machine &&½

1961 A lightweight comedy about two American sailors and a computer scam. McQueen and Mullaney hook up with computer expert Hutton to use their ship's computer to beat the gambling odds at an Italian casino. Their commander misinterprets the signals and thinks the ship is being attacked. Fast paced and the computer angle was new territory in '61. **87m/C VHS.** Steve McQueen, Jack Mullaney, Jim Hutton, Dean Jagger, Paula Prentiss, Brigid Bazlen, Jack Weston; **D:** Richard Thorpe. MGM, MOV

The Honeymooners "Classic 39": TV or Not TV/Honeymooners Highlights

1955 Captain Video and his video rangers are a Kramden household name after Ralph and Ed pool their resources to buy a television. Also includes clips from each of the remaining 38 episodes in "The Honeymooners" series. Video cover illustration by C.F. Payne. This 20 volumes series contains two episodes per tape. **60m/C VHS.** FXV

Honeymooners Hidden Episodes, Vol. 1

The Honeymooners: The Lost Episodes **1953** Three recently-retrieved episodes of the Honeymooners sketches, which were initially aired live as part of the "Jackie Gleason Show." In "Letter to the Boss," Jackie sends some nasty correspondence to his employer when he mistakenly believes that he has been canned. In "Suspense," Ralph fears that Alice is planning his murder when he eavesdrops on her acting practice. In "Dinner Guest," Ralph's plans to suck up to his supervisor meet with hilarious disaster. This "Honeymooners" series contains 28 volumes, which are available separately for purchase. **53m/ B VHS, Beta, Closed Caption.** Jackie Gleason, Audrey Meadows, Art Carney, Joyce Randolph. MPI, FOX, MOV

Honeysuckle Rose &&½

On the Road Again **1980 (PG)** A road-touring country-Western singer whose life is a series of one night stands, falls in love with an adoring young guitar player who has just joined his band. This nearly costs him his marriage with his wife, who while waiting patiently for him at home, decides she's had enough. Easygoing performance by Nelson, essentially playing himself. **120m/C VHS, Beta, LV.** Willie Nelson, Dyan Cannon, Amy Irving, Slim Pickens, Joey Floyd, Charles Levin, Priscilla Pointer; **D:** Jerry Schatzberg; **W:** William D. Wittliff, John Binder, Carol Sobieski; **M:** Willie Nelson, Richard Baskin. Golden Raspberry Awards '80: Worst Supporting Actress (Irving); Nominations: Academy Awards '80: Best Song ("On the Road Again"). WAR, MVD

Hong Kong Nights &&½

1935 Two agents attempt to break up a Chinese smuggling ring run by an unscrupulous madman. Good, action-packed low-budget film. **59m/B VHS, Beta.** Tom Keene, Wera Engels, Warren Hymer, Tetsu Komai, Cornelius Keefe; **D:** E. Mason Hopper. SNC

Hong Kong '97 &&

1994 (R) On the eve of China's takeover of Hong Kong from Great Britain, special agent Reg Cameron (Patrick) murders a Chinese general. With a $10 million bounty on his head, Cameron tries to escape with his partners and girlfriend in tow. Lots of action, good use of Hong Kong setting. **CW:** Language; nudity; violence. **91m/C VHS, LV, Closed Caption.** Robert Patrick, Ming-Na Wen, Brion James, Tim Thomerson; **D:** Albert Pyun. THV

Honky &½

1971 (R) An innocent friendship between a black woman and a white man develops into a passionate romance that has the whole town talking. **92m/C VHS, Beta.** Brenda Sykes, John Nielson, Maria Donzinger; **D:** William A. Graham; **M:** Quincy Jones. UNI

Honky Tonk &&&

1941 A western soap opera in which ne'er do well Clark marries Lana and tries to live a respectable life. In this, the first of several MGM teamings between Gable and Turner, the chemistry between the two is evident. So much so in fact that Gable's then wife Carole Lombard let studio head Louis B. Mayer know that she was not at all thrilled. The public was pleased however, and made the film a hit. **106m/B VHS, Beta.** Clark Gable, Lana Turner, Frank Morgan, Claire Trevor, Marjorie Main, Albert Dekker, Chill Wills, Henry O'Neill, John Maxwell, Morgan Wallace, Betty Blythe, Francis X. Bushman, Veda Ann Borg; **D:** Jack Conway. MGM, CCB

Honky Tonk Freeway &

1981 (PG) An odd assortment of people become involved in a small town Mayor's scheme to turn a dying hamlet into a tourist wonderland. You can find better things to do with your evening than watch this accident. **107m/C VHS, Beta.** Teri Garr, Howard Hesseman, Beau Bridges, Hume Cronyn, William Devane, Beverly D'Angelo, Geraldine Page; **D:** John Schlesinger; **W:** Edward Clinton; **C:** John Bailey; **M:** Elmer Bernstein, Stephen Dorff. NO

Honky Tonk Girl 🎬 1937 Hilarious exploitation film about a hitch-hiking prostitution ring. Also known as "Highway Hell." **?m/C VHS.** Mary Chauning. *SNC*

Honkytonk Man 🎬🎬 1982 (PG) Unsuccessful change-of-pace Eastwood vehicle set during the Depression. Aging alcoholic country singer tries one last time to make it to Nashville, hoping to perform at the Grand Ole Opry. This time he takes his nephew (played by Eastwood's real-life son) with him. **123m/C VHS, Beta, LV.** Clint Eastwood, Kyle Eastwood, John McIntire, Alexa Kenin, Verna Bloom; *D:* Clint Eastwood; *W:* Clancy Carlile; *C:* Bruce Surtees; *M:* Stephen Dorff. *WAR*

Honkytonk Nights 🎬 197? (R) A honkytonkin' romp through an evening in a country/western bar, featuring legendary topless dancer Carol Doda, Georgina ("Devil in Mrs. Jones") Spelvin, and the music of The Hot Licks (minus front man Dan Hicks). **90m/C VHS, Beta.** Carol Doda, Georgina Spelvin, Ramblin' Jack Elliot. *TPV*

Honolulu 🎬🎬½ 1939 A screwball comedy with Powell providing the musical numbers. Young takes on the dual role of a Hollywood star who meets his exact double, a Hawaii plantation owner. They decide to switch identities to give their lives a little oomph. The star sails to Hawaii, falling for fellow passenger Powell, only to discover he's expected to get married upon his arrival in Honolulu. Anderson and Burns and Allen provide the comic relief. ♫ The Leader Doesn't Like Music; This Night Was Made For Dreaming; Honolulu; Hymn To The Sun. **83m/B VHS.** Robert Young, Eleanor Powell, George Burns, Gracie Allen, Rita Johnson, Eddie Anderson, Clarence Kolb; *D:* Edward Buzzell; *W:* Frank Partos, Herbert Fields; *M:* Franz Waxman. *MGM*

Honor Among Thieves 🎬🎬½ *Farewell, Friend* 1968 (R) Two former mercenaries reteam for a robbery that doesn't come off as planned. Not as fast paced as others in Bronson canon. **115m/C VHS, Beta.** *FR IT* Charles Bronson, Alain Delon, Brigitte Fossey, Olga Georges-Picot, Bernard Fresson; *D:* Jean Herman. *CCB, MPI, VTR*

Honor and Glory 🎬🎬 1992 (R) Tracy Pride, an FBI agent and martial arts expert, teams up with an Interpol agent, who doubles as a TV anchorwoman, to stop an international banker from getting his greedy hands on the key to a nuclear arsenal. These fighting gals are up against a team of assassins but they can more than handle themselves. *CW:* Martial arts violence. **90m/C VHS, LV, Closed Caption.** Cynthia Rothrock, Donna Jason, Chuck Jeffreys, Gerald Klein, Robin Shou, Richard Yuen; *D:* Godfrey Hall; *W:* Herb Borkland. *IMP*

Honor of the Range 🎬🎬 1934 The good sheriff's lady is whisked away by his evil twin brother and the sheriff must go undercover to get her back. Odd plot twists for a seemingly normal western. **60m/B VHS.** Ken Maynard, Cecilia Parker, Fred Kohler Sr.; *D:* Ken Maynard. *NOS, DVT, HEG*

Honor Thy Father 🎬🎬 1973 The everyday life of a real-life Mafia family as seen through the eyes of Bill Bonanno, the son of mob chieftain Joe Bonanno. Adapted from the book by Gay Talese. Made for television. **97m/C Beta.** Raf Vallone, Richard Castellano, Brenda Vaccaro, Joseph Bologna; *D:* Paul Wendkos; *M:* George Duning. *PSM*

Honor Thy Father and Mother: The True Story of the Menendez Brothers 🎬🎬½ 1994 First Amy Fisher won the true-sleaze-on-TV award and now its the turn of Lyle and Erik Menendez. Accused of the gruesome 1989 shotgun murders of their wealthy parents, the trial provided numerous sordid details, including alledged sexual abuse of the brothers by both parents. (Both Menendez trials ended in hung juries and will be retried.) Composite characters and compressed time sequences play fast and loose with the facts of the case. Based on public records and on the book "Blood Brothers," by reporters John Johnson and Ronald L. Soble.

Made for television. **90m/C VHS.** Billy Warlock, David Beron, Jill Clayburgh, James Farentino, Susan Blakely, Erin Gray, Elaine Joyce, John Beck, John David Conti, Stanley Kamel; *D:* Paul Schneider; *W:* Michael J. Murray. *AVE*

Hooch 🎬½ 1976 (PG) Comedy about three members of the New York Mafia who get some unexpected southern hospitality when they try to muscle in on a southern family's moonshine operation. **96m/C VHS, Beta.** Gil Gerard, Erika Fox, Melody Rogers, Danny Aiello, Mike Allen, Raymond Serra; *D:* Edward Mann. *PSM*

The Hooded Terror 1938 A merciless group of murderers take on a G-man. **70m/B VHS.** Tod Slaughter, Greta Gynt. *NOS, HEG*

The Hoodlum 🎬🎬 1951 A criminal does his best to rehabilitate and, with a little help from his brother, is able to hold a steady job. However the crime bug dies hard and when he spots an armored car, he just can't resist the temptation. Tierney's real brother, Edward, plays his screen brother. **61m/B VHS, Beta.** Lawrence Tierney, Allene Roberts, Marjorie Riordan, Lisa Golm, Edward Tierney; *D:* Max Nosseck. *SNC*

Hoodlum 🎬🎬½ *Gangster; Hoods* 1996 (R) Director Duke and Fishburne reunite once again (their first union was "Deep Cover") to explore violence in the criminal underworld. Fishburne reprises his role (from "The Cotton Club") as '30s gangster "Bumpy" Johnson, who refuses to allow mobsters Dutch Schultz (Roth) and Lucky Luciano (Garcia) to muscle into the Harlem numbers rackets and starts a bloody turf war. Duke captures the essence of the Depression era gangland saga with an eclectic cast. Roth is ruthless as ever and Garcia, with his small role, is smooth as ever. Fishburne aptly holds his own among the bad guys and bullets. Despite the presence of Tyson and Williams, the women are nothing more than window dressing. Singer Michael McCary from Boyz II Men makes his film debut as Johnson's partner. *CW:* Graphic gangster violence, strong language, a scene of sexuality and some nudity. **?m/C VHS.** Laurence "Larry" Fishburne, Tim Roth, Andy Garcia, Vanessa Williams, Cicely Tyson, Clarence Williams III, William Atherton, Michael McCary; *D:* Bill Duke; *W:* Chris Brancato; *C:* Frank Tidy; *M:* Elmer Bernstein. *NYR*

Hoodlum Empire 🎬🎬 1952 A senator enlists the aid of a former gangster, now a war hero, in his battle against the syndicate. Loosely based on the Kefauver investigations of 1950-51. **98m/B VHS.** Brian Donlevy, Claire Trevor, Forrest Tucker, Vera Ralston, Luther Adler, John Russell, Gene Lockhart, Grant Withers, Taylor Holmes, Roy Barcroft, Richard Jaeckel; *D:* Joseph Kane. *REP*

The Hoodlum Priest 🎬🎬🎬 1961 Biography of the Rev. Charles Dismas Clark (Murray), a Jesuit priest who dedicated his life to working with juvenile delinquents and ex-cons in St. Louis. Dullea made his screen debut as Billy Lee Jackson, a thief who finds the straight and narrow is a hard road with more detours than he can handle. Fine performances with Murray co-scripting under the pseudonym Don Deer. **101m/B VHS, Beta.** Don Murray, Keir Dullea, Larry Gates, Logan Ramsey, Cindi Wood; *D:* Irvin Kershner; *W:* Don Murray, Joseph Landon; *C:* Haskell Wexler. *MGM, FCT*

Hoodoo Ann 🎬🎬 1916 The story of Hoodoo Ann, from her days in the orphanage to her happy marriage. Silent. **27m/B VHS, Beta.** Mae Marsh, Robert "Bobbie" Harron. *CCB*

Hook 🎬🎬 1991 (PG) Although he said he was never gonna to do it, Peter Pan has grown up. Uptight Peter Banning places work before family and has forgotten all about Neverland and the evil Captain Hook, until Hook kidnaps the Banning kids and takes them to Neverland. With the help of Tinkerbell, her magic pixie dust, and happy thoughts, Peter rescues his kids and rediscovers his youth while visiting with the Lost Boys. The sets and special effects are spectacular; the direction less so. Big-budget fantasy lacks the charm it needs to really fly. Still, kids seem to love

it. You'll have to look hard to spot pirates Crosby and Close. Futurizes the J.M. Barrie classic. **142m/C VHS, Beta, LV, 8mm, Closed Caption.** Dustin Hoffman, Robin Williams, Julia Roberts, Bob Hoskins, Maggie Smith, Charlie Korsmo, Caroline Goodall, Amber Scott, Phil Collins, Arthur Malet, Dante Basco, Gwyneth Paltrow; *Cameos:* Glenn Close, David Crosby; *D:* Steven Spielberg; *W:* Nick Castle; *C:* Dean Cundey; *M:* John Williams. Nominations: Academy Awards '91: Best Art Direction/Set Decoration, Best Costume Design, Best Makeup, Best Song ("When You're Alone"), Best Visual Effects. *COL*

Hook, Line and Sinker 🎬🎬 1930 A couple of insurance investigators try to help a young woman restore a hotel, and they find romance and run-ins with crooks. Directed by Cline, who later directed W.C. Fields in "The Bank Dick," "My Little Chickadee," and "Never Give a Sucker an Even Break." **75m/B VHS, LV.** Bert Wheeler, Robert Woolsey, Dorothy Lee, Jobyna Howland, Ralf Harolde, Natalie Moorhead, George F. Marion Sr., Hugh Herbert; *D:* Eddie Cline; *W:* Rod Amateau. *NOS, TTC, FCT*

The Hooked Generation 🎬 1969 (R) A group of drug pushers kidnap defenseless victims, rape innocent girls, and even murder their own Cuban drug contacts (and all without the aid of a cohesive plot). Many gory events precede their untimely deaths; few will be entertained. **92m/C VHS.** Jeremy Slate, Steve Alaimo. *NO*

Hoop Dreams 🎬🎬🎬🎬 1994 (PG-13) Exceptional documentary follows two inner-city basketball phenoms' lives through high school as they chase their dreams of playing in the NBA. We meet Arthur Agee and William Gates as they prepare to enter St. Joseph, a predominantly white Catholic school that has offered them partial athletic scholarships. The coach tabs Gates as the "next Isiah Thomas," alluding to the school's most famous alum. There's plenty of game footage, but the more telling and fascinating parts of the film deal with the kids' families and home life. Both players encounter dramatic reversals of fortune on and off the court, demonstrating the incredibly long odds they face. **169m/C VHS, LV.** Arthur Agee, William Gates; *D:* Steve James; *C:* Peter Gilbert. Chicago Film Critics Awards '94: Best Film; Los Angeles Film Critics Association Awards '94: Best Feature Documentary; MTV Movie Awards '95: Best New Filmmaker Award (James); National Board of Review Awards '94: Best Feature Documentary; New York Film Critics Awards '94: Best Feature Documentary; National Society of Film Critics Awards '94: Best Feature Documentary; Sundance Film Festival '94: Audience Award; Nominations: Academy Awards '94: Best Film Editing. *NLC*

Hooper 🎬🎬½ 1978 (PG) Lightweight behind-the-scenes satire about the world of movie stuntmen. Reynolds is a top stuntman who becomes involved in a rivalry with an up-and-coming young man out to surpass him. Dated good-ole-boy shenanigans. **94m/C VHS, Beta, LV, Closed Caption.** Burt Reynolds, Jan-Michael Vincent, Robert Klein, Sally Field, Brian Keith, John Marley, Adam West; *D:* Hal Needham. Nominations: Academy Awards '78: Best Sound. *WAR*

Hoosiers 🎬🎬🎬 1986 (PG) In Indiana, where basketball is the sport of the gods, a small town high school basketball team gets a new, but surprisingly experienced coach. He makes the team, and each person in it, better than they thought possible. Classic plot rings true because of Hackman's complex and sensitive performance coupled with Hopper's touching portrait of an alcoholic basketball fanatic. **115m/C VHS, Beta, LV, Closed Caption.** Gene Hackman, Barbara Hershey, Dennis Hopper, David Neidorf, Sheb Wooley, Fern Parsons, Brad Boyle, Steve Hollar, Brad Long; *D:* David Anspaugh; *W:* Angelo Pizzo; *C:* Fred Murphy; *M:* Jerry Goldsmith. Los Angeles Film Critics Association Awards '86: Best Supporting Actor (Hopper); Nominations: Academy Awards '86: Best Supporting Actor (Hopper), Best Original Score. *LIV*

Hootch Country Boys 🎬 *Redneck County; The Great Lester Boggs* 1975 (PG) A film packed with moonshine, sheriffs, busty country girls, and chases. **90m/C VHS, Beta.** Alex Karras, Scott MacKenzie, Dean Jagger, Willie Jones, Bob Ridgely, Susan Denbo, Bob Ginnaven, David Haney; *D:* Harry Z. Thomason. *ACA*

Hopalong Cassidy 🐾🐾🐾 *Hopalong Cassidy Enters* **1935** In this first of a long series of "Hopalong Cassidy" films, Hoppy and his pals intervene in a brewing range war. A gang of rustlers is helped by a two-timing foreman who's playing both sides off each other. After a career in silent films, Boyd was pretty much washed up before taking on the role of Cassidy. He was originally asked to play the villain and declined, but agreed to be the good guy if the character was cleaned up. "Gabby" Hayes' stock character was killed off in this episode, but was brought back for later installments. **60m/B VHS.** William Boyd, James Ellison, Paula Stone, Robert Warwick, Charles Middleton, Frank McGlynn, Kenneth Thomson, George "Gabby" Hayes, James Mason, Franklyn Farnum; **D:** Howard Bretherton. *NOS, MRV*

Hopalong Cassidy: Borrowed Trouble 🐾½ **1948** Hoppy must save a righteous teacher from the clutches of kidnappers who plan to place a saloon right next to the school. **61m/B VHS.** William Boyd, Andy Clyde, Rand Brooks, Elaine Riley, John Kellogg, Helen Chapman; **D:** George Archainbaud. *NO*

Hopalong Cassidy: Dangerous Venture 🐾🐾 **1948** "Dangerous Venture" was one of Hoppy's last ventures, produced the final year of the series' 13-year tenure. Hoppy and the gang hunt for Aztec ruins in the great Southwest, and have to deal with renegade Indians and a band of treacherous looters along the way. **55m/B VHS, Beta.** William Boyd, Andy Clyde, Rand Brooks. *NO*

Hopalong Cassidy: False Paradise 🐾🐾 **1948** Another late Hopalong has the noir-clad cowboy rushing to the aid of a girl and her dad when control of their ranch is threatened by swindlers with false mining claims. **59m/B VHS, Beta.** William Boyd, Andy Clyde, Rand Brooks; **D:** George Archainbaud. *NO*

Hopalong Cassidy: Hoppy's Holiday 🐾🐾 **1947** Boyd—the only celluloid incarnation of Clarence Mulford's pulp hero—plays the Hopster yet again. This time, the non-drinking, non-smoking (what does he do for kicks?) hero and a passel of Bar-20 cowboys visit Mesa City for some well-earned R and R, but find themselves caught in a web of corruption. **60m/B VHS, Beta.** William Boyd, Andy Clyde, Rand Brooks, Jeff Corey; **D:** George Archainbaud. *NO*

Hopalong Cassidy: Renegade Trail 🐾🐾 **1939** Hoppy comes to the aid of both a small town sheriff and a widow. **61m/B VHS, Beta.** William Boyd, George "Gabby" Hayes, Russell Hayden, Charlotte Wynters, Russell Hopton, Sonny Bupp, Jack Rockwell, Roy Barcroft, John Merton, Robert F. (Bob) Kortman; **D:** Lesley Selander. *HEG*

Hopalong Cassidy: Riders of the Deadline 🐾🐾 **1943** Hoppy turns into a baddie in this episode in order to infiltrate a treacherous gang and apprehend their leader. **70m/B VHS, Beta.** William Boyd, Andy Clyde, Jimmy Rogers, Robert Mitchum; **D:** Lesley Selander. *NO*

Hopalong Cassidy: Silent Conflict 🐾🐾 **1948** Lucky is tricked and hypnotized by a traveling medicine man who commands him to rob and kill Hoppy. **61m/B VHS, Beta.** William Boyd, Andy Clyde, Rand Brooks; **D:** George Archainbaud. *NO*

Hopalong Cassidy: Sinister Journey 🐾🐾 **1948** Mysterious accidents are plaguing a railroad where an old friend of Hoppy's works, so Hoppy, California, and Lucky take railroad jobs to find out what gives. **58m/B VHS, Beta.** William Boyd, Andy Clyde, Rand Brooks; **D:** George Archainbaud. *NO*

Hopalong Cassidy: The Dead Don't Dream 🐾🐾 **1948** Hoppy's sidekick Lucky decides to get married, but happily-ever-afterdom is threatened when the father of Mrs. Lucky-to-be is murdered. When Hoppy sets out to find the killer, he finds himself suspected of the dastardly deed. **55m/B VHS, Beta.** William Boyd, Andy Clyde, Rand Brooks, John Parrish; **D:** George Archainbaud. *NO*

Hopalong Cassidy: The Devil's Playground 🐾🐾 **1946** Strange things are afoot in a peaceful valley adjacent to a desolate, forbidding wasteland. When Hoppy and a young woman set out across the wasteland to make a gold delivery, they encounter a band of desperados and begin to unravel the secrets of a dishonest political ring. **65m/B VHS.** William Boyd, Andy Clyde, Rand Brooks, Elaine Riley; **D:** George Archainbaud. *NO*

Hopalong Cassidy: The Marauders 🐾🐾 **1947** After seeking shelter in an abandoned church one rainy night, Hoppy and the boys must defend the kirk when it is threatened by a marauder and his gang. **64m/B VHS, Beta.** William Boyd, Andy Clyde, Rand Brooks; **D:** George Archainbaud. *NO*

Hopalong Cassidy: Unexpected Guest 🐾🐾½ **1947** When a small fortune is left to a California family, the head count starts to dwindle, and Hoppy aims to find out why. **59m/B VHS, Beta.** William Boyd, Andy Clyde, Rand Brooks, Una O'Connor; **D:** George Archainbaud. *NO*

Hope and Glory 🐾🐾🐾½ **1987 (PG-13)** Boorman turns his memories of WWII London into a complex and sensitive film. Father volunteers, and mother must deal with the awakening sexuality of her teen-age daughter, keep her son in line, balance the ration books, and try to make it to the bomb shelter in the middle of the night. Seen through the boy's eyes, war creates a playground of shrapnel to collect and wild imaginings come true. Nice companion film to "Empire of the Sun" and "Au Revoir Les Enfants," two more 1987 releases that explore WWII from the recollections of young boys. **97m/C VHS, Beta, LV, 8mm, Closed Caption.** *GB* Sebastian Rice Edwards, Geraldine Muir, Sarah Miles, Sammi Davis, David Hayman, Derrick O'Connor, Susan Wooldridge, Jean-Marc Barr, Ian Bannen, Jill Baker, Charley Boorman, Annie Leon, Katrine Boorman, Gerald James; **D:** John Boorman; **W:** John Boorman; **C:** Philippe Rousselot. British Academy Awards '87: Best Film, Best Supporting Actress (Wooldridge); Golden Globe Awards '88: Best Film—Musical/Comedy; Los Angeles Film Critics Association Awards '87: Best Director (Boorman), Best Film, Best Screenplay; National Board of Review Awards '87: 10 Best Films of the Year; National Society of Film Critics Awards '87: Best Cinematography, Best Director (Boorman), Best Film, Best Screenplay; Nominations: Academy Awards '87: Best Art Direction/Set Decoration, Best Cinematography, Best Director (Boorman), Best Original Screenplay, Best Picture. *FCT, HMV, NLC*

Hoppity Goes to Town *Mr. Bug Goes to Town* **1941** Full-length animated feature from the Max Fleischer studios tells the story of the inhabitants of Bugville, who live in a weed patch in New York City. **77m/C VHS, LV.** **D:** Dave Fleischer; **M:** Frank Loesser, Hoagy Carmichael. *REP, MRV, FCT*

Hoppy Serves a Writ 🐾🐾 **1943** In this last of the series to be based on the writings of the original author, Texas sheriff Cassidy tries to bring a gang of outlaws to justice. Look for a young Robert Mitchum as one of the villains. **67m/B VHS.** William Boyd, Andy Clyde, Jay Kirby, Victor Jory, George Reeves, Hal Taliaferro, Robert Mitchum, Byron Foulger, Earle Hodgins, Roy Barcroft; **D:** George Archainbaud. *NOS, MRV*

Hopscotch 🐾🐾🐾 **1980 (R)** A C.I.A. agent drops out when his overly zealous chief demotes him to a desk job. When he writes a book designed to expose the dirty deeds of the CIA, he leads his boss and KGB pal on a merry chase. Amiable comedy well-suited for Matthau's rumpled talents. **107m/C VHS, Beta, LV.** Walter Matthau, Glenda Jackson, Ned Beatty, Sam Waterston, Herbert Lom; **D:** Ronald Neame. *COL*

Horizons West 🐾🐾½ **1952** Two brothers go their separate ways after the Civil War. One leads a peaceful life as a rancher but the other, corrupted by the war, engages in a violent campaign to build his own empire. Ryan's outstanding performance eclipses that of the young Hudson. **81m/C VHS.** Robert Ryan, Julie Adams, Rock Hudson, Raymond Burr, James Arness, John McIntire, Dennis Weaver, Frances Bavier; **D:** Budd Boetticher; **M:** Henry Mancini. *USH*

The Horizontal Lieutenant 🐾🐾½ **1962** Hutton and Prentiss team up again in this moderately funny romantic-comedy about an officer's escapades during WWII. Based on the novel "The Bottletop Affair" by Gordon Cotler. **90m/C VHS.** Jim Hutton, Paula Prentiss, Jack Carter, Jim Backus, Charles McGraw, Miyoshi Umeki; **D:** Richard Thorpe; **W:** George Wells. *MGM*

The Horn Blows at Midnight 🐾🐾🐾 **1945** A band trumpeter falls asleep and dreams he's a bumbling archangel, on Earth to blow the note bringing the end of the world. But a pretty girl distracts him, and...A wild, high-gloss, well-cast fantasy farce, uniquely subversive in its lighthearted approach to biblical Doomsday. Benny made the film notorious by acting ashamed of it in his later broadcast routines. **78m/B VHS.** Jack Benny, Alexis Smith, Dolores Moran, Allyn Joslyn, Reginald Gardiner, Guy Kibbee, John Alexander, Margaret Dumont; **D:** Raoul Walsh. *MGM, FCT*

Hornet's Nest 🐾🐾½ **1970** Captain Turner (Hudson) is the lone survivor of an Army commando unit which parachuted into the Italian countryside in an effort to blow up a dam being held by the Nazis. He's rescued by a group of boys, the survivors of a German massacre of their nearby town. Turner wants the boys to help him blow up the dam—and they want his help in getting revenge on the Nazis who have occupied their homes. **110m/C VHS.** Rock Hudson, Sylva Koscina, Sergio Fantoni, Jacques Sernas, Giacomo "Jack" Rossi-Stuart, Andrea Bosic, Gerard Herter, Tom Felleghi; **D:** Phil Karlson; **W:** S.S. Schweitzer. *MGM*

The Horrible Dr. Hichcock 🐾🐾½ *L'Orribile Segreto Del Dr. Hichcock* **1962** A sicko doctor, who accidentally killed his first wife while engaged in sexual antics, remarries to bring the first missus back from the dead using his new wife's blood. Genuinely creepy. Sequelled by "The Ghost." **76m/C VHS.** *IT* Robert Flemyng, Barbara Steele; **D:** Riccardo (Robert Hampton) Freda. *SNC*

The Horror Chamber of Dr. Faustus 🐾🐾🐾½ *Eyes without a Face; Les Yeux Sans Visage; Occhi Senza Volto* **1959** A wickedly intelligent, inventive piece of Grand Guignol about a mad doctor who kills young girls so he may graft their skin onto the face of his accidentally mutilated daughter. In French with English subtitles. **84m/B VHS.** *FR* Alida Valli, Pierre Brasseur, Edith Scob, Francois Guerin; **D:** Georges Franju; **C:** Eugene (Eugen Shufftan) Shuftan; **M:** Maurice Jarre. *SNC, TPV, INT*

Horror Express 🐾🐾½ *Panic on the Trans-Siberian Express; Panico en el Transiberiano* **1972 (R)** A creature from prehistoric times, that was removed from its tomb, is transported on the Trans-Siberian railroad. Passengers suddenly discover strange things happening—such as having their souls sucked out of them. **88m/C VHS, Beta.** *SP* Christopher Lee, Peter Cushing, Telly Savalas; **D:** Gene Martin. *SNC, MRV, PSM*

Horror Hospital 🐾 *Computer Killers; Doctor Blood Bath* **1973 (R)** Patients are turned into zombies by a mad doctor in this hospital where no anesthesia is used. Those who try to escape are taken care of by the doctor's guards. **91m/C VHS, Beta.** *GB* Michael Gough, Robin Askwith, Vanessa Shaw, Ellen Pollock, Skip Martin, Dennis Price; **D:** Antony Balch. *GRG*

Horror Hotel 🐾🐾½ *The City of the Dead* **1960** A young witchcraft student visits a small Massachusetts town which has historic ties to witch burnings and discovers a new, and deadly, coven is now active. Well done and atmospheric. **76m/B VHS, LV.** *GB* Christopher Lee, Patricia Jessel, Betta St. John, Dennis Lotis, Venetia Stevenson, Valentine Dyall; **D:** John Llewellyn Moxey; **W:** George L. Baxt. *NOS, MRV, SNC*

Horror House on Highway 5 woof! **1986** Someone in a Nixon mask kills people in this extremely cheap dud. **90m/C VHS, Beta.** *D:* Richard Casey; *W:* Richard Casey. *NO*

The Horror of Dracula 🐾🐾🐾½ *Dracula* **1958** The first Hammer Dracula film, in which the infamous vampire is given a new, elegant and ruthless persona, as he battles Prof. Van Helsing after coming to England. Possibly the finest, most inspired version of Bram Stoker's macabre chestnut, and one that single-handedly revived the horror genre. **82m/C VHS, Beta, LV.** *GB* Peter Cushing, Christopher Lee, Michael Gough, Melissa Stribling, Carol Marsh, John Van Eyssen, Valerie Gaunt; *D:* Terence Fisher; *W:* Jimmy Sangster; *M:* James Bernard. *WAR, FCT, MLB*

The Horror of Frankenstein **1970** Spoof of the standard Frankenstein story features philandering ex-med student Baron Frankenstein, whose interest in a weird and esoteric branch of science provides a shocking and up-to-date rendition of the age-old plot. Preceded by "Frankenstein Must Be Destroyed" and followed by "Frankenstein and the Monster from Hell." **93m/C VHS, Beta.** *GB* Ralph Bates, Kate O'Mara, Dennis Price, David Prowse; *D:* Jimmy Sangster; *W:* Jimmy Sangster. *MLB*

Horror of Party Beach woof! *Invasion of the Zombies* **1964** Considered to be one of the all-time worst films. Features a mob of radioactive seaweed creatures who eat a slew of nubile, surf-minded teenagers. ♫Zombie Stomp. **71m/C VHS, Beta.** John Scott, Alice Lyon, Allen Laurel; *D:* Del Tenney. *PSM*

Horror of the Blood Monsters woof! *Vampire Men of the Lost Planet; Horror Creatures of the Prehistoric Planet; Creatures of the Prehistoric Planet; Creatures of the Red Planet; Flesh Creatures of the Red Planet; The Flesh Creatures; Space Mission of the Lost Planet* **1970** (PG) John Carradine made a career out of being in bad movies, and this one competes as one of the worst. This is an editor's nightmare, made up of black & white film spliced together and colorized. Vampires from outer space threaten to suck all the blood from the people of Earth. **85m/C VHS, Beta.** *PH* John Carradine, Robert Dix, Vicki Volante, Jennifer Bishop; *D:* Al Adamson, George Joseph. *REP*

Horror of the Zombies 🐾 *El Buque Maldito* **1974** (R) Bikinied models are pursued by hooded zombies on board a pleasure yacht...the horror. Effete final installment in the "blind dead" trilogy; see also "Tombs of the Blind Dead" and "Return of the Evil Dead." **90m/C VHS.** *SP* Maria Perschy, Jack Taylor; *D:* Armando de Ossorio; *W:* Armando de Ossorio. *NO*

Horror Planet woof! *Inseminoid* **1980** (R) Alien creature needs a chance to breed before moving on to spread its horror. When a group of explorers disturbs it, the years of waiting are over, and the unlucky mother-to-be will never be the same. Graphic and sensationalistic, capitalizing on the popularity of "Aliens." **93m/C VHS, Beta, LV.** *GB* Robin Clarke, Jennifer Ashley, Stephanie Beacham, Judy Geeson, Steve Grives, Victoria Tennant; *D:* Norman J. Warren.

Horror Rises from the Tomb 🐾🐾 **1972** A 15th century knight and his assistant are beheaded for practicing witchcraft. Five hundred years later, they return to possess a group of vacationers and generally cause havoc. **89m/C VHS, Beta.** *SP* Paul Naschy, Vic Winner, Emma Cohen, Helga Line; *D:* Carlos Aured. *FCT, NLC, LOO*

The Horror Show 🐾 *House 3* **1989** (R) Serial killer fries in electric chair, an event that really steams him. So he goes after the cop who brought him in. Standard dead guy who won't die and wants revenge flick. **95m/C VHS, Beta.** Brion James, Lance Henriksen, Rita Taggart, Dedee Pfeiffer, Aron Eisenberg, Matt Clark; *D:* James Isaac; *W:* Alan Smithee, Leslie Bohem; *C:* Mac Ahlberg. *MGM*

Horrors of Burke & Hare 🐾 **1971** A gory tale about the exploits of a bunch of 19th-century grave robbers. **94m/C VHS, Beta, LV.** Derren Nesbitt, Harry Andrews, Yootha Joyce; *D:* Vernon Sewell. *NWV*

Horrors of Spider Island 🐾 *It's Hot in Paradise; Ein Toter Hing im Netz; A Corpse Hangs in the Web* **1959** D'Arcy is a Hollywood talent scout who sniffs a goldmine in a team of young female dancers whom he schedules to perform for him in Singapore. Their transport plane crashes in the Pacific Ocean and he and the girls are forced to take refuge on an uncharted isle. Upon landing there they discover it is infested with giant crab-sized spiders. Lots of potential for both shock and arousal, which was probably why it was originally released in both "horror" and "girlie" versions. D'Arcy later admitted to taking over for director Bottger and adding all the horror sequences himself. Dubbed from the German. **77m/C VHS.** *GE* Alexander D'Arcy, Ursula Lederstger; *D:* Fritz Bottger. *SMW, TPV*

Horrors of the Red Planet 🐾 *The Wizard of Mars* **1964** Cheapo epic sees astronauts crash on Mars, meet its Wizard, and stumble into a few Oz-like creatures. Technically advised by Forrest J. Ackerman. **81m/C VHS, Beta.** John Carradine, Roger Gentry, Vic McGee; *D:* David L. Hewitt. *GHV, MRV, REP*

The Horse 🐾🐾🐾½ *Horse, My Horse* **1982** A moving, mature Turkish film about a father and son trying to overcome socioeconomic obstacles and their own frailties in order to make enough money to send the boy to school. In Turkish with English subtitles. **116m/C VHS, Beta.** *TU* Ali Ozgenturk. *KIV*

Horse Feathers 🐾🐾🐾½ **1932** Huxley College has to beef up its football team to win the championship game, and the corrupt new college president knows just how to do it. Features some of the brothers' classic routines, and the songs "Whatever It Is, I'm Against It" and "Everyone Says I Love You." **67m/B VHS, Beta, LV.** Groucho Marx, Chico Marx, Harpo Marx, Zeppo Marx, Thelma Todd, David Landau, Nat Pendleton; *D:* Norman Z. McLeod. *USH*

A Horse for Danny 🐾🐾½ **1995** (G) Horse trainer Eddie (Urich), dogged by bad luck, and his 11-year-old niece Danny (Sobieski), come across a thoroughbred named Tom Thumb, who may be their chance at racing's winners circle. TV movie. **92m/C VHS.** Robert Urich, Leelee Sobieski, Ron Brice, Karen Carlson, Gary Basaraba; *D:* Dick Lowry. *HMK*

The Horse in the Gray Flannel Suit 🐾🐾½ **1968** (G) Disney comedy portrays an advertising executive who links his daughter's devotion to horses with a client's new ad campaign. **114m/C VHS, Beta.** Dean Jones, Ellen Janov, Fred Clark, Diane Baker, Lloyd Bochner, Kurt Russell; *D:* Norman Tokar; *M:* George Bruns. *DIS, OM*

The Horse of Pride 🐾🐾½ *Le Cheval D'Orgeuil* **1980** Chabrol takes a telling look at the everyday life of the peasants of Breton—both their pleasures and their sorrows. In French with English subtitles. French script booklet available. **118m/C VHS, Beta.** *FR* Jacques Dufilho, Francois Cluzet; *D:* Claude Chabrol. *INT, APD, AUD*

The Horse Soldiers 🐾🐾½ **1959** An 1863 Union cavalry officer is sent 300 miles into Confederate territory to destroy a railroad junction and is accompanied by a fellow officer who is also a pacifist doctor. Based on a true Civil War incident. **114m/C VHS, Beta, Closed Caption.** John Wayne, William Holden, Hoot Gibson, Anna Lee, Russell Simpson, Strother Martin; *D:* John Ford; *C:* William Clothier. *MGM, FOX*

The Horse Thief 🐾🐾🐾 *Daoma Zei* **1987** Noted as the first movie from the People's Republic of China to be released on video, this epic tells the tale of Norbu, a man who, exiled from his people for horse thievery, is forced to wander the Tibetan countryside with his family in search of work. His son dies while he is in exile, and he, a devout Buddhist, is ultimately forced to accept tribal work in a ritual exorcism, after which he pleads to be accepted back into his clan. Beautiful and image-driven, offering a rare glimpse into the Tibet you won't see in travel brochures. Filmed on location with locals as actors. In Mandarin with English subtitles. **88m/C VHS.** *CH* Tian Zhuang-zhuang. *KIV, FCT*

The Horse Without a Head 🐾🐾½ **1963** Stolen loot has been hidden in a discarded toy horse which is now the property of a group of poor children. The thieves, however, have different plans. Good family fare originally shown on the Disney television show. **89m/C VHS, Beta.** Jean-Pierre Aumont, Herbert Lom, Leo McKern, Pamela Franklin, Vincent Winter; *D:* Don Chaffey. *DIS*

The Horseman on the Roof 🐾🐾½ *Le Hussard sur le Toit* **1995** (R) Lavish costume drama set in Provence in the 1830s, during a cholera epidemic. Italian officer/revolutionary Angelo (Martinez) is on the run and eventually meets up with beautiful Pauline de Theus (Binoche), who hides him in a quarantined French village. Pauline's in search of her husband and Angelo reluctantly agrees to help her. Together they manage to escape a military cordon and travel to another plague town. There's lots of riding through the countryside and hiding out and not much actually happens. Nice scenery, attractive stars. Based on the 1951 novel by Jean Giono. French with subtitles; originally released at 135 minutes.*CW:* A scene of nudity. **119m/C VHS, LV.** *FR* Olivier Martinez, Juliette Binoche, Francois Cluzet, Isabelle Carre, Jean Yanne, Claudio Amendola, Pierre Arditti; *Cameos:* Gerard Depardieu; *D:* Jean-Paul Rappeneau; *W:* Jean-Paul Rappeneau, Jean-Claude Carriere, Nina Companeez; *C:* Thierry Arbogast; *M:* Jean-Claude Petit. Cesar Awards '96: Best Cinematography, Best Sound; Nominations: Cesar Awards '96: Best Actress (Binoche), Best Art Direction/Set Decoration, Best Costume Design, Best Director (Rappeneau), Best Film, Best Film Editing, Best Score. *MAX*

Horsemasters 🐾🐾 **1961** A group of young riders enter a special training program in England to achieve the ultimate equestrian title of horsemaster, with Annette having to overcome her fear of jumping. Originally a two-part Disney television show, and released as a feature film in Europe. **85m/C VHS, Beta.** Tommy Kirk, Annette Funicello, Janet Munro, Tony Britton, Donald Pleasence, Jean Marsh, John Fraser, Millicent Martin; *D:* William Fairchild. *DIS*

The Horsemen 🐾½ **1970** (PG) An Afghani youth enters the brutal buzkashi horse tournament to please his macho-minded father. Beautifully shot in Afghanistan and Spain by Claude Renoir. **109m/C VHS, Beta.** Omar Sharif, Leigh Taylor-Young, Jack Palance, David De, Peter Jeffrey; *D:* John Frankenheimer; *W:* Dalton Trumbo; *M:* Georges Delerue. *COL*

The Horseplayer 🐾½ **1991** (R) A loner is drawn into a mysterious triangle of decadence and desire in this riveting psychothriller. **?m/C VHS, LV, Closed Caption.** Brad Dourif, Sammi Davis, M.K. Harris, Vic Tayback; *D:* Kurt Voss. *REP*

The Horse's Mouth 🐾🐾🐾 *The Oracle* **1958** An obsessive painter discovers that he must rely upon his wits to survive in London. A hilarious adaptation of the Joyce Cary novel. The laserdisc version is accompanied by an episode of the British documentary series "The Art of Film" profiling Guinness and his screen career. **93m/C VHS, Beta, LV.** *GB* Alec Guinness, Kay Walsh, Robert Coote, Renee Houston, Michael Gough; *D:* Ronald Neame. National Board of Review Awards '58: 5 Best Foreign Films of the Year, Best Supporting Actress (Walsh); Nominations: Academy Awards '58: Best Adapted Screenplay. *HMV, ING, NLC*

The Hospital 🐾🐾🐾½ **1971** (PG) Cult favorite providing savage, unrelentingly sarcastic look at the workings of a chaotic metropolitan hospital beset by murders, witchdoctors, madness, and plain ineptitude. **101m/C VHS, Beta, Closed Caption.** George C. Scott, Diana Rigg, Barnard Hughes, Stockard Channing, Nancy Marchand, Richard Dysart; *D:* Arthur Hiller; *W:* Paddy Chayefsky. Academy

Awards '71: Best Story & Screenplay; Berlin International Film Festival '72: Silver Prize; British Academy Awards '72: Best Screenplay; Golden Globe Awards '72: Best Screenplay; Writers Guild of America '71: Best Original Screenplay; Nominations: Academy Awards '71: Best Actor (Scott). *MGM, FOX*

Hospital Massacre woof! *X-Ray; Ward 13; Be My Valentine, Or Else* 1981 (R) Psychopathic killer is loose in a hospital. Seems he holds a grudge against the woman who laughed at his valentine when they were children twenty years earlier, and too bad for her that she just checked in as a patient. Former "Playboy" and Hefner playmate Benton frolics in dangerous health care situation presented by the Cannon organization. 89m/C VHS, Beta. Barbi Benton, Jon Van Ness, Chip Lucio; *D:* Boaz Davidson; *W:* Marc Behm. *MGM*

Hospital of Terror *♂♂* *Nurse Sherri; Terror Hospital; Beyond the Living* 1978 (R) A transmigratory religious fanatic who died on the operating table manages to possess a nurse (Jacobson) before he kicks the bucket, and once in his candystripe incarnation, vents his spleen on the doctors who botched his operation. It's got a little more plasma than Adamson's "AstroZombies," considered by many to be a world-class boner. 88m/C VHS. Jill Jacobson, Geoffrey Land, Marilyn Joi, Mary Kay Pass, Prentiss Moulden, Clayton Foster; *D:* Al Adamson. *NO*

The Hostage *♂♂½* 1967 (PG) A young teenager is witness to a gruesome and clandestine burial. The two murderers responsible take it upon themselves to see that their secret is never told. 84m/C VHS. Don O'Kelly, Harry Dean Stanton, John Carradine, Danny Martins; *D:* Russell S. Doughten Jr. *NO*

Hostage *♂½* 1987 (R) Arab terrorists hijack a plane and the passengers start to fight back. Filmed in South Africa. 94m/C VHS, Beta. Karen Black, Kevin McCarthy, Wings Hauser; *D:* Hanro Mohr; *M:* Brad Fiedel. *COL*

Hostage *♂♂* 1992 (R) British Secret Service agent John Rennie is fed up after a difficult mission in Argentina. He thinks he can walk away clean but his superiors beg to differ. He's marked for murder but Rennie has a dangerous plan that could guarantee his safety—only if he returns to Argentina to set things in motion. Based on the novel "No Place to Hide" by Ted Allbeury.*CW:* Language, violence, and sexuality. 90m/C VHS, Beta, Closed Caption. Sam Neill, Talisa Soto, James Fox; *D:* Robert W. Young. *PAR, PMS*

Hostage for a Day *♂♂½* 1994 Married to a shrew, toiling for an overbearing father-in-law, and suffering a midlife crisis, Wendt decides to fake his own kidnapping, take the ransom money, and head off for a better life. A series of comedic complications abound. Candy's directorial debut. Made for TV. 92m/C VHS, LV. George Wendt, John Vernon, Robin Duke, Peter Torokvei, Don Lake, Frank Moore, John Hemphill, Christopher Templeton; *Cameos:* John Candy; *D:* John Candy; *W:* Peter Torokvei, Robert Crane, Kari Hildebrand; *M:* Ian Thomas. *THV*

The Hostage Tower *♂♂* 1980 (PG) In France, a group of international crime figures capture the visiting U.S. president's mother, hold her hostage in the Eiffel Tower and demand $30 million in ransom. Made for television. 97m/C VHS, Beta, LV. Peter Fonda, Maud Adams, Britt Ekland, Billy Dee Williams, Keir Dullea, Douglas Fairbanks Jr., Rachel Roberts, Celia Johnson; *D:* Claudio Guzman.

Hostages *♂* 1979 A gang of criminals kidnap a family on vacation at a Caribbean island. 93m/C VHS, Beta. Stuart Whitman, Marisa Mell. *NO*

Hostages *♂♂♂* 1993 (R) Harrowing docudrama about the Beirut hostage crisis combines acutal news footage with scenes of the prisoners and their families. Under desperate conditions hostages John McCarthy, Brian Keenan, Terry Anderson, Thomas Sutherland, Frank Reed, and Terry Waite try to hold on to their sanity and humanity as their families struggle for their release. Filmed on location in England, Israel, and Lebanon. Made for cable TV.*CW:* Strong language.

90m/C VHS, Closed Caption. Colin Firth, Ciaran Hinds, Jay O. Sanders, Josef Sommer, Harry Dean Stanton, Kathy Bates, Natasha Richardson, Conrad Asquith; *D:* David Wheatley; *W:* Bernard MacLaverty. *IMP*

Hostile Guns *♂♂½* 1967 A law man discovers a woman he once loved is now an inmate he is transporting across the Texas badlands. Routine with the exception of cameos by veteran actors. Based on a story by Sloan Nibley and James Edward Grant. 91m/C VHS, LV, Closed Caption. George Montgomery, Yvonne De Carlo, Tab Hunter, John Russell; *Cameos:* Brian Donlevy, Richard Arlen, Fuzzy Knight, Donald (Don "Red") Barry; *D:* R.G. Springsteen; *W:* Steve Fisher, Sloan Nibley. *PAR*

Hostile Intentions *♂♂* 1995 (R) Three girlfriends head for a wweekend of fun in the sun in Tijuana and find themselves turned into fugitives through a series of misunderstandings. In order to get home, they must risk a night border crossing with a group of illegal immigrants.*CW:* Language, violence, sexual situations. 90m/C VHS, Closed Caption. Tia Carrere, Lisa Dean Ryan, Tricia Leigh Fisher, Carlos Gomez; *D:* Catherine Cyran; *W:* Catherine Cyran. *AVE*

Hostile Takeover *♂½* *Office Party* 1988 (R) A mild-mannered accountant finally cracks and takes his co-workers hostage. He faces the police in a tense showdown. 93m/C VHS, Beta, LV. David Warner, Michael Ironside, Kate Vernon, Jayne Eastwood; *D:* George Mihalka. *LIV*

Hot Blood *♂* 1989 Two bank robbers take an innocent woman hostage and thrust her in the midst of a huge family battle. Another lukewarm entry from the director of "The Arrogant." 89m/C VHS, Beta. Sylvia Kristel, Alicia Moro, Aldo Sambrel, Gaspar Cano; *D:* Philippe Blot. *CAN*

Hot Box woof! 1972 (R) A Filipino-shot, low budget woofer. Prison flick about women who break out and foment a revolution. 85m/C VHS, Beta. Andrea Cagan, Margaret Markov, Rickey Richardson, Laurie Rose; *D:* Joe Viola; *W:* Joe Viola, Jonathan Demme.

Hot Bubblegum *♂* 1981 (R) Three teenagers discover sex, the beach, rock 'n' roll, sex, drag racing, and sex. 94m/C VHS, Beta. Jonathan Segall, Zachi Noy, Yftach Katzur. *NO*

Hot Child in the City *♂* 1987 A country girl goes to Los Angeles and searches through the city's fleshpots for her sister's killer. Music by Nick Glider, Lou Reed, Billy Idol, and Fun Boy Three. 85m/C VHS, Beta. Leah Ayres Hendrix, Shari Shattuck, Geof Pryssir; *D:* John Florea. *PSM, PAR*

Hot Chocolate *♂♂* 1992 (PG-13) Derek is a sultry Texas tycoon who wants to buy out the French chocolate factory run by Hays. After getting a look at her, work isn't all that's on his mind. 93m/C VHS, LV. Bo Derek, Robert Hays. *LIV*

Hot Dog...The Movie! *♂½* 1983 (R) There's an intense rivalry going on between an Austrian ski champ and his California challenger during the World Cup Freestyle competition in Squaw Valley. Snow movie strictly for teens or their equivalent. 96m/C VHS, Beta, Closed Caption. David Naughton, Patrick Houser, Shannon Tweed, Tracy N. Smith; *D:* Peter Markle; *M:* Peter Bernstein. *MGM, FOX*

Hot Foot/A Happy Married Couple 1920 Two silent comedies: "Hot Foot" (1920), is about Dunn's hobo character in the Chaplin mold; "A Happy Married Couple" (1916), is about a young married couple whose puppy, as described in a letter, is mistaken for a baby by their parents. 51m/B VHS, Beta, 8mm. Bobbie Dunn, Neal Burns, Betty Compson. *VYY*

Hot Lead *♂♂* 1951 Typical Holt oater which has the cowpoke and his sidekick Martin trying to avenge the death of a close friend who was killed by a gang of train robbers. 60m/B VHS. Tim Holt, Joan Dixon, Ross Elliott, John Dehner; *D:* Stuart Gilmore. *MOV*

Hot Lead & Cold Feet *♂♂* 1978 (G) Twin brothers (one a gunfighter, the other meek and mild) compete in a train race where the winner will take ownership of a small western town.

Dale not only plays both brothers, but also their tough father. Standard Disney fare. 89m/C VHS, Beta. Jim Dale, Don Knotts, Karen Valentine; *D:* Robert Butler; *W:* Arthur Alsberg; *M:* Buddy Baker. *DIS*

The Hot Line *♂½* *The Day the Hot Line Got Hot; Le Rouble a Deux Faces; El Rublo de las dos Caras* 1969 The world's two superpowers become befuddled when the hot line connecting Washington and Moscow breaks down. Taylor's final film. 87m/C VHS. Robert Taylor, Charles Boyer, George Chakiris, Dominique Fabre, Gerard Tichy; *D:* Etienne Perier. *REP*

Hot Millions *♂♂♂* 1968 Hysterical comedy about high-class swindling operation with Ustinov as a refined embezzler. Excellent cast and sharp script. Although it didn't do well at the box office, this amusing romp became one of the biggest sleepers of the year. 106m/C VHS, Closed Caption. GB Peter Ustinov, Maggie Smith, Karl Malden, Bob Newhart, Robert Morley, Cesar Romero, Melinda May, Ann Lancaster, Margaret Courtenay, Lynda Baron, Billy Milton, Peter Jones, Raymond Huntley, Kynaston Reeves; *D:* Eric Till; *W:* Ira Wallach, Peter Ustinov. Nominations: Academy Awards '68: Best Story & Screenplay. *MGM*

Hot Money *♂* 1979 A small-town drama about an ex-con who poses as an assistant sheriff and plots a million-dollar robbery during the town's 4th of July parade. Made shortly before Welles' death, and kept on the shelf for more than five years. 78m/C VHS, Beta. Orson Welles, Michael Murphy, Bobby Pickett, Michelle Finney. *THV*

Hot Moves *♂* 1984 (R) Four high school boys make a pact to lose their virginity before the end of the summer. 89m/C VHS, Beta. Michael Zorek, Adam Silbar, Jill Schoelen, Deborah Richter, Monique Gabrielle, Tami Holbrook, Virgil Frye; *D:* Jim Sotos. *VES*

Hot Potato *♂* 1976 (PG) Black Belt Jones rescues a senator's daughter from a megalomaniacal general by using skull-thwacking footwork. 87m/C VHS, Beta. Jim Kelly, George Memmoli, Geoffrey Binney; *D:* Oscar Williams. *WAR*

Hot Pursuit *♂½* 1984 (PG) A woman who has been framed for murder runs from the law and a relentless hitman. 94m/C VHS, Beta. Mike Preston, Dina Merrill, Kerrie Keane. *THV*

Hot Pursuit *♂½* 1987 (PG-13) A prep-school bookworm resorts to Rambo-like tactics in tracking down his girlfriend and her family after being left behind for a trip to the tropics. 93m/C VHS, Beta, LV. John Cusack, Robert Loggia, Jerry Stiller, Wendy Gazelle; *D:* Steven Lisberger; *W:* Steven W. Carabatsos. *PAR*

Hot Resort *♂½* 1985 (R) Young American lads mix work and play when they sign on as summer help at an island resort. Typical teen sex fantasy. 92m/C VHS, Beta. Bronson Pinchot, Tom Parsekian, Michael Berz, Linda Kenton, Frank Gorshin; *D:* John Robins; *W:* Boaz Davidson, John Robins. *MGM*

The Hot Rock *♂♂♂* *How To Steal a Diamond in Four Easy Lessons* 1970 (PG) A motley crew of bumbling thieves conspire to steal a huge, priceless diamond; a witty, gritty comedy that makes no moral excuses for its characters and plays like an early-'70s crime thriller gone awry. Adapted from the novel by Donald E. Westlake. The sequel, 1974's "Bank Shot," stars George C. Scott in the role created by Redford. 97m/C VHS, Beta, LV. Robert Redford, George Segal, Ron Leibman, Zero Mostel, Moses Gunn, William Redfield, Charlotte Rae, Topo Swope; *M:* Quincy Jones. Nominations: Academy Awards '72: Best Film Editing. *FOX*

Hot Rod *♂* *Rebel of the Road* 1979 A young California hotrodder battles the evil sponsor of a drag race championship. 97m/C VHS, Beta. Greg Henry, Robert Culp, Pernell Roberts, Robin Mattson, Grant Goodeve; *D:* George Armitage. *NLC*

Hot Rod Girl *♂* *Hot Car Girl* 1956 A concerned police officer (Conners) organizes supervised drag racing after illegal drag racing gets out of hand in his community. 75m/B VHS. Lori Nelson, Chuck Connors, John W. Smith; *D:* Leslie Martinson; *W:* John McGreevey. *SNC, NOS, MRV*

Hot Shot 🎬½ 1986 (PG) An inspirational tale involving a young soccer player who goes to great lengths to take training from a soccer star, played - of course - by Pele. 90m/C VHS, Beta. Pele, Jim Youngs, Billy Warlock, Weyman Thompson, Mario Van Peebles, David Groh; **D:** Rick King. *WAR, MVD*

Hot Shots! 🎬🎬🎬 1991 (PG-13) Another entry from "The Naked Gun" team of master movie parodists, this has lots of clever sight gags but the verbal humor often plummets to the ground. Spoofs "Top Gun" and similar gung-ho air corps adventures but doesn't forget other popular films including "Dances with Wolves" and "The Fabulous Baker Boys." Sheen is very funny as ace fighter pilot Sean "Topper" Harley who's to avenge the family honor. Great when you're in the mood for laughs that don't require thought. 83m/C VHS, Closed Caption. Charlie Sheen, Cary Elwes, Valeria Golino, Lloyd Bridges, Kevin Dunn, Jon Cryer, William O'Leary, Kristy Swanson, Efrem Zimbalist Jr., Bill Irwin, Heidi Swedberg, Judith Kahan, Pat Proft; *Cameos:* Charles Barkley, Bill Laimbeer; **D:** Jim Abrahams; **W:** Pat Proft, Jim Abrahams; **C:** Bill Butler; **M:** Sylvester Levay. *FXV*

Hot Shots! Part Deux 🎬🎬½ 1993 (PG-13) Second "Hot Shots" outing doesn't live up to the first, but it's not bad either. Admiral Tug Benson (Bridges) is elected President (yes, of the U.S.) and calls on Sheen's newly pumped-up Topper to take on Saddam Hussein Rambo-style. Love interest Ramada (Golino), returns but this time she's competing with Michelle (Bakke), a sexy CIA agent. Crenna spoofs his role in the "Rambo" films as Sheen's mentor; look for real-life dad Martin in a take-off of "Apocalypse Now." Shtick flies as fast and furious as the bodies, with Bridges getting a chance to reprise his glory days of "Sea Hunt." Don't miss the credits. **CW:** Language and sexual spoofs. 89m/C VHS, LV, Closed Caption. Charlie Sheen, Lloyd Bridges, Valeria Golino, Brenda Bakke, Richard Crenna, Miguel Ferrer, Rowan Atkinson, Jerry Haleva, Mitchell Ryan, Gregory Sierra, Ryan Stiles, Michael Colyar; *Cameos:* Martin Sheen, Bob Vila; **D:** Jim Abrahams; **W:** Pat Proft, Jim Abrahams; **M:** Basil Poledouris. *FXV, BTV*

Hot Spell 🎬½ 1958 In an attempt to repair her marriage and unify her family, a mother plans a reunion-birthday party for her husband. Despair reigns in this sultry, Southern melodrama. 86m/B VHS, Beta. Shirley Booth, Anthony Quinn, Shirley MacLaine, Earl Holliman, Eileen Heckart; **D:** Daniel Mann; **C:** Loyal Griggs; **M:** Alex North. *BAR*

The Hot Spot 🎬🎬½ 1990 (R) An amoral drifter arrives in a small Texas town and engages in affairs with two women, including his boss's over-sexed wife and a young woman with her own secrets. Things begin to heat up when he decides to plot a bank robbery. Based on Charles Williams' 1952 novel "Hell Hath No Fury." 120m/C VHS, LV, Closed Caption. Don Johnson, Virginia Madsen, Jennifer Connelly, Charles Martin Smith, William Sadler, Jerry Hardin, Barry Corbin, Leon Rippy, Jack Nance; **D:** Dennis Hopper; **W:** Charles Williams, Nona Tyson; **M:** Jack Nitzsche. *ORI, FCT*

Hot Stuff 🎬 1980 (PG) Officers on a burglary task force decide the best way to obtain convictions is to go into the fencing business themselves. 91m/C VHS, Beta, LV. Dom DeLuise, Jerry Reed, Suzanne Pleshette, Ossie Davis; **D:** Dom DeLuise; **W:** Donald E. Westlake, Michael Kane. *COL*

Hot Summer in Barefoot County 🎬🎬 1974 (R) A state law enforcement officer on the search for illegal moonshiners finds more than he bargained for. 90m/C VHS, Beta. Sherry Robinson, Tonia Bryan, Dick Smith; **D:** Will Zens. *NO*

Hot T-Shirts woof! 1979 (R) A small town bar owner needs a boost for business, finding the answer in wet T-shirt contests. Softcore trash. 86m/C VHS, Beta. Ray Holland, Stephanie Lawlor, Pauline Rose, Corinne Alphen; **D:** Chuck Vincent. *USH*

Hot Target 🎬 1985 (R) An ideal mother becomes obsessed with the stranger who seduced her, even after she finds out he's a thief planning to rob her home. 93m/C VHS, Beta, LV. *NZ* Simone Griffeth, Steve Marachuk; **D:** Denis Lewiston. *LIV, VES*

The Hot, the Cool, and the Vicious 198? A quiet town turns into a bloody, martial arts playground when three hombres trade blows in a tavern. ?m/C VHS. Wang Tao, Tommy Lee, Sun Chia-Lin. *MGI*

Hot Times 🎬 1974 (R) Low-budget comedy about a high school boy who, after striking out with the high school girls, decides to go to New York and have the time of his life. 80m/C VHS, Beta. Gail Lorber, Amy Farber, Henry Cory; **D:** Jim McBride; **W:** Jim McBride. *MON*

Hot to Trot! 🎬 1988 (PG) A babbling idiot links up with a talking horse in an updated version of the "Francis, the Talking Mule" comedies, by way of Mr. Ed. The equine voice is provided by Candy. Some real funny guys are wasted here. 90m/C VHS, Beta, LV, Closed Caption. Bob(cat) Goldthwait, Dabney Coleman, Virginia Madsen, Jim Metzler, Cindy Pickett, Tim Kazurinsky, Santos Morales, Barbara Whinnery, Garry Kluger; **D:** Michael Dinner; **W:** Charlie Peters; **M:** Danny Elfman; **V:** John Candy. *WAR*

Hot Touch woof! 198? An art forger with a large heist is besieged by a slashing maniac, and must discover the culprit. 92m/C VHS, Beta. Wayne Rogers, Samantha Eggar, Marie-France Pisier, Melvyn Douglas. *TWE, HHE*

Hot Under the Collar 🎬½ 1991 (R) Jerry is a weasel who tries to seduce the luscious Monica by using hypnosis. But his plans backfire and instead Monica enters a convent and takes a vow of chastity. This isn't going to stop Jerry, he tries posing as a priest and even dressing as a nun in order to get her out. Things get even more complicated when a mobster, looking for a fortune in stolen diamonds, sneaks into the convent. **CW:** Sensuality. 87m/C VHS. Richard Gabai, Angela Visser, Daniel Friedman, Mindy Clarke, Tane McClure; **D:** Richard Gabai. *HBO*

Hot Water/Safety Last 1924 Two classic Harold Lloyd silent comedies, "Hot Water" (1924) and "Safety Last" (1923). "Safety Last" features one of Lloyd's most famous stunt scenes, where he is hanging from the hands of a giant clock on the side of a building, high above the city. 81m/B VHS, Beta. Harold Lloyd. *TLF*

Hot Wire 🎬½ 197? Tired comedy about the unscrupulous side of the car repossession racket. 92m/C VHS, Beta. George Kennedy, Strother Martin. *NO*

Hotel 🎬½ 1967 (PG) A pale rehash of the "Grand Hotel" formula about an array of rich characters interacting in a New Orleans hotel. From the Arthur Hailey potboiler; the basis for the television series. 125m/C VHS, Beta. Rod Taylor, Catherine Spaak, Karl Malden, Melvyn Douglas, Merle Oberon, Michael Rennie, Richard Conte, Kevin McCarthy; **D:** Richard Quine; **W:** Wendell Mayes; **C:** Charles B(ryant) Lang. *WAR*

Hotel Colonial 🎬½ 1988 (R) A young Italian idealist ventures to Columbia to retrieve the body of his brother, who reportedly killed himself. Once there, he finds the dead man is not his brother, and decides to investigate. 103m/C VHS, Beta, LV, 8mm. *IT* Robert Duvall, John Savage, Rachel Ward, Massimo Troisi; **D:** Cinzia Torrini; **W:** Ira Barmak, Enzo Monteleone; **M:** Pino Donaggio. *NLC*

Hotel de Love 🎬🎬½ 1996 (R) Seventeen-year-old fraternal twin brothers Rick (Young) and Stephen Dunne (Bossell) both fall for beautiful Melissa (Burrows) and she has a short-lived romance with the more-aggressive Rick. Ten years later, mopey stockbroker Stephen shows up at the tacky theme honeymoon hotel Rick now manages and who should show up (besides the twins bickering parents) but Melissa and her fiance Norman (O'Brien). So the twins renew their competition while Melissa decides if Norman is the right guy for her, Mrs. Dunne gets mash notes from a secret admirer, and fortuneteller Alison (Grandi-

son), who happens to be Rick's ex-girlfriend, offers romantic advice to Stephen. **CW:** Sexuality. 93m/C VHS, LV, Closed Caption. *AU* Aden Young, Simon Bossell, Saffron Burrows, Julia Blake, Ray Barrett, Pippa Grandison, Alan Hopgood, Peter O'Brien; **D:** Craig Rosenberg; **W:** Craig Rosenberg; **C:** Stephen Windon; **M:** Brett Rosenberg. *LIV*

Hotel du Lac 🎬🎬 1986 A made-for-British-television adaptation of the Anita Brookner novel about a woman writer languishing at a Swiss lakefront hotel. 110m/C VHS, Beta. *GB* Anna Massey, Denholm Elliott, Googie Withers; **D:** Giles Foster; **M:** Carl Davis. *FOX, TVC, VCO*

Hotel Imperial 🎬🎬 1927 Set in 1917 Budapest, six Hungarian soldiers ride into a frontier town and find it occupied by Russians. Hall plays Lieutenant Almasy, who takes refuge in the Hotel Imperial. Orchestra scored. 84m/B VHS, Closed Caption. Pola Negri, James Hall, George Siegmann, Max Davidson; **D:** Mauritz Stiller. *GPV*

The Hotel New Hampshire 🎬🎬 1984 (R) The witless, amoral adaptation of John Irving's novel about a very strange family's adventures in New Hampshire, Vienna and New York City, which include gang rape, incest, and Kinski in a bear suit. 110m/C VHS, Beta, LV. Jodie Foster, Rob Lowe, Beau Bridges, Nastassia Kinski, Wallace Shawn, Wilford Brimley, Amanda Plummer, Anita Morris, Matthew Modine, Lisa Banes, Seth Green; **D:** Tony Richardson; **W:** Tony Richardson; **C:** David Watkin. *VES*

Hotel Paradiso 🎬🎬½ 1966 Slightly amusing bedroom farce has timid Guinness trying to carry on affair with Italian sexpot Lollibrigida. Guinness fans won't be disappointed, although it's not a top-rate production. Based on the play "L'Hotel du Libre Exchange" by Georges Feydeau and Maurice Desvalliers. 100m/C VHS. *GB* Alec Guinness, Gina Lollobrigida, Akim Tamiroff, Marie Bell, Derek Fowlds; **D:** Peter Glenville; **W:** Peter Glenville, Jean-Claude Carriere. *MGM*

Hotel Reserve 🎬🎬🎬 1944 A Nazi spy is reportedly afoot in a French resort during WWII, and tension mounts as the guests attempt to flush him out. Critical response to this film is wildly split; some find it obvious, while others call it well-done and suspenseful. Based on the novel "Epitaph for a Spy" by Eric Ambler. 79m/B VHS, Beta. *GB* James Mason, Lucie Mannheim, Raymond Lovell, Julien Mitchell, Martin Miller, Herbert Lom, Frederick Valk, Valentine Dyall, Patricia Medina; **D:** Victor Hanbury, Lance Comfort, Max Greene. *TTC, RXM*

Hotel Room 🎬🎬½ David Lynch's Hotel Room 1993 A trilogy of stories set in the same drab New York hotel room in three different time periods. "Getting Rid of Robert," set in 1992, has three girlfriends swilling champagne and discussing Sasha's slick, movie exec boyfriend whom she wants to dump. "Tricks," set in 1969, features Darlene, a bored, druggy prostitute; her client, Moe; and the sudden appearance of Moe's talkative friend, Lou. "Blackout" is set in 1936 and features a young husband trying to cope with the madness of his beautiful wife. Unfortunately, all three stories are rambling and lacking in energy. Made for cable television. 100m/C VHS, Closed Caption. Deborah Unger, Mariska Hargitay, Chelsea Field, Griffin Dunne, Glenne Headly, Harry Dean Stanton, Freddie Jones, Crispin Glover, Alicia Witt, Clark Heathcliffe Brolly, Camilla Overbye Roos; **D:** James Signorelli, David Lynch; **W:** Barry Gifford, Jay McInerney; **M:** Angelo Badalamenti. *WOV, FCT*

Hothead 🎬🎬 Coup de Tete 1978 A heedless, impulsive soccer player's behavior gets him cut from the team, fired from his mill job, and booted out of his favorite bar. In French with English subtitles or dubbed. 98m/C VHS, Beta. *FR* Patrick Dewaere, Jean Bouise, Michel Aumont, France Dougnac; **D:** Jean-Jacques Annaud; **W:** Francis Veber. Cesar Awards '80: Best Supporting Actor (Bouise). *COL*

Hotline 🎬🎬 1982 After taking a job answering phones at a crisis center, a woman becomes the next target of a psychotic killer. Made for television. 96m/C VHS. Lynda Carter, Steve Forrest, Granville

Van Dusen, Monte Markham, James Booth; **D:** Jerry Jameson. *NO*

H.O.T.S. ♂ *T & A Academy* 1979 (R) A sex-filled sorority rivalry film, starring a slew of ex-Playboy Playmates in wet shirts. Screenplay co-written by exploitation star Caffaro. 95m/C **VHS, Beta.** Susan Kiger, Lisa London, Kimberly Cameron, Danny Bonaduce, Steve Bond; **D:** Gerald Seth Sindell; **W:** Cheri Caffaro. *LIV, VES*

Houdini ♂♂½ 1953 Historically inaccurate but entertaining biopic of the infamous magician and escapologist. Chronicles his rise to stardom, his efforts to contact his dearly departed mother through mediums (a prequel to "Ghost"?) and his heart-stopping logic-defying escapes. First screen teaming of Leigh and Curtis, who had already been married for two years. 107m/C **VHS, Closed Caption.** Tony Curtis, Janet Leigh, Torin Thatcher, Angela Clark, Stefan Schnabel, Ian Wolfe, Sig Rumann, Michael Pate, Connie Gilchrist, Mary Murphy, Tor Johnson; **D:** George Marshall; **W:** Philip Yordan. *PAR, FCT*

The Hound of London ♂♂½ *Sherlock Holmes in The Hound of London* 1993 Inspector Lestrade brings Sherlock Holmes (Macnee) his latest case, a double murder that has taken place at the Strand Theatre. And among the suspects is the only woman Holmes has ever admired, the lovely Irene Adler. Eccentric characters, a sword duel, backstage mischief, and Holmes and Watson together once more. Based on the play by Craig Bowlsby. 72m/C **VHS. CA** Patrick Macnee, John Scott-Paget, Colin Skinner, Jack McCreath, Carolyn Wilkinson, Sophia Thornley, Drew Kemp, Ned Lemley, Craig Bowlsby; **D:** Gil Letourneau, Peter Reynolds-Long; **W:** Craig Bowlsby. *IPI*

The Hound of the Baskervilles ♂♂♂ 1939 The curse of a demonic hound threatens descendants of an English noble family until Holmes and Watson solve the mystery. Also available with "Sherlock Holmes Faces Death" on Laser Disc. 80m/B **VHS, Beta, Closed Caption.** *GB* Basil Rathbone, Nigel Bruce, Richard Greene, John Carradine, Wendy Barrie, Lionel Atwill, E.E. Clive; **D:** Sidney Lanfield. *FOX*

The Hound of the Baskervilles ♂♂½ 1959 Cushing's not half bad as Sherlock Holmes as he investigates the mystery of a supernatural hound threatening the life of a Dartmoor baronet. Dark and moody. 86m/C **VHS, Beta, LV, Closed Caption.** *GB* Peter Cushing, Christopher Lee, Andre Morell; **D:** Terence Fisher; **M:** James Bernard. *MGM, MLB, FOX*

The Hound of the Baskervilles woof! 1977 Awful spoof of the Sherlock Holmes classic with Cook as Holmes and Moore as Watson (and Holmes' mother). Even the cast can't save it. 84m/C **VHS.** Dudley Moore, Peter Cook, Denholm Elliott, Joan Greenwood, Spike Milligan, Jessie Matthews, Roy Kinnear; **D:** Paul Morrissey; **W:** Dudley Moore, Peter Cook, Paul Morrissey; **M:** Dudley Moore. *NO*

The Hound of the Baskervilles ♂♂ 1983 Another remake of the Sherlock Holmes story which finds the great detective investigating the murder of Sir Charles Baskerville and a mysterious haunted moor. 100m/C **VHS, Beta, Closed Caption.** *GB* Ian Richardson, Donald Churchill, Martin Shaw, Nicholas Clay, Denholm Elliott, Brian Blessed, Ronald Lacey; **D:** Douglas Hickox. *PAR*

Hour of Decision ♂½ 1957 When a newspaper columnist turns up dead, a reporter investigates the murder. Things get hairy when he finds the prime suspect is his own wife. 81m/B **VHS, Beta.** *GB* Jeff Morrow, Hazel Court, Lionel Jeffries, Anthony Dawson, Mary Laura Wood; **D:** C.M. Pennington-Richards. *SNC*

Hour of the Assassin ♂½ 1986 (R) A mercenary is hired to assassinate a South American ruler, and a CIA operative is sent to stop him. Shot in Peru. 96m/C **VHS, Beta.** Erik Estrada, Robert Vaughn; **D:** Luis Llosa. *MGM*

Hour of the Gun ♂♂ 1967 Western saga chronicles what happens after the gunfight at the OK Corral. Garner plays the grim Wyatt Earp on the trail of vengeance after his brothers are killed. Robards is excellent as the crusty Doc Holliday. 100m/C **VHS.** James Garner, Jason Robards Jr., Robert Ryan, Albert Salmi, Charles Aidman, Steve Ihnat, Jon Voight; **D:** John Sturges; **W:** Edward Anhalt; **M:** Jerry Goldsmith. *MGM*

The Hour of the Star ♂♂♂½ *A Hora Da Estrela* 1985 The poignant, highly acclaimed feature debut by Amaral, about an innocent young woman moving to the city of Sao Paulo from the impoverished countryside of Brazil, and finding happiness despite her socioeconomic failures. Based on Clarice Lispector's novel. In Portuguese with English subtitles. 96m/C **VHS, Beta.** *BR* Marcelia Cartaxo; **D:** Suzana Amaral. Berlin International Film Festival '85: Best Actress (Cartaxo). *KIV, FCT*

Hour of the Wolf ♂♂♂½ 1968 An acclaimed, surreal view into the tormented inner life of a painter as he and his wife are isolated on a small northern island. Cinematography by Sven Nykvist. In Swedish with English subtitles. 89m/B **VHS, Beta.** *SW* Max von Sydow, Liv Ullmann, Ingrid Thulin, Erland Josephson, Gertrud Fridh, Gudrun Brost; **D:** Ingmar Bergman; **W:** Ingmar Bergman; **C:** Sven Nykvist. National Board of Review Awards '68: Best Actress (Ullmann); National Society of Film Critics Awards '68: Best Director (Bergman). *MGM, MRV, FCT*

Hourglass ♂♂ 1995 (R) Fashion industry honcho risks his reputation and his life when he becomes involved with a potentially deadly seductress. **CW:** Strong sexuality, and for violence, language and drug use. 91m/C **VHS, LV, Closed Caption.** C. Thomas Howell, Sofia Shinas, Ed Begley Jr., Timothy Bottoms, Anthony Clark; **D:** C. Thomas Howell; **W:** C. Thomas Howell, Darren Dalton; **C:** John Lambert; **M:** Chris Saranec. *LIV*

The Hours and Times ♂♂♂ 1992 A concise drama based on one point of fact used to quietly evoke differences in class, talent, sexual orientation, and unrequited love. The fact is that in the spring of 1963 Brian Epstein, the Beatles brilliant homosexual manager, shared a four-day Barcelona vacation with John Lennon. Director Munch speculates that the sophisticated Epstein was hopelessly in love with the younger, working-class Lennon who is friendly but unresponsive to the courtship. A tender and rueful depiction of friendship longing to be something more. 60m/B **VHS.** David Angus, Ian Hart, Stephanie Pack, Robin McDonald, Sergio Moreno, Unity Grimwood; **D:** Christopher Munch; **W:** Christopher Munch. Sundance Film Festival '92: Special Jury Prize. *FXL, BTV*

House ♂♂♂ 1986 (R) A horror novelist moves into his dead aunt's supposedly haunted house only to find that the monsters don't necessarily stay in the closets. His worst nightmares come to life as he writes about his Vietnam experiences and is forced to relive the tragic events, but these aren't the only visions that start springing to life. It sounds depressing, but is actually a funny, intelligent "horror" flick. Followed by several lesser sequels. 93m/C **VHS, Beta, LV, Closed Caption.** William Katt, George Wendt, Richard Moll, Kay Lenz, Michael Ensign, Mary Stavin, Susan French; **D:** Steve Miner; **W:** Ethan Wiley; **C:** Mac Ahlberg; **M:** Harry Manfredini. *NWV, VTR*

House 2: The Second Story ♂ 1987 (PG-13) The flaccid sequel to the haunted-house horror flick concerns two innocent guys who move into the family mansion and discover Aztec ghosts. Has none of the humor which helped the first movie along. 88m/C **VHS, Beta, LV, Closed Caption.** John Ratzenberger, Arye Gross, Royal Dano, Bill Maher, Jonathan Stark; **D:** Ethan Wiley; **W:** Ethan Wiley; **C:** Mac Ahlberg. *NWV, VTR*

House 4: Home Deadly Home ♂½ 1991 (R) Another bad real estate epic on a par with the other unusually inept "House" efforts. When her husband (Katt) is killed in an auto accident, a young woman and her daughter move into a mysterious old house. Terror begins to confront them at every turn, threatening to destroy them both. We can only hope. **CW:** Language and fantasy/horror violence. 93m/C **VHS, LV, Closed Caption.** Terri Treas, Scott Burkholder, Melissa Clayton, William Katt, Ned Romero; **D:** Lewis Abernathy. *COL, NLC*

House Across the Bay ♂♂½ 1940 Raft, an imprisoned nightclub owner, finds that he is being duped by his attorney who's eager to get his hooks into the lingerie-clad prisoner's wife. But prison isn't going to stop the bitter husband from getting his revenge. 88m/B **VHS, Beta.** George Raft, Walter Pidgeon, Joan Bennett, Lloyd Nolan, Gladys George; **D:** Archie Mayo. *NO*

House Arrest ♂½ 1996 (PG) Another tired kids-think-they-know-best formula film. When Grover Beindorf (Howard) and his younger sister learn that their constantly fighting parents (Curtis and Pollak) are separating, they lock them in the basement so they'll be forced to sort things out. Word gets around and some school pals kidnap their problem parents and stash them in the basement with the Beindorfs. Most of the movie was actually shot in a basement; watch for Curtis hanging upside down in a laundry chute "True Lies" style. 107m/C **VHS.** Jamie Lee Curtis, Kevin Pollak, Christopher McDonald, Jennifer Tilly, Caroline Aaron, Wallace Shawn, Sheila McCarthy, Ray Walston, Kyle Howard, Jennifer Love Hewitt; **D:** Harry Winer; **W:** Michael Hitchcock; **C:** Ueli Steiger; **M:** Bruce Broughton. *HBO*

The House by the Cemetery ♂ *Quella Villa Accanto Al Cimitero* 1983 (R) When a family moves into a house close to a cemetery, strange things start to happen to them. 84m/C **VHS, Beta.** *IT* Katherine MacColl, Paolo Malco; **D:** Lucio Fulci. *LIV, VES*

House Calls ♂♂♂ 1978 (PG) A widowed surgeon turns into a swinging bachelor until he meets a witty but staid English divorcee. Wonderful dialogue. Jackson is exceptional. Made into a short-lived TV series. 98m/C **VHS, Beta, LV.** Walter Matthau, Glenda Jackson, Art Carney, Richard Benjamin, Candice Azzara; **D:** Howard Zieff; **W:** Charles Shyer; **M:** Henry Mancini. *USH*

The House in Marsh Road ♂♂ 1960 A faithless husband decides to rid himself of She Who Must Be Obeyed, but his wife's ghost-friend intervenes. 70m/B **VHS.** *GB* Tony Wright, Patricia Dainton, Sandra Dorne, Derek Aylward, Sam Kydd; **D:** Montgomery Tully. *SNC*

A House in the Hills ♂♂ 1993 (R) A struggling actress is housesitting at a luxurious estate and innocently lets in the exterminator. Except he's an ex-con looking for revenge on the home's current occupant (whom the actress is pretending to be) and may just exterminate her instead. 91m/C **VHS, LV, Closed Caption.** Helen Slater, Michael Madsen, Jeffrey Tambor, James Laurenson, Elyssa Davalos, Terri Barry; **D:** Ken Wiederhorn; **W:** Ken Wiederhorn; **C:** Josep Civit; **M:** Richard Einhorn. *LIV*

House of Angels ♂♂ *Anglagard; Colin Nutley's House of Angels* 1992 (R) Charming comedy, with some serious overtones, about what happens to the gossipy inhabitants of a small Swedish village when two free-spirited newcomers come to stay. Fanny and her friend Zac, who are cabaret performers, show up at the funeral of eccentric Erik, who turns out to be the grandfather Fanny never knew. With her outrageous clothes and attitude, Fanny has most of the neighbors scandalized but what the generous Fanny wants is some information about her past, including who her father might be. What the neighbors want is for Fanny and Zac to leave as quickly as possible. In Swedish with English subtitles. 119m/C **VHS.** *SW* Helena Bergstrom, Rikard Wolff, Sven Wollter, Jakob Eklund, Viveka Seldahl, Ernst Gunter, Reine Brynolfsson, Per Oscarsson; **D:** Colin Nutley; **W:** Susanne Falck. *COL, FCT*

House of Cards ♂♂♂ 1990 Depicts the political machinations of Machiavellian Tory whip Francis Urquhart (Richardson), who schemes to bring down the present government so that he can become the next Prime Minister. And there's absolutely nothing "F.U." (as he's appropriately known) won't do to achieve power. Followed by "To Play the King" and "The Final Cut," based on the novel Michael Dobbs. On 2 cassettes. **200m/C VHS, Closed Caption.** *GB* Ian Richardson, Susannah Harker. *FOX, TVC*

House of Cards 🐾🐾½ 1992 (PG-13) Precocious 6-year-old Sally (Menina) suddenly stops talking after her father is killed in an accident at an archeological site in Mexico. Mom Ruth (Turner) fights to bring her daughter out of her fantasy world and seeks medical advice from a psychiatrist (a sympathetic Jones) but ignores it when it clashes with her own theories. The ethereal Menina, in her acting debut, gives the best performance in this weakly plotted and confusing family saga. *CW:* Mild profanity. **109m/C VHS, LV, Closed Caption.** Kathleen Turner, Asha Menina, Tommy Lee Jones, Shiloh Strong, Esther Rolle, Park Overall, Michael Horse, Anne Pitoniak; *D:* Michael Lessac; *W:* Michael Lessac. *LIV, BTV, FCT*

House of Dark Shadows 🐾🐾 1970 (PG) A 150-year-old vampire, accidentally released by a handyman, wreaks havoc on the inhabitants of the Collinswood mansion. Based on the TV daytime soap. **97m/C VHS, Beta.** Jonathan Frid, Joan Bennett, Grayson Hall, Kathryn Leigh Scott, Roger Davis, Nancy Barrett, John Karlen, Thayer David; *D:* Dan Curtis. *MGM, FUS*

House of Death 🐾 1982 (R) The ex-Playmate of the Year runs in hysterical fear from a knife-wielding lunatic. **88m/C VHS, Beta.** Susan Kiger, William T. Hicks, Jody Kay, Martin Tucker, Jennifer Chase. *GEM*

The House of Dies Drear 1988 A modern-day African American family moves into an old house that turns out to be haunted by the ghost of a long dead abolitionist. The family is transported back to the days of slavery as they interact with the ghost. Based on the story by Virginia Hamilton. Aired on PBS as part of the "Wonderworks" family movie series. **107m/C VHS.** Howard E. Rollins Jr., Moses Gunn, Shavar Ross, Gloria Foster, Clarence Williams III; *D:* Allan Goldstein. *HMV, PME, FCT*

House of Dracula 🐾🐾 1945 Sequel to "House of Frankenstein" features several of the Universal monsters. Overly ambitious story gets a bit hokey, but it's entertaining, nonetheless. **67m/B VHS, LV, Closed Caption.** Lon Chaney Jr., Martha O'Driscoll, John Carradine, Lionel Atwill, Onslow Stevens, Glenn Strange, Jane Adams, Ludwig Stossel; *D:* Erle C. Kenton; *W:* Edward T. Lowe. *USH, FCT*

House of Dreams 🐾 1964 Berry is a blocked writer coping with domestic difficulties whose dreams reveal a disturbing future. Contains a bit part for Goodnow, now a CNN talking head. **80m/B VHS.** Robert Berry, Pauline Elliott, Charlene Bradley, Lance Bird, David Goodnow; *D:* Robert Berry. *LSV*

The House of Eliott 1992 BBC miniseries set in 1920s London finds the orphaned Beatrice and Evangeline Eliott struggling to begin their fashion business as couturiers to the rich and influential, which eventually leads to their founding of the House of Eliott. Lots of romance and intrigue along the way. Boxed set of six cassettes. **600m/C VHS.** *GB* Stella Gonet, Louise Lombard, Aden Gillett, Richard Lintern. *SIG, AAE, VCO*

House of Errors 🐾½ 1942 Two delivery-men pose as reporters to safeguard a prototype machine gun from the bad guys. Contrived plot consisting of outdated comic routines. This was Marsh's last film. **63m/B VHS.** Harry Langdon, Marcia Marsh, Ray Walker, Betty Blythe, John Holland; *D:* Bernard B. Ray. *NOS*

House of Fear 🐾🐾½ 1945 Holmes and Watson investigate the murders of several members of the Good Comrades Club, men who were neither good nor comradely. **69m/B VHS, Beta, Closed Caption.** Basil Rathbone, Nigel Bruce, Dennis Hoey, Aubrey Mather, Paul Cavanagh, Gavin Muir; *D:* Roy William Neill. *FOX*

House of Frankenstein 🐾🐾½ 1944 An evil scientist (Karloff) escapes from prison, and, along with his hunchback manservant, revives Dracula, Frankenstein's monster, and the Wolfman to carry out his dastardly deeds. An all-star cast helps this horror fest along. **71m/B VHS, LV.** Boris Karloff, J. Carrol Naish, Lon Chaney Jr., John Carradine, Elena Verdugo, Anne Gwynne, Lionel Atwill, Peter Coe, George Zucco, Glenn Strange, Sig Rumann; *D:* Erle C. Kenton. *USH*

House of Games 🐾🐾🐾 1987 (R) The directorial debut of playwright Mamet is a tale about an uptight female psychiatrist who investigates the secret underworld of con-artistry and becomes increasingly involved in an elaborate con game. She's led along her crooked path by smooth-talking con-master Mantegna. A taut, well plotted psychological suspense film with many twists and turns. Stylishly shot, with dialogue which has that marked Mamet cadence. Most of the leads are from Mamet's theater throng (including his wife, Crouse). **102m/C VHS, Beta, LV.** Joe Mantegna, Lindsay Crouse, Lilia Skala, J.T. Walsh, Meshach Taylor, Ricky Jay, Mike Nussbaum, Willo Hausman; *D:* David Mamet; *W:* David Mamet; *C:* Juan Ruiz-Anchia; *M:* Alaric Jans. *HBO, CRC*

House of Horrors 🐾🐾½ 1946 Deformed murderer "The Creeper" (Hatton) is used by a mad sculptor in a twisted revenge plot. Marcel De Lange (Kosleck) believes his work has been vilely abused by art critics so he uses his friend's homicidal urges to get rid of anyone who stands in his way. **76m/B VHS, Closed Caption.** Martin Kosleck, Rondo Hatton, Robert Lowery, Virginia Grey, Bill Goodwin, Alan Napier, Joan Shawlee, Howard Freeman; *D:* Jean Yarbrough; *W:* George Bricker. *USH*

The House of Lurking Death 🐾½ 1984 Detectives Tommy and Tuppence find a box of chocolates laced with arsenic at the home of Lois Hargreaves, and the mad old maid is the prime suspect. Based on the Agatha Christie story. Made for British television. **60m/C VHS, Beta.** *GB* James Warwick, Francesca Annis. *TPV*

House of Mystery 🐾🐾 1934 For a shot at some priceless jewels stolen by the host from a Hindu princess, several guests gather for a weekend in a spine-tingling mansion. A creepy curse keeps them looking over their shoulders. **62m/C VHS.** Ed Lowry, Verna Hillie, Brandon Hurst, George "Gabby" Hayes; *D:* William Nigh. *SNC, DVT, MLB*

House of Mystery 🐾🐾½ At the Villa Rose 1941 Splendid British remake of 1934 film in which the detective does some true sleuthing to catch the culprits. An old widow is killed for her jewels, but the murderers can't locate the goods. After they try a series of fiendish plans to retrieve them, the detective must work to stop the crooks. **61m/B VHS.** *GB* Kenneth Kent, Judy Kelly, Peter Murray Hill, Walter Rilla, Ruth Maitland; *D:* Walter Summers. *NOS, DVT*

The House of 1000 Dolls 🐾 Haus Der Tausend Freuden 1967 Doleful, not dollful, exploitation thriller as magician Price drugs young girls and sells them to slavery rings. An international production set in Tangiers; dialogue is dubbed. **79m/C VHS, Beta.** *GE SP GB* Vincent Price, Martha Hyer, George Nader, Ann Smyrner, Maria Rohm; *D:* Jeremy Summers. *HBO*

House of Psychotic Women woof! Los Ojos Azules de la Muneca Rota 1973 (R) Naschy, Spain's premier horror movie star, plays a studly drifter who winds up in the home of three sisters, one with an artifical arm, one confined to a wheelchair and the other a nymphomaniac. No problemo thinks the hirsute Spaniard, until a series of bizarre murders—in which the victims eyes are ripped out—spoils his fun. Naschy, who usually sprouts fur and fangs, actually doesn't turn into a werewolf. Catchy but inappropriate score. A must for Naschy/bad movie fans. **87m/C VHS, Beta.** *SP* Paul Naschy, Maria Perschy, Diana Lorys, Eva Leon, Ines Morales, Tony Pica; *D:* Carlos Aured; *W:* Paul Naschy. *NO*

The House of Secrets 🐾🐾 1937 A Yank travels to Britain to collect an inheritance and stays in a dusty old mansion filled with an odd assortment of characters. **70m/B VHS, Beta.** Leslie Fenton, Muriel Evans, Noel Madison, Sidney Blackmer, Morgan Wallace, Holmes Herbert; *D:* Roland D. Reed. *SNC*

The House of Seven Corpses 🐾🐾 1973 (PG) A crew attempts to film a horror movie in a Victorian manor where seven people died in a variety of gruesome manners. Things take a turn for the ghoulish when a crew member becomes possesed by the house's evil spirits. Good, low budget fun with a competent "B" cast. Filmed in what was the Utah governor's mansion. **90m/C VHS.** John Ireland, Faith Domergue, John Carradine, Carole Wells; *D:* Paul Harrison. *GEM, MRV, CNG*

House of Shadows 🐾½ 1983 A 20-year-old murder comes back to haunt the victim's friends in this tale of mystery and terror. **90m/C VHS, Beta.** John Gavin, Yvonne De Carlo, Leonor Manso; *D:* Richard Wulicher. *MED*

House of Strangers 🐾🐾🐾½ 1949 Conte, in a superb performance, swears vengeance on his brothers, whom he blames for his father's death. Robinson, in a smaller part than you'd expect from his billing, is nevertheless excellent as the ruthless banker father who sadly reaps a reward he didn't count on. Based on Philip Yordan's "I'll Never Go There Again." **101m/B VHS, Closed Caption.** Edward G. Robinson, Susan Hayward, Richard Conte, Luther Adler, Efrem Zimbalist Jr., Debra Paget; *D:* Joseph L. Mankiewicz; *W:* Philip Yordan; *C:* Milton Krasner. Cannes Film Festival '49: Best Actor (Robinson). *FOX, FCT*

House of Terror 🐾 1987 A woman and her boyfriend plot to kill her rich boss, while they too are being stalked by some undefined horror. **91m/C VHS, Beta.** Jennifer Bishop, Arell Blanton, Jacquelyn Hyde. *TWE*

The House of the Arrow 🐾🐾🐾 1953 Investigating the murder of a French widow, who was killed by a poisoned arrow, a detective must sort through a grab bag of potential suspects. Superior adaptation of the A.E.W. Mason thriller. **73m/B VHS, Beta.** *GB* Oscar Homolka, Yvonne Furneaux, Robert Urquhart; *D:* Michael Anderson Sr. *NOS, SNC*

House of the Black Death 🐾½ Blood of the Man Devil; Night of the Beast 1965 Horror titans Chaney and Carradine co-star in this as warring warlocks, yet they share no scenes together! Chaney is the evil warlock (the horns are a giveaway) holding people hostage in the title edifice. **89m/B VHS.** Lon Chaney Jr., John Carradine, Katherine Victor, Tom Drake, Andrea King; *D:* Harold Daniels, Reginald LeBorg. *NOS, LOO*

House of the Damned 🐾½ 1971 A young woman, a mental hospital, a murdered father, a priceless gold statue—mix together and you get a mystery horror movie. A woman tries to solve her father's murder. **89m/C VHS, Beta.** Donald Pleasence, Michael Dunn; *D:* Gonzolo Suarez. *NO*

House of the Dead 🐾 1980 Man is trapped inside a haunted house. Scary. **100m/C VHS.** John Ericson, Charles Aidman, Bernard Fox, Ivor Francis. *NO*

House of the Living Dead 🐾 Doctor Maniac 1973 (PG) Brattling Manor harbors a murderous and flesh-eating secret ready to lure the unsuspecting. Don't you be one. **87m/C VHS, Beta.** *SA* Mark Burns, Shirley Anne Field, David Oxley; *D:* Ray Austin. *VCI, HHE*

House of the Long Shadows 🐾½ 1982 (PG) Comedy mixes with gore, as four of the horror screen's best leading men team up for the first time, although they have only minor roles. Might have been a contender, but Arnaz is miscast as author who stays in spooky house on a bet with Todd. Nice start but not enough. Based on the play "Seven Keys to Baldpate" by George M. Cohan (and novel by Earl Derr Biggers). **96m/C VHS, Beta.** Vincent Price, Christopher Lee, Peter Cushing,

John Carradine, Desi Arnaz Jr., Sheila Keith, Richard Todd; *D:* Pete Walker; *W:* Michael Armstrong. *MGM*

House of the Rising Sun ♂♂½ 1987 A Los Angeles reporter goes under cover for a story on an exclusive brothel only to discover the owner is a psychopath who has very permanent ways of dealing with troublesome employees. **86m/C VHS, Beta.** John York, Bud Davis, Deborah Wakeham, Frank Annese; *D:* Greg Gold; *M:* Tina Turner, Bryan Ferry. *PSM, PAR*

The House of the Spirits ♂♂ 1993 (R) Star-studded adaptation of the novel by Isabel Allende is a multi-generational saga following the fortunes of the powerful Trueba family. The ambitious Esteban (Irons) marries the clairvoyant Clara (Streep), exploits the peasants on his property, and becomes a conservative senator. Their rebellious daughter Blanca (Ryder) falls for rabble-rousing peasant Pedro (Banderas), and the country undergoes a bloody revolution. Magical realism of the novel is lost in screen melodrama, with the international cast ill-served by tepid direction. The child Clara is played by Streep's daughter, Mary Willa (listed in the credits as Jane Gray).*CW:* Brief nudity, graphic and disturbing violence, and strong sexuality. **109m/C VHS, LV, Closed Caption.** Meryl Streep, Jeremy Irons, Glenn Close, Winona Ryder, Antonio Banderas, Armin Mueller-Stahl, Vanessa Redgrave, Sarita Choudhury, Maria Conchita Alonso, Vincent Gallo, Miriam Colon, Jan Niklas, Teri Polo, Jane Gray; *D:* Bille August; *W:* Bille August; *M:* Hans Zimmer. *LIV*

House of the Yellow Carpet ♂½ 1984 A couple try to sell an ancient Persian carpet heirloom, and in doing so transgress some unwritten mystical law. Havoc ensues. **90m/C VHS, Beta.** Roland Josephson, Beatrice Romand; *D:* Carlo Lizzani. *LIV*

The House of Usher ♂ *Edgar Allen Poe's House of Usher* 1988 (R) Some serious overacting by Reed (as Roderick) and Pleasence (as his balmy brother) almost elevate this Poe retread to "so bad it's good" status, and there are a few admirably grisly moments. But, without other camp virtues, it's merely dreary. Adapted by Michael J. Murray and filmed in South Africa. **92m/C VHS, LV.** Oliver Reed, Donald Pleasence, Romy Windsor; *D:* Alan Birkinshaw; *W:* Michael J. Murray; *M:* Gary Chang. *COL*

House of Wax ♂♂♂ 1953 (PG) A deranged sculptor (Price, who else?) builds a sinister wax museum which showcases creations that were once alive. A remake of the early horror flick "Mystery of the Wax Museum," and one of the 50s' most popular 3-D films. This one still has the power to give the viewer the creeps, thanks to another chilling performance by Price. Look for a very young Charles Bronson, as well as Carolyn "Morticia Addams" Jones as a victim. **88m/C VHS, Beta, LV.** Vincent Price, Frank Lovejoy, Carolyn Jones, Phyllis Kirk, Paul Cavanagh, Charles Bronson; *D:* Andre de Toth. *WAR, MLB*

House of Whipcord woof! 1975 Beautiful young women are kidnapped and tortured in this British gore-o-rama. Awful and degrading. **102m/C VHS, Beta.** *GB* Barbara Markham, Patrick Barr, Ray Brooks, Penny Irving, Anne Michelle; *D:* Pete Walker. *MON, LIV*

The House on Carroll Street ♂½ 1988 (PG) New York 1951, the middle of the McCarthy era. A young woman overhears a plot to smuggle Nazi war criminals into the U.S. She's already lost her job because of accusations of subversion, and it's not easy persuading FBI agent Daniels that she knows what she's talking about. Contrived plot and melodramatic finale help sink this period piece. **111m/C VHS, Beta, LV, Closed Caption.** Kelly McGillis, Jeff Daniels, Mandy Patinkin, Jessica Tandy; *D:* Peter Yates; *W:* Walter Bernstein; *C:* Michael Ballhaus; *M:* Georges Delerue. *HBO*

The House on Chelouche Street ♂♂½ 1973 In Tel-Aviv, during the summer of 1946, 15-year-old Sami, an Egyptian immigrant, tries to help support his mother and family during the upheavals of Palestine under the British mandate. A well thought-out story detailing the struggles of a North African Jewish family before the creation of the country of Israel. In Hebrew with English subtitles. **111m/C VHS, Beta.** *IS* Gila Almagor, Michal Bat-Adam, Shai K. Ophir; *D:* Moshe Mizrahi. Nominations: Academy Awards '73: Best Foreign Language Film. *VYY, NCJ, AUD*

The House on Garibaldi Street ♂♂½ 1979 Spy drama about the capture of Nazi war criminal Adolph Eichmann in Argentina and his extradition to Israel for trial. Based on the book by Isser Harel. Made for television. **96m/C VHS, Beta.** Chaim Topol, Nick Mancuso, Martin Balsam, Janet Suzman, Leo McKern, Charles Gray, Alfred Burke; *D:* Peter Collinson; *M:* Charles Bernstein. *FRH, SWC*

House on Haunted Hill ♂♂½ 1958 A wealthy man throws a haunted house party and offers ten thousand dollars to anyone who can survive the night there. Vintage cheap horror from the master of the macabre Castle. Remembered for Castle's in-theater gimmick of dangling a skeleton over the audiences' heads in the film's initial release. Also available with "Attack of the 50-Foot Woman" on laserdisc. **75m/B VHS, Beta, LV, Closed Caption.** Vincent Price, Carol Ohmart, Richard Long, Alan Marshal; *D:* William Castle. *FOX, SNC, FCT*

House on 92nd Street ♂♂♂ 1945 Documentary-style thriller finds federal investigator George Briggs (Nolan) contacted by German-American student Bill Dietrich (Eythe), who's been sought out by Nazi spies. Briggs encourages Dietrich to play along and report their nefarious activities to the feds. What Dietrich discovers is that a scientist, working on the atomic bomb project, is actually a Nazi agent. Lots of atmosphere and action, with director Hathaway incorporating newsreel footage to highlight the true-to-life feel. Title refers the house where the head of the Nazi spies resides. **89m/B VHS, Closed Caption.** William Eythe, Lloyd Nolan, Signe Hasso, Gene Lockhart, Leo G. Carroll, William Post Jr., Harry Bellaver; *D:* Henry Hathaway; *W:* Barre Lyndon, John Monks Jr., Charles G. Booth; *C:* Norbert Brodine; *M:* David Buttolph. Academy Awards '45: Best Story. *FXV*

The House on Skull Mountain ♂½ 1974 (PG) The four surviving relatives of a deceased voodoo priestess are in for a bumpy night as they gather at the House on Skull Mountain for the reading of her will. **85m/C VHS, Beta, Closed Caption.** Victor French, Janee Michelle, Mike Evans, Jean Durand; *D:* Ron Honthaner. *FOX*

The House on Sorority Row ♂½ *House of Evil; Seven Sisters* 1983 Less-than-harrowing story of what happens when seven sorority sisters have a last fling and get back at their housemother at the same time. **90m/C VHS, Beta, LV.** Eileen Davidson, Kathy McNeil, Robin Meloy; *D:* Mark Rosman; *M:* Richard Band. *VES*

The House on Straw Hill ♂½ *Expose* 1976 (R) A successful novelist is intrigued by an attractive woman who lives in an isolated farmhouse. Her presence induces gory hallucinations, lust and violence. **84m/C VHS, Beta.** Udo Kier, Linda Hayden, Fiona Richmond; *D:* James Kenelm Clarke. *NWV, MED*

House on the Edge of the Park woof! *La Casa Nel Parco* 1984 A frustrated would-be womanizer takes revenge on a parade of women during an all-night party. **91m/C VHS, Beta.** *IT* David Hess, Annie Belle, Lorraine De Selle; *D:* Ruggero Deodato. *LIV, VES*

The House on Todville Road ♂ 1995 (R) Fact-based story about a dangerous cult and its followers. **94m/C VHS.** David Harrod, Terri Harrel, Lisa Marie Newmeyer. *TCE*

The House on Tombstone Hill ♂½ 1992 An old, abandoned mansion seems like a good investment to a group of friends. Wrong! The original owner is still around and doesn't like strangers coming to visit. **95m/C VHS.** Doug Gibson, John Cerna, Sarah Newhouse; *D:* J. Riffel; *W:* J. Riffel. *AIP*

House Party ♂♂♂ 1990 (R) Light-hearted, black hip-hop version of a '50s teen comedy with rap duo Kid 'n' Play. After his father grounds him for fighting, a high-schooler attempts all sorts of wacky schemes to get to his friend's party. Sleeper hit features real-life music rappers and some dynamite dance numbers. **100m/C VHS, Beta, LV.** Christopher Reid, Christopher Martin, Martin Lawrence, Tisha Campbell, Paul Anthony, A.J. Johnson, Robin Harris; *D:* Reginald Hudlin; *W:* Reginald Hudlin; *M:* Marcus Miller. Sundance Film Festival '90: Best Cinematography. *NLC, FCT*

House Party 2: The Pajama Jam ♂♂½ 1991 (R) Rap stars Kid 'N' Play are back in this hip-hop sequel to the original hit. At Harris University Kid 'N' Play hustle up overdue tuition by holding a campus "jammie jam jam." A stellar cast shines in this rap-powered pajama bash.*CW:* Language and sensuality. **94m/C VHS, LV, Closed Caption.** Christopher Reid, Christopher Martin, Tisha Campbell, Iman, Queen Latifah, Georg Stanford Brown, Martin Lawrence, Eugene Allen, George Anthony Bell, Kamron, Tony Burton, Helen Martin, William Schallert; *D:* Doug McHenry, George Jackson; *W:* Rusty Cundieff, Daryl G. Nickens; *M:* Vassal Benford. *NLC*

House Party 3 ♂ 1994 (R) Kid is engaged to be married and Play tries to set up a blowout bachelor party. The duo are also working on their record producer careers by trying to sign a feisty female rap group (real life TLC). Strikes out early for easy profanity while never coming within spitting distance of first two flicks.*CW:* Strong language and sexual suggestiveness. **93m/C VHS, LV, Closed Caption.** Christopher Reid, Christopher Martin, Angela Means, Tisha Campbell, Bernie Mac, Barbara Edwards, Michael Colyar, David Edwards, Betty Lester, Chris Tucker; *D:* Eric Meza; *W:* Takashi Bufford; *M:* David Allen Jones. *COL, IME*

The House that Bled to Death ♂ 1981 Strange things happen to a family when they move into a run-down house where a murder occurred years before. **60m/C VHS, Beta.** Nicholas Ball, Rachel Davies, Brian Croucher, Pat Maynard, Emma Ridley. *LIV*

The House that Dripped Blood ♂♂½ 1971 (PG) A Scotland Yard inspector discovers the history of an English country house while investigating an actor's disappearance. Four horror tales comprise the body of this omnibus creeper, following the successful "Tales from the Crypt" mold. Duffell's debut as director. **101m/C VHS, Beta.** *GB* Christopher Lee, Peter Cushing, Jon Pertwee, Denholm Elliott, Ingrid Pitt, John Bennett, Tom Adams, Joss Ackland, Chloe Franks; *D:* Peter Duffell; *W:* Robert Bloch. *PSM*

The House that Vanished ♂ *Scream and Die* 1973 (R) Semi-exploitative fare about a beautiful young model who witnesses a murder in a house but later can't find the place. Her boyfriend is skeptical. **84m/C VHS, Beta.** *GB* Andrea Allan, Karl Lanchbury, Judy Matheson, Maggie Walker; *D:* Joseph Larraz. *MED, LIV*

House Where Evil Dwells ♂½ 1982 (R) An American family is subjected to a reign of terror when they move into and old Japanese house possessed by three deadly samurai ghosts. The setting doesn't upgrade the creepiness of the plot. **88m/C VHS, Beta.** Edward Albert, Susan George, Doug McClure, Amy Barett; *D:* Kevin Connor. *MGM*

A House Without a Christmas Tree ♂♂½ 1972 A frustrated middle-aged man denies his young daughter her one desire—a Christmas tree. Charming made for cable television holiday fare. **90m/C VHS, Beta.** Jason Robards Jr., Lisa Lucas, Mildred Natwick; *D:* Paul Bogart. *FXV, FCT*

Houseboat ♂♂½ 1958 Widower Grant with three precocious kids takes up residence on a houseboat with Italian maid Loren who is actually a socialite, incognito. Naturally, they fall in love.

Light, fun Hollywood froth. **110m/C Beta, LV.** Cary Grant, Sophia Loren, Martha Hyer, Eduardo Ciannelli, Murray Hamilton, Harry Guardino; **D:** Melville Shavelson; **W:** Melville Shavelson, Jack Rose; **M:** George Duning. Nominations: Academy Awards '58: Best Song ("Almost in Your Arms (Love Song from Houseboat)"), Best Story & Screenplay.**PAR**

Houseguest 🎞🎞 **1994 (PG)** Dumb comedy about mistaken identity finds hard luck dreamer Kevin Franklin (Sinbad) on the run from loan sharks. Fortunately, while trying to make a getaway at the airport, he's mistaken for the childhood buddy (who's also an eminent dentist prompting some hygiene humor) of family guy/lawyer Gary Young (Hartman), who opens his suburban home to his long lost pal. Street smart Kevin naturally manages to solve every dysfunctional family problem that arises while avoiding some inept Mafia thugs. Everyone is oh-so-good-natured but there's nothing new to hold much interest. **109m/C VHS, LV, Closed Caption.** Sinbad, Phil Hartman, Jeffrey Jones, Kim Greist, Stan Shaw, Tony Longo, Mason Adams, Paul Ben-Victor, Chauncey Leopardi, Ron Glass, Talia Seider, Kim Murphy; **D:** Randall Miller; **W:** Michael J. Di Gaetano, Laurence Gay; **C:** Jerzy Zielinski; **M:** John Debney. **TOU**

Household Saints 🎞🎞🎞 **1993 (R)** Chronicling one family from post-WWII Little Italy through the 1970's, this is a quirky little story about sausage, religion, women, and families (not necessarily in that order). Joseph (D'Onofrio) wins his bride (Ullman) in a pinochle game, much to his superstitious Catholic mother's (Malina) chagrin. The product of that union is a slightly obsessive girl (Taylor), who sees visions and wants to be a saint. Interesting study of Italian-American families, and the roles religion and food play in the culture of Little Italy. **124m/C VHS, Closed Caption.** Tracey Ullman, Vincent D'Onofrio, Lili Taylor, Judith Malina, Michael Rispoli, Victor Argo, Michael Imperioli, Rachael Bella, Illeana Douglas, Joe Grifasi, Sebastien Roche; **D:** Nancy Savoca; **W:** Nancy Savoca, Richard Guay; **C:** Bobby Bukowski; **M:** Stephen Endelman. Independent Spirit Awards '94: Best Supporting Actress (Taylor); Nominations: Independent Spirit Awards '94: Best Actor (D'Onofrio), Best Screenplay. **COL**

The Householder 🎞🎞 *Gharbar* **1963** An early Merchant-Ivory collaboration featuring a young Indian schoolteacher whose widowed mother arranges his marriage to a woman he doesn't know. The immature couple find their adjustment to marriage fraught with, sometimes amusing, complications. **101m/B VHS, LV.** **IN** Shashi Kapoor, Leela Naidu, Durga Khote; **D:** James Ivory; **W:** Ruth Prawer Jhabvala. **CVC**

The Housekeeper 🎞🎞 *A Judgement in Stone* **1986 (R)** Tushingham's portrayal of a deranged housekeeper brings this movie to life even as she kills off her employers. **97m/C VHS, Beta, LV, Closed Caption.** **CA** Rita Tushingham, Ross Petty, Jackie Burroughs, Tom Kneebone, Shelly Peterson, Jessica Stern, Jonathan Crombie; **D:** Ousama Rawi. **WAR**

Housekeeping 🎞🎞🎞 **1987 (PG)** A quiet but bizarre comedy by Forsyth (his first American film). A pair of orphaned sisters are cared for by their newly arrived eccentric, free-spirited aunt in a small and small-minded community in Oregon in the 1950s. Conventional townspeople attempt to intervene, but the sisters' relationship with their offbeat aunt has become strong enough to withstand the coercion of the townspeople. May move too slowly for some viewers. Based on novel by Marilynne Robinson. **117m/C VHS, Beta, Closed Caption.** Christine Lahti, Sarah Walker, Andrea Burchill; **D:** Bill Forsyth; **W:** Bill Forsyth; **C:** Michael Coulter; **M:** Michael Gibbs. **COL**

Housemaster 🎞🎞½ **1938** In a British boys' school the housemaster is kind and understanding of his sometimes-unruly charges. The stern new headmaster is not, and the students conspire against him. An okay but dated comedy, featuring characters with names like Bimbo and Button. Based on "Bachelor Born" by Ian Hay, a London

stage hit at the time. **95m/B VHS.** Otto Kruger, Diana Churchill, Phillips Holmes, Rene Ray, Walter Hudd, George L. Baxt, Cecil Parker, Michael Shepley, Jimmy Hanley, Rosamund Barnes; **D:** Herbert Brenon. **NOS, MLB**

Housesitter 🎞🎞½ **1992 (PG)** Newton Davis (Martin), an architect/dreamer, builds his high school sweetheart (Delany) a beautiful house and surprises her with a marriage proposal. Delany says no, he has a one-night stand with Gwen (Hawn), and Hawn moves into his empty house and assumes the position of Davis's wife, unbeknownst to him. Gwen spins whoppers of lies and soon has the entire town, including Davis's parents and ex-girlfriend, believing her wacky stories. This romantic screwball comedy is a delight, not only because of Martin and Hawn, but also because of the array of other characters who complicate the stories they spin. **102m/C VHS, Beta, LV, Closed Caption.** Steve Martin, Goldie Hawn, Dana Delany, Julie Harris, Donald Moffat, Peter MacNicol, Richard B. Shull, Laurel Cronin, Christopher Durang; **D:** Frank Oz; **W:** Mark Stein, Brian Grazer; **C:** John A. Alonzo; **M:** Miles Goodman. **USH, PMS, BTV**

Housewife 🎞🎞 **1972 (R)** A vengeful black man holds an unhappily married Beverly Hills couple hostage in their home. **96m/C VHS, Beta.** Yaphet Kotto, Andrew Duggan, Joyce Van Patten, Jeannie Berlin; **D:** Larry Cohen. **NWV**

How Come Nobody's On Our Side? 🎞 **1973 (PG)** Two out-of-work stuntmen try astrology to find the best time to make some easy money smuggling marijuana out of Mexico. **84m/C VHS, Beta.** Adam Roarke, Larry Bishop, Alexandra Hay, Rob Reiner, Penny Marshall; **W:** Leigh Chapman. **NO**

How Funny Can Sex Be? 🎞🎞 **1976 (R)** Eight risque sketches about love and marriage Italian style. **97m/C VHS, Beta.** **IT** Giancarlo Giannini, Laura Antonelli, Dulio Del Prete; **D:** Dino Risi. **FOX**

How Green Was My Valley 🎞🎞🎞🎞 **1941** Compelling story of the trials and tribulations of a Welsh mining family, from the youthful perspective of the youngest child (played by a 13-year-old McDowall). Spans 50 years, from the turn of the century, when coal mining was a difficult but fair-paying way of life, and it ends, after unionization, strikes, deaths, and child abuse, with the demise of a town and its culture. Considered by many to be director Ford's finest work. When WWII prevented shooting on location, producer Zanuck built a facsimile Welsh valley in California (although Ford, born Sean Aloysius O'Fearna, was said to have been thinking of his story as taking place in Ireland rather than Wales). Based on the novel by Richard Llewellyn. **118m/C VHS, Beta.** Walter Pidgeon, Maureen O'Hara, Donald Crisp, Anna Lee, Roddy McDowall, John Loder, Sara Allgood, Barry Fitzgerald, Patric Knowles, Rhys Williams, Arthur Shields, Ann Todd, Mae Marsh; **D:** John Ford; **W:** Philip Dunne; **C:** Arthur C. Miller; **M:** Alfred Newman. Academy Awards '41: Best Black and White Cinematography, Best Director (Ford), Best Interior Decoration, Best Picture, Best Supporting Actor (Crisp); New York Film Critics Awards '41: Best Director (Ford); Nominations: Academy Awards '41: Best Film Editing, Best Screenplay, Best Sound, Best Supporting Actress (Allgood), Original Dramatic/Comedy Score. **FOX, FUS, BTV**

How I Got into College 🎞🎞 **1989 (PG-13)** A slack, uninspired satire about a high school senior who barely manages to get into a local college so he may pursue the girl of his dreams. **87m/C VHS, Beta, LV, Closed Caption.** Corey Parker, Lara Flynn Boyle, Christopher Rydell, Anthony Edwards, Phil Hartman, Brian Doyle-Murray, Nora Dunn, Finn Carter, Charles Rocket; **D:** Steve Holland; **W:** Terrel Seltzer; **C:** Robert Elswit. **FOX**

How I Learned to Love Women 🎞 **196?** A British comedy of errors involving a carloving youth who learns about women and love. **95m/C VHS, Beta.** **GB** Anita Ekberg. **NO**

How I Won the War 🎞🎞 **1967 (PG)** An inept officer must lead his battalion out of England into the Egyptian desert to conquer a cricket field. Indulgent, scarcely amusing Richard Lester com-

edy; Lennon, in a bit part, provides the brightest moments. **111m/C VHS, Beta, LV.** **GB** John Lennon, Michael Crawford, Michael Hordern; **D:** Richard Lester; **W:** Charles Wood; **C:** David Watkin. **MGM**

How Many Miles to Babylon? 🎞🎞 **1982** During WWI, two young men become friends despite their different backgrounds. But one is court-martialed for desertion, and the other is supposed to oversee his execution. Made for British television. **106m/C VHS, Beta.** **GB** Daniel Day-Lewis, Christopher Fairbank; **D:** Moira Armstrong. **FOX, TVC, FUS**

How Sweet It Is! 🎞 **1968** Typical American family takes a zany European vacation. Looks like a TV sitcom and is about as entertaining. National Lampoon's version is a lot more fun. **99m/C VHS.** James Garner, Debbie Reynolds, Maurice Ronet, Paul Lynde, Erin Moran, Marcel Dalio, Terry-Thomas; **D:** Jerry Paris; **W:** Jerry Belson; **C:** Lucien Ballard. **WAR**

How Tasty Was My Little Frenchman 🎞🎞 *Como Era Gostoso O Meu Frances* **1971** French explorer is captured by a cannibal tribe in the jungles of Brazil. He's treated very well and attempts to learn tribal customs to avoid his fate—he's going to be the main course in a ceremonial dinner. French and Tupi with subtitles. **80m/C VHS.** **BR** Arduino Colasanti, Ana Maria Magalhaes, Ital Natur, Eduardo Embassahy; **D:** Nelson Pereira dos Santos. **NYF**

How the Grinch Stole Christmas 🎞🎞🎞 **1965** Classic television Christmas special from the Dr. Seuss book about a Christmas-hating grinch who steals Christmas from the town of Whoville. Fun for the whole family. **26m/C VHS, Beta. V:** Boris Karloff. **MGM, KUI, TVC**

How the West was Fun 🎞🎞½ **1995** The Olsen gals are visiting great godmother Natty's dude ranch, which is in financial difficulty, and must outsmart her greedy son Bart (Mull), a land grabber who wants to turn the ranch into an environmentally unfriendly western theme park. Made for TV. **93m/C VHS, Closed Caption.** Mary-Kate Olsen, Ashley Olsen, Martin Mull, Michelle Greene, Patrick Cassidy, Leon Pownall, Peg Phillips; **D:** Stuart Margolin; **M:** Richard Bellis. **WAR**

How the West Was Won 🎞🎞🎞 **1963 (G)** A panoramic view of the American West, focusing on the trials, tribulations and travels of three generations of one family, set against the background of wars and historical events. Particularly notable for its impressive cast list and expansive western settings. **165m/C VHS, Beta, LV.** John Wayne, Carroll Baker, Lee J. Cobb, Spencer Tracy, Gregory Peck, Karl Malden, Robert Preston, Eli Wallach, Henry Fonda, George Peppard, Debbie Reynolds, Carolyn Jones, Richard Widmark, James Stewart, Walter Brennan, Andy Devine, Raymond Massey, Agnes Moorehead, Harry (Henry) Morgan, Thelma Ritter, Russ Tamblyn; **D:** John Ford, Henry Hathaway, George Marshall; **W:** James R. Webb; **C:** Milton Krasner, Charles B(ryant) Lang. Academy Awards '63: Best Film Editing, Best Sound, Best Story & Screenplay; National Board of Review Awards '63: 10 Best Films of the Year; Nominations: Academy Awards '63: Best Art Direction/Set Decoration (Color), Best Color Cinematography, Best Costume Design (Color), Best Picture, Best Original Score. **MGM**

How to Be a Perfect Person in Just Three Days **1984** Fun comedy for the whole family shows the efforts of a kid striving for perfection before realizing that individuality is more fun. Based on the book by Stephen Mane. Aired on PBS as part of the "Wonderworks" series. **58m/C VHS, Closed Caption.** Wallace Shawn, Ilan Mitchell-Smith, Hermione Gingold, Joan Micklin Silver. **PME, FCT, HMV**

How to Beat the High Cost of Living 🎞½ **1980 (PG)** Three suburban housewives decide to beat inflation by taking up robbery, and they start by planning a heist at the local shopping mall. Comedic talent can't salvage whipped script and direction. **105m/C VHS, Beta.** Jessica Lange, Susan St. James, Jane Curtin, Richard Benjamin, Eddie Albert, Dabney Coleman, Fred Willard, Cathryn Damon, Art Metrano; **D:** Robert Scheerer. **LIV, VES**

How to Break Up a Happy Divorce 🐾🐾 1976

A divorced woman starts a vigorous campaign to win her ex-husband back by dating another man to make him jealous. Lightweight made-for-television comedy. **74m/C VHS, Beta.** Barbara Eden, Hal Linden, Peter Bonerz, Marcia Rodd, Harold Gould; **D:** Jerry Paris. *WOV*

How to Commit Marriage 🐾🐾½ 1969

(PG) Hope and Wyman have been married for 20 years when they decide to divorce—just when their daughter (Cameron) decides to marry her college boyfriend (Matheson). His father (Gleason) tries to stop the wedding, fails, but sticks around to cause more trouble. Subplots involve the divorced duo's new loves and the fact that they're about to become grandparents but the comedy is completely uninspired. **96m/C VHS.** Bob Hope, Jane Wyman, Jackie Gleason, Joanna Cameron, Tim Matheson, Beatrice Arthur, Leslie Nielsen, Tina Louise, Paul Stewart, Prof. Irwin Corey; **D:** Norman Panama; **W:** Ben Starr, Michael Kanin; **M:** Joseph J. Lilley. *COL*

How to Frame a Figg 🐾🐾½ 1971 (G)

Bookkeeper Hollis A. Figg (Knotts) is working at Dalton's corrupt city hall where he's setup to be the patsy in the fradulent doings of the mayor and city council. But his best friends Prentiss (Welker) and Ema Letha (Joyce) set out to prove the bumbler's innocence. **103m/C VHS.** Don Knotts, Elaine Joyce, Frank Welker, Joe Flynn, Edward Andrews, Yvonne Craig, Parker Fennelly, Fay DeWitt; **D:** Alan Rafkin; **W:** George Tibbles; **C:** William Margulies; **M:** Vic Mizzy. *USH*

How to Get Ahead in Advertising 🐾🐾🐾 1989 (R)

A cynical, energetic satire about a manic advertising idea man who becomes so disgusted with trying to sell a pimple cream that he quits the business. Ultimately he grows a pimple of his own that talks and begins to take over his life. Acerbic and hilarious. **95m/C VHS, Beta, LV.** *GB* Richard E. Grant, Rachel Ward, Susan Wooldridge, Mick Ford, Richard Wilson, John Shrapnel, Jacqueline Tong; **D:** Bruce Robinson; **W:** Bruce Robinson; **M:** David Dundas, Rick Wentworth. *FCT*

How to Kill 400 Duponts 🐾 1965

Bumbling Scotland Yard detective is off to France to stop a master criminal from trying to kill off the rich Dupont family. Why? So he'll be the only one left with any claim to the remaining family fortune. **98m/C VHS, Beta.** Terry-Thomas, Johnny Dorelli, Margaret Lee. *VCD*

How to Make a Doll 🐾 1968

Lewis' sex farce about an extremely shy professor whose ineptness with women inspires him to invent android females to satisfy his sexual needs. **?m/C VHS.** Robert Wood, Jim Vance, Pamela Rhea; **D:** Herschell Gordon Lewis. *MOV, TPV*

How to Make a Monster 🐾🐾 1958

In-joke from the creators of youth-oriented '50s AIP monster flicks; a mad makeup man's homebrew greasepaint brainwashes the actors. Disguised as famous monsters, they kill horror-hating movie execs. Mild fun if—and only if—you treasure the genre. Conway repeats his role as Teenage Frankenstein, but the studio couldn't get Michael Landon for the Teenage Werewolf. **73m/B VHS.** Robert Harris, Paul Brinegar, Gary Conway, Gary Clarke, Malcolm Atterbury, Dennis Cross, John Ashley, Morris Ankrum, Walter Reed, Heather Ames; **D:** Herbert L. Strock. *COL, MLB*

How to Make an American Quilt 🐾🐾½ 1995 (PG-13)

Slow-moving take on female friendship and marriage revolves around perennial grad student Finn (the mopey Ryder), who is frantic to both finish her third attempted thesis and to answer a marriage proposal from practically perfect beau Sam (Mulroney). She takes a summer refuge with her grandmother (Burstyn), where a variety of family friends work on her wedding quilt as they tell stories of loves lost and won. Lots of (somewhat overextended) flashbacks and with so many characters, naturally some get the short end of the script. Based on the novel by Whitney Otto.**CW:** Scene of drug use, some sensuality and nudity. **109m/C VHS, LV, Closed Caption.** Winona Ryder, Ellen Burstyn, Anne Bancroft, Lois Smith, Jean Simmons, Kate Nelligan, Maya Angelou, Alfre Woodard, Dermot Mulroney, Kate Capshaw, Rip Torn, Derrick O'Connor, Loren Dean, Samantha Mathis, Joanna Going, Tim Guinee, Johnathon Schaech, Claire Danes, Jared Leto, Esther Rolle, Melinda Dillon, Alicia (Lecy) Goranson, Maria Celedonio, Mykel T. Williamson; **D:** Jocelyn Moorhouse; **W:** Jane Anderson; **C:** Janusz Kaminski; **M:** Thomas Newman. Nominations: MTV Movie Awards '96: Best Kiss (Winona Ryder/Dermot Mulroney); Screen Actors Guild Award '95: Cast. *USH*

How to Marry a Millionaire 🐾🐾½ 1953

Three models pool their money and rent a lavish apartment in a campaign to trap millionaire husbands. Clever performances by three lead women salvage a vehicle intended primarily to bolster Monroe's career. The opening street scene, with the accompanying theme music, was a state-of-the-art achievement of screen and sound in the first movie to be filmed in CinemaScope. Remake of "The Greeks Had a Word for Them." **96m/C VHS, Beta, LV.** Lauren Bacall, Marilyn Monroe, Betty Grable, William Powell, David Wayne, Cameron Mitchell; **D:** Jean Negulesco; **W:** Nunnally Johnson; **M:** Alfred Newman. Nominations: Academy Awards '53: Best Costume Design (Color). *FOX*

How to Murder Your Wife 🐾🐾🐾 1964

While drunk, a cartoonist marries an unknown woman and then frantically tries to think of ways to get rid of her — even contemplating murder. Frantic comedy is tailored for Lemmon. **118m/C VHS, Beta, LV, Closed Caption.** Jack Lemmon, Terry-Thomas, Virna Lisi, Eddie Mayehoff, Sidney Blackmer, Claire Trevor, Mary Wickes, Jack Albertson; **D:** Richard Quine; **W:** George Axelrod; **C:** Harry Stradling. *MGM*

How to Pick Up Girls 🐾🐾 1978

Comic tale based on Eric Weber's bestseller follows the exploits of a small-town boy who moves to New York City and finds the secret to picking up women. Made for television. **93m/C VHS, Beta.** Desi Arnaz Jr., Bess Armstrong, Fred McCarren, Polly Bergen, Richard Dawson, Alan King, Abe Vigoda, Deborah Raffin; **D:** Bill Persky. *TWE*

How to Seduce a Woman woof! 1974

A playboy attempts to bed five supposedly unattainable women. **108m/C VHS, Beta.** Angus Duncan, Marty Ingels, Lillian Randolph. *PSM*

How to Steal a Million 🐾🐾🐾 1966

Sophisticated comedy-crime caper involving a million-dollar heist of a sculpture in a Paris art museum. Hepburn and O'Toole are perfectly cast as partners in crime and Griffith gives a good performance as Hepburn's art-forging father. A charming, lightweight script and various Parisian locales combine for fun, above-average fluff. Original title was "How to Steal a Million Dollars and Live Happily Ever After." Based on the story "Venus Rising" by George Bradshaw. **127m/C VHS, Closed Caption.** Audrey Hepburn, Peter O'Toole, Eli Wallach, Hugh Griffith, Charles Boyer, Fernand Gravet, Marcel Dalio, Jacques Marin; **D:** William Wyler; **W:** Harry Kurnitz; **C:** Charles B(ryant) Lang; **M:** John Williams. *FXV, MGM*

How to Stuff a Wild Bikini 🐾🐾 1965

Tired next to last feature in the overlong tradition of Frankie and Annette doing the beach thing, featuring a pregnant Funicello (though this is hidden and not part of the plot). Avalon actually has only a small role as the jealous boyfriend trying to see if Annette will remain faithful while he's away on military duty. Keaton is the witch doctor who helps Frankie keep Annette true. "Playboy" playmates wander about in small swimsuits, garage band extraordinare "The Kingsmen" play themselves, and Brian Wilson of the "Beach Boys" drops by. Followed by "Ghost in the Invisible Bikini," the only movie in the series that isn't on video. ♪After the Party; Better Be Ready; Follow Your Leader; Give Her Lovin'; How About Us?; How to Stuff a Wild Bikini; I'm the Boy Next Door; Madison Avenue; The Perfect Boy. **90m/C VHS, Beta.** Annette Funicello, Dwayne Hickman, Frankie Avalon, Beverly Adams, Buster Keaton, Harvey Lembeck, Mickey Rooney, Brian Donlevy, Jody McCrea, John Ashley, Marianne Gaba, Len Lesser, Irene Tsu, Bobbi Shaw, Luree Holmes; **D:** William Asher; **W:** William Asher, Leo Townsend; **C:** Floyd Crosby; **M:** Les Baxter. *NO*

How to Succeed in Business without Really Trying 🐾🐾🐾½ 1967

Classic musical comedy about a window-washer who charms his way to the top of a major company. Robert Morse repeats his Tony winning Broadway role. Loosely based on a non-fiction book of the same title by Shepherd Mead, whose book Morse purchases on his first day of work. Excellent transfer of stage to film, with choreography by Moreda expanding Bob Fosse's original plan. Dynamite from start to finish. ♪I Believe In You; The Company Way; Coffee Break; The Brotherhood of Man; A Secretary Is Not A Toy; Grand Old Ivy; Been A Long Day; Rosemary; Finch's Frolic. **121m/C VHS, LV.** Robert Morse, Michele Lee, Rudy Vallee, Anthony Teague, George Fenneman, Maureen Arthur; **D:** David Swift; **W:** David Swift, Abe Burrows; **C:** Burnett Guffey; **M:** Frank Loesser. *MGM*

How to Succeed with Girls 🐾 1964

Marginally funny comedy about pious wax salesman (Leder) with a secret fantasy life who unwittingly enlists the aid of his wife's lover (Schrier) to help him overcome his shyness. Several fantasy sequences (in color; the rest of the film is black and white) include an Arabian harem, an old West saloon, and a science laboratory. Brubaker's secretary (Mathes) was Playboy's Miss June 1962. Pete's girlfriend (McClanahan of television's Golden Girls) is credited as either Patty Leder or Helen Goodman. **83m/C VHS.** Marissa Mathes, Rue McClanahan, Paul Leder, Leon Schrier; **D:** Edward A. Biery. *SMW, TPV*

How U Like Me Now? 🐾🐾🐾 1992 (R)

Comedy set on Chicago's south side focuses on Thomas, an attractive but unmotivated guy with low earning potential, and his girl Valerie, a pretentious overachiever who wants much more than he's able to offer. Robert's second directorial effort offers a fresh look at African Americans on film with plenty of lively supporting characters and witty dialogue. Filmed on a $600,000 budget.**CW:** Strong language and sexuality. **109m/C VHS, LV, Closed Caption.** Darnell Williams, Salli Richardson, Daniel Gardner, Raymond Whitefield, Debra Crable, Jonelle Kennedy, Byron Stewart, Charnele Brown, Daryll Roberts; **D:** Daryll Roberts; **W:** Daryll Roberts; **M:** Kahil El Zabar, Chuck Webb. *USH*

Howard the Duck 🐾 1986 (PG)

A big-budget Lucasfilm adaptation of the short-lived Marvel comic book about an alien, resembling a cigar-chomping duck, who gets sucked into a vortex, lands on Earth and saves it from the Dark Overlords. While he's at it, he befriends a nice young lady in a punk rock band and starts to fall in love. A notorious box-office bomb and one of the '80s' worst major films, although it seems to work well with children, given the simple story line and good special effects. **111m/C VHS, Beta, LV, Closed Caption.** Lea Thompson, Jeffrey Jones, Tim Robbins; **D:** Willard Huyck; **W:** Willard Huyck, Gloria Katz; **M:** Sylvester Levay, John Barry. Golden Raspberry Awards '86: Worst Picture, Worst Screenplay.*USH*

Howard's End 🐾🐾🐾🐾 1992 (PG)

E.M. Forster's 1910 novel about property, privilege, class differences, and Edwardian society is brought to enchanting life by the Merchant Ivory team. A tragic series of events occurs after two impulsive sisters become involved with a working class couple and a wealthy family. Tragedy aside, this is a visually beautiful effort with subtle performances where a glance or a gesture says as much as any dialog. The winner of numerous awards and wide critical acclaim. Thompson is especially notable as the compassionate Margaret, while Hopkins plays the repressed English gentleman brilliantly. **143m/C VHS, LV, 8mm, Closed Caption.** *GB* Anthony Hopkins, Emma Thompson, Helena Bonham Carter, Vanessa Redgrave, James Wilby, Sam West, Jemma Redgrave, Nicola Duffett, Prunella Scales,

Joseph Bennett; **Cameos:** Simon Callow; **D:** James Ivory; **W:** Ruth Prawer Jhabvala; **C:** Tony Pierce-Roberts. Academy Awards '92: Best Actress (Thompson), Best Adapted Screenplay, Best Art Direction/Set Decoration; British Academy Awards '92: Best Actress (Thompson); Chicago Film Critics Awards '92: Best Actress (Thompson); Golden Globe Awards '93: Best Actress—Drama (Thompson); Los Angeles Film Critics Association Awards '92: Best Actress (Thompson); National Board of Review Awards '92: Best Actress (Thompson), Best Director (Ivory), Best Film; New York Film Critics Awards '92: Best Actress (Thompson); National Society of Film Critics Awards '92: Best Actress (Thompson); Nominations: Academy Awards '92: Best Cinematography, Best Costume Design, Best Director (Ivory), Best Picture, Best Supporting Actress (Redgrave), Best Original Score. *COL, CRC, MOV*

The Howards of Virginia 🎬🎬½ *Tree of Liberty* 1940 A lavish Hollywood historical epic, detailing the adventures of a backwoodsman and the rich Virginia girl he marries as their families become involved in the Revolutionary War. 117m/B VHS, Beta. Cary Grant, Martha Scott, Cedric Hardwicke, Alan Marshal, Richard Carlson, Paul Kelly, Irving Bacon, Tom Drake, Anne Revere, Ralph Byrd, Alan Ladd; **D:** Frank Lloyd. Nominations: Academy Awards '40: Best Sound, Best Original Score. *COL*

The Howling 🎬🎬🎬 1981 (R) A pretty television reporter takes a rest at a clinic and discovers slowly that its denizens are actually werewolves. Crammed with inside jokes, this horror comedy pioneered the use of the body-altering prosthetic make-up (by Rob Bottin) now essential for on-screen man-to-wolf transformations. At last count, followed by five sequels. 91m/C VHS, Beta, LV. Dee Wallace Stone, Patrick Macnee, Dennis Dugan, Christopher Stone, Belinda Balaski, Kevin McCarthy, John Carradine, Slim Pickens, Elisabeth Brooks, Robert Picardo, Dick Miller; **D:** Joe Dante; **W:** John Sayles, Terence H. Winkless; **M:** Pino Donaggio. *COL*

Howling 2: Your Sister Is a Werewolf 🎬 1985 (R) A policeman (the brother of one of the first film's victims) investigates a Transylvanian werewolf-ridden castle and gets mangled for his trouble. Followed by four more sequels. 91m/C VHS, Beta, LV. *FR IT* Sybil Danning, Christopher Lee, Annie McEnroe, Marsha Hunt, Reb Brown, Ferdinand "Ferdy" Mayne; **D:** Philippe Mora; **W:** Gary Brandner. *REP*

Howling 3: The Marsupials 🎬🎬 1987 (PG-13) Australians discover a pouch-laden form of lycanthrope. Third "Howling" (surprise), second from Mora and better than his first. 94m/C VHS, Beta, LV. *AU* Barry Otto, Imogen Annesley, Dasha Blahova, Max Fairchild, Ralph Cotterill, Leigh Biolos, Frank Thring Jr., Michael Pate; **D:** Philippe Mora. *LIV*

Howling 4: The Original Nightmare 🎬 1988 (R) A woman novelist hears the call of the wild while taking a rest cure in the country. This werewolf tale has nothing to do with the other sequels. 94m/C VHS, Beta, LV. Romy Windsor, Michael T. Weiss, Antony Hamilton, Susanne Severeid, Lamya Derval; **D:** John Hough. *LIV*

Howling 5: The Rebirth 🎬 1989 (R) The fifth in the disconnected horror series, in which a varied group of people stranded in a European castle are individually hunted down by evil. 99m/C VHS, Beta, LV. Philip Davis, Victoria Catlin, Elizabeth She, Ben Cole, William Shockley; **D:** Neal Sundstrom; **C:** Arledge Armenaki. *LIV*

Howling 6: The Freaks 🎬½ 1990 (R) Hideous werewolf suffers from multiple sequels, battles with vampire at freak show, and discovers that series won't die. Next up: "Howling 7: The Nightmare that Won't Go Away."**CW:** Graphic horror violence. 102m/C VHS, LV. Brendan Hughes, Michelle Matheson, Sean Gregory Sullivan, Antonio Fargas, Carol Lynley, Jered Barclay, Bruce Martyn Payne; **D:** Hope Perello. *LIV, IME*

The Howling: New Moon Rising 🎬½ 1995 (R) Small desert town is plagued by a series of terrifying murders believed to be the work of a werewolf, whose victims then join his vicious pack. 92m/C VHS, LV, Closed Caption. **D:** Clive Turner; **W:** Clive Turner. *NLC*

H.P. Lovecraft's Necronomicon: Book of the Dead 🎬🎬 *Necronomicon* 1993 (R) Trilogy of stories: Payne encounters a demon who resurrects his late wife and son in "The Drowning;" "The Cold" finds a reporter investigating a series of murders and uncovers crazed doctor Warner, who's discovered the secret to immortality; female cop discovers a subterranean alien in "Whispers." Combs serves as narrator, Lovecraft. 96m/C VHS, LV, Closed Caption. Bruce Payne, Belinda Bauer, Bess Meyer, David Warner, Signy Coleman, Richard Lynch, Dennis Christopher, Jeffrey Combs, Maria Ford, Don Calfa; **D:** Christophe Gans, Shusuke Kaneko, Brian Yuzna; **W:** Kazunori Ito, Christophe Gans, Brent Friedman, Brian Yuzna; **C:** Gerry Lively, Russ Brandt; **M:** Joseph Lo Duca, Daniel Light. *NLC*

Huck and the King of Hearts 🎬🎬½ 1993 (PG) When a cardshark and his young friend Huck travel the country searching for Huck's long-lost grandfather, they find adventure everywhere from Hannibal, Missouri to L.A. to Vegas. Loose, contemporary adaptation of Mark Twain's "The Adventures of Huckleberry Finn." 103m/C VHS, Beta, LV. Chauncey Leopardi, Graham Greene, Dee Wallace Stone, Joe Piscopo, John Astin, Gretchen Becker; **D:** Michael Keusch; **W:** Christopher Sturgeon; **M:** Chris Saranec. *PSM*

Huckleberry Finn 🎬🎬 1974 (G) The musical version of the Mark Twain story about the adventures a young boy and a runaway slave encounter along the Mississippi River. 114m/C VHS, Beta, LV, Closed Caption. Jeff East, Paul Winfield, Harvey Korman, David Wayne, Arthur O'Connell, Gary Merrill, Natalie Trundy, Lucille Benson; **D:** J. Lee Thompson. *MGM, FOX, FCT*

Huckleberry Finn 🎬🎬½ 1975 (G) Whitewashed version of the Twain classic features post Opie Howard as the incredible Huck and Dano as the sharp witted short storyist. Stars four members of the Howard clan. Made for TV. 74m/C VHS, Beta. Ron Howard, Donny Most, Royal Dano, Antonio Fargas, Jack Elam, Merle Haggard, Rance Howard, Jean Howard, Clint Howard, Shug Fisher, Sarah Selby, Bill Erwin; **D:** Robert Totten. *KUI, FXV, FCT*

Huckleberry Finn 🎬½ 1981 A version of the classic Mark Twain novel about the adventures a young boy and a runaway slave encounter as they travel down the Mississippi River. 72m/C VHS, Beta. *LIV*

The Hucksters 🎬🎬🎬 1947 Account of a man looking for honesty and integrity in the radio advertising world and finding little to work with. All performances are excellent; but Greenstreet, as the tyrannical head of a soap company, is a stand out. Deborah Kerr's American debut. 115m/B VHS, Beta, Closed Caption. Clark Gable, Deborah Kerr, Sydney Greenstreet, Adolphe Menjou, Ava Gardner, Keenan Wynn, Edward Arnold; **D:** Jack Conway. *MGM, FCT*

Hud 🎬🎬🎬🎬 1963 Newman is a hard-driving, hard-drinking, woman-chasing young man whose life is a revolt against the principles of stern father Douglas. Neal is outstanding as the family housekeeper. Excellent photography. Based on the Larry McMurtry novel "Horseman, Pass By." 112m/B VHS, Beta, LV. Paul Newman, Melvyn Douglas, Patricia Neal, Brandon de Wilde, John Ashley; **D:** Martin Ritt; **W:** Irving Ravetch, Harriet Frank Jr.; **C:** James Wong Howe; **M:** Elmer Bernstein. Academy Awards '63: Best Actress (Neal), Best Black and White Cinematography, Best Supporting Actor (Douglas); British Academy Awards '63: Best Actress (Neal); National Board of Review Awards '63: 10 Best Films of the Year, Best Actress (Neal), Best Supporting Actor (Douglas); New York Film Critics Awards '63: Best Actress (Neal), Best Screenplay; Nominations: Academy Awards '63: Best Actor (Newman), Best Adapted Screenplay, Best Art Direction/Set Decoration (B & W), Best Director (Ritt). *PAR, BTV*

Hudson Hawk 🎬 1991 (R) A big-budget star vehicle with little else going for it. Willis plays a master burglar released from prison, only to find himself trapped by the CIA into one last theft. Ev-eryone in the cast tries to be extra funny, resulting in a disjointed situation where no one is. Weakly plotted, poorly paced.**CW:** Language. 95m/C VHS, Beta, LV, 8mm, Closed Caption. Bruce Willis, Danny Aiello, Andie MacDowell, James Coburn, Sandra Bernhard, Richard E. Grant, Frank Stallone; **D:** Michael Lehmann; **W:** Steven E. de Souza, Daniel Waters. Golden Raspberry Awards '91: Worst Picture, Worst Director (Lehmann), Worst Screenplay. *COL*

The Hudsucker Proxy 🎬🎬🎬 1993 (PG) In an effort to scare off would-be investors in a public stock offering dim bulb mailboy Robbins is installed as the Prez of Hudsucker Industries (in 1958) by Board Director Newman after corporate magnate Hudsucker (Durning) takes a swan dive from the 44th floor. First truly mainstream effort from the maverick Coen brothers is peppered with obscure references to numerous points on the historical map of cinematic style, and trots out an equally old but instantly recognizable story. Will delight Coen fans, but may be too dark for others. Destined to keep art history profs busy for decades. 115m/C VHS, LV, Closed Caption. Tim Robbins, Paul Newman, Jennifer Jason Leigh, Charles Durning, John Mahoney, Jim True, Bill Cobbs, Bruce Campbell, Steve Buscemi; **Cameos:** Peter Gallagher; **D:** Joel Coen; **W:** Ethan Coen, Joel Coen, Sam Raimi; **C:** Roger Deakins; **M:** Carter Burwell. *WAR*

Hue and Cry 🎬🎬🎬 1947 Nobody believes a young boy when he discovers crooks are sending coded messages in a weekly children's magazine. A detective writer finally believes his story and they set off to capture the crooks. 82m/B VHS. *GB* Alastair Sim, Jack Warner, Frederick Piper, Jack Lambert, Joan Dowling; **D:** Charles Crichton. *SNC, NOS, FCT*

Hugh Hefner: Once Upon a Time 1992 (R) Fascinating look at the "Bunny" king and Playboy Enterprises. His celebrated life of isolation and excess at the Playboy mansions is portrayed as is the founding of "Playboy" magazine in 1953 and the Playboy clubs (with their notorious Bunnies). Includes interviews, home movies, and photographs. Admiring yet not without a few sharp edges.**CW:** Language and nudity. 91m/C VHS, LV. Hugh Hefner; **D:** Robert Heath. *UND, BTV*

Hughes & Harlow: Angels in Hell 🎬 1977 (R) The story of the romance that occurred between Howard Hughes and Jean Harlow during the filming of "Hell's Angels" in 1930. 94m/C VHS, Beta. Lindsay Bloom, Victor Holchak, David McLean, Royal Dano, Adam Roarke, Linda Cristal; **D:** Larry Buchanan. *NO*

Hugo the Hippo 🎬🎬 1976 (G) Animated musical about a forlorn baby hippo who struggles to survive in the human jungle of old Zanzibar. 90m/C VHS, Beta. **W:** Thomas Baum; **V:** Paul Lynde, Burl Ives, Robert Morley, Marie Osmond. *FOX*

Hula 🎬½ 1928 Unflappable flapper Bow and her gang frolic on a Pacific island. 64m/B VHS, Beta. Clara Bow, Clive Brook, Patricia Dupont, Arnold Kent, Agaslino Borgato; **D:** Victor Fleming. *GPV, FCT, DVT*

Hullabaloo Over Georgie & Bonnie's Pictures 🎬🎬½ 1978 A young maharajah has inherited a priceless collection of Indian miniature paintings he doesn't appreciate and which his greedy sister is anxious for him to sell. They're beseiged by art dealers and collectors who learn about the treasure trove and will do anything to possess it. Among them are the British Ashcroft, who wants the art for the British Museum, and competing American collector Pine. Made for British television. 85m/C VHS, Beta. *GB* Victor Banerjee, Aparna Sen, Larry Pine, Saeed Jaffrey, Peggy Ashcroft; **D:** James Ivory; **W:** Ruth Prawer Jhabvala; **C:** Walter Lassally. *NLC*

Human Beasts 🎬 1980 Jewel robbers face a tribe of hungry cannibals. 90m/C VHS, Beta. *SP JP* Paul Naschy, Eiko Nagashima; **D:** Paul Naschy; **W:** Paul Naschy. *NO*

The Human Comedy ✔✔✔½ **1943** A small-town boy experiences love and loss and learns the meaning of true faith during WWII. Straight, unapologetically sentimental version of the William Saroyan novel. 117m/B VHS, Beta, LV. Mickey Rooney, Frank Morgan, James Craig, Fay Bainter, Ray Collins, Donna Reed, Van Johnson, Barry Nelson, Robert Mitchum, Jackie "Butch" Jenkins; **D:** Clarence Brown; **W:** William Saroyan; **C:** Harry Stradling. Academy Awards '43: Best Story; Nominations: Academy Awards '43: Best Actor (Rooney), Best Black and White Cinematography, Best Director (Brown), Best Picture. *MGM*

The Human Condition: A Soldier's Prayer ✔✔✔ **1961** A Japanese pacifist escapes from his commanders and allows himself to be captured by Russian troops, hoping for better treatment as a P.O.W. The final part of the trilogy preceded by "The Human Condition: No Greater Love" and "The Human Condition: Road to Eternity." In Japanese with English subtitles. 190m/B VHS, Beta. *JP* Tatsuya Nakadai, Michiyo Aratama, Yusuke Kawazu, Tamao Nakamura, Chishu Ryu, Taketoshi Naito, Reiko Hitomi, Kyoko Kishida, Keijiro Morozumi, Koji Kiyomura, Nobuo Kaneko, Fujio Suga; **D:** Masaki Kobayashi. *NO*

The Human Condition: No Greater Love ✔✔✔ **1958** First of a three-part series of films. A pacifist is called into military service and subsequently sent to a run a military mining camp. A gripping look at one man's attempt to retain his humanity in the face of war. Followed by "The Human Condition: Road to Eternity" and "The Human Condition: A Soldier's Prayer." In Japanese with English subtitles. 200m/B VHS, Beta. *JP* Tatsuya Nakadai, Michiyo Aratama, So Yamamura, Eitaro Ozawa, Akira Ishihara, Chikage Awashima, Ineko Arima, Keiji Sada, Shinji Nambara, Seiji Miyaguchi, Toru Abe, Masao Mishima, Eijiro Tono, Yasushi Nagata, Yoshio Kosugi; **D:** Masaki Kobayashi. *NO*

The Human Condition: Road to Eternity ✔✔✔ *No Greater Love; Ningen No Joken* **1959** A Japanese pacifist is on punishment duty in Manchuria where he is beaten by sadistic officers who try to destroy his humanity. The second part of the trilogy, preceded by "The Human Condition: No Greater Love" and followed by "The Human Condition: A Soldier's Prayer." In Japanese with English subtitles. 180m/B VHS, Beta. *JP* Tatsuya Nakadai, Michiyo Aratama, Kokinji Katsura, Jun Tatara, Michio Minami, Keiji Sada, Minoru Chiaki, Ryohei Uchida, Kan Yanagidani, Kenjiro Uemura, Yusuke Kawazu, Susumu Fujita; **D:** Masaki Kobayashi. *NO*

Human Desire ✔✔½ **1954** Femme fatale Grahame and jealous husband Crawford turn out the lights on Crawford's boss (seems there's some confusion about how Miss Gloria managed to convince the guy to let her hubby have his job back). Ford's wise to them but plays see no evil because he's gone crackers for Grahame, who by now has decided she'd like a little help to rid herself of an unwanted husband. Bleak, melodramatic, full of big heat, its Lang through and through. Based on the Emile Zola novel "La Bete Humaine," which inspired Renoir's 1938 telling as well. 90m/B VHS. Glenn Ford, Gloria Grahame, Broderick Crawford, Edgar Buchanan, Kathleen Case; **D:** Fritz Lang; **C:** Burnett Guffey. *GKK*

The Human Duplicators ✔½ **1964** Kiel is an alien who has come to Earth to make androids out of important folk, thus allowing the "galaxy beings" to take over. Cheap stuff, but earnest performances make this more fun than it should be. 82m/C VHS, Beta. George Nader, Barbara Nichols, George Macready, Dolores Faith, Hugh Beaumont, Richard Kiel, Richard Arlen; **D:** Hugo Grimaldi. *LIV*

Human Experiments ✔ **1979 (R)** Psychiatrist in a women's prison conducts a group of experiments in which he destroys the "criminal instinct" in the inmates through brute fear. 82m/C VHS, Beta. Linda Haynes, Jackie Coogan, Aldo Ray; **D:** Gregory Goodell. *NO*

The Human Factor ✔½ **1975 (R)** Kennedy stars as a computer expert who tracks down his family's murderers using technology. Bloody and violent. 96m/C VHS, Beta. *GB IT* George Kennedy, John Mills, Raf Vallone, Rita Tushingham, Barry Sullivan, Arthur Franz; **D:** Edward Dmytryk; **M:** Ennio Morricone. *LIV*

The Human Factor ✔✔½ **1979 (R)** Unexciting spy caper has a British Secret Service agent (Williamson) betraying his country in order to aid a friend. As a result of his actions an innocent man is killed and Williamson is forced to defect to the Soviet Union. Based on a novel by Graham Greene. 115m/C VHS. *GB* Nicol Williamson, Richard Attenborough, John Gielgud, Derek Jacobi, Robert Morley, Ann Todd, Richard Vernon, Iman; **D:** Otto Preminger; **W:** Tom Stoppard. *MGM*

Human Gorilla ✔ *Behind Locked Doors* **1948** A thriller involving a mad scientist, an insane asylum, a reporter, and various other mysterious trappings. 58m/B VHS, Beta. Richard Carlson, Lucille Bremer, Tor Johnson. *NO*

Human Hearts ✔✔ **1922** A creaky old silent starring "Phantom of the Opera" leading lady Philbin. A family is torn apart by a con man and his femme fatale. 99m/B VHS, Beta, 8mm. House Peters Sr., Russell Simpson, Mary Philbin. *VYY*

The Human Monster ✔✔½ *Dark Eyes of London* **1939** Scotland Yard inspector investigates five drownings of the blind patients a phony Dr. Orloff (Lugosi) is exploiting for insurance money. Superior Lugosi effort that's modestly violent and tasteless. Based on the Edgar Wallace novel. 73m/B VHS, Beta. *GB* Bela Lugosi, Hugh Williams, Greta Gynt; **D:** Walter Summers; **W:** Walter Summers. *NOS, MRV, SNC*

The Human Shield ✔✔ **1992 (R)** A man risks his life on a mission to save his brother during the Persian Gulf War. **CW:** War violence. 88m/C VHS, LV, Closed Caption. Michael Dudikoff, Tommy Hinkley, Steve Inwood; **D:** Ted Post. *WAR, CAN*

The Human Vapor ✔ *Gasu Ningen Daiichigo* **1968** A normal human being has the ability to vaporize himself at will and use it to terrorize Tokyo. 81m/C VHS, Beta. *JP* GEM, PSM, CNG

Humanoid Defender ✔✔ **1985** A made-for-television film about a scientist and an android rebelling against the government that wants to use the android as a warfare prototype. 94m/C VHS, Beta. Terence Knox, Gary Kasper, Aimee Eccles, William Lucking; **D:** William Lucking. *USH*

Humanoids from the Deep woof! *Monster* **1980 (R)** Mutated salmon-like monsters rise from the depths of the ocean and decide to chomp on some bikinied babes. Violent and bloody. 81m/C VHS, Beta. Doug McClure, Ann Turkel, Vic Morrow, Cindy Weintraub, Anthony Penya, Denise Balik; **D:** Barbara Peeters; **W:** Frank Arnold; **M:** James Horner. *NHO*

Humongous woof! **1982 (R)** Brain-dead bevy of teens shipwreck on an island where they encounter a deranged mutant giant who must kill to survive. You'll be rooting for the monster. 93m/C VHS, Beta. *CA* Janet Julian, David Wallace, Janet Baldwin; **D:** Paul Lynch. *NLC*

Humoresque ✔✔✔½ **1946** A talented but struggling young musician finds a patron in the married, wealthy, and older Crawford. His appreciation is not as romantic as she hoped. Stunning performance from Crawford, with excellent supporting cast, including a young Robert Blake. Fine music sequences (Isaac Stern dubbed the violin), and lush production values. Laserdisc version features the original movie trailer. 123m/B VHS, LV. Joan Crawford, John Garfield, Oscar Levant, J. Carrol Naish, Joan Chandler, Tom D'Andrea, Peggy Knudsen, Ruth Nelson, Craig Stevens, Paul Cavanagh, Richard Gaines, John Abbott, Robert (Bobby) Blake; **D:** Jean Negulesco. Nominations: Academy Awards '46: Original Dramatic/Comedy Score. *MGM, BTV, FCT*

The Hunchback of Notre Dame ✔✔✔ **1923** The first film version of Victor Hugo's novel about the tortured hunchback bellringer of Notre Dame Cathedral, famous for the contortions of Lon Chaney's self-transformations via improvised makeup. Also available at 68 minutes. 100m/B VHS, LV. Lon Chaney Sr., Patsy Ruth Miller, Norman Kerry, Ernest Torrence; **D:** Wallace Worsley. *KIV, MRV, NOS*

The Hunchback of Notre Dame ✔✔✔✔ **1939** Best Hollywood version of the Victor Hugo classic, infused with sweep, sadness and an attempt at capturing a degree of spirited, Hugoesque detail. Laughton is Quasimodo, a deformed Parisian bellringer, who provides sanctuary to a young gypsy woman accused by church officials of being a witch. The final scene of the townspeople storming the cathedral remains a Hollywood classic. Great performances all around; the huge facade of the Notre Dame cathedral was constructed on a Hollywood set for this film. Remake of several earlier films, including 1923's Lon Chaney silent. Remade in 1957 and later for television. 117m/B VHS, Beta, LV. Charles Laughton, Maureen O'Hara, Edmond O'Brien, Cedric Hardwicke, Thomas Mitchell, George Zucco, Alan Marshal, Walter Hampden, Harry Davenport, Curt Bois, George Tobias, Rod La Rocque; **D:** William Dieterle; **W:** Sonya Levien, Bruno Frank; **M:** Alfred Newman. Nominations: Academy Awards '39: Best Sound, Best Score. *TTC, MED, CCB*

The Hunchback of Notre Dame ✔✔½ *Notre Dame de Paris* **1957 (PG)** Slow retelling of the Victor Hugo novel, filmed entirely in France in CinemaScope. Quinn's the tragic Quasimodo with bombshell Lollobrigida appropriatley hotblooded as gypsy Esmerelda. 104m/C VHS, LV, Closed Caption. *FR* Anthony Quinn, Gina Lollobrigida, Alain Cuny, Jean Danet, Robert Hirsch, Jean Tissier; **D:** Jean Delannoy; **W:** Jacques Prevert, Jean Aurenche; **C:** Michel Kelber; **M:** Georges Auric. *TOU*

The Hunchback of Notre Dame ✔✔✔ *Hunchback* **1982 (PG)** It's not often that a classic novel is remade into a classic movie that's remade into a made-for-TV reprise, and survives its multiple renderings. But it's not often a cast so rich in stage trained actors is assembled on the small screen. Hopkins gives a textured, pre-Hannibal Lecter interpretation of Quasimodo, the Hunchback in Hugo's eponymous novel. Impressive model of the cathedral by production designer John Stoll. 102m/C VHS. Anthony Hopkins, Derek Jacobi, Lesley-Anne Down, John Gielgud, Tim Pigott-Smith, Rosalie Crutchley, Robert Powell; **D:** Michael Tuchner. *THV*

The Hunchback of Notre Dame ✔✔✔ **1996 (G)** Animated/musical version of Victor Hugo's story about deformed bellringer Quasimodo (Hulce) and his love for the beautiful gypsy Esmerelda (Moore). The original isn't exactly fun fare but you expect Disney to find a way to leave everybody humming and happy. The sweeping music was provided by "Pocahontas" tunesmiths Menken and Schwartz. Comic relief is supplied by three gargoyles, companions to Quasimodo, who are voiced wonderfully by Alexander, Kimbrough and Wickes. Wickes, 85, died six weeks after voicing her role. Looks like another boatload of box office, merchandising, and video sale cash is making its way into old Walt's vaults. 91m/C VHS, Closed Caption. **V:** Kirk Wise, Gary Trousdale; **M:** Stephen Schwartz, Alan Menken; **V:** Tom Hulce, Demi Moore, Kevin Kline, Tony Jay, Charles Kimbrough, Jason Alexander, Mary Wickes, David Ogden Stiers. Nominations: Academy Awards '96: Best Original Score; Golden Globe Awards '97: Best Score. *TOU*

Hundra ✔ **1985** A warrior queen vows revenge when her all-female tribe is slain by men. Nothing can stop her fierce vendetta—except love. 96m/C VHS, Beta. *IT* Laurene Landon, John Gaffari, Ramiro Oliveros, Marissa Casel; **D:** Matt Cimber; **M:** Ennio Morricone. *MED*

A Hungarian Fairy Tale ✔✔✔ *Hol Volt, Hol Nem Volt* **1987** Political satire meets fantasy in a magical tale of a fatherless young boy searching for a surrogate dad. Unusual characters as well as an homage to Mozart's "The Magic Flute." In Hungarian with English subtitles. 97m/B

VHS. **HU** Arpad Vermes, Maria Varga, Frantisek Husak, Eszter Csakanyi, Szilvia Toth, Judith Pogany, Geza Balkay; **D:** Gyula Gazdag. *FXL, EVD*

Hungarian Rhapsody 🎬🎬🎬 *1978* In 1911, a Hungarian nobleman joins the ranks of the rebelling peasants in order to oppose his brother, who represents aristocratic repression. One of Jancso's clearest political films, and one that continues the filmmaker's experiments with long, uncut sequences and dynamic mise-en-scene. In Hungarian with English subtitles. 101m/C VHS, Beta. **HU** Gyorgy Cserhalmi, Lajos Balaszovits, Gabor Koncz, Bertalan Solti; **D:** Miklos Jancso. *FCT, AUD*

Hunger 🎬🎬 *Sult 1966* In the late 1800's a starving Norwegian writer, unable to sell his work, rejects charity out of pride, and retains his faith in his talent. Based on a novel "Sult" by Knut Hamsun. In Danish with English subtitles. 100m/B VHS. **DK** Per Oscarsson, Gunnel Lindblom; **D:** Henning Carlsen; **W:** Henning Carlsen. Cannes Film Festival '66: Best Actor (Oscarsson); National Society of Film Critics Awards '68: Best Actor (Oscarsson). *FCT, CVC*

The Hunger 🎬🎬 *1983 (R)* A beautiful 2000-year-old vampire needs new blood when she realizes that her current lover, Bowie, is aging fast. Visually sumptuous but sleepwalking modern vampire tale, complete with soft-focus lesbian love scenes between Deneuve and Sarandon. Features a letterboxed screen and original movie trailer on the laserdisc format. 100m/C VHS, Beta, LV. Catherine Deneuve, David Bowie, Susan Sarandon, Cliff DeYoung, Ann Magnuson, Dan Hedaya, Willem Dafoe; **D:** Tony Scott; **W:** Michael Thomas, Ian Davis. *MGM*

Hunk 🎬🎬 *1987 (PG)* A computer nerd sells his soul to the devil for a muscular, beach-blonde physique. Answers the question, "Was it worth it?" 102m/C VHS, Beta, LV. John Allen Nelson, Steve Levitt, Deborah Shelton, Rebecca Bush, James Coco, Avery Schreiber; **D:** Lawrence Bassoff; **W:** Lawrence Bassoff; **C:** Bryan England. *COL*

The Hunt 🎬🎬🎬 *La Caza 1967* A teenage boy accompanies three Spanish Civil War veterans on what is supposed to be a friendly rabbit hunt. Things turn violent, however, when old rivalries and tensions begin to surface. In Spanish with English subtitles. 93m/B VHS. **SP** Alfredo Mayo, Ismael Merlo, Jose Maria Prada, Emilio Gutierrez-Caba, Fernando Sanchez Polack; **D:** Carlos Saura. *TPV, CVC, FCT*

The Hunt for Red October 🎬🎬🎬 *1990 (PG)* Based on Tom Clancy's blockbuster novel, a high-tech Cold War yarn about a Soviet nuclear sub turning rogue and heading straight for U.S. waters, as both the U.S. and the U.S.S.R. try to stop it. Complicated, ill-plotted potboiler that succeeds breathlessly due to the cast and McTiernan's tommy-gun direction. Introduces the character of CIA analyst Jack Ryan who returns in "Patriot Games," though in the guise of Harrison Ford. 137m/C VHS, Beta, LV, 8mm, Closed Captioned. Sean Connery, Alec Baldwin, Richard Jordan, Scott Glenn, Joss Ackland, Sam Neill, James Earl Jones, Peter Firth, Tim Curry, Courtney B. Vance, Jeffrey Jones, Fred Dalton Thompson; **D:** John McTiernan; **W:** Larry Ferguson, Donald Stewart; **C:** Jan De Bont; **M:** Basil Poledouris. Academy Awards '90: Best Sound Effects Editing; Nominations: Academy Awards '90: Best Film Editing, Best Sound. *PAR*

The Hunt for the Night Stalker 🎬🎬 *1991 (PG-13)* Another one of those True-Detective quickies so beloved by network TV, following two hardworking L.A. cops who tracked down satanic serial killer Richard Ramirez in the mid-1980s. It originally aired (under the title "Manhunt: The Search for the Night Stalker") on the date of the killer's death-sentence verdict; the videotape lacks that particular timely sparkle. 95m/C VHS, LV. Richard Jordan, A. Martinez, Lisa Eilbacher, Julie Carmen, Alan Feinstein; **D:** Bruce Seth Green. *ACA*

Hunt the Man Down 🎬🎬½ *1950* An innocent man is charged with murder, and a public defender must find the real killer before time runs out. 68m/B VHS, Beta. Gig Young, Lynn (Mary Hart) Roberts, Gerald Mohr; **D:** George Archainbaud. *NO*

Hunt the Man Down/Smashing the Rackets 🎬🎬½ *1950* A double feature: In "Hunt the Man Down" (1950) a public defender tries to clear a captured fugitive's name, and in "Smashing the Rackets" (1938) a special prosecutor takes on the gangsters who have corrupted a big city. 137m/B VHS, Beta. Gig Young, Lynn (Mary Hart) Roberts, Chester Morris, Frances Mercer, Willard Parker, Gerald Mohr, Paul Frees; **D:** George Archainbaud. *NO*

Hunted 🎬🎬 *1988 (PG)* WWII prisoner attempts to escape from demented officer who seems to enjoy bugging him. Hunted by the MPs, he relies on unorthodox guide to sustain feature length footage. 75m/C VHS. Andrew Buckland, Richard Carlson, Ron Smerczak, Mercia Van Wyk; **D:** David Lister. *ACA*

The Hunted 🎬½ *1994 (R)* American businessman in Japan meets, beds, and witnesses the assassination of a mysterious woman and is forced on the run by the modern-day ninja clan that committed the crime. Only a notch above the low-budget, badly dubbed martial arts flicks of the 70's, this shameless bloodfest features unintentionally campy performances by Lambert and Lone and lots of silly dialogue. Beware, the cliches pile up as quickly as the bodies. **CW:** Bloody ninja violence; some sexuality. 110m/C VHS. Christopher Lambert, John Lone, Joan Chen, Yoshio Harada, Yoko Shimada, Maria Natsuki, Tak Kubota; **D:** Jonathan Lawton; **W:** Jonathan Lawton; **C:** Jack Conroy; **M:** Motofumi Yamaguchi. *USH*

The Hunted Lady 🎬½ *1977* In this television pilot, Mills is an undercover policewoman who is framed by the mob. Tired and predictable. 100m/C VHS. Donna Mills, Robert Reed, Lawrence Casey, Andrew Duggan, Will Sampson, Alan Feinstein; **D:** Richard Lang. *WOV*

Hunter 🎬½ *1973* Pilot for a television series that never emerged. A government agent uncovers an enemy brainwashing scam. 90m/C VHS. John Vernon, Steve Ihnat, Fritz Weaver, Edward Binns, Sabrina Scharf, Barbara Rhoades; **D:** Leonard Horn. *ORI*

Hunter 🎬 *1977* An attorney is falsely accused of a crime and imprisoned. Released after eight years, he sets out to even the score with the mysterious millionaire who set him up. Made for television. 120m/C VHS, Beta. James Franciscus, Linda Evans, Broderick Crawford. *ORI, WAR*

The Hunter 🎬🎬½ *1980 (PG)* Action drama based on the real life adventures of Ralph (Papa) Thorson, a modern day bounty hunter who makes his living by finding fugitives who have jumped bail. McQueen's last. 97m/C VHS, Beta, LV. Steve McQueen, Eli Wallach, Kathryn Harrold, LeVar Burton; **D:** Buzz Kulik; **W:** Peter Hyams; **C:** Fred W. Koenekamp; **M:** Charles Bernstein. *PAR*

Hunter in the Dark 🎬🎬 *1980* Set in 18th-century Japan, where power, betrayal, and corruption are the dark side of the samurai world. Tanuma is a powerful shogunate minister who becomes involved with Gomyo, the leader of a secret underworld organization of thieves and murderers with a violent honor code. In Japanese with English subtitles. 138m/C VHS, LV. **JP** Tatsuya Nakadai, Tetsuro Tamba, Sonny Chiba; **D:** Hideo Gosha. *NO*

The Hunters 🎬🎬½ *1958* A motley crew of pilots learn about each other and themselves in this melodrama set during Korean war. Incredible aerial photography sets this apart from other films of the genre. 108m/C VHS. Robert Mitchum, Robert Wagner, Richard Egan, May Britt, Lee Philips; **D:** Dick Powell; **W:** Wendell Mayes. *NO*

Hunter's Blood 🎬½ *1987 (R)* Five urbanites plunge into the Southern wilderness to hunt deer, and are stalked by maniacal hillbillies. 102m/C VHS, Beta, LV, Closed Caption. Sam Bottoms, Kim Delaney, Clu Gulager, Mayf Nutter, Eugene Glazer; **D:** Robert C. Hughes; **W:** Emmett Alston. *NLC*

Hunters of the Golden Cobra 🎬 *1982 (R)* Two American soldiers plot to recover the priceless golden cobra from the Japanese general who stole the prized relic during the last days of WWII. 95m/C VHS, Beta. David Warbeck, Almanta Suska, Alan Collins, John Steiner; **D:** Anthony (Antonio Margheriti) Dawson. *LIV, VES*

The Hunting 🎬🎬 *1992 (R)* A married woman falls for a ruthless businessman and is drawn into a web of blackmail and murder in this low-budget erotic thriller. **CW:** Language, violence and drug use, and strong sensuality. 97m/C VHS, Beta. John Savage, Kerry Armstrong, Guy Pearce, Rebecca Rigg; **D:** Frank Howson; **W:** Frank Howson. *PAR*

The Hurricane 🎬🎬 *1937* A couple on the run from the law are aided by a hurricane and are able to build a new life for themselves on an idyllic island. Filmed two years before the Academy's "special effects" award came into being, but displaying some of the best effects of the decade. Boringly remade in 1979. 102m/B VHS, Beta, LV. Jon Hall, Dorothy Lamour, Mary Astor, Sir C. Aubrey Smith, Raymond Massey, Thomas Mitchell, John Carradine; **D:** John Ford. Academy Awards '37: Best Sound; Nominations: Academy Awards '37: Best Supporting Actor (Mitchell), Best Original Score.

Hurricane 🎬 *1974* Television's answer to the disaster movie craze of the early 1970s. Realistic hurricane footage and an adequate cast cannot save this catastrophe. 78m/C VHS. Larry Hagman, Martin Milner, Jessica Walter, Barry Sullivan, Will Geer, Frank Sutton; **D:** Jerry Jameson. *NO*

Hurricane woof! *Forbidden Paradise 1979 (PG)* And the wind cried, "turkey." Robards is the governor of a tropical island beset with environmental and personal concerns. Virginal daughter Farrow falls for hunky native, standard colonial power/indigenous people complications ensue, vital explanatory footage is cut, and overacting reaches epidemic heights. Then too late the big wind blows in, leveling the place. Expensive (most of the $22 million must have gone to catering) and essentially misdirected remake of the 1937 semiclassic. 120m/C VHS, Beta. Mia Farrow, Jason Robards Jr., Trevor Howard, Max von Sydow, Timothy Bottoms, James Keach; **D:** Jan Troell; **C:** Sven Nykvist; **M:** Nino Rota. *PAR*

Hurricane Express *1932* Twelve episodes of the vintage serial, in which the Duke pits his courage against an unknown, powerful individual out to sabotage a railroad. 223m/B VHS, Beta. John Wayne, Joseph Girard, Conway Tearle, Shirley Grey; **D:** J.P. McGowan, Armand Schaefer. *SNC, NOS, RHI*

Hurricane Smith 🎬🎬 *1992 (R)* Weathers stars as a roughneck Texan who travels to Australia's Gold Coast in search of his missing sister. While in the land of Oz, he gets entangled in a Mafia-style drug and prostitution ring around the "Surfer's Paradise" section of the Gold Coast. Packed with mind-blowing stunts and a good performance from Weathers, this fast-paced action thriller won't disappoint fans of this genre. **CW:** Language, action violence, and sensuality. 86m/C VHS, Closed Caption. Carl Weathers, Juergen Prochnow, Tony Bonner, Cassandra Delaney; **D:** Colin Budds. *WAR*

Hurricane Streets 🎬🎬½ *Hurricane 1996* Freeman's directorial debut centers on a group of young teenagers getting into trouble in lower Manhattan. 15-year-old Marcus (Sexton) is on the edge—his dad is dead, his mother's in jail, he's being ineffectually looked after by his working grandma, and the authorities are already eyeing this petty thief. He hangs with three buddies, one of whom, Chip (Frank), wants to start them stealing cars. Meanwhile, Marcus falls for 14-year-old Melena (Vega), whose father is both possessive and abusive, and tries to plan an escape for them both. 89m/C VHS. Brendan Sexton III, Isidra Vega, David Roland Frank, L.M. Kit Carson, Jose Zuniga, Lynn Cohen, Edie Falco, Shawn Elliot, Heather Matarazzo; **D:** Morgan J. Freeman; **W:** Morgan J. Freeman; **C:** Enrique Chediak. Sundance Film Festival '97: Best Cinematography, Best Director (Freeman), Audience Award. *NYR*

Hurricane Sword ♂♂½ 197? Thriller sets savage sword play against a background of murder, betrayal, prostitution, and reunion. 86m/C VHS, Beta. Chen Sau Kei, Li Tai Shing. NO

Hurry, Charlie, Hurry ♂ 1941 Husband gets in trouble when he bows out of a trip with his social-climber wife when he tells her he must travel to Washington to see the Vice President. 65m/B VHS, Beta. Leon Errol. MLB

Hurry Up or I'll Be Thirty ♂♂ 1973 A Brooklyn bachelor celebrates his thirtieth birthday by becoming morose, depressed, and enraged. His friends try to help; they fail, but he finds love anyway. For those seeking a better life through celluloid. 87m/C VHS, Beta. Danny DeVito, John Lefkowitz, Steve Inwood, Linda DeCoff, Ronald Anton, Maureen Byrnes, Francis Gallagher; D: Joseph Jacoby. LIV, VES

Husband Hunting ♂ 196? Working girls hit the beach in search of husbands, and find that love isn't easy to find or hold on to. 90m/C VHS, Beta. IT Walter Chiari. NO

Husbands and Lovers ♂♂ 1991 (R) Controversial and confusing film focuses on a couple's unfraditional marriage. Stephen (Sands) and Alina (Pacula) have agreed to be totally honest with each other and when Alina decides to take a lover, Stephen agrees on the condition that she report back to him every intimate detail of her affair. In the confusion and excitement of this kinky love triangle, everyone starts losing control as sexual boundaries are pushed to the limit. Also available in an unrated version.**CW:** Language and strong sensuality. 91m/C VHS, Closed Caption. Julian Sands, Joanna Pacula, Tcheky Karyo; D: Mauro Bolognini; W: Sergio Bazzini; M: Ennio Morricone. COL

Husbands and Wives ♂♂♂½ 1992 (R) Art imitates life as Allen/Farrow relationship dissolves onscreen (and off) and Woody becomes involved with young student. Mature, penetrating look at modern pair bonding and loneliness offers more painful honesty and sadness than outright laughs, though still retains essential Allen charm. Stylistically burdened by experiment with pseudo-documentary telling of tale and spasmodic hand-held cameras that annoy more than entertain. Excellent, intriguing cast, notably Davis as the overwhelming, overbearing wife/friend. Trailers became unintentionally funny in light of the highly publicized personal problems of Allen and Farrow.**CW:** Language and one sexual scene. 107m/C VHS, LV, Closed Caption. Woody Allen, Mia Farrow, Judy Davis, Sydney Pollack, Liam Neeson, Juliette Lewis, Lysette Anthony, Blythe Danner; D: Woody Allen; W: Woody Allen; C: Carlo DiPalma. British Academy Awards '92: Best Original Screenplay; Chicago Film Critics Awards '93: Best Supporting Actress (Davis); Los Angeles Film Critics Association Awards '92: Best Supporting Actress (Davis); National Board of Review Awards '92: Best Supporting Actress (Davis); National Society of Film Critics Awards '92: Best Supporting Actress (Davis); Nominations: Academy Awards '92: Best Original Screenplay, Best Supporting Actress (Davis). COL, MOV

Husbands, Wives, Money, and Murder ♂ 1986 A couple is pushed over the edge by a nosey census taker and then must dispose of the consequences. 92m/C VHS, Beta. Garrett Morris, Greg Mullavey, Meredith MacRae, Timothy Bottoms; D: Bruce Cook Jr. TWE, HHE

Hush, Hush, Sweet Charlotte ♂♂♂ 1965 A fading southern belle finds out the truth about her fiance's murder when the case is reopened thirty-seven years later by her cousin in an elaborate plot to drive her crazy. Grisly, superbly entertaining Southern Gothic horror tale, with vivid performances from the aging leads. 134m/B VHS, Beta, LV, Closed Caption. Bette Davis, Olivia de Havilland, Joseph Cotten, Agnes Moorehead, Mary Astor, Bruce Dern; D: Robert Aldrich; C: Joseph Biroc. Edgar Allan Poe Awards '64: Best Screenplay; Golden Globe Awards '65: Best Supporting Actress (Moorehead); Nominations: Academy Awards '64: Best Art Direction/Set Decoration (B & W), Best Black and White Cinematography, Best Cos-

tume Design (B & W), Best Film Editing, Best Song ("Hush, Hush, Sweet Charlotte"), Best Supporting Actress (Moorehead), Best Original Score. FOX

Hush Little Baby, Don't You Cry ♂ 1986 A made-for-television drama about a seemingly normal middle-aged family man who is in actuality a child abuser/murderer. 110m/C VHS, Beta. Emery L. Kedocia, Gary Giem, Tony Grant, Burt Douglas; D: Don Hawks. PSM

Hussy ♂ 1980 (R) Hooker and her boyfriend find themselves trapped in a web of gangsters and drugs. 95m/C VHS, Beta, LV. GB Helen Mirren, John Shea, Jenny Runacre; D: Matthew Chapman; W: Matthew Chapman; M: George Fenton. VES

The Hustle ♂♂ 1975 (R) Gritty urban adventure with Reynolds as an L.A. detective investigating a young call girl's death. He becomes romantically entangled with high-priced call girl Deneuve. 120m/C VHS, Beta. Burt Reynolds, Catherine Deneuve; D: Robert Aldrich; C: Joseph Biroc. PAR

The Hustler ♂♂♂♂ 1961 The original story of Fast Eddie Felsen and his adventures in the seedy world of professional pool. Newman plays the naive, talented and self-destructive Felsen perfectly, Laurie is outstanding as his lover, and Gleason epitomizes the pool great Minnesota Fats. Rivetingly atmospheric, and exquisitely photographed. Parent to the reprise "The Color of Money," made 25 years later. 134m/B VHS, Beta, LV, Closed Caption. Paul Newman, Jackie Gleason, Piper Laurie, George C. Scott, Myron McCormick, Murray Hamilton, Michael Constantine, Jake La Motta, Vincent Gardenia; D: Robert Rossen; W: Robert Rossen; C: Eugene (Eugen Shufftan) Shuftan. Academy Awards '61: Best Art Direction/Set Decoration (B & W), Best Black and White Cinematography; British Academy Awards '61: Best Actor (Newman), Best Film; National Board of Review Awards '61: 10 Best Films of the Year, Best Supporting Actor (Gleason); New York Film Critics Awards '61: Best Director (Rossen); Nominations: Academy Awards '61: Best Actor (Newman), Best Actress (Laurie), Best Adapted Screenplay, Best Director (Rossen), Best Picture, Best Supporting Actor (Gleason, Scott). FOX, FCT

Hustler Squad ♂ 1976 (R) U.S. Army major and Philippine guerrilla leader stage a major operation to help rid the Philippines of Japanese Occupation forces: they have four combat-trained prostitutes infiltrate a brothel patronized by top Japanese officers. Verrrrry clever. 98m/C VHS, Beta. John Ericson, Karen Ericson, Lynda Sinclaire, Nory Wright; D: Ted V. Mikels. VCI, MRV

Hustling ♂♂♂ 1975 A reporter writing a series of articles on prostitution in New York City takes an incisive look at their unusual and sometimes brutal world. Notable performance by Remick as the reporter and Clayburgh as a victimized hooker. Made for TV and based on a novel by Gail Sheehy. 96m/C VHS, Beta. Jill Clayburgh, Lee Remick, Alex Rocco, Monte Markham; D: Joseph Sargent. WOV

Hyena of London ♂♂ 1962 A doctor steals the hyena of London's corpse and injects the rabid protoplasm into his own brain with deadly results. ?m/C VHS. Diana Martin, Bernard Price. LOO

Hyper-Sapien: People from Another Star ♂½ 1986 (PG) Two cuddly aliens run away from home, are befriended by a lonely farmboy, and are chased all over the wilds of Wyoming. 93m/C VHS, Beta, LV. Sydney Penny, Keenan Wynn, Gail Strickland, Ricky Paull Goldin, Peter Jason, Talia Shire; D: Peter Hunt; W: Richard Adcock, Christopher Blue. WAR

The Hypothesis of the Stolen Painting ♂♂ L'Hypothese du Tableau Vole 1978 An art collector guides an interviewer around six paintings by Frederic Tonnerre, an academic 19th century painter, in an attempt to solve the mysterious disappearance of a seventh painting. The film presents the paintings as tableaux vivants in which the actors hold poses as they are examined. Based on the novel "Baphomet" by Pierre Klossowski. In French with English subtitles. 87m/B VHS. D: Raul Ruiz; W: Raul Ruiz. WAC

Hysteria ♂½ 1964 (PG) When an American becomes involved in an accident and has amnesia, a mysterious benefactor pays all his bills and gives the man a house to live in. But a series of murders could mean he's the murderer—or the next victim. 85m/B VHS, Beta. GB Robert Webber, Sue Lloyd, Maurice Denham; D: Freddie Francis; W: Jimmy Sangster; M: Don Banks. MGM, MLB

Hysterical ♂♂ 1983 (PG) Odd little attempt at a horror flick parody features the Hudson Brothers and involves a haunted lighthouse occupied by the vengeful spirit of a spurned woman. Late-night fun. 86m/C VHS, Beta, LV. Brett Hudson, William Hudson, Mark Hudson, Cindy Pickett, Richard Kiel, Julie Newmar, Bud Cort; D: Chris Bearde; M: Robert Alcivar.

I Accuse My Parents ♂½ 1945 Juvenile delinquent tries to blame a murder and his involvement in a gang of thieves on his mom and dad's failure to raise him properly. 70m/B VHS, Beta. Mary Beth Hughes, Robert Lowell, John Miljan. SNC, NOS, DVT

I Am a Camera ♂♂♂ 1955 A young English writer develops a relationship with a reckless young English girl in Berlin during the 1930s. Based on the Berlin stories by Christopher Isherwood, later musicalized as "Cabaret." 99m/B VHS, Beta. GB Julie Harris, Shelley Winters, Laurence Harvey, Patrick McGoohan; D: Henry Cornelius; C: Guy Green; M: Malcolm Arnold. MON

I Am a Fugitive from a Chain Gang ♂♂♂♂ I Am a Fugitive From the Chain Gang 1932 WWI veteran Muni returns home with dreams of traveling across America. After a brief stint as a clerk, he strikes out on his own. Near penniless, Muni meets up with a tramp who takes him to get a hamburger. He becomes an unwilling accomplice when the bum suddenly robs the place. Convicted and sentenced to a Georgia chain gang, he's brutalized and degraded, though he eventually escapes and lives the life of a criminal on the run. Based on the autobiography by Robert E. Burns. Brutal docu-details combine with powerhouse performances to create a classic. Timeless and thought-provoking. 93m/B VHS, Beta. Paul Muni, Glenda Farrell, Helen Vinson, Preston Foster, Edward Ellis, Allen Jenkins; D: Mervyn LeRoy; W: Howard J. Green. National Board of Review Awards '32: 10 Best Films of the Year; Nominations: Academy Awards '33: Best Actor (Muni), Best Picture, Best Sound. MGM, FOX, CCB

I Am Cuba ♂♂ 1964 Agitprop Russian-Cuban co-production illustrates different aspects of the Cuban revolution from the toppling of Batista's decadent Havana to idealistic soldiers and student revolutionaries. Lots of oratory and deliberate artificiality combined with cinematographer Urusevky's stunning high-contrast photography. Spanish and Russian with subtitles. 141m/B VHS. CU RU Luz Maria Collazo, Jose Gallardo, Sergio Corrieri, Jean Bouise, Raul Garcia, Celia Rodriguez; D: Mikhail Kalatozov; W: Yevgeny Yevtushenko, Enrique Pineda Barnet; C: Sergei Urusevsky; M: Carlos Farinas. Nominations: Independent Spirit Awards '96: Best Foreign Film. MIL, FCT

I Am Curious (Yellow) ♂♂½ 1967 A woman sociologist is conducting a sexual survey on Swedish society, which leads her to have numerous sexual encounters in all sorts of places. Very controversial upon its U.S. release because of the nudity and sexual content but tame by today's standards. Followed by "I Am Curious (Blue)" which was filmed at the same time. In Swedish with English subtitles. 95m/B VHS. SW Lena Nyman, Peter Lindgren; D: Vilgot Sjoman. HTV

I Am the Cheese ♂♂ 1983 An institutionalized boy undergoes psychiatric treatment; with the aid of his therapist (Wagner) he relives his traumatic childhood and finds out the truth about the death of his parents. A bit muddled, but with its moments. Adapted from a Robert Cormier teen novel. 95m/C VHS, Beta. Robert MacNaughton, Hope Lange, Don Murray, Robert Wagner, Sudie Bond; D: Robert Jiras. LIV, VES

I Am the Law �465✮✮ 1938 Robinson is given the task of stopping gangster activity in the city. Although regularly a law professor, he is made special prosecutor and starts canvassing for people to testify. His witnesses become murder victims as an enemy on the inside attempts to thwart the game plan. Robinson is dismissed from the case but continues to pursue justice in street-clothes. Fine performances but somewhat predictable. 83m/B VHS, Beta, LV. Edward G. Robinson, Otto Kruger, John Beal, Barbara O'Neil, Wendy Barrie, Arthur Loft, Marc Lawrence, Charles Halton; **D:** Alexander Hall; **W:** Jo Swerling. COL

I Beheld His Glory 1953 Story based on the experience of Cornelius, the Roman centurion who guarded Christ's tomb. George Macready, Robert Wilson, Virginia Wave. REP, MVC

I Bombed Pearl Harbor ✮✮ 1960 Mifune stars in this epic that shows events of WWII through Japanese eyes. Dramatic battle scenes boast the most ships destroyed per minute of film. Dubbed from Japanese. 98m/C VHS. JP Toshiro Mifune; **D:** Shue Matsubayashi. IVY, FCT

I Bury the Living ✮✮✮ 1958 A cemetery manager sticks pins in his map of a graveyard and people mysteriously start to die. Well-done suspense film. 76m/B VHS. Richard Boone, Theodore Bikel, Peggy Maurer; **D:** Albert Band. SNC, MRV

I Can't Escape ✮✮ 1934 A man attempts to piece his life back together after serving time for a crime he didn't commit. To prove himself to his girlfriend, he tries to break up an illegal stock scam. 60m/B VHS, Beta. Onslow Stevens, Lila Lee, Russell Gleason, Otis Harlan, Hooper Atchley, Clara Kimball Young; **D:** Otto Brower. SNC

I Can't Sleep ✮✮ J'ai Pas Sommeil 1993 Serial killers, French style. Gay, black Camille (Courcet), an immigrant from Martinique, and his white lover Raphael (Dupont) live in a Paris hotel and murder elderly women. Though they also rob them, the motive for their horrific crimes is vague (seemingly even to themselves). Not much actually happens—Camille visits his brother, who longs to return home, and their status as outsiders is juxtaposed against another immigrant, Daiga (Golubeva) from Lithuania, who takes little interest in the crimes but unwittingly crosses paths with Camille. Atmospheric if nothing else. Based on the 1987 "Granny Killer" slayings of 20 women. French with subtitles. 110m/C VHS. FR Richard Courcet, Vincent Dupont, Katerina Golubeva, Alex Descas, Beatrice Dalle, Laurent Grevill; **D:** Claire Denis; **W:** Claire Denis, Jean-Pol Fargeau; **C:** Agnes Godard. NYF

I, Claudius, Vol. 1: A Touch of Murder/Family Affairs 1991 Award-winning Masterpiece Theatre series tells the true story of the Roman Empire and the people determined to rule it. In these first two episodes, Augustus tries to control his conniving second wife, the beautiful Livia, who is determined that her son Tiberius will be the next Roman ruler. Her manipulations lead to bloody mayhem. Brilliant acting. Based on the books of Robert Graves. Also available as a seven-volume set. Made for television. 120m/C VHS. GB Sian Phillips, Brian Blessed, Derek Jacobi; **D:** Herbert Wise. PBS, FCT, SIG

I, Claudius, Vol. 2: Waiting in the Wings/What Shall We Do With Claudius? 1980 Continuation of the Masterpiece Theatre series portraying the true story of the Roman Empire and its rulers. In the third and fourth episodes, Tiberius and his mother Livia attempt to capture the throne with a series of brutal manipulations. Young cousin Claudius, considered an ugly dimwit, watches from afar. Based on the books of Robert Graves. Also available as a seven-volume set. Made for television. 120m/C VHS. Derek Jacobi, Sian Phillips, Brian Blessed; **D:** Herbert Wise. PBS, FCT, SIG

I, Claudius, Vol. 3: Poison is Queen/Some Justice 1980 Episodes 5 and 6 see Emperor Augustus murdered and Tiberius on the throne he's coveted for so long. But how long can he stay, hiding the treachery that brought him there? Good question. Agrippina, wife of his latest victim, is determined to see him punished, and the Roman masses, not so stupid after all, have begun to see a pattern in the deaths of their best and brightest. Based on the books of Robert Graves. Also available as a seven-volume set. Made for television. 120m/C VHS. Derek Jacobi, Sian Phillips, Brian Blessed; **D:** Herbert Wise. PBS, FCT, SIG

I, Claudius, Vol. 4: Queen of Heaven/Reign of Terror 1980 In episodes 7 and 8, Caligula begins his evil manipulation of Tiberius, involving him in a wide variety of amoral activities and creating a trail of blood. Based on the books of Robert Graves. Also available as a seven-volume set. Made for television. 120m/C VHS. Derek Jacobi, Sian Phillips; **D:** Herbert Wise. PBS, FCT, SIG

I, Claudius, Vol. 5: Zeus, By Jove!/Hail Who? 1980 Caligula's schemes result in his rise to the throne after Tiberius. Debauchery rules and murder is a standard procedure that returns to remove the emperor. At last, patient Claudius, the only remaining heir, thought too foolish to be dangerous, ascends the throne. Award-winning Masterpiece Theatre production created by the BBC. Based on the books of Robert Graves. The first episode on this cassette contains the graphic scene of Caligula's evisceration of his sister, as he enacts the life of Zeus in demented belief that he is the god—be forewarned. Also available as a seven-volume set. Made for television. 120m/C VHS. Derek Jacobi, John Hurt; **D:** Herbert Wise. PBS, FCT, SIG

I, Claudius, Vol. 6: Fool's Luck/A God in Colchester 1980 Episodes 11 and 12 see Emperor Claudius wise in the ways of statesmanship, but foolish in the ways of love. His young wife Messalina creates a furor when her sexual practices become known. In spite of his love, the emperor must punish her. Award-winning BBC production, shown in U.S. on Masterpiece Theatre. Based on the books of Robert Graves. Also available as a seven-volume set. 120m/C VHS. Derek Jacobi; **D:** Herbert Wise. PBS, FCT, SIG

I, Claudius, Vol. 7: Old King Log 1980 Claudius, aging and sad, resigns himself to his destiny, as his wife makes plans for his death. Claudius wants only the time to complete the journal of his life. Brilliant acting from Jacobi in this BBC production shown in the U.S. on Masterpiece Theatre. Based on the books of Robert Graves. Also available as a seven-volume set. 60m/C VHS. Derek Jacobi; **D:** Herbert Wise. PBS, FCT, SIG

I Come in Peace ✮✮ Dark Angel 1990 (R) A tough, maverick Texas cop embarks on a one-way ride to Nosebleed City when he attempts to track down a malevolent alien drug czar who kills his victims by sucking their brains. Mindless thrills. 92m/C VHS, Beta, LV, Closed Caption. Dolph Lundgren, Brian Benben, Betsy Brantley, Jesse Vint, Michael J. Pollard; **D:** Craig R. Baxley; **M:** Jan Hammer. MED, VTR

I Confess ✮✮½ 1953 When a priest (Clift) hears a murderer's confession, the circumstances seem to point to him as the prime suspect. Tepid, overly serious and occasionally interesting mid-career Hitchcock. Adapted from Paul Anthelme's 1902 play. 95m/B VHS, Beta, LV. Montgomery Clift, Anne Baxter, Karl Malden, Brian Aherne; **D:** Alfred Hitchcock; **C:** Robert Burks. WAR, FCT, MLB

I Conquer the Sea ✮½ 1936 Two brothers, who works as whalers, cast their affection on the same woman. Drowns in its own melodrama. 68m/B VHS, Beta, 8mm. Steffi Duna, Dennis (Stanley Morner) Morgan, Douglas Walton, George Cleveland, Johnny Pirrone; **D:** Victor Halperin. VYY

I Could Go on Singing ✮✮½ 1963 An aging American songstress, on a tour in Britain, becomes reacquainted with her illegitimate son and his British father, but eventually goes back to the footlights. Garland's last film. Songs include "By Myself" and "It Never Was You." A must for Garland fans. Letterboxed. 99m/C VHS, Beta, LV. Judy Garland, Dirk Bogarde, Jack Klugman, Aline MacMahon; **D:** Ronald Neame. MGM

I Cover the Waterfront ✮✮½ 1933 A reporter is assigned to write about a boatman involved in a fishy scheme to smuggle Chinese immigrants into the country wrapped in shark skins. While trying to get the story, the journalist falls in love with the fisherman's daughter. Torrance passed away before its release. 70m/B VHS, Beta. Claudette Colbert, Ben Lyon, Ernest Torrence, Hobart Cavanaugh; **D:** James Cruze. NOS, MRV, VYY

I Died a Thousand Times ✮✮ 1955 Aging gangster Mad Dog Earle (pushup prince Palance) plans one last death-defying heist while hiding from police in the mountains. Meanwhile, the hard boiled gangster softens a bit thanks to surgery-needing girlfriend, but moll Winters doesn't seem to think that three's company. A low rent "High Sierra." From the novel by W.R. Burnett. 109m/C VHS, LV, Closed Caption. Jack Palance, Shelley Winters, Lori Nelson, Lee Marvin, Earl Holliman, Lon Chaney Jr., Howard St. John; **D:** Stuart Heisler; **W:** W.R. Burnett. WAR, FCT

I Dismember Mama woof! Poor Albert and Little Annie 1974 (R) Classless story of an asylum inmate who escapes to kill his mother. Although he hates women, he likes little girls as evidenced by his nine-year-old love interest. Notably lacking in bloody scenes. 81m/C VHS, Beta. Zooey Hall, Joanne Moore Jordan, Greg Mullavey, Marlene Tracy; **D:** Paul Leder. GEM

I Do! I Do! 1984 This Los Angeles production of the Broadway musical covers 50 years of a marriage, beginning just before the turn of the century. 116m/C VHS, Beta. Lee Remick, Hal Linden. TTC

I Don't Buy Kisses Anymore ✮✮½ 1992 (PG) Heartwarming story starring Alexander and Peeples as two mismatched lovers who end up realizing that they're made for each other. Alexander plays Bernie Fishbine, an overweight Jewish shoe store owner who falls for a psychology graduate student (Peeples). Little does he know, but Peeples is studying him for her term paper, appropriately titled "The Psychological Study of an Obese Male." Alexander gives a great performance, as do Kazan and Jacobi who play Bernie's parents. 112m/C VHS, Beta, Closed Caption. Jason Alexander, Nia Peeples, Lainie Kazan, Lou Jacobi, Eileen Brennan, Larry Storch, Arleen Sorkin; **D:** Robert Marcarelli; **W:** Jonnie Lindsell; **C:** Michael Ferris; **M:** Cobb Bussinger. PAR

I Don't Give a Damn ✮✮ 1988 (R) An embittered wounded soldier returns home to his loved ones, rejects them, and becomes more and more uninterested in life itself. Subtitled. 94m/C VHS, Beta. IS Ika Sohar, Anat Waxman; **D:** Shmuel Imberman. TWE

I Don't Want to Be Born ✮ The Devil Within Her 1975 (R) It's got all the right ingredients for overnight camp: a spurned dwarf, a large, howling baby-thing, slice and dice murder and mayhem, and Collins. It could've been so bad. Instead, this "Rosemary's Baby" rehash is just stupid bad. 90m/C VHS. GB Joan Collins, Eileen Atkins, Donald Pleasence, Ralph Bates, Caroline Munro; **D:** Peter Sasdy. NO

I Don't Want to Talk About It ✮✮½ De Eso No Se Habla 1994 Fable set in a small South American town in the '30s. The widowed Leonor (Brando) is the community leader, a woman determined to see that her daughter Charlotte (Podesta) be as happy and accomplished as possible. Leonor refuses to acknowledge Charlotte is a dwarf and size is never permitted to be mentioned in her presence. Her zealous protectiveness is challenged by worldly and charming newcomer Ludovico (Mastroianni) who becomes entranced by Charlotte. Mastroianni is masterly as always but the moody film proves slight. Based on story by Julio Llinas. Spanish with subtitles. **102m/C VHS, LV.** *AR* Marcello Mastroianni, Luisina Brando, Alejandra Podesta; **D:** Maria-Luisa Bemberg; **W:** Maria-Luisa Bemberg, Jorge Goldenberg. COL

I Dood It 🎞🎞 *By Hook or By Crook* 1943 Young tailor's assistant Skelton falls hard for young actress Powell working near his shop. She agrees to date, and eventually marry him, but only to spite her boyfriend who has just run off with another woman. All's well however, when Skelton stumbles across a spy ring, is hailed a hero and helps Powell realize she really loves him. ♫ Star Eyes; Taking a Chance on Love; Jericho; One O'Clock Jump; So Long Sarah Jane; Hola E Pae; Swing the Jinx Away. **102m/B VHS.** Red Skelton, Eleanor Powell, Richard Ainley, Patricia Dane, Sam Levene, Thurston Hall, Lena Horne, Butterfly McQueen; **D:** Vincente Minnelli. MGM, CCB

I Dream of Jeannie 🎞 1952 The third and worst bio of Stephen Foster has Foster as a bookkeeper-cum-songwriter alternating between writing tunes and chasing Lawrence. When she dumps him, he goes into a funk. Will he be able to complete the title song? The suspense will kill you. Lots of singing, but not much else. **90m/C VHS.** Ray Middleton, Bill Shirley, Muriel Lawrence, Lynn Bari, Rex Allen; **D:** Allan Dwan. NOS, VEC

I Dream Too Much 🎞🎞 1935 A musical vehicle for opera star Pons, as a French singer who marries an American composer played by Fonda. Songwriter falls into wife's shadow after pushing her into a singing career; she then raises his spirits a couple of octaves by helping him sell a musical comedy. Went into production after a rival company, Columbia, launched opera singer Grace Moore's acting career. Ball later bought this studio, where she was given her second starring role. ♫ The Jockey on the Carousel; I'm the Echo; I Got Love; I Dream Too Much; Bell Song; Caro Nome. **90m/B VHS, Beta.** Lily Pons, Henry Fonda, Eric Blore, Lucille Ball, Mischa Auer, Scotty Beckett; **D:** John Cromwell; **M:** Max Steiner. Nominations: Academy Awards '35: Best Sound. HHT, TTC

I Drink Your Blood 🎞½ 1971 (R) Hippie satanists looking for kicks spike an old man's drink with LSD. To get revenge, the old codger's grandson sells the nasty flower children meat pies injected with the blood of a rabid dog. The hippies then turn into cannibalistic maniacs, infecting anyone they bite. From the man responsible for "I Spit on Your Grave," originally played on a double bill with "I Eat Your Skin." **83m/C VHS.** Bhasker, Jadine Wong, Ronda Fultz, Elizabeth Marner-Brooks, George Patterson, Riley Mills, Iris Brooks, John Damon; **D:** David E. Durston. FRG, TPV

I Eat Your Skin woof! *Zombies; Voodoo Blood Bath; Zombie* 1964 Cannibalistic zombies terrorize a novelist and his girlfriend on a Caribbean island. Blood and guts, usually shown on a gourmet double bill with "I Drink Your Blood." **82m/B VHS.** William Joyce, Heather Hewitt, Betty H. Lindon; **D:** Del Tenney. RHI, SNC, FCT

I Hate Blondes 🎞🎞½ *Odio le Bionde* 1983 A group of criminals use a ghostwriter's burglaring stories as instructional manuals. The writer becomes involved with the gang. Relies heavily on visual humor. Notably among the comedy scenes is the author's search for jewels at a get-together. **90m/C VHS, Beta.** *IT* **D:** Giorgio Capitani, Giorgio Capitani. NO

I Heard the Owl Call My Name 🎞🎞½ 1973 Poignant story of an Anglican priest who is relocated to an Indian fishing village on the ouskirts of Vancouver, British Columbia. Made for television and based on a Mar-

garet Craven book. **74m/C Beta.** Tom Courtenay, Dean Jagger, Paul Stanley; **D:** Daryl Duke. PSM

I Killed Rasputin 🎞½ 1967 The "Mad Monk" who rose to power before the Russian Revolution lost his life in a bizarre assassination by Felix Youssoupoff. Film deals with the friendship between the men that ended in betrayal. Well-intentioned, but overwrought. Dubbed. **95m/C VHS, Beta.** *FR IT* Geraldine Chaplin, Gert Frobe, Peter McEnery; **D:** Robert Hossein; **M:** Don Banks. NO

I Killed That Man 🎞🎞½ 1942 A prisoner scheduled to die in the electric chair is given an early ticket out when he is found poisoned. Evidence points to an unusual group of suspects. Effective low-budget thriller offers a few unexpected surprises. **72m/B VHS, Beta.** Ricardo Cortez, Joan Woodbury, Iris Adrian, George Pembroke, Herbert Rawlinson, Pat Gleason, Ralf Harolde, Jack Mulhall, Vince Barnett, Gavin Gordon, John Hamilton; **D:** Phil Rosen. SNC

I Know Where I'm Going 🎞🎞🎞 1945 A young woman (Hiller), who believes that money brings happiness, is on the verge of marrying a rich old man, until she meets a handsome naval officer (Livesey) and finds a happy, simple life. Early on the female lead appears in a dream sequence filmed in the mode of surrealist painter Salvador Dali and avant garde director Luis Bunuel. Scottish setting and folk songs give a unique flavor. Brown provides a fine performance as a native Scot. **91m/B VHS, Beta, LV.** *GB* Roger Livesey, Wendy Hiller, Finlay Currie, Pamela Brown; **D:** Michael Powell. HMV, LCA

I Know Why the Caged Bird Sings 🎞🎞🎞 1979 A black writer's memories of growing up in the rural South during the 1930s. Strong performances from Rolle and Good. Made-for-television film is based on the book by Maya Angelou. **100m/C VHS, Beta.** Diahann Carroll, Ruby Dee, Esther Rolle, Roger E. Mosley, Paul Benjamin, Constance Good; **D:** Fielder Cook. KUI, LIV

I Like Bats 1985 Can a psychiatrist help a vampire become a human? Polish dialogue with English subtitles. **90m/C VHS. D:** Grzegorz Warchol. FCT

I Like It Like That 🎞🎞🎞 1994 (R) Chaotic family life and loves in the Bronx are the setting for this tale of a Cinderella in the record industry. Strong-willed black-Latina Lisette (Velez) has been married for 10 years to macho Latin, Chino (Seda), who has a wandering eye. When Chino is jailed for looting during a blackout, Lisette, needing to support their three kids, talks her way into a job with WASP record promoter Stephen Price (Dunne). When local gossips make it seem Lisette is having an affair, the newly sprung Chino retaliates by turning to lusty Magdalena (Vidal). Lisette, meanwhile, gathers support from her transvestite brother and proves to have inner resources previously unnoticed. Great Latino soundtrack illuminates the complications. Modest-budget sleeper quickly exited the theater but proves to be a strong debut for director/writer Martin, reputed to be the first African American woman to be given the reins by a major studio. **CW:** Brief, graphic sexual activity; scattered profanity; slight violence. **106m/C VHS, LV, Closed Caption.** Lauren Velez, Jon Seda, Lisa Vidal, Jesse Borrego, Griffin Dunne, Rita Moreno, Tomas Melly, Desiree Casado, Isaiah Garcia; **D:** Darnell Martin; **W:** Darnell Martin; **C:** Alexander Grusynski; **M:** Sergio George. Nominations: Independent Spirit Awards '95: Best Actor (Seda), Best Actress (Velez), Best Cinematography, Best First Feature. COL

I Like to Play Games 🎞½ 1995 (R) Michael is looking for a woman who enjoys playing sexual games—and he seems to have the perfect partner in Suzanne. But just how far will their kinks take them? Also available unrated. **95m/C VHS, LV.** Lisa Boyle, Ken Steadman; **D:** Moctezuma Lobato. APX

I Live in Fear 🎞🎞🎞 *Record of a Living Being; Kimono No Kiroku* 1955 Nakajima, an elderly, wealthy owner of a foundry, becomes increasingly fearful of atomic war and the threats to his family's safety. He tries to persuade them to leave Japan and move with him to Brazil but they fear the family will be ruined financially. Nakajima then burns down his foundry to force his children to move but instead they go to court and have him declared mentally incompetent. He is placed in an institution where he finds peace in the delusion that he has escaped to another planet and that the Earth has indeed suffered a nuclear holocaust. Provocative look at the fear of atomic warfare and radiation. In Japanese with English subtitles. **105m/C VHS.** *JP* Toshiro Mifune, Takashi Shimura, Eiko Miyoshi, Haruko Togo; **D:** Akira Kurosawa. FCT

I Live in Grosvenor Square 🎞🎞 *A Yank In London* 1946 An American soldier in Great Britain falls in love with a major's fiancee. Entertaining if a bit drawn out. **106m/B VHS.** *GB* Anna Neagle, Rex Harrison, Dean Jagger, Robert Morley, Jane Darwell; **D:** Herbert Wilcox. NOS, DVT

I Live My Life 🎞½ 1935 Stylish glossy flick with Crawford playing a bored New York debutante who travels to Greece and meets a dedicated archaeologist (Aherne). A love/hate relationship ensues in this typical Crawford vehicle where she is witty and parades around in sophisticated fashions, but there is little substance here. **92m/B VHS, Closed Caption.** Joan Crawford, Brian Aherne, Frank Morgan, Aline MacMahon, Eric Blore, Fred Keating, Jessie Ralph, Arthur Treacher, Frank Conroy, Sterling Holloway, Vince Barnett, Hedda Hopper, Lionel Stander; **D:** Woodbridge S. Van Dyke; **W:** Joseph L. Mankiewicz, Gottfried Reinhardt, Ethel B. Borden. MGM

I Live with Me Dad 🎞½ 1986 A vagrant drunk and his son fight the authorities for the right to be together. **86m/C VHS, Beta, Closed Caption.** *AU* Peter Hehir, Haydon Samuels; **D:** Paul Maloney. FOX

I Love All of You 🎞🎞 1983 Deneuve relives experiences with three former lovers - a composer, a well-intentioned nobody, and a rock star - as she enters into a relationship with a widower. **103m/C VHS, Beta.** *FR* Catherine Deneuve, Jean-Louis Trintignant, Gerard Depardieu, Serge Gainsbourg; **D:** Claude Berri. NO

I Love Lucy 1952 Everyone's favorite redhead in scrape after scrape, along with her Cuban bandleader husband, Ricky Ricardo, and their neighbors Fred and Ethel Mertz. Episodes on this tape are "Lucy Does a TV Commercial" and "Lucy's Italian Movie." Other episodes available. **51m/B VHS, LV.** Lucille Ball, Desi Arnaz Sr., Vivian Vance, William Frawley. FOX, MOV

I Love Melvin 🎞🎞½ 1953 Reynolds wants to be a Tinseltown goddess, and O'Connor just wants Reynolds; so he passes himself off as chief lenseman for a famous magazine and promises her a shot at the cover of "Look." Seems he has a little trouble on the follow through. Choreographed by Robert Alton, it's got a best ever football ballet (with Reynolds as pigskin). ♫ A Lady Loves; Saturday Afternoon Before The Game; I Wanna Wander; We Have Never Met As Of Yet; Life Has Its Funny Little Ups And Downs; Where Did You Learn To Dance?; And There You Are. **77m/C VHS.** Donald O'Connor, Debbie Reynolds, Una Merkel, Richard Anderson, Jim Backus, Allyn Joslyn, Les Tremayne, Noreen Corcoran, Robert Taylor, Howard Keel; **D:** Don Weis. MGM, TTC, FCT

I Love My...Wife 🎞🎞 1970 (R) A medical student plays doctor with hospital nurses when he and his wife stop having sex during her pregnancy. The marriage becomes more strained when their son is born and his mother-in-law moves in. A comedy without the proper dosage of laughs. **98m/C VHS, Beta.** Elliott Gould, Brenda Vaccaro, Angel Tompkins; **D:** Mel Stuart. USH

I Love N.Y. 🎬 1987 A young metropolitan couple struggles to find true love amidst disapproving parents and doubting friends. Choppy direction and poor writing contribute to its failure. **100m/C VHS, Beta, LV.** Scott Baio, Kelley Van Der Velden, Christopher Plummer, Jennifer O'Neill, Jerry Orbach, Virna Lisi; **D:** Alan Smithee; **M:** Bill Conti. **NO**

I Love Trouble 🎬🎬½ 1994 (PG) Veteran reporter Peter Brackett (sexy veteran Nolte) and ambitious cub reporter Sabrina Petersen (young and sexy Roberts) are competitors working for rival Chicago newspapers. When they begin to secretly exchange information on a big story, they find their lives threatened and their rivalry turning to romance. Some action, simplistic retro script, one big star, one sorta big star, and you've got the perfect movie package for the Prozac decade. Written, produced and directed by husband/wife team Meyers and Shyer. **123m/C VHS, LV, Closed Caption.** Julia Roberts, Nick Nolte, Saul Rubinek, Robert Loggia, James Rebhorn; **D:** Charles Shyer; **W:** Nancy Meyers, Charles Shyer; **C:** John Lindley. **TOU**

I Love You 🎬½ 1981 (R) Man down on his luck mistakenly assumes that a woman he meets is a hooker. She plays along, only to find that they are becoming emotionally involved. Pretentious cat-and-mouse game. **104m/C VHS, Beta.** **BR** Sonia Braga, Paulo Cesar Pereio, Vera Fischer, Tarcisio Meria; **D:** Arnaldo Jabor. **MGM**

I Love You Again 🎬🎬🎬½ 1940 A classic screwball comedy with Powell and Loy working together (wonderfully) in something other than their "Thin Man" series. Powell is a gloomy businessman who's about to be divorced by Loy. But after an accident it turns out Powell had been suffering from amnesia and has now regained his memory (which he keeps a secret). It seems Mr. Respectable used to be a con man and he decides to revert to his criminal ways. He also doesn't remember Loy but falls instantly in love with her and must decide what kind of life he wants. Witty dialog, amusing situations, fine direction. **97m/B VHS, LV.** William Powell, Myrna Loy, Frank McHugh, Edmund Lowe; **D:** Woodbridge S. Van Dyke. **MGM**

I Love You, Alice B. Toklas! 🎬🎬½ *Kiss My Butterfly* 1968 A straight uptight lawyer decides to join the peace and love generation in this somewhat maniacal satire of the hippie culture. Authored by Paul Mazursky and Larry Tucker. Incidentally, the title's Alice B. Toklas was actually the lifemate of "Lost Generation" author Gertrude Stein. **94m/C VHS, Beta, LV.** Peter Sellers, Jo Van Fleet, Leigh Taylor-Young, Joyce Van Patten; **D:** Hy Averback; **W:** Paul Mazursky; **M:** Elmer Bernstein. **WAR, FCT**

I Love You ... Goodbye 🎬🎬 1973 A frustrated housewife, fed up with the constant role of wife and mother, leaves her family in an effort to find a more challenging and fulfilling life. A good performance by Lange compensates for some of its muddledness. **74m/C VHS, Beta.** Hope Lange, Earl Holliman. **LCA**

I Love You Rosa 🎬🎬½ 1972 Rosa, a young Jewish widow, wrestles big time with old world values. Required by custom to marry her dearly departed's eldest brother, she's not enamored with her newly betrothed. Not that he's not a nice guy; he seems to plan to take his marital duties very seriously. It's just that he's a tad youthful (eleven years old, to be exact). Much rabbi consulting and soul searching. **90m/C VHS.** Michal Bat-Adam, Gabi Oterman, Yoseph Shiloah; **D:** Moshe Mizrahi; **W:** Moshe Mizrahi. Nominations: Academy Awards '72: Best Foreign Language Film. **FCT, NCJ**

I Love You to Death 🎬🎬½ 1990 (R) Dry comedy based on a true story, concerns a woman who tries to kill off her cheating husband. Lots of stars, but they never shine. Hurt and Reeves are somewhat amusing as drugged up hit men who struggle with the lyrics to the National Anthem. Watch for director Kasdan as Devo's lawyer. Cates, Kline's real-life wife, has an un-

billed part as one of his one-night stands. **110m/C VHS, Beta, LV, Closed Caption.** Kevin Kline, Tracey Ullman, Joan Plowright, River Phoenix, William Hurt, Keanu Reeves, James Gammon, Victoria Jackson, Miriam Margolyes, Heather Graham; *Cameos:* Phoebe Cates; **D:** Lawrence Kasdan; **W:** John Kostmayer; **C:** Owen Roizman; **M:** James Horner. **COL**

I, Madman 🎬🎬 1989 (R) A novel-loving horror actress is stalked by the same mutilating madman that appears in the book she's presently reading. We call that bad luck. **90m/C VHS, Beta, LV.** Jenny Wright, Clayton Rohner, William Cook; **D:** Tibor Takacs; **W:** David Chaskin; **C:** Bryan England. **MED**

I Married a Centerfold 🎬🎬 1984 Television movie fluff about a young man's amorous pursuit of a model. **100m/C VHS, Beta, LV.** Teri Copley, Timothy Daly, Diane Ladd, Bert Remsen, Anson Williams; **D:** Peter Werner. **NO**

I Married a Monster from Outer Space 🎬🎬½ 1958 The vintage thriller about a race of monster-like aliens from another planet who try to conquer earth. Despite its head-shaking title, an effective '50s sci-fi creeper. **78m/B VHS, Beta.** Tom Tryon, Gloria Talbott, Maxie "Slapsie" Rosenbloom, Mary Treen, Ty Hardin, Ken Lynch, John Eldridge; **D:** Gene Fowler Jr. **PAR, MLB**

I Married a Vampire 🎬🎬 1987 A country girl in the city is romanced and wed by a dashing vampire. Troma-produced hyper-camp. **85m/C VHS, Beta.** Rachel Gordon, Brendan Hickey; **D:** Jay Raskin. **PSM**

I Married a Witch 🎬🎬🎬 1942 A witch burned at the stake during the Salem witch trials comes back to haunt the descendants of her accusers and gets romantic with one of them. Wonderfully played fantasy/comedy. **77m/B VHS, Beta, LV.** Veronica Lake, Fredric March, Susan Hayward, Robert Benchley, Cecil Kellaway, Elizabeth Patterson, Robert Warwick, Eily Malyon, Mary Field, Nora Cecil, Emory Parnell, Helen St. Rayer, Aldrich Bowker, Emma Dunn, Harry Tyler, Ralph Peters, Ann Carter; **D:** Rene Clair; **W:** Robert Pirosh, Marc Connelly; **C:** Ted Tetzlaff; **M:** Roy Webb. Nominations: Academy Awards '42: Original Dramatic/Comedy Score. **MLB, WAR**

I Married a Woman 🎬🎬 1956 Advertising executive marries beautiful blonde woman, but finds it very difficult to balance his career and marriage. Low on laughs. Shot in black and white, but includes a fantasy scene in color that features John Wayne. Pay attention to see young Angie Dickinson. **84m/B VHS, Beta, LV.** George Gobel, Diana Dors, Adolphe Menjou, Nita Talbot; **D:** Hal Kanter. **NO**

I Married an Angel 🎬½ 1942 The last MacDonald/Eddy film. A playboy is lured away from his usual interests by a beautiful angel. Adapted from Rodgers and Hart Broadway play. Strange and less than compelling. 🎵I Married An Angel; I'll Tell the Man in the Street; Spring is Here; Tira Lira La; A Twinkle in Your Eye; Aloha Oe; Caprice Viennoise; Chanson Boheme; Anges Purs. **84m/C VHS, Beta.** Jeanette MacDonald, Nelson Eddy, Binnie Barnes, Edward Everett Horton, Reginald Owen, Mona Maris, Janis Carter, Inez Cooper, Douglass Dumbrille, Leonid Kinskey, Marion Rosamond, Anne Jeffreys, Marek Windheim, Veda Ann Borg; **D:** Woodbridge S. Van Dyke; **W:** Anita Loos; **M:** Richard Rodgers, Lorenz Hart. **MGM, MVD**

I Met a Murderer 🎬🎬½ 1939 A man kills his nagging wife after a bitter argument and flees from her vengeful brother. Fine fugitive drama with a number of interesting twists. **79m/B VHS.** James Mason, Pamela Kellino, Sylvia Coleridge, William Devlin, Esma Cannon, James Harcourt; **D:** Roy Kellino. **SNC, NOS, DVT**

I, Mobster 🎬🎬½ 1958 Cochran tells a Senate Sub-Committee of his rise in the ranks of the Underworld—from his humble beginning as a bet collector for a bookie to his position as kingpin of the crime syndicate. **80m/B VHS.** Steve Cochran, Lita Milan, Robert Strauss, Celia Lovsky; **D:** Roger Corman; **C:** Floyd Crosby. **NO**

I Never Promised You a Rose Garden 🎬🎬🎬 1977 (R) A disturbed 16-year-old girl spirals down into madness and despair while a hospital psychiatrist struggles to bring her back to life. Based on the Joanne Greenberg bestseller. Compelling and unyielding exploration of the clinical treatment of schizophrenia. **90m/C VHS, Beta.** Kathleen Quinlan, Bibi Andersson, Sylvia Sidney, Diane Varsi; **D:** Anthony Page; **W:** Gavin Lambert, Lewis John Carlino. Nominations: Academy Awards '77: Best Adapted Screenplay. **WAR, OM**

I Never Sang For My Father 🎬🎬🎬½ 1970 (PG) A devoted son must choose between caring for his cantankerous but well-meaning father, and moving out West to marry the divorced doctor whom he loves. While his mother wants him to stay near home, his sister, who fell out of her father's favor by marrying out of the family faith, argues that he should do what he wants. An introspective, stirring story based on the Robert Anderson play. **90m/C VHS, Beta, LV.** Gene Hackman, Melvyn Douglas, Estelle Parsons, Dorothy Stickney; **D:** Gilbert Cates; **W:** Robert Anderson. National Board of Review Awards '70: 10 Best Films of the Year; Writers Guild of America '70: Best Adapted Screenplay; Nominations: Academy Awards '70: Best Actor (Douglas), Best Adapted Screenplay, Best Supporting Actor (Hackman). **COL**

I Only Want You to Love Me 🎬🎬 *Ich Will Doch Nur, Dass Ihr Mich Liebt* 1976 Peter's (Zeplichal) been denigrated by his family his entire life, so he decides to move with his wife (Aberle) to Munich and show them he can make something of himself. But his desires become compulsions and he falters under the strain of work and marriage, leading to a terrifying crackup. A true story, based on the book "Life Sentence" by Klaus Antes and Christine Eberhardt. Originally produced for TV; German with subtitles. **104m/C VHS.** **GE** Vitus Zeplichal, Elke Aberle, Ernie Mangold, Joanna Hofe, Alexander Allerson; **D:** Rainer Werner Fassbinder; **W:** Rainer Werner Fassbinder; **C:** Michael Ballhaus; **M:** Peer Raben. **WBF**

I Ought to Be in Pictures 🎬🎬 1982 (PG) After hitch-hiking from New York to Hollywood to break into the movies, a teen-aged actress finds her father, a screenwriter turned alcoholic-gambler. Late, desperately unfunny Neil Simon outing, adapted from a Simon play. **107m/C VHS, Beta.** Walter Matthau, Ann-Margret, Dinah Manoff, Lance Guest, Michael Dudikoff; **D:** Herbert Ross; **W:** Neil Simon; **M:** Marvin Hamlisch. **FOX**

I Posed for Playboy 🎬🎬 1991 (R) Three women—one a college co-ed, one a stockbroker, and one a 37-year-old mother—quench their private passions by posing for Playboy Magazine. Made for television with additional footage added to give it an "R" rating. **CW:** Nudity and sexual scene. **98m/C VHS, LV, Closed Caption.** Lynda Carter, Michelle Greene, Amanda Peterson, Brittany York; **D:** Stephen Stafford. **REP**

I Remember Mama 🎬🎬🎬½ 1948 A true Hollywood heart tugger chronicling the life of a Norwegian immigrant family living in San Francisco during the early 1900s. Dunne triumphs as the mother, with a perfect Norwegian accent, and provides her family with wisdom and inspiration. A kindly father and four children round out the nuclear family. A host of oddball characters regularly pop in on the household—three high-strung aunts and an eccentric doctor who treats a live-in uncle. Adapted from John Van Druten's stage play, based on Kathryn Forbes memoirs, "Mama's Bank Account;" a TV series came later. **95m/B VHS, Beta, LV.** Irene Dunne, Barbara Bel Geddes, Oscar Homolka, Ellen Corby, Cedric Hardwicke, Edgar Bergen, Rudy Vallee, Barbara O'Neil, Florence Bates; **D:** George Stevens. Golden Globe Awards '49: Best Supporting Actress (Corby); Nominations: Academy Awards '48: Best Actress (Dunne), Best Black and White Cinematography, Best Supporting Actor (Homolka), Best Supporting Actress (Corby, Bel Geddes). **CCB, TTC**

I See a Dark Stranger 🎬🎬🎬 *The Adventuress* 1946 Cynical yet whimsical postwar British spy thriller about an angry Irish lass who agrees to steal war plans for the Nazis in order to battle her native enemies, the British—then she falls in love with a British officer. A sharply performed, decidedly jaded view of nationalism and wartime "heroism." 112m/B VHS, Beta. *GB* Deborah Kerr, Trevor Howard, Raymond Huntley; *D:* Frank Launder. NO

I Sent a Letter to My Love 🎬🎬🎬 1981 An aging spinster, faced with the lonely prospect of the death of her paralyzed brother, places a personal ad for a companion in a local newspaper, using a different name. Unknown to her, the brother is the one who answers it, and they begin a romantic correspondence. Well-acted, touching account of relationships that change lives, but it takes its time in telling the story. 102m/C VHS, Beta. *FR* Simone Signoret, Jean Rochefort, Delphine Seyrig; *D:* Moshe Mizrahi; *W:* Moshe Mizrahi, Gerard Brach; *C:* Ghislan Cloquet. NO

I Shot a Man in Vegas 🎬½ 1996 (R) Low-budget variation of "Rashomon." Drinking buddies Johnny (Cubitt) and Grant (Stockwell) wind up in a back alley brawl and Johnny takes a bullet, supposedly shot dead by Grant. Only their friends, Gale (Garofalo), Martin (Drillinger), and Amy (Lippman), who witnessed the fight all saw it differently. So they decide to stash the corpse in their car trunk and head out across the desert to California. There's a last-minute revelation and a big finale but the strain shows. *CW:* Pervasive strong language, violence and a scene of sexuality. 84m/C VHS. John Stockwell, Janeane Garofalo, Brian Drillinger, Noelle Lippman, David Cubitt; *D:* Keoni Waxman; *W:* Keoni Waxman; *C:* Steve Firestone. AVI

I Shot Andy Warhol 🎬🎬🎬 1996 (R) Based on a true story, this black comedy focuses on the 15 minutes of fame achieved by Valerie Solanas, the woman who shot pop artist Andy Warhol for ignoring her in 1968. Taylor manages to recreate the more unpleasant aspects of Solanas without making her completely unsympathetic. Writer/director Harron, making her feature film debut, does a wonderful job of recreating the drugged-out world Warhol and his cohorts inhabited. Her script succeeds by attempting to understand Solanas's actions, while not excusing or sensationalizing them. Features music by former Velvet Underground member, John Cale. *CW:* Strong sexual content, language, drug use and brief violence. 100m/C VHS. Lili Taylor, Jared Harris, Stephen Dorff, Martha Plimpton, Donovan Leitch, Tahnee Welch, Michael Imperioli, Lothaire Bluteau, Anna Thompson, Peter Friedman, Jill Hennessey, Craig Chester, James Lyons, Reginald Rodgers, Jamie Harrold, Edoardo Ballerini, Lynn Cohen, Miriam Cyr, Isabel Gillies, Eric Mabius; *D:* Mary Harron; *W:* Mary Harron, Daniel Minahan; *C:* Ellen Kuras; *M:* John Cale. Nominations: Independent Spirit Awards '97: Best First Feature. HMK

I Shot Billy the Kid 🎬½ 1950 Billy the Kid decides to turn over a new leaf and live a decent life. The cards are stacked against him though: He's killed a man for nearly every year of his life, and old habits are hard to break. 58m/B VHS, Beta, LV. Donald (Don "Red") Barry, Robert Lowery, Tom Neal, Jack Perrin; *D:* William (Lester Williams) Berke. NO

I Shot Jesse James 🎬🎬🎬 1949 In his first film, director Fuller breathes characteristically feverish, maddened fire into the story of Bob Ford (Ireland) after he killed the notorious outlaw. An essential moment in Fuller's unique, America-astabloid-nightmare canon, and one of the best antiwesterns ever made. 83m/B VHS, Beta. John Ireland, Barbara Britton, Preston Foster, Reed Hadley; *D:* Samuel Fuller; *W:* Samuel Fuller. RXM

I Spit on Your Corpse woof! *Girls For Rent* 1974 (R) A vicious female hired killer engages in a series of terrorist activities. Stars Spelvin in a non-pornographic role. 90m/C VHS, Beta. Georgina Spelvin, Susan McIver, Kent Taylor; *D:* Al Adamson. REP

I Spit on Your Grave woof! *Day of the Woman* 1977 (R) Woman vacationing at an upstate New York lake house is brutally attacked and raped by four men. Left for dead, she recovers and seeks revenge. Not to be confused with the 1962 film of the same title, this one is worth zero as a film; lots of violent terror and gory death, totally irresponsibly portrayed. Also available in a 102-minute version. 98m/C VHS, Beta, LV. Camille Keaton, Eron Tabor, Richard Pace, Gunter Kleeman; *D:* Mier Zarchi; *W:* Mier Zarchi. VES

I Stand Condemned 🎬🎬½ *Moscow Nights* 1936 A Russian officer is tricked into borrowing money from a spy and is condemned for treason. He's saved when a girl who loves him gives herself to a profiteer. Worth seeing only for young Olivier's performance. 90m/B VHS, Beta, 8mm. *GB* Laurence Olivier, Penelope Dudley Ward, Robert Cochran; *D:* Anthony Asquith. NOS, MRV, VYY

I Take This Oath 🎬 1940 A cop is shocked to discover that his uncle is a wanted mobster, responsible for the death of a man. Hackneyed plot. 64m/B VHS, Beta. Gordon Jones, Joyce Compton, Craig Reynolds, J. Farrell MacDonald, Robert E. Homans, Veda Ann Borg; *D:* Sam Newfield. SNC

I, the Jury 🎬🎬 1982 (R) A remake of the 1953 Mike Hammer mystery in which the famed PI investigates the murder of his best friend. Assante mopes around as Hammer and looks out of place in this slowed-down version. 111m/C VHS, Beta. Armand Assante, Barbara Carrera, Laurene Landon, Alan King, Geoffrey Lewis, Paul Sorvino, Jessica James, Leigh Anne Harris, Lynette Harris; *D:* Richard T. Heffron; *W:* Larry Cohen; *M:* Bill Conti. CCB

I, the Worst of All 🎬🎬 *Yo, la Peor de Todas* 1990 Portrayal of 17-century Mexican poet, Sister Juana Ines de la Cruz (Serna). She develops a passionate but chaste friendship with Maria Luisa (Sanda), the wife of the Spanish viceroy in Mexico, and writes love poems to her. However, the newly-appointed archbishop (Murua) is a religious fanatic who condemns Juana's work, burns her books, and proceeds to persecute her. Adapted from the novel, "The Traps of Faith," by Octavio Paz. Spanish with subtitles. 105m/C VHS. *SP* Assumpta Serna, Dominique Sanda, Lautaro Murua, Hector Alterio; *D:* Maria-Luisa Bemberg; *W:* Maria-Luisa Bemberg, Antonio Larreta; *C:* Felix Monti; *M:* Luis Maria Serra. FRF

I Vitelloni 🎬🎬🎬½ *The Young and the Passionate; Vitelloni; Spivs* 1953 Fellini's semi-autobiographical drama, argued by some to be his finest work. Five young men grow up in a small Italian town. As they mature, four of them remain in Romini and limit their opportunities by roping themselves off from the rest of the world. The characters are multi-dimensional, including a loafer who is supported by his sister and a young stud who impregnates a local woman. The script has some brilliant insights into youth, adulthood and what's in between. 104m/B VHS, LV. *IT* Alberto Sordi, Franco Interlenghi, Franco Fabrizi, Leopoldo Trieste; *D:* Federico Fellini; *W:* Federico Fellini, Ennio Flaiano; *M:* Nino Rota. Nominations: Academy Awards '57: Best Story & Screenplay. MOV, APD

I Wake Up Screaming 🎬🎬🎬 *Hot Spot* 1941 An actress' promoter is accused of her murder. Entertaining mystery with a surprise ending. Remade as "Vicki." 82m/B VHS, Beta, Closed Caption. Betty Grable, Victor Mature, Carole Landis, Laird Cregar, William Gargan, Alan Mowbray, Allyn Joslyn; *D:* H. Bruce Humberstone. FOX

I Walked with a Zombie 🎬🎬🎬½ 1943 The definitive and eeriest of the famous Val Lewton/Jacques Tourneur horror films. Dee, a young American nurse, comes to Haiti to care for the catatonic matriarch of a troubled family. Local legends bring themselves to bear when the nurse takes the ill woman to a local voodoo ceremony for "healing." Superb, startling images and atmosphere create a unique context for this serious "Jane Eyre"-like story; its reputation has grown through the years. 69m/B VHS, Beta, LV. Frances Dee,

Tom Conway, James Ellison, Christine Gordon, Edith Barrett, Darby Jones, Sir Lancelot; *D:* Jacques Tourneur. MED, FCT, MLB

I Wanna Be a Beauty Queen 1985 Divine hosts the "Alternative Miss World" pageant featuring all sorts of bizarre contestants. 81m/C VHS, Beta. Divine, Little Nell, Andrew Logan. AHV, FCT, HHE

I Wanna Hold Your Hand 🎬🎬½ 1978 (PG) Teenagers try to crash the Beatles' appearance on the Ed Sullivan show. 104m/C VHS, Beta, LV, Closed Caption. Nancy Allen, Bobby DiCicco, Wendie Jo Sperber, Marc McClure, Susan Kendall Newman, Theresa Saldana, Eddie Deezen, William Jordan; *D:* Robert Zemeckis; *W:* Robert Zemeckis. WAR, FCT

I Want to Live! 🎬🎬🎬 1958 Based on a scandalous true story, Hayward gives a riveting, Oscar-winning performance as a prostitute framed for the murder of an elderly woman and sentenced to death in the gas chamber. Producer Walter Wanger's seething indictment of capital punishment. 120m/B VHS, Beta, LV. Susan Hayward, Simon Oakland, Theodore Bikel; *D:* Robert Wise; *C:* Lionel Lindon; *M:* Johnny Mandel. Academy Awards '58: Best Actress (Hayward); Golden Globe Awards '59: Best Actress—Drama (Hayward); New York Film Critics Awards '58: Best Actress (Hayward); Nominations: Academy Awards '58: Best Adapted Screenplay, Best Black and White Cinematography, Best Director (Wise), Best Film Editing, Best Sound. MGM, BTV, CCB

I Want What I Want 🎬🎬 1972 (R) A young Englishman wants a sex-change, lives as a woman, falls in love, complications ensue. Not as shocking to watch as it might seem, but more a melodramatic gender-bender. 91m/C VHS, Beta. *GB* Anne Heywood, Harry Andrews, Jill Bennett; *D:* John Dexter. PSM

I Was a Male War Bride 🎬🎬🎬 1949 Hilarious WWII comedy. French officer Grant falls in love with and marries WAC lieutenant Sheridan in occupied Europe. Planning to leave the continent and settle down in the U.S., the couple hits a roadblock of red tape and Grant must cross-dress in order to accompany his bride on the troop ship taking her home. Worth watching for Grant's performance alone. Based on the novel by Henri Rochard. 105m/B VHS. Cary Grant, Ann Sheridan, Randy Stuart, Kenneth Tobey, William Neff, Marion Marshall; *D:* Howard Hawks; *W:* Charles Lederer, Leonard Spigelgass, William Neff; *M:* Cyril Mockridge. FXV

I Was a Teenage TV Terrorist woof! *Amateur Hour* 1987 Two teenagers pull on-the-air pranks at the local cable television, blaming it all on an imaginary terrorist group. Poorly acted, cheaply made, and pointless. 85m/C VHS, Beta. Adam Nathan, Julie Hanlon; *D:* Stanford Singer; *W:* Kevin McDonough. LIV

I Was a Teenage Werewolf 🎬🎬½ 1957 "Rebel Without a Cause" meets "The Curse of the Werewolf" in this drive-in rock'n'roll horror. A troubled young man (pre-Bonanza Landon, in his first feature film appearance) suffers from teen angst and low production values, and falls victim to shrink Bissel. The good doctor turns out to be a bad hypnotist, and Landon's regression therapy takes him beyond childhood into his, gasp, primal past, where he sprouts a premature beard and knuckle hair. Misconstrued and full of terrible longings, the hairy highschooler is understood only by girlfriend Lime and misunderstood hair-sprouting teen viewers. Directorial debut of Fowler. 70m/B VHS. Michael Landon, Yvonne Lime, Whit Bissell, Tony Marshall, Dawn Richard, Barney Phillips, Ken Miller, Cindy Robbins, Michael Rougas, Robert Griffin, Joseph Mell, Malcolm Atterbury, Eddie Marr, Vladimir Sokoloff, Louise Lewis, S. John Launer, Guy Williams, Dorothy Crehan; *D:* Gene Fowler Jr.; *W:* Ralph Thornton. COL, FCT, MLB

I Was a Teenage Zombie 🎬 1987 Spoof of high school horror films features a good zombie against a drug-pushing bear. Forget the story and listen to the music by Los Lobos, the Fleshtones, the Waitresses, Dream Syndicate and Violent Femmes. **92m/C VHS, Beta, LV.** Michael Rubin, Steve McCoy, Cassie Madden, Allen Rickman; **D:** John E. Michalakis. *NLC*

I Was a Zombie for the FBI 🎬½
1982 Intelligence agency toughens its hiring criteria. Much McCarthyian mirth. **105m/B VHS, Beta.** James Raspberry, Larry Raspberry, John Gillick, Christina Wellford, Anthony Isbell, Laurence Hall, Rick Crowe; **D:** Maurice Penczner; **C:** Rick Dupree. *NO*

I Will Fight No More Forever 🎬🎬🎬
1975 A vivid recounting of the epic true story of the legendary Chief Joseph who led the Nez Perce tribe on a 1,600-mile trek to Canada in 1877. Disturbing and powerful. Made for television. **106m/C VHS, Beta.** James Whitmore, Ned Romero, Sam Elliott; **D:** Richard T. Heffron. *CNG, MRV, GEM*

I Will, I Will for Now 🎬🎬 **1976 (R)**
Tacky sex clinic comedy with Keaton and Gould trying to save their marriage through kinky therapy. **109m/C VHS, Beta.** Diane Keaton, Elliott Gould, Paul Sorvino, Victoria Principal, Robert Alda, Warren Bellinger; **D:** Norman Panama; **W:** Norman Panama; **C:** John A. Alonzo. *MED*

I Wonder Who's Killing Her Now? 🎬🎬 **1976**
Husband pays to have his wife murdered, then changes his mind. On-again, off-again comedy. **87m/C VHS.** Bob Dishy, Joanna Barnes, Bill Dana, Vito Scotti; **D:** Steven Hilliard Stern. *LIV*

Ice 🎬🎬½ **1993 (R)**
Charley and Ellen Reed are thieves whose latest heist is $60 million in diamonds from mob boss Vito Malta. There's trouble when they try to fence the goods and Ellen is left with the merchandise and on the run from Malta's henchmen.**CW:** Language, gangster violence, and scene of sexuality. **91m/C VHS, LV, Closed Caption.** Traci Lords, Phillip Troy, Zach Galligan, Jorge Rivero, Michael Bailey Smith, Jamie Alba, Jean Pflieger, Floyd Levine; **D:** Brook Yeaton; **W:** Sean Dash. *PMH*

Ice Castles 🎬🎬 **1979 (PG)**
A young figure skater's Olympic dreams are dimmed when she is blinded in an accident, but her boyfriend gives her the strength, encouragement, and love necessary to perform a small miracle. Way too schmaltzy. **110m/C VHS, Beta.** Robby Benson, Lynn-Holly Johnson, Tom Skerritt, Colleen Dewhurst, Jennifer Warren, David Huffman; **D:** Donald Wrye; **W:** Donald Wrye, Gary L. Bain; **C:** Bill Butler; **M:** Marvin Hamlisch. Nominations: Academy Awards '79: Best Song ("Theme from Ice Castles-Through the Eyes of Love").*COL*

Ice Cream Man 🎬 **1995 (R)**
Quite disgusting horror tale of a dweeby, demented ice cream man who delivers gore and death along with his frozen treats.**CW:** Strong horror/terror and gore. **96m/C VHS.** Clint Howard, Sandahl Bergman, Olivia Hussey, Lee Majors II, David Naughton, Jan-Michael Vincent, David Warner, Steve Garvey; **D:** Norman Apstein. *APX*

The Ice Flood 🎬🎬 **1926**
Silent family type comedy of a son who proves to the old man that he wrote the book on life, wagering the successful supervision of dad's lumberjacks. **63m/B VHS, Beta.** Kenneth Harlan, Viola Dana; **D:** George B. Seitz. *GPV*

Ice House 🎬 **1989**
A sophisticated young lady flees Texas for Hollywood, searching for a better life. When her ex-lover shows up and wants her to go back, the lackless turmoil begins. Pairs real-life couple Gilbert and Brinkman. **81m/C VHS, Beta.** Melissa Gilbert, Bo Brinkman, Andreas Manolikakis, Buddy Quaid; **D:** Bo Brinkman, Eagle Pennell; **W:** Bo Brinkman. *NO*

Ice Palace 🎬🎬 **1960**
Two rugged adventurers maintain a lifelong rivalry in the primitive Alaskan wilderness, their relationship dramatizing the development of the 49th state. Silly but entertaining. Based on Edna Ferber's novel. **143m/C VHS, Beta.** Richard Burton, Robert Ryan, Carolyn Jones, Shirley Knight, Martha Hyer, Jim Backus, George Takei; **D:** Vincent Sherman; **C:** Joseph Biroc; **M:** Max Steiner. *WAR*

Ice Pawn 🎬🎬 **1992**
Alex Dalton may finally get to realize his dream of becoming a gold medal ice skater if he can beat Misha, his Russian rival. He soon finds out that Misha isn't his only problem, as he unknowingly becomes a pawn in a

---

game of corruption and greed that could totally ruin his career. **102m/C VHS.** Paul Cross, Dan Haggerty, Robert Budaska, Chris Thomas; **D:** Barry Samson; **W:** Paul Cross. *NO*

Ice Pirates 🎬½ **1984 (PG)**
Space pirates in the far future steal blocks of ice to fill the needs of a thirsty galaxy. Cool plot has its moments. **91m/C VHS, Beta, LV.** Robert Urich, Mary Crosby, Michael D. Roberts, John Matuszak, Anjelica Huston, Ron Perlman, John Carradine, Robert Symonds; **D:** Stewart Raffill; **W:** Stewart Raffill; **M:** Bruce Broughton. *MGM*

The Ice Runner 🎬🎬½ **1993 (R)**
Low-key Cold War thriller, filmed in 1991, about a U.S. spy who escapes from the Soviet gulag. Jeffrey West (Albert) gets caught in a botched payoff to a Soviet minister and when the diplomats wash their hands of him a rigged trial has West sentenced to 12 years hard labor. A convenient train wreck lets him assume a different prisoner's name which gets him to a minimum security camp under the eyes of a suspicious commander. Now West needs to escape and cross 39 miles of icy tundra separating his Russian prison from American freedom.**CW:** Violence and scene of sexuality. **116m/C VHS.** Edward Albert, Eugene Lazarev, Olga Kabo, Victor Wong, Alexander Kuznitsov, Basil Hoffman, Bill Bordy, Sergei Ruban; **D:** Barry Samson; **W:** Joyce Warren, Clifford Coleman, Joshua Stallings. *MNC*

Ice Station Zebra 🎬🎬½ **1968 (G)**
A nuclear submarine races Soviet seamen to find a downed Russian satellite under a polar ice cap. Suspenseful Cold War adventure based on the novel by Alistair MacLean. **148m/C VHS, Beta, LV.** Rock Hudson, Ernest Borgnine, Patrick McGoohan, Jim Brown, Lloyd Nolan, Tony Bill; **D:** John Sturges; **C:** Daniel F. Fapp; **M:** Michel Legrand. Nominations: Academy Awards '68: Best Cinematography. *MGM*

Icebox Murders woof! **198?**
A crazed, motiveless, faceless killer hangs his victims in a walk-in freezer. Store this one. **90m/C VHS, Beta.** Jack Taylor, Mirta Miller. *NO*

Iced 🎬 **1988**
Wild fun turns to horror on a ski trip as a group of college friends are hunted by a maniac on the loose. It's all downhill. **86m/C VHS, Beta.** Debra Deliso, Doug Stevenson, Ron Kologie, Elizabeth Gorcey, Alan Johnson; **D:** Jeff Kwitny. *PSM*

Iceland **1942**
Labored romance of an Iceland girl and a Marine with plenty of skating thrown in for good measure. Skating and singing interludes are the best part of an otherwise average film. ♫You Can't Say No to a Soldier; There Will Never Be Another You; Lover's Knot; Let's Bring New Glory to Old Glory; I Like a Military Tune. **79m/B VHS.** Sonja Henie, John Payne, Jack Oakie, Felix Bressart, Osa Massen, Fritz Feld; **D:** H. Bruce Humberstone; **W:** Robert Ellis, Helen Logan. *FXV*

Iceman 🎬🎬🎬 **1984 (PG)**
A frozen prehistoric man is brought back to life, after which severe culture shock takes hold. Underwritten but nicely acted, especially by Lone as the primal man. **101m/C VHS, Beta, LV. CA** Timothy Hutton, Lindsay Crouse, John Lone, David Strathairn, Josef Sommer, Danny Glover; **D:** Fred Schepisi; **W:** Chip Proser; **C:** Ian Baker; **M:** Bruce Smeaton. *USH*

The Icicle Thief 🎬🎬🎬 *Ladri di Saponette* **1989** "The Naked Gun" for the art-house crowd. As a stark, black-and-white neo-realist tragedy airs on TV, bright color commercials disrupt the narrative. Soon ads invade the the movie itself, and the film's director jumps into his picture to fix the damage. Study up on your postwar Italian cinema and this'll seem hilarious; otherwise the real fun doesn't kick in until the halfway point. In Italian with English subtitles. **93m/C VHS. IT** Maurizio Nichetti, Cateria Sylos Labini, Claudio G. Fava, Renato Scarpa, Heidi Komarek; **D:** Maurizio Nichetti. *FXL, FCT, APD*

Icy Breasts 🎬🎬🎬 **1975**
A French psychiatrist tries to prevent his beautiful but psychotic patient from continuing her murdering spree. Dubbed. **105m/C VHS, Beta. FR** Alain Delon, Mireille Darc; **D:** Georges Lautner. *FCT*

I'd Climb the Highest Mountain 🎬🎬🎬 **1951**
Sincere, sentimental piece of Americana about a country preacher (Lundigan) and his city wife (Hayward) as they adjust to life in a small town in Southern hill country. Filmed on location in Georgia. Film was a big hit, especially in the South. Based on the novel by Corra Harris. **88m/C VHS.** Susan Hayward, William Lundigan, Rory Calhoun, Gene Lockhart, Ruth Donnelly, Barbara Bates, Lynn Bari, Alexander Knox; **D:** Henry King; **W:** Lamar Trotti. *FXV*

I'd Give My Life 🎬½ **1936**
A gangster's ex-wife is presently married to the governor. He tries to use their honest but framed son to blackmail her. **73m/B VHS, Beta.** Guy Standing, Frances Drake, Tom Brown, Janet Beecher; **D:** Edwin L. Marin. *VYY*

Idaho 🎬½ **1943**
On a mission to close down houses of ill repute, Rodgers teams up with Autry's old sidekick Burnette. **70m/B VHS, Beta.** Roy Rogers, Harry Shannon, Virginia Grey, Smiley Burnette, Ona Munson; **D:** Joseph Kane. *NOS, VDM, VCN*

Idaho Transfer woof! *Deranged* **1973 (PG)**
Fonda's second directorial effort; Carradine's first screen appearance. An obnoxious group of teens travel through time to Idaho in the year 2044. Environmental wasteland story is dull and confused. **90m/C VHS, Beta.** Keith Carradine, Kelley Bohanan; **D:** Peter Fonda. *MPI, FCT*

Identity Crisis 🎬 **1990 (R)**
Campy fashion maven and flamboyant rapper switch identities causing much tedious overacting. Lifeless murder comedy from father and son Van Peebles.**CW:** Language and some sensuality. **98m/C VHS, LV.** Mario Van Peebles, Ilan Mitchell-Smith, Nicholas Kepros, Shelly Burch, Richard Clarke; **D:** Melvin Van Peebles. *ACA*

Identity Unknown 🎬🎬½ **1945**
Shell-shocked veteran goes AWOL to discover who he is, meeting grieving relatives along the way. Interesting premise is sometimes moving. **70m/B VHS, Beta, 8mm.** Richard Arlen, Cheryl Walker, Roger Pryor, Bobby Driscoll; **D:** Walter Colmes. *VYY*

The Idiot 🎬🎬🎬🎬 **1951**
Dostoevski's Russian novel is transported by Kurosawa across two centuries to post-war Japan, where the madness and jealousy continue to rage. In Japanese with English subtitles. **166m/B VHS.** Toshiro Mifune, Masayuki Mori, Setsuko Hara, Yoshiko Kuga, Takashi Shimura; **D:** Akira Kurosawa. *NYF*

Idiot's Delight 🎬🎬🎬 **1939**
At an Alpine hotel, a song and dance man meets a gorgeous Russian countess who reminds him of a former lover. Incredibly, Gable sings and dances through "Puttin' on the Ritz," the film's big highlight. Based on the Pulitzer Prize-winning play by Robert Sherwood. **107m/B VHS, Beta, LV.** Clark Gable, Norma Shearer, Burgess Meredith, Edward Arnold, Charles Coburn, Joseph Schildkraut; **D:** Clarence Brown; **C:** William H. Daniels. *CCB, MGM*

The Idol Dancer 🎬🎬½ **1920**
Romance and adventure in the South Seas with a drunken American beachcomber inspired by love to change his ways. There's also a native uprising for added excitement. Minor Griffith but nice Nassau scenery. **93m/B VHS.** Richard Barthelmess, Clarine Seymour, Creighton Hale, George MacQuarrie, Kate Bruce, Anders Randolf, Walter James, Thomas Carr; **D:** D.W. Griffith. *GPV, GVV*

Idolmaker 🎬🎬½ **1980 (PG)**
A conniving agent can make a rock star out of anyone. Well-acted fluff with Sharkey taking a strong lead. The first film by hack-meister Hackford and somewhat based on true-life teen fab Fabian. **119m/C VHS, Beta, LV.** Ray Sharkey, Tovah Feldshuh, Peter Gallagher, Paul Land, Joe Pantoliano, Maureen McCormick, John Aprea, Richard Bright, Olympia Dukakis, Steven Apostlee Peck; **D:** Taylor Hackford; **C:** Adam Holender; **M:** Jeff Barry. Golden Globe Awards '81: Best Actor—Musical/Comedy (Sharkey). *MGM*

If... 🎬🎬🎬🎬 **1969 (R)**
Three unruly seniors at a British boarding school refuse to conform. A popular, anarchic indictment of staid British society, using the same milieu as Vigo's "Zero de Con-

duite," with considerably more violence. The first of Anderson and McDowell's trilogy, culminating with "O Lucky Man!" and "Britannia Hospital." In color and black and white. **111m/C VHS, Beta, LV.** *GB* Malcolm McDowell, David Wood, Christine Noonan, Richard Warwick, Robert Swann, Arthur Lowe, Mona Washbourne, Graham Crowden, Hugh Thomas, Guy Rose, Peter Jeffrey, Geoffrey Chater, Mary MacLeod, Anthony Nicholls, Ben Aris, Charles Lloyd Pack, Rupert Webster, Brian Pettifer, Sean Bury, Michael Cadman; *D:* Lindsay Anderson; *W:* David Sherwin; *C:* Miroslav Ondricek; *M:* Marc Wilkinson. Cannes Film Festival '69: Best Film. *PAR*

If Ever I See You Again 🐾 **1978 (PG)** The creator of "You Light Up My Life" stars in the sentimental melodrama. Two adolescent lovers meet again years later and try to rekindle old passions. Done with as much skill as "Light" minus a hit song. **105m/C VHS, Beta.** Joseph Brooks, Shelley Hack, Jerry Keller, Jimmy Breslin; *D:* Joseph Brooks; *W:* Joseph Brooks; *M:* Joseph Brooks. *COL*

If I Were Rich 🐾🐾 *Cash; For Love or Money* **1933** Gwenn is arranging a meeting at his home for a group of financiers he hopes will back a scheme to save his ailing business. Meanwhile he has to dodge bill collectors and others determined to ruin his plans. **63m/B VHS, Beta.** *GB* Edmund Gwenn, Wendy Barrie, Robert Donat, Clifford Heatherly; *D:* Zoltan Korda. *VYY, FCT, NOS*

If It's a Man, Hang Up 🐾½ **1975** A model is terrified by harrowing telephone calls from a stranger. **71m/C VHS, Beta.** Carol Lynley, Gerald Harper. *LIV*

If It's Tuesday, This Must Be Belgium 🐾🐾🐾 **1969 (G)** A fast-paced, frantic, and funny look at a group of Americans on a whirlwind European tour. The group does a nine-country, 18-day bus tour with clashing, comic personalities and lots of romantic possibilities. Remade as a 1987 television movie. **99m/C VHS, LV.** Suzanne Pleshette, Ian McShane, Mildred Natwick, Norman Fell, Michael Constantine, Peggy Cass, Murray Hamilton, Marty Ingels, Sandy Baron, Pamela Britton, Luke Halpin; *D:* Mel Stuart. *MGM, MOV*

If Looks Could Kill 🐾🐾 **1986 (R)** Would-be film noir about a man spying on a female embezzler and falling in love. **90m/C VHS.** Alan Fisler, Tim Gail, Kim Lambert, Jeanne Marie; *D:* Chuck Vincent. *REP*

If Looks Could Kill 🐾🐾½ **1991 (PG-13)** TV stud Grieco makes film debut as a high school class cutup who travels to France with his class to parlez vous for extra credit. Mistaken for a CIA agent, he stumbles into a plot to take over all the money in the whole wide world, and much implausible action and eyelash batting follows. Extra kibbles for supporting characterizations. Oh, and don't be put off by the fact that the Parisian scenes were shot in Montreal. **89m/C VHS, Beta, LV, 8mm, Closed Caption.** Richard Grieco, Linda Hunt, Roger Rees, Robin Bartlett, Gabrielle Anwar, Roger Daltrey, Geraldine James, Carole Davis; *D:* William Dear; *W:* Fred Dekker; *M:* David Foster. *WAR*

If Lucy Fell 🐾 **1995 (R)** Schaeffer serves as writer/director/star of this predictable 90s-style romantic comedy. Ludicrous premise has psychotherapist Lucy (Parker) bent on realizing a 10-year-old pact with longtime friend Joe (Schaeffer) that stipulates they both jump off the Brooklyn Bridge if neither one has found true love by age 30. With the big birthday approaching, Lucy takes a desperate shot with eccentric painter Bwick (Stiller), while Joe finally goes for the object of his desire, asking beautiful neighbor Jane (MacPherson) to a showing of his paintings. Highlights come in the casting, with Parker a solid and energetic neurotic and MacPherson showing that there's something beyond her more obvious talents.*CW:* Language and some sexuality. **92m/C VHS, LV, Closed Caption.** Sarah Jessica Parker, Eric Schaeffer, Ben Stiller, Elle Macpherson, James Rebhorn, Dominic Luchese; *D:* Eric Schaeffer; *W:* Eric Schaeffer; *C:* Ron Fortunato; *M:* Amanda Kravat, Charles Pettis. *COL*

If These Walls Could Talk 🐾🐾½ **1996 (R)** Cable movie covers four decades, from the '50s to the present, in telling the stories of three women and the different ways they deal with unexpected pregnancies. "1952" finds recently widowed nurse Claire (Moore) discovering she's pregnant—and it's not her late husband's. In some graphic scenes she tries to end the pregnancy herself with a knitting needle and later through a back-alley abortion. Happily married Barbara (Spacek) already has four children in "1974" and has just returned to college. Then she discovers she's pregnant again. Abortion's an option but does Barbara want one? Finally, college student Christine (Heche) gets pregnant by her married professor in "1996" and reluctantly opts for an abortion at a family planning clinic, which is besieged by pro-lifers and on the edge of some violent confrontations.*CW:* Realistic depiction of abortions, a graphic shooting and some language. **109m/C VHS, Closed Caption.** Demi Moore, Catherine Keener, Jason London, Shirley Knight, Kevin Cooney, CCH Pounder, Robin Gammell, Sissy Spacek, Xander Berkeley, Joanna Gleason, Harris Yulin, Anne Heche, Jada Pinkett, Cher, Diana Scarwid, Lindsay Crouse, Lorraine Toussaint, Rita Wilson, Eileen Brennan, Craig T. Nelson; *D:* Cher, Nancy Savoca; *W:* Nancy Savoca, Susan Manus, I. Marlene King; *C:* Ellen Kuras, Bobby Bukowski, John Stanier; *M:* Cliff Eidelman. *HBO*

If Things Were Different 🐾½ **1979** Feisty woman struggles to hold her family together after her husband is hospitalized with a nervous breakdown. **96m/C VHS, Beta.** Suzanne Pleshette, Tony Roberts, Arte Johnson, Chuck McCann, Don Murray; *D:* Robert Lewis. *WOV*

If You Could See What I Hear 🐾½ **1982 (PG)** Irritatingly upbeat true-life story of blind singer-musician, Tom Sullivan. Covers his life from college days to marriage. Sophomoric comedy centers around the hero's irresponsible, and often life-endangering, behavior. **103m/C VHS, Beta, LV.** *CA* Marc Singer, R.H. Thomson, Sarah Torgov, Shari Belafonte; *D:* Eric Till. Genie Awards '83: Best Supporting Actor (Thomson). *VES*

If You Don't Stop It...You'll Go Blind 🐾½ **1977 (R)** A series of gauche and tasteless vignettes from various little-known comedians. **80m/C VHS, Beta.** Pat McCormick, George Spencer, Patrick Wright; *D:* I. Robert Levy, Keefe Brasselle. *MED*

If You Knew Susie 🐾🐾 **1948** Two retired vaudeville actors find a letter from George Washington which establishes them as descendants of a colonial patriot and the heirs to a seven billion dollar fortune. 🎵If You Knew Susie; My Brooklyn Love Song; What Do I Want With Money?; We're Living the Life We Love; My, How the Time Goes By. **90m/B VHS, Beta.** Eddie Cantor, Joan Davis, Allyn Joslyn, Charles Dingle, Charles Halton; *D:* Gordon Douglas. *CCB*

Igor & the Lunatics 🐾 **1985 (R)** Tasteless tale of a cannibal cult leader released from prison who picks up where he left off. **79m/C VHS, Beta.** Joseph Eero, Joe Niola, T.J. Michaels; *D:* Billy Parolini. *LIV*

Iguana 🐾🐾 **1989** The videocassette box art makes this look like a horror movie, but it's really a stiff, solemn period drama about a deformed sailor with lizardlike features. After a life of mistreatment he reigns mercilessly over a handful of island castaways. An international coproduction with mostly English dialogue, some Spanish and Portuguese with subtitles. **?m/C VHS.** Everett McGill; *D:* Monte Hellman. *IMP*

Ike 🐾🐾½ *Ike: The War Years* **1979** Duvall is top brass in this made-for television epic biography tracing Eisenhower's career during WWII. Previously a six-hour mini-series; also titled "Ike: The War Years." **291m/C VHS, Beta, LV.** Robert Duvall, Lee Remick, Darren McGavin, Dana Andrews, Laurence Luckinbill; *D:* Melville Shavelson. *THV*

Ikiru 🐾🐾🐾🐾 *To Live* **1952** When a clerk finds out he is dying of cancer, he decides to build a children's playground and give something of himself back to the world. Highly acclaimed, heartbreaking drama from the unusually restrained Kurosawa; possibly his most "eastern" film. In Japanese with English subtitles. **134m/B VHS, Beta, LV.** *JP* Takashi Shimura, Nobuo Kaneko, Kyoko Seki, Miki Odagari, Yunosuke Ito; *D:* Akira Kurosawa. *HMV, CRC, FCT*

Il Bell'Antonio 🐾🐾½ **1960** The boastful Antonio has a reputation as a womanizer but when he finally marries, to a lovely young woman, he faces the loss of his libido. Satire of machismo, marriage, and Catholicism. In Italian with English subtitles. **115m/C VHS.** *IT* Marcello Mastroianni, Claudia Cardinale, Pierre Brasseur; *D:* Mauro Bolognini; *W:* Pier Paolo Pasolini, Gino Vissentini. *KIV, FCT*

Il Grido 🐾🐾 *The Cry; The Outcry* **1957** A jilted husband takes his young daughter from village to village in search of the woman who deserted them for another man. Set in the desolate Po Valley of director Antonioni's childhood. In Italian with English subtitles. **116m/B VHS.** *IT* Steve Cochran, Alida Valli, Dorian Gray, Betsy Blair, Gabriella Pallotti; *D:* Michelangelo Antonioni, Ennio de Concini; *M:* Giovanni Fusco. *KIV, FCT*

Il Sorpasso 🐾🐾½ **1963** A braggart, who has failed at everything, spends all his time traveling around Italy in his sportscar. He takes a repressed law student under his wing and decides to teach him how to have fun. In Italian with English subtitles. **116m/B VHS.** *IT* Vittorio Gassman, Jean-Louis Trintignant; *D:* Dino Risi. *NO*

I'll Cry Tomorrow 🐾🐾🐾 **1955** Hayward brilliantly portrays actress Lillian Roth as she descends into alcoholism and then tries to overcome her addiction. Based on Roth's memoirs. 🎵Sing You Sinners; When The Red Red Robin Comes Bob Bob Bobbin' Along; Happiness Is Just a Thing Called Joe; Vagabond King Waltz. **119m/B VHS, Beta, LV.** Susan Hayward, Richard Conte, Eddie Albert, Jo Van Fleet, Margo, Don Taylor, Ray Danton, Veda Ann Borg; *D:* Daniel Mann; *M:* Alex North. Academy Awards '55: Best Costume Design (B & W); Cannes Film Festival '56: Best Actress (Hayward); Nominations: Academy Awards '55: Best Actress (Hayward), Best Art Direction/Set Decoration (B & W), Best Black and White Cinematography.*MGM*

I'll Do Anything 🐾🐾½ **1993 (PG-13)** Hollywood satire finds unemployed actor Matt (Nolte) suddenly forced to care for his six-year-old daughter Jeannie (Wright), whom he hasn't seen in three years. Matt also finally gets a job—as a chauffeur to an obnoxious producer (well-played by Brooks) whose company winds up making the manipulative demon Jeannie into a hot child star. Great work by Kavner as the owner of a test-screening service who romances Brooks. Originally intended as a musical, the test screenings were so disastrous that the numbers were axed. What's left is less jerky than expected; Brooks reportedly based his character in part on mega-mogul Joel Silver.*CW:* Sexual language and sexual situations. **115m/C VHS, LV, 8mm, Closed Caption.** Nick Nolte, Albert Brooks, Julie Kavner, Whittni Wright, Joely Richardson, Tracey Ullman; *D:* James L. Brooks; *W:* James L. Brooks; *C:* Michael Ballhaus; *M:* Hans Zimmer. *COL*

I'll Get You 🐾🐾 *Escape Route* **1953** An FBI agent goes to England on the trail of a kidnapping ring. **79m/B VHS, Beta, LV.** George Raft, Sally Gray, Clifford Evans; *D:* Seymour Friedman. *RXM*

I'll Name the Murderer 🐾🐾 **1936** Suspense film in which a gossip columnist starts his own investigation into the murder of a club singer. **?m/C VHS.** Ralph Forbes, Marion Shilling; *D:* Raymond K. Johnson. *SNC*

I'll See You in My Dreams 🐾🐾½ **1951** Hokey but fun musical biography of songwriter Gus Kahn (Thomas) and his wife Grace LeBoy (Day). Kahn gets his start in Ziegfeld shows but loses both his career and wife after the 1929 crash. However, she soon returns and everything ends happily ever after. ♫ Ain't We Got Fun; Ukelele Lady; The One I Love Belongs To Somebody Else; I'll See You In My Dreams; It Had To Be You; Swingin' Down the Lane; My Buddy; Makin' Whoopee!; Yes Sir, That's My Baby. **109m/B VHS.** Danny Thomas, Doris Day, Frank Lovejoy, Patrice Wymore, James Gleason, Mary Wickes, Jim Backus, Minna Gombell, William Forrest; **D:** Michael Curtiz; **W:** Melville Shavelson, Jack Rose. *WAR, MVD*

I'll Take Sweden 🐾🐾½ 1965 Overprotective father Hope disapproves of teenaged daughter Weld's guitar-playing boyfriend (Avalon). So to keep her out of harm's way he finagles a company transfer to Sweden. Dad falls for an interior decorator (Merrill) while Weld gets involved with a Swedish playboy (Slate). Deciding Avalon is the lesser of two evils, Hope schemes to get the two back together. **96m/C VHS, Beta, Closed Caption.** Bob Hope, Tuesday Weld, Frankie Avalon, Dina Merrill, Jeremy Slate, Walter Sande, John Qualen, Roy Roberts, Maudie Prickett; **D:** Fred de Cordova; **W:** Arthur Marx, Bob Fisher, Nat Perrin; **C:** Daniel F. Fapp. *MGM, FCT*

Illegal 🐾🐾½ 1955 Crime melodrama stars Robinson as an attorney who risks all to acquit his assistant of murder. Early Mansfield appearance. Remake of "The Mouthpiece." **88m/B VHS.** Edward G. Robinson, Nina Foch, Hugh Marlowe, Jayne Mansfield, Albert Dekker, Ellen Corby, DeForest Kelley, Howard St. John; **D:** Lewis Allen. *NO*

Illegal Entry: Formula for Fear 🐾½ 1993 Tracie's scientist father has invented a formula that could change the world. When he's murdered the formula falls into her unsuspecting hands. Tracie might not know what she has but that doesn't stop some very ruthless efforts to get the information others want. **88m/C VHS.** Sabryn Gene't, Barbara Lee Alexander, Gregory Vignolle, Arthur Roberts, Carol Hoyt; **D:** Henri Charr; **W:** John B. Pfeifer. *PMH*

Illegal in Blue 🐾🐾 1995 (R) Chris (Gauthier) the cop falls for sultry blues singer Kari (Dash) and then realizes she could be a suspect in the murder he's investigating. Will libido win out over loyalty to the job? Also available unrated.**CW:** Sexual content, violence, and language. **94m/C VHS, LV.** Dan Gauthier, Stacey Dash, Louis Giambalvo, Michael Durrell, David Groh; **D:** Stu Segall; **W:** Noel Hynd; **M:** Steve Edwards. *ORI*

Illegally Yours 🐾 1987 (PG) Miscast comedy about a college student serving on the jury in trial of old girlfriend. Bring down the gavel on this one. **94m/C VHS, Beta, Closed Caption.** Rob Lowe, Colleen Camp, Kenneth Mars; **D:** Peter Bogdanovich. *MGM*

Illicit 🐾🐾 1931 In love, Stanwyck fears that marrying Rennie will only ruin their wonderful relationship. Two years after their marriage her fears are realized when each searches for happiness with a past lover. A melodramatic performance that doesn't quite hit its mark. Remade two years later as "Ex-Lady" with Bette Davis in the lead. Based on the play by Edith Fitzgerald and Robert Riskin. **76m/B VHS.** Barbara Stanwyck, Ricardo Cortez, Natalie Moorhead, Charles Butterworth, Joan Blondell, Claude Gillingwater; **D:** Archie Mayo; **W:** Harvey Thew. *MGM*

Illicit Behavior 🐾🐾½ 1991 (R) A dangerous manipulative woman (Severance) is out to claim a $2 million inheritance in this intricate and seductive police thriller. Included among her victims are her husband; a Hollywood vice cop suspended for use of excessive force; his partner; his internal affairs adversary; and her own psychiatrist. Also available in an uncut, unrated version.**CW:** Language, violence, and strong sensuality. **101m/C VHS, Closed Caption.** Joan Severance, Robert Davi, James Russo, Jack Scalia, Kent McCord; **D:** Worth Keeter. *PSM*

Illicit Dreams 🐾½ 1994 A lonely housewife fantasizes about a dream lover who then becomes real. Too bad her possessive and vicious tycoon hubby would rather kill her than lose her. **93m/**

C VHS, Closed Caption. Shannon Tweed, Andrew Stevens. *REP*

Illumination 🐾🐾 *Illuminacja* 1973 Cryptic drama about a young scientist who believes that rational analysis can solve every crisis. Until he must confront the accidental death of a close friend and his problematic affair with an older woman. Intercutting of documentary material can prove disconcerting. Polish with subtitles. **91m/C VHS. PL** Stanislaw Latallo, Monika Denisiewicz-Olbrzychska, Malgorzata Pritulak, Edward Zebrowski; **D:** Krzysztof Zanussi; **W:** Krzysztof Zanussi; **C:** Edward Klosinski; **M:** Wojciech Kilar. *FCT*

The Illusion Travels by Streetcar 🐾🐾🐾 *La Ilusion en Travnia* 1953 Odd but enchanting story of two men who restore a streetcar, only to find that it will not be used by the city. In a gesture of defiance, they steal the streetcar and take it for one last ride, picking up an interesting assortment of characters along the way. In Spanish with English subtitles. Not released in the U.S. until 1977. **90m/B VHS. MX** Lilia Prado, Carlos Navarro, Domingo Soler, Fernando Soto, Agustin Isunza, Miguel Manzano; **D:** Luis Bunuel. *CVC, FCT*

Illusions 🐾🐾 1991 (R) Jan (Locklear) is trying to recover from a nervous breakdown and improve her crumbling marriage when her husband's sexy sister arrives and things start to heat up. Jan thinks her husband and sister-in-law are just a little too close, but when she lets her landlord in on her suspicions, he reacts quite strangely. Will Jan have another nervous breakdown? Mysterious with lots of plot twists. Based on Colley's play "I'll Be Back Before Midnight."**CW:** Language and sexuality. **95m/C VHS, Beta, Closed Caption.** Robert Carradine, Heather Locklear, Emma Samms, Ned Beatty; **D:** Victor Kulle; **W:** Peter Colley. *PSM*

The Illustrated Man 🐾🐾🐾 1969 (PG) A young drifter meets a tattooed man. Each tattoo causes a fantastic story to unfold. A strange, interesting, but finally limited attempt at literary sci-fi. Based on the story collection by Ray Bradbury. **103m/C VHS, Beta.** Rod Steiger, Claire Bloom, Robert Drivas, Don Dubbins; **D:** Jack Smight; **M:** Jerry Goldsmith. *WAR, FCT, MLB*

Ilsa, Harem Keeper of the Oil Sheiks woof! 1976 (R) The naughty Ilsa works for an Arab sheik in the slave trade. More graphic violence and nudity. Plot makes an appearance. **45m/C VHS, LV.** Dyanne Thorne, Michael Thayer. *CIC*

Ilsa, She-Wolf of the SS woof! 1974 (R) The torture-loving Ilsa runs a medical camp for the Nazis. Plot is incidental to nudity and violence. **45m/C VHS, LV.** Dyanne Thorne, Greg Knoph; **D:** Don Edmunds. *CIC*

Ilsa, the Tigress of Siberia woof! 1979 Everyone's favorite torturer has been working her wiles on political prisoners in Russia. After escaping to Canada, her past threatens to catch up with her. As usual, no plot, violence. **85m/C VHS.** Dyanne Thorne, Michel Morin, Tony Angelo, Terry Coady, Howard Mauer; **D:** Jean LaFleur. *NO*

Ilsa, the Wicked Warden woof! *Ilsa, the Absolute Power; Greta the Mad Butcher* 1978 (R) Ilsa is now a warden of a woman's prison in South America, behaving just as badly as she always has, until the prisoners stage an uprising. Lots of skin, no violence, no acting. Also: no plot. **90m/C VHS, LV.** Dyanne Thorne, Lina Romay, Jess (Jesus) Franco; **D:** Jess (Jesus) Franco. *CIC*

I'm All Right Jack 🐾🐾🐾 1959 Sellers plays a pompous communist union leader in this hilarious satire of worker-management relations. Based on Alan Hackney's novel "Private Life." **101m/B VHS, Beta.** Peter Sellers, Ian Carmichael, Terry-Thomas, Victor Maddern; **D:** John Boulting. British Academy Awards '59: Best Actor (Sellers), Best Screenplay; National Board of Review Awards '60: 5 Best Foreign Films of the Year.*FCT*

I'm Dancing as Fast as I Can 🐾🐾 1982 (R) A successful television producer hopelessly dependent on tranquilizers tries to stop cold turkey. Good story could be better; based on Barbara Gordon's memoirs. **107m/C VHS, Beta, LV.** Jill Clayburgh, Nicol Williamson, Dianne West, Joe Pesci, Geraldine Page, John Lithgow, Daniel Stern; **D:** Jack Hofsiss; **W:** David Rabe; **C:** Jan De Bont. *PAR*

I'm Dangerous Tonight 🐾½ 1990 (R) Wallflower Amick (Shelley the Waitress in Twin Peaks) turns into party monster when she dons red dress made from evil ancient Aztec cloak. Many dead soldiers when this girl parties. Based on a Cornell Woolrich short story, it's another in a series of ever more disappointing entries from Hooper, whose cult fave "Texas Chainsaw Massacre" had low as they come production values, but far better scares. Originally cable fare.**CW:** Violence. **92m/C VHS.** Madchen Amick, Corey Parker, R. Lee Ermey, Mary Frann, Dee Wallace Stone, Anthony Perkins; **D:** Tobe Hooper; **W:** Alice Wilson. *USH*

I'm from Arkansas 🐾🐾 1944 The little town of Pitchfork, Arkansas, goes nuts when a pig gives birth to ten piglets. **68m/B VHS, Beta.** El Brendel, Slim Summerville, Iris Adrian, Harry Harvey, Bruce (Herman Brix) Bennett; **D:** Lew (Louis Friedlander) Landers. *NOS, MRV, DVT*

I'm Gonna Git You Sucka 🐾🐾🐾 1988 (R) Parody of "blaxploitation" films popular during the '60s and '70s. Funny and laced with out-right bellylaughs. A number of stars who made "blaxploitation" films, including Jim Brown, take part in the gags. **89m/C VHS, Beta, LV.** Keenen Ivory Wayans, Bernie Casey, Steve James, Isaac Hayes, Jim Brown, Ja'net DuBois, Anne-Marie Johnson, Antonio Fargas, Eve Plumb, John Vernon, Clu Gulager, Kadeem Hardison, Damon Wayans, Gary Owens, Clarence Williams III, David Alan Grier, Kim Wayans, Robin Harris, Chris Rock, Dawnn Lewis, Jester Hairston, Eugene Glazer; *Cameos:* Robert Townsend; **D:** Keenen Ivory Wayans; **W:** Keenen Ivory Wayans; **M:** David Michael Frank. *MGM*

I'm No Angel 🐾🐾🐾 1933 "Beulah, peel me a grape." Well, you'd be hungry too if you spent your time eyeing playboy Grant as West does. She's a circus floozy who's prone to extorting money from her men (after hashing over their shortcomings with her seen-it-all-maid, the aforementioned Beulah). However, after wooing Grant, she sues for breach of promise. This leads to a comic courtroom scene with Grant bringing in all West's ex-lovers as witnesses. Grant's second film with West, following "She Done Him Wrong." **88m/B VHS.** Mae West, Cary Grant, Gregory Ratoff, Edward Arnold, Ralf Harolde, Kent Taylor, Gertrude Michael, Russell Hopton, Dorothy Peterson, William B. Davidson, Gertrude Howard; **D:** Wesley Ruggles; **W:** Mae West. *USH, BTV*

I'm Not Rappaport 🐾🐾 1996 (PG-13) Matthau does some comic grump schtick as irascible, unrepentent 81-year-old New York Jewish radical Nat. He likes to vent his considerable opinions in Central Park and carries on a grumbling friendship with fellow octogenarian Midge (Davis), who stills works as a building superintendent, tending an equally ancient boiler. But Nat's fed-up daughter Clara (Irving) is threatening to put him in a home and Midge seems likely to lose his job when the boiler is scheduled for replacement. Gardner's 1986 stage play tends to show its weaknesses on the big screen.**CW:** Drug content and momentary violence. **135m/C VHS, LV, Closed Caption.** Walter Matthau, Ossie Davis, Amy Irving, Martha Plimpton, Craig T. Nelson, Boyd Gaines, Guillermo Diaz, Elina Lowensohn, Ron Rifkin; **D:** Herb Gardner; **W:** Herb Gardner; **C:** Adam Holender; **M:** Gerry Mulligan. *USH*

I'm on My Way/The Non-Stop Kid 1918 Two classic shorts: "I'm on My Way" (1919), in which Lloyd's dreams of an idyllic marriage are shattered; and "The Non-Stop Kid" (1918), in which Lloyd must contend with a rival for the affection of his beloved. **30m/B VHS, Beta.** Harold Lloyd, Snub Pollard, Bebe Daniels; **D:** Harold Lloyd. *CCB, GVV*

I'm the Girl He Wants to Kill 🐾½

1974 A woman sees a murder committed, and the murderer sees her. Now he's after her. **71m/C VHS, Beta.** Julie Sommars, Anthony Steel. *NO*

I'm the One You're Looking For 🐾🐾½

1988 A famous model obsessively combs Barcelona for the man who raped her. Suspenseful thriller based on a short story by Gabriel Garcia Marquez. In Spanish with English subtitles. **85m/C VHS, LV.** *SP* Patricia Adriani, Chus Lampreave, Ricard Borras, Toni Canto, Angel Alcazar, Marta Fedz, Frank Muro, Miriam DeMaeztu; *D:* Jaime Chavarri. *FXL, FCT, IME*

The Image 🐾🐾½

1989 Anchorman Finney, the unscrupulous czar of infotainment, does a little soul delving when a man he wrongly implicated in a savings and loan debacle decides to check into the hereafter ahead of schedule. Seems the newsmonger's cut a few corners en route to the bigtime, and his public is mad as hell and...oops, wrong movie (need we say there are not a few echoes of "Network"?). Finney's great. Made for cable. **91m/C VHS.** Albert Finney, John Mahoney, Kathy Baker, Swoosie Kurtz, Marsha Mason, Spalding Gray; *D:* Peter Werner; *M:* James Newton Howard. *HBO*

Image of Bruce Lee 🐾

197? (G) Martial arts fight scenes prevail in this story about a jeweler who is swindled out of $1 million worth of diamonds. **88m/C VHS, Beta.** Bruce Li, Chang Wu Lang, Chang Lei, Dana. *MED*

Image of Death 🐾

1977 Woman plots to take the life of an old school chum, assume her identity, and then blow up the Capitol. **83m/C VHS, Beta.** Cathy Paine, Cheryl Waters, Tony Banner, Barry Pierce, Sheila Helpmann, Pennie Hackforth-Jones; *D:* Kevin Dobson. *NO*

Image of Passion 🐾

1986 Weak account of male stripper/lovely advertising executive romance. **90m/C Beta.** James Horan, Susan Damante Shaw, Edward Bell; *D:* Susan Orlikoff-Simon. *PSM*

Imagemaker 🐾½

1986 (R) Uneven story of a presidential media consultant who bucks the system and exposes corruption. **93m/C VHS, Beta, LV.** Michael Nouri, Jerry Orbach, Jessica Harper, Farley Granger; *D:* Hal Wiener. *LIV, VES*

Imaginary Crimes 🐾🐾🐾

1994 (PG) Ray Weiler (Keitel) is a well-meaning salesman with dreams much bigger than his reach. After the death of his wife (Lynch), Ray tries to raise his two daughters, Sonya (Balk) and Greta (Moss). But gifted high school senior (in 1962) Sonya is resentful of being her sister's maternal anchor and having her father's schemes come to nothing even as she acknowledges how much Ray cares and how she wants to improve their lives. Remarkable performances by Keitel and Balk. From the novel by Sheila Ballantyne. **106m/C VHS, Closed Caption.** Harvey Keitel, Fairuza Balk, Kelly Lynch, Vincent D'Onofrio, Elissabeth Moss, Diane Baker, Christopher Penn, Seymour Cassel, Annette O'Toole; *D:* Tony Drazan; *W:* Kristine Johnson, Davia Nelson; *M:* Stephen Endelman. *WAR*

Imitation of Life 🐾🐾🐾

1959 Remake of the successful 1939 Claudette Colbert outing of the same title, and based on Fanny Hurst's novel, with a few plot changes. Turner is a single mother, more determined to achieve acting fame and fortune than function as a parent. Her black maid, Moore, is devoted to her own daughter (Kohner), but loses her when the girl discovers she can pass for white. When Turner discovers that she and her daughter are in love with the same man, she realizes how little she knows her daughter, and how much the two of them have missed by not having a stronger relationship. Highly successful at the box office. **124m/C VHS, Beta.** Lana Turner, John Gavin, Troy Donahue, Sandra Dee, Juanita Moore, Susan Kohner; *D:* Douglas Sirk; *C:* Russell Metty. Golden Globe Awards '60: Best Supporting Actress (Kohner); Nominations: Academy Awards '59: Best Supporting Actress (Kohner), Best Supporting Actress (Moore). *USH, FCT*

Immediate Family 🐾🐾½

1989 (PG-13) Childless couple contact a pregnant, unmarried girl and her boyfriend in hopes of adoption. As the pregnancy advances, the mother has doubts about giving up her baby. A bit sugar-coated in an effort to woo family trade. **112m/C VHS, Beta, LV, Closed Caption.** Glenn Close, James Woods, Kevin Dillon, Mary Stuart Masterson, Kevin Dillon, Linda Darlow, Jane Greer, Jessica James, Mimi Kennedy; *D:* Jonathan Kaplan; *W:* Barbara Benedek; *M:* Brad Fiedel. National Board of Review Awards '89: Best Supporting Actress (Masterson). *COL*

The Immigrant 🐾🐾🐾½

1917 Chaplin portrays a newly arrived immigrant who falls in love with the first girl he meets. Silent with musical soundtrack added. **20m/B VHS, Beta.** Charlie Chaplin; *D:* Charlie Chaplin. *CAB, GVV*

Immortal Bachelor 🐾½

1980 (PG) Good cast can't overcome the silliness of this one. A juror daydreams about the dead husband of a cleaning woman on trial for killing her adulterous spouse. She decides the dead man seems a lot more exciting than her own dull and tiresome husband. **94m/C VHS, Beta.** *IT* Giancarlo Giannini, Monica Vitti, Claudia Cardinale, Vittorio Gassman; *D:* Marcello Fondato; *C:* Pasquale De Santos. *NO*

Immortal Battalion 🐾🐾🐾

The Way Ahead **1944** Entertaining wartime psuedo-documentary follows newly recruited soldiers as they are molded from an ordinary group of carping civilians into a hardened battalion of fighting men by Niven. Some prints run to 116 minutes. **89m/B VHS, Beta.** David Niven, Stanley Holloway, Reginald Tate, Raymond Huntley, William Hartnell, James Donald, Peter Ustinov; *D:* Carol Reed; *W:* Peter Ustinov, Eric Ambler; *C:* Guy Green. *NOS, MRV, VYY*

Immortal Beloved 🐾🐾

1994 (R) The death of Ludwig van Beethoven prompts his loyal secretary to seek the identity of a mystery love to whom the composer has bequeathed his estate. While Beethoven's genius is awesome and his music breathtaking, his lovelife is neither, and the ensuing confessions of the maestro's former loves only get in the way of flashbacks that hint at his torment and triumph. Oldman is darkly intense, and a scene in which the aged Beethoven remembers his terrifying childhood amid the strains of "Ode to Joy" is simply stunning, but an unfocused script undoes what might have been a fine tribute to the master. The London Symphony Orchestra and soloists Murray Perahia, Emanuel Ax, and Yo Yo Ma contributed to the splendid soundtrack. *CW:* Sexual situations, rape. **121m/C VHS, LV, Closed Caption.** Gary Oldman, Jeroen Krabbe, Isabella Rossellini, Johanna Ter Steege, Marco Hofschneider, Miriam Margolyes, Barry Humphries, Valeria Golino, Christopher Fulford; *D:* Bernard Rose; *W:* Bernard Rose. *COL*

Immortal Combat 🐾½

1994 (R) An army of men trained in ninja and guerilla warfare have seemingly immortal powers. Can our two violent heroes find an equally destructive way to stop the killing? **109m/C VHS, LV.** Roddy Piper, Sonny Chiba, Tiny Lister, Meg Foster; *D:* Daniel Neira. *APX*

Immortal Sergeant 🐾🐾½

1943 After the battle death of the squad leader, an inexperienced corporal takes command of North African troops during WWII. Fonda gives a strong performance. Based on a novel by John Brody. **91m/B VHS, Beta, Closed Caption.** Henry Fonda, Thomas Mitchell, Maureen O'Hara, Allyn Joslyn, Reginald Gardiner, Melville Cooper, Morton Lowry; *D:* John M. Stahl; *W:* Lamar Trotti; *C:* Clyde De Vinna. *FOX*

Immortal Sins 🐾

1991 (R) Michael and Susan inherited an old Spanish Castle, complete with its own curse, which comes in the form of a seductive women that has haunted families for centuries. *CW:* Horror violence and strong sensuality. **80m/C VHS.** Cliff DeYoung, Maryam D'Abo; *W:* Thomas McKelvey Cleaver. *NO*

The Immortalizer 🐾

1989 (R) A mad doctor transfers people's brains into young bodies for a price, although it's not as simple as it sounds. **85m/C VHS, Beta, LV.** Ron Kay, Chris Crone, Melody Patterson, Clarke Lindsley, Bekki Armstrong; *D:* Joel Bender. *COL*

The Immortals 🐾🐾

1995 (R) Nightclub owner recruits eight terminally ill criminals in an elaborate heist that calls for simultaneously hitting targets citywide. But when they compare notes, the team fear a doublecross. *CW:* Strong bloody violence, strong language, nudity, and some drug use. **92m/C VHS, Closed Caption.** Eric Roberts, Tia Carrere, William Forsythe, Joe Pantoliano, Clarence Williams III, Tony Curtis, Chris Rock, Kieran Mulroney, Kevin Bernhardt; *D:* Brian Grant; *W:* Kevin Bernhardt. *HMK*

Impact 🐾🐾🐾

1949 A woman and her lover plan the murder of her rich industrialist husband, but the plan backfires. More twists and turns than a carnival ride. **83m/B VHS, Beta.** Brian Donlevy, Ella Raines, Charles Coburn, Helen Walker, Anna May Wong, Philip Ahn, Art Baker, Tony Barrett, Harry Cheshire, Lucius Cooke, Sheilah Graham, Tom Greenway, Hans Herbert, Linda Johnson, Joe Kirk, Clarence Kolb, Mary Landa, Mae Marsh; *D:* Arthur Lubin; *W:* Dorothy Reid, Jay Dratler; *C:* Ernest Laszlo; *M:* Michel Michelet. *NOS, MRV, DVT*

The Imperial Japanese Empire 🐾🐾

1985 Epic of the WWII Pacific seen through Japanese eyes. **130m/C VHS, Beta.** *JP* Tetsuro Tamba, Tomokazu Miura, Teruhiko Saigo, Teruhiko Aoi, Saburo Shinoda, Keiko Sekine, Masako Natsume, Akiko Kana. *VCD*

Imperial Navy 🐾🐾

198? A WWII epic as seen from the Japanese perspective, concentrating on their great navy and its suicide squadrons. Dubbed. **145m/C VHS, Beta.** *JP D:* Paul Aaron. *MOV*

Imperial Venus 🐾🐾

1971 (PG) Biography of Napoleon's sister, Paolina Bonaparte—with particular focus on her many loves, lusts and tribulations. **121m/C VHS, Beta.** Gina Lollobrigida, Stephen Boyd, Raymond Pellegrin; *D:* Jean Delannoy. *NO*

Importance of Being Earnest 🐾🐾🐾

1952 Fine production of classic Oscar Wilde comedy-of-manners. Cast couldn't be better or the story funnier. **95m/C VHS, Beta.** Michael Redgrave, Edith Evans, Margaret Rutherford, Michael Denison, Joan Greenwood; *D:* Anthony Asquith. *PAR, HMV*

The Imported Bridegroom 🐾🐾

1989 A comedy set at the turn of the century about a man who returns to Poland in order to find his daughter a proper husband. **93m/C VHS.** Eugene Troobarck, Avi Hoffman, Greta Cowan, Annette Miller; *D:* Pamela Berger; *W:* Pamela Berger. *ERG*

The Impossible Spy 🐾🐾🐾

1987 True story of Elie Cohen, an unassuming Israeli who doubled as a top level spy in Syria during the 1960s. Cohen became so close to Syria's president that he was nominated to become the Deputy Minister of Defense before his double life was exposed. Well-acted spy thriller made for cable and is worth a look for espionage fans. **96m/C VHS.** *GB* John Shea, Eli Wallach, Michal Bat-Adam, Rami Danon, Sasson Gabray, Chaim Girafi; *D:* Jim Goddard. *NCJ, FCT*

The Impossible Years 🐾

1968 Unattractive, leering sex farce about psychiatrist Nivens who has problems with his own young daughter. Dismal adaptation of the hit Broadway play by Bob Fisher and Arthur Marx. **97m/C VHS.** David Niven, Lola Albright, Chad Everett, Ozzie Nelson, Christina Ferrare, Jeff Cooper, John Harding; *D:* Michael Gordon; *W:* George Wells. *MGM*

The Imposter 🐾½

1984 Improbable tale of a con artist/ex-con who impersonates a high school principal in order to regain his estranged girlfriend, who works as a teacher. Complications ensue when he tackles the school's drug problems. Made for television. **95m/C VHS, Beta.** Anthony Geary, Billy Dee Williams, Lorna Patterson; *D:* Michael Pressman. *PSM*

Imposters 🎬🎬 **1984** A comedy centering on the romantic problems between a self-indulgent young man and the woman who cheats on him. **110m/C VHS, Beta.** Ellen McElduff, Charles Ludlam, Lisa Todd, Peter Evans. *NO*

Impromptu 🎬🎬🎬 **1990 (PG-13)** A smart, sassy, romantic comedy set in 1830s Europe among the era's artistic greats—here depicted as scalawags, parasites and early beatniks. The film's ace is Davis in a lusty, dynamic role as mannish authoress George Sand, obsessively in love with the dismayed composer Chopin. Though he's too pallid a character for her attraction to be credible, a great cast and abundant wit make this a treat. Beautiful score featuring Chopin and Liszt. Film debut of stage director Lapine; screenplay written by his wife, Sarah Kernochan. **108m/C VHS, LV.** Judy Davis, Hugh Grant, Mandy Patinkin, Bernadette Peters, Julian Sands, Ralph Brown, Georges Corraface, Anton Rodgers, Emma Thompson, Anna Massey, John Savident, Elizabeth Spriggs; *D:* James Lapine; *W:* Sarah Kernochan; *C:* Bruno de Keyzer. Independent Spirit Awards '92: Best Actress (Davis). *TVC, MOV*

Improper Channels 🎬🎬 **1982 (PG)** Mediocre comedy about a couple trying to recover their daughter after being accused of child abuse. **91m/C VHS, Beta, LV.** Monica Parker, Alan Arkin, Mariette Hartley; *D:* Eric Till; *W:* Adam Arkin. *VES*

Improper Conduct 🎬🎬 **1994 (R)** Ad agency employee is sexually harassed by her boss but loses her court case. Her sister decides to get revenge by getting hired and setting the slimeball up for a fall. *CW:* Strong sexuality; violence and language. **95m/C VHS.** Steven Bauer, Lee Ann Beaman, John Laughlin, Kathy Shower, Tahnee Welch, Nia Peeples, Stuart Whitman, Adrian Zmed, Patsy Pease; *D:* Jag Mundhra; *W:* Carl Austin. *MNC*

Impulse 🎬½ **1955** When his wife leaves for a visit with her mother, a young man is thrust into cahoots with gangsters, and wrapped up in an affair with another woman. **81m/B VHS.** *GB* Arthur Kennedy, Constance Smith, Joy Shelton; *D:* Charles De Latour. *FCT*

Impulse woof! *Want a Ride, Little Girl?; I Love to Kill* **1974 (PG)** Shatner, a crazed killer, is released from prison and starts to kill again in this low-budget, predictable, critically debased film about child-molesting. **85m/C VHS, Beta.** William Shatner, Ruth Roman, Harold Sakata, Kim Nicholas, Jennifer Bishop, James Dobbs; *D:* William Grefe. *LIV, VES*

Impulse 🎬🎬 **1984 (R)** Small town residents can't control their impulses, all because of government toxic waste in their milk. A woman worried about her mother's mental health returns to town with her doctor boyfriend to discover most of the inhabitants are quite mad. Starts strong but... **95m/C VHS, Beta, LV.** Tim Matheson, Meg Tilly, Hume Cronyn, John Karlen, Bill Paxton, Amy Stryker, Claude Earl Jones, Sherri Stoner; *D:* Graham Baker; *W:* Bart Davis. *PAR*

Impulse 🎬🎬½ **1990 (R)** A beautiful undercover vice cop poses as a prostitute, and gives in to base desires. Russell gives a fine performance in this underrated sleeper. **109m/C VHS, Beta, LV, Closed Caption.** Theresa Russell, Nicholas Mele, Eli Danker, Charles McCaughan, Jeff Fahey, George Dzundza, Alan Rosenberg, Lynne Thigpen, Shawn Elliott; *D:* Sondra Locke; *W:* John DeMarco, Leigh Chapman; *M:* Michel Colombier. *WAR*

Impure Thoughts 🎬🎬 **1986 (PG)** Four friends meet in the afterlife and discuss their Catholic school days. Odd premise never catches fire. **87m/C VHS, Beta.** Brad Dourif, Lane Davies, John Putch, Terry Beaver; *D:* Michael A. Simpson. *NLC*

In a Glass Cage 🎬🎬 *Tras el Cristal* **1986** A young boy who was tortured and sexually molested by a Nazi official seeks revenge. Years after the war, he shows up at the Nazi's residence in Spain and is immediately befriended by his tormentor's family. Confined to an iron lung, the official is at the mercy of the young man who tortuously acts out the incidents detailed in the Nazi's

journal. Suspenseful and extremely graphic, it's well crafted and meaningful but may be just too horrible to watch. Sexual and violent acts place it in the same league as Pasolini's infamous "Salo, or The 120 Days in Sodom." Definitely not for the faint of heart. In Spanish with English subtitles. **110m/C VHS.** *SP* Gunter Meisner, David Sust, Marisa Paredes, Gisela Echevarria; *D:* Agustin Villaronga; *W:* Agustin Villaronga. *CCN, FCT, TPV*

In a Lonely Place 🎬🎬🎬½ **1950** Bogart is outstanding as a volatile Hollywood screenwriter who has an affair with starlet Grahame while under suspicion of murder. Offbeat, yet superb film noir entry became one of the most memorable of the genre. Expertly directed by Ray. Based on the novel by Dorothy B. Hughes and an adaptation by Edmund H. North. **93m/B VHS, Beta.** Humphrey Bogart, Gloria Grahame, Frank Lovejoy, Carl Benton Reid, Art Smith, Jeff Donnell; *D:* Nicholas Ray; *W:* Andrew Solt; *C:* Burnett Guffey. *COL*

In a Moment of Passion 🎬½ **1993 (R)** A two-bit actor wants to be a star—in the worst way possible. So he kills off the lead actor of a new film, takes his place, and proceeds to eliminate any obstacle that gets in his way. The problem comes in when an aspiring actress falls for the actor and then figures out what's going on. *CW:* Language, some violence, and sexuality. **100m/C VHS, Closed Caption.** Maxwell Caulfield, Chase Masterson, Vivian Schilling, Julie Araskog, Joe Estevez, Robert Z'Dar, Zbigniew Kaminski; *Cameos:* Jeff Conaway; *W:* Charles Haigh. *HMD*

In a Shallow Grave 🎬🎬 **1988 (R)** Shallow treatment of James Purdy's novel about a WWII veteran, badly disfigured in combat at Guadalcanal, who returns to Virginia in an attempt to return to the life he once had with the woman he still loves. Handsome Biehn plays the disfigured vet, Mueller's his ex-fiancee, and Dempsey's the drifter who adds a bisexual hypotenuse to the love triangle. Pokey American Playhouse coproduction. **92m/C VHS.** Michael Biehn, Maureen Mueller, Patrick Dempsey, Michael Beach, Thomas Boyd Mason; *D:* Kenneth Bowser; *W:* Kenneth Bowser. *WAR*

In a Stranger's Hand 🎬🎬½ **1992** Urich stars a respected businessman who happens to find a doll which belongs to a kidnapped young girl. The police have their suspicions but Urich teams up with the child's mother to find the girl and winds up uncovering a child-selling ring. Made for television. **93m/C VHS, Closed Caption.** Robert Urich, Megan Gallagher, Brett Cullen, Vondie Curtis-Hall, Dakin Matthews, Alan Rosenberg, Maria O'Brien; *D:* David Greene. *TTC*

In a Year of 13 Moons 🎬🎬 *In a Year with 13 Moons; In Einem Jahr Mit 13 Monden* **1978** Notorious Fassbinder tale of Erwin who becomes Elvira and is subjected to a series of humiliating relationships with men. Finally, with the aid of his/her ex-wife and a prostitute, Elvira looks into the past in an effort to resolve the present. Alternatingly depressing and pretentious. German with subtitles. **119m/C VHS.** *GE* Volker Spengler, Ingrid Caven, Gottfried John, Elisabeth Trissenaar, Eva Mattes; *D:* Rainer Werner Fassbinder; *W:* Rainer Werner Fassbinder; *M:* Peer Raben. *NYF*

In an Old Manor House 🎬🎬½ **1984** Residents of an old house are tormented by the vindictive ghost of a murdered adultress whose husband didn't approve of the, uh, affection she showed his son from a previous marriage. Based on the play by Stanislaw Witkiewicz. In Polish with English subtitles. **90m/C VHS.** *PL D:* Jerzy Kotkowski. *FCT*

In Between 🎬🎬½ **1992 (PG-13)** When Margo, Jack, and Amy wake up they expect it to be another average day. Instead, these three strangers find themselves together in a peculiar house. An angel informs them that the house is a way station between life and the hereafter. The three must look at their pasts, imagine their futures, and decide whether to return to their old lives or ac-

cept death and go on to an afterlife. *CW:* Mature subject matter. **92m/C VHS.** Wings Hauser, Robin Mattson, Alexandra Paul, Robert Forster. *NO*

In Celebration 🎬🎬🎬 **1975 (PG)** Three successful brothers return to the old homestead for their parents' 40th wedding celebration. Intense drama but somewhat claustrophobic. Based on a play by David Storey. **131m/C VHS.** *GB CA* Alan Bates, James Bolam, Brian Cox, Constance Chapman, Gabrielle Daye, Bill Owen; *D:* Lindsay Anderson; *C:* Dick Bush. *NO*

In Cold Blood 🎬🎬🎬½ **1967** Truman Capote's supposedly factual novel provided the basis for this hard-hitting docu-drama about two ex-cons who ruthlessly murder a Kansas family in 1959 in order to steal their non-existent stash of money. Blake is riveting as one of the killers. **133m/B VHS, Beta, LV.** Robert (Bobby) Blake, Scott Wilson, John Forsythe; *D:* Richard Brooks; *W:* Richard Brooks; *C:* Conrad Hall; *M:* Quincy Jones. National Board of Review Awards '67: 10 Best Films of the Year, Best Director (Brooks); Nominations: Academy Awards '67: Best Adapted Screenplay, Best Cinematography, Best Director (Brooks), Best Original Score. *COL*

In Cold Blood 🎬🎬 **1996** Tv miniseries version of the Truman Capote true crime classic, which follows the 1959 murders of the four members of the Clutter family in Holcomb, Kansas by ex-cons Dick Hickock (Edwards) and Perry Smith (Roberts). The TV version covers more of the background of both the killers and the Holcombs, the relentless hunt by Al Dewey (Neill) of the Kansas Bureau of Investigation, and the duo's time on death row. **180m/C VHS, Closed Caption.** Anthony Edwards, Eric Roberts, Sam Neill, Kevin Tighe, Gillian Barber, Robbie Bowen, Margot Finley, Bethel Leslie, Gwen Verdon, Stella Stevens, L.Q. Jones, Louise Latham, Campbell Lane, Leo Rossi; *D:* Jonathan Kaplan; *W:* Benedict Fitzgerald. *CAF*

In Country 🎬🎬½ **1989 (R)** Based on Bobbie Ann Mason's celebrated novel, the story of a young Kentuckian high schooler (perfectly played by Lloyd) and her search for her father, killed in Vietnam. Willis plays her uncle, a veteran still struggling to accept his own survival, and crippled with memories. Moving scene at the Vietnam Veterans Memorial. **116m/C VHS, Beta, LV, 8mm.** Bruce Willis, Emily Lloyd, Joan Allen, Kevin Anderson, Richard Hamilton, Judith Ivey, Peggy Rea, John Terry, Patricia Richardson, Jim Beaver; *D:* Norman Jewison; *W:* Frank Pierson, Cynthia Cidre; *C:* Russell Boyd; *M:* James Horner. *WAR, MVD*

The In Crowd 🎬🎬 **1988 (PG)** A bright high school student gets involved with a local television dance show circa 1965, and must choose between uncertain fame and an Ivy League college. A fair nostalgic look at the period. Leitch is the son of psychedelic folk singer Donovan. **96m/C VHS, Beta, LV, Closed Caption.** Donovan Leitch, Jennifer Runyon, Scott Plank, Joe Pantoliano; *D:* Mark Rosenthal; *W:* Mark Rosenthal. *ORI*

In Custody 🎬🎬 *Hifazaat* **1994 (PG)** Producer Merchant makes his feature directorial debut with this dreamy tale of small-town teacher Deven (Puri) who's urged by a publishing friend to interview Nur (Kapoor), the greatest living poet in the disappearing Urdu language. The worshipful Deven is dismayed to find his idol a wreck, surrounded by sycophants and a shrewish second wife who's plagiarizing her husband's work, and soon finds himself hopelessly entangled in the writer's life. Unabashedly literary (the poetry recited is by Faiz Ahmed Faiz) with a star cast. Based on the 1987 novel by Anita Desai. Urdu with subtitles. **123m/C VHS.** *IN* Shashi Kapoor, Om Puri, Shabana Azmi, Sushma Seth, Neena Gupta, Ajay Sahni, Tinnu Anand; *D:* Ismail Merchant; *W:* Anita Desai, Shahrukh Husain; *C:* Larry Pizer; *M:* Zakir Hussain, Ustad Sultan Khan. *COL*

In Dangerous Company 🎬 **1988 (R)** Beautiful babe balances beaux and battles abound. A brow lowering experience. **92m/C VHS.** Tracy Scoggins, Cliff DeYoung, Chris Mulkey, Henry Darrow, Steven Keats, Richard Portnow; **D:** Ruben Preuss; **W:** Mitch Brown; **C:** James L. Carter. *NO*

In Deadly Heat ♂ 1987 Crime, revenge, murder, and urban warfare are done once again. 98m/C VHS, Beta. William Dame, Catherine Dee, M.R. Murphy; **D:** Don Nardo. *JEF*

In Desert and Wilderness ♂♂½ 1973 Two kidnapped children escape and are thrust into the wilds of Africa, where they must survive with wits and courage. Based on a novel by Nobel prize-winning author Henyk Sienkiewicz. In Polish with English subtitles. 144m/C VHS. **PL D:** Wladyslaw Slesicki. *FCT*

In for Treatment ♂♂♂ 1982 A terminally ill cancer patient, lost in the bureaucracy of the hospital, fights to rediscover the joy of life. Strong and disturbing story. In Dutch with English subtitles. 92m/C VHS, Beta. **NL** Helmut Woudenberg, Frank Groothof, Hans Man Int Veld; **D:** Eric Van Zuylen, Marja Kok. *NO*

In Gold We Trust ♂½ 1991 Vincent leads an elite battalion of fighters against a group of rogue American MIAs (!) laying waste to the Vietnemese countryside. 89m/C VHS. Jan-Michael Vincent, Sam Jones; **D:** P. Chalong; **M:** Hummie Mann. *AIP*

In Harm's Way ♂♂ 1965 Overdone story about two naval officers and their response to the Japanese attack at Pearl Harbor. Even the superb cast members (and there are plenty of them) can't overcome the incredible length and overly intricate plot. 165m/B VHS, Beta, LV, Closed Caption. John Wayne, Kirk Douglas, Tom Tryon, Patricia Neal, Paula Prentiss, Brandon de Wilde, Burgess Meredith, Stanley Holloway, Henry Fonda, Dana Andrews, Franchot Tone, Jill Haworth, George Kennedy, Carroll O'Connor, Patrick O'Neal, Slim Pickens, Bruce Cabot, Larry Hagman, Hugh O'Brian, Jim Mitchum, Barbara Bouchet; **D:** Otto Preminger; **W:** Wendell Mayes; **C:** Loyal Griggs; **M:** Jerry Goldsmith. British Academy Awards '65: Best Actress (Neal); Nominations: Academy Awards '65: Best Black and White Cinematography. *PAR*

In Hot Pursuit ♂½ 1982 Convicted for drug smuggling, two young men stage a daring but not too exciting escape from a southern prison. 90m/C VHS, Beta. Bob Watson, Don Watson, Debbie Washington. *NO*

The In-Laws ♂♂♂ 1979 (PG) A wild comedy with Falk, who claims to be a CIA agent, and Arkin, a dentist whose daughter is marrying Falk's son. The fathers foil a South American dictator's counterfeiting scheme in a delightfully convoluted plot. 103m/C VHS, Beta, LV. Peter Falk, Alan Arkin, Richard Libertini, Nancy Dussault, Penny Peyser, Arlene Golonka, Michael Lembeck, Ed Begley Jr., Rosana De Soto, Art Evans; **D:** Arthur Hiller; **W:** Andrew Bergman; **M:** John Morris. *WAR*

In Like Flint ♂♂½ 1967 Sequel to "Our Man Flint" sees our dapper spy confronting an organization of women endeavoring to take over the world. Spy spoofery at its low-level best. 107m/C VHS, Beta, LV. James Coburn, Lee J. Cobb, Anna Lee, Andrew Duggan, Jean Hale; **D:** Gordon Douglas; **C:** William H. Daniels; **M:** Jerry Goldsmith. *FOX*

In Love and War ♂♂½ 1991 (R) Woods plays Navy pilot Jim Stockdale, whose plane was grounded over hostile territory and who endured nearly eight years of torture as a POW. Meanwhile, wife Sybil is an organizer of POW wives in the States. Low octane meeting of the US Navy Commander's true story. Aaron earlier directed "The Miracle Worker," and you may recognize Ngor from "The Killing Fields." 96m/C VHS, LV. James Woods, Jane Alexander, Haing S. Ngor, Concetta Tomei, Richard McKenzie, James Pax; **D:** Paul Aaron; **W:** Carol Schreder. *THV*

In Love and War ♂½ 1996 (PG-13) Tells the story of 19-year-old Ernest Hemingway's (O'Donnell) romance with 27-year-old Red Cross nurse Agnes (Bullock) while both were stationed in Italy during WWI. This romance later served as the basis for Hemingway's novel "A Farewell to Arms." Here's a thought. Read the book instead.

The boyish O'Donnell is so miscast as testosterone-junkie Hemingway, the only analogy would be having Sylvester Stallone play Truman Capote. The lack of passion and chemistry between the two stars is unsettling, and the action is just plain clunky. Bullock looks great in a nurse's uniform, though. Adapted from "Hemingway in Love and War: The Lost Diary of Agnes Von Kurowsky" by Henry Villard and James Nagel. **CW:** Graphic war injuries and some sensuality. 115m/C VHS, LV, Closed Caption. Chris O'Donnell, Sandra Bullock, MacKenzie Astin, Ingrid Lacey, Emilio Bonucci, Margot Steinberg, Colin Stinton, Ian Kelly; **D:** Richard Attenborough; **W:** Clancy Sigal, Dimitri Villard, Allan Scott, Anna Hamilton Phelan; **C:** Roger Pratt; **M:** George Fenton. *NLC*

In Love with an Older Woman ♂♂ 1982 Ritter takes fewer pratfalls than usual in this film; after all, it's a romantic comedy. Adapted from "Six Months with an Older Woman," the novel by David Kaufelt. Made for television. 100m/C VHS, Beta. John Ritter, Karen Carlson, Jamie Rose, Robert Mandan, Jeff Altman, George Murdock; **D:** Jack Bender. *FRH*

In Memoriam ♂♂½ 1976 Tragic and gripping drama about one man's ability, albeit too late, to cope with his unforgettable past. Based on a story by Adolfo Bioy Casares. In Spanish with English subtitles. 96m/C VHS. **SP** Geraldine Chaplin, Jose Luis Gomez; **D:** Enrique Braso. *FCT*

In 'n Out ♂½ 1986 An American loser ventures to Mexico to recover a long-lost inheritance, meeting with mildly comic obstacles along the way. 85m/C VHS, Beta. Sam Bottoms, Pat Hingle. *VTR, NWV*

In Name Only ♂♂½ 1939 Somber drama about a heartless woman who marries for wealth and prestige and holds her husband to a loveless marriage. Based on "Memory of Love" by Bessie Brewer. 102m/B VHS, Beta, LV. Carole Lombard, Cary Grant, Kay Francis; **D:** John Cromwell. *CCB, MLB, TTC*

In Old Caliente ♂½ 1939 Rogers battles the bad guys in the frontier town of Caliente. 60m/B VHS, Beta. Roy Rogers, Lynn (Mary Hart) Roberts, George "Gabby" Hayes. *NOS, VCN, DVT*

In Old California ♂♂½ 1942 Plucky story of a young Boston pharmacist who searches for success in the California gold rush and runs into the local crime boss. Also available colorized. 88m/B VHS. John Wayne, Patsy Kelly, Binnie Barnes, Albert Dekker, Charles Halton; **D:** William McGann. *REP*

In Old Cheyenne ♂½ 1941 Bank holdups, cattle rustling, fist fights, and even car crashes mix with some good ol' guitar plunking in this western. 60m/B VHS, Beta. Roy Rogers, George "Gabby" Hayes. *NOS, CAB, TIM*

In Old Chicago ♂♂♂ 1937 The O'Leary family travels to Chicago to seek their fortune, with mom working as a washerwoman to support her sons. Brothers Power and Ameche become power-broking rivals and when mom comes to break up a brawl between the two, she neglects to properly restrain the family cow. This leads to the great Chicago fire of 1871, supposedly started when the cow kicks over a latern and sets the barn ablaze. The city burns down in a spectacular 20-minute sequence. Based on the story "We the O'Learys" by Niven Busch. 115m/B VHS. Tyrone Power, Alice Faye, Don Ameche, Alice Brady, Andy Devine, Brian Donlevy, Phyllis Brooks, Tom Brown, Sidney Blackmer, Gene Reynolds, Berton Churchill, Bobs Watson; **D:** Henry King; **W:** Lamar Trotti, Sonya Levien. Academy Awards '37: Best Supporting Actress (Brady); Nominations: Academy Awards '37: Best Picture, Best Sound, Best Story. *FXV*

In Old Colorado ♂♂½ 1941 Ankrum and his cronies try to stir up trouble over water rights, but Boyd and his pals ride to the rescue. 67m/B VHS. William Boyd, Russell Hayden, Andy Clyde, Margaret Hayes, Morris Ankrum, Sarah Padden, Cliff Nazarro, Stanley Andrews, James Seay, Morgan Wallace; **D:** Howard Bretherton. *NOS*

In Old Montana ♂ 1939 A Cavalry lieutenant tries to settle a cattleman vs. sheep-herding war. 60m/B VHS, Beta. Fred Scott, Jeanne Carmen, Harry Harvey, John Merton; **D:** Raymond K. Johnson. *VDM, GPV*

In Old New Mexico ♂ 1945 The Cisco Kid and Pancho reveal the murder of an old woman—a mysterious doctor who was after an inheritance. 60m/B VHS, Beta. Duncan Renaldo, Martin Garralaga, Gwen Kenyon, Pedro de Cordoba. *NOS, VCI, VYY*

In Old Santa Fe ♂♂½ 1934 Cowboy star Maynard's best western, and the first film ever with Autry and Burnette. Maynard is framed for murder and his pals save him. 60m/B VHS, Beta. Ken Maynard, Gene Autry, Smiley Burnette, Evalyn Knapp, George "Gabby" Hayes, Kenneth Thomson, Wheeler Oakman, George Chesebro; **D:** David Howard, Joseph Kane. *NOS, VCN, DVT*

In Person ♂♂½ 1935 Spry comedy about a movie star who disguises herself to take a vacation incognito and falls in love with a country doctor who is unaware of her identity. ♫Don't Mention Love To Me; Out of Sight, Out of Mind; Got a New Lease on Life. 87m/B VHS, Beta, LV. Ginger Rogers, George Brent, Alan Mowbray, Grant Mitchell; **D:** William A. Seiter; **M:** Oscar Levant. *TTC*

In Praise of Older Women ♂♂ 1978 Berenger is just right as a young Hungarian who is corrupted by WWII and a large number of older women. Based on a novel by Stephen Vizinczey. 110m/C VHS, Beta, LV. **CA** Karen Black, Tom Berenger, Susan Strasberg, Helen Shaver, Alexandra Stewart; **D:** George Kaczender. *FOX*

In Pursuit of Honor ♂♂½ 1995 (PG-13) Based on the true story of five American cavalry soldiers who find themselves being phased out in the 1935 Army. Ordered by General Douglas MacArthur to destroy their horses, they instead try to outrun an elite tank division to get some 400 horses to safety in Canada. Rugged performances and the violence towards the horses is aptly disturbing. Filmed on location in Australia and New Zealand; made for cable TV. **CW:** Depiction of violence against animals. ?m/C VHS. Don Johnson, Craig Sheffer, Gabrielle Anwar, Bob Gunton, Rod Steiger, James B. Sikking, John Dennis Johnston, Robert Coleby; **D:** Ken Olin; **W:** Dennis Lynton Clark; **C:** Stephen Windon; **M:** John Debney. *HBO*

In Search of a Golden Sky ♂♂ 1984 (PG) Following their mother's death, a motley group of children move in with their secluded cabin-dwelling uncle, much to the righteous chagrin of the welfare department. 94m/C VHS, Beta, Closed Caption. Charles Napier, George Flower, Cliff Osmond; **D:** Jefferson Richard. *FOX*

In Search of Anna woof! 1979 When a convict is released from jail, he hits the road with a flighty model in search of the girlfriend who corresponded with him in prison. There auto be a law. 90m/C VHS, Beta. **AU** Judy Morris, Richard Moir, Chris Hayward, Bill Hunter; **D:** Esben Storm. *AHV*

In Search of the Castaways ♂♂♂ 1962 Stirring adventure tale of a teenage girl and her younger brother searching for their father, a ship's captain lost at sea years earlier. Powerful special effects and strong cast make this a winning Disney effort. Based on a story by Jules Verne. 98m/C VHS, Beta, Closed Caption. **GB** Hayley Mills, Maurice Chevalier, George Sanders, Wilfrid Hyde-White, Michael Anderson Jr.; **D:** Robert Stevenson. *DIS*

In Self Defense ♂½ 1993 (PG) Purl is supposed to be protected from the killer she testified against but it doesn't quite work out that way. 94m/C VHS, Closed Caption. Linda Purl, Yaphet Kotto, Billy Drago; **D:** Bruce Seth Green; **M:** Patrick Gleeson. *TTC*

In Society ♂♂½ 1944 The duo play dimwitted plumbers who are mistakenly invited to a high society party, where they promptly create catastrophe. 84m/B VHS. Bud Abbott, Lou Costello, Marion Hutton, Kirby Grant, Ann Gillis, Arthur Treacher, Thomas Gomez, Steve Geray, Margaret Irving, Thurston Hall; *Cam-*

eos: Sid Fields; **D:** Jean Yarbrough; **W:** Sid Fields, Hal Fimberg, Edmund Hartmann, John Grant. USH, FCT

In the Aftermath: Angels Never Sleep 🐾½ 1987 Mix of animation and live-action in this post-nuclear wasteland tale never quite works. 85m/C VHS, Beta. Tony Markes, Rainbow Dolan; **D:** Carl Colpaert. VTR, NWV

In the Army Now 🐾 1994 (PG) Pauly dude gets his head shaved, man. Service comedy about a slacker who joins the Army hoping to cash in on military benefits but who winds up in combat instead. Shore drops the Valley Guy shtick and ventures into the land of action when he gets sent on a mission to the Sahara. Strictly for Shore's fans. 92m/C VHS, LV, Closed Caption. Pauly Shore, Esai Morales, Lori Petty, David Alan Grier, Ernie Hudson, Andy Dick; **D:** Dan Petrie Jr.; **W:** Dan Petrie Jr., Ken Kaufman, Fax Bahr, Stu Krieger, Adam Small; **M:** Robert Folk. HPH

In the Cold of the Night 🐾 1989 (R) Another drowsy entry into the "to sleep perchance to have a nightmare genre." A photographer with a vivid imagination dreams he murders a woman he doesn't know, and when said dream girl rides into his life on the back of a Harley, Mr. Foto's faced with an etiquette quandary: haven't they met before? Cast includes Hedren (Hitchcock's Marnie and Melanie Griffith's mother). 112m/C VHS, LV, Closed Caption. Jeff Lester, Adrienne Sachs, Shannon Tweed, David Soul, John Beck, Tippi Hedren, Marc Singer; **D:** Nico Mastorakis. REP

In the Company of Men 🐾🐾 1996 (R) A couple of dissatisfied Yuppies, Chad (Eckhart) and Howard (Malloy), are sent on a six-week job out of town by their home office. Grumbling about the lack of control in their lives, they formulate a nasty plan—they'll deliberately get involved with the same girl, secretary Christine (Edwards), string her along, and then abandon her when their job is done. Think misogynistic comedy. **CW:** Language and emotional abuse. 93m/C VHS. Matt Malloy, Aaron Eckhart, Stacy Edwards, Mark Rector; **D:** Neil LaBute; **W:** Neil LaBute; **C:** Anthony P. Hettinger. Sundance Film Festival '97: Filmmakers Trophy. NYR

In the Custody of Strangers 🐾🐾🐾 1982 A teenager's parents refuse to help when he is arrested for being drunk and he ends up spending the night in jail. Realistic handling of a serious subject. Sheen and Estevez play the father and son, mimicking their real-life relationship. Made for television. 100m/C VHS. Martin Sheen, Jane Alexander, Emilio Estevez, Kenneth McMillan, Ed Lauter, Matt Clark, John Hancock; **D:** Robert Greenwald. MOV

In the Days of the Thundering Herd & the Law & the Outlaw 1914 In the first feature, a pony express rider sacrifices his job to accompany his sweetheart on a westward trek to meet her father. In the second show, a fugitive falls in love with a rancher's daughter and risks recognition. 76m/B VHS, Beta. Tom Mix, Myrtle Stedman; **D:** Colin Campbell. CCB, GPV

In the Deep Woods 🐾🐾 1991 Children's author Joanna Warren (Arquette) gets too close to mayhem when a childhood friend is murdered by the Deep Woods Killer. A mysterious private detective (Perkins) is on the killer's trail but when Joanna comes into the picture will she be a suspect or a victim? Based on the book by Nicholas Conde. ?m/C VHS. Rosanna Arquette, Anthony Perkins, Will Patton, D.W. Moffett, Christopher Rydell, Harold Sylvester, Kimberly Beck; **D:** Charles Correll; **W:** Robert Nathan, Robert Rosenbaum; **C:** James Glennon. AEL

In the Gloaming 🐾🐾🐾 1997 Twenty-something Danny (Leonard) bitterly returns home to his suburban, wealthy, emotionally cold family because he is dying of AIDS. He and mother Janet (Close) renew their strained family ties but his businessman dad (Strathairn) doesn't know how to cope except with distance, and his sullen sister Anne (Fonda) is resentful. Wrenching story with fine work by all, including Goldberg in the small

role of live-in nurse, Myrna. Based on a short story by Alice Elliot Dark. Made for cable TV; Reeve's directorial debut. 60m/C VHS. Robert Sean Leonard, Glenn Close, David Strathairn, Bridget Fonda, Whoopi Goldberg; **D:** Christopher Reeve; **W:** Will Scheffer; **C:** Frederick Elmes; **M:** Dave Grusin. HBO

In the Good Old Summertime 🐾🐾🐾 1949 This pleasant musical version of "The Shop Around the Corner" tells the story of two bickering co-workers who are also anonymous lovelorn pen pals. Minnelli made her second screen appearance at 18 months in the final scene. 🎵 I Don't Care; Meet Me Tonight In Dreamland; Play That Barbershop Chord; In the Good Old Summertime; Put Your Arms Around Me Honey; Wait Till the Sun Shines Nellie; Chicago; Merry Christmas. 104m/C VHS, Beta, LV. Judy Garland, Van Johnson, S.Z. Sakall, Buster Keaton, Spring Byington, Liza Minnelli, Clinton Sundberg; **D:** Robert Z. Leonard; **C:** Harry Stradling. MGM

In the Heat of Passion 🐾½ 1991 (R) A low-budget ripoff of "Body Heat" and "Fatal Attraction" starring Kirkland as a married woman who involves a much younger man in a very steamy affair that leads to murder. This movie wants to be a thriller, but is little more than a softcore sex flick. Also available in an unrated version that contains explicit footage. **CW:** Language, violence, and sensuality. 84m/C VHS, LV. Sally Kirkland, Nick Corri, Jack Carter, Michael Greene; **D:** Rodman Flender; **W:** Rodman Flender. COL

In the Heat of Passion 2: Unfaithful 🐾½ 1994 (R) Philip Donovan (Bostwick) is having an affair with his stepdaughter Casey (Hill) and the duo murder hapless wife/mother (Down) to get her money. But it seems someone else knows about their crime. **CW:** Some language and violence; strong sexuality. 88m/C VHS, LV. Barry Bostwick, Teresa Hill, Lesley-Anne Down, Michael Gross; **D:** Catherine Cyran. NHO

In the Heat of the Night 🐾🐾🐾½ 1967 A wealthy industrialist in a small Mississippi town is murdered. A black homicide expert is asked to help solve the murder, despite resentment on the part of the town's chief of police. Powerful script with underlying theme of racial prejudice is served well by taut direction and powerhouse performances. Poitier's memorable character Virgil Tibbs appeared in two more pictures, "They Call Me Mister Tibbs" and "The Organization." 109m/C VHS, Beta, LV. Sidney Poitier, Rod Steiger, Warren Oates, Lee Grant; **D:** Norman Jewison; **W:** Stirling Silliphant; **C:** Haskell Wexler; **M:** Quincy Jones. Academy Awards '67: Best Actor (Steiger), Best Adapted Screenplay, Best Film Editing, Best Picture, Best Sound; British Academy Awards '67: Best Actor (Steiger); Golden Globe Awards '67: Best Screenplay; Golden Globe Awards '68: Best Actor—Drama (Steiger), Best Film—Drama, Best Screenplay; New York Film Critics Awards '67: Best Actor (Steiger), Best Director (Nichols), Best Film; National Society of Film Critics Awards '67: Best Actor (Steiger), Best Cinematography; Nominations: Academy Awards '67: Best Director (Jewison). MGM, FOX, BTV

In the King of Prussia 🐾½ 1983 Recreation of the trial of the "Plowshares Eight" radicals who were jailed for sabotaging two nuclear missiles at an electric plant in Pennsylvania. 92m/C VHS, Beta. Martin Sheen, Rev. Daniel Berrigan. MPI, BUL

In the Kingdom of the Blind the Man with One Eye is King 🐾🐾 1994 (R) The title doesn't seem to mean anything and you may feel the same way about this standard crime drama, despite a strong cast. Mobster Tony (Petersen) gets police assistance from detective Al (Vallelonga) in discovering who murdered a mob boss' brother. **CW:** Language, violence, brief nudity. 99m/C VHS. Nick Vallelonga, William L. Petersen, Michael Biehn, Paul Winfield, James Quarter; **D:** Nick Vallelonga; **W:** Nick Vallelonga. AVI

In the Land of the Owl Turds 1987 The story of a decidedly eccentric young man who drives a dada art gallery on wheels while searching for love. Blank's senior thesis film. 30m/C VHS, Beta. **D:** Harrod Blank. FFM

In the Line of Duty: A Cop for the Killing 🐾🐾 *A Cop for the Killing* 1990 (R) Undercover L.A. narcotics squad is about to bust the city's biggest drug lord when their sting operation goes bad and one of the team is brutally murdered. So, squad leader Ray Wiltern (Farentino) decides to get even. One in a series of TV movies under the "In the Line of Duty" banner. 95m/C VHS. James Farentino, Steven Weber, Charles Haid, Tony Crane, Harold Sylvester, Dan Lauria, Tony Plana; **D:** Dick Lowry; **W:** Philip Rosenberg; **C:** Frank Beasoechea; **M:** Mark Snow. NHO

In the Line of Duty: Ambush in Waco 🐾🐾½ *Ambush in Waco* 1993 (R) Insta-television movie made by NBC even before the fire which engulfed the Texas compound and ended the standoff between self-proclaimed "prophet" David Koresh and the federal government. Daly does well as the manipulative, charasmatic Branch Davidian cult leader whose stockpiling of illegal weapons lead to an investigation by the Bureau of Alchohol, Tobacco and Firearms and a botched raid which caused the ultimately fatal siege. Filmed on location outside Tulsa, Oklahoma. **CW:** Graphic depiction of a shootout. 93m/C VHS, Closed Caption. Timothy Daly, Dan Lauria, William O'Leary; **D:** Dick Lowry; **W:** Phil Penningroth. REP

In the Line of Duty: The FBI Murders 🐾🐾🐾 *The FBI Murders* 1988 A fact-based chiller about the bloody 1986 shootout between Miami FBI agents and a pair of violent killers (Soul and Gross playing against type). This made for television drama was shown on TV as "In the Line of Duty: The FBI Murders." 95m/C VHS, Closed Caption. David Soul, Michael Gross, Ronny Cox, Bruce Greenwood, Doug Sheehan, Teri Copley; **D:** Dick Lowry; **W:** Tracy Keenan Wynn. CAF

In the Line of Fire 🐾🐾🐾½ 1993 (R) Aging Secret Service agent meets his match in a spooky caller who threatens his honor and the president in an exciting, fast paced cat and mouse game. Terrific performance by Eastwood includes lots of dry humor and an unscripted emotional moment, but is nearly overshadowed by Malkovich's menacing bad guy. Eerie special effects add to the mood. The Secret Service cooperated and most scenes are believable, with a few Hollywood exceptions; the end result clearly pays homage to the agents who protect our presidents. Intriguing trailer showed the number "6" in "1963" slowly turning to "9" to become "1993." The seventh highest grossing movie of 1993. **CW:** Language and violence. 128m/C VHS, LV, 8mm, Closed Caption, DVD. Clint Eastwood, John Malkovich, Rene Russo, Dylan McDermott, Gary Cole, Fred Dalton Thompson, John Mahoney, Gregory Alan Williams; **D:** Wolfgang Petersen; **W:** Jeff Maguire; **C:** John Bailey; **M:** Ennio Morricone. Nominations: Academy Awards '93: Best Film Editing, Best Original Screenplay, Best Supporting Actor (Malkovich); British Academy Awards '93: Best Original Screenplay, Best Supporting Actor (Malkovich); Golden Globe Awards '94: Best Supporting Actor (Malkovich); MTV Movie Awards '94: Best Villain (Malkovich); Writers Guild of America '93: Best Original Screenplay. COL, BTV

In the Money 🐾 1934 Veteran vaudevillian "Skeets" Gallagher introduces a muddled mass of acts, including a poor imitator of boxing great Gene Tunney, a mad scientist who talks to rabbits and writes rubber checks, and a limp-wristed lisper. 66m/B VHS. Lois Wilson, Warren Hymer, Arthur Hoyt, Frank "Junior" Coghlan, Louise Beavers; **D:** Frank Strayer. NOS

In the Mood 🐾🐾½ 1987 (PG-13) Based on fact, this is the story of teenager Sonny Wisecarver, nicknamed "The Woo Woo Kid," who in 1944, seduced two older women and eventually landed in jail after marrying one of them. Look for Wisecarver in a cameo role as a mailman in the

film. **98m/C VHS, Beta, LV, Closed Caption.** Patrick Dempsey, Beverly D'Angelo, Talia Balsam, Michael Constantine, Betty Jinnette, Kathleen Freeman, Peter Hobbs, Edith Fellows; *Cameos:* Ellsworth Wisecarver; *D:* Phil Alden Robinson; *W:* Phil Alden Robinson; *M:* Ralph Burns. *WAR, ORI, BAR*

In the Mouth of Madness ♂♂ 1995
(R) Standard horror flick pays homage to or pokes fun at Stephen King (you decide) with story of successful horror novelist whose fans become a bit too engrossed in his stories—seems his readers tend to slip into dementia and carry out the grisly acts depicted within the pages. Neill plays an insurance investigator who must track down the missing author while combating the psychotic, axe-wielding residents of the seemingly quiet east coast hamlet where the author resides. Worth a look for the above average special effects and makeup provided by Industrial Light and Magic (ILM). **95m/C VHS, LV, Closed Caption.** Sam Neill, Juergen Prochnow, Julie Carmen, Charlton Heston, David Warner, John Glover, Bernie Casey, Peter Jason, Francis Bay; *D:* John Carpenter; *W:* Michael De Luca; *M:* John Carpenter, Jim Lang. *TTC, NLC*

In the Name of the Father ♂♂♂½
1993 **(R)** Compelling true story of Gerry Conlon and the Guildford Four, illegally imprisoned in 1974 by British officials after a tragic IRA bombing near London. The British judicial system receives a black eye, but so does the horror and cruelty of IRA terrorism. Politics and family life in a prison cell share the focus, as Sheridan captures superior performances from Day-Lewis and Postlethwaite (beware the thick Belfast brogue). Thompson was accused of pro-IRA sympathies in the British press for her role as the lawyer who believed in Conlon's innocence. Adapted from "Proved Innocent," Conlon's prison memoirs; reunites Sheridan and Day-Lewis after "My Left Foot." Includes original songs by U2's Bono, with a haunting theme sung by Sinead O'Connor.*CW:* Language and politically-generated violence. **127m/C VHS, LV, Closed Caption.** *GB IR* Daniel Day-Lewis, Pete Postlethwaite, Emma Thompson, John Lynch, Corin Redgrave, Beatie Edney, John Benfield, Paterson Joseph, Marie Jones, Gerard McSorley, Frank Harper, Mark Sheppard, Don Baker, Britta Smith, Aidan Grennell, Daniel Massey, Bosco Hogan, Daniel Massey; *D:* Jim Sheridan; *W:* Jim Sheridan, Terry George; *C:* Peter Biziou; *M:* Trevor Jones, Bono, Sinead O'Connor. Berlin International Film Festival '94: Golden Berlin Bear; Nominations: Academy Awards '93: Best Actor (Day-Lewis), Best Adapted Screenplay, Best Director (Sheridan), Best Film Editing, Best Picture, Best Supporting Actor (Postlethwaite), Best Supporting Actress (Thompson); British Academy Awards '93: Best Actor (Day-Lewis), Best Adapted Screenplay; Golden Globe Awards '94: Best Actor—Drama (Day-Lewis), Best Film—Drama, Best Song ("(You Made Me) Thief of Your Heart"), Best Supporting Actress (Thompson); Writers Guild of America '93: Best Adapted Screenplay. *USH*

In the Name of the Pope-King ♂♂♂ 1985 An acclaimed historical epic about the politics and warfare raging around the 1867 Italian wars that made the Pope the sole ruler in Rome. In Italian with English subtitles. **115m/C VHS, Beta.** Nino Manfredi, Danilo Mattei, Carmen Scarpitta, Giovannella Grifea, Carlo Bagno; *D:* Luigi Magni. *WBF, TPV, FCT*

In the Navy ♂♂½ *Abbott and Costello in the Navy* 1941 Abbott and Costello join the Navy in one of four military-service comedies they cranked out in 1941 alone. The token narrative involves about a singing star (Powell) in uniform to escape his female fans, but that's just an excuse for classic A & C routines. With the Andrews Sisters. ♫*Starlight, Starbright; You're Off To See The World; Hula Ba Lua; Gimme Some Skin; A Sailor's Life For Me; We're In The Navy; Anchors Aweigh (instrumental); You're A Lucky Fellow, Mr. Smith (instrumental).* **85m/B VHS, LV, Closed Caption.** Lou Costello, Bud Abbott, Dick Powell, The Andrews Sisters; *D:* Arthur Lubin; *C:* Joseph Valentine. *USH*

In the Presence of Mine Enemies ♂♂½ 1997 **(PG-13)** Cable remake of Rod Serling's 1960 script for "Playhouse 90." Rabbi Adam Heller (Mueller-Stahl) and his daughter Rachel (Lowensohn) are living in the Warsaw ghetto in 1942, trying to deal with Nazi oppression. But the Rabbi's faith is put the test when his son Paul (McKellar), who's escaped from the Treblinka labor camp, returns for vengeance and Rachel becomes the sexual victim of a vicious German officer (Dance).*CW:* Thematic elements and some scenes of violence. **100m/C VHS.** Armin Mueller-Stahl, Elina Lowensohn, Don McKellar, Charles Dance, Chad Lowe; *D:* Joan Micklin Silver; *W:* Rod Serling. *EVE*

In the Realm of Passion ♂♂ *Empire of Passion* 1980 **(R)** A wife and her lover murder her husband and dump the body in an abandoned well. Guilt over their actions drive the lovers to return to the scene where they are greeted by the vengeful ghost of the betrayed husband—or is it only their consciences torturing them? In Japanese with English subtitles. **108m/C VHS.** Kazuko Yoshiyuki, Takahiro Tamura, Tatsuya Fuji; *D:* Nagisa Oshima. *FXL*

In the Realm of the Senses ♂♂♂
1976 **(NC-17)** Taboo-breaking story of a woman and man who turn their backs on the militaristic rule of Japan in the mid-1930s by plunging into an erotic and sensual world all their own. Striking, graphic work that was seized by U.S. customs when it first entered the country. Violent with explicit sex, and considered by some critics as pretentious, while others call it Oshima's masterpiece. In Japanese with English subtitles.*CW:* Sexually explicit. **105m/C VHS.** *JP FR* Tatsuya Fuji, Eiko Matsuda, Aio Nakajima, Meika Seri; *D:* Nagisa Oshima. *FXL, CVC*

In the Region of Ice ♂♂♂ 1976 Award-winning short reveals the complexities of the relationship between a nun and a disturbed student. **38m/B VHS, Beta.** Fionnula Flanagan, Peter Lempert; *D:* Peter Werner. *BFA*

In the Secret State ♂♂ 19?? Inspector Strange finds himself faced with the apparent suicide of a colleague on the day of his own retirement from the force. His private investigation into the case finds him mired in murder and espionage. **107m/C VHS.** Frank Finlay, Matthew Marsh, Thorley Walters. *MOV*

In the Shadow of Kilimanjaro woof!
1986 **(R)** A pack of hungry baboons attacks innocent people in the wilderness of Kenya. Based on a true story but the characters are contrived and just plain stupid at times. Quite gory as well. Filmed on location in Kenya. **105m/C VHS, Beta.** *GB* John Rhys-Davies, Timothy Bottoms, Michele Carey, Irene Miracle, Calvin Jung, Donald Blakely; *D:* Raju Patel. *LIV*

In the Soup ♂♂½ 1992 **(R)** Adolpho is a naive New York filmmaker barely scraping by. He decides to sell his script in a classified ad which is answered by the fast-talking Joe, a would-be film producer who's true profession is as a con artist. The two then try numerous (and humorous) ways to raise the money to begin filming. Also available colorized.*CW:* Language. **93m/B VHS, LV, Closed Caption.** Steve Buscemi, Seymour Cassel, Jennifer Beals, Will Patton, Pat Moya, Stanley Tucci, Sully Boyar, Rockets Redglare, Elizabeth Bracco, Ruth Maleczech, Debi Mazar, Steven Randazzo, Francesco Messina; *Cameos:* Jim Jarmusch, Carol Kane; *D:* Alexandre Rockwell; *W:* Tim Kissell, Alexandre Rockwell; *C:* Phil Parmet; *M:* Mader. Sundance Film Festival '92: Grand Jury Prize.*ACA*

In the Spirit ♂♂½ 1990 **(R)** New Age couple move from Beverly Hills to New York, where they meet an air-headed mystic and are forced to hide from a murderer. Falk gives solid performance in sometimes rocky production. Berlin is the real-life daughter of May. **94m/C VHS, Beta.** Elaine May, Marlo Thomas, Jeannie Berlin, Peter Falk, Melanie Griffith, Olympia Dukakis, Chad Burton, Thurn Hoffman, Michael Emil, Christopher Durang, Laurie Jones; *D:*

Sandra Seacat; *W:* Jeannie Berlin, Laurie Jones; *M:* Patrick Williams. *ACA*

In the Steps of a Dead Man ♂♂½
1974 A family grieving for a fallen soldier is earmarked for evil by a young man who bears an uncanny resemblance to the dead man. A friend of the family has her suspicions and must find out the truth before something terrible happens. **71m/C VHS, Beta.** Skye Aubrey, John Nolan. *NO*

In the White City ♂♂♂ *Dans la Ville Blanche* 1983 A sailor jumps ship in Lisbon and uses a movie camera to record himself and his search through the twisted streets and alleys of the city for something or someone to connect to. In French, Portuguese, and German with English subtitles. **108m/C VHS.** *PT SI* Bruno Ganz, Teresa Madruga; *D:* Alain Tanner. *NYF*

In This House of Brede ♂♂♂ 1975
A sophisticated London widow turns her back on her worldly life to become a cloistered Benedictine nun. Rigg is outstanding as the woman struggling to deal with the discipline of faith. Made for television and based on the novel by Rumer Godden. **105m/C VHS, Beta.** Diana Rigg; *D:* George Schaefer. *LCA, OM*

In This Our Life ♂♂½ 1942 Histrionic melodrama handled effectively by Huston about a nutsy woman who steals her sister's husband, rejects him, manipulates her whole family and eventually leads herself to ruin. Vintage star vehicle for Davis, who chews scenery and fellow actors alike. Adapted by Howard Koch from the Ellen Glasgow novel. **101m/B VHS, Beta.** Bette Davis, Olivia de Havilland, Charles Coburn, Frank Craven, George Brent, Dennis (Stanley Morner) Morgan, Billie Burke, Hattie McDaniel, Lee Patrick, Walter Huston, Ernest Anderson; *D:* John Huston; *M:* Max Steiner. *MGM*

In Too Deep ♂½ 1990 **(R)** A rock star and a beautiful woman are physically drawn to one another in spite of the fact that any contact between them could have disastrous results.*CW:* Strong language, some violence, and strong sensuality. **106m/C VHS, Beta.** Hugo Race, Santha Press, Rebekah Elmaloglou, John Flaus, Dominic Sweeney; *D:* Colin South. *PAR*

In Trouble woof! 1967 Hard-to-follow and frequently aimless story of a pregnant girl who invents a fake rape story that her dull-witted brothers take seriously, embarking on a cross-country search for the culprit. **82m/C VHS, Beta.** *CA* Julie LaChapelle, Katherine Mousseau, Daniel Pilon; *D:* Gilles Carle. *NVV*

In Which We Serve ♂♂♂½ 1943
Much stiff upper-lipping in this classic that captures the spirit of the British Navy during WWII. The sinking of the destroyer HMS Torrin during the Battle of Crete is told via flashbacks, with an emphasis on realism that was unusual in wartime flag-wavers. Features the film debuts of Johnson and Attenborough, and the first Lean directorial effort. Coward received a special Oscar for his "outstanding production achievement," having scripted, scored, codirected and costarred. **114m/B VHS, Beta.** *GB* Noel Coward, John Mills, Bernard Miles, Celia Johnson, Kay Walsh, James Donald, Richard Attenborough; *D:* Noel Coward, David Lean; *W:* Noel Coward; *M:* Noel Coward. National Board of Review Awards '42: 10 Best Films of the Year; New York Film Critics Awards '42: Best Film; Nominations: Academy Awards '43: Best Original Screenplay, Best Picture. *NOS*

In Your Face ♂½ *Abar, the First Black Superman* 1977 **(R)** Little known blaxploitation film about a black family harrassed in a white suburb. A black motorcycle gang comes to their rescue. **90m/C VHS.** J. Walter Smith, Tobar Mayo, Roxie Young, Tina James; *D:* Frank Packard. *XVC, HHE*

The Incident ♂♂½ 1967 A gritty, controversial (at-the-time) drama about two abusive thugs who take over a New York subway car late at night, humiliating and terrorizing each passenger in turn. Film debut for Sheen and Musante as the thugs. **99m/B VHS, Beta, LV.** Martin Sheen, Tony

Musante, Beau Bridges, Ruby Dee, Jack Gilford, Thelma Ritter, Brock Peters, Ed McMahon, Gary Merrill, Donna Mills, Jan Sterling, Mike Kellin, Bob Bannard, Diana Van Der Vlis, Victor Arnold, Robert Fields; **D:** Larry Peerce; **W:** Charles Fox, Nicholas E. Baehr; **M:** Charles Fox. *FOX*

The Incident 🐾🐾🐾 1989 Political thriller set during WWII in Lincoln Bluff, Colorado. Matthau is excellent in his TV debut as a small-town lawyer who must defend a German prisoner of war accused of murder at nearby Camp Bremen. An all-star cast lends powerful performances to this riveting made for TV drama. **95m/C VHS, Closed Caption.** Walter Matthau, Susan Blakely, Harry (Henry) Morgan, Robert Carradine, Barnard Hughes, Peter Firth, William Schallert; **D:** Joseph Sargent. *CAF*

Incident at Channel Q 🐾½ 1986 A heavy-metal rock musical about a suburban neighborhood declaring war on a chain-and-leather deejay. **85m/C VHS, Beta, LV.** Al Corley. *MVD, BMG*

Incident at Deception Ridge 🐾🐾½ 1994 (R) After five years in prison, Jack Bolder (O'Keefe) is finally a free man, and headed for Seattle by bus. Unfortunately, also aboard is weasely bank manager Jack Davis (Begley, Jr.) who's bolted with the ransom money for his kidnapped wife, Helen (Purl). Now Helen is left at the mercy of her kidnappers, who've discovered where their money is and decide to go after it—no matter who gets in their way. Filmed in Vancouver, British Columbia. Made for cable.**CW:** Some violence. **94m/C VHS, LV, Closed Caption.** Michael O'Keefe, Ed Begley Jr., Linda Purl, Miguel Ferrer, Colleen Flynn, Michelle Johnson, Ian Tracey; **D:** John McPherson, John McPherson; **W:** Ken Hixon, Randy Kornfield; **C:** David Geddes. *USH*

Incident at Oglala: The Leonard Peltier Story 🐾🐾🐾 1992 (PG) Offers a detailed account of the violent events leading to the murder of two FBI agents in Oglala, South Dakota in 1975. American Indian activist Leonard Peltier was convicted of the murders and is presently serving two consecutive life sentences, but he's cited as a political prisoner by Amnesty International. The documentary examines the highly controversial trial and the tensions between the government and the Oglala Nation stemming back to the Indian occupation of Wounded Knee in 1973. Director Apted is sympathetic to Peltier and offers reasons why he should be allowed a retrial; he examined similar incidents in his film "Thunderheart." **90m/C VHS. D:** Michael Apted; **M:** John Trudell, Jackson Browne. *LIV, FCT*

An Inconvenient Woman 🐾🐾 1991 When an older married man has an affair with a young seductress, there's suicide, murder, a nasty gossip columnist, a reporter, a knowing society wife, and a lot of cover-ups among the rich and famous. From the novel by Dominick Dunne and based on the Alfred Bloomingdale scandal. Originally a made for television mini-series. **126m/C VHS, Beta, Closed Caption.** Rebecca DeMornay, Jason Robards Jr., Jill Eikenberry, Peter Gallagher, Roddy McDowall, Chad Lowe. *ABC, PSM*

The Incredible Hulk 🐾🐾½ 1977 Bixby is a scientist who achieves superhuman strength after he is exposed to a massive dose of gamma rays. But his personal life suffers, as does his wardrobe. Ferrigno is the Hulkster. The pilot for the television series is based on the Marvel Comics character. **94m/C VHS, Beta.** Bill Bixby, Susan Sullivan, Lou Ferrigno, Jack Colvin; **D:** Kenneth Johnson. *USH*

The Incredible Hulk Returns 🐾½ 1988 The beefy green mutant is back and this time he wages war against a Viking named Thor. Very little substance in this made for television flick, so be prepared to park your brain at the door. Followed by "The Trial of the Incredible Hulk." **100m/C VHS, LV.** Bill Bixby, Lou Ferrigno, Jack Colvin, Lee Purcell, Charles Napier, Steve Levitt; **D:** Nick Corea. *VTR, NWV*

The Incredible Journey 🐾🐾½ 1963 A labrador retriever, bull terrier and Siamese cat mistake their caretaker's intentions when he leaves for a hunting trip, believing he will never return. The three set out on a 250 mile adventure-filled trek across Canada's rugged terrain. Entertaining family adventure from Disney taken from Sheila Burnford's book. **80m/C VHS, Beta, LV. D:** Fletcher Markle. *DIS*

The Incredible Journey of Dr. Meg Laurel 🐾🐾🐾 1979 A young doctor returns to her roots to bring modern medicine to the Appalachian mountain people during the 1930's. Made for television featuring Wagner in a strong performance. **143m/C VHS, Beta.** Lindsay Wagner; Jane Wyman, Dorothy McGuire, James Woods, Gary Lockwood; **D:** Guy Green. *COL*

Incredible Master Beggars 🐾🐾 1982 (R) Against all odds, the Beggars challenge the Great Iron Master, using "Tam Leg" tactics versus the "Iron Cloth" fighting style. **88m/C VHS, Beta.** Tan Tao Liang, Ku Feng, Han Kuo Tsai, Li Tang Ming, Li Hai Sheng, Lui I. Fan, Pan Yao Kun. *GEM*

Incredible Melting Man woof! 1977 (R) Two transformations change an astronaut's life after his return to earth. First, his skin starts to melt, then he displays cannibalistic tendencies. Hard to swallow. Special effects by Rick Baker. Look for director Jonathan Demme in a bit part. **85m/C VHS, Beta.** Alex Rebar, Burr de Benning, Cheryl "Rainbeaux" Smith; **D:** William Sachs. *LIV, VES*

The Incredible Mr. Limpet 🐾🐾 1964 Limp comedy about a nebbish bookkeeper who's transformed into a fish, fulfilling his aquatic dreams. Eventually he falls in love with another fish, and helps the U.S. Navy find Nazi subs during WWII. Partially animated, beloved by some, particularly those under the age of seven. Based on Theodore Pratt's novel. **99m/C VHS, Beta, LV, Closed Caption.** Don Knotts, Jack Weston, Carole Cook, Andrew Duggan, Larry Keating, Elizabeth McRae; **D:** Arthur Lubin; **W:** Jameson Brewer. *WAR*

The Incredible Petrified World woof! 1958 Divers are trapped in an underwater cave when volcanic eruptions begin. Suffocating nonsense. **78m/B VHS.** John Carradine, Allen Windsor, Phyllis Coates, Lloyd Nelson, George Skaff; **D:** Jerry Warren. *NOS, SNC*

The Incredible Rocky Mountain Race 🐾🐾 1977 The townspeople of St. Joseph, fed up with Mark Twain's destructive feud with a neighbor, devise a shrewd scheme to rid the town of the troublemakers by sending them on a road race through the West. Made for television comedy starring the F-Troop. **97m/C VHS, Beta.** Christopher Connelly, Forrest Tucker, Larry Storch, Mike Mazurki; **D:** James L. Conway. *VTR*

The Incredible Sarah 🐾🐾 1976 (PG) A limp adapted stage biography from "Reader's Digest" of the great actress Sarah Bernhardt. Jackson chews scenery to no avail. **105m/C VHS, Beta, LV.** Glenda Jackson, Daniel Massey, Yvonne Mitchell, Douglas Wilmer; **D:** Richard Fleischer; **M:** Elmer Bernstein. Nominations: Academy Awards '76: Best Art Direction/Set Decoration, Best Costume Design.*IME*

The Incredible Shrinking Man 🐾🐾🐾½ 1957 Adapted by Richard Matheson from his own novel, the sci-fi classic is a philosophical thriller about a man who is doused with radioactive mist and begins to slowly shrink. His new size means that everyday objects take on sinister meaning and he must fight for his life in an increasingly hostile, absurd environment. A surreal, suspenseful allegory with impressive special effects. Endowed with the tension usually reserved for Hitchcock films. **81m/B VHS, Beta, LV.** Grant Williams, Randy Stuart, April Kent, Paul Langton, Raymond Bailey; **D:** Jack Arnold; **W:** Richard Matheson. *USH, MLB*

The Incredible Shrinking Woman 🐾🐾½ 1981 (PG) "...Shrinking Man" spoof and inoffensive social satire finds household cleaners producing some strange side effects on model homemaker Tomlin, slowly shrinking her to doll-house size. She then encounters everyday happenings as big tasks and not so menial. Her advertising exec husband has a hand in the down-sizing. Sight gags abound but the cuteness wears thin by the end. **89m/C VHS, Beta, LV.** Lily Tomlin, Charles Grodin, Ned Beatty, Henry Gibson; **D:** Joel Schumacher; **W:** Jane Wagner. *USH*

The Incredible Two-Headed Transplant woof! 1971 (PG) Mad scientist Dern has a criminal head transplanted on to the shoulder of big John Bloom and the critter runs amuck. Low-budget special effects guaranteed to give you a headache or two. Watch for onetime Pat "Marilyn Munster" Priest in a bikini. **88m/C VHS.** Bruce Dern, Pat Priest, Casey Kasem, Albert Cole, John Bloom, Berry Kroeger; **D:** Anthony M. Lanza; **M:** John Barber. *NO*

Incredibly Strange Creatures Who Stopped Living and Became Mixed-Up Zombies woof! *The Teenage Psycho Meets Bloody Mary; The Incredibly Strange Creatures* 1963 The infamous, super-cheap horror spoof that established Sheckler (for whom Cash Flagg is a pseudonym), about a carny side show riddled with ghouls and bad rock bands. Assistant cinematographers include the young Laszlo Kovacs and Vilmos Zsigmond. A must-see for connoisseurs of cult and camp. **90m/C VHS, Beta.** Cash Flagg, Carolyn Brandt, Brett O'Hara, Atlas King, Sharon Walsh; **D:** Ray Dennis Steckler. *NO*

The Incredibly True Adventure of Two Girls in Love 🐾🐾½ 1995 (R) Gentle low-budget romantic comedy about first love between two high school girls. Tomboyish working-class Randy (Holloman) lives with her lesbian aunt and works part-time at the local gas station where she spots the rich and beautiful Evie (Parker), one of the popular girls in school. Some sparks fly but Evie's confused, though she's willing to be wooed and, later, defend her new relationship. The issue of race (Randy's white, Evie's black) is only briefly alluded to—more is made of the differences between the girls' social classes and their vulnerability. Directorial debut for Maggenti.**CW:** Strong sex scene involving teen girls; language; some drug use. **95m/C VHS.** Laurel Holloman, Nicole Parker, Kate Stafford, Stephanie Berry; **D:** Maria Maggenti; **W:** Maria Maggenti. *NLC*

Incubus woof! 1982 (R) A doctor and his teenaged daughter settle in a quiet New England community, only to encounter the incubus, a terrifying, supernatural demon who enjoys sex murders. Offensive trash. **90m/C VHS, Beta, LV.** CA John Cassavetes, Kerrie Keane, Helen Hughes, Erin Flannery, John Ireland; **D:** John Hough; **C:** Conrad Hall. *VES*

Indecency 🐾🐾 1992 (PG-13) Ellie (Beals) is still recovering from a mental breakdown when she goes to work for Marie (Clarkson) at her ad agency. There Ellie must deal with manipulative associate Nia (Davis) and Marie's charming, estranged husband Mick (Remar), who draws the fragile Ellie into an affair. Then Marie commits suicide—or maybe it was murder.**CW:** Violence and sensual scenes. **88m/C VHS, LV, Closed Caption.** Jennifer Beals, James Remar, Sammi Davis, Barbara Williams, Christopher John Fields, Ray McKinnon; **D:** Marisa Silver; **W:** Amy Holden Jones, Holly Goldberg Sloan, Alan Ormsby. *USH*

Indecent Behavior 🐾🐾 1993 (R) Tweed is a sex therapist who's accused of murder when one of her clients overdose's on the latest designer drug. Hudson, who plays the genre's hard-boiled cop figure, gets very personally involved investigating the allegations, which really upsets Tweed's hubby, Vincent. Also available in an unrated version.**CW:** Strong language, some violence, and strong sexuality. **93m/C VHS.** Shannon

Tweed, Gary Hudson, Jan-Michael Vincent, Michelle Moffett, Lawrence-Hilton Jacobs, Penny Peyser; **D:** Lawrence Lanoff. *AVE*

Indecent Behavior 2 🎞½ 1994 (R) Sex
therapist Rebecca is targeted for blackmail as she finds out all sorts of unhealthy things about her patients. Meanwhile, she's practicing her technique with a fellow therapist. Also available unrated.**CW:** Strong sexuality; violence; language. **96m/C VHS.** Shannon Tweed, James Brolin, Chad McQueen, Elizabeth Sandifer, Craig Stepp, Rochelle Swanson; **D:** Carlo Gustaff. *AVE*

Indecent Behavior 3 🎞 1995 (R) Sex
therapist becomes the obsessed object of desire for a decidedly deadly client. Also available unrated.**CW:** Strong sexuality, and for language and violence. **90m/C VHS.** Shannon Tweed, Sam Hennings, Colleen Coffey, Doug Jeffrey, Beau Billingslea, Laura Rogers; **D:** Kelley Cauthen; **W:** Hel Styverson. *AVE*

An Indecent Obsession 🎞🎞½ 1985
Colleen McCullough's bestseller about WWII Australian soldiers recuperating in a field hospital mental ward. Hughes plays the nurse everyone's in love with. **100m/C VHS, Beta.** *AU* Wendy Hughes, Gary Sweet, Richard Moir, Jonathan Hyde, Bill Hunter, Bruno Lawrence; **D:** Lex Marinos; **W:** Denise Morgan. *NO*

Indecent Proposal 🎞🎞½ 1993 (R) High-
gloss movie that had couples everywhere discussing the big question: Would you let your wife sleep with a billionaire in exchange for a million bucks? Probably, if all were as goodlooking as the weathered, yet ever gorgeous Redford. Moore and Harrelson are the financially down on their luck, but happy, couple who venture to Vegas on a last-ditch gambling effort. Surreally slick direction from Lyne, but an ultimately empty film that explores the values of marriage in a terribly angst-ridden fashion. Based on the novel by Jack Engelhard. Proof that average movies can make a killing at the box office, landing in sixth place for 1993.**CW:** Language and sexuality. **119m/C VHS, Beta, CD-I, Closed Caption.** Robert Redford, Demi Moore, Woody Harrelson, Seymour Cassel, Oliver Platt, Billy Bob Thornton, Rip Taylor, Billy Connolly, Joel Brooks; *Cameos:* Sheena Easton, Herbie Hancock; **D:** Adrian Lyne; **W:** Amy Holden Jones; **C:** Howard Atherton; **M:** John Barry. MTV Movie Awards '94: Best Kiss (Demi Moore/Woody Harrelson); Golden Raspberry Awards '93: Worst Picture, Worst Supporting Actor (Harrelson), Worst Screenplay; Nominations: MTV Movie Awards '94: Best Actress (Moore), Most Desirable Female (Moore). *PAR*

Independence Day 🎞🎞 *Follow Your*
Dreams 1983 (R) Uneven romantic drama about a small-town photographer, yearning for the big city, who falls in love with a racing car enthusiast, whose sister is a battered wife. Strong cast, particularly Wiest as the abused wife, is left occasionally stranded by a script reaching too hard for social significance. **110m/C VHS, Beta.** Kathleen Quinlan, David Keith, Frances Sternhagen, Dianne Wiest, Cliff DeYoung, Richard Farnsworth, Josef Sommer, Cheryl "Rainbeaux" Smith; **D:** Robert Mandel; **M:** Charles Bernstein. *WAR, CCB*

Independence Day 🎞🎞🎞 1996 (PG-13)
The biggest of the new wave of disaster flicks paying tribute to the Irwin Allen celebrity-fests of the '70s finds an alien armada descending on Earth to create some fireworks on the July 4th weekend. The fate of the world rests in the hands of an unlikely band of Earthlings led by President Whitmore (Pullman), a computer expert (Goldblum), and a Marine fighter pilot (Smith). Special effects, despite forgoing some of the more expensive newer technology, don't disappoint. Strong (if not A-list) cast and plenty of action. Devlin and Emmerich wrote the script while promoting "Stargate," after a reporter asked Emmerich if he believed in aliens.**CW:** Sci-fi destruction and violence. **135m/C VHS, Closed Caption.** Bill Pullman, Will Smith, Jeff Goldblum, Judd Hirsch, Margaret Colin, Randy Quaid, Mary McDonnell, Robert Loggia, Brent Spiner, James Rebhorn, Vivica A. Fox, James Duval, Harry Connick Jr., Harvey Fierstein; **D:** Roland Emmerich; **W:** Dean Devlin,

Roland Emmerich; **C:** Karl Walter Lindenlaub; **M:** David Arnold. Academy Awards '96: Best Visual Effects; MTV Movie Awards '97: Best Kiss (Vivica A. Fox/Will Smith); Nominations: Academy Awards '96: Best Sound; MTV Movie Awards '97: Best Film, Best Male Performance (Smith), Breakthrough Performance (Fox), Best Action Sequence. *FXV*

The Indestructible Man 🎞 1956 Chaney, electrocuted for murder and bank robbery, is brought back to life by a scientist. Naturally, he seeks revenge on those who sentenced him to death. Chaney does the best he can with the material. **70m/B VHS.** Lon Chaney Jr., Marian Carr, Max Casey Adams Showalter; **D:** Jack Pollexfen. *NOS, MRV, SNC*

The Indian Fighter 🎞🎞🎞 1955 Exciting
actioner has Douglas as a scout hired to lead a wagon train to Oregon in 1870. The train must past through dangerous Sioux territory and Douglas tries to make peace with the Sioux leader but a secret Indian gold mine and romance cause friction and keep things lively. **88m/C VHS.** Kirk Douglas, Elsa Martinelli, Walter Abel, Walter Matthau, Diana Douglas, Lon Chaney Jr., Eduard Franz, Alan Hale Jr., Elisha Cook Jr., Harry Landers; **D:** Andre de Toth; **W:** Ben Hecht. *MGM*

The Indian in the Cupboard 🎞🎞½
1995 (PG) On his ninth birthday, Omri receives a three-inch plastic indian named Little Bear and an old wooden medicine cabinet. (Guess they were out of Power Rangers.) When placed in the cabinet, Little Bear magically comes to life, taking Omri on adventures and teaching him important lessons. Blue screen techniques allow them appear together on-screen although they were actually shot together only once. Based on the bestselling children's book by Lynne Reid Banks. **97m/C VHS, LV, 8mm, Closed Caption.** Hal Scardino, Litefoot, Lindsay Crouse, Richard Jenkins, Rishi Bhat; **D:** Frank Oz; **W:** Melissa Mathison; **C:** Russell Carpenter; **M:** Miles Goodman. *COL*

Indian Paint 🎞🎞 1964 A pleasant children's film about an Indian boy's love for his horse and his rite of passage. Silverheels was Tonto on television's "The Lone Ranger," while Crawford was the "Rifleman's" son. **90m/C VHS, Beta.** Jay Silverheels, Johnny Crawford, Pat Hogan, Robert Crawford Jr., George Lewis; **D:** Norman Foster. *NO*

The Indian Runner 🎞🎞 1991 (R) In
Penn's debut as a writer-director, he brings us the story of two brothers in Nebraska during the late '60s, who are forced to change their lives with the loss of their family farm. Joe is a good cop and family man who can't deal with the rage of his brother Frank, who has just returned from Vietnam and is turning to a life of crime. Penn does a decent job of representing the struggle between the responsible versus the rebellious side of human nature. Based on the song "Highway Patrolman" by Bruce Springsteen.**CW:** Language and violence and drug use. **127m/C VHS, LV, Closed Caption.** David Morse, Viggo Mortensen, Sandy Dennis, Charles Bronson, Valeria Golino, Patricia Arquette, Dennis Hopper; **D:** Sean Penn; **W:** Sean Penn. *MGM*

The Indian Scarf 🎞🎞 1963 Heirs to a
dead man's fortune are being strangled one by one at the benefactor's country estate. An Edgar Wallace suspense tale. **85m/C VHS.** *GE* Heinz Drache, Gisela Uhlen, Klaus Kinski; **D:** Alfred Vohrer. *SNC*

Indian Summer 🎞🎞 1993 (PG-13) Yet another addition to the growing 30-something nostalgia genre. Delete the big house, add a crusty camp director (Arkin), change the characters' names (but not necessarily their lives) and you feel like you're experiencing deja vu. This time seven friends and the requisite outsider reconvene at Camp Tamakwa, the real-life summer camp to writer/director Binder. The former campers talk. They yearn. They save Camp Tamakwa and experience personal growth. A must see for those who appreciate listening to situational jokes that are followed by "I guess you had to be there."**CW:** Some language, some drug content,

and some sensuality. **108m/C VHS, Beta, LV, Closed Caption.** Alan Arkin, Matt Craven, Diane Lane, Bill Paxton, Elizabeth Perkins, Kevin Pollak, Sam Raimi, Vincent Spano, Julie Warner, Kimberly Williams, Richard Chevolleau; **D:** Mike Binder; **W:** Mike Binder; **M:** Miles Goodman. *TOU, FCT*

Indian Uprising 🎞🎞 1951 An army captain tries to keep local settlers from causing trouble with Geronimo and his people when gold is discovered on their territory. **75m/C VHS, Beta.** George Montgomery, Audrey Long, Carl Benton Reid, John Baer, Joseph Sawyer; **D:** Ray Nazarro. *GKK*

Indiana Jones and the Last
Crusade 🎞🎞🎞 1989 (PG) In this, the third and last (?) Indiana Jones adventure, the fearless archaeologist is once again up against the Nazis in a race to find the Holy Grail. Connery is perfectly cast as Indy's father; opening sequence features Phoenix as a teenage Indy and explains his fear of snakes and the origins of the infamous fedora. Returns to the look and feel of the original with more adventures, exotic places, dastardly villains, and daring escapes than ever before; a must for Indy fans. **126m/C VHS, Beta, LV, 8mm, Closed Caption.** Harrison Ford, Sean Connery, Denholm Elliott, Alison Doody, Julian Glover, John Rhys-Davies, River Phoenix, Michael Byrne, Alex Hyde-White; **D:** Steven Spielberg; **W:** Jeffrey Boam; **M:** John Williams. Nominations: Academy Awards '89: Best Sound, Best Original Score. *PAR, TLF*

Indiana Jones and the Temple of
Doom 🎞🎞🎞 1984 (PG) Daredevil archaeologist Indiana Jones is back. This time he's on the trail of the legendary Ankara Stone and a ruthless cult that has enslaved hundreds of children. More gore and violence than the original; Capshaw's whining character is an irritant, lacking the fresh quality that Karen Allen added to the original. Enough action for ten movies, special effects galore, and the usual booming Williams score make it a cinematic roller coaster ride, but with less regard for plot and pacing than the original. Though second in the series, it's actually a prequel to "Raiders of the Lost Ark." Followed by "Indiana Jones and the Last Crusade." **118m/C VHS, Beta, LV, 8mm, Closed Caption.** Harrison Ford, Kate Capshaw, Ke Huy Quan, Amrish Puri; **D:** Steven Spielberg; **W:** Willard Huyck; **M:** John Williams. Academy Awards '84: Best Visual Effects; Nominations: Academy Awards '84: Best Original Score. *PAR, APD*

Indictment: The McMartin
Trial 🎞🎞🎞 1995 (R) Woods stars as attorney Danny Davis, who has the unenviable task of providing a defense in the notorious McMartin child molestation trial. In 1983, Manhattan Beach, California was rocked by reports that some 60 preschoolers had been abused at a day-care center. Seven defendants were accused thanks to lurid videotaped interviews with the children. The trial lasted six years (the longest and most expensive on record) and all charges were eventually dismissed. It's clear from this telepic that public hysteria and media hype lead to a grave miscarriage of justice that put the legal system on trial as well.**CW:** Nudity; strong language. **132m/C VHS, LV, Closed Caption.** James Woods, Henry Thomas, Mercedes Ruehl, Shirley Knight, Sada Thompson, Mark Blum, Alison Elliott, Chelsea Field, Richard Bradford, Lolita Davidovich; **D:** Mick Jackson; **W:** Abby Mann, Myra Mann; **C:** Rodrigo Garcia; **M:** Peter Melnick. *HBO*

Indio 🎞 1990 (R) A Marine-trained half-breed
takes it on himself to save the Amazon rain forest. Not a peaceful demonstrator, his tactics are violent ones. **94m/C VHS, Beta, LV, Closed Caption.** Marvin Hagler, Francesco Quinn, Brian Dennehy; **D:** Anthony (Antonio Margheriti) Dawson. *MED, VTR*

Indio 2: The Revolt 🎞 1992 (R) Greedy
developers are cutting a highway into the Amazon jungle, destroying everything in their path. All is not lost though, because U.S. Marine Sgt. Iron is on top of things, continuing his struggle to unite the Amazon tribes and save the rainforest, no matter what it takes.**CW:** Language and violence.

104m/C VHS. Marvin Hagler, Charles Napier; **M:** Pino Donaggio. *LIV*

Indiscreet ♫♫½ **1931** Empty-headed romantic comedy about a fashion designer whose past catches up with her when her ex-lover starts romancing her sister. No relation to the classic 1958 film with Cary Grant and Ingrid Bergman. ♫Come To Me; If You Haven't Got Love. **81m/B VHS, Beta.** Gloria Swanson, Ben Lyon, Barbara Kent; **D:** Leo McCarey. *NOS, MRV, REP*

Indiscreet ♫♫♫ **1958** A charming American diplomat in London falls in love with a stunning actress, but protects himself by saying he is married. Needless to say, she finds out. Stylish romp with Grant and Bergman at their sophisticated best. Adapted by Norman Krasna from his stage play "Kind Sir." **100m/C VHS, Closed Caption.** Cary Grant, Ingrid Bergman, Phyllis Calvert; **D:** Stanley Donen; **C:** Frederick A. (Freddie) Young; **M:** Richard Rodney Bennett. *REP, MLB*

Indiscreet ♫♫½ **1988 (PG)** Indistinctive made for TV rehash of the charming 1958 Grant/Bergman romantic comedy in which a suave American falls for an English actress. Both versions derive from the play "Kind Sir" by Norman Krasna, but this one suffers by comparison. **94m/C VHS, Closed Caption.** Robert Wagner, Lesley-Anne Down, Maggie Henderson, Robert McBain, Jeni Barnett; **D:** Richard Michaels. *REP*

Indiscretion of an American Wife ♫♫ *Indiscretion; Terminus Station; Terminal Station Indiscretion* **1954** Set almost entirely in Rome's famous Terminal Station, where an ill-fated couple say goodbye endlessly while the woman tries to decide whether to join her husband in the States. Trimmed down from 87 minutes upon U.S. release. **63m/C VHS, Beta.** *IT* Jennifer Jones, Montgomery Clift, Richard Beymer; **D:** Vittorio De Sica; **W:** Truman Capote; **C:** Oswald Morris. Nominations: Academy Awards '54: Best Costume Design (B & W). *NOS, FOX, HEG*

Indochine ♫♫♫ **1992 (PG-13)** Soapy melodrama follows the fortunes of Eliane (Deneuve), a Frenchwoman born and reared in Indochina, from 1930 to the communist revolution 25 years later. She contends with the changes to her country as well as her adopted daughter as she grows up and becomes independent. Deneuve's controlled performance (and unchanging beauty) is eminently watchable. Filmed on location in Vietnam with breathtaking cinematography by Francois Catonne. In French with English subtitles. *CW:* Some violence/drug-related scenes and some sensuality. **155m/C VHS, LV, 8mm, Closed Caption.** *FR* Catherine Deneuve, Linh Dan Pham, Vincent Perez, Jean Yanne, Dominique Blanc, Henri Marteau, Carlo Brandt, Gerard Lartigau; **D:** Regis Wargnier; **W:** Erik Orsenna, Louis Gardel, Catherine Cohen, Regis Wargnier; **C:** Francois Catonne; **M:** Patrick Doyle. Academy Awards '92: Best Foreign Language Film; Cesar Awards '93: Best Actress (Deneuve), Best Art Direction/Set Decoration, Best Cinematography, Best Sound, Best Supporting Actress (Blanc); Golden Globe Awards '93: Best Foreign Film; National Board of Review Awards '92: Best Foreign Film; Nominations: Academy Awards '92: Best Actress (Deneuve); British Academy Awards '93: Best Foreign Film. *COL, FCT, BTV*

Indomitable Teddy Roosevelt ♫♫½ **1983** Entertaining mix of newsreel footage and staged scenes traces the career of the feisty president. **93m/C VHS, Beta. D:** Harrison Engle. *PSM, CHF*

Infamous Crimes ♫♫ *Philo Vance Returns* **1947** Philo investigates the murders of a playboy and his girlfriends. One of the last of the series whose character was based on the S.S. Van Dine stories. **64m/B VHS, Beta, 8mm.** William Wright, Terry Austin, Leon Belasco, Clara Blandick, Iris Adrian, Frank Wilcox; **D:** William Beaudine. *VYY*

Infernal Trio ♫♫½ **1974** An attorney comes up with a plan involving two sisters (who are his lovers) which will make them both wealthy; but it will also make them both murderers. Sophisticated black comedy based on a true story. In French with English subtitles or dubbed. **100m/C**
VHS. *FR IT* Romy Schneider, Michel Piccoli, Mascha Gonska; **D:** Francois Girod. *CVC*

Inferno ♫♫ **1978 (R)** Uneven occult horror tale about a young man who arrives in New York to investigate the mysterious circumstances surrounding his sister's death. Dubbed. **83m/C VHS, Beta.** *IT* Leigh McCloskey, Elenora Giorgi, Irene Miracle, Sacha Pitoeff; **D:** Dario Argento; **W:** Dario Argento; **M:** Keith Emerson. *FOX*

Inferno in Paradise ♫ **1988** Mucho macho firefighter and bimbous gal pal photographer get hot while trailing a murderous pyromaniac. More like purgatory in the living room (that is, unless you thought Forsyth's earlier "Chesty Anderson, US Navy" was divine comedy). **115m/C VHS.** Richard Young, Betty Ann Carr, Jim Davis, Andy Jarrell, Dennis Chun; **D:** Ed Forsyth. *ACA*

The Infiltrator ♫♫½ **1995 (R)** Based on the true story of Yaron Svoray (Platt), an Israeli journalist and the son of Holocaust survivors, whose latest assignment is to go to Berlin and investigate the rising Neo-Nazi movement. Eventually, Svoray manages to meet leaders of the Nationalist Front and then finds himself enmeshed in a worldwide political network. Based on the book "In Hitler's Shadow" by Yaron Svoray and Nick Taylor. Made for cable TV. *CW:* Violence, strong language, some sexuality. **102m/C VHS.** Oliver Platt, Arliss Howard, Peter Riegert, Alan King, Tony Haygarth, Michael Byrne, Julian Glover, Alex Kingston; **D:** John MacKenzie; **W:** Guy Andrews; **M:** Hal Lindes. *HBO*

Infinity ♫♫½ **1996 (PG)** Based on memoirs covering the early years of Nobel Prize-winning physicist Richard Feynman (Broderick) and his romance with aspiring artist Arline Greenbaum (Arquette). They marry despite the fact that Arline is diagnosed with tuberculosis, at this time in the thirties, a contagious and incurable disease. Richard's recruited to work on the Manhattan Project at Los Alamos, New Mexico and the narrative travels between his scientific endeavors and Arline's worsening illness in an Albuquerque hospital. Problem is it's neither a character study or a love story but a weak combo. Directing debut of Broderick; screenplay is written by his mother. **119m/C VHS.** Matthew Broderick, Patricia Arquette, James LeGros, Peter Riegert, Dori Brenner, Peter Michael Goetz, Zeljko Ivanek; **D:** Matthew Broderick; **W:** Patricia Broderick; **C:** Toyomichi Kurita; **M:** Bruce Broughton. *BMG*

The Informer ♫♫½ **1929** Hanson wants to flee Ireland's poverty for America, using the reward money he gets for turning in an IRA comrade. But things don't turn out as planned and instead he's haunted by the guilt of his betrayal. Based on the novel by Liam O'Flaherty and filmed to much greater effect by John Ford in 1935. **83m/B VHS.** *GB* Lars Hanson, Lya de Putti, Warwick Ward, Dennis Wynham; **D:** Arthur Robison; **W:** Benn W. Levy, Rolfe E. Vanlo. *GPV*

The Informer ♫♫♫♫ **1935** Based on Liam O'Flaherty's novel about the Irish Sinn Fein Rebellion of 1922, it tells the story of a hard-drinking Dublin man (McLaglen) who informs on a friend (a member of the Irish Republican Army) in order to collect a 20-pound reward. When his "friend" is killed during capture, he goes on a drinking spree instead of using the money, as planned, for passage to America. Director Ford allowed McLaglen to improvise his lines during the trial scene in order to enhance the realism, leading to excruciating suspense. Wonderful score. **91m/B VHS, Beta, LV.** Victor McLaglen, Heather Angel, Wallace Ford, Margot Grahame, Joseph Sawyer, Preston Foster, Una O'Connor, J.M. Kerrigan, Donald Meek; **D:** John Ford; **W:** Dudley Nichols; **M:** Max Steiner. Academy Awards '35: Best Actor (McLaglen), Best Director (Ford), Best Screenplay, Best Original Score; National Board of Review Awards '35: 10 Best Films of the Year; New York Film Critics Awards '35: Best Director (Ford), Best Film; Nominations: Academy Awards '35: Best Film Editing, Best Picture. *MED, BTV, TTC*

Infra-Man woof! *The Super Inframan; The Infra Superman* **1976 (PG)** If you're looking for a truly bad, hokey flick, this could be it. Infra-man is a superhero who must rescue the galaxy from the clutches of the evil Princess Dragon Mom and her army of prehistoric monsters. Outlandish dialogue (delivered straight) combines with horrible special effects and costumes to create what may well be one of the best camp classics to date. Poorly dubbed in English. **92m/C VHS, Beta.** *HK* Li Hsiu-hsien, Wang Hsieh, Yuan Man-tzu, Terry Liu, Tsen Shu-yi, Huang Chien-lung, Lu Sheng; **D:** Hua-Shan; **W:** Peter Fernandez. *PSM*

Inherit the Wind ♫♫♫½ **1960** Powerful courtroom drama, based on the Broadway play, is actually a fictionalized version of the infamous Scopes "Monkey Trial" of 1925. Tracy is the defense attorney for the schoolteacher on trial for teaching Darwin's Theory of Evolution to a group of students in a small town ruled by religion. March is the prosecutor seeking to put the teacher behind bars and restore religion to the schools. **128m/B VHS, Beta, LV.** Spencer Tracy, Fredric March, Florence Eldridge, Gene Kelly, Dick York; **D:** Stanley Kramer; **W:** Nedrick Young, Harold Jacob Smith; **C:** Ernest Laszlo; **M:** Ernest Gold. Berlin International Film Festival '60: Best Actor (March); National Board of Review Awards '60: 10 Best Films of the Year; Nominations: Academy Awards '60: Best Actor (Tracy), Best Adapted Screenplay, Best Black and White Cinematography, Best Film Editing. *FOX, FCT*

Inheritance ♫♫♫ *Uncle Silas* **1947** Victorian-era melodrama of a young heiress endangered by her guradian, who plots to murder his charge for her inheritance. Chilling and moody story based on a novel by Sheridan Le Fanu. **103m/B VHS, Beta.** *GB* Jean Simmons, Katina Paxinou, Derrick DeMarney, Derek Bond; **D:** Charles Frank. *DVT*

The Inheritance ♫♫½ *L'Eredita Ferramonti* **1976 (R)** Wealthy partiarch becomes sexually involved with scheming daughter-in-law. Tawdry tale is nonetheless engaging. **121m/C VHS, Beta.** *IT* Anthony Quinn, Fabio Testi, Dominique Sanda; **D:** Mauro Bolognini; **M:** Ennio Morricone. Cannes Film Festival '76: Best Actress (Sanda). *NO*

The Inheritor ♫♫ **1990 (R)** Set in a small New England town, this mystery centers on the death of a young woman and her sister's attempts to uncover the murderer. The local celebrity, a writer, seems to be at the heart of the mystery and the sister finds herself growing interested. Keeps you guessing. **83m/C VHS.** Dan Haggerty; **D:** Brian Savegar. *NO*

The Inheritors ♫♫½ **1985** Not-too-subtle tale of a young German boy who becomes involved with a Nazi youth group as his home life deteriorates. Heavy-going anti-fascism creates more message than entertainment. In German with English subtitles or dubbed. **89m/C VHS, Beta.** *GE* Nikolas Vogel, Roger Schauer, Klaus Novak, Johanna Tomek; **D:** Walter Bannert; **W:** Walter Bannert. *APD, GLV, SWC*

Inhibition ♫ **1986** A beautiful heiress has lots of sex with different people in exotic locales. Softcore soap. **90m/C VHS, Beta.** Claudine Beccaire, Ilona Staller. *MED*

The Initiation ♫ **1984 (R)** Trying to rid herself of a troublesome nightmare, a coed finds herself face-to-face with a psycho. Gory campus slaughterfest. **97m/C VHS, Beta.** Vera Miles, Clu Gulager, James Read, Daphne Zuniga; **D:** Larry Stewart. *VTR*

Initiation of Sarah ♫ **1978** College freshman joins a sorority, undergoes abusive initiation, and gains a supernatural revenge. Made-for-television "Carrie" rip-off. **100m/C VHS, Beta.** Kay Lenz, Shelley Winters, Kathryn Crosby, Morgan Brittany, Tony Bill, Tisa Farrow, Robert Hays, Morgan Fairchild; **D:** Robert Day. *WOV*

The Inkwell ♫♫½ **1994 (R)** Quiet teenager Drew Tate finds first love when his family spends their vacation with relatives on Martha's Vineyard. Drew is drawn into the party atmosphere of the

Inkwell, the area where affluent black professionals have summered for decades. Meanwhile, political differences between Drew's former Black Panther father and his conservative uncle threaten family harmony. Everything about the film has a sugary aura, with conflicts handled tastefully. Rich directs broadly, leading to some overacting. Film is set in 1976. **112m/C VHS, LV, Closed Caption.** Larenz Tate, Joe Morton, Phyllis Stickney, Jada Pinkett; *D:* Matty Rich; *W:* Paris Qualles, Tom Ricostronza; *C:* John L. Demps Jr.; *M:* Terence Blanchard. *TOU*

Inn of Temptation 🎬 1986 A bunch of bowling buddies take off for Bangkok on an impulsive weekend, and meet lots of Oriental women. **72m/C VHS, Beta.** Michael Jacot, Claude Martin. *MED*

Inn of the Damned 🎬½ 1974 Detective looks into an inn where no one ever gets charged for an extra day; they simply die. Anderson is watchable. **92m/C VHS, Beta.** *AU* Alex Cord, Judith Anderson, Tony Bonner, Michael Craig, John Meillon; *D:* Terry Burke. *NO*

The Inn of the Sixth Happiness 🎬🎬🎬 1958 Inspiring story of Gladys Aylward, an English missionary in 1930s China, who leads a group of children through war-torn countryside. Donat's last film. **158m/C VHS, Beta.** Ingrid Bergman, Robert Donat, Curt Jurgens; *D:* Mark Robson; *C:* Frederick A. (Freddie) Young; *M:* Malcolm Arnold. National Board of Review Awards '58: Best Actress (Bergman); Nominations: Academy Awards '58: Best Director (Robson). *FXV*

Inn on the River 🎬🎬½ 1962 Scotland Yard investigates a series of murders taking place on the waterfront by the "Shark's" gang. Remake of "The Return of the Frog." **95m/C VHS.** *GE* Klaus Kinski, Joachim Fuchsberger, Brigitte Grothum, Richard Much; *D:* Alfred Vohrer. *SNC*

The Inner Circle 🎬½ 1946 A private detective, framed for murder by his secretary, has a limited amount of time to find the real murderer. Confusing. **57m/B VHS, Beta.** Adele Mara, Warren Douglas, William Frawley, Ricardo Cortez, Virginia Christine; *D:* Philip Ford. *SNC*

The Inner Circle 🎬🎬🎬 1991 (PG-13) Ivan Sanshin is a meek, married man working as a movie projectionist for the KGB in 1935 Russia. Sanshin is taken by the KGB to the Kremlin to show movies, primarily Hollywood features, to leader Joseph Stalin, a job he cannot discuss with anyone, even his wife. Under the spell of Stalin's personality, Sanshin sees only what he's told and overlooks the oppression and persecution of the times. Based on the life of the projectionist who served from 1935 until Stalin's death in 1953. Filmed on location at the Kremlin. **122m/C VHS, LV, 8mm, Closed Caption.** Tom Hulce, Lolita Davidovich, Bob Hoskins, Alexandre Zbruev, Maria Baranova, Feodor Chaliapin Jr, Bess Meyer; *D:* Andrei Konchalovsky; *W:* Andrei Konchalovsky, Anatoli Usov; *M:* Eduard Artemyev. *COL*

Inner Sanctum 🎬🎬 1948 Adequate tale of a young girl accosted by a gypsy who claims that tragedy awaits her. Based on a radio show of the same name. **62m/B VHS.** Chuck Russell, Mary Beth Hughes, Lee Patrick, Nana Bryant; *D:* Lew (Louis Friedlander) Landers. *SNC*

Inner Sanctum woof! 1991 (R) Cheating husband hires sensuous nurse to tend invalid wife. You can guess the rest; in fact, you have to because the plot ultimately makes no sense. Available in R-rated and sex-drenched unrated editions. *CW:* Language, violence, and strong sensuality. **87m/C VHS, LV, Closed Caption.** Tanya Roberts, Margaux Hemingway, Joseph Bottoms, Valerie Wildman, William Butler, Brett Clark; *D:* Fred Olen Ray. *COL*

Inner Sanctum 2 🎬½ 1994 (R) Jennifer Reed (Swope) had a breakdown and killed her husband in the first film. Now under a doctor's (Warner) care, Jennifer is under siege from her brother-in-law's (Nouri) plot to send her over the edge again and claim her fortune. As if that's not enough, Jennifer's also being stalked by a murderer. Also available in an unrated version. **90m/C VHS, LV, Closed Caption.** Michael Nouri, Tracy Brooks Swope, Sandahl Bergman, David Warner, Jennifer Ciesar, Margaux Hemingway; *D:* Fred Olen Ray; *W:* Sherman Scott; *M:* Chuck Cirino. *COL*

Innerspace 🎬🎬½ 1987 (PG) A space pilot, miniaturized for a journey through a lab rat a la "Fantastic Voyage," is accidentally injected into a nebbish supermarket clerk, and together they nab some bad guys and get the girl. Award-winning special effects support some funny moments between micro Quaid and nerdy Short, with Ryan producing the confused romantic interest. **120m/C VHS, Beta, LV, 8mm, Closed Caption.** Dennis Quaid, Martin Short, Meg Ryan, Kevin McCarthy, Fiona Lewis, Henry Gibson, Robert Picardo, John Hora, Wendy Schaal, Orson Bean, Chuck Jones, William Schallert, Dick Miller, Vernon Wells, Harold Sylvester, Kevin Hooks, Kathleen Freeman, Kenneth Tobey; *D:* Joe Dante; *W:* Jeffrey Boam, Chip Proser; *M:* Jerry Goldsmith. Academy Awards '87: Best Visual Effects. *WAR*

Innocence Unprotected 🎬🎬½ 1968 A film collage that contains footage from the 1942 film "Innocence Unprotected," the story of an acrobat trying to save an orphan from her wicked stepmother, newsreels from Nazi-occupied Yugoslavia, and interviews from 1968 with people who were in the film. Confiscated by the Nazis during final production, "Innocence Unprotected" was discovered by director Makavejev, who worked it into the collage. Filmed in color and black and white; in Serbian with English subtitles. **78m/C VHS.** *YU* Dragoljub Aleksic, Ana Milosavljevic, Vera Jovanovic; *D:* Dusan Makavejev; *W:* Dusan Makavejev. *FCT*

The Innocent 🎬🎬🎬½ 1976 (R) L'Innocente The setting: turn of the century Rome, ablaze with atheism and free love. The story: Giannini's a Sicilian aristocrat who ignores wife Antonelli and dallies with scheming mistress O'Neill. Discovering his wife's infidelity, he's profoundly disillusioned, and his manly notion of self disintegrates. Visconti's last film, it was an art house fave and is considered by many to be his best. Lavishly photographed, well set and costumed, and true to the Gabrielle D'Annunzio's novel. In Italian with English subtitles. **125m/C VHS, Beta.** *IT* Laura Antonelli, Jennifer O'Neill, Giancarlo Giannini; *D:* Luchino Visconti; *C:* Pasquale De Santos. *VES, FCT, CVC*

The Innocent 🎬🎬½ 1993 (R) Cold War thriller has naive British engineer Leonard Markham (Scott) sent to Berlin in 1955 by Brits who are warily cooperating with the U.S. forces. He's turned over to CIA operator Bob Glass (Hopkins) and asked to intercept communications between East Germany and the Soviet Union. Glass continually warns Markham not to trust anyone, including Maria (Rossellini), the married German woman with whom he begins an affair. Failure to build necessary suspense and performances leads to disappointing one-note display. Based on the novel by McEwan. *CW:* Sexuality, brief language, and a sequence of violence. **97m/C VHS, LV, Closed Caption.** *GE GB* Anthony Hopkins, Campbell Scott, Isabella Rossellini, Hart Bochner, James Grant, Jeremy Sinden, Ronald Nitschke; *D:* John Schlesinger; *W:* Ian McEwan; *M:* Gerald Gouriet. *MAX*

Innocent Blood 🎬🎬 1992 (R) A mediocre modern-day vampire/gangster combo with the beautiful (though red-eyed) Parillaud as the woman with a taste for someone "Italian." Unfortunately, she doesn't finish off her latest meal—mobster Loggia—who finds being undead very useful to his vicious work. LaPaglia plays the bewildered, love-struck cop involved with the vamp. Parillaud appears nude in several scenes and the gore and violence are stomach-turning. *CW:* Language, vampire violence, and sexuality. **112m/C VHS, Beta, LV, Closed Caption.** Anne Parillaud, Anthony LaPaglia, Robert Loggia, David Proval, Don Rickles, Rocco Sisto, Kim Coates; *D:* John Landis; *C:* Mac Ahlberg; *M:* Ira Newborn. *WAR, PMS*

Innocent Lies 🎬🎬½ 1995 (R) In 1938, British policeman Alan Cross (Dunbar) heads for an island off the French coast to look into the suicide of a colleague who was investigating the expatriate Graves family. There are family tensions, skeletons in the closet, and some Nazi-sympathizers all mixed together in an old-fashioned but satisfying stew. *CW:* Sexual situations, violence. **88m/C VHS.** *FR GB* Adrian Dunbar, Stephen Dorff, Gabrielle Anwar, Joanna Lumley; *D:* Patrick Dewolf; *W:* Kerry Crabbe, Patrick Dewolf; *C:* Patrick Blossier; *M:* Alexandre Desplat. *PGV*

An Innocent Man 🎬🎬½ 1989 (R) Uneven story of Selleck, an ordinary family man and airline mechanic, framed as a drug dealer and sent to prison. **113m/C VHS, Beta, LV, Closed Caption.** Tom Selleck, F. Murray Abraham, Laila Robins, David Rasche, Richard Young, Badja Djola; *D:* Peter Yates; *W:* Larry Brothers; *M:* Howard Shore. *TOU*

Innocent Prey 🎬🎬 1988 (R) When a woman finally summons the courage to bid hasta la vista to her abusive husband, it turns out he's not so quick to say ciao. Definitely not a highlight in Balsam's career. *CW:* Violence and sensuality. **88m/C VHS, Closed Caption.** *AU* P.J. Soles, Martin Balsam, Kit Taylor, Grigor Taylor, John Warnock, Susan Stenmark, Richard Morgan; *D:* Colin Eggleston. *NO*

Innocent Sorcerers 🎬🎬 1960 Niewinni Czarodzieje Ironic comedy about aimless sixties Polish youth that finds a young doctor having trouble committing himself to his superficial girlfriend and coping with the problems of his cynical friends. Polish with subtitles. **86m/B VHS.** *PL* Tadeusz Lomnicki, Zbigniew Cybulski, Roman Polanski, Krystyna Stypulkowska, Jerzy Skolimowski; *D:* Andrzej Wajda; *W:* Jerzy Skolimowski, Andrzej Wajda; *M:* Krzysztof Komeda. *FCT*

Innocent Victim 🎬 The Tree of Hands 1990 (R) Convoluted tale of revenge and madness. Bacall plays a mad grandmother who kidnaps a boy to take the place of her dead grandson. The kidnapped boy's stepfather then is accused of murdering him, and starts murdering others to get the boy back. **100m/C VHS.** Lauren Bacall, Helen Shaver, Paul McGann, Peter Firth; *D:* Giles Foster. *ACA*

The Innocents 🎬🎬🎬½ 1961 Incredibly creepy version of Henry James' "The Turn of the Screw." Minister's daughter, Miss Giddens (Kerr), is hired by Redgrave (known only as "The Uncle") as governess to young Flora (Franklin) and her brother Miles (Stephens) at his country estate. Miss Giddens begins to see the specters of a man and a woman and is told her descriptions match that of former estate manager Peter Quint and the last governess, his mistress, whose influence on the children was thought to be malevolent. Indeed, Miss Giddens believes the children are possessed by evil—but is it true or a product of her own hysteria? **85m/B VHS, Closed Caption.** *GB* Deborah Kerr, Michael Redgrave, Pamela Franklin, Martin Stephens, Peter Wyngarde, Megs Jenkins, Clytie Jessop, Isla Cameron, Eric Woodburn; *D:* Jack Clayton; *W:* Truman Capote, William Archibald, John Mortimer; *C:* Freddie Francis; *M:* Georges Auric. *FXV*

The Innocents Abroad 🎬🎬½ 1984 Entertaining adaptation of Mark Twain's novel about a group of naive Americans cruising the Mediterranean. Ensemble cast offers some surprising performances. Originally produced for PBS. **116m/C VHS.** Craig Wasson, Brooke Adams, David Ogden Stiers. *USH*

Innocents in Paris 🎬🎬½ 1953 A group of seven Britons visit Paris for the first time. A bit long but enough ooo-la-la to satisfy. **89m/B VHS, Beta.** *GB* Alastair Sim, Laurence Harvey, Jimmy Edwards, Claire Bloom, Margaret Rutherford; *D:* Gordon Parry. *NO*

The Inquiry 🎬🎬½ 1987 A new twist on the resurrection of Christ. Carradine senses a cover-up when he's sent from Rome to investigate the problem of Christ's missing corpse. He retraces Christ's final days to solve the case in this interesting, offbeat film. Dubbed. **107m/C VHS.** *IT* Keith

Carradine, Harvey Keitel, Phyllis Logan, Angelo Infanti, Lina Sastri; **D:** Damiano Damiani. *NO*

Inquisition 🎬½ 1976 Naschy is a 16th century witch hunting judge who finds himself accused of witchcraft. **85m/C VHS, Beta.** *SP* Paul Naschy, Daniela Giordano, Juan Gallardo; **D:** Paul Naschy; **W:** Paul Naschy. *VCD*

Insanity 🎬 1982 A film director becomes violently obsessed with a beautiful actress. **101m/C VHS, Beta.** Terence Stamp, Fernando Rey, Corinne Clery. *NO*

The Insect Woman 🎬🎬🎬 *The Insect; Nippon Konchuki* 1963 Chronicles 45 years in the life of a woman who must work with the diligence of an ant in order to survive. Thoughtfully reflects the exploitation of women and the cruelty of human nature in Japanese society. Beautiful performance from Hidari, who ages from girlhood to middle age. In Japanese with English subtitles. **123m/B VHS.** *JP* Sachiko Hidari, Yitsuko Yoshimura, Hiroyuki Nagaes, Sumie Sasaki; **D:** Shohei Imamura. *CVC*

Inserts 🎬 1976 (R) A formerly successful director has been reduced to making porno films in this pretentious, long-winded effort set in a crumbling Hollywood mansion in the 1930s. Affected, windbaggish performances kill it. **99m/C VHS.** *GB* Richard Dreyfuss, Jessica Harper, Veronica Cartwright, Bob Hoskins; **D:** John Byrum; **W:** John Byrum. *FOX*

Inside 🎬🎬🎬 1996 (R) Harrowing anti-apartheid drama finds university professor and white Afrikaaner Peter Martin Strydom (Stoltz) being held in a Johannesburg government prison. He's being interrogated by Colonel Kruger (Hawthorne), head of the prison security force, supposedly for conspiracy against the South African regime. Tortured, Strydom's will begins to break as the drama flashes forward ten years, with Colonel Kruger now subjected to interrogation by a nameless black questioner (Gossett, Jr.) investigating human rights crimes, including Strydom's fate. Made for cable. **CW:** Political violence and torture, language and a brief sex scene. **94m/C VHS, Closed Caption.** Eric Stoltz, Nigel Hawthorne, Louis Gossett Jr.; **D:** Arthur Penn; **W:** Bima Stagg; **C:** Jan Weincke; **M:** Robert Levin. *EVE*

Inside Daisy Clover 🎬🎬½ 1965 Wood is the self-sufficient, junior delinquent waif who becomes a teenage musical star and pays the price for fame in this Hollywood saga set in the 1930s. Discovered by tyrannical studio head Plummer, Daisy is given her big break and taken under his wing for grooming as Swan Studio's newest sensation. She falls for fellow performer, matinee idol Redford, who has some secrets of his own, and eventually has a breakdown from the career pressure. Glossy melodrama is filled with over-the-top performances but its sheer silliness makes it amusing. **128m/C VHS, LV.** Natalie Wood, Christopher Plummer, Robert Redford, Ruth Gordon, Roddy McDowall, Katharine Bard; **D:** Robert Mulligan; **W:** Gavin Lambert; **C:** Charles B(ryant) Lang; **M:** Andre Previn. Golden Globe Awards '66: Best Supporting Actress (Gordon); Nominations: Academy Awards '65: Best Art Direction/Set Decoration (Color), Best Costume Design (Color), Best Supporting Actress (Gordon). *WAR*

Inside Edge 🎬🎬 1992 (R) Urban crime thriller is a complex yet surprisingly uninteresting story of a police officer who falls for the girlfriend of the drug lord he is chasing. Filled with the standard genre violence. **CW:** Strong language, strong violence, and strong sexuality. **84m/C VHS.** Michael Madsen, Richard Lynch, Rosie Vela, Tony Peck, George Jenesky, Branscombe Richmond; **D:** Warren Clark; **W:** William Tannen. *ATV*

Inside Information 🎬 1934 With Tarzan's help, a cop searches out the leader of a ring of jewel thieves. **51m/B VHS, Beta, LV.** Rex Lease, Marion Shilling, Philo McCullough. *NO*

The Inside Man 🎬🎬½ 1984 Double agents struggle to find a submarine-detecting laser device. Based on true incidents in which a soviet sub ran aground in Sweden. Made in Swe-

den; dubbed. **90m/C VHS, Beta.** *SW* Dennis Hopper, Hardy Kruger, Gosta Ekman, David Wilson; **D:** Tom Clegg. *CEL, VTR*

Inside Monkey Zetterland 🎬🎬 1993 (R) Monkey Zetterland (Antin) is a screenwriter and former actor with an eccentric family. His actress mother is neurotically insecure and a nag; his father is an aging hippie who only shows up at Thanksgiving; his lesbian sister Grace is trying to get over a failed relationship; and his brother Brent is totally self-absorbed. Add to this menage his equally lunatic friends: Imogene, the compulsive talker and exhibitionist; his vicious girlfriend Daphne; and frightening married couple Sophie and Sasha. Meanwhile, Monkey tries to survive amidst the chaos. Interesting cast but lots of camera tricks do not a successful film make and the effort to be hip is all too apparent. **CW:** Language. **92m/C VHS, LV.** Steve Antin, Patricia Arquette, Sandra Bernhard, Sofia Coppola, Tate Donovan, Katherine Helmond, Bo Hopkins, Debi Mazar, Martha Plimpton, Rupert Everett, Ricki Lake, Lance Loud, Francis Bay, Luca Bercovici; **D:** Jefery Levy; **W:** John Boskovich, Steve Antin; **C:** Christopher Taylor; **M:** Rick Cox, Jeff Elmassian. Nominations: Independent Spirit Awards '94: Best Supporting Actor (Donovan). *PSM*

Inside Moves 🎬🎬½ 1980 (PG) A look at handicapped citizens trying to make it in everyday life, focusing on the relationship between an insecure, failed suicide and a volatile man who is only a knee operation away from a dreamed-about basketball career. **113m/C VHS, Beta, LV.** John Savage, Diana Scarwid, David Morse, Amy Wright; **D:** Richard Donner; **W:** Valerie Curtin, Barry Levinson; **M:** John Barry. Nominations: Academy Awards '80: Best Supporting Actress (Scarwid). *FOX*

Inside Out 🎬🎬½ *The Golden Heist; Hitler's Gold* 1975 (PG) An ex-GI, a jewel thief and a German POW camp commandant band together to find a stolen shipment of Nazi gold behind the Iron Curtain. To find the gold, they help a Nazi prisoner who knows the secret to break out of prison. Good action caper. **97m/C VHS, Beta.** *GB* Telly Savalas, Robert Culp, James Mason, Aldo Ray, Doris Kunstmann; **D:** Peter Duffell. *WAR*

Inside Out 🎬🎬½ 1991 (R) Hiding in his apartment from a world which terrifies him, Jimmy doesn't feel he's missing much—since he has the necessary women and bookies come to him. He soon finds he's not quite as safe as he thought, and the only way out is "out there." Fine performance from Gould, suspenseful pacing. **87m/C VHS.** Elliott Gould, Jennifer Tilly, Howard Hesseman, Beah Richards, Timothy Scott, Sandy McPeak, Dana Elcar, Meshach Taylor, Nicole Norman; **D:** Robert Taicher; **W:** Robert Taicher. *NO*

Inside the Law 🎬🎬 1942 A gang of crooks takes over a bank and must stay "inside the law" and resist their natural inclinations. Lots of comic situations. **65m/B VHS.** Wallace Ford, Frank Sully, Harry Holman, Luana Walters, Lafayette McKee, Danny Duncan, Earle Hodgins; **D:** Hamilton MacFadden. *NOS*

Inside the Lines 🎬🎬 1930 A WWI tale of espionage and counter-espionage. **73m/B VHS, Beta.** Betty Compson, Montagu Love, Mischa Auer, Ralph Forbes. *VYY*

Inside the Third Reich 🎬🎬½ 1982 A made-for-television mini-series detailing the rise to power within the Third Reich of Albert Speer, top advisor to Hitler. Based on Speer's rather self-serving memoires. **250m/C VHS, Beta, LV.** Derek Jacobi, Rutger Hauer, John Gielgud, Blythe Danner, Maria Schell, Ian Holm, Trevor Howard, Randy Quaid, Viveca Lindfors, Robert Vaughn, Stephen Collins, Elke Sommer, Renee Soutendijk; **D:** Marvin J. Chomsky. *GLV*

Insignificance 🎬🎬🎬 1985 A film about an imaginary night spent in a New York hotel by characters who resemble Marilyn Monroe, Albert Einstein, Joe McCarthy, and Joe DiMaggio. Entertaining and often amusing as it follows the characters as they discuss theory and relativity, the Russians, and baseball among other things.

110m/C VHS, Beta, LV. *GB* Gary Busey, Tony Curtis, Theresa Russell, Michael Emil, Will Sampson; **D:** Nicolas Roeg; **W:** Terry Johnson; **M:** Hans Zimmer. *ORI, WAR*

The Inspector General 🎬🎬🎬 *Happy Times* 1949 Classic Kaye craziness of mistaken identities with the master comic portraying a carnival medicine man who is mistaken by the villagers for their feared Inspector General. If you like Kaye's manic performance, you'll enjoy this one. ♫The Gypsy Drinking Song; Onward Onward; The Medicine Show; The Inspector General; Lonely Heart; Soliloquy For Three Heads; Happy Times; Brodny. **103m/C VHS, Beta.** Danny Kaye, Walter Slezak, Barbara Bates, Elsa Lanchester, Gene Lockhart, Walter Catlett, Alan Hale; **D:** Henry Koster. Golden Globe Awards '50: Best Score. *MGM, MRV, NOS*

The Inspector General 🎬🎬½ 1954 The filmed performance of Gogol's great play by the Moscow Art Theatre, wherein a provincial town panics when they mistake a wandering moron for the Inspector come to check up on them. In Russian with English subtitles. **128m/B VHS, Beta.** *RU* Vladimir Petrov. *FCT, AUD*

Inspector Hornleigh 🎬🎬½ 1939 A pair of bumbling detectives arrive on the scene when a Chancellor's fortune is stolen. Fine comedy, although the Scottish and British accents can be rather thick now and again. **76m/B VHS, Beta.** *GB* Gordon Harker, Alastair Sim, Miki Hood, Wally Patch, Steve Geray, Edward Underdown, Hugh Williams, Gibb McLaughlin; **D:** Eugene Forde. *NOS, SNC*

Instant Justice 🎬½ *Marine Issue* 1986 (R) A professional Marine jeopardizes his military career by avenging his sister's murder, vigilante style. Exclusive action. **101m/C VHS, Beta, Closed Caption.** *GB* Michael Pare, Tawny Kitaen, Charles Napier; **D:** Craig T. Rumar. *WAR*

Instant Karma 🎬½ 1990 Would be comedy depicts young man's far fetched attempts to score babewise. Ask no more what happened to erstwhile teen heart throb Cassidy; he suffers from a major bout of bad karma. **94m/C VHS, Beta, Closed Caption.** Craig Sheffer, Chelsea Noble, David Cassidy, Alan Blumenfeld, Glen Hirsch, Marty Ingels, Orson Bean; **D:** Roderick Taylor. *MGM*

Instant Kung-Fu Man 🎬 1984 Twin brothers get involved in a case of mistaken identity in this martial arts effort. **104m/C VHS, Beta.** John Liu, Hwang Jang Lee, Yeh Fei Yang. *WVE*

The Instructor 🎬 1983 The head of a karate school proves the value of his skill when threatened by the owner of a rival school. **91m/C VHS, Beta.** Don Bendell, Bob Chaney, Bob Saal, Lynday Scharnott; **D:** Don Bendell. *LIV, VES*

Interceptor 🎬🎬 1992 (R) Hijackers attempt to steal a Stealth Bomber in this action-adventure saga which features virtual reality computer-generated imagery in its combat sequences. **CW:** Language and violence. **92m/C VHS, LV, Closed Caption.** Juergen Prochnow, Andrew Divoff, Elizabeth Morehead; **D:** Michael Cohn; **W:** John Brancato. *THV*

Interface 🎬½ 1984 A computer game gets out of hand at a university, turning the tunnels beneath the campus into a battleground of good and evil. **88m/C VHS, Beta.** John Davies, Laura Lane, Matthew Sacks. *LIV, VES*

Interiors 🎬🎬🎬½ 1978 (R) Ultra serious, Bergmanesque drama about three neurotic adult sisters, coping with the dissolution of their family. When Father decides to leave mentally unbalanced mother for a divorcee, the daughters are shocked and bewildered. Depressing and humorless, but fine performances all the way around, supported by the elegant camera work of Gordon Willis. Original theatrical trailer available on the laserdisc format. **95m/C VHS, Beta, LV.** Diane Keaton, Mary Beth Hurt, E.G. Marshall, Geraldine Page, Richard Jordan, Sam Waterston, Kristin Griffith, Maureen Stapleton; **D:** Woody Allen; **W:** Woody Allen; **C:** Gordon Willis. British Academy Awards '78: Best Supporting Actress (Page); Los Angeles Film Critics Association Awards '78: Best Supporting Actress (Stapleton); Nominations: Academy Awards '78: Best Actress (Page), Best Art Direction/Set Decoration, Best Director (Allen), Best Original Screenplay, Best Supporting Actress (Stapleton). *MGM*

Intermezzo 🎬🎬🎬 *Interlude* 1936
Married violinist Ekman meets pianist Bergman and they fall in love. He deserts his family to tour with Bergman, but the feelings for his wife and children become too much. When Bergman sees their love won't last, she leaves him. Shakily, he returns home and as his daughter runs to greet him, she is hit by a truck and he realizes that his family is his true love. One of the great grab-your-hanky melodramas. In Swedish with English subtitles. 1939 English re-make features Bergman's American film debut. **88m/B VHS, LV.** *SW* Gosta Ekman, Inga Tidblad, Ingrid Bergman, Bullen Berglund; **D:** Gustaf Molander. *WAC, TPV, LUM*

Intermezzo 🎬🎬🎬 *Intermezzo: A Love Story* 1939
Fine, though weepy, love story of a renowned, married violinist who has an affair with his stunningly beautiful protege (Bergman), but while on concert tour realizes that his wife and children hold his heart, and he returns to them. A re-make of the 1936 Swedish film, it's best known as Bergman's American debut. Howard's violin playing was dubbed by Jascha Heifetz. **70m/B VHS, Beta, LV.** *IT* Ingrid Bergman, Leslie Howard, Edna Best, Ann Todd; **C:** Gregory Ratoff; **M:** Max Steiner. Nominations: Academy Awards '39: Best Black and White Cinematography, Best Score. *FOX, FCT*

Internal Affairs 🎬🎬½ 1990 (R)
Wild, sexually charged action piece about an Internal Affairs officer for the L.A.P.D. (Garcia) who becomes obsessed with exposing a sleazy, corrupt street cop (Gere). Drama becomes illogical, but boasts excellent, strung out performances, especially Gere as the creepy degenerate you'd love to bust. **114m/C VHS, Beta, LV, 8mm, Closed Caption.** Richard Gere, Andy Garcia, Laurie Metcalf, Ron Vawter, Marco Rodriguez, Nancy Travis, William Baldwin, Richard Bradford, Annabella Sciorra, Michael Beach; **D:** Mike Figgis; **W:** Henry Bean; **C:** John A. Alonzo; **M:** Brian Banks, Mike Figgis. *PAR*

International Crime 🎬🎬 1937
Radio hero The Shadow solves a tough crime in this adventure film. **62m/B VHS, Beta.** Rod La Rocque, Astrid Allwyn, William von Brinken; **D:** Charles Lamont. *SNC, NOS, AOV*

International House 🎬🎬½ 1933
A wacky Dada-esque Hollywood farce about an incredible array of travelers quarantined in a Shanghai hotel where a mad doctor has perfected television. Essentially a burlesque compilation of skits, gags, and routines. Guest stars Rudy Vallee, Baby Rose Marie and Cab Calloway appear on the quaint "television" device, in musical sequences. ♫ Tea Cup; Thank Heaven For You; My Bluebirds are Singing the Blues; Reefer Man. **72m/B VHS, Beta, LV.** W.C. Fields, Peggy Hopkins Joyce, Rudy Vallee, George Burns, Cab Calloway, Sari Maritza, Gracie Allen, Bela Lugosi, Sterling Holloway, Baby Rose Marie; **D:** Edward Sutherland. *USH, MLB*

International Velvet 🎬🎬½ 1978 (PG)
In this long overdue sequel to "National Velvet," adult Velvet, with live-in companion (Plummer), grooms her orphaned niece (O'Neal) to become an Olympic champianion horsewoman. Good photography and performances by Plummer and Hopkins manage to keep the sentiment at a trot. **126m/C VHS, Beta.** *GB* Tatum O'Neal, Anthony Hopkins, Christopher Plummer; **D:** Bryan Forbes. *MGM*

Internecine Project 🎬🎬½ 1973 (PG)
Stylistic espionage tale with Coburn's English professor acting as the mastermind behind an unusual series of murders where industrial spies kill each other, so Coburn can garner a top government job in D.C. Unexpected ending is worth the viewing. Based on Mort Elkind's novel. **89m/C VHS, Beta, Closed Caption.** *GB* James Coburn, Lee Grant, Harry Andrews, Keenan Wynn; **D:** Ken Hughes; **W:** Barry Levinson; **C:** Geoffrey Unsworth. *FOX*

Internes Can't Take Money 🎬🎬½ 1937
With the help of McCrea and gangster Nolan, widow Stanwyck is desperately trying to find the daughter her bank robber husband hid before he died. Young doctor McCrea must save the life of another gangster who knows the whereabouts of the toddler. The first film featuring writer Max Brand's Dr. Kildare characters, which later became part of a series starring Lew Ayres and Laraine Day. **79m/B VHS, Closed Caption.** Barbara Stanwyck, Joel McCrea, Lloyd Nolan, Stanley Ridges, Lee Bowman, Irving Bacon; **D:** Alfred Santell; **W:** Rian James, Theodore Reeves; **C:** Theodor Sparkuhl; **M:** Gregory Stone. *USH*

The Interns 🎬🎬½ 1962
Finessed hospital soaper about interns on the staff of a large city hospital, whose personal lives are fraught with trauma, drugs, birth, death, and abortion. Good performances and direction keep this medical melodrama moving in a gurney-like manner. Followed by the "The New Interns" and the basis for a television series. Adapted from a novel by Richard Frede. **120m/C VHS, Beta, LV.** Cliff Robertson, James MacArthur, Michael Callan, Nick Adams, Stefanie Powers, Suzy Parker, Buddy Ebsen, Telly Savalas, Haya Harareet; **D:** David Swift. *COL*

The Interrogation 🎬🎬🎬 *Przesluchanie* 1982
Grueling depiction of Stalin-era Poland proves that nobody makes anticommunist movies better than those who knew tyranny firsthand. A 1950s cabaret starlet is arrested on false charges and endures years of torment in custody. Banned under Polish martial law in 1982, it circulated illegally in the country until 1989. Janda won an award at Cannes for her transformation from showgirl floozy to defiant heroine. In Polish with English subtitles. **118m/C VHS.** *PL* Krystyna Janda, Janusz Gajos, Adam Ferency, Agnieszka Holland, Anna Romantowska; **D:** Richard Bugajski. *KIV, FCT*

Interrupted Journey 🎬🎬½ 1949
A married man runs away to start a new life with another woman. When she is killed in a train accident, he becomes the prime suspect in her murder. Lots of action and speed, but a disappointing ending. **80m/B VHS.** *GB* Richard Todd, Valerie Hobson; **D:** Daniel Birt. *NOS, SNC*

Interrupted Melody 🎬🎬🎬 1955
True story of opera diva Marjorie Lawrence's courageous battle with polio and her fight to appear once more at the Metropolitan Opera. Parker was nominated for an Oscar in her excellent portrayal of the Australian singer who continues her career despite her handicap. Vocals dubbed by opera star Eileen Farrell. Based on the book by Marjorie Lawrence. **106m/C VHS.** Glenn Ford, Eleanor Parker, Roger Moore, Cecil Kellaway, Evelyn Ellis, Walter Baldwin; **D:** Curtis Bernhardt; **W:** William Ludwig, Sonya Levien; **C:** Paul Vogel. Academy Awards '55: Best Story & Screenplay; Nominations: Academy Awards '55: Best Actress (Parker), Best Costume Design (Color), Best Screenplay. *MGM*

Intersection 🎬½ 1993 (R)
Successful architect Vincent (Gere) is torn between his aloof wife/partner, Sally (Stone), and a sexy journalist mistress, Olivia (Davidovitch). Who to choose? Since he's a completely self-involved boor, you won't care either way. Another retooling of a French film ("Les Choses de la Vie") as a Hollywood star vehicle that doesn't work. Lousy dialogue doesn't help. Does boast some nice location shots of Vancouver, BC. *CW:* Some language and some sexuality. **98m/C VHS, Beta, LV, Closed Caption.** Richard Gere, Sharon Stone, Lolita Davidovich, Martin Landau, David Selby, Jenny Morrison; **D:** Mark Rydell; **W:** Marshall Brickman, David Rayfiel; **C:** Vilmos Zsigmond; **M:** James Newton Howard. Golden Raspberry Awards '94: Worst Actress (Stone). *PAR*

Interval 🎬½ 1973 (PG)
A middle-aged, globe-trotting woman becomes involved with a young American painter while running from her past. Oberon, 62 at the time, produced and played in this, her last film. Filmed in Mexico. **84m/C VHS, Beta.** Merle Oberon, Robert Wolders; **D:** Daniel Mann. *NLC*

Interview with the Vampire 🎬🎬 1994 (R)
Portrayal of the elegantly decadent world of vampires and their prey, which features the perverse Lestat (Cruise) who decides to make 18th-century New Orleans aristocrat Louis (Pitt) his latest recruit. Only problem is Louis is horrified by his blood-sucking nature and whines about it for 200 years (it does get tedious). Lestat even makes a child-vampire, Claudia (Dunst), for their own very dysfunctional family but this doesn't turn out well. Director Jordan brings some much needed humor to the dark mix along with some overdone gore. The first book in Anne Rice's "The Vampire Chronicles" was a 17-year film project beset by controversy, including the casting of Cruise (who looks nothing like Rice's description of the character, although Pitt does), leading to an outcry among the cult book's fans though Rice finally came around. Slater replaced the late River Phoenix as the interviewer. *CW:* Language; sensuality; nudity; violence. **123m/C VHS, LV, Closed Caption, DVD.** Tom Cruise, Brad Pitt, Kirsten Dunst, Christian Slater, Antonio Banderas, Stephen Rea, Domiziana Giordano; **D:** Neil Jordan; **W:** Anne Rice; **C:** Philippe Rousselot; **M:** Elliot Goldenthal. Chicago Film Critics Awards '94: Most Promising Actress (Dunst); MTV Movie Awards '95: Best Male Performance (Pitt), Breakthrough Performance (Dunst), Most Desirable Male (Pitt); Nominations: Academy Awards '94: Best Art Direction/Set Decoration, Best Original Score; Golden Globe Awards '95: Best Supporting Actress (Dunst), Best Original Score; MTV Movie Awards '95: Best Film, Most Desirable Male (Slater, Cruise), Best On-Screen Duo (Tom Cruise/Brad Pitt), Best Villain (Cruise). *WAR*

Intervista 🎬🎬🎬 *Federico Fellini's Intervista* 1987
A pseudo-documentary look at director Fellini's love of the movies, "Intervista" is a mixture of recollection, parody, memoir, satire, self-examination and fantasy. Fellini himself is the master of ceremonies in this joyous celebration of the studio community that features actors, actresses, bit players, make-up artists, scene painters, publicity agents, technicians, and gate-crashers. The high point of the film arrives with the stars of "La Dolce Vita" re-screening the Fellini masterpiece as Ekberg's country villa. It's a special moment of fantasy vs. reality in this glorious tribute to cinema history. In Italian with English subtitles. **108m/C VHS.** *IT* Marcello Mastroianni, Anita Ekberg, Federico Fellini, Sergio Rubini, Lara Wendell, Antonio Cantafora, Antonella Ponziani, Maurizio Mein, Paola Liguori, Nadia Ottaviani; **D:** Federico Fellini; **W:** Federico Fellini, Gianfranco Angelucci; **C:** Tonino Delli Colli; **M:** Nicola Piovani. *TRI*

Interzone 🎬½ 1988
Humans battle mutants in a post-holocaust world. **97m/C VHS, Beta.** Bruce Abbott; **D:** Deran Sarafian. *MED*

Intimate Contact 🎬🎬🎬 1987 (PG)
Top executive discovers he has AIDS after a business trip fling. Powerful drama as he and his wife try to cope. Excellent, understated performances from Massey and Bloom. Originally made for cable television. **140m/C VHS, Beta.** *GB* Claire Bloom, Daniel Massey, Abigail Cruttenden, Mark Kingston, Sylvia Syms, Sally Jane Jackson; **D:** Waris Hussein; **W:** Alma Cullen. *HBO*

Intimate Power 🎬🎬½ 1989 (R)
True story of French schoolgirl sold into slavery to an Ottoman sultan who becomes the harem queen. She bears an heir and begins to teach her son about his people's rights, in the hope that he will bring about reform in Turkey where he grows up to be a sultan. Good cast supports the exotic storytelling in this made for cable drama. **104m/C VHS, Beta, LV, Closed Caption.** F. Murray Abraham, Maud Adams, Amber O'Shea; **D:** Jack Smight. *HBO*

Intimate Relations 🎬🎬½ 1995 (R)
Fifties family dysfunction—British style. Harold Guppy (Graves) is an orphaned merchant marine who winds up in an English coastal town where he takes rooms with the seemingly respectable Beasleys. Stanley Beasley (Walker) is a quiet nonentity whose life is run by homemaker extraordinaire Marjorie (Walters), with 14-year-old daughter Joyce (Sadler) rounding out the family.

The needy Harold fits in fine, especially to the sexually hungry Marjorie who's soon offering her boarder unexpected services. But young Joyce won't be left out and then there's a blackmailing tug of war between the threesome. Based on the true story of a crime of passion that shocked Great Britain. **CW:** Disturbing sexual situations, a scene of related violence and some language. **105m/C VHS.** *GB* Julie Walters, Rupert Graves, Laura Sadler, Matthew Walker, Holly Aird, Les Dennis, Liz McKechnie; **D:** Philip Goodhew; **W:** Philip Goodhew; **C:** Andres Garreton; **M:** Lawrence Shrag. Montreal World Film Festival '95: Best Actor (Graves). *NYR*

Intimate Story 🐾🐾½ 1981 Intimate story of a husband and wife trying unsuccessfully to have a baby, amid the lack of privacy in a Kibbutz. Each blames the other for the problem and tries to escape the problems by focusing on personal fantasies. In Hebrew with English subtitles. **95m/C VHS, Beta, LV.** *IS* Chava Alberstein, Alex Peleg; **D:** Israeli Nadav Levitan. *ERG, TPV*

Intimate Stranger 🐾½ 1991 (R) Sexy, would-be rock star by day, Harry sets out in search of a steadier source of income. Rather than wait on tables all day, she chooses instead to become a phone-sex girl. This turns out to be an unwise career move, as she promptly finds herself the target of a phone-psycho who just can't take "no" for an answer. Will Debbie be able to shake this loser, or will he put a permanent end to her life-long dreams? Made for television. **CW:** Sex-related dialogue, violence, and sensuality. **96m/C VHS, Beta, LV, Closed Caption.** Deborah Harry, James Russo, Tim Thomerson, Paige French, Grace Zabriskie; **D:** Allan Holzman. *PAR*

Intimate Strangers 🐾🐾½ 1977 Taut made-for-television expose on battering and its effects on the family. Weaver and Struthers outshine the material, but the finest performance is a cameo by Douglas as Weaver's irascible aged father. **96m/C VHS, Beta.** Dennis Weaver, Sally Struthers, Quinn Cummings, Tyne Daly, Larry Hagman, Rhea Perlman; **Cameos:** Melvyn Douglas; **D:** John Llewellyn Moxey. *WOV*

Into the Badlands 🐾🐾 1992 (R) Mild made for cable TV thriller presents three suspense tales in "Twilight Zone" fashion, linked by the appearance of a mysterious Man in Black. No, it's not Johnny Cash, but Dern as a sinister bounty hunter in the old west, who inspires strange events on the trail. **CW:** Strong violence. **89m/C VHS.** Bruce Dern, Mariel Hemingway, Helen Hunt, Dylan McDermott, Lisa Pelikan, Andrew (Andy) Robinson; **D:** Sam Pillsbury; **W:** Dick Beebe, Marjorie David, Gordon Dawson. *USH*

Into the Darkness 🐾½ 1986 In the world of fashion models, a maniacal, demented killer stalks his prey. **90m/C VHS, Beta.** Donald Pleasence, Ronald Lacey. *NO*

Into the Fire 🐾 1988 (R) Thriller about a young drifter who, against the backdrop of a Canadian winter, happens upon a roadside lodge and diner, where he gets involved in sex and murder. Title gives a good idea of what to do with this one. **88m/C VHS, Beta, LV.** *CA* Susan Anspach, Art Hindle, Olivia D'Abo, Lee Montgomery; **D:** Graeme Campbell. *LIV, VES*

Into the Homeland 🐾🐾 1987 Seasoned ex-cop (Boothe) infiltrates a white supremacist group which had kidnapped his teenage daughter. Failed "message" about neo-nazi ethics, but good confrontation between Boothe and his son (Howell) make this so-so viewing. Made for cable television. **95m/C VHS, Beta, LV.** Powers Boothe, C. Thomas Howell, Paul LeMat; **D:** Leslie Linka Glatter. *BAR, ORI, WAR*

Into the Night 🐾🐾 1985 (R) Campy, offbeat thriller about a middle-aged, jilted deadbeat (Goldblum), who meets a beautiful woman (Pfeiffer) when she suddenly drops onto the hood of his car, with a relentless gang of Iranians pursuing. During their search through L.A. and other parts

of California for the one person who can help her out of this mess, a whole crew of Hollywood directors make cameo appearances, making this a delight for film buffs, but occasionally tedious for general audiences. B.B. King sings the title song. **115m/C VHS, Beta, LV, Closed Caption.** Jeff Goldblum, Michelle Pfeiffer, David Bowie, Carl Perkins, Richard Farnsworth, Dan Aykroyd, Paul Mazursky, Roger Vadim, Irene Papas, Bruce McGill, Vera Miles, Clu Gulager, Don Steel, Kathryn Harrold; **Cameos:** Jim Henson, Paul Bartel, David Cronenberg, Jack Arnold, Jonathan Demme, Lawrence Kasdan, Amy Heckerling, Donald Siegel, Richard Franklin, Colin Higgins, Andrew Marton; **D:** John Landis; **W:** Ron Koslow; **M:** Ira Newborn. *USH*

Into the Sun 🐾½ 1992 (R) Hall plays a Hollywood star who encounters real-life danger while hanging out with an Air Force pilot (Pare) to prepare for an upcoming role. Spectacular aerial scenes steal the show, which isn't hard to do in this lackluster movie. **CW:** Language. **101m/C VHS, LV, Closed Caption.** Anthony Michael Hall, Michael Pare, Terry Kiser, Deborah Maria Moore; **D:** Fritz Kiersch; **W:** John Brancato. *THV*

Into the West 🐾🐾🐾 1992 (PG) Enchanting horse tale set amid the mystic isle of Eire. Brooding, drunken Riley (Byrne), once the leader of a band of travelers (the Irish version of gypsies), leaves the road after his wife's death and settles in a Dublin slum with his two boys. The boys are enraptured when their grandfather turns up with a beautiful white horse, but their happiness is shattered when the police take it away. Boys and horse eventually escape in a wild ride across Ireland and into the west. Spiritual and mythic, with an awe-inspiring performance by the horse. Fitzgerald and Conroy make a run at best performances by kids, while Byrne is convincingly sodden and sulky. Meany and Barkin shine in small parts as sibling travellers. **97m/C VHS, LV, Closed Caption.** *IR* Gabriel Byrne, Ellen Barkin, Ciaran Fitzgerald, Ruaidhri Conroy, David Kelly, Colm Meaney; **D:** Mike Newell; **W:** Jim Sheridan; **M:** Patrick Doyle. *TOU*

Into Thin Air 🐾🐾🐾 1985 A mother searches tirelessly for her college bound son who disappeared on a cross-country drive. Well-done television drama with a good performance from Burstyn. **100m/C VHS, Beta, LV.** Ellen Burstyn, Robert Prosky, Sam Robards, Caroline McWilliams, Nicholas Pryor, John Dennis Johnston; **D:** Roger Young; **W:** George Rubio, Larry Cohen; **M:** Brad Fiedel. *VTR*

Intolerance 🐾🐾🐾🐾 1916 Griffith's largest film in every aspect. An interwoven, four-story epic about human intolerance, with segments set in Babylon, ancient Judea, and Paris. One of the cinema's grandest follies, and greatest achievements. Silent with music score. Laserdisc version contains supplemental material including cuts from other Griffith works. Black and white with some restored color footage. **175m/B VHS, LV.** Lillian Gish, Mae Marsh, Constance Talmadge, Bessie Love, Elmer Clifton, Erich von Stroheim, Eugene Pallette, Seena Owen, Alfred Paget; **D:** D.W. Griffith. *GPV, MRV, KIV*

Intrigue 🐾🐾½ 1990 (PG) Former CIA agent (Loggia) defects to the KGB, but wants to return to the US when he realizes he has a progressive illness. Underground agent and old buddy (Glenn) is recruited with orders to smuggle his former colleague out. Tension continues throughout as murder comes along with the orders. Loads of suspense and twist ending in this made for television nail-biter. **96m/C VHS, LV.** Scott Glenn, Robert Loggia, William Atherton, Martin Shaw, Cherie Lunghi, Eleanor Bron; **D:** David Drury. *THV*

Intruder 🐾🐾 1977 A man and his stepson are terrorized by a stranger in a panel truck as they travel from Rome to Paris. **98m/C VHS, Beta.** Jean-Louis Trintignant, Mireille Darc, Adolfo Celi. *NO*

Intruder 🐾🐾 1988 (R) A psychotic killer stalks an all-night convenience store shopping for fresh meat (customers beware). Slasher movie fans should get a kick out of the plot twist at the end. **90m/C VHS, Beta, LV, Closed Caption.** Elizabeth

Cox, Renee Estevez, Alvy Moore; **D:** Scott Spiegel; **W:** Lawrence Bender. *PAR*

Intruder in the Dust 🐾🐾🐾½ 1949 A small southern community develops a lynch mob mentality when a black man is accused of killing a white man. Powerful, but largely ignored portrait of race relations in the South. Solid performances from the whole cast; filmed in Mississippi. Adapted from a novel by William Faulkner. **87m/B VHS.** David Brian, Claude Jarman Jr., Juano Hernandez, Porter Hall, Elizabeth Patterson; **D:** Clarence Brown; **C:** Robert L. Surtees. *MGM, MOV, BTV*

Intruder Within 🐾 1981 Half-baked thriller about crew on an isolated oil rig in Antarctica who, while drilling, unearth a nasty creature that goes around terrorizing the frost-bitten men and occasional stray woman. Made for television. **91m/C VHS, Beta.** Chad Everett, Joseph Bottoms, Jennifer Warren; **D:** Peter Carter. *TWE*

Intruders 🐾🐾 1992 Follows the story of three people who have unexplained lapses of time in their lives which they eventually believe are connected to visits by aliens. The three are brought together by a skeptical psychiatrist. The aliens are your typical bugged-eyed, white-faced spooks but part of the film is genuinely unsettling. **162m/C VHS, Closed Caption.** Richard Crenna, Mare Winningham, Susan Blakely, Ben Vereen, Steven Berkoff, Daphne Ashbrook; **D:** Dan Curtis. *FXV*

Intruso 🐾🐾½ *Intruder* 1993 Gloomy story set in a coastal city in northern Spain. Luisa (Abril) spots her destitute ex-husband Angel (Arias) and persuades him to stay with her and her new family, husband Ramiro (Valero)—once Angel's good friend—and their two young children. Angel turns out to be terminally ill and decides to wreak vengeance on Ramiro by reclaiming Luisa for himself. In Spanish with English subtitles. **85m/C VHS.** *SP* Victoria Abril, Imanol Arias, Antonio Valero; **D:** Vicente Aranda; **W:** Vicente Aranda, Alvaro del Amo. *NYF*

Invader 🐾🐾 1991 (R) When a news reporter is sent to cover a mysterious massacre, he begins to realize that the culprits are vicious aliens thirsty for blood...and now they're after him! **CW:** Language and violence. **95m/C VHS, LV.** Hans Bachman, A. Thomas Smith, Rich Foucheux, John Cooke, Robert Diedermann, Allison Sheehy, Ralph Bluemke; **D:** Phillip Cook. *THV*

The Invaders 🐾🐾 *Erik the Conqueror; Gli Invasori; La Ruee Des Vikings; Fury of the Vikings* 1963 Two Viking brothers battle each other and the Britons. **88m/C VHS, Beta.** *FR IT* Cameron Mitchell, George Ardisson, Andrea Checchi, Francoise Christophe, Joe Robinson; **D:** Mario Bava; **M:** Les Baxter. *NO*

The Invaders 1967 The popular science fiction series created by Larry Cohen stars Thinnes, as David Vincent, who attempts to convince people he has witnessed an alien landing and that they want to take over Earth. "Beach Head" is the pilot episode. Additional episodes available. **53m/C VHS.** Roy Thinnes, Kent Smith, Diane Baker, J.D. Cannon, James Daly, John Milford, Ellen Corby, Vaughn Taylor; **D:** Joseph Sargent. *GKK, MOV*

The Invaders 🐾🐾½ 1995 TV mini is an updated continuation of the 1967 sci-fi series that finds the pollution-loving aliens gradually conquering Earth by allowing humans to destroy their own ecosystem (which we're so good at anyway). Bewildered hero Nolan Wood (Bakula) is trying to get everyone to believe in the alien invasion but since he's just gotten out of prison, it's an uphill climb. Still, the aliens (lead by effectively evil Thomas) would like to permanently shut Nolan up. Thinnes, who starred in the original series, briefly reprises his role as David Vincent. **180m/C VHS, LV, Closed Caption.** Scott Bakula, Richard Thomas, DeLane Matthews, Terence Knox, Elizabeth Pena, Raoul Trujillo, Richard Belzer, Jon Polito, Roy Thinnes, Jon Cypher, Todd Susman, Jack Kehler, Elinor Donahue; **D:** Paul Shapiro; **W:** James Dott; **C:** Alan Kivilo; **M:** Joseph Vitarelli. *REP*

Invaders from Mars ⅆⅆ½ **1953** Young boy cries "martian" in this sci-fi cheapy classic. He can't convince the townspeople of this invasion because they've already been possessed by the alien beings. His parents are zapped by the little green things first, making this perhaps an allegory for the missing Eisenhower/Stepford years. Includes previews of coming attractions from classic science fiction films. Remade in 1986 by Tobe Hooper. **78m/C VHS, Beta.** Helena Carter, Arthur Franz, Jimmy Hunt, Leif Erickson; *D:* William Cameron Menzies. *MED, MLB*

Invaders from Mars ⅆ½ **1986 (PG)** A high-tech remake of Menzies' 1953 semi-classic about a Martian invasion perceived only by one young boy and a sympathetic (though hysterical) school nurse, played by mother and son Black and Carson. Instant camp. **102m/C VHS, Beta, LV, Closed Caption.** Hunter Carson, Karen Black, Louise Fletcher, Laraine Newman, Timothy Bottoms, Bud Cort; *D:* Tobe Hooper; *W:* Dan O'Bannon, Don Jakoby. *MED, IME*

Invasion ⅆⅆ½ **1965** A hospital opens its doors to an accident victim, and his attractive female visitors don't seem sympathetic to the idea of a long hospital stay. Turns out he's an escaped alien prisoner, and the alien babes, intent on intergalactic extradition, place a force field around the hospital and demand his return. Early effort of director Bridges, who later did "The Shooting Party." Interesting, creepy, atmospheric, with very cool camera moves. **82m/B VHS.** *GB* Edward Judd, Yoko Tani, Valerie Gearon, Lyndon Brook, Tsai Chin, Barrie Ingham; *D:* Alan Bridges. *MOV*

Invasion Earth: The Aliens Are Here! ⅆ **1987** A cheap spoof of monster movies, as an insectoid projectionist takes over the minds of a movie audience. Clips of Godzilla, Mothra and other beasts are interpolated. **84m/C VHS, Beta, LV.** Janice Fabian, Christian Lee; *D:* George Maitland. *VTR, NWV*

Invasion Force ⅆ **1990** A terrorist army parachutes into a remote region where a film crew is preparing to set up for an action movie. The moviemakers must scare away the terrorists with their smokepots and blanks. Sounds promising, but proves to be as empty as the movie props used to scare the terrorists. **93m/C VHS.** Richard Lynch, David Shark, Renee Cline, Douglas Hartier, Graham Times, Angie Synodis; *D:* David A. Prior. *AIP*

The Invasion of Carol Enders ⅆ½ **1974** A woman, almost killed by a prowler, awakens with an expanded consciousness, and tries to convince her near husband that her death wasn't an accident. **72m/C VHS, Beta.** Meredith Baxter, Christopher Connelly, Charles Aidman. *LIV*

Invasion of Privacy ⅆⅆ **1992 (R)** Alex is a psycho prison inmate obsessed with high profile journalist, Hilary. When Hilary interviews Alex for a magazine cover story, his obsession only grows stronger. Then Alex gets paroled and goes to work for Hilary. When he discovers Hilary isn't interested in him, Alex turns his fantasies to her daughter, who has no notion what she's getting into. An unrated version is also available. Made for cable television.*CW:* Language, violence, and sexuality. **95m/C VHS, Closed Caption.** Robby Benson, Jennifer O'Neill, Lydie Denier, Ian Ogilvy; *D:* Kevin Meyer; *W:* Kevin Meyer. *PSM*

Invasion of Privacy ⅆⅆ **1996 (R)** Some hot-button topics take the thriller route. When Theresa (Avital) becomes pregnant, she discovers her boyfriend Josh (Schaech) is seriously unbalanced. She decides on an abortion but retreats for some quiet time to an isolated lakeside cabin. Mistake—the expectant dad shows up and holds her prisoner until Theresa is too far along to terminate the pregnancy. When Josh finally releases her, Theresa heads for the cops and charges him with kidnapping. He gets a hot female lawyer (Rampling), who turns the media attention to making him a cause celebre for parental rights. Once the baby is born, Josh is also determined to

gain custody—by whatever means necessary.*CW:* Language and some violence and terror. **94m/C VHS.** Johnathon Schaech, Mili Avital, David Keith, Charlotte Rampling, Naomi Campbell, Tom Wright, R.G. Armstrong; *D:* Anthony Hickox; *W:* Larry Cohen; *C:* Peter Wunstorf; *M:* Angelo Badalamenti. *THV*

Invasion of the Animal People woof! *Terror in the Midnight Sun; Space Invasion of Lapland; Horror in the Midnight Sun; Space Invasion from Lapland* **1962** Hairy monster from outer space attacks Lapland. Narrated by Carradine, the only American in the cast. Pretty silly. **73m/C VHS.** *SW* Robert Burton, Barbara Wilson, John Carradine; *D:* Virgil W. Vogel, Jerry Warren. *THV, SNC, NOS*

Invasion of the Bee Girls ⅆⅆⅆ *Graveyard Tramps* **1973** California girls are mysteriously transformed into deadly nymphomaniacs in this delightful campy science fiction romp. Written by Meyer who later directed "Star Trek II: The Wrath of Khan." **85m/C VHS.** Victoria Vetri, William Smith, Anitra Ford, Cliff Osmond, Wright King, Ben Hammer; *D:* Denis Sanders; *W:* Nicholas Meyer; *M:* Charles Bernstein.

Invasion of the Blood Farmers woof! **1972 (PG)** In a small New York town, members of an ancient Druidic cult murder young women, taking their blood in the hope of finding the precise, rare blood type to keep their queen alive. A real woofer. **86m/C VHS, Beta.** Norman Kelley, Tanna Hunter, Bruce Detrick, Jack Neubeck, Cythia Fleming, Paul Craig Jennings; *D:* Ed Adlum. *NO*

Invasion of the Body Snatchers ⅆⅆⅆ **1956** The one and only post-McCarthy paranoid sci-fi epic, where a small California town is infiltrated by pods from outer space that replicate and replace humans. A chilling, genuinely frightening exercise in nightmare dislocation. Based upon a novel by Jack Finney. Remade in 1978. The laserdisc version contains commentary by Maurice Yacowar, the text of an interview with Siegel, and the original theatrical trailer. The film itself is presented in its original wide-screen format. **80m/B VHS, LV, Closed Caption.** Kevin McCarthy, Dana Wynter, Carolyn Jones, King Donovan, Donald Siegel; *D:* Don Siegel; *W:* Sam Peckinpah; *C:* Ellsworth Fredericks. *REP, CRC, MLB*

Invasion of the Body Snatchers ⅆⅆⅆ½ **1978 (PG)** One of the few instances where a remake is an improvement on the original, which was itself a classic. This time, the "pod people" are infesting San Francisco, with only a small group of people aware of the invasion. A ceaselessly inventive, creepy version of the alien-takeover paradigm, with an intense and winning performance by Sutherland. **115m/C VHS, Beta, LV.** Donald Sutherland, Brooke Adams, Veronica Cartwright, Leonard Nimoy, Jeff Goldblum, Kevin McCarthy, Donald Siegel, Art Hindle; *D:* Philip Kaufman; *W:* W.D. Richter; *C:* Michael Chapman. *MGM*

Invasion of the Body Stealers woof! *Thin Air; The Body Stealers* **1969 (PG)** Aliens are thought to be the captors when sky-divers begin vanishing in mid-air. Uneven sci-fi with nothing going for it. **115m/C VHS, Beta.** *GB* George Sanders, Maurice Evans, Patrick Allen; *D:* Gerry Levy. *LIV*

Invasion of the Flesh Hunters woof! *Cannibals in the Streets; Savage Apocalypse; The Slaughterers; Cannibals in the City; Virus* **1982** Group of tortured Vietnam veterans returns home carrying a cannibalistic curse with them. Smorgasbord of gore and sensationalism is not for discriminating tastes. **90m/C VHS, Beta.** *IT* John Saxon, Elizabeth Turner; *D:* Anthony (Antonio Margheriti) Dawson; *W:* Anthony (Antonio Margheriti) Dawson. *LIV, VES*

Invasion of the Girl Snatchers woof! **1973** Aliens from another planet, in cahoots with a cult kingpin, subdue young earth girls and force them to undergo bizarre acts that may just rob them of their dignity.

Save a bit of your own dignity by staying away. Cheap look, cheap feel, cheap thrills. **90m/C VHS, Beta.** Elizabeth Rush, Ele Grigsby, David Roster; *D:* Lee Jones. *NO*

Invasion of the Saucer Men ⅆ **1957** Suburban teenagers (Terrell, Castillo) are detained by a little green man at lovers lane. When they return with police to the scene, only the corpse of the town drunk (Gorshin) remains. Fortunately, the dead man's roommate (Osborn) believes them but the trio must convince authorities before the alien creatures multiply and take over the world. **69m/B VHS.** Steven Terrell, Gloria Castillo, Frank Gorshin, Lyn Osborn, Ed Nelson, Angelo Rossitto; *D:* Edward L. Cahn; *M:* Ronald Stein. *COL*

Invasion of the Space Preachers **1990** Hideous creatures from outer space arrive on Earth with plans for conquest. Led by the seemingly human Reverend Lash, they prey on the innocent and trusting, fleecing God-fearing folk out of their hard earned cash! **100m/C VHS, Beta.** Jim Wolfe, Guy Nelson, Eliska Hahn, Gary Brown, Jesse Johnson, John Riggs; *D:* Daniel Boyd; *W:* Daniel Boyd. *RHI*

Invasion of the Vampires ⅆ *La Invasion de Los Vampiros* **1961** Burrito bat fest has Count Frankenhausen doing his vampire thing in a small, 16th century village. Atmospheric sets are highlight. Not a good substitute for No Doze. **78m/B VHS.** *MX* Carlos Agosti, Rafael Etienne, Bertha Moss, Tito Junco, Erna Martha Bauman, Fernando Soto, Enrique Garcia Alvarez, David Reynoso; *D:* Miguel Morayta; *W:* Miguel Morayta. *SNC*

Invasion of the Zombies ⅆ **1961** Bare-fisted wrestler Santo faces of brace of zombies in order to prove that men with short necks can hug other men and still be mucho macho. **85m/B VHS.** *MX* Santo; *D:* Benito Alazraki. *SNC, HHT*

Invasion U.S.A. ⅆ½ **1952** Cheap Red Scare movie using tons of stock footage showing actual bombings and air battles. O'Herlihy is a stranger who visits a New York bar and convinces the patrons that the H-bomb has been unleashed on America, while Mohr romances Castle. Full of propaganda and overacting. Based on a story by Robert Smith and Franz Spencer. **73m/B VHS.** Gerald Mohr, Peggy Castle, Dan O'Herlihy, Robert Bice, Tom Kennedy, Phyllis Coates; *D:* Alfred E. Green; *W:* Robert Smith. *SNC*

Invasion U.S.A. ⅆ **1985 (R)** A mercenary defends nothing less than the entire country against Russian terrorists landing in Florida and looking for condos. A record-setting amount of people killed. Count them—it's not like you'll miss anything important. Norris is a bit less animated than a wooden Indian, and the acting is more painful to endure than the violence. Glasnost saved the movie industry from additional paranoia movies of this kind. **108m/C VHS, Beta, LV.** Chuck Norris, Richard Lynch, Melissa Prophet, Alex Colon, Billy Drago; *D:* Joseph Zito; *W:* James Bruner. *MGM*

Inventing the Abbotts ⅆⅆ **1997 (R)** Appealing cast populates this sleepy, bittersweet coming-of-age story set in small town Illinois in 1957. Alice (Going), Eleanor (Connelly) and Pamela (Tyler) are the lovely daughters of wealthy Lloyd Abbott (Patton) who's determined that they'll marry well despite the temptations offered by the two working-class Holt boys. Surly stud Jacey (Crudup) holds a grudge against Lloyd for possibly cheating his deceased father in a business deal and causing whispers about his schoolteacher mother Helen's (Baker) reputation, while sweet-natured younger brother Doug (Phoenix) has his romantic ideals fixed on Pamela, who loves him in return. Not memorable, but not a complete waste of time, either. Based on the story by Sue Miller.*CW:* Sexuality and language. **110m/C VHS, Closed Caption.** Billy Crudup, Joaquin Rafael (Leaf) Phoenix, Liv Tyler, Will Patton, Kathy Baker, Jennifer Connelly, Joanna Going, Barbara Williams; *D:* Pat

O'Connor; **W:** Ken Hixon; **C:** Kenneth Macmillan; **M:** Michael Kamen. *FXV*

Investigation 🎦🎦½ 1979 A Frenchman plans to murder his wife so he can marry his pregnant mistress, guaranteeing an heir. Subtle study of small town people so concerned with their own welfare that the dirty deeds of the lead character might be overlooked. Fine performances and story development make this worth investigating. In French with English subtitles. **116m/C VHS, Beta.** *FR* Victor Lanoux, Valerie Mairesse; **D:** Etienne Perier.

Invincible 🎦½ 1980 (R) Martial arts student must find and correct another student who has turned evil. For Bruce Lee fans, as if they haven't already memorized all the memorable lines-"hiyaah," "ugh," "oof," etc. **93m/C VHS, Beta.** Chen Sing, Ho Chung Dao. *GEM*

Invincible Barbarian woof! 1983 A young man leads a tribe of amazing Amazon warriors in a sneak attack against the tribe that annihilated his native village. One of those movies that presumes "primitivism" can be recreated through bad acting. **92m/C VHS, Beta.** Diana Roy, David Jenkins. *PSM*

The Invincible Gladiator 🎦½ *Il Gladiatore Invincibile* 1963 A gladiator who saves the evil man ruling a land for a boy-king is given command of an army. He eventually leads the army in revolt when the evil man tries to take over the throne. Plodding with stock characters. **96m/C VHS.** *IT SP* Richard Harrison, Isabel Corey, Livio Lorenzon; **D:** Frank Gregory. *SNC*

Invincible Gladiators woof! 1964 The sons of Hercules labor to aid a prince whose bride had been kidnapped by an evil queen. Laborious to watch. **87m/C VHS, Beta.** Richard Lloyd, Claudia Lange, Tony Freeman; **D:** Robert Mauri. *NO*

Invincible Mr. Disraeli 🎦🎦½ 1963 Presentation from "George Schaefer's Showcase Theatre" deals with the life and career of Benjamin Disraeli, novelist, philosopher, first Earl of Beaconsfield, statesman, and Prime Minister. Basically a tribute. Made for television. **76m/C VHS, Beta.** Trevor Howard, Greer Garson, Hurd Hatfield, Kate Reid; **D:** George Schaefer. *FHS*

The Invincible Six 🎦🎦 1968 An unlikely band of thieves running from the law winds up protecting a small village from marauding bandits. Plenty of action, as you would expect when thieves take on bandits, but with no scene-stealers or sympathetic characters the story lacks interest. Unremarkable choreography by ballet great Rudolf Nureyev. Filmed in Iran. **96m/C VHS, Beta.** Stuart Whitman, Elke Sommer, Curt Jurgens, Jim Mitchum, Ian Ogilvy; **D:** Jean Negulesco. *NO*

Invisible Adversaries 🎦🎦 1977 A photographer uncovers an extra-terrestrial plot to cause excessive aggression in humans. She and her lover attempt to hold on to their crumbling humanity. Movies like this make you mad enough to tear something up. Enjoyed a meek cult following. In German with English subtitles. **112m/C VHS, Beta.** *GE* Susanne Widl, Peter Weibel; **D:** Valie Export. *FCT*

Invisible Agent 🎦🎦 1942 Hall plays an agent using the secret formula to outwit the Nazis in this third sequel to "The Invisible Man." Especially enjoyable for the kids. Based on characters suggested in H.G. Well's "The Invisible Man." **83m/B VHS, Closed Caption.** Ilona Massey, Jon Hall, Peter Lorre, Cedric Hardwicke, J. Edward Bromberg, Albert Basserman, John Litel, Holmes Herbert; **D:** Edwin L. Marin; **W:** Curt Siodmak. *USH, FCT*

The Invisible Avenger 🎦🎦 *Bourbon St. Shadows* 1958 Based on the vintage radio character "The Shadow." A detective who can make himself invisible investigates the murder of a New Orleans jazz musician. The mysterious element successful on radio is lost on film, and only the Shadow knows why. **60m/B VHS, Beta.** Richard Derr, Mark Daniels, Helen Westcott, Jeanne Neher; **D:** John Sledge, Ben Parker. *SNC, SMW, RXM*

The Invisible Boy 🎦🎦½ 1957 (G) Science fiction story about a young boy and his robot (Robby the Robot from "Forbidden Planet"). Kids will enjoy this adventure as told through the viewpoint of the child. Based on a story by Edmund Cooper. **89m/C VHS.** Richard Eyer, Diane Brewster, Philip Abbott, Harold J. Stone; **D:** Herman Hoffman; **W:** Cyril Hume; **M:** Les Baxter. *MGM, FCT*

The Invisible Dead 🎦 *Orloff Against the Invisible Man* 1970 So many invisible man movies, so little time. A scientist creates an invisible man, imprisons and tortures him. A bit miffed with his host, he who can't be seen escapes, and vents his invisible spleen. **90m/C VHS.** *IT* Howard Vernon, Britt Carva; **D:** Jess (Jesus) Franco. *NO*

The Invisible Dr. Mabuse 🎦🎦🎦 *The Invisible Horror; Die Unsichtbaren Krallen des Dr. Mabuse* 1962 Possibly the best of the Dr. Mabuse series sees the mad scientist using an invisibility agent in an attempt to take over the world. Preiss also played the title villian in Fritz Lang's "The Thousand Eyes of Dr. Mabuse." **89m/B VHS, Beta.** *GE* Lex Barker, Karin Dor, Siegfried Lowitz, Wolfgang Preiss, Rudolf Fernau; **D:** Harald Reinl. *SNC*

The Invisible Ghost 🎦½ 1941 A man carries out a series of grisly stranglings while under hypnosis by his insane wife. Typically bad low-budget exploiter about a fun-lovin' crazy couple bringing down property values in the neighborhood. **70m/B VHS, Beta.** Bela Lugosi, Polly Ann Young; **D:** Joseph H. Lewis. *VYY, MRV, SNC*

Invisible Invaders 🎦 1959 Short, cheap, and silly aliens-try-to-take-over-the-earth flick. This time they're moonmen who use the bodies of dead earthlings (ugh) to attack the living until Agar can save the day. Carradine has a brief role as a formerly-dead scientist. **67m/B VHS, Closed Caption.** John Agar, Robert Hutton, Hal Torey, Jean Byron, Philip Tonge, John Carradine; **D:** Edward L. Cahn; **W:** Samuel Newman; **C:** Maury Gertsman. *MGM*

The Invisible Kid 🎦 1988 A shy teen manages to make himself invisible, a feat which ironically permits him to get people to notice him. Now he can visit places he's only dreamed of, including the girls' locker room. For those who have dreamed of girls' locker rooms. **95m/C VHS, Beta, LV.** Karen Black, Jay Underwood, Chynna Phillips, Wally Ward, Brother Theodore; **D:** Avery Crounse; **W:** Avery Crounse. *MED, VTR*

The Invisible Killer 🎦½ 1940 Someone is killing folks by sending poison through telephone lines. A detective and a reporter team up to find the scoundrel by setting up an answering machine that automatically plays back messages to the caller. Bad connection of events leads to a static resolution. **61m/B VHS, Beta.** Grace Bradley, Roland Drew, William Newell; **D:** Sam Newfield. *SNC, MLB*

The Invisible Man 🎦🎦🎦🎦 1933 The vintage horror-fest based on H. G. Wells' novella about a scientist whose formula for invisibility slowly drives him insane. His mind definitely wandering, he plans plans to use his recipe to rule the world. Rains' first role; though his body doesn't appear until the final scene, his voice characterization is magnificent. The visual detail is excellent, setting standards that are imitated because they are difficult to surpass; with special effects by John P. Fulton. **71m/B VHS, Beta, LV.** Claude Rains, Gloria Stuart, Dudley Digges, William Harrigan, Una O'Connor, E.E. Clive, Dwight Frye; **D:** James Whale; **W:** R.C. Sherriff. *USH, MLB*

The Invisible Man Returns 🎦🎦🎦 1940 Price stars as the original invisible man's brother. Using the same invisibility formula, Price tries to clear himself after being charged with murder. He reappears at the worst times, and you gotta love that floating gun. Fun sequel to 1933's classic "The Invisible Man." **81m/B VHS.** Cedric Hardwicke, Vincent Price, John Sutton, Nan Grey; **D:** Joe May; **C:** Milton Krasner. *USH, MLB*

The Invisible Maniac woof! 1990 (R) A crazy voyeur perfects a serum for invisibility and promptly gets a job as a physics teacher in a high school. There he leers at girls taking showers and slaughters students when he is caught. For voyeurs. Get outta here, you maniac. **87m/C VHS.** Noel Peters, Shannon Wilsey, Melissa Moore, Robert Ross, Rod Sweitzer, Eric Champnella, Alan Curtis, Leon Errol, Doris Lloyd; **D:** Rif Coogan; **W:** Rif Coogan. *REP*

The Invisible Man's Revenge 🎦🎦½ 1944 Left for dead on a safari five years before, Hall seeks revenge against Sondergaard and Matthews, aided by scientist Carradine who renders Hall invisible. Only problem is Hall doesn't stay that way. Fifth in Universal's "Invisible Man" film series. **78m/B VHS, Closed Caption.** Jon Hall, John Carradine, Gale Sondergaard, Lester Matthews, Evelyn Ankers, Alan Curtis, Leon Errol, Doris Lloyd; **D:** Ford Beebe; **W:** Bertram Millhauser; **C:** Milton Krasner. *USH*

Invisible Mom 🎦🎦½ 1996 (PG) Dad (Livingston) invents an invisibility potion that his 10-year-old son decides will make him popular at school. Too bad Mom (Wallace Stone) accidentally swallows the concoction instead. **82m/C VHS.** Dee Wallace Stone, Barry Livingston, Trenton Knight, Russ Tamblyn, Stella Stevens; **D:** Fred Olen Ray. *NHO*

The Invisible Monster *Slaves of the Invisible Monster* 1950 Special investigators Lane Carlson and Carol Richards battle a mad scientist ready to take over the world with his invisible army. 12 episodes of the original serial edited onto two cassettes. **167m/B VHS.** Richard Webb, Aline Towne, Lane Bradford, Stanley Price, John Crawford, George Meeker; **D:** Fred Brannon. *REP*

The Invisible Ray 🎦🎦½ 1936 For a change, this horror film features Lugosi as the hero, fighting Karloff, a scientist who locates a meteor that contains a powerful substance. Karloff is poisoned and becomes a murdering megalomaniac. Watching Karloff and Lugosi interact, and the great special effects—including a hot scene where a scientist bursts into flames—helps you ignore a generally hokey script. **82m/B VHS, Beta, LV.** Boris Karloff, Bela Lugosi, Frances Drake, Frank Lawton, Beulah Bondi, Walter Kingsford; **D:** Lambert Hillyer. *USH, MLB*

The Invisible Strangler 🎦½ 1976 (PG) A death-row murderer can make himself invisible and rubs out witnesses who helped put him away; woman risks her life to expose him when the police fail to see the problem. Very violent collection of brutal scenes. Not released theatrically until 1984. **85m/C VHS, Beta.** Robert Foxworth, Stefanie Powers, Elke Sommer, Sue Lyon, Leslie Parrish, Marianna Hill; **D:** John Florea. *TWE*

The Invisible Terror 🎦🎦 1963 A maniac steals a mad scientist's invisibility formula and uses it on a number of innocent victims. **?m/C VHS.** Herbert Stass, Ellen Scheirs. *SNC*

Invisible: The Chronicles of Benjamin Knight 🎦🎦½ 1993 (R) Scientist Benjamin Knight is rendered invisible during a terrible laboratory accident. His only hope of regaining his visible form is a desperate search by Knight and his fellow scientists for just the right chemical antidote. *CW:* Violence and strong sexuality. **80m/C VHS, Beta, Closed Caption.** Brian Cousins, Jennifer Nash, Michael DellaFemina, Curt Lowens, David Kaufman, Alan Oppenheimer, Aharon Ipale; **D:** Jack Ersgard; **W:** Earl Kenton. *PAR*

The Invisible Woman 🎦🎦🎦 1940 Above average comedy about zany professor Barrymore discovering the secret of invisibility and making luscious model Bruce transparent. Great cast makes this a very likeable movie. Based on a story by Curt Siodmak and Joe May, the same team that wrote "The Invisible Man Returns." **73m/B VHS, Closed Caption.** John Barrymore, Virginia Bruce, John Howard, Charlie Ruggles, Oscar Homolka, Margaret Hamilton, Donald MacBride, Edward Brophy, Shemp Howard, Charles Lane, Thurston Hall; **D:** Edward

Sutherland; **W:** Robert Lees, Frederic Rinaldo, Gertrude Purcell. *USH, FCT*

Invitation au Voyage 🎬🎬½ 1982 (R)
Follows the journey of a twin who refuses to accept the death of his sister, a rock singer. The obsession is played fairly well, but it's a no-twin situation, even though the guy can't admit it. Perversity is played to the point of overkill. From the novel "Moi, Ma Soeur Images," by Jean Bany. In French with English subtitles. **90m/C VHS, Beta.** *FR* Laurent Malet, Nina Scott, Aurore Clement, Mario Adorf; **D:** Peter Del Monte. *COL*

Invitation to a Gunfighter 🎬🎬 1964
Small town politics change when a paid assassin ambles into town and creates a lot of talk among the neighbors. Like a long joke in which the teller keeps forgetting the important details, the plot grows confusing though it's not complicated. Brynner is interesting as an educated, half-black/half-creole, hired gun. **92m/C VHS, Beta, Closed Caption.** Yul Brynner, George Segal, Strother Martin, William Hickey, Janice Rule, Mike Kellin, Pat Hingle; **D:** Richard Wilson. *MGM, HHE*

Invitation to Hell WOOF! 1984
Tormented maiden has a devil of a time discovering a secret power that can enable her to gracefully decline a satanic summoning. The cliched evil is tormenting. **100m/C VHS, Beta.** Becky Simpson, Joseph Sheahan, Colin Efford, Stephen Longhurst. *NO*

Invitation to Hell 🎬½ 1984
"Faust" meets "All My Children" in celluloid suburbia. Never Emmied Lucci is the devil's dirty worker, persuading upwardly mobile suburbanites to join a really exclusive country club in exchange for a little downward mobility. Urich, a space scientist, and family are new in town, and soul searching Lucci's got her devil vixen sights set on space jock and brood. Bound to disappoint both fans of Craven's early independent work ("Last House on the Left") and his later high gloss ("Nightmare on Elm Street") formulas. Made for the small screen. **100m/C VHS, Beta.** Susan Lucci, Robert Urich, Joanna Cassidy, Kevin McCarthy, Patty McCormack, Joe Regalbuto, Soleil Moon Frye; **D:** Wes Craven. *NO*

Invitation to the Dance 🎬🎬½ 1956
Three classic dance sequences, "Circus," "Ring Around the Rosy," and "Sinbad the Sailor." For dance lovers, featuring excellent performances by Kelly. **93m/C VHS, Beta.** Gene Kelly, Igor Youskevitch, Tamara Toumanova; **D:** Gene Kelly. Berlin International Film Festival '56: Golden Berlin Bear. *MGM, CCB*

Invitation to the Wedding 1973 (PG)
When the best friend of a bridegroom falls in love with the bride, he stops at nothing to halt the wedding. Not exactly the Gielgud movie of the year, but there are some excellent scenes between him and Richardson. **89m/C VHS, Beta.** John Gielgud, Ralph Richardson, Paul Nicholas, Elizabeth Shepherd; **D:** Joseph Brooks; **M:** Joseph Brooks. *VES*

The Ipcress File 🎬🎬🎬 1965
The first of the Harry Palmer mysteries that made Caine a star. Based upon the bestseller by Len Deighton, it features the flabby, nearsighted spy investigating the kidnapping of notable British scientists. Solid scenes, including a scary brainwashing session, and tongue-firmly-in-British-cheek humor. Lots of camera play to emphasize Caine's myopia. Two sequels: "Funeral in Berlin" and "Billion Dollar Brain." **108m/C VHS, Beta.** *GB* Michael Caine, Nigel Green, Guy Doleman, Sue Lloyd; **D:** Sidney J. Furie; **M:** John Barry. British Academy Awards '65: Best Film. *USH*

Iphigenia 🎬🎬🎬 1977
Based on the classic Greek tragedy by Euripides, this story concerns the Greek leader Agamemnon, who plans to sacrifice his lovely daughter, Iphigenia, to please the gods. Mere mortals protest and start a save-the-babe movement, but Euripides' moral—you can't please 'em all—is devastatingly realized. Fine adaptation that becomes visually extravagant at times, with an equally fine musical score. In Greek with English subtitles. **130m/C VHS, Beta.** *GR* Irene Papas, Costa Kazakos, Tatiana Papamoskou, Costas

Carras, Christos Tsangas, Panos Michalopoulas; **D:** Michael Cacoyannis; **W:** Michael Cacoyannis; **C:** Yorgos Arvanitis; **M:** Mikis Theodorakis. Nominations: Academy Awards '77: Best Foreign Language Film. *COL, FHS*

I.Q. 🎬🎬½ 1994 (PG)
Albert Einstein (the irascible Matthau) thinks his co-ed niece (Ryan) is in need of a little romance, so he engineers a plan to get her into the arms of Robbins, a local auto mechanic. Robbins and Ryan are comfortable in their comic roles, although they're both above the material. Matthau shines as the famous physicist. Plot gets a little farfetched with its central contrivance of making Robbins look like a brilliant scientist, which leaves second half of story flat. However, chemistry between leads is undeniable and you can't help but cheer on the inevitable. Visually pleasing with Ryan costumed in cool, elegant '50s fashions. Filmed in Princeton, New Jersey. **95m/C VHS, Beta, Closed Caption.** Tim Robbins, Meg Ryan, Walter Matthau, Lou Jacobi, Gene Saks, Joseph Maher, Stephen Fry, Tony Shalhoub, Frank Whaley; **D:** Fred Schepisi; **W:** Michael Leeson, Andy Breckman; **C:** Ian Baker; **M:** Jerry Goldsmith. *PAR*

Iran: Days of Crisis 🎬🎬½ 1991
An insightful made-for-cable-TV miniseries recounts America's humiliation at the hands of Iranian radicals in 1979, told from the vantage of a U.S. embassy official married to a Tehran woman. Former Carter administration aides Hamilton Jordan and Gerald Rafshoon devised the docudrama, which spares neither them nor their president in showing how bungled and shortsighted policies led to 52 Americans held hostage for over a year. **185m/C VHS.** Arliss Howard, Alice Krige, George Grizzard, Jeff Fahey, Tony Goldwyn, Ronald Guttman, Valerie Kaprisky, Daniel Gelin; **D:** Kevin Connor. *TTC*

Irezumi 🎬🎬🎬 Spirit of Tattoo 1983
A Japanese woman has her body elaborately tattooed to please her lover. Things start off well enough. He's an inept lover, so she has directions tattooed, but then he discovers a "Dear John" letter on her foot just as she gives him the boot. Actually proves an interesting study in obsession and eroticism, with the tattoos drawing the lovers deeper and deeper until they get under each other's skin. In Japanese with English subtitles. **88m/C VHS, Beta, LV.** *JP NO*

Iris 🎬🎬 1989
Drama follows the passionate and tragic life of New Zealand writer Iris Wilkinson, an international novelist, poet, and journalist. Wilkinson achieved a great deal of acclaim as a writer, but suffered many personal tragedies, and eventually took her own life at age 33. Well intentioned but clunky treatment of powerful subject matter. **90m/C VHS, Beta.** *NZ* Helen Morse. *WOM*

Irish Cinderella 🎬🎬 1922
A silent version of the Cinderella legend set in Ireland, with thematic stress on Irish politics and patriotism. **72m/B VHS, Beta, 8mm.** Pattie MacNamara. *VYY*

Irish Luck 🎬🎬 1939
A bellhop turns detective to figure out the mysterious happenings in his hotel. Becomes terminally cute by playing on a luck o' the Irish theme. **58m/B VHS.** Frankie Darro, Dick Purcell, Sheila Darcy, Grant Withers; **D:** Howard Bretherton. *NOS, DVT, HEG*

The Irishman 🎬🎬½ 1978
Set in 1920s Australia, the tale of a proud North Queensland family and their struggles to stay together. The Irish immigrant father is a teamster whose horse-drawn wagons are threatened by progress. His fight to preserve old ways is impressive, but gives way to sentimentality. **108m/C VHS, Beta.** *AU* Lou Brown, Michael Craig, Simon Burke, Robyn Nevin, Bryan Brown; **D:** Donald Crombie. *VES*

Irma La Douce 🎬🎬½ 1963
A gendarme pulls a one-man raid on a back-street Parisian joint and falls in love with one of the hookers he arrests. Lemmon is great as a well-meaning, incompetent boob, and MacLaine gives her all as the hapless hooker. A plodding pace, however, robs it of the original's zip, though it was a box office smash. Broadway musical is lost without

the music. **144m/C VHS, Beta, LV, Closed Caption.** Jack Lemmon, Shirley MacLaine, Herschel Bernardi; **D:** Billy Wilder; **W:** Billy Wilder, I.A.L. Diamond; **M:** Andre Previn. Academy Awards '63: Best Adapted Score; Golden Globe Awards '64: Best Actress—Musical/Comedy (MacLaine); Nominations: Academy Awards '63: Best Actress (MacLaine), Best Color Cinematography. *MGM, IME, FOX*

Iron & Silk 🎬🎬½ 1991 (PG)
A young American searches for himself while he teaches English and learns martial arts in mainland China. Based on the true story of Salzman's travels. His studies of martial arts and Chinese culture provide a model for his students in their studies of American language and culture. Beautiful photography. Fine performances. **94m/C VHS, LV.** Mark Saltzman, Pan Qingfu, Jeanette Lin Tsui, Vivian Wu; **D:** Shirley Sun; **W:** Mark Saltzman, Shirley Sun; **M:** Michael Gibbs. *LIV*

Iron Angel 🎬½ 1964
During the Korean War a squadron sets out to silence North Korean guns. They do. Judging by their eternal bickering they must have put the enemy to sleep. **84m/B VHS.** Jim Davis, Margo Woode, Donald (Don "Red") Barry, L.Q. Jones; **D:** Ken Kennedy; **W:** Ken Kennedy. *NOS, LOO*

Iron Cowboy 🎬🎬 1968
Actor finds romance with film editor while audience stifles yawns. Filmed on the set of "Blue," this pre-"Deliverance" Reynolds comedy never made it to the theaters. (Smithee is actually director Jud Taylor.) **86m/C VHS.** Burt Reynolds, Barbara Loden, Terence Stamp, Noam Pitlik, Ricardo Montalban, Patricia Casey, Jane Hampton, Joseph Perry; **D:** Alan Smithee. *ACE*

The Iron Crown 🎬🎬 1941
A 13th-century legend inspired this sometime violent spectacle involving the title totem, a symbol of justice ignored by a powerful king at his peril. There's wonderful pagentry and a notable Tarzan imitator, but the pace is terribly slow. Italian dialogue with English subtitles. **100m/C VHS. D:** Alessandro Blasetti. *FST*

Iron Dragon Strikes Back 🎬 1984
Man seeks out the men who murdered his martial arts instructor. **90m/C VHS, Beta.** Bruce Li. *TWE*

The Iron Duke 🎬🎬½ 1934
Fair to middlin' historical account of the life of the Duke of Wellington, victor over Napoleon at Waterloo. **88m/B VHS, Beta.** *GB* George Arliss, Gladys Cooper, A.E. Matthews, Emlyn Williams, Felix Aylmer; **D:** Victor Saville. *NOS, WFV, BAR*

Iron Eagle 🎬🎬½ 1986 (PG-13)
A teenager teams with a renegade fighter pilot to rescue the youth's father from captivity in the Middle East. Predictable but often exciting. Followed by two sequels. **117m/C VHS, Beta, LV, Closed Caption.** Louis Gossett Jr., Jason Gedrick, Tim Thomerson, David Suchet, Larry B. Scott, Caroline Lagerfelt, Jerry Levine, Michael Bowen, Robbie Rist, Bobby Jacoby, Melora Hardin; **D:** Sidney J. Furie; **W:** Kevin Elders, Sidney J. Furie; **M:** Basil Poledouris. *FOX*

Iron Eagle 2 🎬🎬 1988 (PG)
Lower-budget extended adventures of a maverick fighter pilot after he is reinstated in the Air Force. This time he links with an equally rebellious commie fighter and blasts away at nuke-happy Ivan. Yahoo fun for all overt Yankees! Followed by "Aces: Iron Eagle 3." Available in Spanish. **102m/C VHS, Beta, LV.** *CA IS* Louis Gossett Jr., Mark Humphrey, Stuart Margolin, Alan Scarfe, Maury Chaykin, Sharon H. Brandon; **D:** Sidney J. Furie; **W:** Sidney J. Furie, Kevin Elders; **C:** Alan Dostie; **M:** Amin Bhatia. *LIV*

Iron Eagle 4 🎬½ 1995 (PG-13)
Series has gotten old and tired though Gossett, Jr. shows professionalism in his father figure role of retired Air Force General "Chappy" Sinclair. He's running the Iron Eagle Flight School—a training center/holding cell for troubled teens—along with pilot Doug Masters (Cadieux). Masters and his would-be pilots discover suspicious activities at a local air base, leading to biological weapons and an Air Force conspiracy. **CW:** Military violence, brief strong language, some drug references. **95m/C VHS, LV.** *CA* Louis Gossett Jr., Jason Cadieux, Al Waxman, Joanne Vannicola, Rachel Blanchard, Sean McCann, Ross

Hill, Karen Gayle; **D:** Sidney J. Furie; **W:** Michael Stokes; **C:** Curtis Petersen; **M:** Paul Zaza. THV

Iron Horsemen ⅃ J.C 1971 (R) A motorcycle gang leader has a prophetic vision while tripping on LSD, and returns to his former town to challenge its religious establishment. Also available on video under its original title "J.C." 97m/C VHS, Beta. William F. McGaha, Hannibal Penny, Joanna Moore, Burr de Benning, Slim Pickens, Pati Delaney; **D:** William F. McGaha. NLC

The Iron Major ⅃⅃½ 1943 Frank Cavanaugh, a famous football coach, becomes a hero in WWI. Standard flag-waving biography to increase morale back home, but fairly well-made. 85m/B VHS, Beta. Pat O'Brien, Ruth Warrick, Robert Ryan, Leon Ames, Russell Wade, Bruce Edwards; **D:** Ray Enright. TTC

The Iron Mask ⅃⅃½ 1929 Early swashbuckling extravaganza with a master swordsman defending the French king from a scheme involving substitution by a lookalike. Still fairly exciting, thanks largely to director Dwan's flair. Based on Alexandre Dumas' "Three Musketeers" and "The Man in the Iron Mask" with talking sequences. 87m/B VHS, Beta. Douglas Fairbanks Sr., Nigel de Brulier, Marguerite de la Motte; **D:** Allan Dwan. Nominations: Academy Awards '29: Best Interior Decoration. KIV, CCB, DVT

Iron Maze ⅃½ 1991 (R) A fascinating notion forms the center of this dramatic scrapheap; the classic Japanese "Rashomon" plot shifted to a rusting Pennsylvania steel town. When a Tokyo businessman is found bludgeoned, witnesses and suspects (including his American-born wife) tell contradictory stories. It's too convoluted and contrived to work, with a hollow happy ending tacked on. Oliver Stone helped produce. **CW:** Language and sensuality. 102m/C VHS, LV, Closed Caption. Jeff Fahey, Bridget Fonda, Hiroaki Murakami, J.T. Walsh, Gabriel Damon, John Randolph, Peter Allas; **D:** Hiroaki Yoshida; **W:** Tim Metcalfe. ACA

Iron Thunder ⅃½ 1989 Liberty is in peril and only much kicking and pec flexing will make the world a kinder gentler place. A thundering bore. 85m/C VHS. Iron "Amp" Elmore, George M. Young, Julius Dorsey. XVC, HHE

The Iron Triangle ⅃⅃ 1989 (R) A U.S. officer taken prisoner by the Viet Cong forms a bond with one of his captors. Film lends the viewer an opportunity to see things from the other sides perspective. 94m/C VHS, Beta, LV. Beau Bridges, Haing S. Ngor, Liem Whatley; **D:** Eric Weston; **W:** John Bushelman. LIV

Iron Warrior ⅃ 1987 (R) A barbarian hacks his way through a fantastical world to get to a beautiful princess. 82m/C VHS, Beta, Closed Caption. Miles O'Keeffe, Savina Gersak, Tim Lane; **D:** Al Bradley; **W:** Al Bradley. MED, VTR

Iron Will ⅃⅃½ 1993 (PG) Okay Disney family movie based on a true story. Will Stoneman is a 17-year-old farm kid from South Dakota. It's 1917 and because of his father's death there's no money to send Will to college. So he decides to enter the 500 mile winner-take-all dog sled race, with its $10,000 prize. Lots of obstacles, several villains, but Will perseveres. 109m/C VHS, LV, Closed Caption. MacKenzie Astin, Kevin Spacey, David Ogden Stiers, August Schellenberg, George Gerdes, John Terry; **D:** Charles Haid; **W:** John Michael Hayes, Jeffrey Arch, Djordje Milicevic; **M:** Joel McNeely. DIS

Ironclads ⅃⅃½ 1990 Memorable dramatization of the five-hour naval battle between the Confederate's Merrimac and the Union's Monitor during the Civil War. The special effects are the only thing worth watching in this overlong tale that includes standard subplots of loyalty, lost loves, and death from war. 94m/C VHS, Closed Caption. Virginia Madsen, Alex Hyde-White, Reed Edward Diamond, E.G. Marshall, Fritz Weaver, Philip Casnoff; **D:** Delbert Mann. TTC

Ironheart ⅃½ 1992 Slimy Milverstead and his henchman meet lovely young women at dance clubs, drug them, and sell them into slavery. But the trouble really starts when they kill a cop and his former partner, John Keem (Lee), lashes out with his blazing martial arts skill to still the perpetrators. **?m/C VHS, LV, Closed Caption.** Britton Lee, Bolo Yeung, Richard Norton, Karman Kruschke; **D:** Robert Clouse; **W:** Lawrence Riggins. IMP

Ironmaster ⅃ 1983 When a primitive tribesman is exiled from his tribe, he discovers a mysteriously power-filled iron staff on a mountainside. 98m/C VHS, Beta. George Eastman, Pamela Field. PSM

Ironweed ⅃⅃⅃ 1987 (R) Grim and gritty drama about bums living the hard life in Depression-era Albany. Nicholson excels as a former ballplayer turned drunk bothered by visions of the past, and Streep is his equal in the lesser role of a tubercular boozer. Waits also shines. Another grim view from "Pixote" director Babenco. Kennedy scripted based on his Pulitzer Prize-winning tragedy. 135m/C VHS, Beta, LV, Closed Caption. Jack Nicholson, Meryl Streep, Tom Waits, Carroll Baker, Michael O'Keefe, Fred Gwynne, Diane Venora, Margaret Whitton, Jake Dengel, Nathan Lane, James Gammon, Joe Grifasi, Bethel Leslie, Ted Levine, Frank Whaley; **D:** Hector Babenco; **W:** William Kennedy; **M:** John Morris. Los Angeles Film Critics Association Awards '87: Best Actor (Nicholson); New York Film Critics Awards '87: Best Actor (Nicholson); Nominations: Academy Awards '87: Best Actor (Nicholson), Best Actress (Streep). LIV

Irreconcilable Differences ⅃⅃½ 1984 (PG) When her Beverly Hills parents spend more time working and fretting than giving hugs and love, a ten-year-old girl sues them for divorce on the grounds of "irreconcilable differences." The media has a field day when they hear that she would rather go live with the maid. Well cast, with well-developed characterizations. The script, by the creators of "Private Benjamin," is humanely comic rather than uproariously funny. 112m/C VHS, Beta, LV, Closed Caption. Ryan O'Neal, Shelley Long, Drew Barrymore, Sam Wanamaker, Allen (Goorwitz) Garfield, Sharon Stone, Luana Anders; **D:** Charles Shyer; **W:** Charles Shyer, Nancy Meyers. LIV, VES

Irresistible Impulse ⅃⅃½ 1995 Sleazy real estate agent Jeffrey allows himself to become entangled in a wild scheme with bad girl Beaman. 107m/C VHS. Doug Jeffrey, Lee Anne Beavan; **D:** Jag Mundhra. YHV

Irving Berlin's America 1986 A documentary depicting Berlin's legacy of patriotic pop tunes, shown in a variety of film and performance clips, plus interviews with the stars who sang them. 83m/C Beta. Ginger Rogers, Mary Martin, Howard Keel, Kate Smith, Fred Astaire. CMR

Is Paris Burning? ⅃⅃⅃ Paris Brule-t-il? 1966 A spectacularly star-studded but far too sprawling account of the liberation of Paris from Nazi occupation. The script, in which seven writers had a hand, is based on Larry Collins and Dominique Lapierre's best-seller. 173m/C VHS, Closed Caption. FR Jean-Paul Belmondo, Charles Boyer, Leslie Caron, Jean-Pierre Cassel, George Chakiris, Claude Dauphin, Alain Delon, Kirk Douglas, Glenn Ford, Gert Frobe, Daniel Gelin, E.G. Marshall, Yves Montand, Anthony Perkins, Claude Rich, Simone Signoret, Robert Stack, Jean-Louis Trintignant, Pierre Vaneck, Orson Welles, Bruno Cremer, Suzy Delair, Michael Lonsdale; **D:** Rene Clement; **W:** Gore Vidal, Francis Ford Coppola; **M:** Maurice Jarre. Nominations: Academy Awards '66: Best Art Direction/Set Decoration (B & W), Best Black and White Cinematography. PAR, FCT

Is There Life Out There? ⅃⅃½ 1994 Wife, mother, and waitress Lily Marshall (McEntire) decides it's time to do something for herself—so she goes to work on her college degree. But there's unexpected family resentments, a breast cancer scare, and the interest of a young teaching assistant to turn her head away from her studies. Filmed in Nashville, Tennessee. Based on a song by McEntire; made for TV. 92m/C VHS. Reba McEntire, Keith Carradine, Mitchell Anderson, Donald

Moffat, Genia Michaela; **D:** David Jones; **W:** Dalene Young. CAF

Is There Sex After Death? ⅃⅃⅃ 1971 (R) Often funny satire on the sexual revolution is constructed as a behind-the-scenes view of the porn film world. Odd cast includes Henry and Warhol superstar Woodlawn. Originally rated "X." 97m/C VHS, Beta. Buck Henry, Alan Abel, Marshall Efron, Holly Woodlawn, Earl Doud; **D:** Alan Abel, Jeanne Abel. FRF

Is This Goodbye, Charlie Brown? 1983 Charlie Brown and the gang struggle to understand their loss when a friend moves away. 25m/C VHS. MED, VTR

Isadora ⅃⅃⅃ The Loves of Isadora 1968 A loose, imaginative biography of Isadora Duncan, the cause celebre dancer in the 1920s who became famous for her scandalous performances, outrageous behavior, public love affairs, and bizarre, early death. Redgrave is exceptional in the lead, and Fox provides fine support. Restored from its original 131-minute print length by the director. 153m/C VHS, Beta. Vanessa Redgrave, Jason Robards Jr., James Fox, Ivan Tchenko, John Fraser, Bessie Love; **D:** Karel Reisz; **W:** Melvyn Bragg; **M:** Maurice Jarre. Cannes Film Festival '69: Best Actress (Redgrave); National Board of Review Awards '69: 10 Best Films of the Year; National Society of Film Critics Awards '69: Best Actress (Redgrave); Nominations: Academy Awards '68: Best Actress (Redgrave). USH, HEG

Ishtar ⅃⅃ 1987 (PG-13) Two astoundingly untalented performers have a gig in a fictional Middle Eastern country and become involved in foreign intrigue. A big-budget box-office bomb produced by Beatty offering few laughs, though it's not as bad as its reputation. Considering the talent involved, though, it's a disappointment, with Beatty and Hoffman laboring to create Hope and Crosby chemistry. Anyone for a slow night? 107m/C VHS, Beta, LV, Closed Caption. Dustin Hoffman, Warren Beatty, Isabelle Adjani, Charles Grodin; **D:** Elaine May; **W:** Elaine May; **M:** Dave Grusin. Golden Raspberry Awards '87: Worst Director (May). COL

The Island ⅃⅃⅃½ Hadaka No Shima; Naked Island 1961 Poetic examination of a peasant family's daily struggle for existence on a small island. No dialogue in this slow but absorbing work by one of Japan's master directors. 96m/B VHS, Beta, LV, 8mm. JP Nobuko Otowa, Taiji Tonoyama, Shinji Tanaka, Masanori Horimoto; **D:** Kaneto Shindo. National Board of Review Awards '62: 5 Best Foreign Films of the Year. IHF, VYY, HHT

The Island woof! 1980 (R) New York reporter embarks on a Bermuda triangle investigation, only to meet with the murderous but sterile descendants of seventeenth century pirates on a deserted island. Caine is designated as stud service for the last remaining fertile woman. Almost surreal in its badness. Adapted by Benchley from his novel. 113m/C VHS, Beta, LV. Michael Caine, David Warner, Angela Punch McGregor, Frank Middlemass, Don Henderson; **D:** Michael Ritchie; **W:** Peter Benchley; **C:** Henri Decae; **M:** Ennio Morricone. USH

The Island at the Top of the World ⅃⅃½ 1974 (G) A rich Englishman, in search of his missing son, travels to the Arctic Circle in 1908. The rescue party includes an American archeologist, a French astronaut, and an Eskimo guide. Astonishingly, they discover an unknown, "lost" Viking kingdom. This Jules Verne-style adventure doesn't quite measure up, but kids will like it. 93m/C VHS, Beta, LV. David Hartman, Donald Sinden, Jacques Marin, Mako, David Gwillim; **D:** Robert Stevenson; **M:** Maurice Jarre. Nominations: Academy Awards '74: Best Art Direction/Set Decoration. DIS

Island Claw woof! Night of the Claw 1980 A group of marine biologists experimenting on a tropical island discover the "Island Claw," who evolved as the result of toxic waste seeping into the ocean. A festering, oozing woofer. 91m/C VHS, Beta. Barry Nelson, Robert Lansing; **D:** Hernan Cardenas. LIV, VES

Island in the Sun ✂✂ 1957 Racial tension pulls apart the lives of the residents of a Caribbean island. Good cast, but a very poor adaptation of Alec Waugh's novel. Marvelous location shots. 119m/C VHS. James Mason, Joan Fontaine, Dorothy Dandridge, John Williams, Harry Belafonte; **D:** Robert Rossen; **C:** Frederick A. (Freddie) Young; **M:** Malcolm Arnold. *TCF*

Island Monster ✂½ 1953 Also called "Monster of the Island," this film deals with ruthless, kidnapping drug-smugglers led by "monster" Karloff, and the efforts to bring them to justice. 87m/B VHS, Beta. *IT* Boris Karloff, Renata Vicario, Franco Marzi; **D:** Robert Montero. *SNC, HHT, LSV*

Island of Blood ✂½ 1986 Buckets of blood abound on a remote island when a film crew's beset by berserk butcher. 84m/C VHS. Jim Williams, Dean Richards. *AIP, MOV*

Island of Desire ✂ *Saturday Island* 1952 An Army nurse, a doctor, and a young Navy Adonis are trapped on a deserted island. Not surprisingly, a love triangle develops. 93m/C VHS, Beta. *GB* Tab Hunter, Linda Darnell, Donald Gray; **D:** Stuart Heisler. *MLB*

Island of Dr. Moreau ✂✂½ 1977 (PG) This remake of the "Island of the Lost Souls" (1933) is a bit disappointing but worth watching for Lancaster's solid performance as the scientist who has isolated himself on a Pacific island in order to continue his chromosome research—he can transform animals into near-humans and humans into animals. Neat-looking critters. Adaptation of the H.G. Wells novel of the same title. 99m/C VHS, Beta. Burt Lancaster, Michael York, Nigel Davenport, Barbara Carrera, Richard Basehart; **D:** Don Taylor. *WAR, OM*

The Island of Dr. Moreau ✂½ 1996 (PG-13) What were they thinking? Not even the frightening "manimals" could prevent the unintentional laughs from this abomination of the horrifying 1896 H.G. Wells novel. Brando's enormous presence as the mad scientist Moreau walks a tight rope between puzzling and campy, especially as he explains his ghastly DNA experiments on a remote Pacific to a miscast Thewlis. A wasted Kilmer is the doctors's right-hand hybrid who often seems to be acting in a different movie. Filming hit some big rocks when "creative differences" caused original director Richard Stanley to be replaced and Rob Morrow (originally the lawyer) to ask for his release. Previously filmed under the same title in 1977 and (terrifically) as "Island of Lost Souls" in 1933. **CW:** Sci-fi violence, horror and gore involving mutant creatures. 91m/C VHS, LV, Closed Caption. Marlon Brando, Val Kilmer, David Thewlis, Fairuza Balk, Marco Hofschneider, Temuera Morrison, Ron Perlman; **D:** John Frankenheimer. Nominations: Golden Raspberry Awards '96: Best Director (Frankenheimer), Worst Picture, Worst Supporting Actor (Kilmer, Brando), Worst Screenplay. *NLC*

Island of Lost Girls WOOF! 1973 (R) Young women are taken to an unknown location in the Far East to be sold as part of a white slave ring. 85m/C VHS, Beta. Brad Harris, Tony Kendall, Monica Pardo. *SNC*

Island of Lost Souls ✂✂✂½ 1932 Horrifying adaptation of H.G. Wells "The Island of Dr. Moreau" was initially banned in parts of the U.S. because of its disturbing contents. Laughton is a mad scientist on a remote island obsessed with making men out of jungle animals. When a shipwreck survivor gets stranded on the island, little does he know that Laughton wants to mate him with Lota, the Panther Woman, to produce the first human-animal child. As unsettling today as it was in the '30s. Burke beat out more than 60,000 young women in a nationwide search to play the Panther Woman, winning the role because of her "feline" look. Remade as "The Island of Dr. Moreau." 71m/B VHS, Closed Caption. Charles Laughton, Bela Lugosi, Richard Arlen, Leila Hyams, Kathleen Burke, Stanley Fields, Robert F. (Bob) Kortman; **Cameos:** Alan Ladd, Randolph Scott, Buster Crabbe; **D:**

Erle C. Kenton; **W:** Philip Wylie, Waldemar Young; **C:** Karl Struss. *USH, FCT, BTV*

The Island of Nevawuz 1980 A beautiful island is in trouble when J.B. Trumphorn decides to make lots of money by building factories and refineries on it. Will the Island of Nevawuz end up a polluted mess? 50m/C VHS, Beta.

Island of Terror ✂✂✂ *Night of the Silicates; The Creepers* 1966 First-rate science fiction chiller about an island overrun by shell-like creatures that suck the bones out of their living prey. Good performances and interesting twists make for prickles up the spine. 90m/C VHS, Closed Caption. *GB* Peter Cushing, Edward Judd, Carole Gray, Sam Kydd, Niall MacGinnis; **D:** Terence Fisher. *USH, SNC, MLB*

Island of the Blue Dolphins ✂✂½ 1964 Based on a popular children's book by Scott O'Dell, this is a true story of a young Native American girl who, with her brother, are stranded on a deserted island when their people accidentally leave them. When the boy is killed, the girl learns to survive by her skills and by befriending the leader of a pack of wild dogs. Good family fare. 99m/C VHS, Beta. Celia Kaye, Larry Domasin, Ann Daniel, George Kennedy; **D:** James B. Clark. *USH*

Island of the Burning Doomed ✂✂½ *Island of the Burning Damned; Night of the Big Heat* 1967 A brutal heat wave accompanies invading aliens in this British-made outing. Lee and Cushing carry the picture. 94m/C VHS. *GB* Christopher Lee, Peter Cushing, Patrick Allen, Sarah Lawson, Jane Merrow; **D:** Terence Fisher. *NO*

Island of the Lost ✂½ 1968 An anthropologist's family must fight for survival when they become shipwrecked on a mysterious island. 92m/C VHS. Richard Greene, Luke Halpin; **D:** John Florea; **M:** George Bruns. *REP, GHV*

Island Trader ✂ 1971 Young lad battles pirates and a crooked tug captain who seek hidden gold that he knows about. 95m/C VHS, Beta. John Ewart, Ruth Cracknell, Eric Oldfield; **D:** Harold Rubie. *NO*

The Islander ✂ 1988 Sixteen-year-old Inga comes of age among the commercial fishermen of Lake Michigan. 99m/C VHS, Beta. Kit Wholihan, Jeff Weborg, Celia Klehr, Jacob Mills, Julie Johnson, Mary Ann McHugh, Michael Rock, Sheri Parish; **D:** Phyllis Berg-Pigorsch. *NO*

Islands ✂✂ 1987 A made-for-television drama about a middle-aged ex-hippie and a young rebellious punk who clash during a summer together on a secluded island. 55m/C VHS, Beta. Louise Fletcher. *NWV*

Islands in the Stream ✂✂½ 1977 (PG) Based on Ernest Hemingway's novel, this film is actually two movies in one. An American painter/sculptor, Thomas Hudson, lives a reclusive life on the island of Bimini shortly before the outbreak of WWII. The first part is a sensitive story of a broken family and the coming of the artist's three sons to live with their father after a four year separation. The second part is a second rate action-adventure. 105m/C VHS, Beta, LV. George C. Scott, David Hemmings, Claire Bloom, Susan Tyrrell, Gilbert Roland; **D:** Franklin J. Schaffner; **C:** Fred W. Koenekamp; **M:** Jerry Goldsmith. Nominations: Academy Awards '77: Best Cinematography. *PAR*

Isle of Forgotten Sins ✂✂ 1943 Deep sea divers and an evil ship's captain vie for treasure. Good cast and direction but unremarkable material. Also released under the title "Monsoon." 82m/B VHS, Beta, 8mm. John Carradine, Gale Sondergaard, Sidney Toler, Frank Fenton, Veda Ann Borg; **D:** Edgar G. Ulmer. *SNC, VYY*

Isle of Secret Passion ✂ 1985 A romance novel comes to video life as two lovers thrash out their problems on a Greek island. 90m/C VHS, Beta. Patch MacKenzie, Michael MacRae, Zohra Lampert. *PSM*

Isle of the Dead ✂✂½ 1945 A Greek general is quarantined with seemingly all manner of social vermin on a plague-infested island in the early 1900s. The fear is that vampires walk among them. Characteristically spooky Val Lewton production with some original twists. 72m/B VHS, Beta, LV. Boris Karloff, Ellen Drew, Marc Cramer; **D:** Mark Robson. *TTC, MED, FCT*

Isn't Life Wonderful ✂✂✂✂ 1924 Inga's (Dempster) a Polish war orphan who struggles to provide for her family in post-WWI Germany. It means giving up her dream to marry former soldier, Paul (Hamilton), but he has a secret plan to reunite them. Filmed on location. 118m/B VHS, Beta. Carol Dempster, Neil Hamilton, Lupino Lane, Hans von Schlettow; **D:** D.W. Griffith; **W:** D.W. Griffith. *KIV, GVV, GPV*

Istanbul ✂✂½ 1957 Adventurer Jim Brennan (Flynn) finds a fortune in smuggled diamonds, which he hides in a hotel room. Unfortunately, he's deported before he can retrieve the gems and it takes him five years to make it back to Istanbul. Then he's hounded by the original smugglers who want their gems back and discovers his lost love Stephanie (Borchers). Cole croons a couple of songs in his role as a lounge singer. Remake of 1947's "Singapore." ♫ When I Fall In Love; I Was a Little Too Lonely. 85m/C VHS, Closed Caption. Errol Flynn, Cornell Borchers, John Bentley, Torin Thatcher, Leif Erickson, Peggy Knudsen, Martin Benson, Nat King Cole, Werner Klemperer; **D:** Joseph Pevney; **W:** Seton I. Miller, Barbara Gray; **C:** William H. Daniels. *USH*

Istanbul ✂ 1985 (R) An American charms a Belgian student into taking part in a kidnap scheme. 90m/C VHS, Beta. *FR* Brad Dourif, Dominique Deruddere, Ingrid De Vos, Francois Beukelaers; **D:** Marc Didden. *NO*

Istanbul ✂ *Istanbul, Keep Your Eyes Open* 1990 (PG-13) Believing he has stumbled upon the best story of his career, a journalist soon discovers that he has been pulled into a world of guns and violence. 88m/C VHS, Beta, LV. *TU SW* Robert Morley, Timothy Bottoms, Twiggy; **D:** Mats Arehn. *IME*

It ✂✂½ 1927 A department store clerk with plenty of sex appeal desires her rich boss. Established Bow as a prominent screen siren. Otherwise, it's not particularly interesting. Silent. Adapted by Elinor Glyn from her own story; Glyn also makes an appearance. 71m/B VHS, Beta, LV. Clara Bow, Gary Cooper, Antonio Moreno; **D:** Clarence Badger. *GPV, CRC, CCB*

It Came from Beneath the Sea ✂✂✂ 1955 A giant octopus arises from the depths of the sea to scour San Francisco for human food. Ray Harryhausen effects are special. 80m/B VHS, Beta, LV. Kenneth Tobey, Faith Domergue, Ian Keith, Donald Curtis; **D:** Robert Gordon. *GKK, MLB*

It Came from Hollywood 1982 (PG) A compilation of scenes from "B" horror and science fiction films of the 1950s, highlighting the funny side of these classic schlock movies. Some sequences in black and white. 87m/C VHS, Beta, LV. **D:** Malcolm Leo. *PAR*

It Came From Outer Space ✂✂✂ 1953 Aliens take on the form of local humans to repair their spacecraft in a small Arizona town. Good performances and outstanding direction add up to a fine science fiction film. Based on the story "The Meteor" by Ray Bradbury, who also wrote the script. Originally filmed in 3-D. 81m/B VHS, Closed Caption. Richard Carlson, Barbara Rush, Charles Drake, Russell Johnson; **D:** Jack Arnold; **W:** Ray Bradbury, Harry Essex; **M:** Herman Stein. *USH, MLB, GKK*

It Came from Outer Space 2 ✂½ 1995 (PG-13) Poorly updated cable version of the sci-fi film finds photographer Jack Putnam (Kerwin) heading home to his isolated desert community. A freakish blue lightning storm causes big changes amongst the desert dwellers who are sucked into a glowing ground mass and re-emerge possessed by shape-shifting aliens, who need the human bodies to rebuild their crashed space ship. Based on a story by Ray Bradbury and the 1953 screenplay by Harry Essex. **CW:** Sci-fi violence. **85m/C VHS, Closed Caption.** Brian Kerwin, Elizabeth Pena, Bill McKinney, Jonathan Carrasco, Adrian Sparks, Howard Morris, Mickey Jones, Lauren Tewes; **D:** Roger Duchonwny; **W:** Jim Wheat, Ken Wheat. *USH*

It Came Upon a Midnight Clear 🎬½ 1984
A heavenly miracle enables a retired (and dead) New York policeman to keep a Christmas promise to his grandson. Made for television. **96m/C VHS, Beta, Closed Caption.** Mickey Rooney, Scott Grimes, George Gaynes, Annie Potts, Lloyd Nolan, Barrie Youngfellow; **D:** Peter H. Hunt; **C:** Dean Cundey. *GKK*

It Conquered the World 🎬🎬½ 1956
Vegetable critters from Venus follow a probe satellite back to Earth and drop in on scientist Van Cleef, who'd been their intergalactic pen pal (seems he thought a Venusian invasion would improve the neighborhood). Their travelling companions, little bat creatures, turn earth dwellers into murderous zombies, and it starts to look like the Venusians are trying to make earth their planetary exurbia. Early- vintage zero-budget Corman, for schlock connoisseurs. Remade for television as "Zontar, the Thing from Venus." **68m/B VHS.** Peter Graves, Beverly Garland, Lee Van Cleef, Sally Fraser, Charles B. Griffith, Russ Bender, Jonathan Haze, Dick Miller, Karen Kadler, Paul Blaisdell; **D:** Roger Corman. *COL, FCT, MLB*

It Could Happen to You 🎬½ 1937
Stepbrothers raised by a gentle immigrant take different paths in life. When one ends up killing someone during a botched robbery, the other—a lawyer—defends him. Standard '30s morality play. **64m/B VHS.** Alan Baxter, Andrea Leeds, Owen Davis Jr., Astrid Allwyn, Walter Kingsford, Al Shear; **D:** Phil Rosen. *NOS, BAR*

It Could Happen to You 🎬🎬 1939
A drunken advertising executive is charged with murder after a dead nightclub singer is found in his car. His wife sets out to clear him. **64m/C VHS, Beta.** Stuart Erwin, Gloria Stuart, Raymond Walburn, Douglas Fowley, June Gale, Paul Hurst, Richard Lane; **D:** Alfred Werker. *NO*

It Could Happen to You 🎬🎬½ *Cop Tips Waitress $2 Million* 1994
(PG) NYC cop Charlie Lang (Cage) doesn't have any change to leave coffee shop waitress Yvonne (Fonda) a tip, so he promises to split his lottery ticket with her. When he nets four million dollars, he makes good on the promise, much to the chagrin of his upwardly mobile wife (Perez). Capra-corn for the X-crowd is pleasant dinnertime diversion as Cage and Perez shine as henpecked nice guy and the wife committed to making him miserable. Don't look for the diner on your next trip to NYC; it was specially built in TriBeCa and dismantled after the shoot. **101m/C VHS, LV, 8mm, Closed Caption.** Bridget Fonda, Nicolas Cage, Rosie Perez, Red Buttons, Isaac Hayes, Seymour Cassel, Stanley Tucci, J.E. Freeman, Richard Jenkins, Ann Dowd, Wendell Pierce; **D:** Andrew Bergman; **W:** Jane Anderson, Andrew Bergman; **C:** Caleb Deschanel. *COL*

It Couldn't Happen Here 🎬 1988
(PG-13) Fans of the techno-pop duo The Pet Shop Boys can test their loyalty by enduring this feature music-video that actually played a few theaters. The dour pair journey across a surreal England, encountering a sinister blind priest, a philisophical ventriloquist's dummy, and more. Songs, sometimes presented only as muted incidental music, include the title track, "West End Girls," "It's a Sin" and "Always on My Mind." **87m/C VHS, LV.** *GB* Neil Tennant, Chris Lowe, Joss Ackland, Neil Dickson, Carmen Du Sautoy, Gareth Hunt; **D:** Jack Bond. *COL, MVD*

It Happened at Nightmare Inn 🎬🎬
A Candle for the Devil 1970 Average thriller in which Geeson travels to Spanish inn and confronts two mad sisters who run the hotel. Also known as

"Nightmare Hotel." **95m/C VHS.** *SP* Judy Geeson, Aurora Bautista, Esperanza Roy, Victor Alcocer, Lone Fleming; **D:** Eugenio Martin. *SNC*

It Happened at the World's Fair 🎬🎬½ 1963
Fun and light romance comedy has Elvis and a companion (O'Brien) being escorted through the Seattle World's Fair by a fetching Chinese girl. ♫I'm Falling In Love Tonight; They Remind Me Too Much Of You; Take Me To The Fair; Relax; How Would You Like To Be; Beyond the Bend; One Broken Heart For Sale; Cotton Candy Land; A World Of Our Own. **105m/C VHS, Beta.** Elvis Presley, Joan O'Brien, Gary Lockwood, Kurt Russell, Edith Atwater, Yvonne Craig; **D:** Norman Taurog. *MGM*

It Happened in Brooklyn 🎬🎬 1947
Former sailor with blue eyes bunks with janitor with big nose in Brooklyn. Sailor and cronies encounter many musical opportunities. Lots of songs and falling in love, little entertainment. **104m/B VHS.** Frank Sinatra, Kathryn Grayson, Jimmy Durante, Peter Lawford, Gloria Grahame; **D:** Richard Whorf. *MGM, FCT*

It Happened in New Orleans 🎬½
Rainbow on the River 1936 A young boy is cared for by a former slave in post-Civil War New Orleans until his Yankee grandmother claims him and takes him to New York. The boy is resented by his family but manages to overcome their hostilities. **86m/B VHS, Beta.** Bobby Breen, May Robson, Alan Mowbray, Benita Hume. *VYY*

It Happened in the Park 🎬🎬½ 1956
A rare film exercise for De Sica, wherein the patrons of the Villa Borghese parks are surveyed for a 24-hour period. In French with English dialogue. **72m/B VHS, Beta.** *FR* **D:** Vittorio De Sica. *NOS, FCT*

It Happened One Night 🎬🎬🎬🎬 1934
Classic Capra comedy about an antagonistic couple determined to teach each other about life. Colbert is an unhappy heiress who runs away from her affluent home in search of contentment. On a bus she meets newspaper reporter Gable, who teaches her how "real" people live. She returns the favor in this first of the 1930s screwball comedies. The plot is a framework for an amusing examination of war between the sexes. Colbert and Gable are superb as affectionate foes. Remade as the musicals "Eve Knew Her Apples" and "You Can't Run Away From It." **105m/B VHS, Beta, LV, Closed Caption.** Clark Gable, Claudette Colbert, Roscoe Karns, Walter Connolly, Alan Hale, Ward Bond; **D:** Frank Capra; **W:** Robert Riskin. Academy Awards '34: Best Actor (Gable), Best Actress (Colbert), Best Adapted Screenplay, Best Director (Capra), Best Picture; National Board of Review Awards '34: 10 Best Films of the Year. *COL, BTV, HMV*

It Happens Every Spring 🎬🎬🎬½ 1949
A chemistry professor, working on a bug repellant for trees, accidentally invents a potion that repels any kind of wood that it comes in contact with. Since he needs some big bucks to pop the question to his sweetie, the prof, who also loves baseball, gets a tryout as a pitcher with a major league team and uses the solution on the baseballs he pitches. Naturally, it's strikeout time and the prof becomes a pitching phenom. Now, if he can only keep his little secret. Wacky baseball footage is a highlight. **87m/B VHS.** Ray Milland, Jean Peters, Paul Douglas, Ed Begley Sr., Ted de Corsia, Ray Collins, Jessie Royce Landis, Alan Hale Jr., Gene Evans; **D:** Lloyd Bacon; **W:** Valentine Daviès; **M:** Leigh Harline. Nominations: Academy Awards '49: Best Story. *FXV*

It Means That to Me 🎬🎬 1963
Espionage thriller in which Constantine plays a reporter who's hired by the government to transport top secret micro-film. **?m/C VHS.** *FR* Eddie Constantine, Jean-Louis Richard. *SNC*

It Rained All Night the Day I Left 🎬🎬 1978 **(R)**
Two drifters find their fortunes change when they are hired by a wealthy widow. Interesting romance adventure. **100m/C**

VHS, Beta. Louis Gossett Jr., Sally Kellerman, Tony Curtis; **D:** Nicolas Gessner. *NO*

It Should Happen to You 🎬🎬🎬 1954
An aspiring model attempts to boost her career by promoting herself on a New York City billboard. The results, however, are continually surprising. Fine comedy teamwork from master thespians Holliday and Lemmon in this, the latter's first film. **87m/B VHS, Beta, LV.** Judy Holliday, Jack Lemmon, Peter Lawford; **D:** George Cukor; **W:** Ruth Gordon, Garson Kanin; **C:** Charles B(ryant) Lang. Nominations: Academy Awards '54: Best Costume Design (B & W). *GKK*

It Started in Naples 🎬🎬🎬 1960
Good performances by both Gable and Loren in this comedy-drama about an American lawyer in Italy who, upon preparing his late brother's estate, finds that his brother's nephew is living with a stripper. A custody battle ensues, but love wins out in the end. Loren is incredible in nightclub scenes. **100m/C VHS, Closed Caption.** Clark Gable, Sophia Loren, Marietto, Vittorio De Sica, Paolo Carlini, Claudio Ermelli, Giovanni Filidoro; **D:** Melville Shavelson; **W:** Melville Shavelson, Jack Rose. Nominations: Academy Awards '60: Best Art Direction/Set Decoration (Color). *PAR*

It Started with a Kiss 🎬🎬½ 1959
Reynolds plays a showgirl who impulsively marries an Air Force sargeant (Ford). When he's transfered to Spain they try to make a go of their hasty marriage among numerous comic complications. Flimsy farce with likeable leads. **104m/C VHS.** Debbie Reynolds, Glenn Ford, Eva Gabor, Gustavo Rojo, Fred Clark, Edgar Buchanan, Robert Warwick, Harry (Henry) Morgan, Frances Bavier; **D:** George Marshall. *MGM, MOV*

It Started with Eve 🎬🎬🎬 1941
Funny comedy about a grumpy old millionaire (Laughton) whose dying wish is to meet the young lady his son Johnny is to wed. Unfortunately, the bride-to-be is unavailable, so Johnny (Cummings) finds a replacement in hatcheck girl Durbin. Of course, Durbin steals the old man's heart and he miraculously makes a full-blown recovery, which means big trouble for Cummings. Remade in 1964 as "I'd Rather Be Rich." Based on the story "Almost An Angel" by Hans Kraly. ♫Clavelitos; Going Home. **92m/B VHS.** Deanna Durbin, Charles Laughton, Robert Cummings, Guy Kibbee, Margaret Tallichet, Catherine Doucet, Walter Catlett, Charles Coleman, Clara Blandick; **D:** Henry Koster; **W:** Norman Krasna, Leo Townsend. Nominations: Academy Awards '42: Scoring of a Musical. *USH*

It Takes a Thief 🎬🎬 *The Challenge* 1959
Tough cookie Jayne's a buxom gangstress who does the hokey pokey with her criminal minions. A former lover who's been released from the big house seems to think she's been minding the mint for him. Au contraire. **93m/B VHS.** *GB* Jayne Mansfield, Anthony Quayle, Carl Mohner, Peter Reynolds, John Bennett; **D:** John Gilling. *BBF*

It Takes Two 🎬🎬 1988 **(PG-13)**
A young man spends his last ten days of bachelorhood cruising down Texas highways with a beautiful car saleswoman. Meanwhile, back at the altar, his bride waits patiently. Upbeat with some genuinely funny moments. From the director of "Pass the Ammo." **79m/C VHS, Beta, Closed Caption.** George Newbern, Leslie Hope, Kimberly Foster, Barry Corbin; **D:** David Beaird; **M:** Carter Burwell. *MGM*

It Takes Two 🎬 1995 **(PG)**
Vapid sugary comedy finds the nine-year-old Olsen twins playing a duo from opposite sides of the tracks who change identities in an effort to get their respective adults (Guttenberg and Alley) together. See "The Parent Trap" instead. **100m/C VHS, LV, Closed Caption.** Ashley Olsen, Mary-Kate Olsen, Kirstie Alley, Steve Guttenberg, Philip Bosco, Jane Sibbett, Lawrence Dane, Gerard Parkes; **D:** Andy Tennant; **W:** Deborah Dean Davis; **C:** Kenneth Zunder; **M:** Sherman Foote, Ray Foote. *WAR*

It! The Terror from Beyond Space 🎬½ *It! The Vampire From Beyond Space* 1958
The sole survivor of a Martian expedition is believed to have murdered his colleagues. He's arrested and brought back to Earth via space

ship. En route, a vicious alien, the actual culprit, is discovered on board and begins killing the crew members. A fun science fiction thriller which, 20 years later, would provide Ridley Scott with the plot for "Alien." 68m/B VHS, Beta. Marshall Thompson, Shawn Smith, Kim Spalding, Ann Doran, Dabbs Greer, Paul Langton, Ray Corrigan; **D:** Edward L. Cahn. *MGM, MLB*

It Was a Short Summer, Charlie Brown 1969 The Peanuts gang enjoys the summer until it's time to go back to school. 26m/C VHS. **D:** Bill Melendez.

Italian 1915 The story of an Italian immigrant family living in the slums of New York during the turn of the century. 78m/B VHS, Beta. George Beban, Clara Williams, Leo Wills, J. Frank Burke, Fanny Midgley. *GPV, GVV*

The Italian Job 🐾🐾½ 1969 (G) Caine and Coward pair up to steal $4 million in gold by causing a major traffic jam in Turin, Italy. During the jam, the pair steals the gold from an armored car. Silliness and chases through the Swiss mountains ensue, culminating in a hilarious ending. 99m/C VHS, LV, Closed Caption. *GB* Michael Caine, Noel Coward, Benny Hill, Raf Vallone, Tony Beckley, Rossano Brazzi, Margaret Blye; **D:** Peter Collinson; **M:** Quincy Jones. *PAR*

The Italian Stallion 🐾 1973 Stallone plays a man with only one thing on his mind...sex! 90m/C VHS, Beta. Sylvester Stallone, Henrietta Holm. *JEF*

Italian Straw Hat 🐾🐾🐾 1927 *Un Chapeau de Paille d'Italie* Classic silent about the chain of errors that ensues when a man's horse eats a woman's hat. His vast, unending struggle to replace the hat is the source of continual comedy. From Eugene Labiche's play. 72m/B VHS, Beta. *FR* Albert Prejean; **D:** Rene Clair. *VYY, MRV, INT*

Italianamerican/The Big Shave 19?? Two shorts by Scorsese. "Italianamerican" (1974) features dinner and conversation with his parents in their Little Italy (New York) apartment. In "The Big Shave," (1967) a young man nicks himself shaving and suddenly has a frightening religious experience. 54m/C VHS. **D:** Martin Scorsese. *HMV*

It's a Bundyful Life 1992 The outrageous family from television's "Married with Children" does Christmas in their own inimitable fashion. This parody of "It's a Wonderful Life" features Kinison earning his wings as father Al's guardian angel. See what the family would have been like if Al had never been born...and what Al decides to do about it. Those seeking traditional family fare should look elsewhere. 47m/C VHS. Ed O'Neill, Katey Sagal, Christina Applegate, David Faustino, Sam Kinison, Amanda Bearse, Ted McGinley; **D:** Gerry Cohen. *COL*

It's a Date 🐾🐾 1940 A mother and daughter, both actresses, continually get their professional and romantic lives intertwined. It begins when Durbin (the daughter) is offered Kay's (the mother) Broadway role. It continues in Hawaii where the man that Kay is in love with tries to court Durbin. As it's a comedy, of course, all is put right in the end. ♫ Musetta's Waltz; Ave Maria; Loch Lomond; Love Is All; It Happened in Kaloha; Rhythm of the Islands; Hawaiian War Chant. 103m/B VHS. Deanna Durbin, Kay Francis, Walter Pidgeon, Samuel S. Hinds, S.Z. Sakall, Henry Stephenson, Charles Lane, Leon Belasco; **D:** William A. Seiter; **W:** Norman Krasna; **C:** Joseph Valentine. *FOX, FCT, MLB*

It's a Dog's Life 🐾🐾½ *The Bar Sinister* 1955 The hero and narrator of this story is a wily bull terrier called Wildfire. Wildfire is a tough dog on the mean streets of the Bowery in turn-of-the-century New York. His master has him in dog fights in the local saloon but eventually abandons him. Wildfire is then taken in by the kindly employee of the rich and dog-hating Jagger but naturally manages to win the codger over. Based on the short story "The Bar Sinister" by Richard Harding Davis. 87m/C VHS. Jeff Richards, Edmund Gwenn, Dean Jagger; **D:** Herman Hoffman; **W:** John Michael Hayes; **M:** Elmer Bernstein. *FCT*

It's A Gift 🐾🐾🐾½ 1934 A grocery clerk moves his family west to manage orange groves in this classic Fields comedy. Several inspired sequences. The supporting cast shines too. A real find for the discriminating comedy buff. Remake of the silent "It's the Old Army Game." 71m/B VHS, Beta, LV. W.C. Fields, Baby LeRoy, Kathleen Howard; **D:** Norman Z. McLeod. *USH, BAR*

It's a Great Feeling 🐾🐾½ 1949 Another Carson and Day team-up where Carson plays a camera-hogging show-off whom no one wants to direct. He's such an industry piranha that he ends up directing himself! He cons Day, a waitress and would-be actress, by promising her a part in his new film. Some executives hear her sing before she heads back home to Wisconsin, fed up with Hollywood. They make Carson track her down to star in the new picture, but when he arrives she is at the altar with her high school sweetheart. 85m/C VHS, LV. Dennis (Stanley Morner) Morgan, Doris Day, Jack Carson, Bill Goodwin, Errol Flynn, Gary Cooper, Joan Crawford, Ronald Reagan, Sydney Greenstreet, Danny Kaye, Eleanor Parker, Edward G. Robinson, Jane Wyman; **D:** David Butler. Nominations: Academy Awards '49: Best Song ("It's a Great Feeling"). *FOX, FCT, MLB*

It's a Great Life 🐾🐾½ 1943 Blondie wants Dagwood to buy a house but instead he buys a horse. He's scheming to impress a client of Mr. Dither's by participating in a fox hunt. Blondie comes to the rescue. 13th entry in series. 75m/B VHS. Penny Singleton, Arthur Lake, Larry Simms, Hugh Herbert, Jonathan Hale, Danny Mummert, Alan Dinehart, Irving Bacon, Douglas Leavitt, Marjorie Ann Mutchie; **D:** Frank Strayer; **W:** Karen De Wolf, Connie Lee. *MOV*

It's a Joke, Son! 🐾🐾 1947 Follows the fictional politician, Senator Claghorn from the Fred Allen radio show, during his first run for the U.S. Senate. 67m/B VHS. Kenny Delmar, Una Merkel; **D:** Ben Stoloff. *NOS, MRV, DVT*

It's a Mad, Mad, Mad, Mad World 🐾🐾 1963 Overblown epic comedy with a cast of notables desperately seeking the whereabouts of stolen money. Ultimately exhausting film undone by its length and overbearing performances. Laserdisc contains 20 minutes of supplemental footage, including interviews with some of the surviving cast members. 155m/C VHS, Beta, LV. Spencer Tracy, Sid Caesar, Milton Berle, Ethel Merman, Jonathan Winters, Jimmy Durante, Buddy Hackett, Mickey Rooney, Phil Silvers, Dick Shawn, Edie Adams, Dorothy Provine, Buster Keaton, Terry-Thomas, Moe Howard, Larry Fine, Joe DeRita, Jim Backus, William Demarest, Peter Falk, Leo Gorcey, Edward Everett Horton, Joe E. Brown, Carl Reiner, ZaSu Pitts, Eddie Anderson, Jack Benny, Jerry Lewis; **D:** Stanley Kramer; **M:** Ernest Laszlo; **M:** Ernest Gold. Academy Awards '63: Best Sound Effects Editing; Nominations: Academy Awards '63: Best Color Cinematography, Best Film Editing, Best Song ("It's a Mad, Mad, Mad World"), Best Sound, Best Original Score. *MGM, FOX, FCT*

It's a Mystery, Charlie Brown 1987 Peanuts adventure in which Snoopy interrogates everyone on the disappearance of Woodstock's birdhouse. 30m/C VHS, Beta. **D:** Phil Roman. *BAR*

It's a Wonderful Life 🐾🐾🐾🐾 1946 American classic about a man saved from suicide by a considerate angel, who then shows the hero how important he's been to the lives of loved ones. Corny but inspirational and heartwarming, with an endearing performance by Travers as angel Clarence. Stewart and Reed are typically wholesome. Perfect film for people who want to feel good, joyfully teetering on the border between Hollywood schmaltz and genuine heartbreak. Also available colorized. The laserdisc version includes production and publicity stills, the theatrical trailer, and commentary by film professor Jeanine Basinger. Also available in a 160-minute Collector's Edition with original preview trailer, "The Making of 'It's a Wonderful Life,'" and a new digital transfer from the original negative. 125m/B VHS, LV, Closed Caption. James Stewart, Donna Reed, Henry Travers, Thomas Mitchell, Lionel Barrymore, Samuel S. Hinds, Frank Faylen, Gloria Grahame, H.B. Warner, Ellen Corby, Sheldon Leonard, Beulah Bondi, Ward Bond, Frank Albertson, Todd Karns, Mary Treen, Charles Halton; **D:** Frank Capra; **W:** Frances Goodrich, Albert Hackett, Jo Swerling; **M:** Dimitri Tiomkin. Golden Globe Awards '47: Best Director (Capra); Nominations: Academy Awards '46: Best Actor (Stewart), Best Director (Capra), Best Film Editing, Best Picture, Best Sound. *IGP, MRV, CNG*

It's Alive! 🐾 1968 Slow-moving dud about a farmer feeding passersby to the area's cave-dwelling lizard man. The ping pong ball-eyed monster puts in a belated appearance that's not worth the wait. 80m/C VHS. Tommy Kirk, Shirley Bonne, Bill Thurman; **D:** Larry Buchanan; **W:** Larry Buchanan. *NOS, LOO*

It's Alive 🐾🐾🐾 1974 (PG) Cult film about a mutated baby that is born to a normal Los Angeles couple, who escapes and goes on a bloodthirsty, murderous rampage, is a sight to behold. Fantastic score by Bernard Herrmann makes this chilling film a memorable one. 91m/C VHS, Beta. John P. Ryan, Sharon Farrell, Andrew Duggan, Guy Stockwell, James Dixon, Michael Ansara; **D:** Larry Cohen; **W:** Larry Cohen. *WAR, FCT*

It's Alive 2: It Lives Again woof! 1978 (R) In this sequel to "It's Alive," the original hellspun baby meets up with two more of the same and all three terrorize the city, murdering everyone they can find. Truly horrendous. 91m/C VHS, Beta. Frederic Forrest, Kathleen Lloyd, John P. Ryan, Andrew Duggan, John Marley, Eddie Constantine; **D:** Larry Cohen. *WAR, FCT*

It's Alive 3: Island of the Alive 🐾 1987 (R) The second sequel to the tongue-in-cheek horror film, in which the infant mutant of the previous films has been left with other mutations to spawn on a desert island. 94m/C VHS, Beta. Michael Moriarty, Karen Black, Laurene Landon, Gerrit Graham, James Dixon, Neal Israel, MacDonald Carey; **D:** Larry Cohen; **W:** Larry Cohen. *WAR*

It's All True 🐾🐾 1993 (G) A look at auteur Welles' ill-fated WWII filmmaking project. Welles served as a special cultural ambassador to South America and, in 1942, began a documentary covering the area's complex political and social issues. Includes footage from "Four Men on a Raft," Welles' recreation about the peasant fishermen of Brazil; surviving excerpts from "The Story of Samba," a Technicolor musical about Carnaval in Rio de Janeiro; and footage from "My Friend Bonito," set against a backdrop of bullfighting in Mexico. 85m/C VHS, LV. **D:** Richard Wilson, Bill Krohn, Myron Meise, Orson Welles; **W:** Richard Wilson, Bill Krohn, Myron Meise; **M:** Jorge Arriagada. *PAR*

It's Always Fair Weather 🐾🐾 1955 Three WWII buddies meet again at a 10-year reunion and find that they don't like each other very much. A surprisingly cynical film. Director Donen produced "Seven Brides for Seven Brothers" the previous year. ♫ Stillman's Gym; March, March; Why Are We Here? (Blue Danube); Music Is Better Than Words; Once Upon A Time; The Time For Parting; I Like Myself; Baby You Knock Me Out; Thanks A Lot But No Thanks. 102m/C VHS, Beta, LV. Gene Kelly, Cyd Charisse, Dan Dailey, Michael Kidd; **D:** Stanley Donen; **W:** Betty Comden, Adolph Green; **M:** Betty Comden, Adolph Green, Andre Previn. Nominations: Academy Awards '55: Best Story & Screenplay, Scoring of a Musical. *MGM, FHE*

It's an Adventure, Charlie Brown! 1983 A collection of six vignettes featuring Charlie Brown and the whole Peanuts gang. 50m/C VHS, Beta. **D:** Bill Melendez. *SHL, VTR*

It's Arbor Day, Charlie Brown 1983 Tribulations aplenty for Charlie Brown as his baseball team turns his field into an Arbor Day garden. 26m/C VHS, Beta. *BAR*

It's Called Murder, Baby 🎬 1982 (R)
The famed porn star gives the viewer a lesson in English vocabulary in this tale of a blackmailed movie queen. 94m/C VHS, Beta. John Leslie, Cameron Mitchell, Lisa Trego; *D:* Sam Weston. LIV

It's Flashbeagle, Charlie Brown/ She's a Good Skate, Charlie Brown 1984 A Peanuts double header: In "It's Flashbeagle Charlie Brown," Snoopy infects the Peanuts gang with dance fever, and in "She's a Good Skate Charlie Brown," Snoopy trains Peppermint Patty to become a figure skating champion. 55m/C VHS, Beta. *D:* Bill Melendez. SHL

It's Good to Be Alive 🎬 1974 The true story of how Brooklyn Dodgers' catcher Roy Campanella learned to face life after an automobile accident left him a quadriplegic. Good performances in this television drama. 100m/C VHS, Beta. Paul Winfield, Ruby Dee, Louis Gossett Jr.; *D:* Michael Landon. PSM

It's in the Bag 🎬🎬½ *The Fifth Chair* 1945 A shiftless flea circus owner sells chairs he has inherited, not knowing that a fortune is hidden in one of them. 87m/B VHS, LV. Fred Allen, Don Ameche, Jack Benny, William Bendix, Binnie Barnes, Robert Benchley; *D:* Richard Wallace. REP, MED

It's Love Again 🎬🎬½ 1936 A streetwise chorus girl poses as a fictional socialite in a light music-hall comedy. ♪It's Love Again; Heaven In Your Arms. 83m/B VHS, Beta. GB Jessie Matthews, Robert Young, Sonnie Hale; *D:* Victor Saville. NOS, DVT, HEG

It's Magic, Charlie Brown/Charlie Brown's All Star 1981 In the first of these two stories, Snoopy, "The Great Houndini," makes Charlie Brown disappear. Problems begin when Snoopy finds it difficult conjuring his master back to reality. In the second story, Charlie Brown's baseball team has lost 999 games in a row, and prospects are bleak. New hope arrives when he gets an offer to have the team sponsored in a real league. 55m/C VHS, Beta. *D:* Phil Roman. SHL, VTR

It's My Party 🎬🎬½ 1995 (R) When L.A. architect Nick Stark (Roberts) learns that he's developed untreatable brain lesions from AIDS that will essentially leave him helpless, he decides to throw himself a monumental farewell bash before taking a drug overdose. Friends and family all turn up as does, awkwardly enough, Brandon Theis (Harrison), Nick's former live-in who couldn't handle his HIV-positive diagnosis but would like a last reapproachment. Fine, sympathetic performances, espcially by the two leads, and yes, it's a weepie. Based on a true story.*CW:* Language and brief nudity. 120m/C VHS, LV, Closed Caption. Eric Roberts, Gregory Harrison, Marlee Matlin, Lee Grant, George Segal, Bronson Pinchot, Bruce Davison, Devon Gummersall, Roddy McDowall, Margaret Cho, Paul Regina, Olivia Newton-John, Christopher Atkins, Dennis Christopher, Ron Glass, Eugene Glazer; *D:* Randal Kleiser; *W:* Randal Kleiser; *C:* Bernd Heinl; *M:* Basil Poledouris. MGM

It's My Turn 🎬🎬 1980 (R) A mathematics professor (Clayburgh) struggles in her relationship with live-in lover (Grodin) who sells real-estate in Chicago. She meets retired baseball player (Douglas) and falls in love. "Ho-hum" just about describes the rest. 91m/C VHS, Beta, LV. Jill Clayburgh, Michael Douglas, Charles Grodin, Beverly Garland, Steven Hill, Dianne Wiest, Daniel Stern; *D:* Claudia Weill; *W:* Eleanor Bergstein; *C:* Bill Butler. COL

It's Not the Size That Counts woof! *Percy's Progress* 1974 After the Earth's drinking water is contaminated, Lawson is the only man on Earth not to be struck by impotency. Limp sequel to "Percy," the British comedy about the first man to receive a penis transplant. Promising comedy doesn't deliver. 90m/C VHS. Leigh Lawson, Elke Sommer, Denholm Elliott, Vincent Price; *D:* Ralph Thomas.

It's Pat: The Movie woof! 1994 (PG-13)
This movie is so bad, let's pray it sounds the death knell to big-screen versions of "Saturday Night Live" sketch characters— who possessed little humor to begin with. For what it's worth, the androgynous Pat (Sweeney) falls for the equally gender-suspect Chris (Foley, from Canada's version of SNL, "Kids in the Hall") and all sorts of embarrassing situations arise. Pat's quest to find Pat's self is sketch material stretched see-through thin.*CW:* Bizarre gender-related humor. 78m/C VHS, Closed Caption. Julia Sweeney, Dave Foley, Charles Rocket, Kathy Griffin, Julie Haydon, Tim Meadows, Arleen Sorkin; *Cameos:* Sally Jesse Raphael, Kathy Najimy; *D:* Adam Bernstein; *W:* Julia Sweeney, Jim Emerson, Stephen Hibbert. Nominations: Golden Raspberry Awards '95: Worst Picture, Worst New Star (Sweeney). TOU

It's the Great Pumpkin, Charlie Brown 1988 It's Halloween, and Charlie Brown and his friends are going trick-or-treating, but Linus faithfully awaits the arrival of the Great Pumpkin. 25m/C VHS, Beta. PAR, MED, VTR

It's the Old Army Game 1926 Classic Fields gags in three of his best Ziegfeld Follies sketches: "The Drug Store," "A Peaceful Morning," and "The Family Flivver." The beautiful Brooks serves as his comic foil. 75m/B VHS, Beta. W.C. Fields, Louise Brooks, Blanche Ring, William Gaxton; *D:* Edward Sutherland. GPV

It's Three Strikes, Charlie Brown 1986 Misfortunes abound in the baseball diamond for the Peanuts gang. 41m/C VHS, Beta. *D:* Bill Melendez, Phil Roman, Robert E. Balzer, Sam Nicholson. BAR

It's Your First Kiss, Charlie Brown/ Someday You'll Find Her, Charlie Brown 1977 In "It's Your First Kiss, Charlie Brown," our hero has to escort the school's homecoming queen to the ball. What's worse, he actually has to kiss her in front of everyone! In "Someday You'll Find Her, Charlie Brown," Charlie Brown sees "the most beautiful girl in the world" on television and, after recruiting Linus, embarks upon a door-to-door search to find her. 55m/C VHS, Beta. *D:* Phil Roman. SHL, VTR

Ivan and Abraham 🎬🎬 1994 Abraham (Alexandrovitch) is a 9-year-old Jewish boy, living on a shtetl in 1930s eastern Poland, with his best friend being the family's 14-year-old Christian apprentice Ivan (Iakovlev). The boys sense the increasing family tensions and escape into the nearby forest, only to find politics and prejudice sweeping over them all. In Yiddish, Russian, Polish, and Romany, with English subtitles. 105m/B VHS. Roma Aleksandrovitch, Sacha Iakovlev, Vladimir Machkov, Maria Lipkina, Rolan Bykov, Daniel Olbrychski; *D:* Yolande Zauberman; *W:* Yolande Zauberman; *C:* Jean-Marc Fabre. NYF

Ivan the Terrible, Part 1 🎬🎬🎬🎬 1944 Contemplative epic of Russia's first czar is a classic, innovative film from cinema genius Eisenstein. Visually stunning, with a fine performance by Cherkassov. Ivan's struggles to preserve his country is the main concern of the first half of Eisenstein's masterwork (which he originally planned as a trilogy). In Russian with English subtitles. 96m/B VHS, Beta, 8mm. RU Nikolai Cherkassov, Ludmila Tselikovskaya, Serafina Birman, Piotr Kadochnikev; *D:* Sergei Eisenstein; *W:* Sergei Eisenstein; *M:* Sergei Prokofiev. NOS, MRV, WST

Ivan the Terrible, Part 2 🎬🎬🎬½ 1946 Landed gentry conspire to dethrone the czar in this continuation of the innovative epic. More stunning imagery from master Eisenstein, who makes no false moves in this one. Slow going, but immensely rewarding. Russian dialogue with English subtitles; contains color sequences. 84m/B VHS, Beta, 8mm. RU Nikolai Cherkassov, Ludmila Tselikovskaya, Serafina Birman, Piotr Kadochnikev; *D:* Sergei Eisenstein. NOS, MRV, WST

Ivanhoe 🎬🎬🎬 1952 Knights fight each other and woo maidens in this chivalrous romance derived from the Sir Walter Scott classic. Taylor is suitably noble, while Sanders is familiarly serpentine. Remade in 1982. 107m/C VHS, Beta. Robert Taylor, Elizabeth Taylor, Joan Fontaine, George Sanders, Finlay Currie, Felix Aylmer; *D:* Richard Thorpe; *C:* Frederick A. (Freddie) Young; *M:* Miklos Rozsa. Nominations: Academy Awards '52: Best Color Cinematography, Best Picture, Original Dramatic/Comedy Score. MGM

Ivanhoe 🎬🎬½ 1982 A version of Sir Walter Scott's classic novel of chivalry and knighthood in 12th century England. Made for television. Remake of the 1953 film classic. 142m/C VHS, Beta. Anthony Andrews, James Mason, Lysette Anthony, Sam Neill, Olivia Hussey, Michael Hordern, Julian Glover, George Innes, Ronald Pickup, John Rhys-Davies, Chloe Franks; *D:* Douglas Camfield. TVC, COL

Ivanhoe 🎬🎬🎬 1997 TV miniseries version of Sir Walter Scott's epic tale of knights, chivalry, romance, and daring. Saxon knight Wilfred of Ivanhoe (Waddington), having fought for Richard the Lionheart (Edwards) during the Crusades, returns to England to battle the scheming Prince John (Brown) and sinister Grand Master of the Templars, Lucas De Beaumanoir (Lee) in order to regain his honor. His childhood sweetheart, Saxon heiress Rowena (Smurfit), is betrothed to another but Ivanhoe's also drawn to Jewish healer Rebecca (Lynch) as is scheming Knight Templar, Sir Brian Bois-Guilbert (Hinds). Lots of action. On six cassettes. 300m/C VHS, Closed Caption. GB Steven Waddington, Susan Lynch, Ciaran Hinds, Victoria Smurfit, Ralph Brown, Rory Edwards, Ronald Pickup, David Horovitch, Trevor Cooper, Valentine Pelka, Nick Brimble, Jimmy Chisholm, Christopher Lee, Aden Gillett, James Cosmo, Sian Phillips, Nick Brimble, Ciaran Madden; *D:* Stuart Orme; *W:* Deborah Cook; *C:* Clive Tickner; *M:* Colin Towns. AAE, VIF, PBS

I've Always Loved You 🎬🎬½ *Concerto* 1946 The drama of love and jealousy explored in an extravagant production filled with classical music. 117m/C VHS, LV. Philip Dorn, Catherine McLeod; *D:* Frank Borzage; *C:* Gaetano Antonio "Tony" Gaudio. REP, FCT

I've Heard the Mermaids Singing 🎬🎬🎬 1987 Independent Canadian semi-satiric romantic comedy details the misadventures of a klutzy woman who suddenly obtains a desirable job in an art gallery run by a lesbian on whom she develops a crush. Good-natured tone helped considerably by McCarthy's winning performance. 81m/C VHS, Beta, LV. CA Sheila McCarthy, Paule Baillargeon, Ann-Marie MacDonald, John Evans; *D:* Patricia Rozema; *M:* Mark Korven. Genie Awards '88: Best Actress (McCarthy), Best Supporting Actress (Baillargeon). NLC, FCT

Ivory Hunters 🎬🎬½ *The Last Elephant* 1990 Conservationists team up to thwart a massacre of elephants by poachers. Predictable made-for-cable entertainment co-produced by the National Audubon Society. 94m/C VHS, Beta, Closed Caption. John Lithgow, Isabella Rossellini, James Earl Jones, Tony Todd, Olek Krupa; *D:* Joseph Sargent; *W:* Richard Guttman, Bill Bozzone; *M:* Charles Bernstein. TTC

Izzy & Moe 🎬🎬½ 1985 Carney and The Great One are reunited for the last time on screen as former vaudevillians who become federal agents and create havoc amid speak-easies and bathtub gin during Prohibition. A made-for-television movie based on true stories. 92m/C VHS, Beta, LV. Jackie Gleason, Art Carney, Cynthia Harris, Zohra Lampert, Drew Snyder, Dick Latessa; *D:* Jackie Cooper. THV

J. Edgar Hoover 🎬🎬 1987 Made for cable adaptation from "My 30 years in Hoover's FBI" by William G. Sullivan and William S. Brown. Biographical drama deals with Hoover's fifty-five year career with the government. Included are his FBI days. 110m/C VHS, Beta. Treat Williams, Rip Torn, David Ogden Stiers, Andrew Duggan, Art Hindle, Louise Fletcher; *D:* Robert Collins. MCG

J-Men Forever! 🐾🐾🐾 **1979 (PG)** A spoof on early sci-fi/spy serials in which an alien takeover is attempted via rock-n-roll (your parents warned you). Employs an amusing technique of dubbing footage from dozens of Republic dramas intercut with new film featuring the "Firesign Theater" crew. **73m/B VHS, Beta.** Peter Bergman, Phil Proctor; **D:** Richard Patterson. *VES*

Jabberwalk 🐾🐾 **1979 (R)** A "Mondo Cane," American-style. A reckless and funny view of the bizarre in U.S. life. **110m/C VHS, Beta.** *VCD*

Jabberwocky 🐾🐾½ **1977 (PG)** Pythonesque chaos prevails in the medieval cartoon kingdom of King Bruno the Questionable, who rules with cruelty, stupidity, lust and dust. Jabberwocky is the big dragon mowing everything down in its path until hero Palin decides to take it on. Uneven, but real funny at times. **104m/C VHS, Beta, LV.** *GB* Michael Palin, Eric Idle, Max Wall, Deborah Fallender, Terry Jones, John Le Mesurier; **D:** Terry Gilliam; **W:** Terry Gilliam. *COL*

Jacare 🐾🐾 **1942** First adventure thriller filmed in the Amazon jungle. **?m/C VHS.** Frank Buck; **M:** Miklos Rozsa. *SNC, VYY*

J'Accuse 🐾🐾🐾 *I Accuse; That They May Live* **1937** A Frenchman creates a device he believes will stop the war but it is confiscated by the government and used as part of the national defense. Subsequently, he goes mad. Gance (known for his 1927 "Napoleon"), remade his 1919 silent film, retelling the powerful anti-war message with great sensitivity. Banned in Nazi Germany. **125m/B VHS.** *FR* Victor Francen, Jean Max, Deltaire, Renee Devillers; **D:** Abel Gance. *CVC, SNC, FCT*

Jack 🐾🐾½ **1996 (PG-13)** Ten-year-old Jack Powell (Williams) suffers from a rare genetic disorder that causes him to age at four times the normal rate so he looks like a 40-year-old. His family, fearing ridicule, has kept him isolated but since Jack's so lonely, they finally agree to let him attend school. This new fourth grader isn't the only one with a lot to learn. **CW:** Some sexual references. **111m/C VHS, LV, Closed Caption.** Robin Williams, Bill Cosby, Diane Lane, Brian Kerwin, Fran Drescher, Michael McKean, Jennifer Lopez, Don Novello; **D:** Francis Ford Coppola; **W:** James DeMonaco, Gary Nadeau; **C:** John Toll; **M:** Michael Kamen. *TOU*

Jack and His Friends 🐾🐾 **1992 (R)** Comic satire of the tribulations of Jack the shoe salesman (Garfield), who is shown the front door by his unfaithful wife. Beset by grief, he drives the streets aimlessly until he is kidnapped by a young couple (Rockwell and Reyes) on the run from the law, who force Jack to take them to his summer house where they all try to decide what to do with their lives. **93m/C VHS.** Allen (Goorwitz) Garfield, Sam Rockwell, Judy Reyes; **D:** Bruce Ornstein. *FCT*

Jack and Sarah 🐾🐾½ **1995 (R)** Widowed London lawyer (Grant) hires American waitress (Mathis), to help raise his infant daughter Sarah. Complications arise because Amy has no child rearing skills and Jack's parents and in-laws disapprove of the whole situation. Performances are nice (especially the scene-stealing infants), and there's some fine moments combining tragedy with romance, but the plot is a little thin and the whole film is slow moving (it takes more than half the movie to get the three protagonists in place). An edited version is rated PG. **CW:** Profanity. **110m/C VHS.** *GB* Richard E. Grant, Samantha Mathis, Ian McKellen, Judi Dench, Cherie Lunghi, Eileen Atkins, Imogen Stubbs; **D:** Tim Sullivan; **W:** Tim Sullivan; **C:** Jean-Yves Escoffier; **M:** Simon Boswell. *PGV*

Jack & the Beanstalk 🐾🐾 **1952** While baby-sitting, Lou falls asleep and dreams he's Jack in this spoof of the classic fairy tale. **78m/C VHS, Beta, LV.** Bud Abbott, Lou Costello, Buddy Baer; **D:** Jean Yarbrough. *NOS, VTR*

Jack & the Beanstalk 🐾🐾 **1976** An animated musical version of the familiar story of Jack, the young boy who climbs a magic beanstalk up into the clouds, where he meets a fear-some giant. **80m/C VHS, Beta.** **D:** Peter J. Solmo; **W:** Peter J. Solmo. *COL*

Jack & the Beanstalk **1983** From the "Faerie Tale Theatre" comes this classic tale of Jack, who sells his family's cow for 5 magic beans, climbs the huge beanstalk that sprouts from them, and encounters an unfriendly giant. **60m/C VHS, Beta, LV, Closed Caption.** Dennis Christopher, Katherine Helmond, Elliott Gould, Jean Stapleton, Mark Blankfield; **D:** Lamont Johnson. *KUI, FOX, FCT*

Jack Be Nimble 🐾🐾 **1994 (R)** Siblings Jack (Arquette) and Dora (Kennedy) were separated as children and adopted by different families. Jack's family turns out to be sadistic and he suffers much abuse, until he enacts a violent revenge; Dora begins to hear voices and soon realizes it's Jack crying out to her. The duo finally reunite but between Jack's rage and Dora's telepathic abilities, life takes on further bizarre twists. Much psychological terror rather than gore. **CW:** Disturbing violent behavior and abuse; some sexuality and language. **93m/C VHS.** *NZ* Alexis Arquette, Sarah Kennedy, Bruno Lawrence; **D:** Garth Maxwell; **W:** Garth Maxwell; **M:** Chris Neal. *TRI*

Jack Frost 🐾🐾½ **1943** Moving biographical drama that follows a man from the sweat factories of London to his eventual rise to success. **89m/B VHS, Beta, 8mm.** Michael O'Shea, Susan Hayward. *VYY*

The Jack Knife Man 🐾🐾🐾 **1920** Sentimental silent treatment of the relationship between a boy and a man. A new mother close to death hands over her bundle of joy to a kindly old river man, and the two bond in a familial way despite incessant adversity. Made the year following Vidor's debut as a feature film director. **70m/B VHS, Beta.** Fred Turner, Harry Todd, Bobby Kelso, Willis Marks, Lillian Leighton, James Corrigan; **D:** King Vidor; **W:** William Parker. *VYY, GPV, FCT*

Jack London 🐾½ *The Adventures of Jack London; The Life of Jack London* **1944** Dramatizes London's most creative years during his careers as oyster pirate, prospector, war correspondent and author. Based on "The Book of Jack London" by Charmian London. **94m/B VHS, Beta.** Michael O'Shea, Susan Hayward, Harry Davenport, Virginia Mayo, Frank Craven; **D:** Alfred Santell. Nominations: Academy Awards '44: Original Dramatic/Comedy Score. *NOS, MRV, DVT*

Jack-O 🐾½ **1995 (R)** Halloween nightmares in the small town of Oakmoor Crossing. When warlock Walter Machen (Carradine) was hung 100 years before, he invoked a demon creature to take his revenge. Now partyers, fooling around in the local cemetery, have stumbled onto horrific Jack-O's remains and manage to once again unleash the evil within. Cheesy grade-Z horror features old footage of deceased actors Carradine and Mitchell incorporated into what little plot there is. **CW:** Violence, nudity. **90m/C VHS, LV.** Linnea Quigley, Ryan Latshaw, Cameron Mitchell, John Carradine; **D:** Steve Latshaw. *TRI, IME*

Jack the Bear 🐾½ **1993 (PG-13)** Exercise in misery centers on a father and his two sons, trying to pick up the pieces after the death of wife and mother Marcovicci. Dad DeVito is the host of a late-night horror show who's cuddly as a bear—when he's not drinking. While the talent and circumstances might have been enough to create a sensitive study, the emotion is completely overwrought by contrived plot twists, including a kidnapping by the local Nazi. TV's "thirtysomething" director Herskovitz creates an effect not unlike a cement block being dropped on a card house. Point made, but so much for subtlety. Based on a novel by Dan McCall. **CW:** Thematic elements and some horror. **98m/C VHS, LV, Closed Caption.** Danny DeVito, Robert J. Steinmiller Jr., Miko Hughes, Gary Sinise, Art LaFleur, Andrea Marcovicci, Julia Louis-Dreyfus, Reese Witherspoon; **D:** Marshall Herskovitz; **W:** Steven Zaillian; **C:** Fred Murphy; **M:** James Horner. *FXV*

Jack the Giant Killer 🐾🐾🐾 **1962 (G)** A young farmer joins a medieval princess on a journey to a distant convent. Along the way, they combat an evil wizard, dragons, sea monsters and other mystical creatures, and are assisted by leprechauns, a dog and a chimp. Generally considered a blatant rip-off of "The Seventh Voyage of Sinbad," the film nonetheless delivers plenty of fun and excitement. Jim Danforth of "Gumby" fame provided the stop-motion animation. **95m/C VHS, Beta, LV.** Kerwin Mathews, Judi Meredith, Torin Thatcher, Walter Burke, Roger Mobley, Barry Kelley, Don Beddoe, Anna Lee, Robert Gist; **D:** Nathan (Hertz) Juran. *MGM, FCT*

Jack the Ripper 🐾🐾 **1960** An American detective joins Scotland Yard in tracking down the legendary and elusive Jack the Ripper. More gory than most. The last scene is in color. **88m/B VHS.** *GB* Lee Patterson, Betty McDowall, Barbara Burke, John Le Mesurier, George Rose; **D:** Monty Berman, Robert S. Baker; **M:** Stanley Black. *SNC, PAR*

Jack the Ripper 🐾🐾 **1980 (R)** The inimitable Kinski assumes the role of the most heinous criminal of modern history—Jack the Ripper. **82m/C VHS, Beta.** Klaus Kinski, Josephine Chaplin; **D:** Jess (Jesus) Franco. *VES*

Jack the Ripper 🐾🐾🐾 **1988** Another retelling of the life of the legendary serial killer. Caine is the Scotland Yard inspector who tracks down the murderer. Ending is based on recent evidence found by director/co-writer Wickes. Extremely well done made-for-television film. **200m/C VHS.** Michael Caine, Armand Assante, Ray McNally, Susan George, Jane Seymour, Lewis Collins, Ken Bones; **D:** David Wickes; **W:** David Wickes. *VES, LIV*

Jackie Chan's First Strike 🐾🐾🐾 *First Strike; Police Story 4* **1996 (PG-13)** Plot, schmot. The human hurricane that is Jackie Chan is once again amazing in this kung-fu comedy homage to 60s James Bond movies. Half Bruce Lee and half Charlie Chaplin, Chan reprises the role of the Hong Kong supercop named Jackie, who is this time loaned out by his superior officer "Uncle Bill" (Tung) to the CIA. He is sent to the Ukraine to spy on a beautiful young woman involved in smuggling nuclear weapons along with rogue CIA agent Tsui (Lou). He follows the villains to Australia, where he secures justice, peace and sharp blows to the head. Enough about the plot. Listen to this! He holds bad guys at bay by whirling an aluminum stepladder like it was a drum major's baton! He kicks somebody off of a second story ledge while on stilts! He sings and dances while wearing koala bear underwear! Dubbed in English. **CW:** Plentiful action/violence. **87m/C VHS, LV, Closed Caption.** *HK* Jackie Chan, Bill Tung, Jackson Lou, Chen Chun Wu, Jouri Petrov, Grishajeva Nonna; **D:** Stanley Tong; **W:** Stanley Tong, Nick Tramontane, Elliot Tong, Greg Mellott; **C:** Jingle Ma; **M:** J. Peter Robinson. Nominations: MTV Movie Awards '97: Best Fight (Jackie Chan/A ladder). *NLC*

Jackie Chan's Police Force 🐾🐾½ *The Police Story; Police Force; Jackie Chan's Police Story* **1985 (PG-13)** Chopsocker Chan's assigned to protect a witness in a drug case. Faced by unsavory thugs, he flies through the air with the greatest of ease. Very cool stunts. **89m/C VHS.** *HK* Jackie Chan, Bridget Lin, Maggie Cheung, Cho Yuen, Bill Tung, Kenneth Tong; **D:** Jackie Chan. *TAI*

The Jackie Robinson Story 🐾🐾🐾 **1950** Chronicles Robinson's rise from UCLA to his breakthrough as the first black man to play baseball in the major league. Robinson plays himself; the film deals honestly with the racial issues of the time. **76m/B VHS, Beta.** Jackie Robinson, Ruby Dee, Minor Watson, Louise Beavers, Richard Lane, Harry Shannon, Joel Fluellen, Ben Lessy; **D:** Alfred E. Green. *MGM, MRV, MOV*

Jacknife 🐾🐾🐾 **1989 (R)** The well-crafted story of a Vietnam veteran who visits his old war buddy and tries to piece together what's happened to their lives since their homecoming. During his visit he encounters anger and hostility from the other veteran, and tenderness from his friend's sister. A masterfully acted, small-scale drama, adapted by Stephen Metcalfe from his play. **102m/C VHS, Beta, LV, Closed Caption.** Robert De Niro, Kathy Baker, Ed Harris, Loudon Wainwright III, Charles S. Dutton; **D:** David Jones; **W:** Stephen Metcalfe; **M:** Bruce Broughton. *HBO, IME*

Jacko & Lise 🐾🐾 1982 (R) A French lad falls in love with a young girl, and abandons his previously decadent lifestyle to win her. Available with English subtitles or dubbed. **92m/C VHS, Beta.** FR Laurent Malet, Annie Girardot; **D:** Walter Bal.

The Jackpot 🐾🐾 1950 An average Joe wins a bushel of money from a radio quiz show but can't pay the taxes. Maybe that was funny before the age of read-my-lips economics, but the all-star cast doesn't deliver on its promise. Lang, noted for mostly mediocre pictures, went on to direct "The King and I." **87m/C VHS.** James Stewart, Natalie Wood, Barbara Hale, James Gleason, Fred Clark, Patricia Medina; **D:** Walter Lang; **C:** Joseph LaShelle. *FXV*

Jack's Back 🐾🐾🐾 1987 (R) When a lunatic is killing Los Angeles prostitutes Jack-the-Ripper style, twin brothers get mistakenly involved (Spader in both roles). One of the brothers is accused of the murders and it is up to the other either to clear his name or to provide the final evidence of guilt. A well thought out story with enough twists and turns for any suspense buff. **97m/C VHS, Beta, LV, Closed Caption.** James Spader, Cynthia Gibb, Rod Loomis, Rex Ryon, Robert Picardo, Jim Haynie, Chris Mulkey, Danitza Kingsley; **D:** Rowdy Herrington. *PAR*

Jackson County Jail 🐾🐾½ 1976 (R) While driving cross-country, a young woman is robbed, imprisoned, and raped by a deputy, whom she kills. Faced with a murder charge, she flees, with the law in hot pursuit. Also known by its later remade-for-television name, "Outside Chance," this is a minor cult film. **84m/C VHS.** Yvette Mimieux, Tommy Lee Jones, Robert Carradine, Severn Darden, Howard Hesseman, Mary Woronov; **D:** Michael Miller; **W:** Donald Stewart. *NHO*

The Jacksons: An American Dream 🐾🐾½ 1992 Made for television miniseries covering the career of the Jackson 5, the working-class family from Gary, Indiana which became a celebrated show business success. The series begins with the courtship of Joseph and Katherine Jackson and ends with the group's farewell tour in 1984, covering both family and career turmoils. Simplistic, glossy biography. **225m/C VHS.** Lawrence-Hilton Jacobs, Angela Bassett, Wylie Draper, Angel Vargas, Jacen Wilkerson, Terrence DaShon Howard, Jason Weaver, Jermaine Jackson II, Billy Dee Williams, Vanessa Williams, Holly Robinson, Margaret Avery; **D:** Karen Arthur. *PGV*

Jacob 🐾🐾½ 1994 Jacob (Modine), second son of Isaac (Ackland), tricks his father into giving him the blessing meant for eldest son Esau (Bean). Jacob is forced to run away to his Uncle Laban (Giannini), where he promptly falls in love with his cousin Rachel (Boyle). But Laban tricks Jacob into marrying eldest daughter Leah (Aubrey), before allowing his marriage to Rachel. Finally, Jacob settles on his own land with his wives and children (who will become the tribes of Israel). Dignified retelling of the Biblical story; filmed on location in Morocco. Made for cable TV. **120m/C VHS.** Matthew Modine, Lara Flynn Boyle, Sean Bean, Juliet Aubrey, Giancarlo Giannini, Joss Ackland, Irene Papas, Christoph Waltz; **D:** Peter Hall; **W:** Lionel Chetwynd; **M:** Marco Frisina. *TTC*

Jacob Have I Loved 1988 A teenage girl struggles to overcome her jealousy of her twin sister and find her own place in life as she comes of age on a Chesapeake island. Based on the book by Katherine Paterson. Part of the "Wonderworks" family movie series from PBS. **57m/C VHS.** Bridget Fonda, Jenny Robertson, John Kellogg; **D:** Victoria Hochberg. *PME, WNE, RHU*

Jacob's Ladder 🐾🐾½ 1990 (R) A man struggles with events he experienced while serving in Vietnam. Gradually, he becomes unable to separate reality from the strange, psychotic world into which he increasingly lapses. His friends and family try to help him before he's lost forever. Great story potential is flawed by too many flashbacks, leaving the viewer more confused than the characters. **116m/C VHS, Beta, LV, Closed Caption.** Tim Robbins, Elizabeth Pena, Danny Aiello, Matt Craven, Pruitt Taylor Vince, Jason Alexander, Patricia Kalember, Eriq La Salle, Ving Rhames, Macaulay Culkin; **D:** Adrian Lyne; **W:** Bruce Joel Rubin; **M:** Maurice Jarre. *LIV, FCT*

Jacqueline Bouvier Kennedy 🐾½ 1981 A made-for-television biography of the former First Lady, from her childhood to "Camelot," the glorious years with JFK in the White House. Smith bears a physical resemblance to Jackie, but this drama is far too glossy. **150m/C VHS, Beta.** Jaclyn Smith, James Franciscus, Rod Taylor, Donald Moffat, Dolph Sweet, Stephen Elliott; **D:** Steven Gethers; **M:** Billy Goldenberg. *THV*

Jacquot 🐾🐾 *Jacquot de Nantes* 1991 (PG) Director Varda offers a loving tribute to her husband, filmmaker Jacques Demy. Based on the memoirs of her husband's childhood as a boy obsessed with movies, Varda re-stages scenes and also uses clips from various Demy films to illustrate her points. In French with English subtitles. **118m/C VHS.** FR Philippe Maron, Edouard Joubeaud, Laurent Monnier, Brigitte de Villepoix, Daniel Dublet; **D:** Agnes Varda; **W:** Agnes Varda; **C:** Patrick Blossier; **M:** Joanne Bruzdowicz. *COL*

Jade 🐾½ 1995 (R) Sleazy whodunnit scraped from the bottom of the Eszterhas barrel (and it's a deep one) has hot-shot San Francisco Assistant D.A. David Corelli (Caruso) tracking a trail of pubic hairs across San Francisco. Seems he's caught up in the murder of a millionaire that points to his ex-lover, psychologist Katrina Gavin (Fiorentino), as the killer. Oh yeah, she's also a kinky call girl of choice to California's rich and famous, and happens to be married to Corelli's best friend (Palminteri). Psycho-thriller with little of either injects lots of lurid details (and a car chase scene that Friedkin has done much better elsewhere) in an attempt to curtail boredom; it doesn't work. Combine it with "Showgirls" for the No Self-Respect Film Festival, then go to confession.*CW:* Grisly afterviews of murder victims, violence, language, and strong scenes of aberrant sexuality. **94m/C VHS, Closed Caption.** David Caruso, Linda Fiorentino, Chazz Palminteri, Michael Biehn, Richard Crenna, Kenneth King; **D:** William Friedkin; **W:** Joe Eszterhas; **C:** Andrzej Bartkowiak; **M:** James Horner. *PAR*

The Jade Mask 🐾½ 1945 Chan discovers a murderer and his wife use puppets and masks to make it appear their victims are still alive. Another in the detective series with nothing noteworthy about it. Luke, the brother of actor Keye Luke, takes on the role of Chan's Number Four son. **66m/B VHS.** Sidney Toler, Mantan Moreland, Edwin Luke, Janet Warren, Hardie Albright, Edith Evanson; **D:** Phil Rosen. *MGM*

JAG 🐾🐾½ 1995 TV pilot episode features Navy pilot-turned-lawyer Lt. Harmon Rabb, Jr. (Elliott) assigned to investigate the case of a young female pilot who disappears from an aircraft carrier. Seems some of her fellow sailors resented having women on board so was it an accident or murder? JAG stands for the office of the Judge Advocate General, whose Navy lawyers serve as investigators, prosecutors, and defense attorneys. **94m/C VHS, Closed Caption.** David James Elliott, Andrea Parker, Terry O'Quinn; **D:** Donald P. Bellisario; **W:** Donald P. Bellisario; **M:** Bruce Broughton. *PAR*

The Jagged Edge 🐾🐾½ 1985 (R) The beautiful wife of successful newspaper editor, Jack Forester, is killed and the police want to point the guilty finger at Jack. Attorney Teddy Barnes is brought in to defend him and accidentally falls in love. Taut murder mystery will keep you guessing "whodunit" until the very end. **108m/C VHS, Beta, LV, 8mm, Closed Caption.** Jeff Bridges, Glenn Close, Robert Loggia, Peter Coyote, John Dehner, Leigh Taylor-Young, Lance Henriksen, James Karen, Karen Austin, Michael Dorn, Guy Boyd, Marshall Colt, Louis Giambalvo; **D:** Richard Marquand; **W:** Joe Eszterhas; **M:** John Barry. Nominations: Academy Awards '85: Best Supporting Actor (Loggia). *COL*

Jaguar 1956 Three men leave their homes in Niger in order to find jobs in the cities. When they return to their village, they bring back with them their experiences. **93m/C VHS.** **D:** Jean Rouch; **M:** Van Alexander. *INT*

Jaguar Lives 🐾 1979 (PG) A high-kicking secret agent tracks down bad boy drug kings around the world. **91m/C VHS, Beta.** Joe Lewis, Barbara Bach, Christopher Lee, Woody Strode, Donald Pleasence, Joseph Wiseman, John Huston, Capucine; **D:** Ernie Pintoff. *TWE*

Jail Bait 🐾½ *Hidden Face* 1954 Early Wood film about a group of small-time crooks who are always in trouble with the law; they blackmail a plastic surgeon into using his talents to help them ditch the cops. Not as "bad" as Wood's "Plan 9 From Outer Space," but still bad enough for camp fans to love (check the cheesy score leftover from an equally cheesy Mexican mad-scientist flick). **80m/B VHS, Beta.** Timothy Farrell, Clancy Malone, Lyle Talbot, Steve Reeves, Herbert Rawlinson; **D:** Edward D. Wood Jr. *SNC, AOV, LSV*

Jailbait 🐾🐾 1993 (R) A cop gets involved with an alleged murder witness, a teenaged runaway named Kyle. What they discover is an international crime syndicate that kidnaps runaways to exploit as sex slaves. Now they know too much. An unrated version is also available. **100m/C VHS, Closed Caption.** C. Thomas Howell, Renee Humphrey; **D:** Rafal Zielinksi; **W:** Robert Vincent O'Neil, Alien Castle. *PAR*

Jailbait: Betrayed By Innocence 🐾½ 1986 (R) A man is on trial for statutory rape. Made-for-television. **90m/C VHS, Beta.** Barry Bostwick, Lee Purcell, Paul Sorvino, Cristen Kauffman, Isaac Hayes; **D:** Elliot Silverstein. *HHE*

Jailbird Rock 🐾½ 1988 We'd like to tell you that this isn't really a sweet-young-thing-in-prison musical, but it is. When Antin shoots her stepfather (he told her to turn that damn noise down?) she tries to bring down the Big House with song and dance. No kidding. **90m/C VHS, Beta.** Ronald Lacey, Rhonda Aldrich, Robin Antin; **D:** Phillip Schuman. *TWE*

Jailbird's Vacation 🐾🐾 *Les Grandes Gueules* 1965 Two ex-cons pose as lumberjacks in order to exact revenge on the bum that put them away. In French with English subtitles. **125m/C VHS, Beta.** FR Lino Ventura, Bourvil, Marie DuBois; **D:** Robert Enrico. *FCT, BAR*

Jailbreakin' 🐾 1972 A faded country singer and a rebellious youth team up to break out of jail. **90m/C VHS, Beta.** Erik Estrada. *GEM*

Jailhouse Rock 🐾🐾🐾 1957 (G) While in jail for manslaughter, a teenager learns to play the guitar. After his release, he slowly develops into a top recording star. Probably the only film that captured the magnetic power of the young Elvis Presley; an absolute must for fans. Also available in a colorized version. 🎵 Jailhouse Rock; Treat Me Nice; Baby, I Don't Care; Young and Beautiful; Don't Leave Me Now; I Wanna Be Free; One More Day. **96m/B VHS, Beta, LV.** Elvis Presley, Judy Tyler, Vaughn Taylor, Dean Jones, Mickey Shaughnessy, William Forrest, Glenn Strange; **D:** Richard Thorpe. *MGM*

Jakarta 🐾½ 1988 (R) A love-hardened CIA operative is whisked away to Jakarta for reasons unknown, only to find his thought-to-be-dead lover still alive and caught in a deadly game of espionage. **94m/C VHS, Beta, LV.** Christopher Noth, Sue Francis Pai, Ronald Hunter; **D:** Charles Kaufman. *NO*

Jake Speed 🎬½ 1986 (PG) Comic-book mercenary Jake and his loyal associate Remo rescue a beautiful girl from white slave traders. Supposedly a parody of the action adventure genre. **93m/C VHS, Beta, LV, Closed Caption.** Wayne Crawford, John Hurt, Karen Kopins, Dennis Christopher; **D:** Andrew Lane; **W:** Wayne Crawford. *NWV, VTR*

Jamaica Inn 🎬 1939 In old Cornwall, an orphan girl becomes involved with smugglers. Remade in 1982; based on the story by Daphne Du Maurier. **98m/B VHS, Beta.** *GB* Charles Laughton, Maureen O'Hara, Leslie Banks, Robert Newton; **D:** Alfred Hitchcock; **C:** Harry Stradling. *KIV, NOS, CAB*

Jamaica Inn 🎬½ 1982 A made-for-television mini-series based on the old Daphne Du Maurier adventure about highwaymen and moorlurking thieves in Cornwall. Remake of the 1939 Hitchcock film. **192m/C VHS, Beta.** Patrick McGoohan, Jane Seymour; **D:** Lawrence Gordon Clark. *VTR, NWV*

James and the Giant Peach 🎬🎬🎬 1996 (PG) Terrific combo of live action and stop-motion animation highlights this adaptation of Roald Dahl's 1961 children's book. Orphaned James is sent to live with his wicked aunts. When magic "crocodile tongues," given to James by a hobo, spill at the base of a peach tree, one fruit grows to such a tremendous size that James crawls inside, meets six insect friends, and goes on numerous adventures, all the while trying to face his fears. Dahl's books are creepy and since the people who brought you "Nightmare Before Christmas" are also doing "James," expect the visuals to be astonishing but too scary for the wild ones. **80m/C VHS, Closed Caption.** Paul Terry, Pete Postlethwaite, Joanna Lumley, Miriam Margolyes; **D:** Henry Selick; **C:** Pete Kozachik, Hiro Narita; **M:** Randy Newman; **V:** Richard Dreyfuss, Susan Sarandon, David Thewlis, Simon Callow, Jane Leeves. Nominations: Academy Awards '96: Best Original Score.*TOU*

James Dean 🎬🎬 *The Legend* 1976 Dean's friend Bast wrote this behind-the-scenes look at the short life of the enigmatic movie star. Made for television. **99m/C VHS, Beta.** Stephen McHattie, Michael Brandon, Candy Clark, Amy Irving, Brooke Adams, Dane Clark, Jayne Meadows, Meg Foster; **D:** William Bast, Robert Butler; **W:** William Bast; **M:** Billy Goldenberg. *NWV*

James Dean Story 1957 An intimate portrait of James Dean presented by Robert Altman. The program includes never-before-seen outtakes from "East of Eden" and rare footage from the Hollywood premiere of "Giant" and the infamous Highway Public Safety message Dean made for television. **80m/B VHS, Beta, LV.** James Dean; **D:** George W. George. *FCT, PMS, VEC*

James Dean: The First American Teenager 1976 (PG) A look at the life and legend of the charismatic filmstar, with scenes from his films and comments from those who knew him best. **83m/C VHS, Beta.** James Dean, Elizabeth Taylor, Sammy Davis Jr., Rock Hudson, Sal Mineo, Natalie Wood, Julie Harris, Jack Larson, Nicholas Ray. *NO*

James Joyce: A Portrait of the Artist as a Young Man 1977 A moving, lyrical adaptation of the author's autobiography, told through the character of Stephen Dedalus. Joyce's characterizations, words, and scenes are beautifully translated to the medium of film. Excellent casting. **93m/C VHS.** John Gielgud, T.P. McKenna, Bosco Hogan. *MFV*

James Joyce's Women 🎬🎬🎬 1985 (R) Adapted from her one-woman stage show as well as produced by Flanagan, this acclaimed film features enacted portraits of three real-life Joyce associates, including his wife (Nora Barnacle) and three of his famous characters. **91m/C VHS, Beta.** Fionnula Flanagan, Timothy E. O'Grady, Chris O'Neill; **D:** Michael Pearce; **W:** Fionnula Flanagan. *USH*

Jamon, Jamon 🎬🎬 *Ham Ham* 1993 Comedic melodrama satirizing various aspects of the Spanish character, including machismo, sex, and food. A small Spanish town is dominated by two businesses—an underwear factory and a broth-el—both run by strong-minded women. The brothel's Carmen and the factory's Conchita clash when Carmen's daughter, Silvia, becomes pregnant by Conchita's son, Manuel. Conchita's appalled and hires stud Raul to seduce Silvia—only to fall for him herself. Oh yes, Raul attributes his sexual prowess to a steady diet of ham and garlic. In Spanish with English subtitles. **95m/C VHS, LV.** *SP* Penelope Cruz, Anna Galiena, Javier Bardem, Stefania Sandrelli, Juan Diego, Jordi Molla; **D:** Bigas Luna; **W:** Bigas Luna, Cuca Canals; **M:** Nicola Piovani. *ACA*

Jane & the Lost City 🎬🎬½ 1987 (PG) A British farce based on the age-old, barely dressed comic-strip character, Jane, as she stumbles on ancient cities, treasures, villains, and blond/blue-eyed heroes. Low-budget camp fun. **94m/C VHS, Beta.** *GB* Kristen Hughes, Maud Adams, Sam Jones; **D:** Terry Marcel; **W:** Mervyn Haisman; **M:** Harry Robertson. *NWV, VTR*

Jane Austen in Manhattan 🎬½ 1980 Two acting-teachers vie to stage a long-lost play written by a youthful Jane Austen. Dreary, despite the cast. Hodiak is the real-life daughter of Baxter. **108m/C VHS, Beta.** Anne Baxter, Robert Powell, Michael Wager, Sean Young, Kurt Johnson, Katrina Hodiak; **D:** James Ivory; **W:** Ruth Prawer Jhabvala. *NLC*

Jane Doe 🎬🎬½ 1983 Valentine plays a young amnesia victim who is linked to a series of brutal slayings. Quite suspenseful for a television movie. **100m/C VHS, Beta.** Karen Valentine, William Devane, Eva Marie Saint, Stephen E. Miller, Jackson Davies; **D:** Ivan Nagy. *LIV*

Jane Eyre 🎬🎬 1934 Stiff, early version of Charlotte Bronte's classic gothic romance. English orphan grows up to become the governess of a mysterious manor. Notable as the first talkie version. Remade several times. **67m/B VHS.** Virginia Bruce, Colin Clive, Beryl Mercer, Jameson Thomas, Aileen Pringle, David Torrence; **D:** Christy Cabanne. *SNC*

Jane Eyre 🎬🎬🎬 1944 Excellent adaptation of the Charlotte Bronte novel about the plain governess with the noble heart and her love for the mysterious and tragic Mr. Rochester. Fontaine has the proper backbone and yearning in the title role but to accommodate Welles' emerging popularity the role of Rochester was enlarged. Excellent bleak romantic-Gothic look. Taylor, in her third film role, is seen briefly in the early orphanage scenes. **97m/B VHS.** Joan Fontaine, Orson Welles, Margaret O'Brien, Peggy Ann Garner, John Sutton, Sara Allgood, Henry Daniell, Agnes Moorehead, Aubrey Mather, Edith Barrett, Barbara Everest, Hillary Brooke, Elizabeth Taylor; **D:** Robert Stevenson; **W:** John Houseman, Aldous Huxley, Robert Stevenson; **C:** George Barnes; **M:** Bernard Herrmann. *FXV, FCT, BTV*

Jane Eyre 🎬🎬🎬 1983 A made-for-British-television mini-series based on the famed Charlotte Bronte novel about the maturation of a homeless English waif, her love for the tormented Rochester, and her quest for permanent peace. **239m/C VHS, Beta, LV, Closed Caption.** *GB* Timothy Dalton, Zelah Clarke; **D:** Julian Aymes. *PBS, FOX, SIG*

Jane Eyre 🎬🎬🎬 1996 (PG) Zeffirelli creates an eloquent yet spare interpretation of Charlotte Bronte's 1847 masterpiece, about a meek governess and her mysterious employer, in its fourth film incarnation. Everything about it, from the lighting to the score, is muted and somber. Still a beautiful film, it seems to lack a certain passion that earlier versions (especially the 1944 classic) brought to the screen. Strong performances all around, including Oscar-winner Paquin and French star Gainsbourg as the younger and older Jane, and Hurt as the tormented Rochester. **116m/C VHS, LV, Closed Caption.** William Hurt, Anna Paquin, Charlotte Gainsbourg, Joan Plowright, Elle Macpherson, Geraldine Chaplin, Fiona Shaw, John Wood, Amanda Root, Maria Schneider, Josephine Serre, Billie Whitelaw; **D:** Franco Zeffirelli; **W:** Franco Zeffirelli, Hugh Whitemore; **C:** David Watkin; **M:** Alessio Vlad, Claudio Capponi. *TOU*

Janis: A Film 🎬🎬½ 1974 (R) The famous biographical film about Janis Joplin, from her Texas origins to Woodstock and superstardom, featuring performances with Big Brother and the Holding Company and rare interviews. **79m/C VHS, Beta.** **D:** Howard Alk. *MVD, USH, FCT*

The January Man 🎬🎬 1989 (R) An unorthodox cop, previously exiled by a corrupt local government to the fire department, is brought back to the force in New York City to track down a serial killer. Written by the "Moonstruck" guy, Shanley, who apparently peaked with the earlier movie. **97m/C VHS, Beta, LV, Closed Caption.** Kevin Kline, Susan Sarandon, Mary Elizabeth Mastrantonio, Harvey Keitel, Rod Steiger, Alan Rickman, Danny Aiello; **D:** Pat O'Connor; **W:** John Patrick Shanley, Pat O'Connor; **M:** Marvin Hamlisch. *MGM, FXV*

Japanese Connection 🎬 1982 Warring crime chiefs fight furiously with deadly kung-fu action until end of movie. **96m/C VHS, Beta.** Li Chao, Yang Wei, Wu Ming-Tsai. *GEM*

The Jar 1984 A recluse discovers a disgusting creature in a jar. He keeps it, only to discover that it is out to kill him. **90m/C VHS, Beta.** Gary Wallace, Karen Sjoberg; **D:** Bruce Toscano. *NO*

Jason and the Argonauts 🎬🎬🎬 1963 (G) Jason, son of the King of Thessaly, sails on the Argo to the land of Colchis, where the Golden Fleece is guarded by a seven-headed hydra. Superb special effects and multitudes of mythological creatures; fun for the whole family. **104m/C VHS, Beta, LV, 8mm.** *GB* Todd Armstrong, Nancy Kovack, Gary Raymond, Laurence Naismith, Nigel Green, Michael Gwynn, Honor Blackman; **D:** Don Chaffey; **W:** Jan Read, Beverley Cross. *COL, MLB, FUS*

Jason Goes to Hell: The Final Friday woof! 1993 (R) The supposed last, at least so far, in the "Friday the 13th" gore series. Only through the bodies—dead or alive—of his Vorhees kin can supernatural killer Jason be reborn, and only at their hands can he truly die. One can only hope that this is finally true. An unrated, even gorier, version is also available.*CW:* Language, strong violence and gore, and sexuality. **89m/C VHS, LV, Closed Caption.** Kane Hodder, John D. LeMay, Kari Keegan, Steven Williams, Steven Culp, Erin Gray, Richard Gant, Leslie Jordan, Billy Green Bush, Rusty Schwimmer; **D:** Adam Marcus; **W:** Dean Lorey, Jay Huguely-Cass; **M:** Harry Manfredini. *NLC, IME*

Jason's Lyric 🎬🎬 1994 (R) A romantic triangle, sibling rivalry, family bonds, and neighborhood violence all set on the wrong side of the Houston tracks. Jason (Payne) is the responsible young man who works hard and helps out his mom; younger brother Joshua (Woodbine) has just gotten out of jail and is headed straight for more trouble. Between the two is Lyric (Pinkett), a soul-food waitress whose bad news half-brother Alonzo (Treach) is naturally one of Joshua's homies. Good-looking but ultimately empty storytelling.*CW:* Language; strong violence; drug use; sexuality. **119m/C VHS.** Allen Payne, Bokeem Woodbine, Jada Pinkett, Suzanne Douglas, Forest Whitaker, Treach; **D:** Doug McHenry; **W:** Bobby Smith Jr.; **M:** Matt Noble. *PGV*

Java Head 🎬🎬🎬 1935 Young Chinese wife commits suicide so her husband can marry an English girl. Set in mid-1800s England. Based on the novel by Joseph Hergesheimer. **70m/B VHS, Beta, 8mm.** *GB* Anna May Wong, Elizabeth Allan, John Loder, Edmund Gwenn, Ralph Richardson, George Curzan; **D:** J. Walter Ruben. *VYY*

Jaws 🎬🎬🎬½ 1975 (PG) Early directorial effort by Spielberg from the Peter Benchley potboiler. A tight, very scary, and sometimes hilarious film about the struggle to kill a giant great white shark that is terrorizing an eastern beach community's waters. The characterizations by Dreyfuss, Scheider, and Shaw are much more endurable than the shock effects. Memorable score. Sequeled by "Jaws 2" in 1978, "Jaws 3" 1983, and "Jaws: the Revenge" in 1987. Look for Benchley as a TV reporter. **124m/C VHS, Beta, LV.** Roy Scheider,

Robert Shaw, Richard Dreyfuss, Lorraine Gary, Murray Hamilton, Carl Gottlieb; *Cameos:* Peter Benchley; *D:* Steven Spielberg; *W:* Carl Gottlieb, Peter Benchley; *C:* Bill Butler; *M:* John Williams. Academy Awards '75: Best Film Editing, Best Sound, Best Original Score; Golden Globe Awards '76: Best Score; People's Choice Awards '76: Best Film; Nominations: Academy Awards '75: Best Picture. *USH*

Jaws 2 🐶🐶½ **1978 (PG)** Unsatisfactory sequel to "Jaws." It's been four years since the man-eating shark feasted on the resort town of Amity; suddenly a second shark stalks the waters and the terror returns. Scheider—who must by now wonder at his tendency to attract large aquatic carnivores with lunch on their minds— battles without his compatriots from the original. And we haven't seen the last of the mechanical dorsal fin yet; two more sequels follow. 116m/C VHS, Beta, LV. Roy Scheider, Lorraine Gary, Murray Hamilton; *D:* Jeannot Szwarc; *W:* Carl Gottlieb; *M:* John Williams. *USH*

Jaws 3 🐶🐶 *Jaws 3-D* **1983 (PG)** Same monster, new setting: in a Sea World-type amusement park, a great white shark escapes from its tank and proceeds to cause terror and chaos. Little connection to the previous "Jaws" sagas. Followed by one more sequel, "Jaws: The Revenge." 98m/C VHS, Beta, LV. Dennis Quaid, Bess Armstrong, Louis Gossett Jr., Simon MacCorkindale, Lea Thompson; *D:* Joe Alves; *W:* Richard Matheson, Carl Gottlieb; *M:* John Williams. *USH*

Jaws of Death 🐶🐶 *Mako: The Jaws of Death* **1976** "Jaws"-like saga of shark terror. Jaeckel illogically strikes out to protect his "friends," the sharks. 91m/C VHS, Beta. Richard Jaeckel, Harold Sakata, Jennifer Bishop, John Chandler, Buffy Dee; *D:* William Grefe. *NO*

Jaws of Justice 🐶½ **1933** A Canadian Mountie and his trusty German shepherd track down outlaws in the Canadian Northwest. 55m/B VHS, Beta, 8mm. Richard Terry, Lafe McKee. *VYY*

Jaws of Satan woof! *King Cobra* **1981 (R)** Weaver is terrorized by a slimy snake who is, in actuality, the Devil. Not released for 2 years after it was filmed, and generally considered a bomb of the first caliber. Unfortunate work for usually worthwhile Weaver. 92m/C VHS. Fritz Weaver, Gretchen Corbett, Jon Korkes, Norman Lloyd, Christina Applegate; *D:* Bob Claver; *C:* Dean Cundey. *NO*

Jaws: The Revenge 🐶 **1987 (PG-13)** The third sequel, in which Mrs. Brody is pursued the world over by a seemingly personally motivated Great White Shark. Includes footage not seen in the theatrical release. Each sequel in this series is progressively inferior to the original. 87m/C VHS, Beta, LV, Closed Caption. Lorraine Gary, Lance Guest, Karen Young, Mario Van Peebles, Michael Caine, Judith Barsi, Lynn Whitfield; *D:* Joseph Sargent; *W:* Michael deGuzman. *USH*

The Jayhawkers 🐶🐶 **1959** Chandler and Parker battle for power and women in pre-Civil War Kansas. 100m/C VHS, Closed Caption. Jeff Chandler, Fess Parker, Nicole Maurey, Henry Silva, Herbert Rudley, Frank De Kova, Don Megowan, Leo Gordon; *D:* Melvin Frank. *PAR, FCT*

The Jayne Mansfield Story 🐶 *Jayne Mansfield: A Symbol of the '50s* **1980** Television movie recounting the blond bombshell's career from her first career exposure, through her marriage to a bodybuilder, to the famous car crash that beheaded her. 97m/C VHS, Beta. Loni Anderson, Arnold Schwarzenegger, Raymond Buktenica, Kathleen Lloyd, G.D. Spradlin, Dave Shelley; *D:* Dick Lowry. *LIV*

The Jazz Singer 🐶🐶½ **1927** A Jewish cantor's son breaks with his family to become a singer of popular music. Of historical importance as the first successful part-talkie, very early Loy performance. With the classic line "You ain't heard nothing yet!" Remade several times. 🎵Toot, Toot, Tootsie Goodbye; Blue Skies; My Gal Sal; Waiting for the Robert E. Lee; Dirty Hands, Dirty Face; Mother, I Still Have You; Kol Nidre; Yahrzeit; My Mammy. 89m/B VHS, Beta, LV. Al Jolson, May McAvoy, Warner Oland, William Demarest,

Eugenie Besserer, Myrna Loy; *D:* Alan Crosland; *C:* Hal Mohr. Nominations: Academy Awards '28: Best Adapted Screenplay. *FOX, FCT, MLB*

The Jazz Singer woof! **1980 (PG)** Flat and uninteresting (if not unintentionally funny) remake of the 1927 classic about a Jewish boy who rebels against his father and family tradition to become a popular entertainer. Stick with the original, this is little more than a vehicle for Diamond to sing. 🎵America; You Baby Baby; Jerusalem; Love on the Rocks; Summer Love; On the Robert E. Lee; Louise; Songs of Life; Hello Again. 115m/C VHS, Beta, LV, 8mm. Neil Diamond, Laurence Olivier, Lucie Arnaz, Catlin Adams, Franklin Ajaye; *D:* Richard Fleischer. Golden Raspberry Awards '80: Worst Actor (Diamond), Worst Supporting Actor (Olivier). *REP, PAR*

Jazzman 🐶🐶🐶 **1984** A comedy set in the late 1920s with a young musician forming a jazz band with two street musicians and a saxophonist who played in the czar's marching band. Their music is condemned as a product of bourgeois society but that doesn't stop them. In Russian with English subtitles. 80m/C VHS. *RU* Igor Sklyar, Alexander Chorny; *D:* Karen Chakhnazarov. *KIV*

J.D.'s Revenge 🐶🐶½ **1976 (R)** Attorney in training Glynn Turman is possessed by the spirit of a gangster who was murdered on Bourbon Street in the early 1940s and grisly blaxploitation results. Ever so slightly better than others of the genre. Shot in New Orleans, with a soundtrack by a then-unknown Prince. 95m/C VHS. Louis Gossett Jr., Glynn Turman; *D:* Arthur Marks; *M:* Prince. *ORI, FCT*

Je Tu Il Elle 🐶🐶½ *I You She He* **1974** A hyperactive young woman desperately seeking the answers to life gradually gains experience and maturity as she travels around France. The directorial debut of Ackerman. In French with English subtitles. 90m/B VHS. *FR* Niels Arestrup, Claire Wauthion, Chantal Akerman; *D:* Chantal Akerman. *WAC, FCT, TPV*

Jealousy **1984** Three dramatic episodes dealing with jealousy. Made for TV. 95m/C VHS, Beta. Angie Dickinson, Paul Michael Glaser, David Carradine, Bo Svenson; *D:* Jeffrey Bloom. *IMP*

Jean de Florette 🐶🐶🐶½ **1987 (PG)** The first of two films (with "Manon of the Spring") based on Marcel Pagnol's novel. A single spring in drought-ridden Provence, France is blocked by two scheming countrymen (Montand and Auteuil). They await the imminent failure of the farm nearby, inherited by a city-born hunchback, whose chances for survival fade without water for his crops. A devastating story with a heartrending performance by Depardieu as the hunchback. Lauded and awarded; in French with English subtitles. 122m/C VHS, Beta, LV. *FR* Gerard Depardieu, Yves Montand, Daniel Auteuil, Elisabeth Depardieu, Ernestine Mazurowna; *D:* Claude Berri; *W:* Gerard Brach, Claude Berri. British Academy Awards '87: Best Adapted Screenplay, Best Film, Best Supporting Actor (Auteuil); Cesar Awards '87: Best Actor (Auteuil), Best Supporting Actress (Beart); National Board of Review Awards '87: 5 Best Foreign Films of the Year. *ORI, IME, FCT*

Jeeves & Wooster: Jeeves' Arrival **1991** Based on P.G. Wodehouse's spoofs of upper-crust British life in the 1920s. The bungling Bertie Wooster, a young man who just can't stay out of trouble, is taken in hand by the unflappable "gentleman's gentleman," Jeeves. Wonderful period detail and fine acting add up to a charming and funny hour. Additional episodes available. 60m/C VHS, Closed Caption. *GB* Hugh Laurie, Stephen Fry. *MOV, TVC, PBS*

Jefferson in Paris 🐶🐶½ **1994 (PG-13)** Costume drama explores the impact Thomas Jefferson's (Nolte) five years in pre-revolutionary Paris (as American ambassador to Versailles) had on his private life. Jefferson confronts the personal and political issues of slavery in America, as well as his feelings for Sally Hemings (Newton), a Monticello slave brought to Paris by Jefferson's daughter. The Jefferson-Hemings leg-

end may or may not be true (more likely not, according to many historians), but it seems to be the central theme here. Merchant Ivory's trademark tasteful production values and earnest characters can't camouflage the fact that they're playing fast and loose with the historical facts. *CW:* Contains mature theme, some images of violence, and a bawdy puppet show. 139m/C VHS, LV, Closed Caption. Nick Nolte, Greta Scacchi, Gwyneth Paltrow, Thandie Newton, Jean-Pierre Aumont, Seth Gilliam, Todd Boyce, James Earl Jones; *D:* James Ivory; *W:* Ruth Prawer Jhabvala; *M:* Richard Robbins. *TOU*

Jeffrey 🐶🐶½ **1995 (R)** AIDS-fearing Jeffrey (Weber) decides to give celibacy a try until a trip to the gym brings Mr. Right into the picture. Steve (Weiss) is a hunk, but he happens to be HIV-positive, which prompts Jeffrey to do some serious soul-searching. Hence the message: AIDS sucks, but don't let it destroy life's joys. Musical fantasy numbers, phallic fireworks, and a game show are a bit crass and the high theatrics can get annoying, but wicked barbs and one-liners score lots of laughs. Scene-stealer Stewart is caustically funny as Jeffrey's flamboyantly effeminate best friend Sterling, who works as an interior decorator and dates a "Cats" chorus boy. Adapted from the Paul Rudnick play. *CW:* Strong sexuality and language. 92m/C VHS, LV, Closed Caption. Steven Weber, Patrick Stewart, Michael T. Weiss, Bryan Batt, Sigourney Weaver, Olympia Dukakis, Kathy Najimy, Nathan Lane; *D:* Christopher Ashley; *W:* Paul Rudnick; *C:* Jeffery Tufano; *M:* Stephen Endelman. *ORI*

Jekyll and Hyde 🐶🐶½ **1990** Unmemorable remake of the Robert Louis Stevenson tale of a doctor whose scientific experiments lead to a horrifyingly violent split personality. Caine does have a good time with his dual role. Made for TV. 100m/C VHS. Michael Caine, Cheryl Ladd, Joss Ackland, Ronald Pickup, Kim Thomson, Lionel Jeffries, Kevin McNally, Lee Montague; *D:* David Wickes; *W:* David Wickes. *THV*

Jekyll & Hyde...Together Again 🐶🐶 **1982 (R)** New Wave comic version of the classic story. This time, a serious young surgeon turns into a drug-crazed punk rocker after sniffing a mysterious powder. Mad scientist Blankfield fires and misfires, occasionally eliciting a snort. 87m/C VHS, Beta. Mark Blankfield, Bess Armstrong, Krista Errickson, Tim Thomerson; *D:* Jerry Belson; *W:* Monica Johnson, Michael Leeson, Harvey Miller, Jerry Belson. *PAR*

Jennifer 🐶½ *Jennifer (The Snake Goddess)* **1978 (PG)** Elaboration of that old "Carrie" theme: a teen-age girl outcast who likes snakes wreaks havoc on her catty classmates in this supernatural thriller. 90m/C VHS, Beta. Lisa Pelikan, Bert Convy, Nina Foch, John Gavin, Wesley Eure; *D:* Brice Mack. *LIV, VES*

Jennifer 8 🐶🐶 **1992 (R)** Mix of familiar genres results in a film about a burned-out cop moving to the suburbs where he finds the eighth victim of a serial killer and falls in love with the chief witness. Garcia is John Berlin, the cop who discovers the hand of the blind female victim, which leads him to her school and Helena Robertson (Thurman), another blind woman who may have the information he needs. Dark and mysterious atmosphere is dramatic, but plot lacks logic and sense of thrill. *CW:* Language, nudity, and violence and terror. 127m/C VHS, Beta, LV, Closed Caption. Andy Garcia, Uma Thurman, Lance Henriksen, Kathy Baker, Graham Beckel, Kevin Conway, John Malkovich; *D:* Bruce Robinson; *W:* Bruce Robinson. *PAR, BTV*

Jenny 🐶 **1970 (PG)** A loveless marriage of convenience between a draft-dodger and a film buff gets turned around as they fall in love despite themselves. 90m/C VHS, Beta. Marlo Thomas, Alan Alda, Marian Hailey, Elizabeth Wilson, Vincent Gardenia, Charlotte Rae; *D:* George Bloomfield. *FOX*

Jenny Lamour 🐶🐶 *Quai des Orfevres* **1947** A dark mystery thriller about a singer accused of murdering a man he thought was stealing his woman. Acclaimed genre piece, dubbed into English. 95m/B VHS, Beta. *FR* Louis Jouvet, Suzy Delair, Bernard Blier, Simone Renant; *D:* Henri-Georges Clouzot. *NOS, FCT*

Jenny's War �'t✟½ 1985 (PG) An unbelievable WWII adventure story of an American teacher (Cannon) who outwits the Gestapo and infiltrates a Nazi POW camp in search of her missing soldier son. Actually based on a true story. From the book by Jack Stoneley. Made for television. **192m/C VHS.** Dyan Cannon, Elke Sommer, Robert Hardy, Nigel Hawthorne, Christopher Cazenove, Patrick Ryecart, Hartmut Becker; **D:** Steven Gethers; **W:** Steven Gethers. *COL*

Jeremiah Johnson ✟✟✟ 1972 (PG) The story of a man who turns his back on civilization, circa 1850, and learns a new code of survival in a brutal land of isolated mountains and hostile Indians. In the process, he becomes part of the mountains and their wildlife. A notable and picturesque film. **107m/C VHS, Beta, LV.** Robert Redford, Will Geer; **D:** Sydney Pollack; **W:** Edward Anhalt, John Milius. *WAR, FCT*

Jericho ✟✟ *Dark Sands* 1938 Adventures in Africa occur as a court-martialed captain pursues a murderous deserter. **77m/B VHS, Beta.** *GB* Paul Robeson, Henry Wilcoxon, Wallace Ford; **D:** Thornton Freeland. *NOS, HHT, DVT*

Jericho Fever ✟✟½ 1993 (PG-13) A group of terrorists assassinate Palestinian and Israeli negotiators engaged in peace talks in Mexico. Infected with a deadly disease they escape to the U.S., tracked by Israeli Mossad agents, a border patrolman, and two investigators from the Centers for Disease Control who want to stop the spread of the plague. **88m/C VHS, Beta, Closed Caption.** Stephanie Zimbalist, Perry King, Branscombe Richmond, Alan Scarfe, Elyssa Davalos, Ari Barak; **D:** Sandor Stern; **W:** I.C. Rapoport; **M:** Cameron Allan. *PAR*

The Jericho Mile ✟✟ 1979 A made-for-television drama about a track-obsessed convicted murderer who is given a chance at the Olympics. **97m/C VHS, Beta.** Peter Strauss, Roger E. Mosley, Brian Dennehy; **D:** Michael Mann. *NLC*

The Jerk ✟✟½ 1979 (R) A jerk tells his rags-to-riches-to-rags story in comedic flashbacks, from "I was born a poor Black child," through his entrepreneurial success in his invention of the "Optigrab," to his inevitable decline. Only film in history with a dog named "Shithead." Martin's first starring role, back in his wild and crazy days; his ridiculous misadventures pay tribute to Jerry Lewis movies of the late sixties. Followed by a TV version released in 1984 as "The Jerk Too," with Mark Blankfield as the Jerk. **94m/C VHS, Beta, LV.** Steve Martin, Bernadette Peters, Catlin Adams, Bill Macy, Jackie Mason; **D:** Carl Reiner; **W:** Steve Martin, Carl Gottlieb, Michael Elias. *USH*

The Jerky Boys WOOF! 1995 (R) Quick! Let's make a Jerky Boys movie and exploit their popularity before everyone realizes what a lame, one-joke act it is! Too late, guys. In what passes for a plot, Johnny and Kamal prank call an irritable mob boss (Arkin), pretending to be Chicago hitmen in need of a hideout. The wiseguys soon figure out the truth, but the requisite dumb cop (Sullivan) pads the film by not catching on. All these "twists" serve only one purpose—to get our heroes to the next phone. Don't accept the charges for this one.**CW:** Continuous use of strong language. **82m/C VHS, LV, Closed Caption.** Johnny Brennan, Kamal Ahmed, Alan Arkin, William Hickey, Alan North, James Lorinz, Brad Sullivan, Vinny Pastore, Ozzy Osbourne, Paul Bartel, Suzanne Shepherd; **Cameos:** Tom Jones; **D:** James Melkonian; **W:** Johnny Brennan, Kamal Ahmed, Rich Wilkes, James Melkonian. *TOU*

Jerry Maguire ✟✟✟½ 1996 (R) Romantic sports comedy focuses on the off-field action and makes an agent the good guy. Risky business in an era of strikes, lockouts, and astronomical salaries, but writer/director Crowe manages to pull it off. Cruise is well-used as the title character in the story of a shark-like sports agent who sees the error of his ways and transforms into...a more moral sports agent. Somewhat regretting his momentary twinge of honor (which gets him fired from his ultra-huge agency), he allies himself with his obnoxious and least important client Rod Tidwell (Gooding, Jr.), as well as Dorothy, an adoring young accountant (Zellweger) with a lovable young son (Lipnicki, making a strong bid for Culkin-like stardom). Famously well-researched, film sports great dialogue, talented leads, great supporting cast and a mega-star currently riding a wave of $100-million-plus films (talk about "Show me the money!"). Pop culture bonus points for coining 1996's most memorable catch phrase, which Crowe took from real life ex-Phoenix Cardinal Tim McDonald, and is now being used to sell everything from magazines to t-shirts.**CW:** Language and sexuality. **135m/C VHS, LV, Closed Caption, DVD.** Tom Cruise, Cuba Gooding Jr., Renee Zellweger, Kelly Preston, Bonnie Hunt, Jerry O'Connell, Jay Mohr, Regina King, Glenn Frey, Jonathan Lipnicki, Todd Louiso, Mark Pellington; **Cameos:** Eric Stoltz; **D:** Cameron Crowe; **W:** Cameron Crowe; **C:** Janusz Kaminski; **M:** Nancy Wilson. Academy Awards '96: Best Supporting Actor (Gooding); Golden Globe Awards '97: Best Actor—Musical/Comedy (Cruise); MTV Movie Awards '97: Best Male Performance (Cruise); National Board of Review Awards '96: Best Actor (Cruise); Screen Actors Guild Award '96: Best Supporting Actor (Gooding); Broadcast Film Critics Association Awards '96: Best Supporting Actor (Gooding); Nominations: Academy Awards '96: Best Actor (Cruise), Best Film Editing, Best Original Screenplay, Best Picture; Directors Guild of America Awards '96: Best Director (Crowe); Golden Globe Awards '97: Best Actor—Musical/Comedy (Cruise), Best Film—Musical/Comedy, Best Supporting Actor (Gooding); MTV Movie Awards '97: Best Film, Breakthrough Performance (Zellweger); Screen Actors Guild Award '96: Best Actor (Cruise), Best Supporting Actress (Zellweger); Writers Guild of America '96: Best Original Screenplay. *COL*

Jersey Girl ✟✟½ 1992 (PG-13) Toby Mastellone (Gertz) is a bright single gal from the Jersey shore who wants something better in her life. Her hard-working dad (Bologna) has fixed her up with an apprentice plumber but she wants a Manhattan guy. And then Toby meets cute with Sal (McDermott), who seems just the ticket, but can you really take the Jersey out of the girl? **95m/C VHS, Closed Caption.** Jami Gertz, Dylan McDermott, Joseph Bologna, Aida Turturro, Star Jasper, Sheryl Lee, Joseph Mazzello, Molly Price; **D:** David Burton Morris; **W:** Gina Wendkos; **M:** Stephen Bedell. *COL*

Jerusalem ✟✟ 1996 (PG-13) Charismatic fundamentalist preacher Hellgum (Taube) travels to a small turn-of-the-century Swedish village preaching the end of the world and encouraging the people in his belief that all Christians should move to the Holy Land in order to build the new Jerusalem. He manages to convince the wealthy Karin (August) and to tempt young Gertrud (Bonnevie), whose fiance Ingmar (Friberg) is away trying to earn money so they can get married. Based on the novel by Selma Lagerlof who was inspired by Swedes who made a move to Palestine in 1900. Swedish with subtitles.**CW:** Some violence and a scene of sensuality. **166m/C VHS.** *SW* Maria Bonnevie, Ulf Friberg, Lena Endre, Pernilla August, Olympia Dukakis, Max von Sydow; **D:** Bille August; **W:** Bille August; **C:** Jorgen Persson; **M:** Stefan Nilsson. *NYR*

Jesse ✟✟ 1988 (PG) A heroic nurse ministers to remote Death Valley residents, and state bureaucats hound her for practicing medicine without a license. Although based on a true case and well-acted, this made-for-TV drama just lacks import and impact. **94m/C VHS, Closed Caption.** Lee Remick, Scott Wilson, Leon Rippy, Priscilla Lopez, Albert Salmi; **D:** Glenn Jordan; **M:** David Shire. *REP*

Jesse James ✟✟✟ 1939 A Hollywood biography of the famed outlaw. One of director King's best efforts. **105m/C VHS, Beta, LV.** Henry Fonda, Tyrone Power, Randolph Scott, Henry Hull, Jane Darwell, Brian Donlevy, Charles Halton; **D:** Henry King. *FOX*

Jesse James at Bay ✟✟ 1941 Rogers is the do-good Jesse who's warring against some crooked railroad execs. Interesting perspective. **54m/B VHS, Beta.** Roy Rogers, George "Gabby" Hayes, Sally Payne; **D:** Joseph Kane. *NOS, MRV, VCN*

Jesse James Meets Frankenstein's Daughter ✟½ 1965 The gunslinger and Frankenstein's granddaughter, Maria, meet up in the Old West in this wacky combination of western and horror genres. **95m/C VHS, Beta.** John Lupton, Cal Bolder, Narda Onyx, Steve Geray, Estelita, Jim Davis, William "Bill" Fawcett, Nestor Paiva; **D:** William Beaudine. *NOS*

Jesse James Rides Again 1947 Originally a serial, this feature depicts the further adventures of the West's most notorious outlaw. **181m/B VHS.** Clayton Moore, Linda Stirling, Roy Barcroft, Tristram Coffin; **D:** Fred Brannon, Thomas Carr. *REP, MLB*

Jesse James Under the Black Flag ✟✟½ 1921 An interesting western/pseudo biography/flashback in which Coates and James Jr. (the outlaw's son) play themselves. As Coates attempts to gather information from Jesse's decendants, a stranger appears and falls for Jesse's granddaughter, who shuns him. He proceeds to read the Coates biography and the flashback begins, in the Jesse was really a good guy forced off the straight and narrow vein. **59m/B VHS, Beta.** Jesse James Jr., Franklin Coates, Diana Reed, Marguerite Hungerford; **D:** Franklin Coates. *GPV, FCT*

The Jesse Owens Story ✟✟ 1984 The moving story of the four-time Olympic Gold medal winner's triumphs and misfortunes. A made-for-television movie. **174m/C VHS, Beta.** Dorian Harewood, Debbi Morgan, Georg Stanford Brown, LeVar Burton, George Kennedy, Tom Bosley, Ben Vereen; **D:** Richard Irving. *PAR, FCT*

Jessie's Girls ✟½ *Wanted Women* 1975 (R) In retaliation for the murder of her husband, an angry young woman frees three female prisoners, and they embark on a bloody course of revenge. Together, they track down the killers, and one by one, they fight to even the score. **86m/C VHS, Beta.** Sondra Currie, Regina Carrol, Jennifer Bishop; **D:** Al Adamson. *MON*

Jesus ✟✟ 1979 (G) A supposedly authenticated life of Christ, using real artifacts. **118m/C VHS, Beta.** Brian Deacon; **D:** Peter Sykes, John Kirsh. *VBL*

Jesus Christ, Superstar ✟✟✟ 1973 (G) A rock opera that portrays, in music, the last seven days in the earthly life of Christ, as reenacted by young tourists in Israel. Outstanding musical score was the key to the success of the film. Based on the stage play by Tim Rice and Andrew Lloyd Webber, film is sometimes stirring while exhibiting the usual heavy-handed Jewison approach. ♫Jesus Christ, Superstar; I Don't Know How To Love Him; What's The Buzz?; Herod's Sdng; Heaven On Their Minds; Strange Thing, Mystifying; Then We Are Decided; Everything's Alright; This Jesus Must Die. **108m/C VHS, Beta, LV.** Ted Neeley, Carl Anderson, Yvonne Elliman, Josh Mostel; **D:** Norman Jewison; **W:** Melvin Bragg. Nominations: Academy Awards '73: Original Song Score and/or Adaptation. *USH*

Jesus of Montreal ✟✟✟½ *Jesus de Montreal* 1989 (R) A vagrant young actor (stage-trained Canadian star Bluteau) is hired by a Montreal priest to produce a fresh interpretation of an Easter passion play. Taking the good book at its word, he produces a contemporized literal telling that captivates audiences, inflames the men of the cloth, and eventually wins the players' faith. Quebecois director Arcand (keep an eye out for him as the judge) tells a compelling, acerbically satirical and haunting story that never forces its Biblical parallels. In French with English subtitles. **119m/C VHS, LV.** *FR CA* Gilles Pelletier, Lothaire Bluteau, Catherine Wilkening, Robert Lepage, Johanne-Marie Tremblay, Remy Girard, Marie-Christine Barrault; **D:** Denys Arcand; **W:** Denys Arcand. Cannes Film Festival '89: Special Jury Prize; Genie Awards '90: Best Actor (Girard), Best Director (Arcand), Best Film, Best Supporting Actor (Girard); Nominations: Academy Awards '89: Best Foreign Language Film. *ORI, FCT*

Jesus of Nazareth 🎬🎬½ **1928** A dramatic recreation of the life of Christ from the Annunciation through the Ascension. The film titles are taken from descriptive biblical passages. **85m/ B VHS, Beta, 8mm.** Philip Van Loan, Anna Lehr, Charles McCaffrey. *VYY, FCT*

Jesus of Nazareth 🎬🎬🎬 **1977** An all-star cast vividly portrays the life of Christ in this made-for-television mini-series. Wonderfully directed and sensitively acted. On three cassettes. **371m/C VHS, Beta.** Robert Powell, Anne Bancroft, Ernest Borgnine, Claudia Cardinale, James Mason, Laurence Olivier, Anthony Quinn; **D:** Franco Zeffirelli; **M:** Maurice Jarre. *LIV, FOX, IGP*

The Jesus Trip 🎬½ **1971** Hunted motorcyclists take a young nun hostage in the desert. **86m/C VHS, Beta.** Robert Porter, Tippy Walker; **D:** Russ Mayberry. *UNI*

Jet Attack/Paratroop Command 🎬🎬 **1958** A double feature of "B" war movies. "Jet Attack" is a bad movie about a scientist whose plane gets shot down over Korea. He amazingly survives, only to be taken to a hospital and brainwashed. Enter a squad of soldiers leading a rescue mission who meet up with a beautiful Russian aide and some life-saving guerillas. This movie is so bad it's funny. In "Paratroop Command," a paratrooper accidentally kills a member of his squadron. In order to regain his dignity, the paratrooper sets off land mines in North Africa to prove himself. **139m/B VHS.** John Agar, Audrey Totter, Gregory Walcott, James Dobson, Richard Bakalayan, Jack Hogan, Jimmy Murphy, Ken Lynch; **D:** Edward L. Cahn, William Witney. *COL*

Jet Benny Show 1986 A Buck Rogers/Star Wars-style spoof of Jack Benny's classic TV show. **76m/C VHS, Beta.** Steve Norman, Kevin Dees, Polly MacIntyre, Ted Luedemann; **D:** Roger Evans. *NLC*

Jet Over the Atlantic 🎬½ **1959** Dangerous situation arises as a bomb is discovered aboard a plane en route from Spain to New York. **92m/B VHS, Beta.** Guy Madison, George Raft, Virginia Mayo, Brett Halsey; **D:** Byron Haskin. *NO*

Jet Pilot 🎬🎬 **1957** An American Air Force colonel (Wayne) in charge of an Alaskan Air Force base falls in love with a defecting Russian jet pilot (Leigh). They marry, but Wayne suspects Leigh is a spy planted to find out top U.S. secrets. He pretends to defect with her back to Russia to see what he can find out, but they again flee. Ludicrous plot is saved only by spectacular flying scenes, some performed by Chuck Yeager. Although this was filmed in 1950, it took seven more years to be released because producer Hughes couldn't keep his hands off it. **112m/B VHS, LV, Closed Caption.** John Wayne, Janet Leigh, Jay C. Flippen, Paul Fix, Richard Rober, Roland Winters, Hans Conried, Ivan Triesault; **D:** Josef von Sternberg; **C:** Winton C. Hoch. *USH*

The Jetsons Meet the Flintstones 1988 Trouble arises when young Elroy Jetson's time machine takes him and his family back to the 25th century B.C. There they meet the Flintstones and the Rubbles, who accidentally get transported into the future. Will either family ever get back home? **100m/C VHS, Beta, LV, 8mm.** V: Mel Blanc, Daws Butler, Jean VanDerPyl, George O'Hanlon, Penny Singleton. *TTC, IME*

Jetsons: The Movie 🎬🎬 **1990 (G)** The famous outer space family of '60s TV is given a new silver-screened life. George gets a promotion that puts him in charge of an asteroid populated by furry creatures. Ecological concerns are expressed; while this is rare for a cartoon, the story is overall typical. **82m/C VHS, Beta, LV, Closed Caption.** **D:** William Hanna, Joseph Barbera; **M:** John Debney; **V:** George O'Hanlon, Mel Blanc, Penny Singleton, Tiffany, Patric Zimmerman, Don Messick, Jean VanDerPyl, Ronnie Schell, Patti Deutsch, Dana Hill, Russi Taylor, Paul Kreppel, Rick Dees. *USH, APD*

The Jewel in the Crown 1984 Epic saga of the last years of British rule in India from 1942-1947 concentrating on a controversial love affair between the Indian Hari Kumar and the English Daphne Manners, which profoundly affects the lives of many. Based on "The Raj Quartet" by Paul Scott. Originally shown on British television, it aired in the United States on the PBS series "Masterpiece Theatre." An excellent mini-series that was shown in fourteen segments. Available on eight cassettes. **750m/C VHS, Beta.** *GB* Charles Dance, Susan Wooldridge, Art Malik, Tim Pigott-Smith, Geraldine James, Peggy Ashcroft, Judy Parfitt; **D:** Christopher Morahan, Jim O'Brien; *AAE, VCO, NEW*

The Jewel of the Nile 🎬🎬½ **1985 (PG)** Sequel to "Romancing the Stone" with the same cast but new director. Romance novelist Joan thought she found her true love in Jack but finds that life doesn't always end happily ever. After they part ways, Jack realizes that she may be in trouble and endeavors to rescue her from the criminal hands of a charming North African president. Of course, he can always check out this "jewel" at the same time. Chemistry is still there, but the rest of the film isn't quite up to the "Stone's" charm. **106m/C VHS, Beta, LV, Closed Caption.** Michael Douglas, Kathleen Turner, Danny DeVito, Avner Eisenberg, The Flying Karamazov Brothers, Spiros Focas, Holland Taylor; **D:** Lewis Teague; **M:** Mark Rosenthal, Larry Konner; **C:** Jan De Bont; **M:** Jack Nitzsche. *FOX*

The Jeweller's Shop 🎬🎬 **1990** A highly spiritual tale of two married couples in Poland whose children meet and fall in love much later in Canada. Based on a play by Karol Wojtyla—who later became Pope Jean-Paul II. Adapted under strict Vatican supervision. **90m/C VHS.** Burt Lancaster, Ben Cross, Olivia Hussey. *IGP*

Jezebel 🎬🎬🎬½ **1938** Davis is a willful Southern belle who loses fiance Fonda through her selfish and spiteful ways in this pre-Civil War drama. When he becomes ill, she realizes her cruelty and rushes to nurse him back to health. Davis' role won her an Oscar for Best Actress, and certainly provided Scarlett O'Hara with a rival for most memorable female character of all time. **105m/B VHS, LV.** Bette Davis, George Brent, Henry Fonda, Margaret Lindsay, Fay Bainter, Donald Crisp, Spring Byington, Eddie Anderson; **D:** William Wyler; **M:** Max Steiner. Academy Awards '38: Best Actress (Davis), Best Supporting Actress (Bainter); National Board of Review Awards '38: 10 Best Films of the Year; Nominations: Academy Awards '38: Best Cinematography, Best Picture, Best Score. *MGM, FCT, BTV*

Jezebel's Kiss 🎬🎬 **1990 (R)** A sizzling young beauty returns to the town where she grew up and proceeds to destroy any man she pleases. **96m/C VHS, LV.** Meg Foster, Malcolm McDowell, Meredith Baxter, Everett McGill, Katherine Barrese; **D:** Harvey Keith; **W:** Harvey Keith. *COL*

JFK 🎬🎬🎬½ **1991 (R)** Highly controversial examination of President John F. Kennedy's 1963 assassination, from the viewpoint of New Orleans district attorney Jim Garrison. Hotly debated because of Stone's conspiracy theory, it sparked new calls to open the sealed government records from the 1977 House Select Committee on Assassinations investigation. Outstanding performances from all-star principal and supporting casts, stunning cinematography, and excellent editing. Even Garrison himself shows up as Chief Justice Earl Warren. Considered by some to be a cinematic masterpiece, others see it as revisionist history that should be taken with a grain of salt. Extended version adds 17 minutes. **189m/C VHS, Beta, LV, Closed Caption, DVD.** Kevin Costner, Sissy Spacek, Kevin Bacon, Tommy Lee Jones, Laurie Metcalf, Gary Oldman, Michael Rooker, Jay O. Sanders, Beata Pozniak, Joe Pesci, Donald Sutherland, John Candy, Jack Lemmon, Walter Matthau, Ed Asner, Vincent D'Onofrio, Sally Kirkland, Brian Doyle-Murray, Wayne Knight, Tony Plana, Tomas Milian, Sean Stone; **Cameos:** Lolita Davidovich, Frank Whaley, Jim Garrison; **D:** Oliver Stone; **W:** Oliver Stone, Zachary Sklar; **C:** Robert Richardson; **M:** John Wil-

liams. Academy Awards '91: Best Cinematography, Best Film Editing; Golden Globe Awards '92: Best Director (Stone); Nominations: Academy Awards '91: Best Adapted Screenplay, Best Director (Stone), Best Picture, Best Sound, Best Supporting Actor (Jones), Best Original Score. *WAR*

The JFK Conspiracy 1991 Did Lee Harvey Oswald act alone? Opinions of government officials, eyewitnesses, and director Oliver Stone, in addition to testimony, photographs, documents, and other evidence, address the perennial American question. Includes footage from the House Select Committee on Assassination. Made for television. **98m/C VHS, LV, BMG, VTR**

JFK: Reckless Youth 🎬🎬½ **1993** Glossy made for TV docudrama details the youthful exploits of Kennedy as both ladies man and emerging leader and comes perilously close to being a tacky soap. Follows the president-to-be from his party-hearty years at prep school, through his naval career (and PT-109 heroics), and his first forays into politics. Excellent portrayal by Dempsey details JFK's chronic ill health, his ambitions, and the family ties that provided both friction and support. Based on the controversial biography by Nigel Hamilton. **182m/C VHS, Closed Caption.** Patrick Dempsey, Terry Kinney, Loren Dean, Diana Scarwid, Yolanda Jilot, Robin Tunney, Andrew Lowery, Stan Cahill, James Rebhorn, Malachy McCourt; **D:** Harry Winer; **W:** William Broyles Jr.; **M:** Cameron Allan. *CAF*

Jigsaw 🎬🎬🎬 *Gun Moll* **1949** Crime drama with a smattering of cameos by Hollywood favorites. A newspaper reporter is murdered. The dead man's friend, an assistant district attorney, seeks the punks responsible. They send in a seductress to keep the D.A. busy, but she too is murdered. Action and tension in a well-made flick. Based on a story by John Roeburt. **70m/B VHS.** Franchot Tone, Jean Wallace, Myron McCormick, Marc Lawrence, Winifred Lenihan, Betty Harper, Robert Gist; **Cameos:** Marlene Dietrich, Henry Fonda, Burgess Meredith, John Garfield; **D:** Fletcher Markle. *SNC, DVT*

Jigsaw 🎬🎬 *Man on the Move* **1971** Missing persons lawman is lured into a cover-up more complex than he had bargained for. A tense drama originated as the pilot for a series. **100m/C VHS.** James Wainwright, Vera Miles, Richard Kiley, Andrew Duggan, Edmond O'Brien; **D:** William A. Graham. *LIV*

Jigsaw 🎬🎬 **1990** A developer is found dead the day after his wedding. His widow and a cop team up to find out who, what, where, and why. Lukewarm Australian mystery export. **85m/C VHS.** Rebecca Gibney, Dominic Sweeney, Michael Coard. *ATL*

The Jigsaw Man 🎬🎬 **1984 (PG)** A British-Russian double agent is sent back to England to retrieve a list of Soviet agents which he hid there many years before. **90m/C VHS, Beta, LV.** *GB* Michael Caine, Laurence Olivier, Susan George, Robert Powell, Charles Gray, David Patrick Kelly, Michael Medwin; **D:** Terence Young. *REP*

Jigsaw Murders 1989 A macho detective is out to solve a grisly murder, but the only available leads are a jigsaw puzzle and the victim's severed, tattooed lower limb. **98m/C VHS, Beta.** Chad Everett, Michelle Johnson, Yaphet Kotto; **D:** Jag Mundhra. *MGM*

Jim Thorpe: All American 🎬🎬½ *Man of Bronze* **1951** The life story of Thorpe, a Native American athlete who gained international recognition for his excellence in many different sports. A must for sports fans. **105m/B VHS, Beta.** Burt Lancaster, Phyllis Thaxter, Charles Bickford, Steve Cochran, Dick Wesson; **D:** Michael Curtiz; **W:** Douglas S. Morrow; **M:** Max Steiner. *WAR*

Jimmy Hollywood 🎬½ **1994 (R)** Wannabe Hollywood actor Pesci has never acted in his life but longs for stardom—which he gets after he accidentally becomes a community vigilante. Burned-out sidekick Slater helps create the videotapes that will bring Jimmy his 15 minutes of fame. Although appropriately desperate, Pesci's role comes off as mostly shtick; two dogs in a row for the usually talented Levinson (after "Toys"). *CW:* Language and violence. **118m/C VHS, Beta, LV, Closed Caption.** Joe Pesci, Christian Slater, Victoria Abril; *Cameos:* Barry Levinson, Rob Weiss; *D:* Barry Levinson; *W:* Barry Levinson; *C:* Peter Sova; *M:* Robbie Robertson. PAR

Jimmy, the Boy Wonder *𝄞½* 1966
Goremeister Lewis' attempt at a "family" film turns out just as weird as expected. A young boy goes on a magical trip to find out who stopped time and meets an absent-minded astronomer, the evil Mr. Fig, and then discovers what happens at world's end. **?m/C VHS.** *D:* Herschell Gordon Lewis. MOV, TPV

Jimmy the Kid *𝄞𝄞* 1982 (PG) A young boy becomes the unlikely target for an improbable gang of would-be crooks on a crazy, "fool-proof" crime caper. Kiddie comic caper. **95m/C VHS, Beta.** Gary Coleman, Cleavon Little, Fay Hauser, Ruth Gordon, Dee Wallace Stone, Paul LeMat, Don Adams; *D:* Gary Nelson; *W:* Sam Bobrick. NO

Jingle All the Way *𝄞𝄞* 1996 (PG) Producer Chris Columbus grabs the reins of the slapstick and sentiment sleigh from mentor John Hughes in this farce of holiday capitalism. Any parent who has searched frantically for that Mighty Morphin' Cabbage Elmo will understand hapless Howard Langston (Schwarzenegger), a workaholic dad who was supposed to secure the coveted Turbo Man action figure for his son Jamie (Lloyd). Unfortunately, it slips his mind until Christmas Eve and all the Turbo Men have blasted off with more mindful parents. In his panic-stricken quest for the toy, he is confronted by a crazed postman (Sinbad) hunting Turbo Man, a pack of sleazy Santas, and a vicious reindeer attack. Meanwhile, Howard's slimy neighbor Ted (Hartman) is attempting to get into his wife Liz's (Wilson) stockings with great care. Although aimed at a younger audience, there's a definite lack of kids; which leaves it too grown-up for the kids and too childish for the adults. There is some satisfaction in seeing the Mall of America torn to shreds, however. Ho ho hum. **88m/C VHS.** Arnold Schwarzenegger, Jeff Hartman, Sinbad, Rita Wilson, James Belushi, Robert Conrad, Martin Mull, Jake Lloyd, Harvey Korman, Laraine Newman; *D:* Brian Levant; *W:* Randy Kornfield; *C:* Victor Kemper; *M:* David Newman. Nominations: Golden Raspberry Awards '96: Worst Director (Levant). NYR

Jinxed *𝄞𝄞* 1982 (R) Las Vegas nightclub singer tries to convince a gullible blackjack dealer to murder her crooked boyfriend, but the plan backfires when the gangster electrocutes himself while taking a shower. Offscreen cast disputes were probably much more interesting than on-screen comedy. **104m/C VHS, Beta.** Bette Midler, Ken Wahl, Rip Torn; *D:* Donald Siegel; *W:* David Newman, Frank D. Gilroy; *M:* Miles Goodman. MGM

Jit *𝄞𝄞* 1994 Unpretentious romantic comedy finds the easy-going U.K., who runs errands for his uncle in a Zimbabwe town, falling in love with the beautiful Sofi, who already has a boyfriend. But U.K. won't be stopped by this or Sofi's greedy father. "Jit" refers to the infectious local music, a fusion of traditional African rhythms and reggae-pop. **98m/C VHS.** Dominic Makuvachuma, Sibongile Nene, Faria Sevenzo, Winnie Ndemera; *D:* Michael Raeburn. HMV

The Jitters *𝄞* 1988 (R) The murdered dead turn into zombies and seek revenge on their killers. **80m/C VHS, Beta.** Sal Viviano, Marilyn Tokuda, James Hong, Frank Dietz; *D:* John Fasano. PSM

Jive Junction *𝄞𝄞* 1943 A group of patriotic teenagers convert a barn into a canteen for servicemen and name it "Jive Junction." **62m/B VHS, Beta.** Dickie Moore, Tina Thayer, Gerra Young, Johnny Michaels, Jan Wiley, Beverly Boyd, William Halligan; *D:* Edgar G. Ulmer. NOS, GVV

Jive Turkey *𝄞½* 1976 Cool dude busts heads. **?m/C VHS.** Paul Harris, Frank De Kova, Serena; *D:* Bill Brame. MOV

Jo Jo Dancer, Your Life is Calling *𝄞𝄞½* 1986 (R) Pryor directed and starred in this semi-autobiographical price-of-fame story of a comic, hospitalized for a drug-related accident, who must re-evaluate his life. A serious departure from Pryor's slapstick comedies that doesn't quite make it as a drama; Pryor nevertheless deserves credit for the honesty he demonstrates in dealing with his real-life problems. **97m/C VHS, Beta, LV, Closed Caption.** Richard Pryor, Debbie Allen, Art Evans, Fay Hauser, Barbara Williams, Paula Kelly, Wings Hauser, Carmen McRae, Diahnne Abbott, Scoey Mitchell, Billy Eckstine, Virginia Capers, Dennis Farina; *D:* Richard Pryor; *W:* Richard Pryor, Rocco Urbisci; *C:* John A. Alonzo; *M:* Herbie Hancock. COL

Joan of Arc *𝄞𝄞½* 1948 A touching and devout look at the life of Joan of Arc. Perhaps unfortunately, the film is accurately based on the play by Maxwell Anderson, and adds up to too much talk and too little action. **100m/C VHS, Beta, LV.** Ingrid Bergman, Jose Ferrer, John Ireland, Leif Erickson; *D:* Victor Fleming; *C:* Joseph Valentine. Academy Awards '48: Best Color Cinematography, Best Costume Design (Color); National Board of Review Awards '48: 10 Best Films of the Year; Nominations: Academy Awards '48: Best Actress (Bergman), Best Art Direction/Set Decoration (Color), Best Film Editing, Best Supporting Actor (Ferrer), Original Dramatic/Comedy Score. IGP, HMV

Joan of Paris *𝄞𝄞𝄞½* 1942 A French resistance leader dies so that Allied pilots can escape from the Nazis. A well done, but obviously dated propaganda feature. **91m/B VHS, Beta.** Michele Morgan, Paul Henreid, Thomas Mitchell, Laird Cregar, May Robson, Alexander Granach, Alan Ladd; *D:* Robert Stevenson; *W:* Charles Bennett. Nominations: Academy Awards '42: Original Dramatic/Comedy Score. TTC

Jock Petersen *𝄞* Petersen 1974 (R) A light-hearted story about a blonde hunk who enrolls in college, cavorting and seducing his way to questionable fame and fortune. **97m/C VHS, Beta.** Jack Thompson, Wendy Hughes; *D:* Tim Burstall. NLC

Jocks *𝄞½* 1987 (R) A whiz-kid tennis team competes in a pro meet in Las Vegas, and paints the town red. **90m/C VHS, Beta.** Christopher Lee, Perry Lang, Richard Roundtree, Scott Strader; *D:* Steve Carver; *W:* Jeff Buhai. COL

Joe *𝄞𝄞½* 1970 (R) An odd friendship grows between a businessman and a blue-collar worker as they search together for the executive's runaway daughter. Thrust into the midst of the counter-culture, they react with an orgy of violence. **107m/C VHS, Beta, LV.** Peter Boyle, Susan Sarandon, Dennis Patrick; *D:* John G. Avildsen. Nominations: Academy Awards '70: Best Story & Screenplay. MGM, VES

Joe Kidd *𝄞𝄞½* 1972 (PG) A land war breaks out in New Mexico between Mexican natives and American land barons. Eastwood, once again portraying the "mysterious stranger," must decide with whom he should side, all the while falling in love with Garcia. Lackluster direction results in a surprisingly tedious western, in spite of the cast. One of Eastwood's lowest money grossers. The laserdisc edition is letterboxed and features chapter stops, the original trailer and digital sound. **88m/C VHS, Beta, LV.** Clint Eastwood, Robert Duvall, John Saxon, Don Stroud, Stella Garcia, James Wainwright, Paul Koslo, Gregory Walcott, Dick Van Patten, Lynn Marta; *D:* John Sturges; *W:* Elmore Leonard; *C:* Bruce Surtees; *M:* Lalo Schifrin. USH

The Joe Louis Story *𝄞𝄞* 1953 The story of Joe Louis' rise to fame as boxing's Heavyweight Champion of the world. **88m/B VHS, Beta.** Coley Wallace, Paul Stewart, Hilda Simms; *M:* George Bassman. NOS, DVT, FCT

Joe Panther *𝄞𝄞𝄞* 1976 (G) Family drama about a young Seminole Indian who stakes his claim in the Anglo world by wrestling alligators. Montalban plays a wise old chieftain who helps the youth handle the conflict between Indian and white societies. **110m/C VHS, Beta.** Brian Keith, Ricardo Montalban, Alan Feinstein, Cliff Osmond, A. Martinez, Robert Hoffman; *D:* Paul Krasny. WAR

Joe Versus the Volcano *𝄞𝄞* 1990 (PG) Expressionistic goofball comedy about a dopey guy who, after finding out he has only months to live, contracts with a millionaire to leap into a volcano alive. Imaginative farce with great "Metropolis"-pastiche visuals that eventually fizzle out. Watch for Ryan in not one, but three roles, and mysterious symbolism throughout. Special effects courtesy of Industrial Light and Magic. **106m/C VHS, Beta, LV, 8mm.** Tom Hanks, Meg Ryan, Lloyd Bridges, Robert Stack, Amanda Plummer, Abe Vigoda, Dan Hedaya, Barry McGovern, Ossie Davis; *D:* John Patrick Shanley; *W:* John Patrick Shanley; *M:* Georges Delerue. WAR

Joe's Apartment *𝄞𝄞* 1996 (PG-13) Fresh-from-Iowa Joe (O'Connell) comes to New York, finds a squalid apartment, and then discovers its other occupants are hordes of singing, joking cockroaches. Lucky for Joe, his unwelcome roommates are on his side, even helping out with his love life, when necessary. Gross but interesting, throw in Vaughn as a panty-wearing politician and you've got yourself a potential cult-movie favorite. Neat freaks probably won't enjoy it much. Flick took three years to finish as computer-animated roaches had to do all the dancing and singing. Feature directorial debut for writer Payson, who created the original 1992 live-action/animation MTV short. *CW:* Crude humor and a brief drug reference. **82m/C VHS, LV, Closed Caption.** Jerry O'Connell, Megan Ward, Robert Vaughn, Jim Turner, Don Ho, Sandra "Pepa" Denton, Shiek Mahmud-Bey; *D:* John Payson; *W:* John Payson; *C:* Peter Deming; *V:* Billy West, Reginald Hudlin. MGM

Joe's Bed-Stuy Barbershop: We Cut Heads *𝄞𝄞½* 1983 Lee's first film takes place inside a neighborhood landmark, the corner barbershop. Lee displays the social awareness and urban humor that he honed in his later, bigger films. **60m/C VHS, Beta.** Leon Errol, Morris Carnovsky, Elyse Knox, Billy House, Trudy Marshall; *D:* Spike Lee; *W:* Spike Lee. ICA

Joey *𝄞½* 1985 (PG) Daddy, a former doo-wopper, looks back on his years of musical success as a waste of time. His son takes to the world of rock guitar with blind fervor. Their argument plays against the backdrop of the "Royal Doo-Wopp Show" at New York City's Radio Music Hall. Features multi-generational rock songs. **90m/C VHS, Beta.** Neill Barry, James Quinn. NO

Joey Breaker *𝄞𝄞𝄞* 1993 (R) Joey (cult-fave Edson) is a hot-shot Manhattan talent agent who's consumed by his job. A series of encounters (romantic and otherwise) expands his outlook, first among them with Cyan (Marley), a young Jamaican waitress. Joey also meets AIDS-stricken Fondren, who helps Joey see another side of life. Quirky with a reggae beat, small pic works large message with sense of humor and sincere performances. Dedicated to Fondren, who died of AIDS in 1992. Marley, daughter of late reggae superstar Bob, shares a tune on the soundtrack with brother Ziggy. Filmed in da Big Apple and St. Lucia, West Indies. *CW:* Language. **92m/C VHS, Beta, Closed Caption.** Richard Edson, Cedella Marley, Erik King, Gina Gershon, Philip S. Hoffman, Fred Fondren; *D:* Steven Starr; *W:* Steven Starr; *C:* Joe DeSalvo; *M:* Paul Aston. PAR, FCT

John and the Missus *𝄞½* 1987 (PG) After the discovery of a copper mine threatens to destroy a nearby town, the Canadian government begins a relocation process. However, one man refuses to give up his generations-old home. Canadian Pinsent's directorial debut, adapting his own 1973 novel. **98m/C VHS, Beta.** CA Gordon Pinsent, Jackie Burroughs, Randy Follet, Jessica Steen; *D:* Gordon Pinsent. Genie Awards '87: Best Actor (Pinsent). NO

John & Yoko: A Love Story *𝄞* 1985 Appalling television movie version of the rock legend's life and marriage. With original Beatles tunes. **146m/C VHS, Beta, LV.** Mark McGann, Kim Miyori,

Kenneth Price, Peter Capaldi, Richard Morant, Philip Walsh; **D:** Sandor Stern. *IME*

John Cleese on How to Irritate People
How to Irritate People 1968 Cleese, a master at causing irritation, demonstrates how to take care of all those annoying people who irritate you, including job interviewers, bank clerks, waiters, and salesmen. Monty Python alumni Palin and Chapman also join Cleese in the "Airline Pilots" sketch about bored pilots deliberately trying to terrify their passengers. 65m/C VHS. John Cleese, Michael Palin, Graham Chapman, Connie Booth. *WST, FUS*

John Paul Jones 🐾🐾½ 1959 Big bio of the Revolutionary War naval hero ("I have not yet begun to fight!") who wins a lot of battles but can't convince Congress to maintain a strong navy at war's end. He's sent to win sea battles for the Empress Catherine the Great of Russia and then spends his last years in France. Great action scenes, otherwise tedious. 126m/C VHS. Robert Stack, Charles Coburn, MacDonald Carey, Marisa Pavan, Jean-Pierre Aumont, Peter Cushing, Erin O'Brien, Bruce Cabot, David Farrar, Basil Sydney, John Crawford; **Cameos:** Bette Davis; **D:** John Farrow; **W:** John Farrow, Jesse Lasky Jr.; **M:** Max Steiner. *WAR*

John Wayne Anthology: Star Packer/Lawless Range 1934 In addition to two of Wayne's films, this program captures 40 years of the actor's career. 156m/B VHS. John Wayne; **D:** Robert North Bradbury. *SIM*

Johnnie Gibson F.B.I. 🐾 *Johnnie Mae Gibson: FBI* 1987 Supposedly based on a true story, the adventures of a beautiful, black FBI agent who falls in love with a man she's investigating. 96m/C VHS, Beta. Howard E. Rollins Jr., Lynn Whitfield, William Allen Young, Richard Lawson; **D:** Bill Duke; **M:** Billy Goldenberg. *ACA, PTB*

Johnny Angel 🐾🐾🐾 1945 Merchant Marine captain unravels mystery of his father's murder aboard a ship. Tense film noir. 79m/B VHS, Beta, LV. George Raft, Claire Trevor, Signe Hasso, Lowell Gilmore, Hoagy Carmichael; **D:** Edwin L. Marin. *CCB, TTC*

Johnny Apollo 🐾🐾½ 1940 Upright college student Power keeps his nose clean until Dad's sent to jail for playing with numbers. Scheming to free his old man (Arnold) from the big house, he decides crime will pay for the stiff price tag of freedom. Predictable and melodramatic, but well directed. 93m/B VHS, Beta. Tyrone Power, Dorothy Lamour, Lloyd Nolan, Edward Arnold, Charley Grapewin, Lionel Atwill; **D:** Yves Allegret; **C:** Arthur C. Miller. *FOX, FCT*

Johnny Appleseed 1986 True story of the legendary American who spent his life planting apple trees across the country. Comedy the entire family will enjoy from Shelly Duvall's "Tall Tales and Legends" series. Originally broadcast on cable television. 60m/C VHS, Closed Caption. Martin Short, Rob Reiner, Molly Ringwald. *FOX*

Johnny Be Good 🐾 1988 (R) A too-talented high school quarterback is torn between loyalty to his best friend and to his girlfriend amid bribery and schemings by colleges eager to sign him up. 91m/C VHS, Beta, LV, Closed Caption. Anthony Michael Hall, Robert Downey Jr., Paul Gleason, Uma Thurman, John Pankow, Steve James, Seymour Cassel, Michael Greene, Marshall Bell, Deborah May; **D:** Bud Smith; **W:** Jeff Buhai; **M:** Jay Michael Ferguson. *ORI*

Johnny Belinda 🐾🐾🐾 1948 A compassionate physician cares for a young deaf mute woman and her illegitimate child. Tension builds as the baby's father returns to claim the boy. 103m/B VHS, Beta. Jane Wyman, Lew Ayres, Charles Bickford, Agnes Moorehead; **D:** Jean Negulesco; **M:** Max Steiner. Academy Awards '48: Best Actress (Wyman); Golden Globe Awards '49: Best Actress—Drama (Wyman), Best Film—Drama; Nominations: Academy Awards '48: Best Actor (Ayres), Best Art Direction/Set Decoration (B & W), Best Black and White Cinematography, Best Director (Negulesco), Best Film Editing, Best Picture, Best Screenplay, Best Sound, Best Supporting Actor (Bickford), Best Supporting Actress (Moorehead), Original Dramatic/Comedy Score. *MGM, BTV, CCB*

Johnny Belinda 🐾🐾 1982 A television movie adaptation of the Elmer Harris weepie about a small town doctor who befriends an abused deaf girl. Remake of the 1948 film. 95m/C VHS, Beta. Richard Thomas, Rosanna Arquette, Dennis Quaid, Candy Clark, Roberts Blossom, Fran Ryan; **D:** Anthony Page. *LIV*

Johnny Come Lately 🐾🐾½ *Johnny Vagabond* 1943 An elderly editor helps out an ex-newspaperman with a police charge. The two then team up to expose political corruption despite threats from a rival newspaperman. 97m/B VHS, LV. James Cagney, Grace George, Marjorie Main, Marjorie Lord, Hattie McDaniel, Ed McNamara; **D:** William K. Howard. Nominations: Academy Awards '43: Original Dramatic/Comedy Score. *REP*

Johnny Dangerously 🐾🐾 1984 (PG-13) A gangster spoof about Johnny Dangerously, who turned to crime in order to pay his mother's medical bills. Now, Dangerously wants to go straight, but competitive crooks would rather see him dead than law-abiding and his mother requires more and more expensive operations. Crime pays in comic ways. 90m/C VHS, Beta, Closed Caption. Michael Keaton, Joe Piscopo, Danny DeVito, Maureen Stapleton, Marilu Henner, Peter Boyle, Griffin Dunne, Glynnis O'Connor, Dom DeLuise, Richard Dimitri, Ray Walston, Dick Butkus, Alan Hale Jr., Bob Eubanks; **D:** Amy Heckerling; **W:** Norman Steinberg, Harry Colomby. *FOX*

Johnny Eager 🐾🐾🐾 1942 Glossy crime melodrama starring Taylor as an unscrupulous racketeer and Turner as the daughter of D.A. Arnold who falls for him and ends up becoming a pawn in his schemes. Heflin won an Oscar for his outstanding performance as Taylor's alcoholic confidant. Excellent direction by LeRoy makes this a top-rate gangster film. Based on a story by James Edward Grant. 107m/B VHS. Robert Taylor, Lana Turner, Edward Arnold, Van Heflin, Robert Sterling, Patricia Dane, Glenda Farrell, Barry Nelson, Henry O'Neill, Charles Dingle, Cy Kendall; **D:** Mervyn LeRoy; **W:** James Edward Grant, John Lee Mahin. Academy Awards '42: Best Supporting Actor (Heflin). *MGM*

Johnny Firecloud 🐾 1975 A modern Indian goes on the warpath when the persecution of his people reawakens his sense of identity. 94m/C VHS, Beta. Victor Mohica, Ralph Meeker, Frank De Kova, Sacheen Little Feather, David Canary, Christina Hart; **D:** William Allen Castleman. *PSM*

Johnny Frenchman 🐾🐾 1946 Rival fishing groups battle it out, complicated by a romance across the water. Featured in the cast are real fishermen and villagers from Cornwall, as well as authentic Free French Resistance fighters from WWII. 104m/B VHS. *GB* Francoise Rosay, Tom Walls, Patricia Roc, Ralph Michael, Frederick Piper, Pierre Richard, Carroll O'Connor; **D:** Charles Frend. *NOS*

Johnny Got His Gun 🐾🐾🐾 1971 (R) Dalton Trumbo's story of a young WWI veteran (Bottoms) who meets a bomb with his name on it and is rendered armless, legless, and more or less faceless, as well as deaf, dumb, and blind. Regarded as a vegetable and stuck in a lightless hospital utility room, he dreams and fantasizes about life before and after the bomb, and tries vainly to communicate with the staff. Wrenching and bleak anti-war diatribe made at the climax of the Vietnam War. 111m/C VHS, Beta, LV. Timothy Bottoms, Jason Robards Jr., Donald Sutherland, Diane Varsi, Kathy Field; **D:** Dalton Trumbo. Cannes Film Festival '71: Grand Jury Prize. *MED*

Johnny Guitar 🐾🐾🐾½ 1953 Women strap on six-guns in Nicholas Ray's unintentionally hilarious, gender-bending western. A guitar-playing loner wanders into a small town feud between lovelorn saloon owner Crawford and McCambridge, the town's resident lynch mob-leading harpy. This fascinating cult favorite has had film theorists arguing for decades: is it a parody, a political McCarthy-era allegory, or Freudian exercise? The off-screen battles of the two female stars are equally legendary. Stick around for the end credits to hear Peggy Lee sing the title song.

116m/C VHS, LV, Closed Caption. Joan Crawford, Ernest Borgnine, Sterling Hayden, Mercedes McCambridge, Scott Brady, Ward Bond, Royal Dano, John Carradine; **D:** Nicholas Ray; **W:** Philip Yordan; **C:** Harry Stradling. *REP*

Johnny Handsome 🐾🐾🐾 1989 (R) An ugly, deformed hood, after he's been double-crossed and sent to prison, volunteers for a reconstructive surgery experiment and is released with a new face, determined to hunt down the scum that set him up. A terrific modern B-picture based on John Godey's "The Three Worlds of Johnny Handsome." 96m/C VHS, Beta, LV, Closed Caption. Mickey Rourke, Ellen Barkin, Lance Henriksen, Elizabeth McGovern, Morgan Freeman, Forest Whitaker, Scott Wilson, Blake Clark; **D:** Walter Hill; **W:** Ken Friedman; **M:** Ry Cooder. *LIV*

Johnny Mnemonic 🐾🐾 1995 (R) Robo-yuppie data courier Johnny (Reeves), has over extended the storage capacity in his head and must download his latest job before his brain turns to applesauce. Aided by an implant-enhanced bodyguard (Meyer), underground hacker rebels called LoTeks, and a former doctor (Rollins) battling a technology-induced epidemic, Johnny is on the run from the corporation that wants his head (literally). Freshman director Longo can't seem to get a handle on the plot and doesn't get much help from Gibson, who combined characters and scenarios from his other books. Action sequences and computer effects are appropriately spiffy, preventing a total system crash. *CW:* Strong sci-fi violence; language. 98m/C VHS, LV, 8mm, Closed Caption. Keanu Reeves, Dina Meyer, Ice-T, Takeshi, Dolph Lundgren, Henry Rollins, Udo Kier, Barbara Sukowa, Denis Akiyama; **D:** Robert Longo; **W:** William Gibson; **C:** Francois Protat; **M:** Brad Fiedel. *COL*

Johnny Nobody 🐾🐾½ 1961 A mysterious stranger murders a writer who has been taunting the residents of a quaint Irish town. A sleeper of a thriller, especially in the treatment of the town's reaction to this murder. 88m/B VHS, Beta. *GB* William Bendix, Aldo Ray, Nigel Patrick, Yvonne Mitchell, Cyril Cusack; **D:** Nigel Patrick. *NO*

Johnny 100 Pesos 🐾🐾½ 1993 Seventeen-year-old Johnny (Araiza) walks into a video store that is a front for an illegal currency exchange operation. He's the advance man for a quartet of criminals who are planning to rob the place but before they can escape with the cash, the police show up and the crooks take the store's inhabitants hostage. Now there's a standoff, with the media shamelessly broadcasting all events and the Chilean authorities struggling to control the escalating situation. Based on a true 1990 incident. Spanish with subtitles. 90m/C VHS. Armando Araiza, Patricia Rivera, Willy Semler, Sergio Hernandez; **D:** Gustavo Graef-Marino; **W:** Gustavo Graef-Marino, Gerardo Caceres; **C:** Jose Luis Arredondo; **M:** Andres Pollak. *FXL*

Johnny Reno 🐾½ 1966 Laughable western that has U.S. Marshal Andrews trying to save an accused killer from lynching. Of interest for star-watching only. Based on a story by Steve Fisher, A.C. Lyles, and Andrew Craddock. 83m/C VHS. Dana Andrews, Jane Russell, Lon Chaney Jr., John Agar, Lyle Bettger, Tom Drake, Richard Arlen, Robert Lowery; **D:** R.G. Springsteen; **W:** Steve Fisher. *PAR*

Johnny Shiloh 🐾🐾 1963 An underage youth becomes a heroic drummer during the Civil War. Originally a two-part Disney television show. 90m/C VHS, Beta. Kevin Corcoran, Brian Keith, Darryl Hickman, Skip Homeier; **D:** James Neilson. *DIS*

Johnny Stecchino 🐾🐾🐾 1992 (R) A breathless, charming comedy about mistaken identity, with Benigni starring as both Dante, a mild-mannered Roman bus driver, and his double, a notorious Mafioso known as "Johnny Toothpick." Dante happens to meet a lovely woman who takes exceptional interest in him, even inviting him to visit her home in Palermo. The reason she's interested is that Dante is the exact double of her husband, who has ratted on his fellow mobsters and needs a patsy to take the fall. Benigni's

expressive body language and sweetness of character is well-showcased. In Italian with English subtitles. **CW:** Language and drug-related humor. 100m/C VHS, LV. *IT* Roberto Benigni, Nicoletta Braschi, Paolo Bonacelli, Ignazio Pappalardo, Franco Volpi; *D:* Roberto Benigni; *W:* Roberto Benigni, Vincenzo Cerami; *M:* Evan Lurie. NLC, IME, FCT

Johnny Suede ♂♂ 1992 (R) Hip kid with big hair wanders the city seeking an identity via retro black suede elevator shoes. Sleepy surreal comedy walks Pitt through two romantic entanglements and a rendezvous with his own rock idol in his quest for musical talent and pop singer nirvana (not necessarily in that order). Candidate for induction into the David Lynch Movie Musuem of the Weird. **CW:** Language and sexual elements. 97m/C VHS, LV, Closed Caption. Brad Pitt, Calvin Levels, Nick Cave, Wilfredo Giovanni Clark, Alison Moir, Peter McRobbie, Tina Louise, Michael Mulheren, Catherine Keener, Samuel L. Jackson; *D:* Tom DiCillo; *W:* Tom DiCillo; *M:* Jim Farmer. PAR

Johnny Tiger ♂♂½ 1966 A teacher has his hands full when he arrives at the Seminole Reservation in Florida to instruct the Indian children. 100m/C VHS, Beta. Robert Taylor, Geraldine Brooks, Chad Everett, Brenda Scott; *D:* Paul Wendkos. REP

Johnny Tremain & the Sons of Liberty ♂♂ 1958 The story of the gallant American patriots who participated in the Boston Tea Party. 85m/C VHS, Beta. Sebastian Cabot, Hal Stalmaster, Luana Patten, Richard Beymer; *D:* Robert Stevenson. DIS

Johnny We Hardly Knew Ye ♂♂½ 1977 Well-made biographical drama recounts John F. Kennedy's first political campaign for local office in Boston in 1946. Made for television. 90m/C VHS, Beta. Paul Rudd, Kevin Conway, William Prince, Burgess Meredith, Tom Berenger, Brian Dennehy, Kenneth McMillan; *D:* Gilbert Cates. TLF

Johnny's Girl ♂♂½ 1995 After her mom's death, a 16-year-old (Kirshner) moves to Anchorage, Alaska to live with her wayward dad (Williams). He's a kinda con man involved in shady deals, who tries to go legit in order to give his daughter a proper home. TV movie based on the novel by Kim Rich. 92m/C VHS. Mia Kirshner, Treat Williams, Ron White, Gloria Reuben, Shirley Douglas, Janne Mortil; *D:* John Kent Harrison. HMK

A Joke of Destiny, Lying in Wait Around the Corner Like a Bandit ♂♂ *A Joke of Destiny* 1984 (PG) A irreverent satire about a Minister of the Interior (Tognazzi, of "La Cage aux Folles" fame) who becomes trapped in his high-tech limousine before a vital press conference. An exaggerated vision of Italian bureaucracy. With English subtitles. 105m/C VHS, Beta. *IT* Ugo Tognazzi, Piera Degli Esposti, Gastone Moschin, Renzo Montagnani, Valeria Golino; *D:* Lina Wertmuller; *W:* Lina Wertmuller. ORI, APD

Jokes My Folks Never Told Me ♂ 1977 Series of blackouts and sketches featuring a bevy of beautiful women. 82m/C VHS, Beta. Sandy Johnson, Mariwin Roberts; *D:* Gerry Woolery.

The Jolly Paupers ♂♂½ *Freylekhe Kabtsonim* 1938 A pre-war comedy made in Warsaw about two small-town Jews who try to achieve fame and fortune in the face of setbacks, community quarrels, and insanity. In Yiddish with English subtitles. 62m/B VHS, Beta. Shimon Dzigan, Yisroel Shumacher, Max Bozyk, Menasha Oppenheim; *D:* Zygmund Turkow. ALD

Jolson Sings Again ♂♂ 1949 This sequel to "The Jolson Story" brings back Larry Parks as the ebullient entertainer, with Jolson himself dubbing Parks's voice for the songs. Picking up where the other film ended, the movie chronicles Jolson's comeback in the 1940s and his tireless work with the USO overseas during WWII and the Korean War. ♫ After You've Gone; Chinatown, My Chinatown; Give My Regards to Broadway; I Only Have Eyes For You; I'm Just

Wild About Harry; You Made Me Love You; I'm Looking Over a Four-Leaf Clover; Is It True What They Say About Dixie?; Ma Blushin' Rose. 96m/C VHS, Beta, LV. Larry Parks, William Demarest, Barbara Hale, Bill Goodwin; *D:* Henry Levin; *M:* George Duning. Nominations: Academy Awards '49: Best Color Cinematography, Best Story & Screenplay, Scoring of a Musical. COL

The Jolson Story ♂♂♂ 1946 A smash Hollywood bio of Jolson, from his childhood to super-stardom. Features dozens of vintage songs from Jolson's parade of hits. Jolson himself dubbed the vocals for Parks, rejuvenating his own career in the process. ♫ Swanee; You Made Me Love You; By the Light of the Silvery Moon; I'm Sitting On Top of the World; There's a Rainbow Round My Shoulder; My Mammy; Rock-A-Bye Your Baby With a Dixie Melody; Liza; Waiting for the Robert E. Lee. 128m/C VHS, Beta, LV. Larry Parks, Evelyn Keyes, William Demarest, Bill Goodwin, Tamara Shayne, John Alexander, Jimmy Lloyd, Ludwig Donath, Scotty Beckett; *D:* Alfred E. Green; *M:* Morris Stoloff. Academy Awards '46: Best Sound, Scoring of a Musical; Nominations: Academy Awards '46: Best Actor (Parks), Best Color Cinematography, Best Film Editing, Best Supporting Actor (Demarest). COL

Jon Jost's Frameup ♂♂ *Frameup* 1993 Cocky ex-con Ricky Lee hooks up with dizzy waitress Beth Ann and they head out on a 3000-mile nightmare road trip to California. Free-form story shot in 10 days. 91m/C VHS. Howard Swain, Nancy Carlin; *D:* Jon Jost; *W:* Jon Jost. WAC

Jonah Who Will Be 25 in the Year 2000 ♂♂♂½ *Jonas—Qui Aura 25 Ans en l'An 2000* 1976 A group of eight friends, former 60s radicals, try to adjust to growing older and coping with life in the 70s. The eccentric octet include a disillusioned journalist turned gambler, an unorthodox teacher, and a grocery store cashier who gives away food to the elderly. Wonderful performances highlight this social comedy. In French with English subtitles. 110m/C VHS. *SI* Jean-Luc Bideau, Myriam Meziere, Miou-Miou, Jacques Denis, Rufus, Dominique Labourier, Roger Jendly, Miriam Boyer, Raymond Bussieres, Jonah; *D:* Alain Tanner; *W:* Renato Berta; *M:* Jean-Marie Senia. National Society of Film Critics Awards '76: Best Screenplay. NYF

Jonathan Livingston Seagull ♂♂½ 1973 (G) Based on the best-selling novella by Richard Bach, this film quietly envisions a world of love, understanding, achievement, hope and individuality. 99m/C VHS, Beta. James Franciscus, Juliet Mills; *D:* Hall Bartlett; *M:* Neil Diamond. Golden Globe Awards '74: Best Score; Nominations: Academy Awards '73: Best Cinematography, Best Film Editing. PAR, WSH

Joni ♂♂ 1979 (G) An inspirational story based on the real life of Tada (playing herself) who was seriously injured in a diving accident, and her conquering of the odds. A born-again feature film based on the book by Tada. 75m/C VHS, Beta. Joni Eareckson Tada, Bert Remsen, Katherine De Hetre, Cooper Huckabee; *D:* James F. Collier. LIV

Jornada de Muerte ♂ 198? An ex-cop is hired to bring an important anti-Mob witness to trial via transcontinental train, and must fend off Mob attack squads in the process. In Spanish. 90m/C VHS, Beta. *SP* Fred Williamson, Bernie Kuby, Heidi Dobbs. UNI

Jory ♂♂ 1972 (PG) A young man's father is killed in a saloon fight, and he must grow up quickly to survive. 96m/C VHS, Beta. Robby Benson, B.J. Thomas, John Marley; *D:* Jorge Fons. COL

Joseph ♂♂½ 1995 Following "Abraham" and "Jacob" comes the Old Testament story of young Joseph (Mercurio), beloved son of Jacob, who's sold into slavery by his envious older brothers. Joseph is bought by the Pharoah's chief steward, Potiphar (Kingsley), and, after a long series of tribulations, rises to become a power in Egypt, which unexpectedly leads Joseph to hold the fate of his long-lost family in his hands. Filmed in Morocco. 240m/C VHS, Closed Caption. Paul Mercurio, Ben Kingsley, Martin Landau, Lesley Ann Warren, Warren Clarke, Alice Krige, Dominique Sanda, Stefano Dionisi,

Valeria Cavalli, Peter Eyre, Timothy Bateson, Jamie Glover, Mike Attwell; *D:* Roger Young; *W:* Lionel Chetwynd, James Carrington; *C:* Raffaele Mertes; *M:* Marco Frisina. TTC

Joseph & His Brethren ♂ *The Story of Joseph and His Brethren; Joseph Sold by His Brothers* 1960 A full-length dramatization of the Old Testament story. 103m/C VHS, Beta. Geoffrey Horne, Robert Morley; *D:* Irving Rapper. VCI, KEP

Joseph Andrews ♂♂ 1977 (R) This adaptation of a 1742 Henry Fielding novel chronicles the rise of Joseph Andrews from servant to personal footman (and fancy) of Lady Booby. 99m/C VHS, Beta. *GB* Ann-Margret, Peter Firth, Jim Dale, Michael Hordern, Beryl Reid; *D:* Tony Richardson; *W:* Chris Bryant, Allan Scott; *C:* David Watkin; *M:* John Addison. PAR

Josepha ♂♂♂ 1982 (R) A husband and wife, both actors, are forced to re-examine their relationship when the wife finds a new love while on a film location. In French with English subtitles. 114m/C VHS, Beta. *FR* Miou-Miou, Claude Brasseur, Bruno Cremer; *D:* Christopher Frank. COL

The Josephine Baker Story ♂♂♂ 1990 (R) Made-for-cable bio of exotic entertainer/activist Josephine Baker, an Afro-American woman from St. Louis who found superstardom in pre-WWII Europe, but repeated racism and rejection in the U.S. At times trite treatment turns her eventful life into a standard rise-and-fall showbiz tale, but a great cast and lavish scope pull it through. Whitfield recreates Baker's (sometimes topless) dance routines; Carol Dennis dubs her singing. Filmed on location in Budapest. **CW:** Sensuality. 129m/C VHS, Closed Caption. Lynn Whitfield, Ruben Blades, David Dukes, Craig T. Nelson, Louis Gossett Jr., Kene Holliday, Vivian Bonnell; *D:* Brian Gibson; *M:* Ralph Burns. Emmy Awards '91: Best Actress (Whitfield), Best Director (Gibson). HBO, FCT

Josh and S.A.M. ♂♂ 1993 (PG-13) Road movie for youngsters with a twist: the driver can barely see over the dashboard. Josh and Sam are brothers whose parents are splitting. They cope by taking off on their own. Sam, meanwhile has been convinced by Josh that he's not a real boy at all, but rather a S.A.M.: Strategically Altered Mutant. Weber's directorial debut will appeal to young kids, but adults will see over the dashboard and through the transparent plot. **CW:** Kids in jeopardy. 97m/C VHS, LV, Closed Caption. Jacob Tierney, Noah Fleiss, Martha Plimpton, Joan Allen, Christopher Penn, Stephen Tobolowsky, Ronald Guttman; *D:* Billy Weber; *W:* Frank Deese; *C:* Don Burgess; *M:* Thomas Newman. NLC

Josh Kirby...Time Warrior: Chapter 1, Planet of the Dino-Knights ♂♂½ 1995 (PG) Time-traveling 14-year-old Josh Kirby is accidently zapped to the 25th-century where fierce warriors ride dinosaurs and a madman is out to destroy the universe. The first tale in a fantasy series designed as an old-fashioned movie serial, complete with cliff-hanger ending. 88m/C VHS, Beta, Closed Caption. Corbin Allred, Jennifer Burns, Derek Webster, John De Mita; *D:* Ernest Farino; *W:* Ethan Reiff, Cyrus Voris, Paul Callisi. PAR

Josh Kirby...Time Warrior: Chapter 2, The Human Pets ♂♂½ 1995 (PG) Josh and his friends now find themselves in the year 70,370—held hostage by the enormous Fatlings, who regard their human finds as pet-like action toys. 90m/C VHS, Beta, Closed Caption. Corbin Allred, Jennifer Burns; *D:* Frank Arnold; *W:* Ethan Reiff, Cyrus Voris, Paul Callisi. PAR

Josh Kirby...Time Warrior: Chapter 3, Trapped on Toyworld ♂♂½ 1995 (PG) Josh is stranded away from his friends on the strange planet of Toyworld and must rely on the lifelike creations of a toy magnate to defend himself from the villainous Dr. Zoetrope. 90m/C VHS, Beta, Closed Caption. Corbin Allred, Jennifer Burns, Derek Webster, Sharon Lee Jones, Buck Kartalian, Barrie Ingham; *D:* Frank Arnold; *W:* Nick Paine. PAR

Josh Kirby...Time Warrior: Chapter 4, Eggs from 70 Million B.C. 🎬🎬½ 1995 (PG) Josh and his pals finds themselves in a military compound that is under attack and encounter some very hungry alien worms. 93m/C VHS, Beta, Closed Caption. Corbin Allred, Jennifer Burns, Derek Webster, Gary Kasper, Barrie Ingham; *D:* Mark Manos. *PAR*

Josh Kirby...Time Warrior: Chapter 5, Journey to the Magic Cavern 🎬🎬½ 1996 (PG) Josh and pals find themselves in the center of a planet where they are befriended by the weird Mushroom People who are under siege by a monster known as "the Muncher." 93m/C VHS, Beta, Closed Caption. Corbin Allred, Jennifer Burns, Derek Webster, Michael Hagiwara, Barrie Ingham; *D:* Ernest Farino; *W:* Ethan Reiff, Cyrus Voris. *PAR*

Josh Kirby...Time Warrior: Chapter 6, Last Battle for the Universe 🎬🎬½ 1996 (PG) Josh is ready to get back to his own time but first he must survive a battle between long-feuding rivals of the timebelt. 90m/C VHS, Beta, Closed Caption. Corbin Allred, Jennifer Burns, Derek Webster, Barrie Ingham; *D:* Frank Arnold; *W:* Ethan Reiff, Cyrus Voris. *PAR*

Joshua 🎬 *Black Rider 1976* (R) Western drama about a vigilante who tracks down the group of outlaws that killed his mother. 75m/C VHS. Fred Williamson, Isela Vega; *D:* Larry Spangler. *NO*

Joshua Then and Now 🎬🎬🎬 1985 (R) When a Jewish-Canadian novelist (Woods) is threatened by the breakup of his marriage to his WASPy wife, compounded by a gay scandal, he re-examines his picaresque history, including his life with his gangster father (Arkin). A stirring story that is enhanced by a strong performance by Woods, as well as a picturesque Canadian backdrop. Adapted by Mordecai Richler from his own novel. 102m/C VHS, Beta, Closed Caption. *CA* James Woods, Gabrielle Lazure, Alan Arkin, Michael Sarrazin, Chuck Shamata, Linda Sorensen, Alan Scarfe, Alexander Knox, Robert Joy, Ken Campbell; *D:* Ted Kotcheff; *W:* Mordecai Richler; *M:* Philippe Sarde. Genie Awards '86: Best Supporting Actor (Arkin), Best Supporting Actress (Sorensen). *FOX*

Jour de Fete 🎬🎬🎬½ *The Big Day; Holiday 1948* Tati's first film, dealing with a French postman's accelerated efforts at efficiency after viewing a motivational film of the American post service. Wonderful slapstick moments. In French with English subtitles. 79m/B VHS, Beta, LV. *FR* Jacques Tati, Guy Decomble, Paul Fankeur; *D:* Jacques Tati. *VDM, CRC, NLC*

Journey 🎬 1977 (PG) Violent story of a girl who is rescued from the Sagueney River and falls in love with her rescuer. Choosing to remain in the remote pioneer community of this "hero," she brings everyone bad luck and misery. 87m/C VHS, Beta. *CA* Genevieve Bujold, John Vernon; *D:* Paul Almond. *NO*

Journey 🎬🎬½ 1995 (PG) Eleven-year-old Journey (Pomeranc) and his teenaged sister Cat (Dushku) are abandoned by their unhappy, restless mother Min (Tilly) at the home of her parents, Marcus (Robards) and Lottie (Fricker). Marcus is an amatuer photographer and Journey searches through the family photo albums to find reasons for his mother's leaving as he and his grandfather slowly build their relationship. Based on the book by Patricia MacLachlan. 98m/C VHS. Max Pomeranc, Jason Robards Jr., Brenda Fricker, Eliza Dushku, Meg Tilly; *D:* Tom McLoughlin; *W:* Patricia MacLachlan; *C:* Kees Van Oostrum. *HMK*

Journey Back to Oz 1971 Animated special features Dorothy and Toto returning to visit their friends in the magical land of Oz. 90m/C VHS, Beta. *V:* Liza Minnelli, Ethel Merman, Paul Lynde, Milton Berle, Mickey Rooney, Danny Thomas. *FHE, KAR, HHE*

Journey Beneath the Desert 🎬🎬 *Antinea, l'Amante Della Citta Sepolta 1961* Three engineers discover the lost-but-always-found-in-the-movies kingdom of Atlantis when their helicopter's forced down in the sunny Sahara. A poor hostess with a rotten disposition, the mean sub-saharan queen doesn't roll out the welcome mat for her grounded guests, so a beautiful slave babe helps them make a hasty exit. Dawdling Euro production with adequate visuals. 105m/C VHS, Beta. *FR IT* Haya Harareet, Jean-Louis Trintignant, Brad Fulton, Amedeo Nazzari, George Riviere, Giulia Rubini, Gabriele Tinti, Gian Marie Volonte; *D:* Edgar G. Ulmer, Giuseppe Masini, Frank Borzage. *SNC*

Journey for Margaret 🎬🎬🎬 1942 Young and Day star as an expectant American couple living in London during WWII so Young can cover the war for a newspaper back home. After she loses her baby during an air raid, Day heads back to the States. Young stays in London where he meets two young orphans and takes them under his wing. He decides to take them back to the United States and adopt them, but problems arise. A real tearjerker and a good story that shows the war through the eyes of children. O'Brien's first film. Based on the book by William L. White. 81m/B VHS. Robert Young, Laraine Day, Fay Bainter, Signe Hasso, Margaret O'Brien, Nigel Bruce, G.P. Huntley Jr., William Severn, Doris Lloyd, Halliwell Hobbes, Jill Esmond; *D:* Woodbridge S. Van Dyke. *MGM, FCT*

Journey into Fear 🎬🎬🎬 1942 During WWII, an American armaments expert is smuggled out of Istanbul, but Axis agents are close behind. From the novel by Eric Ambler; remade for television in 1974. 71m/B VHS, Beta, LV. Joseph Cotten, Dolores Del Rio, Orson Welles, Agnes Moorehead, Norman Foster; *D:* Norman Foster; *C:* Karl Struss. *MED, RXM, TTC*

Journey into Fear 🎬½ *Burn Out 1974* A remake of the 1942 Orson Welles classic about a geologist ensnared in Turkish intrigue and murder. 96m/C VHS, Beta. *CA* Sam Waterston, Vincent Price, Shelley Winters, Donald Pleasence, Zero Mostel, Yvette Mimieux, Ian McShane; *D:* Daniel Mann; *M:* Alex North. *LIV*

The Journey of August King 🎬🎬½ 1995 (PG-13) Adapted by Ehle from his own 1971 novel, set in 1815, about a runaway slave (Newton) protected by a lonely farmer against the landowner and posse tracking her down. August King (Patric), a widower on his way home from town, comes upon Annalees (Newton), prize possession of powerful slaveowner Olaf Singletary (Drake). August, a highly principled man, resists helping her at first, for fear of breaking the law and losing his farm and only remaining possessions. But he rises to higher moral ground, deciding to help her find freedom, whatever the consequences. Director Duigan ("Sirens") crafts a thoughtful, but not particularly suspenseful, period piece of early American history. Patric/Newton relationship reflects the gradual feel of the film. Drake booms as slaveowner. Includes brief brutal scene of slave torture. *CW:* Scene of shocking violence. 91m/C VHS, LV, Closed Caption. Jason Patric, Thandie Newton, Larry Drake, Sam Waterston; *D:* John Duigan; *W:* John Ehle; *C:* Slawomir Idziak; *M:* Stephen Endelman. *TOU*

Journey of Honor 🎬🎬½ 1991 (PG-13) During a civil war in 17th century Japan, a nearly defeated Shogun sends his son, Lord Mayeda, to Spain to buy guns from King Phillip III. Along the way he must fight shipboard spies and fierce storms, and once Mayeda arrives in Spain, he is confronted by the evil Duke Don Pedro. In defeating Don Pedro, Mayeda saves King Phillip, gets his guns, and wins the love of Lady Cecilia. To get revenge, Don Pedro plots to capture the Japanese ship and enslave everyone on board. Lots of action and fine acting. Based on a story by martial artist Sho Kosugi. 107m/C VHS, Beta, LV, Closed Caption. Sho Kosugi, David Essex, Kane Kosugi, Christopher Lee, Norman Lloyd, Ronald Pickup, John Rhys-Dav-

ies, Dylan Kussman, Toshiro Mifune; *D:* Gordon Hessler. *USH*

Journey of Hope 🎬🎬🎬½ 1990 (PG) Powerful drama about Kurdish family that sells its material possessions in hopes of emigrating legally to Switzerland, where life will surely be better. During the perilous journey, smugglers take their money and the family must attempt crossing the formidable slopes of the Swiss Mountains on foot. Based on a true story. In Turkish with English subtitles. 111m/C VHS, LV. *SI* Necmettin Cobanoglu, Nur Surer, Emin Sivas, Yaman Okay, Mathias Gnaedinger, Dietmar Schoenherr; *D:* Xavier Koller; *W:* Xavier Koller. Academy Awards '90: Best Foreign Language Film. *WAR, HBO*

The Journey of Natty Gann 🎬🎬🎬½ 1985 (PG) With the help of a wolf (brilliantly portrayed by a dog) and a drifter, a 14-year-old girl travels across the country in search of her father in this warm and touching film. Excellent Disney representation of life during the Great Depression. 101m/C VHS, Beta, LV. Meredith Salenger, John Cusack, Ray Wise, Scatman Crothers, Lainie Kazan, Verna Bloom; *D:* Jeremy Paul Kagan; *W:* Jeanne Rosenberg; *M:* James Horner. Nominations: Academy Awards '85: Best Costume Design. *DIS*

Journey Through Rosebud 1972 A reenactment of the 1970s protest at Wounded Knee by Native Americans. 93m/C VHS, Beta. Robert Forster, Eddie Little Sky; *D:* Tom Giles. *NLC*

Journey to Spirit Island 🎬🎬½ 1992 (PG) A young Native American girl dreams of her ancestors who are buried on Spirit Island, an ancient burial ground. However, the island is now scheduled to be developed into a resort. With the help of three friends the girl tries to protect the land. Filmed in the Pacific Northwest. 93m/C VHS. Brandon Douglas, Gabriel Damon, Tony Acierto, Nick Ramus, Marie Antoinette Rodgers, Tarek McCarthy; *D:* Laszlo Pal. *ACA*

Journey to the Center of the Earth 🎬🎬🎬 1959 A scientist and student undergo a hazardous journey to find the center of the earth and along the way they find the lost city of Atlantis. Based upon the Jules Verne novel. 132m/C VHS, Beta, LV, Closed Caption. James Mason, Pat Boone, Arlene Dahl, Diane Baker, Thayer David, Alan Napier, Peter Ronson; *D:* Henry Levin. Nominations: Academy Awards '59: Best Art Direction/Set Decoration (Color), Best Sound. *FXV, FCT, FUS*

Journey to the Center of the Earth 1976 An animated version of the Jules Verne classic adventure about a scientist's quest to reach the earth's core. 50m/C VHS, Beta. *MGM*

Journey to the Center of the Earth 1988 (PG) A young nanny and two teenage boys discover Atlantis while exploring a volcano. 83m/C VHS, Beta, LV. Nicola Cowper, Paul Carafotes, Ilan Mitchell-Smith; *D:* Rusty Lemorande; *W:* Rusty Lemorande, Kitty Chalmers. *CAN*

Journey to the Center of Time 🎬½ 1967 A scientist and his crew are hurled into a time trap when a giant reactor explodes. 83m/C VHS, Beta. Lyle Waggoner, Scott Brady, Gigi Perreau, Anthony Eisley; *D:* David L. Hewitt. *ACA, GHV*

Journey to the Far Side of the Sun 🎬🎬🎬 *Doppelganger 1969* (G) Chaos erupts in the Earth's scientific community when it is discovered that a second, identical Earth is on the other side of the Sun. Both planets end up sending out identical exploratory missions. The denouement is worth the journey. 92m/C VHS, Beta, LV. *GB* Roy Thinnes, Ian Hendry, Lynn Loring, Patrick Wymark, Loni von Friedl, Herbert Lom, Ed Bishop; *D:* Robert Parrish; *W:* Gerry Anderson. *USH*

Journey to the Lost City 🎬½ *Tiger of Bengal 1958* Architect living in India happens upon a lost city, the rulership of which is being contested by two brothers. In the midst of fighting snakes and tigers, he falls in love with Paget, a beautiful dancer. This feature is actually a poorly edited hybrid of two Lang German adventures, "Der Ti-

ger von Eschnapur" and "Das Indische Grabmal" merged for U.S. release. 95m/C VHS, Beta. **FR IT GE** Debra Paget, Paul Christian, Walter Reyer, Claus Holm, Sabine Bethmann, Valeri Inkizhinov, Rene Deltgen, Luciana Paluzzi; **D:** Fritz Lang. **SNC**

Journeys from Berlin/1971 ♂♂½
1984 This is the true story about a woman who tries to find a solution to her own problems in life. **125m/C VHS, Beta. NO**

Joy House ♂♂ *The Love Cage; Les Felins* **1964** An American woman befriends a handsome French playboy when her husband sends gangsters to kill him. **98m/B VHS, Beta.** Jane Fonda, Alain Delon, Lola Albright; **D:** Rene Clement; **W:** Rene Clement. **NO**

The Joy Luck Club ♂♂♂ **1993 (R)** Universal themes in mother/daughter relationships are explored in a context Hollywood first rejected as too narrow, but which proved to be a modest sleeper hit. Tan skillfully weaves the plot of her 1989 best-seller into a screenplay which centers around young June's going-away party. Slowly the stories of four Chinese women, who meet weekly to play mah-jongg, are unraveled. Each vignette reveals life in China for the four women and the tragedies they survived, before reaching into the present to capture the relationships between the mothers and their daughters. Powerful, relevant, and moving.**CW:** Strong thematic material. **136m/C VHS, LV, Closed Caption.** Tsai Chin, Kieu Chinh, France Nuyen, Rosalind Chao, Tamlyn Tomita, Lisa Lu, Lauren Tom, Ming-Na Wen, Michael Paul Chan, Andrew McCarthy, Christopher Rich, Russell Wong, Victor Wong, Vivian Wu, Jack Ford, Diane Baker; **D:** Wayne Wang; **W:** Amy Tan, Ronald Bass. Nominations: Writers Guild of America '93: Best Adapted Screenplay. **TOU, HPH**

The Joy of Knowledge ♂½ **1965** Godard's experimental use of language and image in a plotless narrative. Berto and Leaud sit together on a bare sound stage and are exposed to popular culture through images, word association, and conversation. In French with English subtitles. Also known as "Le Gai Savoir." **96m/C VHS. FR** Juliet Berto, Jean-Pierre Leaud; **D:** Jean-Luc Godard; **W:** Jean-Luc Godard. **FCT**

Joy of Living ♂♂♂ **1938** Vintage screwball farce about a randy playboy trying to win over a pragmatic songstress. ♪You Couldn't Be Cuter; A Heavenly Party; What's Good About Goodnight; Just Let Me Look At You. **90m/B VHS, Beta, LV.** Irene Dunne, Douglas Fairbanks Jr., Alice Brady, Guy Kibbee, Jean Dixon, Eric Blore, Lucille Ball, Warren Hymer, Billy Gilbert, Frank Milan; **D:** Tay Garnett; **M:** Jerome Kern, Dorothy Fields. **TTC**

Joy of Sex ♂ **1984 (R)** An undercover narcotics agent is sent to Southern California's Richard M. Nixon High School to investigate the school's extracurricular activities. Typical teen sex flick; no relation to the book. **93m/C VHS, Beta.** Cameron Dye, Michelle Meyrink, Colleen Camp, Christopher Lloyd, Ernie Hudson, Lisa Langlois; **D:** Martha Coolidge; **W:** Kathleen Rowell. **PAR**

Joy Ride to Nowhere ♂ **1978 (PG)** Two young women steal a Cadillac with two million dollars in the trunk and ride away with the owner hot on their tail. **86m/C VHS, Beta.** Leslie Ackerman, Sandy Serrano, Len Lesser, Mel Welles, Ron Ross, Speed Stearns. **NO**

Joy Sticks woof! **1983 (R)** Joy sticks in question are down at the arcade. Businessman wants to shut down local video game industry. Inhabitants just say no. **88m/C VHS, Beta, LV.** Joe Don Baker, Leif Green, Jim Greenleaf, Scott McGinnis, Jonathan Gries; **D:** Greydon Clark. **VES**

Joyful Laughter ♂♂ **1954** The dreary life of an Italian movie bit player draws strength from Magnani's powerful emotions as she repeatedly comes near to success only to find disappointment. Set in Rome. With English subtitles. **106m/C VHS. IT D:** Mario Monicelli. **FST**

Joyless Street ♂♂♂½ *Street of Sorrow; Die Freudlose Gasse* **1925** Silent film focuses on the dismal life of the middle class in Austria during an economic crisis. Lovely piano score accompanies the film. **96m/B VHS, Beta, LV. GE** Greta Garbo, Werner Krauss, Asta Nielson, Jaro Furth, Loni Nest, Max Kohlhase, Silva Torf, Karl Ettlinger, Ilka Gruning, Agnes Esterhazy, Alexander Musky, Valeska Gert; **D:** G.W. Pabst; **W:** Willi Haas; **C:** Guido Seeber, Curt Oertel, Walter Robert Lach. **VYY, MRV, FST**

Joyride ♂½ **1977 (R)** Mistreated by a union official, three friends steal a car for a joy ride and plummet into a life of crime. **91m/C VHS, Beta.** Desi Arnaz Jr., Robert Carradine, Melanie Griffith, Anne Lockhart; **D:** Joseph Ruben. **LIV, VES**

Ju Dou ♂♂♂♂ **1990 (PG-13)** Breath-taking story of an aging factory owner in search of an heir. He takes a third wife, but she finds caring in the arms of another man, when her husband's brutality proves too much. Beautiful color cinematography, excellent acting and epic story. Oscar nominee for Best Foreign Film. In Chinese with English subtitles. **98m/C VHS, LV. CH** Gong Li, Li Bao-Tian, Li Wei, Zhang Yi; **D:** Zhang Yimou; **C:** Gu Changwei. Nominations: Academy Awards '90: Best Foreign Language Film. **LIV, BTV**

Juarez ♂♂ **1939** A revolutionary leader overthrows the Mexican government and then becomes President of the country. Based on the true story of Benito Pablo Juarez. **132m/B VHS, Beta.** Paul Muni, John Garfield, Bette Davis, Claude Rains, Gale Sondergaard, Charles Halton; **D:** William Dieterle; **C:** Gaetano Antonio "Tony" Gaudio. Nominations: Academy Awards '39: Best Black and White Cinematography, Best Supporting Actor (Aherne). **MGM, FCT**

Jubal ♂♂ **1956** A rancher (Borgnine) seeks advice from a cowhand (Ford) about pleasing his wife, but another cowhand (Steiger) implies that Ford is "advising" Borgnine's wife, as well. A western take on "Othello." **101m/C VHS, Beta, LV.** Glenn Ford, Rod Steiger, Ernest Borgnine, Felicia Farr, Charles Bronson, Valerie French, Noah Beery Jr.; **D:** Delmer Daves. **IME**

Jubilee Trail ♂♂½ **1954** Wagon trail western follows the lives of a group of pioneers from New Orleans to California. A woman goes through a marriage, a baby, and her husband's death. Ralston has some good tunes in this lush picture. **103m/C VHS.** Vera Ralston, Joan Leslie, Forrest Tucker, John Russell, Ray Middleton, Pat O'Brien; **D:** Joseph Kane. **REP**

Jud ♂½ **1971 (PG)** Society's refusal to understand a young soldier returning from the Vietnam conflict leads to violence and tragedy. Jennings' first film; music by Phillips of Creedence Clearwater Revival. **80m/C VHS, Beta.** Joseph Kaufmann, Robert Deman, Alix Wyeth, Norman Burton, Claudia Jennings, Maurice Sherbanee, Vic Dunlop, Bonnie Bittner; **D:** Gunther Collins; **M:** Stu Phillips. **PSM**

Jud Suess ♂♂♂ **1940** Classic, scandalous Nazi anti-Semitic tract about a Jew who rises to power under the duchy of Wuerttemberg by stepping on, abusing, and raping Aryans. A film that caused riots at its screenings and tragedy for its cast and crew, and the Third Reich's most notorious fictional expression of policy. In German with English subtitles. **100m/B VHS, Beta. GE** Ferdinand Marian, Werner Krauss, Heinrich George, Kristina Soderbaum, Eugene Klopfer; **D:** Veit Harlan. **NOS, VCD, IHF**

The Judas Project: The Ultimate Encounter ♂½ **1994 (PG-13)** Religious fantasy finds Jesse battling corruption and pseudo-religious figures in a fight to save a violent and decaying world. But Jesse's destroyed by his own disciple, Jude. Sound familiar? (There's even a cruxifixion scene.) **98m/C VHS.** John O'Bannion, Ramy Zada, Richard Herd; **D:** James H. Barden; **C:** Bryan England. **HMD**

Jude ♂♂♂ *Jude the Obscure* **1996 (R)** Engrossing retelling of Thomas Hardy's depressing 1896 novel "Jude the Obscure," set in his fictional Wessex. Country stonemason Jude (Eccleston)

hopes to improve his impoverished lot in life by becoming a student at Christminster University. But first he's distracted into an unwise marriage with lively Arabella (Griffiths), who soon leaves him, and then into an ill-fated romance with his capricious cousin Sue Brideshead (Winslet). Class and societal barriers prove impossible for the couple to overcome and lead to a shocking tragedy. Hardy's book was so badly received by critics that he never wrote another novel and stuck to poetry for the rest of his life.**CW:** Strong sexuality and intense depictions of death and birth. **123m/C VHS. GB** Christopher Eccleston, Kate Winslet, Liam Cunningham, Rachel Griffiths; **D:** Michael Winterbottom; **W:** Hossein Amini; **C:** Eduardo Serra; **M:** Adrian Johnston. **PGV**

Jude the Obscure ♂♂½ **1971** Thomas Hardy's last novel is a tragic, bleak story of mismatched lovers and blighted ambitions. Jude is a poor stonemason whose dream is to get a proper education and marry his beloved cousin. Failing to get into Oxford he is seduced by a farm girl, whom he marries and fathers a child by (a gnome-like creature named "Father Time"). Meanwhile, his cousin marries a schoolteacher who disgusts her. Finally, the two thwarted lovers marry, only to find themselves living in poverty and hopelessness. After this novel (said to be Hardy's favorite), he devoted the rest of his long life to poetry. On three cassettes. **262m/C VHS. GB** Robert Powell, Daphne Heard, Alex Marshall, John Franklyn-Robbins, Fiona Walker; **D:** Hugh David; **W:** Harry Green. **FOX, FCT, VCO**

Judex ♂♂½ **1964** Judex, a sensitive cloaked hero-avenger, fights master criminal gangs. In French with English subtitles. Remake of the silent French serial. **103m/B VHS, Beta. FR IT** Channing Pollock, Francine Berge, Jacques Jouanneau; **D:** Georges Franju; **M:** Maurice Jarre. **NOS, SNC, HHT**

The Judge ♂½ **1949** A courtroom crime-drama about the consequences of infidelity. A lawyer sends an acquitted hit man to kill his wife and her lover. Things go amiss and the lawyer winds up dead. **69m/B VHS.** Milburn Stone, Katherine DeMille, Paul Guilfoyle, Jonathan Hale; **D:** Elmer Clifton. **SNC**

Judge & Jury ♂½ **1996 (R)** Convicted killer Joseph Miller (Keith) dies in the electric chair but then manages to return from the dead to get revenge. So how do you kill someone who's already dead? Well, Michael Silvano (Kove) will have to find a way to send Miller back where he belongs.**CW:** Continuous strong violence and language. **98m/C VHS, LV.** David Keith, Martin Kove, Laura Johnson, Thomas Ian Nichols, Paul Koslo; **D:** John Eyres; **W:** John Eyres, John Cianetti, Amanda I. Kirpaul; **C:** Bob Paone; **M:** Johnathon Flood. **APX**

The Judge and the Assassin ♂♂♂½ *Le Juge et L'assassin* **1975** Intriguing courtroom drama. A prejudiced judge has his values challenged when he must decide if a child-killer is insane or not. The relationship that develops between the judge and the killer is the film's focus. Excellent direction by Tavernier. In French with English subtitles. **130m/C VHS, Beta. FR** Philippe Noiret, Michel Galabru, Isabelle Huppert, Jean-Claude Brialy; **D:** Bertrand Tavernier; **W:** Bertrand Tavernier. Cesar Awards '77: Best Writing, Best Score. **CVC, IME, TPV**

Judge Dredd ♂½ **1995 (R)** Futuristic lawman Dredd (Stallone), who acts as cop, judge, jury, and executioner, is framed for murder by his "brother" Rico (Assante), a renegade misfit. With the help of a female Judge (Lane) and an ex-con (Schneider), Dredd fights to clear his name and save the people of Mega City One. Big names, big budget—big disappointment. Dialogue makes "Rambo" sound like Shakespeare, and the choppy, convoluted plot doesn't help. Schneider provides a rare bright spot while acting circles around Sly, who hoped (in vain) that the project would provide him with another profitable

action franchise. The source comic book has been a cult favorite in England for 20 years. *CW:* Continuous violent action. **96m/C VHS, LV, Closed Caption.** Sylvester Stallone, Armand Assante, Diane Lane, Rob Schneider, Joan Chen, Juergen Prochnow, Max von Sydow; *D:* Danny Cannon; *W:* Steven E. de Souza, Michael De Luca, William Wisher; *M:* Alan Silvestri. Nominations: Golden Raspberry Awards '95: Worst Actor (Stallone). *TOU*

Judge Horton and the Scottsboro Boys 🐾🐾½ 1976 A courtroom drama focusing on a famous 1931 trial. A courageous judge must battle the South in the case of nine black men charged with gang-raping two white women. Made for television. **100m/C VHS.** Arthur Hill, Vera Miles, Ken Kercheval, Suzanne Lederer, Tom Ligon; *D:* Fielder Cook. *LIV*

Judge Priest 🐾🐾🐾 1934 Small-town judge in the old South stirs up the place with stinging humor and common-sense observances as he tangles with prejudices and civil injustices. Funny, warm slice-of-life is occasionally defeated by racist characterizations. Ford remade it later as "The Sun Shines Bright." Taken from the Irvin S. Cobb stories. **80m/B VHS, Beta.** Will Rogers, Stepin Fetchit, Anita Louise, Henry B. Walthall; *D:* John Ford. *NOS, MRV, PSM*

Judge Roy Bean 1955 This western series set in Langtry, Texas in 1870 starred Buchanan as the self-appointed "Law West of the Pecos," trying to maintain order in a lawless territory. Two episodes per tape. **55m/B VHS, Beta.** Edgar Buchanan, Jack Beutel, Jackie Loughery. *MOV, MVC*

The Judge Steps Out 🐾🐾½ 1949 Pleasant, light comedy about a hen-pecked, Bostonian judge who decides he's had enough and heads for balmy California. There he finds a job in a restaurant and, more importantly, a sympathetic friend in its female owner. He soon finds himself falling for the woman, and realizes he faces an important decision. **91m/B VHS.** Alexander Knox, Ann Sothern, George Tobias, Sharyn Moffett, Florence Bates, Frieda Inescort, Myrna Dell, Ian Wolfe, H.B. Warner; *D:* Boris Ingster. *TTC*

Judgment 🐾🐾🐾 1990 (PG-13) A devout Catholic couple are shocked to learn that their young son has been molested by the popular priest of their small Louisiana parish. When they find out their son is not the first victim, and other families have been coerced into silence, they vow to fight back. Tasteful treatment of a real court case. Made for cable. **89m/C VHS, Closed Caption.** Keith Carradine, Blythe Danner, Jack Warden, David Strathairn, Bob Gunton, Mitchell Ryan, Michael Faustino; *D:* Tom Topor; *W:* Tom Topor. *HBO*

Judgment at Nuremberg 🐾🐾🐾🐾 1961 It's 1948 and a group of high-level Nazis are on trial for war crimes. Chief Justice Tracy must resist political pressures as he presides over the trials. Excellent performances throughout, especially by Dietrich and Garland. Considers to what extent an individual may be held accountable for actions committed under orders of a superior officer. Consuming account of the Holocaust and WWII; deeply moving and powerful. Based on a "Playhouse 90" television program. **178m/B VHS, Beta, LV.** Spencer Tracy, Burt Lancaster, Richard Widmark, Montgomery Clift, Maximilian Schell, Judy Garland, Marlene Dietrich, William Shatner; *D:* Stanley Kramer; *W:* Abby Mann; *C:* Ernest Laszlo; *M:* Ernest Gold. Academy Awards '61: Best Actor (Schell), Best Adapted Screenplay; Golden Globe Awards '62: Best Actor—Drama (Schell), Best Director (Kramer); National Board of Review Awards '61: 10 Best Films of the Year; New York Film Critics Awards '61: Best Actor (Schell), Best Screenplay; Nominations: Academy Awards '61: Best Actor (Tracy), Best Art Direction/Set Decoration (B & W), Best Black and White Cinematography, Best Costume Design (B & W), Best Director (Kramer), Best Film Editing, Best Picture, Best Supporting Actor (Clift), Best Supporting Actress (Garland). *MGM, FOX, BTV*

Judgment Day 🐾 1988 (PG-13) Four college buddies pick the wrong New England town for their vacation. It seems that the town made a deal with the Devil in 1689 to save themselves

from the plague, and now the Dark Master is here to collect. **93m/C VHS, Beta.** Kenneth McLeod, David Anthony Smith, Monte Markham, Gloria Hayes, Peter Mark Richman, Cesar Romero; *D:* Ferde Grofe Jr. *NO*

Judgment in Berlin 🐾🐾½ *Escape to Freedom* 1988 (PG) East German family hijacks a U.S. airliner into West Germany, and then must stand trial in Berlin before a troubled American judge. Based on a true 1978 incident and the book by Herbert J. Stern. **92m/C VHS, Beta, LV.** Martin Sheen, Sam Wanamaker, Max Gail, Sean Penn, Heinz Hoenig, Carl Lumbly, Max Volkert Martens, Harris Yulin, Jutta Speidel, Juerger Hemrich; *D:* Leonard Penn; *W:* Joshua Sinclair; *M:* Peter Goldfoot. *COL*

Judgment Night 🐾🐾 1993 (R) Four macho buddies on their way to a boxing match detour a highway traffic jam via surface streets and find themselves witnesses to a murder. The rest of their guys-night-out is spent trying to escape a gloomy ghetto and determined killer (played convincingly by Leary). All of the action takes place after dark on the streets and in the sewers and, subsequently, the scenes are extremely dark with only a burnt orange lighting. Lots of action and a little oomph. Based on a story by Lewis Colick and Jere Cunningham. *CW:* Language and strong violence and brutality. **109m/C VHS, LV, Closed Caption.** Emilio Estevez, Cuba Gooding Jr., Stephen Dorff, Denis Leary, Jeremy Piven, Peter Greene; *D:* Stephen Hopkins; *W:* Lewis Colick; *M:* Alan Silvestri. *USH*

Judicial Consent 🐾🐾½ 1994 Gwen Warwick (Bedelia) is an accomplished criminal court judge with a bland husband (Patton) and a lot of unfulfilled desires. At least one desire is taken care of when Gwen succumbs to the charms of handsome law clerk Martin (Wirth). Then her colleague Charles (Coleman) is murdered and all the evidence points to Gwen. She knows she's been set up but can Gwen prove her innocence? Familiar plot, good performances although Patton gets stuck in an underwritten role. **101m/C VHS.** Bonnie Bedelia, Dabney Coleman, Billy Wirth, Will Patton, Lisa Blount; *D:* William Bindley; *W:* William Bindley; *M:* Christopher Young. *AVE*

Judith of Bethulia 🐾🐾🐾 1914 A young widow uses her charm and wits to save her city from attack by the Assyrians. Based on the Apocrypha, this is the last film Griffith directed for Biograph. It was re-released as "Her Condoned Sin" in 1971, including two reels of Griffith's outtakes. **65m/B VHS, LV.** Blanche Sweet, Henry B. Walthall, Mae Marsh, Robert "Bobbie" Harron, Lillian Gish, Dorothy Gish, Kate Bruce, Harry Carey Sr.; *D:* D.W. Griffith; *W:* D.W. Griffith. *GPV, NOS, VYY*

Juggernaut 🐾½ 1937 Not the classic disaster film of the '70s. A young woman hires a sinister doctor (Karloff) to murder her wealthy husband. The doctor, who happens to be insane, does away with the husband and then goes on a poisoning spree. Seems to drag on forever. **64m/B VHS, Beta, Closed Caption.** Boris Karloff, Mona Goya, Arthur Margetson. *NOS, SNC, VYY*

Juggernaut 🐾🐾🐾 1974 (PG-13) Well-done drama about a doomed luxury liner. A madman plants bombs aboard a cruise ship and mocks the crew about his plan over the wireless. The countdown ensues, while the bomb experts struggle to find the explosives. Suspenseful with good direction. **109m/C VHS.** GB Richard Harris, Omar Sharif, David Hemmings, Anthony Hopkins, Shirley Knight, Ian Holm, Roy Kinnear, Freddie Jones; *D:* Richard Lester. *MGM, FOX*

The Juggler of Notre Dame 🐾🐾½ 1984 A hobo and a street juggler embark on an unusual journey that will change the lives of the people they meet. Based on a medieval folktale about the special gift given to the Virgin Mary on Christmas morning. **110m/C VHS, Beta.** Carl Carlson, Patrick Collins, Melinda Dillon, Merlin Olsen, Gene Roche. *PAU*

Juice 🐾🐾½ 1992 (R) Day-to-day street life of four Harlem youths as they try to earn respect ("juice") in their neighborhood. Q, an aspiring deejay, is talked into a robbery by his friends but everything turns for the worse when one of the others, Bishop, gets hold of a gun. The gritty look and feel of the drama comes naturally to Dickerson in his directorial debut. Prior to his first film, Dickerson served as cinematographer for Spike Lee's "Do the Right Thing" and "Jungle Fever." *CW:* Some violence and strong language. **95m/C VHS, Closed Caption.** Omar Epps, Jermaine Hopkins, Tupac Shakur, Khalil Kain, Cindy Herron, Vincent Laresca, Samuel L. Jackson; *D:* Ernest R. Dickerson; *W:* Gerard Brown, Ernest R. Dickerson; *C:* Larry Banks. *PAR*

Juke Joint 🐾½ 1947 "Amos 'n Andy" star Spencer Williams acted in and directed this tale of two men who arrive in Hollywood with only 25 cents between them. Features an all-black cast and musical numbers. **60m/B VHS, Beta.** Spencer Williams Jr., Judy Jones, Mantan Moreland; *D:* Spencer Williams Jr. *NOS, VCN, DVT*

Jules and Jim 🐾🐾🐾🐾 *Jules et Jim* 1962 Beautiful film with perfect casting, particularly Moreau. Spanning from 1912 to 1932, it is the story of a friendship between two men and their twenty-year love for the same woman. Werner is the shy German Jew and Serre the fun-loving Frenchman, who meet as students. The two men discover and woo the bohemian, destructive Moreau, although it is Werner she marries. After WWI, the friends are reunited but the marriage of Moreau and Werner is in trouble and she has an affair with Serre, which leads to tragedy for all three. Adapted from the novel by Henri-Pierre Roche. In French with English subtitles. **104m/B VHS, Beta, LV.** FR Jeanne Moreau, Oskar Werner, Henri Serre, Marie DuBois, Vanna Urbino; *D:* Francois Truffaut; *W:* Jean Gruault; *M:* Georges Delerue. *HMV, APD, FOX*

Julia 🐾🐾🐾½ 1977 (PG) The story recounted in Lillian Hellman's fictional memoir "Pentimento." Fonda plays Hellman as she risks her life smuggling money into Germany during WWII for the sake of Julia, her beloved childhood friend (Redgrave), who is working in the Resistance. All cast members shine in their performances; watch for Streep in her screen debut. **118m/C VHS, Beta, LV.** Jane Fonda, Jason Robards Jr., Vanessa Redgrave, Maximilian Schell, Hal Holbrook, Rosemary Murphy, Meryl Streep, Lisa Pelikan; *D:* Fred Zinnemann; *W:* Alvin Sargent; *M:* Georges Delerue. Academy Awards '77: Best Adapted Screenplay, Best Supporting Actor (Robards), Best Supporting Actress (Redgrave); British Academy Awards '78: Best Actress (Fonda), Best Film, Best Screenplay, Best Supporting Actress (Redgrave); Golden Globe Awards '78: Best Actress—Drama (Fonda), Best Supporting Actress (Redgrave); Los Angeles Film Critics Association Awards '77: Best Cinematography, Best Supporting Actor (Robards), Best Supporting Actress (Redgrave); National Board of Review Awards '77: 10 Best Films of the Year; New York Film Critics Awards '77: Best Supporting Actor (Schell); Writers Guild of America '77: Best Adapted Screenplay; Nominations: Academy Awards '77: Best Actress (Fonda), Best Cinematography, Best Costume Design, Best Director (Zinnemann), Best Film Editing, Best Picture, Best Supporting Actor (Schell), Best Original Score. *FOX, BTV*

Julia and Julia 🐾🐾½ 1987 (R) A beautiful American woman in Trieste is tossed between two seemingly parallel dimensions, one in which her husband died six years earlier in a car crash, and the other in which he didn't. A purposefully obscure Italian-made psychological thriller, filmed in high-definition video and then transferred to film stock, it has a very different look and feel from other films of the genre. Intriguing and engaging most of the time, slow moving and confusing some of the time, it ultimately challenges but fails adequately to reward the viewer. **98m/C VHS, Beta, LV, Closed Caption.** Kathleen Turner, Sting, Gabriel Byrne, Gabriele Ferzetti, Angela Goodwin; *D:* Peter Del Monte; *W:* Peter Del Monte; *C:* Giuseppe Rotunno; *M:* Maurice Jarre. *FOX*

Julia Has Two Lovers �△△ 1991 (R) Minimalist comedy-drama about a woman torn between two men—her dull fiance and a mysterious phone caller. Mostly a long phone conversation; don't expect blistering action.**CW:** Sexual dialogue and sensuality. 87m/C **VHS.** Daphna Kastner, David Duchovny, David Charles; **D:** Bashar Shbib. HMD

Julia Misbehaves �△△△ 1948 Charming comedy that has Garson returning to ex-husband Pidgeon and daughter Taylor after an 18-year absence. Taylor is about to be married at a chateau in France and wants Garson to be there. While traveling to France from England, Garson encounters a bunch of colorful circus characters who are taking their act to Paris. Wonderful slapstick scenes give the stars a chance to have some real fun. Based on the novel "The Nutmeg Tree" by Margery Sharp. 99m/B **VHS.** Greer Garson, Walter Pidgeon, Peter Lawford, Cesar Romero, Elizabeth Taylor, Lucile Watson, Nigel Bruce, Mary Boland, Reginald Owen, Veda Ann Borg, Joi Lansing; **D:** Jack Conway. MGM

Juliet of the Spirits �△△△ Giulietta Degli Spiriti 1965 Fellini uses the sparse story of a woman (Fellini's real-life wife) deliberating over her husband's possible infidelity to create a wild, often senseless surrealistic film. With a highly symbolic internal logic and complex imagery, Fellini's fantasy ostensibly elucidates the inner life of a modern woman. In Italian with English subtitles. 142m/C **VHS, Beta, LV.** IT Giulietta Masina, Valentina Cortese, Sylva Koscina, Mario Pisu; **D:** Federico Fellini; **W:** Federico Fellini, Tullio Pinelli, Ennio Flaiano, Brunello Rondi; **M:** Nino Rota. National Board of Review Awards '65: 5 Best Foreign Films of the Year; New York Film Critics Awards '65: Best Foreign Film; Nominations: Academy Awards '66: Best Art Direction/Set Decoration (Color), Best Costume Design (Color). VYY, MRV, VDM

Julius Caesar �△△△½ 1953 All-star version of the Shakespearean tragedy, heavily acclaimed and deservedly so. Working directly from the original Shakespeare, director Mankiewicz produced a lifelike, yet poetic production. 121m/B **VHS, Beta, LV.** James Mason, Marlon Brando, John Gielgud, Greer Garson, Deborah Kerr, Louis Calhern, Edmond O'Brien, George Macready, John Hoyt, Michael Pate; **D:** Joseph L. Mankiewicz; **W:** Joseph L. Mankiewicz; **C:** Joseph Ruttenberg; **M:** Miklos Rozsa. Academy Awards '53: Best Art Direction/Set Decoration (B & W); British Academy Awards '53: Best Actor (Brando), Best Actor (Gielgud); National Board of Review Awards '53: 10 Best Films of the Year, Best Actor (Mason); Nominations: Academy Awards '53: Best Actor (Brando), Best Black and White Cinematography, Best Picture, Original Dramatic/Comedy Score. MGM

Julius Caesar �△△ 1970 Subpar adaptation of the Shakespeare play about political greed and corruption within the Roman Empire. 116m/C **VHS, Beta.** GB Charlton Heston, John Gielgud, Jason Robards Jr., Richard Chamberlain, Robert Vaughn, Diana Rigg; **D:** Stuart Burge. NOS, REP, APD

July Group �△½ 197? A Quaker family's peaceful existence is threatened when kidnappers invade their home and hold them for ransom. 75m/C **VHS, Beta.** Nicholas Campbell, Calvin Butler, Maury Chaykin. TWE

Jumanji ✄✄½ 1995 (PG) For the past 26 years Alan Parish (Williams) has been stuck in the netherworld of Jumanji, a jungle-themed board game that sucks players into its alternate universe. When unsuspecting youngsters Judy (Dunst) and Peter (Pierce) happen upon the game and begin to play, they release Williams and a jungle full of rampaging beasts from the game and into the present. Loosely based on Chris Van Allsburg's children's book, the film version relies too heavily on cutting-edge special effects to make up for a thin story. Many of the creatures and effects are utterly too bizarre and unsettling for younger audiences. With a $65 million pricetag, Jumanji is definitely a roll of the dice. 104m/C **VHS, LV, Closed Caption, DVD.** Robin Williams, Kirsten Dunst, Bonnie Hunt, Bradley Michael Pierce, Bebe Neuwirth, Jonathan Hyde, David Alan Grier; **D:** Joe John-ston; **W:** Jonathan Hensleigh; **C:** Thomas Ackerman; **M:** James Horner. COL

The Jumper ✄✄½ Der Toderspringer 1985 An abstract, theatrical narrative about a cast of tragicomic characters floundering through their meaningless lives. In German with English subtitles. 90m/C **VHS, Beta.** GE **D:** Benno Trachtmann. FCT, VCD, GLV

Jumpin' at the Boneyard ✄✄ 1992 (R) Gritty family drama about the trials of two dispossessed brothers, set on the streets of New York. Deeply depressed, out-of-work, divorced Manny hates his recently deceased father, adores his mother, and is estranged from his younger brother, Danny. Danny is a scared crack addict who's supported by a hooker/girlfriend. The two brothers reunite for a trip into their scarred past when Danny tries to rob his brother's apartment to get dope money. Manny starts to believe that the only way to redeem his own life is to get his brother into a rehab program. Good acting helps to overcome some script weaknesses but this is one depressing movie. 107m/C **VHS, LV.** Tim Roth, Alexis Arquette, Danitra Vance, Samuel L. Jackson, Kathleen Chalfant, Luis Guzman; **D:** Jeff Stanzler; **W:** Jeff Stanzler. FXV

Jumpin' Jack Flash ✄✄½ 1986 (R) A bank worker is humorously embroiled in international espionage when her computer terminal picks up distress signals from a British agent in Russia. Marshall's directing debut. Good performances from a fun cast and a particularly energetic effort by Goldberg are held back by an average and predictable script. 98m/C **VHS, Beta, LV, Closed Caption.** Whoopi Goldberg, Stephen Collins, Carol Kane, Annie Potts, Jonathan Pryce, James Belushi, Jon Lovitz, John Wood; **Cameos:** Michael McKean, Tracey Ullman, Roscoe Lee Browne, Sara Botsford, Jeroen Krabbe, Phil Hartman, Tracy Reiner, Paxton Whitehead, Jamey Sheridan, Garry Marshall, Peter Michael Goetz; **D:** Penny Marshall; **W:** David Franzoni; **C:** Jan De Bont; **M:** Thomas Newman. FOX, OM

Jumping Jacks ✄✄ 1952 Martin and Lewis are a couple of nightclub performers who wind up in the paratroop corps instead of performing their act for the soldiers. Martin gets to sing and Lewis gets to parachute into enemy territory and capture a general. 96m/B **VHS, LV, Closed Caption.** Dean Martin, Jerry Lewis, Mona Freeman, Don DeFore, Robert Strauss, Ray Teal; **D:** Norman Taurog; **C:** Daniel F. Fapp. PAR

Junction 88 ✄ 1940 Early all-black musical chock full of great dancing and hot music. 60m/B **VHS, Beta.** Noble Sissle, Bob Howard. NOS, DVT

June Bride ✄✄✄ 1948 Fast-paced and entertaining comedy in which Davis and Montgomery are teamed up as magazine writers. A hilarious battle of the sexes erupts as they're sent to Indiana to do a feature story on June brides. Look for Debbie Reynolds in her film debut. 97m/B **VHS, Closed Caption.** Bette Davis, Robert Montgomery, Fay Bainter, Betty Lynn, Tom Tully, Barbara Bates, Jerome Cowan, Mary Wickes; **D:** Bretaigne Windust; **W:** Ranald MacDougall. MGM

June Night ✄✄ Juninatten 1940 A woman who was victimized by a shooting incident cannot escape the public eye due to her former promiscuous behavior. In Swedish with English subtitles. 90m/C **VHS, Beta, LV.** SW Ingrid Bergman, Marianne Lofgren, Gunnar Sjoberg, Olaf Widgren; **D:** Per Lindberg. WAC, TPV, LUM

Jungle ✄ 1952 A princess and an American adventurer lead an expedition into the Indian wilds to discover the source of recent elephant attacks. 74m/B **VHS, Beta, LV.** Rod Cameron, Cesar Romero, Marie Windsor; **D:** William (Lester Williams) Berke; **C:** Clyde De Vinna. NO

Jungle Assault ✄ 1989 Two Vietnam vets with nothing left to lose are called back into the bloodiest action of their lives. Their assignment is to locate and destroy a terrorist base and bring back an American general's brainwashed daughter. 86m/C **VHS, Beta.** William Smith, Ted Prior, William Zipp; **D:** David A. Prior. AIP

The Jungle Book ✄✄ Rudyard Kipling's Jungle Book 1942 A lavish version of Rudyard Kipling's stories about Mowgli, the boy raised by wolves in the jungles of India. 109m/C **VHS, LV.** Sabu, Joseph Calleia, Rosemary DeCamp, Ralph Byrd, John Qualen; **D:** Zoltan Korda; **C:** Lee Garmes; **M:** Miklos Rozsa. Nominations: Academy Awards '42: Best Color Cinematography, Original Dramatic/Comedy Score. CNG, MRV, REP

The Jungle Book ✄✄✄ 1967 Based on Kipling's classic, a young boy raised by wolves must choose between his jungle friends and human "civilization." Along the way he meets a variety of jungle characters including zany King Louie, kind-hearted Baloo, wise Bagherra and the evil Shere Khan. Great, classic songs including "Trust in Me," "I Wanna Be Like You," and Oscar-nominated "Bare Necessities." Last Disney feature overseen by Uncle Walt himself and a must for kids of all ages. 78m/C **VHS, Beta, LV, Closed Caption.** **D:** Wolfgang Reitherman; **V:** Phil Harris, Sebastian Cabot, Louis Prima, George Sanders, Sterling Holloway, J. Pat O'Malley, Verna Felton, Darlene Carr. Nominations: Academy Awards '67: Best Song ("The Bare Necessities"). DIS, TOU, FCT

Jungle Bride ✄✄½ 1933 Three people are shipwrecked and one of them is a suspected murderer. 66m/B **VHS, Beta, LV.** Anita Page, Charles Starrett. SNC, NOS, VYY

Jungle Drums of Africa U-238 and the Witch Doctor 1953 Jungle adventures abound as Moore and Coates encounter lions, wind tunnels, voodoo and enemy agents in deepest Africa. A 12-episode serial re-edited onto two cassettes. 167m/B **VHS.** Clayton Moore, Phyllis Coates, Roy Glenn, John Cason; **D:** Fred Brannon. REP, MLB

Jungle Fever ✄✄✄ 1991 (R) Married black architect's affair with his white secretary provides the backdrop for a cold look at interracial love. Focuses more on the discomfort of friends and families than with the intense world created by the lovers for themselves. Provides the quota of humor and fresh insight we expect from Lee, but none of the joyous sexuality experienced by the lovers in "She's Gotta Have It." In fact, Lee tells viewers that interracial love is unnatural, never more than skin deep, never more than a blind obsession with the allure of the opposite race. Very fine cast but if you don't agree with Lee, a real disappointment as well. **CW:** Violence and drug content and sensuality. 131m/C **VHS, Beta, LV, Closed Caption.** Wesley Snipes, Annabella Sciorra, John Turturro, Samuel L. Jackson, Ossie Davis, Ruby Dee, Lonette McKee, Anthony Quinn, Spike Lee, Halle Berry, Tyra Ferrell, Veronica Webb, Frank Vincent, Tim Robbins, Brad Dourif; **D:** Spike Lee; **W:** Spike Lee; **M:** Terence Blanchard. National Board of Review Awards '91: 10 Best Films of the Year; New York Film Critics Awards '91: Best Supporting Actor (Jackson). USH, CCB, FCT

Jungle Goddess ✄½ 1949 Two mercenaries set out for the reward offered for finding a wealthy heiress last seen in the jungles of Africa. 61m/B **VHS, Beta, LV.** George Reeves, Wanda McKay, Ralph Byrd, Armida; **D:** Lewis D. Collins. NO

Jungle Heat ✄½ Dance of the Dwarfs 1984 (PG) While searching for a pygmy tribe, an anthropologist and her pilot run into a pack of anthropoid mutants. 93m/C **VHS, Beta.** Peter Fonda, Deborah Raffin; **D:** Gus Trikonis. TWE

Jungle Hell ✄✄ 1955 Sabu comes to the rescue of an Indian tribe being harassed by flying saucers, death rays and radioactive debris. ?m/B **VHS, Beta.** Sabu, David Bruce, George E. Stone, K.T. Stevens; **D:** Norman A. Cerf. SNC

Jungle Inferno ✄ 197? Nature boy, a fugitive from the government, fights lions, tigers and pursuing feds in this story of escape and survival. 90m/C **VHS, Beta.** Brad Harris. NO

Jungle Master 🎬 1956 Noble British types hunt for Karzan, the jungle's number one guy, with the aid of a tribal priestess and a lovely photo-journalist. Must see for trash movie fans. **90m/C VHS, Beta.** John Kitzmiller, Simone Blondell, Edward Mann; **D:** Miles Deem. *NO*

Jungle Patrol 🎬½ 1948 In 1943 New Guinea, a squadron of entrapped fliers are confronted with a beautiful USO entertainer. Romance and show tunes follow. **72m/B VHS, Beta.** Kristine Miller, Arthur Franz, Richard Jaeckel, Ross Ford, Tommy Noonan, Gene Reynolds; **D:** Joseph M. Newman. *NO*

Jungle Raiders 🎬½ *Legenda Del Rudio Malese; Captain Yankee* 1985 **(PG-13)** An Indiana Jones-esque mercenary searches the steamy jungles of Malaysia for a valuable jewel, the Ruby of Gloom. **102m/C VHS, Beta.** Lee Van Cleef, Christopher Connelly, Marina Costa; **D:** Anthony (Antonio Margheriti) Dawson. *MGM*

Jungle Siren 🎬🎬 1942 Nazis in Africa try to foment rebellion amongst the black natives against the white residents. Crabbe and a white woman raised in the jungle set things right. **68m/B VHS, Beta.** Ann Corio, Buster Crabbe, Evelyn Wahl, Milton Kibbee; **D:** Sam Newfield. *SNC, MLB*

Jungle 2 Jungle 🎬🎬½ 1996 **(PG)** Remake of French farce released as "Little Indian, Big City," changes little of the "wild child" premise. Workaholic Wall Streeter Michael Cromwell (Allen) decides to finalize the divorce from his long-estranged doctor wife, Patricia (Williams), who happens to have been ministering to a tribe in the Amazon rain forest for many years. He gets more than the divorce when he meets the 13-year-old son, Mimi-Siku (Huntington), he never knew he had. Although the boy speaks English, he's been raised as a tribal native, which causes quite a culture shock when he returns with Michael to the jungles of Manhattan. Of course the kid's more than a match for any situation. **105m/C VHS.** Tim Allen, Sam Huntington, Martin Short, JoBeth Williams, Lolita Davidovich, David Ogden Stiers, Bob Dishy, Valerie Mahaffey, Leelee Sobieski, Luis Avalos, Frankie J. Galasso; **D:** John Pasquin; **W:** Bruce A. Evans, Raynold Gideon; **C:** Tony Pierce-Roberts; **M:** Michael Convertino. *DIS*

The Jungle Trap 🎬🎬 1954 Steve Davis thought he could escape his past living in Africa. However, when the judge who wrongly sentenced his brother to death arrives, he plots revenge. **30m/B VHS.** Ronald Reagan. *RHI*

Jungle Warriors 🎬½ 1984 **(R)** Seven fashion models are abducted by a Peruvian cocaine dealer. To escape him, they must become Jungle Warriors. **96m/C VHS, Beta.** *GE MX* Sybil Danning, Marjoe Gortner, Nina Van Pallandt, Paul Smith, John Vernon, Alex Cord, Woody Strode, Kai Wulff; **D:** Ernst R. von Theumer. *MED*

Jungleground 🎬½ 1995 **(R)** Jungleground is a urban wasteland controlled by rival gangs. Lt. Jake Cornel (Piper) gets caught in a shoot-out when a sting operation goes bad and winds up before psychotic gang leader Odin. Odin offers him one chance—Cornel's going to be hunted in Jungleground's abandoned streets and if he can escape before dawn, he gets to live.**CW:** Strong violence; language; some drug content. **90m/C VHS, LV.** Roddy Piper, Torri Higginson, Peter Williams; **D:** Don Allan; **W:** Michael Stokes. *TRI*

Junior woof! 1986 A raving, drooling lunatic cuts up girls with a chainsaw. **80m/C VHS, Beta.** Suzanne DeLaurentis, Linda Singer, Jeremy Ruthford, Michael McKeever. *PSM*

Junior 1994 **(PG-13)** Out of the way women! Schwarzenegger trades the war room for the delivery room to experience the miracle of birth. As scientists, he and DeVito take a dip in the gene pool once again to test an anti-miscarriage drug. Thompson provides the egg and some surprisingly good physical comedy as the klutzy cryogenics expert who moves into their university

digs. Every pregnancy cliche is explored as Schwarzenegger and DeVito bring the concept to term. Sorry, action fans...nothing blows up except Arnold.**CW:** Contains sex-related humor and some profanity. **109m/C VHS, LV, Closed Caption.** Arnold Schwarzenegger, Danny DeVito, Emma Thompson, Frank Langella, Pamela Reed, Judy Collins, James Eckhouse, Aida Turturro; **D:** Ivan Reitman; **W:** Kevin Wade, Chris Conrad; **M:** James Newton Howard. Nominations: Academy Awards '94: Best Song ("Look What Love Has Done"); Golden Globe Awards '95: Best Actor—Musical/Comedy (Schwarzenegger), Best Actress—Musical/Comedy (Thompson), Best Song ("Look What Love Has Done"). *USH*

Junior Bonner 🎬🎬🎬 1972 **(PG)** A rowdy modern-day western about a young drifting rodeo star who decides to raise money for his father's new ranch by challenging a formidable bull. **100m/C VHS, Beta.** Steve McQueen, Robert Preston, Ida Lupino, Ben Johnson, Joe Don Baker, Barbara Leigh; **D:** Sam Peckinpah; **C:** Lucien Ballard. *FOX*

Junior G-Men 1940 The Dead End Kids fight Fifth Columnists who are trying to sabotage America's war effort. Twelve episodes. **237m/B VHS, Beta.** Billy Halop, Huntz Hall. *VYY, VCN, NOS*

Junior G-Men of the Air 🎬½ 1942 The Dead End Kids become teen-age flyboys in this twelve-episode serial adventure. **215m/B VHS, Beta.** Billy Halop, Huntz Hall. *SNC, NOS, MED*

Junior High School 🎬🎬½ 1978 A comically, on target film detailing the romantic yearnings, petty cruelties, and claustrophobia of 8th grade existence. **60m/C VHS, Beta.** Paula Abdul. *PIC*

The Juniper Tree 🎬½ 1987 Based on a tale by the Brothers Grimm, this Icelandic curio finds sisters Margit (Bjork) and Katla (Bragadottir) fleeing across the medieval countryside after their mother is burned at the stake for witchcraft. The sisters have their own special powers, which they turn on each other when they become romantic rivals over a young widower (Flygenring). **78m/B VHS.** *IC* Bjork, Bryndis Petra Bragadottir, Vladimar Orn Flygenring; **D:** Nietzchka Keene. *RHI*

The Junkman 🎬½ 1982 **(R)** Movie maker whose new film is about to be premiered is being chased by a mysterious killer. Promoted as "the ultimate car chase film" since the production used and destroyed over 150 automobiles. From the makers of "Gone in 60 Seconds." **97m/C VHS, Beta.** H.B. Halicki, Christopher Stone, Susan Shaw, Hoyt Axton, Lynda Day George; **D:** H.B. Halicki. *TWE*

Juno and the Paycock 🎬🎬½ 1930 Perhaps if Hitchcock hadn't been so faithful to O'Casey this early effort would have been less stagey and more entertaining. In Dublin during the civil uprising, a poor family is torn apart when they receive news of an imminent fortune. Hitchcock's reported to have said that "drama is life with the dull bits left out," though here too many dull bits remain. **96m/B VHS.** Sara Allgood, Edward Chapman, John Longden, John Laurie, Maire O'Neill; **D:** Alfred Hitchcock; **W:** Alfred Hitchcock. *NOS, VEC, HHT*

Jupiter's Darling 🎬🎬 1955 This spoof of Hannibal (Keel) and Amytis (Williams) gravely misses the mark in making funny the world of the Roman Empire. Amytis has the job of distracting Hannibal from attacking the Eternal City, and does so through musical interludes and unfunny jokes. ♫ I Have A Dream; If This Be Slav'ry; I Never Trust A Woman; Hannibal's Victory March; Don't Let This Night Get Away; The Life Of An Elephant; Horatio's Narration. **96m/C LV.** Esther Williams, Howard Keel, George Sanders, Gower Champion, Marge Champion, Norma Varden, Richard Haydn, William Demarest, Douglass Dumbrille, Michael Ansara, Martha Wentworth, Chris Alcaide, William Tannen; **D:** George Sidney; **C:** Charles Rosher. *MGM*

Jupiter's Thigh 🎬🎬½ 1981 A madcap married pair of treasure-hunters honeymoon in Greece in search of an ancient statue's lost thigh. Available in French with English subtitles, or

dubbed into English. **96m/C VHS, Beta.** *FR* Annie Girardot, Philippe Noiret; **D:** Philippe de Broca. *FCT*

Jurassic Park 🎬🎬🎬½ 1993 **(PG-13)** Crichton's spine-tingling thriller translates well (but not faithfully) due to its main attraction: realistic, rampaging dinosaurs. Genetically cloned from prehistoric DNA, all is well until they escape from their pens—smarter and less predictable than expected. Contrived plot and thin characters (except Goldblum), but who cares? The true stars are the dinos, an incredible combination of models and computer animation. Violent, suspenseful, and realistic with gory attack scenes. Not for small kids, though much of the marketing is aimed at them. Spielberg knocked his own "E.T." out of first place as "JP" became the highest grossing movie of all time. Also available in a letterbox version.**CW:** Intense science fiction violence. **127m/C VHS, LV, Closed Caption.** Sam Neill, Laura Dern, Jeff Goldblum, Richard Attenborough, Bob Peck, Martin Ferrero, B.D. Wong, Joseph Mazzello, Ariana Richards, Samuel L. Jackson, Wayne Knight; **D:** Steven Spielberg; **W:** David Koepp, Michael Crichton; **C:** Dean Cundey; **M:** John Williams; **V:** Richard Kiley. Awards '93: Best Sound, Best Sound Effects Editing, Best Visual Effects; Nominations: MTV Movie Awards '94: Best Film, Best Villain (T-Rex), Best Action Sequence. *USH*

The Juror 🎬½ 1996 **(R)** Plucky single mom (Moore) ends up on the jury in the trial of a powerful mobster and draws the attention of the smooth enforcer (Baldwin) who muscles her into providing a certain verdict. The usual good-vs.-evil, family-in-danger action ensues. Despite boasting a fine cast and impressive attention to detail, flick is guilty of ludicrous situations, a mechanical plot and a dopey ending. Based on the novel by George Dawes Green.**CW:** Violence, profanity, nudity and sexual situations. **107m/C VHS, LV, 8mm, Closed Caption.** Demi Moore, Alec Baldwin, Joseph Gordon-Levitt, Anne Heche, James Gandolfini, Lindsay Crouse, Tony LoBianco, Michael Constantine, Matt Craven; **D:** Brian Gibson; **W:** Ted Tally; **C:** Jamie Anderson; **M:** James Newton Howard. Nominations: Golden Raspberry Awards '96: Worst Actress (Moore). *COL*

Jury Duty 🎬 1995 **(PG-13)** Mama's boy loser Tommy Collins (Shore) gets jury duty on a serial-killer case and tries to keep what seems to be an open-and-shut case going so he can continue to get free room and board. He falls for babe juror Monica (Carrere) and really drags the trial (and the film) out in a pathetic attempt to woo her. Shore is even more annoying and unfunny than ever. Low-rent bastardization of "Twelve Angry Men" tries to pass off lame O.J references and Shore falling out of chairs as humor. Creates reasonable doubt as to Shore's talent and movie execs' judgement.**CW:** Crude sex-related humor. **88m/C VHS, LV, Closed Caption.** Pauly Shore, Tia Carrere, Shelley Winters, Brian Doyle-Murray, Abe Vigoda, Stanley Tucci, Charles Napier; **Cameos:** Andrew Dice Clay; **D:** John Fortenberry; **W:** Barbara Williams, Fax Bahr. Golden Raspberry Awards '95: Worst Actor (Shore). *COL*

Just a Gigolo 🎬🎬½ 1979 **(R)** Bowie stars in this unusual melodrama about a Prussian war vet turned male prostitute. He spends most of his time working for the sexiest of women. Splendid cast, but a bit incoherent. **105m/C VHS, LV.** *GE* David Bowie, Sydne Rome, Kim Novak, David Hemmings, Maria Schell, Curt Jurgens, Marlene Dietrich; **D:** David Hemmings. *MOV, LUM*

Just Another Girl on the I.R.T. 🎬🎬½ 1993 **(R)** Double debut from two African American women, writer/director Harris, and actress Johnson, captures the sass and wit of a girl from the projects. Seventeen-year-old Chantal has a plan for her life and challenges authority with assurance, even after an unexpected pregnancy puts a twist into her plan. Strong initial statement tends to become weak and cloudy as Chantal loses her focus. This doesn't dismiss the remarkable realism and raw talent portrayed in a picture filmed in just seventeen days for $130,000. Winner of a special jury prize at the Sundance Film Festival. *CW:* Language and sexuality. **96m/C VHS, LV.** Ariyan Johnson, Kevin Thigpen, Ebony Jerido, Jerard Washington, Chequita Jackson, William Badget; *D:* Leslie Harris; *W:* Leslie Harris; *C:* Richard Conners. Sundance Film Festival '93: Special Jury Prize; Nominations: Independent Spirit Awards '94: Best Actress (Johnson). *LIV, FCT*

Just Another Pretty Face 🎬🎬½ *Be Beautiful but Shut Up* 1958 An aging detective catches a gang of jewel smugglers, and gets involved with their young moll. In French with English subtitles. **110m/B VHS, Beta.** *FR* Henri Vidal, Mylene Demongeot, Isa Miranda; *D:* Henri Verneuil. *FCT*

Just Around the Corner 🎬½ 1938 (G) Temple helps her Depression-poor father get a job after she befriends a cantankerous millionaire. Temple duets with Bill "Bojangles" Robinson with the fourth time. Also available colorized. 🎵 This Is A Happy Ditty; I'm Not Myself Today; I'll Be Lucky With You; Just Around the Corner; I Love To Walk in the Rain; Brass Buttons and Epaulets. **71m/B VHS, Closed Caption.** Shirley Temple, Charles Farrell, Bert Lahr, Joan Davis, Bill Robinson, Cora Witherspoon, Franklin Pangborn; *D:* Irving Cummings. *FXV*

Just Before Dawn 🎬🎬 1980 (R) Another murderers stalk campers story; humans resort to their animal instincts in their struggle for survival. Not to be confused with the William Castle film (1946) from the "Crime Doctor" series. **90m/C VHS, Beta.** Chris Lemmon, Deborah Benson, Greg Henry, George Kennedy; *D:* Jeff Lieberman; *M:* Brad Fiedel. *NO*

Just Between Friends 🎬🎬 1986 (PG-13) Two women become friends, not knowing that one is having an affair with the husband of the other. Allan Burns directorial debut. **110m/C VHS, Beta.** Mary Tyler Moore, Christine Lahti, Sam Waterston, Ted Danson, Jim MacKrell, Jane Greer; *D:* Allan Burns; *W:* Allan Burns; *C:* Jordan Cronenweth. *NO*

Just Cause 🎬🎬 1994 (R) Incoherent mystery/thriller set in the Florida Everglades. Retired attorney, Paul Armstrong, now a Harvard law professor, decides to defend Bobby Earl (Underwood), on death row for the murder of a white girl. As Armstrong investigates the case, he discovers that the arresting officer Tanny Brown, (Fishburne) is corrupt and tortured the confession out of Bobby. Starts off promising with the electricity of Connery's and Fishburne's presence and a frightening cameo by Ed Harris as an incarcerated serial killer, but once the barrage of plot twists start, creating gator size holes in the plot, the movie drifts into a murkey swamp of absurdity. Adapted from the legal thriller by John Katzenbach. *CW:* Violence; strong language. **102m/C VHS, LV, Closed Caption.** Sean Connery, Laurence "Larry" Fishburne, Kate Capshaw, Blair Underwood, Ruby Dee, Daniel J. Travanti, Ned Beatty, Lynne Thigpen, George Plimpton, Chris Sarandon, Kevin McCarthy, Ed Harris; *D:* Arne Glimcher; *W:* Jeb Stuart, Robert Stone; *C:* Lajos Koltai; *M:* James Newton Howard. *WAR*

Just for the Hell of It WOOF! *Destruction, Inc* 1968 A quartet of teenage punks ruthlessly terrorize their suburban Miami 'hood while an innocent kid gets blamed. More exploitation from schlock king Lewis, who also wrote the theme song, "Destruction Inc" (pic's alternate title). Essentially the same cast as the director's "She Devils on Wheels," filmed simultaneously. **85m/C VHS.** Rodney Bedell, Ray Sager, Nancy Lee Noble, Agi Gyenes, Steve White; *D:* Herschell Gordon Lewis. *NO*

Just for You 🎬🎬½ 1952 Entertaining musical about producer Crosby who doesn't have time for his kids until Wyman steps in and shows him the way. Based on Stephen Vincent Benet's novel "Famous." 🎵 Zing a Little Zong; He's Just Crazy For Me; The Live Oak Tree; A Flight of Fancy; I'll Si-Si Ya In Bahia; On the 10:10; Just for You. **95m/C VHS, Closed Caption.** Bing Crosby, Jane Wyman, Ethel Barrymore, Robert Arthur, Natalie Wood, Cora Witherspoon; *D:* Elliott Nugent; *W:* Robert Carson. Nominations: Academy Awards '52: Best Song ("Zing a Little Zong"). *PAR*

Just Like a Woman 🎬🎬 1995 (R) Sweet-natured film about an unlikely romance with some decided quirks. Young American Gerald (Pasdar) is working for a London bank and renting a flat from lonely older divorcee Monica (Walters). Ideal tenant Gerald is also recently divorced and a mutual attraction develops, in fact Gerald trusts Monica enough to confess his darkest secret—seems his marriage broke up over women's lingerie—the ones Gerald likes to wear when he cross-dresses in his female persona of Geraldine. Does this put Monica off? Well, she turns out to be very understanding indeed. Based on the memoir "Geraldine" by Monica Jay. *CW:* Adult sexual themes, nudity, some language. **102m/C VHS.** *GB* Adrian Pasdar, Julie Walters, Paul Freeman, Susan Wooldridge, Gordon Kennedy, Ian Redford, Shelley Thompson; *D:* Christopher Monger; *W:* Nick Evans; *C:* Alan Hume; *M:* Michael Storey. *HMK*

Just Like Weather 🎬🎬🎬 1986 Contemporary Hong Kong and the city's looming return to control by mainland China provide the backdrop for the troubled marriage of a young couple. Couple endure abortion, arrest, and veterinarian episodes before departing for on U.S. trip with high hopes. **98m/C VHS.** *HK* Christine Lee, Lee Chi-Keung, Allen Fong; *D:* Allen Fong. *FCT*

Just Me & You 🎬½ 1978 An "It Happened One Night" made-for-television tale of an unlikely couple who fall in love with each other when chance brings them together on a cross-country drive. **100m/C VHS, Beta.** Louise Lasser, Charles Grodin; *D:* Charles Erman; *W:* Louise Lasser. *NO*

Just One of the Girls 🎬½ 1993 (R) Teen star Haim transfers to a new high school where he dresses in drag in order to avoid the itinerant leader of the school's toughest gang whom he has unwittingly enraged. Palling around with Eggert becomes one of his costume's unexpected perks. Sort of a cross between "Some Like It Hot" and "90210." *CW:* Nudity. **94m/C VHS, LV.** Corey Haim, Nicole Eggert, Cameron Bancroft; *D:* Michael Keusch; *M:* Amin Bhatia. *THV*

Just One of the Guys 🎬🎬 1985 (PG-13) When the school newspaper refuses to accept the work of an attractive young girl, she goes undercover as a boy to prove that her work is good. She goes on to befriend the school's nerd, and even helps him grow out of his awkward stage, falling for him in the process. Very cute, but predictable. **100m/C VHS, Beta, LV, Closed Caption.** Joyce Hyser, Clayton Rohner, Billy Jacoby, Toni Hudson, Leigh McCloskey, Sherilyn Fenn; *D:* Lisa Gottlieb. *COL*

Just Suppose 🎬🎬½ 1926 Prince in waiting decides he'd prefer the simple life, travels to the land of the free in search of honest work and is felled by cupid's arrow. All's well 'til duty calls, and his princely presence is expected back in the royal fold. Features beautiful boy Barthelmess, whom Lillian Gish described as having "the most beautiful face of any man who ever went before a camera." Silent. **90m/B VHS, Beta.** Richard Barthelmess, Lois Moran, Geoffrey Kerr, Henry Vibart, George Spelvin; *D:* Kenneth Webb. *GPV*

Just Tell Me What You Want 🎬🎬½ 1980 (R) A wealthy, self-made married man finally drives his longtime mistress away when he refuses to let her take over the operation of a failing movie studio he has acquired. After she falls for another man, the tycoon does everything he can to win her back. The department store battle between MacGraw and King is priceless. **112m/C VHS, Beta.** Alan King, Ali MacGraw, Myrna Loy, Keenan Wynn, Tony Roberts; *D:* Sidney Lumet; *W:* Jay Presson Allen; *C:* Oswald Morris. *WAR*

Just Tell Me You Love Me 🎬 1980 (PG) Three budding con artists plot to make easy money in this Hawaiian romp. **90m/C VHS, Beta.** Robert Hegyes, Debralee Scott, Lisa Hartman Black, Ricci Martin, June Lockhart; *D:* Tony Mordente. *LIV, VES*

Just the Way You Are 🎬 1984 (PG) An attractive musician struggles to overcome a physical handicap and winds up falling in love while on vacation in the French Alps. **96m/C VHS, Beta, Closed Caption.** Kristy McNichol, Kaki Hunter, Michael Ontkean, Alexandra Paul, Lance Guest, Timothy Daly, Patrick Cassidy; *D:* Edouard Molinaro; *W:* Allan Burns; *M:* Vladimir Cosma. *MGM*

Just William's Luck 🎬🎬 1947 A precocious English brat sneaks into an old mansion, which just happens to be the headquarters for a gang of thieves. Based on British series of children's books. **87m/B VHS, Beta.** *GB* William A. Graham, Garry Marsh; *D:* Val Guest. *VYY*

Just Your Luck 🎬½ 1996 (R) The New Sudka Cafe II, owned by the high strung Nick (Polito), is the setting for one wild night. An old man promptly keels over dead upon learning that his lottery ticket is a $6 million prize-winner. Customer Kim (Madsen) tries to convince Nick and her fellow diners that they should keep the ticket and split the winnings. *CW:* Strong language and some violence. **86m/C VHS.** Virginia Madsen, Sean Patrick Flanery, Ernie Hudson, Jon Polito, Alanna Ubach, Jon Favreau, Mike Starr, Carroll Baker; *D:* Gary Auerbach; *W:* Gary Auerbach. *PGV*

Justice 🎬🎬 1955 A crusading attorney tries to keep a waterfront kangaroo court from applying its harsh justice to an admitted killer. A television crime-drama also titled "Flight from Fear." **26m/B VHS, Beta.** William Prince, Jack Klugman, Biff McGuire, Jack Warden. *VYY*

Justice of the West 🎬 1961 The Lone Ranger and his sidekick, Tonto, perform good deeds in the Old West, including helping to retrieve stolen gold, helping to build an Indian school, and giving a blind man a fresh perspective on life. **71m/C VHS, Beta.** Clayton Moore, Jay Silverheels; *D:* Earl Bellamy. *MGM*

Justice Rides Again 🎬½ 193? Mix tries to uphold law and order, but he's up against some very tough outlaws. **55m/B VHS, Beta.** Tom Mix. *VCN*

Justin Morgan Had a Horse 🎬🎬 1981 The true story of a colonial school teacher in post-Revolutionary War Vermont who first bred the Morgan horse, the first and most versatile American breed. **91m/C VHS, Beta.** Don Murray, Lana Wood, Gary Crosby; *D:* Hollingsworth Morse. *DIS*

Justine 🎬🎬 1969 In the 1930s, a prostitute who marries an Egyptian banker becomes involved with a variety of men and a plot to arm Palestinian Jews in their revolt against English rule. A condensed film version of Lawrence Durrell's "The Alexandria Quartet." **115m/C VHS, Beta, Closed Caption.** *IS* Anouk Aimee, Michael York, Dirk Bogarde, Philippe Noiret, Michael Constantine, John Vernon, Jack Albertson; *D:* George Cukor; *W:* Lawrence B. Marcus; *C:* Leon Shamroy; *M:* Jerry Goldsmith. *FOX, HHE*

K-9 🎬🎬½ 1989 (PG-13) After having his car destroyed by a drug dealer, "I work alone" Belushi is forced to take on a partner—a German Shepherd. Together they work to round up the bad guys and maybe chew on their shoes a little. Sometimes amusing one-joke comedy done in by a paper-thin script. Both the dog and Belushi are good, however. **111m/C VHS, Beta, LV, Closed Caption.** James Belushi, Mel Harris, Kevin Tighe, Ed O'Neill, Cotter Smith, James Handy, Jerry Lee; *D:* Rod Daniel; *W:* Steven Siegel, Scott Myers; *M:* Miles Goodman. *USH*

K-9000 🎬🎬 1989 The Hound salutes the idea behind this standard sci-fi crime-fighter; a cyberdog fights the forces of evil with the aid of a cop, a lady reporter, and the usual cliches. Made For television. **96m/C VHS, Closed Caption.** Chris Mulkey, Catherine Oxenberg; *D:* Kim Manners; *M:* Jan Hammer. *FRH*

Kafka 🎬½ 1991 (PG-13) Disappointing and gloomy Soderbergh film that serves no purpose whatsoever. Irons plays Kafka, an insurance workers by day and a writer by night. The movie exists largely without interest until Kafka uncovers an office conspiracy and makes his way to the enemy's castle headquarters. From then on, "Kafka" is nothing but a conventional horror film. Irons is wasted in a role that requires nothing but an impeccable British accent. On the plus side, the film is exquisitely shot in black and white until the castle scenes, when the cinematography is switched to color. **100m/C VHS, Beta, LV, Closed Caption.** Jeremy Irons, Theresa Russell, Joel Grey, Ian Holm, Jeroen Krabbe, Armin Mueller-Stahl, Alec Guinness, Brian Glover, Robert Flemyng, Keith Allen, Simon McBurney; **D:** Steven Soderbergh; **W:** Lem Dobbs; **C:** Walt Lloyd; **M:** Cliff Martinez. Independent Spirit Awards '92: Best Cinematography. *PAR, PMS*

Kagemusha 🐾🐾🐾½ *The Shadow Warrior; The Double* 1980 **(PG)** A thief is rescued from the gallows because of his striking resemblance to a warlord in 16th Century Japan. When the ambitious warlord is fatally wounded, the thief is required to pose as the warlord. In Japanese with English subtitles. **160m/C VHS, Beta, LV.** JP Tatsuya Nakadai, Tsutomu Yamazaki, Kenichi Hagiwara; **D:** Akira Kurosawa. British Academy Awards '80: Best Director (Kurosawa); Cannes Film Festival '80: Best Film; Cesar Awards '81: Best Foreign Film; National Board of Review Awards '80: 5 Best Foreign Films of the Year; Nominations: Academy Awards '80: Best Art Direction/Set Decoration, Best Foreign Language Film.*FOX, APD*

Kalifornia 🐾🐾½ 1993 **(R)** "Badlands" meets the '90s in a road trip with the hitchhikers from hell. Early Grayce (Pitt) is your average slimeball who murders his landlord and hops a ride with his waifish girlfriend Adele (Lewis) from Kentucky to California with Brian (Duchovny), a yuppie writer interested in mass murderers, and his sultry photographer girlfriend Carrie (Forbes). Pitt and Lewis were still an item when they made this. Pitt reportedly wanted to play against type, and as pretty boy gone homicidal, he succeeds. Extremely violent and disturbing. Also available in an unrated version.*CW:* Nudity and graphic and disturbing violence. **117m/C VHS, LV, Closed Caption.** Brad Pitt, Juliette Lewis, David Duchovny, Michelle Forbes, Sierra Pecheur, Lois Hall, Gregory Mars Martin; **D:** Dominic Sena; **W:** Tim Metcalfe; **C:** Bojan Bazelli; **M:** Carter Burwell. *PGV, BTV*

Kama Sutra: A Tale of Love 🐾🐾 1996 Erotic but flawed fantasy covering the sexual and political wiles of palace life in 16th-century India. Princess Tara (Choudhury) and girlhood friend/servant Maya (Varma) are close until the Princess becomes jealous of the even-more beautiful Maya. In revenge for a public humiliation, Maya seduces Tara's dissolute fiance, Raj Singh (Andrews), and is banished from the palace after the wedding. She becomes involved with handsome royal sculptor Jai Kumar (Tikaram) and later learns the sexual arts of the Kama Sutra, becoming the chief courtesan to the Raj. Messy, somewhat overwrought plot, extremely attractive cast. Also available in an R-rated version. **117m/C VHS, LV, Closed Caption.** IN Indira Varma, Sarita Choudhury, Ramon Tikaram, Naveen Andrews, Devi Rekha; **D:** Mira Nair; **W:** Mira Nair, Helena Kriel; **C:** Declan Quinn; **M:** Mychael Danna. *THV*

Kameradschaft 🐾🐾🐾½ 1931 A great, early German sound film about Germans struggling to free themselves and French miners trapped underground on the countries' border. In German and French with English subtitles. **80m/B VHS, Beta.** GE Ernst Busch, Alexander Granach, Fritz Kampers; **D:** G.W. Pabst. National Board of Review Awards '32: 10 Best Films of the Year. *MRV, IHF, NLC*

Kamikaze '89 🐾🐾🐾 1983 German director Fassbinder has the lead acting role (his last) in this offbeat story of a police lieutenant in Berlin, circa 1989, who investigates a puzzling series of bombings. In German with English subtitles. **90m/C VHS, Beta.** GE Rainer Werner Fassbinder, Gunther Kaufman, Boy Gobert; **D:** Wolf Gremm; **M:** Tangerine Dream. *MGM, FCT, GLV*

Kamikaze Hearts 🐾🐾 1991 A quasi-documentary set in the world of two lesbian-junkies (Sharon the actress and Tina the director/producer) making underground X-rated movies. **80m/C VHS.** Sharon Mitchell, Tina "Tigr" Mennett; **D:** Juliet Bashore; **W:** Tina "Tigr" Mennett. *FCT*

Kanal 🐾🐾🐾½ *They Loved Life* 1956 Wajda's first major success, a grueling account of Warsaw patriots, upon the onset of the Nazis toward the end of the war, fleeing through the ruined city's sewers. Highly acclaimed. Part 2 of Wajda's "War Trilogy," preceded by "A Generation" and followed by "Ashes and Diamonds." In Polish with English subtitles or dubbed. **96m/B VHS, Beta.** PL Teresa Izewska, Tadeusz Janczar; **D:** Andrzej Wajda. Cannes Film Festival '57: Grand Jury Prize. *ING, NLC, HMV*

Kandyland 🐾 1987 **(R)** An over-the-hill stripper takes a young innocent stripper under her wing. **94m/C VHS, Beta, LV.** Sandahl Bergman, Kimberly Evenson, Charles Laulette, Bruce Baum; **D:** Robert Allen Schnitzer; **C:** Robert Brinkmann. *VTR, NWV*

Kangaroo 🐾🐾🐾 1986 **(R)** An Australian adaptation of the semi-autobiographical D.H. Lawrence novel. A controversial English novelist and his wife move to the Outback in 1922, and are confronted with all manner of prejudice and temptation. **115m/C VHS, Beta.** AU Judy Davis, Colin Friels, John Walton, Hugh Keays-Byrne, Julie Nihill; **D:** Tim Burstall; **W:** Evan Jones; **C:** Dan Burstall; **M:** Nathan Waks. Australian Film Institute '86: Best Actress (Davis). *USH*

The Kansan 🐾🐾 1943 The marshall in a Kansas town won't rest until he's stamped out all traces of corruption. **79m/B VHS, Beta.** Richard Dix, Victor Jory, Albert Dekker; **D:** George Archainbaud. Nominations: Academy Awards '43: Original Dramatic/Comedy Score. *NOS, MRV, HEG*

Kansas 🐾 1988 **(R)** Two young men, one a lawless rebel, the other a rational loner, stage a bank heist, and then go on the lam. Lame plot and very weak acting combine to make this film a dud. **111m/C VHS, Beta, LV.** Matt Dillon, Andrew McCarthy, Leslie Hope, Kyra Sedgwick; **D:** David Stevens; **C:** David Eggby; **M:** Pino Donaggio. *MED*

Kansas City 🐾🐾🐾 1995 **(R)** Altman mixes music, politics, crime and the movies in this bittersweet homage to his hometown, set in the jazz-driven 1930s. Star-struck, tough-talking Blondie (Leigh) kidnaps Carolyn Stilton (Richardson), a self-sedating wife of a political shaker (Murphy), in a hair-brained scheme to save her husband from a local mobster (Belafonte). Styled to imitate the brilliant jazz scores played by the likes of Joshua Redman and James Carter, the action can become a bit confusing and Leigh is beyond irritating with her derivative dame routine. Belafonte, however, is brilliant, relishing the part of the legendary Seldom Seen, a real-life K.C. gangster.*CW:* Language, and for some violence and drug use. **110m/C VHS, LV, Closed Caption.** Jennifer Jason Leigh, Miranda Richardson, Harry Belafonte, Michael Murphy, Dermot Mulroney, Steve Buscemi, Brooke Smith, Jane Adams; **D:** Robert Altman; **W:** Frank Barhydt, Robert Altman; **C:** Oliver Stapleton; **M:** Hal Willner. New York Film Critics Awards '96: Best Supporting Actor (Belafonte). *NLC*

Kansas City Confidential 🐾🐾🐾 1952 An ex-cop on the wrong side of the law launches a sophisticated armored car heist. A disgruntled ex-con gets arrested for the crime on circumstantial evidence. When released, he scours the underworld for the real thieves. **98m/B VHS.** John Payne, Coleen Gray, Preston Foster, Neville Brand, Lee Van Cleef, Jack Elam; **D:** Phil Karlson. *NOS, MGM, RXM*

Kansas City Massacre 🐾½ 1975 A made-for-television film chronicling the efforts of Melvin Purvis, as he tracked down Depression-era hoods. First called "Melvin Purvis, G-Man." **99m/C VHS, Beta.** Dale Robertson, Sally Kirkland, Bo Hopkins, Scott Brady, Lynn Loring, Matt Clark, Mills Watson, Robert Walden; **D:** Dan Curtis. *THV*

Kansas Pacific 🐾🐾 1953 A group of Confederate sympathizers try to stop the Kansas Pacific Railroad from reaching the West Coast in the 1860s. **73m/C VHS, Beta.** Sterling Hayden, Eve Miller, Barton MacLane, Reed Hadley, Douglas Hadley; **D:** Ray Nazarro. *NOS, MRV, DVT*

The Kansas Terrors 🐾🐾 1939 The "Three Mesquiters" head for the Caribbean to deliver a herd of horses and wind up in a battle against local despot. **57m/B VHS.** Bob Livingston, Raymond Hatton, Duncan Renaldo, Jacqueline Wells, Yakima Canutt, Richard Alexander, Maureen McCormack; **D:** George Sherman. *NOS*

Kaos 🐾🐾🐾 *Chaos-Kaos* 1985 **(R)** The Taviani brothers adaptation of four stories by Luigi Pirandello ("The Other Son," "Moonstruck," "The Jar," and "Requiem"), which look at peasant life in Sicily, ranging from the comic to the tragic. A fictional epilog, "Conversing with Mother," has Pirandello talking with the spirit of his dead mother. As with any anthology some stories are stronger than others but all possess the Taviani's great visual style and some fine acting. In Italian with English subtitles. **188m/C VHS.** IT Margarita Lozano, Claudio Bigagli, Massimo Bonetti, Omero Antonutti, Enrica Maria Modugno, Ciccio Ingrassia, Franco Franchi, Biagio Barone, Salvatore Rossi, Franco Scaldati, Pasquale Spadola, Regina Bianchi; **D:** Paolo Taviani, Vittorio Taviani; **W:** Paolo Taviani, Vittorio Taviani, Tonino Guerra. *MGM, BTV*

Kapo 🐾🐾🐾 1959 A 14-year-old Jewish girl and her family are imprisoned by the Nazis in a concentration camp. There, the girl changes identities with the help of the camp doctor, and rises to the position of camp guard. She proceeds to become taken with her power until a friend commits suicide and jolts the girl back into harsh reality. An Academy Award nominee for Best Foreign Film (lost to "The Virgin Spring"). Primarily English dialogue, with subtitles for foreign language. **116m/B VHS.** IT FR YU Susan Strasberg, Laurent Terzieff, Emmanuelle Riva, Gianni "John" Garko; **D:** Gillo Pontecorvo; **W:** Gillo Pontecorvo. Nominations: Academy Awards '60: Best Foreign Language Film.*DVT, HEG*

Karate Cop 🐾½ 1993 **(R)** In a future without law or order John Travis (Marchini) is the last cop on earth. He saves Rachel, a beautiful scientist, from a band of scavengers and together they hunt for a hidden crystal with mysterious powers. Only first John has to defeat a gladiator in a martial arts fight to the death. **?m/C VHS, LV, Closed Caption.** Ron Marchini, Carrie Chambers, David Carradine, Michael Bristow, D.W. Landingham, Michael Foley, Dana Bentley; **D:** Alan Roberts. *IMP, IME, VTR*

The Karate Kid 🐾🐾🐾½ 1984 **(PG)** A teen-age boy finds out that Karate involves using more than your fists when a handyman agrees to teach him martial arts. The friendship that they develop is deep and sincere; the Karate is only an afterthought. From the director of the original "Rocky," this movie is easy to like. **126m/C VHS, Beta, LV, 8mm, Closed Caption.** Ralph Macchio, Noriyuki "Pat" Morita, Elisabeth Shue, Randee Heller, Martin Kove, Chad McQueen; **D:** John G. Avildsen; **W:** Robert Mark Kamen; **M:** Bill Conti. Nominations: Academy Awards '84: Best Supporting Actor (Morita). *COL*

The Karate Kid: Part 2 🐾🐾½ 1986 **(PG)** Sequel to the first film wherein our high-kicking hero tests his mettle in real-life karate exchanges in Okinawa, and settles a long-standing score. Followed by a second sequel. **95m/C VHS, Beta, LV, 8mm, Closed Caption.** Ralph Macchio, Noriyuki "Pat" Morita, Danny Kamekona, Martin Kove, Tamlyn Tomita, Nobu McCarthy, Yuji Okumoto; **D:** John G. Avildsen; **W:** Robert Mark Kamen; **M:** Bill Conti. Nominations: Academy Awards '86: Best Song ("Glory of Love"). *COL*

The Karate Kid: Part 3 🐾½ 1989 **(PG)** Second sequel takes a tired plot and doesn't do much to perk it up. Macchio again battles an evil nemesis and learns about himself, but this time Morita refuses to be a part of his training until, of course, Macchio desperately needs his help. Followed by "The Next Karate Kid" which introduces a new kid—a girl. **105m/C VHS, Beta, LV, 8mm,**

Closed Caption. Ralph Macchio, Noriyuki "Pat" Morita, John G. Avildsen, Thomas Ian Griffith, Martin Kove, Sean Kanan, Robyn Elaine; **D:** John G. Avildsen; **W:** Robert Mark Kamen; **M:** Bill Conti. COL

Karate Polish Style 🎞️ **1982** Polish painter duo paint, plaster and draw blood. A sort of "Dances with Poles" in Warsaw's Mazurian Lake District. In Polish with English subtitles. Not a Polish joke. **91m/C VHS.** PL **D:** Jerzy Wojcik. FCT

Karate Warrior 🎞️½ **1988** Young martial artist is beaten and left for dead by Filipino crime syndicate. Bones mended, he prescribes a dose of their medicine. Plenty of rest and retaliation. **90m/C VHS, Beta.** Jared Martin, Ken Watanabe. IMP

Karate Warriors 🎞️ **197?** Chiba takes his battle against crime to the streets. **90m/C VHS, Beta.** Sonny Chiba. NO

Kashmiri Run 🎞️ **1969 (R)** Action adventure about trio on the lam from Chinese communists chasing them through Tibet. **101m/C VHS.** SP Pernell Roberts, Alexandra Bastedo, Julian Mateos, Gloria Gamata; **D:** John Peyser. LIV

Kaspar Hauser 🎞️🎞️ **1993** Historical epic based on the true story of Kaspar Hauser (Eisermann), a 16-year-old found abandoned in Nuremberg, Germany in 1828, who was unable to walk, write, or speak. Entrusted to the scientific concerns of Professor Daumer (Samel), rumors begin to circulate that the boy is actually the Crown Prince of Baden. Supposedly, Kaspar was abducted as a baby and substituted for a child who died so his Uncle Ludwig (Oscsenknecht) could become Grand Duke. Court intrigue and threats abound as Kaspar struggles to survive. German with subtitles. **137m/C VHS.** GE Andre Eisermann, Jeremy Clyde, Katharina Thalbach, Udo Samel, Uwe Ochsenknecht; **D:** Peter Sehr; **W:** Peter Sehr; **C:** Gernot Roll; **M:** Nikos Mamangakis. KIV

Katherine 🎞️ The Radical **1975** A young heiress rejects her pampered lifestyle and becomes a violent revolutionary, rebelling against social injustices and the system that spawned them. Made for television. **98m/C VHS, Beta, LV.** Sissy Spacek, Art Carney, Jane Wyatt, Henry Winkler, Julie Kavner, Hector Elias, Jenny Sullivan; **D:** Jeremy Paul Kagan. VTR, NWV, IME

Kavanagh Q.C. **1994** James Kavanagh (Thaw), Queen's Council, is a respected Manchester criminal advocate, who may act for the prosecution in some cases and for the defense in others. In this four-tape set from the TV series, Kavanagh represents a man accused of rape, a porno star, a vigilante, and a prostitute accused of murder. **330m/C VHS.** GB John Thaw, Lisa Harrow, Alison Steadman. VCO, VIF

Kavik the Wolf Dog 🎞️½ The Courage of Kavik, the Wolf Dog **1984** Heartwarming story of a courageous dog's love and suffering for the boy he loves. Made for television. **99m/C VHS, Beta.** Ronny Cox, Linda Sorensen, Andrew Ian McMillian, Chris Wiggins, John Ireland; **D:** Peter Carter. MED

Kazaam 🎞️ **1996 (PG)** Twelve-year-old Max (Capra) is having problems—bullies are chasing him and his single mom's just found a new boyfriend. But his luck seems ready to change when a battered boombox reveals a seven-foot rappin' genie named Kazaam (O'Neal). The kid's beyond obnoxious and Shaq shouldn't plan to give up b-ball anytime soon (at least for an acting career), even though director Glaser did think up the part for the tall guy just before he met him at an NBA All-Star Game. **93m/C VHS, LV, Closed Caption.** Francis Capra, Shaquille O'Neal, Ally Walker, John Costelloe, Marshall Manesh, James Acheson; **D:** Paul Michael Glaser; **W:** Christian Ford, Roger Soffer; **C:** Charles Minsky; **M:** Christopher Tyng. TOU

Keaton's Cop 🎞️ **1990 (R)** Another cheap cop comedy involving the mistaken identity of an important mob witness. **95m/C VHS, Beta, LV.** Lee Majors, Abe Vigoda, Don Rickles; **D:** Robert Burge. MGM, OM

The Keep 🎞️🎞️ **1983 (R)** At the height of the Nazi onslaught, several German soldiers unleash an unknown power from a medieval stone fortress. Technically impressive but lacking in all other aspects. **96m/C VHS, Beta, LV.** Scott Glenn, Alberta Watson, Juergen Prochnow, Robert Prosky, Gabriel Byrne; **D:** Michael Mann; **W:** Michael Mann, Dennis Lynton Clark. PAR

Keep 'Em Flying 🎞️🎞️ **1941** Bud and Lou star in the this wartime morale-booster that hasn't aged well. The duo follow their barnstorming friend into flight academy; a not-too-taxing plot includes five musical numbers and two Martha Rayes (she plays twins). ♫ Pig Foot Pete; Together; I'm Looking for the Boy with the Wistful Eyes; Let's Keep 'Em Flying; I'm Getting Sentimental Over You. **86m/B VHS, LV, Closed Caption.** Bud Abbott, Lou Costello, Martha Raye; **D:** Arthur Lubin. USH

Keep My Grave Open 🎞️🎞️ The House Where Hell Froze Over **1980 (R)** A woman lives in an isolated house where a series of strange murders take place. She attributes them to her brother, but does he really exist? Made cheaply, but not without style; filmed in Harrison County, Texas. **85m/C VHS, Beta.** Camilla Carr, Gene Ross, Stephen Tobolowsky, Ann Stafford, Sharon Bunn, Chelcie Ross; **D:** S.F. Brownrigg. UNI

Keep Punching 🎞️🎞️ **1939** A gambler/boxer is almost destroyed by life in the fast lane, as well as by a seductive woman. **80m/C VHS.** Henry Armstrong, Mae Johnson; **Cameos:** Canada Lee; **D:** John Clein. FCT

Keep Talking Baby 🎞️🎞️ **1961** Action-packed thriller that finds Eddie in prison after being framed for murder. He escapes and is out for revenge on the organization that put him there. **?m/C VHS.** Eddie Constantine. SNC

Keep the Change 🎞️🎞️ **1992 (PG-13)** Joe Starling is an artist with painter's block, living in California with his girlfriend Astrid. He decides to revisit the family ranch in Deadrock, Montana, and his crackpot Uncle Smitty and saintly Aunt Lureen. The family ranch is coveted by the evil Overstreet (typecasting for Palance), whose daughter was once loved by Joe but is now married to his ex-best friend. Character more than plot rules this moody, low-key story based on a novel by Thomas McGuane. Made for cable television. **95m/C VHS, LV, Closed Caption.** William L. Petersen, Lolita Davidovich, Rachel Ticotin, Buck Henry, Jack Palance, Fred Dalton Thompson, Jeff Kober, Lois Smith; **D:** Andy Tennant. TTC

Keeper 🎞️🎞️ **1984** Wealthy patients at Underwood Asylum suffer unspeakable horrors while under the care of Lee. Detective Dick Driver investigates. Obscure horror spoof. **96m/C VHS, Beta.** CA Christopher Lee, Tell Schreiber, Sally Gray; **D:** Tom Drake; **W:** Tom Drake. TWE, HHE

Keeper of the City 🎞️🎞️½ **1992 (R)** Gossett stars as a tough detective out to get a vigilante (LaPaglia) who is roaming the streets of Chicago. LaPaglia turns in a good performance as the son of a Mafia operative who wants to rid himself of the Mafia ties that have controlled him. As he pursues his deadly course of action, a newspaper journalist tags him "The Gangster Killer." Coyote plays the crusading journalist who is always interfering in Gossett's business. Good performances and an intriguing story line combine to make this action-packed thriller worthwhile, although the script isn't as good as Di Pega's novel, which he adapted himself. **CW:** Language and violence. **95m/C VHS, Beta, LV, Closed Caption.** Louis Gossett Jr., Peter Coyote, Anthony LaPaglia, Renee Soutendijk, Aeryk Egan, Tony Todd; **D:** Bobby Roth; **W:** Gerald Di Pega. FXV, VTR

Keeper of the Flame 🎞️🎞️½ **1942** Tracy and Hepburn manage to keep the murk of this story at bay as war correspondent Steven O'Malley (Tracy) is assigned to write about super patriot Robert V. Forrest, who's just died in an accident. Reclusive widow Christine Forrest (Hepburn) finally agrees to help O'Malley out but what our intrepid reporter discovers is that the hero was really a heel—something Christine still doesn't want known. Based on the novel by I.A.R. Wylie. **100m/B VHS.** Spencer Tracy, Katharine Hepburn, Richard Whorf, Margaret Wycherly, Donald Meek, Stephen McNally, Audrey Christie, Frank Craven, Forrest Tucker, Percy Kilbride, Howard da Silva, Darryl Hickman; **D:** George Cukor; **W:** Donald Ogden Stewart; **C:** William H. Daniels; **M:** Bronislau Kaper. TTC

Keeping On 🎞️🎞️½ **1981** Television movie with a pro-union stance. A preacher, who is also a millworker, teams up with an organizer to try to unionize the mill. Originally produced for the PBS "American Playhouse" series. **75m/C VHS.** Dick Anthony Williams, Carol Kane, James Broderick, Marcia Rodd, Rosalind Cash, Carl Lee, Danny Glover, Guy Boyd; **D:** Barbara Kopple. TWE

Keeping Track 🎞️🎞️ **1986 (R)** Two tourists witness a murder and robbery and find the stolen $5 million on a New York-bound train. The two are relentlessly pursued by everyone, including the CIA and Russian spies. **102m/C VHS, Beta, LV, Closed Caption.** Michael Sarrazin, Margot Kidder, Alan Scarfe, Ken Pogue, Vlasta Vrana, Donald Pilon; **D:** Robin Spry. NLC

Keetje Tippel 🎞️🎞️ Katie's Passion; Cathy Tippel; Hot Sweat **1975 (R)** In 1881 Amsterdam, a young Dutch prostitute works her way out of poverty and enters a world of education and wealth. A Victorian tale of exploitation with a tough and intelligent Cinderella heroine. In Dutch with English subtitles. **104m/C VHS, Beta, LV.** NL Monique Van De Ven, Rutger Hauer, Eddie Brugman, Hannah De Leeuwe, Andrea Domburg; **D:** Paul Verhoeven; **C:** Jan De Bont. TPV, CVC, IME

Kelly of the Secret Service 🎞️🎞️ **1936** Agent tries to find out who stole the plans for a guided missile system. Fast-pace rides over the silliness of the plot. **69m/B VHS.** Lloyd Hughes, Sheila Mannors, Fuzzy Knight, Syd Saylor, Jack Mulhall, Forrest Taylor; **D:** Robert F. "Bob" Hill; **W:** Al Martin. SNC

Kelly the Second 🎞️🎞️½ **1936** Slow-moving boxing comedy about a punch-drunk fighter trying to win again with the encouragement of his trainer and manager. **70m/B VHS.** Guinn "Big Boy" Williams, Patsy Kelly, Charley Chase, Pert Kelton, Edward Brophy, Maxie "Slapsie" Rosenbloom, Harold Huber, DeWitt Jennings, Billy Gilbert, Syd Saylor; **D:** Gus Meins. RXM

Kelly's Heroes 🎞️🎞️½ **1970 (PG)** A misfit band of crooks are led by Eastwood on a daring mission: to steal a fortune in gold from behind enemy lines. In the process, they almost win WWII. Sutherland is superb, as is McLeod, in his pre-Love Boat days. **145m/C VHS, Beta, LV.** Clint Eastwood, Donald Sutherland, Telly Savalas, Gavin MacLeod, Don Rickles, Carroll O'Connor, Stuart Margolin, Harry Dean Stanton; **D:** Brian G. Hutton; **M:** Lalo Schifrin. MGM, TLF

Kemek 🎞️ **1988 (R)** An eccentric chemical company owner has his mistress push a new mind-control drug on an American writer, and has them killed after discovering their subsequent affair. Unfortunately, he didn't count on the woman's ex-husband seeking revenge. **82m/C VHS, Beta.** David Hedison, Helmut Snider, Mary Woronov, Alexandra Stewart, Cal Haynes. GHV

Kennedy 🎞️🎞️ **1983** The long television miniseries biography of JFK from his inauguration to assassination. **278m/C VHS, Beta.** Martin Sheen, Blair Brown, Vincent Gardenia, Geraldine Fitzgerald, E.G. Marshall, John Shea; **D:** Richard Hartley. PSM

The Kennel Murder Case 🎞️🎞️ **1933** Debonair detective Philo Vance suspects that a clear-cut case of suicide is actually murder. Fourth Vance mystery starring Powell. Remade as "Calling Philo Vance" in 1940. **73m/B VHS, Beta.** William Powell, Mary Astor, Jack LaRue, Ralph Morgan, Eugene Pallette; **D:** Michael Curtiz. SNC, NOS, HHT

Kenny Rogers as the Gambler 🎞🎞½ 1980 Rogers stars as Brady Hawkes, debonair gambler searching for a son he never knew he had. Based on the Rogers song of the same name. One of the highest rated TV movies ever. Followed by several sequels. **94m/C VHS.** Kenny Rogers, Christine Belford, Bruce Boxleitner, Harold Gould, Clu Gulager, Lance LeGault, Lee Purcell, Noble Willingham; **D:** Dick Lowry. NO

Kenny Rogers as the Gambler, Part 2: The Adventure Continues 🎞½ 1983 The surprise success of the made-for-TV western based on the popular Kenny Rogers' song spawned this equally popular sequel. Rogers returns as Brady Hawkes, this time searching for his kidnapped son. Followed by two more sequels. **195m/C VHS, Beta, 8mm.** Kenny Rogers, Bruce Boxleitner, Linda Evans, Harold Gould, David Hedison, Clu Gulager, Johnny Crawford; **D:** Dick Lowry. NO

Kenny Rogers as the Gambler, Part 3: The Legend Continues 🎞🎞 1987 Roger's third attempt at humanizing the gambler from his hit '70s song. This time, the Gambler gives a hand with the mediating between the warring U.S. government and the Sioux nation. Sitting Bull and Buffalo Bill add credibility to this average undertaking. Made for TV. **90m/C VHS, Beta.** Kenny Rogers, Bruce Boxleitner, Linda Gray, Melanie Chartoff, Matt Clark, George Kennedy, Dean Stockwell, Charles Durning, Jeffrey Jones, George American Horse; **D:** Dick Lowry. NO

Kent State 🎞🎞 1981 Made-for-television drama recounts the tragic events that took place at Kent State University in 1970, when student demonstrators faced National Guardsmen. Goldstone won an Emmy for Outstanding Direction. **120m/C VHS, Beta.** Talia Balsam, Ellen Barkin, Jane Fleiss, John Getz, Keith Gordon; **D:** James Goldstone. USH

The Kentuckian 🎞🎞½ 1955 Burt Lancaster stars as a rugged frontiersman who leaves with his son to go to Texas. On their journey the two are harassed by fighting mountaineers. **104m/C VHS, Beta.** Burt Lancaster, Walter Matthau, Diana Lynn, John McIntire, Dianne Foster, Una Merkel, John Carradine; **D:** Burt Lancaster; **C:** Ernest Laszlo. MGM

Kentucky Blue Streak 🎞½ 1935 Young jockey is framed for murder while riding at an "illegal" racetrack. Later, almost eligible for parole, he escapes from jail to ride "Blue Streak" in the Kentucky Derby. **61m/B VHS, Beta.** Eddie Nugent, Frank "Junior" Coghlan, Patricia Scott, Ben Carter. VYY

Kentucky Fried Movie 🎞🎞🎞 1977 (R) A zany potpourri of satire about movies, television, commercials, and contemporary society. Written by Abrahams and the Zuckers, who were later known for "Airplane!" **85m/C VHS, Beta, LV.** Bill Bixby, Jerry Zucker, Jim Abrahams, David Zucker, Donald Sutherland, Henry Gibson, George Lazenby; **D:** John Landis; **W:** Jerry Zucker, Jim Abrahams, David Zucker. MED

Kentucky Jubilee 🎞½ 1951 At the jubilee, a movie director is kidnapped and the master of ceremonies, among others, decides to find him. **67m/B VHS, Beta, LV.** Jerry Colonna, Jean Porter, James Ellison, Raymond Hatton, Fritz Feld. RXM

Kentucky Kernels 🎞🎞 Triple Trouble 1934 A pair of down and out magicians (thirties comic duo Wheeler and Woolsey) happen upon a young boy (Little Rascal Spanky) who happens to be heir to a fortune. The three head for the rascal's Kentucky home, where they're welcomed with southern inhospitality. Much feuding and slapsticking. **75m/B VHS, LV.** Bert Wheeler, Robert Woolsey, Mary Carlisle, George "Spanky" McFarland, Noah Beery Sr., Lucille LaVerne, Willie Best; **D:** George Stevens; **M:** Max Steiner. TTC, FCT, GVV

Kentucky Rifle 🎞½ 1955 A Comanche Indian tribe will let a group of stranded pioneers through their territory only if they agree to sell the Kentucky rifles aboard their wagon. **80m/C VHS, Beta.** Chill Wills, Lance Fuller, Cathy Downs, Jess Barker,
Sterling Holloway, Jeanne Cagney; **D:** Carl K. Hittleman. MON, HHE

Kept Husbands 🎞🎞 1931 A factory worker saves two lives in an industrial accident, and the boss invites him home to dinner. When he meets the boss' daughter, romance blooms. But their different backgrounds cause difficulties. A bit dull, and dated by its chauvinism. **76m/B VHS.** Dorothy Mackaill, Joel McCrea, Robert McWade, Florence Roberts, Clara Kimball Young, Mary Carr, Ned Sparks, Bryant Washburn; **D:** Lloyd Bacon; **M:** Max Steiner. NOS, HEG

The Kettles in the Ozarks 🎞🎞½ 1956 Since Kilbride retired after the seventh comedy, Hunnicutt played a new male character, Uncle Sledge, in the eighth film. Ma (Main) takes the young'uns to visit their uncle in the Ozarks and finds she must help him and fiancee Bedelia (Merkel) save the failing farm from bootleggers. **81m/B VHS, Closed Caption.** Marjorie Main, Arthur Hunnicutt, Una Merkel, Ted de Corsia, Richard Eyer, Joseph Sawyer, Richard Deacon; **D:** Charles Lamont; **W:** Kay Lenard. USH

The Kettles on Old MacDonald's Farm 🎞🎞½ 1957 The ninth and last in the series finds Ma (Main in her final film) and Pa (Kennelly replacing the retired Kilbride) playing matchmakers for humble lumberman Brad (Smith). Seems he wants to marry the boss' spoiled daughter, Sally (Talbott), whom Ma decides needs a little backwoods seasoning before she'll make the proper wife. **82m/B VHS, Closed Caption.** Marjorie Main, Parker Fennelly, John Smith, Gloria Talbott, Claude Akins, Roy Barcroft, Patricia Morrow, George Dunn; **D:** Virgil W. Vogel; **W:** Herbert Margolis, William Raynor. USH

The Key 🎞🎞½ 1958 A long, slow WWII drama about the key to an Italian girl's apartment that gets passed from tugboat skipper to tugboat skipper before dangerous missions. Ultimately she finds true love, or does she? Based on the novel "Stella" by Jan de Hartog. **134m/B VHS, Beta, LV.** GB William Holden, Sophia Loren, Trevor Howard, Oscar Homolka, Kieron Moore; **D:** Carol Reed; **W:** Carl Foreman; **C:** Oswald Morris; **M:** Malcolm Arnold. British Academy Awards '58: Best Actor (Howard). COL

Key Exchange 🎞🎞½ 1985 (R) Kevin Scott and Paul Kurta based this contemporary look at love and commitments on Kevin Wade's popular play. Two New York City "yuppies" have reached a point in their relationship where an exchange of apartment keys commonly occurs—but they are hesitant. **96m/C VHS, Beta, Closed Caption.** Brooke Adams, Ben Masters, Daniel Stern, Tony Roberts, Danny Aiello, Annie Golden, Nancy Mette; **D:** Barnet Kellman; **W:** Kevin Scott, Paul Kurta; **M:** Jonathan Elias. FOX

Key Largo 🎞🎞🎞½ 1948 A gangster melodrama set in Key West, Florida, where hoods take over a hotel in the middle of a hurricane. Based on a play by Maxwell Anderson. **101m/B VHS, Beta, LV.** Humphrey Bogart, Lauren Bacall, Claire Trevor, Edward G. Robinson, Lionel Barrymore; **D:** John Huston; **W:** Richard Brooks, John Huston; **C:** Karl Freund; **M:** Max Steiner. Academy Awards '48: Best Supporting Actress (Trevor). MGM, FOX, TLF

The Key Man 🎞½ Life at Stake 1957 A radio show host manages to get mixed up with gangsters after recreating a crime on the air. He uses his knowledge of crime to thwart the crooks. **63m/B VHS, Beta.** GB Lee Patterson, Hy Hazell, Colin Gordon, Philip Leaver, Paula Byrne; **D:** Montgomery Tully; **M:** Les Baxter. NOS, SNC

The Key to Rebecca 🎞🎞½ 1985 The Nazis and the British go head-to-head in war torn North Africa. As the Germans push their way across Egypt, they find an unexpected ally in a half-German/half-Arab killer behind the British lines. Tense, well made thriller, originally a miniseries. On two cassettes. Made for television. **190m/C VHS.** David Soul, Cliff Robertson, Robert Culp, Season Hubley, Lina Raymond, Anthony Quayle, David Hemmings; **D:** David Hemmings. WOV

Key to the City 🎞🎞½ 1950 Light comedy featuring Gable and Young as two small town mayors who meet and fall in love at a convention in San Francisco. Throw in some sharp lines, a little slapstick, and a bit of satire for an amusing picture. Based on the story by Albert Beich. **99m/B VHS.** Clark Gable, Loretta Young, Frank Morgan, Marilyn Maxwell, Raymond Burr, James Gleason, Lewis Stone, Raymond Walburn; **D:** George Sidney; **W:** Robert Riley Crutcher. MGM

The Keys of the Kingdom 🎞🎞🎞 1944 An earnest adaptation of A.J. Cronin's novel about a young Scottish missionary spreading God's word in 19th Century China. **137m/B VHS, Beta, LV, Closed Caption.** Gregory Peck, Thomas Mitchell, Edmund Gwenn, Vincent Price, Roddy McDowall, Cedric Hardwicke, Peggy Ann Garner, James Gleason, Anne Revere, Rose Stradner, Sara Allgood, Abner Biberman, Arthur Shields; **D:** John M. Stahl; **W:** Joseph L. Mankiewicz, Nunnally Johnson; **C:** Arthur C. Miller. Nominations: Academy Awards '45: Best Actor (Peck), Best Black and White Cinematography, Best Interior Decoration, Original Dramatic/Comedy Score. FOX, IGP

Keys to Tulsa 🎞🎞½ 1996 (R) After losing his job as a lowly movie reviewer (gasp!), Richter Bourdreau (Stoltz), the black-sheep son of a wealthy Tulsa family, is lured into a blackmail scheme by his ex-flame Vicky (Unger) and her perpetually stoned husband Ronnie (Spader). When the tables are turned on him, Richter finally gets up off of his slacker butt for some revenge. Excellent cast includes Moore as his flinty mother and Coburn as a wealthy redneck patriarch. Stoltz's performance holds the spiraling story of class distinction, murder and deceit together, and Spader's Elvis-helmeted loser is fun to watch. Based on the novel by Brian Fair Berkey. **CW:** Strong sexuality and language, some drug use and violence. **112m/C VHS.** Eric Stoltz, James Spader, Mary Tyler Moore, Joanna Going, Cameron Diaz, James Coburn, Michael Rooker, Peter Strauss, Deborah Unger; **D:** Leslie Greif; **W:** Harley Peyton; **C:** Robert Fraisse; **M:** Stephen Endelman. NYR

The KGB: The Secret War 🎞½ Lethal 1986 (PG-13) Reheated Cold War fare. **90m/C VHS, LV.** Sally Kellerman, Michael Ansara, Michael Billington; **W:** Sandra K. Bailey; **D:** Peter Collister. HHE

Khartoum 🎞🎞½ 1966 A sweeping but talky adventure epic detailing the last days of General "Chinese" Gordon as the title city is besieged by Arab tribes in 1884. **134m/C VHS, Beta, LV.** Charlton Heston, Laurence Olivier, Ralph Richardson, Richard Johnson, Alexander Knox, Hugh Williams, Nigel Green, Michael Hordern, Johnny Sekka; **D:** Basil Dearden. Nominations: Academy Awards '66: Best Story & Screenplay. MGM, CCB

The Kick Fighter 🎞 1991 Would you believe the hero has to kickbox to finance his kid sister's operation? Grungy, Bangkok-set chopsocky cheapie leaves no cliche untouched, but fights are well-staged. A strange end credit lauds real-life champ Urquidez, here a bad guy. **92m/C VHS.** Richard Norton, Benny "The Jet" Urquidez, Glen Ruehland, Franco Guerrero, Erica Van Wagener, Steve Rackman; **D:** Anthony Maharaj. AIP

Kick of Death: The Prodigal Boxer 🎞 198? (R) A young boxer is accused of a murder he didn't commit, and fights a battle to the death to prove it. **90m/C VHS, Beta.** Mang Sei, Suma Wah Lung, Pa Hung; **D:** Chai Yang Min. GEM

Kickboxer 🎞½ 1989 (R) The brother of a permanently crippled kickboxing champ trains for a revenge match. **97m/C VHS, Beta, LV.** Jean-Claude Van Damme, Rochelle Ashana, Dennis Chan, Dennis Alexio; **D:** Mark DiSalle; **W:** Jean-Claude Van Damme, Mark DiSalle, Glenn A. Bruce. HBO, WAR

Kickboxer 2: The Road Back 🎞½ 1990 (R) Mitchell takes over for Van Damme in this action sequel which finds our athletic hero seeking revenge on the kickboxer who murdered his brother. **90m/C VHS, LV.** Sasha Mitchell, Peter Boyle, John Diehl; **D:** Albert Pyun. WAR, MOV, HBO

Kickboxer 3: The Art of War *1/2
1992 (R) Mitchell returns in this second sequel. This time the American kickboxing champ flies to Rio for a big match which turns out to be fixed by a local mobster. For a little more fun our hero saves a kidnapped girl and fights a hired killer.**CW:** Some strong violence. **92m/C VHS, Closed Caption.** Sasha Mitchell, Dennis Chan, Richard Comar, Noah Verduzco, Althea Miranda, Ian Jacklin; **D:** Rick King. *LIV*

Kickboxer 4: The Aggressor **1/2
1994 (R) Martial arts expert David Sloan (Mitchell) was framed by sworn enemy Tong Po but now he's back and looking for revenge. **90m/C VHS, LV, Closed Caption.** Sasha Mitchell, Kamal Krifia, Nicholas Guest, Deborah Mansy, Brad Thornton; **D:** Albert Pyun. *LIV*

Kickboxer the Champion *1991
The opium trade is in for a kick to the stomach when Archer challenges the big man in charge to a deathly duel. **?m/C VHS.** Don Murray, Wayne Archer; **D:** Alton Cheung. *WLA*

Kicking and Screaming ***1995
(R) Baumbach's deft, though slightly self-conscious directorial debut examines the post-college grad angst of Grover (Hamilton) and his three other slacker roomies. In denial of their recently achieved non-student status, the four bond together in pursuit of the inane and trivial, while their various girlfriends slip more easily into adulthood. Funny and tender flashback scenes of Grover and girlfriend Jane (D'Abo) add depth without all the dialogue; well-written though it is. Hilarious highlight occurs as roommate Otis interviews for that most popular of low-budget, Gen-X movie jobs—video store clerk.**CW:** Strong language and some sexuality. **96m/C VHS.** Josh Hamilton, Olivia D'Abo, Carlos Jacott, Christopher Eigeman, Eric Stoltz, Jason Wiles, Parker Posey, Cara Buono, Elliott Gould; **D:** Noah Baumbach; **W:** Oliver Berkman, Noah Baumbach; **C:** Steven Bernsein; **M:** Phil Marshall. *THV*

Kicks *1/2 1985
Two well-off San Francisco professionals play high-risk games with each other, culminating in a life-or-death hunt. Made for television. **97m/C VHS, Beta.** Anthony Geary, Shelley Hack, Tom Mason, Ian Abercrombie, James Avery; **D:** William Wiard; **M:** Peter Bernstein. *NO*

The Kid ***1921
Sensitive and sassy film about a tramp who takes home an orphan. Chaplin's first feature. Also launched Coogan as the first child superstar. **60m/B VHS.** Charlie Chaplin, Jackie Coogan, Edna Purviance; **D:** Charlie Chaplin. *FCT, MLB*

Kid **1/2 1990 (R)
Young guy carries grudge for the murder of his parents and seeks pound of flesh. Enter mysterious beautiful woman and copious complications. Good sound FX. **94m/C VHS, Beta, LV, Closed Caption.** C. Thomas Howell, R. Lee Ermey, Brian Austin Green, Sarah Trigger; **D:** John Mark Robinson. *LIV, IME*

Kid and the Killers *198? (PG)
Young orphan and a hardened criminal band together to pursue a villain. **90m/C VHS, Beta.** Jon Cypher. *NO*

The Kid Brother ***1/2 1927
The shy, weak son of a tough sheriff, Harold fantasizes about being a hero like his father and big brothers, falls in love with a carnival lady, and somehow saves the day. Classic silent comedy. **84m/B VHS, Beta.** Harold Lloyd, Walter James, Jobyna Ralston; **D:** Ted Wilde. *TLF*

Kid Colter **1/2 1985
Enjoyable family film about a city kid who goes to visit his dad in a remote wilderness area of the Pacific Northwest. While there he is abducted by two grizzly mountain men and left for dead, but survives and pursues his abductors relentlessly. Received the Film Advisory Board Award of Excellence and the Award of Merit from the Academy of Family Films. **101m/C VHS, Beta, Closed Caption.** Jim Stafford, Jeremy Shamos, Hal Terrance, Greg Ward, Jim Turner; **D:** David O'Malley; **W:** David O'Malley. *FOX*

Kid Courageous *1935
An athlete goes west, tracks ore mine thieves and prevents a hot-blooded spitfire from marrying the wrong man. **53m/B VHS, Beta.** Bob Steele. *NOS*

Kid Dynamite *Queen of Broadway* 1943
A Bowery Boys series episode. Gorcey is a boxer who is kidnapped to prevent his participation in a major fight. The real fighting occurs when his brother is substituted, and Gorcey is smitten. **73m/B VHS.** Leo Gorcey, Huntz Hall, Bobby Jordan, Gabriel Dell, Pamela Blake; **D:** Wallace Fox. *NOS, HEG*

A Kid for Two Farthings **1/2 1955
An episodic, sentimental portrait of the Jewish quarter in London's East End, centered on a boy with a malformed goat he thinks is a magic unicorn capable of granting wishes and bringing happiness to his impoverished 'hood. Acclaimed adaptation of a novel by screenwriter Wolf Mankowitz, also on tape in a shorter rehash as "The Unicorn." **96m/C VHS.** Jonathan Ashmore; **D:** HMV, FCT

Kid from Brooklyn **1946
A shy, musically inclined milkman becomes a middleweight boxer by knocking out the champ in a street brawl. Remake of "The Milky Way" by Harold Lloyd. Available with digitally remastered stereo and original movie trailer. ♫Sunflower Song; Hey, What's Your Name; You're the Cause Of It All; Welcome, Burleigh; I Love An Old-Fashioned Song; Josie. **113m/C VHS, Beta, LV.** Danny Kaye, Virginia Mayo, Eve Arden, Fay Bainter, Walter Abel; **D:** Norman Z. McLeod; **C:** Gregg Toland. *HBO*

Kid from Gower Gulch *1947
A singing, non-horse-riding cowboy enters a rodeo through a clever ruse. **56m/B VHS, Beta, LV.** Spade Cooley. *NOS*

The Kid from Left Field **1979
Bat boy for the San Diego Padres transforms the team from losers to champions when he passes on the advice of his father, a "has-been" ballplayer, to the team members. A made-for-television remake of the 1953 classic. **80m/C VHS, Beta.** Gary Coleman, Robert Guillaume, Ed McMahon, Tab Hunter; **D:** Adell Aldrich. *VES*

Kid from Not-So-Big **1978 (G)
A family film that tells the story of Jenny, a young girl left to carry on her grandfather's frontier-town newspaper. When two con-men come to town, Jenny sets out to expose them. **87m/C VHS, Beta.** Jennifer McAllister, Veronica Cartwright, Robert Viharo, Paul Tulley; **D:** William Crain. *WAR, OM*

Kid Galahad ***1937
The Battling Bellhop Well acted boxing drama with Robinson playing an honest promoter who wants to make Morris into a prize fighter. Davis plays the girl they both want. Remade as "The Wagons Roll at Night" and then made again as an Elvis Presley vehicle. Shown on television. **101m/B VHS, Closed Caption.** Edward G. Robinson, Bette Davis, Humphrey Bogart, Wayne Morris, Jane Bryan, Harry Carey Sr., Veda Ann Borg; **D:** Michael Curtiz; **W:** Seton I. Miller; **C:** Gaetano Antonio "Tony" Gaudio; **M:** Max Steiner. *MGM*

Kid Galahad **1962
The King plays a young boxer who weathers the fight game, singing seven songs along the way. ♫King of the Whole Wide World; This Is Living; I Got Lucky; A Whistling Tune; Home Is Where The Heart Is; Riding the Rainbow; Love Is For Loves. **95m/C VHS, Beta, LV.** Elvis Presley, Lola Albright, Charles Bronson, Ned Glass, Joan Blackman, Ed Asner, Gig Young; **D:** Phil Karlson; **C:** Burnett Guffey. *MGM*

The Kid/Idle Class ***1921
The Little Tramp adopts a homeless orphan in "The Kid," Chaplin's first feature-length film. This tape also includes "The Idle Class," a rare Chaplin short. **85m/B VHS, Beta.** Charlie Chaplin, Jackie Coogan, Edna Purviance, Chuck Reisner, Lita Grey Chaplin; **D:** Charlie Chaplin. *FOX*

A Kid in King Arthur's Court *1/2
1995 (PG) Lame adaptation of Mark Twain's "A Connecticut Yankee in King Arthur's Court" finds insecure California teen Calvin Fuller (Nicholas), falling down a hole created by an earthquake and landing in Camelot. Arthur's (Ackland) a doddering old man with a cute teen daughter, Princess Katey (Baeza), who needs some help in defeating the evil Lord Belasco (Malik). Naturally, Calvin helps out and gains confidence in himself. Okay time-waster for the kids. **91m/C VHS, Closed Caption.** Thomas Ian Nicholas, Joss Ackland, Art Malik, Paloma Baeza, Kate Winslet, Ron Moody, Daniel Craig; **D:** Michael Gottlieb; **W:** Michael Part, Robert L. Levy; **C:** Elemer Ragalyi; **M:** J.A.C. Redford. *TOU*

Kid Millions **1/2 1934
Vintage musical comedy in which a dull-witted Brooklyn boy must travel to exotic Egypt to collect an inherited fortune. The finale is filmed in early three-strip Technicolor. Lucille Ball appears as a Goldwyn Girl. ♫Your Head on My Shoulder; Ice Cream Fantasy; An Earful of Music; When My Ship Comes In; Okay Toots; I Want to be a Minstrel Man; Mandy. **90m/B VHS, Beta.** Eddie Cantor, Ethel Merman, Ann Sothern, George Murphy; **D:** Roy Del Ruth.

Kid 'n' Hollywood and Polly Tix in Washington 1933
These two "Baby Burlesks" shorts star a cast of toddlers, featuring the most famous moppet of all time, Shirley Temple, in her earliest screen appearances. **20m/B VHS, Beta.** Shirley Temple. *CCB*

Kid Ranger *1936
A ranger shoots an innocent man, but later sets things straight by bringing the real culprit to justice. **57m/B VHS, Beta.** Bob Steele, William Farnum; **D:** Robert North Bradbury. *VYY*

Kid Sister **1/2 1945
A young girl is determined to grab her sister's boyfriend for herself, and enlists the aid of a burglar to do it. **56m/B VHS, Beta.** Roger Pryor, Judy Clark, Frank Jenks, Constance Worth. *VYY*

Kid Vengeance **1/2 1975 (R)
After witnessing the brutal slaying of his family, a boy carries out a personal vendetta against the outlaws. **90m/C VHS, Beta.** Leif Garrett, Jim Brown, Lee Van Cleef, John Marley, Glynnis O'Connor; **D:** Joseph Manduke. *NO*

The Kid Who Loved Christmas **1990
After his adoptive mother is killed in a car accident, a young boy is taken from his adoptive father. The boy, upset about being removed from his new family, writes to Santa Claus for help. A touching yuletide drama. Made for television. This was Sammy Davis, Jr.'s last film. **118m/C VHS, Closed Caption.** Cicely Tyson, Michael Warren, Sammy Davis Jr., Gilbert Lewis, Ken Page, Della Reese, Esther Rolle, Ben Vereen, Vanessa Williams, John Beal, Trent Cameron; **D:** Arthur Seidelman; **C:** Hanania Baer. *PAR*

The Kid with the Broken Halo **1982
Coleman and Guillaume are paired again in this unsuccessful pilot for a TV series. A young angel, out to earn his wings, must try to help three desperate families, with the help of an experienced angel. **100m/C VHS.** Gary Coleman, Robert Guillaume, June Allyson, Mason Adams, Ray Walston, John Pleshette, Kim Fields, Georg Stanford Brown, Telma Hopkins; **D:** Leslie Martinson. *NO*

The Kid with the 200 I.Q. **1983
When an earnest boy genius enters college at age 13, predictable comic situations arise that involve his attempts at impressing his idolized astronomy professor (Guillaume), as well as an equally unrequited bout of first love. Harmless comedy, one of a series of squeaky-clean made-for-TV family fare starring Coleman. **96m/C VHS, Beta.** Gary Coleman, Robert Guillaume, Harriet Hilliard Nelson, Dean Butler, Karli Michaelson, Christina Murrull, Mel Stewart; **D:** Leslie Martinson. *LIV*

Kidco **1983 (PG)
The true story of a money-making corporation headed and run by a group of children ranging in age from nine to sixteen. **104m/C VHS, Beta, Closed Caption.** Scott Schwartz, Elizabeth Gorcey, Cinnamon Idles, Tristine Skyler; **D:** Ronald F. Maxwell.

Kidnap Syndicate *1/2 1976 (R)
Kidnappers swipe two boys, releasing one—the son of a wealthy industrialist who meets their ransom demands. When they kill the other boy, a mechan-

ic's son, the father goes on a revengeful killing spree. 105m/C VHS, Beta. *IT* James Mason, Valentina Cortese; **D:** Fernando Di Leo. *NO*

Kidnapped 🐾🐾½ 1960 A young boy is sold by his wicked uncle as a slave, and is helped by an outlaw. A Disney film based on the Robert Louis Stevenson classic. 94m/C VHS, Beta, Closed Caption. Peter Finch, James MacArthur, Peter O'Toole; **D:** Robert Stevenson. *DIS*

Kidnapped woof! 1987 (R) When a teenage girl is kidnapped by pornographers, her sister seeks help from a tough cop and together they go undercover to find her. Plot is flimsy cover for what is actually an exploitative piece. 100m/C VHS, Beta, LV. David Naughton, Barbara Crampton, Lance Le-Gault, Chick Vennera, Charles Napier; **D:** Howard (Hikmet) Avedis; **W:** Howard (Hikmet) Avedis. *NO*

Kidnapped 🐾🐾½ 1995 Cable TV adaptation of Robert Louis Stevenson's 1886 novel. In 1751 shanghaied young David Balfour (McCardie) and Highland patriot Aln Breck Stewart (Assante) escape from a slave ship and return to Scotland to battle the British. ?m/C VHS. Armand Assante, Brian McCardie, Michael Kitchen, Brian Blessed, Patrick Malahide; **D:** Ivan Passer; **W:** John Goldsmith. *CAF*

Kidnapping of Baby John Doe 1988 Tragedy strikes a family's newborn, and they must make the terrifying decision between life and death. A doctor and nurse, however, take matters into their own hands to save the baby. 90m/C VHS, Beta. Helen Hughes, Jayne Eastwood, Janet-Laine Green, Geoffery Boues, Peter Gerretsen. *NO*

The Kidnapping of the President 🐾🐾½ 1980 (R) The U.S. president is taken hostage by Third World terrorists. The Secret Service is on the ball trying to recover the nation's leader. Well-integrated subplot involves the vice president in a scandal. Engrossing political thriller. Based on novel by Charles Templeton. 113m/C VHS, Beta. *CA* William Shatner, Hal Holbrook, Van Johnson, Ava Gardner, Miguel Fernandez; **D:** George Mendeluk. *NO*

Kids 🐾🐾 1995 Very controversial docudrama about 24 hours in the lives of some aimless New York teenagers. The sullen Telly (Fitzpatrick) enjoys bragging about his skill in deflowering virgins but his promiscuity has lead Jennie (Sevigny) to test H.I.V. positive—something Telly is as yet unaware of. Telly'd rather hang around with best friend Casper (Pierce) anyway, out on the streets, being generally profane and obnoxious. Can either be regarded as a brutally realistic look at teen life today or a lot of fuss about nothing. Korine was 19 when he wrote the screenplay. The MPAA rated the film NC-17, after a protest the distributors chose to release it unrated. 90m/C VHS, LV, Closed Caption. Leo Fitzpatrick, Justin Pierce, Chloe Sevigny, Rosario Dawson, Sarah Henderson, Harold Hunter, Yakira Peguero, Joseph Knafelmacher; **D:** Larry Clark; **W:** Harmony Korine; **C:** Eric Alan Edwards; **M:** Louis Barlow. Independent Spirit Awards '96: Debut Performance (Pierce); Nominations: Independent Spirit Awards '96: Best First Feature, Best Supporting Actress (Sevigny). *THV*

Kid's Auto Race/Mabel's Married Life 🐾🐾 *Kid Auto Races at Venice* 1915 "Kid's Auto Race" (1914) concerns a kiddie-car contest; "Mabel's Married Life" (1915) is about flirtations in the park between married individuals. Piano and organ scores. 21m/B VHS, Beta. Charlie Chaplin, Mabel Normand, Mack Swain; **D:** Mack Sennett. *CCB, GVV*

Kids In the Hall: Brain Candy 🐾🐾 1996 (R) The Canadian Kids bring their Monty Python-meets-SCTV humor to the big screen with moderate success. Dr. Cooper (McDonald), facing corporate downsizing, allows his new, untested anti-depressant to be released to the public after it shows promise. The drug, Gleemonex, sweeps the country by forcing the user's mind to focus on a favorite memory. As befits the troupe's twisted vision, these happy memories aren't always pleasant to the "Family Values" crowd. The easily offended should be warned—there's a

character named "Cancer Boy." The story wanders a bit, giving everyone a chance to show their versatility (these Kids collectively play 32 different roles). Sophomore director Makin served the same duty on many of the TV episodes. *CW:* Language and sexual humor. 88m/C VHS, Beta, Closed Caption. Dave Foley, Bruce McCulloch, Kevin McDonald, Scott Thompson, Mark McKinney, Janeane Garofalo; **D:** Kelly Makin; **W:** Bruce McCulloch, Kevin McDonald, Scott Thompson, Mark McKinney, Norm Hiscock; **C:** David Makin; **M:** Craig Northey. Nominations: Genie Awards '96: Best Costume Design, Best Song ("Some Days It's Black"), Best Sound. *PAR*

Kid's Last Ride 🐾 1941 Three tough guys come into town to settle a feud. 55m/B VHS. Ray Corrigan, John "Dusty" King, Max Terhune, Luana Walters, Edwin Brian; **D:** S. Roy Luby. *NOS, DVT*

Kids of the Round Table 🐾🐾½ 1996 Eleven-year-old Alex (Morina) and his buddies like to have mock sword battles, pretending to be King Arthur and his knights. When their games are broken up by the local bully, Alex takes off into the woods where he discovers a sword in a stone. It's the legendary Excalibur and when Alex removes it, Merlin (McDowell) appears, explaining the sword will give the boy special powers. Of course, Alex abuses his newfound strength until he comes to the rescue of his friends. 89m/C VHS. *CA* Johnny Morina, Michael Ironside, Malcolm McDowell, Peter Aykroyd, Rene Simard; **D:** Robert Tinnell; **W:** David Sherman; **C:** Roxanne Di Santo; **M:** Normand Corbeil. *CAF*

Kika 🐾🐾 1994 Another flamboyant comedy from Almodovar finds irrepressible beautician Kika (Forque) involved with kinky photographer Ramon (Casanovas) and his stepfather Nicholas (Coyote), a sinister American pulp novelist. There's also Andrea Scarface (Jean-Paul Gaultier-costumed Abril), the host of a vile tabloid TV show called "Today's Worst," and Kika's lesbian maid Juana (de Palma) whose brother happens to be an escaped con/porn star, leading to an outlandish rape and...well, it's all pretty nonsensical, anyway. Spanish with subtitles. 115m/C VHS. *SP* Veronica Forque, Peter Coyote, Victoria Abril, Alex Casanovas, Rossy de Palma; **D:** Pedro Almodovar; **W:** Pedro Almodovar. *THV*

The Kill 🐾🐾½ 1973 A rough, cynical, hard-boiled, womanizing detective tracks down stolen cash in downtown Macao. 81m/C VHS, Beta. Richard Jaeckel, Henry Duval, Judy Washington. *NWV*

Kill Alex Kill woof! 1983 A Vietnam POW returns to find his family murdered, and uses the crime underworld to take revenge. 88m/C VHS, Beta. Tony Zarindast, Tina Bowmann, Chris Ponti. *GEM*

Kill and Go Hide 🐾 *The Child* 1976 A young girl visits her mother's grave nightly to communicate with and command the ghoul-like creatures that haunt the surrounding woods. 95m/C VHS, Beta. *NO*

Kill and Kill Again 🐾🐾½ 1981 (PG) A martial arts champion attempts to rescue a kidnapped Nobel Prize-winning chemist who has developed a high-yield synthetic fuel. Colorful, tongue-in-cheek, and fun even for those unfamiliar with the genre. 100m/C VHS, Beta. James Ryan, Anneline Kriel, Stan Schmidt, Bill Flynn, Norman Robinson, Ken Gampu, John Ramsbottom; **D:** Ivan Hall; **W:** John Crowther. *MED*

Kill, Baby, Kill 🐾🐾🐾 *Curse of the Living Dead; Operacione Paura* 1966 A small Transylvania town is haunted by the ghost of a seven-year-old witchcraft victim, and the town's suicide victims all seem to have hearts of gold (coins, that is). Lots of style and atmosphere in this Transylvanian tale from horror tongue in cheekster Bava. Considered by many genre connoisseurs to be the B man's finest, except that it bears early symptoms of the director's late onset infatuation with the zoom shot. 83m/C VHS. *IT* Erika Blanc, Giacomo "Jack" Rossi-Stuart, Fabienne Dali, Giana Vivaldi; **D:** Mario Bava. *SNC, FRG*

Kill Castro 🐾 1980 (R) Ever hear the one about the exploding cigar? Key West boat skipper is forced to carry a CIA agent to Cuba on a mission to assassinate Castro. Low-budget adventure that's deadly dull. 90m/C VHS, Beta. Sybil Danning, Albert Salmi, Michael V. Gazzo, Raymond St. Jacques, Woody Strode, Stuart Whitman, Robert Vaughn, Caren Kaye; **D:** Chuck Workman. *NO*

Kill Cruise 🐾🐾 1990 (R) The depressed and alcoholic skipper of the yacht Bella Donna gives up sailing until he meets two beautiful young women who want to sail to Bermuda for a taste of the good life. The calm of the Atlantic is disturbed when they are plagued by bad weather and fierce storms, and tensions rise as the two women's jealousies erupt. Will it set the climate for murder? *CW:* Language, one violent scene, and sexuality. 99m/C VHS, Beta, LV, Closed Caption. Juergen Prochnow, Patsy Kensit, Elizabeth Hurley; **D:** Peter Keglevic; **W:** Peter Keglevic. *USH*

Kill Factor woof! *Death Dimension; Black Eliminator; The Freeze Bomb* 1978 (R) Something stupid about a killer bomb tht could freeze the planet. So inept your brain cells will also be frozen if you watch it. 91m/C VHS, Beta. Jim Kelly, George Lazenby, Aldo Ray, Harold Sakata, Terry Moore; **D:** Al Adamson. *ACA*

Kill Line 🐾🐾 1991 (R) Kim stars as Joe, a street fighter who seeks to clear his name after serving a 10-year prison sentence for a crime he didn't commit. When he finds his brother's family has been murdered by criminals looking for the millions he supposedly stole, Joe wages a one-man martial arts war against a corrupt police force and the gang of thugs who are looking for the money. 93m/C VHS. Bobby Kim, Michael Parker, Marlene Zimmerman, H. Wayne Lowery, C.R. Valdez, Mark Williams, Ben Pfeifer; **D:** Richard H. Kim; **W:** Richard H. Kim. *HMD*

Kill Me Again 🐾🐾½ 1989 (R) Director Dahl does the contemporary noir thing through the Nevada desert with Whalley-Kilmer as a beautiful femme fatale. She asks a detective (real-life husband Kilmer) to fake her death, which gets him targeted not only by the police, but also the mob and her psycho-boyfriend (Madsen). Fun and full of plot twists that will satisfy fans of the noir persuasion. 93m/C VHS, Beta, Closed Caption. Val Kilmer, Joanne Whalley, Michael Madsen, Jonathan Gries, Bibi Besch; **D:** John Dahl; **W:** John Dahl, David Warfield. *MGM*

Kill My Wife...Please! 🐾🐾 19?? Comic adventure of a despicable husband trying to bump off his wife in order to cash in on her insurance policy. 90m/C VHS. Bob Dishy, Joanna Barnes, Bill Dana; **D:** Steven Hilliard Stern. *HHE*

The Kill-Off 🐾🐾 1990 (R) Bedridden Luanne (Gross), married to janitor Ralph (Monroe), manages to cause dissension in her isolated New Jersey community with her vicious gossip. But when Luanne learns Ralph's involved with a stripper (Haase), it puts her own life in danger. Based on a story by Jim Thompson. *CW:* Mature themes, language, violence, partial nudity. 100m/C VHS. Loretta Gross, Steve Monroe, Cathy Haase, Jackson Sims; **D:** Maggie Greenwald. *XVC*

Kill or Be Killed 🐾🐾 1980 (PG) Martial arts champion is lured to a phony martial arts contest by a madman bent on revenge. 90m/C VHS, Beta. James Ryan, Charlotte Michelle, Norman Combes; **D:** Ivan Hall. *MED*

Kill or Be Killed 🐾½ 1993 Michael Julian just spent eight years in jail for saving his brother Charlie's life. He must wonder why he bothered since Charlie has stolen his girl Beth and set up a drug empire. Michael ambushes Charlie's men and steals a million dollars to use as leverage but Charlie thinks rival drug lords are out to get him and starts a street war. 97m/C VHS. David Heavener, Joseph Nuzzolo, Paulo Tocha, Lynn Levand; **D:** Joe Straw; **W:** Joseph Nuzzolo. *AIP*

The Kill Reflex ⚔ 1989 (R) A tough black cop and his beautiful rookie partner battle the mob and corruption. 90m/C VHS, Beta, LV. Maud Adams, Fred Williamson, Bo Svenson, Phyllis Hyman; **D:** Fred Williamson. *COL*

Kill Slade ⚔ 1989 (PG-13) When a United Nations food-aid diversion conspiracy is uncovered by a beautiful journalist, a plan to kidnap her is put into action. Romance follows. 90m/C VHS, Beta, LV. *SA* Patrick Dollaghan, Lisa Brady, Anthony Fridjhon, Danny Keogh, Alfred Nowke; **D:** Bruce McFarlane. *NLC*

Kill Squad ⚔ 1981 (R) Squad of martial arts masters follow a trail of violence and bloodshed to a vengeful, deadly battle of skills. 85m/C VHS, Beta. Jean Claude, Jeff Risk, Jerry Johnson, Bill Cambra, Cameron Mitchell. *VTR*

Kill the Golden Goose ⚔ 1979 (R) Two martial arts masters work on opposite sides of a government corruption and corporate influence peddling case. 91m/C VHS, Beta. Brad von Beltz, Ed Parker, Master Bong Soo Han; **D:** Elliot Hong. *GEM*

Killcrazy ⚔ 1989 (R) On the way to a weekend camping trip, five Vietnam vets released from a mental hospital are slowly massacred by a group of dangerous killers until one of the vets decides to fight back. 94m/C VHS, LV. David Heavener, Danielle Brisebois, Burt Ward, Lawrence-Hilton Jacobs, Bruce Glover, Gary Owens, Rachelle Carson; **W:** David Heavener; **W:** David Heavener. *MED, IME*

Killer ⚔ 197? An ex-convict sets up an ingenious bank robbery, and gets double-crossed himself. 87m/C VHS, Beta. Henry Silva. *NO*

The Killer ⚔⚔⚔½ *Die Xue Shuang Xiong* 1990 (R) Jeffrey Chow is a gangster gunman who wants out. He's hired by his best friend to perform one last killing, but it doesn't go as smoothly as he wanted. He's almost caught by "Eagle" Lee, a detective who vows to hunt him down using Jennie, a singer blinded by Chow in crossfire. Lots of action and gunfights, but also pretty corny and sentimental. Very similar to American action movies, but using Chinese and Asian cultural conventions. A good introduction to the Chinese gangster-flick genre. Available with subtitles or dubbed in English. 110m/C VHS. *HK* Chow Yun-Fat, Sally Yeh, Danny Lee, Kenneth Tsang, Chu Kong; **D:** John Woo; **W:** John Woo. *FXL, BTV, FCT*

Killer: A Journal of Murder ⚔⚔ 1995 (R) Young, idealistic Jewish guard Henry Lesser (Leonard) befriends prisoner Carl Panzram (Woods) and encourages the man to write his life story. Then he must deal with the consequences of discovering the brutality behind Panzram's murderous crimes. The leads do fine but there's nothing new here. Inspired by true events and set in the 1920s. **CW:** Strong language and brutal violence, including a rape. 91m/C VHS, LV, Closed Caption. James Woods, Robert Sean Leonard, Ellen Greene, Cara Buono, Robert John Burke, Steve Forrest, John Bedford Lloyd, Harold Gould; **D:** Tim Metcalfe; **C:** Ken Kelsch. *REP*

Killer Bait ⚔⚔½ 1949 Muddled drama about an innocent couple who find a large sum of money accidentally dropped into their car by mobsters. Possession of the money leads the greedy wife to ruin when she gets involved with gangsters, blackmail, and murder. Also known as "Killer Bait." 99m/C VHS. Lizabeth Scott, Don DeFore, Dan Duryea, Arthur Kennedy, Kristine Miller, Barry Kelley; **D:** Byron Haskin. *SNC*

Killer Commandos ⚔ 19?? Mercenaries go to the rescue of an oppressed African nation to overthrow the sinister white supremacy dictator. 87m/C VHS. Cameron Mitchell, Anthony Eisley. *NO*

Killer Dill ⚔½ 1947 Also killer dull. A meek salesman is misidentified as a death-dealing gangster, and the comic mixups begin. 71m/B VHS. Stuart Erwin, Anne Gwynne, Frank Albertson, Mike Mazurki, Milburn Stone, Dorothy Granger; **D:** Lewis D. Collins. *NOS, VYY*

Killer Diller ⚔½ 1948 All-black musical revue featuring Nat King Cole and his Trio. 70m/B VHS, Beta. Dusty Fletcher, Nat King Cole, Butterfly McQueen, Moms Mabley, George Wiltshire; **D:** Josh Binney. *MVD, NOS, DVT*

Killer Elephants ⚔⚔ 1976 A Thai man struggles to save his plantation, his wife, and his baby from the terrorists hired by a land baron to drive him away from his property. 83m/C VHS, Beta. Sung Pa, Alan Yen, Nai Yen Ne, Yu Chien. *UNI*

The Killer Elite ⚔⚔½ 1975 (PG) Straight-ahead Peckinpah fare examining friendship and betrayal. Two professional assassins begin as friends but end up stalking each other when they are double-crossed. This minor Peckinpah effort is murky and doesn't have a clear resolution, but is plenty bloody. Lots of Dobermans roam through this picture too. 120m/C VHS, Beta, LV. James Caan, Robert Duvall, Arthur Hill, Gig Young, Burt Young, Mako, Bo Hopkins, Helmut Dantine; **D:** Sam Peckinpah; **W:** Marc Norman, Stirling Silliphant. *MGM*

Killer Fish ⚔ *Deadly Treasure of the Piranha* 1979 (PG) A scheme to steal and then hide a fortune in emeralds at the bottom of a tank full of piranhas backfires as the criminals find it impossible to retrieve them...as if that took a lot of foresight. Director Dawson is AKA Antonio Margheriti. Filmed in Brazil. 101m/C VHS, Beta, Closed Caption. *BR GB* Lee Majors, James Franciscus, Margaux Hemingway, Karen Black, Roy Brocksmith, Marisa Berenson; **D:** Anthony (Antonio Margheriti) Dawson. *FOX*

Killer Force ⚔½ 1975 (R) Predictable adventure involving international diamond smuggling. 100m/C VHS, Beta. Telly Savalas, Peter Fonda, Maud Adams, Hugh O'Brian; **D:** Val Guest. *LIV, VES*

Killer Image ⚔ 1992 (R) A photographer unwittingly sees more than he should and becomes involved in a lethal political coverup. At the same time a wealthy senator targets him and he must fight for his life. Viewers might feel they have to fight their boredom. **CW:** Some language, violence, and sensuality. 97m/C VHS, Beta, LV, Closed Caption. John Pyper-Ferguson, Michael Ironside, M. Emmet Walsh, Krista Errickson; **D:** David Winning. *PAR*

A Killer in Every Corner ⚔ 1974 Three psychology students visit a loony professor and succumb to his hair-raising shenanigans. 80m/C VHS, Beta. Joanna Pettet, Patrick Magee, Max Wall, Eric Flynn. *LIV*

Killer Inside Me ⚔⚔ 1976 (R) The inhabitants of a small Western town are unaware that their mild-mannered deputy sheriff is actually becoming a crazed psychotic murderer. From the novel by Jim Thompson. 99m/C VHS, Beta. Stacy Keach, Susan Tyrrell, Tisha Sterling, Keenan Wynn, John Dehner, John Carradine, Don Stroud, Charles McGraw, Julie Adams, Royal Dano; **D:** Burt Kennedy; **W:** Robert Chandlee. *WAR, OM*

Killer Instinct ⚔⚔ 1992 (R) Two brothers do bloody warfare with notorious mobster kingpins in prohibition-era New York City. **CW:** Some language, violence, and some sensuality. 101m/C VHS, LV, Closed Caption. Christopher Bradley, Bruce Nozick, Rachel York; **D:** Greydon Clark, Ken Stein. *THV*

Killer Klowns from Outer Space ⚔⚔½ 1988 (PG-13) Bozo-like aliens resembling demented clowns land on earth and set up circus tents to lure Earthlings in. Visually striking, campy but slick horror flick that'll make you think twice about your next visit to the big top. Mood is heightened by a cool title tune by the Dickies. Definitely has cult potential! 90m/C VHS, Beta, LV, Closed Caption. Grant Cramer, Suzanne Snyder, John Allen Nelson, Royal Dano, John Vernon, Peter Licassi, Michael Siegel; **D:** Stephen Chiodo; **W:** Charles Chiodo, Stephen Chiodo; **M:** John Massari. *MED, CDV*

Killer Likes Candy ⚔ 1978 An assassin stalks the King of Kafiristan, and a CIA operative tries to stop him. 86m/C VHS, Beta. Kerwin Mathews, Marilu Tolo; **D:** Richard Owens. *GEM, MRV*

Killer Looks ⚔½ 1994 (R) Phil likes to watch his wife Diane seduce strangers. Then they meet Mickey, a charmer with ideas of his own. Soon Diane and Phil find their kinky world threatened. Unrated version contains 13 minutes of additional footage. **CW:** Strong sexuality and language. 87m/C VHS, LV, Closed Caption. Michael Artura, Sara Suzanne Brown, Len Donato; **D:** Toby Phillips. *IMP*

Killer on Board ⚔⚔ 1977 Folks spending their holiday on a cruise ship are afflicted by a fatal virus and subsequently quarantined. Typical made-for-TV disaster flick. 100m/C VHS, Beta. Claude Akins, Beatrice Straight, George Hamilton, Patty Duke, Frank Converse, Jane Seymour, William Daniels; **D:** Philip Leacock. *LIV*

Killer Party woof! 1986 (R) Three coeds pledge a sorority and are subjected to a hazing that involves a haunted fraternity house. Standard horror plot; Paul Bartel ("Eating Raoul"; "Lust in the Dust") is the only significant element. 91m/C VHS, Beta. Elaine Wilkes, Sherry Willis-Burch, Joanna Johnson, Paul Bartel, Martin Hewitt, Ralph Seymour; **D:** William Fruet; **W:** Barney Cohen; **M:** John Beal. *FOX*

The Killer Shrews ⚔⚔ 1959 Lumet (Sidney's father) creates a serum that causes the humble shrew to take on killer proportions. The creatures are actually dogs in makeup. Goude was 1957's Miss Universe. 70m/B VHS. James Best, Ingrid Goude, Baruch Lumet, Ken Curtis; **D:** Ray Kellogg. *SNC, MRV, HHT*

Killer Tomatoes Eat France ⚔½ 1991 Professor Gangrene takes his tomato fetish to France, where the giant vegetables try to take over the streets. The fourth in the killer-vegetable series. 94m/C VHS, LV. John Astin, Marc Price, Steve Lundquist; **D:** John DeBello. *FXV*

Killer Tomatoes Strike Back ⚔⚔ 1990 The third "Killer Tomatoes" movie isn't in the league of "The Naked Gun" satires, but it's still bright parody for the Mad Magazine crowd, as tomato-mad scientist Astin harnesses the powers of trash-TV in a planned vegetable invasion. Perhaps due to a 'Killer Tomatoes' cartoon series at the time, this isn't as saucy as its predecessors and is acceptable for family audiences. Followed by "Killer Tomatoes Eat France." 87m/C VHS, Closed Caption. John Astin, Rick Rockwell, Crystal Carson, Steve Lundquist, John Witherspoon; **D:** John DeBello. *FXV, IME*

Killer with Two Faces ⚔ 1974 A woman is terrorized by the evil twin of her boyfriend. Made for television. 70m/C VHS, Beta. Donna Mills, Ian Hendry, David Lodge, Roddy McMillian. *LIV*

Killer Workout ⚔ *Aerobicide* 1986 (R) A murderer stalks the clients of a sweat/sex/muscle-filled gym. 89m/C VHS, Beta. David James Campbell, Ted Prior; **D:** David A. Prior. *ACA*

The Killers ⚔⚔ *Ernest Hemingway's the Killers* 1964 After two hired assassins kill a teacher, they look into his past and try to find leads to a $1,000,000 robbery. Reagan's last film. Remake of 1946 film of the same name, which was loosely based on a short story by Ernest Hemingway. Originally intended for television, but released to theaters instead due to its violence. 95m/C VHS, Beta. Lee Marvin, Angie Dickinson, John Cassavetes, Ronald Reagan, Clu Gulager, Claude Akins, Norman Fell; **D:** Donald Siegel; **M:** John Williams. *USH*

Killers ⚔ 1988 Remote jungles of southern Africa are the scene of a military coup. 83m/C VHS, Beta. Cameron Mitchell, Alicia Hammond, Robert Dix; **D:** Ewing Miles Brown. *GHV*

The Killer's Edge ⚔½ *Blood Money* 1990 (R) Cop is caught between rock and hard place in L.A. when he's forced to confront criminal who once saved his life in 'Nam. Plenty of gut busting and soul wrenching. **CW:** Language, violence, and sensuality. 90m/C VHS, LV. Wings Hauser, Robert Z'Dar, Karen Black. *PMH*

Killers from Space WOOF! **1954** Cheap sci-fi flick in which big-eyed men from beyond Earth bring scientist Graves to life to assist them with their evil plan for world domination. **80m/B VHS, Beta.** Peter Graves, Barbara Bestar, James Scay; **D:** W. Lee Wilder. *NOS, MRV, RHI*

Killer's Kiss 🐾🐾½ **1955** A boxer and a dancer set out to start a new life together when he saves the woman from an attempted rape. Gritty, second feature from Kubrick was financed by friends and family and shows signs of his budding talent. **67m/C VHS.** Frank Silvera, Jamie Smith, Irene Kane, Jerry Jarret; **D:** Stanley Kubrick; **W:** Stanley Kubrick. *FCT*

The Killing 🐾🐾🐾 **1956** The dirty, harsh, street-level big heist epic that established Kubrick and presented its genre with a new and vivid existentialist aura, as an ex-con engineers the rip-off of a racetrack with disastrous results. Displays characteristic nonsentimental sharp-edged Kubrick vision. Cinematography by Lucien Ballard. Based on the novel "Clean Break" by Lionel White. **83m/B VHS, Beta, LV.** Sterling Hayden, Marie Windsor, Elisha Cook Jr., Jay C. Flippen, Vince Edwards, Timothy Carey, Coleen Gray, Joseph Sawyer, Ted de Corsia; **D:** Stanley Kubrick. *MGM*

A Killing Affair 🐾 **1985 (R)** Set in West Virginia, 1943, this is the story of a widow who takes in a drifter who she believes is the man who killed her husband. She begins to fall for him, but cannot be sure if she should trust him. Vague and melodramatic. From the novel "Monday, Tuesday, Wednesday" by Robert Houston. Saperstein's directorial debut. **100m/C VHS, Beta, LV.** Peter Weller, Kathy Baker, John Glover, Bill Smitrovich; **D:** David Saperstein; **M:** John Barry. *VTR, PSM*

Killing at Hell's Gate 🐾½ **1981** A made-for-television movie about a group of whitewater rafters being picked off by snipers as they travel down river. **96m/C VHS, Beta, Closed Caption.** Robert Urich, Deborah Raffin, Lee Purcell; **D:** Jerry Jameson; **M:** David Bell. *FOX*

The Killing Beach 🐾🐾 *Turtle Beach* **1992 (R)** Australian photojournalist Judith Wilkes (Scacchi) travels to Malaysia in the late 1970s to report on the plight of the Vietnamese boat people seeking refuge there. She befriends the wife of the Australian ambassador, a former callgirl from Saigon, who hopes to find her own children among the refugees. But the native Malays resent the foreign intrusion and are determined to stop the boat people—no matter what the cost in blood. Based on the novel "Turtle Beach" by Blanche D'Alpuget. **CW:** Language, violence, and sensuality. **105m/C VHS, Closed Caption.** *AU* Greta Scacchi, Joan Chen, Jack Thompson, Art Malik, Norman Kaye; **D:** Stephen Wallace; **W:** Ann Turner; **C:** Russell Boyd. *COL*

Killing Cars 🐾½ **1985 (R)** A German car designer's pet project, a car that runs without gas, is halted by the influence of an Arab conglomerate. He nevertheless tries to complete it, and is hunted down. **104m/C VHS, Beta.** Juergen Prochnow, Senta Berger, William Conrad, Agnes Soral; **D:** Michael Verhoeven. *THV, HHE, VTR*

The Killing Device 🐾½ **1992** Two government scientists lose their funding on a covert political assassination project and decide to eliminate the government officials responsible. When two journalists attempt to solve the murders they become the next targets. **93m/C VHS.** Clu Gulager, Antony Alda, Gig Rauch. *VCI*

The Killing Edge 🐾½ **1986** In post-nuclear holocaust Earth, a lone warrior seeks justice, and his family, in a lawless land. **85m/C VHS.** Bill French, Marv Spencer; **D:** Lindsay Shonteff. *VCD, HHE*

Killing 'em Softly 🐾 **1985** Segal portrays a down-on-his-luck musician who accidentally murders a music manager during an argument. Cara's boyfriend is accused and to clear his name, the singer moonlights as a detective. She and Segal end up falling in love. Disappointing.

90m/C VHS, Beta. *CA* George Segal, Irene Cara; **D:** Max Fischer. *PSM, HHE*

The Killing Fields 🐾🐾🐾½ **1984 (R)** Based on the New York Times' Sydney Schanberg's account of his friendship with Cambodian interpreter Dith Pran. They separated during the fall of Saigon, when Western journalists fled, leaving behind countless assistants who were later accused of collusion with the enemy by the Khmer Rouge and killed or sent to re-education camps during the bloodbath known as "Year Zero." Schanberg searched for Pran through the Red Cross and U.S. government, while Pran struggled to survive, finally escaping and walking miles to freedom. Ngor's own experiences echoed those of his character Pran. Malkovich's debut is intense. Joffe's directorial debut shows a generally sure hand, with only a bit of melodrama at the end. **142m/C VHS, Beta, LV, Closed Caption.** *GB* Sam Waterston, Haing S. Ngor, John Malkovich, Athol Fugard, Craig T. Nelson, Julian Sands, Spalding Gray, Bill Paterson; **D:** Roland Joffe; **W:** Bruce Robinson; **C:** Chris Menges. Academy Awards '84: Best Cinematography, Best Film Editing, Best Supporting Actor (Ngor); British Academy Awards '84: Best Actor (Ngor), Best Adapted Screenplay, Best Film; Golden Globe Awards '85: Best Supporting Actor (Ngor); Los Angeles Film Critics Association Awards '84: Best Cinematography; New York Film Critics Awards '84: Best Cinematography; National Society of Film Critics Awards '84: Best Cinematography; Writers Guild of America '84: Best Adapted Screenplay; Nominations: Academy Awards '84: Best Actor (Waterston), Best Adapted Screenplay, Best Director (Joffe), Best Picture. *WAR, BTV, HMV*

Killing Floor 🐾🐾 **1985 (PG)** During WWI, black sharecropper Frank Custer (Leake) travels to Chicago to get work in the stockyards and becomes a voice in the growing labor movement. The tensions in the factories lead to to bloody race riots of 1919. Made for television. **118m/C VHS, Beta, LV.** Damien Leake, Alfre Woodard, Moses Gunn, Clarence Felder, Bill Duke; **D:** William Duke. *KIV, COL, FCT*

The Killing Game 🐾🐾½ *All Weekend Lovers; Jeu de Massacre* **1967** A husband-wife cartoonist team link up with an unhinged playboy and act out a murder-mystery comic they produce together. In French with subtitles. **90m/C VHS, Beta.** *FR* Jean-Pierre Cassel, Claudine Auger, Michael Duchaussoy, Anna Gaylor; **D:** Alain Jessua. *FCT*

The Killing Game 🐾 **1987** A slew of Californians kill and betray each other for lustful reasons. **90m/C VHS, Beta.** Chad Hayward, Cynthia Killion, Geoffrey Sadwith; **D:** Joseph Merhi. *NO*

Killing Grandpa 🐾🐾 *Matar al Abuelito* **1991** Wealthy family patriarch Don Mariano Aguero (Luppi) has lost the will to live and attempted suicide, which has left him comatose. His three greedy children are anxious for their inheritance but the Don's loyal handyman enlists the aid of his half-sister Rosita (Esteves), who possesses healing powers, to give his aged employer the strength to recover. Spanish with subtitles. **114m/C VHS.** *SP AR* Federico Luppi, Ines Estevez; **D:** Luis Cesar D'Angiolillo; **W:** Luis Cesar D'Angiolillo, Ariel Sienra; **C:** Miguel Abal. *NYF*

Killing Heat 🐾½ *The Grass is Singing* **1984 (R)** An independent career woman living in South Africa decides to abandon her career to marry a struggling jungle farmer. Based on Doris Lessing's novel "The Grass is Singing." **104m/C VHS, Beta.** *GB SW* Karen Black, John Thaw, John Kani, John Moulder-Brown; **D:** Michael Raeburn. *FOX*

Killing Hour 🐾🐾 *The Clairvoyant* **1984 (R)** A psychic painter finds that the visions she paints come true in a string of grisly murders. Her ability interests a television reporter and a homicide detective. **97m/C VHS, Beta, Closed Caption.** Elizabeth Kemp, Perry King, Norman Parker, Kenneth McMillan; **D:** Armand Mastroianni. *FOX*

A Killing in a Small Town 🐾🐾🐾 **1990 (R)** Candy Morrison seems like the perfect member of her small Texas community—but appearances can be deceiving, particularly after she's charged with killing a fellow church-goer by striking her 41 times with an axe (shades of Lizzie Borden)! Dennehy is her skeptical lawyer who isn't sure if it was self-defense or a peculiar sort of revenge. Good performances by Hershey and Dennehy lift this above the usual tawdry made for TV level. Based on a true story; originally a television miniseries. **CW:** Violence. **95m/C VHS, LV, Closed Caption.** Barbara Hershey, Brian Dennehy, Hal Holbrook, Richard Gilliland, John Terry, Lee Garlington; **D:** Stephen Gyllenhaal; **C:** Robert Elswit; **M:** Richard Gibbs. *THV*

Killing in the Sun 🐾 **19?? (R)** Gripping struggle for prosperous smuggling in the Mediterranean consume mobsters from three countries. **90m/C VHS.** Henry Silva, Michael Constantine. *NO*

The Killing Jar 🐾🐾½ **1996 (R)** Michael Sanford (Cullen) has taken his pregnant wife Diane (Tomita) back to the California wine country to take over the failing family vineyard. A series of vicious murders occur in the area, one of which Michael may have witnessed. Hypnosis brings up a lot of Michael's repressed childhood memories, he begins to unravel, and becomes the prime suspect in the killings. **CW:** Graphic violence, a strong sex scene and language. **101m/C VHS, LV, Closed Caption.** Brett Cullen, Tamlyn Tomita, Wes Studi, Brion James, M. Emmet Walsh, Tom Bower, Xander Berkeley; **D:** Evan Crooke; **W:** Mark Mullin; **C:** Michael G. Wojciechowski; **M:** David Williams. *APX*

The Killing Kind 🐾🐾½ **1973** Man released from prison is obsessed with wreaking vengeance on his daft lawyer and his accuser. His vendetta eventually draws his mother into the fray as well. Fine performance by Savage. **95m/C VHS.** Ann Sothern, John Savage, Ruth Roman, Luana Anders, Cindy Williams; **D:** Curtis Harrington; **M:** Andrew Belling. *NO*

The Killing Man 🐾🐾 **1994** Former mobster tries going legit by changing his identity and working for the government. **100m/C VHS.** Jeff Wincott. *APX*

The Killing Mind **1990** A young girl witnesses a grisly murder that is never solved. Twenty years later she (Zimbalist) becomes a cop who specializes in trapping psychos. Haunted by her memories, she and a reporter (Bill) team up to find the killer, never suspecting that she is his next victim. Originally made-for-cable-television. **96m/C VHS.** Stephanie Zimbalist, Tony Bill, Daniel Roebuck; **D:** Michael Rhodes. *WOV*

Killing Obsession 🐾½ **1994** Albert (Savage) has been locked in the Parkview State Psychiatric Facility for 20 years, ever since he murdered 11-year-old Annie's mother. Annie is Albert's obsession and in his mind she's always remained a young girl. So when Albert is released, he goes looking for Annie—murdering along the way. Now that the real Annie is an adult will Albert finally accept the passage of time or will she be just another victim? **95m/C VHS, LV.** John Savage, Kimberly Chase, John Saxon, Bernie White; **D:** Paul Leder; **W:** Paul Leder. *TRI*

The Killing of a Chinese Bookie 🐾🐾 **1976 (R)** Gazzara runs a Sunset Strip nightclub and is in hock to loan sharks. When he can't come up with the cash, he's offered a deal—get rid of a troublesome Chinese bookie and all debts will be forgiven. But it turns out the bookie is highly connected in the Asian mob and nothing goes as planned. Cassavetes's improv technique reaches for a self-indulgent and endless film. **109m/C VHS, Beta, Closed Caption.** Ben Gazzara, Jean-Pierre Cassel, Zizi Johari, Soto Joe Hugh, Robert Phillips, Timothy Carey, Morgan Woodward; **D:** John Cassavetes; **W:** John Cassavetes; **C:** Frederick Elmes. *TOU, FCT*

Killing of Angel Street 🐾🐾 **1981 (PG)** A courageous young woman unwittingly becomes the central character in an escalating nightmare about saving a community from corrupt politicians and organized crime. **101m/C VHS, Beta.** *AU* Liz Alexander, John Hargreaves; **D:** Donald Crombie; **W:** Evan Jones; **M:** Brian May. FCT

Killing of Randy Webster ♂♂½ 1981 A
father attempts to prove that his son did not die as a criminal when Texas policemen shot him after transporting a stolen van across state lines. **90m/C VHS, Beta.** Hal Holbrook, Dixie Carter, Sean Penn, Jennifer Jason Leigh; **D:** Sam Wanamaker. NO

The Killing of Sister George ♂♂
1969 (R) Racy, sensationalized film based on the Frank Marcus black comedy/melodrama about a lesbian love triangle between a television executive and two soap opera stars. Things get a little uncomfortable when they learn one of their characters is to be written out of the show. Shot in England. **138m/C VHS, Beta.** Beryl Reid, Susannah York, Coral Browne, Ronald Fraser, Patricia Medina, Hugh Paddick, Cyril Elaine Church, Brandan Dillon; **D:** Robert Aldrich; **C:** Joseph Biroc. FOX

Killing Stone ♂♂ 1978 A freelance writer
uncovers a small town sheriff's plot to cover up a scandalous homicide. Made for television. **120m/C VHS, Beta.** Gil Gerard, J.D. Cannon, Jim Davis, Nehemiah Persoff; **D:** Michael Landon; **W:** Michael Landon. PSM

Killing Streets ♂♂ 1991 A commando
learns that his twin brother is being held hostage in Lebanon and plans a rescue mission. A standard farfetched actioner; noteworthy for a real sense of despair over the endless carnage in the Mideast. Some dialogue in Arabic with subtitles. **109m/C VHS.** Michael Pare, Lorenzo Lamas; **D:** Stephen Cornwell; **W:** Stephen Cornwell. VES, LIV

The Killing Time ♂♂ 1987 (R) A minor,
effective murder thriller about a quiet small resort town suddenly beset by a web of murder, double-crossings, blackmail, and infidelity. They seem to coincide with the appearance of a mysterious stranger posing as the town's deputy sheriff just as the new sheriff is about to take up the badge. **94m/C VHS, Beta, LV.** Kiefer Sutherland, Beau Bridges, Joe Don Baker, Wayne Rogers; **D:** Rick King; **W:** Dan Bohlinger. NWV, VTR

Killing Zoe ♂♂ 1994 (R) American safe-
cracker travels to Paris for a little rest, recreation, and robbery. At the request of a childhood friend, he involves himself in an ill-conceived daytime bank heist, but not before enjoying a night with a local call girl and participating in some good ol' fashioned heroin-induced debauchery with the other bank robbers on the night before the job. Surprising no one (except maybe the still-stoned crooks), things don't go exactly as planned. Visually impressive debut for Tarantino collaborator Avary, who had his actors read "Beowulf" for its portrayal of Viking excess. **CW:** extreme violence, nudity, profanity, drug use **97m/C VHS, LV.** Eric Stoltz, Julie Delpy, Jean-Hugues Anglade, Gary Kemp, Bruce Ramsay, Kario Salem, Carlo Scandiuzzi; **D:** Roger Roberts Avary; **W:** Roger Roberts Avary; **C:** Tom Richmond. LIV

The Killing Zone ♂♂½ 1990 Convict
nephew of onetime Drug Enforcement agent rewrites zoning ordinances to hunt for Mexican drug lord south of the border. **90m/C VHS.** Daron McBee, James Dalesandro, Melissa Moore, Armando Silvestre, Augustine Beral, Sydne Squire, Deborah Dare; **D:** Addison Randall. PMH

Killings at Outpost Zeta ♂ 1980
Earthmen investigate a barren planet where previous expeditions have disappeared, and find hordes of aliens. **92m/C VHS, Beta.** Gordon Devol, Jackie Ray, James A. Watson Jr. VCI

Killjoy ♂♂½ Who Murdered Joy Morgan? 1981 A
sleazy surgeon's daughter is the prey in this television thriller. The plot twists are led by the array of people who become involved. A clever suspense mystery. Made for television. **100m/C VHS, Beta.** Kim Basinger, Robert Culp, Stephen Macht, Nancy Marchand, John Rubinstein, Ann Dusenberry, Ann Wedgeworth; **D:** John Llewellyn Moxey; **M:** Bruce Broughton. LIV

Killpoint ♂♂½ 1984 (R) Special task force is
assembled to catch the criminals who robbed a National Guard armory for its weapons. **89m/C VHS, Beta, LV.** Leo Fong, Richard Roundtree, Cameron Mitchell; **D:** Frank Harris. LIV, VES

Killzone ♂ 1985 A brainwashed Vietnam vet
breaks down during a training exercise and embarks on a psychotic killing spree. **86m/C VHS, Beta.** Ted Prior, David James Campbell, Richard Massery; **D:** David A. Prior. VES

Kilma, Queen of the
Amazons woof! **1986** A shipwrecked sailor finds himself on an island populated by man-hating Amazons. When a shipload of lusty sailors arrive to rescue him, carnage ensues. **90m/C VHS, Beta.** NO

Kim ♂♂♂ 1950 A colorful Hollywood adapta-
tion of the Rudyard Kipling classic about an English boy disguised as a native in 19th Century India, and his various adventures. **113m/C VHS, Beta.** Errol Flynn, Dean Stockwell, Paul Lukas, Cecil Kellaway; **D:** Victor Saville; **M:** Andre Previn. MGM

Kim ♂♂½ 1984 Kim (Sheth) is a 15-year-old
boy living by his wits on the streets of 1890s India. Trying to discover his true identity, Kim's befriended by a Buddhist monk who wishes the boy to be his disciple and a British spy, who trains him for a daring mission against the Russians. Rousing TV adaptation of the Rudyard Kipling novel. **135m/C VHS.** Ravi Sheth, Peter O'Toole, Bryan Brown, John Rhys-Davies, Julian Glover; **D:** John Davies. PME

Kind Hearts and Coronets ♂♂♂½
1949 Black comedy in which an ambitious young man sets out to bump off eight relatives in an effort to claim a family title. Guinness is wonderful in his role as all eight of the fated relations. Based on Roy Horiman's novel. **104m/B VHS, Beta, LV.** GB Alec Guinness, Dennis Price, Valerie Hobson, Joan Greenwood, Audrey Fildes, Miles Malleson, Clive Morton, Cecil Ramage, John Penrose, Hugh Griffith, John Salew, Eric Messiter, Anne Valery, Arthur Lowe, Jeremy Spenser; **D:** Robert Hamer; **W:** Robert Hamer, John Dighton; **C:** Douglas Slocombe; **M:** Ernest Irving. National Board of Review Awards '50: 5 Best Foreign Films of the Year. REP, FCT, HMV

A Kind of Loving ♂♂♂ 1962 Two
North English young people marry rashly as a result of pregnancy, find they really didn't like each other all that much, but manage to adjust. **107m/B VHS, Beta.** GB Alan Bates, Thora Hird, June Ritchie; **D:** John Schlesinger. NO

Kindergarten ♂♂♂ 1984 Endearing tale
based on a true story of a young Russian street violinist. During WWII, the boy meets a variety of interesting people as he travels throughout the Soviet Union. In Russian with English subtitles. **143m/C VHS.** RU Klaus Maria Brandauer; **D:** Yevgeny Yevtushenko. KIV

Kindergarten Cop ♂♂½ 1990 (PG-13)
Pectoral perfect cop Kimble (Schwarzenegger) stalks mama's boy/criminal Crisp (Tyson) by locating the drug lord's ex and his six-year-old son. When the pec man's female partner succumbs to a nasty bout of food poisoning, he's forced to take her place as an undercover kindergarten teacher in the drowsy Pacific northwest community where mother and son reside incognito. A cover all the bases Christmas release; it's got romance, action, comedy and cute. And box office earnings to match Arnie's chest measurements. A bit violent for the milk and cookie set. **111m/C VHS, Beta, LV, Closed Caption.** Arnold Schwarzenegger, Penelope Ann Miller, Pamela Reed, Linda Hunt, Richard Tyson, Carroll Baker, Cathy Moriarty, Park Overall, Richard Portnow, Jayne Brook; **D:** Ivan Reitman; **W:** Murray Salem, Herschel Weingrod, Timothy Harris; **C:** Michael Chapman; **M:** Randy Edelman. USH, CCB

The Kindred ♂♂½ 1987 (R) A young stu-
dent discovers that his mother the biologist has created a hybrid creature using his body tissue. Naturally, he is horrified and begins to search for his test-tube brother; the problem is, this brother

likes eating people. Not too bad; boasts some good acting. **92m/C VHS, Beta, LV.** Rod Steiger, Kim Hunter, David Allan Brooks, Timothy Gibbs, Amanda Pays, Talia Balsam, Amy Obrow, Peter Frechette, Julia Montgomery; **D:** Jeffrey Obrow, Stephen Carpenter; **W:** Jeffrey Obrow, Stephen Carpenter, Joseph Stefano, John Penney, Earl Ghaffari; **M:** David Newman. LIV, VES

King ♂♂♂ 1978 Docudrama with terrific cast
follows the life and career of one of the greatest non-violent civil rights leaders of all time, Martin Luther King. Made for television. **272m/C VHS, Beta.** Paul Winfield, Cicely Tyson, Roscoe Lee Browne, Ossie Davis, Art Evans, Ernie Banks, Howard E. Rollins Jr., William Jordan, Cliff DeYoung; **D:** Abby Mann; **W:** Abby Mann; **M:** Billy Goldenberg. NO

King and Country ♂♂♂ 1964 Aristo-
cratic army officer, Capt. Hargreaves (Bogarde), serves as the defense lawyer for troubled Private Arthur Hamp (Courtenay), whose wartime experiences have caused him to desert. Hargreaves at first ignores the uneducated Hamp's obvious shell-shock but soon begins to feel sympathy for his confused client. Director Losey shows the effects of war rather than the war itself and provides a sincere and bitter condemnation of military mentality. Based on the play "Hamp" by John Wilson. **86m/B VHS.** GB Dirk Bogarde, Tom Courtenay, Leo McKern, Barry Foster, James Villiers, Peter Copley; **D:** Joseph Losey; **W:** Evan Jones; **C:** Denys Coop; **M:** Larry Adler. KIT

The King and Four Queens ♂♂½
1956 Gable, on the run from the law, happens upon a deserted town, deserted, that is, except for a woman and her three daughters. Clark soon discovers that the women are looking for $100,000 in gold that one of their missing husbands had stolen. True to form, conniving Clark wastes no time putting the moves on each of them to find the whereabouts of the loot. **86m/C VHS, Beta.** Clark Gable, Eleanor Parker, Jo Van Fleet, Jean Wiles, Barbara Nichols, Sara Shane, Roy Roberts, Arthur Shields, Jay C. Flippen; **D:** Raoul Walsh; **M:** Alex North. MGM, CCB

The King and I ♂♂♂♂ 1956 Wonderful
adaptation of Rodgers and Hammerstein's Broadway play based on the novel "Anna and the King of Siam" by Margaret Landon. English governess Kerr is hired to teach the King of Siam's many children and bring them into the 20th century. She has more of a job than she realizes, for this is a king, a country, and a people who value tradition above all else. Features one of Rodgers and Hammerstein's best-loved scores. Brynner made this role his, playing it over 4,000 times on stage and screen before his death. Kerr's voice was dubbed when she sang; the voice you hear is Marni Nixon, who also dubbed the star's singing voices in "West Side Story" and "My Fair Lady." ♫Shall We Dance?; Getting To Know You; Hello, Young Lovers; We Kiss in a Shadow; I Whistle a Happy Tune; March of the Siamese Children; I Have Dreamed; A Puzzlement; Something Wonderful. **133m/C VHS, Beta, LV, Closed Caption.** Deborah Kerr, Yul Brynner, Rita Moreno, Martin Benson, Terry Saunders, Rex Thompson, Alan Mowbray, Carlos Rivas; **D:** Walter Lang; **W:** Ernest Lehman; **M:** Richard Rodgers, Oscar Hammerstein, Leon Shamroy. Academy Awards '56: Best Actor (Brynner), Best Art Direction/Set Decoration (Color), Best Costume Design (Color), Best Sound, Scoring of a Musical; Golden Globe Awards '57: Best Actress—Musical/Comedy (Kerr), Best Film—Musical/Comedy; Nominations: Academy Awards '56: Best Actress (Kerr), Best Color Cinematography, Best Director (Lang), Best Picture. FOX, BTV, RDG

King Arthur, the Young
Warlord ♂♂ 1975 (PG) The struggle that was the other side of Camelot—the campaign against the Saxon hordes. The early, somewhat violent years of King Arthur. **90m/C VHS, Beta.** Oliver Tobias, Michael Gothard, Jack Watson, Brian Blessed, Peter Firth; **D:** Sidney Hayers, Pat Jackson, Peter Sasdy. GEM

King Boxer 🎬 1990 A famous martial arts school is taken over by a menacing gang. When a student-to-be finds this out, he enlists himself to take on the best individual of the gang in a deadly match. 106m/C VHS. Lo Lieh, Wang Ping. *HMD*

King Boxers 🎬🎬 1980 (R) Kurate stars in this tale of elephant hunts, warding off Triad Society gangs, and personal combat. Nainam is a former Thailand fists and kick boxing champion. 90m/C VHS, Beta. Yasuka Kurata, Johnny Nainam. *GEM*

King Creole 🎬🎬½ 1958 The King goes film noir as a teenager with a criminal record who becomes a successful pop singer in New Orleans but is threatened by his ties to crime, represented by Walter Matthau. One of the better Elvis films, based on Harold Robbins' "A Stone for Danny Fisher." Features Elvis' last film appearance before his service in the Army. ♫King Creole; Banana; New Orleans; Turtles, Berries and Gumbo; Crawfish; Don't Ask Me Why; As Long As I Have You; Trouble; Hard-Headed Woman. 115m/B VHS, Beta, LV. Elvis Presley, Carolyn Jones, Walter Matthau, Dean Jagger, Dolores Hart, Vic Morrow, Paul Stewart; **D:** Michael Curtiz. *MVD, FOX*

King David 🎬½ 1985 (PG-13) The story of David, the legendary Biblical hero whose acts of bravery paved the way for him to become king of Israel. 114m/C VHS, Beta, LV, Closed Caption. Richard Gere, Alice Krige, Cherie Lunghi, Hurd Hatfield, Edward Woodward; **D:** Bruce Beresford; **W:** Andrew Birkin, James Costigan; **M:** Carl Davis. *PAR*

King Dinosaur 🎬½ 1955 A new planet arrives in the solar system, and a scientific team checks out its giant iguana-ridden terrain. 63m/B VHS, Beta, LV. Bill Bryant, Wanda Curtis, Patti Gallagher, Douglas Henderson. *MLB*

A King in New York 🎬🎬 1957 Chaplin plays the deposed king of a European mini-monarchy who comes to the United States in hope of making a new life. Looks critically at 1950s-era America, including Cold War paranoia and over reliance on technology. Containing Chaplin's last starring performance, this film wasn't released in the U.S. until 1973. Uneven but interesting. 105m/B VHS, Beta. **GB** Charlie Chaplin, Dawn Addams, Michael Chaplin, Oliver Johnston, Maxine Audley, Harry Green; **D:** Charlie Chaplin; **C:** Georges Perinal. *FOX*

King Kelly of the U.S.A. 🎬 1934 Robertson carries on a forgettable romance with a princess aboard a trans-Atlantic line. 64m/B VHS. Guy Robertson, Irene Ware, Edgar Kennedy, Franklin Pangborn, Joyce Compton, Ferdinand Gottschalk, William von Brinken, Otis Harlan; **D:** Leonard Fields. *NOS*

King Kong 🎬🎬🎬🎬 1933 The original beauty and the beast film classic tells the story of Kong, a giant ape captured in Africa and brought to New York as a sideshow attraction. Kong falls for Wray, escapes from his captors and rampages through the city, ending up on top of the newly built Empire State Building. Moody Steiner score adds color, and Willis O'Brien's stop-motion animation still holds up well. Remade numerous times with various theme derivations. Available in a colorized version. The laserdisc, produced from a superior negative, features extensive liner notes and running commentary by film historian Ronald Haver. 105m/B VHS, Beta, LV, 8mm, Closed Caption. Fay Wray, Bruce Cabot, Robert Armstrong, Frank Reicher, Noble Johnson, Sam Hardy, James Flavin; **D:** Ernest B. Schoedsack; **M:** Max Steiner. *TTC, MED, FUS*

King Kong 🎬🎬 1976 (PG) Oil company official travels to a remote island to discover it inhabited by a huge gorilla. The transplanted beast suffers unrequited love in classic fashion: monkey meets girl, monkey gets girl and brandishes her while atop the World Trade Center. An updated remake of the 1933 movie classic that also marks the screen debut of Lange. Impressive sets and a believable King Kong romp around New York City in this film. Watch for Joe Piscopo, and quickly for Corbin Bernsen as a reporter. 135m/C VHS, Beta, LV, 8mm. Jeff Bridges, Charles Grodin, Jessica Lange,

Rene Auberjonois, John Randolph, Ed Lauter, Jack O'Halloran; **D:** John Guillermin; **M:** John Barry. Academy Awards '76: Best Visual Effects; Nominations: Academy Awards '76: Best Cinematography, Best Sound. *PAR, HMV*

King Kong Lives 🎬 1986 (PG-13) Unnecessary sequel to the 1976 remake of "King Kong," in which two scientists get the big ape, now restored after his asphalt-upsetting fall, together with a lady ape his size and type. 105m/C VHS, Beta, LV, Closed Caption. Brian Kerwin, Linda Hamilton, John Ashton, Peter Michael Goetz; **D:** John Guillermin; **W:** Steven Pressfield. *MED, WAR*

King Kong vs. Godzilla 🎬🎬½ King Kong Tai Godzilla 1963 The planet issues a collective shudder as the two mightiest monsters slug it out for reasons known only to themselves. Humankind can only stand by and watch in impotent horror as the tide of the battle sways to and fro, until one monster stands alone and victorious. 105m/C VHS. **JP** Inoshiro Honda, Michael Keith, Tadao Takashima; **D:** Thomas Montgomery. *GKK*

King Kung Fu 🎬 1987 (G) A karate master raises a gorilla, and sends it from Asia to the U.S. There, two out-of-work reporters decide to release it from captivity and then recapture it so they can get the story and some needed recognition. The background they don't have on the gorilla is that its master taught it kung fu. 90m/C VHS. John Balee, Tom Leahy, Maxine Gray, Bill Schwartz; **D:** Bill Hayes. *NO*

King Lear 🎬🎬🎬½ 1971 Brook's version of Shakespeare tragedy. The king drives away the only decent daughter he has, and when he realizes this, it is too late. Powerful performances and interesting effort at updating the bard. 137m/B VHS. **GB** Paul Scofield, Irene Worth, Jack MacGowran, Alan Webb, Cyril Cusack, Patrick Magee; **D:** Peter Brook. *NOS, DVT*

King Lear 🎬½ 1987 Loosely adapted from Shakespeare's tragedy of a king who loses everything. A fragmented French existential reading with gangster undercurrent. This updated version is dark, ominous, wandering, strange, and quite unlike the other 1984 remake. Or any other remake, for that matter. 91m/C VHS. **SI** Peter Sellers, Burgess Meredith, Molly Ringwald, Jean-Luc Godard, Woody Allen; **D:** Jean-Luc Godard; **W:** Norman Mailer. *CAN*

The King Murder 🎬🎬 1932 High-society sleuth Tearle tries to solve the mysterious death of a beautiful, yet dangerous extortionist. Looks a lot like murder, although no weapon can be found. 67m/B VHS. Conway Tearle, Natalie Moorhead, Marceline Day, Dorothy Revier; **D:** Richard Thorpe; **W:** Charles Reed Jones. *SNC*

King of America 🎬 1980 A Greek sailor and a local labor agent battle over who will become King of America. 90m/C VHS, Beta. **D:** Dezso Magyar. *NO*

King of Comedy 🎬🎬🎬 1982 (PG) An unhinged would-be comedian haunts and eventually kidnaps a massively popular Johnny Carson-type television personality. A cold, cynical farce devised by Scorsese seemingly in reaction to John Hinckley's obsession with his film "Taxi Driver." Controlled, hard-hitting performances, especially by De Niro and Lewis. 101m/C VHS, Beta, LV. Robert De Niro, Jerry Lewis, Sandra Bernhard, Tony Randall, Diahnne Abbott, Shelley Hack, Liza Minnelli; **D:** Martin Scorsese. British Academy Awards '83: Best Original Screenplay; National Society of Film Critics Awards '83: Best Supporting Actress (Bernhard). *COL, FCT*

The King of Hearts 🎬🎬🎬 Le Roi de Coeur 1966 In WWI, a Scottish soldier finds a battle-torn French town evacuated of all occupants except a colorful collection of escaped lunatics from a nearby asylum. The lunatics want to make him their king, which is not a bad alternative to the insanity of war. Bujold is cute as ballerina wannabe; look for Serrault ("La Cage aux Folles") as, not surprisingly, a would-be effeminate hairdresser. Light-hearted comedy with a serious message; definitely worthwhile. 101m/C VHS, Beta, LV.

FR GB Alan Bates, Genevieve Bujold, Adolfo Celi, Francoise Christophe, Micheline Presle; **D:** Philippe de Broca; **M:** Georges Delerue. *MGM, TVC, HMV*

King of Jazz 🎬🎬½ 1930 A lavish revue built around the Paul Whiteman Orchestra with comedy sketches and songs by the stars on Universal Pictures' talent roster. (Though billed as the King of Jazz, Whiteman was never as good as jazz's real royalty.) Filmed in two-color Technicolor with a cartoon segment by Walter Lantz. ♫Rhapsody in Blue; So the Bluebirds and the Blackbirds Got Together; Mississippi Mud; It Happened in Monterey; Ragamuffin Romeo; Happy Feet; Song of the Dawn; A Bench in the Park. 93m/C VHS, Beta. Paul Whiteman, John Boles, Jeanette Loff, Bing Crosby; **D:** John Murray Anderson. Academy Awards '30: Best Interior Decoration.*USH, MLB, RXM*

King of Kings 🎬🎬½ 1927 DeMille depicts the life of Jesus Christ in this highly regarded silent epic. The resurrection scene appears in color. Remade by Nicholas Ray in 1961. 115m/B VHS, Beta. H.B. Warner, Dorothy Cumming, Ernest Torrence, Joseph Schildkraut, Jacqueline Logan, Victor Varconi, William Boyd; **D:** Cecil B. DeMille. *MSP*

The King of Kings 🎬🎬🎬 1961 The life of Christ is intelligently told, with an attractive visual sense and a memorable score. Remake of Cecil B. DeMille's silent film, released in 1927. Laserdisc format features a special letterboxed edition of this film. 170m/C VHS, Beta, LV. Jeffrey Hunter, Siobhan McKenna, Hurd Hatfield, Robert Ryan, Rita Gam, Viveca Lindfors, Rip Torn; **D:** Nicholas Ray; **W:** Philip Yordan; **C:** Milton Krasner; **M:** Miklos Rozsa. *MGM, IGP*

King of Kong Island woof! 1978 Intent on world domination, a group of mad scientists implant receptors in the brains of gorillas on Kong Island, and the monster apes run amok. 92m/C VHS, Beta. **SP** Brad Harris, Marc Lawrence; **D:** Robert Morris. *NO*

The King of Marvin Gardens 🎬🎬½ 1972 (R) Nicholson stars as a Midwest radio jock who prefers to reminisce about his life and family back in Atlantic City, New Jersey to playing records. When Nicholson returns for a visit he finds brother Dern, king of the get-rich-quick schemers, working for a black crime syndicate. Dern is involved in another scheme which means embezzling money from his boss—not a smart idea although Nicholson can't disuade him. Talky drama also features Burstyn as Dern's neglected girlfriend. 104m/C VHS. Jack Nicholson, Bruce Dern, Ellen Burstyn, Scatman Crothers, Julia Anne Robinson, Charles Lavine, Arnold Williams, Josh Mostel; **D:** Bob Rafelson; **W:** Jacob Brackman. *COL, BTV*

King of New York 🎬🎬🎬 1990 (R) Drug czar Frank White (Walken), recently returned from a prison sabbatical, regains control of his New York drug empire with the aid of a loyal network of black dealers. How? Call it dangerous charisma, an inexplicable sympatico. Headquartered in Manhattan's chic Plaza hotel, he ruthlessly orchestrates the drug machine, while funneling the profits into a Bronx hospital for the poor. As inscrutable as White himself, Walken makes the drug czar's power tangible, believable, yet never fathomable. 106m/C VHS, LV, Closed Caption. Christopher Walken, Laurence "Larry" Fishburne, David Caruso, Victor Argo, Wesley Snipes, Janet Julian, Joey Chin, Giancarlo Esposito, Steve Buscemi; **D:** Abel Ferrara; **W:** Nicholas St. John; **C:** Bojan Bazelli; **M:** Joe Delia. *LIV*

King of the Airwaves 🎬🎬½ Louis 19, le Roi des Ondes 1994 Louis (Drainville) is a dull salesman who spends his days working in an electronics store and his nights in front of the TV. This leads Louis to enter (and win) a contest sponsored by the local TV station, which promises to provide 24-hour-a-day coverage of the winner's every move. Now, ordinary Louis is a media celebrity who must deal with constant intrusion and the soap opera-ish changes wrought upon his life. 93m/C VHS. **CA FR** Martin Drainville, Agathe de la Fontaine, Dominique Michel, Patricia Tulasne, Gilbert Lachance; **D:** Michel Poulette; **W:** Michael Michaud, Emile

Gaudreault, Sylvie Bouchard; *M:* Jean-Marie Benoit. Nominations: Genie Awards '94: Best Actor (Drainville), Best Film. *NYR*

King of the Bullwhip 🎬½ 1951 Two undercover U.S. Marshals are sent to Tioga City to stop the killing and looting of a masked bandit, whose whip is as dangerous as his gun. 59m/B **VHS, Beta.** Lash LaRue, Al "Fuzzy" St. John, Anne Gwynne, Tom Neal, Jack Holt, Dennis Moore, Michael Whalen, George Lewis; *D:* Ron Ormond. *NOS, VCN, DVT*

King of the Congo 🎬½ 1952 Crabbe, in his last serial, as a pilot who is frantically searching for an important piece of film. In 15 parts. ?m/B **VHS.** Buster Crabbe, Gloria Dee; *D:* Spencer Gordon Bennet, Wallace Grissell. *MLB*

King of the Cowboys 🎬🎬 1943 Roy fights a gang of saboteurs and saves a defense installation. 54m/B **VHS.** Roy Rogers, Smiley Burnette, James Bush. *NOS, VCN, DVT*

King of the Damned 🎬 1936 On an island prison Veidt leads a convict's revolt against the cruel administrator (Hallard), who gets killed. Before he dies, Hallard alerts a convenient warship, which begins shelling the island. Hallard's daughter, who has fallen for Veidt, pleads for the men and everyone is given a fair trial. Miscast and ineptly performed, although Veidt retains some dignity. 81m/B **VHS.** *GB* Conrad Veidt, Helen Vinson, C.M. Hallard, Noah Beery Sr., Percy Walsh, Raymond Lovell, Cecil Ramage, Peter Croft; *D:* Walter Forde; *W:* Charles Bennett, Sidney Gilliat, Noel Langley. *HCV*

King of the Forest Rangers 1946 Ranger Steve King must stop an evil archaeologist from finding a treasure whose secret lies within an ancient Indian rug pattern. Edited from an original, 12 episode serial on two cassettes. 167m/B **VHS, Beta.** Larry Thompson, Helen Talbot, Stuart Hamblen, Anthony Warde. *REP, MLB*

King of the Grizzlies 🎬½ 1969 (G) The mystical relationship between a Cree Indian and a grizzly cub is put to the acid test when the full grown bear attacks a ranch at which the Indian is foreman. 93m/C **VHS, Beta.** Chris Wiggins, John Yesno; *D:* Ron Kelly. *DIS*

King of the Gypsies 🎬🎬½ 1978 (R) Interesting drama. A young man, scornful of his gypsy heritage, runs away from the tribe and tries to make a life of his own. He is summoned home to his grandfather's deathbed where he is proclaimed the new king of the gypsies, thus incurring the wrath of his scorned father. From Peter Maas's best-selling novel. 112m/C **VHS, Beta, LV.** Sterling Hayden, Eric Roberts, Susan Sarandon, Brooke Shields, Shelley Winters, Annie Potts, Annette O'Toole, Judd Hirsch, Michael V. Gazzo, Roy Brocksmith; *D:* Frank Pierson; *W:* Frank Pierson; *C:* Sven Nykvist. *PAR, CCB*

King of the Hill 🎬🎬🎬½ 1993 (PG-13) Quiet depression-era drama focuses on Aaron, a 12-year-old who lives in a seedy hotel in St. Louis. The family is barely scraping by: his mother is in a tuberculosis sanitarium, his younger brother has been sent away to live with relatives, and Aaron must fend for himself when his father gets work as a traveling salesman. Aaron excels at school and his efforts there, as well as his hotel friends, manage to provide him with some semblance of a regular life. Soderberg's third directorial effort is unsentimental but admiring of his character's resourcefulness and imagination during difficult times. Based on the book by A.E. Hochner describing his own childhood. *CW:* Thematic elements. 102m/C **VHS, LV, Closed Caption.** Jesse Bradford, Jeroen Krabbe, Lisa Eichhorn, Karen Allen, Spalding Gray, Elizabeth McGovern, Joseph Chrest, Adrien Brody, Cameron Boyd, Chris Samples, Katherine Heigl, Amber Benson, John McConnell, Ron Vawter, John Durbin, Lauryn Hill, David Jensen; *D:* Steven Soderbergh; *W:* Steven Soderbergh; *M:* Cliff Martinez. *USH*

The King of the Kickboxers woof! 1991 (R) The villains make kung-fu snuff movies with unwitting actors killed on camera. Otherwise, same old junk about a karate cop back in Bang-

kok to get the dude who squashed his brother. Pretty racist at times. *CW:* Language, strong violence, and sensuality. 90m/C **VHS, Closed Caption.** Loren Avedon, Richard Jaeckel, Billy Blanks, Don Stroud, Keith Cooke; *D:* Lucas Lowe. *IMP*

King of the Kongo 🎬🎬 1929 A handsome young man is sent by the government to Nuhalla, deep in the jungle, to break up a gang of ivory thieves. Serial was made in silent and sound versions. 213m/B **VHS, Beta.** Jacqueline Logan, Boris Karloff, Richard Tucker; *D:* Richard Thorpe. *VYY, NOS, MLB*

King of the Mountain 🎬½ 1981 (PG) The "Old King" and the "New King" must square off in this tale of daredevil road racers who zoom through the streets of Hollywood. Interesting cast trapped by tired script. 92m/C **VHS, Beta.** Richard Cox, Harry Hamlin, Dennis Hopper, Joseph Bottoms, Deborah Van Valkenburgh, Dan Haggerty; *D:* Noel Nosseck; *W:* Roger Christian.

King of the Pecos 🎬🎬½ 1936 A young lawyer (who's also adept at the shootin' iron) exacts revenge on his parents' killers in the courtroom. Well made early Wayne outing, with good character development, taut pacing and beautiful photography. 54m/B **VHS.** John Wayne, Muriel Evans, Cy Kendall, Jack Clifford, John Beck, Yakima Canutt; *D:* Joseph Kane. *REP, MLB*

The King of the Roaring '20s: The Story of Arnold Rothstein 🎬🎬½ *The Big Bankroll* 1961 "True" story of infamous gangster, Arnold Rothstein, a brilliant and ruthless gambler who practically ran New York in the twenties. This version of his life focuses on his rise to power, the dealings with his enemies, and his crumbling personal life. Superficial due mostly to the weak screenplay. Adapted from the book "The Big Bankroll" by Leo Katcher. 106m/B **VHS, Beta.** David Janssen, Dianne Foster, Mickey Rooney, Jack Carson, Diana Dors, Dan O'Herlihy, Mickey Shaughnessy, Keenan Wynn; *D:* Joseph M. Newman. *FOX, FCT*

King of the Rocketmen 1949 Jeff King thwarts an attempt by traitors to steal government scientific secrets. Serial in twelve episodes. Later released as a feature titled "Lost Planet Airmen." 156m/B **VHS, LV.** Tristram Coffin, Mae Clarke, I. Stanford Jolley; *D:* Fred Brannon. *MED, VCN, REP*

King of the Rodeo 🎬🎬 1928 Cowpoke Hoot wins a rodeo and catches a thief in the Windy City. Hoot's final silent ride into the sunset. 54m/B **VHS, Beta.** Hoot Gibson, Kathryn Crawford, Slim Summerville, Charles French, Monte Montague, Joseph Girard; *D:* Henry MacRae. *GPV*

King of the Sierras 🎬½ 1938 Bosworth tells his nephew the story of a white horse that protected his mares from a black stallion. The acting of the horses is better than that of the humans. 58m/B **VHS.** Hobart Bosworth, Harry Harvey, Harry Harvey Jr., Jim Campeau; *D:* Samuel Diege; *W:* W. Scott Darling. *GPV*

King of the Stallions 🎬½ 1942 A dangerous stallion is a menacing threat to the herd and the cowboys and Indians and other scattered wildlife. Chief Thundercloud is the only one capable of tackling the matter. Largely Indian cast, including Iron Eyes Cody, famed for the anti-litter campaign. 63m/B **VHS.** Chief Thundercloud, Princess Bluebird, Chief Yowlachie, Rick Vallin, Dave O'Brien, Barbara Felker, Iron Eyes Cody; *D:* Edward Finney. *NOS, DVT*

King of the Texas Rangers 1941 Tom King, Texas Ranger, finds that his father's killers are a group of saboteurs who have destroyed American oil fields. This twelve episode serial comes on two tapes. 195m/B **VHS.** Sammy Baugh, Neil Hamilton; *D:* William Witney, John English. *REP, MRV, MLB*

King of the Wild Horses 🎬🎬🎬 1924 Engaging children's story about a wild stallion that comes to the rescue. Terrific action photography of Rex going through his paces. Look for Chase in a rare dramatic role. Silent. 50m/B **VHS, Beta.** Rex, Edna Murphy, Leon Barry, Pat Hartigan, Frank Butler, Charley Chase; *D:* Fred Jackman. *NO*

King of the Wind 🎬🎬½ 1993 (PG) An epic adventure featuring the true story of a legendary Arabian horse and a poor stable boy who gave the most precious gift of all: love. 101m/C **VHS, Closed Caption.** Richard Harris, Glenda Jackson. *FHE*

King of the Zombies woof! 1941 Mad scientist creates his own zombies without souls, to be used as the evil tools of a foreign government. Zombie nonsense. 67m/B **VHS, Beta.** John Archer, Dick Purcell, Mantan Moreland, Henry Victor, Joan Woodbury; *D:* Jean Yarbrough. Nominations: Academy Awards '41: Original Dramatic/Comedy Score. *VYY, MRV, SNC*

The King on Main Street 🎬🎬½ 1925 A king on vacation in America finds romance. ?m/B **VHS, Beta.** Adolphe Menjou, Bessie Love. *NO*

King, Queen, Knave *Herzbube* 1972 Sexy black comedy about a shy, awkward 19-year-old boy, keenly aware that his interest in girls is not reciprocated. He has to go live with his prosperous uncle and his much younger wife when his parents are killed. Based on the Vladimir Nabokov novel. 94m/C **VHS, Beta.** *GE* Gina Lollobrigida, David Niven, John Moulder-Brown; *D:* Jerzy Skolimowski; *W:* David Seltzer.

King Ralph 🎬🎬 1991 (PG) When the rest of the royal family passes away in a freak accident, lounge lizard Ralph finds himself the only heir to the throne. O'Toole is the long-suffering valet who tries to train him for the job. Funny in spots and Goodman is the quintessential good sport, making the whole outing pleasant. Sometimes too forced. 96m/C **VHS, Beta, LV, Closed Caption.** John Goodman, Peter O'Toole, Camille Coduri, Joely Richardson, John Hurt; *D:* David S. Ward; *W:* David S. Ward; *M:* James Newton Howard. *USH, CCB*

King Rat 🎬🎬🎬 1965 Drama set in a WWII Japanese prisoner-of-war camp. Focuses on the effect of captivity on the English, Australian, and American prisoners. An American officer bribes his Japanese captors to live more comfortably than the rest. Based on James Clavell's novel. 134m/B **VHS, Beta.** George Segal, Tom Courtenay, James Fox, James Donald, Denholm Elliott, Patrick O'Neal, John Mills; *D:* Bryan Forbes; *C:* Burnett Guffey; *M:* John Barry. Nominations: Academy Awards '65: Best Art Direction/Set Decoration (B & W), Best Black and White Cinematography. *COL*

King Richard and the Crusaders 🎬½ 1954 Laughable costume epic with Sanders as Richard the Lionheart, who survives an assassination attempt during the Crusades. Harvey is a loyal knight sworn to find the traitors with Harrison as the noble leader of the Arab forces. Mayo plays Harvey's object of affection. Even the battle scenes are boring. Based on "The Talisman" by Sir Walter Scott. 113m/C **VHS.** George Sanders, Rex Harrison, Laurence Harvey, Virginia Mayo, Robert Douglas, Michael Pate, Paula Raymond, Lester Matthews; *D:* David Butler; *W:* John Twist; *M:* Max Steiner. *FCT, MOV, WAR*

King Solomon's Mines 🎬🎬🎬 1937 The search for King Solomon's Mines leads a safari through the treacherous terrain of the desert, fending off sandstorms, Zulus, and a volcanic eruption. Adapted from the novel by H. Rider Haggard and remade twice. 80m/B **VHS, Beta.** Cedric Hardwicke, Paul Robeson, Roland Young, John Loder, Anna Lee; *D:* Robert Stevenson. *SNC, NOS, HMV*

King Solomon's Mines 🎬🎬🎬 1950 A lavish version of the classic H. Rider Haggard adventures about African explorers searching out a fabled diamond mine. Remake of the 1937 classic; remade again in 1985. 102m/C **VHS, Beta.** Stewart Granger, Deborah Kerr, Richard Carlson, Hugo Haas, Lowell Gilmore; *D:* Compton Bennett; *C:* Robert L. Surtees. Academy Awards '50: Best Color Cinematography, Best Film Editing; Nominations: Academy Awards '50: Best Picture. *MGM*

King Solomon's Mines 🗡️½ 1985
(PG-13) The third remake of the classic H. Rider Haggard novel about a safari deep into Africa in search of an explorer who disappeared while searching for the legendary diamond mines of King Solomon. Updated but lacking the style of the previous two films. Somewhat imperialistic, racist point of view. **101m/C VHS, Beta.** Richard Chamberlain, John Rhys-Davies, Sharon Stone, Herbert Lom; **D:** J. Lee Thompson; **W:** Gene Quintano; **M:** Jerry Goldsmith. MGM

King Solomon's Treasure 🗡️ 1976
The great white adventurer takes on the African jungle, hunting for hidden treasure in the Forbidden City. Ekland stars as a Phoenician Queen—need we say more?? **90m/C VHS, Beta.** CA GB David McCallum, Britt Ekland, Patrick Macnee, Wilfrid Hyde-White; **D:** Alvin Rakoff. VCI

The Kingdom 🗡️🗡️½ 1995 Danish director von Trier serves up what must be the first four and a half hour-long hospital soap opera/ghost story/comedy/satire. Elderly Mrs. Drusse checks herself into a hospital known as the Kingdom, which is inhabited by the usual medical suspects: Pompous surgeons, incompetent buraucrats, and quirky residents. She hears the ghostly call of a child from an elevator shaft and sticks around to investigate. Made for Danish TV but released theatrically there and in the States, film owes a great deal to "Twin Peaks" and B-movie horror flicks. Doesn't take itself too seriously, but probably can't be watched all in one sitting. Danish and Swedish with subtitles. **279m/C VHS.** DK Kirsten Rolffes, Ghita Norby, Udo Kier, Ernst Hugo Jarogard, Soren Pilmark, Holger Juul Hansen, Baard Owe, Birgitte Raabjerg, Peter Mygind; **D:** Lars von Trier; **W:** Lars von Trier, Tomas Gislason; **C:** Eric Kress; **M:** Joachim Holbek. HMK

Kingdom of the Spiders 🗡️🗡️½ 1977
(PG) A desert town is invaded by swarms of killer tarantulas, which begin to consume townspeople. **90m/C VHS, Beta.** William Shatner, Tiffany Bolling, Woody Strode; **D:** John Cardos; **W:** Alan Cailou. FCT

Kingfish: A Story of Huey P. Long 🗡️🗡️½ 1995 Charismatic political kingpin of Louisiana, Huey P. Long is brought to vivid life with Goodman's swaggering portrayal. Story is told in flashback, beginning with Long's assassination in 1935. A champion of the working man, Long parlayed charm and corruption into a Depression-era political career as governor and U.S. Senator. But naturally, the hard-drinking, hard-loving Long makes a lot of enemies along the way. Long's life was also memorably recreated in Robert Penn Warren's "All the King's Men," as was that of his younger brother, Governor Earl Long, in the film "Blaze." **97m/C VHS.** John Goodman, Matt Craven, Anne Heche, Ann Dowd, Jeffery Perry, Bob Gunton, Hoyt Axton, Kirk Baltz, Bill Cobbs; **D:** Thomas Schlamme; **W:** Paul Monash; **M:** Patrick Williams. TTC

Kingfisher Caper 🗡️🗡️ 1976 **(PG)** A power struggle between a businessman, his brother, and a divorced sister is threatening to rip a family-owned diamond empire apart. **90m/C VHS, Beta.** Hayley Mills, David McCallum; **D:** Dirk DeVilliers. MED

Kingfisher the Killer 🗡️ 198? Charles, the Raging Titan of Ninja skill, stalks the bad gang that killed his mother and hits them with nunchakos. **90m/C VHS, Beta.** Sho Kosugi. TWE

Kingpin woof! 1996 **(PG-13)** It's got an IQ lower than "Dumb & Dumber," which lately has been a good thing, but when no one laughs at a comedy movie's trailer—beware. Roy Munson's (Harrelson) a former bowling champ who, thanks to his sleazy ways, lost a hand and is reduced to selling bowling equipment. That is until he meets innocent Amish phenom Ishmael (Quaid), whom he persuades to hit the road to a big money tournament in Vegas where Roy can confront an old nemesis (Murray). There's lots of stupidity about introducing Quaid to beer, girls, and various debauchery. Wonder if the Amish can sue for defamation of character? **CW:** Crude sex-related humor and a drug scene. **107m/C VHS, LV, Closed Caption.** Woody Harrelson, Randy Quaid, Vanessa Angel, Bill Murray, Chris Elliott; **D:** Peter Farrelly, Bobby Farrelly; **W:** Bobby Farrelly, Mort Nathan; **C:** Mark Irwin; **M:** Freedy Johnston. MGM

Kings and Desperate Men 🗡️½ 1983 Apprentice terrorists plea their case at a public forum when they take a rakish talk show host hostage. **118m/C VHS.** Patrick McGoohan, Alexis Kanner, Andrea Marcovicci, Robin Spry, Frank Moore; **D:** Alexis Kanner. NO

Kings Go Forth 🗡️🗡️½ 1958 Hormones and war rage in this love triangle set against the backdrop of WWII France. Sinatra loves Wood who loves Curtis. When Sinatra asks for her hand in marriage she refuses because she is mixed—half black, half white. He says it doesn't matter, but she still declines because she's in love with Curtis. When Sinatra tells Curtis that Wood is mixed, Curtis says that it doesn't matter to him either because he'd never planned on marrying her. Meanwhile, the war continues. Not particularly satisfying on either the war or race front. Based on a novel by Joe David Brown. **109m/B VHS, Beta.** Frank Sinatra, Tony Curtis, Natalie Wood, Leora Dana; **D:** Delmer Daves; **C:** Daniel F. Fapp; **M:** Elmer Bernstein. MGM

Kings of the Road—In the Course of Time 🗡️🗡️🗡️½ 1976 A writer and a film projectionist travel by truck across Germany. The film stands out for its simple and expressive direction, and truly captures the sense of physical and ideological freedom of being on the road. A landmark Wenders epic. In German with English subtitles. **176m/B VHS, Beta.** GE Ruediger Vogler, Hanns Zischler, Elisabeth Kreuzer; **D:** Wim Wenders; **W:** Wim Wenders. FCT, GLV, TPV

Kings, Queens, Jokers 193? Package includes a foolish lover and ghosts in "Haunted Spooks," an escaped convict in "Dangerous Females," and a search for lost jewels in "Stolen Jools." **60m/B VHS, Beta.** Harold Lloyd, Marie Dressler, Polly Moran, Edward G. Robinson, Gary Cooper, Joan Crawford. NO

King's Ransom woof! 1991 When the Japanese Emperor's Pearl is stolen, the underworld is abuzz with excitement. But only the wealthiest individuals are invited to bid for the jewel at Cameron King's secret casino. There, untold pleasures, and dangers, await them. **?m/C VHS.** Miles O'Keeffe, Dedee Pfeiffer, Christopher Atkins; **D:** Hugh Parks. NO

The King's Rhapsody 🗡️🗡️ 1955 Flynn is an heir who abdicates his throne in order to be with the woman he loves. But when the king dies, Flynn sacrifices love for honor and goes back to marry a princess. Very dated and Flynn is long past his swashbuckling-romantic days. **93m/C VHS.** GB Errol Flynn, Anna Neagle, Patrice Wymore, Martita Hunt, Finlay Currie, Frank Wolff, Joan Benham, Reginald Tate, Miles Malleson; **D:** Herbert Wilcox. FCT

Kings Row 🗡️🗡️🗡️ 1941 The Harry Bellamann best-selling Middle American potboiler comes to life. Childhood friends grow up with varying degrees of success, in a decidedly macabre town. All are continually dependent on and inspired by Parris (Cummings) a psychiatric doctor and genuine gentleman. Many cast members worked against type with unusual success. Warner held the film for a year after its completion, in concern for its dark subject matter, but it received wide acclaim. Shot completely within studio settings—excellent scenic design by William Cameron Menzies, and wonderful score. **127m/B VHS, Beta, Closed Caption.** Ann Sheridan, Robert Cummings, Ronald Reagan, Betty Field, Charles Coburn, Claude Rains, Judith Anderson, Nancy Coleman, Karen Verne, Maria Ouspenskaya, Harry Davenport, Ernest Cossart, Pat Moriarity, Scotty Beckett; **D:** Sam Wood; **C:** James Wong Howe; **M:** Erich Wolfgang Korngold. Nominations: Academy Awards '42: Best Black and White Cinematography, Best Director (Wood), Best Picture. MGM, FOX, CCB

The King's Thief 🗡️🗡️½ 1955 Costume swashbuckler with Niven as the bad guy. He's a duke at the court of 17th-century English King Charles II and is involved in a plot to steal the crown jewels. **78m/C VHS.** David Niven, Edmund Purdom, George Sanders, Ann Blyth, Roger Moore, John Dehner, Sean McClory, Melville Cooper, Alan Mowbray; **D:** Robert Z. Leonard; **W:** Christopher Knopf; **M:** Miklos Rozsa. MGM

The King's Whore 🗡️🗡️ 1990 **(R)** Dalton stars as a 17th-century king who falls obsessively in love with the wife of one of his courtiers. His passions lead him to make a decision between the woman and the throne. Good-looking costume epic with obligatory sword fights. **CW:** Sexuality. **111m/C VHS, LV, Closed Caption.** Timothy Dalton, Valeria Golino, Feodor Chaliapin Jr, Margaret Tyzack; **W:** Daniel Vigne, Frederic Raphael. THV

Kinjite: Forbidden Subjects 🗡️🗡️
1989 **(R)** A cop takes on a sleazy pimp whose specialty is recruiting teenage girls, including the daughter of a Japanese business man. Slimy, standard Bronson fare. **97m/C VHS, Beta, LV.** Charles Bronson, Juan Fernandez, Peggy Lipton; **D:** J. Lee Thompson. MGM, CAN

A Kink in the Picasso 🗡️🗡️ 1990 MTV personality Daddo joins a cast of criminals who chase after a Picasso artwork and a counterfeit. Artless Australian production. **84m/C VHS.** Peter O'Brien, Jon Finlayson, Jane Clifton, Andrew Daddo; **D:** Marc Gracie. ATL

Kino Pravda/Enthusiasm 1931 Two famous documentaries by Vertov, the first a prime example of his pioneering avant-garde newsreels that helped establish Soviet montage aesthetic, and the second the famous portrait of Don Basin coal miners, augmented by the famous use of sound editing/montage. In Russian with English titles. **120m/B VHS, Beta.** RU **D:** Dziga Vertov. FCT, FST

Kipperbang 🗡️🗡️ Ptang, Yang, Kipperbang 1982 **(PG)** During the summer of 1948, a 13-year-old boy wishes he could kiss the girl of his dreams. He finally gets the chance in a school play. Not unsatisfying, but falls short of being the bittersweet coming-of-age drama it could have been. **85m/C VHS.** GB John Albasiny, Abigail Cruttenden, Alison Steadman; **D:** Michael Apted. MGM

Kipps 🗡️🗡️🗡️ The Remarkable Mr. Kipps 1941 Based on H.G. Wells' satirical novel. A young British shopkeeper inherits a fortune and tries to join high society while neglecting his working-class girlfriend. Set the stage for the musical "Half a Sixpence." **95m/B VHS, Beta.** GB Michael Redgrave, Phyllis Calvert, Michael Wilding; **D:** Carol Reed. NOS, HHT, CAB

The Kirlian Witness 🗡️ The Plants Are Watching 1978 **(PG)** A woman uses the power of telepathic communication with house plants to solve her sister's murder. **88m/C VHS, Beta.** Nancy Snyder, Joel Colodner, Ted Leplat; **D:** Jonathan Sarno. NO

Kismet 🗡️🗡️🗡️ 1920 Original screen version of the much filmed lavish Arabian Nights saga (remade in '30, '44 and '55). A beggar is drawn into deception and intrigue among Bagdad uppercrusters. Glorious sets and costumes; silent with original organ score. **98m/B VHS.** Otis Skinner, Elinor Fair, Herschel Mayall; **D:** Louis Gasnier; **C:** Gaetano Antonio "Tony" Gaudio. VYY

Kismet 🗡️🗡️ 1955 A big budget Arabian Nights musical drama of a Baghdad street poet who manages to infiltrate himself into the Wazir's harem. The music was adapted from Borodin by Robert Wright and George Forrest. Original trailer and letterboxed screen available in special laserdisc edition. ♫ Fate; Not Since Ninevah; Baubles, Bangles, and Beads; Stranger in Paradise; Bored; Night of My Nights; The Olive Tree; And This Is My Beloved; Sands of Time. **113m/C VHS, Beta, LV, Closed Caption.** Howard Keel, Ann Blyth, Dolores Gray, Vic Damone; **D:** Vincente Minnelli; **W:** Charles Lederer, Luther Davis; **C:** Joseph Ruttenberg; **M:** Andre Previn. MGM, FCT

The Kiss *♂♂♂* 1929 Garbo, the married object of earnest young Ayres' lovelorn affection, innocently kisses him nighty night since a kiss is just a kiss. Or so she thought. Utterly misconstrued, the platonic peck sets the stage for disaster, and murder and courtroom anguish follow. French Feyder's direction is stylized and artsy. Garbo's last silent and Ayres' first film. **89m/B VHS.** Greta Garbo, Conrad Nagel, Holmes Herbert, Lew Ayres, Anders Randolf; **D:** Jacques Feyder; **C:** William H. Daniels. MGM, FCT

The Kiss *♂* 1988 (R) A kind of "Auntie Mame from Hell" story in which a mysterious aunt visits her teen-age niece in New York, and tries to apprentice her to the family business of sorcery, demon possession, and murder. Aunt Felicity's kiss will make you appreciate the harmless cheek-pinching of your own aunt; your evening would be better spent with her, rather than this movie. **98m/ C VHS, Beta, LV.** Pamela Collyer, Peter Dvorsky, Joanna Pacula, Meredith Salenger, Mimi Kuzyk, Nicholas Kilbertus, Jan Rubes; **D:** Pen Densham; **W:** Tom Ropelewski. COL, IME

Kiss and Be Killed *♂½* 1991 (R) Crazy guy with knife cuts short couple's wedding night. Shortchanged widow is mighty miffed. Will she have to return the wedding gifts? **CW:** Language, violence, and sensuality. **89m/C VHS, Beta, 8mm.** Caroline Ludvik, Crystal Carson, Tom Reilly, Chip Hall, Ken Norton, Jimmy Baio; **D:** Tom Milo. NO

Kiss and Kill *♂♂* *Blood of Fu Manchu; Against All Odds* 1968 (R) Lee returns in his fourth outing as Fu Manchu. This time the evil one has injected beautiful girls with a deadly poison that reacts upon kissing. They are then sent out to seduce wealthy leaders. Not on par with the previous movies, but still enjoyable. Sequel to "Castle of Fu Manchu." **91m/C VHS.** Christopher Lee, Richard Greene, Shirley Eaton, Tsai Chin, Maria Rohm, H. Marion Crawford; **D:** Jess (Jesus) Franco. MRV

A Kiss Before Dying *♂♂* 1991 (R) Botched adaptation of Ira Levin's cunning thriller novel (filmed before in 1956). This flick serves up an exploded head in the first few minutes. So much for subtlety. The highlight is Dillon's chilly role as a murderous opportunist bent on marrying into a wealthy family. Young plays two roles (not very well) as lookalike sisters on his agenda. The ending was hastily reshot and it shows. **CW:** Some language, strong violence, and graphic sensuality. **93m/C VHS, Beta, LV, Closed Caption.** Matt Dillon, Sean Young, Max von Sydow, Diane Ladd, James Russo, Martha Gehman, Ben Browder, Joy Lee, Adam Horovitz; **D:** James Dearden; **W:** James Dearden. Golden Raspberry Awards '91: Worst Actress (Young), Worst Supporting Actress (Young). USH

Kiss Daddy Goodbye *♂½* 1981 (R) A widower keeps his two children isolated in order to protect their secret telekinetic powers. When he is killed by bikers, the kids attempt to raise him from the dead. Also on video as "Revenge of the Zombie" and "The Vengeful Dead." **81m/C VHS, Beta.** Fabian, Marilyn Burns, Jon Cedar, Marvin Miller; **D:** Patrick Regan. MRV, GHV

Kiss Daddy Goodnight *♂* 1987 (R) A Danish-made thriller about a beautiful young girl who seduces men, drugs them and takes their money. One man turns the tables on her, however, and decides that she will only belong to him. **89m/C VHS, Beta.** **DK** Uma Thurman, Paul Dillon, Paul Richards, David Brisbin; **D:** P.I. Huemer; **C:** Bobby Bukowski. ACA

A Kiss for Mary Pickford *♂♂½* 1927 A rare, hilarious cinematic oddity, a film formulated from Kuleshov montage techniques from footage of the famous American couple's visit to Russia in 1926, wherein a regular guy tries to win a girl through friendship with the stars. Fairbanks and Pickford didn't know of their role in this film, being spliced in later according to montage theory. **70m/B VHS, Beta.** Mary Pickford, Douglas Fairbanks Sr., Igor Ilinsky; **D:** Sergei Komarov. FCT

A Kiss Goodnight *♂♂½* 1994 (R) Natalie (Trickey) has a romp in the sheets with ad exec Kurt (Corley) when regular beau Michael (Moses) ignores her for work. But when Natalie decides to break things off, Kurt won't take no for an answer. **CW:** Language; some violence; sexuality. **88m/C VHS.** Paula Trickey, Al Corley, Mark Moses, Lawrence Tierney, Brett Cullen, James Karen, Robert Wuhl, Sydney Walsh; **D:** Daniel Raskov; **W:** Daniel Raskov; **C:** Glenn Kershaw. ACA

Kiss Me a Killer *♂♂* 1991 (R) The ancient thriller plot about a young wife and her lover who scheme to kill her middle-aged husband. It's set in L.A.'s Latino community, but extensive shots of salsa music and ethnic cooking hardly raise this above the mediocre. **CW:** Language, violence, and strong sensuality. **91m/C VHS, LV.** Julie Carmen, Robert Beltran, Guy Boyd, Ramon Franco, Charles Boswell; **D:** Marcus De Leon; **W:** Marcus De Leon. COL

Kiss Me Deadly *♂♂♂½* 1955 Aldrich's adaptation of Mickey Spillane's private eye tale takes pulp literature high concept. Meeker, as Mike Hammer, is a self interested rough and tumble all American dick (detective, that is). When a woman to whom he happened to give a ride is found murdered, he follows the mystery straight into a nuclear conspiracy. Aldrich, with tongue deftly in cheek, styles a message through the medium; topsy turvy camerawork and rat-a-tat-tat pacing tell volumes about Hammer, the world he orbits, and that special 50s kind of paranoia. Now a cult fave, it's considered to be the American grandaddy to French New Wave. **105m/B VHS, LV, Closed Caption.** Ralph Meeker, Albert Dekker, Paul Stewart, Wesley Addy, Cloris Leachman, Strother Martin, Marjorie Bennett, Jack Elam, Maxine Cooper, Gaby Rodgers, Nick Dennis, Jack Lambert, Percy Helton; **D:** Robert Aldrich; **C:** Ernest Laszlo. MGM, FCT

Kiss Me Goodbye *♂♂* 1982 (PG) Young widow Fields can't shake the memory of her first husband, a charismatic but philandering Broadway choreographer, who's the antithesis of her boring but devoted professor fiance. She struggles with the charming ghost of her first husband, as well as her domineering mother, attempting to understand her own true feelings. Harmless but two-dimensional remake of "Dona Flor and Her Two Husbands." **101m/C VHS, Beta.** Sally Field, James Caan, Jeff Bridges, Paul Dooley, Mildred Natwick, Claire Trevor; **D:** Robert Mulligan; **W:** Charlie Peters; **M:** Ralph Burns. FOX

Kiss Me Kate *♂♂♂* 1953 A married couple can't separate their real lives from their stage roles in this musical-comedy screen adaptation of Shakespeare's "Taming of the Shrew," based on Cole Porter's Broadway show. Bob Fosse bursts from the screen—particularly if you see the 3-D version—when he does his dance number. ♫Out of This World; From This Moment On; Wunderbar; So In Love; I Hate Men; Were Thine That Special Face; I've Come To Wive It Wealthily In Padua; Where Is The Life That Late I Led?; Always True To You Darling In My Fashion. **110m/C VHS, Beta, LV.** Kathryn Grayson, Howard Keel, Ann Miller, Tommy Rall, Bob Fosse, Bobby Van, Keenan Wynn, James Whitmore; **D:** George Sidney; **C:** Charles Rosher; **M:** Andre Previn. Nominations: Academy Awards '53: Scoring of a Musical. MGM, FCT

Kiss Me, Kill Me *♂½* 1969 (R) Confused woman is on the run after she may have murdered someone. **91m/C VHS, Beta.** Carroll Baker, George Eastman, Isabelle DeFunes, Ely Gallo; **W:** Nick Castle. NO

Kiss Me, Stupid! *♂♂* 1964 (PG-13) Once condemned as smut, this lesser Billy Wilder effort now seems no worse than an average TV sitcom. Martin basically plays himself as a horny Vegas crooner stranded in the boondocks. A local songwriter wants Dino to hear his tunes but knows the cad will seduce his pretty wife, so he hires a floozy to pose as the tempting spouse. It gets along as it goes along, but the whole thing suffers from

staginess, being an adaptation of an Italian play "L'Ora Della Fantasia" by Anna Bonacci. **CW:** Sex-related plot material. **126m/B VHS, Beta, LV.** Dean Martin, Kim Novak, Ray Walston, Felicia Farr, Cliff Osmond, Barbara Pepper, Doro Merande, Howard McNear, Henry Gibson, John Fiedler, Mel Blanc; **D:** Billy Wilder; **W:** Billy Wilder, I.A.L. Diamond; **C:** Joseph LaShelle; **M:** Andre Previn. MGM

KISS Meets the Phantom of the Park *♂½* *Attack of the Phantoms* 1978 The popular '70s rock band is featured in this Dr. Jekyll-esque Halloween horror tale, interspersed with musical numbers. **96m/C VHS, Beta.** Gene Simmons, Paul Stanley, Peter Criss, Ace Frehley, Anthony Zerbe, Deborah Ryan, John Dennis Johnston; **D:** Gordon Hessler. MVD, WOV

Kiss My Grits *♂* 1982 (PG) A good ole boy hightails it to Mexico with his girlfriend and son, chased by mobsters and the law. **101m/C VHS, Beta.** Bruce Davison, Anthony (Tony) Franciosa, Susan George, Bruno Kirby; **D:** Jack Starrett. MED

Kiss of a Killer *♂♂½* 1993 O'Toole is a mousy miss living a dead-end life with her nagging mother. But she has a secret—she spends weekends in a hotel, dressed to entice and picking up strangers. Involved in an auto mishap she's aided by a handsome mechanic, who turns out to be a rapist. When she accidentally kills his latest victim, she realizes our mystery woman can identify him and tries to find her. Based on the novel "The Point of Murder" by Margaret Yorke. Made for television. **93m/C VHS.** Annette O'Toole, Brian Wimmer, Eva Marie Saint, Greg Henry, Vic Polizos; **D:** Larry Elikann; **W:** David Warfield. ABC

Kiss of Death *♂♂♂* 1947 Paroled when he turns state's evidence, Mature must now watch his back constantly. Widmark, in his film debut, seeks to destroy him. Police chief Donlevy tries to help. Filmed on location in New York, this gripping and gritty film is a vision of the most terrifying sort of existence, one where nothing is certain, and everything is dangerous. Excellent. **98m/B VHS, Closed Caption.** Victor Mature, Richard Widmark, Anne Grey, Brian Donlevy, Karl Malden, Coleen Gray; **D:** Henry Hathaway. Nominations: Academy Awards '47: Best Story, Best Supporting Actor (Widmark). FXV, FCT

Kiss of Death *♂♂* 1977 Weird comedy about a shy undertaker's assistant and his attempts at first romance. Made for British television. **80m/C VHS.** **GB** David Threlfall, John Wheatley, Kay Adshead, Angela Curran; **D:** Mike Leigh; **W:** Mike Leigh. WBF

Kiss of Death *♂♂½* 1994 (R) Very loose contemporary remake of the 1947 film noir classic of the same name. Jimmy Kilmartin (Caruso) is a paroled car thief turned informant. He soon finds himself trapped in a web of deceit involving corrupt district attorneys and ruthless hoodlums like Little Junior (Cage, pumped up and playing against type), with no one to trust. Crime drama keeps the far-fetched genre conventions in check until the end. Caruso makes the transition from TV cop on "NYPD Blue" by not straying far from his small screen persona. Cage's standout performance may not be as chilling as Widmark's unforgettable debut in the original, but he's able to convey a level of mercilessness and depth that'll make you wince. **CW:** Violence; nudity; strong language. **100m/C VHS, LV, Closed Caption.** David Caruso, Nicolas Cage, Samuel L. Jackson, Helen Hunt, Stanley Tucci, Michael Rapaport, Ving Rhames, Anthony Heald, Anne Meara; **D:** Barbet Schroeder; **W:** Richard Price; **M:** Trevor Jones. Nominations: Golden Raspberry Awards '95: Worst New Star (Caruso). FXV

Kiss of the Spider Woman *♂♂♂* 1985 (R) From the novel by Manuel Puig, an acclaimed drama concerning two cell mates in a South American prison, one a revolutionary, the other a homosexual. Literate, haunting, powerful. **119m/C VHS, Beta, LV, 8mm, Closed Caption.** **BR** William Hurt, Raul Julia, Sonia Braga, Jose Lewgoy, Milton Goncalves, Nuno Leal Maia, Denise Dumont; **D:** Hector Babenco; **W:** Leonard Schrader; **M:** John Neschling, Wally Badarou. **Academy Awards '85:** Best Actor (Hurt); **British Academy Awards '85:** Best Actor (Hurt); **Cannes Film Festival '85:** Best Actor (Hurt); **Independent Spirit Awards '86:** Best Foreign Film; **Los Angeles Film Critics Association Awards '85:** Best Actor (Hurt); **National Board of Review Awards '85:** Best Actor (Hurt), Best Actor (Julia); **Nominations: Academy Awards '85:** Best Adapted Screenplay, Best Director (Babenco), Best Picture. **COL, BTV, NLC**

Kiss of the Tarantula 🎞️ 1975 (PG)
Teen girl who lives with her family in a mortuary battles inner torment and vents anxiety by releasing her deadly pet spiders on those whom she despises. Eight-legged "Carrie" rip-off. **85m/C VHS, Beta.** Eric Mason; **D:** Chris Munger; **W:** Warren Hamilton. **MPI, FCT**

Kiss of the Vampire 🎞️🎞️½ Kiss of Evil
1962. Newlywed couple is stranded in Bavaria near a villa of vampires and are invited in by its charmingly evil owner. Fortunately, hubby manages to escape and finds a knowledgeable professor who unleashes a horde of bats to rout the bloodsuckers. Properly creepy; producer Hinds used the pseudonym John Elder for his screenplay. **88m/C VHS, Closed Caption.** GB Clifford Evans, Noel Willman, Edward De Souza, Jennifer Daniel, Barry Warren, Jacqueline Wallis; **D:** Don Sharp; **W:** Anthony John Elder Hinds; **C:** Alan Hume; **M:** James Bernard. **USH**

Kiss Shot 🎞️🎞️ 1989 Goldberg is a struggling single mother who loses her job but still must make the mortgage payments. She takes a job as a waitress but realizes it isn't going to pay the bills so she tries her hand as a pool hustler. Frantz is the promoter who finances her bets and Harewood, the pool-shooting playboy whose romantic advances are destroying her concentration. **88m/C VHS, Beta, Closed Caption.** Whoopi Goldberg, Dennis Franz, Dorian Harewood, David Marciano, Teddy Wilson; **D:** Jerry London; **M:** Stephen Dorff. **ACA, MOV**

Kiss the Night 1987 (R) An unfortunate hooker falls head over heels for a man she had the pleasure of doing business with. To her chagrin, it is much harder to leave the street than she thought. A dramatic and timely presentation. **99m/C VHS.** Patsy Stephens, Warwick Moss, Gary Aron Cook; **D:** James Ricketson. **MCG**

Kiss Tomorrow Goodbye 🎞️🎞️ 1950 A brutal, murderous escaped convict rises to crimelord status before his inevitable downfall. Based on a novel by Horace McCoy. **102m/B VHS, LV.** James Cagney, Barbara Payton, Ward Bond, Luther Adler, Helena Carter, Steve Brodie, Rhys Williams; **D:** Gordon Douglas. **REP**

Kissed 🎞️🎞️ 1996 The subject matter (necrophilia) is sure to give one pause though debut director Stopkewich hardly dwells on the prurient. Sandra Larson (Parker) has been obsessed with death and its rituals since childhood. So as a young adult it seems natural when she gets a job in a funeral home, preparing the bodies for embalming. Only Sandra's obsession leads her to begin making love (shown through a gauzy white light) to the corpses. She does attract the attentions of a very alive medical student, Matt (Outerbridge), who becomes fascinated by Sandra's fetish and determined to make himself as appealing to her as the dead. Adapted from Barbara Gowdy's short story "We So Seldom Look on Love." **78m/C VHS.** CA Molly Parker, Peter Outerbridge, Jay Brazeau; **D:** Lynne Stopkewich; **W:** Lynne Stopkewich, Angus Fraser; **C:** Gregory Middleton; **M:** Don MacDonald. **NYR**

Kisses for My President 🎞️🎞️½ 1964
Silly comedy about the first woman elected President and her trials and tribulations. MacMurray is the husband who has to adjust to the protocol of being "First Man." Bergen is miscast, but the other performances are just fine. **113m/C VHS.** Fred MacMurray, Polly Bergen, Arlene Dahl, Edward Andrews, Eli Wallach, Donald May; **D:** Curtis Bernhardt. **Nominations: Academy Awards '64:** Best Costume Design (B & W). **WAR**

Kissin' Cousins 🎞️½ 1964 Air Force officer on a secluded base in the South discovers a local hillbilly is his double. Presley quickie that includes country tunes such as "Smokey Mountain Boy" and "Barefoot Ballad" as well as the title song. **96m/C VHS, Beta.** Elvis Presley, Arthur O'Connell, Jack Albertson, Glenda Farrell, Pam Austin, Yvonne Craig, Cynthia Pepper, David Woods, Tommy Farrell, Beverly Powers; **D:** Gene Nelson. **MGM**

The Kissing Place 1990 A woman who abducted her "son" years ago tracks the boy to New York City to prevent him from finding his biological family. **90m/C VHS, Beta, Closed Caption.** Meredith Baxter, David Ogden Stiers; **D:** Tony Wharmby; **W:** Richard Altabef, Cynthia A. Cherbak. **PAR**

Kissinger and Nixon 🎞️🎞️½ 1996 Intrigue, ambition, and backbiting politics consume the 18 weeks leading up to the signing of the Vietnam peace accords in Paris in January, 1973. Egotistical Kissinger (Silver) is prepared to sacrifice South Vietnam for the sake of his own ambitions (and an end to the conflict) while a distrustful Nixon (Bridges) lurks uneasily in the background. TV docudrama offers little insight; based on Walter Isaacson's biography "Kissinger." **94m/C VHS.** Ron Silver, Beau Bridges, Matt Frewer, Ron White, George Takei, Kenneth Welsh; **D:** Daniel Petrie; **W:** Lionel Chetwynd. **TTC**

Kit Carson 🎞️🎞️ 1940 Frontiersman Kit Carson leads a wagon train to California, fighting off marauding Indians all the way. **97m/B VHS, Beta.** Jon Hall, Dana Andrews, Ward Bond, Lynn Bari; **D:** George B. Seitz. **MED, VTR**

The Kitchen Toto 🎞️🎞️🎞️ 1987 (PG-13)
Set in 1950 Kenya as British rule was being threatened by Mau Mau terrorists. A young black boy is torn between the British for whom he works and the terrorists who want him to join them. Complex and powerful story of the Kenyan freedom crusade. **96m/C VHS, Beta, LV, Closed Caption.** GB Bob Peck, Phyllis Logan, Robert Urquhart, Edward Judd, Edwin Mahinda, Kirsten Hughes; **D:** Harry Hook; **W:** Harry Hook; **C:** Roger Deakins; **M:** John Keane. **WAR**

Kitty and the Bagman 🎞️🎞️ 1982 (R) A comedy about two rival madames who ruled Australia in the 1920s. **95m/C VHS, Beta.** AU Liddy Clark; **D:** Donald Crombie.

Kitty Foyle 🎞️🎞️🎞️ 1940 From the novel by Christopher Morley, Rogers portrays the white-collar working girl whose involvement with a married man presents her with both romantic and social conflicts. **108m/B VHS, Beta.** Ginger Rogers, Dennis (Stanley Morner) Morgan, James Craig, Gladys Cooper, Ernest Cossart, Eduardo Ciannelli; **D:** Sam Wood. **Academy Awards '40:** Best Actress (Rogers); **Nominations: Academy Awards '40:** Best Director (Wood), Best Picture, Best Screenplay, Best Sound. **MED, CCB, FCT**

The Klansman 🎞️ Burning Cross; KKK 1974
(R) Race relations come out on the short end in this film about a sheriff trying to keep the lid on racial tensions in a southern town. Even the big-name cast can't save what comes off as a nighttime soaper rather than a serious drama. **112m/C VHS, Closed Caption.** Lee Marvin, Richard Burton, Cameron Mitchell, Lola Falana, Luciana Paluzzi, Linda Evans, O.J. Simpson; **D:** Terence Young; **W:** Samuel Fuller. **PAR, FCT**

Klondike Annie 🎞️🎞️½ 1936 West stars as a woman on the lam for a murder (self-defense) who heads out for the Yukon aboard McLaglen's ship. He falls for her, finds out about her problems, and helps her with a scam to pass herself off as a missionary, only she begins to take her saving souls seriously (although in her own risque style). **77m/B VHS.** Mae West, Victor McLaglen, Philip Reed, Helen Jerome Eddy, Harry Beresford, Harold Huber, Conway Tearle, Esther Howard; **D:** Raoul Walsh; **W:** Mae West. **USH, BTV**

Klondike Fever 🎞️½ Jack London's Klondike Fever 1979 (PG) Join the young Jack London as he travels from San Francisco to the Klondike fields during the Great Gold Rush of 1898. **118m/C VHS,**

Beta. Rod Steiger, Angie Dickinson, Lorne Greene; **D:** Peter Carter; **M:** Hagood Hardy. **NO**

Klute 🎞️🎞️🎞️½ 1971 (R) A small-town policeman (Sutherland) comes to New York in search of a missing friend and gets involved with a prostitute/would-be actress (Fonda) being stalked by a killer. Intelligent, gripping drama. **114m/C VHS, Beta, LV.** Jane Fonda, Donald Sutherland, Charles Cioffi, Roy Scheider, Rita Gam, Jean Stapleton; **D:** Alan J. Pakula; **C:** Gordon Willis. **Academy Awards '71:** Best Actress (Fonda); **Golden Globe Awards '72:** Best Actress—Drama (Fonda); **New York Film Critics Awards '71:** Best Actress (Fonda); **National Society of Film Critics Awards '71:** Best Actress (Fonda); **Nominations: Academy Awards '71:** Best Story & Screenplay. **WAR, BTV**

The Klutz 🎞️🎞️ 1973 A bumbling fool, on the way to visit his girlfriend, becomes accidentally embroiled in a bank robbery and other ridiculous mishaps. Light French comedy; dubbed. **87m/C VHS, Beta.** FR Claude Michaud, Louise Portal, Guy Provost; **D:** Pierre Rose. **NWV**

The Knack 🎞️🎞️🎞️ The Knack...and How to Get It 1965 Amusing, fast-paced adaptation of the play by Ann Jellicoe. Schoolteacher Crawford is baffled by his tenant Brooks' extreme luck with the ladies so Brooks decides to teach him the "knack" of picking up women. Crawford promptly falls for the first woman (Tushingham) he meets. Swinging London at its most mod. **84m/B VHS.** GB Michael Crawford, Ray Brooks, Rita Tushingham, Donal Donnelly; **D:** Richard Lester; **W:** Charles Wood; **C:** David Watkin; **M:** John Barry. **MGM**

Knife in the Head 🎞️🎞️ Messer Im Kopf 1978 Biogeneticist Berthold Hoffman (Ganz) is meeting his wife (Winkler) at the left-wing youth centre where she works when there's a police raid and Berthold is shot in the head. He awakens in the hospital having lost both his memory and all physical co-ordination. Determined to battle his disabilities, Berthold also becomes the pawn in a political game between the police and political dissidents. In German with English subtitles. **108m/C VHS.** GE Bruno Ganz, Angela Winkler, Hans Honig, Hans Brenner, Udo Samel, Carla Egerer; **D:** Reinhard Hauff; **W:** Peter Schneider. **NYF**

Knife in the Water 🎞️🎞️🎞️🎞️ Noz w Wodzie 1962 A journalist, his wife and a hitchhiker spend a day aboard a sailboat. Sex and violence can't be far off. Tense psychological drama. Served as director Polanski's debut. In Polish with English subtitles. **94m/B VHS, Beta, LV.** PL Leon Niemczyk, Jolanta Umecka, Zygmunt Malandowicz; **D:** Roman Polanski; **W:** Jerzy Skolimowski, Roman Polanski. **Venice Film Festival '62:** International Critics Award; **Nominations: Academy Awards '63:** Best Foreign Language Film. **HMV, FOX, BTV**

Knight Moves 🎞️🎞️ 1993 (R) Suspenseful thriller about a series of murders which take place at an international resort where a championship chess match is underway. The prime suspect is a chess master who has an unlikely affair with a beautiful police psychologist called in to decipher the mind of the murderer. Filmed in the Pacific Northwest. **CW:** Language, strong violence, and sexuality. **105m/C VHS, LV, Closed Caption.** Christopher Lambert, Diane Lane, Tom Skerritt, Daniel Baldwin; **D:** Carl Schenkel; **W:** Brad Mirman; **M:** Anne Dudley. **REP**

Knight Without Armour 🎞️🎞️🎞️ 1937 A journalist opposed to the Russian monarchy falls in love with the daughter of a czarist minister in this classic romantic drama. **107m/B VHS, Beta.** GB Marlene Dietrich, Robert Donat; **D:** Jacques Feyder; **C:** Harry Stradling; **M:** Miklos Rozsa.

Knightriders 🎞️🎞️½ 1981 (R) The story of a troupe of motorcyclists who are members of a traveling Renaissance Fair and look and act like modern-day Knights of the Round Table. Their battles center around who is the bravest and strongest, and who deserves to be king. **145m/C VHS, Beta, LV.** Ed Harris, Gary Lahti, Tom Savini, Amy Ingersoll; **D:** George A. Romero; **W:** George A. Romero. **FUS, MED**

Knights ⚔️½ 1993 (R) In a futuristic waste-land a young martial-arts warrior (Long) and a cyborg (Kristofferson) team up to battle rebel cyborgs that have discovered a new source of fuel—human blood.**CW:** Futuristic violence. 89m/C VHS, Beta, Closed Caption. Kathy Long, Kris Kristofferson, Lance Henriksen, Scott Paulin, Gary Daniels; **D:** Albert Pyun; **W:** Albert Pyun. PAR

Knights & Emeralds ⚔️½ 1987 (PG) Cross-cultural rivalries and romances develop between members of two high school marching bands in a British factory town as the national band championships draw near. 90m/C VHS, Beta, Closed Caption. **GB** Christopher Wild, Beverly Hills, Warren Mitchell; **D:** Ian Emes; **M:** Colin Towns. WAR

Knights of the City ⚔️ 1985 (R) Miami street gangs fight each other over their "turf." One leader decides to opt out, using music. ♫ Let the Music Play; Cry of the City; Jailhouse Rap; T.K. and Jessie Rap; Kurtis Blow Rap; Bounce; My Part of Town; Can You Feel It; Love Goes Up and Down. 87m/C VHS, Beta. Nicholas Campbell, John Mengatti, Wendy Barry, Stoney Jackson, Janine Turner, Michael Ansara; **D:** Leon Isaac Kennedy, Dominic Orlando; **W:** Leon Isaac Kennedy. NWV, VTR

Knights of the Range ⚔️½ 1940 Vintage western. 66m/B VHS, Beta. Russell Hayden, Victor Jory, Jean Parker, Britt Wood, J. Farrell MacDonald, Eddie Dean; **D:** Lesley Selander. VCN, MLB, GPV

Knights of the Round Table ⚔️⚔️½ 1953 The story of the romantic triangle between King Arthur, Sir Lancelot and Guinevere during the civil wars of sixth century England. 106m/C VHS, Beta, LV. Robert Taylor, Ava Gardner, Mel Ferrer, Anne Crawford, Felix Aylmer, Stanley Baker; **D:** Richard Thorpe; **C:** Frederick A. (Freddie) Young; **M:** Miklos Rozsa. Nominations: Academy Awards '53: Best Art Direction/Set Decoration (Color), Best Sound. MGM

Knock on Any Door ⚔️⚔️ 1949 A young hoodlum from the slums is tried for murdering a cop. He is defended by a prominent attorney who has known him from childhood. 100m/B VHS, Beta, LV. Humphrey Bogart, John Derek, George Macready; **D:** Nicholas Ray; **W:** Daniel Taradash, John Monks Jr.; **C:** Burnett Guffey. COL

Knock Outs ⚔️ 1992 Samantha not only loses her shirt at a sorority strip poker marathon but she loses her tuition money to a gang of biker chicks. Then Samantha and a bevy of bikini-clad friends decide to pose for a swimsuit calendar to earn some cash but are secretly videotaped in the nude by some local sleaze promoters. Tired of being taken advantage of these lovelies take up martial arts and challenge their nefarious girl biker rivals to a winner-take-all wrestling match, not forgetting about the purveyors of the not-so-secret videotape. 90m/C VHS. Chona Jackson, Cindy Rome, Brad Zutaut; **D:** John Bowen. HMD

The Knockout/Dough and Dynamite ⚔️⚔️⚔️ 1914 Two Chaplin shorts: "The Knockout" (1914), in which Charlie referees a big fight; "Dough and Dynamite" (1914), in which a labor dispute at a bake shop leaves Charlie in charge when the regular baker walks out. 54m/B VHS, Beta. Charlie Chaplin, Fatty Arbuckle, Mabel Normand, The Keystone Cops; **D:** Charlie Chaplin, Sydney Chaplin. VYY

Knute Rockne: All American ⚔️⚔️⚔️ A Modern Hero 1940 Life story of Notre Dame football coach Knute Rockne, who inspired many victories with his powerful speeches. Reagan, as the dying George Gipp, utters that now-famous line, "Tell the boys to win one for the Gipper." 96m/B VHS, Beta. Ronald Reagan, Pat O'Brien, Gale Page, Donald Crisp, John Qualen; **D:** Lloyd Bacon. MGM, FHE

Kojak: The Belarus File ⚔️⚔️ 1985 The bald-headed detective of prime-time television fame searches for a neo-Nazi who is killing Holocaust survivors in New York. Made for television. 95m/C VHS, Beta. Telly Savalas, Suzanne Pleshette, Max von Sydow, George Savalas; **D:** Robert Markowitz. USH

Kojiro ⚔️⚔️⚔️ 1967 A sprawling epic by prolific Japanese director Inagaki about a dashing rogue's bid for power in feudal times. With English subtitles. 152m/C VHS, Beta. **JP** Kikunosuke Onoe, Tatsuya Nakadai; **D:** Hiroshi Inagaki. VDA

Kolberg ⚔️ Burning Hearts 1945 The true story of a Prussian town heroically withstanding Napoleon. Produced by Joseph Goebbels in the last days of the Third Reich, it is best remembered as the film whose expensive production and momentous use of real German soldiers, supplies, and ammunition eventually helped to fell the Axis war machine. In German with English subtitles. 118m/C VHS, Beta. **GE** Kristina Soderbaum, Heinrich George, Horst Caspar, Paul Wegener; **D:** Veit Harlan. FCT, IHF, GLV

Kolya ⚔️⚔️⚔️ 1996 (PG-13) Set in the late '80s, just before the Velvet Revolution ended Soviet domination of Czechoslovakia, womanizing Prague cellist Louka (Sverak) agrees to marry (for money) the Russian Klara (Safrankova) who wants Czech papers. She soon clears out to join her lover in Berlin and Louka finds himself saddled with her five-year-old son, Kolya (Chaliman). Grumpy Louka isn't obvious dad material and they don't even speak the same language but the kid (who's adorable without being cloying) manages to worm his way into his new life. Czech with subtitles.**CW:** Some sensuality. 111m/C VHS. **CZ** Zdenek Sverak, Andrej Chalimon, Libuse Safrankova; **D:** Jan Sverak; **W:** Zdenek Sverak; **C:** Vladimir Smutny; **M:** Ondrej Soukup. Academy Awards '96: Best Foreign Language Film; Golden Globe Awards '97: Best Foreign Language Film; Nominations: British Academy Awards '96: Best Foreign Language Film. NYR

Konrad 199? Konrad, an "instant" child made in a factory, is accidentally delivered to an eccentric woman. The factory wants him back when the mistake is discovered, but Konrad stands up against it. Includes a viewers' guide. Part of the "Wonderworks" series. 110m/C VHS. Ned Beatty, Polly Holliday, Max Wright, Huckleberry Fox; **D:** Neil Cox; **W:** Malcolm Marmorstein. PME, HMV, BTV

Korczak ⚔️⚔️⚔️ 1990 Based on the life of Dr. Janusz Korczak, an outspoken critic of the Nazis, who ran the Jewish orphanage in Warsaw, Poland and accompanied 200 children to to the Treblinka concentration camp. Harshly poetic film quietly details Polish resistance to the Nazi terror. Criticized for end scenes of the children romping in the countryside, implying that they were somehow freed—since the director did not want to show the children actually entering the gas chambers he used this allegory to imply that their souls were freed. In Polish with English subtitles. 118m/C VHS. **PL** Wojtek Pszoniak, Ewa Dalkowska, Piotr Kozlowski, Marzena Trybala, Wojciech Klata, Adam Siemion; **D:** Andrzej Wajda; **W:** Agnieszka Holland. NYF, FCT

Koroshi ⚔️½ 1967 Secret Agent John Drake is dispatched to Hong Kong to disband a secret society who is killing off international political figures. 100m/C VHS, Beta. Patrick McGoohan, Kenneth Griffith, Yoko Tani; **D:** Michael Truman, Peter Yates. MPI

Kostas ⚔️⚔️ 1979 (R) A migrant Greek taxi driver romantically pursues a wealthy Australian divorcee in England. 88m/C VHS, Beta. Takis Emmanuel, Wendy Hughes; **D:** Paul Cox. LIV, VES

Kotch ⚔️⚔️⚔️ 1971 (PG) An elderly man resists his children's attempts to retire him. Warm detailing of old age with a splendid performance by Matthau. Lemmon's directorial debut. 113m/C VHS. Walter Matthau, Deborah Winters, Felicia Farr; **D:** Jack Lemmon; **M:** Marvin Hamlisch. Golden Globe Awards '72: Best Song ("Life Is What You Make It"); Writers Guild of America '71: Best Adapted Screenplay; Nominations: Academy Awards '71: Best Actor (Matthau), Best Film Editing, Best Song ("Life Is What You MaKe It"), Best Sound. FOX

Kounterfeit ⚔️⚔️ 1996 (R) Hopscotch (Hawkes) finds three million in counterfeit cash and tries to get some real cash for the fake stuff with his topless-bar owner buddy Frankie (Payne) serving as muscle. But things go bad. Bernsen has little more than a cameo role.**CW:** Language, violence, sexual situations. 87m/C VHS, LV, Closed Caption. Andrew Hawkes, Bruce Payne, Hilary Swank, Michael Gross, Mark Paul Gosselaar, Corbin Bernsen; **D:** John Mallory Asher; **W:** Jay Irwin, David Chase; **C:** Karl Herrmann. LIV

Kowloon Assignment ⚔️ 1977 Comic book superhero Golgo 13 comes to life in this action film dealing with a drug war in the Hong Kong underground. 93m/C VHS, Beta. Sonny Chiba. NO

Koyaanisqatsi ⚔️⚔️⚔️ 1983 A mesmerizing film that takes an intense look at modern life (the movie's title is the Hopi word for "life out of balance"). Without dialogue or narration, it brings traditional background elements, landscapes and cityscapes, up front to produce a unique view of the structure and mechanics of our daily lives. Riveting and immensely powerful. A critically acclaimed score by Glass, and Reggio's cinematography prove to be the perfect match to this brilliant film. Followed by "Powaqqatsi." 87m/C VHS, Beta, LV. **D:** Godfrey Reggio; **M:** Philip Glass. Los Angeles Film Critics Association Awards '83: Best Score. MVD, FCT, MLB

Kramer vs. Kramer ⚔️⚔️⚔️½ 1979 (PG) Highly acclaimed family drama about an advertising executive husband and child left behind when their wife and mother leaves on a quest to find herself, and the subsequent courtroom battle for custody when she returns. Hoffman and Streep give exacting performances as does young Henry. Successfully moves you from tears to laughter and back again. Based on the novel by Avery Corman. 105m/C VHS, Beta, LV, Closed Caption. Dustin Hoffman, Meryl Streep, Jane Alexander, Justin Henry, Howard Duff, JoBeth Williams; **D:** Robert Benton; **W:** Robert Benton; **C:** Nestor Almendros. Academy Awards '79: Best Actor (Hoffman), Best Adapted Screenplay, Best Director (Benton), Best Picture, Best Supporting Actress (Streep); Directors Guild of America Awards '79: Best Director (Benton); Golden Globe Awards '80: Best Actor—Drama (Hoffman), Best Film—Drama, Best Screenplay, Best Supporting Actress (Streep); Los Angeles Film Critics Association Awards '79: Best Actor (Hoffman), Best Director (Benton), Best Film, Best Screenplay, Best Supporting Actress (Streep); National Board of Review Awards '79: 10 Best Films of the Year, Best Supporting Actress (Streep); New York Film Critics Awards '79: Best Actor (Hoffman), Best Film, Best Supporting Actress (Streep); National Society of Film Critics Awards '79: Best Actor (Hoffman), Best Director (Benton), Best Supporting Actress (Streep); Writers Guild of America '79: Best Adapted Screenplay; Nominations: Academy Awards '79: Best Cinematography, Best Film Editing, Best Supporting Actor (Henry), Best Supporting Actress (Alexander). COL, BTV

The Krays ⚔️⚔️⚔️½ 1990 (R) An account of British gangsters Reggie and Ronnie Kray, the brothers who ruled London's East End with brutality and violence, making them bizarre celebrities of the sixties. The leads are portrayed by Gary and Martin Kemp, founders of the British pop group Spandau Ballet. 119m/C VHS, LV, 8mm, Closed Caption. **GB** Gary Kemp, Martin Kemp, Billie Whitelaw, Steven Berkoff, Susan Fleetwood, Charlotte Cornwell, Jimmy Jewel, Avis Bunnage, Kate Hardie, Alfred Lynch, Tom Bell, Steven Berkoff, Victor Spinetti, Barbara Ferris, Julia Migenes-Johnson, John McEnery, Sadie Frost, Norman Rossington, Murray Melvin; **D:** Peter Medak; **W:** Philip Ridley; **M:** Michael Kamen. COL, FCT

Kriemhilde's Revenge ⚔️⚔️⚔️ Die Nibelungen 1924 The second film, following "Siegfried," of Lang's "Die Nibelungen," a lavish silent version of the Teutonic legends Wagner's "Ring of the Nibelungen" was based upon. In this episode, Kriemhilde avenges Siegfried's death by her marriage to the Kings of the Huns, thus fulfilling a prophecy of destruction. 95m/B VHS, LV. **GE** Paul Richter, Margareta Schoen, Theodore Loos, Hanna Ralph, Rudolf Klein-Rogge; **D:** Fritz Lang. CCB, IHF, REP

Kronos ⚔️⚔️½ 1957 A giant robot from space drains the Earth of all its energy resources. A good example of this genre from the 50s. Includes previews of coming attractions from classic science fiction films. 78m/B VHS, Beta, LV. Jeff Morrow,

Barbara Lawrence, John Emery; **D:** Kurt Neumann. *MED, MLB*

Krull ✓✓ 1983 (PG) Likeable fantasy adventure set in a world peopled by creatures of myth and magic. A prince embarks on a quest to find the Glaive (a magical weapon) and then rescues his young bride, taken by the Beast of the Black Fortress. 121m/C VHS, Beta, LV, **Closed Caption.** *GB* Ken Marshall, Lysette Anthony, Freddie Jones, Francesca Annis, Liam Neeson; **D:** Peter Yates; **M:** James Horner. *GKK*

Krush Groove ✓ 1985 (R) The world of rap music is highlighted in this movie, the first all-rap musical. "King of Rock; Don't You Dog Me; A Love Bizarre; Pick Up the Pace; If I Ruled the World; Holly Rock; It's Like That; Feel the Spin; I Can't Live Without My Radio. 95m/C VHS, Beta, LV, **Closed Caption.** Blair Underwood, Eron Tabor, Kurtis Blow, Sheila E; **D:** Michael A. Schultz. *WAR*

K2: The Ultimate High ✓✓ 1992 (R) Two men, one a skirt-chasing lawyer, the other a happily married physicist, tackle the world's second largest mountain—the K-2 in Kashmir, northern Pakistan. They encounter a number of dangers, including an ascent of sheer rock face, an avalanche, and a fall down perpendicular mountain ice, but even the exciting mountain-climbing scenes can't hold up this watered down movie. The film was actually shot on Canada's Mount Waddington. Based on the play by Patrick Meyers. 104m/C VHS, Beta, **Closed Caption.** Michael Biehn, Matt Craven, Raymond J. Barry, Luca Bercovici, Patricia Charbonneau, Julia Nickson-Soul, Hiroshi Fujioka, Jamal Shah; **D:** Franc Roddam; **W:** Patrick Meyers, Scott Roberts. *PAR*

Kuffs ✓✓ 1992 (PG-13) Slater stars as George Kuffs, a young guy who reluctantly joins his brother's highly respected private security team in this original action comedy. After his brother is gunned down in the line of duty, George finds himself the new owner of the business. Out to avenge his brother, George pursues a crooked art dealer as he battles crime on the streets of San Francisco. Worthwhile premise is hampered by a predictable plot and mediocre acting. 102m/C VHS, Beta, LV, **Closed Caption.** Christian Slater, Tony Goldwyn, Milla Jovovich, Bruce Boxleitner, Troy Evans, George de la Pena, Leon Rippy; **D:** Bruce A. Evans; **W:** Bruce A. Evans, Raynold Gideon; **M:** Harold Faltermeyer. *USH*

Kull the Conqueror ✓✓½ 1997 (PG-13) Sorbo goes from TV's heroic Hercules to action-fantasy hero Kull, a slave who becomes the warrior or king of a mythic land. Overthrown by a corrupt nobility, Kull begins a perilous journey to find a magic weapon to help him regain his kingdom and his love. Lots of action, although the PG-13 rating keeps some of the mayhem less bloody than might be expected for this genre. Based on the '30s character created by pulp writer Robert E. Howard, who also originated "Conan the Barbarian." **CW:** Fantasy action violence and sensuality. ?m/C VHS. Kevin Sorbo, Tia Carrere, Thomas Ian Griffith, Karina Lombard, Litefoot, Harvey Fierstein, Roy Brocksmith; **D:** John Nicolella; **W:** Charles Edward Pogue, Don Mancini. *NYR*

Kung Fu ✓✓½ 1972 A fugitive Buddhist quasi-Asian martial arts master accused of murder in his native land, roams across the Old West fighting injustice. Served as a pilot for the successful television series and was reincarnated 14 years later in the sequel, "Kung Fu: The Movie." 75m/C VHS, Beta. Keith Carradine, David Carradine, Barry Sullivan, Keye Luke; **D:** Jerry Thorpe. *WAR*

Kung Fu Avengers ✓ 1985 On his way to a karate show at Madison Square Garden, our hero Li confronts the abominable Mr. Chin and his deadly henchman. Another foot-stomper. 90m/C VHS, Beta. Bruce Li, Carl Scott, Jim James, Ku Feng. *PSM*

Kung Fu Commandos ✓ 1980 (R) Five martial arts masters must face an evil warlord's army to rescue a captured agent. 90m/C VHS, Beta. John Liu, Shangkuan Ling-Feng. *PSM, GEM*

Kung Fu Massacre ✓ 1982 (R) Farmers hire hard-handed mercenaries to fight evil war lords. 90m/C VHS, Beta. Yangzi, Pi Li Lee. *LIV*

Kung Fu Rebels ✓½ 1980 Rebels are fearsome enough, but when they're kung fu masters, the establishment has real trouble on its hands. 90m/C VHS, Beta. Wang Chung, Wen Ching Lung, Chang Mei. *NO*

Kung Fu: The Movie ✓✓½ 1986 Carradine reprises his role as Kwai Chang Caine from the television show of the '70s. In this made-for-television fare he's hunted by evil warlord Mako, who's involved in the California opium trade. Mako sends assassin Lee (son of martial-arts star Bruce) after Caine. Luke appears in flashbacks as the young Grasshopper's blind mentor, Master Po. 93m/C VHS, Beta. David Carradine, Mako, Brandon Lee, Keye Luke, Kerrie Keane, Martin Landau, William Lucking, Luke Askew, Benson Fong; **D:** Richard Lang. *WAR*

Kuni Lemel in Tel Aviv ✓✓½ 1977 The bungling folk-hero of the shtetl of 100 years ago is updated to the present. Grandpa Kuni is now 80 and living in Brooklyn. Anxious to see the family line continue, he offers five million dollars to the first of his twin grandsons to marry a nice Jewish girl and settle in Israel. However, the grandsons have plans of their own which conflict with Grandpa's. In Hebrew with English subtitles. 90m/C VHS. *IS* Mike Burstyn, Mandy Rice-Davies; **D:** Yoel Silberg. *ERG*

Kurt Vonnegut's Harrison Bergeron ✓✓½ *Harrison Bergeron* 1995 (R) In the year 2053 the American government has gone to absurd lengths to ensure equality. Mediocrity is championed and everyone is forced to wear metallic headbands that stifle intellect through electronic impulses. Too bad for Harrison Bergeron (Astin), a smart young man being punished for his intelligence. But there's a secret underground elite offering Harrison the chance to think freely, though this power comes with a price. Adapted from Vonnegut's 1961 short story; made for cable TV. **CW:** Language, and for some sexuality and violence. 99m/C VHS, **Closed Caption.** Sean Astin, Christopher Plummer, Miranda de Pencier, Nigel Bennett, Buck Henry, Eugene Levy, Howie Mandel, Andrea Martin; **D:** Bruce Pittman; **W:** Arthur Crimm. *REP*

Kurt Vonnegut's Monkey House ✓✓ 199? Dramatization of four short stories from Vonnegut's "Welcome to the Monkey House" collection, including a twist on the familiar Frankenstein tale. Made for cable television. 100m/C VHS. Frank Langella. *PBS*

Kwaidan ✓✓✓✓ 1964 A haunting, stylized quartet of supernatural stories, each with a surprise ending. Adapted from the stories of Lafcadio Hearn, an American author who lived in Japan just before the turn of the century. The visual effects are splendid. In Japanese with English subtitles. 164m/C VHS, Beta, LV. *JP* Michiyo Aratama, Rentaro Mikuni, Katsuo Makamura, Keiko Kishi, Tatsuya Nakadai, Takashi Shimura; **D:** Masaki Kobayashi; **M:** Toru Takemitsu. Cannes Film Festival '65: Grand Jury Prize; Nominations: Academy Awards '65: Best Foreign Language Film. *VYY, NOS, SNC*

L.627 ✓✓✓ 1992 Melancholy police procedural about dedicated veteran narcotics cop Lulu (Bezace) who works with a small and ill-equipped Parisian drug squad prone to taking the law into their own hands. Lulu constantly finds himself thwarted by obtuse bureaucrats while his life is disturbed by an informant—a young, drug-addicted prostitute who has disappeared and whom Lulu desires to protect. Film title refers to the French anti-drug statute. French with subtitles. 145m/C VHS. *FR* Didier Bezace, Jean-Paul Comart, Cecile Garcia-Fogel, Lara Guiraud, Charlotte Kady, Jean-Roger

Milo, Philippe Torreton, Nils Tavernier; **D:** Bertrand Tavernier; **W:** Bertrand Tavernier, Michel Alexandre; **M:** Philippe Sarde. *KIV*

L.A. Bad ✓ 1985 (R) A Puerto Rican street thug learns he has cancer, and must come to terms with his own impending death. 101m/C VHS, Beta. Esai Morales, Janice Rule, John Phillip Law, Chuck Bail, Carrie Snodgress. *VTR, PSM*

La Balance ✓✓✓ 1982 (R) An underworld stool pigeon is recruited by the Parisian police to blow the whistle on a murderous mob. Baye, as a prostitute in love with the pimp-stoolie, is a standout. Critically acclaimed; French with subtitles. 103m/C VHS, Beta, **Closed Caption.** *FR* Philippe Leotard, Nathalie Baye, Bob Swaim; **D:** Reymond LePlont; **M:** Roland Bocquet. Cesar Awards '83: Best Actor (Leotard), Best Actress (Baye), Best Film. *FOX*

La Bamba ✓✓✓ 1987 (PG-13) A romantic biography of the late 1950s pop idol Ritchie Valens, concentrating on his stormy relationship with his half-brother, his love for his WASP girlfriend, and his tragic, sudden death in the famed plane crash that also took the lives of Buddy Holly and the Big Bopper. Soundtrack features Setzer, Huntsberry, Crenshaw, and Los Lobos as, respectively, Eddie Cochran, the Big Bopper, Buddy Holly, and a Mexican bordello band. 99m/C VHS, Beta, LV, 8mm, **Closed Caption.** Lou Diamond Phillips, Esai Morales, Danielle von Zerneck, Joe Pantoliano, Brian Setzer, Marshall Crenshaw, Howard Huntsberry, Rosana De Soto, Elizabeth Pena, Rick Dees; **D:** Luis Valdez; **W:** Luis Valdez; **M:** Carlos Santana, Miles Goodman. *COL*

La Belle Noiseuse ✓✓✓½ *Divertimento* 1990 The connections between art and life are explored in this beautiful (and long) drama. Creatively crippled, an aging painter has left unfinished a masterpiece work, entitled "La Belle Noiseuse," for ten years. When an admiring younger artist and his beautiful lover arrive for a visit, the painter is newly inspired by the young woman and makes her the model and muse for his masterwork. The film details every nuance of the work from the first to the last brushstroke and the battle of wills between artist and model over the symbiotic creative process. Based on a novella by Honore Balzac. French with subtitles. "Divertimento" is actually a recut and shortened version (126 minutes) of the original film. 240m/C VHS. *FR* Michel Piccoli, Emmanuelle Beart, Jane Birkin, David Bursztein, Marianne Denicourt; **D:** Jacques Rivette. Cannes Film Festival '91: Grand Jury Prize; Los Angeles Film Critics Association Awards '91: Best Foreign Film. *NYF, FCT, ING*

La Bete Humaine ✓✓✓½ *The Human Beast* 1938 A dark, psychological melodrama about human passion and duplicity, as an unhinged trainman plots with a married woman to kill her husband. Wonderful performances and stunning photography. Based on the Emile Zola novel. In French with English subtitles. 1954 Hollywood remake, "Human Desire," was directed by Fritz Lang. 90m/B VHS, Beta, 8mm. *FR* Jean Gabin, Simone Simon, Julien Carette, Fernand Ledoux; **D:** Jean Renoir. *NOS, HHT, CAB*

La Boca del Lobo ✓✓ *The Lion's Den* 1989 Peru's civil strife inspired this sluggish drama about government troops occupying a jungle village. Tormented by unseen communist guerillas, the stressed-out soldiers reach the breaking point. Spanish with subtitles. 111m/C VHS. *AR* Gustavo Bueno, Tono Vega, Jose Tejada; **D:** Francisco J. Lombardi. *CCN, APD, TPV*

La Boum ✓✓½ 1981 A teenager's adjustment to the changes brought about by a move to Paris is compounded by her parents' marital problems. Followed by "La Boum 2." 90m/C VHS, Beta. *FR* Sophie Marceau, Claude Brasseur, Brigitte Fossey, Denise Grey, Bernard Giraudeau; **D:** Claude Pinoteau; **M:** Vladimir Cosma. *COL*

L.A. Bounty ✓½ 1989 (R) A beautiful cop and a bounty hunter go after the same murderer. Hauser steals the show as a psychopath who has completely blown a gasket. 85m/C VHS, Beta, LV.

Sybil Danning, Wings Hauser, Henry Darrow, Lenore Kasdorf, Robert Hanley; **D:** Worth Keeter. NO

La Cage aux Folles 🐾🐾🐾½ 1978 (R)

Adaption of the popular French play. A gay nightclub owner and his transvestite lover play it straight when Tognazzi's son from a long-ago liaison brings his fiancee and her conservative parents home for dinner. Charming music and lots of fun. So successful, it was followed by two sequels, "La Cage Aux Folles II & III" and also a Broadway musical. In French with English subtitles. **91m/C VHS, Beta, LV.** *FR* Ugo Tognazzi, Michel Serrault, Michel Galabru, Claire Maurier, Remy Laurent, Benny Luke; **D:** Edouard Molinaro; **W:** Francis Veber; **M:** Ennio Morricone. Cesar Awards '79: Best Actor (Serrault); Golden Globe Awards '80: Best Foreign Film; Nominations: Academy Awards '79: Best Adapted Screenplay, Best Costume Design, Best Director (Molinaro). *MGM, FOX, CRC*

La Cage aux Folles 2 🐾🐾½ 1981 (R)

Albin sets out to prove to his companion that he still has sex appeal, and gets mixed up in some espionage antics. This sequel to the highly successful "La Cage aux Folles" loses some steam, but is still worth seeing. Followed by "La Cage Aux Folles 3: The Wedding." **101m/C VHS, Beta, LV.** *FR* Ugo Tognazzi, Michel Serrault, Marcel Bozzuffi, Michel Galabru, Benny Luke; **D:** Edouard Molinaro; **W:** Francis Veber; **M:** Ennio Morricone. *MGM, FCT, FOX*

La Cage aux Folles 3: The Wedding 🐾½ 1986 (PG-13)

The flamboyant drag queen Albin must feign normalcy by marrying and fathering a child in order to collect a weighty inheritance. Final segment of the trilogy; inferior to the previous films. In French with English subtitles. **88m/C VHS, Beta, LV.** *FR* Michel Serrault, Ugo Tognazzi, Michel Galabru, Benny Luke, Stephane Audran; **D:** Georges Lautner; **M:** Ennio Morricone. *COL*

La Ceremonie 🐾🐾🐾 A Judgment in Stone 1995

Sullen maid Sophie (Bonnaire) is hired by the rich Lelievre family to work at their country estate. She's befriended by independent postmistress Jeanne (Huppert), who's disliked by Sophie's employers, and who encourages Sophie into small defiant actions. Something's off about the entire situation and there's violence beneath the seemingly calm surface. Based on Ruth Rendell's chiller "Judgement in Stone." French with subtitles. **111m/C VHS.** *FR* Sandrine Bonnaire, Isabelle Huppert, Jacqueline Bisset, Jean-Pierre Cassel; **D:** Claude Chabrol; **W:** Claude Chabrol, Caroline Eliacheff. Cesar Awards '96: Best Actress (Huppert); Los Angeles Film Critics Association Awards '96: Best Foreign Film; National Society of Film Critics Awards '96: Best Foreign Film; Nominations: Cesar Awards '96: Best Actress (Bonnaire), Best Director (Chabrol), Best Film, Best Screenplay, Best Supporting Actor (Cassel), Best Supporting Actress (Bisset). *NYF*

La Chartreuse de Parme 🐾🐾½ Charterhouse at Parma 1948

Nineteenth century period piece featuring an Archbishop willing to break his vows for the woman he loves, and the aunt who will make sure that if she can't have him only God will. French adaptation of the novel. Available dubbed. **?m/C VHS.** *FR* Gerard Philipe, Maria Casares, Rene Faure. *FRA, FCT*

La Chevre 🐾🐾🐾½ The Goat 1981

A screwball French comedy about two policemen (Richard and Depardieu—picture Nick Nolte and Gene Wilder with accents) stumbling along the path of a missing heiress who suffers from chronic bad luck. Contains a hilarious scene with chairs used to test the luck of the investigative team; based on one partner's ability to sit on the only broken chair in a rather large collection, he is judged to be sufficiently jinxed to allow them to recreate the same outrageous misfortunes that befell the heiress in her plight. In French with English subtitles. **91m/C VHS, Beta.** *FR* Gerard Depardieu, Pierre Richard, Corynne Charbit, Michel Robin, Pedro Armendariz Jr.; **D:** Francis Veber; **M:** Vladimir Cosma. *FCT, TPV*

La Chienne 🐾🐾🐾🐾 Isn't Life A Bitch?; The Bitch 1931

Dark, troubling tale of a bedraggled husband whose only excitement is his painting hobby until he becomes consumed by the ever-tempting prostitute Lulu. Director Renoir broke ground with his use of direct sound and Paris shooting locations, and the experiment was a hit. Portrays marriage with acidity; Renoir's own marriage broke up as a result of this film's casting. Mareze died shortly after the filming was complete in a car crash. Based on the novel by Georges de la Fouchardiere. Produced in 1931, but didn't reach American theaters until 1975. In French with English subtitles. Remade in 1945 as "Scarlet Street." **93m/B VHS, Beta, LV.** *FR* Michel Simon, Janie Mareze, Georges Flament, Madeleine Berubet; **D:** Jean Renoir; **W:** Andre Girard, Jean Renoir. *INT, TPV*

La Chute de la Maison Usher 🐾🐾🐾½ The Fall of the House of Usher 1928

An expressionistic, abstracted adaptation of the Poe story "The Fall of the House of Usher" about an evil mansion and its ruined denizens. Epstein used slow motion, superimpressions, and weird camera angles to obtain the proper atmosphere. **48m/B VHS, Beta.** *FR* Marguerite Gance, Jean Debucourt, Charles Lamy; **D:** Jean Epstein. *FCT, GVV*

La Cicada 🐾½ The Cricket 1983

The sparks fly when a woman and her seventeen-year-old daughter become rivals for the affections of the same man. **90m/C VHS, Beta.** *IT* Clio Goldsmith, Virna Lisi, Anthony (Tony) Franciosa, Renato Salvatori; **D:** Alberto Lattuada.

La Collectionneuse 🐾🐾 The Gentleman Tramp 1967

The third of Rohmer's "Moral Tales" finds an artist (Bachau) and an antiques dealer (Pommereulle) vacationing in St. Tropez and sharing a villa with a young woman (Politoff) who picks a different man to sleep with each night. Both try to resist the sexual temptations of being added to her collection of lovers. French with subtitles. **88m/C VHS.** *FR* Patrick Bauchau, Daniel Pommereulle, Haydee Politoff, Alain Jouffroy; **D:** Eric Rohmer; **C:** Nestor Almendros. *FXL*

L.A. Crackdown 🐾 1987

A ruthless yet compassionate policewoman goes after crack dealers and pimps who are exploiting women. Pretty trashy fare; followed by "L.A. Crackdown 2." Made for video. **90m/C VHS, Beta.** Pamela Dixon, Tricia Parks, Kita Harrison, Jeffrey Olson, Michael Coon; **D:** Joseph Merhi. NO

L.A. Crackdown 2 🐾 1988

A woman cop goes undercover as a dancer in a dance hall to try to catch a psychotic killer who stalks hookers in this silly sequel to "L.A. Crackdown." **90m/C VHS, Beta.** Pamela Dixon, Anthony Gates, Joe Vance, Cynthia Miguel, Lisa Anderson, Bo Sabato; **D:** Joseph Merhi. HHE

La Discrete 🐾🐾 The Discreet 1990

Antoine (Luchini) is a cocky writer who is not the lothario he imagines himself to be—in fact his girlfriend has just dumped him. He and his publisher plan a sexist revenge with Antoine advertising for a young female typist whom he will seduce and abandon—all the while keeping a diary of the experience which will be published. The self-possessed Catherine (Henry) answers the ad and even though Antoine protests that she is not his type he finds himself falling in love. Then Catherine discovers Antoine's original scheme. Vincent's directorial debut. In French with English subtitles. **95m/C VHS.** *FR* Fabrice Luchini, Judith Henry, Maurice Garrel, Marie Bunel, Francois Toumarkine; **D:** Christian Vincent; **W:** Jean-Pierre Ronssin, Christian Vincent; **M:** Jay Gottlieb. Cesar Awards '91: Best Writing. *NYF, FCT*

La Dolce Vita 🐾🐾🐾🐾 1960

In this influential and popular work a successful, sensationalistic Italian journalist covers the show-biz life in Rome, and alternately covets and disdains its glitzy shallowness. The film follows his dealings with the "sweet life" over a pivotal week. A surreal, comic tableaux with award-winning costuming; one of Fellini's most acclaimed films. In this film Fellini called his hungry celebrity photographers the Paparazzo—and it is as the paparazzi they have been ever since. In Italian with English subtitles. **174m/B VHS, LV.** *IT* Marcello Mastroianni, Anita Ekberg, Anouk Aimee, Alain Cuny, Lex Barker, Yvonne Furneaux, Barbara Steele, Nadia Gray, Magali Noel, Walter Santesso, Jacques Sernas, Annabelle Ninchi; **D:** Federico Fellini; **W:** Tullio Pinelli, Ennio Flaiano, Federico Fellini; **M:** Nino Rota. Academy Awards '61: Best Costume Design (B & W); Cannes Film Festival '60: Best Film; National Board of Review Awards '61: 5 Best Foreign Films of the Year; New York Film Critics Awards '61: Best Foreign Film; Nominations: Academy Awards '61: Best Art Direction/Set Decoration (B & W), Best Director (Fellini), Best Story & Screenplay. *REP, APD*

La Femme Nikita 🐾🐾🐾 1991 (R)

Stylish French noir version of Pygmalion. Having killed a cop during a drugstore theft gone awry, young French sociopath Nikita (Parillaud) is reprieved from a death sentence in order to enroll in a government finishing school, of sorts. Trained in etiquette and assasination, she's released after three years, and starts a new life with a new beau, all the while carrying out agency-mandated assassinations. Parillaud is excellent as the once-amoral street urchin transformed into a woman of depth and sensitivity—a bitterly ironic moral evolution for a contract killer. Remade as "Point of No Return." **117m/C VHS.** *FR* Anne Parillaud, Jean-Hugues Anglade, Tcheky Karyo, Jeanne Moreau, Jean Reno, Jean Bouise; **D:** Luc Besson; **W:** Luc Besson; **C:** Thierry Arbogast; **M:** Eric Serra. Cesar Awards '91: Best Actress (Parillaud). *THV, FCT, BTV*

L.A. Gangs Rising 🐾🐾 1989

The streets of Los Angeles run red with blood as a gang war explodes into bloody fury. **87m/C VHS, Beta.** David Kyle, Steve Bond, John Ashton; **D:** John Bushelman. NO

L.A. Goddess 🐾½ 1992 (R)

A hard-living, and drinking, movie star and her beautiful stunt double both fall for a studio head. Both of these women know what they want and the man in the middle hasn't got a clue. Also available in an unrated version. **CW:** Language and strong sexuality. **92m/C VHS.** Kathy Shower, Jeff Conaway, David Heavener, Wendy McDonald, Joe Estevez, James Hong; **D:** Jag Mundhra; **W:** Jerry Davis. PSM

La Grande Bouffe 🐾🐾🐾 The Blow-Out 1973

Four middle-aged men, bored with life, meet at a secluded mansion for one last excessive fling and to literally eat themselves to death. Four very fine actors in a vulgar feast. French with subtitles. **125m/C VHS.** *FR* Marcello Mastroianni, Philippe Noiret, Michel Piccoli, Ugo Tognazzi, Andrea Ferreol; **D:** Marco Ferreri; **W:** Marco Ferreri, Rafael Azcona; **C:** Mario Vulpiani; **M:** Philippe Sarde. WBF

La Grande Bourgeoise 🐾🐾½ The Murri Affair 1974

Historical romance about the clash of aristocratic society and the new bourgeoisie in 1897 Italy. Great cast tries to save the true tale of murder and political intrigue from film's slow pacing, but in the end it's the movie's visual polish that shines forth. In Italian with subtitles. **115m/C VHS, Beta.** *IT* Catherine Deneuve, Giancarlo Giannini, Fernando Rey, Tina Aumont; **D:** Mauro Bolognini; **M:** Ennio Morricone. *FCT*

La Grande Vadrouille 🐾🐾🐾 Don't Look Now, We've Been Shot At 1966

In 1943 German-occupied France, three Allied parachutists drop in on a Paris Opera conductor and a house painter. If the pair wish to find some peace, they must help the trio get to the free zone. France's number one box office hit for almost thirty years. Also available dubbed. **122m/C VHS.** *FR* Louis de Funes, Bourvil, Terry-Thomas; **D:** Gerard Oury. *FRA, FCT*

L.A. Heat 🐾½ 1988

When a vice cop's partner is killed, he seeks revenge on the murderers, only to find that his own department may have been involved. Followed by "L.A. Vice." **90m/C VHS, Beta.** Jim Brown, Lawrence-Hilton Jacobs; **D:** Joseph Merhi. PAR, HHE

L.A. Law 🐾🐾🐾 1986

The pilot episode of the acclaimed dramatic series, in which the staff of a Los Angeles law firm tries a variety of cases. **97m/C VHS, Beta, Closed Caption.** Michael Tucker, Jill Eikenberry, Harry Hamlin, Richard Dysart, Jimmy Smits, Alan Rachins, Susan Ruttan, Susan Dey, Corbin Bernsen; **D:** Gregory Hoblit. FOX

La Lectrice 🎬🎬½ *The Reader* 1988 **(R)** Artesian landscapes, Beethoven sonatas, and a Raymond Jean novel titled "La Lectrice" provide the backdrop for Constance (Miou-Miou) to read aloud to her boyfriend in bed, and from there she imagines herself the novel's heroine, who hires out her services as a reader to various odd characters. She reads from "L'Amant," "Alice," "War and Peace," and "Les Fleurs du Mal." Richly textured and not overly intellectual. In French with English subtitles. 98m/C VHS, Beta, LV. *FR* Miou-Miou, Christian Ruche, Sylvie Laporte, Michael Raskine, Brigitte Catillon, Regis Royer, Maria Casares, Pierre Dux, Patrick Chesnais; *D:* Michel DeVille; *W:* Rosalinde DeVille, Michel DeVille. Cesar Awards '89: Best Supporting Actor (Chesnais); Montreal World Film Festival '88: Best Film. *ORI*

La Marseillaise 🎬🎬🎬½ 1937 Sweeping epic by Renoir titled before he hit his stride with "Grand Illusion." It details the events of the French Revolution in the summer of 1789 using a cast of thousands. The opulent lifestyle of the French nobility is starkly contrasted with the peasant lifestyle of poverty and despair. The focus is on two new recruits who have joined the Marseilles division of the revolutionary army as they begin their long march to Paris, the heart of France. As they travel, they adopt a stirring and passionate song that embodies the spirit and ideals of the revolution known as "La Marseillaise," now France's national anthem. In French with English subtitles. 130m/B VHS, Beta. *FR* Pierre Renoir, Lisa Delamare, Louis Jouvet, Aime Clairmond, Andrex Armstrong, Paul Dullac; *D:* Jean Renoir; *W:* Jean Renoir; *C:* Jean Bourgoin. *NOS, INT, HHT*

La Merveilleuse Visite 🎬🎬½ *The Marvelous Visit* 1974 Bittersweet fantasy about an angel that falls from the sky and is found unconscious by a priest. He's nursed back to health but causes problems for his host when he wanders into the nearby village and his curiosity is misunderstood. Adapted from a short story by H.G. Wells. In French with English subtitles. 102m/C VHS. *FR* Gilles Kohler, Deborah Berger, Jean-Pierre Castaldi; *D:* Marcel Carne; *W:* Marcel Carne. *HTV, FCT*

La Nuit de Varennes 🎬🎬🎬 1982 **(R)** This semi-historical romp is based on an actual chapter in French history when King Louis XVI and Marie Antoinette fled from revolutionary Paris to Varennes in 1791. On the way they meet an unlikely group of characters, including Cassanova and Thomas Paine. At times witty and charming, the melange of history and fiction is full of talk, sometimes profane, punctuated by sex and nudity. Director Scola's imagination stretches to light up this night. In French with English subtitles. 133m/C VHS, Beta, LV. *FR IT* Marcello Mastroianni, Harvey Keitel, Jean-Louis Barrault, Hanna Schygulla, Jean-Claude Brialy; *D:* Ettore Scola; *W:* Ettore Scola. *COL, IME, APD*

La Passante 🎬🎬🎬 *La Passante du Sans Souci; The Passerby* 1983 An otherwise peace-loving man murders the Paraguayan ambassador to France. In somewhat clumsy flashback style the murderer's orphaned childhood and other memories provide motives for the murder. Though posed more slowly than typical intrigue plots, the movie blends love and the legacy of Nazism, passion and politics in an engaging way, spiced with nudity and some violence. In her last screen appearance Schneider movingly portrays dual roles. In French with English subtitles. 106m/C VHS, Beta, LV. *FR GE* Romy Schneider, Michel Piccoli, Helmut Griem, Gerard Klein, Matthieu Carriere, Maria Schell; *D:* Jacques Rouffio; *M:* Georges Delerue. Cesar Awards '83: Best Sound. *TPV*

La Petite Sirene 🎬🎬 *The Little Mermaid* 1980 Isabelle is a 14-year-old schoolgirl, obssessed with the story of the Little Mermaid, who tries to ingratiate herself to Georges, a 40-year-old garage mechanic. Seeing him as her prince charming, she persists in trying to make him a part of her life, in spite of his resistance. In French with English subtitles. 104m/C VHS. *FR* Laura Alexis,

Philippe Leotard, Evelyne Dress, Marie DuBois; *D:* Roger Andrieux; *W:* Roger Andrieux. *WAC, FCT, TPV*

La Puritaine 🎬🎬½ 1986 Before his planned reconciliation with his daughter, the artistic manager of a theater has young actresses portray different sides of the daughter's personality. In French with English subtitles. 90m/C VHS. Michel Piccoli, Sandrine Bonnaire; *D:* Lou Doillon. *FCT*

La Ronde 🎬🎬🎬½ 1951 A classic comedy of manners and sharply witty tour-de-farce in which a group of people in 1900 Vienna keep changing romantic partners until things wind up where they started. Ophuls' swirling direction creates a fast-paced farce of desire and regret with wicked yet subtle style. Based on Arthur Schnitzler's play and remade as "Circle of Love." In French with English subtitles. 97m/B VHS, Beta. *FR* Simone Signoret, Anton Walbrook, Simone Simon, Serge Reggiani, Daniel Gelin, Danielle Darrieux, Jean-Louis Barrault, Fernand Gravet, Odette Joyeux, Isa Miranda, Gerard Philipe; *D:* Max Ophuls. British Academy Awards '51: Best Film; Nominations: Academy Awards '51: Best Art Direction/Set Decoration (B & W), Best Screenplay. *APD, NLC, HMV*

La Rupture 🎬🎬½ *The Breakup* 1970 Thriller about a wife trying to protect her child from her husband's unsavory family. Audran and her son are attacked by her husband (Drouot), who's high on drugs. She fights back and he winds up in the hospital. Her father-in-law (Bouquet), who wants his grandson to live with him, then hires a seedy investigator (Cassel) to spy on Audran. Based on the Charlotte Armstrong novel. In French with English subtitles. 124m/C VHS. *FR* Stephane Audran, Jean-Claude Drouot, Michel Bouquet, Jean-Pierre Cassel, Catherine Rouvel, Jean Carmet, Annie Cordy; *D:* Claude Chabrol; *W:* Claude Chabrol; *M:* Pierre Jansen. *CVC, FCT*

La Salamandre 🎬🎬 *The Salamander* 1971 Non-conformist Rosemonde, suspected of shooting her guardian, is being interviewed by a novelist and a journalist trying to write a television script about the incident. The more they supposedly learn, the more they are both intimately drawn towards her. French with subtitles. 119m/B VHS. *SI* Bulle Ogier, Jean-Luc Bideau, Jacques Denis; *D:* Alain Tanner; *W:* Alain Tanner, John Berger; *M:* Patrick Moraz. *FCT*

La Scorta 🎬🎬🎬½ *The Bodyguards; The Escorts* 1994 Slick, fact-based political thriller focuses on four carabinieri (state police officers) who struggle to maintain some semblance of their normal lives after they are assigned to protect a judge investigating government corruption and a related murder in a Sicilian town. A crackling alternative to Americanized mobster melodrama, marked by taut direction, meaty characters, and coolly understated performances that seamlessly portray brotherhood, heroism, suspicion, and betrayal amid the battle for power between the Italian state and the Mafia. In Italian with English subtitles. 92m/C VHS. *IT* Claudio Amendola, Enrico Lo Verso, Tony Sperandeo, Ricky Memphis, Carlo Cecchi, Leo Gullotta; *D:* Ricardo Tognazzi; *W:* Graziano Diana, Simona Izzo; *M:* Ennio Morricone. *NYF*

La Signora di Tutti 🎬🎬🎬 1934 An early Italian biography of Gaby Doriot, a movie star whose professional success is paired by personal misery. Prestigious director Ophuls, working in exile from his native Germany, was unable to complete many projects in the years leading up to and during WWII. This is one of the few. Watch for innovative camera work intended to underscore the film's mood. In Italian with English subtitles. 92m/B VHS, Beta. *IT* Isa Miranda; *D:* Max Ophuls. *CVC, FCT*

La Silence de la Mer 🎬🎬🎬 *The Silence of the Sea* 1947 An old French farmer (Robian) and his niece (Stephane) are forced to billet a German officer (Vernon) in their home during the Occupation. They've vowed never to speak to him but the German continues to pour out his thoughts on music, war, and his love of France into their silence. Melville's first feature; French with subti-

tles. 86m/B VHS. *FR* Howard Vernon, Jean-Marie Robian, Nicole Stephane; *D:* Jean-Pierre Melville; *W:* Jean-Pierre Melville; *C:* Henri Decae; *M:* Edgar Bischoff. *WBF*

L.A. Story 🎬🎬🎬 1991 **(PG-13)** Livin' ain't easy in the city of angels. Harris K. Telemacher (Martin), a weatherman in a city where the weather never changes, wrestles with the meaning of life and love while consorting with beautiful people, distancing from significant other Henner, cavorting with valley girl Parker, and falling for newswoman Tennant (Martin's real life wife). Written by the comedian, the story's full of keen insights into the everyday problems and ironies of living in the Big Tangerine. (It's no wonder the script's full of so much thoughtful detail: Martin is said to have worked on it intermittently for seven years.) Charming, fault forgiving but not fault ignoring portrait. 98m/C VHS, Beta, LV, **Closed Caption.** Steve Martin, Victoria Tennant, Richard E. Grant, Marilu Henner, Sarah Jessica Parker, Sam McMurray, Patrick Stewart, Iman, Kevin Pollak; *D:* Mick Jackson; *W:* Steve Martin; *M:* Peter Melnick. *LIV, WAR*

La Strada 🎬🎬🎬🎬 *The Road* 1954 Simple-minded girl, played by Fellini's wife, Masina, is sold to a brutal, coarse circus strong-man and she falls in love with him despite his abuse. They tour the countryside and eventually meet up with a gentle acrobat, played by Basehart, who alters their fate. Fellini masterwork was the director's first internationally acclaimed film, and is, by turns, somber and amusing as it demonstrates the filmmaker's sensitivity to the underprivileged of the world and his belief in spiritual redemption. Subtitled in English. 107m/B VHS, Beta, LV. *IT* Giulietta Masina, Anthony Quinn, Richard Basehart, Aldo Silvani; *D:* Federico Fellini; *W:* Ennio Flaiano, Brunello Rondi, Tullio Pinelli, Federico Fellini; *M:* Nino Rota. Academy Awards '56: Best Foreign Language Film; National Board of Review Awards '56: 5 Best Foreign Films of the Year; New York Film Critics Awards '56: Best Foreign Film; Nominations: Academy Awards '56: Best Original Screenplay. *IME, APD, HMV*

La Symphonie Pastorale 🎬🎬🎬½ 1946 A Swiss pastor takes in an orphan blind girl who grows up to be beautiful. The pastor then competes for her affections with his son. Quiet drama based on the Andre Gide novel, with breathtaking mountain scenery as the backdrop for this tragedy rife with symbolism. 105m/B VHS. *FR* Pierre Blanchar, Michele Morgan, Jean Desailly, Line Noro, Andree Clement; *D:* Jean Delannoy. Cannes Film Festival '46: Best Actress (Morgan). *FLI*

La Terra Trema 🎬🎬🎬½ *Episoda Del Mare; The Earth Will Tremble* 1948 The classic example of Italian neo-realism, about a poor Sicilian fisherman, his family and their village. A spare, slow-moving, profound and ultimately lyrical tragedy, this semi-documentary explores the economic exploitation of Sicily's fishermen. Filmed on location with the villagers playing themselves; highly acclaimed though not commercially successful. In Sicilian with English subtitles. Some radically cut versions may be available, but are to be avoided. Franco Zeffirelli was one of the assistant directors. 161m/B VHS, Beta. *IT* Antonio Pietrangeli; *D:* Luchino Visconti. *FCT*

La Truite 🎬🎬🎬 *The Trout* 1983 **(R)** A young woman leaves her family's rural trout farm and a loveless marriage to seek her fortune in high finance and corporate mayhem. The complicated plot, full of intrigue and sexual encounters, sometimes lacks focus. Slickly filmed. 80m/C VHS, Beta. *FR* Isabelle Huppert, Jean-Pierre Cassel, Daniel Olbrychski, Jeanne Moreau, Jacques Spiesser, Ruggero Raimondi, Alexis Smith, Craig Stevens; *D:* Joseph Losey. Cesar Awards '83: Best Cinematography. *COL*

La Vengeance d'une Femme 🎬🎬 A *Woman's Revenge* 1989 Refined Cecile and sultry Suzy are two sides of a love triangle whose third member, Cecile's husband, has just died. Cecile decides to get to know his mistress better, which naturally has Suzy worried. Is Cecile out for revenge or does she sincerely want to befriend the "other woman." Based on Dostoyevski's "The Eternal Husband." In French with English subtitles. **133m/C VHS.** *FR* Isabelle Huppert, Beatrice Dalle; *D:* Jacques Doillon; *W:* Jean-Francois Goyet, Jacques Doillon. *FCT*

L.A. Vice 🎬½ **1989** A detective is transferred to the vice squad, where he must investigate a series of murders. Sequel to "L.A. Heat." **90m/C VHS, Beta.** Jim Brown, Lawrence-Hilton Jacobs, William Smith; *D:* Joseph Merhi. *PAR*

La Vie Continue 🎬🎬½ **1982** A middle-aged woman suddenly finds herself widowed after 20 years of marriage and tries to build a new life for herself and her children. Girardot's performance can't quite dispel melodramatic suds. Loosely and more effectively remade as "Men Don't Leave." In French with English subtitles or dubbed. **93m/C VHS, Beta, LV, 8mm, Closed Caption.** *IT* Annie Girardot, Jean-Pierre Cassel, Michel Aumont, Pierre Dux, Guilia Salvatori, Emmanuel Goyet, Rivera Andres; *D:* Moshe Mizrahi; *W:* Moshe Mizrahi; *M:* Georges Delerue. *COL*

La Vie de Boheme 🎬🎬🎬 *Bohemian Life* **1993** Comedy takes a mocking look at art and romantic love. A trio of hapless but dedicated comrades, Rodolfo (Pellonpaa) the painter, Marcel (Wilms) the poet, and Schaunard (Vaananen), must scrounge around the mealy edges of modern Paris because their art isn't filling their stomachs. Meanwhile, they experience the pangs of love like everyone else, although each is devoutly committed to his art as well. Starkly different from the lush, operatic version by Puccini, but based on the same source, a 19th century novel by Henri Mullet. French with subtitles. **100m/C VHS.** Matti Pellonpaa, Andre Wilms, Kari Vaananen, Jean-Pierre Leaud, Samuel Fuller, Louis Malle, Evelyne Didi, Christine Murillo, Laika, Carlos Salgado, Alexis Nitzer, Sylvie van den Elsen, Gilles Charmant, Dominique Marcas; *D:* Aki Kaurismaki; *W:* Aki Kaurismaki. *FXL*

La Vie est Belle 🎬🎬 *Life is Rosy* **1987** The rags to riches story of a poor rural musician from Zaire who goes to the city to break into radio and television. He uses his wit and talent to foil a greedy boss, win a beautiful wife, and make himself a singing sensation. French with subtitles. **85m/C VHS.** *D:* Nagangura Mweze, Bernard Lamy. *KIV*

L.A. Wars 🎬½ **1994 (R)** A Latin American drug dealer moves into the territory of an Italian mobster, causing a turf war. When a cop rescues the mobster's daughter from the scuzzball, his boss forces him to infiltrate the mobster's organization. Abundant body count, lots of T&A. *CW:* Language, gangster violence, and sexuality. **94m/C VHS.** Vince Murdocco, Mary Zilba, A.J. Stevens, Rodrigo Obregon; *D:* Martin Morris, Tony Kandah. *MNC*

Laboratory 🎬 **1980** Things go awry when the earthling subjects of an alien experiment revolt against their captors. **93m/C VHS, Beta.** Camille Mitchell, Corinne Michaels, Garnett Smith. *VCI*

Labyrinth 🎬🎬🎬 **1986 (PG)** While baby-sitting her baby brother Froud, Connelly is so frustrated she asks the goblins to take him away. When the Goblin King, played by Bowie, comes to answer her idle wish, she must try to rescue Froud by solving the fantastic labyrinth. If she does not find him in time, Froud will become one of the goblins forever. During her journey, Connelly is befriended by all sorts of odd creatures created by Henson, and she grows up a little along the way. A fascinating adventure movie for the whole family. **90m/C VHS, Beta, LV, 8mm, Closed Caption.** David Bowie, Jennifer Connelly, Toby Froud; *D:* Jim Henson; *W:* Terry Jones; *M:* David Bowie, Trevor Jones. *NLC*

Labyrinth of Passion 🎬🎬½ *Laberinto de Pasiones* **1982** A screwball farce, directed by Almodovar, featuring a host of strange characters running around Madrid in search of sex and laughter. They find plenty of both. An early film by an influential director. In Spanish with English subtitles. **100m/C VHS.** *SP* Antonio Banderas, Imanol Arias, Cecilia Roth; *D:* Pedro Almodovar; *W:* Pedro Almodovar. *CCN, IME, TPV*

The Lacemaker 🎬🎬🎬½ *La Dentielliere* **1977** Huppert's first shot at stardom, on videodisc with digital sound and a letterboxed print. A young beautician and a university student fall in love on vacation but soon begin to realize the differences in their lives. Adapted from the novel by Pascal Laine. In French with English subtitles. **107m/C LV.** *FR SI GE* Isabelle Huppert, Yves Beneyton, Florence Giorgetti, Anna Marie Duringer; *D:* Claude Goretta. *HMV, CRC, APD*

L'Addition 🎬🎬½ *The Patsy; Caged Heart* **1985 (R)** According to some cinematic code, the male lead always gets in lots of trouble whenever he tries to help a beautiful stranger. This time, Berry, as Bruno Windler, winds up arrested for shoplifting when he attempts to help Abril. Jailed and on the verge of parole, Windler unwittingly becomes involved in a prison break and is accused of helping a crime don mastermind the escape and of shooting a guard. That's where that gallic flair for capturing the sado-masochistic underbelly of humanity comes in, as Windler is viciously pursued by the malevolent guard. **85m/C VHS, Beta.** Richard Berry, Victoria Abril, Richard Bohringer, Farid Chopel, Fabrice Eberhard; *D:* Denis Amar; *W:* Jean Curtelin; *C:* Robert Fraisse; *M:* Jean-Claude Petit. *NWV, MOR*

The Ladies Club 🎬½ **1986 (R)** A group of rape victims get together and begin to victimize rapists. **86m/C VHS, Beta.** Bruce Davison, Karen Austin, Diana Scarwid, Shera Danese, Beverly Todd; *D:* A.K. Allen. *MED*

The Ladies' Man 🎬🎬 **1961** Piecemeal Lewis farce, with Jerry playing a clutzy handyman working at a girls' boarding house. Some riotous routines balanced by slow pacing. **106m/C VHS, Beta, LV, Closed Caption.** Jerry Lewis, Helen Traubel, Jack Kruschen, Doodles Weaver, Gloria Jean; *D:* Jerry Lewis; *W:* Jerry Lewis. *PAR*

Ladies Man 🎬🎬 **1962** Spy adventure with Constantine playing super sleuth/agent, Lemmy Caution, on the French Riviera. **?m/C VHS.** Eddie Constantine. *SNC*

The Ladies of the Bois de Bologne 🎬🎬 *Les Dames du Bois de Bologne; Ladies of the Park* **1944** Beware the woman scorned—as Jean (Bernard) learns. He ends his longtime relationship with Helene (Casares), although they vow to stay friends, but she secretly plots revenge and finds it in the person of Agnes (Labourdette), a former prostitute. Helene introduces Agnes to Jean, hoping they'll be attracted to one another. They are but after the wedding ceremony Helene reveals the truth about Agnes' sordid past. Updated adaptation of a story in Diderot's "Jacques Le Fatalist." French with subtitles. **83m/B VHS.** *FR* Maria Casares, Paul Bernard, Elina Labourdette; *D:* Robert Bresson; *W:* Robert Bresson, Jean Cocteau. *HTV*

Ladies of the Chorus 🎬🎬 **1949** Monroe stars as a burlesque chorus girl who shares the stage with her mom (Jergens) and a handful of other beauties. She meets and falls in love with a wealthy socialite (Brooks), but her mother completely disapproves of the relationship. Monroe later learns that her mother was in love with the same man several years before. Although only her second film appearance, Monroe's talents are already quite apparent in this low-budget musical romance. 🎵Every Baby Nees a Da Da Daddy; Anyone Can Tell I Love You; Crazy For You; You're Never Too Old; Ladies of the Chorus. **61m/B VHS, Closed Caption.** Adele Jergens, Marilyn Monroe, Rand Brooks, Nana Bryant, Steve Geray, Bill Edwards; *D:* Phil Karlson. *COL*

Ladies of the Lotus 🎬 **1987** Blood-thirsty Vancouver gangsters raid Lotus, Inc., a modeling agency, and sell beautiful young women into slavery. As bad as it sounds. **120m/C VHS, Beta.** *CA* Richard Dale, Angela Read, Patrick Bermel, Darcia Carnie; *D:* Lloyd A. Simanol, Douglas C. Nicolle. *NO*

Ladies on the Rocks 🎬🎬½ *Koks I Kulissen* **1983** Aspiring comediennes Micha and Laura pack up their van and take their bizarre cabaret act on the road through rural Denmark. They find their private lives disintegrating but turn each disaster into new material for their act. In Danish with English subtitles. **100m/C VHS.** *DK* Helle Ryslinge, Anne Marie Helger, Flemming Quist Moller; *D:* Christian Braad Thomsen. *NYF*

Ladies They Talk About 🎬🎬½ *Women in Prison* **1933** Stanwyck stars as a tough-talking gun moll who belongs to a gang of bank robbers. They get caught and Stanwyck is sent to the female division of San Quentin. The acting is great in this pre-Code prison movie, but the film gets a bit punchy at times. Based on the true-life experiences of actress Dorothy Mackaye, who went to jail after her husband was killed in a fight with actor Paul Kelley, who was also sent to prison. Adapted from the play "Women in Prison" by Dorothy Mackaye and Carlton Miles. **69m/B VHS, Closed Caption.** Barbara Stanwyck, Preston Foster, Lyle Talbot, Dorothy Burgess, Lillian Roth, Maude Eburne, Harold Huber, Ruth Donnelly; *D:* Howard Bretherton, William Keighley. *MGM*

Ladies Who Do 🎬🎬½ **1963** A group of cleaning ladies band together against the unscrupulous businessman who wants to tear down their homes in order to build an office tower. Along with a retired colonel, they use the stock market secrets gleaned from the rubbish they toss away to make a killing in the market and save the day. **90m/B VHS.** *GB* Peggy Mount, Robert Morley, Harry H. Corbett, Miriam Karlin, Avril Elgar, Dandy Nichols, Jon Pertwee, Nigel Davenport; *D:* C.M. Pennington-Richards; *W:* Michael Pertwee. *FCT*

The Lady and the Highwayman 🎬🎬½ **1989** TV adaptation of the Barbara Cartland historical romance finds a rogue falling for the lady he's sworn to protect. Naturally, there's a happy ending. **100m/C VHS.** *GB* Hugh Grant, Emma Samms, Oliver Reed, Michael York, Robert Morley, John Mills; *D:* John Hough. *FUS*

Lady and the Tramp 🎬🎬🎬🎬 **1955 (G)** The animated Disney classic about two dogs who fall in love. Tramp is wild and carefree; Lady is a spoiled pedigree who runs away from home after her owners have a baby. They just don't make dog romances like this anymore. 🎵He's a Tramp; La La Lu; Siamese Cat Song; Peace on Earth; Bella Notte. **76m/C VHS, Beta, LV.** *D:* Hamilton Luske; *M:* Peggy Lee, Sonny Burke; *V:* Larry Roberts, Peggy Lee, Barbara Luddy, Stan Freberg, Alan Reed, Bill Thompson, Bill Baucon, Verna Felton, George Givot, Dallas McKennon, Lee Millar. *DIS, APD*

Lady Avenger 🎬 **1989 (R)** A woman is bent on getting revenge on her brother's killers. **90m/C VHS, Beta.** Peggie Sanders, Michelle (McClellan) Bauer, Daniel Hirsch; *D:* David DeCoteau; *C:* Thomas Callaway. *NO*

Lady Be Good 🎬🎬½ **1941** Adapted from the 1924 Gershwin Broadway hit, the plot's been revamped, much to the critics' distaste ("Variety" called it "molasses paced"). Sothern and Young play a tunesmith duo who excel at musical harmony and marital strife. Applauded for its music (the critics loved Hammerstein's and the Gershwins' tunes), the show's Academy Award winning song was, ironically, written by Jerome Kern. And if that's not enough, levity man Skelton and hoofer Powell are thrown in for good measure. 🎵The Last Time I Saw Paris; So Am I; Oh Lady Be Good; Fascinating Rhythm; Hang On To Me; You'll Never Know; You're Words, My Music; Saudades. **111m/B VHS.** Eleanor Powell, Ann Sothern, Robert Young, Lionel Barrymore, John Carroll, Red Skelton, Dan Dailey, Virginia O'Brien, Tom Conway, Phil Silvers, Doris Day; *D:* Norman Z. McLeod; *M:* Oscar Hammerstein, George Gershwin, Ira Gershwin, Jerome Kern, George Bassman. Academy Awards '41: Best Song ("The Last Time I Saw Paris"). *MGM, TTC, FCT*

Lady Beware 🐾🐾 1987 (R) A psychotic doctor becomes obsessed with a beautiful store-window dresser who specializes in steamy, erotic fantasies. When he wages a campaign of terror against her, she realizes that she must stop him before he kills her. **108m/C VHS, Beta, LV.** Diane Lane, Michael Woods, Cotter Smith, Viveca Lindfors, Tyra Ferrell, Peter Nevargic, Edward Penn; **D:** Karen Arthur; **W:** Charles Zev Cohen. *LIV*

Lady by Choice 🐾🐾½ 1934 Lombard stars as a beautiful young fan dancer who is arrested for a lewd public performance. Taking the advice of her press agent, she hires an old bag lady to pose as her mother on Mother's Day. Robson portrays her "mother" and comes to think of Lombard as her own daughter. Robson encourages Lombard to give up fan dancing and to strive for greater things in life. She also pushes her into romance with a wealthy young man (Pryor). Robson is excellent in her role as "mother" and Lombard shows great comic talent in this charming film. **78m/C VHS, Closed Caption.** Carole Lombard, May Robson, Roger Pryor, Walter Connolly, Raymond Walburn, James Burke; **D:** David Burton; **W:** Jo Swerling. *COL*

Lady Caroline Lamb 🐾 1973 Lady Caroline is a passionate young lady in 19th-century England, who, although the wife of a member of Parliament, has an affair with Lord Byron and brings about her own downfall. Costume drama that never quite goes anywhere. **123m/C Beta.** *GB IT* Sarah Miles, Richard Chamberlain, Jon Finch, Laurence Olivier, John Mills, Ralph Richardson; **D:** Robert Bolt; **W:** Robert Bolt; **C:** Oswald Morris; **M:** Richard Rodney Bennett. *PSM*

Lady Chatterley's Lover 🐾½ *L'Amant de Lady Chatterley* 1955 Englishwoman has bad luck to have husband shot up during WWI and sent home paralyzed. In her quest for sexual fulfillment, she takes a new lover, the estate's earthy gamekeeper. Limp adaptation of D.H. Lawrence's novel. In French with English subtitles. **102m/B VHS, Beta, LV.** *FR* Danielle Darrieux, Erno Crisa, Leo Genn; **D:** Marc Allegret. *NOS, MRV, HHT*

Lady Chatterley's Lover 🐾½ 1981 (R) Remake of the 1955 film version of D.H. Lawrence's classic novel of an English lady who has an affair with the gamekeeper of her husband's estate. Basically soft-focus soft porn. **107m/C VHS, Beta, LV.** *GB FR* Sylvia Kristel, Nicholas Clay, Shane Briant; **D:** Just Jaeckin; **C:** Robert Fraisse. *MGM*

Lady Cocoa 🐾½ 1975 (R) Routine story of a young woman who gets released from jail for 24 hours and sets out for Las Vegas to find the man who framed her. **93m/C VHS, Beta.** Lola Falana, Joe "Mean Joe" Greene, Gene Washington, Alex Dreier; **D:** Matt Cimber. *UNI*

The Lady Confesses 🐾🐾 1945 Average mystery that involves Hughes trying to clear her boyfriend of murder. Independently produced. "Leave it to Beaver" fans will want to watch for "Ward Cleaver" Beaumont. **66m/B VHS.** Mary Beth Hughes, Hugh Beaumont, Edmund MacDonald, Claudia Drake, Emmett Vogan, Barbara Slater, Edward Howard, Dewey Robinson, Carol Andrews; **D:** Sam Newfield; **W:** Helen Martin, Irwin H. Franklyn; **M:** Lee Zahler. *NOS, SNC*

Lady Dragon 🐾🐾 1992 (R) A woman and her husband are viciously attacked and only she survives. Found by an old man, she learns a number of martial arts tricks and goes out to get her revenge. **CW:** Language, strong violence, and sexuality. **89m/C VHS, LV, Closed Caption.** Cynthia Rothrock, Richard Norton, Robert Ginty, Bella Esperance, Hengko Tornando; **D:** David Worth; **W:** David Worth. *IMP*

Lady Dragon 2 🐾🐾 1993 (R) Martial arts queen Rothrock returns in another saga of kickboxing vengeance. Susan Morgan seeks revenge on the three killers who terrorized her family. When she unleashes the power of the dragon they don't stand a chance. **CW:** Language and plentiful martial arts violence. **?m/C VHS, Closed Caption.** Cynthia Rothrock, Billy Drago, Sam Jones, Greg

Stuart, Bella Esperance, George Rudy, Adisoerya Abdi; **D:** David Worth; **W:** Clifford Mohr; **M:** Jim West. *PSM*

The Lady Eve 🐾🐾🐾🐾 1941 Two con artists, out to trip up wealthy beer tycoon Fonda, instead find themselves tripped up when one falls in love with the prey. Ridiculous situations, but Sturges manages to keep them believable and funny. With a train scene that's every man's nightmare. Perhaps the best Sturges ever. Based on the story "The Faithful Heart" by Monckton Hoffe. Later remade as "The Birds and the Bees." **93m/B VHS, Beta, LV.** Barbara Stanwyck, Henry Fonda, Charles Coburn, Eugene Pallette, William Demarest, Eric Blore, Melville Cooper; **D:** Preston Sturges; **W:** Preston Sturges; **C:** Victor Milner. National Board of Review Awards '41: 10 Best Films of the Year; Nominations: Academy Awards '41: Best Story. *USH*

Lady for a Day 🐾🐾🐾½ 1933 Delightful telling of the Damon Runyon story, "Madame La Gimp," about an apple peddler (Robson) down on her luck, who is transformed into a lady by a criminal with a heart. "Lady By Choice" is the sequel. **96m/B VHS, Beta, LV.** May Robson, Warren William, Guy Kibbee, Glenda Farrell, Ned Sparks, Jean Parker, Walter Connolly; **D:** Frank Capra. Nominations: Academy Awards '33: Best Actress (Robson), Best Adapted Screenplay, Best Director (Capra), Best Picture. *CVC, CRC, MLB*

Lady for a Night 🐾🐾 1942 The female owner of a gambling riverboat does her best to break into high society, when murder threatens to spoil her plans. Cast and costumes burdened by pacing. **88m/B VHS.** John Wayne, Joan Blondell, Ray Middleton, Philip Merivale, Blanche Yurka, Edith Barrett, Leonid Kinskey, Montagu Love; **D:** Leigh Jason. *REP*

Lady Frankenstein 🐾½ *La Figlia di Frankenstein; The Daughter of Frankenstein; Madame Frankenstein* 1972 (R) Frankenstein's lovely daughter graduates from medical school and returns home. When she sees what her father's been up to, she gets some ideas of her own. Good fun for fans of the genre. **84m/C VHS, Beta.** *IT* Joseph Cotten, Rosalba (Sara Bay) Neri, Mickey Hargitay, Paul Muller; **D:** Mel Welles. *SNC, HEG*

Lady from Louisiana 🐾🐾 1942 A lawyer in old New Orleans out to rid the city of corruption falls in love with the daughter of a big-time gambler. Great storm scene. **84m/B VHS.** John Wayne, Ona Munson, Dorothy Dandridge, Ray Middleton, Henry Stephenson, Helen Westley, Jack Pennick; **D:** Bernard Vorhaus. *REP*

Lady from Nowhere 🐾🐾 1936 A woman is the only witness to a gangland rub-out and is subsequently pursued by both the mob and the police. Unfortunately for her, the gangsters catch up with her first. **60m/B VHS.** Mary Astor, Charles Quigley, Thurston Hall, Victor Kilian, Spencer Charters; **D:** Gordon Wiles. *SNC*

The Lady from Shanghai 🐾🐾🐾½ 1948 An unsuspecting seaman becomes involved in a web of intrigue when a woman hires him to work on her husband's yacht. Hayworth (a onetime Mrs. Orson Welles), in her only role as a villainess, plays a manipulative, sensual schemer. Wonderful and innovative cinematic techniques from Welles, as usual, including a tense scene in a hall of mirrors. Filmed on a yacht belonging to Errol Flynn. **87m/B VHS, Beta, LV.** Orson Welles, Rita Hayworth, Everett Sloane, Glenn Anders, Ted de Corsia, Erskine Sanford, Gus Schilling; **D:** Orson Welles. *COL, MLB*

Lady from Yesterday 🐾 1985 An American couple's life is shattered by the appearance of the husband's Vietnamese mistress and her 10-year-old son. Made for television. **87m/C VHS, Beta.** Wayne Rogers, Bonnie Bedelia, Pat Hingle, Barrie Youngfellow, Blue Dedeort, Tina Chen; **D:** Robert Day. *NO*

Lady Godiva 🐾½ 1955 The lovely O'Hara is wasted in the title role as a Saxon noblewoman married to Leofric (Nader). They're trying to stem Norman influence and Godiva vows to ride naked through the streets of Canterbury to prove the Saxon people's loyalty to King Edward (Franz).

Cardboard costumer. Clint Eastwood has a bit as a Saxon soldier. **89m/C VHS.** Maureen O'Hara, George Nader, Eduard Franz, Leslie Bradley, Victor McLaglen, Torin Thatcher, Rex Reason; **D:** Arthur Lubin; **W:** Oscar Brodney, Harry Ruskin; **C:** Carl Guthrie. *USH*

Lady Godiva Rides 1968 A bad, campy version of the story of Lady Godiva. Godiva comes to the United States with a bevy of scantily clad maidens and winds up in the Old West. When the town villain threatens to compromise her, Tom Jones comes to the rescue. The film (of course) features Godiva's naked ride on horseback through the town. **88m/C VHS.** Marsha Jordan, Forman Shane; **D:** A.C. Stephen. *VDM*

Lady Grey 🐾 1982 A poor farmer's daughter rises to the top of the country music charts, but at a price. **111m/C VHS, Beta.** Ginger Alden, David Allen Coe; **D:** Worth Keeter. *NO*

Lady Ice 🐾🐾 1973 (PG) Sutherland, as an insurance investigator on the trail of jewel thieves, follows them to Miami Beach and the Bahamas. After stealing a diamond he enters into partnership with a crook's daughter. Worth seeing for the cast. **93m/C VHS, Beta.** Donald Sutherland, Jennifer O'Neill, Robert Duvall, Eric (Hans Gudegast) Braeden; **D:** Tom Gries; **W:** Alan R. Trustman; **M:** Perry Botkin. *NO*

Lady in a Cage 🐾🐾🐾 1964 A wealthy widow is trapped in her home elevator during a power failure and becomes desperate when hoodlums break in. Shocking violence ahead of its time probably plays better than when first released. Young Caan is a standout among the star-studded cast. **95m/B VHS, Beta.** Olivia de Havilland, Ann Sothern, James Caan, Jennifer Billingsley, Jeff Corey, Scatman Crothers, Rafael Campos; **D:** Walter Grauman; **W:** Luther Davis. *PAR*

Lady in Cement 🐾½ 1968 (R) The second Tony Rome mystery, in which the seedy Miami dick finds a corpse with cement shoes while swimming. **93m/C VHS, Beta.** Frank Sinatra, Raquel Welch, Richard Conte, Martin Gabel, Lainie Kazan, Pat Henry, Steve Peck, Joe E. Lewis, Dan Blocker; **D:** Gordon Douglas; **C:** Joseph Biroc. *FOX*

Lady in Distress 🐾🐾½ *A Window in London* 1939 A British drama about an unhappily married man who witnesses an apparent murder. He discovers, however, it was actually the prank of an illusionist and his flirtatious wife. He soon finds himself becoming increasingly involved with their lives. **59m/B VHS, Beta.** *GB* Michael Redgrave, Paul Lukas, Sally Gray; **D:** Herbert Mason. *SNC, VYY, MLB*

The Lady in Question 🐾½ *It Happened in Paris* 1940 A Parisian shopkeeper, played by Aherne, sits on a jury that acquits Hayworth of murder. His interest doesn't end with the trial, however, and matters heat up when his son also becomes involved. Remake of a melodramatic French release. **81m/B VHS, Beta, LV.** Rita Hayworth, Glenn Ford, Brian Aherne, Irene Rich, Lloyd Corrigan, George Coulouris, Evelyn Keyes, Curt Bois, Edward Norris; **D:** Charles Vidor. *COL, CCB*

Lady in Red 🐾🐾 *Guns, Sin and Bathtub Gin* 1979 A story of America in the '30s, and the progress through the underworld of the woman who was Dillinger's last lover. **90m/C VHS, Beta.** Pamela Sue Martin, Louise Fletcher, Robert Conrad, Christopher Lloyd; **D:** Lewis Teague; **W:** John Sayles; **M:** James Horner. *LIV, VES*

Lady in the Death House 🐾🐾 1944 A framed woman is set to walk the last mile, as a scientist struggles to find the real killer in time. **57m/B VHS, Beta.** Jean Parker, Lionel Atwill, Marcia Mae Jones. *VYY*

Lady in the Lake 🐾🐾½ 1946 Why is it everyone wants to get artsy with pulp fiction? Actor Montgomery directs himself in this Philip Marlowe go-round, using a subjective camera style to imitate Chandler's first person narrative (that means the only time we get to see Marlowe/Montgomery's mug is in a mirror. That pretty well says it all). Having decided to give up eyeing privately, Marlowe turns to the pen to tell the tangled tale of the lady in the lake: once upon a time, a detective was hired to watch the wicked wife of a paying client...Some find the direction clever. Others consider MGM chief Louis B. Mayer, who made sure this was Montgomery's last project with MGM, to be a wise man. 103m/B VHS, Beta. Robert Montgomery, Lloyd Nolan, Audrey Totter, Tom Tully, Leon Ames, Jayne Meadows; **D:** Robert Montgomery; **C:** Paul Vogel. MGM, FCT

Lady in Waiting 🎬🎬 1994 (R) Detective Jimmy Scavetti (Nouri) is hunting down a serial kill preying on call girls when he meets the seductive Lori (Whirry). Then he discovers his ex-wife's new hubby was the lawyer for each of the victims—only the lawyer turns up dead and Jimmy becomes a suspect. Also available in an unrated version.**CW:** Language; violence; strong sexuality. 85m/C VHS. Michael Nouri, Shannon Whirry, William Devane, Karen Kopins, Crystal Chappell, Robert Costanzo, Meg Foster, Charles Grant; **D:** Fred Gallo. AVE

The Lady in White 🎬🎬🎬 1988 (PG-13) Small-town ghost story about murder and revenge. When young Haas is locked in school one night, he's visited by the ghost of a little girl who wants his help in discovering who murdered her. Well-developed characters, interesting style, and suspenseful plot make for a sometimes slow but overall exceptional film. 92m/C VHS, Beta, LV, **Closed Caption.** Lukas Haas, Len Cariou, Alex Rocco, Katherine Helmond, Jason Presson, Renata Vanni, Angelo Bertolini, Jared Rushton, Joelle Jacob; **D:** Frank Laloggia; **W:** Frank Laloggia; **C:** Russell Carpenter; **M:** Frank Laloggia. NO

The Lady is Willing 🎬🎬½ 1942 Dietrich is a stage star who longs for a baby and when an abandoned infant comes her way she decides to keep the child. Only she hasn't a clue about any of the practical aspects. Lucky for her MacMurray is a friendly pediatrician who gives her some advice. Dietrich finds out she can't adopt as a single parent and persuades MacMurray to marry her, in name only, but since this is a romantic comedy the two eventually fall in love. 91m/B VHS. Marlene Dietrich, Fred MacMurray, Aline MacMahon, Stanley Ridges, Arline Judge, Roger Clark, Ruth Ford, Sterling Holloway, Harvey Stephens, Harry Shannon, Elisabeth Risdon, Charles Halton; **D:** Mitchell Leisen; **W:** James Edward Grant, Albert McCleery. FCT

Lady Jane 🎬🎬🎬½ 1985 (PG-13) An accurate account of the life of 15-year-old Lady Jane Grey, who secured the throne of England for 9 days in 1553 as a result of political maneuvering by noblemen and the Church-of-England. A wonderful film even for non-history buffs. Carter's first film. 140m/C VHS, Beta, LV, **Closed Caption.** GB Helena Bonham Carter, Cary Elwes, Sara Kestelman, Michael Hordern, Joss Ackland, Richard Johnson, Patrick Stewart; **D:** Trevor Nunn. PAR, TVC

Lady Killer 🎬🎬🎬 1933 Racy, pre-Code comedy with mobster Cagney hiding out in Hollywood. He gets discovered and becomes a big star, but his old gang turns up to blackmail him. Lots of movie "in" jokes and Clarke (of "Public Enemy" fame) is great as a wisecracking moll. Based on the story "The Finger Man" by Rosalind Keating Shaffer. 74m/B VHS, **Closed Caption.** James Cagney, Mae Clarke, Leslie Fenton, Margaret Lindsay, Henry O'Neill, Raymond Hatton, George Chandler; **D:** Roy Del Ruth; **W:** Ben Markson, Lillie Hayward. MGM

Lady L 🎬½ 1965 Silly turn-of-the-century farce about a sexy laundress (Loren), married to a French anarchist (Newman!), who also marries the aristocratic Niven (in name only). Elaborate sets and Paris and London backgrounds couldn't overcome the odd casting and weak script. Adapted from the novel by Romain Gary. 107m/C VHS, Beta. FR IT Sophia Loren, Paul Newman, David Niven, Cecil Parker, Claude Dauphin, Marcel Dalio, Philippe Noiret, Michel Piccoli, Daniel Emilfork, Eugene Deckers; **Cameos:** Peter Ustinov; **D:** Peter Ustinov; **W:** Peter Ustinov. MGM, FCT

Lady Mobster 🎬 1988 (PG-13) When her parents are murdered a young girl is taken in by a Mafia family. She grows up to be a shrewd lawyer but winds up working in her adoptive family's crime syndicate in order to take revenge on her parents' murderers. Exaggerated and silly but watchable for its so-bad-it's-good qualities. Made for television. 94m/C VHS, Beta, LV, Closed Caption. Susan Lucci, Michael Nader, Roscoe Born, Joseph Wiseman; **D:** John Llewellyn Moxey. TTC

Lady of Burlesque 🎬🎬½ Striptease Lady 1943 Burlesque dancer is found dead, strangled with her own G-string. Clever and amusing film based on "The G-String Murders" by Gypsy Rose Lee. 91m/B VHS, Beta. Barbara Stanwyck, Michael O'Shea, Janis Carter, Pinky Lee; **D:** William A. Wellman. Nominations: Academy Awards '43: Original Dramatic/Comedy Score. MRV, NOS, VCN

Lady of the Evening 🎬🎬 1979 (PG) A prostitute and a crook team up to seek revenge against the mob. 110m/C VHS, Beta. IT Sophia Loren, Marcello Mastroianni. NO

Lady of the House 🎬🎬 1978 A true story about a madame who rose from operator of a brothel to become a political force in San Francisco. 100m/C VHS, Beta. Dyan Cannon, Susan Tyrrell, Colleen Camp, Armand Assante; **D:** Ralph Nelson. PSM

Lady of the Lake 🎬🎬 1928 Rare silent adventure film in which an exiled girl saves the king from outlaws in Scotland. Orchestra score. 47m/B VHS. GB Percy Marmont, Benita Hume, Huddon Mason, Lawson Butt; **D:** James A. Fitzpatrick. GPV, FCT, GVV

Lady On a Train 🎬🎬🎬 1945 Travelling at Christmas, wealthy young Nicky Collins (Durbin) thinks she sees a murder from her train window but when she arrives in New York she can't get anyone to believe her. But not willing to give up, Nicky turns to Wayne Morgan (Bruce), a mystery writer for help. Recognizing the victim from a newspaper photo, Nicky checks out his family and gets mistaken for a nightclub singer (so Durbin can vamp a torch song). Lots of comedy amidst the mystery and romance, and some surprizes as well. Based on a story by Leslie Charteris. ♫Gimme a Little Kiss, Will You, Huh?; Night and Day; Silent Night. 95m/B VHS, **Closed Caption.** Deanna Durbin, David Bruce, Ralph Bellamy, Dan Duryea, Edward Everett Horton, Allen Jenkins, Elizabeth Patterson, William Frawley, Jacqueline DeWit, George Coulouris; **D:** Charles David; **W:** Robert O'Brien, Edmund Beloin; **C:** Woody Bredell; **M:** Miklos Rozsa. Nominations: Academy Awards '45: Best Sound. USH

Lady on the Bus 🎬🎬 1978 (R) Sexually frustrated newlywed bride rides the city buses looking for men to satisfy her. This bothers her husband. Shot in Rio de Janeiro. In Portuguese with English subtitles. 102m/C VHS, Beta, LV. BR Sonia Braga; **D:** Neville D'Almeida. LIV, VES

The Lady Refuses 🎬🎬 1931 A stuffy Victorian father is disappointed in his wastrel son and decides a poor but honest young woman could be the making of him. Problems arise when the girl falls for the father instead. 70m/B VHS, Beta. Betty Compson, John Darrow, Margaret Livingston, Gilbert Emery; **D:** George Archainbaud. DVT, VYY

The Lady Says No 🎬🎬 1951 A photographer must photograph an attractive author who has written a book uncomplimentary toward the male sex. 80m/B VHS. Joan Caulfield, David Niven, James Robertson Justice, Frances Bavier, Henry Jones, Jeff York, John Wood; **D:** Frank Ross. FCT

Lady Scarface 🎬🎬 1941 Murderous mobster queen breaks the law, bats men around, and takes the cops on a merry chase. Cheap, fast-paced action. 66m/B VHS, Beta. Mildred Coles, Dennis O'Keefe, Frances Neal, Judith Anderson, Eric Blore, Charles Halton; **D:** Frank Woodruff. NO

Lady Scarface/The Threat 1949 A crime double feature: "Lady Scarface" (1941), a clever cop is on the trail of a dangerous gunwoman; and "The Threat" (1949), a ruthless killer escapes from prison intent on murdering those who convicted him. 132m/B VHS, Beta. Dennis O'Keefe, Judith Anderson, Robert Knapp, Eric Blore, Charles McGraw, Michael O'Shea, Virginia Grey; **D:** Frank Woodruff. TTC

Lady Sings the Blues 🎬🎬½ 1972 (R) Jazz artist Billie Holiday's life becomes a musical drama depicting her struggle against racism and drug addiction in her pursuit of fame and romance. What could be a typical price-of-fame story is saved by Ross' inspired performance as the tragic singer. ♫My Man; Strange Fruit; God Bless the Child; Don't Explain; T'Ain't Nobody's Business If I Do; Lady Sings the Blues; All Of Me; The Man I Love; Our Love Is Here to Stay. 144m/C VHS, Beta, LV. Diana Ross, Billy Dee Williams, Richard Pryor, James Callahan, Paul Hampton, Sid Melton; **D:** Sidney J. Furie; **C:** John A. Alonzo. Nominations: Academy Awards '72: Best Actress (Ross), Best Art Direction/Set Decoration, Best Costume Design, Best Story & Screenplay, Original Song Score and/or Adaptation. PAR, FCT

Lady Street Fighter 🎬 1986 A well-armed female combat fighter battles an organization of assassins to avenge her sister's murder. 73m/C VHS, Beta. Renee Harmon, Joel McCrea Jr. UNI

Lady Takes a Chance 🎬🎬 1943 A romantic comedy about a New York working girl with matrimonial ideas and a rope-shy rodeo rider who yearns for the wide open spaces. Fine fun on the range. 86m/B VHS, Beta. John Wayne, Jean Arthur, Phil Silvers, Charles Winninger; **D:** William A. Seiter. REP

Lady Terminator 🎬½ 1989 (R) A student on an anthropology expedition digs up more than she bargained for when she is possessed by an evil spirit and goes on a rampage. 83m/C VHS, Beta. Barbara Constable, Christopher Hart, Joseph McGlynn, Claudia Rademaker; **D:** Jalil Jackson. HTV

The Lady Vanishes 🎬🎬🎬🎬 1938 When a kindly old lady disappears from a fast-moving train, her young friend finds an imposter in her place and a spiraling mystery to solve. Hitchcock's first real winner, a smarmy, wit-drenched British mystery that precipitated his move to Hollywood. Along with "39 Steps," considered an early Hitchcock classic. From the novel "The Wheel Spins," by Ethel Lina White. Special edition contains short subject on Hitchcock's cameos in his films. Remade in 1979. 99m/B VHS, Beta, LV. GB Margaret Lockwood, Paul Lukas, Michael Redgrave, May Whitty, Googie Withers, Basil Radford, Naunton Wayne, Cecil Parker, Linden Travers, Catherine Lacey; **Cameos:** Alfred Hitchcock; **D:** Alfred Hitchcock; **W:** Sidney Gilliat, Frank Launder; **M:** Louis Levy. New York Film Critics Awards '38: Best Director (Hitchcock). SNC, NOS, MED

The Lady Vanishes 🎬½ 1979 In this re-working of the '38 Alfred Hitchcock film, a woman on a Swiss bound train awakens from a nap to find that the elderly woman seated next to her was kidnapped. Falls short of the original movie due to the "screwball" nature of the main characters, Gould and Shepherd. Based on Ethel Lina White's novel "The Wheel Spins." 95m/C VHS, Beta, LV. GB Elliott Gould, Cybill Shepherd, Angela Lansbury, Herbert Lom; **D:** Anthony Page; **W:** George Axelrod. MED, MRV

Lady Windermere's Fan 🎬🎬½ 1926 The silent, Lubitsch adaptation of the Oscar Wilde tale concerning an upper-class couple's marriage being almost destroyed by suspected adultery. 66m/B VHS, Beta, 8mm. Ronald Colman, May McAvoy, Bert Lytell; **D:** Ernst Lubitsch. VYY, GPV, GVV

The Lady with the Dog 🎬🎬🎬 1959 A bittersweet love story based on the Anton Chekhov story, about two married Russians who meet by chance in a park, fall in love, and realize they are fated to a haphazard, clandestine affair. In Russian with English titles. 86m/B VHS, Beta. RU Ilya Savvina, Alexei Batalov, Ala Chostakova, N. Alisova; **D:** Yosif Heifitz. WST, FCT, TPV

The Lady Without Camelias 🎬🎬½ 1953 A young woman is discovered by a film producer who casts her in a successful movie and eventually marries her. Convinced that she can sustain a career as a serious actress, the producer is dismayed by the job offers that come her way, usually of a sexually exploitive nature. What follows is a tragic decline for both. 106m/C VHS, Beta. *IT CIG*

Ladybird, Ladybird 🐾🐾🐾 1993 (R) Loach's emotionally bruising look at working-class life and family in the '90s. Maggie (Rock) is a tough unmarried mother of four who's been battered by her lovers and has come under the overwatchful eye of Britain's social services. She meets Jorge (Vega), a gentle Paraguayan, and just when things are looking up, Jorge gets immigration heat, Maggie's insecurities surface, and her baby daughter is taken into care by child welfare. Rock has a no-nonsense manner and acerbic wit that precludes any hand-wringing for her character, even as you hope she'll win out over circumstance. Based on a true story.*CW:* Strong language and intense depiction of domestic abuse. 102m/C VHS. *GB* Crissy Rock, Vladimir Vega, Ray Winstone, Sandie Lavelle, Mauricio Venegas, Clare Perkins, Jason Stracey, Luke Brown, Lily Farrell; *D:* Ken Loach; *W:* Rona Munro; *C:* Barry Ackroyd; *M:* George Fenton. Berlin International Film Festival '94: Best Actress (Rock); Nominations: Independent Spirit Awards '95: Best Foreign Film. *HMK*

Ladybugs 🐾½ 1992 (PG-13) Hangdog salesman Dangerfield would like to move up the corporate ladder, but must first turn the company-sponsored girl's soccer team into winners. Routine Dangerfield vehicle exploits nearly everything for laughs, including dressing an athletic boy as a girl so he can play on the team. Obvious fluff. 91m/C VHS, Beta, Closed Caption. Rodney Dangerfield, Jackee, Jonathan Brandis, Ilene Graff, Vinessa Shaw, Tom Parks, Jeanetta Arnetta, Nancy Parsons, Blake Clark, Tommy Lasorda; *D:* Sidney J. Furie; *W:* Curtis Burch; *C:* Dan Burstall; *M:* Richard Gibbs. *PAR*

Ladyhawke 🐾🐾½ 1985 (PG-13) In medieval times, a youthful pickpocket befriends a strange knight who is on a mysterious quest. This unlikely duo, accompanied by a watchful hawk, are enveloped in a magical adventure. 121m/C VHS, Beta, LV, Closed Caption. Matthew Broderick, Rutger Hauer, Michelle Pfeiffer, John Wood, Leo McKern, Alfred Molina, Ken Hutchison; *D:* Richard Donner; *W:* Edward Khmara, Michael Thomas, Tom Mankiewicz; *M:* Andrew Powell. Nominations: Academy Awards '85: Best Sound. *WAR*

Ladykiller 🐾🐾 1992 (R) Rogers stars as a burned-out cop who goes to a dating service to find a man who'll give her the attention she craves. When she meets wealthy professional Shea she thinks he's the one but her cop's curiosity about her lover's past may cost her her life.*CW:* Sexuality. 92m/C VHS, LV, Closed Caption. Mimi Rogers, John Shea, Alice Krige, Tom Irwin; *D:* Michael Scott; *W:* Shelley Evans. *USH*

The Ladykillers 🐾🐾🐾½ *The Lady Killers* 1955 A gang of bumbling bank robbers is foiled by a little old lady. Hilarious antics follow, especially on the part of Guinness, who plays the slightly demented-looking leader of the gang. 87m/C VHS, Beta. *GB* Alec Guinness, Cecil Parker, Katie Johnson, Herbert Lom, Peter Sellers, Danny Green, Jack Warner, Kenneth Connor, Edie Martin, Jack Melford; *D:* Alexander MacKendrick; *W:* William Rose; *C:* Otto Heller; *M:* Tristram Cary. British Academy Awards '55: Best Actress (Johnson), Best Screenplay; Nominations: Academy Awards '56: Best Original Screenplay. *REP, FCT, HMV*

Ladykillers 🐾🐾 1988 At the glitzy L.A. club Ladykillers, men strip as the women cheer. At the climax of the performance, one of the dancers is brutally murdered, live on stage. In this decadent world of glitter and sex, the women are the hunters and the men are the reward. 97m/C VHS, Beta, Closed Caption. Marilu Henner, Susan Blakely, Lesley-Anne Down, Thomas Calabro; *D:* Robert Lewis; *W:* Greg Dinallo. *PSM*

The Lady's Not for Burning 🐾🐾½ 1987 Romantic comedy, set in a medieval English village, finds ex-soldier Thomas Mendip (Branagh) invading the home of querulous Mayor Heb-

ble Tyson (Hepton), demanding to be hanged. He says he's murdered the local rag and bone merchant but the townspeople insist Jennet Jourdemayne (Lunghi), who's seeking refuge at the mayor's, has turned him into a dog. They demand she be burned as a witch (hence the title, since Thomas, unwillingly but strongly, objects to this action). Adapted by Fry from his play; made for TV. 90m/C VHS. Kenneth Branagh, Cherie Lunghi, Bernard Hepton, Tim Watson, Susannah Harker, Angela Thorne, Shaun Scott; *D:* Julian Amyes; *W:* Christopher Fry. *VCO, FUS*

Lafayette Escadrille 🐾🐾½ *Hell Bent for Glory* 1958 Action and romance in WWI via the famed flying unit manned by American volunteers. Hunter is banal in the lead role as is his romance with a reformed prostitute (Choreau). Director Wellman actually was a member of the squadron and his son plays him in the film but the director regarded the film as a failure because of studio interference. 92m/B VHS. Tab Hunter, Etchika Choureau, William Wellman Jr., Joel McCrea, Dennis Devine, Marcel Dalio, David Janssen, Paul Fix, Will Hutchins, Clint Eastwood; *D:* William A. Wellman; *W:* A.S. Fleischman; *C:* William Clothier; *M:* Leonard Rosenman. *WAR*

L'Age D'Or 🐾🐾🐾🐾 *Age of Gold* 1930 Bunuel's first full-length film and his masterpiece of sex, repression, and of course, death. A hapless man is prevented from reaching his beloved by middle-class morality, forces of the establishment, the Church, government and every bastion of modern values. Banned for years because of its anti-religious stance. Co-scripted by Dali. A mercilessly savage, surreal satire, the purest expression of Bunuel's wry misanthropy. In French with English subtitles. 62m/B VHS, Beta, LV. *FR* Gaston Modot, Lya Lys, Max Ernst, Pierre Prevert, Marie Berthe Ernst, Paul Eluard; *D:* Luis Bunuel; *W:* Salvador Dali, Luis Bunuel. *FCT, IME, GVV*

Laguna Heat 🐾½ 1987 A tired LA cop investigates a series of murders that are related to an old friend of his father's. Based on a novel by T. Jefferson Parker. Made for television. 110m/C VHS, Beta, LV. Harry Hamlin, Jason Robards Jr., Catherine Hicks, Rip Torn, Anne Francis; *D:* Simon Langton. *ORI, WAR*

Lai Shi: China's Last Eunuch 1988 A starving Chinese child becomes a eunuch in order to garner wealth in the Emperor's palace. But he is castrated at a historically inopportune moment (as if there's a good time for such modification), just prior to the turbulent 1920s. In Cantonese with English subtitles. 100m/C VHS. *CH D:* Chan Tsiliang. *FCT*

The Lair of the White Worm 🐾🐾🐾 1988 (R) Scottish archaeologist uncovers a strange skull, and then a bizarre religion to go with it, and then a very big worm. An unusual look at the effects of Christianity and paganism on each other, colored with sexual innuendo and, of course, giant worms. A cross between a morality play and a horror film. Adapted from Bram Stoker's last writings, done while he was going mad from Bright's disease. Everything you'd expect from Russell. 93m/C VHS, Beta, LV. *GB* Amanda Donohoe, Sammi Davis, Catherine Oxenberg, Hugh Grant, Peter Capaldi, Stratford Johns, Paul Brooke, Christopher Gable; *D:* Ken Russell; *W:* Ken Russell; *M:* Stanislas Syrewicz. *VES, LIV, TPV*

Lake Consequence 🐾🐾 1992 (R) Severance plays a suburban housewife who accidentally gets locked in the camper of the tree-trimmer stud (Zane) she's been eyeing while he's been working in her neighborhood. Next thing she knows they wind up at a distant lake where the bored housewife is more than willing to give into her growing sexual fantasies. An unrated version at 90 minutes is also available. 85m/C VHS, LV, Closed Caption. Joan Severance, Billy Zane, May Karasun; *D:* Rafael Eisenman; *W:* Zalman King, Melanie Finn, Henry Cobbold; *M:* George S. Clinton. *REP*

Lakota Woman: Siege at Wounded Knee 🐾🐾½ 1994 Autobiography of Mary Crow Dog (Bedard) and her coming of age during the American Indian Movement's 1973 occupation of Wounded Knee. Tangled loyalties and the battle between Native Americans and U.S. troops make for strong drama. Bedard is remarkable in her film debut. Based on the book by Mary Crow Dog and Richard Erdoes. Filmed on location in South Dakota. 113m/C VHS, Closed Caption. Irene Bedard, August Schellenberg, Joseph Runningfox, Floyd "Red Crow" Westerman, Tantoo Cardinal, Michael Horse, Lawrence Bayne, Nancy Parsons; *D:* Frank Pierson; *W:* Bill Kerby; *C:* Toyomichi Kurita; *M:* Richard Horowitz. *TTC*

The Lamb 🐾🐾½ 1915 Intent on proving to his sweetheart that he's not the coward people say he is, a guy heads west to engage in various manly activities, including fisticuffs, karate and Indian kidnapping. Fairbanks' debut on film (he was already an established Broadway star) set the mold for the American leading man: moral, cheerful, physical, and not hard to look at. A popular guy with the public, Fairbanks formed his own film company the following year. Story's based on D.W. Griffith's book, "The Man and the Test." 60m/B VHS, Beta. Douglas Fairbanks Sr., Seena Owen, Lillian Langdon, Monroe Salisbury, Kate Toncray, Alfred Paget, William E. Lowery; *D:* Christy Cabanne. *GPV, FCT*

Lamb 🐾🐾 1985 Troubled 10-year-old epileptic Owen Kane (Kane) has been dumped by his abusive mother at a Catholic-run institution for wayward boys in Ireland, run by self-righteous headmaster Brother Benedict (Bannen). Owen becomes Benedict's scapegoat—much to the dismay of Brother Michael Lamb (Neeson). When Lamb claims a small family inheritance, he decides to take Owen and head to London, posing as father and son, where they live in increasingly depressed surroundings while Michael tries painfully to make them into a real family. Based on the novel by MacLaverty, who also wrote the screenplay. 110m/C VHS. *IR* Liam Neeson, Hugh O'Conor, Ian Bannen, Frances Tomelty; *D:* Colin Gregg; *W:* Bernard MacLaverty; *C:* Mike Garfath; *M:* Van Morrison. *CTL, FCT, TPV*

Lambada 🐾 1989 (PG) By day, he's a high school teacher in Beverly Hills; by night, a Latin dirty dancer cum tutor of ghetto teens. The very first of several films based on the short-lived dance craze. 92m/C VHS, Beta, LV, Closed Caption. J. Eddie Peck, Melora Hardin, Adolfo "Shabba Doo" Quinones, Ricky Paull Goldin, Basil Hoffman, Dennis Burkley; *D:* Joel Silberg. *MGM*

Lamerica 🐾🐾🐾 1995 Two Italian hustlers, Fiore (Placido) and his younger partner Gino (Lo Verso), head for poverty-stricken Albania in 1991, the first year after the collapse of the Communist dictatorship. They intend to set up a phony corporation and scam money from government grants but they need an Albanian figurehead. The duo find simple-minded, elderly Spiro (Di Mazzarelli), who's spent most of his life in prison camps, and stash him in an orphanage for safe keeping. Only when Spiro gets away, Gino heads for the countryside to find him and discovers some secrets about Spiro's past and just how the wily Albanians have been surviving. Italian with subtitles. 120m/C VHS. *IT* Enrico Lo Verso, Michele Placido, Carmelo Di Mazzarelli, Piro Milkani; *D:* Gianni Amelio; *W:* Gianni Amelio, Andrea Porporati, Alessandro Sermoneta; *C:* Luca Bigazzi; *M:* Franco Piersanti. Nominations: Independent Spirit Awards '97: Best Foreign Film. *NYR*

L'Amour en Herbe 🐾🐾 *Budding Love; Tender Love* 1977 His parents realize Pascal has something on his mind when he fails school. It turns out to be lovely Martine, whom he is then forbidden to see. But Pascal remains true—until betrayed. French with subtitles. 100m/C VHS. *FR* Pascal Meynier, Guilhaine Dubos, Bruno Raffaeli, Michel Galabru, Francoise Prevost, Alix Mahieux; *D:* Roger Andrieux; *W:* Roger Andrieux, Jean-Marie Benard; *C:* Ramon Suarez; *M:* Maxime Le Forestier. *FCT*

Lamp at Midnight ✔✔½ 1966 Presentation from "George Schaefer's Showcase Theatre" deals with three critical periods in the life of Italian astronomer Galileo Galilei, from his invention of the telescope, through his appearance at the Holy Office of the Inquisition, to the publication of his "Dialogue on the Two Systems of the World." For those in a planetary state of mind. **76m/C VHS, Beta.** Melvyn Douglas, David Wayne, Michael Hordern, Hurd Hatfield, Kim Hunter; **D:** George Schaefer. *FHS*

Lana in Love ✔✔ 1992 A lonely woman places an ad in the personal section in hopes of finding her Mr. Right. **90m/C VHS, Beta.** Daphna Kastner, Clark Gregg. *NO*

Lancelot of the Lake ✔✔ *Lancelot du Lac; The Grail; Le Graal* 1974 The Knights of the Round Table return to the court of King Arthur after a long, bloody, and fruitless search for the Holy Grail. Rivalries and jealousies debase the heroes as Lancelot struggles with his feelings for Arthur's Queen Guinevere. Austere acting but the film's rich visuals provide a sensuous air. French with subtitles. **85m/C VHS.** *FR* Luc Simon, Laura Duke Condominas, Vladimir Antolek-Oresek, Humbert Balsan, Patrick Bernard, Arthur De Montalembert; **D:** Robert Bresson; **W:** Robert Bresson; **C:** Pasquale De Santos; **M:** Philippe Sarde. *NYF*

Land and Freedom ✔✔✔ 1995 Earnestly talky drama focusing on idealist Liverpudlian communist David Carr (Hart), who heads to Spain in 1937 to fight against Franco's fascists. What David learns is that the Republican forces, made up of independent militia, are bitterly divided, with much infighting and betrayal from the Stalinist forces within David's own party. He falls for socialist Blanca (Pastor) and learns how terrifying and haphazard war can be (with timeout for ideological discussions). Sympathetic characters and sweeping action help to compensate for the political polemics. **109m/C VHS.** *GB SP GE* Ian Hart, Rosana Pastor, Iciar Bollain, Tom Gilroy, Frederic Pierrot, Marc Martinez; **D:** Ken Loach; **W:** Jim Allen; **C:** Barry Ackroyd; **M:** George Fenton. Cesar Awards '96: Best Foreign Film; Nominations: British Academy Awards '95: Best Film. *PGV*

The Land Before Time ✔✔✔ 1988 (G) Lushly animated children's film about five orphaned baby dinosaurs who band together and try to find the Great Valley, a paradise where they might live safely. Works same parental separation theme as Bluth's "American Tail." Charming, coy, and shamelessly tearjerking; producers included Steven Spielberg and George Lucas. **67m/C VHS, LV, Closed Caption. D:** Don Bluth; **M:** James Horner; **V:** Pat Hingle, Helen Shaver, Gabriel Damon, Candice Houston, Burke Barnes, Judith Barsi, Will Ryan. *USH, FCT, APD*

The Land Before Time 2: The Great Valley Adventure ✔✔½ 1994 (G) Sequel to 1988's animated adventure finds dinosaur pals Littlefoot, Cera, Ducky, Petrie, and Spike happily settled in the Great Valley. But their adventures don't stop as they chase two egg-stealing Struthiomimuses and retrieve an egg of unknown origin from the Mysterious Beyond. **75m/C VHS, LV, Closed Caption.** *USH*

The Land Before Time 3: The Time of the Great Giving ✔✔½ 1995 (G) Littlefoot and his pals try to find a new source of water when the Great Valley experiences a severe water shortage. **71m/C VHS, LV, Closed Caption. D:** Roy Allen Smith. *USH*

The Land Before Time 4: Journey Through the Mists ✔✔½ 1996 The little dinosaurs travel through the land of the mists in search of a rejuvenation flower that can save the life of Litefoot's sick grandpa. **74m/C VHS, LV, Closed Caption. D:** Roy Allen Smith. *USH*

Land of Doom ✔ 1984 An amazon and a warrior struggle for survival in a post-holocaust fantasy setting. **87m/C VHS, Beta.** Deborah Rennard, Garrick Dowhen; **D:** Peter Maris. *LIV*

The Land of Faraway ✔✔ 1987 (G) A Swedish boy is whisked off to a magical land where he does battle with evil knights and flies on winged horses. Dubbed; based on a novel by Astrid Lindgren. **95m/C VHS, Beta.** Timothy Bottoms, Christian Bale, Susannah York, Christopher Lee, Nicholas Pickard; **D:** Vladimir Grammatikov. *PSM*

Land of Fury ✔✔ *The Seekers* 1955 British naval officer Hawkins steps on New Zealand's shore and into trouble when he accidently walks on sacred Maori burial ground. Very British, very dated colonial saga, based on the novel "The Seekers" by John Guthrie. **90m/C VHS.** *GB* Jack Hawkins, Glynis Johns, Noel Purcell, Ian Fleming; **D:** Ken Annakin. *NOS*

Land of Hunted Men ✔ 1943 The Range Busters are on the case as they track down the hideout of terrorizing gunmen. **58m/B VHS, Beta.** Ray Corrigan, Dennis Moore, Max Terhune. *NOS, DVT*

Land of Promise ✔✔½ *Ziemia Obiecana* 1974 At the turn of the century three men build a textile factory in Lodz, Poland. They each represent a particular ethnic group: a Pole (Olbrychski), a German (Seweryn), and a Jew (Pszoniak). Class conflicts threaten to overwhelm as their overworked and underpaid workers plan a revolt. Based on the novel by Wladyslav Reymont. In Polish with English subtitles. **178m/C VHS.** *PL* Daniel Olbrychski, Wojciech Pszoniak, Andrzej Seweryn, Anna Nehrebecka; **D:** Andrzej Wajda; **W:** Andrzej Wajda; **M:** Wojciech Kilar. Nominations: Academy Awards '75: Best Foreign Language Film. *FCT*

Land of the Lawless ✔ 1947 A group of outlaws rule over a barren wasteland. What's the point? **54m/B VHS.** Rachel Brown, Raymond Hatton, Christine McIntyre, Tristram Coffin; **D:** Lambert Hillyer. *NOS, DVT*

Land of the Minotaur ✔✔ *The Devil's Men* 1977 (PG) Small village is the setting for horrifying ritual murders, demons, and disappearances of young terrorists. Fans of Pleasence and Cushing won't want to miss this. **88m/C VHS, Beta.** *GB* Donald Pleasence, Peter Cushing, Luan Peters; **D:** Costa Carayiannis; **M:** Brian Eno. *VCI, MRV*

Land of the Pharaohs ✔✔½ 1955 An epic about the building of Egypt's Great Pyramid. Hawkins is the extremely talkative pharoah and Collins plays his sugary-sweet yet villainous wife. Sort of campy, but worth watching for the great surprise ending. **106m/C VHS, LV, Closed Caption.** Jack Hawkins, Joan Collins, James Robertson Justice, Dewey Martin, Alexis Minotis, Sydney Chaplin; **D:** Howard Hawks; **W:** Harold Jack Bloom; **C:** Lee Garmes. *WAR*

Land Raiders ✔✔ 1969 Savalas plays a man who hates Apaches and wants their land, but is distracted when his brother arrives on the scene, igniting an old feud. **101m/C VHS, Beta.** Telly Savalas, George Maharis, Arlene Dahl, Janet Landgard; **D:** Nathan (Hertz) Juran. *GKK*

The Land that Time Forgot ✔✔ 1975 (PG) A WWI veteran, a beautiful woman, and their German enemies are stranded in a land outside time filled with prehistoric creatures. Based on the 1918 novel by Edgar Rice Burroughs. Followed in 1977 by "The People that Time Forgot." **90m/C VHS, Beta.** *GB* Doug McClure, John McEnery, Susan Penhaligon, Keith Barren, Anthony Ainley, Godfrey James, Bobby Parr, Declan Mulholland, Colin Farrell, Ben Howard, Roy Holder, Andrew McCulloch, Ron Pember, Steve James; **D:** Kevin Connor; **W:** James Cawthorn, Michael Moorcock; **C:** Alan Hume; **M:** Douglas Gamley. *LIV, VES*

The Land Unknown ✔✔½ 1957 A Naval helicopter is forced down in a tropical land of prehistoric terror, complete with ferocious creatures from the Mesozoic Era. While trying to make repairs, the crew discovers the sole survivor of a previous expedition who was driven to madness by life in the primordial jungle. Good performances from cast, although monsters aren't that believable. Based on a story by Charles Palmer. **78m/B VHS, Closed Caption.** Jock Mahoney, Shawn Smith, William Reynolds, Henry Brandon, Douglas Kennedy; **D:** Virgil W. Vogel; **W:** Laszlo Gorog; **M:** Henry Mancini. *USH*

Landlord Blues 1987 A trashy slumlord without morals or a conscience goes one step too far, and a tenant retaliates with munitions. **96m/C VHS, Beta.** Mark Boone, Raye Dowell, Richard Litt, Bill Rice, Mary Schultz, Gigi Williams; **D:** Jacob Burckhardt. *NO*

Landscape in the Mist ✔✔✔ *Topio Stin Omichli* 1988 A stark Greek landscape in a rainy winter sets the scene for a tragic search by two children for their unknown father. Relies heavily on symbolism to make its point about unfulfilled desire (including the film's imaginary German-Greek border). In Greek with English subtitles. **126m/C VHS.** *GR IT* Tania Palaiologou, Michalis Zeke, Stratos Tzortzoglou, Eva Kotamanidou, Alika Georgouli; **D:** Theo Angelopoulos; **W:** Thanassis Valtinos, Tonino Guerra, Theo Angelopoulos. *NYF, FCT, BTV*

Landslide ✔✔ 1992 (PG-13) As a geologist, suffering from memory loss, comes closer to discovering his identity his life is endangered by a sinister plot. **95m/C VHS, LV, Closed Caption.** Anthony Edwards, Tom Burlinson, Joanna Cassidy, Melody Anderson, Ronald Lacey, Ken James, Lloyd Bochner; **D:** Jean-Claude Lord. *REP*

L'Anne Sainte ✔✔½ *Pilgrimage to Rome* 1978 In his last film, Gabin is an escaped convict returning to his hidden loot in Rome when his plane is hijacked by international terrorists. Available dubbed. **?m/C VHS.** *FR* Jean Gabin, Jean-Claude Brialy, Paul Giusti, Danielle Darrieux. *FRA, FCT*

L'Annee des Meduses ✔½ *The Year of the Jellyfish* 1986 (R) An 18-year-old girl tries to seduce the local Monsieur Beefcake she meets on her vacation. When he doesn't return her interest, she decides to teach him a lesson. In French with English subtitles, or dubbed. **110m/C VHS, Beta.** *FR* Valerie Kaprisky, Barnard Giradeau; **D:** Christopher Frank; **C:** Renato Berta. *FCT, TPV*

Lantern Hill ✔✔½ 1990 (G) During the Depression, a 12-year-old girl attempts to fan the embers between her estranged parents. Made for cable Wonderworks production, filmed partly on Canada's Prince Edward Island. Based on a story by Lucy Maud Montgomery, whose "Anne of Green Gables" is also part of the Wonderworks series. **112m/C VHS, LV, Closed Caption.** *CA* Sam Waterston, Colleen Dewhurst, Sarah Polley, Marion Bennett, Zoe Caldwell; **D:** Kevin Sullivan. *TOU, FCT*

Lap Dancing woof! 1995 (R) What hath "Showgirls" wrought? Small town gal Angie Parker moves to Hollywood to become an actress and, when the money runs out, winds up as an exotic dancer. Also available unrated. **CW:** Nudity, violence, sexual situations, language. **90m/C VHS, LV.** Lorissa McComas, Tane McClure, C.T. Miller; **D:** Mike Sedan. *TRI*

L'Appat ✔✔ *Fresh Bait; Live Bait; The Bait* 1994 Deglamourizing, if familiar, look at amoral teens and violence. 18-year-old salesgirl Nathalie (Gillain) supports her unemployed boyfriend Eric (Sitruk) and his dim-bulb buddy Bruno (Putzulu). The guys hang out, watch too many gangster videos, and try to be tough, deciding to get rich by dangling Nathalie as bait. She goes to a man's home (presumably for sex) but Eric and Bruno will break in and rob the mark instead. Plan goes awry when their first victim is killed. What's truly disturbing is the trio's blase attitude that crime is a viable way to obtain money or that anything would happen to them should they be caught. Based on the book by Morgan Sportes, which recounted the 1984 crime. French with subtitles. **117m/C VHS.** *FR* Marie Gillain, Olivier Sitruk, Bruno Putzulu, Philippe Duclos, Richard Berry; **D:** Bertrand Tavernier; **W:** Bertrand Tavernier, Colo Tavernier O'Hagan; **M:** Philippe Haim. Berlin International Film Festival '94: Best Film. *NYR*

Laramie Kid 🎬 1935 A vintage Tyler sagebrush saga. **60m/B VHS, Beta.** Tom Tyler, Alberta Vaughn, Al Ferguson, Murdock McQuarrie, George Chesebro; **D:** Harry S. Webb. *NOS, DVT, RXM*

L'Argent 🎬🎬 1983 When a young man's parents refuse to lend him any money a friend helps out by giving him a counterfeit 500-franc note. This sets off a chain of events, with every passing of the money leading to another lie, betrayal, and increasingly violent crime. Austere and stylized vision is not for all tastes. In French with English subtitles. **82m/C VHS.** *FR* Christian Patey, Sylvie van den Elsen, Michel Briguet, Caroline Lang; **D:** Robert Bresson; **W:** Robert Bresson; **C:** Pasquale De Santos. Cannes Film Festival '83: Best Director (Bresson); National Society of Film Critics Awards '84: Best Director (Bresson). *NYF, FCT*

Larger Than Life 🎬½ *Nickel and Dime; Large as Life* 1996 (PG) The pitch for this movie (Murray takes an elephant on a cross-country trip) must have sounded terrific. Unfortunately, the pitch was fouled off. Murray is his usual smarmy self as cut-rate motivational speaker Jack Corcoran, who inherits the pachyderm and a pile of bills after his circus clown father dies. Following the "road movie" formula, he encounters wacky characters along the way, including a speed-freak trucker (McConaughey), a sexy animal trainer (Fiorentino) and a strait-laced zookeeper (Garofalo). In a piece of brilliant casting, Tai, the star of "Operation Dumbo Drop" appears as...the elephant. **93m/C VHS, Closed Caption.** Bill Murray, Janeane Garofalo, Linda Fiorentino, Matthew McConaughey, Keith David, Pat Hingle, Jeremy Piven, Lois Smith, Anita Gillette, Maureen Mueller, Harve Presnell, Tracey Walter; **D:** Howard Franklin; **W:** Roy Blount Jr.; **C:** Elliot Davis; **M:** Miles Goodman. *MGM*

Larks on a String 🎬🎬🎬½ 1968 Banned for 23 years, this wonderful film is Menzel's masterpiece, even better than his Oscar winning "Closely Watched Trains." Portrays the story of life in labor camps where men and women are re-educated at the whim of the government. No matter what the hardships, these people find humor, hope and love. Their individuality will not be lost, nor their humanity dissolved. Excellent performances, tellingly directed with a beautiful sense of composition and tone. Screenplay written by Menzel and Bohumil Hrabil, author of the short story on which it is based. In Czech with English subtitles. **96m/C VHS.** *CZ* Vaclav Neckar, Jitka Zelenohorska, Jaroslav Satoransky, Rudolf Hrusinsky; **D:** Jiri Menzel; **W:** Jiri Menzel. *FXL*

Larry 🎬🎬 1974 Based on the Nevada State Hospital case history of a 26-year-old man, institutionalized since infancy, who is discovered to be of normal intelligence and must learn to live the life he has always been capable of living. Made for television. **80m/C VHS, Beta.** Frederic Forrest, Tyne Daly, Katherine Helmond, Michael McGuire, Robert Walden; **D:** William A. Graham. *LCA*

Larry McMurtry's Dead Man's Walk 🎬🎬½ *Dead Man's Walk* 1996 (PG-13) McMurtry's prequel to "Lonesome Dove" focuses on the teenaged Gus McCrae (Arquette) and Woodrow Call (Miller) and their first adventures as Texas Rangers in the 1840s. They're involved in the ill-fated Texas-Santa Fe Expedition, led by parrot-owning former seafarer Caleb Cobb (Abraham), to take Santa Fe and make New Mexico part of the Texas Republic. Instead, a Mexican Army detachment led by Capt. Salazar (Olmos), captures the rag-tag group, which is then forced to march across a deadly stretch of desert that few survive. Likeable leads but the supporting actors, including Carradine and Stanton as scouts, steal the show.*CW:* Violence and thematic elements involving the frontier experience. **271m/C VHS, Closed Caption.** Jonny Lee Miller, David Arquette, Keith Carradine, Harry Dean Stanton, F. Murray Abraham, Edward James Olmos, Eric Schweig, Patricia Childress, Jennifer Garner, Haviland Morris, Brian Dennehy, Joaquin de Almeida, Ray McKinnon, Akosua Busia; **D:** Yves Simoneau; **W:** Larry McMurtry, Diana Ossana; **C:** Edward Pei; **M:** David Bell. *CAF*

Larry McMurtry's Streets of Laredo 🎬🎬🎬 *Streets of Laredo* 1995 Texas Ranger-turned-bounty hunter Woodrow F. Call (a splendid Garner) is hired by the railroad to track down ruthless Mexican bandit Joey Garza (Cruz), pitting an old man's skills against a young man's daring, and driving both men across Texas, deep into Mexican territory. Call's old friend Pea Eye Parker (Shepard) reluctantly comes along, with ex-prostitute Lorena (Spacek), who's Parker's wife, and Maria (Braga), Joey's tough-but-deluded mom, providing strong support. Casual cruelty and violence are the norm in the sunset days of both Call's life and that of the west itself. Third in the TV sagas, following "Return to Lonesome Dove." **227m/C VHS.** James Garner, Alexis Cruz, Sam Shepard, Sissy Spacek, Sonia Braga, Wes Studi, Randy Quaid, Charles Martin Smith, Kevin Conway, George Carlin, Ned Beatty, James Gammon, Tristan Tait, Anjanette Comer; **D:** Joseph Sargent; **W:** Larry McMurtry, Diana Ossana; **C:** Edward Pei; **M:** David Shire. *CAF, VIF*

Las Vegas Hillbillys 🎬 *Country Music* 1966 A pair of country-singing hillbillies inherit a saloon in Las Vegas and enjoy wine, moonshine, and song. These two make the Clampetts look like high society. Followed, believe it or not, by "Hillbillys in a Haunted House." ♫ *Money Greases the Wheel.* **85m/C VHS, Beta.** Mamie Van Doren, Jayne Mansfield, Ferlin Husky, Sonny James; **D:** Arthur C. Pierce. *NLC*

Las Vegas Lady 🎬 1976 (PG) Three shrewd casino hostesses plot a multi-million dollar heist in the nation's gambling capital. Non-captivating caper. **90m/C VHS, Beta.** Stella Stevens, Stuart Whitman, George de Cecenzo, Andrew Stevens; **D:** Noel Nosseck; **W:** Walter Dallenbach; **M:** Alan Silvestri. *PSM*

Las Vegas Serial Killer woof! 1986 A serial killer, let out of prison on a technicality, starts killing again. Made for video by Camp. **90m/C VHS, Beta.** Pierre Agostino, Ron Jason, Tara MacGowran, Kathryn Downey. *NO*

The Las Vegas Story woof! 1952 Gambling, colorful sights, and a murder provide the framework for this non-compelling fictional guided-tour of the city. Save your money for the slots. **88m/B VHS, Beta.** Victor Mature, Jane Russell, Vincent Price, Hoagy Carmichael, Brad Dexter; **D:** Robert Stevenson. *NO*

Las Vegas Weekend 🎬 1985 A computer nerd goes to Las Vegas and discovers fun. **83m/C VHS, Beta.** Barry Hickey, Macka Foley, Ray Dennis Steckler; **D:** Dale Trevillion; **W:** Dale Trevillion. *VTR, NWV*

Laser Mission 🎬🎬½ 1990 When it is discovered that the Soviets have laser weapon capabilities, an agent is given the task of destroying the weapon and kidnapping the scientist who developed it. **83m/C VHS, LV, Closed Caption.** Brandon Lee, Debi Monahan, Ernest Borgnine, Werner Pochat, Graham Clarke, Maureen Lahoud, Pierre Knoessen; **D:** Beau Davis. *TTC*

Laser Moon 🎬🎬 1992 A serial killer uses a surgical laser beam to kill his beautiful victims, and he strikes at every full moon. When he announces his next attack on a late-night radio talk show the police call in a beautiful rookie cop (Lords) to use as bait. **90m/C VHS.** Traci Lords, Crystal Shaw, Harrison Leduke, Bruce Carter; **D:** Bruce Carter. *HMD*

Laserblast woof! 1978 (PG) Standard wimpgets-revenge story in which a frustrated young man finds a powerful and deadly laser which was left near his home by aliens; upon learning of its devastating capabilities, his personality changes and he seeks revenge against all who have taken advantage of him. **87m/C VHS, Beta, LV.** Kim Milford, Cheryl "Rainbeaux" Smith, Keenan Wynn, Roddy McDowall; **D:** Michael Raeburn; **M:** Richard Band, Joel Goldsmith. *MED*

The Laserman 🎬🎬 1990 (R) Exotic black comedy about a Chinese-American scientist who, when not fending off his overbearing Jewish mother or having telepathic orgasms, is contending with a band of political terrorists. **92m/C VHS.** Marc Hayashi, Peter Wang, Tony Leung, Sally Yeh, Maryann Urbano, Joan Copeland; **D:** Peter Wang; **W:** Peter Wang; **M:** Mason Daring. *HTV*

Lassie 🎬🎬½ 1994 (PG) Everyone's favorite collie returns as the Turner family moves to Virginia's Shenandoah Valley to take up sheep ranching. However, because this is the '90s, Dad meets financial disaster, and junior can't stand his stepmom. Can Lassie meet the challenges of dysfunctional family living? "What is it girl? Call a therapist?" This Lassie is a direct descendant of Pal, the original 1943 star. **92m/C VHS, Beta, Closed Caption.** Helen Slater, Jon Tenney, Tom Guiry, Brittany Boyd, Richard Farnsworth, Frederic Forrest; **D:** Daniel Petrie; **W:** Matthew Jacobs, Gary Ross, Elizabeth Anderson. *PAR*

Lassie: Adventures of Neeka 1968 America's best friend joins her Native American buddy, Neeka, for a journey through a forest in the Pacific Northwest. They camp out in a deserted settlement, pull an elderly gentleman out of a frigid pond, and risk their lives to release horses from a stable during a raging wildfire. **75m/B VHS, Beta.** Jed Allan, Mark Miranda, Robert Rockwell, Lassie; **D:** Richard Moder, Jack B. Hively. *NO*

Lassie, Come Home 🎬🎬½ 1943 (G) In first of the Lassie series, the famed collie is reluctantly sold and makes a treacherous cross-country journey back to her original family. **90m/C VHS, Beta, LV.** Roddy McDowall, Elizabeth Taylor, Donald Crisp, Edmund Gwenn, May Whitty, Nigel Bruce, Elsa Lanchester, J. Pat O'Malley, Lassie; **D:** Fred M. Wilcox. National Board of Review Awards '43: 10 Best Films of the Year; Nominations: Academy Awards '43: Best Color Cinematography. *MGM*

Lassie from Lancashire 🎬🎬 1938 Not the famous Collie—but here, a Colleen. A pair of struggling lovebirds try to make it in show biz against all odds, including the girl's lunatic aunt, who locks her away before an audition. **67m/B VHS, Beta.** Marjorie Brown, Hal Thompson, Marjorie Sandford, Lassie, Mark Daly. *VYY*

Lassie: The Miracle 🎬 1975 A TV-movie featuring the faithful collie saving new-born pups and befriending a mute boy. **90m/C VHS, Beta.** Lassie. *MGM*

Lassie: Well of Love 1990 Various installments of the classic television series featuring the heroic collie are combined to create a movie-length presentation for home video. Lassie takes two young pups under her paw and, in the process, loses her way. As she tries to get home, she brings joy back into the lives of two despondent children. Finally, the old girl faces death when she tumbles into an abandoned well and must depend on humans for rescue. **76m/C VHS, Beta.** Lassie, Mary Gregory, Robert Donner. *NO*

Lassie's Great Adventure 🎬🎬½ 1962 Lassie and her master Timmy are swept away from home by a runaway balloon. After they land in the Canadian wilderness, they learn to rely on each other through peril and adventure. Made for television. **104m/C VHS, Beta.** June Lockhart, Jon Provost, Hugh Reilly; **D:** William Beaudine; **W:** Charles "Blackie" O'Neal. *MGM*

Lassiter 🎬🎬½ 1984 (R) Selleck plays a jewel thief who is asked to steal diamonds from the Nazis for the FBI. Supporting cast adds value to what is otherwise a fairly ordinary adventure drama. **100m/C VHS, Beta, LV.** Tom Selleck, Jane Seymour, Lauren Hutton, Bob Hoskins, Joe Regalbuto, Ed Lauter, Warren Clarke; **D:** Roger Young. *WAR*

Last Action Hero 🎬🎬 1993 (PG-13) Newcomer O'Brien finds himself in a movie starring his idol Jack Slater, the kind of guy who never loses a fight and is impervious to gunfire and explosions (and he has a really cool car and a really big gun). Disappointing action/spoof of movies within a movie (rumored to have cost $80 million) was critically maimed and never recovered. The concept isn't new and has been done better before, though Ah-nold possesses his usual self-mocking charm, which is more than can be said for the movie. Look for lots of big stars in small roles and cameos. Cluttered with inside Hollywood gags, the script was given uncredited assistance from William Goldman. **CW:** Strong action sequences. **131m/C VHS, Beta, LV, 8mm, Closed Caption.** Arnold Schwarzenegger, Austin O'Brien, Mercedes Ruehl, F. Murray Abraham, Charles Dance, Anthony Quinn, Robert Prosky, Tom Noonan, Frank McRae, Art Carney, Brigitte Wilson; **Cameos:** Sharon Stone, Hammer, Chevy Chase, Jean-Claude Van Damme, Tori Spelling, Joan Plowright, Adam Ant, James Belushi, James Cameron, Tony Curtis, Timothy Dalton, Tony Danza, Edward Furlong, Little Richard, Damon Wayans, Robert Patrick; **D:** John McTiernan; **W:** David Arnott, Shane Black; **C:** Dean Semler; **M:** Michael Kamen. *COL, BTV*

The Last American Hero 🎬🎬🎬 *Hard Driver* 1973 (PG)
The true story of how former moonshine runner Junior Johnson became one of the fastest race car drivers in the history of the sport. Entertaining slice of life chronicling whiskey running and stock car racing, with Bridges superb in the lead. Based on a series of articles written by Tom Wolfe. **95m/C VHS, Beta.** Jeff Bridges, Valerie Perrine, Gary Busey, Art Lund, Geraldine Fitzgerald, Ned Beatty; **D:** Lamont Johnson; **W:** William Roberts; **M:** Charles Fox. National Board of Review Awards '73: 10 Best Films of the Year. *FOX*

Last American Virgin 🎬🎬 1982 (R)
Usual brainless teen sex comedy about three school buddies who must deal with a plethora of problems in their search for girls who are willing. Music by Blondie, The Cars, The Police, The Waitresses, Devo, U2, Human League, and Quincy Jones. **92m/C VHS, Beta.** Lawrence Monoson, Diane Franklin, Steve Antin, Louisa Moritz; **D:** Boaz Davidson; **W:** Boaz Davidson. *MGM*

The Last Angry Man 🎬🎬🎬½ 1959 An
old, idealistic Brooklyn doctor attracts a television producer wanting to make a documentary about his life and career, and the two conflict. Muni was Oscar-nominated for this, his last film. **100m/B VHS, Beta.** Paul Muni, David Wayne, Betsy Palmer, Luther Adler, Dan Tobin; **D:** Daniel Mann; **C:** James Wong Howe. Nominations: Academy Awards '59: Best Actor (Muni), Best Art Direction/Set Decoration (B & W). *COL*

The Last Bastion 🎬🎬 1984 A WWII drama emphasizing the political struggle between Churchill, MacArthur, Roosevelt, and Australia's John Curtin. **160m/C VHS, Beta.** *AU* Robert Vaughn, Timothy West. *ACA*

The Last Best Year 🎬🎬½ 1990 (PG)
Basic TV tearjerker has lonely psychologist Wendy (Moore) befriending patient Jane (Peters), who has a terminal illness. **88m/C VHS.** Mary Tyler Moore, Bernadette Peters, Brian Bedford, Dorothy McGuire, Kate Reid, Kenneth Welsh; **D:** John Erman; **W:** David W. Rintels. *NHO*

The Last Boy Scout 🎬🎬 1991 (R) Are
you ready for some gunplay? This formula thriller stars Willis as a private eye and Wayans as an ex-quarterback teaming up against a pro-football team owner who will stop at nothing to get political backing for a bill promoting legalized gambling on sports. Another variation of the violent buddy-picture by "Lethal Weapon" screenwriter Black. **CW:** Very strong language and graphic violence. **105m/C VHS, LV, Closed Caption.** Bruce Willis, Damon Wayans, Halle Berry, Chelsea Field, Noble Willingham, Taylor Negron, Danielle Harris, Bruce McGill; **D:** Tony Scott; **W:** Shane Black. *WAR*

Last Bullet 🎬🎬 1950 A young westerner chases after a band of outlaws to avenge the cold-blooded murder of his parents. **55m/B VHS, Beta, LV.** James Ellison, Russell Hayden, John Cason. *NO*

The Last Butterfly 🎬🎬 1992 Quiet Holocaust movie set in Theresienstadt, the Czechoslovak ghetto city used by the Nazis to persuade the outside world of their humane treatment of the Jews. Noted French mime Antoine Moreau (Courtenay) has fallen under suspicion by the Gestapo. He's "persuaded" to give a performance in Theresienstadt for the benefit of the visiting Red Cross but decides to subvert Nazi propaganda with his own version of "Hansel and Gretel." This time the witch feeds the children into her oven. Muted performances and screenplay (adapted from the Michael Jacot novel) heightened the film's surreal calmness. **106m/C VHS, LV.** *CZ* Tom Courtenay, Brigitte Fossey, Freddie Jones, Ingrid Held, Linda Jablonska; **D:** Karel Kachyna; **W:** Karel Kachyna, Ota Hofman; **M:** Alex North. *NLC*

Last Call 🎬 1990 (R) Clearly, Joe Sixpack won't rent this bimbo fest for its subtle plot. Katt, a mafiosi-cheated real estate guy, decides to even the score with the assistance of gal pal/playmate of the year Tweed, who's more than willing to compromise her position. A direct to video release, it also features the talents of playboy emerita Stevens. Available in rated and unrated versions. **90m/C VHS, Beta.** William Katt, Shannon Tweed, Joseph Campanella, Stella Stevens, Matt Roe; **D:** Jag Mundhra. *PSM*

The Last Chance 🎬🎬🎬 1945 A realistic look at the efforts of three WWII Allied officers to help a group of refugees escape across the Alps from Italy to Switzerland. The officers are played by former pilots who were shot down over Switzerland. In spite of this—or perhaps because of it—the acting is superb. Watch for inspirational scene of refugees singing. **105m/B VHS.** E.G. Morrison, John Hoy, Ray Reagan, Odeardo Mosini, Sigfrit Steiner, Emil Gerber; **D:** Leopold Lindtberg. *NOS*

Last Chase 🎬½ 1981 (PG) Famed race car driver becomes a vocal dissenter against the sterile society that has emerged, in this drama set in the near future. Made for television. Screenplay written by Christopher Crowe under the pseudonym C.R. O'Cristopher. **106m/C VHS, Beta.** *CA* Lee Majors, Burgess Meredith, Chris Makepeace, Alexandra Stewart; **D:** Martyn Burke; **W:** Christopher Crowe, Martyn Burke. *VES*

Last Command 🎬🎬🎬🎬 1928 Famous powerful silent film by Sternberg about a expatriate Czarist general forging out a pitiful living as a silent Hollywood extra, where he is hired by his former adversary to reenact the revolution he just left. Next to "The Last Laugh," this is considered Jannings' most acclaimed performance. Deeply ironic, visually compelling film with a new score by Gaylord Carter. **88m/B VHS, Beta.** Emil Jannings, William Powell, Evelyn Brent, Nicholas Soussanin, Michael Visaroff, Jack Raymond, Fritz Feld; **D:** Josef von Sternberg; **W:** Warren Duff; **M:** Max Steiner, Gaylord Carter. Academy Awards '28: Best Actor (Jannings); Nominations: Academy Awards '28: Best Picture, Best Story. *PAR, FCT, BTV*

The Last Command 🎬🎬½ 1955 Jim Bowie and his followers sacrifice their lives in defending the Alamo. A good cast holds its own against a mediocre script; battle scenes are terrific. **110m/C VHS.** Sterling Hayden, Richard Carlson, Ernest Borgnine, J. Carrol Naish, Virginia Grey, Anna Maria Alberghetti; **D:** Frank Lloyd. *REP, FCT*

The Last Contract 🎬🎬 1986 (R) An artist who pays his bills by working as a hitman, kills the wrong man. As a result, he must fear for his life since a counterhit is inevitable. **85m/C VHS.** Jack Palance, Rod Steiger, Bo Svenson, Richard Roundtree, Ann Turkel; **D:** Allan A. Buckhantz. *ACA*

Last Cry for Help 🎬½ 1979 A psychiatrist helps a seventeen-year-old high school coed who, fearing she has disappointed her parents, attempts suicide. Typical made-for-television melodrama that attempts to make a statement, but falls short. Definitely not the "Partridge Family." **98m/C VHS, Beta.** Linda Purl, Shirley Jones, Tony LoBian-

co, Murray Hamilton, Grant Goodeve; **D:** Hal Sitowitz; **M:** Miles Goodman. *UNI*

Last Dance 🎬½ 1991 Five scantily-clad exotic dancers are ready to compete for the title of Miss Dance-TV, but trouble ensues when the dancers start turning up dead. **86m/C VHS, Beta, LV.** Cynthia Bassinet, Elaine Hendrix, Kurt T. Williams, Allison Rhea, Erica Ringston; **D:** Anthony Markes. *PSM*

The Last Dance *Sista Dansen* 1993
Two couples, Claus and Tove (Brynolfsson, Bergstrom) and best friends Lennart and Liselott (Andersson, Froling), have a shared obsession with ballroom dance competitions and some secret desires. Seems Claus and Tove have a rocky marriage and think their friends have the perfect union. Instead, Lennart is tired of his overbearing wife and longs for Tove, to whom he was once engaged. Then Liselott's body is found beneath the pier after a competition. Swedish with subtitles. **109m/C VHS.** *SW* Helena Bergstrom, Reine Brynolfsson, Ewa Froling, Peter Andersson; **D:** Colin Nutley; **W:** Colin Nutley; **C:** Jens Fischer. *HTV*

Last Dance 🎬🎬 1996 (R) Following closely on the heels of "Dead Man Walking," this deathrow drama suffered from bad timing and was dubbed by some as "Bad Hair Walking." Stone plays a convicted murderess condemned to die in an unnamed Southern state. Morrow's the rookie attorney for the state's clemency office assigned to her case. As a bond grows between the two, he uncovers errors in her trial that his bosses would rather have him ignore. The movie makes its big mistake by centering on Morrow's callow lawyer instead of Stone's embittered con. The clock-ticking countdown to the execution (which will amuse fans of "The Player") even fails to hold attention. **CW:** Violence, language and some drug content. **103m/C VHS, LV, Closed Caption.** Sharon Stone, Rob Morrow, Randy Quaid, Peter Gallagher, Jack Thompson, Jayne Brook, Pamela Tyson, Skeet Ulrich, Don Harvey, Diane Sellers; **D:** Bruce Beresford; **W:** Ron Koslow; **C:** Peter James; **M:** Mark Isham. *TOU*

Last Day of the War 🎬½ 1969 (PG) A German scientist is chased by Americans and Germans as WWII winds to its conclusion. Filmed in Spain. **96m/C VHS, Beta.** *SP* George Maharis, Maria Perschy, James Philbrook, Gerard Herter; **D:** Juan Antonio Bardem. *LIV*

The Last Days of Chez Nous 🎬🎬½
1992 (R) Armstrong's dramatic comedy about a family falling apart has Ganz as a homesick Frenchman married to controlling, successful Australian writer Harrow. Trouble starts when his wayward sister-in-law Fox returns home to live with them and his wife decides to take an extended holiday with her father. Ganz suddenly finds himself only too involved in Fox's complicated life. Self-involved characters with messy emotional lives leave viewers feeling rather distant, though cast, and particularly Ganz, strive for intimacy. **CW:** A moment of strong sexual language. **96m/C VHS, LV, Closed Caption.** *AU* Bruno Ganz, Lisa Harrow, Kerry Fox, Kiri Paramore, Bill Hunter, Miranda Otto; **D:** Gillian Armstrong; **W:** Helen Garner; **M:** Paul Grabowsky. Australian Film Institute '92: Best Actress (Harrow); Nominations: Australian Film Institute '92: Best Director (Armstrong), Best Film, Best Supporting Actor (Hunter). *NLC, IME, COL*

The Last Days of Dolwyn 🎬🎬½
Woman of Dolwyn; Dolwyn 1949 A man banned for thievery from his Welsh village returns bent upon revenge. He plans to buy the entire district when it is designated part of a water reservoir project, but finds plans thwarted by a dowager and her stepson. Burton's first film was based on a true story. **95m/B VHS.** *GB* Edith Evans, Emlyn Williams, Richard Burton, Anthony James, Barbara Couper, Alan Aynesworth, Hugh Griffith, Roddy Hughes, Tom Jones; **D:** Emlyn Williams; **W:** Emlyn Williams. *FCT, DVT*

Last Days of Frank & Jesse James 🎬½ 1986 A tired television-movie rehash of the well-known western legend in which the famous brothers try to be like others after their

personal war against society ends. **100m/C VHS, Beta.** Johnny Cash, Kris Kristofferson, June Carter Cash, Willie Nelson, Margaret Gibson, Gail Youngs; **D:** William A. Graham. *THV*

The Last Days of Patton 🐾½ 1986 A made-for-television movie depicting the aging general's autumn years as a controversial ex-Nazi defender and desk-bound WWII historian. Scott reprises his feature-film role. **146m/C VHS, Beta, Closed Caption.** George C. Scott, Ed Lauter, Eva Marie Saint, Richard Dysart, Murray Hamilton, Kathryn Leigh Scott; **D:** Delbert Mann. *FOX*

Last Days of Planet Earth woof! *Prophecies of Nostradamus; Catastrophe 1999; Nostradamus No Daiyogen* 1974 Really stinky Japanese doomsday movie about a scientist who charges that a build-up of pollution is responsible for giant mutant sea slugs and other environmental disasters. Dubbed. **88m/C VHS, Closed Caption.** *JP* Tetsuro Tamba, So Yamamura, Takashi Shimura; **D:** Toshio Masuda. *PAR*

Last Days of Pompeii 🐾🐾½ 1935 Vintage DeMille-style epic based on Lord Lytton's book, where the eruption of Vesuvius threatens noblemen and slaves alike. State-of-the-art special effects still look fantastic today. Remade in 1960; available colorized. **96m/B VHS, Beta, LV, Closed Caption.** Preston Foster, Alan Hale, Basil Rathbone, George L. Baxt, Louis Calhern, David Holt, Dorothy Wilson, Wryley Birch, Gloria Shea; **D:** Ernest B. Schoedsack; **C:** Jack Cardiff. *TTC*

The Last Days of Pompeii 🐾🐾 *Ultimi Giorni di Pompeii* 1960 Superman Reeves plays a gladiator trying to clean up the doomed town of Pompeii in this remake of the 1935 classic. Some spectacular scenes, including the explosive climax when the mountain blows its top. **105m/C VHS.** *IT* Steve Reeves, Christine Kaufmann, Barbara Carroll, Anne Marie Baumann, Mimmo Palmara; **D:** Mario Bonnard; **W:** Sergio Leone. *GKK*

The Last Detail 🐾🐾🐾🐾 1973 (R) Two hard-boiled career petty officers (Nicholson and Young) are commissioned to transfer a young sailor facing an eight-year sentence for petty theft from one brig to another. In an act of compassion, they attempt to show the prisoner a final good time. Nicholson shines in both the complexity and completeness of his character. Adapted from a Daryl Ponicsan novel. **104m/C VHS, Beta, LV.** Jack Nicholson, Otis Young, Randy Quaid, Clifton James, Michael Moriarty, Carol Kane, Nancy Allen; *Cameos:* Gilda Radner; **D:** Hal Ashby; **W:** Robert Towne; **C:** Michael Chapman; **M:** Johnny Mandel. British Academy Awards '74: Best Actor (Nicholson), Best Screenplay; Cannes Film Festival '74: Best Actor (Nicholson); National Board of Review Awards '74: 10 Best Films of the Year; New York Film Critics Awards '74: Best Actor (Nicholson); National Society of Film Critics Awards '74: Best Actor (Nicholson); Nominations: Academy Awards '73: Best Actor (Nicholson), Best Adapted Screenplay, Best Supporting Actor (Quaid). *COL, WME*

The Last Don 🐾🐾½ *Mario Puzo's The Last Don* 1997 Re-edited version of the TV miniseries finds author Puzo, of 'Godfather' fame, sticking to what he knows best. The Don in question is Domenico Clericuzo (Aiello), a ruthless patriarch who wipes out the rival family his pregnant daughter Rose Marie marries into (and doesn't spare her hubby). Carrying out the Don's orders is nephew Pippi (Mantegna), an enforcer who weds Vegas showgirl Nalene (Miller) and who gets involved in the casino business. The years pass with the Don manipulating the next generation, as bloodthirsty grandchild Dante (Cochrane) fights for control with Pippi's cool-headed son Cross (Gedrick). Divided loyalties abound. A complete five-hour version of the saga is also available. **150m/C VHS.** Danny Aiello, Joe Mantegna, Jason Gedrick, Rory Cochrane, Penelope Ann Miller, Daryl Hannah, Kirstie Alley, Michelle Rene Thomas, David Marciano, Robert Wuhl, k.d. lang, John Colicos, Cliff DeYoung, Michael Massee; **D:** Graeme Clifford; **W:** Joyce Eliason; **C:** Gordon C. Lonsdale; **M:** Angelo Badalamenti, Roger Bellon. *THV*

The Last Dragon 🐾½ *Berry Gordy's The Last Dragon* 1985 (PG-13) It's time for a Motown kung fu showdown on the streets of Harlem, for there is scarcely enough room for even one dragon. **108m/C VHS, Beta, Closed Caption.** Taimak, Vanity, Christopher Murney, Julius J. Carry III, Faith Prince; **D:** Michael A. Schultz. *FOX*

Last Embrace 🐾🐾🐾 1979 (R) A feverish thriller in the Hitchcock style dealing with an ex-secret serviceman who is convinced someone is trying to kill him. **102m/C VHS, Beta.** Roy Scheider, Janet Margolin, Christopher Walken, John Glover, Charles Napier, Mandy Patinkin; **D:** Jonathan Demme; **M:** Miklos Rozsa. *MGM, FOX*

The Last Emperor 🐾🐾🐾🐾 1987 (PG-13) Deeply ironic epic detailing life of Pu Yi, crowned at the age of three as the last emperor of China before the onset of communism. Follows Pu Yi from childhood to manhood (sequestered away in the Forbidden City) to fugitive to puppet-ruler to party proletariat. O'Toole portrays the sympathetic Scot tutor who educates the adult Pu Yi (Lone) in the ways of the western world after Pu Yi abdicates power in 1912. Shot on location inside the People's Republic of China with a cast of thousands; authentic costumes. Rich, visually stunning movie. The Talking Heads' David Byrne contributed to the score. Cinematography by Vittorio Storaro. **140m/C VHS, Beta, LV, 8mm, Closed Caption.** *IT* John Lone, Peter O'Toole, Joan Chen, Victor Wong, Ryuichi Sakamoto, Dennis Dun, Maggie Han, Ying Ruocheng, Ric Young; **D:** Bernardo Bertolucci; **C:** Vittorio Storaro; **M:** Ryuichi Sakamoto, David Byrne. Academy Awards '87: Best Adapted Screenplay, Best Art Direction/Set Decoration, Best Cinematography, Best Costume Design, Best Director (Bertolucci), Best Film Editing, Best Picture, Best Sound, Best Original Score; British Academy Awards '88: Best Film; Cesar Awards '88: Best Foreign Film; Directors Guild of America Awards '87: Best Director (Bertolucci); Golden Globe Awards '88: Best Director (Bertolucci), Best Film—Drama, Best Screenplay, Best Score; Los Angeles Film Critics Association Awards '87: Best Cinematography; National Board of Review Awards '87: 10 Best Films of the Year; New York Film Critics Awards '87: Best Cinematography. *COL, FCT, BTV*

Last Exit to Brooklyn 🐾🐾🐾½ 1990 (R) Hubert Selby, Jr.'s shocking book comes to the screen in a vivid film. Leigh gives a stunning performance as a young Brooklyn girl caught between the Mafia, union men, and friends struggling for something better. Set in the 1950s. Fine supporting cast; excellent pacing. **102m/C VHS, LV.** Jennifer Jason Leigh, Burt Young, Stephen Lang, Ricki Lake, Jerry Orbach, Maia Danziger, Stephen Baldwin; **D:** Uli Edel; **C:** Stefan Czapsky. New York Film Critics Awards '89: Best Supporting Actress (Leigh). *COL, FCT*

The Last Fight 🐾½ 1982 (R) Boxer risks his life and his girlfriend for a shot at the championship title. Watch and see if he could've been a contender. **85m/C VHS, Beta.** Fred Williamson, Willie Colon, Ruben Blades, Joe Spinell, Darlanne Fluegel; **D:** Fred Williamson. *NO*

The Last Five Days 🐾🐾 1982 Based on the true story of a girl and her brother who, in 1943 Munich, were arrested for distributing anti-Nazi propaganda. The film covers the five days between their capture and execution. In German with English subtitles. **112m/C VHS.** *GE* Lena Stolze, Irm Hermann; **D:** Percy Adlon. *CVC*

The Last Flight of Noah's Ark 🐾🐾½ 1980 (G) Disney adventure concerns a high-living pilot, a prim missionary, and two stowaway orphans who must plot their way off a deserted island following the crash landing of their broken-down plane. **97m/C VHS, Beta.** Elliott Gould, Genevieve Bujold, Rick Schroder, Vincent Gardenia, Tammy Lauren; **D:** Charles Jarrott; **W:** George Arthur Bloom, Steven W. Carabatsos; **M:** Maurice Jarre. *DIS*

Last Flight Out: A True Story 🐾🐾 1990 Hours before Saigon fell to the Vietcong in 1975, Vietnamese and Americans rushed to board the last commercial flight out of Vietnam.

Lukewarm account of a true story. **99m/C VHS, 8mm.** James Earl Jones, Richard Crenna, Haing S. Ngor, Eric Bogosian. *NO*

Last Flight to Hell 🐾🐾 19?? When a drug lord is kidnapped, Brown is sent to South America to rescue the slimeball. His interest in the job picks up when the drug lord's 11-on-a-scale-of-ten daughter joins him for the chase. **94m/C VHS.** Reb Brown, Chuck Connors; **D:** Paul D. Robinson. *AIP*

The Last Fling 🐾½ 1986 When Selleca has her mind set on a romantic fling, Ritter is headed for trouble. She wants love for one night, he wants it forever. Will they solve this difference of opinion? Will true love prevail? Will Ritter consent to being used as a one-night stand? Weakly plotted and poorly acted comedy. Made for television. **95m/C VHS, LV.** John Ritter, Connie Sellecca, Scott Bakula, Shannon Tweed, Paul Sand, John Bennett Perry; **D:** Corey Allen; **M:** Charles Bernstein. *ACA*

Last Four Days 🐾🐾 1977 (PG) A chronicle of the final days of Benito Mussolini. **91m/C VHS, Beta.** Rod Steiger, Henry Fonda, Franco Nero; **D:** Carlo Lizzani. *LIV*

Last Frontier 🐾🐾½ 1932 Serial of 12 chapters contains shades of spectacular figures in Western history: Custer, Hickok, and others in a background of grazing buffalo, boom towns, and covered wagon trails. **216m/B VHS, Beta.** Lon Chaney Jr., Yakima Canutt, Francis X. Bushman; **D:** Spencer Gordon Bennet, Thomas L. Story. *VCN, VYY, DVT*

Last Game 🐾🐾 1980 A college student is torn between his devotion to his blind father and going out for the college's football team. **107m/C VHS, Beta.** Howard Segal, Ed L. Grady, Terry Alden; **D:** Martin Beck. *NO*

The Last Good Time 🐾🐾½ 1994 (R) Old-world violinist Joseph Kopple (Mueller-Stahl), retired and living in a small Brooklyn apartment, has his world turned upside down when his streetsmart neighbor Charlotte (d'Abo) seeks refuge from her abusive boyfriend Eddie (Pasdar). An unsentimental friendship develops between the two inspite of the differences in their ages, educations, and lifestyles. Terrific performance from Mueller-Stahl as the lonely but dignified old man. Based on the novel by Richard Bausch. *CW:* Language and some sexuality. **90m/C VHS.** Armin Mueller-Stahl, Olivia D'Abo, Maureen Stapleton, Lionel Stander, Adrian Pasdar; **D:** Bob Balaban; **W:** Bob Balaban, John McLaughlin; **C:** Claudia Rashke. *HMK*

Last Gun 1964 A legendary gunman on the verge of retirement has to save his town from a reign of terror before turning his gun in. **98m/C VHS, Beta.** Cameron Mitchell. *NO*

The Last Hit 🐾🐾½ 1993 (R) Michael Grant (Brown) is a professional assassin, working for the CIA, who's very good at his job. But now he's burned out and ready to retire to New Mexico for some peace and quiet. He buys a house from the widowed Anna (Adams), naturally falling in love with her. Then one last assignment comes along and, wouldn't you know, his target turns out to be Anna's father (Yulin). Based on the novel 'The Large Kill' by Patrick Ruell. **93m/C VHS, LV, Closed Caption.** Bryan Brown, Brooke Adams, Harris Yulin; **D:** Jan Egleson; **W:** Walter Klenhard, Alan Sharp; **M:** Gary Chang. *USH*

Last Holiday 🐾🐾🐾 1950 A man who is told he has a few weeks to live decides to spend them in a posh resort where people assume he is important. **89m/B VHS, Beta.** *GB* Alec Guinness, Kay Walsh, Beatrice Campbell, Wilfrid Hyde-White, Bernard Lee; **D:** Henry Cass; **W:** J.B. Priestley. *HMV, RXM, LCA*

The Last Horror Film woof! *The Fanatic* 1982 (R) Beautiful queen of horror films is followed to the Cannes Film Festival by her number one fan who, unbeknownst to her, is slowly murdering members of her entourage in a deluded and vain attempt to capture her attentions. Title refers to lack of plans for a sequel. **87m/C VHS, Beta.** Caroline Munro, Joe Spinell, Judd Hamilton; **D:** David Winters. *MED*

The Last Hour 🐾 1991 (R) A Wall Street crook crosses a Mafia punk, so the latter holds the former's wife hostage in an unfinished skyscraper. Fortunately the lady's first husband is a gung-ho cop eager to commence the DIE HARD-esque action. Undistinguished fare that gives away the climax in an opening flash-forward. **CW:** Language, graphic violence, and sensuality. 85m/ C VHS, Beta, LV. Michael Pare, Shannon Tweed, Bobby DiCicco, Robert Pucci; **D:** William Sachs. *ACA*

Last House on Dead End Street woof! *The Fun House* 1977 (R) Gore galore as actors die for their art in this splatter flick about snuff films. 90m/C VHS. Steven Morrison, Dennis Crawford, Lawrence Bornman, Janet Sorley; **D:** Victor Janos. *SUN*

Last House on the Left 🐾🐾 1972 (R) Two girls are kidnapped from a rock concert by a gang of escaped convicts; the girls' parents exact bloody revenge when the guilty parties pay an intended housecall. Controversial and grim low-budget shocker; loosely based on Bergman's "The Virgin Spring." 83m/C VHS, Beta, LV. David Hess, Lucy Grantham, Sandra Cassel, Mark Sheffler, Fred J. Lincoln; **D:** Wes Craven. *LIV, VES, HHE*

The Last Hunt 🐾🐾½ 1956 Well-performed western starring Taylor as a seedy buffalo hunter who gains his identity from senseless acts of murder. When personalities clash, he seeks revenge on fellow buffalo hunter Granger. Shot in Custer National Park, the buffalo scenes were real-life attempts at keeping the animals controlled. Based on the novel by Milton Lott. 108m/C VHS, **Closed Caption.** Robert Taylor, Stewart Granger, Lloyd Nolan, Debra Paget, Russ Tamblyn, Constance Ford, Ainslie Pryor, Ralph Moody, Fred Graham, Dan White, Bill Phillips, Roy Barcroft; **D:** Richard Brooks; **W:** Richard Brooks; **M:** Daniele Amfitheatrof. *MGM*

The Last Hunter 🐾 *Hunter of the Apocalypse* 1980 (R) A soldier fights for his life behind enemy lines during the Vietnam War. 97m/C VHS, Beta. IT Tisa Farrow, David Warbeck, Tony King, Bobby Rhodes, Margit Evelyn Newton, John Steiner, Alan Collins; **D:** Anthony (Antonio Margheriti) Dawson. *LIV, VES*

Last Hurrah 🐾🐾½ 1958 An aging Irish-American mayor battles corruption and political backbiting in his effort to get re-elected for the last time. Semi-acclaimed heart warmer, based on the novel by Edwin O'Connor. 121m/B VHS, Beta, LV. Spencer Tracy, Basil Rathbone, John Carradine, Jeffrey Hunter, Dianne Foster, Pat O'Brien, Edward Brophy, James Gleason, Donald Crisp, Ricardo Cortez, Wallace Ford, Frank McHugh, Jane Darwell; **D:** John Ford. National Board of Review Awards '58: Best Actor (Tracy), Best Director (Ford). *COL*

Last Hurrah for Chivalry 🐾🐾 1978 An honorable man cannot defend his family from a ruthless enemy and turns to two swordsmen-for-hire for help. Chinese with subtitles or dubbed. 108m/C VHS, LV. HK Damian Lau, Wei Pei; **D:** John Woo. *TAI*

The Last Innocent Man 🐾🐾½ 1987 An attorney who quit law due to a guilty conscience is lured into defending a suspected murderer. Things become even more complicated when he begins having an affair with his client's seductive wife. A well-acted and suspense-filled flick. Made for cable television. 113m/C VHS, Beta. Ed Harris, Roxanne Hart, Bruce McGill, Clarence Williams III, Rose Gregorio, David Suchet, Darrell Larson; **D:** Roger Spottiswoode; **W:** Dan Bronson; **M:** Brad Fiedel. *ORI, WAR*

The Last Laugh 🐾🐾🐾½ *Der Letzte Mann* 1924 An elderly man, who as the doorman of a great hotel was looked upon as a symbol of "upper class," is demoted to washroom attendant due to his age. Important due to camera technique and consuming performance by Jannings. Silent with music score. A 91-minute version is also available. 77m/B VHS, Beta. GE Emil Jannings, Maly Delshaft, Max Hiller; **D:** F.W. Murnau. *NOS, FCT, IHF*

Last Light 🐾🐾 1993 (R) A prison guard (Whitaker) on death row forms a tenuous bond with an incorrigible inmate (Sutherland) who's about to be executed. Disturbing, especially the execution scene. Filmed on location at California's Soledad Prison. Sutherland's directorial debut. Made for cable television. **CW:** Strong language, partial nudity, and violence. 95m/C VHS, LV, **Closed Caption.** Kiefer Sutherland, Forest Whitaker, Clancy Brown, Lynne Moody, Kathleen Quinlan, Amanda Plummer; **D:** Kiefer Sutherland. *THV*

The Last Man on Earth 🐾🐾 *L'Ultimo Uomo Della Terra* 1964 Price is the sole survivor of a plague which has turned the rest of the world into vampires, who constantly harass him. Uneven U.S./Italian production manages to convey a creepy atmosphere of dismay. 86m/B VHS. IT Vincent Price, Franca Bettoya, Giacomo "Jack" Rossi-Stuart, Emma Danieli; **D:** Ubaldo Ragona, Sidney Salkow. *SNC, MRV*

Last Man Standing 🐾 1987 (R) A cheap, gritty drama about bare-knuckle fist fighting. Wells stars as a down-on-his-luck prizefighter trying to find work that doesn't involve pugilism. 89m/C VHS, Beta. William Sanderson, Vernon Wells, Franco Columbo; **D:** Damian Lee. *ACA*

Last Man Standing 🐾🐾 1995 (R) L.A. police officer Wincott discovers corruption after his partner Banks is murdered. **CW:** Constant violence; strong language; some sexuality. 96m/C VHS, **Closed Caption.** Jeff Wincott, Jillian McWhirter, Jonathan Banks, Steve Eastin, Jonathan Fuller, Michael Greene, Ava Fabian; **D:** Joseph Merhi; **W:** Joseph Merhi; **M:** Louis Febre. *PMH*

Last Man Standing 🐾🐾½ *Welcome to Jericho* 1996 (R) Engaging, but not terribly original gangster/western features a plot taken from Clint Eastwood's career-making "Fistful of Dollars" (in turn, an adaptation of Akira Kurosawa's "Yojimbo"). The producers and credits claim lineage directly from the Kurosawa film, but this story's been around for a while, folks. In the small 1930s border town of Jericho, Texas, Willis, under the pseudonym John Smith, hires himself out to both sides of a bootlegging war in an effort to make some quick cash. Bigger roles for Walken, the flinty trigger man for Irish boss Doyle (Kelly), and Dern, the town sheriff on the mob payroll, could have perked things up a bit. Willis nicely injects his smirking brand of wit into a film that may have benefitted from more of the dark "Yojimbo" humor. Hill provides his trademark visually exciting action sequences. **CW:** Pervasive strong violence and some sexuality. 101m/C VHS, LV, **Closed Caption.** Bruce Willis, Bruce Dern, Christopher Walken, Karina Lombard, William Sanderson, David Patrick Kelly, Alexandra Powers, Leslie Mann, Michael Imperioli, R.D. Call, Ken Jenkins, Ned Eisenberg; **D:** Walter Hill; **W:** Walter Hill; **C:** Lloyd Ahern; **M:** Ry Cooder. *NLC*

The Last Married Couple in America 🐾🐾 1980 (R) A couple fight to stay happily married amidst the rampant divorce epidemic engulfing their friends. 103m/C VHS, Beta. George Segal, Natalie Wood, Richard Benjamin, Valerie Harper, Dom DeLuise, Priscilla Barnes; **D:** Gilbert Cates; **M:** Charles Fox. *USH*

Last Mercenary woof! 1984 An angry ex-soldier kills everyone who makes him mad. 90m/C VHS, Beta. Tony Marsina, Malcolm Duff, Kitty Nichols, Louis Walser. *NO*

The Last Metro 🐾🐾🐾 *Le Dernier Metro* 1980 Truffaut's alternately gripping and touching drama about a theater company in Nazi-occupied Paris. In 1942, Lucas Steiner (Bennent) is a successful Jewish theater director who is forced into hiding. He turns the running of the theater over to his wife, Marion (the always exquisite Deneuve), who must contend with a pro-Nazi theater critic (Richard) and her growing attraction to the company's leading man (Depardieu), who is secretly working with the Resistance. In French with English subtitles. 135m/C VHS, Beta, LV. FR Catherine Deneuve, Gerard Depardieu, Heinz Bennent, Jean-Louis Richard, Jean Poiret, Andrea Ferreol, Paulette Dubost, Sabine Haudepin; **D:** Francois Truffaut; **W:** Suzanne Schiffman; **C:** Nestor Almendros; **M:** Georges Delerue. Cesar Awards '81: Best Actor (Depardieu), Best Actress (Deneuve), Best Art Direction/Set Decoration, Best Cinematography, Best Director (Truffaut), Best Film, Best Sound, Best Writing, Best Score; Nominations: Academy Awards '80: Best Foreign Language Film. *HMV, FOX, APD*

The Last Mile 🐾🐾 1932 The staff of a prison prepares for the execution of a celebrated murderer. 70m/B VHS, Beta. Preston Foster, Howard Phillips, George E. Stone; **D:** Sam Bischoff. *NOS, MRV, BAR*

The Last Movie 🐾½ *Chinchero* 1971 (R) A movie stunt man stays in a small Peruvian town after his filming stint is over. Hopper's confused, pretentious follow-up to "Easy Rider," has a multitude of cameos but little else. Given an award by the Italians; nobody else understood it. Kristofferson's film debut; he also wrote the music. Based on a story by Hopper and Stern. 108m/C VHS. Dennis Hopper, Julie Adams, Peter Fonda, Kris Kristofferson, Sylvia Miles, John Phillip Law, Russ Tamblyn, Rod Cameron; **D:** Dennis Hopper; **W:** Stewart Stern; **M:** Kris Kristofferson. *NO*

Last Night at the Alamo 🐾🐾🐾 1983 Patrons fight to stop the destruction of their Houston bar, the Alamo, which is about to be razed to make room for a modern skyscraper. Insightful comedy written by the author of "The Texas Chainsaw Massacre." 80m/B VHS. Sonny Carl Davis, Lou Perry, Steve Matilla, Tina Hubbard, Doris Hargrave; **D:** Eagle Pennell; **W:** Ken Henkel; **M:** Wayne Bell. *NO*

The Last of England 🐾🐾🐾½ 1987 A furious non-narrative film by avant-garde filmmaker Jarman, depicting the modern British landscape as a funereal, waste-filled rubble-heap—as depleted morally as it is environmentally. 87m/C VHS, Beta, LV. GB Tilda Swinton, Spencer Leigh; **D:** Derek Jarman. *MFV, TPV*

The Last of His Tribe 🐾🐾 1992 (PG-13) In 1911 an anthropologist befriends an Indian and discovers that Ishi is the last surviving member of California's Yahi tribe. Ishi then becomes a media and scientific society darling, spending the remainder of his remaining life in captivity to academia. A good portrayal of the Native American plight. Based on a true story; made for cable television. 90m/C VHS, LV, **Closed Caption.** Jon Voight, Graham Greene, David Ogden Stiers, Jack Blessing, Anne Archer, Daniel Benzali; **D:** Harry Hook. National Academy of Cable Programming ACE Awards '93: Best Actor (Voight). *WAR*

The Last of Mrs. Cheyney 🐾🐾🐾 1937 Remake of Norma Shearer's 1929 hit, based on the play by Frederick Lonsdale, about a sophisticated jewel thief in England. Crawford stars as the jewel thief who poses as a wealthy woman to get into parties hosted by London bluebloods. Dripping with charm, she works her way into Lord Drilling's mansion where she plans a huge heist. The film is handled well, and the cast gives solid performances throughout. This chic comedy of high society proved to be one of Crawford's most popular films of the '30s. 98m/B VHS, **Closed Caption.** Joan Crawford, Robert Montgomery, William Powell, Frank Morgan, Nigel Bruce, Jessie Ralph; **D:** Richard Boleslawski, George Fitzmaurice. *MGM*

The Last of Mrs. Lincoln 🐾🐾½ 1976 Intimate made for TV portrayal of the famous first lady. Film focuses on Mary Todd Lincoln's life from the assassination of her husband, through her autumn years, and her untimely downfall. 118m/C VHS, Beta. Julie Harris, Robby Benson, Patrick Duffy. *NO*

The Last of Philip Banter 🐾½ 1987 (R) An alcoholic writer is terrified to learn events in his life exactly match a mysterious manuscript. 105m/C VHS. Tony Curtis, Gregg Henry, Irene Miracle, Scott Paulin, Kate Vernon; **D:** Herve Hachuel. *REP*

The Last of Sheila 🎬🎬½ 1973 (PG) A movie producer invites six big-star friends for a cruise aboard his yacht, the "Sheila." He then stages an elaborate "Whodunnit" parlor game to discover which one of them murdered his wife. 119m/C VHS, Beta. Richard Benjamin, James Coburn, James Mason, Dyan Cannon, Joan Hackett, Raquel Welch, Ian McShane; D: Herbert Ross; W: Anthony Perkins, Stephen Sondheim; M: Billy Goldenberg. Edgar Allan Poe Awards '73: Best Screenplay. WAR

Last of the Clintons 🎬½ 1935 A range detective tracks an outlaw gang amid spur jinglin', sharp shootin' and cow punchin'. 64m/B VHS, Beta, LV. Harry Carey Sr. NOS

Last of the Comanches 🎬🎬 The Sabre and the Arrow 1952 Cavalry and Indians fight for water when both are dying of thirst in the desert. 85m/C VHS, Beta. Broderick Crawford, Barbara Hale, John Stewart, Lloyd Bridges, Mickey Shaughnessy, George Mathews; D: Andre de Toth. GKK

The Last of the Dogmen 🎬🎬½ 1995 (PG) Cliched modern western with an intriguing premise and good actors. Montana bounty hunter Lewis Gates (Berenger) is recruited to nab three escaped cons but finds them dead and a Cheyenne arrow nearby. Gates does some investigating (in a library no less!) and discovers that maybe some descendants of the 1864 Sand Creek massacre are existing in the woods. He gets anthropologist Lillian Sloan (Hershey) involved, discovers a tribe of modern-day dog soldiers, and finds a very angry sheriff (Smith) on their trail. Alberta, Canada passes for Big Sky country. 117m/C VHS. Tom Berenger, Barbara Hershey, Kurtwood Smith, Steve Reevis, Andrew Miller, Gregory Scott Cummins; D: Tab Murphy; W: Tab Murphy; C: Karl Walter Lindenlaub; M: David Arnold. HBO

The Last of the Finest 🎬½ Street Legal; Blue Heat 1990 (R) Overzealous anti-drug task force cops break the rules in trying to put dealer-drug lords in prison; ostensibly a parallel on the Iran-Contra affair. 106m/C VHS, Beta, LV, Closed Caption. Brian Dennehy, Joe Pantoliano, Jeff Fahey, Bill Paxton, Deborra-Lee Furness, Guy Boyd, Henry Darrow, Lisa Jane Persky, Michael C. Gwynne; D: John MacKenzie; W: George Armitage, Jere P. Cunningham; M: Jack Nitzsche. ORI

The Last of the Mohicans 🎬🎬🎬 1920 Color tints enhance this silent version of the James Fenimore Cooper rouser. Beery is the villanious Magua, with Bedford memorable as the lovely Cora and Roscoe as the brave Uncas. Fine action sequences, including the Huron massacre at Fort Henry. Director credit was shared when Tourneur suffered an on-set injury and was off for 3 months. 75m/B VHS, LV. Wallace Beery, Barbara Bedford, Albert Roscoe, Lillian Hall-Davis, Henry Woodward, James Gordon, George Hackathorne, Harry Lorraine, Nelson McDowell, Theodore Lorch, Boris Karloff; D: Maurice Tourneur, Clarence Brown; W: Robert Dillon. LUM, FCT, MIL

The Last of the Mohicans 1932 Serial based on James Fenimore Cooper's novel of the life-and-death struggle of the Mohican Indians during the French and Indian War. Twelve chapters, 13 minutes each. Remade as a movie in 1936 and 1992 and as a television movie in 1977. 230m/B VHS, Beta. Edwina Booth, Harry Carey Sr., Hobart Bosworth, Frank "Junior" Coghlan; D: Ford Beebe, B. Reeves Eason. VYY, VCN, NOS

The Last of the Mohicans 🎬🎬½ 1936 James Fenimore Cooper's classic about the French and Indian War in colonial America is brought to the screen. Remake of the 1932 serial was remade itself in 1977 for television. 91m/B VHS, Beta. Randolph Scott, Binnie Barnes, Bruce Cabot, Henry Wilcoxon, Heather Angel, Hugh Buckler; D: George B. Seitz. LIV, MED, CCB

The Last of the Mohicans 🎬🎬 1985 The classic novel by James Fenimore Cooper about the scout Hawkeye and his Mohican companions, Chingachgook and Uncas during the French and Indian war, comes to life in this made-for-television film. Remake of a 1932 serial and a 1936 film. 97m/C VHS, Beta. Steve Forrest, Ned Romero, Andrew Prine, Don Shanks, Robert Tessier, Jane Actman; D: James L. Conway. VCI

The Last of the Mohicans 🎬🎬🎬 1992 (R) It's 1757, at the height of the French and English war in the American colonies, with various Native American tribes allied to each side. Hawkeye (Day-Lewis), a white frontiersman raised by the Mohicans, wants nothing to do with either "civilized" side, until he rescues the beautiful Cora (Stowe) from the revenge-minded Huron Magua (Studi in a powerful performance). Graphically violent battle scenes are realistic, but not gratuitous. The real pleasure in this adaptation, which draws from both the James Fenimore Cooper novel and the 1936 film, is in its lush look and attractive stars. Means is terrific in his film debut as Hawkeye's foster-father. Released in a letterbox format to preserve the original integrity of the film. CW: Violence. 114m/C VHS, LV. Daniel Day-Lewis, Madeleine Stowe, Wes Studi, Russell Means, Eric Schweig, Jodhi May, Steven Waddington, Maurice Roeves, Colm Meaney, Patrice Chereau; D: Michael Mann; W: Christopher Crowe, Michael Mann; C: Dante Spinotti; M: Trevor Jones, Randy Edelman. Academy Awards '92: Best Sound. FXV, BTV

Last of the Pony Riders 🎬½ 1953 When the telegraph lines linking the East and West Coasts are completed, Gene and the other Pony Express riders find themselves out of a job. Autry's final feature film. 59m/B VHS, Beta. Gene Autry, Smiley Burnette, Kathleen Case; D: George Archainbaud. CCB

Last of the Red Hot Lovers 🎬½ 1972 (PG) Not so funny adaptation of Neil Simon's Broadway hit. Middle-aged man decides to have a fling and uses his mother's apartment to seduce three very strange women. 98m/C VHS, Beta, LV. Alan Arkin, Paula Prentiss, Sally Kellerman, Renee Taylor; D: Gene Saks; W: Neil Simon. PAR

The Last of the Redmen 🎬½ 1947 An adaptation of James Fenimore Cooper's "The Last of the Mohicans" geared toward youngsters. Hall must lead three children of a British general through dangerous Indian territory. They have a number of adventures including meeting up with Uncas, the last of the Mohicans, who's a villain in this mangled version. 79m/B VHS. Jon Hall, Michael O'Shea, Evelyn Ankers, Julie Bishop, Buster Crabbe, Rick Vallin, Frederick Worlock, Guy Hedlund; D: George Sherman; W: Herbert Dalmas. COL

Last of the Warrens 🎬 1936 A cowboy returns home after WWI to discover that an unscrupulous storekeeper has stolen his property. 56m/C VHS, Beta. Bob Steele, Charles "Blackie" King, Lafe McKee, Margaret Marquis, Horace Murphy; D: Robert North Bradbury. NOS, DVT, GPV

Last of the Wild Horses 🎬½ 1949 Range war almost starts when ranch owner is accused of trying to force the small ranchers out of business. 86m/B VHS, Beta. Mary Beth Hughes, James Ellison, Jane Frazee. NO

The Last Outlaw 🎬🎬 1927 Action-packed western with Cooper following his success of "Wings" with Paramount. Most excellent equine stunts. 61m/B VHS, Beta. Gary Cooper, Jack Luden, Betty Jewel; D: Arthur Rosson. GPV, FCT

Last Outlaw 🎬🎬 1936 The last of the famous badmen of the old West is released from jail and returns home to find that times have changed. The action climaxes in an old-time blazing shoot-out. 79m/B VHS, Beta. Harry Carey Sr., Hoot Gibson, Henry B. Walthall, Tom Tyler, Russell Hopton, Alan Curtis, Harry Woods, Barbara Pepper; D: Christy Cabanne. VCN

The Last Outlaw 🎬🎬½ 1993 (R) Rourke stars as an ex-Confederate officer who leads a gang of outlaws until his violent excesses leave even them disgusted. The gang shoots Rourke but of course he doesn't die and then he sets out for revenge. Made for cable television. 90m/C VHS. Mickey Rourke, Dermot Mulroney, Ted Levine, John C. McGinley, Steve Buscemi, Keith David; D: Geoff Murphy; W: Eric Red. HBO, FCT

The Last Picture Show 🎬🎬🎬🎬 1971 (R) Slice of life/nostalgic farewell to an innocent age, based on Larry McMurtry's novel. Set in Archer City, a backwater Texas town, most of the story plays out at the local hangout run by ex-cowboy Sam the Lion. Bridges is hooked up with spoiled pretty girl Shepherd, while Bottoms, a sensitive guy, is having an affair with the coach's neglected wife (Leachman). Loss of innocence, disillusionment and confusion are played out against the backdrop of a town about to close its cinema. Shepherd's and Bottoms' film debut. Stunningly photographed in black and white (Bogdanovich claimed he didn't want to "prettify" the picture by shooting in color) by Robert Surtees. Available in a laserdisc special edition with 17 minutes restored. Followed by a weak sequel, "Texasville." A boxed set featuring both films is also available. CW: Language, nudity, and sexuality. 118m/B VHS, LV, 8mm, Closed Caption. Jeff Bridges, Timothy Bottoms, Ben Johnson, Cloris Leachman, Cybill Shepherd, Ellen Burstyn, Eileen Brennan, Clu Gulager, Sharon Taggart, Randy Quaid, Sam Bottoms, John Hillerman; D: Peter Bogdanovich; W: Larry McMurtry, Peter Bogdanovich; C: Robert L. Surtees. Academy Awards '71: Best Supporting Actor (Johnson), Best Supporting Actress (Leachman); British Academy Awards '72: Best Screenplay, Best Supporting Actor (Johnson), Best Supporting Actress (Leachman); Golden Globe Awards '72: Best Supporting Actor (Johnson); National Board of Review Awards '71: Best Supporting Actor (Johnson), Best Supporting Actress (Leachman); New York Film Critics Awards '71: Best Screenplay, Best Supporting Actor (Johnson), Best Supporting Actress (Burstyn); National Society of Film Critics Awards '71: Best Supporting Actress (Burstyn); Nominations: Academy Awards '71: Best Adapted Screenplay, Best Cinematography, Best Director (Bogdanovich), Best Picture, Best Supporting Actor (Bridges), Best Supporting Actress (Burstyn). COL, CRC, FCT

The Last Place on Earth 1994 Saga of bitter hardship and ambition depicting the 1911 race between the British Antarctic Expedition, led by Captain Robert Falcon (Shaw), and his Norwegian rival Roald Amundsen (Ousdal) to conquer the South Pole. On 7 cassettes. 385m/C VHS. CA Martin Shaw, Sverre Anker Ousdal, Max von Sydow, Susan Wooldridge. TVC, VCO

Last Plane Out 🎬½ 1983 (R) A Texas journalist sent out on assignment to Nicaragua falls in love with a Sandanista rebel. Based on producer Jack Cox's real-life experiences as a journalist during the last days of the Samosa regime. Low-budget propaganda. 90m/C VHS, Beta, Closed Caption. Jan-Michael Vincent, Lloyd Batista, Julie Carmen, Mary Crosby, David Huffman, William Windom; D: David Nelson. VTR, FOX

The Last Polka 🎬🎬🎬 1984 SCTV vets Candy and Levy are Yosh and Stan Schmenge, polka kings interviewed for a "documentary" on their years in the spotlight and on the road. Hilarious spoof on Martin Scorsese's "The Last Waltz," about The Band's last concert. Several fellow Second City-ers keep the laughs coming. If you liked SCTV or "This is Spinal Tap," you'll like this. Made for cable (HBO). 54m/C VHS, Beta. John Candy, Eugene Levy, Rick Moranis, Robin Duke, Catherine O'Hara; D: John Blanchard. LIV, VES

The Last Porno Flick 🎬 1974 (PG) A pornographic movie script winds up in the hands of a couple of goofy cab drivers. The twosome sneak the movie's genre past the producers, families, and police. 90m/C VHS. Michael Pataki, Marianna Hill, Carmen Zapata, Mike Kellin, Colleen Camp, Tom Signorelli, Antony Carbone; D: Ray Marsh. NO

The Last Prostitute 🎬🎬 1991 (PG-13) Two teenage boys search for a legendary prostitute to initiate them into manhood, only to discover that she has retired. They hire on as laborers on her horse farm, and one of them discovers the meaning of love. Made for cable TV. 93m/C VHS.

Sonia Braga, Wil Wheaton, David Kaufman, Woody Watson, Dennis Letts, Cotter Smith; **D:** Lou Antonio; **W:** Carmen Culver. *USH*

The Last Remake of Beau Geste

🐾🐾 **1977 (PG)** A slapstick parody of the familiar Foreign Legion story from the Mel Brooksish school of loud genre farce. Gary Cooper makes an appearance by way of inserted footage from the 1939 straight version. 85m/C VHS, Beta. Marty Feldman, Ann-Margret, Michael York, James Earl Jones; **D:** Marty Feldman; **W:** Marty Feldman, Chris Allen. *USH*

Last Resort

🐾🐾 *She Knew No Other Way* **1986 (R)** A married furniture executive unknowingly takes his family on vacation to a sex-saturated, Club Med-type holiday spot, and gets more than he anticipated.**CW:** Language, violence, and graphic sensuality. 80m/C VHS, Beta, LV. Charles Grodin, Jon Lovitz; **D:** Zane Buzby; **W:** Jeff Buhai. *LIV, VES*

The Last Reunion

🐾½ **1980** The only witness to a brutal killing of a Japanese official and his wife during WWII seeks revenge on the guilty American platoon, thirty-three years later. Violent. 98m/C VHS. Cameron Mitchell, Leo Fong, Chanda Romero, Vic Silayan, Hal Bokar, Philip Baker Hall; **D:** Jay Wertz. *SNC*

The Last Ride

🐾 **1991** Another movie probing the dark side of hitchhiking. This time our hero thumbs a ride with a truck driver who plans to bypass the next city...for hell. 84m/C VHS. Dan Ranger, Michael Hilow. *AIP*

The Last Ride

🐾🐾 *F.T.W* **1994 (R)** Frank T. Wells (Rourke) is out of prison after 10 years and free to try to recapture his former rodeo glory. Hellcat Scarlett Stuart's on the run from a botched bank job/murder perpetrated by her vicious brother Clem (Berg). Scarlett manages to hook up with Frank and decides to help him out financially by robbing convenience stores. Frank's not too happy when he finds out. Rourke is surprisingly subdued and Singer's properly unsympathetic but they don't seem to be working in the same movie. Nice Montana scenery though. 102m/C VHS, Closed Caption. Mickey Rourke, Lori Singer, Brion James, Peter Berg, Rodney Grant, Aaron Neville; **D:** Michael Karbelnikoff; **W:** Mari Kornhauser; **C:** James L. Carter; **M:** Gary Chang. *HMK*

The Last Ride of the Dalton Gang

🐾🐾 **1979** A long-winded retelling of the wild adventures that made the Dalton gang legendary among outlaws. 146m/C VHS, Beta. Larry Wilcox, Jack Palance, Randy Quaid, Cliff Potts, Dale Robertson, Don Collier; **D:** Dan Curtis. *WAR, OM*

The Last Riders

🐾 **1990 (R)** Motorcycle centaur Estrada revs a few motors fleeing from cycle club cronies and crooked cops. Full throttle foolishness. 90m/C VHS, LV. Erik Estrada, William Smith, Armando Silvestre, Kathrin Lautner; **D:** Joseph Merhi. *PMH, HHE*

Last Rites

🐾🐾 **1988 (R)** A priest at St. Patrick's Cathedral in New York allows a young Mexican woman to seek sanctuary from the Mob, who soon come after both of them. 103m/C VHS, Beta, LV, Closed Caption. Tom Berenger, Daphne Zuniga, Chick Vennera, Dane Clark, Carlo Pacchi, Anne Twomey, Paul Dooley, Vassili Lambrinos; **D:** Donald P. Bellisario; **W:** Donald P. Bellisario; **C:** David Watkin; **M:** Bruce Broughton. *FOX*

The Last Safari

🐾🐾½ **1967** A young man on safari in Africa befriends a bitter professional guide in a drama hampered by a poor script. Granger and Garas set out to hunt the rampaging elephant which killed Granger's friend. Granger thinks killing the beast will restore his courage and help him overcome the guilt he feels. Based on the novel "Gilligan's Last Elephant" by Gerald Hanley. 111m/C VHS, Closed Caption. Stewart Granger, Kaz Garas, Gabriella Licudi, Johnny Sekka, Liam Redmond; **D:** Henry Hathaway; **W:** John Gay; **C:** Ted Moore. *PAR*

The Last Samurai

🐾 **1990 (R)** Arab arms dealer Saxon arranges a fake kidnapping by rebel military leader Cele in order to keep their weapons deal a secret. But among the other hostages is mercenary Hendricksen, who escapes and wrecks havoc on their plotting.**CW:** Violence, language, and some nudity. 94m/C VHS. Lance Henriksen, John Saxon, Henry Cele, Arabella Holzbog, John Fujioka, James Ryan, Duncan Regehr, Lisa Eilbacher; **D:** Paul Mayersberg. *AVI*

The Last Season

woof! **1987** Shoot 'em up involving a bunch of hunters. Their aimless destruction provokes the good guy to save the forest they are demolishing. A battle ensues. 90m/C VHS. Christopher Gosch, Louise Dorsey, David Cox; **D:** Raja Zahr. *NO*

The Last Seduction

🐾🐾🐾🐾 **1994 (R)** Dahl, the master of modern noir, delivers another stylish hit exploring the darker side of urban life. Fiorentino gives the performance of her life as the most evil, rotten femme fatale to ever hit the big screen. Bridget (Fiorentino) rips off the money her husband Clay (Pullman) made in a pharmaceutical drug deal and leaves Manhattan for a small town in Upstate New York. Once there, she takes nice, naive Mike (Berg) as her lover, while Clay tries to ferret her out and get his money back. Lots of dry humor and a wickedly amusing heroine make for a devilishly entertaining film.**CW:** Language; nudity; sexual situations; violence. 110m/C VHS, LV, Closed Caption. Linda Fiorentino, Peter Berg, J.T. Walsh, Bill Nunn, Bill Pullman; **D:** John Dahl; **W:** Steve Barancik; **M:** Joseph Vitarelli. Independent Spirit Awards '95: Best Actress (Fiorentino); New York Film Critics Awards '94: Best Actress (Fiorentino). *PGV*

The Last Slumber Party

woof! **1987** A slumber party is beset by a homicidal maniac. Heavy metal soundtrack. 89m/C VHS, Beta. Jan Jensen, Nancy Meyer. *VCI*

Last Song

🐾½ **1980 (PG)** A singer's husband discovers a plot to cover up a fatal toxic-waste accident, and is killed because of it. It's up to her to warn the authorities before becoming the next victim. 96m/C VHS, Beta, Closed Caption. Lynda Carter, Ronny Cox, Nicholas Pryor, Paul Rudd, Jenny O'Hara; **D:** Alan J. Levi. *FOX*

Last Stand at Saber River

🐾🐾½ **1996** Cable adaptation of Elmore Leonard's 1959 western novel finds Confederate Civil War vet Paul Cable (Selleck) coming home to his wife Martha's (Amis) family in Texas, having been wounded in the fighting. However, Martha was informed he was dead, so imagine her surprise. What Cable wants to do now is return to his prewar life—a horse ranch in Arizona—but after making the journey the family discovers their ranch has been taken over by Union sympathizer Duane Kidston (Carradine) and he's not intending to let it go. Selleck was born to ride tall in the saddle. 95m/C VHS, Closed Caption. Tom Selleck, Suzy Amis, David Carradine, Keith Carradine, David Dukes, Tracey Needham, Rachel Duncan, Haley Joel Osment, Harry Carey Jr., Lumi Cavazos, Patrick Kilpatrick; **D:** Dick Lowry; **W:** Ronald M. Cohen; **C:** Ric Waite; **M:** David Shire. *WAR*

The Last Starfighter

🐾🐾 **1984 (PG)** A young man who becomes an expert at a video game is recruited to fight in an inter-galactic war. Listless adventure which makes all those video games come from. Watch for O'Herlihy disguised as a lizard. 100m/C VHS, Beta, LV. Lance Guest, Robert Preston, Barbara Bosson, Dan O'Herlihy, Catherine Mary Stewart, Cameron Dye, Kimberly Ross, Wil Wheaton; **D:** Nick Castle; **W:** Jonathan Betuel. *USH*

Last Summer

🐾🐾½ **1969 (R)** Three teenagers discover love, sex, and friendship on the white sands of Fire Island, N.Y. The summer vacation fantasy world they create shatters when a sweet but homely female teenager joins their group. Based on a novel by Evan Hunter. 97m/C VHS, Beta. Barbara Hershey, Richard Thomas, Bruce Davison, Cathy Burns; **D:** Frank Perry. Nominations: Academy Awards '69: Best Supporting Actress (Burns). *FOX*

Last Summer In the Hamptons

🐾🐾🐾½ **1996 (R)** In her last film, Lindfors stars as Helena Mora, the matriarch of a charming three generation theatrical clan that gets together one weekend a year at her spacious, slightly run-down estate to participate in drama workshops and perform plays. When Helena is forced to sell the estate, the family reunites for one last weekend of bickering and performing. Featuring fine performances from the entire ensemble (including Lindfors' son and Jaglom's wife), Jaglom's touching and engaging tribute to his family gives nepotism a good name.**CW:** Mature language. 105m/C VHS. Victoria Foyt, Viveca Lindfors, Jon Robin Baitz, Andre Gregory, Melissa Leo, Martha Plimpton, Roddy McDowall, Nick Gregory, Savannah Smith Boucher, Roscoe Lee Browne, Ron Rifkin, Diane Salinger, Brooke Smith, Kristopher Tabori, Holland Taylor, Henry Jaglom; **D:** Henry Jaglom; **W:** Victoria Foyt, Henry Jaglom; **C:** Hanania Baer; **M:** Johnny Mercer, Harold Arlen. *NYR*

The Last Supper

🐾🐾🐾 **1976** A repentant Cuban slave-owner in the 18th-century decides to cleanse his soul and convert his slaves to Christianity by having twelve of them reenact the Last Supper. Based on a true story. In Spanish with English subtitles. 110m/C VHS, Beta. CU Nelson Villagra, Silvano Rey, Lamberto Garcia, Jose Antonio Rodriguez, Samuel Claxton, Mario Balmasada; **D:** Tomas Gutierrez Alea. *NYF, FCT*

The Last Supper

🐾🐾½ **1996 (R)** First-time feature director Title dishes out an extremely black comedy about a group of liberal roommates who accidentally kill a racist marine they've invited to dinner. This leads to the devious plan of inviting more right wingers over, baiting them into arguments about controversial topics, then killing and burying them in a vegetable garden. Somehow manages to avoid excessive preachiness despite taking on all political comers. Not exactly a great feast, but there's enough tasty snacks to be satisfying. Performances are good and the victims (led by Perlman's Limbaugh turn) really shine. Too bad their characters aren't on screen very long before they become tomato fertilizer.**CW:** Violence, profanity and sexual situations. 91m/C VHS, LV, Closed Caption. Cameron Diaz, Annabeth Gish, Ron Eldard, Jonathan Penner, Courtney B. Vance; **Cameos:** Ron Perlman, Jason Alexander, Charles Durning, Mark Harmon, Bill Paxton; **D:** Stacy Title; **W:** Dan Rosen; **C:** Paul Cameron; **M:** Mark Mothersbaugh. *COL*

Last Tango in Paris

🐾🐾🐾½ **1973 (R)** Brando plays a middle-aged American who meets a French girl and tries to forget his wife's suicide with a short, extremely steamy affair. Bertolucci proves to be a master; Brando gives one of his best performances. Very controversial when made, still quite explicit. Visually stunning. The X-rated version, at 130 minutes, is also available. 126m/C VHS, Beta, LV. IT FR Marlon Brando, Maria Schneider, Jean-Pierre Leaud; **D:** Bernardo Bertolucci; **W:** Bernardo Bertolucci; **C:** Vittorio Storaro; **M:** Gato Barbieri. New York Film Critics Awards '73: Best Actor (Brando); National Society of Film Critics Awards '73: Best Actor (Brando); Nominations: Academy Awards '73: Best Actor (Brando), Best Director (Bertolucci).*MGM, FOX*

The Last Temptation of Christ

🐾🐾🐾½ **1988 (R)** Scorsese's controversial adaptation of the Nikos Kazantzakis novel, portraying Christ in his last year as an ordinary Israelite tormented by divine doubt, human desires and the voice of God. The controversy engulfing the film, as it was heavily protested and widely banned, tended to divert attention from what is an exceptional statement of religious and artistic vision. Excellent score by Peter Gabriel. 164m/C VHS, Beta, LV. Willem Dafoe, Harvey Keitel, Barbara Hershey, Harry Dean Stanton, Andre Gregory, David Bowie, Verna Bloom, Juliette Caton, John Lurie, Roberts Blossom, Irvin Kershner, Barry Miller, Tomas Arana, Nehemiah Persoff, Paul Herman; **D:** Martin Scorsese; **W:** Paul Schrader; **C:** Michael Ballhaus; **M:** Peter Gabriel. Nominations: Academy Awards '88: Best Director (Scorsese).*USH*

The Last Time I Committed Suicide ⚐⚐ 1996 (R) Based on a Beat-era letter from Neal Cassady to Jack Kerouac and set in the late '40s, this insubstantial pic follows a 20-year-old Cassady (Jane) as he drifts into Denver's bars, and a friendship with poolhall regular Harry (Reeves), in order to escape dealing with girlfriend Joan's (Forlani) attempted suicide. Joan's eventual recovery leads Neal to consider settling down but he blows a job interview thanks to a drunken Harry and decides to take off instead. No background is provided on the characters so their actions are inexplicable although Jane offers some appeal. 93m/C VHS, Closed Caption. Thomas Jane, Keanu Reeves, Tom Bower, Adrien Brody, Claire Forlani, Marg Helgenberger, Gretchen Mol; **D:** Stephen Kay; **W:** Stephen Kay; **C:** Bobby Bukowski. USH

The Last Time I Saw Paris ⚐⚐½ 1954 A successful writer reminisces about his love affair with a wealthy American girl in post-WWII Paris. 116m/C VHS, Beta, LV. Elizabeth Taylor, Van Johnson, Walter Pidgeon, Roger Moore, Donna Reed, Eva Gabor; **D:** Richard Brooks; **W:** Richard Brooks, Julius J. Epstein, Philip C. Epstein; **C:** Joseph Ruttenberg. MGM, MRV, NOS

Last Time Out ⚐⚐½ 1994 (PG-13) Danny Dolan (Conrad) is a hard-partying college wide receiver who gets a shock when the father who abandoned him enrolls at his school to finish a college degree. Seems Joe (Beck) had his pro quarterback career cut short by a drinking problem and he's worried his son will follow in his unsteady footsteps. **CW:** Mature themes; mild violence; drug content. 92m/C VHS, LV, Closed Caption. John Beck, Christian Conrad, Lori Werner, Gail Strickland, Betty Buckley; **D:** Don Fox Greene. IMP

The Last Tomahawk ⚐⚐ 1965 Colorful and action packed reworking of Cooper's "Last of the Mohicans." ?m/C VHS. GE IT Anthony Steffen, Karin Dor, Dan Martin, Joachim Fuchsberger. SNC

The Last Train 1974 Romance most hopeless in the heart of France during zee beeg war. During the 1940 invasion of Paris a man and woman turn to each other for comfort when separated from their families while trying to escape the city. French, very French. 101m/C VHS. FR Romy Schneider, Jean-Louis Trintignant, Maurice Biraud; **D:** Pierre Granier-Deferre. NO

Last Train from Gun Hill ⚐⚐⚐ 1959 An all-star cast highlights this suspenseful story of a U.S. marshall determined to catch the man who raped and murdered his wife. Excellent action packed western. 94m/C VHS. Kirk Douglas, Anthony Quinn, Carolyn Jones, Earl Holliman, Brad Dexter, Brian Hutton, Ziva Rodann; **D:** John Sturges; **C:** Charles B(ryant) Lang. NO

The Last Tycoon ⚐⚐⚐ 1976 (PG) An adaptation of the unfinished F. Scott Fitzgerald novel about the life and times of a Hollywood movie executive of the 1920s. Confusing and slow moving despite a blockbuster conglomeration of talent. Joan Collins introduces the film. 123m/C VHS, Beta, LV. Robert De Niro, Tony Curtis, Ingrid Boulting, Jack Nicholson, Jeanne Moreau, Peter Strauss, Robert Mitchum, Theresa Russell, Donald Pleasence, Ray Milland, Dana Andrews, John Carradine, Anjelica Huston; **D:** Elia Kazan; **W:** Harold Pinter; **M:** Maurice Jarre. National Board of Review Awards '76: 10 Best Films of the Year; Nominations: Academy Awards '76: Best Art Direction/Set Decoration. PAR, FCT

The Last Unicorn ⚐⚐½ 1982 (G) Peter Beagle's popular tale of a beautiful unicorn who goes in search of her lost, mythical "family." 95m/C VHS, Beta, LV, Closed Caption. **D:** Jules Bass; **W:** Peter S. Beagle; **M:** Jim Webb; **V:** Alan Arkin, Jeff Bridges, Tammy Grimes, Angela Lansbury, Mia Farrow, Robert Klein, Christopher Lee, Keenan Wynn. FOX, KAR, LIV

The Last Valley ⚐⚐ 1971 (PG) A scholar tries to protect a pristine 17th century Swiss valley, untouched by the Thirty Years War, from marauding soldiers. Historical action with an intellectual twist. 128m/C VHS. Michael Caine, Omar Sharif, Florinda Bolkan, Nigel Davenport, Per Oscarsson, Arthur

O'Connell; **D:** James Clavell; **W:** James Clavell; **M:** John Barry. NO

The Last Voyage ⚐⚐½ 1960 Suspenseful disaster film in which Stack and Malone play a married couple in jeopardy while on an ocean cruise. To make the film more realistic, the French liner Ile de France was actually used in the sinking scenes. Although a bit farfetched, film is made watchable because of fine performances and excellent camerawork. 91m/C VHS, LV, Closed Caption. Robert Stack, Dorothy Malone, George Sanders, Edmond O'Brien, Woody Strode, Jack Kruschen; **D:** Andrew L. Stone; **W:** Andrew L. Stone; **C:** Hal Mohr. MGM

The Last Waltz ⚐⚐ 1978 (PG) Martin Scorsese filmed this rock documentary featuring the farewell performance of The Band, joined by a host of musical guests that they have been associated with over the years. Songs include: "Up On Cripple Creek," "Don't Do It," "The Night They Drove Old Dixie Down," "Stage Fright" (The Band), "Helpless" (Young), "Coyote" (Mitchell), "Caravan" (Morrison), "Further On Up the Road" (Clapton), "Who Do You Love" (Hawkins), "Mannish Boy" (Waters), "Evangeline" (Harris), "Baby, Let Me Follow You Down" (Dylan). 117m/C VHS, Beta, LV, Closed Caption. **D:** Martin Scorsese; **C:** Michael Chapman. MVD, MGM

Last War ⚐ 1968 A nuclear war between the United States and Russia triggers Armageddon. 79m/C VHS, Beta. Frankie Sakai, Nobuko Otowa, Akira Takarada, Yuriko Hoshi; **D:** Shue Matsubayashi. GEM

The Last Warrior ⚐½ Coastwatcher 1989 (R) A good-looking but exploitive "Hell in the Pacific" rip-off, as an American and a Japanese soldier battle it out alone on a remote island during WWII. 94m/C VHS, Beta, LV. Gary Graham, Cary-Hiroyuki Tagawa, Maria Holvoe; **D:** Martin Wragge. COL

The Last Wave ⚐⚐⚐ 1977 (PG) An Australian attorney takes on a murder case involving an aborigine and he finds himself becoming distracted by apocalyptic visions concerning tidal waves and drownings that seem to foretell the future. Weir's masterful creation and communication of time and place are marred by a somewhat pat ending. 109m/C VHS, Beta. AU Richard Chamberlain, Olivia Hamnett, David Gulpilil, Frederick Parslow; **D:** Peter Weir; **W:** Peter Weir; **C:** Russell Boyd. FCT, RHI

The Last Winter ⚐⚐ 1984 (R) An American woman fights to find her Israeli husband who has disappeared in the 1973 Yom Kippur War. Trouble is, an Israeli woman thinks the man she's looking for is really her husband too. 92m/C VHS, Beta. IS Kathleen Quinlan, Yona Elian, Zipora Peled, Michael Schnider; **D:** Riki Shelach. COL

The Last Winter ⚐⚐ 1989 (PG) Ten-year-old Will (Murray) has always lived in the country and finds it hard to accept his parents' decision to move to the city. But with the help of his grandfather (Parkes), Will begins to understand about change and growing up. 103m/C VHS, Closed Caption. CA Joshua Murray, Gerard Parkes, David Ferry, Wanda Cannon, Marsha Moreau, Nathaniel Moreau, Katie Murray; **D:** Aaron Kim Johnston; **W:** Aaron Kim Johnston; **C:** Ian Elkin; **M:** Victor Davies. FXV

The Last Winters ⚐⚐½ 1971 From Jean Charles Tacchella, writer-producer-director of "Cousin Cousine," comes his first short film about an old couple's bittersweet romance. In French with English subtitles. 23m/C VHS, Beta. FR **D:** Jean-Charles Tacchella. INT, MTI

Last Witness ⚐ 1988 A man on the run from the government claims that he is innocent and was unjustly persecuted, but the government sees him as a dangerous threat. Nothing will stop the hunt for the escaped man, no matter what it costs. 85m/C VHS, Beta. Jeff Henderson. TWE

The Last Woman on Earth woof! 1961 Two men vie for the affections of the sole surviving woman after a vague and unexplained disaster of vast proportions. Robert Towne, who appears herein under the pseudonym Edward Wain, wrote the script (his first screenwriting ef-

fort). You might want to watch this if it were the last movie on earth, although Corman fans will probably love it. 71m/C VHS. Antony Carbone, Edward Wain, Betsy Jones-Moreland; **D:** Roger Corman; **W:** Robert Towne. NOS, MRV, SNC

The Last Word ⚐⚐ Danny Travis 1980 (PG) Comedy drama about struggling inventor Harris fighting to protect his home, family, and neighbors from a corrupt real estate deal involving shady politicians, angry policemen, and a beautiful television reporter. 103m/C VHS, Beta. Richard Harris, Karen Black, Martin Landau, Dennis Christopher, Bill McGuire, Christopher Guest, Penelope Milford, Michael Pataki; **W:** Michael Varhol, L.M. Kit Carson.

The Last Word ⚐⚐ 1995 (R) Journalist Martin (Hutton) writes a newspaper column, often featuring characters based on hometown Detroit mob figures, with info supplied to him by his friend, Doc (Pantoliano), who owes the gangsters some big bucks. Doc also introduces Martin to his latest column subject—stripper Caprice (Burke)—and, thanks again to Doc, a Hollywood studio gets interested in filming her story but wants more sex and violence, which means Martin will be betraying her deepest secrets. Now, he must choose between love, success, or friendship. **CW:** Language, sexuality and some violent images. 95m/C VHS. Timothy Hutton, Joe Pantoliano, Michelle Burke, Chazz Palminteri, Tony Goldwyn; **Cameos:** Richard Dreyfuss, Cybill Shepherd, Jimmy Smits; **D:** Tony Spiridakis. THV

Last Year at Marienbad ⚐⚐⚐ L'Anee Derniere a Marienbad 1961 A young man tries to lure a mysterious woman to run away with him from a hotel in France. Once a hit on the artsy circuit, it's most interesting for its beautiful photography. In French with English subtitles. 93m/B VHS, Beta, 8mm. FR IT Delphine Seyrig, Giorgia Albertazzi, Sacha Pitoeff, Luce Garcia-Ville; **D:** Alain Resnais; **C:** Sacha Vierny. Nominations: Academy Awards '62: Best Story & Screenplay. VYY, MRV, NOS

L'Atalante ⚐⚐⚐½ 1934 Vigo's great masterpiece, a slight story about a husband and wife quarreling, splitting, and reuniting around which has been fashioned one of the cinema's greatest poetic films. In French with English subtitles. 82m/B VHS, Beta. FR Dita Parlo, Jean Daste, Michel Simon; **D:** Jean Vigo. NOS, HHT, PMS

Late Chrysanthemums ⚐⚐ Bangiku 1954 A middle-aged geisha has settled into comfortable retirement as a money lender. When she hears a former lover wants to visit her, she tries to recapture her old glamour only to be disillusioned. Based on a short story by Fumiko Hayashi. In Japanese with English subtitles. 101m/B VHS. JP Haruko Sugimura, Chikako Hosokawa, Sadako Sawahura; **D:** Mikio Naruse. WAC

Late Extra ⚐⚐ 1935 A novice reporter attempts to track down a notorious bank robber and gets some help from a savvy female journalist. Mason's first role of substance. 69m/B VHS, Beta. GB Virginia Cherrill, James Mason, Alastair Sim, Ian Colin, Clifford McLaglen, Cyril Cusack, David Horne, Antoinette Cellier, Donald Wolfit, Michael Wilding; **D:** Albert Parker. SNC

Late for Dinner ⚐⚐ 1991 (PG) In 1962 Willie, a young, married man, and his best friend Frank are framed by a sleazy land developer. On the run, the two decide to become guinea pigs in a cryonics experiment and wind up frozen for 29 years. It's now 1991 and Willie wakes to find his family—only his wife is middle-aged and his daughter is all grown-up. Can he make a life with them again or has time indeed passed him by? 93m/C VHS, LV. Brian Wimmer, Peter Berg, Marcia Gay Harden, Peter Gallagher, Ross Malinger; **D:** W.D. Richter; **W:** Mark Andrus. COL, NLC

The Late Shift ⚐⚐½ 1996 (R) Cable adaptation of Bill Carter's book chronicling the follies surrounding NBC's "The Tonight Show" succession battle between Jay Leno (Roebuck) and Dave Letterman (Higgins). It's the behind-the-scenes dealmakers that really steal the show, however, including Jay's profane manager Helen Kushnick (Bates) and superagent Michael Ovitz (Williams), who ultimately orchestrated Dave's move to rival CBS. Both Letterman and Leno made the movie/book fodder for their opening monlogues. **CW:** Language. **96m/C VHS.** Daniel Roebuck, John Michael Higgins, Kathy Bates, Treat Williams, Bob Balaban, Ed Begley Jr., Rich Little, Sandra Bernhard, Peter Jurasik, Reni Santoni, John Kapelos, John Getz, Lawrence Pressman; **D:** Betty Thomas; **W:** Bill Carter, George Armitage; **C:** Mac Ahlberg; **M:** Ira Newborn. *HBO*

The Late Show ⦇⦇⦇ 1977 (PG) A veteran private detective finds his world turned upside down when his ex-partner comes to visit and winds up dead, and a flaky woman whose cat is missing decides to become his sidekick. Carney and Tomlin are fun to watch in this sleeper. A tribute to the classic detective film noirs. **93m/C VHS, Beta, LV, Closed Caption.** Art Carney, Lily Tomlin, Bill Macy, Eugene Roche, Joanna Cassidy, John Considine; **D:** Robert Benton; **W:** Robert Benton. Edgar Allan Poe Awards '77: Best Screenplay; National Board of Review Awards '77: 10 Best Films of the Year; National Society of Film Critics Awards '77: Best Actor (Carney); Nominations: Academy Awards '77: Best Original Screenplay. *WAR*

Late Spring ⦇⦇⦇⦇ 1949 An exquisite Ozu masterpiece. A young woman lives with her widowed father for years. He decides to remarry so that she can begin life for herself. Highly acclaimed, in Japanese with English subtitles. Reworked in 1960 as "Late Autumn." **107m/B VHS, Beta.** JP Setsuko Hara, Chishu Ryu, Jun Usami, Haruko Sugimura; **D:** Yasujiro Ozu. *NYF, FCT*

Late Summer Blues ⦇⦇ *Blues La-Chofesh Ha-Godol* 1987 Experience the life and death decisions of seven teenagers who have finished their finals and face now a more difficult test: serving in the Israeli Armed Forces in the Suez Canal. In Hebrew with English subtitles. **101m/C VHS.** IS Dor Zweigenbom, Shahar Segal, Yoav Zafir; **D:** Renen Schorr. *ERG, AUD, HMV*

Lathe of Heaven ⦇⦇½ 1980 In a late twentieth century world suffocating from pollution, a young man visits a dream specialist. He then dreams of a world free from war, pestilence, and overpopulation. At times, these dreams have disastrous side effects. Based on futuristic novel by Ursula K. LeGuin; produced for PBS. **120m/C VHS, Beta.** Bruce Davison, Kevin Conway, Margaret Avery; **D:** David Loxton. *WNE*

Latin Lovers ⦇⦇½ 1953 Turner plays a wealthy heiress who can't decide if men love her for herself or her money in this festive Brazilian romp. Lund and Montalban portray the suitors vying for her affection. Although not one of MGM's best musicals, the music is good because of the Brodszky-Robin tunes. ♫Night and You; Carlotta, You Gotta Be Mine; A Little More of Your Armor; Come To My Arms; I Had To Kiss You. **104m/C VHS.** Lana Turner, Ricardo Montalban, John Lund, Louis Calhern, Jean Hagen, Eduard Franz, Beulah Bondi; **D:** Mervyn LeRoy; **W:** Isobel Lennart. *MGM*

Latino ⦇⦇½ 1985 The self-tortured adventures of a Chicano Green Beret who, while fighting a covert U.S. military action in war-torn Nicaragua, begins to rebel against the senselessness of the war. **108m/C VHS, Beta, LV, Closed Caption.** Robert Beltran, Annette Cardona, Tony Plana, James Karen, Ricardo Lopez, Luis Torrentes, Juan Carlos Ortiz, Julio Medina; **D:** Haskell Wexler; **W:** Haskell Wexler; **M:** Diane Louie. *FOX*

Lauderdale woof! 1989 (R) Two college schmoes hit the beach looking for beer and babes. Few laughs for the sober and mature. Surf's down in this woofer. **91m/C VHS, Beta, LV.** Darrel Gilbeau, Michelle Kemp, Jeff Greenman, Lara Belmonte; **D:** Bill Milling. *PSM*

Laugh with Linder! 1913 Compilation of Linder shorts, including "Max Learns to Skate" and "Max and His Dog." **70m/B VHS, Beta.** Max Linder. *GVV*

Laughfest 191? Five classic slapstick shorts: "It's a Gift" (1923), with Snub Pollard, "Barney Oldfield's Race for a Life" (1913), "Kid Auto Races" and "Busy Day" (1914), both with Charlie Chaplin, and "Daredevil" (1923), starring Ben Turpin. **59m/B VHS, Beta.** Ben Turpin, Barney Oldfield, Mabel Normand, Charlie Chaplin, Snub Pollard. *CCB*

Laughing at Danger ⦇⦇½ 1924 Talmadge is the supposedly playboy son of a Washington politician. In reality, he's the dashing "Mr. Pep" who comes to the rescue of a scientist who has invented a death ray and is being stalked by agents of a sinister foreign power. Talmadge was a fine silent-screen action star, though his heavy German action proved a barrier with sound films. **45m/B VHS.** Richard Talmadge, Joseph Girard, Eva Novak, Joe Harrington, Stanhope Wheatcroft; **D:** James W. Horne. *GPV*

Laughing at Life ⦇⦇½ 1933 A mercenary leaves his family to fight in South America. Years later, when he is the leader of said country, he meets a man who turns out to be his son. Rehashed plot has been done better. **72m/B VHS.** Victor McLaglen, William "Stage" Boyd, Lois Wilson, Henry B. Walthall, Regis Toomey; **D:** Ford Beebe. *NOS, DVT, HEG*

The Laughing Policeman ⦇⦇½ *An Investigation of Murder* 1974 (R) Two antagonistic cops embark on a vengeful hunt for a mass murderer through the seamy underbelly of San Francisco. Adapted from the Swedish novel by Per Wahloo and Maj Sjowallo. **111m/C VHS, Beta, Closed Caption.** Walter Matthau, Bruce Dern, Louis Gossett Jr.; **D:** Stuart Rosenberg; **M:** Charles Fox. *FOX*

Laughing Sinners ⦇⦇ 1931 Society girl Crawford attempts suicide after Hamilton dumps her and is rescued by Gable—a Salvation Army worker! Predictable drama with some unintentionally funny moments. Gable and Crawford were having an off-screen romance at the time which accounts for the sparks generated on-screen. Based on the play "Torch Song" by Kenyon Nicholson. **71m/B VHS.** Joan Crawford, Neil Hamilton, Clark Gable, Marjorie Rambeau, Guy Kibbee, Cliff Edwards, Roscoe Karns; **D:** Harry Beaumont; **C:** Charles Rosher. *MGM*

Laura ⦇⦇⦇⦇ 1944 A detective assigned to the murder investigation of the late Laura Hunt finds himself falling in love with her painted portrait. Superb collaboration by excellent cast and fine director. Superior suspense yarn, enhanced by a love story. Based on the novel by Vera Caspary. Rouben Mamoulian was the original director, then Preminger finished the film. **85m/B VHS, Beta, LV.** Gene Tierney, Dana Andrews, Clifton Webb, Lane Chandler, Vincent Price, Judith Anderson, Grant Mitchell, Dorothy Adams; **D:** Otto Preminger; **C:** Joseph LaShelle; **M:** David Raksin. Academy Awards '44: Best Black and White Cinematography; Nominations: Academy Awards '44: Best Director (Preminger), Best Interior Decoration, Best Screenplay, Best Supporting Actor (Webb).*FXV, PMS, BTV*

Laurel & Hardy and the Family 1933 Four zany comedies seeing the boys in all kinds of trouble involving homelife. Includes "Brats," "Perfect Day," "Their First Mistake" and "Twice Two." **85m/B VHS.** Stan Laurel, Oliver Hardy. *VTR, FCT*

Laurel & Hardy: Another Fine Mess 1930 The boys find themselves the owners of a magnificent Beverly Hills mansion. Yeah right. Lots of physical comedy and hilarious dialogue with a "special appearance" by Laurel in drag as a maid. Based on a sketch written by Laurel's father. Colorized. **25m/C VHS.** Stan Laurel, Oliver Hardy. *CAF*

Laurel & Hardy: At Work 1932 Three short films collected here. Includes "Towed in a Hole," "Busy Bodies," and "The Music Box." **70m/B VHS.** Oliver Hardy, Stan Laurel. *VTR, FCT*

Laurel & Hardy: Be Big 1931 Stan and Ollie ditch their wives to go to a swinging stag party at their club. Of course everything goes wrong in their quest for lascivious fun. Filled with tons of sight gags. Colorized. **25m/C VHS.** Stan Laurel, Oliver Hardy. *CAF, MOV*

Laurel & Hardy: Below Zero 1930 It's the Great Depression of 1929, and Laurel and Hardy are about as depressed as you can get, working for pennies as street musicians. Their luck changes when they find a full wallet lying in the snow. But, as the saying goes, a fool and his money are soon parted. Colorized. **25m/C VHS.** Stan Laurel, Oliver Hardy. *CAF, MOV*

Laurel & Hardy: Berth Marks 1929 Laurel & Hardy take a hilarious train trip to Pottsville for a vaudeville performance. Colorized. **25m/ C VHS.** Stan Laurel, Oliver Hardy. *CAF*

Laurel & Hardy: Blotto 1930 Laurel and Hardy want to get drunk, but they can't get any alcohol and their wives won't let them get away. When they finally do escape, they wind up at the swanky Rainbow Club, where they're drastically out of their element. Colorized. **25m/C VHS.** Stan Laurel, Oliver Hardy. *CAF*

Laurel & Hardy: Brats 1930 Stan and Ollie play not only themselves but also their children when their wives go away and they have to babysit. The children, of course, wreak havoc wherever they go, playing on the hilariously oversized props and sets. One of the few films in which only Laurel and Hardy appear. Colorized. **25m/C VHS.** Stan Laurel, Oliver Hardy. *CAF, MOV*

Laurel & Hardy: Chickens Come Home 1931 Ollie is running for mayor, but things go crazy when an ex-girlfriend shows up and blackmails him with a compromising photo. Stan, acting as Ollie's campaign manager, tries to help, but things just get worse. A remake of their own film "Love 'Em and Weep." Colorized. **25m/C VHS.** Stan Laurel, Oliver Hardy, James Finlayson. *CAF, MOV*

Laurel & Hardy Comedy Classics, Vol. 1 1933 A collection of four classic comedy shorts starring Laurel and Hardy: "The Music Box," which won an Academy Award for Best Short Subject, "Country Hospital," "The Live Ghost," and "Twice Two," all from 1932-33. **84m/B VHS, Beta.** Stan Laurel, Oliver Hardy, Mae Busch, May Wallace, Charlie Hall, Billy Gilbert. Academy Awards '31: Best Comedy Short ("The Music Box"). *MED*

Laurel & Hardy Comedy Classics, Vol. 2 1930 A collection of four Laurel and Hardy shorts from 1930 including "Blotto," "Towed in a Hole," "Brats," and "Hog Wild." **75m/B VHS, Beta.** Stan Laurel, Oliver Hardy, Billy Gilbert, Tiny Sandford, Anita Garvin. *MED*

Laurel & Hardy Comedy Classics, Vol. 3 1934 Laurel and Hardy star in four separate comedy shorts, including "Oliver the 8th," "Busy Bodies," "Their First Mistake," and "Dirty Work," all from 1933-34. **75m/B VHS, Beta.** Stan Laurel, Oliver Hardy, Billy Gilbert, Mae Busch, Tiny Sandford. *MED*

Laurel & Hardy Comedy Classics, Vol. 4 1932 Laurel and Hardy star in four of their comedy shorts from 1931-32. Included are "Another Fine Mess," "Come Clean," "Laughing Gravy," and "Any Old Part." **75m/B VHS, Beta.** Stan Laurel, Oliver Hardy, Jacqueline Wells, James Finlayson, Thelma Todd. *MED*

Laurel & Hardy Comedy Classics, Vol. 5 1931 Four classic comedy shorts starring Laurel and Hardy. Included are "Be Big," "The Perfect Day," "Night Owls," and "Help Mates," from 1929-31. **84m/B VHS, Beta.** Stan Laurel, Oliver Hardy, Edgar Kennedy, James Finlayson, Blanche Payson. *MED*

Laurel & Hardy Comedy Classics, Vol. 6 1935 Laurel and Hardy comedy shorts are presented in this package: "Our Wife," "The Fixer Uppers," "Them Thar Hills," and "Tit for Tat," from 1932-35. **75m/B VHS, Beta.** Stan Laurel, Oliver Hardy, Charlie Hall, Billy Gilbert, Ben Turpin, Mae Busch, James Finlayson. *MED*

Laurel & Hardy Comedy Classics, Vol. 7 193? Four Laurel and Hardy two-reelers are combined on this tape: "Me and My Pal" (1933), "The Midnight Patrol" (1933), "Thicker than Water" (1935), and the classic "Below Zero" (1930). 90m/B VHS, Beta. Stan Laurel, Oliver Hardy, Mae Busch, Daphne Pollard, James Finlayson. MED

Laurel & Hardy Comedy Classics, Vol. 8 193? Compilation of Laurel and Hardy shorts includes: "Men O' War" (1929), "Scram" (1932), "Laurel and Hardy Murder Case" (1930) and "One Good Turn" (1931). 90m/B VHS, Beta. Stan Laurel, Oliver Hardy, Lewis R. Foster, James W. Horne, James Parrott. MED

Laurel & Hardy Comedy Classics, Vol. 9 193? Includes the shorts: "Beau Hunks" (1931), "Chickens Come Home" (1931), "Going Bye-Bye" (1934), and "Berth Marks" (1929). 100m/B VHS, Beta. Stan Laurel, Oliver Hardy. MED

Laurel & Hardy: Hog Wild 1930 Hilarity ensues when Laurel and Hardy try to fix the radio antenna on Hardy's roof. It may sound easy, but come on, this is Laurel and Hardy. Colorized. 25m/C VHS. Stan Laurel, Oliver Hardy. CAF, MOV

Laurel & Hardy: Laughing Gravy 1931 The boys' pet dog, oddly named Laughing Gravy, gets them into trouble with their landlord who keeps trying to evict them. So funny even the mashed potatos will laugh. Colorized. 25m/C VHS. Stan Laurel, Oliver Hardy. CAF, MOV

Laurel & Hardy: Men O'War 1929 Laurel & Hardy star as two sailors on shore leave trying to impress the ladies. Things go from bad to worse when they take two ladies out on a date. Features the memorable soda fountain and canoe scenes. Colorized. 25m/C VHS. Stan Laurel, Oliver Hardy, Gloria Greer, Anne Cornwall. CAF

Laurel & Hardy: Night Owls 1930 When a cop needs to capture some crooks to save his job, he sets up a fake break-in and catches two bungling burglars—Laurel and Hardy. Lots of sight gags and slapstick. Colorized. 25m/C VHS. Stan Laurel, Oliver Hardy, Edgar Kennedy. CAF, MOV

Laurel & Hardy On the Lam 1930 Four Laurel & Hardy classics are collected, including "Scram," "Another Fine Mess," "One Good Turn," and "Going Bye-Bye." 90m/B VHS. Oliver Hardy, Stan Laurel. VTR, FCT

Laurel & Hardy: Perfect Day 1929 Laurel & Hardy plan a quiet picnic with their wives, but car trouble turns their day into a disaster. Colorized. 25m/C VHS. Stan Laurel, Oliver Hardy, Edgar Kennedy. CAF

Laurel & Hardy Special 🐾🐾½ 19?? A unique program of Laurel and Hardy films including the first film they appeared in together–"Lucky Dog" (1918), "The Soilers," a wild Laurel spoof of The Spoilers, "Kill or Cure," "Near Dublin," "The Sleuths," "Laurel and Hardy's Trip to Britain," and "Stan Visits Ollie," a color home movie of their last visit together. 60m/B VHS, Beta. Stan Laurel, Oliver Hardy. GVV

Laurel & Hardy Spooktacular 1934 Stan and Ollie scream through four spooky comedies, including "The Live Ghost," "The Laurel-Hardy Murder Case," "Oliver the Eighth" and "Dirty Work." 95m/B VHS. VTR, FCT

Laurel & Hardy: Stan "Helps" Ollie 1933 Four Stan and Ollie classics including "County Hospital," "Me and My Pal," "Hog Wild" and "Helpmates." 85m/B VHS. Stan Laurel, Oliver Hardy. VTR, FCT

Laurel & Hardy: The Hoose-Gow 1929 Laurel and Hardy are mistakenly picked up by the police and sent to prison to do hard labor. Hilarity ensues when they try to convince the warden that they're innocent. Colorized. 25m/C VHS. CAF, MOV

Laurel Avenue 🐾🐾½ 1993 Looks at the life of an extended working-class black family in St. Paul, Minnesota, over a busy weekend. Large cast includes family heads Jake and Maggie who live with their basketball coach son, teenage daughter, and elderly uncle. Other children include fraternal twin Yolanda, a cop married to a white man, who knows sister Rolanda's (a recovering drug addict) son is a dealer. Their brother Marcus manages a Mafia-controlled clothing store and is involved in some shady deals while brother Woody is an aspiring musician. The four households are all united at a disasterous Sunday afternoon party. Made for cable television. 156m/C VHS, Closed Caption. Mary Alice, Mel Winkler, Scott Lawrence, Malinda Williams, Jay Brooks, Juanita Jennings, Rhonda Stubbins White, Monte Russell, Vonte Sweet; D: Carl Franklin; W: Michael Henry Brown, Paul Aaron. HBO

The Lavender Hill Mob 🐾🐾🐾½ 1951 A prim and prissy bank clerk schemes to melt the bank's gold down and re-mold it into miniature Eiffel Tower paper-weights for later resale. The foolproof plan appears to succeed, but then develops a snag. An excellent comedy that is still a delight to watch. Also available with "The Man in the White Suit" on laserdisc. 78m/B VHS, Beta, LV. GB Alec Guinness, Stanley Holloway, Sidney James, Alfie Bass, Marjorie Fielding, John Gregson; Cameos: Audrey Hepburn; D: Charles Crichton; W: T.E.B. Clarke. Academy Awards '52: Best Story & Screenplay; British Academy Awards '51: Best Film; Nominations: Academy Awards '52: Best Actor (Guinness). REP, FCT, HMV

L'Avventura 🐾🐾🐾½ The Adventure 1960 A stark, dry and minimalist exercise in narrative by Antonioni, dealing with the search for a girl on an Italian island by her lethargic socialite friends who eventually forget her in favor of their own preoccupations. A highly acclaimed, innovative film; somewhat less effective now, in the wake of many film treatments of angst and amorality. Subtitled in English. Laser edition features the original trailer, commentary and a collection of still photographs from Antonioni's work. 145m/C VHS, Beta, LV. IT Monica Vitti, Gabriele Ferzetti, Lea Massari, Dominique Blanchar, James Addams; D: Michelangelo Antonioni; W: Tonino Guerra, Michelangelo Antonioni. Cannes Film Festival '60: Special Jury Prize. CVC, VDM, APD

Law and Disorder 🐾🐾🐾 1974 (R) Two average Joes, fed up with the rate of rising crime, start their own auxiliary police group. Alternately funny and serious with good performances from the leads. 103m/C VHS. Carroll O'Connor, Ernest Borgnine, Ann Wedgeworth, Anita Dangler, Leslie Ackerman, Karen Black, Jack Kehoe; D: Ivan Passer; M: Angelo Badalamenti. NO

The Law and Jake Wade 🐾🐾½ 1958 Gripping western starring Taylor as a former bank robber turned marshal. His old partner (Widmark) turns up and forces Taylor to lead him to buried loot. 86m/C VHS, Closed Caption. Robert Taylor, Richard Widmark, Patricia Owens, Robert Middleton, Henry Silva, DeForest Kelley, Burt Douglas, Eddie Firestone; D: John Sturges. MGM

Law and Lawless 🐾 1933 A roving cowboy brings justice to a gang of cattle thieves in this film. 58m/B VHS, Beta. Jack Hoxie. NOS, DVT

Law and Order 🐾🐾 1942 Billy the Kid impersonates a Cavalry lieutenant in order to swindle his aunt out of her money. Also called "Billy the Kid's Law and Order." 58m/B VHS, Beta. Buster Crabbe, Al "Fuzzy" St. John. VDM, MRV

Law of Desire 🐾🐾🐾½ La Ley del Deseo 1986 A wicked, Almodovarian attack-on-decency farce about a love-obsessed gay Madridian and his transsexual brother-sister, among others, getting hopelessly entangled in cross-gender relationships. Unlike the work of any other director; in Spanish with English subtitles. 100m/C VHS, Beta, LV. SP Carmen Maura, Eusebio Poncela, Antonio Banderas, Bibi Andersson, Miguel Molina, Manuela Velasco, Nacho Martinez; D: Pedro Almodovar; W: Pedro Almodovar. CCN, TPV

Law of the Jungle 🐾½ 1942 A lady scientist and a fugitive team up to uncover a secret Nazi radio base in the jungle. 61m/B VHS, Beta. Arline Judge, John "Dusty" King, Mantan Moreland, Martin Wilkins, Arthur O'Connell; D: Jean Yarbrough. SNC

Law of the Land 🐾 1976 A made-for-television sagebrush epic with the author/artist of "Garfield" portraying an accused but innocent man searching for a murderer. 100m/C VHS, Beta. Jim Davis, Don Johnson, Barbara Parkins, Charles Martin Smith. WOV

Law of the Lash 🐾 1947 Cowboys and rustlers battle it out. 54m/B VHS, Beta. Lash LaRue, Al "Fuzzy" St. John. NOS, MRV, VCN

Law of the Pampas 🐾🐾 1939 Boyd and Hayden ride off to South America to deliver some cattle, but the bad guys intervene. This is Toler's first outing as Hoppy's sidekick, briefly replacing "Gabby" Hayes. 72m/B VHS. William Boyd, Russell Hayden, Steffi Duna, Sidney Toler, Sidney Blackmer, Pedro de Cordoba, Eddie Dean, Glenn Strange; D: Nate Watt. NOS

Law of the Saddle 🐾½ 1945 The Lone Rider pits himself against a gang of outlaws. 60m/B VHS, Beta. Bob Livingston. VCN, MLB

Law of the Sea 🐾 1938 A family on a sinking ship is rescued by a lecherous sea captain who makes advances on the wife and blinds the husband in a fight. Twenty years later, the husband meets him again, recognizes his laugh and exacts revenge. 63m/B VHS, Beta, LV. Priscilla Dean, Sally Blane, Ralph Ince, Rex Bell, William Farnum. VYY

Law of the Texan 🐾½ 1938 Jones goes undercover to stop Harlan and his gang from stealing a town's store of silver bullion. 54m/B VHS. Buck Jones, Dorothy Fay, Kenneth Harlan, Don Douglas, Matty Kemp, Robert F. (Bob) Kortman, Dave O'Brien; D: Elmer Clifton. GPV

Law of the Underworld 🐾½ 1938 An innocent couple is framed for the robbery of a jewelry store which resulted in the death of a clerk. When they are arrested, their fate lies in the hands of the gangster responsible for the crime. Will he let them fry in the electric chair, or will his conscience get the better of him? 58m/B VHS, Beta. Chester Morris, Anne Shirley, Eduardo Ciannelli, Walter Abel, Richard Bond, Lee Patrick, Paul Guilfoyle, Frank M. Thomas Sr., Eddie Acuff, Jack Arnold; D: Lew (Louis Friedlander) Landers. SNC

Law of the Wild 1934 The search for a magnificent stallion that was hijacked by race racketeers before a big sweepstakes race is shown in this 12 chapter serial. 230m/B VHS. Bob Custer, Ben Turpin, Lucille Browne, Lafe McKee; D: B. Reeves Eason, Armand Schaefer. GPV, NOS, VCN

The Law Rides 🐾 1936 Rush of gold claims causes an outbreak of murder and robbery. 57m/B VHS, Beta. Bob Steele. DVT

The Law Rides Again 🐾 1943 Prairie lawmen bring a cheating Indian agent to justice. 56m/B VHS. Ken Maynard, Hoot Gibson, Betty Miles, Jack LaRue; D: William Castle. NOS, MRV, DVT

Law West of Tombstone 🐾🐾½ 1938 A former outlaw moves to a dangerous frontier town in order to restore the peace. 73m/B VHS, Beta. Tim Holt, Harry Carey Sr., Evelyn Brent; D: Glenn Tryon. MED

Lawless Frontier 🐾½ 1935 In the early West, the Duke fights for law and order. 53m/B VHS, Beta. John Wayne, George "Gabby" Hayes, Sheila Terry, Earl Dwire; D: Robert North Bradbury. COL, NOS, VYY

The Lawless Land 🐾🐾 1988 (R) Postholocaust America is ruled by a tyrant. Two young lovers who can't take it anymore go on the lam to escape the despotic rule. 81m/C VHS, Beta. Leon Berkeley, Xander Berkeley, Nick Corri, Amanda Peterson; D: Jon Hess; W: Tony Cinciripini, Larry Leahy. MGM

The Lawless Nineties 🎬🎬 1936
Wayne plays a government agent sent to guarantee honest elections in the Wyoming territory. Hayes is exceptional as the newspaper editor who backs him up. Re-made in 1940 as "The Dark Command." **55m/B VHS.** John Wayne, Ann Rutherford, Lane Chandler, Harry Woods, George "Gabby" Hayes, Charles "Blackie" King, Sam Flint; **D:** Joseph Kane. *REP*

Lawless Range 🎬½ 1935 Wayne and the marshal's posse save the ranchers from trouble. **56m/B VHS.** John Wayne, Sheila Mannors, Jack Curtis, Earl Dwire; **D:** Robert North Bradbury. *REP, NOS, MRV*

A Lawless Street 🎬🎬½ 1955 Scott portrays a sheriff who rides the Colorado Territory cleaning up lawless towns. His dedication to duty has caused his wife to leave him and she won't come back until he lays down his guns forever, which may come sooner than they think after he rides into the corrupt town of Medicine Bend. Based on the novel "Marshal of Medicine Bend" by Brad Ward. **78m/B VHS.** Randolph Scott, Angela Lansbury, Warner Anderson, Jean Parker, Wallace Ford, John Emery, James Bell, Ruth Donnelly, Michael Pate, Don Megowan, Jeanette Nolan; **D:** Joseph H. Lewis; **W:** Kenneth Gamet; **C:** Ray Rennahan. *COL*

Lawman 🎬🎬🎬 1971 (PG) Brutal western about a fanatical U.S. marshall (Lancaster) who rides into town after Cobb and his six ranch hands. The cowboys have accidentally killed a man and Lancaster is determined to bring them to justice no matter what the cost. Though the entire town is against him that doesn't stop his mission. Brooding and relentless with fine performances, particularly by Ryan as the local marshall living on past glories. **95m/C VHS.** Burt Lancaster, Robert Ryan, Lee J. Cobb, Sheree North, Joseph Wiseman, Robert Duvall, Albert Salmi, J.D. Cannon, John McGiver, Richard Jordan, John Beck, Ralph Waite, John Hillerman, Richard Bull; **D:** Michael Winner; **W:** Gerald Wilson. *MGM*

A Lawman Is Born 🎬🎬🎬 1937 A tough-as-nails marshal goes gunning for a pack of no-good, land-stealing varmits in this installment of the Johnny Mack Brown movie serials. Be sure to count the number of bullets each cowboy can fire from a six-shooter before being forced to reload; you may be surprised. **58m/B VHS, Beta.** Johnny Mack Brown, Iris Meredith, Warner Richmond, Mary MacLaren, Dick Curtis, Earle Hodgins, Charles "Blackie" King, Frank LaRue; **D:** Sam Newfield. *NOS, MOV, MRV*

Lawmen 🎬½ 1944 Government agents fight to enforce the law in the badlands. **55m/B VHS, Beta.** Johnny Mack Brown, Raymond Hatton. *NOS, DVT*

The Lawnmower Man 🎬🎬 1992 (R) Brosnan is a scientist who uses Fahey, a dim-witted gardener, as a guinea pig to test his experiments in "virtual reality," an artificial computer environment. With the use of drugs and high-tech equipment, Brosnan is able to increase Fahey's mental powers—but not necessarily for the better. Fantastic special effects and a memorable "virtual reality" sex scene. Available in an unrated version which contains 32 more minutes of footage. So minimally based on a short story by Stephen King that the author sued (and won) to have his name removed from the film. **CW:** Language, violence, and sensuality. **108m/C VHS, LV, Closed Caption.** Jeff Fahey, Pierce Brosnan, Jenny Wright, Mark Bringleson, Geoffrey Lewis, Jeremy Slate, Dean Norris; **D:** Brett Leonard; **W:** Brett Leonard, Gimel Everett; **C:** Russell Carpenter. *COL, FCT, MOV*

Lawnmower Man 2: Beyond Cyberspace 🎬🎬 *Lawnmower Man 2: Jobe's War* 1995 (PG-13) Resurrecting Jobe (the title character from number one) was easy. So was blowing off his face to explain the new actor (Frewer in for Fahey) playing him. The hard part was tring to make an original movie with a decent script and believable characters. Better luck next time. Corporate baddie Walker (Conway) enlists Jobe to (what else?) take over the world using Virtual Reality. To the rescue comes one burned-out com-

puter expert (Bergin) and a group of VR-addicted kids living in an abandoned subway. Techno-babble abounds but nothing interesting ever happens. Mann and Frewer must've raided their old "Max Headroom" set for the dreary near-future L.A. landscape scenes. **CW:** Sci-fi action/violence and brief language. **93m/C VHS, LV, Closed Caption.** Patrick Bergin, Matt Frewer, Austin O'Brien, Kevin Conway, Ely Pouget, Camille Cooper; **D:** Farhad Mann; **W:** Farhad Mann; **C:** Ward Russell; **M:** Robert Folk. *NLC*

Lawrence of Arabia 🎬🎬🎬🎬 1962 (PG) Exceptional biography of T.E. Lawrence, a British military "observer" who strategically aids the Bedouins battle the Turks during WWI. Lawrence, played masterfully by O'Toole in his first major film, is a hero consumed more by a need to reject British tradition than to save the Arab population. He takes on Arab costume and a larger-than-life persona. Stunning photography of the desert in all its harsh reality. Blacklisted co-writer Wilson had his screen credit restored by the Writers Guild of America in 1995. Laser edition contains 20 minutes of restored footage and a short documentary about the making of the film. Available in letterboxed format. **221m/C VHS, Beta, LV, Closed Caption.** *GB* Peter O'Toole, Omar Sharif, Anthony Quinn, Alec Guinness, Jack Hawkins, Claude Rains, Anthony Quayle, Arthur Kennedy, Jose Ferrer; **D:** David Lean; **W:** Robert Bolt, Michael Wilson; **C:** Frederick A. (Freddie) Young; **M:** Maurice Jarre. Academy Awards '62: Best Art Direction/Set Decoration (Color), Best Color Cinematography, Best Director (Lean), Best Film Editing, Best Picture, Best Sound, Best Original Score; British Academy Awards '62: Best Actor (O'Toole), Best Film, Best Screenplay; Directors Guild of America Awards '62: Best Director (Lean); Golden Globe Awards '63: Best Director (Lean), Best Film—Drama, Best Supporting Actor (Sharif); National Board of Review Awards '62: 10 Best Films of the Year, Best Director (Lean); Nominations: Academy Awards '62: Best Actor (O'Toole), Best Adapted Screenplay, Best Supporting Actor (Sharif). *COL, CRC, BTV*

The Lawrenceville Stories 🎬🎬½ 198? Chronicles the life and times of a group of young men at the prestigious Lawrenceville prep school in 1905. Galligan plays William Hicks, alias "The Prodigious Hickey," the ringleader of their obnoxious stunts. Based on the stories of Owen Johnson, which originally ran in the Saturday Evening Post. Shown on "American Playhouse" and The Disney Channel. Tapes are available separately or as a set. **180m/C VHS.** Zach Galligan, Edward Herrmann, Nicholas Rowe, Allan Goldstein, Robert Joy, Stephen Baldwin; **D:** Robert Iscove. *MON, BTV*

Laws of Gravity 🎬🎬🎬 1992 (R) Critically acclaimed debut film from 29-year-old writer/director Gomez is a three day slice of life set in Brooklyn. Hotheaded Jon (Trese) and married friend Jimmy (Greene) channel violent energy into their relationships and illegal activities. Camera follows "cinema verite" style and captures urban tension as it trails them through a gun heist and subsequent arrest. **CW:** Pervasive strong language. **100m/C VHS.** Peter Greene, Edie Falco, Adam Trese, Arabella Field, Paul Schulzie; **D:** Nick Gomez; **W:** Nick Gomez; **C:** Jean De Segonzac. *TRI*

Lazarillo 🎬🎬 *El Lazarillo de Tormes* 1959 In 17th-century Castille, a fatherless boy, abandoned by his mother, finds work with a strange succession of employers, including a blind beggar, fake nobleman, and traveling band of performers. They all teach him lessons in survival as well as cunning and deception. Spanish with subtitles. **109m/B VHS.** *SP* Marco Paoletti, Juan Jose Menendez, Carlos Casaravilla, Margarita Lozano; **D:** Cesar Ardavin; **W:** Cesar Ardavin; **M:** Ruiz De Luna. Berlin International Film Festival '60: Best Film. *FCT*

The Lazarus Man 🎬🎬½ 1996 Pilot episode of the TV series finds the amnesiac Urich discovering he's linked to the assassination of President Lincoln. In 1865 Texas he literally claws his way out of the grave and is taken in by a farming family. This back from the dead Lazarus may not remember who he is but a trip to town

demonstrates his gunslinger skills and images from his dreams may provide clues to his past. Now, he has to stay alive long enough to figure them out. **90m/C VHS.** Robert Urich, Elizabeth Dennehy, David Marshall Grant, John Diehl, Wayne Grace, Brion James; **D:** Johnny E. Jensen; **W:** Dick Beebe; **C:** Gary Holt; **M:** John Debney. *TTC*

The Lazarus Syndrome 1979 Astute doctor teams up with an ex-patient of the chief of surgery in an effort to expose the chief's unethical surgical procedures. **90m/C VHS, Beta.** Louis Gossett Jr., E.G. Marshall. *NO*

LBJ: A Biography 1991 Produced for the PBS series "The American Experience," this four-hour revisionist look at LBJ is one of the most critically acclaimed political documentaries of our time. Divided into four segments. "Beautiful Texas" chronicles Johnson's rise to power. "My Fellow Americans" focuses on his years as an unelected president. The Great Society and and the escalation of war in Vietnam are covered in "We Shall Overcome." "The Last Believer" highlights events leading to Johnson's withdrawal from politics. **240m/C VHS.** **D:** David Grubin; **W:** David Grubin. *PBS, SIG*

LBJ: The Early Years 🎬🎬🎬 1988 The early years of President Lyndon Baines Johnson's political career are dramatized in this made-for-television movie. Winning performances hoist this above other biographies. **144m/C VHS, Beta.** Randy Quaid, Patti LuPone, Morgan Brittany, Pat Hingle, Kevin McCarthy, Barry Corbin, Charles Frank; **D:** Peter Werner. *FRH*

Le Bal 🎬🎬🎬 1982 You won't find many films with the music of Paul McCartney and Chopin in the credits, and even fewer without dialogue. With only music and dancing the film uses a French dance hall to illustrate the changes in French society over a fifty-year period. Based on a French play. 🎵La Vie en Rose; In the Mood; Michelle; Top Hat White Tie and Tails; Let's Face the Music and Dance; Harlem Nocturne; Shuffle Blues; Tutti Frutti; One You. **112m/C VHS.** *IT FR D:* Ettore Scola; **M:** Irving Berlin, Paul McCartney, John Lennon, Frederic Chopin, Vladimir Cosma. Cesar Awards '84: Best Director (Scola), Best Film, Best Score; Nominations: Academy Awards '83: Best Foreign Language Film. *WAR, FCT*

Le Beau Mariage 🎬🎬🎬 *A Good Marriage; The Well-Made Marriage* 1982 (R) An award-winning comedy from the great French director about a zealous woman trying to find a husband and the unsuspecting man she chooses to marry. In French with English subtitles. **97m/C VHS, Beta.** *FR* Beatrice Romand, Arielle Dombasle, Andre Dussollier; **D:** Eric Rohmer; **W:** Eric Rohmer. Venice Film Festival '82: Best Actress (Romand). *NO*

Le Beau Serge 🎬🎬🎬 *Handsome Serge* 1958 Young theology student Francois returns to his home village and discovers his friend Serge, in despair of ever changing his life, has become a hopeless drunk. So Francois meddles in his life (with the best of intentions) and only causes Serge further disaster. Chabrol's first film, and a major forerunner of the nouvelle vague. In French with English subtitles. **97m/B VHS.** *FR* Gerard Blain, Jean-Claude Brialy, Michele Meritz, Bernadette LaFont; **D:** Claude Chabrol; **W:** Claude Chabrol. *HTV, FCT*

Le Bonheur 🎬🎬½ *Happiness* 1965 A seemingly happily married carpenter (Drouot) takes a vacation with his wife and children where he meets the local postal clerk and the two begin a passionate affair. Unwilling to leave his family, Drouot believes the two women can share him but when his wife discovers his infidelity she kills herself. His grief does not cause Drouot to stop the affair, instead he moves in with his mistress. An uninvolving, unbelievable tale with a lovely Mozart score. In French with English subtitles. **87m/C VHS.** *FR* Jean-Claude Drouot, Claire Drouot, Marie-France Boyer; **D:** Agnes Varda; **W:** Agnes Varda. *FCT*

Le Bonheur Est Dans le Pre 🎬🎬
Happiness Is In the Fields; Happiness 1995 Francis (Serrault) is the harried owner of a toilet brush-making business that is about to undergo a tax audit and is threatened by a workers strike. His wife and daughter are never happy and Francis' one relief is to have lunch with his macho, easy-going friend, Gerard (Mitchell). One day, he watches a TV show about missing persons and sees that a woman is looking for her husband who disappeared 28 years before—a man who looks suspiciously like Francis. The plot's convoluted and the comedy's flat. French with subtitles. 105m/C VHS. *FR* Michel Serrault, Sabine Azema, Eddy Mitchell, Carmen Maura, Alexandra London; *D:* Etienne Chatiliez; *W:* Florence Quentin; *C:* Philippe Welt; *M:* Pascal Andreaccchio. Cesar Awards '95: Best Supporting Actor (Mitchell); Nominations: Cesar Awards '95: Best Actress (Azema), Best Director (Chatiliez), Best Film, Best Screenplay, Best Supporting Actress (Maura). *NYR*

Le Boucher 🎬🎬🎬 *The Butcher* 1969 In a provincial French town a sophisticated schoolmistress is courted by the shy local butcher—who turns out to be a sex murderer. A well-played thriller that looks at sexual frustration. In French with English subtitles. 94m/C VHS, LV. *FR* Stephane Audran, Jean Yanne, Antonio Passallia; *D:* Claude Chabrol; *W:* Claude Chabrol. *CVC*

Le Cas du Dr. Laurent 🎬🎬🎬 1957 A country doctor in a small French town tries to introduce methods of natural childbirth to the native women, but meets opposition from the superstitious villagers. Fine performance by Gabin. 88m/B VHS, Beta. *FR* Jean Gabin, Nicole Courcel; *D:* Jean-Paul LeChanois. *NOS, VYY, DVT*

Le Cavaleur 🎬🎬 *Practice Makes Perfect* 1978 A light hearted comedy about a philandering concert pianist. 90m/C VHS, Beta. *FR* Jean Rochefort, Lila Kedrova, Nicole Garcia, Annie Girardot, Danielle Darrieux; *D:* Philippe de Broca; *M:* Georges Delerue. *NO*

Le Chat 🎬🎬🎬½ *The Cat* 1975 A middle-aged couple's marriage dissolves into a hate-filled battle of wits, centering around the husband's love for their cat. In French with English subtitles. 88m/C VHS, Beta, LV. *FR* Jean Gabin, Simone Signoret, Annie Cordy, Jacques Rispal; *D:* Pierre Granier-Deferre. Berlin International Film Festival '71: Best Actor (Gabin). *FCT, LUM*

Le Complot 🎬🎬🎬 *The Conspiracy* 1973 When de Gaulle announces his intention to abandon Algeria, several army officers, feeling that their service has been in vain, stage a coup. There's suspense aplenty as the Gaulists, the leftists, and the police spy and are spied upon. In French with English subtitles. 120m/C VHS. *FR* Michel Bouquet, Jean Rochefort; *D:* Rene Gainville. *CVC, FCT*

Le Corbeau 🎬🎬🎬 *The Raven* 1943 A great, notorious drama about a small French village whose everyday serenity is ruptured by a series of poison pen letters that lead to suicide and despair. The film was made within Nazi-occupied France, sponsored by the Nazis, and has been subjected to much misdirected malice because of it. In French with English subtitles. 92m/B VHS, Beta. *FR* Pierre Fresnay, Noel Roquevort, Ginette LeClerc, Pierre Larquey, Antoine Belpetre; *D:* Henri-Georges Clouzot. *NOS, HHT, GVV*

Le Crabe Tambour 🎬🎬🎬 1977 Rochefort plays a dying naval captain remembering his relationship with his first officer. Revealed via flashbacks, the recollections concern the adventures which transpired on a North Atlantic supply ship. Great performances from all and award-winning cinematography by Raoul Coutard. Winner of several French Cesars. A French script booklet is available. 120m/C VHS, LV. *FR* Jean Rochefort, Claude Rich, Jacques Dufilho, Jacques Perrin, Odile Versois, Aurore Clement; *D:* Pierre Schoendoerffer. Cesar Awards '78: Best Actor (Rochefort), Best Cinematography, Best Supporting Actor (Dufilho). *INT, IME, APD*

Le Dernier Combat 🎬🎬🎬 *The Last Battle* 1984 (R) A stark film about life after a devastating nuclear war marks the directorial debut of Besson. The characters fight to survive in a now speechless world by staking territorial claims and forming new relationships with other survivors. An original and expressive film made without dialogue. 93m/B VHS, Beta. *FR* Pierre Jolivet, Fritz Wepper, Jean Reno, Jean Bouise, Christiane Kruger; *D:* Luc Besson; *W:* Luc Besson. *COL, OM*

Le Doulos 🎬🎬🎬 1961 Compelling story of an ex-convict and his buddy, a man who may be a police informant. Chronicles the efforts of the snitch (the "doulos" of the title) to bring the criminal element before the law. Melville blends in several plot twists and breathes a new-French life into the cliche-ridden genre. 108m/B VHS, Beta. *FR* Serge Reggiani, Jean-Paul Belmondo, Michel Piccoli; *D:* Jean-Pierre Melville. *INT, TPV*

Le Gendarme de Saint-Tropez 🎬🎬½ 1967 Officer Ludovic Cruchot's plans for career advancement are on shaky ground after he is transferred to St. Tropez where his daughter has a little too much fun at the beach. Also available dubbed. ?m/C VHS. *FR* Louis de Funes, Michel Galabru, Genevieve Grad, Jean LeFevre, Christian Marin. *FRA, FCT*

Le Gentleman D'Epsom 🎬🎬 1962 A French comedy about a breezy con man who scams everyone around him in order to keep up his upwardly mobile appearance and to put his bets down at the racetrack. Subtitled in English. 83m/B VHS, Beta. *FR* Jean Gabin, Paul Frankeur. *BAR*

Le Grand Chemin 🎬🎬 *The Grand Highway* 1987 A sweet, slice-of-life French film about a young boy's idyllic summer on a family friend's farm while his mother is having a baby. Hubert's son plays the boy Louis in this retelling of the director's own childhood. In French with English subtitles. Remade with an American setting in 1991 as "Paradise." 107m/C VHS, Beta, LV. *FR* Anemone, Richard Bohringer, Antoine Hubert, Vanessa Guedj, Christine Pascal, Raoul Billerey, Pascale Roberts; *D:* Jean-Loup Hubert; *W:* Jean-Loup Hubert; *M:* Georges Granier. Cesar Awards '88: Best Actor (Bohringer), Best Actress (Anemone). *FCT, IME, PBS*

Le Joli Mai 🎬🎬 1962 A famous documentary that established Marker, depicting the everyday life of Paris denizens on the occasion of the end of the Algerian War, May 1962, when France was at peace for the first time since 1939. In French with English subtitles. 180m/B VHS, Beta. *FR D:* Chris Marker. *FCT*

Le Jour Se Leve 🎬🎬🎬½ *Daybreak* 1939 The dark, expressionist film about a sordid and destined murder/love triangle that starts with a police stand-off and evolves into a series of flashbacks. The film that put Carne and Gabin on the cinematic map. Highly acclaimed. French with English subtitles. Remade in 1947 as "The Long Night." 89m/B VHS. *FR* Jean Gabin, Jules Berry, Arletty, Jacqueline Laurent; *D:* Marcel Carne. *HMV, APD, GVV*

Le Magnifique 🎬🎬 *The Magnificent One* 1976 Belmondo is a master spy and novelist who mixes fantasy with reality when he chases women and solves cases. 84m/C VHS, Beta. *FR* Jean-Paul Belmondo, Jacqueline Bisset; *W:* Francis Veber; *M:* Claude Bolling. *PSM*

Le Mans 🎬🎬🎬 1971 (G) The famous 24-hour sports car race sets the stage for this tale of love and speed. McQueen (who did his own driving) is the leading race driver, a man who battles competition, fear of death by accident, and emotional involvement. Excellent documentary-style race footage almost makes up for weak plot and minimal acting. 106m/C VHS, LV, Closed Caption. Steve McQueen, Elga Andersen, Ronald Leigh-Hunt, Luc Merenda; *D:* Lee H. Katzin; *C:* Robert B. Hauser. *FOX, FCT*

Le Million 🎬🎬🎬½ 1931 A comedy/musical masterpiece of the early sound era which centers on an artist's adventures in searching for a winning lottery ticket throughout Paris. Highly ac-

claimed member of the Clair school of subtle French farce. In French with English subtitles. 89m/B VHS, Beta. *FR* Annabella, Rene Lefevre, Paul Olivier, Louis Allibert; *D:* Rene Clair. National Board of Review Awards '31: 5 Best Foreign Films of the Year. *VYY, NOS, DVT*

Le Petit Amour 🎬🎬🎬 *Kung Fu Master* 1987 (R) A popular French comedy about the fateful romance between a 40-year-old divorced woman and a 15-year-old boy obsessed with a kung fu video game. In French with English subtitles. 80m/C VHS, Beta. *FR* Jane Birkin, Mathieu Demy, Charlotte Gainsbourg, Lou Doillon; *D:* Agnes Varda. *PSM*

Le Plaisir 🎬🎬½ *House of Pleasure* 1952 An anthology of three Guy de Maupassant stories, "Le Masque," "Le Modele," and "La Maison Teillier," about the search for pleasure. In French with English subtitles. 97m/B VHS, Beta. *FR* Claude Dauphin, Simone Simon, Jean Gabin, Danielle Darrieux; *D:* Max Ophuls. Nominations: Academy Awards '54: Best Art Direction/Set Decoration (B & W). *NOS, DVT, GVV*

Le Polygraphe 🎬🎬 *The Lie Detector* 1996 Francois (Goyette) is still a suspect in the murder of his girlfriend, Marie-Claire, two years after her death. The murder has so affected her friend Judith (Descenes) that she's written a screenplay about the unsolved crime (blaming the crime on a rogue cop). Meanwhile, actress Lucie (Brassard), who auditions for the role of Marie-Claire, gets involved with mystery man Christof (Stormare). English and French with subtitles. 97m/C VHS. *CA* Patrick Goyette, Jose Descenes, Marie Brassard, Peter Stormare, Maria De Medeiros; *D:* Robert Lepage; *W:* Marie Brassard, Robert Lepage; *C:* Georges Dufaux. Nominations: Genie Awards '96: Best Actress (Brassard), Best Adapted Screenplay, Best Cinematography, Best Director (Lepage), Best Film, Best Sound, Best Supporting Actress (Descenes, De Medeiros). *NYR*

Le Repos du Guerrier 🎬🎬 *Warrior's Rest* 1962 Star vehicle for Bardot in which she plays a respectable woman who abandons societal norms to pursue an unbalanced lover. In French with English subtitles. 100m/C VHS, Beta. *FR* Brigitte Bardot, Robert Hossein, James Robertson Justice, Jean-Mark Bory; *D:* Roger Vadim. *BAR*

Le Schpountz 🎬🎬 *Heartbeat* 1938 Satire on filmmaking and film-loving fans finds a small town grocer (Fernandel) in southern France becoming the victim of a practical joke when a visiting film crew promises to make him a star (signing him to a phony contract) if he'll come to Paris. Naturally, the joke's on them when the naive grocer arrives in the City of Light and becomes a successful movie comic. French with subtitles. 135m/B VHS. *FR* Fernandel, Charpin, Orane Demazis, Odette Roger, Jean Castan, Leon Belieres; *D:* Marcel Pagnol; *W:* Marcel Pagnol; *C:* Willy; *M:* Casimir Oberfeld. *INT*

Le Secret 🎬🎬🎬 1974 This classic French thriller with a shocking ending finds an escaped convict seeking shelter with a reclusive couple in the mountains. His tales of abuse and torture create tension for the pair as one believes the woeful story and the other doesn't. Dubbed in English. 103m/C VHS, Beta. *FR* Jean-Louis Trintignant, Philippe Noiret, Jean-Francois Adam; *D:* Robert Enrico; *M:* Ennio Morricone. *NO*

Le Sex Shop 🎬🎬🎬 1973 (R) A man turns his little book store into a porn equipment palace, to make ends meet. When his relationship with his wife gets boring, they begin to use their erotic merchandise and adopt a swinging lifestyle. 92m/C VHS, Beta. *FR* Claude Berri, Juliet Berto, Daniel Auteuil, Nathalie Delon; *D:* Claude Berri; *M:* Serge Gainsbourg. *COL*

Le Sexe des Etoiles 🎬🎬 *The Sex of the Stars* 1993 Curiously uninvolving film about 12-year-old Camille who discovers that the father who abandoned her is now a transsexual. Pierre walked out years before and Camille has always dreamed of his return but though they reach a tentative relationship, it's not what Camille hoped for. Title refers to Camille's obsession with astronomy because stars have no sex. Based on the novel by Proulx (who also wrote the screenplay). In French with English subtitles. **100m/C VHS.** *CA* Marianne-Coquelicot Mercier, Denis Mercier, Tobie Pelletier, Sylvie Drapeau; **D:** Paule Baillargeon; **W:** Monique Proulx. Genie Awards '93: Best Sound. *ICA*

Leader of the Band 🎬🎬 **1987 (PG)** An out-of-work musician tries to train the world's worst high school band. Landesberg helps this attempted comedy along. **90m/C VHS, Beta, LV.** Steve Landesburg, Gailard Sartain, Mercedes Ruehl, James Martinez, Calvert Deforest; **D:** Nessa Hyams; **M:** Dick Hyman. *LIV*

The League of Gentlemen 🎬🎬🎬½ **1960** An ex-Army officer plots a daring bank robbery using specially skilled military personnel and irreproachable panache. Hilarious British humor fills the screen. **115m/B VHS, Beta.** *GB* Jack Hawkins, Nigel Patrick, Richard Attenborough, Roger Livesey, Bryan Forbes; **D:** Basil Dearden. *HMV, FCT*

A League of Their Own 🎬🎬🎬 **1992 (PG)** Charming look at sports history and the Rockford Peaches, one of the teams in the real-life All American Girls Professional Baseball League, formed in the 40s when the men were off at war. Main focus is on sibling rivalry between Davis, the beautiful, crackerjack catcher, and Petty, the younger, insecure pitcher. Boozy coach Hanks is wonderful as he reluctantly leads the team; he also gets credit for the classic "There's no crying in baseball" scene. Great cast of supporting characters, including sarcastic talent scout Lovitz, opinionated, sleazy taxi dancer Madonna, loud-mouthed O'Donnell, and shy, homely Cavanagh. Lots of baseball for the sports fan. **127m/C VHS, Beta, LV, Closed Caption, DVD.** Tom Hanks, Geena Davis, Madonna, Lori Petty, Jon Lovitz, David Strathairn, Garry Marshall, Bill Pullman, Rosie O'Donnell, Megan Cavanagh, Tracy Reiner, Bitty Schram, Ann Cusack, Anne Elizabeth Ramsay, Freddie Simpson, Renee Coleman; **D:** Penny Marshall; **W:** Lowell Ganz, Babaloo Mandel; **M:** Hans Zimmer. *COL*

Lean on Me 🎬🎬🎬 **1989 (PG-13)** The romanticized version of the career of Joe Clark, a tough New Jersey teacher who became the principal of the state's toughest, worst school and, through controversial hard-line tactics, turned it around. **109m/C VHS, Beta, LV, 8mm, Closed Caption.** Morgan Freeman, Robert Guillaume, Beverly Todd, Alan North, Lynne Thigpen, Robin Bartlett, Michael Beach, Ethan Phillips, Regina Taylor; **D:** John G. Avildsen; **W:** Michael Schiffer; **M:** Bill Conti. *WAR, FCT*

Leap of Faith 🎬🎬½ **1992 (PG-13)** Jonas Nightengale (Martin) is a traveling evangelist/scam artist whose tour bus is stranded in an impoverished farm town. Nevertheless he sets up his show and goes to work, aided by the technology utilized by accomplice Winger. Both Martin and Winger begin to have a change of heart after experiencing love—Winger with local sheriff Neeson and Martin after befriending a waitress (Davidovich) and her crippled brother (Haas). Martin is in his element as the slick revivalist with the hidden heart but the film is soft-headed as well as soft-hearted.**CW:** Some language. **110m/C VHS, Beta, LV, Closed Caption.** Steve Martin, Debra Winger, Lolita Davidovich, Liam Neeson, Lukas Haas, Meat Loaf, Philip S. Hoffman, M.C. Gainey, La Chanze, Delores Hall, John Toles-Bey, Albertina Walker, Ricky Dillard; **D:** Richard Pearce; **W:** Janus Cercone; **M:** Cliff Eidelman. *PAR, BTV*

Leap Year 🎬🎬½ **1921** Made at the apex of the 300 pound comedian's career, "Leap Year" wasn't released in the States until the sixties. Tried for manslaughter in 1921 (with two hung juries), Fatty was forced off camera and his films were taken out of circulation (although he did return to cinema behind the camera using the pseudonym William Goodrich). **60m/B VHS, Beta.** Fatty Arbuckle. *GPV, FCT*

Leapin' Leprechauns 🎬🎬½ **1995 (PG)** John Dennehy's dad Michael has arrived from Ireland for a visit, accompanied by some "wee folk" who are invisible to all non-believers. Seems the little leprechauns are just in time to rescue their ancestral home from a plot by John to turn their Irish land into a theme park and make believers out of a family of skeptics. **84m/C VHS, Beta, Closed Caption.** Grant Cramer, John Bluthal, Sharon Lee Jones, Gregory Edward Smith, Sylvester McCoy, James Ellis, Godfrey James, Tina Martin, Erica Nicole Hess; **D:** Ted Nicolaou; **W:** Ted Nicolaou, Michael McGann. *PAR*

The Learning Tree 🎬🎬 **1969 (PG)** A beautifully photographed adaptation of Parks' biographical novel about a fourteen-year-old black boy in the 1920s South, living on the verge of manhood, maturity, love, and wisdom. **107m/C VHS, Beta.** Kyle Johnson, Alex Clarke, Estelle Evans, Dana Elcar; **D:** Gordon Parks; **C:** Burnett Guffey. *WAR, FCT, AFR*

Leather Boys 🎬🎬 **1963** A teen-aged girl marries a mechanic and then begins to look beyond the boundaries of marriage. Considered very controversial in the 60s, but less so now. **103m/C VHS, Beta.** *GB* Rita Tushingham, Dudley Sutton, Gladys Henson, Colin Campbell, Avice Landon, Lockwood West, Betty Marsden, Johnny Briggs, Geoffrey Dunn, Dandy Nichols; **D:** Sidney J. Furie. *NO*

Leather Burners 🎬🎬 **1943** Hoppy goes under cover to get the goods on a suspected rustler. When his cover is blown, the bad guys frame him for murder. Look for Robert Mitchum in his third bit part in this series. **66m/B VHS.** William Boyd, Andy Clyde, Jay Kirby, Victor Jory, George Givot, Bobby Larson, George Reeves, Hal Taliaferro, Forbes Murray, Robert Mitchum; **D:** Joseph Henabery. *NOS, MRV*

Leather Jackets 🎬🎬 **1990 (R)** Sweeney plays a nice guy who lets involvement with a childhood pal destroy his life. Elwes is the friend, now gang member, in trouble with both the cops and members of a rival gang, who needs Sweeney's help to escape. Fonda plays Sweeney's girlfriend caught between the two men. Essentially a routine fugitive pic with an attractive cast.**CW:** Language, violence, and sensuality. **90m/C VHS, LV, Closed Caption.** D.B. Sweeney, Bridget Fonda, Cary Elwes, Christopher Penn, Marshall Bell, James LeGros, Jon Polito, Craig Ng, Ginger Lynn Allen; **D:** Lee Drysdale; **W:** Lee Drysdale. *COL*

Leatherface: The Texas Chainsaw Massacre 3 🎬 **1989 (R)** The human-skin-wearing cannibal is at it again in this, the second sequel to the Tobe Hooper proto-mess. This one sports a bit more humor and is worth seeing for that reason. **81m/C VHS, Beta, LV.** Kate Hodge, William Butler, Ken Foree, Tom Hudson, R.A. Mihailoff; **D:** Jeff Burr; **W:** David J. Schow; **C:** James L. Carter. *COL*

The Leatherneck 🎬🎬 **1928** Love unrequited in a faraway place starring soon to be cowboy (Hopalong Cassidy) matinee idol Boyd and Hale, the real life dad of Gilligan Island's skipper. **65m/B VHS, Beta.** William Boyd, Alan Hale, Diane Ellis. Nominations: Academy Awards '29: Best Writing. *GPV, FCT*

Leave 'Em Laughing 🎬🎬 **1981** Rooney plays Chicago clown Jack Thum in this based-on-real-life TV movie. Thum takes in orphans even though he cannot find steady work, and then discovers he has cancer. **103m/C VHS, Beta, Closed Caption.** Mickey Rooney, Anne Jackson, Allen (Goorwitz) Garfield, Elisha Cook Jr., William Windom, Red Buttons, Michael Le Clair; **D:** Jackie Cooper. *FRH*

Leave Her to Heaven 🎬🎬🎬 **1945** Beautiful neurotic Tierney takes drastic measures to keep hubby all to herself and will do anything to get what she wants. Tierney, in a departure from her usual roles, is excellent as this pathologically possessive creature. Oscar-winner Leon Shamroy's photography (in Technicolor) is breathtaking. Based on the novel by Ben Ames Williams. **110m/C VHS.** Gene Tierney, Cornel Wilde, Jeanne Crain, Vincent Price, Mary Philips, Ray Collins, Darryl Hickman, Gene Lockhart; **D:** John M. Stahl; **W:** Jo Swerling; **C:** Leon Shamroy; **M:** Alfred Newman. Academy Awards '45: Best Color Cinematography; Nominations: Academy Awards '45: Best Actress (Tierney), Best Sound. *FXV*

Leave It to Beaver 🎬🎬 **1997 (PG)** Gee, Mrs. Cleaver, that's an awful nice updating of an old TV favorite you have there. Cut the crap, Eddie. The "let's plop a lovable sitcom family into the dysfunctional 90s" bit has had its run. This time the victims are the Cleavers: wise dad Ward (McDonald), perfect mom June (Turner), popular older brother Wally (von Detten)...and newcomer Cameron Finley as the Beaver. Unlike the Bradys, the modern world has made some impact here. Beav has an African American friend while Mom wears jeans and owns a business. Gosh Wally, do you really think America was anxiously awaiting the return of the impossible-to-live-up-to clan? Don't be such a little dope. **?m/C VHS.** Christopher McDonald, Janine Turner, Erik von Detten, Cameron Finley; **D:** Andy Cadiff; **W:** Brian Levant. *NYR*

Leave It to the Marines 🎬½ **1951** A jerky guy wanders into a recruiting office instead of a marriage license bureau and unwittingly signs on for military service. **66m/B VHS, Beta, LV.** Sid Melton, Mara Lynn. *NO*

Leaves from Satan's Book 🎬🎬½ **1919** Impressionistic episodes of Satan's fiddling with man through the ages, from Christ to the Russian Revolution. An early cinematic film by Dreyer, with ample indications of his later brilliance. Silent. **165m/B VHS, Beta.** *DK* Helge Milsen, Halvart Hoft, Jacob Texiere; **D:** Carl Theodor Dreyer. *GPV, FCT, GVV*

Leaving Las Vegas 🎬🎬🎬½ **1995 (R)** Ben Sanderson (Cage) is a hopeless alcoholic who goes to Vegas to drink himself to death and meets Sera (Shue), a lonely hooker who loves him enough not to stop him. Definitely as depressing as it sounds, but still manages to have both a subtle sense of humor and compassion. Cage tops his best work and Shue proves she deserves better than the lightweight roles she's had in the past. Not for everyone, but worth the effort for people who like to see honest emotion and hate Hollywood's insistence on happy endings. Based on the semi-autobiographical novel by John O'Brien, who committed suicide shortly before pre-production began.**CW:** Strong sexuality and language, violence, pervasive alcohol abuse. **120m/C VHS, LV, Closed Caption.** Nicolas Cage, Elisabeth Shue, Julian Sands, Laurie Metcalf, David Brisbin, Richard Lewis, Valeria Golino, Steven Weber; **D:** Mike Figgis; **W:** Mike Figgis; **C:** Declan Quinn; **M:** Mike Figgis. Academy Awards '95: Best Actor (Cage); Golden Globe Awards '96: Best Actor—Drama (Cage); Independent Spirit Awards '96: Best Actress (Shue), Best Cinematography, Best Director (Figgis), Best Film; Los Angeles Film Critics Association Awards '95: Best Actor (Cage), Best Actress (Shue), Best Director (Figgis), Best Film; National Board of Review Awards '95: Best Actor (Cage); New York Film Critics Awards '95: Best Actor (Cage), Best Film; National Society of Film Critics Awards '95: Best Actor (Cage), Best Actress (Shue), Best Director (Figgis); Screen Actors Guild Award '95: Best Actor (Cage); Nominations: Academy Awards '95: Best Actress (Shue), Best Adapted Screenplay, Best Director (Figgis); British Academy Awards '95: Best Actor (Cage), Best Actress (Shue), Best Adapted Screenplay; Directors Guild of America Awards '95: Best Director (Figgis); Golden Globe Awards '96: Best Actress—Drama (Shue), Best Director (Figgis), Best Film—Drama; Independent Spirit Awards '96: Best Actor (Cage), Best Screenplay; Screen Actors Guild Award '95: Best Actress (Shue); Writers Guild of America '95: Best Adapted Screenplay. *MGM*

Leaving Normal 🎬½ **1992 (R)** Darly, a fed-up waitress, and Marianne, an abused housewife, meet at a bus stop in Normal, Wyoming and decide to blow town. They travel across the American West, through Canada, and up to Alaska. Because both women have made bad choices all their lives, they decide to leave their futures to chance, and end up finding their nirvana. Plot is similar to "Thelma & Louise," but "Leaving Normal" doesn't come close to the innovativeness of the former. Sappy and sentimental to the point of annoyance at times.**CW:** Language. **110m/C VHS, LV, Closed Caption.** Christine Lahti, Meg Tilly, Lenny Von

Dohlen, Maury Chaykin, James Gammon, Patrika Darbo, Eve Gordon, James Eckhouse, Brett Cullen, Rutanya Alda; *D:* Edward Zwick; *W:* Edward Solomon; *C:* Ralf Bode. *USH*

L'Ecole Buisoniere 🎬🎬½ 1951 In a provincial French school a teacher with modern ideas inspires his students with a passion for learning until the suspicious parents are aroused. In French with English subtitles. 108m/C VHS. *FR D:* Jean-Paul LeChanois. *FCT, WBF*

The Leech Woman 🎬🎬 1959 While in Africa, an older woman (Gray) discovers how to restore her youth through a tribal ritual. The only problem is it requires the pineal gland of males, which causes her to go on a killing spree to keep that youthful look. Based on a story by Ben Pivar and Francis Rosenwald. 77m/B VHS, Closed Caption. Coleen Gray, Grant Williams, Gloria Talbot, Phillip Terry; *D:* Edward Dein; *W:* David Duncan. *USH*

Left for Dead 🎬½ 1978 A millionaire is accused of brutally killing his wife, and discovers in his search for an alibi that he is the victim of a conspiracy. 82m/C VHS, Beta. Elke Sommer, Donald Pilon; *D:* Murray Markowitz. *LIV, VES*

The Left Hand of God 🎬🎬🎬 1955 After an American pilot escapes from a Chinese warlord in post-WWII, he disguises himself as a Catholic priest and takes refuge in a missionary hospital. Bogie is great as the flyboy/cleric. 87m/C VHS, Beta. Humphrey Bogart, E.G. Marshall, Lee J. Cobb, Agnes Moorehead, Gene Tierney; *D:* Edward Dmytryk. *FOX*

The Left-Handed Gun 🎬🎬🎬 1958 An offbeat version of the exploits of Billy the Kid, which portrays him as a 19th-century Wild West juvenile delinquent. Newman's role, which he method-acted, was originally intended for James Dean. Based on a 1955 Philco teleplay by Gore Vidal. 102m/B VHS, Beta. Paul Newman, Lita Milan, John Dehner; *D:* Arthur Penn. *WAR, TLF*

The Legacy 🎬½ *The Legacy of Maggie Walsh* 1979 (R) An American couple become privy to the dark secrets of an English family gathering in a creepy mansion to inherit an eccentric millionaire's fortune. Death and demons abound. 100m/C VHS, Beta. *GB* Katharine Ross, Sam Elliott, John Standing, Roger Daltrey, Ian Hogg; *D:* Richard Marquand. *USH*

A Legacy for Leonette woof! 1985 A girl is led into a web of murder and love in this torrid romance novel brought to video. 90m/C Beta. Loyita Chapel, Michael Anderson Jr., Dinah Anne Rogers. *PSM*

Legacy of Horror woof! 1978 (R) A weekend at the family's island mansion with two unfriendly siblings sounds bad enough, but when terror, death, and a few family skeletons pop out of the closets, things go from bad to weird. All-round poor effort with substantial gore. A remake of the director's own "The Ghastly Ones." 83m/C VHS, Beta. Elaine Boies, Chris Broderick, Marilee Troncone, Jeannie Cusik; *D:* Andy Milligan. *MPI*

Legacy of Lies 🎬🎬½ 1992 (R) Zack Resnick is a serious, honest Chicago cop assigned to a murder investigation. He first discovers the killers got the wrong man and then finds out a lot of family secrets he wishes he didn't know. His cop-father is on the take to the Mob, which is really no surprise since Zack's grandfather turns out to be a retired gangland boss, all of which leaves Zack wondering where his loyalties lie. Too intricate plot hampers the story's flow but the cast performances are well worth watching. Made for cable television. *CW:* Gangster violence. 94m/C VHS, LV, Closed Caption. Michael Ontkean, Martin Landau, Eli Wallach, Joe Morton, Patricia Clarkson, Gerry Becker, Chelcie Ross, Ron Dean; *D:* Jason Meshover-Iorg; *W:* David Black. National Academy of Cable Programming ACE Awards '93: Best Supporting Actor (Landau). *USH*

Legal Eagles 🎬🎬½ 1986 (PG) An assistant D.A. faces murder, mayhem, and romance while prosecuting a girl accused of stealing a portrait painted by her father. Redford sparkles in this otherwise convoluted tale from Reitman, while Hannah lacks depth as the daffy thief. 116m/C VHS,

Beta, LV, Closed Caption. Robert Redford, Debra Winger, Daryl Hannah, Brian Dennehy, Terence Stamp, Steven Hill, David Clennon, Roscoe Lee Browne, John McMartin, Jennie Dundas, Ivan Reitman; *D:* Ivan Reitman; *W:* Jim Cash, Jack Epps Jr.; *M:* Elmer Bernstein. *USH*

Legal Tender 🎬½ 1990 (R) Rude talk-show host Downey as a corrupt S & L chief? Big, menacing Davi as a romantic hero? Give this often-inept thriller credit for creative casting, if little else. Roberts adds steamy sex appeal as a lovely saloon-keeper imperiled by deadly bank fraud. *CW:* Language, graphic violence and drug use, and graphic sensuality. 93m/C VHS, Beta. Robert Davi, Tanya Roberts, Morton Downey Jr.; *D:* Jag Mundhra. *PSM*

Legend 🎬🎬 1986 (PG) A colorful, unabashedly Tolkien-esque fantasy about the struggle to save an innocent waif from the Prince of Darkness. Set in a land packed with unicorns, magic swamps, bumbling dwarves and rainbows. Produced in Great Britain. 89m/C VHS, Beta, LV, Closed Caption. *GB* Tom Cruise, Mia Sara, Tim Curry, David Bennett, Billy Barty, Alice Playten; *D:* Ridley Scott; *M:* Jerry Goldsmith. Nominations: Academy Awards '86: Best Makeup. *FOX*

Legend of Alfred Packer 🎬½ 1980 The true story of how a guide taking five men searching for gold in Colorado managed to be the sole survivor of a blizzard. 87m/C VHS, Beta. Patrick Dray, Ron Haines, Bob Damon, Dave Ellingson; *D:* Jim Roberson. *NO*

Legend of Big Foot 🎬 1982 Facing a spree of killings, a local town mobilizes to stop the legendary beast. 92m/C VHS, Beta. Stafford Morgan, Katherine Hopkins. *NO*

Legend of Billie Jean 🎬🎬 1985 (PG-13) Billie Jean believed in justice for all. When the law and its bureaucracy landed hard on her, she took her cause to the masses and inspired a generation. 92m/C VHS, Beta, Closed Caption. Helen Slater, Peter Coyote, Keith Gordon, Christian Slater, Richard Bradford, Yeardley Smith, Dean Stockwell; *D:* Matthew Robbins; *W:* Mark Rosenthal. *FOX*

The Legend of Black Thunder Mountain 🎬½ 1979 (G) A children's adventure in the mold of "Grizzly Adams" and "The Wilderness Family." 90m/C VHS, Beta. Holly Beeman, Steve Beeman, Ron Brown, F.A. Milovich; *D:* Tom Beeman. *NO*

The Legend of Blood Castle 🎬 *The Female Butcher; Blood Ceremony; Ceremonia Sangrienta* 1972 (R) Another version of the Countess of Bathory legend, in which an evil woman bathes in the blood of virgins in an attempt to keep the wrinkles away. Released hot on the heels of Hammer's "Countess Dracula." 87m/C VHS, Beta. *IT SP* Lucia Bose, Ewa Aulin; *D:* Jorge Grau. *NO*

Legend of Boggy Creek 🎬½ 1975 (G) A dramatized version of various Arkansas Bigfoot sightings. 87m/C VHS, Beta. Willie E. Smith, John P. Nixon, John W. Gates, Jeff Crabtree, Buddy Crabtree; *D:* Charles B. Pierce; *W:* Charles B. Pierce. *LIV, MRV*

Legend of Earl Durand 🎬½ 1974 In Wyoming 1939, a man spends his life searching for freedom and justice. His Robin Hood actions cause a manhunt of massive proportions. 90m/C VHS. Martin Sheen, Peter Haskell, Keenan Wynn, Slim Pickens, Anthony Caruso; *D:* John D. Patterson. *NO*

The Legend of Frank Woods 🎬🎬 1977 Gunslinger returns to the land of the free after an extended holiday south of the border. Mistaken for an expected preacher in a small town, he poses as the padre and signs on the dotted line to take out a new lease on life. 88m/C VHS. Troy Donahue, Brad Steward, Kitty Vallacher, Michael Christian; *D:* Deno Paoli. *SIM*

Legend of Frenchie King 🎬½ *Petroleum Girls* 1971 When prospectors discover oil on disputed land, two families feud over their conflicting claims to the property. Adult western still working out the kinks has Bardot heading a band of female outlaws. 96m/C VHS, Beta. Brigitte Bardot, Claudia

Cardinale, Michael J. Pollard, Micheline Presle; *D:* Christian-Jaque. *NO*

The Legend of Gator Face 🎬½ 1996 (PG) Hermit Winfield fills three youngsters in on their small community's legend of Gator Face— half-man, half-alligator. Kids being kids, they decide to wade through the swamps in search of the creature, which they find and also realize is harmless. Too bad the local folk don't believe the same thing and call out the national guard to destroy it. 100m/C VHS. Paul Winfield, John White, Dan Warry-Smith, C. David Johnson, Gordon Michael Woolvett; *D:* Vic Sarin. *HMK*

The Legend of Hell House 🎬🎬🎬 1973 (PG) A multi-millionaire hires a team of scientists and mediums to investigate his newly acquired haunted mansion. It seems that the creepy house has been the site of a number of deaths and may hold clues to the afterlife. A suspenseful, scary screamfest. Matheson wrote the screenplay from his novel "Hell House." 94m/C VHS, Beta, LV, Closed Caption. Roddy McDowall, Pamela Franklin, Clive Revill, Gayle Hunnicutt; *D:* John Hough; *W:* Richard Matheson. *FOX*

The Legend of Hillbilly John 🎬 *Who Fears the Devil; My Name is John* 1973 (G) Hillbilly John holds off the devil with a strum of his six-string. While demons plague the residents of rural America, the hayseed messiah wanders about saving the day. 86m/C VHS, Beta, LV. Severn Darden, Denver Pyle, Susan Strasberg, Hedge Capers; *D:* John Newland. *NWV*

The Legend of Jedediah Carver 🎬🎬 197? A rancher battles desert elements and hostile Indians in a desperate bid for survival. 90m/C VHS. DeWitt Lee, Joshua Hoffman, Val Chapman, Richard Montgomery, David Terril; *D:* DeWitt Lee. *XVC*

Legend of Lobo 🎬½ 1962 The story of Lobo, a crafty wolf who seeks to free his mate from the clutches of greedy hunters. A Disney wildlife adventure. 67m/C VHS, Beta. *DIS*

The Legend of Sea Wolf 🎬🎬 1975 (PG) A sadistic sea captain forcefully rules his crew in this weak version of Jack London's novel. Also known as "Wolf Larsen." 90m/C VHS, Beta. Chuck Connors, Barbara Bach, Joseph Palmer. *NO*

The Legend of Sleepy Hollow 1949 The story of Ichabod Crane and the legendary ride of the headless horseman by Washington Irving; narrated by Crosby. Also includes two classic short cartoons, "Lonesome Ghosts" (1932) with Mickey Mouse and "Trick or Treat" (1952) with Donald Duck. 45m/C VHS, Beta. *D:* Jack Kinney, Clyde Geronimi, James Algar. *DIS*

The Legend of Sleepy Hollow 🎬🎬½ 1979 (G) Washington Irving's classic tale of the Headless Horseman of Sleepy Hollow is brought to life on the screen. Made for television. 100m/C VHS, Beta, LV. Jeff Goldblum, Dick Butkus, Paul Sand, Meg Foster, James Griffith, John S. White. *NO*

The Legend of Sleepy Hollow 1986 Classic Washington Irving tale is given the Shelly Duvall treatment in her "Tall Tales and Legends" series. When a snooty teacher goes too far, the town blacksmith decides to play the ultimate Halloween trick on him. Made for cable television. 51m/C VHS, Closed Caption. Ed Begley Jr., Beverly D'Angelo, Charles Durning, Tim Thomerson. *FOX*

The Legend of Suram Fortress 🎬🎬 *Legenda Suramskoi Kreposti* 1985 Based on a Georgian folktale about a medieval fortress that collapses as soon as it is built. The village soothsayer tells a young man he must sacrifice himself, by bricking himself up alive within the fortress walls, if the building is every to stand. In Russian with English subtitles. 89m/C VHS. *RU* Levan Outchanechvili, Zourab Kipchidze; *D:* Sergei Paradjanov. *KIV*

Legend

Legend of the Lone Ranger 🎬½ **1981 (PG)** The fabled Lone Ranger (whose voice is dubbed throughout the entire movie) and the story of his first meeting with his Indian companion, Tonto, are brought to life in this weak and vapid version of the famous legend. The narration by Merle Haggard leaves something to be desired as do most of the performances. **98m/C VHS, Beta.** Klinton Spilsbury, Michael Horse, Jason Robards Jr., Richard Farnsworth, Christopher Lloyd, Matt Clark; **D:** William A. Fraker; **W:** William Roberts, Ivan Goff, Michael Kane; **M:** John Barry. Golden Raspberry Awards '81: Worst Actor (Spilsbury), Worst New Star (Spilsbury). **FOX**

Legend of the Lost 🎬🎬 **1957** Two men vie for desert treasure and desert women. Interesting only because of Wayne, but certainly not one of his more memorable films. **109m/C VHS.** John Wayne, Sophia Loren, Rossano Brazzi, Kurt Kasznar, Sonia Moser; **D:** Henry Hathaway; **C:** Jack Cardiff. **MGM**

Legend of the Lost Tomb 🎬🎬½ **1997 (PG)** Made for cable adventure finds Egyptologist Dr. Leonhardt (Rossovich) discovering half of an ancient papyrus that could lead to the riches of the desert tomb of pharaoh Ramses II. But Leonhardt is ambused by his rival Dr. Bent (Keach), who demands the rest of the document, which just happens to be in the hands of Leonhardt's son (Pierce) and his archaeologist associate Karen (Peterson). **90m/C VHS.** Rick Rossovich, Stacy Keach, Kimberlee Peterson, Brock Pierce. **EVE**

Legend of the Northwest 🎬🎬 **1978 (G)** The loyalty of a dog is evidenced in the fierce revenge he has for the drunken hunter who shot and killed his master. **83m/C VHS, Beta.** Denver Pyle. **VTR, GEM, HHE**

The Legend of the Sea Wolf 🎬🎬½ *Wolf Larsen; Larsen, Wolf of the Seven Seas* **1958** Adaptation of Jack London's dramatic adventure novel, "The Sea Wolf." A slave driving ship captain rescues a shipwreck victim and sets to abusing him along with the rest of his crew. A rebellion ensues. Superb musical score benefits the strong acting and good pace. **83m/B VHS.** Barry Sullivan, Peter Graves, Gita Hall, Thayer David; **D:** Harmon Jones; **W:** Jack DeWitt. **NO**

Legend of the Werewolf 🎬🎬 **1975 (R)** A child who once ran with the wolves has forgotten his past, except when the moon is full. **90m/C VHS, Beta.** **GB** Peter Cushing, Hugh Griffith, Ron Moody, David Rintoul, Lynn Dalby; **D:** Freddie Francis. **MRV**

The Legend of the Wolf Woman 🎬🎬½ **1977 (R)** The beautiful Daniella assumes the personality of the legendary wolf-woman, leaving a trail of gruesome killings across the countryside. Genre fans will find this one surprisingly entertaining. Also on video as "Werewolf Woman." **84m/C VHS, Beta.** **IT** Anne Borel, Fred Stafford, Tino Carey, Elliot Zamuto, Ollie Reynolds, Andrea Scotti, Karen Carter; **D:** Raphael D. Silver. **VIP**

Legend of Tom Dooley 🎬🎬 **1959** Somber western about three Confederate soldiers who rob a Union stagecoach and kill two soldiers, not knowing that the Civil War has ended. Landon turns in a good performance as the Rebel soldier turned outlaw. Based on the hit song by the Kingston trio. **79m/B VHS.** Michael Landon, Jo Morrow, Jack Hogan, Richard Rust, Dee Pollock, Ken Lynch; **D:** Ted Post; **M:** Ronald Stein. **COL**

Legend of Valentino 1975 Made-for-television docudrama traces the legendary exploits of one of the silver screen's greatest lovers, Rudolph Valentino. Typical TV-movie fare that lacks the power of the legend's life. **96m/C VHS, Beta.** Franco Nero, Suzanne Pleshette, Lesley Ann Warren, Yvette Mimieux, Judd Hirsch, Milton Berle, Harold J. Stone; **D:** Melville Shavelson. **PSM, MRV, NLC**

The Legend of Valentino 1983 A biographical documentary of perhaps the world's greatest lover, beginning with his immigration to America and ending at his unexpected, sudden death. **71m/B VHS, Beta.**

Legend of Walks Far Woman 🎬 **1982** A made for television film about a proud Sioux woman fighting for survival and her tribe during the American-Indian Wars. Welch is miscast. From Colin Stuart's novel. **120m/C VHS, Beta.** Raquel Welch, Nick Mancuso, Bradford Dillman; **D:** Mel Damski. **NO**

The Legend of Wolf Mountain 🎬🎬½ **1992 (PG)** Three children are held hostage by two prison escapees in the Utah mountains. They are aided in their escape by a Native American "wolf spirit." With the criminals on their trail will the three be able to survive in the wilderness until a search party can find them? **91m/C VHS, LV, Closed Caption.** Mickey Rooney, Bo Hopkins, Don Shanks, Vivian Schilling, Robert Z'Dar, David Shark, Nicole Lund, Natalie Lund, Matthew Lewis, Jonathan Best; **D:** Craig Clyde; **W:** Craig Clyde. **HMD**

Legends of the Fall 🎬🎬 **1994 (R)** Sweeping, meandering, melodramatic family saga set in Montana (though filmed in Alberta, Canada). Patriarch William Ludlow (Hopkins), a retired Army colonel, is raising three sons: reserved Alfred (Quinn), idealistic Samuel (Thomas), and wild middle son Tristan (Pitt). In 1913, Samuel returns from Boston with a fiancee, the lovely and refined Susannah (Ormond). Only problem is Alfred and Tristan take one look and also desire her—a passion that will carry them through some 20 years of heartbreak. Film loses the spare toughness of the Jim Harrison novella but is a visual feast (and not just because the camera seems to drool every time Pitt appears on screen).**CW:** Gory violence; nudity; sexual situations. **134m/C VHS, LV, 8mm, Closed Caption, DVD.** Brad Pitt, Aidan Quinn, Julia Ormond, Anthony Hopkins, Henry Thomas, Gordon Tootoosis, Tantoo Cardinal, Karina Lombard, Paul Desmond, Kenneth Welsh; **D:** Edward Zwick; **W:** Susan Shilliday, William D. Wittliff; **C:** John Toll; **M:** James Horner. Academy Awards '94: Best Cinematography; Nominations: Academy Awards '94: Best Art Direction/Set Decoration, Best Sound; Golden Globe Awards '95: Best Actor—Drama (Pitt), Best Director (Zwick), Best Film—Drama, Best Original Score. **COL**

Legends of the North 🎬🎬½ **1995 (PG)** Crusty prospector Whip Gorman (Quaid) and partner Paul Bel Air are searching for a mythical lake of gold when Paul takes a fall off a mountain. Whip sends for Paul's son Charles so that he can translate his father's diary (it's in French) and get the clues to the gold's whereabouts. Naturally, some rival prospectors, some Indians, and even a feisty gal or two help or hinder our treasure seekers. Based on a story by Jack London. **95m/C VHS.** Randy Quaid. **THV**

Legion of Iron 🎬 **1990 (R)** Adventures in a computer-run, neo-Roman civilization where men and women battle for supremacy. **85m/C VHS, Beta, LV.** Kevin T. Walsh, Erica Nann, Regie De Morton, Camille Carrigan; **D:** Yakov Bentsvi. **COL**

Legion of Missing Men 🎬½ **1937** Professional soldiers of fortune, the French Foreign Legion, fight the evil sheik Ahmed in the Sahara. **62m/B VHS, Beta.** Ralph Forbes, Ben Alexander, Hala Linda, Roy D'Arcy, Paul Hurst, Jimmy Aubrey; **D:** Hamilton MacFadden. **VYY, GPV**

Legion of the Lawless 🎬½ **1940** Group of outlaws band together in order to spread terror and confusion among the populace. **59m/B VHS, Beta.** George O'Brien, Virginia Vale. **MED**

Legs 🎬🎬 **1983** Backstage story of three girls who are competing for a job with Radio City Music Hall's Rockettes. Made for television. **91m/C VHS, Beta.** Gwen Verdon, John Heard, Sheree North, Shanna Reed, Maureen Teefy; **D:** Jerrold Freedman; **C:** Allen Daviau. **PSM**

L'Eleve 🎬🎬 *The Pupil* **1995** In 1897 Europe, an aristocratic family hires inexperienced 25-year-old Julien (Cassel) to tutor their precocious teenaged son, Morgan (Salmon). After a tentative battle for control, the two establish a strong emotional rapport and Julien learns that the family is not only in financial difficulty but is part of an empty, amoral social class only concerned with appearance. Based on a story by Henry James; French with subtitles. **92m/C VHS.** **FR** Vincent Cassel, Caspar Salmon, Caroline Cellier, Jean-Pierre Marielle, Sabine Destailleur, Sandrine Le Berre; **D:** Olivier Schatzky; **W:** Eve Deboise, Olivier Schatzky; **C:** Carlo Varini; **M:** Romano Musumarra. Montreal World Film Festival '95: Best Director (Schatzky). **NYR**

The Lemon Drop Kid 🎬🎬½ **1951** Second version of the Damon Runyon chestnut about a racetrack bookie who must recover the gangster's money he lost on a bet. As the fast-talking bookie, Hope sparkles. ♫Silver Bells; It Doesn't Cost a Dime to Dream; They Obviously Want Me to Sing. **91m/B VHS, Beta, LV.** Bob Hope, Lloyd Nolan, Fred Clark, Marilyn Maxwell, Jane Darwell, Andrea King, William Frawley, Jay C. Flippen, Harry Bellaver; **D:** Sidney Lanfield; **W:** Frank Tashlin, Edmund Hartmann, Robert O'Brien; **C:** Daniel F. Fapp. **COL**

The Lemon Sisters 🎬🎬 **1990 (PG-13)** Three women, friends and performance partners since childhood, struggle to buy their own club. They juggle the men in their lives with less success. Great actresses like these should have done more with this interesting premise, and the excellent male cast has much more potential. **93m/C VHS, LV, Closed Caption.** Diane Keaton, Carol Kane, Kathryn Grody, Elliott Gould, Ruben Blades, Aidan Quinn; **D:** Joyce Chopra. **HBO, FCT**

Lemora, Lady Dracula 🎬 *The Lady Dracula; The Legendary Curse of Lemora* **1973 (PG)** A pretty young church singer is drawn into the lair of the evil Lady Dracula, whose desires include her body as well as her blood. Horror fans will enjoy some excellent atmosphere, particularly in a scence where the girl's church bus is attacked by zombie-like creatures; Smith remains a '70s "B" movie favorite. Perhaps a double feature with "Lady Frankenstein...?" **80m/C VHS.** Leslie Gilb, Cheryl "Rainbeaux" Smith, William Whitton, Steve Johnson, Monty Pyke, Maxine Ballantyne, Parker West, Richard Blackburn; **D:** Richard Blackburn. **FRG**

Lena's Holiday 🎬🎬 **1990 (PG-13)** Fluffy comedy about a winsome East German girl visiting L.A. for the first time, and the culture-shock that ensues. Sharp script and performances. **97m/C VHS, LV.** Felicity Waterman, Chris Lemmon, Noriyuki "Pat" Morita, Susan Anton, Michael Sarrazin, Nick Mancuso, Bill Dana, Liz Torres; **D:** Michael Keusch. **PSM**

L'Enfant d'Eau 🎬🎬 *Water Child; Behind the Blue* **1995** Mentally handicapped twentysomething Emile (La Haye) and precocious 12-year-old Cedrine (Monette) must learn to work together to survive after a plane crash strands them on an island in the Bahamas. Familiar story offers no surprises and the script shies away from any sexual implications, negating two excellent performances. French with subtitles. **103m/C VHS.** **CA** David La Haye, Marie-France Monette; **D:** Robert Menard; **W:** Claire Wojas. Genie Awards '95: Best Actor (La Haye). **NYR**

L'Enfer 🎬🎬🎬 *Jealousy; Torment* **1993** Claustrophobic thriller chronicles the descent into madness of an unstable hotel owner (Cluzet) convinced that his beautiful wife (Beart) is having an affair. Intriguing plot points that blur appearances and reality lead to ambiguous and unsatisfying ending. Clouzot himself began filming his screenplay in 1964, but a heart attack forced him to abandon the project. In French with English subtitles. **103m/C VHS.** **FR** Emmanuelle Beart, Francois Cluzet, Nathalie Cardone, Andre Wilms, Marc Lavoine; **D:** Claude Chabrol; **W:** Claude Chabrol, Henri-Georges Clouzot, Jose-Andre Lacour. **FXL**

Leningrad Cowboys Go America 🎬🎬½ **1989 (PG-13)** An outlandish Finnish band, the Leningrad Cowboys, pack up their electric accordians and their one dead member and go on tour in America. With matching front-swept pompadours and pointy shoes, the group's appearance is the picture's best joke—and one of its only jokes, as the road trip plods in deadpan fashion that may bore viewers. It's best appreciated by fans of comic minimalist Jim Jarmusch (who has a guest role). In Finnish with English subtitles. **78m/C VHS, LV.** *Fl* Jim Jarmusch, Matti Pellonpaa, Kari Vaananen, Nicky Tesco; *D:* Aki Kaurismaki; *W:* Aki Kaurismaki. *ORI, FCT*

Lenny 🐾🐾🐾 1974 (R) Smoky nightclubs, drug abuse, and obscenities abound in Hoffman's portrayal of the controversial comedian Lenny Bruce, whose use of street language led to his eventual blacklisting. Perrine is a gem as his stripper wife. Adapted from the Julian Barry play, this is a visually compelling piece that sharply divided critics upon release. **111m/B VHS, Beta, LV, Closed Caption.** Dustin Hoffman, Valerie Perrine, Jan Miner, Stanley Beck; *D:* Bob Fosse; *W:* Julian Barry; *C:* Bruce Surtees; *M:* Ralph Burns. Cannes Film Festival '75: Best Actress (Perrine); National Board of Review Awards '74: 10 Best Films of the Year, Best Supporting Actress (Perrine); New York Film Critics Awards '74: Best Supporting Actress (Perrine); Nominations: Academy Awards '74: Best Actor (Hoffman), Best Actress (Perrine), Best Adapted Screenplay, Best Cinematography, Best Director (Fosse), Best Picture. *MGM, FOX*

Lensman 1984 In the 25th century space pirates known as the Boskande are threatening the civilized universe. Young Kimall Kenison is chosen by a higher power to become a lensman—and live or die for freedom. Based on the E.E. "Doc" Smith novels, this production is a combination of animation and computer graphics. Dubbed in English. **107m/C VHS, LV.** *JP STP, FUS*

Leo Tolstoy's Anna Karenina 🐾🐾½ *Leo Tolstoy's Anna Karenina* 1996 (PG-13) Well, the third film version of Tolstoy's tempestuous, tragic romance certainly looks good, even if the performances don't engender the passion the story demands. Beautiful married Anna (Marceau) leaves stuffy husband Karenin (Fox) and their son to travel to 1880 Moscow and mend the marriage of her philandering brother Stiva (Huston). But she meets dashing soldier, Count Alexei Vronsky (Bean), who immediately decides to pursue the beauty and the two begin an all-encompassing affair that leads to tragedy. This version also includes the secondary, contrasting romance between young Kitty (Kirshner) and Tolstoy's alter ego, questioning aristo Levin (Molina). Filmed on location in St. Petersburg, Russia. The classical score includes selections from Tschaikovsky, Rachmaninoff and Prokofiev, under the direction of Georg Solti.*CW:* Mature thematic elements and some sensuality/nudity. **120m/C VHS.** Sophie Marceau, Sean Bean, Alfred Molina, Mia Kirshner, Danny Huston, Fiona Shaw, Phyllida Law, David Schofield, Saskia Wickham; *D:* Bernard Rose; *W:* Bernard Rose; *C:* Daryn Okada. *NYR*

Leolo 🐾🐾 1992 Deeply disturbing black-comedy about one of the screen's most dysfunctional families. Leo is a 12-year-old French Canadian from Montreal who is determined to remake himself. He's decided to be a Sicilian lad named Leolo, escaping from his horrific family into his fantasies (and potential madness). His parents are obsessed with toilet training, his cowardly brother with body-building, his sisters are demented, and his grandfather is a sadistic, dirty old man. Not for the faint of heart (or stomach). In French with English subtitles. **107m/C VHS, LV.** *CA* Maxime Collin, Julien Guiomar, Ginette Reno, Pierre Bourgault, Yves Montmarquette, Roland Blouin, Giuditta del Vecchio; *D:* Jean-Claude Lauzon; *W:* Jean-Claude Lauzon. Genie Awards '92: Best Costume Design, Best Film Editing, Best Original Screenplay. *NLC, ING*

Leon Morin, Priest 🐾🐾½ 1961 A young priest and a widow, who happens to be a Communist, fall in love during the WWII German occupation of France. Based on the novel by Beatrix Beck. In French with English subtitles. **118m/B VHS.** *IT FR* Jean-Paul Belmondo, Emmanuelle Riva; *D:* Jean-Pierre Melville. *INT, FCT*

Leon the Pig Farmer 🐾🐾½ 1993 Dry comedic satire about identity. Leon Geller has never quite fitted into his parents' comfortable Jewish society and no wonder—Leon accidentally discovers he is the product of artificial insemination. And what's more, the lab made a mistake and Leon isn't a true Geller after all. His father is actually a genial (and Gentile) Yorkshire pig farmer named Brian Chadwick, who cheerfully welcomes Leon as his long-lost son. All four parents try to cope while Leon moves bewilderedly amongst them. The film tends to be too timid in its satire but still has its witty moments. **98m/C VHS.** *GB* Mark Frankel, Janet Suzman, Brian Glover, Connie Booth, David DeKeyser, Maryam D'Abo, Gina Bellman; *D:* Vadim Jean, Gary Sinyor; *W:* Gary Sinyor, Michael Normand. *ORI, FXL*

Leonard Part 6 🐾 1987 (PG) A former secret agent comes out of retirement to save the world from a crime queen using animals to kill agents. In the meantime, he tries to patch up his collapsing personal life. Wooden and disappointing; produced and co-written by Cosby, who himself panned the film. **83m/C VHS, Beta, LV, Closed Caption.** Bill Cosby, Gloria Foster, Tom Courtenay, Joe Don Baker; *D:* Paul Weiland; *W:* Bill Cosby, Jonathan Reynolds; *C:* Jan De Bont; *M:* Elmer Bernstein. Golden Raspberry Awards '87: Worst Picture, Worst Actor (Cosby), Worst Screenplay. *COL*

Leonor 🐾 1975 Idiotic medieval drivel with Ullmann rising from the dead after husband Piccoli seals her in a tomb. Directed by the son of Luis Bunuel. **90m/C VHS, Beta.** *FR SP IT* Liv Ullmann, Michel Piccoli, Ornella Muti; *D:* Juan Bunuel; *M:* Ennio Morricone. *FOX*

Leopard Fist Ninja 🐾 198? A masked ninja whacks away at American hoodlums in a fit of Maoist, anti-capitalistic fury. Dubbed. **88m/C VHS, Beta.** Willie Freeman, Jack Lam, Chuck Horry. *NO*

Leopard in the Snow 🐾🐾 1978 (PG) The romance between a race car driver allegedly killed in a crash and a young woman is the premise of this film. **89m/C VHS, Beta.** Keir Dullea, Susan Penhaligon, Kenneth More, Billie Whitelaw; *D:* Gerry O'Hara.

The Leopard Man 🐾🐾½ 1943 An escaped leopard terrorizes a small town in New Mexico. After a search, the big cat is found dead, but the killings continue. Minor but effective Jacques Tourneur creepie. Based on Cornell Woolrich's novel "Black Alibi." Another Val Lewton Horror production. **66m/B VHS, Beta, LV.** Jean Brooks, Isabel Jewell, James Bell, Margaret Landry, Dennis O'Keefe, Margo, Rita (Paula) Corday; *D:* Jacques Tourneur. *MED*

The Leopard Son 1996 (G) Beautiful documentary follows the birth and first two years of life for a leopard cub born on Africa's Serengeti plain. Mom leopard shows him how to survive and then he's out into the harsh world on his own. Parents should be forewarned that the hunt-and-kill scenes may upset the little ones. **87m/C VHS.** *D:* Hugo Van Lawick; *W:* Michael Olmert; *C:* Hugo Van Lawick, Matthew Aeberhard; *M:* Stewart Copeland. *HMK*

The Leopard Woman 🐾🐾 1920 Long before the cat lady cut her first claws, there was the leopard woman. Vamp Glaum finds much trouble to meow about on the Equator. **66m/B VHS, Beta.** Louise Glaum. *GPV, FCT, GVV*

Leper 🐾🐾 1976 A melodrama of forbidden love between a wealthy nobleman and a beautiful high school teacher. The townspeople try to destroy the love between the two because of their different social classes. In Polish with English subtitles. Also known as "Tredowata." **100m/C VHS.** *PL* Elzbieta Starostecka, Leszek Teleszynski; *D:* Jerzy Hoffman. *FCT*

Lepke 🐾🐾½ 1975 (R) The life and fast times of Louis "Lepke" Buchalter from his days in reform school to his days as head of Murder, Inc. and his execution in 1944. **110m/C VHS, Beta.** Tony Curtis, Milton Berle, Gianni Russo, Vic Tayback, Michael Callan; *D:* Menahem Golan. *WAR*

Leprechaun WOOF! 1993 (R) A sadistic 600-year-old leprechaun winds up wreaking havoc in North Dakota. If this makes no particular sense, neither does the film which is basic horror story excess. A man goes to Ireland for his mother's funeral, steals the gold belonging to the leprechaun, locks the creature up, and winds up accidentally taking the evil imp back to the States with him. When the leprechaun gets free, he wants a bloodthirsty revenge—and shoes. One of the so-called humorous bits is the leprechaun's shoe fetish. Irish eyes will not be smiling watching this mess.*CW:* Language and horror violence. **92m/C VHS, LV.** Warwick Davis, Jennifer Aniston, Ken Olandt, Mark Holton, John Sanderford, Robert Gorman; *D:* Mark Jones; *W:* Mark Jones. *THV*

Leprechaun 2 🐾🐾½ 1994 (R) Sequel to the Irish horror flick about a malevolent gnome. It seems one of his fairy entitlements is that he can possess any woman he wants if she sneezes three times. Thwarted in his attempt to snare a comely lass one thousand years earlier, he returns to present-day California to exact revenge on her descendant Durkin. Contrary to the popular legend that leprechauns are benign kind-hearted sprites, this nasty combines the treachery of a Gestapo officer with the firepower of Rambo in his attempt to harass the unimpressed Durkin into his clutches. **85m/C VHS, LV, Closed Caption.** Warwick Davis, Sandy Baron, Adam Biesk, James Lancaster, Clint Howard, Kimmy Robertson, Charlie Heath, Shevonne Durkin; *D:* Rodman Flender; *W:* Turi Meyer, Al Septien; *M:* Jonathan Elias. *THV*

Leprechaun 3 🐾 1995 (R) A student steals the nasty little beastie's gold and he's off to Las Vegas to get it back and to kill the gamblers, also after his magic money, in decidedly disgusting ways.*CW:* Some strong horror violence and gore; a scene of sexuality. **93m/C VHS, LV, Closed Caption.** Warwick Davis, John Gatins, Michael Callan, Caroline Williams; *D:* Brian Trenchard-Smith. *THV*

Les Assassins de L'Ordre 🐾🐾 *Law Breakers* 1971 A righteous French judge faces the case of an innocent man killed by police brutality. Subtitled in English. **100m/C VHS, Beta.** *FR* Jacques Brel, Catherine Rouvel, Michael Lonsdale, Charles Denner; *D:* Marcel Carne; *M:* Michel Colombier. *NO*

Les Aventuriers 🐾🐾½ *The Last Adventure* 1977 Two friends find themselves swindled in an insurance scam and set out after the perpetrator who sent them off to Africa in search of a treasure. Available dubbed. **?m/C VHS.** *FR* Alain Delon, Lino Ventura, Joanna Shimkus. *FRA, FCT*

Les Biches 🐾🐾🐾½ *The Heterosexuals* 1968 (R) An exquisite film that became a landmark in film history with its theme of bisexuality and upper class decadence. A rich socialite picks up a young artist drawing on the streets of Paris, seduces her, and then takes her to St. Tropez. Conflict arises when a suave architect shows up and threatens to come between the two lovers. In French with English subtitles. **95m/C VHS, LV.** *FR* Stephane Audran, Jean-Louis Trintignant, Jacqueline Sassard; *D:* Claude Chabrol; *W:* Claude Chabrol. *CVC, LUM*

Les Bonnes Femmes 🐾🐾🐾 *The Good Girls; The Girls* 1960 Four Paris shopgirls dream of escaping the monotony of their lives and finding romance but instead discover broken dreams and danger. Chabrol's New Wave thriller focuses more on character and irony than suspense. French with subtitles. **105m/B VHS.** *FR* Bernadette Lafont, Stephane Audran, Clothilde Joano, Lucile Saint-Simon; *D:* Claude Chabrol; *W:* Paul Geoauff; *C:* Henri Decae; *M:* Pierre Jansen, Paul Misraki. *FCT*

Les Bons Debarras 🐾🐾½ 1981 In French with English subtitles, this Canadian film follows a lonely 13-year-old's effort to win her mother's exclusive love. **114m/C VHS, Beta.** *CA* Marie Tifo, Charlotte Laurier, German Houde; *D:* Francis Mankiewicz. Genie Awards '81: Best Actress (Tifo), Best Director

(Mankiewicz), Best Film, Best Supporting Actor (Houde). *NO*

Les Carabiniers 🎬🎬🎬 *The Soldiers* 1963 A cynical, grim anti-war tract, detailing the pathetic adventures of two young bums lured into enlisting with promises of rape, looting, torture and battle without justification. Controversial in its day, and typically elliptical and non-narrative. In French with English subtitles. **80m/B VHS, Beta.** *GB IT FR* Anna Karina, Genevieva Galea, Marino Mase; **D:** Jean-Luc Godard. *FCT*

Les Comperes 🎬🎬🎬 1983 A woman suckers two former lovers into finding her wayward son by secretly telling each ex he is the natural father of the punk. Depardieu is a streetwise journalist who teams up with a suicidal hypochondriac/wimp (Richard) to find the little brat. Humorous story full of bumbling misadventures. In French with English subtitles. **92m/C VHS, Beta, LV.** *FR* Pierre Richard, Gerard Depardieu, Anny Duperey, Michel Aumont; **D:** Francis Veber; **W:** Francis Veber; **M:** Vladimir Cosma. *MED, FCT*

Les Enfants Terrible 🎬🎬🎬 *The Strange Ones* 1950 The classic, lyrical treatment of adolescent deviance adapted by Cocteau from his own play, wherein a brother and sister born into extreme wealth eventually enter into casual crime, self-destruction, and incest. In French with English subtitles. **105m/B VHS, Beta.** *FR* Edouard Dermithe, Nicole Stephane; **D:** Jean-Pierre Melville; **W:** Jean Cocteau, Jean-Pierre Melville. *FCT, WBF*

Les Girls 🎬🎬½ 1957 When one member of a performing troupe writes her memoirs, the other girls sue for libel. Told through a series of flashbacks, this story traces the girls' recollections of their relationships to American dancer Kelly. Cole Porter wrote the score for this enjoyable "Rashomon"-styled musical. Laserdisc features include the original trailer and letterboxed screen. ♫Les Girls; Flower Song; You're Just Too, Too; Ca C'est L'Amour; Ladies In Waiting; La Habanera; Why Am I So Gone (About That Gal?). **114m/C VHS, Beta, LV.** Gene Kelly, Mitzi Gaynor, Kay Kendall, Taina Elg, Henry Daniell, Patrick Macnee; **D:** George Cukor; **C:** Robert L. Surtees. Academy Awards '57: Best Costume Design; Golden Globe Awards '58: Best Actress—Musical/Comedy (Kendall), Best Film—Musical/Comedy; Nominations: Academy Awards '57: Best Art Direction/Set Decoration, Best Sound. *MGM*

Les Grandes Gueules 🎬🎬½ *Jailbirds' Vacation* 1965 From the director of the classic "An Occurrence at Owl Creek Bridge," comes this comedy-drama about a sawmill owner dealing with two ex-convicts hired as lumberjacks. In French with English subtitles. **125m/C VHS, Beta.** *FR* Lino Ventura, Bourvil, Marie DuBois; **D:** Robert Enrico. *BAR*

Les Grandes Manoeuvres 🎬🎬🎬 *Summer Manoeuvers; The Grand Maneuvers* 1955 Clair's first film in color depicts the romance between a seductive soldier (Philipe) and a divorcee (Morgan) in a pre-WWI garrison town. Gentle comedy has Philipe falling in love but his reputation as a Don Juan comes between them. French with subtitles. **106m/C VHS.** *FR* Gerard Philipe, Michele Morgan, Yves Robert, Brigitte Bardot, Jean Desailly, Pierre Dux; **D:** Rene Clair; **W:** Rene Clair; **M:** Georges Van Parys. *WBF*

Les Miserables 🎬🎬🎬 1935 Victor Hugo's classic novel about small-time criminal Jean Valjean and 18th-century France. After facing poverty and prison, escape and torture, Valjean is redeemed by the kindness of a bishop. As he tries to mend his ways, he is continually hounded by the policeman Javert, who is determined to lock him away. The final act is set during a student uprising in the 1730s. This version is the best of many, finely detailed and well-paced with excellent cinematography by Gregg Toland. **108m/B VHS, Beta, LV.** Fredric March, Charles Laughton, Cedric Hardwicke, Rochelle Hudson, John Beal, Frances Drake, Florence Eldridge, John Carradine, Jessie Ralph, Leonid Kinskey; **D:** Richard Boleslawski; **W:** W.P. Lipscomb; **C:** Gregg Toland; **M:** Alfred Newman. National Board of Review Awards '35: 10 Best Films of the Year; Nominations:

Academy Awards '35: Best Cinematography, Best Film Editing, Best Picture. *FOX, APD*

Les Miserables 🎬🎬½ 1952 Hugo's classic novel done up Italian style with lavish sets and spectacle. Dubbed in English. **119m/B VHS.** *IT* Gino Cervi, Valentina Cortese; **D:** Riccardo (Robert Hampton) Freda; **C:** Joseph LaShelle; **M:** Alex North. *VYY, FCT*

Les Miserables 🎬🎬🎬 1957 An epic French adaptation of the Victor Hugo standard about Valjean, Javert, and injustice. Although this doesn't reach the level of the 1935 classic, it is still worth watching. Dubbed in English. **210m/C VHS, Beta.** *FR GE* Jean Gabin, Daniele Delorme, Bernard Blier, Bourvil, Gianni Esposito, Serge Reggiani; **D:** Jean-Paul LeChanois. *FCT, VEC*

Les Miserables 🎬🎬🎬½ 1978 An excellent made-for-television version of the Victor Hugo classic about the criminal Valjean and the policeman Javert playing cat-and-mouse in 18th-century France. Dauphin's last film role. **150m/C VHS, Beta, LV.** Richard Jordan, Anthony Perkins, John Gielgud, Cyril Cusack, Flora Robson, Celia Johnson, Claude Dauphin; **D:** Glenn Jordan. *FOX, FCT*

Les Miserables 🎬🎬½ 1995 (R) Clever, modern rendering of the famous Victor Hugo novel, set in World War II. Humble furniture mover Fortin (Belmondo), nicknamed Valjean for displaying the same brutish strength as his Hugo counterpart, helps a Jewish family escape German occupation. The family becomes separated in the attempt, with lawyer, Monsieur Ziman (Boujenah), being hidden by farmers in the country, Madame Ziman (Martines) relegated to a Polish concentration camp, and their daughter Salome (Lelouch, daughter of the director) protected by a nun at a Catholic school. Gump-like, the unusually strong but illiterate Fortin becomes involved with the French resistance and joins in D-Day. Events, though obviously updated, mirror experiences of Hugo's characters. In one sequence, the Ziman's even teach Fortin to read the Hugo's "Les Miserables," with actors playing their counterparts in dramatizations. Reportedly France's most expensive film ever.**CW:** Violence, brief language, and sexuality. **174m/C VHS, LV.** Jean-Paul Belmondo, Michel Boujenah, Annie Girardot, Philippe Leotard, Clementine Celarie, Rufus, Alessandra Martines, Salome, Philippe Khorsand; **D:** Claude Lelouch; **W:** Claude Lelouch; **C:** Claude Lelouch; **M:** Francis Lai. Cesar Awards '96: Best Supporting Actress (Girardot); Golden Globe Awards '96: Best Foreign Film; Nominations: British Academy Awards '95: Best Foreign Film. *WAR*

Les Mistons 🎬🎬🎬 1957 This study of male adolescence finds five teen-age boys worshiping a beautiful girl from afar, following her everywhere, spoiling her dates, and finally reaching maturity in light of their mistakes. **18m/C VHS, Beta.** *FR* **D:** Francois Truffaut. *FLI*

Les Nuits Fauves 🎬🎬🎬 *Savage Nights* 1992 Collard's semi-autobiographical film about the emotional and physical havoc an H.I.V.-positive filmmaker visits on the two objects of his violent affections—an innocent 18-year-old girl and a sadomasochistic 20-year-old boy. As Jean displays increasing desperation with his situation, the life around him shows an equally arbitrary violence and humor. In French with English subtitles. Collard died of AIDS shortly before his film won both best first film and best French film at the 1993 Cesars—a first in the ceremony's history. **129m/C VHS.** *FR* Cyril Collard, Romane Bohringer, Carlos Lopez, Maria Schneider; **D:** Cyril Collard; **W:** Cyril Collard. Cesar Awards '93: Best Film. *PGV*

Les Patterson Saves the World 🎬½ 1990 (R) An obnoxious ambassador to an anonymous Middle Eastern country teams up with the singularly distastefully named Dr. Herpes to stop a new killer disease about to engulf the world. **105m/C VHS.** Barry Humphries, Pamela Stephenson, Thaao Penghlis, Andrew Clarke, Joan Rivers; **D:** George Miller; **C:** David Connell. *HMD*

Les Rendez-vous D'Anna 🎬🎬 *The Meetings of Anna* 1978 An independent woman travels through Europe and comes face to face with its post-war modernism. In French with English subtitles. **120m/C VHS.** *FR BE GE* Aurore Clement, Helmut Griem, Magali Noel, Hanns Zischler, Lea Massari, Jean-Pierre Cassel; **D:** Chantal Akerman; **W:** Chantal Akerman. *WAC*

Les Violons du Bal 🎬🎬 1974 Follows the story of a young Jewish boy and his family's attempted escape from Nazi-occupied France during WWII. The boy grows up to be a filmmaker obsessed with making a movie about his childhood experiences. In French with English subtitles. **110m/C VHS.** *FR* Marie-Jose Nat, Jean-Louis Trintignant; **D:** Michael Drach. Cannes Film Festival '74: Best Actress (Nat). *CVC, PMS*

Les Visiteurs du Soir 🎬🎬🎬½ *The Devil's Envoys* 1942 A beautiful, charming fairy tale about the devil's intrepid interference with a particular love affair in 15th-century France, which he cannot squelch. Purportedly also a parable about Hitler's invasion of France. Interestingly, this was released after the Nazi occupation of France, so one assumes that the Germans didn't make the connection. In French with English subtitles. **120m/B VHS.** *FR* Arletty, Jules Berry, Marie Dea, Alain Cuny, Fernand Ledoux, Marcel Herrand; **D:** Marcel Carne; **W:** Jacques Prevert, Pierre Laroche. *HMV, FCT, TPV*

Les Voleurs 🎬🎬🎬 *Thieves* 1996 (R) Unexpected romantic triangle among desperate, lonely people, set against a crime backdrop and told from a variety of viewpoints. Edgy cop Alex (Auteuil) is from a family of thieves, including his older brother Ivan (Bezace) who's been murdered. Alex gets involved with sullen Juliette (Cote) without realizing, at first, that her brother Jimmy (Magimel) is a member of Ivan's gang or that she has another lover, her philosophy teacher, Marie (Deneuve). Events finally force a meeting between Marie and Alex over the unstable Juliette (the scenes between Auteuil and Deneuve being the most interesting in the film). French with subtitles.**CW:** Strong sexuality, some violent moments and language. **116m/C VHS, LV.** *FR* Catherine Deneuve, Daniel Auteuil, Laurence Cote, Benoit Magimel, Didier Bezace, Fabienne Babe, Ivan Desny, Julien Riviere; **D:** Andre Techine; **W:** Andre Techine, Gilles Taurand; **C:** Jeanne Lapoirie; **M:** Philippe Sarde. Nominations: Cesar Awards '97: Best Actress (Deneuve), Best Director (Techine), Best Film. *COL*

L'Escorte 🎬🎬 *The Escort* 1996 Thirty-years-old and long-term lovers, Jean-Marc and Philippe find their relationship in crisis thanks to both the stress caused by their failing Montreal restaurant and the intrusion of a third party. Free-spirited Steve works as an escort and soon becomes an object of desire for both men as well as a catalyst for the revelation of long-held secrets. French with subtitles. **91m/C VHS.** *CA* Eric Cabana, Paul-Antoine Taillefer, Robin Aubert, Marie Lefebvre; **D:** Denis Langlois; **W:** Denis Langlois, Bertrand Lachance; **C:** Yves Beaudoin; **M:** Bertrand Chenier. *CCN*

Less Than Zero 🎬 1987 (R) An adaptation of Bret Easton Ellis' popular, controversial novel about a group of affluent, drug-abusing youth in Los Angeles. McCarthy and Gertz play friends of Downey who try to get him off his self-destructive path—to no avail. Although it tries, the film fails to inspire any sort of sympathy for this self-absorbed and hedonistic group. Mirrors the shallowness of the characters although Downey manages to rise above this somewhat. Music by the Bangles, David Lee Roth, Poison, Roy Orbison, Aerosmith and more. **98m/C VHS, Beta, LV, Closed Caption.** Andrew McCarthy, Jami Gertz, Robert Downey Jr., James Spader; **D:** Marek Kanievska; **M:** Thomas Newman. *FOX*

Lesson in Love 🎬🎬½ *En Lektion i Karlek* 1954 A gynecologist's philandering is discovered by his wife, who then starts an affair of her own. Change of pace for Bergman as he does this modest comedy. In Swedish with English subti-

tles. **95m/B VHS, Beta.** *SW* Gunnar Bjornstrand, Eva Dahlbeck, Harriet Andersson; *D:* Ingmar Bergman; *W:* Ingmar Bergman.

Let 'Em Have It 🐾🐾½ *False Faces* 1935
Exciting action saga loosely based on the newly formed FBI and its bouts with John Dillinger. Car chases and tommy guns abound in this fairly ordinary film. **90m/B VHS.** Richard Arlen, Virginia Bruce, Bruce Cabot, Harvey Stephens, Eric Linden, Joyce Compton, Gordon Jones; *D:* Sam Wood. MGM, NOS, HEG

Let 'er Go Gallegher 🐾🐾 1928 A
youngster sees a murder, tells his newspaper buddy about it, and the guy writes an article about the crime. It's a big hit, the guy's ego starts to overinflate, and his life starts to head downwind until he decides its time for him and the little guy to rope themselves a miscreant. **57m/B VHS, Beta.** Frank "Junior" Coghlan, Elinor Fair, Wade Boteler; *D:* Elmer Clifton. GPV, FCT

Let Freedom Ring 🐾🐾½ 1939 Sappy,
yet enjoyable patriotism that has lawyer Eddy returning to small hometown and fighting corruption. Hokey, but it works largely due to Hecht's fine script. ♫Dusty Road; Love Serenade; Home Sweet Home; When Irish Eyes Are Smiling; America; Pat Sez He; Where Else But Here; Funiculi Funicula; Ten Thousand Cattle Straying. **100m/B VHS, Closed Caption.** Nelson Eddy, Virginia Bruce, Victor McLaglen, Lionel Barrymore, Edward Arnold, Guy Kibbee, Charles Butterworth, H.B. Warner, Raymond Walburn; *D:* Jack Conway; *W:* Ben Hecht. MGM

Let Him Have It 🐾🐾🐾½ 1991 (R) Compelling, controversial film about a miscarriage of British justice. In 1952 Christopher Craig, 16, and Derek Bentley, 19, climbed onto the roof of a warehouse in an apparent burglary attempt. The police arrived and captured Bentley; the police shot and wounded one policeman and killed another. According to testimony Bentley shouted "Let him have it" but did he mean shoot or give the officer the gun? Bentley, whose IQ was 66, was sentenced to death by the British courts—though he didn't commit the murder. The uproar over the sentence was reignited by this release, leading to a request for a reexamination of evidence and sentencing by the British Home Office.*CW:* Language and violence. **115m/C VHS, LV.** *GB* Christopher Eccleston, Paul Reynolds, Tom Bell, Eileen Atkins, Clare Holman, Michael Elphick, Mark McGann, Tom Courtenay, Ronald Fraser, Michael Gough, Murray Melvin, Clive Revill, Norman Rossington, James Villiers; *D:* Peter Medak. NLC

Let It Be 🐾🐾 1970 Documentary look at a
Beatles recording session, giving glimpses of the conflicts which led to their breakup. Features appearances by Yoko Ono and Billy Preston. **80m/C VHS, Beta, LV.** John Lennon, Paul McCartney, George Harrison, Ringo Starr, Billy Preston, Yoko Ono; *D:* Michael Lindsay-Hogg; *M:* The Beatles. Academy Awards '70: Original Song Score and/or Adaptation. FOX

Let It Ride 🐾🐾 1989 (PG-13) Dreyfuss is a
small-time gambler who finally hits it big at the track. Some funny moments but generally a lame script cripples the cast, although the horses seem unaffected. Garr is okay as his wife who slips further into alcoholism with each race. **91m/C VHS, Beta, LV, 8mm, Closed Caption.** Richard Dreyfuss, Teri Garr, David Johansen, Jennifer Tilly, Allen (Goorwitz) Garfield, Ed Walsh, Michelle Phillips, Mary Woronov, Robbie Coltrane, Richard Edson, Cynthia Nixon; *D:* Joe Pytka. PAR

Let It Rock 🐾 1986 A maniacal promoter
makes superstars out of his new band by staging publicity stunts. Not one of Hopper's better efforts. Filmed in Germany, but Roger Corman bought the U.S. rights and added clips from other movies before it was released here. **75m/C VHS, Beta.** GE Dennis Hopper, David Hess; *D:* Roland Klick. MED

L'Etat Sauvage 🐾🐾🐾½ *The Savage State*
1978 This French political thriller finds its heart in the middle of racism. The story unfolds around a newly independent African republic and a love affair between a black cabinet minister and a white Frenchwoman. Corruption abounds in this film

based on George Conchon's award-winning novel. In French with English subtitles. **111m/C VHS, Beta, LV.** *FR* Marie-Christine Barrault, Claude Brasseur, Jacques Dutronc, Doura Mane, Michel Piccoli; *D:* Francois Girod. Cesar Awards '79: Best Sound. INT, TPV

Lethal Charm 🐾🐾 1990 Two power-hungry journalists go head-to-head in the high stakes arena of Washington D.C. **92m/C VHS.** Barbara Eden, Heather Locklear. LIV

Lethal Games 🐾🐾 1990 Stallone and
Vaccaro lead a small community against a bloodthirsty band of criminals. **83m/C VHS.** Frank Stallone, Brenda Vaccaro, Dave Adams, Christopher Whalley, Heidi Paine, Karen Russell; *D:* John Bowen. AIP

Lethal Lolita—Amy Fisher: My Story 🐾🐾 *Amy Fisher: My Story* 1992 The only
made-for-television Amy Fisher story out of three whose cast members even remotely resemble the real people—except of course actress Parker is actually pretty. Minor details aside, this account is Amy's story, purchased by NBC for an undisclosed amount, portraying her as an incest victim who gets involved with an opportunistic married jerk who drags her into prostitution, leading her to take out her frustration on his wife. If this is true, the obvious question is "why?"...to which she answers, "He loves me. We have great sex. And he fixes my car." OK. See also: "The Amy Fisher Story" and "Casualties of Love: The 'Long Island Lolita' Story." **93m/C VHS, Closed Caption.** Noelle Parker, Ed Marinaro, Kathleen Lasky, Boyd Kestner, Mary Ann Pascal, Lawrence Dane, Kate Lynch; *D:* Bradford May. TTC

Lethal Ninja 🐾 1993 (R) Kickboxers Joe
and Pete set out to rescue Joe's wife from some third-world country overrun by ninjas. Hackneyed but lots of action for martial arts fans. **97m/C VHS, LV.** Ross Kettle, David Webb, Karyn Hill, Frank Notaro. THV

Lethal Obsession 🐾½ *Der Joker* 1987 (R)
Two cops battle street crime and a powerful drug ring. Filmed in Germany. **100m/C VHS, Beta.** *GE* Michael York, Elliott Gould, Tahnee Welch, Peter Maffay, Armin Mueller-Stahl; *D:* Peter Patzak; *M:* Tony Carey. THV

Lethal Panther 🐾🐾 1990 A film where the
female is indeed deadlier than the male. Japanese hit woman Ling (Miyamoto) gets involved with drug-smuggling gangsters operating out of the Philippines and is opposed by CIA agent Betty Lee (Hu). Dubbed. **120m/C VHS.** *HK* Yoko Miyamoto, Sibelle Hu, Lawrence Ng; *D:* Godfrey Ho. TAI

Lethal Pursuit 🐾🐾 1988 A popular singer
who returns to the town where she grew up is tormented by her ex-boyfriend, a criminal. **90m/C VHS, Beta.** Mitzi Donahue, Blake Gahner, John Wildman; *D:* Donald M. Jones. HMD

Lethal Weapon 🐾🐾🐾 1987 (R) In Los Angeles, a cop nearing retirement (Glover) unwillingly begins work with a new partner (Gibson), a suicidal, semi-crazed risk-taker who seems determined to get the duo killed. Both Vietnam vets, the pair uncover a vicious heroin smuggling ring run by ruthless ex-Special Forces personnel. Packed with plenty of action, violence, and humorous undertones. Clapton's contributions to the musical score are an added bonus. Gibson and Glover work well together and give this movie extra punch. Followed by (so far) two sequels. **110m/C VHS, Beta, LV, Closed Caption, DVD.** Mel Gibson, Danny Glover, Gary Busey, Mitchell Ryan, Tom Atkins, Darlene Love, Traci Wolfe, Steve Kahan; *D:* Richard Donner; *W:* Shane Black; *M:* Michael Kamen, Eric Clapton. Nominations: Academy Awards '87: Best Sound. WAR

Lethal Weapon 2 🐾🐾🐾 1989 (R) This
sequel to the popular cop adventure finds Gibson and Glover going on a variety of blond South African "diplomats" who try to use their diplomatic immunity status to thwart the duo's efforts to crack their smuggling ring. Gibson finally finds romance, and viewers learn the truth about his late wife's accident. Also features the introduction of obnoxious, fast-talking con artist Leo ("OK, OK") Getz, adeptly played by Pesci, who becomes a third wheel to the crime-fighting team. Followed

by a second sequel. **114m/C VHS, Beta, LV, 8mm, Closed Caption.** Mel Gibson, Danny Glover, Joe Pesci, Joss Ackland, Derrick O'Connor, Patsy Kensit, Darlene Love, Traci Wolfe, Steve Kahan, Mary Ellen Trainor; *D:* Richard Donner; *W:* Jeffrey Boam; *M:* Michael Kamen, Eric Clapton, David Sanborn. WAR

Lethal Weapon 3 🐾🐾½ 1992 (R) Murtaugh and Riggs return for more action in another slam-bang adventure. Murtaugh hopes his last week before retirement will be a peaceful one, but partner Riggs isn't about to let him go quietly. Not many changes from the successful formula with bickering buddies, lots of adventure, exploding buildings, a little comic relief from Pesci, and the addition of Russo as an Internal Affairs cop who proves to be more than a match for Riggs.*CW:* Language and violence. **118m/C VHS, LV, 8mm, Closed Caption.** Mel Gibson, Danny Glover, Joe Pesci, Rene Russo, Stuart Wilson, Steve Kahan, Darlene Love, Traci Wolfe, Gregory Millar, Jason Meshover-Iorg, Delores Hall; *D:* Richard Donner; *W:* Jeffrey Boam, Robert Mark Kamen; *C:* Jan De Bont; *M:* Michael Kamen, Eric Clapton, David Sanborn. MTV Movie Awards '93: Best On-Screen Duo (Mel Gibson/Danny Glover), Best Action Sequence. WAR, PMS

Lethal Woman 🐾½ 1988 A group of beautiful women, all once victimized by rapes, is recruited to an island by the "Lethal Woman," who plots revenge on any man who dares to vacation on the island. **96m/C VHS, Beta, LV.** Shannon Tweed, Merete Van Kamp. NO

Let's Dance 🐾🐾½ 1950 A young widow
tries to protect her son from his wealthy, paternal grandmother, while Fred dances his way into her heart. More obscure Astaire vehicle, but as charming as the rest. Needless to say, great dancing. ♫Tunnel of Love; The Hyacinth; Piano Dance; Jack and the Beanstalk; Can't Stop Talking; Oh, Them Dudes; Why Fight the Feeling?. **112m/C VHS, Beta, LV, Closed Caption.** Betty Hutton, Fred Astaire, Roland Young, Ruth Warrick, Shepperd Strudwick, Lucile Watson, Barton MacLane, Gregory Moffett, Melville Cooper; *D:* Norman Z. McLeod. PAR

Let's Do It Again 🐾🐾 1975 (PG) Atlanta
milkman and his pal, a factory worker, milk two big-time gamblers out of a large sum of money in order to build a meeting hall for their fraternal lodge. Lesser sequel to "Uptown Saturday Night." **113m/C VHS, Beta.** Sidney Poitier, Bill Cosby, John Amos, Jimmie Walker, Ossie Davis, Denise Nicholas, Calvin Lockhart; *D:* Sidney Poitier; *W:* Richard Wesley. WAR

Let's Get Harry 🐾½ *The Rescue* 1987 (R)
Americans led by mercenaries mix it up with a Columbian cocaine franchise in an attempt to rescue their friend, Harry. Never released theatrically, for good reason. **107m/C VHS, Beta, LV, Closed Caption.** Robert Duvall, Gary Busey, Michael Schoeffling, Tom Wilson, Glenn Frey, Rick Rossovich, Ben Johnson, Matt Clark, Mark Harmon, Gregory Sierra, Elpidia Carrillo; *D:* Alan Smithee; *W:* Samuel Fuller, Charles Robert Carner; *M:* Brad Fiedel. HBO

Let's Get Lost 1988 Absorbing documentary of Chet Baker, the prominent '50s "cool" jazz trumpeter (and occasional vocalist) who succumbed, like many of his peers, to drug addiction. Weber's black-and-white, fashion photography style well suits his subject. Downbeat, but rarely less than worthy. **125m/B VHS.** Chet Baker; *D:* Bruce Weber. Nominations: Academy Awards '88: Best Feature Documentary. MVD, COL

Let's Get Married 🐾 1963 A young doctor's weakness under pressure brings him to the brink of babbling idiocy when his wife goes into early labor. **90m/B VHS, Beta.** Anthony Newley, Ann Aubrey. NO

Let's Get Tough 🐾 1942 The East Side
Kids, unable to enlist because of their age, harass local Oriental shopkeepers and eventually get involved with a murder. **52m/B VHS, Beta, 8mm.** Leo Gorcey, Bobby Jordan, Huntz Hall, Gabriel Dell, Sammy Morrison; *D:* Wallace Fox. VYY, NOS, RXM

Let's Go! 🎵½ **1923** The son of a cement company president sets out to prove his worth to the firm by landing a contract with the town of Hillsboro. For some unknown reason, he sets off on an amazing set of stunts. Silent with original organ music. 79m/B **VHS, Beta, 8mm.** Richard Talmadge, Hal Clements, Eileen Percy, Tully Marshall; **D:** William K. Howard. *VYY, GPV, GVV*

Let's Go Collegiate 🎵½ **1941** Two college rowers promise their girlfriends that they'll win the big race, but their plans are almost frustrated when their best oarsman is drafted. Their only hope lies in replacing him with a truck driver. 🎵 Look What You've Done To Me; Sweet 16; Let's Do A Little Dreaming. 62m/B **VHS.** Frankie Darro, Marcia Mae Jones, Jackie Moran, Keye Luke, Mantan Moreland, Gale Storm; **D:** Jean Yarbrough. *NOS*

Let's Kill All the Lawyers 🐾🐾½ **1993** Low-budget satire about one man's angst over whether to become a lawyer is witty, entertaining, and not just for legal eagles. Law-firm intern Foster Merkul (Frederick) is apprenticed to a sleazeball (Vezina) who teaches him that money—not justice—is the name of the game in the law biz. Growing increasingly disillusioned, Foster sets out to reform the system with the help of Satori, a beautiful and mysterious creature of his imagination. Shot at sites in and around Detroit, this independent production features lots of cameos by local media celebrities. ?m/C **VHS.** Rick Frederick, James Vezina, Michelle De Vuono, Maggie Patton, Marty Smith; **D:** Ron Senkowski; **W:** Ron Senkowski. *NYR*

Let's Make It Legal 🐾🐾½ **1951** Amusing comedy of a married couple who decide to get a divorce after 20 years of marriage. Colbert stars as the woman who decides to leave her husband, Carey, because he's a chronic gambler. They part as friends, but soon Colbert's old flame, Scott, is back in town and things get rather complicated. A solid cast serves as the main strength in this film. 77m/B **VHS, Closed Caption.** Claudette Colbert, MacDonald Carey, Zachary Scott, Barbara Bates, Robert Wagner, Marilyn Monroe; **D:** Richard Sale; **W:** F. Hugh Herbert. *FXV*

Let's Make Love 🐾🐾½ **1960** An urbane millionaire discovers he is to be parodied in an off-Broadway play, and vows to stop it—until he falls in love with the star of the show. He then ends up acting in the play. 🎵 My Heart Belongs to Daddy; Let's Make Love; Specialization; Incurably Romantic; Sing Me a Song That Sells; You With the Crazy Eyes; Give Me the Simple Life. 118m/C **VHS, Beta.** Yves Montand, Marilyn Monroe, Tony Randall, Frankie Vaughan, Bing Crosby, Gene Kelly, Milton Berle; **D:** George Cukor; **C:** Daniel F. Fapp. Nominations: Academy Awards '60: Scoring of a Musical. *FOX*

Let's Make Up 🐾🐾½ *Lilacs in the Spring* **1955** When it comes to giving her heart, Neagle can't decide between two dashing men. 94m/C **VHS.** GB Errol Flynn, Anna Neagle, David Farrar, Kathleen Harrison, Peter Graves; **D:** Herbert Wilcox. *GKK, MLB, MRV*

Let's Scare Jessica to Death 🐾🐾 **1971 (PG)** A young woman who was recently released from a mental hospital is subjected to unspeakable happenings at a country home with her friends. She encounters murder, vampires, and corpses coming out of nowhere. A supernatural thriller with quite a few genuine scares. 89m/C **VHS, Beta.** Zohra Lampert, Barton Heyman, Kevin J. O'Connor, Gretchen Corbett, Alan Manson; **D:** John Hancock. *PAR*

Let's Sing Again 🐾🐾 **1936** Eight-year-old singing sensation Bobby Breen made his debut in this dusty musical vehicle, as a runaway orphan who becomes the pal of a washed-up opera star in a traveling show. 🎵 Let's Sing Again; Lullaby; Farmer in the Dell; La Donna e Mobile. 70m/B **VHS.** Bobby Breen, Henry Armetta, George Houston, Vivienne Osborne, Grant Withers, Inez Courtney, Lucien Littlefield; **D:** Kurt Neumann. *NOS, LOO, DVT*

The Letter 🐾🐾🐾🐾 **1940** When a man is shot and killed on a Malaysian plantation, the woman who committed the murder pleads self-defense. Her husband and his lawyer attempt to

free her, but find more than they expected in this tightly-paced film noir. Based on the novel by W. Somerset Maugham. Davis emulated the originator of her role, Jeanne Eagels, in her mannerisms and line readings, although Eagels later went mad from drug abuse and overwork. 96m/B **VHS, Beta, LV.** Bette Davis, Herbert Marshall, James Stephenson, Gale Sondergaard, Bruce Lester, Cecil Kellaway, Victor Sen Yung, Frieda Inescort; **D:** William Wyler; **W:** Howard Koch; **C:** Gaetano Antonio "Tony" Gaudio; **M:** Max Steiner. Nominations: Academy Awards '40: Best Actress (Davis), Best Black and White Cinematography, Best Director (Wyler), Best Film Editing, Best Picture, Best Supporting Actor (Stephenson), Best Original Score. *FOX, MGM*

Letter from an Unknown Woman 🐾🐾🐾 **1948** A woman falls in love with a concert pianist on the eve of his departure. He promises to return but never does. The story is told in flashbacks as the pianist reads a letter from the woman. A great romantic melodrama. 90m/B **VHS, LV.** Joan Fontaine, Louis Jourdan, Mady Christians, Marcel Journet, Art Smith; **D:** Max Ophuls. *REP*

Letter of Introduction 🐾🐾½ **1938** A struggling young actress learns that her father is really a well known screen star and agrees not to reveal the news to the public. 104m/B **VHS, Beta.** Adolphe Menjou, Edgar Bergen, George Murphy, Eve Arden, Ann Sheridan, Andrea Leeds; **D:** John M. Stahl; **C:** Karl Freund. *NOS, MRV, HHT*

Letter to Brezhnev 🐾🐾🐾 **1986 (R)** Acclaimed independent film about two working-class Liverpool girls who fall in love with two furloughed Russian sailors. When the men eventually return to the USSR, one of the girls contacts the Russian Secretary General in an effort to rejoin her lover. Amusing tale of different relationships. 94m/C **VHS, Beta, LV, Closed Caption.** GB Margi Clarke, Alexandra Pigg, Peter Firth, Ken Campbell, Tracy Lea, Alfred Molina, Angela Clarke; **D:** Chris Bernard; **W:** Frank Clarke; **M:** Alan Gill. *ORI, IME, WAR*

Letter to My Killer 🐾🐾½ **1995 (PG-13)** Construction worker Nick Parma (Chinlund) finds an unmailed letter in a demolished building, which he and wife Judy (Winningham) discover is 30 years old. The woman letter writer is describing major fraud and when Judy learns that she was murdered, she and Nick decide to blackmail the probable suspects—a powerful business cartel. But if they killed once..... Made for cable movie. **CW:** Some violence and sexuality. 92m/C **VHS, Closed Caption.** Mare Winningham, Nicholas Chinlund, Rip Torn, Josef Sommer, Eddie Jones, Dey Young; **D:** Janet Meyers; **W:** Norman Strum; **C:** Stephen M. Katz. *USH*

A Letter to Three Wives 🐾🐾🐾🐾 **1949** Crain, Darnell, and Sothern star as three friends who, shortly before embarking on a Hudson River boat trip, each receive a letter from Holm (who's never shown), the fourth member in their set. The letter tells them that she has run off with one of their husbands but does not specify his identity. The women spend the rest of the trip reviewing their sometimes shaky unions which provides some of the funniest and most caustic scenes, including Douglas (as Sothern's husband) ranting against the advertising business which supports his wife's radio soap opera. Sharp dialogue, moving performances. Based on the novel by John Klempner. Remade for television in 1985. 103m/B **VHS, Beta, LV.** Jeanne Crain, Linda Darnell, Ann Sothern, Kirk Douglas, Paul Douglas, Jeffrey Lynn, Thelma Ritter, Barbara Lawrence, Connie Gilchrist, Florence Bates; **D:** Joseph L. Mankiewicz; **W:** Joseph L. Mankiewicz; **C:** Arthur C. Miller; **M:** Alfred Newman; **V:** Celeste Holm. Academy Awards '49: Best Director (Mankiewicz), Best Screenplay; Directors Guild of America Awards '48: Best Director (Mankiewicz); Nominations: Academy Awards '49: Best Picture. *FXV*

Letters from My Windmill 🐾🐾🐾½ **1954** A series of three short stories: "The Three Low Masses," "The Elixir of Father Gaucher," and "The Secret of Master Cornille" from respected director Pagnol. The unique format only enhances this film. In French with English subtitles.

116m/B **VHS.** FR Henri Velbert, Yvonne Gamy, Robert Vattier, Roger Crouzet; **D:** Marcel Pagnol. *NOS, DVT, APD*

Letters from the Park 🐾🐾🐾 **1988** In Cuba, 1913, two taciturn would-be lovers hire a poet, Victor La Place, to write love letters to each other. Normal proboscis aside, the poet follows the fate of Cyrano, and finds himself the unhappy hypotenuse in a triangular romance. Based on an original story by Marquez; made for Spanish television. In Spanish with English subtitles. 85m/C **VHS.** CU Victor Laplace, Ivonne Lopez, Miguel Paneque; **D:** Tomas Gutierrez Alea; **W:** Gabriel Garcia Marquez, Tomas Gutierrez Alea. *FXL, FCT, APD*

Letters to an Unknown Lover 🐾🐾½ *Les Louves* **1984** During WWII, a man and woman engage in sexual and emotional combat. 101m/C **VHS, Beta.** GB Cherie Lunghi, Mathilda May, Yves Beneyton, Ralph Bates; **D:** Peter Duffell. *ACA*

Letting Go 🐾🐾 **1985 (PG)** Made for television comedy-drama about a broken-hearted career woman and a young widower who fall in love. 94m/C **VHS, Beta.** John Ritter, Sharon Gless, Joe Cortese; **D:** Jack Bender. *AIP*

Letting the Birds Go Free **1986** When a stranger is caught stealing from a farmer's barn, the farmer and his son decide to let the villain work off his crime. Some very interesting relationships develop from this arrangement. 60m/C **VHS.** Lionel Jeffries. *PSM*

Leviathan 🐾🐾 **1989 (R)** A motley crew of ocean-floor miners are trapped when they are accidentally exposed to a failed Soviet experiment that turns humans into insatiable, regenerating fish-creatures. 98m/C **VHS, Beta, LV, Closed Caption.** Peter Weller, Ernie Hudson, Hector Elizondo, Amanda Pays, Richard Crenna, Daniel Stern, Lisa Eilbacher, Michael Carmine, Meg Foster; **D:** George P. Cosmatos; **W:** David Peoples, Jeb Stuart; **M:** Jerry Goldsmith. *MGM*

L'Homme Blesse 🐾🐾🐾 *The Wounded Man* **1983** A serious erotic film about 18-year-old Henri (Anglade), cloistered by an overbearing family, and his sudden awakening to his own homosexuality. Anglade's film debut. In French with English subtitles. 90m/C **VHS, Beta.** FR Jean-Hugues Anglade, Roland Bertin, Vittorio Mezzogiorno; **D:** Patrice Chereau; **C:** Renato Berta. Cesar Awards '84: Best Writing; Nominations: Cesar Awards '83: Best Supporting Actor (Anglade). *TPV, CCN*

Liana, Jungle Goddess 🐾🐾 **1956** A variation on the Greystoke legend featuring a beautiful (and topless) jungle goddess who is discovered living in the wilds of Africa. Thinking that she may be the lost granddaughter of a wealthy English nobleman, she's brought back to London for a reunion. Will civilization prove to be as dangerous as the jungle? ?m/C **VHS.** Marion Michael, Hardy Kruger. *SNC*

Lianna 🐾🐾🐾 **1983 (R)** Acclaimed screenwriter/director John Sayles wrote and directed this story of a woman's romantic involvement with another woman. Chronicles an unhappy homemaker's awakening to the feelings of love that she develops for a female professor. Sayles makes an appearance as a family friend. 110m/C **VHS, Beta.** Jon DeVries, Linda Griffiths, Jane Hallaren, Jo Henderson, Jessica Wright MacDonald; **Cameos:** John Sayles; **D:** John Sayles; **W:** John Sayles; **M:** Mason Daring. *VES*

Liar Liar 🐾🐾½ **1996 (PG-13)** Carrey takes on one of his less manic but still appealing personas as compulsive liar and attorney Fletcher Reid. A constant disappointment to his ex-wife Audrey (Tierney) and young son Max (Cooper), Fletcher is forced to tell nothing but the truth for 24 hours, thanks to his son's supernatural birthday wish. This puts a crimp in his legal practice, especially as he tries to defend brazen would-be divorcee Samantha Cole (Tilly). Gets kinda sappy but Carrey can carry almost any situation. **CW:** Sex related humor and language. 87m/C **VHS, LV, Closed Caption.** Jim Carrey, Jennifer Tilly, Maura Tierney, Amanda Donohoe, Swoosie Kurtz, Justin Cooper, Jason Bernard,

Mitchell Ryan, Anne Haney, Chip Mayer, Randall "Tex" Cobb, Cary Elwes; **D:** Tom Shadyac; **W:** Paul Guay, Steve Mazur; **C:** Russell Boyd; **M:** John Debney. *USH*

The Liars 🐾🐾 1964 Mystery in which a Frenchman strikes it rich in Africa, then returns home to Paris in search of a wife. He advertises for a mate, but is set up by con artists instead. In French with English subtitles. 92m/C VHS. Dawn Addams, Jean Servais; **D:** Edmond T. Greville. *FCT*

The Liar's Club 🐾½ 1993 (R) High-school football teammates try to cover up a rape and wind up involved in murder. **CW:** Language, violence, and sexuality. 100m/C VHS. Wil Wheaton, Brian Krause, Soleil Moon Frye, Jennifer Burns, Michael Cudlitz, Bruce Weitz; **D:** Jeffrey Porter. *NHO*

Liar's Edge 🐾🐾 1992 (R) Tweed portrays a single mother whose teenaged son, Mark, is plagued by violent fantasies. When she remarries and her new husband and sleazy brother-in-law move in, Mark's hallucinations become stronger until he believes he's witnessed a murder. The murder turns out to be a fact and his new stepfather is involved but can Mark prove it. Filmed on location in Niagra Falls. **CW:** Language, violence, and sensuality. 97m/C VHS, LV. Shannon Tweed, Nicholas Shields, David Keith, Joseph Bottoms, Christopher Plummer; **D:** Ron Oliver; **W:** Ron Oliver. *NLC, IME*

Liar's Moon 🐾🐾 1982 (PG) A local boy woos and weds the town's wealthiest young lady, only to be trapped in family intrigue. 106m/C VHS, Beta. Cindy Fisher, Matt Dillon, Christopher Connelly, Susan Tyrrell; **D:** David Fisher. *VES*

Libeled Lady 🐾🐾🐾½ 1936 A fast, complicated screwball masterwork, dealing with a newspaper editor's efforts to get something on a bratty heiress with the help of his own fiancee and a reporter he recently fired. One of the era's funniest Hollywood films. Remade in 1946 as "Easy to Wed." 98m/B VHS, Beta, LV. Myrna Loy, Spencer Tracy, Jean Harlow, William Powell, Walter Connolly, Charley Grapewin, Cora Witherspoon, E.E. Clive, Charles Trowbridge, Dennis O'Keefe, Hattie McDaniel; **D:** Jack Conway. Nominations: Academy Awards '36: Best Picture. *MGM*

The Liberation of L.B. Jones 🐾🐾 1970 (R) A wealthy black undertaker wants a divorce from his wife, who is having an affair with a white policeman. Wyler's final film. 101m/C VHS, Beta. Lee J. Cobb, Lola Falana, Barbara Hershey, Anthony Zerbe, Roscoe Lee Browne; **D:** William Wyler; **W:** Stirling Silliphant; **M:** Elmer Bernstein. *COL, FCT*

Liberators 🐾 1977 Kinski stars as a criminal soldier battling with the American authorities, German troops, and his fugitive partner. 91m/C VHS, Beta. Klaus Kinski. *UNI*

Liberty & Bash 🐾 1990 (R) Two boyhood friends who served together in Vietnam reunite to rid their neighborhood of drug pushers and save the life of a friend. 92m/C VHS, Beta, Closed Caption. Miles O'Keeffe, Lou Ferrigno, Mitzi Kapture, Richard Eden, Cheryl Paris, Gary Conway; **D:** Myrl A. Schreibman. *FRH*

License to Drive 🐾🐾 1988 (PG-13) When teen Haim fails the road test for his all-important driver's license, he steals the family car for a hot date with the girl of his dreams. The evening starts out quietly enough, but things soon go awry. If Haim survives the weekend, he'll definitely be able to pass his driving test on Monday morning. Semi-funny in a demolition derby sort of way. 90m/C VHS, Beta, LV. Corey Feldman, Corey Haim, Carol Kane, Richard Masur; **D:** Greg Beeman; **C:** Bruce Surtees; **M:** Jay Michael Ferguson. *FOX*

License to Kill 🐾🐾 1964 Constantine stars as Agent Nick Carter involved with Oriental spies and a new secret weapon. 100m/C VHS. *FR* Eddie Constantine, Yvonne Monlaur, Paul Frankeur; **D:** Henri Decoin. *SNC*

License to Kill 🐾🐾 1984 A young girl is killed by a drunk driver, devastating both families. A made-for-television movie with a strong message against drinking and driving. 96m/C VHS, Beta, LV. James Farentino, Don Murray, Penny Fuller, Millie Per-

kins, Donald Moffat, Denzel Washington, Ari Meyers; **D:** Jud Taylor. *GEM*

License to Kill 🐾🐾🐾 1989 (PG-13) Dalton's second Bond effort, in which drug lords try to kill 007's best friend and former CIA agent. Disobeying orders for the first time and operating without his infamous "license to kill," Bond goes after the fiends. Fine outing for Dalton (and Bond, too). 133m/C VHS, Beta, LV, Closed Caption. *GB* Timothy Dalton, Carey Lowell, Robert Davi, Frank McRae, Talisa Soto, David Hedison, Anthony Zerbe, Everett McGill, Wayne Newton, Benicio Del Toro, Desmond Llewelyn, Priscilla Barnes; **D:** John Glen; **W:** Michael G. Wilson, Richard Maibaum; **M:** Michael Kamen. *FOX, MGM*

L'Idiot 🐾🐾 *The Idiot* 1946 Smooth adaptation of Dostoevsky's novel about noble Prince Mishkin's (Philipe) attempts to bring peace to the life of tormented Nastasia Filipovna (Feuillere). First feature for Lampin; French with subtitles. 98m/B VHS. *FR* Gerard Philipe, Edwige Feuillere, Lucien Coedel, Nathalie Nattier, Marguerite Moreno; **D:** Georges Lampin; **W:** Charles Spaak; **C:** Christian Matras; **M:** Maurice Thiriet. *FCT*

Lie Down with Dogs 🐾 1995 (R) You will wake up with fleas if you watch this dull, very low-budget comedy about young Tommie (White), who heads out of New York for some summer fun in the gay-friendly resort of Provincetown, Massachusetts. There's lots of temporary (discreetly filmed) encounters but no lasting romance and Tommie heads back to the Big Apple at season's end satisfied but no wiser. White's debut film. **CW:** Strong sexuality and language; some drug use. 85m/C VHS. Wally White, Randy Becker, Darren Dryden; **D:** Wally White; **W:** Wally White; **C:** George Mitas. *TOU*

Lie Down with Lions 🐾½ 1994 Long and dull TV adaptation of the Ken Follett spy novel. American nurse Kate Neeson (Helgenberger) is aghast when she discovers her lover, Jack Carver (Dalton), is a CIA agent. She marries Czech doctor Peter Husak (Havers) on the rebound and the newleyweds travel to Azerbijan to run a clinic, where Kate has a baby. But Jack's not out of the picture since his current assignment takes him into the war-torn region—and back into Kate's life, especially when he discovers Peter is not what he seems. On 3 cassettes. 136m/C VHS. Timothy Dalton, Marg Helgenberger, Nigel Havers, Omar Sharif, Kabir Bedi, Juergen Prochnow; **D:** Jim Goddard; **W:** Guy Andrews, Julian Bond; **C:** Eddy van der Enden. *CCB, TVC*

Liebelei 🐾🐾 1932 Fritz (Liebeneiner), a handsome lieutenant, has broken off his romance with a married baroness and fallen for young opera singer Christine (Schneider) in turn-of-the-century Vienna. However, when the jealous baron (Grundgens) learns of his wife's infidelity, he challenges Fritz to a duel. Remade as "Christine" in 1967, with Romy Schneider in her mother's role. In German with English subtitles. 82m/B VHS. *GE* Magda Schneider, Wolfgang Liebeneiner, Gustav Grundgens; **D:** Max Ophuls. *KIV*

Liebestraum 🐾🐾 1991 (R) An architectural expert, his old college friend and the friend's wife form a dangerous triangle of passion and lust that strangely duplicates a situation that led to a double murder forty years earlier. The unrated version clocks in at 116 minutes. **CW:** Langauge and strong sensuality. 109m/C VHS, LV. Kevin Anderson, Bill Pullman, Pamela Gidley, Kim Novak; **D:** Mike Figgis; **W:** Mike Figgis. *MGM*

Lies 🐾🐾½ 1983 (PG) Complicated mystery about a murder/thriller movie plot becoming reality as it is being filmed, revolving around a scam to collect an inheritance from a rich guy in a mental hospital. 93m/C VHS, Beta, Closed Caption. *GB* Ann Dusenberry, Gail Strickland, Bruce Davison, Clu Gulager, Bert Remsen, Dick Miller; **D:** Ken Wheat, Jim Wheat. *FOX*

Lies Before Kisses 🐾🐾 1992 (PG-13) A woman finds out her loving husband has been spending time with a beautiful call girl. When the call girl is murdered the husband is accused. His

wife decides to help him clear his name but she just may have her own type of revenge in mind. 93m/C VHS, Beta, Closed Caption. Jaclyn Smith, Ben Gazzara, Nick Mancuso, Greg Evigan, Penny Fuller, James Karen; **D:** Lou Antonio; **W:** Ellen Weston. *TTC, PMS*

Lies My Father Told Me 🐾🐾🐾 1975 (PG) Simple drama about growing up in the 1920s in a Jewish ghetto. The story revolves around a young boy's relationship with his immigrant grandfather. Quiet and moving. 102m/C VHS. *CA* Yossi Yadin, Len Birman, Marilyn Lightstone, Jeffery Lynas; **D:** Jan Kadar; **W:** Ted Allan. Golden Globe Awards '76: Best Foreign Film; Nominations: Academy Awards '75: Best Original Screenplay. *NO*

Lies of the Twins 🐾🐾 1991 A beautiful model becomes involved with her therapist and his identical, and irresponsible, twin brother. 93m/C VHS. Isabella Rossellini, Aidan Quinn, Iman, John Pleshette; **D:** Tim Hunter. *USH*

Lt. Robin Crusoe, U.S.N. 🐾 1966 (G) A lighthearted navy pilot crash lands amusingly on a tropical island, falls hard for an island babe and schemes intensely against the local evil ruler. Lackluster Disney debacle. 113m/C VHS, Beta. Dick Van Dyke, Nancy Kwan, Akim Tamiroff; **D:** Byron Paul; **M:** Robert F. Brunner. *DIS, OM*

The Life and Adventures of Nicholas Nickleby 🐾🐾🐾½ *Nicholas Nickleby* 1981 Nine-hour performance of the 1838 Dickens' tale by the Royal Shakespeare Company, featuring the work of 39 actors portraying 150 characters. Wonderful performances are characterized by frantic action and smoothly meshing intertwining plots, focusing on the trials and tribulations of the Nickleby family, amidst wealth, poverty, and injustice in Victorian England. Nine cassettes. 540m/C VHS. *GB* Roger Rees, David Thewlis, Emily Richard, John Woodvine; **D:** Jim Goddard; **W:** David Edgar; **M:** Stephen Oliver. *AAE, FOX, FHS*

The Life and Assassination of the Kingfish 1976 Recommended by the NEA, this story of Louisiana politician Huey Long is riveting. Asner gives a profound performance. 96m/C VHS, Beta. Ed Asner, Nicholas Pryor, Diane Kagan; **D:** Robert Collins. *NO*

The Life and Death of Colonel Blimp 🐾🐾🐾 *Colonel Blimp* 1943 Chronicles the life of a British soldier who survives three wars (Boer, WWI, and WWII), falls in love with three women (all portrayed by Kerr), and dances a fine waltz. Fine direction and performance abound. 115m/C VHS, Beta, LV. *GB* Roger Livesey, Deborah Kerr, Anton Walbrook, Ursula Jeans, Albert Lieven; **D:** Michael Powell, Emeric Pressburger; **C:** Georges Perinal. *NO*

The Life and Loves of Mozart 🐾🐾½ 1959 Despite the title, this is really about the great composer's later life at the time of the premiere of "Die Zauberfloete" ("The Magic Flute"). This is only partly saved by a stellar performance from Werner, as well as the music. Other than that, it gets bogged down in titillation about W.A.M.'s romantic life. In German with English subtitles. 87m/C VHS. Oskar Werner, Johanna Matz, Angelika Hauff; **D:** Karl Hartl; **V:** Anton Dermota. *NOS, VEC*

Life and Nothing But 🐾🐾🐾½ *La Vie est Rien d'Autre* 1989 (PG) Two young women search for their lovers at the end of WWI. They're helped by a French officer brutalized by the war and driven to find all of France's casualties. Romantic, evocative, and saddening. In French with English subtitles. 135m/C VHS, Beta. *FR* Philippe Noiret, Sabine Azema, Francoise Perrot; **D:** Bertrand Tavernier; **W:** Bertrand Tavernier; **C:** Bruno de Keyzer. British Academy Awards '89: Best Foreign Film; Cesar Awards '90: Best Actor (Noiret), Best Score; Los Angeles Film Critics Association Awards '90: Best Foreign Film. *ORI, FCT*

Life and Nothing More ... 🐾🐾 *And Life Goes On ...; Zendegi Va Digar Hich ...* 1992 Following Iran's devastating 1990 earthquake, a filmmaker and his son search for the young actors who previously worked with him to see if they've survived, meeting various villagers trying to rebuild their lives. Sequel to Kiarostami's film "Where Is My Friend's House?" and followed by "Through the Olive Trees." Farsi with subtitles. 91m/C VHS. Farhad Kheradmand, Pooya Payvar; **D:** Abbas Kiarostami; **W:** Abbas Kiarostami; **C:** Homayun Payvar. FCT

Life & Times of Grizzly Adams 🐾🐾 1974 (G)
Lightweight family adventure film based on the rugged life of legendary frontiersman, Grizzly Adams, that served as the launching pad for the TV series. Grizzly is mistakenly chased for a crime he didn't commit and along the way befriends a big bear. 93m/C VHS, Beta. Dan Haggerty, Denver Pyle, Lisa Jones, Marjorie Harper, Don Shanks; **D:** Richard Friedenberg. NO

Life & Times of Judge Roy Bean 🐾🐾½ 1972 (PG)
Based on the life of the famed Texas "hanging judge," the film features Newman as the legendary Bean who dispenses frontier justice in the days of the Wild West. Filled with gallows humor. Gardner sparkles as actress Lily Langtry. 124m/C VHS, Beta, LV. Paul Newman, Stacy Keach, Ava Gardner, Jacqueline Bisset, Anthony Perkins, Roddy McDowall, Victoria Principal; **D:** John Huston; **W:** John Milius; **M:** Maurice Jarre. Nominations: Academy Awards '72: Best Song ("Marmalade, Molasses & Honey"). WAR

The Life & Times of the Chocolate Killer 🐾½ 1988
Police turn against the hand that's helped them save property and lives, by framing a good samaritan with deeds done by the "Chocolate Killer." 75m/C VHS. Michael Adrian, Rod Browning, Tabi Cooper. THV

Life Begins for Andy Hardy 🐾🐾🐾 1941
Andy gets a job in New York before entering college and finds the working world to be a sobering experience. Surprisingly downbeat and hardhitting for an Andy Hardy film. Garland's last appearance in the series. 100m/B VHS, Beta. Mickey Rooney, Judy Garland, Lewis Stone, Ann Rutherford, Fay Holden, Gene Reynolds, Ralph Byrd; **D:** George B. Seitz. MGM

A Life in the Theater 🐾🐾½ 1993
Life in the theater as a hammy stage veteran (Lemmon) shares his experiences (and his dressing room) with a callow newcomer (Broderick). Petty squabbles, missed cues, and rare candor are displayed as the two stage scenes from their various repertory. Gentle, slight Mamet play, written when he was 25. Made for television. 78m/C VHS, LV, Closed Caption. Jack Lemmon, Matthew Broderick; **D:** Gregory Mosher; **W:** David Mamet. TTC

Life is a Circus, Charlie Brown/You're the Greatest, Charlie Brown 1980
Two Peanuts favorites appear on this tape. In the Emmy award-winning "Life Is a Circus, Charlie Brown," Snoopy falls in love with Fifi, a French poodle circus performer, and winds up as a member of the traveling circus. In "You're the Greatest, Charlie Brown," our hero has a chance to win a decathlon in the Junior Olympics. With Peppermint Patty coaching, anything can happen! 60m/C VHS, Beta. **D:** Phil Roman. SHL, VTR

Life Is a Long Quiet River 🐾🐾🐾 La Vie Est Une Longue Fleuve Tranquille 1988
Social comedy about a nurse who, infuriated with her married doctor employer/lover, switches two babies at birth. Twelve years later, after her lover's wife has died and he still refuses to marry her, she reveals the swap. The children are returned to their rightful families causing a multitude of confusion and adjustment. Directorial debut of Chatiliez. In French with English subtitles. 89m/C VHS. FR Benoit Magimel, Helene Vincent, Andre Wilms, Daniel Gelin, Catherine Hiegel, Christine Pignet, Patrick Bouchitey, Valerie Lalande, Tara Romer, Jerome Floch, Sylvie Cubertafon; **D:** Etienne Chatiliez; **W:** Florence Quentin, Etienne Chatiliez; **M:** Gerard Kawczynski. Cesar Awards '89: Best Supporting Actress (Vincent), Best Writing. NYF, FCT

Life Is Beautiful 🐾🐾½ 1979
A politically neutral man is arrested and tortured in pre-revolutionary Lisbon, and forced to make, and act on, a political commitment. Dubbed. 102m/C VHS, Beta. PT Giancarlo Giannini, Ornella Muti; **D:** Grigorij Ciukhrai. NWV

Life Is Sweet 🐾🐾🐾½ 1990 (R)
The consuming passions of food and drink focus the lives of an oddball English working-class family beset by hopeless dreams and passions. Mother is always fixing family meals—in between helping her friend open a gourmet restaurant which features such revolting dishes as pork cyst and prune quiche. Dad is a chef who buys a snack truck and dreams of life on the road. Natalie and Nicola, the grown twins, eat their meals in front of the television but Nicola is also a bulimic who binges and purges on chocolate bars behind her bedroom door. (Note the chocolate scene between Nicola and her boyfriend.) An affectionate, if sometimes unattractive, look at a chaotic family. **CW:** Language and one sensual scene. 103m/C VHS, LV, Closed Caption. GB Alison Steadman, Jane Horrocks, Jim Broadbent, Claire Skinner, Timothy Spall, Stephen Rea, David Thewlis; **D:** Mike Leigh; **W:** Mike Leigh. Los Angeles Film Critics Association Awards '91: Best Supporting Actress (Horrocks); National Society of Film Critics Awards '91: Best Actress (Steadman), Best Film, Best Supporting Actress (Horrocks). REP, BTV

The Life of Emile Zola 🐾🐾🐾½ 1937
Writer Emile Zola intervenes in the case of Alfred Dreyfus who was sent to Devil's Island for a crime he did not commit. Well-crafted production featuring a handsome performance from Muni. 117m/B VHS, Beta, LV. Paul Muni, Gale Sondergaard, Gloria Holden, Joseph Schildkraut; **D:** William Dieterle; **C:** Gaetano Antonio "Tony" Gaudio; **M:** Max Steiner. Academy Awards '37: Best Picture, Best Screenplay, Best Supporting Actor (Schildkraut); New York Film Critics Awards '37: Best Actor (Muni), Best Film; Nominations: Academy Awards '37: Best Actor (Muni), Best Director (Dieterle), Best Interior Decoration, Best Sound, Best Original Score. MGM, BTV

A Life of Her Own 🐾🐾½ 1950
Turner stars as a farm girl who takes her dream of becoming a top model to the Big Apple. She signs with an agency and is befriended by Dvorak, an aging model, who acts as her mentor. Turner finds success and is soon the toast of the town until she gets involved with a married man (Milland) and her life starts to crumble. Average soap opera with flimsy script. Turner is good, but Dvorak steals the show in her role as an over-the-hill fashion plate. 108m/B VHS. Lana Turner, Ray Milland, Tom Ewell, Louis Calhern, Ann Dvorak, Barry Sullivan, Jean Hagen, Phyllis Kirk, Sara Haden; **D:** George Cukor; **W:** Isobel Lennart. MGM

Life of Oharu 🐾🐾🐾½ Diary of Oharu; Saikaku Ichidai Onna 1952
A near masterpiece rivaled only by "Ugetsu" in the Mizoguchi canon, this film details the slow and agonizing moral decline of a woman in feudal Japan, from wife to concubine to prostitute. A scathing portrait of social predestination based on a novel by Ibara Saikaku. In Japanese with English subtitles. 136m/B VHS, Beta. JP Kinuyo Tanaka, Toshiro Mifune; **D:** Kenji Mizoguchi. HMV, APD, TPV

A Life of Sin 🐾🐾 1992 (R)
Scandalous drama about an impoverished Caribbean girl who rises to wealth and power as a world-famous madame. Colon stars as the beautiful Isabel, who is betrayed by her childhood friend Paulo (Julia) and rejected by the Catholic bishop (Ferrer) in this tragic story of passion and greed. 112m/C VHS, Closed Caption. Raul Julia, Miriam Colon, Jose Ferrer; **D:** Efrain Lopez Neris; **W:** Emilio Diaz Valcarcel. COL, PMS

Life of Verdi 1984
Epic mini-series biography of the famous composer, with many excerpts of his music sung by Luciano Pavarotti, Renata Telbaldi, and Maria Callas. Made for television. 600m/B VHS, Beta. IT Ronald Pickup, Carla Fracci. HMV, KUL, MVD

Life on a String 🐾🐾 1990
Set in the distant past, this is a lyrical story of a young boy searching for a cure for his blindness. His possible cure involves a myth which requires him to devote his life to music and the breaking of 1000 strings on a banjo. Adapted from a story by Shi Tiesheng. In Chinese with English subtitles. 110m/C VHS. CH **D:** Chen Kaige; **C:** Gu Changwei. FCT, KIV

Life 101 🐾🐾½ 1995
Innocent freshman Haim tries to adjust to college life in the sixties, aided by his hippie roommate Coogan, who introduces Haim to the pleasures of life. Innocuous coming of age comedy. 95m/C VHS. Corey Haim, Keith Coogan, Ami Dolenz; **D:** Redge Mahaffey; **W:** Redge Mahaffey. MNC

Life Stinks 🐾 1991 (PG-13)
So does the film. A grasping tycoon bets he can spend a month living on the street without money, resulting in cheap laughs, heavy-handed sentiment and one musical number. Those expecting the innovative, hilarious Brooks of "Young Frankenstein" or "Blazing Saddles" will be very disappointed—these jokes are stale and the timing is tedious. Those looking for a Chaplinesque tale for modern times should stick with Chaplin. 93m/C VHS, Beta, LV, Closed Caption. Mel Brooks, Jeffrey Tambor, Lesley Ann Warren, Stuart Pankin, Howard Morris, Teddy Wilson, Michael Ensign, Billy Barty, Carmine Caridi, Rudy DeLuca; **D:** Mel Brooks; **W:** Mel Brooks, Rudy DeLuca; **C:** Steven Poster. MGM

Life with Father 🐾🐾🐾½ 1947
Based on the writings of the late Clarence Day, Jr., this is the story of his childhood in New York City during the 1880s. A delightful saga about a stern but loving father and his relationship with his knowing wife and four red-headed sons. 118m/C VHS, Beta. William Powell, Irene Dunne, Elizabeth Taylor, Edmund Gwenn, ZaSu Pitts, Jimmy Lydon, Martin Milner; **D:** Michael Curtiz; **M:** Max Steiner. Golden Globe Awards '48: Best Score; New York Film Critics Awards '47: Best Actor (Powell); Nominations: Academy Awards '47: Best Actor (Powell), Best Art Direction/Set Decoration (Color), Best Color Cinematography, Original Dramatic/Comedy Score. CNG, MRV, NOS

Life with Mikey 🐾🐾½ 1993 (PG-13)
Michael "Mikey" Chapman (Fox) is a washed-up former child star who now half-heartedly runs a minor talent agency for other pint-sized would-be thespians. Ever mindful of his previous glory, he believes he is doomed to obscurity when a 10-year-old Brooklyn pickpocket reanimates his taste for life. Light, sweet comedy is generally predictable, a typical Fox effort. Unbilled cameo from Reuben Blades as Vidal's father. **CW:** Language and thematic elements. 92m/C VHS, Beta, LV, Closed Caption. Michael J. Fox, Christina Vidal, Cyndi Lauper, Nathan Lane, David Huddleston, Victor Garber, David Krumholtz, Tony Hendra; **Cameos:** Ruben Blades; **D:** James Lapine; **W:** Marc Lawrence; **M:** Alan Menken. TOU, BTV

Lifeboat 🐾🐾🐾½ 1944
When a German U-boat sinks a freighter during WWII, the eight survivors seek refuge in a tiny lifeboat. Tension peaks after the drifting passengers take in a stranded Nazi. Hitchcock saw a great challenge in having the entire story take place in a lifeboat and pulled it off with his usual flourish. In 1989, the film "Dead Calm" replicated the technique. From a story by John Steinbeck. Bankhead shines. 96m/B VHS, Beta, LV, Closed Caption. Tallulah Bankhead, John Hodiak, William Bendix, Canada Lee, Walter Slezak, Hume Cronyn, Henry Hull, Mary Anderson; **D:** Alfred Hitchcock. National Board of Review Awards '44: 10 Best Films of the Year; New York Film Critics Awards '44: Best Actress (Bankhead); Nominations: Academy Awards '44: Best Black and White Cinematography, Best Director (Hitchcock), Best Story. HMV, FOX

Lifeforce 🐾🐾½ 1985 (R)
A beautiful female vampire from outer space drains Londoners and before long the city is filled with disintegrating zombies in this hi-tech thriller. Sex was never stranger. 100m/C VHS, Beta, LV. Steve Railsback, Peter Firth, Frank Finlay, Patrick Stewart, Michael Gothard, Nicholas Ball, Aubrey Morris, Nancy Paul, Mathilda May, John

Hallam; **D:** Tobe Hooper; **W:** Dan O'Bannon, Don Jakoby; **M:** Henry Mancini, Michael Kamen. *MGM, LIV, VES*

Lifeform 🎬½ **1996 (R)** Human beings may believe they're tops in the universe but when a Viking spaceship suddenly returns to Earth from a mission to Mars, NASA scientists discover a lifeform that thinks differently.**CW:** Language, violence. 90m/C VHS, Closed Caption. Cotter Smith, Deirdre O'Connell, Ryan Phillippe; **D:** Mark H. Baker. *LIV*

Lifeguard **1975 (PG)** The lifeguard lives by the credo that work is for people who cannot surf. Aging, he questions whether he should give up the beach life and start selling Porsches. Made for television. 96m/C VHS, Beta. Sam Elliott, Anne Archer, Stephen Young, Parker Stevenson, Kathleen Quinlan; **D:** Daniel Petrie. *PAR*

Lifepod 🎬 **1980** A group of intergalactic travelers is forced to evacuate a luxury space liner when a mad computer sabotages the ship. 94m/C VHS, Beta. Joe Penny, Jordan Michaels, Kristine DeBell. *VCI*

Lifepod 🎬🎬½ **1993** Trapped on a ship with a killer—only this time it's a space ship. In the year 2169 an interplanetary liner is sabotaged. Nine people escape in a damaged lifepod emergency craft. The survivors are perilously short of food and water and cannot contact Earth. They also face frightening evidence that the terrorist is among their group and is determined to kill the remaining survivors. Very loose adaptation of Alfred Hitchcock's 1944 film "Lifeboat." Made for television. 120m/C VHS, LV. Ron Silver, Robert Loggia, CCH Pounder, Stan Shaw, Adam Storke, Jessica Tuck, Kelli Williams, Ed Gate; **D:** Ron Silver; **W:** M. Jay Roach, Pen Densham. *CAF*

Lifespan 🎬 **1975** A young American scientist visiting Amsterdam discovers experiments involving a drug that halts aging. 85m/C VHS, Beta. Klaus Kinski, Hiram Keller, Tina Aumont; **D:** Alexander Whitelaw. *VES*

The Lifetaker woof! **1989** A woman lures an unsuspecting young man into her home where she seduces him. Violence and sex ensue. 97m/C VHS. Lea Dregorn, Peter Duncan, Terence Morgan; **D:** Michael Papas. *NO*

The Lift 🎬 **1985 (R)** Unsuspecting passengers meet an unfortunate fate when they take a ride in a demonic elevator in a highrise. In this film the last stop isn't ladies' lingerie, but death. In Dutch with English subtitles. 95m/C VHS, Beta, LV. *NL* Huub Stapel, Willeke Van Ammelrooy; **D:** Dick Maas. *MED*

The Light Ahead 🎬🎬½ **1939** Lovers Fishke and Hodel dream of escaping the poverty and prejudices of their shtetl for the possibilities of big city life in Odessa. They're aided in their quest by enlightened bookseller Mendele who turns the town's superstitions to their advantage. Based on the stories of social satirist Mendele Mokher Seforim. In Yiddish with English subtitles. 94m/B VHS. David Opatoshu, Isadore Cashier, Helen Beverly; **D:** Edgar G. Ulmer. *NCJ, ERG*

Light at the Edge of the World 🎬🎬 **1971 (PG)** A band of pirates torments a lighthouse keeper near Cape Horn after he sees a shipwreck they caused. 126m/C VHS, Beta. Kirk Douglas, Yul Brynner, Samantha Eggar; **D:** Kevin Billington. *MED*

The Light in the Forest 🎬🎬½ **1958** Disney adaptation of the classic Conrad Richter novel about a young man, kidnapped by Indians when he was young, who is forcibly returned to his white family. 92m/C VHS, Beta. James MacArthur, Fess Parker, Carol Lynley, Wendell Corey, Joanne Dru, Jessica Tandy, Joseph Calleia, John McIntire; **D:** Herschel Daugherty; **C:** Ellsworth Fredericks. *DIS*

The Light in the Jungle 🎬🎬½ **1991 (PG)** The biography of Nobel Peace Prize winner Dr. Albert Schweitzer. He established a hospital in Africa and had to overcome many obstacles, including tribal superstitions and European bureaucracy to make it successful and bring health care

to the area. 91m/C VHS, LV. Malcolm McDowell, Susan Strasberg, Andrew Davis; **D:** Gray Hofmeyr. *LIV*

Light of Day 🎬🎬 **1987 (PG-13)** A rock 'n roll semi-musical about a working class brother and sister who escape from their parents and aimless lives through their bar band. Script tends to fall flat although both Fox and Jett are believable. Title song written by Bruce Springsteen. 107m/C VHS, Beta, LV. Michael J. Fox, Joan Jett, Gena Rowlands, Jason Miller, Michael McKean, Michael Rooker, Michael Dolan; **D:** Paul Schrader; **W:** Paul Schrader; **C:** John Bailey; **M:** Thomas Newman. *LIV, VES*

The Light of Faith **1922** A sick young woman is cured when she touches the Holy Grail, which a man stole from her former lover in order to help her. Silent. 33m/C VHS, Beta. Lon Chaney Sr., Hope Hampton; **D:** Clarence Brown. *SNC, BFA, CNM*

The Light of Western Stars 🎬🎬½ **1930** Brian plays a young woman from the east who comes to claim her late brother's ranch. She meets her murdered brother's best friend (Arlen) who is a drunken cowboy, and he falls madly in love with her. Wanting to impress her, he quickly sobers up and prevents a gang from taking over the ranch. This was Paramount's first talking adaptation of a Grey novel and the third version of this particular Grey novel; silent versions were made in 1918 and 1925. 70m/B VHS. Richard Arlen, Mary Brian, Regis Toomey, Harry Green, Syd Saylor, George Chandler; **D:** Otto Brower, Edwin H. Knopf. *GPV*

The Light of Western Stars 🎬 **1940** A proper Eastern woman goes West and falls in love with a drunken lout. 67m/B VHS. Victor Jory, Jo Ann Sayers, Russell Hayden, Morris Ankrum; **D:** Lesley Selander. *GPV, DVT, NOS*

Light Sleeper 🎬🎬 **1992 (R)** Schrader's moody look at upscale drug dealers in New York. Dafoe is John LaTour, a 40 year-old drug courier to the club scene. Since his boss (Sarandon) is giving up the drug business for the safer world of natural cosmetics, John must look to his own future. His life becomes even more complicated when he runs into a bitter ex-flame (Delany) and finds the attraction is still overpowering. Cynical, contemplative, and menacing.**CW:** Strong language, violence and drug content, and one sensual scene. 103m/C VHS, LV. Willem Dafoe, Susan Sarandon, Dana Delany, David Clennon, Mary Beth Hurt; **D:** Paul Schrader; **W:** Paul Schrader; **M:** Michael Been. *LIV*

Light Years 🎬🎬½ **1988 (PG)** Garish animated fantasy epic about an idyllic land suddenly beset by evil mutations and death rays. Based on the novel "Robots Against Gondahar" by Jean-Pierre Andrevan. 83m/C VHS, Beta, LV. **D:** Harvey Weinstein; **W:** Isaac Asimov, Raphael Cluzel; **M:** Gabriel Yared; **V:** Glenn Close, Jennifer Grey, Christopher Plummer, Penn Jillette, John Shea, David Johansen, Bridget Fonda, Paul Shaffer, Terrence Mann, Teller. *THV, FUS*

Lightblast 🎬 **1985** A San Francisco policeman tries to stop a deadly explosive-wielding mad scientist from blowing the city to kingdom come. 89m/C VHS, Beta. Erik Estrada, Michael Pritchard; **D:** Enzo G. Castellari. *LIV*

The Lighthorsemen 🎬🎬🎬 **1987 (PG-13)** Compelling WWI drama follows several battle-hardened men of the Australian Light-Horse mounted infantry stationed in the Middle Eastern desert and the new recruit who joins their ranks and craves acceptance. Superbly filmed, particularly the final battle scene which pits the Aussies against the Turks for control of the wells at Beersheba. Fine performance by Andrews in this epic which contains the essential elements of a good war movie—horses, guns, and more horses. Originally planned at 140 minutes. Good companion film for another Aussie WWI saga: "Gallipoli." 110m/C VHS, Beta, Closed Caption. *AU* Jon Blake, Peter Phelps, Tony Bonner, Bill Kerr, Nick Wateres, John Walton, Tim McKenzie, Sigrid Thornton, Anthony Andrews; **D:** Simon Wincer; **W:** Ian Jones; **M:** Mario Millo. *WAR*

Lightnin' Carson Rides Again 🎬½ **1938** A tough frontier lawman tracks down his payroll-carrying nephew who's been accused of murder and thievery. 58m/B VHS, Beta, 8mm. Tim McCoy, Joan Barclay, Ted Adams, Forrest Taylor; **D:** Sam Newfield. *NOS, VYY*

Lightning Bill 🎬 **1935** Bill champions good in battling rustlers. 46m/B VHS, Beta, LV. Buffalo Bill Jr. *NO*

Lightning Bill Crandall 🎬½ **1937** Gunman heads south for the quiet life. Unfortunately, Arizona proves the scene of a fierce battle between various factions of cattlemen. The gunman aids the good guys, and tries to win the daughter's heart. 60m/B VHS. Bob Steele, Lois January, Charles "Blackie" King, Frank LaRue, Ernie Adams, Earl Dwire, Dave O'Brien; **D:** Sam Newfield. *NOS, DVT*

Lightning Bolt 🎬 *Operazione Goldman* **1967** Someone is stealing moon rockets from Cape Kennedy, and secret agent Harry Sennet must find out who is doing this devilish deed. It leads him to an evil madman who plots to destroy the world from his underwater hideout. Cheap and unintentionally funny. 96m/C VHS. *IT SP* Anthony Eisley, Wandisa Leigh, Folco Lulli, Diana Lorys, Ursula Parker; **D:** Anthony (Antonio Margheriti) Dawson. *SNC*

The Lightning Incident 🎬 **1991 (R)** McKeon plays a young Santa Fe sculptor whose worst nightmares come true when her baby is kidnapped by a devil-worshipping cult. Discovering she has a powerful psychic gift, she pursues the kidnappers across the country in a race to save her baby. Almost as bad as it sounds.**CW:** Terror violence. 90m/C VHS, Beta, Closed Caption. Nancy McKeon, Polly Bergen, Tantoo Cardinal, Elpidia Carrillo, Tim Ryan; **D:** Michael Switzer; **W:** Michael J. Murray. *PAR*

Lightning Jack 🎬½ **1994 (PG-13)** Western comedy about Lightning Jack Kane (Hogan), an aging second-rate outlaw who desperately wants to become a western legend. Mute store clerk Ben (Gooding) winds up as his partner in crime, while barely eluding criticisms of Stepin Fetchitism. Cliches galore, the running gags (including Kane's surreptitious use of his eyeglasses so he can see his shooting targets) fall flat.**CW:** Sexual content. 102m/C VHS, LV. Paul Hogan, Cuba Gooding Jr., Beverly D'Angelo, Kamala Dawson, Pat Hingle, Richard Riehle, Frank McRae, Roger Daltrey, L.Q. Jones, Max Cullen; **D:** Simon Wincer; **W:** Paul Hogan; **C:** David Eggby; **M:** Bruce Rowland. *HBO*

Lightning Over Water **1980** An odd, touching documentary co-arranged by Ray and Wenders, all about Ray's last months dying of cancer in his New York loft, his editing of his final film "We Can't Go Home Again," his film corpus and career in general. 91m/C VHS, Beta, LV. Nicholas Ray, Wim Wenders, Ronee Blakley, Tom Farrel, Gerry Bamman; **D:** Wim Wenders; **W:** Wim Wenders; **M:** Ronee Blakley. *IME*

Lightning Raiders 🎬🎬 **1945** When a stage coach filled with mail gets robbed, Billy Carson (Crabbe) and Fuzzy (St. John) set off to avenge the postal system. One of the last Crabbe/St. John efforts; perhaps they should have called it quits a few films earlier. 61m/C VHS. Buster Crabbe, Al "Fuzzy" St. John, Mady Lawrence, Henry Hall, Steve Darrell, I. Stanford Jolley, Karl Hackett, Roy Brent, Marin Sais, Al Ferguson; **D:** Sam Newfield; **W:** Elmer Clifton. *HEG*

Lightning Range 🎬 **1933** Roosevelt stars as a U.S. Deputy Marshal who continually foils the nefarious plots of a gang of outlaws. 50m/B VHS, Beta. Buddy Roosevelt, Lafe McKee. *NOS, VYY*

Lightning Strikes West 🎬½ **1940** U.S. Marshal trails an escaped convict, eventually catches him, and brings him in to finish paying his debt to society. 57m/B VHS, Beta. Ken Maynard. *VCN, VCI*

Lightning: The White Stallion 🎬½ **1986 (PG)** An old gambler and his two young friends enter a horse race in order to win their beloved white stallion back from thieves. 93m/C

VHS, Beta, Closed Caption. Mickey Rooney, Susan George, Isabel Lorca; *D:* William A. Levey. *MED*

Lightning Warrior 1931 Western suspense about pioneer life and the unraveling of a baffling mystery. Twelve chapters, 13 minutes each. **156m/B VHS, Beta.** George Brent, Frankie Darro; *D:* Armand Schaefer, Ben Kline. *VCN*

Lights! Camera! Murder! 🐾🐾 1989 When a twelve-year-old boy witnesses a filmed murder, he becomes the next target. **89m/C VHS.** John Barrett; *D:* Frans Nel. *ATL*

Lights of Old Santa Fe 🐾½ 1947 A cowboy rescues a beautiful rodeo owner from bankruptcy. The original, unedited version of the film. **78m/B VHS, Beta.** Roy Rogers, Dale Evans, George "Gabby" Hayes, Bob Nolan, The Pioneers. *NOS, DVT, TIM*

The Lightship 🐾🐾 1986 (PG-13) On a stationary lightship off the Carolina coast, the crew rescues three men from a disabled boat, only to find they are murderous criminals. Duvall as a flamboyant homosexual psychopath is memorable, but the tale is pretentious, overdone, and hackneyed. Based on Siegfried Lenz's story. **87m/C VHS, Beta, Closed Caption.** Robert Duvall, Klaus Maria Brandauer, Tom Bower, William Forsythe, Arliss Howard; *D:* Jerzy Skolimowski. *FOX*

Like Father, Like Son 🐾 1987 (PG-13) First and worst of a barrage of interchangeable switcheroo movies that came out in '87-'88. Moore is in top form, but the plot is contrived. **101m/C VHS, Beta, LV.** Dudley Moore, Kirk Cameron, Catherine Hicks, Margaret Colin, Sean Astin; *D:* Rod Daniel; *W:* Steven L. Bloom, Lorne Cameron; *M:* Miles Goodman. *COL*

Like It Never Was Before 🐾🐾 *Pensionat Oskar* 1995 Conventional, middleaged married Rune (Falkman) and Gunnel (Ekblad) Runeberg travel to a seaside hotel for their annual vacation with their three children. Ordinary family man Rune, though dissatisfied, is expecting little until he meets, and falls in love with, young handyman Petrus (Norrthon), and suddenly decides to break free. Swedish with subtitles. **108m/B VHS.** *SW* Loa Falkman, Stina Ekblad, Simon Norrthon, Philip Zanden, Sif Ruud, Ghita Norby; *D:* Suzanne Bier; *W:* Jonas Gardell; *C:* Kjell Lagerroos; *M:* Johan Soderqvist. *CCN*

Like Water for Chocolate 🐾🐾🐾½ *Como Agua para Chocolate* 1993 (R) Magical Mexican fairytale set in the early 1900s about family, love, and the power of food. Formidable Mama Elena is left a widow with three daughters. The youngest, Tita, grows up in the kitchen surrounded by all the magic Nacha, the housekeeper, can impart to her about food. Doomed by tradition to spend her days caring for her mother, Tita escapes by cooking, releasing her sorrows and longings into the food, infecting all who eat it. Wonderfully sensuous and slyly exaggerated. Based on the novel by Esquival who also wrote the screenplay and whose husband, Arau, directed. In Spanish with English subtitles. *CW:* Sexuality. **105m/C VHS, LV.** *MX* Lumi Cavazos, Marco Leonardi, Regina Torne, Mario Ivan Martinez, Ada Carrasco, Yareli Arizmendi, Claudette Maille, Pilar Aranda; *D:* Alfonso Arau; *W:* Laura Esquival; *C:* Steven Bernsein; *M:* Leo Brower. Nominations: British Academy Awards '93: Best Foreign Film; Independent Spirit Awards '94: Best Foreign Film. *TOU*

Li'l Abner 🐾½ *Trouble Chaser* 1940 Al Capp's famed comic strip comes somewhat to life in this low-budget comedy featuring all of the Dogpatch favorites. **78m/C VHS, Beta.** Cranville Owen, Martha Driscoll, Buster Keaton; *D:* Albert Rogell. *NOS, MRV, DVT*

Li'l Abner 🐾🐾½ 1959 High color Dogpatch drama adapted from the Broadway play (with most of the original cast) based on the Al Capp comic strip. When Abner's berg is considered as a site for atomic bomb testing, the natives have to come up with a reason why they should be allowed to exist. Choreography by Michael Kidd and Dee Dee Wood. ♫Jubilation T. Compone; Don't Take That Rag Off'n the Bush; A Typical Day; If I Had My Druthers; Room Enuff for Us; Namely You; The Country's in the Very Best of Hands; Unnecessary Town; I'm Past My Prime. **114m/C VHS, Beta, Closed Caption.** Peter Palmer, Leslie Parrish, Stubby Kaye, Julie Newmar, Howard St. John, Stella Stevens, Billie Hayes, Joe E. Marks; *D:* Melvin Frank; *W:* Norman Panama; *C:* Daniel F. Fapp; *M:* Johnny Mercer, Jean De Paul. Nominations: Academy Awards '59: Scoring of a Musical. *PAR, FCT*

Lili 🐾🐾🐾 1953 Delightful musical romance about a 16-year-old orphan who joins a traveling carnival and falls in love with a crippled, embittered puppeteer. Heartwarming and charming, if occasionally cloying. Leslie Caron sings the films's song hit, "Hi-Lili, Hi-Lo." **81m/C VHS, Beta, Closed Caption.** Leslie Caron, Jean-Pierre Aumont, Mel Ferrer, Kurt Kasznar, Zsa Zsa Gabor; *D:* Charles Walters; *M:* Bronislau Kaper. Academy Awards '53: Original Dramatic/Comedy Score; British Academy Awards '53: Best Actress (Caron); Golden Globe Awards '54: Best Screenplay; National Board of Review Awards '53: 10 Best Films of the Year; Nominations: Academy Awards '53: Best Actress (Caron), Best Art Direction/Set Decoration (Color), Best Color Cinematography, Best Director (Walters), Best Screenplay. *MGM*

Lilian's Story 🐾🐾½ 1995 Aging Lilian (Cracknell) has just been released after spending 40 years in a mental institution, placed there as an adolescent by her controlling, possessive father. The haunted Lilian is given a room at a residential hotel in Sydney's red-light district where the local prostitutes look out for her and she spends her days wandering the streets. Flashbacks reveal what lead the high-strung young Lilian (Collette) to her incarceration. Based on Kate Greville's 1984 novel, which was a fictional account of real-life Sydney eccentric Bea Miles. **94m/C VHS.** *AU* Ruth Cracknell, Barry Otto, Toni Collette, John Flaus, Essie Davis, Susie Lindemann, Anne Louise Lambert, Iris Shand; *D:* Jerzy Domaradzki; *W:* Steve Wright; *C:* Slawomir Idziak; *M:* Cezary Skubiszewski. Australian Film Institute '95: Best Supporting Actress (Collette). *NYR*

Lilies 🐾🐾 *Les Feluettes* 1996 Strange revenge fantasy set in a northern Quebec men's prison in 1952. A bishop (Sabourin) goes to the prison to hear the confession of a dying convict and is taken hostage in the chapel by the prison's homosexual population. There, he's forced to watch a play that recreates a 40-year-old incident in his own life. As the prison walls fade away, the actor/prisoners turn into students Simon (Cadieux) and Vallier (Gilmore), who take the lovers' roles in a pageant about the martyrdom of St. Sebastien too seriously for comfort. The female roles in the flashbacks (which include Vallier's crazy mother and Simon's would-be fiance) are played by men. Adapted from Bouchard's play "Les Feluettes out La Repetition d'un Drame Romantique." **95m/C VHS.** *CA* Marcel Sabourin, Jason Cadieux, Danny Gilmore, Brent Carver, Matthew Ferguson, Alexander Chapman, Aubert Pallascio; *D:* John Greyson; *W:* Michel Marc Bouchard; *C:* Daniel Jobin; *M:* Mychael Danna. Genie Awards '96: Best Art Direction/Set Decoration, Best Costume Design, Best Film, Best Sound; Nominations: Genie Awards '96: Best Actor (Cadieux), Best Actor (Ferguson, Gilmore), Best Adapted Screenplay, Best Cinematography, Best Director (Greyson), Best Film Editing, Best Supporting Actor (Chapman), Best Score. *NYR*

Lilies of the Field 🐾🐾🐾 1963 Five East German nuns enlist the aid of a free-spirited U.S. Army veteran. They persuade him to build a chapel for them and teach them English. Poitier is excellent as the itinerant laborer, holding the saccharine to an acceptable level, bringing honesty and strength to his role. Actress Skala had been struggling to make ends meet in a variety of day jobs until this opportunity. Poitier was the first African-American man to win an Oscar, and the first African-American nominated since Hattie MacDaniel in 1939. Followed by "Christmas Lilies of the Field," (1979). **94m/B VHS, Beta, Closed Caption.** Sidney Poitier, Lilia Skala, Lisa Mann, Isa Crino, Stanley Adams; *D:* Ralph Nelson; *M:* Jerry Goldsmith. Academy Awards '63: Best Actor (Poitier); Berlin International Film Festival '63: Best Actor (Poitier); Golden Globe Awards '64: Best Actor—Drama (Poitier); National Board of Review Awards '63: 10 Best Films of the Year; Nominations: Academy Awards '63: Best Adapted Screenplay, Best Black and White Cinematography, Best Picture, Best Supporting Actress (Skala). *MGM, FOX, BTV*

Liliom 🐾🐾🐾 1935 Boyer goes to heaven and is put on trial to see if he is deserving of his wings. Lang's first film after leaving Nazi Germany is filled with wonderful ethereal imagery, surprising coming from the man responsible for such grim visions as "Metropolis." In French only. **85m/B VHS, Beta.** *FR* Charles Boyer, Madeleine Ozeray, Florelle, Roland Toutain; *D:* Fritz Lang. *SNC, DVT, HEG*

Lilith 🐾🐾🐾 1964 Therapist-in-training Beatty falls in love with beautiful mental patient Seberg and approaches madness himself. A look at the doctor-patient relationship among the mentally ill and at the nature of madness and love. Doesn't always satisfy, but intrigues. Rossen's swan song. **114m/B VHS, Beta.** Warren Beatty, Jean Seberg, Peter Fonda, Gene Hackman, Kim Hunter; *D:* Robert Rossen; *C:* Eugene (Eugen Shufftan) Shuftan. *COL, MLB*

Lillie 🐾🐾🐾 1979 The life of Edwardian beauty Lillie Langtry, known as "The Jersey Lily," is portrayed in this British made-for-television drama. Defying the morals of the times, Lillie was the first publicly acknowledged mistress of the Prince of Wales, only one of her numerous lovers. On seven cassettes. Shown on "Masterpiece Theatre" on PBS. **690m/C VHS.** *GB* Francesca Annis, Cheryl Campbell, John Castle, Dennis Lili, Peter Egan, Anton Rodgers, Ann Firbank. *SIG, TVC, HMV*

Lily Dale 🐾🐾½ 1996 (PG) Nineteen-year-old Horace Robedaux (Guinee) is in Houston to visit his estranged mother Corella (Channing) and sister Lily Dale (Masterson) while his taciturn stepfather Pete Davenport (Shepard) is supposed to be away. Pete dislikes Horace and left the boy behind with relatives when he married Corella and they moved away. Self-centered Lily Dale resents Horace taking away attention from herself and matters only get worse when Pete comes home early and Horace becomes so ill that he can't leave. Set in 1910; Foote wrote the play as a memoir to his father, Horace. Made for TV. **95m/C VHS.** Tim Guinee, Stockard Channing, Mary Stuart Masterson, Sam Shepard, John Slattery, Jean Stapleton; *D:* Peter Masterson; *W:* Horton Foote. *HMK*

Lily in Love 🐾🐾½ *Playing for Keeps; Jatszani Kell* 1985 (PG-13) An aging stage star disguises himself as a suave Italian to star in his playwright wife's new play, and woos her to test her fidelity. Charming, warm, and sophisticated. Loosely based on Molnar's "The Guardsman." Made for television. **100m/C VHS, Beta, LV.** *HU* Maggie Smith, Christopher Plummer, Elke Sommer, Adolph Green; *D:* Karoly Makk; *W:* Frank Cucci. *LIV, VES*

Lily in Winter 🐾🐾½ 1994 (PG) Christmas story about families and the ties that bind, set in 1957. Black nanny Lily (Cole in film debut) works for busy showbiz New Yorkers, the Towlers (Hoffmann and Brown), looking after their neglected 10-year-old son Michael (Bonsall). But Lily thinks she's in trouble, thanks to her no-account brother Booker (Russell), and takes off to her rural Alabama roots without realizing Michael has followed her. His parents, however, think Lily has kidnapped him. Made for cable TV. **120m/C VHS.** Natalie Cole, Brian Bonsall, Dwier Brown, Cecil Hoffmann, Marla Gibbs, Monte Russell, Rae'ven Kelly, Salli Richardson, James Pickens Jr., Matthew Faison; *D:* Delbert Mann; *W:* Robert Eisele; *C:* Charles Mills; *M:* David Shire. *USH*

Lily of Killarney 🐾🐾 *The Bride of the Lake* 1934 A musical comedy romance about a British lord who arranges to pay his debts via horseraces, arranged marriages and inheritances. **82m/B VHS, Beta, 8mm.** *GB* Gina Malo, John Garrick, Stanley Holloway; *D:* Maurice Elvey. *VYY*

Lily Was Here ♫½ **1989 (R)** After her fiancee is senselessly murdered, a young woman named Lily is forced to turn to a life of crime in order to survive. A series of petty thefts evolves into a huge crime wave and Lily soon finds herself the object of a massive manhunt. Lily must make the ultimate choice between freedom and motherhood in this shocking thriller. Soundtrack by Dave Stewart features hit instrumental theme "Lily was Here" by saxophonist Candy Dulfur.**CW:** Strong language and some sexuality. **110m/C VHS.** Marion Van Thijn, Thom Hoffman, Adrian Brine, Dennis Rudge; **D:** Ben Verbong; **W:** Ben Verbong, Sytze Van Der Laan, Willem Jan Otten. *NO*

The Limbic Region ♫♫ **1996** Terminally ill police detective Jon Lucca (Olmos) has spent 20 years tracking a serial killer known as "The Scorekeeper," who likes to shotgun the young inhabitants of smalltown lover's lanes. His most likely suspect is Lloyd Warden (Dzundza) and the duo engage in a deadly cat-and-mouse battle that may destroy them both. Made for cable. **?m/C VHS, Closed Caption.** Edward James Olmos, George Dzundza, Gwynyth Walsh, Patrick Ranahan, Todd Johnson; **C:** Tobias Schliessler. *MGM*

Limelight ♫♫♫ **1952** A nearly washed-up music hall comedian is stimulated by a young ballerina to a final hour of glory. A subtle if self-indulgent portrait of Chaplin's own life, featuring an historic pairing of Chaplin and Keaton. **120m/B VHS, Beta, LV.** Charlie Chaplin, Claire Bloom, Buster Keaton, Nigel Bruce, Sydney Chaplin; **D:** Charlie Chaplin; **C:** Karl Struss. National Board of Review Awards '52: 10 Best Films of the Year. *FOX*

Limit Up ♫♫ **1989 (PG-13)** An ambitious Chicago Trade Exchange employee makes a deal with the devil to corner the market in soybeans. Turgid attempt at supernatural comedy, featuring Charles as God. Catch Sally Kellerman in a cameo as a nightclub singer. **88m/C VHS, Beta, LV, Closed Caption.** Nancy Allen, Dean Stockwell, Brad Hall, Danitra Vance, Ray Charles, Luana Anders; **Cameos:** Sally Kellerman; **D:** Richard Martini; **C:** Peter Collister. *NO*

The Limping Man ♫♫ **1953** Bridges returns to post-WWII London to renew a wartime romance. On the way, he gets caught up in solving a murder. Unexceptional-of-its-era thriller. **76m/B VHS, Beta.** GB Lloyd Bridges, Moira Lister, Leslie Phillips, Helene Cordet, Alan Wheatley; **D:** Charles De Latour. *SNC, RXM, VYY*

Linda ♫♫½ **1929** Linda, a young mountain girl, is forced to marry a much older man though her heart belongs to a young doctor. Her kind husband tries to make the best of the situation. **75m/B VHS.** Helen Foster, Warner Baxter, Noah Beery Sr., Mitchell Lewis, Kate Price, Alan Connor; **D:** Dorothy Davenport Reid. *GPV, FCT*

Linda ♫♫ **1993 (PG-13)** Madsen in her femme fatale mode as treacherous wife Linda who wants to frame her schlump husband (Thomas) for murder. Whose murder? Why the inconvenient wife (Harrington) of her boyfriend (McGinley). The two homicidal lovebirds want to take the insurance money and run—leaving hubby to face the consequences. Based on the novella "Linda" by John D. MacDonald. **88m/C VHS, Beta, Closed Caption.** Virginia Madsen, Richard Thomas, Ted McGinley, Laura Harrington; **D:** Nathaniel Gutman; **W:** Nevin Schreiner; **M:** David Michael Frank. *PAR*

The Lindbergh Kidnapping Case ♫♫♫ **1976** The famous Lindbergh baby kidnapping in 1932 and the trial and execution of Bruno Hauptmann, convincingly portrayed by Hopkins. DeYoung as Lindbergh is blah, but the script is quite good. Made for TV. **150m/C VHS, Beta.** Anthony Hopkins, Joseph Cotten, Cliff DeYoung, Walter Pidgeon, Dean Jagger, Martin Balsam, Laurence Luckinbill, Tony Roberts; **D:** Buzz Kulik; **M:** Billy Goldenberg. *COL*

The Line ♫½ **1980 (R)** Not-so-hot anti-war drama about a sit-down strike at a military installation by Vietnam veteran prison inmates. Leans heavily on recycled footage from director Siegel's

own "Parade" (1971). **94m/C VHS, Beta.** Russ Thacker, David Doyle, Erik Estrada; **D:** Robert Siegel. *NO*

The Linguini Incident ♫♫ **1992 (R)** An inept escape artist, a pathological liar, a lingerie designer, a deaf restaurant hostess who throws out one-liners in sign language, and two sinister, yet chic, restaurant owners get together in this marginal comedy about magic and adventure. **99m/C VHS, LV, Closed Caption.** Rosanna Arquette, David Bowie, Eszter Balint, Andre Gregory, Buck Henry, Viveca Lindfors, Marlee Matlin, Lewis Arquette; **Cameos:** Julian Lennon, Iman; **D:** Richard Shepard; **W:** Richard Shepard, Tamar Brott; **M:** Thomas Newman. *IME*

Link WOOF! **1986 (R)** A primatologist and his nubile assistant find their experiment has gone—you guessed it—awry, and their hairy charges are running—yep, that's right—amok. Run for your life! **103m/C VHS, Beta, Closed Caption.** GB Elisabeth Shue, Terence Stamp; **D:** Richard Franklin; **M:** Jerry Goldsmith. *REP*

The Lion Has Wings ♫♫½ **1940** The story of how Britain's Air Defense was set up to meet the challenge of Hitler's Luftwaffe during their "finest hour." Dated, now-quaint but stirring wartime period piece. "Docudrama" style was original at the time. **75m/B VHS, Beta, LV.** Merle Oberon, Ralph Richardson, Flora Robson, June Duprez; **D:** Michael Powell, Brian Desmond Hurst; **C:** Harry Stradling. *RXM*

The Lion in Winter ♫♫♫♫ **1968 (PG)** Medieval monarch Henry II and his wife, Eleanor of Aquitaine, match wits over the succession to the English throne and much else in this fast-paced film version of James Goldman's play. The family, including three grown sons, and visiting royalty are united for the Christmas holidays fraught with tension, rapidly shifting allegiances, and layers of psychological manipulation. Superb dialogue and perfectly realized characterizations. O'Toole and Hepburn are triumphant. Screen debuts for Hopkins and Dalton. Shot on location, this literate costume drama surprised the experts with its box-office success. **134m/C VHS, LV.** Peter O'Toole, Katharine Hepburn, Jane Merrow, Nigel Terry, Timothy Dalton, Anthony Hopkins, John Castle, Nigel Stock; **D:** Anthony Harvey; **W:** James Goldman; **M:** John Barry. Academy Awards '68: Best Actress (Hepburn), Best Adapted Screenplay, Best Original Score; Directors Guild of America Awards '68: Best Director (Harvey); Golden Globe Awards '69: Best Actor—Drama (O'Toole), Best Film—Drama; National Board of Review Awards '68: 10 Best Films of the Year; New York Film Critics Awards '68: Best Film; Nominations: Academy Awards '68: Best Actor (O'Toole), Best Costume Design, Best Director (Harvey), Best Picture. *COL, BTV, TVC*

A Lion Is in the Streets ♫♫♫ **1953** Cagney stars as a backwoods politician in a southern state who fights on the side of the sharecroppers and wins their support when he exposes the corrupt practices of a powerful businessman. On his way up the political ladder, however, Cagney betrays and exploits the very people who support him. Although this is a familiar storyline, Cagney is riveting as the corrupt politician, and Hale is wonderful as his patient wife. **88m/C VHS.** James Cagney, Barbara Hale, Anne Francis, Warner Anderson, John McIntire, Jeanne Cagney, Lon Chaney Jr., Frank McHugh, Larry Keating, Onslow Stevens; **D:** Raoul Walsh. *WAR*

The Lion King ♫♫♫♫ **1994 (G)** Highest grossing film in Disney history (likely a temporary title) is a winner for kids and their folks. Like his dad Mufasa (Jones), Lion cub Simba (Taylor) is destined to be king of the beasts, until evil uncle Scar (Irons) plots against him and makes him an outcast. Growing up in the jungles of Africa, Simba (now Broderick) learns about life and responsibility, before facing his uncle once again. Supporting characters frequently steal the show, with Sabella's Pumba the warthog and Lane's Timon the meerkat heading the procession (though Chong and Goldberg as hyenas give them a run). Disney epic features heartwarming combo of crowd-

pleasing songs, a story with depth, emotion, and politically correct multiculturalism, and stunning animation. The sound quality is equally spectacular; during the 2 1/2 minute wildebeest stampede scene, you'll swear the animals are running amuck in the house. 32nd Disney animated feature is the first without human characters, the first based on an original story, and the first to use the voices of a well-known, ethnically diverse cast. Scenes of violence in the animal kingdom may be too much for younger viewers. ♫Can You Feel the Love Tonight; The Circle of Life; I Just Can't Wait to Be King; Be Prepared; Hakuna Matata. **88m/C VHS, Closed Caption.** D: Rob Minkoff, Roger Allers; **W:** Jonathan Roberts, Irene Mecchi; **M:** Elton John, Hans Zimmer, Tim Rice; **V:** Matthew Broderick, Jeremy Irons, James Earl Jones, Madge Sinclair, Robert Guillaume, Jonathan Taylor Thomas, Richard "Cheech" Marin, Whoopi Goldberg, Rowan Atkinson, Nathan Lane, Ernie Sabella, Niketa Calame, Moira Kelly, Jim Cummings. Academy Awards '94: Best Song ("Can You Feel the Love Tonight"), Best Original Score; Chicago Film Critics Awards '94: Best Score; Golden Globe Awards '95: Best Film—Musical/Comedy, Best Song ("Can You Feel the Love Tonight?"), Best Score; Blockbuster Entertainment Awards '95: Family Movie, Theatrical, Best Soundtrack; Nominations: Academy Awards '94: Best Song ("Circle of Life"), Best Song ("Hakuna Matata"); Golden Globe Awards '95: Best Song ("Circle of Life"); MTV Movie Awards '95: Best Villain (Irons), Best Song ("Can You Feel the Love Tonight"). *DIS*

The Lion Man ♫♫ **1936** Arabian tale of a boy raised by lions. **?m/B VHS.** Jon Hall, Ted Adams. *LOO*

Lion Man ♫ **1979** Raised by wild animals, the son of King Solomon returns to his father's kingdom and roars his way to the throne. **91m/C VHS, Beta.** Steve Arkin. *BFV*

The Lion of Africa ♫♫ **1987** A down-to-earth woman doctor and an abrasive diamond dealer share a truck ride across Kenya. Filmed on location in East Africa. Fine lead performances in otherwise nothing-special made-for-cable adventure. **115m/C VHS, Beta.** GB Brian Dennehy, Brooke Adams, Joseph Shiloal; **D:** Kevin Connor; **M:** George S. Clinton. *ORI, WAR*

Lion of the Desert ♫♫♫ Omar Mukhtar **1981 (PG)** Bedouin horse militias face-off against Mussolini's armored terror in this epic historical drama. Omar Muktar (Quinn as the "Desert Lion") and his Libyan guerrilla patriots kept the Italian troops of Mussolini (Steiger) at bay for 20 years. Outstanding performances enhanced by the desert backdrop. A British-Libyan co-production. **162m/C VHS, Beta.** GB Anthony Quinn, Oliver Reed, Irene Papas, Rod Steiger, Raf Vallone, John Gielgud; **D:** Moustapha Akkad; **W:** H.A.L. Craig; **C:** Jack Hildyard; **M:** Maurice Jarre.

The Lion of Thebes ♫♫♫ **1964** A muscleman unhesitatingly jumps into the thick of things when Helen of Troy is kidnapped. A superior sword and sandal entry. **?m/C VHS, Beta.** IT Mark Forest, Yvonne Furneaux. *SNC*

Lionheart ♫½ **1987 (PG)** A romantic portrayal of the famous English King Richard the Lionheart's early years. Meant for kids, but no Ninja turtles herein—and this is just as silly, and slow to boot. **105m/C VHS, Beta, LV, Closed Caption.** Eric Stoltz, Talia Shire, Nicola Cowper, Dexter Fletcher, Nicholas Clay, Deborah Barrymore, Gabriel Byrne; **D:** Franklin J. Schaffner; **W:** Richard Outten; **M:** Jerry Goldsmith. *WAR*

Lionheart ♫½ A.W.O.L.; Wrong Bet **1990 (R)** Van Damme deserts the foreign legion and hits the streets when he learns his brother has been hassled. Many fights ensue, until you fall asleep.**CW:** Strong language and graphically violent fight scenes. **105m/C VHS, Beta, LV, Closed Caption.** Jean-Claude Van Damme, Harrison Page, Deborah Rennard, Lisa Pelikan, Brian Thompson; **D:** Sheldon Lettich; **W:** Jean-Claude Van Damme, Sheldon Lettich. *USH*

Lion's Den *✔½* 1936 A night club performer and a detective head west to fight crime in this film. 59m/B VHS, Beta. Tim McCoy, Dave O'Brien. *NOS, DVT*

The Lion's Share *✔* 1979 A gang of bank robbers have their loot stolen and go after the guy who ripped them off. 105m/C VHS, Beta. SP Julio de Grazia, Luisina Brando, Fernanda Mistral, Ulises Dumont, Julio Chavez. *NO*

Lip Service *✔✔✔* 1988 Satirical comedy-drama about the TV news industry. An ambitious young newscaster befriends a veteran reporter. He then manipulates his way to replace him on the reporter's morning program. Dooley as the veteran and Dunne as the upstart are fun to watch in this well-done cable rip-off of "Broadcast News." 67m/C VHS, Beta. Griffin Dunne, Paul Dooley; *D:* William H. Macy. *PSM*

Lipstick woof! 1976 (R) Fashion model Margaux seeks revenge on the man who brutally attacked and raped her, after he preys on her kid sister (real-life sis Mariel, in her debut). Exquisitely exploitative excuse for entertainment. 90m/C VHS, Beta, LV. Margaux Hemingway, Anne Bancroft, Perry King, Chris Sarandon, Mariel Hemingway; *D:* Lamont Johnson; *W:* David Rayfiel; *C:* Bill Butler, William A. Fraker. *PAR*

Lipstick Camera *✔✔* 1993 (R) Keats wants a career in television news and seeks out a successful freelance cameraman (Wimmer) to help her out. She also asks to borrow her techno-friend Feldman's mini-camera and then goes after a story on an ex-spy and his sexy companion. Only no one expects what the camera captures. Weak plot but strong cast and high-end production.*CW:* Language, violence, and sexual situations. 93m/C VHS, LV. Ele Keats, Brian Wimmer, Corey Feldman, Sandahl Bergman, Terry O'Quinn; *D:* Mike Bonifer; *W:* Mike Bonifer. *TRI*

Lipstick On Your Collar 1994 British TV fantasy/drama set in the stuffy confines of the British War Offices during the Suez Crisis of 1956. Two army clerks fantasize about the world outside through daydreams set to original tunes. Last series for the innovative Potter; on 3 cassettes. 360m/C VHS. *GB* Ewan McGregor, Giles Thomas, Louise Germaine; *D:* Renny Rye; *W:* Dennis Potter. *TVC, NEW*

Liquid Dreams *✔✔* 1992 (R) In this fast-paced, futuristic thriller, Daly goes undercover as an erotic dancer in a glitzy strip joint to try and solve her sister's murder. She finds that the owner and clientele deal not only in sexual thrills, but also in a strange brain-sucking ritual that provides the ultimate rush. Also available in an unrated version.*CW:* Language, violence and drug content, and sexuality. 92m/C VHS, Beta. Richard Steinmetz, Candice Daly, Barry Dennen, Juan Fernandez, Tracey Walter, Frankie Thorn, Paul Bartel, Mink Stole; *D:* Mark Manos; *W:* Mark Manos, Zach Davis. *ACA*

Liquid Sky *✔✔✔* 1983 (R) An androgynous bisexual model living in Manhattan is the primary attraction for a UFO, which lands atop her penthouse in search of the chemical nourishment that her sexual encounters provide. Low-budget, highly creative film may not be for everyone, but the audience for which it was made will love it. Look for Carlisle also playing a gay male. 112m/C VHS, Beta, LV. Anne Carlisle, Paula Sheppard, Bob Brady; *D:* Slava Tsukerman; *W:* Anne Carlisle; *C:* Yuri Neyman. *MED*

Lisa *✔* 1990 (PG-13) A young girl develops a crush on the new guy in town and arranges a meeting with him in which she pretends to be her mother. Little does she realize he's a psychotic serial killer. Lock your doors! Don't let anyone in if they have this video! 95m/C VHS, Closed Caption. Staci Keanan, Cheryl Ladd, D.W. Moffett, Tanya Fenmore, Jeffrey Tambor, Julie Cobb; *D:* Gary Sherman; *W:* Karen Clark. *FOX*

Lisa and the Devil woof! *The House of Exorcism; La Casa Dell' Exorcismo* 1975 (R) An unfortunate outing for Savalas and Sommer, about devil worship. Poor quality leaves little room for redemption. Just like on the telly, Telly's sucking on a sucker. A shortened version of the director's original 1972 release, re-edited and with additional footage added by producer Alfred Leone. 93m/C VHS. *IT* Telly Savalas, Elke Sommer, Sylva Koscina, Robert Alda; *D:* Mario Bava. *VDM, MPI*

Lisbon *✔✔* 1956 First film directed by Milland, shot in Portugal, details the adventures of a sea captain entangled in international espionage and crime while attempting to rescue damsel O'Hara's husband from communist doings. A familiar plot told with less-than-average panache. 90m/C VHS, Beta. Ray Milland, Claude Rains, Maureen O'Hara, Francis Lederer, Percy Marmont; *D:* Ray Milland. *NO*

The List of Adrian Messenger *✔✔✔* 1963 A crafty murderer resorts to a variety of disguises to eliminate potential heirs to a family fortune. Solid Huston-directed thriller with a twist: you won't recognize any of the name stars. 98m/B VHS, Beta. Kirk Douglas, George C. Scott, Robert Mitchum, Dana Wynter, Burt Lancaster, Frank Sinatra; *D:* John Huston; *M:* Jerry Goldsmith. *USH*

Listen *✔½* 1996 (R) Sex and violence and a faulty cordless telephone. Krista's (Buxton) suffered a nervous breakdown after her breakup with Sarah (Langton). But now they're friends again and Krista's even encouraging Sarah's new romance with weirdo boyfriend Jake (Currie) who likes phone sex. Then there's the obscene phone caller who seems to live in Sarah's apartment building and a serial killer who preys on women. Lots of nastiness and it's easy to figure out who the real killer is. 104m/C VHS, LV. Brooke Langton, Sarah Buxton, Gordon Currie, Andy Romano, Joel Wyner; *D:* Gavin Wilding; *W:* Jonas Quastel, Michael Bafaro; *C:* Brian Pearson; *M:* David Davidson. *ORI*

Listen, Darling *✔✔½* 1938 Garland is appealing in her first big screen role as Pinky Wingate, who decides to find the perfect husband for her widowed mother (Astor). Pinky and her friend Buzz (Bartholomew) manage to find Pidgeon and have him become the willing objection of everyone's affections. ♫Zing! Went the Strings of My Heart; Ten Pins in the Sky; On the Bumpy Road to Love. 70m/C VHS. Judy Garland, Freddie Bartholomew, Mary Astor, Walter Pidgeon, Alan Hale, Scotty Beckett; *D:* Edwin L. Marin. *MGM, FCT*

Listen to Me *✔½* 1989 (PG-13) A small-town college debate team heads for the big time when they go to a national debate tournament. The usual mutual-distaste-turns-to-romance thing. Cheesy-as-all-get-out climactic abortion debate, in front of supposed real-life Supreme Court justices—yeah, right. And Kirk Cameron: get an accent, will ya? 109m/C VHS, Beta, LV, Closed Caption. Kirk Cameron, Jami Gertz, Roy Scheider, Amanda Peterson, Tim Quill, Christopher Atkins; *D:* Douglas Day Stewart; *C:* Fred W. Koenekamp; *M:* David Foster. Golden Raspberry Awards '89: Worst Supporting Actor (Atkins). *COL*

Listen to Your Heart *✔½* 1983 Office romance in the '80s! Sounds like a mediocre, forgettable made-for-TV comedy-drama—which is exactly what it is. If Jackson was the brainy one on "Charlie's Angels," why wasn't she smart enough to avoid this one? 90m/C VHS, Beta. Tim Matheson, Kate Jackson; *D:* Don Taylor. *FOX*

Lisztomania woof! 1975 (R) Russell's excessive vision of what it must have been like to be classical composer/musician Franz Liszt, who is depicted as the first pop star. Rock opera in the tradition of "Tommy" with none of the sense or music. 106m/C VHS, Beta, LV. *GB* Roger Daltrey, Sara Kestelman, Paul Nicholas, Fiona Lewis, Ringo Starr, Veronica Quilligan, Nell Campbell, John Justin, Andrew Reilly, Anulka Dziubinska, Rick Wakeman, Rikki Howard, Felicity Devonshire, Aubrey Morris, Kenneth Colley, Ken Parry, Otto Diamont, Murray Melvin, Andrew Faulds, Oliver Reed; *D:* Ken Russell; *W:* Ken Russell; *C:* Peter Suschitzky; *M:* Rick Wakeman. *WAR*

The Little American *✔✔½* 1917 German-American Karl Von Austreim leaves behind sweetheart Angela Moore, returning to Germany to fight in WWI. Angela travels to France to care for her dying aunt and discovers her aunt's chateau has been turned into a hospital. She remains in the face of a German advance and is naturally reunited with her much-changed beau. 80m/B VHS, Beta. Mary Pickford, Jack Holt, Raymond Hatton, Walter Long, Hobart Bosworth, Ben Alexander, DeWitt Jennings. *GPV*

Little Annie Rooney *✔✔* 1925 A policeman's tomboy daughter spends her time mothering her father and brother while getting into mischief with street punks. Minor melodrama. Silent. 60m/B VHS, Beta, LV. Mary Pickford, William Haines, Walter James, Gordon Griffith, Vola Vale; *D:* William Beaudine; *C:* Charles Rosher. *NOS, CCB, IME*

Little Ballerina *✔✔* 1947 A young dancer struggles against misfortune and jealousy to succeed in the world of ballet, under the auspices of Fonteyn. 62m/B VHS, Beta. Margot Fonteyn, Anthony Newley, Martita Hunt, Yvonne Marsh. *VYY*

Little Big Horn *✔✔½* *The Fighting Seventh* 1951 Low-budget depiction of Custer et al. at Little Big Horn actually has its gripping moments; solid acting all around helps. 88m/B VHS, Beta. Marie Windsor, John Ireland, Lloyd Bridges, Reed Hadley, Hugh O'Brian, Jim Davis; *D:* Charles Marquis Warren. *MRV*

Little Big League *✔✔½* 1994 (PG) 12-year-old inherits the Minnesota Twins baseball team from his grandfather, appoints himself manager when everyone else declines, and becomes the youngest owner-manager in history. Nothing new about the premise, but kids and America's favorite pastime add up to good clean family fun. Features real-life baseball players, including the Mariners' Griffey and O'Neil from the Yankees. Good cast features TV's Busfield at first base. Screenwriting debut from Pincus, and directorial debut from the executive producer of "Seinfeld," Scheinman. 120m/C VHS, LV, Closed Caption. Luke Edwards, Jason Robards Jr., Kevin Dunn, Dennis Farina, John Ashton, Jonathan Silverman, Wolfgang Bodison, Timothy Busfield, Ashley Crow, Scott Patterson, Billy L. Sullivan, Miles Feulner, Kevin Elster, Leon "Bull" Durham, Brad "The Animal" Lesley; *Cameos:* Don Mattingly, Ken Griffey Jr., Paul O'Neill; *D:* Andrew Scheinman; *W:* Gregory Pincus, Adam Scheinman. *COL*

Little Big Man *✔✔✔½* 1970 (PG) Based on Thomas Berger's picaresque novel, this is the story of 121-year-old Jack Crabb and his quixotic life as gunslinger, charlatan, Indian, ally to George Custer, and the only white survivor of Little Big Horn. Told mainly through flashbacks. Hoffman provides a classic portrayal of Crabb, as fact and myth are jumbled and reshaped. 135m/C VHS, Beta, LV, Closed Caption. Dustin Hoffman, Faye Dunaway, Chief Dan George, Richard Mulligan, Martin Balsam, Jeff Corey, Aimee Eccles; *D:* Arthur Penn; *W:* Calder Willingham; *C:* Harry Stradling Jr. New York Film Critics Awards '70: Best Supporting Actor (George); National Society of Film Critics Awards '70: Best Supporting Actor (George); Nominations: Academy Awards '70: Best Supporting Actor (George). *FOX, HMV*

Little Bigfoot *✔✔½* 1996 (PG) The Shoemaker family are taking a camping vacation when the kids discover a baby bigfoot in the wilderness. They find out the hairy little guy and his mom are threatened by the owner of a logging company, who's hired a group of hunters to get rid of the critters. 99m/C VHS, Closed Caption. Ross Malinger, P.J. Soles, Ken Tigar, Kelly Packard, Don Stroud, Matt McCoy; *D:* Art Camacho; *W:* Richard Preston Jr.; *C:* Ken Blakey; *M:* Louis Febre. *REP*

Little Boy Lost *✔✔* 1978 (G) The true story of the disappearance of a young boy in Australia. 92m/C VHS, Beta. *AU* John Hargreaves, Tony Barry, Lorna Lesley; *D:* Alan Spires. *NO*

Little Buddha 🎬🎬 1993 (PG) Tibetan Lama Norbu informs the Seattle Konrad family that their 10-year-old son Jesse may be the reincarnation of a respected monk. He wants to take the boy back to Tibet to find out and, with some apparently minor doubts, the family head off on their spiritual quest. In an effort to instruct Jesse in Buddhism, this journey is interspersed with the story of Prince Siddhartha, who will leave behind his worldly ways to follow the path towards enlightenment and become the Buddha. The two stories are an ill-fit, the acting awkward (with the exception of Ruocheng as the wise Norbu), but boy, does the film look good (from cinematographer Vittorio Storaro). Filmed on location in Nepal and Bhutan. 123m/C VHS, LV, Closed Caption. Keanu Reeves, Alex Wiesendanger, Ying Ruocheng, Chris Isaak, Bridget Fonda; D: Bernardo Bertolucci; W: Mark Peploe, Rudy Wurlitzer; C: Vittorio Storaro; M: Ryuichi Sakamoto. MAX

Little Caesar 🎬🎬🎬 1930 A small-time hood rises to become a gangland czar, but his downfall is as rapid as his rise. Still thrilling. The role of Rico made Robinson a star and typecast him as a crook for all time. 80m/B VHS, Beta. Edward G. Robinson, Glenda Farrell, Sidney Blackmer, Douglas Fairbanks Jr.; D: Mervyn LeRoy; C: Gaetano Antonio "Tony" Gaudio. Nominations: Academy Awards '31: Best Adapted Screenplay. FOX, FCT

Little Church Around the Corner 🎬🎬½ 1923 Silent small town melodrama about a preacher who falls in love with a mine owner's daughter, but finds he isn't dad's favorite fella when he confronts him about poor mining conditions. When the mine caves in, the preacher man's caught between a rock and hard place when his sweetie's family needs protection from an angry mob. 70m/B VHS, Beta. Kenneth Harlan, Hobart Bosworth, Walter Long, Pauline Starke, Alec B. Francis, Margaret Seddon, George Cooper; D: William A. Seiter. GPV

The Little Colonel 🎬🎬🎬 1935 (PG) After the Civil War, an embittered Southern patriarch turns his back on his family, until his dimple-cheeked granddaughter softens his heart. Hokey and heartwarming. Shirley's first teaming with Bill "Bojangles" Robinson features the famous dance scene. Adapted by William Conselman from the Annie Fellows Johnston best-seller. 80m/B VHS, Beta, Closed Caption. Shirley Temple, Lionel Barrymore, Evelyn Venable, John Lodge, Hattie McDaniel, Bill Robinson, Sidney Blackmer; D: David Butler; C: Arthur C. Miller. FOX

Little Darlings woof! 1980 (R) Distasteful premise has summer campers Kristy and Tatum in a race to lose their virginity. Kristy is better (at acting, that is); but who cares? And just who is meant to be the market for this movie, anyway? 95m/C VHS, Beta, LV. Tatum O'Neal, Kristy McNichol, Matt Dillon, Armand Assante, Margaret Blye; D: Ronald F. Maxwell; M: Charles Fox. PAR

Little Dorrit, Film 1: Nobody's Fault 🎬🎬🎬 1988 The mammoth version of the Dickens tome, about a father and daughter trapped interminably in the dreaded Marshalsea debtors' prison, and the good samaritan who works to free them. Told in two parts (on four tapes), "Nobody's Fault," and "Little Dorrit's Story." 369m/C VHS, Beta, LV, Closed Caption. GB Alec Guinness, Derek Jacobi, Cyril Cusack, Sarah Pickering, Joan Greenwood, Max Wall, Amelda Brown, Daniel Chatto, Miriam Margolyes, Bill Fraser, Roshan Seth, Michael Elphick, Eleanor Bron, Patricia Hayes, Robert Morley, Sophie Ward; D: Christine Edzard; W: Christine Edzard; C: Bruno de Keyzer; M: Giuseppe Verdi. Los Angeles Film Critics Association Awards '88: Best Film, Best Supporting Actor (Guinness); Nominations: Academy Awards '88: Best Adapted Screenplay, Best Supporting Actor (Guinness). WAR, SIG, TVC

Little Dorrit, Film 2: Little Dorrit's Story 🎬🎬🎬 1988 The second half of the monumental adaptation of Dickens' most popular novel during his lifetime tells of Amy Dorrit's rise from debtor's prison to happiness. 369m/C VHS, Beta, LV, Closed Caption. GB Alec Guinness, Derek Jacobi, Cyril Cusack, Sarah Pickering, Joan Greenwood, Max Wall, Amelda Brown, Daniel Chatto, Miriam Margolyes, Bill Fraser, Roshan Seth, Robert Morley, Sophie Ward, Eleanor Bron; D: Christine Edzard; W: Christine Edzard; C: Bruno de Keyzer; M: Giuseppe Verdi. Los Angeles Film Critics Association Awards '88: Best Film, Best Supporting Actor (Guinness). WAR, SIG, TVC

Little Dragons 🎬 1980 A grandfather and two young karate students rescue a family held captive by a backwoods gang. 90m/C VHS, Beta. Ann Sothern, Joe Spinell, Charles Lane, Chris Petersen, Pat Petersen, Sally Boyden, Rick Lenz, Sharon Weber, Tony Bill; D: Curtis Hanson; W: Alan Ormsby. AHV

The Little Drummer Girl 🎬🎬🎬 1984 (R) An Israeli counterintelligence agent recruits an actress sympathetic to the Palestinian cause to trap a fanatical terrorist leader. Solid performances from Keaton as the actress and Kinski as the Israeli counter-intelligence office sustain interest through a puzzling, sometimes boring and frustrating, cinematic maze of espionage. Keaton is at or near her very best. Based on the bestselling novel by John Le Carre. 130m/C VHS, Beta, LV, Closed Caption. Diane Keaton, Klaus Kinski, Yorgo Voyagis, Sami Frey, Michael Cristofer, Anna Massey, Thorley Walters; D: George Roy Hill; M: Dave Grusin. WAR

The Little Foxes 🎬🎬🎬½ 1941 A vicious southern woman will destroy everyone around her to satisfy her desire for wealth and power. Filled with corrupt characters who commit numerous revolting deeds. The vicious matriarch is a part made to fit for Davis, and she makes the most of it. Script by Lillian Hellman from her own play. 116m/B VHS, Beta, LV. Bette Davis, Herbert Marshall, Dan Duryea, Teresa Wright, Charles Dingle, Richard Carlson; D: William Wyler. Nominations: Academy Awards '41: Best Actress (Davis), Best Director (Wyler), Best Film Editing, Best Interior Decoration, Best Picture, Best Screenplay, Best Supporting Actress (Collinge, Wright), Original Dramatic/Comedy Score.

Little Giant 🎬🎬½ 1946 The duo fly separately in this entry, which highlights Costello's comic talents and leaves Abbott in the supporting role. Costello is a country bumpkin come to the big city to get enough money to marry his sweetheart. He's hired to sell vacuum cleaners by Abbott and becomes the butt of everyone's jokes but the joke's on them when Lou becomes the company's top-selling salesman. 92m/B VHS. Bud Abbott, Lou Costello, Brenda Joyce, Jacqueline De Wit, George Cleveland, Elena Verdugo, Mary Gordon, Pierre Watkin; D: William A. Seiter; W: Walter DeLeon. USH

Little Giants 🎬🎬½ 1994 (PG) Familiar kids/sport movie about the klutzy coach (Moranis) of an equally woeful pee-wee football team. Coach Danny is up against his overbearing big brother Kevin (O'Neill), former local football hero and the coach of the best team in town. Naturally, there's the big game between the misfit underdogs and the stars. Predictable, of course, but not without some amusing moments. 106m/C VHS, LV. Rick Moranis, Ed O'Neill, Shawna Waldron, Mary Ellen Trainor, Devon Sawa, Susanna Thompson, John Madden; D: Duwayne Dunham; W: Tommy Swerdlow, Michael Goldberg, James Ferguson, Robert Shallcross; C: Janusz Kaminski; M: John Debney. WAR

Little Girl ... Big Tease 🎬 1975 (R) Teen society girl is kidnapped and exploited (along with the viewer) by a group which includes her teacher. 86m/C VHS, Beta. Jody Ray, Rebecca Brooke; D: Roberto Mitrotti. NO

The Little Girl Who Lives Down the Lane 🎬🎬½ 1976 (PG) Engrossing, offbeat thriller about a strange 13-year-old girl whose father is never home, and who hides something - we won't say what - in her basement. Very young Foster is excellent, as are her supporters. Then there's a child molester who knows what she's hiding. . . 90m/C VHS, Beta, LV. CA Jodie Foster, Martin Sheen, Alexis Smith, Scott Jacoby; D: Nicolas Gessner. LIV, VES

Little Gloria...Happy at Last 🎬🎬½ 1984 Mini series based on the best-selling book about the custody battle over child heiress Gloria Vanderbilt, and her tumultuous youth. Lansberry leads a fine cast as the poor little rich girl's aunt Gertrude, the matriarchal family power broker. Made for television. 180m/C VHS, Beta. Bette Davis, Angela Lansbury, Christopher Plummer, Maureen Stapleton, Martin Balsam, Barnard Hughes, John Hillerman; D: Waris Hussein. PSM, PAR

Little Heroes 🎬🎬½ 1991 (G) An impoverished little girl gets through hard times with the aid of her loyal dog (the Hound can relate). A low-budget family tearjerker that nonetheless works, it claims to be based on a true story. 78m/C VHS. Raeanin Simpson, Katherine Willis, Keith Christensen; D: Craig Clyde; W: Craig Clyde; M: John McCallum. HMD

Little Heroes of Shaolin Temple 🎬 1972 The "Prince of Blood" attacks the Shaolin temple, but the Master's Ninjas await him. 90m/C VHS, Beta. Cheng Tain Syh, Hw-Luen, Li Shuen Hwa, Tang Chen Da. TWE

Little House on the Prairie 🎬🎬🎬 1974 The pilot for the television series based on the life of Laura Ingalls Wilder and her family's struggles on the American plains in the 1860s. Other episodes are also available on tape, including one in which Patricia Neal guest stars as a terminally ill widow seeking a home for her children. Neal's performance earned her a best actress Emmy in 1975. 98m/C VHS, Beta. Michael Landon, Karen Grassle, Victor French, Melissa Gilbert, Melissa Sue Anderson; D: Michael Landon. GKK, TLF

Little Indian, Big City 🎬🎬½ An Indian in the City; Un Indien dans la Ville 1995 (PG) French blockbuster dubbed over with "Americanized" English to give U.S. audiences an appetite for upcoming Disney remake. Lhermitte travels to the Amazon to finalize the divorce of a long-dead marriage, only to find he has a 12-year-old son, Mimi-Siku (Briand). Father and son bond and Dad decides to bring the jungle-bred boy to his home in Paris. Dubbing process unfortunately tomahawks this charming story as loin cloth meets Eiffel Tower, but Lhermitte, Briand and Miou-Miou (as estranged wife Patricia) shine through. Subplot of Russian mobsters who cut the fingers off their victims gives an indication of the French definition of "family fare." 90m/C VHS. FR Thierry Lhermitte, Miou-Miou, Patrick Timsit, Arielle Dombasle, Ludwig Briand; D: Herve Palud; W: Thierry Lhermitte, Herve Palud, Philippe Bruneau, Igor Aptekman; C: Pierre Lorraine; M: Manu Katche. NYR

Little Johnny Jones 1980 George M. Cohan's classic musical is featured in a 1980 revival. Songs include "Yankee Doodle Dandy" and "Give My Regards to Broadway." 93m/C VHS, Beta. WAR, OM

The Little Kidnappers 🎬🎬½ 1990 (G) Embittered man (Heston) is forced to take in his Scottish grandsons when the two boys are orphaned. They settle in with gramps in Nova Scotia but when the duo decide to adopt the abandoned baby they've found, they are accused of being kidnappers. Cable remake of 1953 British film. 100m/C VHS. CA Charlton Heston, Bruce Greenwood, Leah K. Pinsent, Charles Miller, Leo Wheatley, Patricia Gage; D: Donald Shebib. AVE

Little Ladies of the Night 🎬 Diamond Alley 1977 Former pimp tries to save Purl and other teenagers from the world of prostitution. Exploitation posing as "significant drama." 96m/C VHS, Beta. Linda Purl, David Soul, Clifton Davis, Carolyn Jones, Louis Gossett Jr.; D: Marvin J. Chomsky. PSM

Little Laura & Big John 🎬 1973 The true-life exploits of the small-time Ashley Gang in the Florida everglades around the turn of the century. Fabian's comeback vehicle, for what it's worth. 82m/C VHS, Beta. Fabian, Karen Black; D: Luke Moberly. NO

Little Lord Fauntleroy 🎬🎬½ 1936
The vintage Hollywood version of the Frances Hodgson Burnett story of a fatherless American boy who discovers he's heir to a British dukedom. Also available in computer-colorized version. Well cast, charming, remade for TV in 1980. Smith is loveable as the noble tyke's crusty old guardian. **102m/B VHS, Beta, Closed Caption.** Freddie Bartholomew, Sir C. Aubrey Smith, Mickey Rooney, Dolores Costello, Jessie Ralph, Guy Kibbee; **D:** John Cromwell; **C:** Charles Rosher; **M:** Max Steiner. *NOS, MRV, VEC*

Little Lord Fauntleroy 🎬🎬½ 1980 A poor boy in New York suddenly finds himself the heir to his grandfather's estate in England. Lavish remake of the 1936 classic, adapted from Frances Hodgson Burnett's novel. Well-deserved Emmy winner for photography; Guinness is his usual old-pro self. Made for TV. **98m/C VHS, Beta, Closed Caption.** Rick Schroder, Alec Guinness, Victoria Tennant, Eric Porter, Colin Blakely, Connie Booth, Rachel Kempson; **D:** Jack Gold. *FHE*

Little Man Tate 🎬🎬🎬 1991 (PG) A seven-year-old genius is the prize in a tug of war between his mother, who wants him to lead a normal life, and a domineering school director who loves him for his intellect. An acclaimed directorial debut for Foster, with overtones of her own extraordinary life as a child prodigy. **99m/C VHS, Closed Caption.** Jodie Foster, Dianne Wiest, Harry Connick Jr., Adam Hann-Byrd, George Plimpton, Debi Mazar, Celia Weston, David Pierce, Danitra Vance, Josh Mostel, P.J. Ochlan; **D:** Jodie Foster; **W:** Scott Frank; **M:** Mark Isham. *ORI, CCB*

Little Marines 1990 Three young boys journey into the wilderness for three days of fun and instead embark on an incredible adventure. **90m/C VHS.** Stephen Baker, Steve Landers Jr., Noah Williams; **D:** A.J. Hixon. *MHF*

The Little Match Girl 🎬🎬 1984 A musical version of the Hans Christian Andersen classic about a girl whose dying grandmother tells her of the magic in the matches she sells. **54m/C VHS, Beta.** Monica McSwain, Nancy Duncan, Matt McKim, Don Hays; **D:** Mark Hoeger.

The Little Match Girl 🎬🎬 1987 The Hans Christian Andersen Yuletide classic about an orphan selling magical matches this time set in the 1920's, with the littlest "Cosby" kid in the title role. Ain't she cute? **90m/C VHS, Beta, Closed Caption.** GB Roger Daltrey, Twiggy, Natalie Morse; **D:** Michael Custance. *ACA*

Little Men 🎬½ 1940 A modern version of the classic juvenile story by Louisa May Alcott is too cute for words. **86m/B VHS, Beta.** Jack Oakie, Jimmy Lydon, Kay Francis, George Bancroft; **D:** Norman Z. McLeod. *NOS, MRV, VCN*

The Little Mermaid 🎬🎬½ 1978 (G) An animated version of Hans Christian Andersen's tale about a little mermaid who rescues a prince whose boat has capsized. She immediately falls in love and wishes that she could become a human girl. Not to be confused with the 1989 Disney version. **71m/C VHS, Beta. D:** Tim Reid. *VTR, GEM*

The Little Mermaid 1984 From "Faerie Tale Theatre" comes an adaptation of the Hans Christian Andersen tale of a little mermaid who makes a big sacrifice to win the prince she loves. **60m/C VHS, Beta, Closed Caption.** Karen Black, Brian Dennehy, Helen Mirren, Pam Dawber, Treat Williams; **D:** Robert Iscove. *FOX, FCT*

The Little Mermaid 🎬🎬🎬½ 1989 (G) Headstrong teenage mermaid falls in love with a human prince and longs to be human too. She makes a pact with the evil Sea Witch to trade her voice for a pair of legs; based on the famous Hans Christian Andersen tale. Charming family musical, which harks back to the days of classic Disney animation, and hails a new era of superb Disney animated musicals. Sebastian the Crab nearly steals the show with his wit and showstopping number "Under the Sea." ♫Under the Sea; Kiss the Girl; Daughters of Triton; Part of Your World; Poor Unfortunate Souls; Les Poissons. **82m/C VHS, Beta, LV, 8mm, Closed Caption. D:** John Musker, Ron Clements; **W:** John Musker, Ron Clements; **M:** Alan Menken, Howard Ashman; **V:** Jodi Benson, Christopher Daniel Barnes, Pat Carroll, Rene Auberjonois, Samuel E. Wright, Buddy Hackett, Jason Marin, Edie McClurg, Kenneth Mars, Nancy Cartwright. Academy Awards '89: Best Song ("Under the Sea"), Best Original Score; Golden Globe Awards '90: Best Song ("Under the Sea"), Best Score; Nominations: Academy Awards '89: Best Song ("Kiss the Girl"). *DIS, OM*

Little Minister 🎬🎬🎬 1934 An adaptation of the James Barrie novel about a prissy Scottish pastor who falls in love with a free-spirited gypsy...he thinks she is, in fact, the local earl's daughter, played to perfection by the young Hepburn. **101m/B VHS, Beta.** Katharine Hepburn, John Beal, Alan Hale, Donald Crisp; **D:** Richard Wallace; **M:** Max Steiner. *TTC*

Little Miss Broadway 🎬🎬 1938 Orphan Temple brings the residents of a theatrical boarding house together in hopes of getting them into show business. She and Durante give worthwhile performances. Also available in computer-colorized version. ♫Be Optimistic; How Can I Thank You; I'll Build a Broadway For You; If All the World Were Paper; Thank You For the Use of the Hall; We Should Be Together; Swing Me an Old-Fashioned Song; When You Were Sweet Sixteen; Happy Birthday to You. **70m/B VHS, Beta, Closed Caption.** Shirley Temple, George Murphy, Jimmy Durante, Phyllis Brooks, Edna May Oliver, George Barbier, Donald Meek, Jane Darwell; **D:** Irving Cummings; **C:** Arthur C. Miller. *FOX*

Little Miss Innocence 🎬 1973 Recording executive tries to survive the amorous advances of the two attractive female hitchhikers that he drove home. **79m/C VHS, Beta.** John Alderman, Sandy Dempsey, Judy Medford; **D:** Chris Warfield. *AHV*

Little Miss Marker 🎬🎬🎬 *Girl in Pawn* 1934 Heartwarming story starring Temple as the title character, who is left with bookie Sorrowful Jones (Menjou) as the IOU for a gambling debt. But when her father doesn't return, it's up to Jones and his racetrack friends to make little Marky a home. Naturally, Temple steals her way into everyone's heart. Based on a story by Damon Runyon; remade three times as "Sorrowful Jones," as "40 Pounds of Trouble," and in 1980 with the original title. **88m/B VHS, Closed Caption.** Adolphe Menjou, Shirley Temple, Dorothy Dell, Charles Bickford, Lynne Overman; **D:** Alexander Hall. *USH*

Little Miss Marker 🎬½ 1980 (PG) Mediocre remake of the often retold story of a bookie who accepts a little girl as a security marker for a $10 bet. Disappointing performance from Curtis adds to an already dull film. **103m/C VHS, Beta.** Walter Matthau, Julie Andrews, Tony Curtis, Bob Newhart, Lee Grant, Sara Stimson, Brian Dennehy; **D:** Walter Bernstein; **W:** Walter Bernstein; **M:** Henry Mancini. *USH*

Little Miss Millions 🎬🎬½ 1993 (PG) A 12-year-old has run away from her wicked stepmom who hires a bounty hunter to bring her back—for a half a million bucks. Only when he finds the girl stepmom doesn't want to pay up and she tells anyone who will listen that the bounty hunter actually kidnapped the girl. Bounty hunter turns to friends, including the 12-year-old who isn't a fool and knows stepmom is a lying witch, for help. **90m/C VHS, Closed Caption.** Howard Hesseman, Anita Morris, Love Hewitt; **D:** Roger Corman. *NHO*

Little Monsters 🎬🎬 1989 (PG) A young boy (Savage) discovers a monster (Mandel) under his bed and eventually befriends it. The pair embark on adventures that land them in trouble. Hardworking, talented cast hurdles the weak script, but can't save the film. **100m/C VHS, Beta, LV, Closed Caption.** Fred Savage, Howie Mandel, Margaret Whitton, Ben Savage, Daniel Stern, Rick Ducommun, Frank Whaley; **D:** Richard Alan Greenberg; **W:** Ted Elliot, Terry Rossio; **M:** David Newman. *MGM*

Little Moon & Jud McGraw 🎬½ 1978 A wronged Indian woman and a framed cowpoke take their revenge on a small, corrupt town, razing it overnight. Already-weak plot is disabled by too many flashbacks. **92m/C VHS, Beta.** James Caan, Sammy Davis Jr., Stefanie Powers, Aldo Ray; **D:** Bernard Girard. *PSM*

Little Murders 🎬🎬🎬 1971 (PG) Black comedy set in New York City. A woman convinces a passive photographer to marry her. Gardenia gives an excellent performance as the woman's father. A shadow of crime, depression, and strife seem to hangs over the funny parts of this film; more often depressing than anything else. Adapted by Jules Feiffer from his own play. **108m/C VHS, Beta.** Elliott Gould, Marcia Rodd, Vincent Gardenia, Elizabeth Wilson, Jon Korkes, Donald Sutherland, Alan Arkin, Lou Jacobi; **D:** Alan Arkin; **W:** Jules Feiffer; **C:** Gordon Willis. *FOX*

Little Nellie Kelly 🎬🎬½ 1940 Garland plays both mother and daughter in a film based on a musical comedy by George M. Cohan. Garland is married to Irish cop Murphy but dies in childbirth. The film then advances twenty years to daughter Garland who is trying to make good on the stage and have a romance with a young man her father disapproves of. ♫Nellie Kelly I Love You; Nellie is a Darling; It's a Great Day For the Irish; A Pretty Girl Milking Her Cow; Danny Boy; Singing in the Rain. **100m/B VHS.** Judy Garland, George Murphy, Charles Winninger, Douglas McPhail; **D:** Norman Taurog. *MGM, FCT*

Little Nemo: Adventures in Slumberland 🎬🎬½ 1992 (G) A bland animated tale of a young boy whose dreams take him to Slumberland. There, Nemo unwittingly unleashes a monster from Nightmare Land who kidnaps Slumberland's king. Nemo must then rescue the king—aided by the king's daughter, a comic squirrel sidekick, and a mischievous con-frog. Based on Winsor McCay's 1900 comic strip. Has some cute comic moments for the kiddies and, while the animation is better than Saturday-morning cartoon quality, it's not Disney. **85m/C VHS, LV. D:** William T. Hurtz, Masami Hata; **W:** Chris Columbus, Richard Outten; **M:** Tom Chase, Steve Rucker; **V:** Gabriel Damon, Mickey Rooney, Rene Auberjonois, Daniel Mann, Laura Mooney, Bernard Erhard, William E. Martin. *HMD*

A Little Night Music 🎬½ 1977 (PG) Features four interwoven, contemporary love stories adapted from the Broadway play, and based loosely on Bergman's "Smiles of a Summer Night." Taylor's pathetic rendition of "Send in the Clowns" should be banned. Filmed on location in Austria. **110m/C VHS, Beta, LV.** Elizabeth Taylor, Diana Rigg, Hermione Gingold, Len Cariou, Lesley-Anne Down; **D:** Harold Prince. Academy Awards '77: Original Song Score and/or Adaptation; Nominations: Academy Awards '77: Best Costume Design. *NLC*

Little Nikita 🎬🎬 1988 (PG) A California boy (Phoenix) discovers that his parents are actually Soviet spies planted as American citizens for eventual call to duty. Poitier's performance as the FBI agent tracking the spies is about the only spark in this somewhat incoherent thriller. **98m/C VHS, Beta, LV, Closed Caption.** River Phoenix, Sidney Poitier, Richard Bradford, Richard Lynch, Caroline Kava, Lucy Deakins; **D:** Richard Benjamin; **W:** Bo Goldman; **M:** Marvin Hamlisch. *COL*

Little Ninjas 🎬🎬½ 1992 Three topnotch ninja kids go up against the Sarak to rescue their friend who is being held hostage. **85m/C VHS, LV.** Steven Nelson, Jon Anzaldo, Alan Godshaw; **D:** Emmett Alston. *THV*

Little Noises 🎬🎬 1991 Glover stars as an artist who seeks not only fame and fortune, but also the love of his best friend (O'Neal). He finally creates a piece that his agent loves, but problems arise. **91m/C VHS, Beta.** Crispin Glover, Tatum O'Neal, Rik Mayall, Tate Donovan, John C. McGinley; **D:** Jane Spencer; **W:** Jane Spencer. *PSM*

Little Odessa 🎬🎬½ **1994 (R)** Working for the stateside Russian mafia, hitman Joshua Shapira (Roth) returns to his childhood neighborhood to carry out his next assignment. Set in the Russian-Jewish emigre community of Brooklyn's Brighton Beach, Gray's directorial debut explores Joshua's relationship with his family—especially kid brother Reuben (Furlong). Not your typical mob opera, one focuses more on characters than killing. Relationships between family members are explored to the hilt, but the audience is left with too many unanswered questions. Dimly lit and entirely too ambiguous, this family tragedy could spawn a serious case of depression. **CW:** Contains violence, profanity, nudity, and sexual situations. **98m/C VHS, LV, Closed Caption.** Tim Roth, Edward Furlong, Moira Kelly, Vanessa Redgrave, Maximilian Schell, Paul Guilfoyle, Natasha Andreichenko, David Vadim, Mina Bern, Boris McGiver, Mohammed Ghaffari, Michael Khumrov, Dmitry Preyers, David Ross, Ron Brice, Jace Kent, Marianna Lead, Gene Ruffini; **D:** James Gray; **W:** James Gray; **C:** Tom Richmond; **M:** Dana Sano. Nominations: Independent Spirit Awards '96: Best Actor (Roth), Best Cinematography, Best First Feature, Best Supporting Actress (Redgrave). *LIV*

Little Orphan Annie **1918** Surrounded by a group of children, poet James Whitcomb Riley narrates the story of Little Orphant Annie, who loses her mother at an early age and is sent to an orphanage where she charms the other children with her stories of ghosts and elves. **57m/B VHS.** Thomas Santschi, Eugenie Besserer, Ben Alexander, Lillie Hayward, Lafayette McKee, Colleen Moore, Harry Lonsdale, Doris Baker, Lillian Wade, Billy Jacobs, James Whitcomb Riley; **D:** Colin Campbell. *GPV*

Little Orphan Annie 🎬🎬½ **1932** The unjustly forgotten first sound adaptation of the comic strip. Fun score adds a lot, as does the good cast. **60m/B VHS, Beta.** May Robson, Buster Phelps, Mitzie Green, Edgar Kennedy; **M:** Max Steiner. *CCB*

The Little Prince 🎬🎬 **1974 (G)** Disappointing adaptation of the classic children's story by Antoine de Saint-Exupery, about a little boy from asteroid B-612. Lousy Lerner and Loewe score underscores a general lack of magic or spontaneity. ♫It's a Hat; I Need Air; I'm On Your Side; Be Happy; You're a Child; I Never Met a Rose; Why Is the Desert (Lovely to See)?; Closer and Closer and Closer; Little Prince (From Who Knows Where). **88m/C VHS, Beta, LV.** **GB** Richard Kiley, Bob Fosse, Steven Warner, Gene Wilder, Joss Ackland, Clive Revill, Victor Spinetti, Graham Crowden, Donna McKechnie; **D:** Stanley Donen; **W:** Alan Jay Lerner; **C:** Christopher Challis; **M:** Frederick Loewe, Alan Jay Lerner. Golden Globe Awards '75: Best Score; Nominations: Academy Awards '74: Best Song ("Little Prince"), Original Song Score and/or Adaptation. *PAR*

The Little Princess 🎬🎬🎬½ **1939 (G)** Based on the Frances Hodgson Burnett children's classic; perhaps the best of the moppet's films. Shirley is a young schoolgirl in Victorian London sent to a harsh boarding school when her Army officer father is posted abroad. When her father is declared missing, the penniless girl must work as a servant at the school to pay her keep, all the while haunting the hospitals, never believing her father has died. A classic tearjerker. **91m/B VHS, Beta, LV, Closed Caption.** Shirley Temple, Richard Greene, Anita Louise, Ian Hunter, Cesar Romero, Arthur Treacher, Sybil Jason, Miles Mander, Marcia Mae Jones, E.E. Clive; **D:** Walter Lang; **C:** Arthur C. Miller. *CNG, MRV, NOS*

The Little Princess **1987** A three-cassette adaptation of Frances Hodgson Burnett's book. In Victorian England, kind-hearted Sara is forced into poverty when her father suddenly dies. Can his longtime friend find her and restore their happiness? Originally aired on PBS as part of the "Wonderworks" family movie series. **180m/C VHS.** **GB** Amelia Shankley, Nigel Havers, Maureen Lipman; **D:** Carol Wiseman. *FCT, PME, SIG*

A Little Princess 🎬🎬🎬½ **1995 (G)** Compelling fantasy, based on the children's book by Frances Hodgson Burnett, and previously best known for the 1939 Shirley Temple incarnation. Sara (Matthews) has been raised in India by her widowed father (Cunningham). When he's called up to fight in WWI, Sara is taken to New York to be educated at stern Miss Michin's (Bron) school, where her money makes her a favored boarder. However, the irrepressible Sara suffers a severe reversal of fortune when her father is reported killed and Miss Michin promptly makes her a servant to pay her way. But Sara's charm has made her some true friends who become her allies under trying circumstances. Lively script, dazzling visuals, and a welcome lack of sappiness create a classic-in-the-making. **97m/C VHS, LV, Closed Caption.** Liesl Matthews, Eleanor Bron, Liam Cunningham, Rusty Schwimmer, Arthur Malet, Vanessa Lee Chester, Errol Sitahal, Heather DeLoach, Taylor Fry; **D:** Alfonso Cuaron; **W:** Richard LaGravenese, Elizabeth Chandler; **C:** Emmanuel Lubezki; **M:** Patrick Doyle. Nominations: Academy Awards '95: Best Art Direction/Set Decoration, Best Cinematography. *WAR*

The Little Rascals 🎬🎬½ **1994 (PG)** Alfalfa runs afoul of the membership requirements for the "He-Man Womun Haters Club" when he starts to fall for Darla. Charming remake of the short film series, now set in suburban L.A., from Spheeris, who also redid another television favorite, "The Beverly Hillbillies." **83m/C VHS, LV, Closed Caption.** Daryl Hannah, Courtland Mead, Travis Tedford, Brittany Ashton Holmes, Bug Hall, Zachary Mabry, Kevin Jamal Woods, Ross Bagley, Sam Saletta, Blake Collins, Jordan Warkol, Blake Ewing, Juliette Brewer, Heather Karasek; **Cameos:** Whoopi Goldberg; **D:** Penelope Spheeris; **W:** Penelope Spheeris, Paul Guay, Steve Mazur; **C:** Richard Bowen; **M:** David Foster, Linda Thompson. *USH*

Little Rascals, Book 1 **193?** Three "Our Gang" shorts: "Railroadin'" (1929), in which the gang takes off on a runaway train; "A Lad and a Lamp" (1932), wherein they find an Aladdin's lamp; and "Beginner's Luck" (1935), in which Spanky wins a dress for a young actress. Additional volumes are available. **59m/B VHS, Beta.** Farina Hoskins, Joe Cobb, Matthew "Stymie" Beard, George "Spanky" McFarland, Carl "Alfalfa" Switzer, Mary Ann Jackson. *CCB*

Little Rascals Christmas Special **1979** Spanky and the Little Rascals attempt to raise enough money to buy a winter coat for Spanky's mom and learn the true meaning of Christmas along the way. **60m/C VHS, Beta.** Darla Hood, Matthew "Stymie" Beard; **D:** Fred Wolf, Charles Swenson. *FHE*

Little Rascals, Vol. 1 **1929** Here is a collection of three uncut "Little Rascals" short subjects. In "Boxing Gloves" (1929), Chubby and Joe decide two settle their differences over who should have Jean Darling's love by staging a winner-take-all boxing match. In "The Kid from Borneo" (1933), Spanky thinks he's met a crazy relative when he confuses an untamed human from Borneo for his uncle from the circus. In "Roamin' Holiday" (1936), Alfalfa and Spanky lead the gang on a journey fit for a hobo. **50m/B VHS.** Darla Hood, George "Spanky" McFarland, Carl "Alfalfa" Switzer, Matthew "Stymie" Beard. *REP, CCB*

Little Rascals, Vol. 2 **1930** Another uncut compilation of three classic episodes featuring the goofy gang. In "The First Seven Years" (1930), Speck and Jackie battle for the attention of a beautiful Mary Ann. In the award-winning "Bored of Education" (1936), Spanky and Alfalfa devise a plan to play hooky from school by developing very acute tooth problems. In "Rushin' Ballet" (1937), Alfalfa and Spanky establish the Secret Revengers Club and liberate Buckwheat and Porky from the bonds of tyranny. **50m/B VHS.** George "Spanky" McFarland, Carl "Alfalfa" Switzer. Academy Awards '36: Best Comedy Short ("Bored of Education"). *REP, CCB*

Little Red Riding Hood **1983** From "Faerie Tale Theatre" comes the retelling of the story about a girl (Mary Steenburgen) off to give her grandmother a picnic basket, only to get stopped by a wicked wolf McDowell. Not particularly faithful, but fun and scary. **60m/C VHS, Beta, LV, Closed Caption.** Mary Steenburgen, Malcolm McDowell; **D:** Graeme Clifford. *FOX, FCT*

Little Red Schoolhouse 🎬🎬 **1936** A hard-nosed schoolteacher hunts for a truant lad and both of them land in jail. **64m/C VHS, Beta.** Frank "Junior" Coghlan, Dickie Moore, Ann Doran. *NOS, BAR, FCT*

A Little Romance 🎬🎬🎬 **1979 (PG)** An American girl living in Paris falls in love with a French boy; eventually they run away, to seal their love with a kiss beneath a bridge. Olivier gives a wonderful, if not hammy, performance as the old pickpocket who encourages her. Gentle, agile comedy based on the novel by Patrick Cauvin. **110m/C VHS, Beta, LV.** Laurence Olivier, Diane Lane, Thelonious Bernard, Sally Kellerman, Broderick Crawford; **D:** George Roy Hill; **W:** Allan Burns; **M:** Georges Delerue. Academy Awards '79: Best Original Score; Nominations: Academy Awards '79: Best Adapted Screenplay. *WAR*

A Little Sex 🎬🎬 **1982 (R)** Capshaw, in her screen debut, finds herself the wife of womanizer Matheson. Harmless, but pointless, with a TV-style plot. **94m/C VHS, Beta.** Tim Matheson, Kate Capshaw, Edward Herrmann, Wallace Shawn, John Glover; **D:** Bruce Paltrow; **W:** Robert De Laurentis; **C:** Ralf Bode; **M:** Georges Delerue. *USH*

Little Shop of Horrors 🎬🎬🎬½ **1960** The landmark cheapie classic, which Roger Corman reputedly filmed in three days, about a nebbish working in a city florist shop who unknowingly cultivates an intelligent plant that demands human meat for sustenance. Notable for then-unknown Nicholson's appearance as a masochistic dental patient. Hilarious, unpretentious farce—if you liked this one, check out Corman's "Bucket of Blood" for more of the same. Inspired a musical of the same name, remade as a movie again in 1986. Available colorized. **70m/B VHS, Beta, LV.** Jackie Joseph, Jonathan Haze, Mel Welles, Jack Nicholson, Dick Miller; **D:** Roger Corman. *CNG, MRV, NOS*

Little Shop of Horrors 🎬🎬🎬 **1986 (PG-13)** During a solar eclipse, Seymour buys an unusual plant and takes it back to the flower shop where he works. The plant, Audrey 2, becomes a town attraction as it grows at an unusual rate, but Seymour learns that he must feed Audrey fresh human blood to keep her growing. Soon, Audrey is giving the orders ("Feed me") and timid Seymour must find "deserving" victims. Martin's performance as the masochistic dentist is alone worth the price. Song, dance, gore, and more prevail in this outrageous musical comedy. Four Tops Levi Stubbs is the commanding voice of Audrey 2. Based on the Off-Broadway play, which was based on Roger Corman's 1960 horror spoof. ♫Mean Green Mother From Outer Space; Some Fun Now; Your Day Begins Tonight. **94m/C VHS, Beta, LV, Closed Caption.** Rick Moranis, Ellen Greene, Vincent Gardenia, Steve Martin, James Belushi, Christopher Guest, Bill Murray, John Candy; **D:** Frank Oz; **M:** Miles Goodman, Howard Ashman. Nominations: Academy Awards '86: Best Song ("Mean Green Mother from Outer Space"). *WAR, HMV, MVD*

Little Sister 🎬½ **1992 (PG-13)** Prankster Silverman on a dare, dresses up as a girl and joins a sorority. Problems arise when he falls in love with his "big sister" (Milano) in the sorority. What will happen when she finds out the truth? Will we care? **94m/C VHS.** Jonathan Silverman, Alyssa Milano; **W:** Sergio D. Altieri. *LIV*

A Little Stiff 🎬🎬 **1991** Slacker romantic comedy about the unrequited romance between filmmaker Caveh and fellow UCLA student McKim from first meeting, through angst, and grand final gestures. **85m/C VHS.** Erin McKim, Caveh Zahedi; **D:** Caveh Zahedi, Greg Watkins; **M:** Kath Bloom. *WAC*

Little Sweetheart 🐾½ 1990 (R) A reworking of "The Bad Seed," with a nine-year-old girl engaging in murder, burglary, and blackmail, ruining the adults around her. Based on "The Naughty Girls" by Arthur Wise. **93m/C VHS, Beta, LV, 8mm.** John Hurt, Karen Young, Barbara Bosson, John McMartin, Cassie Barasch; **D:** Anthony Simmons.

The Little Theatre of Jean Renoir 🐾🐾🐾 1971 A farewell by director Jean Renoir featuring three short films. In the first, Renoir's humanist beliefs are apparent in "The Last Christmas Dinner," a Hans Christian Andersen-inspired story. Next, "The Electric Floor Waxer" is a comic opera. The third piece is called "A Tribute to Tolerance." Slight but important late statement by a great director. In French with English subtitles. **100m/C VHS, Beta, LV.** Jean Renoir, Fernand Sardou, Jean Carmet, Francoise Arnoul, Jeanne Moreau; **D:** Jean Renoir; **W:** Jean Renoir. INT, FLI, IME

The Little Thief 🐾🐾🐾 1989 (PG-13) Touted as Francois Truffaut's final legacy, this trite minidrama is actually based on a story he cowrote with Claude de Givray about a post-WWII adolescent girl who reacts to the world around her by stealing and petty crime. Truffaut's hand is markedly absent, but this film is a testament to his abruptly and sadly truncated career. Director Miller was Truffaut's longtime assistant. French with subtitles. **108m/C VHS, Beta, LV.** FR Charlotte Gainsbourg, Simon de la Brosse, Didier Bezace, Raoul Billerey, Nathalie Cardone; **D:** Claude Miller; **W:** Annie Miller, Claude Miller; **C:** Dominique Chapuis; **M:** Alain Jomy. HBO

Little Tough Guys 🐾🐾 1938 The Little Tough Guys (a.k.a. Dead End Kids) come to the rescue of Halop, a young tough guy gone bad to avenge his father's unjust imprisonment. First of the "Little Tough Guys" series for the former Dead End Kids, who later became the East Side Kids before eventually evolving into the Bowery Boys. **84m/B VHS, Beta.** Helen Parrish, Billy Halop, Leo Gorcey, Marjorie Main, Gabriel Dell, Huntz Hall; **D:** Harold Young. NOS, MRV, VYY

Little Treasure 🐾½ 1985 (R) A stripper heads for Mexico to search for her long-lost father, but ends up looking for treasure with an American guy. Disappointing effort of director Sharp. **95m/C VHS, Beta, LV, Closed Caption.** Burt Lancaster, Margot Kidder, Ted Danson, Joseph Hacker, Malena Doria; **D:** Alan Sharp; **W:** Alan Sharp. COL

The Little Valentino 🐾🐾 1979 One day in the aimless life of a young punk who gets by on his wits and petty theft. Jeles' directorial debut. In Hungarian with English subtitles. **102m/B VHS.** HU **D:** Andras Jeles. FCT, AUD

Little Vegas 🐾🐾½ 1990 (R) Looks like easy street for a young man who inherits a bundle from his girlfriend, but he's forced to wake up and smell the cappucino when her family and the other residents of the tiny desert berg think there's a gigolo in the woodpile. Much strife with siblings as he wages a battle for the bucks with the son while wooing the woman's daughter, with a measure of mob inflicted plot twists. Mildly amusing, cut from vein of you can't get rich quick and get away with it. **90m/C VHS, LV.** Michael Nouri, Jerry Stiller, John Sayles, Anthony John Denison, Catherine O'Hara, Bruce McGill, Anne Francis, Bob(cat) Goldthwait, Jay Thomas, Perry Lang; **D:** Perry Lang; **W:** Perry Lang; **M:** Mason Daring. COL

Little Vera 🐾🐾🐾 Malenkaya Vera 1988 Extremely well-done Soviet film chronicles the life of a young working-class woman who loves rock music and who has been profoundly affected by Western civilization. Post-glasnost Soviet production gives Westerners a glimpse into the Russian way of life. A box-office bonanza back home. Russian with subtitles. **130m/C VHS, Beta, LV.** RU Natalia Negoda, Andrei Sokolov, Yuri Nazarov, Ludmila Zaisova, Alexander Niegreva; **D:** Vassili Pitchul. FCT, LUM, WBF

Little White Lies 🐾🐾 1989 Jillian and Matheson meet and fall in love during an exotic vacation. But both are traveling under assumed identities—she's a policewoman tracking a jewel thief and he's an incognito doctor. When they reunite stateside they try to stick to their ruses in humdrum comedic fashion. Made for network TV. **88m/C VHS.** Ann Jillian, Tim Matheson; **D:** Anson Williams. RHI

Little Witches 🐾🐾 1996 (R) Rejected group of seniors at Catholic girls' high school are transformed into a witches coven, thanks to a book of spells. A rip-off of "The Craft." **CW:** Violence, nudity, sexual situations. **91m/C VHS.** Mimi Reichmeister, Jack Nance, Jennifer Rubin, Sheeri Rappaport, Melissa Taub, Zoe Alexander, Zelda Rubinstein, Eric Pierpont; **D:** Jane Simpson. APX

Little Women 🐾🐾🐾🐾 1933 Louisa May Alcott's Civil War story of the four March sisters—Jo, Beth, Amy, and Meg—who share their loves, their joys, and their sorrows. Everything about this classic film is wonderful, from the lavish period costumes to the excellent script, and particularly the captivating performances by the cast. A must-see for fans of Alcott and Hepburn, and others will find it enjoyable. Remade in 1949, in 1978 for television, and again in 1994. **107m/B VHS, Beta, 8mm, Closed Caption.** Katharine Hepburn, Joan Bennett, Paul Lukas, Edna May Oliver, Frances Dee, Spring Byington, Jean Parker, Douglass Montgomery; **D:** George Cukor; **W:** Victor Heerman, Sarah Y. Mason; **M:** Max Steiner, Max Steiner. Academy Awards '33: Best Adapted Screenplay; Venice Film Festival '34: Best Actress (Hepburn); Nominations: Academy Awards '33: Best Director (Cukor), Best Picture. MGM, IGP

Little Women 🐾🐾🐾 1949 Stylized color remake of the George Cukor 1933 classic. Topnotch if too obvious cast portrays Louisa May Alcott's story of teenage girls growing up against the backdrop of the Civil War. Remade again, for television in 1978. **121m/C VHS, Closed Caption.** June Allyson, Peter Lawford, Margaret O'Brien, Elizabeth Taylor, Janet Leigh, Mary Astor; **D:** Mervyn LeRoy; **W:** Andrew Solt; **M:** Adolph Deutsch. Academy Awards '49: Best Art Direction/Set Decoration (Color); Nominations: Academy Awards '49: Best Color Cinematography. MGM

Little Women 🐾🐾🐾 1978 The third screen version of Louisa May Alcott's classic story. Lackluster compared to the previous attempts, particularly the sterling 1933 film, but still worthwhile. During the Civil War, four sisters share their loves as they grow up and find romance. Garson's television debut. Followed by a television series. **200m/C VHS, Closed Caption.** Meredith Baxter, Susan Dey, Ann Dusenberry, Eve Plumb, Dorothy McGuire, Robert Young, Greer Garson, Cliff Potts, William Shatner; **D:** David Lowell Rich; **M:** Elmer Bernstein. NO

Little Women 🐾🐾🐾🐾 1994 (PG) Beloved story of the March women is beautifully portrayed in a solid production that blends a seamless screenplay with an excellent cast, authentic period costumes, and lovely cinematography and music. Ryder, perfectly cast as the unconventional Jo, is also the strongest of the sisters: domestically inclined Meg (Alvarado), the fragile Beth (Danes), and the youngest, mischievous Amy (the delightful Dunst) who grows up into a sedate young lady (Mathis). Charming adaptation remains faithful to the spirit of the Alcott classic while adding contemporary touches. Fittingly brought to the big screen by producer Denise Di Novi, writer/co-producer Swicord, and director Armstrong. **118m/C VHS, LV, 8mm, Closed Caption, DVD.** Winona Ryder, Gabriel Byrne, Trini Alvarado, Samantha Mathis, Kirsten Dunst, Claire Danes, Christian Bale, Eric Stoltz, John Neville, Mary Wickes, Susan Sarandon; **D:** Gillian Armstrong; **W:** Robin Swicord; **C:** Geoffrey Simpson; **M:** Thomas Newman. Chicago Film Critics Awards '94: Most Promising Actress (Dunst); Nominations: Academy Awards '94: Best Actress (Ryder), Best Costume Design, Best Original Score; Writers Guild of America '94: Best Adapted Screenplay. COL

Little World of Don Camillo 🐾🐾🐾 Le Petit Monde de Don Camillo 1951 A French-made farce based on the beloved novels of Giovanni Guareschi. Earthy priest Don Camillo clashes repeatedly with his friendly enemy, the communist mayor of a tiny Italian village. The hero talks directly to God, whose voice is provided by Orson Welles, also narrator of the English version. Charming, good-natured approach. **106m/B VHS, Beta, 8mm.** FR IT Fernandel, Gino Cervi, Sylvia, Vera Talqui; **D:** Julien Duvivier. VYY, FCT

The Littlest Angel 🐾🐾 1969 Musical about a shepherd boy who dies falling off a cliff and wants to become an angel. He learns a valuable lesson in the spirit of giving. Made for TV. **77m/C VHS, Beta.** Johnny Whitaker, Fred Gwynne, E.G. Marshall, Cab Calloway, Connie Stevens, Tony Randall. KAR

The Littlest Horse Thieves 🐾🐾½ Escape from the Dark 1976 (G) Good Disney film about three children and their efforts to save some ponies who work in mines. The children take it upon themselves to see that the animals escape the abuse and neglect they are put through. Filmed on location in England with excellent photography. **109m/C VHS, Beta.** Alastair Sim, Peter Barkworth; **D:** Charles Jarrott. DIS

The Littlest Outlaw 🐾🐾½ 1954 A Mexican peasant boy steals a beautiful stallion to save it from being destroyed. Together, they ride off on a series of adventures. Disney movie filmed on location in Mexico. **73m/C VHS, Beta.** Pedro Armendariz Sr., Joseph Calleia, Andres Velasquez; **D:** Roberto Gavaldon. DIS

The Littlest Rebel 🐾🐾½ 1935 (PG) Temple stars in this well-done piece set during the Civil War in the Old South. She befriends a Union officer while protecting her father at the same time. She even goes to Washington to talk with President Lincoln. Nice dance sequences by Temple and Robinson. Available in computer-colored version. **70m/B VHS, Beta, Closed Caption.** Shirley Temple, John Boles, Jack Holt, Bill Robinson, Karen Morley, Willie Best; **D:** David Butler. FOX

The Littlest Viking 🐾🐾½ 1994 (PG) Twelve-year-old Sigurd finds archery practice and mock battles an exciting way to learn to be a Viking. But when his older brother is killed in battle, Sigurd's father expects him to avenge the death, and Sigurd must decide just what being a Viking prince means. Scenic Scandinavian settings; obvious dubbing. **85m/C VHS, LV.** Kristian Tonby, Per Jansen, Terje Stromdahl; **D:** Knut W. Jorfald, Lars Rasmussen, Paul Trevor Bale. HMD

Live a Little, Love a Little 🐾🐾 1968 (PG) Itinerant photographer Elvis juggles two different jobs by running around a lot. Sexually more frank than earlier King vehicles. ♫ Almost in Love; A Little Less Conversation; Edge of Reality; Wonderful World. **90m/C VHS, Beta.** Elvis Presley, Michele Carey, Rudy Vallee, Don Porter, Dick Sargent, Sterling Holloway, Eddie Hodges; **D:** Norman Taurog. MGM

Live and Let Die 🐾🐾 1973 (PG) Agent 007 is out to thwart the villainous Dr. Kananga, a black mastermind who plans to control western powers with voodoo and hard drugs. Moore's first appearance as Bond. Can't we have the real Bond back? Title song by Paul McCartney. **131m/C VHS, Beta, LV.** GB Roger Moore, Jane Seymour, Yaphet Kotto, Clifton James, Julius W. Harris, Geoffrey Holder, David Hedison, Gloria Hendry, Bernard Lee, Lois Maxwell, Madeleine Smith; **D:** Guy Hamilton; **W:** Tom Mankiewicz; **C:** Ted Moore; **M:** George Martin. Nominations: Academy Awards '73: Best Song ("Live and Let Die"). MGM, FOX, TLF

Live Bait 🐾🐾½ 1995 Canadian-flavored Gen-X comedy features suburban 23-year-old virgin Trevor MacIntosh (Scholte) trying for a little romance (or at least sex) but seemingly doomed to failure. At least until he meets much older artist Charlotte (Maunsell). Sweeney handles his debut writing, directing, and producing skills with equal aplomb. **84m/B VHS.** *CA* Tom Scholte, Micki Maunsell, Kevin McNulty, Babz Chula, David Lovgren, Laara Sadiq, Michelle Beaudoin, Kelly Aisenstat; *D:* Bruce Sweeney; *W:* Bruce Sweeney; *C:* David Pelletier. Toronto-City Award '95: Best Canadian Feature Film. *NYR*

Live! From Death Row 🐾🐾 1992 Cassidy plays a tabloid TV host who'll do anything to get ratings. She's set to do a live interview with a condemned serial killer (Davison) shortly before his execution. But Davison and his fellow deathrow inmates take Cassidy and her crew hostage as he decides to use the show for his own media message. **94m/C VHS.** Joanna Cassidy, Bruce Davison, Art LaFleur, Calvin Levels, Michael D. Roberts; *D:* Patrick Duncan; *W:* Patrick Duncan. *ABC, PSM*

Live Nude Girls 🐾🐾 1995 (R) Group of thirty-something girlfriends get together to throw a bachelorette party for one of their number and sit around gossiping about sex, relationships, family, and friends. Not much plot but nice ensemble work.*CW:* Graphic sexual dialogue and scenes of sexuality. **92m/C VHS, LV, Closed Caption.** Dana Delany, Kim Cattrall, Cynthia Stevenson, Laila Robins, Olivia D'Abo, Lora Zane, Glenn Quinn, Tim Choate; *D:* Julianna Lavin; *W:* Julianna Lavin; *C:* Christopher Taylor; *M:* Anton Sanko. *REP*

The Live Wire 🐾🐾 1934 Stunt-ridden action fare featuring Talmadge at his most daring. This adventure is complete with desert island, lost treasure, stowaways, evil-doers, and a race against the clock. **57m/B VHS, Beta.** Richard Talmadge, George Walsh, Charles French, Alberta Vaughn; *D:* Harry S. Webb. *NOS, DVT, GPV*

Live Wire 🐾🐾½ 1992 (R) Brosnan is an FBI bomb expert who needs a new line of work. He's up against a terrorist psychopath who has his greedy hands on a new type of explosive. It's liquid, undetectable, looks as innocent as a glass of water, and is capable of blowing up Washington, D.C. Made for cable television. Also available in an unrated version.*CW:* Language, strong violence, and strong sensuality. **85m/C VHS, Closed Caption.** Pierce Brosnan, Ben Cross, Ron Silver, Lisa Eilbacher; *D:* Christian Duguay; *W:* Bart Baker. *COL, NLC*

Live Wire: Human Timebomb 🐾½ 1995 (R) FBI agent Jim Parker is captured by a Cuban general who implants a computer chip into his neck—turning Parker into a human timebomb.*CW:* Language, violence. **98m/C VHS, Closed Caption.** Bryan Genesse, Joe Lara; *D:* Mark Roper; *W:* Jeff Albert; *C:* Rod Stewart; *M:* Itai Haber. *TTC*

The Lives of a Bengal Lancer 🐾🐾🐾🐾 1935 One of Hollywood's greatest rousing adventures. Three British Lancers, of varying experience, encounter a vicious revolution against colonial rule. Rivaled only by "Gunga Din" as the ultimate 1930s swashbuckler. Swell plot, lotsa action, great comraderie. Based on the novel by Major Francis Yeats-Brown, and remade in 1939 as "Geronimo." **110m/B VHS, Beta.** Gary Cooper, Franchot Tone, Richard Cromwell, Guy Standing, Sir C. Aubrey Smith, Monte Blue, Kathleen Burke, Noble Johnson, Lumsden Hare, Akim Tamiroff, J. Carrol Naish, Douglass Dumbrille; *D:* Henry Hathaway; *W:* Waldemar Young, John Balderston; *C:* Charles B(ryant) Lang; *M:* Milan Roder. National Board of Review Awards '35: 10 Best Films of the Year; Nominations: Academy Awards '35: Best Director (Hathaway), Best Film Editing, Best Interior Decoration, Best Picture, Best Screenplay, Best Sound. *USH*

Livin' Large 🐾🐾 1991 (R) An African-American delivery boy gets the break of his life when a nearby newscaster is shot dead. Grabbing the microphone and continuing the story, he soon finds himself hired by an Atlanta news station as an anchorman, fulfilling a life-long dream. But problems arise when he finds himself losing touch with his friends, his old neighborhood and his roots. Comedy "deals" with the compelling issue of blacks finding success in a white world by trivializing the issue at every turn and resorting to racial stereotypes.*CW:* Language. **96m/C VHS, Closed Caption.** Terrence "T.C." Carson, Lisa Arrindell, Blanche Baker, Nathaniel "Afrika" Hall, Julia Campbell; *D:*

Michael A. Schultz; *C:* Peter Collister; *M:* Herbie Hancock. *HBO*

The Living Coffin 🐾½ *El Grito de la Muerte* 1958 Woman has alarm rigged on her coffin in case she's buried alive. And they called her paranoid. Loosely based on Poe's "Premature Burial." **72m/C VHS.** *MX* Gaston Santos, Maria Duval, Pedro de Aguillon; *D:* Fernando Mendez. *SNC*

The Living Daylights 🐾🐾🐾 1987 (PG) After being used as a pawn in a fake Russian defector plot, our intrepid spy tracks down an international arms and opium smuggling ring. Fine debut by Dalton as 007 in a rousing, refreshing cosmopolitan shoot-em-up. Let's be frank: we were all getting a little fatigued by Roger Moore. **130m/C VHS, Beta, LV, Closed Caption.** Timothy Dalton, Maryam D'Abo, Jeroen Krabbe, John Rhys-Davies, Robert Brown, Joe Don Baker, Desmond Llewelyn, Art Malik, Geoffrey Keen, Walter Gotell, Andreas Wisniewski; *D:* John Glen; *W:* Richard Maibaum, Michael G. Wilson; *M:* John Barry. *MGM, TLF, FOX*

The Living Dead 🐾🐾 *The Scotland Yard Mystery* 1936 An English film about a mad, re-animating scientist. **76m/B VHS.** *GB* Gerald du Maurier, George Curzan. *NOS, SNC, DVT*

The Living End 🐾🐾 1992 Director Araki's radical lovers-on-the-lam story concerns freelance L.A. writer Jon (Gilmore) who has just learned he is H.I.V.-positive. He meets a handsome, violent hustler named Luke (Dytri) and the two begin a desperate road trip along the California coast which can only end in tragedy. Araki not only wrote and directed the film but also served as cinematographer and editor—all on a $23,000 budget. Stylish, tragic, and filled with black humor and frank homoeroticism. **92m/C VHS.** Craig Gilmore, Mike Dytri, Darcy Marta; *D:* Gregg Araki; *W:* Gregg Araki; *C:* Gregg Araki. *ACA*

Living Free 🐾🐾½ 1972 (G) Sequel to "Born Free," based on the nonfictional books by Joy Adamson. Recounts the travails of Elsa the lioness, who is now dying, with three young cubs that need care. Nice and pleasant, but could you pick up the pace? **91m/C VHS, Beta, LV.** Susan Hampshire, Nigel Davenport; *D:* Jack Couffer. *COL, GKK*

The Living Head 🐾½ *La Cabeza Viviente* 1959 Archaeologists discover the ancient sepulcher of the great Aztec warrior, Acatl. Ignoring a curse, they steal his severed head and incur the fury of Xitsliapoli. They should have known better. Dubbed in English. **75m/B VHS, Beta.** *MX* Mauricio Garces, Ana Luisa Peluffo, German Robles, Abel Salazar; *D:* Chano Urueto. *VYY, SNC*

Living in Oblivion 🐾🐾🐾 1994 (R) Humorous tri-part story is an insiders joke on the problems of low-budget filmmaking, including talent, libido, ego, and pervasive chaos. First, director Nick Reve (Buscemi) tries to film an emotional scene with leading lady Nicole (Keener) only to have everything go wrong; then star Chad (LeGros), a dimwit but a "name," arrives to throw his weight around (and seduce Nicole); and finally the leading lady must deal with an overly sensitive dwarf and Nick's mother. A sleeper.*CW:* Strong language. **92m/C VHS, LV, Closed Caption.** Steve Buscemi, Catherine Keener, James LeGros, Dermot Mulroney, Danielle von Zerneck, Robert Wightman, Rica Martens, Hilary Gilford, Peter Dinklage, Kevin Corrigan, Matthew Grace, Michael Griffiths, Ryna Bowker, Francesca DiMauro; *D:* Tom DiCillo; *W:* Tom DiCillo; *C:* Frank Prinzi; *M:* Jim Farmer. Sundance Film Festival '95: Best Screenplay; Nominations: Independent Spirit Awards '96: Best Film, Best Screenplay, Best Supporting Actor (LeGros). *COL*

Living on Tokyo Time 🐾🐾½ 1987 Interesting but often dull, low budget independent comedy about a young Japanese woman who hitches up with a boorish Japanese-American man in order to stay in the United States. An Asian view of Asian-America, filmed on location in San Francisco. **83m/C VHS, Beta.** Minako Ohashi, Ken Nakagawa, Kate Connell, Mitzi Abe, Bill Bonham, Brenda Aoki; *D:* Steven Okazaki; *W:* Steven Okazaki, John McCormick. *NLC*

Living Proof: The Hank Williams Jr. Story 🐾🐾½ 1983 TV biopic focusing on the country singer's hell-raising ways as he seeks to get out from under the shadow of his famous father and into the spotlight on his own right. Based on Williams, Jr.'s autobiography; includes 10 songs by Sr. and Jr. **97m/C VHS, Closed Caption.** Richard Thomas, Clu Gulager, Allyn Ann McLerie, Naomi Judd, Christian Slater; *D:* Dick Lowry; *W:* I.C. Rapoport, Stephen Kandel. *WAR*

Living to Die 🐾½ 1991 (R) Vegas gumshoe is assigned to investigate a blackmailed official, and discovers a woman believed to be dead is alive and beautiful and living incognito. This mystifies him. **84m/C VHS.** Wings Hauser, Darcy Demoss, Asher Brauner, Arnold Vosloo, Jim Williams; *D:* Wings Hauser. *PMH, HHE*

The Lizzies of Mack Sennett 1915 Three quick-paced, hilarious Sennett "Tin Lizzie" comedies: "Lizzies of the Field," "Leading Lizzie Astray" and "Love, Speed and Thrills." Plenty of signature slapstick from the master. **51m/C VHS, Beta.** Billy Bevan, Fatty Arbuckle, Mack Swain, Chester Conklin; *D:* Mack Sennett. *VYY*

Lloyds of London 🐾🐾🐾 1936 If you wonder how the story of a British insurance company can be exciting, just watch this lavish spectacular (which, of course, lacks historical accuracy). Jonathan Blake (Power) has risen in the ranks of the firm, thanks in part to his childhood friendship with Lord Horatio Nelson (Burton), much to the disgust of haughty Lord Everett Stacy (an ever-supercilious Sanders). As Bonaparte comes to power, Blake travels to France to rescue some friends and saves Elizabeth (Carroll), who turns out to be Stacy's wife. Stacy is also spreading rumors about Lloyds' solvency and Nelson's heroics at Trafalgar and his machinations lead to further trouble with Blake. **115m/B VHS, Closed Caption.** Tyrone Power, George Sanders, Madeleine Carroll, John Burton, Guy Standing, Sir C. Aubrey Smith, Freddie Bartholomew, Virginia Field, Montagu Love, Una O'Connor; *D:* Henry King; *W:* Ernest Pascal, Walter Ferris; *C:* Bert Glennon. Nominations: Academy Awards '36: Best Film Editing.*FXV*

Loaded 🐾🐾 *Bloody Weekend* 1994 (R) Writer-director Campion (sister of director Jane) follows a group of teens to an abandoned English mansion as they try to film an amateur horror movie. While there, the group decides to have some fun, with the help of LSD. This leads to some therapeutic and angst-ridden discussions about each of their problems, as well as a tragic accident, which changes the lives of all involved. There's some nice character sketches, unfortunately they're more interesting than the loose plot, which leaves too many questions unanswered. Retitled and recut since its original '94 release.*CW:* Profanity, sexual situations and partial nudity. **95m/C VHS, LV, Closed Caption.** *NZ GB* Thandie Newton, Catherine McCormack, Oliver Milburn, Nick Patrick, Danny Cunningham, Mathew Eggleton, Biddy Hodson; *D:* Anna Campion; *W:* Anna Campion; *C:* Alan Almond; *M:* Simon Fisher Turner. *MAX*

Loaded Guns woof! 1975 Airline stewardess-cum-double agent must totally immobilize a top drug trafficking ring. Pathetic spy tale with plenty of unintended laughs. **90m/C VHS, Beta.** Ursula Andress, Woody Strode; *D:* Fernando Di Leo. *LIV*

Loaded Pistols 🐾 1948 Story set in the old West starring Gene Autry. **80m/B VHS, Beta.** Gene Autry, Jack Holt, Barbara Britton; *D:* John English. *NOS, VCN, DVT*

Loan Shark 🐾🐾 1952 An ex-convict gets a job at a tire company, working undercover to expose a loan shark ring. Hackneyed plot moves quickly. **79m/B VHS, Beta, LV.** George Raft, John Hoyt; *D:* Seymour Friedman. *NO*

Lobster for Breakfast 🐾🐾½ 1982 (R) An Italian gag-fest about a toilet salesman infiltrating his friend's confused marital existence just to make a sale. With English subtitles; also available in a dubbed version. **96m/C VHS, Beta.** *IT* Enrico Montesano, Claude Brasseur, Claudine Auger; **D:** Giorgio Capitani.

Lobster Man from Mars 🐭🐭 **1989 (PG)** When rich movie producer (Curtis) learns from his accountant that he must produce a flop or be taken to the cleaners by the IRS, he buys a homemade horror movie from a young filmmaker. The film is an ultra-low budget production featuring a kooky lobster man and a screaming damsel. The premise peters out about halfway through, but there are enough yuks to keep you going. **84m/C VHS, Beta, LV.** Tony Curtis, Deborah Foreman, Patrick Macnee, Tommy Sledge, Billy Barty, Phil Proctor; **D:** Stanley Shiff. *LIV*

Local Badman 🐭 **1932** A dim-witted cowhand saves the day in this rip-roaring tale of the old west. **60m/B VHS, Beta.** Hoot Gibson. *NOS, VCI, RXM*

Local Hero 🐭🐭🐭🐭 **1983 (PG)** Riegert is a yuppie representative of a huge oil company who endeavors to buy a sleepy Scottish fishing village for excavation, and finds himself hypnotized by the place and its crusty denizens. Back in Texas at company headquarters, tycoon Lancaster deals with a psycho therapist and gazes at the stars looking for clues. A low-key, charmingly offbeat Scottish comedy with its own sense of logic and quiet humor, poetic landscapes, and unique characters, epitomizing Forsyth's original style. **112m/C VHS, Beta, LV, Closed Caption.** *GB* Peter Riegert, Denis Lawson, Burt Lancaster, Fulton Mackay, Jenny Seagrove, Peter Capaldi, Norman Chancer; **D:** Bill Forsyth; **W:** Bill Forsyth; **C:** Chris Menges; **M:** Mark Knopfler. British Academy Awards '83: Best Director (Forsyth); New York Film Critics Awards '83: Best Screenplay; National Society of Film Critics Awards '83: Best Screenplay. *WAR*

Loch Ness 🐭🐭½ **1995 (PG)** American zoologist Jonathan Dempsey (Danson) specializes in hunting legendary animals and his latest assignment is to head for the Scottish highlands and take on the Nessie legend. He gets an assistant (Frain), a potential romance with single mom Laura (Richardson), and a lot of grief from some hostile locals before Laura's young daughter Isabel (Graham) decides to help him out. Jim Henson's Creature Shop takes care of the monster's animatronics. **101m/C VHS.** *GB* Ted Danson, Ian Holm, Joely Richardson, Kirsty Graham, James Frain, Keith Allen, Nick Brimble; **D:** John Henderson; **W:** John Fusco; **C:** Clive Tickner; **M:** Trevor Jones. *PGV*

The Loch Ness Horror woof! **1982** The famed monster surfaces and chomps on the local poachers—and with good reason. Would that it had munched this movie's producer in, say, 1981. **93m/C VHS, Beta.** Barry Buchanan, Miki McKenzie, Sandy Kenyon; **D:** Larry Buchanan. *NO*

Lock 'n' Load 🐭🐭 **1990 (R)** Why are all the soldiers in the 82nd Airborne stealing vast sums, then committing suicide? One of the guys involved wants to know. **?m/C VHS, LV.** Jack Vogel; **D:** David A. Prior. *AIP*

Lock Up 🐭½ **1989 (R)** Peaceful con Stallone, with only six months to go, is harassed and tortured by vicious prison warden Sutherland in retribution for an unexplained past conflict. Lackluster and moronic; semi-color; surely Sutherland can find better roles. **115m/C VHS, Beta, Closed Caption.** Sylvester Stallone, Donald Sutherland, Sonny Landham, John Amos, Darlanne Fluegel, Frank McRae; **D:** John Flynn; **W:** Jeb Stuart; **M:** Bill Conti. *LIV*

Lockdown 🐭½ **1990** Charged with his partner's murder, a detective is forced to ponder the perennial puzzle of life. Not a pretty sight. **90m/C VHS.** Joe Estevez, Mike Farrell, Richard Lynch. *THV*

L'Odeur des Fauves 🐭 **1966** One of a cynical reporter's scandalous stories gets an innocent man killed, compelling the reporter somehow to make restitution. Subtitled in English. **86m/C VHS, Beta.** *FR* Maurice Ronet, Josephine Chaplin, Vittorio De Sica; **D:** Richard Balducci. *BAR*

The Lodger 🐭🐭🐭 *The Case of Jonathan Drew; The Lodger: A Case of London Fog* **1926** A mysterious lodger is thought to be a rampaging mass murderer of young women. First Hitchcock film to explore the themes and ideas that would become his trademarks. Silent. Climactic chase is memorable. Remade three times. Look closely for the Master in his first cameo. **91m/B VHS, Beta.** *GB* Ivor Novello, Marie Ault, Arthur Chesney, Malcolm Keen; **Cameos:** Alfred Hitchcock; **D:** Alfred Hitchcock; **W:** Alfred Hitchcock. *GPV, NOS, VYY*

Logan's Run 🐭🐭½ **1976** In the 23rd century, a hedonistic society exists in a huge bubble and people are only allowed to live to the age of 30. Intriguing concepts and great futuristic sets prevail here. Based on the novel by William Nolan and George Clayton Johnson. **120m/C VHS, Beta, LV.** Michael York, Jenny Agutter, Richard Jordan, Roscoe Lee Browne, Farrah Fawcett, Peter Ustinov, Camilla Carr, Ann Ford; **D:** Michael Anderson Sr.; **W:** David Zelag Goodman; **C:** Ernest Laszlo; **M:** Jerry Goldsmith. Academy Awards '76: Best Visual Effects; Nominations: Academy Awards '76: Best Art Direction/Set Decoration, Best Cinematography. *MGM*

Lois Gibbs and the Love Canal 🐭🐭 **1982** Mason's television movie debut as Lois Gibbs, a housewife turned activist, fighting the authorities over chemical-dumping in the Love Canal area of Niagara Falls, New York. The script doesn't convey the seriousness of developments in that region. **100m/C VHS.** Marsha Mason, Bob Gunton, Penny Fuller, Roberta Maxwell, Jeremy Licht, Louise Latham; **D:** Glenn Jordan. *NO*

Lola 🐭🐭🐭 **1961** A wonderful tale of a nightclub dancer and her amorous adventures. Innovative film that marked the beginning of French New Wave. In French with English subtitles. **90m/B VHS.** *FR* Anouk Aimee, Marc Michel, Elina Labourdette, Jacques Harden; **D:** Jacques Demy. *INT, TPV*

Lola 🐭½ *The Statutory Affair; Twinky* **1969 (PG)** A teenaged girl links up romantically with a considerably older writer of pornographic books. One would expect more from such a good cast, but the film never follows through. British release was originally 98 minutes. **88m/C VHS.** *GB IT* Charles Bronson, Susan George, Trevor Howard, Michael Craig, Honor Blackman, Lionel Jeffries, Robert Morley, Jack Hawkins, Orson Bean, Kay Medford, Paul Ford; **D:** Richard Donner. *FCT, MRV*

Lola Montes 🐭🐭🐭🐭 **1955** Ophuls' final masterpiece recounts the life and sins of the famous courtesan, mistress of Franz Liszt and the King of Bavaria. Ignored upon release, but hailed later by the French as a cinematic landmark. Presented in its original wide-screen format; in French with English subtitles. Also available in a 110 minute version. Adapted from an unpublished novel by Cecil Saint-Laurent. **140m/C Beta, LV.** *FR* Martine Carol, Peter Ustinov, Anton Walbrook, Ivan Desny, Oskar Werner; **D:** Max Ophuls; **W:** Max Ophuls; **M:** Georges Auric. *CRC, NLC*

Lolita 🐭🐭🐭 **1962** A middle-aged professor is consumed by his lust for a teenage nymphet in this strange film considered daring in its time. Based on Vladimir Nabokov's novel. Watch for Winters' terrific portrayal as Lolita's sex-starved mother. **152m/B VHS, Beta, LV.** *GB* James Mason, Shelley Winters, Peter Sellers, Sue Lyon, Gary Cockrell, Jerry Stovin, Diana Decker, Lois Maxwell, Cec Linder, Bill Greene, Shirley Douglas, Marianne Stone, Marion Mathie, James Dyrenforth, C. Denier Warren, Terence Kilburn, John Harrison; **D:** Stanley Kubrick; **C:** Oswald Morris; **M:** Nelson Riddle. Nominations: Academy Awards '62: Best Adapted Screenplay. *MGM, CRC*

London Kills Me 🐭🐭 **1991 (R)** A slice-of-life story London-style. Set at the end of the Thatcher era, Clint is a homeless drifter dealing drugs to get by. He's trying to get enough money for a new pair of shoes which will enable him to get a job in a fancy restaurant and away from his aimless life. His friend Muffdiver leads the group of drug pushers and is obsessed with money and power. Sylvie is the sultry junkie who drifts between Clint, Muffdiver, and her drug needs. The directorial debut of Kureishi is more a collection of characters and situations than a complete film but there are moments of disturbing intensity and odd sweetness. **CW:** Language, nudity, and drug use. **105m/C VHS, LV, Closed Caption.** *GB* Justin Chadwick, Steven Mackintosh, Emer McCourt, Roshan Seth, Fiona Shaw, Brad Dourif, Gordon Warnecke; **D:** Hanif Kureishi; **W:** Hanif Kureishi. *LIV, PMS*

London Melody 🐭½ *Girl in the Street* **1937** Neagle is a spirited Cockney busker who meets a kindly Italian diplomat who decides to finance her musical education. He promptly also falls in love with her. **71m/B VHS, Beta, 8mm.** *GB* Anna Neagle, Tullio Carminati, Robert Douglas, Horace Hodgers; **D:** Herbert Wilcox. *VYY*

The Lone Avenger 🐭🐭 **1933** Average oater centers around a bank panic, with two-gun Maynard clearing up the trouble. **60m/B VHS, Beta.** Ken Maynard, Muriel Gordon, James Marcus. *NOS, VCN, CAB*

Lone Bandit 🐭½ **1933** Vintage western starring Chandler. **57m/B VHS, Beta.** Lane Chandler, Doris Brook, Wally Wales; **D:** J.P. McGowan. *VCN*

The Lone Defender **1932** A dozen episodes of the western serial starring the canine crusader, Rin Tin Tin. **235m/B VHS, Beta.** Walter Miller, June Marlowe, Buzz Barton, Josef Swickard, Frank Lanning, Robert F. (Bob) Kortman; **D:** Richard Thorpe. *VDM, GPV, MLB*

Lone Justice 🐭🐭½ **1993 (R)** Cowboy Ned Blessing has seen and done it all (from outlaw to sheriff) but his wild ways have caught up with him. Now, he's relating his exploits from a jail cell as he awaits his fate at the end of a rope. Beware—this looks like the first chapter of a series and there's no real ending. **CW:** Western violence. **94m/C VHS, LV, Closed Caption.** Daniel Baldwin, Luis Avalos, Chris Cooper, Sean Baca, Taylor Fry, Julia Campbell, Rene Auberjonois, Timothy Scott, Bob Gunton, Miguel Sandoval, Jeff Kober; **D:** Peter Werner; **W:** William D. Wittliff; **M:** Basil Poledouris. *ACA*

Lone Justice 2 🐭🐭½ *Ned Blessing: The Story of My Life and Times* **1993 (PG-13)** Laconic hero Ned Blessing (Johnson), along with Mexican sidekick Crecencio (Avalos), return to Blessing's hometown after a six year absence and find it ruled by six-shooters and fists. The despicable Borgers clan has murdered the local sheriff (who happens to be Blessing's daddy) and rules by intimidation—until Ned gets involved. Cliched but amusing TV movie. **CW:** Some violence. **93m/C VHS.** Brad Johnson, Luis Avalos, Wes Studi, Bill McKinney, Brenda Bakke, Julius Tennon, Richard Riehle, Gregory Scott Cummins, Rob Campbell, Rusty Schwimmer; **D:** Jack Bender; **W:** William D. Wittliff. *TRI*

Lone Justice 3: Showdown at Plum Creek 🐭🐭½ **1996 (PG)** Ex-outlaw-turned-sheriff Ned Blessing (Johnson) finds his enemies, the Borgers, have put a bounty on his head and a gang of assassins on his trail. **94m/C VHS.** Brad Johnson, Wes Studi, Brenda Bakke, William Sanderson, Luis Avalos. *TRI*

The Lone Ranger **1938** Western serial about the masked man and his faithful Indian sidekick. From a long-sought print found in Mexico, this program is burdened by a noisy sound track, two completely missing chapters, an abridged episode #15, and Spanish subtitles. **234m/B VHS, Beta.** Lee Powell; **D:** William Witney, John English. *VYY, NOS, VCN*

Lone Ranger **1956** Tonto and that strange masked man must prevent a war between ranchers and Indians in the first of the "Lone Ranger" series. "Hi-ho Silver!" **87m/C VHS, Beta.** Clayton Moore, Jay Silverheels, Lyle Bettger, Bonita Granville; **D:** Stuart Heisler. *MGM*

Lone Ranger and the Lost City of Gold 🐭🐭 **1958** Three Indian men are found dead, and the Lone Ranger and Tonto set out to discover the killers. **80m/C VHS.** Clayton Moore, Jay

Silverheels, Douglas Kennedy; *D:* Lesley Selander; *M:* Les Baxter. NO

The Lone Rider in Cheyenne 🐎½ **1942** One of the last in the "Lone Rider" series. The Lone Rider is out to clear the name of an innocent man accused of murder. **59m/B VHS.** George Houston, Al "Fuzzy" St. John; *D:* Sam Newfield. *NOS, DVT, HEG*

The Lone Rider in Ghost Town 🐎½ **1941** Outlaws "haunt" a ghost town to protect their hidden mine and the Lone Rider and his pal, Fuzzy, are out to solve the mystery. Installment in the short-lived "Lone Rider" series. **64m/B VHS.** George Houston, Al "Fuzzy" St. John, Budd Buster; *D:* Sam Newfield. *NOS, DVT, HEG*

The Lone Runner woof! **1988 (PG)** An adventurer rescues a beautiful heiress from Arab kidnappers in this dud. **90m/C VHS, Beta, LV.** Miles O'Keeffe, Ronald Lacey, Michael J. Aronin, John Steiner, Al Yamanouchi; *D:* Ruggero Deodato. *MED*

Lone Star 🐎🐎½ **1952** Big stars, big budget western in which Texas fights for independence as good guy Gable and badman Crawford fight each other. Gardner plays a fiery newspaper editor as well as Gable's love interest. Script is chock full of holes, but great action scenes make up for it. Based on the story by Borden Chase. **94m/B VHS.** Clark Gable, Ava Gardner, Broderick Crawford, Lionel Barrymore, Beulah Bondi, Ed Begley Sr., William Farnum, Lowell Gilmore; *D:* Vincent Sherman; *W:* Howard Estabrook, Borden Chase. *MGM*

Lone Star 🐎🐎🐎½ **1995 (R)** Terrific contemporary western set in the border town Frontera, Texas. Sheriff Sam Deeds (Cooper) is still dealing with the legacy of his father, legendary lawman Buddy Deeds (McConaughey) who, 40 years before, wrestled control of the town from his racist, corrupt predecessor Charlie Wade (Kristofferson) and supposedly sent him packing. But when skeletal remains and a sheriff's badge turn up on an abandoned Army rifle range, guess whose bones they turn out to be. Buddy's friends would like Sam to just leave the past lie but he can't and learns some hard home truths. This is only one of the town's stories that Sayles gracefully tells and, as always, his ensemble cast all offer outstanding performances. *CW:* Brief language, sex, and violence. **137m/C VHS, LV, Closed Caption.** Chris Cooper, Matthew McConaughey, Kris Kristofferson, Elizabeth Pena, Joe Morton, Ron Canada, Clifton James, Miriam Colon, Frances McDormand; *D:* John Sayles; *W:* John Sayles; *C:* Stuart Dryburgh; *M:* Mason Daring. *Independent Spirit Awards '97: Best Supporting Actress (Pena); Nominations: Academy Awards '96: Best Writing; British Academy Awards '96: Best Original Screenplay; Golden Globe Awards '97: Best Screenplay; Independent Spirit Awards '97: Best Actor (Cooper), Best Film, Best Screenplay; Writers Guild of America '96: Best Original Screenplay. COL*

Lone Star Kid **1988** 11-year-old Brian Zimmerman lives in Crabb, Texas—population 400. After he witnesses a car accident death because there's no adequate emergency service, he decides to run for mayor and help modernize the town. Based on a true story. Includes a viewers' guide. Presented as part of the "Wonderworks" series. **55m/C VHS.** James Earl Jones, Chad Sheets; *M:* Charlie Daniels. *PME, HMV, BTV*

Lone Star Law Men 🐎 **1942** A U.S. marshal has his hands full in a border town overrun with bandits. Keene stars as the deputy marshal who goes undercover and joins the gang in an attempt to foil their crooked plans. **58m/B VHS.** Tom Keene, Frank Yaconelli, Sugar Dawn, Betty Miles; *D:* Robert Emmett Tansey. *NOS, DVT*

The Lone Star Ranger 🐎½ **1930** Former outlaw O'Brien is trying to go straight by helping to bring a gang of rustlers to justice. Interesting plot twist in the link between his girlfriend and the head of the gang. **64m/B VHS.** George O'Brien, Sue Carol, Walter McGrail, Russell Simpson; *D:* A.F. Erickson. *DVT, HEG*

Lone Wolf 🐎 **1988** A werewolf terrorizes a high school, and a few computerniks track it down. **97m/C VHS, Beta.** Dyann Brown, Kevin Hart, Jamie Newcomb, Ann Douglas; *D:* John Callas. *PSM*

Lone Wolf McQuade 🐎🐎½ **1983** Martial arts action abounds in this modern-day Western which pits unorthodox Texas Ranger Norris against a band of gun-running mercenaries led by Carradine. Oh, and there's a conflict-ridden love interest as well. Violent (and not particularly literary) but worthy entry in chop-socky genre. **107m/C VHS, Beta, LV.** Chuck Norris, Leon Isaac Kennedy, David Carradine, L.Q. Jones, Barbara Carrera; *D:* Steve Carver; *W:* H. Kaye Dyal. *VES*

The Loneliest Runner 🐎🐎 **1976** Based on the true story of an Olympic track star who, as a teenager, suffered humiliation as a bed-wetter. The real-life experiences of producer-director Landon are presented in a touching and sensitive manner. Made for television. **74m/C VHS, Beta.** Michael Landon, Lance Kerwin, DeAnn Mears, Brian Keith, Melissa Sue Anderson; *D:* Michael Landon. *WAR, OM*

The Loneliness of the Long Distance Runner 🐎🐎🐎 *Rebel with a Cause* **1962** Courtenay, in his film debut, turns in a powerful performance as an angry young man infected by the poverty and hopelessness of the British slums. His first attempt at crime is a bust and lands him in a boys reformatory where he is recruited for the running team. While training for the big event with a rival school, Redgrave's obsession with winning the race and Courtenay's continued indifference to the outcome lock the two in an intriguing, seemingly one-sided power struggle. Though widely overlooked when first released, it has since been praised as one of the finest teenage angst films of the '60s. Riveting depiction on a boy's rite of passage into manhood. **104m/B VHS, Beta.** *GB* Tom Courtenay, Michael Redgrave, Avis Bunnage, Peter Madden, James Bolam, Julia Foster, Topsy Jane, Frank Finlay; *D:* Tony Richardson; *C:* Walter Lassally; *M:* John Addison. *WAR, SNC*

Lonely Are the Brave 🐎🐎🐎 **1962** A free-spirited cowboy out of sync with the modern age tries to rescue a buddy from a local jail, and in his eventual escape is tracked relentlessly by modern law enforcement. A compelling, sorrowful essay on civilized progress and exploitation of nature. Adapted from the novel "Brave Cowboy" by Edward Abbey. **107m/C VHS, Beta, LV.** Kirk Douglas, Walter Matthau, Gena Rowlands, Carroll O'Connor, George Kennedy; *D:* David Miller; *M:* Jerry Goldsmith. *USH*

The Lonely Guy 🐎🐎½ **1984 (R)** Romantic comedy with Martin as a jilted writer who writes a best-selling book about being a lonely guy and finds stardom does have its rewards. Based on "The Lonely Guy's Book of Life" by Bruce Jay Friedman. **91m/C VHS, Beta, LV.** Steve Martin, Charles Grodin, Judith Ivey, Steve Lawrence, Robyn Douglass, Merv Griffin, Dr. Joyce Brothers; *D:* Arthur Hiller; *W:* Stan Daniels; *M:* Jerry Goldsmith. *USH*

Lonely Hearts 🐎🐎🐎 **1982 (R)** An endearing Australian romantic comedy about a piano tuner, who at 50 finds himself alone after years of caring for his mother, and a sexually insecure spinster, whom he meets through a dating service. Wonderful performances and a good script make this a delightful film that touches the human heart. **95m/C VHS, Beta.** *AU* Wendy Hughes, Norman Kaye, Jon Finlayson, Julia Blake, Jonathon Hardy; *D:* Paul Cox; *W:* John Clarke, Paul Cox. *Australian Film Institute '82: Best Film.*

Lonely Hearts 🐎½ **1991 (R)** A handsome con man works his wiles on a lonely woman in this erotic thriller. Standard plot wastes a good cast. *CW:* Language, violence, and sensuality. **109m/C VHS.** Eric Roberts, Beverly D'Angelo, Joanna Cassidy; *W:* R.E. Daniels. *LIV*

Lonely in America 🐎🐎½ **1990** Charming romantic comedy of a newcomer in New York City. Arun (Chowdhry) has just arrived from India and has quite a few things to learn about life in the

Big Apple. **96m/C VHS, Closed Caption.** Ranjit Chowdhry, Adelaide Miller, Robert Kessler, Melissa Christopher, David Toney, Tirlok Malik; *D:* Barry Brown; *W:* Barry Brown, Satyajit Joy Palit. *ACA*

The Lonely Lady woof! **1983 (R)** Young writer comes to Hollywood with dreams of success, gets involved with the seamy side of moviemaking, and is driven to a nervous breakdown. Pia needs acting lessons, yet it probably wouldn't have helped this trash. Adapted from the novel by Harold Robbins. **92m/C VHS, Beta, LV.** Pia Zadora, Lloyd Bochner, Bibi Besch, Joseph Cali, Ray Liotta; *D:* Peter Sasdy. *Golden Raspberry Awards '83: Worst Picture, Worst Actress (Zadora), Worst Director (Sasdy), Worst Screenplay, Worst Song ("The Way You Do It"). USH*

Lonely Man 🐎🐎½ **1957** A gunfighter tries to end his career, but is urged into one last battle. Strong performances and tight direction make up for weak plot. **87m/B VHS, Beta.** Jack Palance, Anthony Perkins, Neville Brand, Elaine Aiken; *D:* Henry Levin; *C:* Lionel Lindon. *PAR, BAR*

The Lonely Passion of Judith Hearne 🐎🐎🐎 **1987 (R)** A self-effacing Dublin spinster meets a man who gives her his attention, but she must overcome her own self-doubt and crisis of faith. Adapted from Brian Moore's 1955 novel. Excellent performances from both Hoskins and Smith. **116m/C VHS.** *GB* Maggie Smith, Bob Hoskins, Wendy Hiller, Marie Kean, Ian McNeice, Alan Devlin, Rudi Davies, Prunella Scales; *D:* Jack Clayton; *W:* Peter Nelson; *M:* Georges Delerue. *British Academy Awards '88: Best Actress (Smith). CAN*

The Lonely Sex 🐎½ **1959** Creepy and bizarre film in which a maniac kidnaps a young girl and is then harassed by her psychotic housemate. **?m/C VHS.** Jean Evans, Karl Light, Mary Gonzales. *SNC, TPV*

Lonely Trail/Three Texas Steers **1939** Double your pleasure with two early Duke operas. In "Lonely Trail," Wayne dukes it out with dastardly carpetbaggers after the Civil War, while "Three Texas Steers," part of the "Three Mesquiteers" series, has Wayne and company spare a gal rancher/major babe from certain peril. **112m/B VHS.** John Wayne, George "Gabby" Hayes, Ray Corrigan, Raymond Hatton; *D:* George Sherman. *REP*

Lonely Wives 🐎🐎 **1931** A lawyer hires an entertainer to serve as his double because of his marital problems. **86m/B VHS, Beta.** Edward Everett Horton, Patsy Ruth Miller, Esther Ralston; *D:* Russell Mack. *NOS, VYY*

Lonelyhearts 🐎🐎½ **1958** Clift plays a reporter who is assigned the lovelorn column of his paper and gets too immersed in the problems of his readers. Given the superior cast and excellent material, this is a somewhat disappointing adaptation of the brilliant Nathanael West novel "Miss Lonelyhearts." Film debuts of both Stapleton and director Donehue. **101m/B VHS.** Montgomery Clift, Robert Ryan, Myrna Loy, Dolores Hart, Maureen Stapleton, Frank Maxwell, Jackie Coogan, Mike Kellin; *D:* Vincent J. Donehue. *Nominations: Academy Awards '58: Best Supporting Actress (Stapleton). MGM*

Loners 🐎🐎 **1972 (R)** Three teenagers run from the Southwest police after they are accused of murdering a highway patrolman. **80m/C VHS, Beta.** Dean Stockwell, Gloria Grahame, Scott Brady, Alex Dreier, Pat Stich; *D:* Sutton Roley; *W:* Barry Sandler. *NO*

Lonesome Dove 🐎🐎🐎½ **1989** Classic western saga with Duvall and Jones in outstanding roles as two aging ex-Texas Rangers who decide to leave their quiet lives for a last adventure—a cattle drive from Texas to Montana. Along the way they encounter a new love (Lane), a lost love (Huston), and a savage renegade Indian (well-played by Forrest). Based on Larry McMurtry's Pulitzer Prize winning novel, this handsome television miniseries is a finely detailed evocation of the Old West, with a wonderful cast and an equally fine production. Available in a four volume boxed set. Followed by "Return to Lonesome Dove." **480m/C VHS, LV, Closed Caption.** Robert Duvall,

Tommy Lee Jones, Anjelica Huston, Danny Glover, Diane Lane, Rick Schroder, Robert Urich, D.B. Sweeney, Frederic Forrest; **D:** Simon Windsor; **W:** William D. Wittliff; **M:** Basil Poledouris. *CAF, TVC, IME*

Lonesome Trail 🎬½ 1955 Routine Western that differs from the average oater by having the good guys use bows and arrows to fight their battles. **73m/B VHS, Beta.** Jimmy Wakely, Lee White, Lorraine Miller, John James; **D:** Richard Bartlett. *NO*

Long Ago Tomorrow 🎬🎬 *The Raging Moon* 1971 (PG) A paralyzed athlete enters a church-run home for the disabled rather than return to his family as the object of their pity. A love affair with a woman, who shares the same disability, helps the athlete to adapt. **90m/C VHS, Beta.** *GB* Malcolm McDowell, Nanette Newman, Bernard Lee, Georgia Brown, Gerald Sim; **D:** Bryan Forbes. *COL*

The Long Dark Hall 🎬🎬½ 1951 Courtroom drama in which an innocent man is brought to trial when his showgirl mistress is found dead. **86m/B VHS, Beta.** *GB* Rex Harrison, Lilli Palmer, Denis O'Dea, Raymond Huntley, Patricia Wayne, Anthony Dawson; **D:** Anthony Bushell, Reginald Beck. *SNC*

The Long Day Closes 🎬🎬🎬 1992 (PG) It's 1956 Liverpool and 11-year-old Bud (McCormack) is part of a working-class Catholic family who longs to escape from his humdrum life. And how? By going to the movies of course and filling his head with pop songs. Nostalgic view of family life filled with sweet, small everyday moments set in a dreary postwar England. Sequel to Davies's also autobiographical film "Distant Voices, Still Lives." **84m/C VHS, Closed Caption.** *GB* Leigh McCormack, Marjorie Yates, Anthony Watson, Ayse Owens; **D:** Terence Davies; **W:** Terence Davies; **C:** Michael Coulter. *COL*

Long Day's Journey into Night 🎬🎬🎬🎬 1962 A brooding, devastating film based on Eugene O'Neill's most powerful and autobiographical play. Depicts a day in the life of a family deteriorating under drug addiction, alcoholism, and imminent death. Hepburn's performance is outstanding. In 1988, the Broadway version was taped and released on video. **174m/C VHS, LV.** Ralph Richardson, Katharine Hepburn, Dean Stockwell, Jeanne Barr, Jason Robards Jr.; **D:** Sidney Lumet; **W:** Eugene O'Neill; **C:** Boris Kaufman; **M:** Andre Previn. Cannes Film Festival '62: Best Actress (Hepburn); National Board of Review Awards '62: 10 Best Films of the Year, Best Supporting Actor (Robards); Nominations: Academy Awards '62: Best Actress (Hepburn). *REP*

Long Day's Journey into Night 🎬🎬 1988 A taped version of the Broadway production of the epic Eugene O'Neill play about a Southern family deteriorating under the weight of terminal illness, alcoholism and drug abuse. In 1962 a movie adaptation of the play was released with outstanding performances from its cast. **169m/C VHS, Beta.** Jack Lemmon, Bethel Leslie, Peter Gallagher, Kevin Spacey, Jodie Lynne McLintock; **D:** Jonathan Miller. *LIV, VES*

Long Day's Journey Into Night 🎬🎬🎬 1996 Eugene O'Neill's autobiographical play about his family is adapted from Canada's Stratford Festival production. The Tyrones are a troubled Irish-American family: bullying James (Hutt) was a once-great Shakespearean actor who has been typecast in a popular stage potboiler; wife Mary (Henry) is a morphine addict; elder son James, Jr. (Donaldson) is an alcoholic; and O'Neill's alter-ego is Edmund (McCamus), an overly sensitive, consumptive writer. Fine performances, excellent production. **174m/C VHS.** *CA* William Hutt, Martha Henry, Tom McCamus, Peter Donaldson, Martha Burns; **D:** David Wellington; **W:** Eugene O'Neill; **C:** David Franco; **M:** Ron Sures. Genie Awards '96: Best Actor (Hutt), Best Actress (Henry), Best Supporting Actor (Donaldson), Best Supporting Actress (Burns); Toronto-City Award '96: Best Canadian Feature Film; Nominations: Genie Awards '96: Best Actor (McCamus), Best Film, Best Film Editing. *NYR*

The Long Days of Summer 🎬🎬 1980 Set in pre-WWII America, this film portrays a Jewish attorney's struggle against the prejudices of the New England town where he lives. Sequel to "When Every Day Is the Fourth of July." Made for television. **105m/C VHS.** Dean Jones, Joan Hackett, Louanne, Donald Moffat, Andrew Duggan, Michael McGuire; **D:** Dan Curtis. *LIV*

Long Gone 🎬🎬½ 1987 In the fifties, an over-the-hill minor-league player/manager is given a last lease on life and the pennant with two talented rookies and a sexy baseball groupie. Made for cable television. **113m/C VHS, Beta, LV.** William L. Petersen, Henry Gibson, Katy Boyer, Virginia Madsen; **D:** Martin Davidson. *ORI, WAR*

The Long Good Friday 🎬🎬🎬½ 1980 Set in London's dockland, this is a violent story of a crime boss who meets his match. Hoskin's world crumbles over an Easter weekend when his buildings are bombed and his men murdered. He thinks its the work of rival gangsters only to discover an even deadlier threat is behind his troubles. One of the best of the crime genre, with an exquisitely charismatic performance by Hoskins. **109m/C VHS, Beta.** *GB* Bob Hoskins, Helen Mirren, Dave King, Bryan Marshall, George Coulouris, Pierce Brosnan, Derek Thompson, Eddie Constantine, Brian Hall, Stephen Davies, P. H. Moriarty, Paul Freeman, Charles Cork, Paul Barber, Patti Love, Ruby Head, Dexter Fletcher, Roy Alon; **D:** John MacKenzie; **W:** Barrie Keefe; **C:** Phil Meheux; **M:** Francis Monkman. Edgar Allan Poe Awards '82: Best Screenplay. *VTR*

The Long Goodbye 🎬🎬🎬 1973 (R) Raymond Chandler's penultimate novel with the unmistakable Altman touch—which is to say that some of the changes to the story have pushed purist noses out of joint. Gould is cast as an insouciant anti-Marlowe, the film noir atmosphere has been transmuted into a Hollywood film neon, genre jibing abounds, and the ending has been rewritten. But the revamping serves a purpose, which is to make Marlowe a viable character in a contemporary world. Handsomely photographed by Vilmos Zsigmond. Don't miss bulky boy Arnold's cameo (his second film appearance). **112m/C VHS, Beta, LV.** Elliott Gould, Nina Van Pallandt, Sterling Hayden, Henry Gibson, Mark Rydell, David Arkin, Warren Berlinger; **Cameos:** Arnold Schwarzenegger, David Carradine; **D:** Robert Altman; **W:** Leigh Brackett; **C:** Vilmos Zsigmond; **M:** John Williams. National Society of Film Critics Awards '73: Best Cinematography. *MGM, FCT*

The Long Gray Line 🎬🎬🎬 1955 Power gives an outstanding performance as Marty Maher, a humble Irish immigrant who became an institution at West Point. This is the inspiring story of his rise from an unruly cadet to one of the academy's most beloved instructors. O'Hara does a fine job of playing his wife, who like her husband, adopts the young cadets as her own. Director Ford gracefully captures the spirit and honor associated with West Point in this affectionate drama. **138m/C VHS, Closed Caption.** Tyrone Power, Maureen O'Hara, Robert Francis, Donald Crisp, Ward Bond, Betsy Palmer, Phil Carey; **D:** John Ford. *COL*

The Long Haul 🎬🎬 1957 A truck driver becomes involved with crooks as his marriage sours. **88m/C VHS.** Victor Mature, Diana Dors, Patrick Allen, Gene Anderson; **D:** Ken Hughes. *GKK*

The Long, Hot Summer 🎬🎬🎬½ 1958 A tense, well-played adaptation of the William Faulkner story about a wanderer latching himself onto a tyrannical Mississippi family. The first on-screen pairing of Newman and Woodward, and one of the best. Remade for television in 1986. **117m/C VHS, Beta.** Paul Newman, Orson Welles, Joanne Woodward, Lee Remick, Anthony (Tony) Franciosa, Angela Lansbury, Richard Anderson; **D:** Martin Ritt; **W:** Harriet Frank Jr., Irving Ravetch; **C:** Joseph LaShelle; **M:** Alex North. Cannes Film Festival '58: Best Actor (Newman). *FOX*

The Long, Hot Summer 🎬🎬🎬½ 1986 A made-for-television version of the William Faulkner story, "The Hamlet," about a drifter taken under a Southern patriarch's wing. He's bribed

into courting the man's unmarried daughter. Wonderful performances from the entire cast, especially Ivey and surprisingly, Johnson. Remake of the 1958 film with Paul Newman and Joanne Woodward that is on par with the original. **172m/C VHS, Beta, Closed Caption.** Don Johnson, Cybill Shepherd, Judith Ivey, Jason Robards Jr., Ava Gardner, William Russ, Wings Hauser, William Forsythe, Albert Hall; **D:** Stuart Cooper; **M:** Charles Bernstein. *FOX*

The Long Island Four 🎬🎬½ 1980 Four Nazi saboteurs are smitten by the decadent nightlife of the Big Apple in 1942. The late Grafstrom's Super-8 film, based on a true story, was an underground hit. **100m/C VHS.** **D:** Anders Grafstrom. *MWF*

Long John Silver 🎬½ *Long John Silver Returns to Treasure Island* 1953 Famed pirate John Silver plans a return trip to Treasure Island to search for the elusive treasure; unofficial sequel to "Treasure Island" by Disney. **106m/C VHS, Beta.** *AU* Robert Newton, Connie Gilchrist, Kit Taylor, Grant Taylor, Rod Taylor; **D:** Byron Haskin. *GEM, MRV, CAB*

Long Journey Back 🎬🎬 1978 The biographical story of a young woman's rehabilitation after her injury in a school bus accident. Produced for television. **100m/C VHS.** Mike Connors, Cloris Leachman, Stephanie Zimbalist, Katy Kurtzman; **D:** Mel Damski. *LIV*

The Long Kiss Goodnight 🎬🎬½ 1996 (R) Audience-pleasing, blood-soaked, foul-mouthed, and action-packed. Davis obviously has a career as a '90s action star (female division), displaying the proper bravado, and muscles, necessary for her dual role. As mild-mannered, brown-haired Samantha Caine, she's a school-teacher with an eight-year-old daughter, Caitlin (Zima), a nice boyfriend, Hal (Amandes), and amnesia. Sam begins having flashbacks to her past—and what a past it turns out to be. With the help of seedy PI Mitch Henessey (Jackson), she discovers her name is Charly Baltimore and she's a highly trained and very deadly CIA assassin. And the now bleached-blonde, beyond-tough Charly must match her quickly regained lethal abilities with ruthless former nemesis Timothy (Bierko). The body count's high, the blood flows freely, and there's some spectacular stunts. If you're not squeamish it's a guaranteed wild ride. Black got $4 million for his script.**CW:** Substantial amount of strong bloody violence, and for strong language. **120m/C VHS, LV, Closed Caption.** Geena Davis, Samuel L. Jackson, Craig Bierko, Patrick Malahide, Brian Cox, David Morse, Yvonne Zima, Tom Amandes, Melina Kanakaredes, G.D. Spradlin; **D:** Renny Harlin; **W:** Shane Black; **C:** Guillermo Navarro; **M:** Alan Silvestri. *NLC*

The Long, Long Trailer 🎬🎬½ 1954 A couple on their honeymoon find that trailer life is more than they bargained for. Lots of fun with charming direction from Minelli, and Ball's incredible slapstick style. **97m/C VHS, LV, Closed Caption.** Desi Arnaz Sr., Lucille Ball, Marjorie Main, Keenan Wynn; **D:** Vincente Minnelli. *MGM, FCT, BTV*

Long Pants 🎬🎬🎬 1927 Langdon, in a typical man/child role, plays a naive young man who gets his first pair of long pants, which officially ushers him into adulthood. He immediately falls for the wrong gal (Bonner), a drug runner who winds up in jail. So he breaks her out and they go on the lam. **58m/B VHS.** Harry Langdon, Priscilla Bonner, Alma Bennett; **D:** Frank Capra. *KIV*

The Long Riders 🎬🎬🎬 1980 (R) Excellent mythic western in which the Jesse James and Cole Younger gangs raid banks, trains, and stagecoaches in post-Civil War Missouri. Stylish, meticulous and a violent look back, with one of the better slow-motion shootouts in Hollywood history. Notable for the portrayal of four sets of brothers by four Hollywood brother sets. Complimented by excellent Cooder score. **100m/C VHS, Beta, LV.** Stacy Keach, James Keach, Randy Quaid, Dennis Quaid, David Carradine, Keith Carradine, Robert Carradine, Christopher Guest, Nicholas Guest, Pamela Reed, Savannah Smith, James Whitmore Jr., Harry Carey Jr.; *D:* Walter Hill; *W:* Stacy Keach, James Keach, Bill Bryden; *M:* Ry Cooder. MGM

Long Road Home 🎬🎬½ **1991 (PG)** Migrant family must decide between working under inhumane conditions or risk losing everything by joining the labor movement during the depression. TV movie. **?m/C VHS.** Mark Harmon, John Evans, Adam Horovitz, Lee Purcell, Leon Russom, Donald Sutherland, Morgan Weisser; *D:* John Korty. *NHO*

Long Shadows 🎬½ **1986** An analysis of how the resonating effects of the Civil War can still be felt on society, via interviews with a number of noted writers, historians, civil rights activists and politicians. **88m/C VHS, Beta.** Robert Penn Warren, Studs Terkel, Jimmy Carter, Robert Coles, Tom Wicker. *JAF*

The Long Ships 🎬 **1964** Silly Viking saga finds brothers Rolfe (Widmark) and Orm (Tamblyn) stealing a ship and heading off in search of a solid-gold bell. Among their trials are a mutinous crew and battling Moorish Prince El Mansuh (Poitier). Something to be left off the resume. **125m/C VHS.** Richard Widmark, Russ Tamblyn, Sidney Poitier, Oscar Homolka, Rosanna Schiaffino, Beba Loncar, Lionel Jeffries, Edward Judd; *D:* Jack Cardiff; *W:* Beverley Cross, Berkely Mather; *C:* Christopher Challis; *M:* Dusan Radic. *COL*

Long Shot **1981** Two foosball enthusiasts work their way through local tournaments to make enough money to make it to the World Championships in Tahoe. **100m/C VHS, Beta.** Ian Giatti. *NO*

Long Time Gone 🎬 **1986** An over-the-hill detective tries to solve a murder while dealing with his bratty, alienated 11-year-old son. Made for television. **97m/C VHS, Beta.** Paul LeMat, Wil Wheaton, Ann Dusenberry, Barbara Stock; *D:* Robert Butler. *NO*

The Long Voyage Home 🎬🎬🎬½ **1940** A talented cast performs this must-see screen adaptation of Eugene O'Neill's play about crew members aboard a merchant steamer in 1939. Wayne plays a young lad from Sweden who is trying to get home and stay out of trouble as he and the other seaman get shore leave. **105m/B VHS, Beta, LV.** John Wayne, Thomas Mitchell, Ian Hunter, Barry Fitzgerald, Mildred Natwick, John Qualen; *D:* John Ford; *C:* Gregg Toland. National Board of Review Awards '40: 10 Best Films of the Year; New York Film Critics Awards '40: Best Director (Ford); Nominations: Academy Awards '40: Best Black and White Cinematography, Best Film Editing, Best Picture, Best Screenplay, Best Original Score. *WAR*

The Long Walk Home 🎬🎬🎬 **1989 (PG)** In Montgomery Alabama, in the mid 1950s, sometime after Rosa Parks refused to sit in the black-designated back of the bus, Martin Luther King Jr. led a bus boycott. Spacek is the affluent wife of a narrow-minded businessman while Goldberg is their struggling maid. When Spacek discovers that Goldberg is supporting the boycott by walking the nine-mile trek to work, she sympathizes and tries to help, antagonizing her husband. The plot marches inevitably toward a white-on-white showdown on racism while quietly exploring gender equality between the women. Outstanding performances by Spacek and Goldberg, and a great 50s feel. **95m/C VHS, LV, Closed Caption.** Sissy Spacek, Whoopi Goldberg, Dwight Schultz, Ving Rhames, Dylan Baker; *D:* Richard Pearce; *W:* John Cork; *C:* Roger Deakins; *M:* George Fenton. *LIV, IME, FCT*

A Long Way Home 🎬🎬 **1981** A television movie about a grown man searching for his long-lost siblings, after the three of them were given up for adoption after birth. **97m/C VHS, Beta.** Timothy Hutton, Brenda Vaccaro, Rosanna Arquette, Paul Regina, George Dzundza, John Lehne, Bonnie Bartlett; *D:* Robert Markowitz; *C:* Ralf Bode; *M:* William Goldstein. *LIV*

The Long Weekend 🎬 **1986** When a vacationing couple goes camping and carelessly destroys a forest, Mother Nature turns her powers of retribution on them. **95m/C VHS, Beta.** *AU TWE*

The Longest Day 🎬🎬🎬½ **1962** The complete story of the D-Day landings at Normandy on June 6, 1944, as seen through the eyes of American, French, British, and German participants. Exhaustively accurate details and extremely talented cast make this one of the all-time great Hollywood epic productions. The first of the big budget, all-star war productions; based on the book by Cornelius Ryan. Three directors share credit. Also available in a colorized version. **179m/C VHS, Beta, LV.** John Wayne, Richard Burton, Red Buttons, Robert Mitchum, Henry Fonda, Robert Ryan, Paul Anka, Mel Ferrer, Edmond O'Brien, Fabian, Sean Connery, Roddy McDowall, Richard Beymer, Curt Jurgens, Rod Steiger, Jean-Louis Barrault, Peter Lawford, Robert Wagner, Sal Mineo, Leo Genn, Richard Beymer, Jeffrey Hunter, Stuart Whitman, Eddie Albert, Tom Tryon, Alexander Knox, Ray Danton, Kenneth More, Richard Todd, Gert Frobe, Christopher Lee; *D:* Ken Annakin; *W:* Bernhard Wicki; *M:* Maurice Jarre. Academy Awards '62: Best Black and White Cinematography, Best Special Effects; National Board of Review Awards '62: 10 Best Films of the Year; Nominations: Academy Awards '62: Best Art Direction/Set Decoration (B & W), Best Film Editing, Best Picture. *FXV, TLF, HMV*

The Longest Drive 🎬🎬 *The Quest* **1976** Two brothers comb the wildest parts of the West for their sister, whom they believe is living with Indians. A made for television movie originally titled "The Quest," which became a brief television series. Highlights include colorful performances from the veteran actors and a unique horse/camel race. A continuation of the series is available on video as "The Captive: The Longest Drive 2." **92m/C VHS, LV.** Kurt Russell, Tim Matheson, Brian Keith, Keenan Wynn, Neville Brand, Cameron Mitchell, Morgan Woodward, Iron Eyes Cody, Luke Askew; *D:* Lee H. Katzin. *THV*

The Longest Yard 🎬🎬½ **1974 (R)** A one-time pro football quarterback, now an inmate, organizes his fellow convicts into a football team to play against the prison guards. Filmed on location at Georgia State Prison. **121m/C VHS, Beta, LV.** Burt Reynolds, Eddie Albert, Bernadette Peters, Ed Lauter, Richard Kiel; *D:* Robert Aldrich; *W:* Tracy Keenan Wynn; *C:* Joseph Biroc. Golden Globe Awards '75: Best Film—Musical/Comedy; Nominations: Academy Awards '74: Best Film Editing. *PAR*

The Longshot woof! **1986 (PG-13)** Four bumblers try to raise cash to put on a sure-bet racetrack tip in this sorry comedy. Mike Nichols is the executive producer. **89m/C VHS, Beta.** Tim Conway, Harvey Korman, Jack Weston, Ted Wass, Jonathan Winters, Stella Stevens, Anne Meara; *D:* Paul Bartel; *W:* Tim Conway, John Myhers; *M:* Charles Fox. *CNG*

Longtime Companion 🎬🎬🎬½ **1990 (R)** Critically acclaimed film follows a group of gay men and their friends during the 1980s. The closely knit group monitors the progression of the AIDS virus from early news reports until it finally hits home and begins to take the lives of their loved ones. One of the first films to look at the situation in an intelligent and touching manner. Produced by the PBS "American Playhouse" company. **100m/C VHS.** Stephen Caffrey, Patrick Cassidy, Brian Cousins, Bruce Davison, John Dossett, Mark Lamos, Dermot Mulroney, Mary-Louise Parker, Michael Schoeffling, Campbell Scott, Robert Joy, Brad O'Hara; *D:* Norman Rene; *W:* Craig Lucas; *C:* Tony Jennelli. Golden Globe Awards '91: Best Supporting Actor (Davison); Independent Spirit Awards '91: Best Supporting Actor (Davison); New York Film Critics Awards '90: Best Supporting Actor (Davison); National Society of Film Critics Awards '90: Best Supporting Actor (Davison); Sundance Film Festival '90: Audience Award; Nominations: Academy Awards '90: Best Supporting Actor (Davison). *THV, FCT, BTV*

Look Back in Anger 🎬🎬🎬½ **1958** Based on John Osbourne's famous play, the first British "angry young man" film, in which a squalor-living lad takes out his anger on the world by seducing his friend's wife. **99m/B VHS, Beta, LV, GB** Richard Burton, Claire Bloom, Mary Ure, Edith Evans, Gary Raymond; *D:* Tony Richardson; *W:* John Osborne; *C:* Oswald Morris; *M:* John Addison. National Board of Review Awards '59: 10 Best Films of the Year.

Look Back in Anger 🎬🎬 **1980** A working class man angered by society's hypocrisy lashes out at his upper class wife, his mistress, and the world. Inferior remake of 1958 film version starring Richard Burton, based on '50s stage hit. **100m/C VHS, Beta.** Malcolm McDowell, Lisa Banes, Fran Brill, Raymond Hardie, Lindsay Anderson. *WAR, OM*

Look Back in Anger 🎬🎬🎬 **1989** There's something about John Osborne's play that brings out the angry young man in British leads. Richard Burton played Osborne's irascible guy in 1958, Malcom McDowell looked back angrily in '80, and now Branagh convincingly vents his spleen on wife and mistress in this made for British TV production. Director Jones earlier filmed "84 Charing Cross Road" and "Jacknife." **114m/C VHS.** *GB* Kenneth Branagh, Emma Thompson, Gerard Horan, Siobhan Redmond; *D:* David Jones. *HBO*

Look for the Silver Lining 🎬🎬½ **1949** Insipid musical biography of Broadway star Marilyn Miller (Haver). Bolger is the highlight as Miller's mentor from vaudeville to the Great White Way. 🎵Look for the Silver Lining; Whip-Poor-Will; A Kiss in the Dark; Pirouette; Just a Memory; Time On My Hands; Wild Rose; Shine On Harvest Moon; Back, Back, Back to Baltimore. **100m/C VHS, Beta.** June Haver, Ray Bolger, Charlie Ruggles, Rosemary DeCamp, S.Z. Sakall; *D:* David Butler; *W:* Phoebe Ephron, Henry Ephron, Marian Spitzer. Nominations: Academy Awards '49: Scoring of a Musical. *MGM, FCT, BTV*

Look Out Sister 🎬🎬🎬 **1948** Jordan and an all-black cast star in this musical satire of westerns. "Two Gun" Jordan saves a dude ranch from foreclosure and wins the girl. Lots of black culture, slang and music from the '40s. Broad but enjoyable humor. 🎵Caldonia; Don't Burn the Candle at Both Ends. **64m/B VHS.** Louis Jordan, Suzette Harbin, Monte Hawley, Maceo B. Sheffield; *D:* Bud Pollard. *NOS*

Look Who's Laughing 🎬🎬 **1941** Bergen's plane lands in a town conveniently populated by radio stars. Not much plot here, but it might be worth a look to fans of the stars including Jim and Marion Jordan, better known as Fibber McGee and Molly. **79m/B VHS, Beta, LV.** Edgar Bergen, Jim Jordan, Marian Jordan, Lucille Ball, Harold Peary, Lee Bonnell, Charles Halton; *D:* Allan Dwan. *TTC, MLB*

Look Who's Talking 🎬🎬🎬 **1989 (PG-13)** When Alley bears the child of a married, and quite fickle man, she sets her sights elsewhere in search of the perfect father; Travolta is the cabbie with more on his mind than driving Alley around and babysitting. All the while, the baby gives us his views via the voice of Bruce Willis. A very light comedy with laughs for the whole family. **90m/C VHS, Beta, LV, Closed Caption.** John Travolta, Kirstie Alley, Olympia Dukakis, George Segal, Abe Vigoda; *D:* Amy Heckerling; *W:* Amy Heckerling; *M:* David Kitay; *V:* Bruce Willis. People's Choice Awards '90: Best Film—Musical/Comedy. *COL, RDG*

Look Who's Talking Now 🎬½ **1993 (PG-13)** Continuing to wring revenue from a tired premise, the family dogs throw in their two cents in the second sequel to "Look Who's Talking." For anyone who thinks Diane Keaton's hair makes her look a little like a hound dog, here's a chance to visualize her as a similarly long-eared poodle with an attitude. DeVito is also cast in character as the voice of a rough street-smart mutt, who happens to get thrown into the same household as the bosses' pure-bred poodle. Sparks, Alpo, and butt jokes fly as the dogs mark their territory. Meanwhile, dimwit wife Alley is worried that husband Travolta is having an affair, and is determined to get him back. **CW:** Off-color dialogue. **95m/C VHS, LV, 8mm, Closed Caption.** John Travolta, Kirstie Alley, Olympia Dukakis, George Segal, Lysette Anthony; *D:* Tom Ropelewski; *W:* Tom Ropelewski, Leslie Dixon; *M:* William Ross; *V:* Diane Keaton, Danny DeVito. *COL*

Look Who's Talking, Too ✂ 1990

(PG-13) If Academy Awards for Stupidest Sequel and Lamest Dialogue existed, this diaper drama would have cleaned up. The second go-round throws the now married accountant-cabbie duo into a marital tailspin when Alley's babysitting brother moves in and the Saturday Night dancer moves out. Meanwhile, Willis cum baby smartasses incessantly. A once-clever gimmick now unencumbered by plot; not advised for linear thinkers. The voice of Arnold, though, is a guarantee you'll get one laugh for your rental. **81m/C VHS, LV, 8mm, Closed Caption.** Kirstie Alley, John Travolta, Olympia Dukakis, Elias Koteas; **D:** Amy Heckerling; **V:** Bruce Willis, Mel Brooks, Damon Wayans, Roseanne. *COL*

The Lookalike ✂✂ 1990 (PG-13)

A made for cable adaptation of Kate Wilhelm's novel. Bereaved mother Gilbert questions her sanity when she thinks she sees her daughter after she was killed in an automobile accident. Could this girl provide answers to questions about her past? **88m/C VHS, Closed Caption.** Melissa Gilbert, Diane Ladd, Frances Lee McCain, Jason Scott Lee, Thaao Penghlis; **D:** Gary Nelson; **W:** Linda J. Bergman. *USH*

Looker ✂½ 1981 (PG)

Stunning models are made even more beautiful by a plastic surgeon, but one by one they begin to die. Finney plays the Beverly Hills surgeon who decides to investigate when he starts losing all his clients. **94m/C VHS, Beta, LV, Closed Caption.** Albert Finney, James Coburn, Susan Dey, Leigh Taylor-Young; **D:** Michael Crichton; **W:** Michael Crichton. *WAR*

Lookin' to Get Out ✂✂½ 1982 (R)

Comedy about two gamblers running from their debts. They wind up at the MGM Grand in Las Vegas trying to get out of a mess. **70m/C VHS, Beta.** Ann-Margret, Jon Voight, Burt Young; **D:** Hal Ashby; **W:** John Beal, Miles Goodman. *FOX*

Looking for Miracles ✂✂½ 1990 (G)

Two brothers, separated during the Depression because of poverty, get a chance to cultivate brotherly love when they're reunited in 1935. A Wonderworks production based on the A.E. Hochner novel. **104m/C VHS, LV, Closed Caption.** Zachary Bennett, Greg Spottiswood, Joe Flaherty. *TOU, DIS, FCT*

Looking for Mr. Goodbar ✂✂ 1977

(R) Young teacher Keaton seeks companionship and love by frequenting single's bars and furthers her self-destruction by her aimless intake of drugs and alcohol. In need of a father figure, she makes herself available to numerous men and eventually regrets her hedonistic behavior. Unpleasant, aimless characters do little for this dreary film, whose sexual theme sparked a bit of public conversation when first released. Based on the bestselling novel by Judith Rossner. Oscar nominations for supporting actress Weld, and cinematography. **136m/C VHS, Beta, LV.** Diane Keaton, Tuesday Weld, Richard Gere, Tom Berenger, William Atherton, Richard Kiley; **D:** Richard Brooks; **W:** Richard Brooks; **C:** William A. Fraker. Nominations: Academy Awards '77: Best Cinematography, Best Supporting Actress (Weld). *PAR*

Looking for Richard ✂✂✂ 1996 (PG-13)

A Shakespearean "Vanya on 42nd Street," "Richard" is the first semi-documentary addition to the barrage of Bard adaptations. Pacino's protracted pic dwells on a filmmaker's struggles to understand the play. Punctuated with comic relief, Pacino makes a pilgrimage to the Globe Theatre, taps Brit theater heavyweights Gielgud and Redgrave for thoughts on interpreting Shakespeare, and combs New York for candid "man in the street" impressions in a quest to bring his subject to a wider public. Over the course of four years, Pacino, in various stages of facial hair growth, plays the deformed usurper with a cast of worthy Americans (Spacey, Kline, Ryder, Baldwin, and Quinn), illustrating key scenes of the play.**CW:** Brief strong language and some scenes of violence. **108m/C VHS, Closed Caption.** Alec Baldwin, Winona Ryder, Kevin Spacey, Aidan Quinn, F. Murray Abraham, Kenneth Branagh, Kevin Conway, John Gielgud, James Earl Jones, Kevin Kline, Estelle Parsons, Vanessa Redgrave, Harris Yulin, Penelope Allen, Al Pacino; **D:** Al Pacino; **C:** Robert Leacock; **M:** Howard Shore. Directors Guild of America Awards '96: Best Feature Documentary (Pacino). *FXV*

The Looking Glass War ✂✂ 1969

(PG) Polish defector is sent behind the Iron Curtain on a final mission to photograph a rocket in East Berlin. He's guided by frustrated British security officers Rogers and Richardson, who both offer sly turns. An otherwise slow-moving adaptation of John Le Carre's bestselling spy novel. **108m/C VHS, Beta.** GB Christopher Jones, Ralph Richardson, Pia Degermark, Anthony Hopkins, Susan George; **D:** Frank Pierson; **W:** Frank Pierson. *COL, MLB*

Looney Looney Looney Bugs Bunny Movie ✂✂✂ 1981 (G)

Friz Freleng's Looney Looney Looney Bugs Bunny Movie 1981 (G) A feature-length compilation of classic Warner Brothers cartoons tied together with new animation. Cartoon stars featured include Bugs Bunny, Elmer Fudd, Porky Pig, Yosemite Sam, Duffy Duck and Foghorn Leghorn. **80m/C VHS, Beta.** **D:** Isadore "Friz" Freleng, Chuck Jones, Bob Clampett; **V:** Mel Blanc, June Foray. *WAR, FCT*

Loophole ✂✂

Break In 1983 An out-of-work architect, hard pressed for money, joins forces with an elite team of expert criminals, in a scheme to make off with millions from the most established holding bank's vault. **105m/C VHS, Beta.** GB Albert Finney, Martin Sheen, Susannah York, Robert Morley, Colin Blakely, Jonathan Pryce; **D:** John Quested. *MED, HHE, MTX*

Loose Cannons ✂ 1990 (R)

Yet another mismatched-cop-partner comedy, wherein a mystery is ostensibly solved by a veteran cop and a schizophrenic detective. **95m/C VHS, Beta, LV, Closed Caption.** Gene Hackman, Dan Aykroyd, Dom DeLuise, Ronny Cox, Nancy Travis, David Alan Grier; **D:** Bob (Benjamin) Clark; **W:** Bob (Benjamin) Clark, Richard Matheson. *COL*

Loose Connections ✂✂ 1987

A feminist driving to a convention in Europe advertises for a travelmate, and gets a hopeless chauvinist who is masquerading as a gay man in this offbeat cult comedy. **90m/C VHS, Beta.** GB Lindsay Duncan, Stephen Rea, Robbie Coltrane; **D:** Richard Eyre. *TPV*

Loose in New York ✂✂ 198?

Much to her surprise, a cynical socialite begins to fall for her computer-arranged mate. **91m/C VHS, Beta.** Rita Tushingham, Aldo Maccione; **D:** Gian Polidoro. *NO*

Loose Screws ✂ 1985 (R)

Four perverted teenagers are sent to a restrictive academy where they continue their lewd ways in this stupid sequel to "Screwballs." **75m/C VHS, Beta.** CA Bryan Genesse, Karen Wood, Alan Deveau, Jason Warren; **D:** Rafal Zeilinski; **W:** Michael Cory. *LIV*

Loose Shoes ✂✂

Coming Attractions 1980 (R) A collection of vignettes that satirize movie trailers, teasers and special announcements. Murray's film debut. **84m/C VHS, Beta.** Bill Murray, Howard Hesseman, Jaye P. Morgan, Buddy Hackett, Misty Rowe, Susan Tyrrell; **D:** Ira Miller. *FOX*

Loot...Give Me Money, Honey! ✂✂½ 1970

Black comedy about a motley crew of greed-driven golddiggers who chase after a heisted fortune in jewels, which is hidden in a coffin belonging to one of the thieves' mother. From Joe Orton's play. **101m/C VHS, Beta.** GB Richard Attenborough, Lee Remick, Hywel Bennett, Milo O'Shea, Roy Holder; **D:** Silvio Narizzano. *NO*

Lord Jim ✂✂✂ 1965

A ship officer (O'Toole) commits an act of cowardice that results in his dismissal and disgrace, which leads him to the Far East in search of self-respect. Excellent supporting cast. Based on Joseph Conrad's novel. **154m/C VHS, Beta.** Peter O'Toole, James Mason, Curt Jurgens, Eli Wallach, Jack Hawkins, Paul Lukas, Akim Tamiroff, Daliah Lavi, Andrew Keir, Jack MacGowran, Walter Gotell; **D:** Richard Brooks; **W:** Richard Brooks; **C:** Frederick A. (Freddie) Young. *COL, TVC*

Lord of Illusions ✂✂½

Clive Barker's Lord of Illusions 1995 (R) New York P.I. Harry D'Amour (Bakula), who has an affinity for the occult, becomes involved with Dorothea (Janssen), the supposed widow of magician Philip Swann (O'Connor). As Harry investigates he discovers some terrifying secrets, including resurrected cult leader Nix (Von Bargen). Gruesome effects rather than excessive gore but you'll feel like you've been dropped in the middle of a plot without a clear idea what's happening. Bakula's Harry obviously has more stories to tell but Janssen's Dorothea, while attractive, is just around to cower. Barker directs from his own short story "The Last Illusion." The unrated director's cut clocks in at 120 minutes.**CW:** Strong violence and gore; language; sexuality. **109m/C VHS, LV, Closed Caption.** Scott Bakula, Famke Janssen, Kevin J. O'Connor, Daniel von Bargen, Joel Swetow, Barry Sherman, Jordan Marder, Joseph Latimore, Vincent Schiavelli; **D:** Clive Barker; **W:** Clive Barker; **C:** Ronn Schmidt. *MGM*

Lord of the Flies ✂✂✂½ 1963

Proper English schoolboys stranded on a desert island during a nuclear war are transformed into savages. A study in greed, power, and the innate animalistic/survivalistic instincts of human nature. Based on William Golding's novel, which he described as a journey to the darkness of the human heart. The laser disc version contains outtakes, the film trailer, and additional material. **91m/B VHS, Beta, LV.** GB James Aubrey, Tom Chapin, Hugh Edwards, Roger Elwin, Tom Gamen; **D:** Peter Brook; **W:** Peter Brook. National Board of Review Awards '63: 10 Best Films of the Year. *HMV, FUS*

Lord of the Flies ✂✂ 1990 (R)

Inferior second filming of the famed William Golding novel about schoolboys marooned on a desert island who gradually degenerate into savages. Lushly photographed, yet redundant and poorly acted. **90m/C VHS, Beta, LV, 8mm, Closed Caption.** Balthazar Getty, Danuel Pipoly, Chris Furrh, Badgett Dale, Edward Taft, Andrew Taft; **D:** Harry Hook. *COL, TVC, NLC*

The Lord of the Rings ✂✂ 1978 (PG)

An animated interpretation of Tolkien's classic tale of the hobbits, wizards, elves, and dwarfs who inhabit Middle Earth. Animator Ralph Bakshi used live motion animation (roto-scoping) to give his characters more life-like and human motion. Well done in spite of the difficulty of adapting from Tolkien's highly detailed and lengthy works. **128m/C VHS, Beta.** **D:** Ralph Bakshi; **W:** Peter S. Beagle, J.C. (Chris) Conkling; **V:** Christopher Guard, John Hurt. *REP, FCT*

The Lords of Discipline ✂✂½ 1983

(R) A military academy cadet is given the unenviable task of protecting a black freshman from racist factions at a southern school circa 1964. Based on Pat Conroy's autobiographical novel. **103m/C VHS, Beta, LV.** David Keith, Robert Prosky, Barbara Babcock, Judge Reinhold, G.D. Spradlin, Rick Rossovich, Michael Biehn; **D:** Franc Roddam; **C:** Brian Tufano; **M:** Howard Blake. *PAR*

The Lords of Flatbush ✂✂½ 1974

(PG) Four street toughs battle against their own maturation and responsibilities in 1950s Brooklyn. Winkler introduces the leather-clad hood he's made a career of and Stallone introduces a character not unlike Rocky. Interesting slice of life. **88m/C VHS, Beta, LV.** Sylvester Stallone, Perry King, Henry Winkler, Susan Blakely, Armand Assante, Paul Mace; **D:** Stephen Verona, Martin Davidson; **M:** Joseph Brooks. *COL*

Lords of Magick ✂ 1988 (PG-13)

Two warriors chase an evil sorcerer and the princess he's kidnapped across time to the 20th century. **98m/C VHS, Beta.** Jarrett Parker, Matt Gauthier, Brendan Dillon Jr.; **D:** David Marsh. *PSM*

Lords of the Deep

woof! 1989 (PG-13) A Roger Corman cheapie about underwater technicians trapped on the ocean floor with a race of aliens. A film rushed out to capitalize on the undersea sci-fi subgenre highlighted by "The Abyss." **95m/C VHS, Beta.** Bradford Dillman, Priscilla

Barnes, Melody Ryane, Eb Lottimer, Daryl Haney; **D:** Mary Ann Fisher; **W:** Daryl Haney, Howard R. Cohen. *MGM*

Lorenzo's Oil 🐾🐾🐾 1992 **(PG-13)** Based on the true story of Augusto and Michaela Odone's efforts to find a cure for their 5-year-old, Lorenzo, diagnosed with the rare and incurable disease ALD (Adrenoleukodystrophy). Confronted by a slow-moving and clinically cold medical community, the Odones embark on their own quest for a cure. Sarandon delivers an outstanding and emotionally charged performance as Lorenzo's determined mother. Nolte is his equally devoted Italian father, complete with black hair and hand gestures. They are a powerful presence in a film which could have easily degenerated into a made-for-TV movie, but is instead a tribute to what love and hope can accomplish. **CW:** Thematic elements. 135m/C **VHS, Beta, LV, Closed Caption.** Nick Nolte, Susan Sarandon, Zach O'Malley-Greenberg, Peter Ustinov, Kathleen Wilhoite, Gerry Bamman, Margo Martindale, James Rebhorn, Ann Hearn; **D:** George Miller; **W:** Nick Enright, George Miller; **C:** John Seale. Nominations: Academy Awards '92: Best Actress (Sarandon), Best Original Screenplay. *USH, MOV, BTV*

The Loretta Young Show 🐾🐾 1954 Two enchanting episodes of the popular fifties series "The Loretta Young Show," entitled "Somebody Else's Dream" and "So Bright the Light." Other episodes are also available, two per tape. 60m/C **VHS, Beta.** Loretta Young. *MVC*

Lorna Doone 🐾🐾½ 1922 A young girl of royal descent is kidnapped and raised by the bandit Doone family in the highlands of Scotland. Adapted from the novel by R.D. Blackmore. 79m/B **VHS.** Madge Bellamy, John Bowers; **D:** Maurice Tourneur. *GPV*

Lorna Doone 🐾🐾½ 1934 Early version of the R.D. Blackmore novel about an English farmer who falls in love with the daughter of an outlaw family. Set in rural England in the 1600s; remade in 1951 and 1990. 90m/B **VHS.** **GB** Victoria Hopper, John Loder, Margaret Lockwood, Roy Emerton, Mary Clare, Edward Rigby, Roger Livesey; **D:** Basil Dean; **W:** Miles Malleson. *FCT*

Lorna Doone 🐾🐾½ 1990 **(PG)** Classic romance set in 17th-century England and based on the novel by R.D. Blackmore. John Ridd (Bean) vows to destroy the land-grabbing Doone family, whom he blames for the death of his parents. Then he meets, and immediately falls in love with, the beautiful and innocent Lorna Doone (Walker). Made for British television. 90m/C **VHS, Beta, Closed Caption. GB** Sean Bean, Polly Walker, Clive Owen, Billie Whitelaw; **D:** Andrew Grieve; **W:** Matthew Jacobs. *PAR*

Los Olvidados 🐾🐾🐾½ *The Young and the Damned* 1950 From surrealist Bunuel, a powerful story of the poverty and violence of young people's lives in Mexico's slums. In Spanish with English subtitles. 81m/B **VHS, Beta, 8mm. MX** Alfonso Mejias, Roberto Cobo; **D:** Luis Bunuel. Cannes Film Festival '51: Best Director (Bunuel), Best Film. *VYY, HHT, DVT*

The Losers 🐾½ 1970 **(R)** Four motorcyclists are hired by the U.S. Army to rescue a presidential advisor who is being held captive by Asian bad guys. 96m/C **VHS, Beta.** William Smith, Bernie Hamilton, Adam Roarke, Houston Savage, Brad Johnson, Vernon Wells; **D:** Jack Starrett. *ACA*

Losin' It 🐾🐾 1982 **(R)** Four teens travel across the Mexican border to Tijuana on a journey to lose their virginity. Cruise meets a married woman who says she is in town for a divorce, while the others become caught up in frenzied undertakings of their own. 104m/C **VHS, Beta, LV.** Tom Cruise, John Stockwell, Shelley Long, Jackie Earle Haley; **D:** Curtis Hanson. *NLC*

Losing Chase 🐾🐾½ 1996 **(R)** Bacon makes his directorial debut in this cable drama that features wife Sedgwick as Elizabeth, mother's helper to Chase (Mirren) and Richard Philips (Bridges) at their summer home on Martha's Vineyard. Chase is still recovering from a mental breakdown, having spent several months in an institution, and she resents Elizabeth's presence, constantly criticizing her. But when the two women are alone together a confusing and emotional bond gradually begins to form between them. **CW:** Brief language. 95m/C **VHS, Closed Caption.** Helen Mirren, Kyra Sedgwick, Beau Bridges; **D:** Kevin Bacon; **W:** Anne Meredith; **C:** Dick Quinlan; **M:** Michael Bacon. *EVE*

Losing Isaiah 🐾🐾🐾 1994 **(R)** "Kramer vs. Kramer" meets the movie-of-the-week in this controversial and emotionally moving story of a social worker (Lange) who adopts the title character, an African American baby abandoned by his drug-addicted mother (Berry). Courtroom battle ensues when four years later mom, now clean and sober, discovers Isaiah is alive. She enlists the aid of a lawyer (Jackson) known for his high-profile, racially charged cases. Lange and Berry lead the parade of fine performances. Taking on some volatile issues, director Gyllenhaal manages (for the most part) to refrain from melodrama. Based on the novel by Seth Margolis. **CW:** Drug related material; brief strong language. 108m/C **VHS, Beta, Closed Caption.** Jessica Lange, Halle Berry, David Strathairn, Samuel L. Jackson, Cuba Gooding Jr., Latanya Richardson; **D:** Stephen Gyllenhaal; **W:** Naomi Foner; **C:** Andrzej Bartkowiak; **M:** Mark Isham. *PAR*

Lost 🐾½ 1983 A young girl runs away into the wilderness because of the resentment she feels toward her new stepfather. 92m/C **VHS, Beta.** Sandra Dee, Don Stewart, Ken Curtis, Jack Elam, Sheila Newhouse. *PSM*

Lost 🐾🐾 1986 When their boat capsizes in the Pacific, three sailors desperately cling to life, drifting aimlessly for 74 days. Based on a true story, this film is adult-fare. 93m/C **VHS, Beta.** **CA** Michael Hogan, Helen Shaver, Kenneth Welsh; **D:** Peter Rowe. *HHE, BMV*

Lost and Found 🐾🐾½ 1979 **(PG)** An American professor of English and an English film production secretary fall in love on a skiing vacation. Good cast but Segal and Jackson did romance better in "A Touch of Class." 104m/C **VHS, Beta.** George Segal, Glenda Jackson, Maureen Stapleton, Hollis McLaren, John Cunningham, Paul Sorvino, John Candy, Martin Short; **D:** Melvin Frank; **W:** Jack Rose. *GKK*

Lost Angels 🐾🐾½ 1989 **(R)** A glossy "Rebel Without a Cause" '80s reprise providing a no-holds-barred portrait of life in the fast lane. A wealthy, disaffected San Fernando Valley youth immerses himself in sex, drugs and rock 'n' roll. Ultimately he is arrested and sent by his parents to a youth home, where a dedicated therapist assists his tortuous road back to reality. 116m/C **VHS, Beta, LV, Closed Caption.** Donald Sutherland, Adam Horovitz, Amy Locane, Kevin Tighe, John C. McGinley, Graham Beckel, Park Overall, Don Bloomfield, Celia Weston; **D:** Hugh Hudson; **W:** Michael Weller; **M:** Philippe Sarde. *ORI*

Lost Boundaries 🐾🐾½ 1949 Respected physician Scott Carter (debut role for Ferrer) and his family live and work in a small New Hampshire town, hiding the fact that they are black, passing for white, in their segregated society. But then the truth becomes known. Strong, if slow-moving, and based on a true story; the use of white leads for black roles was common casting. 99m/B **VHS.** Mel Ferrer, Beatrice Pearson, Richard Hylton, Susan Douglas, Canada Lee, Carleton Carpenter, Seth Arnold, Wendell Holmes; **D:** Alfred Werker; **W:** Virginia Shaler, Eugene Ling, Charles A. Palmer, Furland de Kay; **C:** William J. Miller; **M:** Louis Applebaum. *WAR*

The Lost Boys 🐾🐾 1987 **(R)** Santa Cruz seems like a dull town when Michael, his younger brother, and their divorced mom move into their eccentric grandfather's home. But when Michael falls for a pretty girl with some hard-living friends he takes on more than he imagines—these partying teens are actually a group of vampires. Some humor, some bloodletting violence, and an attractive cast help out this updated vampire tale. Rock-filled soundtrack. 97m/C **VHS, Beta, LV, 8mm, Closed Caption.** Jason Patric, Kiefer Sutherland, Corey Haim, Jami Gertz, Dianne Wiest, Corey Feldman, Barnard Hughes, Edward Herrmann, Billy Wirth; **D:** Joel Schumacher; **W:** Jeffrey Boam; **C:** Michael Chapman; **M:** Thomas Newman. *WAR, FUS*

Lost Canyon 🐾🐾 1943 Hoppy tries to help a fugitive who's been framed for bank robbery. This is the second installment distributed by United Artists. The song "Jingle, Jangle, Jingle" is sung by the Sportsman Quartet. 61m/B **VHS.** William Boyd, Jay Kirby, Andy Clyde, Lola Lane, Douglas Fowley, Herbert Rawlinson; **D:** Lesley Selander. *NOS*

The Lost Capone 🐾🐾🐾 1990 **(PG-13)** Made for cable TV version of the story of Al Capone's youngest brother, a clean living small town sheriff who struggles with his sibling's reputation at every turn. 93m/C **VHS, Beta, Closed Caption.** Ally Sheedy, Eric Roberts, Adrian Pasdar, Titus Welliver, Jimmie F. Skaggs, Maria Pitillo, Anthony Crivello; **D:** John Gray; **W:** John Gray; **C:** Paul Elliott. *TTC*

The Lost City 🐾🐾 1934 A feature version of the rollicking vintage movie serial about a lost jungle city, adventurers and mad scientists. 74m/B **VHS, Beta.** William "Stage" Boyd, Kane Richmond, George "Gabby" Hayes, Claudia Dell; **D:** Harry Revier. *NOS, SNC, DVT*

Lost City of the Jungle 1945 13-chapter serial focusing on a crazed Atwill, in his last screen role, believing that he can rule the world from the heart of a deep, dark jungle by utilizing a special mineral. The final Universal serial. 169m/B **VHS, Beta.** Russell Hayden, Lionel Atwill, Jane Adams; **D:** Ray Taylor, Lewis D. Collins. *NOS, GPV, DVT*

The Lost Command 🐾🐾½ 1966 A French colonel, relieved of his command, endeavors to regain power by battling a powerful Arab terrorist with his own specially trained platoon of soldiers. Crisp adventure set in post-WWII North Africa. Based on "The Centurions" by Jean Larteguy. 129m/C **Beta.** Anthony Quinn, Michele Morgan, George Segal, Alain Delon, Maurice Ronet, Claudia Cardinale; **D:** Mark Robson; **C:** Robert L. Surtees. *COL*

The Lost Continent 🐾½ 1951 An expedition searching for a lost rocket on a jungle island discovers dinosaurs and other extinct creatures. 82m/B **VHS, Beta, LV.** Cesar Romero, Hillary Brooke, Chick Chandler, John Hoyt, Acquanetta, Sid Melton, Whit Bissell, Hugh Beaumont; **D:** Sam Newfield. *MRV, MLB*

Lost Diamond 🐾 1974 Bumbling spies search for a smuggled gem. 83m/C **VHS, Beta.** Juan Ramon, Sonia Rivas, Ricardo Bauleo. *MED*

The Lost Empire 🐾 1983 **(R)** Three bountiful and powerful women team up to battle the evil Dr. Syn Do. 86m/C **VHS, Beta.** Melanie Vincz, Raven De La Croix, Angela Aames, Paul Coufos, Robert Tessier, Angus Scrimm, Angelique Pettyjohn, Kenneth Tobey; **D:** Jim Wynorski; **W:** Jim Wynorski. *LIV*

Lost Highway 🐾🐾 1996 **(R)** Welcome once again to Lynch-world—that parallel universe understood only by master David. Jazz musician Fred Madison (Pullman) is on Death Row—supposedly for the murder of his wife Renee (Arquette). Only why does young mechanic Pete Dayton (Getty) wind up in Fred's cell (with Fred missing)? Oh, and why does gangster Mr. Eddy (Loggia) have a girlfriend named Alice (Arquette again) who looks just like Renee? And is she real—or did Fred conjure her up? Who's the Mystery Man (Blake), who literally looks like death warmed over. And.....well, you get the idea. Or maybe you're not supposed to. **CW:** Bizarre violent and sexual content, and for strong language. 135m/C **VHS, LV, Closed Caption.** Bill Pullman, Patricia Arquette, Balthazar Getty, Robert Loggia, Robert (Bobby) Blake, Gary Busey, Jack Nance, Richard Pryor, Natasha Gregson Wagner, Lisa Boyle, Michael Massee, Jack Kehler, Henry Rollins, Gene Ross, Scott Coffey; **D:** David Lynch; **W:** David Lynch, Barry Gifford; **C:** Peter Deming; **M:** Angelo Badalamenti. *PGV*

Lost Honeymoon 🐾🐾 1947 Monkeyshines abound as a soldier marries a girl while in a state of amnesia, and then wakes up to find twin daughters. 70m/B VHS, Beta. Franchot Tone, Ann Richards; **D:** Leigh Jason. NOS, DVT, HEG

The Lost Honor of Katharina Blum 🐾🐾🐾 Die Verlorene Ehre Der Katharina Blum 1975 (R) A woman becomes involved with a man who's under police surveillance and finds her life open to public scrutiny and abuse from the media and the government. Based on Heinrich Böll's prize-winning novel. In German with English subtitles. Remade for television as "The Lost Honor of Kathryn Beck." 97m/C VHS, Beta. GE Angela Winkler, Mario Adorf, Dieter Laser, Juergen Prochnow; **D:** Volker Schlondorff, Margarethe von Trotta. APD, GLV

Lost Horizon 🐾🐾🐾🐾 1937 A group of strangers fleeing revolution in China are lost in the Tibetan Himalayas and stumble across the valley of Shangri La. The inhabitants of this Utopian community have lived for hundreds of years in kindness and peace—but what will the intrusion of these strangers bring? The classic romantic role for Colman. Capra's directorial style meshed perfectly with the pacifist theme of James Hilton's classic novel, resulting in one of the most memorable films of the 1930s. This version restores more than 20 minutes of footage which had been cut from the movie through the years. 132m/B VHS, Beta, LV. Ronald Colman, Jane Wyatt, H.B. Warner, Sam Jaffe, Thomas Mitchell, Edward Everett Horton, Isabel Jewell, John Howard, Margo; **D:** Frank Capra; **W:** Robert Riskin; **M:** Dimitri Tiomkin. Academy Awards '37: Best Film Editing, Best Interior Decoration; Nominations: Academy Awards '37: Best Picture, Best Sound, Best Supporting Actor (Warner), Best Original Score. COL, RDG

The Lost Idol/Shock Troop 198? In "The Lost Idol," a lone soldier raids a sacred temple in order to retrieve a golden idol. "Shock Troop" tells of top secret mission to destroy a powerful computer that lies behind enemy lines. 219m/C VHS. Danny Aiello, Lyle Alzado, Erik Estrada. NO

Lost in a Harem 🐾🐾 1944 Abbott & Costello play magicians in a theatrical troupe stranded in a desert kingdom ruled by an evil sheik. The sheik's nephew (and rightful heir) hires the two to steal some magic rings and the pretty Maxwell to play footsie with his susceptible uncle in an attempt to regain his kingdom. Average comedy with musical numbers by Jimmy Dorsey and His Orchestra. 89m/B VHS. Bud Abbott, Lou Costello, Marilyn Maxwell, John Conte, Douglass Dumbrille, Lottie Harrison; **D:** Charles Riesner. MGM

Lost in Alaska 🐾🐾½ 1952 Up in the Alaskan wilderness, Abbott & Costello save Ewell from a greedy saloon owner and his cohorts who are trying to get their hands on Ewell's fortune. 87m/B VHS. Bud Abbott, Lou Costello, Tom Ewell, Mitzie Green, Bruce Cabot, Emory Parnell, Jack Ingram, Rex Lease; **D:** Jean Yarbrough; **W:** Martin Ragaway, Leonard Stern; **M:** Henry Mancini. USH, FCT

Lost in America 🐾🐾🐾 1985 (R) After deciding that he can't "find himself" at his current job, advertising executive David Howard and his wife sell everything they own and buy a Winnebago to travel across the country. This Albert Brooks comedy is a must-see for everyone who thinks that there is more in life than pushing papers at your desk and sitting on "Mercedes leather." Available in widescreen on laserdisc. 91m/C VHS, Beta, LV, Closed Caption. Albert Brooks, Julie Hagerty, Michael Greene, Tom Tarpey, Garry Marshall, Art Frankel; **D:** Albert Brooks; **W:** Albert Brooks, Monica Johnson; **M:** Arthur B. Rubinstein. National Society of Film Critics Awards '85: Best Screenplay. WAR

Lost in the Barrens 🐾🐾 1991 Two young boys, one a Canadian Indian and the other a rich white boy, get lost in the wilderness of the Canadian north. Out of necessity and common need they become close and form a lifelong friendship. Based on the book by Farley Mowat. 95m/C VHS. CA Graham Greene, Nicholas Shields. NO

Lost in Yonkers 🐾🐾½ Neil Simon's Lost in Yonkers 1993 (PG) Arty and Jay are two teenage brothers who, while their widowed father looks for work, are sent to live with their stern grandmother, small-time gangster uncle, and childlike aunt in 1942 New York. Ruehl reprises her Tony award-winning performance as Aunt Bella, who loses herself in the movies while trying to find a love of her own, out from under the oppressive thumb of her domineering mother (Worth). Performances by the adults are more theatrical than necessary but the teenagers do well in their observer roles. Based on the play by Neil Simon, which again chronicles his boyhood. 114m/C VHS, LV, 8mm, Closed Caption. Mercedes Ruehl, Irene Worth, Richard Dreyfuss, Brad Stoll, Mike Damus, David Strathairn, Robert Miranda, Jack Laufer, Susan Merson; **D:** Martha Coolidge; **W:** Neil Simon; **M:** Elmer Bernstein. COL, FCT

The Lost Jungle 1934 Circus legend Beatty searches for his girl and her dad in the jungle. Animal stunts keep it interesting. Serial in 12 chapters, 13 minutes each. 156m/B VHS, Beta. Clyde Beatty, Cecilia Parker, Syd Saylor, Warner Richmond, Wheeler Oakman; **D:** Armand Schaefer, David Howard. NOS, VCN, VDM

The Lost Language of Cranes 🐾🐾🐾 1992 David Leavitt's novel is transported from New York to present-day London but the wrenching emotional drama remains the same. A family is in crisis as long-hidden secrets concerning homosexuality and infidelity are finally revealed. The title refers to one character's social worker's thesis on a young boy from a dysfunctional family who imitates the movements of the building cranes he sees. Fine performances by all. Adult sexual situations. 90m/C VHS. GB Brian Cox, Eileen Atkins, Angus MacFadyen, Corey Parker, Cathy Tyson; **Cameos:** John Schlesinger, Rene Auberjonois; **D:** Nigel Finch; **C:** Remi Adefarasin. FOX, BTV

Lost Legacy: A Girl Called Hatter Fox 🐾🐾½ 1977 Tradition and technology are at odds in the life of a young Indian girl. Strong cast makes this work. Made for television and better than average. 100m/C VHS. Ronny Cox, Joanelle Romero, Conchata Ferrell; **D:** George Schaefer. GEM

Lost, Lonely, and Vicious 🐾 1959 Clayton is a suicidal Hollywood actor who spends much of his time indulging his penchant for women, figuring he may as well enjoy what little time he has left. Then he meets Wilson, a drugstore clerk who moves him to reconsider his self-destructive ways. 73m/B VHS. Ken Clayton, Barbara Wilson, Lilyan Chauvin, Richard Gilden, Carole Nugent, Sandra Giles, Allen Fife, Frank Stallworth, Johnny Erben, Clint Quigley, T. Earl Johnson; **D:** Frank Myers; **W:** Norman Graham. SMW, TPV

The Lost Missile 🐾🐾 1958 A lost, alien missile circles the Earth, causing overheating and destruction on the planet's surface. A scientist works to find a way to save the planet before it explodes into a gigantic fireball. Director Burke's last film. 70m/B VHS. Robert Loggia, Ellen Parker, Larry Kerr, Phillip Pine, Marilee Earle; **D:** William (Lester Williams) Berke. FRG

Lost Moment 🐾🐾 1947 A publisher travels to Italy to search for a valuable collection of a celebrated author's love letters, but finds a neurotic woman in his way. Based on Henry James' "Aspern Papers." 89m/B VHS. Robert Cummings, Agnes Moorehead, Susan Hayward; **D:** Martin Gabel; **C:** Hal Mohr. REP

The Lost One 🐾🐾 Der Verlone 1951 A German scientist's lover is suspected of selling his findings to England during WWII. Based on a true story; Lorre's only directorial outing. 97m/B VHS. GE Peter Lorre, Karl John, Renate Mannhardt; **D:** Peter Lorre. NO

The Lost Patrol 🐾🐾🐾½ 1934 WWI British soldiers lost in the desert are shot down one by one by Arab marauders as Karloff portrays a religious soldier convinced he's going to die. The usual spiffy Ford exteriors peopled by great char-

acters with a stirring score. Based on the story, "Patrol" by Philip MacDonald. 66m/B VHS, Beta, LV. Victor McLaglen, Boris Karloff, Reginald Denny, Wallace Ford, Alan Hale; **D:** John Ford; **M:** Max Steiner. National Board of Review Awards '34: 10 Best Films of the Year; Nominations: Academy Awards '34: Best Score. CCB, MED, RXM

Lost Planet Airmen 🐾½ 1949 A feature-length condensation of the 12-part sci-fi serial "King of the Rocket Men." Rocket Man is pitted against the sinister Dr. Vulcan in this intergalactic battle of good and evil. 65m/B VHS, Beta. Tristram Coffin, Mae Clarke, Dale Van Sickel; **D:** Fred Brannon. AOV, DVT, RXM

The Lost Platoon 1989 (R) A troop of soldiers are transformed into vampires. 120m/C VHS, Beta, LV. David Parry, William Knight, Sean Heyman; **D:** David A. Prior. AIP

Lost Squadron 🐾🐾½ 1932 A look at the dangers stuntmen go through in movie-making. 79m/B VHS, Beta, LV. Richard Dix, Erich von Stroheim; **D:** George Archainbaud; **M:** Max Steiner. RXM

The Lost Stooges 1933 From the trio's one year at MGM, rare clips of them performing their famous slapstick gags. In black and white and color. 68m/B VHS, Beta. Moe Howard, Curly Howard, Larry Fine, Clark Gable, Joan Crawford, Jimmy Durante, Robert Montgomery. TTC

The Lost Tribe 🐾 1989 A man takes his wife on a trek through the jungle to find his lost brother. 96m/C VHS, Beta. John Bach, Darien Teakle; **D:** John Laing. MED

The Lost Weekend 🐾🐾🐾🐾 1945 The heartrending Hollywood masterpiece about alcoholism, depicting a single weekend in the life of a writer, who cannot believe he's addicted. Except for its pat ending, it is an uncompromising, startlingly harsh treatment, with Milland giving one of the industry's bravest lead performances ever. Acclaimed then and now. 100m/B VHS, Beta, LV. Ray Milland, Jane Wyman, Phillip Terry, Howard da Silva, Doris Dowling, Frank Faylen, Mary Young; **D:** Billy Wilder; **W:** Charles Brackett, Billy Wilder; **M:** Miklos Rozsa. Academy Awards '45: Best Actor (Milland), Best Director (Wilder), Best Picture, Best Screenplay; Cannes Film Festival '46: Best Actor (Milland), Best Film; Golden Globe Awards '46: Best Actor—Drama (Milland), Best Director (Wilder), Best Film—Drama; National Board of Review Awards '45: 10 Best Films of the Year, Best Actor (Milland); New York Film Critics Awards '45: Best Actor (Milland), Best Director (Wilder), Best Film; Nominations: Academy Awards '45: Best Black and White Cinematography, Best Film Editing, Original Dramatic/Comedy Score. USH, PAR, BTV

The Lost World 🐾🐾½ 1925 A zoology professor leads a group on a South American expedition in search of the "lost world," where dinosaurs roam in this silent film. Based on a story by Sir Arthur Conan Doyle. A 90-minute version includes the film's original trailer and a recreation of some of the missing footage (the film was released at 108 minutes). 62m/B VHS, Beta, LV. Wallace Beery, Lewis Stone, Bessie Love, Lloyd Hughes; **D:** Harry Hoyt. NOS, MIL, VYY

The Lost World 🐾🐾½ 1992 "Land of the Lost"/"Jurassic Park" themes, based on the story by Sir Arthur Conan Doyle. A scientific team ventures deep into uncharted African jungles where they find themselves confronted by dinosaurs and other dangers. 99m/C VHS, Closed Caption. John Rhys-Davies, David Warner; **D:** Timothy Bond. WOV

The Lost World: Jurassic Park 2 🐾🐾½ Jurassic Park 2 1997 (PG-13) Sequel to "Jurassic Park," proves only that Spielberg has tapped this well one too many times. It's four years after the first adventure and the surviving dinos have peacefully set up house on a deserted island near Costa Rica. Mathematician Ian Malcolm (Goldblum, reprising his role) reluctantly becomes part of an expedition to monitor the beasts, only because his paleontologist girlfriend (Moore) is so gung-ho. Other characters exist, but are reduced to the role of entrees. More dinos (two T-Rexs, a clan of Raptors, and bite-sized newcomers Compsognathus), thrilling special effects, and more gore make up for thin subplots involving a rich businessman who wants to use the dinosaurs for a new zoo and another who hunts them for sport. Ironically, Spielberg's predictablity owes much to better films such as "King Kong," "Aliens" and "Godzilla." Still, T-Rex and buddies, the true stars, rise to the occasion to entertain in an otherwise lackluster sequel. Based on Michael Crichton's book. **CW:** Intense sci-fi terror and violence. **134m/C VHS.** Jeff Goldblum, Julianne Moore, Vince Vaughn, Arliss Howard, Pete Postlethwaite, Peter Stormare, Vanessa Lee Chester; **D:** Steven Spielberg; **W:** David Koepp; **M:** John Williams. *NYR*

Lost Zeppelin *♂♂* **1929** A dirigible becomes lost in the wastes of Antarctica, forcing its passengers to combat the elements. Impressive special effects and miniatures for its time. **73m/B VHS, Beta.** Conway Tearle, Virginia Valli, Ricardo Cortez, Duke Martin, Kathryn McGuire; **D:** Edward Sloman. *SNC, GPV*

Lotna *♂♂½* **1964** Wadja's first color film serves as a tribute to the Polish calvary who fought against the Germans in WWII. The story is told through the trials of a horse that passes to various military officials until it breaks a leg and must be shot. Wadja himself is the son of a cavalryman killed in the war. Polish with subtitles. **89m/C VHS.** *PL* Bozena Kurowska, Jerzy Pichelski, Jerzy Moes, Adam Pawlikowski; **D:** Andrzej Wajda; **W:** Andrzej Wajda, Wojciech Zukrowski; **C:** Jerzy Lipman; **M:** Tadeusz Baird. *FCT*

Lots of Luck *♂♂* **1985** A knee-slapping comedy about a family that wins the million-dollar lottery and sees that money doesn't solve all problems. Disney made for cable. **88m/C VHS, Beta.** Martin Mull, Annette Funicello, Fred Willard, Polly Holliday, Hamilton Camp, Vincent Schiavelli; **D:** Peter Baldwin; **M:** William Goldstein. *DIS*

Lottery Bride *♂♂½* **1930** In this charming musical, Jeanette MacDonald is the lottery bride who is won by the brother of the man she really loves. A fine outing for all involved, particularly the supporting cast. ♫You're an Angel; My Northern Lights; Come Drink to the Girl That You Love; Yubla; Round She Whirls; Shoulder to Shoulder; High and Low; Napoli; Two Strong Men. **85m/B VHS, Beta.** Jeanette MacDonald, Joe E. Brown, ZaSu Pitts, John Garrick, Carroll Nye; **D:** Paul Stein. *NO*

Lotto Land *♂♂½* **1995** Looks at the lives of black and Hispanic characters from the same Brooklyn neighborhood. Ambitious high school grad Hank (Gilliard, Jr.) works stocking shelves at the local liquor store for manager Flo (Costallos), who's raised Hank's girlfriend, the college-bound Joy (Gonzalez). The neighborhood's abuzz when someone in their area holds the winning ticket for a $27 million lottery, which was sold from Flo's store, but just who it is and what happens when the money is claimed leads to a dramatic twist. Debut for Rubino, who shows real affection for his characters. **90m/C VHS.** Larry Gilliard Jr., Barbara Gonzalez, Suzanne Costallos, Wendell Holmes, Jamie Tirelli, Luis Guzman, Paul Calderone; **D:** John Rubino; **W:** John Rubino; **C:** Rufus Standefer. *BMG*

The Lotus Eaters *♂♂* **1993** (PG-13) Sensitive family drama set in British Columbia in the 1960s about a wife who discovers her husband has fallen in love with their childrens' new teacher. Domestic angst done with naturalism and not without humor. **CW:** Nudity; children exposed to parental infidelities. **100m/C VHS.** *CA* Sheila McCarthy, R.H. Thomson, Michelle-Barbara Pelletier, Frances Hyland, Paul Soles; **D:** Paul Shapiro; **W:** Peggy Thompson. Genie Awards '93: Best Actress (McCarthy), Best Screenplay, Best Sound. *SDE, FCT*

Louisiana *♂* **1987** A belle of the Old South tries to get back the family plantation by romancing the new owner, even though she loves someone else. Oh, and then the Civil War breaks out. Made for television. **130m/C VHS, Beta.** Ian Charleson, Margot Kidder, Victor Lanoux, Len Cariou, Lloyd Bochner; **D:** Philippe de Broca. *PSM*

Louisiana Purchase *♂♂½* **1941** Successful screen adaptation of the Broadway musical features several performers from the original cast, lavish costumes, and great musical numbers. As usual, Hope's comedy is extremely funny, especially his famous filibuster scene in Congress. Based on the stage musical by Morrie Ryskind and B. G. DeSylva. **95m/C VHS.** Bob Hope, Vera Zorina, Victor Moore, Dona Drake, Irene Bordoni, Raymond Walburn, Maxie "Slapsie" Rosenbloom, Frank Albertson, Barbara Britton; **D:** Irving Cummings. Nominations: Academy Awards '41: Best Color Cinematography, Best Interior Decoration. *USH, BTV*

Louisiana Story *♂♂♂* **1948** The final effort by the master filmmaker, depicting the effects of oil industrialization on the southern Bayou country as seen through the eyes of a young boy. One of Flaherty's greatest, widely considered a premiere achievement. **77m/B VHS, Beta.** **D:** Robert Flaherty; **M:** Virgil Thomson. National Board of Review Awards '48: 10 Best Films of the Year; Nominations: Academy Awards '48: Best Story. *HMV, VYY, DVT*

Loulou *♂♂♂½* **1980** (R) A woman leaves her middle-class husband for a leather-clad, uneducated jock who is more attentive. Romantic and erotic. In French with English subtitles. **110m/C VHS, Beta.** *FR* Isabelle Huppert, Gerard Depardieu, Guy Marchand; **D:** Maurice Pialat. *NYF*

The Lovable Cheat *♂♂* **1949** Pretty lame adapatation of Balzac's play "Mercadet Le Falseur," about a father who cons money from his friends in order to line up a marriage suitable for his daughter. **75m/B VHS.** Charlie Ruggles, Peggy Ann Garner, Richard Ney, Alan Mowbray, Iris Adrian, Ludwig Donath, Fritz Feld; **D:** Richard Oswald. *FCT*

Love *♂♂♂½* **1971** Torocsik, touted as Hungary's leading actress in the '70s, plays a young woman whose husband has been imprisoned for political crimes. Living in a cramped apartment with her mother-in-law, she keeps the news from the aged and dying woman (Darvas) by reading letters she's fabricated to keep alive the woman's belief that her son is a successful movie director in America. The story is punctuated by the older woman's dreamy remembrances of things past. Exceptional performances by both women, it was Darvas' final film. Based on two novellas by Tibor Dery, it won a special jury prize at the 1973 Cannes film festival. In Hungarian with English subtitles. **100m/C VHS, LV.** *HU* Lili Darvas, Mari Torocsik, Ivan Darvas; **D:** Karoly Makk. *CVC, IME*

Love Affair *♂♂♂½* **1939** Multi-kleenex weepie inspired countless romantic dreams of true love atop the Empire State Building. Dunn and Boyer fall in love on a ship bound for NYC, but they're both involved. They agree to meet later at, guess where, to see if their feelings hold true, but tragedy intevenes. Excellent comedy-drama is witty at first, more subdued later, with plenty of romance and melodrama. Remade in 1957 (by McCarey) as "An Affair to Remember," a lesser version whose popularity overshadows the original. Look for fleeting glimpses of Leslie, Beckett, and Mohr. Ignore the public domain video, which replaces the original music. Remade again in 1994 as "Love Affair." **87m/B VHS.** Irene Dunne, Charles Boyer, Maria Ouspenskaya, Lee Bowman, Astrid Allwyn, Maurice Moscovich, Scotty Beckett, Joan Leslie, Gerald Mohr, Dell Henderson, Carol Hughes; **D:** Leo McCarey; **W:** Delmer Daves, Leo McCarey, Donald Ogden Stewart. Nominations: Academy Awards '39: Best Actress (Dunne), Best Interior Decoration, Best Picture, Best Song ("Wishing"), Best Story, Best Supporting Actress (Ouspenskaya). *NOS, MRV, TTC*

Love Affair *♂♂* **1994** (PG-13) Second remake of the timeless classic has a contemporary look and feel but doesn't justify a new version. The photogenic leads may meet on a plane, but never fear, the Empire State Building and a tragedy are still the main plot devices. The problem is viewers never feel drawn into their lives. Hepburn has a small but moving role as Beatty's aunt. Superb cinematography makes it easy on the eyes

and Morricone's lush romantic score makes it easy on the ears, but ultimately, it's all gloss with little substance. Watch this one, but then set aside time to see the superior original (made in 1939) or the better known 1957 attempt "An Affair to Remember." **CW:** Mild language. **108m/C VHS, LV, Closed Caption.** Warren Beatty, Annette Bening, Katharine Hepburn, Garry Shandling, Chloe Webb, Pierce Brosnan, Kate Capshaw, Paul Mazursky, Brenda Vaccaro, Glenn Shadix, Barry Miller, Harold Ramis; **D:** Glenn Gordon Caron; **W:** Warren Beatty, Robert Towne; **M:** Ennio Morricone. *WAR*

The Love Affair, or The Case of the Missing Switchboard Operator *♂♂♂* *Switchboard Operator; Case of the Missing Switchboard Operator; Ljubarni Slucaj; An Affair of the Heart* **1967** Makavejev's second film, a dissertation on the relationship between sex and politics, involving an affair between a switchboard operator and a middle-aged ex-revolutionary, is told in the director's unique, farcically disjointed manner. In Serbian with English subtitles. **73m/B VHS, Beta.** *YU* Eva Ras, Slobodan Aligrudic, Ruzica Sokic; **D:** Dusan Makavejev; **W:** Dusan Makavejev. *FCT*

Love Affair: The Eleanor & Lou Gehrig Story *♂♂♂* **1977** The true story, told from Mrs. Gehrig's point of view, of the love affair between baseball great Lou Gehrig and his wife Eleanor from his glory days as a New York Yankee, to his battle with an incurable disease. A television drama that is supported by Herrmann and Danner's convincing portrayals. **96m/C VHS, Beta.** Blythe Danner, Edward Herrmann, Patricia Neal, Ramon Bieri, Lainie Kazan; **D:** Fielder Cook. *WOV*

Love After Love *♂♂* *Apres l'Amour* **1994** A look at sex and relationships among thirtysomething professionals in Paris. Lola (Huppert), a successful romance novelist, is suffering a crisis in both her career and, ironically, her love life. She is involved with two men who, in turn, are involved with different women who happen to have borne them children. The movie starts off with so much mate switching and secret sexual rendezvous, that by the second half, you really don't care who Lola ends up with. French with English subtitles. **104m/C VHS.** *FR* Isabelle Huppert, Hippolyte Girardot, Lio; **D:** Diane Kurys; **W:** Diane Kurys, Antoine Lacomblez; **C:** Fabio Conversi; **M:** Yves Simon, Serge Perathone, Jannick Top. *ORI*

Love Among the Ruins *♂♂♂* **1975** A made-for-television romance about an aging, wealthy widow who, after being scandalously sued for breach of promise by her very young lover, turns for aid to an old lawyer friend who has loved her silently for more than forty years. **100m/C VHS, Beta, LV, Closed Caption.** Laurence Olivier, Katharine Hepburn, Leigh Lawson, Colin Blakely; **D:** George Cukor; **M:** John Barry. *FOX*

Love and a .45 *♂♂* **1994** (R) Satirical and violent road movie finds petty career criminal Watty Watts (Bellows) living in a Texas trailer park with gal Starlene (Zellweger), for whom he's just purchased an expensive engagement ring. But he's borrowed the money from some crazed gangster types who want the loan repaid in a timely fashion. Soon, the dippy duo are on the run to Mexico with a trail of dead bodies behind them and the media just delighted to make them the next tabloid darlings. **CW:** Ugly, graphic violence; sexual situations. **101m/C VHS, LV, Closed Caption.** Gil Bellows, Renee Zellweger, Rory Cochrane, Ann Wedgeworth, Peter Fonda, Jeffrey Combs, Jace Alexander; **D:** C.M. Talkington; **W:** C.M. Talkington; **M:** Tom Verlaine. Nominations: Independent Spirit Awards '95: Debut Performance (Zellweger). *THV*

Love and Anarchy *♂♂♂* *Film d'Amore et d'Anarchia* **1973** An oppressed peasant vows to assassinate Mussolini after a close friend is murdered. Powerful drama about the rise of Italian facism. In Italian with English subtitles. **108m/C VHS, Beta.** *IT* Giancarlo Giannini, Mariangela Melato; **D:** Lina Wertmuller; **W:** Lina Wertmuller; **M:** Nino Rota. Cannes Film Festival '73: Best Actor (Giannini). *COL, APD*

Love and Bullets 🎬½ 1979 (PG) An Arizona homicide detective is sent on a special assignment to Switzerland to bring a mobster's girlfriend back to the United States to testify against him in court. **95m/C VHS, Beta, Closed Caption.** *GB* Charles Bronson, Jill Ireland, Rod Steiger, Strother Martin, Bradford Dillman, Henry Silva, Michael V. Gazzo; *D:* Stuart Rosenberg; *W:* Wendell Mayes; *C:* Fred W. Koenekamp; *M:* Lalo Schifrin. FOX

Love and Death 🎬🎬🎬 1975 (PG) In 1812 Russia, a condemned man reviews the follies of his life. Woody Allen's satire on "War and Peace," and every other major Russian novel. **89m/C VHS, Beta, LV.** Woody Allen, Diane Keaton, Georges Adel, Despo Diamantidou, Frank Adu, Harold Gould; *D:* Woody Allen; *W:* Woody Allen; *C:* Ghislain Cloquet. MGM, FOX

Love and Faith 🎬🎬🎬 1978 Two lovers are torn between their love for each other and their faiths during sixteenth-century Japan. English subtitles. **154m/C VHS, Beta.** *JP* Toshiro Mifune, Takashi Shimura, Yoshiko Nakana; *D:* Kei Kumai. VDA

Love and Hate: A Marriage Made in Hell 🎬🎬½ *Love and Hate: The Story of Colin and Joanne Thatcher* 1990 Marital murder mystery based on a true Canadian case. Joanne (Nelligan), the wife of wealthy rancher-politico Colin (Walsh), leaves her publicly charismatic and privately abusive husband with two thirds of their brood. A bitter battle for custody is waged, and Joanne is soon found savagely slain. The number one suspect: philandering ex-spouse Colin. Based on Maggie Siggins' "A Canadian Tragedy," the faux biography originally aired in two parts on Canadian TV. **156m/C VHS, Beta, LV.** Kate Nelligan, Ken Walsh, Leon Pownall, John Colicos, Noam Zylberman, Victoria Snow, Cedric Smith, R.H. Thomson, Victoria Wauchope, Doris Petrie, Duncan Ollenenshaw; *D:* Francis Mankiewicz; *W:* Suzette Couture. PAR

Love and Human Remains 🎬🎬🎬 1993 (R) Director Arcand's first English-language film features a group of late 20ish urbanites trying to come to grips with their place in the world (and their sexuality). David (Gibson) is an ammoral Lothario who doesn't believe in love and can only manage casual gay relationships. He hangs out with a variety of friends, all of whom are trying to cope with their varying sexual natures. Melodramatic framing story about a serial murderer who may, or may not, be one of the principal characters proves somewhat of a distraction. Lots of caustically witty dialogue and some fine performances (particularly Gibson's); filmed in Montreal. Adaptation of the play "Unidentified Human Remains and the True Nature of Love" by Fraser, who also did the screenplay. *CW:* Strong sexual content; language; violence; some drug use. **100m/C VHS, LV.** *CA* Thomas Gibson, Ruth Marshall, Cameron Bancroft, Mia Kirshner, Joanne Vannicola, Matthew Ferguson, Rick Roberts; *D:* Denys Arcand; *W:* Brad Fraser; *C:* Paul Sarossy. Genie Awards '94: Best Adapted Screenplay. COL

Love & Murder 🎬½ 1991 (R) Poorly developed tale of a photographer and his bevy of with beautiful models involved with murder and love, not necessarily in that order. *CW:* Language. **87m/C VHS.** Todd Waring, Kathleen Lasky, Ron White, Wayne Robson; *D:* Steven Hilliard Stern. HMD

Love and Other Catastrophes 🎬🎬 1995 (R) Short, low-budget first feature from 23-year-old Croghan engagingly focuses on 24 hours in the lives of five confused college students. Film students Alice (Garner) and Mia (O'Connor) need a third roommate for their new apartment. Danni (Mitchell), Mia's girlfriend, is upset that Mia doesn't want them living together, while Alice is eyeing potential boyfriends, including shy med student Michael (Day) and womanizing Ari (Dyktynski). Meanwhile, both Alice and Mia try to cope with various academic frustrations. *CW:* Sexuality, language, and some drug use. **76m/C VHS, Closed Caption.** *AU* Frances O'Connor, Alice Garner, Matt Day, Radha Mitchell, Matthew Dyktynski, Suzi Dougherty, Kim Gyngell; *D:* Emma-Kate Croghan; *W:* Emma-Kate Croghan,

Yael Bergman, Helen Bandis; *C:* Justin Brickle; *M:* Oleh Witer. Nominations: Australian Film Institute '96: Best Actress (O'Connor), Best Film, Best Supporting Actress (Garner). FXV

Love and the Frenchwoman 🎬🎬🎬 *La Francaise et L'Amour* 1960 A French tale tracing the nature of love through stages. Deals with a story about where babies come from, puppy love, saving sex for marriage, and the way some men treat women. **135m/B VHS, Beta.** *FR* Jean-Paul Belmondo, Pierre-Jean Vaillard, Marie-Jose Nat, Annie Girardot; *D:* Jean Delannoy; *M:* Georges Delerue. DVT, MRV, HEG

Love at First Bite 🎬🎬½ 1979 (PG) Intentionally campy spoof of the vampire film. Dracula is forced to leave his Transylvanian home as the Rumanian government has designated his castle a training center for young gymnasts. Once in New York, the Count takes in the night life and falls in love with a woman whose boyfriend embarks on a campaign to warn the city of Dracula's presence. Hamilton of the never-fading tan is appropriately tongue-in-cheek in a role which resurrected his career. **93m/C VHS, Beta, LV.** George Hamilton, Susan St. James, Richard Benjamin, Dick Shawn, Arte Johnson, Sherman Hemsley, Isabel Sanford; *D:* Stan Dragoti; *M:* Charles Bernstein. ORI, WAR

Love at First Sight 🎬 *Love is Blind; At First Sight* 1976 A pre-"Saturday Night Live" hack job for Aykroyd, playing a blind man who falls in love with a girl he bumps into. ♫Love at First Sight. **86m/C VHS, Beta.** Dan Aykroyd, Mary Ann McDonald, George Murray, Barry Morse; *D:* Rex Bromfield. NO

Love at Large 🎬🎬🎬 1989 (R) Hired by a beautiful woman, a private detective accidentally follows the wrong man and winds up being followed himself. He vies with a female detective in solving this case of mistaken identity. **90m/C VHS, Beta, LV, Closed Caption.** Tom Berenger, Elizabeth Perkins, Anne Archer, Ann Magnuson, Annette O'Toole, Kate Capshaw, Ted Levine, Kevin J. O'Connor, Ruby Dee, Neil Young, Barry Miller; *D:* Alan Rudolph; *W:* Alan Rudolph; *C:* Elliot Davis. ORI, FCT

Love at Stake 🎬🎬½ 1987 (R) It's condo owners versus the witches in this charming parody that features a hilarious cameo by Dr. Joyce Brothers and a very sexy performance from Carrera. **83m/C VHS, LV.** Patrick Cassidy, Kelly Preston, Bud Cort, Barbara Carrera, Stuart Pankin, Dave Thomas, Georgia Brown, Annie Golden; *Cameos:* Dr. Joyce Brothers; *D:* John Moffitt; *M:* Charles Fox. NLC

Love at the Top 🎬🎬½ 1986 Ladies' foundation designer falls in love with her boss's son-in-law, jeopardizing her career. **90m/C Beta.** Janis Paige, Richard Young, Jim MacKrell; *D:* John Bowab. PSM

The Love Boat 1977? All aboard! Love's waiting for you in this special movie presentation of the immensely popular television series. Captain Stuebing, Julie, Gopher, Isaac (your bartender) and a whole host of celebrities at the end of their careers, fall in and out of love as they sail back and forth between expensive resorts. **?m/C VHS.** Gavin MacLeod, Bernie Kopell, Ted Lange, Lauren Tewes. GKK

The Love Bug 🎬🎬½ 1968 (G) A race car driver (Jones) is followed by Herbie, a white Volkswagen with a mind of its own. Eventually, Jones follows the "Love Bug" to a life of madcap fun. Followed by several sequels. **110m/C VHS, Beta, LV, Closed Caption.** Dean Jones, Michele Lee, Hope Lange, Robert Reed, Bert Convy; *D:* Robert Stevenson; *C:* Edward Colman; *M:* George Bruns. DIS

Love Butcher 1982 (R) A crippled old gardener kills his female employers with his garden tools and cleans up neatly afterward. **84m/C VHS, Beta.** Erik Stern, Kay Neer, Robin Sherwood; *D:* Mikel Angel, Donald M. Jones. NO

Love by Appointment 🎬 1976 An unlikely romantic comedy with a very unlikely cast has two businessmen meeting up with European prostitutes. Made for television. **96m/C VHS, Beta.**

Ernest Borgnine, Robert Alda, Francoise Fabian, Corinne Clery. NLC

Love Camp 🎬 1976 A woman is invited to a swinger's holiday camp, frolics for a while, then is told she can never leave. Suspenseful hijinks ensue. **100m/C VHS, Beta.** Laura Gemser, Christian Anders, Gabriele Tinti. AHV

Love, Cheat & Steal 🎬🎬 1993 (R) Convicted murderer Reno Adams (Roberts) breaks out of prison when he hears that his luscious ex (Amick) has just married another man (Lithgow). He turns up on her door, threatening to destroy her new life, but things aren't exactly what they seem. Faux noir. **95m/C VHS, Closed Caption.** Eric Roberts, Madchen Amick, John Lithgow, Richard Edson, Donald Moffat, David Ackroyd, Dan O'Herlihy; *D:* William Curran; *W:* William Curran. COL

Love Child 🎬🎬 1982 (R) The story of a young woman in prison who becomes pregnant by a guard and fights to have and keep her baby. **97m/C VHS, Beta.** Amy Madigan, Beau Bridges, MacKenzie Phillips, Albert Salmi; *D:* Larry Peerce; *M:* Charles Fox. WAR

Love Crazy 🎬🎬🎬½ 1941 Powell and Loy team once again for a non-"Thin Man" romp through a married-people farce. Via a nosy mother-in-law and a series of misunderstandings, Powell and Loy squabble almost to the point of divorce. Not the wry wit the team was known for, but zany, high-action comedy at its best. **99m/B VHS.** William Powell, Myrna Loy, Gail Patrick, Jack Carson, Florence Bates, Sidney Blackmer, Sig Rumann; *D:* Jack Conway. MGM

Love Crimes 🎬 1992 (R) A con man (Bergin) poses as a photographer who sexually intimidates women while playing on their erotic fantasies. Young is the Atlanta district attorney who sets out to nail him when none of his victims will testify against him, only she may be enjoying her undercover work more than she realizes. Implausible and sleazy. Also available in an unrated version. *CW:* Langauge and strong sensuality. **84m/C VHS, LV.** Sean Young, Patrick Bergin, Arnetia Walker, James Read; *D:* Lizzie Borden; *C:* Phedon Papamichael; *M:* Graeme Revell. HBO

Love Desperados 🎬 1986 Cowboys and ranchers' wives mix it up in a lot of softcore hay. **99m/C VHS, Beta.** Virginia Gordon, James Arena. MED

Love 'Em and Leave 'Em 🎬🎬🎬 1926 Two sisters, with opposite personalities, are department store sales clerks. Brent is the "good" girl and Brooks the "bad" flirt who, under the influence of Perkins, bets the store's welfare benefit money on the horses and loses it all. Brent manages to make things right, while keeping boyfriend Gray from her sister's clutches. Brooks' baby vamp (the actress was 19) stole the picture. Introduced the "Black Bottom" shimmy dance to the screen. Remade in 1929 as "The Saturday Night Kid" with Clara Bow and Jean Arthur. **70m/B VHS, Beta.** Louise Brooks, Evelyn Brent, Lawrence Gray, Osgood Perkins; *D:* Frank Tuttle. GPV

The Love Factor 🎬 1969 A secret agent tries to foil the plans of a race of topless female aliens in this sleazy softcore sci-fi film. Also known as "Zeta One." **?m/C VHS.** *GB* Robin Hawdon, James Robertson Justice, Yutte Stensgaard. SNC

Love Field 🎬🎬½ 1991 (PG-13) Pfeiffer is a Jackie Kennedy-obsessed hairdresser who decides to travel by bus to D.C. when she hears about President Kennedy's assassination. Along the way she gets involved in an interracial friendship with the secretive Haysbert, who's traveling with his young daughter. Pfeiffer's Lurene is basically a sweet dim bulb and Haysbert has an unfortunately written one-note character (mainly exasperation). The 6-year-old McFadden (in her debut) makes the most impact. **104m/C VHS, LV, Closed Caption.** Michelle Pfeiffer, Dennis Haysbert, Stephanie McFadden, Brian Kerwin, Louise Latham, Peggy Rea, Beth Grant, Cooper Huckabee, Mark Miller, Johnny Rae McGhee; *D:* Jonathan Kaplan; *W:* Don Roos; *C:* Ralf

Bode; **M:** Jerry Goldsmith. Nominations: Academy Awards '92: Best Actress (Pfeiffer). *ORI, MOV*

Love Film 🎬🎬 **1970** A train trip from Budapest, Hungary to Lyon, France leads a young man to recall his past as he journeys to visit a childhood sweetheart. Jancsi and Kata's friendship has been disrupted by the 1956 uprising and Jancsi wonders if the love once developing between them has been broken by distance and time. In Hungarian with English subtitles. 130m/C **VHS.** *HU* Andras Balint, Judit Halasz; **D:** Istvan Szabo. *TPV*

Love Finds Andy Hardy 🎬🎬🎬 **1938** Young Andy Hardy finds himself torn between three girls before returning to the girl next door. Garland's first appearance in the acclaimed Andy Hardy series features her singing "In Between" and "Meet the Best of my Heart." Also available with "Andy Hardy Meets Debutante" on Laser Disc. 90m/B **VHS, Beta, LV, Closed Caption.** Mickey Rooney, Judy Garland, Lana Turner, Ann Rutherford, Fay Holden, Lewis Stone, Marie Blake, Cecilia Parker, Gene Reynolds; **D:** George B. Seitz. *MGM*

The Love Flower 🎬🎬½ **1920** A man kills his second wife's lover and escapes with his daughter to a tropical island, pursued by a detective and a young adventurer. Interesting ending wraps things up nicely. Silent. 70m/B **VHS, Beta.** Carol Dempster, Richard Barthelmess, George MacQuarrie, Anders Randolf, Florence Short; **D:** D.W. Griffith; **W:** D.W. Griffith. *NO*

Love for Lydia 🎬🎬🎬 **1979** Made for British television miniseries following wayward beauty Lydia, orphaned heiress to a manufacturing fortune, through the high-spirited 1920s. Set in the industrial Midlands and farming communities of England, Lydia dazzles every man she meets, often to an unhappy end. Based on the novel by H.E. Bates. Available as a seven cassette boxed set. 657m/C **VHS.** *GB* Mel Martin, Christopher Blake, Peter Davison, Jeremy Irons, Michael Aldridge, Rachel Kempson, Beatrix Lehmmann; *FCT, SIG, VIF*

Love from a Stranger 🎬🎬 **1937** Thriller about a working woman who wins a lottery. Soon she is charmed by and marries a man whom she later suspects may be trying to kill her. Remade in 1947. 90m/B **VHS.** *GB* Ann Harding, Basil Rathbone, Binnie Hale, Bruce Seton, Bryan Powley, Jean Cadell; **D:** Rowland V. Lee. *NOS, SNC, NWV*

Love from a Stranger 🎬🎬½ *A Stranger Walked In* **1947** In this remake of the 1937 film, a young newlywed bride fears that the honeymoon is over when she suspects that her husband is a notorious killer and that she will be his next victim. 81m/B **VHS, Beta, LV.** Sylvia Sidney, John Hodiak, John Howard, Ann Richards, Isobel Elsom, Ernest Cossart; **D:** Richard Whorf. *NWV*

The Love God? 🎬½ **1970 (PG-13)** Very silly comedy finds mild-mannered Abner Peacock (Knotts) trying on Hugh Hefner's mantle. With his bird-watcher's magazine in financial trouble, Abner takes on a couple of shifty partners who change it into a different kind of bird watching magazine (the nude female kind) that gets Abner charged with pornography and finds him becoming a (very) unlikely sex symbol. 103m/C **VHS, Closed Caption.** Don Knotts, Edmond O'Brien, Anne Francis, Maureen Arthur, James Gregory, Margaret (Maggie) Peterson, Marjorie Bennett; **D:** Nat Hiken; **W:** Nat Hiken; **C:** William Margulies; **M:** Vic Mizzy. *USH*

The Love Goddesses **1965** A sixty-year examination of some of the most beautiful women on the silver screen, reflecting with extraordinary accuracy the customs, manners and mores of the times. Released theatrically in 1972. 83m/B **VHS, Beta, LV.** Marlene Dietrich, Greta Garbo, Jean Harlow, Gloria Swanson, Mae West, Betty Grable, Rita Hayworth, Elizabeth Taylor, Marilyn Monroe, Theda Bara, Claudette Colbert, Dorothy Lamour; **D:** Saul J. Turell. *COL*

Love Happy 🎬🎬½ **1950** A group of impoverished actors accidentally gain possession of valuable diamonds. Unfortunately for them, detective Groucho is assigned to recover them! 85m/B **VHS, LV.** Groucho Marx, Harpo Marx, Chico Marx, Vera-Ellen, Ilona Massey, Marion Hutton, Raymond Burr, Marilyn Monroe; **D:** David Miller; **C:** William Mellor. *REP*

Love Has Many Faces 🎬🎬½ **1965** Judith Crist was too kind when she said this was for connoisseurs of truly awful movies. Playgal Turner marries beachboy Robertson and many faces come between them. Much melodrama. Filmed on location. 104m/C **VHS, Beta.** Lana Turner, Cliff Robertson, Hugh O'Brian, Ruth Roman, Stefanie Powers, Virginia Grey, Ron Husmann; **D:** Alexander Singer. *GKK*

Love Hurts 🎬🎬 **1991 (R)** A guy looking for romance finds his hands full with a number of beautiful women. Will he find the love he craves, or will the pain be too much to bear? 110m/C **VHS, Closed Caption.** Jeff Daniels, Judith Ivey, John Mahoney, Cynthia Sikes, Amy Wright; **D:** Bud Yorkin; **W:** Ron Nyswaner. *LIV, VES*

Love in Bloom 🎬🎬 **1935** Predictable romance, with Burns and Allen providing some much-needed comic relief. Carnival gal Violet Downey (Lee) falls for struggling songwriter Larry Deane (Morrison) but thinks her tawdry background will ruin his chances and takes off. After Larry becomes successful he searches for Violet, still determined to marry her. 75m/B **VHS, Closed Caption.** George Burns, Gracie Allen, Joe Morrison, Dixie Lee, Lee Kohlmar, Richard Carle; **D:** Elliott Nugent; **W:** J.P. McEvoy, Keene Thompson; **C:** Leo Tover. *USH*

A Love in Germany 🎬🎬½ *Un Amour En Allemagne; Eine Liebe in Deutschland* **1984 (R)** A tragic love affair develops between a German shopkeeper's wife and a Polish prisoner-of-war in a small German village during WWII. In German with English subtitles. 110m/C **VHS, Beta, Closed Caption.** *FR GE* Hanna Schygulla, Piotr Lysak, Elisabeth Trissenaar, Armin Mueller-Stahl; **D:** Andrzej Wajda; **W:** Andrzej Wajda, Agnieszka Holland, Boleslaw Michalek. *COL, APD, GLV*

Love in the Afternoon 🎬🎬½ **1957** A Parisian private eye's daughter (Hepburn) decides to investigate a philandering American millionaire (Cooper) and winds up falling in love with him. Cooper's a little old for the Casanova role but Hepburn is always enchanting. 126m/B **VHS, Beta, Closed Caption.** Gary Cooper, Audrey Hepburn, John McGiver, Maurice Chevalier; **D:** Billy Wilder; **W:** Billy Wilder, I.A.L. Diamond; **C:** William Mellor. *FOX, IME*

Love in the City 🎬🎬🎬 **1953** Five stories of life, love and tears in Rome. In Italian with English subtitles and narration. 90m/B **VHS, Beta.** *IT* Ugo Tognazzi, Maresa Gallo, Caterina Rigoglioso, Silvia Lillo; **D:** Michelangelo Antonioni, Federico Fellini, Dino Risi, Carlo Lizzani, Alberto Lattuada, Francesco Maselli, Cesare Zavattini; **W:** Federico Fellini. *NOS, FCT, APD*

Love in the Present Tense 🎬 **1985** A woman's romantic novel on video, dealing with an affair that reawakens the torpid, tragic life of a beautiful ex-model. 90m/C **VHS, Beta.** *PSM*

Love Is a Gun 🎬½ **1994 (R)** A police photographer (Roberts) begins having violent and erotic hallucinations that begin to affect his fiancee (Garrett). Things get even weirder when a femme fatale model (Preston) enters the picture. **CW:** Sexual situations; language; violence. 92m/C **VHS, LV, Closed Caption.** Eric Roberts, Kelly Preston, Eliza Garrett, R. Lee Ermey; **D:** David Hartwell. *THV*

Love Is a Many-Splendored Thing 🎬🎬½ **1955** A married American war correspondent and a beautiful Eurasian doctor fall in love in post-WWII Hong Kong. They struggle with racism and unhappiness, until he's sent to Korea to observe the Army's activities there. Based on the novel by Han Suyin. The extensive LA Asian acting community got some work out of this film, although the leads are played by Caucasians. Oscar winning song was a very big popular hit. 🎵Love is a Many-Splendored Thing. 102m/C **VHS, Beta, LV, Closed Caption.** William Holden, Jennifer Jones, Torin Thatcher, Isobel Elsom, Jorja Curtright, Virginia Gregg, Richard Loo; **D:** Henry King; **W:** Leon Shamroy; **M:** Alfred Newman. Academy Awards '55: Best Costume De-

sign (Color), Best Song ("Love Is a Many-Splendored Thing"), Original Dramatic/Comedy Score; Nominations: Academy Awards '55: Best Actress (Jones), Best Art Direction/Set Decoration (Color), Best Color Cinematography, Best Picture, Best Sound. *FXV, BTV*

Love Is All There Is 🎬🎬½ **1996 (R)** It's a kind of comedic (happy-ending) version of "Romeo and Juliet," set in the Bronx, about rival restaurant families. Beautiful Gina's (Jolie) a finishing-school grad and Rosario's (Marston) the local boy too handsome for his own good. Both sets of parents are crazy. Oddly enough, Sorvino also plays the heroine's dad in the '96 "William Shakespeare's Romeo & Juliet." 98m/C **VHS.** Angelina Jolie, Nathaniel Marston, Paul Sorvino, Renee Taylor, Joseph Bologna, Lainie Kazan, Barbara Carrera, William Hickey, Abe Vigoda, Dick Van Patten, Connie Stevens; **D:** Renee Taylor, Joseph Bologna; **W:** Renee Taylor, Joseph Bologna; **C:** Alan Jones; **M:** Jeff Beal. *EVE*

Love Is Better Than Ever 🎬🎬½ *The Light Fantastic* **1952** Lightweight romantic-comedy casts Taylor as a dancing instructor who travels to the Big Apple for a convention. Once there, she meets and falls for talent agent Parks. Carefree, bachelor Parks is too busy to be bothered by small town Taylor, but Liz is determined to land her man. Release of this picture was held back because of Parks' blacklisting by the McCarthy committee. 81m/B **VHS.** Larry Parks, Elizabeth Taylor, Josephine Hutchinson, Tom Tully, Ann Doran, Elinor Donahue, Kathleen Freeman; **Cameos:** Gene Kelly; **D:** Stanley Donen; **W:** Ruth Brooks Flippen. *MGM*

Love Jones 🎬🎬🎬 **1996 (R)** A contemporary Chicago nightclub, the Sanctuary, is the gathering spot for middle-class black urbanites looking for romance. Would-be writer/poet Darius (Tate) spouts provocative verse to beautiful photographer Nina (Long), who's not too happy with men at the moment (she's just been dumped). But they make a connection, with both protesting a little too much that it's just a "sex thing." Funny what happens when love clearly enters the picture. Witcher's directorial debut features fine lead performances. **CW:** Language and sexuality. 105m/C **VHS.** Larenz Tate, Nia Long, Isaiah Washington, Lisa Nicole Carson, Khalil Kain, Bill Bellamy, Leonard Roberts, Bernadette L. Clarke; **D:** Theodore Witcher; **W:** Theodore Witcher; **C:** Ernest Holzman; **M:** Darryl Jones. Sundance Film Festival '97: Audience Award. *NYR*

Love Kills 🎬 **1991 (PG-13)** Is the man a beautiful heiress falls in love with actually an assassin hired by her husband to kill her? Find out in this steamy suspenser. 92m/C **VHS, Beta, LV, Closed Caption.** Virginia Madsen, Lenny Von Dohlen, Erich Anderson, Kate Hodge, Jim Metzler; **D:** Brian Grant. *PAR*

Love Laughs at Andy Hardy 🎬🎬 **1946** Andy Hardy, college boy, is in love and in trouble. Financial and romantic problems come to a head when Andy is paired with a six-foot tall blind date. One in the series. 93m/B **VHS, Beta.** Mickey Rooney, Lewis Stone, Sara Haden, Lina Romay, Bonita Granville, Fay Holden; **D:** Willis Goldbeck. *NOS, MRV, HHT*

Love Leads the Way 🎬🎬 **1984** The true story of how Morris Frank established the seeing-eye dog system in the 1930s. 99m/C **VHS, Beta.** Timothy Bottoms, Eva Marie Saint, Arthur Hill, Susan Dey, Ralph Bellamy, Ernest Borgnine, Patricia Neal; **D:** Delbert Mann. *DIS*

Love Letters 🎬🎬🎬 *Passion Play; My Love Letters* **1983 (R)** A young disc jockey falls under the spell of a box of love letters that her mother left behind which detailed her double life. She, in turn, begins an affair with a married man. Thoughtful treatment of the psychology of infidelity. 102m/C **VHS, Beta, LV.** Jamie Lee Curtis, Amy Madigan, Bud Cort, Matt Clark, Bonnie Bartlett, Sally Kirkland, James Keach; **D:** Amy Holden Jones. *LIV, VES, IME*

Love, Lies and Murder 🎬🎬½ **1991 (PG-13)** Shocking psychological thriller in which a businessman convinces his daughter and sister-in-law to murder his wife and then sends his daughter to prison for the crime. The "perfect murder" is not so perfect, however, when the daughter learns that her father has remarried and is now living an insurance-rich lifestyle. She decides to fight back in this true made-for-television story of bizarre murder and deception. **CW:** Mature themes and one violent scene. **190m/C VHS, LV, Closed Caption.** Clancy Brown, John Ashton, Sheryl Lee, Moira Kelly, Ramon Bieri, Ken Walsh, Tom Bower, John M. Jackson; **D:** Robert Markowitz. REP

The Love Machine 𝒵½ 1971 (R) A power-hungry newscaster climbs the corporate ladder by sleeping with many, including the president's wife. An adaptation of Jacqueline Susann's novel. **108m/C VHS, Beta.** John Phillip Law, Dyan Cannon, Robert Ryan, Jackie Cooper, David Hemmings, Jodi Wexler, William Roerick, Maureen Arthur, Shecky Greene, Clinton Greyn, Sharon Farrell, Alexandra Hay, Eve Bruce, Greg Mullavey, Edith Atwater, Gene Baylos, Claudia Jennings, Mary Collinson, Madeleine Collinson, Ann Ford, Gayle Hunnicutt; **D:** Jack Haley Jr.; **C:** Charles B(ryant) Lang; **M:** Artie Butler. COL, MLB

Love Matters 𝒵𝒵 1993 (R) Tom and Julie's fast-track marriage is hovering on the brink when Tom's best friend Geoff, who's also married, shows up on their doorstep with his sexy mistress and announces he's getting a divorce. Reluctantly, Tom and Julie allow the X-rated lovebirds to stay the night but all that heat only shows up the flaws in their own marriage even more. An unrated version at 103 minutes is also available. **97m/C VHS, LV, Closed Caption.** Griffin Dunne, Tony Goldwyn, Annette O'Toole, Gina Gershon, Kate Burton; **D:** Eb Lottimer; **W:** Eb Lottimer; **M:** Simon Boswell. REP

Love Me Deadly 𝒵 1976 (R) A young woman tries to get her husband interested in her new hobby–necrophilia. **95m/C VHS, Beta.** Mary Wilcox, Lyle Waggoner, Christopher Stone, Timothy Scott. GEM

Love Me or Leave Me 𝒵𝒵𝒵 1955 A hard-hitting biography of '20s torch singer Ruth Etting and her rise and fall at the hand of her abusive, gangster husband, a part just made for Cagney. Day emotes and sings expressively in one of the best performances of her career. ♫I'll Never Stop Loving You; Never Look Back; Shaking the Blues Away; Mean to Me; Love Me or Leave Me; Sam, the Old Accordian Man; At Sundown; Everybody Loves My Baby; Five Foot Two. **122m/C VHS, Beta, LV, Closed Caption.** Doris Day, James Cagney, Cameron Mitchell, Robert Keith, Tom Tully, Veda Ann Borg; **D:** Charles Vidor. Academy Awards '55: Best Story; Nominations: Academy Awards '55: Best Actor (Cagney), Best Screenplay, Best Song ("I'll Never Stop Loving You"), Best Sound, Scoring of a Musical.MGM

Love Me Tender 𝒵𝒵 1956 A Civil War-torn family is divided by in-fighting between two brothers who both seek the affections of the same woman. Presley's first film. Songs include "Poor Boy," "We're Gonna Move," and the title tune. **89m/B VHS, Beta.** Elvis Presley, Richard Egan, Debra Paget, Neville Brand, Mildred Dunnock, James Drury, Barry Coe; **D:** Robert D. Webb. MVD, FOX

Love Meetings Comizi d'Amore 1964 Pasolini acts as director and interviewer to query a wide-range of individuals on their experiences at love, including homosexuality, prostitution, marital and non-marital interludes. In Italian with English subtitles. **90m/B VHS, LV.** **IT D:** Pier Paolo Pasolini. WBF

Love Nest 𝒵𝒵 1951 Lundigan stars as Jim Scott, the landlord of an apartment building brimming with wacky tenants, including Monroe, Paar, and Fay. He dreams of becoming a famous writer, but his time is always filled with fixing up the building and trying to pay the mortgage. When one of the tenants ends up in jail because he was living off wealthy widows, Scott's luck changes. This moderately funny film is a good look at the early careers of Monroe and Paar. **84m/B VHS.** William Lundigan, June Haver, Frank Fay, Marilyn Monroe, Jack Paar; **D:** Joseph M. Newman. FXV

Love Notes 1988 Three short vignettes of soft core fantasy, in the life of an ordinary guy. **60m/C VHS, Beta.** Jeff Daniels, Christine Veronica. AHV

The Love of Three Queens 𝒵½ 1954 The loves, on and off stage, of a beautiful actress in a European traveling theatre group. **80m/C VHS, Beta.** Gerard Oury, Massimo Serato, Robert Beatty, Cathy O'Donnell, Terence Morgan, Hedy Lamarr; **D:** Marc Allegret. FCT, VDM

Love on the Dole 𝒵𝒵𝒵 1941 In a gloomy industrial section of England during the early '30s a family struggles to survive and maintain dignity. Grim Depression drama salvaged by great acting. **89m/B VHS, Beta.** GB Deborah Kerr, Clifford Evans, George Carney; **D:** John Baxter. NOS, VYY

Love on the Run 𝒵𝒵½ 1936 Enjoyable romantic comedy starring Crawford as a rich American heiress and Gable and Tone (Crawford's real husband at the time) as journalists stationed in Europe. Gable and Tone are assigned to cover an international aviator, who turns out to be an evil spy, as well as the upcoming wedding of flighty Crawford. When Crawford asks for help in getting out of her marriage, Gable and Tone steal a plane and the trio is chased across Europe by spies. Wild and farfetched plot, but the stars make it worthwhile. Based on the story "Beauty and the Beast" by Alan Green and Julian Brodie. **80m/B VHS.** Joan Crawford, Clark Gable, Franchot Tone, Reginald Owen, Mona Maris, Ivan Lebedeff, Charles Judels, William Demarest; **D:** Woodbridge S. Van Dyke; **W:** John Lee Mahin, Manuel Seff, Gladys Hurlbut. MGM

Love on the Run 𝒵𝒵𝒵 L'Amour en Fuite 1978 The further amorous adventures of Antoine Doinel, hero of "The 400 Blows," "Stolen Kisses," and "Bed and Board." Doinel is now in his thirties and newly divorced. He renews affairs with several women from his past but, after his mother's death, must contend with his emotional immaturity and his inability to sustain a relationship. In French with English subtitles. **95m/C VHS, Beta.** FR Jean-Pierre Leaud, Marie-France Pisier, Claude Jade; **D:** Francois Truffaut; **C:** Nestor Almendros; **M:** Georges Delerue. Cesar Awards '80: Best Score. HMV, WAR

Love on the Run 𝒵½ 1985 A beautiful lawyer helps a wrongly-accused convict escape from prison, then they both evade the law. Made for television. **102m/C VHS, Beta.** Stephanie Zimbalist, Alec Baldwin, Constance McCashin, Howard Duff; **D:** Gus Trikonis; **M:** Billy Goldenberg. COL

Love or Money? 𝒵½ 1988 (PG-13) A small comedy about a yuppie who must choose between a woman and a real estate deal. **90m/C VHS, Beta, LV, Closed Caption.** Timothy Daly, Haviland Morris, Kevin McCarthy, Shelley Fabares, David Doyle, Allen Havey; **D:** Todd Hallowell; **W:** Bart Davis. NO

Love Potion #9 𝒵½ 1992 (PG-13) Two nerdy biochemists procure a love potion that they test on animals. Meeting with success they agree to test it on themselves. Predictably, the scientists are transformed and fall in love with each other. Features a talented young cast, with an amusing cameo by Bancroft, but the script is a real disappointment because of its shallow characters and lame gags. Inspired by the song by Jerry Leiber and Mike Stoller. **96m/C VHS, LV, Closed Caption.** Tate Donovan, Sandra Bullock, Mary Mara, Dale Midkiff, Hillary Bailey Smith, Dylan Baker; **Cameos:** Anne Bancroft; **D:** Dale Launer; **W:** Dale Launer. FXV

Love Songs 𝒵𝒵 1985 (R) A mother of two is confronted with her husband's abandonment and a subsequent romance with a younger man. In French with English subtitles or dubbed. ♫Leave It to Me; Psychic Flash; I Am With You Now; Human Race; We Can Dance; One More Moment; From the Heart; This Must Be Heaven. **107m/C VHS, Beta.** FR CA Catherine Deneuve, Christopher Lambert; **D:** Elie Chouraqui; **C:** Robert Alazraki. LIV, VES

Love Story 𝒵𝒵𝒵 1970 (PG) Melodrama had enormous popular appeal. O'Neal is the son of Boston's upper crust at Harvard; McGraw's the daughter of a poor Italian on scholarship to study music at Radcliffe. They find happiness, but only for a brief period. Timeless story, simply told, with

artful direction from Hiller pulling exceptional performances from the young duo (who have never done as well since). The end result is perhaps better than Segal's simplistic novel, which was produced after he sold the screenplay and became a best-seller before the picture's release—great publicity for any film. Remember: "Love means never having to say you're sorry." **100m/C VHS, Beta, LV.** Ryan O'Neal, Ali MacGraw, Ray Milland, John Marley, Tommy Lee Jones; **D:** Arthur Hiller; **W:** Erich Segal. Academy Awards '70: Best Original Score; Golden Globe Awards '71: Best Actress—Drama (MacGraw), Best Director (Hiller), Best Film—Drama, Best Screenplay, Best Score; National Board of Review Awards '70: 10 Best Films of the Year; Nominations: Academy Awards '70: Best Actor (O'Neal), Best Actress (MacGraw), Best Director (Hiller), Best Picture, Best Story & Screenplay, Best Supporting Actor (Marley). PAR

Love Strange Love 𝒵½ 1982 A young boy develops a bizarre relationship with his mother who works in a luxurious bordello. Also available in an unedited 120-minute version. **97m/C VHS, Beta.** Vera Fischer, Mauro Mendonca. LIV, VES

Love Streams 𝒵𝒵½ 1984 (PG-13) A quirky character drama about a writer and his sister who struggle to find love despite their personal problems. **122m/C VHS, Beta.** Gena Rowlands, John Cassavetes, Diahnne Abbott, Seymour Cassel; **D:** John Cassavetes; **W:** Ted Allan. Berlin International Film Festival '84: Golden Berlin Bear. MGM

Love Thrill Murders woof! 1971 (R) A film about a Mansonesque lunatic who is worshipped and obeyed by a mob of runaways and dropouts. **89m/C VHS, Beta.** Troy Donahue. LIV, VES

Love Under Pressure 𝒵𝒵 198? Man and woman's marriage starts to evaporate when they realize their son is seriously disturbed. **92m/C VHS.** Karen Black, Keir Dullea. ACA

Love! Valour! Compassion! 𝒵𝒵½ 1996 (R) Follows eight gay men, longtime friends, who spend summer holiday weekends together at a beach house. Excellent cast features Alexander as Buzz, who has a severe show tune fixation, and Glover playing a pair of twins with very different personalities (and they're actually named Jeckyll). Together they wander through the turmoil of AIDS, infidelity, rage and impromptu ballet practice. Excellent cast only occasionally swerves from humor and genuine pathos into maudlin. Intermittent periods of stagy claustrophobia betray pic's Broadway origin. Based on the play by Terrence McNally. **CW:** Graphic nudity, some sexuality and brief violence. **115m/C VHS.** Jason Alexander, John Glover, Randy Becker, John Benjamin Hickey, Stephen Bogardus, Stephen Spinella, Justin Kirk; **D:** Joe Mantello; **W:** Terrance McNally; **C:** Alik Sakharov; **M:** Harold Wheeler. NYR

Love with a Perfect Stranger 1986 This Harlequin Romance takes place in Italy where a young widow meets a dashing Englishman. He changes her life forever. **102m/C VHS, Beta.** Marilu Henner, Daniel Massey; **M:** John Du Prez. PAR

Love with the Proper Stranger 𝒵𝒵𝒵 1963 A quiet, gritty romance about an itinerant musician and a young working girl in Manhattan awkwardly living through the consequences of their one night stand. Moved Wood well into the realm of adult roles, after years playing teen-agers and innocents. Although the story is about an Italian neighborhood and family, an exceptional number of the cast members were Jewish, as was the screenwriter. Story does not conclude strongly, although this did not hamper the box office returns. **102m/B VHS, Beta, LV, Closed Caption.** Natalie Wood, Steve McQueen, Edie Adams, Herschel Bernardi, Tom Bosley, Harvey Lembeck, Penny Santon, Virginia Vincent, Nick Alexander, Augusta Ciolli; **D:** Robert Mulligan; **W:** Arnold Schulman; **C:** Milton Krasner; **M:** Elmer Bernstein. Nominations: Academy Awards '63: Best Actress (Wood), Best Art Direction/Set Decoration (B & W), Best Black and White Cinematography, Best Costume Design (B & W), Best Story & Screenplay. PAR

Love Without Fear 1990 A dramatic, heart-rendering look at children with AIDS. Story focuses on the lives of three women from completely different backgrounds who adopt babies with AIDS and develop a special love for these children. Also shows their confrontations with a society which fears the disease and the women's strength to reach out and make a difference. **?m/C VHS.** *NO*

Love Without Pity ✯✯½ 1991 Rochant's theatrical debut is a modern romance, with more distance and alienation than joy. A lovely, successful grad student loses her heart to a jobless, unambitious layabout who wants total commitment from her. Untypical, sardonic love story may be too cynical for sentimental types. In French with English subtitles. **95m/C VHS.** *FR* Hippolyte Girardot, Mireille Perrier, Jean Marie Rollin; *D:* Eric Rochant; *W:* Eric Rochant; *M:* Gerard Torikian. *ORI*

Love Your Mama ✯✯½ 1989 (PG-13) An urban black drama about the strong Dorothy whose faith helps her cope with her many family complications, including her drunken husband, car thief son, and pregnant teenage daughter. Believable role models and good performances help out this amatuer filmmaking effort. **93m/C VHS.** Audrey Morgan, Carol E. Hall, Andre Robinson, Ernest Rayford, Kearo Johnson, Jacqueline Williams; *D:* Ruby L. Oliver; *W:* Ruby L. Oliver. *HMD, BTV, FCT*

The Loved One ✯✯✯ 1965 A famously outlandish, death-mocking farce based on Evelyn Waugh's satire about a particularly horrendous California funeral parlor/cemetery and how its denizens do business. A shrill, protracted spearing of American capitalism. **118m/B VHS, Beta, LV.** Robert Morse, John Gielgud, Rod Steiger, Liberace, Anjanette Comer, Jonathan Winters, James Coburn, Dana Andrews, Milton Berle, Tab Hunter, Robert Morley, Lionel Stander, Margaret Leighton, Roddy McDowall, Bernie Kopell, Alan Napier; *D:* Tony Richardson; *W:* Terry Southern, Christopher Isherwood; *C:* Haskell Wexler; *M:* John Addison. *MGM*

Loveless ✯✯ 1983 (R) A menacing glance into the exploits of an outcast motorcycle gang. In the 50s, a group of bikers on their way to the Florida Cycle Races stop for lunch in a small-town diner. While repairs are being made on their motorcycles, they decide to take full advantage of their situation. **85m/C VHS, Beta, LV.** Robert Gordon, Willem Dafoe, J. Don Ferguson; *D:* Kathryn Bigelow; *W:* Kathryn Bigelow. *MED*

Lovelines ✯ 1984 (R) Two rock singers from rival high schools meet and fall in love during a panty raid. Laughs uncounted ensue. **93m/C VHS, Beta, Closed Caption.** Greg Bradford, Michael Winslow, Mary Beth Evans, Don Michael Paul, Tammy Taylor, Stacey Toten, Miguel Ferrer, Shecky Greene, Aimee Eccles, Sherri Stoner; *D:* Rod Amateau. *FOX*

Lovely ... But Deadly ✯½ 1982 (R) Young girl wages a war against the drug dealers in her school after her brother dies of an overdose. **95m/C VHS, Beta.** Lucinda Dooling, John Randolph, Richard Herd, Susan Mechsner, Mel Novak; *D:* David Sheldon. *LIV, VES*

Lovely to Look At ✯✯✯ 1952 Three wanna-be Broadway producers (Skelton, Keel, Champion) go to gay Paree to peddle Skelton's half interest in Madame Roberta's, a chi chi dress shop. There, they meet the shop's other half interest, two sisters (Champion and Miller), and together they stage a fashion show to finance the floundering hospice of haute couture. Lavish production, light plot. Filmed in Technicolor based on Kern's 1933 Broadway hit (inspired by Alice Duer Miller's "Gowns by Roberta"). Vincent Minelli staged the fashion show, with gowns by Adrian (watch for cop-beater Zsa Zsa as a model). Laserdisc format features the original motion picture trailer. ♫Opening Night; Smoke Gets in Your Eyes; Lovely to Look At; The Touch of Your Hand; Yesterdays; I Won't Dance; You're Devastating; The Most Exciting Night; I'll Be Hard to Handle.

105m/C VHS, LV. Kathryn Grayson, Red Skelton, Howard Keel, Gower Champion, Marge Champion, Ann Miller, Zsa Zsa Gabor, Kurt Kasznar, Marcel Dalio, Diane Cassidy; *D:* Mervyn LeRoy; *M:* Jerome Kern. *MGM, TTC, FCT*

The Lover ✯✯ *L'Amant* 1992 (R) Portrays the sexual awakening of a French teenager and her older Chinese lover in Indochina in 1929. The characters, who remain nameless, meet on a ferry where the man is smitten by the girl's beauty. Detached, determined, and unromantic (the opposite of her indolent lover), she allows herself to be seduced for the experience, and money, he offers. The film is equally detached, including the beautifully photographed but uninvolving sex scenes. Moreau narrates as an adult looking back on her life. March's debut; filmed on location in Vietnam. Based on the semi-autobiographical novel by Marguerite Duras who reputiated director Annuad's film when it was released in France. Also available in an unrated, letterbox version at 115 minutes. **103m/C VHS, Beta, LV, Closed Caption.** *FR* Jane March, Tony Leung, Frederique Meininger, Arnaud Giovianietti, Melvil Poupaud, Lisa Faulkner, Xiem Mang; *D:* Jean-Jacques Annaud; *W:* Gerard Brach, Jean-Jacques Annaud; *C:* Robert Fraisse. Cesar Awards '93: Best Score; Nominations: Academy Awards '92: Best Cinematography. *MGM, BTV*

Lover Come Back ✯✯½ 1961 More Day-Hudson antics in which an advertising executive falls in love with his competitor but that doesn't stop him from stealing her clients. Is there no shame? **107m/C VHS, Beta.** Rock Hudson, Doris Day, Tony Randall, Edie Adams, Joe Flynn, Ann B. Davis, Jack Oakie, Jack Albertson, Jack Kruschen, Howard St. John; *D:* Delbert Mann. Nominations: Academy Awards '61: Best Story & Screenplay. *USH, MOV*

Loverboy ✯ 1989 (PG-13) A college schnook takes a summer job as a Beverly Hills pizza delivery boy and is preyed upon by many rich and sex-hungry housewives. **105m/C VHS, Beta, LV, Closed Caption.** Patrick Dempsey, Kate Jackson, Barbara Carrera, Kirstie Alley, Carrie Fisher, Robert Ginty; *D:* Joan Micklin Silver; *W:* Tom Ropelewski, Leslie Dixon; *M:* Michel Colombier. *COL*

The Lovers ✯✯✯ 1959 Chic tale of French adultery with Moreau starring as a provincial wife whose shallow life changes overnight when she meets a young man. Had a controversial American debut because of the film's tender eroticism and innocent view of adultery. In French with English subtitles. **90m/B VHS.** *FR* Jeanne Moreau, Alain Cuny, Jose-Luis De Villalonga, Jean-Mark Bory; *D:* Louis Malle; *W:* Louis Malle. Venice Film Festival '59: Special Jury Prize. *NYF, FCT, ING*

Lovers: A True Story ✯✯✯ 1990 (R) Erotic love triangle in 1950s Madrid, while Spain is under the suffocating dictatorship of Franco. Naive, young Paco has a virginal, hardworking fiancee named Trini. Things would seem to be headed for an average life until Paco rents a room from young widow Luisa and they embark on a sexual affair bordering on obsession. When Trini discovers what's going on she turns out to have a more passionate, and violent, nature than even Paco could imagine. Steamy and highly dramatic with excellent performances. Based on a true story. In Spanish with English subtitles. An unrated version is also available.***CW:*** Language and sexuality. **105m/C VHS.** *SP* Victoria Abril, Jorge Sanz, Maribel Verdu; *D:* Vicente Aranda. Berlin International Film Festival '91: Best Actress (Abril).*REP*

Lovers and Liars ✯✯ *Travels with Anita; A Trip with Anita* 1981 (R) A romantic adventure in Rome turns into a symphony of zany mishaps when the man forgets to tell the woman that he is married!! **93m/C VHS, Beta.** *IT* Goldie Hawn, Giancarlo Giannini, Laura Betti; *D:* Mario Monicelli; *M:* Ennio Morricone.

Lovers and Other Strangers ✯✯✯ 1970 (R) Two young people decide to marry after living together for a year and a half. Various tensions surface between them and among their families as the wedding day approaches. Good

comedy features some charming performances. Keaton's first film. ♫For All We Know. **106m/C VHS.** Gig Young, Beatrice Arthur, Bonnie Bedelia, Anne Jackson, Harry Guardino, Michael Brandon, Richard Castellano, Bob Dishy, Marian Hailey, Cloris Leachman, Anne Meara, Diane Keaton; *D:* Cy Howard; *W:* Renee Taylor, Joseph Bologna, David Zelag Goodman. Academy Awards '70: Best Song ("For All We Know"); Nominations: Academy Awards '70: Best Adapted Screenplay, Best Supporting Actor (Castellano). *FOX*

Lover's Knot ✯✯½ 1996 (R) Cutesy romantic comedy has Curry as an angel whose heavenly mission is to get the proper romantic couples together. His current pair are poetic college English prof Steve (Campbell) and practical pediatrician Megan (Grey). Steve's imaginative courtship wins Megan but day-to-day living takes its toll and the duo separate, leaving their angelic guide to get them back together.***CW:*** Sexuality. **82m/C VHS, Closed Caption.** Bill Campbell, Jennifer Grey, Tim Curry, Adam Baldwin; *Cameos:* Adam Ant, Anne Francis; *D:* Peter Shaner; *W:* Peter Shaner; *C:* Garett Griffin; *M:* Laura Karpman. *CAF*

Lovers Like Us ✯✯½ *Le Sauvage; The Savage* 1975 Two people each leave their spouses, meet one another, and fall in love. **103m/C VHS, Beta.** *FR* Catherine Deneuve, Yves Montand, Luigi Vannucchi, Tony Roberts, Dana Wynter; *D:* Jean-Paul Rappeneau; *W:* Jean-Paul Rappeneau. *NO*

Lovers' Lovers ✯½ 1994 All sorts of bizarre and erotic adventures ensue when Blaire the jilted narcissist meets Michael, who doesn't want to commit to girlfriend Teri. Michael plans an affair with Blaire without realizing that Teri is already having a fling with Ray, Blaire's ex. Some funny situations but too many talky scenes stop the film cold. **90m/C VHS, LV.** Serge Rodnunsky, Jennifer Ciesar, Cindy Parker, Ray Bennett; *D:* Serge Rodnunsky; *W:* Serge Rodnunsky; *M:* Pierre Rodnunsky. *TRI*

Lovers of Their Time ✯✯ 1985 A romantic novel on tape, about forbidden love and other problems. **60m/C Beta.** Edward Petherbridge, Cheryl Prime, Lynn Farleigh; *D:* Robert Knights. *PSM*

Loves & Times of Scaramouche ✯½ *Scaramouche* 1976 Eighteenth-century rogue becomes involved in a plot to assassinate Napoleon and winds up seducing Josephine in the process. Dubbed. **92m/C VHS, Beta.** *IT* Michael Sarrazin, Ursula Andress, Aldo Maccione; *D:* Enzo G. Castellari. *COL*

Loves of a Blonde ✯✯✯½ *A Blonde in Love; Lasky Jedne Plavovlasky* 1965 A shy teenage factory girl falls in love with a visiting piano player when the reservist army comes to her small town. But when she goes to visit his family, she discovers things aren't as she imagined. Touching look at the complications of love and our expectations. Czech with subtitles. **88m/B VHS, Beta.** *CZ* Jana Brejchova, Josef Sebanek, Vladimir Pucholt; *D:* Milos Forman. Nominations: Academy Awards '66: Best Foreign Language Film. *HMV, COL*

The Loves of Carmen ✯✯½ 1948 Film version of the classic Prosper Merrimee novel about a tempestuous Spanish gypsy and the soldier who loves her. Hayworth is great to look at and the film's main selling point. **98m/C VHS, Beta.** Rita Hayworth, Glenn Ford, Ron Randell, Victor Jory, Arnold Moss, Luther Adler, Joseph Buloff; *D:* Charles Vidor. Nominations: Academy Awards '48: Best Color Cinematography. *COL*

The Loves of Edgar Allen Poe ✯✯ 1942 A bland biographical drama about young Poe's adoption, his treatment at the hands of his foster father, his rejection by a woman for a more well-off man, his marriage to his first cousin, and his early death from alcoholism. **67m/B VHS.** Linda Darnell, Shepperd Strudwick, Virginia Gilmore, Jane Darwell, Mary Howard; *D:* Harry Lachman. *TCF*

The Loves of Hercules woof! *Hercules and the Hydra* 1960 The mythic mesomorph finds a mate with equiponderant chest measurements, and must save her from an evil queen. Somehow it eludes him that both queen and maiden are Miss Jayne in red and black wigs. Kudos for worst dubbing and special effects; a must see for connoisseurs of kitsch. **94m/C VHS.** *IT FR* Jayne Mansfield, Mickey Hargitay; *D:* Carlo L. Bragaglia. *SNC, VDM*

The Loves of Irina 💣 198? Franco's dreamy, sanguine, produced-on-a-dime tale of a vampiress. She cruises the Riviera, seducing and nibbling on a variety of men and women. Spanish release known as "Erotikill," not for most tastes. **95m/C VHS, Beta.** Lina Romay, Monica Swin, Jack Taylor, Alice Arno; *D:* Jess (Jesus) Franco. *MED*

Love's Savage Fury woof! 1979 Two escapees from a Union prison camp seek out a hidden treasure that could determine the outcome of the Civil War. A bad made-for-television "Gone With the Wind" rip-off. **100m/C VHS, Beta.** Jennifer O'Neill, Perry King, Robert Reed, Raymond Burr, Connie Stevens, Ed Lauter; *D:* Joseph Hardy; *M:* John Addison. *PSM*

Lovesick 💿💿 1983 (PG) A very-married New York psychiatrist goes against his own best judgment when he falls in love with one of his patients. **98m/C VHS, Beta, LV.** Dudley Moore, Elizabeth McGovern, Alec Guinness, John Huston, Ron Silver; *D:* Marshall Brickman; *W:* Marshall Brickman. *WAR*

Lovespell 💿 *Tristan and Isolde* 1979 A retelling of the legend of Isolde and Tristan. Stilted direction and writing, but another chance to reminisce on Richard Burton. **91m/C VHS.** Richard Burton, Kate Mulgrew, Nicholas Clay, Cyril Cusack, Geraldine Fitzgerald, Niall Toibin, Diana Van Der Vlis, Niall O'Brien; *D:* Tom Donovan. *NO*

Lovey: A Circle of Children 2 💿💿 1982 Teacher for special children takes in a terrified girl diagnosed as brain damaged or schizophrenic, and discovers love and intelligence in the girl as well as finding some important insights into her own life. **120m/C VHS, Beta.** Jane Alexander, Kris McKeon; *D:* Jud Taylor. *TLF*

Loving 💿💿½ 1984 The full-length, shot-on-video pilot for the daytime television soap opera, with various guest stars. Exteriors shot at C.W. Post Center on Long Island. **120m/C VHS, Beta.** Lloyd Bridges, Geraldine Page. *NO*

Loving Couples 💿💿 1980 (PG) Two happily married couples meet at a weekend resort...and switch partners. Tired and predictable but it has its moments. **120m/C VHS, Beta.** Shirley MacLaine, James Coburn, Susan Sarandon, Stephen Collins, Sally Kellerman; *D:* Jack Smight. *VES*

Loving You 💿💿 1957 A small town boy with a musical style all his own becomes a big success thanks to the help of a female press agent. Features many early Elvis hits. ♫Loving You; Teddy Bear; Lonesome Cowboy; Got a Lot of Livin' To Do; Party; Mean Woman Blues; Hot Dog. **101m/C VHS, Beta, LV.** Elvis Presley, Wendell Corey, Lizabeth Scott, Dolores Hart, James Gleason; *D:* Hal Kanter; *W:* Hal Kanter. *WAR, OM*

Low Blow 💿 1985 A kung fu expert tracks down a mind-bending cult. **88m/C VHS, Beta.** Cameron Mitchell, Leo Fong; *D:* Frank Harris. *LIV, VES*

A Low Down Dirty Shame 💿💿 1994 (R) Shame (Wayans) is a down-on-his-luck private eye, with the obligatory wisecracking secretary, Peaches (Pinkett), who's hired by an old friend to find a vicious drug lord, a sultry ex-girlfriend, and $20 million. Lots of fun stunts and one liners can't make up for major plot holes.*CW:* Violence; strong lanuage; brief sexuality. **100m/C VHS, LV, Closed Caption.** Keenen Ivory Wayans, Jada Pinkett, Salli Richardson, Charles S. Dutton, Andrew Divoff, Corwin Hawkins; *D:* Keenen Ivory Wayans; *W:* Keenen Ivory Wayans. *TOU*

The Low Life 💿💿½ 1995 (R) A "day in the life" sort of story about aspiring writer John (Cochrane) who comes to L.A. with high hopes but instead gets stuck in the low life of awful temp jobs, a lousy landlord (LeGros), and now, his newly arrived loser cousin Andrew (Astin). He tries to cozy up to looker Sedgwick but he

doesn't seem too interested—so what's a would-be cool guy to do?*CW:* Language, sexuality and some drug use. **96m/C VHS, Closed Caption.** Rory Cochrane, Kyra Sedgwick, Sean Astin, James LeGros, Christian Meoli, Shawnee Smith, J.T. Walsh, Renee Zellweger; *D:* George Hickenlooper; *W:* George Hickenlooper, John Enbom; *C:* Richard Crudo; *M:* Bill Boll. *CAF*

The Lower Depths 💿💿💿½ *Les Bas Fonds; Underground* 1936 Renoir's adaptation of the Maxim Gorky play about a thief and a financially ruined baron learning about life from one another. In French with English subtitles. **92m/B VHS, Beta.** *FR* Jean Gabin, Louis Jouvet, Vladimir Sokoloff, Robert Le Vigan, Suzy Prim; *D:* Jean Renoir. National Board of Review Awards '37: 10 Best Films of the Year. *FCT, DVT, GVV*

The Lower Depths 💿💿💿 1957 Kurosawa sets the Maxim Gorky play in Edo during the final Tokugawa period, using Noh theatre elements in depicting the lowly denizens of a low-rent hovel. In Japanese with English subtitles. **125m/B VHS, Beta.** *JP* Toshiro Mifune, Isuzu Yamada, Ganjiro Nakamura, Kyoko Kagawa, Bokuzen Hidari; *D:* Akira Kurosawa. *FCT, COL, NLC*

Lower Level 💿 1991 (R) While working late, an attractive business woman becomes trapped in an office building by her psychotic secret admirer.*CW:* Language, violence, and sensuality. **88m/C VHS, LV, Closed Caption.** David Bradley, Elizabeth Gracen, Jeff Yagher; *D:* Kristine Peterson. *REP*

Loyalties 💿💿½ 1986 (R) A strong treatment of the issue of sexual abuse of girls by men, and of an upper-class woman's willingness to establish a true friendship with a woman of a so-called lower economic class. **98m/C VHS.** *CA* Kenneth Welsh, Tantoo Cardinal, Susan Wooldridge, Vera Martin, Christopher Barrington-Leigh; *D:* Anne Wheeler; *W:* Sharon Riis; *M:* Michael Conway Baker. *NO*

Loyola, the Soldier Saint 1952 A biography of the founder of the Jesuits from his years as a page in the Spanish court to his daring exploits on the battle field and, finally, his spiritual awakening at the University of Paris. Narrated by Father Alfred J. Barrett. **99m/B VHS.** Rafael Duran, Maria Rosa Jiminez; *D:* Jose Diaz Morales. *IVY, KEP*

Lucas 💿💿💿 1986 (PG-13) A high school brain falls in love with the new girl in town, and tries to win her by trying out for the football team. Genuine film about the perils of coming of age. Thoughtful, non-condescending, and humorous. **100m/C VHS, Beta, Closed Caption.** Corey Haim, Kerri Green, Charlie Sheen, Winona Ryder, Courtney Thorne-Smith, Thomas E. Hodges; *D:* David Seltzer; *W:* David Seltzer; *M:* Dave Grusin. *FXV, FOX*

The Lucifer Complex 💿 1978 Nazi doctors are cloning exact duplicates of such world leaders as the Pope and the President of the United States on a remote South American island in the year 1996. **91m/C VHS, Beta.** Robert Vaughn, Merrie Lynn Ross, Keenan Wynn, Aldo Ray; *D:* David L. Hewitt, Kenneth Hartford. *VCI*

Lucky Cisco Kid 💿💿½ 1940 Romero takes over from Warner Baxter in the fourth entry in the series, with Martin as his loyal sidekick. This time a rustler and his gang are stealing cattle and using the Kid's name to place the blame. Fast-paced with Romero appropriately debonair. Andrews screen debut. **67m/B VHS.** Cesar Romero, Chris-Pin Martin, Mary Beth Hughes, Dana Andrews, Evelyn Venable, Joseph Sawyer, Francis Ford; *D:* H. Bruce Humberstone; *W:* Robert Ellis, Helen Logan. *GPV*

Lucky Devil 💿½ 1925 Lucky devil wins car and motors around the country to the tune of organ music. **63m/B VHS, Beta.** Richard Dix, Esther Ralston, Edna May Oliver, Tom Findley; *D:* Frank Tuttle. *GPV, FCT*

Lucky Jim 💿💿½ 1958 A junior lecturer in history at a small university tries to get himself in good graces with the head of his department, but is doomed from the start by doing the wrong things at the worst possible times. Minus the social satire of the Kingsley Amis novel on which it was based; what's left is a cheerful comedy. **91m/**

B VHS, Beta. *GB* Ian Carmichael, Terry-Thomas, Hugh Griffith, Sharon Acker, Jean Anderson, Maureen Connell, Clive Morton, John Welsh, Reginald Beckwith, Kenneth Griffith, Jeremy Hawk, Harry Fowler; *D:* John Boulting; *W:* Jeffrey Dell, Patrick Campbell; *M:* John Addison. *NO*

Lucky Luciano 💿💿 *A Proposito Luciano; RE: Lucky Luciano* 1974 (R) A violent depiction of the final years of Lucky Luciano, gangster kingpin. **108m/C VHS, Beta.** *IT FR* Edmond O'Brien, Rod Steiger, Vincent Gardenia, Gian Marie Volonte; *D:* Francesco Rosi; *C:* Pasquale De Santos. *NLC*

Lucky Luke 💿💿½ 1994 (PG) Fastest gun in the west brings the law to Daisy Town, aided by his horse, Jolly Jumper—who can talk. Not exactly John Wayne material but amusing. **91m/C VHS.** Terence Hill, Nancy Morgan, Ron Carey; *D:* Terence Hill; *V:* Roger Miller. *APX, ACA*

Lucky Luke: The Ballad of the Daltons 1978 Easygoing cowboy hero Lucky Luke gets involved in a wild feud with the bumbling Dalton Brothers gang in this animated feature. **82m/C VHS, Beta, LV.** *D:* Rene Goscinny. *DIS*

Lucky Me 💿💿 1954 A group of theater entertainers are stranded in Miami and are forced to work in a hotel kitchen. They soon acquire the support of a wealthy oilman (Goodwin) who invests in their show, but not before his spoiled daughter tries to thwart all plans. ♫Lucky Me; Superstition Song; I Speak to the Stars; Take a Memo to the Moon; Love You Dearly; Bluebells of Broadway; Parisian Pretties; Wanna Sing Like an Angel; High Hopes. **100m/C VHS, LV.** Doris Day, Robert Cummings, Phil Silvers, Eddie Foy Jr., Nancy Walker, Martha Hyer, Bill Goodwin, Marcel Dalio, James Burke, Jack Shea, William "Billy" Bakewell, Charles Cane, Ray Teal, Tom Powers, Angie Dickinson, Dolores Dorn; *D:* Jack Donohue. *WAR, CCB, MVD*

Lucky Partners 💿💿 1940 When an artist and an errand girl share a winning lottery ticket, funny complications arise as they embark on a fantasy honeymoon. Although Rogers' innocence and Coleman's savoir faire provide an interesting contrast, the script isn't equal to the status of its stars. **101m/B VHS, Beta.** Ronald Colman, Ginger Rogers, Jack Carson, Spring Byington, Harry Davenport; *D:* Lewis Milestone. *TTC*

Lucky Stiff 💿💿 1988 (PG) A fat, unpopular dweeb has the shock of his life when a radiant woman falls in love with him, the strangeness of which becomes evident when he meets her very weird family. **93m/C VHS, Beta, LV.** Donna Dixon, Joe Alaskey, Jeff Kober, Elizabeth Arlen, Charles Frank, Barbara Howard; *D:* Anthony Perkins; *W:* Pat Proft. *COL*

Lucky Terror 💿 1936 Routine Hoot cowboy drama. **60m/B VHS, Beta.** Hoot Gibson, Kone Andre, Charles "Blackie" King; *D:* Alan James. *NOS, GPV, VCN*

Lucky Texan 💿½ 1934 Wayne plays a tough easterner who goes West and finds himself involved in a range war. **61m/B VHS, Beta.** John Wayne, George "Gabby" Hayes, Yakima Canutt; *D:* Robert North Bradbury. *COL, REP, MRV*

Lucy and Desi: Before the Laughter 💿💿½ 1991 (PG-13) The meeting and early married life of actress/comedian Lucille Ball and Cuban bandleader Desi Arnaz is depicted in this routine biopic. Film depicts Desi's womanizing, their struggles with fame, and their efforts to get their television show on the air. Fisher does well as television's favorite redhead but this made-for-television effort is melodramatic. Daughter Lucy Arnaz vehemently opposed this depiction of her parents life.*CW:* Language and sensuality. **95m/C VHS, LV, Closed Caption.** Frances Fisher, Maurice Benard, John Wheeler, Robin Pearson Rose; *D:* Charles Jarrott; *W:* William Luce. *REP, PMS*

L'Udienza 💿💿½ 1971 A bizarre black comedy about a guy who does anything he can, at any criminal cost, to obtain an audience with the Pope. In Italian with subtitles. **111m/C VHS, Beta.** *IT* Claudia Cardinale, Ugo Tognazzi; *D:* Marco Ferreri. *FCT*

Luggage of the Gods ✗✗ 1987 (G) A lost tribe of cave people are confronted with civilization when suitcases fall from an airplane. Low-budget comedy reminiscent of "The Gods Must Be Crazy." 78m/C VHS, Beta. Mark Stolzenberg, Gabriel Barre, Gwen Ellison; **D:** David Kendall. ACA

Lullaby of Broadway ✗✗½ 1951 Many songs highlight this flimsy musical about a girl (Day) who ventures from England to the Big Apple in search of an acting career. She soon discovers that her mom has become a has-been actress now performing in a Greenwich Village dive. Day struggles to gain her own success while coping with her mother's downfall. ♫Lullaby of Broadway; You're Getting to Be a Habit With Me; Just One of Those Things; Somebody Loves Me; I Love the Way You Say Goodnight; Fine and Dandy; Please Don't Talk About Me When I'm Gone; A Shanty in Old Shanty Town; We'd Like to Go On A Trip. 93m/C VHS. Doris Day, Gene Nelson, S.Z. Sakall, Billy DeWolfe, Gladys George, Florence Bates; **D:** David Butler. WAR, CCB, MVD

Lumiere ✗✗½ 1976 (R) An acclaimed drama about four actresses who, during the course of one night together, make pivotal decisions about their lives and relationships. Moreau's first directorial effort; dubbed. 101m/C VHS, Beta. FR Jeanne Moreau, Lucia Bose, Francine Racette, Caroline Cartier, Keith Carradine, Francois Simon, Francis Huster, Bruno Ganz, Rene Feret, Niels Arestrup, Jerome Lapperrousaz; **D:** Jeanne Moreau; **C:** Ricardo Aronvich; **M:** Astor Piazzolla.

Luna e L'Altra ✗✗ 1996 Dizzy schoolteacher Luna (Forte) is the butt of practical jokes by her students and ignored by the other faculty. Dutiful and self-effacing, she's also the secret crush of school custodian Angelo (Nichetti). But Luna has a hidden side that comes to the surface thanks to magician Igor's magic latern and it turns out to be a sexy one. Italian with subtitles. 92m/C VHS. IT Iaia Forte, Maurizio Nichetti, Aurelio Fierro, Luigi Burruano; **D:** Maurizio Nichetti; **W:** Maurizio Nichetti; **C:** Luca Bigazzi; **M:** Carlo Siliotto. Nominations: Golden Globe Awards '97: Best Foreign Language Film. NYR

Luna Park ✗✗ 1991 In contemporary Russia, Andrei (Goutine) is the leader of a gang of body-builder, right-wing skinheads who beat up Jews, foreigners, and anyone else they dislike. Then the anti-Semitic Andrei learns his father is Jewish and he frantically searches through Moscow to find him and discover his past. In Russian with subtitles. 105m/C VHS. RU Oleg Borisov, Andrei Goutine, Natalya Yegorova; **D:** Pavel Lounguine; **W:** Pavel Lounguine. NYF

Lunatic ✗ 1991 "Some minds should be wasted" according to the film promo and if you're in the mood for an amateur mind (and time) waster, this is for you. High schoolers in the woods encounter mayhem in the best horror tradition as the innocents are slaughtered by an escapee from the local lunatic asylum. 90m/C VHS. Rocky Tucker, Ondrea Tucker, Brian D'Lawrence, Keith Vallot, Bronwyn St. John, Cameron Derrick, Ernest Jackson, Rookie Macpherson, Susan Spain; **D:** James Tucker; **W:** James Tucker. CTD

The Lunatic ✗✗ 1992 (R) A robust, oversexed, and scheming German tourist travels to Jamaica where she meets the village idiot, a man who regularly holds conversations with the local plants. The two hook up with a butcher, and the three live happily in the hills, that is until the money is gone. The Jamaican scenery, a few bawdy laughs, and a great reggae soundtrack make this one worthwhile.**CW:** Sensuality. 93m/C VHS, Beta. GB Julie Wallace, Paul Campbell, Reggie Carter, Carl Bradshaw; **D:** Lol Creme; **M:** Wally Badarou. ACA

Lunatics: A Love Story ✗✗✗ 1992 (PG-13) Hank (Raimi) is an ex-mental patient poet suffering from hallucinations and afraid to leave his Los Angeles apartment. For companionship he dials a party-line until, one day, he misdials and insteads gets the number of a local pay tele-phone, which is answered by a naive woman dumped by her boyfriend. When Nancy (Foreman) decides to visit Hank you learn she's as crazy as he is—so it only makes sense they would fall in love. A well-acted fable of how love fragilely connects even the most unlikely of people. 87m/C VHS, LV. Theodore (Ted) Raimi, Deborah Foreman, Bruce Campbell, Brian McCree, Eddie Rosmaya, Michele Stacey; **D:** Josh Becker; **W:** Josh Becker; **M:** Joseph Lo Duca. NO

Lunatics & Lovers ✗½ 1976 (PG) Musician meets a bizarre nobleman who is in love with an imaginary woman. 92m/C VHS, Beta. IT Marcello Mastroianni, Lino Toffalo; **D:** Flavio Mogherini. FOX

Lunch Wagon ✗✗ Come 'n' Get It; Lunch Wagon Girls 1981 (R) Two co-eds are given a restaurant to manage during summer vacation and wind up involved in a hilarious diamond chase and sex romp. 88m/C VHS, Beta. Rick Podell, Candy Moore, Pamela Bryant, Rosanne Katon; **D:** Ernie Pintoff. MED

Lupo ✗✗ 1970 (G) When threatened with the loss of his home and the separation of his family, an exuberant Greek man challenges the modern world. 99m/C VHS, Beta. Yuda Barkan, Gabi Armoni, Esther Greenberg; **D:** Menahem Golan. MGM

Lure of the Islands ✗ 1942 Federal agents track wanted criminals to an island retreat in this highly predictable low-budget thriller. 61m/B VHS, Beta. Margie Hart, Robert Lowery, Guinn "Big Boy" Williams, Warren Hymer, Gale Storm; **D:** Jean Yarbrough. NOS, SNC

Lure of the Sila ✗✗½ 1949 Italian melodrama about a young peasant girl infiltrating a landowner's home in order to avenge the death of her brother and mother. Dubbed and more interesting than it sounds. 72m/B VHS, Beta, 8mm. IT Silvana Mangano, Amedeo Nazzari, Vittorio Gassman; **D:** Duilio Coletti. VYY

Lurkers woof! 1988 (R) An unappealing metaphysical morass about a woman who has been haunted throughout her life by...something. 90m/C VHS. Christine Moore, Gary Warner, Marina Taylor, Carissa Channing, Tom Billett; **D:** Roberta Findlay. MED

Lurking Fear ✗✗ 1994 (R) The town of Lefferts Corner has suffered from generations of horror thanks to man-eating ghouls that dwell beneath the local graveyard and arise whenever a storm breaks out. The inhabitants prepare to fight back but their plan is hindered by the arrival of a group of criminals who are after a fortune supposedly hidden in one of the graves. Based on a story by H.P. Lovecraft.**CW:** Language and violence. 78m/C VHS, Beta, LV. Jon Finch, Blake Bailey, Ashley Lauren, Jeffrey Combs, Paul Mantee, Allison Mackie, Joe Leavengood, Vincent Schiavelli; **D:** C. Courtney Joyner; **W:** C. Courtney Joyner; **M:** Jim Manzie. PAR

Lush Life ✗✗✗ 1994 (R) New York jazz session musicians Al (Goldblum) and Buddy (Whitaker) roam the city's musical scene until dawn, on the prowl for food, women, and ever more music. When trumpeter Buddy is diagnosed with an inoperable brain tumor, saxophonist Al decides on a grand final gesture—a Park Avenue farewell bash, though no one is to know just how final the farewell is to be. Great jazz soundtrack, fine acting, and atmospheric use of the Big Apple. And it avoids overt tearjerking. Made for cable.**CW:** Strong language. 96m/C VHS, Closed Caption. Jeff Goldblum, Forest Whitaker, Kathy Baker, Lois Chiles, Don Cheadle; **D:** Michael Elias; **W:** Michael Elias. COL

Lust for a Vampire ✗✗ To Love a Vampire 1971 (R) The sanguine tale of a deadly vampire who indiscriminately preys on pupils and teachers when she enrolls at a British finishing school. Moody and erotically charged, with an impressive ending. Quasi-sequel to "The Vampire Lovers." 95m/C VHS, Beta, LV. GB Ralph Bates, Barbara Jefford, Suzanna Leigh, Michael Johnson, Yutte Stensgaard, Pippa Steele; **D:** Jimmy Sangster. MLB

Lust for Freedom ✗ 1987 An undercover cop decides to hit the road after she sees her partner gunned down. She winds up near the California-Mexico border, where she is wrongly imprisoned with a number of other young women in a white slavery business. This low-budget film includes lots of steamy women-behind-bars sex scenes. 92m/C VHS. Melanie Coll, William J. Kulzer; **D:** Eric Louzil. AIP, MOV

Lust for Gold ✗✗ 1949 Ford battles against greedy former lover Lupino and her husband for control of the Lost Dutchman gold mine. 90m/B VHS, Beta. Ida Lupino, Glenn Ford, Gig Young, William Prince, Edgar Buchanan, Will Geer, Paul Ford, Jay Silverheels; **D:** Sylvan Simon; **M:** George Duning. GKK

Lust for Life ✗✗✗½ 1956 Absorbing, serious biography of Vincent Van Gogh, from his first paintings to his death. Remarkable for Douglas' furiously convincing portrayal. Featuring dozens of actual Van Gogh works from private collections. Based on an Irving Stone novel, produced by John Houseman. 122m/C VHS, Beta, LV. Kirk Douglas, Anthony Quinn, James Donald, Pamela Brown, Everett Sloane, Henry Daniell, Niall MacGinnis, Noel Purcell, Lionel Jeffries, Jill Bennett; **D:** Vincente Minnelli; **M:** Miklos Rozsa. Academy Awards '56: Best Supporting Actor (Quinn); Golden Globe Awards '57: Best Actor—Drama (Douglas); National Board of Review Awards '56: 10 Best Films of the Year; New York Film Critics Awards '56: Best Actor (Douglas); Nominations: Academy Awards '56: Best Actor (Douglas), Best Adapted Screenplay, Best Art Direction/Set Decoration (Color). MGM, BTV

Lust in the Dust ✗✗✗ 1985 (R) When part of a treasure map is found on the derriere of none other than Divine, the hunt is on for the other half. This comedy western travels to a sleepy town called Chile Verde (green chili for those who don't speak Spanish) and the utterly ridiculous turns comically corrupt. Deliciously distasteful fun. Features Divine singing a bawdy love song in his/her break from John Waters. 85m/C VHS, Beta, LV, Closed Caption. Tab Hunter, Divine, Lainie Kazan, Geoffrey Lewis, Henry Silva, Cesar Romero, Gina Gallego, Courtney Gains, Woody Strode, Pedro Gonzalez-Gonzalez; **D:** Paul Bartel; **W:** Philip John Taylor; **M:** Peter Matz. NWV, VTR, HHE

The Lusty Men ✗✗✗ 1952 Two rival rodeo champions, both in love with the same woman, work the rodeo circuit until a tragic accident occurs. Mitchum turns in a fine performance as the has-been rodeo star trying to make it big again. 113m/B VHS, Beta, LV. Robert Mitchum, Susan Hayward, Arthur Kennedy, Arthur Hunnicutt; **D:** Nicholas Ray; **C:** Lee Garmes. NO

Luther ✗✗½ 1974 (G) A well-acted characterization of Martin Luther's development from a young seminarian to his leadership of the Reformation Movement. 112m/C VHS. Stacy Keach, Patrick Magee, Hugh Griffith, Robert Stephens, Alan Badel, Julian Glover, Judi Dench, Leonard Rossiter, Maurice Denham, Peter Cellier, Thomas Heathcote, Malcolm Stoddard, Bruce Carstairs; **D:** Guy Green; **C:** Frederick A. (Freddie) Young; **M:** John Addison. NO

Luther the Geek woof! 1990 Little Luther's visit to the circus is dramatically changed when he sees the geek, a sideshow freak. Since then Luther has taken to biting off chicken's heads and drinking their blood in his small Illinois town; the town will never be the same. (And neither will you if you watch this stupid film.) 90m/C VHS. Edward Terry, Joan Roth, J. Jerome Clarke, Tom Mills; **D:** Carlton J. Albright. NO

Luv ✗½ 1967 (PG) Although good cast tries hard, they can't do much with this comic farce. Three intellectuals, including one that's suicidal, discuss the trials and tribulations of their middle-class New York existence. 95m/C VHS, Beta, LV. Jack Lemmon, Peter Falk, Elaine May; **D:** Clive Donner; **W:** Murray Schisgal; **C:** Ernest Laszlo. GKK

Luzia ✗✗½ 1988 Ohana stars as a tough and sexy Brazilian cowgirl who is caught in the middle of a class struggle where the personal is definitely political. Her horseriding skills and beauty give her options in both lifestyles. Will she choose to side with the squatters or the wealthy landowners? In Portuguese with English subtitles. **112m/C VHS.** *BR* Claudia Ohana, Thales Pan Chacon, Jose de Abreu, Luiza Falcao; *D:* Fabio Barreto. *FXL, FCT*

Lydia ✓✓✓ **1941** Sentimental drama in which an elderly lady (Oberon) gets to relive her romantic past when she has a reunion with four of her lost loves. Well acted and directed, Oberon gives one of her best performances ever. Adapted from the highly regarded French film "Un Carnet de Bal." **98m/B VHS, Beta, LV.** Merle Oberon, Joseph Cotten, Alan Marshal, George Reeves; *D:* Julien Duvivier; *C:* Lee Garmes; *M:* Miklos Rozsa. Nominations: Academy Awards '41: Original Dramatic/Comedy Score.

Lying Lips ✓½ **1939** All-black detective mystery about a young nightclub singer framed for murder. Her boyfriend then turns detective to clear her name. **60m/B VHS, Beta.** Edna Mae Harris, Carmen Newsome, Earl Jones, Amanda Randolph; *D:* Oscar Micheaux. *FCT, VCN, DVT*

M ✓✓✓✓ **1931** The great Lang dissection of criminal deviance, following the tortured last days of a child murderer, and the efforts of both the police and the underground to bring him to justice. Poetic, compassionate, and chilling. Inspired by real-life serial killer known as "Vampire of Dusseldorf," Lang also borrowed story elements from Jack the Ripper's killing spree. Lorre's screen debut. Lang's personal favorite among his own films. In German with English subtitles. Remade in 1951. **99m/B VHS, Beta, LV, 8mm.** *GE* Peter Lorre, Ellen Widmann, Inge Landgut, Gustav Grundgens, Otto Wernicke, Ernest Stahl-Nachbaur, Franz Stein, Theodore Loos, Fritz Gnass, Fritz Odemar, Paul Kemp, Theo Lingen, Georg John, Karl Platen, Rosa Valetti, Hertha von Walther, Rudolf Blumner; *D:* Fritz Lang; *W:* Fritz Lang, Thea von Harbou; *C:* Fritz Arno Wagner, Gustav Rathje; *M:* Edvard Grieg. National Board of Review Awards '33: 10 Best Films of the Year. *SNC, NOS, HHT*

M. Butterfly ✓✓ **1993 (R)** Disappointing adaptation of Hwang's award-winning play, which was based on a true story. Irons is Rene Gallimard, a minor French diplomat sent to China in 1964. Taken in by the exoticism of the mysterious east, he falls for a Chinese opera performer, Song Liling (Lone). Only she's no lady and the oblivious diplomat turns out to be a patsy as Song Liling uses him to gather information. The story only works if the passion, however deceptive, between Gallimard and Song Liling is believable, passion which is noticeably lacking between Irons and Lone. Irons comes across as too intelligent to be gullible and the usually excellent Lone does not make his role believable.*CW:* Brief bloody sequence and sexuality. **101m/C VHS, Beta, LV, Closed Caption.** Jeremy Irons, John Lone, Ian Richardson, Barbara Sukowa, Vernon Dobtcheff, Annabel Leventon, Shizuko Hoshi, Richard McMillan; *D:* David Cronenberg; *W:* David Henry Hwang; *M:* Howard Shore. *WAR*

Ma and Pa Kettle ✓✓½ *The Further Adventures of Ma and Pa Kettle* **1949** The hillbilly couple were supporting characters in "The Egg and I" but their popularity found them spun off into their own cornpone series. This first feature finds the couple and their 15 children about to be evicted only to have Pa win a tobacco slogan contest. The prize is a brand-new fully-automated house whose futuristic contraptions get the better of Pa. **76m/B VHS, Closed Caption.** Marjorie Main, Percy Kilbride, Richard Long, Meg Randall, Esther Dale, Barry Kelley, Patricia Alphin; *D:* Charles Lamont; *W:* Al Lewis, Herbert Margolis, Louis Morheim. *USH*

Ma and Pa Kettle at Home ✓✓½ **1954** Elwin, one of the Kettle's 15 children, is a finalist in an essay contest that could win him a college scholarship. Then Pa Kettle hears the two judges plan to visit each of the finalists' homes so he tries to spruce-up the family's tumbled-down farm. **80m/B VHS, Closed Caption.** Marjorie Main, Percy Kilbride, Alan Mowbray, Ross Elliott, Brett Halsey, Mary Wickes, Irving Bacon, Emory Parnell; *D:* Charles Lamont; *W:* Kay Lenard. *USH*

Ma and Pa Kettle at the Fair ✓✓½ **1952** The Kettle's eldest daughter Rosie wants to go to college so Ma enters the county fair baking contest to win some money and Pa buys a decrepit old nag to enter in the fair's horse race. Somehow things just have a way of working out for the Kettles. **79m/B VHS, Closed Caption.** Marjorie Main, Percy Kilbride, Lori Nelson, James Best, Esther Dale, Russell Simpson, Emory Parnell; *D:* Charles T. Barton; *W:* John Grant, Richard Morris. *USH*

Ma and Pa Kettle at Waikiki ✓✓½ **1955** Ma (Main) and Pa (Kilbride), as well as oldest daughter Rosie (Nelson), head for Hawaii to help out cousin Rodney's (Smith) pineapple factory. Seems he's old and about to go bankrupt and he thinks Pa is some kind of financial whiz who can bail him out. Pa accidentally does help the business and then gets kidnapped by some sleazy competitors. But it's Ma to the rescue (and the bad guys don't stand a chance). Kilbride retired after his seventh take as Pa in the comedy series. **79m/B VHS, Closed Caption.** Marjorie Main, Percy Kilbride, Lori Nelson, Loring Smith, Russell Johnson, Byron Palmer, Mabel Albertson, Hilo Hattie, Fay Roope, Oliver Blake, Lowell Gilmore, Teddy Hart; *D:* Lee Sholem; *W:* Jack Henley, Harry Clork, Elwood Ullman. *USH*

Ma and Pa Kettle Back On the Farm ✓✓½ **1951** First-time grandparents, the Kettles have to deal with their daughter-in-law's snobby Bostonian parents and their parenting ideas. The family's also moved back to their ramshackle farm where Pa thinks he's found uranium, leading to all sorts of problems. **81m/B VHS, Closed Caption.** Marjorie Main, Percy Kilbride, Richard Long, Meg Randall, Ray Collins, Barbara Brown, Emory Parnell; *D:* Edward Sedgwick; *W:* Jack Henley. *USH*

Ma and Pa Kettle Go to Town ✓✓½ **1950** Ma and Pa head off for New York City when Pa wins a jingle-writing contest, unknowingly leaving their brood in the care of on the lam mobster Mike, who asks the Kettles to deliver a package to his brother. This gets both the crooks and the cops trailing the hillbilly couple, whose backwoods ways are more than a match for any city slicker. **80m/B VHS, Closed Caption.** Marjorie Main, Percy Kilbride, Richard Long, Meg Randall, Charles McGraw, Ray Collins, Esther Dale, Ellen Corby, Barbara Brown; *D:* Charles Lamont; *W:* Martin Ragaway, Leonard Stern. *USH*

Ma and Pa Kettle on Vacation ✓✓½ *Ma and Pa Kettle Go to Paris* **1953** Ma and Pa visit Paris as guests of their son's wealthy in-laws and Pa unwittingly gets involved with spies and shady ladies. **79m/B VHS, Closed Caption.** Marjorie Main, Percy Kilbride, Ray Collins, Sig Rumann, Bodil Miller, Barbara Brown, Peter Brocco, Jay Novello; *D:* Charles Lamont; *W:* Jack Henley. *USH*

Ma Barker's Killer Brood ✓✓ **1960** Biography of the infamous American criminal and her four sons, edited together from a television serial. The shoot-em-up scenes and Tuttle's performance keep the pace from slackening. **82m/B VHS, Beta.** Lurene Tuttle, Tristram Coffin, Paul Dubov, Nelson Leigh, Myrna Dell, Vic Lundin, Donald Spruance; *D:* Bill Karn. *SNC, DVT, HEG*

Ma Saison Preferee ✓✓✓ *My Favorite Season* **1993** Focuses on the intense relationship between a middleaged brother (Auteuil) and sister (Deneuve). When the elderly Berthe (Villalonga) collapses, she goes to stay with daughter Emilie and her family, which provides Emilie with an excuse to invite her estranged brother Antoine for Christmas. It's a disaster with numerous family fights, that leads Emilie to declare her marriage over and to an eventual reapproachment with Antoine. Film is divided into four parts, to coincide with the four seasons, beginning with autumn and ending with summer. French with subtitles. Deneuve and Auteuil reteamed for Techine's "Les Voleurs." **124m/C VHS.** *FR* Daniel Auteuil, Catherine Deneuve, Marthe Villalonga, Jean-Pierre Bouvier, Chiara Mastroianni, Anthony Prada, Carmen Chaplin; *D:* Andre Techine; *W:* Andre Techine; *C:* Thierry Arbogast; *M:* Philippe Sarde. *NYR*

Mabel & Fatty **1916** Three silent shorts featuring the two stars, made with Mack Sennett: "He Did and He Didn't," "Mabel and Fatty Viewing The World's Fair at San Francisco" (with scenes of the actual 1914 World's Fair) and "Mabel's Blunder." **61m/B VHS, Beta, 8mm.** Mabel Normand, Fatty Arbuckle, Al "Fuzzy" St. John. *VYY*

Mac ✓✓✓ **1993 (R)** It's a family affair. Immigrant carpenter's funeral is the starting point for the story of his three sons, construction workers who live in Queens, New York in the 1950s. The passionate bros battle, bitch, and build, with Turturro as the eldest summing up the prevailing philosophy: "It's the doing, that's the thing." Turturro's directorial debut is a labor of love and a tribute to his own dad. Filmed on location in New York City. Fine performances from newcomers Badalucco and Capototo are complemented by smaller roles from Amos, Barkin, and Turturro's real-life wife Borowitz and brother Nick.*CW:* Strong language and some sexuality. **118m/C VHS, LV, Closed Caption.** John Turturro, Carl Capotorto, Michael Badalucco, Katherine Borowitz, John Amos, Olek Krupa, Ellen Barkin, Joe Paparone, Nicholas Turturro, Dennis Farina, Steven Randazzo; *D:* John Turturro; *W:* Brandon Cole, John Turturro; *C:* Ron Fortunato; *M:* Richard Termini, Vin Tese. Nominations: Independent Spirit Awards '94: Best Director (Turturro), Best First Feature. *COL, FCT*

Mac and Me ✓ **1988 (PG)** Lost E.T.-like alien stranded on Earth befriends a wheelchairbound boy. Aimed at young kids, it's full of continual product plugs, most notably for McDonald's. Make the kids happy and stick to the real thing. **94m/C VHS, Beta, LV, Closed Caption.** Christine Ebersole, Jonathan Ward, Katrina Caspary, Lauren Stanley, Jade Calegory; *D:* Stewart Raffill; *W:* Stewart Raffill; *M:* Alan Silvestri. Golden Raspberry Awards '88: Worst Director (Raffill). *ORI*

Macabre ✓✓ **1977** A beautiful woman, lustful and precocious, kills her husband and his twin brother. **89m/C VHS, Beta.** Larry Ward, Teresa Gimpera, Giacomo "Jack" Rossi-Stuart. *NO*

Macao ✓✓✓ **1952** On the lam for a crime he didn't commit, an adventurer sails to the exotic Far East, meets a buxom cafe singer, and helps Interpol catch a notorious crime boss. A strong film noir entry. Russell sneers, Mitchum wise cracks. Director von Sternberg's last film for RKO. **81m/B VHS, Beta, LV.** Robert Mitchum, Jane Russell, William Bendix, Gloria Grahame; *D:* Josef von Sternberg. *MED*

Macaroni ✓½ *Maccheroni* **1985 (PG)** An uptight American businessman returns to Naples forty years after being stationed there in WWII. Comedic situations abound when he is reunited with his Italian war buddy, brother of his lover. Pleasant acting can't save irritating script. **104m/C VHS, Beta, LV, Closed Caption.** *IT* Jack Lemmon, Marcello Mastroianni, Daria Nicolodi, Isa Danieli; *D:* Ettore Scola; *W:* Ettore Scola. *PAR*

MacArthur ✓✓ **1977 (PG)** General Douglas MacArthur's life from Corregidor in 1942 to his dismissal a decade later in the midst of the Korean conflict. Episodic sage with forceful Peck but weak supporting characters. Fourteen minutes were cut from the original version; intended to be Peck's "Patton," it falls short of the mark. **130m/C VHS, Beta, LV.** Gregory Peck, Ivan Bonar, Ward Costello, Nicolas Coster, Dan O'Herlihy; *D:* Joseph Sargent; *W:* Matthew Robbins, Hal Barwood; *M:* Jerry Goldsmith. *USH, TLF*

MacArthur's Children ✓✓ **1985** A poignant evocation of life in a Japanese fishing village as it faces the end of WWII and American occupation. Not as good as some of the other Japanese films, but it is an interesting look at the changes in culture caused by their defeat in the war. In Japanese with English subtitles. **115m/C VHS, Beta, LV.** *JP* Masako Natsume, Shima Iwashita, Hiromi Go, Takaya Yamauuchi, Shiori Sakura, Ken Watanabe, Juzo Itami, Yoshiyuka Omori; *D:* Masahiro Shinoda; *W:* Takeski Tamura. *FCT, TPV*

Macbeth 🎬🎬🎬½ 1948 Shakespeare's classic tragedy is performed with a celebrated lead performance by Welles, who plays the tragic king as a demonic leader of a barbaric society. A low budget adaptation with cheap sets, a three-week shooting schedule, lots of mood, and an attempt at Scottish accents. After making this film, Welles took a 10-year break from Hollywood. 111m/B VHS, LV. Orson Welles, Jeanette Nolan, Dan O'Herlihy, Roddy McDowall, Robert Coote; **D:** Orson Welles. REP, TVC

Macbeth 🎬🎬🎬 1971 (R) Polanski's notorious adaptation of the Shakespearean classic, marked by realistic design, unflinching violence, and fatalistic atmosphere. Contains stunning fight scenes and fine acting. Polanski's first film following the grisly murder of his pregnant wife, actress Sharon Tate, was torn apart by critics. It is in fact a worthy continuation of his work in the horror genre. Very well made. First film made by Playboy Enterprises. Originally rated X. 139m/C VHS, Beta, LV. Jon Finch, Nicholas Selby, Martin Shaw, Francesca Annis, Terence Baylor; **D:** Roman Polanski. National Board of Review Awards '71: 10 Best Films of the Year. COL, HMV, PBS

Macbeth 🎬🎬🎬 1976 An extraordinary version of Shakespeare's "Macbeth" in which all the fire, ambition and doom of his text come brilliantly to life. 137m/C VHS Eric Porter, Janet Suzman. TLF

Macbeth 🎬🎬 1990 Another production of the classic tragedy by Shakespeare. Produced as part of HBO's Thames Collection. 110m/C VHS, Beta. Michael Jayston, Leigh Hunt. HBO

The Machine 🎬🎬 1996 Psychiatrist and inventor Marc Lacroix (Depardieu) is obsessed with the brain. He develops a brain transfer machine and decides to test it on himself (naturally) by fusing his psyche with that of his patient, cold-blooded killer Michael Zyto (does this sound like a good idea to you?). Naturally, the experiment causes terrifying consequences for Lacroix and his family. 96m/C VHS. Gerard Depardieu, Nathalie Baye, Didier Boundon, Natalia Woerner, Erwan Baynaud; **D:** Francois Dupeyron. PGV

Machine Gun Blues 🎬🎬 Black Rose of Harlem 1995 (R) 1930s jazz singer Williams sings at a black-owned club that mobster Viterelli wants to take over. Right-hand man Cassavettes is sent to help things along and makes the mistake of falling for the chanteuse amidst a scene of moonshine, gunrunning and racketeering. **CW:** Violence, sexuality and language. 80m/C VHS. Cynda Williams, Nick Cassavetes, Joe Viterelli, Maria Ford, Lawrence Monoson, Garrett Morris, Richard Brooks; **D:** Fred Gallo. NHO

Machine Gun Kelly 🎬🎬½ 1958 Corman found Euro-appeal with this thirties style gangster bio. Bronson, who was just gaining a reputation as an action lead, stars as criminal Kelly, who's convinced by his moll to give up bank robbery for kidnapping. Amsterdam, the wisecracking writer from "The Dick Van Dyke Show," is the fink who turns him in. 80m/B VHS. Charles Bronson, Susan Cabot, Morey Amsterdam, Barboura Morris, Frank De Kova, Jack Lambert, Wally Campo; **D:** Roger Corman; **W:** Mike Werb; **C:** Floyd Crosby. COL, FCT

Machine to Kill Bad People 🎬🎬 La Macchina Ammazzacattivi 1948 In a small Italian village, a photographer receives a magical camera that has the power to terrify and kill anyone it photographs. The photographer decides to get rid of all the village's evil people but soon learns the difficulty of distinguishing between the grey areas of good and bad. Italian with subtitles. 80m/B VHS. IT Gennaro Pisano, Giovanni Amato, Marilyn Buferd; **D:** Roberto Rossellini; **W:** Roberto Rossellini. FCT

Macho Callahan 🎬🎬 1970 (R) A Civil War convict escapes from a frontier jail bent on tracking down the man who imprisoned him. (The escaped prisoner bit is a recurring theme in Janssen's oeuvre.) Confused script even has a one-armed Carradine! 99m/C VHS, Beta. David Janssen, Jean Seberg, David Carradine, Lee J. Cobb; **D:** Bernard L. Kowalski. COL, NLC

Machoman 🎬 197? The matchless, peerless, Machoman knows all the best killing methods including: Lizard Fists, Crane Kung Fu, and the Drunken Fist. 94m/C VHS, Beta. Araujo, Enyaw Liew, Jerry Rages. NO

Maciste in Hell 🎬½ Witch's Curse 1960 Inexplicably living in 17th century Scotland, Italian hero Maciste pursues a witch into the depths of Hell. She's placed a curse on the world and he wants her to remove it. 78m/C VHS. IT Kirk Morris, Helene Chanel, Vira Silenti, Andrea Bosic, Angelo Zanolli, John Karlsen; **D:** Riccardo (Robert Hampton) Freda. UNI, SNC

The Mack 🎬½ 1973 (R) The Mack is a pimp who comes out of retirement to reclaim a piece of the action in Oakland, California. Violent blaxploitation flick was box office dynamite at time of release. Early Pryor appearance. 110m/C VHS, Beta. Max Julien, Richard Pryor, Don Gordon, Roger E. Mosley, Carol Speed; **D:** Michael Campus. NLC

Mack & Carole 1928 Lombard began her screen career, in earnest, as a Mack Sennett comedienne. These three shorts represent her earliest screen work. 60m/B VHS, Beta. Carole Lombard. GVV

Mack Sennett Comedies: Vol. 1 1921 Four Sennett films are included: "The Eyes Have It," "The Cannon Ball," "The Desperate Scoundrel," and "Pride of Pikeville." Ben Turpin and the Keystone Cops at their manic best. 85m/B VHS. Ben Turpin, Chester Conklin, Ford Sterling, Minta Durfee; **D:** Mack Sennett. REP

Mack Sennett Comedies: Vol. 2 1916 Four more Sennett shorts are featured: "Mabel and Fatty Adrift," "Mabel, Fatty, and the Law," "Fatty's Tin-Type Tangle," and "Our Congressman." The last film features Will Rogers in a lampoon of Capitol Hill. 84m/B VHS. Fatty Arbuckle, Mabel Normand, Will Rogers, Madge Hunt; **D:** Mack Sennett. REP

Mack the Knife woof! The Threepenny Opera 1989 (PG-13) Terrible adaptation of the Brecht and Weill's "Threepenny Opera," detailing the adventures of a master thief in love with an innocent girl. Too much music, too much dancing, too much emoting. 121m/C VHS, Beta, LV. Raul Julia, Roger Daltrey, Richard Harris, Julie Walters, Clive Revill, Erin Donovan, Rachel Robertson, Julia Migenes-Johnson; **D:** Menahem Golan. COL

MacKenna's Gold 🎬🎬½ 1969 (PG) Grim desperados trek through Apache territory to uncover legendary cache of gold in this somewhat inflated epic. Subdued stars Peck and Shariff vie for attention here with such overactors as Cobb, Meredith, and Wallach. Meanwhile, Newmar (Catwoman of TV's Batman) swims nude. A must for all earthquake buffs. 128m/C VHS, Beta, LV. Gregory Peck, Omar Sharif, Telly Savalas, Julie Newmar, Edward G. Robinson, Keenan Wynn, Ted Cassidy, Eduardo Ciannelli, Eli Wallach, Raymond Massey, Lee J. Cobb, Burgess Meredith, Anthony Quayle, John David Garfield; **D:** J. Lee Thompson; **M:** Quincy Jones. GKK

Mackintosh Man 🎬🎬½ 1973 (PG) An intelligence agent must undo a communist who has infiltrated the free world's network in this solid but somewhat subdued thriller. Good cast keeps narrative rolling, but don't look here for nudity-profanity-violence fix. 100m/C VHS, Beta. Paul Newman, Dominique Sanda, James Mason, Ian Bannen, Nigel Patrick, Harry Andrews, Leo Genn, Peter Vaughan, Michael Hordern; **D:** John Huston; **W:** Walter Hill; **M:** Maurice Jarre. WAR

Macon County Line 🎬🎬½ 1974 (R) A series of deadly mistakes and misfortunes lead to a sudden turn-around in the lives of three young people when they enter a small Georgia town and find themselves accused of brutally slaying the sheriff's wife. Sequelled by "Return to Macon County" in 1975, starring Don Johnson and Nick Nolte. 89m/C VHS, Beta. Alan Vint, Jesse Vint, Cheryl Waters, Geoffrey Lewis, Joan Blackman, Max Baer Jr.; **D:** Richard Compton.

Macumba Love 🎬 1960 An author journeys to Brazil to prove a connection between mysterious murders and voodoo. A tedious suspense exploitation travelogue with generous servings of cheesecake and calypso music. 86m/C VHS. Walter Reed, Ziva Rodann, William Wellman Jr., June Wilkinson, Ruth de Souza; **D:** Douglas Fowley. NO

Mad About Money 🎬🎬 He Loved an Actress; Stardust 1930 An early sound comedy about a bespectacled mild-mannered fellow who runs up against a Mexican spitfire. ♫ Oh So Beautiful; Perpetual Motion; Little Lost Tune; Dustin' The Stars. 80m/B VHS, Beta. Lupe Velez, Wallace Ford, Ben Lyon, Harry Langdon, Jean Colin; **D:** Melville Brown. NOS, DVT

Mad About Music 🎬🎬🎬 1938 On the advice of her publicist, film star Gwen Taylor (Patrick) sends her teenaged daughter Gloria (Durbin) off to a Swiss boarding school and keeps her identity a secret. So Gloria invents an exciting world-traveler father that envious schoolmate Felice (Parrish) insists upon meeting. Gloria manages to persuade a complete stranger, composer Richard Todd (Marshall), into playing the role (he's charmed by her singing). Naturally, there's lots of confusion, especially when mother and "father" finally meet. ♫ Love to Whistle; Chapel Bells; Serenade to the Stars; There Isn't a Day Goes By. 92m/B VHS, Closed Caption. Deanna Durbin, Herbert Marshall, Gail Patrick, Arthur Treacher, Helen Parrish, William Frawley, Marcia Mae Jones, Jackie Moran; **D:** Norman Taurog; **W:** Bruce Manning, Felix Jackson; **C:** Joseph Valentine. Nominations: Academy Awards '38: Best Cinematography, Best Story, Best Score. USH

Mad About You woof! 1990 (PG) Millionaire helps his daughter measure prospective suitors. Adam West is not the fourth man in the Montgomery Clift-James Dean-Marlon Brando chain of American acting greats. 90m/C VHS, Beta, LV. Claudia Christian, Joseph Gian, Adam West, Shari Shattuck; **D:** Lorenzo Doumani. ACA

Mad at the Moon 🎬🎬 1992 (R) Western thriller in which a young bride (Masterson) discovers that the man she married is less than human with the rising of the full moon. The only one who can protect her is her husband's half-brother played by Bochner. Masterson gives a great performance as a woman torn apart by a terrifying family secret out on the American plains. **CW:** Sexuality. 98m/C VHS, LV, Closed Caption. Mary Stuart Masterson, Hart Bochner, Fionnula Flanagan, Cec Verrell; **D:** Martin Donovan; **W:** Martin Donovan, Richard Pelusi. REP

The Mad Bomber woof! Police Connection; Detective Geronimo 1972 Grim lawman Edwards tracks deranged bomber Connors, who is determined to blow up anyone who ever offended him. A must for all connoisseurs of acting that is simultaneously overblown and flat. 80m/C VHS, Beta. Vince Edwards, Chuck Connors, Neville Brand; **D:** Bert I. Gordon. MRV

Mad Bull 🎬 1977 Sensitive wrestler finds meaning in life when he falls in love. If you ever cared about Karras, then you probably already saw this. If you never cared about Karras, then you probably never heard of this. If you ever cared about Anspach, rent "Five Easy Pieces" instead. 96m/C VHS, Beta. Alex Karras, Susan Anspach, Nicholas Colasanto, Tracey Walter; **D:** Walter Doniger. NO

The Mad Butcher 🎬 1972 (R) Typically unhinged mental patient seeks teenage flesh for his various instruments of torture and death. Buono has never been more imposing. 90m/C VHS, Beta. IT Victor Buono, Karin Field, Brad Harris; **D:** John Zuru. GHV, MRV

Mad Death 🎬🎬 1985 The British Isles take extreme steps to quarantine themselves against rabies from the European continent. This condensed TV miniseries preys on fears of the worst, as an outbreak of the virus spreads from dogs and other pets to humans, and special commandoes are mobilized. 120m/C VHS. GB FCT, VCO

Mad Doctor of Blood Island woof! *Tomb of the Living Dead; Blood Doctor* **1969** Dull band of travelers arrive on mysterious tropical island and encounter bloodthirsty creature. Warning: This film is not recognized for outstanding achievements in acting, dialogue, or cinematography. 110m/C VHS, Beta. John Ashley; *D:* Gerardo (Gerry) De Leon. NO

Mad Dog woof! **1984** An escaped convict seeks revenge on the cop responsible for his imprisonment. 90m/C VHS, Beta. Helmut Berger, Marisa Mell; *D:* Sergio Grieco. VDC

Mad Dog and Glory 🐾🐾🐾 **1993 (R)** Cast against type, Murray and De Niro play each other's straight man in this dark romantic comedy. Meek "Mad Dog" (De Niro) is an off-duty police photographer who happens upon a convenience store robbery and manages to save the life of Frank (Murray), obnoxious gangster by day, obnoxious stand-up comic by night. To settle up, Frank offers him Glory (Thurman), for a week. Eventually, Frank wants Glory back, forcing wimpy Mad Dog to either confront or surrender. Directed by McNaughton, who established himself with "Henry: Portrait of a Serial Killer." Uneven and not of the knee-slapper ilk, but the performances are tight, including "NYPD Blue" Caruso as a cop buddy of De Niro's. *CW:* Language, violence and drug content, and sexuality. 97m/C VHS, LV, Closed Caption. Robert De Niro, Uma Thurman, Bill Murray, David Caruso, Mike Starr, Tom Towles, Kathy Baker, Derek Anunciation, J.J. Johnston, Richard Belzer; *D:* John McNaughton; *W:* Richard Price; *M:* Elmer Bernstein. USH, FCT

Mad Dog Morgan 🐾🐾½ *Mad Dog* **1976 (R)** Hopper delivers an engaging outlaw roaming outlands of nineteenth-century Australia. Quirky and violent G'day man. Based on a true story. 93m/C VHS, Beta. AU Dennis Hopper, David Gulpilil; *D:* Philippe Mora. SIM

The Mad Executioners 🐾🐾 *Der Henker Von London* **1965** Scotland Yard inspector searches for a sex maniac who decapitates women. In the meantime, a group of vigilantes capture criminals and sentence them without a trial. Confusing film with a predictable ending. Based on the book "White Carpet" by Bryan Edgar Wallace. 92m/B VHS. GE Hansjorg Felmy, Maria Perschy, Dieter Borsche, Rudolph Forster, Chris Howland, Wolfgang Preiss; *D:* Edwin Zbonek. SNC

The Mad Ghoul 🐾🐾½ **1943** Mad scientist (is there any other kind?) Dr. Morris (Zucco) is researching an ancient Egyptian gas that causes paralysis, turning victims into obedient zombies. Morris exposes his innocent assistant Ted (Bruce) to the gas, making Ted dependent on the antidote serum made from newly dead hearts. Poor Ted's fiance Isabel (Ankers) just can't understand what's the matter. 66m/B VHS, Closed Caption. George Zucco, David Bruce, Evelyn Ankers, Turhan Bey, Robert Armstrong, Milburn Stone, Charles McGraw, Rose Hobart; *D:* James Hogan; *W:* Brenda Weisberg, Paul Gangelin. USH

Mad Love 🐾🐾🐾 *The Hands of Orlac* **1935** A brilliant surgeon (Lorre) falls madly in love with an actress, who she rebuffs him. When her pianist husband's hands are cut off in a train accident, Lorre agrees to attach new hands, using those of a recently executed murderer. Lorre then kills the man's stepfather, and to drive him crazy uses psychological terror to make the pianist think he killed him. There's also an appearance by the supposedly executed murderer who shows up to reclaim his hands. A real chiller about obsessive love and psychological fear. The only downfall to this one is the unnecessary comic relief by Healy. Lorre's first American film. 70m/B VHS. Peter Lorre, Colin Clive, Frances Drake, Ted Healy, Edward Brophy, Sara Haden, Henry Kolker; *D:* Karl Freund. MGM

Mad Love 🐾½ **1995 (PG-13)** Teen love has rarely been so insipid. Impulsive, fragile, and annoyingly melodramatic Casey (Barrymore) bewitches responsible, straightlaced Matt (O'Donnell) with her kewpie-doll charm and penchant for mischief. When Casey's bipolar ways land her in a mental hospital, Matt breaks her out and the unconvincing duo hit the road, where their supposedly free-spirited, passion-filled escapades grow increasingly inconsistent and silly, eventually halted by Casey's clinical crash. Slightly redeemed by a cool soundtrack and decent acting, but otherwise dull and insignificant, with an ending that may induce involuntary eyerolling. You've been warned. *CW:* Brief strong language; issues of an emotionally disturbed teen, including risk-taking situations and sexuality. 95m/C VHS, LV, Closed Caption. Chris O'Donnell, Drew Barrymore, Joan Allen, Kevin Dunn, Jude Ciccolella, Amy Sakasitz, T.J. Lowther; *D:* Antonia Bird; *W:* Paula Milne; *C:* Fred Tammes. TOU

Mad Max 🐾🐾🐾½ **1980 (R)** Set on the stark highways of the post-nuclear future, an ex-cop seeks personal revenge against a rovin' band of vicious outlaw bikers who killed his wife and child. Futuristic scenery and excellent stunt work make for an exceptionally entertaining action-packed adventure. Followed by "The Road Warrior" (also known as "Mad Max 2") in 1981 and "Mad Max Beyond Thunderdome" in 1985. 93m/C VHS, Beta, LV. Mel Gibson, Joanne Samuel, Hugh Keays-Byrne, Steve Bisley, Tim Burns, Roger Ward; *D:* George Miller; *W:* George Miller; *C:* David Eggby; *M:* Brian May. LIV, VES

Mad Max: Beyond Thunderdome 🐾🐾½ **1985 (PG-13)** Max drifts into evil town ruled by Turner and becomes gladiator, then gets dumped in desert and is rescued by band of feral orphans. Third in a bleak, extremely violent, often exhilirating series. 107m/C VHS, Beta, LV, 8mm, Closed Caption. AU Mel Gibson, Tina Turner, Helen Buday, Frank Thring Jr., Bruce Spence, Robert Grubb, Angelo Rossitto, Angry Anderson, George Spartels, Rod Zuanic; *D:* George Miller, George Ogilvie; *W:* George Miller, Terry Hayes; *M:* Maurice Jarre. WAR

Mad Miss Manton 🐾🐾 **1938** A socialite turns detective to solve murder. Pleasant comedy-mystery provides occasional laughs and suspense. 80m/B VHS, Beta, LV. Barbara Stanwyck, Henry Fonda, Hattie McDaniel, Sam Levene, Miles Mander, Charles Halton; *D:* Leigh Jason. TTC

Mad Mission 3 🐾½ **1984** Chinese man vacationing in Paris becomes involved in plot to recover precious jewels stolen from England's royal crown. Has there already been "Mad Mission" and "Mad Mission 2"? 81m/C VHS, Beta. Richard Kiel, Sam Kui, Karl Muka, Sylvia Chang, Tsuneharu Sugiyama. NO

The Mad Monster 🐾½ **1942** This "Wolf Man"-inspired cheapie looks like a misty relic today. A mad scientist furthers the war effort by injecting wolf's blood into a handyman, who becomes hairy and anti-social. 77m/B VHS. Johnny Downs, George Zucco, Anne Nagel, Sarah Padden, Glenn Strange, Gordon DeMain, Mae Busch; *D:* Sam Newfield. NOS, LOO, VCN

Mad Monster Party 🐾🐾½ **1968** Frankenstein is getting older and wants to retire from the responsibilities of being senior monster, so he calls a convention of creepy creatures to decide who should take his place—The Wolfman, Dracula, the Mummy, the Creature, It, the Invisible Man, or Dr. Jekyll and Mr. Hyde. Animated feature using the process of "Animagic." 94m/C VHS, Beta. *D:* Jules Bass; *V:* Boris Karloff, Ethel Ennis, Phyllis Diller. COL

Mad Wax: The Surf Movie 🐾 **1990** A flimsy plot about a window-cleaner who discovers a magical surfing wax serves as a framework for lots and lots of scenes of surfin' dudes. 45m/C VHS, Beta. Richard Cram, Marvin Foster, Aaron Napolean, Tom Carroll, Bryce Andrews, Ross Clarke-Jones; *D:* Michael Hohensee. FCT

The Mad Whirl 🐾½ **1925** The Roarin' Twenties are a mad mad whirl in this silent silent piece of period period. 80m/B VHS, Beta. Myrtle Stedman, Barbara Bedford, Alec B. Francis, George Fawcett, Joseph Singleton. GPV, FCT

Mad Youth woof! **1940** A teenage girl falls in love with a man whom her slutty, alcoholic mother had been chasing. Bottom of the barrel production provides many unintentional laughs. Extraneous South American dance sequences included as character development. 61m/B VHS, Beta. Mary Ainslee, Betty Atkinson, Willy Castello, Betty Compson, Tommy Wonder; *D:* Melville Shyer; *W:* Willis Kent. SNC

Madagascar Skin 🐾🐾 **1995 (R)** Harry (Hannah) is a young gay man who's disfigured by a large port-wine birthmark on one side of his face (in the shape of Madagascar). Suicidally depressed he drives to a deserted beach on the Welsh coast but before making any final decisions, he picks up an overturned bucket lying on the sand. To his shock, it's covering the head of the very much alive middle-aged Flint (Hill), who's been buried up to his neck in sand and left to drown by some fellow crooks. Flint knows of a deserted beach shack, the oddly-matched duo move in, and Harry falls in love. Deliberately dreamlike in some respects, the leads provide a bittersweet, adult romance. 95m/C VHS. GB John Hannah, Bernard Hill; *D:* Chris Newby; *W:* Chris Newby; *C:* Oliver Curtis. NYR

Madam Satan 🐾🐾½ **1930** Extremely bizarre DeMille film highlighted by lavish musical numbers and outrageous costumes. Wealthy socialite realizes she's losing her husband to a young showgirl, so she disguises herself as a sultry French tramp and entices her husband at a masquerade party aboard a zeppelin—surely one of the wildest party scenes ever captured on film. Chorus girls perform several exotic dance numbers inside the airship that are nothing short of fantastic. A storm breaks out and the floating dirigible is struck by lightning—leading viewers to wonder if the mad party-goers will make it to safety or crash and burn like this pic did at the box office. 115m/B VHS, Closed Caption. Kay Johnson, Reginald Denny, Lillian Roth, Roland Young, Boyd Irwin, Elsa Peterson; *D:* Cecil B. DeMille. MGM

Madame Bovary 🐾🐾🐾 **1934** A young adultress with delusions of romantic love finds only despair in this offbeat adaptation of Flaubert's masterpiece. In French with English subtitles. 102m/B VHS, Beta. FR Pierre Renoir, Valentine Tessier, Max Dearly; *D:* Jean Renoir. HTV

Madame Bovary 🐾🐾🐾 **1949** Young adultress with delusions of romantic love finds only despair, even in this Hollywood version of Flaubert's classic. Mason/Flaubert is put on trial for indecency following publication of the novel, with the story told from the witness stand. While this device occasionally slows the narrative, astute direction helps the plot along. Minnelli's handling of the celebrated ball sequence is superb. 115m/B VHS, Beta. Jennifer Jones, Van Heflin, Louis Jourdan, James Mason, Gene Lockhart, Gladys Cooper, George Zucco; *D:* Vincente Minnelli; *M:* Miklos Rozsa. Nominations: Academy Awards '49: Best Art Direction/Set Decoration (B & W). MGM, CCB

Madame Bovary 🐾🐾🐾½ **1991 (PG-13)** Provincial 19th century France is the setting for the tragedy of a romantic woman. Emma Bovary is bored by her marriage to an unsuccessful country doctor and longs for passion and excitement. She allows herself to be seduced (and abandoned) by a local aristocrat and herself seduces a young banker. She also struggles with an increasing burden of debt as she continues her quest for luxury. Realizing she will never find the passion she desires, Emma takes drastic, and tragic, measures. Sumptuous-looking film, with an extraordinary performance by Huppert. In French with English subtitles. Based on the novel by Gustave Flaubert. **130m/C VHS, LV.** *FR* Isabelle Huppert, Jean-Francois Balmer, Christophe MaLavoy, Jean Yanne; *D:* Claude Chabrol; *W:* Claude Chabrol; *M:* Matthieu Chabrol. Nominations: Academy Awards '91: Best Costume Design.*REP, BTV*

Madame Butterfly *♂♂* **1995** A French production, filmed in Tunisia, with a Chinese soprano, and Italian subtitles. Mitterrand takes on Puccini's opera, setting it in 1904 Nagasaki, but playing most of the story straight (he adds some documentary footage of old Japan between the acts). 15-year-old Butterfly (Huang) is a geisha who makes the mistake of falling in love and marrying deceitful American naval officer Pinkerton (Troxell). She's disowned by her family, he eventually sails away, and when he does return, it's with an American bride. Tragedy ensues. Newcomer Huang's fine but the handsome Troxell's a little stiff. **129m/C VHS.** *FR* Ying Huang, Richard Troxell, Ning Liang, Richard Cowan; *D:* Frederic Mitterrand; *W:* Frederic Mitterrand; *C:* Philippe Welt. *COL*

Madame Curie *♂♂♂* **1943** The film biography of Madame Marie Curie, the woman who discovered Radium. A deft portrayal by Garson, who is reteamed with her "Mrs. Miniver" co-star, Pidgeon. Certainly better than most biographies from this time period and more truthful as well. **124m/B VHS, LV.** Greer Garson, Walter Pidgeon, Robert Walker, May Whitty, Henry Travers, Sir C. Aubrey Smith, Albert Basserman, Victor Francen, Reginald Owen, Van Johnson; *D:* Mervyn LeRoy; *C:* Joseph Ruttenberg. Nominations: Academy Awards '43: Best Actor (Pidgeon), Best Actress (Garson), Best Black and White Cinematography, Best Interior Decoration, Best Picture, Best Sound, Original Dramatic/Comedy Score. *MGM, CCB*

Madame Rosa *♂♂♂* *La Vie Devant Soi* **1977 (PG)** An aging Jewish prostitute tends prostitutes' offspring in this warmhearted work. A survivor of the Holocaust, the old woman finds her spirit revived by one of her charges—an abandoned Arab boy. In French with English subtitles. **105m/C VHS, Beta.** *FR IS* Simone Signoret, Claude Dauphin; *D:* Moshe Mizrahi; *C:* Nestor Almendros. Academy Awards '77: Best Foreign Language Film; Cesar Awards '78: Best Actress (Signoret); Los Angeles Film Critics Association Awards '78: Best Foreign Film. *HTV, VES*

Madame Sin *♂♂* ½ **1971** Aspiring world dominator enlists former CIA agent in scheme to obtain nuclear submarine. Davis is appealing as evil personified, in her first television feature. **91m/C VHS, Beta.** Bette Davis, Robert Wagner; *D:* David Greene; *M:* Michael Gibbs. *CCB, FOX*

Madame Sousatzka *♂♂♂* **1988 (PG-13)** Eccentric, extroverted piano teacher helps students develop spiritually as well as musically. When she engages a teenage Indian student, however, she finds herself considerably challenged. MacLaine is perfectly cast in this powerful, winning film. **113m/C VHS, Beta, LV.** Shirley MacLaine, Peggy Ashcroft, Shabana Azmi, Twiggy, Leigh Lawson, Geoffrey Bayldon, Navin Chowdhry, Lee Montague; *D:* John Schlesinger; *W:* Ruth Prawer Jhabvala, John Schlesinger; *M:* Gerald Gouriet. Golden Globe Awards '89: Best Actress—Drama (MacLaine); Venice Film Festival '88: Best Actress (MacLaine), Best Actress (MacLaine); National Media Owl Awards '89: First Prize. *USH*

Madame X *♂♂* ½ **1937** Fourth version of this classic tearjerker finds diplomat's wife George having a fling with a playboy. There's a murder and she turns to her nasty mother-in-law for aid. She arranges for daughter-in-law-dearest's "death" in order to prevent a scandal. Then George is on the slippery path to alcoholism and prostitution. Adapted from the play by Alexandre Bisson. Run-of-the-mill; Lana Turner's 1966 version is still the one to watch. **96m/B VHS.** Gladys George, John Beal, Warren William, Reginald Owen, William Henry, Henry Daniell, Philip Reed, Lynne Carver, Emma Dunn, Ruth Hussey; *D:* Sam Wood; *W:* John Meehan. *MGM*

Madame X *♂♂* *Absinthe* **1966** Turner is perfectly cast in this oft-filmed melodrama about a social outcast who is tried for murder and defended by her unknowing son, who believes her long dead. Bennett's last film. **100m/C VHS, Beta.** Lana Turner, John Forsythe, Ricardo Montalban, Burgess Meredith, Virginia Grey, Constance Bennett, Keir Dullea; *D:* David Lowell Rich; *C:* Russell Metty. *USH*

M.A.D.D.: Mothers Against Drunk Driving *♂♂* ½ **1983** Emotionally gripping television movie recounts the story of Candy Lightner, who, after her daughter was killed in a drunk driving accident, founded M.A.D.D. and built it into a nationwide organization. Similar to "License to Kill," which dramatized the effect that a drunk driving accident can have on the families of those involved. **97m/C VHS, Beta.** Mariette Hartley, Paula Prentiss, Bert Remsen; *D:* William A. Graham; *C:* Dean Cundey; *M:* Bruce Broughton. *USH*

The Maddening *♂* ½ **1995 (R)** When their car breaks down in a remote area, Cassie (Sara) and daughter Samantha find refuge at the home of Roy Scudder (Reynolds) and his wife Georgina (Dickinson). At least Cassie thought it was a refuge—until she realizes the Scudders are crazy killers.*CW:* Violence and terror; some language. **97m/C VHS, LV, Closed Caption.** Burt Reynolds, Angie Dickinson, Mia Sara, Brian Wimmer, Josh Mostel, William Hickey; *D:* Danny Huston. *THV*

Made for Each Other *♂♂♂* **1939** Newlyweds must overcome meddlesome in-laws, poverty, and even serious illness in this classic melodrama. Dated but appealing. **85m/B VHS, Beta, Closed Caption.** James Stewart, Carole Lombard, Charles Coburn, Lucile Watson; *D:* John Cromwell; *C:* Leon Shamroy. *CNG, MRV, NOS*

Made for Love *♂* ½ **1926** Couple journeys romantically in Egypt until disaster strikes: they fall into a tomb and can't get out. **65m/B VHS, Beta.** Leatrice Joy, Edmund Burns, Ethel Wales, Brandon Hurst, Frank Butler; *D:* Paul Sloane. *GPV, FCT*

Made in America *♂♂* **1993 (PG-13)** High-energy, lightweight comedy stars Whoopi as a single mom whose daughter Long discovers her birth was the result of artifical insemination. More surprising is her biological dad: white, obnoxious, country-western car dealer Danson. Overwrought with obvious gags, basically a one-joke movie. Nonetheless, Goldberg and Danson chemically connect onscreen (and for a short time offscreen as well) while supporting actor Smith grabs comedic attention as Teacake, Long's best friend. Both Goldberg and Danson deserve better material.*CW:* Language and sexual situations. **111m/C VHS, Beta, LV, Closed Caption.** Whoopi Goldberg, Ted Danson, Will Smith, Nia Long, Paul Rodriguez, Jennifer Tilly, Peggy Rea, Clyde Kusatsu; *D:* Richard Benjamin; *W:* Holly Goldberg Sloan; *C:* Ralf Bode; *M:* Mark Isham. *WAR*

Made in Argentina *♂♂* **1986** An Argentinean couple living in New York decide to return for a visit. Having left for political reasons, they still harbor bitterness. **90m/C VHS, Beta.** *AR* Luis Brandoni, Marta Bianchi, Leonor Manso; *D:* Juan Jose Jusid. *VES*

Made in Heaven *♂♂* **1952** Arid comedy in which British newlyweds try to sustain honeymoon for entire year. The bride, however, eventually suspects her husband of shenanigans with the maid. If this sounds good, then you may like it. **90m/C VHS, Beta, Closed Caption.** *GB* Petula Clark, David Tomlinson, Sonja Ziemann, A.E. Matthews; *D:* John Paddy Carstairs. *HMV*

Made in Heaven *♂♂* ½ **1987 (PG)** Two souls in heaven fall in love and must find each other after being reborn on Earth if they are to remain eternal lovers. Contains ethereal interpretations of heaven and several cameo appearances by famous actors and musicians. **105m/C VHS, Beta, LV, Closed Caption.** Timothy Hutton, Kelly McGillis, Maureen Stapleton, Mare Winningham, Ann Wedgeworth, Don Murray, Amanda Plummer, Timothy Daly, Marj Dusay; *Cameos:* Ellen Barkin, Neil Young, Tom Petty, Ric Ocasek, Tom Robbins, Debra Winger, Gary Larsen,

David Rasche; *D:* Alan Rudolph; *W:* Raynold Gideon, Bruce A. Evans; *M:* Mark Isham. *WAR, ORI*

Made in USA *♂* ½ **1988 (R)** Wayward dudes engage vixen while cruising Midwest. Trouble, however, awaits. Note: This is not Godard's mid-sixties classic. **82m/C VHS, Beta, LV.** Adrian Pasdar, Lori Singer, Christopher Penn; *D:* Ken Friedman; *W:* Ken Friedman. *NLC*

Madeleine *♂♂* ½ *The Strange Case of Madeleine* **1950** Courtroom drama of woman charged with poisoning her French lover in 1850s Scotland. Directed by the same David Lean who made "Bridge on the River Kwai" and "Lawrence of Arabia". Here, though, he was merely trying to provide a vehicle for his wife, actress Todd. Intrigued? **114m/B VHS, Beta.** Ann Todd, Leslie Banks, Ivan Desny, Norman Wooland, Barbara Everest, Susan Stranks, Patricia Raine, Elizabeth Sellars, Edward Chapman, Jean Cadell, Eugene Deckers, Amy Veness, John Laurie, Henry Edwards, Ivor Barnard, Barry Jones, David Morne, Andree Morell, Douglas Barr; *D:* David Lean; *W:* Nicholas Phipps, Stanley Haynes; *C:* Guy Green; *M:* William Alwyn. *LCA*

Mademoiselle *♂♂* **1966** Moreau is a psychotic, sexually repressed schoolteacher in a small village who manages to keep herself under control until studly woodcutter Manni and his son take up residence. The locals distrust the stranger but Moreau can't wait to get her hands on him. Suddenly, the village is battered by a rash of poisonings, fires, and floods, all of which are blamed on Manni, leading the locals to exact a terrible vengeance. In French with English subtitles. **105m/B VHS.** *FR GB* Jeanne Moreau, Ettore Manni, Umberto Orsini, Keith Skinner, Jane Berretta, Mony Rey; *D:* Tony Richardson; *W:* Jean Genet. *MGM, FCT*

Mademoiselle Fifi *♂* ½ **1944** Simon stars as a French laundress in 1870 France who refuses to give in to her small town's Prussian oppressors. The film title is the nickname of the most brutal of the Prussian officers, played by Kreuger. An unsuccessful attempt at political allegory for the devastation of WWII. **69m/B VHS, LV.** Simone Simon, John Emery, Kurt Kreuger, Alan Napier, Jason Robards Sr.; *D:* Robert Wise. *FCT*

Mademoiselle Striptease *♂♂* ½ *Please! Mr. Balzac; While Plucking the Daisy; En Effeuillant la Marguerite* **1957** Bardot stars as a young woman who finds a valuable stolen book. Her attempts to disassociate herself from the actual theft are supposed to be funny. Bardot is characteristically appealing. **100m/B VHS, Beta.** Brigitte Bardot, Robert Hirsch, Daniel Gelin; *D:* Marc Allegret. *STV, MRV*

Madhouse *♂♂* **1974** A troubled horror film star tries to bring his "Dr. Death" character to television, but during production people begin dying in ways remarkably similar to the script. A strong genre cast should hold the fans' attention during this mild adaptation of Angus Hall's novel "Devilday." **92m/C VHS, Beta.** *GB* Vincent Price, Peter Cushing, Robert Quarry, Adrienne Corri, Natasha Pyne, Linda Hayden, Michael Parkinson; *D:* Jim Clark. *HBO*

Madhouse *♂♂* **1987** A woman has bizarre recollections of her twin sister whom she finally meets when she escapes from a mental hospital. Lots of violence and gore, has definite cult potential. **90m/C VHS, Beta.** Trish Everly, Michael MacRae, Dennis Robertson, Morgan Hart; *D:* Ovidio G. Assonitis. *NO*

Madhouse *♂♂* **1990 (PG-13)** New homeowners find themselves unable to expel loathsome, boorish guests. Presumably, a comedy cashing in on two of sitcom's brightest lights. **90m/C VHS, Beta, LV, Closed Caption.** John Larroquette, Kirstie Alley, Alison La Placa, John Diehl, Jessica Lundy, Bradley Gregg, Dennis Miller, Robert Ginty; *D:* Tom Ropelewski; *W:* Tom Ropelewski; *M:* David Newman. *ORI*

Madhouse Mansion *♂♂* ½ *Ghost Story* **1974 (PG)** A horror actor revives his career and becomes embroiled in murder. Plenty of in-jokes and clips from older movies. **86m/C VHS.** *GB* Marianne Faithfull, Leigh Lawson, Anthony Bate, Larry Dann,

Sally Grace, Penelope Keith, Vivian Mackerell, Murray Melvin, Barbara Shelley; *D:* Stephen Weeks. *NO*

Madigan 🎬🎬🎬 1968 Realistic and exciting and among the best of the behind-the-scenes urban police thrillers. Hardened NYC detectives (Widmark and Guardino) lose their guns to a sadistic killer and are given 72 hours to track him down. Fonda is the police chief none to pleased with their performance. Adapted by Howard Rodman, Abraham Polonsky, and Harry Kleiner from Richard Dougherty's "The Commissioner." 101m/C VHS, Beta. Richard Widmark, Henry Fonda, Inger Stevens, Harry Guardino, James Whitmore, Susan Clark, Michael Dunn, Don Stroud; *D:* Donald Siegel; *W:* Abraham Polonsky; *C:* Russell Metty. *USH*

Madigan's Millions woof! 1967 (G) Incompetent Treasury agent treks to Italy to recover funds swiped from deceased gangster. This is Hoffman's first film, and is to his career what "The Last Chalice" was to Paul Newman's and "Studs and Kitty" was Sylvester Stallone. Recommended only to the terminally foolhardy. 89m/C VHS, Beta. Dustin Hoffman, Elsa Martinelli, Cesar Romero; *D:* Stanley Prager. *RHI*

Madman 🎬 1979 (R) Deranged Soviet Jew joins Israeli army to more effectively fulfill his desire to kill loathsome Soviets. Good date movie for those nights when you're home alone. Weaver's first starring role. 95m/C VHS, Beta. *IS* Sigourney Weaver, Michael Beck, F. Murray Abraham; *D:* Dan Cohen. *CNG*

Madman 🎬 1982 (R) Camp leader prompts terror when he revives legend regarding ax murderer. Seems that when you call his name, he appears. Buffoon does not believe story and calls out madman's name. Madman hears the call and emerges from forest, says hi, and hacks everyone to death. Lesson learned, case closed. Filmed on Long Island. 89m/C VHS, Beta. Alexis Dubin, Tony Fish. *HHE*

The Madness of King George 🎬🎬🎬½ 1994 (R) Poor King George is a monarch with problems—his 30 years of royal authority are being usurped by Parliament, his American colonies have been lost, and, in 1788, he's begun to periodically lose his mind. So what do you do when a ruler becomes irrational? The royal physicians are baffled, his loving Queen Charlotte (Mirren) is in despair, but the noxious Prince of Wales (Everett) can barely contain his glee at finally having a chance at the throne. A last resort is offered by Dr. Willis (Holm), a former clergyman with some unusual and sadistic ideas about treating the mentally ill (even if they do have royal blood). Brilliant performance by Hawthorne (who originated the stage role in Bennett's 1991 play "The Madness of George III"). Screen note explains that King George suffered from the metabolic disorder known as porphyria. A Tony Award-winner for his Broadway productions of "Miss Saigon" and "Carousel," Hytner makes his feature-film directing debut.*CW:* Adult themes and situations; profanity. 110m/C VHS, LV, Closed Caption. *GB* Nigel Hawthorne, Helen Mirren, Ian Holm, Rupert Everett, Amanda Donohoe, Rupert Graves, Julian Wadham, John Wood, Julian Rhind-Tutt; *D:* Nicholas Hytner; *W:* Alan Bennett; *M:* George Fenton. Academy Awards '94: Best Art Direction/Set Decoration; British Academy Awards '95: Best Actor (Hawthorne); Cannes Film Festival '95: Best Actress (Mirren); Nominations: Academy Awards '94: Best Actor (Hawthorne), Best Adapted Screenplay, Best Supporting Actress (Mirren); British Academy Awards '95: Best Actress (Mirren), Best Adapted Screenplay, Best Cinematography, Best Director (Hytner), Best Film, Best Supporting Actor (Holm), Best Score; Writers Guild of America '94: Best Adapted Screenplay. *HMK*

Mado 🎬🎬🎬 1976 A middle-aged businessman's life is undone when he falls for a mysterious woman. Piccoli and Schneider are, as usual, convincing. Another of underrated director Sautet's effective, low-key works. In French with subtitles. 130m/C VHS, Beta. Romy Schneider, Michel Piccoli,

Charles Denner; *D:* Claude Sautet. Cesar Awards '77: Best Sound. *FCT*

Madonna: Innocence Lost 🎬½ 1995 Tacky TV movie focusing on the ambitious singer and would-be actress who made wearing underwear as outerwear almost acceptable. Tawdry gossip highlights this laughfest as the trash talker hustles her way to the top of the heap, uncaring of whom she steps on along the way. Toronto substitutes for New York City grit. 90m/C VHS, Closed Caption. Terumi Matthews, Wendie Malick, Jeff Yagher, Dean Stockwell, Nigel Bennett, Don Francks, Rod Wilson, Tom Melissis; *D:* Bradford May; *W:* Michael J. Murray. *FXV*

Madron 🎬½ 1970 (PG) Road western filmed in the Israel desert, complete with menacing Apaches, wagon train massacre, a nun and a gunslinger. 93m/C VHS, Beta. Richard Boone, Leslie Caron, Paul Smith; *D:* Jerry Hopper. Nominations: Academy Awards '70: Best Song ("Till Love Touches Your Life"). *NO*

The Madwoman of Chaillot 🎬½ 1969 (G) Four men conspire to drill for oil which they believe lurks under Paris. Hepburn finds out about their plot and tells each man that oil is bubbling up through her basement. Before the men can arrive at her house to confirm this, she and her three cronies hold a mock trial and sentence the men to death. Features a stellar cast, but this modern-day adaptation of Jean Giraudoux's play "La Folle de Chaillot" falls flat. 142m/C VHS, LV. Katharine Hepburn, Charles Boyer, Claude Dauphin, Edith Evans, John Gavin, Paul Henreid, Oscar Homolka, Margaret Leighton, Giulietta Masina, Nanette Newman, Richard Chamberlain, Yul Brynner, Donald Pleasence, Danny Kaye, Fernand Gravet; *D:* Bryan Forbes; *W:* Edward Anhalt. *WAR*

Mae West 🎬🎬½ 1984 This made-for-television film details West's life from her humble beginnings to her racy film stardom. Jillian does a good job bringing the buxom legend back to life. 97m/C VHS, Beta. Ann Jillian, James Brolin, Piper Laurie, Roddy McDowall; *D:* Lee Philips; *M:* Brad Fiedel. *ORI*

Maedchen in Uniform 🎬🎬🎬½ *Girls in Uniform* 1931 A scandalous early German talkie about a rebellious schoolgirl who falls in love with a female teacher and commits suicide when the teacher is punished for the relationship. A controversial criticism of lesbianism and militarism that impelled the Nazis, rising to power two years later, to exile its director. It was also banned in the United States. In German with English subtitles. Remade in 1965. 90m/B VHS, Beta. *GE* Dorothea Wieck, Ellen Schwannecke, Hertha Thiele; *D:* Leontine Sagan. National Board of Review Awards '32: 5 Best Foreign Films of the Year. *MRV, NLC*

Mafia Princess 🎬🎬 1986 The daughter of a Mafia boss tries to discover her own identity despite her father's involvement in crime. Based on a best-selling autobiography by a real-life member of a Mob family, Antoinette Giancana. Made for television. 100m/C VHS. Tony Curtis, Susan Lucci, Kathleen Widdoes, Chuck Shamata, Louie Dibianco; *D:* Robert Collins. *NO*

Mafia vs. Ninja 🎬½ 1984 The mob wants to control the city, but the Ninja has other ideas. 90m/C VHS, Beta. Alexander Lou, Silvio Azzolini, Wang Hsia, Charlema Hsu, Eugene Trammel. *NO*

Magdalene 🎬½ 1988 (PG) Somewhere in medieval Europe, a violent Baron seeks revenge on a beautiful whore that spurned him. Small-budget costumer. 89m/C VHS, Beta, LV. Steve Bond, Nastassia Kinski, David Warner, Gunter Meisner, Ferdinand "Ferdy" Mayne, Anthony Quayle, Franco Nero, Janet Agren; *D:* Monica Teuber. *PAR, FCT*

Magee and the Lady 🎬🎬 *She'll Be Sweet* 1978 (PG) The crusty captain of a rusty ship must warm up to a spoiled debutante or lose his ship to a foreclosure firm. Could be better. Made for TV. 92m/C VHS, Beta. *AU* Tony LoBianco, Sally Kellerman; *D:* Gene Levitt. *ACA*

Magic 🎬🎬½ 1978 (R) Ventriloquist Hopkins and his dummy, an all-too-human counterpart, get involved with a beautiful but impressionable woman lost between reality and the irresistible world of

illusion. Spine-chilling psycho-drama with a less-than-believable premise. Screenplay by Goldman from his novel. 106m/C VHS, Beta, LV. Anthony Hopkins, Ann-Margret, Burgess Meredith, Ed Lauter; *D:* Richard Attenborough; *W:* William Goldman; *M:* Jerry Goldsmith. *NLC*

The Magic Bow 🎬½ 1947 Typically ridiculous musical bio—this time of violinist Nicolo Paganini (Granger). He's the talented poor boy who falls for the wealthy Jeanne (Calvert) but his one true love is for his Stradivarius. Yehudi Menuhim plays the solos. Based on the novel by Manuel Komroff. 105m/B VHS. *GB* Stewart Granger, Phyllis Calvert, Jean Kent, Dennis Price, Cecil Parker, Felix Aylmer, Frank Cellier, Marie Lohr; *D:* Bernard Knowles; *W:* Roland Pertwee, Norman Ginsburg; *C:* Jack Asher, Jack Cox. *HMK*

The Magic Bubble 🎬🎬½ 1993 (PG-13) On her 40th birthday, Julia Cole finds the fountain of youth...inside a bottle of enchanted bubbles. Ageless and timeless, she begins to know the meaning of true happiness.*CW:* Brief nudity and mild sensuality. 90m/C VHS. Diane Salinger, John Calvin, Priscilla Pointer, Colleen Camp, Tony Peck, Wallace Shawn; *D:* Alfredo Ringel, Deborah Taper Ringel; *W:* Meredith Baer, Geof Pryssir. *MNC*

The Magic Christian 🎬🎬🎬 1969 (PG) A series of related skits about a rich man (Sellers) and his son (Starr) who try to prove that anyone can be bought. Raucous, now somewhat dated comedy; music by Badfinger, including Paul McCartney's "Come and Get It." 101m/C VHS, Beta, LV. *GB* Peter Sellers, Ringo Starr, Isabel Jeans, Wilfrid Hyde-White, Graham Chapman, John Cleese, Peter Graves, John Lennon, Yoko Ono, Richard Attenborough, Leonard Frey, Laurence Harvey, Christopher Lee, Spike Milligan, Yul Brynner, Roman Polanski, Raquel Welch; *D:* Joseph McGrath; *W:* Terry Southern; *C:* Geoffrey Unsworth. *REP, MRV*

The Magic Flute 🎬🎬🎬½ 1973 (G) Bergman's acclaimed version of Mozart's famous comic opera, universally considered one of the greatest adaptations of opera to film ever made. Staged before a live audience for Swedish television. In Swedish with English subtitles. 134m/C VHS, Beta, LV. *SW* Josef Kostlinger, Irma Urrila, Hakan Hagegard, Elisabeth Erikson; *D:* Ingmar Bergman. Nominations: Academy Awards '75: Best Costume Design. *HMV, PAR, MVD*

The Magic Fountain 🎬🎬 1961 Three princes search for a magic fountain whose waters will cure their ailing father. Two of them, however, take the evil course and are turned into ravens by a wicked dwarf. Based on the fairy tale "Das Wasser des Lebens" by the Brothers Grimm. 82m/C VHS. Peter Nestler, Helmo Kinderman, Josef Marz, Catherine Hansen, Cedric Hardwicke; *D:* Allan David. *SNC*

Magic in the Mirror: Fowl Play 🎬🎬½ 1996 (G) Young Mary Margaret (Smith) does an "Alice Through the Looking Glass" when she steps through an antique mirror bequeathed to her by her grandmother and discovers an enchanted kingdom run by giant ducks. But just how will MM find her way back? 86m/C VHS, Beta, Closed Caption. Jaime Renee Smith, Kevin Wixted, Saxon Trainor, David Brooks, Godfrey James; *D:* Ted Nicolaou; *W:* Frank Dietz, Ken Carter Jr.; *C:* Adolfo Bartoli; *M:* Richard Kosinski. *PAR*

Magic in the Water 🎬½ 1995 (PG) Divorced, obnoxious radio shrink and neglectful dad Dr. Jack Black (Harmon) takes the kiddies on a summer jaunt to a Canadian lake, where they begin to explore the legend of Orky, Canada's answer to the Loch Ness monster. Dad becomes a believer when Orky possesses his body and (New Age Alert!) releases his inner child. Harmless fun for the kids, but parents will gag at the attempt to provide a meaningful and symbolic message, which arrives with all the subtlety of an Oliver Stone history lesson. Sort of an "E.T." meets "Free Willy" with Orky shilling for the EPA. Beautiful cinematography showcasing the British Columbia landscape helps, but not enough. 100m/C VHS, Closed Caption. Mark Harmon, Joshua Jackson,

Magic Island 🎬🎬½ 1995 (PG) Thirteen-year-old Jack (Bryan) gets sucked into the pages of a pirate book and finds himself with Blackbeard and his scurvy crew. They're on a treasure hunt and figure Jack's book contains some missing clues. Naturally, Jack finds himself in lots of trouble. 88m/C VHS, Closed Caption. Zachery Ty Bryan, Edward Kerr, Lee Armstrong, French Stewart, Abraham Benrubi, Jessie-Ann Friend, Oscar Dillon, Sean O'Kane, Schae Harrison, Ja'net DuBois, Andrew Divoff; D: Sam Irvin; W: Neil Ruttenberg, Brent Friedman; C: James Lawrence Spencer; M: Richard Band. PAR

Magic Kid 🎬🎬½ Ninja Dragons 1992 (PG) Thirteen-year-old martial-arts champ Kevin and his older sister vacation in L.A., staying with their shady Uncle Bob, a second-rate talent agent. Kevin wants to meet his martial arts movie idol and his sister her favorite soap opera hunk. But they wind up being chased by the mobsters Uncle Bob owes money to. 91m/C VHS, LV, Closed Caption. Ted Jan Roberts, Shonda Whipple, Stephen Furst, Joseph Campanella, Billy Hufsey, Sondra Kerns, Pamela Dixon, Lauren Tewes, Don "The Dragon" Wilson; D: Joseph Merhi; W: Stephen Smoke; M: Jim Halfpenny. PMH

Magic Kid 2 🎬🎬½ 1994 (PG) The young star of a popular martial arts program wants to quit and go to high school like a normal teenager. But the studio execs have other ideas. 90m/C VHS, LV. Ted Jan Roberts, Stephen Furst, Donald Gibb, Jennifer Savidge; D: Stephen Furst. PMH

Magic Moments 🎬🎬½ 199? Ambitious British TV exec Melanie James (Seagrove) is about to score the coup of her career. She's persuaded charismatic American illusionist Troy Gardner (Shea) to recreate his death-defying act on TV—but only if Melanie will produce the show herself. Too bad her power-hungry boss is out to cause trouble. Made for British TV. 103m/C VHS. GB Jenny Seagrove, John Shea. VCO

Magic of Lassie 🎬🎬 1978 (G) Stewart is engaging as the nice grandpa who refuses to sell his land to mean rich guy Roberts. Innocuous, pleasant remake of "Lassie Come Home." Stewart sings, as do Pat Boone and daughter Debby. 100m/C VHS, Beta. James Stewart, Mickey Rooney, Stephanie Zimbalist, Alice Faye, Pernell Roberts, Lassie; D: Don Chaffey. Nominations: Academy Awards '78: Best Song ("When You're Loved"). MGM

The Magic of the Golden Bear: Goldy 3 🎬 Goldy 3 1994 (G) Down-on-his-luck magician (Marin) tries to buy Goldy to save his failing act and Jessie (Morgan) is torn between wanting to keep the bear or return her to the wild. An animal-loving holy man (Mr. T.) tries to help her decide. 104m/C VHS, Closed Caption. Bonnie Morgan, Richard "Cheech" Marin, Mr. T; D: John Quinn. FHE

Magic on Love Island 🎬 1980 Romantic misadventures ensue when eight ladies go on vacation to Love Island, a tropical paradise. 96m/C VHS, Beta. Adrienne Barbeau, Bill Daily, Howard Duff, Dody Goodman, Dominique Dunne, Lisa Hartman Black, Janis Paige; D: Earl Bellamy. NO

Magic Serpent 🎬🎬🎬 1966 Fantasy set in medieval Japan features a grand duel in magic between a good hero and evil sorcerer who transform into a giant dragon and a giant frog to do battle. ?m/C VHS. Hiroki Matsukata, Tomoko Ogawa, Ryutaro Otomo, Bin Amatsu; D: Tetsuya Yamauchi. SMW

The Magic Stone 🎬🎬½ Kilian's Chronicle 1995 Kilian is the 10th-century Irish slave of brutish Viking Ivar, who decides to sacrifice him to the Norse god Thor when the Vikings become lost while sailing off the North American coast. Kilian manages to escape and make it to shore where he's rescued by a Native American tribe and falls in love with local beauty, Turtle. But Ivar goes after Kilian to steal his magic stone, which can navigate a ship through the worst weather, and

begins a Viking war with the tribe. 95m/C VHS. Christopher Johnson, Robert McDonough, Eva Kim, Jonah Ming Lee; D: Pamela Berger; W: Pamela Berger; C: John Hoover; M: R. Carlos Nakai, Bevan Manson. MNC

The Magic Sword 🎬🎬 1962 A family-oriented adventure film about a young knight who sets out to rescue a beautiful princess who is being held captive by an evil sorcerer and his dragon. 80m/C VHS, Beta. Basil Rathbone, Estelle Winwood, Gary Lockwood; D: Bert I. Gordon. MGM, MRV, VYY

Magic Town 🎬🎬½ 1947 An opinion pollster investigates a small town which exactly reflects the views of the entire nation, making his job a cinch. The publicity causes much ado in the town with ensuing laughs. Uneven but entertaining. 103m/B VHS. Jane Wyman, James Stewart, Kent Smith, Regis Toomey, Donald Meek; D: William A. Wellman; C: Joseph Biroc. REP

The Magic Voyage 🎬🎬½ 1993 (G) Animated tale of a friendly woodworm named Pico who voyages with Columbus to the new world and convinces him that the world is indeed round. He then comes to the aid of a magical firefly named Marilyn who helps Columbus find gold to bring back to Spain. 82m/C VHS, LV. V: Dom DeLuise, Mickey Rooney, Corey Feldman, Irene Cara, Dan Haggerty, Samantha Eggar. HMD

The Magic Voyage of Sinbad 🎬🎬 Sadko 1952 Sinbad embarks on a fantastic journey after promising the people of his Covasian home that he will find the elusive Phoenix, the bird of happiness. Unreleased in the U.S. until 1962; rewritten for the American screen by a young Coppola. 79m/C VHS. RU Sergey Stolyarov, Alla Larionova, Mark Troyanovsky; D: Alexander Ptushko; W: Francis Ford Coppola. SNC

Magical Mystery Tour 🎬🎬 1967 On the road with an oddball assortment of people, the Beatles experience a number of strange incidents around the English countryside. Originally made for British television. ♫Magical Mystery Tour; Blue Jay Way; Your Mother Should Know; The Fool on the Hill. 55m/C VHS, Beta, LV. GB John Lennon, George Harrison, Ringo Starr, Paul McCartney, Victor Spinetti. MPI, MED, WFV

Magical Wonderland 1985 Join a handsome prince and his fair young maiden as they venture through such fairy tale classics as "Beauty and the Beast" and "Sleeping Beauty." 90m/C VHS, Beta. VCI

The Magician 🎬🎬🎬 1958 A master magician in 19th century Sweden (von Sydow) wreaks ill in this darkly comical, supernatural parable. Dark, well photographed early Bergman effort. In Swedish with English subtitles. 101m/B VHS, Beta, LV. SW Max von Sydow, Ingrid Thulin, Gunnar Bjornstrand, Bibi Andersson, Naima Wifstrand; D: Ingmar Bergman; W: Ingmar Bergman. Venice Film Festival '59: Special Jury Prize. HMV, MRV, HHT

The Magician of Lublin 🎬½ 1979 (R) Based on an unusual story by Issac Bashevis Singer. Follows the exploits of a magician/con man in turn-of-the-century Poland whose personal flaws kill his career, until a chance emerges for one last trick. A good example of movie not as good as book; this rendering is superficial, badly acted and unsatisfying. Made soon after Singer won the Nobel Prize for literature in 1978. 105m/C VHS, Beta. Alan Arkin, Valerie Perrine, Louise Fletcher, Lou Jacobi, Shelley Winters; D: Menahem Golan; M: Maurice Jarre. NO

Magnificent Adventurer 🎬 1976 Ostensibly a biography of Benvenuto Cellini, the Florentine sculptor, with a concentration on his love life and swordplay. 94m/C VHS, Beta. Brett Halsey. UNI

The Magnificent Ambersons 🎬🎬🎬🎬 1942 Welles' second film. A fascinating, inventive translation of the Booth Tarkington novel about a wealthy turn of the century family collapsing under the changing currents of progress. Pure Welles, except the glaringly bad tacked-on ending that the studio

shot (under the direction of the great Robert Wise and Fred Fleck), after taking the film from him. It seems they wanted the proverbial happy ending. Also available on laserdisc, with interviews and the original story boards. 88m/B VHS, Beta, LV, Closed Caption. Joseph Cotten, Anne Baxter, Tim Holt, Richard Bennett, Dolores Costello, Erskine Sanford, Ray Collins, Agnes Moorehead; D: Freddie Fleck, Robert Wise, Orson Welles; W: Orson Welles; M: Bernard Herrmann, Roy Webb. New York Film Critics Awards '42: Best Actress (Moorehead); Nominations: Academy Awards '42: Best Black and White Cinematography, Best Interior Decoration, Best Picture, Best Supporting Actress (Moorehead). CRC, MLB, TTC

The Magnificent Dope 🎬🎬½ 1942 Fonda is likeable, as usual, as the hapless yokel in the big city. A trip to New York to take a course on being successful is his prize for winning a "laziest man" contest. He falls for his teacher; she uses his crush to motivate him. Funny and entertaining. 83m/B VHS. Henry Fonda, Lynn Bari, Don Ameche, Edward Everett Horton, Hobart Cavanaugh, Pierre Watkin; D: Walter Lang. TCF

The Magnificent Matador 🎬🎬½ The Brave and the Beautiful 1955 The story of an aging matador who faces death in the bullring to win the love of a woman. Quinn is the bullfighter on the horns of a dilemma. Lots of bull in script carried by harried bull in ring. 94m/C VHS, Beta. Anthony Quinn, Maureen O'Hara, Thomas Gomez; D: Budd Boetticher. VHE

Magnificent Obsession 🎬🎬½ 1954 A drunken playboy (Hudson) kills a man and blinds his wife in an automobile accident. Plagued by guilt, he devotes his life to studying medicine in order to restore the widow's sight. Well-acted melodrama lifted Hudson to stardom. Faithful to the 1935 original, based on a novel by Lloyd C. Douglas. 108m/C VHS, Beta. Jane Wyman, Rock Hudson, Barbara Rush, Agnes Moorehead; D: Douglas Sirk; W: Robert Blees; C: Russell Metty. Nominations: Academy Awards '54: Best Actress (Wyman). USH

The Magnificent Seven 🎬🎬🎬🎬 1960 Western remake of Akira Kurosawa's classic "The Seven Samurai." Mexican villagers hire gunmen to protect them from the bandits who are destroying their town. Most of the actors were relative unknowns, though not for long. Sequelled by "Return of the Seven" in 1966, "Guns of the Magnificent Seven" in 1969, and "The Magnificent Seven Ride" in 1972. Excellent score. Uncredited writing by Walter Newman and Walter Bernstein. 126m/C VHS, Beta, LV. Yul Brynner, Steve McQueen, Robert Vaughn, James Coburn, Charles Bronson, Horst Buchholz, Eli Wallach, Brad Dexter; D: John Sturges; W: William Roberts; C: Charles B(ryant) Lang; M: Elmer Bernstein. Nominations: Academy Awards '60: Original Dramatic/Comedy Score. MGM, FOX, TLF

The Magnificent Yankee 🎬🎬🎬 The Man with Thirty Sons 1950 Adaptation of Emmet Lavery's Broadway play on the life of Supreme Court Justice Oliver Wendell Holmes, starring Calhern (who also did the stage version). America's foremost legal mind was well-served by Calhern, with Harding as his ever-patient wife. 80m/B VHS, Beta. Louis Calhern, Ann Harding, Eduard Franz, Philip Ober, Ian Wolfe, Edith Evanson, Richard Anderson, Jimmy Lydon, Robert Sherwood, Hugh Sanders; D: John Sturges; W: Emmet Lavery. Nominations: Academy Awards '50: Best Actor (Calhern), Best Costume Design (B & W). MGM, FCT, BTV

Magnum Force 🎬🎬 1973 (R) Eastwood's second "Dirty Harry" movie. Harry finds a trail leading from a series of gangland killings straight back to the P.D. Less gripping than "Dirty Harry" (1971); followed by "The Enforcer" (1976), "Sudden Impact" (1983), and "The Dead Pool" (1988). Holbrook is cast intriguingly against type, and the premise is good, but little else recommends this too-violent installment. 124m/C VHS, Beta, LV. Clint Eastwood, Hal Holbrook, Mitchell Ryan, David Soul, Robert Urich, Tim Matheson, Kip Niven; D: Ted Post; W: Michael Cimino, John Milius; M: Lalo Schifrin. WAR, TLF

Magnum Killers ✨ 1976 A young man becomes involved in a web of deadly intrigue when he sets out to find who cheated him out of a small fortune during a card game. 92m/C VHS, Beta. Sombat Methance, Prichela Lee. *UNI*

Magnum P.I.: Don't Eat the Snow in Hawaii 1980 Series pilot finds Vietnam-vet-turned-private-eye Thomas Sullivan Magnum (Selleck) living in Hawaii (in the guest house of never-seen mystery writer Robin Masters) and investigating the death of a wartime buddy. Hillerman excels as autocratic major domo Higgins. 99m/C VHS. Tom Selleck, John Hillerman, Roger E. Mosley, Larry Manetti; *D:* Roger Young; *W:* Donald P. Bellisario, Glen Larson. *USH*

The Mahabharata 1989 Adapted from the myths and folklore of ancient India, the screen version of the original 9 hour stage play is the story of a devastating war between two powerful clans. Initially broadcast on public television, the 6 hour movie is divided into three 2 hour tapes, "The Game of Dice," "Exile in the Forest," and "The War." 318m/C VHS, LV. *GB FR* Robert Langton-Lloyd, Antonin Stahly-Vishwanadan, Bruce Myers; *D:* Peter Brook; *W:* Jean-Claude Carriere; *M:* Toshi Tsuchitori. *BTV, WSH, FCT*

Mahler ✨✨✨ 1974 (PG) Strange Russell effort on the life of the great composer Gustav Mahler. Imperfect script is rescued by fine acting. 110m/C VHS, Beta. Robert Powell, Georgina Hale, Richard Morant, Lee Montague, Terry O'Quinn; *D:* Ken Russell; *W:* Ken Russell. *NO*

Mahogany ✨½ 1975 (PG) Poor girl becomes world-famous high fashion model and designer, ditches boyfriend in the old neighborhood, gets a career boost when she daringly appears in a dress of her own creation at a Roman fashion show, and still yearns for the boy back home. Motown attempt to make mainstream hit that's glossy and predictable. 109m/C VHS, Beta, LV. Diana Ross, Billy Dee Williams, Jean-Pierre Aumont, Anthony Perkins, Nina Foch; *D:* Berry Gordy; *W:* John Byrum; *C:* David Watkin. Nominations: Academy Awards '75: Best Song ("Theme from Mahogany"). *PAR, CCB, FCT*

The Maid ✨✨½ 1990 (PG) An offbeat comedy romance with Sheen as the house husband to Bisset's female executive character. Nice acting; charming, if unoriginal, premise. 91m/C VHS, LV, Closed Caption. Martin Sheen, Jacqueline Bisset, Jean-Pierre Cassel, James Faulkner, Victoria Shalet; *D:* Ian Toynton. *MED, VTR*

Maid to Order ✨½ 1987 (PG) Rich girl Sheedy's fairy godmother puts her in her place by turning her into a maid for a snooty Malibu couple. Good-natured and well-acted if rather mindless Cinderella story. 92m/C VHS, Beta, LV. Ally Sheedy, Beverly D'Angelo, Michael Ontkean, Dick Shawn, Tom Skerritt, Valerie Perrine; *D:* Amy Holden Jones; *M:* Georges Delerue. *LIV*

Maid's Night Out ✨✨ 1938 Pleasant, simple-minded mistaken-identity comedy. Fontaine is an heiress; rich-guy posing-as-milkman Lane thinks she is a maid. They fall in love, of course. 64m/B VHS. Joan Fontaine, Allan "Rocky" Lane, Hedda Hopper, George Irving, William Brisbane, Billy Gilbert, Cecil Kellaway; *D:* Ben Holmes. *MLB*

Maids of Wilko ✨✨ *The Young Ladies of Wilko; Panny z Wilka* 1979 Wajda's adaptation of Jaroslav Iwaszkiewicz's memoirs set in the late '20s. Viktor Ruben (Olbrychski) reexamines his life following the death of a friend. He returns to the home of his aunt and uncle in Wilko where he renews friendships with five sisters on a neighboring estate in an attempt to resurrect a happier past. Lots of fruitless romantic yearning. In French and Polish with English subtitles. 118m/C VHS. *PL FR* Daniel Olbrychski, Christine Pascal, Maja Komorowska, Anna Seniuk, Krystyna Zachwatowicz, Stanislawa Celinska, Zofia Jaroszewska, Tadeusz Bialoszczynski; *D:* Andrzej Wajda; *W:* Zbigniew Kaminski. Nominations: Academy Awards '79: Best Foreign Language Film. *FCT*

The Main Event ✨✨ 1979 (PG) Streisand plays a wacky—and bankrupt—cosmetic executive who must depend on the career of washed-up boxer O'Neal to rebuild her fortune. Desperate (and more than a little smitten), she badgers and bullies him back into the ring. Lame, derivative screwball comedy desperate to suggest chemistry of Streisand and O'Neal's "What's Up, Doc?" (1972). Streisand sings the title song. 109m/C VHS, Beta. Barbra Streisand, Ryan O'Neal; *D:* Howard Zieff. *WAR*

Main Street to Broadway ✨✨ 1953 Superficial story of a struggling playwright. Interesting mainly for abundant big-name cameos. Based on a story by Robert E. Sherwood. 102m/B VHS, Beta. Tom Morton, Mary Murphy, Agnes Moorehead, Herb Shriner, Rosemary DeCamp, Clinton Sundberg; *Cameos:* Lionel Barrymore, Ethel Barrymore, Tallulah Bankhead, Shirley Booth, Cornel Wilde, Rex Harrison, Joshua Logan, Helen Hayes, Mary Martin; *D:* Tay Garnett. *MPI, MLB*

Maitresse ✨✨½ 1976 An examination of the sexual underworld in the same vein as "Blue Velvet" and "Crimes of Passion." Director Schroeder also created "Reversal of Fortune." In French with English subtitles. 112m/C VHS. Gerard Depardieu; *D:* Barbet Schroeder; *C:* Nestor Almendros. *WAR, BTV, FCT*

Major Barbara ✨✨✨½ 1941 A wealthy, idealistic girl joins the Salvation Army against her father's wishes. Based on the play by George Bernard Shaw. The excellent adaptation of the original and the cast make this film a winner. Deborah Kerr's film debut. 90m/B VHS, Beta. *GB* Wendy Hiller, Rex Harrison, Robert Morley, Sybil Thorndike, Deborah Kerr; *D:* Gabriel Pascal. *FCT, HMV*

Major Dundee ✨✨½ 1965 A Union army officer (Heston) chases Apaches into Mexico with a motley collection of prisoner volunteers. Too long and flawed; would have been better had Peckinpah been allowed to finish the project. Excellent cast. 124m/C VHS, Beta. Charlton Heston, Richard Harris, James Coburn, Jim Hutton, Ben Johnson, Slim Pickens; *D:* Sam Peckinpah; *C:* Sam Leavitt. *GKK*

Major League ✨✨½ 1989 (R) Comedy about a pathetic major league baseball team whose new owner schemes to lose the season and relocate the team to Miami. Sheen is okay as the pitcher with control problems (both on and off the field), while Bernsen seems to be gazing affectionately at "L.A. Law" from a distance. Predictable sports spoof is good for a few laughs, particularly those scenes involving Haysbert as a slugger with voodoo on his mind (and in his locker) and Snipes as a base stealer whose only problem is getting on base. 107m/C VHS, Beta, LV, 8mm, Closed Caption. Tom Berenger, Charlie Sheen, Corbin Bernsen, James Gammon, Margaret Whitton, Bob Uecker, Rene Russo, Wesley Snipes, Dennis Haysbert, Charles Cyphers, Chelcie Ross; *D:* David S. Ward; *W:* David S. Ward; *C:* Reynaldo Villalobos; *M:* James Newton Howard. *PAR*

Major League 2 ✨½ 1994 (PG) It's been five years since they won the series, and this plodding sequel finds the wacky championship Cleveland Indians ruined by success and once again struggling in last place. Limited charm of original is lost; dull and filled with so many lame jokes that you won't care if they manage to make it to the top again. Cast returns, with the exception of Wesley Snipes as Willie Mays Hays (now played by Epps). 105m/C VHS, LV, Closed Caption. Charlie Sheen, Tom Berenger, Corbin Bernsen, James Gammon, Dennis Haysbert, Omar Epps, David Keith, Bob Uecker, Alison Doody, Michelle Burke, Margaret Whitton, Eric Bruskotter, Takaaki Ishibashi; *D:* David S. Ward; *W:* R.J. Stewart; *M:* Michel Colombier. *WAR*

Major Payne ✨½ 1995 (PG-13) When the marines have no more use for killing-machine Major Payne (Wayans), he reluctantly agrees to train the inept junior ROTC cadets at academically-challenged Madison Academy. The misfit brigade contains the usual assortment of stock loser-types who follow the predictable "outcasts get even" plot to the letter. Wayans shows flashes of comic genius, but not nearly enough to make up for the one-dimensional characters and indifferent writing. Most of the showcase jokes involve the humiliation and degradation of the kids, always a laugh-riot. Sub-moronic remake of 1955's "The Private War of Major Benson."*CW:* Some crude humor and behavior. 97m/C VHS, LV, Closed Caption. Damon Wayans, Karyn Parsons, William Hickey, Albert Hall, Steven Martini, Andrew Harrison Leeds, Scott "Bam Bam" Bigelow; *D:* Nick Castle; *W:* Damon Wayans, Dean Lorey, Gary Rosen; *C:* Richard Bowen. *USH*

The Majorettes ✨ 1987 (R) Eek! Someone is lurking around a high school murdering the majorettes with their own batons. A bare-bones plot lurks within this otherwise worthless pic. 93m/C VHS, Beta. Kevin Kindlan, Terrie Godfrey, Mark V. Jevicky; *D:* John Russo. *LIV, VES, TEM*

A Majority of One ✨✨½ 1956 Dated comedy about late-in-life romance and prejudice. Russell stars as Jewish Brooklyn widow Mrs. Jacoby, who tags along with her daughter and diplomat son-in-law on their shipboard trip to Japan. She meets the charming Koichi Asano (a surprisingly effective Guinness), who's with the Japanese diplomatic corp, runs into problems with her family, and decides she must give up her chance at romance. Adapted from the play by Leonard Spigelgass. 149m/C VHS. Rosalind Russell, Alec Guinness, Ray Danton, Madlyn Rhue, Mae Questel, Frank Wilcox, Alan Mowbray; *D:* Mervyn LeRoy; *W:* Leonard Spigelgass. *WAR*

Make a Million ✨✨ 1935 The Depression is played (successfully) for yuks in this tale of an economics professor fired from his post for advocating radical income redistribution. He doesn't get mad, he gets even: he makes a million by advertising for money. 66m/B VHS, Beta. Charles Starrett, Pauline Brooks. *VYY*

Make a Wish ✨✨ 1937 A noted composer goes stale in this colorful musical about backstage life. The comic relief provides the films best moments. ♫Music In My Heart; My Campfire Dreams; Make a Wish; Old Man Rip. 80m/B VHS, Beta. Basil Rathbone, Leon Errol, Bobby Breen, Ralph Forbes; *D:* Kurt Neumann; *M:* Oscar Straus. Nominations: Academy Awards '37: Best Original Score. *VYY*

Make Haste to Live ✨✨½ 1954 Good, scary thriller. A woman survives attempted murder by her husband; moves far away to raise their infant daughter. He does time, then returns for revenge. McGuire is good as the terrorized wife. 90m/B VHS. Dorothy McGuire, Stephen McNally, Edgar Buchanan, John Howard; *D:* William A. Seiter; *M:* Elmer Bernstein. *REP*

Make Me an Offer ✨✨ 1955 Somewhat slow-moving comedy centering on an antique dealer who attempts to buy an expensive vase from an old man. From the novel by Wolf Mankowitz. 88m/C VHS. *GB* Peter Finch, Adrienne Corri, Rosalie Crutchley, Finlay Currie; *D:* Cyril Frankel.

Make Me an Offer ✨½ 1980 Made-for-TV movie about selling real estate in Hollywood. Better than similar efforts. 97m/C VHS, Beta. Susan Blakely, Stella Stevens, Patrick O'Neal; *D:* Jerry Paris; *M:* Ralph Burns. *NLC*

Make Mine Mink ✨✨✨ 1960 Oft-hilarious British comedy about guests at an elegant but run-down mansion who become unlikely thieves, stealing furs for charity. Good cast headed by Terry-Thomas. 100m/C VHS, Beta. *GB* Terry-Thomas, Billie Whitelaw, Hattie Jacques; *D:* Robert Asher. *NO*

Make Room for Tomorrow ✨✨ 1981 (R) Subtle, somewhat funny French comedy about generations in a family. A man in mid-life crisis has to cope with his father, son, and grandfather on the grandfather's 90th birthday. 106m/C VHS, Beta. *FR* Victor Lanoux, Jane Birkin, George Wilson; *D:* Peter Kassovitz.

Make-Up 🐾🐾 1937 A doctor turned circus clown uses his medical skills when an elephant renders a society girl unconscious. After she awakens the two become involved. The clown's daughter objects, but is soon caught up in an accusation that she murdered the lion tamer. Her father the clown tries to save the day. Predictable doctor/clown relationship. **72m/b VHS.** Nils Asther, June Clyde, Judy Kelly, Kenne Duncan, John Turnbull; **D:** Alfred Zeisler. *NOS, DVT, HEG*

Making Contact 🐾🐾½ 1986 (PG) A small boy's telekinetic powers enable him to bring to life his favorite toys. The ridicule he endures because of this leads him to set off on terrifying adventures with only his toys and a friend for company. **83m/C VHS, Beta.** Joshua Morrell, Eve Kryll; **D:** Roland Emmerich. *NWV, VTR*

Making Love 🐾🐾 1982 (R) A closet homosexual risks his 8-year marriage by getting involved with a carefree writer. What could be a powerful subject gets only bland treatment. **112m/C VHS, Beta.** Kate Jackson, Harry Hamlin, Michael Ontkean, Wendy Hiller, Arthur Hill, Nancy Olson, Terry Kiser, Camilla Carr, Michael Dudikoff; **D:** Arthur Hiller; **W:** Barry Sandler. *FOX*

Making Mr. Right 🐾🐾½ 1986 (PG-13) Under-rated satire about a high-powered marketing and image consultant who falls in love with the android that she's supposed to be promoting. Unbelievable comedy is shaky at times, but Magnuson and Malkovich create some magic. **95m/C VHS, Beta, LV.** John Malkovich, Ann Magnuson, Glenne Headly, Ben Masters, Laurie Metcalf, Polly Bergen, Hart Bochner, Polly Draper, Susan Anton; **D:** Susan Seidelman; **W:** Floyd Byars. *HBO*

Making the Grade 🐾🐾 *Preppies* 1984 (PG) Jersey tough kid owes the mob; attends prep school in place of a rich kid who can't be bothered. Better than similar '80s teen flicks, but not by much. **105m/C VHS, Beta.** Judd Nelson, Joanna Lee, Dana Olsen, Ronald Lacey, Scott McGinnis, Gordon Jump, Carey Scott, Andrew Dice Clay; **D:** Dorian Walker; **W:** Gene Quintano; **M:** Basil Poledouris. *MGM*

The Makioka Sisters 🐾🐾🐾 1983 Much praised drama centering around the lives of four Japanese sisters who are heiresses to the family fortune and, hence, must be found proper husbands. The efforts of the older sisters to "match" their younger siblings are entwined with a gradual realization on the part of the elders that the quiet way of life representative of their own formative years is passing away with the advent of WWII. The movie is as visually stunning as it is poignant. In Japanese with English subtitles. **140m/C VHS, LV.** *JP* Keiko Kishi, Yoshiko Sakuma, Sayuri Yoshinaga; **D:** Kon Ichikawa. *FCT, TPV*

Malarek 🐾🐾 1989 (R) Tough Montreal journalist Victor Malarek exposed abuse in that city's teen detention center in his book "Hey, Malarek." Compelling lead performance from Koteas in decent though not great screen adaptation. **95m/C VHS, Beta, LV.** Michael Sarrazin, Elias Koteas, Al Waxman, Kerrie Keane; **D:** Roger Cardinal. *COL*

Malaya 🐾🐾½ *East of the Rising Sun* 1949 Hokey adventure tale set in WWII that's based on a true story. Stewart and Tracy are hired to smuggle a huge shipment of rubber out of Malaya to waiting U.S. ships without the Japanese finding out. Greenstreet does his usual shifty role. **98m/B VHS, Beta.** Spencer Tracy, James Stewart, Sydney Greenstreet, Valentina Cortese, John Hodiak, Lionel Barrymore, Gilbert Roland, Richard Loo, Roland Winters; **D:** Richard Thorpe; **W:** Frank Fenton; **M:** Bronislau Kaper. *MGM*

Malcolm 🐾🐾½ 1986 (PG-13) An offbeat comedy about a slightly retarded young man who is mechanically inclined and his unusual entry into a life of crime. Directorial debut for actress Tass, whose husband Parker wrote the screenplay (and designed the Tinkertoys). Music score performed by The Penguin Cafe Orchestra. **86m/C VHS, Beta, LV.** *AU* Colin Friels, John Hargreaves, Lindy Davies, Chris Haywood, Charles Tingwell, Beverly Phillips, Judith Stratford; **D:** Nadia Tass; **W:** David Parker; **M:** Simon Jeffes.

Australian Film Institute '86: Best Actor (Friels), Best Film. *LIV, VES*

Malcolm X 🐾🐾🐾 1992 (PG-13) Stirring tribute to the controversial black activist, a leader in the struggle for black liberation. Hitting bottom during his imprisonment in the 50s, he became a Black Muslim and then a leader in the Nation of Islam. His assassination in 1965 left a legacy of black nationalism, self-determination, and racial pride. Marked by strong direction from Lee and good performances (notably Freeman Jr. as Elijah Muhammad), it is Washington's convincing performance in the title role that truly brings the film alive. Based on "The Autobiography of Malcolm X" by Malcolm X and Alex Haley. **CW:** Some language and some violence and drug content. **201m/C VHS, Beta, LV, 8mm, Closed Caption.** Denzel Washington, Angela Bassett, Albert Hall, Al Freeman Jr., Delroy Lindo, Spike Lee, Theresa Randle, Kate Vernon, Lonette McKee, Tommy Hollis, James McDaniel, Ernest Thompson, Jean LaMarre, Giancarlo Esposito, Craig Wasson, John Ottavino, David Patrick Kelly, Shirley Stoler; **Cameos:** Christopher Plummer, Karen Allen, Peter Boyle, William Kunstler, Bobby Seale, Al Sharpton; **D:** Spike Lee; **W:** Spike Lee, Arnold Perl, James Baldwin; **M:** Terence Blanchard. Chicago Film Critics Awards '93: Best Actor (Washington), Best Film; MTV Movie Awards '93: Best Male Performance (Washington); New York Film Critics Awards '92: Best Actor (Washington); Nominations: Academy Awards '92: Best Actor (Washington), Best Costume Design. *WAR, MOV, BTV*

Malcolm X: Make It Plain 1995 In-depth portrait of the life of Malcolm X as told through the memories of many of Malcolm's close personal friends and individuals who had worked closely with him. Contains footage of Malcolm X speaking at rallies, meetings, and interviews with Maya Angelou, Ossie Davis, Alex Haley, Mike Wallace, and his family. **136m/C VHS.** *MPI*

Male and Female 🐾🐾🐾🐾 1919 A group of British aristocrats is shipwrecked on an island and must allow their efficient butler (Meighan) to take command for their survival. Swanson is the spoiled rich girl who falls for her social inferior. Their rescue provides a return to the rigid British class system. Based on the play "The Admirable Crichton" by James M. Barrie. **110m/B VHS, Beta.** Gloria Swanson, Thomas Meighan, Lila Lee, Raymond Hatton, Bebe Daniels; **D:** Cecil B. DeMille. *GPV*

Malibu Beach 🐾½ 1978 (R) The California beach scene is the setting for this movie filled with bikini clad girls, tanned young men, and instant romances. For connoisseurs of the empty-headed teen beach movie. **93m/C VHS, Beta.** Kim Lankford, James Daughton; **D:** Robert J. Rosenthal; **C:** Jamie Anderson. *PSM*

The Malibu Beach Vampires 1991 (R) Three unscrupulous yuppies, Congressman Teri Upstart, Col. Ollie West and Rev. Timmy Fakker, keep beautiful mistresses in their Malibu beach house. What they don't know is, the girls are all really vampires who have injected them with a serum that compels them to tell the truth! Will our "heroes" continue to dupe the American Public, or will the sexy blood suckers cause their downfall? **90m/C VHS.** Angelyne, Becky Le Beau, Joan Rudelstein, Marcus A. Frishman, Rod Sweitzer, Francis Creighton, Anet Anatelle, Yvette Buchanan, Cherie Romaors, Kelly Galindo; **D:** Francis Creighton. *NO*

Malibu Bikini Shop 🐾 1986 (R) Two brothers manage a beachfront bikini shop in Malibu, and spend their time ogling the customers and arguing about running the "business." Just another excuse for parading babes in bathing suits across the naked screen. **90m/C VHS, Beta, Closed Caption.** Michael David Wright, Bruce Greenwood, Barbara Horan, Debra Blee, Jay Robinson, Galyn Gorg, Ami Julius, Frank Nelson, Kathleen Freeman, Rita Jenrette; **D:** David Wechter; **W:** David Wechter. *FOX*

Malibu Express 🐾 1985 (R) Mystery/adventure plot about a P.I. is the excuse; babes in swimsuits is the reason for this waste of time. **101m/C VHS, Beta.** Darby Hinton, Sybil Danning, Art Me-

trano, Shelley Taylor Morgan, Niki Dantine, Barbara Edwards; **D:** Andy Sidaris. *USH*

Malibu High 🐾 1979 (R) The accidental death of a young prostitute's client leads her to a new series of illegal activities of the "sex and hit" variety. Dark, sleazy, and antisocial; belies Beach Boys-esque title. **92m/C VHS, Beta.** Jill Lansing, Stuart Taylor; **D:** Irvin Berwick. *NO*

Malibu Hot Summer 🐾 *Sizzle Beach U.S.A* 1974 (R) Three aspiring young actresses want a shot at becoming famous and travel to Los Angeles where they spend their time at the beach with little budget and no particular purchase. Re-released and renamed in 1986 when Costner (in his film debut) became more well-known. **89m/C VHS.** Terry Congie, Leslie Brander, Roselyn Royce, Kevin Costner; **D:** Richard Brander. *VHE, THV, VTR*

Malice 🐾🐾½ 1993 (R) In a sleepy little college town, strange things sure do happen. Too bad rumpled college dean Andy Safian (Pullman) didn't see "Pacific Heights." If he did, he would know that sometimes roommates are more trouble than they're worth, even if renovation on that old Victorian is getting expensive. Routine thriller throws out an inventive twist to keep things moving, but manages to be fairly predictable anyway. **CW:** Language, some violence, and sexuality. **107m/C VHS, LV, Closed Caption.** Alec Baldwin, Nicole Kidman, Bill Pullman, Bebe Neuwirth, Anne Bancroft, George C. Scott, Peter Gallagher, Josef Sommer; **D:** Harold Becker; **W:** Aaron Sorkin, Scott Frank; **C:** Gordon Willis; **M:** Jerry Goldsmith. *NLC*

Malicious 🐾🐾 *Malizia* 1974 (R) A housekeeper hired for a widower and his three sons becomes the object of lusty affection of all four men. As Papa makes plans to court and marry her, his fourteen-year-old son plots to have her as a companion on his road to sensual maturity. Dubbed in English. **98m/C VHS, Beta.** *IT* Laura Antonelli, Turi Ferro, Alessandro Momo, Tina Aumont; **D:** Salvatore Samperi. *PAR*

Malicious 🐾🐾 1995 (R) College athlete Doug Gordon (McGaw) impulsively has what he thinks is a one-nighter with mystery lady, Melissa (Ringwald). Only she's not willing to give him up and his rejection sends her on the road to revenge. **CW:** Scenes of strong sexuality; language; some violence. **92m/C VHS, LV, Closed Caption.** Molly Ringwald, Patrick McGaw, Sarah Lassez, John Vernon, Mimi Kuzyk, Rick Henrickson; **D:** Ian Corson; **W:** George Saunders; **C:** Michael Slovis; **M:** Graeme Coleman. *REP*

Mallrats 🐾🐾½ 1995 (R) Smith's better-financed follow-up to the legendary "Clerks" (the second in the "Lord of the Rings" trilogy) follows Jersey slackers T.S. (London) and Brodie (Lee) to the mall, where they intend to wallow in food-court cookies and reclaim their girlfriends, who recently dumped them. While wandering the mall in low-key and confused pursuit of their women and self respect, they encounter the usual band of bizarre inhabitants, including Ivannah, the topless psychic, and Silent Bob (Smith) and stoner Jay (Mewes), the guys who hung out in front of the video shop during "Clerks." Dialogue and sight-gags are director/writer Smith's strong point; moving the plot forward is not high on the priority list. The ensemble cast, featuring Doherty as the boring babe who spurns Brodie, is up to the often funny sidebits and gen-x references. Ribald humor is not for young teens with virgin ears, unless mom and dad are out for the evening. Slick packaging with alternative soundtrack insures return on investment. **CW:** Strong language, including sexual dialogue, and scenes of sexuality and drug content. **95m/C VHS, LV, Closed Caption.** Shannen Doherty, Jeremy London, Jason Lee, Claire Forlani, Michael Rooker, Priscilla Barnes, Renee Humphrey, Ben Affleck, Joey Lauren Adams, Jason Mewes, Brian O'Halloran, David Brinkley, Kevin Smith; **Cameos:** Stan Lee; **D:** Kevin Smith; **W:** Kevin Smith; **C:** David Klein; **M:** Ira Newborn. *USH*

Malone 🎞½ **1987 (R)** A burnt-out secret agent stumbles into a real-estate swindle/murder plot in Oregon and sets out to stop it. Film tries hard but doesn't succeed in being believable. **92m/C VHS, Beta, LV, Closed Caption.** Burt Reynolds, Lauren Hutton, Cliff Robertson, Kenneth McMillan, Scott Wilson, Cynthia Gibb; **D:** Harley Cokliss; **M:** David Newman. ORI

Malou 🎞🎞 **1983 (R)** A young French woman tries to uncover the truth about her late mother's life, sifting through wildly contradictory evidence in the desire to discover her own identity and avoid her mother's mistakes. A feminist story. In German with English subtitles. **95m/C VHS, Beta.** GE Grischa Huber, Ingrid Caven, Helmut Griem; **D:** Jeanine Meerapfel; **C:** Michael Ballhaus. GLV

Malta Story 🎞🎞½ **1953** A British WWII flier becomes involved with the defense of Malta. **103m/B VHS, Beta.** Alec Guinness, Jack Hawkins, Anthony Steel, Flora Robson, Muriel Pavlow; **D:** Brian Desmond Hurst.

The Maltese Falcon 🎞🎞🎞 *Dangerous Female* **1931** A good first screen version of the Dashiell Hammett story about private detective Sam Spade's search for the elusive Black Bird. Remade five years later as "Satan Met a Lady" with Bette Davis. Its most famous remake, however, occurred in 1941 with Humphrey Bogart in the lead. **80m/B VHS, Beta.** Bebe Daniels, Ricardo Cortez, Dudley Digges, Thelma Todd, Una Merkel, Dwight Frye, Robert Elliott; **D:** Roy Del Ruth. MLB

The Maltese Falcon 🎞🎞🎞 **1941** After the death of his partner, detective Sam Spade finds himself enmeshed in a complicated, intriguing search for a priceless statuette. "It's the stuff dreams are made of," says Bogart of the Falcon. Excellent, fast-paced film noir with outstanding performances, great dialogue, and concentrated attention to details. Director Huston's first film and Greenstreet's talky debut. First of several films by Bogart and Astor. Based on the novel by Dashiell Hammett. Also available colorized. **101m/B VHS, Beta, LV, Closed Caption.** Humphrey Bogart, Mary Astor, Peter Lorre, Sydney Greenstreet, Ward Bond, Barton MacLane, Gladys George, Lee Patrick, Elisha Cook Jr., Jerome Cowan; **Cameos:** Walter Huston; **D:** John Huston; **W:** John Huston; **M:** Adolph Deutsch. Nominations: Academy Awards '41: Best Picture, Best Screenplay, Best Supporting Actor (Greenstreet). MGM, FOX, TLF

Mama Dracula woof! **1980** Fletcher stars in this poor satire of the horror genre. She's a vampire who needs the blood of virgins to stay young. Her son helps out—what good son wouldn't? **90m/C VHS.** FR Louise Fletcher, Bonnie Schneider, Maria Schneider, Marc-Henri Wajnberg, Alexander Wajnberg, Jess Hahn; **D:** Boris Szulzinger. TWE

Mama, There's a Man in Your Bed 🎞🎞🎞 *Romuald et Juliet* **1989 (PG)** When a powerful executive is framed for insider trading, the only witness to the crime and his only hope is an earthy cleaning woman named Juliette. Together they plot revenge and takeovers in her tiny apartment, filled with children. Soon, he regains his former position of power but realizes his life isn't complete without his co-conspirator. In French with English subtitles. **111m/C VHS, Beta, LV.** FR Daniel Auteuil, Firmine Richard, Pierre Vernier, Maxime LeRoux, Gilles Privat, Muriel Combeau, Catherine Salviat, Sambou Tati; **D:** Coline Serreau; **W:** Coline Serreau. HBO, FCT

Mama Turns a Hundred 🎞🎞🎞 **1979 (R)** A baronial family (a bizarre set of characters) is celebrating their mother's 100th birthday at her estate. One of the daughter's seduces her brother-in-law, another has a uniform fetish, a religious zealot is desperate to hang-glide, and several of them are trying to kill poor Mama. But of course she prevails, although sick and ailing. Slow-paced yet uproarious film full of inept characters who bumble along. In Spanish with English subtitles. **100m/C VHS, Beta.** SP Geraldine Chaplin, Fernando Gomez, Amparo Munoz; **D:** Carlos Saura. Nominations: Academy Awards '79: Best Foreign Language Film. INT, AUD, TPV

Mama's Dirty Girls **1974 (R)** A gangster mom's daughters take over where their mother left off and have the time of their lives. **82m/C VHS, Beta.** Gloria Grahame, Paul Lambert, Sondra Currie, Candice Rialson, Mary Stoddard; **D:** John Hayes; **M:** Don Bagley. TWE

Mambo 🎞🎞½ **1955** A poor young dancer inspires patronage and lust by dancing the Mambo. Although attracted to Gassman, she marries Rennie for his money. Technically weak but artistically interesting, though Rennie and Mangano have done their roles somewhat better elsewhere. **94m/B VHS.** Silvana Mangano, Michael Rennie, Vittorio Gassman, Shelley Winters, Katherine Dunham, Mary Clare, Eduardo Ciannelli; **D:** Robert Rossen; **M:** Nino Rota. NOS, HTV

The Mambo Kings 🎞🎞🎞 **1992 (R)** Armand and Banderas (in his first English speaking role) are Cesar and Nestor Castillo, two brothers who flee Cuba for New York City with dreams of hitting it big with their mambo music. Desi Arnaz Jr. gets to play his own dad in a funny and technical scene that leads to a climactic confrontation between the brothers. Good cast and great music make this one worthwhile. Based on the Pulitzer prizewinning novel "The Mambo Kings Play Songs of Love" by Oscar Hijuelos. **100m/C VHS, LV, 8mm, Closed Caption.** Armand Assante, Antonio Banderas, Cathy Moriarty, Maruschka Detmers, Desi Arnaz Jr., Celia Cruz, Roscoe Lee Browne, Vondie Curtis-Hall, Tito Puente, Talisa Soto; **D:** Arne Glimcher; **W:** Cynthia Cidre; **C:** Michael Ballhaus; **M:** Robert Kraft, Carlos Franzetti. Nominations: Academy Awards '92: Best Song ("Beautiful Maria of My Soul"). WAR, FCT, MVD

Mame 🎞🎞 **1974 (PG)** In an adaptation of the Broadway musical "Auntie Mame" by Jerry Herman, Ball plays a dynamic woman who takes it upon herself to teach a group of eccentrics how to live life to the fullest. Arthur plays Mame's friend just as splendidly as she did in the Broadway version, but Ball in her last feature film is a lame Mame. Overly ambitious production avoids reaching goal. ♫Mame; We Need a Little Christmas; If He Walked Into My Life; Bosom Buddies; It's Today; Loving You; My Best Girl; What Do I Do Now? (Gooch's Son); Open a New Window. **132m/C VHS, Beta, LV.** Lucille Ball, Beatrice Arthur, Robert Preston, Joyce Van Patten, Bruce Davison; **D:** Gene Saks. WAR, MVD

Mamele 🎞½ *Little Mother* **1938** Picon prematurely becomes the "mother" of her seven siblings when their mother dies. Quintessential Yiddish musical with the usual shimmering performance from Picon. In Yiddish with English subtitles. **95m/B VHS, Beta.** PL Molly Picon, Max Bozyk, Edmund Zayenda; **D:** Joseph Green. ERG, TPV

Mamma Roma 🎞🎞🎞½ **1962** Pasolini's second film is a heartbreaking story of family ties, escaping the past, and dreams of the future. The title character (Magnani) is a former prostitute who attempts respectability for herself and her teenaged son (Garofolo). But her ex-pimp (Citti) threatens her new life and Rome's big-city temptations prove to be a pathway to crime and tragedy for the boy. Magnani gives one of her finest performances. Italian with subtitles. **110m/B VHS.** IT Anna Magnani, Ettore Garofolo, Franco Citti, Silvana Corsini, Luisa Loiano; **D:** Pier Paolo Pasolini; **W:** Pier Paolo Pasolini; **C:** Tonino Delli Colli. MFI

A Man, a Woman, and a Bank 🎞🎞½ **1979 (PG)** Two con-men plan to rob a bank by posing as workers during the bank's construction. An advertising agency woman snaps their picture for a billboard to show how nice the builders have been, then becomes romantically involved with one of the would-be thieves. Nice performances, but wacky touches aren't plentiful enough or well-timed to sustain comedy. Also called "A Very Big Weekend." **100m/C VHS, Beta.** CA Donald Sutherland, Brooke Adams, Paul Mazursky; **D:** Noel Black; **W:** Bruce A. Evans, Raynold Gideon; **C:** Jack Cardiff; **M:** Bill Conti. NLC

A Man, a Woman and a Killer 🎞🎞½ **19??** Unusual film within a film shows the actual making of a movie while unfolding a story of a hired killer. A joint project from the directors of the well-received "Emerald Cities" and "Chan is Missing." **75m/C VHS. D:** Rick Schmidt, Wayne Wang. FCT

A Man About the House 🎞🎞½ **1947** Two unmarried English sisters move into the Italian villa they have inherited. There, one marries the caretaker, who secretly plans to regain the property that once belonged to his family. When the newly married sister is found dead, her sibling sets out to solve the murder. **83m/B VHS.** GB Kieron Moore, Margaret Johnston, Dulcie Gray, Guy Middleton, Felix Aylmer; **D:** Leslie Arliss. NOS, SNC

A Man Alone 🎞🎞 **1955** Man falsely accused of robbing a stagecoach hides not alone but with comely sheriff's daughter. Milland's debut behind the camera. **96m/C VHS.** Ray Milland, Ward Bond, Mary Murphy, Raymond Burr, Lee Van Cleef; **D:** Ray Milland; **C:** Lionel Lindon. REP

A Man and a Woman 🎞🎞🎞 *Un Homme et Un Femme* **1966** When a man and a woman, both widowed, meet and become interested in one another but experience difficulties in putting their past loves behind them. Intelligently handled emotional conflicts within a well-acted romantic drama, acclaimed for excellent visual detail. Remade in 1977 as "Another Man, Another Chance." Followed in 1986 with "A Man and A Woman: 20 Years Later." Dubbed. **102m/C VHS, Beta, Closed Caption.** FR Anouk Aimee, Jean-Louis Trintignant, Pierre Barouh, Valerie Lagrange; **D:** Claude Lelouch; **W:** Claude Lelouch. Academy Awards '66: Best Foreign Language Film, Best Story & Screenplay; British Academy Awards '67: Best Actress (Aimee); Cannes Film Festival '66: Best Film; Golden Globe Awards '67: Best Actress—Drama (Aimee), Best Foreign Film; Nominations: Academy Awards '66: Best Actress (Aimee), Best Director (Lelouch). WAR, APD, HMV

A Man and a Woman: 20 Years Later 🎞½ *Un Homme Et Une Femme: Vingt Ans Deja* **1986 (PG)** Slouchy sequel to the highly praised "A Man and a Woman" that catches up with a couple after a long separation. The sad romantic complications of the original are more mundane in this sequel, which is burdened by a film-within-a-film script as well as shots from the original. In French with English subtitles. **112m/C VHS, Beta.** FR Jean-Louis Trintignant, Anouk Aimee, Richard Berry; **D:** Claude Lelouch; **W:** Claude Lelouch. WAR

Man & Boy 🎞🎞 *Ride a Dark Horse* **1971 (G)** A black Civil War veteran, played by Bill Cosby, encounters bigotry and prejudice when he tries to set up a homestead in Arizona. An acceptable family film, some might be disappointed that Cosby is not playing this one for laughs. **98m/C VHS, Beta.** Bill Cosby, Gloria Foster, George Spell, Henry Silva, Yaphet Kotto; **D:** E.W. Swackhamer; **M:** Quincy Jones. COL

The Man and the Monster 🎞½ **1965** When a concert pianist sells his soul to the devil, he fails to realize that part of the deal has him turning into a hideous beast every time he hears a certain piece of music. Maybe it was "Stairway to Heaven." **78m/B VHS.** MX Enrique Rambal, Abel Salazar, Martha Roth; **D:** Rafael Baledon. SNC

Man Bait 🎞🎞½ *The Last Page* **1952** A complex web of intrigue and mystery surrounds a blackmailed book dealer when he allows a blonde woman to catch his eye. A competently made film. **78m/B VHS, Beta, LV.** GB George Brent, Marguerite Chapman, Diana Dors; **D:** Terence Fisher. RXM, MLB

Man Beast 🎞 **1955** The abominable snowman is sought and found in this grade-Z '50s monster movie. **65m/B VHS, Beta.** Rock Madison, Virginia Maynor, George Skaff, Lloyd Nelson, Tom Maruzzi; **D:** Jerry Warren. NOS, MRV, RHI

Man Bites Dog 🎞🎞 **1991 (NC-17)** A pseudo-documentary about a serial killer, filled with ever-mounting violence. Ben is the killer being followed by a two-man camera/sound crew (which he's hired), who record his casual carnage without lifting a finger to stop him. Indeed his continued killing and robbing is to pay for financing the documentary about himself. This satire on film violence, as well as reality-based television shows, is both appalling and humorous in a sick way. In French with English subtitles. Also available in an unrated edited version. 95m/B VHS. *BE* Benoit Poelvoorde, Remy Belvaux, Andre Bonzel; *D:* Benoit Poelvoorde, Remy Belvaux, Andre Bonzel; *W:* Benoit Poelvoorde, Remy Belvaux, Andre Bonzel, Vincent Tavier. *FXL, FCT*

A Man Called Adam 🐾½ 1966 A jazz musician is tortured by prejudice and the guilt created by his having accidentally killed his wife and baby years before. Davis is appropriately haunted, but the film is poorly produced. 103m/B VHS, Beta. Sammy Davis Jr., Louis Armstrong, Ossie Davis, Cicely Tyson, Frank Sinatra Jr., Lola Falana, Mel Torme, Peter Lawford; *D:* Leonard Penn; *C:* Jack Priestley. *COL, NLC*

A Man Called Horse 🐾🐾🐾 1970 (PG) After a wealthy Britisher is captured and tortured by the Sioux Indians in the Dakotas, he abandons his formal ways and discovers his own strength. As he passes their torture tests, he is embraced by the tribe. In this very realistic and gripping portrayal of American Indian life, Harris provides a strong performance. Sequelled by "Return of a Man Called Horse" (1976) and "Triumphs of a Man Called Horse" (1983). 114m/C VHS, Beta, LV, Closed Caption. Richard Harris, Judith Anderson, Jean Gascon, Stanford Howard, Manu Tupou, Dub Taylor; *D:* Elliot Silverstein; *W:* Jack DeWitt; *C:* Robert B. Hauser. *FOX*

A Man Called Peter 🐾🐾🐾 1955 A biographical epic about Peter Marshall, a Scottish chaplain who served the U.S. Senate. Todd does his subject justice by sensitively showing all that was human in Marshall, and a talented supporting cast makes for a thoroughly watchable film. 119m/C VHS, Beta, Closed Caption. Richard Todd, Jean Peters, Marjorie Rambeau, Jill Esmond, Les Tremayne, Robert Burton; *D:* Henry Koster. Nominations: Academy Awards '55: Best Color Cinematography. *FOX*

A Man Called Rage woof! 1984 Rage is the only man capable of safely escorting a group of pioneers through a nuclear wasteland infested with mutants and cannibals. 90m/C VHS, Beta. *IT* Stelio Candelli, Conrad Nichols; *D:* Anthony Richmond. *LIV*

A Man Called Sarge 🐾½ 1990 (PG-13) Sophomoric comedy about a daffy WWII sergeant leading his squad against the Germans at Tobruk. 88m/C VHS, Beta, LV. Gary Kroeger, Marc Singer, Gretchen German, Jennifer Runyon; *D:* Stuart Gillard. *WAR, OM*

A Man Called Sledge 🐾🐾 1971 Garner fans might be surprised to see the star play a villain in this violent story of a gang of outlaws who wind up fighting each over a cache of gold. This is mainstream Western entertainment. 93m/C VHS. James Garner, Dennis Weaver, Claude Akins, John Marley, Laura Antonelli; *D:* Vic Morrow. *COL, GKK*

A Man Escaped 🐾🐾🐾½ *Un Condamne a Mort s'est Echappe; The Wind Bloweth Where it Listeth* 1957 There's an excruciating realism about Bresson's account of a WWII Resistance fighter's escape from a Nazi prison just before he was to be executed by the Gestapo. It's the sounds and lingering camera shots, not the wham bam variety of action, that create and sustain the film's suspense. Bresson, who had been a Nazi prisoner, solicited the supervision of Andre Devigny, whose true story the film tells. Contributing to the realistic feel was the use of non professional actors. An award-wiining film that fellow director Truffaut lauded as the most crucial French film of the previous ten years. In French with English subtitles. 102m/B VHS. Francois Leterrier; *D:* Robert Bresson. Cannes Film Festival '57: Best Director (Bresson); National Board of Review Awards '57: 5 Best Foreign Films of the Year. *NYF*

Man Facing Southeast 🐾🐾🐾½ *Hombre Mirando Al Sudeste; Man Looking Southeast* 1986 (R) The acclaimed Argentinean film about the sudden appearance of a strange man in an asylum who claims to be an extraterrestrial, and a psychologist's attempts to discover his true identity. The sense of mystery intensifies when the new patient indeed seems to have some remarkable powers. Although the pace at times lags, the story intriguingly keeps one guessing about the stranger right to the end. In Spanish, with English subtitles. 105m/C VHS, Beta, LV. *AR* Lorenzo Quinteros, Hugo Soto, Ines Vernengo; *D:* Eliseo Subiela; *C:* Ricardo De Angelis; *M:* Pedro Aznar. *VTR, NWV, IME*

A Man for All Seasons 🐾🐾🐾🐾 1966 (G) Sterling, heavily Oscar-honored biographical drama concerning the life and subsequent martyrdom of 16th-century Chancellor of England, Sir Thomas More (Scofield). Story revolves around his personal conflict when King Henry VIII (Shaw) seeks a divorce from his wife, Catherine of Aragon, so he can wed his mistress, Anne Boleyn—events that ultimately lead the King to bolt from the Pope and declare himself head of the Church of England. Remade for television in 1988 with Charlton Heston in the lead role. 120m/C VHS, Beta, LV, Closed Caption. Paul Scofield, Robert Shaw, Orson Welles, Wendy Hiller, Susannah York, John Hurt, Nigel Davenport, Vanessa Redgrave; *D:* Fred Zinnemann; *W:* Constance Willis, Robert Bolt; *C:* Ted Moore; *M:* Georges Delerue. Academy Awards '66: Best Actor (Scofield), Best Adapted Screenplay, Best Color Cinematography, Best Costume Design (Color), Best Director (Zinnemann), Best Picture; British Academy Awards '67: Best Actor (Scofield), Best Film, Best Screenplay; Directors Guild of America Awards '66: Best Director (Zinnemann); Golden Globe Awards '67: Best Actor—Drama (Scofield), Best Director (Zinnemann), Best Film—Drama, Best Screenplay; National Board of Review Awards '66: 10 Best Films of the Year, Best Actor (Scofield), Best Director (Zinnemann), Best Supporting Actor (Shaw); New York Film Critics Awards '66: Best Actor (Scofield), Best Director (Zinnemann), Best Film, Best Screenplay; Nominations: Academy Awards '66: Best Supporting Actor (Shaw), Best Supporting Actress (Hiller). *COL, BTV, TVC*

A Man for All Seasons 🐾🐾🐾 1988 Fresh from the London stage, Heston directs and stars in this version of Robert Bolt's play depicting the conflict between Henry VIII and his chief advisor, Sir Thomas More. Strong supporting cast. Made for cable TV. 150m/C VHS, LV. Charlton Heston, Vanessa Redgrave, John Gielgud, Richard Johnson, Roy Kinnear, Martin Chamberlain; *D:* Charlton Heston. *TTC*

Man Friday 🐾🐾 1975 (PG) Stranded on a deserted island, a man forces a native from a neighboring island to be his slave. Based on the classic story "Robinson Crusoe" by Daniel Defoe, this adaptation charts the often-brutal treatment the native receives as his captor tries to civilize him. Through his intelligence, the enslaved man regains his freedom and returns home with his former captor, who then seeks acceptance from the native's tribe. A sometimes confusing story line and excessive blood and guts detract from this message-laden effort. 115m/C VHS. *GB* Peter O'Toole, Richard Roundtree, Peter Cellier, Christopher Cabot, Joel Fluellen; *D:* Jack Gold; *M:* Carl Davis. *FOX*

The Man from Atlantis 🐾🐾 1977 Patrick Duffy stars as the water-breathing alien who emerges from his undersea home, the Lost City of Atlantis. The made-for-TV movie led to a brief television series. 60m/C VHS, Beta. Patrick Duffy, Belinda J. Montgomery, Victor Buono; *D:* Lee H. Katzin. *WOV*

The Man from Beyond 🐾🐾½ 1922 Frozen alive, a man returns 100 years later to try and find his lost love. Silent. 50m/B VHS, Beta. Harry Houdini, Arthur Maude, Nita Naldi; *D:* Burton King. *SNC, VYY, DVT*

Man from Button Willow 🐾🐾 1965 (G) Classic animated adventure is the story of Justin Eagle, a man who leads a double life. He is a respected rancher and a shrewd secret agent for the government, but in 1869 he suddenly finds

himself the guardian of a four-year-old Oriental girl, leading him into a whole new series of adventures. Strictly for younger audiences. 79m/C VHS, Beta. *M:* George Bruns; *V:* Dale Robertson, Edgar Buchanan, Barbara Jean Wong, Howard Keel. *NO*

Man from Cairo 🐾🐾 1954 An American in Algiers is mistaken for a detective in search of gold lost during WWII and decides to play along. 82m/B VHS, Beta, LV. *IT* George Raft, Gianna Maria Canale; *D:* Ray Enright. *NO*

Man from Cheyenne 🐾 1942 Cowboy comes home to find his town under a siege of terror from a lawless gang of cattle rustlers. He gets mad and seeks some frontier justice. 54m/B VHS, Beta. Roy Rogers, Gale Storm, George "Gabby" Hayes, Sally Payne. *NOS, DVT, RXM*

Man from Colorado 🐾🐾½ 1949 An odd Technicolor western about two Civil War vets at odds, one an honest marshall, the other a sadistic judge. Solid Western fare with a quirky performance by Ford. 99m/C VHS, Beta. William Holden, Glenn Ford, Ellen Drew, Ray Collins, Edgar Buchanan, Jerome Courtland, James Millican, Jim Bannon; *D:* Henry Levin; *M:* George Duning. *COL*

Man from Deep River woof! 1977 (R) A photographer is captured by a savage tribe in Thailand and forced to undergo a series of grueling initiation rites. Full of very violent and sickening tortures inflicted on both human and animal victims. 90m/C VHS, Beta. *IT* Ivan Rassimov; *D:* Umberto Lenzi. *NO*

The Man from Gun Town 🐾½ 1936 McCoy comes to the rescue of a woman who has been framed by an evil gang for the murder of her brother. 58m/B VHS. Tim McCoy, Billie Seward, Rex Lease, Jack Clifford, Wheeler Oakman, Bob McKenzie; *D:* Ford Beebe. *NOS, DVT*

Man from Headquarters 🐾🐾 1928 Good silent mystery in which a U.S. agent takes on a gang of foreign operatives. ?m/B VHS. Cornelius Keefe, Edith Roberts. *SNC*

The Man from Hell 🐾 1934 Sheriff Russell goes undercover to expose the head of a gang of outlaws. Low-budget fare. 55m/B VHS. Reb Russell, Fred Kohler Jr., Ann Darcy, George "Gabby" Hayes, Jack Rockwell, Charles French, Charles "Slim" Whitaker, Yakima Canutt; *D:* Lewis D. Collins. *DVT, HEG, GPV*

Man from Hell's Edges 🐾½ 1932 An innocent cowpoke escapes from jail and brings the real baddy to justice. 63m/B VHS, Beta. Bob Steele, Nancy Drexel, Julian Rivero, Robert E. Homans, George "Gabby" Hayes; *D:* Robert North Bradbury. *NOS, DVT*

The Man from Laramie 🐾🐾🐾½ 1955 A ranch baron who is going blind worries about which of his two sons he will leave the ranch to. Into this tension-filled familial atmosphere rides Stewart, a cow-herder obsessed with hunting down the men who sold guns to the Indians that killed his brother. Needless to say, the tension increases. Tough, surprisingly brutal western, the best of the classic Stewart-Mann films. 104m/C VHS, Beta, Closed Caption. James Stewart, Arthur Kennedy, Donald Crisp, Alex Nicol, Cathy O'Donnell, Aline MacMahon, Wallace Ford, Jack Elam; *D:* Anthony Mann; *W:* Philip Yordan; *C:* Charles B(ryant) Lang. *COL*

The Man from Left Field 🐾½ 1993 Homeless man winds up coaching a little league baseball team, inspiring the kids, and turning his life around. Made for TV. 96m/C VHS, Closed Caption. Burt Reynolds, Reba McEntire; *D:* Burt Reynolds; *M:* Bobby Goldsboro. *CAF*

Man from Montana 🐾½ *Montana Justice* 1941 Brown is a sheriff who battles outlaws trying to stir up trouble between ranchers and homesteaders. 56m/B VHS. Johnny Mack Brown, Fuzzy Knight, William Gould, Kermit Maynard, Nell O'Day, Billy Lenhart, Kenneth Brown, Murdock McQuarrie, Ray Taylor. *GPV*

Man from Monterey ♂♂ 1933 South-of-the-border Western has U.S. Army captain Wayne trying to get Mexican landowners to register their property under Spanish land grants or lose them to public domain. Wayne's last series western for Warner Bros. **59m/B VHS, Closed Caption.** John Wayne, Ruth Hall, Luis Alberni, Francis Ford, Lafe McKee, Lillian Leighton, Charles "Slim" Whitaker; **D:** Mack V. Wright; **W:** Lesley Mason. *MGM*

The Man from Music Mountain ♂♂ 1938 Worthless mining stock is sold in a desert mining town, but Gene and Smiley clear that up, with a little singing as well. **54m/B VHS, Beta.** Gene Autry, Smiley Burnette, Carol Hughes, Polly Jenkins. *NOS, VDM, HHT*

Man from Nowhere ♂♂½ 1937 A henpecked man gets the break of his life when his domineering wife and mother-in-law believe he's dead. Based on the novel by Luigi Pirandello. In French with English subtitles. **98m/B VHS, Beta.** *FR* Pierre Blanchar, Ginette LeClerc; **D:** Pierre Chenal. *FCT, AUD*

The Man from Painted Post ♂ 1917 Fairbanks plays a Cattlemen's Association detective who comes to the range to stop the cattle rustlers as well as to find the man who murdered his sister. **?m/B VHS.** Douglas Fairbanks Sr., Eileen Percy, Frank Campeau, Monte Blue; **D:** Joseph Henabery. *GVV*

The Man from Snowy River ♂♂½ 1982 (PG) Stunning cinematography highlights this otherwise fairly ordinary adventure story set in 1880's Australia. A young man comes of age in the outback while taming a herd of wild horses. In a dual role, Douglas portrays battling brothers, one a rich landowner and the other a one-legged prospector. Based on the epic poem by A.B. "Banjo" Paterson and followed by "Return to Snowy River Part II." A big hit in Australia and not directed by "Mad Max's" Miller, but another Miller named George. **104m/C VHS, Beta, LV.** *AU* Kirk Douglas, Tom Burlinson, Sigrid Thornton, Terence Donovan, Tommy Dysart, Jack Thompson, Bruce Kerr; **D:** George Miller. *FOX, TVC, HMV*

Man from Texas ♂♂ 1939 Singing and gun-slinging Tex defends a kid accused of horse thieving until the kid turns bad and Tex must bring him in. **55m/B VHS, Beta.** Tex Ritter, Hal Price, Charles B. Wood, Vic Demourelle Sr.; **D:** Al(bert) Herman. *NOS, VDM*

Man from the Alamo ♂♂♂ 1953 A soldier sent from the Alamo during its last hours to get help is branded as a deserter, and struggles to clear his name. Well acted, this film will satisfy those with a taste for action. **79m/C VHS, Closed Caption.** Glenn Ford, Julie Adams, Chill Wills, Victor Jory, Hugh O'Brian; **D:** Budd Boetticher. *USH*

The Man from the Pru ♂♂½ 1989 Shocking 1931 murder case follows insurance agent William Wallace (Pryce) who was sentenced to hang for the murder of his wife, Julia. Wallace insisted he was called from home on a possible insurance sale and returned home to find his wife dead. His case made British legal history when the appeals court overturned the verdict. Made for TV. **90m/C VHS.** *GB* Jonathan Pryce, Anna Massey, Susannah York; **D:** Rob Rohrer. *TVC, AAE*

Man from Thunder River ♂♂ 1943 A group of cowboys uncover a plot to steal gold ore and wind up saving a young girl's life in the process. Standard western with lots of action. **55m/B VHS, Beta.** Wild Bill Elliott, George "Gabby" Hayes, Anne Jeffreys, Ian Keith, John James; **D:** John English. *DVT*

The Man from U.N.C.L.E. 1964 Vaughn and McCallum star as Napoleon Solo and Illya Kuryakin, two super-cool super-agents battling the evil forces of THRUSH. The series ran from 1964-1968. Two episodes per tape; additional episodes available. On this tape: "The Project Strigas Affair" has Solo and Illya against a Balkan intelligence agent. In "The Never Never Affair" an innocent translator is captured by a ruthless THRUSH operator who's after some valuable microfilm. **110m/B VHS, Beta.** Robert Vaughn, David McCallum, Leo G. Carroll, Leonard Nimoy, William Shatner, Barbara Feldon, Cesar Romero. *MGM, MOV*

Man from Utah ♂½ 1934 The Duke tangles with the crooked sponsor of some rodeo events who has killed several of the participants. Also available with "Blue Steel" on laserdisc. **55m/B VHS, Beta, LV.** John Wayne, George "Gabby" Hayes, Polly Ann Young, Yakima Canutt, Lafe McKee; **D:** Robert North Bradbury. *COL, NOS, MRV*

The Man I Love ♂♂♂ 1946 Slick drama about nightclub singer Lupino falling for no-good mobster Alda. Enjoyable and well-acted, although script doesn't make sense. Great selection of tunes. This film inspired Scorsese's "New York, New York." Based on the novel "Night Shift" by Maritta Wolff. ♪Body and Soul; Why Was I Born; Bill; The Man I Love; Liza; If I Could Be With You. **96m/B VHS, Closed Caption.** Ida Lupino, Robert Alda, Andrea King, Martha Vickers, Bruce (Herman Brix) Bennett, Alan Hale, Dolores Moran, John Ridgely, Don McGuire, Warren Douglas, Craig Stevens; **D:** Raoul Walsh, John Maxwell; **W:** Catherine Turney, Jo Pagano; **M:** Max Steiner. *MGM, FCT*

The Man in Grey ♂♂♂ 1945 In a story of romantic intrigue set in nineteenth-century England, a Marquis's wife is betrayed by her vile husband and the schoolmate she once befriended who has an affair with him. Stunning costumes and fine performances compensate for the overly extravagant production values in a work that helped bring stardom to Mason. **116m/B VHS, Beta.** *GB* James Mason, Margaret Lockwood, Stewart Granger, Phyllis Calvert; **D:** Leslie Arliss. *NO*

A Man in Love ♂♂♂ *Un Homme Amoureux* 1987 (R) An international romantic melodrama set during the Italian filming of a biography of suicidal author Cesar Pavese. The self-important lead actor and a beautiful supporting actress (Coyote and Scacchi) become immersed in the roles and fall madly in love, overlooking the fact that Coyote is married and Scacchi's engaged. The two make a steamy pair, to the detriment of friends, family, and the movie they're making. Kurys' first English-language film is visually appealing with a lush, romantic score, seamlessly weaving the story lines among vivid characters. **110m/C VHS, Beta, LV.** *FR* Peter Coyote, Greta Scacchi, Jamie Lee Curtis, Peter Riegert, Jean Pigozzi, John Berry, Claudia Cardinale, Vincent Lindon; **D:** Diane Kurys; **W:** Diane Kurys, Olivier Schatzky, Israel Horovitz; **M:** Georges Delerue. *COL*

The Man in the Attic ♂½ 1994 (R) Harris certainly leaves his "Doogie Howser" past behind as he takes a grownup turn in an erotic thriller based on a true case history from the early 20th century, gathered from the book "Sex and the Criminal Mind." Teenaged Edward (Harris) has a blazing affair with married, mature Krista (Archer), who does indeed hide her young lover in the family attic when her clueless husband (Cariou) returns home at night. But such consuming passion can hardly be kept a secret for long—and takes a decidedly deadly turn. Made for cable.*CW:* Sexuality and a murder scene. **97m/C VHS, Beta, Closed Caption.** Anne Archer, Neil Patrick Harris, Len Cariou, Alex Carter; **D:** Graeme Campbell; **W:** Duane Poole, Tom Swale; **M:** Lou Natale. *PAR*

The Man in the Glass Booth ♂♂♂ 1975 (PG) In this adaptation of a play written by actor Robert Shaw, a successful Jewish businessman is suspected of being a Nazi war criminal. Loosely based on the life of death camp commandant Otto Adolf Eichmann, the film depicts the arrest and subsequent trial of the former Nazi by the Israelis. The film's title is derived from the fact that Eichmann sat in a glass booth during his trial. Schell's performance is outstanding. **117m/C VHS.** Maximilian Schell, Lois Nettleton, Luther Adler, Lawrence Pressman, Henry Brown, Richard Rasof; **D:** Arthur Hiller; **W:** Edward Anhalt; **C:** Sam Leavitt. Nominations: Academy Awards '75: Best Actor (Schell).*NO*

The Man in the Gray Flannel Suit ♂♂½ 1956 A very long and serious adaptation of the Sloan Wilson novel about a Madison Avenue advertising exec trying to balance his life between work and family. The Hollywood treatment falls short of the adaptation potential of the original story. **152m/C VHS, Beta, LV, Closed Caption.** Gregory Peck, Fredric March, Jennifer Jones, Ann Harding, Arthur O'Connell, Henry Daniell, Lee J. Cobb, Marisa Pavan, Gene Lockhart, Keenan Wynn, Gigi Perreau, Joseph Sweeney, Kenneth Tobey, DeForest Kelley; **D:** Nunnally Johnson. *FOX*

The Man in the Iron Mask ♂♂♂ 1939 Swashbuckling tale about twin brothers separated at birth. One turns out to be King Louis XIV of France, and the other a carefree wanderer and friend of the Three Musketeers. Their eventual clash leads to action-packed adventure and royal revenge. Remake of the "The Iron Mask" (1929) with Douglas Fairbanks. Remade for television in 1977 with Richard Chamberlain. **110m/B VHS, Beta.** Louis Hayward, Alan Hale, Joan Bennett, Warren William, Joseph Schildkraut, Walter Kingsford, Marion Martin; **D:** James Whale. Nominations: Academy Awards '39: Best Original Score. *CCB, MED*

The Man in the Iron Mask ♂♂♂ 1977 A tyrannical French king kidnaps his twin brother and imprisons him on a remote island. Chamberlain, the king of the miniseries, is excellent in a dual role in this big production swashbuckler. Adapted from the Dumas classic. Made for television. **105m/C VHS, Beta, Closed Caption.** Richard Chamberlain, Patrick McGoohan, Louis Jourdan, Jenny Agutter, Ian Holm, Ralph Richardson; **D:** Mike Newell. *LIV, FUS, FOX*

The Man in the Mist 1983 Private investigators Tommy and Tuppence Beresford find themselves trying to solve a murder while on vacation in a provincial hotel. Made for British television and based upon the Agatha Christie story. **51m/C VHS, Beta.** *GB* Francesca Annis, James Warwick. *TPV*

The Man in the Moon ♂♂♂½ 1991 (PG-13) Beautifully rendered coming-of-age tale. On a farm outside a small Louisiana town in the 1950s, 14 year-old Dani wonders if she will ever be as pretty and popular as her 17 year-old sister Maureen. This becomes especially important as Dani is beginning to notice boys, particularly Court, the 17 year-old young man she meets when swimming. Although Dani and Maureen have always been especially close a rift develops between the sisters after Court meets Maureen. Intelligently written, excellent direction, lovely cinematography, and exceptional acting make this a particularly worthwhile and entertaining film. **100m/C VHS, Closed Caption.** Reese Witherspoon, Emily Warfield, Jason London, Tess Harper, Sam Waterston, Gail Strickland; **D:** Robert Mulligan. *MGM*

The Man in the Raincoat ♂♂ 1957 French film about a bumbling clarinet player who is erroneously tracked down as a murderer. Strenuous efforts to evoke laughter usually fail. Dubbed. **97m/B VHS, Beta, 8mm.** *FR* Fernandel, John McGiver, Bernard Blier; **D:** Julien Duvivier. *VYY*

Man in the Saddle ♂♂½ *The Outcast* 1951 Western star Scott gets roped in a romantic triangle out on the range, leading to some exciting gunplay. As usual, justice triumphs in this above average oater. Based on the novel by Ernest Haycox. **87m/C VHS.** Randolph Scott, Joan Leslie, Ellen Drew, Alexander Knox, Richard Rober, John Russell; **D:** Andre de Toth; **W:** Kenneth Gamet. *COL*

The Man in the Santa Claus Suit ♂♂ 1979 A costume shop owner has an effect on three people who rent Santa Claus costumes from him. Astaire plays seven different roles in this made for television film. Average holiday feel-good movie. **96m/C VHS, Beta.** Fred Astaire, Gary Burghoff, John Byner, Nanette Fabray, Bert Convy; **D:** Corey Allen. *MED*

Man in the Silk Hat 🎬🎬 1915 A collection of the nearly-forgotten French comic's early silent comedy shorts, made in France before his resettlement in America. 96m/B VHS, Beta. *FR* Max Linder; *D:* Maud Linder. *NO*

Man in the Silk Hat 🎬🎬🎬 1983 Gabriel-Maximilien Leuvielle, known in films as Max Linder, is now credited with developing the style of silent-movie slapstick comedy that Mack Sennett, Charlie Chaplin, and others became more famous for in their time. Here, Linder's daughter has done a fine job writing and directing a film full of historic footage of her father's work. 99m/B VHS, Beta. Mack Sennett, Buster Keaton, Charlie Chaplin, Max Linder. *XVC, MED*

The Man in the White Suit 🎬🎬🎬½ 1951 A humble laboratory assistant in a textile mill invents a white cloth that won't stain, tear, or wear out, and can't be dyed. The panicked garment industry sets out to destroy him and the fabric, resulting in some sublimely comic situations and a variety of inventive chases. Also available with "Lavender Hill Mob" on Laser Disc. 82m/B VHS, Beta. *GB* Alec Guinness, Joan Greenwood; *D:* Alexander MacKendrick. National Board of Review Awards '52: 10 Best Films of the Year; Nominations: Academy Awards '52: Best Screenplay. *REP, HMV*

Man in the Wilderness 🎬🎬½ 1971 (PG) Harris is part of an expedition traveling through the Northwest Territory. He's mauled by a grizzly and left for dead by leader Huston. While Harris fights for survival, he also plots revenge. Blood and violence is somewhat offset by good lead performances. 108m/C VHS. Richard Harris, John Huston, Henry Wilcoxon, Percy Herbert, Dennis Waterman, Prunella Ransome, Norman Rossington, James Doohan; *D:* Richard Sarafian; *W:* Jack DeWitt; *M:* Johnny Harris. *WAR*

A Man in Uniform 🎬🎬 *I Love a Man in Uniform* 1993 (R) A look at the making of a sociopath. Henry (McCamus) is a quiet bank employee who moonlights as an actor. Then he gets his big break in the role of a self-righteous cop in a TV series. Only the lines between his make-believe cop and the real world begin to blur and Henry's intensity turns to violence. Fine performances lead to an unsatisfying film conclusion. 99m/C VHS. *CA* Tom McCamus, Brigitte Bako, Kevin Tighe, David Hemblen, Alex Karzis, Graham McPherson; *D:* David Wellington; *W:* David Wellington. Genie Awards '93: Best Actor (McCamus), Best Supporting Actor (Tighe). *APX*

The Man Inside 🎬½ 1976 Undercover agent infiltrates a powerful underworld narcotics ring and finds his honesty tested when $2 million is at stake. 96m/C VHS, Beta. *CA* James Franciscus, Stefanie Powers, Jacques Godin; *D:* Gerald Mayer. *TWE*

The Man Inside 🎬🎬 1990 (PG) Lukewarm Cold War saga based on the true story of Gunther Wallraff, a West German journalist who risked all to expose the corruption behind a large European newspaper. 93m/C VHS, LV. *NL GE* Juergen Prochnow, Peter Coyote, Nathalie Baye, Dieter Laser, Monique Van De Ven, Sylvie Granotier; *D:* Bobby Roth; *W:* Bobby Roth. *COL*

Man Is Not a Bird 🎬🎬½ 1965 Follows the destructive love of a factory engineer and a hairdresser in a small Yugoslavian mining town. In Serbian with English subtitles. 80m/B VHS, Beta. *YU* Eva Ras, Milena Dravic, Janez Urhovec; *D:* Dusan Makavejev; *W:* Dusan Makavejev. *FCT*

A Man Like Eva 🎬🎬🎬 *Ein Mann wie Eva* 1983 A weird, morbid homage to and portrait of Rainer Werner Fassbinder after his inevitable death, detailing his work-obsessed self-destruction. Mattes, one of Fassbinder's favorite actresses, plays him in drag, in an eerie gender-crossing transformation. In German with English subtitles. 92m/C VHS, Beta. *GE* Eva Mattes, Elisabeth Kreuzer, Charles Regnier, Werner Stocker; *D:* Radu Gabrea. *FCT, APD, GLV*

Man Made Monster 🎬🎬½ 1941 Chaney stars as carnival performer "Dynamo" Dan McCormick, whose act has caused Dan to build up an immunity to electrical charges. Dan falls prey to the mad Dr. Rigas (Atwill) who seeks to create a race of electro-men who'll do his bidding. Experiments on the hapless Dan turn him into a glowing monster whose every touch can kill. Chaney's first role in the horror genre led to Universal's casting him in "The Wolf Man" and "The Ghost of Frankenstein." 61m/B VHS, Closed Caption. Lon Chaney Jr., Lionel Atwill, Anne Nagel, Frank Albertson, Samuel S. Hinds; *D:* George Waggner; *W:* Joseph West. *USH*

Man of a Thousand Faces 🎬🎬🎬½ 1957 A tasteful and touching portrayal of Lon Chaney, from his childhood with his deaf and mute parents to his success as a screen star. Recreates some of Chaney's most famous roles, including the Phantom of the Opera and Quasimodo in "Notre Dame." Cagney is magnificent as the long-suffering film star who was a genius with makeup and mime. 122m/B VHS, LV. James Cagney, Dorothy Malone, Jane Greer, Marjorie Rambeau, Jim Backus, Roger Smith, Robert Evans; *D:* Joseph Pevney; *W:* Ivan Goff; *C:* Russell Metty. Nominations: Academy Awards '57: Best Story & Screenplay. *USH*

Man of Action 🎬½ 1933 Texas Ranger McCoy is out to solve the mystery of what happened to money, recovered from a robbery, which has vanished once again. 56m/B VHS. Tim McCoy, Wheeler Oakman, Walter Brennan, Stanley Blystone, Charles French; *D:* George Melford. *GPV*

Man of Aran 🎬🎬🎬 1934 Celebrated account of a fisherman's struggle for survival on a barren island near the west coast of Ireland, featuring amateur actors. Three years in the making, it's the last word in man against nature cinema, and a visual marvel. A former explorer, Flaherty became an influential documentarian. Having first gained fame with "Nanook of the North," he compiled an opus of documentaries made for commercial release. 132m/B VHS. *D:* Robert Flaherty. *HMV, GVV*

Man of Destiny 🎬🎬½ 1973 Bonaparte (Keach) and a mysterious woman battle good-humoredly over a collection of love letters. From a Bernard Shaw story. Charming and well-acted. 60m/C VHS, Beta. Stacy Keach, Samantha Eggar. *NO*

Man of Evil 🎬🎬 *Fanny by Gaslight* 1948 The hard times of the illegitimate daughter of a member of the British Parliament in the early 1900s, told with an astonishing number of plot twists and a plodding melodramtic style. Based on the novel "Fanny by Gaslight." 108m/B VHS. *GB* Phyllis Calvert, James Mason, Wilfred Lawson, Stewart Granger, Margaretta Scott, Jean Kent, John Laurie, Stuart Lindsell, Nora Swinburne, Amy Veness, Ann Wilton, Helen Haye, Cathleen Nesbitt, Guy le Feuvre, John Turnbull, Peter Jones; *D:* Anthony Asquith. *FCT*

Man of Flowers 🎬🎬½ 1984 Because of his puritan upbringing, a reclusive art collector has trouble coping with his feelings of sexuality. He pays a woman to disrobe in front of him, but is never able to bring himself to see her naked. A moody piece with overtones of black humor, this work has limited audience appeal. 91m/C VHS, Beta, LV. *AU* Norman Kaye, Alyson Best, Chris Haywood, Sarah Walker, Julia Blake, Bob Ellis, Werner Herzog; *D:* Paul Cox; *W:* Bob Ellis, Paul Cox. Australian Film Institute '83: Best Actor (Kaye). *LIV, VES*

Man of Iron 🎬🎬🎬 *Człowiek z Zelaza* 1981 (PG) Director Wajda's follow-up to "Man of Marble" deals with a reporter (Odania) who is expected to tow the government line when writing about the Gdansk shipyard strike of 1980. He meets the harassed laborer son (Radziwilowicz) of worker-hero Birkut, about whom Odania is expected to conduct a smear campaign, and finds his loyalties tested. In Polish with English subtitles. 116m/C VHS. *PL* Jerzy Radziwilowicz, Marian Opania, Krystyna Janda; *D:* Andrzej Wajda; *W:* Aleksander Scibor-Rylski; *M:* Andrzej Korzynski. Cannes Film Festival '81: Best Film; Nominations: Academy Awards '81: Best Foreign Language Film. *MGM*

Man of La Mancha 🎬½ 1972 (PG) Arrested by the Inquisition and thrown into prison, Miguel de Cervantes relates the story of Don Quixote. Not nearly as good as the Broadway musical it is based on. ♫It's All the Same; The Impossible Dream; Barber's Song; Man of La Mancha; Dulcinea; I'm Only Thinking of Him; Little Bird, Little Bird; Life as It Really Is; The Dubbing. 129m/C VHS, Beta, LV. Peter O'Toole, Sophia Loren, James Coco, Harry Andrews, John Castle, Brian Blessed; *D:* Arthur Hiller. National Board of Review Awards '72: 10 Best Films of the Year, Best Actor (O'Toole); Nominations: Academy Awards '72: Original Song Score and/or Adaptation. *FOX, FCT*

Man of Legend 🎬🎬 1971 (PG) An adventure-romance filmed in Morocco; a WWI German soldier flees to the Foreign Legion and fights with nomadic rebels, ultimately falling in love with their chief's beautiful daughter. An unoriginal desert saga. 95m/C VHS, Beta. *IT SP* Peter Strauss, Tina Aumont, Pier Paola Capponi; *D:* Sergio Grieco. *NO*

Man of Marble 🎬🎬🎬 1976 A satire on life in post-WWII Poland. A young filmmaker sets out to tell the story of a bricklayer who, because of his exceptional skill, once gained popularity with other workers. He became a champion for worker rights, only to then find himself being persecuted by the government. The conclusion was censored by the Polish government. Highly acclaimed and followed by "Man of Iron" in 1981. In Polish with English subtitles. 160m/C VHS. *PL* Krystyna Janda, Jerzy Radziwilowicz, Tadeusz Lomnicki, Jacek Lomnicki, Krystyna Zachwatowicz; *D:* Andrzej Wajda; *W:* Aleksander Scibor-Rylski; *M:* Andrzej Korzynski. *NYF, FCT*

A Man of No Importance 🎬🎬🎬 1994 (R) Touching and entertaining saga of lovable Alfie Byrne (Finney), a 1960's Dublin bus conductor with a passion for the work of Oscar Wilde, who successfully represses his own homosexuality. He also moonlights as director of a community theatre, where he sets out to produce Wilde's controversial play "Salome" starring fetching new bus passenger Adele (Fitzgerald), who further confuses Alfie's take on his identity. Finney is both delightful and heartbreaking in this character study of an innocent soul whose life is tested by the social code of his day. Equally affecting and charming supporting performances round out this witty but sad tale.*CW:* Contains a nude scene, some violence, and complex adult themes. 98m/C VHS, LV, Closed Caption. *GB* Albert Finney, Brenda Fricker, Michael Gambon, Tara Fitzgerald, Rufus Sewell, Patrick Malahide, David Kelly; *D:* Suri Krishnamma; *W:* Barry Devlin; *M:* Julian Nott. *COL*

A Man of Passion 🎬🎬 199? (R) Quinn plays an aging artist living pleasurably on a Mediterranean isle. His summer guest is his uptight grandson, a classical pianist. Naturally, Gramps is about to teach the kid to loosen up, including appreciating one of his lovely artist's models. Another variation for Quinn on his "Zorba" personality but it works. 90m/C VHS. Anthony Quinn, Ramon Sheen, Maud Adams, Elizabeth Ashley, R.J. Williams, Ray Walston, Victoria Vera; *D:* J. Anthony Loma; *W:* J. Anthony Loma. *ATV*

Man of the Forest 🎬🎬 1933 A cowboy goes to the aid of a damsel in distress and he winds up being framed for murder for his efforts. Based on Zane Grey's novel. 59m/B VHS. Randolph Scott, Verna Hillie, Harry Carey Sr., Noah Beery Sr., Barton MacLane; *D:* Henry Hathaway. *NOS, DVT, MLB*

Man of the House 🎬🎬 1995 (PG) Kids' comedy about a boy's scheme to sabotage his mother's new love interest. Ben (Thomas) concocts a plan to join the YMCA Indian Guides to discourage daddy wannabe Jack (Chase), while mom (Fawcett) stands idly by tolerating her son's bratty behavior. Subplot involves a screwy gangster theme that deteriorates into a "Home Alone"-ish ending. Film attempts to play off of Chase's knack for physical comedy, but falls short. And what's with the mime? Wendt is amusing as the

Indian Guide leader. Will probably appeal more to younger crowds as Thomas' scheming teen upstages Chase's deadpan dad-to-be. **97m/C VHS, LV, Closed Caption.** Chevy Chase, Farrah Fawcett, Jonathan Taylor Thomas, George Wendt, David Shiner, Art LaFleur, Richard Portnow, Richard Foronjy, Spencer Vrooman, John Disanti, Chief Leonard George, Peter Appel, George Greif, Chris Miranda, Ron Canada, Zachary Browne, Nicholas Garrett; **D:** James Orr; **W:** James Orr, Jim Cruickshank; **C:** Jamie Anderson; **M:** Mark Mancina. DIS

Man of the West ♂♂½ 1958 Reformed bad guy Cooper is asked to deliver a tidy hunk of cash to another city to recruit a school marm. Ambushed en route by his former partners in crime (who are led by his wacko uncle) he's forced to revert to his wanton ways in order to survive and save innocent hostages. There's a raging debate among Cooper fans whether this late effort has been unduly overlooked or duly ignored. A number of things conspire to give it a bad rap: Cooper does little but look mournful until the very end; there's no hiding the fact that he's older than Cobb, who plays his uncle; and the acting is in general more befitting of a B-grade slice and dicer. You be the judge. **100m/C VHS, Beta, Closed Caption.** Gary Cooper, Julie London, Lee J. Cobb, Arthur O'Connell, Jack Lord, John Dehner, Royal Dano, Guy Wilkerson, Emory Parnell; **D:** Anthony Mann; **W:** Reginald Rose. MGM, FCT

Man of Violence ♂ The Sex Racketeers 1971 A vulgar, tasteless man spends the worthless hours of his wasted life lurking about the more wretched entrance-ways of his native land. **107m/C VHS, Beta.** Michael Latimer, Luan Peters; **D:** Pete Walker. NO

Man on a String ♂♂½ 1971 (PG) In order to bring down a Mob boss the feds first frame cop Peter King and send him to the pen. When he gets out, King uses his prison contacts to get in with the Mob and winds up pitting two rival gangs against each other in order to destroy them both. Made for television. **73m/C VHS.** Christopher George, Jack Warden, Keith Carradine, Joel Grey, William Schallert, Kitty Winn; **D:** Joseph Sargent. COL

Man on Fire ♂ 1987 (R) Told via flashback, a cynical ex-CIA man is hired as a bodyguard for the daughter of a wealthy Italian couple, who is soon thereafter kidnapped by terrorists. He goes to her rescue with all the subtlety of a wrecking ball. Decent cast goes down the tubes in this botched thriller. **92m/C VHS, Beta, LV.** FR Scott Glenn, Brooke Adams, Danny Aiello, Joe Pesci, Paul Shenar, Jonathan Pryce, Jade Malle; **D:** Elie Chouraqui. LIV, VES

The Man on the Box ♂♂½ 1925 Chaplin is a wealthy bachelor who takes a job as a gardener to be near his girl. He overhears a plot by the butler, who's an enemy agent, to steal the secret plans for a helicopter from his sweetie's father. In order to thwart the dastardedly scheme Chaplin dresses as a maid to infiltrate the household. **58m/B VHS.** Sydney Chaplin, David Butler, Alice Calhoun, Kathleen Calhoun, Helene Costello, Theodore Lorch; **D:** Charles F. Reisner. GPV, GVV

Man on the Eiffel Tower ♂♂♂ 1948 Laughton plays Inspector Maigret, the detective created by novelist Georges Simenon, in a highly suspenseful and cerebral mystery about a crazed killer who defies the police to discover his identity. This is the first film Meredith directed. **82m/C VHS, Beta.** Charles Laughton, Burgess Meredith, Franchot Tone, Patricia Roc; **D:** Burgess Meredith. NOS, MRV, GEM

Man on the Run ♂♂ 1949 A robbery takes place in the store where an Army deserter is trying to sell his gun, and he ends up taking the rap. It's up to a lovely lady lawyer to prove his innocence. Efficiently told "B" crime drama. **82m/B VHS, Beta.** GB Derek Farr, Joan Hopkins, Edward Chapman, Laurence Harvey, H. Marion Crawford, Alfie Bass, John Bailey, John Stuart, Edward Underdown, Leslie Perrins, Kenneth More, Martin Miller, Eleanor Summerfield; **D:** Lawrence Huntington; **W:** Lawrence Huntington. SNC

Man on the Run ♂½ 1974 (R) After an unwitting involvement with a small robbery, a teenager finds himself the object of a police manhunt for a murder suspect. **90m/C VHS, Beta.** Kyle Johnson, James B. Sikking, Terry Carter; **D:** Herbert L. Strock. PSM

Man or Gun ♂½ 1958 Standard western yarn involving a drifter who rides into a town operated by a powerful family and liberates the cowardly townsfolk. **79m/B VHS.** MacDonald Carey, Audrey Totter, James Craig, James Gleason, Warren Stevens, Harry Shannon; **D:** Albert C. Gannaway; **W:** Vance Skarstedt, James C. Cassity. MOV

The Man Outside ♂♂ 1968 (R) After a CIA agent is fired for allegedly assisting another agent in defecting to the East, he becomes involved in further intrigue. A Russian spy is looking to defect. In the process, the ex-agent is framed for murder. Straightforward espionage tale taken from Gene Stackleborg's novel "Double Agent." **98m/C VHS.** GB Van Heflin, Heidelinde Weis, Pinkas Braun, Peter Vaughan, Charles Gray, Ronnie Barker; **D:** Samuel Gallu. NO

Man Outside ♂ 1988 (PG-13) Logan is an ex-lawyer who takes to the Arkansas outback after his wife dies. Anthropologist/teacher Quinlan takes a shine to him. He seems like an okay guy, but bad guy Dillman has made it look like he's a child snatcher. Slick on the outside but empty inside independent effort. Look for former members of The Band in supporting roles. **109m/C VHS, LV.** Robert F. Logan, Kathleen Quinlan, Bradford Dillman, Rick Danko, Levon Helm; **D:** Mark Stouffer. NO

The Man They Could Not Hang ♂♂½ 1939 A good doctor tinkering with artificial hearts is caught by police while experimenting on a willing student. When the doctor is convicted and hanged for a murder, his assistant uses the heart to bring him back to life. No longer a nice guy, he vows revenge against the jurors that sentenced him. Karloff repeated the same story line in several films, and this one is representative of the type. **70m/B VHS, Beta.** Boris Karloff, Adrian Booth, Roger Pryor, Robert Wilcox; **D:** Nick Grinde. GKK

Man Trouble ♂♂ 1992 (PG-13) A divorcing opera singer (Barkin) seeks the help of a sleazy attack-dog trainer (Nicholson) when she becomes the victim of a stalker. Nicholson hits on her, first because that's one of his habits, and then because he is being paid to by a billionaire who wants her to steal the manuscript of a tell-all book about him written by Barkin's sister. Although both Nicholson and Barkin are excellent actors, they lack the electricity to make the romance credible, and the jokes are weak. Supporting cast, including D'Angelo, Stanton, and McKean, provide the funny parts in this otherwise dull film. **100m/C VHS, LV, Closed Caption.** Jack Nicholson, Ellen Barkin, Harry Dean Stanton, Beverly D'Angelo, Michael McKean, Saul Rubinek, Viveka Davis, David Clennon, John Kapelos, Paul Mazursky; **D:** Bob Rafelson; **W:** Adrien (Carole Eastman) Joyce; **C:** Stephen Burum; **M:** Georges Delerue. FXV

The Man Upstairs ♂♂½ 1993 Escaped con Moony Polaski (O'Neal) hides out in the home of crotchety spinster Victoria Brown (Hepburn). When she finds the crook in her attic, instead of turning him in, Victoria befriends the slob and soon the two are sharing dinner and secrets. Meanwhile, the manhunt for Moony is intensifying and, oh yes, Christmas is coming as well. Made for television cornpone barely saved by some professional performances. Executive producer Burt Reynolds was hoping for a part until scheduling made it impossible. **95m/C VHS, Closed Caption.** Katharine Hepburn, Ryan O'Neal, Henry Beckman, Helen Carroll, Brenda Forbes; **D:** George Schaefer; **W:** James Prideaux. CAF

The Man Who Broke 1,000 Chains ♂♂ 1987 A made-for-television movie about a man who is committed to a chain gang after WWII for a petty crime, and his efforts, after escaping, in making a new life for himself. An unimaginative plot is occasionally highlighted by a good scene or two. **113m/C VHS, Beta.** Val Kilmer, Charles Durning, Sonia Braga; **D:** Daniel Mann; **M:** Charles Bernstein. ORI, WAR

The Man Who Came to Dinner ♂♂♂½ 1941 Based on the Moss Hart-George S. Kaufman play, this comedy is about a bitter radio celebrity (Woolley) on a lecture tour (a character based on Alexander Woolcott). He breaks his hip and must stay in a quiet suburban home for the winter. While there, he occupies his time by barking orders, being obnoxious and generally just driving the other residents nuts. Woolley reprises his Broadway role in this film that succeeds at every turn, loaded with plenty of satiric jabs at the Algonquin Hotel Roundtable regulars. **112m/B VHS, Beta, LV.** Monty Woolley, Bette Davis, Ann Sheridan, Jimmy Durante, Reginald Gardiner, Richard Travis, Billie Burke, Grant Mitchell, Mary Wickes, George Barbier, Ruth Vivian, Elisabeth Fraser; **D:** William Keighley; **W:** Julius J. Epstein, Philip C. Epstein; **C:** Gaetano Antonio "Tony" Gaudio. MGM

The Man Who Captured Eichmann ♂♂½ 1996 In 1960 Israeli Mossad agents prepare to capture Adolf Eichmann (Duvall), who organized the transport of millions of Jews to the concentration camps, from his home in Argentina. Peter Malkin (Howard), the agent responsible for the kidnapping, holds Eichmann in a Buenos Aires safe house before smuggling him into Israel as Eichmann tries to ingratiate himself with Malkin, refusing to accept responsibility and constantly maintaining his innocence. Cable movie based on the book "Eichmann In My Hands" by Peter Z. Malkin and Harry Stein. **96m/C VHS, Closed Caption.** Robert Duvall, Arliss Howard, Jeffrey Tambor, Jack Laufer, Nicolas Surovy, Joel Brooks, Sam Robards, Michael Tucci; **D:** William A. Graham; **W:** Lionel Chetwynd; **C:** Robert Steadman; **M:** Laurence Rosenthal. WAR

The Man Who Could Work Miracles ♂♂♂½ 1937 A mild-mannered draper's assistant becomes suddenly endowed with supernatural powers to perform any feat he wishes. Great special effects (for an early film) and fine performances result in a classic piece of science fiction. **82m/B VHS, Beta, LV.** Ralph Richardson, Joan Gardner, Roland Young; **D:** Lothar Mendes.

The Man Who Cried ♂♂½ 1993 Abel Mason (Hinds) is an unhappily married man with a vindictive wife (Walsh) and a young son he's desperate to provide for. When an affair with a married woman ends in murder, Mason and his son travel in search of a new life. Desperate for a home, Mason enters into a bigamous marriage with a widow—only to find himself falling in love with her sister. Based on the novel by Catherine Cookson. Set in the years between England's depression and WW2. **156m/C VHS.** GB Ciaran Hinds, Amanda Root, Kate Buffery, Angela Walsh. VCO, FCT

The Man Who Envied Women ♂½ 1985 The non-narrative feminist story of a smug womanizer: the man "who knows almost too much about women." **125m/C VHS, Beta.** Bill Raymond, Larry Loonin, Trisha Brown; **D:** Yvonne Rainer; **W:** Yvonne Rainer. NO

The Man Who Fell to Earth ♂♂♂½ 1976 (R) Entertaining and technically adept cult classic about a man from another planet (Bowie, in a bit of typecasting) who ventures to earth in hopes of finding water to save his family and drought-stricken planet. Instead he becomes a successful inventor and businessman, along the way discovering the human vices of booze, sex, and television. Also available in a restored version at 138 minutes. Remade for television in 1987 and based on Walter Tevis' novel. **118m/C VHS,**

Beta, LV. *GB* David Bowie, Candy Clark, Rip Torn, Buck Henry, Bernie Casey; *D:* Nicolas Roeg. COL

The Man Who Guards the Greenhouse

1988 Tracy must come to terms with her attraction for Jeff as well as once again trying to write a meaningful novel. 150m/C VHS. Christopher Cazenove, Rebecca Dewey. ORI

Man Who Had Power Over Women

♂♂ 1970 (R) Disappointing sex farce about the exploits of a carnally insatiable (and married) talent executive (Taylor) who has an affair with every woman he meets and creates problems aplenty. Adapted from a novel by Gordon Williams. 89m/C VHS, Beta. *GB* Rod Taylor, James Booth, Carol White, Penelope Horner, Clive Francis; *D:* John Krish; *W:* Chris Bryant, Allan Scott.

The Man Who Haunted Himself

♂♂ 1970 While a man lies in critical condition on the operating table after a car accident, his alter-ego emerges and turns his ideal life into a nightmare until the man recovers and moves toward a fateful encounter. An expanded version of an episode of the television series "Alfred Hitchcock Presents," this was Moore's first movie after having starred in the TV series "The Saint," and it was Dearden's last film; he died in a car accident the following year. Appeals primarily to those fascinated by "Hitchcock" or "The Twilight Zone"—where mystery matters most. Filmed in London. 94m/C VHS, **Closed Caption**. *GB* Roger Moore, Hildegarde Neil, Olga Georges-Picot; *D:* Basil Dearden. REP, FCT

The Man Who Knew Too Much

♂♂♂ 1934 Hitchcock's first international success. A British family man on vacation in Switzerland is told of an assassination plot by a dying agent. His daughter is kidnapped to force his silence. In typical Hitchcock fashion, the innocent person becomes caught in a web of intrigue; the sticky situation culminates with surprising events during the famous shootout in the final scenes. Remade by Hitchcock in 1956. 75m/B VHS, Beta. *GB* Leslie Banks, Edna Best, Peter Lorre, Nova Pilbeam, Pierre Fresnay, Frank Vosper, Hugh Wakefield, Cicely Oates, D. A. Clarke-Smith, George Curzon, Henry Oscar, Wilfrid Hyde-White; *D:* Alfred Hitchcock; *W:* Emlyn Williams, Charles Bennett, A.H. Rawlinson, Edwin Greenwood, D. B. Wyndham-Lewis. SNC, MRV, NOS

The Man Who Knew Too Much

♂♂ 1956 (PG) Hitchcock's remake of his 1934 film, this time about an American doctor and his family vacationing in Marrakech. They become involved in a complicated international plot involving kidnapping and murder. While Doris tries to save the day by singing "Que Sera, Sera," Stewart tries to locate his abducted son. More lavish settings and forms of intrigue make this a less focused and, to some, inferior version. ♫Que Sera, Sera. 120m/C VHS, Beta, LV. *GB* James Stewart, Doris Day, Brenda de Banzie, Bernard Miles, Ralph Truman, Daniel Gelin, Alan Mowbray, Carolyn Jones, Hillary Brooke; *D:* Alfred Hitchcock; *W:* John Michael Hayes; *C:* Robert Burks. Academy Awards '56: Best Song ("Que Sera, Sera"). USH, HHE

The Man Who Laughs

♂♂♂½ 1927 Veidt's sensitive performance highlights this silent classic. He plays a young man whose features are surgically altered into a permanent smile because his family are political enemies of the current ruler. The man is befriended by the owner of a sideshow who first exhibits him as a freak but later finds Veidt gaining fame as a clown. A beautiful blind girl in the show loves Veidt for who he is and the two find happiness. 110m/B VHS. Conrad Veidt, Mary Philbin, Olga Baclanova, Josephine Crowell, George Siegmann, Brandon Hurst; *D:* Paul Leni. GPV

The Man Who Lived Again

♂♂½ The Man Who Changed His Mind; The Brainsnatchers; Dr. Maniac 1936 Boris strives to be a brain-switcher, and suspense builds around the question of whether or not he will change his mind. Shot in England with fine sets and a definite Anglo feel to

the proceedings, with Karloff doing one of his better mad scientist routines. 61m/B VHS, Beta, 8mm. *GB* Boris Karloff, Anna Lee, John Loder, Frank Cellier, Lyn Harding, Cecil Parker; *D:* Robert Stevenson. SNC, VYY, MLB

Man Who Loved Cat Dancing

♂♂ 1973 (PG) Reynolds is an outlaw on the run after avenging his wife's murder and robbing a safe with pals Hopkins and Warden, and Miles has recently escaped from her abusive husband. It's love on the run as Burt and Sarah are pursued by bounty hunters and their tragic pasts—coming close to making us care, but close doesn't mean as much in movies as it does in dancing. Based on Marilyn Durham's novel. 114m/C VHS, Beta. Burt Reynolds, Sarah Miles, Jack Warden, Lee J. Cobb, Jay Silverheels, Robert Donner; *D:* Richard Sarafian; *C:* Harry Stradling Jr.; *M:* John Williams. MGM, FCT

The Man Who Loved Women

♂♂♂ L'Homme Qui Aimait les Femmes 1977 An intelligent, sensitive bachelor writes his memoirs and recalls the many, many, many women he has loved. Truffaut couples sophistication and lightheartedness, the thrill of the chase and, when it leads to an accidental death, the wondering what-it's-all-about in the mourning after. In French with English subtitles. Remade in 1983. 119m/C VHS, Beta, LV, **Closed Caption**. *FR* Charles Denner, Brigitte Fossey, Leslie Caron, Nelly Borgeaud, Genevieve Fontanel, Nathalie Baye, Sabine Glaser; *D:* Francois Truffaut; *W:* Francois Truffaut, Suzanne Schiffman, Michel Fermaud; *C:* Nestor Almendros; *M:* Maurice Jaubert. National Board of Review Awards '77: 5 Best Foreign Films of the Year. MGM, BTV

The Man Who Loved Women

♂♂ 1983 (R) A remake of the 1977 French film, this is slower, tries to be funnier, and is less subtle than the original. Reynolds is a Los Angeles sculptor whose reputation as a playboy leads him to a psychoanalyst's couch, where a lot of talk slows the action—though Burt & Julie (the shrink) do share the couch. 110m/C VHS, Beta, **Closed Caption**. Burt Reynolds, Julie Andrews, Kim Basinger, Marilu Henner, Cynthia Sikes, Jennifer Edwards; *D:* Blake Edwards; *W:* Blake Edwards; *M:* Henry Mancini. COL

The Man Who Never Was

♂♂♂ 1955 Tense true story (with melodramatic embroidery) from WWII shows in step-by-step detail how Britain duped the Axis by letting them find an Allied corpse bearing phony invasion plans. Based on the book by the scheme's mastermind Ewen Montagu, played by Webb; Peter Sellers provides the voice of an offscreen Winston Churchill. 102m/C VHS, Beta. *GB* Clifton Webb, Gloria Grahame, Robert Flemyng, Josephine Griffin, Stephen Boyd, Andre Morell, Laurence Naismith, Geoffrey Keen, Michael Hordern; *D:* Ronald Neame; *C:* Oswald Morris. British Academy Awards '56: Best Screenplay. FOX, FCT, TVC

The Man Who Shot Liberty Valance

♂♂♂½ 1962 Tough cowboy Wayne and idealistic lawyer Stewart join forces against dreaded gunfighter Liberty Valance, played leatherly by Marvin. While Stewart rides to Senatorial success on his reputation as the man who shot the villain, he suffers moral crises about the act, but is toughened up by Wayne. Wayne's use of the word "pilgrim" became a standard for his impersonators. Strong character acting, great Western scenes, and value judgements to ponder over make this last of Ford's black and white westerns among his best. 123m/B VHS, Beta, LV, **Closed Caption**. James Stewart, John Wayne, Vera Miles, Lee Marvin, Edmond O'Brien, Andy Devine, Woody Strode, Ken Murray, Jeanette Nolan, John Qualen, Strother Martin, Lee Van Cleef, John Carradine, Carleton Young; *D:* John Ford; *W:* William Clothier. Nominations: Academy Awards '62: Best Costume Design (B & W). PAR, HMV

The Man Who Skied Down Everest

♂♂½ 1975 (G) Documentary about a Japanese athlete who undertakes a demanding downhill run, and the cost (human and financial) of getting there. 86m/C VHS. Academy Awards '75: Best Feature Documentary. NO

The Man Who Wagged His Tail

♂♂½ An Angel Passed Over Brooklyn; Un Angelo e Sceso a Brooklyn 1957 A mean slumlord is turned into a dog as the result of a curse cast upon him. In order to return to his human form, he must be loved by someone. Despite his attempts to be loved, the dog alienates his only friend and must try to redeem himself. Played for fun, this is a mildly amusing fantasy filmed in Spain and Brooklyn. Not released in the U. S. until 1961. 91m/B VHS. *IT SP* Peter Ustinov, Pablito Calvo, Aroldo Tieri, Silvia Marco; *D:* Ladislao Vajda. SNC, VYY

The Man Who Wasn't There

♂ 1983 (R) A member of the State department receives a formula from a dying spy that can render him invisible, see? He has to use the formula to protect himself from the police and other spies, becoming a comic "Invisible Man," see? Generally chaotic tale that's bad, but not so bad that it's worth seeing, though you might want to see what invisibility looks like in 3-D. 111m/C VHS, Beta. Steve Guttenberg, Jeffrey Tambor, Art Hindle, Lisa Langlois; *D:* Bruce Malmuth; *M:* Miles Goodman. PAR

The Man Who Would Be King

♂♂♂ 1975 (PG) A grand, old-fashioned adventure based on the classic story by Rudyard Kipling about two mercenary soldiers who travel from India to Kafiristan in order to conquer it and set themselves up as kings. Splendid characterizations by Connery and Caine, and Huston's royal directorial treatment provides it with adventure, majestic sweep, and well-developed characters. 129m/C VHS, Beta, LV, **Closed Caption**. Sean Connery, Michael Caine, Christopher Plummer, Saeed Jaffrey, Shakira Caine; *D:* John Huston; *W:* Gladys Hill, John Huston; *C:* Oswald Morris; *M:* Maurice Jarre. Nominations: Academy Awards '75: Best Adapted Screenplay, Best Art Direction/Set Decoration, Best Costume Design, Best Film Editing. FOX

The Man Who Would Not Die

♂♂ Target in the Sun 1975 (PG) During his investigation of several deaths, a man discovers that all of the deceased were actually the same man. It seems the deaths were part of a intricate scheme to cover up a million dollar heist. Two of the top three actors are killed early on; it's not very suspenseful. It's more like the mystery that would not die. From Charles Williams' novel "The Sailcloth Shroud." 83m/C VHS, Beta. Dorothy Malone, Keenan Wynn, Aldo Ray; *D:* Robert Arkless. WAR, OM

Man with a Cross

♂♂ 1943 Archaeologists of the cinema may want to unearth this early Rossellini, made by the future father of neo-realist cinema as a propaganda piece for the fascist war effort. A heroic Italian chaplain on the Russian front ministers to foe and friend alike, and even converts a few commies to Christ. Not as awful as it sounds—but never forget where this came from. 88m/B VHS. *IT D:* Roberto Rossellini. FST

Man with a Gun

♂♂½ 1995 (R) Hitman John Hardin (Madsen) is asked by mobster employer Jack Rushton (Busey) to kill his ex-girlfriend Rena (Tilly) and get a CD-ROM filled with info he doesn't want to get out. Rena now happens to be John's gal pal but isn't too upset since she figures they'll substitute Rena's goody two-shoes twin sister Kathy for the needed corpse. Too bad John starts to fall for the intended victim, leaving the plan to unravel. It's a connect-the-dots plot with a creditable cast. Based on the novel "The Shroud Society" by Hugh C. Rae. *CW:* Violence, language, and some sexuality. 100m/C VHS, **Closed Caption**. Michael Madsen, Jennifer Tilly, Gary Busey, Robert Loggia, Ian Tracey, Bill Cobbs; *D:* David Wyles; *W:* Laurie Finstad-Knizhik; *C:* Jan Kiesser; *M:* George Blondheim. HMK

A Man with a Maid

♂ 1973 A bizarre British exploitation pic mixes spookhouse cliches and sex, as a young man finds his new bachelor pad haunted by Jack the Ripper. Originally shot in 3-D and known variously as "The Groove Room" and "What the Swedish Butler Saw." It didn't

help. **83m/C VHS.** Sue Longhurst, Martin Long, Diana Dors; **D:** Vernon Becker. *VDM*

The Man with a Movie Camera 🐾🐾🐾½ 1929
A plotless, experimental view of Moscow through the creative eye of the cameraman Dziga Vertov, founder of the Kino Eye. The editing methods and camera techniques used in this silent film were very influential and still stand up to scrutiny today. **69m/B VHS, Beta.** *RU* **D:** Dziga Vertov. *IHF, MRV, DVT*

The Man with Bogart's Face 🐾🐾
Sam Marlowe, Private Eye 1980 (PG) Sacchi is no Bogart, but he does imitate him well. Bogart fans will enjoy this fond tribute to the late great actor, but the story uncertainly wavers between genuine detective story and detective spoof. **106m/C VHS, Beta.** Robert Sacchi, Misty Rowe, Sybil Danning, Franco Nero, Herbert Lom, Victor Buono, Olivia Hussey; **D:** Robert Day; **W:** Andrew J. Fenady; **M:** John Beal, George Duning. Golden Raspberry Awards '80: Worst Song ("The Man with Bogart's Face"). *FOX*

The Man with One Red Shoe 🐾🐾
1985 (PG) Hanks is a lovable clod of a violinist who ensnares himself in a web of intrigue when CIA agents, both good and evil, mistake him for a contact by his wearing one red shoe. Sporadically funny remake of the French "The Tall Blond Man with One Black Shoe." **92m/C VHS, Beta, Closed Caption.** Tom Hanks, Dabney Coleman, Lori Singer, Carrie Fisher, James Belushi, Charles Durning, Edward Herrmann, Tom Noonan, Gerrit Graham, David Lander, David Ogden Stiers; **D:** Stan Dragoti; **M:** Thomas Newman. *FXV, OM*

The Man with the Golden Arm 🐾🐾🐾 1955
A gripping film version of the Nelson Algren junkie melodrama, about an ex-addict who returns to town only to get mixed up with drugs again. Considered controversial in its depiction of addiction when released. Sinatra's performance as Frankie Machine is a stand-out. **119m/B VHS, Beta.** Frank Sinatra, Kim Novak, Eleanor Parker, Arnold Stang, Darren McGavin, Robert Strauss, George Mathews, John Conte, Doro Merande; **D:** Otto Preminger; **C:** Sam Leavitt; **M:** Elmer Bernstein. Nominations: Academy Awards '55: Best Actor (Sinatra), Best Art Direction/Set Decoration (B & W), Original Dramatic/Comedy Score. *WAR, MRV, NOS*

The Man with the Golden Gun 🐾🐾½ 1974 (PG)
Roger Moore is the debonair secret agent 007 in this ninth James Bond flick. Assigned to recover a small piece of equipment which can be utilized to harness the sun's energy, Bond engages the usual bevy of villains and beauties. **134m/C VHS, Beta, LV.** *GB* Roger Moore, Christopher Lee, Britt Ekland, Maud Adams, Herve Villechaize, Clifton James, Soon-Teck Oh, Richard Loo, Marc Lawrence, Bernard Lee, Lois Maxwell, Desmond Llewelyn; **D:** Guy Hamilton; **W:** Tom Mankiewicz; **C:** Ted Moore; **M:** John Barry. *MGM, FOX*

The Man with the Perfect Swing 🐾🐾½ 1995
Middle-aged ex-baseball player-turned-business entrepreneur Anthony "Babe" Lombardo (Black) is deep in debt and having trouble with the IRS even as he schemes to find success with his latest endeavor—designing specialty golf equipment. But Babe's latest design is a radically new golf swing (combining putting with his baseball expertise) featured in a how-to video with a budding PGA star. Naturally, given Babe's woeful record, the money just doesn't seem to be coming his way. **94m/C VHS.** James Black, Suzanne Savoy, Marco Perella, James Belcher, Richard Bradshaw; **D:** Michael Hovis; **W:** Michael Hovis; **C:** Jim Barham; **M:** Paul English. *MNC*

The Man with Two Brains 🐾🐾🐾
1983 (R) Did you hear the one about the brilliant neuro-surgeon who falls in love with a woman in his laboratory? He only has two problems: dealing with his covetous wife and finding a body for his cerebral lover. Plenty of laughs in this spoof of mad scientist movies that is redeemed from potential idiocy by the cast's titillating performances. Listen closely and you'll recognize the voice of Spacek as the brain-in-the-jar of Martin's dreams.

91m/C VHS, Beta, LV. Steve Martin, Kathleen Turner, David Warner, Sissy Spacek; **D:** Carl Reiner; **W:** Steve Martin, George Gipe, Carl Reiner; **C:** Michael Chapman; **M:** Joel Goldsmith. *WAR*

Man with Two Heads 🐾 1972 (R)
Doctor Jekyll gets in touch with his innermost feelings when his muffed experiments turn him into, gasp, Mr. Blood. Another forlorn addition to the Dr. Jekyll retread collection. **80m/C VHS.** **D:** Andy Milligan; **W:** Andy Milligan. *NO*

The Man with Two Lives 🐾🐾½ 1942
Well done horror thriller about a wealthy young man who's killed in a car accident, then brought back to life by a mad scientist. At precisely the moment his life is restored, a murderous gangster is executed and his soul enters the young man's body. **?m/C VHS.** Edward Norris, Addison Richards, Marlo Dwyer. *SNC*

The Man Without a Face 🐾🐾½ 1993
(PG-13) Gibson plays a badly scarred recluse in Maine who develops a mentor relationship with a lonely, fatherless boy. Chuck (Stahl) wants to go away to military school, but flunks the entrance exam, and enlists former teacher McLeod as a tutor. First foray for Gibson into the director's chair tends to be overly melodramatic. Adapted from a novel by Isabelle Holland. *CW:* Sex talk; adult themes and sexual situations. **115m/C VHS, Beta, LV, Closed Caption.** Mel Gibson, Nick Stahl, Margaret Whitton, Fay Masterson, Richard Masur, Gaby Hoffman, Geoffrey Lewis, Jack DeMave; **D:** Mel Gibson; **W:** Malcolm MacRury; **M:** James Horner. *WAR*

Man Without a Star 🐾🐾🐾 1955
A cowboy helps ranchers stop a ruthless cattle owner from taking over their land. The conflict between freedom in the wild west and the need for order and settlements is powerfully internalized in Douglas, whose fight for justice will tame the cowboy code he lives by. You'll shed a tear for the fading frontier. **89m/B VHS, Beta.** Kirk Douglas, Jeanne Crain, Claire Trevor, William Campbell; **D:** King Vidor. *USH*

Man, Woman & Child 🐾🐾 1983 (PG)
A close, upscale California family is shocked when a child from the husband's long-ago affair with a Frenchwoman appears at their door. Pure sentimentalism, as the family confronts this unexpected development. Two hankies—one each for fine performances by Sheen and Danner. Based on a sentimental novel by Erich Segal of "Love Story" fame, who co-wrote the script. **99m/C VHS, Beta.** Martin Sheen, Blythe Danner, Craig T. Nelson, David Hemmings; **D:** Dick Richards; **W:** Erich Segal; **M:** Georges Delerue. *PAR*

Manchurian Avenger 🐾 1984 (R)
Desperados have wrested control of a Colorado gold rush town from Joe Kim's family, but he'll put an end to that, chop chop. **87m/C VHS, Beta.** Bobby Kim, Bill Wallace; **D:** Ed Warnick. *NO*

The Manchurian Candidate 🐾🐾🐾🐾
1962 Political thriller about an American Korean War vet who suspects that he and his platoon may have been brainwashed during the war, with his highly decorated, heroic friend programmed by commies to be an operational assassin. Loaded with shocks, conspiracy, inventive visual imagery, and bitter political satire of naivete and machinations of the left and right. Excellent performances by an all-star cast, with Lansbury and Gregory particularly frightening. Based on the Richard Condon novel. Featuring a special interview with Sinatra and Frankenheimer in which Sinatra is deified. **126m/B VHS, Beta, LV, Closed Caption.** Frank Sinatra, Laurence Harvey, Angela Lansbury, Janet Leigh, James Gregory, Leslie Parrish, John McGiver, Henry Silva, Khigh Deigh; **D:** John Frankenheimer; **W:** George Axelrod, John Frankenheimer; **C:** Lionel Lindon; **M:** David Amram. Golden Globe Awards '63: Best Supporting Actress (Lansbury); National Board of Review Awards '62: Best Supporting Actress (Lansbury); Nominations: Academy Awards '62: Best Film Editing, Best Supporting Actress (Lansbury). *MGM*

The Mandarin Mystery 🐾½ 1937
In the process of trying to retrieve a stolen Mandarin stamp, detective Ellery Queen uncovers a counterfeiting ring. Some fine performances, but a muddled script creates a mystery as to whether or not the action is played for laughs. **65m/B VHS, Beta.** Eddie Quillan, Charlotte Henry, Rita La Roy, Wade Boteler, Franklin Pangborn, George Irving, Kay Hughes, William Newell; **D:** Ralph Staub. *NOS, SNC*

Mandela 🐾🐾🐾 1987
A gripping, powerful drama about human rights and dignity, tracing the real-life trials of Nelson and Winnie Mandela. The story focuses on the couple's early opposition to South African apartheid, as well as the events leading up to Nelson's life-imprisonment sentencing in 1964. Excellent, restrained performances from Glover and Woodard. Made for cable television. **135m/C VHS, Beta.** Danny Glover, Alfre Woodard, John Matshikiza, Warren Clarke, Allan Corduner, Julian Glover; **D:** Philip Saville. *KUI, FCT*

Mandela and de Klerk 🐾🐾½ 1997 (PG)
Cable docudrama about the two men who changed South Africa. White Afrikaaner president F.W. de Klerk (Caine) declared an end to apartheid in 1992 and two years later was succeeded as the country's president by Nelson Mandela (Poitier), a black activist imprisoned on treason charges for 27 years before his release. Both men shared the Nobel Peace Prize for their efforts to unite South Africa. **114m/C VHS, Closed Caption.** Sidney Poitier, Michael Caine, Tina Lifford, Ian Roberts, Gerry Maritz, Jerry Mofokeng; **D:** Joseph Sargent; **W:** Richard Wesley; **C:** Tobias Schliessler; **M:** Cedric Gradus-Samson. *EVE*

Mandinga 🐾 1977
A plantation owner develops an obsession for one of his female slaves. Made to cash in on the already exploitive "Mandingo"; two wrongs don't make a right. **100m/C VHS, Beta.** Anthony Gismond; **D:** Mario Pinzauti. *PAR*

Mandingo 🐾🐾 1975 (R)
Overheated southern-fried tale of slavery in the Deep South, circa 1840, dealing with the tangled loves and hates of a family and their slaves. Heavyweight boxer Norton made his screen debut in the title role as the slave who makes his master money with his boxing prowess. King is the wastrel son who makes Norton's wife, another slave, his mistress. Followed by 1975's "Drum." Based on the novel by Kyle Onstott. **127m/C VHS, Beta, LV.** James Mason, Susan George, Perry King, Richard Ward, Ken Norton, Ben Masters, Brenda Sykes, Paul Benedict, Ji Tu Cumbuka; **D:** Richard Fleischer; **M:** Maurice Jarre. *PAR*

Mandroid 🐾½ 1993 (R)
Two scientists design a high-tech robot, Mandroid, to handle a powerful new element they've discovered. Dr. Zimmer and daughter Zanna want to use their creation to help mankind while mad scientist Dr. Drago wants the power Mandroid can give him. When a laboratory accident leaves Drago horribly disfigured it also gives him the chance to steal Mandroid and put his evil plan into action. Filmed on location in Romania. *CW:* Violence and sex scene. **81m/C VHS, Beta, Closed Caption.** Brian Cousins, Jane Caldwell, Michael DellaFemina, Curt Lowens, Patrick Ersgard, Robert Symonds; **D:** Joakim Ersgard; **W:** Jackson Barr, Earl Kenton. *PAR*

Mandy 🐾🐾🐾
Crash of Silence 1953 Poignant drama of a deaf child and the family who must come to terms with her deafness. Well-developed plot and well performed; an intelligent treatment in all. **93m/B VHS, Beta.** *GB* Phyllis Calvert, Jack Hawkins, Mandy Miller; **D:** Alexander MacKendrick. *LCA*

Manfish 🐾½ 1956
Two men venture out in a boat, the Manfish, to hunt for sunken treasure in the Caribbean. Only one survives the trip, as his greed destroys the other. The scenes off the Jamaican coast are lovely, but the story fails to take hold. Though there is a star aboard in Chaney, you'll look astern and bow out with a sinking feeling. Derived from two Edgar Allan Poe stories, "The Gold Bug" and "The Tell-Tale Heart." **76m/C**

VHS. John Bromfield, Lon Chaney Jr., Victor Jory, Barbara Nichols; **D:** W. Lee Wilder. *NOS, SNC*

The Mangler &⁄ 1994 (R) Laundry machine munches workers in a small-town Maine industrial plant. Bossman Englund's only concern (besides huge workman's comp premiums) is keeping the machine well-fed. Weak attempt at horror by veteran Tobe "If it's worth doing, it's worth overdoing" Hooper ("The Texas Chainsaw Massacre") that tries to capitalize on the popularity of story originator Stephen King. Offers little in plot or scare, but fans of the gore genre will enjoy the overuse of chunky-style blood and guts spewed from the monstrous steam ironer and folder that is apparently possesed by the devil. About 45 minutes too long for anybody to suspend their disbelief.**CW:** Language; gory horror violence, mostly mangling. 106m/C VHS, LV, Closed Caption. Robert Englund, Ted Levine, Daniel Matmor, Vanessa Pike, Demetre Phillips, Lisa Morris, Ashley Hayden, Vera Blacker; **D:** Tobe Hooper; **W:** Tobe Hooper, Peter Welbeck, Stephen Brooks; **C:** Amnon Salomon; **M:** Barrington Pheloung. *NLC, TTC, IME*

The Mango Tree &&½ 1977 A young man comes of age in a small Australian town during the 1920s. Everything is well done, if not dramatic or fascinating. 93m/C VHS, Beta. *AU* Geraldine Fitzgerald, Robert Helpmann, Diane Craig, Gerald Kennedy, Christopher Pate; **D:** Kevin Dobson. *NO*

Manhandled &&½ 1924 Department store clerk Swanson is the hit of an artist's party with her impersonations and is asked by Morgan to impersonate a Russian countess to lend some class to his store. She winds up with lots of suitors. 67m/B VHS. Gloria Swanson, Frank Morgan, Tom Moore, Lilyan Tashman, Ian Keith, Arthur Houseman; **D:** Allan Dwan. *GPV*

The Manhandlers &⁄ 1973 (R) After the uncle of a young woman is killed by the mob, she goes after them for revenge. For your entertainment pleasure, best stick with the soup commercial of the same name. 87m/C VHS, Beta. Cara Burgess, Judy Brown, Vince Cannon, Rosalind Miles; **D:** Lee Madden. *TWE*

Manhattan &&&& 1979 (R) Successful TV writer Allen yearns to be a serious writer. He struggles through a series of ill-fated romances, including one with high school senior Hemingway, about 25 years younger, and another with Keaton, who's also having an on-again, off-again affair with Murphy, Allen's best friend. Scathingly serious and comic view of modern relationships in urban America and of the modern intellectual neuroses. Shot in black-and-white to capture the mood of Manhattan and mated with an excellent Gershwin soundtrack, the video version preserves the widescreen effect adding yet another impressive element to the overall production. 96m/B VHS, Beta, LV. Woody Allen, Diane Keaton, Meryl Streep, Mariel Hemingway, Michael Murphy, Wallace Shawn, Anne Byrne, Tisa Farrow, Mark Linn-Baker, David Rasche, Karen Allen; **D:** Woody Allen; **W:** Woody Allen, Marshall Brickman; **C:** Gordon Willis; **M:** George Gershwin. British Academy Awards '79: Best Film, Best Screenplay; Cesar Awards '80: Best Foreign Film; Los Angeles Film Critics Association Awards '79: Best Supporting Actress (Streep); National Board of Review Awards '79: 10 Best Films of the Year; New York Film Critics Awards '79: Best Director (Allen), Best Supporting Actress (Streep); National Society of Film Critics Awards '79: Best Director (Allen), Best Supporting Actress (Streep); Nominations: Academy Awards '79: Best Original Screenplay, Best Supporting Actress (Hemingway). *MGM*

Manhattan Baby &⁄ 1982 Unscary horror film about an archaeologist who digs up a relic that draws evil into the world and infects an American girl with powers that lead to many deaths. Advice to you that might have saved the archaeologist: don't dig this. 90m/C VHS, Beta. *IT* Christopher Connelly, Martha Taylor; **D:** Lucio Fulci. *LIV*

Manhattan Melodrama &&&½ 1934 Powell and Gable are best friends from childhood, growing up together in an orphanage. Their adult lives take different paths, however, as Powell becomes a respected prosecuting attorney while Gable becomes a notorious gambler/racketeer. Lovely Loy is Gable's girl who comes between the two. Eventually, Powell must prosecute his lifelong friend for murder in order to win the governorship. One of Gable's toughest roles; Powell's character, however, is a bit unbelievable as his ethics seem to extend beyond love and friendship. This is the first film to team Powell and Loy, who would go on to make 13 more films together, including the "Thin Man" series. 93m/B VHS, Beta, LV. Clark Gable, William Powell, Myrna Loy, Leo Carrillo, Nat Pendleton, George Sidney, Isabel Jewell, Muriel Evans, Claudelle Kaye, Frank Conroy, Jimmy Butler, Mickey Rooney, Edward Van Sloan; **D:** Woodbridge S. Van Dyke; **C:** James Wong Howe. Academy Awards '34: Best Story. *MGM, CCB*

Manhattan Merenque! &&½ *Rice, Beans and Ketchup* 1995 (R) Young mambo dancer Miguel (Perez) has been unable to get a visa to come to the U.S. from the Dominican Republic so he stows away and eventually makes it to New York with new friend Carmello (Leonardi), who's searching for an old girlfriend and their son. While Miguel tries for dance work on Broadway, he makes a friend in dance instructor Susan (Reed) and locates long-lost girlfriend Rosita (Cavazos). Too bad Carmello's luck isn't as good. Sweetly cornball and romantic.**CW:** Language and brief violence. 100m/C VHS. George Perez, Lumi Cavazos, Marco Leonardi, Alyson Reed; **D:** Joseph B. Vasquez; **W:** Joseph B. Vasquez, Rue Kent Wildman; **C:** David Castillo; **M:** Lalo Schifrin. *BMG*

Manhattan Merry-Go-Round &&
1937 One of the movies where a corrupt boss—in this case a record producer—threatens a bunch of good people as a pretense for a plot when the movie simply serves as a showcase for stars. Features many singing stars of the thirties ("where have you gone Cab Calloway?") plus Joltin' Joe, who ended up having a hit-streak in another genre. ♫Mama I Wanna Make Rhythm; Manhattan Merry-Go-Round; Heaven?; I Owe You; It's Round Up Time in Reno. 89m/B VHS, Beta. Cab Calloway, Louis Prima, Ted Lewis, Ann Dvorak, Phil Regan, Kay Thompson, Gene Autry, Joe DiMaggio; **D:** Charles Riesner. Nominations: Academy Awards '37: Best Interior Decoration. *NOS, VCN, HHT*

Manhattan Murder Mystery &&&
1993 (PG) Keaton and Allen team up again as two New Yorkers who get involved in a mystery when their neighbor dies under strange circumstances. Light, entertaining comedy steers clear of some of Allen's heavier themes and should keep audiences laughing till the end. Allen, writing with Brickman for the first time since "Annie Hall" and "Manhattan," makes viewers fall in love with the magic of NYC all over again. 105m/C VHS, LV, 8mm, Closed Caption. Woody Allen, Diane Keaton, Anjelica Huston, Alan Alda, Jerry Adler, Ron Rifkin, Joy Behar, Lynn Cohen, Melanie Norris; **D:** Woody Allen; **W:** Woody Allen, Marshall Brickman; **C:** Carlo DiPalma. Nominations: Golden Globe Awards '94: Best Actress—Musical/Comedy (Keaton).*COL*

The Manhattan Project && *Manhattan Project: The Deadly Game* 1986 (PG-13) An exceptionally bright teenager decides to build a nuclear bomb for his project at the New York City science fair. He's out to prove how dangerously easy it is to build big bombs. When he steals plutonium from a local government installation, the feds attempt to nab the precocious youngster. Light moral overtones abound. Director Brickman once similarly titled "Manhattan." 112m/C VHS, Beta, LV. John Lithgow, Christopher Collet, Cynthia Nixon, Jill Eikenberry, John Mahoney, Sully Boyer, Richard Council, Robert Schenkkan, Paul Austin; **D:** Marshall Brickman; **W:** Marshall Brickman, Thomas Baum; **C:** Billy Williams. *REP*

Manhunt && *The Italian Connection; La Mala Ordina* 1973 (R) A man marked for execution by the mob launches his own assault on the organization's headquarters. Action and Italian food, but not much else. Dubbed. 93m/C VHS, Beta. *IT* Henry Silva, Mario Adorf, Woody Strode, Luciana Paluzzi; **D:** Fernando Di Leo. *MED, AIP*

The Manhunt && 1986 A framed cowhand escapes from prison to prove his innocence. Made-for-TV movie. 89m/C VHS, Beta. Ernest Borgnine, Bo Svenson, John Ethan Wayne; **D:** Larry Ludman. *MED*

Manhunt &⁄½ 1995 (R) Fugitive Jim Trudell (Wilson) rescues a woman from a gang of thugs and winds up in a net of police corruption. Now he needs to survive long enough to figure out what's going on. ?m/C VHS, LV. Don "The Dragon" Wilson, Jillian McWhirter. *NHO*

Manhunt for Claude Dallas && 1986 Mountain man uses game wardens for firing practice, ticks off local sheriff Torn, is tossed behind bars, checks out ahead of schedule and becomes a legend in his own time. Mediocre made-for-TV macho man melodrama. From the novel "Outlaw" by Jeff Long. 93m/C VHS, Beta. Matt Salinger, Rip Torn, Claude Akins, Pat Hingle, Lois Nettleton, Beau Starr, Frederick Coffin; **D:** Jerry London; **W:** John Gay; **M:** Stephen Dorff. *PSM*

Manhunt in the African Jungle 1954 An American undercover agent battles Nazi forces in Africa. A serial in fifteen episodes. 240m/B VHS, LV. Rod Cameron, Joan Marsh, Duncan Renaldo. *VCN, REP, MLB*

Manhunt of Mystery Island *Captain Mephisto and the Transformation Machine* 1945 Serial about the super-powered Captain Mephisto. 100m/C VHS, Beta, LV. Linda Stirling, Roy Barcroft, Richard Bailey, Kenne Duncan; **D:** Spencer Gordon Bennet. *MED, MLB*

Manhunter &⁄ 1974 A made-for-television escapade about a WWI Marine who returns home from China in 1933 to track down a bunch of gangsters headed by his sister. 78m/C VHS, Beta, LV, Closed Caption. Ken Howard, Stefanie Powers, Gary Lockwood, Tim O'Connor, L.Q. Jones; **D:** Walter Grauman. *WAR, TWE*

Manhunter &&½ 1983 A mercenary sets out to disengage organized crime from high-level politics. Produced by Owensby. 92m/C VHS, Beta. Earl Owensby, Johnny Popwell, Doug Hale, Elizabeth Upton; **D:** Earl Owensby. *MED*

Manhunter &&& *Red Dragon* 1986 (R) FBI forensic specialist—who retired after a harrowing pursuit of a serial killer—is called back to duty to find a psychotic family killer. His technique: to match the thought processes of serial killers and thus anticipate their moves. Intense thriller, based on the Thomas Harris novel "Red Dragon." Harris also wrote "The Silence of the Lambs," whose most notorious character Hannibal ("The Cannibal") Lecter, appears in this movie as well. Director Mann applies the slick techniques he introduced in the popular television series "Miami Vice," creating a quiet, moody intensity broken by sudden onslaughts of violence. Available in widescreen on laserdisc. 100m/C VHS, Beta, LV, Closed Caption. William L. Petersen, Kim Greist, Joan Allen, Brian Cox, Dennis Farina, Stephen Lang, Tom Noonan; **D:** Michael Mann; **W:** Michael Mann. *WAR*

Mania &&½ *The Flesh and the Fiends; Fiendish Ghouls; Psycho Killers* 1960 Fine adaptation of the Burke and Hare grave robbing legend. Cushing is the doctor who needs corpses and Pleasence and Rose provide them by any means. Highly atmospheric representation of dismal, 19th century Edinburgh. Very graphic for its time. 87m/B VHS. *GB* Peter Cushing, June Laverick, Donald Pleasence, George Rose, Dermot Walsh, Renee Houston, Billie Whitelaw, John Cairney, Michael Balfour; **D:** John Gilling; **M:** Stanley Black. *SNC, DVT, MLB*

Mania 🗡🗡 198? Four suspense/murder stories set in a sleazy urban milieu. 120m/C Beta. Deborah Grover, Stephen Hunter, Lenore Zann, Wayne Robson. *NO*

Maniac woof! 1934 A scientist has designs on raising the dead and searches for victims on which to experiment. Bizarre "adults only" exploitation feature was considered very risque for its time, and includes eaten eyeballs, a cat fight with syringes and a rapist who thinks he's an orangutan. A must for genre aficionados. 67m/B VHS, **Beta**. Bill Woods, Horace Carpenter, Ted Edwards, Thea Ramsey, Jennie Dark, Marcel Andre, Celia McGann; *D:* Dwain Esper. *VDM, SNC, MRV*

Maniac 🗡🗡 1963 An American artist living in France becomes involved with the daughter of a cafe owner, not suspecting that murder will follow. Seems that the old man is locked up in an insane asylum for torching the daughter's rapist several years earlier. 86m/B VHS, Beta. *GB* Kerwin Mathews, Nadia Gray, Donald Houston, Liliane Brousse; *D:* Michael Carreras; *W:* Jimmy Sangster; *M:* Stanley Black. *COL, MLB*

Maniac 🗡 *Ransom; Assault on Paradise; The Town That Cried Terror* 1977 (PG) A New York cop hunts down an arrow-shooting and obviously crazed Vietnam veteran who endeavors to hold an entire Arizona town for ransom. Which is entirely appropriate, since the cast is in it only for the money. 87m/C VHS, Beta. Oliver Reed, Deborah Raffin, Stuart Whitman, Jim Mitchum, Edward Brett, John Ireland, Richard Compton, Paul Koslo; *D:* Richard Compton. *LIV, VES*

Maniac woof! 1980 A psycho murderer slaughters and scalps his victims, adding the "trophies" to his collection. Carries a self-imposed equivalent "X" rating due to its highly graphic gore quotient. For extremely strong stomachs only. 91m/C VHS, Beta. Joe Spinell, Caroline Munro, Gail Lawrence, Kelly Piper, Tom Savini; *D:* William Lustig; *W:* Joe Spinell, C.A. Rosenberg. *MED*

Maniac Cop 🗡 1988 (R) In New York city, a cop goes beyond the realm of sanity and turns vigilante. Low-budget slasher/thriller that too often sags. 92m/C VHS, Beta. Tom Atkins, Bruce Campbell, Laurene Landon, Richard Roundtree, William Smith, Robert Z'Dar, Sheree North; *D:* William Lustig; *W:* Larry Cohen. *TWE, HHE*

Maniac Cop 2 🗡 1990 (R) Everyone thought he was dead but you can't keep a bad guy down so this grossly disfigured policeman forms a one-man vigilante squad, seeking revenge (why never matters—just the body count). Blood and guts fly as any plot shortcomings are cleverly disguised by an array of violent video deaths. Sequel to "Maniac Cop." 90m/C VHS, LV, **Closed Caption**. Robert Davi, Claudia Christian, Michael Lerner, Bruce Campbell, Laurene Landon, Robert Z'Dar, Clarence Williams III, Leo Rossi; *D:* William Lustig; *W:* Larry Cohen. *LIV*

Maniac Cop 3: Badge of Silence 🗡 1993 (R) The grossly disfigured policeman returns yet again to exact gory vengeance as the good guys try to get rid of him once and for all. 85m/C VHS, **Closed Caption**. Robert Z'Dar, Robert Davi, Gretchen Becker, Paul Gleason, Doug Savant, Caitlin Dulany; *D:* William Lustig, Joel Soisson; *W:* Larry Cohen; *M:* Jerry Goldsmith. *ACA*

Maniac Warriors 🗡 199? A nuclear apocalypse has caused some strange changes in the population—and not for the better. Blood-crazed mutants attack the heavily armed inhabitants of New State Idaho and there's lots of mayhem in store. 91m/C VHS. Tom Schioler, John Wood, Melanie Kilgour. *AIP, MOV*

The Manions of America 🗡🗡½ 1981 The long and sometimes interesting rags-to-riches tale of Rory O'Manion, a feisty Irish patriot who leaves his native land during the potato famine of 1845 to settle in America. Originally a television miniseries. 290m/C VHS, **Beta**. Pierce Brosnan, Kate Mulgrew, Linda Purl, David Soul, Kathleen Beller, Simon MacCorkindale; *D:* Joseph Sargent, Charles S. Dubin. *WMI, PAR, PSM*

Manipulator 🗡 1971 (R) A deranged ex-movie makeup man (Rooney, playing to type) kidnaps a young actress and holds her prisoner in a deserted Hollywood sound stage. 91m/C VHS, Beta. Mickey Rooney, Luana Anders, Keenan Wynn; *D:* Yabo Yablonsky. *LIV, VES*

The Manitou 🗡🗡 1978 (PG) A San Francisco woman suffers from a rapidly growing neck tumor which eventually grows into a 400-year-old Indian witch doctor. (I hate when that happens.) Redeemed only by good special effects, especially those that kept Curtis, Strasberg, and Meredith from laughing. 104m/C VHS, Beta, LV. Susan Strasberg, Tony Curtis, Stella Stevens, Ann Sothern, Burgess Meredith, Michael Ansara; *D:* William Girdler; *M:* Lalo Schifrin. *COL, NLC*

Mankillers 🗡 1987 A group of tough female convicts are enlisted to hunt down and rub out a psycho drug dealer, all the while displaying their feminine charms. 90m/C VHS, Beta. Edd Byrnes, Gail Fisher, Edy Williams, Lynda Aldon, William Zipp, Christopher Lunde, Susanne Tegman, Marilyn Stafford, Paul Bruno, Byron Clark; *D:* David A. Prior. *COL*

Mannequin 🗡🗡½ 1937 Tracy and Crawford star in this romantic story of a poor girl who finds temporary happiness with a wealthy man after ditching her con-artist husband. Somewhat predictable, the movie reads like a "People" magazine story on The Donald and Ivana. Tracy and Crawford keep the story afloat (in their only film together), with an able assist from Curtis. 95m/B **VHS**. Joan Crawford, Spencer Tracy, Alan Curtis, Ralph Morgan, Leo Gorcey, Elisabeth Risdon, Paul Fix; *D:* Frank Borzage; *W:* Lawrence Hazard. Nominations: Academy Awards '38: Best Song ("Always and Always"). *MGM, MED*

Mannequin 🗡🗡 1987 (PG) A young artist creates a store window display using various mannequins, one of which contains the spirit of an ancient Egyptian woman. She comes to life when he is around, and naturally none of his co-workers believe her. Very light comedy, featuring two pretty stars and music by Jefferson Starship. 90m/C VHS, Beta, LV, **Closed Caption**. Andrew McCarthy, Kim Cattrall, Estelle Getty, James Spader, Meshach Taylor, Carole Davis, G.W. Bailey; *D:* Michael Gottlieb; *W:* Ed Rugoff. Nominations: Academy Awards '87: Best Song ("Nothing's Gonna Stop Us Now"). *CCB, MED, VTR*

Mannequin 2: On the Move woof! 1991 (PG) Less of a sequel, more of a lame rehash proving that the first "Mannequin" could have been even dumber. At this rate part three will be off the scale. Now it's a lovesick Teutonic princess frozen for 1,000 years who revives in a department store. Taylor reprises his grotesque gay role. 95m/C VHS, LV. Kristy Swanson, William Ragsdale, Meshach Taylor, Terry Kiser, Stuart Pankin; *D:* Stewart Raffill; *W:* Ed Rugoff. *LIV*

Manny & Lo 🗡🗡🗡 1996 (R) Krueger's directorial debut features fine performances in a story about three misfits forming a unique family bond. Surly 16-year-old Lo (Palladino) and her serious 11-year-old sister Manny (Johansson) have run away from their foster homes and hit the road together. Living hand-to-mouth, it's Manny who persuades her irresponsible pregnant sister that they need a home and they settle into an isolated cabin. When the sisters visit a baby store, eccentric clerk Elaine (Place) seems such a font of wisdom that the girls kidnap her and hold her as a hostage to help with the pregnancy. But Elaine's not trying to escape and has an agenda of her own.*CW:* Mild profanity and a brief sexual situation. 90m/C VHS, LV, **Closed Caption**. Mary Kay Place, Scarlett Johansson, Aleksa Palladino, Paul Guilfoyle, Glenn Fitzgerald, Cameron Boyd, Novella Nelson, Angie Phillips; *D:* Lisa Krueger; *W:* Lisa Krueger; *C:* Tom Krueger; *M:* John Lurie. Nominations: Independent Spirit Awards '97: Best Actress (Johansson), Best First Feature, Best Supporting Actress (Place). *COL*

Manny's Orphans 🗡 *Here Come the Tigers* 1978 (PG) An out-of-work teacher takes on a lovable home for orphaned boys. Dull remake of "Bad News Bears." 92m/C VHS, Beta. Richard Lincoln, Ma-

lachy McCourt, Sel Skolnick; *D:* Sean S. Cunningham. *LIV, VES*

Manon 🗡🗡 1950 Tragic tale of a French woman condemned for her affair with a Resistance fighter. They flee to Paris, where her brother forces her into prostitution. Based on the novel "Manon Lescaut" by Abbe Antoine-Francois Prevost. In French with English subtitles. 91m/B VHS. Cecile Aubry, Michel Auclair, Serge Reggiani, Henri Vilbert, Daniel Ivernel; *D:* Henri-Georges Clouzot. *NOS*

Manon of the Spring 🗡🗡🗡½ *Manon des Sources; Jean de Florette 2* 1987 (PG) In this excellent sequel to "Jean de Florette," the adult daughter of the dead hunchback, Jean, discovers who blocked up the spring on her father's land. She plots her revenge, which proves greater than she could ever imagine. Montand is astonishing. Based on a Marcel Pagnol novel. In French with English subtitles. 113m/C VHS, Beta, LV. *FR* Yves Montand, Daniel Auteuil, Emmanuelle Beart, Hippolyte Girardot; *D:* Claude Berri; *W:* Gerard Brach, Claude Berri. National Board of Review Awards '87: 5 Best Foreign Films of the Year. *ORI, APD, HMV*

Manos, the Hands of Fate woof! 1966 Horrible acting and laughable special effects elevate this story of a family ensnared by a satanic cult a notch above your average bad horror film. Highlights include a Satan-like character who can't stop laughing; the dreaded "hounds of hell" (or are those mangy dogs with big ears glued on?); and Torgo the monstrous henchman, who you know is evil because he has giant kneecaps (a sure sign of the devil's work). Notable as the one of the most often requested movies on Comedy Central's satiric "Mystery Science Theatre 3000," this one is good for a laugh. 74m/C VHS. Tom Nayman, Diane Mahree, Hal P. Warren, John Reynolds; *D:* Hal P. Warren; *W:* Hal P. Warren. *SNC*

Man's Best Friend 🗡½ 1993 (R) A guard dog is the object of a genetic experiment that has given him the aggressiveness of other creatures, including a cobra and a leopard. Since Max is an enormous Tibetan mastiff this means big trouble for everyone but the reporter (Sheedy) who rescued him—and even she better watch out.*CW:* Profanity, terror, and sexual situations. 87m/C VHS, LV, **Closed Caption**. Ally Sheedy, Lance Henriksen, Frederic Lehne, Robert Costanzo, John Cassisi, J.D. Daniels; *D:* John Lafia; *W:* John Lafia; *M:* Joel Goldsmith. *NLC*

Man's Country 🗡🗡 1938 A rip-roarin' western saga filled with the usual action and danger, as ranger Randall leads the fight against a band of nasties headed by Long, in a dual role as twin brothers. 55m/B VHS, Beta. Jack Randall, Ralph Peters, Marjorie Reynolds, Walter Long; *D:* Robert F. "Bob" Hill. *NOS, DVT*

Man's Favorite Sport? 🗡🗡½ 1963 A slapstick comedy about a renowned fishing expert author who actually hates fishing, but is forced to compete in a major tournament by a romantically inclined publicity agent. Very funny in spots. 121m/C VHS, Beta. Rock Hudson, Paula Prentiss, Charlene Holt, Maria Perschy, John McGiver; *D:* Howard Hawks; *M:* Henry Mancini. *USH, CCB*

Man's Land 🗡½ 1932 A ranch needs savin', and Hoot's the guy to do it in this formulaic Gibson epic. 65m/B VHS, Beta. Hoot Gibson, Marion Shilling, Skeeter Bill Robbins, Alan Bridge; *D:* Phil Rosen. *VCI*

Mansfield Park 🗡🗡½ 1985 Fanny is an impoverished young woman, snubbed by society, who earns the respect and love of her cousin in a BBC mini-series adaptation of the Jane Austen classic set in 19th century England. 261m/C VHS, Beta, **Closed Caption**. *GB* Sylvestria Le Touzel, Bernard Hepton, Anna Massey, Donald Pleasence; *D:* David Giles. *FOX, TVC, HMV*

The Manster 🗡 *The Manster—Half Man, Half Monster; The Split* 1959 Another masterpiece from the director who brought us "Monster from Green Hell." Womanizing, whiskey swilling American journalist receives mysterious injection from crazed scientist and sprouts unsightly hair and extra head. Although shot in the land of the rising sun, lips move in sync with dialogue. **72m/B VHS.** *JP* Peter Dyneley, Jane Hylton, Satoshi Nakamura, Terri Zimmern; **D:** Kenneth Crane, George Breakston. *SNC, MRV*

Mantis in Lace 🎬½ *Lila* 1968 (R) A go-go dancer slaughters men while tripping on LSD. Cinematography by pre-"Easy Rider" Laslo Kovacs. Watch it for the "hep" dialogue. **68m/C VHS.** Susan Stewart, Steve Vincent, M.K. Evans, Vic Lance, Pat Barrington, Janu Wine, Stuart Lancaster, John Carrol, Judith Crane, Cheryl Trepton; **D:** William Rotsler. *TPV*

Mantrap 🎬🎬½ 1926 Early silent success by Fleming, who later directed "Gone with the Wind" and "The Wizard of Oz." Fabled flapper Bow tempts a lawyer on retreat in the woods. **66m/B VHS, Beta.** Clara Bow, Ernest Torrence, Percy Marmont, Eugene Pallette, Tom Kennedy; **D:** Victor Fleming. *GPV, FCT*

The Manxman 🎬🎬½ 1929 Hitchcock's last silent film, a romantic melodrama about ambition and infidelity on the Isle of Man. **129m/B VHS, Beta.** *GB* Carl Brisson, Anny Ondra; **D:** Alfred Hitchcock. *VYY, MRV, MLB*

The Many Adventures of Winnie the Pooh 1977 (G) Disney's 22nd animated feature with A.A. Milne's beloved characters and their adventures in the Hundred Acre Wood. Includes a behind-the-scenes featurette with the original creators, animators, and voices. **83m/C VHS, Closed Caption.** *TOU*

Many Faces of Sherlock Holmes 1986 A documentary look at the various incarnations of the famous sleuth from A. Conan Doyle's stories to various film portrayals. **58m/C VHS, Beta.** Christopher Plummer, Basil Rathbone, Christopher Lee. *PSM*

Map of the Human Heart 🎬🎬 1993 (R) Thirty-year saga told in flashback. Young Eskimo Avik (Lee) and his Metis love interest Albertine (Parillaud) struggle with racism in a white world. They meet and become friends as children and years later meet again in Dresden during WWII, but now Albertine is married to Avik's once close friend, denying her heritage and living in the white world that he has been fighting for so long. Mediocre movie with extraordinary Arctic scenery. **CW:** Some language and one sexual scene. **109m/C VHS, Closed Caption.** Jason Scott Lee, Anne Parillaud, Patrick Bergin, Robert Joamie, Annie Galipeau, John Cusack, Jeanne Moreau; **D:** Vincent Ward; **W:** Vincent Ward, Louis Nowra. *HBO, FCT, BTV*

Mapp & Lucia 🎬🎬½ 1985 British TV adaptation of H.E. Benson's stories of provincial English society in the fictional village of Tilling-on-Sea in the 1920s. Miss Mapp (Scales) holds local court but finds a potential usurper when elegant widow Lucia (McEwan) comes to town. Battle lines are formed between the two women in this sharp-tongued satire. On 5 cassettes. **270m/C VHS.** *GB* Prunella Scales, Geraldine McEwan, Nigel Hawthorne. *WMI, VIF*

Marat/Sade 🎬🎬🎬½ *Persecution and Assassination of Jean-Paul Marat as Performed by the Inmates of the Asylum of Charenton Under the Direction of the Marquis De Sade* 1966 (R) A theatrical production presented by patients at a mental institution is directed by the Marquis de Sade. Well directed and visually effective, featuring Jackson's first film performance. Based on a play by Peter Weiss. Some theaters were forced to add extensions to the marquee when the film was first released. **115m/C VHS, LV.** *GB* Patrick Magee, Clifford Rose, Glenda Jackson, Ian Richardson, Brenda Kempner, Ruth Baker, Michael Williams; **D:** Peter Brook; **C:** David Watkin. *WBF, MGM, LUM*

Marathon 🎬🎬 1980 When a middle-aged jogger's ego gets a boost through the attention of a beautiful young woman, he takes up marathon running. Light comedy. Made for television. **100m/**

C **VHS.** Bob Newhart, Leigh Taylor-Young, Herb Edelman, Dick Gautier, Anita Gillette, John Hillerman; **D:** Jackie Cooper. *LIV*

Marathon Man 🎬🎬🎬 1976 (R) Nightmarish chase-thriller in which a graduate student becomes entangled in a plot involving a murderous Nazi fugitive. As student Hoffman is preparing for the Olympic marathon, he is reunited with his secret-agent brother, setting the intricate plot in motion. Courtesy of his brother, Hoffman becomes involved with Olivier, an old crazed Nazi seeking jewels taken from concentration camp victims. Non-stop action throughout, including a torture scene sure to set your teeth on edge. Goldman adapted the screenplay from his novel. **125m/C VHS, Beta, LV.** Dustin Hoffman, Laurence Olivier, Marthe Keller, Roy Scheider, William Devane, Fritz Weaver; **D:** John Schlesinger; **W:** William Goldman; **C:** Conrad Hall. Golden Globe Awards '77: Best Supporting Actor (Olivier); Nominations: Academy Awards '76: Best Supporting Actor (Olivier). *PAR*

Marauder 🎬🎬 1965 The prince of Venice leads a sea-faring onslaught against ransacking pirates and enemy fleets. **90m/C VHS, Beta.** *IT* Gordon Scott, Gianna Maria Canale, Franca Bettoya; **D:** Luigi Capuano. *NO*

Marbella 🎬½ 1985 A luxury resort in Spain is the setting for a big caper heist of three million dollars from a monarchical tycoon. **96m/C VHS, Beta.** Rod Taylor, Britt Ekland; **D:** Miguel Hermoso. *LIV*

March of the Wooden Soldiers 🎬🎬🎬 *Babes in Toyland* 1934 The classic Mother Goose tale about the secret life of Christmas toys, with Laurel and Hardy as Santa's helpers who must save Toyland from the wicked Barnaby. A Yuletide "must see." Also available in a colorized version. **73m/B VHS, LV.** Stan Laurel, Oliver Hardy, Charlotte Henry, Henry Kleinbach (Brandon), Felix Knight, Jean Darling, Johnny Downs, Marie Wilson; **D:** Charles R. Rogers, Gus Meins. *NOS, GKK, IME*

March or Die 🎬🎬½ 1977 (PG) Great potential, unrealized. An American joins the French Foreign Legion during WWI after his dismissal from West Point. Following the brutality of training, he is assigned to guard an archeological expedition in Morocco, where he pulls together a rag-tag outfit for the mission. Hackman proves once again the wide range of his acting abilities, surmounting the cliched and fairly sadistic plot. Shot on location in the Sahara Desert. **104m/C VHS.** *GB* Gene Hackman, Terence Hill, Max von Sydow, Catherine Deneuve, Ian Holm; **D:** Dick Richards; **W:** David Zelag Goodman; **M:** Maurice Jarre. *FOX*

Marciano 🎬🎬 1979 A made-for-television version of the great boxer's life. Average fight movie. **97m/C VHS, Beta.** Tony LoBianco, Vincent Gardenia; **D:** Bernard L. Kowalski; **M:** Ernest Gold. *NLC*

Marco 🎬🎬 1973 Entertaining musical adventure of Marco Polo's life casts Arnaz as Marco Polo and Mostel as Kublai Khan. A couple of cutups, right? One of the first films to combine animation with live action. Shot partially on location in the Orient. ♫By Damn; Walls; A Family Man; Spaghetti. **109m/C VHS, Beta.** Desi Arnaz Jr., Zero Mostel, Jack Weston, Cie Cie Win; **D:** Seymour Robbie. *PSM*

Marco Polo, Jr. 🎬 1972 Marco Polo, Jr., the daring descendant of the legendary explorer, travels the world in search of his destiny in this song-filled, feature-length, but poorly animated, fantasy. **82m/C VHS, Beta.** **D:** Eric Porter; **V:** Bobby Rydell. *FHE*

Mardi Gras for the Devil 🎬🎬 *Night Trap* 1993 (R) Black magic and the occult combine as a New Orleans cop tries to catch a killer who strikes only at Mardi Gras. The cop's got his work cut out for him since the killer is no mere mortal but a demon who believes in human sacrifice. **95m/C VHS, Beta.** Robert Davi, Michael Ironside, Lesley-Anne Down, Lydie Denier, Mike Starr, Margaret Avery, John Amos; **D:** David A. Prior; **W:** David A. Prior. *PSM*

Mardi Gras Massacre woof! *Crypt of Dark Secrets* 1978 Aztec priest arrives in New Orleans during Mardi Gras to revive the blood ritual of human sacrifice to an Aztec god. A police detective relentlessly pursues him. Much gore and gut-slicing, with no redeeming social value. **92m/C VHS, Beta.** Curt Dawson, Gwen Arment, Wayne Mack, Laura Misch; **D:** Jack Weis. *VHE*

Margaret's Museum 🎬🎬🎬½ 1995 (R) The museum of the title is the bizarre shrine Margaret (Bonham Carter) dedicates to the family members who have been killed in the coal mines that dominate her small (1940s) Cape Breton, Nova Scotia town. Both Margaret and her mother, Catherine (Nelligan), are embittered by their tragedies and when Margaret finds romance with eccentric bagpiper Neil (Russell), she makes him promise he'll never return to mine work. But with a bad economy, Neil is forced back to the pits and inevitable disaster. It's Bonham Carter's picture all the way and she shows a wide (and welcome) range of emotions and strength. Adapted from a story by Sheldon Currie. **CW:** Strong language and some sexuality. **114m/C VHS.** *CA GB* Helena Bonham Carter, Clive Russell, Kate Nelligan, Kenneth Welsh, Craig Olejnik; **D:** Mort Ransen; **W:** Mort Ransen, Gerald Wexler; **C:** Vic Sarin; **M:** Milan Kymlicka. Genie Awards '95: Best Actress (Bonham Carter), Best Costume Design, Best Supporting Actor (Welsh), Best Supporting Actress (Nelligan), Best Writing, Best Score. *CAF*

Margin for Murder 🎬🎬 *Mickey Spillane's Margin for Murder* 1981 Mike Hammer investigates a mysterious accident that killed his best friend. Made for television. **98m/C VHS, Beta.** Kevin Dobson, Cindy Pickett, Donna Dixon, Charles Hallahan; **D:** Daniel Haller. *PSM*

Maria Candelaria 🎬🎬 *Portrait of Maria; Xochimilco* 1946 Society rejects a woman because people don't like her mother. (She posed nude for an artist, and the town responds by stoning her to death, proving that going against small-town morals can be lethal.) Eventually, time and circumstance push daughter onto mother's path in this tragic soaper. Del Rio portrays the scorned young woman, although she was 40 years old. **96m/B VHS, Beta.** *MX* Dolores Del Rio, Pedro Armendariz Sr., Margarita Cortes; **D:** Emilio Fernandez. *MAD*

Maria Chapdelaine 🎬🎬🎬 1934 An early film from the renowned French director, in which a brutish trapper and a sophisticate battle for the love of a girl in the Canadian wilderness. English subtitles. Remade in 1984. **75m/B VHS, Beta.** *FR* Jean Gabin, Jean-Pierre Aumont, Madeleine Renaud; **D:** Julien Duvivier. *HHT*

Maria Chapdelaine 🎬🎬½ 1984 Around the turn of the century, a young girl in the Northern Canadian wilderness endures a year of passion, doomed love, and tragedy. In French with subtitles. Remake of a 1935 French film. **108m/C VHS, Beta.** *FR CA* Nick Mancuso, Carole Laure, Claude Rich, Pierre Curzi; **D:** Gilles Carle. *MED*

Marianne and Juliane 🎬🎬🎬½ 1982 Powerful combination of relationships and politics in West Germany as experienced through the lives of two sisters—Juliane, a feminist editor, and Marianne, a political terrorist. Based on the lives of Gudrun and Christiane Ensslin. German with subtitles. **106m/C VHS.** *GE* Jutta Lampe, Barbara Sukowa, Ruediger Vogler, Doris Schade, Franz Rudnick; **D:** Margarethe von Trotta. *NYF*

Maria's Child 🎬🎬½ 1993 Light comedy about a dancer who becomes pregnant and must decide whether or not to keep the baby. When her live-in boyfriend (not the father) admits he cheated on her, she kicks him out. Unable to make up her mind, she imagines a dialogue with the fetus. Second of a trilogy by British television screenwriter Malcolm McKay on the subject of forgiveness. **97m/C VHS.** *GB* Yolanda Vasquez, David O'Hara, Fiona Shaw, Alec McCowen, Sophie Okenado, Linda Davidson, Rudi Davies, Nicholas Woodeson, Anita Zagaria; **D:** Malcolm McKay; **W:** Malcolm McKay; **M:** Philip Appleby. *NYR*

Maria's Day *√√√* **1984** Chronicles the plague-riddled downfall of a formerly aristocratic and wealthy Hungarian family in the years following the failed 1849 Revolution. In Hungarian with English subtitles. **113m/C VHS, Beta.** *D:* Judit Elek. *FCT, AUD*

Maria's Lovers *√√½* **1984 (R)** The wife (Kinski) of an impotent WWII veteran (Savage) succumbs to the charms of a rakish lady-killer (Spano). Savage turns to the charms of an older woman, finds love again with Kinski, but is still impotent; she gets pregnant by a wandering minstrel (Carradine) and on we go to film climax. Offbeat and uneven, representing Russian director Konchalovsky's first American film and one of Kinski's better roles. **103m/C VHS, Beta.** Nastassia Kinski, John Savage, Robert Mitchum, Keith Carradine, Anita Morris, Bud Cort, Karen Young, Tracy Nelson, John Goodman, Vincent Spano; *D:* Andrei Konchalovsky; *W:* Marjorie David, Andrei Konchalovsky, Gerard Brach; *C:* Juan Ruiz-Anchia. *MGM*

Maricela **1988** Young Maricela Flores and her mother have come to the U.S. from El Salvador to escape the fighting. Living with a Southern Californian family, Maricela has a hard time adjusting to American life and, in particular, dealing with prejudice. An entry in the PBS "Wonderworks" series. **55m/C VHS.** Linda Lavin, Carlina Cruz. *PME, HMV, BTV*

Marie *√√√* **1985 (PG-13)** In this true story, a divorced (and battered) mother works her way through school and the system to become the first woman to head the Parole Board in Tennessee. Finding rampant corruption, she blows the whistle on her bosses, who put her life in jeopardy. Spacek gives a powerful performance, as does first-time actor Thompson, portraying himself as the abused woman's attorney. Based on the book by Peter Maas. **113m/C VHS, Beta, Closed Caption.** Sissy Spacek, Jeff Daniels, Keith Szarabajka, John Cullum, Morgan Freeman, Fred Dalton Thompson, Don Hood, Lisa Banes, Vincent Irizarry; *D:* Roger Donaldson; *W:* John Briley; *C:* Chris Menges; *M:* Francis Lai. *MGM*

Marie Antoinette *√√½* **1938** An elephantine costume drama chronicling the French queen's life from princesshood to her final days before the Revolution. A Shearer festival all the way, and a late example of MGM's overstuffed period style and star-power. Overlong, but engrossing for the wrong reasons. Morley, in his first film, plays Louis XVI. Power's only MGM loan-out casts him as a Swedish count and Marie's romantic dalliance. Based on a book by Stephan Zweig, with script assistance from (among others) F. Scott Fitzgerald. **160m/B VHS, Beta, LV.** Norma Shearer, Tyrone Power, John Barrymore, Robert Morley, Gladys George, Anita Louise, Joseph Schildkraut, Henry Stephenson, Reginald Gardiner, Peter Bull, Albert Dekker, Joseph Calleia, George Zucco, Cora Witherspoon, Barry Fitzgerald, Mae Busch, Harry Davenport, Scotty Beckett; *D:* Woodbridge S. Van Dyke; *W:* F. Scott Fitzgerald; *C:* William H. Daniels. Nominations: Academy Awards '38: Best Actress (Shearer), Best Interior Decoration, Best Supporting Actor (Morley), Best Original Score. *MGM*

Marie Galante *√√√* **1934** Fine spy drama has Tracy running into Gallien in Panama (years earlier he had been left there after a kidnapping). He finds her most helpful in his attempt to thwart the bombing of the Panama Canal. It's the performances that raise this otherwise standard thriller up a few notches. **88m/B VHS, Beta.** Spencer Tracy, Katie Galian, Ned Sparks, Helen Morgan, Sig Rumann, Leslie Fenton, Jay C. Flippen; *D:* Henry King. *NOS, SNC, HEG*

Marihuana *√* *Marijuana: The Devil's Weed* **1936** An unintentionally hilarious, "Reefer Madness"-type cautionary film about the exaggerated evils of pot smoking. A real dopey film favored by right-winger zealots. **57m/B VHS, Beta.** Harley Wood, Hugh McArthur, Pat Carlyle; *D:* Dwain Esper. *SNC, VYY, HEG*

Marilyn & Bobby: Her Final Affair *√½* **1994** Sordid account of the alleged romance between movie star Monroe (Anderson) and Attorney General Robert Kennedy (Kelly). Culminates in a silly scene at Marilyn's home, on the night of her death, where various men all try to find her tell-all diary while keeping out of sight of each other. Made for cable TV. **95m/C VHS.** Melody Anderson, James F. Kelly, Richard Dysart, Thomas Wagner, Raymond Serra, Kristopher Tabori, Jonathan Banks, Geoffrey Blake, Ian Buchanan; *D:* Bradford May. *AVE*

Marilyn: The Untold Story *√√√* **1980** Nominated for an Emmy, Hicks elevates what could easily have been a dull made-for-TV movie with her remarkable performance as Marilyn Monroe. Based on the book by Norman Mailer. **156m/C VHS.** Catherine Hicks, Richard Basehart, Frank Converse, John Ireland, Sheree North, Anne Ramsey, Viveca Lindfors, Jason Miller, Bill Vint; *D:* Jack Arnold, John Flynn, Lawrence Schiller; *M:* William Goldstein. *ABC*

Marine Raiders *√√* **1943** Marines train and then fight at Guadalcanal. A typical flag-waver, watchable but not particularly engaging. **90m/B VHS, Beta.** Pat O'Brien, Robert Ryan, Ruth Hussey, Frank McHugh, Barton MacLane; *D:* Harold Schuster. *TTC*

Marius *√√√√* **1931** This is the first of Marcel Pagnol's trilogy ("Fanny" and "Cesar" followed), about the lives and adventures of the people of Provence, France. Marius is a young man who dreams of going away to sea. When he acts on those dreams, he leaves behind his girlfriend, Fanny. Realistic dialogue and vivid characterizations. Adapted by Pagnol from his play. The musical play and film "Fanny" (1961) were adapted from this trilogy. **125m/B VHS, Beta, LV.** *FR* Raimu, Pierre Fresnay, Charpin, Orane Demazis; *D:* Alexander Korda; *W:* Marcel Pagnol; *M:* Francis Gromon. *NOS, MRV, INT*

Marjoe *√√* **1972 (PG)** Documentary follows the career of rock-style evangelist Marjoe Gortner, who spent 25 years of his life touring the country as a professional preacher. Marjoe later went on to become an actor and professional fundraiser. **88m/C VHS, Beta.** Marjoe Gortner; *D:* Howard Smith, Sarah Kernochan. Academy Awards '72: Best Feature Documentary. *COL*

Marjorie Morningstar *√√* **1958** A tempered Hollywood adaptation of the Herman Wouk story of a young actress who fails to achieve stardom and settles on being a housewife. Wood slipped a bit in this story. **123m/C VHS.** Natalie Wood, Gene Kelly, Martin Balsam, Claire Trevor, Ed Wynn, Everett Sloane, Carolyn Jones; *D:* Irving Rapper; *C:* Harry Stradling; *M:* Max Steiner. Nominations: Academy Awards '58: Best Song ("A Very Precious Love"). *REP*

The Mark *√√√½* **1961** Story of a convicted child molester who cannot escape his past upon his release from prison. Whitman gives a riveting performance as the convict. **127m/B VHS, Beta.** *GB* Stuart Whitman, Maria Schell, Rod Steiger, Brenda de Banzie, Maurice Denham, Donald Wolfit, Paul Rogers, Donald Houston, Amanda Black, Russell Napier, Marie Devereux; *D:* Guy Green; *W:* Sidney Buchman, Raymond Stross; *M:* Richard Rodney Bennett. Nominations: Academy Awards '61: Best Actor (Whitman). *NO*

Mark of Cain *√√½* **1984** Twin brothers, one normal, the other a raving lunatic with murderous tendencies, confuse the authorities who imprison the nice guy, allowing the nutcase to chase after his beautiful sister-in-law. **90m/C VHS, Beta.** Robin Ward, Wendy Crewson, August Schellenberg; *D:* Bruce Pittman; *W:* Peter Colley. *LIV, VES*

Mark of the Beast *√* **19??** Two students inadvertently videotape an assassination, and are then relentlessly pursued by the killer. **90m/C VHS.** Carolyn Guillet, David Smulker; *D:* Robert Stewart. *NO*

Mark of the Devil *√* *Burn, Witch, Burn; Brenn, Hexe, Brenn* **1969 (R)** Witchcraft and romance don't mix, as a Medieval witch hunter and a sexy girl accused of witchery discover. Notoriously graphic torture scenes add to the mayhem but the weird part is that this is based on true stories. **96m/**

C VHS, Beta. *GB GE* Herbert Lom, Olivera Vuco, Udo Kier, Reggie Nalder, Herbert Fux, Michael Maien, Ingeborg Schoener, Johannes Buzalski, Gaby Fuchs; *D:* Michael Armstrong. *VES, LIV, TPV*

Mark of the Devil 2 *√* **1972 (R)** Sadistic witchhunters torture satan's servants and torch sisters of mercy, whilst trying to horn in on a nobleman's fortune. It's just not as gross without the vomit bags. **90m/C VHS.** *GB GE* Erika Blanc, Anton Diffring, Reggie Nalder; *D:* Adrian Hoven. *VDM*

The Mark of the Hawk *√√√* *The Accused* **1957** A uniquely told story of African nations struggling to achieve racial equality after gaining independence. Songs include "This Man Is Mine," sung by Kitt. **83m/C VHS.** *GB* Sidney Poitier, Eartha Kitt, Juano Hernandez, John McIntire; *D:* Michael Audley. *MRV*

Mark of the Spur *√½* **1932** The mark on an injured man's face is used to track down his attacker. **60m/B VHS, Beta.** Bob Custer, Lillian Rich, Franklyn Farnum, Bud Osborne; *D:* J.P. McGowan. *NOS, DVT, GPV*

Mark of the Vampire *√√√* **1935** A murder in a small town is solved through the use of vaudeville actors who pose as vampires. Great cast, surprise ending. **61m/B VHS, Beta.** Lionel Barrymore, Bela Lugosi, Elizabeth Allan; *D:* Tod Browning; *C:* James Wong Howe. *MGM, MLB*

Mark of Zorro *√√√* **1920** Fairbanks plays a dual role as the hapless Don Diego and his dashing counterpart, Zorro, the hero of the oppressed. Silent film. **80m/B VHS, LV.** Douglas Fairbanks Sr., Marguerite de la Motte, Noah Beery Sr.; *D:* Fred Niblo. *REP, MRV, GPV*

The Mark of Zorro *√√√½* **1940** The dashing Power swashbuckles his way through this wonderfully acted and directed romp. He plays the foppish son of a 19th-century California aristocrat who is secretly the masked avenger of the oppressed peons. Bromberg plays the wicked governor, with the beautiful niece (Darnell) beloved by Power, and Rathbone is supremely evil as his cruel minion. Lots of swordplay with a particularly exciting duel to the death between Rathbone and Power. Based on the novel "The Curse of Capistrano" by Johnston McCulley. Remake of the 1921 silent film and followed by a number of other Zorro incarnations. **93m/B VHS, Beta.** Tyrone Power, Linda Darnell, Basil Rathbone, Gale Sondergaard, Eugene Pallette, J. Edward Bromberg, Montagu Love, Janet Beecher; *D:* Rouben Mamoulian; *W:* John Taintor Foote; *C:* Arthur C. Miller; *M:* Alfred Newman. Nominations: Academy Awards '40: Best Original Score. *FXV, BTV*

Mark Twain and Me *√√½* **1991** Robards portrays the aging and irascible Mark Twain, attended by a neglected but devoted daughter, and befriended by 11-year-old Dorothy Quick, as they travel on the same ship. Based on a true story. Made for television. **93m/C VHS.** Jason Robards Jr., Talia Shire, Amy Stewart, Chris Wiggins, R.H. Thomson, Fiona Reid; *D:* Daniel Petrie. *DIS, BTV*

Marked for Death *√½* *Screwface* **1990 (R)** Having killed a prostitute, DEA agent Seagal decides it's time to roll out the white picket fence in the 'burbs with the little woman and brood. Trouble is, a bunch of guys with dreadlocks don't approve of his early retirement, and the Jamaican gangsters plan to send him and his family to the great Rasta playground in the sky. Whereupon the Stevester kicks and punches and wags his ponytail. Much blood flows, mon. Tunes by Jimmy Cliff. **93m/C VHS, LV, Closed Caption.** Steven Seagal, Joanna Pacula, Basil Wallace, Keith David, Tom Wright, Danielle Harris, Arlen Dean Snyder, Teri Weigel; *D:* Dwight Little; *W:* Mark Victor, Michael Grais. *FXV, CCB*

Marked for Murder *√½* **1945** Another in the Texas Ranger series. In this entry, the Rangers come to the rescue when a rancher war appears inevitable. **58m/B VHS, LV.** Tex Ritter, Dave O'Brien, Guy Wilkerson; *D:* Elmer Clifton; *W:* Elmer Clifton. *THV*

Marked for Murder 🎬½ 1989 (R) Two TV station employees are framed for murder after being sent out to find a missing videocassette. Renee Estevez is part of the Sheen/Estevez dynasty. 88m/C VHS, Beta. Renee Estevez, Wings Hauser, Jim Mitchum, Ross Hagen, Ken Abraham; **D:** Rick Sloane. THV

Marked Man 🎬🎬 1996 (R) After auto mechanic Frank Stanton (Piper) witnesses a murder he finds himself accused of the crime and on the run, trying to prove his innocence.**CW:** Violence and language. 94m/C VHS, LV, Closed Caption. Roddy Piper, Jane Wheeler, Alina Thompson, Miles O'Keeffe; **D:** Marc Voizard; **W:** Thomas Ritz; **C:** Stephen Reizes; **M:** Marty Simon. LIV

Marked Money 🎬🎬 1928 Amiable captain takes in boy who'll soon roll in the dough and swindlers show up on the scene. The captain's courageous girl and her pilot beau step in to right the rookery. 61m/B VHS, Beta. Frank "Junior" Coghlan, George Duryea, Tom Kennedy, Bert Woodruff, Virginia Bradford, Maurice Black, Jack Richardson; **D:** Spencer Gordon Bennet. GPV, FCT

Marked Trails 🎬 1944 One clue stamps out the guilty parties in this wild west saga. 59m/B VHS, Beta. Hoot Gibson, Bob Steele, Veda Ann Borg. NOS, DVT

Marked Woman 🎬🎬🎬 1937 Gangster drama about crusading District Attorney who persuades a group of clipjoint hostesses to testify against their gangster boss. A gritty studio melodrama loosely based on a true story. 97m/B VHS, Beta, LV, Closed Caption. Bette Davis, Humphrey Bogart, Eduardo Ciannelli, Isabel Jewell, Jane Bryan, Mayo Methot, Allen Jenkins, Lola Lane; **D:** Lloyd Bacon; **C:** George Barnes. Venice Film Festival '37: Best Actress (Davis). MGM

Marlowe 🎬🎬½ 1969 (PG) Updated telling by Stirling Silliphant of Chandler's "The Little Sister" sports retro guy Garner as Philip Marlowe, gumshoe. Hired by a mystery blonde to find her misplaced brother, rumpled sleuth Marlowe encounters kicking Bruce Lee in his first film. Slick looking, but the story's a bit slippery. 95m/C VHS, Beta. James Garner, Gayle Hunnicutt, Carroll O'Connor, Rita Moreno, Sharon Farrell, William Daniels, Bruce Lee; **D:** Paul Bogart; **W:** Stirling Silliphant; **C:** William H. Daniels. MGM, FCT

Marnie 🎬🎬🎬½ 1964 A lovely blonde with a mysterious past robs her employers and then changes her identity. When her current boss catches her in the act and forces her to marry him, he soon learns the puzzling aspects of Marnie's background. Criticized at the time of its release, the movie has since been accepted as a Hitchcock classic. 130m/C VHS, Beta, LV. Tippi Hedren, Sean Connery, Diane Baker, Bruce Dern, Louise Latham; **D:** Alfred Hitchcock; **W:** Jay Presson Allen; **C:** Robert Burks. USH

Maroc 7 🎬 1967 Slow story of a secret agent after a thief suffering from a split personality. 92m/C VHS, Closed Caption. Gene Barry, Elsa Martinelli, Cyd Charisse, Leslie Phillips; **D:** Gerry O'Hara. PAR

Marooned 🎬🎬 1969 (G) Tense thriller casts Crenna, Hackman, and Franciscus as astronauts stranded in space after a retro-rocket misfires and their craft is unable to return to earth. 134m/C VHS, Beta, LV. Gregory Peck, David Janssen, Richard Crenna, James Franciscus, Gene Hackman, Lee Grant; **D:** John Sturges; **C:** Daniel F. Fapp. Academy Awards '69: Best Visual Effects; Nominations: Academy Awards '69: Best Cinematography, Best Sound. GKK

Marquis 🎬🎬 1990 A bizarre satire combining sex, lust, and the French Revolution, based on the writings of the Marquis de Sade. Amusing, decadent, and not for the prudish. In French with English subtitles. 88m/C VHS. FR **D:** Henri Xhonneux. FRF

The Marriage Circle 🎬🎬🎬 1924 A pivotal silent comedy depicting the infidelity of several married couples in Vienna. Director Lubitsch's first American comedy. Remade as a musical, "One Hour With You," in 1932. Silent. 90m/B VHS. Florence Vidor, Monte Blue, Marie Prevost, Creighton Hale, Adolphe Menjou, Harry Myers, Dale Fuller; **D:** Ernst Lubitsch. NOS, MOV, GVV

Marriage Is Alive and Well 🎬 1980 A wedding photographer reflects on the institution of marriage from his unique perspective. Made for television. 100m/C VHS. Joe Namath, Jack Albertson, Melinda Dillon, Judd Hirsch, Susan Sullivan, Fred McCarren, Swoosie Kurtz; **D:** Russ Mayberry. LIV

Marriage Italian Style 🎬🎬🎬 1964 When an engaged man hears that his mistress is on her death bed, he goes to her side and, in an emotional gesture, promises to marry her if she survives. She does; and holds him to his promise. After they're married, however, she gives him a big surprise—three grown sons. A silly film, but DeSica's direction keeps it from being too fluffy. Lots of fun. Based on the play "Filumena Marturano" by Eduardo De Filippo. 102m/C VHS. IT Sophia Loren, Marcello Mastroianni, Aldo Puglisi, Tecla Scarano, Marilu Tolo; **D:** Vittorio De Sica. Golden Globe Awards '65: Best Foreign Film; Nominations: Academy Awards '64: Best Actress (Loren). VTR

The Marriage of Maria Braun 🎬🎬🎬🎬 Die Ehe Der Maria Braun 1979 (R) In post-WWII Germany, a young woman uses guile and sexuality to survive as the nation rebuilds itself into an industrial power. The first movie in Fassbinder's trilogy about German women in Germany during the post war years, it is considered one of the director's finest films, and an indispensable example of the New German Cinema. In German with English subtitles. 120m/C VHS, Beta. GE Hanna Schygulla, Klaus Lowitsch, Ivan Desny, Gottfried John, Gisela Uhlen; **D:** Rainer Werner Fassbinder; **W:** Rainer Werner Fassbinder; **C:** Michael Ballhaus; **M:** Peer Raben. Berlin International Film Festival '79: Best Actress (Schygulla); National Board of Review Awards '79: 5 Best Foreign Films of the Year. NYF, COL, GLV

Married? 🎬½ 1926 Couple endures 365 days of marital bliss in order to inherit big bucks. Some do it for less. 65m/B VHS, Beta. Owen Moore, Constance Bennett; **D:** George Terwilliger. GPV, FCT

A Married Man 🎬🎬 1984 Story focusing on a bored British lawyer who begins cheating on his wife. Amid the affair, someone gets murdered. Made for television. 200m/C VHS, Beta. GB Anthony Hopkins, Ciaran Madden, Lise Hilboldt, Yvonne Coulette, John Le Mesurier, Sophie Ashton; **D:** John Davies. LIV

Married People, Single Sex 🎬🎬½ 1993 (R) Three couples decide to spread their sexual wings. Shelly takes a new lover; Artie makes obscene phone calls; and Beth and Mike, who end their relationship, still can't keep out of bed. An unrated version is also available.**CW:** Sex-related dialogue and strong sexuality. 110m/C VHS. Chase Masterson, Joseph Pilato, Darla Slavens, Shelley Michelle, Wendi Westbrook, Robert Zachar, Samuel Mongiello, Teri Thompson; **D:** Mike Sedan; **W:** Catherine Tavel. TRI

Married People, Single Sex 2: For Better or Worse 🎬🎬½ 1994 (R) Three women are faced with sexual unhappiness: Carol's hubby has an affair, Valerie wants a baby but her spouse doesn't, and Karen's husband is just too darn nice (she wants some spice in her life). So, there's lots of sexual encounters to solve their problems. Also available unrated.**CW:** Language; nudity; strong sexuality. 93m/C VHS. Kathy Shower, Monique Parent, Liza Smith, Craig Stepp, Doug Jeffrey; **D:** Mike Sedan. TRI

Married to It 🎬🎬 1993 (R) Three vastly different couples work together to plan a pageant at a private school. The oil and water group includes struggling hippie leftovers Bridges and Channing, '80s-era corporate cutthroats Shepherd and Silver, and starry-eyed newlyweds Masterson and Leonard. Contrived plot offers few humourous moments, with the main focus revolving around coping rather than comedy. And the coping is slow business, done by characters you don't really care with about problems that don't really matter.**CW:** Language and one sensual scene. 112m/C VHS, LV, Closed Caption. Beau Bridges, Stockard Channing, Robert Sean Leonard, Mary Stuart Masterson, Cybill Shepherd, Ron Silver; **D:** Arthur Hiller; **W:** Janet Kovalcik; **M:** Henry Mancini. ORI

Married to the Mob 🎬🎬🎬 1988 (R) After the murder of her husband, an attractive Mafia widow tries to escape "mob" life, but ends up fighting off amorous advances from the current mob boss while being wooed by an undercover cop. A snappy script and a spry performance by Pfeiffer pepper this easy-to-watch film. 102m/C VHS, Beta, LV, Closed Caption. Michelle Pfeiffer, Dean Stockwell, Alec Baldwin, Matthew Modine, Mercedes Ruehl, Anthony J. Nici, Joan Cusack, Ellen Foley, Chris Isaak, Trey Wilson, Charles Napier, Tracey Walter, Al Lewis, Nancy Travis, David Johansen, Jonathan Demme; **D:** Jonathan Demme; **W:** Mark Burns, Barry Strugatz; **C:** Tak Fujimoto; **M:** David Byrne. New York Film Critics Awards '88: Best Supporting Actor (Stockwell); National Society of Film Critics Awards '88: Best Supporting Actor (Stockwell), Best Supporting Actress (Ruehl); Nominations: Academy Awards '88: Best Supporting Actor (Stockwell). ORI

Married Too Young 🎬🎬 I Married Too Young 1962 High school honeys elope, despite disapproval from the parental units. When the boy groom trades his med school plans for a monkey wrench in order to support the little missus, he finds much trouble with the hot rod heavies. 76m/B VHS. Harold Lloyd Jr., Jana Lund, Anthony Dexter, Marianna Hill, Trudy Marshall, Brian O'Hara, Nita Loveless; **D:** George Moskov. HHT, SNC

A Married Woman 🎬🎬🎬 La Femme Mariee 1965 Dramatizes a day in the life of a woman who has both a husband and a lover. One of Godard's more mainstream efforts. 94m/B VHS, Beta, 8mm. FR Macha Meril, Phillippe LeRoy, Bernard Noel; **D:** Jean-Luc Godard; **W:** Jean-Luc Godard. VYY, MRV, DVT

Marry Me, Marry Me 🎬🎬🎬 Mazel Tov Ou le Mariage 1969 (R) While in Paris, a Jewish encyclopedia salesman falls in love with a pregnant Belgian woman. A sensitive story about European Jewish families. Berri wrote, produced, directed, and starred in this romantic comedy. 87m/C VHS. FR Elisabeth Wiener, Regine, Claude Berri, Louisa Colpeyn; **D:** Claude Berri; **C:** Ghislan Cloquet. NO

The Marrying Kind 🎬🎬½ 1952 Marrieds Florence (Holliday) and Chet (Ray) Keefer are in the chambers of Judge Carroll (Kennedy) talking about why they want a divorce. They flashback to their courtship and marriage and the bumps they've endured along the way, and then realize they still love each other. Holliday reunited with Cukor and scriptwriters Gordon and Kanin after their triumph with "Born Yesterday." 92m/B VHS. Judy Holliday, Aldo Ray, Madge Kennedy, Sheila Bond, John Alexander, Peggy Cass, Rex Williams; **D:** George Cukor; **W:** Ruth Gordon, Garson Kanin; **C:** Joseph Walker; **M:** Hugo Friedhofer. COL

The Marrying Man 🎬½ 1991 (R) Young man meets his match when his buddies take him to Las Vegas for his bachelor party. He falls like a ton of bricks for the singer, not knowing she belongs to the local crime lord, who catches them together and forces them to marry. They immediately divorce, can't forget each other and eventually re-marry, again and again and again. Silly story supposedly based on the story of Harry Karl (eventual husband of Debbie Reynolds) and Marie MacDonald. Basinger and Baldwin's off-stage romance created quite a stir but their chemistry onscreen is zilch. Ineffective, not funny, poorly paced and acted: a good example of what happens when egotistical stars get their way.**CW:** Language and sensuality. 116m/C VHS, LV, Closed Caption. Alec Baldwin, Kim Basinger, Robert Loggia, Armand Assante, Elisabeth Shue, Paul Reiser, Fisher Stevens, Peter Dobson, Gretchen Wyler; **D:** Jerry Rees; **W:** Neil Simon; **M:** David Newman. HPH

Mars Attacks! 🎬🎬½ 1996 (PG-13) Only director Burton could make a movie based on a series of 1960s trading cards. Intentionally tacky, this huge scale epic spoof of monster, sci-fi, and disaster flicks finds moronic President Dale (Nicholson), his frigid wife (Close) and a cast of thousands battling the green-skinned invaders. Jack's back for a second role as Vegas hotel developer Art Land, who tries to cash in on the opportunities the invasion brings. Plot is relatively nonexistent and zig-zags wildly throughout, but the gist is that the aliens are bent on destroying the population, and have little trouble battling the bumbling humans. Brosnan is the hilariously deluded alien-hugger, Professor Kessler. A semi-lampoon of fellow alien flick competitor "Independence Day," this film goes all out for the camp laugh, but its big budget effects, way over-the-top style and all-star cast can't conquer the audience. **CW:** Sci-fi fantasy violence and brief sexuality. **106m/C VHS, LV, Closed Caption, DVD.** Jack Nicholson, Glenn Close, Martin Short, Pierce Brosnan, Lukas Haas, Sarah Jessica Parker, Michael J. Fox, Natalie Portman, Rod Steiger, Paul Winfield, Annette Bening, Sylvia Sidney, Danny DeVito, Tom Jones, Pam Grier, Jim Brown, Lisa Marie; **D:** Tim Burton; **W:** Jonathan Gems; **C:** Peter Suschitzky; **M:** Danny Elfman. Nominations: MTV Movie Awards '97: Best Fight (Jim Brown/A Martian). *WAR*

Mars Needs Women 🎬 1966

When the Martian singles scene starts to drag, Mars boys cross the galaxy in search of fertile earth babes to help them repopulate the planet. Seems Batgirl Craig, the go-go dancing lady scientist, is at the top of their dance cards. **80m/C VHS.** Tommy Kirk, Yvonne Craig; **D:** Larry Buchanan; **W:** Larry Buchanan. *SNC*

Marshal Law 🎬🎬 1996 (R)

Highland Glen is a gated community in L.A. that seems very secure, especially for ex-Texas Marshal Jack Coleman (Smits) and his family. But an earthquake leaves the neighborhood prey to a vicious gang unless Coleman can find a way to outwit them. **CW:** Strong violence and language and for some sexuality and drug use. **96m/C VHS, Closed Caption.** Jimmy Smits, James LeGros, Vonte Sweet, Scott Plank, Kristy Swanson, Channon Roe, Michael Cavalieri, Rodney Rowland, Tai Thai; **D:** Stephen Cornwell; **W:** Stephen Cornwell, Nick Gregory; **C:** Levie Isaacks; **M:** Tim Truman. *MGM*

Marshal of Cedar Rock 🎬🎬 1953

Marshal Rocky Lane sets a prisoner free, thinking the guy will lead him to a stash of stolen bank funds. Seems he miscalculates, but by way of consolation, he routs a rotten railroad agent who's rooking innocent people. Features the equine talent of Black Jack. **54m/B VHS.** Allan "Rocky" Lane, Phyllis Coates, Roy Barcroft, William Henry, Robert Shayne, Eddy Waller; **D:** Harry Keller. *HEG, DVT, NOS*

Marshal of Heldorado 🎬 1950

An outlaw-infested town needs an injection of law and order. **53m/B VHS.** James Ellison, Russell Hayden, Raymond Hatton, Fuzzy Knight; **D:** Thomas Carr. *NOS, DVT*

The Marshal's Daughter 🎬½ 1953

A father and daughter team up to outwit an outlaw. Features many cowboy songs, including the title track by Tex Ritter. **71m/B VHS.** Tex Ritter, Ken Murray, Laurie Anders, Preston Foster, Hoot Gibson; **D:** William (Lester Williams) Berke. *NOS, MOV, HEG*

Martha and I 🎬🎬🎬 1991

In 1934 Czechoslovakia, distinguished Jewish doctor Ernest Paul Fuchs (Piccoli), having divorced his unfaithful wife, impulsively marries his lower-class gentile German maid Martha (Sagebrecht). What turns out to be a true love match is witnessed through the adolescent eyes of nephew Emil (Chalupa), who comes to live with the couple. With the rise of Nazism and increased Jewish persecution the devoted Martha begins to fear for her husband and makes a futile attempt to find a safe haven. Stirring drama based on the director's childhood (he's the semi-fictionalized Emil). German with subtitles. **107m/C VHS.** *GE* Marianne Saegebrecht, Michel Piccoli, Vaclav Chalupa, Ondrej Vetchy; **D:** Jiri Weiss; **W:** Jiri Weiss; **C:** Viktor Ruzicka; **M:** Jiri Stivin. *NYR*

Martial Law 🎬½ 1990 (R)

A film solely for martial arts fans. Two cops use their hands, feet, and other body parts to fight crime. **90m/C VHS.** Chad McQueen, Cynthia Rothrock, David Carradine, Andy McCutcheon; **D:** S.E. Cohen; **W:** Richard Brandes. *MED, FOX, VTR*

Martial Law 2: Undercover 🎬½ 1991 (R)

Two cops, martial arts experts and part of an elite police force called Martial Law, go undercover to investigate the murder of a colleague. They uncover a fast-growing crime ring headed by a bad cop and a nightclub owner. The nightclub is host to the city's rich and powerful, who are treated to a bevy of beautiful women, protected by martial arts experts, and entertained by martial arts fights to the death. Lots of high-kicking action. **CW:** Language, violence, and one sensual scene. **92m/C VHS, LV, Closed Caption.** Jeff Wincott, Cynthia Rothrock, Paul Johansson, Evan Lurie, L. Charles Taylor, Sherrie Rose, Billy Drago; **D:** Kurt Anderson; **W:** Richard Brandes, Jiles Fitzgerald. *USH*

Martial Outlaw 🎬🎬 1993 (R)

DEA man Kevin White (Wincott) has been following a drug-dealing ex-KGB kingpin from Moscow to San Francisco. The Russian's latest move takes him to Los Angeles where Kevin meets up with his older brother Jack (Hudson), a maverick LA cop. Jack persuades Kevin to let him in on the action but Kevin begins to suspect Jack is playing both sides and their sibling rivalry could lead to death. **89m/C VHS, LV, Closed Caption.** Jeff Wincott, Gary Hudson, Richard Jaeckel, Krista Errickson, Vladimir Skomarovsky, Liliana Komorowska, Gary Wood; **D:** Kurt Anderson; **W:** Thomas Ritz. *REP*

The Martian Chronicles: Part 1 1979

Series episode "The Explorers." Adapted from Ray Bradbury's critically acclaimed novel. Futuristic explorations of the planet Mars. Strange fates of the discovery teams make everything more curious. Made for television. **120m/C VHS, Beta.** Rock Hudson, Bernie Casey, Nicholas Hammond, Darren McGavin; **D:** Michael Anderson Sr. *FRH*

The Martian Chronicles: Part 2 🎬½ 1979

Episode following the television movie. This part is called "The Settlers." The planet Mars meets with its first colonization and the settlers watch the Earth explode. **97m/C VHS, Beta.** Rock Hudson, Fritz Weaver, Roddy McDowall, Bernie Casey, Darren McGavin, Gayle Hunnicutt, Barry Morse, Bernadette Peters; **D:** Michael Anderson Sr. *FRH*

The Martian Chronicles: Part 3 🎬🎬½ 1979

In the final chapter of this space saga, the Martian's secrets become known and will forever change man's destiny. Adapted from Ray Bradbury's classic novel; made-for-television. **97m/C VHS, Beta.** Rock Hudson, Bernadette Peters, Christopher Connelly, Fritz Weaver, Roddy McDowall, Bernie Casey, Nicholas Hammond, Darren McGavin, Gayle Hunnicutt, Barry Morse; **D:** Michael Anderson Sr. *FRH*

Martians Go Home! 🎬½ 1990 (PG-13)

Joke-loving Martians come to earth and pester a nerdy composer. **89m/C VHS, Beta, LV.** Randy Quaid, Margaret Colin, Anita Morris, John Philbin, Ronny Cox, Gerrit Graham, Barry Sobel, Vic Dunlop; **D:** David Odell. *NO*

Martin 🎬🎬🎬 1977 (R)

Martin is a charming young man, though slightly mad. He freely admits of the need to drink blood. Contemporary vampire has found a new abhorrent means of killing his victims. **96m/C VHS, Beta, LV.** John Amplas, Lincoln Maazel; **D:** George A. Romero; **W:** George A. Romero. *NO*

Martin Chuzzlewit 🎬🎬½ 1994

Martin Chuzzlewit (Scofield) is a rich and elderly man with a lot of greedy relatives just waiting for him to die so they can get their hands on his money. The only exceptions being his already disinherited namesake grandson and his young orphaned nurse, Mary Graham. Adapted from the Charles Dickens novel. On 3 cassettes. **288m/C VHS, Closed Caption.** Paul Scofield, John Mills, Pete Postlethwaite, Tom Wilkinson, Julia Sawalha; **D:** Pedr James. *PBS, FOX, VIF*

Martin Luther 🎬½ 1953

French-made biography of the 16th century reformer who began the Protestant Reformation. **105m/B VHS, Beta.** *FR* Niall MacGinnis, John Ruddock, Pierre Leeavre, Guy Verney. Nominations: Academy Awards '53: Best Art Direction/Set Decoration (B & W), Best Black and White Cinematography. *NOS, VCI, ECU*

Martin's Day 🎬🎬 1985 (PG)

An unusual friendship develops between an escaped convict and the young boy he kidnaps. **99m/C VHS, Beta, Closed Caption.** *CA* Richard Harris, Lindsay Wagner, James Coburn, Justin Henry, Karen Black, John Ireland; **D:** Alan Gibson; **W:** Chris Bryant, Allan Scott. *MGM, FOX*

Marty 🎬🎬🎬½ 1955

Marty is a painfully shy bachelor who feels trapped in a pointless life of family squabbles. When he finds love, he also finds the strength to break out of what he feels is a meaningless existence. A sensitive and poignant film from the writer of "Altered States." Remake of a television version that originally aired in 1953. Notable for Borgnine's sensitive portrayal, one of his last quality jobs before sinking into the B-Movie sludge pit. **91m/B VHS, Beta, LV, Closed Caption.** Ernest Borgnine, Betsy Blair, Joe De Santis, Esther Minciotti, Jerry Paris, Karen Steele; **D:** Delbert Mann; **W:** Paddy Chayefsky; **C:** Joseph LaShelle. Academy Awards '55: Best Actor (Borgnine), Best Director (Mann), Best Picture, Best Screenplay; British Academy Awards '55: Best Actor (Borgnine), Best Actress (Blair); Directors Guild of America Awards '55: Best Director (Mann); Golden Globe Awards '56: Best Actor—Drama (Borgnine); National Board of Review Awards '55: 10 Best Films of the Year, Best Actor (Borgnine); New York Film Critics Awards '55: Best Actor (Borgnine), Best Film; Nominations: Academy Awards '55: Best Art Direction/Set Decoration (B & W), Best Black and White Cinematography, Best Supporting Actor (Mantell), Best Supporting Actress (Blair). *MGM, FOX, BTV*

Marvelous Stunts of Kung Fu 🎬 1983

Beautiful woman, fortune teller, and martial arts hero team up to seek vengeance against the evil empire. **86m/C VHS, Beta.** Ling Yun, Wei Ping Line, Lung Fei. *TWE*

Marvin & Tige 🎬🎬½ 1984 (PG)

A deep friendship develops between an aging alcoholic and a street-wise 11-year-old boy after they meet one night in an Atlanta park. **104m/C VHS, Beta.** John Cassavetes, Gibran Brown, Billy Dee Williams, Fay Hauser, Denise Nicholas-Hill; **D:** Eric Weston; **W:** Eric Weston, Wanda Dell.

Marvin's Room 🎬🎬½ 1996 (PG-13)

Guaranteed sobfest with a gifted set of performers. Sensitive spinster Bessie (Keaton) is living in Orlando where she's been caring for her bedridden father, Marvin (Cronyn), who's been dying for the last 20 years, and her eccentric aunt Ruth (Verdon). When she's stricken with leukemia and needs a bone marrow donor, Bessie must rely on tough, estranged sister Lee (Streep) to help out. But divorcee Lee's got her hands full with rebellious teenaged son Hank (DiCaprio) and his geeky younger bro Charlie (Scardino) and is none too eager to renew the family ties. Based on Scott McPherson's 1991 Off-Broadway play. **CW:** Thematic elements and brief language. **98m/C VHS, LV, Closed Caption.** Diane Keaton, Meryl Streep, Leonardo DiCaprio, Hume Cronyn, Gwen Verdon, Hal Scardino, Robert De Niro, Dan Hedaya, Margo Martindale, Cynthia Nixon; **D:** Jerry Zaks; **W:** Scott McPherson; **M:** Rachel Portman. Nominations: Academy Awards '96: Best Actress (Keaton); Golden Globe Awards '97: Best Actress—Drama (Streep); Screen Actors Guild Award '96: Best Actress (Keaton), Best Supporting Actress (Verdon), Cast. *TOU*

The Marx Brothers in a Nutshell 🎬🎬🎬½ 1990

A tribute to the Marx Brothers, narrated by Gene Kelly. Contains clips from "Duck Soup," "Horse Feathers," "Animal Crackers," "Cocoanuts," and "Room Service." Also contains rare outakes and interviews with the brothers, plus guest appearances by Dick Cavett, Robert Klein, David Steinberg, and others. Indispensible. **100m/B VHS, LV.** Groucho Marx, Chico Marx, Harpo Marx, Zeppo Marx, Robert Klein, David Steinberg, George Fenneman, Dick Cavett. *FCT*

Mary and Joseph: A Story of Faith ✻✻½ 1979
A speculative look at the experiences and courtship of Mary and Joseph before the birth of Jesus. Made for television. **100m/C VHS, Beta.** Blanche Baker, Jeff East, Colleen Dewhurst, Stephen McHattie, Lloyd Bochner, Paul Hecht; **D:** Eric Till. *LIV, WAR*

Mary, Mary, Bloody Mary ✻ 1976 (R)
Young beautiful artist ravages Mexico with her penchant for drinking blood. Turns out she's a bisexual vampire. When even her friends become victims, her father steps in to end the bloodbath. **85m/C VHS, Beta.** Christina Ferrare, David Young, Helena Rojo, John Carradine; **D:** Juan Lopez Moctezuma; **M:** Tom Bahler. *NO*

Mary of Scotland ✻✻✻ 1936
The historical tragedy of Mary, Queen of Scots and her cousin, Queen Elizabeth I of England is enacted in this classic film. Traces Mary's claims to the throne of England which ultimately led to her execution. Based on the Maxwell Anderson play. **123m/B VHS, Beta, LV.** Katharine Hepburn, Fredric March, Florence Eldridge, Douglas Walton, John Carradine, Robert Barrat, Gavin Muir, Ian Keith, Moroni Olsen, William Stack, Alan Mowbray; **D:** John Ford. *TTC*

Mary Poppins ✻✻✻½ 1964
Magical English nanny arrives one day on the East Wind and takes over the household of a very proper London banker. She introduces her two charges to her friends and family, including Bert, the chimney sweep (Van Dyke), and eccentric Uncle Albert (Wynn). She also changes the lives of everyone in the family. From her they learn that life can always be happy and joyous if you take the proper perspective. Film debut of Andrews. Based on the books by P.L. Travers. A Disney classic that hasn't lost any of its magic. Look for the wonderful sequence where Van Dyke dances with animated penguins. ♫Chim Chim Cheree; A Spoonful of Sugar; The Perfect Nanny; Sister Suffragette; The Life I Lead; Stay Awake; Feed the Birds; Fidelity Feduciary Bank; Let's Go Fly a Kite. **139m/C VHS, Beta, LV, Closed Caption.** Ed Wynn, Hermione Baddeley, Julie Andrews, Dick Van Dyke, David Tomlinson, Glynis Johns; **D:** Robert Stevenson; **C:** Edward Colman. Academy Awards '64: Best Actress (Andrews), Best Film Editing, Best Song ("Chim Chim Cher-ee"), Best Visual Effects, Best Original Score; Golden Globe Awards '65: Best Actress—Musical/Comedy (Andrews); Nominations: Academy Awards '64: Best Adapted Screenplay, Best Art Direction/Set Decoration (Color), Best Color Cinematography, Best Costume Design (Color), Best Director (Stevenson), Best Picture, Best Sound, Best Original Score. *DIS, APD, BTV*

Mary Reilly ✻✻ 1995 (R)
Mary (Roberts) is an innocent maid whose employer happens to be the infamous Dr. Jekyll (Malkovich). They both seem to be employed by Dr. Freud in this dank, dreary psychosexual thriller. Mary is torn between the repressed affection of the doctor and the oily sexuality of his alter ego, who conjures up images of her abusive father. Reuniting the crew and some of the cast of "Dangerous Liaisons" (Glenn Close appears as a bawdy brothel owner), they fail to reach their previous heights. Most of the gloomy sets will make you wish you were wearing galoshes. Release date was bumped several times as the ending of the film was reshot (more than once). Based on the novel by Valerie Martin.**CW:** Notable gore and some strong violence. **108m/C VHS, LV, Closed Caption.** Julia Roberts, John Malkovich, George Cole, Michael Gambon, Kathy Staff, Glenn Close, Michael Sheen, Bronagh Gallagher, Linda Bassett, Henry Goodman, Ciaran Hinds, Sasha Hanav; **D:** Stephen Frears; **W:** Christopher Hampton; **C:** Philippe Rousselot; **M:** George Fenton. Nominations: Golden Raspberry Awards '96: Worst Actress (Roberts), Worst Director (Frears). *COL*

Mary Shelley's Frankenstein ✻✻½ 1994 (R)
Frankenstein Branagh turns from Shakespeare to another form of literary classic with his operatic (and loose) adaptation of the Shelley novel. He also plays Victor, the overwrought medical student who decides that death can be vanquished and sets out to prove his theories by making a man. De Niro is sufficently grisly (though lacking in pathos) as the reanimated corpse with Bonham Carter alternately suffering and excitable as Victor's fiancee Elizabeth. Visually arresting—particularly the Creature's birth scene—pic doesn't engender audience sympathy for the characters' trials and final fates.**CW:** Horrific images; violence; gore. **123m/C VHS, LV, 8mm, Closed Caption.** Kenneth Branagh, Robert De Niro, Helena Bonham Carter, Tom Hulce, Aidan Quinn, John Cleese, Ian Holm, Robert Hardy, Cherie Lunghi, Celia Imrie, Trevyn McDowell; **D:** Kenneth Branagh; **W:** Frank Darabont, Steph Lady; **M:** Patrick Doyle. Nominations: Academy Awards '94: Best Makeup. *COL*

Mary White ✻✻ 1977
The true story of Mary White, the sixteen-year-old daughter of a newspaper editor who rejects her life of wealth and sets out to find her own identity. **102m/C VHS, Beta.** Ed Flanders, Kathleen Beller, Tim Matheson, Donald Moffat, Fionnula Flanagan; **D:** Jud Taylor; **C:** Bill Butler. *PAR*

Masada ✻✻✻ 1981
Based on Ernest K. Gann's novel "The Antagonists," this dramatization recreates the first-century A.D. Roman siege of the fortress Masada, headquarters for a group of Jewish freedom fighters. Abridged from the original television presentation. **131m/C VHS, Beta.** Peter O'Toole, Peter Strauss, Barbara Carrera, Anthony Quayle, Giulia Pagano, David Warner; **D:** Boris Sagal; **M:** Jerry Goldsmith. *USH*

Masala ✻✻ 1991
An experiment in a variety of genres, including glitzy musical-comedy numbers, erotic fantasy sequences, and all manner of kitsch. Krishna (who both stars and directs in his feature film debut) is a violence-prone, ex-junkie still trying to recover from the deaths of his family in a plane crash as they travelled from Toronto to a vacation in India. Jaffrey has multi-roles as Krishna's unscrupulous uncle and cousin as well as the blue-skinned Indian deity, Lord Krishna, who appears to an Indian grandmother on her television set. Multicultural confusion. **105m/C VHS.** CA Srinivas Krishna, Saeed Jaffrey, Zohra Segal, Sakina Jaffrey; **D:** Srinivas Krishna; **W:** Srinivas Krishna. *FXL, FCT*

Mascara ✻✻ 1987 (R)
A group inspecting a transvestite's death are led into the seedy underground world of Belgian nightlife. **99m/C VHS, Beta, Closed Caption.** BE Derek De Lint, Charlotte Rampling, Michael Sarrazin; **D:** Patrick Conrad. *WAR*

Masculine Feminine ✻✻✻½ 1966
Masculin Feminin A young Parisian just out of the Army engages in some anarchistic activities when he has an affair with a radical woman singer. Hailed as one of the best French New Wave films. In French with English subtitles. **103m/B VHS, Beta.** FR Jean-Pierre Leaud, Chantal Goya, Marlene Jobert; **D:** Jean-Luc Godard. Berlin International Film Festival '66: Best Actor (Leaud). *NYF, DVT, VDM*

M*A*S*H ✻✻✻✻ 1970 (R)
Hilarious, irreverent, and well-cast black comedy about a group of surgeons and nurses at a Mobile Army Surgical Hospital in Korea. The horror of war is set in counterpoint to their need to create havoc with episodic late-night parties, practical jokes, and sexual antics. An all-out anti-war festival, highlighted by scenes that starkly uncover the chaos and irony of war, and establish Altman's influential style. Watch for real-life football players Fran Tarkenton, Ben Davidson, and Buck Buchanan in the game. Loosely adapted from the novel by the pseudonymous Richard Hooker (Dr. H. Richard Hornberger and William Heinz). Subsequent hit TV series moved even further from the source novel. **116m/C VHS, Beta, LV.** Donald Sutherland, Elliott Gould, Tom Skerritt, Sally Kellerman, JoAnn Pflug, Robert Duvall, Rene Auberjonois, Roger Bowen, Gary Burghoff, Fred Williamson, John Schuck, Bud Cort, G. Wood; **D:** Robert Altman; **W:** Ring Lardner Jr.; **M:** Johnny Mandel. Academy Awards '70: Best Adapted Screenplay; Cannes Film Festival '70: Best Film; Golden Globe Awards '71: Best Film—Musical/Comedy; National Society of Film Critics Awards '70: Best Film; Writers Guild of America '70: Best Adapted Screenplay; Nominations: Academy Awards '70: Best Director (Altman), Best Film Editing, Best Picture, Best Supporting Actress (Kellerman). *FOX*

M*A*S*H: Goodbye, Farewell & Amen ✻✻✻½ 1983
The final two-hour special episode of the television series "M*A*S*H" follows Hawkeye, B.J., Colonel Potter, Charles, Margaret, Klinger, Father Mulcahy, and the rest of the men and women of the 4077th through the last days of the Korean War, the declaration of peace, the dismantling of the camp, and the fond and tearful farewells. **120m/C VHS, Beta, LV.** Alan Alda, Mike Farrell, Harry (Henry) Morgan, David Ogden Stiers, Loretta Swit, Jamie Farr, William Christopher, Allan Arbus. *FOX, OM*

M*A*S*H: The Collector's Edition 1972
Join Hawkeye, Trapper John, Radar, Klinger, and the rest of the loonies of the 4077th Mobile Army Surgical Hospital, located three miles from the frontline of the Korean conflict, as they battle military regulations (and sometimes each other). Three episodes per cassette from the television series which lasted 11 seasons. Additional episodes available. **?m/C VHS.** Alan Alda, Wayne Rogers, McLean Stevenson, Gary Burghoff, Loretta Swit, Larry Linville, Jamie Farr, William Christopher. *CMB*

The Mask ✻✻ 1961
Eyes of Hell; The Spooky Movie Show A deservedly obscure gory horror film about a masked killer, filmed mostly in 3-D. With special 3-D packaging and limited edition 3-D glasses. **85m/B VHS, Beta, LV.** CA Paul Stevens, Claudette Nevins, Bill Walker, Anne Collings, Martin Lavut; **D:** Julian Roffman. *RHI, MLB*

Mask ✻✻✻ 1985 (PG-13)
A dramatization of the true story of a young boy afflicted with craniodiaphyseal dysplasia (elephantiasis). The boy overcomes his appearance and revels in the joys of life in the California bikers' community. Well acted, particularly the performances of Stoltz and Cher. A touching film, well-directed by Bogdanovich, that only occasionally slips into maudlin territory. **120m/C VHS, Beta, LV, Closed Caption, DVD.** Cher, Sam Elliott, Eric Stoltz, Estelle Getty, Richard Dysart, Laura Dern, Harry Carey Jr., Lawrence Monoson, Marsha Warfield, Barry Tubb, Andrew (Andy) Robinson, Alexandra Powers; **D:** Peter Bogdanovich; **W:** Anna Hamilton Phelan. Academy Awards '85: Best Makeup; Cannes Film Festival '85: Best Actress (Cher). *USH*

The Mask ✻✻✻ 1994 (PG-13)
Adolescent supernatural comedy with lollapalooza special effects is Carrey's follow-up to "Ace Ventura." Mild-mannered bank clerk Carrey discovers an ancient mask that has supernatural powers. Upon putting on the mask, he turns into one truly animated guy. He falls for a dame mixed up with gangsters and from there on, our hero deals not only with the incredible powers of the mask, but with hormones and bad guys as well. Based on the Dark Horse comic book series and originally conceived as a horror flick, director Russell, who gave Freddy Krueger a sense of humor, recast this one as a hellzapoppin' cartoon-action black comedy. Carrey's rubber face is an asset magnified by the breakthrough special effects courtesy of Industrial Light and Magic.**CW:** Some stylized violence. **100m/C VHS, Closed Caption.** Jim Carrey, Cameron Diaz, Peter Greene, Peter Riegert, Amy Yasbeck, Orestes Matacena, Richard Jeni; **D:** Chuck Russell; **W:** Mike Werb; **M:** Randy Edelman. Blockbuster Entertainment Awards '95: Comedy Actor, Theatrical (Carrey), Female Newcomer, Theatrical (Diaz); Blockbuster Entertainment Awards '96: Comedy Actor, Video (Carrey); Nominations: Academy Awards '94: Best Visual Effects; Golden Globe Awards '95: Best Actor—Musical/Comedy (Carrey); MTV Movie Awards '95: Breakthrough Performance (Diaz), Most Desirable Female (Diaz), Best Comedic Performance (Carrey), Best Dance Sequence (Jim Carrey/Cameron Diaz). *NLC*

Mask of Death ✻✻ 1997 (R)
Detective Dan McKenna's (Lamas) wife is killed by Frank Dallio (Dunn) during the criminal's escape from the FBI and he's shot in the face by Dallio's buddy Mason, who happens to be a ringer for McKenna

and conveniently dies in a car crash. Since the FBI want Dallio, Agent Jeffries (Williams) persuades McKenna to pose as Mason, which he does in order to get revenge. **125m/C VHS, LV, Closed Caption.** Lorenzo Lamas, Billy Dee Williams, Rae Dawn Chong, Conrad Dunn. *TOU*

The Mask of Dijon *♪♪½* 1946
A mad magician suspects that his wife is cheating on him and tries to hypnotize her into killing her supposed paramour. The plan goes awry when the wife uses a gun loaded with blanks. Von Stroheim's performance makes it worthwhile. **73m/B VHS.** Erich von Stroheim, Jeanne Bates, William Wright, Edward Van Sloan, Denise Vernac; *D:* Lew (Louis Friedlander) Landers. *NOS*

The Mask of Fu Manchu *♪♪½* 1932
The evil Dr. Fu Manchu and his equally evil daughter set out to capture the scimitar and golden mask of Genghis Khan. With them, they will be able to destroy all white men and rule the world. Although a detective from Scotland Yard tries to stop them, the pair obtain the treasures and begin sadistically torturing their victims to death. Can they be stopped before they destroy the earth? One of the creepiest entries in the Fu Manchu series, and Loy's last oriental role. Based on the novel by Sam Rohmer. **72m/B VHS.** Boris Karloff, Lewis Stone, Karen Morley, Charles Starrett, Myrna Loy, Jean Hersholt, Lawrence Grant, David Torrence; *D:* Charles Brabin; *C:* Gaetano Antonio "Tony" Gaudio. *MGM*

Mask of the Dragon *♪* 1951
A soldier's friend and girlfriend track down his killer after he delivers a golden curio to a shop in Los Angeles. **54m/B VHS, Beta, LV.** Richard Travis, Sheila Ryan, Richard Emory, Jack Reitzen. *NO*

The Masked Marvel *Sakima and the Masked Marvel* 1943
The Masked Marvel saves America's war industries from sabotage. Serial in twelve episodes. **195m/B VHS.** William Forrest, Louise Currie, Johnny Arthur; *D:* Spencer Gordon Bennet. *VCN, REP, MLB*

The Masked Rider *♪♪½* 1941
Drifters Brown and Knight head south of the border and find themselves trying to solve crimes committed by a mysterious masked rider. Latin American dancers and singers provide a nice change of pace from the usual cowpoke musical relief. Based on a story by Sam Robins. **57m/B VHS.** Johnny Mack Brown, Fuzzy Knight, Nell O'Day, Grant Withers; *D:* Ford Beebe; *W:* Sherman Lowe, Victor McLeod. *MOV*

Masks of Death *♪♪* 1986
New adventure for Sherlock Holmes, as he is pulled from retirement to find the murderer of three unidentified corpses found in London's East End. **80m/C VHS, Beta, LV.** Peter Cushing, John Mills, Anne Baxter, Ray Milland; *D:* Roy Ward Baker. *ORI, IME, WAR*

Mason of the Mounted *♪* 1932
Harmless enough western in which a Canadian Mountie tracks down a murderer in the U.S. **58m/B VHS.** Bill Cody, Nancy Drexel, Art Mix, Nelson McDowell; *D:* Harry Fraser. *NOS, DVT, HEG*

Masque of the Red Death *♪♪♪* 1965
An integral selection in the famous Edgar Allan Poe/Roger Corman canon, it deals with an evil prince who traffics with the devil and playfully murders any of his subjects not already dead of the plague. Photographed by Nicholas Roeg. Remade in 1989 with Corman as producer. **88m/C VHS, Beta.** *GB* Vincent Price, Hazel Court, Jane Asher, Patrick Magee; *D:* Roger Corman. *ORI, LIV, MLB*

Masque of the Red Death *♪♪* 1989
(R) Roger Corman's second attempt at Edgar Allan Poe's horror tale pales compared to his Vincent Price version made 25 years earlier. Underaged cast adds youth appeal but subtracts credibility from the fable of a sadistic prince and his sycophants trying to ignore the plague outside castle walls. Only late in the plot does veteran actor Macnee add proper note of doom. **90m/C VHS, Beta, LV.** Patrick Macnee, Jeffery Osterhage, Adrian Paul, Tracy Reiner, Maria Ford; *D:* Larry Brand; *W:* Larry Brand, Daryl Haney. *MGM, IME*

Masque of the Red Death *♪♪½* 1990
(R) Unrecognizable Poe mutation has guests invited to the mansion of a dying millionaire, only to be murdered by an unknown stalker. One scene features a pendulum, and that's it for literary faithfulness. **94m/C VHS, LV.** Frank Stallone, Brenda Vaccaro, Herbert Lom, Michelle McBride, Christine Lunde; *D:* Alan Birkinshaw. *COL*

Masque of the Red Death/Premature Burial 1965
Double feature of horror classics adapted from Edgar Allan Poe's work. Price stars in "Masque of the Red Death" as a satan worshipper. Millard plays a man obsessed with the fear of catastrophe in "Premature Burial." **175m/C VHS, LV.** Vincent Price, Hazel Court, Jane Asher, Patrick Magee, Nigel Green, Ray Milland; *D:* Roger Corman. *IME*

Masquerade *♪♪♪* 1988
(R) A lonely young heiress meets a handsome "nobody" with a mysterious background and it is love at first sight. The romance distresses everyone in the circle of the elite because they assume that he is after her money and not her love. At first it seems decidedly so, then definitely not, and then nothing is certain. A real romantic thriller, with wonderful scenes of the Hamptons. *CW:* Strong sexuality. **91m/C VHS, Beta, LV, Closed Caption.** Rob Lowe, Meg Tilly, John Glover, Kim Cattrall, Doug Savant, Dana Delany, Eric Holland; *D:* Bob Swaim; *W:* Dick Wolf; *C:* David Watkin; *M:* John Barry. *FOX*

Mass Appeal *♪♪* 1984
(PG) An adaptation of the Bill C. Davis play about the ideological debate between a young seminarian and a complacent but successful parish pastor. Lemmon has had better roles and done better acting. **99m/C VHS, Beta, LV, Closed Caption.** Jack Lemmon, Zeljko Ivanek, Charles Durning, Louise Latham, James Ray, Sharee Gregory, Talia Balsam; *D:* Glenn Jordan; *W:* Bill Davis; *M:* Bill Conti. *USH*

Massacre at Central High *♪♪½* 1976
(R) A new student takes matters into his own hands when gang members harass other students at a local high school. Other than some silly dialogue, this low-budget production is above average. **85m/C VHS.** Derrel Maury, Andrew Stevens, Kimberly Beck, Robert Carradine, Roy Underwood, Steve Bond; *D:* Renee Daalder; *W:* Renee Daalder. *MPI*

Massacre in Dinosaur Valley *♪½* 1985
A dashing young paleontologist and his fellow explorers go on a perilous journey down the Amazon in search of the Valley of the Dinosaur. **98m/C VHS, Beta.** Michael Sopkiw, Suzanne Carvall. *LIV*

Massacre in Rome *♪♪½* 1973
(PG) A priest opposes a Nazi colonel's plan to execute Italian civilians in retaliation for the deaths of 33 German soldiers. Strong drama based on a real event. **110m/C VHS, Beta.** Richard Burton, Marcello Mastroianni, Leo McKern, John Steiner, Anthony Steel; *D:* George P. Cosmatos; *W:* George P. Cosmatos; *M:* Ennio Morricone. *NO*

Masseuse *♪* 1995
(R) Kristy (Drew) decides to get back at cheating fiance Jack (Abell), who's out of town on a business trip, by turning their house into a massage parlor. *CW:* Language, nudity, sexual situations. **90m/C VHS.** Griffin Drew, Monique Parent, Tim Abell; *D:* Daniel Peters. *TRI*

Massive Retaliation *♪* 1985
Hordes of pesky villagers seek refuge within the secluded safety of a family's country house as WWIII approaches. **90m/C VHS.** Tom Bower, Peter Donat, Karlene Crockett, Jason Gedrick, Michael Pritchard; *D:* Thomas A. Cohen. *LIV, VES*

Master Blaster *♪½* 1985
(R) Friendly game of survival with paintball guns goes awry when one of the contestants exchanges the play guns for deadly weapons. **94m/C VHS.** Jeff Moldovan, Donna Rosae, Joe Hess, Peter Lunblad; *D:* Glenn Wilder. *MVD, PSM*

Master Harold and the Boys *♪♪♪* 1984
Stagey cable presentation of South African Athol Fugard's play about relationship between white man and two black servants. Occasionally

provocative. **90m/C VHS, Beta.** Matthew Broderick; *D:* Michael Lindsay-Hogg. *ORI, WAR*

Master Key *♪½* 1944
Federal agents battle Nazis in this action-packed 12-chapter serial. **169m/B VHS, Beta.** Jan Wiley, Milburn Stone, Lash LaRue, Dennis Moore; *D:* Ray Taylor, Lewis D. Collins. *NOS, DVT, MLB*

Master Killer *♪* *The Thirty-Sixth Chamber* 1984
(R) Master Killers are made, not born. Liu trains as he readies himself for an attack on the brutal Manchu assassins. **109m/C VHS, Beta.** Liu Chia Hui; *D:* Liu Chia Liang. *FXL*

Master Mind *♪♪* 1973
A renowned Japanese super sleuth attempts to solve the theft of a sophisticated midget android. **86m/C VHS, Beta.** Zero Mostel, Keiko Kishi, Bradford Dillman, Herbert Berghof, Frankie Sakai; *D:* Alex March. *UNI*

Master Minds *♪½* 1949
The Bowery Boys run into trouble when Hall gets a toothache and can suddenly predict the future. He takes a job at a carnival where a mad scientist wants to transplant his brain into that of a monster ape man. **64m/B VHS.** Leo Gorcey, Huntz Hall, Glenn Strange, Gabriel Dell, Alan Napier, Billy Benedict, Bennie Bartlett, David Gorcey; *D:* Jean Yarbrough. *GPV*

Master Ninja *♪½* *The Master* 1978
First in the continuing adventures of the Master and Max (Van Cleef and Van Patten) follow the pair across the US in their search for the Master's long-lost daughter. They're pursued by Kosugi. Originally filmed for television; each tape includes two programs. **93m/C VHS, Beta.** Lee Van Cleef, Sho Kosugi, Timothy Van Patten. *QVD, TWE*

The Master of Ballantrae *♪♪* 1953
Flynn plays James Durrisdear, the heir to a Scottish title, who gets involved in a rebellion with Bonnie Prince Charlie against the English crown. When the rebellion fails, Flynn heads for the West Indies where he and his partner amass quite a fortune through piracy. Flynn eventually returns to Scotland where he finds that his brother has taken over his title as well as his longtime love. Based on the novel by Robert Louis Stevenson. Flynn's riotous life had put him long past his peak swashbuckling days, as this film unfortunately demonstrates. **89m/C VHS, Beta, LV.** Errol Flynn, Roger Livesey, Anthony Steel, Beatrice Campbell, Yvonne Furneaux, Jacques Berthier, Felix Aylmer, Mervyn Johns; *D:* William Keighley; *C:* Jack Cardiff. *WAR*

Master of Dragonard Hill *♪½* 1989
A low-rent swashbuckling romance-novel pastiche. **92m/C VHS, Beta.** Oliver Reed, Eartha Kitt; *W:* R.J. Marx. *MED*

Master of Kung Fu *♪* 1977
A Kung Fu instructor calls upon his former teacher to help him fend off loan sharks who want to take over his school. **88m/C VHS, Beta.** Yu Chan Yuan, Chi Hsiao Fu. *FOX*

Master of the House *♪♪♪* *Thou Shalt Honour Thy Wife* 1925
Story of a spoiled husband, a type extinct in this country but still in existence abroad. Silent with titles in English. **118m/B VHS, Beta.** *D:* Carl Theodor Dreyer. *VYY, FCT*

Master of the World *♪♪½* 1961
Visionary tale of a fanatical 19th century inventor who uses his wonderous flying fortress as an antiwar weapon. Adapted from "Robur, the Conqueror" and "Master of the World," both by Jules Verne. **95m/C VHS, Beta.** Vincent Price, Charles Bronson, Henry Hull; *D:* William Witney; *W:* Richard Matheson; *M:* Les Baxter. *ORI, WAR*

Master Race *♪♪½* 1944
Absorbing cautionary tale of a German officer who escapes retribution when the Nazis collapse, continuing to hold control over the inhabitants of a small town through intimidation. **98m/B VHS, Beta.** George Coulouris, Lloyd Bridges, Osa Massen, Nancy Gates, Stanley Ridges; *D:* Herbert Biberman; *C:* Russell Metty. *TTC*

Master Touch ⚔️½ *Hearts and Minds; Un Uomo da Rispettare* 1974 **(PG)** When a legendary safecracker is released from prison, he attempts one last heist at a Hamburg insurance company. 96m/C VHS, Beta. **GE IT** Kirk Douglas, Florinda Bolkan, Giuliano Gemma; **D:** Michele Lupo; **M:** Ennio Morricone. **PSM**

The Masters of Menace ⚔️½ 1990 **(PG-13)** The men in blue are mighty miffed when a bunch of bikers break parole to pay their last respects to a comrade in leather. Comic bits by Candy, Belushi, Aykroyd and Wendt provide little relief. 97m/C VHS, LV. David Rasche, Catherine Bach, Dan Aykroyd, James Belushi, John Candy, George Wendt, Tino Insana; **D:** Daniel Raskov; **W:** Tino Insana. **COL**

Masters of the Universe ⚔️⚔️ 1987 **(PG)** A big-budget live-action version of the cartoon character's adventures, with He-Man battling Skeletor for the sake of the universe. 109m/C VHS, Beta, LV, Closed Caption. Dolph Lundgren, Frank Langella, Billy Barty, Courteney Cox, Meg Foster; **D:** Gary Goddard; **C:** Hanania Baer; **M:** Bill Conti. **WAR**

Masters of Venus ⚔️½ 1959 Eight-part serial about spaceships, space maidens and the like. 121m/B VHS, Beta. Ferdinand "Ferdy" Mayne. **SNC, VDM**

Master's Revenge ⚔️½ 1971 When a girl is kidnapped by a violent motorcycle gang, martial artists are called in to rescue her. Originally released as "Devil Rider." 78m/C VHS. Sharon Mahon, Ridgely Abele, Johnny Pachivas. **ACA**

Mata Hari ⚔️⚔️⚔️ 1932 During WWI, a lovely German spy steals secrets from the French through her involvement with two military officers. Lavish production and exquisite direction truly make this one of Garbo's best. Watch for her exotic pseudo-strip tease. 90m/B VHS. Greta Garbo, Ramon Novarro, Lionel Barrymore, Lewis Stone, C. Henry Gordon, Karen Morley, Alec B. Francis; **D:** George Fitzmaurice; **C:** William H. Daniels. **MGM, FCT**

Mata Hari ⚔️⚔️ 1985 **(R)** Racy, adventure-prone story of WWI's most notorious spy, Mata Hari, who uses her seductive beauty to seduce the leaders of Europe. Stars "Emmanuelle" Kristel. 105m/C VHS, Beta. Sylvia Kristel, Christopher Cazenove, Oliver Tobias, Gaye Brown, Gottfried John; **D:** Curtis Cunningham. **MGM**

Matador ⚔️⚔️½ 1986 Bizarre, entertaining black comedy about a retired matador who finds a new way to satiate his desire to kill. He meets his match in an equally deadly woman and the two are drawn closer together by a young bullfighting student who confesses to a series of murders. Not for all tastes, but fine for those who like the outrageous. In Spanish with English subtitles. 90m/C VHS, Beta, LV. **SP** Assumpta Serna, Antonio Banderas, Nacho Martinez, Eva Cobo, Carmen Maura, Julieta Serrano, Chus Lampreave, Eusebio Poncela; **D:** Pedro Almodovar; **W:** Pedro Almodovar, Jesus Ferrere; **M:** Bernardo Bonazzi. **CCN, TPV**

The Match Factory Girl ⚔️⚔️⚔️ *Tulitkkutehtaan Tytto* 1990 Kaurismak's final segment of his "working class" trilogy. Iris, a plain, shy outsider shares a drab dwelling with her one-dimensional mother and stepfather, works in a match factory, and hopes desperately for romantic love. Her world is transformed when the extraordinary occurs—she spots a brightly colored party dress in a shop window, buys it, wears it to a bar, and meets the Scandinavian creep who will soon get her pregnant and dump her. Angry at the world, Iris seeks revenge, and in so doing the audience learns that she has become very real and human. Kaurismaki makes his point that beauty can exist in ugly places. In Finnish with English subtitles. 70m/C VHS. **SW FI** Kati Outinen, Elina Salo, Esko Nikkari, Vesa Vierikko; **D:** Aki Kaurismaki; **W:** Aki Kaurismaki. **KIV, BTV, FCT**

The Matchmaker ⚔️⚔️ 1958 An adaptation of the Thornton Wilder play concerning two young men in search of romance in 1884 New York. Later adapted as "Hello Dolly." An amusing diversion. 101m/B VHS, Beta, LV, Closed Caption. Shirley Booth, Anthony Perkins, Shirley MacLaine, Paul Ford, Robert Morse, Perry Wilson, Wallace Ford, Russell Collins, Rex Evans, Gavin Gordon, Torben Meyer; **D:** Joseph Anthony; **W:** John Michael Hayes; **C:** Charles B(ryant) Lang. **PAR, FCT**

Maternal Instincts ⚔️⚔️½ 1996 **(PG-13)** Tracy (Burke) is a childless woman who undergoes an emergency hysterectomy without her consent. But she badly wants a baby and decides to get revenge on anyone thwarting her plans. Made for cable.**CW:** Some violent content. 92m/C VHS, Beta, Closed Caption. Delta Burke, Beth Broderick, Garwin Sanford, Sandra Nelson, Gillian Barber, Kevin McNulty, Tom Butler, Tom Mason; **D:** George Kaczender. **PAR**

Matewan ⚔️⚔️⚔️½ 1987 **(PG-13)** An acclaimed dramatization of the famous Matewan massacre in the 1920s, in which coal miners in West Virginia, reluctantly influenced by a young union organizer, rebelled against terrible working conditions. Complex and imbued with myth, the film is a gritty, moving, powerful drama with typically superb Sayles dialogue and Haskell Wexler's beautiful and poetic cinematography. Jones delivers an economical yet intense portrayal of the black leader of the miners. The director makes his usual on-screen appearance, this time as an establishment-backed reactionary minister. Partially based on the Sayles novel "Union Dues." 130m/C VHS, Beta, LV, Closed Caption. Chris Cooper, James Earl Jones, Mary McDonnell, William Oldham, Kevin Tighe, David Strathairn, Jace Alexander, Gordon Clapp, Mason Daring, Joe Grifasi, Bob Gunton, Jo Henderson, Jason Jenkins, Ken Jenkins, Nancy Mette, Josh Mostel, Michael B. Preston, Maggie Renzi, Frank Hoyt Taylor, Tom Wright; **Cameos:** John Sayles; **D:** John Sayles; **W:** John Sayles; **C:** Haskell Wexler; **M:** Mason Daring. Independent Spirit Awards '88: Best Cinematography; Nominations: Academy Awards '87: Best Cinematography. **ORI, WAR**

Matilda ⚔️⚔️ 1978 **(PG)** Family fare about a entrepreneur who decides to manage a boxing kangaroo, which nearly succeeds in defeating the world heavyweight champion. Uneven and occasionally engaging. Based on Paul Gallico's novel. 103m/C VHS, Beta. Elliott Gould, Robert Mitchum, Harry Guardino, Clive Revill; **D:** Daniel Mann. **LIV, VES**

Matilda ⚔️⚔️⚔️ 1996 **(PG)** Intelligent child Matilda Wormwood (Wilson) is oppressed by both her monstrous parents (DeVito and Perlman) and awful school principal, Trunchbull (Ferris). However, her first grade teacher, appropriately-named Miss Honey (Davidtz), believes in her, which is enough to make Matilda plot an appropriate fate for the miserable people in her life. Excellent adaptation of a typically subversive book by Roald Dahl. Director DeVito, who wanted to create the illusion of a live-action cartoon, built among other things a "Carrot-cam" to capture the flying food of a food fight. 93m/C VHS, LV, Closed Caption, DVD. Mara Wilson, Danny DeVito, Rhea Perlman, Embeth Davidtz, Pam Ferris, Paul (Pee Wee Herman) Reubens, Tracey Walter; **D:** Danny DeVito; **W:** Robin Swicord, Nicholas Kazan; **C:** Stefan Czapsky; **M:** David Newman. **COL**

Matinee ⚔️⚔️½ 1992 **(PG)** "MANT: Half-man, Half-ant, All Terror!" screams from the movie marquee after Lawrence Woolsey, promoter extraordinaire, and Ruth Corday, his leading lady, roll into Key West circa 1962. Meanwhile, teen Gene Loomis listens to his health teacher push the benefits of red meat and his girlfriend question life, while worrying about his dad, stationed in Cuba. Builds sly parallels between real life and movie horror by juxtaposing Woolsey (modeled after B-movie king William Castle) hyping his schlock, shown in "Atomo-Vision," against JFK solemnly announcing the Russian's approach. Fun, nostalgic look at days gone by—and the matinees that died with them. 98m/C VHS, Beta, LV, Closed Caption. John Goodman, Cathy Moriarty, Simon Fenton, Omri Katz, Lisa Jakub, Kellie Martin, Jesse Lee, Lucinda Jenney, James Villemaire, Robert Picardo, Dick Miller, John Sayles, Mark McCracken,

Jesse White, David Clennon, Luke Halpin; **D:** Joe Dante; **M:** Jerry Goldsmith. **USH, BTV**

The Mating Game ⚔️⚔️⚔️ 1959 A fast-paced comedy about a tax collector, a beautiful girl, and a wily farm couple. Randall is the strait-laced IRS agent who finds out that the farming Larkins have never paid taxes and use a complicated barter system to get along. Randall falls for farm daughter Reynolds, gets drunk with her Pa, and decides to help the family out of their government dilemma—to the dismay of his superiors. Randall has a terrific drunk scene among his many comedic capers and Reynolds is a highlight. 96m/C VHS. Tony Randall, Debbie Reynolds, Paul Douglas, Una Merkel, Fred Clark, Philip Ober, Charles Lane; **D:** George Marshall; **W:** William Roberts. **MGM**

Mating Season ⚔️⚔️ 1981 Successful female attorney Arnaz meets good-natured laundromat owner Luckinbill at a bird-watching retreat. Romance ensues. Made for television. 96m/C VHS, Beta. Lucie Arnaz, Laurence Luckinbill; **D:** John Llewellyn Moxey. **LCA**

Matrimaniac ⚔️⚔️ 1916 A man goes to great lengths to marry a woman against her father's wishes. Silent with music score. 48m/B VHS, Beta. Douglas Fairbanks Sr., Constance Talmadge. **VYY, GPV**

A Matter of Degrees ⚔️⚔️ 1990 **(R)** Weeks before his graduation, a beatnik-type college senior finally acquires a goal: romancing a mystery girl...or maybe saving the student radio station...or not. The hero's aimlessness permeates the script, which never goes anywhere in its exploration of campus ennui. Good photography and a great stratum of alternative music groups on the soundtrack: Dream Syndicate, Pere Ubu, Schooly D, Pixies, Poi Dog Pondering, Minutemen, and Throwing Muses.**CW:** Language. 89m/C VHS, Beta. Arye Gross, Judith Hoag, Tom Sizemore, John Doe; **Cameos:** John F. Kennedy Jr., Fred Schneider, Kate Pierson; **D:** W.T. Morgan. **PSM**

A Matter of Dignity ⚔️⚔️ 1957 Young girl, forced into marriage with millionaire, eventually brings ruin to the entire family. Why? In Greek with English subtitles. 104m/B VHS, Beta. **GR** Georges Pappas, Ellie Lambetti, Athena Michaelidou, Eleni Zafirou; **D:** Michael Cacoyannis. **FCT**

A Matter of Honor ⚔️⚔️ 1995 **(PG)** Rugby player is killed during match and his coach gets blamed. So, to clear his name, said coach takes up an unusual challenge with the captain of the opposing team. 95m/C VHS. Jackson Bostwick, Allen Arkus, Rebecca Gray, David Michie; **D:** Frederick P. Watkins. **AVI**

A Matter of Life and Death ⚔️⚔️ 1981 True story follows the real-life experiences of nurse Joy Ufema who has devoted her life to helping terminally ill patients. Exceptional work from Lavin. Made for television. 98m/C VHS. Linda Lavin, Salome Jens, Gail Strickland, Gerald S. O'Loughlin, Ramon Bieri, Tyne Daly, Larry Breeding, John Bennett Perry; **D:** Russ Mayberry. **NO**

A Matter of Love ⚔️ 1978 **(R)** Two couples indulge in spouse swapping while vacationing at the beach. 89m/C VHS, Beta. Michelle Harris, Mark Anderson, Christy Neal, Jeff Alin; **D:** Chuck Vincent. **LIV, VES**

A Matter of Principle 1983 The perennial Christmas special about a Scrooge-like character's yuletide change of heart. He decides it's time to shape up when he realizes he may lose his family permanently. 60m/C VHS, Beta. Alan Arkin, Barbara Dana, Tony Arkin; **D:** Gwen Arner. **ACA**

A Matter of Time *WOOF!* 1976 **(PG)** Maid is taught to enjoy life by an eccentric, flamboyant contessa, then finds the determination to become an aspiring actress. Often depressing and uneven, arguably Minnelli's worst directing job and his last film. Also Boyer's last appearance and first bit for Bergman's daughter Rosellini, in a small part as a nun. 97m/C VHS, Beta. Liza Minnelli, Ingrid Bergman, Charles Boyer, Tina Aumont, Spiros Andros, Anna Proclemer, Isabella Rossellini; **D:** Vincente Minnelli; **C:** Geoffrey Unsworth. *VES*

A Matter of WHO 🐾🐾 1962 A detective for the World Health Organization, or WHO, investigates the disease related deaths of several oil men. Travelling to the Middle East, he uncovers a plot by an unscrupulous businessman to control the oil industry by killing off its most powerful members. Although intended as a comedy, the subject matter is too grim to be taken lightly. 92m/B **VHS, Beta.** *GB* Terry-Thomas, Alex Nicol, Sonja Ziemann, Richard Briers, Clive Morton, Vincent Ball, Honor Blackman, Carol White, Martin Benson, Geoffrey Keen; **D:** Don Chaffey; **M:** Edwin Astley. *SNC*

Matters of the Heart 🐾🐾 1990 Young pianist searches for an opportunity to display his talents, much to the disapproval of his veteran father. He meets a successful but embittered musician who takes him under her wing and passion between the two soon flares. Made for cable TV and based on "The Country of the Heart" by Barbara Wershba. 94m/C **VHS, Closed Caption.** Jane Seymour, Christopher Gartin, James Stacy, Geoffrey Lewis, Nan Martin, Allen Rich, Clifford David, Kathy Cannon; **D:** Michael Rhodes; **W:** Linda J. Bergman. *USH*

Maurice 🐾🐾🐾 1987 (R) Based on E.M. Forster's novel about a pair of Edwardian-era Cambridge undergraduates who fall in love, but must deny their attraction and abide by British society's strict norms regarding homosexuality. Maurice finds, however, that he cannot deny his nature, and must come to a decision regarding family, friends, and social structures. A beautiful and stately film of struggle and courage. 139m/C **VHS, Beta, LV, Closed Caption.** *GB* James Wilby, Hugh Grant, Rupert Graves, Mark Tandy, Ben Kingsley, Denholm Elliott, Simon Callow, Judy Parfitt, Helena Bonham Carter, Billie Whitelaw, Phoebe Nicholls, Barry Foster; **D:** James Ivory; **W:** James Ivory, Kit Hesketh-Harvey; **M:** Richard Robbins. Nominations: Academy Awards '87: Best Costume Design. *ORI, IME, WAR*

Mausoleum 🐾🐾 1983 (R) Only one man can save a woman from eternal damnation. 96m/C **VHS, Beta, LV.** Marjoe Gortner, Bobbie Bresee, Norman Burton, LaWanda Page, Shari Mann; **D:** Michael Dugan.

Mauvaise Graine 🐾🐾 *Bad Seed* 1933 Wilder (in his debut) filmed this comedy-drama (along with Esway) before heading off to Hollywood. Parisian wastrel Henri Pasquier (Mingand) impulsively steals a car when his disgusted wealthy father cuts him off. This lands Henri in with a professional gang of thieves, headed by Jean (Galle), who uses his pretty teenaged sister Jeannette (Darrieux) as a decoy. Henri enjoys his new career (and Jeannette) until jealousy gets in the way. French with subtitles. 76m/B **VHS.** *FR* Pierre Mingand, Danielle Darrieux, Raymond Galle, Jean Wall; **D:** Billy Wilder, Alexander Esway; **W:** Billy Wilder, Alexander Esway; **C:** Paul Cotteret, Maurice Delattre; **M:** Franz Waxman, Walter Gray. *KIV*

Maverick 🐾🐾½ 1994 (PG) Entertaining remake of the popular ABC series is fresh and funny, with sharp dialogue and a good cast. Everybody looks like they're having a great time, not difficult for the charming Gibson, but a refreshing change of pace for the usually serious Foster and Greene. In a fun bit of casting, Garner, the original Maverick, shows up as Marshal Zane Cooper. Lightweight, fast-paced comedy was reportedly highly improvised, though Donner retained enough control to keep it coherent. The end is left wide open so a sequel seems likely. Keep your eyes peeled for cameos from country stars, old time Western actors, and an unbilled appearance from Glover. 127m/C **VHS, LV, Closed Caption.** Mel Gibson, Jodie Foster, James Garner, Graham Greene, James Coburn, Alfred Molina, Paul Smith, Geoffrey Lewis, Max Perlich; **Cameos:** Dub Taylor, Dan Hedaya, Robert Fuller, Doug McClure, Bert Remsen, Denver Pyle, Will Hutchins, Waylon Jennings, Kathy Mattea, Danny Glover, Clint Black; **D:** Richard Donner; **W:** William Goldman; **C:** Vilmos Zsigmond; **M:** Randy Newman. Blockbuster Entertainment Awards '95: Comedy Actress, Theatrical (Foster);

Nominations: Academy Awards '94: Best Costume Design. *WAR*

The Maverick Queen 🐾🐾½ 1955 Barbara Stanwyck, owner of a gambling casino and a member of the "Wild Bunch" outlaw gang, is torn between going straight for the love of a lawman or sticking with the criminals. Stanwyck is perfectly cast in this interesting Western. 90m/C **VHS.** Barbara Stanwyck, Barry Sullivan, Wallace Ford, Scott Brady, Jim Davis, Mary Murphy; **D:** Joseph Kane. *REP*

Maverick: The Collector's Edition 195? Offbeat television western starring Garner as conniving gambler Bret Maverick. The premiere show, "War of the Silver Kings," finds Maverick falling out with the richest man in town over a card game. "Point Blank" features Connors as a conniving bank clerk. Additional episodes are available. 100m/B **VHS.** James Garner, Mike Connors. *WAR, MOV*

Max 1922 Compilation of hilarious Linder shorts plus two features, "Seven Years Bad Luck" and "The Three Must-Get-Theres" 90m/B **VHS, Beta.** Max Linder. *GVV*

Max 🐾🐾 1979 A night watchman watches an aspiring actress who is working on her performance in a Broadway play. He tells her she would be better off marrying a doctor. 20m/C **VHS, Beta.** Jack Gilford, Lynn Lipton; **D:** Joseph Gilford, Jennifer Lax. *NO*

Max and Helen 🐾🐾½ 1990 Uneven, but sensitive and at times highly moving made for TV story of two lovers who are victims of the holocaust. Max (Williams) survives both Nazi and Stalinist camps out of both love for his fiancee and guilt for having lived while she did not. 94m/C **VHS, Beta, Closed Caption.** *GB* Treat Williams, Alice Krige, Martin Landau, Jodhi May, John Phillips, Adam Kotz; **D:** Philip Saville; **W:** Corey Blechman. *TTC*

Max Dugan Returns 🐾🐾 1983 (PG) A Simon comedy about an ex-con trying to make up with his daughter by showering her with presents bought with stolen money. Sweet and light, with a good cast. 98m/C **VHS, Beta, LV.** Jason Robards Jr., Marsha Mason, Donald Sutherland, Matthew Broderick, Kiefer Sutherland; **D:** Herbert Ross; **W:** Neil Simon; **M:** David Shire. *FOX*

Max Fleischer's Documentary Features 1923 Two scientific films, "Evolution" and "Einstein's Theory of Relativity," from Fleischer's early studio were made to finance their cartoons. Features animated sequences. 60m/B **VHS, Beta.** **D:** Max Fleischer. *GVV*

Max Headroom, the Original Story 🐾🐾½ 1986 The computer-generated, British Channel-4 comedy personality stars in his first film, actually a shot-on-video feature about an innocent reporter who is transformed by an evil futuristic TV station into Headroom, the perfect (read: artificial) talk show host. 60m/C **VHS, Beta, LV, Closed Caption.** *GB* Matt Frewer, Nickolas Grace, Hilary Tindall, Amanda Pays, Rocky Morton, Annabel Jankel. *ORI, WAR*

Max is Missing 🐾🐾½ 1995 (PG) 12-year-old Max (Caudell) gets separated from his father, is given a priceless Incan artifact by a dying man, and joins with a local lad to guard it from fortune hunters. Set in the ruins of Machu Picchu in the Peruvian Andes. Made for cable. 95m/C **VHS, Closed Caption.** Toran Caudell, Victor Rojas, Matthew Sullivan, Rick Dean, Charles Napier; **D:** Mark Griffiths. *HMK*

Max, Mon Amour 🐾🐾 *Max, My Love* 1986 A very refined British diplomat in Paris discovers his bored wife has become involved with Max, who happens to be a chimpanzee. Instead of being upset, the husband decides Max should live with them. Very strange menage a trois manages to avoid the obvious vulgarities. In French with English subtitles. 97m/C **VHS.** *FR* Anthony Higgins, Charlotte Rampling, Victoria Abril, Christopher Hovik, Anne-Marie Besse, Pierre Etaix; **D:** Nagisa Oshima; **W:** Jean-Claude Carriere; **M:** Michel Portal. *CVC, ING*

Maxie 🐾🐾 1985 (PG) Highly predictable, and forgettable, comedy where a ghost of a flamboyant flapper inhabits the body of a modern-day secretary, and her husband is both delighted and befuddled with the transformations in his spouse. Close is okay, but the film is pretty flaky. 98m/C **VHS, Beta, LV.** Glenn Close, Ruth Gordon, Mandy Patinkin, Barnard Hughes, Valerie Curtin, Harry Hamlin; **D:** Paul Aaron; **W:** Patricia Resnick; **M:** Georges Delerue. *NO*

Maxim Xul woof! 1991 A professor of the occult is forced to tangle with a beast from Hell that possesses enormous strength and an insatiable appetite for human blood. 90m/C **VHS.** Adam West, Jefferson Leinberger, Hal Strieb, Mary Schaeffer; **D:** Arthur Egeli. *NO*

Maximum Breakout 🐾½ 1991 A beautiful and wealthy girl is kidnapped, her boyfriend left for dead. But he recovers and leads a posse of mercenaries to the rescue. 93m/C **VHS.** Sydney Coale Phillips; **D:** Tracy Lynch Britton. *AIP*

Maximum Force 🐾½ 1992 (R) Three renegade cops join together to infiltrate the underworld and bring to justice both the city's leading crime king and their own corrupt chief of police. **CW:** Language, violence, and sexuality. 90m/C **VHS, LV.** Sam Jones, Sherrie Rose, Jason Lively, John Saxon, Richard Lynch, Mickey Rooney, Jeff Langton; **D:** Joseph Merhi. *PMH*

Maximum Overdrive 🐾 1986 (R) Based upon King's story "Trucks," recounts what happens when a meteor hits Earth and machines run by themselves, wanting only to kill people. Score by AC/DC. 97m/C **VHS, Beta, LV.** Emilio Estevez, Pat Hingle, Laura Harrington, Jonathan Murphy, Yeardley Smith; **D:** Stephen King; **W:** Stephen King. *ORI, WAR*

Maximum Risk 🐾🐾½ 1996 (R) Like we need two of them? Van Damme, in a deja vu storyline (see "Double Impact") plays identical twins—a good French guy and a bad Russian guy—and when the bad guy gets killed, his brother takes over his life to find out whodunit. Risk and danger aside, the ruse is not all that bad, what with Henstridge as his sib's squeeze, unaware that the man she has in a lip lock is not her beloved. Has all the action you'd expect from a pic with "The Muscles from Brussels" and more guns, fists, and car chases is, of course, the major reason to invest your entertainment dollars here. Hong Kong action auteur Lam's stateside debut ensures that fast-paced chases and full-throttle combat is well done and visually appealing. 100m/C **VHS, LV, Closed Caption.** Jean-Claude Van Damme, Natasha Henstridge, Jean-Hugues Anglade, Stephane Audran, Paul Ben-Victor, Zach Grenier, Frank Senger; **D:** Ringo Lam; **W:** Larry Ferguson; **C:** Alexander Grusynski; **M:** Robert Folk. *COL*

Maximum Security 🐾 1987 A small-budget prison film detailing the tribulations of a model prisoner struggling to resist mental collapse. 113m/C **VHS, LV.** Geoffrey Lewis, Jean Smart, Robert Desiderio; **D:** Bill Duke. *VTR, NWV*

Maximum Thrust woof! *Waldo Warren: Private Dick Without a Brain* 1988 A few white men confront a deadly Caribbean voodoo tribe. 80m/C **Beta.** Rick Gianisi, Joe Derrig, Jennifer Kanter, Mizan Nunes; **D:** Tim Kincaid. *NO*

May Fools 🐾🐾🐾 *Milou en Mai; Milou in May* 1990 (R) Malle portrays individuals collectively experiencing personal upheaval against the backdrop of unrelated social upheaval. An upper-crust family gathers at a country estate for the funeral of the clan's matriarch, while the May of '68 Parisian riots unfold. Few among the family members mourn the woman's passing, save her son Milou (Piccoli) who leads a pastoral existence tending grapes on the estate. Milou's daughter (Miou-Miou), like the others, is more concerned with her personal gain, suggesting, to her father's horror, that they divide the estate in three. Touching, slow, keenly observed. In French with English subtitles. **CW:** Adult situations, nudity, and sexual situations. 105m/C **VHS, LV.** *FR* Michel Piccoli, Miou-

Miou, Michael Duchaussoy, Dominique Blanc, Harriet Walter, Francois Berleand, Paulette Dubost, Bruno Carette, Martine Gautier; **D:** Louis Malle; **W:** Jean-Claude Carriere, Louis Malle; **M:** Stephane Grappelli. Cesar Awards '91: Best Supporting Actress (Blanc). *ORI, FXL, FCT*

May Wine 🎞🎞 1990 (R) A sexy, romantic comedy starring "Twin Peaks" alumna, Boyle. **85m/C VHS, LV, Closed Caption.** Guy Marchand, Lara Flynn Boyle, Joanna Cassidy. *MED, VTR*

Maya 🎞½ 1966 After the death of his mother, young Terry (North) goes to join his big-game hunting father in India. After a quarrel Terry runs off and meets an Indian boy who has promised his dying father he will deliver a sacred white elephant to a jungle temple. The two lads join forces for the trek and have all sorts of adventures along the way. Basis for a short-lived television series. **91m/C VHS.** Jay North, Clint Walker, Sajid Kahn, I.S. Johar; **D:** John Berry; **W:** John Fante. *MGM, FCT*

Maya woof! 1982 A teacher of fashion in a high school becomes the object of a student's devotion and another teacher's insane jealousy. **114m/C VHS, Beta.** Berta Dominguez, Joseph D. Rosevich; **D:** Agust Agustsson. *NO*

Mayalunta 1986 A young artist is emotionally tortured by a dying older couple. **90m/C VHS.** SP Federico Luppi, Miguel Angel Sola, Barbara Mujica. *VES*

Maybe I'll Be Home in the Spring 🎞🎞½ *Deadly Desire* 1970 (PG) Denise (Field) is estranged from her family and decides to leave home for life on a commune where she becomes involved with drugs. When she decides to return home everyone finds it hard to adjust. Made for television. **90m/C VHS.** Sally Field, Jackie Cooper, Eleanor Parker, David Carradine, Lane Bradbury; **D:** Joseph Sargent. *VTR*

Maybe...Maybe Not 🎞🎞 *Der Bewegte Mann; The Most Desired Man* 1994 (R) The German title refers to a man who moves between both sexual preferences although the film takes a straighter line. Hunky-but-dumb Axel (Schweiger) has cheated on girlfriend Dorothy (Riemann) once too often and she kicks him out. Axel winds up staying with gay pal Norbert (Krol), who would like to go from friendship to lovers, which Axel doesn't pick up on. Dorothy does, however, and wonders if Axel is really gay, but when she discovers she's pregnant, Dorothy decides to marry him anyway. Warm-hearted and campy, with some blatantly sexual dialogue. Based on two gay comic books by Ralf Koenig. German with subtitles or dubbed. **CW:** Sexuality and language, including some explicit sexual dialogue. **93m/C VHS, LV, Closed Caption.** GE Til Schweiger, Katja Riemann, Joachim Krol, Rufus Beck; **D:** Soenke Wortmann; **W:** Soenke Wortmann; **C:** Gernot Roll; **M:** Torsten Breuer. *LIV*

Mayerling 🎞🎞🎞½ 1936 Considered one of the greatest films about doomed love. Story of the tragic and hopeless affair between Crown Prince Rudolf of Hapsburg and young Baroness Marie Vetsera. Heart wrenching and beautiful, with stupendous acting. Remade in 1968. In French with English subtitles. **95m/B VHS, Beta, LV.** Charles Boyer, Danielle Darrieux; **D:** Anatole Litvak. New York Film Critics Awards '37: Best Foreign Film. *HMV, MRV, FCT*

Mayerling 🎞🎞½ 1968 (PG-13) Based on the tragic romance between Crown Prince Rudolf of Hapsburg (Sharif) and the teenaged Baroness Maria Vetsera (Deneuve). Set in 1888, the royal Rudolf defies his father, the Emperor Franz Josef (Mason), to take part in a student revolt for the liberation of Hungary and to fall for the common-born Maria (despite his political marriage). No doubt meant to be a sweeping combo of politics and love ala "Doctor Zhivago," it's mostly tedious; see the 1936 version instead. **CW:** Sex-related scenes. **140m/C VHS.** GB FR Omar Sharif, Catherine Deneuve, James Mason, Ava Gardner, James Robertson Justice, Genevieve Page, Ivan Desny, Fabienne Dali; **D:** Terence Young; **W:** Terence Young; **C:** Henri Alekan; **M:** Francis Lai. *MGM*

Mayflower Madam 🎞🎞 1987 (R) Fairly unsexy and uninteresting made-for-TV movie recounting the business dealings and court battles of the real-life Sydney Biddle Barrows. Barrows/Bergen is a prominent New York socialite and madam of an exclusive escort service whose clientele includes businessmen and dignitaries. **93m/C VHS, Beta.** Candice Bergen, Chris Sarandon, Chita Rivera; **D:** Lou Antonio; **M:** David Shire. *THV*

Mayhem 🎞 1987 Two loners in Hollywood confront all types of urban low-life murderers, drug pushers, and child molesters. **90m/C VHS, Beta.** Raymond Martino, Pamela Dixon, Robert Gallo, Wendy MacDonald. *NO*

Maytime 🎞🎞🎞 1937 Lovely story of an opera star (MacDonald) and penniless singer (Eddy) who fall in love in Paris, but her husband/teacher (Barrymore) interferes. One of the best films the singing duo ever made. ♫Maytime Finale; Virginia Ham and Eggs; Vive l'Opera; Student Drinking Song; Carry Me Back to Old Virginny; Reverie; Jump Jim Crow; Road to Paradise; Page's Aria. **132m/B VHS, LV.** Jeanette MacDonald, Nelson Eddy, John Barrymore, Herman Bing, Tom Brown, Lynne Carver; **D:** Robert Z. Leonard; **W:** Noel Langley. Nominations: Academy Awards '37: Best Sound, Best Original Score. *MGM*

Maytime in Mayfair 🎞🎞 1952 A dress shop owner's rival is getting all the goodies first, for which he takes the heat from his partner. When he finds out how the rival is doing it, the partners up and head for a vacation in the south of France. Overly simplistic but charming kitsch, helped along by Technicolor shots of the fashions and sets. **94m/C VHS.** Anna Neagle, Michael Wilding, Peter Graves, Nicholas Phipps, Tom Walls, Tom Walls Jr.; **D:** Herbert Wilcox. *NOS*

The Maze 🎞🎞🎞 1985 Made-for-British-television mystery about a young girl who meets the ghost of her mother's first love in her garden estate. **60m/C VHS, Beta.** GB Francesca Annis, James Bolam, Sky McCatskill. *PSM*

Mazes and Monsters 🎞🎞½ *Rona Jaffe's Mazes and Monsters; Dungeons and Dragons* 1982 A group of university students becomes obsessed with playing a real life version of the fantasy role-playing game, Dungeons and Dragons (known in the film as Mazes & Monsters since D&D is trademarked). Early Hanks appearance is among the film's assets. Adapted for television from the book by Rona Jaffe. **100m/C VHS, Beta.** CA Tom Hanks, Wendy Crewson, David Wallace, Chris Makepeace, Lloyd Bochner, Peter Donat, Murray Hamilton, Vera Miles, Louise Sorel, Susan Strasberg, Anne Francis; **D:** Steven Hilliard Stern; **M:** Hagood Hardy. *ORI, HHE, WAR*

McBain 🎞🎞🎞 1991 (R) In this exciting fast-paced action-thriller, POW Robert McBain (Walken) leads a group of veterans into battle against the Columbian drug cartel. Stunning cinematography and superb performances combine to make this a riveting action film you won't soon forget. **CW:** Language and strong war violence and drug use. **104m/C VHS, Closed Caption.** Christopher Walken, Maria Conchita Alonso, Michael Ironside, Steve James, Jay Patterson, Thomas G. Waites; **D:** James Glickenhaus; **W:** James Glickenhaus. *USH*

McCabe & Mrs. Miller 🎞🎞🎞🎞 1971 (R) Altman's characteristically quirky take on the Western casts Beatty as a self-inflated entrepreneur who opens a brothel in the Great North. Christie is the madame who helps stabilize the haphazard operation. Unfortunately, success comes at a high price, and when gunmen arrive to enforce a business proposition, Beatty must become the man he has, presumably, merely pretended to be. A poetic, moving work, and a likely classic of the genre. Based on the novel by Edmund Naughton. **121m/C VHS, Beta, LV.** Warren Beatty, Julie Christie, William Devane, Keith Carradine, John Schuck, Rene Auberjonois, Shelley Duvall, Bert Remsen, Michael Murphy, Hugh Millais, Jack Riley; **D:** Robert Altman; **W:** Robert Altman; **C:** Vilmos Zsigmond; **M:** Leonard Cohen. Nominations: Academy Awards '71: Best Actress (Christie). *WAR*

The McConnell Story 🎞🎞½ *Tiger in the Sky* 1955 True story of ace flyer McConnell, his heroism during WWII and the Korean conflict, and his postwar aviation pioneer efforts. Fine acting from Allyson and Ladd, with good support from Whitmore and Faylen. **107m/C VHS, Beta, LV, Closed Caption.** Alan Ladd, June Allyson, James Whitmore, Frank Faylen; **D:** Gordon Douglas; **M:** Max Steiner. *WAR, FCT*

The McGuffin 🎞🎞 1985 A film critic's inquisitiveness about the activities of his neighbors gets him caught up in murder and a host of other problems. A takeoff of Alfred Hitchcock's 1954 classic "Rear Window." **95m/C VHS.** GB Charles Dance, Ritza Brown, Francis Matthews, Brian Glover, Phyllis Logan, Jerry Stiller, Anna Massey; **D:** Colin Bucksey. *NO*

McHale's Navy 🎞½ 1997 (PG) Yet another (unsuccessful) attempt to take a TV series and let it loose on the big screen. Retired Navy skipper McHale (Arnold) has set up his scheming ways on the Caribbean island of San Ysidro, where he can be a thorn in the side of Capt. Binghampton (Stockwell), the newly transferred commanding officer of the island's sleepy naval base. McHale's former cronies aid their leader when he's reluctantly reunited with the Navy in order to prevent the terrorist threats of his former Soviet nemesis Vladakov (Curry). A shining example of "why bother?" moviemaking. TV's original McHale, Borgnine, has a cameo (and gets a promotion to admiral). **108m/C VHS, LV, Closed Caption.** Tom Arnold, Tim Curry, Dean Stockwell, David Alan Grier, Debra Messing, Thomas Chong, Bruce Campbell, French Stewart, Brian Haley, Danton Stone; **Cameos:** Ernest Borgnine; **D:** Bryan Spicer; **W:** Peter Crabbe; **C:** Buzz Feitshans IV; **M:** Dennis McCarthy. *USH*

McKenzie Break 🎞🎞🎞 1970 Irish intelligence agent John Connor (Keith) is sent to Scotland to Camp McKenzie, a prison for German POWs during WWII. Captured U-boat commander Schluetter (Griem) is suspected of planning a mass escape and Connor is supposed to stop the action. The battle of wills between the hard-headed Connor and wily Schluetter provides taut, suspenseful drama. Adapted from "The Bowmanville Break" by Sidney Shelley. **106m/C VHS.** Brian Keith, Helmut Griem, Ian Hendry, Jack Watson, Horst Janson, Patrick O'Connell; **D:** Lamont Johnson; **W:** William W. Norton Sr. *MGM*

McLintock! 🎞🎞🎞 1963 Rowdy western starring Wayne as a tough cattle baron whose refined wife (O'Hara) returns from the east after a two-year separation. She wants a divorce and custody of their 17-year-old daughter (Powers), who's been away at school. In the meantime, he's hired a housekeeper (De Carlo), whose teenage son (real-life son Patrick) promptly falls for Powers. It's a battle royal between the feisty wife and cantankerous husband but no one out-dukes the Duke. Other Wayne family members involved in the production include daughter Aissa (as the housekeeper's daughter) and son Michael who produced the film. **127m/C VHS, LV.** John Wayne, Maureen O'Hara, Yvonne De Carlo, Patrick Wayne, Stefanie Powers, Jack Kruschen, Chill Wills, Jerry Van Dyke, Edgar Buchanan, Bruce Cabot, Perry Lopez, Michael Pate, Strother Martin, Gordon Jones; **D:** Andrew V. McLaglen; **W:** James Edward Grant; **C:** William Clothier. *MPI, GKK, ING*

The McMasters 🎞🎞 *The Blood Crowd; The McMasters...Tougher Than the West Itself* 1970 (PG) Set shortly after the Civil War, the film tells the story of the prejudice faced by a black soldier who returns to the southern ranch on which he was raised. Once there, the rancher gives him half of the property, but the ex-soldier has difficulty finding men who will work for him. When a group of Native Americans assist him, a band of bigoted men do their best to stop it. The movie was released in two versions with different endings: in one, prejudice prevails; in the other, bigotry is defeated. **89m/C VHS.** Burl Ives, Brock Peters, David Carradine, Nancy Kwan, Jack Palance, Dane Clark, L.Q. Jones, Alan Vint, John Carradine; **D:** Alf Kjellin. *VTR, XVC*

McQ 🐾🐾½ **1974 (PG)** After several big dope dealers kill two police officers, a lieutenant resigns to track them down. Dirty Harry done with an aging Big Duke. **116m/C VHS, Beta, LV, Closed Caption.** John Wayne, Eddie Albert, Diana Muldaur, Clu Gulager, Colleen Dewhurst, Al Lettieri, Julie Adams, David Huddleston; **D:** John Sturges; **C:** Harry Stradling Jr.; **M:** Elmer Bernstein. *WAR*

McVicar 🐾🐾½ **1980 (R)** A brutish and realistic depiction of crime and punishment based on the life of John McVicar, who plotted to escape from prison. From the book by McVicar. **90m/C VHS, Beta, LV.** *GB* Roger Daltrey, Adam Faith, Cheryl Campbell; **D:** Tom Clegg; **W:** Tom Clegg. *VES*

Me and Him 🐾½ *Ich und Er* **1989 (R)** An unsuspecting New Yorker finds himself jockeying for position with his own instincts when his libido decides it wants a life of its own. **94m/C VHS, LV, Closed Caption.** *GE* Griffin Dunne, Carey Lowell, Ellen Greene, Craig T. Nelson; **D:** Doris Dorrie; **M:** Mark Linn-Baker. *COL*

Me and the Colonel 🐾🐾½ **1958** Average satire finds Jewish refugee S.L. Jacobowsky (Kaye) trying to get out of Paris to Spain before the Nazis occupy the city. He gets stuck travelling with anti-Semitic Polish colonel Prokoszny (Jurgens), who's also not eager to fall into German hands. If the trip went smoothly, there wouldn't be a story, so naturally the men are forced to put aside their differences to survive. Adapted from Franz Werfel's play "Jacobowsky and the Colonel." **110m/B VHS.** Danny Kaye, Curt Jurgens, Akim Tamiroff, Nicole Maurey, Francoise Rosay, Martita Hunt, Alexander Scourby, Liliane Montevecchi; **D:** Peter Glenville; **W:** S.N. Behrman, George Froeschel; **C:** Burnett Guffey; **M:** George Duning. *COL*

Me and the Kid 🐾🐾½ **1993 (PG)** Minor career criminals Aiello and Pantoliano try a robbery on a ruthless financier's (Dukes) home and wind up kidnapping his 10-year-old son instead. But dad doesn't want to pay the ransom and Aiello dumps his partner (who wants to kill the kid) and heads out on the road with the boy. **97m/C VHS, LV, Closed Caption.** Danny Aiello, Joe Pantoliano, Alex Zuckerman, Cathy Moriarty, David Dukes, Anita Morris; **D:** Dan Curtis. *ORI*

Me and the Mob 🐾½ *Who Do I Gotta Kill?* **1994 (R)** Writer Jimmy Corona (Lorinz) thinks the way to get some colorful stories is to join up with his mobster uncle (Darrow). But Jimmy's no tough guy and the feds coerce him into wearing a wire to bust the local godfather. Low-budget comedy is a lesson in tedium.*CW:* Profanity; sexual situations. **85m/C VHS.** James Lorinz, Tony Darrow, John Costelloe, Sandra Bullock, Anthony Michael Hall, Stephen Lee, Ted Sorel; *Cameos:* Steve Buscemi; **D:** Frank Rainone; **W:** James Lorinz, Frank Rainone. *AVI*

Me & Veronica 🐾🐾 **1993 (R)** Two estranged sisters try to come to terms with each other and their dead end lives. Good sister Fanny (McGovern) is a divorced waitress living in a rundown seaside town in New Jersey. One day bad sister Veronica (Wettig) shows up, announcing she's about to be sent to jail for welfare fraud. Veronica asks Fanny to look after her two kids while she's in jail and it is while visiting Veronica in prison that Fanny comes to realize her seemingly flamboyant sister is actually mentally ill and possibly suicidal. Grim little film with good lead performances. **97m/C VHS.** Elizabeth McGovern, Patricia Wettig, Michael O'Keefe, John Heard; **D:** Don Scardino; **W:** Leslie Lyles; **M:** David Mansfield. *COL*

Me, Myself & I 🐾🐾½ **1992 (R)** Segal is a successful New York writer who falls in love with next-door neighbor Williams. But the road to romance is never smooth—particularly when your paranoid gal suffers from multiple personality disorder. Fun leads, dumb movie.*CW:* Strong language, some drug use, and some sexuality. **97m/C VHS.** George Segal, JoBeth Williams, Shelley Hack, Don Calfa, Bill Macy, Betsey Lynn George, Sharon McNight, Ruth Gilbert; **D:** Pablo Fero; **W:** Julian Barry. *COL*

The Meal 🐾🐾 *Deadly Encounter* **1975 (R)** During a dinner party held by a wealthy woman, the rich and powerful guests divulge each others' secrets with reckless disregard for the consequences. **90m/C VHS.** Dina Merrill, Carl Betz, Leon Ames, Susan Logan, Vicki Powers, Steve Potter; **D:** R. John Hugh. *MOV*

Mean Dog Blues 🐾🐾½ **1978 (PG)** A musician is convicted of hit-and-run driving after hitching a ride with an inebriated politician. **108m/C VHS, Beta.** George Kennedy, Kay Lenz, Scatman Crothers, Greg Henry, Gregory Sierra, Tina Louise, William Windom; **D:** Mel Stuart; **C:** Robert B. Hauser. *LIV, VES*

Mean Frank and Crazy Tony 🐾🐾 **1975 (R)** A mobster and the man who idolizes him attempt a prison breakout in this fun, action-packed production. **92m/C VHS, Beta.** *IT* Lee Van Cleef, Tony LoBianco, Jean Rochefort, Jess Hahn; **D:** Michele Lupo. *LIV*

Mean Johnny Barrows 🐾½ **1975** When Johnny Barrows returns to his home town after being dishonorably discharged from the Army he is offered a job as a gang hitman. **83m/C VHS, Beta.** Fred Williamson, Roddy McDowall, Stuart Whitman, Luther Adler, Jenny Sherman, Elliott Gould; **D:** Fred Williamson. *UNI*

Mean Machine 🐾🐾 **1973 (R)** A man and his beautiful cohort plot revenge on organized crime for the murder of his father. **89m/C VHS, Beta.** Chris Mitchum, Barbara Bouchet, Arthur Kennedy. *NO*

Mean Season 🐾🐾 **1985 (R)** A vicious mass murderer makes a Miami crime reporter his confidante in his quest for publicity during his killing spree. In time, the madman's intentions become clear as the tensions and headlines grow with each gruesome slaying. Then the reporter must come to terms with the idea that he is letting himself be used due to the success that the association is bringing him. Suspenseful story with a tense ending. Good performance from Russell as the reporter. Screenplay written by Christopher Crowe under the pseudonym Leon Piedmont. **106m/C VHS, Beta, LV.** Kurt Russell, Mariel Hemingway, Richard Jordan, Richard Masur, Andy Garcia, Joe Pantoliano, Richard Bradford, William Smith; **D:** Phillip Borsos; **W:** Christopher Crowe; **M:** Lalo Schifrin. *NO*

Mean Streets 🐾🐾🐾🐾 **1973 (R)** A grimy slice of street life in Little Italy among lower echelon Mafiosos, unbalanced punks, and petty criminals. A riveting, free-form feature film, marking the formal debut by Scorsese (five years earlier he had completed a student film, "Who's That Knocking At My Door?"). Unorthodox camera movement and gritty performances by De Niro and Keitel, with underlying Catholic guilt providing the moral conflict. Excellent early '60s soundtrack. **112m/C VHS, Beta, LV, Closed Caption.** Harvey Keitel, Robert De Niro, David Proval, Amy Robinson, Richard Romanus, David Carradine, Robert Carradine, Cesare Danova, George Memmoli; **D:** Martin Scorsese; **W:** Mardik Martin, Martin Scorsese. National Society of Film Critics Awards '73: Best Supporting Actor (De Niro).*WAR*

The Meanest Men in the West 🐾 **1976 (PG)** Two criminal half-brothers battle frontier law and each other. **92m/C VHS, Beta.** Charles Bronson, Lee Marvin, Lee J. Cobb, James Drury, Albert Salmi, Charles Grodin; **D:** Samuel Fuller; **W:** Charles S. Dubin. *USH*

Meatballs 🐾🐾 **1979 (PG)** The Activities Director at a summer camp who is supposed to organize fun for everyone prefers his own style of "fun." If you enjoy watching Murray blow through a movie, you'll like this one even as it lapses into box office sentimentality. **92m/C VHS, Beta, LV, Closed Caption.** *CA* Bill Murray, Harvey Atkin, Kate Lynch; **D:** Ivan Reitman; **W:** Len Blum, Harold Ramis, Janis Allen; **M:** Elmer Bernstein. Genie Awards '80: Best Actress (Lynch). *PAR*

Meatballs 2 🐾½ **1984 (PG)** The future of Camp Sasquatch is in danger unless the camp's best fighter can beat Camp Patton's champ in a boxing match. The saving grace of Bill Murray is absent in this one. **87m/C VHS, Beta, LV, 8mm, Closed Caption.** Archie Hahn, John Mengatti, Tammy Taylor, Kim Richards, Ralph Seymour, Richard Mulligan, Hamilton Camp, John Larroquette, Paul (Pee Wee Herman) Reubens, Misty Rowe, Elayne Boosler; **D:** Ken Wiederhorn. *COL*

Meatballs 3 woof! **1987 (R)** Second sequel to the teen-age sex/summer camp comedy. Enough is enough! **95m/C VHS, Beta.** Sally Kellerman, Shannon Tweed, George Buza, Isabelle Mejias, Al Waxman, Patrick Dempsey; **D:** George Mendeluk. *LIV*

Meatballs 4 🐾½ **1992 (R)** Feldman stars as a water skier hired to serve as recreation director of Lakeside Water Ski Camp. His enemy is Monica (Douglas) of a nearby rival camp who wants to buy out Lakeside's owner and use the land for real estate development. Lame plot only serves to showcase some good water skiing stunts.*CW:* Nudity and sensual scene. **87m/C VHS, Closed Caption.** Corey Feldman, Jack Nance, Sarah Douglas, Bojesse Christopher; **D:** Bob Logan. *HBO*

The Meateater woof! **1979** Disgusting horror flick of a disfigured hermit who inhabits a closed-up movie house. When it is reopened he turns into a stereotypical slasher. Vegetarians beware: references throughout about eating meat. **84m/C VHS, Beta.** Arch Jaboulian, Diane Davis, Emily Spendler; **D:** Derek Savage. *NO*

The Mechanic 🐾🐾 *Killer of Killers* **1972 (R)** Bronson stars as Arthur Bishop, a wealthy professional killer for a powerful organization. He has innumerable ways to kill. **100m/C VHS, Beta, LV.** Charles Bronson, Jan-Michael Vincent, Keenan Wynn, Jill Ireland, Linda Ridgeway; **D:** Michael Winner; **W:** Lewis John Carlino. *MGM, FOX*

Medea **1959** Medea, who betrayed her homeland for Jason, is becoming wary of his boredom with her. The classic story of love and revenge ensues thereafter in unbridled fury and passion. **107m/B VHS.** Colleen Dewhurst, Zoe Caldwell, Judith Anderson; **D:** Jose Quintero. *IVY, FHS*

Medea **1970** Cinema poet Pasolini directs opera diva Callas in this straightforward adaptation of Euripides's classic about a sorceress whose escapades range from assisting in the theft of the Golden Fleece to murdering her own children. Not Pasolini at his best, but still better than most if what you're looking for is something arty. In Italian with English subtitles. **118m/C VHS, Beta.** *IT* Maria Callas, Guiseppi Gentile, Laurent Terzieff; **D:** Pier Paolo Pasolini. *HMV, VAI, APD*

Medicine Man 🐾½ **1930** Benny stars as a con-man who fronts a medicine show in this early talkie comedy. **57m/B VHS, Beta.** Jack Benny, Betty Bronson, E. Alyn Warren, George E. Stone, Tom Dugan; **D:** Scott Pembroke. *NOS, DVT, VYY*

Medicine Man 🐾🐾 **1992 (PG-13)** Connery's usual commanding presence and the beautiful scenery are the only things to recommend in this lame effort. Dr. Robert Campbell (Connery) is a biochemist working in the Amazon rain forest on a cancer cure. Bracco is Dr. Rae Crane, a fellow researcher sent by the institute sponsoring Campbell to see how things are going. Although Crane is uptight and Campbell is gruff, they fall in love (supposedly), but they're sorely lacking in chemistry. Oh, Campbell's cancer cure is made from a rare flower being eradicated by the destruction of the rain forest. This politically correct cause meets romance falls short of ever being truly entertaining. **105m/C VHS, Beta.** Sean Connery, Lorraine Bracco, Jose Wilker, Rodolfo de Alexandra, Francisco Tsirene Tsere Rereme, Elias Monteiro da Silva; **D:** John McTiernan; **M:** Jerry Goldsmith. *HPH*

Medicine River 🐾🐾½ **1994 (PG)** A Native American photojournalist returns to his hometown after a 20-year absence and winds up in hot water with newfound friend Harlen Bigbear. **96m/C VHS.** Graham Greene, Tom Jackson, Sheila Tousey, Jimmy Herman, Raoul Trujillo; **D:** Stuart Margolin. *ACA*

The Mediterranean in Flames ♂½ 1972 In Nazi-occupied Greece, a small but brave resistance is formed to fight its captors. One of the women within the group is forced to seduce a Nazi officer in an attempt to learn enemy secrets. 85m/C VHS, Beta. *GR* Costas Karras, Costas Precas; *D:* Dimis Dadiras. *NO*

Mediterraneo ♂♂♂ 1991 (R) Languid, charming comedy based on the premise that love does make the world go 'round—especially in wartime. In 1941, eight misfit Italian soldiers are stranded on a tiny Greek island and are absorbed into the life of the island, finding love and liberty in the idyllic setting. Lighthearted fun. In Italian with English subtitles. *CW:* Language, drug content, and sexuality. 90m/C VHS, Beta, LV, Closed Caption. *IT* Diego Abatantuono; Giuseppe Cederna, Claudio Bigagli, Vanna Barba, Claudio Bisio, Luigi Alberti, Ugo Conti, Memo Dini, Vasco Mirandola, Luigi Montini, Irene Grazioli, Antonio Catania; *D:* Gabriele Salvatores. Academy Awards '91: Best Foreign Language Film. *TOU, IME*

The Medium ♂♂ 1951 A phony medium is done in by her own trickery in this filmed version of the Menotti opera. 80m/B VHS, Beta. Marie Powers, Anna Maria Alberghetti, Leo Coleman; *D:* Gian-Carlo Menotti; *W:* Gian-Carlo Menotti. Nominations: Academy Awards '52: Scoring of a Musical. *MVD, VAI*

Medium Cool ♂♂♂½ 1969 Commentary on life in the '60s focuses on a television news cameraman and his growing apathy with the events around him. His involvement with a Appalachian woman and her young son reawakens his conscience, leading to the three getting caught up in the turbulence of the 1968 Chicago Democratic convention. A frightening depiction of detachment in modern society. 111m/C VHS, Beta, Closed Caption. Robert Forster, Verna Bloom, Peter Bonerz, Marianna Hill, Peter Boyle; *D:* Haskell Wexler; *W:* Haskell Wexler; *C:* Haskell Wexler. *PAR*

Medusa ♂ *Twisted* 1974 A bizarre series of events occur when an abandoned yacht containing two lifeless bodies is found on the Aegean Sea. 103m/C VHS, Beta. George Hamilton, Cameron Mitchell, Luciana Paluzzi, Theodore Roubanis; *D:* Gordon Hessler. *SNC, PSM*

Medusa Against the Son of Hercules ♂ *Perseus the Invincible* 1962 This time the strongman takes on the evil Medusa and her deadly army of rock men. ?m/C VHS, Beta. *IT* Richard Harrison. *SNC*

The Medusa Touch ♂ 1978 (R) A man is struck over the head and is admitted to a hospital. Meanwhile, strange disasters befall the surrounding city. It seems that despite his unconscious state, the man is using his telekinetic powers to will things to happen.... 110m/C VHS. *GB* Richard Burton, Lino Ventura, Lee Remick, Harry Andrews, Alan Badel, Marie-Christine Barrault, Michael Hordern, Derek Jacobi, Jeremy Brett; *D:* Jack Gold; *W:* Jack Gold, John Briley. *FOX*

Meet Danny Wilson ♂♂½ 1952 Talented New York singer Wilson (Sinatra) and his pianist buddy Mike Ryan (Nicol) head out to Hollywood to try their luck. Danny meets club singer Joy Carroll (Winters) who introduces him to gangster owner Nick Driscoll (Burr). Nick manages Danny for a hefty percentage and makes him a star at his club but Danny's lovelife goes south when Joy picks Mike over him. Then Driscoll demands his money. Sinatra gets to croon some great tunes. ♫I've Got a Crush on You; How Deep Is the Ocean; When You're Smiling; All of Me; She's Funny That Way; That Old Black Magic; You're a Sweetheart; Lonesome Man Blues; A Good Man Is Hard to Find. 88m/B VHS, Closed Caption. Frank Sinatra, Alex Nicol, Shelley Winters, Raymond Burr, Tommy Farrell, Vaughn Taylor, Jack Kruschen, Donald MacBride; *D:* Joseph Pevney; *W:* Don McGuire. *USH*

Meet Dr. Christian ♂½ 1939 The good old doctor settles some problems. Part of a series. 72m/B VHS, Beta. Jean Hersholt, Robert Baldwin, Paul Harvey; *D:* Bernard Vorhaus. *NOS, DVT, VYY*

Meet John Doe ♂♂♂ 1941 A social commentary about an unemployed, down-and-out man selected to be the face of a political goodwill campaign. Honest and trusting, he eventually realizes that he is being used to further the careers of corrupt politicians. Available in colorized version. 123m/B VHS, LV. Gary Cooper, Barbara Stanwyck, Edward Arnold, James Gleason, Walter Brennan, Spring Byington, Gene Lockhart, Regis Toomey, Ann Doran, Rod La Rocque; *D:* Frank Capra; *C:* George Barnes. Nominations: Academy Awards '41: Best Story. *NOS, MRV, PSM*

Meet Me in Las Vegas ♂♂ 1956 Compulsive gambler/cowboy Dailey betters his luck when he hooks up with hoofer girlfriend Charisse. Much frolicking and dancing and cameo appearances by a truckload of stars. A little more entertaining than a game of solitaire. ♫The Girl With the Yaller Shoes; If You Can Dream; Hell Hath No Fury; Lucky Charm; I Refuse to Rock 'n Roll; Rehearsal Ballet; Sleeping Beauty Ballet; Frankie and Johnny. 112m/C VHS, LV. Dan Dailey, Cyd Charisse, Agnes Moorehead, Lili Darvas, Jim Backus, Cara Williams, Betty Lynn, Oscar Karlweis, Liliane Montevecchi, Jerry Colonna, Frankie Laine; *Cameos:* Debbie Reynolds, Frank Sinatra, Peter Lorre, Vic Damone, Tony Martin, Elaine Stewart; *D:* Roy Rowland; *W:* Isobel Lennart. Nominations: Academy Awards '56: Scoring of a Musical. *MGM, TTC, FCT*

Meet Me in St. Louis ♂♂♂½ 1944 Wonderful music in this charming tale of a St. Louis family during the 1903 World's Fair. One of Garland's better musical performances. ♫You and I; Skip to My Lou; Over the Bannister; Meet Me In St. Louis; Brighten the Corner; Summer In St. Louis; All Hallow's Eve; Ah, Love; The Horrible One. 113m/C VHS, Beta, LV, 8mm. Judy Garland, Margaret O'Brien, Mary Astor, Lucille Bremer, Tom Drake, June Lockhart, Harry Davenport; *D:* Vincente Minnelli. National Board of Review Awards '44: 10 Best Films of the Year; Nominations: Academy Awards '44: Best Color Cinematography, Best Screenplay, Best Song ("The Trolley Song"), Scoring of a Musical. *MGM, TLF, HMV*

Meet Sexton Blake ♂♂ 1944 A detective is hired to find a ring and some secret papers that were stolen from the corpse of a man killed in an air raid. He discovers that the papers contained the plans for a new metal alloy to be used in planes. Entertaining for its melodramatic elements. 80m/B VHS, Beta. *GB* David Farrar, John Varley, Magda Kun, Gordon McLeod, Manning Whiley; *D:* John Harlow; *W:* John Harlow. *SNC*

Meet the Feebles ♂♂ 1989 Sex and violence gorefest perpetuated by puppets—and the dementia of director Jackson. A TV variety show, populated by animal puppets and humans in costume, is the setting for backstage mayhem, including sex, drugs, and a shooting spree. Among the characters are a sleazy walrus producer, his slinky Siamese cat mistress, a junkie frog, and a manic-depressive elephant. There's also several musical production numbers, if things aren't strange enough for you already. 94m/C VHS. *NZ* D: Peter Jackson; *W:* Peter Jackson, Danny Mulheron, Frances Walsh. *MTH*

Meet the Hollowheads ♂½ 1989 (PG-13) Family situation comedy set in a futuristic society. 89m/C VHS, LV, Closed Caption. John Glover, Nancy Mette, Richard Portnow, Matt Shakman, Juliette Lewis, Anne Ramsey; *D:* Tom Burman; *W:* Tom Burman. *MED, IME*

Meet the Mob ♂♂ 1942 A country spinster visits her son in the big city and is mistaken for a notorious murderess. Complications arise when she tries to keep the boy honest. Could have worked better. 62m/B VHS. ZaSu Pitts, Roger Pryor, Warren Hymer, Gwen Kenyon, Douglas Fowley, Elizabeth Russell, Tristram Coffin, Lester Dorr, Wheeler Oakman, Bud McTaggart; *D:* Jean Yarbrough. *NOS*

Meet the Navy ♂♂ 1946 Post-war musical revue about a pianist and a dancer. 81m/B VHS, Beta. Joan Pratt, Margaret Hurst, Lionel Murton. *VYY*

Meet the Parents ♂♂ 1991 A young man visits his fiance's parents and every nightmare, every tragedy that can possibly happen, does. From the minds of "National Lampoon," with an appearance by beyond-bizarre comedian Emo Phillips. ?m/C VHS. Greg Glionna, Jacqueline Cahill, Dick Galloway, Carol Wheeler, Mary Ruth Clarke, Emo Phillips; *D:* Greg Glionna; *W:* Mary Ruth Clarke. *NO*

Meet Wally Sparks ♂♂ 1997 (R) No-brow "Man Who Came to Dinner." Smutty TV shock-talk host Sparks (Dangerfield) is given one week to save his failing show when producer Reynolds (with a noticeably bad rug) puts him on notice. Opportunity knocks when he is invited to a party at the governor's mansion to interview the conservative head honcho (Stiers). Once there, a freak accident with a drunken horse prevents Sparks from leaving, and the new guest makes himself right at home by turning the fancy digs into a broadcast studio. Dangerfield's machine gun spray of one liners occasionally hits, as do his sometimes lengthy and elaborately set up jokes that do little to propel the plot along but are pure Dangerfield. Not much beyond Rodney makes lackluster "Sparks" fly. *CW:* Continuous sexual humor and partial nudity. 107m/C VHS. Rodney Dangerfield, David Ogden Stiers, Burt Reynolds, Debi Mazar, Cindy Williams, Alan Rachins; *D:* Peter Baldwin; *W:* Rodney Dangerfield, Harry Basil; *C:* Richard Kline; *M:* Michel Colombier. *THV*

Meeting at Midnight ♂♂ 1944 Charlie Chan is invited to a seance to solve a perplexing mystery. Chan discovers that they use mechanical figures and from there on solving the murder is easy. 67m/B VHS, Beta. Sidney Toler, Joseph Crehan, Mantan Moreland, Frances Chan, Ralph Peters, Helen Beverly; *D:* Phil Rosen. *MGM, VCN, MRV*

Meeting Venus ♂♂½ 1991 (PG-13) Backstage drama featuring Close as Karin Anderson, a world-famous Swedish opera diva. An international cast of characters adds to this sophisticated film of romance, rivalry and political confrontation set amidst a newly unified Europe. 121m/C VHS, Beta, LV. Glenn Close, Niels Arestrup, Erland Josephson, Johanna Ter Steege, Maria De Medeiros, Ildiko Bansagi, Macha Meril, Dorottya Udvaros, Jay O. Sanders, Victor Poletti; *D:* Istvan Szabo; *W:* Istvan Szabo, Michael Hirst; *C:* Lajos Koltai; *V:* Kiri Te Kanawa. *WAR*

Meetings with Remarkable Men ♂♂½ 1979 An acclaimed, visually awesome film version of the memoir by Gurdjieff, about his wanderings through Asia and the Middle East searching for answers and developing his own spiritual code. Mildly entertaining but only of true interest to those familiar with the subject. 108m/C VHS, Beta. Terence Stamp, Dragan Maksimovic, Mikica Dmitrijevic; *D:* Peter Brook. *WSH*

Megaforce woof! 1982 (PG) Futuristic thriller directed by stuntman Needham follows the adventures of the military task force, Megaforce, on its mission to save a small democratic nation from attack. Bostwick leads the attack. 'Nuff said. 99m/C VHS, Beta. Barry Bostwick, Persis Khambatta, Edward Mulhare, Henry Silva, Michael Beck, Ralph Wilcox; *D:* Hal Needham. *FOX*

Megaville ♂♂ 1991 (R) Set in the not too distant future, corrupt politician Travanti struggles to corner the market on the evil technology "Dream-a-Life," which aims to control the rebellious "riff-raff" of Megaville. He does all of his dealings while up against a hitman who has a defective memory chip in his brain. 96m/C VHS. Billy Zane, Daniel J. Travanti, J.C. Quinn, Grace Zabriskie; *D:* Peter Lehner; *W:* Peter Lehner. *LIV*

Mein Kampf: Hitler's Rise and Fall 1960 The rise and fall of German fascism and its impact upon the world is examined in this documentary. 120m/C VHS, Beta, LV. *D:* Erwin Leiser. *MRV, CCP, FCT*

Melanie 🎬🎬½ 1982 (PG) Drama tells the tale of one poor woman's courage, determination, and optimism, as she tries to regain her child from her ex-husband. She befriends musician Cummings (a founding member of "Guess Who" rock band) who helps. Usual cliches balanced by good performances. 109m/C VHS, Beta. *CA* Glynnis O'Connor, Paul Sorvino, Don Johnson, Burton Cummings; *D:* Rex Bromfield. *VES*

Melodie en Sous-Sol 🎬🎬 *Any Number Can Win* 1963 Two ex-convicts, one old and one young, risk their lives and freedom for one last major heist: a gambling casino. In French with English subtitles. 118m/B VHS, Beta. *FR* Jean Gabin, Alain Delon, Viviane Romance; *D:* Henri Verneuil. *BAR*

Melody 🎬🎬 1971 (G) Sensitive but slow study of a special friendship which enables two pre-teens to survive in a regimented and impersonal world. Features music by the Bee Gees. 106m/C VHS, Beta. *GB* Tracy Hyde, Jack Wild, Mark Lester, Colin Barrie, Roy Kinnear; *D:* Waris Hussein; *W:* Alan Parker.

Melody Cruise 🎬🎬 1932 Boring musical romantic comedy that can't stay with any one of those three things for more than a minute without careening into one of the other two. 🎵I Met Her at a Party; He's Not the Marrying Kind; Isn't This a Night For Love; This is the Hour. 75m/B VHS, Beta. Phil Harris, Charlie Ruggles, Greta Nissen, Helen Mack, Chick Chandler; *D:* Mark Sandrich; *M:* Max Steiner. *TTC*

Melody for Three 🎬🎬 1941 In the tradition of matchmaker, Doctor Christian aids in the reuniting of music-teacher mother and great-conductor father, who have been divorced for years, in order to help the couple's son, a violin prodigy. 69m/B VHS, Beta, 8mm. Jean Hersholt, Fay Wray; *D:* Erle C. Kenton. *NOS, VYY, DVT*

Melody in Love 🎬 1978 A young girl visits her cousin and her swinging friends on a tropical island. Dubbed. 90m/C VHS, Beta, Closed Caption. Melody O'Bryan, Sasha Hehn; *D:* Hubert Frank. *FOX*

Melody Master 🎬🎬 *New Wine* 1941 Romanticized biography of composer Franz Schubert, chronicling his personal life and loves, along with performances of his compositions. If you just have to know what drove the composer of "Ave Maria" it may hold your interest, but otherwise not very compelling. 80m/B VHS, Beta. Alan Curtis, Ilona Massey, Binnie Barnes, Albert Basserman, Billy Gilbert, Sterling Holloway; *M:* Miklos Rozsa. *NOS, VYY, DVT*

Melody of the Plains 🎬 1937 Singing cowpoke teams up with a young girl for some cattle-rustlin' adventure. Substandard horse opry due to poor direction and haphazard lensing. 53m/B VHS. Fred Scott, Louise Small, Al "Fuzzy" St. John, David Sharpe, Lafe McKee, Charles "Slim" Whitaker, Hal Price, Lew Meehan; *D:* Sam Newfield; *W:* Bennett Cohen. *MOV*

Melody Ranch 🎬🎬½ 1940 Gene returns to his home town as an honored guest and appointed sheriff. But gangster MacLane is determined to drive him out of town. 🎵Melody Ranch; Call of the Canyon; We Never Dream the Same Dream Twice; Vote for Autry; My Gal Sal; Torpedo Joe; What Are Cowboys Made Of?; Rodeo Rose; Back in the Saddle Again. 84m/C VHS, Beta. Gene Autry, Jimmy Durante, George "Gabby" Hayes, Ann Miller, Barton MacLane, Joseph Sawyer, Horace McMahon, Veda Ann Borg; *D:* Joseph Santley. *CCB, VCN*

Melody Trail 🎬 1935 Autry wins $1000 in a rodeo, loses the money to a gypsy, gets a job, falls for his employer's daughter...and in the end captures a kidnapper and cattle rustlers. 🎵Hold On, Little Doggie, Hold On; On the Prairie; Lookin for the Lost Chord; The Hurdy Gurdy Man; My Prayer For Tonight; End of the Trail; I'd Love a Home in the Mountains. 60m/B VHS, Beta. Gene Autry, Smiley Burnette, Ann Rutherford; *D:* Joseph Kane. *CCB, VCN*

Melvin and Howard 🎬🎬🎬½ 1980 (R) Story of Melvin Dummar, who once gave Howard Hughes a ride. Dummar later claimed a share of Hughes's will. Significant for Demme's direction and fine acting from Steenburgen/LeMat, and Robards in a small role as Hughes. Offbeat and very funny. 95m/C VHS, Beta, LV. Paul LeMat, Jason Robards Jr., Mary Steenburgen, Michael J. Pollard, Dabney Coleman, Elizabeth Cheshire, Pamela Reed, Cheryl "Rainbeaux" Smith; *D:* Jonathan Demme; *W:* Bo Goldman. Academy Awards '80: Best Original Screenplay, Best Supporting Actress (Steenburgen); Golden Globe Awards '81: Best Supporting Actress (Steenburgen); Los Angeles Film Critics Association Awards '80: Best Supporting Actress (Steenburgen); National Board of Review Awards '80: 10 Best Films of the Year; New York Film Critics Awards '80: Best Director (Demme), Best Screenplay, Best Supporting Actress (Steenburgen); National Society of Film Critics Awards '80: Best Film, Best Screenplay, Best Supporting Actress (Steenburgen); Writers Guild of America '80: Best Original Screenplay; Nominations: Academy Awards '80: Best Supporting Actor (Robards).*USH, BTV*

Melvin Purvis: G-Man 🎬🎬 *The Legend of Machine Gun Kelly* 1974 Mediocre action film has dedicated federal agent tracking killer Machine Gun Kelly across American Midwest during Depression. Made for television. 78m/C VHS. Dale Robertson, Harris Yulin, Margaret Blye, Matt Clark, Elliot Street, Dick Sargent, John Karlen, David Canary; *D:* Dan Curtis. *HBO*

The Member of the Wedding 🎬🎬🎬 1952 While struggling through her adolescence, a twelve-year-old girl growing up in 1945 Georgia seeks solace from her family's cook. Based on Carson McCullers's play, this story of family, belonging, and growth is well acted and touching. 90m/C VHS, Beta. Ethel Waters, Julie Harris, Brandon de Wilde, Arthur Franz; *D:* Fred Zinnemann; *W:* Edward Anhalt; *C:* Hal Mohr; *M:* Alex North. Nominations: Academy Awards '52: Best Actress (Harris). *NO*

The Member of the Wedding 🎬🎬 1983 TV rehash of Carson McCuller's play about a young girl who finds she's got some growing up to do when big brother marries. No match for Zinnemann's '52 version, or for Mann's earlier "All Quiet on the Western Front" and "Marty." 90m/C VHS. Dana Hill, Pearl Bailey, Howard E. Rollins Jr.; *D:* Delbert Mann. *VHE*

Memoirs of an Invisible Man 🎬½ 1992 (PG-13) Nick Halloway, a slick and shallow stock analyst, is rendered invisible by a freak accident. When he is pursued by a CIA agent-hit man who wants to exploit him, Nick turns for help to Alice, a documentary filmmaker he has just met. Naturally, they fall in love along the way. Effective sight gags, hardworking cast can't overcome pitfalls in script, which indecisively meanders between comedy and thrills. 99m/C VHS, LV, Closed Caption. Chevy Chase, Daryl Hannah, Sam Neill, Michael McKean, Stephen Tobolowsky, Jim Norton, Patricia Heaton, Rosalind Chao; *D:* John Carpenter; *W:* Robert Collector. *WAR*

Memorial Day 🎬🎬 1983 Good cast highlights this made-for-television outing covering a Vietnam veterans reunion. With the old memories come new problems for the men and their families. 120m/C VHS. Mike Farrell, Shelley Fabares, Keith Mitchell, Bonnie Bedelia, Robert Walden, Edward Herrmann, Danny Glover; *D:* Joseph Sargent; *M:* Billy Goldenberg. *NO*

Memorial Valley Massacre 🎬 1988 (R) When campers settle for a weekend in a new, unfinished campground, they're slaughtered in turn by a nutty hermit. 93m/C VHS, Beta, LV. Cameron Mitchell, William Smith, John Kerry, Mark Mears, Lesa Lee, John Caso; *D:* Robert C. Hughes. *NLC*

Memories of a Marriage 🎬🎬🎬 1990 A nostalgic look at a couple's many years of marriage, from the husband's point of view, as they face their most trying times. Touchingly reminiscent as it spans the youthful years of new love and marriage to the more quiet, solid years of matured love. In Danish with English subtitles.

90m/C VHS. *DK* Ghita Norby, Frits Helmuth, Rikke Bendsen, Henning Moritzen; *D:* Kaspar Rostrup. *ORI, FXL*

Memories of Hell 1987 Examines the special bonds of friendship that have been maintained among the New Mexicans who survived one of WWII's most brutal battles and subsequent prisoner experiences. 57m/C VHS, Beta. *NO*

Memories of Me 🎬🎬 1988 (PG-13) A distraught doctor travels to L.A. to see his ailing father and make up for lost time. Both the doctor and his father learn about themselves and each other. Story of child/parent relationships attempts to pull at the heartstrings but only gets as far as the liver. Co-written and co-produced by Crystal, this film never quite reaches the potential of its cast. 103m/C VHS, Beta, LV, Closed Caption. Billy Crystal, Alan King, JoBeth Williams, David Ackroyd, Sean Connery, Janet Carroll; *D:* Henry Winkler; *W:* Billy Crystal, Eric Roth; *M:* Georges Delerue. *FOX*

Memories of Murder 1990 A woman suffering from amnesia is stalked by a merciless killer, apparently seeking revenge. Can she regain her memory and understand why she is being hunted, before it's too late? 104m/C VHS, Beta. Vanity, Nancy Allen, Robin Thomas; *D:* Robert Lewis; *W:* John Kent Harrison, Nevin Schreiner. *PSM*

Memories of Underdevelopment 🎬🎬½ 1968 Set in the early 1960s. An anti-revolutionary, Europeanized intellectual takes a stand against the new government in Cuba. In Spanish with English subtitles. 97m/B VHS. *CU* Sergio Corrieri, Daisy Granados; *D:* Tomas Gutierrez Alea; *W:* Tomas Gutierrez Alea. *NYF, FCT*

Memory of Us 🎬🎬 1974 (PG) Still-relevant story of a married, middle-aged woman who starts to question her happiness as a wife and mother. Written by its star Geer, whose father, Will, plays a bit part. 93m/C VHS. Ellen Geer, Jon Cypher, Barbara Colby, Peter Brown, Robert Hogan, Rose Marie, Will Geer; *D:* H. Kaye Dyal. *ACA*

Memphis 🎬🎬½ 1991 (PG-13) In 1957 three white drifters (two men and a woman) decide to secure some easy money by kidnapping the young grandson of the richest black businessman in Memphis. They think it's an easy job since, given the prejudice of the times, the police will do little or nothing but they reckon without the resources of the black community itself. Based on the novel "September, September" by Shelby Foote. Originally made for cable. 92m/C VHS, Beta, LV, Closed Caption. Cybill Shepherd, John Laughlin, J.E. Freeman, Richard Brooks, Moses Gunn, Vanessa Bell, Martin C. Gardner; *D:* Yves Simoneau; *W:* Cybill Shepherd, Larry McMurtry; *M:* David Bell. *TTC*

Memphis Belle 🎬🎬🎬 1990 (PG-13) Satisfying Hollywood version of the documentary of the same name captures the true story of the final mission of a WWII bomber crew stationed in England. The boys of the Memphis Belle were the first group of B-17 crewmen to complete a 25 mission tour—no small feat in an air war that claimed many lives. Good ensemble cast of up and coming young actors; Lithgow has a nice turn as an army PR guy determined to exploit their boyish good looks on the homefront. Caton-Jones effectively uses 1940s film techniques and some original footage, making up for a rather hokey script. Film debut of singer Connick. Produced by Catherine Wyler, whose father made the original. *CW:* Language; adult situations and violence. 107m/C VHS, Beta, LV, 8mm, Closed Caption. Matthew Modine, John Lithgow, Eric Stoltz, Sean Astin, Harry Connick Jr., Reed Edward Diamond, Tate Donovan, D.B. Sweeney, Billy Zane, David Strathairn, Jane Horrocks, Courtney Gains, Neil Giuntoli; *D:* Michael Caton-Jones; *W:* Monte Merrick; *C:* David Watkin; *M:* George Fenton. *WAR, VYY, FCT*

Memphis Belle: A Story of a Flying Fortress 1944 The entire final mission of the B-25 bomber "Memphis Belle" and its daring daylight attack on the submarine pens at Wilhelmshaven, Germany is captured through newsreel footage. The crew was the first to complete a 25 run mission. A film version of the story was released in 1990 as "Memphis Belle." Produced by William Wyler. **43m/C VHS, Beta.** *TPV, NOS, HHT*

The Men *♂♂♂½* *Battle Stripe* 1950 A paraplegic WWII veteran sinks into depression until his former girlfriend manages to bring him out of it. Marlon Brando's first film. A thoughtful story that relies on subtle acting and direction. **85m/B VHS.** Marlon Brando, Teresa Wright, Everett Sloane, Jack Webb; **D:** Fred Zinnemann. National Board of Review Awards '50: 10 Best Films of the Year; Nominations: Academy Awards '50: Best Story & Screenplay. *REP*

Men... *♂♂♂½* 1985 A funny and insightful satire about a man who discovers his loving wife has been having an affair with a young artist. In a unique course of revenge, the husband ingratiates himself with the artist and gradually turns him into a carbon copy of himself. In German with English subtitles or dubbed. **96m/C VHS.** *GE* Heiner Lauterbach, Uwe Ochsenknecht, Ulrike Kriener, Janna Marangosoff; **D:** Doris Dorrie. *ING, NYF*

Men Are Not Gods *♂♂½* 1937 Verbose film (precursor to "A Double Life") about an actor playing Othello who nearly kills his wife during Desdemona's death scene. **90m/B VHS, Beta, LV.** *GB* Rex Harrison, Miriam Hopkins, Gertrude Lawrence; **D:** Walter Reisch.

Men at Work *♂♂* 1990 (PG-13) Garbage collectors Sheen and Estevez may not love their work, but at least it's consistent from day to day. That is, until they get wrapped up in a very dirty politically-motivated murder. And who will clean up the mess when the politicians are through trashing each other? A semi-thrilling semi-comedy that may leave you semi-satisfied. **98m/C VHS, Beta, LV, Closed Caption.** Charlie Sheen, Emilio Estevez, Leslie Hope, Keith David; **D:** Emilio Estevez; **W:** Emilio Estevez. *COL, FOX*

Men Don't Leave *♂♂½* 1989 (PG-13) A recent widow tries to raise her kids single-handedly, suffers big city life, and takes a chance at a second love. Good performances by all, especially Cusack as the sweet seducer of teenaged O'Donnell. By the director of "Risky Business." **115m/C VHS, Beta, LV, 8mm, Closed Caption.** Jessica Lange, Arliss Howard, Joan Cusack, Kathy Bates, Charlie Korsmo, Corey Carrier, Chris O'Donnell, Tom Mason, Jim Haynie; **D:** Paul Brickman; **W:** Barbara Benedek, Paul Brickman; **C:** Bruce Surtees; **M:** Thomas Newman. *WAR*

Men in Black *♂♂♂* *MIB* 1997 (PG-13) Charm, wit and some outrageous insect-type aliens make a winning cosmic combination. K (Jones) and J (Smith) are top-secret government operatives, investigating alien visitations on Earth, who must stop terrorist extraterrestrial D'Onofrio from causing a galactic disaster. Excellent chemistry between deadpan Jones and hip-hop Smith is strengthened by a very funny script. Director Sonnenfeld tops it off with just enough detail and human element to keep the special effects from stealing the show, and with Rick Baker around, that's not easy to do. Box office hit that should spawn a sequel or two. Adapted from the Marvel comic book.**CW:** Language and sci-fi violence. **98m/C VHS.** Tommy Lee Jones, Will Smith, Linda Fiorentino, Rip Torn, Vincent D'Onofrio, Tony Shalhoub, Carel Struycken, Sergio Calderon; **D:** Barry Sonnenfeld; **W:** Edward Solomon; **C:** Don Peterman; **M:** Danny Elfman. *NYR*

Men in Love *♂♂* 1990 A young San Franciscan travels to Hawaii with the cremated remains of his lover, who has succumbed to AIDS. There he encounters a supportive group of men who nurse him back to sexual and spiritual wholeness. **93m/C VHS.** Doug Self, Joe Tolbe, Emerald Starr, Kutira Decosterd, Scott Catamas; **D:** Marc Huestis; **C:** Fawn Yacker. *WBF, FCT*

Men in War *♂♂½* 1957 Korean War drama about a small platoon trying to take an enemy hill by themselves. A worthwhile effort with some good action sequences. **100m/B VHS, Beta.** Robert Ryan, Robert Keith, Aldo Ray, Vic Morrow; **D:** Anthony

Mann; **W:** Philip Yordan; **M:** Elmer Bernstein. *FGF, MRV, BMV*

Men of Boys Town *♂♂½* 1941 Sequel to 1938's "Boys Town" has the same sentimentality, even more if that's possible. Father Flanagan's reformatory faces closure, while the kids reach out to an embittered new inmate. Worth seeing for the ace cast reprising their roles. **106m/B VHS.** Spencer Tracy, Mickey Rooney, Darryl Hickman, Henry O'Neill, Lee J. Cobb, Sidney Miller; **D:** Norman Taurog. *MGM, FCT*

Men of Ireland *♂♂* 1938 A Dublin medical student cavorts with islanders off the Irish coast. Uninspired programmer with authentic native folk of the Blasket Islands, plus their songs and dances. **62m/B VHS, Beta, 8mm.** *IR* Cecil Ford, Eileen Curran, Brian O'Sullivan, Gabriel Fallon; **D:** Richard Bird. *VYY*

Men of Respect *♂♂* 1991 (R) Shakespeare meets the mafia in this misbegotten gangster yarn. Turturro, a gangster MacBeth, is prodded by wife and psychic to butcher his way to the top o' the mob. Well acted but ill conceived, causing Bard's partial roll over in grave. **113m/C VHS, LV, 8mm, Closed Caption.** John Turturro, Katherine Borowitz, Peter Boyle, Dennis Farina, Chris Stein, Steven Wright, Stanley Tucci; **D:** William Reilly; **W:** William Reilly; **C:** Bobby Bukowski. *COL*

Men of Sherwood Forest *♂♂½* 1957 Robin Hood and his band take it to the sheriff et al in this colorful Hammer version of the timeless legend. **77m/C VHS.** *GB* Don Taylor, Reginald Beckwith, Eileen Moore, Davis King-Wood, Patrick Holt, John Van Eyssen, Douglas Wilmer; **D:** Val Guest. *NOS, SNC, DVT*

Men of Steel *♂* 1988 (PG) Two Canadian military officers, one French and one English, must struggle to survive when their plane crashes in the wilderness. Besides contending with the surroundings, they must deal with one another's instilled bitterness and underlying prejudices. **91m/C VHS, Beta.** Allan Royal, Robert Lalonde, David Ferry, Mavor Moore, Yvan Ponton; **D:** Donald Shebib. *TWE*

Men of the Fighting Lady *♂♂♂½* 1954 Action-adventure offers plenty of exciting battle footage. Features the stories of selected pilots stationed on a U.S. aircraft carrier in the Pacific during the Korean War. The stories, told to Calhern as writer James A. Michener, center around the lead pilot Johnson. Dramatic airlifts include a scene in which Johnson helps a blinded Martin land his plane safely on the carrier deck. Gene Ruggero's editing of the war footage was so expertly done that he was questioned by the Pentagon when they had a hard time believing the scenes were achieved by skillful editing and painted backdrops. Look for "Beaver" Mathers as one of Wynn's sons. **81m/C VHS, Beta.** Van Johnson, Walter Pidgeon, Louis Calhern, Dewey Martin, Keenan Wynn, Frank Lovejoy, Robert Horton, Bert Freed, Jerry Mathers; **D:** Andrew Marton; **M:** Miklos Rozsa. *MGM*

Men of Two Worlds *♂♂* *Witch Doctor; Kisenga, Man of Africa* 1946 Classical musician raised in Africa is the toast of Europe until he finds out he's got a voodoo curse, and suddenly he's got the heebie jeebies too bad to play chopsticks. **90m/C VHS, Beta.** *GB* Robert Adams, Eric Portman, Orlando Martins, Phyllis Calvert, Arnold Marle, Cathleen Nesbitt, David Horne, Cyril Raymond; **D:** Thorold Dickinson. *SNC*

Men of War *♂½* 1994 (R) Ex-Special Forces mercenaries decide to defend, rather than destroy, the inhabitants of an exotic island, whose land is wanted by a suspicious company interested in mining rights.**CW:** Non-stop violence; strong language; some sexuality. **102m/C VHS, LV, Closed Caption.** Dolph Lundgren, Charlotte Lewis, B.D. Wong, Anthony John Denison, Tim Guinee, Don Harvey, Tiny Lister, Tom Wright, Kevin Tighe; **D:** Perry Lang; **W:** John Sayles, Ethan Reiff, Cyrus Voris; **C:** Ronn Schmidt; **M:** Gerald Gouriet. *TOU*

The Men Who Tread on the Tiger's Tail *♂♂½* 1945 Twelfth-century Japan is the setting for this struggle of power between two brothers, one a reigning shogun, the other on the run. English subtitles. **60m/B VHS, Beta.** *JP* **D:** Akira Kurosawa. *IHF*

Menace on the Mountain *♂♂* 1970 (G) Family-oriented drama about a father and son who battle carpetbagging Confederate deserters during the Civil War. **89m/C VHS, Beta.** Patricia Crowley, Albert Salmi, Charles Aidman; **D:** Vincent McEveety. *DIS*

Menace II Society *♂♂♂½* 1993 (R) Portrayal of black teens lost in inner-city hell is realistically captured by 21-year-old twin directors, in their big-screen debut. Caine (Turner) lives with his grandparents and peddles drugs for spending money, from the eve of his high school graduation to his decision to escape south-central Los Angeles for Atlanta. Bleak and haunting, with some of the most unsettling, bloodiest violence ever shown in a commercial film. Disturbing to watch, but critcally acclaimed. The Hughes' make their mark on contemporary black cinema with intensity, enhanced by an action-comics visual flair. Based on a story by the Hughes' and Tyger Williams.**CW:** Language and strong violence and drug use. **104m/C VHS, LV, Closed Caption.** Tyrin Turner, Larenz Tate, Samuel L. Jackson, Glenn Plummer, Julian Roy Doster, Bill Duke, Charles S. Dutton, Jada Pinkett, Vonte Sweet, Ryan Williams; **D:** Allen Hughes, Albert Hughes; **W:** Tyger Williams; **C:** Lisa Rinzler. Independent Spirit Awards '94: Best Cinematography; MTV Movie Awards '94: Best Film; Nominations: Independent Spirit Awards '94: Best Actor (Turner), Best First Feature. *COL, NLC, IME*

Menage *♂♂♂* *Tenue de Soiree* 1986 Depardieu is the homosexual crook who breaks into the home of an impoverished couple—the dominating Miou-Miou and her submissive husband, Blanc. An unrepentant thief, he begins to take over their lives, introducing them to the wonderful world of crime, among other, more kinky, pastimes. Gender-bending farce that doesn't hold up to the end but is worth watching for sheer outrageousness. In French with English subtitles. **84m/C VHS.** *FR* Gerard Depardieu, Michel Blanc, Miou-Miou, Bruno Cremer, Jean-Pierre Marielle; **D:** Bertrand Blier; **W:** Bertrand Blier; **M:** Serge Gainsbourg. Cannes Film Festival '86: Best Actor (Blanc). *TRI, FCT*

The Men's Club *♂½* 1986 (R) Seven middle-aged buddies get together for a single night, and bare their respective souls and personal traumas, talking about women and eating and drinking. Banal. Based on novel by Leonard Michael. **100m/C VHS, Beta, LV.** Harvey Keitel, Roy Scheider, Craig Wasson, Frank Langella, David Dukes, Richard Jordan, Treat Williams, Stockard Channing, Jennifer Jason Leigh, Ann Dusenberry, Cindy Pickett, Gwen Welles; **D:** Peter Medak. *PAR*

Menschenfrauen *♂♂½* 1980 A philandering journalist is put in his place by the four women with whom he is simultaneously having relationships. In German with English subtitles. **100m/C VHS, Beta.** *GE* **D:** Valie Export. *FCT*

Mephisto *♂♂♂½* 1981 An egomaniacal actor, compellingly played by Brandauer, sides with the Nazis to further his career, with disastrous results. The first of three brilliant films by Szabo and Brandauer exploring the price of power and personal sublimation in German history. Critically hailed. In German with English subtitles. From the novel by Klaus Mann. Followed by "Colonel Redl" and "Hanussen." **144m/C VHS, Beta.** *HU* Klaus Maria Brandauer, Krystyna Janda, Ildiko Bansagi, Karin Boyd, Rolf Hoppe, Christine Harbort, Gyorgy Cserhalmi, Christiane Graskoff, Peter Andorai, Ildiko Kishonti; **D:** Istvan Szabo; **C:** Lajos Koltai. Academy Awards '81: Best Foreign Language Film. *REP, SWC, GLV*

The Mephisto Waltz *♂♂♂* 1971 (R) Journalist gets more than a story when he is granted an interview with a dying pianist. It turns out that he is a satanist and the cult he is a part of wants the journalist. Chilling adaptation of the Fred Mustard Stewart novel features a haunting musical score. 108m/C VHS. Alan Alda, Jacqueline Bisset, Barbara Parkins, Curt Jurgens, Bradford Dillman, William Windom, Kathleen Widdoes; **D:** Paul Wendkos; **M:** Jerry Goldsmith. FOX

The Mercenaries 🎬½ 1965 Romantic warrior fights to save the lives and honor of his people who are under attack from mercenaries murdering and raping their way across Europe. 98m/C Beta. Debra Paget. AIP

The Mercenaries 🎬 *Cuba Crossing; Kill Castro; Assignment: Kill Castro; Key West Crossing; Sweet Dirty Tony* 1980 A tough guy, given the assignment to kill Fidel Castro, encounters all sorts of adversity along the way. Key West scenery is the only thing of interest. 92m/C VHS, Beta. Stuart Whitman, Robert Vaughn, Caren Kaye, Raymond St. Jacques, Woody Strode, Sybil Danning, Albert Salmi, Michael V. Gazzo; **D:** Chuck Workman. ACA, JEF

Mercenary 🎬🎬 1996 Ex-Commando-turned-mercenary Alex Hawks (Gruner) is hired by wealthy businessman Jonas Ambler (Ritter) to avenge his wife's death at the hands of terrorists. Only Ambler's desk jockey doesn't want to stay on the sidelines and watch—he wants to do. So, Hawks is forced to take him along to Iraq when he goes after the bad guys. 97m/C VHS. Olivier Gruner, John Ritter, Robert Culp, Ed Lauter, Martin Kove. PGV

Mercenary Fighters 🎬½ 1988 (R) An American soldier-of-fortune fights for both sides of an African revolution. Shot in South Africa. 90m/C VHS, Beta, LV. Peter Fonda, Reb Brown, Ron O'Neal, Jim Mitchum; **D:** Riki Shelach. MED, VTR

The Merchant of Four Seasons 🎬🎬🎬 1971 Story focuses on the depression and unfulfilled dreams of an average street merchant. Direction from Fassbinder is slow, deliberate, and mesmerizing. In German with English subtitles. 88m/C VHS, Beta. Hans Hirschmuller, Irm Hermann, Hanna Schygulla, Andrea Schober, Gusti Kreissl; **D:** Rainer Werner Fassbinder; **W:** Rainer Werner Fassbinder. NYF

The Merchant of Venice 🎬🎬🎬 1973 Shakespeare's tragedy of prejudice, vengeance, and sacrifice stars Olivier as the persecuted money lender Shylock, who demands his payment of a pound of flesh for a defaulted loan. 131m/C VHS. GB Laurence Olivier, Joan Plowright, Jeremy Brett. FUS, FCT

Merchants of War 🎬 1990 (R) Sent out by the CIA on a mission, two best friends are soon the target of one of the most dangerous terrorists in the world. The fanatical Islamic terrorist soon casts his wrath upon the two men. 100m/C VHS. Asher Brauner, Jesse Vint, Bonnie Beck; **D:** Peter M. MacKenzie. THV

Mercy Mission 🎬🎬½ 1993 Young pilot Bakula runs into trouble over the Pacific with his small plane and it's upto Air New Zealand airline pilot Loggia, who risks the lives of his passengers and crew, to come to his rescue. 92m/C VHS. Scott Bakula, Robert Loggia; **D:** Roger Young. HMK

Meridian: Kiss of the Beast 🎬½ 1990 (R) A beautiful heiress is courted, kidnapped and loved by a demonic man-beast. 90m/C VHS, Beta, LV, Closed Caption. Sherilyn Fenn, Malcom Jamieson, Hilary Mason, Alex Daniels, Phil Fondacaro; **D:** Charles Band; **M:** Pino Donaggio. PAR

Merlin 🎬🎬½ 1992 (PG-13) In a remote California town reporter Christy Lake is stunned to discover her ancient heritage. Turns out she's the reincarnated daughter of legendary Merlin the magician and it is her duty to protect the Sword of Power from the evil sorcerer Pendragon. And aided by a handsome warrior and an ancient sage, that's just what she intends to do.**CW:** Action/adventure violence. 112m/C VHS. Nadia Cameron, Peter Phelps, Richard Lynch, James Hong, Ted Markland, Desmond Llewelyn; **D:** Paul Hunt; **W:** Nick McCarty. HMD

Merlin and the Sword 🎬 *Arthur the King* 1985 Poor use of a good cast in this treatment of the legend of Merlin, Arthur and Excalibur. 94m/C VHS, Beta. Malcolm McDowell, Edward Woodward, Candice Bergen, Dyan Cannon; **D:** Clive Donner. LIV, VES

Merlin of the Crystal Cave 🎬🎬½ 1991 Depicts the adventures of the young boy Merlin as he learns the ways of magic in the days before Camelot and King Arthur. Made for British television. 159m/C VHS. GB FOX

Mermaids 🎬🎬🎬 1990 (PG-13) Mrs. Flax (Cher) is the flamboyant mother of two who hightails out of town every time a relationship threatens to turn serious. Having moved some eighteen times, her daughters, Charlotte (Ryder), 15, and Kate (Ricci), 8, are a little worse for the wear, psychologically speaking. One aspires to be a nun though not Catholic, and the other holds her breath under water. Now living in Massachusetts, Mrs. Flax starts having those "I got you, babe" feelings for Hoskins, a shoestore owner. Amusing, well-acted multi-generational coming of ager based on a novel by Patty Dann.**CW:** Adult situations; language and sexual situations. 110m/C VHS, Beta, LV, Closed Caption. Cher, Winona Ryder, Bob Hoskins, Christina Ricci, Michael Schoeffling, Caroline McWilliams, Jan Miner; **D:** Richard Benjamin; **W:** June Roberts; **C:** Howard Atherton; **M:** Jack Nitzsche. National Board of Review Awards '90: Best Supporting Actress (Ryder). ORI

The Mermaids of Tiburon 🎬 *The Aqua Sex* 1962 A marine biologist and a criminal travel to a remote island off Mexico in search of elusive, expensive "fire pearls." There they encounter a kingdom of lovely mermaids who promptly liven things up. Filmed in "Aquascope" for your viewing pleasure. 77m/C VHS. Diane Webber, George Rowe, Timothy Carey, Jose Gonzalez-Gonzalez, John Mylong, Gil Baretto, Vicki Kantenwine, Nani Morrissey, Judy Edwards, Jean Carroll, Diana Cook, Karen Goodman, Nancy Burns; **D:** John Lamb; **W:** John Lamb. FRG

Merrill's Marauders 🎬🎬½ 1962 Chandler is the commander of a battle-hardened regiment fighting in the jungles of Burma in 1944. The exhausted unit gains their latest objective and expects to be relieved, only to be continuously pushed into more fighting down the line. Director Fuller excels at showing the confusion of battle; Chandler's last film role (he died before the film was released). 98m/C VHS. Jeff Chandler, Ty Hardin, Peter Brown, Andrew Duggan, Will Hutchins, Claude Akins; **D:** Samuel Fuller; **W:** Milton Sperling, Samuel Fuller; **C:** William Clothier; **M:** Howard Jackson. WAR

Merry Christmas, Mr. Lawrence 🎬🎬🎬 1983 (R) An often overlooked drama about a WWII Japanese POW camp. Taut psychological drama about clashing cultures and physical and emotional survival focusing on the tensions between Bowie as a British POW and camp commander Sakamato, who also composed the outstanding score. A haunting and intense film about the horrors of war. Based on the novel by Laurens van der Post. 124m/C VHS, Beta. JP GB David Bowie, Tom Conti, Ryuichi Sakamoto, Takeshi, Jack Thompson; **D:** Nagisa Oshima. National Board of Review Awards '83: Best Actor (Conti). USH

Merry-Go-Round 🎬🎬🎬 1923 A handsome Austrian count is engaged to a woman of his class when he meets the beautiful Agnes, who works as an organ grinder for the local merry-go-round. He disguises himself to woo her but finally decides to marry his fiance, although Agnes continues to love him. But the story doesn't end for the two lovers who are destined to be together. Producer Thalberg and director von Stroheim battled over the expense and length of the film until Thalberg had the director replaced. However, much of the film still shows the von Stroheim brilliance and attention to lavish detail. 110m/B VHS. Norman Kerry, Mary Philbin, Cesare Gravina, Edith Yorke, George Hackathorne; **D:** Rupert Julian, Erich von Stroheim. FCT, HEG

The Merry Widow 🎬🎬🎬½ *The Lady Dances* 1934 The first sound version of the famous Franz Lehar operetta, dealing with a playboy from a bankrupt kingdom who must woo and marry the land's wealthy widow or be tried for treason. A delightful musical comedy, with a sterling cast and patented Lubitschian gaiety. Made as a silent in 1912 and 1925; remade in color in 1952. ♫Girls, Girls, Girls; Vilia; Tonight Will Teach Me to Forget; Melody of Laughter; Maxim's; The Girls at Maxim's; The Merry Widow Waltz; If Widows are Rich; Russian Dance. 99m/B VHS, Beta, LV. Maurice Chevalier, Jeanette MacDonald, Edward Everett Horton, Una Merkel, George Barbier, Minna Gombell, Ruth Channing, Sterling Holloway, Henry Armetta, Barbara Leanard, Donald Meek, Akim Tamiroff, Herman Bing; **D:** Ernst Lubitsch; **M:** Franz Lehar, Lorenz Hart. Academy Awards '34: Best Interior Decoration. MGM

The Merry Widow 🎬🎬½ 1952 Rich widow Turner travels to her husband's homeland of Marshovia to dedicate a statue to his memory. The country is deeply in debt and the king would like the widow to marry a local count and remain (along with her fortune). Lamas is charming as the intended bridegroom but Turner, though lovely looking, is miscast; her singing was dubbed by Erwin. Uninspired remake of the 1934 film only benefits from being shot in color and the lavish production values. Based on the operetta by Lehar. ♫The Merry Widow Waltz; Can-Can; Girls, Girls, Girls; I'm Going to Maxim's. 105m/C VHS. Lana Turner, Fernando Lamas, Una Merkel, Richard Haydn, Thomas Gomez, John Abbott, Marcel Dalio, King Donovan, Robert Coote, Joi Lansing; **Cameos:** Gwen Verdon; **D:** Curtis Bernhardt; **W:** Sonya Levien, William Ludwig; **C:** Robert L. Surtees; **M:** Franz Lehar; **V:** Trudy Erwin. Nominations: Academy Awards '52: Best Art Direction/Set Decoration (Color), Best Costume Design (Color). MGM

Merton of the Movies 🎬🎬½ 1947 Skelton stars as star-struck, small town theater usher Merton Gill who wins a trip to Hollywood. He's befriended by stunt double Phyllis (O'Brien) who recognizes his comedic talents and works to get him that big break. Based on the play by George S. Kaufman and Marc Connelly and previously filmed in 1924 and 1932 (as "Make Me a Star"). 82m/B VHS, Beta, Closed Caption. Red Skelton, Virginia O'Brien, Gloria Grahame, Leon Ames, Alan Mowbray, Charles D. Brown, Hugo Haas, Harry Hayden; **D:** Robert Alton; **W:** George Wells, Lou Breslow. MGM, FCT

Mesa of Lost Women woof! *Lost Women; Lost Women of Zarpa* 1952 Mad scientist creates brave new race of vicious women with long fingernails. So bad it's a wanna-B. Addams Family buffs will spot the Fester in Coogan. 70m/B VHS. Jackie Coogan, Richard Travis, Allan Nixon, Mary Hill, Robert Knapp, Tandra Quinn, Lyle Talbot, Katherine Victor, Angelo Rossitto; **D:** Herbert Tevos, Ron Ormond; **W:** Herbert Tevos; **C:** Gilbert Warrenton, Karl Struss. NOS, MRV, SNC

Mesmerized 🎬🎬 *Shocked* 1984 Based on the work by Jerzy Skolimowski, the film is a dramatization of the Victoria Thompson murder case in 1880's New Zealand. A teenaged orphaned girl marries an older man and decides after years of abuse to kill him through hypnosis. An unengaging drama, though the lovely New Zealand landscape serves as a fitting contrast to the film's ominous tone. 90m/C VHS, Beta. GB NZ AU John Lithgow, Jodie Foster, Michael Murphy, Dan Shor, Harry Andrews; **D:** Michael Laughlin. LIV, VES

Mesquite Buckaroo 🎬 1939 Two cowboys bet over who is the better bronco buster, but one of them gets kidnapped. 59m/B VHS, Beta. Bob Steele, Carolyn Curtis, Frank LaRue, Juanita Fletcher, Charles "Blackie" King; **D:** Harry S. Webb. NOS, DVT

Messalina vs. the Son of Hercules 🎬 1964 A Roman slave leads a rebellion against the emperor Messalina. Italian; dubbed into English. 105m/C VHS, Beta. IT Richard Harrison, Marilu Tolo, Lisa Gastoni; **D:** Umberto Lenzi. SNC, NLC

The Messenger ⅋ 1987 (R) A man right out of prison sets out to avenge his wife's murder by an Italian drug syndicate. 95m/C VHS, Beta. Fred Williamson, Sandy Cummings, Christopher Connelly, Cameron Mitchell. *FCT*

Messenger of Death ⅋⅋½ 1988 (R) A tough detective investigates the slaughter of a Mormon family, and uncovers a conspiracy centering around oil-rich real estate. 90m/C VHS, Beta, LV, Closed Caption. Charles Bronson, Trish Van Devere, Laurence Luckinbill, Daniel Benzali, Marilyn Hassett, Jeff Corey, John Ireland, Penny Peyser, Gene Davis; *D:* J. Lee Thompson; *W:* Paul Jarrice; *M:* Robert O. Ragland. *MED, VTR*

The Messenger of the Blessed Virgin ⅋⅋ 1930 When his beloved niece Dorothy is tragically paralyzed Uncle John makes a trip to the shrine at Lourdes to pray for a miracle. The story of the original vision of Bernadette and the blessed virgin in 1856 is also related to Uncle John for inspiration. 105m/B VHS. *VYY*

The Messiah ⅋⅋⅋½ 1975 Rossellini's final film, a rarely-seen version of the life of Christ, completely passed over any notions of divinity to portray him as a morally perfect man. In Italian with subtitles. 145m/C VHS, Beta. *IT D:* Roberto Rossellini. *FCT, MVD*

Messiah of Evil ⅋ *Dead People; Return of the Living Dead; Revenge of the Screaming Dead; The Second Coming* 1974 (R) California coastal town is invaded by zombies. Confusing low-rent production from the writers of "American Graffiti." 90m/C VHS, Beta. Marianna Hill, Joy Bang, Royal Dano, Elisha Cook Jr., Michael Greer; *D:* Gloria Katz, Willard Huyck; *W:* Gloria Katz, Willard Huyck. *GEM, MRV*

Messidor ⅋⅋ 1977 Bored university student Jeanne (Amouroux) and shop assistant Marie (Retore) meet while hitchhiking and decide to travel together through Europe—committing robberies when they run out of money. French with subtitles. 118m/C VHS. *SI* Clementine Amouroux, Catherine Retore, Franziskus Abgottspon, Gerald Battiaz, Hansjorg Bedschard; *D:* Alain Tanner; *W:* Alain Tanner; *C:* Renato Berta; *M:* Arie Dzierlatka. *NYF, FCT*

Metallica ⅋ 1985 Alien warmongers endeavor to conquer Earth and scientists try to stop them. 90m/C VHS, Beta. Anthony Newcastle, Sharon Baker; *D:* Al Bradley. *NO*

Metalstorm: The Destruction of Jared Syn ⅋ 1983 (PG) It's the science fiction battle of the ages with giant cyclops and intergalactic magicians on the desert planet of Lemuria. 84m/C VHS, Beta, LV. Jeffrey Byron, Mike Preston, Tim Thomerson, Kelly Preston, Richard Moll; *D:* Charles Band; *W:* Alan J. Adler; *C:* Mac Ahlberg; *M:* Richard Band. *USH*

Metamorphosis ⅋ 1990 (R) Novice scientist foolishly uses himself as the guinea pig for his anti-aging experiments. He quickly loses control of the project. 90m/C VHS, Beta. Gene Le Brock, Catherine Baranov, Stephen Brown, Harry Cason, Jason Arnold; *D:* G.L. Eastman. *IMP, THV*

Metamorphosis: The Alien Factor ⅋⅋½ 1993 (R) Gerard is a genetic engineer who is bitten by a frog injected with a mutation sample from outer space. He turns into a slimy virus that infects everything he touches. 92m/C VHS. George Gerard, Tony Gigante, Katharine Romaine; *D:* Glen Takakjian. *THV*

Meteor woof! 1979 (PG) American and Soviet scientists attempt to save the Earth from a fast-approaching barrage of meteors from space in this disaster dud. Destruction ravages parts of Hong Kong and the Big Apple. 107m/C VHS, Beta, LV. Sean Connery, Natalie Wood, Karl Malden, Brian Keith, Martin Landau, Trevor Howard, Henry Fonda, Joseph Campanella, Richard Dysart; *D:* Ronald Neame. Nominations: Academy Awards '79: Best Sound. *WAR, OM*

The Meteor Man ⅋⅋½ 1993 (PG) Townsend is a school teacher who reluctantly becomes a hero when he acquires semi-super powers after being hit by a meteor. Meteor Man flies only four feet off the ground (because he's afraid of heights) and wears costumes fashioned by his mother. Funny premise satires "superhero" movies, but is inconsistent with some hilarious gags and others that fall flat. Includes interesting cameos by Cosby, Sinbad, Vandross, and Page. 100m/C VHS, LV, Closed Caption. Robert Townsend, Robert Guillaume, Marla Gibbs, James Earl Jones, Frank Gorshin; *Cameos:* Bill Cosby, Sinbad, Luther Vandross, LaWanda Page; *D:* Robert Townsend; *W:* Robert Townsend; *C:* John A. Alonzo. *MGM*

Meteor Monster woof! *Teenage Monster* 1957 A young boy is hit by a meteor and is somehow transformed into a raving, slime-covered maniac. 73m/C VHS, Beta. Anne Gwynne, Stuart Wade, Gloria Castillo, Chuck Courtney; *D:* Jacques Marquette. *SNC*

Metro ⅋⅋½ 1996 (R) Murphy has now officially made this exact movie a kajillion times. He plays fast-talking, fast-shooting cop Axel Fo...er.. Scott Roper, who's forced to accept a partner that he doesn't want, played by Nick...um...Judge...uh...Michael Rapaport! When a villain kills his best friend, he vows revenge. He and his sidekick are involved in car chases, shoot-outs and a tense situation where his girlfriend is taken hostage. Any of this ring a bell? Maybe it was in that "Another 48 Beverly Hills Cop Movies." *CW:* Strong violence and language. 117m/C VHS, LV, Closed Caption. Eddie Murphy, Michael Rapaport, Michael Wincott, Carmen Ejogo, Denis Arndt, Art Evans, Donal Logue, Paul Ben-Victor, Kim Miyori; *D:* Thomas Carter; *W:* Randy Feldman; *C:* Fred Murphy; *M:* Steve Porcaro. *TOU*

Metropolis ⅋⅋⅋⅋ 1926 Now a classic meditation on futurist technology and mass mentality, this fantasy concerns mechanized society. Original set design and special effects made this an innovative and influential film in its day. Is now considered one of the hippest films of the sci-fi genre. Silent, with musical score. The 1984 re-release features some color tinting, reconstruction, and a digital score with songs by Pat Benatar, Bonnie Tyler, Giorgio Moroder, and Queen. 115m/B VHS, Beta, LV. *GE* Brigitte Helm, Alfred Abel, Gustav Froehlich, Rudolf Klein-Rogge, Fritz Rasp, Heinrich George, Theodore Loos, Erwin Biswanger, Olaf Storm, Hans Leo Reich, Heinrich Gotho; *D:* Fritz Lang; *W:* Fritz Lang, Thea von Harbou; *C:* Karl Freund, Gunther Rittau, Eugene Schufftan; *M:* Gottfried Huppertz. *SNC, NOS, MRV*

Metropolitan ⅋⅋⅋ 1990 (PG-13) The Izod set comes of age on Park Avenue during Christmas break. Tom Townsend (Clements), a member of the middle class, finds himself drawn into a circle of self-proclaimed urban haute bourgeoisie types. They're embarrassingly short on male escorts for the holiday season's parties so he stands in and gets an inside look at life within the brat pack. Intelligently written and carefully made, it transcends the flirting-with-adulthood genre. *CW:* Adult situations; profanity and substance abuse. 98m/C VHS, LV. Carolyn Farina, Edward Clements, Taylor Nichols, Christopher Eigeman, Allison Rutledge-Parisi, Dylan Hundley, Isabel Gillies, Bryan Leder, Will Kempe, Elizabeth Thompson; *D:* Whit Stillman; *W:* Whit Stillman; *M:* Mark Suozzo. Independent Spirit Awards '91: Best First Feature; New York Film Critics Awards '90: Best Director (Stillman); Nominations: Academy Awards '90: Best Original Screenplay. *COL, FCT*

Mexican Bus Ride ⅋⅋½ *Ascent to Heaven; Subida Al Cielo* 1951 A good-natured Bunuel effort about a newlywed peasant who travels to the big city to attend to his mother's will. While en route, he encounters a diversity of people on the bus and some temptation. In Spanish with English subtitles. 85m/B VHS, Beta. *MX* Lilia Prado, Esteban Marquez, Carmelita Gonzalez; *D:* Luis Bunuel. *FCT, APD, AUD*

Mexican Hayride ⅋⅋ 1948 Bud heads a gang of swindlers and Lou is the fall guy. When things up north get too hot, the boys head south of the border to cool off and start a mining scam. Watch for the hilarious bullfighting scene. Believe it or not, this is based on a Cole Porter musical—minus the music. 77m/B VHS. Bud Abbott, Lou Costello, Virginia Grey, Luba Malina, John Hubbard, Pedro de Cordoba, Fritz Feld, Tom Powers, Pat Costello, Frank Fenton; *D:* Charles T. Barton; *W:* Oscar Brodney. *USH*

Mexican Spitfire at Sea ⅋⅋½ 1942 The feisty wife from South of the Border heads for Hawaii to close a deal for her husband. He goes along to help her, impersonating nobility. The thin story line keeps it from being quite as good as the first "Mexican Spitfire" film. Most of the action takes place aboard ship. 73m/B VHS. Lupe Velez, Leon Errol, Charles "Buddy" Rogers, ZaSu Pitts, Elisabeth Risdon, Florence Bates, Marion Martin, Eddie Dunn, Harry Holman; *D:* Leslie Goodwins. *NOS*

Mexican Spitfire/Smartest Girl in Town 1940 A comedy double feature: In "Mexican Spitfire," a man impersonates an English lord in order to save a contract for the spitfire's husband. In "The Smartest Girl in Town," a photographer's model mistakes a millionaire for a fellow magazine model. 125m/B VHS, Beta. Lupe Velez, Leon Errol, Donald Woods, Ann Sothern, Gene Raymond. *TTC*

MGM: When the Lion Roars 1992 Three-part documentary covers the history and films of the Metro-Goldwyn-Mayer (MGM) studio from its beginnings in 1924 with the release of the studio's first film ("He Who Gets Slapped"), through its glory years, to the studio's gradual decline and ever-changing leadership. MGM brought out such films as "The Wizard of Oz," "Gone With the Wind," the Andy Hardy series, and the Thin Man films. Features clips of films and stars as well as footage of studio executives, including Louis B. Mayer and legendary studio chief and producer Irving Thalberg. Tapes are also available individually for $19.98. Originally made for cable TV. 360m/C VHS, LV. *MGM*

MGM's The Big Parade of Comedy 1992 An anthology of more than 50 of MGM's stars and comedians in some of their funniest screen moments. Looks at Laurel & Hardy, the Marx Brothers, W.C. Fields, Clark Gable, Jean Harlow, Greta Garbo, and others. 100m/C VHS. *MGM*

Mi Vida Loca ⅋⅋ *My Crazy Life* 1994 (R) Looks at the lives of Latina gang members from L.A.'s Echo Park. The women talk about their romantic dreams, friendships, families, and raising children amidst the pervasive violence and despair of their tough neighborhood. Small budget and some unpolished performances don't lessen film's impact—about the stupidity of violence and how "average" the hopes and dreams of these women are. 92m/C VHS. Angel Aviles, Jacob Vargas, Jesse Borrego, Seidy Lopez, Marlo Marron, Neilida Lopez, Bertilla Damas, Art Esquer, Christina Solis, Salma Hayek, Magali Alvarado, Julian Reyes, Panchito Gomez; *D:* Allison Anders; *W:* Allison Anders; *M:* John Taylor. *HBO*

Miami Beach Cops ⅋½ 1993 Two vets return home expecting life to be routine when they become sheriff's deputies. But when bad guys murder a local merchant things heat up fast. 97m/C VHS. Frank Maldonatti, Salvatore Rendino, William Childers, Joyce Geier, Raff Baker, Dan Preston, Deborah Daniels; *D:* James R. Winburn. *AIP*

Miami Blues ⅋⅋½ 1990 (R) Cold-blooded killer plays cat-and-mouse with bleary cop while diddling with an unflappable prostitute. Violent and cynical, with appropriate performances from three leads. Based on the novel by Charles Willeford. *CW:* Nudity, violence; drug use, and sexual situations. 97m/C VHS, Beta, LV, Closed Caption. Fred Ward, Alec Baldwin, Jennifer Jason Leigh, Nora Dunn, Charles Napier, Jose Perez, Paul Gleason, Obba Babatunde, Martine Beswick, Shirley Stoler; *D:* George Armitage; *W:* George Armitage; *M:* Gary Chang. New York Film Critics Awards '90: Best Supporting Actress (Leigh). *ORI, IME*

Miami Cops ⅋ 1989 When a cop's father is killed by a drug smuggler, he and his partner pursue the murderer over two continents. Italian-made adventure is a bit drawn-out. 103m/C VHS,

Beta. *IT* Richard Roundtree, Harrison Muller, Dawn Baker, Michael J. Aronin; **D:** Al Bradley. *CAN*

Miami Horror ✗ 1987 A Florida scientist is experimenting with bacteria from space, trying to recreate a human only to have his efforts stolen by a crook. His intentions for the use of the experiment are not exactly for the furtherance of science. 85m/C VHS, Beta. *IT* David Warbeck, Laura Trotter, Lawrence Loddi, John Ireland; **D:** Martin Herbert. *NO*

Miami Hustle ✗✗½ 1995 (R) Con artist Marsha (Ireland) is forced by a sleazy lawyer to impersonate a bar waitress (England) who's about to inherit a fortune. But when things turn sour, she gets a computer mogul (Enos) to figure out who's setting her up. Made for cable. **CW:** Erotic dance nudity. 81m/C VHS, **Closed Caption.** Kathy Ireland, John Enos, Audie England, Richard Sarafian; **D:** Lawrence Lanoff. *REP*

Miami Rhapsody ✗✗ 1995 (PG-13) Woody Allen-ish romantic comedy about a young, neurotic copywriter who becomes disillusioned with the idea of marriage as she discovers every member of her family is having an affair. Parker plays the newly-engaged Gwyn who is not entirely sure if she wants to marry her cute, zoologist boyfriend. Most of the characters come across as annoying, self-absorbed whiners, except for Banderas, who charms as a sexy Cuban nurse. Film moves along with its light-hearted narrative, but never reaches the comic or emotional depth of Allen's work. Director/writer Frankel shows promise, but should come out from behind the Woodman's shadow. Filmed on location in Miami. **CW:** Profanity and sexual situations. 95m/C VHS, LV, **Closed Caption.** Sarah Jessica Parker, Gil Bellows, Antonio Banderas, Mia Farrow, Paul Mazursky, Kevin Pollak, Barbara Garrick, Carla Gugino, Bo Eason, Naomi Campbell, Jeremy Piven, Kelly Bishop; **D:** David Frankel; **W:** David Frankel; **C:** Jack Wallner; **M:** Mark Isham. *TOU*

Miami Supercops ✗✗½ 1985 Two goofy policemen strike out against such threats as a gang that hassles buses, the attempted kidnapping of an Orange Bowl quarterback, and a multi-million-dollar robbery. 97m/C VHS, Beta. Terence Hill, Bud Spencer, Jackie Castellano, C.V. Wood Jr.; **D:** Bruno Corbucci. *WAR*

Miami Vendetta ✗ 1987 L.A. vice cop risks it all to avenge his friend's death at the hands of Cuban drug smugglers. 90m/C VHS, Beta. Sandy Brooke, Frank Gargani, Maarten Goslins, Barbara Pilavin; **D:** Steven Seemayer. *NO*

Miami Vice ✗✗½ 1984 Pilot for the popular television series paired Crockett and Tubbs for the first time on the trail of a killer in Miami's sleazy underground. Music by Jan Hammer and other pop notables. 99m/C VHS, Beta, LV. Don Johnson, Philip Michael Thomas, Saundra Santiago, Michael Talbott, John Diehl, Gregory Sierra; **D:** Thomas Carter. *USH*

Miami Vice 2: The Prodigal Son ✗✗ 1985 The second full-length television movie spawned by the popular series, following the laconic Floridians to the gritty streets of New York. 99m/C VHS, Beta, LV. Don Johnson, Philip Michael Thomas, Edward James Olmos, Penn Jillette. *USH*

Michael ✗✗½ 1996 (PG) Following up "Phenomenon" with another celestial storyline, Travolta tries on the giant, molting wings of Michael, an atypical archangel with an amazing joie de vivre and an appetite for alcohol, women, and sugar. Residing in Iowa with the elderly Pansy (Stapleton), Michael is being tracked by a cynical tabloid reporter (Hurt) and an angel expert (MacDowell), so he figures he might as well play cupid. The now standard dance sequence in Travolta movies takes place in a bar to the tune of "Chain of Fools" and is one of the movie's stand-outs. While Travolta gives another stellar performance, Hurt and MacDowell have little to do but play out their tired romantic subplot in a script that could've used some inspiration from its lead character. 105m/C VHS, LV, **Closed Caption, DVD.** John Travolta, William Hurt, Andie MacDowell, Bob Hoskins, Robert

Pastorelli, Jean Stapleton, Teri Garr; **D:** Nora Ephron; **W:** Nora Ephron, Delia Ephron, Pete Dexter; **C:** John Lindley; **M:** Randy Newman. *WAR*

Michael Collins ✗✗✗ 1996 (R) Collins (Neeson) was a revolutionary leader with the Irish Volunteers, a guerilla force (an early version of the IRA) dedicated to freeing Ireland from British rule by any means necessary. After a number of successful moves against British intelligence, Collins is unwillingly drawn into a statesman's role as negotiations for an Anglo-Irish Treaty begin in 1921, ultimately dividing the country in two and leading to Collins' own assassination. Controversy surrounded the film as historians, politicians, and the media took potshots at director Jordan's admittedly personal look at the complexities of Irish life and one of its equally complicated heroes. **CW:** Violence and language. 117m/C VHS, DVD. Liam Neeson, Aidan Quinn, Alan Rickman, Stephen Rea, Julia Roberts, Ian Hart, Sean McGinley, Gerard McSorley, Stuart Graham, Brendan Gleeson, Charles Dance, Jonathan Rhys Myers; **D:** Neil Jordan; **W:** Neil Jordan; **C:** Chris Menges; **M:** Elliot Goldenthal. Los Angeles Film Critics Association Awards '96: Best Cinematography; Venice Film Festival '96: Golden Lion, Best Actor (Neeson); Nominations: Academy Awards '96: Best Cinematography, Original Dramatic/Comedy Score; British Academy Awards '96: Best Supporting Actor (Rickman); Golden Globe Awards '97: Best Actor—Drama (Neeson), Best Score. *WAR*

The Michigan Kid ✗✗ 1928 Two boys fight for the same girl in this silent love triangle set in Alaska. Film's most notable scene is of a raging forest fire, considered a classic even today. 62m/B VHS, Beta. Conrad Nagel, Renee Adoree, Fred Esmelton, Virginia Grey, Adolph Milar, Lloyd Whitlock; **D:** Irvin Willat. *GPV*

Mickey ✗✗ 1917 Spoof on high society as a penniless young woman moves in with relatives and works as the family's maid. Silent film. 105m/B VHS, Beta. Mabel Normand, Lew Cody, Minta Durfee; **D:** Mack Sennett. *NOS, VYY, DVT*

Mickey ✗ 1948 A tomboy becomes a woman even as she plays matchmaker for her own father and sings a few songs. Not too exciting; you may fall asleep if you're slipped this "Mickey." Based on the novel "Clementine," by Peggy Goodin. 87m/C VHS. Lois Butler, Bill Goodwin, Irene Hervey, John Sutton, Hattie McDaniel; **D:** Ralph Murphy. *NOS*

Mickey One ✗✗½ 1965 Nightclub comic Mickey (Beatty) gets into trouble when he can't pay his gambling debts. So he hides out in Chicago under an assumed name, working as a janitor, but can't live without the applause. His agent finds him a club job but Mickey panics, thinking the place is under mob control, and spends a lot of time running around, trying to clear his debts. Finally, returning to the club, Mickey resigns himself to a bleak fate. Beatty's jumpy character is an acquired taste—as is the film. 93m/B LV. Warren Beatty, Hurd Hatfield, Alexandra Stewart, Franchot Tone, Teddy Hart, Jeff Corey; **D:** Arthur Penn; **W:** Alan M. Surgal; **C:** Ghislain Cloquet; **M:** Jack Shaindlin, Eddie Sauter. *FCT*

Mickey the Great 1939 Stitched together from several late 20's Mickey McGuire shorts, starring 10-year-old Mickey Rooney. 70m/B VHS, Beta. Billy Barty, Mickey Rooney. *VYY, DVT, NOS*

Mickey's Christmas Carol ✗✗✗ 1983 (G) Mickey Mouse returns along with all the other Disney characters in this adaptation of the Charles Dickens classic. Includes a documentary on how the featurette was made. 25m/C VHS, Beta, LV. **V:** Alan Young, Hal Smith, Will Ryan, Wayne Alline, Clarence Nash, Eddie Carroll, Pat Parris, Susan Sheridan. *DIS, MTI, DSN*

Micki & Maude ✗✗ 1984 (PG-13) When a man longs for a baby, he finds that his wife, Micki, is too busy for motherhood. Out of frustration, he has an affair with Maude that leads to her pregnancy. Still shocked by the news of his upcoming fatherhood, the man learns that his wife is also expecting. 117m/C VHS, Beta, LV, **Closed Caption.** Dudley Moore, Amy Irving, Ann Reinking, Richard Mulligan,

Wallace Shawn, George Gaynes, Andre the Giant; **D:** Blake Edwards; **W:** Jonathan Reynolds; **C:** Harry Stradling Jr. Golden Globe Awards '85: Best Actor—Musical/Comedy (Moore). *COL*

Microcosmos ✗✗✗ 1996 (G) Warning: Do not attempt to smash the bugs on the screen with your shoe. They're supposed to be there. This French documentary uses special cameras and sound recording devices to explore the world of insects like never before. The editing and score also add a human dimension to the creepy-crawly world under the lawn, making amorous snails and workaholic beetles seem like people you know (well, if they had an extra set of legs and a shell-like carapace). Of course, if you don't like bugs, then this is just a 77-minute gross out. Cameo appearances by some birds and frogs. 77m/C VHS. *FR* D: Claude Nuridsany, Marie Perennou; **C:** Claude Nuridsany, Marie Perennou, Hughes Ryffel, Thierry Machado; **M:** Bruno Coulais. Nominations: Cesar Awards '97: Best Film. *NYR*

Microwave Massacre ✗ 1983 (R) Killer kitchen appliances strike again as late lounge comic Vernon murders nagging wife and 'waves her. Overcome by that Betty Crocker feeling, he goes on a microwave murdering/feeding spree of the local ladies. Lots of Roger Corman copying. 80m/C VHS. Jackie Vernon, Loren Schein, Al Troupe; **D:** Wayne Berwick. *RHI, FCT*

Mid-Channel ✗✗½ 1920 A married couple become bored with each other and the wife seeks diversion with other men. Surprise ending. 70m/B VHS, Beta. Clara Kimball Young, J. Frank Glendon, Edward M. Kimball, Bertram Grassby, Eileen Robinson, Helen Sullivan, Katherine Griffith, Jack Livingston; **D:** Harry Garson. *NOS, MRV, GPV*

Mid Knight Rider ✗ 1984 Penniless actor becomes a male prostitute at the service of bored, rich women. At an all-night orgy, he suddenly goes on a rampage, nearly killing one of his customers. 76m/C VHS, Beta. Michael Christian, Keenan Wynn. *TWE*

The Midas Touch ✗✗ 1989 A flea market merchant in 1956 Budapest has the ability to turn items into gold. In Hungarian with English subtitles. 100m/C VHS, Beta. *HU* D: Geza Beremenyi; **W:** Geza Beremenyi. *EVD, FCT*

Middle Age Crazy ✗✗½ 1980 (R) Story of a Texas building contractor who takes life pretty lightly until his own father dies. Then he becomes immersed in a mid-life crisis and has an affair with a Dallas Cowboys' cheerleader. Ann-Margret plays the victim wife of the middle aged swingin' guy. 95m/C VHS. *CA* Bruce Dern, Ann-Margret, Graham Jarvis, Eric Christmas, Deborah Wakeham; **D:** John Trent. *FOX*

Middlemarch ✗✗✗ 1993 Stylish British TV costume drama, adapted from George Eliot's 1872 novel, finds idealistic Dorothea Brooke (Aubrey) determined to be a helpmate to the older scholar, the Rev. Edward Casaubon (Malahide), whom she marries. Too bad that he takes so little interest in her ability (or in Dorothea herself). This leads Casaubon's distant cousin, young and handsome Will Ladislaw (Sewell), to discreetly make his interest clear. Naturally, Eliot has a number of other plots (some dealing with the impact of the Industrial Revolution on 19th-century life) and romances worked into the mix. Filmed in Stamford, England. On 3 cassettes. 360m/C VHS, **Closed Caption.** *GB* Juliet Aubrey, Patrick Malahide, Rufus Sewell, Douglas Hodge, Trevyn McDowell, Michael Hordern, Robert Hardy, John Savident, Jonathan Firth, Peter Jeffrey, Simon Chandler, Julian Wadham; **D:** Anthony Page; **W:** Andrew Davies, Stanley Myers; **C:** Brian Tufano. *FOX, TVC*

Midnight ✗✗½ *Call it Murder* 1934 A jury foreman's daughter is romantically involved with a gangster who is interested in a particular case before it appears in court. The foreman, who sentenced a girl to death, faces a dilemma when his own daughter is arrested for the same crime. An early Bogart appearance in a supporting role led to a re-release of the film as "Call it Murder" after Bogart made it big. Weak melodrama. **74m/B VHS, Beta.** Humphrey Bogart, Sidney Fox, O.P. Heggie, Henry Hull, Richard Whorf, Margaret Wycherly, Lynne Overman; *D:* Chester Erskine. *CCB, DVT, BAR*

Midnight 🐾🐾🐾½ 1939 Struggling showgirl Colbert masquerades as Hungarian countess in sophisticated comedy of marital conflicts. Near-classic film scripted by Wilder and Brackett. Based on a story by Edwin Justus Mayer and Franz Schulz. Remade as "Masquerade in Mexico." **94m/B VHS, Closed Caption.** Claudette Colbert, Don Ameche, John Barrymore, Francis Lederer, Mary Astor, Hedda Hopper, Rex O'Malley; *D:* Mitchell Leisen; *W:* Billy Wilder, Charles Brackett; *C:* Charles B(ryant) Lang. *USH*

Midnight 🐾 *Backwoods Massacre* 1981 (R) Russo, who cowrote the original "Night of the Living Dead," wrote and directed this film about a runaway girl who is driven out of her home by a lecherous stepfather and meets two young thieves and then a family of cultists. Russo adapted his own novel. He also attains some of "Night of the Living Dead's" low-budget ambience. **88m/C VHS, Beta.** Lawrence Tierney, Melanie Verliin, John Hall, John Amplas; *D:* John Russo. *THV*

Midnight 🐾 1989 (R) Murder-thriller involving the vampirish hostess of a television horror movie showcase and a fanatical fan. **90m/C VHS, Beta, LV.** Lynn Redgrave, Tony Curtis, Steve Parrish, Rita Gam, Gustav Vintas, Karen Witter, Frank Gorshin, Wolfman Jack; *D:* Norman Thaddeus Vane. *VTR*

Midnight 2: Sex, Death, and Videotape 🐾 1993

Sequel to "Midnight" finds the sole surviving member of the crazed family stalking a beautiful unsuspecting teller with a video camera. Only she's teamed up with a detective to solve the murder of her best friend—even if it means she's bait for a psycho. **70m/C VHS.** Matthew Jason Walsh, Jo Norcia; *D:* John Russo. *TEM, MOV*

Midnight at the Wax Museum 🐾

Midnight at Madame Tussaud's 1936 A man attempts to spend an evening in a wax museum's chamber of horrors, only to find that he is the target of a murder plot. **66m/B VHS.** Lucille Lisle, James Carew, Charles Oliver, Kim Peacock; *D:* George Pearson. *NOS, DVT, SNC*

Midnight Auto Supply 🐾½ 1978 Dealers in hot car parts, working out of the garage behind the local brothel, become persuaded to donate some of their profits to the cause of Mexican farm workers. Also called "Love and the Midnight Auto Supply." **91m/C VHS.** Michael Parks, Rory Calhoun, Scott Jacoby, Rod Cameron, Colleen Camp, Linda Cristal, John Ireland; *D:* James Polakof. *NO*

Midnight Blue 🐾 1996 (R) Martin Blake (Chapa) is a lonely banker on a trip to Atlanta where he meets prostitute Martine (Schofield). They have a one-nighter and Martin later decides he loves her and hires a detective (Stockwell) to find her—only Martine has disappeared. After Martin has moved to L.A., he discovers his new boss' wife, Georgine, just happens to be a double for Martine. Naturally, Martin becomes obsessed and this leads to big trouble. *CW:* Nudity, language, sexual situations, violence. **95m/C VHS, LV.** Damian Chapa, Annabel Schofield, Steve Kanaly, Dean Stockwell, Harry Dean Stanton, Jennifer Jostyn; *D:* Skott Snider. *ORI*

Midnight Cabaret woof! 1990 (R) A New York nightclub-based Satanic cult selects a child actress to bear Satan's child. **94m/C VHS, Beta, LV.** Michael Des Barres, Thom Mathews, Carolyn Seymour, Leonard Termo, Norbert Weisser, Lydie Denier; *D:* Pece Dingo; *W:* Pece Dingo; *M:* Michel Colombier. *WAR*

A Midnight Clear 🐾🐾🐾 1992 (PG) Sensitive war drama that takes place in the Ardennes Forest, near the French-German border in December 1944. It's Christmastime and six of the remaining members of a 12-member squad are sent on a dangerous mission to an abandoned house to locate the enemy. Filmed in a dreamy

surreal style, the setting is somewhat reminiscent of a fairytale, although a sense of anguish filtrates throughout the picture. A solid script, excellent direction, and a good cast make this a worthwhile film that pits the message of peace against the stupidity of war. Adapted from the novel by William Wharton. **107m/C VHS, LV, Closed Caption.** Peter Berg, Kevin Dillon, Arye Gross, Ethan Hawke, Gary Sinise, Frank Whaley, John C. McGinley, Larry Joshua, Curt Lowens; *D:* Keith Gordon; *W:* Keith Gordon; *M:* Mark Isham. *COL, PMS*

Midnight Confessions 🐾 1995 (R) Provocative night-time DJ Vannesse (Hoyt) lures her listeners into revealing their sexual fantasies. But when an obsessed fan begins killing women just how deeply is she involved? *CW:* Strong, lurid sexuality and sex-related dialogue. **98m/C VHS, LV.** Carol Hoyt, Julie Strain, Monique Parent, Richard Lynch. *TRI*

Midnight Cop 🐾 1988 (R) A young woman gets tangled up in a web of murder, intrigue, prostitution and drugs, and she enlists the aid of a cop to help get her out of it. **100m/C VHS, Beta, LV.** Michael York, Morgan Fairchild, Frank Stallone, Armin Mueller-Stahl; *D:* Peter Patzak. *THV, HHE*

Midnight Cowboy 🐾🐾🐾½ 1969 (R) Drama about the relationship between a naive Texan hustler and a seedy derelict, set in the underbelly of New York City. Graphic and emotional character study is brilliantly acted and engaging. Shocking and considered quite risque at the time of its release, this film now carries an "R" rating. It is the only film carrying an "X" rating ever to win the Best Picture Oscar. From James Leo Herlihy's novel. Laserdisc version features: audio commentary by director John Schlesinger and producer Jereome Hellman, behind the scenes production photos, and original movie trailer. **113m/C VHS, Beta, LV, DVD.** Dustin Hoffman, Jon Voight, Sylvia Miles, Brenda Vaccaro, John McGiver, Bob Balaban, Barnard Hughes; *D:* John Schlesinger; *W:* Waldo Salt; *C:* Adam Holender; *M:* John Barry. Academy Awards '69: Best Adapted Screenplay, Best Director (Schlesinger), Best Picture; British Academy Awards '69: Best Actor (Hoffman), Best Director (Schlesinger), Best Film, Best Screenplay; Directors Guild of America Awards '69: Best Director (Schlesinger); New York Film Critics Awards '69: Best Actor (Voight); National Society of Film Critics Awards '69: Best Actor (Voight); Writers Guild of America Awards '69: Best Adapted Screenplay; Nominations: Academy Awards '69: Best Actor (Hoffman), Best Actor (Voight), Best Film Editing, Best Supporting Actress (Miles). *MGM, CRC, BTV*

Midnight Crossing 🐾🐾 1987 (R) Two married couples are subjected to jealousy, betrayal and uncloseted-skeletons as their pleasure cruise on a yacht turns into a ruthless search for sunken treasure. **96m/C VHS, Beta, LV.** Faye Dunaway, Daniel J. Travanti, Kim Cattrall, John Laughlin, Ned Beatty; *D:* Roger Holzberg. *LIV, VES*

Midnight Dancer 🐾🐾 1987 A young ballerina is forced to work as an erotic dancer. **97m/C VHS, Beta.** *AU* Deanne Jeffs, Mary Regan; *D:* Pamela Gibbons. *ACA*

Midnight Dancers 🐾🐾 1994 Seamy look at Manila's gay subculture and male prostitution. Sonny and his older brothers Dennis and Joel work as dancers at a sleazy club whose upstairs apartments are used for prostitution. The boys need the money to help their impoverished family survive in the slums but the emotional wear and tear (not to mention police raids and assorted brutalities) provide lots of melodrama. Filipino with subtitles. **115m/C VHS.** *PH* Alex Del Rosario, Gandong Cervantes, Laurence David, Perla Bautista, Soxy Topacio; *D:* Mel Chionglo; *W:* Ricardo Lee; *C:* George Tutanes; *M:* Nonong Buenoamino. *FRF*

Midnight Edition 🐾🐾 1993 (R) Investigative reporter Jack Travers (Patton) returns to his Georgia hometown newspaper just in time to write the story of his life. Nineteen-year-old Darryl Weston (DeLuise) massacres a local family for no apparent reason, is tried, convicted, and sentenced to die. Jack's death row interviews with

Darryl become hot news but his reporter's objectivity is lost and he becomes a pawn in an escape plan. Good interplay between the charming sociopath and the self-deluded reporter in a sometimes confusing thriller. Based on the autobiography "Escape of My Dead Men" by Charles Postell. *CW:* Strong language; violence; sexual situations. **98m/C VHS, Closed Caption.** Will Patton, Michael DeLuise, Clare Wren, Nancy Moore Atchison, Sarabeth Tucek, Judson Vaughn, Ji Tu Cumbuka, Jay Bernard; *D:* Howard Libov; *W:* Howard Libov, Yuri Zeltser, Michael Stewart; *M:* Murray Attaway. *USH*

Midnight Express 🐾🐾🐾 1978 (R) Gripping and powerful film based on the true story of Billy Hayes. Davis plays Hayes as a young American in Turkey who is busted trying to smuggle hashish. He is sentenced to a brutal and nightmarish prison for life. After enduring tremendous mental and physical torture, he seeks escape along the "Midnight Express." Not always easy to watch, but the overall effect is riveting and unforgettable. **120m/C VHS, Beta, LV, 8mm.** John Hurt, Randy Quaid, Brad Davis, Paul Smith, Bo Hopkins, Oliver Stone; *D:* Alan Parker; *W:* Oliver Stone; *M:* Giorgio Moroder. Academy Awards '78: Best Adapted Screenplay, Best Original Score; British Academy Awards '78: Best Director (Parker), Best Supporting Actor (Hurt); Golden Globe Awards '79: Best Film—Drama, Best Screenplay, Best Supporting Actor (Hurt), Best Score; National Board of Review Awards '78: 10 Best Films of the Year; Writers Guild of America '78: Best Adapted Screenplay; Nominations: Academy Awards '78: Best Director (Parker), Best Film Editing, Best Picture, Best Supporting Actor (Hurt). *COL*

Midnight Faces 🐾🐾 1926 Mysterious doings abound in a house in the Florida bayous, recently inherited by Bushman. Silent, with original organ music. **72m/B VHS, Beta, 8mm.** Francis X. Bushman, Jack Perrin, Kathryn McGuire. *SNC, VYY, LSV*

Midnight Fear 🐾½ 1990 When a sexually demented killer skins a woman alive, Sheriff Hanley sets out to find whodunit. He suspects two weird brothers, who turn out to be holding a woman hostage, but the situation may not be so simple. Carradine plays the good-guy sheriff in this creeper. **90m/C VHS.** David Carradine, Craig Wasson; *D:* William Crain. *RHI*

Midnight Girl 🐾½ 1925 A fading opera impresario plots to steal a family's fortune. Lugosi before he became Dracula. Silent. **84m/B VHS, Beta, 8mm.** Bela Lugosi, Lila Lee. *GPV, VYY, DVT*

Midnight Heat 🐾🐾½ 1995 (R) Football player is the prime suspect when his lover's husband (who happens to be the team owner) is murdered. **97m/C VHS.** Tim Matheson, Stephen Mendel, Mimi Craven; *D:* Harvey Frost. *AVE*

The Midnight Hour 🐾½ 1986

A group of high schoolers stumbles upon a vintage curse that wakes up the dead. Made for television. More humor than horror. **97m/C VHS.** Shari Belafonte, LeVar Burton, Lee Montgomery, Dick Van Patten, Kevin McCarthy, Jonelle Allen, Peter DeLuise, Dedee Pfeiffer, Mark Blankfield; *D:* Jack Bender; *M:* Brad Fiedel. *THV*

Midnight Kiss 🐾🐾½ 1993 (R) When a woman police detective investigates a mysterious series of deaths—women whose blood has been drained—she gets more than she bargains for. She's attacked by a vampire and is herself turned into a reluctant bloodsucker. Quick moving and some gross special effects. Also available in an unrated version. **85m/C VHS.** Michelle Owens, Gregory A. Greer; *D:* Joel Bender; *W:* John Weidner, Ken Lamplugh. *ACA*

Midnight Lace 🐾🐾½ 1960 Acceptable thriller about a woman in London who is being harassed by a telephone creep. Day is at her frantic best, and Harrrison is suitably charming. Handsome Gavin later became American ambassador to Mexico. Adapted from the play "Matilda Shouted Fire." **108m/C VHS, Beta.** Doris Day, Rex Harrison, John Gavin, Myrna Loy, Roddy McDowall; *D:* David Miller; *W:* Ivan Goff; *C:* Russell Metty. Nominations: Academy Awards '60: Best Costume Design (Color). *USH*

Midnight Limited ✉✉ 1940 A detective sets out to thwart the criminals who would rob the "Midnight Limited" train on its route from New York to Montreal. 61m/B VHS, **Beta.** John "Dusty" King, Marjorie Reynolds, George Cleveland, Edward Keane, Pat Flaherty, Monty Collins, I. Stanford Jolley; **D:** Howard Bretherton. *SNC*

Midnight Madness ✉ 1980 (PG) Five teams of college students search the city of Los Angeles for clues leading to hundreds and thousands of dollars in buried treasure. 110m/C VHS, **Beta.** David Naughton, Stephen Furst, Debra Clinger, Eddie Deezen, Michael J. Fox, Maggie Roswell; **D:** David Wechter; **W:** David Wechter. *TOU, OM*

Midnight Movie Massacre ✉✉½ 1988 Retro splatterama has really gross alien land outside a movie theater in 1956, and the really weird movie patrons try to terminate it. 86m/C VHS. Robert Clarke, Ann Robinson; **D:** Mark Stock. *NO*

Midnight Murders ✉✉½ *Manhunt in the Dakotas; In the Line of Duty: Manhunt in the Dakotas* 1991 (R) Steiger stars as a farmer and Posse Commitatus member whose paramilitary pretensions lead to a bloody confrontation with federal marshals. Gross is the FBI agent sent to hunt him down. Made for TV.**CW:** Language. 95m/C VHS. Rod Steiger, Michael Gross, Gary Basaraba, Christopher Rich, Henderson Forsythe; **D:** Dick Lowry. *NHO*

The Midnight Phantom ✉✉ 1935 Incredibly rare horror film featuring a bizarre murder at a midnight lecture. ?m/B VHS. Reginald Denny. *SNC*

Midnight Ride ✉½ 1992 Lots of silly action fails to save this slight tale of a cop (Dudikoff) chasing after his runaway wife (Gersak), who has made the mistake of picking up a psycho hitchhiker (Hamill, gleefully overacting). 95m/C VHS. Michael Dudikoff, Mark Hamill, Savina Gersak; *Cameos:* Robert Mitchum; **D:** Robert Bralver. *CAN*

Midnight Run ✉✉✉ 1988 (R) An ex-cop, bounty hunter must bring in an ex-mob accountant who has embezzled big bucks from his former boss. After he catches up with the thief, the hunter finds that bringing his prisoner from New York to Los Angeles will be very trying, especially when it is apparent that the Mafia and FBI are out to stop them. The friction between the two leads—De Niro and Grodin—is fun to watch, while the action and comic moments are enjoyable. 125m/C VHS, **Beta, LV.** Robert De Niro, Charles Grodin, Yaphet Kotto, John Ashton, Dennis Farina, Joe Pantoliano, Richard Foronjy, Wendy Phillips; **D:** Martin Brest; **W:** George Gallo; **C:** Donald E. Thorin; **M:** Danny Elfman. *USH*

Midnight Tease ✉½ 1994 Strip bar, the Club Fugazi, is having trouble with its help—the dancers keep getting murdered. Dancer Samantha (Leigh) actually dreams about the murders before they occur, so naturally she becomes the prime suspect. Leigh can actually do more than look fetching but plot is barely apparent. 87m/C VHS, **LV.** Cassandra Leigh, Rachel Reed, Edmund Halley, Ashlie Rhey, Todd Joseph; **D:** Scott Levy; **W:** Daniella Purcell. *NHO*

Midnight Tease 2 ✉ 1995 (R) Jen Brennan (Kelly) goes undercover at an L.A. strip club to find out who's been murdering the dancers, including her sister.**CW:** Pervasive sex-related material, and for violence. 93m/C VHS. Kimberly Kelley, Tane McClure, Ross Hagen; **D:** Richard Styles; **W:** Richard Styles; **C:** Gary Graver. *NHO*

Midnight Warning ✉✉½ 1932 A woman thinks she's going off the deep-end when her brother and all records of his existence disappear. Based on an urban legend that appeared somewhere around the time of the 1893 World's Fair. Remade in 1952 as "So Long at the Fair." 63m/B VHS. William Boyd, Claudia Dell, Henry Hall, John Harron, Hooper Atchley; **D:** Spencer Gordon Bennet. *SNC, NOS, DVT*

Midnight Warrior ✉ 1989 A reporter strikes it big when he investigates the underside of L.A. nightlife, but things go terribly wrong when he becomes wrapped up in the sleaze. 90m/C VHS,

Beta. Bernie Angel, Michelle Berger, Kevin Bernhardt, Lilly Melgar; **D:** Joseph Merhi. *PAR*

Midnight Witness ✉½ 1993 (R) Guy finds himself on the run when after he videotapes the beating of a young drug dealer by corrupt cops. Plot bears more than a little resemblance to the Rodney King incident, but according to writer Foldy it was written before it took place. Low budget thriller went direct to video.**CW:** Language, violence, and strong sexuality. 90m/C VHS. Maxwell Caulfield, Jan-Michael Vincent, Paul Johansson, Karen Moncrieff, Mark Pellegrino, Virginia Mayo; **D:** Peter Foldy; **W:** Peter Foldy; **M:** Graydon Hillock. *ACA*

Midnight's Child ✉½ 1993 Another Nanny-from-Hell story, only this time it's literal. D'Abo is the Nanny in question, who belongs to a Satanic cult. Her mission is to select the young daughter in her care as a bride for the devil, even if the girl's parents don't approve of the match. 89m/C VHS, **Beta.** Olivia D'Abo, Marcy Walker, Cotter Smith, Elisabeth Moss, Jim Norton, Judy Parfitt, Roxann Biggs-Dawson, Mary Larkin; **D:** Colin Bucksey; **W:** David Chaskin. *PSM*

Midnite Spares ✉✉ 1985 A young man's search for the men who kidnapped his father leads him into the world of car thieves and chopshops. 90m/C VHS, **Beta.** Bruce Spence, Gia Carides, James Laurie; **C:** Geoff Burton; **D:** Cameron Allan. *NO*

A Midsummer Night's Dream ✉✉✉ 1935 Famed Reinhardt version of the Shakespeare classic, featuring nearly every star on the Warner Brothers lot. The plot revolves around the amorous battle between the king and queen of a fairy kingdom, and the humans who are drawn into their sport. Features de Havilland's first film role. Classic credit line: Dialogue by William Shakespeare. 117m/B VHS, **Beta.** James Cagney, Dick Powell, Joe E. Brown, Hugh Herbert, Olivia de Havilland, Ian Hunter, Mickey Rooney, Victor Jory, Arthur Treacher, Billy Barty; **D:** Max Reinhardt, William Dieterle; **C:** Hal Mohr. Academy Awards '35: Best Cinematography, Best Film Editing; Nominations: Academy Awards '35: Best Picture. *MGM, FOX, FCT*

A Midsummer Night's Dream ✉✉½ 1968 Fine acting from the Royal Shakespeare Company cast in this filmed version of the play. Makes very little use of the Athens, Greece scenery. 124m/C VHS. **GB** David Warner, Diana Rigg, Ian Richardson, Judi Dench, Ian Holm, Barbara Jefford, Nicholas Selby, Helen Mirren, Michael Jayston, Derek Godfrey, Hugh Sullivan, Paul Rogers, Sebastian Shaw, Bill Travers; **D:** Peter Hall. *WBF, WAR, DARK*

A Midsummer Night's Sex Comedy ✉✉✉½ 1982 (PG) Allen's homage to Shakespeare, Renoir, Chekhov, Bergman, and who knows who else is an engaging ensemble piece about hijinks among friends and acquaintances gathered at a country house at the turn of the century. Standouts include Ferrer as pompous professor and Steenburgen as Allen's sexually repressed wife. Mia's first for the Woodman. 88m/C VHS, **Beta.** Woody Allen, Mia Farrow, Mary Steenburgen, Tony Roberts, Julie Hagerty, Jose Ferrer; **D:** Woody Allen; **W:** Woody Allen; **C:** Gordon Willis. *WAR*

Midway ✉✉ 1976 (PG) The epic WWII battle of Midway, the turning point in the war, is retold through Allied and Japanese viewpoints by a big all-star cast saddled with dumpy dialogue and enough weaponry to seize Hollywood on any given Wednesday. 132m/C VHS, **Beta, LV.** Charlton Heston, Henry Fonda, James Coburn, Glenn Ford, Hal Holbrook, Robert Mitchum, Cliff Robertson, Robert Wagner, Kevin Dobson, Christopher George, Toshiro Mifune, Tom Selleck; **D:** Jack Smight; **C:** Harry Stradling Jr.; **M:** John Williams. *USH, TLF*

A Midwinter's Tale ✉✉½ *In the Bleak Midwinter* 1995 (R) Branagh assembles a largely unknown cast in this low-budget backstage saga about an out-of-work thesp, Joe Harper (Maloney), who assembles a shaggy crew of actors to stage an alternative "Hamlet" in a small English country church. The diverse cast squabble, stumble, and emote their way through rehearsals, fi-

nally pulling together for the big show. Funny and interesting performances manage to show through the dense and somewhat cliched script. Maloney's Joe, who exhibits the proper frustration of being forced to deal with amateurs and Sessions as a camp queen playing the Queen (Gertrude, that is) stand out.**CW:** Some language. 98m/B VHS, LV, **Closed Caption.** *GB* Michael Maloney, Richard Briers, Mark Hadfield, Nicholas Farrell, Gerard Horan, John Sessions, Celia Imrie, Hetta Charnley, Julia Sawalha, Joan Collins, Jennifer Saunders; **D:** Kenneth Branagh; **C:** Roger Lanser; **M:** Jimmy Yuill. *COL*

Mighty Aphrodite ✉✉½ 1995 (R) Neurotic (Surprise!) New York sportswriter Lenny Weinrib (Allen) is trapped in an unhappy marriage to art dealer Amanda (Bonham-Carter), who talks him into adopting a child. Film comes alive when Lenny tracks down his son's biological mother, consummate dumb blond and hooker/porno actress Linda, played with over-the-top (in a good way) gusto by Sorvino. Lenny attempts to reform his son's real mother while a Greek chorus (including Abraham and Dukakis) provide a running commentary on the tragedy/comedy of Lenny's predicaments. Allen's 31st film treads into familiar Woodman waters but falls short of his past comic genius.**CW:** Language and sex-related material. 95m/C VHS, LV, **Closed Caption.** Woody Allen, Helena Bonham Carter, Mira Sorvino, F. Murray Abraham, Michael Rapaport, Jack Warden, Olympia Dukakis, Peter Weller, Claire Bloom, David Ogden Stiers; **D:** Woody Allen; **W:** Woody Allen; **C:** Carlo DiPalma; **M:** Dick Hyman. Academy Awards '95: Best Supporting Actress (Sorvino); Golden Globe Awards '96: Best Supporting Actress (Sorvino); National Board of Review Awards '95: Best Supporting Actress (Sorvino); New York Film Critics Awards '95: Best Supporting Actress (Sorvino); Broadcast Film Critics Association Awards '95: Best Supporting Actress (Sorvino); Nominations: Academy Awards '95: Best Screenplay; British Academy Awards '95: Best Supporting Actress (Sorvino); Screen Actors Guild Award '95: Best Supporting Actress (Sorvino); Writers Guild of America '95: Best Original Screenplay. *TOU*

The Mighty Ducks ✉✉½ 1992 (PG) Bad News Bears on skates. Selfish yuppie lawyer is arrested for drunk driving and as part of his community service sentence, he is forced to coach an inner-city hockey team full of the usual misfits and underachievers. Although sarcastic and skeptical, Coach Gordon Bombay (Estevez) eventually bonds with the Ducks and learns to treat them with respect. Dual themes of teamwork and redemption are repeated constantly, and it gets a bit hokey at times, but the kids won't mind with this fun Disney film, while adults will appreciate the sarcasm. Followed by "D2: The Mighty Ducks." 114m/C VHS, **Beta, LV, Closed Caption.** Emilio Estevez, Joss Ackland, Lane Smith, Heidi Kling, Josef Sommer, Matt Doherty, Steven Brill, Joshua Jackson, Elden Ratliff, Shaun Weiss; **D:** Stephen Herek; **W:** Steven Brill, Brian Hohlfield; **M:** David Newman. *TOU, BTV*

Mighty Joe Young ✉✉½ 1949 Tongue-in-cheek King Kong variation features giant ape brought to civilization and exploited in a nightclub act, whereupon things get darned ugly. Bullied and given the key to the liquor cabinet, mild-mannered Joe goes on a drunken rampage, but eventually redeems himself by rescuing orphans from a fire. Special effects (courtesy of Willis O'Brien and the great Ray Harryhausen) probably film's greatest asset. Also available colorized. 94m/B VHS, **Beta, LV.** Terry Moore, Ben Johnson, Robert Armstrong, Frank McHugh; **D:** Ernest B. Schoedsack. Academy Awards '49: Best Special Effects. *TTC*

Mighty Jungle ✉✉ 1964 Lost in the Amazon jungle, a hunter must fight off killer iguanas, man-eating crocodiles and bloodthirsty natives who perform human sacrifices. 90m/C VHS, **Beta.** Marshall Thompson, David Dalie. *NO*

Mighty Morphin Power Rangers: The Movie ✉✉ 1995 (PG) From the living room onto the big screen, these six suburban teenagers with super powers battle the evil Ivan Ooze to save Earth. Offers more special effects, new Zord animals, more ooze and more growth to the retail toy industry than the small screen could provide. A child's dream come true, but a parent's nightmare. 93m/C VHS. Paul Freeman, Jason Harold Yost, Amy Jo Johnson, Jason David Frank, John Yong Bosch, Stephen Antonio Cardenas; **D:** Bryan Spicer; **W:** Arne Olsen, John Camps; **C:** Paul Murphy; **M:** Graeme Revell. *FXV*

The Mighty Pawns 1987 Inner-city kids turn to chess when their teacher inspires them to stay off the streets. Originally aired on PBS as part of the "Wonderworks" family movie series. 58m/C VHS, Closed Caption. Paul Winfield, Alfonso Ribeiro, Terence Knox, Rosalind Cash, Teddy Wilson; **D:** Eric Laneuville. *PME, HMV, FCT*

The Mighty Quinn 🦮🦮½ 1989 (R) While investigating the local murder of a rich white guy, the black Jamaican head of police becomes convinced that the prime suspect, a childhood friend, is innocent. As the police chief, Denzel is good in this off-beat comedy mystery. 98m/C VHS, Beta, LV. Denzel Washington, Robert Townsend, James Fox, Mimi Rogers, M. Emmet Walsh, Sheryl Lee Ralph, Esther Rolle, Art Evans, Norman Beaton, Keye Luke; **D:** Carl Schenkel; **W:** Hampton Fancher; **M:** Anne Dudley. *MGM, FOX*

The Migrants 🦮🦮🦮 1974 Adaptation of the Tennessee Williams play about the hardscrabble world of a migrant family yearning for a better life. Made for TV. 83m/C VHS. Cloris Leachman, Ron Howard, Sissy Spacek, Cindy Williams, Ed Lauter, Lisa Lucas, Mills Watson, Claudia McNeil, Dolph Sweet; **D:** Tom Gries; **W:** Lanford Wilson. *MON*

Mike's Murder 🦮½ 1984 (R) Disjointed drama about a shy bank teller who falls for a slick tennis player. When he is murdered, she investigates the circumstances, placing herself in dangerously close contact with his seedy, drug-involved buddies. The twists and confused plot leave the viewer bewildered. 109m/C VHS, Beta. Debra Winger, Mark Keyloun, Paul Winfield, Darrell Larson, Dan Shor, William Ostrander; **D:** James Bridges; **W:** James Bridges; **M:** John Barry. *WAR*

Mikey 🦮½ 1992 (R) Mikey seems like such a sweet little boy—but these awful things keep happening all around him. At every foster home and every school people have such dreadful, and deadly, accidents. But innocent Mikey couldn't be to blame—or could he. 92m/C VHS, Closed Caption. Brian Bonsali, John Diehl, Lyman Ward, Josie Bissett; **D:** Dennis Dimster. *IMP*

Mikey & Nicky 🦮🦮½ 1976 (R) Quirky, uneven film about longtime friends dodging a hit man during one long night. Bears little evidence of time and money invested. Cassavetes and Falk, however, provide some salvation. 105m/C VHS, Beta. John Cassavetes, Peter Falk, Ned Beatty, Oliver Clark, William Hickey; **D:** Elaine May; **W:** Elaine May. *FRF*

The Milagro Beanfield War 🦮🦮🦮½ 1988 (R) Redford's endearing adaptation of John Nichols's novel about New Mexican townfolk opposing development. Seemingly simple tale provides plenty of insight into human spirit. Fine cast, with especially stellar turns from Blades, Braga, and Vennera. 118m/C VHS, Beta, LV. Chick Vennera, John Heard, Ruben Blades, Sonia Braga, Daniel Stern, Julie Carmen, Christopher Walken, Richard Bradford, Carlos Riquelne, James Gammon, Melanie Griffith, Freddy Fender, M. Emmet Walsh; **D:** Robert Redford; **W:** David S. Ward; **C:** Robbie Greenberg; **M:** Dave Grusin. Academy Awards '88: Best Original Score. *USH*

Mildred Pierce 🦮🦮🦮½ 1945 Gripping melodrama features Crawford as hard-working divorcee rivaling daughter for man's love. Things, one might say, eventually get ugly. Adaptation of James M. Cain novel is classic of its kind. 113m/B VHS, Beta, LV, Closed Caption. Joan Crawford, Jack Carson, Zachary Scott, Eve Arden, Ann Blyth, Bruce (Herman Brix) Bennett; **D:** Michael Curtiz; **W:** Ranald MacDougall; **M:** Max Steiner. Academy Awards '45: Best Actress (Crawford); Nominations: Academy Awards '45: Best Black and White Cinematography, Best Picture, Best Screenplay, Best Supporting Actress (Arden, Blyth). *MGM, FOX, BTV*

Miles from Home 🦮🦮 *Farm of the Year* 1988 (R) Times are tough for farmers Frank and Terry Roberts. The brothers are about to have another bad harvest and the bank is threatening to foreclose. In a symbolic last ditch effort to save their pride, they decide to burn the farm and leave. On their journey, they meet strangers who recognize the pair and help them escape the police. A melodrama with many members of Chicago's Steppenwolf Theater. 113m/C VHS, Beta, Closed Caption. Richard Gere, Kevin Anderson, John Malkovich, Brian Dennehy, Judith Ivey, Penelope Ann Miller, Laurie Metcalf, Laura San Giacomo, Daniel Roebuck, Helen Hunt; **D:** Gary Sinise; **W:** Chris Gerolmo; **C:** Elliot Davis; **M:** Robert Folk. *WAR*

Miles to Go 🦮½ 1986 A successful businesswoman tries to enjoy her last days after learning she has terminal cancer. 88m/C VHS, Beta. Mimi Kuzyk, Tom Skerritt, Jill Clayburgh; **D:** David Greene. *NO*

Miles to Go before I Sleep 🦮🦮½ 1974 A retired, lonely man and a delinquent girl distrust each other but eventually reach out in mutual need. 78m/C VHS, Beta. Martin Balsam, MacKenzie Phillips, Kitty Winn, Elizabeth Wilson; **D:** Fielder Cook. *LCA*

Milk Money 🦮½ 1994 (PG-13) Twelve year-old Frank (Carter) talks his pals into pooling their milk money and heading to the big city so they can get a look at a naked woman. They find a prostitute (Griffith) for the job, whom Frank decides would be perfect to bring home to his widower dad (Harris). Although Griffith is generally adorable and the movie is actually less salacious than the premise might suggest, overall, it's sappy and another in the long line of cute-hooker/Cinderella fairytales.**CW:** Sexual themes involving adolescents. 110m/C VHS, Beta, Closed Caption. Michael Patrick Carter, Melanie Griffith, Ed Harris, Malcolm McDowell, Casey Siemaszko, Anne Heche, Philip Bosco; **D:** Richard Benjamin; **W:** John Mattson; **M:** Michael Convertino. *PAR*

Milky Way 🦮🦮½ 1936 Loopy comedy about milkman who finds unhappiness after accidentally knocking out champion boxer. Adequate, but not equal to Lloyd's fine silent productions. 89m/B VHS, Beta, LV. Harold Lloyd, Adolphe Menjou, Verree Teasdale, Helen Mack, William Gargan; **D:** Leo McCarey. *VYY, MRV, NOS*

The Milky Way 🦮🦮🦮 1968 Wicked anticlerical farce. Two bums team on religious pilgrimage and encounter seemingly all manner of strangeness and sacrilege in this typically peculiar Bunuel work. Perhaps the only film in which Jesus is encouraged to shave. In French with English subtitles. 102m/C VHS, Beta, LV. *FR* Laurent Terzieff, Paul Frankeur, Delphine Seyrig, Alain Cuny, Bernard Verley, Michel Piccoli, Edith Scob; **D:** Luis Bunuel; **W:** Jean-Claude Carriere. *XVC, MED, FCT*

Mill of the Stone Women 🦮🦮½ Ⅱ *Mulino Delle Donne di Pietra; Horror of the Stone Women; The Horrible Mill Women* 1960 Sculpture-studying art student encounters strange carousel with beautiful babes rather than horsies. And soon finds out that the statues contain shocking secrets. Filmed in Holland, it's offbeat and creepy. 94m/C VHS. *FR IT* Pierre Brice, Scilla Gabel, Danny Carrel, Wolfgang Preiss, Herbert Boenne, Liana Orfei; **D:** Giorgio Ferroni. *SNC*

The Mill on the Floss 🦮🦮 1937 Based on George Eliot's classic novel, this film follows the course of an ill-fated romance and family hatred in rural England. Underwhelming, considering the source. 77m/B VHS, Beta. *GB* James Mason, Geraldine Fitzgerald, Frank Lawton, Victoria Hopper, Fay Compton, Griffith Jones, Mary Clare; **D:** Tim Whelan. *NOS, MRV, DVT*

Mille Bolle Blu 🦮🦮 1993 Follows the lives of the inhabitants of a single block in Rome on the eve of a solar eclipse. The nieghborhood children take the opportunity to spy on their elders, including the engaged Elvira, whose old boyfriend Antonio wants her back, escaped convict Caligiuri who returns to his loving wife, and blind Guido, who's undergone an operation to restore his sight. Italian with subtitles. 83m/C VHS. *IT* Stefano Dionisi, Claudio Bigagli, Paolo Bonacelli, Nicoletta Boris; **D:** Leone Pompucci. *NYF*

Millenium 🦮🦮½ 1989 (PG-13) The Earth of the future is running out of time. The people are sterile and the air is terrible. To keep the planet viable, Ladd and company must go back in time and yank people off planes that are doomed to crash. Great special effects and well-thought out script make this a ball of fun. 108m/C VHS, Beta, LV, Closed Caption. Kris Kristofferson, Cheryl Ladd, Daniel J. Travanti, Lloyd Bochner, Robert Joy, Brent Carver, Maury Chaykin, David McIlwraith, Al Waxman; **D:** Michael Anderson Sr.; **W:** John Varley; **M:** Eric N. Robertson. *CCB*

Miller's Crossing 🦮🦮🦮½ 1990 (R) From the Coen brothers (makers of "Blood Simple" and "Raising Arizona") comes this extremely dark entry in the gangster movie sweepstakes of 1990. Jewish, Italian, and Irish mobsters spin webs of deceit, protection, and revenge over themselves and their families. Byrne is the protagonist, but no hero, being as deeply flawed as the men he battles. Harden stuns as the woman who sleeps with Byrne and his boss, Finney, in hopes of a better life and protection for her small-time crook brother. Visually exhilarating, excellently acted and perfectly paced. 115m/C VHS, Beta, LV, Closed Caption. Albert Finney, Gabriel Byrne, Marcia Gay Harden, John Turturro, Jon Polito, J.E. Freeman; **D:** Joel Coen; **W:** Ethan Coen, Joel Coen; **M:** Carter Burwell. *FXV, FCT*

Millie 🦮½ 1931 Creaky melodrama about a divorcee who wants every man but one. He pursues her teenage daughter instead, leading to tragedy and courtroom hand-wringing. Twelvetrees still stands out in this hokum, based on a Donald Henderson novel considered daring in its day. 85m/B VHS. Helen Twelvetrees, Robert Ames, Lilyan Tashman, Joan Blondell, John Halliday, James Hall, Anita Louise, Frank McHugh; **D:** John Francis Dillon. *NOS*

Million Dollar Duck 🦮½ 1971 (G) A family duck is dosed with radiation and begins to lay gold eggs. Okay Disney family fare, especially for youngsters. 92m/C VHS, Beta. Dean Jones, Sandy Duncan, Joe Flynn, Tony Roberts; **D:** Vincent McEveety; **M:** Buddy Baker. *DIS, OM*

Million Dollar Haul 🦮 1935 Tarzan sniffs out a ring of warehouse thieves. 60m/B VHS, Beta, LV. Reed Howes, Janet Chandler, William Farnum. *NO*

Million Dollar Kid 🦮🦮 1944 When a group of thugs wreak havoc in the neighborhood, the East Side Kids try to help a wealthy man put a stop to it. They face an even greater dilemma when they discover that the man's son is part of the gang. Part of the "Bowery Boys" series. 65m/B VHS. Leo Gorcey, Huntz Hall, Gabriel Dell, Louise Currie, Noah Beery Jr., Iris Adrian, Mary Gordon; **D:** Wallace Fox. *VYY, DVT, NOS*

Million Dollar Mermaid 🦮🦮 1952 The prototypical Williams aquashow, with the requisite awesome Berkeley dance numbers. As a biography of swimmer Annette Kellerman it isn't much, but as an MGM extravaganza, it fits the bill. 115m/C VHS, Beta. Esther Williams, Victor Mature, Walter Pidgeon, Jesse White, David Brian, Maria Tallchief, Howard Freeman, Busby Berkeley; **D:** Mervyn LeRoy. Nominations: Academy Awards '52: Best Color Cinematography. *MGM*

Million Dollar Mystery 🦮½ 1987 (PG) A dying man's last words indicate that several million dollars have been stashed near a diner. Chaos breaks out as nearly everyone in town tries to dig up the loot. 95m/C VHS, LV, Closed Caption. Eddie Deezen, Penny Baker, Tom Bosley, Rich Hall, Wendy Sherman, Rick Overton, Mona Lyden; **D:** Richard Fleischer; **W:** Rudy DeLuca, Tim Metcalfe; **C:** Jack Cardiff. *HBO, CNG*

A Million to Juan 🦮🦮½ 1994 (PG) Familiar rags-to-riches tale, this time set in a Los Angeles barrio, centers on Juan Lopez (Rodriguez), an uneducated good guy struggling to raise his son. Juan gets his lucky break when a stranger hands him a check for one million dollars, explains it's a loan, and if Juan can use the money properly for a month, he'll get a reward. Juan remains incredibly noble; the movie remains mushy. Loose adaptation of the Mark Twain story "The Million Pound Bank Note." Directorial debut for Rodriguez. 97m/C VHS, Closed Caption. Paul Rodriguez, Polly Draper, Pepe Serna, Bert Rosario, Jonathan Hernandez, Gerardo, Victor Rivers, Edward James Olmos, Paul Williams; Cameos: Tony Plana, Ruben Blades, Richard "Cheech" Marin, David Rasche, Liz Torres; D: Paul Rodriguez; W: Francisca Matos, Robert Grasmere. PSM

A Million to One ♂½ 1937 An athlete trains for the Olympic decathlon, and catches the eye of an upper-class woman in the process. The lead Bennett was actually a shot-putter in the 1932 Olympic Games. 60m/B VHS. Bruce (Herman Brix) Bennett, Joan Fontaine, Monte Blue, Kenneth Harlan, Reed Howes; D: Lynn Shores. VYY

The Millionairess ♂♂½ 1960 Loren is an incredibly rich woman who has ended a bad marriage, and feels that the only thing she still needs to fulfill her life is a good husband. She meets a humble doctor from India, in the person of Sellers, and finds he evades her every effort to snare him. In the process she learns that money can't buy everything. From a play by George Bernard Shaw. 90m/C VHS. GB Sophia Loren, Peter Sellers, Alastair Sim, Vittorio De Sica, Dennis Price; D: Anthony Asquith; C: Jack Hildyard. FXL

Millions ♂½ 1990 (R) To a family of millionaires, money is everything, and the heir to the family fortune is willing to do anything to get his hands on all that money. Even if it means sleeping with his sister-in-law and cousin! Lucky for him they happen to be beautiful models.CW: Some language, drug content, and sexuality. 118m/C VHS, Beta, Closed Caption. IT Billy Zane, Lauren Hutton, Carol Alt, Alexandra Paul, Catherine Hickland, Donald Pleasence; D: Carlo Vanzina. PSM

Milo & Otis ♂♂½ 1989 (G) Charming tale of a kitten named Milo and his best friend, a puppy named Otis. The two live on a farm and, when exploring the countryside, Milo is swept down a rushing river. Otis goes after to rescue his friend and the two begin a series of adventures as they try to return home. 76m/C VHS, Closed Caption. COL

Milo Milo ♂♂ 196? Comedy about some very silly French people who propose to steal the Venus de Milo from the Louvre. 110m/C VHS, Beta. Antonio Fargas, Joe Higgins. VCD

The Milpitas Monster ♂ 1975 (PG) Creature spawned in a Milpitas, California, waste dump terrorizes the town residents. 80m/C VHS, Beta. Doug Hagdahl, Scott A. Henderson, Scott Parker; D: Robert L. Burrill. VCI

Mimi ♂♂ 1935 Melodrama with a down-on-his-luck playwright falling for a poor lass who provides him with the needed inspiration to be a winner. The question is, will she die before he hits the big time? Loosely based on "La Vie de Boheme" by Henri Murger. 98m/B VHS. GB Douglas Fairbanks Jr., Gertrude Lawrence, Diana Napier, Harold Warrender, Carol Goodner, Richard Bird, Austin Trevor, Lawrence Hanray, Paul Graetz, Martin Walker; D: Paul Stein. VYY, FCT

Mimic ♂♂♂ 1997 (R) Married biotech scientists Sorvino and Northam upset the balance of nature when they cure a plague only to have their concoction unleashed in the New York subways. This causes giant cockroaches to mimic, and kill, humans. Far-fetched story is forgiven with a unique script (both John Sayles and Steven Soderbergh made additions) and original kills and thrills. Plenty of gore also makes it a worthy addition to the horror genre.CW: Terror/violence and language. ?m/C VHS. Jeremy Northam, Mira Sorvino, Josh Brolin, Charles S. Dutton; D: Guillermo del Toro; W: John Sayles, Steven Soderbergh, Matthew Robbins; M: Marco Beltrami. NYR

Min & Bill ♂♂ 1930 Patchy early talkie about two houseboat dwellers fighting to preserve their waterfront lifestyle and keep their daughter from being taken to a "proper" home. 66m/B VHS,

Beta. Marie Dressler, Wallace Beery, Marjorie Rambeau, Dorothy Jordan; D: George Roy Hill. Academy Awards '31: Best Actress (Dressler). MGM, BTV, FHE

Mina Tannenbaum ♂♂ 1993 Touching but unsentimental look at the 25-year friendship between two Jewish women in Paris. Mina (Bohringer) and Ethel (Zylberstein) meet as seven-year-olds and go through various childhood and teenage tramas together, including the desperate pangs of first love. Mina becomes an intense artist while flirty Ethel works as a freelance journalist. And, naturally, their friendship undergoes its own relentless changes. Pacing problems cause something of a letdown. Directorial debut for cinematographer Dugowson. French with subtitles. 128m/C VHS. FR Romane Bohringer, Elsa Zylberstein, Nils Tavernier, Florence Thomassin, Jean-Philippe Ecoffey, Stephane Slima; D: Martine Dugowson; W: Martine Dugowson; C: Dominique Chapuis. NYF

Minbo—Or the Gentle Art of Japanese Extortion ♂♂ 1992 Satire on Japanese mobsters, known as the Yakuza, focusing on the blackmail and intimidation that gives these criminals a great deal of their power. The ill-mannered group likes to congregate at a local hotel—much to the detriment of business—and hotel management finally hire a hardball-playing female lawyer to solve their problems with the thugs. Japanese with subtitles. 123m/C VHS. JP Nobuko Miyamoto, Akira Takarada, Takehiro Murata, Yasuo Daichi, Hideji Otaki; D: Juzo Itami; W: Juzo Itami; C: Yonezo Maeda; M: Toshiyuki Honda. HMV

Mind, Body & Soul ♂♂ 1992 (R) When a woman witnesses a human sacrifice performed by her boyfriend's satanic cult, she goes to the police. The cops, however, believe she is part of the cult, so she is forced to rely on the public defender to protect her from angry cult members. Pretty dull, but Hauser and Allen add some spice to this hokey thriller. 93m/C VHS. Wings Hauser, Ginger Lynn Allen, Jay Richardson, Ken Hill, Jesse Kaye, Tami Bakke; D: Rick Sloane. AIP

Mind Games ♂♂½ 1989 (R) A young couple and their ten-year-old son pick up a hitcher in their mobile home, never suspecting that he's a deranged psychology student ready to pit the family against each other as an experiment. 93m/C VHS, Beta. Edward Albert, Shawn Weatherly, Matt Norero, Maxwell Caulfield; D: Bob Yari. FOX, HHE

Mind Snatchers ♂♂½ 1972 (PG) An American G.I. becomes involved in U.S. Army experimental psychological brain operations when he is brought into a western European hospital for treatment. Also know as "The Happiness Cage." 94m/C VHS, Beta. Christopher Walken, Ronny Cox, Ralph Meeker, Joss Ackland; D: Bernard Girard. PSM

A Mind to Kill ♂♂ 1995 When a murdered girl is found in a small English seaside town, the crime is linked to a previous death. Police call on a university professor for help but then a new victim, with ties to the professor, is discovered and the police detective in charge finds that his own loved ones are now in danger. 95m/C VHS. GB Hywel Bennett, Philip Madoc, Sue Jones-Davies, Nicola Beddoe; D: Peter Edwards. FCT

A Mind to Murder ♂♂½ P.D. James: A Mind to Murder 1996 Scotland Yard Commander Adam Dalgliesh (Marsden) is still depressed over the murder of a colleague some months earlier when he's discreetly called in to investigate the stabbing death of the administrator of the Steen Clinic, located in East Anglia. The exclusive psychiatric facility is home to some politically sensitive patients and Dalgleish is under pressure to solve the crime quickly and quietly. His work would go a lot easier if people cooperated, but naturally the investigation doesn't go smoothly at all. Based on the 1963 novel by P.D. James and updated for the TV movie. 100m/C VHS. GB Roy Marsden, Sean Scanlan, Robert Pugh, Mairead Carty, Frank Finlay, Cal Macaninch, Ann-Gisel Glass, Sian Thomas, Jerome Flynn, Suzanne Burden, Donald Douglas,

Christopher Ravenscroft; Cameos: David Hemmings; D: Gareth Davies; C: Bill Broomfield. VCO, AAE

Mind Trap ♂½ 1991 A beautiful movie star's family is killed due to her father's involvement with naval research. The government wants no part of her troubles so she is forced to take the law into her own hands. 90m/C VHS. Dan Haggerty, Lyle Waggoner, Martha Kincare, Thomas Elliot, Samuel Steven; D: Eames Demetrios. NO

Mind Twister ♂½ 1993 (R) Erotic thriller finds a tough police detective on the trail of a sadistic killer with a twist. An unrated version is available at 94 minutes. 87m/C VHS. Telly Savalas, Gary Hudson, Richard Roundtree, Erica Nann, Suzanne Slater; D: Fred Olen Ray. VCI

Mind Warp ♂½ Grey Matter; The Brain Machine 1972 (R) A future society exercises mental control and torture over its citizens. 92m/C VHS, Beta. James Best, Barbara Burgess, Gil Peterson, Gerald McRaney, Marcus J. Grapes, Doug Collins, Anne Latham; D: Joy Houck Jr. COL

Mindfield ♂½ 1989 (R) An innocent man gets trapped by the CIA and is used by them in mind control experiments. 91m/C VHS, Beta, LV. CA Michael Ironside, Lisa Langlois, Christopher Plummer, Stefan Wodoslowsky, Sean McCann; D: Jean-Claude Lord. NO

Mindkiller ♂½ 1987 A tongue-in-cheek gore-fest about a shy young guy who develops his brain in an effort to be socially accepted. Unfortunately, he overdoes it and his brain mutates, bursts from his head and runs around on its own. An aspiring cult classic. 84m/C VHS, Beta. Joe McDonald, Christopher Wade, Shirley Ross, Kevin Hart; D: Michael Krueger. PSM

Mindwalk: A Film for Passionate Thinkers ♂♂♂ 1991 (PG) A feature-length intellectual workout; a physicist, poet and politician stroll the ancient grounds of Mont St. Michel monastery in France and discuss the need to change mankind's view of the universe. Uncinematic? Perhaps, but it entertainingly conveys the epochal ideas of scientist/author Fritjof Capra (whose book was adapted for the screen by younger brother Bernt). 111m/C VHS, Beta, Closed Caption. Liv Ullmann, Sam Waterston, John Heard, Ione Skye; D: Bernt Capra; W: Fritjof Capra, Floyd Byars; M: Philip Glass. PAR, WSH

Mindwarp ♂♂ 1991 (R) After an ecological disaster, residents of Earth move to a sterile haven known as "Inworld." When survivor Judy (Alicia) seeks answers about her missing father (accidentally killing her mother in the process), she is cast from "Inworld" into Earth's wasteland, where she and human compatriot Stover (Campbell) are left to fight the elements and learn the awful truth about Judy's father.CW: Horror violence and gore. 91m/C VHS, LV, Closed Caption. Marta Alicia, Bruce Campbell, Angus Scrimm, Elizabeth Kent, Mary Becker; D: Steve Barnett; W: Henry Dominick. COL

Mine Own Executioner ♂♂♂ 1947 Determined but unstable psychologist in postwar London struggles to treat schizophrenic who suffered torture by Japanese while wartime prisoner. Strong, visually engrossing fare. 102m/B VHS. GB Burgess Meredith, Kieron Moore, Dulcie Gray, Christine Norden, Barbara White, John Laurie, Michael Shepley; D: Anthony Kimmins. FCT, DVT, HHT

Mines of Kilimanjaro ♂½ 1987 (PG-13) An archaeology student heads for Africa to investigate his professor's murder and comes up with a heap of trouble. 88m/C VHS, Beta. Christopher Connelly, Tobias Hoels, Gordon Mitchell, Elena Pompei; D: Mino Guerrini. IMP

Ministry of Vengeance ♂ 1989 (R) A psychotic murderer who hates grapes of any kind finds the woman of his dreams—she's a psychotic murderer who hates grapes! Together they find bliss—until the plumber discovers their secret! 90m/C VHS, Beta, LV. John Schneider, Ned Beatty, George Kennedy, Yaphet Kotto, James Tolkan, Apollonia. LIV, VTR

The Miniver Story 🐾🐾 1950 Weepy sequel to "Mrs. Miniver" reunites the family in post-WWII England, but clearly lacks the inspiration of the original. Garson is again Mrs. Miniver and she's secretly suffering from a never-named fatal disease. She decides to straighten out the family troubles before her time is up, including her daughter's love life and her husband's plan to move to Brazil. Depressing and glum. **104m/B VHS.** *GB* Greer Garson, Walter Pidgeon, John Hodiak, Leo Genn, Cathy O'Donnell, Reginald Owen, Anthony Bushell; **D:** H.C. Potter; **W:** Ronald Millar, George Froeschel; **C:** Joseph Ruttenberg; **M:** Miklos Rozsa. **MGM**

Minnesota Clay 🐾½ *L'Homme du Minnesota* 1965 A blind gunman, who aims by sound and smell, is marked by two rival gangs and a tempestuous tramp. **89m/C VHS, Beta, LV.** *FR IT* Cameron Mitchell, Diana Martin; **D:** Sergio Corbucci. **NO**

A Minor Miracle 🐾🐾 1983 (G) Tender family fare about a group of orphaned children who band together under the loving guidance of their guardian (Huston) to save St. Francis School for boys from the town planners. Warms the cockles. **100m/C VHS, Beta, LV.** John Huston, Pele, Peter Fox; **D:** Terrell Tannen. **COL**

Minsky's Follies 1983 Recreation of an old time burlesque revue complete with strippers. **60m/C VHS, Beta.** Phyllis Diller, Rip Taylor, Stubby Kaye. **NO**

A Minute to Pray, A Second to Die 🐾🐾 *Un Minuto Per Pregare, Un Istante Per Morire; Dead or Alive; Outlaw Gun* 1967 A notorious, wanted-dead-or-alive gunman retreats to the amnesty of the New Mexico Territory, but finds he cannot shake his past. **100m/C VHS, Beta.** *IT* Robert Ryan, Arthur Kennedy, Alex Cord; **D:** Franco Giraldi. **FOX**

The Miracle 🐾🐾🐾 *Ways of Love* 1948 An innocent peasant woman is seduced by a shepherd and becomes convinced that her pregnancy will produce a second Christ. Controversial, compelling film derived from a story by Federico Fellini. In Italian with English subtitles. **43m/B VHS, Beta.** *IT* Anna Magnani, Federico Fellini; **D:** Roberto Rossellini; **W:** Federico Fellini. **NOS, FCT, APD**

The Miracle 🐾🐾½ 1991 (PG) Irish teens, whose strong friendship is based upon their equally unhappy home lives, find both tested when a secretive American woman turns up in town. Excellent debuts from Byrne and Pilkington but tedious pacing in a dreamy script that tells too much too soon. Worth watching just for D'Angelo's smouldering rendition of "Stardust." **97m/C VHS, LV.** *GB* Beverly D'Angelo, Donal McCann, Niall Byrne, Lorraine Pilkington, J.G. Devlin; **D:** Neil Jordan; **W:** Neil Jordan; **M:** Anne Dudley. **LIV**

Miracle at Moreaux 1986 Three Jewish children fleeing from Nazis find sanctuary with a nun and her wards. Based on Clare Huchet Bishop's book "Twenty and Ten." Originally aired on PBS as part of the "Wonderworks" family movie series. **58m/C VHS.** Loretta Swit, Marsha Moreau, Robert Joy, Ken Pogue, Robert Kosoy, Talya Rubin; **D:** Paul Shapiro. **PME, HMV, IGP**

Miracle Beach 🐾½ 1992 (PG-13) Scotty McKay has lost his job, his apartment, and his girl. Then he gets rejected by Dana, the super model he's secretly adored. Can things get any worse? Scotty decides to take a walk along the beach and sort things out when he stumbles across a girl genie, named Jeanie, who has been sent to Earth on a good will mission. Scotty gets Jeanie to grant his every material wish in order to dazzle model Dana. But when Jeanie falls in love with Scotty can she get him to recognize the difference between true love and fantasy? **CW:** Nudity and sexual situations. **88m/C VHS, LV.** Dean Cameron, Felicity Waterman, Ami Dolenz, Alexis Arquette, Martin Mull, Noriyuki "Pat" Morita, Vincent Schiavelli; **D:** Skott Snider. **COL**

Miracle Down Under 🐾🐾 1987 A family endures arduous times in 1890s Australia before a Christmas miracle changes their fortunes. Inoffensive Disney-produced drama. Australia has

two directors named George Miller—one directs Mad Max movies; the other directs family fare such as "The Man from Snowy River." This Miller is the latter. **101m/C VHS, Beta, Closed Caption.** *AU* Dee Wallace Stone, John Waters, Charles Tingwell, Bill Kerr, Andrew Ferguson; **D:** George Miller. **TOU, IGP**

Miracle in Harlem 🐾🐾 1948 A gang tries to take over a candy shop and when the gang leader is killed, the evidence points to the foster daughter of the shop owner. The script suffers from cliched dialog and less-than-believable situations, but the all-black cast turns in good performances. **69m/B VHS.** Sheila Guyse, Stepin Fetchit, Hilda Offley, Lawrence Criner, Monte Hawley; **D:** Jack Kemp. **NOS**

Miracle in Milan 🐾🐾🐾 *Miracolo a Milano* 1951 An innocent, child-like fantasy about heavenly intervention driving capitalists out of a Milanese ghetto and helping the poor to fly to a new Utopia. Happy mixture of whimsy and neo-realism. In Italian with English subtitles. **95m/B VHS, Beta, LV.** *IT* Francesco Golisano, Brunella Bova, Emma Gramatica, Paolo Stoppa; **D:** Vittorio De Sica; **W:** Cesare Zavattini. Cannes Film Festival '51: Best Film; National Board of Review Awards '51: 5 Best Foreign Films of the Year; New York Film Critics Awards '51: Best Foreign Film. **HMV, FCT, APD**

Miracle in Rome 🐾🐾½ *Milagro en Roma* 1988 Margarito Duarte digs up his dead daughter and finds her body in perfect condition despite 12-year internment. Attempting to convince the local clergy that she's miracle material, he finds them less than eager to elect her to sainthood. Based on a story by Gabriel Garcia marquez; made for Spanish TV. In Spanish with English subtitles. **76m/C VHS, LV.** *SP* Frank Ramirez, Gerardo Arellano, Amalia Duque Garcia, Lisandro Duque, Daniel Priolett; **D:** Lisandro Duque Naranjo; **W:** Lisandro Duque Naranjo, Gabriel Garcia Marquez. **FXL, FCT, APD**

Miracle in the Wilderness 🐾🐾½ 1991 A Christmas western based on Paul Gallico's novella, "The Snow Goose." Kristofferson stars as Jericho Adams, a former Indian fighter, who turns to farming to support his wife and child. When they are captured by a raiding party of Blackfeet, Adams discovers they have never heard the story of the Nativity. **88m/C VHS, LV.** Kris Kristofferson, Kim Cattrall, John Dennis Johnston, Joanelle Romero, Dennis Olvers, Sheldon Peters Wolfchild; **D:** Kevin Dobson; **W:** Jim Byrnes. **TTC, FCT**

Miracle Kid 🐾🐾 1942 Standard story of a young boxer who'd rather be something else. His romance is interrupted when he becomes successful in the ring. **66m/B VHS.** Tom Neal, Carol Hughes, Betty Blythe, Minta Durfee, Gertrude Messinger; **D:** William Beaudine. **NOS**

Miracle Mile 🐾🐾🐾 1989 (R) A riveting, apocalyptic thriller about a mild-mannered misfit who, while inadvertently standing on a street corner at 2 a.m., answers a ringing pay phone. The caller is a panicked missile-silo worker who announces that the bombs have been launched for an all-out nuclear war. With about an hour left before the end, he decides to head into the city and rendezvous with his new girlfriend. A surreal, wicked farce sadly overlooked in theatrical release. Music by Tangerine Dream. **87m/C VHS, Beta, LV, Closed Caption.** Anthony Edwards, Mare Winningham, John Agar, Denise Crosby, Lou Hancock, Mykel T. Williamson, Kelly Jo Minter, Kurt Fuller, Robert DoQui, Danny De La Paz, O-lan Jones, Alan Rosenberg, Claude Earl Jones; **D:** Steve DeJarnatt; **W:** Steve DeJarnatt; **M:** Tangerine Dream. **HBO**

Miracle of Morgan's Creek 🐾🐾🐾🐾 1944 The breakneck comedy that stands as Sturges' premier achievement. Details the misadventures of a wartime floozy who gets drunk, thinks she marries a soldier on leave, gets pregnant by him, forgets the whole thing, and then tries to evade scandal by getting a local schnook to marry her again. And she's expecting sextuplets. Hilarious, out-to-make-trouble farce that shouldn't have, by all rights, made it past the cen-

sors of the time. Sturges' most scathing assault on American values earned him an Oscar nomination for writing. Remade as "Rock-A-Bye Baby" in 1958. **98m/B VHS, Beta.** Eddie Bracken, Betty Hutton, Diana Lynn, Brian Donlevy, Akim Tamiroff, Porter Hall, Emory Parnell, Alan Bridge, Julius Tannen, Victor Potel, Almira Sessions, Chester Conklin, William Demarest, Jimmy Conlin; **D:** Preston Sturges; **W:** Preston Sturges; **M:** Leo Shuken, Charles Bradshaw. Nominations: Academy Awards '44: Best Original Screenplay. **PAR, CCB**

Miracle of Our Lady of Fatima 🐾🐾 *The Miracle of Fatima* 1952 Slick cold-war version of the supposedly true events surrounding the sighting of a holy vision by three children in Portugal during WWI. **102m/C VHS, Beta, LV.** Gilbert Roland, Susan Whitney, Sherry Jackson, Sammy Ogg, Angela Clark, Frank Silvera, Jay Novello; **D:** John Brahm; **M:** Max Steiner. Nominations: Academy Awards '52: Original Dramatic/Comedy Score. **WAR, IGP, KEP**

The Miracle of the Bells 🐾🐾 1948 A miracle occurs after a dead movie star is buried in the cemetary of her modest hometown. Given the premise, the casting is all the more peculiar. Adapted by Ben Hecht from Russell Janney's novel. **120m/B VHS, Beta.** Fred MacMurray, Alida Valli, Frank Sinatra, Lee J. Cobb; **D:** Irving Pichel. **REP, IGP**

Miracle of the Heart: A Boys Town Story 🐾🐾 1986 A television movie based on the story of Boys Town, and an old priest who sticks up for Boys Town's principles in the face of a younger priest with rigid ideas. **100m/C VHS, Beta.** Art Carney, Casey Siemaszko, Jack Bannon; **D:** Georg Stanford Brown. **COL**

The Miracle of the White Stallions 🐾½ *The Flight of the White Stallions* 1963 A disappointing Disney adventure about the director of a Viennese riding academy who guides his prized Lipzzan stallions to safety when the Nazis occupy Austria in WWII. **92m/C VHS, Beta.** Robert Taylor, Lilli Palmer, Eddie Albert, Curt Jurgens; **D:** Arthur Hiller; **W:** A.J. Carothers. **DIS**

Miracle on Ice 🐾🐾½ 1981 Occasionally stirring television film recounts the surprise triumph of the American hockey team over the touted Soviet squad during the 1980 Winter Olympics at Lake Placid. **150m/C VHS, Beta.** Karl Malden, Steve Guttenberg, Andrew Stevens, Lucinda Dooling, Jessica Walter; **D:** Steven Hilliard Stern. **NO**

Miracle on 34th Street 🐾🐾🐾🐾 *The Big Heart* 1947 The actual Kris Kringle is hired as Santa Claus for the Macy's Thanksgiving parade but finds difficulty in proving himself to the cynical parade sponsor. When the boss's daughter also refuses to acknowledge Kringle, he goes to extraordinary lengths to convince her. Holiday classic equal to "It's a Wonderful Life," with Gwenn and Wood particularly engaging. Also available colorized. **97m/B VHS, Beta, LV, Closed Caption.** Maureen O'Hara, John Payne, Edmund Gwenn, Natalie Wood, William Frawley, Porter Hall, Gene Lockhart, Thelma Ritter, Jack Albertson; **D:** George Seaton; **W:** George Seaton; **M:** Cyril Mockridge. Academy Awards '47: Best Screenplay, Best Story, Best Supporting Actor (Gwenn); Golden Globe Awards '48: Best Screenplay, Best Supporting Actor (Gwenn); Nominations: Academy Awards '47: Best Picture. **CCB, FOX, HMV**

Miracle on 34th Street 🐾🐾½ 1994 (PG) Updated remake of the 1947 Christmas classic in which a jolly, bearded gent (Attenborough) claiming to be Santa Claus brings happiness to a doubting girl (Wilson) and her jaded mother (Perkins). Before he can prove himself to the precocious child, he must prove himself in a court of law with the help of Perkins's impossibly perfect neighbor (McDermott), a lawyer with a heart of gold (talk about your Christmas miracles!). This version can't compete with the original's "classic" status, but Attenborough and Wilson bring soul and substance to this otherwise average adaptation. **114m/C VHS.** Richard Attenborough, Elizabeth Perkins, Dylan McDermott, J.T. Walsh, Mara Wilson, Joss Ackland, James Remar, Jane Leeves, Simon Jones, Robert

Prosky, William Windom; **D:** Les Mayfield; **W:** John Hughes, George Seaton; **M:** Bruce Broughton. *FXV*

The Miracle Rider 1935 A 15-chapter serial finds the bad guys trying to run the Indians off their lands in this saga of the old west. **295m/B VHS.** Tom Mix, Joan Gale, Charles Middleton, Jason Robards Sr., Pat O'Malley, Robert Frazer, Wally Wales, Tom London, George Chesebro, Lafe McKee; **D:** B. Reeves Eason, Armand Schaefer. *GPV, MRV, VCN*

The Miracle Woman 🎬🎬½ 1931 Stanwyck's particularly fine as evangelist Florence "Faith" Fallon, who becomes very successful thanks to her way with words, some fake miracles, and the talents of shady promoter Hornsby (Hardy). After blind ex-pilot John Carson (Manners) hears her on the radio, he decides Faith might be able to cure him. Florence winds up falling in love with John but Hornsby starts to worry she's going soft and will end their scam. Even Capra apparently thought this film was corny but it still works. Based on the play "Bless You Sister" by John Meehan and Robert Riskin. **90m/B VHS.** Barbara Stanwyck, David Manners, Sam Hardy, Beryl Mercer, Russell Hopton, Charles Middleton, Eddie Boland; **D:** Frank Capra; **W:** Dorothy Howell, Jo Swerling; **C:** Joseph Walker. *COL*

The Miracle Worker 🎬🎬🎬½ 1962 Depicts the unconventional methods that teacher Anne Sullivan used to help the deaf and blind Helen Keller adjust to the world around her and shows the relationship that built between the two courageous women. An intense, moving experience. William Gibson adapted his own play for the screen. **107m/B VHS, Beta.** Anne Bancroft, Patty Duke, Victor Jory, Inga Swenson, Andrew Prine, Beah Richards; **D:** Arthur Penn. Academy Awards '62: Best Actress (Bancroft), Best Supporting Actress (Duke); British Academy Awards '62: Best Actress (Bancroft); National Board of Review Awards '62: 10 Best Films of the Year, Best Actress (Bancroft); Nominations: Academy Awards '62: Best Adapted Screenplay, Best Costume Design (B & W), Best Director (Penn). *MGM, BTV, CCB*

The Miracle Worker 🎬🎬🎬 1979 Remade for television story of blind, deaf and mute Helen Keller and her teacher, Annie Sullivan, whose patience and perseverance finally enable Helen to learn to communicate with the world. Duke was Keller in the 1962 original, but plays the teacher in this version. **98m/C VHS, Beta.** Patty Duke, Melissa Gilbert; **D:** Paul Aaron; **M:** Billy Goldenberg. *WAR, OM*

Miracles 🎬½ 1986 (PG) Comedic misfire pairs a recently divorced couple as reluctant adventurers dodging jewel thieves and peculiar tribes in South America. In a desperate move to create a plot, Mexican jewel thieves, strange tribal rites, and some outrageously unlikely coincidences reunite the family. If this sounds good, see "Romancing the Stone" instead. **90m/C VHS, Beta, LV.** Tom Conti, Teri Garr, Paul Rodriguez, Christopher Lloyd, Jorge Russek, Charles Rocket, Bob Nelson; **D:** Jim Kouf; **M:** Peter Bernstein. *IME*

Mirage 🎬🎬🎬 1966 An amnesiac finds himself the target of a dangerous manhunt in New York City in this offbeat thriller. Peck is particularly sympathetic in the lead, and McCarthy, Matthau, and Kennedy all shine in supporting roles. Worth it just to hear that Kennedy grunt, "I owe this man some pain!" **108m/B VHS, Beta.** Gregory Peck, Diane Baker, Walter Matthau, Jack Weston, Kevin McCarthy, Walter Abel, George Kennedy; **D:** Edward Dmytryk; **M:** Quincy Jones. *BAR, MLB*

Mirage 🎬½ 1994 (R) Neo-noir with plot problems has former Palm Springs cop Matteo Juarez (Olmos) hired to protect Jennifer (Young), the wife of wealthy environmentalist Donald Gale (Williams). But Jennifer just happens to suffer from multiple personality disorder, leading a not-so-secret second life as a stripper and having trouble always on her heels. **CW:** Sexuality, language, and some shootings. **106m/C VHS.** Edward James Olmos, Sean Young, James Andronica, Paul W. Williams; **D:** Paul W. Williams; **W:** James Andronica. *USH*

Mirele Efros 🎬🎬½ 1938 A widowed but successful businesswoman finds herself at odds with her daughter-in-law in this film set in the turn of the century. In Yiddish with English subtitles. **80m/B VHS, Beta.** Berta Gersten, Michael Rosenberg, Ruth Elbaum, Albert Lipton, Sarah Krohner, Moishe Feder; **D:** Joseph Berne. *ERG*

The Mirror 🎬🎬🎬 *Zerkalo; A White White Boy* 1975 Wonderful child's view of life in Russia during WWII. Black and white flashbacks of important events in the country's history are interspersed with scenes of day-to-day family life. In Russian with English subtitles. **106m/C VHS.** *RU* Margarita Terekhova, Philip Yankovsky, Ignat Danilitsev, Oleg Yankovsky; **D:** Andrei Tarkovsky. *TPV, KIV*

The Mirror Crack'd 🎬🎬 1980 (PG) While filming a movie in the English countryside, an American actress is murdered and Miss Marple must discover who the killer is. Based on the substantially better Agatha Christie novel. **105m/C VHS, Beta, LV.** *GB* Elizabeth Taylor, Kim Novak, Tony Curtis, Edward Fox, Geraldine Chaplin, Charles Gray, Pierce Brosnan; **D:** Guy Hamilton; **W:** Barry Sandler. *REP*

The Mirror Has Two Faces 🎬🎬 1996 (PG-13) Gregory (Bridges) is a hunky, but flustered, professor (nutty professor?) looking for romance without all that complicated sex, which shortly leads him to plain but soulful Rose (Streisand), the ugly duckling of her family. Rose's mother (Bacall) seems more happy with her much married sister (Rogers), who is headed down the aisle again with gorgeous Alex (Brosnan). Rose decides it's her turn, despite Gregory's protests, and she weds the bow-tied (and perhaps hogtied?) educator anyway. When Gregory leaves her on a promotional book tour, frumpy Babs decides a big makeover is in order. Her newfound outer beauty, however, becomes the beast on the inside. Premise is marred by Streisand's unwillingness to look bad, and there's a too-subtle transformation between the "ugly" Rose and the updated version. Bacall gives a memorable, Oscar-nominated performance. Remake of 1959 French film. La Streisand added to her reputation for being a "difficult" perfectionist with her constant reshoots and personnel firings that extended the film's schedule. **CW:** Language, sensuality and some mature thematic material. **127m/C VHS, LV, Closed Caption.** Barbra Streisand, Jeff Bridges, Pierce Brosnan, Mimi Rogers, Lauren Bacall, Brenda Vaccaro, Austin Pendleton, George Segal, Elle Macpherson; **D:** Barbra Streisand; **W:** Richard LaGravenese; **C:** Dante Spinotti, Andrzej Bartkowiak; **M:** Barbra Streisand, Marvin Hamlisch. Golden Globe Awards '97: Best Supporting Actress (Bacall); Screen Actors Guild Award '96: Best Supporting Actress (Bacall); Nominations: Academy Awards '96: Best Song ("I've Finally Found Someone"), Best Supporting Actress (Bacall); British Academy Awards '96: Best Supporting Actress (Bacall); Golden Globe Awards '97: Best Actress—Musical/Comedy (Streisand), Best Song ("I've Finally Found Someone"), Best Score. *COL*

Mirror Images 🎬½ 1991 (R) Although sexy twins Kaitlin and Shauna may look alike, they couldn't have more diverse personalities. Yet the gorgeous twins find their lives thrown together in a mad tornado of passion and danger when they each encounter a handsome, mysterious stranger. Could it be that this guy has something more on his mind than love, something like... murder? Also available in an even steamier unrated version. **CW:** Drug content and strong sensuality. **94m/C VHS.** Delia Sheppard, Jeff Conaway, Richard Arbolino, John O'Hurley, Korey Mall, Julie Strain, Nels Van Patten; **D:** Alexander Gregory Hippolyte. *USH*

Mirror Images 2 🎬🎬 1993 Direct-to-video erotic thriller features identical twins Carrie and Terrie (Whirry in a dual role). Carrie's Miss Goody Two-Shoes and Terrie's a murderous nympho who likes Carrie's guys. Terrie dies in a mysterious fire and Carrie sets out to investigate. Sex and nudity sells. **92m/C VHS.** Shannon Whirry, Luca

Bercovici, Tom Reilly; **D:** Alexander Gregory Hippolyte. *ACA*

Mirror, Mirror 🎬🎬 1990 (R) The prolific Ms. Black turns on the ol' black magic when her daughter's classmates decide it's open season for taunting shrinking violets. Thanks to a magical mirror on the wall, the cheerleading classmates are willed to the great pep rally in the sky. **105m/C VHS, LV.** Karen Black, Rainbow Harvest, Kristin Datillo, Ricky Paull Goldin, Yvonne De Carlo, William Sanderson; **D:** Marina Sargenti. *ACA*

Mirror, Mirror 2: Raven Dance 🎬½ 1994 (R) Teenaged Marlee (Wells) and her brother are temporarily housed in a convent after the death of their parents. The mystery mirror is discovered and looking into it causes Marlee to become partially blind. Meanwhile, her inheritance is threatened and a mysterious stranger, living in the convent's basement, may be Marlee's only hope. **91m/C VHS, LV.** Tracy Wells, Roddy McDowall, Sally Kellerman, Veronica Cartwright, William Sanderson, Lois Nettleton; **D:** Jimmy Lifton; **W:** Jimmy Lifton, Virginia Perfili. *ORP*

Mirror Mirror 3 🎬½ 1996 Artist discovers a mirror in an abandoned mansion and sees that it reflects the presence of his lost lover, who is now able to manipulate his dreams. **?m/C VHS.** Billy Drago, Monique Parent, David Naughton, Mark Ruffalo, Elizabeth Baldwin, Richard Cansino; **D:** Rachel Gordon, Virginia Perfili; **W:** Steve Tymon; **C:** Nils Erickson. *MTH*

Mirror of Death 🎬 1987 A woman subject to physical abuse gets more than she bargains for when she seeks revenge by unleashing the gruesome Queen of Hell. Watch this if you dare! **85m/C VHS, Beta.** Julie Merrill, Kuri Browne, John Reno, Deryn Warren. *NO*

Mirrors 🎬 1978 Woman finds that her dreams lead to death and destruction in New Orleans. **83m/C VHS, Beta.** Kitty Winn, Peter Donat, William Swetland, Mary-Robin Redd, William Burns; **D:** Noel Black. *NO*

Mirrors 🎬🎬½ 1985 A Detroit-born ballerina goes to the Big Apple in search of fame and glory, leaving behind her journalist boyfriend. This upbeat love story features some spectacular dance routines and a behind-the-scenes look at a Broadway dancer's lifestyle. Originally made for television. **99m/C VHS, Closed Caption.** Timothy Daly, Marguerite Hickey, Antony Hamilton; **D:** Harry Winer. *THV*

The Misadventures of Merlin Jones 🎬½ 1963 (G) A pair of college sweethearts become embroiled in a rollicking chimpnapping scandal. Disney pap done appropriately. A sequel, "The Monkey's Uncle," followed. **90m/C VHS, Beta.** Tommy Kirk, Annette Funicello, Leon Ames, Stuart Erwin, Connie Gilchrist; **D:** Robert Stevenson; **W:** Alfred Lewis Levitt, Helen Levitt; **C:** Edward Colman; **M:** Buddy Baker. *DIS*

The Misadventures of Mr. Wilt 🎬🎬 *Wilt* 1990 (R) Bumbling college lecturer has to convince inept inspector that he murdered a blowup doll, not his mean missing wife. Based on Tom Sharpe's bestseller. **CW:** Language and cosmic sexual situations. **84m/C VHS.** *GB* Griff Rhys Jones, Mel Smith, Alison Steadman, Diana Quick; **D:** Michael Tuchner; **M:** Anne Dudley. *THV*

Misbehaving Husbands 🎬½ 1941 Weak story finds store-owner Langton suspected of being untrue by wife Blythe—thanks to rumors spread by a shyster lawyer only to happy to console the lady after the divorce. **65m/B VHS.** Harry Langdon, Betty Blythe, Ralph Byrd, Esther Muir, Luana Walters; **D:** William Beaudine. *GPV*

Mischief 🎬🎬 1985 (R) Alienated youths form a friendship during James Dean's heyday. Warning: this film offers a fairly convincing recreation of the 1950s. **97m/C VHS, Beta, LV, Closed Caption.** Doug McKeon, Catherine Mary Stewart, Kelly Preston, Chris Nash, D.W. Brown, Jami Gertz, Margaret Blye, Graham Jarvis, Terry O'Quinn; **D:** Mel Damski; **W:** Noel Black. *FOX*

Misery 🐾🐾🐾 **1990 (R)** Author Caan decides to chuck his lucrative but unfulfilling pulp novels and write seriously by finishing off his most popular character, Misery Chastain. However, fate intervenes when he crashes his car near the home of Bates, his "biggest fan ever," who saves his life, but then tortures him into resurrecting her favorite character. Bates is chillingly glib and calmly brutal—watch your ankles. Based on the novel by Stephen King. **CW:** Language and violence. **107m/C VHS, Beta, LV, Closed Caption.** James Caan, Kathy Bates, Lauren Bacall, Richard Farnsworth, Frances Sternhagen, Graham Jarvis; **D:** Rob Reiner; **W:** William Goldman; **M:** Marc Shaiman. Academy Awards '90: Best Actress (Bates); Golden Globe Awards '91: Best Actress—Drama (Bates). *COL, NLC, BTV*

The Misfit Brigade 🐾🐾 *Wheels of Terror* **1987 (R)** Variation on the "Dirty Dozen" finds German misfits recruited for warfare by desperate Nazis during WWII. **99m/C VHS, Beta.** Bruce Davison, Oliver Reed, David Carradine, David Patrick Kelly, D.W. Moffett, Keith Szarabajka; **D:** Gordon Hessler. *TWE*

The Misfits 🐾🐾🐾 **1961** A cynical floozy befriends grim cowboys in this downbeat drama. Compelling performances from leads Clift, Monroe (screenwriter Miller's wife), and Gable. Last film for the latter two performers, and nearly the end for Clift. **124m/B VHS, Beta, LV.** Clark Gable, Marilyn Monroe, Montgomery Clift, Thelma Ritter, Eli Wallach, James Barton, Estelle Winwood; **D:** John Huston; **W:** Arthur Miller; **C:** Russell Metty; **M:** Alex North. *MGM, FOX, FCT*

Misfits of Science 🐾 **1985** Pilot for a failed television series about a group of teens with special powers who fight to save the world. **96m/C VHS, Beta.** Dean Paul Martin, Kevin Peter Hall, Mark Thomas Miller, Kenneth Mars, Courteney Cox; **D:** Philip DeGuere. *USH*

Mishima: A Life in Four Chapters 🐾🐾🐾 **1985 (R)** Somewhat detached account and indulgent portrayal of the narcissistic Japanese author (and actor, filmmaker, and militarist) alternates between stylized interpretations of his books and a straightforward account of his life. Culminates in a pseudo-military operation that, in turn, resulted in Mishima's ritualistic suicide. A U.S./Japanese production. Innovative design by Eiko Ishioka. In Japanese with English subtitles. **121m/C VHS, Beta, Closed Caption.** Ken Ogata, Kenji Sawada, Yasosuke Bando; **D:** Paul Schrader; **W:** Leonard Schrader, Paul Schrader; **C:** John Bailey; **M:** Philip Glass. *WAR*

Miss A & Miss M 🐾 **1986** A young girl is shocked when she realizes that two teachers she has befriended also live together. **60m/C VHS.** Kika Markham, Jennifer Hilary. *PSM*

Miss All-American Beauty 🐾1/2 **1982** A behind-the-scenes look at a smalltime Texas beauty pageant. Lane stars as a contestant who comes to realize her self-respect is more important than winning an award. Meadow's mean pageant director adds an ironic edge that the movie as a whole lacks. Made for television. **96m/C VHS, Beta.** Diane Lane, Cloris Leachman, David Dukes, Jayne Meadows, Alice Hirson, Brian Kerwin; **D:** Gus Trikonis. *LIV*

Miss Annie Rooney 🐾🐾 **1942 (G)** Intended to bill the child star in a more mature role, Temple receives her first screen kiss in this story about a poor Irish girl who falls in love with a wealthy young man. The well-worn plot is weighed down by lifeless dialogue. **86m/B VHS, Beta.** Shirley Temple, Dickie Moore, William Gargan, Guy Kibbee, Peggy Ryan, June Lockhart; **D:** Edwin L. Marin. *LIV, MED*

Miss Evers' Boys 🐾🐾1/2 **1997 (PG)** Wrenching cable docudrama covers a 40-year U.S. Public Health Service study in which black men suffering from syphillis were monitored but not treated for the disease. Eunice Evers (Woodard) is a nurse at Alabama's Tuskegee Hospital in 1932, assisting Dr. Brodus (Morton) in the care of the afflicted men. White Dr. Douglas (Sheffer) first has a funded government program for treat-ment but when the program is cut, he's offered funding only for the study of syphilitic black men and establishing whether the disease affects blacks and whites differently. Brodus and Evers both lie to their patients as each comes to realize that treatment will never be re-established and only the deaths of their patients will provide the final information for the study. Based on the play by David Feldshuh. **120m/C VHS.** Alfre Woodard, Laurence "Larry" Fishburne, Joe Morton, Craig Sheffer, Obba Babatunde, Ossie Davis, E.G. Marshall; **D:** Joseph Sargent; **W:** Walter Bernstein; **C:** Donald M. Morgan; **M:** Charles Bernstein. *HBO*

Miss Firecracker 🐾🐾🐾 **1989 (PG)** Hunter, longing for love and self-respect, decides to change her promiscuous image by entering the local beauty pageant in her conservative southern hometown. The somewhat drippy premise is transformed by a super script and cast into an engaging and upbeat film. Henley's script was adapted from her own Off-Broadway play where Hunter created the role. Actress Lahti, wife of director Schlamme, makes a brief appearance. **102m/C VHS, Beta, LV, Closed Caption.** Holly Hunter, Scott Glenn, Mary Steenburgen, Tim Robbins, Alfre Woodard, Trey Wilson, Bert Remsen, Ann Wedgeworth, Christine Lahti, Amy Wright; **D:** Thomas Schlamme; **W:** Beth Henley; **C:** Arthur Albert; **M:** David Mansfield. *HBO*

Ms. 45 🐾🐾🐾 *Angel of Vengeance* **1981 (R)** Rough, bristling cult favorite about a mute girl who, in response to being raped and beaten twice in one night, goes on a man-killing murder spree. Wild ending. **84m/C VHS, Beta, LV.** Zoe Tamerlis, Steve Singer, Jack Thibeau, Peter Yellen, Darlene Stuto, Editta Sherman, Albert Sinkys, Jimmy Laine; **D:** Abel Ferrara. *LIV, FCT*

Miss Grant Takes Richmond 🐾🐾 *Innocence is Bliss* **1949** Zipperhead secretary finds herself in hot water a la Lucy when she finds out the company she's been working for is really the front for a gambling getup. Only Lucy fans need apply. **87m/B VHS.** Lucille Ball, William Holden, Janis Carter, James Gleason, Gloria Henry, Frank McHugh, George Cleveland, Arthur Space, William Wright, Jimmy Lloyd; **D:** Lloyd Bacon. *COL, FCT*

Miss Julie 🐾🐾 **1950** Melodramatic stew adapted from from the August Strindberg play about a confused noblewoman who disgraces herself when she allows a servant to seduce her. In Swedish with English subtitles. **90m/B VHS, Beta.** *SW* Anita Bjork, Ulf Palme, Anders Henrikson; **D:** Alf Sjoberg. Cannes Film Festival '51: Best Film. *HMV, COL*

Miss Mary 🐾🐾1/2 **1986 (R)** A compassionate English governess in Buenos Aires conflicts with the honor-obsessed family she works for and Argentina's tumultuous history. Christie gives a wonderful performance. **CW:** Some profanity and nudity. **100m/C VHS, Beta.** *AR* Julie Christie, Donald McIntire, Sofia Viruboff, Luisina Brando; **D:** Maria-Luisa Bemberg; **W:** Jorge Goldenberg, Maria-Luisa Bemberg. *VTR, NWV*

Miss Melody Jones 🐾 **1973** A beautiful young black woman's dreams of stardom unravel as she is forced to pander to prurient men by disrobing publicly for financial recompense. **86m/C VHS.** Philomena Nowlin, Ronald Warren, Jacqueline Dalya, Peter Jacob; **D:** Bill Brame; **W:** Bill Brame. *XVC*

Miss Right 🐾 **1981 (R)** A young man determines to find the ideal woman for himself and casts aside his other romantic interests. Sputtering lightweight comedy. **98m/C VHS, LV.** William Tepper, Karen Black, Virna Lisi, Margot Kidder, Marie-France Pisier; **D:** Paul Williams. *IME*

Miss Rose White 🐾🐾🐾 **1992 (PG)** Sedgwick is Rose, a modern young career woman in post-WWII New York, as American as apple pie, who lives two very separate lives. Born Rayzel Weiss, a Polish Jew, she immigrated to the U.S. with her father as a very young girl, before the holocaust devastated her remaining family in Poland. After the war her older sister, thought dead, comes to America. The haunted Luisa causes Rose to question whether she can ever leave her past behind. Above average Hallmark Hall of Fame presentation has a good cast, particularly Plummer as Luisa. Based on the play "A Shayna Maidel" by Barbara Lebow. **95m/C VHS, Closed Caption.** Kyra Sedgwick, Amanda Plummer, Maximilian Schell, D.B. Sweeney, Penny Fuller, Milton Selzer, Maureen Stapleton; **D:** Joseph Sargent; **W:** Anna Sandor. *REP, BTV*

Miss Sadie Thompson 🐾🐾🐾 **1953** Based on the novel "Rain" by W. Somerset Maugham. Promiscuous tart Hayworth arrives on a Pacific island occupied by a unit of Marines and a sanctimonious preacher played by Ferrer While Hayworth parties with the Marines and becomes involved with Ray's Sgt. O'Hara, Ferrer moralizes and insists she return to the mainland to face moral charges. Quasi-musical with a scattering of dubbed songs by Hayworth includes a memorable erotic dance scene complete with tight dress and dripping sweat. Hayworth's strong performance carries the picture with Ferrer and Ray turning in cardboard versions of their Maugham characters. Originally filmed in 3-D. **91m/C VHS, Beta, LV.** Rita Hayworth, Jose Ferrer, Aldo Ray, Charles Bronson; **D:** Curtis Bernhardt. Nominations: Academy Awards '53: Best Song ("Sadie Thompson's Song (Blue Pacific Blues)"). *COL*

Missile to the Moon 🐾1/2 **1959** First expedition to the moon encounters not acres of dead rock but a race of gorgeous women in lingerie and high heels. A bad but entertaining remake of "Cat Women of the Moon," featuring a bevy of beauty contest winners from New Hampshire to Yugoslavia. Who says truth is stranger than fiction. **78m/B VHS, Beta.** Gary Clarke, Cathy Downs, K.T. Stevens, Laurie Mitchell, Michael Whalen, Nina Bara, Richard Travis, Tommy Cook, Marjorie Hellen; **D:** Richard Cunha. *RHI, SNC, CNM*

Missiles of October 🐾🐾🐾 **1974** Telling the story of the October 1962 Cuban Missile crisis, this made-for-TV drama keeps you on the edge of your seat while unfolding the sequence of events within the U.S. government. Well written, with a strong cast including Devane, who turns in a convincing performance as—guess who—J.F.K. **155m/C VHS, Beta.** William Devane, Ralph Bellamy, Martin Sheen, Howard da Silva; **D:** Anthony Page. *MPI, LCA*

Missing 🐾🐾🐾1/2 **1982 (PG)** At the height of a military coup in Chile (never named in the movie), a young American writer (Shea) disappears. His right-wing father Lemmon tries to get to the bottom of his disappearance while bickering with Shea's wife, played by Spacek, a bohemian who is the political opposite of her father-in-law. Outstanding performances by Spacek and Lemmon along with excellent writing and direction result in a gripping and thought-provoking thriller. Based on the book by Thomas Hauser from the true story of Charles Horman. **122m/C VHS, Beta, LV.** Jack Lemmon, Sissy Spacek, John Shea, Melanie Mayron, David Clennon, Charles Cioffi, Joe Regalbuto, Richard Venture, Janice Rule; **D:** Constantin Costa-Gavras; **W:** Constantin Costa-Gavras, Donald Stewart; **M:** Vangelis. Academy Awards '82: Best Adapted Screenplay; British Academy Awards '82: Best Screenplay; Cannes Film Festival '82: Best Actor (Lemmon), Best Film; Writers Guild of America '82: Best Adapted Screenplay; Nominations: Academy Awards '82: Best Actor (Lemmon), Best Actress (Spacek), Best Picture. *USH*

The Missing Corpse 🐾🐾 **1945** When a newspaper publisher's worst rival is murdered, he fears that he will be implicated. He decides the only thing to do is hide the body to prevent its being discovered. Enjoyable, light comedy/mystery. **62m/B VHS.** J. Edward Bromberg, Eric Sinclair, Frank Jenks, Isabelle Randolph, Paul Guilfoyle, John Shay, Lorell Sheldon; **D:** Al(bert) Herman. *NOS, MRV, SNC*

Missing in Action 🐾🐾 **1984 (R)** An army colonel returns to the Vietnam jungle to settle some old scores and rescue some POWs while on an MIA fact-finding mission. Box office smash. **101m/C VHS, Beta, LV.** Chuck Norris, M. Emmet Walsh; **D:**

Joseph Zito; **W:** James Bruner; **C:** Joao Fernandes. *MGM, TLF*

Missing in Action 2: The Beginning ✄ 1985 (R) Set in Vietnam, this prequel to the original "Missing in Action" provides some interesting background on Norris's rocky relationship with communism. Packed with violence, bloodshed and torture. **96m/C VHS, Beta, LV.** Chuck Norris, Soon-Teck Oh, Cosie Costa, Steven Williams; **D:** Lance Hool; **W:** Steve Bing. *MGM*

Missing Link ✄✄½ 1988 (PG) A strange, meditative quasi-documentary depicting the singular adventures of a humanoid silently transversing the African wilderness and confronting various natural phenomena. Beautifully photographed. Make-up by Rick Baker. **92m/C VHS, Beta.** Peter Elliott, Michael Gambon; **D:** David Hughes. *USH*

Missing Pieces ✄✄½ 1983 A woman takes a job as a private investigator in order to find her journalist husband's killer. Effective made-for-television mystery taken from the novel "A Private Investigation" by Karl Alexander. **96m/C VHS.** Elizabeth Montgomery, Louanne, John C. Reilly, Ron Karabatsos, Robin Gammell, Julius W. Harris; **D:** Mike Hodges. *LIV*

Missing Pieces ✄✄½ 1991 (PG) Goof-ups Wuhl and Idle find out about a potential inheritance thanks to a fortune cookie. Now if they can jut figure out what the riddle means. **93m/C VHS.** Eric Idle, Robert Wuhl, Lauren Hutton; **D:** Leonard Stern; **W:** Leonard Stern. *HBO*

The Mission ✄✄✄ 1986 (PG) Sweeping, cinematically beautiful historical drama about an 18th-century Jesuit mission in the Brazilian jungle. The missionaries struggle against the legalized slave trade of Portugal and political factions within the church. Written by Bolt (of "A Man for All Seasons" fame), its visual intensity is marred by length and so much overt symbolism that an emotional coolness surfaces when the action slows. Nonetheless, epic in ambition and nearly in quality. Magnificent musical score. **125m/C VHS, Beta, LV, 8mm, Closed Caption.** Robert De Niro, Jeremy Irons, Ray McAnally, Philip Bosco, Aidan Quinn, Liam Neeson, Cherie Lunghi, Rev. Daniel Berrigan, Ronald Pickup; **D:** Roland Joffe; **W:** Robert Bolt; **C:** Chris Menges; **M:** Ennio Morricone. Academy Awards '86: Best Cinematography; British Academy Awards '86: Best Supporting Actor (McAnally); Cannes Film Festival '86: Best Film; Golden Globe Awards '87: Best Screenplay, Best Score; Los Angeles Film Critics Association Awards '86: Best Cinematography; Nominations: Academy Awards '86: Best Art Direction/Set Decoration, Best Costume Design, Best Director (Joffe), Best Film Editing, Best Picture, Best Original Score. *WAR*

Mission Batangas ✄½ 1969 Unremarkable adventure-war-heist movie tells the story of a shallow American WWII pilot (Weaver) and a missionary nurse (Miles), who team up to steal the Philippine government's entire stock of gold bullion from the Japanese who captured it. Beautiful scenery, shot in the Philippines, adds something to an otherwise vacant effort. **100m/C VHS, Beta, LV.** Dennis Weaver, Vera Miles, Keith Larsen; **D:** Keith Larsen. *VTR, NWV*

Mission Corbari ✄ 197? One heavily armed and ill-tempered hombre takes on the Nazis, with indifferent results. **88m/C VHS, Beta.** *NO*

Mission Galactica: The Cylon Attack ✄✄ 1979 Spaceship Battlestar Galactica is stranded in space without fuel and open to attack from the chrome-plated Cylons. Adama (Greene) is forced to stop Commander Cain's (Bridges) efforts to launch an attack against the Cylons, while countering the attacks of the Cylon leader. Warmed over made-for-television sci-fi. **108m/C VHS, Beta, LV.** Lorne Greene, Lloyd Bridges, Richard Hatch, Dirk Benedict. *USH*

Mission Impossible 1966 Six-volumes (containing 2 episodes each) follow the adventures of a team of highly specialized government agents known as the Impossible Missions Force, under the leadership of Jim Phelps (Graves), who

took on top-secret assignments. The original TV series ran from 1966-1973 and was briefly revived in 1988-1990. The show's distinctively jazzy theme by Lalo Schifrin was a hit single in 1968. **102m/C VHS, Beta, Closed Caption.** Peter Graves, Barbara Bain, Martin Landau, Greg Morris, Peter Lupus, Steven Hill, George Takei, Pernell Roberts, Martin Sheen, Lee Meriwether. *PAR*

Mission: Impossible ✄✄✄ 1996 (PG-13) Cruise and director DePalma did not completely succeed or fail in their mission to create a blockbuster hit based on the popular '60's TV series. Cruise (one of the film's producers) is Ethan Hunt, pointman extraordinaire of the IMF team headed by Jim Phelps (Jon Voight). Their team is sent to recover a computer disk with devastating information from a mercenary Russian spy. Smelling a double cross, Hunt confronts his conniving agency boss Kitteridge (the perfectly cast Czerny) and creates his own team of crack agents to get to the truth, mind-boggling plot twists and crazy train rides be damned. The plotline may have self-destructed two-thirds into the movie and the absence of a truly sinister villain causes some damage, but with solid acting talent, tight pacing, alluring European locales, and tension-inducing special effects, who has time to notice? $100 million gross in the first two weeks would seem to indicate a sequel is in order. **CW:** Some intense action violence. **110m/C VHS.** Tom Cruise, Jon Voight, Emmanuelle Beart, Ving Rhames, Henry Czerny, Emilio Estevez, Vanessa Redgrave, Jean Reno; **D:** Brian DePalma; **W:** Robert Towne, David Koepp; **C:** Stephen Burum; **M:** Danny Elfman. Nominations: MTV Movie Awards '97: Best Action Sequence. *PAR*

Mission in Morocco ✄ 1959 When an oilman scouting for oil fields in the Sahara is killed, his partner, Barker, hops a jet to Morocco to find the whereabouts of a microfilm that gives the location of a valuable oil deposit. The search for the secret microfilm is complicated by competing parties also interested in the black gold. Ho-hum action adventure. **79m/C VHS.** Lex Barker, Juli Reding. *REP*

Mission Manila ✄ 1987 (R) An ex-CIA operative and Manila-based drug addict is called by his ex-lover to return to Manila to help his brother, who has gotten in much the same trouble he had. **98m/C VHS, Beta, LV.** Larry Wilcox. *NO*

Mission Mars ✄ 1967 American astronauts McGavin and Adams, on a mission to the red planet, discover the bodies of two cosmonauts floating in space. After landing on the planet's surface, they find a third cosmonaut, this one in a state of suspended animation. While putting the viewer to sleep, they proceed to revive the third cosmonaut and have at it with the sinister alien force responsible for all the trouble. **87m/C VHS, Beta.** Darren McGavin, Nick Adams, George DeVries; **D:** Nicholas Webster. *UNI*

Mission: Monte Carlo ✄✄ 1975 An episode from the television series "The Persuaders," wherein our two vacationing adventurers discover a girl's drowned body and try to solve the case. **102m/C VHS, Beta.** Roger Moore, Tony Curtis, Susan George, Annette Andre, Alfred Marks, Laurence Naismith; **D:** Basil Dearden, Roy Ward Baker. *FOX*

Mission of Justice ✄✄ 1992 (R) Revel in non-stop martial arts action with this tale of a cop who goes undercover to get the goods on a corrupt female politico, who also happens to run her own ruthless private army. **CW:** Language and strong martial arts violence. **?m/C VHS, LV, Closed Caption.** Jeff Wincott, Brigitte Nielsen, Matthias Hues, Luca Bercovici, Cyndi Pass, Billy "Sly" Williams, Tony Burton; **D:** Steve Barnett; **W:** John Bryant. *REP*

Mission of the Shark ✄✄✄ 1991 A top secret naval mission leads to a scandal-ridden court martial in this true WWII saga, based on the worst sea disaster in naval history. The U.S.S. Indianapolis has just completed a secret mission when it is torpedoed by enemy subs. The survi-

vors spend five days in shark-infested waters awaiting rescue and, when the Navy points fingers, the ship's highly decorated and well-respected Captain McVay accepts responsibility for the good of the service. Contains some harrowing scenes of sailors versus sharks. Made for television. **92m/C VHS.** Stacy Keach, Richard Thomas, Steve Landesburg, Carrie Snodgress, Bob Gunton, Andrew Prine, Stacy Keach Sr., Don Harvey; **D:** Robert Iscove. *TRI*

Mission Phantom ✄ 1979 A group of spies on a mission in Russia plans to steal some diamonds and help a woman get to the United States. **90m/C VHS, Beta.** Andrew Ray, Ingrid Sholder, Peter Martell; **D:** James Reed. *NO*

Mission Stardust ✄½ 4...3...2...1...Morte 1968 An internationally produced but thoroughly unambitious adaptation of the once-popular Perry Rhodan sci-fi serial, in which Rhodan and his team bring ill aliens back to Earth and defend them against evil spies. Dubbed. **90m/C VHS, Beta.** *GE IT SP* Essy Persson, Gianni Rizzo, Lang Jeffries, Pinkas Braun; **D:** Primo Zeglio. *RHI*

Mission to Death 1966 An adventure extravaganza in which a group of friends must risk their very lives. **76m/C VHS.** Jim Brewer, James E. McLarty, Jim Westerbrook, Robert Stolper, Dudley Hafner, Jerry Lasater. *LBD*

Mission to Glory ✄✄ The Father Kino Story 1980 (PG) This docudrama tells the story of Father Francisco "Kino" Kin, a tough, seventeenth-century priest in California who took on the Apaches and murderous Conquistadors in defense of his people. **100m/C VHS, Beta.** Richard Egan, John Ireland, Cesar Romero, Ricardo Montalban, Rory Calhoun, Michael Ansara, Keenan Wynn, Aldo Ray; **D:** Ken Kennedy. *IGP*

Mission to Kill ✄½ 1985 (R) An American demolitions expert, Ginty, joins a Latin American guerrilla force in battling tyrannical junta forces. This action-packed, fast-paced thriller is big on revenge and violence but not much else. **97m/C VHS, Beta.** Robert Ginty, Olivia D'Abo, Cameron Mitchell; **D:** David Winters. *MED*

Mission to Venice ✄✄ 1963 Flynn plays a sleuth attempting to find a missing husband when he accidentally stumbles upon a ring of spies. **?m/C VHS.** Sean Flynn, Madeleine Robinson. *SNC*

The Missionary ✄✄½ 1982 (R) A mild-mannered English missionary returns to London from his work in Africa and is recruited into saving the souls of a group of prostitutes. Aspiring to gentle comedy status, it's often formulaic and flat, with Palin and Smith fighting gamely to stay above script level. Still, good for some laughs, particularly during the near classic walking butler sequence. **86m/C VHS, Beta.** *GB* Michael Palin, Maggie Smith, Trevor Howard, Denholm Elliott, Michael Hordern; **D:** Richard Loncraine; **W:** Michael Palin. *PAR, TVC, FCT*

Mississippi Burning ✄✄✄ 1988 (R) Hard-edged social drama centers around the civil rights movement in Mississippi in 1964. When three activists turn up missing, FBI agents Hackman and Dafoe are sent to head up the investigation. Unfortunately, this is another example of a "serious" film about racial conflict in which white characters predominate and blacks provide background. **127m/C VHS, Beta, LV, Closed Caption.** Gene Hackman, Willem Dafoe, Frances McDormand, Brad Dourif, R. Lee Ermey, Gailard Sartain, Stephen Tobolowsky, Michael Rooker, Pruitt Taylor Vince, Badja Djola, Kevin Dunn, Frankie Faison, Tom Mason, Park Overall; **D:** Alan Parker; **W:** Chris Gerolmo; **C:** Peter Biziou; **M:** Trevor Jones. Academy Awards '88: Best Cinematography; Berlin International Film Festival '88: Best Actor (Hackman); National Board of Review Awards '88: 10 Best Films of the Year, Best Actor (Hackman), Best Director (Parker), Best Supporting Actress (McDormand); Nominations: Academy Awards '88: Best Actor (Hackman), Best Director (Parker), Best Film Editing, Best Picture, Best Sound, Best Supporting Actress (McDormand). *ORI*

Mississippi Masala ✲✲✲ 1992 (R) "Masala" is an Indian seasoning blending different-colored spices, as this film is a blend of romance, comedy, and social conscience. An interracial romance sets off a cultural collision and escalates racial tensions in a small Southern town when Mina, a sheltered young Indian woman, falls in love with Demetrius, an ambitious black man with his own carpet-cleaning business. Washington and Choudhury are engaging as the lovers with Seth, as Mina's unhappy father, especially watchable. **CW:** Language and sensuality. 118m/C VHS, LV, Closed Caption. Denzel Washington, Sarita Choudhury, Roshan Seth, Sharmila Tagore, Charles S. Dutton, Joe Seneca, Ranjit Chowdhry; **Cameos:** Mira Nair; **D:** Mira Nair; **W:** Sooni Taraporevala; **M:** L. Subramaniam. NAACP Image Awards '93: Best Actor (Washington). COL, FCT

Mississippi Mermaid ✲✲✲ 1969 (PG) Truffaut generally succeeds in merging his own directorial style with Hitchcockian suspense, but this is not considered one of his best. Millionaire tobacco planter Belmondo looks for a bride in the personals and finds Deneuve. Belmondo feels lucky landing this beauty until she leaves him and takes his money with her. A lookalike, also played by Deneuve, takes over his wife's role and attempts to poison Belmondo. Look for numerous references to the movies, including Bogart, Balzac and Cocteau. Based on the Cornell Woolrich novel "Waltz into Darkness." In French with English subtitles. 110m/C VHS, LV. **FR IT** Jean-Paul Belmondo, Catherine Deneuve, Michel Bouquet, Nelly Borgeaud, Marcel Berbert, Martine Ferriere; **D:** Francois Truffaut; **W:** Francois Truffaut; **M:** Antoine Duhamel. MGM, FCT

Missouri Breaks ✲✲ 1976 (PG) Thomas McGuane wrote the screenplay for this offbeat tale of Montana ranchers and rustlers fighting over land and livestock in the 1880s. Promising combination of script, cast and director unfortunately yields rather disappointing results, though both Brando and Nicholson chew up scenery to their hearts' content. 126m/C VHS, Beta. Jack Nicholson, Marlon Brando, Randy Quaid, Kathleen Lloyd, Frederic Forrest, Harry Dean Stanton; **D:** Arthur Penn; **W:** Thomas McGuane; **M:** John Williams. FOX

Missouri Traveler ✲✲✲ 1958 An orphan boy struggles to get his own farm in Missouri. Family fare based on John Buress' novel. 103m/C VHS, Beta. Lee Marvin, Gary Merrill, Brandon de Wilde, Paul Ford. MRV

Missourians ✲✲½ 1950 Small-town sheriff Hale helps a Polish rancher overcome ethnic prejudice among the townspeople. The situation worsens with the arrival in town of the rancher's outlaw brother. Strong direction and engaging storyline. 60m/B VHS, Beta. Monte Hale, Paul Hurst. DVT

Mrs. 'Arris Goes to Paris ✲✲½ 1992 Ada Harris (Lansbury) is a widowed charwoman, living in '50s London, whose one dream is to visit Paris and buy a Christian Dior gown at the designer's own salon. Naturally, her dream comes true—and she even finds a little romance too. Adapted from the Paul Gallico novel; made for TV. 90m/C VHS. Angela Lansbury, Omar Sharif, Diana Rigg, Lothaire Bluteau, Lila Kaye, John Savident. TVC, CCB

Mrs. Brown, You've Got a Lovely Daughter ✲½ 1968 (G) The Herman's Hermits gang inherits a greyhound and attempts to make a racer out of him while singing their songs. For the Brit group's diehard fans only. ♫It's Nice To Be Out in the Morning; Ooh, She's Done It Again; Lemon and Lime; The World is for the Young; Holiday Inn; The Most Beautiful Thing in My Life; Daisy Chain; Mrs. Brown, You've Got a Lovely Daughter; There's a King of Hush. 95m/C VHS, Beta. Peter Noone, Stanley Holloway, Mona Washbourne; **D:** Saul Swimmer. MGM

Mrs. Doubtfire ✲✲½ 1993 (PG-13) Williams is an unemployed voiceover actor going through a messy divorce. When his wife gets custody, the distraught father decides to dress up as a woman and become a nanny to his own children. He also has to deal with the old flame who re-enters his ex-wife's life. Williams schtick extraordinaire with more than a little sugary sentimentality. Based on the British children's book "Madame Doubtfire" by Anne Fine. **CW:** Sexual references. 120m/C VHS, LV, Closed Caption. Robin Williams, Sally Field, Pierce Brosnan, Harvey Fierstein, Robert Prosky, Mara Wilson; **D:** Chris Columbus; **W:** Randi Mayem Singer, Leslie Dixon; **M:** Howard Shore. Academy Awards '93: Best Makeup; Golden Globe Awards '94: Best Actor—Musical/Comedy (Williams), Best Film—Musical/Comedy; MTV Movie Awards '94: Best Comedic Performance (Williams); Nominations: MTV Movie Awards '94: Best Actor (Williams). FXV

Mrs. Miniver ✲✲✲✲ 1942 A moving tale of a courageous, gentle middle-class British family and its struggle to survive during WWII. A classic that garnered six Academy Awards, it's recognized for contributions to the Allied effort. Contains one of the most powerful orations in the film history, delivered by Wilcoxon, who portrayed the vicar. Followed by "The Miniver Story." Adapted from Jan Struther's book. 134m/B VHS, Beta, LV. Greer Garson, Walter Pidgeon, Teresa Wright, May Whitty, Richard Ney, Henry Travers, Reginald Owen, Henry Wilcoxon, Helmut Dantine, Aubrey Mather, Rhys Williams, Tom Conway, Peter Lawford; **D:** William Wyler; **W:** George Froeschel, James Hilton, Arthur Wimperis, Claudine West; **C:** Joseph Ruttenberg; **M:** Herbert Stothart. Academy Awards '42: Best Actress (Garson), Best Black and White Cinematography, Best Director (Wyler), Best Picture, Best Screenplay, Best Supporting Actress (Wright); National Board of Review Awards '42: 10 Best Films of the Year; Nominations: Academy Awards '42: Best Actor (Pidgeon), Best Film Editing, Best Sound, Best Supporting Actor (Travers), Best Supporting Actress (Whitty). MGM, BTV

Mrs. Munck ✲✲ 1995 (R) Creepy cable thriller finds widowed Rose Munck (Ladd) agreeing to care for bitter father-in-law Patrick Leary (Dern, Ladd's real-life ex-hubby), who's suffered a debilitating stroke. But they share a nasty past—seems he seduced a teenaged Rose (played by Preston), she had a child, Patrick refused any responsibilty, and the child died. So whacked-out Rose is really out for revenge. Based on a novel by Ella Leffland. Ladd's debut as writer/director. **CW:** Strong sex scene. 99m/C VHS, Closed Caption. Diane Ladd, Bruce Dern, Kelly Preston, Shelley Winters; **D:** Diane Ladd; **W:** Diane Ladd; **C:** James Glennon; **M:** Leonard Rosenman. REP

Mrs. Parker and the Vicious Circle ✲✲½ 1994 (R) *Mrs. Parker and the Round Table* Bio of witty, suicidal writer Dorothy Parker and her equally witty friends, including theater critics, playwrights, and novelists, who lunched together at New York's Algonquin Hotel for most of the 1920's. An irreverant band known as the Algonquin Round Table, their numerous bon mots were regularly reported in the papers. Their private lives were often less than happy with alcohol, drug addiction and depression prominent factors. Parker's downward spiral is depressing though compelling to watch, thanks to Leigh's performance (in spite of much criticism for her lockjawed accent) but many of the characters come and go so quickly they make little impression. 124m/C VHS, LV, Closed Caption. Jennifer Jason Leigh, Matthew Broderick, Andrew McCarthy, Campbell Scott, Jennifer Beals, Tom McGowan, Nick Cassavetes, Sam Robards, Rebecca Miller, Wallace Shawn, Martha Plimpton, Gwyneth Paltrow, Peter Gallagher, Lili Taylor; **D:** Alan Rudolph; **W:** Rudolph Coburn, Randy Sue Coburn; **C:** Jan Kiesser; **M:** Mark Isham. Chicago Film Critics Awards '94: Best Actress (Leigh); National Society of Film Critics Awards '94: Best Actress (Leigh); Nominations: Golden Globe Awards '95: Best Actress—Drama (Leigh), Independent Spirit Awards '95: Best Actor (Scott), Best Actress (Leigh), Best Director (Rudolph), Best Film, Best Screenplay. NLC, IME

Mrs. Parkington ✲✲½ 1944 Overblown epic drama spanning six decades tells the story of the rise and fall of an American dynasty made on easy money. Garson plays the woman who goes from working as a maid in a boarding house to living a life of luxury when she marries a multimillionaire. This was the fifth pairing of Garson and Pidgeon and although it's not one of their best, it proved to be a big hit with audiences. Lavish costumes and good performances by Garson and Moorehead. Based on the novel by Louis Bromfield. 124m/B VHS. Greer Garson, Walter Pidgeon, Edward Arnold, Frances Rafferty, Agnes Moorehead, Selena Royle, Gladys Cooper, Lee Patrick; **D:** Tay Garnett; **W:** Robert Thoeren, Polly James; **C:** Joseph Ruttenberg. Golden Globe Awards '45: Best Supporting Actress (Moorehead); Nominations: Academy Awards '44: Best Actress (Garson), Best Supporting Actress (Moorehead). MGM

Mrs. R's Daughter ✲✲ 1979 An outraged mother fights the judicial systems in order to bring her daughter's rapist to trial. Based on a true story and made for television. 97m/C VHS, Beta. Cloris Leachman, Season Hubley, Donald Moffat, John McIntire, Stephen Elliott, Ron Rifkin; **D:** Dan Curtis. WAR, OM

Mrs. Santa Claus ✲✲½ 1996 (G) Who better than Lansbury to star as the title character in this sweet TV musical set in 1910. Vivacious Mrs. C is tired of being left home during Santa's (Durning) annual trip and decides to borrow the sleigh for a test drive just before the big day. But bad weather and an injured reindeer force an emergency landing in New York City where she befriends the young sweatshop workers at villainous toy-maker A.P. Tavish's (Mann) factory and does a little matchmaking too. But Mrs. Claus still must make it back to the North Pole by Christmas Eve. ♫Avenue A; Almost Jolly; We Don't Go Together; Suffragette March; He Needs Me. 90m/C VHS. Angela Lansbury, Charles Durning, Terrence Mann, David Norona, Debra Wiseman, Rosalind Harris, Bryan Murray, Lynsey Bartilson, Michael Jeter; **D:** Terry Hughes; **W:** Mark Saltzman; **C:** Stephen M. Katz; **M:** Jerry Herman. HMK

Mrs. Silly ✲ 1985 Romance novel on tape, following the exploits of an aging woman who in losing material wealth, gains contentment. 60m/C Beta. Maggie Smith, James Villiers, Cyril Luckham. PSM

Mrs. Soffel ✲✲½ 1984 (PG-13) Falling in love with a convicted murderer and helping him flee confinement occupies the time of the prison warden's wife. Effectively captures the 1901 setting, yet a dark pall fairly strangles any emotion. Based on a true story. 110m/C VHS, Beta, LV, Closed Caption. Diane Keaton, Mel Gibson, Matthew Modine, Edward Herrmann, Trini Alvarado, Terry O'Quinn, Jennie Dundas, Danny Corkill, Maury Chaykin, Dana Wheeler-Nicholson; **D:** Gillian Armstrong; **W:** Ron Nyswaner; **C:** Russell Boyd; **M:** Mark Isham. MGM

Mrs. Wiggs of the Cabbage Patch ✲✲½ 1942 A warm, funny, and altogether overdone story of a mother whose husband abandons her, leaving the woman to raise their four children alone. It's Thanksgiving, so the rich visit the poor household to deliver a turkey dinner, and in the end all live happily ever after. Not one of Fields' larger roles; he doesn't even make an appearance until midway through the schmaltz. 80m/B VHS. Pauline Lord, ZaSu Pitts, W.C. Fields, Evelyn Venable, Donald Meek, Barbara Britton; **D:** Norman Taurog. GKK

Mrs. Winterbourne ✲✲ 1996 (PG-13) Pregnant loser Connie Doyle (Lake) is whisked into the lap of luxury when she's assumed to be the widowed Patricia Winterbourne after a train wreck. The grieving family (who had never met the bride) take her in and accept her and her baby as part of the household. Since her life is now going well, Connie decides to keep her true identity a secret while she falls for faux-brother-in-law Bill (Fraser). MacLaine is brilliant as the spirited matriarch of the family. Retooled as a comedy, the story is actually based on the noirish novel "I Married a Dead Man" by Cornell Woolrich and a remake of the equally dark "No Man of Her Own" from 1950. **CW:** Some thematic elements and brief strong language. 106m/C VHS, LV, Closed Caption. Ricki Lake, Brendan Fraser, Shirley MacLaine,

Miguel Sandoval, Loren Dean, Susan Haskell, Paula Prentiss; *D:* Richard Benjamin; *W:* Phoef Sutton, Lisa-Marie Rodano; *C:* Alex Nepomniaschy; *M:* Patrick Doyle. COL

Mistaken Identity 🎬½ 1936 A swank hotel is the setting for this so-so comedy about three con men who wind up conning each other as much as their supposed victims. A couple of light romances are also thrown in for good measure. 75m/B VHS. Chick Chandler, Evalyn Knapp, Berton Churchill, Patricia Farr, Richard Carle, Bradley Page, Lew Kelly; *D:* Phil Rosen. VYY

Mistaken Identity 🎬½ 1941 All-black mystery set against the background of a nightclub, and featuring a production number, "I'm a Bangi from Ubangi." 60m/B VHS, Beta. Nellie Hill, George Oliver. VCN, DVT, RXM

Mr. Ace 🎬½ 1946 A congresswoman decides to run for governor without the approval of the loyal political kingpin, Mr. Ace. 85m/B VHS, Beta, LV. George Raft, Sylvia Sidney, Sara Haden, Stanley Ridges; *D:* Edwin L. Marin. COL

Mr. & Mrs. Bridge 🎬🎬🎬 1990 (PG-13) Set in the thirties and forties in Kansas City, Ivory's adaptation of Evan S. Connell's novels painstakingly portrays an upper middle-class family struggling to survive within an emotional vacuum. Newman and Woodward, together for the first time in many years as Walter and Ivory Bridge, bring a wealth of experience and insight to their characterizations. Many consider this to be Newman's best, most subtle and nuanced performance. 127m/C VHS, LV, Closed Caption. Joanne Woodward, Paul Newman, Kyra Sedgwick, Blythe Danner, Simon Callow, Diane Kagan, Robert Sean Leonard, Saundra McClain, Margaret Welsh, Austin Pendleton, Gale Garnett, Remak Ramsay; *D:* James Ivory; *W:* Ruth Prawer Jhabvala; *C:* Tony Pierce-Roberts. New York Film Critics Awards '90: Best Actress (Woodward), Best Screenplay; Nominations: Academy Awards '90: Best Actress (Woodward). FCT

Mr. & Mrs. Loving 🎬🎬🎬 1996 (PG-13) Fact-based cable movie, set in the 1960s, follows the romance, marriage, and struggle of Richard Loving (Hutton) and Mildred "Bean" Jeter (Rochon). Growing up in rural Central Point, Virginia, their interracial relationship isn't considered uncommon. But when Bean gets pregnant, they aren't allowed to marry and live together because of Virginia's racial laws. Instead, the Lovings start a life in Washington, DC, but desperately homesick and increasingly aware of the civil rights movement, Bean writes a letter to the Attorney General's office. What results is young ACLU lawyer Bernie Cohen (Parker) taking on their case—which eventually leads to a landmark Supreme Court decision about miscegenation laws. *CW:* Some sexuality. 95m/C VHS, LV. Timothy Hutton, Lela Rochon, Corey Parker, Ruby Dee, Isaiah Washington, Bill Nunn, Charles Gray; *D:* Richard Friedenberg; *W:* Richard Friedenberg; *C:* Kenneth Macmillan; *M:* Branford Marsalis. HMK

Mr. & Mrs. Smith 🎬🎬🎬½ 1941 Hitchcock's only screwball comedy, an underrated, endearing farce about a bickering but happy modern couple who discover their marriage isn't legitimate and go through courtship all over again. Vintage of its kind, with inspired performances and crackling dialogue. 95m/B VHS, Beta, LV. Carole Lombard, Robert Montgomery, Gene Raymond, Jack Carson, Lucile Watson, Charles Halton; *D:* Alfred Hitchcock; *W:* Norman Krasna. MED, TTC

Mr. Arkadin 🎬🎬🎬 *Confidential Report* 1955 Screenwriter, director, star Welles, adapting from his own novel, gave this plot a dry run on radio during early 1950s. Welles examines the life of yet another ruthless millionaire, but this one can't seem to remember the sordid source of all that cash. Investigator Arden follows the intriguing and descending trail to a surprise ending. As in "Citizen Kane," oblique camera angles and layered dialogue prevail, but this time only serve to confuse the story. Shot over two years around Europe, required seven years of post production be-

fore finding distribution in 1962. 99m/B VHS, Beta, LV. *GB* Orson Welles, Akim Tamiroff, Michael Redgrave, Patricia Medina, Mischa Auer; *D:* Orson Welles; *C:* Jean Bourgoin. VDM, HTV, HEG

Mr. Baseball 🎬🎬 1992 (PG-13) Washed-up American baseball player tries to revive his career by playing in Japan and experiences cultures clashing under the ballpark lights. Semi-charmer swings and misses often enough to warrant return to minors. Film drew controversy during production when Universal was bought by the Japanese Matsushita organization and claims of both Japan- and America-bashing were thrown about. *CW:* Language and sensuality. 109m/C VHS, Beta, LV, Closed Caption. Tom Selleck, Ken Takakura, Toshi Shioya, Dennis Haysbert, Aya Takanashi; *D:* Fred Schepisi; *W:* Gary Ross, Kevin Wade, Monte Merrick; *C:* Ian Baker; *M:* Jerry Goldsmith. USH

Mr. Billion 🎬🎬 1977 (PG) Engaging chase adventure comedy about an Italian mechanic who stands to inherit a billion dollar fortune if he can travel from Italy to San Francisco in twenty days. Of course, things get in his way. Hill made his American debut in this film. 89m/C VHS, Beta, Closed Caption. Jackie Gleason, Terence Hill, Valerie Perrine, Slim Pickens, Chill Wills; *D:* Jonathan Kaplan; *W:* Jonathan Kaplan, Ken Friedman; *M:* Dave Grusin. FOX

Mr. Bill's Real Life Adventures 1986 A made-for-television live-action adventure for the "Saturday Night Live" clay star, portrayed by Scolari, who is victimized as usual by his nemesis, Mr. Sluggo. 43m/C VHS, Beta. Peter Scolari, Valerie Mahaffey, Lenore Kasdorf, Michael McManus; *D:* Jim Drake. PAR

Mr. Blandings Builds His Dream House 🎬🎬🎬½ 1948 Classic comedy features Grant as an adman who tires of city life and moves his family to the country, where his troubles really begin. Grant is at his funniest. Loy and Douglas provide strong backup. A must for all homeowners. 93m/B VHS, Beta, LV. Cary Grant, Myrna Loy, Melvyn Douglas, Lex Barker, Reginald Denny, Louise Beavers; *D:* H.C. Potter; *W:* Norman Panama. TTC, MED, MLB

Mr. Boggs Steps Out 🎬½ 1938 A pencil-pusher wins a bundle and invests it in a barrel factory. Trouble arises when a slickster tries to close it down. Even with the usual romantic entanglements, the film has trouble staying interesting. 68m/B VHS. Stuart Erwin, Helen Chandler, Toby Wing, Tully Marshall, Spencer Charters, Otis Harlan, Walter Byron, Milburn Stone; *D:* Gordon Wiles. NOS, VYY

Mr. Corbett's Ghost 🎬🎬 1990 A young man, displeased with his boss's managerial finesse, cuts a deal with a soul collector who pink slips the guy to the great unemployment line in the sky. Once a boss always a boss, and the guy's ghost stops in to say boo, while the soul collector is hot to get his hands on his part of the bargain. Huston's final film appearance. Made for television. 60m/C VHS, Closed Caption. John Huston, Paul Scofield, Burgess Meredith. MON, KAR

Mr. Deeds Goes to Town 🎬🎬🎬½ 1936 Typical Capra fare offers Cooper as philanthropic fellow who inherits $20 million and promptly donates it to the needy. He also manages to find time to fall in love with a beautiful reporter. Arthur is the hard-edged reporter determined to fathom the good guy's motivation. Superior entertainment. Based on Clarence Budington Kelland's play "Opera Hut." 118m/B VHS, Beta, LV. Gary Cooper, Jean Arthur, Raymond Walburn, Walter Catlett, Lionel Stander, George Bancroft, H.B. Warner, Ruth Donnelly, Douglass Dumbrille, Margaret Seddon, Margaret McWade; *D:* Frank Capra; *W:* Robert Riskin. Academy Awards '36: Best Director (Capra); National Board of Review Awards '36: 10 Best Films of the Year; New York Film Critics Awards '36: Best Film; Nominations: Academy Awards '36: Best Actor (Cooper), Best Picture, Best Screenplay, Best Sound. COL, BTV

Mr. Destiny 🎬🎬 1990 (PG-13) Mid-level businessman Belushi has a mid-life crisis of sorts when his car dies. Wandering into an empty bar, he encounters bartender Caine who serves cocktails and acts omniscient before taking him on the ten-cent tour of life as it would've been if he hadn't struck out in a high school baseball game. Less than wonderful rehash of "It's a Wonderful Life." 110m/C VHS, Beta, LV, Closed Caption. James Belushi, Michael Caine, Linda Hamilton, Jon Lovitz, Bill McCutcheon, Hart Bochner, Rene Russo, Jay O. Sanders, Maury Chaykin, Pat Corley, Douglas Seale, Courteney Cox, Kathy Ireland; *D:* James Orr; *W:* James Orr, Jim Cruickshank. TOU, FCT

Mr. Emmanuel 🎬🎬½ 1944 An elderly Jewish widower leaves his English home in 1935 in quest of the mother of a German refugee boy, and is subjected to shocking treatment in Germany. 97m/B VHS, Beta. Felix Aylmer, Greta Gynt, Walter Rilla, Jean Simmons. LCA

Mr. Frost 🎬 1989 (R) Goldblum feigns fascination in this lackluster tale of the devil incarnate, who is imprisoned after owning up to a series of grisly murders, and who hides his true identity until approached by a woman psychiatrist. 92m/C VHS, Closed Caption. Jeff Goldblum, Kathy Baker, Alan Bates, Roland Giraud, Jean-Pierre Cassel; *D:* Phillip Setbon; *W:* Phillip Setbon, Brad Lynch. FCT, IME

Mister Halpren & Mister Johnson 🎬🎬 1983 Gleason attends the funeral of a longtime friend and one time flame, and becomes acquainted with the woman's husband (Olivier). Heavyweight cast wasted on flimsy script...and away we go! 57m/C VHS, Beta. Laurence Olivier, Jackie Gleason; *D:* Alvin Rakoff. NO

Mr. Hobbs Takes a Vacation 🎬🎬🎬 1962 Good-natured comedy in which beleaguered parents try to resolve family squabbles while the entire brood is on a seaside vacation. Stewart and O'Hara are especially fine and funny as the well-meaning parents. 116m/C VHS, Beta, Closed Caption. James Stewart, Maureen O'Hara, Fabian, John Saxon, Marie Wilson, John McGiver, Reginald Gardiner; *D:* Henry Koster; *M:* Henry Mancini. Berlin International Film Festival '62: Best Actor (Stewart). FOX, HMV

Mr. Holland's Opus 🎬🎬🎬 1995 (PG) Well-done Disney tearjerker begins in 1965 as musician Glenn Holland (Dreyfuss) takes a teaching job to get himself off the wedding reception circuit and help support his wife, Iris (Headley), and their deaf son. Spanning three decades, with actual newsreel footage thrown in to highlight time passing, Holland sets aside his dream of composing a great symphony and finds his true calling—mentoring and inspiring young minds. Holland's son being deaf might have proved corny, but their rocky relationship is deeply rooted to the storyline. Dreyfuss turns in his most vibrant performance in years and, while sentimental buttons are definitely pushed, director Herek avoids falling into sappiness. 142m/C VHS, LV, Closed Caption. Richard Dreyfuss, Glenne Headly, Jay Thomas, Olympia Dukakis, William H. Macy, Alicia Witt, Jean Louisa Kelly, Anthony Natale; *D:* Stephen Herek; *W:* Patrick Sheane Duncan; *C:* Oliver Wood; *M:* Michael Kamen. Nominations: Academy Awards '95: Best Actor (Dreyfuss); Golden Globe Awards '95: Best Actor—Drama (Dreyfuss), Best Screenplay. TOU

Mr. Horn 🎬🎬 1979 Based on the William Goldman western novel, this slow-paced film about folk-hero Scott Tom Horn capturing the famous Apache warrior, Geronimo, is average at best. 200m/C VHS. David Carradine, Richard Widmark, Karen Black, Jeremy Slate, Enrique Lucero, Jack Starrett; *D:* Jack Starrett. LIV

Mr. Hulot's Holiday 🎬🎬🎬½ *Les Vacances de Monsieur Hulot; Monsieur Hulot's Holiday* 1953 Superior slapstick details the misadventures of a dullard's seaside holiday. Inventive French comedian Tati at his best. Light-hearted and natural, with magical mime sequences. Followed by "Mon Oncle." 86m/B VHS, Beta, LV, 8mm. *FR* Jacques Tati, Natalie Pascaud, Michelle Rolla; *D:* Jacques Tati. National Board of Review Awards '54: 5 Best Foreign Films of the

Year; Nominations: Academy Awards '55: Best Story & Screenplay. **NOS, MRV, VYY**

Mr. Inside, Mr. Outside ♂½ 1974 A television movie about two New York City cops, one undercover, one not, trying to infiltrate a tough diamond-smuggling ring. **74m/C VHS, Beta.** Tony LoBianco, Hal Linden; *D:* William A. Graham. **THV**

Mister Johnson ♂♂♂ 1991 (PG-13) In 1923 Africa, an educated black man working for the British magistrate constantly finds himself in trouble, thanks to backfiring schemes. This highly enjoyable film from the director of "Driving Miss Daisy" suffers only from the underdevelopment of the intriguing lead character. Based on the novel by Joyce Cary. **105m/C VHS, Closed Caption.** Pierce Brosnan, Edward Woodward, Maynard Eziashi, Beatie Edney, Denis Quilley, Nick Reding; *D:* Bruce Beresford; *W:* Bruce Beresford, William Boyd; *M:* Georges Delerue. **VES, LIV**

Mr. Jones ♂½ 1993 (R) Psychiatrist (Olin) falls in love with her manic-depressive patient (Gere). Head case Mr. Jones (Gere) is a charmer who gets a rush from tightrope walking a high beam on a construction site, yet is prone to bad moods when he fails to remember his own name. He can't resist flirting with the seductive Dr. Bowen, who eagerly leaps past professional boundaries while trying to coax him out of his illness. Wastes the talents of its stars with Gere showy, Olin brittle, and the whole story as contrived as their prefunctory love affair. Psychiatrists are getting as bad a rep professionally as lawyers in their recent film appearances. *CW:* Language. **110m/C VHS, LV, Closed Caption.** Richard Gere, Lena Olin, Anne Bancroft, Tom Irwin, Delroy Lindo, Bruce Altman, Lauren Tom; *D:* Mike Figgis; *W:* Michael Cristofer, Eric Roth; *M:* Maurice Jarre. **COL**

Mr. Kingstreet's War ♂♂½ *Heroes Die Hard* 1971 An idealistic game warden and his wife defend the wildlife of Africa against the fighting Italian and British armies at the dawn of WWII. **92m/C VHS, Beta.** John Saxon, Tippi Hedren, Rossano Brazzi, Brian O'Shaughnessy; *D:* Percival Rubens. **VCI**

Mr. Klein ♂♂♂ 1975 (PG) Cleverly plotted script and fine direction in this dark and intense film about a French-Catholic merchant who buys valuables from Jews trying to escape Nazi occupied France in 1942, paying far less than what the treasures are worth. Ironically, he's later mistaken for a Jew by the same name who has been using this man's reputation as a cover. **122m/C VHS, Beta.** Alain Delon, Jeanne Moreau; *D:* Joseph Losey. **COL, SWC**

Mr. Love ♂♂½ 1986 (PG-13) A meek gardener is perceived by neighbors as a fool until he dies and numerous women arrive for his funeral. Is it his cologne? The radishes? **91m/C VHS, Beta, Closed Caption.** GB Barry Jackson, Maurice Denham, Margaret Tyzack, Linda Marlowe; *D:* Roy Battersby; *M:* Ially Russell. **WAR**

Mr. Lucky ♂♂♂ 1943 Likeable wartime drama about a gambler who hopes to swindle a philanthropic organization, but then falls in love and determines to help the group in a fundraising effort. Grant is, no surprise, excellent as the seemingly cynical con artist who actually has a heart of gold. Cliched, but nonetheless worthwhile. Later developed into a television series. **99m/B VHS, Beta, LV, Closed Caption.** Cary Grant, Laraine Day, Charles Bickford, Gladys Cooper, Paul Stewart, Henry Stephenson, Florence Bates; *D:* H.C. Potter; *C:* George Barnes. **MED, RXM, TTC**

Mr. Majestyk ♂♂½ 1974 (PG) When a Vietnam veteran's attempt to start an honest business is thwarted by Mafia hitmen and the police, he goes after them with a vengeance. **103m/C VHS, Beta.** Charles Bronson, Al Lettieri, Linda Cristal, Lee Purcell; *D:* Richard Fleischer; *W:* Elmore Leonard; *M:* Charles Bernstein. **MGM**

Mister Mean ♂ 1977 A man who once worked for a mafia don is now given the task of rubbing him out. For Cosa Nostra diehards and gluttons for Roman scenery. **98m/C VHS, Beta.** IT Fred Williamson; *D:* Fred Williamson. **NO**

Mr. Mike's Mondo Video ♂♂ 1979 (R) A bizarre, outrageous comedy special declared too wild for television conceived by the "Saturday Night Live" alumnus Mr. Mike. **75m/C VHS, Beta.** Michael O'Donoghue, Dan Aykroyd, Jane Curtin, Carrie Fisher, Teri Garr, Joan Haskett, Deborah Harry, Margot Kidder, Bill Murray, Laraine Newman, Gilda Radner, Julius LaRosa, Paul Shaffer, Sid Vicious; *W:* Mitch Glazer. **NO**

Mr. Mom ♂♂♂ 1983 (PG) A tireless auto exec loses his job and stays home with the kids while his wife becomes the breadwinner. He's forced to cope with the rigors of housework and child care, resorting to drugs, alcohol and soap operas. Keaton's hilarious as the homebound dad chased by killer appliances and poker buddy to the ladies in the neighborhood. **92m/C VHS, Beta, LV, Closed Caption.** Michael Keaton, Teri Garr, Christopher Lloyd, Martin Mull, Ann Jillian, Jeffrey Tambor, Edie McClurg, Valri Bromfield; *D:* Stan Dragoti; *W:* John Hughes. **LIV, VES**

Mr. Moto's Last Warning ♂♂♂ 1939 One of the better in the series of Mr. Moto, the wily detective! Lorre is convincing in the title role and gets good support from character villains Carradine and Sanders in this story of saboteurs converging on the Suez Canal plotting to blow up the French Fleet. **71m/B VHS, Beta.** Peter Lorre, George Sanders, Ricardo Cortez, John Carradine, Virginia Field, Robert Coote; *D:* Norman Foster. **SNC, NOS, CAB**

Mr. Moto's Last Warning/Meeting at Midnight 1944 The first film finds Moto at the Suez Canal trying to save France's flotilla from a deadly conspiracy. The second feature is classic Charlie Chan fare. This time his driver, Birmingham, gets Chan caught in the midst of the occult. **130m/B VHS, Beta.** Sidney Toler, Peter Lorre, Mantan Moreland. **AOV**

Mr. Music ♂♂½ 1950 Crosby is a successful songwriter who would rather enjoy life on the golf course than pen any more tunes. He's persuaded by his secretary to help out an old-time producer who's fallen on hard times by writing a new Broadway show. Light-hearted fluff. Based on the play "Accent on Youth" by Samson Raphaelson which had been filmed in 1935. ♫Life is So Precious; Accidents Will Happen; High on the List; Wouldn't It Be Funny; Wasn't I There?; Mr. Music; Once More the Blue and White; Milady; Then You'll Be Home. **113m/B VHS, Closed Caption.** Bing Crosby, Nancy Olson, Charles Coburn, Robert Stack, Tom Ewell, Ruth Hussey, Charles Kemper, Donald Woods, Gower Champion, Marge Champion; *Cameos:* Groucho Marx, Peggy Lee; *D:* Richard Haydn. **PAR**

Mr. Nanny ♂♂ 1993 (PG) For those who fear change, this predictable plot should serve as comforting assurance that Hollywood will still sacrifice substance for the quick buck. Basic story line has the child-hating Hulkster playing nanny/bodyguard to a couple of bratty kids. Meanwhile, his arch rival (Johansen) hatches a scheme to gain world domination by kidnapping the kids for the ransom of their father's top secret computer chip. Never fear—in this world, the good guys kick butt, naturally, and everyone learns a lesson. **85m/C VHS, Closed Caption.** Hulk Hogan, Sherman Hemsley, Austin Pendleton, Robert Gorman, Madeline Zima, Mother Love, David Johansen; *D:* Michael Gottlieb; *W:* Ed Rugoff, Michael Gottlieb; *M:* David Johansen, Brian Koonin. **COL**

Mr. Nice Guy ♂ 1986 (PG-13) In the near future, a hired gun strives for national recognition as the best of his now legitimate profession. Comedy with few laughs. **92m/C VHS, Beta.** Michael MacDonald, Jan Smithers, Joe Silver. **VTR, NWV**

Mr. North ♂♂½ 1988 (PG) Capra-corn fable about a charming, bright Yale graduate who encounters admiration and disdain from upper-crust Rhode Island residents when news of his miraculous "cures" spreads. Marks the directorial debut of Danny Huston, son of John Huston, who cowrote the script and served as executive producer before dying several weeks into shooting. Set in the 1920s and adapted from Thornton Wilder's "Theophilus North." **90m/C VHS, Beta, LV, Closed Caption.** Anthony Edwards, Robert Mitchum, Lauren Bacall, Harry Dean Stanton, Anjelica Huston, Mary Stuart Masterson, Virginia Madsen, Tammy Grimes, David Warner, Hunter Carson, Christopher Durang, Mark Metcalf, Katharine Houghton, Christopher Lawford; *D:* Danny Huston; *W:* John Huston, Janet Roach, James Costigan; *M:* David McHugh. **NO**

Mr. Peabody & the Mermaid ♂♂½ 1948 Lightweight fish story about a middle-aged married man who hooks a beautiful mermaid while fishing in the Caribbean and eventually falls in love with her. Powell is smooth as always, though hampered by the unrestrained absurdity of it all. Based on the novel by Guy and Constance Jones. Also available colorized. **89m/B VHS.** William Powell, Ann Blyth, Irene Hervey, Andrea King, Clinton Sundberg, Art Smith; *D:* Irving Pichel; *W:* Nunnally Johnson. **REP**

Mr. Peek-A-Boo ♂♂½ *Garou Garou le Passe Muraille* 1950 A French clerk discovers he has the ability to walk through walls. Although friends try to coax him into a life of crime, he instead comes to the aid of an English girl who is being blackmailed. Good-natured French comedy was shot with English dialogue for the American market. **74m/B VHS, Beta.** FR Joan Greenwood, Bourvil, Marcel Arnold, Roger Treville; *D:* Jean Boyer. **SNC**

Mr. Reeder in Room 13 ♂♂ 1938 Based on the mystery stories created by Edgar Wallace, Mr. Reeder (a cultured English gentleman who fights crime) enlists the aid of a young man to get evidence on a gang of counterfeiters. **66m/B VHS, Beta.** Gibb McLaughlin. **VYY**

Mr. Reliable: A True Story ♂♂ 1995 (R) A "truth is stranger than fiction" comedy about Australia's first hostage situation. During the summer of 1968, recently released car thief Wally Mellish (Friels) rents a rundown cottage in a Sydney suburb. He finds a girlfriend in Beryl Muddle (McKenzie), who moves in with her 2-year-old daughter. When Wally steals some trifles to brighten up the place, the cops come 'round and Wally, who's still on probation, pulls a gun. The authorities think Beryl and the baby are hostages and are afraid to storm the cottage while the standoff becomes hot media news. Wally and Beryl are thrilled with the attention but there's increasing political pressure to put an end to the farcical situation. *CW:* Language and a sex scene involving teenagers. **112m/C VHS.** AU Colin Friels, Jacqueline McKenzie, Paul Sonkkila, Frank Gallacher, Barry Otto, Lisa Hensley, Ken Radley, Neil Fitzpatrick; *D:* Nadia Tass; *W:* Terry Hayes, Don Catchlove; *C:* David Parker; *M:* Phil Judd. Nominations: Australian Film Institute '96: Best Film. **PGV**

Mister Roberts ♂♂♂♂ 1955 Crew of a Navy cargo freighter in the South Pacific during WWII relieves the boredom of duty with a series of elaborate practical jokes, mostly at the expense of their long-suffering and slightly crazy captain, who then determines that he will get even. The ship's cargo officer, Mr. Roberts, longs to be transferred to a fighting vessel and see some action. Originally a hit Broadway play (based on the novel by Thomas Heggen) which also featured Fonda in the title role. Great performance from Lemmon as Ensign Pulver. Powell's last film. Sequelled in 1964 by "Ensign Pulver," and later a short-lived TV series as well as a live TV special. Newly transferred in 1988 from a pristine stereo print. **120m/C VHS, Beta.** Henry Fonda, James Cagney, Jack Lemmon, William Powell, Betsy Palmer, Ward Bond, Harry Carey Jr., Nick Adams, Phil Carey, Ken Curtis, Martin Milner, Jack Pennick, Perry Lopez, Patrick Wayne; *D:* John Ford, Mervyn LeRoy; *W:* Frank Nugent, Joshua Logan; *C:* Winton C. Hoch; *M:* Franz Waxman. Academy Awards '55: Best Supporting Actor (Lemmon); National Board of Review

Awards '55: 10 Best Films of the Year; Nominations: Academy Awards '55: Best Picture, Best Sound. WAR, BTV

Mr. Robinson Crusoe 🎬🎬½ **1932 (R)** Rollicking adventure in the South Seas as Fairbanks makes a bet that he can live on a desert island for a year without being left any refinements of civilization. Lucky for him, a woman arrives. Also written by Fairbanks. **76m/B VHS, Beta, LV.** Douglas Fairbanks Sr., William Farnum, Maria Alba, Earle Brown; **D:** Edward Sutherland; **W:** Douglas Fairbanks Sr.; **M:** Alfred Newman. NOS, GPV, CCB

Mr. Saturday Night 🎬🎬½ **1992 (R)** Crystal, in his directorial debut, stars as Buddy Young, Jr., a self-destructive comedian whose career spans five decades. His nasty one-liners and witty jokes combine with poignancy in this satisfying comedy/drama. Paymer is excellent as Young's long-suffering, faithful brother and manager. Watch for Lewis in a cameo role. Expectations were very high and the box office results were disappointing, but fans of Crystal shouldn't miss this one. The video also includes additional footage and outtakes selected and hosted by Crystal. **CW:** Language. **118m/C VHS, LV, Closed Caption.** Billy Crystal, David Paymer, Julie Warner, Helen Hunt, Mary Mara, Jerry Orbach, Ron Silver, Sage Allen, Jackie Gayle, Carl Ballantine, Slappy (Melvin) White, Conrad Janis; **Cameos:** Jerry Lewis; **D:** Billy Crystal; **W:** Billy Crystal, Babaloo Mandel, Lowell Ganz; **M:** Marc Shaiman. Nominations: Academy Awards '92: Best Supporting Actor (Paymer). COL, IME, MOV

Mr. Scarface 🎬½ **1977 (R)** A young man searches for the man who murdered his father years earlier in a dark alley. **85m/C VHS, Beta.** Jack Palance, Edmund Purdom, Al Cliver, Harry Baer, Gisela Hahn; **D:** Fernando Di Leo. CNG

Mr. Skeffington 🎬🎬🎬 **1944** A super-grade soap opera spanning 26 years in the life of a ravishing, spoiled New York socialite. The beauty with a fondness for bedrooms marries for convenience, abuses her husband, then enjoys a highly equitable divorce settlement. Years later when diphtheria leaves her totally deformed and no man will have her, she is saved by her former husband. Based on the novel by "Elizabeth" (Mary Annette Beauchamp Russell) and adapted by "Casablanca's" Julius and Philip Epstein. **147m/B VHS, Beta.** Bette Davis, Claude Rains, Walter Abel, Richard Waring, George Coulouris, John Alexander; **D:** Vincent Sherman. Nominations: Academy Awards '44: Best Actress (Davis), Best Supporting Actor (Rains). MGM

Mr. Skitch 🎬🎬 **1933** Weak Rogers offering. Couple loses their farm and begins cross country jaunt with mishaps at every turn. All ends well when their daughter meets an Army cadet, but few laughs and lots of loose ends. **70m/B VHS.** Will Rogers, ZaSu Pitts, Rochelle Hudson, Charles Starrett; **D:** James Cruze. FOX, FCT

Mr. Smith Goes to Washington 🎬🎬🎬🎬 **1939** Another classic from Hollywood's golden year of 1939. Jimmy Stewart is an idealistic and naive young man selected to fill in for an ailing Senator. Upon his arrival in the Capitol, he is inundated by a multitude of corrupt politicians. He takes a stand for his beliefs and tries to denounce many of those he feels are unfit for their positions, meeting with opposition from all sides. Great cast is highlighted by Stewart in one of his most endearing performances. Quintessential Capra tale sharply adapted from Lewis Foster's story. Outstanding in every regard. **130m/B VHS, Beta, LV.** James Stewart, Jean Arthur, Edward Arnold, Claude Rains, Thomas Mitchell, Beulah Bondi, Eugene Pallette, Guy Kibbee, Harry Carey Sr., H.B. Warner, Porter Hall, Jack Carson, Charles Lane; **D:** Frank Capra; **W:** Sidney Buchman; **M:** Dimitri Tiomkin. Academy Awards '39: Best Story; National Board of Review Awards '39: 10 Best Films of the Year; New York Film Critics Awards '39: Best Actor (Stewart); Nominations: Academy Awards '39: Best Actor (Stewart), Best Director (Capra), Best Film Editing, Best Interior Decoration, Best Picture, Best Sound, Best Supporting Actor (Rains, Carey), Best Score. COL, HMV

Mr. Stitch 🎬 **1995 (R)** Demented scientist (Hauer) plays Frankenstein and makes a creature, named Lazarus (Wheaton), from the body parts of more than 80 men and women. Unfortunately, the sensitive Lazarus has retained the collective memories of all these people and becomes obsessed with finding the reason for his existence. He receives compassion from a shrink (Peeples) but his maker has less-than-honorable plans for Lazarus. **CW:** Mature themes, violence, language. **98m/C VHS.** Rutger Hauer, Wil Wheaton, Nia Peeples, Taylor Negron, Ron Perlman, Michael Harris; **Cameos:** Tom Savini; **D:** Roger Roberts Avary. AVE

Mr. Superinvisible 🎬🎬 *Mr. Invisible; L'Inafferrabile Invincible* **1973 (G)** Searching to cure the common cold, a bumbling scientist invents a bizarre virus, then strives to keep it from falling into the wrong hands. The Disney-like plot, featuring enemy agents and invisibilty may appeal to youngsters. **90m/C VHS, Beta.** IT GE SP Dean Jones, Ingeborg Schoener, Gastone Moschin; **D:** Anthony (Antonio Margheriti) Dawson. NO

Mr. Sycamore 🎬½ **1974** A sappy mail carrier escapes his badgering wife by sprouting into a tree. A potentially whimsical piece that wilts. **90m/C VHS, Beta.** Jason Robards Jr., Jean Simmons, Sandy Dennis; **D:** Pancho Kohner; **M:** Maurice Jarre. WOV

Mr. Walkie Talkie 🎬🎬 **1952** Tired of a sargeant's jabber-jaws, a soldier requests to be relocated to the front lines, only to find his catty comrade has followed. Set during the Korean War and featuring some truly amusing escapades set between the lulls in the war. **65m/B VHS, Beta, LV.** William Tracy, Joseph Sawyer; **D:** Fred Guiol. NO

Mr. Winkle Goes to War 🎬🎬 **1944** A weak, nerdy former banker is drafted for service during WWII and proves himself a hero by bulldozing a Japanese foxhole. Bits of genuine war footage add a measure of realism to an otherwise banal flag-waving comedy that is based on a novel by Theodore Pratt. **80m/B VHS, Beta.** Edward G. Robinson, Ruth Warrick, Richard Lane, Robert Armstrong; **D:** Alfred E. Green. COL

Mr. Wise Guy 🎬🎬 **1942** The East Side Kids break out of reform school to clear one of the Kids' brother of a murder charge. Typical pre-Bowery Boys vehicle. **70m/B VHS, Beta.** Leo Gorcey, Huntz Hall, Billy Gilbert, Guinn "Big Boy" Williams, Benny Rubin, Douglas Fowley, Ann Doran, Jack Mulhall, Warren Hymer, David Gorcey; **D:** William Nigh. NOS, DVT, HEG

Mr. Wonderful 🎬🎬½ **1993 (PG-13)** Bittersweet (rather than purely romantic) look at love and romance. Divorced Con Ed worker Gus (Dillon) is hard up for cash and tries to marry off ex-wife Lee (Sciorra) so he can use her alimony to invest in a bowling alley with his buddies. Routine flick's saved by the cast, who manage to bring a small measure of believability to a transparent plot. Minghella was a hit with his first film "Truly, Madly, Deeply" but may find that fame can be fleeting with this second effort. **99m/C VHS, Beta, LV, Closed Caption.** Matt Dillon, Annabella Sciorra, William Hurt, Mary-Louise Parker, Luis Guzman, Dan Hedaya, Vincent D'Onofrio; **D:** Anthony Minghella; **M:** Amy Schor, Vicki Polon; **M:** Michael Gore. WAR

Mr. Wong, Detective 🎬🎬 **1938** The first in the Mr. Wong series, the cunning detective traps a killer who feigns guilt to throw suspicion away from himself. The plot is loaded with the usual twists and villains. However, Karloff is a standout. **69m/B VHS, Beta.** Boris Karloff, Grant Withers; **D:** William Nigh. NOS, MRV, HHT

Mr. Wong in Chinatown 🎬½ **1939** Third of the Mr. Wong series finds James Lee Wong investigating the murder of a wealthy Chinese woman. She had been helping to fund the purchase of airplanes to equip China in its 1930s' struggle with Japan. **70m/B VHS.** Boris Karloff, Grant Withers, William Royle, Marjorie Reynolds, Peter George Lynn, Lotus Long, Richard Loo; **D:** William Nigh. VYY, MRV, SNC

Mr. Write 🎬🎬 **1992 (PG-13)** Modest advertising satire mixed with romance. Aspiring writer Charlie (Reiser) decides to make some money by acting in commercials. He falls for ad exec Nicole (Tuck) but there are some complications to be overcome first, including her dim bulb boyfriend and obnoxious father. Adapted from the play by Howard J. Morris. **89m/C VHS, LV, Closed Caption.** Paul Reiser, Jessica Tuck, Doug Davidson, Martin Mull, Wendie Jo Sperber, Eddie Barth, Darryl M. Bell, Tom Wilson, Jane Leeves, Calvert Deforest; **D:** Charles Loventhal; **W:** Howard J. Morris; **C:** Elliot Davis. USH

Mr. Wrong 🎬🎬 **1995 (PG-13)** In her feature film debut, DeGeneres plays Martha, a thirty-something single woman with wacky friends who's being pressured by parents toward marriage while having little luck in the dating scene. Hmm...sounds familiar. Pullman plays Whitman, her dreamboat who quickly turns into the Titanic. Along the relationship road to ruin she is forced to deal with bad poetry, charades and...gum in her hair!! The usually entertaining DeGeneres is given little to do but react lamely to the wild events going on around her. Those that have had an experience with "the ex that would not go away" might want to rent something more calming, such as "Psycho." **CW:** Crude language, some sex related scenes and drug content. **97m/C VHS, LV, Closed Caption.** Ellen DeGeneres, Bill Pullman, Joan Cusack, Dean Stockwell, Joan Plowright, John Livingston, Robert Goulet, Ellen Cleghorne, Brad Henke, Polly Holliday, Briant Wells; **D:** Nick Castle; **W:** Chris Matheson, Kerry Ehrin, Craig Munson; **C:** John Schwartzman; **M:** Craig Safan. Nominations: Golden Raspberry Awards '96: Worst New Star (DeGeneres). TOU

Mistral's Daughter 🎬½ **1984** Frothy miniseries, based on the Judith Krantz novel, about a French artist and his relationship with three beautiful women. Formulaic TV melodrama offers sexual scenes and revealing glimpses. Produced, like other Krantz miniseries, by author's hubby, Steve. **390m/C VHS, Beta.** Stefanie Powers, Lee Remick, Stacy Keach, Robert Urich, Timothy Dalton; **D:** Douglas Hickox; **M:** Vladimir Cosma. LIV

Mistress 🎬🎬🎬 *Wild Geese* **1953** A classic Japanese period piece about an innocent woman who believes she's married to a ruthless industrialist, only to find he is already married and she is but his mistress. Her love for a medical student unleashes tragedy. Subtly moving in a low-key way; starkly beautiful in black and white. In Japanese, with English subtitles. **106m/B VHS, Beta.** JP Hideko Takamine, Hiroshi Akutagawa; **D:** Shiro Toyoda. NO

Mistress 🎬½ **1987** Weepy made-for-television melodrama about a woman who makes a living as a mistress. When her lover dies, she must learn to stand on her own two feet. **96m/C VHS.** Victoria Principal, Alan Rachins, Don Murray; **D:** Michael Tuchner; **M:** Michael Convertino. REP

Mistress 🎬 **1991 (R)** A weak script does in a formidable cast in a behind-the-scenes look at movie making. Wuhl plays Marvin Landisman, a failed director/screenwriter, who's approached by has-been producer Jack Roth (Landau) who says he's found a backer to finance a movie from one of Marvin's old scripts. It turns out Roth has three men (De Niro, Aiello, and Wallach) ready to finance the film as long as each of their mistresses, who all have acting ambitions, gets the starring role. Double-dealing at a bargain basement level sets up the rest of this lifeless comedy. **CW:** Language. **100m/C VHS, LV, Closed Caption.** Robert Wuhl, Martin Landau, Robert De Niro, Eli Wallach, Danny Aiello, Sheryl Lee Ralph, Jean Smart, Tuesday Weld, Jace Alexander, Laurie Metcalf; **Cameos:** Christopher Walken, Ernest Borgnine; **D:** Barry Primus; **W:** J.F. Lawton, Barry Primus. LIV, PMS

Mistress of the Apes woof! **1979 (R)** A woman searches for her missing husband in Africa with a group of scientists and discovers a tribe of near-men, who may be the missing link in evolution (or perhaps, a professional football team). Into their little group she is accepted, becoming their queen. Buchanan earned his reputation as a maker of horrible films honestly. Includes the songs "Mistress of the Apes" and "Ape Lady." **88m/C VHS, Beta.** Jenny Neumann, Barbara Leigh, Garth Pillsbury, Walt Robin, Stuart Lancaster, Suzy Mandel; **D:** Larry Buchanan; **W:** Larry Buchanan. *MON*

Mistress of the World 🎬🎬 1959 A scientist, aided by Swedish Intelligence agent Ventura, works to protect his gravity-altering invention from Chinese agents. Partly based on a German serial from the silent film era, but not up to director Dieterle's usual fare. A must-see for Ventura fans and Mabuse mavens. **107m/C VHS, Beta.** Martha Hyer, Micheline Presle, Gino Cervi, Lino Ventura, Sabu, Wolfgang Preiss; **D:** William Dieterle. *THV*

Mistress Pamela 🎬½ 1974 (R) When young Pamela goes to work in the household of handsome Lord Devonish, he sets about in wild pursuit of her virginity. Loosely based on the 1740 work "Pamela" by Samuel Richardson, considered the first modern English novel. Read the book unless you only have 95 minutes to spend finding out who gets what. **95m/C VHS, Beta.** Anne Michelle, Julian Barnes, Anna Quayle, Rosemary Dunham; **D:** Jim O'Connor. *NO*

Mistrial 🎬🎬 1996 (R) NYC cop Steve Donohue (Pullman) is incensed when accused cop killer Eddie Rios (Seda) is acquitted and Donohue himself is about to be charged in the wrongful deaths of the suspect's wife and brother, which occurred during his pursuit. So he takes the entire courtroom hostage. Made for cable. **90m/C VHS.** Bill Pullman, Robert Loggia, Jon Seda, Blair Underwood; **D:** Heywood Gould; **W:** Heywood Gould. *HBO*

Misty 🎬🎬½ 1961 Ladd and Smith are two kids who capture a wild pony and teach it to run around in circles and step over things. Based on Marguerite Henry's bestselling "Misty of Chincoteague," and filmed on an island off the coast of Virginia. **92m/C VHS, Closed Caption.** David Ladd, Arthur O'Connell, Pam Smith; **D:** James B. Clark. *PAR, WAX, FCT*

Misunderstood 🎬🎬½ 1984 (PG) A former black market merchant has to learn how to relate to his sons after his wife dies. The father, now a legitimate businessman, is more concerned with running his shipping business than growing closer to his boys. Fine acting can't overcome a transparent plot. **92m/C VHS, Beta.** Gene Hackman, Susan Anspach, Henry Thomas, Rip Torn, Huckleberry Fox; **D:** Jerry Schatzberg; **C:** Pasquale De Santos. *MGM*

Misunderstood 1987 A father learns his lonely son is full of love and sensitivity when a tragedy reveals that it is this son who takes the blame for all the wrongs his brother commits. **101m/C VHS, Beta.** Anthony Quayle, Stefano Colagrande, Simone Gianozzi, John Sharp; **D:** Luigi Comencini. *IMP*

Mitchell 🎬 1975 (R) Tough cop battles drug traffic and insipid script. Big screen release with that certain TV look. **90m/C VHS.** Joe Don Baker, Linda Evans, Martin Balsam, John Saxon, Merlin Olsen, Harold J. Stone; **D:** Andrew V. McLaglen. *VTR*

Mixed Blood 🎬🎬½ 1984 (R) From the renowned underground film-maker, a dark comedy that examines the seedy drug subculture in New York. Violent, fast, and funny. **98m/C VHS, Beta.** Marilia Pera, Richard Vlacia, Linda Kerridge, Geraldine Smith, Angel David; **D:** Paul Morrissey; **W:** Paul Morrissey. *MED*

Mixed Nuts 🎬 *Lifesavers* 1994 (PG-13) Misfits man a suicide hotline on Christmas Eve in this unfunny, pathetic comedy that's a real downer. Director/writer Ephron (along with her co-writer sister Delia) try way too hard to fashion a hip, racy, madcap farce reminiscent of the screwball comedies that Hollywood churned out in the 1930s and '40s. Film never finds its style and the story line is very weak. Most of the performances are over the top, although Martin, Shandling, and Kahn are good for a few amusing scenes. Ephron and the cast are capable of doing so much better, it's a shame their talents are virtually wasted here.

Adapted from the French film "Le Pere Noel Est Une Ordure."**CW:** Sex-related humor, profanity, mature themes. **97m/C VHS, LV, Closed Caption.** Steve Martin, Madeline Kahn, Robert Klein, Anthony LaPaglia, Juliette Lewis, Rob Reiner, Adam Sandler, Rita Wilson, Garry Shandling, Liev Schreiber; **D:** Nora Ephron; **W:** Nora Ephron, Delia Ephron; **M:** George Fenton. *COL*

M'Lady's Court 🎬 198? A lawyer searching for an heiress in a convent of lusty maidens has loads of fun. None too captivating. **92m/C VHS, Beta.** Sonia Jeanine, Maja Hoppe. *MED*

Mo' Better Blues 🎬🎬½ 1990 (R) Not one of his more cohesive or compelling works, Lee's fourth feature is on the surface a backstage jazz biopic. But all Lee features are vitally concerned with complicated racial issues, and though subtle, this is no exception. Bleek Gilliam is a handsome, accomplished jazz trumpeter who divides his limited extra-curricular time between Clarke (newcomer Williams) and Indigo (junior Lee sibling Joie). What's interesting is not so much the story of self-interested musician and ladies' man Gilliam, but the subtle racial issues his life draws into focus. The Branford Marsalis Quartet provides the music for Bleek's group, scored by Lee's dad Bill (on whose life the script is loosely based).**CW:** Adult situations; language, nudity, violence, and sexual situations. **129m/C VHS, Beta, LV, Closed Caption.** Denzel Washington, Spike Lee, Joie Lee, Wesley Snipes, Cynda Williams, Giancarlo Esposito, Robin Harris, Bill Nunn, John Turturro, Dick Anthony Williams, Ruben Blades, Nicholas Turturro, Samuel L. Jackson, Abbey Lincoln, Tracy C. Johns, Joe Seneca; **D:** Spike Lee; **W:** Spike Lee; **M:** Branford Marsalis, Bill Lee. *USH, FCT*

Mo' Money 🎬🎬½ 1992 (R) Damon Wayans is a small-time con-artist who is inspired to go straight by a beautiful woman (Dash). He lands a job at the credit card company she works for, but temptation overcomes him, he swipes some plastic, and the scamming begins anew. With the help of his younger brother (played by real-life younger brother Marlon), they get involved in an even bigger, more dangerous scam being operated by the credit card company's head of security. Crude formula comedy driven by energetic, inventive performances by the brothers Wayans. Needless to say, will be especially enjoyed by fans of TV's "In Living Color."**CW:** Language and violence. **97m/C VHS, Beta, LV, 8mm.** Damon Wayans, Marlon Wayans, Stacey Dash, Joe Santos, John Diehl, Harry J. Lennix, Mark Beltzman, Quincy Wong, Larry Brandenburg, Almayvonne; **D:** Peter Macdonald; **W:** Damon Wayans; **C:** Don Burgess; **M:** Jay Gruska. *COL*

Moana, a Romance of the Golden Age 🎬🎬🎬½ 1926 An early look through American eyes at the society of the people of Samoa, in the Pacific Islands. Picturesque successor to Flaherty's "Nanook of the North." **76m/B VHS.** Ta'avale, Fa'amgase, Moana; **D:** Robert Flaherty. *GPV, FCT*

Mob Boss 🎬 1990 (R) Gangster films spoof starring Hickey as the head of a successful California crime ring. When his beautiful wife conspires to have him killed, he is left just breaths away from his demise. He calls his nerdy son to his bedside to ask him to take over the family business. But this kid thinks that money laundering requires detergent! Take this one down for a walk by the river in its new cement shoes. **93m/C VHS.** Eddie Deezen, Morgan Fairchild, William Hickey, Stuart Whitman; **D:** Fred Olen Ray. *THV*

Mob Story 🎬½ 1990 (R) Vernon stars as a big-wig mob boss on the run from the government and a few of his "closest" friends. He plans to disappear into Canada, but if his girl (Kidder) and best friend (Waxman) find him first he'll be traveling in a body-bag. Very silly, but fun. **98m/C VHS, Beta, LV.** John Vernon, Margot Kidder, Al Waxman, Kate Vernon; **D:** Gabriel Markiw, Jancarlo Markiw. *IME*

Mob War 🎬½ 1988 (R) A war breaks out between the head of New York's underworld and a media genius. After deciding to become partners, the "family" tries to take over. For fun, count how many times the word "respect" pops up in the script. Tries hard but fails. **96m/C VHS, Beta.** John Christian, David Henry Keller, Jake La Motta, Johnny Stumper; **D:** J. Christian Ingvordsen. *MCG*

Mobsters 🎬½ 1991 (R) It sounded like a great idea, casting the hottest young actors of the '90s as youthful racketeers "Lucky" Luciano, Meyer Lansky, Bugsy Siegel, and Frank Costello. But it would take an FBI probe to straighten out the blood-choked plot, as the pals' loyalties get tested the hard way in a dismembered narrative. Sicker than the violence is a seeming endorsement of the glamorous hoods.**CW:** Language and violence. **104m/C VHS, Beta, LV, Closed Caption.** Christian Slater, Patrick Dempsey, Richard Grieco, Costas Mandylor, Anthony Quinn, F. Murray Abraham, Lara Flynn Boyle, Michael Gambon, Christopher Penn; **D:** Michael Karbelnikoff; **W:** Nicholas Kazan; **C:** Lajos Koltai. *USH, CCB*

Moby Dick 🎬🎬🎬 1956 This adaptation of Herman Melville's high seas saga features Peck as Captain Ahab. His obsession with desire for revenge upon the great white whale, Moby Dick, isn't always believable, but the moments that click, however, make the film more than worthwhile. **116m/C VHS, Beta, LV, Closed Caption.** Gregory Peck, Richard Basehart, Orson Welles, Leo Genn, Harry Andrews, Friedrich Ledebur; **D:** John Huston; **W:** Ray Bradbury, John Huston; **C:** Oswald Morris. National Board of Review Awards '56: 10 Best Films of the Year, Best Director (Huston); New York Film Critics Awards '56: Best Director (Huston). *MGM*

Mockery 🎬🎬½ 1927 Chaney plays a peasant working for a Russian countess. He becomes involved in a peasant revolution against the rich and threatens the countess but eventually saves her from the mob. **75m/B VHS.** Lon Chaney Sr., Barbara Bedford, Ricardo Cortez, Emily Fitzroy; **D:** Benjamin Christiansen. *FCT*

The Mod Squad 1968 The ultimate sixties series features a trio of young misfits who are recruited by a gruff police captain in Southern California. Their undercover assignments take them into the counter-culture. The series was created by former L.A. police officer Bud Ruskin, and was based on his own experiences. Two episodes per tape: "Teeth of the Barracuda" explains the formation of the Mod Squad, and "Mother of Sorrow" finds a generation gap leading to murder. Additional episodes are available. **60m/C VHS.** Michael Cole, Clarence Williams III, Peggy Lipton, Tige Andrews, Lee Grant, Richard Dreyfuss. *MOV*

Model Behavior 🎬½ 1982 Fresh from college, an aspiring photographer pines for a glamorous model. **86m/C VHS, Beta.** Richard Bekins, Bruce Lyons, Cindy Harrel; **D:** Bud Gardner. *LIV*

Model by Day 🎬½ 1994 (R) When New York model Janssen's father is murdered, she takes up martial arts training and becomes the vengeful "Lady X." Then she becomes the prime suspect in a murder and finds herself falling for a plainsclothes cop. Fair amount of action, somewhat less exploitive than usual for the genre. **89m/C VHS, Beta, LV, Closed Caption.** Famke Janssen, Stephen Shellan, Shannon Tweed, Sean Young; **D:** Christian Duguay. *ACA*

A Modern Affair 🎬½ *Mr. 247* 1994 (R) Single executive Grace Rhodes' (Eichorn) biological clock is ringing and without Mr. Right in sight, she decides to visit a sperm bank. Grace gets pregnant and also very curious about her anonymous donor—who of course doesn't stay anonymous. Grace even manages to fall for photographer Peter Kessler (Tucci) but how does she tell him she's carrying his baby when they haven't even had sex yet?**CW:** Language. **91m/C VHS, Closed Caption.** Lisa Eichhorn, Stanley Tucci, Caroline Aaron, Tammy Grimes, Robert Joy, Wesley Addy, Cynthia Martells, Mary Jo Salerno; **D:** Vern Oakley; **W:** Paul Zimmerman; **C:** Rex Nicholson; **M:** Jan Hammer. *COL*

Modern Girls ◻½ 1986 (PG-13) Teen comedy about three bubble-headed LA rock groupies and their various wild adventures during a single night on the town. Surprising in that the three lead actresses waste their talents in this lesson in exploitation. Bruce Springsteen's younger sister portrays a drug user. 82m/C VHS, Beta, LV. Cynthia Gibb, Daphne Zuniga, Virginia Madsen; **D:** Jerry Kramer; **W:** Laurie Craig; **M:** Eddie Arkin. PAR

Modern Love ◻ 1990 (R) An average slob realizes that marriage, fatherhood and in-law-ship isn't quite what he expected. Benson stars, directs and produces as well as co-starring with real-life wife DeVito. A plotless hodgepodge of bits that were more successful in "Look Who's Talking" and "Parenthood." 89m/C VHS, Beta, Closed Caption. Robby Benson, Karla DeVito, Rue McClanahan, Kaye Ballard, Frankie Valli, Cliff Bemis, Louise Lasser, Burt Reynolds, Lyric Benson; **D:** Robby Benson; **W:** Robby Benson. NO

Modern Problems ◻◻ 1981 (PG) A man involved in a nuclear accident discovers he has acquired telekinetic powers, which he uses to turn the tables on his professional and romantic rivals. A fine cast but an unsuccessful fission trip. 93m/C VHS, Beta. Chevy Chase, Patti D'Arbanville, Mary Kay Place, Brian Doyle-Murray, Nell Carter, Dabney Coleman; **D:** Ken Shapiro. FOX

Modern Romance ◻◻◻ 1981 (R) The romantic misadventures of a neurotic film editor who is hopelessly in love with his girlfriend but can't seem to maintain a normal relationship with her. Smart and hilarious at times and always simmering with anxiety. Offers an honest look at relationships as well as an accurate portrait of filmmaking. 102m/C VHS, Beta, LV. Albert Brooks, Kathryn Harrold, Bruno Kirby, George Kennedy, James L. Brooks, Bob Einstein; **D:** Albert Brooks; **W:** Albert Brooks, Monica Johnson. COL

Modern Times ◻◻◻◻ 1936 This "mostly" silent film finds Chaplin playing a factory worker who goes crazy from his repetitious job on an assembly line and his boss' demands for greater speed and efficiency. Ultimately encompassing the tyranny of machine over man, this cinematic masterpiece has more relevance today than ever. Chaplin wrote the musical score which incorporates the tune "Smile." Look for a young Gloria De Haven as one of Goddard's sisters; she's the real-life daughter of Chaplin's assistant director. 87m/B VHS, Beta, LV. Charlie Chaplin, Paulette Goddard, Henry Bergman, Stanley Sandford, Gloria De Haven, Chester Conklin; **D:** Charlie Chaplin; **W:** Charlie Chaplin; **M:** Charlie Chaplin. National Board of Review Awards '36: 10 Best Films of the Year. FOX, HMV

The Moderns ◻◻◻ 1988 (R) One of the quirkier directors around, this time Rudolph tries a comedic period piece about the avant-garde art society of 1920s Paris. Fleshed out with some familiar characters (Ernest Hemingway, Gertrude Stein) and some strange art-world types. The tone is not consistently funny but, instead, romantic as the main characters clash over art and love. 126m/C VHS, Beta, 8mm. Keith Carradine, Linda Fiorentino, John Lone, Genevieve Bujold, Geraldine Chaplin, Wallace Shawn, Kevin J. O'Connor; **D:** Alan Rudolph; **W:** Alan Rudolph; **M:** Mark Isham. Los Angeles Film Critics Association Awards '88: Best Supporting Actress (Bujold). NLC

Modigliani ◻◻½ Montparnasse 19; The Lovers of Montparnasse; Modigliani of Montparnasse 1958 Life of dissolute 19th-century painter Modigliani (Philipe), which tracks his affairs with British poet Beatrice Hastings (Palmer) and later mistress Jeanne (Aimee), who commits suicide shortly before his death. Female performances make up for the lackluster lead. Becker inherited the film from director Max Ophuls, who co-wrote the screenplay but who died before the start of production. In French with English subtitles. 110m/B VHS. FR Gerard Philipe, Lilli Palmer, Anouk Aimee, Gerard Sety, Lino Ventura, Lila Kedrova, Lea Padovani; **D:** Jacques Becker; **W:** Max Ophuls, Henri Jeanson, Jacques Becker. FCT

Mogambo ◻◻◻ 1953 Remake of "Red Dust," this is the steamy story of a love triangle between an African game hunter, a proper British lady, and an American showgirl in the jungles of Kenya. 115m/C VHS, Beta. Clark Gable, Ava Gardner, Grace Kelly; **D:** John Ford; **C:** Robert L. Surtees. Golden Globe Awards '54: Best Supporting Actress (Kelly); National Board of Review Awards '53: 10 Best Films of the Year; Nominations: Academy Awards '53: Best Actress (Gardner), Best Supporting Actress (Kelly). MGM, FCT, CCB

Mohammed: Messenger of God ◻◻ The Message; Al-Ris-Alah 1977 (PG) Sprawling saga of the genesis of the religion of Islam, with Quinn portraying Mohammad's uncle, Hamza, an honored warrior. The story behind the movie might prove much more successful as a sequel than did the movie itself. The filming itself created a religious controversy. 180m/C VHS. GB Damien Thomas, Anthony Quinn, Irene Papas, Michael Ansara, Johnny Sekka, Michael Forest, Neville Jason; **D:** Moustapha Akkad; **C:** Jack Hildyard; **M:** Maurice Jarre. Nominations: Academy Awards '77: Best Original Score. NO

Mohawk ◻½ 1956 A cowboy and his Indian maiden try to stop a war between Indian tribes and fanatical landowners. 80m/C VHS, Beta. Rita Gam, Neville Brand, Scott Brady, Lori Nelson; **D:** Kurt Neumann; **C:** Karl Struss. NOS, MRV, GEM

Mole Men against the Son of Hercules ◻ 1961 Italian muscleman Maciste battles the pale-skinned denizens of an underground city. ?m/C VHS, Beta. IT Mark Forest. SNC

The Mole People ◻ 1956 A really bad fifties creature feature which finds two archeologists accidentally discovering an underground civilization of albinos who shun all forms of light. They've also enslaved the local populace of half-human, half-mole creatures who decide to help the good guys escape by rising up in a revolt against their evil masters. When the weapon of choice is a flashlight you know not to expect much. 78m/B VHS, Closed Caption. John Agar, Cynthia Patrick, Hugh Beaumont, Alan Napier, Nestor Paiva, Phil Chambers; **D:** Virgil W. Vogel; **W:** Laszlo Gorog. USH

Moll Flanders ◻◻½ 1996 Rousing, bawdy retelling of Daniel Defoe's 1722 novel about the wickedly seductive Moll (Kingston). Born in London's Newgate prison, Moll becomes a house servant, embarks on her first marriage, is soon widowed, and decides to make her own way (and fortune). She becomes a thief, a whore, marries several more times, and eventually winds up back in prison and a likely candidate for the gallows. But the ever-enterprising Moll always finds her way. TV miniseries on two cassettes. 210m/C VHS, Closed Caption. GB Alex Kingston, Daniel Craig, Diana Rigg, Colin Buchanan, Christopher Fulford, James Fleet, Ian Driver, Tom Ward; **D:** David Attwood; **W:** Andrew Davies; **C:** Ivan Strasburg. VTR, PBS, VIF

Moll Flanders ◻◻½ 1996 (PG-13) Writer/director Densham takes only the title character and the 18th-century London setting from Daniel Defoe's 1722 novel in telling of spirited heroine Moll Flanders' (Wright) life. Orphaned Moll eventually finds herself working at the brothel of greedy, scheming Mrs. Allworthy (Channing). Her life as a prostitute leads her to drink and near suicide—despite the unwavering friendship of Hibble (Freeman), Allworthy's dignified servant—until she falls for an impoverished artist (Lynch) and briefly finds happiness. Wright's heartfelt performance holds everything together (with help from a talented supporting cast) but things get dreary. CW: Violence, nudity and sex-related material. 120m/C VHS, LV, Closed Caption. Robin Wright, Morgan Freeman, Stockard Channing, John Lynch, Brenda Fricker, Aisling Corcoran, Geraldine James, Jim Sheridan, Jeremy Brett, Britta Smith, Ger Ryan; **D:** Pen Densham; **W:** Pen Densham; **C:** David Tattersall; **M:** Mark Mancina. MGM

Molly and Gina ◻◻ 1994 (R) The very different lives of Molly and Gina intersect suddenly when their boyfriends are killed in the street by gunfire. They are drawn into the underworld of gun-runners and violence, as they seek justice for the men they loved. CW: Language, violence, and sexuality. 90m/C VHS. Frances Fisher, Natasha Gregson Wagner, Bruce Weitz, Stella Stevens, Peter Fonda; **D:** Paul Leder; **W:** Reuben Leder; **M:** Dana Walden. APX

Molly & Lawless John ◻◻ 1972 Average western, with Miles the wife of a sadistic sheriff who helps a prisoner escape the gallows so they can run away together. Enough cliches for the whole family to enjoy. 90m/C VHS, Beta. Sam Elliott, Vera Miles; **D:** Gary Nelson. NO

Molly Maguires ◻◻½ 1970 (PG) Dramatization based on a true story, concerns a group of miners called the Molly Maguires who resort to using terrorist tactics in their fight for better working conditions during the Pennsylvania Irish coal mining rebellion in the 1870s. During their reign of terror, the Mollies are infiltrated by a Pinkerton detective who they mistakenly believe is a new recruit. It has its moments but never fully succeeds. Returned less than fifteen percent of its initial eleven million dollar investment. 123m/C VHS, Beta. Sean Connery, Richard Harris, Samantha Eggar, Frank Finlay; **D:** Martin Ritt; **W:** Walter Bernstein; **C:** James Wong Howe; **M:** Henry Mancini. Nominations: Academy Awards '70: Best Art Direction/Set Decoration. PAR, CCB

The Mollycoddle ◻◻ 1920 Fairbanks is a British-educated American whom everyone thinks is less-than-manly until he brings a smuggler to justice. ?m/B VHS. Douglas Fairbanks Sr., Wallace Beery, Ruth Renick; **D:** Victor Fleming; **W:** Douglas Fairbanks Sr. KIV

Mom woof! 1989 (R) When his mother is bitten by a flesh-eater, Clay Dwyer is at a loss as to what to do. How do you tell your own mother that she must be destroyed, lest she continue to devour human flesh? A campy horror/comedy. 95m/C VHS, LV, Closed Caption. Mark Thomas Miller, Art Evans, Mary McDonough, Jeanne Bates, Brion James, Stella Stevens, Claudia Christian; **D:** Patrick Rand. COL

Mom & Dad ◻◻ 1947 An innocent young girl's one night of passion leads to an unwanted pregnancy. Stock footage of childbirth and a lecture on the evils of syphilis concludes this campy schlock that features the national anthem. Banned or denied release for years, this movie is now a cult favorite for its time-capsule glimpse at conventional 1940s sexual attitudes. 97m/B VHS, Beta. Hardie Albright, Sarah Blake, George Eldridge, June Carlson, Jimmy Clark, Bob Lowell; **D:** William Beaudine. VDM

Mom and Dad Save the World ◻½ 1992 (PG) A suburban housewife (Garr) is transported along with her husband in the family station wagon to the planet Spengo, ruled by King Tod Spengo (Lovitz), who has fallen in love with her and wants to save her from his plans to blow up Earth. While trying to prevent the king from marrying her and killing them, Garr and Jones wind up in many goofy situations and wind up saving the Earth from its imminent doom. Uninspired comedy just isn't funny, and the excellent cast is misused, especially Idle and Shawn. Save this one for the kiddies. 87m/C VHS, LV, Closed Caption. Teri Garr, Jeffrey Jones, Jon Lovitz, Eric Idle, Wallace Shawn, Dwier Brown, Kathy Ireland, Thalmus Rasulala; **D:** Greg Beeman; **M:** Jerry Goldsmith. HBO

Mom, the Wolfman and Me ◻◻½ 1980 An 11-year-old girl arranges and manages the love affair of her mother, an ultra-liberated photographer, and an unemployed teacher, who is also the owner of an Irish wolfhound. Charming adaptation of a novel by Norma Klein. 100m/C VHS, Beta. Patty Duke, David Birney, Danielle Brisebois, Keenan Wynn, Viveca Lindfors, John Lithgow; **D:** Edmond Levy. TLF

Moment in Time *🗡* 1984 A romantic novel on tape, about a guy, a girl, and their various troubles. **60m/C Beta.** Jean Simmons. *PSM*

Mommie Dearest *🗡🗡* 1981 (PG) Film based on Christina Crawford's memoirs of her incredibly abusive and violent childhood at the hands of her adoptive mother, actress Joan Crawford. The story is controversial and sometimes trashy, but fairly well done nevertheless. **129m/C VHS, Beta, LV.** Faye Dunaway, Diana Scarwid, Steve Forrest, Mara Hobel, Rutanya Alda, Harry Goz, Howard da Silva; *D:* Frank Perry; *W:* Robert Getchell; *M:* Henry Mancini. Golden Raspberry Awards '81: Worst Picture, Worst Actress (Dunaway), Worst Supporting Actor (Forrest), Worst Supporting Actress (Scarwid), Worst Screenplay. *PAR*

Mommy *🗡🗡½* 1995 Schoolteacher is stalked by murderous mom who'll do anything for her daughter. Mommy McCormack was the original "Bad Seed" child. Filmed in Muscatine, Iowa. **89m/C VHS.** Patty McCormack, Majel Barrett, Jason Miller, Brinke Stevens, Rachel Lemieux, Mickey Spillane, Michael Cornelison, Sarah Jane Miller; *D:* Max Allan Collins; *W:* Max Allan Collins; *C:* Phillip W. Dingeldein; *M:* Richard Lowry. *MNC*

Mommy 2: Mommy's Day *🗡🗡½* 1996 Murderous Mommy (McCormack) returns as does her beloved daughter (now rebellious teenager), Jessica Ann (Lemieux). Mommy's on Death Row, awaiting execution after her murder spree but the Mommy-style killings continue. Shot on location in Iowa. **89m/C VHS.** Patty McCormack, Rachel Lemieux, Brinke Stevens, Michael Cornelison, Sarah Jane Miller, Mickey Spillane, Gary Sandy, Paul Petersen, Arlen Dean Snyder, Todd Eastland, Del Close; *D:* Max Allan Collins; *W:* Max Allan Collins; *C:* Phillip W. Dingeldein; *M:* Richard Lowry. *EAG*

Mon Amie Max *🗡🗡* 1994 Marie-Alexandrine (Max) Babant (Bujold) is a middle-aged former pianist who returns to her native Quebec City after 25 years of self-imposed exile. Pregnant at 15, Max was forced to give her son up for adoption and ran away from friends and family. Now, she's meet former best friend Catherine (Keller), who's had the concert career Max never did, who's also agreed to help Max find her son. Slow-going melodrama with little emotional impact. **107m/C VHS.** *CA FR* Genevieve Bujold, Marthe Keller, Michel Rivard, Johanne McKay; *D:* Michel Brault; *W:* Jefferson Lewis. Nominations: Genie Awards '94: Best Actress (Bujold), Best Film. *NYR*

Mon Oncle *🗡🗡🗡🗡* My Uncle; My Uncle, Mr. Hulot 1958 Tati's celebrated comedy contrasts the simple life of Monsieur Hulot with the technologically complicated life of his family when he aids his nephew in war against his parents' ultramodern, push-button home. An easygoing, delightful comedy, this is the director's first piece in color. Sequel to "Mr. Hulot's Holiday," followed by "Playtime." In French with English subtitles. **110m/C VHS, Beta, LV, 8mm.** *FR* Jacques Tati, Jean-Pierre Zola, Adrienne Serrantie, Alain Bacourt; *D:* Jacques Tati; *C:* Jean Bourgoin. Academy Awards '58: Best Foreign Language Film; Cannes Film Festival '58: Grand Jury Prize; National Board of Review Awards '58: 5 Best Foreign Films of the Year; New York Film Critics Awards '58: Best Foreign Film. *HMV, MRV, HHT*

Mon Oncle Antoine *🗡🗡🗡½* 1971 A splendid tale of young Benoit, who learns about life from a surprisingly compassionate uncle, who works as everything from undertaker to grocer in the depressed area where they live. **104m/C VHS.** *CA* Jean Duceppe, Olivette Thibault; *D:* Claude Jutra. *HMV, FLI, APD*

Mon Oncle D'Amerique *🗡🗡🗡½* Les Somnambules 1980 (PG) Three French characters are followed as they try to find success of varying kinds in Paris, interspersed with ironic lectures by Prof. Henri Laborit about the biology that impels human behavior. Their disappointments lead them to dream of a legendary American uncle, who could make their desires come true. An acclaimed, witty comedy by former Nouvelle Vague filmmaker, dubbed into English. **123m/C VHS, Beta.**

FR Gerard Depardieu, Nicole Garcia, Roger-Pierre, Marie DuBois; *D:* Alain Resnais; *W:* Jean Gruault; *C:* Sacha Vierny. Cannes Film Festival '80: Grand Jury Prize; New York Film Critics Awards '80: Best Foreign Film; Nominations: Academy Awards '80: Best Original Screenplay. *NYF, BTV*

Mona Lisa *🗡🗡🗡½* 1986 (R) Jordan's wonderful, sad, sensitive story of a romantic, small-time hood who gets personally involved with the welfare and bad company of the high-priced whore he's been hired to chauffeur. Hoskins is especially touching and Caine is chilling as a suave gangster. Fine film debut for Tyson. Brilliantly filmed and critically lauded. **104m/C VHS, Beta, LV.** *GB* Bob Hoskins, Cathy Tyson, Michael Caine, Clarke Peters, Kate Hardie, Robbie Coltrane, Zoe Nathenson, Sammi Davis, Rod Bedall, Joe Brown, Pauline Melville; *D:* Neil Jordan; *W:* David Leland, Neil Jordan; *M:* Michael Kamen. British Academy Awards '86: Best Actor (Hoskins); Cannes Film Festival '86: Best Actor (Hoskins); Golden Globe Awards '87: Best Actor—Drama (Hoskins); Los Angeles Film Critics Association Awards '86: Best Actor (Hoskins), Best Supporting Actress (Tyson); New York Film Critics Awards '86: Best Actor (Hoskins); National Society of Film Critics Awards '86: Best Actor (Hoskins); Nominations: Academy Awards '86: Best Actor (Hoskins). *VTR*

Monaco Forever *🗡🗡* 1983 An enigmatic American meets a mysterious Frenchwoman and they set off on a string of unusual romantic adventures. Set around the 1956 marriage of Grace Kelly to Prince Rainier of Monaco. Film debut of Van Damme. **79m/C VHS.** Charles Pitt, Martha Farris, Sydney Lassick, Jean-Claude Van Damme; *D:* William A. Levey; *W:* C. William Pitt, William A. Levey. *VHE, FCT*

Mondo Balardo *🗡* 1964 Translated as "Crazy World," this is crude sensationalism masked as a horror story. Karloff guides the viewer through a curious mixture of society's fringe elements. A loosely connected series of sketches includes portraits of a reincarnated Rudolph Valentino, practitioners of transvestism, Roman coke whores, and an Italian-Japanese rock 'n roll midget (Drago) in director Montero's unusual vision of an anti-paradise. Includes standard lesbian club scene. Volume 11 of Frank Henenlotter's Sexy Shockers. **86m/C VHS.** Franz Drago; *D:* Robert Montero; *W:* Albert T. Viola. *SMW, FCT*

Mondo Cane *🗡🗡* 1963 (R) A documentary showcasing the eccentricities of human behavior around the world, including cannibalism, pig killing and more. Dubbed in English. Inspired a rash of "shockumentaries" over the next several years. The song "More" made its debut in this film. **105m/C VHS, Beta.** *IT D:* Gualtiero Jacopetti. Nominations: Academy Awards '63: Best Song ("More"). *SNC, VDC, VDM*

Mondo Cane 2 *🗡* Mondo Pazzo 1964 (R) More documentary-like views of the oddities of mankind and ethnic rituals around the world. Enough, already. **94m/C VHS, Beta.** *IT D:* Gualtiero Jacopetti. *VDC, HHE, TPV*

Mondo Magic *🗡½* 1976 A compilation of tribal rituals offering viewers a look on the darker side of matters magical. **100m/C VHS, Beta.** *D:* Melvin Ashford. *NO*

Mondo Trasho WOOF! 1969 A major trasho film of the last day in the life of a most unfortunate woman, complete with sex and violence. First full length effort from cult filmmaker Waters, who was also writer, producer, and editor. **95m/B VHS, Beta.** Divine, Mary Vivian Pearce, John Leisenring, Mink Stole, David Lochary, Chris Atkinson; *D:* John Waters; *W:* John Waters. *NO*

The Money *🗡🗡* 1975 (R) The quest for money drives a young man to kidnap the child that his girlfriend is baby-sitting. Average but Workman's direction is right on the money. **88m/C VHS.** Laurence Luckinbill, Elizabeth Richards, Danny DeVito, Graham Beckel; *D:* Chuck Workman. *GHV, VTR*

Money for Nothing *🗡🗡* 1993 (R) $1.2 million falls off a truck in the warehouse district of Philadelphia where a simple-minded unemployed longshoreman (Cusack) finds the chance of a lifetime. Indiscreetly leaving behind a trail of spending, he soon has a detective (Madsen) snooping

around dangerously close. But he only digs himself deeper by enlisting the assistance of the mob to help him launder the money. At this point the film disintegrates into a limp diatribe on the injustice of capitalism on society's downtrodden. Mazar plays Joey's ex-girlfriend who double-times it back to the fold after his find. Based on a true story. *CW:* Language and a scene of sexuality. **100m/C VHS, LV, Closed Caption.** John Cusack, Michael Madsen, Benicio Del Toro, Michael Rapaport, Debi Mazar, Fionnula Flanagan, Maury Chaykin, James Gandolfini, Elizabeth Bracco, Ashleigh Dejon, Lenny Venito; *D:* Ramon Menendez; *W:* Ramon Menendez, Carol Sobieski, Tom Musca; *M:* Craig Safan. *TOU*

Money Madness *🗡🗡* 1947 Beaumont (Ward Cleaver) plays a taxi driver turned thief in this curiosity. **?m/C VHS.** Hugh Beaumont, Frances Rafferty, Harlan Warde, Cecil Weston, Ida Moore, Danny Morton, Joel Friedkin, Lane Chandler; *D:* Peter Stewart, Sam Newfield; *W:* Al Martin; *C:* Jack Greenhalgh. *SNC*

Money Movers *🗡🗡* 1978 Aussie thieves plan megabuck bank robbery but heist and plot go sour. An oft told tale based on a true story. Features early appearance from burly boy Brown. **94m/C VHS.** *AU* Terence Donovan, Ed Devereaux, Tony Bonner, Lucky Grills, Charles Tingwell, Candy Raymond, Bryan Brown, Alan Cassell; *D:* Bruce Beresford; *W:* Bruce Beresford. *IMP*

The Money Pit *🗡🗡* 1986 (PG) A young yuppie couple encounter sundry problems when they attempt to renovate their newly purchased, seemingly self-destructive, Long Island home. However, the collapse of their home leads directly to the collapse of their relationship as well. Somewhat modeled after "Mr. Blandings Builds His Dream House." Hanks and Long fail to jell as partners and the many sight gags are on the predictable side. A Spielberg production. **91m/C VHS, Beta, LV, Closed Caption.** Tom Hanks, Shelley Long, Alexander Godunov, Maureen Stapleton, Philip Bosco, Joe Mantegna, Josh Mostel; *D:* Richard Benjamin; *C:* Gordon Willis; *M:* Michel Colombier. *USH*

Money to Burn *🗡🗡* 1983 Aging high school counselor and two senior citizens develop a plan to steal $50 million dollars from the Federal Reserve Bank. Harmless bit of fun. **90m/C VHS, Beta.** Jack Kruschen, Meegan King, David Wallace, Phillip Pine; *D:* Virginia Lively Stone. *NO*

Money to Burn *🗡½* 1994 (R) Two buddies go off on a wild spending spree when $2 million in cash falls into their laps. Only one problem—a crazy cop who's determined to stop them squandering the money. **96m/C VHS, LV.** Chad McQueen, Don Swayze, Joe Estevez, Julie Strain, Sydney Lassick; *D:* John Sjogren; *W:* John Sjogren, Scott Ziehl. *NLC, COL*

Money Train *🗡½* 1995 (R) Snipes and Harrelson team up again, this time as New York City transit cops (and foster brothers) who decide to rob the money train—a subway car that collects all the cash accrued from the transit system each day. To complicate matters, they're both in love with their new Latina partner (Lopez). Lame attempt to cash in on the Snipes and Harrelson chemistry leaves out one important ingredient—a competent script. The movie is almost over before the train actually becomes part of the plot line. Film came under criticism when it was blamed for a series of "copycat" arsons in which a New York City subway clerk was killed. *CW:* Contains strong language, violence, and a sex scene. **110m/C VHS, LV, 8mm, Closed Caption.** Woody Harrelson, Wesley Snipes, Jennifer Lopez, Robert (Bobby) Blake, Chris Cooper, Joe Grifasi; *D:* Joseph Ruben; *W:* Doug Richardson, David Loughery; *C:* John Lindley; *M:* Mark Mancina. *COL*

The Moneytree *🗡½* 1993 A carefree would-be actor decides to make some money by harvesting a huge marijuana crop in the California hills, all the while fending off his girlfriend, the cops, and some wild boars. **92m/C VHS.** Christopher Dienstag; *D:* Alan Dienstag. *TPV*

A Mongolian Tale ✓✓ *Hei Ma* 1994 Nai Nai has raised her granddaughter Somiya and the abandoned Bayingbulag among the Mongolian steppes. Eventually, Bayingbulag leaves to get an education but promises to return and marry Somiya. Away three years, he comes back only to discover Somiya pregnant, so he takes off, finds success as a folk singer, and doesn't return for 12 years. Somiya now has a drunken husband, four sons, and an illegitimate 12-year-old daughter who is desperate for a father. Mongolian dialogue. Adapted by Chengzhi from his story "A Song of the Grassland." 105m/C VHS. *CH HK* Narenhua, Tengger; *D:* Xie Fei; *W:* Zhang Chengzhi. Montreal World Film Festival '95: Best Director (Fei). *NYR*

The Mongols ✓✓½ *Les Mongols* 1960 Splashy Italian production has Genghis Khan's son repelling invading hordes while courting buxom princess. Pairing of Palance and Ekberg makes this one worthy of consideration. 105m/C VHS. *IT FR* Jack Palance, Anita Ekberg, Antonella Lualdi, Franco Silva, Gianni "John" Garko, Roldano Lupi, Gabriella Pallotti; *D:* Andre de Toth, Leopoldo Savona, Riccardo (Robert Hampton) Freda. *SNC*

Mongrel woof! 1983 El-cheapo kennel horror about a man who dreams he's a wild murderous mutt. His relief upon waking up is short-lived, however, when he discovers the people he killed in his dreams are actually dead. Flick will make you want to gnaw on a bone. 90m/C VHS, Beta. Aldo Ray, Terry Evans; *D:* Robert Burns. *NO*

Monika ✓✓½ *Summer with Monika* 1952 Two teenagers who run away together for the summer find the winter brings more responsibility than they can handle when the girl becomes pregnant and gives birth. Lesser, early Bergman, sensitively directed, but dull. Adapted by Bergman from a Per Anders Fogelstrom novel. In Swedish with English subtitles. *SW* Harriet Andersson, Lars Ekborg, John Harryson, Georg Skarsted, Dagmar Ebbesen, Ake Gronberg; *D:* Ingmar Bergman; *W:* Ingmar Bergman; *M:* Les Baxter. HMV, CVC, TPV

Monique ✓ 1983 A sophisticated career woman is about to unleash a terrifying secret on her new husband. 96m/C VHS, Beta. Florence Giorgetti, John Ferris. *NO*

Monkey Boy ✓✓½ 1990 Decent sci-fi horror from Britain, about a cunning human-ape hybrid that escapes from a genetics lab after massacring the staff. Not excessively gruesome or vulgar, and some sympathy is aroused for the killer mutant. Based on the novel "Chimera." 104m/C VHS, Beta. John Lynch, Christine Kavanagh, Kenneth Cranham; *D:* Lawrence Gordon Clark. *PSM*

Monkey Business ✓✓✓½ 1931 Marx Brothers run amok as stowaways on ocean liner. Fast-paced comedy provides seemingly endless amount of gags, quips, and pratfalls, including the fab four imitating Maurice Chevalier at Immigration. This film, incidentally, was the group's first to be written—by noted humorist Perelman—directly for the screen. 77m/B VHS, Beta, LV. Groucho Marx, Harpo Marx, Chico Marx, Zeppo Marx, Thelma Todd, Ruth Hall, Harry Woods; *D:* Norman Z. McLeod. *USH*

Monkey Business ✓✓ 1952 A scientist invents a fountain-of-youth potion, a lab chimpanzee mistakenly dumps it into a water cooler, and then grown-ups start turning into adolescents. Top-flight crew occasionally labors in this screwball comedy, though comic moments shine. Monroe is the secretary sans skills, while absent-minded Grant and sexy wife Rogers race hormonally as teens. 97m/B VHS, Beta, LV. Cary Grant, Ginger Rogers, Charles Coburn, Marilyn Monroe, Hugh Marlowe, Larry Keating, George Winslow; *D:* Howard Hawks; *W:* Ben Hecht, Charles Lederer, I.A.L. Diamond; *C:* Milton Krasner. FOX

Monkey Grip ✓✓✓ 1982 An unmarried woman copes with parenthood and a drug-addicted boyfriend while working on the fringe of Australia's music business. Grim but provocative, based on Helen Graham's novel. 101m/C VHS. *AU*

Noni Hazlehurst, Colin Friels, Alice Garner, Harold Hopkins, Candy Raymond; *D:* Ken Cameron; *W:* Ken Cameron. Australian Film Institute '82: Best Actress (Hazlehurst).

Monkey Hustle ✓ 1977 (PG) Vintage blaxploitation has trouble hustling laffs. The Man plans a super freeway through the ghetto, and law abiding do gooders join forces with territorial lords of vice to fight the project. Shot in the Windy City. 90m/C VHS. Yaphet Kotto, Rudy Ray Moore, Rosalind Cash, Debbi Morgan, Thomas Carter; *D:* Arthur Marks. ORI, FCT

Monkey Shines ✓✓ *Monkey Shines: An Experiment in Fear* 1988 (R) Based on the novel by Michael Stuart, this is a sick, scary yarn about a quadriplegic who is given a specially trained capuchin monkey as a helpmate. However, he soon finds that the beast is assuming and acting on his subconscious rages. 108m/C VHS, Beta, LV, Closed Caption. Jason Beghe, John Pankow, Melanie Parker, Christine Forrest, Stephen Root, Kate McNeil, Joyce Van Patten, Stanley Tucci, Janine Turner; *D:* George A. Romero; *W:* George A. Romero; *M:* David Shire. ORI

Monkey Trouble ✓✓½ 1994 (PG) Lonely schoolgirl Birch is feeling abandoned when mom and stepdad shower attention on her new baby brother. Then a monkey trained as a pickpocket enters her life. Keitel is the organ grinder turned bad who must answer to the mob when the monkey scampers off to suburbia. Stakes a lot of its entertainment wallop on the considerable talents of the slippery-fingered monkey, who steals the show. Birch is amusing as the youngster caught in all sorts of uncomfortable situations. Formula abounds, but the milk and cookies set won't notice; fine family fare. 95m/C VHS, LV, Closed Caption. Thora Birch, Harvey Keitel, Mimi Rogers, Christopher McDonald; *D:* Franco Amurri; *W:* Franco Amurri, Stu Krieger; *M:* Mark Mancina. COL

Monkeys, Go Home! ✓½ 1966 Dumb Disney yarn about young American who inherits a badly neglected French olive farm. When he brings in four chimpanzees to pick the olives, the local townspeople go on strike. People can be so sensitive. Based on "The Monkeys" by G. K. Wilkinson. Chevalier's last film appearance. 89m/C VHS, Beta. Dean Jones, Yvette Mimieux, Maurice Chevalier, Clement Harari, Yvonne Constant; *D:* Andrew V. McLaglen; *M:* Robert F. Brunner. DIS

Monkey's Uncle ✓½ 1965 A sequel to Disney's "The Misadventures of Merlin Jones" and featuring more bizarre antics and scientific hoopla, including chimps and a flying machine. 90m/C VHS, Beta. Tommy Kirk, Annette Funicello, Leon Ames, Arthur O'Connell; *D:* Robert Stevenson; *W:* Alfred Lewis Levitt, Helen Levitt; *C:* Edward Colman; *M:* Buddy Baker. DIS

The Monocle ✓✓ 1964 Steele plays a seductive villainess in this rare, spy/comedy thriller. ?m/C VHS. *FR* Paul Meurisse, Barbara Steele, Marcel Dalio. SNC

Monolith ✓✓½ 1993 (R) Tucker (Paxton) and Flynn (Frost) are unlikely partners on the LAPD. But they're teamed up on an unlikely case: a Russian scientist commits a seemingly senseless murder and is taken away by a mystery man (Hurt) before she can be interrogated. What the curious duo discover is a lethal alien force capable of posessing any living creature and whose objective is the destruction of the planet. 96m/C VHS, LV, Closed Caption. Bill Paxton, Lindsay Frost, John Hurt, Louis Gossett Jr.; *D:* John Eyres; *W:* Stephen Lister. USH

The Monolith Monsters ✓✓ 1957 A geologist investigates a meteor shower in Arizona and discovers strange crystals. The crystals attack humans and absorb their silicone, causing them to grow into monsters. Good "B" movie fun. 76m/B VHS, Closed Caption. Grant Williams, Lola Albright, Les Tremayne, Trevor Bardette; *D:* John Sherwood; *W:* Norman Jolley, Robert M. Fresco; *M:* Joseph Gershenson. USH, MLB, FRG

Monsieur Beaucaire ✓½ 1924 The Duke of Chartres ditches France posing as a barber, and once in Britain, becomes a lawman. Not a classic Valentino vehicle. 100m/B VHS, Beta. Rudolph Valentino, Bebe Daniels, Lois Wilson, Doris Kenyon, Lowell Sherman, John Davidson; *D:* Sidney Olcott. GPV

Monsieur Beaucaire ✓✓✓ 1946 Entertaining Hope vehicle that casts him as a barber impersonating a French nobleman in the court of Louis XV. He's set to wed a Spanish princess in order to prevent a full-scale war from taking place. However, he really wants to marry social-climber chambermaid Caulfield. Director Marshall was at his best here. Based on the novel by Booth Tarkington. 93m/B VHS, Closed Caption. Bob Hope, Joan Caulfield, Patric Knowles, Marjorie Reynolds, Cecil Kellaway, Joseph Schildkraut, Reginald Owen, Constance Collier; *D:* George Marshall; *W:* Melvin Frank, Norman Panama; *C:* Lionel Lindon. USH, BTV

Monsieur Hire ✓✓✓½ *M. Hire* 1989 (PG-13) The usual tale of sexual obsesssion and suspense. Mr. Hire spends much of his time trying to spy on his beautiful young neighbor woman, alternately alienated and engaged by her love affairs. The voyeur soon finds his secret desires have entangled him in a vicious intrigue. Political rally set-piece is brilliant. Excellent acting, intense pace, elegant photography. Based on "Les Fiancailles de M. Hire" by Georges Simenone and adapted by Leconte and Patrick Dewolf. In French with English subtitles. 81m/C VHS, LV. *FR* Michel Blanc, Sandrine Bonnaire, Luc Thuillier, Eric Berenger, Andre Wilms; *D:* Patrice Leconte; *W:* Patrice Leconte. Cesar Awards '90: Best Sound. FXL, FCT, IME

Monsieur Verdoux ✓✓✓ 1947 A thorough Chaplin effort, as he produced, directed, wrote, scored and starred. A prim and proper bank cashier in Paris marries and murders rich women in order to support his real wife and family. A mild scandal in its day, though second-thought pacifism and stale humor date it. A bomb upon release (leading Chaplin to shelve it for 17 years) and a cult item today, admired for both its flaws and complexity. Raye fearlessly chews scenery and croissants. Initially based upon a suggestion from Orson Welles. 123m/B VHS, Beta, LV. Charlie Chaplin, Martha Raye, Isobel Elsom, Mady Correll, Marilyn Nash, Irving Bacon, William Frawley, Allison Roddan, Robert Lewis; *D:* Charlie Chaplin; *W:* Charlie Chaplin. National Board of Review Awards '47: 10 Best Films of the Year; Nominations: Academy Awards '47: Best Original Screenplay.FOX

Monsieur Vincent ✓✓✓ 1948 True story of 17th century French priest who became St. Vincent de Paul. He forsakes worldly possessions and convinces members of the aristocracy to finance his charities for the less fortunate. Inspirational. In French with English subtitles or dubbed. 100m/B VHS, Beta. *FR* Pierre Fresnay, Lisa Delamare, Aime Clarimond; *D:* Maurice Cloche. Academy Awards '48: Best Foreign Language Film. HTV, MRV, DVT

Monsignor woof! 1982 (R) Callow, ambitious priest befriends mobsters and even seduces a nun while managing Vatican's business affairs. No sparks generated by Reeve and Bujold (who appears nude in one scene), and no real conviction related by most other performers. Absurd, ludicrous melodrama best enjoyed as unintentional comedy. Based on Jack Alain Leger's book. 121m/C VHS, Beta. Christopher Reeve, Fernando Rey, Genevieve Bujold, Jason Miller; *D:* Frank Perry; *W:* Abraham Polonsky, Wendell Mayes; *C:* Billy Williams; *M:* John Williams. USH

Monsignor Quixote ✓✓½ 1991 A small town priest takes on the persona of his ancestor, Don Quixote, and prepares to battle the evil he sees around him. Based on the novel by Graham Greene. 118m/C VHS. Alec Guinness, Ian Richardson, Graham Crowden, Maurice Denham, Philip Stone, Rosalie Crutchley, Valentine Pelka, Don Fellows, Leo McKern; *D:* Rodney Bennett. FCT

The Monster ♂♂♂ 1925 This silent horror film has all the elements that would become genre standards. A mad scientist (Chaney), working in an asylum filled with lunatics, abducts strangers to use in his fiendish experiments to bring the dead back to life. There's the obligatory dungeon and even a lovely heroine that needs rescuing. Great atmosphere and Chaney's usual spine-tingling performance. **86m/B VHS.** Lon Chaney Sr., Gertrude Olmsted, Johnny Arthur, Charles Sellon; **D:** Roland West. *FCT*

Monster ♂ 1978 (R) Bloodthirsty alien indiscriminately preys on gaggle of teens in wilds of civilization. Performers struggle with dialogue and their own self-esteem. **98m/C VHS, Beta.** Jim Mitchum, Diane McBain, Roger Clark, John Carradine, Phil Carey, Anthony Eisley, Keenan Wynn; **D:** Herbert L. Strock. *GHV, MRV*

The Monster ♂♂½ *Il Mostre* 1996 (R) Italian impresario of comedy Benigni co-wrote, directed and starred in this film that has become the highest grossing film in Italian history to date. Jaded American audiences, however, may find the broad comedy of errors all too familiar territory with Loris (Benigni) as a criminal Clouseau, an incompetent petty thief whom police mistake for a serial murderer on the loose. Cops install an attractive female detective (Braschi, Benigni's wife) in the sexually strained shyster's apartment to tempt him into striking again. Sight gags aplenty populate Benigni's highly physical performance, including: being pulled wildly around a garage attached to an out-of-control chainsaw; contending with a lit cigarette down his pants; and scores of pratfalls, all of which garner comparisons to American comedy phenom, Jim Carrey. French director and actor Blanc ("Dead Tired") is great as the loony police psychiatrist. **110m/C VHS.** *IT* Roberto Benigni, Nicoletta Braschi, Michel Blanc, Dominque Lavanant, Jean-Claude Brialy, Ivano Marescotti, Laurent Spielvogel, Massimo Girotti, Franco Mescolini; **D:** Roberto Benigni; **W:** Roberto Benigni, Vincenzo Cerami; **C:** Carlo Di Palma; **M:** Evan Lurie. *COL*

Monster a Go-Go! woof! 1965 Team of go-go dancers battle a ten-foot monster from outerspace whose mass is due to a radiation mishap. He can't dance, either. **70m/B VHS, Beta.** Phil Morton, June Travis, Bill Rebane, Sheldon Seymour; **D:** Herschell Gordon Lewis. *VCI*

The Monster and the Girl ♂♂½ 1941 It's the mob vs. the ape in this tale of revenge. Scott (Terry) discovers innocent sister Susan (Drew) is being lead down the path to prostitution by suave mobster Reed (Paige). But Reed manages to frame Scott for murder and he's executed, although not before donating his brain to science. Then scientist Parry (Zucco) decides to transplant the brain into the body of an ape who goes on a rampage aimed at the mobster. **65m/B VHS, Closed Caption.** Ellen Drew, Robert Paige, Phillip Terry, Paul Lukas, Joseph Calleia, Onslow Stevens, Rod Cameron, George Zucco, Marc Lawrence, Gerald Mohr; **D:** Stuart Heisler; **W:** Stuart Anthony; **C:** Victor Milner. *USH*

The Monster Club ♂♂ 1985 Price and Carradine star in this music-horror compilation, featuring songs by Night, B.A. Robertson, The Pretty Things and The Viewers. Soundtrack music by John Williams, UB 40 and The Expressos. **104m/C VHS, Beta, LV.** *GB* Vincent Price, Donald Pleasence, John Carradine, Stuart Whitman, Britt Ekland, Simon Ward, Patrick Magee; **D:** Roy Ward Baker. *LIV*

The Monster Demolisher ♂♂ 1960 Nostradamus' descendent shares the family penchant for sanguine cocktails, and threatens a professor who protects himself with an electronic wonder of modern technology. Edited from a sombrero serial; if you make it through this one, look up its Mexican siblings, "Curse of Nostradamus" and "Genie of Darkness." **?m/B VHS.** *MX* German Robles; **D:** Frederick Curiel. *NOS, LOO*

Monster Dog woof! 1982 A rock band is mauled, threatened, and drooled upon by an untrainable mutant canine. Rock star Cooper plays the leader of the band. No plot, but the German shepherd is worth watching. **88m/C VHS, Beta.** Alice Cooper, Victoria Vera; **D:** Clyde Anderson. *TWE*

Monster from Green Hell ♂ 1958 An experimental rocket containing radiation-contaminated wasps crashes in Africa, making giant killer wasps that run amok. Stinging big bug horror. **71m/B VHS, Beta.** Jim Davis, Robert Griffin, Barbara Turner, Eduardo Ciannelli; **D:** Kenneth Crane. *NOS, MRV, SNC*

Monster from the Ocean Floor ♂ *It Stalked the Ocean Floor; Monster Maker* 1954 An oceanographer in a deep-sea diving bell is threatened by a multi-tentacled creature. Roger Corman's first production. **66m/C VHS, Beta.** Anne Kimball, Stuart Wade; **D:** Wyott Ordung. *THV*

Monster High ♂ 1989 (R) Bloodthirsty alien indiscriminately preys on gaggle of teens in wilds of civilization. Even the people who made this one may not have seen it all the way through. **89m/C VHS, Beta, LV.** David Marriott, Dean Iandoli, Diana Frank, D.J. Kerzner; **D:** Rudiger Poe. *COL*

Monster in a Box ♂♂♂ 1992 (PG-13) Master storyteller Gray spins a wonderful tale about his life, including stories about his adventures at a Moscow film festival, a trip to Nicaragua, and his first experience with California earthquakes. Filled with wit, satire, and hilarity. Filmed before an audience, this is based on Gray's Broadway show of the same title. By the way, the monster in the box is a 1,900-page manuscript of his autobiography and the box in which he lugs it around. **88m/C VHS, LV, Closed Caption.** Spalding Gray; **D:** Nick Broomfield; **W:** Spalding Gray; **C:** Michael Coulter; **M:** Laurie Anderson. *NLC, COL, BTV*

Monster in the Closet ♂♂ 1986 (PG) A gory horror spoof about a rash of San Francisco murders that all take place inside closets. A news reporter and his scientist friend decide they will be the ones to protect California from the evil but shy creatures. From the makers of "The Toxic Avenger." **87m/C VHS, Beta, Closed Caption.** Donald Grant, Claude Akins, Denise DuBarry, Stella Stevens, Howard Duff, Henry Gibson, Jesse White, John Carradine; **D:** Bob Dahlin; **W:** Bob Dahlin. *ORI, WAR*

The Monster Maker ♂♂ 1944 Low-budget gland fest in which deranged scientist develops serum that inflates heads, feet, and hands. He recklessly inflicts others with this potion, then must contend with deformed victims while courting a comely gal. **65m/B VHS, Beta.** J. Carrol Naish, Ralph Morgan, Wanda McKay, Terry Frost; **D:** Sam Newfield. *NOS, MRV, SNC*

The Monster of London City ♂½ *Das Ungeheuer von London City* 1964 During a stage play about Jack the Ripper, murders occur paralleling those in the production. The lead actor finds himself to be the prime suspect. Lightweight horror from Germany. **87m/B VHS, Beta.** *GE* Hansjorg Felmy, Marianne Koch, Dietmar Schoenherr, Hans Nielsen; **D:** Edwin Zbonek. *SNC*

The Monster of Piedras Blancas woof! 1957 During a seaside festival, two fisherman are killed by a bloodthirsty oceanic critter with no respect for holidays. The fishing village is determined to find it and kill it. Low-budget, with amateurish effects and poor acting. **72m/B VHS.** Les Tremayne, Jeanne Carmen, Forrest Lewis; **D:** Irvin Berwick. *VDM, MRV, REP*

Monster on the Campus ♂♂½ 1959 Science-fiction thriller about the blood of a prehistoric fish turning college professor into murderous beast. Will the halls of Dunsfield University ever be safe again? **76m/B VHS, Closed Caption.** Arthur Franz, Joanna Moore, Judson Pratt, Nancy Walters, Troy Donahue; **D:** Jack Arnold; **W:** David Duncan. *USH*

The Monster Squad ♂♂½ 1987 (PG-13) Youthful monster enthusiasts find their community inundated by Dracula, Frankenstein creature, Wolf Man, Mummy, and Gill Man(!?!), who are all searching for a life-sustaining amulet. Somewhat different, but still somewhat mediocre. **82m/C VHS, Beta, LV.** Andre Gower, Stephen Macht, Tom Noonan, Duncan Regehr; **D:** Fred Dekker; **W:** Fred Dekker, Shane Black; **M:** Bruce Broughton. *LIV, VES*

The Monster That Challenged the World ♂♂½ 1957 Huge, ancient eggs are discovered in the Salton Sea and eventually hatch into killer, crustaceous caterpillars. Superior monster action. **83m/B VHS.** Tim Holt, Audrey Dalton, Hans Conried, Harlen Ward, Max Casey Adams Showalter, Mimi Gibson, Gordon Jones; **D:** Arnold Laven. *MGM, FRG, MLB*

The Monster Walks ♂♂ *The Monster Walked* 1932 A whodunit thriller, complete with stormy nights, suspicious cripples, weird servants, a screaming gorilla, and a spooky house. Not unique but entertaining. **60m/B VHS, Beta.** Rex Lease, Vera Reynolds, Mischa Auer, Willie Best; **D:** Frank Strayer. *SNC, NOS, CCB*

Monsters Crash the Pajama Party ♂♂ 1965 Mad scientist is discovered conducting weird experiments by a group of teens who enter a supposedly haunted house. This one was much better in the theater, because "monsters" would run through the audience and select a victim. Then the monsters and the victim would magically appear on the screen. Weird. **?m/C VHS.** Peter J. D'Noto; **D:** David L. Hewitt. *SNC*

Montana ♂♂½ 1990 (PG) Hoyce and Bess Guthrie are long-married and strong-willed ranchers who are at odds over the family ranch in Montana. He wants to sell the land to a power company for oil drilling but she wants to keep the land in the family. Made for cable television. **91m/C VHS, Beta, Closed Caption.** Gena Rowlands, Richard Crenna, Lea Thompson, Justin Deas, Elizabeth Berridge, Scott Coffey, Darren Dalton; **D:** William A. Graham; **W:** Larry McMurtry. *TTC, FCT*

Montana Belle ♂♂ 1952 A buxom bandit teams with the notorious Dalton Brothers before embarking on a life of reform. In the cardgame of life, Russell is always holding a pair. **81m/C VHS, Beta.** Jane Russell, George Brent, Scott Brady, Forrest Tucker, Andy Devine, Jack Lambert, John Litel, Ray Teal; **D:** Allan Dwan. *TTC*

Monte Carlo ♂♂ 1986 A sexy Russian woman aids the Allies by relaying important messages during WWII. Fun, made for television production featuring Collins at her seductive best. **200m/C VHS, Beta, Closed Caption.** Joan Collins, George Hamilton, Lisa Eilbacher, Lauren Hutton, Robert Carradine, Malcolm McDowell; **D:** Anthony Page. *VTR, NWV*

Monte Carlo Nights ♂½ 1934 Wrongly convicted murderer determines to prove his innocence even as he is tracked by police. **60m/B VHS, Beta.** Mary Brian, John Darrow, Kate Campbell, Robert Frazer, Astrid Allwyn, George "Gabby" Hayes, George Cleveland; **D:** William Nigh. *SNC*

Monte Walsh ♂♂♂ 1970 (PG) Aging cowboy sees declining of Old West, embarks on mission to avenge best friend's death. Subdued, moving western worthy of genre greats Marvin and Palance. Cinematographer Fraker proves himself a proficient director in this, his first venture. Based on Jack Schaefer's novel. **100m/C VHS, Beta, Closed Caption.** Lee Marvin, Jack Palance, Jeanne Moreau, Jim Davis, Mitchell Ryan; **D:** William A. Fraker; **W:** David Zelag Goodman; **M:** John Barry. *FOX*

Montenegro ♂♂♂½ *Montenegro—Or Pigs and Pearls* 1981 Offbeat, bawdy comedy details experiences of bored, possibly mad housewife who lands in a coarse, uninhibited ethnic community. To its credit, this film remains unpredictable to the end. And Anspach, an intriguing, resourceful—and attractive—actress, delivers what is perhaps her greatest performance. **97m/C VHS.** *SW* Susan Anspach, Erland Josephson; **D:** Dusan Makavejev; **W:** Dusan Makavejev. *FXL*

Monterey Pop 🎬🎬🎬½ **1968** This pre-Woodstock rock 'n roll festival in Monterey, California features landmark performances by some of the most popular sixties rockers. Compelling for the performances, and historically important as the first significant rock concert film. Appearances by Jefferson Airplane, Janis Joplin, Jimi Hendrix, Simon and Garfunkel, The Who, and Otis Redding. **72m/C VHS, Beta, LV, 8mm.** *MVD, COL*

A Month by the Lake 🎬🎬½ **1995 (PG)** Redgrave takes the plunge into highly familiar romantic comedy of the Proper English sort and glides effortlessly through this slow-moving but often charming adaptation of an H. E. Bates short story. Set in pre-WWII northern Italy, Miss Bentley (Redgrave) sets her spinster's eye on the somewhat wooden, but gradually warming, English Major Wilshaw (Fox). Petulant American nanny Thurman arrives to provide an arresting diversion for Wilshaw, while Gassman proves an unwitting pawn for Miss Bentley's game of "get the major." Touching and lighthearted performances, especially by heavyweight Redgrave, are complemented by glorious cinematography. **92m/C VHS, LV, Closed Caption.** Vanessa Redgrave, Edward Fox, Uma Thurman, Alida Valli, Alessandro Gassman, Carlo Cartier; *D:* John Irvin; *W:* Trevor Bentham; *C:* Pasquale De Santos; *M:* Nicola Piovani. Nominations: Golden Globe Awards '96: Best Actress—Musical/Comedy (Redgrave). *TOU*

A Month in the Country 🎬🎬🎬 **1987** The reverently quiet story of two British WWI veterans, one an archaeologist and the other a church painting restorer, who are working in a tiny village while trying to heal their emotional wounds. Based on the novel by J.L. Carr. **92m/C VHS, Beta, LV.** *GB* Colin Firth, Natasha Richardson, Kenneth Branagh, Patrick Malahide, Tony Haygarth, Jim Carter; *D:* Pat O'Connor; *W:* Simon Gray; *M:* Howard Blake. *ORI, WAR*

Monty Python and the Holy Grail 🎬🎬🎬½ **1975 (PG)** Britain's famed comedy band assaults the Arthurian legend in a cult classic replete with a Trojan rabbit and an utterly dismembered, but inevitably pugnacious, knight. Fans of manic comedy—and graphic violence—should get more than their fill here. **90m/C VHS, Beta, LV, 8mm.** *GB* Graham Chapman, John Cleese, Terry Gilliam, Eric Idle, Terry Jones, Michael Palin, Carol Cleveland, Connie Booth, Neil Innes, Patsy Kensit; *D:* Terry Gilliam, Terry Jones; *W:* Graham Chapman, John Cleese, Terry Gilliam, Eric Idle, Terry Jones, Michael Palin. *COL, SIG, TVC*

Monty Python Live at the Hollywood Bowl 🎬🎬🎬 **1982** The revered comedy group perform many of their most celebrated routines in this uproarious performance documentary. A must-see for all Python aficionados. **78m/C VHS, Beta, LV, Closed Caption.** *GB* Eric Idle, Michael Palin, John Cleese, Terry Gilliam, Terry Jones, Graham Chapman; *D:* Terry Hughes; *W:* John Cleese, Terry Gilliam; *M:* John Du Prez. *PAR*

Monty Python's Flying Circus 1971 The original classic irreverant BBC comedy series that introduced the gang of six comics to the world. Two episodes per tape. Four skits: "The Architect's Sketch," "The Naughty Chemist," "Ministry of Silly Walks," and "The Piranha Brothers." **60m/C VHS, Beta, LV.** *GB* Michael Palin, Graham Chapman, Eric Idle, John Cleese, Terry Jones, Terry Gilliam, Carol Cleveland, Connie Booth, Neil Innes; *D:* Ian MacNaughton. *MOV, PAR*

Monty Python's Life of Brian 🎬🎬🎬½ *Life of Brian* **1979 (R)** Often riotous spoof of Christianity tracks hapless peasant mistaken for the messiah in 32 A.D. Film reels from routine to routine, and only the most pious will remain unmoved by a chorus of crucifixion victims. Probably the group's most daring, controversial venture. **94m/C VHS, Beta, LV, Closed Caption.** *GB* Graham Chapman, John Cleese, Terry Gilliam, Eric Idle, Michael Palin, George Harrison, Terry Jones; *D:* Terry Jones; *W:* Graham Chapman, John Cleese, Terry Gilliam,

Eric Idle, Michael Palin, Terry Jones; *C:* Peter Biziou; *M:* Geoffrey Burgon. *PAR, SIG*

Monty Python's Parrot Sketch Not Included 1990 To celebrate their 20th anniversary, the crazy guys of Monty Python put together this collection of some of their funniest sketches. The parrot was pretty disappointed that he wasn't included. **75m/C VHS, LV, Closed Caption.** Graham Chapman, John Cleese, Terry Gilliam, Eric Idle, Terry Jones, Michael Palin. *PAR, SIG, TVC*

Monty Python's The Meaning of Life 🎬🎬🎬 **1983 (R)** Funny, technically impressive film conducts various inquiries into the most profound questions confronting humanity. Notable among the sketches here are a live sex enactment performed before bored schoolboys, a student-faculty rugby game that turns quite violent, and an encounter between a physician and a reluctant, untimely organ donor. Another sketch provides a memorable portrait of a glutton prone to nausea. And at film's end, the meaning of life is actually revealed. **107m/C VHS, Beta, LV.** *GB* Graham Chapman, John Cleese, Terry Gilliam, Eric Idle, Terry Jones, Michael Palin, Carol Cleveland; *D:* Terry Jones; *W:* Graham Chapman, John Cleese, Terry Gilliam, Eric Idle, Terry Jones, Michael Palin; *M:* John Du Prez. Cannes Film Festival '83: Grand Jury Prize. *USH, CCB, SIG*

The Moon and Sixpence 🎬🎬🎬 **1943** Stockbroker turns ambitious painter in this adaptation of W. Somerset Maugham's novel that was, in turn, inspired by the life of artist Paul Gauguin. Fine performance from Sanders. Filmed mainly in black and white, but uses color sparingly to great advantage. Compare this one to "Wolf at the Door," in which Gauguin is played by Donald Sutherland. **89m/B VHS.** George Sanders, Herbert Marshall, Steve Geray, Doris Dudley, Eric Blore, Elena Verdugo, Florence Bates, Albert Basserman, Heather Thatcher; *D:* Albert Lewin. Nominations: Academy Awards '43: Original Dramatic/Comedy Score. *MGM, IVY*

Moon 44 🎬🎬½ **1990 (R)** A space prison is overrun by thugs who terrorize their fellow inmates. Fine cast, taut pacing. Filmed in Germany. **102m/C VHS, LV, Closed Caption.** *GE* Malcolm McDowell, Lisa Eichhorn, Michael Pare, Stephen Geoffreys, Roscoe Lee Browne, Brian Thompson, Dean Devlin, Mechmed Yilmaz, Leon Rippy; *D:* Roland Emmerich. *LIV, IME, BTV*

Moon in Scorpio 🎬½ **1986** Three Vietnam-vet buddies go sailing and are attacked by the back-from-the-dead victims of a bloody war crime. **90m/C VHS, Beta.** John Phillip Law, Britt Ekland, William Smith; *D:* Gary Graver. *TWE*

Moon in the Gutter 🎬½ *La Lune Dans le Caniveau* **1983 (R)** In a ramshackle harbor town, a man searches despondently for the person who killed his sister years before. Various sexual liaisons and stevedore fights intermittently spice up the action. Nasty story that doesn't make much sense on film; adapted from a book by American pulp writer David Goodis. In French with English subtitles. **109m/C VHS, Beta.** *IT FR* Gerard Depardieu, Nastassia Kinski, Victoria Abril, Vittorio Mezzogiorno, Dominique Pinon; *D:* Jean-Jacques Beineix; *W:* Jean-Jacques Beineix; *C:* Philippe Rousselot. Cesar Awards '84: Best Art Direction/Set Decoration. *COL*

The Moon Is Blue 🎬🎬½ **1953** A young woman flaunts her virginity in this stilted adaptation of F. Hugh Herbert's play. Hard to believe that this film was once considered risque. Good performances, though, from Holden and Niven. **100m/B Beta, LV.** William Holden, David Niven, Maggie McNamara, Tom Tully; *D:* Otto Preminger. Golden Globe Awards '54: Best Actor—Musical/Comedy (Niven); Nominations: Academy Awards '53: Best Actress (McNamara), Best Film Editing, Best Song ("The Moon Is Blue"). *WAR*

Moon of the Wolf 🎬 **1972** A small town in bayou country is terrorized by a modern-day werewolf that rips its victims to shreds. Made-for-television. **74m/C VHS, Beta.** David Janssen, Barbara Rush, Bradford Dillman, John Beradino; *D:* Daniel Petrie. *WOV, GKK*

Moon over Harlem 🎬½ **1939** A musical melodrama about a widow who unwittingly marries a fast-talking gangster involved in the numbers racket. The film features 20 chorus girls, a choir, and a 60-piece orchestra. **67m/B VHS, Beta.** Bud Harris, Cora Green, Alec Lovejoy, Sidney Bechet; *D:* Edgar G. Ulmer. *FCT, DVT, NOS*

Moon over Miami 🎬🎬🎬 **1941** Manhunting trio meet their match in this engaging musical. A remake of 1938's "Three Blind Mice," this was later remade in 1946 as "Three Little Girls in Blue." ♫ Moon Over Miami; I've Got You All To Myself; What Can I Do For You?; Kindergarten Congo; You Started Something; Oh Me Oh Mi-Am-Mi; Solitary Seminole; Is That Good?; Loveliness and Love. **91m/C VHS, Beta, Closed Caption.** Don Ameche, Betty Grable, Robert Cummings, Carole Landis, Charlotte Greenwood, Jack Haley; *D:* Walter Lang; *W:* Mitch Glazer; *C:* Leon Shamroy. *FOX*

Moon over Parador 🎬🎬½ **1988 (PG-13)** An uneven comedy about a reluctant American actor who gets the role of his life when he gets the chance to pass himself off as the recently deceased dictator of a Latin American country. A political strongman wants to continue the charade until he can take over, but the actor begins to enjoy the benefits of dictatorship. Look for a cameo by director/writer Mazursky in drag. **103m/C VHS, Beta, LV.** Richard Dreyfuss, Sonia Braga, Raul Julia, Jonathan Winters, Fernando Rey, Ed Asner, Dick Cavett, Michael Greene, Sammy Davis Jr., Polly Holliday, Charo, Marianne Saegebrecht, Dana Delany, Ike Pappas; *Cameos:* Paul Mazursky; *D:* Paul Mazursky; *W:* Leon Capetanos, Paul Mazursky; *M:* Maurice Jarre. *USH*

Moon Pilot 🎬🎬 **1962** An astronaut on his way to the moon encounters a mysterious alien woman who claims to know his future. **98m/C VHS, Beta.** Tom Tryon, Brian Keith, Edmond O'Brien, Dany Saval, Tommy Kirk; *D:* James Neilson. *DIS*

The Moon-Spinners 🎬🎬 **1964 (PG)** Lightweight Disney drama featuring Mills as a young tourist traveling through Crete who meets up with a young man, accused of being a jewel thief, and the two work together to find the real jewel thieves. Watch for silent film star Pola Negri. **118m/C VHS, Beta.** Hayley Mills, Peter McEnery, Eli Wallach, Pola Negri; *D:* James Neilson. *DIS, OM*

The Moon Stallion 🎬🎬½ **1985** A charming tale of mystery and fantasy for children and adults. Professor Purwell is researching King Arthur. His blind daughter soon becomes involved with supernatural events and a white horse that appears to lead her into adventures not of this age. **95m/C VHS.** *GB* Sarah Sutton, David Haig, James Greene, John Abineri, Caroline Goodall; *D:* Dorothea Brooking. *VCO, HMV*

Mooncussers 🎬½ **1962** A children's film detailing the exploits of a precocious 12-year-old determined to exact revenge upon a band of ruthless pirates. **85m/C VHS, Beta.** Kevin Corcoran, Rian Garrick, Oscar Homolka; *D:* James Neilson. *DIS*

Moonfleet 🎬🎬½ **1955** Follows the adventures of an 18th century buccaneer who tries to swindle a young lad in his charge of a valuable diamond. From J. Meade Falkner's novel. **89m/C VHS, LV.** Stewart Granger, Jon Whiteley, George Sanders, Viveca Lindfors, Joan Greenwood, Ian Wolfe; *D:* Fritz Lang; *M:* Miklos Rozsa. *MGM*

Moonlight and Valentino 🎬🎬 **1995 (R)** To help her recover from the death of her husband, Rebecca turns to the comfort of flaky neighbor Sylvie (Goldberg), self-destructive sis Lucy (Paltrow) and overbearing ex-stepmother Alberta (Turner). Together they sit around and talk some of the more contrived and clichéd "women talk" ("Chicken soup is the most womanly thing on the face of the planet") in recent film history. The finale, a hokey ritual in a cemetery, will have you pulling out hair rather than hankies. Rock star Bon Jovi makes his screen debut as the beefcake (discussion of his butt takes up about two-thirds of the dialogue) who puts the fire back into Rebecca's life. Not for the estrogen impaired. **CW:** Brief strong language. **104m/C VHS, LV.** Elizabeth Perkins, Whoopi Goldberg, Gwyneth Paltrow, Kathleen Turner, Jon Bon Jovi, Jeremy Sisto, Josef Sommer, Peter Coyote; **D:** David Anspaugh; **W:** Ellen Simon; **C:** Julio Macat; **M:** Howard Shore. *PGV*

Moonlight Sonata 🐾🐾½ 1938 Professional concert pianist Paderewski performs his way through a confusing soap-opera of a film. Includes performances of Franz Liszt's "Second Hungarian Rhapsody" and Frederic Chopin's "Polonaise." **80m/B VHS.** *GB* Ignace Jan Paderewski, Charles Farrell, Marie Tempest, Barbara Greene, Eric Portman; **D:** Lothar Mendes. *NOS, DVT*

Moonlighting 🐾🐾🐾½ 1982 (PG) Compelling drama about Polish laborers illegally hired to renovate London flat. When their country falls under martial law, the foreman conceals the event and pushes workers to complete project. Unlikely casting of Irons as foreman is utterly successful. **97m/C VHS, Beta, LV.** *PL GB* Jeremy Irons, Eugene Lipinski, Jiri Stanislav, Eugeniusz Haczkiewicz; **D:** Jerzy Skolimowski; **C:** Tony Pierce-Roberts; **M:** Hans Zimmer. *USH*

Moonlighting 🐾🐾🐾½ 1985 The television-pilot for the popular detective show, where Maddie and David, the daffy pair of impetuous private eyes, meet for the first time and solve an irrationally complex case. **93m/C VHS, Beta, Closed Caption.** Cybill Shepherd, Bruce Willis, Allyce Beasley; **D:** Robert Butler. *WAR, OM*

The Moonraker 🐾🐾½ 1958 Compelling action scenes highlight this tale set at the end of the English Civil War, as the Royalists attempt to sneak the king out of England and into France. **82m/C VHS.** *GB* George Baker, Sylvia Syms, Peter Arne, Marius Goring, Clive Morton, Gary Raymond, Richard Leech, Patrick Troughton; **D:** David MacDonald. *NOS*

Moonraker 🐾🐾 1979 (PG) Uninspired Bond fare has 007 unraveling intergalactic hijinks. Bond is aided by a female CIA agent, assaulted by a giant with jaws of steel, and captured by Amazons when he sets out to protect the human race. Moore, Chiles, and Lonsdale all seem to be going through the motions only. **136m/C VHS, Beta, LV, Closed Caption.** *GB* Roger Moore, Lois Chiles, Richard Kiel, Michael Lonsdale, Corinne Clery, Geoffrey Keen, Emily Bolton, Michael Gothell, Bernard Lee, Lois Maxwell, Desmond Llewelyn; **D:** Lewis Gilbert; **M:** John Barry. *MGM, TLF*

Moonrise 🐾🐾 1948 A melodramatic tale about the son of an executed murderer who becomes the object of derision in the small town where he lives. One tormentor finally attacks him, and the young man must make a split-second decision that may affect his own mortality. **90m/B VHS, LV.** Dane Clark, Gail Russell, Ethel Barrymore, Allyn Joslyn, Harry (Henry) Morgan, Lloyd Bridges, Selena Royle, Rex Ingram, Harry Carey Jr.; **D:** Frank Borzage. Nominations: Academy Awards '48: Best Sound. *REP*

The Moon's Our Home 🐾🐾½ 1936 A fast-paced, breezy, screwball comedy about an actress and adventurer impulsively marrying and then bickering through the honeymoon. Silliness at its height. Fonda and Sullavan were both married and then divorced before filming this movie. **80m/B VHS, Beta.** Margaret Sullavan, Henry Fonda, Beulah Bondi, Charles Butterworth, Margaret Hamilton, Walter Brennan; **D:** William A. Seiter; **C:** Joseph Valentine. *BAR*

Moonshine County Express 🐾½ 1977 (PG) Three sexy daughters of a hillbilly moonshiner set out to run the still and avenge their father's murder. **97m/C VHS, Beta.** John Saxon, Susan Howard, William Conrad, Morgan Woodward, Claudia Jennings, Jeff Corey, Dub Taylor, Maureen McCormick, Albert Salmi, Candice Rialson; **D:** Gus Trikonis. *WAR*

Moonshine Highway 🐾🐾 1996 (PG-13) Redneck alert! '50s Tennessee moonshiner Jed Muldoon (MacLachlan) clashes with Sheriff Miller (Quaid), who's not only aggrieved about Jed's illegal liquor running but is not happy that his estranged wife Ethel (Del Mar) has taken up with the miscreant. Lots of backwoods car chases. Made for cable. **CW:** Some scenes of violence. **96m/C VHS, Beta, Closed Caption.** Kyle MacLachlan, Randy

Quaid, Maria Del Mar, Gary Farmer, Jeremy Ratchford; **D:** Andy Armstrong; **W:** Andy Armstrong; **C:** Dick Quinlan. *PAR*

Moonshine Mountain woof! *White Trash on Moonshine Mountain* 1964 A country-western star travels with his girlfriend to the singer's home in backwoods Carolina. When the girl is killed by a lusting resident, all hell breaks loose. One of gore-meister Lewis' excursions into the dramatic. **90m/C VHS, Beta.** Chuck Scott, Adam Sorg, Jeffrey Allen, Bonnie Hinson, Carmen Sotir, Ben Moore, Pat Patterson, Mark Douglas; **D:** Herschell Gordon Lewis. *SNC*

Moonstruck 🐾🐾🐾½ 1987 (PG-13) Winning romantic comedy about widow engaged to one man but falling in love with his younger brother in Little Italy. Excellent performances all around, with Cher particularly fetching as attractive, hapless widow. Unlikely casting of usually dominating Aiello, as unassuming mama's boy also works well, and Cage is at his best as a tormented one-handed opera lover/baker. **103m/C VHS, Beta, LV, Closed Caption.** Cher, Nicolas Cage, Olympia Dukakis, Danny Aiello, Vincent Gardenia, Julie Bovasso, Louis Guss, Anita Gillette, Feodor Chaliapin Jr, John Mahoney; **D:** Norman Jewison; **W:** John Patrick Shanley; **C:** David Watkin. Academy Awards '87: Best Actress (Cher), Best Original Screenplay, Best Supporting Actress (Dukakis); Berlin International Film Festival '87: Best Director (Jewison); Golden Globe Awards '88: Best Actress—Musical/Comedy (Cher), Best Supporting Actress (Dukakis); Los Angeles Film Critics Association Awards '87: Best Supporting Actress (Dukakis); National Board of Review Awards '87: Best Supporting Actress (Dukakis); Writers Guild of America '87: Best Original Screenplay; Nominations: Academy Awards '87: Best Director (Jewison), Best Picture, Best Supporting Actor (Gardenia). *MGM, BTV, HMV*

Moontrap 🐾🐾 1989 An astronaut discovers an alien frozen in space and returns to Earth with it. Once thawed, the creature reveals its horrible secret. **92m/C VHS, LV.** Walter Koenig, Bruce Campbell, Leigh Lombardi; **D:** Robert Dyke. *MOV, IME*

Morals for Women 🐾½ 1931 This soap-opera's so old it almost predates soap. A secretary becomes the Kept Woman of her boss in the Big Bad City. She escapes, but not for long. **65m/B VHS.** Bessie Love, Conway Tearle, John Holland, Natalie Moorhead, Emma Dunn, June Clyde; **D:** Mort Blumenstock. *NOS, LOO*

Moran of the Lady Letty 🐾🐾½ 1922 Seaweed saga of Ramon Laredo (Valentino), a high society guy who's kidnapped aboard a pirate barge. When the salty dogs rescue/capture Moran (a theme ahead of its time?) from a ship fuming with burning coal, Ramon is smitten in a big way with the boyish girl and battles contagiously to prevent the pirates from selling her as a slave. Excellent fight scenes with much hotstepping over gangplanks and swinging from masts, with a 60-foot death dive from above. Little known Dalton was a celluloid force in the 'teens and twenties, and Valentino is atypically cast as a man's man. The sheik himself is said not to have like this one because it undermined his image as a ladies' man. **71m/B VHS, Beta.** Dorothy Dalton, Rudolph Valentino, Charles Brinley, Walter Long, Emil Jorgenson; **D:** George Melford. *GPV, FCT*

More 🐾🐾½ 1969 Smells like teen angst in the sixties when a German college grad falls for an American in Paris, to the tune of sex, drugs, and Pink Floyd. Schroeder's first effort as director, it's definitely a sixties pic. In French with English subtitles. **110m/C VHS, Beta.** Mimsy Farmer, Klaus Grunberg, Heinz Engelmann, Michel Chanderli; **D:** Barbet Schroeder; **C:** Nestor Almendros. *WAR, BTV, FCT*

More American Graffiti 🐾½ 1979 (PG) Sequel to 1973's acclaimed '50s homage "American Graffiti" charts various characters' experiences in the more radical '60s. George Lucas didn't direct, Richard Dreyfuss didn't reprise. Ron Howard doesn't direct, he acts. B.W.L. Norton doesn't direct either, though he's credited. Pass on this one and have that root canal done instead. **111m/C VHS, LV, Closed Caption.** Candy Clark, Bo Hopkins, Ron Howard, Paul LeMat, MacKenzie Phillips, Charles

Martin Smith, Anna Bjorn, Richard Bradford, Cindy Williams, Scott Glenn; **D:** Bill W.L. Norton; **C:** Caleb Deschanel. *USH*

More! Police Squad 1982 More episodes from the seminal spoof of television cop shows, episodes entitled "Revenge and Remorse," "The Butler Did It" and "Testimony of Evil." **75m/C VHS, Beta, LV.** Leslie Nielsen, Alan North, Rex Hamilton, Peter Lupus. *PAR*

The More the Merrier 🐾🐾🐾 1943 Likeable romantic comedy in which working girl must share apartment with two bachelors in Washington, D.C., during WWII. Arthur is especially endearing as a young woman in male company. **104m/B VHS, Beta, LV.** Joel McCrea, Jean Arthur, Charles Coburn, Richard Gaines, Bruce (Herman Brix) Bennett, Ann Savage, Ann Doran, Frank Tully, Grady Sutton; **D:** George Stevens. Academy Awards '43: Best Supporting Actor (Coburn); New York Film Critics Awards '43: Best Director (Stevens); Nominations: Academy Awards '43: Best Actress (Arthur), Best Director (Stevens), Best Picture, Best Screenplay, Best Story. *COL, BTV*

More Wild, Wild West 🐾🐾 1980 Another feature-length continuation of the satirical television western series, with Winters taking on Conrad and Martin. Made for television. **94m/C VHS, Beta.** Robert Conrad, Ross Martin, Jonathan Winters, Victor Buono; **D:** Burt Kennedy. *FOX*

Morgan! 🐾🐾½ *Morgan: A Suitable Case for Treatment; A Suitable Case for Treatment* 1966 Offbeat comedy in which deranged artist copes with divorce by donning ape suit. Some laughs ensue. Based on David Mercer's play. **93m/B VHS, Beta, LV.** *GB* Vanessa Redgrave, David Warner, Robert Stephens, Irene Handl, Bernard Bresslaw, Arthur Mullard, Newton Blick, Nan Munro, Graham Crowden, John Rae, Peter Collingwood, Edward Fox; **D:** Karel Reisz; **W:** David Mercer. British Academy Awards '66: Best Screenplay; Cannes Film Festival '66: Best Actress (Redgrave); Nominations: Academy Awards '66: Best Actress (Redgrave), Best Costume Design (B & W). *HMV*

Morgan Stewart's Coming Home 🐾 *Home Front* 1987 (PG-13) When Dad needs a good family image in his political race, he brings Morgan home from boarding school. Fortunately, Morgan can see how his parents are using him and he doesn't approve at all. He decides to turn his family's life upside down while pursuing the love of his life. **96m/C VHS, Beta, LV.** Jon Cryer, Lynn Redgrave, Nicholas Pryor, Viveka Davis, Paul Gleason, Andrew Duncan, Savely Kramorov, John Cullum, Robert Sedgwick, Waweru Njenga, Sudhir Rad; **D:** Alan Smithee; **M:** Peter Bernstein. *NO*

Morgan the Pirate 🐾🐾 *Capitaine Morgan; Morgan il Pirata* 1960 Steve Reeves is at his finest as Morgan, an escaped slave who becomes a notorious pirate in the Caribbean and is wrongly condemned to death in this brisk, sea-going adventure. **93m/C VHS, Beta, LV.** *FR IT* Steve Reeves, Valerie Lagrange; **D:** Andre de Toth. *FCT*

Morituri 🐾🐾🐾 *Saboteur: Code Name Morituri; The Saboteur* 1965 Gripping wartime drama in which an Allied spy tries to persuade German gunboat captain to surrender his vessel. Brando is—no surprise—excellent. **123m/C VHS, Beta, Closed Caption.** Marlon Brando, Yul Brynner, Trevor Howard, Janet Margolin, Wally Cox, William Redfield; **D:** Bernhard Wicki; **W:** Daniel Taradash; **C:** Conrad Hall; **M:** Jerry Goldsmith. Nominations: Academy Awards '65: Best Black and White Cinematography, Best Costume Design (B & W). *FOX*

Mork & Mindy 1978 Williams struts his comedic stuff in this 1978-1981 sitcom as a mixed-up alien from the planet Ork who lands in Boulder, Colorado and manages to convince Mindy McConnell (Dawber) to let him stay with her while he studies human behavior (and tries to adapt). And a good "Nanu, nanu" to you too! Two episodes per tape. **50m/C VHS, Closed Caption.** Robin Williams, Pam Dawber, Conrad Janis. *PAR*

A Mormon Maid 🐾½ 1917 Young woman and her family, after being saved from an Indian attack by a Mormon group, come to live among them without converting to their beliefs. Considered a shocking expose of controversial Mormon practices, including polygamy. **78m/B VHS, Beta.** Mae Murray, Frank Borzage, Hobart Bosworth, Noah Beery Sr.; *D:* Robert Z. Leonard. *VYY, GVV*

The Morning After ♂♂ 1986 (R) A predictable suspense-thriller about an alcoholic actress who wakes up one morning with a corpse in bed next to her, but cannot remember anything about the night before. She evades the police, accidentally meets up with an ex-cop, and works with him to unravel an increasingly complicated mystery. **103m/C VHS, Beta, LV, Closed Caption.** Jane Fonda, Jeff Bridges, Raul Julia, Diane Salinger, Richard Foronjy, Geoffrey Scott, Kathleen Wilhoite, Frances Bergen, Rick Rossovich, Kathy Bates; *D:* Sidney Lumet; *W:* James Cresson; *C:* Andrzej Bartkowiak. Nominations: Academy Awards '86: Best Actress (Fonda).*ORI, WAR*

Morning Glory ♂♂½ 1933 Small-town girl finds love and fame in the big city. Predictable fare nonetheless boasts fine performances from Hepburn and Fairbanks. Adapted from Zoe Atkins' stage play. **74m/B VHS, Beta, LV.** Katharine Hepburn, Douglas Fairbanks Jr., Adolphe Menjou, Mary Duncan; *D:* Lowell Sherman; *M:* Max Steiner. Academy Awards '33: Best Actress (Hepburn). *CCB, MED, BTV*

Morning Glory ♂♂½ 1993 (PG-13) Sappy romance, set during the Depression, about a pregnant widow (Raffin) trying to survive on her hardscrabble farm in Georgia. Elly Dinsmore advertises for a husband, not for romance but to help with the work, and is answered by Will Parker (Reeve), an ex-con trying to live down his past. When a local floozy who has been eyeing Will is killed the sheriff (Walsh) is only too happy to go after the stranger in town. Light-weight with some unbelievable plot twists. Based on the novel "Morning Glory" by LaVyrle Spencer.*CW:* Sex-related scene. **90m/C VHS.** Deborah Raffin, Christopher Reeve, Lloyd Bochner, Nina Foch, Helen Shaver, J.T. Walsh; *D:* David Hillard Stern; *W:* Deborah Raffin, Charles Jarrott; *M:* Jonathan Elias. *ACA*

Morocco ♂♂♂½ 1930 A foreign legion soldier falls for a world-weary chanteuse along the desert sands. Cooper has never been more earnest, and Dietrich has never been more blase and exotic. In her American film debut, Dietrich sings "What am I Bid?" A must for anyone drawn to improbable, gloriously well-done kitsch. Based on Benno Vigny's novel "Amy Jolly." **92m/B VHS, Beta, LV.** Marlene Dietrich, Gary Cooper, Adolphe Menjou, Ullrich Haupt, Francis McDonald, Eve Southern, Paul Porcasi; *D:* Josef von Sternberg; *C:* Lee Garmes. Nominations: Academy Awards '31: Best Actress (Dietrich), Best Cinematography, Best Director (von Sternberg), Best Interior Decoration. *USH, FCT*

Morons from Outer Space ♂♂ 1985 (PG) Slow-witted aliens from elsewhere in the universe crash onto Earth, but unlike other sci-fis, these morons become internationally famous, despite them acting like intergalactic stooges. Plenty of sight gags. **87m/C VHS.** *GB* Griff Rhys Jones, Mel Smith, James B. Sikking, Dinsdale Landen, Jimmy Nail, Joanne Pearce, Paul Brown; *D:* Mike Hodges; *C:* Phil Meheux; *M:* Peter Brewis. *MGM*

Mortal Danger ♂♂½ *Turn Your Pony Around* 1994 (PG-13) Kathy and Phil are suicidal teens finding different solutions to their difficulties over the same weekend. Comes across like a TV movie but does maintain an honest message with affecting performances.*CW:* Language and drug & alcohol abuse, suicide. **86m/C VHS, LV, Closed Caption.** Ami Dolenz, Noah Hathaway, Paul Coufos, Larry Gatlin, Charles Napier; *D:* Brianne Murphy. *IMP, BPG*

Mortal Kombat 1: The Movie ♂♂ 1995 (PG-13) Inevitable film version of mega popular arcade game intended to cash in fast on the game's popularity. Shameless nirvana for youngin's with permanent joystick scars on their hands. Grown-ups forced to sit through it may get into some of the eye-popping special effects and nifty martial arts sequences if they can block out the contrived plot, lame acting, and Lambert's presence as Thunder God.*CW:* Martial arts combat. **101m/C VHS, Closed Caption, DVD.** Christopher

Lambert, Talisa Soto, Cary-Hiroyuki Tagawa, Brigitte Wilson; *D:* Paul Anderson. *NLC*

Mortal Passions ♂½ 1990 (R) Another "Double Indemnity" rip-off, with a scheming tramp manipulating everyone around her with betrayal, sex, and murder. Her dead husband's brother eventually ignites old flames to steer her away from his money. **96m/C VHS, Beta, Closed Caption.** Zach Galligan, Krista Errickson, Michael Bowen, Luca Bercovici, Sheila Kelley, David Warner; *D:* Andrew Lane. *FOX*

Mortal Sins ♂ 1990 (R) A TV evangelist finds more than salvation at the altar, when bodies begin to turn up. The detective he hires is close-mouthed, but more than a little interested in the preacher's daughter. A tense psycho-sexual thriller. **85m/C VHS.** Brian Benben, Anthony LaPaglia, Debrah Farentino; *D:* Yuri Sivo. *ACA, FXV*

Mortal Sins ♂♂ 1992 (PG-13) Reeve stars as parish priest Thomas Cusack, who hears the confession of a serial killer. What's worse is that the killer is preying on the women of Cusack's parish. Since he can't break the seal of the confessional, the good Father tries to stop the killer himself before another murder takes place.*CW:* Violence. **93m/C VHS, LV, Closed Caption.** Christopher Reeve; *D:* Bradford May. *FXV*

The Mortal Storm ♂♂♂½ 1940 Phyllis Bottome's famous novel comes to life in this extremely well acted film about the rise of the Nazi regime. Stewart and Sullavan are young lovers who risk everything to escape the country after their families are torn apart by the Nazi takeover. Although Germany is never identified as the country, it is obvious in this story about the early days of WWII. Hitler took one look at this and promptly banned all MGM movies in Nazi Germany. **100m/B VHS.** Margaret Sullavan, James Stewart, Robert Young, Frank Morgan, Robert Stack, Bonita Granville, Irene Rich; *D:* Frank Borzage; *W:* Claudine West, George Froeschel, Anderson Ellis; *C:* William H. Daniels. *MGM*

Mortal Thoughts ♂♂½ 1991 (R) Best friends find their relationship tested when the brutal husband of one of them is murdered. Moore and Headly are exceptional, capturing the perfect inflections and attitudes of the hard-working New Jersey beauticians sure of their friendship. Excellent pacing, fine supporting cast, with Keitel and Willis stand-outs.*CW:* Strong language and momentary violence and drug content. **104m/C VHS, Beta, LV, 8mm, Closed Caption.** Demi Moore, Bruce Willis, Glenne Headly, Harvey Keitel, John Pankow, Billie Neal; *D:* Alan Rudolph; *W:* William Reilly, Claude Kerven; *C:* Elliot Davis; *M:* Mark Isham. National Society of Film Critics Awards '91: Best Supporting Actor (Keitel). *COL*

Mortuary ♂ 1981 (R) Young woman's nightmares come startlingly close to reality. **91m/C VHS, Beta.** Christopher George, Lynda Day George, Paul Smith; *D:* Howard (Hikmet) Avedis; *W:* Howard (Hikmet) Avedis. *LIV, VES*

Mortuary Academy ♂ 1991 (R) To win an inheritance two brothers must attend the family mortician school, a situation paving the way for aggressively tasteless jokes on necrophilia. An attempt to recapture the successful black humor of the earlier Bartel/Woronov teaming "Eating Raoul," this one's dead on arrival. **86m/C VHS, LV.** Christopher Atkins, Perry Lang, Paul Bartel, Mary Woronov, Tracey Walter, Lynn Danielson, Cesar Romero, Wolfman Jack; *D:* Michael Schroeder. *COL*

The Mosaic Project ♂½ 1995 (R) Action junkies should be happy with the chases, explosions, and other mayhem engendered by this story of two buddies who find themselves the victims of a mad scientist. Now they have experimental computer chips implanted in their brains that make them skilled in 25 martial arts forms (and some other stuff that doesn't matter much).*CW:* Language, sexual situations, violence. **89m/C VHS.** Jon Tabler, Ben Marley, Joe Estevez; *D:* John Sjogren; *W:* John Sjogren. *MNC*

Mosby's Marauders ♂♂ 1966 A young boy joins a Confederate raiding company during the Civil War and learns about bravery, war, and love. **79m/C VHS, Beta.** Kurt Russell, James MacArthur, Jack Ging, Peggy Lipton, Nick Adams; *D:* Michael O'Herlihy. *DIS*

Moscow Does Not Believe in Tears ♂♂♂ *Moscow Distrusts Tears; Moskwa Sljesam Nje Jerit* 1980 Three Soviet women realize very different fates when they pursue their dreams in 1950's Moscow. Bittersweet, moving fare that seems a somewhat surprising production from pre-Glasnost USSR. Brief nudity and violence. In Russian with English subtitles. A 150-minute version has also been released. **115m/C VHS, Beta, LV.** *RU* Vera Alentova, Irina Muravyova, Raisa Ryazanova, Natalie Vavilova, Alexei Batalov; *D:* Vladimir Menshov. Academy Awards '80: Best Foreign Language Film. *COL, IME, KIV*

Moscow on the Hudson ♂♂♂ 1984 (R) Good-natured comedy has Williams as Soviet defector trying to cope with new life of freedom in fast-paced, freewheeling melting pot of New York City. Williams is particularly winning as naive jazzman, though Alonso also scores as his Hispanic love interest. Be warned though, it's not just played for laughs. **115m/C VHS, Beta, LV, 8mm, Closed Caption.** Robin Williams, Maria Conchita Alonso, Cleavant Derricks, Alejandro Rey, Elya Baskin; *D:* Paul Mazursky; *W:* Leon Capetanos, Paul Mazursky. *COL*

Moscow Parade ♂♂ *Prorva* 1992 Sexy cabaret singer gets caught up in the shifting alliances caused by war. Set in Russia before the Nazi invasion. Russian with subtitles. **103m/C VHS.** *RU* Ute Lemper, Vladimir Simonov; *D:* Ivan Dykhovichny. *FRF*

Moses woof! 1976 (PG) Lancaster goes biblical as Moses, the man with the tablets. Edited from the 360-minute British television series, with no improvement obvious from the economy, except that the bad parts are shorter. Poor chatter and scattered bouts of acting are surpassed in inadequacy only by special effects. **141m/C VHS, Beta.** Burt Lancaster, Anthony Quayle, Ingrid Thulin, Irene Papas, William Lancaster; *D:* Gianfranco DeBosio; *W:* Anthony Burgess, Vittorio Bonicelli; *M:* Ennio Morricone. *FOX, LIV, VES*

Moses ♂♂½ 1996 Another entry in TNT's series of Bible stories finds a humble Moses (Kingsley), raised in the Egyptian court, finding his way to his own people, the Israelites. Chosen by God to be his messenger and lead his people out of bondage, Moses must unleash a series of plagues upon Egypt before pharaoh Mernefta (Langella) will let them go. If you want action, look to "The Ten Commandments," since this is a faithful but tedious retelling. Filmed on location in Morocco; on two cassettes. **185m/C VHS.** Ben Kingsley, Frank Langella, David Suchet, Christopher Lee, Anna Galiena, Enrico Lo Verso, Geraldine McEwan, Maurice Roeves, Anthony Higgins, Anton Lesser; *D:* Roger Young; *W:* Lionel Chetwynd; *C:* Raffaele Mertes; *M:* Marco Frisina. *TTC*

Mosquito ♂ 1995 (R) Alien forces transform the annoying insects into monstrous mutants. Schlocky special effects are good for laughs.*CW:* Sci-fi violence and gore; scene of sexuality/nudity; some language. **92m/C VHS.** Gunnar Hansen, Ron Asheton, Steve Dixon, Rachel Loiselle, Tim Loveface; *D:* Gary Jones; *W:* Gary Jones, Steve Hodge, Tom Chaney; *C:* Tom Chaney; *M:* Allen Lynch, Randall Lynch. *HMD*

The Mosquito Coast ♂♂½ 1986 (PG) Ambitious adaptation of Paul Theroux's novel about an asocial inventor who transplants his family to a rainforest to realize his utopian dream. A nightmare ensues. Ford tries hard, but supporters Mirren and Phoenix are main appeal of only intermittently successful drama. **119m/C VHS, Beta, LV, Closed Caption.** Harrison Ford, Helen Mirren, River Phoenix, Andre Gregory, Martha Plimpton, Conrad Roberts, Butterfly McQueen, Jadrien Steele, Hilary Gordon, Rebecca Gordon, Dick O'Neill, Jason Alexander; *D:* Peter Weir; *W:* Paul Schrader; *C:* John Seale; *M:* Maurice Jarre. *WAR*

The Most Dangerous Game 🎬🎬🎬

The Hounds of Zaroff **1932** Shipwrecked McRae washed ashore on the island of Banks's Count Zaroff, a deranged sportsman with a flair for tracking humans. Guess who becomes the mad count's next target. Oft-told tale is compellingly related in this, the first of many using Richard Connell's famous short story. If deja vu sets in, don't worry. This production used much of the scenery, staff, and cast from its studio cousin, "King Kong." Remade in 1945 as "A Game of Death" and in 1956 as "Run for the Sun." **78m/B VHS, Beta.** Joel McCrea, Fay Wray, Leslie Banks, Robert Armstrong; *D:* Ernest B. Schoedsack, Irving Pichel; *M:* Max Steiner. *SNC, SNC, MED*

Most Wanted 🎬½

1976 A psychopath with a penchant for raping nuns and collecting crucifixes is tracked down by a special police unit in this made-for-television film. Became a TV series. **78m/C VHS, Beta.** Robert Stack, Shelly Novack, Leslie Charleson, Tom Selleck, Sheree North; *D:* Walter Grauman. *WOV*

Motel Hell 🎬½

1980 (R) A completely tongue-in-cheek gore-fest about a farmer who kidnaps tourists, buries them in his garden, and reaps a human harvest to grind into his distinctive brand of smoked, preservative-free sausage. **102m/C VHS, Beta, LV.** Rory Calhoun, Nancy Parsons, Paul Linke, Nina Axelrod, Wolfman Jack, Elaine Joyce, Dick Curtis; *D:* Kevin Connor. *MGM*

Mother 🎬🎬🎬½

1926 Pudovkin's innovative classic about a Russian family shattered by the uprising in 1905. A masterpiece of Russian cinema that established Pudovkin, and rivaled only Eisenstein for supremacy in montage, poetic imagery, and propagandistic ideals. Based on Maxim Gorky's great novel, it's one of cinematic history's seminal works. Striking cinematography, stunning use of montage make this one important. Silent with English subtitles. **70m/B VHS, Beta.** *RU* Vera Baranovskaya, Nikolai Batalov; *D:* Vsevolod Pudovkin. *NOS, IHF, DVT*

Mother 🎬🎬🎬½

Okasan **1952** A Japanese family is undone after the devastation of WWII. An uncharacteristically dramatic, and thus more accessible, film from one of the Japanese cinema's greatest masters. In Japanese with English subtitles. **98m/B VHS, Beta, LV.** *JP* Kinuyo Tanaka, Kyoko Kagawa, Eiji Okada, Akihiko Katayama; *D:* Mikio Naruse. *FCT, IME*

Mother 🎬🎬½

1994 (R) Olivia Hendrix (Ladd) is a very over-protective mom—even though son Tom (Weisser) is nineteen and anxious to untie the apron strings. But Mom thinks she knows best and she's willing to kill to made certain Tom stays home where he belongs.*CW:* Implied violence, language. **90m/C VHS, LV.** Diane Ladd, Olympia Dukakis, Morgan Weisser, Ele Keats; *D:* Frank Laloggia. *TRI*

Mother 🎬🎬½

1996 (PG-13) Yes, you will shake your head in recognition of that parent-child bond. Twice-divorced writer John Henderson (Brooks) decides it all Mom's fault he has problems with women, so he decides to move back home and figure out what went wrong. Mom Beatrice (Reynolds) is exasperated and married younger brother Jeff (Morrow) winds up jealous of mom's attentions to his sibling. Reynolds' first feature film in 25 years.*CW:* Some sexual references. **104m/C VHS, Closed Caption.** Albert Brooks, Debbie Reynolds, Rob Morrow, Lisa Kudrow, John C. McGinley, Isabel Glasser, Peter White; *D:* Albert Brooks; *W:* Albert Brooks, Monica Johnson; *C:* Lajos Koltai; *M:* Marc Shaiman. New York Film Critics Awards '96: Best Screenplay; National Society of Film Critics Awards '96: Best Screenplay; Nominations: Golden Globe Awards '97: Best Actress—Musical/Comedy (Reynolds). *PAR*

Mother & Daughter: A Loving War 🎬½

1980 A made-for-television film about three women experiencing motherhood. Special appearance by Harry Chapin as himself. **96m/C VHS, Beta.** Tuesday Weld, Frances Sternhagen, Kathleen Beller, Jeanne Lang, Ed Winter; *D:* Burt Brinckerhoff. *NLC*

Mother and Son 🎬🎬

1931 Melodrama finds the wayward Young shielding her son from the fact that she runs a gambling hall. He grows up to be a society lad before discovering the devastating truth. **67m/B VHS.** Clara Kimball Young, Bruce Warren, Mildred Golden, John Elliott, Gordon Wood, Ernest Hilliard; *D:* John P. McCarthy. *GPV*

Mother Doesn't Always Know Best 🎬½

1967 A strange relationship between a young count and his widowed mother initiates a strange series of events. **95m/C VHS, Beta.** Senta Berger; *D:* Alfredo Gianelli. *NO*

Mother Goose Rock 'n' Rhyme 🎬🎬

1990 Duvall follows the success of her "Faerie Tale Theatre" series with a new comedic fable, starring some of Hollywood's top names. Great fun for the whole family. **96m/C VHS, Beta, Closed Caption.** Shelley Duvall, Teri Garr, Howie Mandel, Jean Stapleton, Ben Vereen, Bobby Brown, Art Garfunkel, Dan Gilroy, Deborah Harry, Cyndi Lauper, Little Richard, Paul Simon, Harry Anderson, Elayne Boosler, Woody Harrelson, Richard "Cheech" Marin, Garry Shandling. *MED*

Mother Joan of the Angels 🎬🎬🎬

The Devil and the Nun; Matka Joanna Od Aniolow **1960** A priest investigating demonic possession among nuns in a 17th-century Polish convent becomes involved in a mutual attraction with the Mother Superior. A powerful allegory complemented by the stylized narrative and performances. Polish with subtitles. Based on actual events at Loudun and also the subject of a play by John Whiting, an opera by Krzysztof Penderecki, "The Devils of Loudon" novel by Aldous Huxley, and Ken Russell's movie "The Devils." **108m/B VHS.** *PL* Lucyna Winnicka, Mieczyslaw Voit, Anna Ciepielewska, Maria Chwalibog; *D:* Jerzy Kawalerowicz; *W:* Jerzy Kawalerowicz, Tadeusz Konwicki; *M:* Adam Walacinski. Cannes Film Festival '61: Grand Jury Prize. *FCT*

Mother, Jugs and Speed 🎬½

1976 (PG) Black comedy about the day-to-day tragedies encountered by a group of ambulance drivers. Interesting mix of stars. **95m/C VHS.** Bill Cosby, Raquel Welch, Harvey Keitel, Allen (Goorwitz) Garfield, Larry Hagman, Bruce Davison, Dick Butkus, L.Q. Jones, Toni Basil; *D:* Peter Yates; *W:* Tom Mankiewicz. *FOX*

Mother Kusters Goes to Heaven 🎬🎬🎬

Mutter Kusters Fahrt Zum Himmel **1976** Mrs. Kusters's husband is a frustrated factory worker who goes over the edge and kills the factory owner's son and himself. Left alone, she learns that everyone is using her husband's death to further their own needs, including her daughter, who uses the publicity to enhance her singing career. A statement that you should trust no one, not even your family and friends. This film was banned from the Berlin Film Festival because of its political overtones. In German with English subtitles. **108m/C VHS.** *GE* Brigitte Mira, Ingrid Caven, Armin Meier, Irm Hermann, Gottfried John, Margit Carstensen, Karl-Heinz Boehm; *D:* Rainer Werner Fassbinder; *W:* Rainer Werner Fassbinder; *C:* Michael Ballhaus. *NYF*

Mother Lode 🎬½

Search for the Mother Lode; The Last Great Treasure **1982 (PG)** The violent conflict between twin brothers (played by Heston) is intensified by greed, near madness, and the all-consuming lust for gold in this action-adventure. Heston's son, Fraser Clarke Heston, wrote as well as produced the film. **101m/C VHS, Beta.** Charlton Heston, Nick Mancuso, Kim Basinger; *D:* Charlton Heston. *VES*

Mother Night 🎬🎬🎬

1996 (R) American writer Howard Campbell (Nolte) is recruited as a spy in pre-World War II Germany in this adaptation of Kurt Vonnegut's 1962 novel. He poses as a Nazi sympathizer in broadcasts to American troops, but his anti-semitic diatribes are actually coded information crucial to the Allies. After the war, Campbell's life unravels as he loses his young wife (Lee) and the U.S. government refuses to acknowledge his efforts. He is smuggled back to the U.S., where both Israeli Nazi-hunters and twisted neo-Nazis search for him. After being captured, imprisoned in Israel, and conversing with fellow prisoner Adolf Eichmann (Gibson), Campbell realizes the moral of this dark comedy: "We are what we pretend to be." Arkin is excellent as his Greenwich Village neighbor who also has some secrets. If you look closely, you can see author Vonnegut in a cameo.*CW:* Scene of sexuality. **113m/C VHS.** Nick Nolte, Sheryl Lee, Alan Arkin, John Goodman, Kirsten Dunst, David Strathairn, Arye Gross, Frankie Faison, Bernard Behrens; *D:* Keith Gordon; *W:* Robert B. Weide; *C:* Tom Richmond; *M:* Michael Convertino; *V:* Henry Gibson. *NLC*

Mother of Kings 🎬🎬

1982 Livin' ain't easy for a widowed charwoman thanks to WWII and Stalinism. Innovative use of newsreel scenes. In Polish with English subtitles. **126m/C VHS.** *PL* Magda Teresa Wojcik. *FCT*

Mother's Boys 🎬🎬

1994 (R) Estranged mother Curtis attempts to reunite with the family she abandoned only to be snubbed, inspiring in her a ruthless effort to win back the children and oust father Gallagher's new live-in girlfriend Whalley-Kilmer. With an almost psychotic devotion, she terrorizes everyone in the family, including enticing her 12-year-old son Edwards into a nude bathtub game of peek-a-boo. Film lacks the tension necessary to carry suspense. Based on the novel by Bernard Taylor.*CW:* Language and mother's sociopathic inclination. **96m/C VHS, LV, Closed Caption.** Jamie Lee Curtis, Peter Gallagher, Joanne Whalley, Luke Edwards, Vanessa Redgrave, Colin Ward, Joss Ackland, Paul Guilfoyle, John C. McGinley, J.E. Freeman, Ken Lerner, Lorraine Toussaint, Joey Zimmerman, Jill Freedman; *D:* Yves Simoneau; *W:* Richard Hawley, Barry Schneider; *C:* Elliot Davis; *M:* George S. Clinton. *MAX, TOU*

Mother's Day 🎬½

1980 Three women who were former college roommates plan a reunion together in the wilderness. All goes well until they are dragged into an isolated house by two insane boys who constantly watch television, ardently consume the products advertised, and then terrorize and torture people to please their mom. Sanitized gore with black satiric intentions. **98m/C VHS, Beta.** Tiana Pierce, Nancy Hendrickson, Deborah Luee, Holden McGuire, Billy Ray McQuade, Rose Ross; *D:* Charles Kaufman; *W:* Warren Leight, Charles Kaufman. *MED*

A Mother's Prayer 🎬🎬½

1995 (PG-13) Fact-based story about young mom Rosemary Holmstrom (Hamilton), who has AIDS, and is determined to find a home for her 8-year-old son T.J. (Fleiss) before she dies. Guaranteed to make the tear ducts flow, with a determined performance from Hamilton that lessens the sentimentality. Made for cable TV. Holmstrom died at the age of 36 in 1994.*CW:* Emotionally charged subject matter. **90m/C VHS, Closed Caption.** Linda Hamilton, Noah Fleiss, Bruce Dern, Kate Nelligan, S. Epatha Merkerson, Corey Parker, Jenny O'Hara, RuPaul; *D:* Larry Elikann; *W:* Lee Rose. *USH*

Mothra 🎬🎬

1962 Classic Japanese monster shenanigans about an enraged giant caterpillar that invades Tokyo while searching for the Ailenas, a set of very tiny, twin princesses who've been kidnapped by an evil nightclub owner in the pursuit of big profits. After tiring of crushing buildings and wreaking incidental havoc, the enormous crawly thing zips up into a cocoon and emerges as Mothra, a moth distinguished by both its size and bad attitude. Mothra and the wee babes make appearances in later Godzilla epics. **101m/C VHS, Beta.** *JP* Yumi Ito, Frankie Sakai, Lee Kresel, Emi Ito; *D:* Inoshiro Honda. *GKK*

Motor Patrol 🎬½

1950 A cop poses as a racketeer to infiltrate a car-stealing ring. **66m/B VHS, Beta, LV.** Don Castle, Jane Nigh, Charles Victor. *NO*

Motor Psycho woof!

1965 When a motorcycle gang rapes a woman, she and her husband pursue them into the desert to seek their brutal revenge. **73m/B VHS.** Haji, Alex Rocco, Stephen Oliver, Holle K. Winters, Joseph Cellini, Thomas Scott, Coleman Francis, Sharon Lee; *D:* Russ Meyer. *RMF*

Motorama 🐾🐾 1991 (R) A 10-year-old juvenile delinquent becomes obsessed with winning a gas station contest which involves collecting game cards. So he steals a car and hits the road where he gets his first tattoo and encounters a beautiful "older" woman (Barrymore) and lots of trouble. **CW:** Language and sensual scene. 89m/C VHS. Jordan Christopher Michael, Martha Quinn, Flea, Michael J. Pollard, Meat Loaf, Drew Barrymore, Garrett Morris, Robin Duke, Sandy Baron, Mary Woronov, Susan Tyrrell, John Laughlin, John Diehl, Robert Picardo, Jack Nance, Vince Edwards, Dick Miller, Allyce Beasley, Shelley Berman; **D:** Barry Shils; **W:** Joe Minion; **M:** Andy Summers. *COL, BTV*

Motorcycle Gang 🐾 1957 It's the summer of '57, and Randy plans to bring home the title at the Pacific Motorcycle Championships for his club, the "Skyriders." But first his old rival Nick, who's just out of jail, turns up and challenges Randy to an illegal street race. Will Randy succumb to peer pressure and race? Lame plot + lame acting = lame movie. 78m/B VHS. Steven Terrell, John Ashley, Anne Neyland, Carl "Alfalfa" Switzer, Raymond Hatton; **D:** Edward L. Cahn; **W:** Lou Rusoff. *COL*

Motorcycle Squad 🐾½ 1937 A policeman is dishonorably discharged so he can get the "inside" dope on a gang of crooks in this 'B' thriller. 7m/C VHS. Kane Richmond, Wynne Gibson. *SNC*

Mouchette 🐾🐾🐾½ 1967 A lonely 14-year-old French girl, daughter of a drunk father and dying mother, eventually finds spiritual release by committing suicide. Typically somber, spiritual fare from unique master filmmaker Bresson. Perhaps the most complete expression of Bresson's austere, Catholic vision. In French with English subtitles. 80m/B VHS, Beta. *FR* Nadine Nortier, Maria Cardinal, Paul Hebert; **D:** Robert Bresson; **C:** Ghislain Cloquet. *FCT, TPV, HTV*

Moulin Rouge 🐾🐾🐾½ 1952 Colorful, entertaining portrait of acclaimed Impressionist painter Toulouse-Lautrec, more famous for its production stories than on-screen drama, Ferrer delivers one of his most impressive performances as the physically stunted, cynical artist who basked in the seamy Montmartre nightlife. 119m/C VHS, Beta, LV. Jose Ferrer, Zsa Zsa Gabor, Christopher Lee, Peter Cushing, Colette Marchand, Katherine Kath, Michael Balfour, Eric Pohlmann, Suzanne Flon, Claude Nollier, Muriel Smith, Mary Clare, Walter Crisham, Harold Kasket, Jim Gerald, George Lannes, Lee Montague, Maureen Swanson, Tutte Lemkow, Jill Bennett, Theodore Bikel; **D:** John Huston; **W:** John Huston, Anthony Veiller; **C:** Oswald Morris. Academy Awards '52: Best Art Direction/Set Decoration (Color), Best Costume Design (Color); National Board of Review Awards '53: 5 Best Foreign Films of the Year; Nominations: Academy Awards '52: Best Actor (Ferrer), Best Director (Huston), Best Film Editing, Best Picture, Best Supporting Actress (Marchand). *MGM*

The Mountain 🐾🐾 1956 A man and his shady younger brother set out to inspect a Paris-routed plane that crashed in the French Alps. After some harrowing experiences in climbing the peak, it becomes evident that one brother has designs to save whatever he can, while the other intends to loot it. Many real, as well as staged, climbing scenes. Based on Henri Troyat's novel. 105m/C VHS, Beta, Closed Caption. Spencer Tracy, Robert Wagner, Claire Trevor, William Demarest, Richard Arlen, E.G. Marshall; **D:** Edward Dmytryk. *PAR*

Mountain Charlie 🐾½ 1980 Mountain girl's life is destroyed by three drifters. 96m/C VHS, Beta. Denise Neilson, Dick Robinson, Rick Guinn, Lynn Seus; **D:** George Stapleford. *NO*

Mountain Family Robinson 🐾🐾 1979 (G) An urban family, seeking escape from the hassles of city life, moves to the Rockies, determined to get back to nature. They soon find that nature may be more harsh than rush-hour traffic and nasty bosses when a bear comes calling. More "Wilderness Family"-type adventures. 102m/C VHS, Beta. Robert F. Logan, Susan Damante Shaw, Heather Rattray, Ham Larsen, William Bryant, George Flower; **D:** John Cotter. *MED, VTR*

Mountain Justice 🐾🐾½ *Kettle Creek* 1930 Maynard's first all-talkie western finds our hero in search of his father's murderer. Good action sequences (with stunts performed by Maynard), including those aboard a moving train and a buckboard. 73m/B VHS. Ken Maynard, Otis Harlan, Kathryn Crawford, Paul Hurst; **D:** Harry Joe Brown. *GPV*

Mountain Man 🐾🐾½ *Guardian of the Wilderness* 1977 Historically accurate drama about Galen Clark's successful fight in the 1860s to save the magnificent wilderness area that is now Yosemite National Park. Together with naturalist John Muir, he fought a battle against the lumber companies who wanted the timber and won President Lincoln's support for his cause. 96m/C VHS, Beta. Denver Pyle, John Dehner, Ken Berry, Cheryl Miller, Don Shanks, Cliff Osmond, Jack Kruschen, Ford Rainey; **D:** David O'Malley; **W:** David O'Malley. *COL*

The Mountain Men 🐾½ 1980 (R) Dull adventure drama set in the American West of the 1880s. Two trappers argue about life and have trouble with Indians. 102m/C VHS, Beta, LV. Charlton Heston, Brian Keith, John Glover, Seymour Cassel, Victor Jory; **D:** Richard Lang. *COL*

The Mountain Road 🐾½ 1960 Listless drama of an American squadron stationed in China during the last days of WWII. Only Stewart makes this drab film worthwhile. 102m/B VHS. James Stewart, Harry (Henry) Morgan, Glenn Corbett, Mike Kellin; **D:** Daniel Mann. *COL*

Mountains of the Moon 🐾🐾🐾½ 1990 (R) Sprawling adventure detailing the obsessive search for the source of the Nile conducted by famed Victorian rogue/explorer Sir Richard Burton and cohort John Hanning Speke in the late 1800s. Spectacular scenery and images. Director Rafelson, better known for overtly personal films such as "Five Easy Pieces" and "The King of Marvin Gardens," shows considerable skill with this epic. Cinematography by Roger Deakins. From William Harrison's novel "Burton and Speke." 140m/C VHS, Beta, LV, Closed Caption. Patrick Bergin, Iain Glen, Fiona Shaw, Richard E. Grant, Peter Vaughan, Roger Rees, Bernard Hill, Anna Massey, Leslie Phillips, John Savident, James Villiers, Delroy Lindo, Roshan Seth; **D:** Bob Rafelson; **W:** Bob Rafelson; **C:** Roger Deakins. *LIV*

Mountaintop Motel Massacre woof! 1986 (R) A resort motel's hostess is a raving lunatic who regularly slaughters her guests. 95m/C VHS, Beta. Bill Thurman, Anna Chappell, Will Mitchell; **D:** Jim McCullough. *VTR, NWV*

Mouse and His Child 🐾🐾 1977 A gentle animated fantasy adventure about a toy wind-up mouse and his child who fall into the clutches of a villainous rat when they venture into the outside world. 83m/C VHS, Beta. **D:** Fred Wolf; **V:** Peter Ustinov, Cloris Leachman, Andy Devine. *COL*

The Mouse That Roared 🐾🐾🐾 1959 With its wine export business going down the drain, a tiny, desperate country decides to declare war on the United States in hopes that the U.S., after its inevitable triumph, will revive the conquered nation. So off to New York go 20 chain-mail clad warriors armed with bow and arrow. Featured in three roles, Sellers is great as the duchess, less effective (though still funny) as the prime minister, and a military leader. A must for Sellers' fans; maintains a sharp satiric edge throughout. Based on the novel by Leonard Wibberley. 83m/C VHS, Beta. *GB* Peter Sellers, Jean Seberg, Leo McKern, David Kossoff, William Hartnell, Timothy Bateson, MacDonald Parke, Monte Landis; **D:** Jack Arnold; **W:** Roger MacDougall, Stanley Mann; **M:** Edwin Astley. *COL*

Mouth to Mouth 🐾🐾 *Boca a Boca* 1995 (R) Budding actor Victor (Bardem) is working in Madrid as a phone sex operator while waiting to hear about his big break on an American picture. Victor's regularly called by repressed gay surgeon Ricardo (Flotats) and Amanda (Sanchez-Gijon), who says she's Ricardo's wife. Naive Victor falls for Amanda—who of course isn't Ricardo's wife but seems to be involved in a plot to kill Ricardo masterminded by his real wife Angela (Barranco) and her lover David (Gutierrez Caba). The plot's a little tangled but there's lots of visual gags and bedroom farce and the virile Bardem turns out to be a gifted comedian. Spanish with subtitles. **CW:** Sexuality and language. 105m/C VHS. *SP* Javier Bardem, Aitana Sanchez-Gijon, Josep Maria Flotats, Maria Barranco, Emilio Gutierrez-Caba, Fernando Guillen, Myriam Meziere; **D:** Manuel Gomez Pereira; **W:** Manuel Gomez Pereira, Joaquin Oristrell, Naomi Wise, Juan Luis Iborra; **C:** Juan Amoros; **M:** Bernardo Bonazzi. *NYR*

Mouvements du Desir 🐾🐾 *Desire in Motion* 1994 Sex-on-a-train sequences add more than a little steam to this romantic drama. Catherine (Kaprisky) is travelling with her young daughter on the Montreal to Vancouver train in order to forget a failed relationship. She meets shy Vincent (Pichette), who is supposed to be on his way to meet his lover, but somewhere on the journey the sexual sparks start igniting. There are some eccentric fellow passengers to contend with (and director Pool drops in some surreal dream sequences as well) but the heat generated by the leads is genuine enough. 94m/C VHS. *CA SI* Valerie Kaprisky, Jean-Francois Pichette, Jolianne L'Allier-Matteau, Matthew Mackay, William Jacques; **D:** Lea Pool; **W:** Lea Pool; **C:** Pierre Mignot; **M:** Zbigniew Preisner. Nominations: Genie Awards '94: Best Actress (Kaprisky), Best Director (Pool). *NYR*

Movers and Shakers 🐾½ 1985 (PG) An irreverent spoof of Hollywood depicting a filmmaker's attempt to render a best-selling sex manual into a blockbuster film. Fails to live up to its potential and wastes a star-studded cast. 100m/C VHS, Beta. Walter Matthau, Charles Grodin, Gilda Radner, Vincent Gardenia, Bill Macy, Tyne Daly, Steve Martin, Penny Marshall, Luana Anders; **D:** William Asher; **W:** Charles Grodin. *MGM*

The Movie House Massacre 🐾 1978 A psychopath runs rampant in a theatre killing and maiming moviegoers. No refunds are given. 80m/C VHS, Beta. Mary Woronov. *AHV, MRV*

Movie ... In Your Face 🐾 1990 Japanese mobsters want to take over a movie studio. This supposed comedy comes with a "PU-13" rating—"Stinks to anyone with an I.Q. over 13," make of that what you will and be forewarned that it's also sophomoric and tasteless. 85m/C VHS. Tommy Sledge. *HTV*

Movie Maker 🐾 *Smart Alec* 1986 A young filmmaker ineptly raises money for his next film. 87m/C VHS, Beta. Zsa Zsa Gabor, Antony Alda, Orson Bean, Bill Henderson; **D:** Jim Wilson. *LIV*

Movie, Movie 🐾🐾½ 1978 (PG) Acceptable spoof of 1930s films features Scott in twin-bill of black and white "Dynamite Hands," which lampoons boxing dramas, and "Baxter's Beauties," a color send-up of Busby Berkeley musicals. There's even a parody of coming attractions. Wholesome, mildly entertaining. 107m/B VHS. Stanley Donen, George C. Scott, Trish Van Devere, Eli Wallach, Red Buttons, Barbara Harris, Barry Bostwick, Harry Hamlin, Art Carney; **D:** Stanley Donen; **W:** Larry Gelbart; **M:** Ralph Burns. Writers Guild of America '78: Best Original Screenplay. *FOX*

A Movie Star's Daughter 1979 The daughter of a famous movie star moves to a new town and school. She is afraid her popularity is due to her famous father. She must make choices and learn the real meaning of friendship. Also available in a 33-minute edited version. 46m/C VHS, Beta. Frank Converse, Trini Alvarado; **D:** Robert Fuest. *LCA*

Movie Stuntmen 🐾 *Hollywood Thrillmakers; Hollywood Stunt Man* 1953 A retired Hollywood stunt man takes a job for a dead friend so that the friend's widow can receive the fee. Good stunt work taken mostly from old Richard Taldmadge movies almost makes up for poor production. 56m/B VHS. James Gleason, William Henry; **D:** Bernard B. Ray. *NOS*

Movies Money Murder 🐾🐾 1996
Ruthless actress Lee McNight (Purcell) seduces Dr. Jim (Mull) into helping her produce a movie and then invites the moviemakers, including the writer (Black), to his beach house. Too bad the doc's wife (Kazan) shows up unexpectedly and the doc kills her. And when Dr. Jim hears the plot of the movie (about a murder in a doctor's house), he figures he's being blackmailed and decides to get rid of the suspects. **?m/C VHS.** Martin Mull, Lee Purcell, Karen Black, Lainie Kazan; **D:** Arthur Webb. *MTH*

Moving 🐾 1988 (R) An engineer must relocate his family from New Jersey to Idaho in order to get his dream job. Predictable calamities ensue. Not apt to move you. **89m/C VHS, Beta, LV, 8mm, Closed Caption.** Richard Pryor, Randy Quaid, Dana Carvey, Dave Thomas, Rodney Dangerfield, Stacey Dash; **D:** Alan Metter; **W:** Andy Breckman; **M:** Howard Shore. *WAR*

Moving Out 🐾🐾 1983 Adolescent migrant Italian boy finds it difficult to adjust to his new surroundings in Melbourne, Australia. **91m/C VHS, Beta.** Vince Colosimo, Sally Cooper, Maurice Devincentis, Tibor Gyapjas; **D:** Michael Pattinson. *NO*

Moving Target 🐾½ 1989 (R) A young woman witnesses the brutal murder of her boyfriend by mobsters and flees to Florida. Unbeknownst to her, the thugs are still after her. Although top-billed, Blair's role is actually a supporting one. **85m/C VHS, Beta.** *IT* Linda Blair, Ernest Borgnine, Stuart Whitman, Charles Pitt, Jainine Linde, Kurt Woodruff; **D:** Marius Mattei. *HMD*

Moving Target 🐾🐾 1996 (R) Sonny McClean (Dudikoff) is a bounty hunter. But his latest job has him framed for murder and caught up in the middle of mob rivalries. So in order to clear his name, Sonny has to avoid getting killed by violent gangs and quick-draw cops. **106m/C VHS, LV.** Michael Dudikoff, Billy Dee Williams, Michelle Johnson, Aaron Bess, Tom Harvey, Len Doncheff, Noam Jenkins; **D:** Damien Lee; **W:** Mark Sevi, Kevin Mcarthy; **C:** David Pelletier; **M:** David Lawrence. *APX*

Moving Targets 🐾🐾 1987 A young girl and her mother find themselves tracked by a homicidal maniac. **95m/C VHS, Beta.** *AU* Michael Aitkens, Carmen Duncan, Annie Jones, Shane Briant; **D:** Chris Langman. *ACA*

Moving Violation 🐾🐾 1976 (PG) Crooked cops chase two young drifters who have witnessed the local sheriff commit a murder. Corman car chase epic. **91m/C VHS, Beta, LV.** Eddie Albert, Kay Lenz, Stephen McHattie, Will Geer, Lonny Chapman; **D:** Charles S. Dubin; **W:** William W. Norton Sr. *FOX*

Moving Violations 🐾 1985 (PG-13) This could be entitled "Adventures in Traffic Violations School." A wise-cracking tree planter is sent to traffic school after accumulating several moving violations issued to him by a morose traffic cop. Bill Murray's little brother in feature role. **90m/C VHS, Beta, LV, Closed Caption.** John Murray, Jennifer Tilly, James Keach, Brian Backer, Sally Kellerman, Fred Willard, Clara Peller, Wendie Jo Sperber; **D:** Neal Israel; **W:** Pat Proft; **M:** Ralph Burns. *FOX*

Mozart: A Childhood Chronicle 🐾🐾🐾 1976 An experimental, semi-narrative portrait of the immortal composer, from the ages of seven to twenty, filmed on authentic locations and with the original instruments of the era. Entire soundtrack is composed of Mozart's music. In German with English subtitles. **224m/B VHS, Beta, LV.** *GE D:* Klaus Kirschner. *KIV, IME, GLV*

The Mozart Brothers 🐾🐾🐾 1986 An angst-ridden Swedish opera director decides to break all the rules while doing an innovative production of Mozart's "Don Giovanni." At first he horrifies his conservative opera company but as his vision is gradually realized their resistance breaks down. A wonderful look at behind-the-scenes chaos and not just for opera aficionados. In Swedish with English subtitles. **111m/C VHS.** *SW*

Etienne Glaser, Philip Zanden, Henry Bronett; **D:** Suzanne Osten. *FRF, TPV*

The Mozart Story 🐾🐾 1948 After Mozart's death, music minister to the Emperor, Antonio Salieri, reflects on how his jealousy and hatred of the musical genius held the great composer back and contributed to his death. Originally filmed in Austria in 1937, scenes were added for the U.S. release in 1948. **91m/B VHS, Beta.** Hans Holt, Winnie Markus, Irene von Meyendorf, Rene Deltgen, Edward Vedder, Wilton Graff, Walther Jansson, Curt Jurgens, Paul Hoerbiger; **D:** Karl Hartl. *VYY, GLV*

Much Ado about Nothing 🐾🐾🐾½ 1993 (PG-13) Shakespeare for the masses details romance between two sets of would-be lovers—the battling Beatrice and Benedick (Thompson and Branagh) and the ingenuous Hero and Claudio (Beckinsdale and Leonard). Washington is the noble warrior leader, Reeves his evil half-dressed half-brother, and Keaton serves comic relief as the officious, bumbling Dogberry. Sunlit, lusty, and revealing about all the vagaries of love, Branagh brings passion to his quest of making Shakespeare more approachable. His second attempt after "Henry V" at breaking the stuffy Shakespearean tradition. Filmed on location in Tuscany, Italy. **CW:** Mild sexual situations. **110m/C VHS, LV, Closed Caption.** *GB* Kenneth Branagh, Emma Thompson, Robert Sean Leonard, Kate Beckinsale, Denzel Washington, Keanu Reeves, Michael Keaton, Brian Blessed, Phyllida Law, Imelda Staunton, Gerard Horan, Jimmy Yuill, Richard Clifford, Ben Elton, Richard Briers; **D:** Kenneth Branagh; **W:** Kenneth Branagh; **C:** Roger Lanser; **M:** Patrick Doyle. Nominations: Golden Globe Awards '94: Best Film—Musical/Comedy; Independent Spirit Awards '94: Best Actress (Thompson), Best Film. *COL*

Mugsy's Girls 🐾 *Delta Pi* 1985 (R) A messy comedy about six sorority women, educated in the refined skills of bar mud wrestling, who wallow in a Las Vegas championship tournament. Features pop singer Laura Branigan. **87m/C VHS, Beta.** Ruth Gordon, Laura Branigan, Eddie Deezen; **D:** Kevin Brodie. *LIV, VES*

Mulholland Falls 🐾🐾½ 1995 (R) Noir meets the nuclear age in this stylish period piece from New Zealand director Tamahori. Nolte plays the leader of the Hat Squad, a vicious group of fedora-sporting detectives assigned to bust organized crime in '50s L.A. at all costs. While investigating the murder of his ex-mistress, Nolte and cohorts Madsen, Palminteri and Penn discover evidence linking the murder to a general (Malkovich) in charge of the top secret nuclear program. Although the cast is dripping with big name stars, the best performance is put in by the glossy set design of Richard Sylbert, who probably had a strong case of deja vu, having previously done "Chinatown." **CW:** Sexuality, violence and language. **107m/C VHS, LV, Closed Caption.** Nick Nolte, Melanie Griffith, Chazz Palminteri, Michael Madsen, Christopher Penn, Treat Williams, Jennifer Connelly, Andrew McCarthy, John Malkovich, Daniel Baldwin, Bruce Dern, Ed Lauter; *Cameos:* William L. Petersen, Rob Lowe; **D:** Lee Tamahori; **W:** Pete Dexter; **C:** Haskell Wexler; **M:** Dave Grusin. Golden Raspberry Awards '96: Worst Supporting Actress (Griffith). *MGM*

Multiple Maniacs 🐾 1970 Waters at his most perverse. Divine's travelling freak show, filled with disgusting side-show sex acts, is the vehicle used for robbing and killing hapless spectators. One of the best scenes of a sordid lot is Divine being raped by Lobstora, a 15-foot broiled lobster. **90m/B VHS.** Divine, David Lochary, Mary Vivian Pearce, Edith Massey, Mink Stole; **D:** John Waters. *NO*

Multiplicity 🐾🐾½ 1996 (PG-13) With too many business and personal responsibilities, construction supervisor Doug Kinney (Keaton) is a prime candidate for the cloning experiments of Dr. Leeds (Yulin). Since the cloning process isn't exactly perfect, each clone (Doug winds up with three) has a different dominant personality trait—a hard-charger, a "Mister Mom," and a dopey slacker. Confusion reigns as wife Laura (MacDo-

well) deals with separation anxiety on a grand scale. Pleasant comedy shows Keaton can still be funny given the chance. Keaton had his choice of cloning comedies and chose this one over Chris Columbus's "More." **CW:** Sexual situations. **117m/C VHS, LV, Closed Caption.** Michael Keaton, Andie MacDowell, Harris Yulin, Richard Masur, Eugene Levy, Obba Babatunde, Ann Cusack, Brian Doyle-Murray; **D:** Harold Ramis; **W:** Lowell Ganz, Babaloo Mandel, Chris Miller, Mary Hale, Harold Ramis; **C:** Laszlo Kovacs; **M:** George Fenton. *COL*

The Mummy 🐾🐾🐾½ 1932 Eerie chills mark this classic horror tale of an Egyptian priest, buried alive nearly 4000 years earlier, who comes back to life after a 1921 archaeological dig. Eight hours of extraordinary makeup transformed Karloff into the macabre mummy, who believes the soul of the long-deceased (and probably long-decayed) lover resides in the body of a young woman. Marked the directing debut of famed German cinematographer Freund. **72m/B VHS, Beta, LV.** Boris Karloff, Zita Johann, David Manners, Edward Van Sloan; **D:** Karl Freund. *USH, TLF*

The Mummy 🐾🐾🐾 1959 A group of British archaeologists discover they have made a grave mistake when a mummy kills off those who have violated his princess' tomb. A summation of all the previous "mummy" films, this one has a more frightening mummy (6'4" Lee) who is on screen much of the time. Additionally, there is pathos in this monster, not merely murder and revenge. An effective remake of the 1932 classic. **88m/C VHS, Beta, LV.** *GB* Peter Cushing, Christopher Lee, Felix Aylmer, Yvonne Furneaux; **D:** Terence Fisher; **W:** Jimmy Sangster. *WAR, MLB*

Mummy & Curse of the Jackal WOOF! 1967 Upon opening the tomb of female mummy, a man is cursed to roam the streets of Las Vegas as a werejackal. Impossibly inept. **86m/C VHS.** Anthony Eisley, Martina Pons, John Carradine, Saul Goldsmith; **D:** Oliver Drake. *ACA*

The Mummy's Curse 🐾🐾 1944 Sequel to "The Mummy's Ghost" and Chaney's last outing as Kharis. Construction by a government order causes Kharis and Ananka to be dug up in a Louisiana bayou and taken to Cajun country for study by archaeologists. The usual havoc ensues. Includes lots of stock footage from earlier mummy movies. Based on a story by Leon Abrams and Dwight V. Babcock. **61m/B VHS, Closed Caption.** Lon Chaney Jr., Peter Coe, Virginia Christine, Kay Harding, Dennis Moore, Martin Kosleck, Kurt Katch; **D:** Leslie Goodwins; **W:** Bernard Schubert. *USH, FCT*

The Mummy's Ghost 🐾🐾 1944 Sequel to "The Mummy's Tomb" has Chaney, Jr. searching for the reincarnation of his ancient love, Princess Ananka. The least interesting entry in the series. Based on a story by Griffith Jay and Henry Sucher. **61m/B VHS, Closed Caption.** Lon Chaney Jr., John Carradine, Ramsay Ames, Robert Lowery, Barton MacLane, George Zucco; **D:** Reginald LeBorg; **W:** Griffin Jay, Henry Sucher, Brenda Weisberg. *USH, FCT*

The Mummy's Hand 🐾🐾½ 1940 Two archaeologists (Foran and Ford) searching for the tomb of ancient Egyptian Princess Ananka discover more than they bargained for when they find that an evil and deadly mummy is the tomb's guardian. From there the plot unravels, but the good cast and a mix of scares and comedy make this worth watching. **70m/B VHS, Closed Caption.** Dick Foran, Wallace Ford, Peggy Moran, Cecil Kellaway, George Zucco, Tom Tyler, Eduardo Ciannelli, Charles Trowbridge; **D:** Christy Cabanne. *USH*

The Mummy's Revenge 🐾 1973 A fanatic revives a mummy with virgin blood. The first mummy movie to feature open gore. **91m/C VHS, Beta.** *SP* Paul Naschy, Jack Taylor, Maria Silva, Helga Line; **D:** Carlos Aured; **W:** Paul Naschy. *UNI*

The Mummy's Tomb 🐾🐾 1942 Chaney, Jr. is in wraps for the first time in this sequel to "The Mummy's Hand." Kharis is transported to America by a crazed Egyptian high priest to kill off surviving members of the expedition. Weakened by a lame script and too much stock footage. Based on a story by Neil P. Varnick. **71m/B VHS, Closed Caption.** Lon Chaney Jr., Dick Foran, John Hubbard, Elyse Knox, George Zucco, Wallace Ford, Turhan Bey; *D:* Harold Young; *W:* Griffin Jay, Henry Sucher. *USH, FCT*

Munchie 🎭½ 1992 (PG) A forgotten alien critter is discovered in a mine shaft by young Gage. Munchie turns out to be a good friend, protecting Gage from bullies and granting other wishes. Frequent sight gags help keep the film moving but it's still awfully slow. Sequel to "Munchies" (1987). **80m/C VHS, Closed Caption.** Loni Anderson, Andrew Stevens, Arte Johnson, Jamie McEnnan; *D:* Jim Wynorski; *V:* Dom DeLuise. *NHO*

Munchies 🎭 1987 (PG) "Gremlins" rip-off about tiny aliens who love beer and fast food, and invade a small town. Lewd and ribald. **83m/C VHS, Beta.** Harvey Korman, Charles Stratton, Nadine Van Der Velde; *D:* Bettina Hirsch. *MGM*

The Munsters' Revenge 🎭🎭 1981 Television movie based on the continuing adventures of the 1960s comedy series characters. Herman, Lily, and Grandpa have to contend with robot replicas of themselves that were created by a flaky scientist. **96m/C VHS, Beta.** Fred Gwynne, Yvonne De Carlo, Al Lewis, Jo McDonnel, Sid Caesar, Ezra Stone, Howard Morris, Bob Hastings, K.C. Martel; *D:* Don Weis. *USH*

The Muppet Christmas Carol 🎭🎭½ 1992 (G) Christmas classic features all the muppet favorites together and in Victorian garb. Storyline is more or less faithful to Dickens original, with pleasant special effects. Gonzo the Great as Dickens narrates the tale as Scrooge (Caine) takes his legendary Christmas Eve journey escorted by three (flannel) spirits. The Cratchits are led by Kermit and Miss Piggy. Directed by Brian Henson, Jim's son, the film is as heartwarming as the Cratchit's crackling fire, but doesn't quite achieve the former muppet magic. Also features some sappy songs by Williams, including "Love is Like a Heatwave" and "Island in the Sun." **120m/C VHS, Beta, Closed Caption.** Michael Caine; *D:* Brian Henson; *C:* John Fenner; *M:* Paul Williams, Miles Goodman; *V:* Dave Goelz, Steve Whitmire, Jerry Nelson, Frank Oz. *JHV*

The Muppet Movie 🎭🎭🎭½ 1979 (G) Seeking fame and footlights, Kermit the Frog and his pal Fozzie Bear travel to Hollywood, and along the way are joined by sundry human and muppet characters, including the lovely Miss Piggy. A delightful cult favorite filled with entertaining cameos, memorable (though somewhat pedestrian) songs and crafty special effects—Kermit rides a bike and rows a boat! A success for the late Jim Henson. 🎵The Rainbow Connection; Frog's Legs So Fine; Movin Right Along; Can You Picture That?; Never Before; Something Better; This Looks Familiar; I'm Going Back There Someday. **94m/C VHS, Beta, LV.** *GB* Jim Henson's Muppets; *Cameos:* Edgar Bergen, Milton Berle, Mel Brooks, Madeline Kahn, Steve Martin, Carol Kane, Paul Williams, Charles Durning, Bob Hope, James Coburn, Dom DeLuise, Elliott Gould, Cloris Leachman, Telly Savalas, Orson Welles; *D:* James Frawley; *W:* Jack Burns; *M:* Paul Williams; *V:* Jim Henson, Frank Oz. Nominations: Academy Awards '79: Best Song ("The Rainbow Connection"), Original Score and/or Adaptation. *JHV, FOX*

Muppet Treasure Island 🎭🎭½ 1996 (G) Literary classic gets its first coat of felt as Kermit the Frog, Miss Piggy and the entire Muppet gang hit the high seas in an adaptation of Robert Louis Stevenson's 1883 well-worn adventure tale. Delightful settings, from an old English tavern to an exotic south sea island, frame the journey of young Jim Hawkins (flesh and blood Bishop), who along with tavern owners Rizzo the Rat (Whitmire) and the Great Gonzo (Goelz) search for buried treasure. Long John Silver is played to the hilt by Curry, master of the over-the-top villain. Helmer Henson steers a steady ship, with over 400 Muppet critters making an appear-

ance. **99m/C VHS.** Tim Curry, Kevin Bishop, Billy Connolly, Jennifer Saunders; *D:* Brian Henson; *W:* Jerry Juhl, Jim V. Hart, Kirk R. Thatcher; *C:* John Fenner; *M:* Hans Zimmer; *V:* Steve Whitmire, Frank Oz, Dave Goelz. *TOU*

The Muppets Take Manhattan 🎭🎭🎭 1984 (G) Following a smashing success with a college musical, the Muppets take their show and talents to Broadway, only to face misfortune in the form of an unscrupulous producer. A less imaginative script than the first two Muppet movies, yet an enjoyable experience with numerous major stars making cameo appearances. **94m/C VHS, Beta, LV, Closed Caption.** Jim Henson's Muppets; *Cameos:* Dabney Coleman, James Coco, Art Carney, Joan Rivers, Gregory Hines, Linda Lavin, Liza Minnelli, Brooke Shields, John Landis; *D:* Frank Oz; *M:* Ralph Burns; *V:* Jim Henson, Frank Oz. Nominations: Academy Awards '84: Original Song Score and/or Adaptation. *FOX, HMV*

Murder 🎭🎭🎭 1930 Believing in a young woman's innocence, one jurist begins to organize the pieces of the crime in order to save her. Fine early effort by Hitchcock based on play "Enter Sir John," by Clemense Dane and Helen Simpson. **92m/B VHS, Beta.** Herbert Marshall, Nora Baring, Phyllis Konstam, Miles Mander; *D:* Alfred Hitchcock; *W:* Alfred Hitchcock. *REP, NOS, HHT*

Murder Ahoy 🎭🎭½ 1964 Miss Marple looks perplexed when dead bodies surface on a naval cadet training ship. Dame Marge is the dottie detective in the final, and least appealing, of her four Agatha Christie films of the sixties (although it was released in the States prior to "Murder Most Foul"). **74m/B VHS, Beta.** Margaret Rutherford, Lionel Jeffries, Charles Tingwell, William Mervyn, Francis Matthews; *D:* George Pollock. *MGM, FCT*

Murder at 45 R.P.M. 🎭🎭 *Meurtre en 45 Tours* 1965 A singer and her lover suspect each other of her husband's murder. Things become sticky when she receives a recorded message from her dead husband. Average. **98m/C VHS.** *FR* Danielle Darrieux, Michel Auclair, Jean Servais, Henri Guisol; *D:* Etienne Perier. *SNC*

Murder at Midnight 🎭🎭 1931 The killings begin with a game of charades in which the gun wasn't supposed to be loaded, and continue as members of English high society die one by one. "Blondie" director Strayer still working on his change of pace. **69m/B VHS, Beta, 8mm.** Alice White, Leslie Fenton, Aileen Pringle, Hale Hamilton, Robert Elliott, Clara Blandick, Brandon Hurst; *D:* Frank Strayer. *SNC, NOS, DVT*

Murder at 1600 🎭🎭 1997 (R) Jaded D.C. detective Harlan Regis (Snipes) is called to investigate the murder of Carla Town (Moore), a secretary found dead in a White House bathroom. He's reluctantly assisted by hard-boiled Secret Service agent Chance (Lane), while head of security Nick Spikings (Benzali) wants the whole matter wrapped up quickly and quietly—justice not being his main concern. Cliche-fest script gives stereotypical characters a little more development than you may be used to seeing, but doesn't give them anything new or interesting to say or do. Snipes and Lane make a good team, however, and Miller fulfills his usual wise-cracking sidekick role effortlessly. *CW:* Sexuality, violence and some language. **107m/C VHS, LV, Closed Caption.** Wesley Snipes, Diane Lane, Daniel Benzali, Dennis Miller, Alan Alda, Ronny Cox, Tate Donovan, Diane Baker, Mary Moore; *D:* Dwight Little; *W:* Wayne Beach, David Hodgin; *C:* Steve Bernstein; *M:* Christopher Young. *WAR*

Murder at the Baskervilles 🎭🎭 *Silver Blaze* 1937 Sherlock Holmes is invited to visit Sir Henry Baskerville at his estate, but then finds that Baskerville's daughter's fiance is accused of stealing a race horse and murdering its keeper. Based on Sir Arthur Conan Doyle's story "Silver Blaze." **67m/B VHS, Beta.** *GB* Arthur Wontner, Ian Fleming, Lyn Harding; *D:* Thomas Bentley. *SNC, CCB, REP*

Murder at the Gallop 🎭🎭🎭½ 1963 Snooping Miss Marple doesn't believe a filthy rich old-timer died of natural causes, despite the dissenting police point of view. Wheedling her way into the police investigation, she discovers the secret of the Gallop club, a place where people bounce up and down on top of horses. Much mugging between Dame Margaret and Morley. Marple's assistant, Mr. Stringer, is the real life Mr. Dame Margaret. Based on Christie's Poirot mystery "After the Funeral." **81m/B VHS, Beta.** Margaret Rutherford, Robert Morley, Flora Robson, Charles Tingwell, Duncan Lamont; *D:* George Pollock. *MGM, FCT*

Murder at the Vanities 🎭🎭½ 1934 Vintage murder mystery set against a musical revue format, in which a tough detective must find a killer before the Earl Carroll-based cabaret ends and he or she will escape with the exiting crowd. Also featured is a mind-boggling production number based on the song "Marijuana." 🎵Marijuana; Lovely One; Where Do They Come From Now; Live and Love Tonight; Cocktails for Two; Ebony Rhapsody. **91m/B VHS, Beta.** Victor McLaglen, Kitty Carlisle Hart, Jack Oakie, Duke Ellington, Carl Brisson; *D:* Mitchell Leisen. *USH*

Murder by Death 🎭🎭½ 1976 (PG) Capote is an eccentric millionaire who invites the world's greatest detectives to dinner, offering one million dollars to the one who can solve the evening's murder. Entertaining and hammy spoof of Agatha Christie's "And Then There Were None" and the earlier "Ten Little Indians." **95m/C VHS, Beta, LV.** Peter Falk, Alec Guinness, David Niven, Maggie Smith, Peter Sellers, Eileen Brennan, Elsa Lanchester, Nancy Walker, Estelle Winwood, Truman Capote, James Coco; *D:* Robert Moore; *W:* Neil Simon; *M:* Dave Grusin. *COL, TVC*

Murder by Decree 🎭🎭🎭 1979 (PG) Realistic and convincing version of the Jack the Ripper story. Sherlock Holmes and Dr. Watson find a vast web of conspiracy when they investigate the murders of Whitechapel prostitutes. Based partially on facts, it's a highly detailed suspenser with interesting camera work and fine performances. **120m/C VHS, Beta.** *CA* Christopher Plummer, James Mason, Donald Sutherland, Genevieve Bujold, Susan Clark, David Hemmings, Frank Finlay, John Gielgud, Anthony Quayle; *D:* Bob (Benjamin) Clark; *W:* John Hopkins. Genie Awards '80: Best Actor (Plummer), Best Director (Clark), Best Supporting Actress (Bujold). *NLC*

Murder by Moonlight 🎭🎭 1991 (PG-13) Rival agents investigate a mysterious murder in a prosperous mining colony on the moon. Not only do they discover a dastardly trail that leads all the way back to Earth, but a strange romantic attraction for each other. Originally broadcast on British TV. **94m/C VHS, Closed Caption.** *GB* Julian Sands, Brigitte Nielsen, Gerald McRaney, Jane Lapotaire, Brian Cox; *D:* Michael Lindsay-Hogg; *M:* Trevor Jones. *THV*

Murder by Natural Causes 🎭🎭🎭 1979 A made-for-TV brain teaser in which a woman and her lover plot to kill her mind-reader husband. Lots of twists make this fun for viewers who enjoy a challenge. **96m/C VHS, Beta.** Hal Holbrook, Barry Bostwick, Katharine Ross, Richard Anderson; *D:* Robert Day. *NO*

Murder by Night 🎭🎭½ 1989 (PG-13) Amnesia victim Urich is found next to a dead body, the result of a gruesome murder. Urich is the only witness and thinks he may be the next victim. Others think he's the killer. Made for cable mystery with enough twists to make it worthwhile. **95m/C VHS, Beta.** Robert Urich, Kay Lenz, Jim Metzler, Richard Monette, Michael Ironside, Michael Williams; *D:* Paul Lynch. *USH*

Murder by Numbers 🎭½ 1989 (PG-13) Murder in the art world stumps a detective. What might have been a good suspense story is ruined by bad editing and a lack of continuity, resulting in confusion rather than suspense. **91m/C VHS, Beta, LV.** Sam Behrens, Shari Belafonte, Ronee Blakley, Stanley Kamel, Jayne Meadows, Debra Sandlund, Dick Sargent, Cleavon Little; *D:* Paul Leder; *W:* Paul Leder. *NO*

Murder by Phone 🎬🎬 *Bells; The Calling*
1982 (R) A deranged technician has turned his phone into an instrument of electronic death. Chamberlain is the visiting professor trying to discover who's permanently disconnecting the numbers of his students. Good cast decides to test schlock meter. **79m/C VHS, Beta.** **CA** Richard Chamberlain, John Houseman, Sara Botsford; **D:** Michael Anderson Sr.; **W:** Michael Butler, John Kent Harrison; **M:** John Barry. WAR

Murder by Television 🎬½ *The Houghland Murder Case* **1935** Low-budget murder mystery with Lugosi in a dual role as twins—one good, one not so. When a professor and the evil twin are murdered, the instrument of death suspected is...television. Still an exotic and misunderstood invention when this was made, TV sometimes invoked fear and suspicion in the general public. Historically interesting and Lugosi fans will appreciate seeing him in a non-vampiric role. **55m/B VHS, Beta.** Bela Lugosi, George Meeker; **D:** Clifford Sanforth. VYY, SNC, NOS

Murder by the Book 🎬🎬½ *Alter Ego*
1987 A mystery writer finds that his fictional character, a hard-boiled private eye, has taken control of his life. With his new macho persona the writer solves a crime and saves the obligatory dame. Based on the novel "Alter Ego" by Mel Arrighi. Made for television. **100m/C VHS, Beta.** Robert Hays, Catherine Mary Stewart, Celeste Holm, Fred Gwynne, Christopher Murney; **D:** Mel Damski. NO

Murder Czech Style 🎬🎬 *Vrazda Po Cesky*
1966 Chubby and boring office clerk Frantisek (Hrusinsky) is amazed when a colleague, the beautiful Alice (Fialova), agrees to marry him. He can't believe his good fortune—and he's right—Frantisek soon discovers his wife has a married lover. So, he plots to murder her in several increasingly silly fantasies. Czech with subtitles. **87m/C VHS.** **CZ** Rudolf Hrusinsky, Kveta Fialova, Vaclav Voska, Vladimir Mensik; **D:** Jiri Weiss; **W:** Jiri Weiss, Jan Otcenasek; **C:** Jan Nemecek; **M:** Zdenek Liska. FCT

Murder Elite 🎬½ **1986** A murdering maniac terrorizes the rural English countryside, where MacGraw has returned after losing all her money in America. Poor acting and direction make this one a dust-gatherer. **98m/C VHS, Beta.** Ali MacGraw, Billie Whitelaw, Hywel Bennett; **D:** Claude Whatham. LIV, VES

Murder for Sale 🎬 **1970** Secret Agent 117 stages an elaborate scam in order to infiltrate a ring of terrorists and criminals. Ask for Bond next time. **90m/C VHS, Beta.** John Gavin, Margaret Lee, Curt Jurgens. MED

Murder in Coweta County 🎬🎬½
1983 Griffith and Cash are strong in this true-crime drama based on the book by Margaret Anne Barnes. Griffith is a Georgia businessman who thinks he's gotten away with murder; Cash is the lawman who tenaciously pursues him. Based on an actual 1948 case. Made for television. **100m/ C VHS, Beta.** Johnny Cash, Andy Griffith, Earl Hindman, June Carter Cash, Cindi Knight, Ed Van Nuys; **D:** Gary Nelson; **M:** Brad Fiedel. LIV

Murder-in-Law 🎬 **1992 (R)** Graphic slasher flick about a mother-in-law from hell who escapes from an insane asylum and terrorizes her son-in-law (Estevez) and his family in a series of gruesome killings.**CW:** Language, horror violence, and sexuality. **97m/C VHS.** Marilyn Adams, Joe Estevez, Sandy Snyder, Darrel Guilbeau; **D:** Tony Jiti Gill. MNC

Murder in New Hampshire: The Pamela Smart Story 🎬🎬½ **1991 (PG-13)** A sleazy true story about a young high school teacher who seduces an impressionable student into murdering her husband. Hunt's fine as the seductress but this made-for-television fare is just average. **93m/C VHS, Beta, Closed Caption.** Helen Hunt, Chad Allen, Larry Drake, Howard Hesseman, Ken Howard, Michael Learned; **D:** Joyce Chopra; **M:** Gary Chang. TTC, PMS

Murder in Space 🎬½ **1985** Nine multinational astronauts are stranded aboard a space station when they discover one of them is a murderer. This creates anxiety, particularly since the killer's identity is unknown. Oatmeal salesman Brimley is the earth-bound mission control chief trying desperately to finger a spaceman while the bodies pile up. Made for television. **95m/C VHS, Beta.** Wilford Brimley, Martin Balsam, Michael Ironside; **D:** Steven Hilliard Stern. THV

Murder in Texas 🎬🎬🎬 **1981** Made for television docudrama looks at the strange but true events surrounding the death of society woman Joan Robinson Hill, first wife of prominent plastic surgeon, Dr. John Hill, and daughter of wealthy oilman Ash Robinson. Well-crafted script and effective performances keep your interest. Griffith was Emmy nominated. From the book "Prescription Murder," written by the doctor's second wife. **200m/C VHS, Beta.** Farrah Fawcett, Katharine Ross, Andy Griffith, Sam Elliott, Craig T. Nelson, Barbara Sammeth; **D:** William Hale. VHE, HHE

Murder in the Doll House 🎬½ **1979** Private detective must find out who is systematically killing off the family of a Japanese toy executive. With English subtitles. **92m/C VHS, Beta.** **JP** Yusaku Matsuda, Hiroko Shino, Yoko Nosaki. VDA

Murder In the First 🎬🎬½ **1995 (R)** Hours after leaving a three-year stint in solitary confinement at Alcatraz, petty thief Henri Young (Bacon) kills the inmate he thinks ratted him out. Young, eager-puppy lawyer James Stamphill (Slater) defends Young by claiming that inhumane and brutal prison treatment turned him into a murderer. Heavy-handed and uneven despite excellent performances by top-notch cast. Oldman does his usual fine job with yet another unsympathetic character, the sadistic warden. Major professional landmark for both Slater and Bacon. Loosely based on a true story that led to the closing of Alcatraz.**CW:** Contains profanity, sadistic violence, and mild sexual situations. **123m/C VHS, LV, Closed Caption.** Christian Slater, Kevin Bacon, Gary Oldman, Embeth Davidtz, Bill Macy, Stephen Tobolowsky, Brad Dourif, R. Lee Ermey, Mia Kirshner, Stefan Gierasch, Kyra Sedgwick; **D:** Marc Rocco; **W:** Dan Gordon; **C:** Fred Murphy; **M:** Christopher Young. Broadcast Film Critics Association Awards '95: Best Actor (Bacon); Nominations: Screen Actors Guild Award '95: Best Supporting Actor (Bacon). WAR

Murder in the Footlights 🎬🎬 **1951** Murder drama involving a socialite and a vaudeville team. **?m/C VHS.** **GB** Lesley Brook, David Hutcheson. SNC

Murder in the Old Red Barn 🎬 *Maria Marten* **1936** Based on the real murder of an unassuming girl by a randy squire. Stiff, melodramatic performances are bad enough, but the play-style production, unfamiliar to modern viewers, is the last nail in this one's coffin. **67m/B VHS, Beta.** **GB** Tod Slaughter, Sophie Stewart, D.J. Williams, Eric Portman; **D:** Milton Rosmer. NOS, MRV, SNC

A Murder Is Announced 🎬🎬 *Agatha Christie's Miss Marple: A Murder Is Announced* **1987** From the critically acclaimed BBC television series. While on holiday, super-sleuth Marple encounters a murder that was advertised in the local newspaper one week prior to its occurrence. Based on the 1952 Agatha Christie novel, Hickson shines once again as Christie's detective extraordinaire. **155m/C VHS, Beta, Closed Caption.** **GB** Joan Hickson; **D:** David Giles. FOX, HMV, VCO

Murder Mansion 🎬½ **1970** Some decent scares ensue when a group of travelers is stranded in an old haunted mansion. **84m/C VHS, Beta.** **SP** Evelyn Stewart, Analia Gade; **D:** Francisco Lara Polop. UNI, SNC, FCT

Murder Most Foul 🎬🎬🎬 **1965** Erstwhile school marm Dame Margaret is excellent as the only jury member to believe in the accused's innocence. Posing as a wealthy actress to insinuate herself into the local acting troupe, she sniffs out

the true culprit. Based on the Poirot mystery "Mr. McGinty's Dead." **90m/B VHS, Beta.** Margaret Rutherford, Ron Moody, Charles Tingwell, Megs Jenkins, Dennis Price, Ralph Michael; **D:** George Pollock. MGM, FCT

Murder Motel 🎬 **1974** Inept made-for-television spine-tingler about a motel keeper who makes a practice of killing his customers. There's always a vacancy at the Murder Motel, at least until the fiancee of one of his victims decides to look into the matter. **80m/C VHS, Beta.** Robyn Millan, Derek Francis, Ralph Bates, Edward Judd. LIV

Murder, My Sweet 🎬🎬🎬½ *Farewell, My Love* **1944** Down-on-his-luck private detective Philip Marlowe (Powell) searches for an ex-convict's missing girlfriend through a dark world of murder, mayhem and ever-twisting directions. Classic film noir screen version of Raymond Chandler's tense novel "Farewell, My Lovely," which employs flashback fashion using that crisp Chandler narrative. A breakthrough dramatically for singer Powell; Chandler's favorite version. Remade using the novel's title in 1975. **95m/B VHS, Beta, LV.** Dick Powell, Claire Trevor, Mike Mazurki, Otto Kruger, Anne Shirley, Miles Mander; **D:** Edward Dmytryk. Edgar Allan Poe Awards '45: Best Screenplay. MED, CCB

Murder of a Moderate Man 🎬½ **197?** An Interpol agent sets out for the Alps to apprehend an assassin gunning down political leaders. A British-made effort based on a novel by John Howlett. **165m/C VHS.** **GB** Denis Quilley, Susan Fleetwood. FCT, MOV, VCO

The Murder of Mary Phagan 🎬🎬🎬½ **1987 (PG)** Lemmon stars as John Slaton, governor of Georgia during one of America's most notorious miscarriages of justice. In 1913, timid, Jewish factory manager Leo Frank is accused of the brutal murder of a female worker. Prejudice and a power hungry prosecuting attorney conspire to seal the man's fate at the end of the hangman's noose. Sensing the injustice, Slaton re-opens the case, causing riots in Atlanta. Top notch television drama, featuring a superb recreation of turn of the century atmosphere and a compelling, true story which was not finally resolved until the 1970s. **251m/C VHS.** Jack Lemmon, Peter Gallagher, Richard Jordan, Robert Prosky, Paul Dooley, Rebecca Miller, Kathryn Walker, Charles S. Dutton, Kevin Spacey, Wendy J. Cooke; **D:** Billy Hale; **M:** Maurice Jarre. ORI

Murder on Approval 🎬 *Barbados Quest* **1956** Conway is a carbon-copy Sherlock Holmes, called in to verify the authenticity of a stamp and finds himself involved in murder. Slow-paced, weak and transparent. **70m/B VHS.** Tom Conway, Delphi Lawrence, Brian Worth, Michael Balfour, John Colicos; **D:** Bernard Knowles. NOS

Murder on Flight 502 🎬🎬 **1975** A crisis arises on a 747 flight from New York to London when a terrorist runs amuck. Big cast of TV stars and Stack as the pilot keep this stale television flick from getting lost in the ozone. **97m/C VHS, Beta.** Farrah Fawcett, Sonny Bono, Ralph Bellamy, Theodore Bikel, Dane Clark, Polly Bergen, Laraine Day, Fernando Lamas, George Maharis, Hugh O'Brian, Molly Picon, Walter Pidgeon, Robert Stack; **D:** George McCowan. PSM

Murder on Lenox Avenue 🎬🎬½ **1941** When the leader of the Harlem Better Business Bureau is overthrown, he swears revenge. **60m/C VHS.** Alec Lovejoy. BBE, MOV

Murder on Line One 🎬🎬 **1990** A London murderer films his crimes for his later viewing pleasure. The police arrest a suspect, but the killings continue. Both the police and viewer are soon aware that they've made a mistake. **103m/C VHS, Beta.** Emma Jacobs, Peter Blake, Simon Shepherd, Allan Surtees, Andrew Wilde, Dirkan Tulane, Neil Duncan, Brett Forrest; **D:** Anders Palm; **W:** Anders Palm. ACA, TTC

Murder on the Bayou 🎬🎬🎬 *A Gathering of Old Men* **1991 (PG)** Down on the L'siana bayou, a white guy who thinks civil rights are color coded is murdered, and an elderly black man is accused of the crime. Made for TV, well performed, engaging. From the novel by Ernest J. Gaines. **91m/C VHS, LV.** Louis Gossett Jr., Richard Widmark, Holly Hunter, Woody Strode, Joe Seneca, Papa John Creach, Julius W. Harris, Will Patton; **D:** Volker Schlondorff. *THV*

Murder on the Campus 🐾🐾 *Out of the Shadow* 1952

A reporter investigates the apparent suicide of his brother at Cambridge University. He discovers that a number of other mysterious deaths have occurred as well. Interesting characterizations hampered by predictability. **61m/B VHS, Beta.** *GB* Terence Longdon, Donald Gray, Diane Clare, Robertson Hare, Dermot Walsh; **D:** Michael Winner; **W:** Michael Winner. *NOS, MRV, SNC*

Murder on the High Seas 🐾🐾 1932

Infidelity and murder aboard a cruise ship. **?m/C VHS.** Natalie Moorhead, Jack Mulhall. *SNC*

Murder on the Midnight Express 🐾½ 1974

Made-for-television mystery about spies, thieves, honeymooners and a corpse aboard an all-night train. All aboard. **70m/C VHS, Beta.** Judy Geeson, James Smillie, Charles Gray. *LIV*

Murder on the Orient Express 🐾🐾🐾🐾 1974 (PG)

An Agatha Christie mystery lavishly produced with an all-star cast. In 1934, a trainful of suspects and one murder victim make the trip from Istanbul to Calais especially interesting. Super-sleuth Hercule Poirot sets out to solve the mystery. An entertaining whodunit, ably supported by the remarkable cast. Followed by "Death on the Nile." **128m/C VHS, Beta, LV.** *GB* Albert Finney, Martin Balsam, Ingrid Bergman, Lauren Bacall, Sean Connery, Richard Widmark, Anthony Perkins, John Gielgud, Jacqueline Bisset, Jean-Pierre Cassel, Wendy Hiller, Rachel Roberts, Vanessa Redgrave, Michael York, Colin Blakely, George Coulouris, Denis Quilley, Vernon Dobtcheff, Jeremy Lloyd; **D:** Sidney Lumet; **W:** Paul Dehn; **C:** Geoffrey Unsworth; **M:** Richard Rodney Bennett. Academy Awards '74: Best Supporting Actress (Bergman); British Academy Awards '74: Best Supporting Actor (Gielgud), Best Supporting Actress (Bergman); National Board of Review Awards '74: 10 Best Films of the Year; Nominations: Academy Awards '74: Best Actor (Finney), Best Adapted Screenplay, Best Cinematography, Best Costume Design, Original Dramatic/Comedy Score. *PAR, BTV*

Murder on the Yukon 🐾½ 1940

An installment in the "Renfrew of the Royal Mounted" series. Newill and O'Brien's vacation plans are ruined when they find a corpse in a canoe and must investigate. Lots of action, but a somewhat threadbare production. Based on "Renfrew Rides North" by Lauri York Erskine. **57m/B VHS, Beta.** James Newill, Dave O'Brien, Polly Ann Young; **D:** Louis Gasnier. *VDM*

Murder Once Removed 🐾½ 1971

A private eye discovers that a respectable doctor has a bedside manner that women are dying for. Made for television. **74m/C VHS, Beta.** John Forsythe, Richard Kiley, Barbara Bain, Joseph Campanella; **D:** Charles S. Dubin. *ORI*

Murder One 🐾 1988 (R)

Two half-brothers escape from a Maryland prison and go on a killing spree, dragging their younger brother with them. Low-budget and it shows. Based on a true story. **83m/C VHS, Beta, LV.** Henry Thomas, James Wilder, Stephen Shellan, Errol Slue; **D:** Graeme Campbell. *NLC*

Murder 101 🐾🐾 1991 (PG-13)

Brosnan plays Charles Lattimore, an author and English professor who specializes in murder mysteries. He gives his students a rather unique assignment of planning the perfect murder. When a student is killed right before his eyes and a fellow teacher turns up dead, Lattimore realizes he's being framed for murder. Surprising twists abound in this stylish thriller. **93m/C VHS, Closed Caption.** Pierce Brosnan, Dey Young, Raphael Sbarge, Kim Thomson; **D:** Bill Condon; **W:** Bill Condon. *USH*

Murder or Mercy 🐾🐾½ 1974

Still timely story of a famous doctor accused of killing his terminally ill wife. Focuses on the morality of mercy killing. Made for television. **78m/C VHS.** Melvyn Douglas, Bradford Dillman, David Birney, Denver Pyle, Mildred Dunnock; **D:** Harvey Hart. *WOV*

Murder Ordained 🐾🐾½ 1987

Yet another true-crime network miniseries, this time about a Kansas minister and her lover plotting the demise of their spouses. Good acting for this sort of thing. In two-cassette package. **183m/C VHS, Closed Caption.** Keith Carradine, JoBeth Williams, Terry Kinney, Guy Boyd, Terence Knox, Darrell Larson, M. Emmet Walsh, Kathy Bates; **D:** Mike Robe. *FRH*

Murder over New York 🐾🐾 1940

Episode in the Charlie Chan mystery series. Chan visits New York City and becomes involved in an investigation at the airport. With the aid of his klutzy son, he sleuths his way through a slew of suspects until the mystery is solved. Standard fare for the Chan fan. **65m/B VHS, Beta, Closed Caption.** Sidney Toler, Marjorie Weaver, Robert Lowery, Ricardo Cortez, Donald MacBride, Melville Cooper, Victor Sen Yung; **D:** Harry Lachman. *FOX*

Murder Rap 🐾 1987

An aspiring musician/sound technologist becomes involved with a mysterious woman and her plot to kill her husband. Complications galore, especially for the viewer. **90m/C VHS, Beta.** John Hawkes, Seita Kathleen Feigny; **D:** Kliff Keuhl. *VCI*

Murder She Said 🐾🐾½ *Meet Miss Marple* 1962

Dame Margaret, playing the benign Miss M for the first time, witnesses a murder on board a train, but the authorities don't seem inclined to believe her. Posing as a maid at an estate near where she thought the body was dropped, she solves the murder and lands three more Miss Marple movies. Based on Christy's "4:50 From Paddington," it features Marple-to-be Hickson as the cook. **87m/B VHS, Beta.** Margaret Rutherford, Arthur Kennedy, Muriel Pavlow, James Robertson Justice, Thorley Walters, Charles Tingwell, Conrad Phillips; **D:** George Pollock. *MGM, FCT*

Murder So Sweet 🐾🐾½ *Poisoned by Love: The Kern County Murders* 1993

Hamlin stars as a slick small-town loser, with an apparently limitless appeal to women. He marries five of them but two wives and his mother mysteriously die of poisoning. Then an ex gets suspicious and tries to make certain it'll never happen again. Based on a true story. Made for television. **94m/C VHS.** Harry Hamlin, Helen Shaver, Faith Ford, Daphne Ashbrook, Eileen Brennan, K.T. Oslin, Terence Knox, Ed Lauter. *ACA*

Murder Story 🐾🐾½ 1989 (PG)

An aspiring mystery writer finds himself mixed up in a real murder and winds up involving his mentor as well. An overdone story, but a reasonably enjoyable film. **90m/C VHS, Beta, LV.** Christopher Lee, Bruce Boa; **D:** Eddie Arno, Markus Innocenti; **W:** Eddie Arno. *FHS, ACA*

Murder: Ultimate Grounds for Divorce 🐾 1985

A quiet weekend of camping turns into a night of horror for two couples when one of them plans an elaborate murder scheme. **90m/C VHS, Beta.** Roger Daltrey, Toyah Wilcox, Leslie Ash, Terry Raven. *ORI, WAR*

Murder with Music 🐾🐾 1945

A musical drama featuring an all-black cast. **60m/B VHS, Beta.** Bob Howard, Nellie Sissle, Nellie Hill; **D:** George P. Quigley. *NOS, DVT, VDM*

Murder without Motive 🐾🐾½ 1992

When two African American teenagers harrass an undercover cop, a struggle ensues and one teen ends up dead. Was the struggle racially motivated, or did the police act justifiably? **93m/C VHS.** Curtis McClaren, Anna Maria Horsford, Carla Gugino, Christopher Daniel Barnes, Cuba Gooding Jr., Georg Stanford Brown; **D:** Kevin Hooks. *TTC*

Murdered Innocence 🐾🐾 1994 (R)

In 1972, a rookie New York cop is called to a crime scene where a woman has been stabbed to death. Her young son is hysterical and her husband is holding the knife. When the husband panics and tries to flee, the cop shoots him in the back. Now, it's 1992, the convicted killer is out of prison and out for revenge (seems the son said his mother's lover committed the crime but there was a police coverup).**CW:** Violence; language; some sexuality; drug content. **88m/C VHS, Closed**

Caption. Jason Miller, Ellen Greene, Fred Carpenter; **D:** Frank Coraci; **W:** Diego Matamoros. *COL*

Murderers Among Us: The Simon Wiesenthal Story 🐾🐾🐾 1989

Powerful re-enactment of concentration camp survivor Simon Wiesenthal's search for war criminals. Kingsley's gripping performance drives this made-for-cable film. Be prepared for disturbing death camp scenes. **157m/C VHS, Closed Caption.** Ben Kingsley, Renee Soutendijk, Craig T. Nelson, Paul Freeman, Louisa Haigh, Jack Shepherd; **D:** Brian Gibson; **W:** Abby Mann; **M:** Bill Conti. *HBO, FCT, VIF*

Murderers Are Among Us 🐾🐾 *Die Morder Sind Unter Uns* 1946

In post WWII Germany, Suzanne Wallner (Knef) returns from a concentration camp to her apartment in Berlin only to find it occupied by Dr. Hans Mertens (Borchert). Haunted by his wartime experiences, Mertens has turned to women and alcohol. Suzanne refuses to give up her claim and moves in with Hans, eventually falling in love with him. In turn, Hans decides to face his demons by going after his former superior, Colonel Otto Bruckner (Paulsen), who's living an untroubled life despite the war crimes he committed. German with subtitles. **84m/B VHS.** *GE* Hildegarde Knef, Ernst Borchert, Arno Paulsen; **D:** Wolfgang Staudte; **W:** Wolfgang Staudte; **C:** Friedl Behn-Grund, Eugen Klagemann; **M:** Ernst Roters. *KIV*

Murderer's Keep woof! 1988

Secret ingredients contained in the Central Meat Market's hamburger are discovered by a young, deaf girl. Beware of filler, she learns, particularly if it's someone you know. **89m/C VHS, Beta.** Vic Tayback, Talia Shire, Robert Walden; **D:** Paulmichel Miekhe. *GHV*

Murderers' Row 🐾½ 1966

Daredevil bachelor and former counter-espionage agent Matt Helm is summoned from his life of leisure to ensure the safety of an important scientist. Martin's attempt as a super-spy doesn't wash, and Margret is implausible as the kidnapped scientist's daughter. Unless you want to hear Martin sing "I'm Not the Marrying Kind," don't bother. Second in the "Matt Helm" series. **108m/C VHS, Beta.** Dean Martin, Ann-Margret, Karl Malden, Beverly Adams, James Gregory; **D:** Henry Levin; **M:** Lalo Schifrin. *COL*

Murderlust woof! 1986

Employers in search of a security guard make a poor choice in offering the position to a sexually frustrated man whose hobbies include strangling prostitutes. Poor hiring decisions come into play later when he secures a job at an adolescent crisis center. **90m/C VHS, Beta.** Eli Rich, Rochelle Taylor, Dennis Gannon, Bonnie Schneider, Lisa Nichols; **D:** Donald M. Jones. *PSM*

Murderous Vision 🐾🐾 1991 (R)

Television fixture Boxleitner is a bored detective in this outing. But one day, while tracking a young mother in the missing persons bureau, he stumbles upon the trail of a serial killer. Enter a beautiful psychic who wants to help, add a race to catch the murderer, and Bruce suddenly has his hands full. Made for television. **93m/C VHS, LV, Closed Caption.** Bruce Boxleitner, Laura Johnson, Robert Culp; **D:** Gary Sherman. *PAR*

Murders at Lynch Cross 1985

Made-for-British-television mystery about a weird, isolated hotel on the Yorkshire moors. **60m/C VHS, Beta.** *GB* Jill Bennett, Joanna David, Barbara Jefford, Sylvia Syms. *PSM*

Murders in the Rue Morgue 🐾🐾½ 1932

Lugosi stars as a deranged scientist (what a stretch) who wants to find a female companion for his pet gorilla. He kidnaps a beautiful woman and prepares to make her the gorilla's bride. Very loosely based on the story by Edgar Allan Poe, which has been remade several times. **61m/B VHS, Closed Caption.** Bela Lugosi, Sidney Fox, Leon Ames, Brandon Hurst, Arlene Francis; **D:** Robert Florey; **C:** Karl Freund. *USH*

Murders in the Rue Morgue 🐾🐾½ 1971 (PG) A young woman has frightening dreams inspired by a play that her father is producing in Paris at the turn of the century. After many people associated with the production become murder victims, the girl becomes involved with one of her father's former associates, a man who killed her mother years ago and then faked his own suicide. The fourth film based on Edgar Allan Poe's classic horror story. 87m/C VHS, Beta. Jason Robards Jr., Lilli Palmer, Herbert Lom, Michael Dunn, Christine Kaufmann, Adolfo Celi; *D:* Gordon Hessler. *NO*

The Murders in the Rue Morgue 🐾🐾🐾 1986 (PG) The fifth filmed version of the Edgar Allan Poe story. Set in 19th-century Paris; actors in a mystery play find their roles coming to life. Scott is terrific, with good supporting help. Made for television. 92m/C VHS, Beta. George C. Scott, Rebecca DeMornay, Val Kilmer, Ian McShane, Neil Dickson; *D:* Jeannot Szwarc; *C:* Bruno de Keyzer. *THV*

Murders in the Zoo 🐾🐾½ 1933 Zoologist Atwill has a reason to be insanely jealous since his wife (Burke) has been having lots of extramarital affairs. But his way of dealing with these other men is certainly unique—he feeds them to various zoo animals (after first sewing the victims' lips shut). Censors were outraged and the film underwent various edits for its theatrical release. 62m/B VHS, Closed Caption. Lionel Atwill, Kathleen Burke, Charlie Ruggles, Randolph Scott, Gail Patrick, John Lodge, Harry Beresford; *D:* Edward Sutherland; *W:* Philip Wylie, Seton I. Miller. *USH*

Muriel 🐾🐾🐾½ *Muriel, Ou le Temps d'Un Retour; The Time of Return; Muriel, Or the Time of Return* 1963 A complex, mosaic drama about a middle-aged woman who meets an old lover at Boulogne, and her stepson who cannot forget the needless suffering he caused a young woman named Muriel while he was a soldier at war. Throughout, director Alain Resnais plumbs the essential meanings of memory, age, and the anxieties created from the tension between personal and public actions. Acclaimed; in French with subtitles. 115m/C VHS, Beta. *FR IT* Delphine Seyrig, Jean-Pierre Kerien, Nita Klein, Jean-Baptiste Thierree; *D:* Alain Resnais; *C:* Sacha Vierny; *M:* Georges Delerue. Venice Film Festival '63: Best Actress (Seyrig). *HTV, FCT*

Muriel's Wedding 🐾🐾🐾 1994 (R) Muriel (Collette) can catch a bridal bouquet, but can she catch a husband? Her blonde, bitch-goddess friends don't think so. But dowdy, pathetic, overweight Muriel dreams of a fairy tale wedding anyway. How she fulfills her obsessive fantasy is the basis for this quirky, hilarious, and often touchingly poignant ugly duckling tale with the occasional over-the-top satiric moment. Strong cast is led by sympathetic and engaging performances from Collette (who gained 40-plus pounds for the role) and Griffiths as her best friend, Rhonda. '70s pop supergroup ABBA lends its kitschy but catchy tunes to the plot and soundtrack. Not released in the U.S. until 1995.*CW:* Contains profanity and sexual situations. 105m/C VHS, LV, Closed Caption. *AU* Toni Collette, Bill Hunter, Rachel Griffiths, Jeanie Drynan, Gennie Nevinson Brice, Matt Day, Daniel Lapaine; *D:* P.J. Hogan; *W:* P.J. Hogan; *M:* Peter Best. Australian Film Institute '94: Best Actress (Collette), Best Film, Best Sound, Best Supporting Actress (Griffiths); Nominations: Australian Film Institute '94: Best Director (Hogan), Best Screenplay, Best Supporting Actor (Hunter), Best Supporting Actress (Drynan); British Academy Awards '95: Best Original Screenplay; Golden Globe Awards '96: Best Film—Musical/Comedy (Collette); Writers Guild of America '95: Best Original Screenplay. *MAX*

Murmur of the Heart 🐾🐾🐾½ 1971 (R) Honest treatment of a fourteen-year-old's coming of age. After his older brothers take him to a prostitute for his first sexual experience, he comes down with scarlet fever. He then travels to a health spa with his mom to recover. There they find that their mother-son bond is stronger than most. Music by Charlie Parker is featured in the score. In French with English subtitles. 118m/C

VHS, Beta, LV. *FR* Benoit Ferreux, Daniel Gelin, Lea Massari, Corinne Kersten, Jacqueline Chauveau, Marc Wincourt, Michael Lonsdale; *D:* Louis Malle; *W:* Louis Malle. Nominations: Academy Awards '72: Best Story & Screenplay. *ORI*

Murph the Surf 🐾🐾½ *Live a Little, Steal a Lot; You Can't Steal Love* 1975 (PG) Fact-based, engrossing story of two beach bums turned burglars who grow bored with small-time robbery and plan a trip to New York City to steal the Star of Africa sapphire. Notable among the many action scenes is a boat chase through the inland waterways of Miami, Florida. 102m/C VHS, Beta. Robert Conrad, Don Stroud, Donna Mills, Luther Adler, Robyn Millan, Paul Stewart; *D:* Marvin J. Chomsky. *WAR, OM*

Murphy's Fault 🐾🐾 1988 (PG-13) Dark comedy about a night watchman/writer plagued by a series of bad luck incidents. 94m/C VHS, Beta, LV. Patrick Dollaghan, Anne Curry, Stack Pierce; *D:* Robert J. Smawley. *THV*

Murphy's Law 🐾 1986 (R) A hard-headed cop gets framed for his ex-wife's murder and embarks on a mission to find the actual killer. He is slowed down by a smart-mouthed prostitute who is handcuffed to him during his search. Casting a female in the role of a psycho-killer is unique to the genre. 101m/C VHS, Beta, LV, Closed Caption. Charles Bronson, Carrie Snodgress, Kathleen Wilhoite, Robert F. Lyons, Richard Romanus, Angel Tompkins, Bill Henderson, James Luisi, Janet MacLachlan, Lawrence Tierney; *D:* J. Lee Thompson; *M:* Mark Donohue. *MED, VTR*

Murphy's Romance 🐾🐾🐾 1985 (PG-13) A young divorced mother with an urge to train horses pulls up the stakes and heads for Arizona with her son. There she meets a pharmacist who may be just what the doctor ordered to help her build a new life. 107m/C VHS, Beta, LV, Closed Caption. James Garner, Sally Field, Brian Kerwin, Corey Haim, Dennis Burkley, Charles Lane, Georgann Johnson; *D:* Martin Ritt; *W:* Harriet Frank Jr., Irving Ravetch; *M:* Carole King. Nominations: Academy Awards '85: Best Actor (Garner), Best Cinematography. *COL, HMV*

Murphy's War 🐾🐾 1971 (PG) In WWII, the Germans sink an English ship and gun down most of its crew. An Irishman, however, survives and returns to health with the help of a nurse. He then seeks revenge on those who killed his crewmates, even after he learns the war has ended. O'Toole is interesting as the revenge-minded seaman though saddled with a mediocre script. 106m/C VHS, Beta. *GB* Peter O'Toole, Sian Phillips, Philippe Noiret; *D:* Peter Yates; *W:* Stirling Silliphant; *M:* John Barry. *PAR, CCB*

Murrow 🐾🐾½ 1986 A cable television biography of the renowed chain-smoking journalist who changed broadcasting history by fearlessly voicing his liberal ideas on the air waves. His life was more interesting though Travanti does his best to breathe some life into the script. 114m/C VHS, Beta. Daniel J. Travanti, Dabney Coleman, Edward Herrmann, David Suchet, John McMartin, Robert Vaughn, Kathryn Leigh Scott; *D:* Jack Gold; *W:* Ernest Kinoy; *M:* Carl Davis. *FCT, LIV*

Muscle Beach Party 🐾🐾 1964 Sequel to "Beach Party" finds Frankie and Annette romping in the sand again. Trouble invades teen nirvana when a new gym opens and the hardbodies try to muscle in on surfer turf. Meanwhile, Paluzzi tries to muscle in on Funicello's turf. Good clean corny fun, with the usual lack of script and plot. Lorre appeals in a cameo, his final screen appearance. Watch for "Little" Stevie Wonder in his debut. Rickles' first appearance in the "BP" series; Lupus was credited as Rock Stevens. Followed by "Bikini Beach." 🎵Muscle Beach Party; Runnin' Wild; Muscle Bustle; My First Love; Surfin' Woodie; Surfer's Holiday; Happy Street; A Girl Needs a Boy; A Boy Needs a Girl. 94m/C VHS, Beta, LV. Frankie Avalon, Annette Funicello, Buddy Hackett, Luciana Paluzzi, Don Rickles, John Ashley, Jody McCrea, Morey Amsterdam, Peter Lupus, Candy Johnson, Dolores Wells, Stevie Wonder, Donna Loren, Amadee Cha-

bot; *Cameos:* Peter Lorre; *D:* William Asher; *W:* William Asher, Robert Dillon; *M:* Les Baxter. *NO*

Music Box 🐾🐾½ 1989 (R) An attorney defends her father against accusations that he has committed inhumane Nazi war crimes. If she loses, her father faces deportation. As the case progresses, she must struggle to remain objective in the courtroom and come to terms with the possibility that her father is guilty. Lange's portrayal of an ethnic character is highly convincing. 126m/C VHS, Beta, LV. Jessica Lange, Frederic Forrest, Lukas Haas, Armin Mueller-Stahl, Michael Rooker, Donald Moffat, Cheryl Lynn Bruce; *D:* Constantin Costa-Gavras; *W:* Joe Eszterhas; *C:* Patrick Blossier; *M:* Philippe Sarde. Nominations: Academy Awards '89: Best Actress (Lange). *NO*

Music Box/Helpmates 1932 These two classic, award-winning comedy shorts by the dynamic duo have been color-enhanced by Colorization. 50m/B VHS, Beta. Stan Laurel, Oliver Hardy. *VTR*

Music in My Heart 🐾½ 1940 Two taxi cabs crash and spur the love of Martin and Hayworth. She proceeds to break off her engagement to save Martin from deportation. Hayworth's last low-budget film before becoming a Hollywood goddess. 69m/B VHS. Rita Hayworth, Tony Martin, Edith Fellows, Alan Mowbray, Eric Blore, George Tobias, Joseph Crehan, George Humbert, Phil Tead; *D:* Joseph Santley; *M:* Robert Wright, Chet Forrest. Nominations: Academy Awards '40: Best Song ("It's a Blue World"). *COL, CCB*

The Music Lovers 🐾🐾½ 1971 (R) Russell's version of Tchaikovsky's tormented life and glorious achievements is a shocker, a movie that infuriates professed music lovers but, nonetheless, has introduced many a neophyte to the world of classical music via its sensationalism. Homosexual Tchaikovsky marries an admirer to appease the Russian government and his financial benefactor. Stunned when he discovers his wife is a nymphomaniac, he banishes her to a netherworld of prostitution and eventual insanity which Russell mercilessly explores. Tchaikovsky's own squalid life is hardly better, though he does enjoy success before the bottom falls out. 122m/C VHS, LV. *GB* Richard Chamberlain, Glenda Jackson, Max Adrian, Christopher Gable, Kenneth Colley, Izabella Telezynska, Maureen Pryor; *D:* Ken Russell; *W:* Melvin Bragg. *MGM, MLB, FCT*

The Music Man 🐾🐾🐾🐾 1962 (G) Con man in the guise of a traveling salesman gets off the train in River City, Iowa. After hearing about plans to build a pool hall, he argues it would be the gateway to hell for the young, impressionable males of the town. He then convinces the River Cityians to look toward the future of the community and finance a wholesome children's marching band. Although the huckster plans to take their money and run before the instruments arrive, his feelings for the town librarian cause him to think twice about fleeing the Heartland. This isn't just a slice of Americana; it's a whole pie. Acting and singing are terrific "with a capital 'T' and that rhymes with 'P' and that stands for" Preston, who epitomizes the charismatic pitchman. 🎵Seventy-six Trombones; Trouble; If You Don't Mind; Till There Way You; The Wells Fargo Wagon; Being in Love; Goodnight, My Someone; Rock Island; Iowa Stubborn. 151m/C VHS, Beta, LV, Closed Caption. Robert Preston, Shirley Jones, Buddy Hackett, Hermione Gingold, Paul Ford, Pert Kelton, Ron Howard; *D:* Morton DaCosta; *W:* Marion Hargrove; *C:* Robert Burks. Academy Awards '62: Best Adapted Score; Golden Globe Awards '63: Best Film—Musical/Comedy; Nominations: Academy Awards '62: Best Art Direction/Set Decoration (Color), Best Costume Design (Color), Best Film Editing, Best Picture, Best Sound. *WAR, MVD, TLF*

The Music of Chance 🐾🐾½ 1993 (R) Convoluted story about a smalltime gambler (Spader) and a drifter (Patinkin) who wind up involved in a bizarre high stakes poker game with a Laurel and Hardyish pair (Durning and Grey) who live in an isolated mansion. When Spader and Patinkin lose, their debt forces them into an indentured servitude where they must construct a brick wall around their new masters' estate. Bloated with symbolism, this adaptation from cult fave novelist Auster (who has a small part), loses its eclectic significance in the translation to the big screen. Nonetheless, valiant effort by rookie director Haas. 98m/C VHS, LV, Closed Caption. James Spader, Mandy Patinkin, Joel Grey, Charles Durning, M. Emmet Walsh, Samantha Mathis, Christopher Penn, Pearl Jones, Paul Auster; *D:* Philip Haas; *W:* Philip Haas, Belinda Haas; *C:* Bernard Zitzermann; *M:* Philip Johnston. COL, BTV

Music Shoppe 🎬🎬 1982 (G) Four teenagers form a rock band with the assistance of the local music store proprietor. Interesting cast. 93m/C VHS, Beta. Gary Crosby, Nia Peeples, Benny Medina, Stephen Schwartz, David Jackson, Jesse White, Doug Kershaw, Giselle MacKenzie. GEM

The Music Teacher 🎬🎬½ *Le Maitre de Musique* 1988 (PG) A Belgian costume drama dealing with a famed singer who retires to devote himself to teaching two students exclusively. In time, he sees his prized pupils lured into an international competition by an old rival of his. Although the singing is sharp, the story is flat. In French with yellow English subtitles. 95m/C VHS, Beta, LV. BE Patrick Bauchau, Sylvie Fennec, Phillipe Volter, Jose Van Dam, Johan Leysen, Anne Roussel; *D:* Gerard Corbiau. Nominations: Academy Awards '88: Best Foreign Language Film. ORI

Musica Proibita 🎬🎬½ 1943 A serious opera-spiced drama about a young romance crushed by adultery in the teenage couple's ancestry. In Italian with English subtitles. 93m/B VHS, Beta. Tito Gobbi, Maria Mercader. VYY, APD

Mussolini & I 🎬🎬½ *Mussolini: The Decline and Fall of Il Duce* 1985 Docudramatization of the struggle for power between Italy's Benito Mussolini and his son-in-law, Galeazzo Ciano. Narrated by Sarandon in the role of Il Duce's daughter. Made for cable television. 130m/C VHS, Beta. Bob Hoskins, Anthony Hopkins, Susan Sarandon, Annie Girardot, Barbara DeRossi, Fabio Testi, Kurt Raab; *D:* Alberto Negrin. NLC

Mutant 🎬½ *Night Shadows* 1983 (R) Another argument for the proper disposal of toxic waste. Hazardous materials transform the people of a southern town into monsters. 100m/C VHS, Beta, LV. Wings Hauser, Bo Hopkins, Jennifer Warren, Lee Montgomery; *D:* John Cardos; *M:* Richard Band. LIV, VES

Mutant Hunt woof! *Matt Riker* 1987 Made for video movie about a battle between robots gone haywire and an all-American hero. The detective cyborgs are set free while high on a sexual stimulant called Euphoron to wreak their technological havoc on a rampage in Manhattan. 90m/C Beta. Rick Gianisi, Mary-Anne Fahey; *D:* Tim Kincaid; *W:* Tim Kincaid. HMD

Mutant on the Bounty 🎬½ 1989 A musician, lost in space as a beam of light for 23 years, is transported aboard a spaceship. Once he materializes, it becomes apparent that he has undergone some incredible physical changes. As if that's not enough, the crew then must flee from a couple of thugs who are trying to steal a vial of serum they have on board. A space spoof that never gets into orbit. 93m/C VHS. John Roarke, Deborah Benson, John Furey, Victoria Catlin, John Fleck, Kyle T. Heffner; *D:* Robert Torrance. HMD

Mutant Species 🎬 *Bio-Force I* 1995 (R) Soldier is accidentally exposed to altered DNA and begins to mutate into a remorseless and terrifying killer.*CW:* Violence and language. 100m/C VHS, LV. Leo Rossi, Ted Prior, Grant Gelt, Denise Crosby, Powers Boothe, Wilford Brimley; *D:* David A. Prior; *W:* David A. Prior, William Vigil; *C:* Carlos Gonzalez. LIV

Mutant Video 1976 Six comedic, award-winning short-subject films from Jim Belushi and Rob Riley. Outrageous humor. 60m/B VHS, Beta. James Belushi, Rob Riley. LIV

Mutants In Paradise woof! 1988 Comedy about a human guinea-pig who always gets involved in some sort of mishap. 78m/C VHS, Beta. Brad Greenquist, Robert Ingham, Anna Nicholas. TWE

Mutator 🎬🎬 *Time of the Beast* 1990 (R) A corporation makes a tiny genetic mistake and winds up creating a new life form...a demonic pussycat who preys on humans.*CW:* Language and monster violence and gore. 91m/C VHS, Beta. Brion James, Carolyn Ann Clark, Milton Raphiel Murrill; *D:* John R. Bowey; *W:* Lynn Rose Higgins. PSM

Mute Witness 🎬🎬½ 1995 (R) Low-budget British thriller, lensed in Moscow film studio, about U.S. filmers making a cheap thriller in Moscow film studio. Billy (Sudina) is the mute make-up artist of the title who, returning to the studio for a forgotten item, witnesses some of the crew shooting a snuff film with a real-life stabbing. First-timer Waller mocks both thriller genre and film biz, sometimes relying on, rather than spoofing, cliched elements. Highlight is 20-minute long chase scene with the killers pursuing Billy in the cavernous studio. Guinness makes a surprise appearance in a cameo.*CW:* Violence and a strong scene combining sex and violence. 100m/C VHS, LV, Closed Caption. GB Marina Sudina, Fay Ripley, Evan Richards, Oleg Jankowsky, Igor Volkow, Sergei Karlenkov; *Cameos:* Alec Guinness; *D:* Anthony Waller; *W:* Anthony Waller; *C:* Egon Werdin; *M:* Wilbert Hirsch. COL

The Muthers 🎬🎬 1976 (R) Women prisoners escape from their confinement in a South American jungle. 101m/C VHS, Beta. Jeanne Bell, Rosanne Katon, Jayne Kennedy, Trina Parks; *D:* Cirio H. Santiago. NO

The Mutilator woof! *Fall Break* 1985 (R) After accidentally bumping off his mother, a young man stalks five high school students wanting to cut them up into tiny bits. An unedited version is also available. Bloody boredom. 85m/C VHS, Beta, LV. Jack Chatham, Trace Cooper, Frances Raines, Bill Hitchcock; *D:* Buddy Cooper. LIV, VES

Mutiny 🎬🎬 1952 In the War of 1812, the crew of an American ship carrying $10 million in gold ingots among themselves for a part of France's donation to the war effort. The beautiful photography doesn't make up for the predictability of the storyline. 76m/C VHS, Beta. Mark Stevens, Gene Evans, Angela Lansbury, Patric Knowles; *D:* Edward Dmytryk; *W:* Philip Yordan. NOS, VCI

Mutiny in the Big House 🎬🎬½ 1939 A man is sent to prison for writing a bad ten dollar check and must choose between seeking salvation with the prison chaplain or toughing it out with a hardened convict. Suprisingly good low-budget programmer. 83m/B VHS, Beta. Charles Bickford, Barton MacLane, Pat Moriarity, Dennis Moore, William Royle, Charles Foy, George Cleveland; *D:* William Nigh. SNC

The Mutiny of the Elsinore 🎬 1939 A writer on board an old sailing ship fights mutineers and wins back both the helm and the captain's daughter. Tedious British flotsam that made hash of an oft-filmed Jack London tale, and made news even in 1939 for its use of modern-day slang and clothing in the period setting. 74m/B VHS. Paul Lukas, Lyn Harding, Kathleen Kelly, Clifford Evans, Ben Soutten, Jiro Soneya; *D:* Roy Lockwood. NOS, DVT, FCT

Mutiny on the Bounty 🎬🎬🎬🎬 1935 Compelling adaptation of the true story of sadistic Captain Bligh, Fletcher Christian and their turbulent journey aboard the HMS Bounty. No gray here: Laughton's Bligh is truly a despicable character and extremely memorable in this MGM extravaganza. Remade twice, in 1962 and again in 1984 as "The Bounty." Much, much better than the 1962 remake. 132m/B VHS, Beta, LV, 8mm. Clark Gable, Franchot Tone, Charles Laughton, Donald Crisp, Dudley Digges, Spring Byington, Henry Stephenson, Eddie Quillan, Herbert Mundin, Movita, Ian Wolfe; *D:* Frank Lloyd; *W:* Talbot Jennings, Jules Furthman, Carey Wilson; *M:* Herbert Stothart. Academy Awards '35: Best Picture; National Board of Review Awards '35: 10 Best Films of the Year;

New York Film Critics Awards '35: Best Actor (Laughton); Nominations: Academy Awards '35: Best Actor (Gable), Best Actor (Tone, Laughton), Best Director (Lloyd), Best Film Editing, Best Screenplay, Best Score. MGM, BMV, BTV

Mutiny on the Bounty 🎬🎬 1962 Based on the novel by Charles Nordhoff and James Norman Hall, this account of the 1789 mutiny led by Fletcher Christian against Captain Bligh of the Bounty is highlighted by lavish photography. Can't navigate the same perfect course set by the 1935 classic. Marlon Brando seems miscast, giving a choppy performance as the mutiny leader. 177m/C VHS, Beta, LV. Marlon Brando, Trevor Howard, Richard Harris, Hugh Griffith; *D:* Lewis Milestone; *C:* Robert L. Surtees. Nominations: Academy Awards '62: Best Art Direction/Set Decoration (Color), Best Color Cinematography, Best Film Editing, Best Picture, Best Song ("Love Song (Follow Me)"), Best Original Score. MGM

Mutual Respect 🎬½ 1977 (PG) A dying wealthy man sets out to find the son he never knew. 88m/C VHS, Beta. Lloyd Bridges, Beau Bridges. ACA

My African Adventure woof! 1987 Silly tale of an ambassador's son discovering a talking monkey in Africa and meeting a slew of opportunistic misfits in his travels. A comedy unfortunately short on laughs. Based on Tamar Burnstein's book. 93m/C VHS, Beta. Dom DeLuise, Jimmie Walker; *D:* Sam Firstenberg. MED

My American Cousin 🎬🎬🎬 1985 (PG) Award-winning Canadian coming-of-age comedy about a 12-year-old girl who falls for her rebellious, fun-loving 17-year-old American cousin over summer vacation. Followed by "American Boyfriends." 94m/C VHS, Beta, LV. CA Margaret Langrick, John Wildman, Richard Donat, Jane Mortifee; *D:* Sandy Wilson; *W:* Sandy Wilson. Genie Awards '86: Best Actor (Wildman), Best Actress (Langrick), Best Director (Wilson), Best Film.MED, VTR

My Antonia 🎬🎬½ 1994 (PG) Orphaned teenaged farm boy Jim Burden (Harris) discovers first romance with poor immigrant girl Antonia (Lowensohn) in 1886 Nebraska. They fall in love, separate, but maintain a 30-year friendship. Based on the book by Willa Cather. 92m/C VHS, Beta, Closed Caption. Neil Patrick Harris, Jason Robards Jr., Eva Marie Saint, Elina Lowensohn, Norbert Weisser, Travis Fine, Jan Triska, Anne Tremko, Mira Furlan, Boris Krutonog; *D:* Joseph Sargent; *C:* Robert Primes. PAR

My Apprenticeship 🎬🎬🎬 1939 The second film of Donskoi's trilogy on Maxim Gorky has the writer earning his living, at the age of eight, as an apprentice to a bourgeois family. Although they promise him an education, Gorky is forced to learn to read on his own and eventually sets off on a series of land and sea voyages. He recognizes that the poverty and abuse he has suffered is typical of the lives of most Russians and he encounters the beginnings of revolution. In Russian with English subtitles. Preceded by "My Childhood" and followed by "My Universities." 100m/C VHS. RU D: Mark Donskoi. FCT

My Beautiful Laundrette 🎬🎬🎬 1985 (R) Omar (Warnecke), the nephew of a Pakistani businessman, is given the opportunity to better himself by turning his uncle's run-down laundry into a profitable business. He reunites with Johnny (Day Lewis), a childhood friend and a working-class street punk, and they go into the business together. They find themselves battling the prejudice of each other's families and friends in order to succeed. An intelligent look at the sexuality, race relations and economic problems of Thatcher's London. Great performances by a relatively unknown cast (for contrast, note Day Lewis' performance in "Room with a View," released in the same year.) 93m/C VHS, Beta, LV, Closed Caption. Gordon Warnecke, Daniel Day-Lewis, Saeed Jaffrey, Roshan Seth, Shirley Anne Field, Derrick Branche, Rita Wolf, Souad Faress, Richard Graham, Dudley Thomas, Garry Cooper, Charu Bala Choksi, Neil Cunningham, Walter Donohue, Stephen Marcus, Badi Uzzaman; *D:* Stephen

Frears; **W:** Hanif Kureishi; **C:** Oliver Stapleton; **M:** Ludus Tonalis, Stanley Myers. National Board of Review Awards '86: Best Supporting Actor (Day-Lewis); New York Film Critics Awards '86: Best Screenplay, Best Supporting Actor (Day-Lewis); National Society of Film Critics Awards '86: Best Screenplay; Nominations: Academy Awards '86: Best Original Screenplay.*ORI, WAR*

My Best Friend Is a Vampire 🎬🎬
1988 (PG) Another teenage vampire story, about trying to cope with certain changes that adolescence and bloodsucking bring. Good supporting cast. **90m/C VHS, Closed Caption.** Robert Sean Leonard, Evan Mirand, Cheryl Pollak, Rene Auberjonois, Cecilia Peck, Fannie Flagg, Kenneth Kimmins, David Warner, Paul Wilson; **D:** Jimmy Huston; **M:** Stephen Dorff. *HBO*

My Best Friend's Girl 🎬🎬½ *La Femme De Mon Pote*
1984 Coy, sardonic French romance about a woman who slaloms between two buddies working at a ski resort. Despite fine performances from all, it never quite makes it to the top of the hill. In French with English subtitles. **99m/C VHS, Beta.** *FR* Isabelle Huppert, Thierry Lhermitte, Coluche, Francoise Perrot; **D:** Bertrand Blier; **W:** Bertrand Blier, Gerard Brach. *COL*

My Best Friend's Wedding 🎬🎬½
1997 (PG-13) Yes, it's a romantic comedy, but like director Hogan's previous effort, "Muriel's Wedding," there's some snap among the smiles. Restaurant critic Julianne (Roberts) and sports writer Michael (Mulroney) are best friends who have a pact that they'll marry each other if neither has found someone else by the age of 28. Michael finds sweet, wealthy Kimmy (Diaz) and invites Julianne to his nuptials. Naturally, Julianne realizes she's in love with Michael and she'll stop at nothing to break up the wedding, even enlisting gay friend George (Everett) to pose as her new beau. Roberts appears as the critics prefer her (long hair and smiling) while she extends her range of physical comedy. Diaz gets to be nice, Everett gets to steal every scene he's in, and Mulroney gets to be the lucky object of two lovely women's affections. Shot on location oin Chicago.**CW:** One use of strong language and brief sex-related humor. **105m/C VHS.** Julia Roberts, Dermot Mulroney, Cameron Diaz, Rupert Everett, Philip Bosco, M. Emmet Walsh, Rachel Griffiths, Susan Sullivan, Paul Giamatti; **D:** P.J. Hogan; **W:** Ronald Bass; **C:** Laszlo Kovacs; **M:** James Newton Howard. *NYR*

My Best Girl 🎬🎬
1927 Mary attempts to bring her new sweetheart home for dinner, with disastrous results. A gentle satire on middle-American life in the 1920s. Includes organ score. **78m/B VHS, Beta, LV.** Mary Pickford, Charles "Buddy" Rogers; **D:** Sam Taylor; **C:** Charles Rosher; **M:** Gaylord Carter. Nominations: Academy Awards '28: Best Cinematography. *CCB*

My Bloody Valentine 🎬🎬
1981 (R) Psychotic coal miner visits the peaceful little town of Valentine Bluffs on the night of the yearly Valentine Ball. Many of the townspeople have their hearts removed with a pick axe and sent to the sheriff in candy boxes. The bloodiest scenes were cut out to avoid an X-rating. **91m/C VHS, Beta, LV.** *CA* Paul Kelman, Lori Hallier; **D:** George Mihalka. *PAR*

My Blue Heaven 🎬🎬
1990 (PG-13) After agreeing to rat on the Mafia, Martin is dropped into suburbia as part of the witness protection program. Moranis plays the FBI agent assigned to help the former mobster become an upstanding citizen. Adjusting to life in the slow lane isn't easy for an ex con who has grown accustomed to the big time. Not the typical role for Martin, who plays a brunette with a New York accent and is handcuffed by bad writing. **96m/C VHS, Beta, LV, Closed Caption.** Steve Martin, Rick Moranis, Joan Cusack, Melanie Mayron, Carol Kane, Bill Irwin, William Hickey, Daniel Stern; **D:** Herbert Ross; **W:** Nora Ephron; **C:** John Bailey; **M:** Ira Newborn. *WAR, BTV*

My Bodyguard 🎬🎬🎬
1980 (PG) An undersized high school student fends off attacking bullies by hiring a king-sized, withdrawn lad as his bodyguard. Their "business" relationship, however, develops into true friendship. An adolescent coming of age with more intelligence and sensitivity than most of its ilk, and a pack of up and coming stars as well as old stand-bys Houseman and Gordon. **96m/C VHS, Beta.** Chris Makepeace, Adam Baldwin, Martin Mull, Ruth Gordon, Matt Dillon, John Houseman, Joan Cusack, Craig Richard Nelson; **D:** Tony Bill; **W:** Alan Ormsby; **M:** Dave Grusin. National Board of Review Awards '80: 10 Best Films of the Year. *FOX*

My Boy 🎬🎬½
1921 Coogan stars as a foreign orphan who faces deportation. Instead he escapes and follows an old man home. This rare film includes an organ score. **56m/B VHS, Beta.** Jackie Coogan, Claude Gillingwater, Mathilde Brundage; **D:** Albert Austin. *GPV*

My Boyfriend's Back 🎬 *Johnny Zombie*
1993 (PG-13) Embarassingly dumb flick about a teenage boy who wants to take the prettiest girl in the school to the prom. The only problem is that he's become a zombie. Bits of him keep falling off (his girl thoughtfully glues them back on) and if he wants to stay "alive" long enough to get to the dance he has to munch on human flesh. Yuck.**CW:** Strong language, zombie violence, and teen sex fantasy. **85m/C VHS, LV, Closed Caption.** Andrew Lowery, Traci Lind, Edward Herrmann, Mary Beth Hurt, Danny Zorn, Austin Pendleton, Jay O. Sanders, Paul Dooley, Bob Dishy, Matthew Fox, Paxton Whitehead; **D:** Bob Balaban; **W:** Dean Lorey; **C:** Mac Ahlberg. *TOU*

My Boys Are Good Boys 🎬
1978 (PG) A young foursome steal from an armored car and have to face the consequences. Quirky with an implausible storyline. **90m/C VHS, Beta.** Ralph Meeker, Ida Lupino, Lloyd Nolan, David Doyle; **D:** Bethel Buckalew. *NO*

My Breakfast with Blassie
1983 Kaufman and professional wrestler Blassie meet for breakfast and carry on a comical dialogue. **60m/C VHS, Beta.** Andy Kaufman, Freddie Blassie; **D:** Johnny Legend, Linda Lautrec. *RHI*

My Brilliant Career 🎬🎬🎬½
1979 (G) A headstrong young woman spurns the social expectations of turn-of-the-century Australia and pursues opportunities to broaden her intellect and preserve her independence. Davis is wonderful as the energetic and charismatic community trendsetter. Based on an autobiographical novel by Miles Franklin which has been marvelously transferred to the screen. Armstrong deserves credit for her fine direction. **101m/C VHS, Beta.** *AU* Judy Davis, Sam Neill, Wendy Hughes; **D:** Gillian Armstrong. Australian Film Institute '79: Best Film; British Academy Awards '80: Best Actress (Davis); Nominations: Academy Awards '80: Best Costume Design. *VES*

My Brother Has Bad Dreams 🎬
1988 Young man with sibling tosses and turns in bed. **97m/C VHS.** Nick Kleinholz, Marlena Lustic. *VCI*

My Brother's Wife 🎬🎬½
1989 (PG) Barney (Ritter), the black sheep of a wealthy family, spends two decades pursuing Eleanor (Harris), the woman of his dreams. Unfortunately, she's already married—to the brother he despises. Adapted from the play "The Middle Ages" by A.R. Gurney. Made for television. **94m/C VHS.** John Ritter, Mel Harris, Polly Bergen, Dakin Matthews, David Byron, Lee Weaver; **D:** Jack Bender; **W:** Percy Granger. *APX, TPV*

My Champion 🎬
1984 Chance meeting propels Mike Gorman and Miki Tsuwa into a relationship based on the strong bonds of love and athletic competition. **101m/C VHS, Beta.** Yoko Shimada, Chris Mitchum. *MED*

My Chauffeur 🎬🎬½
1986 (R) When a wise-cracking female is hired on as a chauffeur at an all-male chauffeur service, sparks fly. And when the owner takes a definite liking to her work, things take a turn for the worse. As these sort of sexploitation flicks go, this is one of the better ones. **94m/C VHS, Beta, LV.** Deborah Foreman, Sam Jones, Howard Hesseman, E.G. Marshall, Sean McClory; **D:** David Beaird; **W:** David Beaird. *LIV, VES*

My Childhood 🎬🎬🎬
1938 The first of director Donskoi's trilogy on the life of Maxim Gorky, based on Gorky's autobiographical stories. In this first film, Donskoi depicts Gorky's childhood of abuse and poverty with his grandparents in the 1870s. Eventually, Gorky is forced into the streets and he becomes a wandering beggar. In Russian with English subtitles. Followed by "My Apprenticeship" and "My Universities." **100m/C VHS.** *RU* **D:** Mark Donskoi. *FCT*

My Cousin Vinny 🎬🎬🎬
1992 (R) Vinny Gambini (Pesci), a lawyer who took the bar exam six times before passing, goes to Wahzoo City, Alabama to get his cousin and a friend off the hook when they're accused of killing a store clerk. Leather jackets, gold chains, Brooklyn accents, and his fiancee Tomei's penchant for big hair and bold clothing don't go over well with conservative judge Gwynne, causing plenty of misunderstandings. Surprising hit with simplistic story reaches popular heights via entertaining performances by the entire cast. Tomei in particular steals every scene she's in and has an Oscar to prove it.**CW:** Language. **120m/C VHS, Closed Caption.** Joe Pesci, Ralph Macchio, Marisa Tomei, Mitchell Whitfield, Fred Gwynne, Lane Smith, Austin Pendleton, Bruce McGill; **D:** Jonathan Lynn; **W:** Dale Launer; **M:** Randy Edelman. Academy Awards '92: Best Supporting Actress (Tomei); MTV Movie Awards '93: Breakthrough Performance (Tomei). *FXV, MOV, PMS*

My Darlin' Clementine
1986 Shelly Duvall gives the famous song about a miner who bemoans the loss of his daughter and her size nine shoes her own touch in this entry from the "Tall Tales and Legends" series. Made for cable television. **49m/C VHS, Closed Caption.** Shelley Duvall, Ed Asner, David Dukes, John Matuszak. *FOX*

My Darling Clementine 🎬🎬🎬½
1946 One of the best Hollywood westerns ever made, this recounts the precise events leading up to and including the gunfight at the O.K. Corral. Ford allegedly knew Wyatt Earp and used his stories to recount the details vividly, though not always accurately. Remake of 1939's "Frontier Marshal." **97m/B VHS, Beta, LV, Closed Caption.** Henry Fonda, Victor Mature, Walter Brennan, Linda Darnell, Tim Holt, Ward Bond, John Ireland; **D:** John Ford. *FOX, TLF*

My Daughter's Keeper 🎬🎬
1993 (R) The apparently neglectful nanny of an unsuspecting family reveals her deadly agenda of murder, adultery, and more. **94m/C VHS.** Nicholas Guest, Jocelyn Broderick, Ana Padrao. *LIV*

My Dear Secretary 🎬🎬½
1949 After she marries her boss, a woman grows jealous of the secretary that replaces her. Comedic dialogue and antics result. **94m/C VHS, Beta.** Kirk Douglas, Laraine Day, Keenan Wynn, Rudy Vallee, Florence Bates, Alan Mowbray, Charles Halton; **D:** Charles Martin; **W:** Charles Martin. *NOS, MRV, BAR*

My Demon Lover 🎬🎬
1987 (PG-13) This sex comedy is complicated by the hero's transformation into a demon whenever he is aroused. Saved from complete mediocrity by Family Ties's Valentine in a likable performance. **90m/C VHS, Beta, LV.** Scott Valentine, Michelle Little, Arnold Johnson, Gina Gallego; **D:** Charles Loventhal; **M:** David Newman, Ed Alton. *COL*

My Dinner with Andre 🎬🎬🎬½
1981 Two friends talk about their lives and philosophies for two hours over dinner one night. A wonderful exploration into storytelling, the conversation juxtaposes the experiences and philosophies of nerdish, bumbling Shawn and the globe-trotting spiritual pilgrimage of Gregory, in this sometimes poignant, sometimes comic little movie that starts you thinking. **110m/C VHS, Beta, LV.** Andre Gregory, Wallace Shawn; **D:** Louis Malle. *HMV, TPV*

My Dog Shep 🎬
1946 An orphan and his dog run away and are pursued diligently when it is discovered that he is a wealthy heir. **71m/B VHS, Beta, LV.** Tom Neal, William Farnum, Lannie Rees; **D:** Ford Beebe. *NOS, VYY*

My Dog, the Thief ⅋ 1969 A helicopter weatherman is unaware that the lovable St. Bernard he has adopted is a kleptomaniac. When the dog steals a valuable necklace from a team of professional jewel thieves, the fun begins. 88m/C VHS, Beta. Joe Flynn, Elsa Lanchester, Roger C. Carmel, Mickey Shaughnessy, Dwayne Hickman, Mary Ann Mobley; **D:** Robert Stevenson. DVT

My Dream Is Yours ⅋⅋½ 1949 Day plays an up and coming radio star in this Warner Brothers musical comedy with a cameo from Bugs Bunny in a dream sequence. This fresh, fun remake of "Twenty Million Sweethearts" is often underrated, but is well worth a look. ♫My Dream is Yours; Some Like You; Tic, Tic, Tic; Love Finds a Way; I'll String Along with You; Canadian Capers; Freddie Get Ready; You Must Have Been a Beautiful Baby; Jeepers, Creepers. 101m/C VHS. Jack Carson, Doris Day, Lee Bowman, Adolphe Menjou, Eve Arden, S.Z. Sakall, Selena Royle, Edgar Kennedy; **D:** Michael Curtiz. FOX, FCT, MLB

My Fair Lady ⅋⅋⅋½ 1964 (G) Colorful production of Lerner and Loewe's musical version of "Pygmalion," about an ill-mannered cockney girl who is plucked from her job as a flower girl by Professor Henry Higgins. Higgins makes a bet with a colleague that he can turn this rough diamond into a "lady." Winner of eight Academy Awards. Hepburn's singing voice is dubbed by Marni Nixon, who was also responsible for the singing in "The King and I" and "West Side Story;" the dubbing may have undermined her chance at an Oscar nomination. Typecasting role for Harrison as the crusty, egocentric Higgins. A timeless classic. ♫Why Can't the English?; Wouldn't It be Loverly?; I'm an Ordinary Man; With a Little Bit of Luck; Just You Wait, 'Enry 'Iggins; The Servant's Chorus; The Rain in Spain; I Could Have Danced all Night; Ascot Gavotte. 170m/C VHS, Beta, LV, Closed Caption. Audrey Hepburn, Rex Harrison, Stanley Holloway, Wilfrid Hyde-White, Theodore Bikel, Mona Washbourne, Jeremy Brett, Robert Coote, Gladys Cooper; **D:** George Cukor; **C:** Harry Stradling; **M:** Frederick Loewe, Alan Jay Lerner. Academy Awards '64: Best Actor (Harrison), Best Adapted Score, Best Art Direction/Set Decoration (Color), Best Color Cinematography, Best Costume Design (Color), Best Director (Cukor), Best Picture, Best Sound; British Academy Awards '65: Best Film; Directors Guild of America Awards '64: Best Director (Cukor); Golden Globe Awards '65: Best Actor—Musical/Comedy (Harrison), Best Director (Cukor), Best Film—Musical/Comedy; National Board of Review Awards '64: 10 Best Films of the Year; New York Film Critics Awards '64: Best Actor (Harrison), Best Film; Nominations: Academy Awards '64: Best Adapted Screenplay, Best Film Editing, Best Supporting Actor (Holloway), Best Supporting Actress (Cooper). FOX, FCT, BTV

My Family ⅋⅋⅋½ Mi Familia 1994 (R) Patriarch Jose Sanchez (Rojas) comes to America in the early 1900's from Mexico and soon finds that the grass is not always greener on the other side. Thus begins the multigenerational saga of the Sanchez family in L.A., which chronicles their struggles and hopes over a time span of sixty years. Overlooked in the glut of Hispanic-themed movies released, featuring soulful performances from the ensemble cast, especially Smits and Morales. Their deep-seated need to assimilate matched by a disdain for authority provide most of the family's heartaches. English and Spanish dialogue.**CW:** Strong language; some graphic violence; scene of sexuality. 126m/C VHS, LV, Closed Caption. Jimmy Smits, Esai Morales, Eduardo Lopez Rojas, Jenny Gago, Elpidia Carrillo, Lupe Ontiveros, Jacob Vargas, Jennifer Lopez, Scott Bakula, Edward James Olmos, Michael De Lorenzo, Maria Canals, Leon Singer, Jonathan Hernandez, Constance Marie, Enrique Castillo, Mary Steenburgen; **D:** Gregory Nava; **W:** Gregory Nava, Anna Thomas; **C:** Edward Lachman; **M:** Pepe Avila, Mark McKenzie. Nominations: Academy Awards '95: Best Makeup; Independent Spirit Awards '96: Best Actor (Smits), Best Supporting Actress (Lopez). NLC, TTC

My Family Treasure ⅋⅋½ 1993 Mother tells her children about her dangerous trip into Russia to recover a family legacy—a priceless Faberge egg. 95m/C VHS. Dee Wallace Stone, Theodore Bikel, Alex Vincent, Bitty Schram; **D:** Rolfe Kanefsky, Edward Staroselsky. AVI

My Father Is Coming ⅋⅋ 1991 German immigrant, Vicky, is trying to get an acting career off the ground in New York. She shares her apartment with Ben, a gay man, and generally does more work as a waitress than actress. Vicky's alarmed when her father, Hans, arrives for a visit. She's told him she's married (Vicky's also gay), so Ben agrees to pose as her husband. The rest of the film details Vicky's complicated love life, unsuccessful actor tryouts, and her father's increasing bewilderment. It's meant as a sort of reverse, and perverse, innocents abroad, with the two Germans adrift in zany New York but this only works fitfully. 82m/C VHS, Closed Caption. GE Shelley Kastner, Alfred Edel, David Bronstein, Mary Lou Graulau, Michael Massee, Annie Sprinkle, Bruce Benderson; **D:** Monika Treut; **W:** Monika Treut. FRF

My Father, My Rival ⅋ 1985 A high school student's crush on his teacher leads to emotional complications when his widowed father becomes romantically involved with her. 60m/C VHS, Beta. Lance Guest. NO

My Father the Hero ⅋⅋ 1993 (PG) Another adaptation of a French film ("Mon Pere, Ce Heroes") finds 14-year-old Heigl on an island paradise with divorced dad Depardieu, passing him off as her boyfriend (without his knowledge) to impress a cute boy, causing obvious misunderstandings. Depardieu shows a flair for physical comedy, but his talent is wasted in a role that's vaguely disturbing; one of the few funny moments finds him unwittingly singing "Thank Heaven For Little Girls" to a horrified audience. For the preteen set only, others will probably find it a waste of time. Top notch actress Thompson's surprising (uncredited) cameo is due to her friendship with Depardieu. 90m/C VHS, LV, Closed Caption. Gerard Depardieu, Katherine Heigl, Dalton James, Lauren Hutton, Faith Prince; **Cameos:** Emma Thompson; **D:** Steve Miner; **W:** Francis Veber, Charlie Peters; **M:** David Newman. TOU

My Father's Glory ⅋⅋⅋ La Gloire de Mon Pere 1991 (G) Based on Marcel Pagnol's tales of his childhood, this is a sweet, beautiful memory of a young boy's favorite summer in the French countryside of the early 1900s. Not much happens, yet the film is such a perfect evocation of the milieu that one is carried swiftly into the dreams and thoughts of all the characters. One half of a duo, followed by "My Mother's Castle." In French with English subtitles. 110m/C VHS. FR Julien Ciamaca, Philippe Caubere, Nathalie Roussel, Therese Liotard, Didier Pain; **D:** Yves Robert; **W:** Lucette Andrei; **C:** Robert Alazraki; **M:** Vladimir Cosma. ORI, BTV

My Father's House ⅋⅋ 1975 Magazine editor recounts his youth while recovering from a heart attack. He measures his own quality of life against the life that his father led and begins to question his own choices with regard to his family. 96m/C VHS, Beta. Cliff Robertson, Robert Preston, Eileen Brennan, Rosemary Forsyth. WOV

My Father's Nurse ⅋ 1985 While father convalesces upstairs, the family frolics about the house and plots his dispatch. When his new nurse secretly cures him, he takes to a wheelchair and mounts a comedic covert counter offensive. 97m/C VHS, Beta. VCD, MOV

My Favorite Blonde ⅋⅋⅋ 1942 Beautiful British spy Carroll convinces Hope to aid her in carrying out a secret mission. Lots of fun as Hope and his trained penguin, along with Carroll, embark on a cross-country chase to elude the Nazis. Hope's behavior is hilarious and the pacing of the film is excellent. Based on a story by Melvin Frank and Norman Panama. 78m/B VHS, Closed Caption. Bob Hope, Madeleine Carroll, Gale Sondergaard, George Zucco, Lionel Royce, Walter Kingsford, Victor Varconi; **Cameos:** Bing Crosby; **D:** Sidney Lanfield; **W:** Frank Butler, Don Hartman; **C:** William Mellor. USH, BTV

My Favorite Brunette ⅋⅋½ 1947 Detective parody starring Hope as a photographer turned grumbling private eye. He becomes involved with a murder, a spy caper, and a dangerous brunette (Lamour). 85m/B VHS, Beta, LV. Bob Hope, Dorothy Lamour, Peter Lorre, Lon Chaney Jr., Alan Ladd, Reginald Denny, Bing Crosby; **D:** Elliott Nugent; **C:** Lionel Lindon. CNG, MRV, NOS

My Favorite Wife ⅋⅋⅋ 1940 Handsome widower Grant remarries only to discover that first wife Dunne, shipwrecked seven years earlier and presumed dead, has reappeared. Eventually, a judge must decide what to do in this most unusual situation, completely lacking precedent. Farcical and hilarious story filled with a clever cast. The 1963 remake "Move Over Darling" lacks the style and wit of this presentation. Also available colorized. 88m/B VHS, Beta, LV. Irene Dunne, Cary Grant, Randolph Scott, Gail Patrick, Scotty Beckett; **D:** Garson Kanin; **W:** Samuel Spewack, Bella Spewack, Leo McCarey. Nominations: Academy Awards '40: Best Story, Best Original Score.MED, MLB, TTC

My Favorite Year ⅋⅋⅋ My Favourite Year 1982 (PG) A young writer on a popular live television show in the 1950s is asked to keep a watchful eye on the week's guest star—his favorite swashbuckling movie hero. Through a series of misadventures, he discovers his matinee idol is actually a drunkard and womanizer who has trouble living up to his cinematic standards. Sterling performance from O'Toole, with memorable portrayal from Bologna as the show's host, King Kaiser (a take-off of Sid Caesar from "Your Show of Shows"). 92m/C VHS, Beta, LV. Peter O'Toole, Mark Linn-Baker, Joseph Bologna, Jessica Harper, Lainie Kazan, Bill Macy, Anne DeSalvo, Lou Jacobi, Adolph Green, Cameron Mitchell, Gloria Stuart; **D:** Richard Benjamin; **W:** Norman Steinberg; **M:** Ralph Burns. Nominations: Academy Awards '82: Best Actor (O'Toole). MGM

My Fellow Americans ⅋⅋ 1996 (PG-13) Political "Odd Couple" pits cantankerous conservative Kramer (Lemmon) against womanizing liberal Douglas (Garner) when current President Aykroyd frames his two predecessors for a White House scandal. The age-old adversaries must set aside their differences long enough to clear their names by reaching Kramer's presidential library, where he has vindicating papers. Along the way, they encounter adventure, danger and "the people," the average Americans they used to work for. "Grumpy Old Men" veteran Lemmon is plenty cranky while Garner's charisma is a suitable foil. The ironic "charm" of course banter from the mouths of two ex-Presidents is supposed to carry much of the humor, but instead wears thin. Supporting characters (Aykroyd, Bacall) aren't as well used as the two main characters. Mainly for Lemmon, Garner, and "Grumpy" fans.**CW:** Salty language and innuendo. 96m/C VHS, LV, Closed Caption, DVD. Dan Aykroyd, James Garner, Jack Lemmon, John Heard, Sela Ward, Wilford Brimley, Everett McGill, Bradley Whitford, Lauren Bacall, James Rebhorn, Esther Rolle, Conchata Ferrell, Jack Kehler, Tom Everett, Jeff Yagher; **D:** Peter Segal; **W:** E. Jack Kaplan, Richard Chapman, Peter Tolan; **C:** Julio Macat; **M:** William Ross. WAR

My First Wife ⅋⅋½ 1984 (PG) Strong drama about a self-indulgent man's devastation when his wife abruptly leaves well after ten years of marriage. Realistic and well-acted. 95m/C VHS. AU John Hargreaves, Wendy Hughes, Lucy Angwin, Anna Jemison, David Cameron; **D:** Paul Cox; **W:** Paul Cox, Bob Ellis. Australian Film Institute '84: Best Actor (Hargreaves). NO

My Forbidden Past ⅋⅋½ 1951 Melodrama set in 1890 New Orleans centers on a young woman (Gardner) with an unsavory past who unexpectedly inherits a fortune and vows to break up the marriage of the man (Mitchum) she loves. His wife is murdered and he is charged with doing the deed until Gardner, exposing her past, wins his love and helps to extricate him. 81m/B

VHS, Beta. Ava Gardner, Melvyn Douglas, Robert Mitchum; **D:** Robert Stevenson. *MED*

My Friend Flicka ����✝ 1943 Boy makes friends with four-legged beast. Dad thinks the horse is full of wild oats, but young Roddie trains it to be the best gosh darned horse in pre-Disney family faredom. Based on Mary O'Hara book, followed by "Thunderhead, Son of Flicka," and TV series. 89m/C **VHS, Beta.** Roddy McDowall, Preston Foster, Rita Johnson, James Bell, Jeff Corey; **D:** Harold Schuster. *FXV, FCT, HMV*

My Friend Irma ✝✝½ 1949 An adaptation of the radio series, featuring Wilson as the dumb blonde with boyfriend trouble and Lynn as her sensible pal. The film debut of Martin (singing) and Lewis (mugging) as juice-bar operators. Followed by a sequel, "My Friend Irma Goes West," and later by a television series. 103m/B **VHS, LV, Closed Caption.** Marie Wilson, Diana Lynn, John Lund, Don DeFore, Dean Martin, Jerry Lewis, Hans Conried; **D:** George Marshall. *PAR*

My Friend Walter ✝✝½ 1993 Bess Throckmorten attends a family reunion in London with her Aunt Ellie and discovers one of her ancestors is Sir Walter Raleigh. Visiting the Tower of London, Bess finds Sir Walter's ghost who wants to follow her home to Devon to see how the family is doing. He finds that the Throckmorten's are about to lose the family farm but Sir Walter comes up with a plan to restore their fortunes. Shot on location in England and based on the book by Michael Morpurgo. 87m/C **VHS.** *GB* Polly Grant, Ronald Pickup, Prunella Scales, Louise Jameson, James Hazeldine, Lawrence Cooper, Constance Chapman; **D:** Gavin Millar. *PME, BTV*

My Geisha ✝✝½ 1962 MacLaine and husband experience bad karma because she wants to be in his new film. In pancake makeup and funny shoes, she poses as a geisha girl and is cast as Madame Butterfly. Her husband, however, is one sharp cookie. Filmed in Japan. 120m/C **VHS, Closed Caption.** Shirley MacLaine, Yves Montand, Edward G. Robinson, Robert Cummings; **D:** Jack Cardiff. Nominations: Academy Awards '62: Best Costume Design (Color). *PAR, WAX, FCT*

My Girl ✝✝½ 1991 (PG) Chlumsky is delightful in her film debut as an 11-year old tomboy who must come to grips with the realities of life. Culkin plays her best friend Thomas, who understands her better than anyone else, including her father, a mortician, and his girlfriend, the makeup artist at the funeral parlor. Some reviewers questioned whether young children would be able to deal with some unhappy occurrences in the film, but most seemed to classify it as a movie the whole family would enjoy. 102m/C **VHS, LV, 8mm, Closed Caption.** Dan Aykroyd, Jamie Lee Curtis, Macaulay Culkin, Anna Chlumsky, Griffin Dunne, Raymond Buktenica, Richard Masur, Ann Nelson, Peter Michael Goetz, Tom Villard; **D:** Howard Zieff; **W:** Laurice Elehwany; **C:** Paul Elliott; **M:** James Newton Howard. MTV Movie Awards '92: Best Kiss (Macaulay Culkin/Anna Chlumsky). *COL*

My Girl 2 ✝✝½ 1994 (PG) It's 1974 and Chlumsky is back as Vada (this time without Culkin, given the killer bee attack in MG1) in this innocent coming-of-ager. Portly Ackroyd and flaky Curtis return as parental window dressing who encourage Vada's search for information on her long-dead mother. She tracks down old friends of her mom's (Masur and Rose) who are having difficulties with their obnoxious adolescent son (O'Brien). Predictable, but enjoyable. Certain to fail the credibility test of nit-pickers who may wonder why the only thing Ackroyd can remember of his first wife is that she left behind a paper bag with a date scribbled on it. 99m/C **VHS, LV, 8mm, Closed Caption.** Dan Aykroyd, Jamie Lee Curtis, Austin O'Brien, Richard Masur, Christine Ebersole; **D:** Howard Zieff; **W:** Janet Kovalcik; **C:** Paul Elliott; **M:** Cliff Eidelman. *COL*

My Girl Tisa ✝✝½ 1948 Chronicles the experiences of a young immigrant woman who struggles to survive in the U.S. at the turn of the century and hopes to bring her father over from their home country. Based on a play by Lucille S. Prumbs and Sara B. Smith. 95m/B **VHS.** Lilli Palmer, Sam Wanamaker, Akim Tamiroff, Alan Hale, Hugo Haas, Gale Robbins, Stella Adler; **D:** Elliott Nugent; **M:** Max Steiner. *REP*

My Grandpa is a Vampire ✝½ 1992 (PG) When 12 year-old Lonny and his pal visit Grandpa Cooger in New Zealand Lonny discovers a long-hidden family secret—Grandpa's a vampire! This doesn't stop either boy from joining with Grandpa in lots of scary adventures. 90m/C **VHS, Closed Caption.** Al Lewis, Justin Gocke, Milan Borich, Noel Appleby; **D:** David Blyth. *REP*

My Heroes Have Always Been Cowboys ✝✝½ 1991 (PG) An aging rodeo rider returns to his hometown to recuperate and finds himself forced to confront his past. His ex-girlfriend, his dad and his sister all expect something from him. He learns how to give it, and gains the strength to get back on the bull that stomped him. Excellent rodeo footage, solid performances, but the story has been around the barn too many times to hold much interest. 106m/C **VHS, Beta, LV, Closed Caption.** Scott Glenn, Kate Capshaw, Ben Johnson, Balthazar Getty, Mickey Rooney, Gary Busey, Tess Harper, Clarence Williams III, Dub Taylor, Clu Gulager, Dennis Fimple; **D:** Stuart Rosenberg; **W:** Joel Don Humphreys; **M:** James Horner. *VTR, FXV, COL*

My Lady of Whims ✝ 1925 Clara Bow's dad disapproves of debutante daughter's desire to hang out with the girls who just want to have fun. 42m/B **VHS, Beta.** Clara Bow, Betty Baker, Carmelita Geraghty, Donald Keith, Lee Moran. *GPV, FCT*

My Left Foot ✝✝✝✝ 1989 (R) A gritty, unsentimental drama based on the life and autobiography of cerebral-palsy victim Christy Brown. Considered an imbecile by everyone but his mother (Fricker), in a stunning award-winning performance) until he teaches himself to write. He survives his impoverished Irish roots to become a painter and writer using his left foot, the only appendage over which he has control. He also falls in love and finds some heartaches along the way. Day-Lewis is astounding; the supporting cast, especially Shaw and Cusack, match him measure for measure. 103m/C **VHS, Beta, LV, Closed Caption.** *IR* Daniel Day-Lewis, Brenda Fricker, Ray McAnally, Cyril Cusack, Fiona Shaw, Hugh O'Conor, Adrian Dunbar, Ruth McCabe, Alison Whelan; **D:** Jim Sheridan; **W:** Shane Connaughton, Jim Sheridan; **M:** Elmer Bernstein. Academy Awards '89: Best Actor (Day-Lewis), Best Supporting Actress (Fricker); British Academy Awards '89: Best Actor (Day-Lewis), Best Supporting Actor (McAnally); Independent Spirit Awards '90: Best Foreign Film; Los Angeles Film Critics Association Awards '89: Best Actor (Day-Lewis), Best Supporting Actress (Fricker); Montreal World Film Festival '89: Best Actor (Day-Lewis); New York Film Critics Awards '89: Best Actor (Day-Lewis), Best Film; National Society of Film Critics Awards '89: Best Actor (Day-Lewis); Nominations: Academy Awards '89: Best Adapted Screenplay, Best Director (Sheridan), Best Picture. *HBO, BTV, HMV*

My Life ✝✝½ 1993 (PG-13) Maudlin, sometimes depressing production preaches the power of a well-examined life. Public relations exec Keaton is diagnosed with cancer and the doctors predict he will most likely die before the birth of his first child. Film follows his transition from uncommunicative and angry to acceptance, a role to which Keaton brings a sentimental strength. Kidman is window dressing as the ever-patient, nobly suffering wife, a cardboard character notable mainly for her beauty. **CW:** Mature subject matter. 114m/C **VHS, LV, 8mm, Closed Caption.** Michael Keaton, Nicole Kidman, Haing S. Ngor, Bradley Whitford, Queen Latifah, Michael Constantine, Toni Sawyer, Rebecca Schull, Lee Garlington; **D:** Bruce Joel Rubin; **W:** Bruce Joel Rubin; **M:** John Barry. *COL*

My Life and Times with Antonin Artaud ✝✝✝ *En Compagnie d'Antonin Artaud* 1993 Postwar Parisian bohemia is depicted in the obsessive friendship between ambitious young poet Jacques Prevel (Barbe) and famed intellectual/poet/impressario Antonin Artaud (Frey), who founded the Theatre of Cruelty. Artaud has returned to Paris after spending nine years in an asylum and is suffering from terminal cancer, the misery of which is partially alleviated by the opiates that Prevel can provide. Delusional and paranoid, Artaud makes his self-destruction into genius while Prevel documents Artaud's last two years in diaries, hoping to gain some measure of fame for himself. French with subtitles. Based on Prevel's "En Compagnie d'Antonin Artaud." 93m/B **VHS.** *FR* Sami Frey, Marc Barbe, Valerie Jeannet, Julie Jezequel; **D:** Gerard Mordillat; **W:** Gerard Mordillat, Jerome Prieur; **C:** Francois Catonne; **M:** Jean-Claude Petit. *FXL*

My Life As a Dog ✝✝✝✝ *Mitt Liv Som Hund* 1985 A troublesome boy is separated from his brother and is sent to live with relatives in the country when his mother is taken ill. Unhappy and confused, he struggles to understand sexuality and love and tries to find security and acceptance. Remarkable Swedish film available with English subtitles or dubbed. 101m/C **VHS, Beta, LV.** *SW* Anton Glanzelius, Tomas Van Bromssen, Anki Liden, Melinda Kinnaman, Kicki Rundgren, Ing-mari Carlsson; **D:** Lasse Hallstrom. Golden Globe Awards '88: Best Foreign Film; Independent Spirit Awards '88: Best Foreign Film; New York Film Critics Awards '87: Best Foreign Film; Nominations: Academy Awards '87: Best Adapted Screenplay, Best Director (Hallstrom). *PAR, HMV*

My Life to Live ✝✝✝✝ *Vivre Savie; It's My Life* 1962 A woman turns to prostitution in this probing examination of sexual, and social, relations. Idiosyncratic Godard has never been more starstruck than in this vehicle for the endearing Karina, his wife at the time. A classic. In French with English subtitles. 85m/B **VHS, Beta.** *FR* Anna Karina, Sady Rebbot, Andre S. Labarthe, Guylaine Schlumberger; **D:** Jean-Luc Godard; **W:** Jean-Luc Godard; **M:** Michel Legrand. Venice Film Festival '62: Special Jury Prize. *NOS, NYF, DVT*

My Life's in Turnaround ✝✝ 1994 (R) Amusing low-budget comedy takes a behind-the-scenes, semi-autobiographical look at the lives of two would-be filmmakers. They try for cool but manage only goofy. **CW:** Strong language and some explicit sex-related dialogue. 84m/C **VHS.** Eric Schaeffer, Donal Lardner Ward, Lisa Gerstein, Dana Wheeler-Nicholson, Debra Clein, Sheila Jaffe; **Cameos:** Casey Siemaszko, John Sayles, Martha Plimpton, Phoebe Cates; **D:** Eric Schaeffer, Donal Lardner Ward; **W:** Eric Schaeffer, Donal Lardner Ward; **M:** Reed Hays. *AVI*

My Little Chickadee ✝✝✝ 1940 Classic comedy about a gambler and a fallen woman who marry for convenience so they can respectably enter an unsuspecting town. Sparks fly in their adventures together. Fields and West are both at their best playing their larger-than-life selves. 91m/B **VHS, Beta, LV.** W.C. Fields, Mae West, Joseph Calleia, Dick Foran, Margaret Hamilton, Donald Meek; **D:** Eddie Cline; **C:** Joseph Valentine. *USH, MLB, BTV*

My Little Girl ✝✝ 1987 (R) A rich Philadelphia girl idealistically volunteers her time to help local institutionalized orphans, but meets with opposition. 118m/C **VHS, Beta, LV.** Mary Stuart Masterson, James Earl Jones, Geraldine Page, Anne Meara, Peter Gallagher, George Newbern; **D:** Connie Kaiserman. *PSM*

My Little Pony: The Movie ✝✝½ 1986 Animated tale about the siege of Ponyland by malevolent witches. 87m/C **VHS, Beta, Closed Caption. D:** Michael Joens; **V:** Danny DeVito, Cloris Leachman, Tony Randall, Madeline Kahn.

My Love For Yours ✝✝½ *Honeymoon in Bali* 1939 The romantic tale of a young man hoping to win the love of a beautiful but icy girl. A tad silly in parts, but the clever dialogue moves the story along. 99m/B **VHS, Beta.** Fred MacMurray, Madeleine Carroll; **D:** Edward H. Griffith. *NOS, CAB*

My Lucky Star ⅅⅅ½ **1938** Skating star Henie plays a department store clerk that gets sent off to college to model clothes from the store's sports line. She somehow manages to convince school officials to stage their winter ice show in the department store, where she gets to show off her stuff. Don't miss the grand finale, a performance of "Alice in Wonderland Ice Ballet." Based on the story "They Met in Chicago" by Karl Tunberg and Don Ettlinger. ♫I've Got a Date With a Dream; Could You Pass in Love; This May Be the Night; The All-American Swing; Plymouth University Song. **81m/B VHS.** Sonja Henie, Richard Greene, Joan Davis, Cesar Romero, Buddy Ebsen, Arthur Treacher, George Barbier, Gypsy Rose Lee; **D:** Roy Del Ruth; **W:** Harry Tugend, Jack Yellen. **FXV**

My Man Adam ⅅⅅ **1986 (R)** A dreamy, Mitty-esque high schooler falls in love with a girl (Daryl's auburn-haired sister, Page Hannah), and becomes ensnared in a real life crime, leaving his friend to bail him out. Typical boy-meets-girl, boy-gets-in-trouble yarn. **84m/C VHS, Beta, Closed Caption.** Raphael Sbarge, Veronica Cartwright, Page Hannah, Larry B. Scott, Charlie Barnett, Arthur Pendleton, Dave Thomas; **D:** Roger L. Simon. **FOX**

My Man Godfrey ⅅⅅⅅⅅ **1936** A spoiled rich girl picks up someone she assumes is a bum as part of a scavenger hunt and decides to keep him on as her butler. In the process, he teaches her about life, money, and happiness. Top-notch screwball comedy defines the genre. Lombard is a stunner alongside the equally charming Powell. Watch for Jane Wyman as an extra in the party scene. Remade in 1957 with June Allyson and David Niven. From the novel by Eric Hatch, who also co-scripted. **95m/B VHS, Beta.** William Powell, Carole Lombard, Gail Patrick, Alice Brady, Mischa Auer, Eugene Pallette, Alan Mowbray, Franklin Pangborn, Jane Wyman; **D:** Gregory La Cava; **W:** Morrie Ryskind, Gregory La Cava. Nominations: Academy Awards '36: Best Actor (Powell), Best Actress (Lombard), Best Director (La Cava), Best Screenplay, Best Supporting Actor (Auer), Best Supporting Actress (Brady). **CNG, MRV, NOS**

My Man Godfrey ⅅⅅ½ **1957** Inferior remake of the sophisticated screwball comedy of the 30's about a butler who brings a touch of the common man to the filthy rich. Niven stars as the butler and Allyson plays the rich girl, but nothing compares to the original roles created by Powell and Lombard. **92m/C VHS.** June Allyson, David Niven, Martha Hyer, Jessie Royce Landis, Robert Keith, Eva Gabor, Jay Robinson, Jeff Donnell; **D:** Henry Koster; **W:** Everett Freeman, Peter Berneis, William Bowers; **C:** William H. Daniels. **USH**

My Michael ⅅⅅⅅ **1975** Sensitive adaptation of Amos Oz's novel set in Jerusalem in the late 1950s. A young woman is stifled by marriage and the conventions of her bourgeois life and her fantasies begin to take over. In Hebrew with English subtitles. **90m/C VHS, Beta.** **IS** Efrat Lavie, Oded Kotler; **D:** Dan Wolman. **ERG, FCT, TPV**

My Mom's a Werewolf ⅅ½ **1989 (PG)** An average suburban mother gets involved with a dashing stranger and soon, to her terror, begins to turn into a werewolf. Her daughter and companion must come up with a plan to regain dear, sweet mom. **90m/C VHS, Beta, LV.** Susan Blakely, John Saxon, John Schuck, Katrina Caspary, Ruth Buzzi, Marilyn McCoo, Marcia Wallace, Diana Barrows; **D:** Michael Fischa; **W:** Mark Pirro. **PSM**

My Mother's Castle ⅅⅅⅅ½ **1991 (PG)** Le Chateau de Ma Mere The second half of the two part film series based on the autobiography of Marcel Pagnol. Picking up where "My Father's Glory" left off, the family begins a series of vacations in a beautiful country home. Dynamically acted and tenderly directed, charming and suitable for the entire family. In French with English subtitles. **98m/C VHS.** **FR** Philippe Caubere, Nathalie Roussel, Didier Pain, Therese Liotard, Julien Ciamaca, Victorien Delmare; **D:** Yves Robert; **M:** Vladimir Cosma. **ORI, BTV**

My Mother's Secret Life ⅅ½ **1984** Dull drama focusing on a long-forgotten daughter who suddenly appears on her mother's doorstep and discovers that mom makes a living as a high-priced hooker. **100m/C VHS, Beta.** Loni Anderson, Paul Sorvino, Amanda Wyss, James Sutorius, Sandy McPeak; **D:** Robert Markowitz; **M:** Brad Fiedel. **PSM**

My Name is Ivan ⅅⅅⅅ½ Ivan's Childhood; The Youngest Spy **1962** Tarkovsky's first feature film is a vivid, wrenching portrait of a young Soviet boy surviving as a spy behind enemy lines during WWII. Technically stunning, heralding the coming of modern cinema's greatest formalist. In Russian with English subtitles. **84m/B VHS, Beta, LV.** **RU** Kolya Burlyayev, Valentin Zubkov, Ye Zharikov, S. Krylov; **D:** Andrei Tarkovsky. Venice Film Festival '62: Best Film. **FXL, FCT**

My Name is Nobody ⅅⅅ½ Il Mio Nome e Nessuno **1974 (PG)** Fast-paced spaghetti-western wherein a cocky, soft-hearted gunfighter is sent to kill the famous, retired outlaw he reveres, but instead they band together. **115m/C VHS, Beta.** Henry Fonda, Terence Hill, R.G. Armstrong; **D:** Tonino Valerii; **M:** Ennio Morricone. **BAR, HHE**

My Neighbor Totoro ⅅⅅ½ **1993 (G)** Rather gooey Japanese animated movie about Satsuki and her younger sister Lucy, whose new house in the country is filled with magic, including a friendly creature named Totoro. Totoro is a cuddly, if weird, mix of bear, owl, and seal, with whiskers and a gentle roar. He can fly, has a magic bus, and can only be seen by children. Naturally, every time the two girls get into mischief Totoro is there to rescue them. Dubbed into English. **76m/C VHS, LV.** **JP D:** Hayao Miyazaki; **W:** Hayao Miyazaki. **FXV**

My New Gun ⅅⅅ½ **1992 (R)** Uneven, restless dark comedy about Debbie and Gerald Bender, yuppified suburban couple whose lives are disrupted by a gun. When their newly engaged friends get a gun, Gerry decides they need a gun as well. Debbie is very uncomfortable about having a weapon in the house and doesn't want anything to do with it. When mysterious neighbor LeGros steals the gun, it sets off a bizarre chain of events that culminate at the wedding of their friends. Impressive first effort for writer/director Cochran. **99m/C VHS, LV, Closed Caption.** Diane Lane, Stephen Collins, James LeGros, Tess Harper, Bill Raymond, Bruce Altman, Maddie Corman; **D:** Stacy Cochran; **W:** Stacy Cochran; **M:** Pat Irwin. Cannes Film Festival '92: Best Film. **COL**

My New Partner ⅅⅅ½ Les Ripoux **1984 (R)** Amiable French comedy in which cynical veteran cop is saddled with straight arrow rookie partner. French Cesars for best film and best director, but remember: They like Jerry Lewis too. In French with English subtitles. **106m/C VHS, Beta, LV.** **FR** Philippe Noiret, Thierry Lhermitte, Regine, Grace de Capitani, Claude Brosset, Julien Guiomar; **D:** Claude Zidi; **W:** Claude Zidi. **MED, IME**

My Night at Maud's ⅅⅅⅅ My Night with Maud; Ma Nuit Chez Maud **1969** Typically subtle Rohmer entry concerns quandary of upright fellow who finds himself drawn to comparatively care-free woman. Talky, somewhat arid film is one of director's Six Moral Tales. You'll either find it fascinating or wish you were watching "Rocky XXIV" instead. Cinematography by Nestor Almendros, in French with English subtitles. **111m/B VHS, Beta, LV.** **FR** Jean-Louis Trintignant, Francoise Fabian, Marie-Christine Barrault, Antoine Vitez; **D:** Eric Rohmer; **W:** Eric Rohmer; **C:** Nestor Almendros. New York Film Critics Awards '70: Best Screenplay; National Society of Film Critics Awards '70: Best Cinematography, Best Screenplay; Nominations: Academy Awards '70: Best Foreign Language Film, Best Story & Screenplay. **MED, APD**

My Old Man ⅅⅅ½ **1979** Plucky teen and her seedy horsetrainer father come together over important horse race. Oates makes this one worth watching on a slow evening. A Hemingway story made for television. **102m/C VHS, Beta.** Kristy McNichol, Warren Oates, Eileen Brennan; **D:** John Erman. **CAF**

My Old Man's Place ⅅⅅ **1971 (R)** A veteran, with two war buddies and a girl, returns to his father's run-down farm, hoping to fix it up. Sexual tensions arise and violence erupts. **93m/C VHS, Beta.** Arthur Kennedy, Michael Moriarty, Mitchell Ryan, William Devane, Topo Swope; **D:** Edwin Sherin. **PSM**

My Other Husband ⅅⅅ½ Attention! Une Femme Peut en Cacher une Autre **1985 (PG-13)** A woman has two husbands and families, one in Paris and one in Trouville, who eventually meet each other. Seems silly but grows into a sensitive and sad portrait of married life. In French with English subtitles. **110m/C VHS, Beta.** **FR** Miou-Miou, Rachid Ferrache, Roger Hanin; **D:** Georges Lautner. **COL**

My Outlaw Brother ⅅⅅ My Brother, the Outlaw **1951** A man travelling West to visit his brother in Mexico meets a Texas Ranger on the train. The man discovers that his brother is an outlaw, and teams up with the Ranger to capture him. **82m/B VHS.** Mickey Rooney, Wanda Hendrix, Robert Preston, Robert Stack, Jose Torvay; **D:** Elliott Nugent. **MOV, MRV, VYY**

My Own Private Idaho ⅅⅅⅅ **1991 (R)** Director Van Sant of "Drugstore Cowboy" returns to the underworld to examine another group of outsiders, this time young, homosexual hustlers. On the streets of Seattle, narcoleptic hustler Mike meets slumming rich boy Scott, and together they begin a search for Mike's lost mother, which leads them to Idaho and Italy. Stunning visuals, an elliptical plot, and a terrific performance by Phoenix highlight this search for love, the meaning of life, and power. Van Sant couples these activities with scenes from Shakespeare's "Henry IV" for a sometimes inscrutable, but always memorable film. Look for director Richert's Falstaff role as an aging chickenhawk.**CW:** Language, drug use, and sensuality. **105m/C VHS, LV, Closed Caption.** River Phoenix, Keanu Reeves, James Russo, William Richert, Rodney Harvey, Michael Parker, Flea, Chiara Caselli, Udo Kier, Grace Zabriskie, Tom Troupe; **D:** Gus Van Sant; **W:** Gus Van Sant; **C:** John Campbell, Eric Alan Edwards. Independent Spirit Awards '92: Best Actor (Phoenix), Best Screenplay; National Society of Film Critics Awards '91: Best Actor (Phoenix).**COL, NLC**

My Pal, The King ⅅⅅ½ **1932** Amusing western with Rooney as the boy king of Ruritania, who's bored with his official duties. He meets Mix, the proprietor of a traveling wild west show which just happens to be performing in the country. Good thing too because Rooney has an evil prime minister who wants the throne for himself and kidnaps the kid. Naturally, Mix and his friends arrive to save him in the nick of time. **62m/B VHS.** Tom Mix, Mickey Rooney, Stuart Holmes, Paul Hurst, Noel Francis, James Kirkwood, Jim Thorpe; **D:** Kurt Neumann. **GPV**

My Pal Trigger ⅅⅅ **1946** Roy is unjustly imprisoned in this high adventure on the plains. Better than usual script and direction makes this is one of the more entertaining of the singing cowboy's films. **79m/B VHS, Beta.** Roy Rogers, George "Gabby" Hayes, Dale Evans, Jack Holt; **D:** Frank McDonald. **NOS, MRV, HHT**

My Pleasure Is My Business **1974 (R)** Cinematic autobiography of Xaveria Hollander, the world's most renowned prostitute of the seventies, and the zany occurrences which abound in her profession. **85m/C VHS.** **CA** Xaviera Hollander, Henry Ramer, Colin Fox, Ken Lynch, Jayne Eastwood; **D:** Al Waxman. **NO**

My Samurai ⅅ½ **1992 (R)** When young Peter McCrea witnesses a gang murder he turns to his martial-arts expert friend Young Park to help him. On the run from both the gang and the police Peter learns self-defense and the courage to face his fears.**CW:** Violence. **87m/C VHS, LV, Closed Caption.** Julian Lee, Mako, Terry O'Quinn, Bubba Smith, Jim Turner, Carlos Palomino, John Kallo; **D:** Fred Dresch. **IMP**

My Science Project 🎬½ 1985 (PG)
Teenager Stockwell stumbles across a crystal sphere with a funky light. Unaware that it is an alien time-travel device, he takes it to school to use as a science project in a last-ditch effort to avoid failing his class. Chaos follows and Stockwell and his chums find themselves battling gladiators, mutants, and dinosaurs. Plenty of special effects and a likeable enough, dumb teenage flick. **94m/C VHS, Beta, LV.** John Stockwell, Danielle von Zerneck, Fisher Stevens, Raphael Sbarge, Richard Masur, Barry Corbin, Ann Wedgeworth, Dennis Hopper, Candace Silvers, Beau Dremann, Pat Simmons, Pamela Springsteen; **D:** Jonathan Betuel; **W:** Jonathan Betuel; **M:** Peter Bernstein. *TOU*

My Side of the Mountain 🎬🎬½ 1969
(G) A thirteen-year-old boy decides to emulate his idol, Henry David Thoreau, and gives up his home and his family to live in the Canadian mountains. **100m/C VHS, Beta.** CA Teddy Eccles, Theodore Bikel; **D:** James B. Clark. *PAR*

My Sister Eileen 🎬🎬🎬 1955 Ruth and Eileen are two small-town Ohio sisters who move to Manhattan seeking excitement. They live in a basement apartment in Greenwich Village with an assortment of oddball tenants as they pursue success and romance. Everyone is daffy and charming, as is the film. Fun, but unmemorable songs, however the terrific choreography is by Fosse, who also appears as one sister's suitor. Remake of a 1942 film which was based on a Broadway play, which was based on a series of autobiographical stories published in the New Yorker. The play was later turned into a Broadway musical known as "Wonderful Town," which has nothing to do with this version of the original stories. ♫Give Me a Band and My Baby; It's Bigger Than You and Me; There's Nothing Like Love; As Soon As They See Eileen; I'm Great; Conga; Atmosphere. **108m/C VHS.** Janet Leigh, Betty Garrett, Jack Lemmon, Bob Fosse, Kurt Kasznar, Dick York, Lucy Marlow, Tommy Rall, Barbara Brown, Horace McMahon; **D:** Richard Quine; **W:** Blake Edwards, Richard Quine; **M:** Jule Styne. *COL, MOV, MVD*

My Sister, My Love 🎬½ *The Cage; The Mafu Cage* 1978 (R) Odd tale of two sisters' incestuous relationship and what happens when one of them takes another lover. The cage of the alternate titles refers to the place where their pet apes are kept and seems to symbolize the confining nature of their life together. **102m/C VHS.** Lee Grant, Carol Kane, Will Geer, James Olson; **D:** Karen Arthur. *NO*

My Son, the Vampire 🎬½ *Old Mother Riley Meets the Vampire; The Vampire and the Robot; Vampire Over London; Mother Riley Meets the Vampire* 1952 Last of Britain's Old Mother Riley series in which Lucan plays the Irish housekeeper in drag. Lugosi is a crazed scientist who thinks he's a vampire and wants to take over the world with his giant robot. Mother Riley interferes. Theme song by Alan Sherman. **72m/B VHS.** GB Bela Lugosi, Arthur Lucan, Dora Bryan, Richard Wattis; **D:** John Gilling. *NOS, SNC*

My Song Goes Round the World 🎬½ 1934 Chronicles the romantic foibles of a singing trio and the one girl they decide they all love. **68m/B VHS.** Joseph Schmidt, John Loder, Charlotte Ander; **D:** Richard Oswald. *NO, DVT*

My Stepmother Is an Alien 🎬🎬
1988 (PG-13) When eccentric physicist Aykroyd sends a message beam to another galaxy on a stormy night, the last thing he expects is a visit from beautiful alien Basinger. Unfortunately, he does not realize that this gorgeous blonde is an alien and he continues to court her despite her rather odd habits. Only the daughter seems to notice the strange goings on, and her dad ignores her warnings, enabling Basinger's evil sidekick to continue in its plot to take over the Earth. **108m/C VHS, Beta, LV, Closed Caption.** Dan Aykroyd, Kim Basinger, Jon Lovitz, Alyson Hannigan, Joseph Maher, Seth Green, Wesley Mann, Adrian Sparks, Juliette Lewis, Tanya

Fenmore; **D:** Richard Benjamin; **W:** Herschel Weingrod, Timothy Harris, Jonathan Reynolds; **M:** Alan Silvestri. *COL*

My Summer Story 🎬🎬½ *It Runs in the Family* 1994 (PG) Humorist Shepherd and director Clark re-team for another period family comedy in the tradition of their first collaboration, "A Christmas Story," now a video classic. This time the Parkers find themselves battling their crazy new neighbors, the Bumpus family, Ralphie (Kieran Culkin) has troubles with a neighborhood bully and tries to bond with his dad (Grodin) while fishing, and mom (Steenburgen) goes loopy over gravy boats. Charming family fun. Based on Shepherd's novels "In God We Trust, All Others Pay Cash" and "Wanda Hickey's Night of Golden Memories and Other Disasters." **85m/C VHS, LV, Closed Caption.** Charles Grodin, Mary Steenburgen, Kieran Culkin, Chris Culkin, Al Mancini, Troy Evans, Glenn Shadix, Dick O'Neill, Wayne Grace; **D:** Bob (Benjamin) Clark; **W:** Jean Shepherd, Bob (Benjamin) Clark, Leigh Brown; **C:** Stephen M. Katz; **M:** Paul Zaza. *MGM*

My Sweet Charlie 🎬🎬½ 1970 Unwed, pregnant white woman hides out with black lawyer in backwater Texas. Better than it sounds, with nice performances by Duke and Freeman. Made for television. **97m/C VHS, Beta.** Patty Duke, Al Freeman Jr., Ford Rainey, William Hardy, Chris Wilson, Archie Moore, Noble Willingham; **D:** Lamont Johnson. *USH*

My Sweet Little Village 🎬🎬½ *Vesnicko Ma Strediskova* 1986 Gentle comedy set in a rural village dealing with everyday events, including a romantic teenager who develops a crush on a schoolteacher, an adulterous wife and her boyfriend, the accident-prone doctor, a Laurel and Hardy duo of truck drivers, and others. Czech with subtitles. **100m/C VHS.** CZ Rudolf Hrusinsky, Janos Ban, Marian Labuda, Milena Dvorska, Ladislav Zupanic, Petr Cepek; **D:** Jiri Menzel; **W:** Zdenek Sverak; **C:** Jaromir Sofr; **M:** Jiri Sust. Nominations: Academy Awards '86: Best Foreign Language Film. *HTV*

My Sweet Victim 🎬🎬 1985 A young couple who recently moved to the United States from Poland try to make a go of their own business. The business fails, and so does their marriage. Will it end in murder? **92m/C VHS.** Candice Bergen, Juergen Prochnow. *QVD*

My Therapist woof! 1984 A sex therapist's boyfriend cannot bear the thought of her having intercourse with other men as part of her work. Soft core. **81m/C VHS, Beta.** Marilyn Chambers; **D:** Gary Legon. *NO*

My Tutor 🎬½ 1982 (R) When a high school student is in danger of flunking French, his parents hire a private tutor to help him learn the lessons. It becomes clear that his studies will involve many more subjects, however. Standard teen sex comedy. **97m/C VHS, Beta, LV.** Caren Kaye, Matt Lattanzi, Kevin McCarthy, Clark Brandon, Bruce Bauer, Arlene Golonka, Crispin Glover, Shelley Taylor Morgan, Francesca "Kitten" Natividad, Jewel Shepard, Marilyn Tokuda; **D:** George Bowers; **C:** Mac Ahlberg. *USH*

My Twentieth Century 🎬🎬🎬 *Az en XX. Szazadom* 1990 This quirky gem of a movie is a charming, sentimental journey through the early 1900s. Twins Dora and Lili are separated in early childhood. They reunite as grown, very different women on the Orient Express after they both (unknowingly) have sex with the same man. Dora is a sex kitten, while Lili is a radical equipped with explosives. When the two sisters come together, they both lose their destructive, dependent selves (Dora on men, Lili on politics) and become independent women. Lots of sidelights and subplots that are sure to amuse the viewer. In Hungarian with English subtitles. **104m/B VHS.** HU CA Dortha Segda, Oleg Jankowsky, Peter Andorai, Gabor Mate, Paulus Manker, Laszlo Vidovszky; **D:** Ildiko Enyedi; **W:** Ildiko Enyedi. *FXL*

My Uncle: The Alien 🎬🎬½ 1996 (PG) Kelly, President Sullivan's teenaged daughter, travels to L.A. to visit a children's shelter at Christmas. When she finds out the shelter needs mon-

ey to stay open, she eludes the Secret Service and hatches a plan to raise the funds. But she does have someone watching out for her—no, not a guardian angel, a guardian alien! **90m/C VHS, Closed Caption.** Hailey Foster; **D:** Henri Charr. *PMH*

My Universities 🎬🎬🎬 1940 In the final part of Donskoi's trilogy on Maxim Gorky, Gorky is a young man at university who is introduced to radical politics by several liberal intellectuals. He makes his first attempts at writing and joins the revolution as he leaves his painful past behind. In Russian with English subtitles. Preceded by "My Childhood" and "My Apprenticeship." **100m/C VHS.** RU D: Mark Donskoi. *FCT*

My Wicked, Wicked Ways 🎬🎬½
1984 Cleverly cast, low-budget television drama based on the autobiography of Errol Flynn. **95m/C VHS, Beta.** Duncan Regehr, Barbara Hershey, Hal Linden, Darren McGavin; **D:** Don Taylor. *FOX*

My Wonderful Life 🎬 1990 (R) Softcore gristle about a beautiful tramp climbing the social ladder via the boudoir. **107m/C VHS, Beta, LV.** IT Pierre Cosso, Jean Rochefort, Massimo Venturiello, Carol Alt, Elliott Gould; **D:** Carlo Vanzina. *COL*

Myra Breckinridge woof! 1970 (R) A tasteless version of the Gore Vidal novel. An alleged satire of a film critic who undergoes a sex change operation and then plots the destruction of the American male movie star stereotype. Created an outcry from all sides, and hung out to dry by studio where it's reportedly still blowing in the wind. **94m/C VHS, Beta.** Mae West, John Huston, Raquel Welch, Rex Reed, Farrah Fawcett, Jim Backus, John Carradine, Andy Devine, Tom Selleck; **D:** Michael Sarne. *FOX*

The Mysterians 🎬🎬½ *Earth Defense Forces; Chikyu Boelgun* 1958 A race of gigantic scientific intellects from a doomed planet attempts to conquer Earth. They want to rebuild their race by reproducing with earth women. Earth fights back. From the director of "Godzilla." Dubbed in English from Japanese. **85m/C VHS, Beta.** JP Kenji Sahara, Yumi Shirakawa, Takashi Shimura; **D:** Inoshiro Honda. *MLB*

Mysteries 🎬½ 1984 A rich tourist becomes obsessed by a beautiful local girl. As his obsession grows, his behavior becomes stranger. Interesting and well-acted. The film is an adaptation of the famous love story by Nobel-laureate Knut Hamsun. Suffers from poor dubbing. **100m/C VHS, Beta.** Rutger Hauer, Sylvia Kristel, David Rappaport, Rita Tushingham; **D:** Paul de Lussanet. *NO*

Mysterious Desperado 🎬½ 1949
Young man, about to inherit a large estate, is framed on a murder charge by land grabbers. **61m/B VHS, Beta.** Tim Holt, Richard Martin. *NO*

Mysterious Desperado/Rider From Tucson 🎬🎬½ 1949 A western double feature. In "Mysterious Desperado," a young man is framed for a crime he did not commit. In "Rider From Tucson," evil claim jumpers will resort to murder to gain control of a gold mine. **121m/B VHS, Beta.** Tim Holt, Richard Martin. *TTC*

Mysterious Doctor Satan 🎬🎬 1940 A mad satanic scientist builds an army of mechanical robots to rob and terrorize the nation. In 15 episodes. **250m/B VHS.** Eduardo Ciannelli, Robert Wilcox, Ella Neal; **D:** William Witney. *REP, VCN, MLB*

Mysterious Island 🎬🎬🎬½ 1961 Exhilirating sci-fi classic adapted from Jules Verne's novel about escaping Civil War soldiers who go up in Verne balloon and come down on a Pacific island populated by giant animals. They also encounter two shipwrecked English ladies, pirates, and Captain Nemo (and his sub). Top-rate special effects by master Ray Harryhausen. **101m/C VHS, Beta, LV, Closed Caption.** GB Michael Craig, Joan Greenwood, Michael Callan, Gary Merrill, Herbert Lom, Beth Rogan, Percy Herbert, Dan Jackson, Nigel Green; **D:** Cy Endfield; **M:** Bernard Herrmann. *COL, MLB*

Mysterious Island of Beautiful Women 🎬 1979 A male sextet is stranded on a South Sea island, where they must endure the trials of an angry tribe of conveniently bikini-clad women. 100m/C VHS. Jamie Lyn Bauer, Jayne Kennedy, Kathryn Davis, Deborah Shelton, Susie Coelho, Peter Lawford, Steven Keats, Clint Walker; **D:** Joseph Pevney. *LIV*

Mysterious Jane 🎬 198? Amid soft-focus nudity, a husband and his lover conspire to institutionalize his wife. 90m/C VHS, Beta. Amber Lee, Sandy Carey. *MED*

The Mysterious Lady 🎬🎬½ 1928 Pre-Ninotchka Garbo plays Russian spy who betrays her mother country because she does not want to be alone. 99m/B VHS. Greta Garbo, Conrad Nagel, Gustav von Seyffertitz, Richard Alexander, Albert Pollet, Edward Connelly; **C:** William H. Daniels. *MGM, FCT*

The Mysterious Magician 🎬🎬½ 1965 Entertaining suspense story of the mad murderer known as "The Wizard," who was thought by Scotland Yard to be dead, but the current murder-wave in London suggests otherwise. Based on an Edgar Wallace story. 95m/C VHS. GE Joachim Fuchsberger, Eddi Arent, Sophie Hardy, Karl John, Heinz Drache; **D:** Alfred Vohrer. *SNC*

Mysterious Mr. Wong 🎬½ 1935 The Thirteen Coins of Confucius put San Francisco's Chinatown in a state of terror until Mr. Wong arrives. 56m/B VHS, Beta. Arline Judge, Wallace Ford; **D:** William Nigh. *VYY, MRV, SNC*

The Mysterious Rider 🎬🎬½ *The Fighting Phantom* 1933 A cowboy tries to prevent unscrupulous homesteaders from cheating farmers out of their land. 59m/B VHS. Kent Taylor, Lona Andre, Gail Patrick, Warren Hymer, Berton Churchill; **D:** Fred Allen. *SNC, DVT*

The Mysterious Rider 🎬½ *Mark of the Avenger* 1938 A man framed for murder must help innocent homesteaders from being cheated out of their land. 75m/B VHS. Douglass Dumbrille, Sidney Toler, Russell Hayden, Charlotte Field; **D:** Lesley Selander. *NOS, DVT, RXM*

The Mysterious Rider 🎬🎬 1942 Routine oater has Crabbe and St. John helping a couple of kids protect their inheritance. 56m/B VHS. Buster Crabbe, Al "Fuzzy" St. John, Caroline Burke, John Merton, Kermit Maynard, Jack Ingram, Charles "Slim" Whitaker; **D:** Sam Newfield. *DVT, HEG*

The Mysterious Stranger 🎬🎬 1982 Printer's apprentice is given to bouts of daydreaming about a magic castle in Austria. Based on Twain tale. 89m/C VHS. Chris Makepeace, Lance Kerwin, Fred Gwynne; **D:** Peter H. Hunt. *USH*

Mysterious Two 🎬🎬½ 1982 Two aliens visit the Earth in an effort to enlist converts to travel the universe with them. 100m/C VHS, Beta. John Forsythe, Priscilla Pointer, Noah Beery Jr., Vic Tayback, James Stephens, Karen Werner, Robert Englund, Robert Pine; **D:** Gary Sherman. *LIV*

Mystery at Fire Island 🎬 1981 A clever young girl and her cousin encounter some strange people as they try to find out why their fisherman friend mysteriously vanished. 52m/C VHS, Beta. Frank Converse, Barbara Byrne, Beth Ehlers, Eric Gurry. *NO*

Mystery Date 🎬🎬 1991 (PG-13) A sort of teen version of "After Hours," in which a shy college guy gets a date with the girl of his dreams, only to be mistaken for a master criminal and pursued by gangsters, police and a crazed florist. Not terrible, but if you're old enough to drive you're probably too old to watch with amusement. 98m/C VHS, Closed Caption. Ethan Hawke, Teri Polo, Brian McNamara, Fisher Stevens, B.D. Wong; **D:** Jonathan Wacks; **W:** Terry Runte, Parker Bennett; **M:** John Du Prez. *ORI*

Mystery in Swing 🎬🎬 1940 An all-black mystery with music, about a trumpet player who has snake venom put on his mouthpiece. 66m/B VHS, Beta. F.E. Miller, Monte Hawley, Marguerite Whitten, Tom Moore, Ceepee Johnson; **D:** Arthur Dreifuss. *VYY*

Mystery Island 🎬🎬½ 1981 Beautifully filmed underwater scenes in this children's film about four youths who discover a deserted island which they name Mystery Island, and a retired pirate who lives there. When the children find counterfeit money and the bad guys return for it, the old pirate's clever plans keep the kids safe. 75m/C VHS, Beta. *NO*

Mystery Liner 🎬🎬½ *The Ghost of John Holling* 1934 Dead bodies are found aboard ocean liner and passengers are concerned about it. Slow-moving sea cruise. 62m/B VHS, Beta. Noah Beery Sr., Astrid Allwyn, Cornelius Keefe, Gustav von Seyffertitz, Edwin Maxwell, Boothe Howard, George "Gabby" Hayes; **D:** William Nigh. *NOS, SNC*

The Mystery Man 🎬🎬½ 1935 A Chicago reporter goes on a drinking binge and ends up in St. Louis. There he stumbles upon a mystery which may involve the paper for which he works. He teams up with a beautiful woman to try to crack the case. 65m/B VHS, Beta. Robert Armstrong, Maxine Doyle, Henry Kolker, Leroy Mason, James Burke; **D:** Ray McCarey. *SNC*

Mystery Man 🎬½ 1944 Below-average episode has rancher Hoppy being bothered by rustlers. Boyd solves things in the usual way, while Clyde provides the laughs. 58m/B VHS. William Boyd, Andy Clyde, Jimmy Rogers, Don Costello, Francis McDonald, Forrest Taylor, Eleanor Stewart; **D:** George Archainbaud. *NOS*

Mystery Mansion 🎬🎬 1983 (PG) Fortune in gold and a hundred-year-old mystery lead three children into an exciting treasure hunt. Family fare. 95m/C VHS, Beta. Dallas McKennon, Greg Wynne, Jane Ferguson. *MED*

Mystery Mountain 🎬½ 1934 Twelve episodes depict the villain known as the "Rattler" attempting to stop the construction of a railroad over Mystery Mountain. 156m/B VHS, Beta. Ken Maynard, Gene Autry, Smiley Burnette; **D:** Otto Brower, B. Reeves Eason. *NOS, VCN, CAB*

The Mystery of Alexina 🎬🎬½ *Mystere Alexina* 1986 True story of Herculine Adelaide Barbin, a 19th-century French hermaphrodite, who, after growing up a woman, fell in love with another woman and was actually revealed to be a man. Subtitled. 86m/C VHS, Beta. FR Vuillemin, Valeri Stroh; **D:** Rene Feret; **W:** Jean Gruault. *NLC*

The Mystery of Edwin Drood 🎬🎬½ 1935 Nicely creepy gothic atmosphere highlights this version of Charles Dickens' final novel, which was unfinished at the time of his death. English choirmaster and opium addict John Jasper (Rains) is visited by his nephew Edwin Drood (Manners), who's soon to enter into an arranged marriage with Rosa (Angel). Unbeknownst to anyone, Jasper has long desired Rosa for himself and kills his nephew in a jealous rage. Now that Drood's disappeared, will Jasper have Rosa to himself? 85m/B VHS, Closed Caption. Claude Rains, Heather Angel, Douglass Montgomery, Valerie Hobson, David Manners, Francis L. Sullivan, Ethel Griffies, E.E. Clive; **D:** Stuart Walker; **W:** John L. Balderston, Gladys Unger; **C:** George Robinson; **M:** Edward Ward. *USH*

The Mystery of Edwin Drood 🎬🎬½ 1993 When Edwin Drood vanishes on Christmas Eve, his disappearance leads to a terrifying mystery that unfolds amidst the slums of Victorian England. Adapted from Charles Dickens' last novel, which was left unfinished at his death. 98m/C VHS, Closed Caption. GB Robert Powell, Michelle Evans, Jonathan Phillips, Finty Williams, Rupert Rainsford, Nanette Newman, Freddie Jones, Rosemary Leach, Ronald Fraser; **D:** Timothy Forder; **W:** Timothy Forder. *AAE, TVC*

Mystery of Mr. Wong 🎬½ 1939 The largest star sapphire in the world, the "Eye of the Daughter of the Moon," is stolen from a museum in its home country of China. Mr. Wong becomes involved in trying to trace its trail and the perpetrator of the murders that follow in its wake. One in the series of detective films. 67m/B VHS. Boris Karloff, Grant Withers, Dorothy Tree, Lotus Long; **D:** William Nigh. *VYY, MRV, DVT*

The Mystery of Rampo 🎬🎬🎬 1994 (R) Visually dazzling fantasy that propels mystery writer Edogawa Rampo (Takenaka) into his own stories. Set just before WWII, Rampo is despondent when his latest novel (about a woman suffocating her husband in a trunk) is censored by the government and then amazed when a newspaper story reveals a similar crime. So Rampo decides to meet the widow Shizuko (Hada) and discovers she's a double for his fictional character. He then writes a sequel, again featuring Shizuko, and once again finds reality and fiction blending into the bizarre. Rampo was the pseudonym for renowned writer Hirai Taro, regarded as the Japanese Edgar Allan Poe. The film had its own complications when the version filmed by original director Rentaro Mayusumi was rejected by producer Okuyama, who then reshot much of the film himself. Japanese with subtitles. **CW:** Adult themes, nudity, violence. 96m/C VHS, Beta. JP Naoto Takenaka, Michiko Hada, Masahiro Motoki, Teruyuki Kagawa, Mikijiro Hira; **D:** Kazuyoshi Okuyama; **W:** Kazuyoshi Okuyama, Yuhei Enoki; **C:** Yasushi Sasakibara; **M:** Akira Senju. *HMK*

Mystery of the Hooded Horseman 🎬🎬 1937 Tex finds himself pitted against a very strange adversary. 61m/B VHS, Beta. Tex Ritter, Iris Meredith, Charles "Blackie" King, Joseph Girard, Lafe McKee; **D:** Ray Taylor. *NOS, VDM, DVT*

Mystery of the Leaping Fish/Chess Fever 🎬🎬½ 1925 Two silent shorts. The first, filmed in 1916, is a surreal comedy-mystery about a doped-up detective named Coke Ennyday and his hallucinatory, sped-up adventures. The second, made in 1925 during the Moscow Chess Tournament, is a parody of professional chess playing and the fever with which it grips a country. Pudovkin's second directorial credit. 64m/B VHS, Beta, 8mm. Douglas Fairbanks Sr., Bessie Love, Alma Rubens; **D:** John Emerson, Vsevolod Pudovkin; **W:** Tod Browning. *VYY, MRV*

The Mystery of the Mary Celeste 🎬🎬 *The Phantom Ship; The Mystery of the Marie Celeste* 1937 Tale of terror based on the bizarre case of the "Marie Celeste," an American ship found adrift off the coast of England with her sails set but minus any of her crew on December 5, 1872. 64m/B VHS, Beta. Bela Lugosi, Shirley Grey, Edmund Willard, Arthur Margetson. *NOS, MRV, VYY*

Mystery of the Million Dollar Hockey Puck 🎬½ 198? Sinister diamond smugglers learn a lesson on ice from a pair of orphan lads. Features the National Hockey League's Montreal Canadiens in one of their few film appearances. 88m/C VHS, Beta. Michael MacDonald, Angele Knight; **D:** Jean LaFleur, Peter Svatek. *NO*

Mystery of the Riverboat 🎬🎬½ 1944 Louisiana and the Mississippi River are the background for these 13 episodes of mystery and murder. 90m/B VHS, Beta. Robert Lowery, Eddie Quillan, Lyle Talbot, Francis McDonald, Arthur Hohl; **D:** Ray Taylor, Lewis D. Collins. *VCI, MLB, GPV*

Mystery of the Wax Museum 🎬🎬🎬 1933 Rarely seen, vintage horror classic about a wax-dummy maker who, after a disfiguring fire, resorts to murder and installs the wax-covered bodies of his victims in his museum. Famous for its pioneering use of two-strip Technicolor. Remade in 1953 in 3-D as "House of Wax." 77m/C VHS, Beta, LV. Lionel Atwill, Fay Wray, Glenda Farrell; **D:** Michael Curtiz; **C:** Ray Rennahan. *MGM, MLB*

Mystery Plane 🎬½ 1939 An inventor devises a new bomb-dropping mechanism, and must evade secret agents on his way to deliver it to the government. 60m/B VHS, Beta. John Trent, Marjorie Reynolds, Milburn Stone, Peter George Lynn, Polly Ann Young; **D:** George Waggner. *NOS, DVT, HEG*

Mystery Ranch 🎬½ 1934 A cowboy finds himself in strange predicaments out on the range. 52m/B VHS, Beta. George O'Brien, Charles Middleton, Cecilia Parker; **D:** David Howard. *NOS, DVT, GPV*

Mystery Science Theater 3000: The Movie 🎬🎬½ 1996 (PG-13) Mad scientist Dr. Clayton Forrester (Beaulieu) maroons Mike Nelson on the Satellite of Love, forces him to watch bad movies, and monitors his reactions. Mike and his robotic pals, Tom Servo and Crow T. Robot, save their sanity by wisecracking their way through the movies. Today's experiment is "This Island Earth," an uncharacteristically semi-respectable flick. As regular viewers know, the jokes and snide remarks come fast and in bunches. Not all of them work, but the ones that do will be remembered and repeated often. Audience participation is inevitable. Weekend theme-party status is virtually assured. **CW:** Some sexual humor. 73m/C VHS, LV, Closed Caption. Trace Beaulieu, James Mallon, Michael J. Nelson, Kevin Murphy, John Brady; **D:** James Mallon; **W:** Trace Beaulieu, James Mallon, Michael J. Nelson, Kevin Murphy, Mary Jo Pehl, Paul Chaplin, Bridget Jones; **C:** Jeff Stonehouse; **M:** Billy Barber. *USH*

Mystery Squadron 1933 Twelve chapters, 13 minutes each. Daredevil air action in flight against the masked pilots of the Black Ace. 240m/B VHS, Beta. Bob Steele, Guinn "Big Boy" Williams, Lucille Browne, Jack Mulhall, J. Carrol Naish, Jack Mower; **D:** Colbert Clark. *GPV, VCN, DVT*

Mystery Train 🎬🎬🎬 1989 (R) A run down hotel in Memphis is the scene for three vignettes concerning the visit of foreigners to the U.S. Themes of mythic Americana, Elvis, and life on the fringe pervade this hip and quirky film. The three vignettes all tie together in clever and funny overlaps. Waits fans should listen for his performance as a DJ. 110m/C VHS, LV. Masatoshi Nagase, Youki Kudoh, Jay Hawkins, Cinque Lee, Joe Strummer, Nicoletta Braschi, Elizabeth Bracco, Steve Buscemi, Tom Noonan, Rockets Redglare, Rick Aviles, Rufus Thomas; **D:** Jim Jarmusch; **W:** Jim Jarmusch; **M:** John Lurie; **V:** Tom Waits. *ORI*

Mystery Trooper 🎬🎬 *Trail of the Royal Mounted* 1932 Adventures in the great wilderness full of prospecting, greed, and Indians all being observed by the Royal Mounties. Ten chapters of the serial at 20 minutes each. 200m/B VHS, Beta. Robert Frazer, Buzz Barton. *GPV, NOS, CAB*

Mystic Circle Murder 🎬 1939 Reporter sets out to uncover phony mediums, particularly the Great La Gagge, whose fake apparitions are so convincing that it caused one of his clients to have a heart attack. Cheaply made, and it's obvious. Watch for a cameo by Harry Houdini's wife, who talks about life after death. Also known as "Religious Racketeers." Based on a story by director O'Connor. 69m/B VHS. Betty Compson, Robert Fiske, Helene Le Berthon, Arthur Gardner; **D:** Frank O'Connor. *SNC*

Mystic Pizza 🎬🎬🎬 1988 (R) Intelligent coming of age drama centers on two sisters and their best friend as they struggle with their hopes, loves, and family rivalries in the small town of Mystic, Connecticut. At times predictable, there are enough unexpected moments to keep interest high; definite appeal to young women, but others may not relate. The relatively unknown Roberts got most of the attention, but is the weakest of the three leads, so watch this one for the strong performances from Gish and Taylor. 101m/C VHS, Beta, LV, Closed Caption. Annabeth Gish, Julia Roberts, Lili Taylor, Vincent D'Onofrio, William R. Moses, Adam Storke, Conchata Ferrell, Joanna Merlin; **D:** Donald Petrie; **W:** Amy Holden Jones, Perry Howze, Alfred Uhry; **M:** David McHugh. Independent Spirit Awards '89: Best First Feature. *VTR*

Nabonga 🎬🎬 *Gorilla; Jungle Woman* 1944 The daughter of an embezzler, whose plane crashes in the jungle, befriends a gorilla who protects her. Soon a young man comes looking for the embezzler's cash, meets the woman and the ape, and together they go on a wonderful journey. 72m/

B VHS. Buster Crabbe, Fifi d'Orsay, Barton MacLane, Julie London, Herbert Rawlinson; **D:** Sam Newfield. *SNC, NOS, MOV*

Nadia 🎬🎬½ 1984 Entertaining account of the life of Nadia Comaneci, the Romanian gymnast who earned six perfect tens with her stunning performance at the 1976 Olympic Games. Made for television. 100m/C VHS, Beta. Talia Balsam, Jonathan Banks, Simone Blue, Johann Carlo, Carrie Snodgress; **D:** Alan Cooke. *FHE, STP*

Nadine 🎬🎬½ 1987 (PG) In Austin circa 1954, an almost divorced beautician witnesses a murder and goes undercover with her estranged husband to track down the murderer, before he finds her. Plenty of low-key humor. Well-paced fun; Basinger is terrific. 83m/C VHS, Beta, LV, Closed Caption. Jeff Bridges, Kim Basinger, Rip Torn, Gwen Verdon, Glenne Headly, Jerry Stiller, Jay Patterson; **D:** Robert Benton; **W:** Robert Benton; **C:** Nestor Almendros; **M:** Howard Shore. *FOX*

Nadja 🎬🎬🎬 1995 (R) Fresh, modern comic take on the vampire tale is about family ties and the power of home, with the required AIDS analogy and lesbian sex scenes. Tired of nightly bloodletting, the daughter of the now-deceased Count, Nadja (Lowensohn), lives in New York's East Village, hoping to change her life. She seduces and falls in love with Lucy (Craze), whose husband is the nephew of old family nemesis Van Helsing (Fonda, in a surprisingly comedic role). Manic Fonda Van Helsing sets out to save Lucy and steal the film. Meanwhile, Nadja finds her long lost twin brother (Harris, son of Richard) and Lucy discovers sex with Nadja is draining. Innovative camera work (vampire point-of-view scenes shot with a toy Pixelvision camera and blown up to 35mm for a moody, grainy look) and a great score keep "Nadja" very watchable despite some missteps in the plot. (Director Almereyda pioneered use of the Pixel-vision camera in "Another Girl, Another Planet.") Executive producer David Lynch contributes a cameo as a guard at the morgue where Nadja claims her father's body. **CW:** Some scenes of bizarre vampire sexuality and gore, some language. 92m/B VHS. Elina Lowensohn, Suzy Amis, Galaxy Craze, Martin Donovan, Peter Fonda, Karl Geary, Jared Harris; **Cameos:** David Lynch; **D:** Michael Almereyda; **W:** Michael Almereyda; **C:** Jim Denault; **M:** Simon Fisher Turner. Nominations: Independent Spirit Awards '96: Best Actress (Lowensohn), Best Cinematography, Best Director (Almereyda). *HMK*

Nail Gun Massacre woof! 1986 A crazed killer with a penchant for nailing bodies to just about anything goes on a hammering spree. In horrific, vivid color. 90m/C VHS, Beta. Rocky Patterson, Ron Queen, Beau Leland, Michelle Meyer; **D:** Bill Lesley. *NO*

Nails 🎬½ 1992 (R) Harry "Nails" Niles (Hopper) is a tough, experienced cop whose partner has been killed by drug dealers. Harry doesn't take this well and decides to go on a violent search for revenge. Archer is wasted as Harry's estranged wife and Hopper can sleepwalk through this type of cliched wildman role. Made for cable television. **CW:** Language, strong violence, and sexuality. 96m/C VHS, Beta, LV, Closed Caption. Dennis Hopper, Anne Archer, Tomas Milian, Cliff DeYoung; **D:** John Flynn. *FXV, VTR*

Nairobi Affair 🎬🎬 1988 (PG) Savage and Heston fight poachers and each other in Kenya, when the father has an affair with his son's ex-wife. Mediocre, derivative script, but beautiful scenery. Made for television. 95m/C VHS, Beta. Charlton Heston, John Savage, Maud Adams, John Rhys-Davies, Connie Booth; **D:** Marvin J. Chomsky. *THV*

Nais 🎬🎬🎬 1945 Vintage Pagnolian peasant drama. A hunchback sacrifices himself for the girl he loves. She escapes to another man's arms. Adapted from the Emile Zola novel "Nais Micoulin." In French with English subtitles. 105m/B VHS, Beta, 8mm. FR Fernandel; **D:** Fernand Lauterier; **W:** Marcel Pagnol. *VYY, FCT, DVT*

Naked 🎬🎬🎬 *Mike Leigh's Naked* 1993 (R) Existential angst in a '90s London filled with Leigh's usual eccentrics. The unemployed Johnny (Thewlis) comes to London and bunks with former girlfriend Louise (Sharp). After seducing her flatmate Sophie (Cartlidge), Johnny leaves to wander the streets, exchanging philosophical, if foulmouthed, dialogues with a variety of odd characters. Thewlis gives an explosive performance as the calculatingly brutal and desolate Johnny. Chaotic shifts in mood from comedy to violence to love prove a challenge and the pervasive abuse of all the women characters is very disturbing. Critically acclaimed; see it as a reflection on the mess of modern England. **CW:** Vulgar & profane language, nudity, and explicit & violent sex. 131m/C VHS, LV. GB David Thewlis, Lesley Sharp, Katrin Cartlidge, Greg Cruttwell, Claire Skinner, Peter Wight, Ewen Bremmer, Susan Vidler, Deborah MacLaren, Gina McKee; **D:** Mike Leigh; **W:** Mike Leigh; **C:** Dick Pope; **M:** Andrew Dickson. Cannes Film Festival '93: Best Actor (Thewlis), Best Director (Leigh); New York Film Critics Awards '93: Best Actor (Thewlis); National Society of Film Critics Awards '93: Best Actor (Thewlis); Nominations: British Academy Awards '93: Best Film; Independent Spirit Awards '94: Best Foreign Film. *COL, IME*

The Naked and the Dead 🎬🎬½ 1958 Sanitized adaptation of Norman Mailer's bestselling novel about army life in the Pacific during WWII. Resentment between officers and enlisted men proves to be almost as dangerous as the Japanese. Uneven acting and cliched characterizations make this an average outing. Don't expect to hear the profane language that sensationalized the book, because most of it was edited out of the screenplay. 131m/C VHS, Beta. Aldo Ray, Cliff Robertson, Joey Bishop, Raymond Massey, Lili St. Cyr, James Best; **D:** Raoul Walsh; **C:** Joseph LaShelle. *NO*

The Naked Angels 🎬 1969 (R) Rape, mayhem, beatings, and road-hogging streetbikes highlight this biker film, acted, in part, by actual bikers, and in part by others who were actually (almost) actors. The gang war rages from Los Angeles to Las Vegas. Roger Corman was the executive producer. 83m/C VHS, Beta. Michael Greene, Richard Rust, Felicia Guy; **D:** Bruce Clark; **W:** Bruce Clark. *CRV*

Naked Cage woof! 1986 (R) Brutal women's prison film that is borderline soft-core, about an innocent country woman, a horseriding fanatic, who is framed for a robbery and sent to the slammer. There, she contends with lesbian wardens and inmates. Disgusting. 97m/C VHS, Beta. Shari Shattuck, Angel Tompkins, Lucinda Crosby, Christina Whitaker; **D:** Paul Nicholas. *COL*

The Naked City 🎬🎬🎬½ 1948 Film noir classic makes spectacular use of its NYC locations. Beautiful playgirl is murdered and police detectives Fitzgerald and Taylor are left without clues. They spend most of their time running down weak leads and interviewing various suspects and witnesses. When they finally get a break, it leads to playboy Duff. Spectacular ending on the Brooklyn Bridge between cops and killer. Producer Hellinger provided the hard-boiled narration, patterned after the tabloid newspaper stories he once wrote. Served as the impetus for the TV show of the same name, where Hellinger's film postscript also became the show's noted tagline: "There are eight million stories in the naked city, this has been one of them." 96m/B VHS. Barry Fitzgerald, Don Taylor, Howard Duff, Ted de Corsia, Dorothy Hart; **D:** Jules Dassin; **C:** William H. Daniels; **M:** Miklos Rozsa. Academy Awards '48: Best Black and White Cinematography, Best Film Editing; Nominations: Academy Awards '48: Best Story. *IVY*

The Naked Civil Servant 🎬🎬🎬½ 1975 Remarkable film, based on the life of flamboyant homosexual Quentin Crisp, who came out of the closet in his native England, long before his lifestyle would be tolerated by Britains. For mature audiences. 80m/C VHS, Beta. John Hurt; **D:** Jack Gold; **M:** Carl Davis. *HBO*

The Naked Country ♂½ 1985 (R) In the untamed frontier of Australia rancher bigoted Lance Dillion and his sensual wife Mary are determined to make their way. But when Lance finds out that the neglected Mary is fooling around with a local cop, he goes on a killing spree on land sacred to the Aborigines. Plodding plot. 90m/C VHS, Closed Caption. AU John Stanton, Rebecca Gilling, Ivar Kants; D: Tim Burstall; C: David Eggby; M: Bruce Smeaton. HMD

The Naked Edge ♂♂ 1961 Cooper stars as a middle-aged businessman whose wife suspects him of murder after she begins snooping into his business affairs. Cooper's last film and far from his best. Poor direction and holes in the screenplay divert from what could have been a tight thriller. 99m/C VHS, Closed Caption. GB Gary Cooper, Deborah Kerr, Eric Portman, Diane Cilento, Hermione Gingold, Peter Cushing, Michael Wilding, Ronald Howard; D: Michael Anderson Sr.; W: Joseph Stefano. MGM, MOV

The Naked Face ♂♂ 1984 (R) A psychiatrist tries to find out why his patients are being killed. He gets no help from police, who suspect he is the murderer. A dull affair featuring unusual casting of Moore, while Steiger's suspicious police captain character provides spark. From the novel by Sidney Sheldon. 105m/C VHS, Beta. Roger Moore, Rod Steiger, Elliott Gould, Art Carney, Anne Archer, David Hedison; D: Bryan Forbes. MGM

The Naked Flame woof! 1968 (R) O'Keefe plays an investigator in a strange town inhabited by weird, religious fanatics. After he arrives, the womenfolk shed their clothes in this pitiful, pathetic hilarity. ?m/C VHS. Dennis O'Keefe, Linda Bennett, Kasey Rogers. SNC

The Naked Gun: From the Files of Police Squad ♂♂♂ 1988 (PG-13) More hysterical satire from the creators of "Airplane!" The short-lived television cop spoof "Police Squad" moves to the big screen and has Lt. Drebin uncover a plot to assassinate Queen Elizabeth while she is visiting Los Angeles. Nearly nonstop gags and pratfalls provide lots of laughs. Nielsen is perfect as Drebin and the supporting cast is strong; cameos abound. 85m/C VHS, Beta, LV, 8mm, Closed Caption. Leslie Nielsen, Ricardo Montalban, Priscilla Presley, George Kennedy, O.J. Simpson, Nancy Marchand, John Houseman; Cameos: Weird Al Yankovic, Reggie Jackson, Dr. Joyce Brothers; D: David Zucker; W: Jerry Zucker, Jim Abrahams, Pat Proft, David Zucker; M: Ira Newborn. PAR

Naked Gun 33 1/3: The Final Insult ♂♂ 1994 (PG-13) Ever dumb, crass, and crude, Lt. Drebin returns to the force from retirement to lead an investigation into terrorist activities in Hollywood. Lots of current events jokes—dated as soon as they hit the screen. Sure to satisfy genre fans with a taste for bad puns. Watch for the cameos, especially at the "Oscars."CW: Off-color humor and sexual innuendo. 90m/C VHS, Beta, LV, Closed Caption. Leslie Nielsen, Priscilla Presley, George Kennedy, O.J. Simpson, Fred Ward, George Kennedy, Gary Cooper, Kathleen Freeman, Raquel Welch; Cameos: Pia Zadora, James Earl Jones, Weird Al Yankovic, Ann B. Davis; D: Peter Segal; W: Robert Locash, David Zucker, Pat Proft; M: Ira Newborn. Golden Raspberry Awards '94: Worst Supporting Actor (Simpson), Worst New Star (Smith).PAR

Naked Gun 2 1/2: The Smell of Fear ♂♂½ 1991 (PG-13) Lt. Drebin returns to rescue the world from a faulty energy policy devised by the White House and oil-lords. A notch down from the previous entry but still hilarious cop parody. Nielsen has this character down to a tee, and there's a laugh every minute. Laserdisc version is letterboxed and features dolby surround sound. 85m/C VHS, Beta, LV, 8mm, Closed Caption. Leslie Nielsen, Priscilla Presley, George Kennedy, O.J. Simpson, Robert Goulet, Richard Griffiths, Jacqueline Brookes, Lloyd Bochner, Tim O'Connor, Peter Mark Richman; Cameos: Mel Torme, Eva Gabor, Weird Al Yankovic; D: David Zucker; W: David Zucker, Pat Proft; M: Ira Newborn. PAR

Naked Hills ♂½ 1956 Meandering tale about a man (Wayne) who, suffering from gold fever, searches for 40 years in 19th Century California and ends up out of luck, losing his wife and family. 72m/C VHS. David Wayne, Keenan Wynn, James Barton, Marcia Henderson, Jim Backus, Denver Pyle, Myrna Dell, Frank Fenton, Fuzzy Knight; D: Josef Shaftel; W: Josef Shaftel. NO

Naked in New York ♂♂½ 1993 (R) Aspiring New York playwright Jake Briggs (Stoltz) and his girlfriend Joanne (Parker), an aspiring photographer, find their relationship in jeopardy when their respective careers start to take off. Offspring from the "Annie Hall" school of neurotic romance examines a number of issues, including ambition, commitment, and the societal dynamics of theatre and art. Celebrity appearances abound, including Styron as himself and Goldberg as a tragedy mask on a wall. Directorial debut of Scorsese protege Algrant is uneven but charming. Parker is particularly strong, and Turner's a riot as a sexpot soap star on the prowl for Jake.CW: Language, pot use and sexuality. 89m/C VHS, LV, Closed Caption. Eric Stoltz, Mary-Louise Parker, Ralph Macchio, Jill Clayburgh, Tony Curtis, Kathleen Turner, Timothy Dalton, Lynne Thigpen, Roscoe Lee Browne; Cameos: Whoopi Goldberg, William Styron, Eric Bogosian, Quentin Crisp; D: Dan Algrant; W: Dan Algrant, John Warren; M: Angelo Badalamenti; V: David Johansen. COL

Naked in the Night ♂ 1958 Cheap German exploitation film about the dangers of promiscuous women. Dubbed in English. ?m/C VHS. GE Eva Bartok, Alexander Kerst. SNC, TPV

Naked in the Sun ♂♂ 1957 The true story of events leading to the war between the Osceola and Seminole Indians and a slave trader. Somewhat slow. 95m/C VHS. James Craig, Lita Milan, Barton MacLane, Tony Hunter; D: R. John Hugh. REP

Naked Is Better ♂ 1973 A couple of buffoons pose as hospital workers so they can play doctor with a hospitalized actress. 93m/C VHS, Beta. Alberto Olmedo, Jorge Porcel, Jorge Barreiro, Maria Casan. MED

Naked Jungle ♂♂♂ 1954 Suspenseful, well-done jungle adventure of a plantation owner (Heston) in South America and his North American mail-order bride (Parker), who do battle with a deadly, miles-long siege of red army ants. Realistic and worth watching. Produced by George Pal, shot by Ernest Laszlo and based on the story "Leiningen vs. the Ants" by Carl Stephenson. 95m/C VHS, Beta, LV. Charlton Heston, Eleanor Parker, Abraham Sofaer, William Conrad; D: Byron Haskin; W: Philip Yordan; C: Ernest Laszlo. PAR

Naked Killer ♂ 1992 Kitty (Ching) turns to a female assassin to learn the art of killing so that she may avenge her father's death. When that teacher is herself unceremoniously murdered, Kitty and her policeman boyfriend (Yam) have two scores to settle. Sex and violence. Subtitled in English. 86m/C VHS. CN My Yau Ching, Simon Yam; D: Clarence Fok Yiu Leung. WVE

Naked Kiss ♂♂½ The Iron Kiss 1964 Fuller's most savage, hysterical film noir. A brutalized prostitute escapes her pimp and tries to enter respectable small-town society. She finds even more perversion and sickness there. 92m/B VHS, LV. Constance Towers, Anthony Eisley, Michael Dante, Virginia Grey, Patsy Kelly, Betty Bronson; D: Samuel Fuller. HMV

Naked Lie ♂♂ 1989 A District Attorney and a judge engage in an ultra-steamy affair and inevitably clash when she is assigned as a prosecutor on the politically explosive case over which he is presiding. 89m/C VHS. Victoria Principal, James Farentino, Glenn Withrow, William Lucking, Dakin Matthews; D: Richard A. Colla; M: Robert Alcivar. ING

Naked Lunch ♂♂♂ 1991 (R) Whacked-out movie based on William S. Burroughs's autobiographical account of drug abuse, homosexuality, violence, and weirdness set in the drug-inspired land called Interzone. Hallucinogenic images are carried to the extreme: typewriters metamorphose into beetles, bloblike creatures with sex organs scurry about, and characters mainline insecticide. Some of the characters are clearly based on writers of the Beat generation, including Jane and Paul Bowles, Allen Ginsberg, and Jack Kerouac.CW: Language, violence, and strong sensuality. 117m/C VHS, Closed Caption. Peter Weller, Judy Davis, Ian Holm, Julian Sands, Roy Scheider, Monique Mercure, Nicholas Campbell, Michael Zelniker, Robert A. Silverman, Joseph Scorsiani; D: David Cronenberg; W: David Cronenberg; M: Howard Shore. Genie Awards '92: Best Adapted Screenplay, Best Art Direction/Set Decoration, Best Cinematography, Best Director (Cronenberg), Best Film, Best Sound, Best Supporting Actress (Mercure); New York Film Critics Awards '91: Best Screenplay, Best Supporting Actress (Davis); National Society of Film Critics Awards '91: Best Director (Cronenberg), Best Screenplay. TCF

The Naked Maja ♂♂ 1959 Elaborate, yet dull drama about the tumultuous romance between a Spanish duchess and the legendary painter Francisco Goya. Even the gorgeous costumes and spectacular sets can't overcome the weak script and poor direction that plague the film. Based on a story by Oscar Saul and Talbot Jennings. 111m/C VHS, Closed Caption. Ava Gardner, Anthony (Tony) Franciosa, Amedeo Nazzari, Gino Cervi, Lea Padovani, Massimo Serato, Carlo Rizzo, Renzo Cesana; D: Henry Koster, Mario Russo; W: Norman Corwin, Giorgio Prosperi. MGM, FCT

Naked Massacre ♂ 198? A maniac kills nurses, leaving no clues for the police to follow. 90m/C VHS, Beta. Matthieu Carriere, Carol Laurie; D: Denis Heroux. VDC

Naked Obsession ♂½ 1991 (R) A city councilman running for mayor is mugged in one of the seedier parts of the city. He's found by a homeless man who takes him to a kinky nightclub where the councilman is promptly seduced by a topless bar hostess with secrets of her own. Also available in an unrated version. 93m/C VHS. William Katt, Maria Ford, Rick Dean; D: Dan Golden. VES, MOV

Naked Paradise 1978 (R) A young woman moves in with her mother and step-sister and finds difficulty in adjusting. 86m/C VHS, Beta. Laura Gemser, Annie Belle. NO

The Naked Prey ♂♂♂ 1966 Unnerving African adventure which contains some unforgettably brutal scenes. A safari guide (Wilde), leading a hunting party, must watch as an indigenous tribe murders all his companions, and according to their customs, allows him to be set free, sans clothes or weapons, to be hunted by the best of the tribe. 96m/C VHS, Beta, LV. Cornel Wilde, Gertrude Van Der Berger, Ken Gampu; D: Cornel Wilde. Nominations: Academy Awards '66: Best Story & Screenplay. PAR

Naked Souls ♂ 1995 (R) Anderson must save fiance Krause from the evil experiments of murderous doctor Warner. Like you'll care as long as the Anderson bod is on display.CW: Strong sexuality, and for language and violence. 90m/C VHS. Pamela Anderson Lee, Brian Krause, Clayton Rohner, Justina Vail, David Warner; Cameos: Dean Stockwell; D: Lyndon Chubbuck; W: Frank Dietz; C: Eric Goldstein; M: Nigel Holton. WEA

The Naked Spur ♂♂♂½ 1953 A compulsive bounty hunter tracks down a vicious outlaw and his beautiful girlfriend. An exciting film from the Mann-Stewart team and considered one of their best, infusing the traditional western with psychological confusion. Wonderful use of Rockies locations. 93m/C VHS, Beta. James Stewart, Robert Ryan, Janet Leigh, Millard Mitchell; D: Anthony Mann; C: William Mellor. Nominations: Academy Awards '53: Best Story & Screenplay. MGM, TLF

The Naked Sword of Zorro ♂ 1969 Deadly Don Luis taxes the town by day and violates the women by night, but Zorro takes a stand and saves the town. When he's not dressed as Zorro, he is Don Diego, an inept fool, but when he puts that suit on, look out. The ladies can't keep their hands off of him. There are more lusty females than villains, but there's still lots of sword-play and action. **94m/C VHS.** *VDM*

Naked Tango 🎞️½ 1991 **(R)** A lurid recreation of the Argentinian underworld in 1924. Stephanie is a bored wife with an older husband who, while traveling with her husband on a cruise ship, pretends to fall overboard in order to establish a new identity. The problem is she becomes the supposed mail-order bride of a young man who promptly sells her into white slavery. One of her customers is a charismatic killer named Cholo who isn't interested in Stephanie for sex, he just wants to dance the tango with her. This is meant to be taken seriously but is one of the many pretensions, erotic and otherwise, that hamper the film. **90m/C VHS.** Mathilda May, Vincent D'Onofrio, Esai Morales, Fernando Rey; **D:** Leonard Schrader; **W:** Leonard Schrader; **M:** Thomas Newman. *NO*

The Naked Truth 🎞️🎞️½ *Your Past is Showing* 1958 A greedy publisher tries to get rich quick by publishing a scandal magazine about the "lurid" lives of prominent citizens. Well-drawn characters in an appealing offbeat comedy. **92m/C VHS, Beta.** *GB* Peter Sellers, Terry-Thomas, Shirley Eaton, Dennis Price; **D:** Mario Zampi. *NO*

Naked Vengeance woof! *Satin Vengeance* 1985 **(R)** A woman's husband is murdered, she is beaten and raped, and she becomes a vengeful, vicious killing machine. Gratuitous violence, distasteful to the max. **97m/C VHS, Beta.** Deborah Tranelli, Kaz Garas, Bill McLaughlin; **D:** Cirio H. Santiago. *LIV*

Naked Venus 🎞️½ 1958 Ulmer's last film is a slow-paced tale about an American artist, married to a model who poses in the nude and belongs to a nudist camp, whose wealthy mother tries to tear the marriage apart. Discrimination and intolerance of nudist camps is explored. **80m/B VHS, Beta.** Patricia Conelle; **D:** Edgar G. Ulmer. *VDM, TPV*

Naked Warriors 🎞️🎞️ *The Arena* 1973 **(R)** Ancient Romans capture beautiful women from around the world and force them to compete in gladiatorial games. New World exploitation gem featuring mostly Italian cast, including Bay, who starred in the previous year's "Lady Frankenstein." **75m/C VHS, Beta.** Margaret Markov, Pam Grier, Lucretia Love, Paul Muller, Daniel Vargas, Marie Louise, Mary Count, Rosalba (Sara Bay) Neri, Vic Karis, Sid Lawrence, Peter Cester, Anna Melita; **D:** Steve Carver. *MGM*

The Naked Witch 🎞️ *The Naked Temptress* 1964 College student researching witchcraft digs up the grave of a long-dead witch. She comes back to life and takes revenge on the village that killed her years earlier. The nude shots feature someone's finger over the camera lens to cover the witch's vital organs. **60m/C VHS.** Beth Porter, Robert Burgos, Bryarly Lee, Lee Forbes; **D:** Andy Milligan. *SNC*

Naked Youth woof! *Wild Youth* 1959 Seedy drive-in cheapie about two punks breaking out of juvenile detention and heading south of the border on a trail filled with crime, drugs, and loose women. **80m/B VHS, Beta.** Robert Hutton, John Goddard, Carol Ohmart, Jan Brooks, Robert Arthur, Steve Rowland, Clancy Cooper; **D:** John F. Schreyer. *RHI, SNC*

Nam Angels 🎞️ 1988 **(R)** Hell's Angels enter Southeast Asia and rescue POWs. **91m/C VHS, Beta.** Brad Johnson, Vernon Wells, Kevin Duffis; **D:** Cirio H. Santiago. *MED*

A Name for Evil 🎞️🎞️ 1970 **(R)** Having grown tired of city living, a couple moves to an old family estate out in the country near the Great Lakes. Strange sounds in the night are the first signs of the terror to come. **74m/C VHS, Beta.** Robert Culp, Samantha Eggar, Sheila Sullivan, Mike Lane; **D:** Bernard Girard. *NO*

The Name of the Rose 🎞️🎞️½ 1986 **(R)** An exhaustive, off-center adaptation of the best-selling Umberto Eco novel about violent murders in a 14th-century Italian abbey. An English monk struggles against religious fervor in his quest to uncover the truth. **128m/C VHS, Beta, LV, Closed**

Caption. *IT GE FR* Sean Connery, F. Murray Abraham, Christian Slater, Ron Perlman, William Hickey, Feodor Chaliapin Jr, Elya Baskin, Michael Lonsdale; **D:** Jean-Jacques Annaud; **W:** Andrew Birkin, Gerard Brach, Howard Franklin; **C:** Tonino Delli Colli; **M:** James Horner. British Academy Awards '87: Best Actor (Connery); Cesar Awards '87: Best Foreign Film. *NLC*

Namu, the Killer Whale 🎞️🎞️½ 1966 Based on the true story of a marine biologist (Lansing) who gets the perfect opportunity to study killer whales when one is confined to a small cove. The local fisherman want to kill the creature because it feeds on the salmon they catch but they are persuaded against their baser instincts. Filmed on location in the San Juan Islands of Puget Sound. The real Namu lived at the Seattle Public Aquarium. **89m/C VHS.** Robert Lansing, John Anderson, Robin Mattson, Richard Erdman, Lee Meriwether, Joe Higgins; **D:** Laslo Benedek. *MGM, FCT*

Nana 🎞️🎞️🎞️ 1955 French version of Emile Zola's novel about an actress-prostitute who seduces the high society of Paris in the late 1880s, and suffers a heart-breaking downfall and death. Film has three remakes of the original 1926 version. **118m/C VHS, Beta.** *FR* Charles Boyer, Martine Carol. *NOS, DVT, HEG*

Nana 🎞️🎞️½ 1982 A lavishly photographed, graphic adaptation of the Emile Zola novel about a Parisian whore who acquires power by seducing the richest and politically formidable men. Dubbed. **92m/C VHS, Beta.** *IT* Katya Berger, Jean-Pierre Aumont; **D:** Dan Wolman; **W:** Marc Behm; **M:** Ennio Morricone. *FCT, MGM*

Nancy Astor 🎞️🎞️ 1982 A portrait of the beautiful, spirited Virginian who became a member of the British Parliament. **55m/C VHS, Beta.** *GB* Lisa Harrow, James Fox, Dan O'Herlihy, Sylvia Syms. *TLF*

Nancy Drew, Reporter 🎞️🎞️ 1939 The young sleuth gets to play reporter after winning a newspaper contest. In no time at all, she's involved in a murder mystery. **68m/B VHS.** Bonita Granville, John Litel, Frankie Thomas Jr., Mary Lee, Sheila Bromley, Betty Amann, Dick Jones, Olin Howlin, Charles Halton; **D:** William Clemens. *HTV, NOS*

Nancy Goes to Rio 🎞️🎞️½ 1950 Actresses Powell and Sothern compete for the same part in a play and for the same man. Catch is, they're mother and daughter. Zany consequences ensue. Sothern's last film for MGM. ♫Time and Time Again; Shine On Harvest Moon; Cha Bomm Pa Pa; Yipsee-I-O; Magic is the Moonlight; Musetta's Waltz; Love is Like This; Nancy Goes to Rio. **99m/C VHS.** Ann Sothern, Jane Powell, Barry Sullivan, Carmen Miranda, Louis Calhern, Scotty Beckett, Hans Conried, Glenn Anders; **D:** Robert Z. Leonard; **W:** Sidney Sheldon. *MGM, MLB, CCB*

The Nanny 🎞️🎞️½ 1965 Creepfest stars Davis as a seemingly proper nameless nanny who's been accused by her young charge Joey (Dix) of drowning his sister in the bathtub. But it's Joey who's sent away to a home for disturbed children and when he returns two years later (and just why is the nanny still around a childless home?) it's a battle of wills between the duo over who's responsible for some evil goings-on. Based on a novel by Evelyn Piper. **93m/B VHS, Closed Caption.** *GB* Bette Davis, William Dix, Wendy Craig, Jill Bennett, James Villiers, Pamela Franklin, Jack Watling, Alfred Burke, Maurice Denham; **D:** Seth Holt; **W:** Jimmy Sangster; **C:** Henry Waxman; **M:** Richard Rodney Bennett. *FXV*

Napoleon 🎞️🎞️🎞️🎞️ 1927 A vivid, near-complete restoration of Gance's epic silent masterpiece about the famed conqueror's early years, from his youth through the Italian Campaign. An innovative, spectacular achievement with its use of multiple split screens, montage, color, and triptychs. Given a gala theatrical re-release in 1981. Remade in 1955. **235m/B VHS, Beta, LV.** *FR* Albert Dieudonne, Antonin Artaud, Pierre Batcheff, Gina Manes, Armand Bernard, Harry Krimer, Albert Bras, Abel Gance, Georges Cahuzac; **D:** Abel Gance; **M:** Carmine Coppola. *USH*

Napoleon 🎞️🎞️ 1955 Depicts life story of Napoleon from his days as a soldier in the French army to his exile on the Island of Elba. Falls short of the fantastic 1927 silent classic as it attempts to delve into Napoleon the man, as opposed to his conquests. Some might find it too slow for their tastes. **123m/C VHS, Beta, LV.** *FR* Raymond Pellegrin, Orson Welles, Maria Schell, Yves Montand, Erich von Stroheim, Jean Gabin, Jean-Pierre Aumont; **D:** Sacha Guitry. *NOS, MRV, MPI*

Napoleon 🎞️🎞️½ 1996 Cute pic for young kiddies who like animals. Napoleon is a very curious golden retriever puppy who slips into a hot-air balloon and finds himself airborne across Australia. He lands unexpectedly near Sydney Harbor and is befriended by Birdo the parrot, who becomes his guide when Napoleon decides he wants to meet his wild dog cousins, the dingoes. And it's off into the bush, with kangaroos, koalas, snakes, and lizards to help or hinder along the way. **81m/C VHS.** *AU JP* **D:** Mario Andreacchio; **W:** Mario Andreacchio, Mark Saltzman; **C:** Roger Dowling; **M:** Bill Conti; **V:** Jamie Croft, Philip Quast, Carole Skinner, Anne Lambert, David Argue, Joan Rivers, Steven Vidler, Susan Lyons. *NYR*

Napoleon and Samantha 🎞️🎞️🎞️ 1972 Disney adventure about Napoleon, an orphan (Whitaker), who is befriended by Danny, a college student (Douglas). After the death of his grandfather, Napoleon decides to take Major, his elderly pet lion, and follow Danny, who is herding goats for the summer, across the American northwest mountains and they are joined by Samantha (Foster in her film debut). Worth watching. **91m/C VHS, Beta.** Jodie Foster, Johnny Whitaker, Michael Douglas, Will Geer, Henry Jones; **D:** Bernard McEveety; **W:** Stewart Raffill; **M:** Buddy Baker. Nominations: Academy Awards '72: Original Dramatic/Comedy Score. *DIS*

The Narcotics Story woof! *The Dreaded Persuasion* 1958 Bad film on the same vein as "Reefer Madness." Originally intended as a police training film, this shows the evils and destruction of heroin addiction. Portrayals of drug addicts are hilarious. **75m/C VHS.** Sharon Strand, Darlene Hendricks, Herbert Crisp, Fred Marratto; **D:** Robert W. Larsen. *SNC, TPV*

The Narrow Margin 🎞️🎞️🎞️ 1952 Well-made, harrowing adventure about a cop who is in charge of transporting a gangster's widow to a trial where she is to testify. On the train he must try to keep her safe from the hit-men who would murder her. A real cat and mouse game—one of the best suspense movies of the '50s. **71m/B VHS.** Charles McGraw, Marie Windsor, Jacqueline White, Queenie Leonard, Gordon Gebert, Don Beddoe, Harry Harvey; **D:** Richard Fleischer. Nominations: Academy Awards '52: Best Story. *TTC, MLB, TTC*

Narrow Margin 🎞️🎞️ 1990 **(R)** Archer reluctantly agrees to testify against the mob after witnessing a murder, and Los Angeles D.A. Hackman is assigned to protect her on the train through the Rockies back to L.A. Bad idea, she finds out. No match for its '52 predecessor. **99m/C VHS, LV, Closed Caption.** Gene Hackman, Anne Archer, James B. Sikking, J.T. Walsh, M. Emmet Walsh; **D:** Peter Hyams; **W:** Peter Hyams; **M:** Bruce Broughton. *LIV*

Narrow Trail 🎞️🎞️🎞️½ 1917 A silent classic that still stands as one of the best Westerns ever made. A tough cowboy with a troubled past hopes a good woman can save him. But she's seen trouble, too. They meet up again in San Francisco's Barbary Coast. A horse race might hold the answer. **56m/B VHS, Beta.** William S. Hart, Sylvia Bremer, Milton Ross; **D:** William S. Hart. *NOS, GPV, CCB*

Nashville 🎞️🎞️🎞️🎞️ 1975 **(R)** Altman's stunning, brilliant film tapestry that follows the lives of 24 people during a political campaign/music festival in Nashville. Seemingly extemporaneous vignettes, actors playing themselves (Elliott Gould and Julie Christie), funny, touching, poignant character studies concerning affairs of the heart and despairs of the mind. Repeatedly blurs reality and fantasy. ♫I'm Easy; Two Hundred Years; Keep A'Goin'; One, I Love You; Let Me Be the One; The Day I Looked Jesus in the Eye; For the Sake of the Children; I Never Get Enough; It Don't Worry Me. **159m/C VHS, Beta, LV.** Keith Carradine, Lily Tomlin, Henry Gibson, Ronee Blakley, Keenan Wynn, David Arkin, Geraldine Chaplin, Lauren Hutton, Shelley Duvall, Barbara Harris, Allen (Goorwitz) Garfield, Karen Black, Christina Raines, Michael Murphy, Ned Beatty, Barbara Baxley, Scott Glenn, Jeff Goldblum, Gwen Welles, Bert Remsen, Robert DoQui; *Cameos:* Elliott Gould, Julie Christie; *D:* Robert Altman; *W:* Joan Tewkesbury; *M:* Richard Baskin. Academy Awards '75: Best Song ("I'm Easy"); Golden Globe Awards '76: Best Song ("I'm Easy"); National Board of Review Awards '75: 10 Best Films of the Year, Best Director (Altman), Best Supporting Actress (Blakley); New York Film Critics Awards '75: Best Director (Altman), Best Film, Best Supporting Actress (Tomlin); National Society of Film Critics Awards '75: Best Director (Altman), Best Film, Best Supporting Actor (Gibson), Best Supporting Actress (Tomlin); Nominations: Academy Awards '75: Best Director (Altman), Best Picture, Best Supporting Actress (Blakley, Tomlin). *PAR*

Nashville Beat 🎬🎬 1989 Gang targets the citizens of Nashville, Tennessee, until two tough cops stomp the gang's delusion that Southern folk are easy marks. **110m/C VHS.** Kent McCord, Martin Milner; *D:* Bernard L. Kowalski. *NO*

Nashville Girl 🎬 *Country Music Daughter; New Girl in Town* 1976 (R) Innocent country girl who wants to make good in the country music scene, rises to the top of the Nashville success ladder, by compromising everything and hanging out with stereotyped no-goods in the show biz world. It's as good as a yawn. **90m/C VHS, Beta.** Monica Gayle, Johnny Rodriguez; *D:* Gus Trikonis. *NLC*

The Nasty Girl 🎬🎬🎬½ 1990 (PG-13) A bright young German model plans to enter a national essay contest on the topic of her hometown's history during the Third Reich. While researching the paper, she's harassed and even brutalized, but refuses to cease her sleuthing. Excellent performances, tight direction, with comedic touches that charmingly imparts an important message. Based on a true story. In German with English subtitles. **93m/C VHS.** *GE* Lena Stolze, Monika Baumgartner, Michael Gahr; *D:* Michael Verhoeven; *W:* Michael Vorhoeven. British Academy Awards '91: Best Foreign Film; New York Film Critics Awards '90: Best Foreign Film; Nominations: Academy Awards '90: Best Foreign Language Film. *HBO*

Nasty Habits 🎬🎬 1977 (PG) Broad farce depicting a corrupt Philadelphia convent as a satiric parallel to Watergate, with nuns modeled on Nixon, Dean and Mitchell. Includes cameo appearances by various media personalities. Based on the British novel "The Abbess of Crewe" by Muriel Spark. **92m/C VHS, Beta.** Glenda Jackson, Geraldine Page, Anne Jackson, Melina Mercouri, Sandy Dennis, Susan Penhaligon, Anne Meara, Edith Evans, Rip Torn, Eli Wallach; *Cameos:* Mike Douglas, Bill Jorgensen, Jessica Savitch, Howard K. Smith; *D:* Michael Lindsay-Hogg. *MED*

Nasty Hero 🎬½ 1989 (PG-13) Hard-boiled ex-con comes to Miami to avenge the car thieves who framed him and got him sent to the slammer. This is car-chase scene heaven—little plot or drama. **79m/C VHS, Beta, LV.** Robert Sedgwick, Carlos Palomino, Scott Feraco, Mike Starr, Rosanna DaVon; *D:* Nick Barwood. *COL*

Nasty Rabbit 🎬 *Spies-A-Go-Go* 1964 Ridiculous spoof about Soviet spies intent on releasing a rabbit with a hideous Communist disease into the U.S. Everyone gets in on the chase: Nazi forces, cowboys and indians, sideshow freaks, banditos—what is the point? **88m/C VHS, Beta.** Arch Hall Jr., Micha Terr, Melissa Morgan, John Akana; *D:* James Landis. *RHI*

Natas...The Reflection 🎬 1983 (PG) A reporter persists in validating an Indian demon myth. **90m/C VHS, Beta.** Randy Mulkey, Pat Bolt, Craig Hensley, Kelli Kuhn. *LIV*

Nate and Hayes 🎬🎬½ 1983 (PG) Set during the mid-1800s in the South Pacific, the notorious real-life swashbuckler Captain "Bully" Hayes ("good pirate") helps young missionary Nate recapture his fiancee from a cutthroat gang of evil slave traders. Entertaining "jolly rogers" film. **100m/C VHS, Beta, LV.** *NZ* Tommy Lee Jones, Michael O'Keefe, Max Phipps, Jenny Seagrove; *D:* Ferdinand Fairfax; *M:* Trevor Jones. *PAR*

A Nation Aflame 🎬½ 1937 Anti-Klan film is based on a story by Thomas L. Dixon, the author of "The Clansman," from which D.W. Griffith made "The Birth of a Nation." In this story, a con man gains control of the state's government through an ultra-nationalistic secret society, and eventually pays for his corruption. **70m/B VHS, Beta.** Lila Lee, Noel Madison, Snub Pollard, Norma Trelvar; *D:* Victor Halperin. *SNC, NOS, GVV*

National Lampoon Goes to the Movies 🎬🎬 1981 Parodies of popular Hollywood genres, including cop thrillers, melodramas, and inspirational biographies, done in goofy "Lampoon" style. **89m/C VHS.** Robby Benson, Candy Clark, Diane Lane, Christopher Lloyd, Peter Riegert, Richard Widmark, Henny Youngman; *D:* Henry Jaglom. *MOV*

National Lampoon's Animal House 🎬🎬🎬½ *Animal House* 1978 (R) Classic Belushi vehicle running amuck. Set in 1962 and responsible for launching Otis Day and the Knights and defining cinematic food fights. Every college tradition from fraternity rush week to the homecoming pageant is irreverently and relentlessly mocked in this wild comedy about Delta House, a fraternity on the edge. Climaxes with the homecoming parade from hell. Sophomoric, but very funny, with a host of young stars who went on to more serious work. Remember: "Knowledge is good." **109m/C VHS, Beta, LV.** John Belushi, Tim Matheson, John Vernon, Donald Sutherland, Peter Riegert, Stephen Furst, Bruce McGill, Mark Metcalf, Verna Bloom, Karen Allen, Tom Hulce, Mary Louise Weller, Kevin Bacon; *D:* John Landis; *W:* Harold Ramis; *M:* Elmer Bernstein. People's Choice Awards '79: Best Film. *USH*

National Lampoon's Attack of the 5 Ft. 2 Women 🎬🎬 *Attack of the 5 Ft. 2 Women* 1994 (R) Brown parodies two of 1994's most notorious tabloid material: "Tonya: The Battle of Wounded Knee" and "He Never Give Me Orgasm: The Lenora Babbitt Story." Made for cable TV.*CW:* Language and comic sex-related material. **82m/C VHS, Closed Caption.** Julie Brown, Sam McMurray, Adam Storke, Priscilla Barnes, Lauren Tewes, Dick Miller, Rick Overton, Stanley DeSantis, Anne DeSalvo, Liz Torres, Vicki Lawrence, Stella Stevens, Peter DeLuise; *D:* Julie Brown, Richard Wenk; *W:* Julie Brown, Charlie Coffey; *M:* Christopher Tyng. *PAR*

National Lampoon's Christmas Vacation 🎬🎬½ *Christmas Vacation* 1989 (PG-13) The third vacation for the Griswold family finds them hosting repulsive relatives for Yuletide. The sight gags, although predictable, are sometimes on the mark. Quaid is a standout as the slovenly cousin. **93m/C VHS, Beta, LV, 8mm, Closed Caption.** Chevy Chase, Beverly D'Angelo, Randy Quaid, Diane Ladd, John Randolph, E.G. Marshall, Doris Roberts, Julia Louis-Dreyfus, Mae Questel, William Hickey, Brian Doyle-Murray, Juliette Lewis, Johnny Galecki, Nicholas Guest, Miriam Flynn; *D:* Jeremiah S. Chechik; *W:* John Hughes; *C:* Thomas Ackerman; *M:* Angelo Badalamenti. *WAR*

National Lampoon's Class of '86 *Class of '86* 1986 This is a live stage comedy show written and sponsored by the infamous adult humor magazine, featuring a new cast of comics. **86m/C VHS, Beta.** Rodger Bumpass, Veanne Cox, Andy Annie, John Michael Higgins, Tommy Koenig. *PAR*

National Lampoon's Class Reunion woof! *Class Reunion* 1982 (R) Class reunion with some very wacky guests and a decided lack of plot or purpose. Things go from bad to worse when a crazed killer decides to join in on

the festivities. Disappointing with very few laughs. **85m/C VHS, Beta, LV.** Shelley Smith, Gerrit Graham, Michael Lerner; *D:* Michael Miller; *W:* John Hughes; *M:* Peter Bernstein. *PAR, VES*

National Lampoon's European Vacation 🎬½ *European Vacation* 1985 (PG-13) Sappy sequel to "Vacation" that has witless Chase and his family bumbling around in the land "across the pond." The Griswolds nearly redefine the term "ugly American." Stonehenge will never be the same. **94m/C VHS, Beta, LV, 8mm, Closed Caption.** Chevy Chase, Beverly D'Angelo, Dana Hill, Jason Lively, Victor Lanoux, John Astin; *D:* Amy Heckerling; *W:* John Hughes, Robert Klane, Eric Idle; *M:* Charles Fox. *WAR*

National Lampoon's Favorite Deadly Sins 🎬🎬½ 1995 (R) Three sketches about greed, anger, and lust. In "Lust," Leary plays a security guard who spies on a neighbor; "Anger" finds Clay as an irate convenience store shopper; and Mantegna, in "Greed," stars as a sleazoid producer who helps a young woman kill her wicked stepmother and stepsisters in order to make a movie about it.*CW:* Nudity, strong language, brief violence. **99m/C VHS, Closed Caption.** Joe Mantegna, Denis Leary, Annabella Sciorra, Andrew Dice Clay, Cassidy Rae, Brian Keith, William Ragsdale, Farrah Forke, Tanya Pohlkotte; *D:* Denis Leary, David Jablin; *W:* Michael Barrie, Jim Mulholland, Lee Biondi, Ann Lembeck. *REP*

National Lampoon's Last Resort 🎬½ 1994 (PG-13) Retired film actor finds his long-time movie nemesis can't separate screen life from the real thing anymore and is planning an invasion of the actor's private island. So, he calls on his nephew (who brings along a friend) to help him out. **91m/C VHS, LV, Closed Caption.** Corey Feldman, Corey Haim, Geoffrey Lewis, Robert Mandan; *D:* Rafal Zielinksi. *THV*

National Lampoon's Loaded Weapon 1 🎬½ *Loaded Weapon 1* 1993 (PG-13) Cop Jack Colt (Estevez) and partner Wes Luger (Jackson) attempt to recover a microfilm which contains a formula for turning cocaine into cookies. Essentially a sendup of the popular "Lethal Weapon" series, although other movies and themes make an appearance, well sort of. Short on plot and long on slapstick, but that's the whole point. Tired formula creates nostalgia for the granddaddy of them all, "Airplane." Lots of cameos, including one from sibling spoof star Sheen. The magazine folded while the movie was in production, an ominous sign. **83m/C VHS, LV.** Emilio Estevez, Samuel L. Jackson, Jon Lovitz, Tim Curry, Kathy Ireland, William Shatner; *Cameos:* Dr. Joyce Brothers, James Doohan, Richard Moll, F. Murray Abraham, Denis Leary, Corey Feldman, Phil Hartman, J.T. Walsh, Erik Estrada, Larry Wilcox, Allyce Beasley, Charlie Sheen; *D:* Gene Quintano; *W:* Gene Quintano, Don Holley. *COL, IME*

National Lampoon's Senior Trip 🎬 *Senior Trip* 1995 (R) According to the promotion, "they came, they saw, they passed out." Good dumb fun is hard to come by, particularly here. Latest lesser "Lampoon" effort in a long line of lesser Lampoons is about midwestern high school seniors who take a bus trip to Washington to meet the President. Along the way they have hijinks, including manipulation by a stereotypically corrupt senator out to embarrass his political opponent. Frewer is the inept principal who leads the hopelessly cliched group of misfits through the dopey corridors of power. Somehow, even the Coreys avoided this one.*CW:* Continuous teenage alcohol and drug abuse; crude sexual references. **91m/C VHS, LV, Closed Caption.** Matt Frewer, Valerie Mahaffey, Lawrence Dane, Thomas Chong, Kevin McDonald; *D:* Kelly Makin; *W:* I. Marlene King, Roger Kumble. *NLC*

National Lampoon's Vacation 🎬🎬🎬 *Vacation* 1983 (R) The Clark Griswold (Chase) family of suburban Chicago embarks on a westward cross-country vacation via car to the renowned "Wally World." Ridiculous and hysterical misadventures, including a falling asleep at the wheel sequence and the untimely death of Aunt Edna.

98m/C VHS, Beta, LV. Chevy Chase, Beverly D'Angelo, Imogene Coca, Randy Quaid, Christie Brinkley, James Keach, Anthony Michael Hall, John Candy, Eddie Bracken, Brian Doyle-Murray, Eugene Levy; *D:* Harold Ramis; *W:* John Hughes, Harold Ramis; *M:* Ralph Burns. WAR

National Velvet 🐾🐾🐾🐾 1944 (G) A young English girl wins a horse in a raffle and is determined to train it to compete in the famed Grand National race. Taylor, only 12 at the time, is superb in her first starring role. Rooney also gives a fine performance. Filmed with a loving eye on lushly decorated sets, this is a masterpiece version of the story of affection between a girl and her pet. Based on the novel by Enid Bagnold and followed by "International Velvet" in 1978. 124m/C VHS, LV, Closed Caption. Elizabeth Taylor, Mickey Rooney, Arthur Treacher, Donald Crisp, Anne Revere, Angela Lansbury, Reginald Owen, Norma Varden, Jackie "Butch" Jenkins, Terence Kilburn; *D:* Clarence Brown; *W:* Helen Deutsch, Theodore Reeves; *M:* Herbert Stothart. Academy Awards '45: Best Film Editing, Best Supporting Actress (Revere); Nominations: Academy Awards '45: Best Color Cinematography, Best Director (Brown). MGM, TLF, BTV

Native Son 🐾🐾½ 1951 A young black man from the ghettos of Chicago is hired as a chauffeur by an affluent white family. His job is to drive their head-strong daughter anywhere she wants to go. Unintentionally, he kills her, tries to hide, and is ultimately found guilty. Based on the classic novel by Richard Wright, who also stars. Remade in 1986. Unprofessional direction and low budget work against the strong story. 91m/B VHS. Richard Wright, Jean Wallace, Nicholas Joy, Gloria Madison, Charles Cane; *D:* Pierre Chenal. NOS, XVC, FCT

Native Son 🐾🐾½ 1986 (R) This second film adaptation of the classic Richard Wright novel is chock full of stars and tells the story of a poor black man who accidentally kills a white woman and then hides the body. Changes in the script soft-soap some of the novel's disturbing truths and themes—so-so drama for those who have not read the book. 111m/C VHS, Beta, LV, Closed Caption. Geraldine Page, Oprah Winfrey, Matt Dillon, John Karlen, Elizabeth McGovern, Akosua Busia, Carroll Baker, Victor Love, John McMartin, Art Evans, Willard Pugh, David Rasche; *D:* Jerrold Freedman; *W:* Richard Wesley; *C:* Thomas Burstyn; *M:* James Mtume. MON, KUI, LIV

Nativity 🐾🐾 1978 Unmemorable, made-for-TV portrayal of the romance between Mary and Joseph (of the Bible story), Joseph's response to Mary's pregnancy, and the birthing of Jesus. Not exactly a Bible epic, the direction and acting are uninspired. 97m/C VHS, Beta, Closed Caption. John Shea, Madeleine Stowe, Jane Wyatt, John Rhys-Davies, Kate O'Mara; *D:* Bernard L. Kowalski. FOX

The Natural 🐾🐾🐾 1984 (PG) A beautifully filmed movie about baseball as myth. A young man, whose gift for baseball sets him apart, finds that trouble dogs him, particularly with a woman. In time, as an aging rookie, he must fight against his past to lead his team to the World Series, and win the woman who is meant for him. From the Bernard Malamud novel. 134m/C VHS, Beta, LV, Closed Caption. Robert Redford, Glenn Close, Robert Duvall, Kim Basinger, Wilford Brimley, Barbara Hershey, Richard Farnsworth, Robert Prosky, Darren McGavin, Joe Don Baker, Michael Madsen; *D:* Barry Levinson; *C:* Caleb Deschanel; *M:* Randy Newman. Nominations: Academy Awards '84: Best Art Direction/Set Decoration, Best Cinematography, Best Supporting Actress (Close), Best Original Score. COL

Natural Born Killers 🐾🐾 1994 (R) An old script by (Graphic Screen Violence) Tarantino is resurrected by (Damn the Torpedoes) Stone and invested with its own unique subtle nuance and style. Controversial (natch, considering the director and writer) look at the way the media portrays criminals. Harrelson and Lewis are the lovestruck, white-trash serial killers who become tabloid-TV darlings, thanks to a sensationalistic press led by Downey, Jr. Stone's dark and manic comment on America's fascination and revulsion with violence is strictly of the love it or leave it

variety. Bloodshed galore, dazzling photography, and a dynamite soundtrack (with over 75 selections) add up to sensory overload.CW: Strong language, extreme violence, graphic carnage, and sexuality. 119m/C VHS, LV, Closed Caption. Woody Harrelson, Robert Downey Jr., Juliette Lewis, Tommy Lee Jones, Ashley Judd, Tom Sizemore, Rodney Dangerfield, Rachel Ticotin, Arliss Howard, Russell Means, Denis Leary, Steven Wright, Pruitt Taylor Vince; *D:* Oliver Stone; *W:* Oliver Stone; *C:* Robert Richardson; *M:* Trent Reznor. Nominations: Golden Globe Awards '95: Best Director (Stone); MTV Movie Awards '95: Best On-Screen Duo (Woody Harrelson/Juliette Lewis), Best Kiss (Woody Harrelson/Juliette Lewis). WAR, THV

Natural Causes 🐾½ 1994 (PG-13) Muddled political thriller finds Dr. Jessie McCarthy (Purl) traveling to Thailand to visit her estranged mother Rachel (Paige), only to discover she's just been murdered. Then Jessie learns Rachel had a secret life aiding Vietnamese refugees and a scheme is afoot to sabotage a reconciliation treaty between the U.S. and Vietnam. However, none of this makes much sense, though the Bangkok settings provide a pleasant distraction. 90m/C VHS, Closed Caption. Linda Purl, Cary-Hiroyuki Tagawa, Will Patton, Tim Thomerson, Janis Paige, Ali MacGraw; *D:* James Becket; *W:* Jake Raymond Needham; *C:* Denis Maloney; *M:* Nathan Wang. COL

Natural Enemies 🐾🐾½ 1979 (R) A successful publisher begins to consider suicide and murder as the cure for his family's increasing alienation and despair. Dark and depressing drama. 100m/C VHS, Beta. Hal Holbrook, Louise Fletcher, Jose Ferrer, Viveca Lindfors; *D:* Jeff Kanew; *W:* Jeff Kanew. COL

Natural Enemy 🐾🐾 1996 (R) Unsuspecting married couple become the target of a disturbed man with a big secret. Made for cable.CW: Violence, some strong sexuality and language. ?m/C VHS. Donald Sutherland, William McNamara, Lesley Ann Warren, Joe Pantoliano, Tia Carrere; *D:* Douglas Jackson; *W:* Kevin Bernhardt; *C:* Rodney Gibbons; *M:* Alan Reeves. PMH

The Natural History of Parking Lots 🐾🐾 1994 What's a rich L.A. father to do when his teenage son hot-wires antique cars for kicks? Why pay his gun-running older brother to keep an eye on him. And the whackiness is just beginning. 92m/C VHS. *D:* Everet Lewis. FCT

Nature of the Beast 🐾🐾 1994 (R) A businessman and a drifter are both hiding deadly secrets as police search for both a serial killer and the million dollars missing from a Vegas casino robbery. Just which man is involved in which crime?CW: Hard drug use; a sex scene; strong language; some terror/violence. 91m/C VHS, LV, Closed Caption. Eric Roberts, Lance Henriksen, Brion James; *D:* Victor Salva; *W:* Victor Salva. NLC

Nature's Playmates 🐾 1962 A beautiful private eye tours Florida nudist camps in search of a missing man with a distinctive tattoo on his posterior. One of H.G. Lewis' obscure "nudie" flicks, sexually tame by modern standards, awful by any standards. 56m/B VHS. Vicki Miles, Scott Osborne; *D:* Herschell Gordon Lewis. VDM, TPV

Naughty Knights 🐾 Up the Chastity Belt 1971 (PG) Soft-core romp in a medieval setting. Toss it in the moat. 94m/C VHS, Beta. Frankie Howerd, Graham Crowden, Bill Fraser, Roy Hudd, Hugh Paddick, Anna Quayle, Eartha Kitt, Dave King, Fred Emney; *D:* Bob Kellett; *M:* Carl Davis. ACA

Naughty Marietta 🐾🐾½ 1935 A French princess switches identities with a mail-order bride to escape from her arranged marriage, and is captured by pirates. When she's saved by a dashing Indian scout, it's love at first sight. The first MacDonald-Eddy match-up and very popular in its day. ♫Italian Street Song; Chansonette; Antoinette and Anatole; Prayer; Tramp, Tramp, Tramp; The Owl and the Bobcat; Neath the Southern Moon; Mon Ami Pierrot; Ship Ahoy. 106m/B VHS, Beta, LV. Jeanette MacDonald, Nelson Eddy, Frank Morgan, Elsa Lanchester, Douglass Dumbrille,

Cecilia Parker; *D:* Woodbridge S. Van Dyke; *C:* William H. Daniels. Academy Awards '35: Best Sound; Nominations: Academy Awards '35: Best Picture. MGM

The Naughty Nineties 🐾🐾 1945 Bud and Lou help a showboat owner fend off crooks in the 1890s. Usual slapstick shenanigans, but highlighted by verbal banter. Includes the first on-screen rendition of the classic "Who's on First?" routine. ♫Rolling Down the River; Uncle Tom's Cabin; I Can't Get You Out of My Mind; On a Sunday Afternoon; I'd Leave My Happy Home for You; Nora Malone; Ma Blushin' Rosie; The Showboat's Comin' to Town; A Blarney from Killarney. 72m/B VHS, Beta. Bud Abbott, Lou Costello, Henry Travers, Alan Curtis, Joseph Sawyer, Rita Johnson, Joe Kirk, Lois Collier; *D:* Jean Yarbrough. USH, MLB

Navajo Joe 🐾½ 1967 The sole survivor of a massacre single-handedly kills each person involved in the atrocity, and aids a terrorized, though unappreciative, town in the process. Low-budget Spanish-Italian western only worth watching because of Reynolds. Filmed in Spain. 89m/C VHS. IT SP Burt Reynolds, Aldo Sambrel, Tanya Lopert, Fernando Rey; *D:* Sergio Corbucci; *M:* Ennio Morricone. MGM

The Navigator 🐾🐾🐾 1924 Ever the quick thinker, Keaton actually bought a steamer headed for the scrap heap and used it to film an almost endless string of sight gags. Rejected by a socialite, millionaire Keaton finds himself alone with her on the abandoned boat. As he saves her from various and sundry perils, the gags and thrills abound—including one stunt that was inspired by a near-accident on the set. Too bad they don't make 'em like this anymore. Silent. 60m/B VHS. Buster Keaton, Kathryn McGuire, Frederick Vroom, Noble Johnson, Clarence Burton, H. M. Clugston; *D:* Buster Keaton, Donald Crisp. NO

The Navigator 🐾🐾🐾 1988 (PG) A creative time-travel story of a 14th-century boy with visionary powers who leads the residents of his medieval English village away from a plague by burrowing through the earth's core and into late-20th-century New Zealand. Quite original and refreshing. 92m/C VHS. NZ Hamish McFarlane, Bruce Lyons, Chris Haywood, Marshall Napier, Noel Appleby, Paul Livingston, Sarah Pierse; *D:* Vincent Ward; *W:* Vincent Ward. Australian Film Institute '88: Best Cinematography, Best Director (Ward), Best Film. HTV

Navy Blue and Gold 🐾🐾½ 1937 Three football-playing midshipmen (Young, Stewart, and Brown) at Annapolis share a friendship. Stewart has registered under a false name since his dad was unfairly cashiered from the service. When he hears some slander about his old man he stands up and tells the truth and gets suspended, just before the big game with Army. Naturally, he's reinstated just in time to make the big play and carry the team to victory. Well-done, old-fashioned hokum. 94m/B VHS. James Stewart, Robert Young, Tom Brown, Lionel Barrymore, Florence Rice, Billie Burke, Samuel S. Hinds, Paul Kelly, Frank Albertson, Minor Watson; *D:* Sam Wood; *M:* George Bruce. MGM, MOV

The Navy Comes Through 🐾🐾 1942 Salty sailors aboard a mangy freighter beat the odds and sink Nazi warships and subs with the greatest of ease. Boy meets girl subplot is added for good measure. Morale booster includes newsreel footage. 81m/B VHS. Pat O'Brien, George Murphy, Jane Wyatt, Jackie Cooper, Carl Esmond, Max Baer Sr., Desi Arnaz Sr., Ray Collins, Lee Bonnell, Frank Jenks, Helmut Dantine; *D:* Edward Sutherland. TTC

Navy SEALS 🐾½ 1990 (R) A group of macho Navy commandos, whose regular work is to rescue hostages from Middle Eastern underground organizations, finds a stash of deadly weapons. They spend the balance of the movie attempting to destroy the arsenal. Sheen chews the scenery as a crazy member of the commando team. Lots of action and violence, but simplistic good guys - bad guys philosophy and plot weaknesses keep this from being more than below average. 113m/C VHS, Beta, LV, Closed Caption. Charlie

Sheen, Michael Biehn, Joanne Whalley, Rick Rossovich, Cyril O'Reilly, Bill Paxton, Dennis Haysbert, Paul Sanchez, Ron Joseph, Nicholas Kadi; *D:* Lewis Teague; *W:* Gary Goldman; *C:* John A. Alonzo. ORI

Navy vs. the Night Monsters woof! 1966 When horrifying, acid-secreting plant monsters try to take over the world, Van Doren and the Navy must come to the rescue, with the action taking place in a tropical South Pole setting. Amazing deployment of talents. **87m/C VHS, Beta.** Mamie Van Doren, Anthony Eisley, Pamela Mason, Bobby Van, Russ Bender; *D:* Michael Hoey; *W:* Michael Hoey. NO

Navy Way 🎬 1944 Hurriedly produced war propaganda film in which a boxer gets inducted into the Navy just before his title shot. **74m/B VHS.** Robert Lowery, Jean Parker; *D:* William (Lester Williams) Berke, William C. Thomas. NOS, DVT, HEG

Nazarin 🎬🎬🎬 1958 Bunuel's scathing indictment of Christianity finds its perfect vehicle in the adventures of a defrocked priest attempting to relive Christ's life. Gathering a group of disciples, he wanders into the Mexican desert as a cross between Christ and Don Quixote. Filmed in Mexico, this is Bunuel at his grimmest. In Spanish with English subtitles. **92m/B VHS, Beta, LV.** MX Francesco Rabal, Rita Macedo, Margo Lopez, Rita McLedo, Ignacio Lopez Tarso, Jesus Fernandez; *D:* Luis Bunuel. FCT, MAD, CVC

Nea 🎬🎬½ 1978 (R) Comic drama about a young girl from a privileged home who writes a best selling pornographic novel anonymously. When her book writing talents are made public through betrayal, she gets even in a most unique way. Subtitled "A Young Emmanuelle." Kaplan also performs. Appealing and sophisticated. **101m/C VHS, Beta.** Sami Frey, Ann Zacharias, Heinz Bennent; *D:* Nelly Kaplan. COL

Near Dark 🎬🎬🎬 1987 (R) A farm boy falls in unwillingly with a family of thirsty, outlaw-fringe vampires who roam the West in a van. The first mainstream effort by Bigelow, and a rollicking, blood-saturated, slaughterhouse of a movie, with enough laughs and stunning imagery to revive the genre. **95m/C VHS, Beta, LV.** Adrian Pasdar, Jenny Wright, Bill Paxton, Jenette Goldstein, Lance Henriksen, Tim Thomerson, Joshua Miller; *D:* Kathryn Bigelow; *W:* Kathryn Bigelow, Eric Red; *M:* Tangerine Dream. HBO, DNG

Near Misses 🎬½ 1991 Missable farce with Reinhold as a bigamist in the foreign service. To make time for a mistress he swaps identities with a young Marine in Paris, but then the KGB kidnaps the imposter. Doors slam in hallways all over the place as the performers crank up the mixups to maximum frenzy, but with little effect since you really don't care much about these fools. **93m/C VHS, Beta, LV.** Judge Reinhold, Casey Siemaszko; *D:* Baz Taylor; *W:* Peter Baloff, Dave Wollert. FXV, VTR

Near the Rainbow's End 🎬½ 1930 Cattle rancher Steele (in his first talking western) finds out that rustlers are aggravating the trouble between the cattlemen and the sheep herders. So he goes after the bad guys and then settles the feud by marrying a sheep herder's daughter. **57m/B VHS.** Bob Steele, Lafe McKee, Louise Lorraine, Al Ferguson, Al Hewston; *D:* J.P. McGowan. GPV

'Neath Brooklyn Bridge 🎬🎬 1942 The Boys from the Bowery get tangled up in crime when they try to help a young girl whose guardian was murdered. **61m/B VHS.** Leo Gorcey, Huntz Hall, Bobby Jordan, Sammy Morrison, Ann Gillis, Noah Beery Jr., Marc Lawrence, Gabriel Dell; *D:* Wallace Fox. NOS, MRV, PME

'Neath Canadian Skies 🎬 1946 Mounted lawman who says "eh" a lot tracks murdering gang of mine looters. **41m/B VHS, Beta, LV, 8mm.** CA Russell Hayden, Inez Cooper, Cliff Nazarro, Kermit Maynard, Jack Mulhall. VYY

'Neath the Arizona Skies 🎬🎬 1934 Low budget oater epic about a cowhand who finds all the action he and his friends can handle as they try to rescue a young Indian girl (and oil

heiress) who has been kidnapped. 'Nuff said. **54m/B VHS.** John Wayne, George "Gabby" Hayes, Sheila Terry; *D:* Harry Fraser. COL, NOS, REP

Necessary Parties 1988 Based on Barbara Dana's book that has a 15-year-old boy filing a lawsuit to stop his parents' divorce. Originally aired on PBS as part of the "Wonderworks" family movie series. **120m/C VHS.** Alan Arkin, Mark Paul Gosselaar, Barbara Dana, Adam Arkin, Donald Moffat, Julie Hagerty, Geoffrey Pierson, Taylor Fry; *D:* Gwen Arner. PME, WNE, HMV

Necessary Roughness 🎬🎬 1991 (PG-13) After losing their NCAA standing, the Texas Southern University (passing for the real Texas State) Armadillos football team looks like it's headed for disaster. The once proud football factory is now composed of assorted goofballs instead of stud players. But hope arrives in the form of a 34-year-old farmer with a golden arm, ready to recapture some lost dreams as quarterback. Can this unlikely team rise above itself and win a game, or will their hopes be squashed all over the field? **108m/C VHS, Beta, LV, Closed Caption.** Scott Bakula, Robert Loggia, Harley Jane Kozak, Sinbad, Hector Elizondo, Kathy Ireland, Jason Bateman; *D:* Stan Dragoti; *M:* Bill Conti. PAR

Necromancer: Satan's Servant 🎬🎬 1988 (R) After a woman is brutally raped, she contacts a sorceress and makes a pact with the devil to ensure her successful revenge. Plenty of graphic violence and nudity. **90m/C VHS, Beta, LV.** Elizabeth Cayton, Russ Tamblyn, Rhonda Dorton; *D:* Dusty Nelson. MCG, IME

Necropolis 🎬 1987 (R) A witch burned at the stake 300 years ago is brought back to life as a motorcycle punkette in New York searching for a sacrificial virgin (in New York?). New wave horror should have been watchable. **77m/C VHS, Beta.** Leeanne Baker, Michael Conte, Jacquie Fritz, William Reed, Paul Ruben; *D:* Tim Kincaid. LIV, VES

Ned Kelly 🎬🎬½ *Ned Kelly, Outlaw* 1970 (PG) Dramatizes the life of Australia's most notorious outlaw. Kelly (Jagger) and his family start off as horse thieves and proceed from there. A manhunt results in death and the eventual capture and execution of Kelly. The very contemporary British Jagger was miscast as a period Australian and British director Richardson seems to have lacked an empathy for the material, given his lethargic direction. **100m/C VHS.** GB Mick Jagger, Allen Bickford, Geoff Gilmour, Mark McManus, Serge Lazareff, Ken Shorter, James Elliott, Diane Craig, Sue Lloyd, Clarissa Kaye; *D:* Tony Richardson; *W:* Ian Jones, Tony Richardson; *M:* Shel Silverstein. MGM

Needful Things 🎬🎬½ 1993 (R) Stephen King film adaptations are becoming as prolific as his novels, though few seem to improve in the transition from page to screen. This time a scheming Maine shopkeeper (Von Sydow) sells unsuspecting small towners peculiar items that, not surprisingly, begin to cause horror and mayhem. Harris is the town sheriff who tries to warn everyone that he's the devil in disguise. Big screen directorial debut for Heston (yes, Charlton's son). **120m/C VHS, LV, Closed Caption.** Ed Harris, Bonnie Bedelia, Max von Sydow, Amanda Plummer, J.T. Walsh; *D:* Fraser Heston; *W:* W.D. Richter; *M:* Patrick Doyle. COL

Nefertiti, Queen of the Nile 🎬🎬 1964 Woman, married against her will, turns into Nefertiti. For fans of Italo-Biblical epics only. **97m/C VHS.** IT Jeanne Crain, Vincent Price, Edmund Purdom, Amedeo Nazzari, Liana Orfei; *D:* Fernando Cerchio. NO

Negatives 🎬🎬 1968 A couple indulge in sexual fantasies to dangerous extremes, with the man first impersonating Dr. Crippen, the early 1900s murderer, and later a WWI flying ace. When a photographer friend joins the fun, the action careens off the deep end. **90m/C VHS.** GB Peter McEnery, Diane Cilento, Glenda Jackson, Maurice Denham, Norman Rossington; *D:* Peter Medak. NO

The Neighbor 🎬🎬½ 1993 (R) See nice city couple John and Mary move to small town Vermont. See their nice retired obstetrician neighbor Myron welcome them. See Mary get pregnant and Myron take an obsessional interest. See John arrested for murder. See Mary left alone—except for Myron's tender care.*CW:* Violence and terror. **93m/C VHS.** Linda Kozlowski, Ron Lea, Rod Steiger, Francis Bay, Bruce Boa, Jane Wheeler; *D:* Rodney Gibbons; *W:* Kurt Wimmer. ACA

Neighbors 🎬🎬 1981 (R) The Keeses (Belushi and Walker) live in a quiet, middle-class suburban neighborhood where life is calm and sweet. But their new neighbors, Ramona and Vic (Aykroyd and Moriarty), prove to be loud, obnoxious, crazy, and freeloading. Will Earl and Enid Keese mind their manners as their neighborhood disintegrates? Some funny moments, but as the script fades, so do the laughs. Belushi's last waltz is based on Thomas Berger's novel. **90m/C VHS, Beta, LV.** John Belushi, Dan Aykroyd, Kathryn Walker, Cathy Moriarty; *D:* John G. Avildsen; *W:* Larry Gelbart; *M:* Bill Conti. GKK

Nell 🎬🎬½ 1994 (R) "Wild child" story—adult version. When illiterate, barely verbal backwoods Nell (Foster) is discovered after her stroke-afflicted mother's death, she's placed in the care of a doctor (Neeson) and psychologist (Richardson) who have different ideas about how to bring her into society. Unfairly dismissed by some as self-indulgent, Foster's raw, physical performance is truly mesmerizing; dull script, unconvincingly tidy ending, and gross over-sentimentality are what disappoint. From the play "Idioglossia" by Mark Handley.*CW:* Rated PG-13 for nudity. **114m/C VHS, Closed Caption.** Jodie Foster, Liam Neeson, Natasha Richardson, Richard Libertini; *D:* Michael Apted; *W:* William Nicholson. Screen Actors Guild Award '94: Best Actress (Foster); Nominations: Academy Awards '94: Best Actress (Foster); Golden Globe Awards '95: Best Actress—Drama (Foster), Best Film—Drama, Best Original Score; MTV Movie Awards '95: Best Female Performance (Foster). FXV

Nelly et Monsieur Arnaud 🎬🎬🎬 *Nelly and Mr. Arnaud* 1995 Chatty adult May/December would-be romance between 25-year-old secretary Nelly (Beart) and Pierre Arnaud (Serrault), the mid-60s retired magistrate for whom she's working. The arrogant divorced Arnaud is intrigued by the independent Nelly, whom he finds he can't control, while she comes to appreciate their emotional ties (altogether different from the selfishness of the younger men she knows). Conclusion avoids a neat resolution to a situation beset by bad timing. French with subtitles. **105m/C VHS.** IT GE FR Emmanuelle Beart, Michel Serrault, Jean-Hugues Anglade, Francoise Brion, Claire Nadeau, Michael Lonsdale, Charles Berling, Michele Laroque; *D:* Claude Sautet; *W:* Jacques Fieschi, Claude Sautet; *C:* Jean-Francois Robin; *M:* Philippe Sarde. Cesar Awards '96: Best Actor (Serrault), Best Director (Sautet); Nominations: British Academy Awards '96: Best Foreign Film; Cesar Awards '96: Best Actress (Beart), Best Film, Best Film Editing, Best Screenplay, Best Sound, Best Supporting Actor (Anglade, Lonsdale), Best Supporting Actress (Nadeau), Best Score. NYF

Nemesis 🎬½ 1993 (R) Futuristic thriller that combines cybernetics and cyborgs in post-nuclear Los Angeles. Gruner plays a human (although he's mostly composed of mechanical replacement parts) in a world overwrought with system cowboys, information terrorists, bio-enhanced gangsters, and cyborg outlaws. Film's biggest flaw is the extremely confusing script that makes no attempt at logic whatsoever. Special visual effects are good despite the obviously low f/x budget.*CW:* Strong futuristic violence. **95m/C VHS, LV, Closed Caption.** Olivier Gruner, Tim Thomerson, Cary-Hiroyuki Tagawa, Merele Kennedy, Yuji Okumoto, Marjorie Monaghan, Nicholas Guest, Vincent Klyn; *D:* Albert Pyun; *W:* Rebecca Charles; *M:* Michael Rubini. IMP, UND

Nemesis 2: Nebula ♫½ **1994 (R)** Cyborg goes on a rampage across time with a superhuman in pursuit. **CW:** Sci-fi violence. **83m/C VHS.** Sue Price, Tina Cote, Earl White, Jahi JJ Zuri, Traci Davis; **D:** Albert Pyun. *IMP*

Nemesis 3: Time Lapse ♫½ **1996 (R)** Superhuman mutant Alex is the last hope for mankind as the cyborgs once again prepare to destroy civilization. **CW:** Sci-fi violence and language. **?m/C VHS.** Sue Price, Tim Thomerson, Norbert Weisser, Xavier DeClie, Sharon Bruneau, Debbie Muggli; **D:** Albert Pyun; **W:** Albert Pyun; **C:** George Mooradian; **M:** Tony Riparetti. *IMP*

The Neon Bible ♫♫ **1995** Beautifully crafted, yet thin telling of the struggles of a rural family in 1940's Georgia. The stories unfold in a series of flashbacks, as a 15-year old boy travels alone on a train, reflecting on his dysfunctional early adolescence. An abusive father (Leary) who dies in the war, suicidal mom (Scarwid), and ex-showgirl visiting aunt (Rowlands) provide plenty of opportunities for familial angst. Starts out strong, with some stunning scenes sprinkled throughout, but director Davies never ventures far from the narrative territory he's covered thoroughly in his other films ("Distant Voices, Still Lives" and "The Long Day Closes"). Adapted from the novel by Pulitzer Prize winning author John Kennedy Toole. **92m/C VHS.** Gena Rowlands, Jacob Tierney, Diana Scarwid, Drake Bell, Denis Leary, Leo Burmester, Frances Conroy, Peter McRobbie, Joan Glover, Dana Dick, Virgil Graham Hopkins; **D:** Terence Davies; **W:** Terence Davies; **C:** Michael Coulter. *FXL*

Neon City ♫♫ **1991 (R)** Title refers to a rumored city of refuge in the year 2053, where eight misfit adventurers in an armored transport seek safety from the Earth's toxic environment and "Mad Max" cliches. **CW:** Violence. **99m/C VHS, Closed Caption.** Michael Ironside, Vanity, Lyle Alzado, Valerie Wildman, Nick Klar, Juliet Landau, Arsenio "Sonny" Trinidad, Richard Sanders; **D:** Monte Markham. *THV*

The Neon Empire ♫½ **1989 (R)** Tepid tale of two gangsters battling inner mob opposition and backstabbing to build Las Vegas. Ostensibly based on the story of Bugsy Siegel and Meyer Lansky. Made for cable. **120m/C VHS, Beta, LV.** Martin Landau, Ray Sharkey, Gary Busey, Harry Guardino, Julie Carmen, Linda Fiorentino, Dylan McDermott; **D:** Larry Peerce; **W:** Pete Hamill. *FRH*

Neon Maniacs woof! **1986 (R)** An even half-dozen fetish-ridden zombies stalk the streets at night, tearing their victims into teensy weensy bits. Brave teenagers try to stop the killing. Brave viewers will stop the tape. **90m/C VHS, Beta.** Allan Hayes, Leilani Sarelle Ferrer, Bo Sabato, Donna Locke, Victor Elliot Brandt; **D:** Joseph Mangine. *LIV, VES*

Neptune Factor ♫ *The Neptune Disaster; An Underwater Odyssey* **1973 (G)** Scientists board a special new deep-sea sub to search for their colleagues lost in an undersea earthquake. Diving ever deeper into the abyss that swallowed their friend's Ocean Lab II, they end up trapped themselves. The plot's many holes sink it. **94m/C VHS, Beta, Closed Caption.** Ben Gazzara, Yvette Mimieux, Walter Pidgeon, Ernest Borgnine; **D:** Daniel Petrie; **W:** Jack DeWitt. *FOX*

Neptune's Daughter ♫♫ **1949** A swim-happy bathing suit designer finds romance and deep pools of studio water to dive into. Typically lavish and ridiculous Williams aqua-parade. ♫Baby It's Cold Outside; I Love Those Men; My Heart Beats Faster. **92m/C VHS, Beta, LV, Closed Caption.** Esther Williams, Red Skelton, Ricardo Montalban, Betty Garrett, Keenan Wynn, Xavier Cugat, Ted de Corsia, Mike Mazurki, Mel Blanc, Juan Duvall, George Mann, Joi Lansing; **D:** Edward Buzzell; **C:** Charles Rosher. Academy Awards '49: Best Song ("Baby It's Cold Outside"). *MGM*

Nerolio ♫♫ **1996** Three imagined episodes depicting the final months of an unnamed poet/director (Cavicchioli), who is actually based on homosexual writer/filmmaker Pier Paolo Pasolini. The contradictory, hypocritical, aging Poet is shown buying sex, while extolling the virtues of male beauty in voiceover, and as the maker of his own doom (Pasolini was murdered in 1975). "Nerolio" is a contraction of "nero" (black) and "Petrolio" (oil), which refers to Pasolini's posthumous novel "Petrolio." Italian with subtitles. **82m/B VHS.** *IT* Marco Cavicchioli, Vincenzo Crivello, Salvatore Lazzaro; **D:** Aurelio Grimaldi; **C:** Maurizio Calvesi; **M:** Maria Soldatini. *CCN*

Nervous Ticks ♫♫½ **1993 (R)** Ninety minutes in the life of airline employee York Daley. All he needs to do is get off work, go home, grab his luggage, pick up his married girlfriend, and get back to the airport for a flight to Rio De Janeiro. Simple, right? Not in this movie. **95m/C VHS, Closed Caption.** Bill Pullman, Julie Brown, Peter Boyle, James LeGros, Brent Jennings; **D:** Rocky Lang; **W:** David Frankel. *COL*

The Nervous Wreck ♫♫♫ **1926** Harrison Ford (not the one from "Indiana Jones") heads West, seeking a cure for what he believes is a terminal illness. Once there, he becomes romantically entangled with the sheriff's fiancee, uses a wrench to hold up a gas station, and gets involved in other shenanigans. And then he discovers he's going to live after all. **70m/B VHS, Beta.** Harrison Ford, Phyllis Haver, Chester Conklin, Mack Swain, Hobart Bosworth, Charles Gerrard; **D:** Scott Sidney. *NO*

The Nest ♫♫½ **1980** Tragic romance of an elderly man and a 13-year-old girl is helped along by superior script and directing. **109m/C VHS, Beta.** *SP* Ana Torrent, Hector Alterio, Patriani Adriani; **D:** Jaime de Arminan. Nominations: Academy Awards '80: Best Foreign Language Film. *APD*

The Nest ♫♫½ **1988 (R)** A small island is overcome by giant cockroaches created by, you guessed it, a scientific experiment gone wrong. Special effects make it watchable. **89m/C VHS, Beta.** Robert Lansing, Lisa Langlois, Franc Luz, Terri Treas, Stephen Davies, Diana Bellamy, Nancy Morgan; **D:** Terence H. Winkless; **W:** Robert King; **M:** Rick Conrad. *MGM*

The Nesting ♫½ **1980 (R)** Too-long tale of a neurotic author who rents a haunted Victorian manor and finds herself a pawn in a ghostly plan for revenge. Features Grahame's last performance. **104m/C VHS, Beta.** Robin Groves, John Carradine, Gloria Grahame, Christopher Loomis, Michael Lally; **D:** Armand Weston; **C:** Joao Fernandes. *WAR*

The Net ♫♫½ **1995 (PG-13)** The ever-spunky Bullock gets stuck behind a computer screen rather than the wheel of a bus as reclusive computer systems analyst Angela Bennett. She's puzzled by a mysterious Internet program, which Angela finds can easily access highly classified databases. It's soon apparent that someone knows she knows because every record of her identity has been erased and the conspirators decide to take care of one last detail by eliminating her as well. Miller's the ex she turns to for help and Northam's a seductive British hacker. Techno paranoia. **CW:** Violence, some sexuality, brief strong language. **114m/C VHS, LV, 8mm, Closed Caption.** Sandra Bullock, Jeremy Northam, Dennis Miller, Diane Baker, Ken Howard, Wendy Gazelle, Ray McKinnon; **D:** Irwin Winkler; **W:** John Brancato, Michael Ferris; **C:** Jack N. Green; **M:** Mark Isham. *COL*

Netherworld ♫½ **1990 (R)** A young man investigating his mysterious, dead father travels to his ancestral plantation in the bayou. To his horror, he discovers that his father was involved in the black arts. Now two beautiful young witches are after him. Can he possibly survive this madness? **CW:** Language, strong horror violence, and strong sensuality. **87m/C VHS, LV, Closed Caption.** Michael C. Bendetti, Denise Gentile, Anjanette Comer, Holly Floria, Robert Burr; **D:** David Schmoeller; **W:** Billy Chicago; **M:** Edgar Winter. *PAR*

Network ♫♫♫♫½ **1976 (R)** As timely now as it was then; a scathing indictment of the television industry and its propensity towards self-prostitution. A television newscaster's mental breakdown turns him into a celebrity when the network tries to profit from his illness. The individual characters are startlingly realistic and the acting is excellent. **121m/C VHS, Beta, LV.** Faye Dunaway, Peter Finch, William Holden, Robert Duvall, Wesley Addy, Ned Beatty, Beatrice Straight; **D:** Sidney Lumet; **W:** Paddy Chayefsky; **C:** Owen Roizman. Academy Awards '76: Best Actor (Finch), Best Actress (Dunaway), Best Original Screenplay, Best Supporting Actress (Straight); British Academy Awards '77: Best Actor (Finch); Golden Globe Awards '77: Best Actor—Drama (Finch), Best Actress—Drama (Dunaway), Best Director (Lumet), Best Screenplay; Los Angeles Film Critics Association Awards '76: Best Director (Lumet), Best Film; National Board of Review Awards '76: 10 Best Films of the Year; New York Film Critics Awards '76: Best Screenplay; Writers Guild of America '76: Best Original Screenplay; Nominations: Academy Awards '76: Best Actor (Holden), Best Cinematography, Best Director (Lumet), Best Film Editing, Best Picture, Best Supporting Actor (Beatty). *MGM, BTV*

Neurotic Cabaret ♫½ **1990** Would-be actress dances exotically and finds more exotic ways to roll in dough. **90m/C VHS.** Edwin Neal, Tammy Stone. *AIP*

Neutron and the Black Mask ♫ **1961** Man wears mask with lightning bolts and gains comic book style powers to do deathly battle with a scientist with a neutron bomb up his sleeve. First Neutron feature. **80m/B VHS.** *MX* Wolf Ruvinskis, Julio Aleman, Armando Silvestre, Rosita Arenas, Claudio Brook; **D:** Frederick Curiel. *SNC*

Neutron vs. the Amazing Dr. Caronte ♫ **1961** Dr. Caronte from "Neutron and the Black Mask" just won't give up that neutron bomb and let the series die. **80m/B VHS.** *MX* Wolf Ruvinskis, Julio Aleman, Armando Silvestre, Rosita Arenas, Rodolfo Landa; **D:** Frederick Curiel. *SNC*

Neutron vs. the Death Robots ♫ **1962** Guy with a mask takes on army of killer robots and neutron bomb to protect the world from future sequels. **80m/B VHS.** *MX* Wolf Ruvinskis, Julio Aleman, Armando Silvestre, Rosita Arenas; **D:** Frederick Curiel. *SNC*

Neutron vs. the Maniac ♫ **1962** Man in mask hunts guys who kill people. **80m/B VHS.** *MX* Wolf Ruvinskis. *SNC*

Nevada ♫♫½ **1927** Entertaining silent western with a great cast finds gunslinger Cooper running from the law and winding up on a ranch where he falls for Todd, the rancher's daughter. Naturally, Cooper redeems himself by going after a gang of cattle rustlers, led by Powell. Based on a novel by Zane Grey. **67m/B VHS.** Gary Cooper, Thelma Todd, William Powell, Ernie Adams, Philip Strange; **D:** John Waters. *GPV*

Nevada ♫♫½ **1944** Cowpoke Mitchum is mistaken for the killer of a homesteader and narrowly escapes the rope by finding the real killer. First leading role for Mitchum as the tough but laconic hero. Based on a story by Zane Grey. **62m/B VHS.** Robert Mitchum, Anne Jeffreys, Nancy Gates, Craig Reynolds, Guinn "Big Boy" Williams, Richard Martin, Harry Woods; **D:** Edward Killy. *GPV*

Nevada City ♫½ **1941** Roy outwits a financier who is trying to monopolize transportation in California. **54m/B VHS, Beta.** Roy Rogers. *VCN*

Nevada Smith ♫♫ **1966** The half-breed Nevada Smith (previously introduced in Harold Robbins' story "The Carpetbaggers" and film of same name) seeks the outlaws who killed his parents. Standard western plot, characters. Later remade as a TV movie. **135m/C VHS, Beta, LV.** Steve McQueen, Karl Malden, Brian Keith, Arthur Kennedy, Raf Vallone, Suzanne Pleshette; **D:** Henry Hathaway; **W:** John Michael Hayes. *PAR*

The Nevadan ♫½ *The Man From Nevada* **1950** A marshal goes in search of an outlaw's gold cache, only to be opposed by a crooked rancher. Good scenery and action, but not one of Scott's best. **81m/C VHS, Beta.** Randolph Scott, Dorothy Malone, Forrest Tucker, Frank Faylen, George Macready, Charles Kemper, Jeff Corey, Tom Powers, Jock Mahoney; **D:** Gordon Douglas. *GKK*

Never a Dull Moment 🎬🎬 1950 New York songwriter falls for rodeo Romeo, moves out West, and finds welcome wagon deficient. Mediocre songs; many dull moments. ♫Once You Find Your Guy; Sagebrush Lullaby; The Man With the Big Felt Hat. **89m/B VHS.** Irene Dunne, Fred MacMurray, William Demarest, Andy Devine, Gigi Perreau, Natalie Wood, Philip Ober, Jack Kirkwood, Ann Doran, Margaret Gibson; **D:** George Marshall. *TTC, FCT*

Never a Dull Moment 🎬🎬 1968 (G) Mobsters mistake an actor for an assassin in this gag-filled adventure. They threaten the thespian into thievery, before the trouble really starts when Ace, the actual assassin, arrives. **90m/C VHS, Beta, LV.** Dick Van Dyke, Edward G. Robinson, Dorothy Provine, Henry Silva, Joanna Moore, Tony Bill, Slim Pickens, Jack Elam; **D:** Jerry Paris; **W:** A.J. Carothers; **M:** Robert F. Brunner. *DIS*

Never Cry Wolf 🎬🎬🎬½ 1983 (PG) A young biologist is sent to the Arctic to study the behavior and habitation of wolves, then becomes deeply involved with their sub-society. Based on Farley Mowat's book. Beautifully photographed. **105m/C VHS, Beta, LV.** Charles Martin Smith, Brian Dennehy, Samson Jorah; **D:** Carroll Ballard; **W:** Curtis Hanson, Sam Hamm. National Society of Film Critics Awards '83: Best Cinematography; Nominations: Academy Awards '83: Best Sound. *DIS*

Never Forget 🎬🎬 1991 Made-for-cable-TV true story of California resident Mel Mermelstein (played by Nimoy), a survivor of Hitler's death camps who accepted a pro-Nazi group's challenge to prove in court that the Holocaust of six million Jews really happened. A sincere, well-meaning courtroom drama that just can't surmount the uncinematic nature of the source material. **94m/C VHS, Beta, Closed Caption.** Leonard Nimoy, Blythe Danner, Dabney Coleman; **D:** Joseph Sargent; **M:** Henry Mancini. *TTC*

Never Give a Sucker an Even Break 🎬🎬🎬½ *What a Man* 1941 An almost plotless comedy, based on an idea reputedly written on a napkin by Fields (he took screenplay credit as Otis Criblecoblis), and features Fields at his most unleashed. It's something of a cult favorite, but not for all tastes. Classic chase scene ends it. Fields' last role in a feature-length film. **71m/B VHS, Beta, LV.** W.C. Fields, Gloria Jean, Franklin Pangborn, Leon Errol, Margaret Dumont; **D:** Eddie Cline. *USH, BAR*

Never Let Go 🎬🎬 1960 A man unwittingly tracks down the mastermind of a gang of racketeers. Sellers sheds his comedic image to play the ruthless and brutal gang boss, something he shouldn't have done. **91m/C VHS, Beta.** *GB* Peter Sellers, Richard Todd, Elizabeth Sellars, Carol White; **D:** John Guillermin; **M:** John Barry.

Never Let Me Go 🎬🎬½ 1953 Implausible yet entertaining account of American newsman Gable trying to smuggle ballerina wife Tierney out of Russia. Hard to believe Gable as a one-man assault force infiltrating Russia, but enjoyable nonetheless. Based on the novel "Came the Dawn" by Roger Bax. **94m/B VHS.** Clark Gable, Gene Tierney, Richard Haydn, Bernard Miles, Kenneth More, Karel Stepanek, Theodore Bikel; **D:** Delmer Daves; **W:** Ronald Millar, George Froeschel. *MGM*

Never Love a Stranger 🎬🎬 1958 A young man becomes a numbers runner for a mobster and ultimately winds up heading his own racket. Later he finds himself in conflict with his old boss and the district attorney. No surprises here. Based on the Harold Robbins' novel. **93m/B VHS.** John Blythe Barrymore Jr., Steve McQueen, Lita Milan, Robert Bray; **D:** Robert Stevens. *REP*

Never on Sunday 🎬🎬 1960 An American intellectual tries to turn a Greek prostitute into a refined woman. Fine performances and exhilarating Greek photography. Fun all around. ♫Never on Sunday. **91m/B VHS, Beta.** *GR* Melina Mercouri, Titos Vandis, Jules Dassin, Mitsos Liguisos; **D:** Jules Dassin; **W:** Jules Dassin; **M:** Manos Hadjidakis. Academy Awards '60: Best Song ("Never on Sunday"); Cannes Film Festival '60: Best Actress (Mercouri); Nominations: Acade-

my Awards '60: Best Actress (Mercouri), Best Costume Design (B & W), Best Director (Dassin), Best Story & Screenplay. *MGM, HMV*

Never on Tuesday 🎬½ 1988 (R) Two jerks from Ohio head to California and find themselves stuck midway in the desert with a beautiful girl, who has plans of her own. **90m/C VHS, Beta, LV, Closed Caption.** Claudia Christian, Andrew Lauer, Peter Berg; **Cameos:** Charlie Sheen, Emilio Estevez; **D:** Adam Rifkin; **W:** Adam Rifkin. *PAR*

Never Pick Up a Stranger 🎬½ 1979 When a local hooker is murdered, her cop boyfriend, who never gives up on a case, hunts her killer with a vengeance. Extremely graphic. Also on video as "Bloodrage." **82m/C VHS, Beta.** Ian Scott, Judith-Marie Bergan, James Johnston, Lawrence Tierney; **D:** Joseph Bigwood. *LIV, BFV*

Never Say Die 🎬½ 1990 Two innocents are thrown into a web of international intrigue and acquit themselves rather well. Lots of explosions and car crashes for a film shot in New Zealand. **98m/C VHS, Beta.** *NZ* George Wendt, Lisa Eilbacher; **D:** Geoff Murphy. *JTC*

Never Say Die 🎬🎬 1994 (R) Ex-Special Forces soldier John Blake (Zagarino), ambushed and left to die, returns to seek vengeance on the renegade commander who betrayed him. And he has the perfect opportunity when his nemesis kidnaps a general's daughter. **CW:** Violence, language. **99m/C VHS, LV, Closed Caption.** Frank Zagarino, Billy Drago, Todd Jensen, Jennifer Miller, Robin Smith; **D:** Yossi Wein; **W:** Jeff Albert; **M:** Wendy Oldfield, Adrian Levy. *TTC, NLC*

Never Say Goodbye 🎬🎬 1946 Cliche-ridden story about a man trying to win back his divorce-bound wife. Flynn tries hard, but the material just isn't up to par. Based on the story "Don't Ever Leave Me" by Ben and Norma Barzman. Co-screenwriter Diamond later became famous when he teamed up with Billy Wilder to script "Some Like it Hot" and "The Apartment." **97m/B VHS.** Errol Flynn, Eleanor Parker, Lucile Watson, S.Z. Sakall, Forrest Tucker, Donald Woods, Peggy Knudsen, Tom D'Andrea, Hattie McDaniel; **D:** James V. Kern; **W:** James V. Kern, I.A.L. Diamond, Lewis R. Foster. *MGM*

Never Say Never Again 🎬🎬½ 1983 (PG) James Bond matches wits with a charming but sinister tycoon who is holding the world nuclear hostage as part of a diabolical plot by SPECTRE. Connery's return to the world of Bond after 12 years is smooth in this remake of "Thunderball" hampered by an atrocious musical score. Carrera is stunning as Fatima Blush. Although Connery is back, purists will have qualms considering this part of the "official" Bond series since longtime Bond producer, Albert "Cubby" Broccoli, had nothing to do with this endeavor. **134m/C VHS, Beta, LV, Closed Caption.** Sean Connery, Klaus Maria Brandauer, Max von Sydow, Barbara Carrera, Kim Basinger, Edward Fox, Bernie Casey, Pamela Salem, Rowan Atkinson, Valerie Leon, Prunella Gee, Saskia Cohen Tanugi; **D:** Irvin Kershner. *WAR, TLF*

Never So Few 🎬🎬½ 1959 A military commander and his outnumbered troops overcome incredible odds against the Japanese. There is a lot of focus on romance, but the script and acting make a strong impression nonetheless. Based on the novel by Tom T. Chamales. **124m/C VHS, LV.** Frank Sinatra, Gina Lollobrigida, Peter Lawford, Steve McQueen, Richard Johnson, Paul Henreid, Charles Bronson; **D:** John Sturges; **C:** William H. Daniels. *MGM*

Never Steal Anything Small 🎬½ 1959 A tough union boss pushes everyone as he battles the mob for control of the waterfront. A strange musical-drama combination that will be of interest only to the most ardent Cagney and Jones fans. Based on the Maxwell Anderson/ Rouben Mamoulian play "The Devil's Hornpipe." Largely forgettable songs. ♫I'm Sorry, I Want a Ferrari; I Haven't Got a Thing to Wear; It Takes Love to Make a Home; Never Steal Anything Small; Helping Out Friends. **94m/C VHS, Beta.** James

Cagney, Shirley Jones, Cara Williams; **D:** Charles Lederer; **M:** Henry Mancini. *USH*

Never Talk to Strangers 🎬🎬 1995 (R) Sarah Taylor (DeMornay) is an uptight criminal psychologist who gets involved with handsome stranger Tony Ramirez (Banderas) while working on the case of a serial killer (Stanton). Then Sarah finds herself the target of an increasingly malevolent stalker—and she has lots of suspects to choose from. Typical woman-in-peril film with equally standard frights but the leads certainly look good (and Banderas is a fine sex object in a bit of role reversal). Filmed in Toronto. **CW:** Violence, language and some strong graphic sexuality. **86m/C VHS, LV, Closed Caption.** Rebecca DeMornay, Antonio Banderas, Harry Dean Stanton, Dennis Miller, Len Cariou, Beau Starr; **D:** Peter Hall; **W:** Lewis Green, Jordan Rush; **C:** Elemer Ragaly; **M:** Pino Donaggio. *COL*

Never Too Late to Mend 🎬🎬 1937 Victorian British play about the abuses of the penal system which had, upon its initial London West End run, caused Queen Victoria to institute a sweeping program of prison reform. The movie caused considerably less stir. **67m/B VHS, Beta, 8mm.** *GB* Tod Slaughter, Marjorie Taylor, Jack Livesey, Ian Colin; **D:** David MacDonald. *VYY, MRV, SNC*

Never Too Young to Die 🎬🎬 1986 (R) A young man is drawn into a provocative espionage adventure by his late father's spy associates. Together they try to discover who killed the young man's father. High point may be Simmons as a crazed hermaphrodite plotting to poison L.A. **97m/C VHS, Beta, LV, Closed Caption.** John Stamos, Vanity, Gene Simmons, George Lazenby; **D:** Gil Bettman; **W:** Gil Bettman; **M:** James Newton Howard, Lennie Niehaus. *COL, NLC*

Never Wave at a WAC 🎬🎬½ *The Private Wore Skirts* 1952 A Washington socialite joins the Women's Army Corps hoping for a commission that never comes. She has to tough it out as an ordinary private. A reasonably fun ancestor of "Private Benjamin," with a cameo by Gen. Omar Bradley as himself. **87m/B VHS.** Rosalind Russell, Paul Douglas, Marie Wilson, William Ching, Arleen Whelan, Leif Erickson, Hillary Brooke, Regis Toomey; **Cameos:** Omar Bradley; **D:** Norman Z. McLeod; **M:** Elmer Bernstein. *NOS, DVT, HEG*

Never Weaken/Why Worry? 🎬🎬🎬 1923 Silent comedy shorts from Harold. In "Never Weaken" (1921), Lloyd hustles customers. In "Why Worry?" (1923), he plays a wealthy young man who journeys to South America for his health and gets caught in the middle of a revolution. **78m/B VHS, Beta.** Harold Lloyd. *TLF*

The NeverEnding Story 🎬🎬🎬½ 1984 (PG) A lonely young boy helps a warrior save the fantasy world in his book from destruction by the Nothing. A wonderful, intelligent family movie about imagination, with swell effects and a sweet but not overly sentimental script. Petersen's first English-language film, based on the novel by Michael Ende. **94m/C VHS, Beta, LV, 8mm, Closed Caption.** Barret Oliver, Noah Hathaway, Gerald McRaney, Moses Gunn, Tami Stronach, Patricia Hayes, Sydney Bromley; **D:** Wolfgang Petersen; **W:** Wolfgang Petersen; **M:** Klaus Doldinger, Giorgio Moroder. *WAR, GLV, APD*

NeverEnding Story 2: The Next Chapter 🎬🎬 1991 (PG) Disappointing sequel to the first story that didn't end. Boy Oliver staves off life of couch potatodom reading books and escaping into fantasy land. Even the kids may wander away. But wait: contains the first Bugs Bunny theatrical cartoon in 26 years, "Box Office Bunny." **90m/C VHS, LV, 8mm, Closed Caption.** Jonathan Brandis, Kenny Morrison, Clarissa Burt, John Wesley Shipp, Martin Umbach; **D:** George Miller; **C:** David Connell; **M:** Robert Folk. *WAR, APD*

The Neverending Story 3: escape from Fantasia 🎬🎬 1994 (G) The third time was not the charm in this case. Bastian, on the edge of puberty, is being bullied by a group at school called the Nasties. He seeks refuge in the library and enters the world of Fantasia through the "Neverending Story" tome. When the book is stolen by the Nasties, it is up to Bastian to return it. Unfortunately, the story does not have the charm of the original, trying to incorporate too much reality and not enough of dreamland. **95m/C VHS, Closed Caption.** Jason James Richter, Melody Kay, Freddie Jones, Jack Black, Ryan Bollman, Tracey Ellis, Kevin McNulty; *D:* Peter Macdonald; *C:* Robin Vidgeon; *M:* Peter Wolf. TOU

Nevil Shute's The Far Country 𝄞𝄞½ *The Far Country* 1985 Carl Zlint-
ner (York), once a doctor in Hitler's army, escapes to Australia from postwar Europe to begin a new life with a new identity. Falling in love with the beautiful Jennifer Morton (Thornton), Carl hopes he's left his past behind. But nothing is every that simple. Made-for-television adaptation of the Shute novel. **120m/C VHS, Beta.** AU Michael York, Sigrid Thornton; *D:* George Miller. NO

The New Adventures of Pippi Longstocking 𝄞½ 1988 (G) Decent cast is
trapped in another musical rehashing of the Astrid Lindgren children's books about a precocious redheaded girl and her fantastic adventures with horses, criminals, and pirates. **100m/C VHS, Beta, LV, Closed Caption.** Tami Erin, Eileen Brennan, Dennis Dugan, Dianne Hull, George DiCenzo, John Schuck, Dick Van Patten; *D:* Ken Annakin; *W:* Ken Annakin. COL, TVC

The New Adventures of Tarzan 1935
Twelve episodes, each 22 minutes long, depict the adventures of Edgar Rice Burrough's tree-swinging character—Tarzan. Also known as "Tarzan and the Green Goddess." **260m/B VHS, Beta.** Bruce (Herman Brix) Bennett, Ula Holt, Frank Baker, Dale Walsh, Lewis Sargent; *D:* Edward Kull. SNC, NOS, VCN

The New Age 𝄞𝄞 1994 (R) Illusions in
L.A. centering on talent agent Peter (Weller) and art designer Katherine (Davis) Witner. Katherine loses her job the same day Peter decides to quit his and suddenly the caustic duo are dependent upon each other. The trendy couple decide to open a boutique and quickly find themselves in a fiscal sinkhole and on a downhill slide. The acting is fine but the story is empty.*CW:* Sexuality; language; nudity. **106m/C VHS, LV, Closed Caption.** Peter Weller, Judy Davis, Adam West, Patrick Bauchau, Corbin Bernsen, Jonathan Hadary, Samuel L. Jackson, Patricia Heaton, Audra Lindley, Paula Marshall, Maureen Mueller, Bruce Ramsay, Sandra Seacat, Susan Traylor; *D:* Michael Tolkin; *W:* Michael Tolkin, Mark Mothersbaugh. WAR

The New Centurions 𝄞𝄞½ 1972 (R)
Rookies training for the Los Angeles Police Department get the inside info from retiring cops. Gritty and realistic drama based on the novel by former cop Joseph Wambaugh. Tends to be disjointed at times, but overall is a good adaptation of the bestseller. Scott, excellent as the retiring beat-walker, is supported well by the other performers. **103m/C VHS, Beta, LV.** George C. Scott, Stacy Keach, Jane Alexander, Scott Wilson, Erik Estrada, James B. Sikking; *D:* Richard Fleischer; *W:* Stirling Silliphant; *M:* Quincy Jones. COL, FCT

New Crime City: Los Angeles 2020 𝄞½ 1994 (R) Prisoner Tony Ricks (Ros-
sovich) is executed and then revived thanks to technology. But there's a price to pay for his life and freedom—he must retrieve a biowarfare weapon from a prison gang and he only has 24 hours to do it.*CW:* Violence; language; sexuality. **95m/C VHS, LV.** Rick Rossovich, Stacy Keach, Sherrie Rose; *W:* Rick Rossovich. NHO

New Eden 𝄞𝄞 1994 (R) In the year 2237
wartime prisoners are condemned to a desert planet where they are preyed upon by brutal Sand Pirates. An idealistic engineer falls in love and seeks to protect his new family from a deadly confrontation. **89m/C VHS, LV, Closed Caption.** Stephen Baldwin, Lisa Bonet, Tobin Bell, Michael Bowen, Janet Hubert-Whitten; *D:* Alan Metzger; *W:* Dan Gordon. USH

New Faces of 1952 𝄞𝄞½ 1954 Based
on the hit Broadway revue. The plot revolves around a Broadway show that is about to be closed down, and the performers who fight to keep it open. Lots of hit songs. Mel Brooks is credited as a writer, under the name Melvin Brooks. ♫C'est Si Bon; Santa Baby; Uskadara; Monotonous; Bal Petit Bal; Boston Beguine; I'm in Love with Miss Logan; Penny Candy; Time for Tea. **98m/C VHS, Beta.** Ronny Graham, Eartha Kitt, Robert Clary, Alice Ghostley, June Carroll, Carol Lawrence, Paul Lynde; *D:* Harry Horner. FCT, NOS, VAI

New Fist of Fury 𝄞 1985 During WWII, a
former pickpocket becomes a martial arts whiz with the assistance of his fiancee, and fights the entire Imperial Army. **120m/C VHS, Beta.** Jackie Chan; *D:* Jackie Chan. NO

The New Frontier 𝄞½ 1935 Wayne is a
small-town sheriff whose predecessor, his father, was murdered. The local saloon-keeper and his gang do everything they can to prevent Wayne from bringing the culprit to justice. **59m/B VHS.** John Wayne, Muriel Evans, Murdock McQuarrie, Mary MacLaren, Warner Richmond; *D:* Carl Pierson. NOS, MLB

The New Gladiators WOOf! 1987 In the
future, criminals try to kill each other on television for public entertainment. Two such gladiators discover that the network's computer is using the games in order to take over mankind, and they attempt to stop it. Even if the special effects were any good, they couldn't save this one. **90m/C VHS, Beta.** IT Jared Martin, Fred Williamson, Eleanor Gold, Howard Ross, Claudio Cassinelli; *D:* Lucio Fulci. MED

The New Invisible Man 𝄞𝄞 1958 A
so-so Mexican adaptation of the popular H.G. Wells novel has a prisoner receiving a vanishing drug from his brother, who created it—perhaps to aid an escape attempt. Also called "H.G. Wells' New Invisible Man." **95m/B VHS.** MX Arturo de Cordova, Ana Luisa Peluffo, Jorge Mondragon; *D:* Alfredo B. Crevenna. SNC

New Jack City 𝄞𝄞½ 1991 (R) Just say no
ghetto-melodrama. Powerful performance by Snipes as wealthy Harlem drug lord sought by rebel cops Ice-T and Nelson. Music by Johnny Gill, 2 Live Crew, Ice-T and others.*CW:* Language, strong language and drug content, and sensuality. **101m/C VHS, LV.** Wesley Snipes, Ice-T, Mario Van Peebles, Chris Rock, Judd Nelson, Tracy C. Johns, Allen Payne, Kim Park, Vanessa Williams, Nick Ashford, Thalmus Rasulala, Michael Michele, Bill Nunn, Russell Wong; *D:* Mario Van Peebles; *W:* Keith Critchlow, Barry Michael Cooper; *M:* Roger Bourland, Michel Colombier. WAR, CCB

New Jersey Drive 𝄞𝄞½ 1995 (R) Jason
(Corley) has dreams of life outside the mean streets of Newark, but he jeopardizes his future by stealing cars and joyriding around the neighborhood with his friends. Unblinking realism, provided by credible actors (especially Corley, a former gang member), dialogue, and filming in the projects of Brooklyn and Queens, is nuetralized by stereotypical characters (especially the lily-white, sadistically brutal cops) and lack of a sympathetic point of view. Loosely based on a series of articles by Michel Mariott, a reporter for the "New York Times." **98m/C VHS, LV, Closed Caption.** Sharron Corley, Gabriel Casseus, Saul Stein, Andre Moore, Donald A. Faison, Conrad Meertin Jr., Deven Eggleston, Gwen McGee, Koran C. Thomas, Samantha Brown, Christine Baranski, Robert Jason Jackson, Roscoe Orman, Dwight Errington Myers, Gary DeWitt Marshall; *D:* Nick Gomez; *W:* Nick Gomez, Michel Mariott; *C:* Adam Kimmel; *M:* Wendy Blackstone. Nominations: Independent Spirit Awards '96: Debut Performance (Casseus). USH

The New Kids 𝄞𝄞 1985 (R) An orphaned
brother and sister find out the limitations of the good neighbor policy. A sadistic gang terrorizes them after their move to a relatives' home in Florida. They go after expected revenge. **90m/C VHS, Beta, LV, Closed Caption.** Shannon Presby, Lori Loughlin, James Spader, Eric Stoltz; *D:* Sean S. Cunningham; *W:* Brian Taggert, Stephen Gyllenhaal. COL

A New Kind of Love 𝄞𝄞½ 1963 Ro-
mantic fluff starring real-life couple Newman and Woodward who meet en route to Paris and end up falling in love. Newman plays a reporter and Woodward is a fashion designer in this light comedy set amidst the sights of Paris. **110m/C VHS, Beta, Closed Caption.** Paul Newman, Joanne Woodward, Thelma Ritter, Eva Gabor, Maurice Chevalier, George Tobias; *D:* Melville Shavelson; *W:* Melville Shavelson; *C:* Daniel F. Fapp. Nominations: Academy Awards '63: Best Adapted Score, Best Costume Design (Color). PAR

The New Land 𝄞𝄞𝄞 Nybyggarna 1973
(PG) Sequel to "The Emigrants" follows Von Sydow and his family as they struggle to make their new home in the new world. Hardships include severe weather which devastates the farm, a Sioux indian uprising, and a disastrous trek to the Southwest to search for gold. Sensitive performances and direction. Based on the novels by Vilhelm Moberg. Dubbed into English. **161m/C VHS.** SW Max von Sydow, Liv Ullmann, Allan Edwall, Eddie Axberg, Hans Alfredson, Halvar Bjork, Peter Lindgren, Monica Zetterlund, Pierre Lindstedt, Per Oscarsson; *D:* Jan Troell; *W:* Jan Troell, Bengt Forslund; *M:* Bengt Ernryd, George Oddner. National Board of Review Awards '73: Best Actress (Ullmann); National Society of Film Critics Awards '73: Best Actress (Ullmann). WAR, MOV

A New Leaf 𝄞𝄞½ 1971 (G) A playboy who
has depleted his financial resources tries to win the hand of a clumsy heiress. May was the first woman to write, direct and star in a movie. She was unhappy with the cuts that were made by the studio, but that didn't seem to affect its impact with the public. Even with the cuts, the film is still funny and May's performance is worth watching. **102m/C VHS.** Walter Matthau, Elaine May, Jack Weston, George Rose, William Redfield, James Coco; *D:* Elaine May; *W:* Elaine May. PAR, FCT

A New Life 𝄞𝄞½ 1988 (PG-13) An uptight
stockbroker is abandoned by his wife. The New York singles scene beckons both of them to a new chance at life. Appealing performances cannot completely mask the old story line, but it's definitely worth a look. **104m/C VHS, Beta, LV, Closed Caption.** Alan Alda, Ann-Margret, Hal Linden, Veronica Hamel, John Shea, Mary Kay Place, Cynthia Belliveau, Beatrice Alda; *D:* Alan Alda; *W:* Alan Alda; *M:* Joseph Turrin. PAR

New Mafia Boss 𝄞½ *Crime Boss* 1972 (PG)
Italian-made plodder has Savalas taking over a huge Mafia family and all hell breaks loose. **90m/C VHS, Beta.** IT Telly Savalas, Lee Van Cleef, Antonio Sabato, Paolo Tedesco; *D:* Alberto De Martino. VCD

New Moon 𝄞𝄞½ 1940 An adaptation of
the operetta by Sigmund Romberg and Oscar Hammerstein II. A French heiress traveling on a boat that is captured by pirates falls in love with their leader. Remake of the 1930 film. Includes the 1935 Robert Benchley MGM short "How to Sleep." ♫Dance Your Cares Away; Stranger in Paris; The Way They Do It in Paris; Lover Come Back; Shoes; Softly as in a Morning Sunrise; One Kiss; Troubles of the World; No More Weeping. **106m/B VHS, Beta.** Jeanette MacDonald, Nelson Eddy, Buster Keaton, Joe Yule, Jack Perrin, Mary Boland; *D:* Robert Z. Leonard. MGM

New Orleans After Dark 𝄞𝄞 1958 A
pair of New Orleans detectives tour the city, crime-buster style, and bag a dope ring. Average crime tale, shot on location in the Big Easy. **69m/B VHS.** Stacy Harris, Louis Sirgo, Ellen Moore; *D:* John Sledge. NOS, LOO

New Pastures 𝄞𝄞½ 1962 Three ex-con-
victs run into some humorous situations when they go back to their small hometown. A semi-acclaimed Czech comedy, with subtitles. **92m/B VHS, Beta.** CZ D: Vladimir Cech. IHF

New Year's Day 𝄞𝄞𝄞 1989 (R) Jaglom
continues his look at modern relationships in this story of a man reclaiming his house from three female tenants. Introspective character study lightened by humor and insight. **90m/C VHS, Beta, Closed Caption.** Maggie Jakobson, Gwen Welles, Melanie

Winter, Milos Forman, Michael Emil, David Duchovny, Tracy Reiner, Henry Jaglom; **D:** Henry Jaglom; **W:** Henry Jaglom. PAR, BTV, FCT

New Year's Evil WOOF! 1978 (R) Every hour during a New Year's Eve concert, a madman kills an unsuspecting victim. After each killing, the murderer informs a local disc jockey of his deed. Little does the disc jockey know that she will soon be next on his list. No suspense, bad music makes this slash and crash a holiday wrecker. 88m/C VHS, Beta. Roz Kelly, Kip Niven, Chris Wallace, Louisa Moritz, Grant Kramer, Jed Mills; **D:** Emmett Alston; **W:** Emmett Alston. CAN

New York Cop 𝕴½ 1994 (R) Japanese martial arts expert Toshi (Nakamura) joins the NYPD and is given an undercover assignment to infiltrate a gun-running gang that supplies both drug lords and Japanese mobsters. But internal rivalries force Toshi to bond with gang leader Hawk (McQueen) and the duo to do battle together.**CW:** Gangster violence; language; some sexuality. 88m/C VHS, Closed Caption. Toru Nakamura, Chad McQueen, Mira Sorvino; **D:** Toru Murakawa. COL

New York, New York 𝕴𝕴𝕴 1977 (PG) Tragic romance evolves between a saxophonist and an aspiring singer/actress in this salute to the big-band era. A love of music isn't enough to hold them together through career rivalries and life on the road. Fine performances by De Niro and Minnelli and the supporting cast. Re-released in 1981 with the "Happy Endings" number, which was cut from the original. Look for "Big Man" Clarence Clemons on sax. ♫New York, New York; There Goes the Ball Game; Happy Endings; But the World Goes 'Round; Night in Tunisia; Opus One; Avalon; You Brought a New Kind of Love to Me; I'm Getting Sentimental Over You. 163m/C VHS, Beta, LV, Closed Caption. Robert De Niro, Liza Minnelli, Lionel Stander, Barry Primus, Mary Kay Place, Dick Miller, Diahnne Abbott; **D:** Martin Scorsese; **W:** Mardik Martin; **M:** Ralph Burns. FOX

New York Nights 𝕴 1984 (R) The lives of nine New Yorkers intertwine in a treacherous game of passion and seduction. Liberal borrowing from plot of "La Ronde." 104m/C VHS, Beta. Corinne Alphen, George Auyer, Bobbi Burns, Peter Matthey, Cynthia Lee, Willem Dafoe; **D:** Simon Nuchtern. LIV

New York Ripper WOOF! 1982 A New York cop tracks down a rampaging murderer in this dull, mindless slasher flick. 88m/C VHS, Beta. IT Fred Williamson; **D:** Lucio Fulci. THV

New York Stories 𝕴𝕴𝕴 1989 (PG) Entertaining anthology of three separate short films by three esteemed directors, all set in New York. In "Life Lessons" by Scorsese, an impulsive artist tries to prevent his live-in girlfriend from leaving him. "Life Without Zoe" by Coppola involves a youngster's fantasy about a wealthy 12-year-old who lives mostly without her parents. Allen's "Oedipus Wrecks," generally considered the best short, is about a 50-year-old man who is tormented by the specter of his mother. 124m/C VHS, Beta, LV. Nick Nolte, Rosanna Arquette, Woody Allen, Mia Farrow, Mae Questel, Julie Kavner, Talia Shire, Giancarlo Giannini, Don Novello, Patrick O'Neal, Peter Gabriel, Paul Herman, Deborah Harry, Steve Buscemi, Heather McComb, Chris Elliott, Carole Bouquet, Edward I. Koch; **D:** Woody Allen, Martin Scorsese, Francis Ford Coppola; **W:** Woody Allen, Francis Ford Coppola, Richard Price, Sofia Coppola; **C:** Sven Nykvist, Nestor Almendros; **M:** Carmine Coppola. TOU

New York's Finest 𝕴 1987 (R) Three prostitutes are determined to leave their calling and marry very eligible millonaires. But becoming society ladies is more difficult than they thought. Would-be sophisticated comedy misfires. 80m/C VHS, Beta. Ruth Collins, Jennifer Delora, Scott Thompson Baker, Heidi Paine, Jane Hamilton, Alan Naggar, John Altamura, Alan Fisler, Josey Duval; **D:** Chuck Vincent. ACA

The Newlydeads 𝕴½ 1987 An uptight, conservative, honeymoon resort owner murders one of his guests and finds out that "she" is really a he. Fifteen years later, on his wedding night, all

of his guests are violently murdered by the transvestite's vengeful ghost. Oddball twist to the usual slasher nonsense. 84m/C VHS, Beta. Scott Kaske, Jim Williams, Jean Levine, Jay Richardson; **D:** Joseph Merhi. NO

Newman's Law 𝕴𝕴 1974 (PG) A city detective is implicated in a corruption investigation. While on suspension, he continues with his own investigation of a large drug ring and finds corruption is closer than he thought. Director Heffron's first feature film. 98m/C VHS, Beta. George Peppard, Roger Robinson, Eugene Roche, Gordon Pinsent, Louis Zorich, Abe Vigoda; **D:** Richard T. Heffron. USH

News at Eleven 𝕴𝕴 1986 A fading news anchorman is pressured by his ambitious young boss to expose a touchy local sex scandal, forcing him to consider the public's right to know versus the rights of the individual. About average for made-for-television drama. 95m/C VHS, Beta, LV. Martin Sheen, Peter Riegert, Barbara Babcock, Sheree J. Wilson, Sydney Penny, David S. Sheiner, Christopher Allport; **D:** Mike Robe. TTC

News from Home 𝕴𝕴 1976 Scenes of life in New York are juxtaposed with voiceover from the letters of a mother to her young daughter. Plotless narrative deals with the small details of life. 85m/C VHS. **D:** Chantal Akerman; **W:** Chantal Akerman. WAC, FCT

Newsfront 𝕴𝕴𝕴 1978 A story about two brothers, both newsreel filmmakers, and their differing approaches to life and their craft in the 1940s and '50s. Tribute to the days of newsreel film combines real stories and fictionalized accounts with color and black and white photography. Noyce's feature film debut. 110m/C VHS, LV. *AU* Bill Hunter, Gerard Kennedy, Angela Punch McGregor, Wendy Hughes, Chris Haywood, John Ewart, Bryan Brown; **D:** Phillip Noyce. Australian Film Institute '78: Best Actor (Hunter), Best Film.

Newsies 𝕴½ 1992 (PG) An unfortunate attempt at an old-fashioned musical with a lot of cute kids and cardboard characters and settings. The plot, such as it is, concerns the 1899 New York newsboys strike against penny-pinching publisher Joseph Pulitzer. Bale plays the newsboy's leader and at least shows some charisma in a strictly cartoon setting. The songs are mediocre but the dancing is lively. However, none of it moves the story along. Add a bone for viewers under 12. Choreographer Ortega's feature-film directorial debut. 121m/C VHS, Beta, Closed Caption. Christian Bale, Bill Pullman, Robert Duvall, Ann-Margret, Michael Lerner, Kevin Tighe, Charles Cioffi, Luke Edwards, Max Casella, David Moscow; **D:** Kenny Ortega; **M:** Alan Menken, Jack Feldman. Golden Raspberry Awards '92: Worst Song ("High Times, Hard Times"). DIS

Next Door 𝕴𝕴½ 1994 (R) College professors Matt (Woods) and Karen (Capshaw) have the perfect suburban home—complete with the perfect suburban garden. Then their boorish blue-collar neighbor Lenny (Quaid) takes to enthusiastic lawn watering and ruins their flowers. One thing leads to a full-scale feud. Made for cable TV.**CW:** Strong language; some violence. 95m/C VHS. James Woods, Randy Quaid, Kate Capshaw, Lucinda Jenney; **D:** Tony Bill; **W:** Barney Cohen; **C:** Thomas Del Ruth. COL

The Next Karate Kid 𝕴𝕴½ 1994 (PG) Fourth installment in the "Kid" series finds martial arts expert Miyagi (Morita) training Julie Pierce (Swank), the orphaned tomboy daughter of an old war buddy who saved his life 50 years earlier. He even teaches her the waltz, just in time for the prom, but she's still tough enough to scrap with a guy. A must-see for "Karate Kid" fans, if there are any left. 107m/C VHS, LV, Closed Caption. Noriyuki "Pat" Morita, Hilary Swank; **D:** Christopher Cain; **W:** Mark Lee; **M:** Bill Conti. COL

Next of Kin 𝕴 1982 A daughter moves into her dead mother's retirement home and discovers an unspeakable evil that lurks there. Typical horror stuff has some very creepy moments; filmed in

New Zealand. 90m/C VHS, Beta, LV, 8mm. *AU* Jackie Kerin, John Jarratt, Gerida Nicholson, Alex Scott; **D:** Tony Williams. NO

Next of Kin 𝕴𝕴 1984 A young man experiencing familial difficulties undergoes experimental video therapy where he views a videotape of an Armenian family who gave their son up for adoption. When he discovers the actual family he insinuates himself into their life, determined to be their long-lost son. 72m/C VHS. *CA* Patrick Tierney; **D:** Atom Egoyan; **W:** Atom Egoyan. CVC, FCT

Next of Kin 𝕴𝕴 1989 (R) A Chicago cop returns to his Kentucky home to avenge his brother's brutal murder. Swayze's return to action films after his success in "Dirty Dancing" is unimpressive. 108m/C VHS, Beta, LV, 8mm, Closed Caption. Patrick Swayze, Adam Baldwin, Bill Paxton, Helen Hunt, Andreas Katsulas, Ben Stiller, Michael J. Pollard, Liam Neeson; **D:** John Irvin; **C:** Steven Poster; **M:** Jack Nitzsche. WAR

Next One 𝕴½ 1984 Mysterious visitor from another time winds up on an isolated Greek island as the result of a magnetic storm. The local inhabitants are amazed when the visitor displays some Christ-like characteristics. 105m/C VHS, Beta. Keir Dullea, Adrienne Barbeau, Jeremy Licht, Peter Hobbs; **D:** Nico Mastorakis. VES

Next Stop, Greenwich Village 𝕴𝕴𝕴 1976 (R) An affectionate, autobiographical look by Mazursky at a Brooklyn boy with acting aspirations, who moves to Greenwich Village in 1953. Good performances, especially by Winters as the overbearing mother. 109m/C VHS, Closed Caption. Lenny Baker, Christopher Walken, Ellen Greene, Shelley Winters, Lou Jacobi, Mike Kellin; **D:** Paul Mazursky; **W:** Paul Mazursky; **M:** Bill Conti. FXV

Next Summer 𝕴𝕴𝕴 L'Ete Prochain 1984 A large, character-studded French family pursues power, love and beauty. Excellent performances. In French with English subtitles. 120m/C VHS, Beta. *FR* Jean-Louis Trintignant, Claudia Cardinale, Fanny Ardant, Philippe Noiret, Marie Trintignant; **D:** Nadine Trintignant. CTL, FCT, TPV

Next Time I Marry 𝕴½ 1938 Lucy fraternizes with ditch digger Ellison because she needs to hitch a Yankee in order to inherit $20 mill. Seems she really loves a foreigner, though. Not much to bobaloo about. Director Kanin's second effort. 65m/B VHS. Lucille Ball, James Ellison, Lee Bowman, Granville Bates, Mantan Moreland, Florence Lake; **D:** Garson Kanin. TTC, FCT, MLB

The Next Victim 𝕴 Lo Strano Vizio Della Signora Wardh 1971 (PG) The unfaithful wife of an Austrian diplomat attempts to find out who has been slicing up beautiful jet-setters. Tepid mystery. 87m/C VHS, Beta. George Hilton, Edwige French, Christina Airoldi, Ivan Rassimov; **D:** Sergio Martino. GEM, CNG

Next Victim 𝕴 1974 A beautiful woman confined to a wheelchair is stalked by a lunatic killer. You've seen it before, and done better. 80m/C VHS, Beta. *GB* Carroll Baker, T.P. McKenna, Ronald Lacey, Maurice Kaufman; **D:** James Ormerod. LIV

The Next Voice You Hear 𝕴𝕴½ 1950 Lives are changed forever when a group of people hear the voice of God on the radio. Interesting premise presented seriously. 84m/B VHS, Beta. James Whitmore, Nancy Davis, Gary Gray, Lillian Bronson, Art Smith, Tom D'Andrea, Jeff Corey, George Chandler; **D:** William A. Wellman. MGM

Next Year If All Goes Well 𝕴𝕴½ 1983 Two young lovers struggle to overcome insecurities while establishing a relationship. Dubbed. 95m/C VHS, Beta. *FR* Isabelle Adjani, Thierry Lhermitte, Mariann Chazel; **D:** Jean-Loup Hubert. VTR

Niagara 𝕴𝕴½ 1952 During their honeymoon in Niagara Falls, a scheming wife (Monroe) plans to kill her crazed war-vet husband (Cotten). Little does she know that he is plotting to double-cross her. Steamy, quasi-Hitchcockian mystery ably directed, with interesting performances. Monroes sings "Kiss." 89m/B VHS, Beta, LV. Joseph Cotten,

Jean Peters, Marilyn Monroe, Max Casey Adams Showalter, Don Wilson; **D:** Henry Hathaway. *FOX*

Nice Girl? *♫♫½* 1941
Jane (Durbin) develops a crush on visiting professor Richard Calvert (Tone), much to his embarrassment. But her steady beau Don (Stack) sticks around to provide support while Calvert seeks a way to let Jane down easy. The video includes a 3-minute alternate ending. **96m/B VHS.** Deanna Durbin, Franchot Tone, Robert Stack, Robert Benchley, Walter Brennan, Ann Gillis, Helen Broderick, Anne Gwynne; **D:** William A. Seiter; **W:** Richard Connell, Gladys Lehman; **C:** Joseph Valentine. *USH*

Nice Girl Like Me *♫♫* 1969 (PG)
An orphaned young girl roams Europe, getting pregnant twice by two different men. She eventually finds love in the form of a kind caretaker. Harmless fluff. Based on Anne Piper's novel "Marry At Leisure." **91m/C VHS, Beta.** *GB* Harry Andrews, Barbara Ferris, Gladys Cooper, Bill Hinnant, James Villiers; **D:** Desmond Davis. *NLC*

Nice Girls Don't Explode *♫♫* 1987
(PG) A girl telekinetically starts fires when sexually aroused. This puts a bit of a damper on her relationship with O'Leary, much to her mother's delight. Matchless entertainment. **92m/C VHS, Beta.** Barbara Harris, Wallace Shawn, Michelle Meyrink, William O'Leary; **D:** Chuck Martinez; **M:** Brian Banks. *VTR, NWV*

Nice Neighbor *♫♫♫* 1979
An acclaimed film about an outwardly self-sacrificing neighbor who cold-bloodedly manipulates his fellow rooming house tenants for his own ends. In Hungarian with English subtitles. **90m/C VHS, Beta.** *HU* Laszlo Szabo, Margit Dayka, Agi Margittay; **D:** Zsolt Kedzi-Kovacs. *FCT*

Nicholas and Alexandra *♫♫½* 1971
(PG) Epic chronicling the final years of Tsar Nicholas II, Empress Alexandra and their children. Their lavish royal lifestyle gives way to imprisonment and eventual execution under the new Lenin government. Beautiful but overlong costume epic that loses steam in the second half. Based on the biography by Robert Massie. Available in widescreen format on laserdisc. **183m/C VHS, Beta, LV.** Michael Jayston, Janet Suzman, Tom Baker, Laurence Olivier, Michael Redgrave, Harry Andrews, Jack Hawkins, Alexander Knox, Curt Jurgens; **D:** Franklin J. Schaffner; **C:** Frederick A. (Freddie) Young; **M:** Richard Rodney Bennett. Academy Awards '71: Best Art Direction/Set Decoration, Best Costume Design; National Board of Review Awards '71: 10 Best Films of the Year; Nominations: Academy Awards '71: Best Actress (Suzman), Best Cinematography, Best Picture, Original Dramatic/Comedy Score. *COL, TVC*

Nicholas Nickleby *♫♫♫* The Life and Adventures of Nicholas Nickleby 1946
An ensemble cast works hard to bring to life Charles Dickens' novel about an impoverished family dependent on their wealthy but villainous uncle. Young Nicholas is an apprentice at a school for boys, and he and a student run away to a series of exciting adventures. An enjoyable film, though it is hard to tell the entire story in such a small amount of time. **108m/B VHS.** *GB* Cedric Hardwicke, Stanley Holloway, Derek Bond, Alfred Drayton, Sybil Thorndike, Sally Ann Howes, Bernard Miles, Mary Merrall, Cathleen Nesbitt; **D:** Alberto Cavalcanti; **C:** Georges Perinal. *MRV, PSM, DVT*

Nick Knight *♫♫* 198?
An L.A. cop on the night beat is really a good-guy vampire, who quaffs cattle blood as he tracks down another killer who's draining humans of their plasma. A gimmicky pilot for a would-be TV series that never bit. **92m/C VHS.** Rick Springfield, Michael Nader, Laura Johnson. *VTR*

Nick of Time *♫½* 1995 (R)
A malicious stranger (Walken) and his cohort give ordinary accountant Gene Watson (Depp) 90 minutes to assassinate the governor of California (Mason) or his little girl will be killed. Walken as an evil psycho...now there's a stretch. On the other hand, Depp as a button-down, conservative widower is a bit of a switch after his usually quirky roles of the recent past. This may be the first time Depp's picked up a gun since "21 Jump Street." Illogical

scenarios (even for an action flick) and curiously uneven pacing do this one in. Shot almost entirely in L.A's Bonaventure Hotel in real time with a handheld camera. **CW:** Contains violence and strong language. **98m/C VHS, Beta, Closed Caption.** Johnny Depp, Christopher Walken, Charles S. Dutton, Peter Strauss, Roma Maffia, Gloria Reuben, Marsha Mason, Courtney Chase, Bill Smitrovich, G.D. Spradlin; **D:** John Badham; **W:** Patrick Duncan; **C:** Roy Wagner; **M:** Arthur B. Rubinstein. *PAR*

Nickel & Dime *♫♫* 1992 (PG)
A con artist's luck turns bad when the IRS catches up with him, impounds all his worldly goods, and sticks him with an officious auditor. But if Jack can find the heiress to a fortune, within 48 hours, he can claim a hefty finder's fee and his money worries will be a thing of the past. **96m/C VHS.** C. Thomas Howell, Wallace Shawn, Lise Cutter, Lynn Danielson, Roy Brocksmith; **D:** Ben Moses; **W:** Seth Front, Eddy Polon, Ben Moses. *COL*

Nickel Mountain *♫♫½* 1985
Heartwarming story of a suicidal 40-year-old man who finds a new reason to live when he falls in love with a pregnant 16-year-old girl who works at his diner. Langenkamp particularly appealing. Based on a John Gardner novel. **88m/C VHS, Beta.** Michael Cole, Heather Langenkamp, Ed Lauter, Brian Kerwin, Patrick Cassidy, Grace Zabriskie, Don Beddoe; **D:** Drew Denbaum. *ORI*

Nico Icon *♫♫♫* 1995 (R)
Documentary probes the life of Velvet Underground sensation and Warhol superstar Nico. A pastiche showing V.U. concert footage and movie clips from Nico's most famous film appearances: Fellini's "La Dolce Vita" and Warhol's "The Chelsea Girls." Also features interviews from Warhol's Factory inhabitants, band members, and Nico's grown son Ari. Visually as interesting as the subject herself, film manages to bring the viewer closer to the untouchable Teutonic figure without being sensational or overly flashy. Director Paul Morrissey and musician Jackson Browne make appearances. Some French and German language; subtitled. **75m/C VHS.** *GE* **D:** Susanne Ofteringer; **W:** Susanne Ofteringer. *NYR*

Nicole *♫* 1972 (R)
The downfall of a wealthy woman who is able to buy everything she wants except love. **91m/C VHS, Beta.** Leslie Caron, Catherine Bach, Ramon Bieri; **D:** Itsvan Ventilla. *GHV*

The Night After Halloween *♫* 1983
(R) A young woman gets the shock of her life when she discovers that her boyfriend is a crazed killer. **90m/C VHS, Beta.** *IT* Chantal Contouri, Robert Bruning, Sigrid Thornton. *NO*

Night After Night *♫♫½* 1932
West's screen debut finds her in an unaccustomed secondary role, although a prime scene-stealer. In Raft's first starring role, he's a monied low-life who opens a fancy nightclub and becomes infatuated with Park Avenue beauty Cummings. His problems are compounded by the arrival of raucous ex-flames West and Gleason. When a hatcheck girl cries "Goodness!" over West's diamonds, she replies, in suggestive West-style, "Goodness had nothing to do with it, dearie." Adapted from the novel "Single Night" by Louis Bromfield. **73m/B VHS.** George Raft, Constance Cummings, Mae West, Wynne Gibson, Alison Skipworth, Roscoe Karns, Louis Calhern; **D:** Archie Mayo; **W:** Mae West, Kathryn Scola, Vincent Lawrence. *USH*

Night Ambush *♫♫½* Ill Met By Moonlight 1957
A Nazi general is kidnapped on Crete by British agents, who embark on a dangerous trip to the coast where a ship awaits to take them to Cairo. The general tries to thwart their plans, but they outwit him at every turn. Based on a novel by W. Stanley Moss that details a similar real-life event. **100m/B VHS.** *GB* Dirk Bogarde, Marius Goring, David Oxley, Cyril Cusack, Christopher Lee; **D:** Michael Powell, Emeric Pressburger. *NO*

Night and Day *♫♫½* 1946
Sentimental musical about the life of bon-vivant composer-extraordinaire Cole Porter. His intensity and the motivations for his music are dramatized, but this film succeeds best as a fabulous showcase for Porter's songs. ♫Begin the Beguine; My Heart Belongs to Daddy; You're the Top; I've Got You Under My Skin; Just One of Those Things; I Get a Kick Out of You; Night and Day; What Is This Thing Called Love; Do I Love You. **128m/C VHS, Beta.** Cary Grant, Alexis Smith, Jane Wyman, Eve Arden, Mary Martin, Alan Hale, Monty Woolley, Ginny Simms, Dorothy Malone; **D:** Michael Curtiz; **M:** Max Steiner. Nominations: Academy Awards '46: Scoring of a Musical.*MGM, FCT*

Night and Day *♫♫♫* Nuit et Jour 1991
Charming adult romance about Jack and Julie, young lovers newly arrived in Paris. When Jack gets a night job driving a cab, Julie finds her evenings lonely. But not for long. She meets Joseph, a cab driver on the day shift. Soon, Julie is juggling sexual affairs with both men and everything gets increasingly complicated. Her lovers find out about each other but Julie doesn't want to fully commit to either of them. In French with English subtitles. **90m/C VHS.** *FR BE SI* Guilaine Londez, Thomas Langmann, Francois Negret; **D:** Chantal Akerman; **W:** Pascal Bonitzer, Chantal Akerman; **M:** Marc Herouet. *FXL, ORI, FCT*

Night and the City *♫♫♫½* 1950
A film noir classic about a hustler's money-making schemes. Widmark is Harry Fabian, a small-time promoter working for slimy nightclub owner Sullivan, whose job is to hustle the marks into the club where his girlfriend Tierney is the singer. Widmark also happens to be romancing Sullivan's wife, Withers, and wants her to back his latest con. But his schemes go awry and Fabian's on the run for his life. Widmark gives a riveting performance of a lowlife whose brains don't match his ambitions. Filmed in London with appropriate brooding tawdriness. Adapted from the novel by Gerald Kersh; remade in 1992. **95m/B VHS.** *GB* Richard Widmark, Gene Tierney, Googie Withers, Francis L. Sullivan, Hugh Marlowe, Herbert Lom, Mike Mazurki, Charles Farrell; **D:** Jules Dassin; **W:** Jo Eisinger; **M:** Franz Waxman. *FXV, MOV, RXM*

Night and the City *♫♫♫* 1992 (R)
Harry Fabian (De Niro), a con-artist/ambulance-chaser, concocts a scheme to make it big, and approaches an old boxing great (Warden) to come out of retirement and revive a local boxing night. Problem is, although Harry has energy and ambition, he also has a talent for making enemies out of the wrong people, like the boxer's brother (King), a neighborhood mobster. Filled with details more interesting than the plot; more about fast-living, fast-talking New Yorkers, a fine showcase for De Niro's talent. Winkler's remake of the 1950 Jules Dassin film.**CW:** Strong language. **98m/C VHS, LV, Closed Caption.** Robert De Niro, Jessica Lange, Cliff Gorman, Alan King, Jack Warden, Eli Wallach, Barry Primus, Gene Kirkwood, Pedro Sanchez; **Cameos:** Regis Philbin, Joy Philbin, Richard Price; **D:** Irwin Winkler; **W:** Richard Price; **C:** Tak Fujimoto; **M:** James Newton Howard. *FXV*

Night Angel *♫* 1990 (R)
A beautiful seductress lures men into a deadly trap from which only true love can free them. **90m/C VHS, Beta, LV.** Isa Anderson, Linda Ashby, Debra Feuer, Helen Martin, Karen Black; **D:** Dominique Othenin-Girard; **W:** Joe Augustyn. *FRH*

A Night at the Opera *♫♫♫♫* 1935
The Marx Brothers get mixed up with grand opera in their first MGM-produced epic and their first without Zeppo. Jones, as a budding opera singer warbles "Alone" and "Cosi Cosa." One of their best films, blessed with a big budget—used to reach epic anarchic heights. Some scenes were tested on live audiences before inclusion, including the Groucho/Chico paper-tearing contract negotiation and the celebrated stateroom scene, in which the boys are joined in a small closet by

two maids, the ship's engineer, his assistant, a manicurist, a young woman, a cleaning lady, and four food-laden waiters. Laserdisc includes letterboxing, digital sound, original trailers, production photos, memorabilia, and soundtrack commentary by film critic Leonard Maltin. **92m/B VHS, Beta, LV.** Groucho Marx, Chico Marx, Harpo Marx, Allan Jones, Kitty Carlisle Hart, Sig Rumann, Margaret Dumont, Walter Woolf King; **D:** Sam Wood; **W:** George S. Kaufman, Morrie Ryskind, Bert Kalmar, Harry Ruby, Al Boasberg; **M:** Herbert Stothart. MGM, CRC, CCB

Night Beast *☙* 1983 Alien creature lands his spaceship near a small town and begins a bloody killing spree. Recycled plot. **90m/C VHS, Beta.** Tom Griffith, Dick Dyszel, Jaimie Zemarel; **D:** Donald M. Dohler. NO

Night Beat *☙☙½* 1948 A labored crime drama from postwar Britain. Two army pals pursue diverging careers. One becomes a cop, the other a crook. Want to bet that they meet again? **95m/B VHS.** GB Anne Crawford, Maxwell Reed, Ronald Howard, Christine Norden; **D:** Harold Huth. LOO

The Night Before *☙☙½* 1988 (PG-13) Snobby high school beauty Loughlin loses a bet and has to go to the prom with the school geek Reeves. On the way, they get lost on the wrong side of the tracks, and become involved with pimps, crime and the police. A drunken Reeves loses Loughlin as well as his father's car. Typical teen farce. **90m/C VHS, Beta, Closed Caption.** Keanu Reeves, Lori Loughlin, Trinidad Silva, Michael Greene, Theresa Saldana, Suzanne Snyder, Morgan Lofting, Gwil Richards; **D:** Thom Eberhardt; **W:** Gregory Scherick, Thom Eberhardt. HBO

Night Birds *☙* 1931 Early British thriller about a notorious crook named "Flash Jack," who heads a gang of top-hatted criminals that rob the wealthy. Poor production quality and Raine's standoffish screen presence contribute to this below-average film. **76m/B VHS.** GB Jameson Thomas, Jack Raine, Muriel Angelus, Eve Gray; **D:** Richard Eichberg; **W:** Miles Malleson. SNC

Night Breed *☙½* 1990 (R) A teenager flees a chaotic past to slowly become a member of a bizarre race of demons that live in a huge, abandoned Canadian graveyard; a place where every sin is forgiven. Based on Barker's novel "Cabal," and appropriately gross, nonsensical and strange. Good special effects almost save this one. **102m/C VHS, Beta, LV, Closed Caption.** CA Craig Sheffer, Anne Bobby, David Cronenberg, Charles Haid; **D:** Clive Barker; **W:** Clive Barker. MED

The Night Brings Charlie *☙½* 1990 A disfigured tree surgeon is the prime suspect in some grisly murders committed with a tree trimming saw. Obviously, everyone in the town fears him as a result. Not a sequel to "Roots." **90m/C VHS.** Kerry Knight, Joe Fishback, Aimee Tenalia, Monica Simmons; **D:** Tom Logan. NO

Night Call Nurses *☙☙* 1972 (R) Three gorgeous nurses find danger and intrigue on the night shift at a psychiatric hospital. Third in the "nurse" quintet is back on target, shrugging off the previous film's attempts at "serious" social commentary. Miller provides comic relief. Preceded by "The Student Nurses" and "Private Duty Nurses" and followed by "The Young Nurses," and "Candy Stripe Nurses." Also on video as "Young L.A. Nurses 2." **85m/C VHS, Beta.** Patricia T. Byrne, Alana Collins, Mittie Lawrence, Clinton Kimbrough, Felton Perry, Stack Pierce, Richard Young, Dennis Dugan, Dick Miller; **D:** Jonathan Kaplan; **W:** George Armitage. NLC

Night Caller from Outer Space *☙½* Blood Beast from Outer Space; The Night Caller 1966 When a woman-hunting alien arrives in London, women begin to disappear. At first, incredibly, no one makes the connection, but then the horrible truth comes to light. **84m/B VHS, Beta, LV.** GB John Saxon, Maurice Denham, Patricia Haines, Alfred Burke, Jack Watson, Aubrey Morris; **D:** John Gilling. COL

Night Children *☙* 1989 (R) Tough L.A. cop teams with a parole officer to battle a nasty gang leader. The battle is quite violent and senseless. **90m/C VHS, Beta.** David Carradine, Nancy Kwan, Griffin O'Neal, Tawny Fere; **D:** Norbert Meisel. THV

The Night Club *☙☙½* 1925 Swinging single stands to gain fortune if he weds a certain girl, and, as luck would have it, he falls for her. When the usual hearts and roses don't convince her he's earnest, he tries to prove his love is true by attempting suicide and hiring a hit man. **62m/B VHS, Beta.** Raymond Griffith, Vera Reynolds, Wallace Beery, Louise Fazenda; **D:** Frank Urson. GPV

Night Creature *☙* Out of the Darkness; Fear 1979 (PG) A tough, Hemingway-type writer is determined to destroy the man-eating black leopard which nearly killed him once before. Filmed in Thailand. **83m/C VHS, Beta.** Donald Pleasence, Nancy Kwan, Ross Hagen; **D:** Lee Madden. VCI

Night Cries *☙☙½* 1978 After a woman's baby dies at birth, she has persistent dreams that he is alive and in trouble. No one will believe her when she tells them that something is wrong. Made for television. **100m/C VHS, Beta.** Susan St. James, Michael Parks, William Conrad; **D:** Richard Lang. WOV

Night Crossing *☙☙½* 1981 (PG) The fact-based story of two East German families who launch a daring escape to the West in a home-made hot air balloon. Exciting action for the whole family. **106m/C VHS, Beta.** John Hurt, Jane Alexander, Glynnis O'Connor, Doug McKeon, Beau Bridges; **D:** Delbert Mann; **W:** John McGreevey; **M:** Jerry Goldsmith. DIS

The Night Cry *☙☙* 1926 Silent canine melodrama has sheep-murdering dog sentenced to death row until he saves little girl from unbelievably big bird. **65m/B VHS, Beta.** John Harron, June Marlowe, Mary Louise Miller; **D:** Herman C. Raymaker. GPV, GVV

The Night Evelyn Came Out of the Grave *☙½* La Notte Che Evelyn Usca Dalla Tomba 1971 (R) A wealthy Italian playboy, obsessed with his dead, flame-haired wife, lures living redheads into his castle, where he tortures and kills them. Standard '70s Euro/horror/sex stuff enlivened by the presence of the incredible Erika Blanc as a stripper who works out of a coffin. **99m/C VHS.** IT Anthony Steffen, Marina Malfatti, Rod Murdock, Erika Blanc, Giacomo "Jack" Rossi-Stuart, Umberto Raho; **D:** Emilio P. Miraglio. FRG

Night Eyes *☙* Hidden Vision 1990 (R) Surveillance can be a dangerous profession, especially when your boss happens to be the jealous husband of a very sexy woman. Watching turns to yearning for this professional peeper, but he may just get more than he bargained for. Roberts is worth watching. **95m/C VHS, Beta, LV.** Andrew Stevens, Tanya Roberts, Warwick Sims, Cooper Huckabee; **D:** Emilio P. Miraglio; **W:** Tom Citrano. PSM

Night Eyes 2 *☙½* 1991 (R) A security expert assigned to protect the sultry wife of a foreign diplomat finds himself spending a little too much time eyeing her through his hidden cameras. Soon he can no longer control his desire and he makes a move on her that may have international implications. Also available in an unrated version. **CW:** Language, violence, and sensuality. **97m/C VHS, Beta, Closed Caption.** Andrew Stevens, Shannon Tweed, Tim Russ, Richard Chaves, Geno Silva; **D:** Rodney McDonald. PSM

Night Eyes 3 *☙☙* 1993 (R) Night Eyes Security boss Stevens' latest assignment is to protect the superstar lead (Shannon Tweed) of a top TV cop show from a stalker. They wind up in very close contact but someone is videotaping their private moments which don't stay private for long. Maybe on-screen partner Tracy (Shannon's sister) has something to do with it. Also available in an unrated version. **CW:** Language, violence, and strong sexuality. **97m/C VHS, Beta.** Andrew Stevens, Shannon Tweed, Tracy Tweed, Tristan Rogers; **D:** Andrew Stevens; **W:** Andrew Stevens, Michael W. Potts. PSM

Night Eyes 4: Fatal Passion *☙½* 1995 (R) Beverly Hills shrink gets involved with the bodyguard hired to protect her from a stalker. Also available unrated. **CW:** Some strong sexuality. **101m/C VHS.** Paula Barbieri, Jeff Trachta, Andrew Stevens; **D:** Rodney McDonald; **W:** John Eubanks, Henry Krinkle; **C:** Gary Graver; **M:** Patrick Seymour. PSM

Night Falls on Manhattan *☙☙☙* 1996 (R) One man's search for truth runs into serious problems in this adaptation of "Tainted Evidence" by Robert Daley. Former cop turned junior DA, Sean Casey (Garcia), is chosen to lead the prosecution in a sensational NY trial involving a drug dealer/cop killer, who also seriously wounded Sean's long-time cop father, Liam (Holm). He wins but allegations of police corruption dog the trial, thanks to liberal defense lawyer Vigoda (Dreyfuss), and when Sean rather unexpectedly becomes the new district attorney, the issue becomes a full-blown scandal, leading the naive Sean very close to home. Veteran director Lumet knows this scandal-ridden territory very well and is aided by fine performances from his leads. **CW:** Violence and language. **114m/C VHS.** Andy Garcia, Ian Holm, Richard Dreyfuss, Lena Olin, James Gandolfini, Ron Leibman, Colm Feore, Shiek Mahmud-Bey; **D:** Sidney Lumet; **W:** Sidney Lumet; **C:** David Watkin; **M:** Mark Isham. NYR

Night Fire *☙½* 1994 (R) Barry wants wife Lydia to try to rekindle the passion in their marriage by getting away for the weekend at their remote ranch. But they're interrupted in their leisure by the stranded Cal and Gwen. Only it turns out Barry has hired the duo, who like kinky games, to peak Lydia's interest. She's merely disgusted and Barry gets nasty. Also available unrated. **93m/C VHS.** Shannon Tweed, John Laughlin, Martin Hewitt, Rochelle Swanson; **D:** Mike Sedan; **W:** Catherine Tavel, Helen Haxton. TRI

Night Flight from Moscow *☙☙½* The Serpent 1973 (PG) A Soviet spy defects with a fistful of secret documents that implicate every free government. Then the CIA must decide if he's telling the truth. Complex espionage thriller. **113m/C VHS, Beta.** FR IT GE Yul Brynner, Henry Fonda, Dirk Bogarde, Virna Lisi, Philippe Noiret, Farley Granger, Robert Alda, Marie DuBois, Elga Andersen; **D:** Henri Verneuil; **M:** Ennio Morricone. NLC

A Night for Crime *☙☙* 1942 A movie star disappears during the filming of a movie. When she turns up dead, a bumbling cop suspects everyone on the set. **75m/B VHS.** Glenda Farrell, Lyle Talbot, Lena Basquette, Donald Kirke, Ralph Sanford; **D:** Alexis Thurn-Taxis. NOS, DVT

Night Friend *☙* 1987 (R) A priest sets out to help a young woman caught up in a world of drug abuse and prostitution. Exploitation morality flick. **94m/C VHS, Beta.** Art Carney, Chuck Shamata, Jayne Eastwood, Heather Kjollesdal; **D:** Peter Gerretsen. PSM

A Night Full of Rain *☙½* End of the World (in our Usual Bed in a Night Full of Rain) 1978 (R) Italian communist tries unsuccessfully to seduce vacationing American feminist. They meet again in San Francisco and wedding bells chime. They argue. They argue more. They put all but rabid Wertmuller fans to sleep. The director's first English-language film. **104m/C VHS.** IT Giancarlo Giannini, Candice Bergen, Anne Byrne, Flora Carabella; **D:** Lina Wertmuller; **W:** Lina Wertmuller. WAR, FCT

Night Gallery *☙☙☙* 1969 Serling is the tour guide through an unusual art gallery consisting of portraits that reflect people's greed, desire and guilt. Made for television pilot for the series, which ran from 1969 to 1973. Three stories, including "Eyes," which saw novice Spielberg directing veteran Crawford. **95m/C VHS, Beta.** Joan Crawford, Roddy McDowall, Tom Bosley, Barry Sullivan, Ossie Davis, Sam Jaffe, Kate Greenfield; **D:** Steven Spielberg, Boris Sagal. USH

Night Game 🐾½ 1989 (R) A cop links a string of serial killings to the night games won by the Houston Astros. Brave cast tries hard, but is retired without a hit. **95m/C VHS, Beta, LV.** Roy Scheider, Karen Young, Paul Gleason, Lane Smith, Carlin Glynn; **D:** Peter Masterson; **M:** Pino Donaggio. *HBO*

Night Games 🐾 1980 (R) Raped as a child, California girl Pickett has trouble relating to her husband. To overcome her sexual anxieties, she engages in a number of bizarre fantasies. **100m/C VHS, Beta, LV.** Cindy Pickett, Joanna Cassidy, Barry Primus, Gene Davis; **D:** Roger Vadim; **M:** John Barry.

The Night God Screamed woof! *Scream 198?* (PG) A fanatical cult leader is convicted of murder and the cult goes wild. **85m/C VHS, Beta.** Michael Sugich, Jeanne Crain, James B. Sikking; **D:** Lee Madden. *TWE*

The Night Has Eyes 🐾🐾½ *Terror House* 1942 Tense melodrama concerns a young teacher who disappears on the Yorkshire moors at the same spot where her girlfriend had vanished the previous year. Early film appearance for Mason. **79m/B VHS, Beta.** *GB* James Mason, Joyce Howard, Wilfred Lawson, Mary Clare; **D:** Leslie Arliss. *NOS, SNC, DVT*

Night Hunter 🐾🐾 1995 (R) Jack Cutter's (Wilson) vampire-hunting parents were killed by a group of bloodsuckers so he teams up with a tabloid reporter (Smith) to eliminate the last nine vampires who have gathered together in Los Angeles and plan to multiply. **CW:** Language, violence. **86m/C VHS.** Don "The Dragon" Wilson, Melanie Smith, Nicholas Guest, Maria Ford; **D:** Rick Jacobson. *NHO*

A Night in Casablanca 🐾🐾🐾 1946 Groucho, Harpo and Chico find themselves in the luxurious Hotel Casablanca, going after some leftover Nazis searching for treasure. One of the later Marx Brothers' films, but still loaded with the familiar wisecracks and mayhem. **85m/B VHS, Beta.** Groucho Marx, Harpo Marx, Chico Marx, Charles Drake, Dan Seymour, Sig Rumann; **D:** Archie Mayo. *NO*

A Night in Heaven woof! 1983 (R) A college teacher gets involved with one of her students, who moonlights as a male stripper. Will he earn that extra credit he needs to pass? Uninspired, overly explicit. Look for Denny Terrio of "Dance Fever" fame. **85m/C VHS, Beta, Closed Caption.** Christopher Atkins, Lesley Ann Warren, Carrie Snodgress, Andy Garcia; **D:** John G. Avildsen; **W:** Joan Tewkesbury. Golden Raspberry Awards '83: Worst Actor (Atkins). *FOX*

A Night in the Life of Jimmy Reardon 🐾½ 1988 (R) A high school Casanova watches his friends leave for expensive schools while he contemplates a trip to Hawaii with his rich girlfriend, a ruse to avoid the dull business school his father has picked out. Well photographed, but acting leaves something to be desired. Based on Richert's novel "Aren't You Even Going to Kiss Me Good-bye?" **95m/C VHS, Beta, LV, Closed Caption.** River Phoenix, Meredith Salenger, Matthew L. Perry, Louanne, Ione Skye, Ann Magnuson, Paul Koslo, Jane Hallaren, Jason Court; **D:** William Richert; **M:** Elmer Bernstein, Bill Conti. *FOX*

Night Is My Future 🐾🐾½ *Music in Darkness* 1947 A young musician, blinded in an accident, meets a girl who tries to bring him happiness. Usual somber Bergman, but unimportant story. In Swedish with English subtitles. **89m/B VHS, Beta.** *SW* Mai Zetterling, Birger Malmsten, Naima Wifstrand, Olof Winnerstrand, Hilda Borgstrom; **D:** Ingmar Bergman. *VYY, DVT, HEG*

Night Life 🐾🐾 1990 (R) A teenager gets the all-out, high-stakes ride of his life when four cadavers are re-animated in his uncle's mortuary. **92m/C VHS, LV.** Scott Grimes, John Astin, Cheryl Pollak, Alan Blumenfeld; **D:** David Acomba; **W:** Keith Critchlow; **M:** Roger Bourland. *COL*

Night Life in Reno 🐾🐾 1931 When a man leaves his wife, she sets out for Reno and falls in love with a married man. When her new love is killed by his jealous wife, the woman re-

turns to her husband and they begin their marriage anew. Watchable melodrama. **58m/B VHS, Beta, LV.** Jameson Thomas, Dorothy Christy, Virginia Valli, Carmelita Geraghty. *NO*

Night Master 🐾 1987 A handful of karate students practice their homework with much higher stakes away from the classroom. For them, deadly Ninja games are the only way to study. **87m/C VHS, Beta.** Tom Jennings, Nicole Kidman, Vince Martin; **D:** Mark Joffe. *ACA*

Night Monster 🐾🐾½ *House of Mystery* 1942 A maniac wears artifical limbs to hunt down and murder the doctors responsible for amputating his legs. Picture was shot in 11 days. Fire scene was stock footage from "The Ghost of Frankenstein." **80m/B VHS, Closed Caption.** Ralph Morgan, Lionel Atwill, Leif Erickson, Don Porter, Irene Hervey, Nils Asther, Bela Lugosi; **D:** Ford Beebe. *USH*

'night, Mother 🐾🐾½ 1986 (PG-13) A depressed woman, living with her mother, announces one evening that she is going to kill herself. Her mother spends the evening reliving their lives and trying to talk her out of it, but the outcome seems inevitable. Well acted, though depressing. Based on Marsha Norman's Pulitzer Prize-winning novel. **97m/C VHS, Beta, LV, Closed Caption.** Sissy Spacek, Anne Bancroft, Ed Berke, Carol Robbins, Jennifer Roosendahl; **D:** Tom Moore; **W:** Marsha Norman; **M:** David Shire. *USH*

Night Moves 🐾🐾🐾½ 1975 (R) While tracking down a missing teenager, a Hollywood detective uncovers a bizarre smuggling ring in the Florida Keys. Hackman is realistic as the detective whose own life is unraveling and in one of her early roles, Griffith plays the teenager. The dense, disjointed plot reaches a shocking end. Underrated when released and worth a view. **100m/C VHS, Beta.** Gene Hackman, Susan Clark, Jennifer Warren, Melanie Griffith, Harris Yulin, Edward Binns, Kenneth Mars, James Woods, Dennis Dugan, Max Gail; **D:** Arthur Penn; **C:** Bruce Surtees. *WAR*

Night Nurse 🐾🐾🐾 1931 Stanwyck is a nurse who uncovers a sordid plot involving the murder of two young children for an inheritance. An entertaining, overlooked crime-drama, initially notorious for Stanwyck and roommate Blondell's continual onscreen dressings and undressings. Gable is compelling in an early, villainous role. **72m/B VHS, LV.** Barbara Stanwyck, Ben Lyon, Joan Blondell, Charles Winninger, Charlotte Merriam, Eddie Nugent, Blanche Frederici, Allan "Rocky" Lane, Walter McGrail, Ralf Harolde, Clark Gable; **D:** William A. Wellman. *MGM*

Night Nurse 🐾 1977 Young nurse signs on to care for an aging, wheelchair-ridden opera star, only to find that the house is haunted. **80m/C VHS, Beta.** Davina Whitehouse, Kay Taylor, Gary Day, Kate Fitzpatrick; **D:** Igor Auzins. *NO*

Night of a Thousand Cats 🐾🐾 *La Noche de Los Mil Gatos; Blood Feast* 1972 (R) A reclusive playboy cruises Mexico City in his helicopter, searching for beautiful women. It seems he needs their bodies for his cats who, for some reason, eat only human flesh. He keeps the heads, for some reason, for his private collection. A really odd '70s cannibal cat entry, but it moves along nicely and features some truly groovy fashions (floppy hats, translucent blouses, etc.). Not to be confused with the 1963 film of the same name. From the director of "Night of the Bloody Apes" and "Survive!" **83m/C VHS, Beta.** *MX* Anjanette Comer, Zulma Faiad, Hugo Stiglitz, Christa Linder, Teresa Velasquez, Barbara Ange; **D:** Rene Cardona Jr. *ACA, JEF*

Night of Bloody Horror 🐾½ 1976 (R) Tale of a former mental patient who is believed to be responsible for the brutal murders of his ex-girlfriends. A night of bloody horror indeed, as the gore is liberally spread. **89m/C VHS, Beta.** Gaye Yellen, Evelyn Hendricks, Gerald McRaney. *NO*

Night of Dark Shadows woof! *Curse of Dark Shadows* 1971 (PG) An abominable film which even fans of the TV show have a hard time liking. The last of the Collins family and his new bride

are sent 150 years into the past. Sequel to "House of Dark Shadows." **97m/C VHS, Beta, Closed Caption.** David Selby, Lara Parker, Kate Jackson, Grayson Hall, John Karlen, Nancy Barrett, James Storm; **D:** Dan Curtis. *MGM*

Night of Evil 🐾🐾½ 1962 Girl is released from reform school and promptly wins a beauty contest. Her bid to win the Miss America title is blown to smithereens however, when it is discovered that she has been secretly married all along. From there she resorts to working in strip joints and attempts to pull off an armed robbery. As exploitation fare goes, a winner. **88m/B VHS, Beta.** Lisa Gaye, William Campbell; **D:** Richard Galbreath. *SNC*

Night of Horror 🐾½ 198? (R) Zombies attack four young people stranded in the wilderness. **76m/C VHS, Beta.** Steve Sandkuhler, Gae Schmitt, Rebecca Bach, Jeff Canfield. *GHV, MRV*

A Night of Love 🐾🐾½ *Manifesto* 1987 (R) Because of an assassination threat on the new king, Inspector Avanti (Molina) is charged with rounding up the town's troublemakers. Among them is a beguiling debutante (Soeberg) whose sexual appetites are matched only by her passion to kill the king. Based on a story by Emile Zola. **CW:** Nudity, sexual situations. **97m/C VHS.** Alfred Molina, Camilla Soeberg, Eric Stoltz, Gabrielle Anwar; **D:** Dusan Makavejev. *ORI, FXL*

Night of Terror 🐾🐾 *He Lived to Kill* 1933 A swami, a couple of Hindu servants, a pretty heroine, a reporter, and all stalked by a killer who's after a formula that can put people in a state of suspended animation. Lame chiller. **64m/B VHS.** Bela Lugosi, Sally Blane, Wallace Ford, Tully Marshall, George Meeker, Edwin Maxwell; **D:** Ben Stoloff; **C:** Joseph Valentine. *GPV*

Night of Terror 🐾 1987 A bizarre family conducts brain experiments on themselves and then begins to kill each other. Bloodshed for the whole family. **105m/C VHS.** Renee Harmon, Henry Lewis. *IME*

Night of the Assassin 🐾 1977 Priest leaves his pulpit to become a terrorist. He plans a surprise for a U.N. secretary visiting Greece that would put the U.S. and Greek governments in the palm of his hand. Hard to believe. **98m/C VHS, Beta.** Klaus Kinski, Michael Craig, Eva Renzi; **D:** Robert McMahon. *LIV*

Night of the Blood Beast 🐾½ 1958 An astronaut comes back from space with an alien growing inside his body. The low budget defeats a valiant attempt at a story. Alternative title: "Creature from Galaxy 27." **65m/B VHS.** Michael Emmet, Angela Greene, John Baer, Ed Nelson; **D:** Bernard L. Kowalski. *SNC, MRV*

Night of the Bloody Apes woof! *Gomar the Human Gorilla; La Horriplante Bestia Humana* 1968 (R) When a doctor transplants an ape's heart into his dying son's body, the son goes berserk. Gory Mexican-made horror at its finest. **84m/C VHS, Beta.** *MX* Jose Elias Moreno, Armando Silvestre, Norma Lazareno, Agustin Martinez Solares, Gina Moret, Noelia Noel, Gerard Zepeda; **D:** Rene Cardona Jr. *MPI*

Night of the Bloody Transplant woof! 1986 (R) A lunatic scientist switches hearts from one person to another in this bloody gorefest. Footage of real surgery adds authenticity, but not believeability. **90m/C VHS, Beta.** Dick Grimm; **D:** David W. Hanson. *NO*

Night of the Cobra Woman 🐾 1972 (R) A woman who can turn herself into a cobra needs constant sex and snake venom to keep her eternally young. Shot on location in the Philippines. One-time underground filmmaker Meyer co-wrote the script, for the Corman factory. **85m/C VHS, Beta.** *PH* Joy Bang, Marlene Clark, Roger Garrett, Slash Marks, Vic Diaz; **D:** Andrew Meyer; **W:** Andrew Meyer. *NO*

Night of the Comet 🐾🐾½ 1984 (PG-13) After surviving the explosion of a deadly comet, two California girls discover that they are the last people on Earth. When zombies begin to chase them, things begin to lose their charm. Cute and funny, but the script runs out before the movie does. **90m/C VHS, Beta, Closed Caption.** Catherine Mary Stewart, Kelli Maroney, Robert Beltran, Geoffrey Lewis, Mary Woronov, Sharon Farrell, Michael Bowen; **D:** Thom Eberhardt; **W:** Thom Eberhardt; **C:** Arthur Albert. *FOX*

Night of the Creeps *♫♫½* 1986 (R) In 1958 an alien organism lands on earth and infects a person who is then frozen. Thirty years later he is accidentally unfrozen and starts spreading the infection throughout a college town. B-movie homage contains every horror cliche there is. Director Dekker's first film. **89m/C VHS, Beta, LV, Closed Caption.** Jason Lively, Jill Whitlow, Tom Atkins, Dick Miller, Steve Marshall; **D:** Fred Dekker; **W:** Fred Dekker. *NO*

Night of the Cyclone *♫♫* 1990 (R) A complex but not overly interesting thriller about a big city cop who goes to an island paradise in search of his missing daughter and finds murder. **90m/C VHS, LV, Closed Caption.** Kris Kristofferson, Jeffrey Meek, Marisa Berenson, Winston Ntshona, Gerrit Graham; **D:** David Irving. *REP*

Night of the Death Cult *♫♫* *Night of the Seagulls* 1975 After moving to a quiet seaside community, a young couple is plagued by cult practising human sacrifice in order to appease the Templars, a zombie-like pack of ancient clergymen who rise from the dead and torture the living. Last in a four film series about the Templars. **90m/C VHS, Beta.** *SP* Victor Petit, Julie James, Maria Kosti, Sandra Mozarowsky; **D:** Armando de Ossorio. *NO*

Night of the Demon woof! 1980 Anthropology students are attacked by the legendary Bigfoot. Later they discover that he has raped and impregnated a young woman. Gore and sex prevail. **97m/C VHS, Beta.** Jay Allen, Michael J. Cutt, Bob Collins, Jodi Lazarus; **D:** James C. Watson. *VHE*

Night of the Demons 1988 (R) A gory, special-effects-laden horror farce about teenagers calling up demons in a haunted mortuary. On Halloween, of course. **90m/C VHS, LV.** Linnea Quigley, Cathy Podewell, Alvin Alexis, William Gallo, Mimi Kinkade, Lance Fenton; **D:** Kevin S. Tenney; **W:** Joe Augustyn. *REP*

Night of the Demons 2 *♫♫* 1994 (R) Some humor and reasonable special effects help this rise above the usual teen-slasher horror sequels. The demonic Angela (complete with her skull-shaped lollipops) lives on in legend, handily haunting her creepy old house where a group of dumb teens end up on Halloween (and soon wind up dead). With each casualty, a new victim also joins the ranks of the undead. Funniest parts come with heroic rescuer, yardstick-wielding Sister Gloria, who's not about to let any of Satan's helpers get the better of her. **96m/C VHS, LV, Closed Caption.** Amelia Kinkade, Jennifer Rhodes, Merele Kennedy, Bobby Jacoby, Rod McCary, Zoe Trilling, Cristi Harris, Johnny Moran, Rick Peters, Christine Taylor, Ladd York, Darin Heames; **D:** Brian Trenchard-Smith; **W:** Joe Augustyn; **M:** Jim Manzie. *REP*

The Night of the Following Day *♫♫* 1969 (R) Four professional criminals kidnap a young girl at France's Orly airport, demanding a large ransom from her wealthy father. Each kidnapper turns out to be beset by personal demons, hindering their plans and leading to a bloody climax. Then, there's a final twist to the entire story. Brando and Boone are properly chilling but the plot is muddled and melodramatic. From the novel "The Snatchers" by Lionel White. **93m/C VHS, Closed Caption.** Marlon Brando, Richard Boone, Rita Moreno, Pamela Franklin, Jess Hahn, Jacques Marin, Gerard Buhr, Hughes Wanner; **D:** Hubert Cornfield; **W:** Robert Phippeny, Hubert Cornfield. *USH, FCT*

Night of the Fox *♫♫* 1990 (R) An American officer with top secret knowledge is captured by Germans on the brink of D-day. His home team plans to kill him if he cannot be rescued before spilling the beans. On-location filming adds

much. Made for cable. **95m/C VHS, LV.** Michael York, Deborah Raffin, George Peppard; **D:** Charles Jarrott. *THV*

Night of the Generals *♫♫♫* *La Nuit de Generaux* 1967 (R) A Nazi intelligence officer is pursuing three Nazi generals who may be involved in the brutal murder of a Warsaw prostitute. Dark and sinister, may be too slow for some tastes. Based on Hans Helmut Kirst's novel. **148m/C VHS, Beta, LV.** Peter O'Toole, Omar Sharif, Tom Courtenay, Joanna Pettet, Donald Pleasence, Christopher Plummer, Philippe Noiret, John Gregson; **D:** Anatole Litvak; **M:** Maurice Jarre. *COL, MOV*

Night of the Ghouls woof! *Revenge of the Dead* 1959 Second to last in Wood's celebrated series of inept horror films that began with "Bride of the Monster" and "Plan 9 from Outer Space." This one tells of a phony spiritualist who swindles the grieving by pretending to raise the dead. To his great surprise he actually does enliven some cadavers, who then go after him. Unreleased for over 20 years because Wood couldn't pay the film lab. Not quite as classically bad as his other films, but still a laugh riot. **69m/B VHS, Beta.** Paul Marco, Tor Johnson, Duke Moore, Kenne Duncan, John Carpenter; **D:** Edward D. Wood Jr. *RHI, SNC, MED*

Night of the Grizzly *♫♫* 1966 An ex-lawman's peaceful life as a rancher is threatened when a killer grizzly bear goes on a murderous rampage terrorizing the residents of the Wyoming countryside. **99m/C VHS, Beta.** Clint Walker, Martha Hyer; **D:** Joseph Pevney. *PAR*

Night of the Howling Beast *♫* *The Werewolf and the Yeti* 1975 (R) The selling point of this one is an epic, first-time battle between a werewolf and a Yeti. Unfortunately it lasts about fifteen seconds. Naschy's eighth stint as the wolfman. **87m/C VHS, Beta.** *SP* Paul Naschy, Grace Mills, Castillo Escalona, Silvia Solar, Gil Vidal; **D:** Miguel Iglesias. *REP*

The Night of the Hunter *♫♫♫♫* 1955 The nightmarish story of a psychotic preacher who marries a lonely widow with two children in the hopes of finding the cache of money her thieving husband had stashed. A dark, terrifying tale, completely unique in Hollywood's history. Mitchum is terrific. From novel by Davis Grubb and, sadly, Laughton's only directorial effort. **93m/B VHS, Beta, LV.** Robert Mitchum, Shelley Winters, Lillian Gish, Don Beddoe, Evelyn Varden, Peter Graves, James Gleason, Billy Chapin, Sally Jane Bruce; **D:** Charles Laughton; **W:** James Agee. *REP*

The Night of the Iguana *♫♫♫* 1964 An alcoholic ex-minister acts as a tour guide in Mexico, becoming involved with a spinster and a hotel owner. Based on Tennessee Williams' play. Excellent performances from Burton and Gardner. **125m/B VHS, Beta, LV.** Richard Burton, Deborah Kerr, Ava Gardner, Grayson Hall, Sue Lyon; **D:** John Huston. Academy Awards '64: Best Costume Design (B & W); Nominations: Academy Awards '64: Best Art Direction/Set Decoration (B & W), Best Black and White Cinematography, Best Supporting Actress (Hall). *MGM*

Night of the Juggler *♫♫½* 1980 (R) An ex-cop encounters countless obstacles in trying to track down his daughter's kidnapper in New York City. Just a tad too complicated for some tastes. **101m/C VHS, Beta.** James Brolin, Cliff Gorman, Richard Castellano, Mandy Patinkin, Julie Carmen; **D:** Robert Butler; **W:** William W. Norton Sr. *MED*

Night of the Kickfighters *♫* 1991 A mighty band of martial artists takes on a terrorist group that has in their possession a secret weapon that could destroy the world. **87m/C VHS.** Andy Bauman, Adam West, Marcia Karr; **D:** Buddy Reyes. *AIP*

Night of the Laughing Dead *♫½* *Crazy House; House in Nightmare Park* 1975 Veteran British comedy cast perform unthinkable spoof. Man stands to inherit lotsa money as his family members kick the bucket one by one. **90m/C VHS, LV.** *GB* Ray Milland, Frankie Howerd, Rosalie Crutchley, Kenneth Griffith; **D:** Peter Sykes. *MGM*

Night of the Living Babes woof! 1987 Two yuppie men go looking for fun at a brothel. They get their just deserts in the form of sex-seeking female zombies. **60m/C VHS.** Michelle (McClellan) Bauer, Connie Woods, Andrew Nichols, Louie Bonanno; **D:** Jon Valentine. *NO*

Night of the Living Dead *♫♫♫½* *Night of the Flesh Eaters* 1968 Cult favorite is low budget but powerfully frightening. Space experiments set off a high level of radiation that makes the newly dead return to life, with a taste for human flesh. Handful of holdouts find shelter in a farmhouse. Claustrophobic, terrifying, gruesome, extreme, and yes, humorous. Followed by "Dawn of the Dead" (1979) and "Day of the Dead" (1985). Romero's directorial debut. Available in a colorized version. **90m/B VHS, LV.** Judith O'Dea, Duane Jones, Russell Streiner, Karl Hardman; **D:** George A. Romero. *REP, MRV, NOS*

Night of the Living Dead *♫♫* 1990 (R) A bunch of people are trapped in a farmhouse and attacked by ghouls with eating disorders. Remake of the '68 classic substitutes high tech blood 'n' guts for bona fide frights. **92m/C VHS, LV.** Tony Todd, Patricia Tallman, Tom Towles; **D:** Tom Savini; **W:** George A. Romero. *COL*

Night of the Living Dead, 25th Anniversary Documentary 1993 Features behind the scenes look at low-budget 1968 classic film about legions of dead people who stalk the earth looking for live humans to feed on. **83m/C VHS, LV.** *MTH*

Night of the Running Man *♫½* 1994 (R) Las Vegas cab driver McCarthy finds $1 million stolen from a casino and goes on the run from hit man Glenn, who's been hired to recover the loot. *CW:* Strong sexuality, violence and language. **93m/C VHS, LV, Closed Caption.** Scott Glenn, Andrew McCarthy, John Glover; **D:** Mark L. Lester. *THV*

Night of the Scarecrow *♫♫½* 1995 (R) Hundreds of years before a small town makes a pact with a warlock (Lazar) to ensure prosperity. After regretting the deal, the townspeople kill him and bury the body in a field where it's eventually uncovered. Now the warlock's ghost inhabits the frame of a scarecrow and is off on a murderous rampage. Formula horror with some decent production values. Based on a comic book. *CW:* Strong horror violence; some sexuality and language. **90m/C VHS, Closed Caption.** Elizabeth Barondes, John Mese, Stephen Root, Bruce Glover, Dirk Blocker, Howard Swain, Gary Lockwood, John Lazar, John Hawkes; **D:** Jeff Burr; **W:** Reed Steiner, Dan Mazur; **C:** Thomas Callaway; **M:** Jim Manzie. *REP*

Night of the Sharks woof! 1989 Mercenaries in a downed plane go after a jewel-ridden shipwreck despite a plethora of sharks. **87m/C VHS, Beta, LV.** Treat Williams, Christopher Connelly, Antonio Fargas, Janet Agren; **D:** Anthony Richmond. *LIV, VTR*

The Night of the Shooting Stars *♫♫♫♫* *The Night of San Lorenzo; La Notte di San Lorenzo* 1982 (R) Set in an Italian village during the last days of WWII, this film highlights the schism in the village between those who support the fascists and those who sympathize with the Allies. This division comes to a head in the stunning final scene. A poignant, deeply moving film. **106m/C VHS, Beta.** *IT* Omero Antonutti, Margarita Lozano, Claudio Bigagli, Massimo Bonetti, Norma Martel; **D:** Paolo Taviani, Vittorio Taviani; **W:** Tonino Guerra, Giuliani G. De Negri, Paolo Taviani, Vittorio Taviani; **C:** Franco Di Giacomo; **M:** Nicola Piovani. Cannes Film Festival '82: Grand Jury Prize; National Society of Film Critics Awards '83: Best Director (Taviani), Best Director (Taviani), Best Film. *MGM, APD, AUD*

Night of the Sorcerers woof! 1970 An expedition to the Congo uncovers a bizarre tribe of vampire leopard women who lure young girls to their deaths. **85m/C VHS, Beta.** Jack Taylor, Simon Andrew, Kali Hansa; **D:** Armando de Ossorio. *UNI*

Night of the Strangler ✇✇ 1973 (R) A love affair between a white society girl and a young black man causes a chain of events that end with brutal murders in New Orleans. 88m/C **VHS, Beta.** Mickey Dolenz, James Ralston, Susan McCullough; **D:** Joy Houck Jr. *NO*

Night of the Twisters ✇✇½ 1995 A teenager and his new stepfather must work together to protect the family when tornadoes rip through their small Nebraska town. Based on the book by Ivy Ruckman. Made for cable. **?m/C VHS.** John Schneider, Devon Sawa, Lori Hallier, Helen Hughes. *GKK*

Night of the Warrior ✇ 1991 (R) Music videos and martial arts don't mix...not here, anyway. A hunky exotic-dance-club owner pays his disco bills by fighting in illegal, underground blood matches, but not enough to make it exciting. Lamas stars with real life wife Kinmont and mom Dahl.**CW:** Language, strong violence and drug content, and sensuality. 96m/C **VHS, LV.** Lorenzo Lamas, Anthony Geary, Kathleen Kinmont, Arlene Dahl. *THV*

Night of the Wilding ✇ 1990 Very, very loosely based on the story of the female jogger who was gang-raped and left for dead in New York's Central Park. Made for television, soon after the actual incident occurred. 90m/C **VHS, Beta, LV.** Erik Estrada, Kathrin Lautner; **D:** Joseph Merhi. *NO*

Night of the Zombies ✇ *Gamma 693; Night of the Wehrmacht Zombies* 1981 (R) WWII soldiers with eating disorders shuffle through 88 minutes of gratuitous gore, while pursued by porn star cum intelligence agent. From the director of "Bloodsucking Freaks." 88m/C **VHS.** James Gillis, Ryan Hilliard, Samantha Grey, Joel M. Reed; **D:** Joel M. Reed; **W:** Joel M. Reed. *PSM*

Night of the Zombies woof! *Apocalipsis Canibal; Hell of the Living Dead; Zombie Creeping Flesh* 1983 Staff of a scientific research center are killed and then resurrected as cannibals who prey on the living. The living will suffer again if trapped into watching. Mattei is pseudonym for director Vincent Dawn. Cheap, dubbed, and possessing minimal coherence. 101m/C **VHS, Beta.** *IT SP* Margit Evelyn Newton, Frank Garfield, Selan Karay; **D:** Bruno Mattei. *VES, PSM*

Night on Earth ✇✇✇ 1991 (R) Jarmusch's "road" movie comprises five different stories taking place on the same night in five different cities—Los Angeles, New York, Paris, Rome, and Helsinki—between cabbies and their passengers. As with any anthology some stories work better than others but all have their moments in this ambitious film with its outstanding international cast. Subtitled in English for the three foreign segments.**CW:** Language and sensuality. 125m/C **VHS, LV.** Winona Ryder, Gena Rowlands, Giancarlo Esposito, Armin Mueller-Stahl, Rosie Perez, Beatrice Dalle, Roberto Benigni, Paolo Bonacelli, Matti Pellonpaa, Kari Vaananen, Sakari Kuosmanen, Tomi Salmela, Lisanne Falk, Isaach de Bankole, Alan Randolph Scott, Anthony Portillo, Richard Boes, Pascal Nzonzi, Emile Abossolo-M'Bo; **D:** Jim Jarmusch; **W:** Jim Jarmusch; **C:** Frederick Elmes; **M:** Tom Waits, Kathleen Brennan. Independent Spirit Awards '93: Best Cinematography.*NLC, FAF*

Night Partners ✇½ 1983 Bored housewives assist the police to patrol the streets after the kids have gone to bed. Originally made for television with the intention of turning it into a series, but the script doesn't hold water. 100m/C **VHS, Beta.** Yvette Mimieux, Diana Canova, Arlen Dean Snyder, M. Emmet Walsh, Patricia Davis, Larry Linville; **D:** Noel Nosseck. *NWV*

The Night Patrol ✇✇½ 1926 Talmadge is a cop who winds up arresting his girlfriend's brother for murder. Convinced the boy is innocent, Talmadge disguises himself in order to infiltrate the gang he thinks is actually responsible for the crime. Lots of derring-do and a last-minute rescue from the electric chair. 53m/B **VHS.** Richard Talmadge, Mary Carr, Rose Blossom, Josef Swickard, Gardner James; **D:** Noel Mason Smith. *GPV*

Night Patrol woof! 1985 (R) The streets of Hollywood will never be the same after the night patrol runs amuck in the town. Crude imitation of "Police Academy." 87m/C **VHS, Beta, LV, Closed Caption.** Linda Blair, Pat Paulsen, Jaye P. Morgan, Jack Riley, Murray Langston, Billy Barty, Noriyuki "Pat" Morita, Sydney Lassick, Andrew Dice Clay; **D:** Jackie Kong; **C:** Hanania Baer. Golden Raspberry Awards '85: Worst Actress (Blair). *NWV, VTR*

The Night Porter ✇✇ *Il Portiere de Notte* 1974 (R) Max, an ex-SS concentration camp officer, unexpectedly meets his former lover-victim at the Viennese hotel where he works as the night porter. After they get reacquainted, the couple must hide from the porter's ex-Nazi friends who want the women dead because they fear she will disclose their past. A sado-masochistic voyage not for the faint-hearted. 115m/C **VHS, Beta, LV.** *IT* Dirk Bogarde, Charlotte Rampling, Phillippe LeRoy, Gabriele Ferzetti, Isa Miranda; **D:** Liliana Cavani. *GLV, NLC*

Night Rhythms ✇½ 1992 (R) Nick West is a radio talk show host with a sexy voice that causes his women listeners to reveal their most intimate fantasies and problems to him on the air. When one listener goes too far, it's murder, and Nick must work to prove his innocence in the crime if he intends to save his career—and his life. Also available in an unrated version.**CW:** Sex-related dialogue and strong sexuality. **?m/C VHS, LV, Closed Caption.** Martin Hewitt, Delia Sheppard, David Carradine, Terry Tweed, Sam Jones, Deborah Driggs, Julie Strain; **D:** Alexander Gregory Hippolyte. *IMP, MOV*

Night Rider ✇ 1932 A cowboy posing as a gunman ends a trail of murder and violence in a small western town. 54m/B **VHS, Beta.** Harry Carey Sr., George "Gabby" Hayes. *NOS, DVT*

Night Riders of Montana ✇ 1950 A state ranger helps a group of ranchers to fight off a band of rustlers. 60m/B **VHS, Beta.** Allan "Rocky" Lane. *DVT*

Night Ripper ✇ 1986 A psychopathic killer stalks high fashion models and kills them by carving them up. Lots of violence. 88m/C **VHS, Beta.** James Hansen, April Anne, Larry Thomas; **D:** Jeff Hathcock. *NO*

Night School ✇ *Terror Eyes* 1981 (R) A police detective must find out who has been decapitating the women attending night school at Wendell College. Ward's first film. 89m/C **VHS, Beta.** Edward Albert, Rachel Ward, Leonard Mann, Drew Snyder, Joseph R. Sicari; **D:** Ken Hughes; **W:** Ruth Avergon; **M:** Brad Fiedel. *FOX*

Night Screams ✇ 1987 Violent scaremonger about two escaped convicts who crash a high school house party. Kids and convicts start getting killed, one by one. 85m/C **VHS, Beta.** Joe Manno, Ron Thomas, Randy Lundsford, Megan Wyss; **D:** Allen Plone. *PSM*

Night Shadow ✇ 1990 (R) A woman, returning home after being away for years, picks up a hitchhiker. Soon after her arrival, terrible serial killings begin, and only she has the nerve to track down the killer. 90m/C **VHS.** Brenda Vance, Dana Chan, Tom Boylan; **D:** Randolph Cohlan; **W:** Randolph Cohlan. *NO*

Night Shift ✇✇ 1982 (R) Two morgue attendants, dull Winkler and manic Keaton, decide to spice up their latenight shift by running a call-girl service on the side. Keaton turns in a fine performance in his film debut, and Howard's sure-handed direction almost overcome the silly premise. 106m/C **VHS, Beta, LV.** Henry Winkler, Michael Keaton, Shelley Long, Kevin Costner, Pat Corley, Bobby DiCicco, Nita Talbot, Richard Belzer, Shannen Doherty; **D:** Ron Howard; **W:** Babaloo Mandel, Lowell Ganz; **M:** Burt Bacharach. *WAR*

Night Siege Project: Shadowchaser 2 ✇✇½ *Project Shadowchaser 2* 1994 (R) Smooth actioner finds a terrorist android taking over a nuclear arsenal and threatening to make Washington, D.C. a mushroom cloud. Naturally, there's a hero (and a heroine) to take care of the evildoers. 97m/C **VHS, LV, Closed Caption.** Bryan Genesse, Frank Zagarino, Beth Toussaint; **D:** John Eyres; **W:** Nick Davis; **M:** Steve Edwards. *TTC, NLC*

Night Slasher ✇ 1984 A madman enjoys spilling the innards of London prostitutes with his dagger. 87m/C **VHS, Beta.** Jack May, Linda Marlowe. *UNI*

Night Stage to Galveston ✇½ 1952 Autry leads his Texas Rangers on a mission to uncover corruption in the Texas State Police during the turbulent post-Civil War era. 61m/B **VHS, Beta.** Gene Autry, Pat Buttram, Virginia Huston, Thurston Hall; **D:** George Archainbaud. *CCB*

Night Stalker ✇✇ 1987 (R) A bloodthirsty serial killer is tracked by a detective through the streets in New York. The usual rigamarole of fisticuffs, gunplay, and car chases ensure. Impressive acting from Napier raises the film from the run-of-the-mill. 91m/C **VHS, Beta.** Charles Napier, John Goff, Robert Viharo, Robert Z'Dar, Joseph Gian, Gary Crosby, Joan Chen, Michelle Reese; **D:** Max Cleven; **C:** Don Burgess. *VES*

The Night Stalker: Two Tales of Terror 1974 Two episodes from the television series "Kolchak: The Night Stalker" in which McGavin plays a nosy newspaper reporter who constantly stumbles upon occult phenomenon. Episodes are "Jack the Ripper" and "The Vampire." 98m/C **VHS, Beta.** Darren McGavin, Simon Oakland. *USH*

Night Terror ✇ 1976 Everyone's after a hausfrau who saw a highway patrolman murdered on an expressway...including the psychotic murderer. Pretty standard fare. Made for television. 73m/C **VHS, Beta.** Valerie Harper, Richard Romanus, Michael Tolan, Beatrice Manley, John Quade, Quinn Cummings, Nicholas Pryor; **D:** E.W. Swackhamer. *WOV*

Night Terror ✇✇ 1989 A man wakes up from a nightmare only to find that his terrors are still present. 90m/C **VHS, Beta.** Lloyd B. Mote, Jeff Keel, Guy Ecker, Jon Hoffman, Michael Coopet; **D:** Michael Weaver, Paul Howard. *NO*

The Night the City Screamed ✇✇½ 1980 (PG) It's the hottest day of the year, the city experiences a massive blackout, and nighttime brings out less-than-noble emotions amongst the citizenry. Made for television. 96m/C **VHS.** Raymond Burr, Georg Stanford Brown, Linda Purl, Robert Culp, Clifton Davis, David Cassidy, George DiCenzo, Gary Frank, Don Meredith, Shelley Smith, Vic Tayback, Dick Anthony Williams; **D:** Harry Falk; **W:** Larry Brody. *COL*

The Night the Lights Went Out in Georgia ✇✇ 1981 (PG) Loosely based on the popular hit song, the film follows a brother and sister as they try to cash in on the country music scene in Nashville. McNichol is engaging. 112m/C **VHS, Beta.** Kristy McNichol, Dennis Quaid, Mark Hamill, Don Stroud; **D:** Ronald F. Maxwell; **W:** Bob Bonney; **C:** Bill Butler; **M:** David Shire. *TWE*

The Night They Raided Minsky's ✇✇ *The Night They Invented Striptease* 1969 (PG) Chaotic but interesting period comedy about a young Amish girl who leaves her tyrannical father to come to New York City in the 1920s. She winds up at Minsky's Burlesque and accidentally invents the striptease. Lahr's last performance—he died during filming. ♫The Night They Raided Minsky's; Take Ten Terrific Girls But Only 9 Costumes; How I Love Her; Perfect Gentleman; You Rat, You; Penny Arcade; Wait For Me. 97m/C **VHS, Beta, Closed Caption.** Jason Robards Jr., Britt Ekland, Elliott Gould, Bert Lahr, Norman Wisdom, Denholm Elliott; **D:** William Friedkin; **W:** Norman Lear, Arnold Schulman. *FOX*

The Night They Robbed Big Bertha's 🐾 1983 Bungling burglar attempts to knock off Big Bertha's massage parlor. **83m/C VHS, Beta.** Robert Nichols. *NO*

The Night They Saved Christmas 🐾½ 1987 A Christmas special in which Santa's North Pole headquarters is endangered by the progress of an expanding oil company. Will the attempts of three children be enough to save the day? **94m/C VHS, Beta.** Art Carney, Jaclyn Smith, Paul Williams, Paul LeMat; **D:** Jackie Cooper. *CAF, PSM*

Night Tide 🐾🐾½ 1963 Hopper in another off the wall character study, this time as a lonely sailor. He falls for a mermaid (Lawson) who works at the dock. She may be a descendent of the man-killing Sirens. Interesting and different little love story, sometimes advertised as horror, which it is not. **84m/B VHS.** Dennis Hopper, Gavin Muir, Luana Anders, Marjorie Eaton, Tom Dillon; **D:** Curtis Harrington. *SNC, FRG, TPV*

Night Time in Nevada 🐾🐾½ 1948 Young woman heads West to claim $50,000 trust left by dear old dad, but his crooked lawyer and associate have their hands in the pot. Cowboy Roy rides horse and flexes dimples while helping helpless girl. **67m/B VHS, Beta, 8mm.** Roy Rogers, Adele Mara, Andy Devine, Grant Withers, Joseph Crehan; **D:** William Witney. *NOS, HEG, VYY*

A Night to Remember 🐾🐾🐾 1942 A murder-mystery writer's wife convinces him to move to a new apartment because she thinks the change might help him finish a novel he started long ago. When they find a dead body behind their new building, they try their hands at sleuthing. A clever and witty mystery, indeed, supported by likeable performances. **91m/B VHS.** Loretta Young, Brian Aherne, Sidney Toler, Gale Sondergaard, William Wright, Donald MacBride, Blanche Yurka; **D:** Richard Wallace. *COL*

A Night to Remember 🐾🐾🐾 1958 Gripping tale of the voyage of the Titanic with an interesting account of action in the face of danger and courage amid despair. Large cast is effectively used. Adapted by Eric Ambler from the book by Walter Lord. **119m/B VHS, Beta, LV.** Kenneth More, David McCallum, Anthony Bushell, Honor Blackman, Michael Goodliffe, George Rose, Laurence Naismith, Frank Lawton, Alec McCowen, Jill Dixon, John Cairney, Joseph Tomelty, Jack Watling, Richard Clarke, Ralph Michael, Keneth Kent, C.V. France, Frederick Valk, Morland Graham, Wally Patch, Irene Handl, Alien Lieven, David Horne; **D:** Roy Ward Baker; **W:** Eric Ambler; **C:** Geoffrey Unsworth. Golden Globe Awards '59: Best Foreign Film; National Board of Review Awards '58: 5 Best Foreign Films of the Year. *PAR, HMV*

The Night Train to Kathmandu 🐾🐾 1988 A young girl accompanies her parents on a research expedition to Nepal, where her head is turned by an exotically handsome young Sherpa. Old family without much help from actors or director. Made for cable. **102m/C VHS, Beta, LV, Closed Caption.** Milla Jovovich, Pernell Roberts, Eddie Castrodad; **D:** Robert Wiemer. *PAR*

Night Train to Munich 🐾🐾🐾 1940 *Night Train; Gestapo* There's Nazi intrigue galore aboard a big train when a scientist's daughter joins allied intelligence agents in retrieving some secret documents. From the book "Report on a Fugitive" by Gordon Wellesley. **93m/B VHS, Beta.** *GB* Margaret Lockwood, Rex Harrison, Paul Henreid, Basil Radford, Naunton Wayne, James Harcourt, Felix Aylmer, Roland Culver, Raymond Huntley, Austin Trevor, Keneth Kent, C.V. France, Frederick Valk, Morland Graham, Wally Patch, Irene Handl, Alien Lieven, David Horne; **D:** Carol Reed; **W:** Frank Launder, Sidney Gilliat. *KIV, DVT, HEG*

Night Train to Terror woof! 1984 (R) Strange things start happening on the train where a rock band makes its last appearance. Clips from other horror films were pieced together to make this film that's so bad it's almost good. **98m/C VHS, Beta.** John Phillip Law, Cameron Mitchell, Marc Lawrence, Charles Moll, Ferdinand "Ferdy" Mayne; **D:** Jay Schlossberg-Cohen. *PSM*

Night Train to Venice 🐾½ 1993 (R) Martin (Grant) is aboard the Orient Express on his way to Venice to deliver his book about the rise of neo-Nazism. He meets a mystery man (McDowell) and an actress (Welch) with ties to a neo-Nazi group, who also happen to be aboard the train and anxious to stop Martin from delivering his expose. Extended dream sequences and flashbacks tend to stop the story cold but Grant is a draw (and probably the only reason this mish-mash has been released to video).*CW:* Language; sexuality; violence; drug content. **98m/C VHS, LV, Closed Caption.** Hugh Grant, Malcolm McDowell, Tahnee Welch, Kristina Soderbaum; **D:** Carlo U. Quinterio; **W:** Leo Tichat; **M:** Alexander Bubenheim. *LIV, WEA*

Night Vision 🐾 1987 A young writer in the big city is given a video monitor by a street thief which is equipped with some remarkable features, including the ability to present scenes of future murders and demon worship. **102m/C VHS, Beta.** Ellie Martins, Stacy Carson, Shirley Ross, Tony Carpenter; **D:** Michael Krueger. *PSM*

The Night Visitor 🐾🐾½ 1970 (PG) A man in a prison for the criminally insane seeks violent vengeance on those he believes have set him up. Heavily detailed, slow moving. Ullman and von Sydow can do better. **106m/C VHS, Beta.** *GB DK* Max von Sydow, Liv Ullmann, Trevor Howard, Per Oscarsson, Andrew Keir; **D:** Laslo Benedek; **M:** Henry Mancini. *VCI*

Night Visitor 🐾 *Never Cry Devil* 1989 (R) A retired police detective teams up with a teenage peeping tom to disclose the identity of a satanic serial killer. The killer, of course, is one of the youth's teachers. **95m/C VHS, Beta.** Derek Rydell, Shannon Tweed, Elliott Gould, Allen (Goorwitz) Garfield, Michael J. Pollard, Richard Roundtree, Henry Gibson; **D:** Rupert Hitzig; **W:** Randal Viscovich. *MGM*

The Night Walker 🐾🐾½ 1964 Stanwyck is always worth watching and she has the best moments in this psycho-thriller which suffers from a low-budget and confused script. The basic story has Stanwyck as a rich widow with a recurring nightmare featuring a faceless lover. There's also a too-helpful lawyer (Taylor), a suspicious private detective (Bochner)—and maybe her husband isn't so dead after all. Taylor and Stanwyck, who had once been married, worked together for the first time in 27 years. **86m/B VHS, Closed Caption.** Barbara Stanwyck, Robert Taylor, Lloyd Bochner, Hayden Rorke, Judith Meredith, Rochelle Hudson; **D:** William Castle; **W:** Robert Bloch. *USH, GPV*

Night Warning 🐾🐾 *Nightmare Maker; Butcher Baker (Nightmare Maker)* 1982 (R) A slasher gorefest redeemed by Tyrrell's go-for-broke performance. She plays a sexually repressed aunt who makes up for her problems by going on murderous rampages. Hide the kitchen knives! **96m/C VHS, Beta.** Bo Svenson, Jimmy McNichol, Susan Tyrrell, Julia Duffy; **D:** William Asher; **W:** Stephen Breimer. *NO*

Night Wars 🐾½ 1988 Two ex-POWs who are plagued by their memories turn to dream therapy to relive their escape. Eventually, they rescue a buddy they left behind. **90m/C VHS, Beta.** Dan Haggerty, Brian O'Connor, Cameron Smith; **D:** David A. Prior. *COL*

Night Watch 🐾½ *Le Trou; Il Buco* 1972 A woman recovering from a nervous breakdown witnesses a murder, but no one will believe her. **100m/C VHS, Beta.** Elizabeth Taylor, Laurence Harvey, Billie Whitelaw; **D:** Brian G. Hutton; **C:** Billy Williams. *MED*

The Night We Never Met 🐾🐾½ 1993 (R) Three yuppies bring different visions of romance and a case of mistaken identity to a time-share apartment in New York's Greenwich Village. Sam (Broderick) needs a quiet space to get over being dumped by a flaky performance artist (Tripplehorn). Ellen (Sciorra) is looking for space to paint away from the confines of her thick-headed spouse (Mantell). Brian, the organizer of the living arrangement, wants a space where he can be one of the boys and escape from his cloying fiancee (Bateman). Fairly predictable but enjoyable romantic comedy.*CW:* Language. **98m/C VHS.** Matthew Broderick, Jeanne Tripplehorn, Kevin Anderson, Justine Bateman, Annabella Sciorra, Christine Baranski, Doris Roberts, Dominic Chianese, Michael Mantell, Tim Guinee, Greg Germann, Dana Wheeler-Nicholson, Louise Lasser, Bill Campbell, Ranjit Chowdhry, Garry Shandling, Katharine Houghton, Brooke Smith; **D:** Warren Leight; **W:** Warren Leight; **M:** Evan Lurie. *HBO*

Night Zoo 🐾🐾 *Un Zoo, La Nuit* 1987 A confusing story about a father/son reconciliation and the lurid underworld of drugs and sex in Montreal. The graphic sex and violence undermines the sensitive aspects of the film. **115m/C VHS, Beta, LV.** *CA* Gilles Maheu, Roger Le Bel, Lynne Adams, German Houde; **D:** Jean-Claude Lauzon. Genie Awards '88: Best Actor (Le Bel), Best Director (Lauzon), Best Film, Best Supporting Actor (Houde). *VTR, NWV, IME*

Nightbreaker 🐾🐾🐾 1989 Revelation of the U.S. government's deliberate exposure of servicemen to atomic bomb tests and the resulting radiation, in order to observe the effects on humans. Sheen and his son, Estevez, portray a U.S. doctor in the 1980s and the 1950s, respectively. **100m/C VHS.** Martin Sheen, Emilio Estevez, Lea Thompson, Melinda Dillon, Nicholas Pryor, Joe Pantoliano; **D:** Peter Markle; **W:** T.S. Cook; **M:** Peter Bernstein. *TTC*

The Nightcomers 🐾 1972 (R) A pretend "prequel" to Henry James's "The Turn of the Screw," wherein an Irish gardener trysts with the nanny of two watchful children who believe that lovers unite in death. Don't be fooled: stick to the original. **96m/C VHS, Beta, LV.** *GB* Marlon Brando, Stephanie Beacham, Thora Hird; **D:** Michael Winner. *COL, NLC*

Nightfall 🐾🐾🐾 1956 Ray, accused of a crime he didn't commit, is forced to flee from both the law and the underworld. Classic example of film noir, brilliantly filmed by Tourneur. **78m/B VHS.** Aldo Ray, Brian Keith, Anne Bancroft, Jocelyn Brando, James Gregory, Frank Albertson; **D:** Jacques Tourneur; **W:** Stirling Silliphant. *GKK*

Nightfall 🐾🐾 1988 (PG-13) Television adaptation of the classic Isaac Asimov short story. A planet that has two suns (and therefore no night) experiences an eclipse and its inhabitants go mad. **87m/C VHS, Beta.** David Birney, Sarah Douglas, Alexis Kanner, Andra Millian; **D:** Paul Mayersberg; **C:** Darius Wolski. *MGM*

Nightflyers 🐾½ 1987 (R) Aboard a weathered space freighter, the crew experience a series of deadly accidents caused by an unknown evil presence. From a novella by George R.R. Martin; T.C. Blake is better known as Robert Collector. **88m/C VHS, Beta, LV.** Michael Praed, Michael Des Barres, Catherine Mary Stewart, John Standing, Lisa Blount; **D:** T.C. Blake. *NO*

Nightforce 🐾 1986 (R) Five buddies plunge into Central American jungles to rescue a young girl held by terrorists. **87m/C VHS, Beta.** Linda Blair, James Van Patten, Chad McQueen, Richard Lynch, Cameron Mitchell; **D:** Lawrence Foldes. *NO*

Nighthawks 🐾🐾½ 1981 (R) New York City cops scour Manhattan to hunt down an international terrorist on the loose. They race from disco to subway to an airborne tramway. Exciting and well paced. Hauer's American film debut. **100m/C VHS, Beta, LV, Closed Caption.** Sylvester Stallone, Billy Dee Williams, Rutger Hauer, Lindsay Wagner, Nigel Davenport, Persis Khambatta, Catherine Mary Stewart, Joe Spinell; **D:** Bruce Malmuth; **M:** Keith Emerson. *USH*

The Nightingale 1983 From "Faerie Tale Theatre" comes the story of an Emperor who discovers the value of true friendship and loyalty from his palace kitchen maid who gives him a nightingale. **60m/C VHS, Beta, LV, Closed Caption.** Mick Jagger, Barbara Hershey, Bud Cort, Mako; **D:** Ivan Passer. *KUI, FOX, FCT*

Nightjohn 🐾🐾½ 1996 (PG-13) Nightjohn (Lumbly) is the new slave purchased by Southern plantation owner Clel Walker (Bridges). He moves into the cabin shared by 12-year-old Sarny

(Jones) and Delie (Toussaint). When Sarny finds out that Nightjohn can read and write (illegal for slaves), she's determined to learn from him. And with her new knowledge, Sarny looks for ways to help her fellow slaves. Based on Gary Paulsen's 1993 novel; made for cable and filmed on location at Rip Raps Plantation in Sumter, South Carolina.**CW:** Some scenes of racial oppression and abuse. **96m/C VHS.** Carl Lumbly, Allison Jones, Beau Bridges, Lorraine Toussaint, Bill Cobbs, Kathleen York, Gabriel Casseus, Tom Nowicki, Monica Ford, Joel Thomas Traywick; *D:* Charles Burnett; *W:* Bill Cain; *C:* Elliot Davis; *M:* Stephen James Taylor. *HMK*

Nightkill 𝄢𝄢½ 1980 (R) Simple love affair turns into a deadly game of cat and mouse when a bored wife plots to do away with her wealthy, powerful husband with the aid of her attractive lover. Mitchum is the reluctant investigator pulled into the game. **104m/C VHS, Beta.** Jaclyn Smith, Mike Connors, James Franciscus, Robert Mitchum, Sybil Danning; *D:* Ted Post. *NLC*

Nightlife 𝄢𝄢½ 1990 An ancient vampiress who rises from the dead spends her time haunting a blood clinic, where the Jewish hematologist starts to fall for her. Made for cable. **93m/C VHS, Beta, LV.** Ben Cross, Maryam D'Abo, Keith Szarabajka, Jesse Corti, Oliver Clark, Glenn Shadix, Camille Saviola; *D:* Daniel Taplitz. *USH*

The Nightman 𝄢𝄢 1993 (R) Ex-soldier Marcoux becomes the night manager of a failing southern resort, run by sexy, and lonely, Kerns. They begin an affair, which turns sour when Roberston, Kerns' teenaged daughter, also falls for the stud. Then mom is murdered and Marcoux goes to prison. But 18 years later Robertson's past comes back to haunt her. Just what did happen all those years ago? Made for television thriller with additional footage. **96m/C VHS, LV.** Ted Marcoux, Jenny Robertson, Joanna Kerns; *D:* Charles Haid; *W:* James Poe; *M:* Gary Chang. *APX*

Nightmare 𝄢𝄢½ 1963 As a child, Janet sees her insane mother stab her father to death. Left in the care of two guardians, the now-grown Janet has recurring nightmares and fears she's inherited her mother's madness. Routine, with red herrings galore. **83m/B VHS, Closed Caption.** *GB* Jennie Linden, David Knight, Moira Redmond, Brenda Bruce; *D:* Freddie Francis; *W:* Jimmy Sangster; *C:* John Wilcox; *M:* Don Banks. *USH*

Nightmare woof! *Blood Splash* 1982 (R) Boring splatterthon has a young boy hacking his father and his aggressive mistress to pieces when he discovers them in bed. He grows up to be a psycho who continues along the same lines. Humorless and dreadful, the original ads claimed Tom Savini did the special effects. He had nothing to do with it. **97m/C VHS, Beta.** Baird Stafford, Sharon Smith, C.J. Cooke, Mik Cribben, Kathleen Ferguson, Danny Ronan; *D:* Romano Scavolini; *W:* Romano Scavolini. *NO*

Nightmare 𝄢𝄢 1991 (PG-13) Single mom Linda Hemmings (Principal) takes matters into her own hands when her daughter Dana (Harris) is kidnapped. Though Dana escapes and her assailant, Edward Ryter (Banks), is arrested, he's soon released and threatening Dana to prevent her testifying. So mom teams up with police detective Jake Wilman (Sorvino) to get the goods on the psycho before he can do further harm.**CW:** Mature theme; element of terror. **84m/C VHS.** Victoria Principal, Jonathan Banks, Paul Sorvino, Danielle Harris; *D:* John Pasquin; *W:* Rich Husky; *C:* Denis Lewiston; *M:* Dana Kaproff. *NHO*

Nightmare at Bittercreek 𝄢𝄢 1991 (PG-13) Four babes and a tour guide are pursued by psycho gang in the Sierra mountains. Made for television nightmare in your living room. **92m/C VHS.** Tom Skerritt, Joanna Cassidy, Lindsay Wagner, Constance McCashin, Janne Mortil; *D:* Tim Burstall. *THV*

Nightmare at 43 Hillcrest 1974 A family's life becomes a living hell when the police mistakenly raid their house. Based on a true story. **72m/C VHS, Beta.** Jim Hutton, Mariette Hartley. *NO*

Nightmare at Noon 𝄢 1987 (R) Watered-down thriller about a small desert town beset by violent terrorists (who are really locals gone mad from a chemical experiment dumped into the water system). Only the sheriff's small staff is there to stop them. **96m/C VHS.** Wings Hauser, George Kennedy, Bo Hopkins, Brion James, Kimberly Beck, Kimberly Ross; *D:* Nico Mastorakis. *REP*

The Nightmare Before Christmas 𝄢𝄢𝄢 *Tim Burton's The Nightmare Before Christmas* 1993 (PG) Back when he was an animator trainee at Disney, Burton came up with this adventurous idea but couldn't get it made; subsequent directorial success brought more clout. Relies on a painstaking stop-motion technique that took more than two years to film and is justifiably amazing. The story revolves around Jack Skellington, the Pumpkin King of the dangerously weird Halloweentown. Suffering from ennui, he accidentally discovers the wonders of Christmastown and decides to kidnap Santa and rule over this peaceable holiday. Fast pace is maintained by the equally breathless score. Not cuddly, best appreciated by those with a feel for the macabre. **75m/C VHS, LV, Closed Caption.** *D:* Henry Selick; *W:* Caroline Thompson, Tim Burton; *M:* Danny Elfman; *V:* Danny Elfman, Chris Sarandon, Catherine O'Hara, William Hickey, Ken Page, Ed Ivory, Paul (Pee Wee Herman) Reubens, Glenn Shadix. Nominations: Academy Awards '93: Best Visual Effects; Golden Globe Awards '94: Best Original Score. *TOU*

Nightmare Castle 𝄢𝄢 *Amanti d'Oltretomba; Night of the Doomed; The Faceless Monsters; Lovers From Beyond the Tomb* 1965 Jealous mad scientist murders his wife and her lover. Then he conducts a bizarre experiment, using the dead couple's blood to rejuvenate an old servant. Not quite satisfied with his revenge, he then seeks to marry his late wife's sister after realizing that she has been left the inheritance. In time, the perturbed ghosts of the late lovers appear and seek revenge. A real nightmare. **90m/B VHS, Beta.** *IT* Barbara Steele, Paul Muller, Helga Line; *D:* Allan Grunewald; *M:* Ennio Morricone. *SNC, HHT*

Nightmare in Badham County 𝄢 *Nightmare* 1976 Two girls get arrested on trumped-up charges in a small backwoods town. They soon discover that the prison farm is a front for a slavery ring. Made for television. **100m/C VHS, Beta.** Deborah Raffin, Lynne Moody, Chuck Connors, Della Reese, Robert Reed, Ralph Bellamy, Tina Louise; *D:* John Llewellyn Moxey; *M:* Charles Bernstein. *THV*

Nightmare in Blood 𝄢½ *Horror Convention* 1975 Vampires lurk in San Francisco and wreak havoc on the night life. **90m/C VHS, Beta.** Kerwin Mathews, Jerry Walter, Barrie Youngfellow; *D:* John Stanley. *VCD*

Nightmare in Wax 𝄢½ *Crimes in the Wax Museum* 1969 After suffering disfigurement in a fight with a studio boss, a former make-up man starts a wax museum. For fun, he injects movie stars with a formula that turns them into statues. **91m/C VHS, Beta.** Cameron Mitchell, Anne Helm; *D:* Bud Townsend. *MRV*

A Nightmare on Elm Street 𝄢𝄢½ 1984 (R) Feverish, genuinely frightening horror film about Freddy Krueger (Englund), a scarred maniac in a fedora and razor-fingered gloves who kills neighborhood teens in their dreams and, subsequently, in reality. Of the children-fight-back genre, in which the lead victim (Langenkamp) ingeniously goes to great lengths to destroy Freddy. In the tradition of "Friday the 13th" and "Halloween;" spawned a "Freddy" phenomenon: five sequels (to date); a TV series ("Freddy's Nightmares," a horror anthology show hosted by Englund capitalized on his character); and an army of razor-clawed trick or treaters at Halloween.

92m/C VHS, Beta, LV, Closed Caption. John Saxon, Heather Langenkamp, Ronee Blakley, Robert Englund, Amanda Wyss, Nick Corri, Johnny Depp, Charles Fleischer; *D:* Wes Craven; *W:* Wes Craven; *M:* Charles Bernstein. *MED, CDV, IME*

A Nightmare on Elm Street 2: Freddy's Revenge 𝄢½ 1985 (R) Mediocre sequel to the popular horror film. Freddy, the dream-haunting psychopath with the ginsu knife hands, returns to possess a teenager's body in order to kill again. Nothing new here, however praise is due for the stunning high-tech dream sequence. **87m/C VHS, Beta, LV, Closed Caption.** Mark Patton, Hope Lange, Clu Gulager, Robert Englund, Kim Myers; *D:* Jack Sholder; *W:* David Chaskin. *MED, CDV, IME*

A Nightmare on Elm Street 3: Dream Warriors 𝄢𝄢𝄢 1987 (R) Chapter three in this slice and dice series. Freddy Krueger is at it again, haunting the dreams of unsuspecting suburban teens. Langenkamp, the nightmare-freaked heroine from the first film, returns to counsel the latest victims of Freddy-infested dreams. Noted for the special effects wizardry but little else, Part Three was produced on a $4.5 million shoe string and took in more than $40 million, making it one of the most successful independently produced films in Hollywood. Followed by "Nightmare on Elmstreet 4: Dream Master." **96m/C VHS, Beta, LV, Closed Caption.** Patricia Arquette, Robert Englund, John Saxon, Craig Wasson, Heather Langenkamp, Dick Cavett, Priscilla Pointer, Laurence "Larry" Fishburne; *D:* Chuck Russell; *W:* Chuck Russell, Bruce Wagner, Wes Craven, Frank Darabont; *C:* Roy Wagner; *M:* Angelo Badalamenti. *MED, CDV, IME*

A Nightmare on Elm Street 4: Dream Master 𝄢𝄢½ 1988 (R) Freddy Krueger is still preying on people in their dreams, but he may have met his match as he battles for supremacy with a telepathically talented girl. What Part 4 lacks in substance, it makes up for in visual verve, including scenes of a kid drowning in his waterbed, and a pizza covered with pepperoni-like faces of Freddy's previous victims. This box office bonanza set a new record as the most successful opening weekend of any independently released film. Followed by "A Nightmare on Elm Street: A Dream Child." **99m/C VHS, Beta, LV, Closed Caption.** Robert Englund, Rodney Eastman, Danny Hassel, Andras Jones, Tuesday Knight, Lisa Wilcox, Ken Sagoes, Toy Newkirk, Brooke Theiss, Brooke Bundy; *D:* Renny Harlin; *W:* Scott Pierce, Brian Helgeland; *M:* Craig Safan. *MED, CDV, IME*

A Nightmare on Elm Street 5: Dream Child 𝄢𝄢 1989 (R) The fifth installment of Freddy Krueger's never-ending adventures. Here, America's favorite knife-wielding burn victim, unable to best the Dream Master from the previous film, haunts the dreams of her unborn fetus. Gore fans may be disappointed to discover that much of the blood and guts ended up on the cutting room floor. **90m/C VHS, Beta, LV, Closed Caption.** Robert Englund, Lisa Wilcox, Kelly Jo Minter, Danny Hassel; *D:* Stephen Hopkins; *W:* Leslie Bohem; *M:* Jay Michael Ferguson. Golden Raspberry Awards '89: Worst Song ("Bring Your Daughter to the Slaughter"). *IME, MED, VTR*

Nightmare on the 13th Floor 𝄢 1990 (PG-13) A travel writer at an old hotel glimpses murder on a supposedly non-existent floor. Nasty devil-worshippers are afoot, but the chills in this mild made-for-cable throwaway seldom dip below room temperature. **85m/C VHS, Beta, Closed Caption.** Michael Greene, John Karlen, Louise Fletcher, Alan Fudge, James Brolin; *D:* Walter Grauman. *PAR*

Nightmare Sisters woof! 1987 (R) Three sorority sisters become possessed by a demon and then sexually ravage a nearby fraternity. **83m/C VHS, Beta.** Brinke Stevens, Michelle (McClellan) Bauer, Linnea Quigley; *D:* David DeCoteau. *TWE*

Nightmare Weekend ⚔ **1986 (R)** A professor's evil assistant lures three young women into his lab and performs cruel and vicious experiments that transform the girls and their dates into crazed zombies. **86m/C VHS, Beta.** Dale Midkiff, Debbie Laster, Debra Hunter, Lori Lewis; **D:** Henry Sala. *LIV*

The Nightmare Years **1989** An American reporter in Nazi Germany dares to report the truth to an unbelieving world. Based on a true story. Two cassettes. **237m/C VHS, Beta.** Sam Waterston, Marthe Keller, Kurtwood Smith; **D:** Anthony Page; **M:** Vladimir Cosma. *TTC*

Nightmares ⚔⚔ **1983 (PG)** A less-than-thrilling horror anthology featuring four tales in which common, everyday occurrences take on the ingredients of a nightmare. In the same vein as "Twilight Zone" and "Creepshow". **99m/C VHS, Beta.** Christina Raines, Emilio Estevez, Moon Zappa, Lance Henriksen, Richard Masur, Veronica Cartwright; **D:** Joseph Sargent; **W:** Jeffrey Bloom, Christopher Crowe. *USH*

Nights and Days ⚔⚔½ **1976** Adaptation of writer Maria Dabrowska's tale about a Polish family chronicles the persecution, expulsions, and land grabbing that occurred after the unsuccessful Uprising of 1864. In Polish with English subtitles. **255m/C VHS.** *PL* Jadwiga Baranska, Jerzy Binczycki; **D:** Jerzy Antczak. Nominations: Academy Awards '76: Best Foreign Language Film. *FCT*

Nights in White Satin ⚔½ **1987** A made-for-video Cinderella story about the growing love between a fashion photographer and a young model whose boyfriend has just been murdered. **96m/C VHS, Beta.** Kenneth Gilman, Priscilla Harris; **D:** Michael Bernard. *PSM, PAR*

Nights of Cabiria ⚔⚔⚔½ *Le Notti de Cabiria; Cabiria* **1957** Fellini classic which details the personal decline of a naive streetwalker who thinks she's found true love. In Italian with English subtitles or dubbed. Basis for the musical "Sweet Charity." **111m/B VHS, Beta.** *IT* Giulietta Masina, Amedeo Nazzari; **D:** Federico Fellini; **W:** Federico Fellini, Tullio Pinelli, Ennio Flaiano; **M:** Nino Rota. Academy Awards '57: Best Foreign Language Film; Cannes Film Festival '57: Best Actress (Masina). *NOS, VYY, APD*

Nightscare ⚔⚔ *Night Scare; Beyond Bedlam* **1993 (R)** When Dr. Stephanie Lyell's drug behavior-modification experiment goes wrong it allows serial killer Marc Gilmour (Allen) to get to his victims through their dreams. The doc tries to prove to Detective Inspector Terry Hamilton (Fairbrass) that the drug is safe by injecting them both but things get out of hand. Adapted from the novel by Harry Adam Knight. **CW:** Strong horror violence and gore, sexuality and language. **89m/C VHS, LV, Closed Caption.** *GB* Craig Fairbrass, Elizabeth Hurley, Keith Allen, Jesse Birdsall, Craig Kelly; **D:** Vadim Jean; **W:** Vadim Jean. *LIV*

Nightstalker woof! **1979** A brother and sister who were condemned to eternal death 12,000 years ago must eat virgins to keep their bodies from rotting. Trouble is, while they search for dinner, the movie decomposes. For mature audiences with no fantasies of celluloid nirvana. **90m/C VHS, Beta.** Aldo Ray. *LIV*

Nightstick ⚔⚔½ *Calhoun* **1987 (R)** New York vigilante cop fights nasties who threaten to blow the lid off the city. Worse, they kidnap super cop's girl forcing him to save her along with the city. Lots of violence, predictable plot, and mediocre acting leave this one without much bang. **90m/C VHS, Beta.** Bruce Fairbairn, Kerrie Keane, John Vernon, Robert Vaughn, Isaac Hayes, Leslie Nielsen; **D:** Joseph L. Scanlan. *COL*

Nightwing ⚔½ **1979 (PG)** Suspense drama about three people who risk their lives to exterminate a colony of plague-carrying vampire bats in New Mexican Indian community. From the novel by Martin Cruz Smith and adapted by Smith, Steve Shagan, and Bud Shrake. OK viewing for the undiscriminating palate. **103m/C VHS, Beta, LV.** Nick Mancuso, David Warner, Kathryn Harrold, Strother Martin; **D:** Arthur Hiller; **M:** Henry Mancini. *COL*

Nightwish ⚔½ **1989 (R)** Students do more than homework when a professor leads them into their own horrifying dreams. Soon it becomes impossible to distinguish dreams from reality. **96m/C VHS, LV.** Jack Starrett, Robert Tessier, Clayton Rohner, Elizabeth Kaitan; **D:** Bruce Cook Jr. *VES*

Nijinsky ⚔⚔ **1980 (R)** An opulent biography of the famous ballet dancer. His exciting and innovative choreography gets little attention. The film concentrates on his infamous homosexual lifestyle and his relationship with impresario Sergei Diaghilev (Bates, in a tour-de-force performance). Lovely to look at, but slow and unconvincing. **125m/C VHS, Beta, Closed Caption.** Alan Bates, George de la Pena, Leslie Browne, Alan Badel, Carla Fracci, Colin Blakely, Ronald Pickup, Ronald Lacey, Vernon Dobtcheff, Jeremy Irons, Frederick Jaeger, Janet Suzman, Sian Phillips; **D:** Herbert Ross. *PAR*

Nikki, the Wild Dog of the North ⚔½ **1961 (G)** When a Malemute pup is separated from his Canadian trapper master, he teams up with a bear cub for a series of adventures. Later the pup is reunited with his former master for still more adventures. Adapted from a novel by James Oliver Curwood for Disney. **73m/C VHS, Beta.** *CA* Jean Coutu; **D:** Jack Couffer, Don Haldane. *DIS*

Nil by Mouth ⚔⚔ **1996** Oldman draws on his own dysfunctional working-class London background for his impressive writer/director debut, which casually puts you into the middle of one cockney family's life. There's brutal Ray (Winstone), husband to Val (Burke) and brother-in-law to young addict Billy (Creed-Miles), as well as his tough mother-in-law Janet (Morse) and her mother, Kath (Dore). Billy gets kicked out of the house by Ray and struggles to survive outside his family while a drunken Ray beats the pregnant Val, prompting a display of female solidarity. Formless pic drops into characters' lives at random, showcasing family loyalty and generosity. **120m/C VHS.** *GB* Ray Winstone, Kathy Burke, Charlie Creed-Miles, Laila Morse, Edna Dore, Steve Sweeney, Chrissie Cotterill, Jon Morrison, Jamie Forman; **D:** Gary Oldman; **W:** Gary Oldman; **C:** Ron Fortunato; **M:** Eric Clapton. Cannes Film Festival '97: Best Actress (Burke). *NYR*

Nina Takes a Lover ⚔⚔ **1994 (R)** Romantic comedy finds Nina (San Giacomo) deciding that the passion is gone from her three-year marriage so, while her husband is out of town, she picks up a nameless Welsh photographer (Rhys) and begins an affair. The affair is over as the movie begins but Nina tells her story to a tabloid journalist (O'Keefe) who's writing about adultery. Gimmicky, with shallow if attractive characters and an equally attractive San Francisco setting. **CW:** Language; some strong sexuality. **100m/C VHS, LV, Closed Caption.** Laura San Giacomo, Paul Rhys, Michael O'Keefe, Cristi Conaway, Fisher Stevens; **D:** Alan Jacobs; **W:** Alan Jacobs; **C:** Phil Parmet; **M:** Todd Boekelheide. *COL*

Nine Ages of Nakedness ⚔ **1969** The story of a man whose ancestors have been plagued by a strange problem: beautiful, naked women who create carnal chaos. **88m/C VHS, Beta.** Harrison Marks. *VDM, MED, MRV*

9 1/2 Ninjas ⚔⚔½ **1990 (R)** A cautious and disciplined martial artist trains a young and flirtatious woman in the ways of the ninja. His life becomes exciting in more ways than one, when he realizes she's being followed by ninjas with more on their minds than her training—they want to assassinate her! Crazy mixture of sex, kung fu and humor make this film one surprise after another. **88m/C VHS, Beta, LV, Closed Caption.** Michael Phenicie, Andee Gray, Tiny Lister; **D:** Aaron Worth; **W:** Bill Crounse. *REP*

9 1/2 Weeks ⚔⚔½ **1986 (R)** Chance meeting between a Wall Street exec and an art gallery employee evolves into an experimental sexual relationship bordering on sado-masochism. Video version is more explicit than the theatrical release, but not by much. Strong characterizations by both actors prevent this from being strictly pornography. Well-written, with strength of male and female personalities nicely balanced. Intriguing, but not for all tastes. **114m/C VHS, Beta, LV.** Mickey Rourke, Kim Basinger, Margaret Whitton, Karen Young, David Margulies, Christine Baranski, Roderick Cook, Dwight Weist; **D:** Adrian Lyne; **W:** Patricia Louisiana Knop, Zalman King; **C:** Peter Biziou; **M:** Jack Nitzsche. *MGM*

Nine Days a Queen ⚔⚔⚔ *Lady Jane Grey; Tudor Rose* **1936** An historical drama based on the life of Lady Jane Grey, proclaimed Queen of England after the death of Henry VIII of England and summarily executed for treason by Mary Tudor after a nine-day reign. An obscure tragedy with good performances and absorbing storyline. Remade as "Lady Jane" (1985). **80m/B VHS, Beta.** *GB* John Mills, Cedric Hardwicke, Nova Pilbeam, Sybil Thorndike, Leslie Perrins, Felix Aylmer, Miles Malleson, Frank Cellier, Desmond Tester, Gwen Francon-Davies, Martita Hunt, John Laurie, Roy Emerton, John Turnbull, J.H. Roberts; **D:** Robert Stevenson; **W:** Robert Stevenson, Miles Malleson. *HHT, DVT*

Nine Deaths of the Ninja woof! **1985 (R)** Faceless ninja warrior Kosugi leads a team of commandos on a mission to rescue a group of political prisoners held captive in the Philippine jungles. Features Ozone-depleted plot, incongruous performances, and inane dialogue, not to mention two main villains—a neurotic Nazi in a wheelchair and a black lesbian amazon—who chew jungle and bring bad art to a new level of appreciation. Amazing in its total badness. Produced by Cannon. **93m/C VHS, Beta.** Sho Kosugi, Brent Huff, Emelia Lesniak, Regina Richardson; **D:** Emmett Alston; **W:** Emmett Alston. *MED*

The Nine Lives of Elfego Baca ⚔⚔ **1958** Venerable Western hero Loggia faces a veritable army of gunfighters and bandits. Action-packed but not too violent; family fun. **78m/C VHS, Beta.** Robert Loggia, Robert Simon, Lisa Montell, Nestor Paiva; **D:** Norman Foster. *DVT*

Nine Lives of Fritz the Cat ⚔⚔ **1974** Fritz feels that life's too square in the 70's, so he takes off into some of his other lives for more adventure. Cleaner but still naughty sequel to the X-rated "Fritz the Cat," featuring neither the original's writer/director Ralph Bakshi nor cartoonist Robert Crumb. Tame and lame. Animated. **77m/C VHS, LV.** **D:** Robert Taylor. *VES*

Nine Months ⚔⚔½ **1995 (PG-13)** Happily single Samuel (Grant) gets girlfriend Rebecca (Moore) pregnant and promptly wigs out. He makes amends to the lovely Rebecca, they marry, and true to writer/director Columbus' style, live happily ever after. Bachelor pal Sean (Goldblum) and an expectant couple (Arnold and Cusack) with three kids round out the cast, with Williams offering his usual manic flair as a Russian obstetrician, improvising his scenes with glee. Grant's knack for clumsy befuddlement fits well with the warm, fuzzy style of Columbus. "Nine" doesn't go out on any limbs, but is a pleasant diversion anyway. Film may well have gotten lost in the megabox office summer of '95, till Grant guaranteed publicity when his dalliance with Divine Brown threw him into jail and the headlines. His faux pas causes unintended laughs during a few key scenes. The trailer clip showing Grant during a mug shot is gone—producers claim the segment was deleted before his real-life arrest. Remake of the French film "Neuf Mois." **CW:** Language and sexual innuendo. **103m/C VHS, LV, Closed Caption.** Hugh Grant, Julianne Moore, Tom Arnold, Joan Cusack, Jeff Goldblum; *Cameos:* Robin Williams; **D:** Chris Columbus; **W:** Chris Columbus; **C:** Donald McAlpine; **M:** Hans Zimmer. *TCF*

9 to 5 ⚔⚔½ **1980 (PG)** In this caricature of large corporations and women in the working world, Coleman plays the male chauvinist boss who calls the shots and keeps his employees, all female, under his thumb. Three of the office secretaries daydream of Coleman's disposal and rashly kidnap him after a silly set of occurrences threaten their jobs. While they have him under lock and key, the trio take office matters into their own hands and take a stab at running things their own way, with amusing results. The basis for a television series. 111m/C VHS, Beta, LV. Jane Fonda, Lily Tomlin, Dolly Parton, Dabney Coleman, Sterling Hayden, Norma Donaldson; **D:** Colin Higgins; **W:** Patricia Resnick; **C:** Reynaldo Villalobos; **M:** Charles Fox. Nominations: Academy Awards '80: Best Song ("Nine to Five"). *FOX*

976-EVIL 🐾🐾 1988 (R) Englund (the infamous Freddy from the Nightmare on Elm Street epics) directs this horror movie where a lonely teenager dials direct to demons from hell. 102m/C VHS, Beta, LV, Closed Caption. Stephen Geoffreys, Jim Metzler, Maria Rubell, Sandy Dennis, Robert Picardo, Leslie Deane, Pat O'Bryan; **D:** Robert Englund; **C:** Paul Elliott; **M:** Tom Chase, Steve Rucker. *COL*

976-EVIL 2: The Astral Factor 🐾½ 1991 (R) Satan returns the call in this supernatural thriller that sequels the original film.**CW:** Horror violence. 93m/C VHS, Closed Caption. Pat O'Bryan, Rene Assa, Debbie James; **D:** Jim Wynorski; **W:** Erik Anjou. *LIV, VES*

984: Prisoner of the Future *The Tomorrow Man* 1984 A shocking, futuristic tale of human self-destruction. 70m/C VHS, Beta. Don Francks, Stephen Markle; **D:** Tibor Takacs. *NO*

1900 🐾🐾🐾 1976 (R) Bertolucci's impassioned epic about two Italian families, one land-owning, the other, peasant. Shows the sweeping changes of the 20th century begun by the trauma of WWI and the onslaught of Italian socialism. Edited down from its original 360-minute length and dubbed in English from three other languages, the film suffers somewhat from editing and from its nebulous lack of commitment to any genre. Elegantly photographed by Vittorio Storaro. Also titled "Novecento." 255m/C VHS, Beta, LV. *FR IT GE* Robert De Niro, Gerard Depardieu, Burt Lancaster, Donald Sutherland, Dominique Sanda, Sterling Hayden, Laura Betti, Francesca Bertini, Werner Bruhns, Stefania Sandrelli, Anna Henkel, Alida Valli; **D:** Bernardo Bertolucci; **W:** Giuseppe Bertolucci, Bernardo Bertolucci; **C:** Vittorio Storaro. *PAR*

1918 🐾🐾½ 1985 An adaptation of the Horton Foote play about the effects of WWI and an influenza epidemic on a small Texas town. Slow-moving but satisfying. Score by Willie Nelson. Originally produced for PBS's "American Playhouse." Prequeled by "On Valentine's Day." 89m/C VHS, Beta, Closed Caption. Matthew Broderick, Hallie Foote, William Converse-Roberts, Rochelle Oliver, Michael Higgins, Horton Foote Jr., William Bill McGhee, Jeannie McCarthy; **D:** Ken Harrison; **W:** Horton Foote; **M:** Willie Nelson. *FOX*

1931: Once Upon a Time in New York 🐾🐾 1972 Prohibition-era gangsters war, beat each other up, make headlines, and drink bathtub gin. 90m/C VHS, Beta. Richard Conte, Adolfo Celi, Lionel Stander, Irene Papas. *VCD*

1941 🐾🐾½ 1979 (PG) Proved to be the most expensive comedy of all time with a budget exceeding $35 million. The depiction of Los Angeles in the chaotic days after the bombing of Pearl Harbor combines elements of fantasy and black humor. 120m/C VHS, Beta, LV. John Belushi, Dan Aykroyd, Patti LuPone, Ned Beatty, Slim Pickens, Murray Hamilton, Christopher Lee, Tim Matheson, Toshiro Mifune, Warren Oates, Robert Stack, Nancy Allen, Elisha Cook Jr., Lorraine Gary, Treat Williams, Mickey Rourke, John Candy; **D:** Steven Spielberg; **W:** Robert Zemeckis, Bob Gale; **C:** William A. Fraker; **M:** John Williams. Nominations: Academy Awards '79: Best Cinematography, Best Sound. *USH, CCB*

1969 🐾🐾🐾½ 1989 (R) Three teenage friends during the 1960s become radicalized by the return of one of their friends from Vietnam in a coffin. Critically lambasted directorial debut for "On Golden Pond" author Ernest Thompson. 96m/C VHS, Beta, LV, Closed Caption. Kiefer Sutherland, Robert Downey Jr., Winona Ryder, Bruce Dern, Joanna Cassidy, Mariette Hartley; **D:** Ernest Thompson. *MED*

1984 🐾🐾🐾½ 1984 (R) A very fine adaptation of George Orwell's infamous novel, this version differs from the overly simplistic and cautionary 1954 film because of fine casting and production design. The illegal love affair of a government official becomes his attempt to defy the crushing inhumanity and lack of simple pleasures of an omniscient government. Filmed in London, it skillfully visualizes our time's most central prophetic nightmare. 117m/C VHS, Beta, LV. *GB* John Hurt, Richard Burton, Suzanna Hamilton, Cyril Cusack, Gregory Fisher, Andrew Wilde, Rupert Baderman; **D:** Michael Radford; **C:** Roger Deakins. *LIV*

1990: The Bronx Warriors woof! *1990 I Guerrieri del Bronx; Bronx Warriors* 1983 (R) Good street gang members combat evil corporate powers in a semi-futuristic South Bronx. Lame copy of "Escape from New York." 86m/C VHS, Beta. *IT* Vic Morrow, Christopher Connelly, Fred Williamson; **D:** Enzo G. Castellari. *MED*

1991: The Year Punk Broke 1992 Documents a grunge rock tour of European festivals in 1991 when the alternative bands were largely unknown to all but hardcore fans. Follows Sonic Youth, Nirvana, Dinosaur Jr., Babes in Toyland, Gumball, and grandaddy punk idols, The Ramones, behind-the-scenes and through their performances. 95m/C VHS. **D:** David Markey. *MOV*

90 Days 🐾🐾🐾 1986 Charming independently made Canadian comedy about two young men handling their respective romantic dilemmas—one awaiting an oriental fiancee he's never met, the other who is being kicked out of his house by his wife. 99m/C VHS, Beta, Closed Caption. *CA* Stefan Wodoslowsky, Sam Grana, Christine Pak; **D:** Giles Walker. *FOX*

92 in the Shade 🐾🐾🐾 1976 (R) Based upon McGuane's novel, the film deals with a bored, wealthy rogue who becomes a fishing guide in the Florida Keys, and battles against the competition of two crusty, half-mad codgers. Sloppy, irreverent comedy as only a first-time writer-turned-director can fashion. 91m/C VHS, Beta. Peter Fonda, Warren Oates, Margot Kidder, Burgess Meredith, Harry Dean Stanton; **D:** Thomas McGuane; **W:** Thomas McGuane. *FOX*

99 & 44/100 Dead 🐾 *Call Harry Crown* 1974 (PG) Frankenheimer falters with this silly gangster flick. Harris is hired to kill Dillman, by local godfather O'Brien. Originally written as a satirical look at gangster movies, but it doesn't stick to satire, and as a result is disappointing. 98m/C VHS. Richard Harris, Chuck Connors, Edmond O'Brien, Bradford Dillman, Ann Turkel; **D:** John Frankenheimer; **W:** Robert Dillon; **M:** Henry Mancini. *FOX*

99 Women 🐾½ *Isle of Lost Women* 1969 (R) Sympathetic prison warden attempts to investigate conditions at a women's prison camp. Thin and exploitative view of lesbianism behind bars that sensationalizes the subject. 90m/C VHS, Beta. *GB SP GE IT* Maria Schell, Herbert Lom, Mercedes McCambridge, Luciana Paluzzi; **D:** Jess (Jesus) Franco. *NO*

Ninja 3: The Domination 🐾🐾 1984 (R) Ninja master must remove the spirit of a deadly ninja assassin from a young woman intent on wreaking havoc among the Phoenix police department. Extremely silly super ninja epic utterly uninhibited by the usual plot conventions. 92m/C VHS, Beta. Lucinda Dickey, Sho Kosugi; **D:** Sam Firstenberg; **W:** James R. Silke; **C:** Hanania Baer. *MGM*

Ninja Academy 🐾½ 1990 (R) Seven wimps, losers, and spoiled brats come to the Ninja Academy to learn the art. Will they make it? 93m/C VHS. Will Egan, Kelly Randall, Gerald Okomura, Michael David, Robert Factor, Jeff Robinson; **D:** Nico Mastorakis. *NO*

Ninja: American Warrior 🐾½ 1990 An evil ninja takes on the U.S. Drug Enforcement Agency when the authorities threaten to shut him down. 90m/C VHS, Beta. Joff Houston, John Wilford; **D:** Tommy Cheng. *IMP*

Ninja Brothers of Blood 🐾 1989 A guy falls for a rival gang member's girl. Neither the gang nor the guy's former girlfriend take kindly to this! 90m/C VHS, Beta, LV. Marcus Gibson, Fonda Lynn, Brian McClave, Jonathan Soper; **D:** Raymond Woo. *IMP*

Ninja Champion woof! 198? White-clad and masked ninja heros come to the aid of two Interpol agents tracking down a sleazy diamond smuggler. Invisible storyline features very little actual ninja. Extremely unconvincing and poorly dubbed. 90m/C VHS, Beta. *HK* Bruce Baron, Richard Harrison; **D:** Godfrey Ho; **W:** Godfrey Ho. *TWE*

Ninja Checkmate 🐾 1990 An evil ninja seems indestructible, but finally he meets his match. 90m/C VHS, Beta. Simon Lee, Jack Long, Jeanie Chang. *MGI*

Ninja Commandments 🐾 1987 Everything is at stake when an evil warrior takes on the greatest fighter in the land: the winner will rule the empire! 90m/C VHS, Beta. Richard Harrison, Dave Wheeler; **D:** Joseph Lai. *IMP*

Ninja Condors 🐾 1987 A young man grows up to avenge the murder of his father. 85m/C VHS, Beta. Alexander Lou, Stuart Hugh; **D:** James Wu. *TWE*

Ninja Connection 🐾 1990 Ninja terrorism is employed as a scare tactic to deter a group who wants to break up an international drug ring. 90m/C VHS, Beta. Patricia Greenford, Jane Kingsly, Joe Nelson, Louis Roth, Henry Steele, Stuart Steen; **D:** York Lam. *IMP*

Ninja Death Squad 🐾 1987 A team specializing in political assassinations is hunted down by a special agent. 89m/C VHS, Beta. Glen Carson, Patricia Goodman, Joff Houston, Billy Jones, Wallace Jones, John Wilford; **D:** Tommy Cheng. *IMP*

Ninja Demon's Massacre 🐾 198? Ninja named Willie responds to federal investigations into his spying business by wearing a black robe and slashing feds with long swords. 89m/C VHS, Beta. Ted Brooke, James Lear. *TWE*

Ninja Destroyer 🐾 197? (R) Ninja warriors battle over an emerald mine. 92m/C VHS, Beta. *HK* Bruce Baron, Stuart Smith; **D:** Godfrey Ho; **W:** Godfrey Ho. *TWE*

Ninja Dragon 🐾 198? Two Ninjas are hired in a gang war and dazzle all those who watch by kicking their enemies to death. 92m/C VHS, Beta. Richard Harrison. *TWE*

Ninja Exterminators woof! 1981 Low-grade kung-fu antics mascarading as ninja rib-kicking bonanza. Dubbed. 85m/C VHS, Beta. *HK* Jacky Cheng, Ko Shou Liang, Tai Chen. *NO*

Ninja Fantasy woof! 1986 Ninja drug smugglers and government officials battle over a large drug shipment. Everybody go chop socky. Not much in way of ninja fantasy. Dubbed. 95m/C VHS, Beta. *HK* Adam Nell, Ian Frank, Jordan Heller, Ken Ashley, Jenny Mills, Jack Rodman; **D:** Bruce Lambert; **W:** Anthony Green. *TWE*

Ninja Hunt woof! 198? This time, ninjas kick international terrorists in the head while searching for secret formula. Poorly dubbed pseudo ninja developed by Godfrey Ho. 92m/C VHS, Beta. *HK* Bruce Baron, Stuart Smith; **D:** Joseph Lai; **W:** Stephen Saul. *TWE*

Ninja Massacre 🐾 1984 Gangsters covet a secret manual of kung fu techniques. Heel-splintering battles break out as a result. 87m/C VHS, Beta. Lo Lieh, Pai Ying, Lung Jun Ehr, Tiki Shirtee. *GEM, MRV*

Ninja Masters of Death 🐾 1985 Terrorists reign supreme until the white ninja saves the city. 90m/C VHS, Beta. Mick Jones, Chris Petersen, Daniel Wells, Richard Young; **D:** Bruce Lambert. *IMP*

Ninja Mission 🐾½ 1984 (R) First Scandinavian ninja epic follows CIA agent and his group of ninja fighters as they embark on a hazardous mission to rescue two people from a Soviet prison. They use their fighting skills (Swedish ninjas favor guns more than ninjutsu) against Russian soldiers. Dubbed. 95m/C VHS, Beta. *SW* Christopher Kohlberg, Curt Brober, Hanna Pola; *D:* Mats Helge. *MED*

Ninja Nightmare 🥷 1988 (R) A man seeks revenge for his family's death. 98m/C VHS, Beta. Leo Fong. *PSM*

Ninja of the Magnificence 🥷½ 1989 When the ninja master is killed, factions within his group battle for control. 90m/C VHS, Beta. Sam Baker, Patrick Frbezar, Clive Hadwen, Tim Michael, Renato Sala; *D:* Charles Lee. *IMP*

Ninja Operation: Licensed to Terminate 🥷 1987 Two warriors risk broken noses and twisted limbs to take on the Black Ninja Empire. 89m/C VHS, Beta. Richard Harrison, Paul Marshall, Jack McPeat, Grant Temple; *D:* Joseph Lai. *IMP*

Ninja Phantom Heroes 🥷 1987 Two Vietnam vets are imprisoned for war crimes. One escapes and forms his own secret ninja society. 90m/C VHS, Beta. Glen Carson, George Dickson, Allen Leung, Christine Wells; *D:* Bruce Lambert. *TWE*

The Ninja Pirates 🥷 1990 In the Sung Dynasty, a group of bloodthirsty pirates are hunted down after stealing a golden treasure. 90m/C VHS, Beta. Chi Lan, Lo Lieh, Carter Wong, Nancy Yan. *MGI*

Ninja Powerforce 🥷½ 1990 Two childhood friends end up as members of rival ninja gangs in the midst of a bloody war. Usual assortment of ninja-inflicted injuries result. 90m/C VHS, Beta. Jonathan Bould, Richard Harrison; *D:* Joseph Lai. *IMP*

Ninja Showdown 🥷 1990 A warrior must take on a number of vicious bandits in order to defend his small town. He vows revenge on anyone who threatens his people. 92m/C VHS, Beta. Richard Harrison; *D:* Joseph Lai. *TWE*

Ninja Squad 🥷 198? Empires, families, and honor are at stake in a fierce battle of heel-to-head action. 92m/C VHS, Beta. Dave Wheeler, Richard Harrison, Timalden. *TWE*

Ninja Strike Force 🥷½ 1988 The Black Ninjas steal the powerful "spirit sword," and go on a bloody rampage. 89m/C VHS, Beta. Richard Harrison, Gary Carter; *D:* Joseph Lai. *IMP*

Ninja Supremo 🥷 1990 A rebellious teenager studies Kung-fu, and then returns to his village a hero after he gains expertise in his chosen field. 100m/C VHS, Beta. David Tao, Andrew Kam Yeun Wah, Sun Yueh. *MGI*

Ninja Swords of Death 🥷½ 1990 A noble warrior challenges a vicious assassin who uses a spur-sword. He is nearly decapitated in the process. 90m/C VHS, Beta. Chang Ying Chun, Chia Ling, Tien Pang, Kong Pun. *MGI*

Ninja, the Battalion 🥷 1990 Agents from America, the Soviet Union, and China try to recover germ warfare secrets stolen by the Japanese secret service. 90m/C VHS, Beta, Closed Caption. Roger Crawford, Sam Huxley, Alexander Lou, Dickson Warn; *D:* Victor Sears. *TWE*

Ninja the Protector 🥷 198? A ninja tracks down and kicks the ninja head of a counterfeiting ring. 92m/C VHS, Beta. Richard Harrison. *TWE*

Ninja, the Violent Sorcerer 🥷½ 1986 Murderer, with the help of Chinese vampires, does battle with the ghost of a dead gambling lord's wife and the gambling lord's living brother. Often tedious even with above average production and incredible plot. 90m/C VHS, Beta. *D:* Bruce Lambert; *W:* Daniel Clough. *TWE*

Ninja Turf 🥷 *L.A. Streetfighters* 1986 (R) Teenage kick artists rip off a Hollywood drug dealer and are pursued by a swarm of ninja hitmen. 83m/C VHS, Beta, LV. Jun Chong, Bill Wallace, Rosanna King, James Lew, Phillip Rhee. *COL*

Ninja Vengeance 🥷½ 1993 (R) The corrupt sheriff of a small Texas town, who also leads the KKK, is terrorizing a young African-American local. Then our lone hero rides into town on his trusty motorcycle to save the day. Only this time

instead of your average gunman, he's a ninja. *CW:* Language, violence, and sexuality. 87m/C VHS, Closed Caption. Stephen K. Hayes, Janet K. Pawlak, Craig Boyett, David Paul Lord; *D:* Karl Armstrong; *W:* Carrie Armstrong, Karl Armstrong. *COL*

Ninja vs. Ninja 🥷½ 1990 A scientist has found a cure for heroin addiction, but ninja drug lords won't let his discovery see the light of day! 90m/C VHS, Beta. Hui Hsiao Chiang, Callan Leong. *MGI*

Ninja vs. the Shaolin 🥷½ 1984 Savage fighting between priests and ninjas results in one of the bloodiest pages in history. 90m/C VHS, Beta. Alexander Lou, John Wu; *D:* Jacky Hwong. *MGI*

Ninja's Extreme Weapons 🥷½ 1990 Blue Ninja takes it to the streets when his brother is killed by the underworld. 90m/C VHS, Beta. James Gray, Donald Muir; *D:* Victor Sears. *TWE, HHE*

Ninotchka 🥷🥷🥷½ 1939 (R) Delightful romantic comedy. Garbo is a cold Russian agent sent to Paris to check up on her comrades, who are being seduced by capitalism. She inadvertently falls in love with a playboy, who melts her communist heart. Garbo talks and laughs. Satirical, energetic, and witty. Later a Broadway musical called "Silk Stockings." *CW:* Language and strong sexuality. 110m/B VHS, Beta, LV, 8mm. Greta Garbo, Melvyn Douglas, Ina Claire, Sig Rumann, Felix Bressart, Bela Lugosi; *D:* Ernst Lubitsch; *W:* Billy Wilder; *C:* William H. Daniels. National Board of Review Awards '39: 10 Best Films of the Year; Nominations: Academy Awards '39: Best Actress (Garbo), Best Picture, Best Story. *MGM*

The Ninth Configuration 🥷🥷🥷 *Twinkle, Twinkle, Killer Kane* 1979 (R) Based on Blatty's novel "Twinkle, Twinkle, Killer Kane" (also the film's alternate title), this is a weird and surreal tale of a mock rebellion of high-ranking military men held in a secret base hospital for the mentally ill. Keach is good as the commander who is just as insane as the patients. Available in many different lengths, this is generally considered to be the best. 115m/C VHS, Beta, LV. Stacy Keach, Scott Wilson, Jason Miller, Ed Flanders, Neville Brand, Alejandro Rey, Robert Loggia, George DiCenzo; *D:* William Peter Blatty; *W:* William Peter Blatty. Golden Globe Awards '81: Best Screenplay. *NWV*

Nitti: The Enforcer 🥷🥷 1988 (PG-13) Made-for-TV saga about Al Capone's brutal enforcer and right hand man, Frank Nitti. Diversified cast, (Moriarty in particular) do their best to keep things moving along, and the atmosphere is consistently and appropriately violent. Made to capitalize on the success of 1987's "The Untouchables." 94m/C VHS. Anthony LaPaglia, Vincent Guastaferro, Trini Alvarado, Michael Moriarty, Michael Russo, Louis Guss, Bruno Kirby; *D:* Michael Switzer. *ACA*

Nixon 🥷🥷🥷 1995 (R) Stone again "interprets" historical events of the 60s and 70s with a sprawling, bold bio of Richard Nixon. Covering all the highlights of Nixon's public life, and speculating on his private one, Hopkins convincingly portrays "Tricky Dick" as an embattled, lonely political genius. Gigantic all-star cast is lead by Oscar-caliber performance of Joan Allen as Pat Nixon. Even at over three hours, there isn't nearly enough time to explore the significance of all the events covered here. As usual, Stone has taken some creative license, which lead to the Nixon daughters publicly trashing the film, and Walt Disney's daughter expressing "shame" at being affiliated with it. *CW:* Language. 192m/C VHS, LV, Closed Caption. Anthony Hopkins, Joan Allen, Ed Harris, Bob Hoskins, David Paymer, Paul Sorvino, J.T. Walsh, James Woods, Madeline Kahn, Brian Bedford, Mary Steenburgen, Powers Boothe, E.G. Marshall, David Hyde Pierce, Kevin Dunn, Annabeth Gish, Tony Goldwyn, Larry Hagman, Edward Herrmann, Saul Rubinek, Tony LoBianco; *D:* Oliver Stone; *W:* Christopher Wilkinson, Stephen J. Rivele; *C:* Robert Richardson; *M:* John Williams. Los Angeles Film Critics Association Awards '95: Best Supporting Actress (Allen); National Society of Film Critics Awards '95: Best Supporting Actress (Allen); Nominations: Academy Awards '95: Best Actor (Hopkins), Best Screenplay, Best Supporting Actress (Allen), Original Dramatic/Comedy

Score; British Academy Awards '95: Best Supporting Actress (Allen); Golden Globe Awards '96: Best Actor—Drama (Hopkins); Screen Actors Guild Award '95: Best Actor (Hopkins), Best Actress (Allen), Cast. *TOU*

No Big Deal 🥷½ 1983 (PG-13) Dillon is a streetwise teenager who makes friends at his new school. Blah promise; bad acting makes this no big deal. 86m/C VHS. Kevin Dillon, Sylvia Miles, Tammy Grimes, Jane Krakowski, Christopher Gartin, Mary Joan Negro; *D:* Robert Charlton. *BTV*

No Comebacks 1985 Two British mysteries, made for television from stories by Frederick Forsyth: "A Careful Man," about a dying millionaire who cheats his heirs, and "Privilege," about a clever stamp dealer who exacts revenge upon a libelous gossip columnist. 60m/C VHS, Beta. *GB* Milo O'Shea, Cyril Cusack, Dan O'Herlihy, Gayle Hunnicutt. *PSM*

No Contest 🥷🥷 1994 (R) International terrorists, lead by Oz (Clay), hold the TV host (Tweed) and contestants of the Ms. Galaxy beauty pageant hostage with a $10 million ransom demand. *CW:* Great amount of strong violence; language. 94m/C VHS, Closed Caption. Andrew Dice Clay, Shannon Tweed, Robert Davi, Roddy Piper, Nicholas Campbell; *D:* Paul Lynch; *W:* Robert Cooper. *COL*

No Dead Heroes 🥷 1987 Green Beret Vietnam war hero succumbs to Soviet scheming when they plant a computer chip in his brain. Unoriginal and unworthy. 86m/C VHS, Beta. Max Thayer, John Dresden, Toni Nero; *D:* J.C. Miller. *NO*

No Deposit, No Return 🥷🥷 *Double Trouble* 1976 (G) Tedious, silly, pointless Disney action comedy. Rich brats persuade bumbling crooks to kidnap them, offer them for ransom to millionaire grandfather. 115m/C VHS, Beta. David Niven, Don Knotts, Darren McGavin, Barbara Feldon, Charles Martin Smith; *D:* Norman Tokar; *W:* Arthur Alsberg; *M:* Buddy Baker. *DIS*

No Dessert Dad, 'Til You Mow the Lawn 🥷½ 1994 (PG) Suburban parents Ken and Carol Cochran (Robert Hays and Joanna Kerns) are harassed at home by their annoying offspring, Justin, Monica, and Tyler. When they try hypnosis tapes to quit smoking, the kids discover by doctoring the tapes, they can plant suggestions resulting in parental perks. 80m/C VHS. Robert Hays, Joanna Kerns, Joshua Schaefer, Allison Meek, Jimmy Marsden, Richard Moll, Larry Linville; *D:* Howard McCain. *NHO*

No Drums, No Bugles 🥷½ 1971 (G) A West Virginia farmer and conscientious objector leaves his family to live alone in a cave for three years during the Civil War. Bad direction spoils Sheen's good performance. 85m/C VHS, Beta. Martin Sheen, Davey Davidson, Denine Terry, Rod McCary; *D:* Clyde Ware. *VTR*

No End 🥷🥷 *Bez Konca* 1984 The ghost of a dead lawyer watches as his wife and young son struggle to survive without him, including the widow getting involved in her husband's last case about a worker arrested for organizing a strike. Well-acted but overly solemn and slow; set during Poland's martial law in 1982. In Polish with English subtitles. 108m/C VHS. *PL* Grazyna Szapolowska, Jerzy Radziwilowicz, Maria Pakulnis, Aleksander Bardini, Artur Barcis, Michal Bajor; *D:* Krzysztof Kieslowski; *W:* Krzysztof Piesiewicz, Krzysztof Kieslowski. *NYF, FCT, ING*

No Escape 🥷🥷½ 1994 (R) In 2022, Captain Robbins (Liotta) has been banished to a prison colony island inhabited by the most dangerous criminals. With no walls and no guards, the prisoners are left to kill each other. Then Robbins discovers a relatively peaceful community of prisoners who help each other. But this group is soon bedeviled by the evil nasties on the other side of the island. Attempts at escape define the plot, so the film is filled with superhuman feats of sheer courage, determination, and guts. Adapted from the book "The Penal Colony" by Richard Herley. *CW:* Some language and large amount of strong violence. 118m/C VHS, LV, Closed Caption.

Ray Liotta, Lance Henriksen, Stuart Wilson, Kevin Dillon, Kevin J. O'Connor, Michael Lerner, Ernie Hudson, Ian McNeice, Jack Shepherd; **D:** Martin Campbell; **W:** Joel Gross; **M:** Graeme Revell. *HBO*

No Escape, No Return 🐾🐾½ 1993 (R) An FBI agent (Nouri) and a police captain (Saxon) force three renegade cops (Nguyen, Caulfield, and Loveday) to infiltrate a drug syndicate. But things go from bad to worse when a war breaks out between rival drug gangs, leaving a lot of bodies, and a large chunk of money gone missing. Now the trio is sought by both the cops and the crooks. **93m/C VHS, LV, Closed Caption.** Maxwell Caulfield, Dustin Nguyen, Denise Loveday, John Saxon, Michael Nouri, Kevin Benton; **D:** Charles Kanganis; **W:** Charles Kanganis; **M:** Jim Halfpenny. *PMH*

No Fear, No Die 🐾🐾 1990 To make some quick cash two black immigrants in France train and sell birds for illegal cockfights at a roadside restaurant. Jocelyn, who trains the cocks, pays them lavish, obsessive attention. But cultural conflicts and repressed passions are just waiting to explode. In French with English subtitles. **97m/C VHS.** *FR* Alex Descas, Isaach de Bankole, Jean-Claude Brialy, Solveig Dommartin, Christopher Buchholz; **D:** Claire Denis; **W:** Claire Denis, Jean-Pol Fargeau; **M:** Abdullah Ibrahim. *FRF*

No Greater Love 🐾🐾½ 1943 Capraesque Soviet war movie. A peasant woman mobilizes her village against the Nazis to avenge her family's death. Dubbed into English by the Soviets for Western circulation during WWII. **74m/B VHS, Beta.** *RU* Vera Maretskaya; **D:** Frederic Ermler. *FCT, IHF*

No Highway in the Sky 🐾🐾🐾 1951 Eccentric scientist Theodore Honey (Stewart) works for the Royal Aircraft Establishment, which has just produced a new plane, the Reindeer. But Honey tells his boss Dennis Scott (Hawkins) that the plane has a serious defect. While flying to examine a Reindeer crash site, Honey befriends Monica (Dietrich), a musical star, and stewardess Marjorie (Johns), who support him when his company accuses him of maliciously damaging the aircraft's reputation. Dietrich steals every scene with her Christian Dior wardrobe and star attitude. Based on the novel "No Highway" by Nevil Shute. **98m/B VHS.** *GB* James Stewart, Marlene Dietrich, Glynis Johns, Jack Hawkins, Ronald Squire, Niall MacGinnis, Elizabeth Allan, Kenneth More, David Hutcheson; **D:** Henry Koster; **W:** R.C. Sherriff, Oscar Millard; **M:** Malcolm Arnold. *FXV*

No Holds Barred 🐾½ 1989 (PG-13) Cheesy, campy remake of cheesy, campy 1952 wrestling movie. Hulk Hogan on the big screen, at last. **98m/C VHS, Beta, LV, Closed Caption.** Hulk Hogan, Kurt Fuller, Joan Severance, Tiny Lister; **D:** Thomas J. Wright. *COL*

No Love for Johnnie 🐾🐾🐾 1960 Well acted if unoriginal political drama. Finch is a British M.P. who fails in both public and private life. Based on the novel by Wilfred Fienburgh. **105m/B VHS, Beta.** *GB* Peter Finch, Stanley Holloway, Donald Pleasence, Mary Peach, Mervyn Johns, Dennis Price, Oliver Reed, Billie Whitelaw; **D:** Ralph Thomas; **M:** Mordecai Richler; **M:** Malcolm Arnold. British Academy Awards '61: Best Actor (Finch). *NO*

No Man of Her Own 🐾🐾½ 1932 Gable and Lombard in their only screen pairing. Gambler Babe Stewart (Gable) marries small town librarian (Lombard) on a bet and attempts to hide his secret life from her. Neither star's best film. **81m/B VHS, Beta, LV.** Carole Lombard, Clark Gable, Grant Mitchell, Elizabeth Patterson, Dorothy Mackaill; **D:** Wesley Ruggles. *USH, BAR*

No Man's Land 🐾🐾 1987 (R) Undercover cop Sweeney tails playboy Sheen but is seduced by wealth and glamour. Flashy surfaces, shiny cars, little substance. **107m/C VHS, Beta, LV, Closed Caption.** Charlie Sheen, D.B. Sweeney, Lara Harris, Randy Quaid; **D:** Peter Werner; **W:** Dick Wolf; **M:** Basil Poledouris. *ORI*

No Man's Law 🐾🐾½ 1927 Hardy plays the depraved villian desperate to get the goldmine owned by an old prospector and his beautiful daughter. But the mine is protected by Rex the Wonder Horse! **?m/B VHS.** Oliver Hardy, Barbara Kent, James Finlayson, Theodore von Eltz; **D:** Fred Jackman. *NO*

No Man's Range 🐾 *No Man's Land* 1935 Unremarkable, typical, predictable Western: good guys, bad guys, guns, bullets, horses. **56m/B VHS, Beta.** Bob Steele. *NO*

No Mercy 🐾🐾 1986 (R) A Chicago cop (Gere) plunges into the Cajun bayou in order to avenge the murder of his partner. He falls for a beautiful girl enslaved by the killer, but that doesn't stop him from using her to flush out the powerful swamp-inhabiting crime lord. Absurd story without much plot. **108m/C VHS, Beta, LV.** Richard Gere, Kim Basinger, Jeroen Krabbe, George Dzundza, William Atherton, Ray Sharkey, Bruce McGill; **D:** Richard Pearce; **W:** Jim Carabatsos; **M:** Alan Silvestri. *COL*

No Name On the Bullet 🐾🐾🐾 1959 Aloof gunman John Gant (Murphy) is seeking revenge from someone in the town of Lordsburg, only none of the inhabitants know who the intended victim is. And slowly the town's citizens begin to panic. Great final showdown. **77m/C VHS.** Audie Murphy, Charles Drake, Joan Evans, Edgar Stehli, Warren Stevens, R.G. Armstrong, Whit Bissell, Karl Swenson; **D:** Jack Arnold; **W:** Gene L. Coon; **C:** Harold Lipstein. *USH*

No, No Nanette 🐾½ 1940 Lackluster filming of the Broadway production which fared better on the stage. Stock story of a young woman (Neagle) who rescues her uncle from financial ruin and finds romance in the process. **96m/B VHS.** Anna Neagle, Richard Carlson, Victor Mature, Roland Young, ZaSu Pitts, Eve Arden, Billy Gilbert, Keye Luke; **D:** Herbert Wilcox; **C:** Russell Metty. *NOS*

No One Cries Forever woof! 1985 When a prostitute breaks away from a gangstermadam after finding love, she is tracked down and disfigured. Swedish; dubbed. **96m/C Beta.** Elke Sommer, Howard Carpendale, Zoli Marks; **D:** Jans Rautenbach. *NO*

No Place to Hide 🐾½ 1981 A girl's father drowns and she blames herself. Her mother and psychologist try to convince the girl that her father's spirit isn't stalking her. She doesn't believe them. Made for television. **120m/C VHS, Beta.** Keir Dullea, Mariette Hartley, Kathleen Beller, Arlen Dean Snyder, Gary Graham, John Llewellyn Moxey; **D:** John Llewellyn Moxey. *PSM*

No Place to Hide 🐾🐾½ 1993 (R) Barrymore is the target of a psycho who's already killed her sister. Kristofferson plays the hard-edged cop who's out to protect her and trap the killer. ***CW:*** Language, violence, and sexuality. **90m/C VHS.** Drew Barrymore, Kris Kristofferson, Martin Landau, O.J. Simpson, Dey Young, Bruce Weitz; **D:** Richard Danus; **W:** Richard Danus. *CAN*

No Place to Run 🐾🐾 1972 An elderly man fights for custody of his grandson, then kidnaps him and flees with him to Canada. Made for TV. **78m/C VHS, Beta.** Herschel Bernardi, Larry Hagman, Stefanie Powers, Neville Brand; **D:** Delbert Mann. *THV*

No Prince for My Cinderella 1978 A schizophrenic girl who has turned to prostitution is sought desperately by her social worker. **100m/C VHS, Beta.** Robert Reed. *WOV*

No Problem 🐾🐾 197? A man is pursued, shot, and drops dead in the apartment of an unsuspecting man who doesn't know what to do with the body. Dubbed in English. **94m/C VHS, Beta.** *FR* Miou-Miou. *NO*

No Regrets for Our Youth 🐾🐾🐾 1946 A feminist saga depicting the spiritual growth of a foolish Japanese girl during the tumultuous years of WWII. In Japanese with English subtitles. **110m/B VHS.** *JP* Setsuko Hara; **D:** Akira Kurosawa. *CVC*

No Retreat, No Surrender 🐾 1986 (PG) A young American kick-boxer battles a formidable Russian opponent and wins, quite improbably, after having been tutored by the ghost of Bruce Lee in an abandoned house. Notable as Van Damme's debut, but little else recommends this silly "Rocky" rehash. Followed by "No Retreat, No Surrender II." **85m/C VHS, Beta, LV.** Kurt McKinney, J.W. Fails, Jean-Claude Van Damme; **D:** Corey Yuen. *NWV, VTR*

No Retreat, No Surrender 2 🐾 1989 (R) With help from two karate experts, a man sets out to find his girlfriend who has been kidnapped by Soviets. Has little or nothing to do with the movie to which it is ostensibly a sequel. High level kick-boxing action sequences. **92m/C VHS, Beta.** Loren Avedon, Max Thayer, Cynthia Rothrock; **D:** Corey Yuen; **W:** Maria Elene Cellino. *MCG*

No Retreat, No Surrender 3: Blood Brothers 🐾 1991 (R) Sibling martial arts rivals decide to bond in a manly way when CIA agent dad is most heinously slain by terrorists. Answers the burning question: "Whatever became of Joseph Campanella?"***CW:*** Martial arts violence. **97m/C VHS, Closed Caption.** Keith Vitali, Loren Avedon, Joseph Campanella. *IMP*

No Room to Run 🐾½ 1978 Concert promoter's life turns into a nightmare of deadly corporate intrigue when he arrives in Australia. Luckily, he finds time to fall in love. Made for television hokum. **101m/C VHS, Beta.** *AU* Richard Benjamin, Paula Prentiss, Barry Sullivan; **D:** Robert Lewis. *ACA*

No Safe Haven 🐾 1987 (R) A government agent seeks revenge for his family's death. **92m/C VHS, Beta.** Wings Hauser, Marina Rice, Robert Tessier; **D:** Ronnie Rondell; **M:** Joel Goldsmith. *MCG*

No Secrets 🐾½ 1991 (R) A young man on the run seeks refuge with three girls in an isolated house. His dread secret isn't so dread, leaving this mild teen-oriented thriller starved for lack of menace. **92m/C VHS, LV.** Adam Coleman Howard, Amy Locane, Heather Fairfield, Traci Lind; **D:** Dezso Magyar. *COL*

No Small Affair 🐾🐾 1984 (R) A 16-year-old aspiring photographer becomes romantically involved with a sultry 22-year-old rock star. **102m/C VHS, Beta, LV, Closed Caption.** Jon Cryer, Demi Moore, George Wendt, Peter Frechette, Elizabeth Daily, Tim Robbins, Jennifer Tilly, Rick Ducommun, Ann Wedgeworth; **D:** Jerry Schatzberg; **C:** John A. Alonzo; **M:** Rupert Holmes. *COL*

No Surrender 🐾🐾🐾 1986 (R) An unpredictable, darkly charming comedy about a Liverpool nightclub newly managed by Angelis. On New Year's Eve, a small drunken war is triggered when two groups of irate senior citizens are booked into the club and clash over their beliefs. The group is made up of Protestants and Catholics and the fight resembles the ongoing conflicts in modern-day Northern Ireland, although most of the action takes place in the loo. Watch for Costello as an inept magician. **100m/C VHS, Beta.** *GB* Ray McAnally, Michael Angelis, Avis Bunnage, James Ellis, Tom Georgeson, Mark Mulholland, Joanne Whalley, Elvis Costello, Bernard Hill, Michael Ripper; **D:** Peter Smith; **W:** Alan Bleasdale; **C:** Michael Coulter; **M:** Daryl Runswick. *PSM*

No Survivors, Please 🐾½ *Der Chef Wuenscht Keine Zeugen; The Chief Wants No Survivors* 1963 Aliens from Orion take over politicians in order to rule the Earth. Bizarre, obscure, based on true story. **92m/B VHS.** *GE* Maria Perschy, Uwe Friedrichsen, Robert Cunningham, Karen Blanguernon, Gustavo Rojo; **D:** Hans Albin, Peter Berneis. *MOV*

No Time for Romance 🐾🐾 1948 A sprightly musical with an all-black cast. First such film to be shot in color. **?m/C VHS.** Bill Walker. *FCT*

No Time for Sergeants 🐾🐾🐾 1958 Hilarious film version of the Broadway play by Ira Levin. Young Andy Griffith is excellent as the Georgia farm boy who gets drafted into the service and creates mayhem among his superiors and colleagues. Story also told on an earlier television special and later in a series. Note Don Knotts and Benny Baker in small roles along with Jameel Farah who went on to star in TV's M*A*S*H after changing his name to Jamie Farr. 119m/B VHS, Beta, LV, Closed Caption. Andy Griffith, Nick Adams, Murray Hamilton, Don Knotts, Jamie Farr, Myron McCormick; **D:** Mervyn LeRoy. WAR

No Time to Die 🎬 1978 In Indonesia, two corporate pawns and a beautiful reporter battle for the possession of a new laser cannon. 87m/C VHS, Beta. Chris Mitchum, John Phillip Law, Grazyna Dylong. TWE

No Trace 🎬🎬 1950 A writer who broadcasts his crime stories as part of a radio show is the victim of blackmail. It seems a former associate is aware that the stories are all based in fact. A Scotland Yard detective investigates when murder rears its ugly head. 76m/B VHS, Beta. GB Hugh Sinclair, Dinah Sheridan, John Laurie, Barry Morse, Michael Brennan, Dora Bryan; **D:** John Gilling. SNC

No Way Back 🎬🎬 1974 (R) Way. Writer, director, and producer Williamson portrays Jess Crowder, a man-for-hire who is an expert with guns, fists, and martial arts. An angry look at the white establishment. 92m/C VHS, Beta. Fred Williamson, Charles Woolf, Tracy Reed, Virginia Gregg, Don Cornelius; **D:** Fred Williamson. UNI

No Way Back 🎬🎬 1996 (R) FBI agent Zack Grant (Crowe) has never dealt with the death of his wife in childbirth and his career has suffered. His last professional chance is a sting operation involving the Mafia and the Yakuza. But when the operation goes wrong, Grant has a vendetta on his hands. Mafia boss Serlano (Lerner) kidnaps Zack's young son so Zack will turn over his prisoner—Yuji (Toyokawa), a Yakuza whom Serlano believes is responsible for his own son's death. Zack's only interest is to rescue his son and he doesn't care who gets in his way, including his fellow feds and the gangsters. 92m/C VHS, Closed Caption. Russell Crowe, Helen Slater, Michael Lerner, Etsushi Toyokawa, Ian Ziering; **D:** Frank Cappello; **W:** Frank Cappello; **C:** Richard Clabaugh; **M:** David Williams. COL

No Way Out 🎬🎬🎬 1987 (R) Career Navy man Costner is involved with a beautiful, sexy woman who is murdered. Turns out she was also the mistress of the Secretary of Defense, Costner's boss. Assigned to investigate the murder, he suddenly finds himself the chief suspect. A tight thriller based on 1948's "The Big Clock," with a new surprise ending. 114m/C VHS, Beta, LV. Kevin Costner, Sean Young, Gene Hackman, Will Patton, Howard Duff, George Dzundza, Iman, Chris D, Marshall Bell, Jason Bernard, Fred Dalton Thompson, David Paymer, Eugene Glazer; **D:** Roger Donaldson; **W:** Robert Garland; **M:** Maurice Jarre. HBO

No Way to Treat a Lady 🎬🎬🎬 1968 Steiger is a psychotic master of disguise who stalks and kills various women in this suspenseful cat-and-mouse game. Segal, as the detective assigned to the case, uncovers clues, falls in love, and discovers that his new girl may be the killer's next victim. 108m/C VHS, Beta. Rod Steiger, Lee Remick, George Segal, Eileen Heckart, Murray Hamilton; **D:** Jack Smight; **W:** John Gay; **C:** Jack Priestley. PAR

Noa at Seventeen 🎬🎬🎬 1982 The political/social turmoil of Israel in 1951 is allegorically depicted by the school vs. kibbutz debate within a young girl's middle-class family. In Hebrew with English subtitles. 86m/C VHS, Beta. IS Dalia Shimko, Idit Zur, Shmuel Shilo, Moshe Havazelet; **D:** Isaac Yeshurun. ERG, FCT, TPV

Noble House 1988 Continuation of James Clavell's Hong Kong series, following "Tai-Pan," and set in the present day. Ian Dunross (Brosnan) is the head of Struan and Company, Hong Kong's leading trading company, which is being undermined by the nefarious Quillan Gornt (Rhys-Davies) who plots to destroy his archrival. American businesswoman Casey Tcholok (the bland Raffin)

serves as Dunross' love interest. Originally a four-part TV miniseries partially filmed on location. 350m/C VHS. Pierce Brosnan, John Rhys-Davies, Deborah Raffin, Ben Masters, Julia Nickson-Soul, Khigh Deigh, Tia Carrere, Gordon Jackson. TVC

The Noble Ninja 🎬🎬 1990 In a fantastic prehistoric world, a ninja does battle with foes both real and supernatural. 90m/C VHS, Beta. Tsui Fung, Lo Lieh. MGI

Nobody's Daughter 🎬🎬½ 1976 The tragedy of an eight-year-old orphan shuttled from one family to another, all of whom are only interested in the money the government will pay for her care. In Hungarian with English subtitles. 90m/C VHS. HU Zsuzsi Czinkoczi; **D:** Lazlo Ranody. EVD

Nobody's Fool 🎬🎬 1986 (PG-13) Another entry in the genre of quirky Americana, this romantic comedy concerns a hapless Midwestern waitress suffering from low-self esteem who falls in love with a traveling stage-hand. 107m/C VHS, Beta, LV, Closed Caption. Rosanna Arquette, Eric Roberts, Mare Winningham, Louise Fletcher, Jim Youngs, Gwen Welles, Stephen Tobolowsky, Charlie Barnett, Lewis Arquette; **D:** Evelyn Purcell; **W:** Beth Henley; **C:** Misha Suslov; **M:** James Newton Howard. ORI, WAR

Nobody's Fool 🎬🎬🎬½ 1994 (R) Newman shines as 60-year-old Donald "Sully" Sullivan, a construction worker who, in spite of himself, begins mending his many broken relationships over the course of the holiday season. Seemingly plotless scenario is sprinkled with enough humor, hope, and understated inspiration to become a delightfully modest celebration of a perfectly ordinary man. Character-driven story is blessed with commendable performances by supporting players—obviously inspired by Newman's brilliant portrayal. Based on the novel by Richard Russo.**CW:** Contains some nudity and mild profanity. 110m/C VHS, Beta, Closed Caption. Paul Newman, Jessica Tandy, Bruce Willis, Melanie Griffith, Dylan Walsh, Pruitt Taylor Vince, Gene Saks, Josef Sommer, Philip S. Hoffman, Philip Bosco, Margo Martindale, Jay Patterson; **D:** Robert Benton; **W:** Robert Benton; **C:** John Bailey; **M:** John Bloom. Berlin International Film Festival '94: Best Actor (Newman); New York Film Critics Awards '94: Best Actor (Newman); National Society of Film Critics Awards '94: Best Actor (Newman); Nominations: Academy Awards '94: Best Actor (Newman), Best Adapted Screenplay; Golden Globe Awards '95: Best Actor—Drama (Newman); Screen Actors Guild Award '94: Best Actor (Newman). PAR

Nobody's Perfect 🎬 1990 (PG-13) Where "Tootsie" and "Some Like it Hot" collide (or more likely crash and burn). A lovesick teenager masquerades as a girl and joins the tennis team to be near his dream girl. Takes its title from Joe E. Brown's famous last line in "Some Like it Hot." 90m/C VHS, Beta, LV, Closed Caption. Chad Lowe, Gail O'Grady, Patrick Breen, Kim Flowers, Robert Vaughn; **D:** Robert Kaylor; **W:** Joel Block. MED, VTR

Nobody's Perfekt woof! 1979 (PG) Supposed comedy about three psychiatric patients who decide to extort $650,000 from the city of Miami when their car is wrecked. Lacks laughs and generally considered a turkey. 95m/C VHS, Beta. Gabe Kaplan, Robert Klein, Alex Karras, Susan Clark; **D:** Peter Bonerz. COL

Nocturna woof! 1979 (R) Nocturna, Granddaughter of Dracula 1979 (R) Hard times have fallen upon the house of Dracula. To help pay the taxes on the castle, the owners have converted it to the Hotel Transylvania. In order to increase business and the blood supply at the hotel, Nocturna books a disco group to entertain the guests. Hard times fell on this script, too. It's no wonder that director Tampa hid behind the alias Harry Hurwitz. 82m/C VHS, Beta, LV. Yvonne De Carlo, John Carradine, Tony Hamilton, Nai Bonet; **D:** Harry Tampa; **C:** Mac Ahlberg. MED

Nocturne 🎬🎬½ 1946 A police lieutenant investigates the supposed suicide of a famous composer and uncovers dark secrets that suggest murder is afoot. An overlooked RKO production shines thanks to Raft's inimitable tough guy per-

formance and some offbeat direction. For film noir completists. 88m/B VHS, Beta, LV. George Raft, Lynn Bari, Virginia Huston, Joseph Pevney, Myrna Dell, Edward Ashley, Walter Sande, Mabel Paige; **D:** Edwin L. Marin. TTC

Noir et Blanc 🎬🎬 1986 Antoine (Frappat) is a shy accountant who takes a job in a health club and begins an increasingly sado-masochistic relationship with black masseur, Jacques (Martial). The violence is inferred not actually shown but still makes for some kinky adult fare. Based on a short story by Tennessee Williams; debut film for director Devers. French with subtitles. 82m/B VHS. FR Francis Frappat, Jacques Martial, Josephine Fresson, Marc Berman, Claire Rigollier; **D:** Claire Devers; **W:** Claire Devers. CCN

Noises Off 🎬🎬½ 1992 (PG-13) An Americanization of a British farce about a group of second-rate actors touring in a sex comedy and their convoluted private lives. Wretched rehearsals and equally disasterous preformances, backstage sniping, lovers' quarrels, and a beleaguered director all bumble along together. It worked better on stage, where it was a Broadway hit, but the actors at least have some fun with the material. Based on the play by Michael Frayn. 101m/C VHS, Beta, LV. Michael Caine, Carol Burnett, Denholm Elliott, Julie Hagerty, Marilu Henner, Mark Linn-Baker, Christopher Reeve, John Ritter, Nicolette Sheridan; **D:** Peter Bogdanovich; **W:** Marty Kaplan; **M:** Phil Marshall. TOU, PMS

Nomad Riders 🎬 1981 A la "Mad Max," (though with an even smaller budget and a decided lack of originality) one rugged man goes after the bikers who killed his wife and daughter. 82m/C VHS, Beta. Wayne Chema, Richard Cluck, Ron Gregg; **D:** Frank Roach. LIV, VES

Nomads 🎬🎬½ 1986 (R) A supernatural thriller set in Los Angeles about a French anthropologist who is mysteriously killed, and the woman doctor who investigates and becomes the next target of a band of strange street people with nomadic spirits. Nomad notables include pop stars Adam Ant and Josie Cotton. 91m/C VHS, Beta, LV. Pierce Brosnan, Lesley-Anne Down, Adam Ant, Anna Maria Monticelli, Mary Woronov; **D:** John McTiernan; **M:** Bill Conti. IME, PAR

Nomads of the North 🎬½ 1920 Vintage silent melodrama set in the North Woods with the requisite young girl beset by evil villians, a climactic forest fire, and a dashing Mountie who allows a man wrongly sought by the law to be reunited with the woman he secretly loves. Also available at 75 minutes. 109m/B VHS, Beta, 8mm. Lon Chaney Sr., Lewis Stone, Betty Blythe; **D:** David M. Hartford. SNC, GPV, VYY

Nomugi Pass 🎬🎬½ 1979 A young woman working in a Japanese silk mill in the early 1900s must endure hardship and abuse. English subtitles. 154m/C VHS, Beta. JP Shinobu Otake, Meiko Harada, Rentaro Mikuni, Takeo Jii. VDA

Non-Stop New York 🎬🎬½ 1937 Mystery tale with interesting twist. A wealthy woman can give an alibi for a murder suspect, but no one will listen, and she is subsequently framed. Pays homage to Hitchcock with its photography and humor. Quick and charming. 71m/B VHS. Anna Lee, John Loder, Francis L. Sullivan, Frank Cellier, Desmond Tester, Athene Seyler, William Dewhurst, Drusilla Wills, Jerry Verno, James Pirrie, Ellen Pollock, Arthur Goullet, James Carew, Alf Goddard, Danny Green; **D:** Robert Stevenson; **W:** Curt Siodmak, Roland Pertwee, Derek Twist, J.O.C. Orton, E.V.H. Emmett. NOS, SNC

None But the Brave 🎬🎬 1965 During WWII, an American bomber plane crash-lands on an island already inhabited by stranded Japanese forces. After a skirmish, the two groups initiate a fragile truce, with the understanding that fighting will resume if one or the other sends for help. The Americans repair their radio unit and must decide on their next actions. Sinatra's directorial debut is a poor effort. 105m/C VHS, Beta, LV, Closed Caption. Frank Sinatra, Clint Walker, Tommy Sands, Brad Dexter, Tony Bill, Tatsuya Mihashi, Takeshi Kato, Sammy Jackson; **D:** Frank Sinatra; **M:** John Williams. WAR, FCT

None But the Lonely Heart 🐾🐾🐾 **1944** In the days before WWII, a Cockney drifter (Grant) wanders the East End of London. When his get-rich-quick schemes fail, his dying shop-keeper-mother tries to help and lands in prison. Interesting characterization of life in the slums. Odets not only directed, but wrote the screenplay. **113m/B VHS, Beta.** Cary Grant, Ethel Barrymore, Barry Fitzgerald, Jane Wyatt, Dan Duryea, George Coulouris, June Duprez; **D:** Clifford Odets; **W:** Clifford Odets; **C:** George Barnes. Academy Awards '44: Best Supporting Actress (Barrymore); National Board of Review Awards '44: 10 Best Films of the Year; Nominations: Academy Awards '44: Best Actor (Grant), Best Film Editing, Original Dramatic/Comedy Score. *MED, BTV*

Noon Sunday 🐾 **1971 (PG)** A cold war situation in the Pacific islands explodes into an orgy of death. **104m/C VHS, Beta.** Mark Lenard, John Russell, Linda Avery, Keye Luke. *ACA*

Noon Wine 🐾🐾🐾 **1984** Dramatization of Katherine Anne Porter's classic story about a Swedish worker on a Texas farm who becomes the center of a family battle. Made for PBS' American Playhouse. **60m/C VHS, Beta.** Fred Ward, Lise Hilboldt, Stellan Skarsgard, Jon Cryer; **D:** Michael Fields. *MON, FCT, KAR*

The Noose Hangs High 🐾🐾🐾 **1948** This broad comedy has our heroes as window washers mistaken for gamblers and getting involved with a bunch of gangsters. Much physical and verbal shenanigans as only these two can do it. The bits may be a bit old, but they're done with a fresh twist. Some good word play with the phrase "You can't be here" runs in the same vein as their classic "Who's on first?" routine. Genuinely funny. **77m/B VHS.** Bud Abbott, Lou Costello, Cathy Downs, Joseph Calleia, Leon Errol, Mike Mazurki, Jack Overman, Fritz Feld, Vera Martin, Joe Kirk, Matt Willis, Benny Rubin; **D:** Charles T. Barton. *MGM, NOS*

Norma Jean and Marilyn 🐾🐾½ **1995 (R)** Blonde screen goddess Marilyn Monroe (Sorvino) is haunted by her past, literally, since she never escapes the legacy of ambitious Norma Jean Baker (Judd). As her relationships and career falter, Norma Jean is always there (thanks to drug-induced hallucinations) to remind Marilyn how worthless she is. Cable drama deals with Norma Jean's troubled past and how she was willing to do anything to be in the movies, although it (apparently) brought her little happiness. The dual stars work surprisingly well and director Fywell offers the proper camp flair. **CW:** Sexual situations, strong language, and violence. **133m/C VHS.** Mira Sorvino, Ashley Judd, Josh Charles, Peter Dobson, Ron Rifkin, David Dukes, Taylor Nichols, Lindsay Crouse, John Rubinstein, Steven Culp, Perry Stephens, Earl Boen; **D:** Tim Fywell; **W:** Jill Isaacs; **C:** John Thomas; **M:** Christopher Young. *HBO*

Norma Rae 🐾🐾🐾 **1979 (PG)** A poor, uneducated textile worker joins forces with a New York labor organizer to unionize the reluctant workers at a Southern mill. Field was a surprise with her fully developed character's strength, beauty, and humor; her Oscar was well-deserved. Ritt's direction is top-notch. Jennifer Warnes sings the theme song, "It Goes Like It Goes," which also won an Oscar. 🎵It Goes Like It Goes. **114m/C VHS, Beta, LV.** Sally Field, Ron Leibman, Beau Bridges, Pat Hingle; **D:** Martin Ritt; **W:** Harriet Frank Jr., Irving Ravetch; **C:** John A. Alonzo; **M:** David Shire. Academy Awards '79: Best Actress (Field), Best Song ("It Goes Like It Goes"); Cannes Film Festival '79: Best Actress (Field); Golden Globe Awards '80: Best Actress—Drama (Field); Los Angeles Film Critics Association Awards '79: Best Actress (Field); National Board of Review Awards '79: Best Actress (Field); New York Film Critics Awards '79: Best Actress (Field); National Society of Film Critics Awards '79: Best Actress (Field); Nominations: Academy Awards '79: Best Adapted Screenplay, Best Picture. *FOX, BTV*

Normal Life 🐾🐾 **1996 (R)** Straight-arrow, smalltown Illinois rookie cop Chris Anderson (Perry) comes to the aid of sexy, impetuous biker chick Pam (Judd) and they impulsively marry.

Fast forward two years and the willfully irresponsible Pam has turned their lives into a disaster but for some reason Chris (now a security guard) sticks it out, even pulling bank jobs to afford Pam's luxuries. When she finds out what Chris has been doing, Pam insists on joining in, leading to a bitter end. Based on the true story of Jeffrey and Jill Erickson, who went on a bank robbing spree and were killed in 1991. Great lead performances though character motivation is lacking. **CW:** Scenes of violence, sexuality, drug use and language. **108m/C VHS, LV, Closed Caption.** Luke Perry, Ashley Judd, Bruce A. Young, Jim True, Dawn Maxey, Penelope Milford, Tom Towles; **D:** John McNaughton; **W:** Bob Schneider, Peg Haller; **C:** Jean De Segonzac. *NLC*

Norman Conquest 🐾 **Park Plaza 1953** Conway finds himself drugged and framed for murder in this bargain-basement thriller. Bartok is the leader of a diamond-smuggling operation who may be involved. **75m/B VHS.** **GB** Tom Conway, Eva Bartok, Joy Shelton, Sidney James, Richard Wattis, Robert Adair, Ian Fleming; **D:** Bernard Knowles; **W:** Bernard Knowles. *NOS, SNC*

The Norman Conquests, Part 1: Table Manners 🐾🐾🐾 **1980** Part one of playwright Alan Ayckbourn's comic trilogy of love unfulfilled, as the charmingly unreliable Norman (Conti) works his amorous wiles on three women. **108m/C VHS, Beta.** **GB** Tom Conti, Richard Briers, Penelope Keith. *TVC*

The Norman Conquests, Part 2: Living Together 🐾🐾🐾 **1980** Part two concerns the happenings in the living room during Norman's disastrous weekend of unsuccessful seduction. **93m/C VHS, Beta.** **GB** Tom Conti, Penelope Keith, Richard Briers. *TVC*

The Norman Conquests, Part 3: Round and Round the Garden 🐾🐾🐾 **1980** Part three concerns Norman's furtive appearance in the garden, which suggests that the weekend is going to misfire. **106m/C VHS, Beta.** **GB** Tom Conti, Penelope Keith, Richard Briers. *TVC*

Norman, Is That You? 🐾½ **1976** Unsuccessful film adaptation based on the unsuccessful Broadway play about one family's sexual revolution. Revamped by a host of black stars, it's basically a one-joke affair when Foxx discovers his son is gay and living with his white lover. Shot on videotape and transferred to film. **91m/C VHS.** Redd Foxx, Pearl Bailey, Dennis Dugan, Michael Warren, Tamara Dobson, Vernee Watson-Johnson, Jayne Meadows, George Furth; **D:** George Schlatter; **W:** George Schlatter, Ron Clark, Sam Bobrick; **M:** William Goldstein. *MGM*

Norman Loves Rose 🐾½ **1982 (R)** A precocious 13-year-old and his married sister-in-law join forces in this substandard comedy. When Rose tries to help Norman by teaching him about sex, she learns a little too—she's pregnant. **95m/C VHS, Beta.** **AU** Carol Kane, Tony Owen, Warren Mitchell, Myra de Groot; **D:** Henri Safran. *LIV, VES*

Norman's Awesome Experience woof! **1988 (PG-13)** Three adolescents are transported back in time to the Roman Empire. Bill and Ted, anyone? **90m/C VHS, Beta.** Tom McCamus, Laurie Paton, Jaques Lussier; **D:** Paul Donovan; *

Norseman 🐾½ **1978 (PG)** Leader of a band of Norsemen sets sail for the New World in search of his missing royal father. Low-budget Viking adventure. **90m/C VHS, Beta.** Lee Majors, Cornel Wilde, Mel Ferrer, Christopher Connelly, Jack Elam; **D:** Charles B. Pierce; **W:** Charles B. Pierce. *LIV, VES*

North 🐾🐾½ **1994 (PG)** Some laughs with a message in family fare from Reiner. Eleven-year old ace kid actor Wood divorces his workaholic parents Alexander and Louis-Dreyfus and searches the world for a functional family (good luck). Willis, who's a treat in a pink bunny suit, acts as guardian angel/narrator and shows the kid what's really important. Illustrious comedic cast inhabits story based on a book by original "Satur-

day Night Live" screenwriter (and "Gary Shandling Show" co-creator) Zweibel, who put things in motion ten years ago when he asked Reiner to write a book jacket quote for the novel. **87m/C VHS, LV, Closed Caption.** Elijah Wood, Jason Alexander, Julia Louis-Dreyfus, Bruce Willis, Jon Lovitz, Alan Arkin, Dan Aykroyd, Kathy Bates, Faith Ford, Graham Greene, Reba McEntire, John Ritter, Abe Vigoda, Kelly McGillis, Alexander Godunov, Noriyuki "Pat" Morita; **D:** Rob Reiner; **W:** Andrew Scheinman, Alan Zweibel; **M:** Marc Shaiman. Nominations: Golden Raspberry Awards '94: Worst Picture, Worst Actor (Willis). *NLC*

North and South Book 1 🐾🐾🐾 **1985** Lavish spectacle about a friendship tested by the turbulent times leading up to Civil War. Orry Main (Swayze) is a South Carolina plantation owner while his best friend George Hazard (Read) comes from a Pennsylvania industrial family. Orry is also involved in a doomed romance with the beautiful Madeline (Down), who's forced to marry the odious Justin LaMotte (Carradine). Lots of intrigue and excitement. Based on the novel by John Jakes. Filmed on location in Charleston, South Carolina. Originally broadcast as a six-part TV miniseries. Available on six cassettes. **561m/C VHS, Beta.** Patrick Swayze, James Read, Lesley-Anne Down, David Carradine, Kirstie Alley, Jean Simmons, Inga Swenson, Jonathon Frakes, Genie Francis, Terri Garber, Georg Stanford Brown, Olivia Cole, David Ogden Stiers, Robert Guillaume, Hal Holbrook, Gene Kelly, Robert Mitchum, Johnny Cash, Elizabeth Taylor; **M:** Bill Conti. *WAR, FUS, TVC*

North and South Book 2 🐾🐾🐾 **1986** Equally dramatic sequel follows the southern Main clan and the northern Hazard family into the Civil War as friendship and romance struggle to survive the fighting. Casnoff is a notable presence as the aptly-named Bent, who will go to any length to settle old scores with both families. Based on the John Jakes novel "Love and War." Originally broadcast as a six-part TV miniseries; on six cassettes. The last of the Jakes trilogy, "Heaven and Hell," was finally filmed for TV in '94 but proved a major disappointment. **570m/C VHS.** Patrick Swayze, James Read, Lesley-Anne Down, Terri Garber, Genie Francis, Jean Simmons, Kirstie Alley, Philip Casnoff, Hal Holbrook, Lloyd Bridges, James Stewart, Morgan Fairchild, Nancy Marchand, Parker Stevenson, Lewis Smith; **M:** Bill Conti. *WAR, TVC*

The North Avenue Irregulars 🐾🐾½ **1979 (G)** Slapstick Disney comedy along the same lines as some of their earlier laugh-fests. A priest and three members of the local ladies' club try to bust a crime syndicate. Though the premise is silly, there are still lots of laughs in this family film. **99m/C VHS.** Edward Herrmann, Barbara Harris, Susan Clark, Karen Valentine, Michael Constantine, Cloris Leachman, Melora Hardin, Alan Hale Jr., Ruth Buzzi, Patsy Kelly, Virginia Capers; **D:** Bruce Bilson; **M:** Robert F. Brunner. *DIS*

North by Northwest 🐾🐾🐾🐾 **1959** Self-assured Madison Avenue ad exec Grant inadvertently gets involved with international spies when they mistake him for someone else. His problems are compounded when he's framed for murder. The movie where Grant and Saint dangle from the faces of Mount Rushmore and a plane chases Grant through farm fields. Exceptional performances, particularly Grant's. Plenty of plot twists are mixed with tongue-in-cheek humor. Considered by many to be one of Hitchcock's greatest films. Laserdisc includes letterboxing, digital soundtrack, Hitchcock interview, production and publicity photos, storyboards, and the original trailer. **136m/C VHS, Beta, LV.** Cary Grant, Eva Marie Saint, James Mason, Leo G. Carroll, Martin Landau, Jessie Royce Landis, Philip Ober, Adam Williams, Josephine Hutchinson, Edward Platt; **D:** Alfred Hitchcock; **W:** Ernest Lehman; **C:** Robert Burks; **M:** Bernard Herrmann. Edgar Allan Poe Awards '59: Best Screenplay; Nominations: Academy Awards '59: Best Art Direction/Set Decoration (Color), Best Film Editing, Best Story & Screenplay. *MGM*

North Dallas Forty 🎥🎥🎥½ 1979 (R)
Based on the novel by former Dallas Cowboy Peter Gent, the film focuses on the labor abuses in pro-football. One of the best football movies ever made, it contains searing commentary and very good acting, although the plot is sometimes dropped behind the line of scrimmage. 119m/C VHS, Beta, LV. Nick Nolte, Mac Davis, Charles Durning, Bo Svenson, Brian Dennehy, John Matuszak, Dayle Haddon, Steve Forrest, Dabney Coleman, G.D. Spradlin; D: Ted Kotcheff. National Board of Review Awards '79: 10 Best Films of the Year. PAR

North of the Border 🎥½ 1946 A cowboy in Canada gets involved with back-stabbing and treachery in and around Alberta. 40m/B VHS, Beta, LV. CA Russell Hayden, Lyle Talbot, Inez Cooper, Douglas Fowley, Jack Mulhall; D: B. Reeves Eason. VYY

North of the Great Divide 🎥½ 1950
Standard Rogers programmer, with Roy as a half-breed mediator between salmon fisherman and Indians. 67m/C VHS. Roy Rogers, Penny Edwards, Gordon Jones, Roy Barcroft, Jack Lambert, Douglas Evans, Noble Johnson; D: William Witney. REP

North Shore 🎥½ 1987 (PG) A young surfer from Arizona hits the beaches of Hawaii and discovers love, sex, and adventure. Only redeeming quality is surfing footage. 96m/C VHS, Beta. Matt Adler, Nia Peeples, John Philbin, Gregory Harrison, Christina Raines; D: Will Phelps. USH

The North Star 🎥🎥🎥 Armored Attack 1943
Gripping war tale of Nazis over-running an eastern Russian city, with courageous villagers fighting back. Colorized version available. 108m/B VHS, Beta. Dana Andrews, Walter Huston, Anne Baxter, Farley Granger, Walter Brennan, Erich von Stroheim, Jack Perrin, Dean Jagger; D: Lewis Milestone; M: Aaron Copland. Nominations: Academy Awards '43: Best Black and White Cinematography, Best Interior Decoration, Best Original Screenplay, Best Sound, Original Dramatic/Comedy Score. NOS, MRV, VYY

North Star 🎥½ 1996 (R) Formulaic actioner where no one seems very enthusiastic. Half-breed trapper Hudson Ipsehawk (Lambert) refuses to mine the gold on his Alaskan property because the land is considered sacred. This doesn't concern greedy miner Sean McLennon (Caan) who wants the property for himself. Oh yeah, there's also a babe, Sarah (McCormack), that both men are interested in. Norway substitutes for Alaska. Based on the novel by Will Henry. CW: Some violence and language. 89m/C VHS, Closed Caption. Christopher Lambert, James Caan, Catherine McCormack, Burt Young; D: Nils Gaup; W: Paul Ohl, Sergio Donati, Lorenzo Donati; C: Bruno de Keyzer; M: Bruce Rowland. WAR

North to Alaska 🎥🎥🎥 1960 A gold prospector encounters many problems when he agrees to pick up his partner's fiancee in Seattle to bring her home to Nome, Alaska, in the 1890s. Overly slapstick at times, but great fun nonetheless. Loosely based on Laszlo Fodor's play "The Birthday Gift." 120m/C VHS, Beta, LV, Closed Caption. John Wayne, Stewart Granger, Ernie Kovacs, Fabian, Capucine; D: Henry Hathaway; C: Leon Shamroy. FOX

Northanger Abbey 🎥🎥½ 1987 Catherine is a young woman whose head is turned by her romance readings of dark secrets, sinister castles, dashing heroes, and helpless women. When the handsome Henry Tilney invites her to visit his ancestral home, Northanger Abbey, it seems all her fancies have come to life. A somewhat tepid adaptation of Jane Austen's parody of the popular Gothic romances of her day. 90m/C VHS. GB Peter Firth, Katherine Schlesinger, Googie Withers, Robert Hardy. TVC, VCO, FUS

Northeast of Seoul 🎥 1972 (PG) Three people will stop at nothing to steal a legendary jewel-encrusted sword out of Korea. 84m/C VHS, Beta. Anita Ekberg, John Ireland, Victor Buono; D: David Lowell Rich. MGM

Northern Extremes 🎥½ Buried on Sunday 1993 (PG) Silly comedy about an eccentric Canadian island village whose fishing livelihood is threatened. So the town mayor captures an errant nuclear submarine and uses it as a big bargaining chip. Filmed in Nova Scotia, Canada. 80m/C VHS. CA Paul Gross, Denise Virieux, Henry Czerny, Jeff Leder, Tommy Sexton, Louis Del Grande, Maury Chaykin; D: Paul Donovan; W: Bill Flemming. ACA

Northern Lights 🎥🎥🎥 1979 A small, black-and-white independent drama depicting the struggle of a lowly farmer combating governmental forces in the 1915 heartland. Subtitled. 85m/B VHS, Beta. Robert Behling, Susan Lynch, Joe Spano, Rob Nilsson, Henry Martinson, Marianne Astrom-DeFina, Ray Ness, Helen Ness; D: Rob Nilsson, John Hanson; W: Rob Nilsson. VTR, NWV

Northern Passage 🎥🎥½ 1995 (PG-13)
Cowboy tries to protect a young Native American woman from harm in the wilderness. CW: Some intense violence. 97m/C VHS. Jeff Fahey, Neve Campbell. THV

Northern Pursuit 🎥🎥½ 1943 A Canadian Mountie disguises himself to infiltrate a Nazi spy ring in this exciting adventure film. Based on Leslie White's "Five Thousand Trojan Horses." 94m/B VHS, Beta. Errol Flynn, Helmut Dantine, Julie Bishop, Gene Lockhart, Tom Tully; D: Raoul Walsh. MGM, MLB

Northville Cemetery Massacre 🎥
The Northfield Cemetery Massacre 1976 (R) Gang of bikers comes to town and all hell breaks loose. The result is a horribly bloody war between the townsfolk and the gang. Yup, it was a massacre. 81m/C VHS, Beta. David Hyry, Craig Collicott, Jan Sisk; W: William Dear. NO

Northwest Outpost 🎥½ End of the Rainbow 1947 Eddy is a California cavalry officer in this lightweight operetta. He helps a young woman who is trying to free her husband from jail, and after his death they are able to pursue their relationship. Eddy's last film. ♫ Weary; Raindrops on a Drum; Tell Me With Your Eyes; One More Mile to Go; Russian Easter Hymn; Love is the Time; Nearer and Dearer. 91m/B VHS. Nelson Eddy, Ilona Massey, Hugo Haas, Elsa Lanchester, Lenore Ulric; D: Allan Dwan. REP

Northwest Passage 🎥🎥🎥 1940 The lavish first half of a projected two-film package based on Kenneth Roberts' popular novel, depicting the troop of Rogers' Rangers fighting the wilderness and hostile Indians. Beautifully produced; the second half was never made and the passage itself is never seen. 126m/C VHS, Beta. Spencer Tracy, Robert Young, Ruth Hussey, Walter Brennan, Nat Pendleton, Robert Barrat, Lumsden Hare; D: King Vidor. Nominations: Academy Awards '40: Best Color Cinematography. MGM

Northwest Trail 🎥🎥 1946 Royal Canadian Mountie Steele's assignment is to escort Woodbury across the wilderness. She's carrying a large sum of money to save her uncle's business. Problem is, killers are on their trail. 75m/C VHS, Beta. Bob Steele, Joan Woodbury, John Litel, Raymond Hatton, Madge Bellamy, Charles Middleton; D: Derwin Abrahams. NOS, HHT, VCN

Nosferatu 🎥🎥🎥🎥 Nosferatu, Eine Symphonie des Grauens; Nosferatu, A Symphony of Terror; Nosferatu, A Symphony of Horror; Nosferatu, The Vampire 1922 The first film adaptation of Bram Stoker's "Dracula" remains one of the creepiest and most atmospheric versions. Murnau knew how to add just the right touches to make this one of the best vampire films ever made. All it lacks is the name of Dracula, which was changed due to copyright problems with Stoker's widow. Filmed in Bavaria. Silent with music and English titles. Remade by Werner Herzog in 1979. 63m/B VHS, Beta, LV. GE Max Schreck, Alexander Granach, Gustav von Wagenheim, Greta Schroeder; D: F.W. Murnau. GPV, MRV, NOS

Nostalgia 🎥🎥 1983 Russian academic Jankovsky comes to Tuscany to research the life of an 18th-century composer and meets the mysterious Josephson, who's convinced the end of the world is near. And soon the homesick Russian is in a search for himself. Filled with Christian iconography and some extraordinary images. Tarkovsky's first film outside his native Russia. Russian and Italian with subtitles; the Russian sequences are filmed in B&W. 126m/C VHS. IT Oleg Jankowsky, Erland Josephson, Domiziana Giordano, Delia Boccardo; D: Andrei Tarkovsky; W: Andrei Tarkovsky, Tonino Guerra; C: Giuseppe Lanci. FCT

Nostradamus 🎥🎥 1993 (R) Historical soap opera about unconventional 16th-century French physician and astrologer Michel de Nostradame. Persecuted by the Inquisition, he comes under the protection of Queen Catherine de Medici of France, although his visions of destruction and death continue to haunt him. Nostradamus' prophecies, first published in 1555, have continued to fascinate, being used to predicate everything from the death of historical leaders to WWI. The film, however, is slow going and fails to hold much interest. CW: Some images of violence and strong sexuality. 118m/C VHS, LV, Closed Caption. FR Tcheky Karyo, F. Murray Abraham, Julia Ormond, Rutger Hauer, Amanda Plummer, Assumpta Serna, Anthony Higgins, Diana Quick, Michael Gough; D: Roger Christian; W: Knut Boeser, Piers Ashworth. ORI

The Nostradamus Kid 🎥🎥 1992 (R)
Young man, convinced the world is about to end, decides his last goal will be to make love (for the first time) with his girlfriend. CW: Sexuality and language. 120m/C VHS. Noah Taylor, Miranda Otto, Arthur Dignam; D: Bob Ellis. LIV

Nostromo 🎥🎥 Joseph Conrad's Nostromo 1996
Tediously drawn-out TV adaptation of the 1904 novel by Joseph Conrad takes place in the 1890's in the fictional South American country of Costaguana. Englishman Charles Gould (Firth) is determined to reopen his family's silver mine—a plan supported by the local regime, which is, however, soon to be overthrown. Amidst the revolution is the title character Nostromo (Amendola), a contraction of "nostro uomo" or "our man," an enigmatic Italian immigrant who organizes the dockworkers and is thrust into the role of hero. Filmed on location in Cartagena, Colombia. On 3 cassettes. 360m/C VHS. Colin Firth, Albert Finney, Claudio Amendola, Serena Scott Thomas, Claudia Cardinale, Brian Dennehy, Lothaire Bluteau, Ruth Gabriel, Joaquim de Almeida; D: Alastair Reid; W: John Hale; M: Ennio Morricone. FOX, SIG, WMI

Not as a Stranger 🎥🎥½ 1955 Glossy film about the medical profession and the varying degrees of dedication shown by doctors. Mitchum stars as an medical student who can't afford to pay his tuition, so he marries nurse de Havilland and continues going to school on her money, although their relationship is far from being a loving one. Producer Kramer's directorial debut. Based on the book by Morton Thompson. 135m/B VHS, Closed Caption. Olivia de Havilland, Robert Mitchum, Frank Sinatra, Gloria Grahame, Broderick Crawford, Charles Bickford, Myron McCormick, Lon Chaney Jr.; D: Stanley Kramer; W: Edward Anhalt. Nominations: Academy Awards '55: Best Sound. MGM

Not for Publication 🎥🎥 1984 (R) A woman working as both a tabloid reporter and a mayoral campaign worker uncovers governmental corruption with the help of a shy photographer and a midget. Meant to be on par with older screwball comedies but lacking the wit and subtlety. 87m/C VHS, Beta. Nancy Allen, David Naughton, Richard Paul, Alice Ghostley, Laurence Luckinbill; D: Paul Bartel; W: Paul Bartel. NO

Not My Kid 🎥🎥½ 1985 The 15-year-old daughter of a surgeon brings turmoil to her family when she becomes heavily involved in drugs. Producer Polson, along with Dr. Miller Newton, wrote the original book for this emotional story that is one of the better treatments of this impor-

tant subject. Made for television. **120m/C VHS, Beta.** George Segal, Stockard Channing, Viveka Davis, Andrew (Andy) Robinson, Gary Bayer, Nancy Cartwright, Tate Donovan; *D:* Michael Tuchner; *W:* Christopher Knopf. *SVE*

Not of This Earth 🎬½ 1988 **(R)** In a remake of the 1957 Roger Corman quickie, an alien wearing sunglasses makes an unfriendly trip to Earth. In order to save his dying planet he needs major blood donations from unsuspecting Earthlings. Not a match for the original version, some may nevertheless want to see ex-porn star Lords in her role as the nurse. **92m/C VHS, Beta.** Traci Lords, Arthur Roberts, Lenny Juliano, Rebecca Perle, Ace Mask, Roger Lodge; *D:* Jim Wynorski; *W:* Jim Wynorski, R.J. Robertson. *MGM*

Not of This Earth 🎬🎬 1996 **(R)** Corman cable remake of his own 1957 cheapie is both camp and sexy. Sunglass-wearing mystery millionaire Paul Johnson (York) apparently suffers from a rare condition and must have constant blood transfusions, so he hires a sexy live-in nurse (Barondes) to be at his beck-and-call. Yes, he does turn out to be a vampire but of the space alien-with-telepathic-powers variety who has a particular purpose for coming to earth.*CW:* Language, extreme violence, nudity, gore. **92m/C VHS.** Michael York, Elizabeth Barondes, Richard Belzer, Parker Stevenson; *D:* Terence H. Winkless. *NHO*

Not Quite Human 🎬🎬 1987 When Jonas Carson builds himself an android teenage son, he must keep the technology from falling into the hands of an evil toy manufacturer with plans of his own. Humorous hijinks abound. Based on the book series "Not Quite Human" by Seth McEvoy. Made for cable television; followed by two sequels. **91m/C VHS, Beta, Closed Caption.** Alan Thicke, Robin Lively, Robert Harper, Joseph Bologna, Jay Underwood; *D:* Steven Hilliard Stern. *DIS*

Not Quite Human 2 🎬🎬½ 1989 In this sequel, Dr. Jonas Carson sends his cyber-son off to college where Chip meets the not-quite-human girl of his dreams. Followed by "Still Not Quite Human." Made for cable television. **91m/C VHS, Beta, Closed Caption.** Alan Thicke, Jay Underwood, Robin Lively, Greg Mullavey, Katie Barberi, Mark Arnott; *D:* Eric Luke. *DIS*

Not Quite Paradise 🎬 *Not Quite Jerusalem* 1986 **(R)** A young American medical student falls in love with a young Israeli girl living on a kibbutz. **106m/C VHS, Beta.** Sam Robards, Joanna Pacula; *D:* Lewis Gilbert. *VTR, NWV*

Not Tonight Darling 🎬 1972 **(R)** A bored suburban housewife becomes involved with a fast-talking businessman who leads her into a web of deceit and blackmail. **70m/C VHS, Beta.** Luan Peters, Vincent Ball, Jason Twelvetrees. *GEM*

Not Without My Daughter 🎬🎬½ 1990 **(PG-13)** Overwrought drama shot in Israel about American Field, who travels with her Arab husband and their daughter to his native Iran, where (he must have forgotten to tell her) she has no rights. He decides the family will stay, using beatings and confinement to persuade his uncooperative wife, but she risks all to escape with daughter. Based on the true story of Betty Mahmoody. **116m/C VHS, Beta, LV, 8mm, Closed Caption.** Sally Field, Alfred Molina, Sheila Rosenthal, Roshan Seth, Sarah Badel, Mony Rey, Georges Corraface; *D:* Brian Gilbert. *MGM, FCT*

Notes for an African Orestes 🎬🎬 1970 Director Pasolini's insight into how a filmmaker works and what motivates him, as the camera reveals his plans to film a modern day version of Aeschylus' "Orestes" in Africa. **75m/B VHS.** *D:* Pier Paolo Pasolini; *M:* Gato Barbieri. *MFV, CIG*

Nothing But a Man 🎬🎬½ 1964 Duff Anderson (Dixon) is a black laborer trying to make a life in a small Alabama town. He falls for the daughter of a minister, they marry, and he gets a job at a local sawmill. When he won't bend to his racist white employers, he's fired and labeled a troublemaker. Unsentimental depiction of the

times. **95m/B VHS.** Ivan Dixon, Abbey Lincoln, Gloria Foster, Julius W. Harris, Martin Priest, Yaphet Kotto; *D:* Michael Roemer; *W:* Michael Roemer. *NEW, BTV, AAE*

Nothing But the Night 🎬½ *The Devil's Undead; The Resurrection Syndicate* 1972 **(PG)** Lee's company produced this convoluted story of orphans who are victims of a cult that uses them in their quest for immortality. **90m/C VHS.** *GB* Christopher Lee, Peter Cushing, Diana Dors, Georgia Brown, Keith Barron, Fulton Mackay, Gwyneth Strong; *D:* Peter Sasdy. *SNC*

Nothing But Trouble 🎬🎬½ 1944 Laurel & Hardy's last film for MGM is a complicated tale of two servants who wind up protecting an exiled boy king from the machinations of his power-mad uncle. **70m/B VHS.** Stan Laurel, Oliver Hardy, Henry O'Neill, Mary Boland, David Leland, John Warburton, Connie Gilchrist, Philip Merivale; *D:* Sam Taylor. *MGM*

Nothing But Trouble 🎬 1991 **(PG-13)** Yuppie couple out for weekend drive find themselves smoldering in small town hell thanks to a traffic ticket. Horror and humor mix like oil and water in Aykroyd's debut as director. **93m/C VHS, Beta, LV, 8mm, Closed Caption.** Dan Aykroyd, Demi Moore, Chevy Chase, John Candy, Taylor Negron, Bertila Demas, Valri Bromfield; *D:* Dan Aykroyd; *W:* Dan Aykroyd, Peter Aykroyd; *C:* Dean Cundey. Golden Raspberry Awards '91: Worst Supporting Actor (Aykroyd). *WAR*

Nothing in Common 🎬🎬½ 1986 **(PG)** In his last film, Gleason plays the abrasive, diabetic father of immature advertising agency worker Hanks. After his parents separate, Hanks learns to be more responsible and loving in caring for his father. Comedy and drama are blended well here with the help of satirical pokes at the ad business and Hanks turns in a fine performance, but the unorganized, lengthy plot may lose some viewers. **119m/C VHS, Beta, LV, Closed Caption.** Tom Hanks, Jackie Gleason, Eva Marie Saint, Bess Armstrong, Hector Elizondo, Barry Corbin, Sela Ward, John Kapelos, Jane Morris, Dan Castellaneta, Tracy Reiner; *D:* Garry Marshall; *W:* Rick Podell; *C:* John A. Alonzo; *M:* Patrick Leonard. *WAR*

Nothing Personal 🎬½ 1980 **(PG)** Confused mix of romantic comedy and environmental themes. Lawyer (?) Somers attempts to help college professor Sutherland prevent the slaughter of seals. Enter romance (hey, but what about the baby seals?). Enlivened by appearances of Canadian SCTV vets and Somers's first starring theatrical role. **96m/C VHS, Beta, LV.** Donald Sutherland, Suzanne Somers, Dabney Coleman, John Dehner, Roscoe Lee Browne, Catherine O'Hara; *D:* George Bloomfield. *LIV, VES*

Nothing Personal 🎬🎬🎬 1995 Uncompromising drama about the sectarian violence in northern Ireland that engulfs even the innocent. The IRA bombing of a Protestant pub sets a Loyalist unit, led by dedicated Kenny (Frain) and psychotic Ginger (a terrifying Hart), on an increasingly deadly 24-hour rampage through Belfast (in 1975). Catholic single father Liam Kelly (Lynch) finds himself in the wrong part of town and only wants to return to his two children but is inexorably drawn into the violence, which leads to tragedy for all. Adapted from the novel "All Our Fault" by Mornin, who wrote the screenplay. **86m/C VHS.** *GB IR* Ian Hart, John Lynch, James Frain, Michael Gambon, Ruaidhri Conroy, Jeni Courtney, Gary Lydon, Maria Doyle Kennedy, Gerard McSorley, Gareth O'Hare; *D:* Thaddeus O'Sullivan; *W:* Daniel Mornin; *C:* Dick Pope; *M:* Philip Appleby. *NYR*

Nothing Sacred 🎬🎬🎬½ 1937 Slick, overzealous reporter takes advantage of a small-town girl's situation. As a publicity stunt, his newspaper brings her to the Big Apple to distract her from her supposedly imminent death in order to manipulate the public's sentiment as a means to sell more copy. Innocent young Lombard, however, is far from death's door, and deftly exploits her exploitation. Scathing indictment of the mass media and bovine mentality of the masses. Both hysterically funny and bitterly cynical; boasts

Lombard's finest performance as the small-town rube who orchestrates the ruse. Remade in 1954 as "Living It Up." **75m/C VHS, LV.** Fredric March, Carole Lombard, Walter Connolly, Sig Rumann, Charles Winninger, Margaret Hamilton; *D:* William A. Wellman; *W:* Ben Hecht; *C:* William Howard Greene; *M:* Oscar Levant. *KIV, MRV, VYY*

Nothing to Lose 🎬🎬½ 1996 **(R)** Ad exec Nick Beam (Robbins) is having a very bad day. He loses his job, finds his wife is having an affair, then gets carjacked by street-wise but dim-witted thief T-Paul (Lawrence). T-Paul picked the wrong day to rob Nick, who ironically takes T-Paul hostage. The unlikely pair find they have more in common than realized. Screwball comedy comedy shows its originality in casting, and not much else. Robbins and Lawrence are an inspired pair with great comedic potential but are trapped in a mundane story. Filming was delayed due, in part, to Lawrence's constant run-ins with the law.*CW:* Pervasive strong language and a sex scene. **?m/C VHS.** Tim Robbins, Martin Lawrence, John C. McGinley, Giancarlo Esposito, Kelly Preston; *D:* Steve Oedekerk; *W:* Steve Oedekerk; *C:* Donald E. Thorin; *M:* Robert Folk. *NYR*

Nothing Underneath 🎬½ 1985 An American guy goes to Rome to search for his model twin sister, who may be one of the victims of a series of scissor killings. **95m/C VHS, Beta.** Tom Schanley, Renee Simonsen, Nicola Perring, Donald Pleasence; *D:* Carlo Vanzina. *NO*

Notorious 🎬🎬🎬🎬 1946 Post-WWII story of a beautiful playgirl sent by the US government to marry a suspected spy living in Brazil. Grant is the agent assigned to watch her. Duplicity and guilt are important factors in this brooding, romantic spy thriller. Suspenseful throughout, with a surprise ending. The acting is excellent all around and Hitchcock makes certain that suspense is maintained throughout this classy and complex thriller. Laser edition contains original trailer, publicity photos, and additional footage. **101m/B VHS, Beta, LV, Closed Caption.** Cary Grant, Ingrid Bergman, Claude Rains, Louis Calhern, Madame Konstantin, Reinhold Schunzel, Moroni Olsen; *D:* Alfred Hitchcock; *W:* Ben Hecht. Nominations: Academy Awards '46: Best Original Screenplay, Best Supporting Actor (Rains). *FOX, CRC, MLB*

The Notorious Lady 🎬🎬½ 1927 Englishman Stone kills the man he finds in Bedford's room, believing him to be his wife's lover. He's mistaken but she lies to save him and Stone takes off for the diamond mines in Africa. Bedford hears he's dead and sets out, seeking the truth. **79m/B VHS.** Lewis Stone, Barbara Bedford, Earl Metcalfe, Francis McDonald; *D:* King Baggot; *C:* Gaetano Antonio "Tony" Gaudio. *FCT*

Nous N'Irons Plus au Bois 🎬🎬 1969 On the outskirts of a forest held by the Germans, a small group of French resistance fighters capture a German soldier during WWII. He actually wants to join forces with them, however, after falling in love with a lovely young French girl. In French; subtitled in English. **98m/C VHS, Beta.** *FR* Marie-France Pisier, Siegfried Rauch, Richard Leduc; *D:* Georges Dumoulin. *NO*

Nouvelle Vague 🎬🎬½ *New Wave* 1990 Delon is a philosopher king and Giordano a wealthy countess involved in Godard's usual sexual and political themes, which has society geared toward support of the rich. Dialogue is composed entirely of quotations. In French with English subtitles. **89m/C VHS.** *SI FR* Alain Delon, Domiziana Giordano, Roland Amstutz, Laurence Cote, Christophe Odent; *D:* Jean-Luc Godard; *W:* Jean-Luc Godard. *FCT*

Novel Desires 🎬½ 1992 **(R)** Brian Freedman is a best-selling author who teams up with his writing rival, Vicky Chance. But it isn't just their imaginations they give free reign to, it's all their desires as well.*CW:* Strong sexuality. **80m/C VHS.** Tyler Gains, Caroline Monteith, Mitchell Clark, Lisa Hayland; *D:* Lawrence Unger. *CEL*

November Conspiracy 🎬🎬½ 1996 (R) Journalist Jenny Baron (Turco) is covering the presidential campaign of a senator (Segal) when she uncovers a conspiracy linking a number of assassinations and murder attempts. A computer disk reveals more information but when her lover (Benedict) is murdered during an attempted political assassination, Baron goes on the run to save her own life.**CW:** Nudity, language, violence. 103m/C VHS, Closed Caption. Paige Turco, George Segal, Elliott Gould, Bo Hopkins, Dirk Benedict, Conrad Janis; **D:** Conrad Janis. **MET**

Now and Forever 🎬🎬½ 1934 Penny (Temple) is the young daughter of charming widower and con man Jerry Day (Cooper). Penny's been in the care of her uncle but Jerry's decided to settle down in Paris with his lady love Toni (Lombard) and figures he can give the tyke a home. But the hard-up Jerry can't resist stealing a valuable necklace and there's much trouble ahead (and not your average happy ending). Temple steals the film from her elders. Adapted from the story "Honor Bright" by Jack Kirkland and Melville Baker. Colorized. 82m/C VHS, Closed Caption. Gary Cooper, Carole Lombard, Shirley Temple, Guy Standing, Charlotte Granville, Gilbert Emery; **D:** Henry Hathaway; **W:** Vincent Lawrence, Sylvia Thalberg; **C:** Harry Fischbeck. **USH**

Now and Forever 🎬½ 1982 (R) Young wife's life is shattered when her unfaithful husband is wrongly accused and convicted of rape. After he is sent to prison, she begins drinking and taking drugs. From the novel by Danielle Steel, it will appeal most to those who like their romances a la Harlequin. 93m/C VHS, Beta, LV. **AU** Cheryl Ladd, Robert Coleby, Carmen Duncan, Christine Amor, Aileen Britton; **D:** Adrian Carr. **USH**

Now and Then 🎬🎬 1995 (PG-13) Four women hold a reunion 25 years after their most eventful childhood summer to relive the good ol' days of prepubescent triumphs and tragedies. Flashback, which thankfully comprises about 85% of the movie, explores first kisses, budding breasts, death and divorce. Despite good intentions, this nostalgic coming-of-ager for the girls is a jumbled mass of borrowed formulas that just can't shake that feeling of forced sentimentality. The young actresses are talented and charming, but their less convincing adult counterparts serve mostly as big names to draw crowds and studio support.**CW:** Contains strong language, brief nudity, and adolescent discussions about sex. 97m/C VHS, LV, Closed Caption. Rosie O'Donnell, Melanie Griffith, Demi Moore, Rita Wilson, Christina Ricci, Thora Birch, Gaby Hoffman, Ashleigh Aston Moore, Cloris Leachman, Lolita Davidovich, Bonnie Hunt, Brendan Fraser; **D:** Leslie Linka Glatter; **W:** I. Marlene King; **C:** Ueli Steiger; **M:** Cliff Eidelman. **NLC**

Now, Voyager 🎬🎬🎬½ 1942 Davis plays a lonely spinster who is transformed into a vibrant young woman by therapy. She comes out of her shell to have a romantic affair with a suave European (who turns out to be married) but still utters the famous phrase "Oh, Jerry, we have the stars. Let's not ask for the moon." Definitely melodramatic, but an involving story nonetheless. Based on a novel by Olive Higgins Prouty. 117m/B VHS, Beta, LV. Bette Davis, Gladys Cooper, Claude Rains, Paul Henreid, Bonita Granville; **D:** Irving Rapper; **M:** Max Steiner. Academy Awards '42: Original Dramatic/Comedy Score; Nominations: Academy Awards '42: Best Actress (Davis), Best Supporting Actress (Cooper). **MGM**

Now You See Him, Now You Don't 🎬🎬 1972 (G) Light Disney comedy involving a gang of crooks who want to use a college student's invisibility formula to rob a local bank. Sequel to Disney's "The Computer Wore Tennis Shoes." 85m/C VHS, Beta. Kurt Russell, Joe Flynn, Cesar Romero, Jim Backus; **D:** Robert Butler; **M:** Robert F. Brunner. **DIS**

Nowhere 🎬🎬 1996 (R) Third in Araki's teen trilogy, following "Totally F***ed Up" and "The Doom Generation" is a basic day-in-the-life look at alienated L.A. 18-year-old Dark Smith (Duval), adrift in a world of consumerism and looking for love. He loves Mel (True) but she's torn between Dark and girlfriend Lucifer (Robertson), so Dark turns to Montgomery (Bexton). His friends have their own trials with drugs and sex (in various combos), and violence. Angst to the Nth degree, with Araki's imagination in wild disarray.**CW:** Scenes of strong violence, sexuality and drug use involving teens, and for strong language. 82m/C VHS. James Duval, Rachel True, Kathleen Robertson, Nathan Bexton, Guillermo Diaz, Alan Boyce, Christina Applegate, Jeremy Jordan, Chiara Mastroianni, Debi Mazar, Jordan Ladd, Thyme Lewis, Sarah Lassez, Ryan Phillippe, Heather Graham, Scott Caan; **Cameos:** John Ritter; **D:** Gregg Araki; **W:** Gregg Araki; **C:** Arturo Smith. **NYR**

Nowhere to Hide 🎬🎬 1987 (R) A widow whose Marine officer husband has been assassinated is chased by some bad guys who are after a helicopter part (say what?) and she must fight for survival for herself and her 6-year-old son. 91m/C VHS, Beta, Closed Caption. Amy Madigan, Daniel Hugh-Kelly, Michael Ironside; **D:** Mario Azzopardi; **M:** Brad Fiedel. **ORI, HHE, WAR**

Nowhere to Hide 🎬🎬 19?? A hitman is hired to kill a young boy who witnesses a brutal murder. The hitman, however, decides he's already killed too many people and wants to get out of the business. Will he become the next murder target? 80m/C VHS. Paul Winfield, Rod Taylor. **QVD**

Nowhere to Run 🎬 1988 (R) Slipshod version of a true story about a series of murders in Caddo, Texas in 1960. Carradine, paroled from prison, murders for revenge while six high school seniors get involved in the chase and in the seedy side of politics, police, and their own puberty. 87m/C VHS, Beta. David Carradine, Jason Priestley, Kieran Mulroney, Henry Jones; **D:** Carl Franklin. **MGM**

Nowhere to Run 🎬½ 1993 (R) Kickboxer with heart seeks cross-over movie to establish real acting career. Unfortunately, even if such a movie existed, Van Damme wouldn't know what to do with it. Arquette plays the damsel in distress, facing eviction from the family farm with her two small children. Fortunately for Van Damme's escaped convict character, she is also a very lonely widow (nudge, nudge). He saves the day by abusing the daylights out of the big bad bankers, yet also finds time to play surrogate dad. Whatta guy.**CW:** Language, violence, and sexuality. 95m/C VHS, LV, 8mm, Closed Caption. Jean-Claude Van Damme, Rosanna Arquette, Kieran Culkin, Tiffany Taubman, Joss Ackland, Ted Levine; **D:** Robert Harmon; **W:** Joe Eszterhas, Leslie Bohem, Randy Feldman; **M:** Mark Isham. **COL**

Nuclear Conspiracy 🎬½ 1985 A reporter disappears while investigating a huge nuclear waste shipment, and his wife searches for him. 115m/C VHS, Beta. Birgit Doll, Albert Fortell. **THV**

The Nude Bomb 🎬🎬½ The Return of Maxwell Smart 1980 (PG) Proof that old TV shows never die—they just get made into big screen movies. Maxwell Smart from "Get Smart" (would you believe?) tries to save the world from a bomb intended to destroy clothing and leave everyone in the buff. Old hat lines. Followed by the TV movie "Get Smart, Again!" 94m/C VHS, LV. Don Adams, Dana Elcar, Pamela Hensley, Sylvia Kristel, Norman Lloyd, Rhonda Fleming, Joey Forman; **D:** Clive Donner; **W:** Bill Dana; **M:** Lalo Schifrin. **USH**

Nude on the Moon woof! 1961 Lunar expedition discovers moon inhabited by people who bare skin as hobby. Groovy theme song, "I'm Mooning Over You, My Little Moon Doll." Part of Joe Bob Brigg's "Sleaziest Movies in the History of the World" series. 83m/C VHS. **D:** Doris Wishman. **VTR**

Nudity Required 🎬 1990 Two pals use the casting couch, pretending to be Hollywood producers, to seduce young women. Silly comedy with gratuitous nudity (Ms. Newmar included). Hardly a laugh to be found. 90m/C VHS. Julie Newmar, Troy Donahue, Brad Zutaut, Billy Frank, Ty Randolph, Alvin Silver, Eli Rich, Phil Hock; **D:** John Bown. **NO**

Nudo di Donna 🎬🎬🎬 Portrait of a Woman, Nude 1983 A witty comedy about a Venetian bookseller who is becoming tired of marital struggles with his sexy wife of 16 years. He wanders into a fashion photography shop, sees a backside nude photo of a model who looks like his wife, and he takes off in fiery pursuit to find the subject of the photo. Venetian location photography is quite nice. In Italian with English subtitles. 112m/C VHS, Beta, LV. **IT** Nino Manfredi, Jean-Pierre Cassel, George Wilson, Elenora Giorgi; **D:** Nino Manfredi. **APD, TPV**

Nueba Yol 🎬🎬 1995 Balbuena (Marti) is a recent widower with nothing much to look forward to in his native Dominican Republic, so he's easily persuaded by fast-talking friend Fellito (Carbonell) into immigrating to New York (illegally). He has trouble finding any kind of work, is confused and intimidated by the city, and finds himself at odds with more acclimated immigrants from his homeland. Spanish with subtitles. 105m/C VHS. Luisito Marti, Caridad Ravelo, Raul Carbonell, Joel Garcia; **D:** Angel Muniz; **W:** Angel Muniz; **C:** Chris Norr. **KIT**

Nukie 🎬🎬½ 1993 (G) Brothers from another planet crash land on Earth. The first one is subjected to a dizzying array of scientific experiments in Florida involving electric cattle prods. The other one, Nukie, lands in Africa and is befriended by twins from a remote tribal village. They join him in his quest to free his brother from the sadistic clutches of suntanned professionals who have lost all compassion. Important message for our youth about the dangers of a runaway technocracy. 99m/C VHS, LV. Glynis Johns, Steve Railsback; **D:** Sias Odendal. **THV**

Number One Fan 🎬½ 1994 (R) Hollywood action star Zane Barry (McQueen) is stalked by Blair (Ammann), a fan with whom he had a brief romance. Zane manages to patch things up when fiancee Holly (Stewart) finds out but Blair's determined to be the only woman in his life.**CW:** Some language; strong violence; sexuality. 93m/C VHS, Closed Caption. Chad McQueen, Catherine Mary Stewart, Renee Ammann, Hoyt Axton, Paul Bartel, Eric Da Re, Charles Matthau; **D:** Jane Simpson; **W:** Anthony Laurence Greene. **ORI**

Number 1 of the Secret Service 🎬🎬 1977 (PG) A handsome secret agent must foil the plans of a maniacal industrialist to destroy the economy. Spy spoof that's marginally interesting. 87m/C VHS, Beta. **GB** Nicky Henson, Geoffrey Keen, Sue Lloyd, Aimi MacDonald, Richard Todd; **D:** Lindsay Shonteff. **MGM**

Number One with a Bullet 🎬🎬 1987 (R) Two unorthodox "odd couple" detectives are demoted after losing a key witness, but still set out on their own to unearth a drug czar. Carradine and Williams are better than this standard action material. 103m/C VHS, Beta. Robert Carradine, Billy Dee Williams, Peter Graves, Valerie Bertinelli; **D:** Jack Smight; **W:** James Belushi, Andrew Kurtzman, Rob Riley. **MGM**

No. 17 🎬🎬🎬 1932 A humorous early thriller by the Master Hitchcock, filmed before the likes of "The 39 Steps." An unsuspecting hobo accidentally discovers a jewel thief's cache. The chase is on—superb final chase sequence involving a bus and a train. Based on the play by J. Jefferson Farjeon. 64m/B VHS, Beta, 8mm. **GB** Leon M. Lion, Anne Grey, John Stuart, Donald Calthrop; **D:** Alfred Hitchcock; **W:** Alfred Hitchcock. **REP, NOS, HHT**

Numero Deux 🎬🎬 Number Two 1975 Godard explores politics, sex, and the trials of the modern family. A dissatisfied wife suffers from chronic constipation, her exhausted husband is impotent, they, their children, and grandparents all try to cope with daily life. For nine-tenths of the film Godard only used small portions of the screen (the upper left and lower right corners) to manipulate his message of frustration. It's only at the end that the full-screen is used to offer some sort of relief. In French with English subtitles. **90m/C VHS.** *FR* Sandrine Battistella, Pierre Oudry, Alexandre Rignault, Rachel Stefanopol; **D:** Jean-Luc Godard; **W:** Anne-Marie Mieville, Jean-Luc Godard. *FCT*

The Nun 🐾🐾½ 1966 A young woman, unable to meet financial obligations, is forced into a convent. Victimized by the mother superior and betrayed by a clergyman who befriends her, she escapes from the convent and eventually ends up in a bordello, despairing and suicidal. Not a cheery story. Banned in France for two years. In French with English subtitles. **155m/C VHS.** *FR* Anna Karina, Lilo (Liselotte) Pulver, Micheline Presle, Christine Lenier, Francine Berge, Francesco Rabal, Wolfgang Reichmann, Catherine Diamant, Yori Bertin; **D:** Jacques Rivette. *INT, FCT*

Nuns on the Run 🐾🐾 1990 (PG-13) Idle and Coltrane are two nonviolent members of a robbery gang who double-cross their boss during a hold-up and disguise themselves as nuns while on the run from both the Mob and the police. Catholic humor, slapstick, and much fun with habits dominate. Idle and Coltrane do their best to keep the so-so script moving with its one-joke premise. **95m/C VHS, Beta, LV.** Eric Idle, Robbie Coltrane, Janet Suzman, Camille Coduri, Robert Patterson, Tom Hickey, Doris Hare, Lila Kaye; **D:** Jonathan Lynn; **W:** Jonathan Lynn. *FOX*

The Nun's Story 🐾🐾🐾½ 1959 The melancholy tale of a young nun working in the Congo and Belgium during WWII, and struggling to reconcile her free spirit with the rigors of the order. Highly acclaimed; from the Kathryn Hulme novel. **152m/C VHS, Beta, LV.** Audrey Hepburn, Peter Finch, Edith Evans, Peggy Ashcroft, Mildred Dunnock, Dean Jagger, Beatrice Straight, Colleen Dewhurst; **D:** Fred Zinnemann; **W:** Robert Anderson. British Academy Awards '59: Best Actress (Hepburn); National Board of Review Awards '59: 10 Best Films of the Year, Best Director (Zinnemann), Best Supporting Actress (Evans); New York Film Critics Awards '59: Best Actress (Hepburn), Best Director (Zinnemann); Nominations: Academy Awards '59: Best Actress (Hepburn), Best Adapted Screenplay, Best Color Cinematography, Best Director (Zinnemann), Best Film Editing, Best Picture, Best Sound, Original Dramatic/Comedy Score. *WAR*

Nurse 🐾🐾½ 1980 A recently widowed woman resumes her career as a nurse in a large urban hospital, after her son leaves for college. Based on Peggy Anderson's book. Made for television; became a weekly series. **105m/C VHS, Beta.** Michael Learned, Robert Reed, Antonio Fargas; **D:** David Lowell Rich. *LIV*

The Nurse 🐾½ 1997 (R) Nurse (Zane) seeks revenge from the man she holds responsible for her father's suicide. **94m/C VHS, LV, Closed Caption.** Lisa Zane, John Stockwell, Janet Gunn, William R. Moses, Nancy Dussault, Sherrie Rose, Jay Underwood, Michael Fairman; **D:** Rob Malenfant; **W:** Richard Brandes; **C:** Feliks Parnell; **M:** Richard Bowers. *LIV*

Nurse Edith Cavell 🐾🐾🐾 1939 Fine performances in this true story of Britain's famous nurse who aided the Belgian underground during WWI, transporting wounded soldiers out of the German-occupied country. Decidedly opposes war and, ironically, was released just as WWII began to heat up in 1939. **95m/B VHS, Beta.** George Sanders, Edna May Oliver, ZaSu Pitts, Robert Coote, May Robson, Anna Neagle; **D:** Herbert Wilcox. Nominations: Academy Awards '39: Best Original Score. *NOS, CAB, BAR*

Nurse Marjorie 🐾🐾 1920 Aristocratic nurse Marjorie (Minter) falls in love and marries the leader of the Labor Party, much to her family's dismay. Based on the play by Israel Zangwill. Minter made four films with director Taylor, whose murder in 1922 has never been solved. **?m/B VHS.** Mary Miles Minter, Clyde Fillmore, George Periolat, Mollie McConnell, Frank Leigh, Vera Lewis; **D:** William Desmond Taylor; **W:** Julia Crawford Ivers. *GPV*

Nurse on Call 🐾 1988 A bevy of trampy nurses cavort throughout a big city hospital. Softcore. **80m/C VHS, Beta.** Anne Tilson, Jennie Martinez, Christopher Floyd. *MED*

The Nut 🐾🐾½ 1921 Charlie Jackson (Fairbanks) is a wacky, wealthy inventor who falls for Estrell Wynn (De La Motte), a society gal dedicated to improving the lives of underprivileged children. He tries to aid her in a variety of ways—none of which work out as he expects. The usually swashbuckling Fairbanks does get to rescue the heroine. **61m/B VHS.** Douglas Fairbanks Sr., Marguerite de la Motte, William E. Lowery; **D:** Theodore Reed; **W:** William Parker. *FCT, KIV*

Nutcase 🐾 1983 A trio of young children in New Zealand attempt to thwart a group of terrorists who threaten to reactivate a large city's volcanoes unless they are given a large sum of money. Novel twist there. **49m/C VHS, Beta.** *NZ* Nevan Rowe, Ian Watkin, Michael Wilson; **D:** Roger Donaldson. *NO*

The Nutcracker Prince 🐾🐾 1991 The classic children's Christmas tale comes alive in this feature-length animated special. **75m/C VHS, LV, 8mm, Closed Caption.** *CA* **D:** Paul Schibli; **V:** Kiefer Sutherland, Megan Follows, Michael MacDonald, Phyllis Diller, Peter O'Toole. *WAR*

Nutcracker Sweet 🐾 1984 Ridiculous drama about a beautiful and powerful socialite (Collins) who runs a renowned ballet company with an iron fist. A Russian ballerina defects and infiltrates Collins's company to try out her own treacherous motives. **101m/C VHS, Beta.** Joan Collins, Finola Hughes, Paul Nicholas; **D:** Anwar Kawadri. *LIV, VES*

Nutcracker: The Motion Picture 🐾🐾 1986 A lavish, stage-bound filmization of the Tchaikovsky ballet, designed by Maurice Sendak. **82m/C VHS, Beta.** **D:** Carroll Ballard. *PAR, BAR, KAR*

Nuts 🐾🐾🐾 1987 (R) A high-priced prostitute attempts to prove her sanity when she's accused of manslaughter. Ashamed of her lifestyle, and afraid of her reasons for it, her parents attempt to institutionalize her. A filmed version of Tom Topor's play that manages to retain its mesmerizing qualities. Fine performances, although the funny-girl goes over the top on several occasions. **116m/C VHS, Beta, LV, 8mm, Closed Caption.** Barbra Streisand, Richard Dreyfuss, Maureen Stapleton, Karl Malden, James Whitmore, Robert Webber, Eli Wallach, Leslie Nielsen, William Prince, Dakin Matthews, Hayley Taylor Block; **D:** Martin Ritt; **W:** Tom Topor, Darryl Ponicsan, Alvin Sargent; **C:** Andrzej Bartkowiak; **M:** Barbra Streisand. *WAR*

Nuts in May 🐾🐾 1976 Two smug, middle-aged, middle-class vegetarians go on a camping trip and totally alienate their cynical, working-class fellow campers. Made for British television. **84m/C VHS.** *GB* Alison Steadman; **D:** Mike Leigh. *WBF, BTV*

The Nutt House 🐾½ 1995 (PG-13) Identical twins—separated at birth— grow up to be a slimy politician and a nutcase (living up to the family name) with multiple personalities. Naturally, when the two are reunited it makes for lots of outrageous complications. **CW:** Farcical sex-related scenes. **90m/C VHS, LV.** Stephen Kearney, Traci Lords, Amy Yasbeck; **Cameos:** Stella Stevens, Robert Mandan, Catherine Bach; **D:** Adam Rifkin. *TRI*

The Nutty Professor 🐾🐾🐾 1963 A mild-mannered chemistry professor creates a potion that turns him into a suave, debonair, playboy type with an irresistible attraction to women. Lewis has repeatedly denied the slick character is a Dean Martin parody, but the evidence is quite strong. Easily Lewis's best film. **107m/C VHS, LV.** Jerry Lewis, Stella Stevens, Howard Morris, Kathleen Freeman; **D:** Jerry Lewis; **W:** Jerry Lewis. *PAR*

The Nutty Professor 🐾🐾🐾 1996 (PG-13) Remake of the 1963 Jerry Lewis comedy stars Murphy as Professor Sherman Klump, a severely overweight but bright man whose heft gets in the way of his love life. He takes a swig of his own secret potion and is transformed into the slim

and suave Buddy Love. Only the formula isn't perfect and seems to wear off at the worst possible times. After a string of bad movies, Murphy may have stumbled upon his own formula for a comeback by relinquishing creative control and concentrating on the comedy. Reminiscent of "Coming to America," Murphy plays eight roles. The fat and fart jokes are plentiful and so are the laughs. **CW:** Crude humor and sexual references. **96m/C VHS, LV, Closed Caption.** Eddie Murphy, Jada Pinkett, James Coburn, Dave Chappelle; **D:** Tom Shadyac; **W:** David Sheffield, Barry W. Blaustein, Steve Oedekerk, Tom Shadyac; **C:** Julio Macat; **M:** David Newman. Academy Awards '96: Best Makeup; National Society of Film Critics Awards '96: Best Actor (Murphy); Nominations: Golden Globe Awards '97: Best Actor—Musical/Comedy (Murphy); MTV Movie Awards '97: Best Male Performance (Murphy), Best Comedic Performance (Murphy). *USH*

A Nymphoid Barbarian in Dinosaur Hell woof! 1994 Nuclear holocaust survivors, human and otherwise, vie for the affections of the last woman alive, a voluptuous nymphoid barbarian. **90m/C VHS.** Linda Corwin, Paul Guzzi. *TTV*

Nyoka and the Tigermen *Nyoka and the Lost Secrets of Hippocrates; Perils of Nyoka* 1942 The adventures of the jungle queen Nyoka and her rival Vultura in their search for the lost tablets of Hippocrates. In 15 episodes. **250m/B VHS, LV.** Kay Aldridge, Clayton Moore; **D:** William Witney. *VCN, REP, MLB*

O Lucky Man! 🐾🐾🐾🐾 1973 (R) Surreal, black comedy following the rise and fall and eventual rebirth of a modern British coffee salesman. Several actors play multiple roles with outstanding performances throughout. Price's excellent score combines with the hilarity for an extraordinary experience. **178m/C VHS, Beta.** *GB* Malcolm McDowell, Ralph Richardson, Rachel Roberts, Arthur Lowe, Alan Price, Helen Mirren, Mona Washbourne, Warren Clarke; **D:** Lindsay Anderson; **M:** Alan Price. British Academy Awards '73: Best Supporting Actor (Lowe); National Board of Review Awards '73: 10 Best Films of the Year. *WAR*

O Pioneers! 🐾🐾½ 1991 (PG) Lange plays Alexandra Bergson, an unmarried woman at the turn of the century, who inherits her family's Nebraska homestead because her father knows how much she loves the land. Although the family has prospered through Alexandra's smart investments, her brothers come to resent her influence. When her first love returns after fifteen years and the romance is rekindled, family resentments surface once again. Based on the novel by Willa Cather. A Hallmark Hall of Fame presentation. **99m/C VHS, LV, Closed Caption.** Jessica Lange, David Strathairn, Tom Aldredge, Reed Edward Diamond, Anne Heche, Heather Graham, Josh Hamilton, Leigh Lawson, Graham Beckel; **D:** Glenn Jordan; **W:** Glenn Jordan. *REP, FCT*

O Quatrilho 🐾🐾 1995 Two young couples from Italy immigrate to southern Brazil in the 1910s, hoping to find their fortunes. Thrifty peasant Angelo (Paternost) marries romantic Teresa (Pillar) and goes into business with the equally romantic Massimo (Campos), who's married to the thrifty Pierina (Pires). The grain mill thrives but the romantic half of each couple delve into some illicit amore and decide to flee while their left-behind spouses discover their own attractions. A happy ending is had by all (this must be a fairytale). Lots of high-gloss gush. Based on the novel by Jose Clemente Pozenat. Portuguese and Italian with subtitles. **120m/C VHS.** *BR* Gloria Pires, Patricia Pillar, Bruno Campos, Alexandre Paternost; **D:** Fabio Barreto; **W:** Leopoldo Serran; **C:** Felix Monti; **M:** Caetano Veloso. Nominations: Academy Awards '95: Best Foreign Language Film. *NYR*

The Oak 🐾🐾½ 1993 Morgenstern grieves over the loss of her father until she realizes she can't get rid of the body. Her difficulties in locating adequate medical facilities reflect the nightmarish realities of pre-1990 communist Romania. Potentially farcical aspects of storyline are successfully removed by violence in following scene involving Morgenstern and a band of roaming soldiers. A tragicomic look at obstinate communist bureaucrats and the wily, willful peasants who overcome them. Based on a novel by Ion Baiesu. In Romanian with English subtitles. 105m/C VHS. *RO* Maia Morgenstern, Razvan Vasilescu, Victor Rebenguic, Dorel Visan, Mariana Mihut, Dan Condurache, Virgil Andriescu, Leopoldina Balanuta, Matei Alexandru, Gheorghe Visu, Magda Catone, Ionel Mahailescu; *D:* Lucian Pintilie; *W:* Lucian Pintilie. *NYF*

Oasis of the Zombies 🎬 1982 European students set out to find buried treasure in Saharan oasis but instead find bevy of hungry Nazis with eating disorders. 75m/C VHS, Beta. *SP FR* Manuel Gelin, France Jordan, Jeff Montgomery, Miriam Landson, Eric Saint-Just, Caroline Audret, Henry Lambert; *D:* A.M. Frank. *NO*

Oath of Vengeance 🎬½ 1944 Billy the Kid rides the West once more. 50m/B VHS, Beta. Buster Crabbe, Al "Fuzzy" St. John, Jack Ingram, Charles "Blackie" King; *D:* Sam Newfield. *VCN, RXM*

The Object of Beauty 🎬🎬🎬 1991 (R) Two Americans, trapped in Europe by their love of pleasure and their lack of money, bicker over whether to sell their one object of value - a tiny Henry Moore sculpture. When it disappears, their relationship is challenged. Excellent acting and telling direction. Forces an examination of one's own value placement.*CW:* Language. 105m/C VHS, LV, Closed Caption. Andie MacDowell, John Malkovich, Joss Ackland, Lolita Davidovich, Peter Riegert, Bill Paterson, Rudi Davies, Ricci Harnett; *D:* Michael Lindsay-Hogg; *W:* Michael Lindsay-Hogg; *C:* David Watkin; *M:* Tom Bahler. *LIV*

Object of Obsession 🎬½ 1995 (R) One wrong phone call propels divorcee Margaret into an affair with a stranger that leads to kinky psycho/sexual games and revenge.*CW:* Strong sexual content; sex-related dialogue. 91m/C VHS, LV. Erika Anderson, Scott Valentine; *D:* Alexander Gregory Hippolyte. *APX*

Objective, Burma! 🎬🎬🎬🎬 1945 Deemed by many to be the greatest and most moving WWII production released during the war. American paratroopers are dropped over Burma where their mission is to destroy a Japanese radar station. The Americans led by Flynn are successful in wiping out the station, but they are spotted and descended upon by Japanese forces. Impeded from returning to Allied lines, the American soldiers must try to survive enemy encounters, exhaustion, starvation, and the elements until they are rescued. Splendid performance by Flynn and exceptional direction from Walsh; excellent performances enhanced by energetic score. 142m/B VHS, Beta. Errol Flynn, James Brown, William Prince, George Tobias, Henry Hull, Warner Anderson, Richard Erdman, Mark Stevens, Anthony Caruso, Hugh Beaumont; *D:* Raoul Walsh; *W:* Ranald MacDougall, Lester Cole; *C:* James Wong Howe; *M:* Franz Waxman. Nominations: Academy Awards '45: Best Film Editing, Best Story, Original Dramatic/Comedy Score. *MGM*

Oblivion 🎬🎬½ 1994 (PG-13) In this sci-fi western, set in the year 3031, its cowboys versus the aliens. A sheriff's son (Paul) returns to the town of Oblivion to avenge his father's murder and finds a reptilian extraterrestrial (Divoff) terrorizing the community.*CW:* Language; sci-fi violence; some sensuality. 94m/C VHS, Beta, Closed Caption. Richard Joseph Paul, Andrew Divoff, Jackie Swanson, Meg Foster, Isaac Hayes, Julie Newmar, Carel Struycken, George Takei; *D:* Sam Irvin; *W:* Peter David; *M:* Pino Donaggio. *PAR*

Oblomov 🎬🎬🎬½ *A Few Days in the Life of I.I. Oblomov; Neskolko Dnei iz Zhizni I.I. Oblomov* 1981 A production of the classic Goncharov novel about a symbolically inert Russian aristocrat whose childhood friend helps him find a reason for action. Well made, with fine performances. In Russian with English subtitles. 145m/C VHS, Beta. *RU* Oleg

Tabakov, Elena Solovei; *D:* Nikita Mikhalkov. *TPV, KIV, AUD*

The Oblong Box 🎬🎬 *Edgar Allen Poe's The Oblong Box* 1969 (PG) Coffins, blood, and live corpses fill drawn-out and lifeless adaptation of Edgar Allan Poe story. English aristocrat Price attempts to hide his disfigured brother in an old tower. Brother predictably escapes and rampages through town before being killed. 91m/C VHS, Beta. *GB* Vincent Price, Christopher Lee, Alastair Williamson, Hilary Dwyer, Peter Arne, Harry Baird, Carl Rigg, Sally Geeson, Maxwell Shaw; *D:* Gordon Hessler. *NO*

The Obsessed 🎬🎬 *The Late Edwina Black* 1951 Uninspiring story with Farrar suspected of murdering his wife. Competent performances, but this mystery isn't developed with any sense of style and the killer's real identity will be obvious to anyone watching. Cliches and stereotyped situations don't add anything. 77m/B VHS, LV. *GB* David Farrar, Geraldine Fitzgerald, Roland Culver, Jean Cadell, Mary Merrall, Harcourt Williams, Charles Heslop, Ronald Adam, Sydney Monkton; *D:* Maurice Elvey; *W:* Charles Frank, David Evans. *SNC, NOS, MOV*

Obsessed 🎬½ 1988 (PG-13) Semi-realistic tale of a woman's exhausting desire for revenge against hit-and-run driver who killed her son. Cast acceptable but lack of psychological foundation weakens plot. 100m/C VHS, Beta, LV. Kerrie Keane, Alan Thicke, Colleen Dewhurst, Saul Rubinek, Daniel Pilon, Lynne Griffin; *D:* Robin Spry. Genie Awards '89: Best Supporting Actress (Dewhurst). *NO*

Obsession 🎬🎬½ 1976 (PG) A rich, lonely businessman meets a mysterious young girl in Italy, the mirror image of his late wife who was killed by kidnappers. Intriguing suspense film that's not quite up to comparisons with Hitchcock thrillers. Music by Hitchcock-collaborator Herrmann. 98m/C VHS, Beta, LV. Cliff Robertson, Genevieve Bujold, John Lithgow; *D:* Brian DePalma; *W:* Paul Schrader; *M:* Bernard Herrmann. National Board of Review Awards '76: 10 Best Films of the Year; Nominations: Academy Awards '76: Best Original Score. *COL, HHE*

Obsession: A Taste for Fear 🎬½ 1989 (R) Diane's high fashion models are being killed and although there are plenty of suspects, she can't find the killer. 90m/C VHS, Beta. Virginia Hey, Gerard Darmon, Carlo Mucari; *D:* Piccio Raffanini. *IMP*

Obsessive Love 🎬🎬½ 1984 A lonely, mentally unstable typist (Mimieux) becomes obsessed with her soap opera hero and decides to go to Hollywood to seduce him. She transforms herself into a sleek and stunning Hollywood temptress to woo him, and at first he goes along with her—until he realizes that she is insane. An average made-for-TV movie of the older woman/younger man genre. 97m/C VHS. Yvette Mimieux, Simon MacCorkindale, Kin Shriner, Constance McCashin, Alan Miller, Lainie Kazan; *D:* Steven Hilliard Stern. *LIV*

O.C. and Stiggs 🎬½ 1987 (R) Two teens spend a summer harassing a neighbor and his family. Flimsy attempts at comedy fall flat. A failed adaptation of a National Lampoon short story, it was held for three years before release. 109m/C VHS, Beta, Closed Caption. Daniel H. Jenkins, Neill Barry, Jane Curtin, Tina Louise, Jon Cryer, Dennis Hopper, Paul Dooley, Ray Walston, Louis Nye, Martin Mull, Melvin Van Peebles; *D:* Robert Altman; *W:* Donald Cantrell. *FOX*

An Occasional Hell 🎬🎬½ 1996 (R) Ernest DeWalt (Berenger) is an ex-cop turned writer and college professor. He investigates the death of a fellow professor (Lang) at the behest of the beautiful widow (Golino) and then learns the lady is the prime suspect. Filmed in South Carolina.*CW:* Strong sexuality, violence, language and some drug content. 93m/C VHS, LV. Tom Berenger, Valeria Golino, Kari Wuhrer, Robert Davi, Stephen Lang; *D:* Salome Breziner. *THV*

The Occultist woof! 1989 Satan worshippers do the dance of death as they skin men alive for their evil purposes. 82m/C VHS, Beta. Rick Gianisi; *D:* Tim Kincaid; *W:* Tim Kincaid. *UNI*

An Occurrence at Owl Creek Bridge/Coup de Grace 1962 "Occurrence at Owl Creek Bridge" (1962), from a story by Ambrose Bierce documents the last moments of a man about to be hanged for sabotage. "Coup de Grace" (1978) tells the story of a group of friends who are caught up amongst the turmoil of the Bolshevik revolution. 123m/B VHS, Beta. Margarethe von Trotta, Matthias Habich, Rudiger Kirschstein, Matthieu Carriere, Valeska Gert; *D:* Volker Schlondorff, Robert Enrico. *NO*

Ocean Drive Weekend woof! 1985 (PG-13) Several college students congregate at "Ocean Drive" for a weekend of beer, sex, and dancing. Stereotypical characters, lack of plot, and poor versions of 1960 classics combine for boring and inane comedy. 98m/C VHS, Beta. Robert Peacock, Charles Redmond, Tony Freeman; *D:* Brian Thomas Jones. *LIV, VES*

Ocean's 11 🎬🎬½ 1960 A gang of friends plans to rob five Las Vegas casinos simultaneously. Part of the "A Night at the Movies" series, this tape simulates a 1960 movie evening, with Bugs Bunny cartoon, "Person to Bunny;" a newsreel; and coming attractions for "The Sundowners" and "Sunrise at Campobello." 148m/C VHS, Beta, LV. Frank Sinatra, Dean Martin, Sammy Davis Jr., Angie Dickinson, Peter Lawford; *D:* Lewis Milestone; *C:* William H. Daniels. *WAR*

Oceans of Fire 🎬 1986 (PG) Average rehash of the tension-filled world of oil riggers. Lives of two ex-cons are threatened when they hire on as divers for world's deepest undersea oil rig. 100m/C VHS, Beta, LV. Gregory Harrison, Billy Dee Williams, Cynthia Sikes, Lyle Alzado, Tony Burton, Ray "Boom Boom" Mancini, David Carradine, Ken Norton; *D:* Steve Carver. *THV*

Octagon 🎬🎬 1980 (R) Norris protects a woman from threatening Ninja warriors in average kung-fu adventure. Enough action and violence for fans of the genre. 103m/C VHS, Beta, LV. Chuck Norris, Karen Carlson, Lee Van Cleef, Kim Lankford, Art Hindle, Jack Carter; *D:* Eric Karson; *W:* Paul Aaron, Leigh Chapman. *MED*

Octaman 🎬½ 1971 Comical thriller featuring non-threatening octopus-man discovered by scientists in Mexico. Rip-off of director Essex's own "Creature from the Black Lagoon." Not without its curiosity factor: young Rick Baker designed the octopus man, while actress Angeli died of a drug overdose during filming. 79m/C VHS, Beta. Kerwin Mathews, Pier Angeli, Harry Guardino, David Essex, Jeff Morrow, Norman Fields; *D:* Harry Essex. *GEM, CNG, PSM*

Octavia 🎬 1982 (R) A contemporary fable about a blind girl who befriends a convict and learns about life and love. 93m/C VHS, Beta. Susan Curtis; *D:* David Beaird; *W:* David Beaird. *NLC*

The October Man 🎬🎬🎬 1948 When a model is found murdered, a stranger with mental problems must prove his innocence to others and himself. Strong characters make good, suspenseful mystery reminiscent of Hitchcock. 95m/B VHS. *GB* John Mills, Joan Greenwood, Edward Chapman, Joyce Carey, Kay Walsh, Felix Aylmer, Juliet Mills; *D:* Roy Ward Baker. *FCT*

Octopussy 🎬🎬 1983 (PG) The Bond saga continues as Agent 007 is on a mission to prevent a crazed Russian general from launching a nuclear attack against the NATO forces in Europe. Lots of special effects and gadgets keep weak plot moving. 140m/C VHS, Beta, LV. *GB* Roger Moore, Maud Adams, Louis Jourdan, Kristina Wayborn, Kabir Bedi; *D:* John Glen; *W:* Michael G. Wilson; *M:* John Barry. *MGM, FOX, TLF*

The Odd Angry Shot 🎬🎬½ 1979 Australian soldiers fighting in Vietnam discover the conflict is not what they expected. Ironic perspective of men struggling with their feelings about the war. More of an unremarkable drama with comic overtones than a combat film, it will appeal to those who prefer good direction to bloodshed. 90m/C VHS, Beta. *AU* *D:* Tom Jeffrey. *LIV, VES*

Odd Birds 🐾🐾½ **1985** Coming of age drama set in 1965 California. Shy 15 year old Joy Chan is a Chinese-American dreaming of becoming an actress. Her widowed immigrant mother wants Joy to have a practical profession—like nursing. Longing for someone to understand Joy meets Brother Murphy, a math teacher at the local boys school. Murphy's been trying to reconcile his religious commitment with his unorthodox views. It isn't long before these two individualists recognize a fellow kindred spirit. **87m/C VHS.** Michael Moriarty, Donna Lai Ming Lew, Nancy Lee, Bruce Gray, Karen Maruyama, Scott Crawford; **D:** Jeanne Collachia; **W:** Jeanne Collachia. *WAC*

The Odd Couple 🐾🐾🐾½ **1968 (G)** Two divorced men with completely opposite personalities move in together. Lemmon's obsession with neatness drives slob Matthau up the wall, and their inability to see eye-to-eye results in many hysterical escapades. A Hollywood rarity, it is actually better in some ways than Neil Simon's original Broadway version. Basis for the hit television series. **106m/C VHS, Beta, LV.** Jack Lemmon, Walter Matthau, Herb Edelman, John Fiedler, Monica Evans, Carol Shelley; **D:** Gene Saks; **W:** Neil Simon; **C:** Robert B. Hauser. Nominations: Academy Awards '68: Best Adapted Screenplay, Best Film Editing. *PAR*

The Odd Job 🐾🐾 **1978** Insurance salesman Chapman, depressed after his wife leaves him, hires a hit man to kill him. Chapman then has a hard time shaking his stalker after deciding he wants to live. Monty Python fans will enjoy seeing ex-troupe member Chapman again, but the comic's heart isn't in this unoriginal story. **100m/C VHS, Beta.** *GB* Graham Chapman; **D:** Peter Medak; **M:** Howard Blake. *VES*

Odd Jobs 🐾🐾 **1985 (PG-13)** When five college friends look for jobs during summer break, they wind up running their own moving business with the help of the mob. Good comic talent, but a silly slapstick script results in only a passable diversion. **89m/C VHS, Beta.** Paul Reiser, Scott McGinnis, Rick Overton, Robert Townsend; **D:** Mark Story; **W:** Robert Conte; **C:** Arthur Albert, Peter Collister; **M:** Robert Folk. *NO*

Odd Man Out 🐾🐾🐾½ *Gang War* **1947** An Irish revolutionary is injured during a robbery attempt. Suffering from gunshot wounds and closely pursued by the police, he must rely on the help of others who could betray him at any moment. A gripping tale of suspense and intrigue that will keep the proverbial seat's edge warm until the final credits. Adapted from F.L. Green's novel, previously filmed as "The Last Man." **111m/B VHS, Beta, LV.** *GB* James Mason, Robert Newton, Dan O'Herlihy, Kathleen Ryan, Cyril Cusack; **D:** Carol Reed; **C:** Robert Krasker. British Academy Awards '47: Best Film; National Board of Review Awards '47: 10 Best Films of the Year; Nominations: Academy Awards '47: Best Film Editing. *PAR*

Odd Obsession 🐾🐾½ *The Key* **1960** One of Ichikawa's first films, about an elderly Japanese gentleman with a young wife whose feelings of jealousy and impotence eventually wreak havoc on the marriage. In Japanese with English subtitles. **96m/C VHS, Beta.** *JP* Machiko Kyo, Ganjiro Nakamura; **D:** Kon Ichikawa. Golden Globe Awards '60: Best Foreign Film. *COL*

The Odd Squad 🐾 **1986 (R)** Five GIs in WWII defend a bridge from the enemy, and manage in doing so to have loads of laughs. **82m/C VHS, Beta.** Johnny Dorelli, Vincent Gardenia; **D:** E.B. Clucher. *VTR, PSM*

Oddball Hall 🐾🐾 **1991 (PG)** Two aging jewel thieves hide out in the African wilds, masquerading as powerful "wizards." When they head back to civilization, an African tribe beseeches the phony sorcerers to cure their long drought. **87m/C VHS.** Don Ameche, Burgess Meredith; **D:** Jackson Hunsicker; **W:** Jackson Hunsicker. *WAR, CAN*

Oddballs WOOF! **1984 (PG-13)** In another attempt to capitalize on the success of Bill Murray's "Meatballs," this summer camp story follows three campers and their pathetic attempts to lose their virginity. Brooks has his moments, but there is little else to recommend here. **92m/C VHS, Beta.** Foster Brooks, Jason Sorokin, Wally Wodchis, Konnie Krome; **D:** Miklos Lente. *LIV*

Odds Against Tomorrow 🐾🐾🐾 **1959** Compulsive gambler/nightclub singer Johnny Ingram (Belafonte) owes big money to gangster Bacco (Kuluva). He hooks up with racist ex-con Earl Slater (Ryan) and former policeman Dave Burke (Begley) to rob a bank but everything goes wrong. Ingram and Slater manage to escape to a nearby oil storage area but the racial tensions between the two are proving deadlier than the cops on their trail. Based on the novel by William P. McGivern; because of the blacklist screenwriter Polonsky was "fronted" by John O. Killens. Polonsky officially received credit for his work in 1996. **120m/B VHS, Closed Caption.** Harry Belafonte, Robert Ryan, Shelley Winters, Ed Begley Sr., Gloria Grahame, Will Kuluva, Richard Bright; **D:** Robert Wise; **W:** Abraham Polonsky, Nelson Gidding; **C:** Joseph Brun; **M:** John Lewis. *WAR*

Odds and Evens 🐾½ **1978 (PG)** Italian supercops pretend they don't have badges in order to clean up illegal betting and gambling rings in sunny Miami. Odds are this spaghetti cop-o-rama won't keep Morpheus at bay. **109m/C VHS, Beta.** *IT* Terence Hill, Bud Spencer; **D:** Sergio Corbucci. *WAR*

Ode to Billy Joe 🐾🐾 **1976 (PG)** The 1967 Bobby Gentry hit song of the same title is expanded to tell why a young man jumped to his death off the Tallahatchie Bridge. The problems of growing up in the rural South and teenage romance do not match the appeal of the theme song. Benson and O'Connor, however, work well together. **106m/C VHS, Beta.** Robby Benson, Glynnis O'Connor, Joan Hotchkis, Sandy McPeak, James Best; **D:** Max Baer Jr. *CCB, WAR*

The Odessa File 🐾🐾½ **1974 (PG)** During 1963, a German journalist attempts to track down some SS war criminals who have formed a secret organization called ODESSA. The story, from Frederick Forsyth's novel, drags in some places, but the scene where bad guy Schell and reporter Voight finally confront each other is a high point. **128m/C VHS, Beta, LV, Closed Caption.** *GB GE* Jon Voight, Mary Tamm, Maximilian Schell, Maria Schell, Derek Jacobi, Peter Jeffrey, Klaus Lowitsch, Kurt Meisel, Hannes Meesember, Garfield Morgan, Shmuel Rodensku, Ernst Schroder, Noel Willman, Hans Canineberg, Towje Kleiner, Gunnar Moiler; **D:** Ronald Neame; **W:** Kenneth Ross, George Markstein; **C:** Oswald Morris; **M:** Andrew Lloyd Webber. *GKK*

The Odyssey 🐾🐾½ **1997 (PG-13)** Lavish TV miniseries based on Homer's 2,700-year-old epic poem, relating the adventures of King Odysseus of Ithaca. On the day his son is born to faithful wife Penelope (Scacchi), Odysseus (Assante) is commanded by the goddess Athena (Rossellini) to leave his home and travel to battle the Trojans. Little does he realize that this is the beginning of a 20-year sojourn, where additional trials include sea monsters, the Cyclops, the Kingdom of the Dead, enchantress Circe (Peters), and getting shipwrecked on the isle of Calypso (Williams), who wants to keep the hunk around. But even Odysseus realizes there's no place like home. **165m/C VHS, Closed Caption.** Armand Assante, Greta Scacchi, Geraldine Chaplin, Eric Roberts, Bernadette Peters, Irene Papas, Vanessa Williams, Christopher Lee, Isabella Rossellini, Jeroen Krabbe, Nicholas Clay, Ron Cook, Michael J. Pollard, Paloma Baeza, Alan Cox, Heathcote Williams; **D:** Andrei Konchalovsky; **W:** Andrei Konchalovsky, Chris Solimine; **C:** Sergei Koslov; **M:** Eduard Artemyev. *HMK*

The Odyssey of the Pacific 🐾🐾½ *The Emperor of Peru* **1982** Three young Cambodian refugees encounter retired train engineer Rooney living in the woods where a railway station once thrived. Together they work to restore an old locomotive. The ordinary, inoffensive script will not endanger quality family time. **82m/C VHS, Beta.** *CA* Mickey Rooney, Monique Mercure; **D:** Fernando Arrabal. *USH*

Oedipus Rex 🐾🐾🐾 *Edipo Re* **1967** A new twist on the famous tragedy as Pasolini gives the story a modern prologue and epilogue. The classic plot has Oedipus spiraling downward into moral horror as he tries to avoid fulfilling the prophecy that he will murder his father and sleep with his mother. Cross-cultural curiosities include Japanese music and Lenin-inspired songs, some written by Pasolini, who also stars as the high priest. In Italian with English subtitles. **110m/C VHS.** *IT* Franco Citti, Silvana Mangano, Alida Valli, Julian Beck, Pier Paolo Pasolini; **D:** Pier Paolo Pasolini. *FST, FCT, WBF*

Of Cooks and Kung-Fu 🐾🐾 **198?** A martial arts culinary adventure. **90m/C VHS, Beta.** Jacky Cheng, Chia Kai, Lee Kuen. *MGI*

Of Human Bondage 🐾🐾🐾 **1934** The first movie version of W. Somerset Maugham's classic novel in which a young, handicapped medical student falls in love with a crude cockney waitress, in a mutually destructive affair. Established Davis's role as the tough, domineering woman. Remade in 1946 and 1964. **84m/B VHS, Beta, LV.** Bette Davis, Leslie Howard, Frances Dee, Reginald Owen, Reginald Denny, Alan Hale; **D:** John Cromwell; **M:** Max Steiner. *CNG, MRV, NOS*

Of Human Bondage 🐾🐾 **1964** An essentially decent man falls fatally in love with an alluring but heartless waitress, who subtly destroys him. Based on the W. Somerset Maugham novel. Miscast and least interesting of the three film versions, although Novak gives a good performance. **100m/B VHS, Beta.** *GB* Kim Novak, Laurence Harvey, Robert Morley, Roger Livesey, Siobhan McKenna; **D:** Henry Hathaway, Ken Hughes; **W:** Bryan Forbes; **C:** Oswald Morris. *MGM*

Of Human Hearts 🐾🐾½ **1938** Rural life just before the Civil War sets up this cornpone tale of family strife. Huston is a stern preacher who has his family living in near poverty as an example of sacrifice to his flock. Son Stewart wants to study medicine and Bondi, defying her husband, manages to fund his dream. Only Stewart becomes so engrossed by his ambitions that he ignores the family, even after his father dies and his mother is left poor and alone. Then Stewart joins the Civil War as a doctor where he meets President Lincoln (Carradine), who tells him he should never neglect his mother. Oy. Well, the cast is good. Adapted from the story "Benefits Forgot" by Honore Morrow. **100m/B VHS.** James Stewart, Beulah Bondi, Walter Huston, Guy Kibbee, Charles Coburn, Ann Rutherford, Charley Grapewin, Gene Lockhart; **D:** Clarence Brown; **W:** Bradbury Foote; **C:** Clyde De Vinna. Nominations: Academy Awards '38: Best Supporting Actress (Bondi). *MGM, MOV*

Of Love and Shadows 🐾🐾 **1994 (R)** Political photojournalist Francisco (Banderas) begins investigating the disappearance of a self-proclaimed saint after the bloody 1973 coup in Chile. He's aided by aristocratic Chilean Irene (Connelly), who's engaged to her Army captain cousin Gustavo (Gallardo) but can't resist Francisco's ever-smoldering charms. The intrepid duo naturally find lots of corruption. Based on the novel by Isabel Allende; shot on location in Argentina. *CW:* Scene of strong sexuality and gore for some violence. **103m/C VHS, LV, Closed Caption.** Antonio Banderas, Jennifer Connelly, Stefania Sandrelli, Camillo Gallardo, Patricio Contreras; **D:** Betty Kaplan; **W:** Donald Freed; **C:** Felix Monti; **M:** Jose Nieto. *TOU*

Of Mice and Men ✍✍✍✍ 1939 A powerful adaptation of the classic Steinbeck tragedy about the friendship between two itinerant Southern ranch hands during the Great Depression. Chaney is wonderful as the gentle giant and mentally retarded Lenny, cared for by migrant worker Meredith. They both get into an irreversible situation when a woman is accidentally killed. **107m/C VHS, Beta.** Lon Chaney Jr., Burgess Meredith, Betty Field, Bob Steele, Noah Beery Jr., Charles Bickford; *D:* Lewis Milestone; *M:* Aaron Copland. Nominations: Academy Awards '39: Best Picture, Best Sound, Best Original Score.*NO*

Of Mice and Men ✍✍✍ 1981 Made-for-television remake of the classic Steinbeck tale, casting TV's Baretta (Blake) as George and Quaid as Lenny. Worth watching. **150m/C VHS, Beta.** Robert (Bobby) Blake, Randy Quaid, Lew Ayres, Mitchell Ryan, Ted Neeley, Cassie Yates, Pat Hingle, Whitman Mayo, Dennis Fimple, Pat Corley; *D:* Reza Badiyi. *PSM*

Of Mice and Men ✍✍✍½ 1992 (PG-13) Set on the migratory farms of California, John Steinbeck's novel covers the friendship of the simple-minded Lenny, his protector George, and a flirtatious farm wife who doesn't know Lenny's strength. Director Sinise got permission from Steinbeck's widow to film the novel (actually the third adaptation).*CW:* Violent scenes. **110m/C VHS, LV, Closed Caption.** John Malkovich, Sherilyn Fenn, Casey Siemaszko, Joe Morton, Ray Walston, Gary Sinise, John Terry, Richard Riehle; *D:* Gary Sinise; *W:* Horton Foote. *MGM, PMS, BTV*

Of Unknown Origin ✍✍½ 1983 (R) Weller encounters a mutated rampaging rat in his New York townhouse while his family is away on vacation. His house becomes the battleground in a terror-tinged duel of survival. A well-drawn rat thriller not for those with a delicate stomach. **88m/C VHS, Beta.** *CA* Peter Weller, Jennifer Dale, Lawrence Dane, Kenneth Welsh, Louis Del Grande, Shannon Tweed; *D:* George P. Cosmatos; *W:* Brian Taggert. *WAR*

Off and Running ✍✍½ 1990 (PG-13) Struggling actress Cyd (Lauper) is working as a mermaid at a Miami hotel lounge when her horse trainer boyfriend Woody is suddenly murdered by a psycho thug (Belzer). Turns out he's after a key hidden in a necklace now in Cyd's possession. Cyd goes on the run and gets some help from failed golf pro Jack (Keith) as they try to stay one step ahead of the killer and discover what the key unlocks. **91m/C VHS.** Cyndi Lauper, David Keith, Richard Belzer. *HBO*

Off Beat ✍½ 1986 (PG) A shy librarian unluckily wins a spot in a police benefit dance troupe, and then falls in love with a tough police woman. With a screenplay by playwright Medoff, and a good supporting cast, it still manages to miss the mark. **92m/C VHS, Beta, LV.** Judge Reinhold, Meg Tilly, Cleavant Derricks, Fred Gwynne, John Turturro, Jacques D'Amboise, James Tolkan, Joe Mantegna, Harvey Keitel, Amy Wright, Christopher Noth; *D:* Michael Dinner; *W:* Mark Medoff; *C:* Carlo DiPalma; *M:* James Horner. *TOU*

Off Limits ✍✍½ 1953 When a boxing manager is drafted into the Army, he freely breaks regulations in order to train a fighter as he sees fit. Hope and Rooney, while not in peak form, make a snappy duo in this amusing romp. **89m/B VHS, Beta, LV.** Bob Hope, Mickey Rooney, Marilyn Maxwell, Marvin Miller; *D:* George Marshall. *BAR*

Off Limits ✍½ 1987 (R) A spree of murders involving Vietnamese hookers draws two cops from the Army's Criminal Investigation Department into the sleazy backstreets of 1968 Saigon. There is little mystery as to who the killer is in this tale that seems written more for the sake of foul language and gratuitous gunfights than actual plot. **102m/C VHS, Beta, LV, Closed Caption.** Willem Dafoe, Gregory Hines, Fred Ward, Scott Glenn, Amanda Pays, Keith David, David Alan Grier; *D:* Christopher Crowe; *W:* Christopher Crowe, Jack Thibeau; *M:* James Newton Howard. *FOX*

Off the Mark ✍✍ 1987 (R) Neely is a young athlete suffering from a childhood affliction that causes spasms in his legs. Facing the ultimate challenge, he must overcome his handicap and defeat a talented woman athlete and a Russian student in a triathalon competition. An unremarkable effort, it had a limited one-week run in theaters. **89m/C VHS, Beta.** Mark Neely, Terry Farrell, Jon Cypher, Clarence Gilyard Jr.; *D:* Bill Berry; *C:* Arledge Armenaki. *FRH*

Off the Wall ✍ 1982 (R) Two hitchhikers wind up in a southern maximum security prison after being accused of a crime they did not commit. What follows is a series of shenanigans as they try to escape. This supposed comedy falls flat in every way with the possible exception of Arquette's portrayal of the governor's daughter. **86m/C VHS, Beta.** Paul Sorvino, Rosanna Arquette, Patrick Cassidy, Billy Hufsey, Monte Markham, Mickey Gilley; *D:* Rick Friedberg. *LIV, VES*

Off Your Rocker ✍½ 1980 Representatives of a corporate conglomerate find that the residents of Flo Adler's Mapleview Nursing Home can still muster stiff resistance to a threatened takeover. **99m/C VHS, Beta.** Milton Berle, Red Buttons, Lou Jacobi, Dorothy Malone, Helen Shaver, Sharon Acker, Helen Hughes; *D:* Morley Markson, Larry Pall. *NO*

The Offence ✍✍✍ *Something Like the Truth* 1973 (R) Connery plays a London detective who beats a suspected child molester to death during a police interrogation. Turns out he's reacting to a long-buried molestation incident from his own childhood. A chilling psycho-drama highlighted by a strong lead performance by Connery. **108m/C VHS.** *GB* Sean Connery, Trevor Howard, Vivien Merchant, Ian Bannen, Derek Newark, John Hallam, Peter Bowles; *D:* Sidney Lumet; *W:* John Hopkins. *MGM*

Offerings ✍ 1989 (R) After a boy is tormented by a gang of children who cause him to fall down a well, his resulting brain injuries turn him into a psychopathic killer. Seeking revenge ten years later, he systematically murders his oppressors, offering bits of their anatomy to the one girl who treated him kindly. A typical slasher movie, the plot is only slightly better than the worst examples of the genre. **96m/C VHS, Beta.** G. Michael Smith, Loretta L. Bowman; *D:* Christopher Reynolds. *HMD*

Office Romances ✍✍ 1986 A woman who has moved to London from the country is seduced by her employer. Because of her plain appearance, she is flattered by his attention even though he is married and has no real feelings for her. Competently made, nonetheless hard to watch because of the slow pace. **60m/C VHS, Beta.** *GB* Judy Parfitt, Ray Brooks, Suzanne Burden. *PSM*

An Officer and a Gentleman ✍✍✍½ 1982 (R) Young drifter Gere, who enters Navy Officer Candidate School because he doesn't know what else to do with his life, becomes a better person almost despite himself. Winger is the love interest who sets her sights on marrying Gere, and Gossett is the sergeant who whips him into shape. Strong performances by the whole cast made this a must-see in 1982 that is still appealing, despite the standard Hollywood premise. ♫Up Where We Belong; Hungry for Your Love; An Officer and a Gentleman; Treat Me Right; Tunnel of Love. **126m/C VHS, Beta, LV, 8mm.** Richard Gere, Louis Gossett Jr., David Keith, Lisa Eilbacher, Debra Winger, David Caruso, Robert Loggia, Lisa Blount; *D:* Taylor Hackford; *C:* Donald E. Thorin; *M:* Jack Nitzche. Academy Awards '82: Best Song ("Up Where We Belong"), Best Supporting Actor (Gossett); Golden Globe Awards '83: Best Song ("Up Where We Belong"), Best Supporting Actor (Gossett); Nominations: Academy Awards '82: Best Actress (Winger), Best Film Editing, Best Original Screenplay, Best Original Score. *PAR, FCT, BTV*

Official Denial ✍✍½ 1993 A victim of an alien abduction becomes the only hope for a captured space being. Can Paul help the alien escape from a special Air Force UFO group and what secrets will he uncover if he does? Made for television. **86m/C VHS, Beta, Closed Caption.** Parker Stevenson, Erin Gray, Dirk Benedict, Chad Everett; *D:* Brian Trenchard-Smith; *W:* Bruce Zabel; *M:* Garry McDonald, Laurie Stone. *PAR*

The Official Story ✍✍✍½ *La Historia Oficial; The Official History; The Official Version* 1985 (R) A devastating drama about an Argentinian woman who realizes her young adopted daughter may be a child stolen from one of the thousands of citizens victimized by the country's repressive government. A powerful, important film. In Spanish with English subtitles or dubbed. **112m/C VHS, Beta, LV.** *AR* Norma Aleandro, Hector Alterio, Chunchuna Villafane, Patricio Contreras; *D:* Luis Puenzo; *W:* Luis Puenzo, Aida Bortnik. Academy Awards '85: Best Foreign Language Film; Cannes Film Festival '85: Best Actress (Aleandro); Golden Globe Awards '86: Best Foreign Film; Los Angeles Film Critics Association Awards '85: Best Foreign Film; New York Film Critics Awards '85: Best Actress (Aleandro); Nominations: Academy Awards '85: Best Original Screenplay. *APD, TPV*

The Offspring ✍✍ *From a Whisper to a Scream* 1987 (R) In four stories of past evils Price reveals his hometown can force folks to kill. Not the usual Price material: dismemberment, cannibalism, and necrophilia clash with his presence. Strong yuk factor. **99m/C VHS, Beta, LV.** Vincent Price, Cameron Mitchell, Clu Gulager, Terry Kiser, Susan Tyrrell, Harry Caesar, Rosalind Cash, Martine Beswick, Angelo Rossitto, Lawrence Tierney; *D:* Jeff Burr; *W:* C. Courtney Joyner, Jeff Burr; *M:* John Beal. *LIV*

Oh, Alfie ✍✍ *Alfie Darling* 1975 (R) In every man's life, there comes a time to settle down... but never when you're having as much fun as Alfie! Inadequate sequel to "Alfie". **99m/C VHS, Beta.** *GB* Joan Collins, Alan Price, Jill Townsend; *D:* Ken Hughes; *W:* Ken Hughes. *HHE*

Oh, Bloody Life! ✍✍½ 1988 Young actress faces deportation during the Stalin era in Hungary because of her aristocratic family ties. In Hungarian with English subtitles. **115m/C VHS.** *HU* Udvaros Dorottya, Szacsvay Laszlo, Kern Andras, Bezeredi Zoltan, Oze Lajos, Lukacs Margit; *D:* Peter Bacso; *W:* Peter Bacso. Montreal World Film Festival '88: Best Actress (Dorottya). *EVD, TPV*

Oh! Calcutta! ✍½ 1972 Film version of the first nude musical to play on Broadway, which caused a sensation in the late 1960s. It's really a collection of skits, some of which were written by such notables as John Lennon, Sam Shepard, and Jules Feiffer. And it's really not that funny or erotic. **105m/C VHS, Beta.** Bill Macy, Mark Dempsey, Raina Barrett, Samantha Harper, Patricia Hawkins, Mitchell McGuire; *D:* Guillaume Martin Aucion. *NO*

Oh Dad, Poor Dad (Momma's Hung You in the Closet & I'm Feeling So Sad) ✍✍ 1967 Cult fave black comedy about a bizarre family on a vacation in Jamaica. The domineering mother travels with a coffin containing the stuffed body of her late husband. Additional corpses abound. Based on the play by Arthur L. Kopit. **86m/C VHS, Beta.** Rosalind Russell, Robert Morse, Barbara Harris, Hugh Griffith, Lionel Jeffries, Jonathan Winters; *D:* Richard Quine. *PAR*

Oh, God! ✍✍½ 1977 (PG) God, in the person of Burns, recruits Denver as his herald in his plan to save the world. Despite initial skepticism, Denver, in his film debut, keeps faith and is rewarded. Sincere performances and optimistic end make for satisfying story. Followed by "Oh God! Book 2" and "Oh God! You Devil". **104m/C VHS, Beta, LV.** George Burns, John Denver, Paul Sorvino, Ralph Bellamy, Teri Garr, William Daniels, Donald Pleasence, Barnard Hughes, Barry Sullivan, Dinah Shore, Jeff Corey, David Ogden Stiers; *D:* Carl Reiner; *W:* Larry Gelbart. Writers Guild of America '77: Best Adapted Screenplay; Nominations: Academy Awards '77: Best Adapted Screenplay. *WAR*

Oh, God! Book 2 ✍ 1980 (PG) Burns returns as the "Almighty One" in strained sequel to "Oh God!" This time he enlists the help of a young girl to remind others of his existence. The slogan she concocts saves God's image, but not the movie. Followed by "Oh, God! You Devil." **94m/C VHS, Beta.** George Burns, Suzanne Pleshette, David Birney, Louanne, Conrad Janis, Wilfrid Hyde-White, Hans Conried, Howard Duff; **D:** Gilbert Cates; **M:** Charles Fox. *WAR*

Oh, God! You Devil 🐾🐾 **1984 (PG)** During his third trip to earth, Burns plays both the Devil and God as he first takes a struggling musician's soul, then gives it back. A few zingers and light atmosphere save unoriginal plot. The second sequel to "Oh, God!" **96m/C VHS, Beta, LV, Closed Caption.** George Burns, Ted Wass, Roxanne Hart, Ron Silver, Eugene Roche, Robert Desiderio; **D:** Paul Bogart; **W:** Andrew Bergman; **M:** David Shire. *WAR*

Oh, Heavenly Dog! 🐾🐾 **1980 (PG)** A private eye returns from the dead as a dog to solve his own murder. Man's best friend and intelligent to boot. The famous dog Benji's third film, and his acting improves with each one. Adults may find this movie slow, but kids will probably love it. **104m/C VHS, Beta, Closed Caption.** Chevy Chase, Jane Seymour, Omar Sharif, Robert Morley, Susan Kellerman; **D:** Joe Camp; **W:** Joe Camp, Rod Browning. *FOX*

Oh, Mr. Porter 🐾🐾 **1937** Billeted at an obscure railway post, the stationmaster hero renovates the place and hires a special train to transport the area soccer team. Trouble arises when the train is hijacked by gun smugglers. **85m/B VHS.** *GB* Will Hay, Moore Marriott, Graham Moffatt, Frederick Piper; **D:** Marcel Varnel. *NOS*

Oh Susannah 🐾½ **1938** Robbed and thrown from a train, Autry and the two drifters who rescue him follow the thieves to Mineral Springs. Their journey is plagued by too many songs and the bad guys are predictably punished in the end. **59m/B VHS, Beta.** Gene Autry, Boothe Howard, Smiley Burnette, Frances Grant, Donald Kirke, Clara Kimball Young; **D:** Joseph Kane. *NOS, VDM, HHT*

Oh, What a Night 🐾🐾 **1992 (PG-13)** Bittersweet coming of age tale about a lonely 17-year-old (Haim) who has moved with his father and stepmother to a chicken farm in 1955 Ontario. After struggling with the untimely death of his mother, Haim falls in love with an older woman who has a husband and two kids. Features a great fifties soundtrack and beautiful scenes of the Canadian countryside.**CW:** Elements of teen sexuality. **93m/C VHS, LV, Closed Caption.** *CA* Corey Haim, Barbara Williams, Keir Dullea, Genevieve Bujold, Robbie Coltrane; **D:** Eric Till. *COL, NLC*

O'Hara's Wife 🐾½ **1982** Loving wife Harley continues to care for her family even after her untimely death. Only husband Asner, however, can see her ghost. Lightweight, made-for-television drama traps good cast. **87m/C VHS, Beta.** Ed Asner, Mariette Hartley, Jodie Foster, Tom Bosley, Perry Lang, Ray Walston; **D:** William S. Bartman; **W:** William S. Bartman; **M:** Artie Butler. *VES*

O.H.M.S. 🐾½ **1937** Convoluted story about a New York hood (Ford) who flees to England where he joins the British Army by posing as a Canadian. He buddies up with Mills and they both fall for Lee. His regiment is sent to China, via ship, and Lee just happens to be a stowaway. In China, Ford manages to prove his worth by saving Lee from bandits. Maybe it's not supposed to make sense. **71m/B VHS.** *GB* Wallace Ford, John Mills, Anna Lee, Frank Cellier, Frederick Leister, Peter Croft; **D:** Raoul Walsh. *HCV*

Oil 🐾 **1978 (PG)** Seven men fight a raging oil fire that threatens to destroy an entire country. Unfortunately, the movie is unable to ignite any interest at all. **95m/C VHS, Beta.** Ray Milland, Woody Strode, Stuart Whitman, Tony Kendall, William Berger; **D:** Mircea Dragan. *VCI*

The O.J. Simpson Story 🐾 **1994** Tacky tabloid TV movie follows incredibly exploited story about former gridiron star Simpson (Hosea) who's accused of murdering blonde babe ex-wife Nicole (Tuck). Mainly stolid performances though Weitz is slick as Simpson lawyer Robert Shapiro. Told in flashbacks, the actual murder is

never depicted. Director Jerry Friedman took his name off the credits, leaving the standard Smithee pseudonym as a replacement. **90m/C VHS.** Bobby Hosea, Jessica Tuck, James Handy, Kimberly Russell, David Roberson, Bruce Weitz; **D:** Alan Smithee; **W:** Stephen Harrigan; **M:** Harald Kloser. *FXV*

Oklahoma! 🐾🐾🐾½ **1955 (G)** Jones's film debut; a must-see for musical fans. A cowboy and country girl fall in love, but she is tormented by another unwelcomed suitor. At over two hours, cuteness wears thin for some. Actually filmed in Arizona. Adapted from Rodgers and Hammerstein's broadway hit with original score; choreography by Agnes de Mille. ♫Oh, What a Beautiful Morning; Surrey with the Fringe on Top; I Cain't Say No; Many a New Day; People Will Say We're in Love; Poor Jud Is Dead; All 'Er Nuthin'; Everything's Up to Date in Kansas City; The Farmer and the Cowman. **145m/C VHS, Beta, LV, Closed Caption.** Gordon MacRae, Shirley Jones, Rod Steiger, Gloria Grahame, Eddie Albert, Charlotte Greenwood, James Whitmore, Gene Nelson, Barbara Lawrence, Jay C. Flippen; **D:** Fred Zinnemann; **W:** Sonya Levien, William Ludwig; **C:** Robert L. Surtees; **M:** Richard Rodgers, Oscar Hammerstein. Academy Awards '55: Best Sound, Scoring of a Musical; Nominations: Academy Awards '55: Best Color Cinematography, Best Film Editing. *FOX, RDG, HMV*

Oklahoma Annie 🐾🐾 **1951** Storekeeper Canova joins the new sheriff in booting undesirables out of town, and tries to sing her way into his heart. Amazingly, it works—not for delicate ears. **90m/C VHS, Beta.** Judy Canova, Fuzzy Knight, Grant Withers, John Russell, Denver Pyle, Allen Jenkins, Almira Sessions; **D:** R.G. Springsteen. *MLB*

Oklahoma Badlands 🐾½ **1948** Lane and his horse outsmart a corrupt newspaper publisher trying to steal land from a female rancher. An early directorial work for veteran stuntman Canutt. **59m/B VHS, Beta.** Allan "Rocky" Lane, Mildred Coles; **D:** Yakima Canutt. *DVT*

Oklahoma Bound 🐾 **1981** A feisty farmer tries to save his failing farm through a series of ostensibly comedic, unsuccessful schemes. **92m/C VHS, Beta.** F.E. Bowling, Dan Jones; **D:** Patrick C. Poole. *NO*

Oklahoma Crude 🐾🐾½ **1973 (PG)** Sadistic oil trust rep Palence battles man-hating Dunaway for her well. Drifter Scott helps her resist on the promise of shared profits. In this 1913 setting, Dunaway tells Scott she wishes she could avoid men altogether, but later settles for him. **108m/C VHS.** George C. Scott, Faye Dunaway, John Mills, Jack Palance, Harvey Jason, Woodrow Parfrey; **D:** Stanley Kramer; **W:** Marc Norman; **C:** Robert L. Surtees; **M:** Henry Mancini. *FOX*

Oklahoma Cyclone 🐾½ **1930** A group of bronco busters find action and adventure on the prairie. Second of eight talkies in Steele series, includes his first of few singing roles. **64m/B VHS.** Bob Steele, Al "Fuzzy" St. John, Nita Ray, Charles "Blackie" King; **D:** John P. McCarthy. *NOS, GPV, DVT*

Oklahoma Kid 🐾🐾🐾 **1939** Offbeat, hilarious western with Bogie as the villain and gunfighter Cagney seeking revenge for his father's wrongful death. Highlight is Cagney's rendition of "I Don't Want To Play In Your Yard," complete with six-shooter accompaniment. **82m/B VHS, Beta.** James Cagney, Humphrey Bogart, Rosemary Lane, Ward Bond, Donald Crisp, Charles Middleton, Harvey Stephens; **D:** Lloyd Bacon; **C:** James Wong Howe; **M:** Max Steiner. *MGM, FCT*

The Oklahoman 🐾🐾 **1956** A routine western with some trivia value. Town doc McCrea helps Indian Pate keep his land. Talbott plays Indian maiden in same year as her title role in Daughter of Jekyll. Continuity buffs will note Hale wears the same outfit in m ost scenes. **80m/C VHS, Beta.** Joel McCrea, Barbara Hale, Brad Dexter, Gloria Talbott, Verna Felton, Douglas Dick, Michael Pate, Scotty Beckett; **D:** Francis D. Lyon. *FOX*

Okoge 🐾🐾 **1993** Rueful sexual comedy about a triangular friendship. Sayoko is a single young working woman living in a tiny Tokyo apartment. She meets the gay Noh and his older married lover Tochi and when they become friendly, Sayoko lets them use her apartment as their love nest—to the complications of all concerned. Title is a slang term used to refer to women who prefer the company of gay men. In Japanese with English subtitles. **120m/C VHS.** *JP* Misa Shimizu, Takehiro Murata, Takeo Nakahara, Masayuki Shionoya, Noriko Sengoku, Kyozo Nagatsuka, Toshie Nogishi; **D:** Takehiro Nakajima; **W:** Takehiro Nakajima. *FCT, CCN*

Old Barn Dance 🐾½ **1938** Autry and his singing cowboys are selling horses until a crooked tractor company puts them out of business. They join a radio program, discovers that it is owned by the same company that put them out of the horse-selling business, and runs the crooks out of town. **54m/B VHS, Beta.** Gene Autry, Smiley Burnette, Roy Rogers; **D:** Joseph Kane. *NOS, VCN, DVT*

Old Boyfriends 🐾🐾 **1979 (R)** Shire is weak as a psychologist searching for old boyfriends in order to analyze her past. Strange combination of Carradine and Belushi may draw curious fans. **103m/C VHS, Beta, LV.** Talia Shire, Richard Jordan, John Belushi, Keith Carradine, John Houseman, Buck Henry; **D:** Joan Tewkesbury; **W:** Leonard Schrader, Paul Schrader; **M:** David Shire. *NLC*

Old Corral 🐾🐾 **Texas Serenade 1936** Sheriff Autry protects his love interest, a girl fleeing the Mob. **54m/B VHS, Beta.** Gene Autry, Roy Rogers, Smiley Burnette; **D:** Joseph Kane. *NOS, MRV, VTR*

The Old Curiosity Shop 🐾🐾½ **1935** Webster and Benson are an old gambler and his daughter in this well-made film adaptation of the Dickens tale. Their miserly landlord tries to ruin their lives by evicting them and forcing them into a life of poverty. Remade as "Mr. Quilp" in 1957. **90m/B VHS.** Ben Webster, Elaine Benson, Hay Petrie, Beatrix Thompson, Gibb McLaughlin, Reginald Purdell; **D:** Thomas Bentley. *NOS*

The Old Curiosity Shop 🐾🐾 **Mr. Quilp 1975 (G)** Flat musical version of the Charles Dickens story about an evil man who wants to take over a small antique shop run by an elderly man and his granddaughter. ♫When a Felon Needs a Friend; Somewhere; Love Has the Longest Memory; Happiness Pie; The Sport of Kings; What Shouldn't Happen to a Dog; Quilp. **118m/C VHS, Beta.** *GB* Anthony Newley, David Hemmings, David Warner, Jill Bennett, Peter Duncan, Michael Hordern; **D:** Michael Tuchner; **M:** Elmer Bernstein. *REP*

The Old Curiosity Shop 🐾🐾 **1984 (G)** An animated adaptation of the classic Dickens story about a young girl and her grandfather who are evicted from their curiosity shop by an evil man. **72m/C VHS, Beta, Closed Caption.** **V:** John Benton, Jason Blackwell, Wallas Easton, Pennie Hackforth-Jones, Brian Harrison. *LIV*

The Old Curiosity Shop 🐾🐾½ **1994 (PG)** Another adaptation of Charles Dickens' 1840 tale about Grandfather Trent (Ustinov), an antiques dealer who has lost his fortune through gambling and makes matters worse by borrowing money from the miserable Mr. Quilp (Courtenay). Unable to repay the debt, Trent and young granddaughter Sally (Walsh) try to escape London, which turns Quilp's wrath upon them. Fine performances and a colorful production; made for cable TV. **280m/C VHS.** Peter Ustinov, Tom Courtenay, James Fox, Sally Walsh, William Mannering, Christopher Ettridge, Julia McKenzie, Anne White, Jean Marlow, Cornelia Hayes O'Herlihy, Michael Mears; **D:** Kevin Connor; **W:** John Goldsmith; **C:** Doug Milsome; **M:** Mason Daring. *HMK*

The Old Dark House 🐾🐾🐾 **1932** An atmospheric horror film, with more than a touch of comedy, well-directed by Whale. In an old haunted house live the bizarre Femm family: the 102 year-old patriarch, an atheist son, a religious fanatic daughter, and a crazed pyromanic son, all watched over by the mute, scarred, and psychotic butler (Karloff's first starring role). Into this strange group wander five unsuspecting, stranded travelers who set all sorts of dastardly plots in motion. Based on the novel "Benighted" by J.B. Priestley. **71m/B VHS.** Boris Karloff, Melvyn Douglas, Charles Laughton, Gloria Stuart, Ernest Thesiger, Raymond Massey, Lillian Bond, Eva Moore, Brember Wills, John Dudgeon; *D:* James Whale; *W:* Robert Dillon. *KIV, FCT*

Old Enough 🎬🎬 1984 (PG)
Slow-moving coming-of-age comedy on the rich kid-poor kid friendship theme. Silver's directing debut. **91m/C VHS, Beta.** Sarah Boyd, Rainbow Harvest, Neill Barry, Danny Aiello, Susan Kingsley, Roxanne Hart, Alyssa Milano, Fran Brill, Anne Pitoniak; *D:* Marisa Silver; *W:* Marisa Silver; *C:* Michael Ballhaus. Sundance Film Festival '84: Grand Jury Prize. *MED*

Old Explorers 🎬🎬½ 1990 (PG)
Two old friends refuse to let old age lessen their want for excitement, so they get together on a regular basis to set out on dangerous, imaginary adventures. They search for Atlantis, explore the Himalayan Mountains, and visit the Bermuda Triangle. After one of the men survives a stroke, the two set out on a real-life adventure on a tugboat cruising down the Mississippi River. Although the leads put in strong performances, they can't hide the slow-moving plot or the thin action sequences. Based on the play by James Cada and Mark Keller. **91m/C VHS, LV.** Jose Ferrer, James Whitmore, Jeffrey Gadbois, Caroline Kaiser, William Warfield, Christopher Pohlad, Storm Richardson, Mark M. Pohlad. *ACA*

Old Gringo 🎬🎬½ 1989 (R)
Adapted from Carlos Fuentes' novelization of writer Ambrose Bierce's mysterious disappearance in Mexico during the revolution of 1913. Features Fonda in the unlikely role of a virgin schoolteacher, Smits as her revolutionary lover, and Peck as her hero. Soggy acting by all but Peck, whose presence is wasted in a sketchy character. Technical problems and cheesy sets and costumes—look for the dusk backdrop in the dance scene and Smits' silly moustache. Better to read the book. **119m/C VHS, Beta, LV, 8mm, Closed Caption.** Jane Fonda, Gregory Peck, Jimmy Smits, Patricio Contreras, Jenny Gago, Gabriela Roel, Sergio Calderon, Guillermo Rios, Anne Pitoniak, Pedro Armendariz Jr., Jim Metzler; *D:* Luis Puenzo; *W:* Aida Bortnik, Luis Puenzo; *M:* Lee Holdridge. *COL*

Old Gun 🎬🎬🎬 1976
A grief-plagued doctor finds he must seek out and kill each Nazi involved in the slaughter of his wife and child to ease his pain. Excellent directing and a fully formed main character. **141m/C VHS, Beta.** Philippe Noiret, Romy Schneider, Jean Bouise; *D:* Robert Enrico. *MED*

Old Ironsides 🎬🎬🎬 1926
Silent, black-and-white version of the big budget/important director and stars action-adventure. Merchant marines aboard the famous Old Ironsides battle 19th century Barbary pirates in rousing action scenes. Home video version features an engaging organ score by Gaylord Carter. Based on the poem "Constitution" by Oliver Wendell Holmes. **111m/B VHS, Beta.** Esther Ralston, Wallace Beery, Boris Karloff, Charles Farrell, George Bancroft; *D:* James Cruze; *M:* Gaylord Carter. *PAR*

The Old Lady Who Walked in the Sea 🎬🎬 *La Vieille qui Marchait dans la Mer* 1991
Eccentric Lady M (Moreau) and her equally aging ex-lover Pompilius (Serrault) have spend their lives conning the rich. Summering on the French Riviera, Lady M spots handsome beach boy/thief Lambert (Thuiller) and decides to groom him for their latest caper, a jewel heist. Meanwhile, Pompilius pursues the young Noemie (Danon) and brings her into their menage, where Lambert is instantly smitten. Their lust leads to some unexpected complications but the real drama in the film is watching old pros Moreau and Serrault at work. Based on the novel by San Antonio; French with subtitles. **95m/C VHS.** *FR* Jeanne Moreau, Michel Serrault, Luc Thuillier, Geraldine Danon; *D:* Laurent Heynemann; *W:* Dominique Roulet; *C:* Robert Alazraki; *M:* Philippe Sarde. *HMK*

The Old Maid 🎬🎬🎬 1939
After her beau is killed in the Civil War, a woman allows her cousin to raise her illegitimate daughter, and therein begins a years-long struggle over the girl's affections. High grade soaper based on Zoe Adkin's stage adaptation of Edith Wharton's novel. **96m/B VHS, Beta.** Bette Davis, Miriam Hopkins, George Brent, Donald Crisp, Jane Bryan, Louise Fazenda, Henry Stephenson; *D:* Edmund Goulding; *C:* Gaetano Antonio "Tony" Gaudio; *M:* Max Steiner.. *MGM*

The Old Man and the Sea 🎬🎬½ 1990
Quinn is wonderful as Hemingway's aging Cuban fisherman, Santiago, who battles a band of marauding sharks for a giant marlin in the Gulf Stream. Unfortunately, this made for TV adaptation is ordinary. **97m/C VHS.** Anthony Quinn, Gary Cole, Alexis Cruz, Patricia Clarkson, Francesco Quinn; *D:* Jud Taylor; *W:* Roger O. Hirson; *C:* James Wong Howe; *M:* Bruce Broughton. *VCO*

Old Mother Riley's Ghosts 🎬🎬 1941
A group of spies "haunt" Mother Riley's castle home in a futile attempt to scare her out; she turns the tables. Some good scares and laughs. Part of the Old Mother Riley series. Look for similarities to later Monty Python films. **82m/B VHS, Beta.** *GB* Arthur Lucan, Kitty McShane, John Stuart; *D:* John Baxter. *NOS, SNC*

Old Spanish Custom 🎬 *The Invader* 1936
Only a Keaton fan could love this comedy, set in Spain and filmed in England. One of his rarest—and poorest—sound films. He plays a bumbling rich yachtsman smitten with Tovar, a Spanish maiden who uses him to make her lover jealous. **58m/B VHS, Beta.** *GB* Buster Keaton, Lupita Tovar, Lyn Harding, Esme Percy; *D:* Adrian Brunel. *VYY, GPV, VDM*

Old Swimmin' Hole 🎬 *When Youth Conspires* 1940
Small-town friends Moran and Jones try to bring their single parents together; his mother can't afford to finance his dream to be a doctor. Dull, melodramatic ode to heartland America, reminiscent of "Our Town." **78m/B VHS, Beta.** Marcia Mae Jones, Jackie Moran, Leatrice Joy, Charles D. Brown; *D:* Robert McGowan. *VYY*

Old Yeller 🎬🎬🎬½ 1957 (G)
Disney Studios' first and best boy-and-his-dog film. Fifteen-year-old Kirk is left in charge of the family farm while Parker is away. When his younger brother brings home a stray dog, Kirk is displeased but lets him stay. Yeller saves Kirk's life, but contracts rabies in the process. Kirk is forced to kill him. Keep tissue handy, especially for the kids. Stong acting, effective scenery—all good stuff. Based on the novel by Fred Gipson. Sequel "Savage Sam" released in 1963. **84m/C VHS, Beta, LV, Closed Caption.** Dorothy McGuire, Fess Parker, Tommy Kirk, Kevin Corcoran, Jeff York, Beverly Washburn, Chuck Connors; *D:* Robert Stevenson. *DIS*

Oldest Confederate Widow Tells All 🎬🎬🎬 1995
TV drama starts with the recollections of 99-year-old Lucy Marsden (Bancroft), the widow of the title, who revisits her marriage to troubled Civil War veteran Capt. William Marsden (Sutherland, sporting an impressive set of whiskers). In 1899, the teenaged Lucy (played by Lane) marries the eccentric 50-year-old, who constantly relives battlefield horrors and the loss of his boyhood friend, while she deals with family and various domestic crises. Somewhat meandering story with fine performances and subtle details. Based on Allan Gurganus' novel. **180m/C VHS, Closed Caption.** Diane Lane, Donald Sutherland, Anne Bancroft, Cicely Tyson, Blythe Danner, E.G. Marshall, Gwen Verdon, Maureen Mueller, Wil Horneff; *D:* Ken Cameron; *W:* Joyce Eliason; *M:* Mark Snow. *CAF*

Oldest Living Graduate 🎬🎬🎬½ 1982
Fonda is memorable in his last stage role as the oldest graduate of a Texas military academy. He and his son clash when Fonda refuses to give up his land. Teleplay features strong performances from Leachman and other big-name cast members. **75m/C VHS, Beta.** Cloris Leachman, Henry Fonda,

John Lithgow, Timothy Hutton, Harry Dean Stanton, David Ogden Stiers, George Grizzard, Penelope Milford. *VHE*

Oldest Profession 🎬 *Le Plus Vieux Metier du Monde* 1967
A study of prostitution from prehistoric times to the future. Generally unexciting and unfunny. In six segments meant as vehicles for their directors. **97m/C VHS, Beta, LV.** *FR GE IT* Raquel Welch, Jeanne Moreau, Elsa Martinelli, Michele Mercier; *D:* Jean-Luc Godard, Philippe de Broca, Claude Autant-Lara, Franco Indovina, Mauro Bolognini, Michael Pfleghar; *W:* Jean-Luc Godard. *NWV, IME*

Oleanna 🎬½ 1994
Mamet directs the big-screen version of his controversial play about political correctness, sexual harrassment, and the gender gap. Pompous, burned-out college professor (Macy) is accused of sexual harassment by dense, shrill, academically weak student (Eisenstadt) after she misconstrues a self-important speech as a come-on. Unbalanced perspective, obvious stereotyping of unsympathetic characters, and weak performances remove any hint of the intended drama. **90m/C VHS, LV, Closed Caption.** William H. Macy, Debra Eisenstadt; *D:* David Mamet; *W:* David Mamet; *C:* Andrzej Sekula; *M:* Rebecca Pidgeon. Nominations: Independent Spirit Awards '95: Best Actor (Macy). *HMK*

Oliver! 🎬🎬🎬½ 1968 (G)
Splendid big-budget musical adaptation of Dickens' "Oliver Twist." An innocent orphan is dragged into a life of crime when he is befriended by a gang of pickpockets. ♫Food, Glorious Food; Oliver; Boy For Sale; Where Is Love?; Consider Yourself; Pick a Pocket or Two; I'd Do Anything; Be Back Soon; As Long As He Needs Me. **145m/C VHS, Beta, LV, Closed Caption.** *GB* Mark Lester, Jack Wild, Ron Moody, Shani Wallis, Oliver Reed, Hugh Griffith; *D:* Carol Reed; *C:* Oswald Morris. Academy Awards '68: Best Adapted Score, Best Art Direction/Set Decoration, Best Director (Reed), Best Picture, Best Sound; Golden Globe Awards '69: Best Actor—Musical/Comedy (Moody), Best Film—Musical/Comedy; National Board of Review Awards '69: 10 Best Films of the Year; Nominations: Academy Awards '68: Best Actor (Moody), Best Adapted Screenplay, Best Cinematography, Best Costume Design, Best Film Editing, Best Supporting Actor (Wild). *COL, BTV, HMV*

Oliver & Company 🎬🎬½ 1988 (G)
Animated animal retelling of Dicken's "Oliver Twist"—Disney style. Kitten Oliver (Lawrence) is left to fend for himself on the mean streets of New York until he's taken under the paw of Dodger (Joel) the dog. Dodger heads up a gang of doggy thieves, who help down-and-out human Fagin (DeLuise), who owes money to ruthless loan shark Sykes (Loggia). Out on his first job, Oliver's found by rich little Jenny (Gregory) and happily adopted. But his pals think he's been kidnapped and are off to rescue him. ♫Once Upon a Time in New York City; Why Should I Worry?. **72m/C VHS, Closed Caption.** *D:* George Scribner; *W:* Jim Cox, James Mangold; *V:* Joey Lawrence, Billy Joel, Richard "Cheech" Marin, Bette Midler, Dom DeLuise, Roscoe Lee Browne, Richard Mulligan, Sheryl Lee Ralph, Robert Loggia, Taurean Blacque, Carl Weintraub, Natalie Gregory, William Glover. *TOU*

Oliver Twist 🎬🎬🎬 1922
Silent version of the Dickens classic is a vehicle for young Jackie Coogan. As orphan Oliver Twist, he is subjected to many frightening incidents before finding love and someone to care for him. Remade numerous times, most notably in 1933 and 1948 and as the musical "Oliver!" in 1968. **77m/B VHS, Beta.** Jackie Coogan, Lon Chaney Sr., Gladys Brockwell, George Siegmann, Esther Ralston; *D:* Frank Lloyd. *NOS, CCB, KIV*

Oliver Twist 🎬🎬🎬 1933
The first talking version of Dickens' classic about an ill-treated London orphan involved with youthful gang of pickpockets. Moore was too young—at five—to be very credible in the lead role. The 1948 version is much more believable. **70m/B VHS, Beta, Closed Caption.** Dickie Moore, Irving Pichel, William "Stage" Boyd, Barbara Kent; *D:* William J. Cowen. *NOS, MRV, HHT*

Oliver Twist 🎬🎬🎬🎬 1948 Charles Dickens' immortal story of a workhouse orphan who is forced into a life of crime with a gang of pickpockets. The best of many film adaptations, with excellent portrayals by the cast. 116m/C VHS, Beta, LV. *GB* Robert Newton, John Howard Davies, Alec Guinness, Francis L. Sullivan, Anthony Newley, Kay Walsh, Diana Dors, Henry Stephenson; *D:* David Lean; *W:* David Lean; *C:* Guy Green. PAR, DVT, FHS

Oliver Twist 🎬🎬🎬 1982 Good made-for-television version of the classic Dicken's tale of a boy's rescue from a life of crime. Scott's Fagin is a treat, and period details are on the mark. 100m/C VHS, Closed Caption. George C. Scott, Tim Curry, Michael Hordern, Timothy West, Lysette Anthony, Eileen Atkins, Cherie Lunghi; *D:* Clive Donner; *W:* James Goldman; *M:* Nick Bicat. TVC, VES, REP

Oliver Twist 1985 A British television miniseries adaptation of the Charles Dickens classic about an orphan boy plunging into the underworld of 19th-century London. On two tapes. 333m/C VHS, Beta. *GB* Ben Rodska, Eric Porter, Frank Middlemass, Gillian Martell. FOX, SIG, HMV

Oliver's Story 🎬 1978 (PG) A "not so equal" sequel to "Love Story," where widower O'Neal wallows in grief untils rich heiress Bergen comes along. He falls in love again, this time with money. 90m/C VHS, Beta. Ryan O'Neal, Candice Bergen, Ray Milland, Edward Binns, Nicola Pagett, Charles Haid; *D:* John Korty; *W:* Erich Segal. PAR

Olivia 🎬½ 1983 Abused housewife moonlights as a prostitute and begins killing her customers. She falls in love with an American businessman and flees to America when her husband finds out about the affair. Revenge and murder are the result. 90m/C VHS, Beta. Suzanna Love, Robert Walker Jr., Jeff Winchester; *D:* Ulli Lommel. VHE

Olivier, Olivier 🎬🎬🎬 1992 (R) Holland's directorial follow-up to "Europa, Europa" is based on a 1984 French newspaper story and evokes "The Return of Martin Guerre" and its update, "Sommersby." Beloved nine-year-old boy disappears from his home in a small French town and his dysfunctional family falls apart. Mom obsesses and falls into trances, dad escapes to North Africa, and sister Nadine develops telekinetic powers in order to cope. Six years later a detective brings an amnesiac teenager, who has been working as a hustler in Paris, to the boy's family. Is it the missing Olivier? Spooky, provocative, and emotionally resonate. In French with English subtitles. *CW:* Language and sexuality. 110m/C VHS, LV. *FR* Francois Cluzet, Brigitte Rouan, Gregoire Colin, Marina Golovine, Jean-Francois Stevenin, Emmanuel Morozof, Faye Gatteau, Frederic Quiring; *D:* Agnieszka Holland; *W:* Agnieszka Holland. Los Angeles Film Critics Association Awards '93: Best Score. COL

Ollie Hopnoodle's Haven of Bliss 🎬🎬½ 1988 Humorist Jean Shepherd (of "A Christmas Story" fame) spins another tale of frantic family life with his alter ego, Ralphie. This time the family is off on a summer vacation—with all its inherent problems. Made for cable television. 90m/C VHS, Beta, Closed Caption. James B. Sikking, Dorothy Lyman, Jerry O'Connell; *D:* Dick Bartlett. DIS

Olly Olly Oxen Free 🎬🎬 *The Great Balloon Adventure* 1978 Junkyard owner Hepburn helps two boys fix up and fly a hot-air balloon, once piloted by McKenzie's grandfather, as a surprise for the man's birthday. Beautiful airborne scenes over California and a dramatic landing to the tune of the "1812 Overture," but not enough to make the whole film interesting. 89m/C VHS, Beta. Katharine Hepburn, Kevin McKenzie, Dennis Dimster, Peter Kilman; *D:* Richard A. Colla; *M:* Robert Alcivar. TLF

Olongapo: The American Dream 🎬½ 1989 A young woman works in a cheap bar while waiting for the chance to come to America. 97m/C VHS, Beta. Jacklyn Jose, Susan Africa, Chanda Romero, Joel Torre, Marilou Sadiua; *D:* Chito Rono. TWE

omaha (the movie) 🎬🎬 1995 Gen-Xer Simon (Walkinshaw) flees his native Nebraska and eccentric, dysfunctional family for enlightenment in Tibet. He's instructed in Buddhism and returns home but doesn't find the peace he's seeking and decides to hit the road with former girlfriend Gina (Anderson). 85m/C VHS. Hughston Walkinshaw, Jill Anderson; *D:* Dan Mirvish; *W:* Dan Mirvish; *C:* Oslo Anderson. WAC

Omar Khayyam 🎬🎬 1957 In medieval Persia, Omar (Wilde) becomes involved in a romance with the Shah of Persia's fiancee, while trying to fight off a faction of assassins trying to overthrow the Shah. Although this film has a great cast, the script is silly and juvenile, defeating the cast's fine efforts. 101m/C VHS, Closed Caption. Cornel Wilde, Michael Rennie, Debra Paget, Raymond Massey, John Derek, Yma Sumac, Margaret Hayes, Joan Taylor, Sebastian Cabot; *D:* William Dieterle. PAR

Omega Cop 🎬 *John Travis, Solar Survivor* 1990 (R) In a post-apocalyptic future, there's only one cop left. He uses his martial arts skills and tons of guns attempting to rescue three women, but the violence doesn't cover the poor acting and shoddy production. Fans of TV's Batman might enjoy this for West's presence. 89m/C VHS. Ron Marchini, Adam West, Stuart Whitman, Troy Donahue, Meg Thayer, Jennifer Jostyn, Chrysti Jimenez, D.W. Landingham, Chuck Katzakian; *D:* Paul Kyriazi. HMD

Omega Doom 🎬🎬 1996 (PG-13) Four hundred years after an apocalyptic war the most organic thing around are the cyborgs, who exist along with androids and robots in a world where humans no longer matter. Omega Doom (Hauer) is an android developed as a fighter who has no function except to kill. In a ruined amusement park, the Roms and Droids, two rival cyborg groups, maintain an uneasy truce and when Doom wanders in they unite to destroy the intruder. But they don't know what they're up against. *CW:* Sci-fi violence. 84m/C VHS, Closed Caption. Rutger Hauer, Anna Katarina, Norbert Weisser, Jahi JJ Zuri, Shannon Whirry, Earl White, Tina Cote, Jill Pierce; *D:* Albert Pyun; *W:* Ed Naha. COL

Omega Man 🎬🎬½ 1971 (PG) In post-holocaust Los Angeles, Heston is immune to the effects of a biologically engineered plague and battles those who aren't—an army of albino victims bent on destroying what's left of the world. Strong suspense with considerable violence, despite the PG rating. Based on the science fiction thriller "I Am Legend" by Richard Matheson, which is also the basis for the film "The Last Man on Earth." 98m/C VHS, Beta, LV. Charlton Heston, Anthony Zerbe, Rosalind Cash, Paul Koslo; *D:* Boris Sagal; *C:* Russell Metty. WAR

Omega Syndrome 🎬½ 1987 (R) Neo-Nazis kidnap Wahl's daughter. He and Vietnam buddy DiCenzo get her back. Ho hum. DiCenzo's is the best performance. Tolerable for vigilante film fans. 90m/C VHS, Beta. Ken Wahl, Ron Kuhlman, George DiCenzo, Doug McClure; *D:* Joseph Manduke. NWV, VTR

The Omen 🎬🎬½ *Birthmark* 1976 (R) American diplomat's family adopts a young boy who always seems to be around when bizarre and inexplicable deaths occur. Of course, what else would you expect of Satan's son? The shock and gore prevalent in "The Exorcist" is replaced with more suspense and believable effects. Well-done horror film doesn't insult the viewer's intelligence. Followed by three sequels: "Damien: Omen 2," "The Final Conflict," and "Omen 4." 111m/C VHS, Beta, LV. Gregory Peck, Lee Remick, Billie Whitelaw, David Warner, Holly Palance, Richard Donner; *D:* Richard Donner; *W:* David Seltzer; *M:* Jerry Goldsmith. Academy Awards '76: Best Original Score; Nominations: Academy Awards '76: Best Song ("Ave Satani"). FOX

Omen 4: The Awakening 🎬🎬 1991 It turns out Damien of Omens past had a daughter, Delia, who takes up where dear old devilish Dad left off. Delia is adopted by your basic clueless

couple and proceeds to wreak havoc wherever she goes, including getting rid of several interfering adults. She also plans to make her adoptive father, a U.S. senator, President, so that his delightful child anti-Christ can have him carry out all her evil plans. 97m/C VHS, Closed Caption. Faye Grant, Michael Woods, Michael Lerner, Asia Vieira; *D:* Jorge Montesi, Dominique Othenin-Girard. FXV

Omoo Omoo, the Shark God 🎬 1949 A sea captain is cursed when he removes the black pearls from a stone shark god in this extremely cheap adventure. 58m/B VHS. Ron Randell, Devera Burton, Trevor Bardette, Pedro de Cordoba, Richard Benedict, Rudy Robles, Michael Whalen, George Meeker; *D:* Leo Leonard. SNC

On a Clear Day You Can See Forever 🎬🎬 1970 (G) A psychiatric hypnotist helps a girl stop smoking and finds that in trances she remembers previous incarnations. He falls in love with one of the women she used to be. Alan Jay Lerner of "My Fair Lady" and "Camelot" wrote the lyrics and the book. Based on a musical by Lerner and Burton Lane. ♫On a Clear Day, You Can See Forever; Come Back to Me; What Did I Have That I Don't Have?; He Isn't You; Hurry, It's Lovely Up Here; Go To Sleep; Love with All the Trimmings; Melinda. 129m/C VHS, Beta, LV. Barbra Streisand, Yves Montand, Bob Newhart, Jack Nicholson, Simon Oakland; *D:* Vincente Minnelli; *C:* Harry Stradling. PAR

On an Island with You 🎬🎬½ 1948 Williams plays a movie star who finds romance on location in Hawaii in this musical extravaganza. Contains many of Williams' famous water ballet scenes and a bevy of bathing beauties. ♫On an Island with You; If I Were You; Taking Miss Mary to the Ball; Dog Song; Buenas Noches, Buenos Aires; Wedding Samba; I Can Do Without Broadway, But Can Broadway Do Without Me?. 107m/C VHS. Esther Williams, Peter Lawford, Ricardo Montalban, Jimmy Durante, Cyd Charisse, Leon Ames; *D:* Richard Thorpe. MGM

On Approval 🎬🎬🎬 1944 Hilarious British farce in which two women trade boyfriends. Lillie's performace provides plenty of laughs. Brook runs the show as leading man, co-author, director, and co-producer. Based on the play by Frederick Lonsdale. 80m/B VHS, Beta. *GB* Clive Brook, Beatrice Lillie, Googie Withers, Roland Culver, O.B. Clarence, Lawrence Hanray, Elliot Mason, Hay Petrie, Marjorie Munks, Molly Munks; *D:* Clive Brook; *W:* Terence Young, Clive Brook. KIV, MRV, HHT

On Borrowed Time 🎬🎬🎬 1939 Engrossing tale of Death (Hardwicke) coming for an old man (Barrymore) who isn't ready to die so he traps him in his backyard apple tree. Performances are first rate in this good adaptation of the stage success (originally by Eugene O'Neill). Hardwicke is especially a standout; he gave up theatre for Hollywood after making this film. 99m/B VHS, Closed Caption. Lionel Barrymore, Cedric Hardwicke, Beulah Bondi, Una Merkel, Bobs Watson, Henry Travers; *D:* Harold Bucquet; *C:* Joseph Ruttenberg. MGM

On Dangerous Ground 🎬🎬🎬 1951 A world-weary detective is sent to the countryside to investigate a murder. He encounters the victim's revenge-hungry father and the blind sister of the murderer. In the hateful father the detective sees a reflection of the person he has become, in the blind woman, he learns the redeeming qualities of humanity and compassion. A well-acted example of film noir that features the composer Herrman's favorite score. 82m/B VHS, Beta, LV. Robert Ryan, Ida Lupino, Ward Bond, Ed Begley Sr., Cleo Moore, Charles Kemper; *D:* Nicholas Ray; *M:* Bernard Herrmann. TTC

On Deadly Ground woof! 1994 (R) Seagal nearly destroys Alaska in an effort to save it in this inane, preachy story of an oil-rig roughneck out to protect the landscape from an evil oil company's drilling habits. Directorial debut for Seagal lumbers from scene to scene. Violence is expected, as is silly dialogue—just try to keep from laughing when stoneyfaced Steven intones "What does it take to change the essence of man?" A better script, for one. **CW:** Language, nudity, and strong violence. **102m/C VHS, LV, Closed Caption.** Steven Seagal, Michael Caine, Joan Chen, John C. McGinley; **D:** Steven Seagal; **W:** Ed Horowitz; **M:** Basil Poledouris. Golden Raspberry Awards '94: Worst Director (Seagal); Nominations: Golden Raspberry Awards '94: Worst Picture. *WAR*

On Golden Pond ♂♂♂½ 1981 (PG)
Henry Fonda won his first, and long overdue, Oscar for his role as the curmudgeonly patriarch of the Thayer family. He and his wife have grudgingly agreed to look after a young boy while at their summer home in Maine. Through his gradually affectionate relationship with the boy, Fonda learns to allay his fears of mortality. He also gains an understanding of his semi-estranged daughter. Jane Fonda plays his daughter and Hepburn is his loving wife in this often funny adaptation of Ernest Thompson's 1978 play. Predictable but deeply moving. Henry Fonda's final screen appearance. **109m/C VHS, Beta, LV.** Henry Fonda, Jane Fonda, Katharine Hepburn, Dabney Coleman, Doug McKeon, William Lanteau; **D:** Mark Rydell; **W:** Ernest Thompson; **C:** Billy Williams; **M:** Dave Grusin. Academy Awards '81: Best Actor (Fonda), Best Actress (Hepburn), Best Adapted Screenplay; British Academy Awards '82: Best Actress (Hepburn); Golden Globe Awards '82: Best Actor—Drama (Fonda), Best Film—Drama, Best Screenplay; National Board of Review Awards '81: Best Actor (Fonda); Writers Guild of America '81: Best Adapted Screenplay; Nominations: Academy Awards '81: Best Cinematography, Best Director (Rydell), Best Film Editing, Best Picture, Best Sound, Best Supporting Actress (Fonda), Best Original Score. *FHE, KAR, BTV*

On Her Majesty's Secret Service ♂♂♂ 1969 (PG)
In the sixth 007 adventure, Bond again confronts the infamous Blofeld, who is planning a germ-warfare assault on the entire world. Australian Lazenby took a crack at playing the super spy, with mixed results. Many feel this is the best-written of the Bond films and might have been the most famous, had Sean Connery continued with the series. Includes the song "We Have All the Time In the World," sung by Louis Armstrong. **144m/C VHS, Beta, LV.** GB George Lazenby, Diana Rigg, Telly Savalas, Gabriele Ferzetti, Ilse Steppat, Bernard Lee, Lois Maxwell, Desmond Llewelyn, Catherine Schell, Julie Ege, Joanna Lumley, Mona Chong, Anouska Hempel, Jenny Hanley; **D:** Peter Hunt; **M:** John Barry. *MGM, FOX, TLF*

On Moonlight Bay ♂♂½ 1951
Set in small-town Indiana in 1917 with Day as the tomboyish Marjorie who falls for college man MacRae. Her father (Ames) doesn't approve but the trouble really begins when Marjorie's younger brother gets into trouble at school. The incorrigible Wesley (Gray) blames everything on dear old dad and MacRae feels he must come to Marjorie's rescue! Gray steals the movie as the bratty brother—otherwise its business as usual. Based on Booth Tarkington's "Penrod" stories and followed by "By the Light of the Silvery Moon." ♫Love Ya; On Moonlight Bay; Till We Meet Again; Pack Up Your Troubles In Your Old Kit Bag; I'm Forever Blowing Bubbles; Christmas Story; Tell Me Why Nights Are Lonely; Cuddle Up a Little Closer; Every Little Movement Has a Meaning All Its Own. **95m/C VHS, LV.** Doris Day, Gordon MacRae, Leon Ames, Billy Gray, Rosemary DeCamp, Mary Wickes, Ellen Corby, Esther Dale; **D:** Roy Del Ruth; **W:** Melville Shavelson, Jack Rose; **M:** Max Steiner. *WAR, MVD*

On My Own ♂♂ 1992
Fifteen-year-old Simon Henderson (Ferguson) struggles to cope with his life when he's sent away to school after his mother (Davis) suffers a nervous breakdown. Just as he begins to adjust and make friends, his mother pays a disturbing visit and reveals the source of her troubles. **96m/C VHS.** CA Judy Davis, Matthew Ferguson, David McIlwraith; **D:** Antonio Tibaldi. *FCT, CCN*

On the Air Live with Captain Midnight ♂½ Captain Midnight 1979
Socially challenged teen finds hipness as a rebel DJ operating an illegal radio station from his van. Leading actor is the son of the director/writer/producer but nepotism does not a good film make. **90m/C VHS, Beta.** Tracy Sebastian; **D:** Ferd Sebastian. *NO*

On the Avenue ♂♂♂ 1937
Broadway showman Powell opens up a new musical, starring Faye as the richest girl in the world, in this musical-comedy satirizing upper-crust society. Debutante Carroll is outraged because she realizes it's mocking her actual life. Carroll tries to get Powell to change the show, they fall in love, Faye gets her nose out of joint, and after lots of fuss everything ends happily. Fine Berlin score. ♫He Ain't Got Rhythm; You're Laughing at Me; This Year's Kisses; Slumming on Park Avenue; The Girl on the Police Gazette; I've Got My Love to Keep Me Warm. **90m/B VHS, Beta.** Dick Powell, Madeleine Carroll, Alice Faye, George Barbier, The Ritz Brothers, Alan Mowbray, Cora Witherspoon, Walter Catlett, Stepin Fetchit, Sig Rumann, Douglas Fowley, Joan Davis; **D:** Roy Del Ruth; **W:** Gene Markey; **M:** Irving Berlin. *FXV*

On the Beach ♂♂♂½ 1959
A group of survivors attempt to live normal lives in post-apocalyptic Australia, waiting for the inevitable arrival of killer radiation. Astaire is strong in his first dramatic role. Though scientifically implausible, still a good anti-war vehicle. Based on the best-selling novel by Nevil Shute. **135m/B VHS, Beta, LV.** Gregory Peck, Anthony Perkins, Donna Anderson, Ava Gardner, Fred Astaire; **D:** Stanley Kramer; **C:** Daniel F. Fapp; **M:** Ernest Gold. Golden Globe Awards '60: Best Score; National Board of Review Awards '60: 10 Best Films of the Year; Nominations: Academy Awards '59: Best Film Editing, Original Dramatic/Comedy Score. *FOX, FCT*

On the Comet ♂♂♂ Na Komete; Hector Servadac's Ark 1968
Zeman's fourth fantasy based on Jules Verne stories, about a chunk of the Earth's crust suddenly becoming a comet and giving its passengers a ride through the galaxy. Complete with Zeman's signature animation fantasias. In English. **76m/C VHS, Beta.** CZ Emil Horvath Jr., Magda Vasarykova, Frantisek Filipovsky; **D:** Karel Zeman. *FCT, MRV*

On the Edge ♂ 1982
A narcotics agent tracks down a wealthy Brazilian drug kingpin. **82m/C VHS, Beta.** Anthony Steffen. *NO*

On the Edge ♂♂½ 1986 (PG-13)
A drama about the inevitable Rocky-esque triumph of Dern as an aging marathon runner. Simultaneous to his running endeavor, Dern is trying to make up for lost time with his father. Available in two versions, one rated, the other unrated with a racy appearance by Pam Grier as the runner's interracial lover. **86m/C VHS, Beta.** Bruce Dern, John Marley, Bill Bailey, Jim Haynie, Pam Grier; **D:** Rob Nilsson; **W:** Rob Nilsson. *NO*

On the Edge: The Survival of Dana ♂ 1979
Another entry from the world of low-quality made-for-TV films. A young girl moves with her family to a new town. When she falls in with the "bad" crowd, her ethical standards are challenged. A stinker that may appeal to those with campy tastes. Not for the discriminating palate. **92m/C VHS, Beta.** Melissa Sue Anderson, Robert Carradine, Marion Ross, Talia Balsam, Michael Pataki, Kevin Breslin, Judge Reinhold, Barbara Babcock; **D:** Jack Starrett. *GEM*

On the Fiddle ♂♂½ Operation Snafu; Operation Warhead 1961
Conniving Horace Pope (Lynch) gets his mate Pedlar Pascoe (Connery) to join the Royal Air Force with him during WWII. Horace sets up a number of rackets but, despite their larceny, they become unintentional heroes. Based on the novel "Stop at a Winner" by R.F. Delderfield. **93m/B VHS, Closed Caption.** GB Alfred Lynch, Sean Connery, Cecil Parker, Stanley Holloway, Wilfrid Hyde-White; **D:** Cyril Frankel; **W:** Harold Buchman; **C:** Edward Scaife; **M:** Malcolm Arnold. *REP*

On the Line ♂½ 1983
Two Mexico-US border guards, one hard-bitten, the other sympathetic to the illegal immigrants' plight, battle it out over a beautiful Mexican whore. Disjointed and confusing. **95m/C VHS, Beta, Closed Caption.** SP David Carradine, Victoria Abril, Scott Wilson, Sam Jaffe, Jesse Vint; **D:** Jose Luis Borau; **W:** Jose Luis Borau. *NLC*

On the Nickel ♂♂ 1980 (R)
An ex-alcoholic returns to Fifth Street in Los Angeles to save his friend from a life of despair. Waits' musical score enhances this sentimental skid row drama. Scripted, directed and produced by "The Waltons'" Waite. **96m/C VHS, Beta.** Ralph Waite, Donald Moffat, Hal Williams, Jack Kehoe; **D:** Ralph Waite; **W:** Ralph Waite; **M:** Tom Waits. *VES*

On the Night Stage ♂♂ 1915
Gruff bandit (legendary Hart) loses his girl-of-questionable-values to town preacher. One of the first feature length westerns. **83m/B VHS, Beta, 8mm.** William S. Hart, Robert Edeson, Rhea Mitchell, Shorty Hamilton; **D:** Reginald Barker. *GPV, VYY*

On the Old Spanish Trail ♂½ 1947
Rogers becomes a singing cowboy with a traveling tent show in order to pay off a note signed by the Sons of the Pioneers. **56m/B VHS, Beta.** Roy Rogers, Jane Frazee, Andy Devine, Tito Guizar; **D:** William Witney. *NOS, MRV, VCN*

On the Right Track ♂½ 1981 (PG)
Young orphan living in Chicago's Union Station has the gift of being able to pick winning race horses. May be appealing to fans of Coleman and "Different Strokes" television show, but lacks the momentum to keep most viewers from switching tracks. **98m/C VHS, Beta.** Gary Coleman, Lisa Eilbacher, Michael Lembeck, Norman Fell, Maureen Stapleton, Herb Edelman; **D:** Lee Philips. *FOX*

On the Run ♂ 1985 (R)
An ex-con and his gal cut a law-defying swath through the Bayou. **96m/C VHS, Beta.** Jack Conrad, Rita George, Dub Taylor, David Huddleston. *GEM*

On the Third Day ♂ 1983
A headmaster finds a mysterious stranger in his house who turns out to be his long-lost illegitimate son. **101m/C VHS, Beta.** Richard Marant, Catherine Schell, Paul Williamson. *ORI*

On the Town ♂♂♂½ 1949
Kelly's directorial debut features three sailors on a one day leave search for romance in the Big Apple. Filmed on location in New York City, with uncompromisingly authentic flavor. Based on the successful Broadway musical, with a score composed by Leonard Bernstein, Betty Comden, and Adolph Green. Additional songs by Roger Edens. Available in a deluxe collector's laserdisc edition. ♫New York, New York; I Feel Like I'm Not Out of Bed Yet; Come Up to My Place; Miss Turnstiles Ballet; Main Street; You're Awful; On the Town; You Can Count on Me; Pearl of the Persian Sea. **98m/C VHS, Beta, LV.** Gene Kelly, Frank Sinatra, Vera-Ellen, Ann Miller, Betty Garrett; **D:** Gene Kelly, Stanley Donen; **W:** Betty Comden, Adolph Green. Academy Awards '49: Scoring of a Musical. *MGM*

On the Town ♂♂½ 1991
Bernstein's first big Broadway success in 1944, recorded in a live performance June 1992, at London's Barbican Centre. Follows the story of three sailors on a 24-hour leave in New York City during WWII. This version includes numbers which never made it into the original Broadway show. **110m/C VHS, LV.** Frederica von Stade, Tyne Daly, Marie McLaughlin, David Garrison, Thomas Hampson, Kurt Ollman, Evelyn Lear, Samuel Ramey, Cleo Laine; **M:** Leonard Bernstein, Betty Comden, Adolph Green. *PGV, FCT*

On the Waterfront ♂♂♂♂ 1954
A trend-setting, gritty portrait of New York dock workers embroiled in union violence. Cobb is the gangster union boss, Steiger his crooked lawyer, and Brando, Steiger's ex-fighter brother who "could've been a contender!" Intense performances and excellent direction stand up well today. The picture was a huge financial success. **108m/B VHS, Beta, LV, Closed Caption.** Marlon Brando,

Rod Steiger, Eva Marie Saint, Lee J. Cobb, Karl Malden, Pat Henning, Leif Erickson, Tony Galento, John Hamilton, Nehemiah Persoff; **D:** Elia Kazan; **W:** Budd Schulberg; **C:** Boris Kaufman; **M:** Leonard Bernstein. Academy Awards '54: Best Actor (Brando), Best Art Direction/Set Decoration (B & W), Best Black and White Cinematography, Best Director (Kazan), Best Film Editing, Best Picture, Best Story & Screenplay, Best Supporting Actress (Saint); British Academy Awards '54: Best Actor (Brando); Directors Guild of America Awards '54: Best Director (Kazan); Golden Globe Awards '55: Best Actor—Drama (Brando), Best Director (Kazan), Best Film—Drama; National Board of Review Awards '54: 10 Best Films of the Year; New York Film Critics Awards '54: Best Actor (Brando), Best Director (Kazan), Best Film; Nominations: Academy Awards '54: Best Supporting Actor (Cobb), Best Supporting Actor (Malden, Steiger), Original Dramatic/Comedy Score. *COL, BTV*

On the Yard 🎞🎞 1979 (R) An attempt to realistically portray prison life. Focuses on a murderer who runs afoul of the leader of the prisoners and the system. A fairly typical prison drama with above average performances from Heard and Kellin. 102m/C VHS, Beta. John Heard, Thomas G. Waites, Mike Kellin, Joe Grifasi; **D:** Raphael D. Silver; **W:** Malcolm Braly. *MED*

On Top of Old Smoky 🎞½ 1953 Autry and the Cass County Boys are mistaken for Texas Rangers by a gang of land poachers. 59m/B VHS, Beta. Gene Autry, Smiley Burnette, Gail Davis, Sheila Ryan; **D:** George Archainbaud. *CCB*

On Top of the Whale 🎞🎞 1982 Two scholars move onto the estate of strange but wealthy benefactor to conduct research on the few survivors of a disappearing clan of Indians. Two tribesmen speak bizarre dialect which utilizes only one word while others confound the researchers with stories of ghosts and graveyards. Dutch comedy subtitled in English. 93m/C VHS. NL **D:** Raul Ruiz. *KIV, FCT*

On Valentine's Day 🎞🎞½ *Story of a Marriage* 1986 (PG) Author Horton Foote based this story loosely on his parents' lives. A wealthy young Southern girl marries a poor but decent young man and finds herself ostracized from her family. A prequel to the same author's "1918." Produced with PBS for "American Playhouse." 106m/C VHS, Beta. Hallie Foote, Matthew Broderick, Michael Higgins, Steven Hill, William Converse-Roberts, Rochelle Oliver, Richard Jenkins, Horton Foote Jr., Carol Goodheart; **D:** Ken Harrison; **W:** Horton Foote; **D:** Jonathan Sheffer. *ORI*

On Wings of Eagles 🎞🎞½ 1986 During the 1979 Iranian revolution two American executives are imprisoned by Islamic radicals. Help arrives in the form of covert agents of their boss—Texas tycoon H. Ross Perot (played by Crenna). Don't expect strict historical veracity or insight from this network miniseries (based on the "nonfiction novel" by Ken Follett), an okay but lengthy "mission impossible." It came out in a two-cassette set, just in time for Perot's 1992 presidential campaign. 221m/C VHS. Burt Lancaster, Richard Crenna, Paul LeMat, Esai Morales, Constance Towers, Jim Metzler, James Sutorius, Lawrence Pressman, Karen Carlson, Cyril O'Reilly; **D:** Andrew V. McLaglen. *WOV*

Onassis 🎞½ *The Richest Man in the World: The Story of Aristotle Onassis* 1988 Romanticized biography of Greek shipping magnate Aristotle Onassis, from the poverty of his youth to his later wealth and family and romantic liaisons and tragedies. Julia is adequate as the title character but English actress Annis is badly miscast as Jackie Kennedy Onassis. However, Seymour is terrific as Onassis' lover, opera star Maria Callas. Quinn, who played Onassis in "The Greek Tycoon," plays Onassis' father in this one. Based on the novel by Peter Evans. Originally a made for television miniseries. 120m/C VHS, LV, Closed Caption. Raul Julia, Jane Seymour, Francesca Annis, Anthony Quinn, Anthony Zerbe, Lorenzo Quinn; **D:** Waris Hussein. *TTC*

Once a Hero 🎞🎞 1988 The dregs of society, the Cicero Gang, have taken Captain Justice's number one fan and his mother hostage. Is it really curtains for rosy cheeks, bubble gum, and

apple pie? But wait, it's Captain Justice, the man, the myth, to the rescue! 74m/C VHS. Jeff Lester, Robert Forster, Milo O'Shea; **D:** Claudia Weill. *NWV, VTR*

Once a Thief 🎞🎞🎞 1996 (R) A fun and action-packed TV movie finds adopted children Li Ann (Holt) and Mac (Sergei) being raised along with natural son Michael (Wong) by Hong Kong crime head Tang (Ito) and trained as daring professional thieves. A falling out finds Li Ann in Vancouver, involved with ex-cop Victor (Lea), and both of them working for a covert crime-fighting agency headed by a very tough director (Dale). Then Mac is forced to join the duo in an elaborate heist to bring down Michael and his family's criminal empire. Woo's director's cut contains additional footage.**CW:** Some strong violence. 101m/C VHS, LV. Ivan Sergei, Sandrine Holt, Nicholas Lea, Michael Wong, Robert Ito, Jennifer Dale, Alan Scarfe; **D:** John Woo; **W:** Glenn Davis, William Laurin; **C:** Bill Wong; **M:** Amin Bhatia. *APX*

Once Around 🎞🎞½ 1991 (R) 30ish, lonely Renata Bella (Hunter) meets boisterous, self-assured (read utterly obnoxious) Lithuanian salesman Sam Sharpe (Dreyfuss). He sweeps her off her feet, showers her with affection and gifts, and then tries too hard—too hard—to please her close-knit Italian family. Casting doesn't get much better than the group assembled here and Hallstrom steers everyone to wonderful performances in his American directorial debut. The major flaw is the script, a light romantic comedy that sometimes swerves into heavy drama, so much so that you may need kleenex. 115m/C VHS, Beta, LV, Closed Caption. Richard Dreyfuss, Holly Hunter, Danny Aiello, Gena Rowlands, Laura San Giacomo, Roxanne Hart, Danton Stone, Tim Guinee, Greg Germann, Griffin Dunne; **D:** Lasse Hallstrom; **W:** Malia Scotch Marmo; **M:** James Horner. *USH, FCT*

Once Before I Die 🎞🎞½ 1965 Army soldiers caught in the Philippines during WWII struggle to survive and elude the Japanese. A single woman traveling with them becomes the object of their spare time considerations. A brutal, odd, and gritty war drama. Director/actor Derek was Andress' husband at the time. 97m/C VHS. PH Ursula Andress, John Derek, Richard Jaeckel, Rod Lauren, Ron Ely; **D:** John Derek. *MOV*

Once Bitten 🎞🎞 1985 (PG-13) Centuries-old though still remarkably youthful vampiress comes to LA to stalk male virgins. That may be the wrong city, but she needs their blood to retain her young countenance. Vampire comedy theme was more effectively explored in 1979s "Love at First Bite," notable, however for the screen debut of comic Carrey who would later gain fame for TV's "In Living Color" and "Ace Ventura, Pet Detective." 94m/C VHS, Beta, LV, Closed Caption. Lauren Hutton, Jim Carrey, Cleavon Little, Karen Kopins, Thomas Balltore, Skip Lackey; **D:** Howard Storm; **W:** Jonathan Roberts; **M:** John Du Prez. *LIV, VES*

Once in Paris... 🎞🎞½ 1979 (PG) A bittersweet romance about a scriptwriter working in Paris, the chauffeur who befriends him, and the aristocratic British woman with whom the writer falls in love. Beautiful French scenery and the engaging performance of Lenoir as the chauffeur make this film a diverting piece of entertainment. 100m/C VHS, Beta. Wayne Rogers, Gayle Hunnicutt, Jack Lenoir; **D:** Frank D. Gilroy; **W:** Frank D. Gilroy. *MED*

Once is Not Enough 🎞½ *Jacqueline Susann's Once is Not Enough* 1975 (R) Limp trash-drama concerning the young daughter of a has-been movie producer who has a tempestuous affair with a writer who reminds her of her father. Based on the novel by Jacqueline Susann. 121m/C VHS, Beta. Kirk Douglas, Deborah Raffin, David Janssen, George Hamilton, Brenda Vaccaro, Alexis Smith, Melina Mercouri; **D:** Guy Green; **W:** Julius J. Epstein, Philip C. Epstein; **C:** John A. Alonzo; **M:** Henry Mancini. Golden Globe Awards '76: Best Supporting Actress (Vaccaro); Nominations: Academy Awards '75: Best Supporting Actress (Vaccaro). *PAR*

Once Upon a Brothers Grimm 🎞🎞 1977 An original musical fantasy in which the Brothers Grimm meet a succession of their most famous storybook characters including Hansel and Gretel, the Gingerbread Lady, Little Red Riding Hood, and Rumpelstiltskin. 102m/C VHS, Beta. Dean Jones, Paul Sand, Cleavon Little, Ruth Buzzi, Chita Rivera, Teri Garr. *VCI*

Once Upon a Crime 🎞½ 1992 (PG) Extremely disappointing comedy featuring a high profile cast set in Europe. The plot centers around Young and Lewis finding a dachshund and travelling from Rome to Monte Carlo to return the stray and collect a $5,000 reward. Upon arrival in Monte Carlo, they find the dog's owner dead and they end up getting implicated for the murder. Other prime suspects include Belushi, Candy, Hamilton, and Shepherd. Weak script is made bearable only by the comic genius of Candy. 94m/C VHS, Closed Caption. John Candy, James Belushi, Cybill Shepherd, Sean Young, Richard Lewis, Ornella Muti, Giancarlo Giannini, George Hamilton, Joss Ackland, Elsa Martinelli; **D:** Eugene Levy; **M:** Richard Gibbs. *MGM*

Once Upon a Forest 🎞🎞 1993 (G) Animated tale of three woodland creatures in a daring race against time when their young friend's life is at stake. Ecologically correct story by "American Tail" creator David Kirschner is light on humor and heavy on gloom, as little animals encounter oppressive human society and their big, bad machines. Servicable animation, though not up to Don Bluth standards (and a long, long way from Disney). Crawford, the voice of the wise old uncle, has a song, while Vereen breaks into a fervent gospel number as a marsh bird with a yen for preaching. For an evening of anti-pollution, treat the earth kindly animation, see it with "Ferngully." 80m/C VHS, LV, Closed Caption. **D:** Charles Grosvenor; **W:** Mark Young, Kelly Ward; **V:** Michael Crawford, Ben Vereen. *FXV, FUS*

Once Upon a Honeymoon 🎞🎞½ 1942 Set in 1938, Grant is an American radio broadcaster reporting on the oncoming war. Rogers is the ex-showgirl who unknowingly marries a Nazi. In this strange, uneven comedy, Grant tries to get the goods on him and also rescue Rogers. The plot is basic and uneven with Grant attempting to expose the Nazi and save Rogers. However, the slower moments are offset by some fairly surreal pieces of comedy. 116m/B VHS, Beta, LV. Ginger Rogers, Cary Grant, Walter Slezak, Albert Dekker; **D:** Leo McCarey; **C:** George Barnes. Nominations: Academy Awards '42: Best Sound. *CCB, TTC, FCT*

Once Upon a Midnight Scary 🎞🎞 1990 Price narrates a collection of three tales of terror, "The Ghost Belonged to Me," "The Legend of Sleepy Hollow," and "The House with a Clock in Its Walls." Aimed at the kiddies. 50m/C VHS. Rene Auberjonois, Severn Darden; **D:** Neil Cox. *GEM, MRV*

Once Upon a Scoundrel 🎞🎞½ 1973 (G) A ruthless Mexican land baron arranges to have a young woman's fiancee thrown in jail so he can have her all to himself. 90m/C VHS, Beta. Zero Mostel, Katy Jurado, Titos Vandis, Priscilla Garcia, A. Martinez; **D:** George Schaefer; **M:** Alex North. *PSM*

Once Upon a Time 1976 (G) A pretty girl, her puppy, a charming prince, and a grinch combine for a magical, wondrous animated fantasy. 83m/C VHS, Beta. *GEM*

Once Upon a Time 1987 Two rival tribes spoil the love of a prince and princess in ancient times. Animated. 92m/C VHS, Beta. *MED*

Once Upon a Time in America 🎞🎞🎞½ 1984 (R) The uncut original version of director Leone's saga of five young men growing up in Brooklyn during the '20s who become powerful mob figures. Also available in a 143-minute version. Told from the perspective of De Niro's Noodles as an old man looking back at 50 years of crime, love, and death, told with a sweeping and violent elegance. 225m/C VHS, Beta, LV, Closed Caption. Robert De Niro, James Woods, Elizabeth McGovern, Treat Williams, Tuesday Weld, Burt Young, Joe Pesci, Danny Aiello, Darlanne Fluegel, Jennifer Connelly; **D:** Sergio Leone; **C:** Tonino Delli Colli; **M:** Ennio Morricone. *WAR*

Once Upon a Time in the West 𝄪𝄪½ 1968 (PG)

The uncut version of Leone's sprawling epic about a band of ruthless gunmen who set out to murder a mysterious woman waiting for the railroad to come through. Filmed in John Ford's Monument Valley, it's a revisionist western with some of the longest opening credits in the history of the cinema. Fonda is cast against type as an extremely cold-blooded villain. Brilliant musical score. 165m/C VHS, Beta, LV. *IT* Henry Fonda, Jason Robards Jr., Charles Bronson, Claudia Cardinale, Keenan Wynn, Lionel Stander, Woody Strode, Jack Elam; **D:** Sergio Leone; **W:** Sergio Leone, Bernardo Bertolucci, Dario Argento; **C:** Tonino Delli Colli; **M:** Ennio Morricone. *PAR*

Once Upon a Time ... When We Were Colored 𝄪𝄪𝄪 1995 (PG)

Actor Reid makes a fine directorial debut with the story of a black youngster growing up parentless in 50's Mississippi. His family faces the usual troubles of the time, including poor wages and white bigotry, but manages to provide a positive and loving home life for him. Nostalgic, sensitive, and heartwarming adaptation of Clifton Taulbert's autobiographical book. 112m/C VHS, LV, Closed Caption. Al Freeman Jr., Paula Kelly, Phylicia Rashad, Polly Bergen, Richard Roundtree, Charles Taylor, Willie Norwood, Jr., Damon Hines, Leon; **D:** Tim Reid; **W:** Paul Cooper; **C:** Johnny Simmons; **M:** Steve Tyrell. *REP*

Once Were Warriors 𝄪𝄪𝄪 1994 (R)

Violent story of the struggling Maori Heke family, who have left their rural New Zealand roots to live in the city. Feisty mom Beth (Owen) is struggling with five kids and volatile hubby Jake (Heke), who's continuously out of work, boozing, and fighting. Eldest son Nig (Arahanga) has left home and joined a street gang and the rest of the kids hate Jake for beating up on their mother. They also fall victim to his temper and his habit of bringing his brawling, drunk buddies home-leading to further tragedy. Intense drama showcases great performances, with Owen honored as best actress at the Montreal World Film Festival. Based on the novel by Alan Duff. Feature-film directorial debut of Tamahori.**CW:** Pervasive language; strong depiction of domestic abuse, including sexual violence and substance abuse. 102m/C VHS, LV, Closed Caption. *NZ* Rena Owen, Temuera Morrison, Mamaengaroa Kerr-Bell, Julian (Sonny) Arahanga, Taungaroa Emile, Rachael Morris, Joseph Kairau, Pete Smith; **D:** Lee Tamahori; **W:** Riwia Brown; **C:** Stuart Dryburgh; **M:** Murray Grindlay, Murray McNabb. Australian Film Institute '95: Best Foreign Film; Montreal World Film Festival '94: Best Actress (Owen), Best Film. *NLC*

One Against the Wind 𝄪𝄪𝄪 1991 (PG)

A true story of one woman's courage against great odds. British Mary Liddell and her children are living in Paris during the WWII Nazi occupation. Mary's secret agenda is to smuggle downed Allied pilots out of the country to safety without arousing Nazi suspicions. Great performances by Davis as the resourceful Mary and Neill as one of the pilots she rescues. A Hallmark Hall of Fame presentation. 96m/C VHS, Closed Caption. Judy Davis, Sam Neill, Denholm Elliott, Anthony Higgins, Christien Anholt, Kate Beckinsale, Frank Middlemass; **D:** Larry Elikann. *REP*

One A.M. 1916

Charlie is a drunk who must first battle a flight of stairs in order to get to bed. Silent with music track. 20m/B VHS, Beta. Charlie Chaplin. *CAB, GVV*

The One and Only 𝄪𝄪½ 1978 (PG)

An egotistical young man is determined to make it in show business. Instead, he finds himself in the world of professional wrestling. Most of the humor comes from the wrestling scenes, with Winkler and Darby's love story only serving to dilute the film. 98m/C VHS, Beta. Henry Winkler, Kim Darby, Gene

Saks, William Daniels, Harold Gould, Herve Villechaize; **D:** Carl Reiner. *PAR*

The One and Only, Genuine, Original Family Band 𝄪𝄪𝄪 1968 (G)

A harmonious musical family becomes divided when various members take sides in the presidential battle between Benjamin Harrison and Grover Cleveland, a political era that has been since overlooked. 110m/C VHS, Beta, LV. Walter Brennan, Buddy Ebsen, Lesley Ann Warren, Kurt Russell, Goldie Hawn, Wally Cox, Richard Deacon, Janet Blair; **D:** Michael O'Herlihy. *DIS*

One Arabian Night 𝄪𝄪𝄪 Sumurun 1921

When an exotic dancer in a traveling carnival troupe is kidnapped into a harem, a dwarf acts on his unrequited love and avenges her death by murdering the sheik who killed her. Secured a place in American filmmaking for director Lubitsch. 85m/B VHS, Beta. *GE* Pola Negri, Ernst Lubitsch, Paul Wegener; **D:** Ernst Lubitsch. *VYY, GPV, GLV*

One Armed Executioner 𝄪𝄪 1980 (R)

An Interpol agent seeks revenge on his wife's murderers. 90m/C VHS, Beta. Franco Guerrero, Jody Kay; **D:** Bobby A. Auarez. *NO*

One Away 𝄪 1980 (PG)

Gypsy escapes from a South African prison and the police are in hot pursuit. 83m/C VHS, Beta. Elke Sommer, Bradford Dillman, Dean Stockwell. *NO*

One Body Too Many 𝄪𝄪 1944

A mystery spoof about a wacky insurance salesman who's mistaken for a detective. The usual comedy of errors ensues. A contrived mish-mash—but it does have Lugosi going for it. 75m/B VHS, Beta. Jack Haley, Jean Parker, Bela Lugosi, Lyle Talbot; **D:** Frank McDonald. *NOS, SNC, HHT*

One Brief Summer woof! 1970 (R)

Love triangles and intrigues abound on a spectacular country manor. An aging woman is mortified by her father's interest in a young seductress, who finds herself attracted to the old man, but not only him. 86m/C VHS. Clifford Evans, Felicity Gibson, Jennifer Hilary, Jan Holden, Peter Egan; **D:** John MacKenzie. *NO*

One Cooks, the Other Doesn't 𝄪𝄪 1983

A most unlikely story of a man's ex-wife and his son moving back into his house, where he's now living with his new wife. Made for television. 96m/C VHS, Beta. Suzanne Pleshette, Joseph Bologna, Rosanna Arquette, Oliver Clark; **D:** Richard Michaels. *LIV*

One Crazy Night 𝄪𝄪½ 1993 (PG-13)

In 1964, five Australian teenagers try to get into the Melbourne hotel where the Beatles are staying on tour. They wind up trapped in the basement, swapping secrets, and finding out how much they have in common.**CW:** Language and teen sensuality. 92m/C VHS. *AU* Noah Taylor, Beth Champion, Malcolm Kennard, Danni Minogue, Malcolm Braly; **D:** Michael Pattinson. *THV*

One Crazy Summer 𝄪𝄪½ 1986 (PG)

A group of wacky teens spend a fun-filled summer on Nantucket Island in New England. This follow-up to "Better Off Dead" is offbeat and fairly charming, led by Cusack's perplexed cartoonist and with comic moments delivered by Goldthwait. 94m/C VHS, Beta, LV, Closed Caption. John Cusack, Demi Moore, William Hickey, Curtis Armstrong, Bob(cat) Goldthwait, Mark Metcalf, Joel Murray, Tom Villard, Joe Flaherty; **D:** Steve Holland; **W:** Steve Holland; **M:** Cory Lerios. *WAR*

One Dark Night 𝄪½ 1982 (R)

Two high school girls plan an initiation rite for one of their friends who is determined to shed her "goody-goody" image. West is the caped crusader of TV series "Batman" fame. 94m/C VHS, Beta. Meg Tilly, Adam West, David Mason Daniels, Robin Evans; **D:** Tom McLoughlin. *NO*

One Day in the Life of Ivan Denisovich 𝄪𝄪𝄪 1971

The film version of Nobel Prize-winner Alexander Solzhenitsyn's novel about a prisoner's experiences in a Soviet labor camp. A testament to human endurance. Photography be Sven Nykvist. 105m/C VHS, LV. *NO GB* Tom Courtenay, Alfred Burke, Espen Skjonberg, James

Maxwell, Eric Thompson; **D:** Caspar Wrede; **W:** Ronald Harwood; **C:** Sven Nykvist. *NO*

One Deadly Owner 𝄪 1974

A made-for-television film about a possessed Rolls-Royce torturing its new owner. Quite a vehicle for the usually respectable set of wheels. 80m/C VHS, Beta. Donna Mills, Jeremy Brett, Robert Morris, Laurence Payne. *LIV*

One Deadly Summer 𝄪𝄪𝄪 L'Ete Meurtrier 1983 (R)

Revenge drama about a young girl who returns to her mother's home village to ruin three men who had assaulted her mother years before. Very well acted. From the novel by Sebastien Japrisot. In French with English subtitles. 134m/C VHS, Beta, Closed Caption. *FR* Isabelle Adjani, Alain Souchon, Suzanne Flon; **D:** Jean Becker; **M:** Georges Delerue. Cesar Awards '84: Best Actress (Adjani), Best Supporting Actress (Flon), Best Writing. *USH*

One Down, Two to Go! woof! 1982 (R)

When the mob is discovered to be rigging a championship karate bout, two dynamic expert fighters join in a climactic battle against the hoods. Example of really bad "blaxploitation" that wastes talent, film, and the audience's time. 84m/C VHS, Beta. Jim Brown, Fred Williamson, Jim Kelly, Richard Roundtree; **D:** Fred Williamson. *MED, RHI, HHE*

187 𝄪𝄪𝄪 1997 (R)

Jackson's a Brooklyn high school teacher who is brutally attacked by one of his students. His physical scars are healed, but his emotional state is marred as he takes some pretty unorthodox teaching methods to a troubled L.A. school. Very dark, psychological drama with a powerful performance by Jackson. Tough film whose title refers to the California penal code number for murder. First film from director Reynolds after his "Waterworld" fiasco.**CW:** Violence, strong language, drug use and brief nudity. ?m/C VHS. Samuel L. Jackson, John Heard, Kelly Rowan, Clifton Gonzalez Gonzalez; **D:** Kevin Reynolds; **W:** Scott Yagemann; **C:** Ericson Core. *NYR*

One-Eyed Jacks 𝄪𝄪𝄪½ 1961

An often engaging, but lengthy, psychological western about an outlaw who seeks to settle the score with a former partner who became a sheriff. Great acting by all, particularly Brando, who triumphed both as star and director. Stanley Kubrick was the original director, but Brando took over mid-way through the filming. The photography is wonderful and reflects the effort that went into it. 141m/C VHS, Beta, LV. Marlon Brando, Karl Malden, Katy Jurado, Elisha Cook Jr., Slim Pickens, Ben Johnson, Pina Pellicer, Timothy Carey; **D:** Marlon Brando; **W:** Calder Willingham; **C:** Charles B(ryant) Lang. Nominations: Academy Awards '61: Best Color Cinematography. *PAR*

One-Eyed Soldiers 𝄪 1967

Young woman, criminal, and dwarf follow trail to mysterious key to unlock $15 million treasure. Much cheesy intrigue. 83m/C VHS. *GB YU* Dale Robertson, Luciana Paluzzi; **D:** Jean Christopher. *NO*

One-Eyed Swordsman 𝄪 1963

A handicapped samurai battles shogun warriors. With English subtitles. 95m/C VHS, Beta. *JP* Tetsuro Tamba, Haruko Wanibuchi; **D:** Seiichiro Uchikawa. *VDA*

One False Move 𝄪𝄪𝄪 1991 (R)

Black psycho Pluto, his white-trash partner Ray, and Ray's biracial lover Fantasia are three low-level drug dealers on the streets of Los Angeles who get involved in murder. Fleeing the city for Fantasia's small hometown in Arkansas, they come up against the local sheriff and two L.A. cops sent to bring them back. Not a typical crime thriller, first-time feature director Franklin is more interested in a psychological character study of racism and smalltown mores than in your average shoot 'em up action picture. Good performances, especially by Williams as the deceptive bad girl.**CW:** Strong language and strong violence and drug content. 105m/C VHS, LV, Closed Caption. Bill Paxton, Cynda Williams, Michael Beach, Jim Metzler, Earl Billings, Billy Bob Thornton, Natalie Canderday, Robert Ginnaven, Robert Anthony Bell, Kevin Hunter; **D:** Carl Franklin; **W:** Billy Bob Thornton, Tom Epperson; **C:** James L. Carter. Independent Spirit Awards '93: Best Director (Franklin); MTV Movie

Awards '93: Best New Filmmaker Award (Franklin). *COL, FCT*

One Fine Day ♫♫½ 1996 (PG) Marshmallows. That's what this movie is like—light, fluffy, not much substance, but enjoyable when you're in the mood. Nod to the classic screwball comedies of the '40s and '50s throws harried single mom/architect Pfeiffer and political columnist/weekend dad Clooney together when their kids, who attend the same school, miss a class field trip. Naturally, they take an instant dislike to each other, but are forced to cooperate to solve the daycare situation. An accidental switching of cell phones provides the chance for repeated encounters, and growing mutual interest. Predictable, but pleasantly so. No matter how hard she tries, Pfeiffer always looks good, and Clooney has that cocked head, devilish grin thing working overtime. Screenplay by Neil Simon's daughter Ellen supplies all the elements for a fine date movie. 108m/C **VHS, Closed Caption.** Michelle Pfeiffer, George Clooney, Alex D. Linz, Mae Whitman, Charles Durning, Jon Robin Baitz, Ellen Greene, Joe Grifasi, Pete Hamill, Anna Maria Horsford, Sheila Kelley, Barry Kivel, Robert Klein, George Martin, Michael Massee, Amanda Peet, Bitty Schram, Holland Taylor, Rachel York; **D:** Michael Hoffman; **W:** Terrel Seltzer, Ellen Simon; **C:** Oliver Stapleton; **M:** James Newton Howard. Nominations: Academy Awards '96: Best Song ("For the First Time"); Golden Globe Awards '97: Best Song ("For the First Time"). *TCF*

One Flew Over the Cuckoo's Nest ♫♫♫♫ 1975 (R) Touching, hilarious, dramatic, and completely effective adaptation of Ken Kesey's novel. Nicholson is a two-bit crook, who, facing a jail sentence, feigns insanity to be sentenced to a cushy mental hospital. The hospital is anything but cushy, with a tyrannical head nurse out to squash any vestige of the patients' independence. Nicholson proves to be a crazed messiah and catalyst for these mentally troubled patients and a worthy adversary for the head nurse. Classic performs superbly on numerous levels. 129m/C **VHS, Beta, LV.** Jack Nicholson, Brad Dourif, Louise Fletcher, Will Sampson, William Redfield, Danny DeVito, Christopher Lloyd, Scatman Crothers, Vincent Schiavelli, Michael Berryman, Peter Brocco, Louisa Moritz; **D:** Milos Forman; **W:** Ken Kesey, Bo Goldman; **C:** Haskell Wexler, Bill Butler, William A. Fraker; **M:** Jack Nitzsche. Academy Awards '75: Best Actor (Nicholson), Best Actress (Fletcher), Best Adapted Screenplay, Best Director (Forman), Best Picture; British Academy Awards '76: Best Actor (Nicholson), Best Actress (Fletcher), Best Director (Forman), Best Film, Best Supporting Actor (Dourif); Directors Guild of America Awards '75: Best Director (Forman); Golden Globe Awards '76: Best Actor—Drama (Nicholson), Best Actress—Drama (Fletcher), Best Director (Forman), Best Film—Drama, Best Screenplay; National Board of Review Awards '75: 10 Best Films of the Year, Best Actor (Nicholson); New York Film Critics Awards '75: Best Actor (Nicholson); National Society of Film Critics Awards '75: Best Actor (Nicholson); People's Choice Awards '77: Best Film; Writers Guild of America Awards '75: Best Adapted Screenplay; Nominations: Academy Awards '75: Best Cinematography, Best Film Editing, Best Supporting Actor (Dourif), Best Original Score. *REP, BTV, FCT*

One Frightened Night ♫♫½ 1935 An eccentric millionaire informs his family members that he is leaving each of them one million dollars...as long as his long-lost granddaughter doesn't reappear. Guess who comes to dinner. 69m/B **VHS, Beta.** Mary Carlisle, Wallace Ford, Hedda Hopper, Charley Grapewin; **D:** Christy Cabanne. *NOS, BAR, VYY*

One from the Heart ♫♫ 1982 (R) The film more notable for sinking Coppola's Zoetrope Studios than for its cinematic context. Garr and Forrest are a jaded couple who seek romantic excitement with other people. An extravagant (thus Coppola's finance problems) fantasy Las Vegas set, pretty to look at but does little to enhance the weak plot. Score by Waits, a much-needed plus. 100m/C **VHS, Beta, LV.** Teri Garr, Frederic Forrest, Nastassia Kinski, Raul Julia, Lainie Kazan, Rebecca DeMornay, Harry Dean Stanton; **D:** Francis Ford Coppola; **W:** Armyan Bernstein, Francis Ford Coppola; **M:** Tom Waits, Robert Alcivar. Nominations: Academy Awards '82: Original Song Score and/or Adaptation. *COL*

One Good Cop ♫♫½ 1991 (R) A noble, inconsistent attempt to do a police thriller with a human face, as a young officer and his wife adopt the three little daughters of his slain partner from the force. But it reverts to a routine action wrapup, with 'Batman' Keaton even donning a masked-avenger getup to get revenge. **CW:** Language and violence and drug content. 105m/C **VHS, Beta, LV, Closed Caption.** Michael Keaton, Rene Russo, Anthony LaPaglia, Kevin Conway, Rachel Ticotin, Grace Johnston, Blair Swanson, Rhea Silver-Smith, Tony Plana, Benjamin Bratt, Charlaine Woodard; **D:** Heywood Gould; **W:** Heywood Gould; **C:** Ralf Bode; **M:** William Ross. *HPH*

One Good Turn ♫♫ 1995 (R) Matt Forrest (Von Dohlen) and his wife Laura (Amis) seemingly have it all only to have their fortunes take a radical turn for the worse. Matt "accidentally" runs into Simon Jury (Remar), the man who saved his life 12 years before. But the seemingly friendly Jury is actually intent on destroying everything they have. **CW:** Some strong sexuality and violence. 90m/C **VHS, Closed Caption.** Lenny Von Dohlen, James Remar, Suzy Amis, John Savage; **D:** Tony Randel. *BMG*

100 Men and a Girl ♫♫♫ 1937 Charming musical features Durbin as the daughter of an unemployed musician, who decides she will try to persuade Leopold Stokowski to help her launch an orchestra that will employ her father and his musician friends. Beautiful mix of classical and pop music. Based on a story by Hans Kraly. ♫Hungarian Rhapsody No. 2; Symphony No. 5; Alleluia; It's Raining Sunbeams; A Heart That's Free. 85m/B **VHS.** Deanna Durbin, Leopold Stokowski, Adolphe Menjou, Alice Brady, Eugene Pallette, Mischa Auer, Billy Gilbert, Alma Kruger, Christian Rub, Jed Prouty, Jack Mulhall; **D:** Henry Koster; **C:** Joseph Valentine. Academy Awards '37: Best Score; Nominations: Academy Awards '37: Best Film Editing, Best Picture, Best Sound, Best Story. *USH*

100 Rifles ♫♫ 1969 (R) Native American bank robber and Black American lawman join up with a female Mexican revolutionary to help save the Mexican Indians from annihilation by a despotic military governor. What it lacks in political correctness it makes up for in fits of action. Although quite racy in its day for its interracial sex sizzle of Brown and Rachel, it's tame and overblown by today's standards. 110m/C **VHS, Beta.** Jim Brown, Raquel Welch, Burt Reynolds, Fernando Lamas; **D:** Tom Gries; **M:** Jerry Goldsmith. *FOX, FXV*

101 Dalmatians ♫♫♫½ 1961 (G) Disney classic is one of the highest-grossing animated films in the history of Hollywood. Dogowners Roger and Anita, and their spotted pets Pongo and Perdita are shocked when their puppies are kidnapped by Cruella de Vil, villainess extraordinaire, to make a simply fabulous spotted coat. The aid of various animals including a dog named Colonel, a horse, a cat, and a goose is enlisted to rescue the doomed pups. Imagine their surprise when they find not only their own puppies, but 84 more as well. You can expect a happy ending and lots of spots—6,469,952 to be exact. Based on the children's book by Dodie Smith. Technically notable for the first time use of the Xerox process to transfer the animator's drawings onto celluloid, which made the film's opening sequence of dots evolving into 101 barking dogs possible. ♫Remember When; Cruella de Vil; Dalmation Plantation; Kanine Krunchies Kommercial. 79m/C **VHS, Beta. D:** Clyde Geronimi, Wolfgang Reitherman, Hamilton Luske; **M:** George Bruns; **V:** Rod Taylor, Betty Lou Gerson, Lisa Davis, Ben Wright, Frederick Worlock, J. Pat O'Malley. *DIS, OM*

101 Dalmatians ♫♫½ 1996 (G) Yes, it's the live-action Disney version of their own 1961 animated feature (based on the book by Dodie Smith) about dog-naping villainess Cruella De Vil (Close) and lots of spotted pups. They're absolutely adorable, of course, Cruella's costumes (and hair) are certainly eye-catching, and the bumbling crooks get their proper comeuppance. Daniels and Richardson have the thankless role of the dogs' human owners, Roger and Anita, and get upstaged at every opportunity. Kids familiar with the cartoon pups may be surprised that the live pups don't talk - and keep in mind that Close, while terrific, may be too scary for the little ones. The Hound is always happy to see another dog movie but still feels some classics should be left alone. 103m/C **VHS, Closed Caption.** Glenn Close, Jeff Daniels, Joely Richardson, Joan Plowright, Hugh Laurie, Mark Williams; **D:** Stephen Herek; **W:** John Hughes; **C:** Adrian Biddle; **M:** Michael Kamen. Nominations: Golden Globe Awards '97: Best Actress—Musical/Comedy (Close). *TOU*

125 Rooms of Comfort ♫♫ 1983 A mental patient has bizarre fantasies that create havoc among those who stand in his way. 82m/C **VHS, Beta.** Tim Henry, Jackie Burroughs, Bob Warner, Bob Silverman, Les Barker; **D:** Patrick Loubert; **W:** Patrick Loubert, Bill Freut. *TWE*

One in a Million ♫♫♫ 1936 Debut film of Norwegian skating star Henie centers around a Swiss girl whose father is training her for the Olympics. Features good comedy by the Ritz Brothers and Sparks, as well as the beautiful skating of Henie. ♫One in a Million; We're Back in Circulation Again; Who's Afraid of Love; Lovely Lady in White; The Moonlight Waltz. 95m/B **VHS.** Sonja Henie, Adolphe Menjou, Jean Hersholt, The Ritz Brothers, Arline Judge, Don Ameche, Ned Sparks, Montagu Love, Leah Ray; **D:** Sidney Lanfield; **W:** Leonard Praskins, Mark Kelly. *FXV*

One in a Million: The Ron LeFlore Story ♫♫½ 1978 The true story of Detroit Tigers' star Ron LeFlore, who rose from the Detroit ghetto to the major leagues. Adaptation of LeFlore's autobiography, "Breakout." A well-acted and compelling drama with Burton in a standout performance. 90m/C **VHS, Beta.** LeVar Burton, Madge Sinclair, Billy Martin, James Luisi; **D:** William A. Graham; **C:** Jordan Cronenweth. *NO*

One Last Run ♫½ 1989 It's drama on the slopes as a variety of individuals confront their pasts/fears/personal demons via extreme skiing. Features the performances of champion skiers Franz Weber and Scot Schmidt. 82m/C **VHS, Beta.** Russell Todd, Ashley Laurence, Craig Branham, Jimmy Aleck, Tracy Scoggins, Nels Van Patten, Chuck Connors; **D:** Peter Winograd, Glenn Gebhard; **W:** Peter Winograd, Glenn Gebhard. *PSM*

One Little Indian ♫♫ 1973 An AWOL cavalry man and his Indian ward team up with a widow and her daughter in an attempt to cross the New Mexican desert. A tepid presentation from the usually high quality Disney studio. 90m/C **VHS, Beta.** James Garner, Vera Miles, Jodie Foster, Clay O'Brien, Andrew Prine, Bernard McEveety; **D:** Bernard McEveety; **M:** Jerry Goldsmith. *DIS*

One Magic Christmas ♫♫½ 1985 (G) Disney feel-good film about a disillusioned working woman whose faith in Christmas is restored when her guardian angel descends to Earth and performs various miracles. Somewhat cliched and tiresome, but partially redeemed by Stanton and Steenburgen's presence. 88m/C **VHS, Beta, LV, Closed Caption.** Mary Steenburgen, Harry Dean Stanton, Gary Basaraba, Michelle Meyrink, Arthur Hill, Elisabeth Harnois, Robbie Magwood; **D:** Phillip Borsos; **W:** Thomas Meehan; **M:** Michael Conway Baker. *DIS*

One Man Army ♫½ 1993 (R) Kickboxer goes to visit gramps in small town, only to discover the old guy has been murdered and corruption and cover-ups abound. So he decides to kick some butt and set things right. 95m/C **VHS.** Jerry Trimble; **D:** Cirio H. Santiago. *NHO*

One Man Force ♫ 1989 (R) L.A. narcotics cop Jake Swan goes on a vigilante spree. Huge in body and vengeful in spirit, he makes his partner's murderers pay! 92m/C **VHS, Beta, LV.** John Matuszak, Ronny Cox, Charles Napier, Sharon Farrell, Sam

Jones, Chance Boyer, Richard Lynch, Stacey Q; **D:** Dale Trevillion; **W:** Dale Trevillion; **M:** Charles Fox. ACA

One Man Jury ♂ 1978 (R) LAPD lieutenant, wearied by an ineffective justice system, becomes a one-man vigilante avenger. Pale Dirty Harry rip-off with over acting and an overdose of violence. **95m/C VHS, Beta.** Jack Palance, Chris Mitchum, Joe Spinell, Pamela Shoop; **D:** Charles Martin. VCI

One Man Out ♂ 1989 (R) An ex-CIA agent diverts his psychological problems into his new job: assassin for a South American despot. His jaded view of life changes when he meets and falls in love with an American journalist. Trouble in paradise when he is ordered to kill her. One man out was not enough, they should have done away with the entire crew of this stinker. **90m/C VHS, Beta, LV.** Stephen McHattie, Deborah Van Valkenburgh, Aharon Ipale, Ismael Carlo, Michael Champion, Dennis A. Pratt; **D:** Michael Kennedy. COL

One Man's Justice ♂♂½ 1995 (R) Army drill sergeant John North (Bosworth) heads for the streets of Venice, California to get the drug-dealing, gun-running scum who killed his wife and daughter. And a streetwise 10-year-old may be his best chance for finding them. **100m/C VHS, LV, Closed Caption.** Brian Bosworth, Bruce Payne, Jeff Kober, DeJuan Guy, Hammer; **D:** Kurt Wimmer; **W:** Steven Selling; **M:** Anthony Marinelli. LIV

One Man's War ♂♂½ 1990 (PG-13) A human-rights crusader in repressive Paraguay won't be silenced, even after government thugs torture and murder his son. He fights obsessively to bring the killers to justice. The true story of the Joel Filartiga family is heartfelt but ultimately a dramatic letdown; an epilogue proves that full story hasn't been told. **91m/C VHS, Closed Caption.** Anthony Hopkins, Norma Aleandro, Fernanda Torres, Ruben Blades; **D:** Sergio Toledo. HBO

One Man's Way ♂♂½ 1963 Murray is appropriately devout as charasmatic religious leader Norman Vincent Peale. With the support of his wife (Hyland), he survives the adulations and accusations of blasphemy for his rather unorthodox theological ideas and his book, "The Power of Positive Thinking." Based on the book "Norman Vincent Peale: Minister to Millions" by Arthur Gordon. **105m/B VHS, Beta.** Don Murray, Diana Hyland, William Windom, Virginia Christine, Carol Ohmart, Veronica Cartwright, Liam Sullivan, June Dayton, Ian Wolfe; **D:** Denis Sanders; **W:** Eleanore Griffin, John W. Bloch. MGM, FCT, BTV

One Million B.C. ♂♂½ The Cave Dwellers; Cave Man; Man and His Mate 1940 The strange saga of the struggle of primitive cavemen and their battle against dinosaurs and other monsters. Curiously told in flashbacks, this film provided stock footage for countless dinosaur movies that followed. Portions of film rumored to be directed by cinematic pioneer D. W. Griffith. **80m/B VHS, Beta.** Victor Mature, Carole Landis, Lon Chaney Jr.; **D:** Hal Roach, Hal Roach Jr. Nominations: Academy Awards '40: Best Original Score. MED, RXM

One Million Years B.C. ♂♂½ 1966 (R) It's Welch in a fur bikini and special FX expert Ray Harryhausen doing dinosaurs so who cares about a plot (which involves Welch and her boyfriend, who's from a rival clan). Remake of the 1940 film "One Million B.C." **100m/C VHS, Closed Caption.** Raquel Welch, John Richardson, Percy Herbert, Robert Brown, Martine Beswick; **D:** Don Chaffey. FXV

One Minute Before Death ♂ 1988 A woman is buried in a catatonic state, and returns from the grave to exact retribution. Supposedly based loosely on Poe. **87m/C VHS, Beta.** Giselle MacKenzie. NO

One Minute to Zero ♂♂ 1952 Korean War action film divides its time between an army romance and war action. The lukwarm melodrama features Mitchum as a colonel in charge of evacuating American civilians but who ends up bombing refugees. **105m/B VHS, Beta.** Robert Mitchum, Ann Blyth, William Talman, Charles McGraw, Marga-

ret Sheridan, Richard Egan, Eduard Franz, Robert Osterloh, Robert Gist; **D:** Tay Garnett. TTC

One More Chance ♂½ 1990 While he was in jail, an ex-con's family moves away without leaving a forwarding address. When he's released he strikes up a friendship with a woman from the neighborhood who knows where they've gone. **102m/C VHS, Beta.** Kirstie Alley, John Lamotta, Logan Clarke, Michael Pataki, Hector Maisonette; **D:** Sam Firstenberg. WAR, OM

One More Saturday Night ♂ 1986 (R) Franken and Davis, "Saturday Night Live" alumni, wrote this film about a small town going wild on the weekend. Dry, taxing, and unfunny. Averages about 1 laugh per 1/2 hour—at 1 1/2 hours, it's way too long. **96m/C VHS, Beta, LV, Closed Caption.** Al Franken, Tom Davis, Nan Woods, Dave Reynolds; **D:** Dennis Klein; **W:** Al Franken, Tom Davis. NO

One Night in the Tropics ♂♂½ 1940 The film debut of radio stars Abbott & Costello who play secondary roles to a love triangle (set to music). Jones is an insurance salesman who falls in love with Kelly, the fiance of Cummings. Based on the novel "Love Insurance" by Earl Derr Biggers. ♫Back in My Shell; Remind Me; You and Your Kiss; Your Dream is the Same as My Dream. **83m/B VHS.** Allan Jones, Robert Cummings, Nancy Kelly, Bud Abbott, Lou Costello, Mary Boland, Peggy Moran, William Frawley, Leo Carrillo; **D:** Edward Sutherland; **W:** Kathryn Scola, Gertrude Purcell, Charles Grayson, Francis Martin. USH, FCT

One Night of Love ♂♂♂½ 1934 Moore's best quasi-operetta, about a young American diva rebelling in response to her demanding Italian teacher. "Pygmallion"-like story has her falling in love with her maestro. Despite being nearly 60 years old, this film is still enchanting and fresh. ♫One Night of Love; Ciri-Biri-Bin; Sempre Libera; Sextet; Indian Love Call; 'Tis the Last Rose of Summer; Habanera; Un bel di; None But the Lonely Heart. **95m/B VHS, Beta, LV.** Grace Moore, Tullio Carminati, Lyle Talbot, Jane Darwell, Nydia Westman, Mona Barrie, Jessie Ralph, Luis Alberni; **D:** Victor Schertzinger. Academy Awards '34: Best Sound, Best Score; Nominations: Academy Awards '34: Best Actress (Moore), Best Director (Schertzinger), Best Film Editing, Best Picture. COL

One Night Only 1984 A gorgeous law student decides to make big money by hiring herself and her friends out as hookers to the school football team. **87m/C VHS, Beta.** Lenore Zann, Jeff Braunstein, Grant Alianak; **D:** Timothy Bond. FOX

One Night Stand ♂♂ 1977 Woman's chance encounter with a man in a singles bar leads to an evening of unexpected terror. Adapted from a play for Canadian television. Billed as a horror flick, it is really more of a drama. **90m/C VHS, Beta.** CA Chapelle Jaffe, Brent Carver. TWE

One Night Stand ♂♂♂ 1984 Four young people attempt to amuse themselves at the empty Sydney Opera House on the New Year's Eve, that night WWIII begins. An odd commentary on nuclear war that sees the bomb as the ultimate bad joke. Features an appearance by alternative rock group Midnight Oil. **94m/C VHS, Beta.** Tyler Coppin, Cassandra Delaney, Jay Hackett, Saskia Post; **D:** John Duigan.

One Night Stand ♂♂½ 1995 (R) Lonely Michelle (Sheedy) visits a nightclub and allows herself to be picked up by your basic handsome stranger, Jack (Martinez) in this case. She wakes up alone and learns from building owner Josslyn (Forrest) that the apartment is up for lease. Obsessed with finding her mystery man, Michelle discovers Jack's wife was murdered—possibly by him or maybe by Josslyn, who turns out to be the dead woman's father. Debut feature for director Shire covers familiar territory, with Sheedy giving a strong performance. **CW:** Nudity, language, violence, sexual situations. **92m/C VHS.** Ally Sheedy, A. Martinez, Frederic Forrest, Don Novello, Diane Salinger,

Millie Slavin; **D:** Talia Shire; **W:** Marty Casella; **C:** Arthur Albert; **M:** David Shire. NHO

1-900 ♂♂ 1994 Based on the play "06" by Doesburg, which refers to the Dutch exchange for phone-sex numbers. Sarah (Schluter) and Thomas (van Kempen) are both lonely professionals who "meet" when Thomas answers Sarah's personal ad. Their weekly phone chats lead to descriptions of sexual fantasies but relationship issues begin to intrude as time passes. Dutch with subtitles. **80m/C VHS. NL** Ariane Schluter, Ad van Kempen; **D:** Theo van Gogh; **W:** Ariane Schluter, Ad van Kempen, Johan Doesburg, Marcel Otten; **C:** Tom Erisman; **M:** Ruud Bos. FXL

One of My Wives Is Missing ♂♂½ 1976 An ex-New York cop tries to solve the mysterious disappearance of a newlywed socialite. Things become strange when she reappears but is discovered as an imposter. Above average acting in a film adapted from the play, "The Trap for a Lonely Man." **97m/C VHS, Beta.** Jack Klugman, Elizabeth Ashley, James Franciscus; **D:** Glenn Jordan. ORI

One of Our Aircraft Is Missing ♂♂♂½ 1941 The crew of an R.A.F. bomber downed in the Netherlands, struggle to escape Nazi capture. A thoughtful study of wars and the men who fight them, with an entertaining melodramatic plot. Look for the British version, which runs 106 minutes. Some of the American prints only run 82 minutes. **103m/B VHS. GB** Godfrey Tearle, Eric Portman, Hugh Williams, Pamela Brown, Googie Withers, Peter Ustinov; **D:** Emeric Pressburger, Michael Powell. National Board of Review Awards '42: 10 Best Films of the Year; Nominations: Academy Awards '42: Best Original Screenplay. NOS, MRV, REP

One of Our Dinosaurs Is Missing ♂♂ 1975 (G) An English nanny and her cohorts help British Intelligence retrieve a microfilm—concealing dinosaur fossil from the bad guys that have stolen it. Disney film was shot on location in England. **101m/C VHS, Beta.** Peter Ustinov, Helen Hayes, Derek Nimmo, Clive Revill, Robert Stevenson, Joan Sims; **D:** Robert Stevenson. DIS

One on One ♂♂½ 1977 (PG) A Rocky-esque story about a high school basketball star from the country who accepts an athletic scholarship to a big city university. He encounters a demanding coach and intense competition. Light weight drama that is economically entertaining. **100m/C VHS, Beta.** Robby Benson, Annette O'Toole, G.D. Spradlin, Gail Strickland, Melanie Griffith; **D:** Lamont Johnson; **W:** Robby Benson; **M:** Charles Fox. WAR

One Plus One ♂ Exploring the Kinsey Report 1961 A dramatization, believe it or not, of the Kinsey sex survey of the 1950s. Participants in a sex lecture talk about and demonstrate various "risque" practices, such as premarital sex and extramarital affairs. Despite this film, the sexual revolution went on as planned. **114m/B VHS, Beta.** CA Leo G. Carroll, Hilda Brawner, William Traylor, Kate Reid, Ernest Graves; **D:** Arch Oboler; **W:** Arch Oboler. SNC

One-Punch O'Day ♂ 1926 Boxing boy tries to buy back hometown's oil livelihood by winning prizefight. Much patient waiting by his honey. **60m/B VHS, Beta.** Billy Sullivan, Jack Herrick, Charlotte Merriam; **D:** Harry Joe Brown. GPV, FCT, GVV

One Rainy Afternoon ♂ 1936 A bit-player kisses the wrong girl in a Paris theater causing a massive uproar that brands him as a notorious romantic "monster." Patterned after a German film, the story lacks depth and zest. **80m/B VHS, Beta.** Francis Lederer, Ida Lupino, Hugh Herbert, Roland Young, Donald Meek; **D:** Rowland V. Lee. NOS, MRV, VYY

One Russian Summer woof! 1973 (R) During the Russian Revolution, a cripple seeks revenge on the corrupt land baron who murdered his parents. An unfortunate attempt to dramatize a novel by M. Lermontov. **112m/C VHS, Beta.** Oliver Reed, Claudia Cardinale, John McEnery, Carole Andre, Ray Lovelock; **D:** Antonio Calenda. VCI

One Shoe Makes It Murder 🎬🎬

1982 A shady casino owner hires ex-cop Mitchum to investigate the disappearance of his unfaithful wife. Adapted from Eric Bercovici's novel, the story does little to enhance Mitchum's TV debut. **100m/C VHS, Beta.** Robert Mitchum, Angie Dickinson, Mel Ferrer, Howard Hesseman, Jose Perez; **D:** William Hale; **M:** Bruce Broughton. *LIV*

One Sings, the Other Doesn't 🎬🎬½

L'Une Chante, L'Autre Pas **1977** Seeking contentment, a conservative widow and a liberal extrovert help each other cope in a man's world. Endearing characters, but a superficial treatment of dated feminist issues. In French with English subtitles. **105m/C VHS, Beta.** *FR BE* Valerie Mairesse, Therese Liotard, Robert Dadies, Ali Affi, Jean-Pierre Pellegrin, Francois Wertheimer; **D:** Agnes Varda; **W:** Agnes Varda; **C:** Charlie Van Damme; **M:** Francois Wertheimer. *COL*

One Step Beyond 🎬🎬

1959 This creepy anthology series featured stories of the occult and supernatural which were supposedly based on true incidents. Two episodes per tape. Includes "Message from Clara" starring Barbara Baxley and Robert Ellenstein and "The Sorcerer" with Christopher Lee and Martin Benson. **60m/B VHS. D:** John Newland. *MOV, HEG*

One Step to Hell 🎬½

Caccia Ai Violenti; King of Africa **1968** Good cop rescues gold-miner's widow from three escaped convicts. Beautiful African scenery helps save an otherwise mediocre film. **90m/C VHS, Beta.** Ty Hardin, Rossano Brazzi, Pier Angeli, George Sanders, Tab Hunter, Sandy Howard. *NO*

One Summer Love 🎬½

Dragonfly **1976** Man checks out from loony bin, searches for family ties and befriends beautiful woman who works in a moviehouse. **95m/C VHS.** Beau Bridges, Susan Sarandon, Mildred Dunnock, Ann Wedgeworth, Michael B. Miller, Linda Miller, James Noble, Frederick Coffin; **D:** Gilbert Cates; **W:** N. Richard Nash. *HBO*

One That Got Away 🎬🎬🎬

1957 A loyal German Luftwaffe pilot captured by the British becomes obsessed with escape. Fast paced and exciting. Based on a true story. **111m/B VHS, Beta.** Hardy Kruger, Colin Gordon, Alec Gordon; **D:** Roy Ward Baker. *NO*

One Third of a Nation 🎬🎬½

1939 Depression era film contrasts the conditions of slum life with those in high society. A young entrepreneur inherits a city block in ruins, only to fall in love with a young woman who lives there and help her crippled brother. Timely social criticism. **79m/B VHS.** Sylvia Sidney, Leif Erickson, Myron McCormick, Sidney Lumet; **D:** Dudley Murphy. *NOS, PAR, MLB*

1001 Arabian Nights 🎬🎬½

1959 In this Arabian nightmare, the nearsighted Mr. Magoo is known as "Azziz" Magoo, lamp dealer and uncle of Aladdin. **76m/C VHS, Beta. D:** Jack Kinney; **M:** George Duning; **V:** Jim Backus, Kathryn Grant, Hans Conried, Herschel Bernardi. *COL*

One Too Many 🎬

The Important Story of Alcoholism; Killer With a Label **1951** Exploitation film depicting the evils of alcoholism. Campy, but slick. **?m/C VHS.** Ruth Warrick, Richard Travis, Victor Kilian, Onslow Stevens, Lyle Talbot. *SNC*

One Touch of Venus 🎬🎬½

1948 Love fills a department store when a window dresser kisses a statue of the goddess Venus—and she comes to life. Appealing adaptation of the Broadway musical. 🎵Speak Low; The Trouble with Women; That's Him; Don't Look Now But My Heart Is Showing; My Week. **82m/B VHS.** Ava Gardner, Robert Walker, Eve Arden, Dick Haymes, Olga San Juan, Tom Conway; **D:** William A. Seiter; **M:** Kurt Weill, Ogden Nash. *REP, MLB*

One Trick Pony 🎬🎬½

1980 (R) Once-popular rock singer/songwriter struggles to keep his head above water in a turbulent marriage and in the changing currents of popular taste. Simon wrote the autobiographical screenplay and score, but let's hope he is more sincere in real life. A good story. **100m/C VHS, Beta.** Paul Simon, Blair Brown,

Rip Torn, Joan Hackett, Mare Winningham, Lou Reed, Harry Shearer, Allen (Goorwitz) Garfield, Daniel Stern; **D:** Robert M. Young. *WAR*

One, Two, Three 🎬🎬🎬½

1961 Cagney, an American Coca-Cola exec in Germany, zealously pursues any opportunity to run Coke's European operations. He does the job too well and loses his job to a Communist hippie turned slick capitalist. Fast-paced laughs, wonderful cinematography, and a fine score. **110m/B VHS, Beta, LV.** James Cagney, Horst Buchholz, Arlene Francis; **D:** Billy Wilder; **W:** Billy Wilder, I.A.L. Diamond; **C:** Daniel F. Fapp; **M:** Andre Previn. National Board of Review Awards '61: 10 Best Films of the Year; Nominations: Academy Awards '61: Best Black and White Cinematography. *MGM*

One Way Out 🎬🎬

1995 Frank (Gwaltney) gets out of jail, teams up with Bobby (Monahan) and his stripper girlfriend Eve (Golden), and the trio go to visit Frank's brother, Snooky (Turano). When Frank learns that Snooky's lowlife boss (Ironside) has been ripping him off, they plan to even the score. Naturally, the heist goes wrong and they wind up with a hostage (Gillies) and on the lam. **106m/C VHS.** Jack Gwaltney, Jeff Monahan, Annie Golden, Robert Turano, Michael Ironside, Isabel Gillies; **D:** Kevin Lynn. *AVI*

One Wild Moment 🎬🎬½

1978 (R) Comic complications arise when a divorced man is seduced by his best friend's daughter while vacationing. Warm and charming. Later re-made as "Blame It on Rio." In French with English subtitles. **88m/C VHS, Beta.** *FR* Jean-Pierre Marielle, Victor Lanoux, Agnes Soral, Christine Dejoux, Martine Sarcey; **D:** Claude Berri; **W:** Claude Berri. *COL*

One Wish Too Many 🎬🎬½

1955 A young boy finds a marble that grants wishes. He has the time of his life with his teachers and the school bullies, but runs into trouble when he creates a giant steam roller which overruns London. Winner of Best Children's Film, 1956 Venice Film Festival, but it is hard to say why. **55m/B VHS, Beta.** *GB* Anthony Richmond, Rosalind Gourgey, John Pike; **D:** John Durst. *SNC*

One Woman or Two 🎬🎬½

Une Femme ou Deux **1985 (PG-13)** Paleontologist Depardieu is duped by beautiful ad-exec who plans to use his findings to push perfume. Remake of "Bringing Up Baby," this screwball comedy has a few screws loose. Dubbed. **100m/C VHS, Beta.** *FR* Gerard Depardieu, Sigourney Weaver, Dr. Ruth Westheimer, Michel Aumont, Zabou; **D:** Daniel Vigne; **W:** Elisabeth Rappeneau, Daniel Vigne. *LIV, VES, TPV*

Onibaba 🎬🎬🎬

The Demon; The Devil Woman **1964** A brutal parable about a mother and her daughter-in-law in war-ravaged medieval Japan who subsist by murdering stray soldiers and selling their armor. One soldier beds the daughter, setting the mother-in-law on a vengeful tirade. Review of the film varied widely, hailed by some as a masterpiece and by others as below average; in Japanese with subtitles. **103m/B VHS, Beta.** *JP* Nobuko Otowa, Yitsuko Yoshimura, Kei Sato; **D:** Kaneto Shindo. *HMV, CVC, TPV*

The Onion Field 🎬🎬🎬½

1979 (R) True story about the mental breakdown of an ex-cop who witnessed his partner's murder. Haunted by the slow process of justice and his own feelings of insecurity, he is unable to get his life together. Based on the novel by Joseph Wambaugh, who also wrote the screenplay. Compelling script and excellent acting. **126m/C VHS, Beta, LV.** John Savage, James Woods, Ronny Cox, Franklyn Seales, Ted Danson; **D:** Harold Becker. *NLC*

Only Angels Have Wings 🎬🎬🎬🎬

1939 Melodramatic adventure about a broken-down Peruvian air mail service. Large cast adds to the love tension between Grant, a pilot, and Arthur, a showgirl at the saloon. Nominated for special effects, a category recognized by the academy that year for the first time. William Rankin and Eleanor Griffin are uncredited writers. **121m/B VHS, Beta.** Cary Grant, Thomas Mitchell, Richard

Barthelmess, Jean Arthur, Noah Beery Jr., Rita Hayworth, Sig Rumann, John Carroll, Allyn Joslyn; **D:** Howard Hawks; **W:** Jules Furthman; **M:** Dimitri Tiomkin. Nominations: Academy Awards '39: Best Black and White Cinematography, Best Special Effects. *COL*

Only Once in a Lifetime 🎬

1983 A love story about an Hispanic immigrant painter looking for success in America. **90m/C VHS, Beta.** Miguel Robelo, Estrellita Lopez, Sheree North. *VHE, MOV*

Only One Night 🎬🎬

En Enda Natt **1942** Upon finding out that he's the illegitimate son of an aristocrat, a happy-go-lucky carousel operator in a circus joins high society and is promptly matched with a beautiful but repressed woman. In Swedish with English subtitles. **87m/B VHS, Beta, LV.** *SW* Ingrid Bergman, Edvin Adolphson, Alno Taube, Olof Sandborg, Erik Berglund, Marianne Lofgren, Magnus Kesster; **D:** Gustaf Molander. *WAC, LUM*

Only the Brave 🎬🎬

1994 Gay coming-of-age story about two teenaged, working-class girls living on the seedy fringes of Melbourne. Alex (Manadalis), her wild best friend Vicki (Kaskanis), and their equally tough girlfriends seem to spend most of their time hanging out, smoking dope, and getting into trouble. But Alex slowly recognizes her feelings for Vicki are also sexual, and their friendship drastically changes. **62m/C VHS.** *AU* Elena Mandalis, Dora Kaskanis, Moudo Davey, Bob Bright; **D:** Ana Kokkinos; **W:** Ana Kokkinos, Mira Robertson. *FRF*

Only the Lonely 🎬🎬½

1991 (PG) Middle-aged cop, Candy, falls in love with a shy undertaker's assistant, Sheedy, and is torn between love and dear old Mom, O'Hara, in her first role in years. Candy is an unlikely leading man and even the jokes are forced. But the restaurant scene makes the whole thing well worth seeing. **104m/C VHS, Beta, LV.** John Candy, Ally Sheedy, Maureen O'Hara, Anthony Quinn, Kevin Dunn, James Belushi, Milo O'Shea, Bert Remsen, Macaulay Culkin, Joe V. Greco; **D:** Chris Columbus; **W:** Chris Columbus; **M:** Maurice Jarre. *FXV, OM*

Only the Strong 🎬½

1993 (PG-13) Louis (Dacascos) is a special forces officer who has mastered capoeira, a Brazilian form of kung fu. In Miami, he works with his old teacher (Lewis) to instill discipline in the 12 toughest punks in school by teaching them his martial arts skills. A neighborhood drug lord, related to two of the students, decides to cause trouble for Louis. Dacascos displays some charm along with his physical abilities but the story's ridiculous and the movie hastily put together. **CW:** Gang violence. **96m/C VHS, LV, Closed Caption.** Mark Dacascos, Stacy Travis, Todd Susman, Geoffrey Lewis, Paco Christian Prieto; **D:** Sheldon Lettich; **W:** Sheldon Lettich, Luis Esteban; **M:** Harvey W. Mason. *FXV*

Only the Valiant 🎬🎬

1950 Action-packed story of a cavalry officer who struggles to win his troops respect while warding off angry Apaches. Fast-paced Western fun requires little thought. **105m/B VHS, LV.** Gregory Peck, Ward Bond, Gig Young, Lon Chaney Jr., Barbara Payton, Neville Brand; **D:** Gordon Douglas; **C:** Lionel Lindon. *REP*

Only Two Can Play 🎬🎬🎬

1962 Sellers is a hilarious Casanova librarian who puts the moves on a society lady to get a promotion. Funny, of course, and based on Kingsley Amis' novel "That Uncertain Feeling." **106m/C VHS, Beta.** *GB* Peter Sellers, Virginia Maskell, Mai Zetterling, Richard Attenborough; **D:** Sidney Gilliat; **M:** Richard Rodney Bennett. *COL*

The Only Way 🎬🎬½

1970 (G) A semi-documentary account of the plight of the Jews in Denmark during the Nazi occupation. Despite German insistence, the Danes succeeded in saving most of their Jewish population from the concentration camps. **86m/C VHS, Beta.** Jane Seymour, Martin Potter, Benjamin Christiansen; **M:** Carl Davis. *VCI*

The Only Way Home 🎬🎬

1972 (PG) Two bikers end up in big trouble when one of them kills a wealthy man, and they kidnap his wife. Filmed entirely in Oklahoma. **86m/C VHS,**

Beta. Bo Hopkins, Beth Brickell, Steve Sandor, G.D. Spradlin; **D:** G.D. Spradlin. *NO*

Only When I Laugh 🎬🎬🎬 *It Hurts Only When I Laugh* **1981 (R)** Neil Simon reworked his Broadway flop "The Gingerbread Lady" to produce this poignant comedy about the relationship between an aging alcoholic actress and her teenage daughters. **120m/C VHS, Beta, LV.** Marsha Mason, Kristy McNichol, James Coco, Joan Hackett, David Dukes, Kevin Bacon, John Bennett Perry; **D:** Glenn Jordan; **W:** Neil Simon; **M:** David Shire. Golden Globe Awards '82: Best Supporting Actress (Hackett); Nominations: Academy Awards '81: Best Actress (Mason), Best Supporting Actor (Coco), Best Supporting Actress (Hackett). *COL*

Only with Married Men 🎬 **1974** Carne's hassle-free dating routine is disrupted when a sly bachelor pretends that he's married to get a date. A middle-aged persons answer to a teenage sex comedy. Pretty bad. **74m/C VHS, Beta.** David Birney, Judy Carne, Gavin MacLeod, John Astin; **D:** Jerry Paris. *ORI*

Only You 🎬½ **1992 (PG-13)** A shy guy has always searched for true romance. But his cup runneth over when he meets, and must choose between, two beautiful women—your basic beach babe and a sensible beauty. **85m/C VHS, Closed Caption.** Andrew McCarthy, Kelly Preston, Helen Hunt; **M:** Wendy Blackstone. *LIV*

Only You 🎬🎬½ *Him; Just in Time* **1994 (PG)** According to her ouija board, young Faith's (Tomei) soul mate is named Damon Bradley. But as the years pass, Faith is about to settle for a podiatrist—until an old school friend of her fiance's calls from Venice, Italy, with best wishes. Guess what his name is. So Faith and best friend Kate (Hunt) hop on a plane in search of Mr. Right. Then Faith meets charming shoe salesman Peter Wright (Downey) and wonders if ouija got things wrong. Slight romantic comedy with Jewison creating satisfactory chemistry with charming Downey and the somewhat miscast Tomei (and the Venetian scenery is gorgeous). **108m/C VHS, LV, Closed Caption.** Marisa Tomei, Robert Downey Jr., Bonnie Hunt, Fisher Stevens, Billy Zane, Joaquin de Almeida; **D:** Norman Jewison; **W:** Diane Drake. *COL*

Open All Hours 🎬 **1983** A British television comedy about a small corner shop and its viciously greedy, opportunistic owner. **85m/C VHS, Beta.** **GB** Ronnie Barker, Lynda Baron, David Jason, Stephenie Cole. *FOX*

Open City 🎬🎬🎬🎬 *Roma, Citta Aperta; Rome, Open City* **1945** A leader in the Italian underground resists Nazi control of the city. A stunning film, making Rossellini's realistic style famous. In Italian with English subtitles. **103m/B VHS, Beta, 8mm.** **IT** Anna Magnani, Aldo Fabrizi, Marcel Pagliero, Maria Michi, Vito Annicchiarico, Nando Bruno, Harry Feist; **D:** Roberto Rossellini; **W:** Federico Fellini, Sergio Amidei. National Board of Review Awards '46: 5 Best Foreign Films of the Year; New York Film Critics Awards '46: Best Foreign Film; Nominations: Academy Awards '46: Best Screenplay. *VYY, MRV, NOS*

Open Doors 🎬🎬🎬½ *Porte Aperte* **1989 (R)** Bitter review of Fascist rule and justice. The Fascist regime promises security, safety, and tranquility. So, on the morning that a white collar criminal murders his former boss, murders the man who got his job, and then rapes and murders his wife, tensions rise and the societal structures are tested. The people rally for his death. A judge and a juror struggle to uphold justice rather than serve popular passions. Winner of 4 Donatello Awards, Italian Golden Globes for Best Film, Best Actor, and Best Screenplay, and many international film awards. In Italian with English subtitles. **109m/C VHS.** **IT** Gian Marie Volonte, Ennio Fantastichini, Lidia Alfonsi; **D:** Gianni Amelio; **W:** Gianni Amelio. Nominations: Academy Awards '90: Best Foreign Language Film. *ORI, FCT*

Open Fire 🎬🎬 **1994 (R)** Alex McNeil (Wincott) is an ex-FBI agent, haunted by the death of his partner. But when a group of terrorists threaten to release a cloud of nerve gas over L.A. and

hold McNeil's father hostage, he comes back full force. **93m/C VHS, LV, Closed Caption.** Jeff Wincott, Patrick Kilpatrick, Lee DeBroux, Mimi Craven, Arthur Taxier. *REP*

Open House 🎬 **1986** Radio psychologist and beautiful real estate agent search for the killer of real estate agents and their clients. A mystery-thriller for the very patient. **95m/C VHS, Beta.** Joseph Bottoms, Adrienne Barbeau, Mary Stavin, Rudy Ramos; **D:** Jag Mundhra. *PSM*

Open Season 🎬🎬 **1995 (R)** Stuart Sain (Wuhl) is an ambitious executive at Fielding, a TV ratings company (think Nielsen) whose boxes turn out to be defective. The ratings error causes public television programming to be number one, forcing the networks to counter-program culturally in order to regain their market share. Meanwhile, the public TV executives get overconfident and everything's just up for grabs. Flawed satire. **CW:** Language and some sexuality. **97m/C VHS, Closed Caption.** Robert Wuhl, Rod Taylor, Gailard Sartain, Maggie Han, Joe Piscopo, Helen Shaver, Dina Merrill, Saul Rubinek, Steven C. White, Timothy Arrington, Barry Flatman, Tom Selleck, Alan Thicke, Jimmie Walker; **D:** Robert Wuhl; **W:** Robert Wuhl; **C:** Stephen Lighthill; **M:** Marvin Hamlisch. *REP*

Open Secret 🎬🎬 **1948** Jewish residents are plagued by a gang of anti-semitic thugs. Violence and destruction escalate until a fed up police lieutenant, tenaciously played by Ireland, and a victimized shop owner (Tyne) join forces to just say no more. When the gang learns the shopkeeper has caught their dastardly deeds on camera, the battle begins in earnest. Fast-paced and intriguing suspense. **70m/B VHS, Beta.** John Ireland, Jane Randolph, Roman Bohnen, Sheldon Leonard, George Tyne, Morgan Farley, Ellen Lowe, Anne O'Neal, Arthur O'Connell; **D:** John Reinhardt. *SNC*

Opening Night 🎬🎬½ **1977 (PG-13)** Very long study about an actress (Rowlands) and the play she's about to open in on Broadway. Backstage turmoil increases her own insecurities and the bad luck persists when an adoring fan dies in an accident on opening night. Performances carry this neurotic epic along, including Cassavetes as Rowland's co-star and Blondell as the playwright. **144m/C VHS, Beta, Closed Caption.** Gena Rowlands, John Cassavetes, Joan Blondell, Ben Gazzara, Paul Stewart, Zohra Lampert, Laura Johnson; **D:** John Cassavetes; **W:** John Cassavetes; **C:** Frederick Elmes. *TOU, BTV*

Opera do Malandro 🎬🎬 **1987** A lavish Brazilian take off of "The Threepenny Opera." Married hustler falls for a beautiful entrepreneur longing to get rich off of American goods. Based on Chico Buarque's musical play. In Portuguese, with subtitles. **106m/C VHS, Beta, LV, Closed Caption.** **BR** Edson Celulari, Claudia Ohana, Elba Ramalho, Ney Latorraca; **D:** Ruy Guerra. *NO*

Operation Amsterdam 🎬🎬 **1960** Four agents have fourteen hours to snare $10 million in diamonds from under the noses of local Nazis. Based on a true story. Full of 1940s wartime action and suspense. **103m/B VHS, Beta.** Peter Finch, Eva Bartok, Tony Britton, Alexander Knox; **D:** Michael McCarthy.

Operation C.I.A. 🎬🎬 *Last Message From Saigon* **1965** A plot to assassinate the U.S. ambassador in Saigon inspires brave CIA agent Reynolds to wipe out the bad guys. Action-packed and somewhat exciting. **90m/C VHS, Beta, Closed Caption.** Burt Reynolds, John Hoyt, Kieu Chinh, Danielle Aubry; **D:** Christian Nyby. *FOX, DVT, HEG*

Operation Cross Eagles 🎬🎬 *Unakrsna Vatra* **1969** Routine WWII military thriller with Conte and Calhoun on a mission to rescue an American general in exchange for their German prisoner. Their mission is complicated by a traitor in the group. Conte's only directorship. **90m/C VHS.** **YU** Richard Conte, Rory Calhoun, Aili King, Phil Brown; **D:** Richard Conte. *NO*

Operation Crossbow 🎬🎬🎬 *The Great Spy Mission; Code Name: Operation Crossbow* **1965** Action-packed espionage tale in which a trio of agents are assigned to destroy a Nazi munitions installation. Exciting ending and sensational pyrotechnics. **116m/C VHS, Closed Caption.** Sophia Loren, George Peppard, Trevor Howard, John Mills, Richard Johnson, Tom Courtenay, Jeremy Kemp, Anthony Quayle, Helmut Dantine; **D:** Michael Anderson Sr. *MGM*

Operation Dames 🎬½ **1959** A squadron of soldiers must go behind Korean enemy lines to locate a missing U.S.O. troupe and bring them to safety. Low budget and not very funny for a supposed comedy. **73m/B VHS.** Eve Meyer, Chuck Henderson, Don Devlin, Ed Craig, Cindy Girard; **D:** Louis Clyde Stouman. *COL*

Operation Dumbo Drop 🎬🎬½ *Dumbo Drop* **1995 (PG)** It's 1968 and tough Green Beret captain (Glover), rescued by Vietnamese villagers, promises to replace their prized elephant, which was killed during his mission. He and a group of commandos use land, sea, and air to transport the reluctant beast, learning way more about elephant hygiene and eating habits than they ever wanted to know in the process. Wincer, who also directed "Free Willy," seems to be going for the title of "greatest large mammal director of all time." Anything with good-guy U.S. troops, a paratrooper elephant, and a family-friendly plot should be a Bob Dole favorite. **107m/C VHS, LV, Closed Caption.** Danny Glover, Ray Liotta, Doug E. Doug, Denis Leary, Corin "Corky" Nemec, Thein Le Dihn; **D:** Simon Wincer; **W:** Jim Kouf, Gene Quintano; **C:** Russell Boyd; **M:** David Newman. *DIS*

Operation Golden Phoenix 🎬 **1994 (R)** A security specialist (Mehri) is betrayed in his assignment to protect one half of a valuable medallion. Seems the medal reveals the location in Lebanon of a ancient mountain of gold—desired by a ruthless warlord (Hong). Martial arts fights are well done in this routine actioner. **CW:** Graphic shootings, martial arts violence; some language. **95m/C VHS, LV, Closed Caption.** Jalal Merhi, James Hong, Al Waxman, Loren Avedon; **D:** Jalal Merhi. *USH*

Operation Haylift 🎬🎬 **1950** The true story of the U.S. Air Force's efforts to rescue starving cattle and sheep herds during Nevada's blizzards of 1949. The Air Force provided realism for the film with planes, equipment, and servicemen. **73m/B VHS, Beta, LV.** Bill Williams, Tom Brown, Ann Rutherford, Jane Nigh; **D:** William (Lester Williams) Berke. *NO*

Operation Intercept 🎬½ **1995 (R)** Francesca (Andreichenko) suspects that the government is behind her father's murder after he develops technology that causes enemy planes to crash. So she threatens to destroy civilian aircraft until the killer is brought to justice. **94m/C VHS.** Natasha Andreichenko, Bruce Payne, John Stockwell, Lance Henriksen, Dennis Christopher, Michael Champion, Curt Lowens, Corbin Bernsen; **D:** Paul Levine; **W:** Paul Levine; **C:** John Newby. *THV*

Operation Julie 🎬½ **1985** A detective searches out a huge drug ring that manufactures LSD. **100m/C VHS, Beta.** Colin Blakely, Lesley Nightingale, Clare Powney; **D:** Bob Mahoney. *LIV*

Operation 'Nam 🎬🎬 **1985** A group of bored Vietnam vets return to 'Nam to rescue their leader from a POW camp. Nothing special, but features John Wayne's son. **85m/C VHS.** Oliver Tobias, Christopher Connelly, Manfred Lehman, John Steiner, Ethan Wayne, Donald Pleasence; **D:** Larry Ludman. *IMP*

Operation Orient 🎬½ **19??** A statue laden with drugs is stolen when an international drug smuggler tries to bring it to the U.S. **94m/C VHS, Beta.** Gianni Gori, Gordon Mitchell; **D:** Elia Milonakos. *MED*

Operation Petticoat 🎬🎬🎬½ **1959** Submarine captain Grant teams with wheeler-dealer Curtis to make his sub seaworthy. They're joined by a group of Navy women, and the gags begin. Great teamwork from Grant and Curtis keeps things rolling. Jokes may be considered sexist these days. Later remake and TV series couldn't hold a candle to the original. **120m/C VHS, LV, Closed Caption.** Cary Grant, Tony Curtis, Joan O'Brien, Dina Merrill, Gene Evans, Arthur O'Connell, Virginia Gregg; **D:** Blake Edwards. Nominations: Academy Awards '59: Best Story & Screenplay. *REP*

Operation Thunderbolt 🎬🎬½ 1977 *Entebbe: Operation Thunderbolt* Israeli-produced depiction of Israel's July 14, 1976 commando raid on Entebbe, Uganda to rescue the passengers of a hijacked plane. Better than the American versions "Raid on Entebbe" and "Victory at Entebbe" in its performances as well as the information provided, much of it unavailable to the American filmmakers. **120m/C VHS, Beta.** Yehoram Gaon, Assaf Dayan, Ori Levy, Klaus Kinski; **D:** Menahem Golan. Nominations: Academy Awards '77: Best Foreign Language Film. *MGM*

Operation War Zone 🎬 1989 A platoon of soldiers uncovers a plot by corrupt officers to continue the Vietnam war and sell weapons. **86m/C VHS, Beta.** Joe Spinell. *AIP*

The Oppermann Family 🎬🎬½ 1982 On two tapes, the long epic made for German television about a family trying to survive in Berlin during the rise of Hitler. In German with subtitles. **238m/C VHS, Beta.** *GE* **D:** Egon Monk. *FCT, APD*

The Opponent 🎬🎬 1989 (R) A young boxer saves a young woman's life, not realizing that she has mob connections, thus embroiling him in a world of crime. **102m/C VHS, LV.** *IT* Daniel Greene, Ernest Borgnine, Julian Gemma, Mary Stavin, Kelly Shaye Smith; **D:** Sergio Martino. *THV*

Opportunity Knocks 🎬🎬½ 1990 (PG-13) Carvey's first feature film has him impersonating a friend of a rich suburbanite's family while hiding from a vengeful gangster. They buy it, and give him a job and the daughter. Not hilarious, but not a dud either. **105m/C VHS, Beta, LV, Closed Caption.** Dana Carvey, Robert Loggia, Todd Graff, Milo O'Shea, Julia Campbell, James Tolkan, Doris Belack, Sally Gracie, Del Close; **D:** Donald Petrie; **W:** Mitchel Katlin, Nat Bernstein; **M:** Miles Goodman. *USH*

Opposing Force 🎬🎬½ 1987 (R) *Hellcamp* The commander of an Air Force camp simulates prisoner-of-war conditions for realistic training, but he goes too far, creating all too real torture situations. He preys on the only female in the experiment, raping her as part of the training. A decent thriller. **97m/C VHS, Beta.** Tom Skerritt, Lisa Eichhorn, Anthony Zerbe, Richard Roundtree, Robert Wightman, John Considine, George Kee Chueng, Paul Joynt, Jay Louden, Ken Wright, Dan Hamilton; **D:** Eric Karson; **W:** Gil Cowan; **M:** Mark Donohue. *HBO*

The Opposite Sex 🎬🎬 1956 Bevy of women battle mediocre script in adaptation of 1939's "The Women." Laserdisc includes original trailer and letterboxed screen. 🎵The Opposite Sex; Dere's Yellow Gold on de Trees (De Banana); A Perfect Love; Rock and Roll Tumbleweed; Now! Baby, Now; Jungle Red; Young Man with a Horn. **115m/C VHS, LV.** June Allyson, Joan Collins, Dolores Gray, Ann Sheridan, Ann Miller, Leslie Nielsen, Agnes Moorehead, Joan Blondell; **D:** David Miller; **W:** Fay Kanin, Michael Kanin. *MGM, FCT*

The Opposite Sex and How to Live With Them 🎬 1993 (R) Yuppies (Gross and Cox) from different backgrounds (he's Jewish, she's a WASP) meet, fall in love, fight, break up, and reunite, inspiring yawning disinterest. All this while their two best buddies (Pollak and Brown) offer what are meant to be "candid insights" delivered directly to the camera. Flat and formulaic romantic comedy wants to sparkle, but script lacks both purpose and point, and worse, takes way too much time not getting there. Winner of the annual Grammar Police award for the worst example of a semantically incorrect title in recent years. **CW:** Language and sexual dialogue. **86m/C VHS.** Arye Gross, Courteney Cox, Kevin Pollak, Julie Brown, Mitchell Ryan, Philip Bruns, Mitzi McCall, B.J. Ward; **D:** Matthew Meshekoff; **W:** Noah Stern; **M:** Ira Newborn. *HBO*

Options 🎬🎬 1988 (PG) Nerdy Hollywood agent Salinger treks to Africa to "option" a princess's life story—hence the title. He gets mixed up with her kidnapping and with her. Misplaced cameos by Roberts and Anton drag down the overall comedy content, which isn't to high to begin with. **105m/C VHS, LV.** Matt Salinger, Joanna Pacula, John Kani, James Keach; *Cameos:* Susan Anton, Eric Roberts; **D:** Camilo Vila; **W:** Edward Decter. *LIV, VES*

The Oracle 🎬 1985 A woman takes a new apartment only to find that the previous occupant's spirit is still a resident. The spirit tries to force her to take revenge on his murderers. Not bad for a low-budget thriller, but bad editing is a distraction. **94m/C VHS, Beta.** Caroline Capers Powers, Roger Neil; **D:** Roberta Findlay. *LIV*

Oranges Are Not the Only Fruit 🎬🎬 1989 Lesbian coming of age story about young Jess (Coleman), who must escape her evangelical religious upbringing and mother (McEwan) in order to be true to herself. When the teenaged Jess gets a schoolgirl crush on her friend Melanie, the congregation finds out and condemns the girls until Jess finds the strength to break away. Based on the novel by Winsterson, who also wrote the screenplay. Made for TV. **165m/C VHS.** *GB* Charlotte Coleman, Geraldine McEwan, Cathryn Bradshaw, Kenneth Cranham, Freda Dowie, Richard Henders, Elizabeth Spriggs, Sophie Thursfield; **D:** Beeban Kidron; **W:** Jeanette Winterson; **M:** Rachel Portman. *FOX*

Orca woof! 1977 (PG) *Orca—Killer Whale* Ridiculous premise has a killer whale chasing bounty hunter Harris to avenge the murder of its pregnant mate. Great for gore lovers, especially when the whale chomps Derek's leg off. **92m/C VHS, Beta, LV.** Richard Harris, Charlotte Rampling, Bo Derek, Keenan Wynn, Will Sampson; **D:** Michael Anderson Sr.; **C:** Ted Moore; **M:** Ennio Morricone. *PAR*

Orchestra Wives 🎬🎬🎬 1942 A drama bursting with wonderful Glenn Miller music. A woman marries a musician and goes on the road with the band and the other wives. Trouble springs up with the sultry singer who desperately wants the woman's new husband. The commotion spreads throughout the group. 🎵People Like You and Me; At Last; Serenade in Blue; I've Got a Gal in Kalamazoo. **98m/B VHS, Beta, LV, Closed Caption.** George Montgomery, Glenn Miller, Lynn Bari, Carole Landis, Jackie Gleason, Cesar Romero, Ann Rutherford, Virginia Gilmore, Mary Beth Hughes, Harry (Henry) Morgan; **D:** Archie Mayo. Nominations: Academy Awards '42: Best Song ("I've Got a Gal in Kalamazoo"). *FXV, FCT*

Ordeal by Innocence 🎬½ 1984 (PG-13) Sutherland is an amateur sleuth in 1950s England convinced he has proof that a convicted murderer is innocent, but no one wishes to reopen the case. Big-name cast is essentially wasted. Based on an Agatha Christie story. **91m/C VHS, Beta, LV.** Donald Sutherland, Christopher Plummer, Faye Dunaway, Sarah Miles, Ian McShane, Diana Quick, Annette Crosbie, Michael Elphick; **D:** Desmond Davis; **C:** Billy Williams; **M:** Pino Donaggio. *MGM*

Ordeal in the Arctic 🎬🎬½ 1993 (PG) Military transport plane, piloted by Capt. John Couch (Chamberlain), crashes into the remote glaciers of the Arctic. The survivors face a blizzard and freezing to death unless a rescue team can get to them quickly. Made for cable. **93m/C VHS.** Richard Chamberlain, Melanie Mayron, Catherine Mary Stewart; **D:** Mark Sobel. *THV*

The Ordeal of Dr. Mudd 🎬🎬🎬 1980 His name was Mudd—a fitting moniker after he unwittingly aided President Lincoln's assassin. Dr. Mudd set John Wilkes Boothe's leg, broken during the assassination, and was jailed for conspiracy. He became a hero in prison for his aid during yellow fever epidemics and was eventually released. A strong and intricate performance by Weaver keeps this made-for-television drama interesting. Mudd's descendants are still trying to completely clear his name of any wrongdoing in the Lincoln assassination. **143m/C VHS, Beta.** Dennis Weaver, Susan Sullivan, Richard Dysart, Michael McGuire, Nigel Davenport, Arthur Hill; **D:** Paul Wendkos. *LIV*

Order of the Black Eagle 🎬½ 1987 (R) A Bond-ish spy and his sidekick, Typhoon the Baboon, battle neo-Nazis planning to bring Hitler back to life in this silly tongue-in-cheek thriller. **93m/C VHS, Beta.** *GB* Ian Hunter, Charles K. Bibby, William T. Hicks, Jill Donnellan; **D:** Worth Keeter. *CEL*

Order of the Eagle 🎬½ 1989 An innocent scouting trip turns into a non-stop nightmare when an Eagle Scout uncovers some dangerous information. **88m/C VHS, Beta.** Frank Stallone. *AIP*

Order to Kill 🎬🎬½ 1973 A gambling boss puts out a contract on a hit man. **110m/C VHS, Beta.** Jose Ferrer, Helmut Berger, Sydne Rome, Kevin McCarthy; **D:** Jose Maesso. *NO*

Ordet 🎬🎬🎬½ 1955 *The Word* A man who believes he is Jesus Christ is ridiculed until he begins performing miracles, which result in the rebuilding of a broken family. A statement on the nature of religious faith vs. fanaticism by the profoundly religious Dreyer, and based on the play by Kaj Munk. In Danish with English subtitles. **126m/B VHS, Beta.** *DK* Henrik Malberg; **D:** Carl Theodor Dreyer. Golden Globe Awards '56: Best Foreign Film; National Board of Review Awards '57: 5 Best Foreign Films of the Year; Venice Film Festival '55: Best Film. *NOS, WFV, HEG*

Ordinary Heroes 🎬🎬½ 1985 The story is familiar but the leads make it worthwhile. Anderson is strong as a blinded Vietnam vet readjusting to life at home. Bertinelli's portrayal of his former girlfriend is eloquent. Nice work on an overdone story. **105m/C VHS.** Richard Dean Anderson, Doris Roberts, Valerie Bertinelli; **D:** Peter H. Cooper. *HBO*

Ordinary Magic 🎬🎬½ 1993 Teenaged Jeffrey was raised in India, picking up more than a little eastern wisdom along the way. After the death of his parents Jeffrey comes to the U.S. to live with his aunt where he sticks out not only as the new kid but as a decided oddball. But he manages to make some new friends and teach a few lessons about individuality along the way. Adapted from the novel by Malcolm Bosse. **96m/C VHS.** David Fox, Glenne Headly, Heath Lamberts, Ryan Reynolds; *Cameos:* Paul Anka; **D:** Giles Walker; **W:** Jefferson Lewis. *TRI*

Ordinary People 🎬🎬🎬½ 1980 (R) Powerful, well-acted story of a family's struggle to deal with one son's accidental death and the other's subsequent guilt-ridden suicide attempt. Features strong performances by all, but Moore is especially believable as the cold and rigid mother. McGovern's film debut as well as Redford's directorial debut. Based on the novel by Judith Guest. **124m/C VHS, Beta, LV.** Mary Tyler Moore, Donald Sutherland, Timothy Hutton, Judd Hirsch, M. Emmet Walsh, Elizabeth McGovern, Adam Baldwin, Dinah Manoff, James B. Sikking; **D:** Robert Redford; **W:** Alvin Sargent; **C:** John Bailey; **M:** Marvin Hamlisch. Academy Awards '80: Best Adapted Screenplay, Best Director (Redford), Best Picture, Best Supporting Actor (Hutton); Directors Guild of America Awards '80: Best Director (Redford); Golden Globe Awards '81: Best Actress—Drama (Moore), Best Director (Redford), Best Film—Drama, Best Supporting Actor (Hutton); Los Angeles Film Critics Association Awards '80: Best Supporting Actor (Hutton); National Board of Review Awards '80: 10 Best Films of the Year, Best Director (Redford); New York Film Critics Awards '80: Best Film; Writers Guild of America '80: Best Adapted Screenplay; Nominations: Academy Awards '80: Best Actress (Moore), Best Supporting Actor (Hirsch). *PAR, BTV*

Oregon Trail 1939 A western serial in 15 chapters, each 13 minutes long. **195m/B VHS, Beta.** Johnny Mack Brown, Fuzzy Knight; **D:** Ford Beebe. *VCN, DVT, MLB*

The Organization 🎬🎬🎬 1971 (PG) Poitier's third and final portrayal of Detective Virgil Tibbs, first seen in "In the Heat of the Night." This time around he battles a drug smuggling ring with a vigilante group. Good action scenes and a realistic ending. **108m/C VHS, Beta, Closed Caption.** Sidney Poitier, Barbara McNair, Sheree North, Raul Julia; **D:** Don Medford; **C:** Joseph Biroc. MGM, FOX

Organized Crime & Triad Bureau ♂♂ *Chungon Satluk Linggei* 1993 Determined Lee and his cop team seal off crowded Hong Kong island Cheung Chai to trap mob boss Tung and his tootsie. And the bystanders better just get out of the way. Lots of action; Chinese with subtitles. **91m/C VHS, LV.** *HK* Danny Lee, Anthony Wong, Cecilia Yip; **D:** Kirk Wong. TAI

Orgy of the Dead woof! 1965 Classic anti-canon film scripted by Ed Wood, Jr. from his own novel. Two innocent travelers are forced to watch an even dozen nude spirits dance in a cardboard graveyard. Hilariously bad. **90m/C VHS, Beta.** Criswell, Fawn Silver, William Bates, Pat Barringer; **D:** A.C. Stephen; **W:** Edward D. Wood Jr. RHI

Orgy of the Vampires ♂ *Vampire's Night Orgy* 1973 (R) Tourists wander into village during cocktail hour. **86m/C VHS.** *SP IT* Jack Taylor, Charo Soriano, Dianik Zurakowska, John Richard; **D:** Leon Klimovsky. SNC

Oriane ♂♂ 1985 A troubled Venezuelan woman must leave France for her native soil when her aunt dies. Once there, in the place where she spent youthful summers, she begins to recall her incestuous past. **88m/C VHS.** Daniela Silverio, Doris Wells, Philippe Rouleau, David Crotto; **D:** Fina Torres. NO

The Original Fabulous Adventures of Baron Munchausen ♂♂½ *The Fabulous Baron Munchausen* 1961 An adventure fantasy that takes the hero all over, from the belly of a whale, eventually landing him on the surface of the moon. **84m/C VHS, LV.** *CZ* Milos Kopecky, Jana Brejchova, Rudolph Jelinek, Jan Werich; **D:** Karel Zeman. NO

The Original Flash Gordon Collection 1991 Four vintage Flash Gordon serials from the 1930s were recently re-edited into feature length films and released as this collection. Great stuff, including "Spaceship to the Unknown," "Deadly Ray From Mars," "Peril From Planet Mongo," and "Purple Death From Outer Space." **366m/B VHS.** Buster Crabbe. QHV, FCT

Original Gangstas ♂♂ 1996 (R) In Hollywood everything old eventually becomes new again. John Bookman (Williamson) returns to his old neighborhood in Gary, Indiana after his father is brutally shot by a gang leader. Things have changed from Bookman's days of gang banging, with the streets swarming with young machine gun-toting lowlifes. Bent on revenge, cigar chewing Bookman, aided by childhood friends Jake (Brown), Slick (Roundtree) and Bubba (O'Neal), decide to take back their streets with a little help from Foxy Brown herself (Grier), as a greiving mother. The nostalgia quotient is high watching these '70s blaxploitation stars together in one movie, older, more gray and a little wider, but still able to kick butt. Serious topic (gang violence) is lost in a conventional vigilante vehicle, which sacrifices a message for an all-too-familiar and bloody showdown.**CW:** Non-stop violence and pervasive strong language. **98m/C VHS, LV, Closed Caption.** Jim Brown, Fred Williamson, Pam Grier, Ron O'Neal, Richard Roundtree, Paul Winfield; **D:** Larry Cohen; **W:** Aubrey Rattan; **C:** Carlos Gonzalez; **M:** Vladimir Horunzhy. ORI

Original Intent ♂♂ 1991 (PG) A successful lawyer, facing a mid-life crisis, jeopardizes both his family and career when he decides to defend a homeless shelter from eviction proceedings. What might have been a powerful drama about one man's crusade to help the homeless instead seemed merely melodramtic. Actor/activist Sheen appears briefly as a homeless man. **97m/C VHS, Beta, Closed Caption.** Jay Richardson, Candy Clark, Kris Kristofferson, Vince Edwards, Cindy Pickett, Robert DoQui, Joseph Campanella; **Cameos:** Martin Sheen; **D:** Robert Marcarelli; **W:** Robert Marcarelli. PAR

Orlando ♂♂♂ 1992 (PG-13) Potter's sumptuous film adaptation of Virginia Woolf's 1928 novel, which covers 400 years in the life of an English nobleman, who not only defies death but evolves from a man to a woman in the intervening years. Orlando (Swinton) is first seen as a young man in the court of Queen Elizabeth I (Crisp) but after a deep sleep it's suddenly 40 years later. Things like this just keep happening and by 1750 he is now a she (and remains so), finding and losing love, and eventually gaining fulfillment in the 20th century. Elaborate productions never overwhelm Swinton's serene, self-assured performance.**CW:** Some sensuality. **93m/C VHS, LV, Closed Caption.** *GB* Tilda Swinton, Charlotte Valandrey, Billy Zane, Lothaire Bluteau, John Wood, Quentin Crisp, Heathcote Williams, Dudley Sutton, Thom Hoffman, Peter Eyre, Jimmy Somerville; **D:** Sally Potter; **W:** Sally Potter; **C:** Alexei Rodionov; **M:** Bob Last. Nominations: Academy Awards '93: Best Art Direction/Set Decoration, Best Costume Design; Independent Spirit Awards '94: Best Foreign Film. COL

The Orphan ♂½ 1979 A young orphaned boy seeks revenge against his cruel aunt who is harassing him with sadistic discipline. **80m/C VHS, Beta.** Mark Evans, Joanna Miles, Peggy Feury; **D:** John Ballard. PSM, RHI

An Orphan Boy of Vienna ♂½ 1937 A homeless street urchin with a beautiful singing voice is accepted into the wonderful world of the Choir, but is later unjustly accused of stealing. Performances by the Vienna Boys' Choir redeem the melodramatic plot. In German with English subtitles. **87m/B VHS, Beta.** *GE* **D:** Max Neufeld. VYY, IHF, GLV

Orphan Train ♂♂♂ 1979 A woman realizes her New York soup kitchen can't do enough to help the neighborhood orphans, so she takes a group of children out West in hopes of finding families to adopt them. Their journey is chronicled by a newspaper photographer and a social worker. Based on the actual "orphan trains" of the mid- to late 1800s. From the novel by Dorothea G. Petrie. Made for television. **150m/C VHS.** Jill Eikenberry, Kevin Dobson, Glenn Close, Linda Manz; **D:** William A. Graham. PSM, KAR, HHE

Orphans ♂♂♂ 1977 A sensitive edge-of-glasnost portrait of a young boy's discovery of love, friendship, and literature. In Russian with English subtitles. **97m/C VHS, Beta.** *RU* Nikolai Gubenko, Y. Boudraitis, A. Tcherstvov, A. Kaliaguine, E. Bourkov, J. Bolotova, R. Bikov, E. Evstigneev; **D:** Nikolai Gubenko; **C:** Alexander Kniajinsky. FCT

Orphans ♂♂♂ 1987 (R) A gangster on the run is kidnapped by a young New York orphan but soon takes control by befriending his abductor's maladjusted brother. Eventually each brother realizes his need for the older man, who has become a father figure to them. This very quirky film is salvaged by good performances. Based on the play by Lyle Kessler. **116m/C VHS, Beta, LV, Closed Caption.** Albert Finney, Matthew Modine, Kevin Anderson; **D:** Alan J. Pakula; **W:** Lyle Kessler; **M:** Michael Small. ORI, WAR

Orphans of the North ♂ 1940 The story of Bedrock Brown's search for gold and his lost partner. Filmed on location in Alaska with nonprofessional actors. Impressive footage of America's "last frontier," including the flora and fauna. **56m/C VHS, Beta, 8mm. D:** Norman Dawn; **W:** Susan Denis. VYY

Orphans of the Storm ♂♂♂½ 1921 Two sisters are separated and raised in opposite worlds—one by thieves, the other by aristocrats. Gish's poignant search for her sister is hampered by the turbulent maelstrom preceding the French Revolution. Silent. Based on the French play "The Two Orphans." **190m/B VHS, LV.** Lillian Gish, Dorothy Gish, Monte Blue, Joseph Schildkraut; **D:** D.W. Griffith. KIV, MRV, CCB

Orpheus ♂♂½ *Orphee* 1949 Cocteau's fascinating, innovative retelling of the Orpheus legend in a modern, though slightly askew, Parisian setting. Classic visual effects and poetic imagery. In French with English subtitles. **95m/B VHS, Beta, 8mm.** Jean Marais, Francois Perier, Maria Casares; **D:** Jean Cocteau. SNC, NOS, VYY

Orpheus Descending ♂♂½ 1991 Lust and hatred in small Southern town. Confusing, poorly paced, but interesting for Anderson as Elvis-style drifter and Redgrave as woman addicted to love. Made-for-cable version of the 1989 Broadway revival of Tennessee Williams play. **117m/C VHS, Closed Caption.** Vanessa Redgrave, Kevin Anderson, Anne Twomey, Miriam Margolyes, Brad Sullivan, Sloane Shelton, Patti Allison; **D:** Peter Hall; **W:** Peter Hall, Tennessee Williams. TTC, FCT

Osa ♂½ 1985 Yet another post-nuke flick with the usual devastated landscape, leather-clad survivors, and hokey dialog. It's sometimes funny, despite everyone's effort to make it dramatic. The supposed plot centers on one woman's efforts to break up a man's monopoly on clean water. **94m/C VHS.** Kelly Lynch, Daniel Grimm, Phillip Vincent, Etienne Chicot, John Forristal, Pete Walker, David Hausman, Bill Moseley; **D:** Oleg Egorov; **M:** Mason Daring. NO

Osaka Elegy ♂♂½ *Woman of Osaka* 1936 A study of Japanese cultural rules when society condemns a woman for behavior that is acceptable for a man. In Japanese with English subtitles. **71m/B VHS.** *JP* Isuzu Yamada; **D:** Kenji Mizoguchi. NO

The Oscar ♂½ 1966 (R) Unless you enjoy razzing bad acting, this is not for you. Meant as a comeuppance for Hollywood, by Hollywood, this story of a star climbing the ladder of success and squashing fingers on every rung is too schlocky to succeed. The climax, when the scumbag star thinks he's won an Oscar and stands up, only to find it's for someone else, was based on Frank Capra's embarrassing experience with the same situation. **119m/C VHS, Beta.** Stephen Boyd, Elke Sommer, Jill St. John, Tony Bennett, Milton Berle, Eleanor Parker, Joseph Cotten, Edie Adams, Ernest Borgnine, Ed Begley Sr., Walter Brennan, Broderick Crawford, James Dunn, Peter Lawford, Merle Oberon, Bob Hope, Frank Sinatra; **D:** Russel Rouse; **C:** Joseph Ruttenberg. Nominations: Academy Awards '66: Best Art Direction/Set Decoration (Color), Best Costume Design (Color).

Oscar ♂♂ 1991 (PG) The improbable casting of Stallone in a 1930s style crime farce (an attempt to change his image) is hard to imagine, and harder to believe. Stallone has little to do as he plays the straight man in this often ridiculous story of a crime boss who swears he'll go straight. Cameos aplenty, with Curry's the most notable. Based on a French play by Claude Magnier. **109m/C VHS, LV, Closed Caption.** Sylvester Stallone, Ornella Muti, Peter Riegert, Vincent Spano, Marisa Tomei, Kirk Douglas, Art LaFleur, Ken Howard, Chazz Palminteri, Tim Curry, Don Ameche, Richard Romanus; **D:** John Landis; **W:** Michael Barrie, Jim Mulholland; **C:** Mac Ahlberg; **M:** Elmer Bernstein. COL, IME, TOU

Oscar's Greatest Moments: 1971-1991 1992 Collection of highlights from the Oscar ceremonies, featuring footage from the past 21 years. Proceeds from video sales benefit the Center for Motion Picture Study. **110m/C VHS, LV, 8mm, Closed Caption. D:** Jeff Margolis. COL, BTV

O.S.S. ♂♂♂ 1946 John Martin (Ladd) has been recruited by Commander Brady (Knowles) as a would-be spy for the new Office of Strategic Services. Martin's teamed with Ellen Rogers (Fitzgerald) and they parachute into France with orders to obtain information on German troop movements and destroy an important railroad tunnel. A turncoat Gestapo agent sells them information but German colonel Meister (Hoyt) is after them and it's a race to see if their mission can be completed before they're caught. The O.S.S. allowed Paramount studio a look at their WWII files for story purposes and numerous ex-agents served as technical advisors. **108m/B VHS, Closed Caption.** Alan

Ladd, Geraldine Fitzgerald, Patric Knowles, John Hoyt, Richard Benedict, Gloria Saunders, Bobby Driscoll, Don Beddoe; **D:** Irving Pichel; **W:** Richard Maibaum; **C:** Lionel Linden; **M:** Daniele Amfitheatrof. *USH*

Ossessione 🎬🎬🎬½ 1942 An adaptation of "The Postman Always Rings Twice," transferred to Fascist Italy, where a drifter and an innkeeper's wife murder her husband. Visconti's first feature, which initiated Italian neo-realism, was not released in the U.S. until 1975 due to a copyright dispute. In Italian with English subtitles. 135m/B VHS, Beta. *IT* Massimo Girotti, Clara Calamai, Juan deLanda, Elio Marcuzzo; **D:** Luchino Visconti. *FCT, TPV*

The Osterman Weekend 🎬🎬 1983 (R) Peckinpah was said to have disliked the story and the script in this, his last film, which could account for the convoluted and confusing end result. Adding to the problem is the traditional difficulty of adapting Ludlum's complex psychological thrillers for the screen. The result: cast members seem to not quite "get it" as they portray a group of friends, one of whom has been convinced by the CIA that the others are all Soviet spies. 102m/C VHS, Beta, LV. Burt Lancaster, Rutger Hauer, Craig T. Nelson, Dennis Hopper, John Hurt, Chris Sarandon, Meg Foster, Helen Shaver; **D:** Sam Peckinpah; **M:** Lalo Schifrin. *NO*

Otaku no Video *Fan's Video* 1991 Fictionalized animated history of the famed Japanese animation studio Gainax, including strange interviews with rabid fans who want to "Otakunize" the human race. Contains both episodes: "Otaku no Video" (1982) and "More Otaku no Video" (1985). In Japanese with English subtitles. 100m/C VHS. *JP ANI*

Otello 🎬🎬🎬½ 1986 (PG) An uncommon film treat for opera fans, with a stellar performance by Domingo as the troubled Moor who murders his wife in a fit of jealous rage and later finds she was never unfaithful. Be prepared, however, for changes from the Shakespeare and Verdi stories, necessitated by the film adaptation. Highly acclaimed and awarded; in Italian with English subtitles. 123m/C VHS, Beta, LV. *IT* Placido Domingo, Katia Ricciarelli, Justino Diaz; **D:** Franco Zeffirelli. Nominations: Academy Awards '86: Best Costume Design. *HMV, MED, MVD*

Othello 🎬🎬½ 1922 A silent version of Shakespeare's tragedy, featuring Jannings as the tragic Moor. Titles are in English; with musical score. 81m/B VHS, Beta. *GE* Emil Jannings, Lya de Putti, Werner Krauss; **D:** Dimitri Buchowetzki. *VYY, NOS, DVT*

Othello 🎬🎬🎬 1952 Welles' striking adaptation of the Shakespeare tragedy casts him as the self-deluding Moor, with MacLiammoir as the despicable Iago and Cloutier as innocent victim, Desdemona. Welles filmed his epic over a four-year period due to budget difficulties, which also resulted in his filming in a number of different countries and settings. The film underwent a $1 million restoration, supervised by Welles' daughter, prior to its limited theatrical re-release in 1992. 90m/B VHS, LV. Orson Welles, Michael MacLiammoir, Suzanne Cloutier, Robert Coote, Hilton Edwards, Michael Lawrence, Nicholas Bruce, Fay Compton, Doris Dowling, Jean Davis, Joseph Cotten, Joan Fontaine; **D:** Orson Welles. Cannes Film Festival '52: Best Film. *ACA*

Othello 🎬🎬🎬½ 1965 Olivier (in blackface) gives another towering performance as Shakespeare's tragic Moor, led to disaster by his own jealousy. He's ably supported by Finlay's insinuating performance as Iago, Smith as a sweetly vulnerable Desdemona, and Jacobi as unwitting rival Cassio. The production, however, doesn't stray far from its stage-bound roots. 150m/C VHS. Laurence Olivier, Frank Finlay, Maggie Smith, Derek Jacobi, Joyce Redman, Anthony Nicholls, Sheila Reid, Roy Holder; **D:** Stuart Burge; **W:** Margaret Unsworth; **C:** Geoffrey Unsworth; **M:** Richard Hampton. Nominations: Academy Awards '65: Best Actor (Olivier), Best Supporting Actor (Finlay), Best Supporting Actress (Smith, Redman). *WMI*

Othello 🎬🎬🎬 1995 (R) Fishburne stars as Shakespeare's tragic Moor, with Branagh as silken agitator Iago, and Jacob as the tragic Desdemona. First time director Oliver Parker (brother Nathaniel is also in the film) drastically cut the play, rearranging scenes (and even adding material)—purists will no doubt scream, but performances carry the production. Through the clever use of asides directed at the camera, Branagh's Iago makes the viewer feel like an accomplice in the plot. French-speaking Jacob, however, seems to have a hard time pronouncing the Shakespearean dialogue. Fishburne's imposing performance as Othello is the first by an actor of African descent in a major motion picture. **CW:** Contains violence, sexuality, and nudity. 125m/C VHS, LV, **Closed Caption.** Laurence "Larry" Fishburne, Irene Jacob, Kenneth Branagh, Nathaniel Parker, Michael Maloney, Anna Patrick, Nicholas Farrell, Indra Ove, Michael Sheen, Andre Oumansky, Philip Locke, John Savident, Gabriele Ferzetti, Pierre Vaneck; **D:** Oliver Parker; **W:** Oliver Parker; **C:** David Johnson; **M:** Charlie Mole. Nominations: Screen Actors Guild Award '95: Best Supporting Actor (Branagh). *COL*

The Other 🎬🎬🎬 1972 (PG) Eerie, effective thriller adapted by Tyron from his supernatural novel. Twin brothers represent good and evil in a 1930s Connecticut farm town beset with gruesome murders and accidents. A good scare. 100m/C VHS, Beta. Martin Udvarnoky, Chris Udvarnoky, Uta Hagen, Diana Muldaur, Christopher Connelly, Victor French, John Ritter; **D:** Robert Mulligan; **C:** Robert L. Surtees; **M:** Jerry Goldsmith. *FOX*

Other Hell 🎬 1985 (R) Schlocky Italian-made chiller has the devil inhabiting a convent where he does his damnest to upset the nuns. Gross, but not scary—lots of cliche dark-hallway scenes and fright music. 88m/C VHS, Beta. *IT* Carlo De Meyo, Francesca Carmeno; **D:** Stefan Oblowsky. *LIV, VES*

Other People's Money 🎬🎬½ 1991 (R) DeVito is "Larry the Liquidator," a corporate raider with a heart of stone and a penchant for doughnuts. When he sets his sights on a post-smokestack era, family-owned cable company, he gets a taste of love for the first time in his life. He and Miller, the daughter of the company president and also its legal advisor, court one another while sparring over the fate of the company. Unbelievably clipped ending mars otherwise enterprising comedy about the triumph of greed in corporate America. Based on the off-Broadway play by Jerry Sterner. **CW:** Language and sex-related dialogue. 101m/C VHS, LV, 8mm, **Closed Caption.** Danny DeVito, Penelope Ann Miller, Dean Jones, Gregory Peck, Piper Laurie, Tom Aldredge, R.D. Call; **D:** Norman Jewison; **W:** Alvin Sargent; **C:** Haskell Wexler; **M:** David Newman. *WAR, CCB*

The Other Side of Midnight woof! 1977 (R) The dreary, depressingly shallow life story of a poor French girl, dumped by an American GI, who sleeps her way to acting stardom and a profitable marriage, then seeks revenge for the jilt. Based on Sidney Sheldon's novel, it's not even titillating—just a real downer. 160m/C VHS, Beta, LV. Susan Sarandon, Marie-France Pisier, John Beck, Raf Vallone, Clu Gulager, Sorrell Booke; **D:** Charles Jarrott; **W:** Daniel Taradash; **C:** Fred W. Koenekamp. Nominations: Academy Awards '77: Best Costume Design. *FOX*

The Other Side of Sunday 🎬🎬 1996 A small town in 1959 Norway is the setting for this coming of age comedy. Maria (Thiesen) is the eldest daughter of conservative priest Johannes (Sundquist). Fun doesn't seem to be part of their religion but puberty is hitting Maria hard and she longs to join in with the livelier crowd of her school friend Brigit (Salvesen), who listens to rock 'n' roll, wears makeup, and makes out with boys. Maria does find a compassionate listener in Mrs. Tunheim (Riise), who urges the teenager to learn how to think for herself. Based on the novel "Sunday" by Reidun Nortvedt. Norwegian with subtitles. 103m/C VHS. *NO* Marie Theisen, Bjorn Sundquist, Hilde-

gunn Riise, Sylvia Salvesen; **D:** Berit Nesheim; **W:** Berit Nesheim, Lasse Glomm; **C:** Arne Borsheim; **M:** Geir Bohren, Bent Aserud. Nominations: Academy Awards '96: Best Foreign Language Film. *NYR*

The Other Side of the Law 🎬🎬 1995 (R) Man makes a wilderness hideout with his son after killing his wife's murderer. But when the boy grows up, dad decides to send him back into civilization for education, leading to nothing but trouble. **CW:** Adventure violence. 96m/C VHS. Juergen Prochnow; **D:** Gilles Carle. *THV*

The Other Side of the Mountain 🎬🎬 *A Window to the Sky* 1975 (PG) Tear-jerking true story of Olympic hopeful skier Jill Kinmont, paralyzed in a fall. Bridges helps her pull her life together. A sequel followed two years later. Based on the book "A Long Way Up" by E. G. Valens. 102m/C VHS, Beta. Marilyn Hassett, Beau Bridges, Dabney Coleman, John David Garfield, Griffin Dunne; **D:** Larry Peerce; **W:** David Seltzer; **M:** Charles Fox. Nominations: Academy Awards '75: Best Song ("Richard's Window"). *USH*

The Other Side of the Mountain, Part 2 🎬🎬 1978 (PG) Quadriplegic Jill Kinmont, paralyzed in a skiing accident that killed her hopes for the Olympics, overcomes depression and the death of the man who helped her to recover. In this chapter, she falls in love again and finds happiness. More tears are jerked. 99m/C VHS, Beta. Marilyn Hassett, Timothy Bottoms; **D:** Larry Peerce. *USH*

The Other Woman 🎬🎬½ 1992 (R) Investigative reporter Jessica is working on a murder case when she finds incriminating sex photos showing her husband with another woman. She becomes obsessed with finding the woman in the pictures but it would be dangerous for Jessica to forget there's still a murderer on the loose. **CW:** Language and strong sexuality. 90m/C VHS, **Closed Caption.** Adrian Zmed, Lee Ann Beaman, Daniel Moriarty, Jenna Persaud, Sam Jones; **D:** Jag Mundhra. *IMP*

Oubliette 1914 A peripheral version of Francois Villon, in what is a recently discovered and restored film, the earliest extant Chaney film. 35m/B VHS, Beta. Lon Chaney Sr. *GVV, LSV*

Our Daily Bread 🎬🎬 *Miracle of Life* 1934 Vidor's sequel to the 1928 "The Crowd." A young couple inherit a farm during the Depression and succeed in managing the land. A near-classic, with several sequences highly influenced by directors Alexander Dovshenko and Sergei Eisenstein. Director Vidor also co-scripted this film, risking bankruptcy to finance it. 80m/B VHS, Beta, LV. Karen Morley, Tom Keene, John Qualen, Barbara Pepper, Addison Richards; **D:** King Vidor; **W:** King Vidor. *NOS, BAR, VYY*

Our Dancing Daughters 🎬🎬½ 1928 Flapper (Crawford on the brink of stardom) falls hard for millionaire who's forced into arranged marriage, but obliging little missus kicks bucket so Crawford can step in. 86m/B VHS, Beta. Joan Crawford, Johnny Mack Brown, Nils Asther, Dorothy Sebastian, Anita Page; **D:** Harry Beaumont; **C:** George Barnes. Nominations: Academy Awards '29: Best Cinematography, Best Writing. *MGM, FCT*

Our Family Business 🎬🎬 1981 Made for television and meant as a series pilot, this generally plodding "Godfather"-type story is saved by good performances by Wanamaker and Milland. 74m/C VHS. Sam Wanamaker, Vera Miles, Ray Milland, Ted Danson, Chip Mayer; **D:** Robert Collins. *LIV*

Our Gang 1926 Two silent "Our Gang" comedies, including "Thundering Fleas" and "Shivering Spooks." 57m/B VHS, Beta, 8mm. Joe Cobb, Farina Hoskins, Mary Kornman, Mickey Daniels, Scooter Lowry. *VYY*

Our Gang Comedies 194? The five shorts on this cassette show the gang at their comedic best. They include "The Big Premiere," "Bubbling Troubles," "Clown Princes," "Don't Lie" and "Farm Hands." 53m/B VHS, Beta, LV. Robert (Bobby) Blake, Billie "Buckwheat" Thomas, George

"Spanky" McFarland, Darla Hood, Carl "Alfalfa" Switzer, Tommy "Butch" Bond, Eugene "Porky" Lee, Shirley "Muggsy" Coates, Joe "Corky" Geil, Billy "Froggy" Laughlin. *MGM, VTR*

Our Gang Comedy Festival 1988 A 20-year span of comedy from the Little Rascals, including rare silent features. 45m/B VHS. Joe Cobb, Farina Hoskins, Mary Kornman, Mickey Daniels, Scooter Lowry. *GKK*

Our Gang Comedy Festival 2 1989 More riotous good times with The Little Rascals, including silent footage. 45m/B VHS. Joe Cobb, Farina Hoskins, Mary Kornman, Mickey Daniels, Scooter Lowry. *GKK*

Our Hospitality 🎞🎞🎞🎞 1923 One of Keaton's finest silent films, with all the elements in place. William McKay (Keaton) travels to the American South on a quaint train (a near-exact replica of the Stephenson Rocket), to claim an inheritance as the last survivor of his family. En route, a young woman traveler informs him that her family has had a long, deadly feud with his, and that they intend to kill him. McKay resolves to get the inheritance, depending on the Southern rule of hospitality to guests to save his life until he can make his escape. Watch for the river scene where, during filming, Keaton's own life was really in danger. By the way, Keaton married his leading lady in real life. 74m/B VHS, LV. Buster Keaton, Natalie Talmadge, Joe Keaton, Buster Keaton Jr., Kitty Bradbury, Joe Roberts; *D:* Buster Keaton, John Blystone. *HBO*

Our Little Girl 🎞🎞 1935 (PG) A precocious little tyke tries to reunite her estranged parents by running away to their favorite vacation spot. Sure to please Shirley Temple fans, despite a lackluster script. 65m/B VHS, Beta, Closed Caption. Shirley Temple, Joel McCrea, Rosemary Ames, Lyle Talbot, Erin O'Brien Moore; *D:* John S. Robertson. *FOX*

Our Man Flint 🎞🎞 1966 James Bond clone Derek Flint uses gadgets and his ingenuity to save the world from an evil organization, GALAXY, that seeks world domination through control of the weather. The plot moves quickly around many bikini-clad women, but still strains for effect. Spawned one sequel: "In Like Flint." 107m/C VHS, Beta, LV. James Coburn, Lee J. Cobb, Gila Golan, Edward Mulhare, Benson Fong, Shelby Grant, Sigrid Valdis, Gianna Serra, James Brolin, Helen Funai, Michael St. Clair; *D:* Daniel Mann; *C:* Daniel F. Fapp; *M:* Jerry Goldsmith. *FOX*

Our Miss Brooks 🎞🎞½ 1956 Quietly pleasing version of the television series. Miss Brooks pursues the "mother's boy" biology professor. The father of the child she begins tutoring appears taken with her. The professor takes notice. 85m/B VHS. Eve Arden, Gale Gordon, Nick Adams, Richard Crenna, Don Porter; *D:* Al Lewis. *WAR*

Our Modern Maidens 🎞🎞½ 1929 Scandalous jazz-age drama in which Crawford and Fairbanks both fall in love with other people before their wedding is to take place. This sequel to "Our Dancing Daughters" features beautiful gowns and lush, opulent Art Deco interiors. Based on a story by Josephine Lovett. 75m/B VHS, Closed Caption. Joan Crawford, Rod La Rocque, Douglas Fairbanks Jr., Anita Page, Josephine Dunn; *D:* Jack Conway; *W:* Josephine Lovett. *MGM*

Our Relations 🎞🎞🎞½ 1936 Confusion reigns when Stan and Ollie meet the twin brothers they never knew they had, a pair of happy-go-lucky sailors. Laurel directs the pair through mad-cap encounters with their twins' wives and the local underworld. One of the pair's best efforts, though not well-remembered. Based on a story by W.W. Jacobs. 94m/B VHS, Beta. Stan Laurel, Oliver Hardy, Alan Hale, Sidney Toler, James Finlayson, Daphne Pollard; *D:* Harry Lachman. *MED, CCB, MLB*

Our Sons 🎞🎞½ 1991 Two middle-aged moms strike up an unlikely friendship over their gay sons in this TV weeper. Arkansas waitress Luanna (Ann Margret) hasn't talked to son Donald (Ivanek) in years—now he's dying of AIDS. Successful career woman Audrey (Andrews in her TV-movie debut) has seemingly accepted son James' (Grant) life with Donald and it's James who urges his mother to make contact with Luanna and persuade her to see Donald one last time. 100m/C VHS. Julie Andrews, Ann-Margret, Hugh Grant, Zeljko Ivanek, Tony Roberts; *D:* John Erman; *W:* John Erman, William Hanley. *AEL*

Our Time 🎞🎞½ *Death of Her Innocence* 1974 An exclusive girls finishing school in the fifties is the setting for the friendship of Abby (Martin) and Muffy (Slade) and their first stirrings of romance. But when Muffy gets pregnant, tragedy awaits. Sappy. 91m/C VHS. Pamela Sue Martin, Betsey Slade, Parker Stevenson, George O'Hanlon Jr., Roderick Cook, Edith Atwater, Meg Wyllie, Debralee Scott, Nora Heflin, Kathryn Holcomb, Robert Walden; *D:* Peter Hyams; *W:* Jane C. Stanton. *WAR*

Our Town 🎞🎞🎞 1940 Small-town New England life in Grover's Corners in the early 1900s is celebrated in this well-performed and directed adaptation of the Pulitzer Prize-winning play by Thornton Wilder. Film debut of Scott. 90m/B VHS, Beta. Martha Scott, William Holden, Thomas Mitchell, Fay Bainter, Guy Kibbee, Beulah Bondi, Frank Craven; *D:* Sam Wood; *M:* Aaron Copland. National Board of Review Awards '40: 10 Best Films of the Year; Nominations: Academy Awards '40: Best Actress (Scott), Best Interior Decoration, Best Picture, Best Sound, Best Score. *CNG, MRV, NOS*

Our Town 🎞🎞🎞 1977 Television version of Thornton Wilder's classic play about everyday life in Grovers Corners, a small New England town at the turn of the century. It hews more closely to the style of the stage version than the earlier film version. 120m/C VHS, Beta, LV. Ned Beatty, Sada Thompson, Ronny Cox, Glynnis O'Connor, Robby Benson, Hal Holbrook, John Houseman; *D:* Franklin J. Schaffner. *MAS*

Our Town 🎞🎞½ 1989 Filmed TV version of the Tony Award-winning Lincoln Center production of the Thornton Wilder play focusing on small-town life in Grover's Corners, New Hampshire. Gray is the omniscient Stage Manager, with Stolz and Miller as the young couple brought together by the everyday cycle of happiness and hardship. 104m/C VHS. Eric Stoltz, Penelope Ann Miller, Spalding Gray; *D:* Gregory Mosher. *MAS*

Our Vines Have Tender Grapes 🎞🎞½ 1945 A change of pace role for the volatile Robinson who plays a kind Norwegian farmer, living in Wisconsin with his daughter, the spunky O'Brien. The film is made-up of small-town moments as O'Brien learns a few of life's lessons, eased by the thoughtful compassion of Robinson. Based on the novel "For Our Vines Have Tender Grapes" by George Victor Martin. 105m/B VHS. Edward G. Robinson, Margaret O'Brien, James Craig, Agnes Moorehead, Jackie "Butch" Jenkins, Morris Carnovsky, Frances Gifford, Sara Haden, Louis Jean Heydt; *D:* Roy Rowland; *W:* Dalton Trumbo; *C:* Robert L. Surtees. *MGM, MOV, BTV*

Out 🎞🎞½ 1988 A drifter's travels throughout the U.S. from the sixties to the eighties. Successfully manages to satirize just about every conceivable situation but keeps from posturing by not taking itself too seriously. Adapted from an experimental novel by Ronald Sukenick. 88m/C VHS. Peter Coyote, Danny Glover, O-Lan Shepard, Jim Haynie, Scott Beach, Semu Haute; *D:* Eli Hollander; *W:* Eli Hollander; *M:* David Cope. *NO*

Out Cold 🎞½ 1989 (R) Black comedy follows the misadventures of a butcher who believes he has accidentally frozen his business partner; the iced man's girlfriend, who really killed him; and the detective who tries to solve the crime. Too many poor frozen body jokes may leave the viewer cold. 91m/C VHS, Beta, LV. John Lithgow, Teri Garr, Randy Quaid, Bruce McGill; *D:* Malcolm Mowbray; *M:* Michel Colombier. *HBO*

Out for Blood 🎞🎞 1993 (R) Attorney John Decker is living a happy life until his family is murdered by drug dealers. He turns vigilante, dubbed "Karateman" by the press, and finds himself hunted by the cops and the criminals. ?m/C VHS, Closed Caption. Don "The Dragon" Wilson, Shari Shattuck, Michael Delano, Kenneth McLeod, Todd Curtis, Timothy Baker, Howard Jackson, Bob Schott, Eric Lee; *D:* Richard W. Munchkin; *W:* David S. Green. *PMH*

Out for Justice 🎞🎞½ 1991 (R) A psycho Brooklyn hood goes on a murder spree, and homeboy turned lone-wolf cop Seagal races other police and the mob to get at him. Bloodthirsty and profane, it does try to depict N.Y.C.'s Italian-American community—but 90 percent of them are dead by the end so what's the point? Better yet, why does it open with a quote from Arthur Miller? Better still, what's Daffy Duck doing on this tape peddling Warner Brothers T-shirts to kid viewers?!*CW:* Strong language, strong violence and drug use, and sensuality. 91m/C VHS, Beta, LV, 8mm. Steven Seagal, William Forsythe, Jerry Orbach, Julianna Margulies, Gina Gershon, John Leguizamo, Julie Strain. *WAR*

Out of Africa 🎞🎞🎞 1985 (PG) An epic film of the years spent by Danish authoress Isak Dinesen (her true name is Karen Blixen) on a Kenya coffee plantation. She moved to Africa to marry, and later fell in love with Denys Finch-Hatten, a British adventurer. Based on several books, including biographies of the two lovers. Some critics loved the scenery and music; others despised the acting and the script. A definite "no" for those who love action. 161m/C VHS, Beta, LV, Closed Caption. Meryl Streep, Robert Redford, Klaus Maria Brandauer, Michael Kitchen, Malick Bowens, Michael Gough, Suzanna Hamilton, Rachel Kempson, Graham Crowden, Shane Rimmer, Donal McCann, Iman, Joseph Thiaka, Stephen Kinyanjui; *D:* Sydney Pollack; *W:* Kurt Luedtke; *C:* David Watkin; *M:* John Barry. Academy Awards '85: Best Adapted Screenplay, Best Art Direction/Set Decoration, Best Cinematography, Best Director (Pollack), Best Picture, Best Sound, Best Original Score; British Academy Awards '86: Best Adapted Screenplay; Golden Globe Awards '86: Best Film—Drama, Best Supporting Actor (Brandauer), Best Score; Los Angeles Film Critics Association Awards '85: Best Actress (Streep), Best Cinematography; National Board of Review Awards '85: Best Supporting Actor (Brandauer); New York Film Critics Awards '85: Best Cinematography, Best Supporting Actor (Brandauer); Nominations: Academy Awards '85: Best Actress (Streep), Best Costume Design, Best Film Editing, Best Supporting Actor (Brandauer). *USH, BTV*

Out of Annie's Past 🎞🎞½ 1994 (R) Successful career woman Annie Carver (Stewart) has managed to hide a dreadful secret from family and co-workers for some 10 years. But now the past is back to haunt her—seems Annie was once the prime suspect in a murder. Made for cable.*CW:* Some violence. 91m/C VHS. Catherine Mary Stewart, Dennis Farina, Scott Valentine, Carsten Norgaard, Michel Flynn; *D:* Stuart Cooper; *W:* Pablo F. Fenjves. *USH*

Out of Bounds 🎞½ 1986 (R) An Iowa farmboy picks up the wrong bag at the Los Angeles airport, and is plunged into a world of crime, drugs, and murder. Plenty of action, but the fast pace can't hide huge holes in the script or the silliness of Hall playing a tough kid on the run from the law. 93m/C VHS, Beta, LV, Closed Caption. Anthony Michael Hall, Jenny Wright, Jeff Kober; *D:* Richard Tuggle; *C:* Bruce Surtees; *M:* Stewart Copeland. *COL*

Out of Control 🎞 1985 (R) A plane full of rich teenagers crash on a secluded island and must battle a gang of vicious smugglers to survive. A teen sex theme keeps working its way in, leaving the viewer as confused as the actors and actresses appear to be. 78m/C VHS, Beta, LV. Betsy Russell, Martin Hewitt, Claudia Udy, Andrew J. Lederer; *D:* Allan Holzman; *W:* Vicangelo Bullock; *C:* John A. Alonzo. *NWV, VTR*

Out of Order 🎞½ 1984 A German-made film about people stuck in an office building's malevolent, free-thinking elevator. Dubbed. 87m/C VHS, Beta. GE Renee Soutendijk, Goetz George, Wolfgang Kieling, Hannes Jaenicke; *D:* Carl Schenkel. *LIV, VES*

Out of Season 🎞🎞 *Winter Rates* 1975 (R) Mother and teenage daughter compete for the attentions of the mother's mysterious ex-lover. We never know who wins the man in this enigmatic drama set in an English village, and hints of incest make the story even murkier. Had only a short run in the U.S. **90m/C VHS, Beta.** *GB* Cliff Robertson, Vanessa Redgrave, Susan George; *D:* Alan Bridges. *VCI*

Out of Sight, Out of Her Mind 🐾🐾
1989 (R) After witnessing her daughter burned alive, Alice is released from a mental institution. She tries to start a new life, but her daughter won't let her—she keeps appearing, crying out for help. **94m/C VHS, Beta, LV.** Susan Blakely, Eddie Albert, Wings Hauser. *PSM, PAR*

Out of Sync 🐾½
1995 (R) Deejay Jason St. Julian gets in trouble with his bookies and L.A. detectives, one of whom forces him into an undercover job with a drug-dealing club owner. Then Jason falls for the dealer's girlfriend. Hip-hop soundtrack may provide the only interest. *CW:* Strong sexuality, language and violence. **105m/C VHS, LV, Closed Caption.** L.L. Cool J., Victoria Dillard, Howard Hesseman, Ramy Zada, Don Yesso, Yaphet Kotto; *D:* Debbie Allen; *W:* Robert E. Dorn; *M:* Steve Tyrell. *LIV*

Out of the Blue 🐾🐾½
1947 There's trouble in paradise for a married man when a shady lady passes out in his apartment. Thinking she is dead, he tries to get rid of the body. The antics with his neighbor and wife provide plenty of laughs. **86m/B VHS, Beta, LV.** George Brent, Virginia Mayo, Carole Landis, Turhan Bey, Ann Dvorak; *D:* Leigh Jason. *NWV*

Out of the Blue 🐾🐾🐾
1980 (R) A harsh, violent portrait of a shattered family. When an imprisoned father's return fails to reunite this Woodstock-generation family, the troubled teenage daughter takes matters into her own hands. "Easy Rider" star Hopper seems to have reconsidered the effects of the 1960s. **94m/C VHS, Beta.** Dennis Hopper, Linda Manz, Raymond Burr; *D:* Dennis Hopper. *MED*

Out of the Body 🐾
1988 (R) A man is possessed by a spirit that likes to kill young, beautiful women. This makes him (and the viewer) uncomfortable. **91m/C VHS, LV.** Mark Hembrow, Tessa Humphries; *D:* Brian Trenchard-Smith. *NO*

Out of the Dark 🐾½
1988 (R) The female employees of a telephone-sex service are stalked by a killer wearing a clown mask in this tongue-in-cheek thriller. A few laughs amid the mayhem. Look for Divine. **98m/C VHS, Beta, LV, Closed Caption.** Cameron Dye, Divine, Karen Black, Bud Cort, Lynn Danielson, Geoffrey Lewis, Paul Bartel, Tracey Walter, Silvania Gallardo, Starr Andreeff, Lainie Kazan, Tab Hunter; *D:* Michael Schroeder; *W:* James DeFelice; *M:* Paul Antonelli. *COL*

Out of the Darkness 🐾🐾🐾
1985 (R) A television movie about the personal life of the New York detective who hunted and arrested sexual killer Son of Sam. Sheen shines in a tight suspenser. **96m/C VHS, Beta, LV.** Martin Sheen, Hector Elizondo, Matt Clark, Jennifer Salt, Eddie Egan, Robert Trebor; *D:* Jud Taylor; *W:* T.S. Cook. *VTR, THV*

Out of the Past 🐾🐾🐾½
Build My Gallows High **1947** A private detective gets caught in a complex web of love, murder, and money in this film noir classic. The plot is torturous but clear thanks to fine directing. Mitchum became an overnight star after this film, which was considered low-budget but now considered one of the best in its genre. Based on Geoffrey Homes' novel "Build My Gallows High." Remade in 1984 as "Against All Odds." **97m/B VHS, Beta, LV.** Robert Mitchum, Kirk Douglas, Jane Greer, Rhonda Fleming, Steve Brodie, Dickie Moore; *D:* Jacques Tourneur; *W:* Geoffrey Homes. *MED, TTC*

Out of the Rain 🐾🐾½
1990 (R) A small town becomes a hotbed of deceit and lies due to the influence of drugs. A man and a and a woman engage in a passionate struggle to free themselves from the town's grip. **91m/C VHS, Beta, LV.** Bridget Fonda, Michael O'Keefe, John E. O'Keefe, John Seitz, Georgine Hall, Al Shannon; *D:* Gary Winick; *W:* Shem Bitterman. *CCB, LIV*

Out of the Shadows 🐾🐾½
199? Scotland Yard Chief Inspector Michael Hayden (Dance) investigates a series of international art thefts that lead him to believe the goods are being smuggled out of the country through diplomatic channels. **95m/C VHS.** *GB* Charles Dance, Alexandra Paul, Wanda Ventham. *VCO*

The Out-of-Towners 🐾🐾🐾
1970 (G) A pair of Ohio rubes travels to New York City and along the way everything that could go wrong does. Lemmon's performance is excellent and Simon's script is, as usual, both wholesome and funny. **98m/C VHS, Beta, LV.** Jack Lemmon, Sandy Dennis, Anne Meara, Sandy Baron, Billy Dee Williams; *D:* Arthur Hiller; *W:* Neil Simon. Writers Guild of America '70: Best Original Screenplay. *PAR*

Out on a Limb 🐾🐾
1987 MacLaine plays herself in this made-for-television miniseries based on her best-selling book by the same name. In the midst of love affairs with an unnamed British politician and a mysterious teacher, she learns about her past, present, and future through meditation and her beliefs in reincarnation. Features footage of psychics performing spiritual channeling. Beautiful scenery filmed on location in California, Hong Kong, London, Hawaii, Sweden, and Peru, but the acting is just average, and the movie is slow in some parts. A 234-minute special collector's edition is also available. **160m/C VHS, Beta, Closed Caption.** Shirley MacLaine, Charles Dance, John Heard, Anne Jackson, Jerry Orbach; *D:* Robert Butler. *PSM, WSH*

Out on a Limb 🐾
1992 (PG) Lame comedy follows the misadventures of financial whiz Bill Campbell (Broderick). His young sister is convinced their stepfather is a criminal and persuades her brother to return home. On his way, Bill is robbed and abandoned by a woman hitchhiker, then found by two moronic brothers. It also turns out his stepfather has a twin brother who wants revenge for past crimes. Frantic chase scenes and lots of noise do not a comedy make. Broderick and Jones also appeared together in "Ferris Bueller's Day Off." **82m/C VHS, Beta, LV, Closed Caption.** Matthew Broderick, Jeffrey Jones, Heidi Kling, John C. Reilly, Marian Mercer, Larry Hankin, David Margulies; *D:* Francis Veber. *MGM*

Out on Bail 🐾½
1989 (R) A law-abiding citizen witnesses a murder, only to discover the crooked town council is behind the slaying. **102m/C VHS, Beta.** Robert Ginty, Kathy Shower, Tom Badal, Sydney Lassick; *D:* Gordon Hessler; *W:* Tom Badal, Jason Booth. *TWE*

Out There 🐾🐾½
1995 (PG-13) Cable sci-fi comedy finds photographer Delbert Mosley (Campbell) buying a Brownie camera at a garage sale and discovering the 25-year-old film shows pictures of a UFO encounter. Mosley then tries to verify the photos with a supermarket tabloid, the military, and UFO fanatics all on his trail. Fast-paced amusement with appealing performances. *CW:* Nude images and crude language. **98m/C VHS, Beta, Closed Caption.** Bill Campbell, Wendy Schaal, Julie Brown, David Rasche, Paul Dooley, Bill Cobbs, Bob(cat) Goldthwait, Rod Steiger, June Lockhart, Jill St. John, Carel Struycken, Billy Bob Thornton, P.J. Soles; *D:* Sam Irvin; *W:* Thomas Strelich, Alison Nigh; *C:* Gary Tieche; *M:* Deborah Holland, Frankie Blue. *PAR*

Out to Sea 🐾🐾½
1997 (PG-13) Matthau persuades brother-in-law Lemmon to become a dance instructor aboard a cruise ship so they can meet women and con them out of money. Matthau sets his sights on feisty socialite Cannon, while Lemmon romances a woman tagging along on her daughter's honeymoon. Both of these "salty old dogs" have to avoid the wrath of militaristic cruise director Spiner. The duo still has great comic timing, as they continue to defy the odds that this is the one that's gonna flop. Great supporting cast, which includes O'Connor in a couple of nifty dance scenes, seems to be having a great time. *CW:* Language and sex-related humor. **?m/C VHS.** Walter Matthau, Jack Lemmon, Elaine Stritch, Dyan Cannon, Gloria De Haven, Hal Linden, Donald O'Connor, Rue McClanahan, Estelle Harris; *D:* Martha Coolidge; *W:* Robert Nelson Jacobs, Danny Jacobson; *C:* Lajos Koltai; *M:* David Newman. *NYR*

Outbreak 🐾🐾🐾
1994 (R) Smuggled African monkey spits on someone who kisses someone else who sneezes on a bunch of people, thus initiating the spread of a highly infectious mystery disease in a northern California 'burb. Hoffman leads a team of scientists in a search for the anti-serum, but it's a secret government plot to exterminate the victims that literally sends Hoffman and crew into action movie cliche overdrive (add "helicopter" to the list of chase scene vehicles). Not that that's so bad—if the beat-the-clock tempo doesn't grab you, paranoia certainly will. But Hoffman's hardly a threat to Arnold or Sylvester as the next action hero, and the talented Russo remains suspiciously ravishing even with festering pustules. Based on two books: Richard Preston's "The Hot Zone" and Laurie Garrett's "The Coming Plague." *CW:* Language; ugly sick people. **128m/C VHS, LV, Closed Caption, DVD.** Dustin Hoffman, Rene Russo, Morgan Freeman, Donald Sutherland, Cuba Gooding Jr., Kevin Spacey, J.T. Walsh; *D:* Wolfgang Petersen; *W:* Robert Roy Pool, Laurence Dworet; *C:* Michael Ballhaus; *M:* James Newton Howard. New York Film Critics Awards '95: Best Supporting Actor (Spacey). *WAR*

The Outcast 🐾🐾
1954 A young tough heads west to seize the family ranch wrongfully held by a conniving uncle. Of course he finds love as well, and enjoys gun and fistfights in this exciting though unspectacular western. **90m/C VHS.** John Derek, Jim Davis, Joan Davis; *D:* William Witney. *REP*

The Outcast 🐾½
1984 Story of three brothers who live by the ax, love from the heart, hate with passion, and die violently. Trouble is they have to recite from a script written in crayon. **86m/C VHS.** Ben Dekker, Sandra Prinsloo. *REP*

The Outcasts 🐾🐾🐾
1986 A Taiwanese film about young gay boys in an urban jungle who are given shelter and protection by an aging photographer. In Chinese with English subtitles. **102m/C VHS, Beta.** *TW* D: Yu Kan-Ping. *FCT*

Outcasts of the City 🐾🐾
1958 The sort of negligible film filler that TV killed off. An American officer in post-WWII Germany romances a German girl, then gets blamed for the death of her Boche beau. **61m/B VHS.** Osa Massen, Robert Hutton, Maria Palmer, Nestor Paiva, John Hamilton, George Neise, Norbert Schiller, George Sanders; *D:* Boris L. Petroff. *NOS*

Outcasts of the Trail 🐾½
1949 When Tom White (Gallaudet) is jailed for robbing the stage, his children are shunned by the town even after Tom decides to return the stolen cash after his release. So, it's up to stagecoach driver Pat Garrett (Hale) to clear up the family's trouble. **61m/B VHS, Closed Caption.** Monte Hale, John Gallaudet, Roy Barcroft, Jeff Donnell, T.V. Tommy Ivo, Paul Hurst; *D:* Philip Ford; *W:* Olive Cooper, Stanley Wilson; *C:* Bud Thackery. *REP*

The Outer Limits: Galaxy Being...
1963 "There is nothing wrong with your TV set..." in this sci-fi series which ran from 1963-1965. In the show's pilot episode an obsessed scientist transmits a pure-energy being from Andromeda into our universe, and chaos ensues. Additional episodes are available. **53m/B VHS, Beta.** Cliff Robertson, Jacqueline Scott, Lee Philips, William O. Douglas Jr.; *D:* Leslie Stevens. *MGM, MOV*

The Outer Limits: Sandkings 🐾🐾🐾
Sandkings **1995** Made-for-cable revival of the '60s sci-fi series is creepier than ever with this tale of loony scientist Simon Kress (Bridges). He discovers tiny alien eggs while doing an analysis of Martian soil samples and decides to take his research home with him when the government cuts off funding. Big mistake—the critters he successfully hatches in his barn are mean and hungry. Features both dad Lloyd and Beau's 10-year-old son, Dylan, in roles. **93m/C VHS, Closed Caption.** Beau

Bridges, Lloyd Bridges, Helen Shaver, Dylan Bridges, Kim Coates; **D:** Stuart Gillard; **W:** Melinda M. Snodgrass. *MGM*

The Outfit 🎬🎬½ 1993 (R) It's the 1930s and a mob war is brewing between Lucky Luciano, Legs Diamond and Dutch Schultz. A maverick FBI agent gets in good with Diamond and works to end their reign of crime—only he winds up being the spark to light a war between the rival bosses.**CW:** Language, gangster violence, and sexuality. 92m/C VHS, LV, Closed Caption. John Christian, Billy Drago, Lance Henriksen, Martin Kove, Josh Moby, Rick Washburne; **D:** J. Christian Ingvordsen; **W:** J. Christian Ingvordsen, Steven Kaman, Whitney Ransick. *USH, SGE*

The Outing 🎬🎬 *The Lamp* 1987 (R) A group of high school kids sneaks into a museum at night to party, and get hunted down by a 3,000-year-old genie-in-a-lamp. The genie idea is original enough to make things interesting. Mediocre special effects and run-of-the-mill acting. 87m/C VHS, Beta. Deborah Winters, James Huston; **D:** Tom Daley. *LIV*

Outland 🎬🎬 1981 (R) On a volcanic moon of Jupiter, miners begin suffering from spells of insanity. A single federal marshal begins an investigation that threatens the colony's survival. No more or less than a western in space, and the science is rather poor. Might make an interesting double feature with "High Noon," though. 109m/C VHS, Beta, LV, Closed Caption. Sean Connery, Peter Boyle, Frances Sternhagen, James B. Sikking; **D:** Peter Hyams; **W:** Peter Hyams; **M:** Jerry Goldsmith. Nominations: Academy Awards '81: Best Sound. *WAR*

The Outlaw 🎬🎬 1943 Hughes's variation on the saga of Billy the Kid, which spends more time on Billy's relationship with girlfriend Rio than the climactic showdown with Pat Garrett. The famous Russell vehicle isn't as steamy as it must have seemed to viewers of the day, but the brouhaha around it served to keep it on the shelf for six years. Also available colorized. 123m/B VHS, Beta, LV. Jane Russell, Jack Beutel, Walter Huston, Thomas Mitchell; **D:** Howard Hughes. *CNG, MRV, NOS*

The Outlaw and His Wife 🎬🎬½ 1917 An early silent film about a farmer, accused of a petty crime, who flees with his wife into the mountains to escape the police. This powerful drama was a breakthrough film for the early Swedish movie industry. 73m/B VHS, Beta, LV. SW Victor Sjostrom, Edith Erastoff; **D:** Victor Sjostrom. *KIV, FCT*

The Outlaw Bikers—Gang Wars 🎬 1970 The original road warriors take it to the streets as rival biker gangs square off. 90m/C VHS, Beta. Clancy Syrko, Des Roberts, King John III, Linda Jackson; **D:** Lawrence Merrick. *PSM*

Outlaw Blues 🎬🎬 1977 (PG) An ex-convict becomes a national folk hero when he sets out to reclaim his stolen hit song about prison life. St. James is charming in her first major movie role. A grab bag of action, drama, and tongue-in-cheek humor. 101m/C VHS, Beta. Peter Fonda, Susan St. James, Johnny Crawford, Michael Lerner, James Callahan; **D:** Richard T. Heffron; **M:** Charles Bernstein. *WAR*

Outlaw Country 🎬🎬½ 1949 LaRue has a dual role as the marshal who is after a band of counterfeiters and an outlaw who's part of the gang. 72m/B VHS. Lash LaRue, Al "Fuzzy" St. John, House Peters Jr., Ted Adams, Dan White, Steve Dunhill; **D:** Ray Taylor. *GPV*

The Outlaw Deputy 🎬½ 1935 The law-abiding McCoy is an outlaw! It's really a mistake and Lane helps him clear his name. Based on the story "King of Cactusville" by Johnston McCulley. 55m/B VHS. Tim McCoy, Nora Lane, Bud Osborne, Si Jenks, George Offerman Jr.; **D:** Otto Brower. *GPV*

Outlaw Express 🎬½ 1938 After the annexing of California, a U.S. marshall is sent to stop a gang of outlaws who have been raiding Spanish landowners. 57m/B VHS, Beta. Bob Baker, Cecilia Callejo, Leroy Mason, Don Barclay, Carleton Young; **D:** George Waggner. *DVT*

Outlaw Force 🎬 1987 (R) A Vietnam veteran country singer tracks down the vicious rednecks that kidnapped his daughter and raped and killed his wife. Heavener did all the work in this low-budget, low-quality take-off on "Death Wish." 95m/C VHS, Beta. David Heavener, Frank Stallone, Paul Smith, Robert Bjorklund, Devin Dunsworth; **D:** David Heavener. *TWE*

Outlaw Fury 🎬½ 1950 Another Shamrock Ellison epic, this time dealing with a coward proving himself by killing the bad guys. 55m/B VHS, Beta, LV. James Ellison, Russell Hayden. *NO*

Outlaw Gang 🎬½ 1949 A marshal investigates a rash of rancher killings, leading to a conflict between Indians and local land and water companies. 59m/B VHS, Beta, LV. Donald (Don "Red") Barry, Robert Lowery, Betty Adams. *NO*

The Outlaw Josey Wales 🎬🎬🎬½ 1976 (PG) Eastwood plays a farmer with a motive for revenge—his family was killed and for years he was betrayed and hunted. His desire to play the lone killer is, however, tempered by his need for family and friends. He kills plenty, but in the end finds happiness. Considered one of the last great Westerns, with many superb performances. Eastwood took over directorial chores during filming from Kaufman, who co-scripted. Adapted from "Gone To Texas" by Forest Carter. 135m/C VHS, Beta, LV. Clint Eastwood, Chief Dan George, Sondra Locke, Matt Clark, John Vernon, Bill McKinney, Sam Bottoms; **D:** Clint Eastwood; **W:** Philip Kaufman; **C:** Bruce Surtees. Nominations: Academy Awards '76: Best Original Score. *WAR, TLF*

Outlaw Justice 🎬🎬 1932 Worn oater plot has our hero infiltrating a gang of outlaws to bring them to justice and save the heroine. 56m/C VHS, Beta. Jack Hoxie, Dorothy Gulliver, Donald Keith, Kermit Maynard, Charles "Blackie" King, Tom London; **D:** Armand Schaefer. *GPV*

Outlaw of Gor 🎬½ 1987 (PG) Once again, the mild professor is transported to Gor, where he has new, improved, bloody adventures. Lots of sword-play, but no magic. Sequel to "Gor." From the novel by John Norman. 89m/C VHS, Beta, Closed Caption. Rebecca Ferratti, Urbano Barberini, Jack Palance, Donna Denton; **D:** John Cardos; **W:** R.J. Marx. *WAR*

Outlaw of the Plains 🎬 1946 Another of Crabbe's cowboy pictures in which he played hero Billy Carson, now bailing his trouble-prone sidekick out of a land swindle. Very plain indeed. 56m/B VHS. Buster Crabbe, Al "Fuzzy" St. John, Patti McCarty, Charles "Blackie" King, Karl Hackett, John Cason, Bud Osborne, Budd Buster, Charles "Slim" Whitaker; **D:** Sam Newfield. *NOS*

Outlaw Riders 🎬 1972 (PG) Three outlaw bikers take it on the lam after committing a series of disastrous bank robberies. 84m/C VHS, Beta. Sonny West, Darlene Duralia, Bambi Allen, Bill Bonner; **D:** Tony Houston. *NO*

Outlaw Roundup 🎬 1944 The Texas Rangers battle an outlaw gang. Guess who wins. 51m/B VHS, Beta. Tex O'Brien, James Newill, Guy Wilkerson, Helen Chapman, Jack Ingram, I. Stanford Jolley; **D:** Harry Fraser. *NOS, MRV, VDM*

Outlaw Rule 🎬½ 1936 Standard action-packed western adventure pitting outlaws against the law of the West. 61m/B VHS, Beta. Reb Russell, Betty Mack, Yakima Canutt, Jack Rockwell, John McGuire, Alan Bridge; **D:** S. Roy Luby. *NOS, VCN, HEG*

The Outlaw Tamer 🎬 1933 Even though Chandler is on the run he still helps capture some horse thieves. 56m/B VHS, Beta. Lane Chandler, J.P. McGowan, Janet Morgan, George "Gabby" Hayes; **D:** J.P. McGowan. *GPV, VCN*

Outlaw Trail 🎬½ 1944 The Trail Blazers put an end to a counterfeiter's evil ways. 53m/B VHS, Beta. Hoot Gibson, Bob Steele, Chief Thundercloud, Jennifer Holt, Cy Kendall; **D:** Robert Emmett Tansey. *NOS, DVT*

Outlaw Women 🎬 1952 A western town is run by a woman who won't let male outlaws in—until one wins her heart. 76m/C VHS, Beta. Marie Windsor, Jackie Coogan, Carla Balenda; **D:** Sam Newfield. *NO*

The Outlaws is Coming! 🎬🎬½ 1965 Three magazine staffers (Larry, Moe, and Curly Joe) and their editor (West) encounter Wyatt Earp, Wild Bill Hickock, Jesse James, and Annie Oakley when they journey out West to save the buffalo. Last, and one of the best, of the Three Stooges feature films. 90m/B VHS. Moe Howard, Larry Fine, Joe DeRita, Adam West, Nancy Kovack, Emil Sitka, Henry Gibson; **D:** Norman Maurer. *COL*

Outlaws of Sonora 🎬½ 1938 A man transports money to a neighboring town while his outlaw double tries to steal it from him. 58m/B VHS. Bob Livingston, Ray Corrigan, Max Terhune, Jack Mulhall, Otis Harlan; **D:** George Sherman. *NOS, DVT*

Outlaws of the Desert 🎬½ 1941 Having run out of bad guys in the Old West, Hoppy and his pals head to Arabia to buy some horses. Once there, they get involved in a kidnapping. Russell Hayden is replaced as Hoppy's sidekick by Brad King. Duncan ("The Cisco Kid") Renaldo plays the sheik. 66m/B VHS. William Boyd, Brad King, Andy Clyde, Forrest Stanley, Jean Phillips, Duncan Renaldo, George Lewis; **D:** Howard Bretherton. *NOS*

Outlaws of the Range 🎬½ 1936 Action western featuring outlaws who terrorize the countryside. 60m/B VHS, Beta. Bill Cody, Catherine Cotter, William McCall, Gordon Griffith; **D:** Al(bert) Herman. *VCN*

Outlaw's Paradise 🎬🎬 1939 Cowboy hero McCoy plays not only a lawman out to catch mail thieves, but also the chief outlaw he's hunting! That's one way to keep the budget low. 62m/B VHS. Tim McCoy, Benny Corbett, Joan Barclay, Ted Adams, Forrest Taylor, Bob Terry; **D:** Sam Newfield. *NOS, LOO, RXM*

Outpost in Morocco 🎬½ 1949 A desert soldier is sent to quiet the restless natives and falls for the rebel leader's daughter. The good guys win, but the love interest is sacrificed. Glory before love boys, and damn the story. 92m/B VHS. George Raft, Marie Windsor, Akim Tamiroff, John Litel, Eduard Franz; **D:** Robert Florey. *NOS, MRV, MGM*

Outrage! 🎬🎬½ 1986 An upstanding citizen guns down his daughter's killer and turns himself in to police. His ambitious lawyer fights an open-and-shut homicide case with both fair and foul means. Not a shootout like the cassette box suggests, but an okay courtroom drama attacking excesses of the legal system. From a novel by Henry Denker, made for TV by producer Irwin Allen. 96m/C VHS. Robert Preston, Beau Bridges, Anthony Newley, Mel Ferrer, Burgess Meredith, Linda Purl, William Allen Young; **D:** Walter Grauman. *THV*

Outrage 🎬 *Dispara* 1993 (R) Journalist Marco Vallez's (Banderas) latest assignment is a story about a traveling circus. Bored with the usual acts, he's intrigued by equestrian/sharpshooter Anna (Neri) and asks her for an interview, which leads to passion. While Marco is on assignment in Barcelona, Anna is attacked and raped in her trailer. Rather than calling the police, Anna decides to take her own revenge. Spanish with subtitles or dubbed.**CW:** Violence, including a brutal rape scene; sexuality and language. 108m/C VHS. SP Antonio Banderas, Francesca Neri; **D:** Carlos Saura. *APX*

Outrageous! 🎬🎬🎬 1977 (R) An offbeat, low-budget comedy about the strange relationship between a gay female impersonator and his pregnant schizophrenic friend. The pair end up in New York, where they feel right at home. Russell's impersonations of female film stars earned him the best actor prize at the Berlin Film Festival. 100m/C VHS, Beta. CA Craig Russell, Hollis McLaren, Richard Easley, Allan Moyle, Helen Shaver; **D:** Richard Benner. *COL*

Outrageous Fortune 🎬🎬 1987 (R) Two would-be actresses - one prim and innocent and one wildly trampy - chase after the same two-timing boyfriend and get involved in a dangerous CIA plot surrounding a deadly bacteria. Tired plot. Mediocre acting and formula jokes, but somehow still funny. Disney's first foray into comedy for grownups. 112m/C VHS, Beta, LV, Closed Caption. Shelley Long, Bette Midler, George Carlin, Peter Coyote; *D:* Arthur Hiller; *W:* Leslie Dixon; *M:* Alan Silvestri. TOU

Outside Chance 🎬 1978 A soapy, sanitized remake of Mimieux's film, "Jackson County Jail," wherein an innocent woman is persecuted in a small Southern jail. Made for television. 92m/C VHS, Beta. Yvette Mimieux, Royce D. Applegate; *D:* Michael Miller. NLC

Outside Chance of Maximillian Glick 🎬🎬 1988 (G) A sentimental Canadian comedy about a boy's dreams and his tradition-bound Jewish family. 94m/C VHS, Beta. CA Noam Zylberman, Fairuza Balk, Saul Rubinek; *D:* Allan Goldstein; *C:* Ian Elkin. Toronto-City Award '88: Best Canadian Feature Film. HMD

The Outside Man 🎬🎬 *Un Homme Est Mort* 1973 (PG) A French hit man is called to Los Angeles to knock off a crime boss, which he does. But then an American hit man is hired to do in the Frenchman. The climactic showdown is set around the crime boss' body, which happens to be embalmed in a sitting position. Decidely offbeat. 104m/C VHS. FR Jean-Louis Trintignant, Roy Scheider, Ann-Margret, Angie Dickinson, Georgia Engel, Carlo De Meyo, Umberto Orsini, Ted de Corsia, Felice Orlandi, John Hillerman; *D:* Jacques Deray. MGM

Outside the Law 🎬🎬 1921 Lon Chaney plays dual roles of the underworld hood in "Black Mike Sylva," and a Chinese servant in "Ah Wing." Silent. 77m/B VHS. Lon Chaney Sr., Priscilla Dean, Ralph Lewis, Wheeler Oakman; *D:* Tod Browning. KIV, CCB, VYY

Outside the Law 🎬🎬 1995 (R) Maverick cop Brad Kingsbury (Bradley) crosses the line when he falls for luscious Tanya Borgman (Thomson), who's the prime suspect in a murder investigation. Also available unrated. 94m/C VHS, LV, Closed Caption. David Bradley, Anna Thomson, Ashley Laurence; *D:* Boaz Davidson; *W:* Dennis Dimster Denk; *C:* Avi Karpik; *M:* Blake Leyh. TTC, NLC, IME

The Outsiders 🎬🎬½ 1983 (PG) Based on the popular S.E. Hinton book, the story of a teen gang from the wrong side of the tracks and their conflicts with society and each other. Melodramatic and over-done, but teen-agers still love the story. Good soundtrack and cast ripples with up and coming stars. Followed by a television series. Coppola adapted another Hinton novel the same year, "Rumble Fish." 91m/C VHS, Beta, LV. C. Thomas Howell, Matt Dillon, Ralph Macchio, Patrick Swayze, Diane Lane, Tom Cruise, Emilio Estevez, Rob Lowe, Tom Waits, Leif Garrett; *D:* Francis Ford Coppola; *W:* Kathleen Rowell; *C:* Stephen Burum; *M:* Carmine Coppola. WAR

Outtakes 🎬½ 1985 (R) A piecemeal compilation of comedy skits, concentrating on sex and genre parody. 85m/C VHS, Beta. Forrest Tucker, Bobbi Wexler, Joleen Lutz; *D:* Jack M. Sell. NO

The Oval Portrait 🎬½ 1988 An adaptation of the Edgar Allan Poe suspense tale about a Civil War-era maiden, her illicit love for a Confederate soldier and her eventual death. 89m/C VHS, Beta. Giselle MacKenzie, Barry Coe; *D:* Regelio A. Gonzalez Jr. NO

Over Indulgence 🎬🎬 1987 (R) A young woman witnesses a murder in an affluent society in British East Africa. 95m/C VHS, Beta. Denholm Elliott, Holly Aird, Michael Byrne, Kathryn Pogson; *D:* Ross Devenish. MCG

Over the Brooklyn Bridge 🎬🎬 *My Darling Shiksa* 1983 (R) A young Jewish man (Gould) must give up his Catholic girlfriend (Hemingway) in order to get his uncle (Caesar) to lend him the money he needs to buy a restaurant in Manhattan. Nowhere near as funny as it should be, and potentially offensive to boot. 100m/C VHS, Beta. Elliott Gould, Sid Caesar, Shelley Winters, Margaux Hemingway, Carol Kane, Burt Young; *D:* Menahem Golan; *M:* Pino Donaggio. MGM

Over the Edge 🎬🎬🎬½ 1979 (PG) The music of Cheap Trick, The Cars, and The Ramones highlights this realistic tale of alienated suburban youth on the rampage. Dillon makes his screen debut in this updated, well-done "Rebel Without a Cause." Shelved for several years, the movie was finally released after Dillon made it big. Sleeper with excellent direction and dialogue. 91m/C VHS, Beta. Michael Kramer, Matt Dillon, Pamela Ludwig, Vincent Spano; *D:* Jonathan Kaplan. WAR

Over the Hill 🎬🎬½ 1993 (PG) Dukakis stars as Alma, an eccentric widow who decides to leave her well-meaning son's restrictive home in Maine to visit her estranged daughter Elizabeth in Sydney, Australia. Embarassed by her peculiarities Elizabeth arranges a holiday away but Mom has her own plans. She wants to "loop the loop," and make a complete circuit around the Australian continent. Soon Alma is on the road, meeting fellow eccentrics and experiencing a variety of adventures. 102m/C VHS, LV, Closed Caption. Olympia Dukakis, Sigrid Thornton, Derek Fowlds, Pippa Grandison; *D:* George Miller; *W:* Robert Caswell; *C:* David Connell. NLC, COL, IME

Over the Summer 🎬🎬½ 1985 Strong drama about a troubled teen who escapes the city for a summer with her grandparents. No cliches here—the grandfather lusts after the granddaughter and eventually kills himself, and problems remain at the end. Intelligent and entertaining, though marred by needless nude scenes. 97m/C VHS, Beta. Laura Hunt, Johnson West, Catherine Williams, David Romero; *D:* Teresa Sparks. LIV, VES

Over the Top 🎬½ 1986 (PG) The film that started a nationwide arm-wrestling craze. A slow-witted trucker decides the only way he can retain custody of his estranged son, as well as win the boy's respect, is by winning a big arm-wrestling competition. Stallone is an expert at grinding these movies out by now, and the kid (General Hospital's Mikey) is all right, but the end result is boredom, as it should be with an arm-wrestling epic. 94m/C VHS, Beta, LV, Closed Caption. Sylvester Stallone, Susan Blakely, Robert Loggia, David Mendenhall; *D:* Menahem Golan; *W:* Sylvester Stallone, Gary Conway, Stirling Silliphant. Golden Raspberry Awards '87: Worst Supporting Actor (Mendenhall), Worst New Star (Mendenhall). WAR

Over the Wire 🎬½ 1995 Telephone lineman accidentally overhears a conversation where a woman hires a hitman to kill her sister. He finds out that the sisters live together and tries to figure out just who the target is before it's too late (of course, he has to seduce both of them to accomplish this). 90m/C VHS. Shauna O'Brien, Griffin Drew, Tim Abell. TRI

Overboard 🎬🎬 1987 (PG) A wealthy, spoiled woman falls off of her yacht and into the arms of a low-class carpenter who picks her up and convinces her she is in fact his wife, and mother to his four brats. Just when she learns to like her life, the tables are turned again. Even though it's all been done before, you can't help but laugh at the screwy gags. 112m/C VHS, Closed Caption. Goldie Hawn, Kurt Russell, Katherine Helmond, Roddy McDowall, Edward Herrmann; *D:* Garry Marshall; *W:* Leslie Dixon; *C:* John A. Alonzo; *M:* Alan Silvestri. MGM, HMV, FOX

The Overcoat 🎬🎬🎬½ 1959 An adaptation of Nikolai Gogol's classic story about the dehumanizing life endured in 20th-century bureaucracy. All a menial civil servant wants is a new overcoat. When he finally gets one, this treasured article not only keeps him warm but makes him feel self-satisfied as well. In Russian with English subtitles. 93m/B VHS, Beta. RU Rolan Bykov; *D:* Alexei Batalov. National Board of Review Awards '65: 5 Best Foreign Films of the Year. HTV

Overdrawn at the Memory Bank 🎬🎬 1983 In a futuristic tyranny, a romantic rebel becomes somehow fused with the spirit of Humphrey Bogart in the milieu of "Casablanca," and lives out a cliched version of the film character's adventures. 84m/C VHS, Beta. Raul Julia, Linda Griffiths; *D:* Douglas Williams. VTR, NWV

Overexposed 🎬🎬 1990 (R) All the wackos love the sultry soap star Oxenburg; one is a killer. Eighty minutes and a bunch of bodies later the killer is unmasked. Plenty of suspense and some original gore. Based on the true stories of fans who stalk celebrities. 83m/C VHS. Catherine Oxenberg, David Naughton, Jennifer Edwards, Karen Black; *D:* Larry Brand; *W:* Larry Brand. MGM

Overkill 🎬 1986 (R) A detective and the vengeance-minded brother of a dead Japanese-American fight back against the controlling Yakuza in Little Tokyo. 81m/C Beta. Steve Rally, John Nishio, Laura Burkett, Roy Summerset; *D:* Ulli Lommel. NO

Overland Mail 1941 Fifteen episodes of the vintage serial filled with western action. 225m/B VHS, Beta. Lon Chaney Jr., Helen Parrish. NOS, VCN, MLB

Overland Stage Raiders 🎬🎬🎬 1938 The "Three Mesquiteers" ride again, this time to guard a Greyhound bus! The trio must protect a shipment of gold from hijackers. This is the last film for Brooks, who had starred in the German masterpiece "Pandora's Box" in 1929. 55m/B VHS. John Wayne, Ray Corrigan, Max Terhune, Louise Brooks, John Archer, Frank LaRue, Yakima Canutt; *D:* George Sherman. REP, NOS

Overlanders 🎬🎬🎬 1946 The Japanese may invade, but rather than kill 1,000 head of cattle, these Aussies drive the huge herd across the continent, facing danger along the way. Beautifully photographed, featuring the "Australian Gary Cooper" and a stampede scene to challenge "Dances with Wolves." 91m/B VHS, Beta. AU Chips Rafferty, Daphne Campbell, Jean Blue, John Nugent Hayward; *D:* Harry Watt. NOS, DVT, HEG

Overnight Sensation 🎬🎬 1983 A modern adaptation of the W. Somerset Maugham story about a traditional marriage being tested by the wife's sudden literary success. 30m/C VHS, Beta. Louise Fletcher, Robert Loggia, Shari Belafonte. PYR

Overseas: Three Women with Man Trouble 🎬🎬 1990 Three beautiful sisters in French colonial Algeria surround themselves in a life of luxury to avoid the incredible social changes going on around them. Each sister has a different perspective on her life, and the perspectives are graphically revealed. Lush photography set in the Mediterranean. In French with English subtitles. 96m/C VHS. FR Nicole Garcia, Marianne Basler, Philippe Galland, Pierre Doris, Brigitte Rouan; *D:* Brigitte Rouan; *W:* Brigitte Rouan. Cannes Film Festival '90: Best Film. FXL, BTV, BFV

Overthrow 🎬½ 1982 (R) American sportswriter finds himself caught up in violence and intrigue in Buenos Aires. 90m/C VHS, Beta. John Phillip Law, Lewis Van Bergen, Roger Wilson; *D:* Larry Ludman. IMP, HHE, VTR

Overture 1975 An episode of "The Persuaders." Brett and Danny are tricked into helping a retired judge. This adventure leads them to the Mediterranean and a gorgeous gal. 52m/C VHS. GB Roger Moore, Tony Curtis. NO

Overture to Glory 🎬🎬½ *Der Vilner Shtot Khazn* 1940 A Jewish cantor longs for the world of opera. He leaves his wife and son to fulfill his passion, but eventually he loses his voice and humbly returns home on Yom Kippur, the Jewish Day of Atonement. He learns that his son has passed away. Grief-stricken, he goes to the synagogue. There, the cantor regains his voice as he performs Kol Nidre in a passionate and melodious rendering. In Yiddish with English subtitles. 85m/B VHS, Beta. Helen Beverly, Florence Weiss. ERG, TPV

The Owl and the Pussycat 🐾🐾🐾

1970 (PG) Nerdy author gets the neighborhood hooker evicted from her apartment. She returns the favor, and the pair hit the street—and the sack—in Buck Henry's hilarious adaptation of the Broadway play. Streisand's first non-singing role. **96m/C VHS, Beta, LV.** Barbra Streisand, George Segal, Robert Klein, Allen (Goorwitz) Garfield; **D:** Herbert Ross; **W:** Buck Henry; **C:** Harry Stradling, Andrew Laszlo. *GKK*

The Ox 🐾🐾½

1991 Slow-moving, simple tale, set in rural Sweden in the 1860's during a famine. Desperate to feed his family a tenant farmer kills his employer's ox. Consumed by guilt, the man is quickly found out and sentenced to life imprisonment. Pardoned after six years, the farmer returns to his family, to find out his wife has survived by doing things he finds difficult to forgive. Based on a true story. Directorial debut of Nykvist, the longtime cinematographer for Ingmar Bergman, well displays his familiarity with composition and lighting to heighten mood. In Swedish with English subtitles. **93m/C VHS.** *SW* Stellan Skarsgard, Ewa Froling, Lennart Hjulstrom, Max von Sydow, Liv Ullmann, Bjorn Granath, Erland Josephson; **D:** Sven Nykvist; **W:** Lasse Summanen, Sven Nykvist. Nominations: Academy Awards '91: Best Foreign Language Film. *ACA, ICA, FCT*

The Ox-Bow Incident 🐾🐾🐾🐾 *Strange Incident*

1943 A popular rancher is murdered, and a mob of angry townspeople can't wait for the sheriff to find the killers. They hang the young man, despite the protests of Fonda, a cowboy with a conscience. Excellent study of mob mentality with strong individual characterizations. A brilliant western based on a true story by Walter Van Tilburg Clark. Also see "Twelve Angry Men"—less tragic but just as moving. **75m/B VHS, Beta, LV, Closed Caption.** Henry Fonda, Harry (Henry) Morgan, Dana Andrews, Anthony Quinn, Frank Conroy, Harry Davenport, Jane Darwell, William Eythe, Mary Beth Hughes; **D:** William A. Wellman; **W:** Lamar Trotti; **C:** Arthur C. Miller; **M:** Cyril Mockridge. National Board of Review Awards '43: 10 Best Films of the Year, Best Director (Wellman); Nominations: Academy Awards '43: Best Picture. *FOX*

Oxford Blues 🐾🐾

1984 (PG-13) An American finagles his way into England's Oxford University and onto the rowing team in pursuit of the girl of his dreams. Beautiful scenery, but the plot is wafer-thin. Remake of "Yank at Oxford." **98m/C VHS, Beta, LV, Closed Caption.** Rob Lowe, Ally Sheedy, Amanda Pays, Julian Sands, Michael Gough, Gail Strickland, Cary Elwes; **D:** Robert Boris; **W:** Robert Boris; **M:** John Du Prez. *FOX*

Pace That Kills 🐾

1928 An anti-drug cautionary drama from the Roaring '20s, one of many now marketed on cassette as campy fun. Beware, though, a little bit of this stuff goes a long way. A young man goes to the big city to find his missing sister and winds up hooked on heroin. **87m/B VHS, Beta, 8mm.** Owen Gorin, Virginia Roye, Florence Turner. *GVV*

Pacific Heights 🐾🐾🐾

1990 (R) Young San Francisco couple takes on mammoth mortgage assuming tenants will write their ticket to the American dream, but psychopathic tenant Keaton moves in downstairs and redecorates. He won't pay the rent and he won't leave. Creepy psycho-thriller has lapses but builds to effective climax. It's a treat to watch mother/daughter actresses Hedren and Griffith work together. Watch for D'Angelo as Keaton's lover. **CW:** Adult situations; language, brief nudity, and violence. **103m/C VHS, LV, Closed Caption.** Melanie Griffith, Matthew Modine, Michael Keaton, Mako, Nobu McCarthy, Laurie Metcalf, Carl Lumbly, Dorian Harewood, Luca Bercovici, Tippi Hedren, Sheila McCarthy, Dan Hedaya, Beverly D'Angelo, Nicholas Pryor, Miriam Margolyes; **D:** John Schlesinger; **W:** Daniel Pyne; **M:** Hans Zimmer. *FOX*

Pacific Inferno 🐾🐾

1985 During WWII, American POWs endeavor to break out of a Japanese prison camp in the Philippines. Their goal is to prevent their captors from retrieving millions of dollars worth of sunken U.S. gold. Made for cable television. **90m/C VHS, Beta.** Jim Brown, Richard Jaeckel, Tim Brown; **D:** Rolf Bayer. *NO*

The Pack 🐾🐾½ *The Long, Dark Night*

1977 (R) A group of dogs become wild when left on a resort island. A marine biologist leads the humans who fight to keep the dogs from using vacationers as chew toys. Fine production valves keep it from going to the dogs. Made with the approval of the American Humane Society who helped with the treatment of stage hands. **99m/C VHS, Beta.** Joe Don Baker, Hope Alexander-Willis, R.G. Armstrong, Richard B. Shull; **D:** Robert Clouse; **W:** Robert Clouse. *WAR*

The P.A.C.K. 🐾🐾

1996 The P.A.C.K. are alien warriors who mistakenly land on earth, which doesn't prevent them from killing all but one of a team of government agents sent to investigate. Now lone agent Rachel (Bergman) reluctantly teams up with a second alien who's been sent to destroy the P.A.C.K. **90m/C VHS.** Sandahl Bergman, Ted Prior, Red West. *SWI*

Pack Up Your Troubles 🐾🐾½ *We're In the Army Now*

1932 Laurel and Hardy make good on a promise to help find the grandfather of a girl whose father was killed in WWI. All they know is the grandfather's last name though—Smith. Wholesome R and R. **68m/B VHS, Beta.** Stan Laurel, Oliver Hardy, James Finlayson, Jacquie Lyn; **D:** George Marshall. *MED, FCT, MLB*

The Package 🐾🐾½

1989 (R) An espionage thriller about an army sergeant who loses the prisoner he escorts into the U.S. When he tries to track him down, he uncovers a military plot to start WWIII. Hackman is believable in his role as the sergeant. **108m/C VHS, Beta, LV, Closed Caption.** Gene Hackman, Tommy Lee Jones, Joanna Cassidy, Dennis Franz, Pam Grier, John Heard, Reni Santoni, Thalmus Rasulala, Ike Pappas, Kevin Crowley; **D:** Andrew Davis; **W:** John Bishop; **M:** James Newton Howard. *ORI*

Packin' It In 🐾🐾

1983 A Los Angeles family is in for a rude awakening when they leave the city for a quieter life in the Oregon woods. There they encounter a band of survivalists with semi-comedic results. **92m/C VHS, Beta.** Richard Benjamin, Paula Prentiss, Molly Ringwald, Tony Roberts, Andrea Marcovicci; **D:** Jud Taylor. *NO*

Paco 🐾½

1975 (G) A young, South American boy heads for the city, where he meets his uncle. He discovers his uncle is the leader of a gang of youthful thieves. Predictable and sluggish. **89m/C VHS, Beta.** Jose Ferrer, Panchito Gomez, Allen (Goorwitz) Garfield, Pernell Roberts, Andre Marquis; **D:** Robert Vincent O'Neil. *GHV*

Paddy 🐾🐾 *Goodbye to the Hill*

1970 (PG) A young Irish lad realizes his sexual potential by seducing every woman he can find. Freudians will have a field day. **97m/C VHS, Beta.** *IR* Des Cave, Milo O'Shea, Darbnia Molloy, Peggy Cass; **D:** Daniel Haller. *NO*

Padre Nuestro 🐾🐾½

1985 Religious satire about a dying priest who wishes to reunite his family, who include an atheist brother, a mistress from his youth, and his illegitimate daughter who's a notorious prostitute. In Spanish with English subtitles. **91m/C VHS.** *SP* Fernando Rey, Francesco Rabal, Victoria Abril; **D:** Francisco Regueiro. *CVC, FCT*

Padre Padrone 🐾🐾🐾½ *Father Master; My Father, My Master*

1977 The much acclaimed adaptation of the Gavino Ledda autobiography about his youth in agrarian Sardinia with a brutal, tyrannical father. Eventually he overcomes his handicaps, breaks the destructive emotional ties to his father and successfully attends college. Highly regarded although low budget; in an Italian dialect (Sardinian) with English subtitles. **113m/C VHS, Beta.** *IT* Omero Antonutti, Saverio Marconi, Marcella Michelangeli, Fabrizio Forte; **D:** Paolo Taviani, Vittorio Taviani; **W:** Paolo Taviani, Vittorio Taviani; **C:** Mario Masini; **M:** Egisto Macchi. Cannes Film Festival '77: Best Film. *COL*

Pagan Island 🐾

1960 A man is stranded on a desert island with 30 beautiful girls who tie him up and abandon him. Maki, to be sacrificed by the rest, saves Dew and they fall in love. They go off in search of a reputed treasure, which they find, but at a deadly cost. **67m/B VHS.** Eddie Dew, Nani Maka; **D:** Barry Mahon; **W:** Clelle Mahon. *SMW, TPV*

Pagan Love Song 🐾🐾

1950 A dull musical which finds Keel in Tahiti taking over his uncle's coconut plantation and falling in love with Williams. Surprise! Williams performs one of her famous water ballets, which is the only saving grace in this lifeless movie. ♫The House of Singing Bamboo; Singing in the Sun; Etiquette; Why is Love So Crazy; Tahiti; The Sea of the Moon; Pagan Love Song; Coconut Milk. **76m/C VHS.** Esther Williams, Howard Keel, Minna Gombell, Rita Moreno; **D:** Robert Alton. *MGM*

The Pagemaster 🐾½

1994 (G) Timid Richard (Macauley) is basically scared of his own shadow but, during a storm, he's forced to take refuge in a mysterious library with an even odder librarian, Mr. Dewey (Lloyd). Richard's intrigued by the library's mural, which turns out to be the doorway to an animated universe where the wizardlike Pagemaster (voiced by Lloyd) and other literary characters help Richard discover his strengths and overcome his fears. Mildly amusing but kids may not know who the characters refer to unless they're readers (a good intro, perhaps?) **76m/C VHS, LV.** Macaulay Culkin, Christopher Lloyd, Ed Begley Jr., Mel Harris; **D:** Joe Johnston, Maurice Hunt; **W:** David Casci, David Kirschner, Ernie Contreras; **M:** James Horner; **V:** Christopher Lloyd, Whoopi Goldberg, Patrick Stewart, Frank Welker, Leonard Nimoy. Nominations: Golden Raspberry Awards '94: Worst Actor (Culkin). *FXV*

Paid to Kill 🐾🐾 *Five Days*

1954 A failing businessman hires a thug to kill him in order to leave his family insurance money, but when the business picks up, he can't contact the thug to cancel the contract. The actors' lack of talent is matched only by the characters' lack of motivation. **71m/B VHS, Beta, LV.** *GB* Dane Clark, Paul Carpenter, Thea Gregory; **D:** Montgomery Tully. *RXM*

Pain in the A— 🐾🐾🐾

1977 (PG) A hit man helps a suicidal shirt salesman solve his marital problems in this black comedy that was later Americanized as "Buddy, Buddy." Not for all tastes, but has acquired a reputation for its dark wit. In French with English subtitles. **90m/C VHS, Beta.** *FR* Lino Ventura, Jacques Brel, Caroline Cellier; **D:** Edouard Molinaro; **W:** Francis Veber, Edouard Molinaro. *FRF, COL*

Paint It Black 🐾🐾½

1989 (R) A violent/steamy mystery and action flick from the director of "River's Edge," in which a young man from the silver-spoon set develops a fascination for an artist. **101m/C VHS, Beta, LV.** Sally Kirkland, Rick Rossovich, Martin Landau, Doug Savant, Peter Frechette, Julie Carmen, Jason Bernard, Monique Van De Ven; **D:** Tim Hunter. *LIV, VES*

The Paint Job 🐾🐾

1993 (R) Wesley, the lonely house painter, falls in love with his neighbor, Margaret. Unfortunately, Margaret is married—to Wesley's boss Willy. Margaret is drawn to Wesley and bored with Willy. But one of the men turns out to be a serial killer. What's a gal in love to do? **90m/C VHS.** Will Patton, Bebe Neuwirth, Robert Pastorelli; **D:** Micheal Taav; **W:** Micheal Taav; **M:** John Wesley Harding. *COL*

Paint Your Wagon 🐾🐾½

1969 (PG) Big-budget western musical-comedy about a gold mining boom town, and two prospectors sharing the same Mormon wife complete with a classic Lerner and Lowe score. Marvin chews up the sagebrush and Eastwood attempts to sing, although Seberg was mercifully dubbed. Overlong, with patches of interest, pretty songs, and plenty of panoramic scenery. Adapted from the L & L play. ♫I Talk To the Trees; I Still See Elisa; I'm On My Way; Hand Me Down That Can O' Beans; Whoop-Ti-Ay; They Call the Wind Maria; There's a Coach Comin' In; Wandrin' Star; Best Things. **164m/C VHS, Beta, LV.** Lee Marvin, Clint Eastwood, Jean Seberg, Harve Presnell; **D:** Joshua Logan; **W:** Paddy Chayefsky; **M:** Frederick Loewe, Andre Previn, Alan Jay Lerner. Nominations: Academy Awards '69: Scoring of a Musical. *PAR*

Painted Desert 🐾 1931 Gable's first film role of any consequence came in this early sound western. Gable plays a villain opposite "good guy" William Boyd. 80m/B VHS, Beta. William Boyd, Helen Twelvetrees, George O'Brien, Clark Gable, William Farnum; *D:* Howard Higgin. NOS, MRV, HHT

Painted Hero 🐾½ 1995 (R) Rodeo clown Yoakum has to watch out for more than rampaging bulls when he returns to Waco, where he's accused of murder and reunites with the mother of his dead son.*CW:* Language, some sexuality and violence. 105m/C VHS, Closed Caption. Dwight Yoakam, Bo Hopkins, Cindy Pickett, Michelle Joyner; *D:* Terry Benedict. CAF

The Painted Hills 🐾½ 1951 (G) Lassie outsmarts crooked miners and rescues her friends. Surprise, Surprise! Overly sentimental, but action packed and beautifully shot. Lassie's last outing with MGM. 70m/C VHS, Beta. Paul Kelly, Bruce Cowling, Gary Gray, Art Smith, Ann Doran, Lassie; *D:* Harold F. Kress. MGM, BPG, FCT

The Painted Stallion 1937 This 12-chapter serial features a mysterious figure on a painted stallion who attempts to maintain peace between Mexicans and Indians. 212m/B VHS, LV. Ray Corrigan, Hoot Gibson, Duncan Renaldo, Leroy Mason, Yakima Canutt; *D:* William Witney, Ray Taylor. NOS, VDM, REP

The Painted Veil 🐾½ 1934 Adaptation of a W. Somerset Maugham story. Garbo, once again the disillusioned wife turning to the affections of another man, is magnificent, almost eclipsing the weak script. Lost money at the box office, but for Garbo fans, an absolute must. 83m/B VHS, Beta. Greta Garbo, Herbert Marshall, George Brent, Warner Oland, Jean Hersholt; *D:* Richard Boleslawski; *C:* William H. Daniels. MGM, FCT

Pair of Aces 🐾½ 1990 Kristofferson is a Texas Ranger who's on the trail of a serial killer. His only other problem is being saddled with Nelson, a philosophical safecracker who's awaiting trial and in the reluctant cop's custody. Low-key western with good buddy pairing of Nelson and Kristofferson. Made for television. 94m/C VHS, Closed Caption. Willie Nelson, Kris Kristofferson, Rip Torn, Helen Shaver, Jane Cameron, Sonny Carl Davis, Lash La-Rue, Emily Warfield, Michael Marich; *D:* Aaron Lipstadt. WAR

Paisan 🐾🐾🐾 1946 Six episodic tales of life in Italy, several featuring Allied soldiers and nurses during WWII. One of the stories tells of a man who tries to develop a relationship without being able to speak Italian. Another focuses on a young street robber who is confronted by one of his victims. Strong stories that covers a wide range of emotions. In Italian with English subtitles. 115m/B VHS. IT Maria Michi, Carmela Sazio, Gar Moore, William Tubbs, Harriet White, Robert Van Loon, Dale Edmonds, Carla Pisacane, Dots Johnson; *D:* Roberto Rossellini; *W:* Federico Fellini, Roberto Rossellini. National Board of Review Awards '48: 5 Best Foreign Films of the Year, Best Director (Fellini); New York Film Critics Awards '48: Best Foreign Film; Nominations: Academy Awards '49: Best Story & Screenplay. HTV, HHT, CAB

The Pajama Game 🐾🐾🐾½ 1957 A spritely musical about the striking workers of a pajama factory and their plucky negotiator, who falls in love with the boss. Based on the hit Broadway musical, which was based on Richard Bissell's book "Seven and a Half Cents" and adapted for the screen by Bisell and Abbott. Bob Fosse choreographed the dance numbers. ♫I'm Not at All in Love; Small Talk; There Once Was a Man; Steam Heat; Hernando's Highway; Hey There; Once-a-Year Day; Seven and a Half Cents; I'll Never Be Jealous Again. 101m/C VHS, Beta, LV, Closed Caption. Doris Day, John Raitt, Eddie Foy Jr., Reta Shaw, Carol Haney; *D:* Stanley Donen, George Abbott; *C:* Harry Stradling. WAR

Pajama Party 🐾🐾 1964 Followup to "Bikini Beach" takes the party inside in this fourth entry in the popular "Beach Party" series. Plot is up to beach party realism. Funicello is Avalon-less

(although he does have a cameo) so she falls for Martian Kirk instead. He's scouting for an alien invasion, but after he falls into Annette's lap decides to save the planet instead. Typical fluff with the usual beach movie faces present; look for a young Garr as a dancer. Followed by the classic "Beach Blanket Bingo." ♫It's That Kind of Day; There Has to Be a Reason; Where Did I Go Wrong?; Pajama Party; Beach Ball; Among the Young; Stuffed Animal. 82m/C VHS, LV. Tommy Kirk, Annette Funicello, Elsa Lanchester, Harvey Lembeck, Jesse White, Jody McCrea, Donna Loren, Susan Hart, Bobbi Shaw, Cheryl Sweeten, Luree Holmes, Candy Johnson, Dorothy Lamour, Toni Basil, Teri Garr, Ben Lessy; *Cameos:* Buster Keaton, Frankie Avalon, Don Rickles; *D:* Don Weis; *W:* Louis M. Heyward; *C:* Floyd Crosby; *M:* Les Baxter. NO

Pajama Tops 🐾🐾½ 1983 A stage production of the classic French bedroom farce, taped live at the Music Hall Theatre in Toronto, Canada. Includes all the trials of marriage including adultery and deceit. 105m/C VHS. Robert Klein, Susan George, Pia Zadora. NO

Pal Joey 🐾🐾🐾 1957 Musical comedy about an opportunistic singer who courts a wealthy socialite in hopes that she will finance his nightclub. His play results in comedic complications. Stellar choreography, fine direction, and beautiful costumes complement performances headed by Hayworth and Sinatra. Oscar overlooked his pal Joey when awards were handed out. Songs include some of Rodgers and Hart's best. Based on John O'Hara's book and play. ♫Zip; Bewitched, Bothered and Bewildered; I Could Write a Book; That Terrific Rainbow; Whad Do I Care for a Dame?; Happy Hunting Horn; Plant You Now, Dig You Later; Do It the Hard Way; Take Him. 109m/C VHS, Beta, LV. Frank Sinatra, Rita Hayworth, Kim Novak; *D:* George Sidney; *M:* Richard Rodgers, Lorenz Hart. Golden Globe Awards '58: Best Actor—Musical/Comedy (Sinatra); Nominations: Academy Awards '57: Best Art Direction/Set Decoration, Best Costume Design, Best Film Editing, Best Sound. COL

Palais Royale 🐾½ 1988 Craven plays an ad exec who gets involved in the world of gangsters in the late 50s. 100m/C VHS. CA Matt Craven, Kim Cattrall, Dean Stockwell; *D:* Martin Lavut. REP

Pale Blood 🐾½ 1991 (R) A serial killer in Los Angeles is leaving his victims drained of blood. Could it be that a vampire is stalking the modern American metropolis, or is this merely the workings of a bloodthirsty psychopath? 93m/C VHS, LV. George Chakiris, Wings Hauser, Pamela Ludwig, Diana Frank, Darcy Demoss; *D:* V.V. Dachin Hsu. NO

Pale Rider 🐾🐾🐾 1985 (R) A mysterious nameless stranger rides into a small California gold rush town to find himself in the middle of a feud between a mining syndicate and a group of independent prospectors. Christ-like Eastwood evokes comparisons to "Shane." A classical western theme treated well complemented by excellent photography and a rock-solid cast. 116m/C VHS, Beta, LV, 8mm, Closed Caption. Clint Eastwood, Michael Moriarty, Carrie Snodgress, Sydney Penny, Richard Dysart, Richard Kiel, Christopher Penn, John Russell, Charles Hallahan, Douglas McGrath, Fran Ryan; *D:* Clint Eastwood; *W:* Michael Butler, Dennis Shryack; *C:* Bruce Surtees; *M:* Lennie Niehaus. WAR, TLF

The Paleface 🐾🐾🐾 1948 A cowardly dentist becomes a gunslinging hero when Calamity Jane starts aiming for him. A rip-roarin' good time as the comventions of the Old West are turned upside down. Includes the Oscar-winning song "Buttons and Bows." The 1952 sequel is "Son of Paleface." Remade in 1968 as "The Shakiest Gun in the West." ♫Buttons and Bows; Get a Man!; Meetcha 'Round the Corner. 91m/C VHS, Beta, LV. Jane Russell, Bob Hope, Robert Armstrong, Iris Adrian, Robert Watson; *D:* Norman Z. McLeod; *C:* Ray Rennahan. Academy Awards '48: Best Song ("Buttons and Bows"). USH

The Palermo Connection 🐾🐾 1991 (R) Not the action-thriller the cassette box claims, but a cynical study of a crusading N.Y.C. mayoral candidate who honeymoons in Mafia-haunted Sicily and learns that the war on crime has already been lost. Remote adaptation of "To Forget Palermo" by Edmonde Charles-Roux. 100m/C VHS, LV, Closed Caption. James Belushi, Mimi Rogers, Joss Ackland, Philippe Noiret, Vittorio Gassman, Caroline Rosi; *D:* Francesco Rosi; *W:* Gore Vidal. LIV

The Pallbearer 🐾🐾½ 1995 (PG-13) You probably liked this one better when it was called "The Graduate," as this one shares some key plot points with, but lacks the edge and cultural impact of the 1967 classic. Basset-faced Schwimmer plays Tom, who is asked to be a pallbearer for an old high school classmate whom he can't quite remember. He is then seduced by the mother (Hershey) of the deceased, while trying to kindle a romance with the fabulous Julie DeMarco (Paltrow), an old classmate whom can't quite remember him. The spurned older woman then begins to exact her revenge, while Tom tries to figure out how to court Julie while living at home with his mom. Good performances make it watchable.*CW:* Some sexuality and language. 98m/C VHS, LV, Closed Caption. David Schwimmer, Gwyneth Paltrow, Barbara Hershey, Michael Rapaport, Carol Kane, Toni Collette, Michael Vartan; *D:* Matt Reeves; *W:* Matt Reeves, Jason Katims; *C:* Robert Elswit; *M:* Stewart Copeland. TOU

Palm Beach 🐾🐾 1979 The lives of two petty thieves, a runaway, and a private detective intertwine at Palm Beach Down Under. Best appreciated by fans of things Aussie. 90m/C VHS, Beta. AU Bryan Brown, Nat Young, Ken Brown, Amanda Berry; *D:* Albie Thomas. AHV

The Palm Beach Story 🐾🐾🐾 1942 Colbert and McCrea play a married couple who have everything—except money. The wife decides to divorce her current husband, marry a rich man, and finance her former husband's ambitions. She decides the best place to husband-hunt is Palm Beach. A Sturges classic screwball comedy. 88m/B VHS, Beta, LV. Claudette Colbert, Joel McCrea, Mary Astor, Rudy Vallee, William Demarest, Franklin Pangborn; *D:* Preston Sturges; *C:* Victor Milner. USH

Palm Springs Weekend 🐾🐾½ 1963 A busload of love-hungry kids head south and get involved in routine hijinks. Actually shot in Palm Springs with adove average performances by a handful of stars. 100m/C VHS, Beta, LV. Troy Donahue, Ty Hardin, Connie Stevens, Stefanie Powers, Robert Conrad, Jack Weston, Andrew Duggan; *D:* Norman Taurog. WAR

Palombella Rossa 🐾🐾 1989 Political comedy about the fate of Italian communism. When communist politician Michele loses his memory in a car crash, he finds himself trying to reconstruct his life during a game of water polo as well as trying to answer political questions and keep track of the people from his life who randomly appear and disappear. In Italian with English subtitles. 87m/C VHS. IT D: Nanni Moretti. FXL, ORI, FCT

Palooka 🐾🐾½ Joe Palooka; The Great Schnozzle 1934 (G) Based on the comic strip, this film portrays a fast-talking boxing manager and his goofy, lovable protege. The young scrapper fights James Cagney's little brother. Durante sings his classic tune, "Inka-Dinka-Doo," and packs a punch in the lead. A two-fisted comedy with a witty dialogue and fine direction. Not a part of the Palooka series of the 1940s. 86m/B VHS, Beta. Jimmy Durante, Stuart Erwin, Lupe Velez, Robert Armstrong, Thelma Todd, William Cagney; *D:* Ben Stoloff. NOS, RXM, VYY

Palookaville 🐾🐾🐾 1995 (R) Nostalgic comedy of three under-employed friends who take up crime, temporarily, just until they can secure legit work. Using a little-known 1950's crime movie as their tutor, the trio of criminal cretins encounter a variety of setbacks on their way to financial security. Planning an elaborate scheme to rob an armored car, they decide to use toy guns, so Jerry (Trese) rounds up a most intimidating assortment of the neon orange plastic variety. Later, while chiseling through a wall to a jewelry store, they find themselves in the bakery next door, with Jerry delighted to score some pastries instead. The other two aren't much brighter—Russ (Gallo) is the leader of the three and a small-time ladies man while Sid (Forsythe) is a devout dog lover whose dreams of a taxi service for the aged are shattered when customers are driven away by his kennel on wheels. Adapted from short stories written in the 1940s by the Italian Italo Calvino, modern adaptation manages to retain a 40s feel and charm. *CW:* Language. **92m/C VHS, Closed Caption.** William Forsythe, Vincent Gallo, Adam Trese, Lisa Gay Hamilton, Frances McDormand, David Boulton, James David Hilton; *D:* Alan Taylor; *W:* David Epstein; *C:* John Thomas; *M:* Rachel Portman. *EVE*

Pals 🎬🎬 1987 Old friends stumble across $3 million in cash and learn the predictable lesson that money can't buy happiness. A terribly trite TV-movie with an exceptional cast. **90m/C VHS.** Don Ameche, George C. Scott, Sylvia Sidney, Susan Rinell, James Greene; *D:* Lou Antonio. *THV*

Pals of the Range 🎬 1935 A framed ranch owner breaks out of jail in order to catch the real cattle thieves. Ho hum in the Old West. **55m/B VHS, Beta.** Rex Lease. *NOS*

Pals of the Saddle 🎬🎬½ 1938 The intrepid trio go after enemy agents who are trying to smuggle chemicals for poisonous gas into Mexico. This is the first of the series in which the Duke played the part of Stony Brooke. Somewhat convoluted plot, but nevertheless enjoyable. **55m/B VHS.** John Wayne, Ray Corrigan, Max Terhune, Doreen McKay, Josef Forte, Ted Adams, Curly Dresden; *D:* George Sherman. *NOS*

The Pamela Principle 🎬🎬 1991 (R) A bored, middle-aged man thinks his prayers are answered when he meets a sexy 20-year-old model and begins a sordid affair with her. Soon, however, he finds himself in a tense situation when he must choose between his family or his fantasy. Also available in an unrated version. *CW:* Language and strong sexuality. **?m/C VHS, LV, Closed Caption.** J.K. Dumont, Veronica Cash, Shelby Lane, Troy Donahue, Frank Pesce; *D:* Toby Phillips. *IMP*

Panama Hattie 🎬🎬 1942 Screen adaptation of Cole Porter's delightful Broadway musical. Unfortunately, something (like a plot) was lost in transition. Southern runs a saloon for our boys down in Panama. Among the musical numbers and vaudevillian acts some spies show up. Several screenwriters and directors, including Vincente Minnelli, worked uncredited on this picture, to no avail. Horne's second screen appearance. ♫ It Was Just One of Those Things; Fresh as a Daisy; I've Still Got My Health; Let's Be Buddies; Make It Another Old Fashioned; Hattie from Panama; Good Neighbors; I'll Do Anything for You; The Son of a Gun Who Pick on Uncle Sam. **79m/B VHS.** Ann Sothern, Dan Dailey, Red Skelton, Virginia O'Brien, Rags Ragland, Alan Mowbray, Ben Blue, Carl Esmond, Lena Horne; *D:* Norman Z. McLeod; *M:* George Bassman, Cole Porter. *MGM, CCB*

Panama Lady 🎬½ 1939 Ball stars as the sexy, sultry "Panama Lady" in this old-fashioned romance. She gets involved in some shady business south of the border. A lackluster remake of "Panama Flo." **65m/B VHS, Beta.** Lucille Ball, Evelyn Brent. *NO*

Panama Menace 🎬 *South of Panama* 1941 An agent heads to Panama to thwart spies who are after a special paint that makes things invisible. Poor effort all around, in spite of Beaumont's presence. **68m/B VHS, Beta.** Roger Pryor, Virginia Vale, Lionel Royce, Lucien Prival, Duncan Renaldo, Lester Dorr, Hugh Beaumont; *D:* Jean Yarbrough. *SNC, VYY*

Panama Patrol 🎬🎬½ 1939 Just as they are about to be married, two Army officers are called to duty in Panama. It seems that the Chinese have infiltrated the area with spies and something's got to be done. Too much attention to minor parts of the plot slows the story occasionally, but performances and photography compensate for some of the sluggishness. **67m/B VHS, Beta.** Leon Ames, Charlotte Wynters, Weldon Heyburn, Adrienne Ames, Abner Biberman, Hugh McArthur, Donald (Don "Red") Barry; *D:* Charles Lamont. *SNC*

Panamint's Bad Man 🎬 1938 Ballaw is a poor man's Gary Cooper fighting for justice against stagecoach robbers. Almost as much flavor as tumbleweed. **59m/B VHS, Beta.** Smith Ballew, Evelyn Daw, Noah Beery Sr.; *D:* Ray Taylor. *NOS, VDM, DVT*

Pancho Barnes 🎬🎬½ 1988 (PG) Routine biography of one of the first female pilots of the 1920s. Barnes is a bored debutante who finds her challenge in life when she learns to fly, becoming a barnstormer and movie stunt pilot. Her ambitions naturally get in the way of her romantic life. Good flying scenes. Made for television. **150m/C VHS.** Valerie Bertinelli, Ted Wass, Sam Robards, James Stephens, Cynthia Harris, Geoffrey Lewis; *D:* Richard T. Heffron; *W:* John Michael Hayes. *ORI*

Pancho Villa 🎬½ 1972 (PG) Savalas has the lead in this fictional account of the famous Mexican, He leads his men in a raid on an American fort after being hoodwinked in an arms deal. Connors tries to hold the fort against him. The finale, in which two trains crash head on, is the most exciting event in the whole darn movie. **92m/C VHS.** SP Telly Savalas, Clint Walker, Anne Francis, Chuck Connors, Angel Del Pozo, Luis Davila; *D:* Eugenio Martin; *W:* Julian Zimet. *NO*

Pancho Villa Returns 🎬🎬 1950 It's 1913, and noble Mexican General Pancho Villa leads his merry men against the assassins of President Madera. This Mexican production (filmed in English) paints a partisan portrait of title character as a good-hearted revolutionary folk hero, not the roving bandit later notorious north of the border. **95m/B VHS.** MX Leo Carrillo, Esther Fernandez, Jeanette Comber, Rodolfo Acosta; *D:* Miguel Contreras Torres; *W:* Miguel Contreras Torres. *NOS, LOO*

Pandemonium 🎬🎬½ *Thursday the 12th* 1982 (PG) A spoof of teen slasher films involving murder at Bambi's Cheerleading School. Seems that nationwide, cheerleaders have been brutally eliminated from their squads, leaving Bambi's as the last resort for the terminally perky. Smothers is interesting and more intelligent than his TV persona (although not by much) as the Mountie hero, assisted by Paul Reubens in a pre-Pee-Wee role. Kane steals the show as Candy, a pleasant lass with hyperkinetic powers. **82m/C VHS, Beta.** CA Tom Smothers, Carol Kane, Miles Chapin, Paul (Pee Wee Herman) Reubens, Judge Reinhold, Tab Hunter, Marc McClure, Donald O'Connor, Eve Arden, Eileen Brennan, Edie McClurg; *D:* Alfred Sole. *MGM*

Pandora and the Flying Dutchman 🎬🎬½ 1951 Feverish romantic fantasy has playgirl/nightclub singer Pandora Reynolds (Gardner) living in '30s Spain and being romanced by every man in sight. Naturally, she cares for none of them until she meets enigmatic Dutch captain Hendrick van der Zee (Mason) who is, in fact, the legendary Flying Dutchman—condemned to wander the seas forever unless a woman is willing to give up her life for him. Gardner is, as usual, exotically lovely. **123m/C VHS.** Ava Gardner, James Mason, Nigel Patrick, Sheila Sim, Harold Warrender, Mario Cabre; *D:* Albert Lewin; *W:* Albert Lewin; *C:* Jack Cardiff; *M:* Alan Rawsthorne. *KIV*

Pandora's Box 🎬🎬🎬 *Die Buechse Der Pandora* 1928 This silent classic marked the end of the German Expressionist era and established Brooks as a major screen presence. She plays the tempestuous Lulu, who destroys everyone she comes in contact with, eventually sinking to prostitution and a fateful meeting with Jack the Ripper. Silent with orchestral score. **110m/B VHS, Beta.** GE Louise Brooks, Fritz Kortner, Francis Lederer, Carl Goetz, Alice Roberts, Gustav Diesl; *D:* G.W. Pabst; *W:* G.W. Pabst. *GPV, MRV, VDM*

Panic 🎬½ 1983 A scientist terrorizes a small town when he becomes hideously deformed by one of his bacteria experiments. He should have known better. **90m/C VHS, Beta.** David Warbeck, Janet Agren. *MPI*

Panic Button 🎬½ 1962 Mel Brooks took the plot from this film and made "The Producers," which was much better. Italian gangsters produce a television show and stack the deck so that it will fail. Unbeknownst to them, the star has figured out what they are doing and works to make it a success. Shot in Italy, mainly in Venice and Rome. **90m/B VHS.** IT Maurice Chevalier, Eleanor Parker, Jayne Mansfield, Mike Connors, Akim Tamiroff; *D:* George Sherman. *NO*

Panic in Echo Park 🎬🎬 1977 A doctor races against time to find the cause of an epidemic that is threatening the health of a city. Good performances compensate for a predictable plot. Made for television. **78m/C VHS.** Dorian Harewood, Robin Gammell, Catlin Adams, Ramon Bieri, Movita; *D:* John Llewellyn Moxey. *NO*

Panic in Needle Park 🎬🎬🎬 1975 (R) Drugs become an obsession for a young girl who goes to New York for an abortion. Her new boyfriend is imprisoned for robbery in order to support both their habits. She resorts to prostitution to continue her drug habit, and trouble occurs when her boyfriend realizes she was instrumental in his being sent to jail. Strikes a vein in presenting an uncompromising look at drug use. May be too much of a depressant for some. Pacino's first starring role. **90m/C VHS, LV.** Al Pacino, Kitty Winn, Alan Vint, Richard Bright, Kiel Martin, Warren Finnerty, Raul Julia, Paul Sorvino; *D:* Jerry Schatzberg; *W:* Joan Didion, John Gregory Dunne; *C:* Adam Holender. Cannes Film Festival '71: Best Actress (Winn). *FOX*

Panic in the Streets 🎬🎬🎬 1950 The Black Death threatens New Orleans in this intense tale. When a body is found on the waterfront, a doctor (Widmark) is called upon for a diagnosis. The carrier proves to be deadly in more ways than one. Fine performances, taut direction (this was one of Kazan's favorite movies). Filmed on location in New Orleans. **96m/B VHS, LV, Closed Caption.** Richard Widmark, Jack Palance, Barbara Bel Geddes, Paul Douglas, Zero Mostel; *D:* Elia Kazan; *W:* Edward Anhalt. Academy Awards '50: Best Story. *FOX, FCT*

Panic in the Year Zero! 🎬🎬½ *End of the World* 1962 Milland and family leave Los Angeles for a fishing trip just as the city is hit by a nuclear bomb. Continuing out into the wilderness for safety, the family now must try to survive as their world crumbles around them. Generally considered the best of Milland's five directorial efforts. **92m/B VHS.** Ray Milland, Jean Hagen, Frankie Avalon, Mary Mitchell, Joan Freeman, Richard Garland, Rex Holman; *D:* Ray Milland; *M:* Les Baxter. *FRG*

Panic on the 5:22 🎬🎬 1974 Wealthy commuters are kidnapped and held hostage by terrorist hoodlums in a suburban train club car. Standard made for television vehicle. **78m/C VHS, Beta.** Lynda Day George, Laurence Luckinbill, Ina Balin, Bernie Casey; *D:* Harvey Hart. *WOV*

Panic Station 🎬🎬 *The Plains of Heaven* 1982 Two guys get lonely at remote satellite relay station. **90m/C VHS.** AU Richard Moir, Reg Evans, Gerard Kennedy; *D:* Ian Pringle. *ACA*

Panique 🎬🎬🎬 *Panic* 1947 A study of mob psychology in slums of post-WWII Paris. Two lovers frame a stranger for murder. Dark and tautly paced thriller taken from the novel by Georges Simenon. In French with English subtitles. **87m/B VHS, Beta.** FR Michel Simon, Viviane Romance; *D:* Julien Duvivier. *NOS, HHT, CAB*

Pantaloons 🐾🐾 1957 A man who fancies himself to be irresistible chases women for sport. A quaint and lively period film. **93m/C VHS.** *FR* Fernandel, Carmen Sevilla, Fernando Rey; *D:* John Berry. 𝒱𝒱𝒴

Panther 🐾🐾 1995 (R) The Van Peebles family teaches Oliver Stone History 101 with a fictionalized account of the Black Panthers' emergence as a voice for African Americans and as a fixture on the FBI's most wanted list in the late '60's. Judge (Hardison), a Vietnam vet forced by the FBI to become an informant, chronicles the activities of leaders Bobby Seale (Vance) and Huey P. Newton (Chong) and serves as witness to the Panthers' rise and subsequent fall into corruption and disintegration. Scatter-shot editing is meant to signify the chaos of the times, but instead adds to the action-flick feel and further detracts from the professed intent of being a message movie.**CW:** Strong violence and language. **124m/C VHS.** Kadeem Hardison, Marcus Chong, Courtney B. Vance, Bokeem Woodbine, Joe Don Baker, Anthony Griffith, Nefertiti, James Russo, Richard Dysart, M. Emmet Walsh, Mario Van Peebles; *D:* Mario Van Peebles; *W:* Melvin Van Peebles; *C:* Edward Pei; *M:* Stanley Clarke. *PGV*

Panther Squad 🐾 1984 Litter of sex kittens led by Danning get into major scraps to save world. **77m/C VHS.** Sybil Danning. *NO*

The Panther's Claw 🐾🐾 1942 Murder befalls an opera troupe, but a sleuth with the memorable name of Thatcher Colt is on the case. A quick-moving mystery quickie that delivers on its own modest terms. **72m/B VHS.** Sidney Blackmer, Byron Foulger, Rick Vallin, Herbert Rawlinson; *D:* William Beaudine. *NOS, LOO*

Papa's Delicate Condition 🐾🐾🐾 1963 Based on the autobiographical writings of silent screen star Corinne Griffith. Gleason is Papa whose "delicate condition" is a result of his drinking. His antics provide a constant headache to his family. A paean to turn-of-the-century family life. No I.D.s required as the performances are enjoyable for the whole family. Features the Academy Award-winning song "Call Me Irresponsible." ♫Call Me Irresponsible; Bill Bailey, Won't You Please Come Home?. **98m/C VHS, Beta, Closed Caption.** Jackie Gleason, Glynis Johns, Charlie Ruggles, Laurel Goodwin, Elisha Cook Jr., Murray Hamilton; *D:* George Marshall; *W:* Jack Rose; *M:* Loyal Griggs. Academy Awards '63: Best Song ("Call Me Irresponsible"). *BAR*

The Paper 🐾🐾🐾 1994 (R) Another crowd pleaser from director Howard follows a red letter day in the life of an editor at the tabloid New York Sun (modeled on the trashy Post). Fresh, fast-moving script by the Koepp brothers (who appear as reporters) offers a fairly accurate portrayal of the business of journalism (including the "brisk" language), with a few Hollywood exceptions. Pace suffers from cutaways to life outside, while script and direction sometimes coast past targets. Propelled by a fine cast, with cola-swigging editor Keaton the focus as he juggles his personal and professional lives. Close is both funny and scary. Duvall contributes salt as the old newsroom warhorse. Tons of cameos, though those outside of the business may not notice them.**CW:** Strong language. **112m/C VHS, LV, Closed Caption.** Michael Keaton, Robert Duvall, Marisa Tomei, Glenn Close, Randy Quaid, Jason Robards Jr., Jason Alexander, Spalding Gray, Catherine O'Hara, Lynne Thigpen; *D:* Ron Howard; *W:* David Koepp, Steven Koepp; *M:* Randy Newman. Nominations: Academy Awards '94: Best Song ("Make Up Your Mind"). *USH*

The Paper Brigade 🐾🐾½ 1996 (PG) Fifteen-year-old Gunther (Howard) gets a paper route to pay for the concert tickets he bought to impress a girl. Now he has to contend with his crazy neighbor (Englund) and a gang of bullies, as well as other obstacles. **89m/C VHS, Closed Caption.** Kyle Howard, Robert Englund, Travis Wester; *D:* Blair Treu. *WAR*

The Paper Chase 🐾🐾🐾 1973 (PG) Students at Harvard Law School suffer and struggle through their first year. A realistic, sometimes acidly humorous look at Ivy League ambitions, with Houseman stealing the show as the tough professor. Wonderful adaptation of the John Jay Osborn novel which later became the basis for the acclaimed television series. **111m/C VHS, Beta, LV.** Timothy Bottoms, Lindsay Wagner, John Houseman, Graham Beckel, Edward Herrmann, James Naughton, Craig Richard Nelson, Bob Lydiard; *D:* James Bridges; *W:* James Bridges; *C:* Gordon Willis; *M:* John Williams. Academy Awards '73: Best Supporting Actor (Houseman); Golden Globe Awards '74: Best Supporting Actor (Houseman); National Board of Review Awards '73: Best Supporting Actor (Houseman); Nominations: Academy Awards '73: Best Adapted Screenplay, Best Sound.*FOX, BTV*

Paper Lion 🐾🐾½ 1968 A comedy "documentary" about bestselling writer George Plimpton's tryout game as quarterback with the Detroit Lions. Film debut of Alan Alda. Helped Karras make the transition from the gridiron to the silver screen. Moves into field goal range but doesn't quite score. **107m/C VHS, Beta.** Alan Alda, Lauren Hutton, Alex Karras, Ann Turkel, John Gordy, Roger Brown, "Sugar Ray" Robinson, Roy Scheider, David Doyle; *D:* Alex March. *NO*

Paper Man 🐾🐾 1971 A group of college students create a fictitious person in a computer for a credit card scam. The scheme snowballs, resulting in murder and hints of possible artificial intelligence. But it's just standard network TV fare, with a creepy performance by Stockwell as a computer whiz. **90m/C VHS.** Dean Stockwell, Stefanie Powers, James Stacy, Elliot Street, Tina Chen, James Olson, Ross Elliott; *D:* Walter Grauman. *XVC, VTR*

Paper Marriage 🐾½ 1988 In Canada, a less than successful Chinese boxer agrees to marry a Hong Kong girl for a promise of payment in order that she may become a citizen. The money never comes, but the newly betrothed pair discover that they love each other, after all. In Cantonese with English subtitles. **102m/C VHS.** *CH* Samo Hung, Maggie Cheung; *D:* Alfred Cheung. *FCT, MOV, ACA*

Paper Marriage 🐾🐾½ 1993 Yet another variation on the marriage in order to gain citizenship but yes we're going to fall in love films. A young Polish woman has fallen for an upper-crust English doctor she's met in Warsaw. When Alicja arrives in England, she's promptly dumped by the cad. She's ambitious and wants to stay in England so Alicja arranges a marriage of convenience with small-time crook Aiden, who finds his new bride is more than he bargained for. **88m/C VHS.** *GB PL* Gary Kemp, Joanna Trzepiechinska, Rita Tushingham, Richard Hawley, David Horovitch, William Ilkley, Mark McKellen, Ann Mitchell, Sadie Frost; *D:* Krzysztof Lang; *W:* Marek Kreutz, Krzysztof Lang. *ACA*

Paper Mask 🐾🐾½ 1991 (R) When a promising young doctor is killed in an auto accident, an unscrupulous, psychotic porter assumes his identity. He uses said identity to, among other things, initiate an affair with a sultry co-worker. How long will this madman play his unholy game, and at what cost?**CW:** Language and some sensuality. **105m/C VHS.** *GB* Paul McGann, Amanda Donohoe, Frederick Treves, Barbara Leigh-Hunt, Jimmy Yuill, Tom Wilkinson; *D:* Christopher Morahan; *W:* John Collee; *M:* Richard Harvey. *ACA*

Paper Moon 🐾🐾🐾½ 1973 (PG) Award-winning story set in depression-era Kansas with Ryan O'Neal as a Bible-wielding con who meets up with a nine-year-old orphan. During their travels together, he discovers that the orphan (his daughter, Tatum) is better at "his" game than he is. Irresistible chemistry between the O'Neals, leading to Tatum's Oscar win (she is the youngest actor ever to take home a statue). Cinematically picturesque and cynical enough to keep overt sentimentalism at bay. Based on Joe David Brown's novel, "Addie Pray." The director's version contains a prologue by director Bogdanovich. **102m/B VHS, Beta, LV.** Ryan O'Neal, Tatum O'Neal, Madeline Kahn, John Hillerman, Randy Quaid; *D:* Peter Bogdanovich; *W:* Alvin Sargent. Academy Awards '73: Best Supporting Actress (O'Neal); National Board of Review Awards '73: 10 Best Films of the Year; Writers Guild of America '73: Best Adapted Screenplay; Nominations: Academy Awards '73: Best Adapted Screenplay, Best Sound, Best Supporting Actress (Kahn). *PAR, BTV*

Paper Tiger 🐾🐾 1974 Niven plays an imaginative English tutor who fabricates fantastic yarns fictionalizing his past in order to impress his student, the son of the Japanese ambassador to a Southeast Asian country. Poorly executed karate, misdirection, and a simplistic storyline work against it. **104m/C VHS, Beta.** *GB* David Niven, Toshiro Mifune, Eiko Ando, Hardy Kruger; *D:* Ken Annakin; *W:* Jack Davies. *NO*

A Paper Wedding 🐾🐾🐾 *Les Noces de Papier* 1989 A middle-aged literature professor with a dead-end career and equally dead-end romance with a married man is persuaded by her lawyer sister to marry a Chilean political refugee to avoid his deportation. Of course, they must fool an immigration official and their fake marriage does turn into romance, but this is no light-hearted "Green Card." Bujold shines. In French and Spanish with English subtitles. **90m/C VHS, LV, Closed Caption.** *CA* Genevieve Bujold, Manuel Aranguiz, Dorothee Berryman; *D:* Michel Brault. *CTL, LUM*

Paperback Hero 🐾🐾 1973 A hot-shot hockey player turns to crime when his team loses its financial backing. Choopy storyline could use a Zamboni, while Dullea should be penalized for occasionally losing his rustic accent. Still the supporting actors skate through their roles and, for periods, it works. A slapshot that ultimately clangs off the goal post. **94m/C VHS.** *CA* Keir Dullea, Elizabeth Ashley, John Beck, Dayle Haddon; *D:* Peter Pearson. *NO*

Paperback Romance 🐾🐾½ *Lucky Break* 1996 (R) Carides is a writer of erotica who doesn't act on her own impulses because she's embarrassed by her crippled leg. But when she breaks her leg, she passes the injury off as a skiing accident and decides to go after the man (LaPaglia) of her dreams—who just happens to be engaged.**CW:** Sexuality and related dialogue. **99m/C VHS.** *AU* Gia Carides, Anthony LaPaglia, Rebecca Gibney; *D:* Ben Lewin; *W:* Ben Lewin. *NYR*

The Paperboy 🐾🐾 1994 (R) Melissa Thorpe (Paul) returns to her small hometown to settle her mother's estate, only to become the obsession of Johnny (Marut), the 12-year-old paperboy she mistakenly befriends. Seems he becomes psychotically jealous when Melissa takes up with an old flame (Katt) and dead bodies become as common as old newspapers. **93m/C VHS, LV, Closed Caption.** Alexandra Paul, Marc Marut, William Katt, Brigid Tierney; *D:* Douglas Jackson; *W:* David Peckinpah; *M:* Milan Kymlicka. *REP*

Paperhouse 🐾🐾🐾 1989 An odd fantasy about a young girl plagued by recurring dreams that begin to influence real life. Very obtuse, British-minded film with "Twilight Zone" feel that manages to capture genuine dream-ness. Not for all audiences, but intriguing nonetheless. Based on the novel "Marianne Dreams" by Catherine Storr. **92m/C VHS, Beta, LV.** *GB* Glenne Headly, Ben Cross, Charlotte Burke, Elliott Spiers, Gemma Jones, Sarah Newbold; *D:* Bernard Rose; *W:* Matthew Jacobs; *M:* Hans Zimmer, Stanley Myers. *LIV, VES*

Papillon 🐾🐾🐾 1973 (PG) McQueen is a criminal sent to Devil's Island in the 1930s determined to escape from the Lemote prison. Hoffman is the swindler he befriends. A series of escapes and recaptures follow. Box-office winner based on the autobiographical writings of French thief Henri Charriere. Excellent portrayal of prison life and fine performances from the prisoners. Certain segments would have been better left on the cutting room floor. The film's title refers to the lead's butterfly tattoo. **150m/C VHS, Beta, LV.** Steve McQueen, Dustin Hoffman, Victor Jory, George Coulouris, Anthony Zerbe; *D:* Franklin J. Schaffner; *C:* Fred W. Koenekamp; **M:** Jerry Goldsmith. Nominations: Academy Awards '73: Original Dramatic/Comedy Score. *FOX, WAR*

Parade 🐾🐾🐾 1974 A series of vignettes in a circus, "Parade" is actually a play within a play, meshing the action with events offstage. The laser disc edition includes Rene Clement's 1936 "Soigne Ton Gauche," Tati's inspiration. **85m/C VHS, LV.** *FR* Jacques Tati; **D:** Jacques Tati; **W:** Jacques Tati. *HMV, CRC, FCT*

The Paradine Case 🐾🐾½ 1947 A passable Hitchcock romancer about a young lawyer who falls in love with the woman he's defending for murder, not knowing whether she is innocent or guilty. Script could be tighter and more cohesive. Seventy thousand dollars of the three million budget were spent recreating the original Bailey courtroom. Based on the novel by Robert Hichens. **125m/B VHS, Beta, LV, Closed Caption.** Gregory Peck, Alida Valli, Ann Todd, Louis Jourdan, Charles Laughton, Charles Coburn, Ethel Barrymore, Leo G. Carroll; **D:** Alfred Hitchcock; **C:** Lee Garmes. Nominations: Academy Awards '47: Best Supporting Actress (Barrymore). *FOX*

Paradise 🐾🐾 1982 (R) Young American boy and beautiful English girl on a 19th-century jaunt through the Middle East are the sole survivors when their caravan is massacred. Left to their own devices, they discover a magnificent oasis and the joys of frolicking naked and experience (surprise) their sexual awakening. Do a double-take: it's the "Blue Lagoon" all over, with a bit more nudity and a lot more sand. **96m/C VHS, Beta, LV.** Phoebe Cates, Willie Aames, Richard Curnock, Tuvio Tavi; **D:** Stuart Gillard. *COL*

Paradise 🐾🐾 1991 (PG-13) Young boy is sent to the country to live with his pregnant mother's married friends (real life husband and wife Johnson and Griffith). From the outset it is clear that the couple are experiencing marital troubles, making the boy's assimilation all the more difficult. Help arrives in the form of a sprightly ten-year-old girl, with whom he forms a charming relationship. Largely predictable, this remake of the French film "Le Grand Chemin" works thanks to the surprisingly good work of its ensemble cast, and the gorgeous scenery of South Carolina, where the movie was filmed. **112m/C VHS, Beta, Closed Caption.** Melanie Griffith, Don Johnson, Elijah Wood, Thora Birch, Sheila McCarthy, Eve Gordon, Louise Latham, Greg Travis, Sarah Trigger; **D:** Mary Agnes Donoghue; **W:** Mary Agnes Donoghue; **M:** David Newman. *TOU*

Paradise Alley 🐾🐾 1978 (PG) Rocky tires of boxing, decides to join the WWF. Three brothers brave the world of professional wrestling in an effort to strike it rich and move out of the seedy Hell's Kitchen neighborhood of New York, circa 1946. Stallone wrote, stars in, and makes his directorial debut in addition to singing the title song. He makes a few good moves as director, but is ultimately pinned to the canvas. **109m/C VHS, Beta, LV.** Sylvester Stallone, Anne Archer, Armand Assante, Lee Canalito, Kevin Conway; **D:** Sylvester Stallone; **W:** Sylvester Stallone; **M:** Bill Conti. *USH*

Paradise Canyon 🐾½ 1935 Early Wayne "B" thriller, in which he plays an undercover government agent sent to track down a group of counterfeiters. **59m/B VHS.** John Wayne, Yakima Canutt, Marion Burns. *COL, NOS, REP*

Paradise, Hawaiian Style 🐾½ 1966 Out-of-work pilot returns to Hawaii, where he and a buddy start a charter service with two helicopters. Plenty of gals are wooed by "the Pelvis." Filmed four years after Elvis's first Pacific piece, "Blue Hawaii." Presley, showing the first signs of slow-down, displays no surprises here. 🎵Paradise, Hawaiian Style; Scratch My Back (Then I'll Scratch Yours); Stop Where You Are; This Is My Heaven; House of Sand; Queenie Wahine's Papaya; Datin'; Drums of the Islands; A Dog's Life. **91m/C VHS, Beta.** Elvis Presley, Suzanna Leigh, James Shigeta, Donna Butterworth, Irene Tsu, Julie Parrish, Philip Ahn, Mary Treen, Marianna Hill, John Doucette, Grady Sutton; **D:** Michael Moore. *FOX, MVD*

Paradise in Harlem 🐾½ 1940 All-black musical in which a cabaret performer witnesses a gangland murder, sees his sick wife die, and is pressured into leaving town by the mob. Have a nice day. **83m/B VHS, Beta.** Frank Wilson, Mamie Smith, Edna Mae Harris, Juanita Hall; **D:** Joseph Seiden. *VYY, FCT, VCN*

Paradise Island 🐾 1930 Down-scale musical romance about an ingenue on her way to join her fiance in the South Seas, only to find that he has gambled away his money. The opportunistic saloon owner tries to put the moves on her. Will the two lovers be reunited? 🎵I've Got a Girl in Every Port; Drinking Song; Lazy Breezes; Just Another Dream. **68m/B VHS.** Kenneth Harlan, Marceline Day, Thomas Santschi, Paul Hurst, Victor Potel, Gladden James, Will Stanton; **D:** Bert Glennon. *GPV, NOS*

Paradise Motel 🐾½ 1984 (R) Teen exploitation film centered around a local motel predominantly used for one-night rendezvous. High school heroes and jocks battle for the affections of a beautiful classmate. **87m/C VHS, Beta, Closed Caption.** Bob Basso, Gary Hershberger, Jonna Leigh Stack, Robert Krantz; **D:** Cary Medoway; **C:** James L. Carter. *FOX*

Paradise Park 🐾🐾½ 199? A whimsical comedy about the inhabitants of a West Virginia trailer park who dream of better lives while coping with their depressing surroundings. An English teacher (Groce) wishes he was a writer, an elderly woman (Basquette) dreams of winning a TV quiz show, and a mechanic wants to be a race car driver. Director Boyd sprinkles in appearances of non-Hollywood notables Porter Waggoner, Johnny Paycheck, Webb Wilder, and wrestler Dusty Rhodes. Includes some black and white fantasy sequences. **100m/C VHS.** Lena Basquette, Larry Groce, Jennifer Gurney; *Cameos:* Johnny Paycheck, Webb Wilder, Dusty Rhodes, Porter Waggoner; **D:** Daniel Boyd. *MTH*

Paradise Road 🐾🐾 1997 (R) Fleeing Singapore during WWII, a group of British, American, and Australian women straggle to the shore of Sumatra after their ship is bombed, where they're taken prisoner by the Japanese. Headed by Close, the prisoners form a vocal ensemble that crosses their collective national differences and attempts to lift the spirits of the brutalized women. Familiar ground is trod in this prisoner-of-war saga, but the music is genuinely moving, and excellent performances from the cast help sustain interest. The symphonic choral pieces were taken from actual sheet music used by a similar group of real-life WWII prisoners. **CW:** Prisoner of war brutality and violence. **115m/C VHS.** Glenn Close, Frances McDormand, Julianna Margulies, Pauline Collins, Jennifer Ehle, Elizabeth Spriggs, Tessa Humphries, Sab Shimono; **D:** Bruce Beresford; **W:** Bruce Beresford; **C:** Peter James. *NYR*

Paradisio 🐾½ 1961 (R) Dying inventor wills Oxford professor an authentic pair of X-ray specs. Spies come gunning for the professor, chasing him through Europe. Doc keeps forgetting he's being chased while using the special specs to see (sometimes in 3-D) through the clothing of young women. Meager plot does not get in way of 3-D nudie exploitation. **82m/C VHS, Beta.** Arthur Howard, Eva Waegner. *NWV, VDM*

The Parallax View 🐾🐾🐾½ 1974 (R) A reporter tries to disprove a report which states that a presidential candidate's assassination was not a conspiracy. As he digs deeper and deeper, he uncovers more than he bargained for and becomes a pawn in the conspirators' further plans. Beatty is excellent and the conspiracy is never less than believable. A lesser-known, compelling political thriller that deserves to be more widely seen. **102m/C VHS, Beta.** Warren Beatty, Hume Cronyn, William Daniels, Paula Prentiss, Kenneth Mars, Bill McKinney, Anthony Zerbe, Walter McGinn; **D:** Alan J. Pakula; **C:** Gordon Willis. National Society of Film Critics Awards '74: Best Cinematography. *PAR*

Parallel Corpse 🐾 1983 A mortuary attendant finds a murder victim hidden in a coffin and blackmails the remorseless killer. **89m/C VHS, Beta.** Buster Larsen, Jorgen Kiil, Agneta Ekmanner, Masja Dessau. *MED*

Parallel Lives 🐾🐾½ 1994 (R) Sorority sisters and frat brothers (and their various spouses and lovers) , from the classes of both 1948 and 1973, gather for an on-campus weekend reunion and discover old and new jealousies, rivalries, and lots of lust (requited and not). There's also an unexpected death and a police investigation as well. Director Yellen had her cast improvise much of their dialogue—the same method she used in "Chantilly Lace." Made for cable TV. **CW:** Strong language; scene of sexuality. **105m/C VHS, Beta, Closed Caption.** James Belushi, James Brolin, LeVar Burton, Lindsay Crouse, Jill Eikenberry, Ben Gazzara, Jack Klugman, David Lansbury, Liza Minnelli, Dudley Moore, Gena Rowlands, Ally Sheedy, Helen Slater, Mira Sorvino, Paul Sorvino, Robert Wagner, Patricia Wettig, JoBeth Williams, Treat Williams; **D:** Linda Yellen; **W:** Gisella Bernice; **M:** Patrick Seymour. *PAR*

Paralyzed 🐾🐾 197? An unconscious journalist, mistaken for dead in a hospital emergency room, flashes back to the investigation that embroiled him in his predicament. **90m/C VHS, Beta.** Ingrid Thulin, Jean Sorel, Mario Adorf; **D:** Aldo Lado; **W:** Aldo Lado. *MPI*

Paramedics 🐾½ 1988 (PG-13) A motley crew of cavorting paramedics battle their evil captain. Another parody of people in uniform. A comedy with little pulse. **91m/C VHS, Beta, LV.** George Newbern, Christopher McDonald, John P. Ryan, Ray Walston, Lawrence-Hilton Jacobs; **D:** Stuart Margolin. *LIV, VES*

Paranoia 🐾 *Orgasmo; A Beautiful Place to Kill; A Quiet Place to Kill* 1969 Beautiful jet-set widow is trapped in her own Italian villa by a young couple who drug her to get her to perform in various sex orgies, which are probably the most interesting part of this muddled affair. **94m/C VHS, Beta.** *IT* Carroll Baker, Lou Castel, Colette Descombes; **D:** Umberto Lenzi. *REP*

Paranoiac 🐾🐾½ 1962 Greed and terror set in a country mansion. Simon (Reed) wants the family inheritance all to himself even if it means driving sister Eleanor (Scott) insane. This may not be so hard—she's claiming to see their dead brother Tony. Surprise! Tony (Davion) shows up (really throwing Simon for a loop). Reed's evil is tinged with humor although the numerous plot twists can get confusing. First directorial effort for cinematographer Francis. **80m/B VHS, Closed Caption.** *GB* Oliver Reed, Janette Scott, Alex Davion, Liliane Brousse, Sheila Burell, Maurice Denham; **D:** Freddie Francis; **W:** Jimmy Sangster; **C:** Arthur Grant; **M:** Elisabeth Lutyens. *USH*

Parasite woof! 1982 (R) A small town is beset by giant parasites. An "Alien" ripoff originally filmed in 3-D, during that technique's brief return in the early '80s. Bad films like this killed it both the first and second times. An unpardonable mess that comes off as a stinky sixth-grade film project. **90m/C VHS, Beta, LV, Closed Caption.** Demi Moore, Luca Bercovici, Cherie Currie, Gale Robbins, James Davidson, Al Fann, Cheryl "Rainbeaux" Smith, Vivian Blaine; **D:** Charles Band; **W:** Alan J. Adler; **C:** Mac Ahlberg; **M:** Richard Band. *PAR*

Pardners 🐾🐾½ 1956 Spoiled New York millionaire (Lewis) becomes the sheriff of small western town, with Martin as a ranch foreman. The two team up to rid the town of bad guys and romance two local cuties. Western spoof (with music) is a remake of 1936's "Rhythm on the Range." 🎵Buckskin Beauty; Pardners; The Wind! The Wind!; Me 'N You 'N the Moon. **88m/C VHS, Closed Caption.** Jerry Lewis, Dean Martin, Lori Nelson, Jackie Loughery, Jeff Morrow, John Baragrey, Agnes Moorehead, Lon Chaney Jr., Milton Frome, Lee Van Cleef, Jack Elam, Bob Steele, Emory Parnell; **D:** Norman Taurog; **W:** Sidney Sheldon, Jerry Davis. *PAR* in B. Armstrong; **W:** Robin B. Armstrong. Sundance Film Festival '91: Audience Award. **COL**

Pat and Mike 🐾🐾🐾 1952 War of the sexes rages in this comedy about a leathery sports promoter who futilely attempts to train a woman for athletic competition. Tracy and Hepburn have fine chemistry, but supporting players contribute too. Watch for the first on-screen appearance of Bronson (then Charles Buchinski) as a crook. **95m/B VHS, Beta, LV, Closed Caption.** Spencer Tracy, Katharine Hepburn, Aldo Ray, Jim Backus, William Ching, Sammy White, Phyllis Povah, Charles Bronson, Chuck Connors, Mae Clarke, Carl "Alfalfa" Switzer; **D:** George Cukor; **W:** Ruth Gordon, Garson Kanin; **C:** William H. Daniels. Nominations: Academy Awards '52: Best Story & Screenplay. **MGM**

Pat Garrett & Billy the Kid 🐾🐾🐾 1973 Coburn is Garrett, one-time partner of Billy the Kid (Kristofferson), turned sheriff. He tracks down and eventually kills the outlaw. The uncut director's version which was released on video is a vast improvement over the theatrically released and television versions. Dylan's soundtrack includes the now famous "Knockin' on Heaven's Door." **106m/C VHS, Beta, LV, Closed Caption.** Kris Kristofferson, James Coburn, Bob Dylan, Richard Jaeckel, Katy Jurado, Chill Wills, Charles Martin Smith, Slim Pickens, Harry Dean Stanton; **D:** Sam Peckinpah; **W:** Rudy Wurlitzer; **M:** George Duning. **MGM**

A Patch of Blue 🐾🐾½ 1965 A kind-hearted blind girl falls in love with a black man without acknowledging racial differences. Good performances from Hartman and Poitier are film's strongest assets. **108m/C VHS, Beta.** Sidney Poitier, Elizabeth Hartman, Shelley Winters, Wallace Ford, Ivan Dixon, John Qualen, Elisabeth Fraser, Kelly Flynn; **D:** Guy Green; **C:** Robert Burks; **M:** Jerry Goldsmith. Academy Awards '65: Best Supporting Actress (Winters); Nominations: Academy Awards '65: Best Actress (Hartman), Best Art Direction/Set Decoration (B & W), Best Black and White Cinematography, Best Original Score. **MGM, FXV**

Patchwork Girl of Oz 🐾🐾 1914 A very early silent film production by Baum that brought his own Oz books to the screen. **80m/B VHS, Beta.** **D:** L. Frank Baum. **NOS, DVT, VYY**

Paternity 🐾🐾 1981 (PG) Routine comedy about middle-aged manager of Madison Square Gardens (Reynolds) who sets out to find a woman to bear his child, no strings attached. The predictability of the happy ending makes this a yawner. Steinberg's directorial debut. **94m/C VHS, Beta, LV.** Burt Reynolds, Beverly D'Angelo, Lauren Hutton, Norman Fell, Paul Dooley, Elizabeth Ashley; **D:** David Steinberg; **W:** Charlie Peters; **M:** David Shire. Golden Raspberry Awards '81: Worst Song ("Baby Talk"). **PAR**

Pather Panchali 🐾🐾🐾 The Song of the Road; The Saga of the Road; The Lament of the Path 1954 Somber, moving story of a young Bengali boy growing up in impoverished India. Stunning debut from India's master filmmaker Ray, who continued the story in "Aparajito" and "World of Apu." A truly great work. In Bengali with English subtitles. **112m/B VHS, Beta.** **IN** Kanu Banerjee, Karuna Banerjee, Uma Das Gupta, Subir Banerji, Runki Banerji, Chunibala Devi; **D:** Satyajit Ray; **W:** Satyajit Ray; **M:** Ravi Shankar. **NOS, FCT, MRV**

Pathfinder 🐾🐾🐾½ 1987 A young boy in Lapland of 1,000 years ago comes of age prematurely after he falls in with cutthroat nomads who already slaughtered his family and now want to wipe out the rest of the village. Gripping adventure in the ice and snow features stunning scenery. In Lappish with English subtitles and based on an old Lapp fable. **88m/C VHS.** **NO** Mikkel Gaup, Nils Utsi, Svein Scharffenberg, Helgi Skulason, Sara Marit Gaup, Sverre Porsanger; **D:** Nils Gaup; **W:** Nils Gaup. Nominations: Academy Awards '87: Best Foreign Language Film. **FXL, FXV**

The Pathfinder 🐾🐾½ 1994 (PG-13) TV adaptation of the 1840 James Fenimore Cooper novel that finds legendary woodsman Natty Bumppo, his adoptive Indian father Chingachgook, and lovely Mabel Dunham trying to aid a

beseiged British fort during the French and Indian wars. If this sounds familiar, it's because Cooper's "Leatherstocking Tales" were also the basis for "The Last of the Mohicans." **CW:** Some frontier violence. **104m/C VHS.** Kevin Dillon, Graham Greene, Jaimz Woolvett, Laurie Holden, Russell Means, Stacy Keach; **D:** Donald Shebib; **W:** James Mitchell Miller, Thomas W. Lynch; **M:** Reg Powell. **HMK**

Paths of Glory 🐾🐾🐾🐾 1957 Classic anti-war drama set in WWI France. A vain, ambitious officer imposes unlikely battle strategy on his hapless troops, and when it fails, he demands that three soldiers be selected for execution as cowards. Menjou is excellent as the bloodless French officer, with Douglas properly heroic as the French officer who knows about the whole disgraceful enterprise. Fabulous, wrenching fare from filmmaking great Kubrick, who co-wrote. Based on a true story from Humphrey Cobb's novel of the same name. **86m/B VHS, Beta, LV, Closed Caption.** Kirk Douglas, Adolphe Menjou, George Macready, Ralph Meeker, Richard Anderson, Wayne Morris, Timothy Carey, Susanne Christian, Bert Freed; **D:** Stanley Kubrick; **W:** Calder Willingham, Stanley Kubrick. **MGM, FOX**

Paths to Paradise 🐾🐾🐾 1925 Compson and Griffith share criminal past, reunite at gala event to snatch priceless necklace and head south of the border. Watch- class chase scene. **78m/B VHS, Beta.** Raymond Griffith, Betty Compson, Thomas Santschi, Bert Woodruff, Fred Kelsey; **D:** Clarence Badger. **GPV**

Patrick 🐾½ 1978 (PG) Coma patient suddenly develops strange powers and has a weird effect on the people he comes in contact with. **115m/C VHS, Beta.** **AU** Robert Helpmann, Susan Penhaligon, Rod Mullinar; **D:** Richard Franklin; **M:** Brian May. **NO**

The Patriot 🐾½ 1986 (R) An action film about an ex-Navy commando who battles a band of nuclear-arms smuggling terrorists. Edited via George Lucas' electronic editor, Edit Droid. **88m/C VHS, Beta, LV.** Jeff Conaway, Michael J. Pollard, Leslie Nielsen, Greg Henry, Simone Griffeth; **D:** Frank Harris; **W:** Andy Ruben, Katt Shea Ruben; **M:** Jay Michael Ferguson. **LIV, VES**

Patriot Games 🐾🐾🐾 1992 (R) Jack Ryan, retired CIA analyst, takes his wife and daughter to England on a holiday and ends up saving a member of the Royal Family from assassination by IRA extremists. Ryan, who has killed one of the terrorists, then becomes the target of revenge by the dead man's brother. Good action sequences but otherwise predictable adaptation of the novel by Tom Clancy. Companion to "The Hunt for Red October," with Ford taking over the role of Ryan from Alec Baldwin. Since this movie did well, we can probably expect two more from Ford, who's becoming the king of trilogies. Followed by "Clear and Present Danger." **CW:** Language, violence, and sexuality. **117m/C VHS, Beta, CD-I, Closed Caption.** Harrison Ford, Anne Archer, Patrick Bergin, Thora Birch, Sean Bean, Richard Harris, James Earl Jones, James Fox, Samuel L. Jackson, Polly Walker; **D:** Phillip Noyce; **W:** W. Peter Iliff, Donald Stewart; **M:** James Horner. **PAR**

The Patriots 🐾🐾🐾 1933 A German prisoner works as a shoemaker in a small village during WWI. A lyrical drama in German and Russian with English titles. **82m/B VHS, Beta.** **RU** **D:** Boris Barnet. **FCT, IHF**

The Patsy 🐾🐾 1964 Shady producers attempt to transform a lowly bellboy into a comedy superstar. Not one of Lewis's better efforts. Lorre's last film. **101m/C VHS, Beta.** Jerry Lewis, Ina Balin, Everett Sloane, Phil Harris, Keenan Wynn, Peter Lorre, John Carradine, Hans Conried, Richard Deacon, Scatman Crothers, Del Moore, Neil Hamilton, Buddy Lester, Nancy Kulp, Norman Alden, Jack Albertson; **D:** Jerry Lewis; **W:** Jerry Lewis. **IME**

Pattern for Plunder 🐾½ The Bay of Saint Michel 1962 Ex-commando leader rounds up his former comrades to head back to Normandy in search of buried Nazi plunder. **73m/B VHS.** **GB** Keen-

an Wynn, Mai Zetterling, Ronald Howard, Edward Underdown; **D:** John Ainsworth; **W:** Christopher Davis. **SNC**

Patterns 🐾🐾🐾 Patterns of Power 1956 Realistic depiction of big business. Heflin starts work at a huge New York office that is under the ruthless supervision of Sloane. Serling's astute screenplay (adapted from his TV play) is adept at portraying ruthless, power-struggling executives and the sundry workings of a large corporation. Film has aged slightly, but it still has some edge to it. Originally intended for television. **83m/B VHS.** Van Heflin, Everett Sloane, Ed Begley Sr., Beatrice Straight, Elizabeth Wilson; **D:** Fielder Cook; **W:** Rod Serling; **C:** Boris Kaufman. **NOS, MGM, MRV**

Pattes Blanches 🐾🐾½ White Paws 1949 A reclusive aristocrat always wears white spats, causing ridicule in the small fishing village where he lives. Trouble comes when a local saloon-keeper becomes resentful of the rich man's advances on his girlfriend. Moody, sensual French melodrama exploring class, money and sex. Adaptation of a play by Jean Anouilh. In French with English subtitles. **92m/B VHS.** **FR** Suzy Delair, Fernand Ledoux, Paul Bernard, Michel Bouquet; **D:** Jean Gremillon. **INT, FCT**

Patti Rocks 🐾🐾🐾 1988 (R) Offbeat, realistic independent effort concerns a foul chauvinist who enlists a friend to accompany him on a visit to a pregnant girlfriend who turns out to be less than the bimbo she's portrayed as en route. Mulkey shines as the sexist. Same characters featured earlier in "Loose Ends." **86m/C VHS, Beta, LV.** Chris Mulkey, John Jenkins, Karen Landry, David L. Turk, Stephen Yoakam; **D:** David Burton Morris; **W:** Chris Mulkey, John Jenkins, Karen Landry, David Burton Morris; **M:** Doug Maynard. **NO**

Patton 🐾🐾🐾½ Patton—Lust for Glory; Patton: A Salute to a Rebel 1970 (PG) Lengthy but stellar bio of the vain, temperamental American general who masterminded significant combat triumphs during WWII. "Old Blood and Guts," who considered himself an 18th-century commander living in the wrong era, produced victory after victory in North Africa and Europe, but not without a decided impact upon his troops. Scott is truly magnificent in the title role, and Malden shines in the supporting role of General Omar Bradley. Not a subtle film, but neither is its subject. Interesting match-up with the 1986 made-for-TV movie "The Last Days of Patton," also starring Scott. **171m/C VHS, Beta, LV.** George C. Scott, Karl Malden, Stephen Young, Michael Strong, Frank Latimore, James Edwards, Lawrence Dobkin, Michael Bates, Tim Considine; **D:** Franklin J. Schaffner; **W:** Francis Ford Coppola, Edmund H. North; **C:** Fred W. Koenekamp; **M:** Jerry Goldsmith. Academy Awards '70: Best Actor (Scott), Best Art Direction/Set Decoration, Best Director (Schaffner), Best Film Editing, Best Picture, Best Sound, Best Story & Screenplay; Directors Guild of America Awards '70: Best Director (Schaffner); Golden Globe Awards '71: Best Actor—Drama (Scott); National Board of Review Awards '70: 10 Best Films of the Year, Best Actor (Scott); New York Film Critics Awards '70: Best Actor (Scott); National Society of Film Critics Awards '70: Best Actor (Scott); Writers Guild of America '70: Best Original Screenplay; Nominations: Academy Awards '70: Best Cinematography, Best Original Score. **FXV, TLF, BTV**

Patty Hearst 🐾½ 1988 (R) Less than fascinating, expressionistic portrait of Hearst from her kidnapping through her brainwashing and eventual criminal participation with the SLA. An enigmatic film that seems to only make Hearst's transformation to a Marxist terrorist all the more mysterious. Based on Hearst's book, "Every Secret Thing." **108m/C VHS, Beta, LV.** Natasha Richardson, William Forsythe, Ving Rhames, Frances Fisher, Jodi Long, Dana Delany; **D:** Paul Schrader; **W:** Nicholas Kazan; **C:** Bojan Bazelli. **MED**

Paul and Michelle 🐾 1974 (R) The equally dull sequel to "Friends" finds the two lovers a little older but no wiser. Paul has graduated from his British school and returns to France to seek out Michelle and their child. They try to rekindle their romance but the stresses of everyday life

---

Pardon Mon Affaire 🐾🐾🐾 Un Elephant a Trompe Enormement 1976 (PG) When a middle-aged civil servant gets a look at a model in a parking garage, he decides it's time to cheat on his wife. Enjoyable French farce. Re-made as in the United States "The Woman in Red" and followed by "Pardon Mon Affair, Too!" Subtitled. **107m/C VHS, Beta, LV.** **FR** Jean Rochefort, Claude Brasseur, Guy Bedos, Victor Lanoux, Daniele Delorme, Martine Sarcey, Anny Duperey; **D:** Yves Robert; **M:** Vladimir Cosma. Cesar Awards '77: Best Supporting Actor (Brasseur). **FOX**

Pardon Mon Affaire, Too! 🐾🐾½ We Will All Meet in Paradise 1977 Pale sequel to the first popular French comedy, "Pardon Mon Affair." This time the four fantasy-minded buddies withstand the trials of marriage and middle-class life. With English subtitles or dubbed. **105m/C VHS, Beta.** **FR** Jean Rochefort, Claude Brasseur, Guy Bedos; **D:** Yves Robert; **M:** Vladimir Cosma.

Pardon My Gun 🐾½ 1930 Cowpoke falls for the boss' daughter but has a rival in a wealthy rancher, who isn't above sabotage to get the girl. **64m/B VHS.** George Duryea, Harry Woods, Sally Starr, Lee Moran, Mona Ray; **D:** Robert De Lacy; **W:** Hugh Cummings. **GPV**

Pardon My Sarong 🐾🐾½ 1942 Bud and Lou star as Chicago bus drivers who end up shipwrecked on a South Pacific island when they get involved with notorious jewel thieves. The island natives think Lou is a god! Standard Abbott & Costello fare. **83m/B VHS.** Bud Abbott, Lou Costello, Virginia Bruce, Robert Paige, Lionel Atwill, Leif Erickson, William Demarest, Samuel S. Hinds; **D:** Erle C. Kenton; **C:** Milton Krasner. **USH**

Pardon My Trunk 🐾🐾 Hello Elephant; Bvongiorno, Elefante 1952 Struggling against poverty on his teacher's salary, a man and his family receive a gift from a Hindu prince—an elephant. De Sica carries this silly premise beyond mere slapstick. Dubbed. **85m/B VHS, Beta.** **IT** Sabu, Vittorio De Sica; **D:** Gianni Franciolini. **VYY**

Pardon Us 🐾🐾½ Jail Birds 1931 Laurel and Hardy are thrown into prison for bootlegging. Plot meanders along aimlessly, but the duo have some inspired moments. The first Laurel and Hardy feature. **78m/B VHS, Beta.** Stan Laurel, Oliver Hardy, June Marlowe, James Finlayson; **D:** James Parrott. **MED, CCB, MLB**

The Parent Trap 🐾🐾½ 1961 Mills plays a dual role in this heartwarming comedy as twin sisters who conspire to bring their divorced parents together again. Well-known Disney fluff. Followed by several made-for-television sequels featuring the now grown-up twins. **127m/C VHS, Beta, LV, Closed Caption.** Hayley Mills, Maureen O'Hara, Brian Keith, Charlie Ruggles, Una Merkel, Leo G. Carroll; **D:** David Swift. Nominations: Academy Awards '61: Best Film Editing, Best Sound. **DIS**

Parenthood 🐾🐾🐾 1989 (PG-13) Four grown siblings and their parents struggle with various levels of parenthood. From the college drop-out, to the nervous single mother, to the yuppie couple raising an overachiever, every possibility is explored, including the perspective from the older generation, portrayed by Robards. Genuinely funny with dramatic moments that work most of the time, with an affecting performance from Martin and Wiest. Director Howard has four kids and was inspired to make this film when on a European jaunt with them. **124m/C VHS, Beta, LV, Closed Caption.** Steve Martin, Mary Steenburgen, Dianne Wiest, Martha Plimpton, Keanu Reeves, Tom Hulce, Jason Robards Jr., Rick Moranis, Harley Jane Kozak, Joaquin Rafael (Leaf) Phoenix, Paul Linke, Dennis Dugan; **D:** Ron Howard; **W:** Lowell Ganz, Babaloo Mandel, Ron Howard; **M:** Randy Newman. Nominations: Academy Awards '89: Best Song ("I Love to See You Smile"), Best Supporting Actress (Wiest). **USH**

Parents 🐾🐾🐾 1989 (R) Dark satire of middle class suburban life in the '50s, centering on a young boy who discovers that his parents aren't getting their meat from the local butcher. Gives new meaning to leftovers and boasts a very dis-

turbing barbecue scene. Balaban's debut is a strikingly visual and creative gorefest with definite cult potential. The eerie score is by Badalamenti, who also composed the music for "Blue Velvet," "Wild at Heart," and the television series "Twin Peaks." **81m/C VHS, Beta, LV.** Randy Quaid, Mary Beth Hurt, Sandy Dennis, Kathryn Grody, Deborah Rush, Graham Jarvis, Bryan Madorsky, Juno Mills-Cockell; **D:** Bob Balaban; **W:** Christopher Hawthorne; **M:** Angelo Badalamenti, Jonathan Elias. **LIV, VES, HHE**

Paris Belongs to Us 🐾🐾½ Paris Nous Appartient; Paris is Ours 1960 An early entry in the French "new wave" of naturalistic cinema, this psychological mystery drama has a woman investigating a suicide linked to a possible worldwide conspiracy. Interesting, if somewhat dated by Cold War elements. **120m/B VHS.** **FR** Jean-Claude Brialy, Betty Schneider, Gianni Esposito, Francoise Prevost; **D:** Jacques Rivette; **W:** Jacques Rivette, Jean Gruault. **VDM**

Paris When It Sizzles 🐾🐾 1964 A screenwriter and his secretary fall in love while working on a film in Paris, confusing themselves with the script's characters. Star-studded cast deserves better than this lame script. Shot on location in Paris. Holden's drinking—he ran into a brick wall while under the influence—and some unresolved romantic tension between him and Hepburn affected shooting. Dietrich, Sinatra, Astaire, Ferrer, and Curtis show up for a party on the set. **110m/C VHS, Beta.** William Holden, Audrey Hepburn, Gregoire Aslan, Raymond Bussieres, Tony Curtis, Fred Astaire, Frank Sinatra, Noel Coward, Marlene Dietrich, Mel Ferrer; **D:** Richard Quine; **W:** George Axelrod. **PAR**

Paris Blues 🐾🐾½ 1961 Two jazz musicians, one white, one black, strive for success in Paris and become involved with American tourists who want to take them back to the States. Score by Duke Ellington and an appearance by Armstrong make it a must-see for jazz fans. **100m/B VHS, Beta, Closed Caption.** Paul Newman, Sidney Poitier, Joanne Woodward, Diahann Carroll, Louis Armstrong, Barbara Lange; **D:** Martin Ritt; **W:** Jack Sher, Walter Bernstein; **M:** Duke Ellington. Nominations: Academy Awards '61: Scoring of a Musical. **MGM, FCT**

Paris Express 🐾🐾½ The Man Who Watched Trains Go By 1953 When a man steals money from his employer, he boards the Paris Express to escape from the police. A bit convoluted, but well acted. Based on the George Simenon novel. **82m/C VHS, Beta.** Claude Rains, Herbert Lom, Felix Aylmer, Marius Goring, Anouk Aimee, Marta Toren; **D:** Harold French. **SNC, NOS, MRV**

Paris, France 🐾🐾 1994 (NC-17) Lucy (Hope) is a frustrated writer, living in Toronto, who decides the pursuit of sexual passion will unleash her blocked creative urges. Her main partner is poet Sloan (Outerbridge), the young man Lucy is trying to fashion in the image of a deceased Parisian lover, and also the man whose poetry her husband (and publisher) Michael (Ertmanis) is promoting. Lots of self-delusion and literary pretensions as well as erotic grappling. Adapted from the novel by Tom Walmsley. **CW:** Explicit sexual content. **111m/C VHS.** **CA** Leslie Hope, Peter Outerbridge, Victor Ertmanis, Raoul Trujillo, Dan Lett; **D:** Gerard Ciccoritti; **W:** Tom Walmsley; **M:** John McCarthy. **APX**

Paris Holiday 🐾🐾½ 1957 An actor heading for Paris to buy a noted author's latest screenplay finds mystery and romance. Entertaining chase scenes as the characters try to find the elusive script. **100m/C VHS, Beta.** Bob Hope, Fernandel, Anita Ekberg, Martha Hyer, Preston Sturges; **D:** Gerd Oswald. **UNI**

Paris Is Burning 🐾🐾🐾 1991 (R) Livingston's documentary portrayal of New York City's transvestite balls where men dress up, dance, and compete in various categories. Filmed between 1985 and 1989, this is a compelling look at a subculture of primarily black and Hispanic men and the one place they can truly be themselves. Madonna noted this look and attitude (much watered down) in her song "Vogue." **CW:** Language and sexuality. **71m/C VHS.** Dorian Corey, Pepper Labeija, Venus Xtravaganza, Octavia St. Laurant, Willi Ninja, Anji Xtravaganza, Freddie Pendavis, Junior Labeija; **D:** Jennie Livingston. National Society of Film Critics Awards '91: Best Feature Documentary; Sundance Film Festival '91: Grand Jury Prize. **ACA, FCT**

Paris, Texas 🐾🐾🐾½ 1983 (PG) After four years a drifter returns to find his son is being raised by his brother because the boy's mother has also disappeared. He tries to reconnect with the boy. Introspective script acclaimed by many film critics, but others found it to be too slow. **145m/C VHS, Beta, LV, Closed Caption.** **FR GE** Harry Dean Stanton, Nastassia Kinski, Dean Stockwell, Hunter

Carson, Aurore Clement; **D:** Wim Wenders; **W:** Sam Shepard, L.M. Kit Carson; **M:** Ry Cooder. British Academy Awards '84: Best Director (Wenders); Cannes Film Festival '84: Best Film. **FOX**

Paris Trout 🐾🐾🐾½ 1991 (R) Believing himself above the law, southern Trout (Hopper) shoots the mother and sister of a young black man who reneged on his IOU. Lawyer Harris is forced to defend a man he knows deserves to be punished, and wife Hershey suffers long. Adapted by Pete Dexter from his National Book Award-winning novel. Made for cable. **CW:** Brief language, violence, and sensuality. **98m/C VHS, Beta, LV, Closed Caption.** Dennis Hopper, Barbara Hershey, Ed Harris, Tina Lifford, Darnita Henry, Eric Ware, Ray McKinnon; **D:** Stephen Gyllenhaal; **W:** Pete Dexter; **C:** Robert Elswit. **MED, FXV, FCT**

Park Avenue Logger 🐾½ 1937 Silly story has blue-blood Ingraham believing son O'Brien is a pantly-waist, so he sends him to a lumber camp to prove his manhood. But junior is actually a wrestling champ (known as The Masked Marvel) and manages just fine, even winning the gal. **65m/B VHS.** George O'Brien, Beatrice Roberts, Lloyd Ingraham, Ward Bond, Willard Robertson, Bert Hanlon; **D:** David Howard. **GPV**

The Park is Mine 🐾🐾 1985 A deranged and desperate Vietnam vet takes hostages in Central Park. Semi-infamous film, notable for being the first movie made for HBO on cable and for being filmed in Toronto, before the inexpensive practice of filming in Canada became widespread. **102m/C VHS, Beta, Closed Caption.** Tommy Lee Jones, Yaphet Kotto, Helen Shaver; **D:** Steven Hilliard Stern; **M:** Tangerine Dream. **FOX**

Parker 🐾🐾 1984 An executive is kidnapped, then released, but does not know why. Unable to live with the mystery, he tracks his kidnappers down into a world of blackmail, drugs, and intrigue. **100m/C VHS, Beta.** Bryan Brown, Kurt Raab. **ORI**

Parlor, Bedroom and Bath 🐾🐾 Romeo in Pyjamas 1931 A family tries to keep a young woman from seeing that her love interest is flirting with other prospects. Doesn't live up to the standard Keaton set in his silent films. Keaton spoke French and German for foreign versions. **75m/B VHS, Beta.** Buster Keaton, Charlotte Greenwood, Cliff Edwards, Reginald Denny; **D:** Edward Sedgwick. **NOS, VYY, VDM**

Parole, Inc. 🐾🐾 1949 FBI takes on the underground in this early crime film. Criminals on parole have not served their sentences, and the mob is responsible. A meagerly financed yawner. **71m/B VHS.** Michael O'Shea, Evelyn Ankers, Turhan Bey, Lyle Talbot; **D:** Alfred Zeisler. **NOS, SNC**

Paroled to Die 🐾½ 1937 A man frames a young rancher for a bank robbery and a murder he committed in this wild west saga. Predictable and bland. **66m/B VHS, Beta.** Bob Steele, Kathleen Elliott. **NOS, DVT**

Parrish 🐾🐾 1961 Parrish McLean (Donohue) is a very ambitious young man, determined to make it in the rich world of the tobacco growers of the Connecticut River Valley. But his ruthless tobacco king stepfather (Malden) would like to thwart his plans. As befits Donohue's teen idol status, he also gets to romance three beautiful girls. Very silly and much too long. Based on the novel by Mildred Savage. 138m/C VHS. Troy Donahue, Claudette Colbert, Karl Malden, Dean Jagger, Diane McBain, Connie Stevens, Sharon Hugueny, Dub Taylor, Hampton Fancher, Bibi Osterwald, Madeleine Sherwood, Sylvia Miles, Carroll O'Connor, Vincent Gardenia; **D:** Delmer Daves; **W:** Delmer Daves; **C:** Harry Stradling; **M:** Max Steiner. *WAR*

Parting Glances 🎬🎬🎬 **1986 (R)** Low-budget but acclaimed film shows the relationship between two gay men and how they deal with a close friend's discovery of his exposure to the AIDS virus. Touching and realistic portrayals make this a must see. In 1990 Sherwood died of AIDS without completing any other films. **90m/C VHS, Beta, Closed Caption.** John Bolger, Richard Ganoung, Steve Buscemi, Adam Nathan, Patrick Tull; **D:** Bill Sherwood; **W:** Bill Sherwood. *FOX, FRF*

Partner 🎬 **1968** An extremely shy young man invents a strong alter ego to cope with the world but this second personality comes to dominate—with tragic results. In Italian with English subtitles. **110m/C VHS.** *IT* Pierre Clementi, Stefania Sandrelli, Tina Aumont; **D:** Bernardo Bertolucci; **M:** Ennio Morricone. *TPV*

Partners 🎬🎬 **1982 (R)** A straight, macho cop must pose as the lover of a gay cop to investigate the murder of a gay man in Los Angeles' homosexual community. Sets out to parody "Cruising"; unfortunately, the only source of humor the makers could find was in ridiculous homosexual stereotypes that are somewhat offensive and often unfunny. **93m/C VHS, Beta.** Ryan O'Neal, John Hurt, Kenneth McMillan, Robyn Douglass, Jay Robinson, Rick Jason; **D:** James Burrows; **W:** Francis Veber; **M:** Georges Delerue. *PAR*

Partners of the Trail 🎬½ **1944** U.S. marshals Brown and Hatton try to find out who's murdering ranchers which leads them to gunplay with Ingraham's band of outlaws. **57m/B VHS.** Johnny Mack Brown, Raymond Hatton, Lloyd Ingraham, Christine McIntyre, Robert Frazer; **D:** Lambert Hillyer. *GPV*

The Party 🎬🎬🎬 **1968** Disaster-prone Indian actor wreaks considerable havoc at a posh Hollywood gathering. Laughs come quickly in this quirky Sellers vehicle. **99m/C VHS, Closed Caption.** Peter Sellers, Claudine Longet, Marge Champion, Sharron Kimberly, Denny Miller, Gavin MacLeod, Carol Wayne; **D:** Blake Edwards; **W:** Blake Edwards; **M:** Henry Mancini. *MGM, TVC*

Party Animal 🎬 **1983 (R)** A college stud teaches a shy farm boy a thing or two about the carnal aspects of campus life. **78m/C VHS, Beta.** Timothy Carhart, Matthew Causey, Robin Harlan; **D:** David Beaird; **W:** David Beaird; **C:** Bryan England. *LIV*

Party Camp 🎬 **1987 (R)** A rowdy summer camp counselor endeavors to turn a tame backwoods camp into a non-stop party. Late entry in the "Meatballs"-spawned genre fails to do anything of even minor interest. **96m/C VHS, Beta.** Andrew Ross, Billy Jacoby, April Wayne, Kirk Cribb; **D:** Gary Graver. *LIV*

Party Favors woof! **1989 (R)** Erotic dancing, strip tease acts, and general hilarity are featured in this party tape. **83m/C VHS, Beta.** Jeannie Winters, Marjorie Miller, Gail Thackray; **D:** Ed Hansen. *LIV, VES*

Party Girl 🎬🎬🎬½ **1958** A crime drama involving an attorney representing a 1920s crime boss and his henchmen when they run afoul of the mob. The lawyer falls in love with a nightclub dancer who successfully encourages him to leave the mob, but not before he is wounded in a gang war attack, arrested, and forced to testify against the mob as a material witness. The mob then takes his girlfriend hostage to prevent his testifying, leading to an exciting climax. Must-see viewing for Charisse's steamy dance number. **99m/C VHS, Beta, LV.** Robert Taylor, Cyd Charisse, Lee J. Cobb, John Ireland, Kent Smith, Claire Kelly, Corey Allen; **D:** Nicholas Ray. *MGM*

Party Girl 🎬🎬½ **1994 (R)** In the "girls just wanna have fun" category comes this spritely saga of twenty-something Manhattan club gal Mary (Posey), who needs some steady income after the cops bust her for throwing an illegal rent party. So, since Mary's godmother is a librarian, she gets a job as a library clerk and discovers the wonders of the Dewey Decimal system (no, I'm not joking but presumably director Mayer is). Parker's Mary is a properly flaunting poseur but a little nightlife tends to go a long way. **CW:** Language and drug content. **94m/C VHS, LV, Closed Caption.** Parker Posey, Omar Townsend, Anthony De Sando, Guillermo Diaz, Sasha von Scherler, Liev Schreiber; **D:** Daisy von Scherler Mayer; **W:** Harry Birckmayer, Daisy von Scherler Mayer; **C:** Michael Slovis; **M:** Anton Sanko. *COL*

Party Girls 🎬½ **1929** Escort service girls run afoul of the law in this hokey melodrama. **67m/B VHS, Beta.** Douglas Fairbanks Jr., Jeanette Loff, Judith Barrie, Marie Prevost, John St. Polis, Lucien Prival; **D:** Victor Halperin. *NOS, LOO, SNC*

Party Girls for Sale 🎬🎬 **1954** Mystery thriller in which a young girl's body is found on the beach in Rio de Janeiro. Also known as "Violated." **?m/C VHS.** Raymond Burr, Scott Brady, Johanna Matz. *SNC*

Party Incorporated 🎬 *Party Girls* **1989 (R)** Marilyn Chambers (of "Behind the Green Door" fame) stars as a young widow with a huge tax load who gives parties to pay it off. Also known as "Party Girls." **80m/C VHS, LV.** Marilyn Chambers, Kurt Woodruff, Christine Veronica, Kimberly Taylor; **D:** Chuck Vincent. *VTR, NWV, IME*

Party Line 🎬 **1988 (R)** A veteran police captain and a district attorney team up to track down a pair of killers who find their victims through party lines. **90m/C VHS, Beta.** Richard Hatch, Shawn Weatherly, Richard Roundtree, Leif Garrett, Greta Blackburn; **D:** William Webb; **W:** Richard Brandes. *NO*

Party! Party! 🎬 **1983** A bunch of kids go nuts and have a party when their parents leave. **100m/C VHS.** **GB** M: Sting, David Bowie, Joe Jackson, Elvis Costello. *ACA*

Party Plane 🎬 **1990** Softcore fun-fest about a plane full of oversexed stewardesses. **81m/C VHS, Beta, LV.** Kent Stoddard, Karen Annarino, John Goff, Jill Johnson; **D:** Ed Hansen. *VES*

Pas Tres Catholique 🎬🎬 *Something Fishy* **1993** Pleasant comedy finds 40ish, chain-smoking, unconventional P.I. Maxine (Anemone) investigating her ex-husband for an insurance scram, drawing closer to her estranged son, and trying to decide romantically between long-time friend Florence and handsome economist Jacques. French with subtitles. **100m/B VHS.** *FR* Anemone, Christine Boisson, Michel Didym, Gregoire Colin, Denis Podalydes, Roland Bertin, Bernard Verley, Michel Roux; *Cameos:* Micheline Presle; **D:** Tonie Marshall; **W:** Tonie Marshall; **C:** Dominique Chapuis. Nominations: Cesar Awards '95: Best Actress (Anemone). *NYR*

Pascali's Island 🎬🎬🎬½ **1988 (PG-13)** A Turkish spy becomes involved with an adventurer's plot to steal rare artifacts, then finds himself ensnared in political and personal intrigue. Superior tragedy features excellent performances from Kingsley, Dance, and Mirren. **106m/C VHS, Beta, LV.** **GB** Ben Kingsley, Helen Mirren, Charles Dance, Sheila Allen, Vernon Dobtcheff; **D:** James Dearden; **W:** James Dearden. *LIV*

Pass the Ammo 🎬🎬½ **1988 (R)** Entertaining comedy about a young couple who attempt to steal back $50,000 of inheritance money that a televangelist swindled from the family. One of the more creative satires on this religious TV phenomenon. **93m/C VHS, Beta, LV.** Bill Paxton, Tim Curry, Linda Kozlowski, Annie Potts, Anthony Geary, Dennis Burkley, Glenn Withrow, Richard Paul; **D:** David Beaird; **W:** Neil Cohen, Joel Cohen; **M:** Carter Burwell. *LIV*

A Passage to India 🎬🎬🎬 **1984 (PG)** An ambitious adaptation of E.M. Forster's complex novel about relations between Brits and Indians in the 1920s. Drama centers on a young British woman's accusations that an Indian doctor raped her while serving as a guide in some rather ominous caves. Film occasionally flags, but is usually compelling. Features particularly strong performances from Bannerjee, Fox, and Davis. **163m/C VHS, Beta, LV, Closed Caption.** **GB** Peggy Ashcroft, Alec Guinness, James Fox, Judy Davis, Victor Banerjee, Nigel Havers; **D:** David Lean; **M:** Maurice Jarre. Academy Awards '84: Best Supporting Actress (Ashcroft), Best Original Score; British Academy Awards '85: Best Actress (Ashcroft); Golden Globe Awards '85: Best Foreign Film, Best Supporting Actress (Ashcroft), Best Score; Los Angeles Film Critics Association Awards '84: Best Supporting Actress (Ashcroft); National Board of Review Awards '84: Best Actor (Banerjee), Best Actress (Ashcroft), Best Director (Lean); New York Film Critics Awards '84: Best Actress (Ashcroft), Best Director (Lean), Best Film; Nominations: Academy Awards '84: Best Actress (Davis), Best Adapted Screenplay, Best Art Direction/Set Decoration, Best Cinematography, Best Costume Design, Best Director (Lean), Best Film Editing, Best Picture, Best Sound. *COL, BTV, HMV*

Passage to Marseilles 🎬🎬🎬 **1944** Hollywood propaganda in which convicts escape from Devil's Island and help French freedom fighters combat Nazis. Routine but entertaining. What else could it be with Bogart, Raines, Greenstreet, and Lorre, who later made a pretty good film set in Casablanca? **110m/B VHS, Beta.** Humphrey Bogart, Claude Rains, Sydney Greenstreet, Peter Lorre, Helmut Dantine, George Tobias, John Loder, Eduardo Ciannelli, Michele Morgan; **D:** Michael Curtiz; **C:** James Wong Howe; **M:** Max Steiner. *FOX*

Passed Away 🎬½ **1992 (PG-13)** Family patriarch Jack Scanlan dies and his entire family gets together for the funeral and a big Irish wake. The family, of course, is made up of a weird group of characters, good steadfast son Hoskins, dim-witted but good-looking son Petersen, rebellious daughter Reed, and a left-wing nun who wants to go to Central America and is accompanied by an illegal alien (McDormand). Throw in a mysterious female mourner and a pregnant granddaughter who goes into labor at the graveside and you come up with a movie that manages to use every comic death cliche ever imagined. Talented cast is wasted in a movie that should have passed away. **96m/C VHS, Beta, Closed Caption.** Bob Hoskins, Jack Warden, William L. Petersen, Helen Lloyd Breed, Maureen Stapleton, Pamela Reed, Tim Curry, Peter Riegert, Blair Brown, Patrick Breen, Nancy Travis, Teri Polo, Frances McDormand; **D:** Charlie Peters; **W:** Charlie Peters; **C:** Arthur Albert; **M:** Richard Gibbs. *HPH*

Passenger 🎬🎬🎬 *Pasazerka* **1961** While on a cruise ship Lisa (Slaska), a former camp guard at Auschwitz, realizes that fellow passenger Martha (Ciepielewska) was once one of her prisoners. Their meeting triggers a series of flashbacks to the Holocaust and to domination, suffering, and resistance. Director Munk was killed in a car crash during filming, which was completed by his colleague Witold Lesiewicz. Based on the novel by Zofia Posmysz-Piasecka; Polish with subtitles. **63m/B VHS.** **PL** Aleksandra Slaska, Anna Ciepielewska, Marek Walezewski, Jan Kreczewski, Irena Malkiewicz; **D:** Andrzej Munk; **W:** Andrzej Munk, Zofia Posmysz-Piasecka; **C:** Krzysztof Winiewicz; **M:** Tadeusz Baird. *HTV*

The Passenger 🎬🎬🎬½ *Profession: Reporter* **1975 (PG)** A dissatisfied television reporter changes identities with a dead man while on assignment in Africa, then learns that he is posing as a gunrunner. Mysterious, elliptical production from Italian master Antonioni, who co-wrote. Nicholson is fine in the low-key role, and Schneider is surprisingly winning as the woman drawn to him. The object of much debate, hailed by some as quintessential cinema and by others as slow and unrewarding. **119m/C VHS, Beta.** *IT* Jack Nicholson, Maria Schneider, Ian Hendry, Jenny Runacre, Steven Berkoff; **D:** Michelangelo Antonioni; **W:** Mark Peploe, Michelangelo Antonioni; **M:** Claude Bolling. National Board of Review Awards '75: 10 Best Films of the Year. *WAR*

Passenger 57 🎬 **1992 (R)** Classic movie-of-the-week fare. Anti-terrorist specialist John Cutter (Snipes) leaves his profession because of his wife's murder, and coincidentally boards the same plane as Charles Rane (Payne), an apprehended evil terrorist headed to trial in L.A. Somehow, Rane's thugs have also sneaked aboard with plans to hijack the plane, and it's up to Cutter to use his skills and save the day. Athletic Snipes is convincing in his role but can't make up for the plot's lack of premise. **CW:** Language and terrorist violence. **84m/C VHS, LV, Closed Caption.** Wesley Snipes, Bruce Payne, Tom Sizemore, Alex Datcher, Bruce Greenwood, Robert Hooks, Elizabeth Hurley, Michael Horse; **D:** Kevin Hooks; **W:** David Loughery, Dan Gordon; **M:** Stanley Clarke. *WAR*

The Passing 🎬🎬½ **1988** Two men find themselves trapped in the darker vicissitudes of life. The two lead almost parallel lives until an extraordinary event unites them. **96m/C VHS.** James Plaster, Welton Benjamin Johnson, Lynn Dunn, Albert B. Smith; **D:** John Huckert. *NO*

The Passing of Evil 🎬🎬½ *The Grasshopper; Passions* **1970 (R)** Bisset is a starstruck Canadian undone by the bright lights and big cities of America. By age 22, she's a burnt-out prostitute in Las Vegas. Cheerless but compelling. **96m/C VHS.** Jacqueline Bisset, Jim Brown, Joseph Cotten, Corbett Monica, Ramon Bieri, Christopher Stone, Roger Garrett, Shady Adams, Dick Richards, Tim O'Kelly, Ed Flanders; **D:** Jerry Paris; **C:** Sam Leavitt; **M:** Billy Goldenberg. *WAR*

The Passing of the Third Floor Back 🎬🎬 **1936** Boarding house tenants improve their lives after being inspired by a mysterious stranger. They revert, though, when he leaves. Now you know. Based on a Victorian morality play. **80m/B VHS, Beta.** **GB** Conrad Veidt, Rene Ray, Frank Cellier, Anna Lee, John Turnbull, Cathleen Nesbitt; **D:** Berthold Viertel. *SNC*

Passion 🎬🎬½ **1919** Paris, and the decadent Louis XV falls for the lovely Jeanne, making her his mistress, much to the scandal of the nation. Respectable silent version of "Madame DuBarry" is a relatively realistic costume drama, but it doesn't rate with the best German films of this period. **135m/B VHS, Beta.** **GE** Pola Negri, Emil Jannings, Harry Liedtke; **D:** Ernst Lubitsch. *VYY, GLV, GVV*

Passion 🎬🎬 **1954** When a rancher's young family falls victim to rampaging desperadoes, he enlists an outlaw's aid to avenge the murders of his loved ones. **84m/C VHS, Beta.** Raymond Burr, Cornel Wilde, Yvonne De Carlo, Lon Chaney Jr., John Qualen; **D:** Allan Dwan. *NO*

Passion 🎬½ **1992** Linda decides she married the wrong brother. So she plots to kill her husband and marry her in-law instead. **90m/C VHS.** Kristine Rose, Robert Labrosse, Kristine Frischhertz, Jack Ciolini; **D:** Joe D'Amato. *TSR*

Passion Fish 🎬🎬🎬 **1992 (R)** McDonnell plays May-Alice, a soap opera actress who is paralyzed after a taxi accident in New York. Confined to a wheelchair, the bitter woman moves back to her Louisiana home and alienates a number of live-in nurses until Chantelle (Woodard), who has her own problems, comes along. Blunt writing and directing by Sayles overcome the story's inherent sentimentality as do the spirited performances of the leads, including Curtis-Hall as the rogue romancing Chantelle and Strathairn as the Cajun bad boy McDonnell once loved. The laserdisc is available in letterbox format. **136m/C VHS, Beta, Closed Caption.** Mary McDonnell, Alfre Woodard, David Strathairn, Vondie Curtis-Hall, Nora Dunn, Sheila Kelley, Angela Bassett, Mary Portser, Maggie Renzi, Leo Burmester, Shauntisa Willis, John Henry, Michael Laskin; **D:** John Sayles; **W:** John Sayles; **C:** Roger Deakins; **M:** Mason Daring. Independent Spirit Awards '93: Best Supporting Actress (Woodard); Nominations: Academy Awards '92: Best Actress (McDonnell), Best Original Screenplay. *COL, MOV, BTV*

Passion Flower 🎬🎬 **1986 (PG-13)** A tropical romantic melodrama made for network TV and set in Singapore, where an ambitious banker falls in love with the daughter of island's wealthiest smuggler. The mixture of high finance, low-dealing and lust only proves moderately passionate. **95m/C VHS.** Bruce Boxleitner, Barbara Hershey, Nicol Williamson; **D:** Joseph Sargent; **M:** Miles Goodman. *THV*

Passion for Life 🎬🎬½ *L'Ecole Buissonniere; I Have a New Master* **1948** A new teacher uses revolutionary methods to engage students, but draws ire from staid parents in rural France. Worthwhile drama. In French with English subtitles. **89m/B VHS, Beta.** Bernard Blier, Julliette Faber, Edouard Delmont; **D:** Jean-Paul LeChanois. *FCT*

Passion for Power **1985** Two men involved in a drug-smuggling syndicate attempt to take over the business. Complications arise when they both fall for a beautiful, deceitful woman who turns them against one another. **94m/C VHS.** *SP* Hector Suarez, Sasha Montenegro, Manuel Capetillo, Alejandra Peniche. *NO*

Passion in Paradise 🎬🎬½ **1989** Fact-based mystery set in the Bahamas in 1943. Stewart is a spoiled rich girl who marries a handsome gigolo (Assante) much to daddy big bucks' (Steiger) displeasure. Then daddy is murdered and the son-in-law becomes the key suspect. Trashy, but Assante's fine. Made for television. **100m/C VHS, LV.** Armand Assante, Catherine Mary Stewart, Rod Steiger, Mariette Hartley, Wayne Rogers; **D:** Harvey Hart. *APX*

The Passion of Anna 🎬🎬🎬 **1970 (R)** A complicated psychological drama about four people on an isolated island. Von Sydow is an excon living a hermit's existence when he becomes involved with a crippled widow (Ullmann) and her two friends—all of whom have secrets in their pasts. Brutal and disturbing. Wonderful cinematography by Sven Nykvist. Filmed on the island of Faro. In Swedish with English subtitles. **101m/C VHS.** *SW* Max von Sydow, Liv Ullmann, Bibi Andersson, Erland Josephson, Erik Hell; **D:** Ingmar Bergman; **W:** Ingmar Bergman; **C:** Sven Nykvist. National Society of Film Critics Awards '70: Best Director (Bergman). *MGM, BTV*

The Passion of Darkly Noon 🎬½ **1995** Strange religious/sexual allegory. Running through the woods, Darkly Noon (Fraser) stumbles across the rural home of Callie (Judd) and Clay (Mortensen). Callie sees that the young man is ill and allows him to stay, discovering his parents have recently died and he's escaped from the ultra-religious community where he was raised. The sexy Callie is an uncomfortable attraction for the naive lad and when he meets a crazy old woman, Roxy (Zabriskie), in the woods, he's inclined to listen to her ravings against Callie, leading Darkly to believe he's been sent to punish the transgressors. **106m/C VHS.** **GB GE BE** Brendan Fraser, Ashley Judd, Viggo Mortensen, Grace Zabriskie, Loren Dean; **D:** Philip Ridley; **W:** Philip Ridley; **C:** John de Borman; **M:** Nick Bicat. *TTC*

The Passion of Joan of Arc 🎬🎬🎬 **1928** Masterful silent film relates the events of St. Joan's trial and subsequent martyrdom. Moving, eloquent work features legendary performace by Falconetti. Also rates among master Dreyer's finest efforts. A classic. Silent with music. **114m/B VHS, Beta.** **FR** Maria Falconetti, Eugena Sylvaw, Maurice Schultz, Antonin Artaud; **D:** Carl Theodor Dreyer. *VYY, MRV, NOS*

Passion of Love 🎬🎬🎬 *Passione d'Amore* **1982** Military captain becomes the obsession of his commander's mysterious cousin when he reports to an outpost far from home. Daring and fascinating. An unrelentingly passionate historical romance guaranteed to heat up the VCR. Available dubbed or with subtitles. **117m/C VHS, Beta.** *IT* **FR** Laura Antonelli, Bernard Giraudeau, Valeria D'Obici, Jean-Louis Trintignant; **D:** Ettore Scola; **W:** Ettore Scola. *VES, CIG, KIV*

A Passion to Kill 🎬½ *Rules of Obsession* **1994 (R)** Formulaic thriller finds psychologist David (Bakula) getting sexually involved with his best friend Jerry's (Getz) wife, who has a lurid past. Seems Diana (Field) stuck a kitchen knife into her abusive first husband and now Jerry's prospects don't look too good. **CW:** Strong sexuality; some violence and language. **95m/C VHS.** Scott Bakula, Chelsea Field, Sheila Kelly, John Getz, Rex Smith, France Nuyen, Michael Warren; **D:** Rick King; **W:** William F. Delligan. *APX*

Passionate Thief 🎬🎬½ *Risate de Gioia; Joyous Laughter* **1960** Two pickpockets and a bumbling actress plan to rip off the guests at a posh New Year's Eve party with slightly comic results. Not much to recommend in this slow moving flick. **100m/C VHS, Beta.** *IT* Anna Magnani, Ben Gazzara, Fred Clark, Toto, Edy Vessel; **D:** Mario Monicelli. *NLC*

The Passover Plot 🎬🎬 **1975 (PG)** A controversial look at the crucifixion of Christ which depicts him as a Zealot leader who, aided by his followers, faked his death and then "rose" to win new converts. **105m/C VHS, Beta.** Harry Andrews, Hugh Griffith, Zalman King, Donald Pleasence, Scott Wilson; **D:** Michael Campus; **M:** Alex North. Nominations: Academy Awards '76: Best Costume Design. *CAN*

Passport to Pimlico 🎬🎬½ **1949** Farce about a London neighborhood's residents who discover an ancient charter proclaiming their right to form their own country within city limits. Passable comedy. **81m/B VHS, Beta.** **GB** Stanley Holloway, Margaret Rutherford, Hermione Baddeley, Naunton Wayne, Basil Radford; **D:** Henry Cornelius. Nominations: Academy Awards '49: Best Story & Screenplay. *NOS, PSM, DVT*

Past Midnight 🎬🎬 **1992 (R)** Richardson plays a social worker who believes recently paroled killer Hauer was wrongly convicted. She attempts to prove his innocence while also falling in love—a dangerous combination. Richardson's beautiful and Hauer's making a successful career out of playing handsome psychos. **CW:** Language, violence, and sensuality. **100m/C VHS, LV, Closed Caption.** Natasha Richardson, Rutger Hauer, Clancy Brown, Guy Boyd; **D:** Jan Eliasberg; **W:** Frank Norwood; **M:** Steve Bartek. *COL*

Past Tense 🎬🎬½ **1994 (R)** Complicated thriller about a cop with a gorgeous but mysterious neighbor, a murder to solve, and problems separating reality from his nightmares. Made for cable television. **91m/C VHS, LV, Closed Caption.** Scott Glenn, Lara Flynn Boyle, Anthony LaPaglia, David Ogden Stiers, Sheree J. Wilson, Marita Geraghty, Stephen Graziano; **D:** Graeme Clifford. *REP*

Past the Bleachers 🎬🎬½ **1995 (PG)** Sentimental TV movie finds Anderson starring as Bill Parish—a man still lost by the death of his 11-year-old son. Reluctantly, he agrees to coach the Little League team his son had played on, with the help of an opinionated senior citizen (scene-stealer Hughes), and is drawn to the boy who turns out to be the team's star player. The appropriately named Lucky Diamond (Fricke) is both mute and part of a mysterious family background, and bonding proves therapeutic for both Bill and the youngster. Based on a novel by Christopher A. Bohjalian. **120m/C VHS, LV, Closed Caption.** Richard Dean Anderson, Barnard Hughes, Grayson Fricke, Glynnis O'Connor, Ken Jenkins; **D:** Michael Switzer; **W:** Don Rhymer; **M:** Stewart Levin. *HMK*

Pastime 🎬🎬🎬 *One Cup of Coffee* **1991 (PG)** A bittersweet baseball elegy set in the minor leagues in 1957. A boyish 41-year-old pitcher can't face his impending retirement and pals around with the team pariah, a 17-year-old black rookie. Splendidly written and acted, it's a melancholy treat whether you're a fan of the game or not, and safe for family attendance. The only drawback is a grungy, low-budget look. **94m/C VHS, LV.** William Russ, Scott Plank, Glenn Plummer, Noble Willingham, Jeffrey Tambor, Deirdre O'Connell, Ricky Paull Goldin; *Cameos:* Ernie Banks, Harmon Killebrew, Duke Snider, Bob Feller, Bill Mazeroski, Don Newcombe; **D:** Rob-cause them problems. **102m/C VHS, Closed Caption.** *GB FR* Sean Bury, Anicee Alvina, Keir Dullea, Ronald Lewis, Catherine Allegret, Georges Beller; *D:* Lewis Gilbert; *M:* Michel Colombier. *PAR*

Paul Bartel's The Secret Cinema ⚥⚥½ *The Secret Cinema* 1969 A woman cannot determine whether her life is real or a film by a maniacal director. Offbeat, creative, and a little disturbing. Followed by Bartel's short "Naughty Nurse." **37m/B VHS, Beta.** *D:* Paul Bartel. *RHI*

Paul Robeson ⚥⚥ 197? Major events in the life of the popular actor are recounted in this one-man performance. Originally staged by Charles Nelson Reilly. **118m/C VHS, Beta.** James Earl Jones; *D:* Lloyd Richards. *KAR*

Pauline at the Beach ⚥⚥⚥½ *Pauline a la Plage* 1983 (R) A young woman accompanies her more experienced cousin to the French coast for a summer of sexual hijinks. Contemplative, not coarse, though the leads look great in—and out—of their swimsuits. Breezy, typically talky fare from small-film master Rohmer. Cinematography by Nestor Almendro. In French with English subtitles. **95m/C VHS, Beta, LV.** *FR* Amanda Langlet, Arielle Dombasle, Pascal Greggory, Rosette; *D:* Eric Rohmer; *W:* Eric Rohmer; *C:* Nestor Almendros. *XVC, MED*

The Pawnbroker ⚥⚥⚥½ 1965 A Jewish pawnbroker in Harlem is haunted by his grueling experiences in a Nazi camp during the Holocaust. Powerful and well done. Probably Steiger's best performance. Adapted from a novel by Edward Lewis Wallant. **120m/B VHS, LV, Closed Caption.** Rod Steiger, Brock Peters, Geraldine Fitzgerald, Jaime Sanchez, Thelma Oliver; *D:* Sidney Lumet; *C:* Boris Kaufman; *M:* Quincy Jones. Berlin International Film Festival '65: Best Actor (Steiger); British Academy Awards '66: Best Actor (Steiger); Nominations: Academy Awards '65: Best Actor (Steiger). *REP*

Pawnshop 1916 Charlie is employed as a pawnbroker's assistant. Silent with music track. **20m/B VHS, Beta.** Charlie Chaplin. *CAB, GVV*

Pay Off ⚥ 1989 A lunatic psychiatrist seeks murderous revenge on his ex-patient/girlfriend and her family. **87m/C VHS, Beta.** Michael Fitzpatrick, Veronika Mattson, Margareta Krook; *D:* George Tirl. *TWE*

Pay or Die 1983 (R) A crime boss' men turn on him and kidnap his daughter. **92m/C VHS, Beta.** Dick Adair, Johnny Wilson; *D:* Bobby Suarez. *LIV*

Payback 1989 A brawny young man uses firepower to avenge those who have wronged him. **90m/C VHS, Beta.** Jean Carol. *NO*

Payback ⚥½ 1990 (R) A convict sets out to avenge his brother's death, and creates all sorts of mayhem in the process. Produced by Bob "Newlywed Game" Eubanks and scored by Daryl "Captain and Tennille" Dragon. *CW:* Language and violence. **94m/C VHS, Closed Caption.** Corey Michael Eubanks, Michael Ironside, Teresa Blake, Bert Remsen, Vincent Van Patten, Don Swayze; *D:* Russell Solberg; *M:* Daryl Dragon. *REP*

Payback ⚥⚥½ 1994 (R) An old, dying con (Armstrong) tells fellow inmate Oscar Bonsetter (Howell) the whereabouts of a fortune if he'll promise to kill cruel jail guard Gully (Bell) who made the geezer's life a misery. Years later, the now ex-con finds the ex-guard running a diner near the spot where the money is buried and decides to carry out his plan for revenge. If Oscar doesn't get too distracted by Gully's hot-to-trot wife, Rose (Severance), first. Also available in an unrated version. *CW:* Violence; nudity; language; explicit sex. **92m/C VHS, LV, Closed Caption.** C. Thomas Howell, Joan Severance, Marshall Bell, R.G. Armstrong; *D:* Anthony Hickox; *W:* Sam Bernard; *C:* David Bridges. *THV*

Payday ⚥⚥½ 1972 Torn stars as a declining country music star on tour in this portrayal of the seamy side of show business, from groupies to grimy motels. Well-written script and fine performances make this an engaging, if rather draining, drama not easily found on the big screen. **98m/C**

VHS, Beta. Rip Torn, Ahna Capri, Michael C. Gwynne, Jeff Morris; *D:* Daryl Duke. *NO*

The Payoff ⚥½ 1943 The old-fashioned newspaper-reporter-as-crime-fighter routine. When the city's special prosecutor is murdered a daring newshawk investigates and tracks the bad guys. But will he spell their names right? **74m/B VHS.** Lee Tracy, Tom Brown, Tina Thayer, Evelyn Brent, Jack LaRue, Ian Keith, John Maxwell; *D:* Arthur Dreifuss. *NOS, LOO*

Payoff ⚥⚥ 1991 (R) An ex-cop discovers the identity of gangsters who killed his parents. He traces them to a Lake Tahoe resort and plots revenge. Familiar crime story with a good cast. *CW:* Language, violence, and sensuality. **111m/C VHS, Beta, LV, Closed Caption.** Keith Carradine, Kim Greist, Harry Dean Stanton, John Saxon, Jeff Corey; *D:* Stuart Cooper; *W:* Douglas S. Cook; *M:* Charles Bernstein. *FXV*

P.C.U. ⚥⚥ 1994 (PG-13) Satire on campus political correctness follows freshman Tom Lawrence's (Young) adventures as he navigates the treacherous waters of Port Chester University (PCU). He falls in with the gang from the Pit, the militantly non-PC dorm, who encourage bizarre and offensive behavior. Essentially a modern update of "National Lampoon's Animal House," but without the brilliance; add half a bone for tackling the thorny sensitivity issue in a humorous way that parodies, but shouldn't offend. Actor Bochner's directorial debut. *CW:* Language, drug-content, and some sensuality. **81m/C VHS, LV, Closed Caption.** Jeremy Piven, Chris Young, David Spade, Sarah Trigger, Jessica Walter, Jon Favreau, Megan Ward, Jake Busey, Alex Desert; *Cameos:* George Clinton; *D:* Hart Bochner; *W:* Adam Leff, Zak Penn; *M:* Steve Vai. *FXV*

Peacekillers ⚥½ 1971 A mean bunch of bikers visit a commune to kidnap a young woman. The gang has a big surprise in store for them when the girl escapes. **86m/C VHS, Beta.** Michael Ontkean, Clint Ritchie, Paul Krokop; *D:* Douglas Schwartz. *NWV, VTR*

Peacemaker ⚥ 1990 (R) Two aliens masquerading as human cops stalk each other through a major city. **90m/C VHS, Beta, LV.** Robert Forster, Lance Edwards, Hilary Shepard, Bert Remsen, Robert Davi; *D:* Kevin S. Tenney; *W:* Kevin S. Tenney. *FRH*

The Peacock Fan ⚥½ 1929 The Peacock Fan is protected by a deadly curse, with certain death to anyone who possesses it. **50m/B VHS, Beta.** Lucian Preval. *SNC, VYY*

The Peanut Butter Solution ⚥⚥½ 1985 (PG) An imaginative 11-year-old boy investigates a strange old house which is haunted by friendly ghosts who are in possession of a magic potion. **96m/C VHS, Beta.** Matthew Mackay, Siluck Saysanasy, Alison Podbrey, Michael Maillot, Griffith Brewer, Michael Hogan, Helen Hughes; *D:* Michael Rubbo; *W:* Michael Rubbo; *M:* Lewis Furey. *NWV, VTR, HHE*

The Pearl ⚥⚥⚥ 1948 Based on a John Steinbeck story, a Mexican fisherman, living in poverty, finds a magnificent pearl and he thinks it will improve the lives of his family. He is bewildered by what this pearl really brings—liars and thieves. Simple, yet larger-than-life film, beautifully photographed; a timeless picture capturing human nature. **77m/B VHS.** *MX* Pedro Armendariz Sr., Maria Elena Marques, Fernando Wagner, Charles Rooner; *D:* Emilio Fernandez. *FCT, MAS*

The Pearl of Death ⚥⚥½ 1944 Holmes and Watson investigate the theft of a precious pearl. **69m/B VHS, Beta, Closed Caption.** Basil Rathbone, Nigel Bruce, Dennis Hoey, Miles Mander, Rondo Hatton, Evelyn Ankers; *D:* Roy William Neill. *FOX*

Pearl of the South Pacific ⚥⚥ *South Sea Woman* 1955 A trio of adventurers destroy a quiet and peaceful island when they ransack it for pearl treasures. **85m/C VHS, Beta.** Dennis (Stanley Morner) Morgan, Virginia Mayo, David Farrar; *D:* Allan Dwan; *W:* Edwin Blum. *NO*

The Pebble and the Penguin ⚥⚥½ 1994 (G) Animated musical about a shy, romantic penguin named Hubie (Short), who must present his lady love Marina (Golden) with a beautiful pebble to win her hand forever before the villainous Drake (Curry) can claim her. Hubie is helped along the way by a cantankerous new friend (Belushi) he meets when stranded on a boat to Tahiti. Together the two race back to Antarctica fighting enemies and the elements along the way. Based on a true mating custom of the Adeli penguins, the story is satisfying for younger viewers, but does not have the animation magic of other recent films to keep adults interested. Beware of the sugary Manilow tunes. **74m/C VHS, LV, Closed Caption.** *W:* Rachel Koretsky, Steve Whitestone; *M:* Barry Manilow, Bruce Sussman, Mark Watters; *V:* Martin Short, Annie Golden, Tim Curry, James Belushi. *MGM*

Peck's Bad Boy ⚥⚥ 1921 Impudent, precocious brat causes his parents considerable grief. Someone should lock this kid in a room with W.C. Fields or the Alien. Silent film based on the stories by George Wilbur Peck. **51m/B VHS, Beta, LV.** Jackie Coogan, Thomas Meighan, Raymond Hatton, Wheeler Oakman, Lillian Leighton; *D:* Sam Wood. *NOS, MRV, CCB*

Peck's Bad Boy ⚥⚥½ 1934 A wedge is driven between a young boy and his adoptive father when the man's sister and her son move in. The aunt wants her son to be number one, causing much discord. Cooper is excellent in his role as the adopted son. **70m/B VHS.** Thomas Meighan, Jackie Cooper, Dorothy Peterson, Jackie Searl, O.P. Heggie, Harvey Clark, Lloyd Ingraham; *D:* Eddie Cline. *NOS, MLB*

Peck's Bad Boy with the Circus ⚥⚥ 1938 The circus will never be the same after the mischievous youngster and his buddies get done with it. Gilbert and Kennedy provide the high points. **67m/B VHS, Beta.** Tommy Kelly, Ann Gillis, George "Spanky" McFarland, Edgar Kennedy, Billy Gilbert; *D:* Eddie Cline. *NOS, VYY, DVT*

Pecos Bill 1986 Meet the man who used the Grand Canyon for a swimmin' hole, dug the Rio Grande and used the Texas panhandle for a fryin' pan. From Shelly Duvall's "Tall Tales and Legends" series. Originally made for cable television. **50m/C VHS, Closed Caption.** Steve Guttenberg, Martin Mull, Claude Akins, Rebecca DeMornay. *FOX, COL*

Pecos Kid ⚥ 1935 A child has his parents killed, and grows up embittered, vengeful and thirsty for blood. **56m/B VHS, Beta, LV.** Fred Kohler Jr. *NOS*

Pedale Douce ⚥⚥½ *What a Drag* 1996 Irreverant comedy features a romantic triangle involving content gay businessman Adrien (Timsit), whose confidante is the liberal Eva (Ardant), owner of a trendy Paris eatery with an all-gay staff and predominantly gay clientele. Adrien persuades Eva to pose as his wife in order to close a deal with conservative, married banker Alexandre (Berry). Alexandre becomes enchanted with Eva and begins to pursue her, causing a comedy of errors and unexpected jealousy for Adrien, who tries to derail their affair. French with subtitles. **102m/C VHS.** *FR* Patrick Timsit, Fanny Ardant, Richard Berry, Michele Laroque, Jacques Gamblin; *D:* Gabriel Aghion; *W:* Patrick Timsit, Gabriel Aghion, Pierre Palmade; *C:* Fabio Conversi; *M:* Herve Masini, Philippe Chopin. Cesar Awards '97: Best Actress (Ardant); Nominations: Cesar Awards '97: Best Actor (Timsit), Best Film. *NYR*

Peddlin' in Society ⚥⚥ *Da Bancarella a Bancarotta* 1947 A fruit vendor makes it big on the black market and lives the good life, until poor investments force her back to her old means. Strong perfomances by Magnani and De Sica. In Italian with English subtitles. **85m/B VHS.** *IT* Anna Magnani, Vittorio De Sica, Virgilio Riento, Laura Gore; *D:* Gennaro Righelli. *DVT, HEG*

The Pedestrian 🐾🐾🐾½ *Der Fussgaenger* **1973 (PG)** A prominent German industrialist is exposed as a Nazi officer who supervised the wholesale devastation of a Greek village during WWII. Impressive debut for director Schell, who also appears in a supporting role. **97m/C VHS, Beta.** *GE SI* Maximilian Schell, Peggy Ashcroft, Lil Dagover, Francoise Rosay, Elisabeth Bergner; **D:** Maximilian Schell; **M:** Manos Hadjidakis. Golden Globe Awards '74: Best Foreign Film; National Board of Review Awards '74: 5 Best Foreign Films of the Year; Nominations: Academy Awards '73: Best Foreign Language Film. *GLV, SWC*

The Pee Wee Herman Show **1982** The original HBO special which introduced Pee Wee to the world. Hilarious stuff, with help from Captain Carl (Hartman), Miss Yvonne, and other assorted pals. Warning: Not to be confused with Pee Wee's children's show. **60m/C VHS.** Paul (Pee Wee Herman) Reubens, Phil Hartman, John Paragon. *NO*

Pee Wee's Big Adventure 🐾🐾🐾½ **1985 (PG)** Zany, endearing comedy about an adult nerd's many adventures while attempting to recover his stolen bicycle. Chock full of classic sequences, including a barroom encounter between Pee Wee and several ornery bikers, and a tour through the Alamo. A colorful, exhilarating experience. **92m/C VHS, Beta, LV, Closed Caption.** Paul (Pee Wee Herman) Reubens, Elizabeth Daily, Mark Holton, Diane Salinger, Judd Omen, Cassandra Peterson, James Brolin, Morgan Fairchild, Tony Bill, Jan Hooks; **D:** Tim Burton; **W:** Paul (Pee Wee Herman) Reubens, Phil Hartman, Michael Varhol; **M:** Danny Elfman. *WAR*

Pee Wee's Playhouse Festival of Fun **1988** Five fun-filled episodes of the playhouse! **123m/C VHS, Beta, Closed Caption.** Paul (Pee Wee Herman) Reubens. *MED*

Peephole 🐾 **1993** Prison psychiatrist is asked by the DA to keep Rick, who committed a sex crime against a little girl, in jail any way he can. So he visits Rick's prostitute girlfriend Sheena for info but instead winds up one of her clients. Meanwhile, Rick has been released and a little girl has been found dead, but nothing's that clear cut. Based on director/writer Bitterman's play. **90m/C VHS.** Patrick Husted, Rick Dean, William Dennis Hunt, Kristen Trucksess, Peter Crook; **D:** Shem Bitterman; **W:** Shem Bitterman. *LEO*

Peeping Tom 🐾🐾🐾½ **1960** Controversial, unsettling thriller in which a psychopath lures women before his film camera, then records their deaths at his hand. Unnerving subject matter is rendered impressively by British master Powell. A classic of its kind, but definitely not for everyone. This is the original uncut version of the film, released in the U.S. in 1979 with the assistance of Martin Scorsese. **88m/C VHS, Beta, LV.** Karl-Heinz Boehm, Moira Shearer, Anna Massey, Maxine Audley, Esmond Knight, Shirley Anne Field, Brenda Bruce, Pamela Green, Jack Watson, Nigel Davenport, Susan Travers, Veronica Hurst, Martin Miller; **Cameos:** Michael Powell; **D:** Michael Powell. *HMV, AOV*

Peg O' My Heart 🐾🐾 **1922** Taylor portrays the motherless Irish charmer sent to live with her mother's English relatives during the Irish rebellion. Of course, she must overcome their upper-class English snobbery to become a part of the family. **85m/B VHS.** Laurette Taylor, Mahlon Hamilton, Russell Simpson, Ethel Grey; **D:** King Vidor; **C:** George Barnes. *NO*

Peggy Sue Got Married 🐾🐾½ **1986 (PG-13)** Uneven but entertaining comedy about an unhappily married woman seemingly unable to relive her life when she falls unconscious at a high school reunion and awakens to find herself back in school. Turner shines, but the film flags often, and Cage isn't around enough to elevate entire work. O'Connor scores, though, as a sensitive biker. Look for musician Marshall Crenshaw as part of the reunion band. **103m/C VHS, Beta, LV, Closed Caption.** Kathleen Turner, Nicolas Cage, Catherine Hicks, Maureen O'Sullivan, John Carradine, Helen Hunt, Lisa Jane Persky, Barbara Harris, Joan Allen, Kevin J. O'Connor, Barry Miller, Don Murray, Leon Ames, Sofia Coppola, Sachi Parker, Jim Carrey; **D:** Francis Ford Coppola; **W:** Jerry Leichtling, Arlene Sarner; **C:** Jordan Cronenweth; **M:** John Barry. National Board of Review Awards '86: Best Actress (Turner); Nominations: Academy Awards '86: Best Actress (Turner), Best Cinematography, Best Costume Design. *FOX*

The Peking Blond 🐾½ *The Blonde From Peking; Le Blonde de Pekin* **1968** French-fried spyfilm boasts lousy acting unencumbered by plot. Amnesiac may or may not hold secrets coveted by Americans, Russians and Chinese. **80m/C VHS.** *FR* Mireille Darc, Claudio Brook, Edward G. Robinson, Pascale Roberts; **D:** Nicolas Gessner; **W:** Nicolas Gessner, Marc Behm. *MRV*

The Pelican Brief 🐾🐾½ **1993 (PG-13)** Tulane law student Darby Shaw (Roberts) writes a speculative brief on the murders of two Supreme Court justices that results in more murder and sends her running for her life. Fairly faithful to the Grisham bestseller, but the multitude of characters is confusing. Pakula adds style and star-power, but much will depend on your tolerance for paranoid political thrillers and ability to accept Roberts as the smart cookie who hits on the right answer and then manages to keep herself alive while bodies are dropping all around her. Washington is sharp as reporter Gray Grantham, the guy Roberts looks like she falls hard for (but the book's romance is nowhere to be seen).**CW:** Momentary language and some violence. **141m/C VHS, LV, 8mm, Closed Caption, DVD.** Julia Roberts, Denzel Washington, John Heard, Tony Goldwyn, Stanley Tucci, James B. Sikking, William Atherton, Robert Culp, John Lithgow, Sam Shepard; **Cameos:** Hume Cronyn; **D:** Alan J. Pakula; **W:** Alan J. Pakula; **C:** Stephen Goldblatt; **M:** James Horner. Nominations: MTV Movie Awards '94: Best Actress (Roberts), Most Desirable Male (Washington). *WAR*

Pelle the Conqueror 🐾🐾🐾🐾 **1988** Overpowering tale of a Swedish boy and his widower father who serve landowners in late 19th-century Denmark. Compassionate saga of human spirit contains numerous memorable sequences. Hvenegaard is wonderful as young Pelle, but von Sydow delivers what is probably his finest performance as a sympathetic weakling. American distributors foolishly trimmed the film by some 20 minutes (140 minute version). From the novel by Martin Anderson Nexo. In Swedish with English subtitles. **160m/C VHS, Beta, LV.** *SW DK* Max von Sydow, Pelle Hvenegaard, Erik Paaske, Bjorn Granath, Axel Strobye, Astrid Villaume, Troels Asmussen, John Wittig, Anne Lise Hirsch Bjerrum, Kristina Tornqvist, Morten Jorgensen; **D:** Bille August; **W:** Bille August. Academy Awards '88: Best Foreign Language Film; Cannes Film Festival '88: Best Film; Golden Globe Awards '89: Best Foreign Film; Nominations: Academy Awards '88: Best Actor (von Sydow). *HBO*

The Penalty 🐾🐾½ **1920** Legless madman Blizzard (Chaney) is after revenge on his family, doctor, and society. Chaney's properly creepy. **60m/B VHS.** Lon Chaney Sr., Claire Adams, Kenneth Harlan, Charles Clary; **D:** Wallace Worsley. *FCT*

Penalty Phase 🐾🐾 **1986** An up-for-election judge must decide a murder case in which his future, as well as the defendant's, is in question. Made for television. **94m/C VHS, Beta, Closed Caption.** Peter Strauss, Melissa Gilbert, Jonelle Allen; **D:** Tony Richardson; **M:** Ralph Burns. *VTR, NWV*

Pendulum 🐾🐾 **1969 (PG)** A police captain struggles to prove himself innocent of his wife's—and his wife's lover's—murders. Wow. **106m/C VHS, Beta, LV.** George Peppard, Jean Seberg, Richard Kiley, Madeline Sherwood, Charles McGraw, Marj Dusay; **D:** George Schaefer; **C:** Lionel Lindon. *COL*

The Penitent 🐾🐾 **1988 (PG-13)** A remote village's annual reenactment of the crucifixion of Christ serves as the backdrop for Assante's affair with his friend's (Julia) wife. Quirky little tale that focuses a shade too much on the romantic problems of the trio rather than the intriguing religious practices going on around them. **94m/C VHS, Beta.** Raul Julia, Armand Assante, Rona Freed, Julie Carmen; **D:** Cliff Osmond; **M:** Alex North. *LIV*

Penitentiary 🐾🐾½ **1979 (R)** A realistic story of a black fighter who survives his prison incarceration by winning bouts against the other prisoners. Well-made and executed, followed by two progressively worse sequels. **99m/C VHS, Beta.** Leon Isaac Kennedy, Jamaa Fanaka; **D:** Jamaa Fanaka; **W:** Jamaa Fanaka. *UNI, FCT*

Penitentiary 2 🐾 **1982 (R)** A welterweight fighter is after the man who murdered his girlfriend, who, luckily, is incarcerated in the same prison as Our Hero. Sometimes things just work out right. **108m/C VHS, Beta.** Leon Isaac Kennedy, Mr. T, Leif Erickson, Ernie Hudson, Glynn Turman; **D:** Jamaa Fanaka; **W:** Jamaa Fanaka. *MGM, HHE*

Penitentiary 3 🐾½ **1987 (R)** Once again, Kennedy as the inmate boxer extraordinaire punches his way out of various prison battles. Another punch-drunk sequel. **91m/C VHS, Beta, Closed Caption.** Leon Isaac Kennedy, Anthony Geary, Steve Antin, Ric Mancini, Kessler Raymond, Jim Bailey; **D:** Jamaa Fanaka; **W:** Jamaa Fanaka. *WAR*

Penn and Teller Get Killed 🐾🐾 **1990 (R)** The comedy team with a cult following are pursued by an assassin through dozens of pratfalls in this dark comedy. **91m/C VHS, Beta, LV, Closed Caption.** Penn Jillette, Teller, Caitlin Clarke, Leonardo Cimino, David Patrick Kelly; **D:** Arthur Penn. *WAR*

Pennies From Heaven 🐾🐾🐾½ **1981 (R)** Underrated, one-of-a-kind musical about a horny sheet-music salesman in Chicago and his escapades during the Depression. Extraordinary musical sequences have stars lip-synching to great effect. Martin is only somewhat acceptable as the hapless salesman, but Peters and Harper deliver powerful performances as the women whose lives he ruins. Walken brings down the house in a stunning song-and-dance sequence. Adapted by Dennis Potter from his British television series. ♫The Clouds Will Soon Roll By; Did You Ever See A Dream Walking?; Yes, Yes; Pennies From Heaven; Love Is Good for Anything That Ails You; I Want to Be Bad; Let's Misbehave; Life Is Just a Bowl of Cherries; Let's Face the Music and Dance. **107m/C VHS, Beta, LV.** Steve Martin, Bernadette Peters, Christopher Walken, Jessica Harper, Vernel Bagneris; **D:** Herbert Ross; **W:** Dennis Potter; **C:** Gordon Willis; **M:** Ralph Burns, Marvin Hamlisch. Golden Globe Awards '82: Best Actress—Musical/Comedy (Peters); National Society of Film Critics Awards '81: Best Cinematography; Nominations: Academy Awards '81: Best Adapted Screenplay, Best Costume Design, Best Sound. *MGM, FCT*

Penny Serenade 🐾🐾🐾 **1941** Newlyweds adopt a child, but tragedy awaits. Simplistic story nonetheless proves to be a moving experience. They don't make 'em like this anymore, and no one plays Grant better than Grant. Dunne is adequate. Also available colorized. **120m/B VHS, LV.** Cary Grant, Irene Dunne, Beulah Bondi, Edgar Buchanan; **D:** George Stevens. Nominations: Academy Awards '41: Best Actor (Grant).*CNG, NOS, PSM*

Pentathlon 🐾🐾½ **1994 (R)** East German Olympic athlete Eric Brogar (Lundgren) defects to the U.S. a year before the crash of the Berlin Wall, causing embarassed German authorities to seek revenge on him and his family.**CW:** Violence; language. **101m/C VHS, LV, Closed Caption.** Dolph Lundgren, David Soul, Roger E. Mosley, Renee Coleman; **D:** Bruce Malmuth. *LIV*

Penthouse 🐾🐾🐾 *Crooks in Clover* **1933** Baxter is a corporation lawyer who, for a change of pace, defends a gangland boss (Pendleton). His success loses him his high-society clientele but wins him Pendleton's respect and protection. But Baxter then gets involved in a further series of gang-related crimes, which nearly cost him his life. Also aiding Baxter is Loy, playing a smart-cookie gun moll, who would take her wisecracks to "The Thin Man" the following year. Good combo of melodrama, suspense, and humor. **90m/B LV.** Warner Baxter, Myrna Loy, Nat Pendleton, C. Henry Gordon, Mae Clarke, Charles Butterworth, Phillips Holmes; **D:** Woodbridge S. Van Dyke. *MGM*

The Penthouse 🐾🐾 1992 Givens stars as a wealthy young woman stalked by an old boyfriend who just happens to have escaped from a mental institution. When he traps her in her home, she has two choices—love him or die. Based on the novel by Elleston Trevor. **93m/C VHS, Closed Caption.** Robin Givens, David Hewlett, Cedric Smith, Donnelly Rhodes, Robert Guillaume; **D:** David Greene. *TTC*

The People 🐾🐾½ 1971 A young teacher takes a job in a small town and finds out that her students have telepathic powers and other strange qualities. Adapted from a novel by Zenna Henderson. Good atmosphere, especially for a TV movie. **74m/C VHS, Beta.** Kim Darby, Dan O'Herlihy, Diane Varsi, William Shatner; **D:** John Korty; **M:** Carmine Coppola. *PSM*

People Are Funny 🐾🐾 1946 Battling radio producers vie to land the big sponsor with an original radio idea. Comedy ensues when one of them comes up with a great idea—stolen from a local station. **94m/B VHS, Beta.** Jack Haley, Rudy Vallee, Ozzie Nelson, Art Linkletter, Helen Walker; **D:** Sam White. *NO*

The People Next Door 🐾🐾 1970 Seventies attempt at exposing the drug problems of suburban youth. Typical middle-class parents Wallach and Harris are horrified to discover that daughter Winters is strung out on LSD. They fight to expose the neighborhood pusher while struggling to understand their now-alien daughter. Based on J.P. Miller's television play. **93m/C VHS.** Deborah Winters, Eli Wallach, Julie Harris, Stephen McHattie, Hal Holbrook, Cloris Leachman, Nehemiah Persoff; **D:** David Greene. *NO*

The People That Time Forgot 🐾🐾½ 1977 (PG) Sequel to "The Land That Time Forgot," based on the Edgar Rice Burroughs novel. A rescue team returns to a world of prehistoric monsters to rescue a man left there after the first film. **90m/C VHS, Beta.** *GB* Doug McClure, Patrick Wayne, Sarah Douglas, Dana Gillespie, Thorley Walters, Shane Rimmer; **D:** Kevin Connor.

The People Under the Stairs 🐾🐾½ 1991 (R) Adams is part of a scheme to rob a house in the slums owned by a mysterious couple (Robie and McGill, both of "Twin Peaks" fame). After his friends are killed off in a gruesome fashion, he discovers that the couple aren't the house's only strange inhabitants—homicidal creatures also lurk within. **CW:** Terror/violence. **102m/C VHS, LV, Closed Caption.** Everett McGill, Wendy Robie, Brandon Adams, Ving Rhames, A.J. Langer, Sean Whalen; **D:** Wes Craven; **W:** Wes Craven; **C:** Sandi Sissel; **M:** Don Peake. *USH*

The People vs. Jean Harris 🐾🐾🐾 1981 Follows the trial of Jean Harris. Shortly before this film was released, she had been convicted of murder in the death of Dr. Herman Tarnower, the author of "The Scarsdale Diet." Harris was headmistress in a private school all the while. Made for television. Burstyn was nominated for an Emmy Award for best actress. **147m/C VHS, Beta.** Ellen Burstyn, Martin Balsam, Richard Dysart, Peter Coyote, Priscilla Morrill, Sarah Marshall, Millie Slavin; **D:** George Schaefer; **M:** Brad Fiedel. *NO*

The People vs. Larry Flynt 🐾🐾🐾 1996 (R) Controversy surrounded director Forman's look at unrepentant pornographer and Hustler Magazine publisher, Larry Flynt (Harrelson). While feminists decried what they saw as a whitewash of Flynt's career, Forman insisted his movie was about Flynt's legal battles concerning the First Amendment and freedom of speech. If you can set aside your prejudices, you'll find a master storyteller at work and some great performances from Harrelson as Flynt, Love as his drug-addicted and ultimately tragic wife Althea, and Norton as Flynt's sometimes impatient attorney, Alan Isaacman, who does get his big moment before the U.S. Supreme Court (his speeches are taken from actual court transcripts). **CW:** Strong sexual material, nudity, language and drug use. **130m/C VHS,** LV, Closed Caption. Woody Harrelson, Courtney Love, Edward Norton, James Cromwell, Crispin Glover, Brett Harrelson, James Carville, Vincent Schiavelli, Richard Paul, Donna Hanover, Norm MacDonald, Miles Chapin, Jan Triska; **Cameos:** Larry Flynt; **D:** Milos Forman; **W:** Larry Karaszewski, Scott Alexander; **C:** Philippe Rousselot; **M:** Thomas Newman. Golden Globe Awards '97: Best Director (Forman), Best Screenplay; Los Angeles Film Critics Association Awards '96: Best Supporting Actor (Norton); National Board of Review Awards '96: Best Supporting Actor (Norton); New York Film Critics Awards '96: Best Supporting Actress (Love); Nominations: Academy Awards '96: Best Actor (Harrelson), Best Director (Forman); Golden Globe Awards '97: Best Actor—Drama (Harrelson), Best Actress—Drama (Love), Best Film—Drama; MTV Movie Awards '97: Breakthrough Performance (Love); Screen Actors Guild Award '96: Best Actor (Harrelson). *COL*

People Who Own the Dark woof! 1975 (R) A group of wealthy men and a coterie of call girls are having an orgy in the basement of an old home when a nuclear war breaks out. Everyone outside is blinded by the blast but some survivors manage to make their way to the house where they try to attack the inhabitants. Don't bother. **87m/C VHS.** Paul Naschy, Tony Kendall, Maria Perschy, Terry Kemper, Tom Weyland, Anita Brock, Paul Mackey; **D:** Armando de Ossorio; **W:** Armando de Ossorio. *SUN, MRV*

People Will Talk 🐾🐾🐾½ 1951 Grant plays Dr. Noah Praetorius, a doctor and educator who believes that the mind is a better healer than medicine. Archenemy Cronyn is the fellow instructor with a vengeance. Sickened by Grant's goodwill and the undying attention he receives, Cronyn reports Grant's unconventional medical practices to the higher-ups in hopes of ruining his reputation as doctor/educator. Witty and satirical, this well-crafted comedy-drama is chock-full of interesting characters and finely tuned dialogue. Adapted from the play "Dr. Praetorius" by Curt Goetz. **110m/B VHS.** Cary Grant, Jeanne Crain, Finlay Currie, Hume Cronyn, Walter Slezak, Sidney Blackmer, Basil Ruysdael, Katherine Locke, Margaret Hamilton, Carleton Young, Billy House, Stuart Holmes; **D:** Joseph L. Mankiewicz; **W:** Joseph L. Mankiewicz; **C:** Milton Krasner. *FXV*

People's Choice 🐾🐾 1946 A small town boy suffers laryngitis, becomes a radio personality via his new huskiness, and claims he's a notorious criminal. **68m/B VHS, Beta, LV.** Drew Kennedy, Louise Arthur, George Meeker, Rex Lease, Fred Kelsey. *NO*

Pepe Le Moko 🐾🐾🐾 1937 An influential French film about a notorious gangster holed up in the Casbah, emerging at his own peril out of love for a beautiful woman. Stirring film established Gabin as a matinee idol. Cinematography is particularly fine too. Based upon the D'Ashelbe novel. The basis for both "Algiers," the popular Boyer-Lamarr melodrama, and the musical "The Casbah." In French with English subtitles. **87m/B VHS, Beta, 8mm.** *FR* Jean Gabin, Mireille Balin, Gabriel Gabrio, Lucas Gridoux; **D:** Julien Duvivier. National Board of Review Awards '41: 5 Best Foreign Films of the Year. *VYY, NOS, HHT*

Pepi, Luci, Bom and Other Girls on the Heap 🐾🐾½ *Pepi, Luci, Bom y Otras Chicas del Monton* 1980 Almodovar's low-budget directorial debut will be of interest primarily to the director's aficionados. Pepi (Maura's debut role) is a Madrid heiress who gets in trouble when her neighbor, a policeman, notices her marijuana plants. She offers sexual favors in return for silence but is raped instead. Pepi later decides on revenge by seducing Luci, the policeman's wife, aided by her girlfriend, Bom. There's lots of partying, drugs, promiscuity, and violence, none of it very involving. In Spanish with English subtitles. **80m/C VHS.** *SP* Carmen Maura, Eva Siva, Olivido Gara, Felix Rotaeta; **D:** Pedro Almodovar; **W:** Pedro Almodovar. *FCT, CCN*

Pepper and His Wacky Taxi 🐾½ 1972 (G) Father of four buys a '59 Cadillac and starts a cab company. Time-capsule fun. **79m/C VHS, Beta.** John Astin, Frank Sinatra Jr., Jackie Gayle, Alan Sherman; **D:** Alex Grasshof. *UNI*

Peppermint Soda 🐾🐾🐾 1977 Kurys' affecting directorial debut is a semi-autobiographical tale of two teenaged sisters set in 1963 Paris. Seen through the eyes of the 13-year-old Anne, who lives with 15-year-old sister Frederique and their divorced mother, this is the year of first loves, strict teachers, dreaded family vacations, and a general awareness of growing up. Sweet look at adolescence and all its embarassing tribulations. In French with English subtitles. **97m/C VHS.** *FR* Eleonore Klarwein, Odile Michel, Anouk Ferjac, Tsilla Chelton, Coralie Clement, Marie-Veronique Maurin, Puterflam; **D:** Diane Kurys; **W:** Diane Kurys; **C:** Philippe Rousselot. *NYF, BTV, FCT*

Percy & Thunder 🐾🐾½ 1993 Percy Banks (Jones) is an old-school boxing trainer who believes in hard work and he sees a likely prospect in Wayne "Thunder" Carter (Vance), a middleweight with a chance to be a champ. That is, if big time boxing promotion doesn't get in the way. **90m/C VHS, Closed Caption.** James Earl Jones, Billy Dee Williams, Courtney B. Vance, Robert Wuhl, Gloria Foster, Zakes Mokae, Gloria Reuben; **D:** Ivan Dixon; **W:** Art Washington; **M:** Tom Scott. *TTC*

The Perez Family 🐾🐾½ 1994 (R) Juan Paul Perez (Molina) has spent 20 years in Cuban jails, dreaming of being reunited with wife Carmela (Huston) and daughter Teresa (Alvarado) who successfully escaped to Miami. Part of the 1980 Mariel exodus, Juan meets exuberant Dottie (Tomei), who learns families get sponsored first at the refugee camps. She convinces Juan to pose as her husband, while Carmela, who's being wooed by cop Pirelli (Palminteri), mistakenly believes Juan has literally missed the boat. Tomei's spunky (but with a garish accent), Huston's regal, Palminteri courtly, and Molina morose. The film's inconsistently whimsical, wistful, and clunky. From the novel by Christine Bell. **CW:** Some sexuality, discreet nudity, and language. **135m/C VHS, Closed Caption.** Marisa Tomei, Alfred Molina, Anjelica Huston, Chazz Palminteri, Trini Alvarado, Celia Cruz, Molina; **D:** Mira Nair; **W:** Robin Swicord; **C:** Stuart Dryburgh; **M:** Alan Silvestri. *HMK*

Perfect 🐾½ 1985 (R) A "Rolling Stone" reporter goes after the shallowness of the Los Angeles health club scene, and falls in love with the aerobics instructor he is going to write about. "Rolling Stone" publisher Wenner plays himself. As bad as it sounds. **120m/C VHS, Beta, LV, Closed Caption.** John Travolta, Jamie Lee Curtis, Carly Simon, Marilu Henner, Laraine Newman, Jann Wenner, Anne DeSalvo; **D:** James Bridges, Aaron Latham; **C:** Gordon Willis; **M:** Ralph Burns. *COL*

Perfect Alibi 🐾🐾½ 1994 Woman's suspicions of her husband's affair leads to murder. **90m/C VHS.** Teri Garr, Hector Elizondo, Kathleen Quinlan, Anne Ramsey; **D:** Kevin Meyer. *AVE*

The Perfect Bride 🐾½ 1991 (R) A pretty young nurse prepares to marry her fiance, but his sister thinks she is hiding a secret. Could the bride-to-be have murder on her mind? Made for cable. **95m/C VHS, Beta, LV, Closed Caption.** Sammi Davis, Kelly Preston, Linden Ashby, Marilyn Rockafellow, Ashley Tillman; **D:** Terrence O'Hara; **M:** Richard Bronskill. *FXV, VTR*

Perfect Crime 🐾🐾 1978 A Scotland Yard inspector must find out who has been killing off executives of a powerful world trust. **90m/C VHS, Beta.** Joseph Cotten, Anthony Steel, Janet Agren. *NO*

The Perfect Daughter 🐾🐾½ 1996 (PG-13) A near-fatal hit-and-run accident reintroduces Alexandra Michelson (Gold) to her family—mother, Jill (Armstrong), father, Tom (Joy), and younger brother, Josh (Shulman). They'd cut the ties to the troubled drug abuser and runaway but the accident has erased Alexandra's memory of her recent life. Unfortunately for them all, Alex's sordid and dangerous past will leave neither her nor her family alone. Made for cable.**CW:** Drug content and some violence. **90m/C VHS, Closed Caption.** Tracey Gold, Bess Armstrong, Mark Joy, Michael Shulman, Harold Pruett, Jay Edward Anthony, Brian Gamble; **D:** Harry S. Longstreet. *USH*

Perfect Family 🐶🐶 1992 (R) Standard woman-and-kids-in-peril-from-psycho tale. Maggie is a recent widow with two young daughters who's looking for a nanny and a handyman. She hires brother and sister combo Janice and Alan, who, of course, are too good to be true. One is a sociopath who has murdered a family once before. Guess along with Maggie who the nut might be.**CW:** Violence and terror. **92m/C VHS, Beta, Closed Caption.** Jennifer O'Neill, Bruce Boxleitner, Joanna Cassidy, Juliana Hansen, Shiri Appleby; **D:** E.W. Swackhamer; **W:** Christian Stoianovich, Phoebe Dorin; **M:** Nicholas Pike. *PAR*

Perfect Furlough 🐶🐶½ *Strictly for Pleasure* 1959 A corporal wins a week in Paris with a movie star, accompanied by a female Army psychologist. Pretty bizarre, but it works. **93m/C VHS, Beta.** Tony Curtis, Janet Leigh, Keenan Wynn, Linda Cristal, Elaine Stritch; **D:** Blake Edwards. *BAR, MLB*

The Perfect Gift 🐶🐶 1995 (R) Suzanne decides to fulfill her boyfriend's menage-a-trois fantasy and discovers that the partner they involve just may be the woman of her dreams.**CW:** Strong sexuality; sex-related dialogue. **90m/C VHS.** John McCafferty, Kim Dawson, Monique Parent. *SWI*

Perfect Harmony 🐶🐶½ 1991 Racial conflict at an exclusive Southern boys school in 1950s South Carolina is overcome through friendship and the love of music in this sentimental tale. Made for cable television. **93m/C VHS, Beta, Closed Caption.** Peter Scolari, Darren McGavin, Catherine Mary Stewart, Moses Gunn, Cleavon Little, Justin Whalin, David Faustino, Richie Havens, Eugene Boyd; **D:** Will MacKenzie. *DIS*

Perfect Killer 🐶½ *Satanic Mechanic* 1977 (R) Van Cleef stars as a world weary Mafia hit-man who is double-crossed by his girl, set up by his best friend, and hunted by another hired assassin. **85m/C VHS, Beta.** Lee Van Cleef, Tita Barker, John Ireland, Robert Widmark; **D:** Marlon Sirko. *PSM*

A Perfect Little Murder 🐶🐶½ *A Quiet Little Neighborhood, A Perfect Little Murder* 1990 Marsha is expecting an uneventful life of barbecues and Little League when her family settles down in the suburbs. But then she overhears a murder plot and someone finds out she knows. Made for television. **94m/C VHS, Closed Caption.** Teri Garr, Robert Urich, Susan Ruttan, Jeffrey Tambor, Tom Poston, Florence Stanley, Gail Edwards, Alex Rocco; **D:** Anson Williams; **W:** Mark Stein. *TTC*

The Perfect Marriage 🐶🐶 1946 Tired comedy about a perfect couple who decide they can't stand each other anymore after ten years of marriage. Good cast makes the most of weak script. Based on the play by Samuel Raphaelson. **88m/B VHS, Closed Caption.** Loretta Young, David Niven, Eddie Albert, Charlie Ruggles, ZaSu Pitts, Jerome Cowan, Rita Johnson; **D:** Lewis Allen; **W:** Leonard Spigelgass. *USH*

Perfect Match 🐶🐶 1988 (PG) A timid young woman and an unambitious young man meet each other through the personal ads and then lie to each other about who they are and what they do for a living. **93m/C VHS, Beta.** Marc McClure, Jennifer Edwards, Diane Stilwell, Rob Paulsen, Karen Witter; **D:** Mark Deimel. *MCG*

A Perfect Spy 🐶🐶½ *John Le Carre's A Perfect Spy* 1988 In this BBC miniseries, John Le Carre takes a break from the world of George Smiley to take a look at spying from a personal view. Magnus Pym (Evan) would seem to be the perfect English gentleman; having gone to the right schools he proceeds to join the covert world of espionage. But Magnus hides the secret that his estranged father is a con man par excellence and it leads him to his own betrayals. Adapted from the novel, which Le Carre is said to have drawn from his own past. On three cassettes. **360m/C VHS.** *GB* Peter Egan, Ray McAnally, Frances Tomelty, Benedict Taylor, Tim Healy; **W:** Arthur Hopcraft. *FOX, SIG, VCO*

Perfect Strangers 🐶🐶 *Blind Alley* 1984 (R) Thriller develops around a murder and the child who witnesses it. The killer attempts to kidnap the young boy, but problems arise when he falls in love with the lad's mother. **90m/C VHS, Beta.** Anne Carlisle, Brad Rijn, John Woehrle, Matthew Stockley, Ann Magnuson, Stephen Lack; **D:** Larry Cohen; **W:** Larry Cohen. *NLC*

Perfect Timing woof! 1984 Soft-core film about a fledgling photographer who can't turn his orgy-like photo sessions into anything profitable. **87m/C VHS, Beta.** Stephen Markle, Michelle Scarabelli; **D:** Rene Bonniere. *LIV*

Perfect Victims 🐶 1987 (R) Beautiful models are being hunted by a killer, and a police officer wants to catch the psychopath before he strikes again. **100m/C VHS, Beta, LV.** Deborah Shelton, Clarence Williams III, Lyman Ward; **D:** Shuki Levy. *ACA*

The Perfect Weapon 🐶🐶 1991 (R) Kenpo karate master Speakman severs family ties and wears funny belt in order to avenge underworld murder of his teacher.**CW:** Some language and martial arts violence. **85m/C VHS, Beta, LV, Closed Caption.** Jeff Sanders, Jeff Speakman; **D:** Mark DiSalle; **W:** David Wilson; **C:** Russell Carpenter; **M:** Gary Chang. *PAR*

Perfect Witness 🐶🐶½ 1989 A restaurant owner witnesses a mob slaying and resists testifying against the culprit to save his family and himself. Made for television. Filmed in New York City. **104m/C VHS, Beta, LV.** Brian Dennehy, Aidan Quinn, Stockard Channing, Laura Harrington, Joe Grifasi; **D:** Robert Mandel; **M:** Brad Fiedel. *HBO*

A Perfect World 🐶🐶½ 1993 (PG-13) Butch Haynes (Costner) is an escaped con who takes 8-year-old fatherless Phillip (Lowther) as a hostage in 1963 Texas and is pursued by Texas Ranger Red Garnett (Eastwood). Butch is a bad guy and the film never tries to make him heroic but it also allows him to grow attached to Phillip and acknowledge him as a surrogate son. Costner gives a quiet and strong performance and the remarkable Lowther never goes wrong in his role as the needy little boy. Eastwood's role is strictly secondary as the well-tested lawman who understands justice without seeking vengeance. Somewhat draggy—especially the protracted final scene.**CW:** Language, some violence, and sexual content. **138m/C VHS, LV, Closed Caption.** Kevin Costner, T.J. Lowther, Clint Eastwood, Laura Dern, Keith Szarabajka, Leo Burmester, Paul Hewitt, Bradley Whitford, Ray McKinnon, Wayne Dehart, Jennifer Griffin, Linda Hart; **D:** Clint Eastwood; **W:** John Lee Hancock; **C:** Jack N. Green; **M:** Lennie Niehaus. *WAR*

Perfectly Normal 🐶🐶 1991 (R) Two friends end up in hilarious situations when one opens an eccentric restaurant with a mysterious, newly found fortune.**CW:** Language and sensual scene. **106m/C VHS, Beta, LV.** Michael Riley, Robbie Coltrane, Kenneth Welsh, Eugene Lipinski; **D:** Yves Simoneau; **W:** Eugene Lipinski, Paul Quarrington. *ACA*

Performance 🐶🐶🐶½ 1970 (R) Grim and unsettling psychological account of a criminal who hides out in a bizarre house occupied by a peculiar rock star and his two female companions. Entire cast scores high marks, with Pallenberg especially compelling as a somewhat mysterious and attractive housemate to mincing Jagger. A cult favorite, with music by Nitzsche under the direction of Randy Newman. **104m/C VHS, Beta, LV.** *GB* James Fox, Mick Jagger, Anita Pallenberg; **D:** Donald Cammell, Nicolas Roeg; **W:** Donald Cammell; **M:** Jack Nitzsche. *WAR*

Perfume 🐶½ 1991 Five beautiful, black childhood friends join together to conquer the cosmetics industry with their new perfume, Sassy. But can they resist all the temptations success brings and keep both their company and their friendship? **98m/C VHS.** Cheryl Francis Harrington, Kathleen Bradley Overton, Shy Jefferson, Lynn Marlin, Eugina Wright, Ted Lange; **D:** Roland S. Jefferson. *XVC*

Perfumed Nightmare 🐶🐶🐶 1989 Unique, appealing fable about a Filipino youth who discovers the drawbacks of social and cultural progress when he moves to Paris. Director Tahimik also plays the lead role. Imaginative, yet remarkably economical, this film was produced for $10,000 and received the International Critics Award at the Berlin Film Festival. In Tagalog with English dialogue and subtitles. **93m/C VHS.** *PH* Kidlat Tahimik, Dolores Santamaria, Georgette Baudry, Katrin Muller, Harmut Lerch; **D:** Kidlat Tahimik. *UWA*

Peril 🐶🐶½ *Peril en la Demeure* 1985 (R) From the novel "Sur La Terre Comme Au Ciel" by Rene Belletto. Deals with a music teacher's infiltration into a wealthy family and the sexually motivated, back-stabbing murder plots that ensue. DeVille does poorly with avant-garde technique. In French with English subtitles. **100m/C VHS, Beta.** *FR* Michel Piccoli, Christophe MaLavoy, Richard Bohringer, Nicole Garcia, Anais Jeanneret; **D:** Michel DeVille; **W:** Michel DeVille. Cesar Awards '86: Best Director (DeVille). *NO*

The Perils of Gwendoline 🐶🐶½ *Gwendoline; The Perils of Gwendoline in the Land of the Yik-Yak* 1984 (R) A young woman leaves a convent to search for her long-lost father, in this adaptation of a much funnier French comic strip of the same name. What ends up on the screen is merely a very silly rip-off of the successful "Raiders of the Lost Ark," and of primary interest for its numerous scenes of amply endowed Kitaen in the buff. **88m/C VHS, Beta, LV.** *FR* Tawny Kitaen, Brent Huff, Zabou, Bernadette LaFont, Jean Rougerie; **D:** Just Jaeckin; **M:** Pierre Bachelet. *LIV, VES*

The Perils of Pauline 🐶🐶½ 1934 All 12 episodes of this classic melodrama/adventure serial in one package, featuring dastardly villains, cliff-hanging predicaments, and worldwide chases. **238m/B VHS, Beta.** Evalyn Knapp, Robert Allen, James Durkin, Sonny Ray, Pat O'Malley; **D:** Ray Taylor. *NOS, VYY, MLB*

The Perils of Pauline 🐶🐶 1947 A musical biography of Pearl White, the reigning belle of silent movie serials. Look for lots of silent film stars. **96m/C VHS, Beta.** Betty Hutton, John Lund, Constance Collier, William Demarest, Billy DeWolfe; **D:** George Marshall; **C:** Ray Rennahan; **M:** Frank Loesser. Nominations: Academy Awards '47: Best Song ("I Wish I Didn't Love You So"). *NOS, PSM, HHT*

Perils of the Darkest Jungle 🐶🐶½ *The Tiger Woman; Jungle Gold* 1944 Tiger Woman battles money-mad oil profiteers to protect her tribe. This twelve episode serial comes on two tapes. **180m/B VHS, Beta, LV.** Linda Stirling, Allan "Rocky" Lane, Duncan Renaldo, George Lewis; **D:** Spencer Gordon Bennet. *REP, MLB*

Period of Adjustment 🐶🐶🐶 1962 Heartwarming comedy about young newlyweds adjusting to the pressures of domestic life and trying to help the troubled marriage of an older couple. Based on the play by Tennessee Williams. **112m/B VHS.** Anthony (Tony) Franciosa, Jane Fonda, Jim Hutton, Lois Nettleton, John McGiver, Jack Albertson; **D:** George Roy Hill; **W:** Isobel Lennart. Nominations: Academy Awards '62: Best Art Direction/Set Decoration (B & W).*MGM*

Permanent Record 🐶🐶½ 1988 (PG-13) Hyper-sincere drama about a popular high schooler's suicide and the emotional reactions of those he left behind. Great performance from Reeves. Cinematography by Frederick Elmes. **92m/C VHS, Beta, LV, Closed Caption.** Alan Boyce, Keanu Reeves, Michelle Meyrink, Jennifer Rubin, Pamela Gidley, Michael Elgart, Richard Bradford, Barry Corbin, Kathy Baker, Dakin Matthews; **D:** Marisa Silver; **W:** Jarre Fees, Alice Liddle, Larry Ketron; **C:** Frederick Elmes; **M:** Joe Strummer. *PAR*

Permanent Vacation 🎟🎟½ 1984 A young man disenchanted with New York City decides to escape to Europe to forget about his problems. 80m/C VHS, Beta. John Lurie, Chris Parker; **D:** Jim Jarmusch; **W:** Jim Jarmusch; **M:** John Lurie. NO

Permission To Kill 🎟🎟½ 1975 (PG) Grim spy drama features Bogard as an agent determined to prevent the return of a third-world radical to a totalitarian state. 96m/C VHS, Beta. **GB** Dirk Bogarde, Ava Gardner, Timothy Dalton, Frederic Forrest; **D:** Cyril Frankel; **C:** Frederick A. (Freddie) Young; **M:** Richard Rodney Bennett.

Perry Mason Returns 🎟🎟🎟 1985 Perry Mason returns to solve another baffling mystery. This time he must help his longtime assistant, Della Street, when she is accused of killing her new employer. 95m/C VHS, Beta. Raymond Burr, Barbara Hale, William Katt, Patrick O'Neal, Richard Anderson, Cassie Yates, Al Freeman Jr.; **D:** Ron Satlof. MCG

Perry Mason: The Case of the Lost Love 🎟🎟½ 1987 Super-lawyer Mason defends the husband of a former lover he hadn't seen in 30 years. The solution to the mystery may catch viewer off guard. 98m/C VHS. Raymond Burr, Barbara Hale, William Katt, Jean Simmons, Gene Barry, Robert Walden, Stephen Elliott, Robert Mandan, David Ogden Stiers; **D:** Ron Satlof. VTR

Persona 🎟🎟🎟🎟 1966 A famous actress turns mute and is treated by a talkative nurse at a secluded cottage. As their relationship turns increasingly tense, the women's personalitites begin to merge. Memorable, unnerving—and atypically avant garde—fare from cinema giant Bergman. First of several collaborations between the director and leading lady Ullman. In Swedish with English subtitles. 100m/C VHS, Beta, 8mm. **SW** Bibi Andersson, Liv Ullmann, Gunnar Bjornstrand, Margareta Krook; **D:** Ingmar Bergman; **W:** Ingmar Bergman; **C:** Sven Nykvist. National Board of Review Awards '67: 5 Best Foreign Films of the Year; National Society of Film Critics Awards '67: Best Actress (Andersson), Best Director (Bergman), Best Film. MGM, VYY, VDM

Personal Best 🎟🎟🎟 1982 (R) Lesbian lovers compete while training for the 1990 Olympics. Provocative fare often goes where few films have gone before, but overly stylized direction occasionally overwhelms characterizations. It gleefully exploits locker-room nudity, with Hemingway in her pre-implant days. Still, an ambitious, often accomplished production. Towne's directorial debut. 126m/C VHS, Beta. Mariel Hemingway, Scott Glenn, Patrice Donnelly; **D:** Robert Towne; **W:** Robert Towne; **C:** Michael Chapman; **M:** Jack Nitzsche. WAR

Personal Exemptions 🎟½ 1988 (PG) In this stock comedy a frenzied IRS auditor learns that her daughter is smuggling aliens into the country, her son is brokering with some businessmen she's targeted for tax fraud, and her husband is having an affair with a high-school girl. 100m/C VHS, Beta. Nanette Fabray, John Cotton; **D:** Peter Rowe. HMD

Personal Property 🎟🎟½ The Man in Possession 1937 Taylor tries every trick in the book to win Harlow over in this MGM romantic fluff. Not that big on laughs, but plenty of good shots of Harlow and a beefcake scene of Taylor in a bathtub, who was the darling of the MGM lot and worked with every leading lady. This was the only film Harlow and Taylor made together. Remake of the 1931 film "The Man in Possession." 84m/B VHS, Closed Caption. Robert Taylor, Jean Harlow, Reginald Owen, Una O'Connor, E.E. Clive, Henrietta Crosman, Cora Witherspoon; **D:** Woodbridge S. Van Dyke; **W:** Hugh Mills. MGM

Personal Services 🎟🎟½ 1987 (R) A bawdy satire loosely based on the life and times of Britain's modern-day madam, Cynthia Payne, and her rise to fame in the world of prostitution. Payne's earlier years were featured in the film "Wish You Were Here." 104m/C VHS, Beta, LV. **GB** Julie Walters, Alec McCowen, Shirley Stelfox, Tim Woodward, David Atkins, Danny Schiller, Victoria Hardcastle; **D:**

Terry Jones; **W:** David Leland; **C:** Roger Deakins; **M:** John Du Prez. LIV, VES

The Personals 🎟🎟½ 1983 (PG) A recently divorced young man takes out a personal ad in a newspaper to find the woman of his dreams. But it isn't quite that simple in this independent comedy shot entirely in Minneapolis. 90m/C VHS, Beta. Bill Schoppert, Karen Landry, Paul Eiding, Michael Laskin, Vickie Dakil; **D:** Peter Markle.

Personals 🎟🎟 1990 Chilling drama that casts O'Neill as an unnoticed librarian, until she begins to meet (and kill) the men who answer her ads. Zimbalist is a widow who is determined to learn the truth. Made for television. 93m/C VHS, Beta, LV, Closed Caption. Stephanie Zimbalist, Jennifer O'Neill, Robin Thomas, Clark Johnson, Gina Gallego, Rosemary Dunsmore, Colm Feore; **D:** Steven Hilliard Stern. PAR

The Persuaders 1971 The first two episodes of Moore and Curtis as international playboy crime fighters. 52m/C VHS, Beta. **GB** Roger Moore, Tony Curtis, Alex Scott, Joan Collins, Robert Hutton; **D:** Basil Dearden. NO

Persuasion 🎟🎟🎟½ 1995 (PG) Charming British costume romance, based on Jane Austen's final novel, deals with the constricted life of practical, plain, put-upon Anne Elliot (Root). Thanks to well-meaning interference, Anne refused the marriage proposal of the manly Frederick Wentworth (Hinds) and instead stuck by her snobbish and demanding family. Eight years later, Anne is given a second chance at love when the now-wealthy Wentworth happens back into her life—but she still has her obnoxious relations to contend with. It's wonderful to see Anne blossom from mouse to lioness although the swirl of supporting players (and settings) provide some confusion. 104m/C VHS, LV, Closed Caption. **GB** Amanda Root, Ciaran Hinds, Susan Fleetwood, Corin Redgrave, Fiona Shaw, John Woodvine, Phoebe Nicholls, Sam West, Sophie Thompson, Judy Cornwell, Felicity Dean, Simon Russell Beale, Victoria Hamilton, Emma Roberts; **D:** Roger Mitchell; **W:** Nick Dear, Jeremy Sams; **C:** John Daly. COL

The Perverse Countess 🎟 La Comtesse Perverse 1973 Romay is a bored tourist who spends a free weekend on a fling with Woods, who procures human flesh for the cannibalistic Count and Countess Zaroff (Vernon and Arno). Romay accompanies her lover to the haunted castle on a delivery, not realizing she is the package. When the Countess sees what a succulent bon-bon Romay is, she faces difficult choices. Subtitled in English. 86m/C VHS. **FR** Lina Romay, Robert Woods, Howard Vernon, Alice Arno, Caroline Riviere; **D:** Jess (Jesus) Franco. VSM

The Pest 🎟 1996 (PG-13) Movie certainly lives up to its title. A hyperkinetic Leguizamo stars as Pestario (Pest) Vargas, a smalltime Miami con man, who owes fifty large to the mob. Eccentric German businessman Gustav Shank (Jones) offers the money to Pest—the catch being that Pest will become the human prey for Gustav's private island hunting game. You'll be rooting for the hunter.**CW:** Crude sexual, scatalogical and ethnic humor. 85m/C VHS, Closed Caption. John Leguizamo, Jeffrey Jones, Edoardo Ballerini, Freddy Rodriguez, Joe Morton, Charles Hallahan, Tammy Townsend, Aries Spears; **D:** Paul Miller; **W:** David Bar Katz; **C:** Roy Wagner; **M:** Kevin Kiner. COL

Pet Sematary 🎟🎟 1989 (R) A quirky adaptation of Stephen King's bestseller about a certain patch of woods in the Maine wilderness that rejuvenates the dead, and how a newly located college MD eventually uses it to restore his dead son. Mildly creepy. 103m/C VHS, Beta, LV, 8mm, Closed Caption. Dale Midkiff, Fred Gwynne, Denise Crosby, Stephen King; **D:** Mary Lambert; **W:** Stephen King; **M:** Elliot Goldenthal. PAR

Pet Sematary 2 🎟½ 1992 (R) Lame sequel to original Stephen King flick. After seeing his mother electrocuted, a teen and his veterinarian father move to the Maine town where the legendary Pet Sematary is located. Horror begins when

the boy's friend's dog is shot by his stepfather, and the boys bury the dog in the "sematary." King wasn't involved with this film, so the story isn't very coherent, but shock value and special effects are great. Not recommended for those with a weak stomach.**CW:** Language, strong horror violence, and sexuality. 102m/C VHS, Beta, LV, Closed Caption. Anthony Edwards, Edward Furlong, Clancy Brown, Jared Rushton, Darlanne Fluegel, Lisa Waltz, Jason McGuire, Sarah Trigger; **D:** Mary Lambert; **W:** Richard Outten; **C:** Russell Carpenter. PAR

Pet Shop 🎟🎟½ 1994 (PG) Pair of evil, galaxy-travelling aliens take over the local pet store in a remote desert town and plan to abduct all the kids by bewitching them with a spaceship full of intergalactic creatures. Only Dena (aided by the good alien furballs) can stop the bad guys from making space pets of the earthlings. 88m/C VHS, Beta. Leigh Ann Orsi, Spencer Vrooman, David Wagner, Joanne Baron, Jane Morris, Terry Kiser, Jeff Michalski, Shashawnee Hall, Sabrina Wiener, Cody Burger; **D:** Hope Perello; **W:** Mark Goldstein, Greg Suddeth, Brent Friedman; **M:** Reg Powell. PAR

Pete Kelly's Blues 🎟🎟 1955 A jazz musician in a Kansas City speakeasy is forced to stand up against a brutal racketeer. The melodramatic plot is brightened by a nonstop flow of jazz tunes sung by Lee and Fitzgerald and played by an all-star lineup that includes Dick Cathcart, Matty Matlock, Eddie Miller and George Van Eps. ♫ Sugar; Sombody Loves Me; Bye Bye Blackbird; What Can I Say After I Say I'm Sorry?; He Needs Me; Sing a Rainbow; Pete Kelly's Blues. 96m/C VHS, Beta, LV. Jack Webb, Janet Leigh, Edmond O'Brien, Lee Marvin, Martin Milner, Peggy Lee, Ella Fitzgerald, Jayne Mansfield; **D:** Jack Webb. Nominations: Academy Awards '55: Best Supporting Actress (Lee). WAR

Pete 'n' Tillie 🎟🎟½ 1972 (PG) Amiable comedy turns to less appealing melodrama as couple meets, marries, and endures tragedy. Film contributes little to director Ritt's hitt-and-miss reputation, but Matthau and Burnett shine in leads. Adapted by Julius J. Epstein from a Peter de Vries' story. 100m/C VHS, Beta. Walter Matthau, Carol Burnett, Geraldine Page, Barry Nelson, Rene Auberjonois, Lee Montgomery, Henry Jones, Kent Smith; **D:** Martin Ritt; **W:** Julius J. Epstein; **C:** John A. Alonzo; **M:** John Williams. British Academy Awards '73: Best Actor (Matthau); Nominations: Academy Awards '72: Best Adapted Screenplay, Best Supporting Actress (Page). USH

Pete Townshend: White City 1985 The Who guitarist portrays a musician who helps bring a close friend and and his estranged wife back together. This semi-autobiographical film includes music from Townsend. 60m/C VHS, Beta, LV. Pete Townshend, Andrew Wilde, Frances Barber; **D:** Richard Lowenstein. MVD, VES

Peter and Paul 🎟🎟½ 1981 TV miniseries follows the lives of the two apostles, Peter (Foxworth) and Paul (Hopkins), from the Crucifixion through the next three decades as they travel spreading the word of Christ, until both are executed in Rome. Tries valiantly, but falls a bit short. 194m/C VHS. Anthony Hopkins, Robert Foxworth, Eddie Albert, Raymond Burr, Jose Ferrer, Jon Finch, David Gwillim, Herbert Lom, Jean Peters; **D:** Robert Day; **W:** Christopher Knopf. USH, GFV

Peter Gunn 🎟🎟 1989 Detective Peter Gunn returns, only to find himself being hunted by both the mob and the Feds. A TV movie reprise of the vintage series that has none of the original cast members. 97m/C VHS. Peter Strauss, Barbara Williams, Jennifer Edwards, Charles Cioffi, Pearl Bailey, Peter Jurasik, David Rappaport; **D:** Blake Edwards; **M:** Henry Mancini. VTR

Peter Lundy and the Medicine Hat Stallion 🎟🎟½ The Medicine Hat Stallion; Pony Express 1977 A teenaged Pony Express rider must outrun the Indians and battle the elements in order to carry mail from the Nebraska Territory to the West Coast in this made-for-television film. Good family entertainment. 85m/C VHS, Beta. Leif

Garrett, Mitchell Ryan, Bibi Besch, John Quade, Milo O'Shea; **D:** Michael O'Herlihy. *LIV, VES*

Peter Pan 🎞🎞🎞 **1953 (G)** Disney classic about a boy who never wants to grow up. Based on J.M. Barrie's book and play. Still stands head and shoulders above any recent competition in providing fun family entertainment. Terrific animation and lovely hummable music. **76m/C VHS, Beta, LV, Closed Caption. D:** Hamilton Luske; **V:** Bobby Driscoll, Kathryn Beaumont, Hans Conried, Heather Angel, Candy Candido. *DIS, APD, HMV*

Peter Pan 🎞🎞🎞½ **1960** A TV classic, this videotape of a performance of the 1954 Broadway musical adapted from the J.M. Barrie classic features Mary Martin in one of her most famous incarnations, as the adolescent Peter Pan. Songs include "I'm Flying," "Neverland," and "I Won't Grow Up." **100m/C VHS, Beta, LV, Closed Caption.** Mary Martin, Cyril Ritchard, Sondra Lee, Heather Halliday, Luke Halpin; **D:** Vincent J. Donehue. *GKK, COL, MLT*

Peter the First: Part 1 🎞🎞 **1937** The first half of Petrov's Soviet epic about the early years of Tsar Peter I's reign. Lavish, in Russian with English subtitles. **95m/B VHS, Beta.** *RU* **D:** Vladimir Petrov. *FCT*

Peter the First: Part 2 🎞🎞 **1938** The second half of Petrov's epic, also titled "The Conquests of Peter the Great," covering the triumphs and final years of the famous Tsar. In Russian with English subtitles. **104m/B VHS, Beta.** *RU* **D:** Vladimir Petrov. *FCT*

Peter the Great 🎞🎞🎞 **1986** Dry but eye-pleasing TV mini-series follows the life of Russia's colorful, very tall ruler from childhood on. Much of the interesting cast is wasted in tiny roles. **371m/C VHS.** Maximilian Schell, Laurence Olivier, Omar Sharif, Vanessa Redgrave, Ursula Andress. *VTR*

Peter's Friends 🎞🎞½ **1992 (R)** Peter has recently inherited a grand manor house located outside London and invites some chums to celebrate a New Year's Eve weekend, ten years after they've been at university together. So begins another nostalgic trip down memory lane ala "The Big Chill," but unlike other clones, this one can stand on its own, with a lightweight and sly script by talented comedienne Rudner (in her film debut) and her husband Bergman. If the script sometimes falls a little flat, the fine cast will make up for it. Thompson's mother, actress Law, plays the housekeeper.**CW:** Language and some sexuality. **102m/C VHS, LV, Closed Caption.** *GB* Kenneth Branagh, Rita Rudner, Emma Thompson, Stephen Fry, Hugh Laurie, Imelda Staunton, Alphonsia Emmanuel, Tony Slattery, Alex Lowe, Alex Scott, Phyllida Law, Richard Briers; **D:** Kenneth Branagh; **W:** Rita Rudner, Martin Bergman; **M:** Jacques Offenbach. *HBO, BTV*

Pete's Dragon 🎞🎞½ **1977 (G)** Elliot, an enormous, bumbling dragon with a penchant for clumsy heroics, becomes friends with poor orphan Pete. Combines brilliant animation with the talents of live actors for an interesting effect. **128m/C VHS, Beta, LV, Closed Caption.** Helen Reddy, Shelley Winters, Mickey Rooney, Jim Dale, Red Buttons, Sean Marshall, Jim Backus, Jeff Conaway; **D:** Don Chaffey; **W:** Malcolm Marmorstein; **V:** Charlie Callas. Nominations: Academy Awards '77: Best Song ("Candle on the Water"), Original Song Score and/or Adaptation. *DIS, FCT*

Petit Con 🎞🎞½ **1984 (R)** A live-action version of the popular French comic strip wherein a young rebel drops out of society to live with aging hippies. With English subtitles. **90m/C VHS, Beta.** *FR* Guy Marchand, Michel Choupon, Caroline Cellier, Bernard Brieux, Souadad Amidou; **D:** Gerard Lauzier. *ORI*

Petrified Forest 🎞🎞🎞 **1936** Patrons and employees are held captive by a runaway gangster's band in a desert diner. Often gripping, with memorable performances from Davis, Howard, and Bogart. Based on the play by Robert Sherwood with Howard and Bogart recreating their stage roles. **83m/B VHS, Beta.** Bette Davis, Leslie Howard, Humphrey Bogart, Dick Foran, Charley Grapewin, Porter Hall; **D:** Archie Mayo. *FOX, MGM*

Petulia 🎞🎞🎞🎞 **1968 (R)** Overlooked, offbeat drama about a flighty woman who spites her husband by dallying with a sensitive, recently divorced surgeon. Classic '60s document and cult favorite offers great performance from the appealing Christie, with Scott fine as the vulnerable surgeon. On-screen performances by the Grateful Dead and Big Brother. Among idiosyncratic director Lester's best. Photographed by Nicholas Roeg. From the novel "Me and the Arch Kook Petulia" by John Haase. **105m/C VHS, Beta.** George C. Scott, Richard Chamberlain, Julie Christie, Shirley Knight, Arthur Hill, Joseph Cotten, Pippa Scott, Richard Dysart, Kathleen Widdoes, Austin Pendleton, Rene Auberjonois; **D:** Richard Lester; **W:** Lawrence B. Marcus; **M:** John Barry. *WAR*

Peyton Place 🎞🎞🎞 **1957** Passion, scandal, and deception in a small New England town set the standard for passion, scandal, and deception in soap operadom. Shot on location in Camden, Maine. Performances and themes now seem dated, but produced a blockbuster in its time. Adapted from Grace Metalious' popular novel and followed by "Return to Peyton Place." **157m/C VHS, LV, Closed Caption.** Lana Turner, Hope Lange, Lee Philips, Lloyd Nolan, Diane Varsi, Lorne Greene, Russ Tamblyn, Arthur Kennedy, Terry Moore, Barry Coe, David Nelson, Betty Field, Mildred Dunnock, Leon Ames, Alan Reed Jr.; **D:** Mark Robson; **W:** John Michael Hayes; **C:** William Mellor. Nominations: Academy Awards '57: Best Actress (Turner), Best Adapted Screenplay, Best Cinematography, Best Director (Robson), Best Picture, Best Supporting Actor (Kennedy, Tamblyn), Best Supporting Actress (Lange, Varsi). *FOX, FCT*

Phaedra 🎞🎞 **1961** Loose and updated adaptation of Euripides' "Hipploytus." Mercouri, the second wife of a rich Greek shipping magnate, is dispatched to London to convince her husband's adult son (Perkins) to come home to Greece. Mercouri and Perkins immediately begin a steamy affair but their return home brings problems for all. Dubbed. **116m/B VHS.** *GR FR* Melina Mercouri, Anthony Perkins, Raf Vallone, Elizabeth Ercy; **Cameos:** Jules Dassin; **D:** Jules Dassin; **W:** Jules Dassin, Margaritta Liberaki; **M:** Mikis Theodorakis. Nominations: Academy Awards '62: Best Costume Design (B & W). *FCT*

Phantasm 🎞🎞½ **1979 (R)** A small-budgeted, hallucinatory horror fantasy about two parentless brothers who discover weird goings-on at the local funeral parlor, including the infamous airborne, brain-chewing chrome ball. Creepy, unpredictable nightmare fashioned on a shoestring by young independent producer Coscarelli. Scenes were cut out of the original film to avoid "X" rating. Followed by "Phantasm II." **90m/C VHS, Beta, LV.** Michael Baldwin, Bill Thornbury, Reggie Bannister, Kathy Lester, Terrie Kalbus, Ken Jones, Susan Harper, Lynn Eastman, David Arntzen, Angus Scrimm, Bill Cone; **D:** Don A. Coscarelli; **W:** Don A. Coscarelli. *COL*

Phantasm II 🎞🎞 **1988 (R)** Teen psychic keeps flashing on villainous Tall Man. A rehash sequel to the original, cultishly idiosyncratic fantasy, wherein more victims are fed into the inter-dimensional abyss and Mike discovers that the horror is not all in his head. Occasional inspired gore; bloodier than its predecessor. More yuck for the buck. **97m/C VHS, Beta, LV.** James LeGros, Reggie Bannister, Angus Scrimm; **D:** Don A. Coscarelli; **W:** Don A. Coscarelli. *USH*

Phantasm III: Lord of the Dead 🎞½ **1994 (R)** Murderous mortician The Tall Man and his killer silver spheres return once again in this continuing gore fest. Mike, whose brother Jody was one of The Tall Man's victims, teams up with the cynical Reggie and martial arts expert Rocky to try to defeat the creep. That's if they can get past his zombie cohorts and flesh-eating ghouls. **91m/C VHS, LV, Closed Caption.** Reggie Bannister, A. Michael Baldwin, Bill Thornbury, Gloria Henry, Kevin Connor, Angus Scrimm; **D:** Don A. Coscarelli; **W:** Don A. Coscarelli. *USH*

The Phantom 🎞🎞 **1931** Rare cheapie of a hooded killer terrorizing a group of people in a haunted house. **62m/C VHS.** Guinn "Big Boy" Williams, Wilfrid Lucas, Sheldon Lewis, William Gould; **D:** Alan James. *SNC, GPV*

The Phantom 🎞🎞½ **1996 (PG)** Based on the Lee Falk comic created in 1936. Deep in the Bengalla jungle, a mysterious costumed figure honors a 400-year-old legacy by fighting piracy, greed, and cruelty. With the help of a beautiful newspaper heiress (Swanson), the latest guardian (Zane) must keep an American industrialist (Williams) and a secret brotherhood of pirates from finding three sacred skulls that contain the power to dominate the world. Old-fashioned swashbuckling story is helped along by Zane's enthusiastic portrayal of the stalwart hero. Action set pieces, while done more dynamically elsewhere, are fun and exciting. Older kids (read: teenagers) may find the proceedings a bit hokey, but everyone seems to be having a good time. **100m/C VHS, LV, Closed Caption.** Billy Zane, Kristy Swanson, Treat Williams, Catherine Zeta Jones, James Remar, Jon Tenney, Patrick McGoohan, Samantha Eggar, Cary-Hiroyuki Tagawa, Robert Coleby, David Proval; **D:** Simon Wincer; **W:** Jeffrey Boam; **C:** David Burr; **M:** David Newman. *PAR*

The Phantom Broadcast 🎞🎞½ *Phantom of the Air* **1933** A popular radio crooner is murdered. The main suspect is his hunchbacked accompanist and manager, who had all along secretly pre-recorded his own velvet voice for the crooner to lip-sync along with. A tightly plotted minor thriller that holds up surprisingly well. **63m/B VHS, Beta, 8mm.** Ralph Forbes, Gail Patrick, Vivienne Osborne, Guinn "Big Boy" Williams, George "Gabby" Hayes; **D:** Phil Rosen. *VYY, NOS, FCT*

Phantom Brother 🎞½ **1988** A semi-spoof about a teenager left orphaned by a car crash that wiped out his entire family, and who is subsequently haunted by his dead brother. Even thinner than it sounds. **92m/C VHS, Beta.** Jon Hammer, Patrick Molloy, John Gigante, Mary Beth Pelshaw; **D:** William Szarka. *HMD*

The Phantom Bullet 🎞½ **1926** Hoot wants to holler at his father's murderers. **60m/B VHS, Beta.** Hoot Gibson. *GPV*

The Phantom Chariot 🎞🎞½ **1920** A fantasy depicting the Swedish myth about how Death's coach must be driven by the last man to die each year. Silent. **89m/B VHS, Beta.** *SW* **D:** Victor Sjostrom. *SNC, FCT, GVV*

The Phantom Creeps **1939** Evil Dr. Zorka, armed with a meteorite chunk which can bring an army to a standstill, provides the impetus for this enjoyable serial in 12 episodes. **235m/B VHS, Beta.** Bela Lugosi, Dorothy Arnold, Robert Kent, Regis Toomey; **D:** Ford Beebe, Saul Goodkind. *NOS, SNC, VCN*

The Phantom Empire *Radio Ranch* **1935** Autry faces the futuristic "Thunder Riders" from the subterranean city of Murania, located 20,000 feet beneath his ranch. A complete serial in twelve episodes. If you only see one science fiction western in your life, this is the one. Also available in an edited theatrical version at 80 minutes. **245m/B VHS, Beta.** Gene Autry, Frankie Darro, Betsy King Ross, Smiley Burnette; **D:** B. Reeves Eason, Otto Brower. *NOS, SNC, VYY*

Phantom Empire 🎞🎞 **1987 (R)** A woman who rules over a lost city takes a bunch of scientists prisoner and forces them to be slaves. **85m/C VHS, Beta.** Ross Hagen, Jeffrey Combs, Dawn Wildsmith, Robert Quarry, Susan Stokey, Michelle (McClellan) Bauer, Russ Tamblyn, Sybil Danning; **D:** Fred Olen Ray. *PSM*

Phantom Express 🎞🎞 **1932** Experienced old engineer is dismissed from his job because no one believes his explanation that a mysterious train caused the wreck of his own train. He aims to find justice. **65m/B VHS, Beta.** J. Farrell MacDonald, Sally Blane, William Collier Jr., Hobart Bosworth; **D:** Emory Johnson. *NO*

Phantom Fiend ✄½ 1935 A gentle musician becomes a suspect when a series of Jack-the-Ripper type murders terrorize London. Is he the nice guy known by his girlfriend and the people in his lodging house, or is the musician really JTR? Based on the novel "The Lodger" by Marie Belloc-Lowndes. **70m/B VHS.** *GB* Ivor Novello, Elizabeth Allan, A.W. Baskcomb, Jack Hawkins, Barbara Everest, Peter Gawthorne, P. Kynaston Reeves; **D:** Maurice Elvey. *FCT, RXM*

The Phantom Flyer ✄½ 1928 Stunt pilot helps out a cattle-owning frontier family bedeviled by rustlers. Silent. **54m/B VHS, Beta, 8mm.** Al Wilson. *VYY, GPV, RXM*

Phantom from Space ✄½ 1953 An invisible alien lands on Earth, begins killing people, and is pursued by a pair of scientists. **72m/B VHS, Beta.** Ted Cooper, Rudolph Anders, Noreen Nash, James Seay, Harry Landers; **D:** W. Lee Wilder; **C:** William Clothier. *VYY, SNC, NOS*

The Phantom from 10,000 Leagues ✄ 1956 Slimy sea monster attacks swimmers and fishermen; investigating oceanographer pretends not to notice monster is hand puppet. Early AIP release, when still named American Releasing Company. **80m/B VHS.** Kent Taylor, Cathy Downs, Michael Whalen, Helene Stanton, Phillip Pine; **D:** Dan Milner. *VYY, SNC, MLB*

Phantom Gold ✄½ 1938 The wicked Whitaker claims to have struck it rich but it's really a scam to lure unsuspecting miners to the claim and then rob and murder them. Luden's suspicious and proves Whitaker's a bad guy. **56m/B VHS.** Jack Luden, Charles "Slim" Whitaker, Beth Marion, Hal Taliaferro, Art Davis; **D:** Joseph Levering. *GPV*

The Phantom in the House ✄✄ 1929 A woman commits a murder and has her inventor husband take the rap. While he's in prison, she gets rich off of his work. Things get hairy when he is released fifteen years later and is introduced to his daughter as a friend of the family. Melodramatic film was originally made with and without sound. **64m/B VHS, Beta.** Ricardo Cortez, Nancy Welford, Henry B. Walthall, Grace Valentine; **D:** Phil Rosen. *SNC*

Phantom Killer ✄✄ 1942 A district attorney tries to hang a murder rap on a most improbable suspect. When the man is aquitted, the DA quits his job to find the truth, which takes a disturbing twist. The plot is a thinly veiled rehash of "The Sphinx" (1933). **61m/B VHS.** Dick Purcell, Joan Woodbury, John Hamilton, Warren Hymer, Kenneth Harlan, J. Farrell MacDonald, Mantan Moreland; **D:** William Beaudine. *NOS*

The Phantom Light ✄✄½ 1935 A lighthouse keeper is murdered under strange circumstances and a mysterious light keeps appearing at the scene. Detective Hale joins up with a navy man and another lighthouse keeper to solve the crime. A low-budget mystery with good atmosphere and some humor. **75m/B VHS.** *GB* Binnie Hale, Gordon Harker, Ian Hunter, Donald Calthrop; **D:** Michael Powell. *HCV*

Phantom of Chinatown ✄ 1940 Mr. Wong is called in to solve another murder in the final entry in the series. The first to have an Asian actor portray the lead, as Luke replaced Boris Karloff. **61m/B VHS.** Keye Luke, Lotus Long, Grant Withers, Paul McVey, Charles Miller; **D:** Phil Rosen. *NOS, SNC, HEG*

Phantom of Death ✄½ 1987 (R) A brilliant pianist, stricken by a fatal disease that causes rapid aging, goes on a murderous rampage. **95m/C VHS, Beta.** *IT* Michael York, Donald Pleasence, Edwige Fenech; **D:** Ruggero Deodato; **M:** Pino Donaggio. *THV*

The Phantom of 42nd Street ✄✄ 1945 An actor and a cop team up to find the killer of a wealthy uncle. **58m/B VHS.** Dave O'Brien, Kay Aldridge, Alan Mowbray, Frank Jenks; **D:** Al(bert) Herman. *SNC, NOS, MRV*

Phantom of Liberty ✄✄✄½ *Le Fantome de la Liberte; The Specter of Freedom* 1974 Master surrealist Bunuel's episodic film wanders from character to character and from event to event. Animals wander through a man's bedroom, soldiers conduct military exercises in an inhabited area, a missing girl stands before her parents even as they futilely attempt to determine her whereabouts, and an assassin is found guilty, then applauded and led to freedom. They don't get much more surreal than this. If you think you may like it, you'll probably love it. Bunuel, by the way, is among the firing squad vicitms in the film's opening enactment of Goya's May 3, 1808. In French with English subtitles. **104m/C VHS, Beta, LV.** *FR* Adrianna Asti, Jean-Claude Brialy, Michel Piccoli, Adolfo Celi, Monica Vitti, Milena Vukotic, Michel Lonsdale, Claude Pieplu, Julien Bertheau, Paul Frankeur, Paul Leperson, Bernard Verley; **D:** Luis Bunuel; **W:** Luis Bunuel, Jean-Claude Carriere; **C:** Edmond Richard. National Board of Review Awards '74: 5 Best Foreign Films of the Year. *XVC, APD*

The Phantom of Soho ✄✄ *Das Phantom von Soho* 1964 A Scotland Yard detective investigates the murders of several prominent businessmen and is assisted by a beautiful mystery writer. **92m/B VHS, Beta.** *GE* Dieter Borsche, Barbara Rutting, Hans Sohnker, Peter Vogel, Helga Sommerfeld, Werner Peters; **D:** Franz Gottlieb. *SNC*

Phantom of the Air 1933 Twelve chapters of high-flying adventure with Tom Tyler! **230m/B VHS.** Tom Tyler, Gloria Shea, William Desmond, Leroy Mason, Walter Brennan; **D:** Ray Taylor. *GPV, MLB*

Phantom of the Mall: Eric's Revenge ✄ 1989 A murderous spirit haunts the local mall. Gore flows like water. **91m/C VHS, Beta, LV.** Morgan Fairchild, Kari Whitman, Jonathan Goldsmith, Derek Rydell; **D:** Richard S. Friedman. *FRH*

The Phantom of the Opera ✄✄✄ 1925 Deranged, disfigured music lover haunts the sewers of a Parisian opera house and kills to further the career of an unsuspecting young soprano. First of many film versions still packs a wallop, with fine playing from Chaney, Sr. Silent with two-color Technicolor "Bal Masque" sequence. Versions with different running times are also available, including 79 and 88 minutes. **101m/B VHS.** Lon Chaney Sr., Norman Kerry, Mary Philbin, Gibson Gowland; **D:** Rupert Julian. *KIV, NOS, FUS*

The Phantom of the Opera ✄✄✄ 1943 Second Hollywood version—the first with talking—of Gastron Leroux novel about a madman who promotes fear and mayhem at a Paris opera house. Raines is good in lead; Eddy warbles away. **92m/C VHS, Beta, LV.** Claude Rains, Nelson Eddy, Susanna Foster, Edgar Barrier, Leo Carrillo, Hume Cronyn, J. Edward Bromberg; **D:** Arthur Lubin; **C:** Hal Mohr. Academy Awards '43: Best Color Cinematography, Best Interior Decoration; Nominations: Academy Awards '43: Best Sound, Scoring of a Musical. *USH*

The Phantom of the Opera ✄✄½ 1962 Hammer version of the Gaston Leroux novel transfers the action from Paris to London but keeps the basic story of a young singer (Sears) and her masked benefactor (Lom), who lives in the sewers beneath the opera house. There's also the wimpy fiance (De Souza) to come between them. Good gothic melodrama. Sears' singing was dubbed by opera performer Pat Clark; producer Hinds used the pseudonym John Elder for his screenplay. **85m/C VHS, Closed Caption.** Herbert Lom, Heather Sears, Edward De Souza, Thorley Walters, Michael Gough, Martin Miller, Ian Wilson; **D:** Terence Fisher; **W:** Anthony John Elder Hinds; **C:** Arthur Grant; **M:** Edwin Astley. *USH*

The Phantom of the Opera ✄½ 1989 (R) A gory, "Elm Street"-ish version of the Gaston Leroux classic, attempting to cash in on the success of the Broadway musical. **93m/C VHS, Beta, LV, Closed Caption.** Robert Englund, Jill Schoelen, Alex Hyde-White, Bill Nighy, Terence Harvey, Stephanie Lawrence; **D:** Dwight Little. *COL*

The Phantom of the Opera ✄✄½ 1990 Yet another version of the tragic tale of a disfigured mask-wearing opera lover, who lurks in the depths of the Paris Opera House, and his desire for lovely young singer, Christine. Dance plays the Phantom as doomed romantic, with Lancaster as his protective father. Kopit adapted from his 1983 play. Made for TV drama, originally shown in two parts. **200m/C VHS.** *GB* Charles Dance, Burt Lancaster, Teri Polo, Ian Richardson, Andrea Ferreol, Adam Storke, Jean-Pierre Cassel; **D:** Tony Richardson; **W:** Arthur Kopit; **M:** John Addison. *AVE*

Phantom of the Paradise ✄✄ 1974 (PG) A rock 'n roll parody of "Phantom of the Opera." Splashy, only occasionally horrific spoof in which cruel music executive Williams, much to his everlasting regret, swindles a songwriter. Violence ensues. Not for most, or even many, tastes. Graham steals the film as rocker Beef. A failure at the box office, and now a cult item (small enthusiastic cult with few outside interests) for its oddball humor and outrageous rock star parodies. Williams also wrote the turgid score. ♫Goodbye, Eddie, Goodbye; Faust; Upholstery; Special to Me; Old Souls; Somebody Super Like You; Life At Last; The Hell of It; The Phantom's Theme (Beauty and the Beast). **92m/C VHS, Beta, LV.** Paul Williams, William Finley, Jessica Harper, Gerrit Graham; **D:** Brian De-Palma; **W:** Brian DePalma; **M:** Paul Williams. Nominations: Academy Awards '74: Original Song Score and/or Adaptation. *FOX*

The Phantom of the Range ✄✄½ 1938 Marion is trying to sell her grandfather's ranch only his "ghost" is scaring everyone away. She and cowpoke Tyler find out a group of evil treasure hunters are searching the property for hidden gold. **59m/B VHS.** Tom Tyler, Beth Marion, Charles "Blackie" King, Forrest Taylor, John Elliott, Soledad Jiminez, Sammy Cohen; **D:** Robert F. "Bob" Hill. *GPV*

Phantom of the Ritz ✄✄ 1988 (R) Bizarre accidents begin to take place when Ed Blake and his girlfriend start renovating the old Ritz Theater. It seems the theater is inhabited by a rather angry ghost and somebody's got to deal with it before the Ritz can rock and roll. Featuring the fabulous sounds of the Fifties. **89m/C VHS, Beta, Closed Caption.** Peter Bergman, Deborah Van Valkenburgh; **D:** Allen Plone. *PSM*

Phantom of the West ✄✄ 1931 Ten-episode serial about a rancher who becomes "The Phantom of the West" in order to smoke out his father's killer. **166m/B VHS, Beta.** William Desmond, Thomas Santschi, Tom Tyler; **D:** David Ross Lederman. *VYY, NOS, VCN*

Phantom Patrol ✄½ 1936 A mystery writer is kidnapped and someone impersonates him. Mountie Maynard must come to the rescue. **60m/B VHS, Beta.** Kermit Maynard, Joan Barclay, Paul Fix, Julian Rivero, Eddie Phillips, Roger Williams; **D:** Charles Hutchinson. *DVT, VYY*

The Phantom Planet ✄½ 1961 An astronaut crash-lands on an asteroid and discovers a race of tiny people living there. Having breathed the atmosphere, he shrinks to their diminutive size and aids them in their war against brutal invaders. Infamously peculiar. **82m/B VHS, Beta.** Dean Fredericks, Coleen Gray, Tony Dexter, Dolores Faith, Francis X. Bushman, Richard Kiel; **D:** William Marshall. *NOS, SNC*

Phantom Rancher ✄½ 1939 Roaring melodrama finds Maynard donning a mask to find the real Phantom, who is causing havoc. **61m/B VHS, Beta.** Ken Maynard. *VCI, VCN*

Phantom Ranger ✄½ 1938 A federal agent masquerades as a crook to catch a band of counterfeiters. **54m/B VHS.** Tim McCoy, Suzanne Kaaren, Karl Hackett, John St. Polis, John Merton, Harry Strang; **D:** Sam Newfield. *NOS, DVT*

The Phantom Rider 1937 Mystery fills the old West in this serial composed of fifteen chapters. **152m/B VHS, Beta.** Buck Jones, Marla Shelton. *REP, MLB, VCN*

The Phantom Rider 🎬½ 1946 The masked do-gooder rides the plains protecting the local Indians from some surly settlers. A 12-episode serial. **167m/C VHS.** Robert Kent, Peggy Stewart, Leroy Mason, Chief Thundercloud. *MOV*

Phantom Thunderbolt 🎬½ 1933 A man who has falsely spread the rumor that he's a gunfighter is hired to chase away some good-for-nothings. **62m/B VHS, Beta.** Ken Maynard, Frances Lee, Frank Rice, William Gould, Robert F. (Bob) Kortman; *D:* Alan James. *NOS, DVT, MTX*

Phantom Tollbooth 🎬🎬🎬 1969 (G) A young boy drives his car into an animated world, where the numbers are at war with the letters and he has been chosen to save Rhyme and Reason, to bring stability back to the Land of Wisdom. Completely unique and typically Jonesian in its intellectual level and interests. Bright children will be interested, but this is really for adults who will understand the allegory. Based on Norman Justers' metaphorical novel. **89m/C VHS, Beta.** *D:* Chuck Jones; *V:* Mel Blanc, Hans Conried. *MGM*

Phantom 2040 Movie: The Ghost Who Walks 🎬🎬½ 1995 Teenager Kit Walker discovers his destiny when a mysterious stranger tells him about his late father and how Kit must carry on his father's legacy as a superhero called the Phantom. A purple suit renders Kit invisible and he finds himself battling his dad's old nemesis, Rebecca Madison, who's out to destroy the Earth's resources. Based on the television and comic book series. **97m/C VHS.** *V:* Scott Valentine, Margot Kidder, Ron Perlman, Carrie Snodgress, Mark Hamill. *FHE, LIV*

Phar Lap 🎬🎬½ *Phar Lap: Heart of a Nation* 1984 (PG) Saga of a legendary Australian racehorse who rose from obscurity to win nearly 40 races in just three years before mysteriously dying in 1932. American version runs 10 minutes shorter than the Aussie one. **107m/C VHS, Beta, Closed Caption.** *AU* Ron Leibman, Tom Burlinson, Judy Morris, Celia de Burgh; *D:* Simon Wincer; *W:* David Williamson; *C:* Russell Boyd. *FOX*

Pharaoh 🎬🎬 1966 An expensive Polish epic about the power plays of royalty in ancient Egypt. Dubbed. **125m/B VHS, Beta.** *PL* Jerzy Zelnick; *D:* Jerzy Kawalerowicz. *FCT*

Pharmacist 🎬🎬½ 1932 A day in the life of a hapless druggist undone by disgruntled customers and robbers. Typical Fields effort. **19m/B VHS, Beta.** Elise Cavanna, Babe Kane, W.C. Fields, Grady Sutton. *CCB*

Pharoah's Army 🎬🎬½ 1995 (PG-13) Five Union soldiers are foraging for food at a small Kentucky farm when one young soldier (Fox) is badly injured and his captain, John Abston (Cooper), is forced to stay put while he treats the wounds. The farm is home to Sarah Anders (Clarkson) and her young son (Lucas), while her husband is off fighting for the Confederates. Sarah isn't happy about the arrangement but the decent Alston, a farmer himself in peacetime, begins slowly to win her over. Their friendship, however, doesn't sit well with either his men nor Sarah's son. Fine performances in a restrained drama. *CW:* Brief violence and sexual references. **90m/C VHS.** Chris Cooper, Patricia Clarkson, Kris Kristofferson, Richard Tyson, Huckleberry Fox, Will Lucas; *D:* Robby Henson; *W:* Robby Henson; *C:* Doron Schlair. *ORI*

Phase 4 🎬🎬 1974 (PG) A tale of killer ants retaliating against the humans attempting to exterminate them. **84m/C VHS, Beta, LV.** Nigel Davenport, Michael Murphy, Lynne Frederick; *D:* Saul Bass. *PAR*

Phat Beach 🎬🎬½ 1996 (R) Generic but basically harmless buddies-at-the-beach comedy with a hip-hop beat. Fast-talking, slickster Durrell (Hooks) manipulates sensitive, overweight pal Benny (Hopkins, who's real life nickname is "Huggy") into emptying his savings, "borrowing" his dad's Mercedes convertible, and taking off for some Southern California fun. Scores of scantily-clad beach bunnies aren't the only ones thread-

bare—so's the whole premise of this flick—but that's not the point of this lighthearted romp. The likable Hopkins/Hooks comedy team is a hit with precise, lowbrow humor. Coolio, prominent in the ads, is barely window dressing with minimal screen time. Kickin' soundtrack includes E-40, Biz Markie, and SugaT featuring The Click. *CW:* Sexuality, nudity and strong language. **99m/C VHS.** Jermaine Hopkins, Brian Hooks, Jennifer Lucienne, Claudia Kaleem, Gregg D. Vance, Tiny Lister, Erick Fleeks, Alma Collins, Candice Merideth, Sabrina De Pina; *Cameos:* Coolio; *D:* Doug Ellin; *W:* Doug Ellin, Brian E. O'Neal, Ben Morris; *C:* Jurgen Baum; *M:* Paul Stewart. *LIV*

Phedre 🎬½ 1968 Jean Racine's adaptation of the Greek legend involving Phedre, Theseus, and Hippolyte. Bell is the only one worth watching in this weak and stagy picture. In French with English subtitles. **93m/C VHS, Beta.** Marie Bell; *D:* Pierre Jourdan. *VYY, APD*

Phenomenal and the Treasure of Tutankamen 🎬🎬 1977? (R) Fiendish criminal genius steals priceless golden mask of King Tut. Superhero Phenomenal is less than dry spaghetti sci-fi. **90m/C VHS.** *IT* Mauro Parenti, Lucretia Love. *NO*

Phenomenon 🎬🎬½ 1996 (PG) Average small town schmoe George Malley (Travolta) is turned into a genius when he's struck by a bright light on his 37th birthday. This development brings him to the attention of the scientific community and, of course, the military. The locals scorn him, thus fulfilling the Hollywood stereotype of rural folks fearing anything they don't understand. Good-natured weeper plays the Gump card (but turns too paranoid) and wins as Travolta gets to be the nice guy, while attractive Sedgwick is fine as romantic interest Lace. **123m/C VHS, LV, Closed Caption.** John Travolta, Robert Duvall, Kyra Sedgwick, Forest Whitaker, Richard Kiley, Brent Spiner; *D:* Jon Turteltaub; *W:* Gerald DiPego; *C:* Phedon Papamichael; *M:* Thomas Newman. Nominations: MTV Movie Awards '97: Best Male Performance (Travolta), Best Song ("Change the World"), Best Kiss (John Travolta/Kyra Sedgwick). *TOU*

Phffft! 🎬🎬½ 1954 Holliday and Lemmon are a bored couple who decide to divorce, date others, and take mambo lessons. By no stretch of plausibility, they constantly run into each other and compete in the same mambo contest. **91m/C VHS.** Judy Holliday, Jack Lemmon, Jack Carson, Kim Novak, Luella Gear, Merry Anders; *D:* Mark Robson; *W:* George Axelrod; *C:* Charles B(ryant) Lang. *GKK*

Philadelphia 🎬🎬🎬½ 1993 (PG-13) AIDS goes Hollywood as hot-shot corporate attorney Andrew Beckett (Hanks), fired because he has the disease, hires brilliant but homophobic personal injury attorney Washington as his counsel when he sues for discrimination. Box office winner was criticized by some gay activists as too mainstream, which is the point. It doesn't probe deeply into the gay lifestyle, focusing instead on justice and compassion. Boasts a good script, make-up that transforms Hanks, sure direction, great soundtrack, and a strong supporting cast, but all would mean little without Hanks' superb performance, his best to date. ♫Streets of Philadelphia. **125m/C VHS, LV, 8mm, Closed Caption.** Tom Hanks, Denzel Washington, Antonio Banderas, Jason Robards Jr., Joanne Woodward, Mary Steenburgen, Ron Vawter, Robert Ridgely, Obba Babatunde, Robert Castle, Daniel Chapman, Roger Corman, John Bedford Lloyd, Roberta Maxwell, Warren Miller, Anna Deavere Smith, Kathryn Witt, Andre B. Blake, Ann Dowd, Bradley Whitford, Chandra Wilson, Charles Glenn, Peter Jacobs, Paul Lazar, Dan Olmstead, Joey Perillo, Lauren Roselli, Bill Rowe, Lisa Talerico, Daniel von Bargen, Tracey Walter; *Cameos:* Karen Finley, David Drake, Quentin Crisp; *D:* Jonathan Demme; *W:* Ron Nyswaner; *C:* Tak Fujimoto; *M:* Howard Shore. Academy Awards '93: Best Actor (Hanks), Best Song ("Streets of Philadelphia"); Berlin International Film Festival '94: Best Actor (Hanks); Golden Globe Awards '94: Best Actor—Drama (Hanks), Best Song ("Streets of Philadelphia"); MTV Movie Awards '94: Best Male Performance (Hanks); Blockbuster Entertainment Awards '95: Drama Actor, Video (Hanks); Nominations: Academy Awards '93: Best Makeup, Best Original Screenplay, Best Song ("Philadelphia"); Gold-

en Globe Awards '94: Best Screenplay; MTV Movie Awards '94: Best Film, Best On-Screen Duo (Tom Hanks/Denzel Washington), Best Song ("Streets of Philadelphia"); Writers Guild of America '93: Best Original Screenplay. *COL*

The Philadelphia Experiment 🎬🎬½ 1984 (PG) A WWII sailor falls through a hole in time and lands in the mid-1980s, whereupon he woos a gorgeous woman. Sufficient chemistry between Pare and Allen, but PG rating is an indication of the film's less-than-graphic love scenes. **101m/C VHS, Beta, LV.** Michael Pare, Nancy Allen, Eric Christmas, Bobby DiCicco; *D:* Stewart Raffill; *W:* Don Jakoby. *VTR*

Philadelphia Experiment 2 🎬🎬½ 1993 (PG-13) Melodramatic sci-fi what-ifer has Germany winning WWII by dropping a bomb on Washington. So southern California is now one big labor camp with an evil mad scientist (Graham) and a beleaguered hero (Johnson) who must time-travel back to 1943 to prevent the Germans from dropping that bomb. **98m/C VHS, LV, Closed Caption.** Brad Johnson, Gerrit Graham, Marjean Holden, James Greene, Geoffrey Blake, John Christian Grass, Cyril O'Reilly; *D:* Stephen Cornwell; *W:* Kevin Rock, Nick Paine; *M:* Gerald Gouriet. *THV*

The Philadelphia Story 🎬🎬🎬🎬 1940 A woman's plans to marry again go awry when her dashing ex-husband arrives on the scene. Matters are further complicated when a loopy reporter—assigned to spy on the nuptials—falls in love with the blushing bride. Classic comedy, with trio of Hepburn, Grant, and Stewart all serving aces. Based on the hit Broadway play by Philip Barry, and remade as the musical "High Society" in 1956 (stick to the original). Also available colorized. **112m/B VHS, Beta, LV.** Katharine Hepburn, Cary Grant, James Stewart, Ruth Hussey, Roland Young, John Howard, John Halliday, Virginia Weidler, Henry Daniell, Hillary Brooke, Mary Nash; *D:* George Cukor; *W:* Donald Ogden Stewart; *C:* Joseph Ruttenberg; *M:* Franz Waxman. Academy Awards '40: Best Actor (Stewart), Best Screenplay; New York Film Critics Awards '40: Best Actress (Hepburn); Nominations: Academy Awards '40: Best Actress (Hepburn), Best Director (Cukor), Best Picture, Best Supporting Actress (Hussey). *MGM, BTV, HMV*

Philby, Burgess and MacLean: Spy Scandal of the Century 🎬🎬½ 1984 The true story of the three infamous British officials who defected to the Soviet Union in 1951, after stealing some vital British secrets for the KGB. **83m/C VHS, Beta.** *GB* Derek Jacobi, Anthony Bate, Michael Culver; *D:* Gordon Flemyng. *MTI*

Phobia woof! 1980 (R) Patients at a hospital are mysteriously being murdered. Stupid and unpleasant story that lasts too long and probably should never have started. **91m/C VHS, Beta, Closed Caption.** Paul Michael Glaser, Susan Hogan; *D:* John Huston; *W:* Peter Bellwood, Lew Lehman, Gary Sherman, Ronald Shusett, Jimmy Sangster. *PAR*

Phoenix 🎬½ 1978 Aging queen summons her marksman to find the Phoenix, a mythical bird that she believes will bring her eternal life. With English subtitles. **137m/C VHS, Beta.** *JP* Tatsuya Nakadai, Tomisaburo Wakayama, Raoru Yumi, Reiko Ohara. *VDA*

Phoenix 🎬🎬 1995 The Titus 4 deep-space outpost has problems when the creators of a killing machine are targeted for death by their creation, which has begun to think for itself. **?m/C VHS.** Stephen Nichols, Billy Drago, William Sanderson, Brad Dourif. *MNC*

The Phoenix and the Magic Carpet 🎬🎬½ 1995 (PG) Visiting England to settle her father's estate, Mrs. Wilson and her three children discover an egg from which a phoenix emerges. This mythical firebird proceeds to take the children on a magic adventure. Adapted from the book by Edith Nesbit. **80m/C VHS, Closed Caption.** Dee Wallace Stone, Timothy Hegeman, Nick Klein, Laura Kamrath, Peter Ustinov; *D:* Zoran Perisic; *W:* Florence Fox; *M:* Alan Parker. *PAR*

Phoenix Team ⚐ 1980 Two agents discover their mutual attraction can be deadly in the spy business. 90m/C VHS, Beta. Don Francks, Elizabeth Shepherd. TWE

Phoenix the Ninja ⚐ 198? A young girl grows up to be a ninja warrior and battles everyone who would deign to impede her. 92m/C VHS, Beta. Sho Kosugi. TWE

Phoenix the Warrior ⚐ 1988 Sometime in the future, female savages battle each other for control of the now ravaged earth. A newcomer seeks the tribe most worthy of receiving the last man on the planet, thereby continuing the human race. 90m/C VHS. Persis Khambatta, James H. Emery, Peggy Sands, Kathleen Kinmont; D: Robert Hayes. NO

The Phone Call ⚐ 1989 (R) 900-number morality tale about high-powered executive who calls phone sex line and is connected with escaped homicidal maniac who takes a toll on him and his family. CW: Menacing violence. 95m/C VHS. Michael Sarrazin, Linda Smith, Ron Lea, Lisa Jakub; D: Allan Goldstein. NO

Phone Call from a Stranger ⚐⚐½ 1952 After a plane crash, a survivor visits the families of three of the victims whom he met during the flight. 96m/B VHS, Beta, Closed Caption. Bette Davis, Gary Merrill, Michael Rennie, Shelley Winters, Hugh Beaumont, Keenan Wynn, Eve Arden, Craig Stevens; D: Jean Negulesco; W: Nunnally Johnson; C: Milton Krasner. FOX

Photographer ⚐ 1975 (PG) A photographer turns into a murderer, showing the negative side of his personality. 94m/C VHS, Beta. Michael Callan; D: William B. Hillman. NLC

Physical Evidence ⚐⚐ 1989 (R) A lawyer finds herself falling for an ex-cop turned murder suspect while she tries to defend him for a crime he doesn't remember committing. 99m/C VHS, Beta, LV, Closed Caption. Burt Reynolds, Theresa Russell, Ned Beatty, Kay Lenz, Ted McGinley; D: Michael Crichton; W: Bill Phillips; C: John A. Alonzo; M: Henry Mancini. LIV, VES, HHE

P.I. Private Investigations ⚐ 1987 (R) Corrupt, drug-dealing cops stalk another cop who can finger them. 91m/C VHS, Beta. Martin Balsam. FOX

Piaf 1981 (PG) Musical drama chronicles the life of Edith Piaf, France's legendary singer of the Roaring '20s. Her rise from the streets, bout with temporary blindness, and many self-destructive attempts at experiencing life are retold in music. 114m/C VHS, Beta. Jane Lapotaire. FOX

The Piano ⚐⚐⚐½ 1993 (R) In the 1850s, Ada (Hunter), a mute Scottish widow with a young daughter, agrees to an arranged marriage with Stewart (Neill), a colonial landowner in New Zealand. The way she expresses her feelings is by playing her cherished piano, left behind on the beach by her new husband. Another settler, George, (Keitel) buys it, arranges for lessons with Ada, and soon the duo begin a grand passion leading to a cruelly calculated revenge. Fiercely poetic and well acted (with Keitel in a notably romantic role), though the film may be too dark and intense for some. Fine original score with Hunter doing her own piano playing. CW: Extremely graphic sexuality. 120m/C VHS, LV, Closed Caption. AU Holly Hunter, Harvey Keitel, Sam Neill, Anna Paquin, Kerry Walker, Genevieve Lemon; D: Jane Campion; W: Jane Campion; C: Stuart Dryburgh; M: Michael Nyman. Academy Awards '93: Best Actress (Hunter), Best Original Screenplay, Best Supporting Actress (Paquin); Australian Film Institute '93: Best Actor (Keitel), Best Actress (Hunter), Best Cinematography, Best Costume Design, Best Director (Campion), Best Film, Best Film Editing, Best Sound, Best Original Score; British Academy Awards '93: Best Actress (Hunter); Cannes Film Festival '93: Best Actress, Best Film; Golden Globe Awards '94: Best Actress—Drama (Hunter); Independent Spirit Awards '94: Best Foreign Film; Los Angeles Film Critics Association Awards '93: Best Actress (Hunter), Best Cinematography, Best Director (Campion), Best Screenplay, Best Supporting Actress (Paquin); National Board of Review Awards '93: Best Actress (Hunter); New York Film Critics Awards '93:

Best Actress (Hunter), Best Director (Campion), Best Screenplay; National Society of Film Critics Awards '93: Best Actress (Hunter), Best Screenplay; Writers Guild of America '93: Best Original Screenplay; Nominations: Academy Awards '93: Best Cinematography, Best Costume Design, Best Director (Campion), Best Film Editing, Best Picture; British Academy Awards '94: Best Director (Campion), Best Film, Best Original Screenplay, Best Original Score; Directors Guild of America Awards '93: Best Director (Campion); Golden Globe Awards '94: Best Director (Campion), Best Film—Drama, Best Screenplay, Best Supporting Actress (Paquin), Best Original Score. LIV

A Piano for Mrs. Cimino ⚐⚐⚐ 1982 Declared senile and incompetent, a widowed woman fights for control of her own life. Good script helps this made for TV soaper. 100m/C VHS, Beta. Bette Davis, Keenan Wynn, Alexa Kenin, Penny Fuller, Christopher Guest, George Hearn; D: George Schaefer; M: James Horner. GEM

The Piano Lesson ⚐⚐⚐ 1994 (PG) The prized heirloom of the Charles family is an 80-year-old, ornately carved upright piano, jealously guarded by widowed Berniece (Woodard), and housed in the Pittsburgh home of Uncle Doaker (Gordon). When Berniece's brother Willie Boy (Dutton) visits from Mississippi, it's to persuade her to sell the piano in order to buy some land that their grandfather had worked on as a slave. But the past, carved into the piano's panels, has a strong hold—one that Berniece refuses to give up. Set in 1936. Adaptation by Wilson of his 1990 Pulitzer Prize-winning play. 99m/C VHS, LV, Closed Caption. Alfre Woodard, Charles S. Dutton, Courtney B. Vance, Carl Gordon, Tommy Hollis, Zelda Harris, Lou Myers, Rosalyn Coleman, Tommy La Fitte; D: Lloyd Richards; W: August Wilson; M: Stephen James Taylor, Dwight Andrews. REP

Picasso Trigger ⚐⚐ 1989 (R) An American spy tries to catch an elusive murderer. The sequel to "Hard Ticket to Hawaii" and "Malibu Express." 99m/C VHS. Steve Bond, Dona Speir, John Aprea, Hope Marie Carlton, Guich Koock, Roberta Vasquez, Bruce Penhall; D: Andy Sidaris. WAR

Pick a Star ⚐⚐ Movie Struck 1937 Lawrence is a small-town girl who wins a contest and is off to Hollywood. Only no one pays any attention to her except for publicity man Haley, who arranges her screen test. Naturally, she knocks the studio bosses for a loop and becomes a star. Laurel & Hardy are featured in a couple of comedy segments showing the newcomer some backstage silliness and movie business on the set of a Western they're filming (with Finlayson, better known as a director, cast as the duo's director). 70m/B VHS. Rosina Lawrence, Jack Haley, Patsy Kelly, Mischa Auer, Stan Laurel, Oliver Hardy, Charles Halton, Tom Dugan, Russell Hicks, James Finlayson; D: Edward Sedgwick. MGM, NOS, CAB

The Pick-Up Artist ⚐⚐½ 1987 (PG-13) The adventures of a compulsive Don Juan who finds he genuinely loves the daughter of an alcoholic who's in debt to the mob. Standard story with no surprises. 81m/C VHS, Beta, LV, Closed Caption. Robert Downey Jr., Molly Ringwald, Dennis Hopper, Harvey Keitel, Danny Aiello, Vanessa Williams, Robert Towne, Mildred Dunnock, Lorraine Bracco, Joe Spinell, Victoria Jackson, Polly Draper, Brian Hamill; D: James Toback; W: James Toback; C: Gordon Willis; M: Georges Delerue. FOX

Pick-Up Summer ⚐ Pinball Summer; Pinball Pick-Up 1979 (R) Two suburban boys cruise their town after school lets out, chasing a pair of voluptuous sisters. 99m/C VHS, Beta. CA Michael Zelniker, Carl Marotte; D: George Mihalka. NWV

The Pickle ⚐ 1993 (R) Self-indulgent comedy about a midlife crisis. Aiello stars as a middle-aged manic-depressive director certain that his new film is going to be an abysmal flop (as have all his recent pictures). He seeks comfort and reassurance from various ex-wives, children, lovers, and others, though he abuses them all. This dispirited tale also shows clips of the director's dreadful film about children who launch a giant pickle into space. It couldn't possibly be worse

that what Mazursky actually put up on the screen. CW: Some language and sexual scene. 103m/C VHS, LV, Closed Caption. Danny Aiello, Dyan Cannon, Clothilde Courau, Shelley Winters, Barry Miller, Jerry Stiller, Christopher Penn, Rebecca Miller; Cameos: Ally Sheedy, Little Richard, Spalding Gray, Griffin Dunne, Isabella Rossellini, Dudley Moore; D: Paul Mazursky; W: Paul Mazursky; M: Michel Legrand. COL

Pickpocket ⚐⚐⚐½ 1959 Slow moving, documentary-like account of a petty thief's existence is a moral tragedy inspired by "Crime and Punishment." Ending is particularly moving. Classic filmmaking from Bresson, France's master of austerity. In French with English subtitles. 75m/B VHS. FR Martin LaSalle, Marika Green, Pierre Leymarie; D: Robert Bresson. NYF, FCT, TPV

Pickup on South Street ⚐⚐⚐ 1953 Petty thief Widmark lifts woman's wallet only to find it contains top secret Communist micro-film for which pinko agents will stop at nothing to get back. Intriguing look at the politics of the day. The creme of "B" movies. 80m/B VHS, Beta. Richard Widmark, Jean Peters, Thelma Ritter, Murvyn Vye, Richard Kiley, Milburn Stone; D: Samuel Fuller; W: Samuel Fuller. Nominations: Academy Awards '53: Best Supporting Actress (Ritter). FOX, FCT

The Pickwick Papers ⚐⚐½ 1954 Comedy based on the Dickens classic wherein Mrs. Bardell sues the Pickwick Club for breach of promise. 109m/B VHS, Beta. GB James Hayter, James Donald, Nigel Patrick, Hermione Gingold, Hermione Baddeley, Kathleen Harrison; D: Noel Langley. Nominations: Academy Awards '55: Best Costume Design (B & W). VCI

Picnic ⚐⚐⚐½ 1955 A wanderer arrives in a small town and immediately wins the love a his friend's girl. The other women in town seem interested too. Strong, romantic work, with Holden excelling in the lead. Novak provides a couple pointers too. Lavish Hollywood adaptation of the William Inge play, including the popular tune "Moonglow/Theme from Picnic". 113m/C VHS, Beta, LV. William Holden, Kim Novak, Rosalind Russell, Susan Strasberg, Arthur O'Connell, Cliff Robertson, Betty Field, Verna Felton, Reta Shaw, Nick Adams, Phyllis Newman, Raymond Bailey; D: Joshua Logan; W: Daniel Taradash; C: James Wong Howe; M: George Duning. Academy Awards '55: Best Art Direction/Set Decoration (Color), Best Film Editing; Golden Globe Awards '56: Best Director (Logan); National Board of Review Awards '55: 10 Best Films of the Year; Nominations: Academy Awards '55: Best Director (Logan), Best Picture, Best Supporting Actor (O'Connell), Original Dramatic/Comedy Score. COL

Picnic at Hanging Rock ⚐⚐⚐ 1975 (PG) School outing in 1900 into a mountainous region ends tragically when three girls disappear. Eerie film is strong on atmosphere, as befits mood master Weir. Lambert is extremely photogenic—and suitable subdued—as one of the girls to disappear. Otherwise beautifully photographed on location. From the novel by Joan Lindsey. 110m/C VHS, Beta. AU Margaret Nelson, Rachel Roberts, Dominic Guard, Helen Morse, Jacki Weaver, Vivean Gray, Anne Lambert; D: Peter Weir; C: Russell Boyd; M: Bruce Smeaton. VES, OM

Picnic on the Grass ⚐⚐ Le Dejeuner Sur l'Herbe; Lunch on the Grass 1959 A strange, whimsical fantasy heavily evocative of the director's Impressionist roots; a science-minded candidate for the president of Europe throws a picnic as public example of his earthiness, and falls in love with a peasant girl. In French with English subtitles. 92m/C VHS, Beta. FR Paul Meurisse, Catherine Rouvel, Fernand Sardou, Jacqueline Morane, Jean-Pierre Granval; D: Jean Renoir. FCT, INT, TPV

Picture Bride ⚐⚐½ 1994 (PG-13) Familiar immigrant saga finds 17-year-old Japanese Riyo (Kudoh) setting off for Hawaii in 1918 as a "picture bride" to a husband she's never met but with whom she's exchanged photos (hence the title). Riyo's shocked to discover her intended, sugarcane worker Matsuji (Takayama), has deceived her with an out-of-date picture and is at least 25 years older than she. She refuses to consummate the marriage and goes to work in the fields, intending to earn money for her passage home but of course things don't work out quite as Riyo intends. Japanese with subtitles. **CW:** Partial nudity and sexual situations. **95m/C VHS, LV, Closed Caption. JP** Yoko Sugi, Youki Kudoh, Akira Takayama, Tamlyn Tomita, Cary-Hiroyuki Tagawa; **Cameos:** Toshiro Mifune; **D:** Kayo Hatta; **W:** Kayo Hatta, Mari Hatta, Diane Mark; **C:** Claudio Rocha; **M:** Cliff Eidelman. Sundance Film Festival '95: Audience Award; Nominations: Independent Spirit Awards '96: Best First Feature. *TOU*

Picture Mommy Dead ♂♂ 1966 Well acted melodrama involving a scheming shrew who struggles to drive her mentally disturbed stepdaughter insane for the sake of cold, hard cash. **85m/C VHS, Beta.** Don Ameche, Zsa Zsa Gabor, Martha Hyer, Susan Gordon; **D:** Bert I. Gordon; **C:** Ellsworth Fredericks. *NLC*

Picture of Dorian Gray ♂♂♂ 1945 Hatfield plays the rake who stays young while his portrait ages in this adaptation of Oscar Wilde's classic novel. Lansbury steals this one. **110m/B VHS, Beta, LV.** Hurd Hatfield, George Sanders, Donna Reed, Angela Lansbury, Peter Lawford, Lowell Gilmore; **D:** Albert Lewin; **C:** Harry Stradling. Academy Awards '45: Best Black and White Cinematography; Golden Globe Awards '46: Best Supporting Actress (Lansbury); Nominations: Academy Awards '45: Best Interior Decoration, Best Supporting Actress (Lansbury). *MGM, FHE, TVC*

Picture of Dorian Gray ♂♂♂ 1974 Another version of Wilde's renowned novel about a man who retains his youthful visage while his portrait shows the physical ravages of aging. Davenport is particularly appealing in the lead. Made for television. **130m/C VHS, Beta.** Shane Briant, Nigel Davenport, Charles Aidman, Fionnula Flanagan, Linda Kelsey, Vanessa Howard; **D:** Glenn Jordan. *LIV, MPI*

Picture Perfect ♂♂½ 1996 (PG-13) While trying to impress her new boss, ad exec Aniston claims Mohr, the man standing with her in a photo, is her fiance. Unfortunately, the boss now wants to meet the guy (a stranger who was at the same party) and she must find him and get him to play along. Find him she does—too bad he's engaged. The story's cliched, but Aniston's appealing screen presence perks things up a bit. **CW:** Sensuality and related dialogue. **?m/C VHS.** Jennifer Aniston, Jay Mohr, Kevin Bacon, Illeana Douglas, Olympia Dukakis; **D:** Glenn Gordon Caron; **W:** Glenn Gordon Caron; **M:** Carter Burwell. *NYR*

Picture Windows ♂♂ 1995 (R) Three short cable movies inspired by works of art. "Lightning," based on Frederic Remington sketches and a Zane Grey short story, finds western codger Keith striking gold with the help of his trusty mule. A David Hockney painting suggested "Armed Response," which features a confrontation between a wealthy lawyer (Loggia) and a burglar (Zahn). And an anonymous 16th-century canvas "Two Nudes Bathing" is given an imaginative history. **CW:** Some sexuality/nudity. **95m/C VHS.** Brian Keith, Robert Loggia, Steve Zahn, Charley Boorman; **D:** Joe Dante, Bob Rafelson, John Boorman. *HMK*

Pictures ♂♂½ 198? The silent-film era in England is spoofed in this look at ambitious waitress Ruby Sears, who's determined to be a film star, and writer Bill Trench, who winds up a novice screenwriter. Bill's first movie script is based on Ruby's life and she desperately wants to star in the production, if only she can convince the producer and the drunken male lead that she has the talent. Made for British television; 7 episodes on 4 cassettes. **208m/C VHS.** **GB** Wendy Morgan, Peter McEnery, Harry Towb, Anton Rodgers, Annette Badland, Malcom Jamieson, Marc Smith; **W:** Roy Clarke. *TVC, SIG, VCO*

Pie In the Sky ♂♂½ 1995 (R) Charles Dunlap (Charles) is a traffic geek, fascinated by the flow of cars on the nearby freeway, whose hero is local traffic reporter Alan Davenport (Goodman), with whom he eventually gets a job in L.A. Charles' other interest is dancer/waitress

Amy (Heche)—their first attempt at romance goes awry but persistence pays off. Optimistic and corny. **CW:** Sexuality. **94m/C VHS, LV, Closed Caption.** Josh Charles, Anne Heche, John Goodman, Christine Lahti, Peter Riegert, Christine Ebersole, Wil Wheaton, Bob Balaban, Dey Young; **D:** Bryan Gordon; **W:** Bryan Gordon; **C:** Bernd Heinl; **M:** Michael Covertino. *NLC*

Piece of Cake ♂♂½ 1990 Adaptation of the Derek Robinson novel follows the flyboys of the RAF Hornet Squadron during the early years of WWII. They have trouble taking the war seriously but tangles with the Luftwaffe and increasing casualties put a strain on everyone. Great aerial photography and the British planes are vintage Spitfires not repros. Made for British TV miniseries on 6 cassettes. **312m/C VHS. GB** Tom Burlinson, Tim Woodward, Boyd Gaines, Nathaniel Parker, Neil Dudgeon, David Horovitch, Richard Hope, Jeremy Wortham, Michael Elwyn, Corinne Dacla, Helena Michell. *SIG, VCO*

A Piece of Pleasure ♂♂♂ 1970 Marriage declines due to a domineering husband in this familiar domestic study from French master Chabrol. Good, but not among the director's best efforts. In French with English subtitles. **100m/C VHS, Beta. D:** Claude Chabrol. *FCT*

Piece of the Action ♂♂½ 1977 (PG) An ex-cop beats two con men at their own game when he convinces them to work for a Chicago community center. **135m/C VHS, Beta.** Sidney Poitier, Bill Cosby, James Earl Jones, Denise Nicholas, Hope Clarke, Tracy Reed, Titos Vandis, Ja'net DuBois; **D:** Sidney Poitier; **M:** Curtis Mayfield. *WAR*

Pieces WOOF! 1983 (R) Chain-saw wielding madman roams a college campus in search of human parts for a ghastly jigsaw puzzle. Gory and loathsome. **90m/C VHS, Beta.** *IT SP* Christopher George, Lynda Day George, Paul Smith; **D:** J. Piquer Simon. *VES*

The Pied Piper of Hamelin ♂♂ 1957 The evergreen classic of the magical piper who rids a village of rats and then disappears with the village children into a mountain when the townspeople fail to keep a promise. **90m/C VHS, Beta.** Van Johnson, Claude Rains, Jim Backus, Kay Starr, Lori Nelson; **D:** Bretaigne Windust. *KAR, NOS, MED*

The Pied Piper of Hamelin 1984 From Shelley Duvall's "Faerie Tale Theatre" comes the story of how a man with a magic flute charmed the rats out of Hamelin. **60m/C VHS, Beta, Closed Caption.** Eric Idle; **D:** Nicholas Meyer. *FOX, FCT*

Pier 23 ♂♂ 1951 A private eye is hired to bring a lawless ex-convict to a priest's custody, but gets an imposter instead. A web of intrigue follows. **57m/B VHS, Beta, LV.** Hugh Beaumont, Ann Savage, David Bruce, Raymond Greenleaf, Joi Lansing. *NO*

Pierrot le Fou ♂♂½ 1965 A woman fleeing a gangster joins a man leaving his wife in this stunning, occasionally confusing classic from iconoclast Godard. A hallmark in 1960s improvisational filmmaking, with rugged Belmondo and always-photogenic Karina effortlessly excelling in leads. In French with English subtitles. **110m/C VHS, LV.** *FR IT* Samuel Fuller, Jean-Pierre Leaud, Jean-Paul Belmondo, Anna Karina, Dirk Sanders; **D:** Jean-Luc Godard; **M:** Antoine Duhamel. *INT, FCT, IME*

Pigs ♂½ Daddy's Deadly Darling; The Killers 1973 Young woman who has escaped from a mental hospital teams up with an evil old man to go on a murdering spree. They complement each other beautifully. She kills them and he disposes of the bodies by making pig slop out of them. **90m/C VHS, Beta.** Toni Lawrence, Marc Lawrence, Jesse Vint, Katharine Ross; **D:** Marc Lawrence; **W:** Marc Lawrence; **M:** Charles Bernstein. *MRV*

A Pig's Tale ♂♂ 1994 (PG) Rich kids rule at Kamp Kipperman but one 13-year-old forms the Pig Pen club and the club members decide to turn the tables on their overbearing rivals. **94m/C VHS.** Joe Flaherty, Grack Sack; **D:** Paul Tassie. *PGV*

Pigskin Parade ♂♂½ 1936 Fifteen-year-old Garland's first feature is a lighthearted musical combining college and football. Winston Winters (Haley) coaches the Texas State U team, which has been mistakenly invited to play Yale, and goes to great lengths to give his team a chance by recruiting a farmboy (Erwin) who's a natural phenom. (Garland's the boy's singing sister.) ♪Balboa; The Texas Tornado; It's Love I'm After; You're Simply Terrific; You Do the Darndest Things, Baby; T.S.U. Alma Mater; Hold That Bulldog; Down with Everything; We'd Rather Be In College. **95m/B VHS.** Jack Haley, Patsy Kelly, Stuart Erwin, Judy Garland, Johnny Downs, Betty Grable, Arline Judge, Tony Martin, Fred Kohler Jr., Elisha Cook Jr.; **D:** David Butler; **W:** Harry Tugend, Jack Yellen; **C:** Arthur C. Miller. Nominations: Academy Awards '36: Best Supporting Actor (Erwin). *FXV*

Pilgrim, Farewell ♂♂½ 1982 Dramatic story about a dying woman who needs to tie up loose ends before her death and goes looking for her estranged teenage daughter. Made for television for PBS' "American Playhouse." **110m/C VHS, Beta.** Elizabeth Huddle, Christopher Lloyd, Laurie Pranage, Lesley Paxton, Shelley Wyant, Robert Brown; **D:** Michael Roemer. *FLI*

The Pillow Book ♂♂ 1995 Greenaway's usual chilliness gives way to some true erotic heat that still keeps to arcane subjects, violence, and dazzling visuals. Japanese model Nagiko (Wu) longs for the childhood rituals enacted by her calligrapher father (Ogata) as he literally painted birthday greetings on her face with brush and ink. As an adult, Nagiko searches out calligrapher/lovers willing to use her body as their paper but she's still unsatisfied until she meets bisexual Englishman Jerome (McGregor) and he insists Nagiko write on him. When Nagiko learns Jerome's male lover is the publisher (Oida) who was once involved with her father, her jealousy triggers tragic consequences. Title refers to the 10th century diary "The Pillow Book of Sei Shonagon." English, Japanese, Mandarin, and Cantonese dialogue. **126m/C VHS.** *NL FR GB* Vivian Wu, Ewan McGregor, Ken Ogata; **D:** Peter Greenaway; **W:** Peter Greenaway; **C:** Sacha Vierny. *NYR*

Pillow Talk ♂♂♂½ 1959 Sex comedy in which a man woos a woman who loathes him. By the way, they share the same telephone party line. Narrative provides minimal indication of the film's strengths, which are many. Classic '50s comedy with masters Day and Hudson exhibiting considerable rapport, even when fighting. Lighthearted, constantly funny. **102m/C VHS, Beta, LV.** Rock Hudson, Doris Day, Tony Randall, Thelma Ritter, Nick Adams, Lee Patrick; **D:** Michael Gordon. Academy Awards '59: Best Story & Screenplay; Nominations: Academy Awards '59: Best Actress (Day), Best Art Direction/Set Decoration (Color), Best Supporting Actress (Ritter), Original Dramatic/Comedy Score. *USH, CCB*

Pilot ♂½ 1984 Young girl discovers the debilitating effects of dishonesty when she becomes a break-dancing champion. **27m/C VHS, Beta.** Kelly Jo Minter, Adolph "Oz" Alvarez, Katie Rich. *PAU*

Pimpernel Smith ♂♂½ Mister V 1942 Seemingly scatterbrained archaeology professor is actually a dashing agent rescuing refugees from evil Nazis in WWII France. Howard is well cast, but the film is somewhat predictable, and it's too long. Wonderful scene, though, in which a Nazi officer champions Shakespeare as Aryan. **121m/B VHS, Beta.** *GB* Leslie Howard, Mary Morris, Francis L. Sullivan, David Tomlinson; **D:** Leslie Howard. *VYY*

Pin ♂♂½ 1988 (R) A boy's imaginary friend assists in the slaying of various enemies. Horror effort could be worse. **103m/C VHS, Beta, LV.** Cyndy Preston, David Hewlett, Terry O'Quinn; **D:** Sandor Stern. *VTR, NWV, IME*

Pin Down Girls ♂ 1951 Great schlock about girl wrestlers. Also known as "Racket Girls." **?m/C VHS.** Clara Mortensen, Rita Martinez. *SNC*

Pin-Up Girl 🎬🎬 1944 Grable plays a secretary who becomes an overnight sensation during WWII. Loosely based on her famous pinup poster that was so popular at the time, the movie didn't even come close to being as successful. The songs aren't particularly memorable, although Charlie Spivak and his Orchestra perform. 🎵Once Too Often; Yankee Doodle Dandy; I'll Be Marching to a Love Song; You're My Little Pin Up Girl; Story of the Very Merry Widow; Time Alone Will Tell; Don't Carry Tales Out of School; Red Robins, Bob Whites and Blue Birds. **83m/C VHS, LV, Closed Caption.** Betty Grable, Martha Raye, Jon Harvey, Joe E. Brown, Eugene Pallette, Mantan Moreland; **D:** H. Bruce Humberstone; **C:** Ernest Palmer. FOX, FXV

Ping Pong 🎬🎬½ 1987 (PG) A Chinese patriarch drops dead in London's Chinatown, leaving a young law student to disentangle his will, and get mixed up with his cross-cultured family. **100m/C VHS, Beta, LV.** David Yip, Lucy Sheen, Robert Lee, Lam Fung, Victor Kan, Ric Young; **D:** Po Chich Leong. NO

Pink Cadillac 🎬🎬½ 1989 (PG-13) A grizzled, middle-aged bondsman is on the road, tracking down bail-jumping crooks. He helps the wife and baby of his latest target escape from her husband's more evil associates. Eastwood's performance is good and fun to watch, in this otherwise lightweight film. **121m/C VHS, Beta, LV, 8mm, Closed Caption.** Clint Eastwood, Bernadette Peters, Timothy Carhart, Michael Des Barres, William Hickey, John Dennis Johnston, Geoffrey Lewis, Jim Carrey, Tiffany Gail Robinson, Angela Louise Robinson; **D:** Buddy Van Horn; **W:** John Eskow; **M:** Stephen Dorff. WAR

The Pink Chiquitas 🎬 1986 (PG-13) Sci-fi spoof about a detective battling a mob of meteorite-traveling Amazons. **86m/C VHS, Beta.** Frank Stallone, Eartha Kitt, Bruce Pirrie, McKinlay Robinson, Elizabeth Edwards, Claudia Udy; **D:** Anthony Currie. PSM

Pink Flamingos 🎬 1972 Divine, the dainty 300-pound transvestite, faces the biggest challenge of his/her career when he/she competes for the title of World's Filthiest Person. Tasteless, crude, and hysterical film; this one earned Waters his title as "Prince of Puke." If there are any doubts about this honor—watch through to the end to catch Divine chewing real dog excrement, all the time wearing a you-know-what grin. **95m/C VHS, Beta, LV.** Divine, David Lochary, Mary Vivian Pearce, Danny Mills, Mink Stole, Edith Massey; **D:** John Waters; **W:** John Waters. NO

Pink Floyd: The Wall 🎬🎬 1982 (R) Film version of Pink Floyd's 1979 LP, "The Wall." A surreal, impressionistic tour-de-force about a boy who grows up numb from society's pressures. The concept is bombastic and overwrought, but Geldof manages to remain somewhat likeable as the cynical rock star and the Gerald Scarfe animation perfectly complements the film. Laserdisc edition includes the original theatrical trailer and the letterboxed format of the film. **95m/C VHS, Beta, LV.** GB Bob Geldof, Christine Hargreaves, Bob Hoskins; **D:** Alan Parker; **C:** Peter Biziou; **M:** Michael Kamen. MVD, MGM

Pink Motel woof! Motel 1982 (R) Several people spend a night meant to be romantic at a pink stucco motel which caters to couples. Comic stiff with Diller and Pickens as the owners of said pink motel. **90m/C VHS, Beta.** Phyllis Diller, Slim Pickens, Terri Berland, Squire Fridell; **D:** Mike MacFarland. NO

Pink Nights 🎬 1987 (PG) A high school nebbish is suddenly pursued by three beautiful girls, and his life gets turned upside-down. **87m/C VHS, Beta, LV.** Shaun Allen, Kevin Anderson, Larry King, Johnathan Jamcovic Michaels; **D:** Philip Koch. VTR, NWV

The Pink Panther 🎬🎬🎬 1964 Bumbling, disaster-prone inspector invades a Swiss ski resort and becomes obsessed with capturing a jewel thief hoping to lift the legendary "Pink Panther" diamond. Said thief is also the inspector's wife's lover, though the inspector doesn't know it. Slick slapstick succeeds on strength of Sellers' classic portrayal of Clouseau, who accidentally destroys everything in his path while speaking in a funny French accent. Followed by "A Shot in the Dark," "Inspector Clouseau" (without Sellers), "The Return of the Pink Panther," "The Pink Panther Strikes Again," "Revenge of the Pink Panther," "Trail of the Pink Panther," and "Curse of the Pink Panther." Memorable theme supplied by Mancini. **113m/C VHS, Beta, LV.** GB Peter Sellers, David Niven, Robert Wagner, Claudia Cardinale, Capucine, Brenda de Banzie; **D:** Blake Edwards; **W:** Blake Edwards; **M:** Henry Mancini. Nominations: Academy Awards '64: Best Original Score. MGM, FOX, TVC

The Pink Panther Strikes Again 🎬🎬🎬 1976 (PG) Fifth in the series has the incompetent inspector tracking his former boss, who has gone insane and has become preoccupied with destroying the entire world. A must for Sellers buffs and anyone who appreciates slapstick. **103m/C VHS, Beta, LV.** GB Peter Sellers, Herbert Lom, Lesley-Anne Down, Colin Blakely, Leonard Rossiter, Burt Kwouk; **D:** Blake Edwards; **W:** Edwards Waldman, Frank Waldman; **M:** Henry Mancini. Writers Guild of America '76: Best Adapted Screenplay; Nominations: Academy Awards '76: Best Song ("Come to Me"). FOX, TVC

Pink String and Sealing Wax 🎬🎬 1945 A brutish pub owner in Victorian England is poisoned by his abused wife. She tries to involve the son of a chemist with the idea of blackmailing the father. Fine period flavor. **89m/B VHS, Beta.** GB Mervyn Johns, Mary Merrall, Gordon Jackson, Googie Withers, Sally Ann Howes, Catherine Lacey, Garry Marsh, Frederick Piper, Don Stannard, Valentine Dyall; **W:** Robert Hamer. SNC

Pinky 🎬🎬🎬 1949 Early Hollywood treatment of the tragic choice made by some black Americans to pass as white in order to attain a better life for themselves and their families. The story is still relevant today. Waters and Barrymore also star, but the lead black character is portrayed by a white actress. Based on the novel "Quality" by Cyd Ricketts Sumner. **102m/B VHS.** Jeanne Crain, Ethel Barrymore, Ethel Waters, Nina Mae McKinney, William Lundigan; **D:** Elia Kazan; **W:** Philip Dunne, Dudley Nichols; **M:** Alfred Newman. Nominations: Academy Awards '49: Best Actress (Crain), Best Supporting Actress (Barrymore, Waters). FXV

Pinocchio 🎬🎬🎬🎬 1940 (G) Second Disney animated film featuring Pinocchio, a little wooden puppet, made with love by the old woodcarver Geppetto, and brought to life by a good fairy. Except Pinocchio isn't content to be just a puppet—he wants to become a real boy. Lured off by a sly fox, Pinocchio undergoes a number of adventures as he tries to return safely home. Has some scary scenes, including Geppetto, Pinocchio, and their friend Jiminy Cricket getting swallowed by a whale, and Pleasure Island, where naughty boys are turned into donkeys. An example of animation at its best and a Disney classic that has held up over time. 🎵When You Wish Upon a Star; Give a Little Whistle; Turn on the Old Music Box; Hi-Diddle-Dee-Dee (An Actor's Life For Me); I've Got No Strings. **87m/C VHS, Beta, LV, Closed Caption. D:** Ben Sharpsteen; **V:** Dick Jones, Cliff Edwards, Evelyn Venable, Walter Catlett, Frankie Darro, Charles Judels, Don Brodie, Christian Rub. Academy Awards '40: Best Song ("When You Wish Upon a Star"), Best Original Score. DIS

Pinocchio 🎬🎬 1976 Classic Pinocchio story in musical form. **76m/C VHS, Beta.** Danny Kaye, Sandy Duncan. VCI

Pinocchio 1983 Pee Wee Herman is the puppet who wants to be a real little boy in this "Faerie Tale Theatre" adaptation of this children's classic. **60m/C VHS, Beta, Closed Caption.** Paul (Pee Wee Herman) Reubens, James Coburn, Carl Reiner, Lainie Kazan; **D:** Peter Medak. FOX, FCT

Pinocchio's Revenge 🎬 1996 (R) Man murders his child and buries the body with a wooden Pinocchio puppet. Somehow before his execution, his lawyer, Jennifer Garrick (Allen), and her cute daughter Zoe (Smith) wind up with the grisly toy and Jennifer allows her daughter to keep it. Naturally, this is not a good thing. **96m/C VHS.** Rosalind Allen, Brittany Alyse Smith, Todd Allen, Lewis Van Bergen, Aaron Lustig, Ron Canada; **D:** Kevin S. Tenney. THV

Pinocchio's Storybook Adventures 🎬½ 1979 Pinocchio takes over for an ailing puppet master and puts on a show for a group of children. **80m/C VHS, Beta. D:** Ron Merk. VTR

Pinto Canyon 🎬½ 1940 An honest sheriff does away with a band of cattle rustlers. **55m/B VHS.** Bob Steele, Louise Stanley, Kenne Duncan, Ted Adams, Steve Clark, Budd Buster; **D:** Raymond K. Johnson. NOS, DVT

Pinto Rustlers 🎬½ 1936 A cowboy left orphaned by a gang of rustlers seeks revenge. **52m/C VHS, Beta.** Tom Tyler, Catherine Cotter. NOS, DVT

Pioneer Marshal 🎬 1949 Lawman Hale disguises himself as a criminal to track down an embezzler. **60m/B VHS, Beta.** Monte Hale, Paul Hurst. DVT

Pioneer Woman 🎬🎬 Pioneers 1973 A family encounters hostility when they set up a frontier homestead in Nebraska in 1867. Told from the feminine perspective, the tale is strewn with hurdles, both personal and natural. **74m/C VHS, Beta.** Joanna Pettet, William Shatner, David Janssen; **D:** Buzz Kulik. WOV

The Pioneers 🎬½ 1941 Ritter sets out to protect a wagon train. **59m/B VHS, Beta.** Tex Ritter. VCN

Pipe Dreams 🎬🎬 1976 (PG) A couple tries to repair their broken marriage against the backdrop of the Alaskan pipeline's construction. **89m/C VHS, Beta.** Gladys Knight, Barry Hankerson, Bruce French, Sally Kirkland, Sherry Bain; **D:** Stephen Verona. COL

Pippi Goes on Board 🎬🎬½ 1975 (G) The fourth and last film in the Swedish series finds Pippi's father arriving one day to take her sailing to Taka-Kuka, his island kingdom. She can't bear to leave her friends and jumps off the ship to return home. The series is poorly dubbed and technically flawed, which the kids probably won't notice. Based on the books by Astrid Lindgren. Preceded by "Pippi Longstocking," "Pippi in the South Seas," and "Pippi on the Run." **83m/C VHS, Beta.** SW Inger Nilsson; **D:** Olle Hellbron. GEM, MOV, TPV

Pippi in the South Seas 🎬🎬½ Pippi Langstrump Pa de Sju Haven 1974 (G) Pippi, a fun-loving, independent, red haired little girl, and her two friends decide to rescue her father, who is being held captive by a band of pirates on a South Sea island. Naturally, clever Pippi saves the day. Poorly dubbed and edited. Based on the children's book by Astrid Lindren. Follows "Pippi Longstocking" and precedes "Pippi on the Run" and "Pippi Goes on Board." **99m/C VHS, Beta.** SW Inger Nilsson; **D:** Olle Hellbron. GEM, MOV, TPV

Pippi Longstocking 🎬🎬½ 1973 (G) This little red-headed, pigtailed terror is left alone by her sailor father as he heads out to sea. Not that Pippi minds, since it gives her the chance to create havoc in her town through the antics of her pets, a monkey and a horse. Pippi's antics may amuse the kiddies but adults will find her obnoxious. Poorly dubbed and technically somewhat shaky. Based on the children's book by Astrid Lindgren. Followed by "Pippi in the South Seas," "Pippi on the Run," and "Pippi Goes on Board." **99m/C VHS, Beta.** SW Inger Nilsson; **D:** Olle Hellbron. GEM, MOV, TPV

Pippi on the Run 🎬🎬½ 1974 (G) The third film in the series finds Pippi on the trail of two friends who have run away from home. The three have many adventures before deciding home is best. Preceded by "Pippi Longstocking" and "Pippi in the South Seas," followed by "Pippi Goes on Board." Films lacks technical and dubbing skills. Based on the children's book by Astrid Lindgren. **99m/C VHS, Beta.** SW GEM, MOV, TPV

Pippin ♂♂♂ 1981 Video version of the stage musical about the adolescent son of Charlemagne finding true love. Adequate record of Bob Fosse's Broadway smash. Features Vereen recreating his original Tony Award-winning role. 120m/C VHS, Beta, LV. Ben Vereen, William Katt, Martha Raye, Chita Rivera. VCI, FHE, FCT

Piranha ♂♂½ 1978 (R) A rural Texas resort area is plagued by attacks from ferocious man-eating fish which a scientist created to be used as a secret weapon in the Vietnam War. Spoofy horror film features the now-obligatory Dante film in-jokes in the background. 90m/C VHS, Beta. Bradford Dillman, Heather Menzies, Kevin McCarthy, Keenan Wynn, Barbara Steele, Dick Miller, Paul Bartel; D: Joe Dante; W: John Sayles; C: Jamie Anderson; M: Pino Donaggio. WAR, OM

Piranha ♂♂½ 1995 (R) Genetically-enhanced piranha terrorize the resort community of Lost River. Scientists Katt and Paul have accidentally released the vicious fishies but everyone ignores their warnings until some swimmers become din-din. Remake of Roger Corman's 1978 cult item and based on John Sayles' original screenplay.CW: Violence/gore and some nudity. 81m/C VHS. Alexandra Paul, William Katt, Soleil Moon Frye, Monte Markham, Darlene Carr, James Karen, Lincoln Kilpatrick; D: Scott Levy. NHO

Piranha 2: The Spawning ♂½ Piranha 2: Flying Killers 1982 (R) Diving instructor and a bio-chemist seek to destroy piranha mutations that are murdering tourists at a club. Early Cameron exercise in gore tech that's a step down from original "Piranha." 88m/C VHS, Beta, LV. Steve Marachuk, Lance Henriksen, Ricky Paul; D: James Cameron. NLC

The Pirate ♂♂♂ 1948 A traveling actor poses as a legendary pilot to woo a lonely woman on a remote Caribbean island. Minnelli always scores with this type of fare, and both Garland and Kelly make the most of the Cole Porter score. ♫Be a Clown; Nina; Mack the Black; You Can Do No Wrong; Sweet Ices, Papayas, Berry Man; Sea Wall; Serafin; The Ring; Judy Awakens. 102m/C VHS, Beta, LV. Judy Garland, Gene Kelly, Walter Slezak, Gladys Cooper, George Zucco, Reginald Owen, Nicholas Brothers; D: Vincente Minnelli; C: Harry Stradling. Nominations: Academy Awards '48: Scoring of a Musical.MGM

Pirate Movie ♂♂½ 1982 (PG) Gilbert and Sullivan's "The Pirates of Penzance" is combined with new pop songs in this tale of fantasy and romance. Feeble attempt to update a musical that was fine the way it was. 98m/C VHS, Beta. Kristy McNichol, Christopher Atkins, Ted Hamilton, Bill Kerr, Garry McDonald; D: Ken Annakin; M: Tony Britten. Golden Raspberry Awards '82: Worst Director (Annakin), Worst Song ("Pumpin' and Blowin'").FOX

Pirate Ship ♂½ The Mutineers 1949 Slow-moving story has sailor Hall discovering new captain Reeves is involved in a gang of gun-runners and counterfeiters. 60m/C VHS. Jon Hall, George Reeves, Adele Jergens, Noel Cravat, Tom Kennedy, Lyle Talbot; D: Jean Yarbrough. GPV

Pirate Warrior ♂♂ 1964 Grade-B pirate flick about slavery and the evil Tortuga. 86m/C VHS, Beta. Ricardo Montalban, Vincent Price, Liana Orfei; D: Mary Costa. NO

Pirates ♂½ 1986 (PG-13) Blustery, confused effort at a big-budgeted retro-adventure, about a highly regarded pirate and his gains and losses on the high seas. Broad comedy, no story to speak of. 124m/C VHS, Beta. Walter Matthau, Cris Campion, Damien Thomas, Richard Pearson, Charlotte Lewis, Olu Jacobs, David Patrick Kelly, Roy Kinnear, Bill Fraser, Jose Santamaria; D: Roman Polanski; W: Gerard Brach, Roman Polanski. Cesar Awards '87: Best Art Direction/Set Decoration, Best Costume Design; Nominations: Academy Awards '86: Best Costume Design. LIV

The Pirates of Penzance ♂♂ 1983 (G) Gilbert and Sullivan's comic operetta is the story of a band of fun-loving pirates, their reluctant young apprentice, the "very model of a modern major general," and his lovely daughters. An ad-aptation of Joseph Papp's award-winning Broadway play. 112m/C VHS, Beta, LV. Kevin Kline, Angela Lansbury, Linda Ronstadt, Rex Smith, George Rose; D: Wilford Leach. USH, FOX

Pirates of the Coast ♂½ 1961 A Spanish naval commander teams up with a group of pirates to even the score with an evil governor during the 1500s. 102m/C VHS, Beta. Lex Barker, Estella Blain, Livio Lorenzon, Liana Orfei; D: Domenico Paolella. UNI

Pirates of the High Seas ♂½ 1950 Crabbe helps a friend save his shipping line from sabotage. A serial in fifteen chapters. ?m/C VHS. Buster Crabbe, Lois Hall, Tommy Farrell, Gene Roth, Tristram Coffin; D: Spencer Gordon Bennet, Thomas Carr. MLB

Pirates of the Seven Seas ♂½ 1962 In the further tales of "Sandokan the Great," the pirate hero helps save the heroine's father from an evil English Imperialist. 90m/C VHS, Beta. Steve Reeves, Jacqueline Sassard, Andrea Bosic; D: Umberto Lenzi. NO

Pistol: The Birth of a Legend ♂♂½ 1990 (G) Biography of "Pistol" Pete Maravich, the basketball star who defied age limitations in the 1960s to play on his varsity team. 104m/C VHS, Beta, Closed Caption. Adam Guier, Nick Benedict, Boots Garland, Millie Perkins; D: Frank C. Schroeder; W: Darrel A. Campbell. COL

Pistoleros Asesinos ♂♂ 1987 Plenty of action, plus a little romance, when a man falls in love with a crooked landowner's daughter and must battle her father's henchmen for her hand. 83m/C VHS, Beta. SP Maria de Lourdes, Federico Villa, Victor Alcocer, Arturo Benavides, Polo Ortin, Rosa Gloria. MAD

The Pit ♂½ 1981 (R) Autistic boy gets his chance for revenge. The townspeople who humiliate him are in for a surprise after he stumbles across a huge hole in the forest, at the bottom of which are strange and deadly creatures. 96m/C VHS, Beta. Sammy Snyders, Sonja Smits, Jeannie Elias, Laura Hollingsworth; D: Lew Lehman. VTR

The Pit and the Pendulum ♂♂♂ 1961 A woman and her lover plan to drive her brother mad, and he responds by locking them in his torture chamber, which was built by his loony dad, whom he now thinks he is. Standard Corman production only remotely derived from the classic Poe tale, with the cast chewing on a loopy script. A landmark in Gothic horror. 80m/C VHS, Beta. Vincent Price, John Kerr, Barbara Steele, Luana Anders; D: Roger Corman; W: Richard Matheson; C: Floyd Crosby; M: Les Baxter. WAR, OM

The Pit & the Pendulum ♂♂½ 1991 (R) Retelling of the classic Poe short story, mixed with his "A Cask of Amantillado" and set during the Spanish Inquisition. Great special effects and professional scary guy, Lance Henriksen.CW: Language, nudity, and torture scenes. 97m/C VHS, LV, Closed Caption. Lance Henriksen, Rona De Ricci, Jonathan Fuller, Jeffrey Combs, Tom Towles, Stephen Lee, Francis Bay, Oliver Reed; D: Stuart Gordon; W: Dennis Paoli; M: Richard Band. PAR

Pitfall ♂♂♂ 1948 Gritty tale in which an insurance salesman, bored with his routine suburban life and family, follows his less noble instincts—and finds himself up to his ears in stolen goods, adultery and murder. 85m/B VHS, LV. Dick Powell, Jane Wyatt, Lizabeth Scott, Raymond Burr, John Litel, Byron Barr, Ann Doran, Jimmy Hunt, Selmer Jackson, Margaret Wells, Dick Wassel; D: Andre de Toth; W: Karl Kamb; C: Harry Wild; M: Louis Forbes. REP, FCT

Pittsburgh ♂♂ 1942 Slow-moving drama about a love triangle combined with class differences. Dietrich loves Wayne, but he's more interested in the coal and steel business, so rival Scott steps in. Although limited by standard plot, picture works because of excellent performances by leads. Based on a screen story by George Owen and Tom Reed. 98m/B VHS, Closed Caption. Marlene Dietrich, Randolph Scott, John Wayne, Frank Craven, Louise Allbritton, Shemp Howard, Thomas Gomez, Ludwig Stossel; D: Lewis Seiler; W: Kenneth Gamet, Tom Reed, John Twist. USH, FCT

Pixote ♂♂♂ 1981 Wrenching, documentary-like account of an orphan-boy's life on the streets in a Brazil metropolis. Graphic and depressing, it's not for all tastes but nonetheless masterfully done. In Portuguese with English subtitles. 127m/C VHS, Beta. BR Fernando Ramos Da Silva, Marilia Pera, Jorge Juliao, Gilberto Moura, Jose Nilson dos Santos, Edilson Lino; D: Hector Babenco; W: Hector Babenco; M: John Neschling. Los Angeles Film Critics Association Awards '81: Best Foreign Film; New York Film Critics Awards '81: Best Foreign Film; National Society of Film Critics Awards '81: Best Actress (Pera). FCT, COL

Pizza Man ♂½ 1991 (PG-13) Pizza deliveryman Elmo Bunn is minding his own business, delivering an extra large with anchovies and sausage, when he finds himself mixed up in a political scandal. Lawton directed under alias "J.D. Athens."CW: Violence. 90m/C VHS. Bill Maher, Annabelle Gurwitch; D: J.F. Lawton; W: J.F. Lawton. MNC

P.K. and the Kid ♂♂ 1985 A runaway kid meets up with a factory worker on his way to an arm wrestling competition and they become friends. 90m/C VHS, Beta, LV. Molly Ringwald, Paul LeMat, Alex Rocco, John Madden, Esther Rolle; D: Lou Lombardo; W: Neal Barbera; M: James Horner. ORI, WAR

A Place Called Glory ♂♂ Die Holle von Manitoba 1966 Barker comes to the aid of the local townsfolk in Glory city who have their hands full with a gang of bloodthirsty outlaws. 92m/C VHS. Lex Barker, Pierre Brice, Marianne Koch. SNC

A Place Called Today ♂ 1972 Sordid tale of big city politics where violence and fear in the streets is at the heart of the campaign. Also called "City in Fear." 105m/C VHS, Beta. Cheri Caffaro, J. Herbert Kerr Jr., Lana Wood, Richard Smedley, Tim Brown; D: Don Schain. NO

A Place for Annie ♂♂½ 1994 (PG) Lots of tears in this drama of devoted pediatrics nurse Susan Lansing (Spacek) who decides to become the foster mother of abandoned baby girl Annie, who's been diagnosed as HIV-positive. Then Annie's destitute birth mom (Parker), a former junkie dying of AIDS, resurfaces and decides she wants her daughter back. Sputters into melodrama but good performances by strong women, including Plowright as the nanny and Merkerson as a concerned hospital social worker. Based on a true story. Made for television. 98m/C VHS, Closed Caption. Sissy Spacek, Mary-Louise Parker, Joan Plowright, S. Epatha Merkerson, Jack Noseworthy; D: John Gray; W: Cathleen Young, Lee Guthrie. REP

Place in Hell ♂½ 1965 The Japanese armed forces camouflage a Pacific island beach which they are holding and invite the American forces to invade it during WWII. 106m/C VHS, Beta. Guy Madison, Helene Chanel, Monty Greenwood. UNI

A Place in the Sun ♂♂♂ 1951 Melodramatic adaptation of "An American Tragedy," Theodore Dreiser's realist classic about an ambitious laborer whose aspirations to the high life with a gorgeous debutante are threatened by his lower-class lover's pregnancy. Clift is magnificent in the lead, and Taylor and Winters also shine in support. Burr, however, grossly overdoes his role of the vehement prosecutor. Still, not a bad effort from somewhat undisciplined director Stevens. 120m/B VHS, Beta, LV. Montgomery Clift, Elizabeth Taylor, Shelley Winters, Raymond Burr, Anne Revere; D: George Stevens; C: William Mellor; M: Franz Waxman. Academy Awards '51: Best Black and White Cinematography, Best Costume Design (B & W), Best Director (Stevens), Best Film Editing, Best Screenplay, Original Dramatic/Comedy Score; Directors Guild of America Awards '51: Best Director (Stevens); Golden Globe Awards '52: Best Film—Drama; National Board of Review Awards '51: 10 Best Films of the Year; Nominations: Academy Awards '51: Best Actor (Clift), Best Actress (Winters), Best Picture. PAR, BTV

A Place in the World ♂♂♂ 1995 Returning from exile to their native Argentina during a military dictatorship, Mario and Ana (Luppi and Roth) work to help the less advantaged in their society, determined to make a difference. Story is seen as a flashback from point-of-view of the couples' son Ernesto (Batyi). Well-crafted, finely acted piece exploring political, social, and interpersonal themes. 1993 Oscar bid retracted due to controversy over country of film's origin. **120m/C VHS. AR AR** Jose Sacristan, Federico Luppi, Cecilia Roth, Leonor Benedetto, Gaston Batyi, Lorena Del Rio; **D:** Adolfo Aristarain; **W:** Alberto Lecchi, Adolfo Aristarain; **C:** Ricardo De Angelis; **M:** Emilio Kauderer. *NYF*

Place of Weeping 🐾🐾½ 1986 **(PG)** Early entry in the anti-apartheid sweepstakes (made in South Africa, no less). A South African woman opposes her nation's racist policies. A reporter supports her. **88m/C VHS, Beta. SA** James Whylie, Geini Mhlophe; **D:** Darrell Roodt. *VTR, NWV, FCT*

Places in the Heart 🐾🐾🐾 1984 **(PG)** A young widow determines to make the best of a bad situation on a small farm in Depression-era Texas, fighting poverty, racism, and sexism while enduring back-breaking labor. Support group includes a blind veteran and a black drifter. Hokey but nonetheless moving film is improved significantly by strong performances by virtually everyone in the cast. In his debut, Malkovich shines through this stellar group. Effective dust-bowl photography by Nestor Almendros. **113m/C VHS, Beta, LV, Closed Caption.** Sally Field, John Malkovich, Danny Glover, Ed Harris, Lindsay Crouse, Amy Madigan, Terry O'Quinn; **D:** Robert Benton; **W:** Robert Benton; **C:** Nestor Almendros; **M:** Howard Shore. Academy Awards '84: Best Actress (Field), Best Original Screenplay; Golden Globe Awards '85: Best Actress—Drama (Field); National Board of Review Awards '84: Best Supporting Actor (Malkovich); New York Film Critics Awards '84: Best Screenplay; National Society of Film Critics Awards '84: Best Supporting Actor (Malkovich); Nominations: Academy Awards '84: Best Costume Design, Best Director (Benton), Best Picture, Best Supporting Actor (Malkovich), Best Supporting Actress (Crouse). *FOX, BTV, HMV*

The Plague 🐾½ 1992 **(R)** An outbreak of bubonic plague has turned the South American city of Oran into a prison, with no one permitted to leave until the disease has run its course. Hurt is the doctor trying to balance his duties with his own fears. Necessarily bleak adaptation of the Albert Camus novel is also slow-moving and long-winded—an equally deadly combination for the viewer. **CW:** Some language, nudity, and grim images. **105m/C VHS, Closed Caption. FR SP** William Hurt, Robert Duvall, Raul Julia, Sandrine Bonnaire, Jean-Marc Barr; **D:** Luis Puenzo. *LIV, FCT, BTV*

The Plague Dogs 🐾🐾½ 1982 Two dogs carrying a plague escape from a research center and are tracked down in this unlikely animated film. A bit ponderous. And yes, that is Hurt's voice. From the novel by Richard Adams, author of "Watership Down." **99m/C VHS, Beta, Closed Caption.** **D:** Martin Rosen; **W:** Martin Rosen; **M:** Patrick Gleeson; **V:** John Hurt, Christopher Benjamin, Judy Geeson, Barbara Leigh-Hunt, Patrick Stewart. *NLC*

Plague of the Zombies 🐾🐾½ 1966 The local doctor in a Cornish village gets suspicious when its inhabitants begin suddenly dying off and the local squire refuses to allow any autopsies. That's because he's learned voodoo rites while staying in Haiti and is turning the dead locals into zombies. **90m/C VHS. GB** Andre Morell, John Carson, Diane Clare, Alex Davion, Jacqueline Pearce, Brook Williams; **D:** John Gilling; **W:** Peter Bryan, John Elder; **C:** Arthur Grant; **M:** James Bernard. *VTR*

Plain Clothes 🐾🐾½ 1988 **(PG)** An undercover cop masquerades as a high school student to solve the murder of a teacher. He endures all the trials that made him hate high school the first time around. **98m/C VHS, Beta, Closed Caption.** Arliss Howard, George Wendt, Suzy Amis, Diane Ladd, Seymour Cassel, Larry Pine, Jackie Gayle, Abe Vigoda, Robert Stack; **D:** Martha Coolidge; **M:** Scott Wilk. *PAR*

The Plainsman 🐾🐾½ 1937 Western legends Wild Bill Hickock, Buffalo Bill, and Calamity Jane team up for adventure in this big, empty venture. Just about what you'd expect from

splashy director DeMille. **113m/B VHS, Beta, LV.** Gary Cooper, Jean Arthur, Charles Bickford, Anthony Quinn, George "Gabby" Hayes, Porter Hall, James Mason; **D:** Cecil B. DeMille; **C:** Victor Milner. *USH, MLB*

Plan 9 from Outer Space woof! *Grave Robbers from Outer Space* 1956 Two or three aliens in silk pajamas conspire to resurrect several slow-moving zombies from a cardboard graveyard in order to conquer the Earth. Spaceships that look suspiciously like paper plates blaze across the sky. Pitiful, inadvertently hilarious fright worth a look if you're desperate to kill time since it's in the running for the "dumbest movie ever made" award. Lugosi's actual screen time is under two minutes, since he had the good sense to die before the film was complete. Enjoy the taller and younger replacement (the chiropractor of Wood's wife) they found for Lugosi, who remains hooded to protect his identity. **78m/B VHS, Beta, LV.** Bela Lugosi, Tor Johnson, Lyle Talbot, Vampira, Gregory Walcott, Tom Keene, Dudley Manlove, Mona McKinnon, Duke Moore, Joanna Lee, Bunny Breckinridge, Criswell, Carl Anthony, Paul Marco, Norma McCarty, David DeMering, Bill Ash, Conrad Brooks, Edward D. Wood Jr.; **D:** Edward D. Wood Jr.; **W:** Edward D. Wood Jr.; **C:** William C. Thompson. *NOS, SNC, MED*

Plan 10 from Outer Space 🐾½ 1995 The play on the infamous Ed Wood title is the only connection between the two fringe features as director Harris takes aim at his hometown of Salt Lake City, Utah. Heroine Lucinda (Russell) discovers a mysterious bronze plaque buried near the Great Salt Lake and uncovers a UFO conspiracy loosely conforming to Mormon mythology. There's a basic mass hysteria/alien invasion scene, cheesy special effects, dumb sexual humor, and not much else. **82m/C VHS.** Stefene Russell, Pat Collins, Curtis James, Karen Black; **D:** Trent Harris; **W:** Trent Harris; **C:** Bryan Duggan; **M:** Fred Myrow. *LEO*

Planes, Trains & Automobiles 🐾🐾½ 1987 **(R)** One-joke Hughes comedy saved by Martin and Candy. A straight-laced businessman (played straight by Martin) on the way home for Thanksgiving meets up with a oafish, bad-luck-ridden boor who turns his efforts to get home upside down. Martin and Candy both turn in fine performances, and effectively straddle a thin line between true pathos and hilarious buffoonery. Bacon and McClurg, both Hughes alumni, have small but funny roles. **93m/C VHS, Beta, LV, 8mm, Closed Caption.** Steve Martin, John Candy, Edie McClurg, Kevin Bacon, Michael McKean, William Windom, Laila Robins, Martin Ferrero, Charles Tyner, Dylan Baker; **D:** John Hughes; **W:** John Hughes; **M:** Ira Newborn. *PAR*

Planet Burg 🐾🐾½ 1962 A classic Soviet sci-fi flick about a space exploration team landing on Venus. Their job becomes a rescue mission when one of the crew is stranded. Although there are some silly moments, some good plot twists and acting make up for them. In Russian with English subtitles. **90m/C VHS, Beta. RU** Vladimir Temelianov, Gennadi Vernov, Kyunna Ignatova; **D:** Pavel Klush-antsev. *SNC*

Planet Busters 🐾 1985 Japanimation feature. Haphazardly developed swift-paced science fiction adventure about a magic sword, a royal heir apparent, a couple of bounty hunters, and evil robots. **80m/C VHS. JP STP, TPV**

Planet Earth 🐾🐾½ 1974 In the year 2133, a man who has been in suspended animation for 154 years is revived to lead the troops against a violent group of women (and mutants, too!). **78m/C VHS.** John Saxon, Janet Margolin, Ted Cassidy, Diana Muldaur, Johana DeWinter, Christopher Gary; **D:** Marc Daniels. *UNI*

Planet of Blood 🐾🐾 *Queen of Blood* 1966 Space opera about an alien vampire discovered on Mars by a rescue team. If you've ever seen the Soviet film "Niebo Zowiet," don't be surprised if some scenes look familiar; the script was written around segments cut from that film. **81m/C VHS.**

John Saxon, Basil Rathbone, Judi Meredith, Dennis Hopper, Florence Marly; **D:** Curtis Harrington. *SNC, NOS, MRV*

Planet of Dinosaurs 🐾½ 1980 **(PG)** Survivors from a ruined spaceship combat huge savage dinosaurs on a swampy uncharted planet. **85m/C VHS, Beta.** James Whitworth; **D:** James K. Shea. *AHV, VTR*

Planet of the Apes 🐾🐾🐾½ 1968 **(G)** Astronauts crash land on a planet where apes are masters and humans are merely brute animals. Superior science fiction with sociological implications marred only by unnecessary humor. Heston delivers one of his more plausible performances. Superb ape makeup creates realistic pseudo-simians of McDowall, Hunter, Evans, Whitmore, and Daly. Adapted from Pierre Boulle's novel "Monkey Planet." Followed by four sequels and two television series. **112m/C VHS, Beta, LV, Closed Caption.** Charlton Heston, Roddy McDowall, Kim Hunter, Maurice Evans, Linda Harrison, James Whitmore, James Daly; **D:** Franklin J. Schaffner; **W:** Rod Serling, Michael G. Wilson; **C:** Leon Shamroy; **M:** Jerry Goldsmith. National Board of Review Awards '68: 10 Best Films of the Year; Nominations: Academy Awards '68: Best Costume Design, Best Original Score. *FOX, FUS*

Planet of the Vampires 🐾🐾½ *Terror in Space; Terreur dans l'Espace; Space Mutants; The Demon Planet* 1965 Astronauts search for missing comrades on a planet dominated by mind-bending forces. Acceptable atmospheric filmmaking from genre master Bava, but it's not among his more compelling ventures. **86m/C VHS, Beta. IT** Barry Sullivan, Norman Bengell, Angel Aranda, Evi Marandi; **D:** Mario Bava. *ORI*

Planet on the Prowl 🐾 *War Between the Planets* 1965 A fiery planet causes earthly disasters, so a troop of wily astronauts try to destroy it with the latest technology. They fail, leading one sacrificial soul to do it himself. **80m/C VHS, Beta. IT** Giacomo "Jack" Rossi-Stuart, Amber Collins, Peter Martell, John Bartha, Halina Zalewska, James Weaver; **D:** Anthony (Antonio Margheriti) Dawson. *NO*

Planets Against Us 🐾½ *I Pianeti Contro di Noi; The Man with the Yellow Eyes; Hands of a Killer; The Monster with Green Eyes* 1961 Science fiction tale of escaped alien humanoid robots who take refuge on Earth, but whose touch is fatal. Good special effects. **85m/B VHS. IT FR** Michel Lemoine, Maria Pia Luzi, Jany Clair; **D:** Romano Ferrara. *SNC*

Platinum Blonde 🐾🐾🐾 1931 Screwball comedy in which a newspaper journalist (Williams) marries a wealthy girl (Harlow) but finds that he doesn't like the restrictions and confinement of high society. Yearning for a creative outlet, he decides to write a play and hires a reporter (Young) to collaborate with him. The results are funny and surprising when Young shows up at the mansion flanked by a group of hard-drinking, fun-loving reporters. **86m/B VHS, Closed Caption.** Loretta Young, Robert Williams, Jean Harlow, Louise Closser Hale; **D:** Frank Capra; **W:** Jo Swerling, Dorothy Howell. *COL*

Platinum High School 🐾½ *Trouble at 16; Rich, Young, and Deadly* 1960 Divorced father Rooney is appalled when his son is "accidentally" killed while off at an exclusive military academy. His suspicions are aroused by the prevaricating school commander and he discovers some horrible truths about his son's death and life at the school. **91m/B VHS.** Mickey Rooney, Terry Moore, Dan Duryea, Conway Twitty, Warren Berlinger, Yvette Mimieux, Jimmy Boyd, Richard Jaeckel, Harold Lloyd Jr., Elisha Cook Jr., Jimmy Murphy; **D:** Charles Haas; **W:** Robert Smith; **M:** Van Alexander. *REP*

Platoon 🐾🐾🐾½ 1986 **(R)** A grunt's view of the Vietnam War is provided in all its horrific, inexplicable detail. Sheen is wooden in the lead, but both Dafoe and Berenger are resplendent as, respectively, good and bad soldiers. Strong, visceral filmmaking from fearless director Stone, who based the film on his own GI experiences. Highly acclaimed; considered by many to be the most realistic portrayal of the war on film. **113m/C VHS,**

Beta, LV, Closed Caption. Charlie Sheen, Willem Dafoe, Tom Berenger, Francesco Quinn, Forest Whitaker, John C. McGinley, Kevin Dillon, Richard Edson, Reggie Johnson, Keith David, Johnny Depp; **D:** Oliver Stone; **W:** Oliver Stone; **C:** Robert Richardson; **M:** Georges Delerue. Academy Awards '86: Best Director (Stone), Best Film Editing, Best Picture, Best Sound; British Academy Awards '87: Best Director (Stone); Directors Guild of America Awards '86: Best Director (Stone); Golden Globe Awards '87: Best Director (Stone), Best Film—Drama, Best Supporting Actor (Berenger); Independent Spirit Awards '87: Best Cinematography, Best Director (Stone), Best Film, Best Screenplay; National Board of Review Awards '86: 10 Best Films of the Year; Nominations: Academy Awards '86: Best Cinematography, Best Original Screenplay, Best Supporting Actor (Berenger, Dafoe). *LIV, BTV*

Platoon Leader ♂♂ 1987 (R) A battle-drenched portrait of a West Point lieutenant in Vietnam. When he first arrives, he must win the trust of his men, who have been on their tours for a much longer time. As time goes on, he slowly becomes hardened to the realities of the brutal life in the field. Made on the heels of the widely acclaimed "Platoon," but it doesn't have the same power. Norris is martial arts king Chuck Norris' brother. **97m/C VHS, Beta, LV.** Michael Dudikoff, Brian Libby, Robert F. Lyons, Rick Fitts, Jesse Dabson, William Smith, Michael De Lorenzo; **D:** Aaron Norris; **W:** R.J. Marx; **M:** George S. Clinton. *MED, VTR*

Platoon the Warriors ♂ 1988 The underworld rages with violence when two kingpins, Rex and Bill, become bitter and declare war over a botched drug deal. **90m/C VHS, Beta.** David Coley, Dick Crown, James Miller, Don Richard, Alex Sylvian; **D:** Philip Ko. *NO*

Platypus Cove ♂ 1986 An adopted boy tracks down the culprits responsible for the sabotage of his family's boat, a crime for which he was suspected. Australian. **72m/C VHS, Beta.** Paul Smith; **D:** Peter Maxwell.

Play Dead ♂ *Satan's Dog* 1981 Poor Yvonne De Carlo plays a psychotic woman who trains a dog to rip people to shreds. **89m/C VHS.** Yvonne De Carlo, Stephanie Dunham, David Cullinane, Glenn Kezer, Ron Jackson, Carolyn Greenwood; **D:** Peter Wittman. *ACA*

Play It Again, Charlie Brown 1970 The Peanuts gang goes bananas when Lucy enlists Schroeder to play rock music at a PTA meeting. **25m/C VHS, Beta.** Charles M. Schulz. *SHL, VTR*

Play It Again, Sam ♂♂♂½ 1972 (PG) Allen is—no surprise—a nerd, and this time he's in love with his best friend's wife. Modest storyline provides a framework of endless gags, with Allen borrowing heavily from "Casablanca." Bogey even appears periodically to counsel Allen on the ways of wooing women. Superior comedy isn't hurt by Ross directing instead of Allen, who adapted the script from his own play. **85m/C VHS, Beta, LV, 8mm.** Woody Allen, Diane Keaton, Tony Roberts, Susan Anspach, Jerry Lacy, Jennifer Salt, Joy Bang, Viva, Herbert Ross; **D:** Herbert Ross; **W:** Woody Allen; **C:** Owen Roizman; **M:** Billy Goldenberg. *PAR*

Play Misty for Me ♂♂♂ 1971 (R) A radio deejay obliges a psychotic woman's song request and suddenly finds himself the target of her obsessive behavior, which rapidly turns from seductive to murderous. Auspicious directorial debut for Eastwood, borrowing from the Siegel playbook (look for the director's cameo as a barkeep). Based on a story by Heims. **102m/C VHS, Beta, LV.** Jessica Walter, Donna Mills, John Larch, Irene Hervey, Jack Ging, Clint Eastwood; *Cameos:* Donald Siegel; **D:** Clint Eastwood; **W:** Jo Heims, Dean Riesner; **C:** Bruce Surtees; **M:** Dee Barton. *USH, TLF*

Play Murder for Me ♂♂ 1991 (R) Saxophonist performing in a seedy Buenos Aires nightclub has his world turned upside down when a former lover suddenly re-enters his life. She still has her eye on him, but she's now the woman of a notorious mobster. Soon the musician finds himself drawn into the usual deadly world of crime, deceit, and unharnessed passion. *CW:* Language,

violence, and strong sexuality. **80m/C VHS.** Jack Wagner, Tracy Scoggins; **D:** Hector Olivera. *NHO*

Play Nice ♂♂½ 1992 (R) A detective hunts down a murderous psychopath but is shocked when he discovers his suspect is a woman—and someone he knows. Also available in an unrated version. *CW:* Language, violence, and strong sexuality. **90m/C VHS.** Ed O'Ross. *THV*

Play Time ♂♂ 1994 Jeannie, Lindsay, and their husbands are on vacation in Palm Springs where they get up to some naughty sexual games that test the limits of friendship. Available in an unedited version at 95 minutes. **90m/C VHS.** Monique Parent, Craig Stepp. *TRI*

Playback ♂♂½ 1995 (R) Young couple think they've finally captured the gold ring when hubby David (Grant) gets a chance at a million dollar merger deal. But David's set-up by a sexy co-worker (Whirry) and his slimy boss (Hamilton) tries to seduce his wife. *CW:* Strong sexuality and language. **91m/C VHS, Beta, Closed Caption.** Charles Grant, Shannon Whirry, George Hamilton, Tawny Kitaen, Harry Dean Stanton; **D:** Oley Sassone; **W:** Oley Sassone, David DuBos. *PAR*

Playboy of the Western World ♂♂½ 1962 An innkeeper's daughter is infatuated with a young man who says he murdered his father. Adapted from the classic play by John Millington Synge. **96m/C VHS, Beta.** *IR* Siobhan McKenna, Gary Raymond; **D:** Brian Desmond Hurst. *NO*

The Playboys ♂♂♂ 1992 (PG-13) In 1957 in a tiny Irish village, unmarried Tara Maguire causes a scandal by having a baby. Her beauty attracts lots of men—there's a former beau who kills himself, the obsessive, middle-aged Sergeant Hegarty, and the newest arrival, Tom Castle, an actor with a rag-tag theatrical troupe called the Playboys. Slow-moving and simple story with particularly good performances by Wright as the strong-willed Tara and Finney as Hegarty, clinging to a last chance at love and family. The Playboys' hysterically hammy version of "Gone With the Wind" is a gem. Directorial debut of Mackinnon. Filmed in the village of Redhills, Ireland, the hometown of co-writer Connaughton. **114m/C VHS.** Albert Finney, Aidan Quinn, Robin Wright, Milo O'Shea, Alan Devlin, Niamh Cusack, Ian McElhinney, Niall Buggy, Adrian Dunbar; **D:** Gilles Mackinnon; **W:** Shane Connaughton, Kerry Crabbe; **C:** Jack Conroy; **M:** Jean-Claude Petit. *HBO, FCT*

The Player ♂♂♂½ 1992 (R) Clever, entertaining, and biting satire of the movie industry and the greed that controls it. Robbins is dead-on as Griffin Mill, a young studio exec who becomes the chief suspect in a murder investigation. He personifies Hollywood's ethics (or lack thereof) in a performance both cold and vulnerable, as he looks for the right buttons to push and the proper back to stab. Strong leading performances are supplemented by 65 star cameos. Some viewers may be put off by the inside-Hollywood jokes, but Altman fans will love it. The laserdisc version includes commentary by Altman, interviews with 20 screenwriters, and celebrity cameos that didn't make the final cut. *CW:* Language and sensuality. **123m/C VHS, LV, Closed Caption, DVD.** Tim Robbins, Greta Scacchi, Fred Ward, Whoopi Goldberg, Peter Gallagher, Brion James, Cynthia Stevenson, Vincent D'Onofrio, Dean Stockwell, Richard E. Grant, Dina Merrill, Sydney Pollack, Lyle Lovett, Randall Batinkoff, Gina Gershon; *Cameos:* Michael Tolkin, Louise Fletcher, Dennis Franz, Malcolm McDowell, Ray Walston, Rene Auberjonois, David Alan Grier, Jayne Meadows, Michael Bowen, Steve James, Brian Tochi, Burt Reynolds, Cher, Nick Nolte, Jack Lemmon, Lily Tomlin, Marlee Matlin, Julia Roberts, Bruce Willis, Anjelica Huston, Elliott Gould, Sally Kellerman, Steve Allen, Richard Anderson, Harry Belafonte, Shari Belafonte, Karen Black, Gary Busey, Robert Carradine, James Coburn, Cathy Lee Crosby, John Cusack, Brad Davis, Peter Falk, Teri Garr, Leeza Gibbons, Scott Glenn, Jeff Goldblum, Joel Grey, Buck Henry, Kathy Ireland, Sally Kirkland, Andie MacDowell, Martin Mull, Mimi Rogers, Jill St. John, Susan Sarandon, Rod Steiger, Joan Tewkesbury, Robert Wagner; **D:**

Robert Altman; **W:** Michael Tolkin; **C:** Jean Lepine; **M:** Thomas Newman. British Academy Awards '92: Best Adapted Screenplay; Cannes Film Festival '92: Best Actor (Robbins), Best Director (Altman); Chicago Film Critics Awards '93: Best Director (Altman); Golden Globe Awards '93: Best Actor—Musical/Comedy (Robbins), Best Film—Musical/Comedy; Independent Spirit Awards '93: Best Film; New York Film Critics Awards '92: Best Cinematography, Best Director (Altman), Best Film; Writers Guild of America '92: Best Adapted Screenplay; Nominations: Academy Awards '92: Best Adapted Screenplay, Best Director (Altman), Best Film Editing. *NLC, CRC, MOV*

Players ♂ 1979 (PG) Young tennis hustler touring Mexico hooks up with beautiful and mysterious older woman. They seem to be from different worlds yet their love grows. She inspires him enough to enter Wimbledon. Several tennis pros appear, including Guillermo Vilas, John McEnroe, and Ilie Nastase. Almost as boring as watching a real tennis game. **120m/C VHS, Beta.** Ali MacGraw, Dean Paul Martin, Maximilian Schell, Pancho Gonzales; **D:** Anthony Harvey; **W:** Arnold Schulman; **M:** Jerry Goldsmith. *PAR*

Playgirl Killer ♂ *Decoy for Terror* 1966 After impulsively murdering a restless model, an artist continues to kill indiscriminately, keeping his spoils on ice. Sedaka croons between kills and luxuriates poolside—seemingly oblivious to the plot of the film—while a female decoy is sent to bait the killer for the police. For adult viewers. **86m/C VHS, Beta.** *CA* William Kerwin, Jean Christopher, Andree Champagne, Neil Sedaka; **D:** Erick Santamaria. *NWV*

Playing Away ♂ 1987 A team of Caribbean cricket players meet a team of stuffy Brits on the field in a clash of the cultures. **100m/C VHS, Beta, LV.** *GB* Norman Beaton, Robert Urquhart; **D:** Horace Love. *NLC*

Playing Dead ♂♂½ 1915 Drew and his wife portray a married couple in this silent farce. The insecure husband decides to fake his death so his wife can be with the man he thinks she loves. **58m/B VHS.** Sidney Drew, Lucille Drew, Alice Lake, Donald Hall, Harry English, Isadore Marcil; **D:** Sidney Drew. *GPV*

Playing for Keeps ♂ 1986 (PG-13) Three high school grads turn a dilapidating hotel into a rock 'n roll resort. Music by Pete Townshend, Peter Frampton, Phil Collins, and others. **103m/C VHS, Beta, LV, Closed Caption.** Daniel Jordano, Matthew Penn, Leon Grant, Harold Gould, Jimmy Baio; **D:** Bob Weinstein. *USH*

Playing for Time ♂♂♂ 1980 Compelling, award-winning television drama based on actual experiences of a Holocaust prisoner who survives by leading an inmate orchestra. Strong playing from Redgrave and Mayron. Pro-Palestinian Redgrave's political beliefs made her a controversial candidate for the role of Jewish Fania Fenelon, but her stunning performance is on the mark. **148m/C VHS, Beta.** Vanessa Redgrave, Jane Alexander, Maud Adams, Verna Bloom, Melanie Mayron; **D:** Daniel Mann; **M:** Brad Fiedel. *NO*

Playing with Fire ♂ 197? A young girl gets caught up in drugs, casual sex, and murder. **87m/C VHS, Beta.** Karen Tungay, Danny Keogh, Sam Marais; **D:** Alan Nathanson. *NO*

Playmaker ♂½ 1994 (R) Jaime (Rubin) is a struggling actress whose coach Talbert (Firth) guarantees success as long as she follows his bizarre training methods, which include seduction, abuse, and betrayal. Good chemistry between the leads but a mishmash of a script. *CW:* Language; nudity; sex. **91m/C VHS.** Jennifer Rubin, Colin Firth, John Getz, Jeffery Perry; **D:** Yuri Zeltser; **W:** Yuri Zeltser; **C:** Ross Berryman; **M:** Mark Snow. *ORI*

Playmates ♂ 1941 Barrymore is practically wasted in his last film as a down-on-his-luck actor who agrees to turn bandleader Kyser into a Shakespearean actor. Bizarre comedy is funny at times, but leaves the audience wondering what Barrymore thought he was doing. ♫Humpty Dumpty Heart; How Long Did I Dream?; Que Chi-ca?; Romeo Smith and Juliet Jones; Thank Your Lucky Stars and Stripes. **96m/B VHS, Beta.** Kay Kyser, John Barrymore, Ginny Simms, Lupe Velez, May Robson, Patsy Kelly, Peter Lind Hayes, George Cleveland; **D:** David Butler. *TTC*

Playmates 🎬🎬½ **1972** Two divorced buddies fall in love with each other's ex-wives in this made for television flick. Typical Alda vehicle isn't bad. **78m/C VHS, Beta.** Doug McClure, Alan Alda, Connie Stevens, Barbara Feldon, Eileen Brennan, Tiger Williams, Severn Darden; **D:** Theodore J. Flicker. *THV*

Playroom 🎬🎬 **1990 (R)** Archaeologist McDonald is completing his father's search for the tomb of a medieval boy-prince. But someone, or something, has been waiting for him for a long, long time. When he finally reaches the long-sought-after tomb, he discovers that it is a torture chamber where his worst nightmares become realities. The demonic prince who was buried in the tomb has picked Chris as his playmate, and the rest of the staff as his personal toys. **87m/C VHS, LV, Closed Caption.** Lisa Aliff, Aron Eisenberg, Christopher McDonald, James Purcell, Jamie Rose, Vincent Schiavelli; **D:** Manny Coto; **C:** James L. Carter. *REP*

Playtime 🎬🎬🎬 **1967** Occasionally enterprising comedy in which the bemused Frenchman Hulot tries in vain to maintain an appointment in an urban landscape of glass and steel. The theme of cold, unfeeling civilization is hardly unique, but the film is nonetheless enjoyable. The third in the Hulot trilogy, preceded by "Mr. Hulot's Holiday" and "Mon Oncle." In French with English subtitles. **108m/C VHS, Beta.** *FR* Jacques Tati, Barbara Dennek, Jacqueline Lecomte, Jack Gautier; **D:** Jacques Tati. *HMV, NLC*

Plaza Suite 🎬🎬🎬 **1971 (PG)** Three alternating skits from Neil Simon's play about different couples staying at the New York hotel. Matthau shines in all three vignettes. Some of Simon's funnier stuff, with the first sketch being the best: Matthau and Stapleton are a couple celebrating their 24th anniversary. She's sentimental, while he's yearning for his mistress. Number two has producer Matthau putting the make on old flame Harris, while the finale has father Matthau coaxing his anxious daughter out of the bathroom on her wedding day. **114m/C VHS, Beta, LV.** Walter Matthau, Maureen Stapleton, Barbara Harris, Lee Grant, Louise Sorel; **D:** Arthur Hiller; **W:** Neil Simon; **M:** Maurice Jarre. *PAR*

Please Don't Eat My Mother woof! *Hungry Pets; Glump* **1972** A softcore remake of "Little Shop of Horrors" in which a lonely voyeur plays host to a human-eating plant. **95m/C VHS.** Buck Kartalian, Renee Bond; **D:** Carl Monson. *MOV, VDM, TPV*

Please Don't Eat the Daisies 🎬🎬½ **1960** City couple and kids leave the Big Apple for the country and are traumatized by flora and fauna. Goofy sixties fluff taken from Jean Kerr's book and the basis for the eventual TV series. **111m/C VHS, Beta, LV.** Doris Day, David Niven, Janis Paige, Spring Byington, Richard Haydn, Patsy Kelly, Jack Weston, Margaret Lindsay; **D:** Charles Walters. *MGM, FCT*

Pleasure 🎬🎬 **1931** A saga of love, treachery, and melodrama in English society where self-indulgence held priority and good manners were the rule. **53m/B VHS, Beta, LV.** Conway Tearle, Roscoe Karns, Carmel Myers, Lena Basquette. *NOS*

A Pleasure Doing Business 🎬 **1979 (R)** Three high school buddies, now in their 40s, are reunited at a stag party, where they decide to go into business as managers in "the oldest profession." **86m/C VHS, Beta.** Conrad Bain, John Byner, Alan Oppenheimer, Misty Rowe, Phyllis Diller, Tom Smothers; **D:** Steve Vagnino. *VHE*

Pleasure Palace 🎬🎬 **1980** A gambling lady's-man (Sharif) meets his match when he helps a woman casino owner (Lange). Made for television. **96m/C VHS, Beta.** Omar Sharif, Victoria Principal, J.D. Cannon, Gerald S. O'Loughlin, Jose Ferrer, Hope Lange, Alan King; **D:** Walter Grauman. *LIV*

Pledge Night 🎬🎬 **1990 (R)** Tale of horror and revenge. Killed years before in a fraternity hazing, Sid returns for the brothers who did him in. Gory and violent. **90m/C VHS, LV.** Will Kempe, Shannon McMahon, Todd Eastland; **D:** Paul Ziller. *IMP*

Plenty 🎬🎬½ **1985 (R)** Difficult but worthwhile film with Streep in top form as a former member of the French Resistance, who upon returning to England finds life at home increasingly tedious and banal and begins to fear her finest hours may be behind her. Gielgud is flawless as the aging career diplomat. Adapted by David Hare from his play, an allegory for British decline. **119m/C VHS, Beta, LV.** Meryl Streep, Tracey Ullman, Sting, John Gielgud, Charles Dance, Ian McKellen, Sam Neill, Burt Kwouk; **D:** Fred Schepisi; **W:** David Hare; **C:** Ian Baker; **M:** Bruce Smeaton. Los Angeles Film Critics Association Awards '85: Best Supporting Actor (Gielgud); National Society of Film Critics Awards '85: Best Supporting Actor (Gielgud). *REP*

The Plot Against Harry 🎬🎬🎬 **1969** Jewish racketeer Harry Plotnik checks out of prison, and finds the outside world ain't what it used to be. Attempting to lead an honest life only makes matters worse. Completely overlooked when first released in 1969 (and quickly shelved) because it was considered to have no commercial potential, Roemer's crime comedy found an enthusiastic audience when it was rediscovered twenty years later. **81m/B VHS.** Martin Priest, Ben Lang, Maxine Woods, Henry Nemo; **D:** Michael Roemer; **W:** Michael Roemer. *NYF, FCT*

The Ploughman's Lunch 🎬🎬🎬 **1983** A BBC news reporter claws and lies his way to the top. He then discovers that he is the victim of a far more devious plan. Engrossing and well made, although some of the political views are simplistic. **107m/C VHS, Beta.** Jonathan Pryce, Charlie Dore, Tim Curry, Rosemary Harris, Frank Finlay, Bill Paterson; **D:** Richard Eyre.

Plughead Rewired: Circuitry Man 2 🎬🎬 *Circuitry Man 2* **1994 (R)** Earth's atmosphere has been destroyed and survivors are forced underground, where they're terrorized by the humanoid Plughead, who likes to literally plug into the minds of his victims. Plughead wants to rule what's left of life on Earth and all that stands in his way is the android Circuitry Man and FBI agent Kyle. Special effects are strictly bargain basement level. **97m/C VHS.** Vernon Wells, Deborah Shelton, Jim Metzler, Dennis Christopher, Nicholas Worth, Traci Lords; **D:** Steven Lovy, Robert Lovy; **W:** Steven Lovy, Robert Lovy. *COL*

Plumber 🎬🎬½ **1979** A plumber who makes a house call extends his stay to psychologically torture the woman of the house. Originally made for Australian television. **76m/C VHS, Beta.** *AU* Judy Morris, Ivar Kants, Robert Coleby; **D:** Peter Weir; **W:** Peter Weir. *MED*

Plunder Road 🎬🎬½ **1957** A pair of crooks cook up a plan to rob a train bound for the San Francisco Mint that's carrying a fortune in gold bullion. Top notch B-film noir. **76m/B VHS.** Gene Raymond, Jeanne Cooper, Wayne Morris, Elisha Cook Jr.; **D:** Hubert Cornfield. *REP*

Plunge Into Darkness 🎬½ **1977** Quiet weekend in the mountains turns into a nightmare for an ex-Olympic runner and his family. **77m/C VHS, Beta.** Bruce Barry, Olivia Hamnett, Ashley Greenville, Wallace Eaton, Tom Richards; **D:** Peter Maxwell. *NO*

Plutonium Baby 🎬 **1987** A mutated kid, whose mother was killed by the same radiation exposure that infected him, tracks down the guilty party in New York in this comic-book style film. **85m/C VHS, Beta.** Patrick Molloy, Danny Guerra; **D:** Ray Hirschman. *TWE*

Plutonium Incident 🎬🎬 **1982** A female technician at a nuclear power plant suspects the facility to be less safe than it appears, and faces a diabolical plan of harassment when she attempts to bring attention to the hazards. **90m/C VHS, Beta.** Janet Margolin, Powers Boothe, Bo Hopkins, Joseph Campanella; **D:** Richard Michaels. *TLF*

Pocahontas 🎬🎬🎬 **1995 (G)** It's 1607 and spirited Powhatan maiden Pocahontas and British settler Captain John Smith strike an unlikely but doomed romance in Disney's 33rd animated feature, its first based on the life of a historical figure. Lovely Poca, a virtual post-adolescent Native American superbabe, introduces the roguish captain (spoken and sung by Gibson) to the wonders of unspoiled nature and serves as peacemaker in the clash of European and Native American cultures. Disney puts its spin on history but maintains cultural sensitivity: several characters are voiced by Native American performers, including Chief Powhatan, spoken by American Indian activist Means, who led the 1973 siege at Wounded Knee, and Bedard as Pocahontas. Just don't tell the kids the real Pocahontas married someone else, moved to England, and died of smallpox at 21. Stunningly animated, but its mediocre soundtrack and decidedly somber tone leave it lacking in typical Disney majesty and charm. Premiered at New York's Central Park, for the usual theater crowd of 100,000 or so. **90m/C VHS, Closed Caption. D:** Mike Gabriel, Eric Goldberg; **V:** Carl Binder, Susannah Grant, Philip LaZebnik; **M:** Alan Menken, Stephen Schwartz; **V:** Irene Bedard, Judy Kuhn, Mel Gibson, Joe Baker, Christian Bale, Billy Connolly, James Apaumut Fall, Linda Hunt, John Kassir, Danny Mann, Bill Cobbs, David Ogden Stiers, Michelle St. John, Gordon Tootoosis, Frank Welker. Academy Awards '95: Best Song ("Colors of the Wind"), Best Original Score; Golden Globe Awards '96: Best Song ("Colors of the Wind"); Nominations: Golden Globe Awards '96: Best Score. *DIS*

Pocahontas: The Legend 🎬🎬½ **1995** Live-action version of the increasingly familiar story of the Native American girl who aids Virginia settler, John Smith. **101m/C VHS.** *CA* Sandrine Holt, Miles O'Keeffe, Tony Goldwyn, Gordon Tootoosis; **D:** Daniele Suissa; **W:** Daniele Suissa. *GKK*

The Pocatello Kid 🎬½ **1931** Maynard stretches in a dual role as the wrongly convicted Kid and the Kid's no-good sheriff brother. **60m/B VHS, Beta.** Ken Maynard, Marceline Day, Charles "Blackie" King, Lafe McKee; **D:** Phil Rosen. *NOS, VCN, VDM*

Pocket Money 🎬🎬 **1972 (PG)** Down-on-their-luck cowpokes foolishly do business with crooked rancher in attempt to make comeback in faltering acting careers. Star-powered, moderately entertaining modern western-comedy based on the novel "Jim Kane" by J.K.S. Brown. **100m/C VHS, Beta.** Paul Newman, Lee Marvin, Strother Martin, Christine Belford, Wayne Rogers, Hector Elizondo, Gregory Sierra; **D:** Stuart Rosenberg; **W:** Terence Malick; **M:** Alex North. *WAR, FCT*

Pocketful of Miracles 🎬🎬🎬 **1961** Capra's final film, a remake of his 1933 "Lady for a Day," is just as corny and sentimental but doesn't work quite as well. Davis is delightful as Apple Annie, a down-on-her-luck street vendor who will go to any extreme to hide her poverty from the well-married daughter she adores. Ford is terrific as the man who transforms Annie into a lady in time for her daughter's visit. Touching. Maybe too touching. Also marks Ann-Margret's film debut. **136m/C VHS, Beta, LV, Closed Caption.** Bette Davis, Glenn Ford, Peter Falk, Hope Lange, Arthur O'Connell, Ann-Margret, Thomas Mitchell, Jack Elam, Edward Everett Horton, David Brian, Mickey Shaughnessy; **D:** Frank Capra. Golden Globe Awards '62: Best Actor—Musical/Comedy (Ford); Nominations: Academy Awards '61: Best Costume Design (Color), Best Song ("Pocketful of Miracles"), Best Supporting Actor (Falk). *MGM, FOX, CCB*

A Pocketful of Rye 🎬🎬 *Agatha Christie's Miss Marple: A Pocketful of Rye* **1987** Based on Agatha Christie's novel featuring the sleuthing Miss Marple. She faces another murderous puzzle, this one based on an old nursery rhyme. Made for British television. **101m/C VHS, Beta, Closed Caption.** *GB* Joan Hickson; **D:** Guy Slater. *FOX, HMV, VCO*

Poco 🎬 **1977** The story of Poco, a shaggy little dog who travels across the country to search for the young girl who owns him. **88m/C VHS, Beta.** Chill Wills, Michelle Ashburn, John Steadman. *LIV, VES*

Poetic Justice 🎬🎬½ 1993 **(R)** Justice (Jackson in her movie debut, for better or worse) gives up college plans to follow a career in cosmetology after her boyfriend's brutal murder. She copes with her loss by dedicating herself to poetry writing (provided by no less than poet Maya Angelou) and meets postal worker Shakur. Singleton's second directorial effort is about the girlz n the hood and boasts a lighter script (well, it is about a hairdresser) focusing less on the Boyz-style morality and more on the trials and tribulations of Justice. Production stopped on the South Central L.A. set during the '92 riots, but the aftermath provided poignant pictures for later scenes.**CW:** Strong language, violence, and sex. **109m/C VHS, LV, 8mm, Closed Caption.** Janet Jackson, Tupac Shakur, Tyra Ferrell, Regina King, Joe Torry, Norma Donaldson; **D:** John Singleton; **W:** John Singleton; **C:** Peter Collister; **M:** Stanley Clarke. MTV Movie Awards '94: Best Female Performance (Jackson), Most Desirable Female (Jackson); Golden Raspberry Awards '93: Worst New Star (Jackson); Nominations: Academy Awards '93: Best Song ("Again"); Golden Globe Awards '94: Best Song ("Again"). *COL, BTV*

Pogo for President: "I Go Pogo" 🎬🎬½ 1984 **(PG)** Animated adventure with Walt Kelly's Pogo Possum becoming an unlikely presidential candidate when Howland Owl proclaims him the winner of a election. **120m/C VHS, Beta. V:** Jonathan Winters, Vincent Price, Ruth Buzzi, Stan Freberg, Jimmy Breslin, Arnold Stang. *DIS*

Poil de Carotte 🎬🎬½ *The Red Head* 1931 A semi-famous French melodrama about a young boy harassed by his overbearing mother to the point of disaster, redeemed finally by the love of his father. In French with English subtitles. **90m/B VHS, Beta.** *FR* Harry Baur, Robert Lynen, Catherine Fontenoy; **D:** Julien Duvivier. *NOS, FCT, MRV*

The Point 1971 Charming and sincere made-for-television animated feature about the rejection and isolation of a round-headed child in a world of pointy-headed people. Excellent score. **74m/C VHS, Beta, LV. D:** Fred Wolf; **M:** Harry Nilsson; **V:** Paul Frees. *FHE, VES, MLT*

Point Blank 🎬🎬½ 1967 Adapted from Stark's "The Hunter." The film's techniques are sometimes compared to those of Resnais and Godard. Double-crossed and believed dead, gangster Marvin returns to claim his share of the loot from the Organization. Hard-nosed examination of the depersonalization of a mechanized urban world. **92m/C VHS, Beta, Closed Caption.** Lee Marvin, Angie Dickinson, Keenan Wynn, Carroll O'Connor, Lloyd Bochner, Michael Strong, James B. Sikking; **D:** John Boorman. *MGM*

Point Break 🎬🎬½ 1991 **(R)** If you can suspend your disbelief—and you'd need a crane—then this crime adventure is just dandy. Reeves is a young undercover FBI kid sent to infiltrate a gang of bank-robbing surfer dudes. Swayze is the leader of the beach subculture, a thrillseeker who plays cat-and-mouse with the feds in a series of excellent action scenes. Silly brain candy.**CW:** Language, brief nudity, and violence. **117m/C VHS, LV, Closed Caption.** Patrick Swayze, Keanu Reeves, Gary Busey, Lori Petty, John C. McGinley, Chris Pederson, Bojesse Christopher, Julian Reyes, Daniel Beer, Sydney Walsh, Vincent Klyn, James LeGros, John Philbin; **D:** Kathryn Bigelow; **W:** W. Peter Iliff; **M:** Mark Isham. MTV Movie Awards '92: Most Desirable Male (Reeves). *FXV*

Point of Impact 🎬🎬 1993 **(R)** A Miami customs officer is killed in an explosion and his partner is blamed. He knows a Cuban crime boss was actually behind it and goes undercover to bring the criminal organization down. But there's also the temptation of the the criminal's sexy ladyfriend. Also available in an unrated version.**CW:** Language, strong violence, and strong sexuality. **96m/C VHS, LV, Closed Caption.** Michael Pare, Barbara Carrera, Michael Ironside. *THV*

Point of No Return 🎬🎬½ 1993 **(R)** Fonda is Maggie, a drugged-out loser condemned to death for her part in a murder spree, but if she agrees to work as a government assassin, she'll be given a reprieve. Fonda displays a certain perkiness as the assassin and is better in her early surly scenes; Keitel is creepy as another assassin. Flashy, exacting, but ultimately innocuous remake of the 1990 French thriller "La Femme Nikita."**CW:** Language, strong violence, and sexuality. **108m/C VHS, Beta, LV, Closed Caption.** Bridget Fonda, Gabriel Byrne, Dermot Mulroney, Miguel Ferrer, Anne Bancroft, Olivia D'Abo, Harvey Keitel, Richard Romanus, Lorraine Toussaint, Geoffrey Lewis, Calvin Levels; **D:** John Badham; **W:** Robert Getchell, Alexandra Seros; **C:** Michael Watkins; **M:** Hans Zimmer. *WAR*

Point of Terror 🎬 1971 **(R)** A handsome rock singer seduces a record company executive's wife in order to further his career. **88m/C VHS, Beta.** Peter Carpenter, Dyanne Thorne, Lory Hansen, Leslie Simms; **D:** Alex Nicol. *NO*

The Pointsman 🎬🎬½ *De Wisselwachter* 1986 **(R)** A quirky, small film based on the novel by Jean Paul Franssens. A beautiful Scandinavian woman accidentally gets off a train in Northern Scotland, where the only shelter is a small railway outpost, and the only company is a mysterious pointsman who lives by the comings and goings of the trains. The couple's increasing isolation as winter falls and their lack of a common language persists is portrayed with both humor and poignancy. **95m/C VHS, Beta, LV.** *NL* Jim Van Der Woude, Stephane Excoffier, John Kraaykamp, Josse De Pauw, Ton Van Dort; **D:** Jos Stelling. *LIV, VES*

Poison 🎬🎬🎬 1991 **(R)** A controversial, compelling drama weaving the story of a seven year-old boy's murder of his father with two other tales of obsessive, fringe behavior. From the director of the underground hit "Superstar: The Karen Carpenter Story," which was shot using only a cast of "Barbie" dolls.**CW:** Strong language, sexual violence, and sensuality. **85m/C VHS.** Edith Meeks, Larry Maxwell, Susan Norman, Scott Renderer, James Lyons, Millie White, Buck Smith, Anne Giotta, Al Quagliata, Michelle Sullivan, John R. Lombardi, Tony Pemberton, Andrew Harpending; **D:** Todd Haynes; **W:** Todd Haynes; **C:** Maryse Alberti; **M:** James Bennett. Sundance Film Festival '91: Grand Jury Prize. *FXL*

Poison Ivy 🎬🎬 1985 A routine, made for television comedy about a chaotic and lusty summer camp. **97m/C VHS, Beta.** Michael J. Fox, Nancy McKeon, Robert Klein, Caren Kaye; **D:** Larry Elikann; **M:** Miles Goodman. *NO*

Poison Ivy 🎬🎬 1992 **(R)** Barrymore is right on target as a junior femme fatale in this trashy tale of a wayward teenager and her takeover of her best friend's family. Ivy has no discernable family life and quickly attaches herself to the lonely, neglected Cooper (Gilbert) who ends up watching as she systematically seduces both her mother (emotionally) and her father (physically). But when Ivy's homewrecking turns lethal, Cooper must fight her "friend" to save herself. Glossy, over-done pulp. An unrated version is also available.**CW:** Language and sensuality. **91m/C VHS, LV, Closed Caption.** Drew Barrymore, Sara Gilbert, Tom Skerritt, Cheryl Ladd; **D:** Katt Shea Ruben; **W:** Katt Shea Ruben, Andy Ruben; **C:** Phedon Papamichael. *COL, NLC, PMS*

Poison Ivy 2: Lily 🎬½ 1995 **(R)** Art student Lily (Milano) finds the provocative Ivy's diary and becomes intrigued enough to decide to take a walk on the wild side herself. Also available unrated.**CW:** Strong sexuality, and for language. **110m/C VHS, LV, Closed Caption.** Alyssa Milano, Xander Berkeley, Johnathon Schaech, Belinda Bauer; **D:** Anne Goursaud; **W:** Chloe King; **M:** Joseph Williams. *NLC*

Poison Ivy 3: The New Seduction 🎬½ 1997 **(R)** Now Ivy has a long-lost sister, appropriately named Violet (Pressly), who heads to their childhood home to get revenge on those she believes betrayed them. Naturally, it's all sex and men being led around by their...zippers. Also available unrated.**CW:** Strong

sexuality, and for some language and drug content. **93m/C VHS, LV, Closed Caption.** Jaime Pressly, Megan Edwards, Michael Des Barres, Greg Vaughan; **D:** Kurt Voss. *NLC*

Poker Alice 🎬🎬 1987 A lively Western starring Elizabeth Taylor as a sometime gambler who wins a brothel in a poker game. **100m/C VHS, Beta, Closed Caption.** Elizabeth Taylor, George Hamilton, Tom Skerritt, Richard Mulligan, David Wayne, Susan Tyrrell, Pat Corley; **D:** Arthur Seidelman; **W:** James Lee Barrett. *VTR, NWV*

The Polar Bear King 🎬🎬½ 1994 **(PG)** When a handsome prince refuses to marry the evil witch of Summerland, the wicked woman uses her power to turn him into a polar bear. The polar bear prince embarks on a journey to Winterland where he meets and falls in love with a beautiful princess. Together they return to Summerland and try to break the witch's spell. Filmed on location in Norway and Sweden. **87m/C VHS, LV.** Maria Bonnevie, Jack Fjeldstad, Tobias Hoesl, Anna-Lotta Larsson; **D:** Ola Solum. *HMD*

Poldark 🎬🎬🎬 1975 Tempestuous love, political intrigue, and family struggles all set in 18th-century Cornwall, then the copper-producing center of England. Heroic Ross Poldark has just returned from fighting upstart Americans in the Revolutionary War only to discover that his father has died and the family mines are about to be sold to the scheming Warleggan family. Ross struggles to pay off family debts, reclaim his heritage, resolve his feelings for an old love, and fight his attraction to the beguiling, but completely unsuitable, Demelza. Adapted from the novels by Winston Graham. Made for British television; 12 episodes on 6 cassettes. **720m/C VHS.** *GB* Robin Ellis, Angharad Rees, Jill Townsend, Judy Geeson, Ralph Bates, Richard Morant, Clive Francis, John Baskcomb, Paul Curran, Tilly Tremayne, Mary Wimbush; **D:** Paul Annett, Christopher Barry, Kenneth Ives; **W:** Paul Wheeler, Jack Russell, Peter Draper, Jack Pulman. *TVC, SIG*

Poldark 2 🎬🎬🎬 1975 The further adventures of Ross Poldark, wife Demelza, and assorted family, friends, and enemies, all set in 18th-century Cornwall. Demelza's two meddlesome younger brothers come to live at Nampara, enemy George Warleggan and Ross' old love Elizabeth move too close for comfort, and the uncertainties of the copper mining economy all bring their share of trouble. Adapted from the novels by Winston Graham. Made for British TV; 6 cassettes. **720m/C VHS.** *GB* Robin Ellis, Angharad Rees, Jill Townsend, Judy Geeson, Ralph Bates, Kevin McNally, Brian Stirner, Michael Cadman, Jane Wymark, David Delve, Christopher Biggins, Trudie Styler; **D:** Philip Dudley, Roger Jenkins; **W:** Alexander Baron, John Wiles, Martin Worth. *TVC*

Police 🎬🎬½ 1985 French police drama with the intense Depardieu as a cop hunting an Algerian drug boss. Matters grow complicated when he falls for the elusive crook's girlfriend. Sometimes gripping, but uneven; the actors were encouraged to improvise. Inspired by the novel "Bodies Are Dust" by P.J. Wolfson. In French with English subtitles. **113m/C VHS.** *FR* Gerard Depardieu, Sophie Marceau, Sandrine Bonnaire, Richard Anconina, Pascale Rocard; **D:** Maurice Pialat; **W:** Catherine Breillat. Venice Film Festival '85: Best Actor (Depardieu). *NYF, FCT*

Police Academy 🎬½ 1984 **(R)** In an attempt to recruit more cops, a big-city police department does away with all its job standards. The producers probably didn't know that they were introducing bad comedy's answer to the "Friday the 13th" series, but it's hard to avoid heaping the sins of its successors on this film. Besides, it's just plain dumb. **96m/C VHS, Beta, LV, 8mm, Closed Caption.** Steve Guttenberg, Kim Cattrall, Bubba Smith, George Gaynes, Michael Winslow, Leslie Easterbrook, Georgina Spelvin, Debralee Scott; **D:** Hugh Wilson; **W:** Hugh Wilson, Pat Proft, Neal Israel; **M:** Robert Folk. *WAR*

Police Academy 2: Their First Assignment ⅟ 1985 (PG-13) More predictable idiocy from the cop shop. This time they're determined to rid the precinct of some troublesome punks. No real story to speak of, just more high jinks in this mindless sequel. 87m/C VHS, Beta, LV, Closed Caption. Steve Guttenberg, Bubba Smith, Michael Winslow, Art Metrano, Colleen Camp, Howard Hesseman, David Graf, George Gaynes; D: Jerry Paris; W: Barry W. Blaustein. WAR

Police Academy 3: Back in Training ⅟ 1986 (PG) In yet another sequel, the bumbling cops find their alma mater is threatened by a budget crunch and they must compete with a rival academy to see which school survives. The "return to school" plot allowed the filmmakers to add new characters to replace those who had some scruples about picking up yet another "Police Lobotomy" check. Followed by three more sequels. 84m/C VHS, Beta, LV, Closed Caption. Steve Guttenberg, Bubba Smith, David Graf, Michael Winslow, Marion Ramsey, Art Metrano, Bob(cat) Goldthwait, Leslie Easterbrook, Tim Kazurinsky, George Gaynes, Shawn Weatherly; D: Jerry Paris; W: Gene Quintano; M: Robert Folk. WAR

Police Academy 4: Citizens on Patrol ⅟ 1987 (PG) The comic cop cutups from the first three films aid a citizen's patrol group in their unnamed, but still wacky, hometown. Moronic high jinks ensue. Fourth in the series of five (or is it six?) that began with "Police Academy". 88m/C VHS, Beta, LV, Closed Caption. Steve Guttenberg, Bubba Smith, Michael Winslow, David Graf, Tim Kazurinsky, George Gaynes, Colleen Camp, Bob(cat) Goldthwait, Sharon Stone; D: Jim Drake; W: Gene Quintano; M: Robert Folk. WAR

Police Academy 5: Assignment Miami Beach WOOF! 1988 (PG) The fourth sequel, wherein the misfits-with-badges go to Miami and bumble about in the usual manner. It's about time these cops were retired from the force. 89m/C VHS, Beta, LV, Closed Caption. Bubba Smith, David Graf, Michael Winslow, Leslie Easterbrook, Rene Auberjonois, Marion Ramsey, Janet Jones, George Gaynes, Matt McCoy; D: Alan Myerson; W: Stephen J. Curwick; M: Robert Folk. WAR

Police Academy 6: City Under Siege ⅟ 1989 (PG) In what is hoped to be the last in a series of bad comedies, the distinguished graduates pursue three goofballs responsible for a crime wave. 85m/C VHS, LV, Closed Caption. Bubba Smith, David Graf, Michael Winslow, Leslie Easterbrook, Marion Ramsey, Matt McCoy, Bruce Mahler, G.W. Bailey, George Gaynes; D: Peter Bonerz; W: Stephen J. Curwick; M: Robert Folk. WAR

Police Academy: Mission to Moscow ⅟ 1994 (PG) The seventh in the series is another inept comedy, which finds the chaotic crew tackling a Russian mobster on his Moscow turf—all because of a popular computer game with some sinister software. Like you'll care about the plot anyway. 83m/C VHS. George Gaynes, Michael Winslow, David Graf, Leslie Easterbrook, G.W. Bailey, Charlie Schlatter, Ron Perlman, Christopher Lee; D: Alan Metter; W: Michele S. Chodos, Randolph Davis; M: Robert Folk. WAR

Police Court ⅟⅟ 1937 The son of a faded, alcoholic screen star tries to bring the old fellow back to prominence. 62m/B VHS, Beta, LV. Nat Barry, Henry B. Walthall, Leon Janney. NO

Police Squad! Help Wanted! 1982 Three episodes from the brilliant, short-lived television spoof, with the patented pun-a-second style of humor typical of the makers of "Airplane!" and "The Naked Gun," which was based on this show. Episodes included: "A Substantial Gift," "Ring of Fear," and "Rendezvous at Big Gulch." See also "More! Police Squad." 75m/C VHS, Beta, LV. Leslie Nielsen, Alan North, Ed Williams, William Duell; D: Jerry Zucker, David Zucker, Jim Abrahams; W: Jerry Zucker, David Zucker, Jim Abrahams. PAR

Policewoman Centerfold ⅟ 1983 Exploitative rendering based on the true story of a cop who posed for a pornographic magazine. Anderson is appealing in the lead. 100m/C VHS, Beta. Melody Anderson, Ed Marinaro, Donna Pescow, Bert Remsen, David Spielberg; D: Reza Badiyi. NO

Policewomen ⅟⅟ 1973 (R) Female undercover agent must stop a ring of gold smugglers. 99m/C VHS, Beta. Sondra Currie, Tony Young, Phil Hoover, Elizabeth Stuart, Jeanne Bell; D: Lee Frost. NO

A Polish Vampire in Burbank ⅟⅟ 1980 A shy vampire in Burbank tries again and again to find blood and love. Wacky. 84m/C VHS, Beta. Mark Pirro, Lori Sutton, Eddie Deezen; D: Mark Pirro. NO

Pollyanna ⅟⅟⅟ 1920 A young orphan girl is adopted by her cold, embittered aunt and does her best to bring joy and gladness to all the new people she meets. Silent with music score. 60m/B VHS, Beta, LV. Mary Pickford; C: Charles Rosher. CCB

Pollyanna ⅟⅟⅟⅟ 1960 Based on the Eleanor Porter story about an enchanting young girl whose contagious enthusiasm and zest for life touches the hearts of all she meets. Mills is perfect in the title role and was awarded a special Oscar for outstanding juvenile performance. A distinguished supporting cast is the icing on the cake in this delightful Disney confection. Original version was filmed in 1920 with Mary Pickford. 134m/C VHS, Beta, LV, Closed Caption. Hayley Mills, Jane Wyman, Richard Egan, Karl Malden, Nancy Olson, Adolphe Menjou, Donald Crisp, Agnes Moorehead, Kevin Corcoran; D: David Swift. DIS, BTV

Poltergeist ⅟⅟⅟⅟ 1982 (PG) This production has Stephen Spielberg written all over it. A young family's home becomes a house of horrors when they are terrorized by menacing spirits who abduct their five-year-old daughter...through the TV screen! Roller-coaster thrills and chills, dazzling special effects, and perfectly timed humor highlight this stupendously scary ghost story. 114m/C VHS, Beta, LV, DVD. JoBeth Williams, Craig T. Nelson, Beatrice Straight, Heather O'Rourke, Zelda Rubinstein, Dominique Dunne, Oliver Robbins, Richard Lawson, James Karen; D: Tobe Hooper; W: Steven Spielberg, Michael Grais, Mark Victor; M: Jerry Goldsmith. Nominations: Academy Awards '82: Best Original Score. MGM

Poltergeist 2: The Other Side ⅟⅟⅟ 1986 (PG-13) Adequate sequel to the Spielburg-produced venture into the supernatural, where demons follow the Freeling family in their efforts to recapture the clairvoyant young daughter Carol Anne. The film includes sojourns into Indian lore and a four-foot high agave worm designed by H.R. Giger. The movie was followed by "Poltergeist 3" in 1988. 92m/C VHS, Beta, LV, Closed Caption. Craig T. Nelson, JoBeth Williams, Heather O'Rourke, Will Sampson, Julian Beck, Geraldine Fitzgerald, Oliver Robbins, Zelda Rubinstein; D: Brian Gibson; W: Mark Victor, Michael Grais; M: Jerry Goldsmith. MGM

Poltergeist 3 ⅟⅟ 1988 (PG-13) Wrestling with the supernatural has finally unnerved Carol Ann and she's sent to stay with her aunt and uncle in Chicago where she attends a school for gifted children with emotional disorders. Guess who follows her? Uninspired acting, threadbare premise, and one ghastly encounter too many. Oddly, O'Rourke died suddenly four months before the film's release. 97m/C VHS, Beta, LV, Closed Caption. Tom Skerritt, Nancy Allen, Heather O'Rourke, Lara Flynn Boyle, Zelda Rubinstein; D: Gary Sherman; W: Brian Taggert. MGM

Poltergeist: The Legacy ⅟⅟⅟ 1996 Premiere episode of the cable TV series about a secret international society, the Legacy, which is devoted to the paranormal and to protecting mankind from supernatural evil. Derek Rayne (De Lint), the head of the San Francisco Legacy house, must find the last of five sepulchers containing the evil spirits of five fallen angels. This takes him and his cohorts to Ireland where Rachel Corrigan (Shaver) and her young psychic daugh-

ter Kat (Purvis) come into unwitting possession of the fifth box and untold danger. ?m/C VHS, Closed Caption. Derek De Lint, Helen Shaver, Alexandra Purvis, Martin Cummins, Robbi Chong, Patrick Fitzgerald, Jordan Bayne, William Sadler, Daniel Pilon, Chad Krowchuk; D: Stuart Gillard; W: Brad Wright; C: Manfred Guthe. MGM

Polyester ⅟⅟⅟ 1981 (R) Amusing satire on middle-class life, described by producer, director and writer Waters as "'Father Knows Best' gone berserk." Forlorn housewife Divine pines for the man of her dreams while the rest of her life is falling apart at the seams. Filmed in "Odorama," a hilarious gimmick in which theatre goers were provided with scratch-n-sniff cards, containing specific scents corresponding to key scenes. Video watchers will have to use their imagination in experiencing a wide range of smells. The first of Waters' more mainstream films. Features songs by Murray and Harry. 86m/C VHS, Beta, LV. Divine, Tab Hunter, Edith Massey, Mink Stole, Stiv Bators, David Samson, Mary Garlington, Kenneth King, Joni-Ruth White; D: John Waters; W: John Waters; M: Bill Murray, Deborah Harry, Michael Kamen. NLC

Pom Pom Girls ⅟⅟ 1976 (R) High school seniors, intent on having one last fling before graduating, get involved in crazy antics, clumsy romances, and football rivalries. 90m/C VHS, Beta. Robert Carradine, Jennifer Ashley, Michael Mullins, Cheryl "Rainbeaux" Smith, Dianne Lee Hart, Lisa Reeves, Bill Adler; D: Joseph Ruben. NO

The Pompatus of Love ⅟⅟⅟ 1995 (R) Remember Steve Miller's song "The Joker"?—well, that's where the title comes from—and we still don't know what it means. But the film's about four New York guys and the mystery of women. They may be (reasonably) bright and literate but they still don't have a clue about love or how to grow-up. Naturally, the women they know—or meet—are all too smart for them. CW: Nudity, sexuality and language. 99m/C VHS. Jon Cryer, Tim Guinee, Adrian Pasdar, Adam Oliensis, Kristen Wilson, Dana Wheeler-Nicholson, Paige Turco, Mia Sara, Kristin Scott Thomas, Arabella Field, Jennifer Tilly, Roscoe Lee Browne; D: Richard Schenkman; W: Jon Cryer, Adam Oliensis, Richard Schenkman; C: Russell Fine; M: John Hill. BMG

Ponette ⅟⅟ 1995 Four-year-old Ponette (Thivisol) is hard-pressed to understand what's happening to her family after her mother is killed in a car accident. Her father can't seem to explain it properly, so Ponette comes to her own acceptance with the help of some school friends. Film drew some controversy when the very young Thivisol was awarded the best actress award at the Venice Film Festival—since Thivisol was thought by some critics to be too young to "act," director Doillon was accused of manipulating the youngster in order to get a performance. French with subtitles. 107m/C VHS. FR Victoire Thivisol, Marie Trintignant, Claire Nebout, Xavier Beauvois; D: Jacques Doillon; W: Jacques Doillon. Venice Film Festival '96: Best Actress (Thivisol). NYR

Pontiac Moon ⅟⅟ 1994 (PG-13) Danson plays a high school teacher who takes his son on a road trip to Spires of the Moon National Park hoping to arrive simultaneously with the astronauts' first lunar landing. His wife (Steenburgen) decides to follow them, although she's phobic about leaving the house and hasn't set foot outside in seven years. Sincere yet tedious film about father-son bonding has a few heartfelt moments, but not enough to sustain interest for entire viewing period. Best (and only) reason for watching: Monument Valley scenery. 108m/C VHS, Beta, Closed Caption. Ted Danson, Mary Steenburgen, Ryan Todd, Eric Schweig, Cathy Moriarty, Max Gail, Lisa Jane Persky; D: Peter Medak; W: Finn Taylor, Jeffrey Brown; M: Randy Edelman. PAR

The Pony Express ⅟⅟ 1925 Melodramatic western about an evil senator (Hart) who's out to establish his own empire. His scheme is thwarted by pony express rider Cortez. Based on the novel by Henry James Forman and Walter Woods. 67m/B VHS. Ricardo Cortez, Al Hart, Betty

Compson, Ernest Torrence, Wallace Beery, George Bancroft, Frank Lackteen; **D:** James Cruze; **W:** Walter Woods. *GPV*

Pony Express ♪♪♪ 1953 Buffalo Bill Cody and Wild Bill Hickok join forces to extend the Pony Express mail route west to California through rain and sleet, snow and hail. Far from a factual account but good for extending the myth of the Old West. 101m/C VHS, Beta. Charlton Heston, Rhonda Fleming, Jan Sterling, Forrest Tucker; **D:** Jerry Hopper; **C:** Ray Rennahan. *PAR, BAR, HHE*

Pony Express Rider ♪♪♪ 1976 (G) Young man with a mission joins up with the Pony Express hoping to bag the male responsible for killing his pa. The well-produced script boasts a bevy of veteran western character actors, all lending, solid, rugged performances. 100m/C VHS. Stewart Peterson, Henry Wilcoxon, Buck Taylor, Maureen McCormick, Joan Caulfield, Ken Curtis, Slim Pickens, Dub Taylor, Jack Elam; **D:** Robert Totten. *TPI*

Pony Post ♪♪½ 1940 Standard horse opera has Brown running a pony express station where he battles Indians and typical villains. 59m/B VHS. Johnny Mack Brown, Fuzzy Knight, Nell O'Day, Dorothy Short, Kermit Maynard, Lane Chandler; **D:** Ray Taylor; **W:** Sherman Lowe. *GPV*

Pool Hustlers ♪♪½ 1983 A romantic comedy about an amateur billiards whiz who finds love and successfully defeats the national champ. In Italian with English subtitles. 101m/C VHS, Beta. *IT* Francesco Nuti, Giuliana de Sio, Marcello Loti; **D:** Maurizio Ponzi. *XVC, MED*

Pool Sharks ♪♪½ 1915 W.C. Fields' first film features the comedian's antics while playing a pool game to win the love of a woman. Silent. 10m/B VHS, Beta. W.C. Fields. *FLI, GVV*

Poor Girl, A Ghost Story ♪♪ 1974 A young girl takes a job as a governess at an English mansion and is besieged by all manner of strange goings-on. 52m/C VHS, Beta. *AU* Lynn Miller, Angela Thorne; **D:** Michael Apted. *PSM*

A Poor Little Rich Girl ♪♪♪ 1917 Mary Pickford received raves in this film, in which she portrayed Gwendolyn, with everything money could buy, except the attention of her family. Gwendolyn has a bizarre dream in which she sees a number of horrors and is tempted by death. Elaborate sets and special effects, as well as Pickford's delicate performance, make this one special. Organ score. 64m/B VHS, Beta, **Closed Caption.** Mary Pickford, Madeline Traverse, Charles Wellesley, Gladys Fairbanks; **D:** Maurice Tourneur. *CCB, VYY*

The Poor Little Rich Girl ♪♪½ 1936 A motherless rich girl wanders away from home and is "adopted" by a pair of struggling vaudevillians. With her help, they rise to the big time. Also available with "Heidi" on laserdisc. ♫Oh My Goodness; Buy a Bar of Barry's; Wash Your Neck With a Cake of Peck's; Military Man; When I'm with You; But Definitely; You've Gotta Eat Your Spinach, Baby. 79m/B VHS, Beta, **Closed Caption.** Shirley Temple, Jack Haley, Alice Faye, Gloria Stuart, Michael Whalen, Sara Haden, Jane Darwell; **D:** Irving Cummings. *FOX*

Poor Little Rich Girl: The Barbara Hutton Story ♪♪½ 1987 Bio-drama of the one-time richest woman in America, Woolworth heiress Hutton (Fawcett), and her extravagant lifestyle. She married seven times (including actor Cary Grant) until falling into self-destructive alcohol and drug addictions. Lavishly presented but superficial. Based on the book by C. David Heymann. Originally a two-part television movie. 98m/C VHS. Farrah Fawcett, Bruce Davison, Kevin McCarthy, Burl Ives, James Read, Stephane Audran, Anne Francis, David Ackroyd, Tony Peck, Zoe Wanamaker, Amadeus August; **D:** Charles Jarrott; **W:** Dennis Turner; **M:** Richard Rodney Bennett. *LIV*

Poor Pretty Eddie ♪♪½ 1973 (R) A young black singer gets waylaid and taken in by a twisted white Southern clan. An incredibly sleazy movie which boasts Shelly Winters performing a strip act. Also on video as "Black Vengeance," "Redneck County," and "Heartbreak Motel." 90m/C Beta. Leslie Uggams, Shelley Winters, Michael Christian, Ted Cassidy, Slim Pickens, Dub Taylor; **D:** Richard Robinson. *MRV*

Poor White Trash ♪♪½ *Bayou* 1957 An architect arrives in bayou country with plans to design a new building. He meets with resistance from the locals but falls for the sensual daughter of one of his staunchest detractors. 83m/B VHS, Beta. Peter Graves, Lita Milan, Douglas Fowley, Timothy Carey, Jonathan Haze; **D:** Harold Daniels. *NO*

Poor White Trash 2 ♪ *Scum of the Earth* 1975 (R) A young couple, vacationing in Louisiana's bayou country, are introduced to an unusual brand of southern hospitality by the eponymous group of locals. 90m/C VHS, Beta. Gene Ross, Ann Stafford, Norma Moore, Camilla Carr; **D:** S.F. Brownrigg. *TPV*

Pop Always Pays ♪♪ 1940 A father gets in a jam when he has to make good on a bet with his daughter's boyfriend. 67m/B VHS, Beta. Walter Catlett, Dennis O'Keefe, Leon Errol, Adele Pearce; **D:** Leslie Goodwins. *MLB*

Pop Goes the Cork 1922 Three films by the man Chaplin referred to as his "professor," Max Linder: "Be My Wife," "Seven Years Bad Luck," and "The Three Must-Get-Theres." Linder was the foremost film comedian in early twentieth-century France, and made these three films during a stay in America. 87m/B VHS, Beta. Max Linder. *CCB*

Popcorn ♪♪ 1989 (R) A killer stalks a movie audience who is unaware that his crimes are paralleling those in the very film they are watching.***CW:*** Some language and strong violence. 93m/C VHS, LV, 8mm. Jill Schoelen, Tom Villard, Dee Wallace Stone, Derek Rydell, Elliott Hurst, Kelly Jo Minter, Malcolm Danare, Ray Walston, Tony Roberts; **D:** Mark Herrier; **W:** Alan Ormsby. *COL*

Pope John Paul II ♪♪ 1984 A made-for-television biography of the Pontiff, from childhood to world eminence. 150m/C VHS, Beta. Albert Finney, Michael Crompton, Nigel Hawthorne, John McEnery, Brian Cox; **D:** Herbert Wise. *PSM, IGP*

The Pope Must Diet ♪½ *The Pope Must Die* 1991 (R) Coltrane stars as a misfit who accidentally becomes Pope Dave I. Living up to the benevolence suggested by his title, Pope Dave proposes to use Vatican money to create a children's fund. But there are those in the organization who have different, less noble plans for the cash, and soon Dave finds himself the target of a mob hit. Frantic comedy caused a stir with its original title "The Pope Must Die," with many newspapers refusing to run ads for the film. This, coupled with lukewarm critical reviews, led to a very brief stint at the box office.***CW:*** Language and sensuality. 87m/C VHS, Beta, LV, **Closed Caption.** *GB* Robbie Coltrane, Alex Rocco, Beverly D'Angelo, Herbert Lom, Paul Bartel, Salvatore Cascio, Balthazar Getty; **D:** Peter Richardson; **M:** Anne Dudley. *MED, VTR*

The Pope of Greenwich Village ♪♪½ 1984 (R) A film about two Italian-American cousins who struggle to escape the trap of poverty in New York's Greenwich Village. When a small crime goes wrong in a big way, the two must learn about deception and loyalty. Mostly character study; Page is exceptional. Inferior re-run of the "Mean Streets" idea. 122m/C VHS, Beta, LV. Eric Roberts, Mickey Rourke, Daryl Hannah, Geraldine Page, Tony Musante, M. Emmet Walsh, Kenneth McMillan, Burt Young; **D:** Stuart Rosenberg; **W:** Vincent Patrick; **C:** John Bailey; **M:** Dave Grusin. Nominations: Academy Awards '84: Best Supporting Actress (Page). *CCB, MGM*

Popeye ♪♪ 1980 (PG) The cartoon sailor brought to life is on a search to find his long-lost father. Along the way, he meets Olive Oyl and adopts little Sweet Pea. Williams accomplishes the near-impossible feat of physically resembling the title character, and the whole movie does accomplish the maker's stated goal of "looking like a comic strip," but it isn't anywhere near as funny as it should be. 114m/C VHS, Beta, LV. Robin Williams, Shelley Duvall, Ray Walston, Paul Dooley, Bill Irwin, Paul Smith, Linda Hunt, Richard Libertini; **D:** Robert Altman; **W:** Jules Feiffer; **M:** Harry Nilsson. *PAR*

Popi ♪♪♪ 1969 (G) Arkin is the heart and soul of this poignant charmer in his role as a Puerto Rican immigrant hell-bent on securing a better life outside the ghetto for his two sons. His zany efforts culminate in one outrageous scheme to set them adrift off the Florida coast in hopes they will be rescued and raised by a wealthy family. Far fetched, but ultimately heartwarming. 115m/C VHS, Beta. Alan Arkin, Rita Moreno, Miguel Alejandro, Ruben Figueroa; **D:** Arthur Hiller. *NO*

The Poppy Is Also a Flower ♪½ *Poppies Are Also Flowers; Opium Connection* 1966 (PG) A star-laden, antidrug drama produced by the United Nations. Filmed on location in Iran, Monaco, and Italy. Based on a drug trade thriller by Ian Fleming that explains how poppies, converted into heroin, are brought into the United States. Made for television. 100m/C VHS, Beta. E.G. Marshall, Trevor Howard, Gilbert Roland, Eli Wallach, Marcello Mastroianni, Angie Dickinson, Rita Hayworth, Yul Brynner, Trini Lopez, Bessie Love; **D:** Terence Young. *NO*

Porcile ♪♪♪ *Pigsty* 1969 Pasolini intertwines the story of a soldier cannibal living in a medieval age with the son of an ex-Nazi industrialist in present day Germany. Both the soldier and the young German (who prefers pigs to his fiance) become sacrificial victims of their differing societies. A grotesque fable on Pasolini's hatred of middle class mores and the 20th century. In Italian with English subtitles. 90m/C VHS, LV. *IT* Pierre Clementi, Franco Citti, Jean-Pierre Leaud, Anna Wiazemsky, Ugo Tognazzi, Alberto Lionello; **D:** Pier Paolo Pasolini; **W:** Pier Paolo Pasolini; **C:** Tonino Delli Colli. *WBF*

Pork Chop Hill ♪♪♪ 1959 A powerful, hard-hitting account of the last hours of the Korean War. Peck is totally believable as the man ordered to hold his ground against the hopeless onslaught of Chinese Communist hordes. A chilling, stark look in the face of a no-win situation. Top notch cast and masterful directing. 97m/B VHS, Beta, LV, **Closed Caption.** Gregory Peck, Harry Guardino, Rip Torn, George Peppard, James Edwards, Bob Steele, Woody Strode, Robert (Bobby) Blake, Martin Landau, Norman Fell, Bert Remsen; **D:** Lewis Milestone; **C:** Sam Leavitt. *MGM*

Porky's ♪♪½ 1982 (R) Investigation of teen horniness set in South Florida during the fab '50s. Irreverent comedy follows the misadventures of six youths imprisoned in Angel Beach High School who share a common interest: girls. Their main barrier to sexual success: the no-touch babes they lust after and the incredibly stupid adults who run the world. Fairly dumb and tasteless with occasional big laughs that earned mega bucks at the drive-in and created perceived popular outcry for more porky: "Porky's II: The Next Day" (1983) and "Porky's Revenge" (1985). 94m/C VHS, Beta, LV. *CA* Dan Monahan, Wyatt Knight, Scott Colomby, Tony Ganios, Mark Herrier, Cyril O'Reilly, Roger Wilson, Bob (Benjamin) Clark, Kim Cattrall, Kaki Hunter; **D:** Bob (Benjamin) Clark; **W:** Bob (Benjamin) Clark. *FXV, FOX*

Porky's 2: The Next Day ♪♪ 1983 (R) More tame tomfoolery about teenage sex drives, Shakespeare, fat high school teachers, the Ku Klux Klan, and streaking in the Florida high school where it all began. Outright caricature shares the stage with juvenile humor, some of which may induce laughter. 100m/C VHS, Beta, LV. *CA* Bill Wiley, Dan Monahan, Wyatt Knight, Cyril O'Reilly, Roger Wilson, Tony Ganios, Mark Herrier, Scott Colomby;

D: Bob (Benjamin) Clark; **W:** Alan Ormsby, Bob (Benjamin) Clark. *FOX*

Porky's Revenge 🎬 1985 **(R)** The Angel Beach High School students are out to get revenge against Porky who orders the school basketball coach to throw the championship game. The second of the "Porky's" sequels. 95m/C **VHS, Beta, LV, Closed Caption.** *CA* Dan Monahan, Wyatt Knight, Tony Ganios, Nancy Parsons, Chuck "Porky" Mitchell, Kaki Hunter, Kimberly Evenson, Scott Colomby; **D:** James Komack. *FOX*

The Pornographers 🎬🎬🎬 1966 Bizzare, black comedy focuses on a part-time porno filmmaker lusting after the daughter of the widow he lives with and trying to cope with his family, the world, and himself. A perversely fascinating exploration of contemporary Japanese society and the many facets of sexual emotion. In Japanese with English subtitles. 128m/B **VHS.** *JP* Shoichi Ozawa, Massaomi Konda, Sumiko Sakamota, Haruo Tanaka, Keiko Sagowa; **D:** Shohei Imamura. *CVC, TPV*

Porridge 🎬🎬 *Doing Time* 1991 A British comedy inspired by the popular BBC situation comedy of the title, about a habitual criminal and convict who makes the most of his time in prison. 105m/C **VHS.** *GB* Ronnie Barker, Fulton Mackay, Peter Vaughan, Julian Holloway, Geoffrey Bayldon; **D:** Dick Clement. *VCO*

Port of Call 🎬🎬🎬 1948 Early Bergman drama about a seaman on the docks who falls for a troubled woman whose wild, unhappy past has earned her an unsavory reputation. The hopeful, upbeat tone seems incongruous with the grim harbor/slum setting. It's minor Bergman but the seeds of his trademark themes can be seen taking shape, making it a must-see for avid fans. In Swedish with English subtitles. 100m/B **VHS, Beta.** *SW* Ivine-Christine Jonsson, Bengt Eklund, Erik Hell, Berta Hall, Mimi Nelson; **D:** Ingmar Bergman. *NLC*

The Port of Missing Girls 🎬 1938 A young woman implicated in a murder stows away on a freighter. There she becomes caught up in a waterfront world of pirates, smugglers and other assorted undesirables. 56m/B **VHS, Beta, 8mm.** Harry Carey Sr., Judith Allen, Milburn Stone, Betty Compson; **D:** Karl Brown. *VYY*

Port of New York 🎬🎬 1949 A narcotics gang is smuggling large quantities of drugs into New York. A government agent poses as a gang member in order to infiltrate the mob and get the goods on them. Brynner's film debut. 82m/B **VHS, Beta.** Scott Brady, Yul Brynner, K.T. Stevens; **D:** Laslo Benedek. *NOS, VYY, DVT*

Portfolio 1988 **(R)** Real-life models star in this gritty drama about rising to the top of the fashion heap. Music by Eurythmics, Fun Boy Three and others. 83m/C **VHS, LV.** Paulina Porizkova, Julie Wolfe, Carol Alt, Kelly Emberg. *NO*

Portnoy's Complaint 🎬½ 1972 **(R)** Limp screen adaptation of Philip Roth's novel follows the frustrating experiences of a sexually obsessed young man as he relates them to his psychiatrist. 101m/C **VHS, Beta.** Richard Benjamin, Karen Black, Lee Grant, Jeannie Berlin, Jill Clayburgh; **D:** Ernest Lehman; **W:** Ernest Lehman. *WAR*

The Portrait 🎬🎬🎬 1993 Longtime real-life friends Bacall and Peck on-screen together for the first time in 37 years prove they are still shining stars as they play aging parents to Peck's real-life daughter, Cecilia Peck. The younger Peck is an artist preparing for a exhibition and asks her parents to sit for a portrait. This is the pole around which their relationships and reconciliations swing in this emotional made-for-cable-tv drama based loosely on Tina Howe's 1983 off-Broadway play, "Painting Churches." 89m/C **VHS, LV, Closed Caption.** Lauren Bacall, Gregory Peck, Cecilia Peck, Paul McCrane, Joyce O'Connor, Donna Mitchell, Mitchell Laurance, William Prince, Augusta Dabney; **D:** Arthur Penn; **W:** Lynn Roth, Jack Darcus; **M:** Michael Conway Baker. *TTC, BTV*

Portrait in Black 🎬🎬½ 1960 Invalid shipping magnate Matthew Cabot (Nolan) is contempuous of second wife Sheila (Turner), who can't leave the marriage because of young son Peter (Kohler). She finds comfort in the arms of her husband's doctor, David Rivera (Quinn), and the duo decide the only way to find happiness is to kill off Cabot, which they do. Then Sheila begins to get anonymous letters accusing her of murder. Turner's glamor can't hide the gaping holes in the contrived plot. Adapted from the Goff/Roberts play. 113m/C **VHS, Closed Caption.** Lana Turner, Lloyd Nolan, Anthony Quinn, Richard Basehart, Sandra Dee, John Saxon, Ray Walston, Anna May Wong, Virginia Grey, Dennis Kohler; **D:** Michael Gordon; **W:** Ivan Goff, Ben Roberts; **C:** Russell Metty; **M:** Frank Skinner. *USH*

Portrait in Terror 🎬½ 1966 A master thief and a deranged artist plan a heist of a Titian painting in an oddball suspense piece. Not a great success, but atmospheric and weird. 81m/B **VHS.** Patrick Magee, William Campbell, Anna Pavane; **D:** Jack Hill. *SMW*

Portrait of a Hitman 🎬 *Jim Buck* 1977 Aspiring painter leads a double life as a professional hitman. Ragged feature feels more abandoned than finished, as if most of the movie had been shot and then the money ran out. All leads turn in paycheck performances, no more. 85m/C **VHS, Beta.** Jack Palance, Rod Steiger, Richard Roundtree, Bo Svenson, Ann Turkel; **D:** Allan A. Buckhantz. *NO*

Portrait of a Lady 🎬🎬½ 1967 A spirited young American woman is taken to England and insists on complete freedom to choose her own future and make her own choices. Based on the 1881 novel by Henry James. On 2 cassettes. 240m/C **VHS.** *GB* Richard Chamberlain, Suzanne Neve, Edward Fox. *VCO, TVC*

Portrait of a Lady 🎬🎬🎬 1996 **(PG-13)** Adapted from the century-old Henry James novel, "Portrait" paints the story of independent and newly wealthy American, Isabel Archer (Kidman). Abroad in Europe, she falls under the influence of the bitter, opportunistic Madame Merle (Hershey, in a strong portrayal), who manages to steer the innocent Isabel into a disastrous marriage with Gilbert Osmond (Malkovich). From there, film deals with Isabel's efforts to flee the domineering Osmond and find herself again. Kidman plays her role with never-before-seen efficiency. Malkovich is suitably evil but plays his villain card a bit too early. Director Campion's modern voice carries the film through, but is sometimes out of place, as in the opening segment. Filmed in England and Italy. **CW:** Sensuality and some brief nudity. 142m/C **VHS, LV, Closed Caption, DVD.** *GB* Nicole Kidman, John Malkovich, Barbara Hershey, Martin Donovan, Christian Bale, Shelley Winters, Shelley Duvall, Mary-Louise Parker, Richard E. Grant, John Gielgud, Viggo Mortensen; **D:** Jane Campion; **W:** Laura Jones; **C:** Stuart Dryburgh; **M:** Wojciech Kilar. Los Angeles Film Critics Association Awards '96: Best Supporting Actress (Hershey); National Society of Film Critics Awards '96: Best Supporting Actor (Donovan), Best Supporting Actress (Hershey); Nominations: Academy Awards '96: Best Costume Design, Best Supporting Actress (Hershey); Golden Globe Awards '97: Best Supporting Actress (Hershey). *PGV*

Portrait of a Rebel: Margaret Sanger 🎬🎬½ 1982 TV docudrama about the struggle of Margaret Sanger to repeal the Comstock Act of 1912, which prohibited the distribution of birth control information. 96m/C **VHS, Beta.** Bonnie Franklin, David Dukes, Milo O'Shea; **D:** Virgil W. Vogel. *TLF*

Portrait of a Showgirl 🎬🎬 1982 Inexperienced showgirl learns the ropes of Las Vegas life from a veteran of the Vegas stages. Made for television. 100m/C **VHS, Beta.** Lesley Ann Warren, Rita Moreno, Tony Curtis, Dianne Kay, Howard Morris; **D:** Steven Hilliard Stern. *PSM*

Portrait of a Stripper 🎬 1979 A widowed mother works part-time as a stripper to support her son. Trouble arises when her father-in-law attempts to prove that she is an unfit mother. 100m/C **VHS, Beta.** Lesley Ann Warren, Edward Herrmann, Vic Tayback, Sheree North; **D:** John Alonzo. *VES*

Portrait of a White Marriage 🎬🎬½ 1988 An extended made-for-cable comedy special revamping certain old "Mary Hartman, Mary Hartman" and "Fernwood 2-Night" conventions; a moronic talk show host moves his cheap show to his hometown of Hawkins Falls in order to boost the ratings. 81m/C **VHS, Beta.** Martin Mull, Mary Kay Place, Fred Willard, Michael McKean, Harry Shearer, Jack Riley, Conchata Ferrell; **D:** Harry Shearer. *USH*

Portrait of Grandpa Doc 🎬½ 1977 As a young artist prepares for his first one-man show, he struggles to complete a painting which he especially wants to have ready for the show—a portrait of his grandfather, who died seven years earlier. Well, okay. 28m/C **VHS, Beta.** Melvyn Douglas, Bruce Davison, Barbara Rush, Anne Seymour, Keith Blanchard. *BFA, ECU*

Portrait of Jennie 🎬🎬🎬½ *Jennie; Tidal Wave* 1948 In this haunting, romantic fable, a struggling artist is inspired by and smitten with a strange and beautiful girl who he also suspects may be the spirit of a dead woman. A fine cast works wonders with what could have been a forgettable story. The last reel was tinted green in the original release with the last scene shot in technicolor. Oscar-winning special effects. 86m/B **VHS, Beta, LV, Closed Caption.** Joseph Cotten, Jennifer Jones, Cecil Kellaway, Ethel Barrymore, David Wayne, Lillian Gish, Henry Hull, Florence Bates, Felix Bressart, Anne Francis; **D:** William Dieterle; **C:** Joseph August. Academy Awards '48: Best Special Effects; Venice Film Festival '49: Best Actor (Cotten); Nominations: Academy Awards '48: Best Black and White Cinematography. *FOX*

Portrait of Teresa 🎬🎬🎬 1979 Havana housewife has to balance motherhood, textile job, and cultural group activities without the cooperation of her husband. Vega skillfully portrays the lingering archaic attitudes and insulting assumptions that still confront post-revolution women. A fine eye for the revealing moments and movements of everyday life. In Spanish with English subtitles. 115m/C **VHS.** Daisy Granados, Aldolfo Llaurado, Alina Sanchez, Alberto Molina; **D:** Pastor Vega. *NYF, FCT*

Portraits of a Killer 🎬🎬 1995 Attorney Elaine Taylor (Grey) is getting all hot and bothered by her client—photographer George Kendell (Mandylor), who's suspected in the murders of five hookers. But the detective (Ironside) on the case thinks she's just asking for trouble. 93m/C **VHS, LV, Closed Caption.** Jennifer Grey, Costas Mandylor, Michael Ironside, Patricia Charbonneau, Kenneth Welsh, M. Emmet Walsh; **D:** Bill Corcoran. *LIV*

Posed for Murder 🎬🎬 1989 **(R)** A young centerfold is stalked by a psycho who wants her all for himself. 90m/C **VHS, Beta.** Charlotte J. Helmkamp, Carl Fury, Rick Gianisi, Michael Merrins; **D:** Brian Thomas Jones. *ACA*

The Poseidon Adventure 🎬🎬½ 1972 **(PG)** The cruise ship Poseidon is on its last voyage from New York to Athens on New Year's Eve when it is capsized by a tidal wave. The ten survivors struggle to escape the water-logged tomb. Oscar-winning special effects, such as Shelley Winters floating in a boiler room. Created an entirely new genre of film making—the big cast disaster flick. ♫ The Morning After. 117m/C **VHS, Beta, LV.** Gene Hackman, Ernest Borgnine, Shelley Winters, Red Buttons, Jack Albertson, Carol Lynley, Roddy McDowall; **D:** Ronald Neame; **W:** Wendell Mayes, Stirling Silliphant; **M:** John Williams. Academy Awards '72: Best Song ("The Morning After"), Best Visual Effects; Golden Globe Awards '73: Best Supporting Actress (Winters); Nominations: Academy Awards '72: Best Art Direction/Set Decoration, Best Cinematography, Best Costume Design, Best Film Editing, Best Sound, Best Supporting Actress (Winters), Original Dramatic/Comedy Score. *FOX*

Positive I.D. 🎬🎬 **1987 (R)** A troubled housewife learns that the man who raped her years before is getting released on parole. She devises a second persona for herself with which to entrap him and get her revenge. **96m/C VHS, Beta.** Stephanie Rascoe, John Davies, Steve Fromholz; **D:** Andy Anderson; **W:** Andy Anderson. *USH*

The Positively True Adventures of the Alleged Texas Cheerleader-Murdering Mom 🎬🎬🎬½ **1993 (R)** Satirical melodrama about Texas housewife Wanda Holloway (Hunter), accused of hiring a hitman to murder the mother of her daughter's chief cheerleading rival. She figures the girl will be so distraught that her own daughter can easily replace her. Ruthless and hilarious, this fact-based made-for-cable movie goes way over the top in satirizing suburban life-style excess and media overkill. Hunter, complete with whiney Texas twang, is perfect in her role as self-absorbed Wanda and Bridges is great as her loopy ex-brother-in-law and partner in planned homicide. A riot compared to the usual dramatic movies served up by the networks. **CW:** Language. **99m/C VHS.** Holly Hunter, Beau Bridges, Swoosie Kurtz, Greg Henry, Matt Frewer, Frankie Ingrassia, Elizabeth Ruscio, Megan Berwick; **D:** Michael Ritchie; **W:** Jane Anderson; **M:** Lucy Simon. National Academy of Cable Programming ACE Awards '93: Best Movie/Miniseries, Best Actress (Hunter). *HBO, FCT, BTV*

Posse 🎬🎬🎬 **1975 (PG)** There's a hidden agenda, fueled by political ambition, in a lawman's (Douglas) dauntless pursuit of an escaped bandit (Dern). An interesting contrast between the evil of corrupt politics and the honesty of traditional lawlessness. Well performed, well photographed, and almost insightful. **94m/C VHS, Beta, LV, Closed Caption.** Kirk Douglas, Bruce Dern, James Stacy, Bo Hopkins, Luke Askew, David Canary, Alfonso Arau, Kate Woodville, Mark Roberts; **D:** Kirk Douglas; **W:** William Roberts; **M:** Maurice Jarre. *PAR*

Posse 🎬🎬🎬 **1993 (R)** Big, brawny western shot with MTV in mind that tells the tale in part of how more than 8,000 black cowboys helped tame the American frontier. Or, as the advertising put it, "The untold story of the wild West." Or, spaghetti western meets blaxploitation meets the magnificent seven meets the L.A. riots, with characters actually saying, "No justice, no peace" and "Can't we all get along." However categorized, the intent is to show a side of Americana seldom seen, a goal realized. Strode, perhaps the greatest black Western star, appears at both the beginning and ending, while several other veteran black performers, including Russell, appear in cameos. Hunky Van Peebles is the leader of the usual misfits in the "Dirty Dozen" tradition, infantry deserters holding a load of gold. Between them and freedom is a gang of goons led by Zane. Lots of flash and dash, but lacking soul. **CW:** Language, strong violence, and strong sexuality. **113m/C VHS, LV, Closed Caption.** Mario Van Peebles, Stephen Baldwin, Charles Lane, Tiny Lister, Big Daddy Kane, Billy Zane, Blair Underwood, Tone Loc, Salli Richardson, Reginald Hudlin, Richard Edson, Reginald VelJohnson, Warrington Hudlin; **Cameos:** Melvin Van Peebles, Pam Grier, Isaac Hayes, Robert Hooks, Richard Jordan, Paul Bartel, Nipsey Russell, Woody Strode, Aaron Neville, Stephen J. Cannell; **D:** Mario Van Peebles; **W:** Sy Richardson, Dario Scardapane; **C:** Peter Menzies Jr.; **M:** Michel Colombier. *PGV, FCT*

Possessed 🎬🎬½ **1931** A poor factory girl becomes a wealthy Park Avenue sophisticate when she falls in love with a rich lawyer who wants to be governor. Not to be confused with Crawford's 1947 movie of the same name, but worth a look. Gable and Crawford make a great couple! **77m/B VHS, Beta.** Joan Crawford, Clark Gable, Wallace Ford, Richard "Skeets" Gallagher, John Miljan; **D:** Clarence Brown. *MGM*

The Possessed 🎬🎬🎬 **1947** Crawford is at her melodramatic best as a crazed gal who can't find happiness with either hunk Heflin or bland Massey. First film for Brooks. From the story "One Man's Secret" by Rita Weiman. **109m/B VHS, LV.** Joan Crawford, Van Heflin, Raymond Massey, Geraldine Brooks, Stanley Ridges, John Ridgely, Nana Bryant, Moroni Olsen; **D:** Curtis Bernhardt; **C:** Joseph Valentine. Nominations: Academy Awards '47: Best Actress (Crawford). *MGM*

The Possessed 🎬½ **1977 (PG-13)** Farentino is a priest who loses his faith, but regains it after an apparently fatal auto accident. Hackett is the headmistress of a private girls' school which is in need of an exorcist, since one of her student's appears to be possessed, and Farentino seems just the man for the job. Fairly tame, since originally made for TV. **75m/C VHS, Beta.** James Farentino, Joan Hackett, Diana Scarwid, Claudette Nevins, Eugene Roche, Ann Dusenberry, Dinah Manoff, P.J. Soles; **D:** Jerry Thorpe. *UNI*

Possessed by the Night 🎬🎬 **1993 (R)** Kinky sex games ensue between a married writer and a sexy other woman thanks to a mysterious fetish object. Unrated version also available. **84m/C VHS, LV, Closed Caption.** Ted Prior, Shannon Tweed, Sandahl Bergman, Chad McQueen, Henry Silva; **D:** Fred Olen Ray. *COL*

Possession 🎬 **1981 (R)** Returned from a long mission, a secret agent notices that his wife is acting very strangely. She's about to give birth to a manifestation of the evil within her! Gory, hysterical, over-intellectual and often unintelligible. Originally shown in a longer version in Europe. **97m/C VHS, Beta.** *FR GE* Isabelle Adjani, Sam Neill, Heinz Bennent, Margit Carstensen, Shaun Lawtor; **D:** Andrzej Zulawski. Cesar Awards '82: Best Actress (Adjani). *LIV, VES*

The Possession of Joel Delaney 🎬🎬½ **1972 (R)** Blend of occult horror and commentary on social mores works for the most part, but some viewers may be put off by the low production values and spottiness of the script. MacLaine is a wealthy divorcee who must deal with the mysterious transformations affecting her brother. Skeptical at first, she begins to suspect he is the victim of Caribbean voodoo. **105m/C VHS, Closed Caption.** Shirley MacLaine, Perry King, Michael Hordern, David Elliott, Robert Burr; **D:** Waris Hussein. *PAR*

Possession: Until Death Do You Part 🎬 **1990** When one man's attraction for a beautiful young woman becomes an obsession, a bizarre series of inexplicable events unravels a terrifying account of passion and revenge. **93m/C VHS.** Monica Marko, John R. Johnston, Sharlene Martin, Cat Williamson; **D:** Michael Mazo; **M:** Lloyd A. Simanol. *NO*

Postal Inspector 🎬🎬 **1936** An extraordinary tale of a postal inspector's life. Crime, romance, and natural disaster all overtake this civil servant. Catch the song "Let's Have Bluebirds On All Our Wallpaper." **58m/B VHS.** Carlos Cortez, Patricia Ellis, Michael Loring, Bela Lugosi, David Oliver, Wallis Clark; **D:** Otto Brower. *SNC, LSV*

Postcards from America 🎬🎬 **1995 (R)** Traces the non-artistic aspects of the life of writer/artist David Wojnarowicz, who died of AIDS. Neophyte McLean concentrates on troubled childhood with an abusive father and teen years spent as a street hustler years. Choppy narrative uses little of Wojnarowicz's dialogue, save the voice-over narration by the lead character. Based on two semi-autobiographical novels by the artist. **93m/C VHS.** James Lyons, Michael Tighe, Olmo Tighe, Michael Imperioli, Michael Ringer, Maggie Low; **D:** Steve McLean; **W:** Steve McLean; **C:** Ellen Kuras; **M:** Stephen Endelman. *NYR*

Postcards from the Edge 🎬🎬🎬½ **1990 (R)** Fisher adapted her best-selling novel, tamed and tempered, for the big screen with a tour-de-force of talent. Streep very fine as a delightfully harried actress struggling with her career, her drug dependence, and her competitive, overwhelming show-biz mother. Autobiographical script is bitingly clever and filled with refreshingly witty dialogue. Lots of cameos by Hollywood's hippest. **101m/C VHS, Beta, LV, 8mm, Closed Caption.** Meryl Streep, Shirley MacLaine, Dennis Quaid, Gene Hackman, Richard Dreyfuss, Rob Reiner, Mary Wickes, Conrad Bain, Annette Bening, Michael Ontkean, Dana Ivey; **Cameos:** Robin Bartlett, Annette Heald, Oliver Platt, CCH Pounder; **D:** Mike Nichols; **W:** Carrie Fisher; **C:** Michael Ballhaus. Nominations: Academy Awards '90: Best Actress (Streep), Best Song ("I'm Checkin' Out"). *COL, FCT*

The Postman 🎬🎬🎬½ *Il Postino* **1994 (PG)** Bittersweet, charming film about Mario (Troisi), a shy villager who winds up the personal postman of poet Pablo Neruda (Noiret), who is exiled from his beloved Chile in 1952, granted asylum by the Italian government, and who finds himself living in the tiny Italian community of Isla Negra. The tongue-tied Mario has fallen in love with barmaid Beatrice (Cucinotta) and asks the poet's help in wooing the dark-eyed beauty, striking up an unlikely friendship with the worldly Neruda. Based on the novel "Burning Patience" by Antonio Skarmeta. Italian with subtitles. Troisi, a beloved comic actor in his native Italy, was gravely ill, needing a heart transplant, during the making of the film (all-too apparent from his gaunt appearance) and died the day after filming was completed. **115m/C VHS.** *IT* Massimo Troisi, Philippe Noiret, Maria Grazia Cucinotta, Linda Moretti, Renato Scarpa, Anna Buonaiuto, Mariana Rigillo; **D:** Michael Radford; **W:** Massimo Troisi, Michael Radford, Furio Scarpelli, Anna Pavignano, Giacomo Scarpelli; **C:** Franco Di Giacomo; **M:** Luis Bacalov. Academy Awards '95: Original Dramatic/Comedy Score; British Academy Awards '95: Best Director (Radford), Best Foreign Film, Best Score; Broadcast Film Critics Association Awards '95: Best Foreign Language Film; Nominations: Academy Awards '95: Best Actor (Troisi), Best Adapted Screenplay, Best Director (Radford), Best Picture; British Academy Awards '95: Best Actor (Troisi), Best Adapted Screenplay; Cesar Awards '97: Best Foreign Film; Directors Guild of America Awards '95: Best Director (Radford); Screen Actors Guild Award '95: Best Actor (Troisi). *TOU*

The Postman Always Rings Twice 🎬🎬🎬½ **1946** Even without the brutal sexuality of the James M. Cain novel, Garfield and Turner sizzle as the lust-laden lovers in this lurid tale of fatal attraction. Garfield steals the show as the streetwise drifter who blows into town and lights a fire in Turner. As their affair steams up the two conspire to do away with her husband and circumstances begin to spin out of control. Tense and compelling. A classic. **113m/B VHS, Beta, LV, Closed Caption.** Lana Turner, John Garfield, Cecil Kellaway, Hume Cronyn, Leon Ames, Audrey Totter, Alan Reed; **D:** Tay Garnett; **M:** George Bassman. *MGM*

The Postman Always Rings Twice 🎬🎬 **1981 (R)** It must be true because he's ringing again in Mamet's version of James M. Cain's depression-era novel. This time Nicholson plays the drifter and Lange the amoral wife with an aged husband. Truer to the original story than the 1946 movie in its use of brutal sex scenes, it nevertheless lacks the power of the original. Nicholson works well in this time era and Lange adds depth and realism to the character of Cora. But in the end it remains dreary and easily forgettable. **123m/C VHS, Beta, LV.** Jack Nicholson, Jessica Lange, John Colicos, Anjelica Huston, Michael Lerner, John P. Ryan, Christopher Lloyd; **D:** Bob Rafelson; **W:** David Mamet; **C:** Sven Nykvist. *FOX, WAR*

Postmark for Danger 🎬🎬½ *Portrait of Alison* **1956** Detectives do their best to smash a diamond smuggling ring that operates between Britain and the U.S. Along the way a number of people are killed. **84m/B VHS, Beta.** *GB* Terry Moore, Robert Beatty, William Sylvester, Josephine Griffin, Geoffrey Keen, Henry Oscar; **D:** Guy Green. *SNC*

Postmark for Danger/Quicksand 🎬🎬 **1956** A "film noire" double feature. In "Postmark for Danger," a young actress returns from the dead to find a criminal, while in "Quicksand," a mechanic becomes indebted to the mob when he borrows extra money for a date. **155m/B VHS, Beta.** *GB* Terry Moore, Robert Beatty, Mickey Rooney, Jeanne Cagney, Peter Lorre; **D:** Guy Green. *SNC*

Pot O' Gold 🎬🎬 *The Golden Hour* 1941 Stewart plays a wealthy young man who signs on with a struggling band. He convinces his uncle, who has a radio program, to let the band perform during a radio giveaway show he has concocted. Slight comedy, Stewart notwithstanding. **87m/B VHS, Beta.** Paulette Goddard, James Stewart, Charles Winninger, Horace Heidt, Art Carney; **D:** George Marshall. *NOS, CCB, VYY*

Pot, Parents, and Police 🎬 1971 A 13-year-old boy goes crazy when his dog dies and soon gets in with a hippie crowd, drops acid, and gets in trouble with the cops. **m/C VHS.** Phillip Pine, Robert Mantell, Madelyn Keen; **D:** Phillip Pine; **W:** Phillip Pine. *SMW, MOV, TPV*

Pound Puppies and the Legend of Big Paw 1988 The Pound Puppies, known for breaking dogs out of pounds and delivering them to safe and secure homes, are featured in their first full-length musical (and merchandising effort). Fifties music. **76m/C VHS. D:** Pierre de Celles; **W:** Jim Carlson; **V:** Nancy Cartwright, George Rose, B.J. Ward, Ruth Buzzi, Brennan Howard. *FHE*

Pouvoir Intime 🎬🎬½ 1987 (PG-13) What happens when robbers of an armored car lock the guard in the vehicle, and he decides to fight back? This film offers one possible scenario. Available in dubbed or subtitled versions. **86m/C VHS. FR** Marie Tifo, Pierre Curzi, Yvan Ponton, Jaques Lussier; **D:** Yves Simoneau. *TPV*

P.O.W. Deathcamp 🎬🎬 1989 A combat unit is captured and tortured by the Vietcong in this typical Vietnam story. **95m/C VHS.** Charles Black, Bill Balbridge, Rey Malonzo; **D:** Jett C. Espiritu. *ATL*

The P.O.W. Escape 🎬½ *Behind Enemy Lines* 1986 (R) The adventures of a surly American commander captured as a POW during the final days of the Vietnam War. **90m/C VHS, Beta, LV.** David Carradine, Mako, Charles R. Floyd, Steve James; **D:** Gideon Amir; **W:** Malcolm Barbour, James Bruner, Jeremy Lipp, John Langley. *VTR*

Powaqqatsi: Life in Transformation 🎬🎬🎬½ 1988 (G) Director Reggio's follow-up to "Koyaanisqatsi" doesn't pack the wallop of its predecessor. Still, the cinematography is magnificent and the music of Philip Glass is exquisitely hypnotic as we are taken on a spellbinding video collage of various third world countries and see the price they've paid in the name of progress. Part 2 of a planned trilogy. **95m/C VHS, Beta. D:** Godfrey Reggio; **M:** Philip Glass. *CAN*

Powder 🎬🎬 1995 (PG-13) An electromagnetic albino with an I.Q. off the charts is discovered living in his grandparents' cellar and brought to live in a school for troubled teens. Despite harrassment from the crude locals, Powder (Flanery) manages to exude compassion and electricity all over the place with the help of sensitive school director Steenbergen and wacky science teacher Goldblum. Hyper-sentimentality, convoluted and contradictory writing, absurd messianic overtones, and a cop-out climax barely scratch the surface of film's problems. Revelations of Salva's criminal conviction for child molestation cast some scenes in a disturbing light and caused major headaches for Disney's publicity department. **CW:** Contains intense, sometimes frightening elements of theme and strong language. **111m/C VHS.** Sean Patrick Flanery, Mary Steenburgen, Lance Henriksen, Jeff Goldblum, Brandon Smith, Bradford Tatum, Susan Tyrrell, Missy Crider, Ray Wise, Esteban Louis Powell; **D:** Victor Salva; **W:** Victor Salva; **M:** Jerry Goldsmith. Nominations: MTV Movie Awards '96: Breakthrough Performance (Flanery). *TOU*

Powder Burn 🎬½ 1996 Detective Jack Becker seeks to protect a Beverly Hills client's young daughter when he uncovers unsavory goings-on at her home. And then discovers he's being set up to be the patsy for a murder. **92m/C VHS.** Jay Irwin, Elizabeth Barry. *LEO*

Powder Keg 🎬🎬 1970 Railroad company hires a rowdy team of investigators to retrieve a hijacked train. Action never quits. The idea for the television pilot "The Bearcats" came from this movie. **93m/C VHS, Beta.** Rod Taylor, Dennis Cole, Michael Ansara, Fernando Lamas, Tisha Sterling; **D:** Douglas Heyes. *SIM, WOV*

Powdersmoke Range 🎬½ 1935 Crooked frontier politician plots to steal valuable ranch property. The new owners, however, have other ideas. First in "The Three Mesquiteer" series. **71m/B VHS, Beta.** Harry Carey Sr., Hoot Gibson, Tom Tyler, Guinn "Big Boy" Williams, Bob Steele, Sam Hardy, Patricia "Boots" Mallory, Franklyn Farnum, William Desmond, William Farnum, Buzz Barton, Wally Wales, Art Mix, Buffalo Bill Jr., Buddy Roosevelt; **D:** Wallace Fox. *MED, RXM*

Power 🎬🎬½ 1928 Two dam-building construction workers vie with each other for the local girls. Silent. **60m/B VHS, Beta.** William Boyd, Alan Hale, Carole Lombard, Joan Bennett; **D:** Howard Higgin. *FCT, GPV, GVV*

Power 🎬🎬½ *Jew Suss* 1934 A Jewish ghetto inhabitant in 18th-century Wurtemburg works his way out of the gutter and into some authority by pleasing the whims of an evil duke. Based on the novel by Leon Fuechtwangler. **105m/B VHS. GB** Conrad Veidt, Benita Hume, Frank Vosper, Cedric Hardwicke, Gerald du Maurier, Pamela Ostrer, Joan Maude, Paul Graetz, Mary Clare, Percy Parsons, Dennis Hoey, Gibb McLaughlin, Francis L. Sullivan; **D:** Lothar Mendes. *DVT*

The Power 🎬½ 1980 (R) An ancient clay idol that was created by the Aztecs and possesses incredible destructive power is unleashed on modern man. **87m/C VHS.** Warren Lincoln, Susan Stokey, Lisa Erickson, Jeffrey Obrow; **D:** Stephen Carpenter; **W:** Stephen Carpenter, John Penney. *LIV, VES*

Power 🎬🎬½ 1986 (R) A study of corporate manipulations. Gere plays a ruthless media consultant working for politicians. Fine cast can't find the energy needed to make this great, but it's still interesting. Lumet did better with same material in "Network." **111m/C VHS, Beta, LV, Closed Caption.** Richard Gere, Julie Christie, E.G. Marshall, Gene Hackman, Beatrice Straight, Kate Capshaw, Denzel Washington, Fritz Weaver, Michael Learned, E. Katherine Kerr, Polly Rowles, Matt Salinger, J.T. Walsh; **D:** Sidney Lumet; **W:** David Himmelstein; **C:** Andrzej Bartkowiak; **M:** Cy Coleman. *ORI, WAR*

Power 98 🎬 1996 (R) L.A. shock-jock Karlin Pickett (Roberts) takes inexperienced Jon Price (Gedrick) as his protege, much to the dismay of girlfriend Sharon (Garth). Since Pickett will do anything to get higher ratings, she's right to worry, especially after a caller confesses to murder during Pickett's show. Roberts refrains from scenery-chewing but co-stars Gedrick and Garth give new meaning to bland. **CW:** Strong sexuality, language and some violence. **89m/C VHS.** Eric Roberts, Jason Gedrick, Jennie Garth, Larry Drake, Stephen Tobolowsky; **D:** Jaime Hellman; **W:** Jaime Hellman; **C:** Kent Wakeford; **M:** Jeff Beal. *WAR*

Power of Attorney 🎬🎬 1994 (R) Ambitious up-from-the-streets lawyer Paul Diehl (Koteas) decides to defend Mafia don Joseph Scassi (Aiello) against federal charges of murder and extortion, convincing himself that the mobster is telling the truth. But Scassi decides to make certain his lawyer will do his best by threatening Diehl's drug-dealing brother Frankie (Wilson). **CW:** Sexuality, language. **97m/C VHS.** Danny Aiello, Elias Koteas, Nina Siemaszko, Rae Dawn Chong, Roger Wilson; **D:** Howard Himelstein; **W:** George Erschbamer, Jeff Barmash; **M:** Hal Beckett. *TTC*

The Power of One 🎬🎬 1992 (PG-13) Good cast is generally wasted in liberal white look at apartheid. Set in South Africa during the 1940s, P.K. is a white orphan of British descent who is sent to a boarding school run by Afrikaaners (South Africans of German descent). Humiliated and bullied, particularly when England and Germany go to war, P.K. is befriended by a German

pianist and a black boxing coach who teach him to box and stand up for his rights. Preachy and filled with stereotypes. Based on the novel by Bryce Courtenay. **126m/C VHS, LV, Closed Caption.** Stephen Dorff, Armin Mueller-Stahl, Morgan Freeman, John Gielgud, Fay Masterson, Marius Weyers, Tracy Brooks Swope, John Osborne, Daniel Craig, Dominic Walker, Alois Mayo, Ian Roberts, Maria Marais; **D:** John G. Avildsen; **W:** Robert Mark Kamen. *WAR*

The Power of the Ninjitsu 🎬 1988 A young man inherits the leadership of a martial arts crime gang, the Scorpions, but the elder members muscle him out of his place. He returns for revenge and has the old ones running scared. Power to the Ninjitsu! **90m/C VHS, Beta.** Britton Lee, Adam Frank, Peter Ujaer; **D:** Joseph Lai. *IME*

Power, Passion & Murder 🎬🎬½ 1983 A young, glamorous movie star has an affair with a married man which begins the end of her career in 1930s Hollywood. **104m/C VHS, Beta, LV.** Michelle Pfeiffer, Darren McGavin, Stella Stevens; **D:** Paul Bogart, Leon Ichaso. *THV, IME, HHE*

Power Play 🎬½ *Operation Overthrow* 1981 Young army colonel from a small European country joins forces with rebels to overthrow the government. After the coup, the group discovers that in their midst is a traitor. So who is it? Suspense never builds adequately. **95m/C VHS, Beta.** *CA GB* Peter O'Toole, David Hemmings, Donald Pleasence, Barry Morse; **D:** Martyn Burke; **W:** Martyn Burke. *MED*

The Power Within 🎬🎬½ 1979 An electrified stuntman finds he can send electrical shocks from his hands and becomes the victim of a kidnapping plot. **90m/C VHS, Beta.** Eric (Hans Gudegast) Braeden, David Hedison, Susan Howard, Art Hindle; **D:** John Llewellyn Moxey. *PSM*

The Power Within 🎬🎬½ 1995 (PG-13) Evil Raymond Vonn has stolen an ancient ring of power but to acquire its complete strength he needs to find a second, matching ring. This is in the possession of teenaged Stan Dryer (Roberts), who must discover the ring's power if he expects to defeat Vonn. **CW:** Martial arts violence. **97m/C VHS, Closed Caption.** Ted Jan Roberts, Karen Valentine, Keith Coogan, John O'Hurley, Gary Morgan, Sean Fitzgerald; **D:** Art Camacho; **W:** Susan Bowen, Jacobsen Hart; **M:** Jim Halfpenny. *PMH*

Powwow Highway 🎬🎬🎬½ 1989 (R) Remarkably fine performances in this unusual, thought-provoking, poorly-titled foray into the plight of Native Americans. Farmer shines as the unassuming, amiable Cheyenne traveling to New Mexico in a beat-up Chevy with his Indian activist buddy, passionately portrayed by Martinez. On the journey they are constantly confronted with the tragedy of life on a reservation. A sobering look at government injustice and the lingering spirit of a people lost inside their homeland. **105m/C VHS, Beta.** Gary Farmer, A. Martinez, Amanda Wyss, Rene Handren-Seals, Graham Greene; **D:** Joanelle Romero, Jonathan Wacks; **W:** Janet Heaney, Jean Stawarz; **C:** Toyomichi Kurita; **M:** Barry Goldberg. Sundance Film Festival '89: Filmmakers Trophy. *FCT*

The Practice of Love 🎬🎬 1984 A woman journalist's investigation of a murder casts suspicion on her two male lovers. The film raises the question of whether love is even possible in a world dominated by men's struggles for power. In German with English subtitles. **90m/C VHS. GE D:** Valie Export. *FCT, MOV*

Prairie Badmen 🎬½ 1946 Outlaws are after a treasure map in the possession of the owner of a medicine show. It's up to our hero to stop them. One of the "Billy Carson" western series. **55m/B VHS, Beta.** Buster Crabbe. *VCN*

The Prairie King 🎬½ 1927 Will grants three people the same gold mine but stipulates only one may own it. Silent quandary. **58m/B VHS, Beta.** Hoot Gibson, Barbara Worth, Charles Sellon, Albert Priscoe. *GPV*

Prairie Moon ⅅ½ 1938 Autry becomes the guardian of three tough kids from Chicago after they inherit a ranch. The kids help Autry round up a gang of rustlers. 58m/B **VHS, Beta.** Gene Autry, Smiley Burnette. *CCB, VCN, DVT*

Prairie Pals ⅅ½ 1942 Deputies go undercover to rescue a kidnapped scientist. 60m/B **VHS, Beta.** William Boyd, Lee Powell, Art Davis, Charles "Blackie" King, John Merton, Kermit Maynard, Al "Fuzzy" St. John; **D:** Sam Newfield. *GPV, VCN*

The Prairie Pirate ⅅⅅ½ 1925 Carey is the western hero tracking down the dirty dogs who murdered his sister. Fast-paced. 59m/B **VHS.** Harry Carey Sr., Lloyd Whitlock, Jean Dumas, Trilby Clark; **D:** Edmund Mortimer. *GPV*

Prancer ⅅⅅ 1989 (G) An eight-year-old girl whose mother has recently died thinks an injured reindeer she has found belongs to Santa. She lovingly nurses him back to health. Harmless family entertainment. 102m/C **VHS, Beta, LV, 8mm, Closed Caption.** Sam Elliott, Rebecca Harrell, Cloris Leachman, Rutanya Alda, John Joseph Duda, Abe Vigoda, Michael Constantine, Ariana Richards, Mark Rolston; **D:** John Hancock; **M:** Maurice Jarre. *COL, ORI, FCT*

Pray for Death ⅅⅅ 1985 (R) When a mild-mannered Japanese family is victimized by a crime syndicate in L.A., a master ninja comes to the rescue. Higher quality production than most ninja adventures. 93m/C **VHS, Beta.** James Booth, Robert Ito, Sho Kosugi, Shane Kosugi, Kane Kosugi, Donna Kei Benz; **D:** Gordon Hessler; **W:** James Booth. *NO*

Pray for the Wildcats ⅅ½ 1974 Three advertising executives' promotional trip from (or to?) Hell. Anything to please a client. 96m/C **VHS, Beta.** Andy Griffith, William Shatner, Angie Dickinson, Janet Margolin, Marjoe Gortner, Lorraine Gary; **D:** Robert Lewis. *REP*

Pray TV ⅅⅅ KGOD 1980 (PG) A sly con man turns a failing television station into a profitable one when the station starts to broadcast around-the-clock religious programming. Made for television. 92m/C **VHS, Beta, LV.** Dabney Coleman, Archie Hahn, Joyce Jameson, Nancy Morgan, Roger E. Mosley, Marcia Wallace; **D:** Rick Friedberg; **W:** Nick Castle. *VES*

Pray TV ⅅⅅ 1982 A television movie expose of broadcast religion in which a young preacher chooses between orthodox religion and lots of money. Not as cutting an indictment as it could have been. 100m/C **VHS, Beta.** John Ritter, Ned Beatty, Madolyn Smith, Richard Kiley, Louise Latham, Jonathan Prince, Michael Currie, Lois Areno; **D:** Robert Markowitz.

A Prayer for Katarina Horovitzova ⅅⅅⅅ½ 1969 Stunning tale of a Polish singer who struggles to find the meaning and beauty of life while working to trade Nazi prisoners in U.S. jails for Jews hoping to emigrate. Based on the Arnost Lustig novel. Confiscated by the Czech Communist government and kept from the screen for 21 years. In Czechoslovakian with English subtitles. 60m/C **VHS.** CZ Jiri Adamira, Lenka Fiserova, Cestmir Randa. *FCT*

Prayer for the Dying ⅅⅅ½ 1987 (R) An IRA hitman longs to quit, but he has to complete one last assignment. The hit is witnessed by a priest who becomes an unwitting associate when the hitman hides out at the church. Fine performances from Bates and Rourke, though Hodges and Rourke were not satisfied with finished film. 104m/C **VHS, Beta, LV, Closed Caption.** Mickey Rourke, Alan Bates, Bob Hoskins, Sammi Davis, Liam Neeson, Alison Doody, Christopher Fulford; **D:** Mike Hodges; **W:** Edmund Ward, Martin Lynch; **M:** Bill Conti. *NO*

Prayer of the Rollerboys ⅅⅅ½ 1991 (R) Violent, futuristic, funky action as Haim infiltrates a criminal gang of syncopated roller-blading neo-nazi youth with plans for nationwide domination. Though routinely plotted and predictable, it's got great skating stunts and a wry vision of tomorrow's shattered USA—broke, drug-soaked, homeless, foreign-owned; even sharper when you realize this is a Japanese-American co-produc-

tion. *CW:* Language, violence and drug content, and sensuality. 94m/C **VHS, LV.** Corey Haim, Patricia Arquette, Christopher Collet, Julius W. Harris, J.C. Quinn, Jake Dengel, Devin Clark, Mark Pellegrino, Morgan Weisser; **D:** Rick King. *ACA*

Praying Mantis ⅅⅅ 1983 (PG-13) The professor's scheming nurse murdered his family and plans to marry him for his money. She enlists the aid of the professor's assistant in her evil plot. *CW:* Some violence and terror and scene of sensuality. 119m/C **VHS, Beta.** Jonathan Pryce, Cherie Lunghi, Ann Cropper, Carmen Du Sautoy, Pinkas Braun; **D:** Jack Gold; **M:** Carl Davis. *NO*

Praying Mantis ⅅⅅ½ 1993 (PG-13) Seymour stars as a femme fatale who likes to get married and then, in a rage against her own abusive childhood, kill her new husbands off. So far her total is five dead hubbies with number six (Bostwick) in her sights. Only this time, her almost-sister-in-law (Fisher) is very suspicious of the bride-to-be. Made for cable television. 90m/C **VHS, Beta, Closed Caption.** Jane Seymour, Barry Bostwick, Frances Fisher, Chad Allen; **D:** James Keach; **W:** Duane Poole, William F. Delligan; **M:** John Debney. *PAR*

Pre-Madonnas: Rebels Without a Clue ⅅⅅ½ 1995 (PG-13) Kim Sterling (Sturges) decides to rig the Beverly Hills Las Madonnas debutante ball to teach the snobs a lesson. 98m/C **VHS, LV, Closed Caption.** Shannon Sturges, Bobbie Bresee, Peter Anthony Elliott, Kenn Cooper; **D:** Lawrence Foldes. *AVE*

Preacherman ⅅ½ 1983 (R) Phony preacher travels through the South, fleecing gullible congregations (and providing for their sexual desires) wherever he goes. 90m/C **VHS, Beta.** Amos Huxley, Marian Brown, Adam Hesse, Ilene Kristen, W. Henry Smith; **D:** Albert T. Viola; **W:** Albert T. Viola, Harvey Flaxman; **M:** W. Henry Smith, Roland Pope. *TTV*

The Preacher's Wife ⅅⅅ 1996 (PG) Remake of 1947's "The Bishop's Wife" finds troubled Newark minister Henry Biggs (Vance) praying for heavenly intervention. His prayers are answered with angel Dudley (Washington)—who isn't so holy that he can't appreciate the minister's choir-leading wife Julia (Houston). While trying to save his cash-strapped church from a greedy developer (Hines), Rev. Biggs is so mired in material problems that he is unable to believe that Dudley is actually an angel. Washington is the dictionary definition of debonair as the angel with a touch of the devil in his eye. All problems are, of course, wrapped up neatly with a bow on top in the end. The real stars of this Christmas tale, however, are Houston's vocal cords. Fans of her singing will love this movie, while others may want to rent the original. 124m/C **VHS, LV, Closed Caption.** Denzel Washington, Whitney Houston, Courtney B. Vance, Gregory Hines, Jenifer Lewis, Loretta Devine, Lionel Richie, Paul Bates, Justin Pierre Edmund, Darvel Davis Jr., William James Stiggers Jr.; **D:** Penny Marshall; **W:** Nat Mauldin, Allan Scott; **C:** Miroslav Ondricek; **M:** Hans Zimmer. Nominations: Academy Awards '96: Best Original Score. *TOU*

Precious Find ⅅⅅ 1996 (R) In 2049 there's a new gold rush—this time into outer space. The moon's enclosed city is a staging area for mining operations throughout the solar system and draws the attention of three prospectors: Ben, who can "smell" gold, Crille (Hauer), who has a high-tech treasure map, and Sam (James), who owns a space hauler. They're all anxious to cash in when a newly discovered asteroid turns out to be a literal gold mine as is claim jumper Camilla (Chen). 90m/C **VHS, Closed Caption.** Rutger Hauer, Brion James, Harold Pruett, Joan Chen; **D:** Philippe Mora; **W:** Brian Rix, Jane Ubell, John Remark; **D:** Walter Bal; **M:** Roy Hay. *REP*

Predator ⅅⅅ½ 1987 (R) Schwarzenegger leads a team of CIA-hired mercenaries into the Central American jungles to rescue hostages. They encounter an alien force that begins to attack them one by one. Soon it's just Arnold and the Beast in this attention-grabbing, but some-

times silly, suspense film. 107m/C **VHS, Beta, LV, Closed Caption.** Arnold Schwarzenegger, Jesse Ventura, Sonny Landham, Bill Duke, Elpidia Carrillo, Richard Chaves, Shane Black, Kevin Peter Hall; **D:** John McTiernan; **W:** Jim Thomas, John Thomas; **M:** Alan Silvestri. *FXV*

Predator 2 ⅅⅅ 1990 (R) Tough cop takes time away from battling drug dealers to deal with malicious extraterrestrial who exterminated Arnold's band of commandos in "Predator." Miss-billed as sequel, its only resemblance to the original is that the predator has inexplicably returned (this time to the thick of L.A.). Gory action aplenty, little logic. Fine cast dominated by minority performers can't save this one. *CW:* Strong language, strong violence and drug content, and sensuality. 105m/C **VHS, Beta, LV, Closed Caption.** Danny Glover, Gary Busey, Ruben Blades, Maria Conchita Alonso, Bill Paxton, Robert Davi, Adam Baldwin, Kent McCord, Morton Downey Jr., Calvin Lockhart, Teri Weigel; **D:** Stephen Hopkins; **W:** John Thomas, Jim Thomas. *FXV, CCB*

Prefontaine ⅅⅅ½ 1996 (PG-13) Sports bio has appeal, thanks to lead actor Leto, in covering the brief career of early '70s runner Steve Prefontaine. Cocky and outspoken, the charismatic University of Oregon star soon owns every American record for distances between 2,000 and 10,000 meters. He's expected to gold at the 1972 Munich Olympics but falters, thanks in part to the tragedy surrounding the games. Returning home, the flamboyant Pre becomes a sports activist for athletes' rights before dying in a car crash in 1975 at the age of 24. Relatively straight narrative and little psychological insight make for few lasting impressions. *CW:* Brief strong language. 107m/C **VHS.** Jared Leto, R. Lee Ermey, Ed O'Neill, Amy Locane, Lindsay Crouse, Laurel Holloman, Breckin Meyer, Kurtwood Smith, Brian McGovern, Peter Anthony Jacobs; **D:** Steve James; **W:** Steve James, Eugene Corr; **C:** Peter Gilbert; **M:** Mason Daring. *NYR*

Prehistoric Bimbos in Armageddon City woof! 1993 Trianna and her tribe of Prehistoric Bimbos must prevent post-nuclear domination in Old Chicago City, the last remaining civilization after WWIII, by defeating the evil ruler Nemesis and his cyborgs. "Enough bimbos to fill two post-nuclear action comedies." So bad its gotta be good. 70m/C **VHS.** Robert Vollrath, Tonia Monahan, Deric Bernier. *TEM*

Prehistoric Women woof! *Slave Girls* 1950 A tribe of prehistoric women look for husbands the old-fashioned way—they drag them back to their caves from the jungle. So bad it's almost good. 74m/C **VHS, Beta.** Laurette Luez, Allan Nixon, Mara Lynn, Joan Shawlee, Judy Landon; **D:** Greg Tallas. *FHE, NOS, RHI*

Prehysteria ⅅⅅ½ 1993 (PG) Fantasy/adventure stars a widower, his 11-year-old son and teenage daughter, and what happens when some mysterious eggs from South America accidentally wind up at their farm. Imagine their surprise when the eggs hatch and out pop a brood of pygmy dinosaurs. The dinosaurs are cute (as is the family), the villain is dumb, and the violence minimal. 84m/C **VHS, Beta, LV, Closed Caption.** Brett Cullen, Austin O'Brien, Samantha Mills, Colleen Morris, Tony Longo, Stuart Fratkin, Stephen Lee; **D:** Albert Band, Charles Band; **W:** Greg Suddeth, Mark Goldstein. *PAR*

Prehysteria 2 ⅅⅅ½ 1994 (PG) While their adoptive family is on vacation the pygmy dinosaurs get loose and aid a lonely rich boy whose governess is plotting to send him to military boarding school. 81m/C **VHS, Beta, Closed Caption.** Kevin R. Connors, Jennifer Harte, Dean Scofield, Bettye Ackerman, Larry Hankin, Greg Lewis, Alan Palo, Michael Hagiwara, Owen Bush; **D:** Albert Band; **W:** Brent Friedman, Michael Paul Davis; **M:** Richard Band. *PAR*

Prehysteria 3 ⅅⅅ½ 1995 (PG) The mini-dinos take up miniature golf. Seems Thomas MacGregor's (Willard) putt-putt business is about to sink when his daughter Ella (Anderson) finds the pygmy dinosaurs and a promotional bonanza is born. But Thomas' evil brother Hal (Weitz) hatches a plot to take over the now-successful enterprize. 85m/C VHS, **Closed Caption.** Fred Willard, Bruce Weitz, Whitney Anderson, Pam Matteson; **D:** Julian Breen; **W:** Michael Paul Davis, Neil Ruttenberg. *PAR*

Prelude to a Kiss 🎞🎞 1992 (PG-13) Disappointing screen adaptation of Craig Lucas' hit play features Baldwin and Ryan as young lovers in this romantic fantasy. Ryan is Rita, a free-spirited bartender and Baldwin is Peter, a conservative writer, who decide to marry after a whirlwind courtship. At their wedding reception, Rita obligingly kisses one of their guests, an old man (Walker). Then, on their honeymoon, Peter begins to notice a number of changes to Rita's character and comes to realize this is truly not the girl he married. The delicate fantasy which worked on stage struggles to survive the "opening up" of the screen adaptation though Baldwin (who reprises his stage role) and Ryan are appealing. 106m/C **VHS, LV, Closed Caption.** Alec Baldwin, Meg Ryan, Sydney Walker, Ned Beatty, Patty Duke, Kathy Bates, Stanley Tucci; **D:** Norman Rene; **M:** Howard Shore. *FXV, PMS*

Prelude to War 1942 A compact look at the events of 1931-39; includes a series of contrasts between free societies and totalitarian governments. From the "Why We Fight" series. 53m/B **VHS, Beta. D:** Frank Capra. Academy Awards '42: Best Feature Documentary. *REP, MPI, HHT*

Premature Burial 🎞🎞 1962 A cataleptic Englishman's worst fears come true when he is buried alive. He escapes and seeks revenge on his doctor and his greedy wife. Based upon the story by Edgar Allan Poe. 81m/C **VHS, Beta, LV.** Ray Milland, Richard Ney, Hazel Court, Heather Angel; **D:** Roger Corman; **C:** Floyd Crosby. *LIV, VES, MLB*

Premonition 🎞½ 1971 (PG) Three drug-riddled '60s college students experience similar premonitions of death, and subsequently either die or become tormented. 83m/C **VHS, Beta.** Carl Crow, Tim Ray, Winfrey Hester Hill, Victor Izay; **D:** Alan Rudolph; **W:** Alan Rudolph; **C:** John Bailey. *NO*

The Premonition 🎞🎞½ 1975 (PG) Parapsychologist searching for a missing child is drawn into a frightening maze of dream therapy and communication with the dead. Well-done paranorm tale filmed in Mississippi. 94m/C **VHS, Beta.** Richard Lynch, Sharon Farrell, Jeff Corey, Ellen Barber, Edward Bell, Danielle Brisebois; **D:** Robert Allen Schnitzer; **W:** Anthony Mahon.

Prep School 🎞 1981 (PG-13) A very proper New England prep school is turned topsy-turvy by two rambunctious co-eds. They're determined to break every one of the school's cardinal rules. 97m/C **VHS, Beta.** Leslie Hope, Andrew Sabiston; **D:** Paul Almond. *PSM*

The Preppie Murder 🎞🎞½ 1989 Made for TV crime drama based on the killing of Jennifer Levin in New York City's Central Park in 1987, with Baldwin cast as prep school grad Robert Chambers. Amid sensational headlines, the story told of drugs, sexual games, and idle and disaffected youth. 100m/C **VHS, Closed Caption.** William Baldwin, Lara Flynn Boyle, Danny Aiello, Joanna Kerns, Dorothy Fielding, James Handy, William Devane; **D:** John Herzfeld. *TTC*

Preppies 🎞½ 1982 (R) Yet another teen sex comedy, but this time Ivy Leaguer Drake must pass his exams to receive his $50 million inheritance. Lots of skirt chasing as his conniving cousin leads him astray. 83m/C **VHS, Beta.** Dennis Drake, Peter Brady Reardon, Steven Holt, Nitchie Barrett, Cindy Manion, Katt Shea Ruben, Lynda Wiesmeier; **D:** Chuck Vincent. *LIV, VES*

Prescott Kid 🎞🎞 1936 Legendary western star McCoy plays a law-abiding cowboy mistaken for the new Marshall in the outlaw town of San Lorenzo, which has been targeted by a gang of cattle rustling killers. 58m/B **VHS.** Tim McCoy, Sheila Mannors, Alden Chase, Hooper Atchley, Walter Brennan; **D:** David Selman; **W:** Ford Beebe. *COL*

Presenting Lily Mars 🎞🎞 1943 A small-town girl comes to New York to make it on Broadway. Based on the Booth Tarkington novel. 🎵When I Look at You; Three O'Clock in the Morning; Kulebiaka; Is It Love? (Or The Gypsy in Me); Broadway Rhythm; Sweethearts of America; Where There's Music; Every Little Movement Has a Meaning All Its Own; Tom, Tom the Piper's Son. 105m/B **VHS, Beta.** Judy Garland, Van Heflin, Fay Bainter, Richard Carlson, Tommy Dorsey; **D:** Norman Taurog; **C:** Joseph Ruttenberg. *MGM*

The President's Analyst 🎞🎞🎞½ 1967 A superbly written, brilliantly executed satire from the mind of Theodore J. Flicker, who wrote as well as directed. Coburn steals the show as a psychiatrist who has the dubious honor of being appointed "secret shrink" to the President of the U.S. Pressures of the job steadily increase his paranoia until he suspects he is being pursued by agents and counter agents alike. Is he losing his sanity or...? Vastly entertaining. 104m/C **VHS.** James Coburn, Godfrey Cambridge, Severn Darden, Joan Delaney, Pat Harrington, Will Geer, William Daniels; **D:** Theodore J. Flicker; **W:** Theodore J. Flicker; **M:** Lalo Schifrin. *PAR*

President's Mistress 🎞½ 1978 A security agent searches for his sister's murderer, while trying to obscure the fact that she was having an affair with the President. 97m/C **VHS, Beta.** Beau Bridges, Susan Blanchard, Larry Hagman, Joel Fabiani, Karen Grassle; **D:** John Llewellyn Moxey. *NO*

The President's Mystery 🎞½ One For All 1936 A lawyer decides to turn his back on society by giving up his practice and his marriage. Eventually he meets and falls in love with another woman. The most interesting aspect of the film is that it is based on a story by Franklin D. Roosevelt, which was published in "Liberty" magazine. The story was supposedly better than its screen adaptation. 80m/B **VHS, Beta.** Henry Wilcoxon, Betty Furness, Sidney Blackmer, Evelyn Brent; **D:** Phil Rosen. *SNC*

The President's Plane is Missing 🎞🎞 1971 When Air Force One disappears, the less than trustworthy Vice President takes control. Could there be a dire plot in the making? Based on a novel by Rod Serling's brother Robert J. Serling. 100m/C **VHS.** Buddy Ebsen, Peter Graves, Arthur Kennedy, Rip Torn, Louise Sorel, Raymond Massey, James Wainwright, Mercedes McCambridge, Dabney Coleman, Joseph Campanella; **D:** Daryl Duke. *REP*

President's Target 🎞🎞 1993 An antidrug mission in South America is ambushed and CIA operative Peter Caine is the only survivor. Now he's out to see who planned the doublecross and how best to get his revenge. 82m/C **VHS, Closed Caption.** John Coleman, Martin Kove, Bo Hopkins, Brigitte Audrey; **D:** Yvan Chiffre. *HMD*

The Presidio 🎞🎞 1988 (R) An easy going police detective must investigate a murder on a military base where he and the base commander have sparred before. The commander becomes downright nasty when his daughter shows an interest in the detective. Good action scenes in San Francisco almost covers up script weaknesses, but not quite. 97m/C **VHS, Beta, LV, 8mm, Closed Caption.** Sean Connery, Mark Harmon, Meg Ryan, Jack Warden, Mark Blum, Jenette Goldstein; **D:** Peter Hyams; **W:** Larry Ferguson; **M:** Bruce Broughton. *PAR*

Pressure Point 🎞🎞 1962 Poitier stars as a prison psychiatrist treating an inmate who is a racist and a member of the Nazi party. Darin gives an excellent performance as the Nazi patient in this intelligent drama based on a true case. 87m/B **VHS, Closed Caption.** Sidney Poitier, Bobby Darin, Peter Falk, Carl Benton Reid, Barry Gordon, Howard Caine, Mary Munday; **D:** Hubert Cornfield; **M:** Ernest Gold. *MGM*

Presumed Guilty 🎞 1991 An innocent man is released from prison only to find he is once again a wanted man! So he gets his gal, who happens to be the sheriff's daughter, is beaten up and in the end winds up living happily ever after. 91m/C **VHS, LV.** Jack Vogel, Holly Floria, Sean Holton, Wayne Zanelotti, Bradley Rockwell, Sharon Young, Al Schuerman; **D:** Lawrence L. Simeone; **W:** Lawrence L. Simeone. *AIP*

Presumed Innocent 🎞🎞🎞 1990 (R) Assistant district attorney is the prime suspect when a former lover turns up brutally murdered. Coverups surround him, the political climate changes, and friends and enemies switch sides. Slow-paced courtroom drama with excellent performances for Ford, Julia, and Bedelia. Skillfully adapted from the best-seller by Chicago attorney Scott Turow.**CW:** Adult situations; language; nudity, and sexual situations. 127m/C **VHS, Beta, LV, 8mm, Closed Caption.** Harrison Ford, Brian Dennehy, Bonnie Bedelia, Greta Scacchi, Raul Julia, Paul Winfield, John Spencer, Joe Grifasi, Anna Maria Horsford, Sab Shimono, Christine Estabrook, Michael Tolan, Tom Mardirosian; **D:** Alan J. Pakula; **W:** Frank Pierson, Alan J. Pakula; **C:** Gordon Willis; **M:** John Williams. *WAR, FCT*

Pretty Baby 🎞🎞🎞 1978 (R) Shield's launching pad and Malle's first American film is a masterpiece of cinematography and style, nearly upstaged by the plodding storyline. Carradine manages to be effective but never succeeds at looking comfortable as the New Orleans photographer besotted with, and subsequently married to, an 11-year old prostitute (Shields). Low key, disturbingly intriguing story, beautifully photographed by Sven Nykist. 109m/C **VHS, Beta, LV.** Brooke Shields, Keith Carradine, Susan Sarandon, Barbara Steele, Diana Scarwid, Antonio Fargas; **D:** Louis Malle; **C:** Sven Nykist. National Board of Review Awards '78: 10 Best Films of the Year; Nominations: Academy Awards '78: Original Song Score and/or Adaptation. *PAR*

Pretty in Pink 🎞🎞½ 1986 (PG-13) More teen angst from the pen of Hughes. Poor girl falls for a rich guy. Their families fret, their friends are distressed, and fate conspires against them. If you can suspend your disbelief that a teenager with her own car and answering machine is financially inferior, then you may very well be able to accept the entire premise. Slickly done and adequately, if not enthusiastically, acted. In 1987, Hughes essentially remade this film and put himself in the director's chair with "Some Kind of Wonderful," the same story with the rich/pauper characters reversed by gender. 96m/C **VHS, Beta, LV, 8mm, Closed Caption.** Molly Ringwald, Andrew McCarthy, Jon Cryer, Harry Dean Stanton, James Spader, Annie Potts, Andrew Dice Clay, Margaret Colin, Alexa Kenin, Gina Gershon, Dweezil Zappa; **D:** Howard Deutch; **W:** John Hughes; **C:** Tak Fujimoto; **M:** Michael Gore. *PAR*

Pretty Poison 🎞🎞🎞 1968 You won't need an antidote for this one. Original, absorbing screenplay, top-notch acting, and on target direction combine to raise this low-budget, black comedy above the crowd. Perkins at his eerie best as a burned-out arsonist who cooks up a crazy scheme and enlists the aid of a hot-to-trot high schooler, only to discover too late she has some burning desires of her own. Weld is riveting as the turbulent teen. 89m/C **VHS.** Anthony Perkins, Tuesday Weld, Beverly Garland, John Randolph, Dick O'Neill; **D:** Noel Black. New York Film Critics Awards '68: Best Screenplay. *ING, MLB*

Pretty Smart woof! 1987 (R) Two diametrically opposed sisters at a European finishing school team up against a drug-dealing, voyeuristic teacher. Pretty lame. 84m/C **VHS, Beta.** Tricia Leigh Fisher, Patricia Arquette, Dennis Cole, Lisa Lorient; **D:** Dimitri Logothetis; **M:** Eddie Arkin. *VTR, NWV*

Pretty Woman 🎞🎞🎞 1990 (R) An old story takes a fresh approach as a successful but stuffy business man hires a fun-loving, energetic young hooker to be his companion for a week. The film caused some controversy over its upbeat portrayal of prostitution, but its popularity at the box office catapulted Roberts to stardom.*CW:* Adult situations; language. **117m/C VHS, Beta, LV, Closed Caption.** Richard Gere, Julia Roberts, Ralph Bellamy, Jason Alexander, Laura San Giacomo, Hector Elizondo, Alex Hyde-White, Elinor Donahue, Larry Miller, Jane Morris; *D:* Garry Marshall; *W:* J.F. Lawton; *M:* James Newton Howard. Golden Globe Awards '91: Best Actress—Musical/Comedy (Roberts); People's Choice Awards '91: Best Film, Best Film—Musical/Comedy; Nominations: Academy Awards '90: Best Actress (Roberts). *TOU*

Prettykill woof! **1987 (R)** A confusing storyline with numerous subplots involves detective with a paramour/prostitute (Hubley) attempting to stalk a mad killer while contending with her split personality. **95m/C VHS, Beta, LV.** David Birney, Susannah York, Season Hubley, Yaphet Kotto, Suzanne Snyder, Germane Honde; *D:* George Kaczender; *W:* Sandra K. Bailey; *C:* Joao Fernandes. *WAR*

The Prey ⅋ **1980 (R)** Poorly done horror show about a predator who is looking for a mate in the Colorado Rockies and kills five campers in the process. **80m/C VHS, Beta.** Debbie Thurseon, Steve Bond, Lori Lethin, Jackie Coogan; *D:* Edwin Scott Brown; *W:* Edwin Scott Brown, Summer Brown.

Prey for the Hunter ⅋ **1992 (R)** Four businessmen on a big-game hunt decide they're bored with their usual prey. They persuade a photojournalist to join them in a game with paint pellet guns except they decide to use real bullets and the journalist becomes their new target. An old and tired plot with nothing new to distinguish it.*CW:* Language. **90m/C VHS.** Todd Jensen, Andre Jacobs, Michelle Bestbier, Evan J. Klisser, David Butler, Allan Granville; *D:* John H. Parr. *COL*

Prey of the Chameleon ⅋ **1991 (R)** A female serial killer escapes from her asylum, ready to rip more men to shreds. However a tough lady cop has other ideas and goes all out to put an end to the madwoman's doings. Can she stop this fiend before the man she loves becomes the next victim?*CW:* Violence and strong sensuality. **91m/C VHS, Beta, Closed Caption.** Daphne Zuniga, James Wilder, Alexandra Paul, Don Harvey; *D:* Fleming Fuller. *PSM*

Priceless Beauty ⅋⅋½ **1990 (R)** Musician Lambert was only looking when he spotted the bottle which changed his life. Beautiful genie (Lane) lives inside, and is waiting just for him! Fun premise, good score, nice chemistry between the actors. **94m/C VHS, LV, Closed Caption.** Christopher Lambert, Diane Lane, Francesco Quinn, J.C. Quinn, Claudia Ohana, Monica Scattini, Joaquin D'Almeida; *D:* Charles Finch. *REP*

Prick Up Your Ears ⅋⅋⅋ **1987 (R)** Film biography of popular subversive playwright Joe Orton depicts his rise to fame and his eventual murder at the hands of his homosexual lover in 1967. Acclaimed for its realistic and sometimes humorous portrayal of the relationship between two men in a society that regarded homosexuality as a crime, the film unfortunately pays scant attention to Orton's theatrical success. The occasional sluggishness of the script detracts a bit from the three leads' outstanding performances. **110m/C VHS, Beta, LV.** *GB* Gary Oldman, Alfred Molina, Vanessa Redgrave, Julie Walters, Lindsay Duncan, Wallace Shawn, James Grant, Frances Barber, Janet Dale, David Atkins; *D:* Stephen Frears; *W:* Alan Bennett; *M:* Stanley Myers. New York Film Critics Awards '87: Best Supporting Actress (Redgrave).*NO*

Pride and Prejudice ⅋⅋⅋½ **1940** Classic adaptation of Austen's classic novel of manners as a young marriageable woman spurns the suitor her parents choose for her. Excellent cast vividly recreates 19th century England, aided by the inspired set design that won the film an Oscar. **114m/B VHS, Beta, LV.** Greer Garson, Laurence Olivier, Edmund Gwenn, Edna May Oliver, Mary Boland, Maureen O'Sullivan, Ann Rutherford, Frieda Inescort; *D:* Robert Z. Leonard; *C:* Karl Freund. Academy Awards '40: Best Interior Decoration. *MGM*

Pride and Prejudice ⅋⅋½ **1985** BBC mini-series adaptation of Jane Austen's novel about 19th century British mores and the attempts of five sisters to get married. **226m/C VHS, Beta, LV, Closed Caption.** *GB* Elizabeth Garvie, David Rintoul; *D:* Cyril Coke. *FOX, SIG, TVC*

Pride and Prejudice ⅋⅋⅋ **1995** Lavish TV adaptation of the Jane Austen novel finds bright Elizabeth Bennet (Ehle) unwillingly smitten by the wealthy, mysterious, and arrogant Mr. Darcy (Firth). Her family, filled with unmarried daughters, is rather silly and, of course, Elizabeth should be looking to get married (or at least not hinder her sisters' chances). Filmed on location in Derbyshire. On 6 cassettes. **300m/C VHS.** *GB* Jennifer Ehle, Colin Firth, Susannah Harker, Alison Steadman, Julia Sawalha, Benjamin Whitrow, Crispin Bonham Carter, Anna Chancellor, David Bamber, David Bark-Jones, Polly Maberly, Lucy Briers, Barbara Leigh-Hunt, Adrian Lukis; *D:* Simon Langton; *W:* Andrew Davies; *C:* John Kenway; *M:* Carl Davis. *AAE, PBS, VIF*

The Pride and the Passion ⅋⅋ **1957** A small group of resistance fighters battling for Spanish independence in 1810 must smuggle a 6-ton cannon across the rugged terrain of Spain. Miscasting, especially of Sinatra as a Spanish peasant, hurts this film. **132m/C VHS, Beta.** Cary Grant, Frank Sinatra, Sophia Loren; *D:* Stanley Kramer; *W:* Edward Anhalt. *MGM*

Pride of Jesse Hallum ⅋½ **1981** A made-for-television film about an illiterate man, played by country singer Cash, who learns, after much trial and tribulation, to read. **105m/C VHS, Beta, Closed Caption.** Johnny Cash, Brenda Vaccaro, Eli Wallach; *D:* Gary Nelson. *FOX*

Pride of St. Louis ⅋⅋ **1952** A romanticized and humorous portrait of famed baseball player-turned-commentator Dizzy Dean. **93m/B VHS, Beta.** Dan Dailey, Joanne Dru, Richard Crenna, Richard Haydn, Hugh Sanders; *D:* Harmon Jones; *W:* Herman J. Mankiewicz. Nominations: Academy Awards '52: Best Story. *FOX*

Pride of the Bowery ⅋ *Here We Go Again* **1941** The Dead End Kids versus a boxing hopeful in training camp. **60m/B VHS, Beta.** Leo Gorcey, David Gorcey, Huntz Hall, Gabriel Dell, Billy Halop, Bobby Jordan; *D:* Joseph H. Lewis. *NOS, CAB, DVT*

Pride of the Clan ⅋⅋½ **1918** Silent drama with Pickford and Moore as Scottish sweethearts battling a bit of adversity. When Pickford's father is lost at sea, she moves onto his fishing boat. She meets Moore, a fishing boy, and falls in love. But, he inherits a fortune and his parents forbid him to see Pickford. He goes off to live the good life but comes back to dramatically rescue Pickford. **80m/B VHS, Beta.** Mary Pickford, Matt Moore; *D:* Maurice Tourneur. *GPV*

The Pride of the Yankees ⅋⅋⅋½ **1942** Excellent portrait of baseball great Lou Gehrig. Beginning as he joined the Yankees in 1923, the film follows this great American through to his moving farewell speech as his career was tragically cut short by the disease that bears his name. Cooper is inspiring in the title role. **128m/B VHS, Beta, LV, Closed Caption.** Gary Cooper, Teresa Wright, Babe Ruth, Walter Brennan, Dan Duryea; *D:* Sam Wood. Academy Awards '42: Best Film Editing; Nominations: Academy Awards '42: Best Actor (Cooper), Best Actress (Wright), Best Black and White Cinematography, Best Interior Decoration, Best Picture, Best Screenplay, Best Sound, Best Story, Original Dramatic/Comedy Score. *FOX*

Priest ⅋⅋ **1994 (R)** Father Greg (an intense performance by Roache) is a young, idealistic priest who gets a rude awakening when he's assigned to a tough inner-city Liverpool parish. His superior, Father Matthew (Wilkinson), is a middle-aged rabble rouser who's openly having an affair with their black housekeeper Maria (Tyson). But Father Greg has a secret of his own—despite struggles with his sexuality he gets involved with Graham (Carlyle), a man he meets in the local gay bar. Greg's inner turmoil is heightened when

a young parishoner confesses that her father is sexually abusing her but, because of the seal of the confessional, the priest cannot report the problem. Director Bird walks a fine line between criticism and condemnation of Catholic doctrine. British TV feature provoked a storm of controversy in the U.S.; originally released at 105 minutes.*CW:* Mature themes involving sexuality. **98m/C VHS.** *GB* Linus Roache, Tom Wilkinson, Cathy Tyson, Robert Carlyle, James Ellis, Jim Bennett, Rio Fanning, Jimmy Coleman, Lesley Sharp, Robert Pugh, Christine Tremarco; *D:* Antonia Bird; *W:* Jimmy McGovern; *C:* Fred Tammes; *M:* Andy Roberts. Nominations: Australian Film Institute '95: Best Foreign Film. *TOU*

Priest of Love ⅋⅋ **1981 (R)** Arty account of the final years of the life of then-controversial author D.H. Lawrence, during which time he published "Lady Chatterly's Lover." A slow-moving but interesting portrayal of this complex man and his wife as they grapple with his imminent death from tuberculosis. **125m/C VHS, Beta.** *GB* Ian McKellen, Janet Suzman, John Gielgud, Helen Mirren, Jorge Rivero; *D:* Christopher Miles; *W:* Alan Plater; *C:* Ted Moore. *HBO*

Primal Fear ⅋⅋ **1996 (R)** Chicago defense attorney Martin Vail (Gere) is torn between the fight for justice and the lure of fame. He seems to have found the spotlight when a gentle altar boy (newcomer Norton is a standout) is accused of savagely murdering an archbishop. This leads to some courtroom fireworks due, in part, to the fact that the prosecutor (Linney) is Vail's former lover. Gere turns in a satisfying performance but, except when he's with his client, can't keep the script afloat. Lame plot revelations and an obvious "shocker" ending don't help matters. Feature directorial debut of Hoblit, Emmy winner for TV's "Hill Street Blues," "L.A. Law," and "NYPD Blue." Adapted from the book by William Diehl.*CW:* Profanity, violence, sexual situations and nudity. **130m/C VHS, Beta, Closed Caption.** Richard Gere, Laura Linney, Edward Norton, John Mahoney, Alfre Woodard, Frances McDormand, Terry O'Quinn, Andre Braugher, Steven Bauer, Joe Spano, Tony Plana, Stanley Anderson, Maura Tierney, Jon Seda; *D:* Gregory Hoblit; *W:* Steve Shagan, Ann Biderman; *C:* Michael Chapman; *M:* James Newton Howard. Golden Globe Awards '97: Best Supporting Actor (Norton); Los Angeles Film Critics Association Awards '96: Best Supporting Actor (Norton); National Board of Review Awards '96: Best Supporting Actor (Norton); Nominations: Academy Awards '96: Best Supporting Actor (Norton); British Academy Awards '96: Best Supporting Actor (Norton); MTV Movie Awards '97: Best Villain (Norton). *PAR*

Primal Impulse ⅋½ **1974** An astronaut, stranded on the moon because of a sinister experimental double-cross, unleashes a mental scream which possesses a young woman's mind back on earth. **90m/C VHS, Beta.** Klaus Kinski. *NO*

Primal Rage ⅋ **1990 (R)** A student is bitten by an experimental monkey, and begins to manifest his primal urges physically. Special effects by Carlo Rimbaldi.*CW:* Strong language and strong violence. **92m/C VHS, Beta.** Bo Svenson, Patrick Lowe, Mitch Watson, Cheryl Arutt, Sarah Buxton; *D:* Vittoria Rambaldi. *WAR*

Primal Scream ⅋½ *Hellfire* **1987 (R)** The Year is 1993. Earth's fuel sources are rapidly decaying and the top secret project to mine a revolutionary new energy source is underway—independently managed by a corrupt corporation. **95m/C VHS.** Kenneth John McGregor, Sharon Mason, Julie Miller, Jon Maurice, Mickey Shaughnessy; *D:* William Murray. *NO*

Primal Secrets ⅋⅋½ *Trick of the Eye* **1994** Artist Tilly, who specializes in illusionary trompe l'oeil paintings, is commissioned to paint a mural for reclusive socialite/widow Burstyn but there's a lot of mystery surrounding the job, especially when Burstyn begins to take an overly avid interest in Tilly's life. Based on the novel by Jane Stanton Hitchcock. Made for TV. **93m/C VHS.** Meg Tilly, Ellen Burstyn, Barnard Hughes; *D:* Ed Kaplan. *HMK*

Primary Motive 🎬🎬 **1992 (R)** Taut political thriller with Nelson as Andy Blumenthal, a press secretary who finds that an opposing candidate's campaign is covered by a web of lies. Blumenthal exposes the lies, but the candidate denies them and pulls further ahead in the polls. When the candidate's wife gives Blumenthal an extremely damaging piece of information, will the polls finally turn against him? *CW:* Language. **93m/C VHS, Beta, LV.** Judd Nelson, Richard Jordan, Sally Kirkland, Justine Bateman, John Savage; *D:* Daniel Adams; *W:* William Snowden III, Daniel Adams; *M:* John Cale. *FXV, VTR*

Primary Target 🎬 **1989 (R)** A mercenary reunites his 'Nam guerilla unit to rescue a diplomat's wife kidnapped by a Laotian jungle lord. **85m/C VHS, Beta.** John Calvin, Miki Kim, Joey Aresco, Chip Lucio, John Ericson, Colleen Casey; *D:* Clark Henderson. *MGM*

Prime Cut 🎬🎬½ **1972 (R)** Veritable orgy of drug trafficking, prostitution, extortion, loan sharking, fisticuffs and gangsters getting ground into mincemeat. Sleazy but well-made crime melodrama has its followers, but is best known as Spacek's film debut. **86m/C VHS, Beta, Closed Caption.** Lee Marvin, Gene Hackman, Sissy Spacek, Angel Tompkins, Gregory Walcott; *D:* Michael Ritchie; *W:* Robert Dillon; *M:* Lalo Schifrin. *FOX*

Prime Evil 🎬🎬 **1988 (R)** A brave and determined nun infiltrates a sect of devil worshiping monks in an attempt to end their demonic sacrifices. The question is, will this sister slide beneath Satan's cleaver? **87m/C VHS, LV.** William Beckwith, Christine Moore; *D:* Roberta Findlay. *VTR*

The Prime of Miss Jean Brodie 🎬🎬🎬 **1969 (PG)** Oscar-winning performance by Smith as a forward-thinking teacher in a Scottish Girls' school during the 1920s. She captivates her impressionable young students with her fascist ideals and free-thinking attitudes in this adaptation of the play taken from Muriel Spark's novel. **116m/C VHS, Closed Caption.** *GB* Maggie Smith, Pamela Franklin, Robert Stephens, Celia Johnson, Gordon Jackson, Jane Carr; *D:* Ronald Neame; *W:* Jay Presson Allen; *C:* Ted Moore. Academy Awards '69: Best Actress (Smith); British Academy Awards '69: Best Actress (Smith), Best Supporting Actress (Johnson); Golden Globe Awards '70: Best Song ("Jean"); National Board of Review Awards '69: Best Supporting Actress (Franklin); Nominations: Academy Awards '69: Best Song ("Jean"). *TCF, BTV*

Prime Risk 🎬½ **1984 (PG-13)** A young engineer who discovers an electronic method to break into automated teller machines finds that it leads to more trouble when she discovers that foreign agents are hot on her trail. **98m/C VHS, Beta.** Toni Hudson, Lee Montgomery, Sam Bottoms; *D:* W. Farkas; *C:* Mac Ahlberg. *LIV*

Prime Suspect 🎬🎬 **1982** An honest citizen becomes the prime suspect after the coverage of a murder by an over-ambitious television reporter. **100m/C VHS, Beta.** Mike Farrell, Teri Garr, Veronica Cartwright, Lane Smith, Barry Corbin, James Sloyan, Charles Aidman; *D:* Noel Black. *NO*

Prime Suspect 🎬🎬 **1988** A young man escapes from a mental institution to clear his name after being wrongfully accused of murdering his girlfriend. **89m/C VHS.** Susan Strasberg, Frank Stallone, Billy Drago, Doug McClure; *D:* Mark Rutland. *NO*

Prime Suspect 🎬🎬🎬 **1992** Mirren stars as Detective Chief Inspector Jane Tennison in this British television police procedural. When a male inspector dies of a heart attack while investigating a rape-murder, Tennison, the only woman of senior police status, wants the case. But she runs into multiple obstructions, not the least being the smug male police system. Then the case really takes a turn when it appears Tennison is searching for a serial killer. But Jane is no quitter and she has both the brains and the guts to back up her orders. Adapted from the book by Lynda La Plante, who also wrote the teleplay. **240m/C VHS.** *GB* Helen Mirren, Tom Bell, Zoe Wanamaker, John Bowe, Tom Wilkinson, Ralph Fiennes; *D:* Christopher Menaul; *W:* Lynda La Plante. *SIG, FXL*

Prime Suspect 2 🎬🎬🎬 **1993** DCI Jane Tennison (Mirren) returns in another British made for TV police drama. Jane has been off at a police seminar where she has a brief liaison with a black police detective, Robert Oswalde (Salmon). She is recalled to investigate the decomposed body of a young woman found in one of London's Afro-Caribbean neighborhoods and must deal with their resentment of the police. When detective Oswalde is reassigned to Jane's department, she begins having trouble separating her public and private feelings, while trying to obtain a confession from her most likely suspect. Based on a story by Lynda La Plante. **240m/C VHS.** *GB* Helen Mirren, Colin Salmon, Tom Watson, Ian Fitzgibbon, Philip Wright, Jack Ellis, Craig Fairbrass; *D:* John Strickland; *W:* Allan Cubitt. *SIG, FXL*

Prime Suspect 3 🎬🎬🎬 **1993** The BBC returns Jane Tennison to the beat (as does her portrayer Mirren) in another intriguing police drama. Tennison has transferred from homicide to the vice squad but still can't escape murder investigations—or male chauvinists. Oh yes, Tennison has a new team of macho colleagues to contend with and she's still getting heat from her bosses about her job. Still, this is one copper who lets nothing stand in her way. Made for British TV; on 3 cassettes. **205m/C VHS.** *GB* Helen Mirren, Tom Bell, Peter Capaldi, David Thewlis, Ciaran Hinds, Terrence Hardiman, Mark Strong, Karen Tomlin, Struan Rodger, Liza Sadovy, Andrew Woodall, Kelly Hunter; *D:* David Drury; *W:* Lynda La Plante; *M:* Stephen Warbeck. *TVC, PBS*

Prime Suspect 5: Errors of Judgment 🎬🎬🎬 **1996** Detective Superintendent Jane Tennison (Mirren) has been transferred to Manchester where her first project is to deal with the death of a drug dealer and the problems caused by an arrogant young gang leader, known as "The Street" (Mackintosh). But Jane's making more than her share of professional errors and, as usual, her personal life's a mess of her own making—this time by starting an affair with her married boss, Martin Ballinger (McArdle). **240m/C VHS.** *GB* Helen Mirren, John McArdle, Steven Mackintosh, David O'Hara, Julia Lane, Joseph Jones, Ray Emmet Brown, Marsha Thomson; *D:* Philip Davis; *W:* Guy Andrews; *C:* Barry McCann; *M:* Stephen Warbeck. *PBS, VIF*

Prime Suspect: Inner Circles 🎬🎬½ **1995** Jane Tennison (Mirren) finds herself caught up in suburban fraud and murder and once again on the outs with her bosses. Two drugged-up youths are accused of murdering a country club manager. The powers that be are satisfied but Tennison isn't—and rightly so because the murder is merely the tip of a very large and nasty iceberg. TV movie. **102m/C VHS.** *GB* Helen Mirren, Jill Baker, Anthony Bate, John Benfield, Richard Hawley, James Laurenson, Kelly Reilly, Sophie Stanton, Nick Patrick, Tom Russell; *D:* Sarah Pia Anderson; *W:* Eric Deacon; *C:* David Odd; *M:* Stephen Warbeck. *VTR*

Prime Suspect: The Lost Child 🎬🎬🎬 **1994** Jane Tennison (Mirren), promoted to Detective Chief Inspector, is caught up in a drama that strikes a little too close to her well-schooled emotions. A young mother's (Edney) 14-month-old daughter has been abducted—has the child been kidnapped for ransom or is this the work of a pedophile? Suspicion falls on released sex offender Chris (Glenister) but things aren't that simple—even as tensions rise among Tennison's own detectives. Made for TV. **102m/C VHS.** *GB* Helen Mirren, Beatie Edney, Robert Glenister, Lesley Sharp, Jack Ellis, Stuart Wilson, John Benfield, Richard Hawley; *D:* John Madden; *W:* Paul Billing; *M:* Stephen Warbeck. *VTR*

Prime Suspect: The Scent of Darkness 🎬🎬🎬 **1995** Could this be curtains for the career of the irascible Jane Tennison? Not bloody likely but she's got more than her fair share of trouble when a new wave of murders are in the same modus operandi as multiple killer George Marlow—whom Tennison put away four years before (in "Prime Suspect"). Now Marlow's conviction is called into question, as are Jane's methods, so she's placed on suspension. But that isn't going to stop her from getting to the truth. **102m/C VHS.** *GB* Helen Mirren, Tim Woodward, Stuart Wilson, Richard Hawley, John Benfield, Christopher Fulford, Joyce Redman, Stephen Boxer; *D:* Paul Marcus. *VTR*

Prime Target 🎬🎬 **1991 (R)** Small-town cop John Bloodstone (Heavener) is recruited by the FBI to transfer a mafia boss (Curtis) from a safehouse to the courthouse. He has to keep the former mobster alive long enough to testify against the "family." Their cross-country adventure is heightened by a murderous confrontation with evil forces that want them both dead. *CW:* Violence and sensuality. **87m/C VHS, Closed Caption.** David Heavener, Tony Curtis, Isaac Hayes, Jenilee Harrison, Robert Reed, Andrew (Andy) Robinson, Don Stroud; *D:* David Heavener; *W:* David Heavener; *M:* Chris Boardman. *HMD*

The Prime Time woof! **1960** Horrid film about a teen girl who leaves home and gets involved with a teen gang and a slimy detective. She's also kidnapped by a weird beatnik artist who forces her to pose nude. Black's film debut. Also known as "Hellkitten." **76m/B VHS.** JoAnn LeCompte, Frank Roche, James Brooks, Ray Gronwold, Maria Pavelle, Robert Major, Karen Black; *D:* Herschell Gordon Lewis. *SNC*

Prime Time 🎬½ **1980 (R)** Forgotten satirical comedy about what would happen if the censors took a day off from American television. **73m/C VHS, Beta.** Warren Oates, David Spielberg. *NO*

Prime Time Murder 🎬½ **1992 (R)** Freelance TV journalist hooks up with eccentric ex-cop to trail a psycho stalking street people. *CW:* Graphic stabbings. **95m/C VHS.** Tim Thomerson, Sally Kirkland, Anthony Finetti, Laura Reed; *D:* Gary Skeen Hall. *ACA*

The Primitive Lover 🎬🎬 **1916** Early silent comedy about young wife who decides she deserves more than her marriage is giving her. **67m/B VHS, Beta.** Constance Talmadge, Kenneth Harlan, Harrison Ford; *D:* Sidney Franklin. *GPV*

Primrose Path 🎬🎬½ **1940** Melodramatic soaper with comedic touches about a wrong-side-of-the-tracks girl falling for and then losing an ambitious young go-getter running a hamburger stand. **93m/B VHS, Beta.** Ginger Rogers, Joel McCrea, Marjorie Rambeau, Henry Travers, Miles Mander, Queenie Vasser, Joan Carroll, Vivienne Osborne; *D:* Gregory La Cava. Nominations: Academy Awards '40: Best Supporting Actress (Rambeau). *TTC*

Prince and the Great Race 🎬🎬 **1983** Three Australian children search the outback to find their kidnapped horse who is scheduled to run in the big New Year's Day Race. **91m/C VHS, Beta.** *AU* John Ewart, John Howard, Nicole Kidman. *LIV*

The Prince and the Pauper 🎬🎬🎬 **1937** Satisfying adaptation of the classic Mark Twain story of a young street urchin who trades places with the young king of England. Wonderful musical score by noted composer Korngold who provided the music for many of Flynn's adventure films. Also available in a computer-colorized version. **118m/B VHS, Beta, LV.** Errol Flynn, Claude Rains, Alan Hale, Billy Mauch, Montagu Love, Henry Stephenson, Barton MacLane; *D:* William Keighley; *M:* Erich Wolfgang Korngold. *FOX, MLB, CCB*

The Prince and the Pauper 🎬🎬 **1962** A prince and a poor teenage boy swap their clothes and identities, thus causing a lot of confusion for their families. Based on the story by Mark Twain. **93m/C VHS, Beta.** Guy Williams, Laurence Naismith, Donald Houston, Jane Asher, Walter Hudd. *DIS*

The Prince and the Pauper 🎬🎬½ *Crossed Swords* **1978 (PG)** Remake of the 1937 Errol Flynn film employing lavish sets and a tongue-in-cheek attitude among the all-star cast, who occasionally wander adrift when the director stops for tea. When an English prince and a pauper discover that they have identical appearances, they decide to trade places with each other. From Mark

Twain's classic. **113m/C VHS, Beta.** *GB* Oliver Reed, Raquel Welch, Mark Lester, Ernest Borgnine, George C. Scott, Rex Harrison, Charlton Heston, Sybil Danning; **D:** Richard Fleischer; **C:** Jack Cardiff; **M:** Maurice Jarre. *MED*

The Prince and the Showgirl 🐾🐾½

1957 An American showgirl in 1910 London is wooed by the Prince of Carpathia. Part of the "A Night at the Movies" series, this tape simulates a 1957 movie evening, with a Sylvester the Cat cartoon, "Greedy for Tweety," a newsreel and coming attractions for "Spirit of St. Louis." **127m/C VHS, Beta, LV.** Laurence Olivier, Marilyn Monroe, Sybil Thorndike, Jeremy Spenser, Richard Wattis; **D:** Laurence Olivier; **W:** Terence Rattigan; **C:** Jack Cardiff. *WAR*

Prince Brat and the Whipping Boy 🐾🐾🐾

The Whipping Boy **1995 (G)** Orphaned Jemmy (Munro) is living on the streets of the 18th-century German town of Brattenburg with his younger sister Annyrose (Salt). Neglected, spoiled Prince Horace (Knight) has been causing mischief in the castle but instead of being punished himself, the king's men catch Jemmy and use him as a punishment stand-in. Jemmy escapes the castle to get back to his sister and the Prince decides to go along for the adventure. Filmed on location in North Rhine-Westphalia and Burgundy, Germany. Adventurous TV movie with spunky leads; adapted from Sid Fleischman's novella. **96m/C VHS, LV, Closed Caption.** Truan Munro, Nic Knight, Karen Salt, George C. Scott, Kevin Conway, Vincent Schiavelli, Andrew Bicknell, Jean Anderson, Mathilda May; **D:** Syd Macartney; **W:** Max Brindle; **M:** Lee Holdridge. *COL*

Prince Jack 🐾🐾

1983 Profiles the turbulent political career of President John F. Kennedy. **100m/C VHS, Beta.** Lloyd Nolan, Dana Andrews, Robert Guillaume, Cameron Mitchell; **D:** Bert Lovitt; **M:** Elmer Bernstein. *LIV*

Prince of Bel Air 🐾½

1987 (R) A pool-cleaning playboy who makes a habit of one night stands meets a woman and starts falling in love with her. Originally a made-for-television movie. **95m/C VHS, Beta, LV.** Mark Harmon, Kirstie Alley, Robert Vaughn, Patrick Laborteaux, Deborah Harmon; **D:** Charles Braverman; **M:** Robert Folk. *ACA*

The Prince of Central Park 🐾🐾🐾

1977 Two young orphans are forced by circumstance to live in a tree in New York's Central Park until they are befriended by a lonely old woman. An above-average made for television adaptation of the novel by Evan H. Rhodes, the story was later used for a Broadway play. **76m/C VHS, Beta.** Ruth Gordon, T.J. Hargrave, Lisa Richards, Brooke Shields, Marc Vahanian, Dan Hedaya; **D:** Harvey Hart. *LIV*

Prince of Darkness 🐾½

1987 (R) University students release Satan, in the form of a mysterious chemical, unwittingly on the world. Written by Martin Quatermass (a pseudonym of Carpenter). Strong personnel does not save this dreary and slow-moving cliche plot. **102m/C VHS, Beta, LV.** Donald Pleasence, Lisa Blount, Victor Wong, Jameson Parker, Dennis Dun; **Cameos:** Alice Cooper; **D:** John Carpenter; **W:** John Carpenter; **M:** John Carpenter. *USH*

Prince of Pennsylvania 🐾½

1988 (R) A mild comedy about a spaced-out youth who kidnaps his own father in hopes of nabbing a family inheritance. **113m/C VHS, Beta, LV.** Keanu Reeves, Fred Ward, Amy Madigan, Bonnie Bedelia, Jeff Hayenga; **D:** Ron Nyswaner; **W:** Ron Nyswaner; **M:** Thomas Newman. *COL*

Prince of the City 🐾🐾🐾

1981 (R) Docudrama of a police officer who becomes an informant in an effort to end corruption within his narcotics unit, but finds he must pay a heavy price. Based on the true story told in Robert Daly's book, the powerful script carries the tension through what would otherwise be an overly long film. Excellent performances make this a riveting character study. **167m/C VHS, Beta, LV.** Treat Williams, Jerry Orbach, Lance Henriksen; **D:** Sidney Lumet; **W:** Jay Presson Allen, Sidney Lumet; **C:** Andrzej Bartkowiak. New York Film Critics Awards '81: Best Director (Lumet); Nomi-

nations: Academy Awards '81: Best Adapted Screenplay. *WAR*

The Prince of Thieves 🐾🐾

1948 Robin Hood helps Lady Marian extricate herself from a forced marriage in this adventure made with younger audiences in mind. **72m/C VHS.** Jon Hall, Patricia Morison, Adele Jergens, Alan Mowbray, Michael Duane; **D:** Howard Bretherton. *COL*

The Prince of Tides 🐾🐾🐾½

1991 (R) Conroy's sprawling southern-fried saga is neatly pared down to essentials in this tale of the dysfunctional Wingo family, whose dark tragedies are gradually revealed as twins Tom and Savannah come to grips with personal demons under the ministering aid of psychiatrist Streisand. Bravura performance by Nolte in what may be his best role to date; Streisand is restrained in both her performance and direction although a subplot dealing with her bad marriage and rebellious son is a predictable distraction. The South Carolina low country, and even New York City, never looked better. Conroy adapted the screenplay from his novel of the same name with Johnston's help. **CW:** Strong language and sex-related violence scene. **132m/C VHS, Beta, LV, 8mm, Closed Caption.** Nick Nolte, Barbra Streisand, Blythe Danner, Kate Nelligan, Jeroen Krabbe, Melinda Dillon, George Carlin, Jason Gould, Brad Sullivan; **D:** Barbra Streisand; **W:** Pat Conroy, Becky Johnston; **M:** James Newton Howard. Golden Globe Awards '92: Best Actor—Drama (Nolte); Los Angeles Film Critics Association Awards '91: Best Actor (Nolte); Nominations: Academy Awards '91: Best Actor (Nolte), Best Adapted Screenplay, Best Art Direction/Set Decoration, Best Cinematography, Best Picture, Best Supporting Actress (Nelligan), Best Original Score. *COL*

Prince Valiant 🐾🐾½

1954 When his royal dad is exiled by an evil tyrant, brave young Wagner brushes aside bangs and journeys to Camelot to seek the help of King Arthur. Based on Harold Foster's classic comic strip. **100m/C VHS, Beta.** James Mason, Janet Leigh, Robert Wagner, Debra Paget, Sterling Hayden, Victor McLaglen, Donald Crisp, Brian Aherne, Barry Jones, Mary Philips; **D:** Henry Hathaway; **W:** Dudley Nichols. *FXV, FCT*

Princes in Exile 🐾🐾½

1990 (PG-13) Young people struggle with their life-threatening illnesses at a special summer camp. They find that love and friendship hold the key to dreams about the future. Excellent cast of newcomers. Based on a novel of the same name by Mark Schreiber. **103m/C VHS, Beta, LV, Closed Caption.** Zachary Ansley, Nicholas Shields, Stacy Mistysyn, Alexander Chapman, Chuck Shamata; **D:** Giles Walker. *FRH, FCT*

Princess Academy 🐾

1987 (R) A self-respecting young debutante battles the ways of her elitist finishing school. **91m/C VHS, Beta.** *FR* Eva Gabor, Lu Leonard, Richard Paul, Lar Park Lincoln, Carole Davis; **D:** Bruce Block; **M:** Paul Antonelli, Roger Bellon. *LIV*

The Princess & the Call Girl 🐾🐾

1984 A call girl asks her look-alike roommate to take her place in Monaco for a lavishly erotic weekend. **90m/C VHS, Beta.** Carol Levy, Shannah Hall, Victor Bevine; **D:** Radley Metzger. *MON*

The Princess and the Goblin 🐾🐾½

1994 (G) Little kiddies may enjoy this animated adventure but it's a bland story with mediocre animation. Groups of ugly, underground-dwelling goblins like nothing better than to scare humans, especially castle-dwelling Princess Irene. Brave working-class Curdie helps to save the day. Based on a book by George MacDonald. **82m/C VHS.** *GB HU V:* Sally Ann Marsh, Peter Murray, Claire Bloom. *HMD*

The Princess and the Pea

1983 From "Faerie Tale Theatre" comes the story of a princess who tries to prove that she's a blueblood by feeling the bump of a tiny pea under the thickness of twenty mattresses. **60m/C VHS, Beta, LV, Closed Caption.** Liza Minnelli, Tom Conti, Tim Kazurinsky, Pat McCormick, Beatrice Straight; **D:** Tony Bill. *FOX, FCT*

The Princess and the Pirate 🐾🐾🐾

1944 Hope at his craziest as a vaudvillian who falls for a beautiful princess while on the run from buccaneers on the Spanish Main. Look for Crosby in a closing cameo performance. Available in digitally remastered stereo with original movie trailer. **94m/C VHS, Beta, LV.** Bob Hope, Walter Slezak, Walter Brennan, Virginia Mayo, Victor McLaglen; **Cameos:** Bing Crosby; **D:** David Butler; **C:** Victor Milner. Nominations: Academy Awards '44: Best Interior Decoration, Original Dramatic/Comedy Score. *HBO*

The Princess and the Swineherd 🐾½

1960 A German adaptation of the Brothers Grimm fairy tale about a young suitor who tries to please a materialistic princess. **82m/B VHS, Beta.** *GE VYY*

The Princess Bride 🐾🐾🐾½

1987 (PG) A modern update of the basic fairy tale crammed with all the cliches, this adventurously irreverent love story centers around a beautiful maiden and her young swain as they battle the evils of the mythical kingdom of Florin to be reunited with one another. Great dueling scenes and offbeat satire of the genre make this fun for adults as well as children. Based on William Goldman's cult novel. **98m/C VHS, Beta, LV, 8mm, Closed Caption.** Cary Elwes, Mandy Patinkin, Robin Wright, Wallace Shawn, Peter Falk, Andre the Giant, Chris Sarandon, Christopher Guest, Billy Crystal, Carol Kane, Fred Savage, Peter Cook, Mel Smith; **D:** Rob Reiner; **W:** William Goldman; **M:** Mark Knopfler. Nominations: Academy Awards '87: Best Song ("Storybook Love"). *COL, HMV*

Princess Caraboo 🐾🐾½

1994 (PG) Fluffy quasi-fairy tale (but based on a true story) finds an exotic beauty (Cates) appearing in an English village in 1817. She speaks a language no one understands and is taken under the wing of the local gentry, the Worralls, who believe she is an Asian princess washed ashore during a shipwreck. Meanwhile, the local jouralist (Rea) is suspicious but protective, an Oxford linguist (Lithgow) is determined to prove her a fraud, and she must put up with the Worrall family's pompous Greek butler (Cate's husband Kline at his showy best). **97m/C VHS, LV, Closed Caption.** Phoebe Cates, Stephen Rea, John Lithgow, Kevin Kline, Jim Broadbent, Wendy Hughes, Peter Eyre, Jacqueline Pearce, John Lynch, John Sessions, Arkie Whiteley, John Wells; **D:** Michael Austin; **W:** John Wells, Michael Austin; **M:** Richard Hartley. *COL*

Princess Cinderella 🐾🐾

193? A live-action dramatization of the famous fantasy. Dubbed in English. **75m/B VHS, Beta.** *SP* Silvana Jachino, Roberto Villa. *JEF*

The Princess Comes Across 🐾🐾🐾

1936 Deft comedy-mystery finds Brooklyn actress Lombard deciding to take an ocean voyage and pass herself off as a Swedish princess in the hopes of furthering her career. Bandleader MacMurray is smitten but an old beau recognizes the ruse and demands hush money. Then he turns up dead and the duo fall under the suspicious eye of a German passenger (Rumann) who happens to be a detective. From the novel by Louis Lucien Rogger. **77m/B VHS, Closed Caption.** Carole Lombard, Fred MacMurray, Alison Skipworth, Sig Rumann, Douglass Dumbrille, William Frawley, Porter Hall, George Barbier, Lumsden Hare, Mischa Auer, Tetsu Komai; **D:** William K. Howard; **W:** Walter DeLeon, Francis Martin, Frank Butler, Don Hartman; **C:** Ted Tetzlaff. *USH*

Princess Daisy 🐾

1983 Made for television movie about a beautiful model who claws her way to the top of her profession while trying to find true love and avoid the clutches of her rotten half-brother. Adapted from Judith Krantz's glitzy best-selling novel. **200m/C VHS, Beta.** Merete Van Kamp, Lindsay Wagner, Claudia Cardinale, Stacy Keach, Ringo Starr, Barbara Bach; **D:** Waris Hussein. *VTR, FOX, MOV*

Princess Tam Tam 🐾🐾🐾

1935 Pleasing French adaptation of Shaw's "Pygmalion," as a beautiful native African woman is "westernized" by a handsome writer and then introduced to high society as an exotic princess. A musical notable for its spectacular choreography and on-location

Tunisian scenery. Story by Pepito Abatino, who was then Baker's husband. In French with English subtitles. **77m/B VHS, Beta, LV.** *FR* Josephine Baker, Albert Prejean, Germaine Aussey, Viviane Romance; *D:* Edmond T. Greville. *MVD, TPV, KIV*

The Princess Who Never Laughed
1984 A stern king holds a laugh-off contest to make his morose daughter happy in this adaptation of the Brothers Grimm story from the "Faerie Tale Theatre" series. **60m/C VHS, Beta, Closed Caption.** Ellen Barkin, Howard Hesseman, Howie Mandel, Mary Woronov. *FOX, FCT*

Princess Yang Kwei Fei 🎬🎬🎬 *Yokihi; The Empress Yang Kwei Fei* **1955** Set in 8th-century China and based on the life of the last T'ang emperor and the beautiful servant girl he loves and makes his bride. She falls victim to court jealousy and he to his greedy family, though even death cannot end their love. Beautifully filmed and acted romantic tragedy. In Japanese with English subtitles. **91m/C VHS.** *JP* Machiko Kyo, Masayuki Mori, Sakae Ozawa, So Yamamura; *D:* Kenji Mizoguchi. *NYF*

The Principal 🎬🎬½ **1987 (R)** A tough, down-on-his-luck high school teacher is hired as the principal of a relentlessly violent, uncontrollable high school. Naturally he whips it into shape. **109m/C VHS, Beta, LV.** James Belushi, Louis Gossett Jr., Rae Dawn Chong, Michael Wright, Esai Morales, J.J. Cohen, Troy Winbush; *D:* Christopher Cain; *W:* Frank Deese; *C:* Arthur Albert; *M:* Jay Gruska. *COL*

Prison 🎬½ **1988 (R)** The zombified body of an unjustly executed inmate haunts Creedmore Prison, stalking the guard that killed him. His search is aided by the terrified inmates. **102m/C VHS, Beta, LV, Closed Caption.** Lane Smith, Chelsea Field, Viggo Mortensen, Lincoln Kilpatrick, Tom Everett, Tiny Lister; *D:* Renny Harlin; *W:* C. Courtney Joyner; *C:* Mac Ahlberg; *M:* Richard Band. *NWV*

Prison Break 🎬🎬 **1938** A convict plans a daring prison escape in order to clear his name for a murder he did not commit. **72m/B VHS, Beta.** Barton MacLane, Glenda Farrell, Ward Bond. *SNC, NOS, MRV*

Prison for Children 🎬🎬½ **1993** Sixteen year old Chris is orphaned and put into a boys home where a supervisor sees his potential and helps him achieve it. **96m/C VHS.** Raphael Sbarge, Kenny Ransom, Jonathan Chapin, Josh Brolin, James Callahan, Betty Thomas, John Ritter; *D:* Larry Peerce. *USH*

Prison Planet 🎬½ **1992 (R)** In the year 2200 Earth is under the dictatorship of an evil king, with only a band of intrepid rebels to oppose him. Blaine, one of the rebels, gets himself arrested and sent to prison in search of the true ruler, the king's brother. But the prison is protected by a brutal warlord and his equally sadistic warriors, whom Blaine must battle if he ever hopes to find truth and justice. **90m/C VHS.** James Phillips, Jack Willcox, Michael Foley, Deborah Thompson-Carlin; *D:* Armand Gazarian; *W:* Armand Gazarian. *COL*

Prison Shadows 🎬 **1936** Contrived programmer about a fighter (Nugent) who attempts to make a comeback after having served three years of a five-year sentence for killing an opponent in the boxing ring. He makes his comeback, but deals yet another mortal blow. Turns out that a gambling ring is behind the bizarre murders of the fighters and Nugent is their next victim. **67m/B VHS.** Eddie Nugent, Lucille Lund, Joan Barclay, Forrest Taylor, Syd Saylor, Monte Blue; *D:* Robert F. "Bob" Hill; *W:* Al Martin. *SNC*

Prison Stories: Women on the Inside 🎬🎬🎬 **1991** Three short dramatic stories depict the life of women inside prison walls. "New Chicks," directed by Spheeris, tells the story of two lifelong friends and partners in crime. "Esperanza," directed by Deitch, tells the story of a woman on the inside trying to prevent her family from following the same destructive path. Silver's "Parole Board" features Davidovich as a murderess up for parole but reluctant to leave the security of the prison. Blunt and gritty portrayal of

prison gangs, the lifestyle of female inmates, and their fears of returning to life on the outside. Originally produced for cable TV. **94m/C VHS, Beta, Closed Caption.** Rae Dawn Chong, Annabella Sciorra, Lolita Davidovich, Talisa Soto, Rachel Ticotin, Grace Zabriskie, Silvania Gallardo, Francesca Roberts; *D:* Donna Deitch, Penelope Spheeris, Joan Micklin Silver; *W:* Dick Beebe. *PSM*

Prison Train 🎬🎬½ *People's Enemy* **1938** Travelogue of a convicted murderer's cross-country journey to begin his prison sentence at Alcatraz. **84m/B VHS.** Fred Keating, Linda (Dorothy Comingore) Winters, Clarence Muse, Faith Bacon, Alexander Leftwich, Nestor Paiva, Franklyn Farnum; *D:* Gordon Wiles. *VYY, MOV*

The Prisoner 🎬🎬🎬 **1955** Gritty drama about a Cardinal imprisoned in a Soviet bloc country as his captors attempt to break his determination not to be used as a propaganda tool. Interactions between the prisoner and his interrogator are riveting. Based on the real-life experiences of Cardinal Mindszenty, a Hungarian activist during and after WWII. **91m/B VHS.** *GB* Alec Guinness, Jack Hawkins, Raymond Huntley, Wilfred Lawson; *D:* Peter Glenville. *COL*

The Prisoner: Arrival **1968** Introductory episode of the cult television series. McGoohan stars as a former British spy abducted and held captive in a mysterious village where everyone is assigned a number. As Number 6 he tries to figure out what's going on and how he can get out. Additional episodes available. **52m/C VHS, Beta, LV.** *GB* Patrick McGoohan, Virginia Maskell, Guy Doleman, Paul Eddington, George Baker, Angelo Muscat, Barbara Yu Ling, Stephanie Randall; *D:* Don Chaffey. *MPI, MOV, TVC*

Prisoner Cell Block H **1980** Popular Australian television soap opera set in Wentworth Detention Center, a women's prison. Primary characters include Franky, a violent lesbian biker in for armed robbery; Karen, who murdered her husband and is the object of Franky's affection; and naive Lynn, accused of kidnapping and attempted murder. Two episodes per cassette. **95m/C VHS.** *AU* Carol Burns, Kerry Armstrong, Patsy King, Gerard Maguire, Barry Quin, Mary Ward, Monica Maughan, Fiona Spence, Val Lehman, Pieta Tommano. *MPI, MOV*

Prisoner in the Middle 🎬🎬 **1974 (PG)** Janssen is the only man who can stop a nuclear warhead from falling into the hands of rival Middle East factions. Originally released as "Warhead." **87m/C VHS, Beta, LV, 8mm.** David Janssen, Karin Dor, Christopher Stone, Turia Tan, David Semadar, Art Metrano; *D:* John O'Conner. *ACA, MTX*

Prisoner of Honor 🎬🎬🎬 **1991 (PG)** A made-for-cable-TV retelling of notorious Dreyfus Affair, in which a Jewish officer in the 19th-century French military was accused of treason based on little evidence and lots of bigotry. George Piquart (Dreyfuss), the anti-semitic counterintelligence head, grows to realize Dreyfuss' innocence and fights zealously for the truth. Russell's flamboyant direction takes the heroic tale into the realm of the surreal; this may not be a thoroughly accurate account, but it's one of the more eye-filling. **90m/C VHS.** Richard Dreyfuss, Oliver Reed, Peter Firth, Jeremy Kemp, Brian Blessed, Peter Vaughan, Kenneth Colley, Lindsay Anderson; *D:* Ken Russell. *HBO*

Prisoner of Rio 🎬🎬 **1989** The made-for-cable-TV satire about scruple-less television evangelists and their nefarious schemes at acquiring their audience's money. **90m/C VHS, Beta, LV.** Steven Berkoff, Paul Freeman; *D:* Lech Majewski; *M:* Hans Zimmer. *MOV*

Prisoner of Second Avenue 🎬🎬½ **1974 (PG)** A New Yorker in his late forties faces the future, without a job or any confidence in his ability, with the help of his understanding wife. Based on the Broadway play by Neil Simon. **98m/C VHS, Beta, LV.** Jack Lemmon, Anne Bancroft, Gene Saks, Elizabeth Wilson, Sylvester Stallone, F. Murray Abraham; *D:* Melvin Frank; *W:* Neil Simon; *M:* Marvin Hamlisch. *WAR*

Prisoner of the Mountains 🎬🎬🎬 *Kavkazsky Plennik; Prisoner of the Caucasus* **1996 (R)** A modern-day, freely adapted version of Leo Tolstoy's novella "Prisoner of the Caucasus." Two Russian soldiers find themselves taken hostage in a remote Muslim village high in the Caucasus Mountains. Their captor, Abdul-Mourant (Sikharulidze), wishes to exchange them for his own captive son. Seasoned veteran Sacha (Menshikov) and young recruit Vanya (Bodrov Jr.) slowly form a bond, not only with each other but gradually with their captors. But there's a tragic inevitability to the entire untenable situation. Russian with subtitles. *CW:* Some violence and language. **98m/C VHS, LV.** *RU* Sergei Bodrov Jr., Oleg Menshikov, Djemal Sikharulidze, Susanna Mekhralieva, Alexander Burejev; *D:* Sergei Bodrov; *W:* Sergei Bodrov, Arif Aliev, Boris Giller; *C:* Pavel Lebeshev; *M:* Leonid Desyatnikov. Nominations: Academy Awards '96: Best Foreign Language Film; Golden Globe Awards '97: Best Foreign Film. *ORI*

Prisoner of Zenda 🎬🎬🎬½ **1937** An excellent cast and splendid photography make this the definitive film adaptation of Anthony Hope's swashbuckling novel. A British commoner is forced to pose as his cousin, the kidnapped king of a small European country, to save the throne. Complications of the romantic sort ensue when he falls in love with the queen. Excellent acting, robust sword play, and beautifully designed costumes make this an enjoyable spectacle. **101m/B VHS, Beta, LV.** Ronald Colman, Douglas Fairbanks Jr., Madeleine Carroll, David Niven, Raymond Massey, Mary Astor, Sir C. Aubrey Smith, Montagu Love, Byron Foulger, Alexander D'Arcy, Charles Halton; *D:* John Cromwell; *W:* Donald Ogden Stewart, John Balderston, Wells Root; *C:* James Wong Howe. Nominations: Academy Awards '37: Best Interior Decoration, Best Original Score. *MGM*

Prisoner of Zenda 🎬🎬½ **1952** Less-inspired remake of the 1937 version of Anthony Hope's novel, of a man resembling the monarch of a small country who is forced to pose as King during the coronation ceremony, becomes enamored with the queen, and finds himself embroiled in a murder plot. Worth watching for the luxurious costumes and lavish sets. Cast as a Cardinal here, Stone starred in the 1922 version. **101m/C VHS, Beta, LV.** Stewart Granger, Deborah Kerr, Louis Calhern, James Mason, Jane Greer, Lewis Stone; *D:* Richard Thorpe; *C:* Joseph Ruttenberg. *MGM*

Prisoner of Zenda 🎬🎬 **1979 (PG)** Flat comedic interpretation of Anthony Hope's swashbuckling tale of two identical men who switch places, only to find things complicated by a murder. Sellers stars in the double role of Prince Rudolph of Ruritania and Syd, the cockney cab driver who doubles for Rudolph when the Prince is imprisoned by his jealous brother Michael. **108m/C VHS, Beta.** Peter Sellers, Jeremy Kemp, Lynne Frederick, Lionel Jeffries, Elke Sommer; *D:* Richard Quine; *W:* Dick Clement, Ian LaFrenais; *M:* Henry Mancini. *USH*

Prisoners of Inertia 🎬🎬½ **1989 (R)** Two newlyweds travel to New York city and find themselves caught up in a whirlwind adventure in this well-acted but lazily scripted comedy drama. **92m/C VHS.** Amanda Plummer, Christopher Rich, John C. McGinley; *D:* Jay Noyles Seles. *BTV*

Prisoners of the Lost Universe 🎬½ **1984** Talk-show hostess and her buddy are transported to a hostile universe by a renegade scientist. The two terrified humans search desperately for the dimensional door that is their only hope of escape. Made for television. **94m/C VHS, Beta.** Richard Hatch, Kay Lenz, John Saxon; *D:* Terry Marcel. *NO*

Prisoners of the Sun 🎬🎬 *Blood Oath* **1991 (R)** Right after WWII an Australian captain fights to convict Japanese officers for atrocities against Allied POWs, but he's stonewalled by both the U.S. military and still-defiant enemy prisoners. This fiery drama from Down Under packs a punch as it questions whether wartime justice even exists; similar in that way to Brown's earlier "Breaker Morant." Takei (Sulu of the original "Star Trek") makes an imposing Japanese admi-

ral. **CW:** Momentary strong violence. **109m/C VHS, Beta.** *AU* Bryan Brown, George Takei, Terry O'Quinn, John Back, Toshi Shioya, Deborah Unger; **D:** Stephen Wallace. *PAR*

Private Affairs 🎬 1989 (R)
The mistress of a well-known surgeon becomes jealous when the doctor decides to have a fling with a gorgeous young swim instructor. Italian-made cheapie. **83m/C VHS, Beta.** *IT* Guiliana de Sio, Kate Capshaw, David Naughton, Luca Barbareschi, Michele Placido; **D:** Francesco Massaro. *ACA*

The Private Affairs of Bel Ami 🎬🎬🎬 1947
"This is the story of a scoundrel," proclaims the opening. Sanders is ideally cast as a suave cad who rises in 1880s Parisian society, largely through the strategic seduction of prominent women. Morablistically minded Old Hollywood toned down the talky adaptation of the Guy de Maupassant novel, but it's still drama of a high order. **112m/B VHS.** George Sanders, Angela Lansbury, Ann Dvorak, Frances Dee, John Carradine, Susan Douglas, Hugo Haas, Marie Wilson, Albert Basserman, Warren William, Katherine Emery, Richard Fraser; **D:** Albert Lewin; **W:** Albert Lewin. *REP, FCT*

Private Benjamin 🎬🎬½ 1980 (R)
Lighthearted fare about a pampered New York Jewish princess who impulsively enlists in the U.S. Army after her husband dies on their wedding night. Hawn, who also produced, creates a character loveable even at her worst moments and brings a surprising amount of depth to this otherwise frivolous look at high society attitudes. The basis for the television series. **110m/C VHS, Beta, LV.** Goldie Hawn, Eileen Brennan, Albert Brooks, Robert Webber, Armand Assante, Barbara Barrie, Mary Kay Place, Sally Kirkland, Craig T. Nelson, Harry Dean Stanton, Sam Wanamaker; **D:** Howard Zieff; **W:** Nancy Meyers, Charles Shyer, Harvey Miller; **M:** Bill Conti. Writers Guild of America '80: Best Original Screenplay; Nominations: Academy Awards '80: Best Actress (Hawn), Best Original Screenplay, Best Supporting Actress (Brennan). *WAR*

Private Buckaroo 🎬🎬 1942
War time entertainment in which Harry James and his orchestra get drafted. They decide to put on a show for the soldiers and get help from the Andrews Sisters. ♫ Don't Sit Under the Apple Tree with Anyone Else But Me; Three Little Sisters; Private Buckaroo; Johnny Get Your Gun Again; We've Got a Job to Do; You Made Me Love You; Six Jerks in a Jeep; That's the Moon My Son; I Love the South. **70m/B VHS, Beta.** The Andrews Sisters, Harry James, Joe E. Lewis, Dick Foran, Shemp Howard, Mary Wickes, Donald O'Connor; **D:** Eddie Cline. *NOS, HEG, CAB*

Private Contentment 🎬🎬 1983
This is a drama about a young soldier's experiences before he goes off to war in 1945. **90m/C VHS, Beta.** Trini Alvarado, Peter Gallagher, John McMartin, Kathryn Walker; **D:** Vivian Matalon. *FLI*

Private Duty Nurses 🎬½ 1971 (R)
Three nurses take on racism, war wounds, and a menage-a-trois (between one nurse, a doctor, and a drug addict). Second in Roger Corman's "nurse" quintet takes itself too seriously to be entertaining, but the gals make good use of those exciting new inventions, waterbeds. Preceded by "The Student Nurses" and followed by "Night Call Nurses," "The Young Nurses," and "Candy Stripe Nurses." Also on video as "Young L.A. Nurses 1." **80m/C VHS, Beta.** Kathy Cannon, Joyce Williams, Pegi Boucher, Joseph Kaufmann, Dennis Redfield, Herbert Jefferson Jr., Paul Hampton, Paul Gleason; **D:** George Armitage; **W:** George Armitage. *NLC*

The Private Eyes 🎬½ 1980 (PG)
Light and uneven comedic romp with Knotts and Conway as bungling sleuths engaged to investigate two deaths. They're led on a merry chase through secret passages to a meeting with a ghostly adversary. **91m/C VHS, Beta, LV.** Don Knotts, Tim Conway, Trisha Noble, Bernard Fox; **D:** Lang Elliott; **W:** Tim Conway, John Myhers. *VES*

The Private Files of J. Edgar Hoover 🎬🎬½ 1977 (PG)
Scandal-mongering "biography" of J. Edgar Hoover's private, sex-filled life. **112m/C VHS.** Broderick Crawford, Dan Dailey, Jose Ferrer, Rip Torn, Michael Parks, Raymond St. Jacques, Ronee Blakley; **D:** Larry Cohen; **W:** Larry Cohen. *HBO*

A Private Function 🎬🎬½ 1984 (PG)
A ribald gag-fest dealing with Palin as a Yorkshireman who steals and fattens a wily contraband pig against the backdrop of post-WWII rationing. The satire ranges from biting to downright nasty, but Palin is always likeable in the center of it all. **96m/C VHS, Beta.** *GB* Michael Palin, Maggie Smith, Denholm Elliott, Bill Paterson, Liz Smith; **D:** Malcolm Mowbray; **W:** Alan Bennett; **C:** Tony Pierce-Roberts; **M:** John Du Prez. British Academy Awards '84: Best Actress (Smith), Best Supporting Actor (Elliott), Best Supporting Actress (Smith). *PAR, TVC, FCT*

Private Hell 36 🎬🎬 1954
Two detectives become guilt-ridden after keeping part of some stolen money recovered after a robbery. Co-produced by Lupino. **81m/B VHS, Beta.** Ida Lupino, Howard Duff, Steve Cochran; **D:** Donald Siegel; **W:** Ida Lupino. *REP*

The Private History of a Campaign That Failed 🎬½ 1987
Adaptation of the Mark Twain story about a cowardly troop of Confederate soldiers. **89m/C VHS, Beta.** Pat Hingle, Edward Herrmann. *USH*

Private Investigations 🎬½ 1987 (R)
A made-for-video thriller about a nosey reporter who gets himself and his adult son in trouble while investigating drug-pushing cops. **91m/C VHS, Beta, Closed Caption.** Ray Sharkey, Clayton Rohner, Talia Balsam, Anthony Zerbe, Paul LeMat; **D:** Nigel Dick; **W:** John Dahl, David Warfield. *MGM, FOX*

Private Lessons 🎬🎬 1981 (R)
Teenage boy is left alone for the summer in the care of an alluring maid and a scheming chauffeur. **83m/C VHS, Beta, LV.** Eric Brown, Sylvia Kristel, Howard Hesseman; **D:** Alan Myerson; **C:** Jan De Bont. *USH*

Private Lessons 19??
A boy can't concentrate on his piano lessons when he gets a beautiful new teacher. You won't be able to concentrate on anything but comedy. **90m/C VHS, Beta.** Carroll Baker. *JEF*

Private Lessons, Another Story 🎬½ 1994 (R)
A New York photographer (Morgan) is sick of her philandering husband and decides to experience some sexual excitement of her own by heading off to Miami. All that tropical heat inspires passion with her Cuban chauffeur (Garaza). **CW:** Strong sexuality. **86m/C VHS, Closed Caption.** Mariana Morgan, Ray Garaza, Theresa Morris; **D:** Dominique Othenin-Girard; **W:** William Mernit. *PAR*

Private Life 🎬🎬½ Chastnaya Zhizn 1982
Suddenly with time on his hands, a Soviet official scrutinizes his relationships. After a number of revelations, he is forced to make new choices based on what he has learned. Oscar nominee in 1983. In Russian with English subtitles. **103m/C VHS.** *RU* Mikhail Ulyanov, Ita Sanvina, Irina Gubanova; **D:** Edgar Ryazanov; **W:** Andrew Davies. Nominations: Academy Awards '82: Best Foreign Language Film. *KIV, FCT*

Private Life of Don Juan 🎬🎬 Don Juan 1934
Appropriately slow-moving British costume drama set in 17th-century Spain finds an aging Don Juan struggling to maintain his usual antics in the pursuit of beautiful women. Furthermore, his reputation is being upstaged by a young imposter. Notable only as the last film appearance by Douglas Fairbanks Sr., and based on the play by Henri Bataille. **87m/B VHS, Beta.** *GB* Douglas Fairbanks Sr., Merle Oberon, Binnie Barnes, Melville Cooper, Joan Gardner, Benita Hume, Athene Seyler; **D:** Alexander Korda; **C:** Georges Perinal. *CNG, NOS, GPV*

The Private Life of Henry VIII 🎬🎬🎬🎬 1933
Lavish historical spectacle lustily portraying the life and lovers of notorious British Monarch, King Henry VIII. A tour de force for Laughton as the robust 16th-century king, with outstanding performances by the entire cast. **97m/**

B **VHS, Beta, LV.** *GB* Charles Laughton, Binnie Barnes, Elsa Lanchester, Robert Donat, Merle Oberon, Miles Mander, Wendy Barrie, John Loder, Lady Tree, Franklin Dyall, Claud Allister, William Austin, Gibb McLaughlin, Sam Livesey, Lawrence Hanray, Everley Gregg, Judy Kelly, John Turnbull, Frederick Culley, Hay Petrie, Wally Patch; **D:** Alexander Korda; **W:** Arthur Wimperis, Lajos Biro; **C:** Georges Perinal. Academy Awards '33: Best Actor (Laughton); Nominations: Academy Awards '33: Best Picture. *HBO, NOS, PSM*

The Private Life of Sherlock Holmes 🎬🎬🎬½ 1970 (PG-13)
A unique perspective on the life of the famous detective reveals a complex character. Beautifully photographed, with fine performances by the supporting cast, the film boasts a haunting musical score but received suprisingly little recognition despite Wilder's high caliber direction. **CW:** Brief, drug-related plot material. **125m/C VHS, LV.** *GB* Robert Stephens, Colin Blakely, Genevieve Page, Irene Handl, Stanley Holloway, Christopher Lee, Clive Revill, Catherine Lacey, Tamara Toumanova, Mollie Maureen, Michael Balfour; **D:** Billy Wilder; **W:** Billy Wilder, I.A.L. Diamond; **M:** Miklos Rozsa. *FOX*

Private Lives 🎬🎬🎬½ 1931
Stylish adaptation of Noel Coward play starring Shearer and Montgomery as a couple with a tempestuous relationship. Although once married, they have since divorced and married other mates. While honeymooning at the same french hotel (Quelle coincidence!), they have trouble showing affection to their new spouses and realize they still feel passionately about one another. Excellent acting combined with Coward's witty dialogue makes this film a treat. **92m/B VHS, LV, Closed Caption.** Norma Shearer, Robert Montgomery, Reginald Denny, Una Merkel, Jean Hersholt; **D:** Sidney Franklin. *MGM*

The Private Lives of Elizabeth & Essex 🎬🎬🎬 1939
Cast reads like a Who's Who in Hollywood in this lavishly costumed dramatization of the love affair between Queen Elizabeth I and the Second Earl of Essex. Forced to choose between her Kingdom and her lover, Davis' monarch is the epitome of a regal women. Fobray made her first film appearance as an adult in the adaptation of Maxwell Anderson's "Elizabeth the Queen." **106m/C VHS, Beta.** Bette Davis, Errol Flynn, Vincent Price, Nanette Fabray, Olivia de Havilland, Alan Hale, Donald Crisp, Leo G. Carroll; **D:** Michael Curtiz. Nominations: Academy Awards '39: Best Color Cinematography, Best Sound, Best Special Effects, Best Score. *FOX*

Private Manoeuvres woof! 1983
A comely Swiss military adviser gives her all to uplift the morale of the men at Camp Samantha. **79m/C VHS, Beta.** Zachi Noy, Yoseph Shiloah, Dvora Bekon. *MGM*

A Private Matter 🎬🎬🎬 1992 (PG-13)
Based on the true story of Sherri Finkbine (hostess of TV's "Romper Room") and the controversy surrounding her decision to terminate her pregnancy in 1962. Pregnant with her fifth child, she discovered her sleeping medication contained thalidomide, known to cause severe birth defects. Although technically illegal, her doctor agreed to quietly perform an abortion. Sherri warned a local newspaper reporter about the drug's dangers and her identity was mistakenly revealed. A storm of adverse publicity forced her to Sweden for the abortion. Great performances highlight this complex and traumatic issue. Made for cable television. **89m/C VHS, LV, Closed Caption.** Sissy Spacek, Aidan Quinn, Estelle Parsons, Sheila McCarthy, Leon Russom, William H. Macy; **D:** Joan Micklin Silver; **W:** William Nicholson. *HBO*

Private Obsession 🎬½ 1994 (R)
Model Emanuelle Griffith (Whirry) is missing—kidnapped by obsessed admirer Richard (Christian) who wants the beauty for himself alone. Emanuelle may be blonde but she's not dumb and she decides to turn the tables on her captor. **CW:** Strong sexuality and language. **93m/C VHS.** Shannon Whirry, Michael Christian, Bo Svenson, Rip Taylor; **D:** Lee Frost. *TRI*

Private Parts 🐾🐾 1972 (R) A bizarre first attempt at feature length for Bartel. Black comedy featuring a runaway, a voyeuristic photographer and a hotel full of strange people who participate in murder and a variety of freakish sexual acts. **87m/C VHS.** Ayn Ruymen, Lucille Benson, John Ventantonio, Laurie Main, Stanley Livingston, Charles Woolf; **D:** Paul Bartel. *FRG, MGM*

Private Parts 🐾🐾½ *Howard Stern's Private Parts* 1996 (R) Stern makes his movie debut as...himself! Self-effacing yet self-aggrandizing bio traces Stern's rise from gawky kid to gawky college student to awkward small-market DJ to New York madman to inauguration as self-proclaimed King of All Media. Funny, and at times, touching flick features good performances by the rookie actors in Stern's inner circle, as well as by the pros. Giamatti is exceptional as the young WNBC exec assigned to tame Howard. Script manages to show Stern's outrageousness and still make him likeable. While this is clearly a whitewash job, and under other circumstances Stern himself might make fun of its sentimentality, pic should please everyone but the most rabid Stern-hater.**CW:** Strong language, nudity, and crude sexual humor. **109m/C VHS, Beta, Closed Caption.** Howard Stern, Robin Quivers, Mary McCormack, Paul Giamatti, Fred Norris, Gary Dell'Abate, Bobby Borriello, Michael Maccarone, Matthew Friedman, Jackie Martling, Carol Alt, Richard Portnow, Kelly Bishop, Henry Goodman, Jonathan Hadary, Paul Hecht, Allison Janney, Michael Murphy, James Murtaugh, Reni Santoni, Lee Wilkof, Theresa Lynn, Amber Smith; **D:** Betty Thomas; **W:** Len Blum, Michael Kalesniko; **C:** Walt Lloyd; **M:** Van Dyke Parks. *PAR*

Private Passions 🐾 1985 A sultry woman gives her teenaged cousin a lesson in love during his European vacation. **86m/C VHS, Beta.** Sybil Danning. *PSM*

Private Resort 🐾🐾 1984 (R) Curious house detective and a bumbling thief interrupt the highjinks of two girl-crazy teens on a quest for fun at an expensive Miami hotel. Occasionally funny plodder. **82m/C VHS, Beta, LV.** Johnny Depp, Rob Morrow, Karyn O'Bryan, Emily Longstreth, Tony Azito, Hector Elizondo, Dody Goodman, Leslie Easterbrook, Andrew Dice Clay; **D:** George Bowers. *COL*

Private Road: No Trespassing 1987 (R) A stock car racer and a top engineer compete over a military project, cars and a rich heiress. **90m/C VHS, Beta.** George Kennedy, Greg Evigan, Mitzi Kapture; **D:** Raphael Nussbaum. *TWE*

Private School 🐾½ 1983 (R) Two high school girls from the exclusive Cherryvale Academy for Women compete for the affections of a young man from nearby Freemount Academy for Men, while Cherryvale's headmistress is trying to raise funds to build a new wing. Banal teen sexploitation comedy with better-than-average cast. **89m/C VHS, Beta, LV.** Phoebe Cates, Betsy Russell, Kathleen Wilhoite, Sylvia Kristel, Ray Walston, Matthew Modine, Michael Zorek, Fran Ryan, Jonathan Prince, Kari Lizer, Richard Stahl; **D:** Noel Black; **C:** Walter Lassally. *USH*

The Private Secretary 🐾½ 1935 Horton is a mild-mannered clergyman who finds out his identity has been usurped by a young man with a great many angry creditors. Horton has some amusing comic bits but the film, based on a popular Victorian farce "Der Bibliotheker" by Van Moser, did not translate well to the screen. **70m/B VHS.** GB Edward Everett Horton, Barry Mackay, Oscar Asche, Judy Gunn, Michael Shepley, Alastair Sim; **D:** Henry Edwards. *HCV*

Private War 🐾½ 1990 (R) Training for an elite force turns deadly when the commanding officer makes the rules. Now it's a private war between two brutal fighting machines. Adapted from a Jan Guillou story. **95m/C VHS.** Martin Hewitt, Joe Dallesandro, Kimberly Beck; **D:** Frank De Palma; **W:** Frank De Palma, Terry Borst. *REP*

The Private War of Major Benson 🐾🐾½ 1955 Tough Army officer Major Bernard Benson (Heston) has his work cut out for him when he's ordered to take over an ROTC program at a military academy. First he finds out the school's run by nuns and then he treats his young cadets as he would adult troops, which naturally makes him very unpopular. But he manages to unbend enough to try for a romance with the school's doctor (Adams). And of course the kids teach him how to become a human being. Remade in 1995 as "Major Payne." **104m/C VHS, Closed Caption.** Charlton Heston, Julie Adams, Milburn Stone, Nana Bryant, William Demarest, Tim Considine, Sal Mineo; **D:** Jerry Hopper; **W:** William Roberts, Richard Alan Simmons; **C:** Harold Lipstein. Nominations: Academy Awards '55: Best Story. *USH*

Private Wars 🐾🐾 1993 (R) A law-abiding community falls victim to gangland violence until the inhabitants hire a down-and-out private eye (Railsback) to show them how to fight back. He finds out that a greedy land developer (Whitman) has bribed the Chief of Police (Champion) to let his goons do anything to get the people out so he can redevelop the land. **94m/C VHS, LV, Closed Caption.** Steve Railsback, Michael Champion, Stuart Whitman, Holly Floria, Dan Tullis Jr., Michael Delano, James Lew, Brian Patrick Clark; **D:** John Weidner; **W:** Ken Lamplugh; John Weidner. *PMH, IME*

Privates on Parade 🐾🐾½ 1984 (R) Film centering around the comic antics of an Army song-and-dance unit entertaining the troops in the Malayan jungle during the late '40s. Occasionally-inspired horseplay based on Peter Nichols play. **107m/C VHS, Beta.** GB John Cleese, Denis Quilley, Simon Jones, Joe Melia, Nicola Pagett, Julian Sands; **D:** Michael Blakemore. *PAR, TVC*

Prix de Beaute 🐾½ *Miss Europe* 1930 A woman's boyfriend does not know that she has won a beauty contest. Brooks' last starring role and the only film she did in France. In French with English subtitles. **93m/B VHS, Beta.** FR Louise Brooks, Jean Bradin, George Charlia, Gaston Jacquet; **D:** Augusto Genina. *INT*

The Prize 🐾🐾🐾 1963 Gripping spy story laced with laughs based on a novel by Irving Wallace (adapted by Lehman). In Stockholm, writer accepts the Nobel prize for dubious reasons and then finds himself in the midst of political intrigue. Newman and Sommer turn in great performances in this action drama. **136m/C VHS.** Paul Newman, Edward G. Robinson, Elke Sommer, Leo G. Carroll, Diane Baker, Micheline Presle, Gerard Oury, Sergio Fantoni; **D:** Mark Robson; **W:** Ernest Lehman; **C:** William H. Daniels; **M:** Jerry Goldsmith. *MGM, REP, MLB*

Prize Fighter 🐾🐾 1979 (PG) Comedy team of Knotts and Conway take on Depression-era boxing. Fight manager Knotts and his pugilistic protege Conway unknowingly get involved with a powerful gangster, who convinces them to fight in a fixed championship match. Most enjoyable if intelligence is suspended at onset. **99m/C VHS, Beta.** Tim Conway, Don Knotts; **D:** Michael Preece; **W:** Tim Conway. *MED*

Prize of Peril 🐾🐾 1984 A French television game show rewards it winners with wealth and its losers with execution. Not always the best policy to learn what's behind Door #1. **95m/C VHS, Beta.** FR Michel Piccoli, Marie-France Pisier; **D:** Yves Boisset. *LIV*

The Prize Pulitzer 🐾🐾 1989 Watered-down, made-for-television account of the scandalous divorce between publishing heir Herbert "Pete" Pulitzer and his young wife Roxanne. Based on the book "The Prize Pulitzer" by Roxanne Pulitzer. Also known as "Roxanne: The Prize Pulitzer." **95m/C VHS, Beta.** Perry King, Chynna Phillips, Courteney Cox, Betsy Russell, Sondra Blake, Caitlin Brown; **D:** Richard A. Colla. *CAF*

The Prizefighter and the Lady 🐾🐾🐾 *Every Woman's Man* 1933 In his first film role boxer Baer (who won the heavyweight boxing crown in 1934) is a natural as a fighter who falls for a beautiful nightclub singer (Loy). Baer and Loy get, but don't stay, together but she does turn out to be his lucky charm in the big fight finale. Fellow professional boxer Carnera, Baer's opponent in the climatic fight scene, refused to lose as the script indicated and the film ending was eventually rewritten. The likeable Baer later earned his living as an actor. **102m/B LV.** Max Baer Sr., Myrna Loy, Otto Kruger, Primo Carnera, Walter Huston, Vince Barnett, Jack Dempsey; **D:** Woodbridge S. Van Dyke. Nominations: Academy Awards '33: Best Story. *MGM*

Prizzi's Honor 🐾🐾🐾 1985 (R) Highly stylized, sometimes leaden black comedy about an aging and none-to-bright hit man from a New York mob family who breaks with family loyalties when he falls for an upwardly mobile tax consultant who's also a hired killer. Skirting caricature in every frame, Nicholson is excellent in his portrayal of the thick-skulled mobster, as are Anjelica Huston as the hot-to-trot Mafia daughter and Hickey as the Don. Adapted by Richard Condon and Janet Roach from Condon's novel. **130m/C VHS, Beta, LV, Closed Caption.** Jack Nicholson, Kathleen Turner, Robert Loggia, John Randolph, Anjelica Huston, Lawrence Tierney, William Hickey, Lee Richardson, Michael Lombard, Joseph Ruskin, CCH Pounder; **D:** John Huston; **W:** Richard Condon, Janet Roach; **C:** Andrzej Bartkowiak; **M:** Alex North. Academy Awards '85: Best Supporting Actress (Huston); British Academy Awards '85: Best Adapted Screenplay; Golden Globe Awards '86: Best Actor—Musical/Comedy (Nicholson), Best Actress—Musical/Comedy (Turner), Best Director (Huston), Best Film—Musical/Comedy; Los Angeles Film Critics Association Awards '85: Best Supporting Actress (Huston); New York Film Critics Awards '85: Best Actor (Nicholson), Best Director (Huston), Best Film, Best Supporting Actress (Huston); National Society of Film Critics Awards '85: Best Actor (Nicholson), Best Director (Huston), Best Supporting Actress (Huston); Writers Guild of America '85: Best Adapted Screenplay; Nominations: Academy Awards '85: Best Actor (Nicholson), Best Adapted Screenplay, Best Costume Design, Best Director (Huston), Best Film Editing, Best Picture, Best Supporting Actor (Hickey). *PAR, VES, BTV*

Probable Cause 🐾🐾 1995 (R) A knife-wielding serial killer specializes in murdering cops and the clues seem to point to a troubled veteran cop (Ironside), newly-paired with a beautiful detective (Vernon). Some unexpected twists and a surprise ending.**CW:** Violence; a rape scene; language; some nudity. **90m/C VHS, Closed Caption.** Michael Ironside, Kate Vernon, Kirk Baltz, Craig T. Nelson, M. Emmet Walsh; **D:** Paul Ziller; **W:** Hal Salwen; **C:** Danny Nowak. *LIV*

Probation 🐾🐾 *Second Chances* 1932 A dashing young man in trouble with the law receives an unusual sentence; he must become a chauffeur for a spoiled society girl. Grable's first film role is a small one. **60m/B VHS, Beta.** Sally Blane, J. Farrell MacDonald, Eddie Phillips, Clara Kimball Young, Betty Grable; **D:** Richard Thorpe. *NOS, SNC*

Probe 🐾🐾½ 1972 A detective uses computer-age technology to apprehend criminals. Pilot for the television series "Search." **95m/C VHS.** Hugh O'Brian, Elke Sommer, John Gielgud, Burgess Meredith, Angel Tompkins, Lilia Skala, Kent Smith, Alfred Ryder, Jaclyn Smith; **D:** Russ Mayberry; **W:** Leslie Stevens. *UNI*

Problem Child 🐾½ 1990 (PG) Ritter decides to adopt Oliver out of the goodness of his heart, but it seems young Oliver's already got a father figure named Beelzebub. Potential for laughs is unmet. **81m/C VHS, LV, Closed Caption.** John Ritter, Michael Oliver, Jack Warden, Amy Yasbeck, Gilbert Gottfried, Michael Richards, Peter Jurasik; **D:** Dennis Dugan; **W:** Scott Alexander, Larry Karaszewski; **C:** Peter Collister; **M:** Miles Goodman. *USH*

Problem Child 2 🐾 1991 (PG-13) Ritter and his nasty adopted son are back, but this time there's an equally malevolent little girl. They team up to prevent Ritter's upcoming marriage to a socialite. Low slapstick junk. **91m/C VHS, Beta, LV,**

Closed Caption. John Ritter, Michael Oliver, Laraine Newman, Amy Yasbeck, Jack Warden, Ivyann Schwan, Gilbert Gottfried, James Tolkan, Charlene Tilton, Alan Blumenfeld, Paul Sutera; *D:* Brian Levant; *W:* Scott Alexander, Larry Karaszewski. *USH*

The Prodigal *♂♂½* 1955 Luke's New Testament Bible story of the son seduced by greed slickly transfered to the silver screen by MGM. A colorful cast is the main attraction. 113m/C LV. Lana Turner, Edmund Purdom, Louis Calhern, Audrey Dalton, Neville Brand, Walter Hampden, Taina Elg, Francis L. Sullivan, Joseph Wiseman, Sandy Descher, John Dehner, Cecil Kellaway, Henry Daniell, Paul Cavanagh, Tracey Roberts, Jay Novello, Dorothy Adams, Richard Devon; *D:* Richard Thorpe; *C:* Joseph Ruttenberg. *MGM*

The Prodigal *♂♂* 1983 (PG) A born-again family drama in which a sundered family is brought together by the return of a once-estranged son. 109m/C VHS, Beta, LV. John Hammond, Hope Lange, John Cullum, Morgan Brittany, Ian Bannen, Arliss Howard, Joey Travolta, Billy Graham; *M:* Bruce Broughton. *LIV*

Prodigal Boxer: The Kick of Death *♂* 1973 (R) A son must avenge his father's death by facing two kung fu masters. 90m/C VHS, Beta, LV. Meng Fei, Pa Hung, Suma Wah Lung. *GEM, MRV*

The Prodigal Planet *♂* 1988 Small group of believers continue their struggle against the world government UNTIE by disrupting their communication network. Sequel to "Thief in the Night," "A Distant Thunder," and "Image of the Beast." 67m/C VHS, Beta. William Wellman Jr., Linda Beatie, Cathy Wellman, Thom Rachford; *D:* Donald W. Thompson. *HHE*

The Producers *♂♂♂½* 1968 Considered one of Brooks' best films, this hilarious farce follows an attempted swindle by a con artist and his accountant who attempt to stage a Broadway flop only to have it backfire. Achieving cult status, the film is known for musical interlude "Springtime for Hitler." The phony play was later actually produced by Alan Johnson. 90m/C VHS, Beta, LV, 8mm. Zero Mostel, Gene Wilder, Dick Shawn, Kenneth Mars, Estelle Winwood; *D:* Mel Brooks; *W:* Mel Brooks. Academy Awards '68: Best Story & Screenplay; Writers Guild of America '68: Best Original Screenplay; Nominations: Academy Awards '68: Best Supporting Actor (Wilder). *COL, CRC*

The Professional *♂♂* *Leon* 1994 (R) Leon (Reno) is an eccentric French hit man, working New York's mean streets, when his 12-year-old neighbor Mathilda (Portman) comes knocking. Seems her family has been murdered by minions of crooked drug enforcement agent Stansfield (Oldman) and she'd like Leon to teach her how to be a "cleaner" so she can get revenge. And Leon obliges. The lovely young Portman (in her film debut) is a little too Lolita-ish for comfort as she manipulates the stolid Reno, with Oldman suitably extravagant in the role of sadistic psycho.*CW:* Great deal of graphic violence; language. 109m/C VHS, LV. *FR* Jean Reno, Natalie Portman, Gary Oldman, Danny Aiello, Michael Badalucco, Ellen Greene; *D:* Luc Besson; *W:* Luc Besson; *M:* Eric Serra. Nominations: Cesar Awards '94: Best Actor (Reno), Best Director (Besson), Best Film. *COL*

The Professional: Golgo 13 1983 Animated mystery & suspense film. Leonard Dawson vows revenge for his son's death and must battle Duke Togo, a professional hitman better known as "Golgo 13." Dubbed. 94m/C VHS. *JP*

Professional Killers 1 *♂* 1973 Trio of hired assassins wanders about the countryside killing people during Japan's Feudal Era. 87m/C VHS, Beta. Jiro Tamiya, Koji Takahashi. *NO*

The Professionals *♂♂♂½* 1966 (PG) Action and adventure count for more than a storyline in this exciting western about four mercenaries hired by a wealthy cattle baron to rescue his young wife from Mexican kidnappers. Breathtaking photography recreates turn-of-the-century Mexico in this adaptation of the Frank O'Rourke novel. 117m/C VHS, Beta, LV. Burt Lancaster, Lee Mar-

vin, Claudia Cardinale, Jack Palance, Robert Ryan, Woody Strode, Ralph Bellamy; *D:* Richard Brooks; *W:* Richard Brooks; *C:* Conrad Hall; *M:* Maurice Jarre. Nominations: Academy Awards '66: Best Adapted Screenplay, Best Color Cinematography, Best Director (Brooks). *COL*

Professionals *♂♂* 1976 When the daily rigors of cocaine smuggling begin to dampen their spirits, the "Professionals" plan an exciting plutonium heist. From the British Action Show. 104m/C VHS, Beta, LV. Gordon Jackson, Martin Shaw, Lewis Collins. *TWE*

The Professor *♂♂* 1958 Rare sci-fi thriller featuring a werewolf, an eccentric scientist and a communist plot. Also includes several 'werewolf' oriented movie trailers. 30m/C VHS. Doug Hobart, John Copeland, Irene Barr. *SNC*

Profile *♂♂½* 1954 A newsman gets an editorial job for a magazine called "Profile," and promptly falls in love with the boss's daughter. Complications arise when the boss's wife puts the moves on him. As if that isn't trouble enough, he finds himself accused of embezzlement. Average entertainment with some notable performances and an interesting chase scene. 65m/B VHS. John Bentley, Kathleen Byron, Thea Gregory, Stuart Lindsell; *D:* Francis Searle. *SNC*

Profile for Murder *♂♂* 1996 (R) Psychiatrist-cop-babe gets involved with a businessman who is also a suspected serial killer. Made for cable, with lots of nudity and sex.*CW:* Violence, language and strong sexuality. 95m/C VHS. Joan Severance, Lance Henriksen, Jeff Wincott; *D:* David Winning; *W:* Steve Fisher; *C:* Bruce Worrall; *M:* Barron Abromovitch. *LIV*

The Program *♂♂♂½* 1993 (R) Sensitive tearjerker about college football players getting caught up in the drive for a championship. As the season takes its toll on both mind and body, players prepare for the Big Game. Caan is the team's gruff coach, who's willing to look the other way as long as his boys are winning. Film sparked controversy when the Disney studio pulled and recut it after release because one scene, where Shefer's character lies down in traffic, sparked copycat actions and several deaths. The scene was not restored for the video version.*CW:* Language. 110m/C VHS, Beta, LV, Closed Caption. James Caan, Craig Sheffer, Kristy Swanson, Halle Berry, Omar Epps, Duane Davis, Abraham Benrubi, Jon Maynard Pennell, Andrew Bryniarski, Joey Lauren Adams; *D:* David S. Ward; *W:* David S. Ward, Aaron Latham; *M:* Michel Colombier. *TOU*

Programmed to Kill *♂♂* *Retaliator* 1986 (R) A beautiful terrorist is captured by the CIA and transformed into a buxom bionic assassin. 91m/C VHS, Beta, Closed Caption. Robert Ginty, Sandahl Bergman, James Booth, Louise Caire Clark; *D:* Allan Holzman. *MED*

Project A-ko 1986 Set in the near future, this Japanese animated feature, which is intended for adults, concerns teenagers with strange powers, an alien spaceship, and lots of action. Seventeen year-old A-ko possesses superhuman strength and a ditzy sidekick, C-ko. B-ko, the spoiled and rich daughter of a business tycoon, decides to fight A-ko for C-ko's companionship. Meanwhile, an alien spaceship is headed toward Earth with unknown intentions. Somehow, everything ties together—watch and see how. In Japanese with English subtitles. 86m/C VHS, LV. *JP CPM, FUS, TPV*

Project A: Part 2 1987 Dragon Ma, the only honest cop in Hong Kong with the high seas at the turn of the century is back with a new set of adventures. In Cantonese with English subtitles. 101m/C VHS. *CH* Jackie Chan, Maggie Cheung, Carina Lau, David Lam; *D:* Jackie Chan; *W:* Edward Tang, Jackie Chan. *FCT*

Project: Alien *♂♂* 1989 (R) Science fiction fans in search of a good extraterrestrial flick should avoid this teaser, for it has nothing to do with aliens. As the film begins, Earth is allegedly being attacked by beings from space, and a vast array of scientists, militia and journalists track the

aliens. What's actually happening revolves around the testing of deadly biological weapons. Shot in Yugoslavia. 92m/C VHS, LV. Michael Nouri, Darlanne Fluegel, Maxwell Caulfield, Charles Durning; *D:* Frank Shields; *W:* Anthony Able. *THV*

Project: Eliminator *♂♂½* 1991 (R) A group of terrorists kidnap a designer of "smart" weapons, and it's up to a hard-hitting special forces unit to get him back. Filmed in New Mexico.*CW:* Language, violence, and sensual scene. 89m/C VHS. David Carradine, Frank Zagarino, Drew Snyder, Hilary English, Vivian Schilling; *D:* H. Kaye Dyal; *W:* H. Kaye Dyal, Morris Asgar. *HMD*

Project: Genesis *♂♂½* 1993 Pascal and a beautiful Alien Woman are shipwrecked on a desolate planet in the 23rd century. As they watch the worlds around them clash in war, they know it is up to them to create a new beginning at the end of the Universe. 79m/C VHS, LV. David Ferry, Olga Prokhorova; *D:* Philip Jackson; *W:* Philip Jackson; *M:* Andy McNeill. *PSM*

Project: Kill! *♂* 1977 Head of a murder-for-hire squad suddenly disappears and his former assistant is hired to track him down dead or alive. 94m/C VHS, Beta. Leslie Nielsen, Gary Lockwood, Nancy Kwan. *QVD*

Project Metalbeast: DNA Overload *♂♂½* 1994 (R) A CIA agent, cryogenically frozen for 10 years, becomes the guinea pig when a group of scientists decide to unthaw him for a DNA experiment involving living metallic skin. Too bad he turns into a metal beast by the light of the full moon. Sci-fi take on the werewolf saga.*CW:* Monster violence and gore. 92m/C VHS. Kim Delaney, Barry Bostwick; *D:* Alessandro DeGaetano; *W:* Timothy E. Sabo; *M:* Conrad Pope. *PSM*

Project Moon Base *♂½* 1953 Espionage runs rampant on a spaceship headed by a female officer. Eventually the ship is stranded on the moon. Actually filmed for television series "Ring Around the Moon." A cold-war sexist relic. 64m/C VHS, Beta. Donna Martell, Hayden Rourke; *D:* Richard Talmadge. *THV*

Project: Nightmare *♂½* 1985 Seems not all dreams are wish fulfillment, when these nightmares start coming true. 75m/C VHS. Elly Koslo, Lance Dickson; *D:* Donald M. Jones. *ACA, MOV*

Project: Shadowchaser *♂½* 1992 (R) Action-packed would-be thriller about a billion dollar android who escapes from a top secret government laboratory. Programmed with superhuman strength and no human emotions the android and five terrorists take over a hospital (located in a skyscraper no less). Their hostages include the President's daughter and the terrorists demand a $50 million ransom. With a four-hour deadline the FBI calls in the hospital architect to advise them—only they've got the wrong man—and the android's creator, who wants his creation back—no matter what the cost. A low budget Terminator clone.*CW:* Action violence. 97m/C VHS, Closed Caption. Martin Kove, Meg Foster, Frank Zagarino, Paul Koslo, Joss Ackland; *D:* John Eyres. *PSM*

Project Shadowchaser 3000 *♂½* 1995 (R) Deep space satellite station collides with a mining vessel carrying a killer android. The seven surviving crew are then hunted by the android as the ship's nuclear core is also threatening to explode.*CW:* Language, sci-fi violence and gore. 99m/C VHS, LV, Closed Caption. Frank Zagarino, Sam Bottoms, Christopher Atkins, Musetta Vander, Christopher Neame; *D:* John Eyres; *W:* Nick Davis; *M:* Steve Edwards. *TTC, NLC*

Project Vampire *♂½* 1993 Vampire concocts a serum that will change humans into vampires within three days. His first guinea pig fights to stop the evil from succeeding. 90m/C VHS. Brian Knudson, Mary-Louise Gemmill, Christopher Cho, Myron Natwick; *D:* Peter Flynn. *AIP*

Project X 🎬🎬½ 1987 (PG) A bemused Air Force pilot is assigned to a special project involving chimpanzees. He must decide where his duty lies when he realizes the semi-intelligent chimps are slated to die. 107m/C VHS, Beta, LV, **Closed Caption.** Matthew Broderick, Helen Hunt, William Sadler, Johnny Rae McGhee, Jonathan Stark, Robin Gammell, Stephen Lang, Jean Smart, Dick Miller; **D:** Jonathan Kaplan; **W:** Stanley Weiser, Lawrence Lasker; **C:** Dean Cundey; **M:** James Horner. *FOX*

The Projectionist 🎬🎬🎬 1971 (PG) A must-see for movie buffs, Dangerfield made his screen debut in this story about a projectionist in a seedy movie house whose real-life existence begins to blur into the films he continuously watches. Made on a limited budget, this creative effort by Hurwitz was the first film to utilize the technique of superimposition. 84m/C VHS, Beta. Rodney Dangerfield, Chuck McCann, Ina Balin; **D:** Harry Hurwitz; **W:** Harry Hurwitz. *LIV, VES*

Prom Night 🎬🎬 1980 (R) A masked killer stalks four high school girls during their senior prom as revenge for a murder which occurred six years prior. Sequelled by "Hello Mary Lou: Prom Night II" and "Prom Night III: The Last Kiss." 91m/C VHS, Beta, LV. CA Jamie Lee Curtis, Leslie Nielsen; **D:** Paul Lynch. *NLC*

Prom Night 3: The Last Kiss 🎬 1989 (R) The second sequel, in which the reappearing high school ghoul beguiles a lucky teenager. 97m/C VHS, Beta, LV. Tim Conlon, Cyndy Preston, Courtney Taylor; **D:** Ron Oliver, Peter Simpson. *LIV*

Prom Night 4: Deliver Us From Evil 🎬 1991 (R) Yet another gory entry in the Prom series (one would hope it will be the last). Another group of naive teens decide that they can have more fun at a private party than at the prom. They host the party in a summer home that was once a monastery, but the festive affair soon turns into a night of terror when an uninvited guest crashes the party. For true fans of slasher flicks.**CW:** Language, violence, and sensuality. 95m/C VHS, **Closed Caption.** Nikki DeBoer, Alden Kane, Joy Tanner, Alle Ghadban; **D:** Clay Borris. *LIV*

The Promise 🎬½ *Face of a Stranger* 1979 (PG) Weepie outdated story about star-crossed lovers Michael (Collins) and Nancy (Quinlan). A car accident leaves Michael comatose and Nancy badly disfigured. Michael's mother (Straight), who loathes Nancy, sees her chance to finally break them up. She offers to pay for Nancy's plastic surgery if she'll leave Michael forever, then Mom tells her son his girlfriend's dead. A year later Nancy, with her new face and new identity, and Michael meet. From the novel by Danielle Steele. 97m/C VHS. Stephen Collins, Kathleen Quinlan, Beatrice Straight, Laurence Luckinbill, William Prince, Michael O'Hare; **D:** Gilbert Cates; **W:** Garry Michael White; **M:** David Shire. Nominations: Academy Awards '79: Best Song ("Theme from The Promise: I'll Never Say Goodbye"). *USH*

The Promise 🎬🎬½ *Das Versprechen* 1994 (R) Young lovers Konrad (Zoller and Zirner) and Sophie (Harfouch and Becker) find themselves separated by the Berlin Wall after a botched escape attempt in 1961. The estranged lovers meet only four times during the next three decades as they adjust to the systems under which they're forced to live. Somewhat contrived and cliched, this bittersweet romance uses Konrad and Sophie as symbols of the social and political turmoil and triumphs of the divided Germany. Received some criticism from East Germans who found the film's severe portrayal of Communist rule too harsh. Gets points for being the first post-fall film to explore the Wall's legacy.**CW:** Contains sexual situations and strong language. 115m/C VHS, LV, **Closed Caption.** GE Corinna Harfouch, Meret Becker, August Zirner, Anian Zollner, Jean-Yves Gaultier, Eva Mattes, Suzanne Uge, Hans Kremer, Pierre Besson, Tina Engel, Otto Sander, Hark Bohm; **D:** Margarethe von Trotta; **W:** Peter Schneider, Margarethe von Trotta; **C:** Franz Rath; **M:** Jurgen Knieper. *NLC*

Promise Her Anything 🎬🎬 1966 A widow (Caron) with a baby decides to make her boss (Cummings), a child psychologist who hates kids, her new husband. So she stashes the kid with her upstairs neighbor (Beatty), a would-be filmmaker who earns his living making blue movies. But the filmmaker has romantic designs on the widow and decides the baby may be his way to make a good impression. Beatty isn't very believable in this type of light-romantic comedy and the farcical situations are forced. 98m/C VHS. GB Warren Beatty, Leslie Caron, Robert Cummings, Hermione Gingold, Lionel Stander, Keenan Wynn, Cathleen Nesbitt; **D:** Arthur Hiller; **W:** William Peter Blatty. *PAR*

Promise to Murder 🎬½ 1956 An early murder-drama episode from the "Climax" television series. 60m/B VHS, Beta. Peter Lorre, Louis Hayward, Ann Harding. *NOS, DVT*

Promised a Miracle 🎬🎬½ 1988 (PG) Based on the true story of a religious couple who sought help for their diabetic son through prayer rather than conventional medical means. Following the boy's death in 1974 the couple were charged with manslaughter. From the non-fiction account "We Let Our Son Die" by Larry Parker. Made for television. 94m/C VHS, LV, **Closed Caption.** Rosanna Arquette, Judge Reinhold, Tom Bower, Gary Bayer, Maria O'Brien, Giovanni Ribisi; **D:** Stephen Gyllenhaal; **W:** David Hill; **C:** Thomas Burstyn. *REP*

Promised Land 🎬🎬🎬 *Young Hearts* 1988 (R) Two high school friends from the rural northwestern U.S. come together several years after graduation under tragic circumstances. Writer Hoffman's semi-autobiographical, disillusioned look at the American Dream was re-discovered by movie goers due to its excellent dramatic performances, notable also as the first film produced by Robert Redford's Sundance Institute. 110m/C VHS, Beta, LV. Kiefer Sutherland, Meg Ryan, Tracy Pollan, Jason Gedrick, Googy Gress, Deborah Richter, Sandra Seacat, Jay Underwood, Oscar Rowland; **D:** Michael Hoffman; **W:** Michael Hoffman; **M:** James Newton Howard. *LIV, VES*

Promises in the Dark 🎬🎬½ 1979 (PG) Drama focusing on the complex relationship between a woman doctor and her 17-year-old female patient who is terminally ill with cancer. Hellman's directorial debut. 118m/C VHS, Beta. Marsha Mason, Ned Beatty, Kathleen Beller, Susan Clark, Paul Clemens, Donald Moffat, Michael Brandon; **D:** Jerome Hellman. *WAR*

Promises! Promises! 🎬½ *Promise Her Anything* 1963 Having difficulty getting pregnant, a woman goes on a cruise with her husband. While on board, they meet another couple, all get drunk, and change partners. Of course, both women find themselves pregnant, leaving the paternity in doubt. Famous primarily as the movie Mansfield told "Playboy" magazine she appeared "completely nude" in. 90m/B VHS, Beta. Jayne Mansfield, Marie McDonald, Tommy Noonan, Fritz Feld, Claude Stroud. *NO*

The Promoter 🎬🎬🎬 *The Card* 1952 Horatio Alger comedy stars Guinness as an impoverished student who gives himself a surreptitious leg up in life by altering his school entrance exam scores. Outstanding performances enliven this subtle British comedy of morals. 87m/B VHS, Beta. GB Alec Guinness, Glynis Johns, Petula Clark, Valerie Hobson, Michael Hordern; **D:** Ronald Neame. Nominations: Academy Awards '52: Best Sound. *HMV*

Proof 🎬🎬🎬 1991 (R) Directorial debut of Moorhouse tells a tale of manipulation, friendship, and obsessive love between a blind photographer, Martin, his housekeeper, and the young man he befriends. Martin, mistrustful of the world around him, takes photographs as "proof" of the reality of his life. A chance meeting with Andy provides Martin with his "eyes" and the opportunity to expand his world and emotions—something his housekeeper, Celia, is none too happy to help him with. Unhealthy triangle leads all three to a re-evaluation of their lives. Propelled by terrif-

ic performances and enough humor to balance its emotional content.**CW:** Some language and sensuality. 90m/C VHS, LV, **Closed Caption.** AU Hugo Weaving, Genevieve Picot, Russell Crowe, Heather Mitchell, Jeffrey Walker, Frank Gallacher; **D:** Jocelyn Moorhouse; **W:** Jocelyn Moorhouse. Australian Film Institute '91: Best Actor (Weaving), Best Director (Moorhouse), Best Film, Best Film Editing, Best Supporting Actor (Crowe), Best Writing. *NLC, COL*

Proof of the Man 🎬 1984 A Japanese co-production about a murder in Tokyo that takes on international importance. 100m/C VHS, Beta. JP George Kennedy, Broderick Crawford, Toshiro Mifune. *VCD*

Prophecy 🎬½ 1979 (PG) A doctor and his wife travel to Maine to research the effects of pollution caused by the lumber industry. They encounter several terrifying freaks of nature and a series of bizarre human deaths. Laughable horror film. 102m/C VHS, Beta. Talia Shire, Robert Foxworth, Armand Assante, Victoria Racimo, Richard Dysart; **D:** John Frankenheimer; **W:** David Seltzer; **C:** Harry Stradling Jr. *PAR*

The Prophecy 🎬🎬½ 1995 (R) Modern variation of "Paradise Lost" carries a heavy load including possession, Native American mythology, and Walken as the archangel Gabriel. Not surprisingly, it stumbles under the weight. Gabriel is at odds with good angel Simon (Stolz) over the souls of humans, a battle that has its final showdown in a small Arizona community and crosses the paths of homicide detective Thomas Dagget (Koteas) and school teacher Katherine (Madsen). Successfully mixes humor and horror, but biblical jargon can lose horror fans just looking for a cheap thrill. Directorial debut of screenwriter Widen.**CW:** Violence and gore; some language. 97m/C VHS, LV, **Closed Caption.** Christopher Walken, Eric Stoltz, Elias Koteas, Virginia Madsen, Amanda Plummer, Viggo Mortensen; **D:** Gregory Widen; **W:** Gregory Widen; **C:** Bruce Douglas Johnson, Richard Clabaugh; **M:** David Williams. *MAX*

A Propos de Nice 🎬🎬🎬 1929 First film by French director Vigo, the silent film parodies French travelogues in a manner that indicates the director's later brilliance. 25m/B VHS, Beta. FR **D:** Jean Vigo. *FST, MRV*

The Proposition 🎬🎬½ 1996 (R) Unless widow Catherine Morgan (Russell) can find the money to pay her late husband's gambling debts, she and her two daughters will be evicted from their Welsh farm. She refuses to take the easy way and marry local sheriff Huw (Lynch), instead making a bargain with his rakish, drunken bastard brother Rhys (Bergin) to drive her cattle to Gloucester market. Huw takes exception to this plan and tries every dirty trick he can to thwart them and naturally, Catherine and Rhys become more than antagonistic allies along the rough journey.**CW:** Strong sex scene, partial nudity, violence. 99m/C VHS. Theresa Russell, Patrick Bergin, Richard Lynch, Richard Harrington, Jennifer Vaughan, Ifan Huw Dafydd, Nick McGaughey, Owen Garmon; **D:** Strathford Hamilton; **W:** Paul Matthews; **C:** David Lewis; **M:** Ben Heneghan, Ian Lawson. *APX*

The Proprietor 🎬🎬 1996 (R) Thinly disguised as a returning-to-your-roots and facing-your-ghosts drama, film is actually a celluloid shrine to its Gallic star, the legendary Moreau, who plays a legendary Gallic novelist, Adrienne Mark. Mark, after residing in New York for 30 years, reclaims her Jewish identity and returns to Paris to buy the home in which she grew up with her mother, who was killed in World War II. Famous for writing the novel, "Call Me French" which became a highly acclaimed French film and a current American remake, Mark's primary struggle to come to grips with her mother's death is overshadowed by a bevy of subplots that compete with one another. Young as a sassy and somewhat stereotypical Hollywood producer; Carter as Milly the loyal housekeeper; Waterston, an antique dealer; and Billy, NYC video artist and adoring Mark fan, all add to the confusion. Moreau tries her best to give life to the saintly lead figure, but the coma-inducing sugar level of her character's goodness is overwhelming. Director Merchant's sophomore effort, though well-acted, is a good idea, poorly told.**CW:** Brief sexuality. **105m/C VHS, Closed Caption.** Jeanne Moreau, Sean Young, Sam Waterston, Nell Carter, Austin Pendleton, Pierre Vaneck, Christopher Cazenove, Jean-Pierre Aumont, Josh Hamilton, Marc Tissot; **D:** Ismail Merchant; **W:** Jean-Marie Besset, George Trow; **C:** Larry Pizer; **M:** Richard Robbins. *WAR*

Prospero's Books 🐾🐾🐾 1991 **(R)**
Greenaway's free-ranging adaptation of Shakespeare's "The Tempest" has all his usual hallmarks of the bizarre. Gielgud is the aged Prospero, exiled to a magical island with his innocent daughter Miranda, and 24 beloved books containing the magician's recipe for life, each of which becomes a separate chapter in the film. Greenaway mixes film and high-definition video to create, with cinematographer Sacha Vierny, dazzling visuals that threaten to overwhelm but don't quite, thanks to both Greenaway's skill and the astonishing performance of the then 87-year-old Gielgud.**CW:** Pervasive nudity. **129m/C VHS, Beta, LV.** John Gielgud, Michel Blanc, Erland Josephson, Isabelle Pasco, Tom Bell, Kenneth Cranham, Michael Clark, Mark Rylance; **D:** Peter Greenaway; **W:** Peter Greenaway; **C:** Sacha Vierny; **M:** Michael Nyman. *FXV, FCT, VTR*

Protector 🐾 1985 **(R)** A semi-martial arts cops 'n' robbers epic about the cracking of a Hong Kong-New York heroin route. **94m/C VHS, Beta, LV, Closed Caption.** Jackie Chan, Danny Aiello; **D:** James Glickenhaus. *WAR*

Proteus 🐾🐾 1995 **(R)** Survivors of a boat wreck wash up on an off-shore oil rig that's actually a secret lab financed by loony millionaire Bradley, who's seeking immortality. His DNA experiments have led to the creation of a disgusting parasite that travels from body to body. Naturally, the boat survivors also seek to survive this latest health threat.**CW:** Violence, gore and language. **97m/C VHS, Closed Caption.** Doug Bradley, Craig Fairbrass, Toni Barry; **D:** Bob Keen. *THV*

Protocol 🐾🐾 1984 **(PG)** A series of comic accidents lead a Washington cocktail waitress into the U.S. State Department's employ as a protocol official. Once there she is used as a pawn to make an arms deal with a Middle Eastern country. Typical Hawn comedy with an enjoyable ending. **100m/C VHS, Beta, LV, Closed Caption.** Goldie Hawn, Chris Sarandon, Andre Gregory, Cliff DeYoung, Ed Begley Jr., Gail Strickland, Richard Romanus, Keith Szarabajka, James Staley, Kenneth Mars, Kenneth McMillan, Archie Hahn, Amanda Bearse; **D:** Herbert Ross; **W:** Charles Shyer, Buck Henry, Nancy Meyers, Harvey Miller; **M:** Basil Poledouris. *WAR*

Prototype 🐾🐾🐾 1983 Made-for-television revision of the Frankenstein legend has award-winning scientist Plummer as the creator of the first android. Fearful of the use the military branch of government has in mind for his creation, he attempts to steal back his discovery, in this suspenseful adventure. **100m/C VHS, LV.** Christopher Plummer, David Morse, Frances Sternhagen, James Sutorius; **D:** David Greene; **M:** Billy Goldenberg. *LIV*

Prototype X29A 🐾½ 1992 **(R)** The year is 2057 in a desolate, lawless Los Angeles. A research scientist is conducting experiments on a crippled ex-soldier named Hawkins when they suddenly go awry, turning him into a half-man, half-machine robot. Known as Prototype, the creature goes on a hunting and killing spree. Lame "Terminator" & "Robocop" takeoff.**CW:** Language, strong violence, and strong sexuality. **98m/C VHS, LV, Closed Caption.** Brenda Swanson, Robert Tossberg, Lane Lenhart; **D:** Phillip J. Roth; **W:** Phillip J. Roth. *THV*

The Proud and the Damned 🐾
Proud, Damned, and Dead 1972 **(PG)** Five Civil-War-veteran mercenaries wander into a Latin American war and get manipulated by both sides. **95m/C**

VHS, Beta. Chuck Connors, Aron Kincaid, Cesar Romero; **D:** Ferde Grofe Jr. *NOS, VCI, MRV*

Proud Men 🐾🐾 1987 A cattle rancher and his expatriate son are separated by bitterness toward each other. Good acting from Heston and Strauss, and good action sequences, but ordinary script. **95m/C VHS, Closed Caption.** Charlton Heston, Peter Strauss, Nan Martin, Alan Autry, Belinda Balaski, Red West; **D:** William A. Graham. *TTC*

The Proud Ones 🐾🐾½ *Les Orgueilleux* 1953 An aristocratic French woman and her husband are traveling through Mexico when he suddenly dies of a mysterious illness. Left penniless in a decaying seaside town, she falls for the local doctor who is mourning the death of his wife. Adaptation of the Satre novel "L'Amour Redempteur." In French with English subtitles. **105m/B VHS.** *FR* Gerard Philipe, Michele Morgan, Victor Manuel Mendoza; **D:** Yves Allegret. Nominations: Academy Awards '56: Best Story.*FCT, INT*

Proud Rebel 🐾🐾🐾 1958 A character study of a stubborn widower who searches for a doctor to aid him in dealing with the problems of his mute son, and of the woman who helps to tame the boy. Ladd's real-life son makes his acting debut. **99m/C VHS, Beta.** Alan Ladd, Olivia de Havilland, Dean Jagger, Harry Dean Stanton; **D:** Michael Curtiz.

Providence 🐾🐾🐾 1977 **(R)** An interesting score highlights this British fantasy drama of a dying writer envisioning his final novel as a fusion of the people from his past with the circumstances he encounters on a daily basis. The first English-language effort by French director Resnais. **104m/C VHS, Beta.** *GB* John Gielgud, Dirk Bogarde, Ellen Burstyn, David Warner, Elaine Stritch; **D:** Alain Resnais; **M:** Miklos Rozsa. Cesar Awards '78: Best Art Direction/Set Decoration, Best Director (Resnais), Best Film, Best Sound, Best Writing, Best Score; New York Film Critics Awards '77: Best Actor (Gielgud).*COL*

Provincial Actors 🐾🐾 1979 Ambitious Christopher is the leading actor of a rural theater troupe, who dreams of moving to the city and becoming a star. But his wife Anna is fed up with his dreams and leaves him and Christopher must make a choice between his career and his marriage. Polish with subtitles. **104m/C VHS.** *PL* Tadeysz Huk, Halina Labonarska, Ewa Dalkowska, Jerzy Stuhr; **D:** Agnieszka Holland. *NYF*

Provoked 🐾🐾½ 1989 What would you do if your husband were being held hostage by a gang of ruthless, but stupid, escaped cons? Well, Maranne actually wants her husband back (maybe 'cause they're newlyweds) and no by-the-book police chief (Jones) is gonna stop her. This bride gets her hands on some automatic weaponry and look out! Shot in eight days with a $130,000 budget. **90m/C VHS, Beta.** Cindy Maranne, McKeiver Jones III, Harold W. Jones, Sharon Blair, Bob Fall, Joe Sprosty, Phyllis Durant, Tara Untiedt; **D:** Rick Pamplin; **W:** Tara Untiedt, Steve Pake. *VTR, HHE*

Prowler 🐾🐾½ 1951 Heflin is a cop who responds to a prowler scare and finds the beautiful married Keyes worried about an intruder. He learns she will inherit a lot of money if anything happens to her husband so he seduces her and then "accidentally" kills her husband, supposedly mistaking him for a prowler. Keyes then marries Heflin but when she learns the truth her own life is in danger. Tidy thriller with Heflin doing a good job as the unpredictable villain. **92m/B VHS, Beta.** Van Heflin, Evelyn Keyes, Katherine Warren, John Maxwell; **D:** Joseph Losey; **C:** Arthur C. Miller. *NO*

The Prowler 🐾 *Rosemary's Killer* 1981 **(R)** A soldier returns from duty during WWII, only to find his girl in bed with another guy. He kills them, and for unclear reasons, returns to the same town 35 years later to kill more people. An effects-fest for Tom Savini. **87m/C VHS.** Vicky Dawson, Christopher Goutman, Cindy Weintraub, Farley Granger, John Seitz, Lawrence Tierney; **D:** Joseph Zito; **W:** Neal Barbera; **M:** Richard Einhorn. *VHE*

Prudential Family Playhouse 1950
Presentation of Sinclair Lewis' "Dodsworth." Tells the story of a wealthy American couple who travel from their small town to Europe. **53m/B VHS, Beta.** Ruth Chatterton, Walter Abel, Cliff Hall, Eva Marie Saint. *VYY*

PSI Factor 🐾🐾½ 1980 A civilian researcher working at the NASA space track station observes and records signals coming from planet Serius B. **91m/C VHS.** Peter Mark Richman, Gretchen Corbett, Tommy Martin; **D:** Bryan Trizers; **W:** Quentin Masters. *NO*

Psych-Out 🐾🐾½ 1968 A deaf girl searches Haight-Ashbury for her runaway brother. She meets hippies and flower children during the Summer of Love. Psychedelic score with Strawberry Alarm Clock and The Seeds. Somewhere in the picture, Nicholson whangs on lead guitar. **95m/C VHS, Beta, LV.** Jack Nicholson, Bruce Dern, Susan Strasberg, Dean Stockwell, Henry Jaglom; **D:** Richard Rush; **W:** Richard Rush. *HBO*

The Psychic woof! 1968 An ad executive gains psychic powers after he falls off a ladder and tries to conquer the world. A later effort by gore-king Lewis, notable only for sex scenes inserted by Lewis to make the movie salable. **90m/C VHS, Beta.** Dick Genola, Robin Guest, Bobbi Spencer; **D:** Herschell Gordon Lewis. *NO*

The Psychic 🐾 1978 **(R)** A psychic envisions her own death and attempts to alter the prediction. **90m/C VHS, Beta.** Jennifer O'Neill, Marc Porel, Evelyn Stewart, Gabriele Ferzetti, Gianni "John" Garko; **D:** Lucio Fulci. *NO*

Psychic 🐾½ 1991 **(R)** A college student with psychic powers believes he knows who the next victim of a demented serial killer will be. The problem is: no one will believe him. And the victim is the woman he loves.**CW:** Violence and sensuality. **92m/C VHS, Closed Caption.** Michael Nouri, Catherine Mary Stewart, Zach Galligan. *THV*

Psychic Killer 🐾½ 1975 **(PG)** A wrongfully committed asylum inmate acquires psychic powers and decides to use them in a deadly revenge. Good cast in cheapie horror flick. **89m/C VHS, Beta.** Jim Hutton, Paul Burke, Julie Adams, Neville Brand, Aldo Ray, Rod Cameron, Della Reese; **D:** Ray Danton.

Psycho 🐾🐾🐾🐾 1960 Hitchcock counted on his directorial stature and broke all the rules in this story of violent murder, transvestism, and insanity. Based on Robert Bloch's novelization of an actual murder, Leigh plays a fleeing thief who stops at the secluded Bates Motel where she meets her death in Hitchcock's classic "shower scene." Shot on a limited budget in little more than a month, "Psycho" changed the Hollywood horror film forever. Followed by "Psycho II" (1983), "Psycho III" (1986), and a made-for-television movie. **109m/B VHS, Beta, LV.** Anthony Perkins, Janet Leigh, Vera Miles, John Gavin, John McIntire, Martin Balsam, Simon Oakland, Ted Knight, John Anderson, Frank Albertson, Patricia Hitchcock; **D:** Alfred Hitchcock; **W:** Joseph Stefano; **M:** Bernard Herrmann. Edgar Allan Poe Awards '60: Best Screenplay; Golden Globe Awards '61: Best Supporting Actress (Leigh); Nominations: Academy Awards '60: Best Art Direction/Set Decoration (B & W), Best Black and White Cinematography, Best Director (Hitchcock), Best Supporting Actress (Leigh). *USH, TLF*

Psycho 2 🐾🐾 1983 **(R)** This sequel to the Hitchcock classic finds Norman Bates returning home after 22 years in an asylum to find himself haunted by "mother" and caught up in a series of murders. In a surprisingly good horror film, Perkins and Miles reprise their roles from the original "Psycho." Perkins went on to direct yet another sequel, "Psycho 3." **113m/C VHS, Beta, LV.** Anthony Perkins, Vera Miles, Meg Tilly, Robert Loggia, Dennis Franz; **D:** Richard Franklin; **W:** Tom Holland; **C:** Dean Cundey; **M:** Jerry Goldsmith. *USH*

Psycho 3 🐾🐾 1986 **(R)** The second sequel to Hitchcock's "Psycho" finds Norman Bates drawn into his past by "mother" and the appearance of a woman who reminds him of this original victim. Perkins made his directorial debut in this film that stretches the plausibility of the storyline to its limits, but the element of parody throughout makes this an entertaining film for "Psycho" fans. **93m/C VHS, Beta, LV, Closed Caption.** Anthony Perkins, Diana Scarwid, Jeff Fahey, Roberta Maxwell, Alan Browne; **D:** Anthony Perkins; **W:** Charles Edward Pogue; **C:** Bruce Surtees; **M:** Carter Burwell. *USH*

Psycho 4: The Beginning 🎞🎞 1990 (R) Prequels "Psycho" when, at the behest of a radio talk show host, Norman Bates recounts his childhood and reveals the circumstances that aided in the development of his peculiar neuroses. Stefano wrote the original screenplay and the original score is used, but this doesn't even come close to the original.**CW:** Violence and sensuality. **96m/C VHS, LV.** Anthony Perkins, Henry Thomas, Olivia Hussey, CCH Pounder, Warren Frost, Donna Mitchell; **D:** Mick Garris; **W:** Joseph Stefano; **M:** Bernard Herrmann. *USH*

Psycho Cop 🎞½ 1988 Six college undergrads on a weekend retreat are menaced and picked off one at a time by a crazed local cop. **89m/C VHS, Beta.** Bobby Ray Shafer; **D:** Wallace Potts. *NO*

Psycho Cop 2 🎞½ 1994 (R) Four buddies plan a raunchy bachelor party, commandeering the company conference room for an after-hours orgy. Only Psycho Cop is on their case. Gore. **80m/C VHS.** Bobby Ray Shafer, Barbara Lee Alexander, Julie Strain; **D:** Rif Coogan. *COL*

Psycho from Texas 🎞 *The Butcher* 1983 (R) Quiet Southern town is disrupted by the kidnapping of a wealthy oil man, followed by a string of meaningless murders. **85m/C VHS, Beta.** King John III, Candy Dee, Janel King. *NO*

Psycho Girls 🎞 1986 (R) Very low budget horror flick redeemed by spurts of weird black humor. Crazed woman is released from institution to seek out sister who should have been put away in the first place. She crashes anniversary celebration and, well, let's just say she's not the life of the party. Never released theatrically. **87m/C VHS, Beta.** *CA* John Haslett Cuff, Darlene Mignacco, Agi Gallus, Rose Graham, Silvio Oliviero, Michael Hoole, Pier Giorgia DiCicco, Fernne Kane; **D:** Gerard Ciccoritti; **W:** Gerard Ciccoritti, Michael Boekner. *MGM*

Psychomania 🎞½ *Violent Midnight* 1963 Semi-limpid mystery thriller about a former war hero and painter who is suspected of being the demented killer stalking girls on campus. To prove his innocence, he tracks the killer himself. **95m/C VHS, Beta.** Lee Philips, Shepperd Strudwick, Jean Hale, Dick Van Patten, Sylvia Miles, James Farentino; **D:** Richard Hilliard. *SNC, HHT*

Psychomania 🎞🎞 *The Death Wheelers* 1973 (R) A drama of the supernatural, the occult, and the violence which lies just beyond the conventions of society for a group of dead motorcyclists, the Living Dead, who all came back to life after committing suicide with the help of the devil. **89m/C VHS, Beta.** *GB* George Sanders, Beryl Reid, Nicky Henson, Mary Laroche, Patrick Holt; **D:** Don Sharp. *MED, MRV*

Psychopath 🎞½ 1968 A film about a modern-day, slightly unhinged, Robin Hood and his escapades, stealing from other thieves and giving to the victimized. **90m/C VHS, Beta.** *GB* Klaus Kinski, George Martin, Ingrid Schoeller; **D:** Guido Zurli. *NO*

Psychopath 🎞 *An Eye for an Eye* 1973 (PG) A nutso children's television personality begins to murder abusive parents. Fairly gory, and definitely not for family viewing. **85m/C VHS, Beta.** Tom Basham, Gene Carlson, Gretchen Kanne; **D:** Larry G. Brown; **M:** John Williams. *MED*

Psychos in Love woof! 1987 A psychotic murderer who hates grapes of any kind finds the woman of his dreams—she's a psychotic murderer who hates grapes! Together they find bliss—until the plumber discovers their secret! **90m/C VHS, Beta.** Carmine Capobianco, Debi Thibeault, Frank Stewart; **D:** Gorman Bechard. *NO*

The Psychotronic Man 🎞½ 1991 An innocent man suddenly finds he possesses amazing and dangerous powers, enabling him to control outside events with a thought. **88m/C VHS.** Peter Spelson, Christopher Carbis, Curt Colbert, Robin Newton, Paul Marvel; **D:** Jack M. Sell. *UNI*

PT 109 🎞🎞 1963 The WWII exploits of Lieutenant (j.g.) John F. Kennedy in the South Pacific. Part of the "A Night at the Movies" series, this tape simulates a 1963 movie evening, with a Foghorn Leghorn cartoon ("Banty Raids"), a newsreel on the JFK assassination, and coming attractions for "Critic's Choice" and "Four for Texas." **159m/C VHS, Beta, LV.** Cliff Robertson, Ty Hardin, Ty Hardin, Robert (Bobby) Blake, Robert Culp, James Gregory; **D:** Leslie Martinson. *WAR*

Puberty Blues 🎞🎞½ 1981 (R) Two Australian girls become part of the local surfing scene in order to be accepted by the "in crowd" at their high school. **86m/C VHS, Beta.** *AU* Neil Schofield, Jad Capelja; **D:** Bruce Beresford. *USH*

Public Access 🎞🎞 1993 (R) Newcomer Whitley Pritcher (Marquette) manages to cause trouble in the small town of Brewster when he begins broadcasting a call-in program over a public-access cable station that encourages complaining about the town's problems. Skeletons start falling out of closets, leading to unexpected tragedy. Feature-film directorial debut of Singer.**CW:** Language, brief sexuality and violence. **90m/C VHS.** Ron Marquette, Dina Brooks, Burt Williams, Charles Kavanaugh, Larry Maxwell, Brandon Boyce; **D:** Bryan Singer; **W:** Bryan Singer, Christopher McQuarrie, Michael Feit Dougan; **C:** Bruce Douglas Johnson; **M:** John Ottman. Sundance Film Festival '93: Grand Jury Prize. *TRI*

A Public Affair 🎞½ 1962 Exposes the evils and abuses of collection agencies without even a shred of humor. Certainly gets its point across, but will bore any audience to tears or spontaneous naps. **71m/B VHS, Beta.** Myron McCormick, Edward Binns, Harry Carey Jr. *VYY*

Public Cowboy No. 1 🎞½ 1937 Cattle thieves use a radio, airplanes, and refrigerator trucks in their updated rustling schemes. **54m/B VHS, Beta.** Gene Autry, William Farnum. *NOS, VCN, DVT*

Public Enemies 🎞🎞 1996 (R) It's nefarious Ma Barker (Russell) and her boys on a '30s crime spree that gets even bigger when they hook up with criminal Alvin Karpis (Stallone). But when Ma's lover (Roberts) dreams up a kidnapping plot, it's a fast road to ruin.**CW:** Language, violence, nudity, sexual situations. **95m/C VHS.** Theresa Russell, Eric Roberts, Frank Stallone, Alyssa Milano, Joseph Lindsey; **D:** Mark L. Lester. *THV*

Public Enemy 🎞🎞🎞½ *Enemies of the Public* 1931 Cagney's acting career was launched by this story of two Irish boys growing up in a Chicago shantytown to become hoodlums during the prohibition era. Cagney and Woods hook up with molls Clarke and Blondell on their rise to the top. Considered the most realistic "gangster" film, Wellman's movie is also the most grimly brutal due to its release prior to Hollywood censorship. The scene where Cagney smashes a grapefruit in Clarke's face was credited with starting a trend in abusing film heroines. **85m/B VHS, Beta, LV.** James Cagney, Edward Woods, Leslie Fenton, Joan Blondell, Mae Clarke, Jean Harlow; **D:** William A. Wellman. Nominations: Academy Awards '31: Best Story. *MGM, FOX*

The Public Eye 🎞🎞🎞½ 1992 (R) Underappreciated film noir homage casts Pesci as a crime photographer with an unsuspected romantic streak. It's 1942 in NYC and cynical freelancer Leon "Bernzy" Bernstein's always looking for the perfect shot. Hershey's recent widow whose nightclub-owner husband had mob ties and decides Pesci would be a likely patsy for helping her out. Hershey seems decorative and the romantic angle never quite develops, but Pesci delivers a rich, low-key performance as the visionary, hard-boiled artist. Climatic mob shootout is cinematic bullet ballet. Based loosely on the career of '40s

photog Weegee, who defined New York and its times in his work.**CW:** Violence. **98m/C VHS, Beta, LV.** Joe Pesci, Barbara Hershey, Stanley Tucci, Richard Foronjy, Richard Riehle, Jared Harris, Jerry Adler, Dominic Chianese, Gerry Becker; **D:** Howard Franklin; **W:** Howard Franklin; **M:** John Barry. *USH*

Pucker Up and Bark Like a Dog 🎞 1989 (R) A young artist and his inspirationally lovely actress girl-friend find themselves in strange and crazy situations. Good cast gives this potential. **94m/C VHS, Closed Caption.** Lisa Zane, Jonathan Gries, Paul Bartel, Robert Culp; **D:** Paul S. Parco. *FRH, BTV*

Pudd'nhead Wilson 🎞½ 1987 An adaptation of a Mark Twain story about a small-town lawyer who discovers the illicit exchange of a white infant for a light-skinned negro infant by a slave woman. Made for television as an "American Playhouse" presentation on PBS. **87m/C VHS, Beta.** Ken Howard; **D:** Alan Bridges. *USH*

Pueblo Affair 🎞🎞 1973 A dramatization of the capture of the American spy ship "Pueblo" by the North Koreans, during which time the crew was tortured, imprisoned, and all intelligence documents were confiscated. **99m/C VHS, Beta.** Hal Holbrook, Andrew Duggan, Richard Mulligan, George Grizzard, Gary Merrill, Mary Fickett; **D:** Anthony Page. *NO*

Pulp 🎞🎞½ 1972 (PG) Caine, playing a mystery writer, becomes a target for murder when he ghostwrites the memoirs of a movie gangster from the 1930s, played deftly by Rooney. **95m/C VHS, Beta.** *GB* Michael Caine, Mickey Rooney, Lionel Stander, Lizabeth Scott, Nadia Cassini, Dennis Price, Al Lettieri; **D:** Mike Hodges; **W:** Mike Hodges. *NO*

Pulp Fiction 🎞🎞🎞🎞 1994 (R) Tarantino moves into the cinematic mainstream with his trademark violence and '70s pop culture mindset intact in this stylish crime trilogy. A day in the life of a criminal community unexpectedly shifts from outrageous, esoteric dialogue to violent mayhem with solid scripting that takes familiar stories to unexplored territory. Offbeat cast offers superb performances, led by Travolta, in his best role to date as a hit man whose adventures with partner Jackson tie the seemingly unrelated stories together. Clever, almost gleeful look at everyday life on the fringes of mainstream society. Inspired by "Black Mask" magazine. A special collector's edition includes never-before-seen footage and commentary by Tarantino.**CW:** Ultra-violence, ugly drug overdose (and treatment thereof), language, homosexual rape. **154m/C VHS, LV, Closed Caption.** John Travolta, Samuel L. Jackson, Uma Thurman, Harvey Keitel, Tim Roth, Amanda Plummer, Maria De Medeiros, Ving Rhames, Eric Stoltz, Rosanna Arquette, Christopher Walken, Bruce Willis, Frank Whaley, Steve Buscemi, Quentin Tarantino; **D:** Quentin Tarantino; **W:** Roger Roberts Avary, Quentin Tarantino; **C:** Andrzej Sekula. Academy Awards '94: Best Original Screenplay; British Academy Awards '94: Best Original Screenplay, Best Supporting Actor (Jackson); Cannes Film Festival '94: Best Film; Chicago Film Critics Awards '94: Best Director (Tarantino), Best Screenplay; Golden Globe Awards '95: Best Screenplay; Independent Spirit Awards '95: Best Actor (Jackson), Best Director (Tarantino), Best Film, Best Screenplay; Los Angeles Film Critics Association Awards '94: Best Actor (Travolta), Best Director (Tarantino), Best Film, Best Screenplay; MTV Movie Awards '95: Best Film, Best Dance Sequence (John Travolta/Uma Thurman); National Board of Review Awards '94: Best Director (Tarantino), Best Film; New York Film Critics Awards '94: Best Director (Tarantino), Best Screenplay; National Society of Film Critics Awards '94: Best Director (Tarantino), Best Film, Best Screenplay; Nominations: Academy Awards '94: Best Actor (Travolta), Best Director (Tarantino), Best Film Editing, Best Picture, Best Supporting Actor (Jackson), Best Supporting Actress (Thurman); Australian Film Institute '95: Best Foreign Film; Directors Guild of America Awards '94: Best Director (Tarantino); Golden Globe Awards '95: Best Actor—Drama (Travolta), Best Director (Tarantino), Best Film—Drama, Best Supporting Actor (Jackson), Best Supporting Actress (Thurman); Independent Spirit Awards '95: Best Supporting Actor (Stoltz); MTV Movie Awards '95: Best Male Performance (Travolta), Best Female Performance (Thurman), Best On-Screen Duo (John Travolta/Samuel L. Jackson), Best Song

("Girl, You'll Be A Woman Soon"); Screen Actors Guild Award '94: Best Actor (Travolta). *MAX*

Pulse 🎬🎬 1988 (PG-13) Electricity goes awry in this science-fiction thriller about appliances and other household devices that become super-charged and destroy property and their owners. 90m/C VHS, Beta, LV, Closed Caption. Cliff DeYoung, Roxanne Hart, Joey Lawrence, Charles Tyner, Dennis Redfield, Robert Romanus, Myron Healey; *D:* Paul Golding; *C:* Peter Collister; *M:* Jay Michael Ferguson. *COL*

Pulsebeat WOOF! 1985 Flick about warring health club owners. As boring as it sounds unless you're in the mood for lots of on-screen aerobics. If so, rent Jane Fonda instead. Dubbed. 92m/C VHS, Beta. *SP* Daniel Greene, Lee Taylor Allen, Bob Small, Alice Moore, Helga Line, Alex Intriago, Peter Lupus; *D:* Marice Tobias. *LIV*

The Puma Man WOOF! 1980 Puma Man is a super hero who must stop the evil Dr. Kobras from using an ancient mask in his attempt to become ruler of the world. Unreleased theatrically in the U.S., this low budget Sci fi/ horror mix is so bad one wonders why an actor like Pleasence would sign on. Special effects these days are so extraordinary that the ones employed here are laughable. 80m/C VHS, Beta. *IT* Donald Pleasence, Walter George Alton, Sydne Rome, Miguel Angel Fuentes; *D:* Alberto De Martino. *PSM*

Pump Up the Volume 🎬🎬½ 1990 (R) High school newcomer leads double life as Hard Harry, sarcastic host of an illegal radio broadcast and Jack Nicholson soundalike. Anonymously popular with his peers, he invites the wrath of the school principal due to his less than flattering comments about the school administration. Slater seems to enjoy himself as defiant deejay while youthful cast effectively supports. 105m/C VHS, 8mm, Closed Caption. Christian Slater, Scott Paulin, Ellen Greene, Samantha Mathis, Cheryl Pollak, Annie Ross, Andy Romano, Mimi Kennedy; *D:* Allan Moyle; *W:* Allan Moyle. *COL, FCT, MVD*

Pumping Iron 1976 (PG) A widely acclaimed documentary look at the sport of bodybuilding, following the behind-the-scenes action surrounding the competition for the Mr. Olympia title. The grueling training ritual and the constant striving for perfection are all explored. 90m/C VHS, Beta, LV. Arnold Schwarzenegger, Mike Katz, Franco Columbo, Lou Ferrigno; *D:* George Butler. *COL, SCH, RHI*

Pumping Iron 2: The Women 1985 This sequel to "Pumping Iron" takes an in-depth look at the world of female body building. The documentary also follows the ladies to a competition held at Caesar's Palace in Las Vegas. 107m/C VHS, Beta, LV, Closed Caption. Lori Bowen, Bev Francis, Rachel McLish, Carla Dunlap, Lydia Cheng; *D:* George Butler. *VES*

The Pumpkin Eater 🎬🎬🎬 1964 British housewife Jo (Bancroft) has seemingly found contentment with her third husband, famous and wealthy writer Jake (Finch), and her eight children. But as Jo struggles to face middle age she discovers Jake is chronically unfaithful and goes into an emotional tailspin. Last film for Hardwicke. Slow-paced film with fine performances; based on the novel by Penelope Mortimer. 110m/C VHS, Closed Caption. *GB* Anne Bancroft, Peter Finch, James Mason, Richard Johnson, Cedric Hardwicke, Maggie Smith, Alan Webb, Eric Porter; *D:* Jack Clayton; *W:* Harold Pinter; *C:* Oswald Morris; *M:* Georges Delerue. British Academy Awards '64: Best Screenplay; Nominations: Academy Awards '64: Best Actress (Bancroft). *COL*

Pumpkinhead 🎬🎬½ 1988 (R) A farmer evokes a demon from the earth to avenge his son's death. When it continues on its murdering rampage, the farmer finds he no longer has any control over the vicious killer. 89m/C VHS, Beta, LV, Closed Caption. Lance Henriksen, John DiAquino, Kerry Remsen, Matthew Hurley, Jeff East, Kimberly Ross, Cynthia Bain, Joel Hoffman, Florence Schauffler, Buck Flower, Tom Woodruff Jr.; *D:* Stan Winston; *W:* Gary Gerani, Mark Patrick Carducci; *C:* Bojan Bazelli; *M:* Richard Stone. *MGM*

Pumpkinhead 2: Blood Wings 🎬½ 1994 (R) Five typically stupid teenagers resurrect a demon and the creature goes on a bloodthirsty rampage. His leaves his signature, a calling card in the shape of wings, at each murder scene. 88m/C VHS, LV. Ami Dolenz, Andrew (Andy) Robinson, Kane Hodder, R.A. Mihailoff, Linnea Quigley; *D:* Jeff Burr. *LIV*

Punch the Clock 🎬🎬 1990 (R) Attractive female thief finds her bail bondsman very exciting; he's ready to help her any way he can. 88m/C VHS. Michael Rogan, Chris Moore, James Lorinz; *D:* Eric L. Schlagman. *NO*

Punchline 🎬🎬 1988 (R) A look at the lives of stand-up comics, following the career ups-and-downs of an embittered professional funny-man and a frustrated housewife hitting the stage for the first time. Some very funny and touching moments and some not-so-funny and touching as the movie descends into melodrama without a cause. 100m/C VHS, Beta, LV, Closed Caption. Tom Hanks, Sally Field, John Goodman, Mark Rydell, Kim Greist, Barry Sobel, Paul Mazursky, Pam Matteson, George Michael McGrath, Taylor Negron, Damon Wayans; *D:* David Seltzer; *W:* David Seltzer; *C:* Reynaldo Villalobos. Los Angeles Film Critics Association Awards '88: Best Actor (Hanks). *COL*

The Punisher 🎬 1990 (R) Lundgren portrays Frank Castle, the Marvel Comics anti-hero known as the Punisher. When his family is killed by the mob Castle set his eyes on revenge. Filmed in Australia. 92m/C VHS, Beta, LV, Closed Caption. Dolph Lundgren, Louis Gossett Jr., Jeroen Krabbe, Kim Miyori; *D:* Mark Goldblatt; *C:* Ian Baker. *LIV*

Punk Rock Movie 1978 The musical explosion known as punk rock is documented here in its early days (circa 1977) at the Roxy in England. Includes a look at leading punk rock artists such as the Sex Pistols, the Clash, Slits, and others, and at the entire counterculture that was punk. 80m/C VHS, Beta. *MVD, SUN*

Punk Vacation 🎬 1990 A gang of motorcycle mamas terrorize a small town. The usual biker stuff. 90m/C VHS, Beta, LV. Stephen Falchi, Roxanne Rogers, Don Martin, Sandra Bogan; *D:* Stanley Lewis. *NO*

Puppet Master 🎬🎬½ 1989 (R) Four psychics are sent to investigate a puppet maker who they think may have discovered the secret of life. Before they know it, they are stalked by evil puppets. Great special effects, not-so-great script. 90m/C VHS, Beta, LV, Closed Caption. Paul LeMat, Jimmie F. Skaggs, Irene Miracle, Robin Rates, Barbara Crampton, William Hickey; *D:* David Schmoeller; *M:* Richard Band. *PAR*

Puppet Master 2 🎬🎬 1990 (R) Puppets on a rampage turn hotel into den of special effects. Less effective string pulling than in original. Long live Pinocchio. 90m/C VHS, Beta, LV, Closed Caption. Elizabeth MacLellan, Collin Bernsen, Greg Webb, Charlie Spradling, Nita Talbot, Steve Welles, Jeff Weston; *D:* David Allen; *W:* David Pabian; *M:* Richard Band. *PAR*

Puppet Master 3: Toulon's Revenge 🎬🎬 1990 (R) Prequel about the origin of the whole gory Puppet Master shebang, set in Nazi Germany. The weapon-hungry Third Reich tries to wrest secrets of artificial life from sorceror Andre Toulon, who sics his deadly puppets on them. Toulon's a good guy here, one of many contradictions in the series. Fine cast, but strictly for the followers. *CW:* Violence and sensuality. 86m/C VHS, LV, Closed Caption. Guy Rolfe, Ian Abercrombie, Sarah Douglas, Richard Lynch, Walter Gotell; *D:* David DeCoteau; *M:* Richard Band. *PAR*

Puppet Master 4 🎬🎬 1993 (R) It's the puppets versus the totems, equally loathsome midget creatures who derive their power from the same eternal force as the puppets. No one wants to share and there's lots of gore while they battle for supremacy. *CW:* Language and horror violence. 80m/C VHS, Beta, Closed Caption. Gordon Currie, Chandra West, Jason Adams, Teresa Hill, Guy Rolfe; *D:* Jeff Burr; *W:* Todd Henschell, Steven E. Carr, Jo Duffy, Dough Aarniokoski, Keith Payson; *M:* Richard Band. *PAR*

Puppet Master 5: The Final Chapter 🎬🎬½ 1994 Greedy Dr. Jennings has come to Bodega Bay Inn to capture the puppets and discover the secret formula for their animation so he can sell it to the highest bidder. But he's not the only threat, it seems the demonic Eyad, a being from another dimension, also wants the secret and has sent his own evil puppet to kill the puppet master and steal their magic. 81m/C VHS, Beta, LV, Closed Caption. Gordon Currie, Chandra West, Ian Ogilvy, Teresa Hill, Nicholas Guest, Willard Pugh, Diane McBain, Kaz Garas, Guy Rolfe; *D:* Jeff Burr; *M:* Richard Band. *PAR*

The Puppet Masters 🎬🎬½ *Robert A. Heinlein's The Puppet Masters* 1994 (R) Government official (Sutherland) discovers aliens are taking over the bodies of humans and if he doesn't find a way to stop the parasites they'll soon rule the Earth. Yes, it does sound like "Invasion of the Body Snatchers" but the film is based on Robert A. Heinlein's 1951 novel, written five years before. The parasites are sufficiently yucky but, unfortunately, this adaptation is mediocre and generally wastes a talented cast. 109m/C VHS, Beta, LV, Closed Caption. Donald Sutherland, Eric Thal, Julie Warner, Keith David, Will Patton, Richard Belzer, Yaphet Kotto; *D:* Stuart Orme; *W:* Terry Rossio, David S. Goyer, Ted Elliott; *M:* Colin Towns. *HPH*

Puppet on a Chain 🎬🎬 1972 (PG) American narcotics officer busts an Amsterdam drug ring and the leader's identity surprises him. Slow-moving thriller based on the Alistair MacLean novel. 97m/C VHS, Beta. *GB* Sven-Bertil Taube, Barbara Parkins, Alexander Knox, Patrick Allen, Geoffrey Reeve; *D:* Geoffrey Reeve; *C:* Jack Hildyard. *PSM*

The Puppetoon Movie 1987 (G) A compilation of George Pal's famous Puppetoon cartoons from the 1940s, marking his stature as an animation pioneer and innovator. Hosted by Gumby, Pokey, Speedy Alka Seltzer and Arnie the Dinosaur in newly directed scenes. 80m/C VHS, Beta, LV. *D:* Arnold Leibovit; *M:* Buddy Baker. *FHE*

The Purchase Price 🎬🎬 1932 After a less than amorous beginning, farmer Brent and mail order bride Stanwyck fall into love and financial despair in this drama bordering on comedy. Good neighbor Landau is willing to help the poor agriculturalist out in exchange for Stanwyck. Tragedy strikes again when Stanwyck's bootlegger ex-boyfriend shows up and further disasters continue to test the couple's commitment. Based on the story "The Mud Lark" by Arthur Stringer. 70m/B VHS. Barbara Stanwyck, George Brent, Lyle Talbot, Hardie Albright, David Landau; *D:* William A. Wellman; *W:* Robert Lord. *MGM*

Pure Country 🎬🎬½ 1992 (PG) An easygoing movie about a familiar subject is held together by the charm of Strait (in his movie debut) and the rest of the cast. Strait plays a country music superstar, tired of the career glitz, who decides to get out and go back to his home in Texas. He falls in love with the spunky Glasser and decides to run his career his own way. Warren is effective as his tough manager and old-time cowboy Calhoun is finely weathered as Glasser's gruff dad. 113m/C VHS, Beta, LV, Closed Caption. George Strait, Isabel Glasser, Lesley Ann Warren, Rory Calhoun, Kyle Chandler, John Doe, Molly McClure; *W:* Rex McGee; *C:* Rick Bota; *M:* Stephen Dorff. *WAR, MVD*

Pure Danger 🎬🎬½ 1996 (R) Short order cook Johnny (Howell) and his waitress girlfriend Becky (Linn) stumble upon a bag of diamonds and think all their troubles are over. Wrong—they're just beginning, since some very nasty men want the jewels and don't care who they kill to get them. Howell keeps his directorial debut fast-paced and surprisingly entertaining. *CW:* Action violence, language and some nudity. 90m/C VHS, Closed Caption. C. Thomas Howell, Teri Ann Linn, Leon, Michael Russo; *D:* C. Thomas Howell; *W:* William Applegate Jr., John Barmettler; *C:* Ken Blakey; *M:* K. Alexander Wilkinson. *PMH*

A Pure Formality 🎞🎞 *Una Pura Formalita; Une Pure Formalite* **1994 (PG-13)** Murky psycho-drama finds a disheveled man (Depardieu) winding up at an isolated police station in a nameless country (in the middle of a rainstorm, no less). The Inspector (Polanski) suspects him of a local murder, especially after he claims to be a famous writer named Onoff, yet, can remember nothing. The Inspector wants a confession and spends the night trying to exact one from his guileful suspect. French with subtitles. Film is rated at a much younger level than will possibly understand or enjoy it. **CW:** Brief shocking violence; momentary language. **111m/C VHS, LV. FR IT** Gerard Depardieu, Roman Polanski, Sergio Rubini; **D:** Giuseppe Tornatore; **W:** Giuseppe Tornatore, Pascal Quignard; **C:** Basco Giurato; **M:** Ennio Morricone. *COL*

The Pure Hell of St. Trinian's 🎞🎞½ **1961** In this sequel to "Blue Murder at St. Trinian's," a sheik who desires to fill out his harem tries recruiting at a rowdy girls' school. Although it isn't as funny as the first, due to the lack of Alistair Sim, it is still humorous. Followed by "The Great St. Trinian's Train Robbery." Based on the cartoon by Ronald Searle. **94m/B VHS. GB** Cecil Parker, Joyce Grenfell, George Cole, Thorley Walters; **D:** Frank Launder; **M:** Malcolm Arnold. *FCT*

Pure Luck 🎞½ **1991 (PG)** A who-asked-for-it remake of a 1981 Franco-Italian film called "La Chevre." The premise is the same: an accident-prone heiress disappears in Mexico, and her father tries to locate her using an equally clumsy accountant. The nebbish and an attendant tough private eye stumble and bumble south of the border until the plot arbitrarily ends. Pure awful. **96m/C VHS, Beta, LV, Closed Caption.** Martin Short, Danny Glover, Sheila Kelley, Scott Wilson, Sam Wanamaker, Harry Shearer; **D:** Nadia Tass; **W:** Herschel Weingrod, Timothy Harris. *USH*

Purgatory 🎞 **1989** While travelling abroad, two innocent women find themselves unjustly jailed. During their confinement they are tortured and raped. **90m/C VHS, Beta, LV.** Tanya Roberts, Julie Pop; **D:** Ami Artzi; **W:** Paul Aratow. *NO*

Purlie Victorious 🎞🎞 **1963** Presentation of the award-winning Broadway hit, which takes a look at racial integration. **93m/C VHS, Beta.** Ossie Davis, Ruby Dee, Godfrey Cambridge, Alan Alda; **D:** Nicholas Webster. *NO*

The Purple Heart 🎞🎞½ **1944** An American Air Force crew is shot down over Tokyo and taken into brutal POW camps. Ultimate wartime melodramatics. **99m/B VHS, Beta.** Dana Andrews, Richard Conte, Farley Granger, Donald (Don "Red") Barry, Sam Levene, Kevin O'Shea, Tala Birell, Nestor Paiva, Benson Fong, Marshall Thompson, Richard Loo; **D:** Lewis Milestone; **C:** Arthur C. Miller. *FOX*

Purple Hearts 🎞½ **1984 (R)** Wahl stars as a Navy doctor who falls in love with nurse Ladd against the backdrop of the Vietnam war. Overlong and redundant. **115m/C VHS, Beta.** Cheryl Ladd, Ken Wahl, Stephen Lee, Annie McEnroe, Paul McCrane, Cyril O'Reilly; **D:** Sidney J. Furie; **W:** Sidney J. Furie, Ron Nyswaner; **M:** Robert Folk. *WAR*

The Purple Monster Strikes 🎞🎞 **1945** A martian plots to conquer Earth to save his dying planet. Serial in fifteen episodes. **188m/B VHS.** Dennis Moore, Linda Stirling, Roy Barcroft; **D:** Spencer Gordon Bennet. *REP, VCN, MLB*

Purple Noon 🎞🎞🎞 *Plein Soleil; Lust for Evil* **1960 (PG-13)** Don't let the ratings fool you, this isn't teen fodder. The gorgeous Delon stars as opportunistic Tom Ripley, who's hired by the father of his rich, arrogant playboy friend Philippe (Ronet) to persuade him to return home to San Francisco. Instead, Ripley covets the man's yacht, beautiful girlfriend Marge (Laforet), and money, so when Philippe pushes Tom too far he disposes of him and tries to divert police suspicions. Film noir set in the hedonistic Mediterranean sun. Based on the novel "The Talented Mr. Ripley" by Patricia Highsmith. French with subtitles. **118m/C VHS, LV.**

FR Alain Delon, Maurice Ronet, Marie Laforet, Erno Crisa, Billy Kearns; **D:** Rene Clement; **W:** Rene Clement, Paul Gegauff; **C:** Henri Decae; **M:** Nino Rota. *TOU*

Purple People Eater 🎞 **1988 (PG)** The alien of the title descends to earth to mix with young girls and rock 'n roll. Based on the song of the same name whose performer, Sheb Wooley, appears in the film. Harmless, stupid fun for the whole family. **91m/C VHS, Beta, LV.** Ned Beatty, Shelley Winters, Neil Patrick Harris, Kareem Abdul-Jabbar, Little Richard, Chubby Checker, Peggy Lipton; **D:** Linda Shayne. *MED, VTR*

Purple Rain 🎞🎞½ **1984 (R)** A quasi-autobiographical video showcase for the pop-star Prince. Film tells the tale of his struggle for love, attention, acceptance, and popular artistic recognition in Minneapolis. Not a bad film, for such a monumentally egotistical movie. **113m/C VHS, Beta, LV, Closed Caption, DVD.** Prince, Apollonia, Morris Day, Olga Karlatos, Clarence Williams III; **D:** Albert Magnoli; **W:** William Blinn; **C:** Donald E. Thorin; **M:** Michel Colombier. Academy Awards '84: Original Song Score and/or Adaptation. *MVD, WAR*

The Purple Rose of Cairo 🎞🎞🎞 **1985 (PG)** A diner waitress, disillusioned by the Depression and a lackluster life, escapes into a film playing at the local movie house where a blond film hero, tiring of the monotony of his role, makes a break from the celluloid to join her in the real world. The ensuing love story allows director-writer Allen to show his knowledge of old movies and provide his fans with a change of pace. Farrow's film sister is also her real-life sister Stephanie, who went on to appear in Allen's "Zelig." **82m/C VHS, Beta, LV, Closed Caption.** Mia Farrow, Jeff Daniels, Danny Aiello, Dianne Wiest, Van Johnson, Zoe Caldwell, John Wood, Michael Tucker, Edward Herrmann, Milo O'Shea, Glenne Headly, Karen Akers, Deborah Rush; **D:** Woody Allen; **W:** Woody Allen; **C:** Gordon Willis; **M:** Dick Hyman. British Academy Awards '85: Best Film, Best Original Screenplay; Cesar Awards '86: Best Foreign Film; Golden Globe Awards '86: Best Screenplay; New York Film Critics Awards '85: Best Screenplay; Nominations: Academy Awards '85: Best Original Screenplay. *LIV, VES, HMV*

The Purple Taxi 🎞🎞½ **1977 (R)** Romantic drama revolving around several wealthy foreigners who have taken refuge in beautiful southern Ireland. From Michel Deon's bestselling novel. **93m/C VHS, Beta. FR** Fred Astaire, Charlotte Rampling, Peter Ustinov, Philippe Noiret, Edward Albert; **D:** Yves Boisset. *COL*

Purple Vigilantes 🎞½ *The Purple Riders* **1938** The Three Mesquiteers uncover a gang of vigilantes. Part of the series. **54m/B VHS, Beta.** Bob Livingston, Ray Corrigan, Max Terhune. *VCN, DVT*

Pursued 🎞🎞🎞 **1947** Excellent performances by Mitchum and Wright mark this suspenseful Western drama of a Spanish-American war veteran in search of his father's killer. **105m/C VHS, Closed Caption.** Teresa Wright, Robert Mitchum, Judith Anderson, Dean Jagger, Alan Hale, Harry Carey Jr., John Rodney; **D:** Raoul Walsh; **C:** James Wong Howe; **M:** Max Steiner. *REP, HEG*

Pursuit 🎞🎞🎞 **1972** A terrorist threatens to release a toxic nerve gas throughout a city hosting a political convention. Tension mounts as federal agents must beat the extremists' countdown to zero. Based on the novel by Crichton. **73m/C VHS, Beta.** Ben Gazzara, E.G. Marshall, Martin Sheen, Joseph Wiseman, William Windom; **D:** Michael Crichton; **M:** Jerry Goldsmith. *REP*

Pursuit 🎞🎞 **1990 (R)** A mercenary comes out of retirement to join a renegade team recovering stolen gold. But they turn on him, stealing the treasure and leaving him a hostage. Now he must track them down, or there's no movie. **CW:** Language, violence, and sensuality. **94m/C VHS, Closed Caption.** James Ryan, Andre Jacobs; **D:** John H. Parr. *HBO*

The Pursuit of D.B. Cooper 🎞🎞 **1981 (PG)** Based on an actual hijacking that occurred on Thanksgiving Eve in 1971 in which J.R. Meade (alias D.B. Cooper) parachuted out of an airliner with $200,000 of stolen money. Although

his fate and whereabouts have remained a mystery, this story speculates about what may have happened. **100m/C VHS, Beta, LV.** Robert Duvall, Treat Williams, Kathryn Harrold, Ed Flanders; **D:** Roger Spottiswoode; **C:** Harry Stradling Jr.; **M:** James Horner. *LIV, VES*

The Pursuit of Happiness 🎞🎞½ **1970 (PG)** An idealistic man is convicted of manslaughter after accidentally running down a woman. Once in prison, he's faced with the decision to try to escape. **85m/C VHS, Beta.** Michael Sarrazin, Arthur Hill, E.G. Marshall, Barbara Hershey, Robert Klein; **D:** Robert Mulligan. *NO*

Pursuit of the Graf Spee 🎞🎞½ *The Battle of the River Plate* **1957** Three small British ships destroy the mighty Graf Spee, a WWII German battleship. **106m/C VHS, Beta. GB** Anthony Quayle, Peter Finch, Ian Hunter; **D:** Michael Powell. *NO*

Pursuit to Algiers 🎞🎞 **1945** The modernized Holmes and Watson guard over the King of fictional Rovenia during a sea voyage, during which assassins close in. **65m/B VHS, Beta, Closed Caption.** Basil Rathbone, Nigel Bruce, Martin Kosleck, Marjorie Riordan, Rosalind Ivan, John Abbott; **D:** Roy William Neill. *FOX*

Pushed to the Limit 🎞½ **1992 (R)** Harry Lee, the most feared gangster in Chinatown, is about to meet his match in martial-arts queen Lesseos. She's out for revenge when she learns that Lee is responsible for her brother's murder but first she must get by Lee's lethal bodyguard, the equally skilled Inga. **CW:** Martial arts violence/drug content. **88m/C VHS, LV.** Mimi Lesseos. *IMP*

Pushing Hands 🎞🎞½ **1992** Aging tai chi master Mr. Chu (Lung) leaves Beijing to live with his son Alex (Wang) and daughter-in-law Martha (Snyder) in suburban New York. High-strung Martha doesn't understand her tranquilly stubborn father-in-law, nor does Chu find disposable American society much to his liking. Naturally, and slowly, some accomodations are made. The title is a tai chi reference to keeping your opponent off-balance while maintaining your own equilibrium. Director Lee's debut feature is also the first in his trilogy of family films—followed by the more accomplished "The Wedding Banquet" and "Eat Drink Man Woman." English and Mandarin Chinese with subtitles. **100m/C VHS, LV.** Sihung Lung, Deb Snyder, Bo Z. Wang, Lai Wang; **D:** Ang Lee; **W:** Ang Lee; **C:** Jong Lin; **M:** Xiao-Song Qu. *TRI*

Puss 'n Boots 🎞🎞 **1984** From "Faerie Tale Theatre" comes the story of a cat who makes his poor master a rich land-owning nobleman. **60m/C VHS, Beta, Closed Caption.** Ben Vereen, Gregory Hines; **D:** Robert Iscove. *FOX, FCT*

Putney Swope 🎞🎞🎞 **1969 (R)** Comedy about a token black ad man mistakenly elected Chairman of the board of a Madison Avenue ad agency who turns the company upside-down. A series of riotous spoofs on commercials is the highpoint in this funny, though somewhat dated look at big business. **84m/B VHS, Beta.** Arnold Johnson, Laura Greene, Stan Gottlieb, Mel Brooks; **D:** Robert Downey. *COL*

Puzzle 🎞🎞½ **1978** Franciscus searches for the urn that contains the remains of Buddha but instead finds danger and intrigue. Made for television. **90m/C VHS. AU** James Franciscus, Wendy Hughes, Robert Helpmann, Peter Gwynne, Gerald Kennedy, Kerry McGuire; **D:** Gordon Hessler. *ACA*

Pygmalion 🎞🎞🎞½ **1938** Oscar-winning film adaptation of Shaw's play about a cockney flower-girl who is transformed into a "lady" under the guidance of a stuffy phonetics professor. Shaw himself aided in writing the script in this superbly acted comedy that would be adapted into the musical, "My Fair Lady," first on Broadway in 1956 and for the screen in 1964. **96m/B VHS, Beta, LV. GB** Leslie Howard, Wendy Hiller, Wilfred Lawson, Marie Lohr, Scott Sunderland, David Tree, Everley Gregg, Leueen McGrath, Jean Cadell, Eileen Beldon, Frank Atkinson, O.B. Clarence, Esme Percy, Violet Vanbrugh, Iris Hoey, Viola Tree, Irene Browne, Kate Cutler, Cathleen Nesbitt, Cecil Trouncer, Stephen Murray, Wally Patch, H.F. Maltby; **D:** Anthony Asquith, Leslie Howard; **W:** W.P. Lipscomb, Anatole de Grunwald, Cecil Lewis, Ian Dalyrymple, George Bernard Shaw; **C:** Harry Stradling. Academy Awards '38: Best Screenplay; Venice Film Festival '38: Best Actor (Howard); Nominations: Academy Awards '38: Best Actor (Howard), Best Actress (Hiller), Best Picture. *MON, NOS, COL*

Pyrates 🎬 **1991 (R)** Real life husband-wife team of Bacon and Sedgwick try to provide fireworks as hot, hot lovers in the forgettable one. For the price of this one you can buy a newspaper and chewing gum instead. Use both at the same time and you'll be ahead of everyone involved in this senseless movie.**CW:** Language and sensuality. **98m/C VHS.** Kevin Bacon, Kyra Sedgwick, Bruce Martyn Payne, Kristin Datillo; **D:** Noah Stern. *VES, LIV*

A Pyromaniac's Love Story 🎬🎬 **1995 (PG)** Offbeat tale of romance has a neigborhood bakery burning down and every major character confessing to the crime. Earnest working stiffs, snotty rich kids, and kindly old shop owners all have really confusing reasons for wanting to take the heat, most of which have to do with unrequited love. At times charming, but ultimately too whimsical for its own good. The quirky characters and goofy plot twists sabotage any attempt to ignite much interest. **99m/C VHS, LV, Closed Caption.** John Leguizamo, Sadie Frost, William Baldwin, Erika Eleniak, Michael Lerner, Joan Plowright, Armin Mueller-Stahl, Richard Crenna; **D:** Joshua Brand; **W:** Morgan Ward; **C:** John Schwartzman; **M:** Rachel Portman. *TOU*

Python Wolf 🎬🎬 *C.A.T. Squad: Python Wolf* **1988 (R)** It's non-stop action in South Africa as a counter-terrorist group sets out to thwart a drug smuggler's plans to export plutonium. As usual, intense pacing from director Friedkin. Made for television. Sequel to "C.A.T. Squad" (1986). **100m/C VHS, LV.** Joe Cortese, Jack Youngblood, Steve James, Deborah Van Valkenburgh, Miguel Ferrer, Alan Scarfe; **D:** William Friedkin; **M:** Ennio Morricone. *THV*

The Pyx 🎬🎬🎬 *The Hooker Cult Murders* **1973 (R)** Canadian suspense thriller about the murder of a prostitute with satanic overtones. Poice sergeant investigates the crime and enters a world of devil worship and decadence. Based on the novel by John Buell. **111m/C VHS.** *CA* Karen Black, Christopher Plummer, Donald Pilon; **D:** Harvey Hart. *PSM*

Q & A 🎬🎬 **1990 (R)** Semi-taut thriller with Nolte playing a totally corrupt, hair-trigger cop trying to make his murder of a drug dealer look like self-defense. Assigned to the case is an ex-cop turned assistant DA (Hutton) who's supposed to sweep the case under the rug. Then he finds out another dealer (Assante) is a witness and he happens to be romancing Hutton's former girlfriend (film debut of director Lumet's daughter). Lots of violence and raw language. **132m/C VHS, Beta, LV, Closed Caption.** Nick Nolte, Timothy Hutton, Armand Assante, Patrick O'Neal, Lee Richardson, Luis Guzman, Charles S. Dutton, Jenny Lumet, Paul Calderone, Fyvush Finkel; **D:** Sidney Lumet; **W:** Sidney Lumet; **C:** Andrzej Bartkowiak; **M:** Ruben Blades. *HBO, WAR*

Q Ships 🎬🎬½ **1928** Silent German drama about a submarine commander who has inner conflicts with his country's war effort. Uses actual WWI footage. **78m/B VHS, Beta.** *GE* J.P. Kennedy, Roy Travers, Johnny Butt, Philip Hewland; **D:** Geoffrey Barkas, Michael Barringer. *GPV, DVT, GLV*

Q (The Winged Serpent) 🎬🎬🎬 **1982 (R)** A cult of admirers surrounds this goony monster flick about dragonlike Aztec god Quetzlcoatl, summoned to modern Manhattan by gory human sacrifices, and hungry for rooftop sunbathers and construction teams. Direction and special effects are pretty ragged, but witty script helps the cast shine, especially Moriarty as a lowlife crook who's found the beast's hidden nest. Also called "Q: The Winged Serpent." **92m/C VHS, Beta.** Michael Moriarty, Candy Clark, David Carradine, Richard Roundtree; **D:** Larry Cohen; **W:** Larry Cohen. *USH*

QB VII 🎬🎬🎬½ **1974** A knighted physician brings a suit for libel against a novelist for implicating him in war crimes. Hopkins as the purportedly wronged doctor and Gazzara as the writer are both superb. Ending is stunning. Adapted from the novel by Leon Uris. Over five hours long; made for TV. Available only as a three-cassette set. **313m/C VHS, Beta, LV.** Anthony Hopkins, Ben Gazzara, Lee Remick, Leslie Caron, Juliet Mills, John Gielgud, Anthony Quayle; **D:** Tom Gries; **M:** Jerry Goldsmith. *COL, SWC*

Quackser Fortune Has a Cousin in the Bronx 🎬🎬🎬 *Fun Loving* **1970 (R)** An Irish fertilizer salesman meets an exchange student from the U.S., who finds herself attracted to this unlearned, but not unknowing, man. An original love story with drama and appeal. **88m/C VHS, Beta, LV.** *IR* Gene Wilder, Margot Kidder; **D:** Waris Hussein. *VCI*

Quadrophenia 🎬🎬🎬 **1979 (R)** Pete Townshend's excellent rock opera about an alienated youth looking for life's meaning in Britain's rock scene circa 1963. Music by The Who is powerful and apt. Fine performance by Sting in his acting debut. **115m/C VHS, Beta, LV.** *GB* Phil Daniels, Mark Wingett, Philip Davis, Leslie Ash, Sting; **D:** Franc Roddam; **C:** Brian Tufano. *MVD, COL, RHI*

Quake 🎬½ **1992 (R)** Railsback stars as a stalker who takes advantage of the 1990 San Franscisco earthquake to finally obtain the woman of his dreams. A surveillance expert, he's after a beautiful lawyer (Anderson) and when the earthquake leaves her trapped he rushes to rescue her—only to hold her captive himself.**CW:** Language, violence, and sexuality. **83m/C VHS.** Steve Railsback, Erika Anderson, Eb Lottimer, Dick Miller; **D:** Louis Morneau; **W:** Mark Evan Schwartz. *COL*

Quality Street 🎬🎬 **1937** English lovers Tone and Hepburn are separated when he leaves to fight in the Napoleonic Wars. When Tone returns years later, he's forgotten his erstwhile heartthrob. He also fails to recognize that the 16-year old coquette who's caught his eye is his old beloved in disguise. Cast works hard to overcome the absurd premise, based on the play by Sir James Barrie. **84m/B VHS, LV.** Katharine Hepburn, Franchot Tone, Fay Bainter, Eric Blore, Cora Witherspoon, Estelle Winwood, Florence Lake, Bonita Granville; **D:** George Stevens; **W:** J.M. Barrie. Nominations: Academy Awards '37: Best Original Score. *NOS, FCT, TTC*

Quarantine 🎬🎬½ **1989 (R)** Quarantine camps for carriers of a fatal virus are the serious measures taken by the nation. The solution is clear to a rebel and an inventor; all must be liberated or exterminated. **92m/C VHS.** Beatrice Boepple, Garwin Sanford, Jerry Wasserman, Charles Wilkinson; **D:** Charles Wilkinson; **W:** Charles Wilkinson. *REP*

The Quarrel 🎬🎬½ **1993** Chaim Kovler is a New York poet visiting Montreal in 1948. In a park he notices a group of Orthodox Jews and discovers one is his childhood friend Hersh. Fifteen years earlier their friendship broke over Chaim's decision to give up the religious life for his writing. Having lost their families to the Holocaust in Poland, both men have immigrated to new lives in North America. They immediately pick up their quarrel over religious faith and its value, particularly in light of the Holocaust. The two characters serve too much as careful ideologues to be compelling and the story turns cloyingly sentimental. Based on a short story by Yiddish writer Chaim Grade. **88m/C VHS.** *CA* Saul Rubinek, R.H. Thomson; **D:** Eli Cohen; **W:** David Brandes; **M:** William Goldstein. *BMG*

Quarterback Princess 🎬🎬 **1985** Workaday made-for-TV telling of the real-life girl who goes out for football and becomes homecoming queen. Heartwarming, if you like that kinda stuff, but not exciting. **96m/C VHS, Beta, Closed Caption.** Helen Hunt, Don Murray, John Stockwell, Daphne Zuniga; **D:** Noel Black. *FOX*

Quartet 🎬🎬🎬 **1981 (R)** A young French woman is taken in by an English couple after her husband goes to prison. The husband seduces her, and she becomes trapped emotionally and socially. Superbly acted, claustrophobic drama based on a Jean Rhys novel. **101m/C VHS, Beta.** *GB FR* Isabelle Adjani, Alan Bates, Maggie Smith, Anthony Higgins; **D:** James Ivory; **W:** Ruth Prawer Jhabvala. Cannes Film Festival '81: Best Actress (Adjani). *WAR*

Quartier Mozart 🎬🎬 **1992** Sexual farce presenting the assimilation of African American pop-culture into African traditions. A local sorceress uses witchcraft to give Queen of the 'Hood a first-hand look at sexual politics. The young girl enters the body of a boy struggling to find his place in the male hierarchy established by neighborhood Casanovas. In French with English subtitles. **80m/C VHS.** *D:* Jean-Pierre Bekolo. *KIV*

Quatermass 2 🎬🎬🎬 *Enemy from Space* **1957** In the well-made sequel to "Quatermass Experiment," (also known as "The Creeping Unknown") Professor Quatermass battles blobs and brainwashed zombies to rescue government officials whose bodies have been invaded by aliens. "Five Million Years to Earth" concluded the trilogy. **84m/B VHS, Beta, LV.** *GB* Brian Donlevy, John Longden, Sidney James, Bryan Forbes, William Franklyn, Vera Day, John Van Eyssen, Michael Ripper, Michael Balfour; **D:** Val Guest; **M:** James Bernard. *FCT, CTH, SNC*

Quatermass and the Pit 🎬🎬½ **1958** From the original BBC production. Professor Quatermass is up to his ears in trouble as a Martian spacecraft is found by subway workers. Not long after a monster stalks the streets of London. Remade cinematically in 1968 as "Five Million Years to Earth." **180m/B VHS.** *GB* Andre Morell, Cec Linder. *SNC, MRV*

Quatermass Conclusion 🎬🎬 **1979** An elderly British scientist comes out of retirement to stop an immobilizing death ray from outer space from destroying Earth. Edited version of a television miniseries continues earlier adventures of Quatermass on film and television. **105m/C VHS, Beta.** *GB* John Mills, Simon MacCorkindale, Barbara Kellerman, Margaret Tyzack; **D:** Piers Haggard. *NO*

The Quatermass Experiment 🎬🎬🎬 *The Creeping Unknown* **1956** Excellent British production about an astronaut who returns to Earth carrying an alien infestation that causes him to turn into a horrible monster. Competent acting and tense direction. Followed by "Enemy From Space." **78m/B VHS.** *GB* Brian Donlevy, Margia Dean, Jack Warner, Richard Wordsworth; **D:** Val Guest; **M:** James Bernard. *MGM, SNC, NOS*

Quatorze Juliet 🎬🎬½ **1932** A taxi driver and a flower girl meet on Bastille Day and fall in love. When he becomes involved with gangsters, she steers him back to virtue in this minor French relic from director Clair. **85m/B VHS.** *FR* Anabella Rigaud, Jorge Rigaud; **D:** Rene Clair. *VDM, FCT*

Que Viva Mexico 🎬🎬🎬 **1932** Eisenstein's grand unfinished folly on the history of Mexico, reconstructed and released in 1979 by his protege, Grigori Alexandrov. Divided into four sections: "Sandunga" covers the Tehuantepec jungles and its inhabitants; "Manguei" is about a peasant and his bride; "Fiesta" devotes itself to bullfighting and romance; and "Soldadera" depicts the 1910 Mexican revolution through frescoes. Along with "Greed" and "Napoleon," it remains as one of cinema's greatest irrecoverable casualties. Russian narration with English subtitles. **85m/B VHS, Beta.** *RU* **D:** Sergei Eisenstein, Grigori Alexandrov. *KIV*

Queen Bee 🎬🎬½ **1955** Crawford is at her manipulative best as Southern belle Eva Phillips, married to wealthy Georgia mill owner Avery (Sullivan). The ruthless Eva is despised by her bitter, tippling husband who finds a chance at romance when cousin Jennifer (Marlow) comes to visit. Naturally, Eva can't stand any competition, though she doesn't care about Avery, and tries to break up the duo even as she seeks to renew her own affair with a former lover (Ireland). Based on the novel by Edna Lee. **94m/B VHS, Closed Caption.** Joan Crawford, Barry Sullivan, John Ireland, Lucy Marlow, Betsy Palmer, Fay Wray; *D:* Ranald MacDougall; *W:* Ranald MacDougall; *C:* Charles B(ryant) Lang; *M:* George Duning. Nominations: Academy Awards '55: Best Black and White Cinematography, Best Costume Design (B & W).*COL*

Queen Boxer 🐾 1973 (R) A female kickboxer beats up those who reprehensibly enslaved her family. **92m/C VHS, Beta.** Judy Lee, Peter Yang Kwan. *LIV*

Queen Christina 🐾🐾🐾½ 1933 A stylish, resonant star vehicle for Garbo, portraying the 17th-century Swedish queen from ascension to the throne to her romance with a Spanish ambassador. Alternately hilarious and moving, it holds some of Garbo's greatest and most memorable moments. Gilbert's second to last film and his only successful outing after the coming of sound. **101m/B VHS, Beta, LV.** Greta Garbo, John Gilbert, Lewis Stone, Sir C. Aubrey Smith, Ian Keith, Reginald Owen, Elizabeth Young; *D:* Rouben Mamoulian; *C:* William H. Daniels. *MGM*

Queen for a Day 🐾🐾½ *Horsie* 1951 Three differing vignettes, based on a rather notorious radio and TV game show of the time, in which "deserving" (or sufficiently pathetic) working-class women were rewarded for their selflessness. Part one concerns a perfect suburban family whose son contracts polio. Part two has a teen spooking his immigrant parents by working as a carnival high diver to earn college cash. The finale is a Dorothy Parker farce about a homely but kindhearted nurse caring for the child of an unappreciative couple. So popular was this segment that the film was retitled after the main character. Overall, not bad considering the source. **107m/B VHS.** Phyllis Avery, Darren McGavin, Tristram Coffin, Adam Williams, Tracey Roberts, Jack Bailey, Jim Morgan, Fort Pearson; *D:* Arthur Lubin. *NOS*

Queen Kelly 🐾🐾🐾 1929 The popularly known, slapdash version of von Stroheim's famous final film, in which an orphan goes from royal marriage to white slavery to astounding wealth. Never really finished, the film is the edited first half of the intended project, prepared for European release after von Stroheim had been fired. Even so, a campy, extravagant and lusty melodrama. Silent. **113m/B VHS, Beta, LV, 8mm.** Gloria Swanson, Walter Byron, Seena Owen, Tully Marshall, Madame Sul Te Wan; *D:* Erich von Stroheim. *NOS, KIV, VYY*

Queen Margot 🐾🐾🐾½ *La Reine Margot* 1994 (R) Blood-soaked period of French history is duly rendered on screen in big-budget costume epic. Beautiful Catholic, Marguerite de Valois (Adjani), is the pawn of her devious mother, the widowed queen Catherine de Medici (Lisi) who skillfully manipulates unstable son Charles IX (Anglade), the nominal ruler of 1570's France, while she plots to marry Margot off to Protestant Henri de Navarre (Auteuil). Margot is contemptuous of her new husband, preferring to find her amatory amusements in the Paris streets, where she takes a handsome lover (Perez). But both Margot and Henri are united against the Queen when Catherine's minions order the murder of the rival Huguenots—a notably violent affair known as the St. Bartholomew's Day Massacre. The history's confusing, the violence graphic, the acting flamboyant, and the visuals top-notch. Based on the novel by Alexandre Dumas. French with subtitles; originally released at 161 minutes.*CW:* Nudity; strong sexuality; graphic scenes of massacre. **135m/C VHS, LV.** *FR* Isabelle Adjani, Daniel Auteuil, Virna Lisi, Jean-Hugues Anglade, Vincent Perez, Pascal Greggory, Miguel Bose, Dominique Blanc, Claudio Amendola, Asia Argento, Julien Rassam, Jean-Claude Brialy; *D:* Patrice Chereau; *W:* Patrice Chereau, Daniele Thompson; *M:* Goran Bregovic. Cannes Film Festival '94: Special Jury Prize, Best Actress (Lisi); Cesar Awards '95: Best Actress (Adjani), Best Cinematography, Best Costume Design, Best Supporting Actor (Anglade), Best Supporting Actress (Lisi); Nomina-

tions: Academy Awards '94: Best Costume Design; British Academy Awards '95: Best Foreign Film; Cesar Awards '95: Best Director (Chereau), Best Film, Best Supporting Actress (Blanc); Golden Globe Awards '95: Best Foreign Film. *MAX*

Queen of Diamonds 🐾🐾 198? A woman pulls off the biggest diamond heist of all time. **90m/C VHS, Beta.** Claudia Cardinale, Stanley Baker, Henri Charriere. *NO*

Queen of Diamonds 🐾🐾 1991 The "Queen of Diamonds" is an alienated blackjack dealer in Vegas who, in between dealing cards, casually searches for her missing husband and looks after an old man in a motel. **77m/C VHS.** Tinka Menkes; *D:* Nina Menkes; *W:* Nina Menkes. *FCT*

Queen of Hearts 🐾🐾🐾½ 1989 (PG) Excellent, original romantic comedy is a directorial triumph for Amiel in his first feature. An Italian couple defy both their families and marry for love. Four children later, we find them running a diner in England. Humorous, dramatic, sad—everything a move can and should be. Fine performances. **112m/C VHS, Beta, LV.** *GB* Anita Zagaria, Joseph Long, Eileen Way, Vittorio Duse, Vittorio Amandola, Ian Hawkes; *D:* Jon Amiel; *M:* Michael Convertino. *NO*

The Queen of Mean 🐾½ *Leona Helmsley: The Queen of Mean* 1990 Tabloid TV-movie based on Randsell Pierson's scandal-sheet bio of the hotel magnate and convicted tax cheat. See Leona connive. See Leona bitch. See Leona get hers. What's the point? If you ask that you're too bright to watch. **94m/C VHS, Closed Caption.** Suzanne Pleshette, Lloyd Bridges, Bruce Weitz, Joe Regalbuto; *D:* Richard Michaels; *C:* Hanania Baer. *FRH*

Queen of Outer Space woof! 1958 Notorious male-chauvinist sci-fi cheapie starts out slow, but then the laughs keep coming as the cast plays the hyperdumb material straight. Space cadets crash on Venus, find it ruled by women—and the dolls have wicked plans in store for mankind. Don't be surprised if you've seen the sets before since they were borrowed from "Forbidden Planet," "World Without End," and "Flight to Mars." **80m/C VHS, Beta.** Zsa Zsa Gabor, Eric Fleming, Laurie Mitchell, Paul Birch, Barbara Darrow, Dave Willcock, Lisa Davis, Patrick Waltz, Marilyn Buferd, Marjorie Durant, Lynn Cartwright, Gerry Gaylor; *D:* Edward L. Bernds. *FXV*

The Queen of Spades 🐾🐾🐾 1949 Mystical drama about a Russian soldier who ruins his life searching for winning methods of card playing. Well-made version of the Pushkin story. **95m/B VHS, LV.** *GB* Anton Walbrook, Edith Evans, Ronald Howard, Mary Jerrold, Yvonne Mitchell, Anthony Dawson; *D:* Thorold Dickinson. *NO*

Queen of the Amazons 🐾½ 1947 A girl searches for her fiance and finds him reluctantly held captive by a tribe of women who rule the jungle. **60m/B VHS, Beta, LV.** Robert Lowery, Patricia Morison, J. Edward Bromberg, John Miljan. *SNC, NOS*

Queen of the Jungle 🐾 1935 Re-edited adventure serial featuring a white woman cast off in a hot-air balloon and landing in Africa, where she is hailed as a Queen. High camp, starring ex-Our Ganger Kornman. **85m/B VHS, Beta, 8mm.** Mary Kornman, Reed Howes; *D:* Robert F. "Bob" Hill. *VYY, NOS, MLB*

Queen of the Road 🐾🐾 1984 A feisty Aussie schoolteacher starts a new life as a tractor-trailer driver. **96m/C VHS, Beta.** *AU* Joanne Samuel, Amanda Muggleton; *D:* Bruce Best. *LIV, VES*

Queen of the Stardust Ballroom 🐾🐾🐾 1975 Well-made television drama about a lonely widow who goes to a local dance hall, where she meets a man and begins an unconventional little love. **98m/C Beta.** Maureen Stapleton, Charles Durning, Michael Strong, Charlotte Rae, Sam O'Steen; *D:* Michael Brandon; *M:* Billy Goldenberg. *PSM*

Queenie 🐾🐾½ 1987 Television miniseries loosely based on the life of actress Merle Oberon, exploring her rise to stardom. Based on the best-selling novel by Michael Korda, Oberon's nephew by marriage. Many long, dry passages fit for leav-

ing the room for snacks. **233m/C VHS.** Mia Sara, Kirk Douglas, Martin Balsam, Claire Bloom, Chaim Topol, Joel Grey, Sarah Miles, Joss Ackland; *D:* Larry Peerce; *M:* Georges Delerue. *VTR, NWV*

Queens Logic 🐾🐾½ 1991 (R) Ensemble comedy in the tradition of "The Big Chill" featuring the trials and tribulations of the "old-neighborhood" gang, who gather again on hometurf and reminisce. Most of the film centers around Olin and girlfriend Webb and whether or not he will chicken out of their wedding. Not bad comedy, with Mantegna delivering most of the good lines. **116m/C VHS, LV, Closed Caption.** John Malkovich, Kevin Bacon, Jamie Lee Curtis, Linda Fiorentino, Joe Mantegna, Ken Olin, Tom Waits, Chloe Webb, Ed Marinaro, Kelly Bishop, Tony Spiridakis; *D:* Steve Rash; *W:* Tony Spiridakis; *M:* Joe Jackson. *LIV*

Querelle 🐾🐾½ 1983 (R) Querelle, a handsome sailor, finds himself involved in a bewildering environment of murder, drug smuggling, and homosexuality in the port of Brest. Highly stylized and erotic sets, along with a dark look, give the film an interesting feel. Nice performances by Davis, Nero, and Moreau. Fassbinder's controversial last film, based on the story by Jean Genet. Strange, difficult narrative (such as it is), alternately boring and engrossing. **106m/C VHS, Beta.** *GE* Brad Davis, Jeanne Moreau, Franco Nero, Laurent Malet; *D:* Rainer Werner Fassbinder; *M:* Peer Raben. *COL, APD, GLV*

The Quest 🐾🐾 1986 (PG) Australian film never released theatrically in the United States. A young boy (Thomas, of "E.T." fame) raised in the outback investigates a local Aboriginal superstition about a monster living in an ancient cemetery. Not bad, just dull. **94m/C VHS, Beta, Closed Caption.** *AU* Henry Thomas, Tony Barry, John Ewart, Rachel Friend, Tamsin West, Dennis Miller, Katya Manning; *D:* Brian Trenchard-Smith. *NLC*

The Quest 🐾🐾 1996 (PG-13) In his directorial debut, Van Damme plays pickpocket Christopher Dubois, who finds his adventures just beginning when he hops a freighter heading for the Far East in order to escape police trouble. He learns about a prestigious martial arts competition, where the prize could set him up for life, if he can manage to get into the invitation-only event. After many films set in the future, Van Damme chose to set this one in the 20's, with fairly good results. He piles on the beautiful location shots until the inevitable martial arts melee toward the end. Pacing is sketchy but Van Damme does display directorial talent.*CW:* Adventure violence and martial arts fights. **95m/C VHS, LV, Closed Caption.** Jean-Claude Van Damme, Roger Moore, Aki Aleong, James Remar, Jack McGee, Janet Gunn, Abdel Qissi, Louis Mandylor; *D:* Jean-Claude Van Damme; *W:* Stuart Klein, Paul Mones; *C:* David Gribble; *M:* Randy Edelman. *USH*

Quest for Fire 🐾🐾🐾 1982 (R) An interesting story sans the usual dialogue thing. A group of men during the Ice Age must wander the land searching for fire after they lose theirs fending off an attack. During their quest, they encounter and battle various animals and tribesmen in order to survive. The special language they speak was developed by Anthony Burgess, while the primitive movements were Desmond "The Naked Ape" Morris. Perlman went on to become the Beast in TV's "Beauty and the Beast"; Chong is the daughter of Tommy Chong of the comic duo Cheech and Chong. **75m/C VHS, Beta, LV.** *FR* Everett McGill, Ron Perlman, Nameer El-Kadi, Rae Dawn Chong; *D:* Jean-Jacques Annaud; *W:* Gerard Brach. Academy Awards '82: Best Makeup; Genie Awards '83: Best Actress (Chong). *FOX*

Quest for Love 🐾🐾½ 1971 Quirky sci-fi story of a man who passes through a time warp and finds himself able to maintain two parallel lives. Based on John Wyndham's short story. **90m/C VHS, Beta.** *GB* Joan Collins, Tom Bell, Denholm Elliott, Laurence Naismith; *D:* Ralph Thomas. *NO*

Quest for the Mighty Sword ✍ 1990

(PG-13) A warrior battles dragons, demons and evil wizards. 94m/C VHS, Beta, LV. Eric Allen Kramer, Margaret Lenzey, Donald O'Brien, Dina Marrone, Chris Murphy; D: David Hills. COL

Quest of the Delta Knights ✍✍½

1993 (PG) Swashbuckling fantasy about a kingdom suffering under an evil ruler and his equally sinister queen. They are opposed by the heroic Delta Knights whose only chance to defeat the fiendish powers of darkness is by unearthing a legendary storehouse containing technology from the age of Atlantis and all the powers of the Ancients. 97m/C VHS. David Warner, Olivia Hussey, Corbin Allred, Brigid Conley Walsh, David Kriegel; D: James Dodson; W: Redge Mahaffey. HMD

A Question of Attribution ✍✍½ 1991

Sir Anthony Blunt (Fox) is an internationally respected art expert who also serves as an art adviser to Queen Elizabeth II. His life unravels when an on-going British Intelligence investigation reveals him to be the fourth man in the Burgess-Maclean-Philby scandal involving Englishmen who spied for, and eventually defected to, the USSR. The investigation of Blunt's covert past is paralleled with his own art investigation of a painting attributed to Titian. Three men are depicted in the art work—with a fourth male figure discovered to have been painted over. Alan Bennett adapted his play for the television drama. 90m/C VHS. GB James Fox, David Calder, Geoffrey Palmer, Prunella Scales, Mark Payton, Jason Flemyng, Edward De Souza, Ann Beach; D: John Schlesinger; W: Alan Bennett. FOX

Question of Faith ✍✍½ 1993 A happily

married woman is diagnosed with a rare form of cancer. Much to her family's dismay, she turns to some unconventional medical therapies in order to heal herself. Based on a true story. Basically noble, Archer and Neill lift this tearjerker out of most of its maudlin aspects. 90m/C VHS, Closed Caption. Anne Archer, Jean Neill, Frances Lee McCain, James Tolkan, James Hong, CCH Pounder, Louis Giambalvo, Norman Parker, Michael Constantine; D: Stephen Gyllenhaal; W: Bruce Hart. WOV

A Question of Guilt ✍✍ 1978 When

her child turns up dead, a free-wheeling divorcee is the prime suspect. Made-for-television drama. 100m/C VHS. Tuesday Weld, Ron Leibman, Peter Masterson, Alex Rocco, Viveca Lindfors, Lana Wood; D: Robert Butler. LIV

Question of Honor ✍✍½ 1980 Under

governmental pressures, an honest narcotics cop decides to inform on his department's corruption. Co-written and produced by ex-cop Sonny Grosso, on whom "The French Connection" was based. Made for television and based on the book, "Point Blank," by Grosso and Philip Rosenberg. 134m/C VHS, Beta. Ben Gazzara, Paul Sorvino, Robert Vaughn, Tony Roberts, Danny Aiello, Anthony Zerbe; D: Jud Taylor; W: Budd Schulberg. NO

A Question of Love ✍✍✍ 1978 Fine

performances in this well-done television movie about two lesbians—one of whom is fighting her ex-husband for custody of their child. 100m/C VHS. Gena Rowlands, Jane Alexander, Ned Beatty, Clu Gulager, Bonnie Bedelia, James Sutorius, Jocelyn Brando; D: Jerry Thorpe; M: Billy Goldenberg. NO

Question of Silence ✍✍✍ De Stilte

Rond Christine M 1983 (R) Three women, strangers to each other, stand trial for a murdering a man. Intricately analyzed courtroom drama with much to say about male domination. In Dutch with English subtitles or dubbed. 92m/C VHS, Beta. NL Cox Habrema, Nelly Frijda, Henriette Tol, Edda Barends; D: Marleen Gorris. FRF

Qui Etes Vous, Mr. Sorge? ✍✍

1961 The story of German journalist Richard Sorge, who was hanged by the Japanese in 1944 for being a Soviet spy. Uninteresting docudrama which focuses on the opinions of various witnesses as to the accuracy of the espionage charge. In French with English subtitles. 130m/B

VHS, Beta. FR Thomas Holtzman, Keiko Kishi; D: Andre Girard. BAR

Quick ✍✍½ 1993 (R) Polo stars as Quick, a

professional assassin whose latest job is Herschel (Donovan), a mob accountant turned federal witness. When Quick is double-crossed, she takes off with Herschel as her insurance and a couple of bad guys (Fahey and Davi) on her trail. Not too much sex and lots of violence to go along with the fast pacing. 99m/C VHS. Teri Polo, Martin Donovan, Jeff Fahey, Robert Davi, Tia Carrere; D: Rick King; W: Frederick Bailey; M: Robert Sprayberry. ACA

The Quick and the Dead ✍✍ 1987

Based on a Louis L'Amour story, this made-for-cable western features a lone gunslinger who protects a defenseless settler's family from the lawless West, only to become a source of sexual tension for the wife. 91m/C VHS, Beta. Sam Elliott, Tom Conti, Kate Capshaw, Kenny Morrison, Matt Clark; D: Robert Day; M: Stephen Dorff. ORI, WAR

The Quick and the Dead ✍✍ 1994

(R) Stone is a tough gal gunslinger (ala a female Clint Eastwood) out to avenge the murder of her father. Ellen arrives in the frontier town of Redemption where arch-villain Herod (Hackman) rules by means of violence and intimidation. Director Raimi packs in so many cliches that you're amazed that it's not a parody of the spaghetti westerns it tries to emulate. Maybe if Stone and Raimi didn't take this film so seriously, it would have been a better movie. One redeeming quality of the film is its wildly staged gunfights. CW: Extreme gunplay violence. 105m/C VHS, LV, 8mm, Closed Caption. Sharon Stone, Gene Hackman, Leonardo DiCaprio, Russell Crowe, Kevin Conway, Lance Henriksen, Roberts Blossom, Pat Hingle, Keith David, Michael Stone; Cameos: Gary Sinise; D: Sam Raimi; W: Simon Moore; C: Dante Spinotti. COL

Quick Change ✍✍½ 1990 (R) Murray,

Davis, and Quaid form bumbling trio of New York bank robbers who can't seem to exit the Big Apple with loot. Based on Jay Cronley's book, it's Murray's directing debut (with help from screenwriter Franklin). Engaging minor caper comedy displaying plenty of NYC dirty boulevards. 89m/C VHS, Beta, LV, 8mm, Closed Caption. Bill Murray, Geena Davis, Randy Quaid, Jason Robards Jr., Bob Elliott, Victor Argo, Kathryn Grody, Philip Bosco, Phil Hartman, Kurtwood Smith, Jamey Sheridan; D: Bill Murray, Howard Franklin; W: Howard Franklin; C: Michael Chapman; M: Randy Edelman, Howard Shore. WAR

Quick, Let's Get Married woof! 1971

Seven Different Ways; The Confession Quick, let's not watch this movie. Even the people who made it must have hated it: they waited seven years to release it. Rogers runs a whorehouse; Eden is a gullible, pregnant prostitute; Gould in his big-screen debut(!) is a deaf-mute. A must-not see. 96m/C VHS, Beta, LV. Ginger Rogers, Ray Milland, Barbara Eden, Carl Schell, Michael Ansara, Walter Abel, Scott Meyer, Cecil Kellaway, Elliott Gould; D: William Dieterle. NO

Quicker Than the Eye ✍✍ 1988 When

a magician gets mixed up in an assassination plot, he must use his wit, cunning, and magic to get out of it. 94m/C VHS, Beta. Ben Gazzara, Mary Crosby, Catherine Jarrett, Ivan Desny, Eb Lottimer, Sophie Carle, Wolfram Berger, Dinah Hinz, Jean Yanne; D: Nicolas Gessner. ACA

Quicksand ✍✍½ 1950 Mechanic Rooney

borrows $20 from his boss's cash register, intending to return it. One thing leads to another, the plot thickens, and it's downhill (for Rooney) from there. Good, tense suspense drama. 79m/B VHS, Beta. Mickey Rooney, Peter Lorre, Jeanne Cagney; D: Irving Pichel. NOS, MRV, SNC

Quicksand: No Escape ✍✍ 1991

(PG-13) Scott Reinhardt (Matheson) is a successful architect whose partner decides to secure a building contract by bribing a city official. When his partner is murdered Reinhardt is approached by a former cop (Sutherland) asking a lot of money for some incriminating evidence. Reinhardt is

then drawn ever deeper into the illicit dealings, endangering his life. 93m/C VHS, Beta, LV, Closed Caption. Tim Matheson, Donald Sutherland, Jay Acovone, Timothy Carhart, John Finn, Marc Alaimo, Felicity Huffman, Al Pugliese; D: Michael Pressman; W: Peter Baloff, Dave Wollert. USH

Quicksilver ✍½ 1986 (PG) A young stock-

broker loses all, then quits his job to become a city bicycle messenger. Pointless, self-indulgent yuppie fantasy. 106m/C VHS, Beta, LV, Closed Caption. Kevin Bacon, Jami Gertz, Paul Rodriguez, Rudy Ramos, Andrew Smith, Gerald S. O'Loughlin, Laurence "Larry" Fishburne, Louie Anderson; D: Tom Donnelly; W: Tom Donnelly; M: Tony Banks. COL

Quiet Cool ✍ 1986 (R) When his former girl-

friend's family is killed, a New York cop travels to a sleepy California town run by a pot-growing tycoon. He subsequently kills the bad guys in a Rambo-like fit of vengeance. Dopey exercise in sleepy-eyed bloodshed. 80m/C VHS, Beta, LV. James Remar, Daphne Ashbrook, Adam Coleman Howard, Jared Martin, Fran Ryan; D: Clay Borris; W: Clay Borris; M: Jay Michael Ferguson. COL

Quiet Day In Belfast ✍✍✍ 1974 Trag-

edy occurs when northern Irish patriots and British soldiers clash in an Irish betting parlor. Kidder plays a duel role: an Irish woman in love with a British soldier and the woman's twin sister. Convincingly adapted from a Canadian stage play. 92m/C VHS, Beta. CA Barry Foster, Margot Kidder; D: Milad Bessada. MED

A Quiet Duel ✍✍ A Silent Duel; Shizuka Naru

Ketto 1949 Kyoji (Mifune), a young, idealistic doctor working as an army surgeon, contracts syphillis from the blood of a patient during an operation. Because the disease was virtually incurable at the time, the tormented Kyoji abandons his fiance and decides to dedicate himself to his work. Based on a play by Kazuo Kikuta. Japanese with subtitles. 95m/B VHS. JP Toshiro Mifune, Takashi Shimura, Kenjiro Uemura; D: Akira Kurosawa; W: Senkichi Taniguhi, Akira Kurosawa; M: Akira Ifukube. FCT

The Quiet Earth ✍✍✍ 1985 (R) Serious

science fiction film about a scientist who awakens to find himself seemingly the only human left on earth as the result of a misfired time/space government experiment. He later finds two other people, a girl and a Maori tribesman, and must try to repair the damage in order to save what's left of mankind. 91m/C VHS, Beta, LV, Closed Caption. NZ Bruno Lawrence, Alison Routledge, Peter Smith; D: Geoff Murphy; W: Bruno Lawrence, Sam Pillsbury, Bill Baer; M: John Charles. FOX

Quiet Fire ✍½ 1991 (R) A health-club owner

tries to get the goods on the arms-dealing congressman who killed his best friend. Hilton-Jacobs looks properly pumped up since his sweat-hog days on TV's "Welcome Back Kotter." 100m/C VHS. Lawrence-Hilton Jacobs, Robert Z'Dar, Nadia Marie, Karen Black, Lance Lindsay; D: Lawrence-Hilton Jacobs. PMH

The Quiet Man ✍✍✍✍ 1952 The classic

incarnation of Hollywood Irishness, and one of Ford's best, and funniest films. Wayne is Sean Thornton, a weary American ex-boxer who returns to the Irish hamlet of his childhood and tries to take a spirited lass as his wife, despite the strenuous objections of her brawling brother (McLaglen). Thornton's aided by the leprechaun-like Fitzgerald and the local parish priest, Bond. A high-spirited and memorable film filled with Irish stew, wonderful banter, and shots of the lush countryside. Listen for the Scottish bagpipes at the start of the horse race, a slight geographic inaccuracy. 129m/C VHS, LV, Closed Caption. John Wayne, Maureen O'Hara, Barry Fitzgerald, Victor McLaglen, Arthur Shields, Jack MacGowran, Ward Bond, Mildred Natwick, Ken Curtis, Mae Marsh, Sean McClory, Francis Ford; D: John Ford; W: Frank Nugent; C: Archie Stout; M: Victor Young. Academy Awards '52: Best Color Cinematography, Best Director (Ford); Directors Guild of America Awards '52: Best Director (Ford); National Board of Review Awards '52: 10 Best Films of the Year; Venice Film Festival

'52: Best Director (Ford); Nominations: Academy Awards '52: Best Art Direction/Set Decoration (Color), Best Picture, Best Screenplay, Best Sound, Best Supporting Actor (McLaglen). *REP, TLF, CCB*

Quiet Thunder 🎬 1987 (PG-13)
A hard-drinking bush pilot in Africa and a beautiful senator's wife are thrown together on the run after both witness an assassination. Mindless, thoroughly derivative "adventure." **94m/C VHS, Beta, LV.** Wayne Crawford, June Chadwick, Victor Steinbach; *D:* David Rice. *LIV*

Quigley Down Under 🎬🎬½ 1990
(PG-13) A Western sharpshooter moves to Australia in search of employment. To his horror, he discovers that he has been hired to kill aborigines. Predictable action is somewhat redeemed by the terrific chemistry between Selleck and San Giacomo and the usual enjoyable theatrics from Rickman as the landowner heavy. **121m/C VHS, Beta, LV, 8mm, Closed Caption.** *AU* Tom Selleck, Laura San Giacomo, Alan Rickman, Chris Haywood, Ron Haddrick, Tony Bonner, Roger Ward, Ben Mendelsohn, Jerome Ehlers, Conor McDermottroe; *D:* Simon Wincer; *W:* John Hill; *C:* David Eggby; *M:* Basil Poledouris. *MGM*

The Quiller Memorandum 🎬🎬🎬 1966
An American secret agent travels to Berlin to uncover a deadly neo-Nazi gang. Refreshingly different from other spy tales of its era. Good screenplay adapted from Adam Hall's novel, "The Berlin Memorandum." **103m/C VHS, Beta, Closed Caption.** George Segal, Senta Berger, Alec Guinness, Max von Sydow, George Sanders; *D:* Michael Anderson Sr.; *W:* Harold Pinter; *M:* John Barry. *FOX*

Quilombo 🎬🎬½ 1984
The title refers to a legendary settlement of runaway slaves in 17th-century Brazil; an epic chronicles its fortunes as leadership passes from a wise ruler to a more militant one who goes to war against the government. Stunning scenery, tribal images, and folk songs, but the numerous characters seldom come to life as personalities. One of Brazil's most expensive films, in Portuguese with English subtitles. **114m/C VHS.** *BR* Vera Fischer, Antonio Pompeo, Zeze Motta, Toni Tornado; *D:* Carlos Diegues; *W:* Carlos Diegues. *NYF, FCT*

Quintet 🎬🎬 1979
Atypical Altman sci-fi effort. The stakes in "Quintet," a form of backgammon, are high—you bet your life. Set during the planet's final ice age. Newman and wife Fossey wander into a dying city and are invited to play the game, with Fossey losing quickly. Bizarre and pretentious with heavy symbolic going. **118m/C VHS, Beta.** Paul Newman, Bibi Andersson, Fernando Rey, Vittorio Gassman, David Langton, Nina Van Pallandt, Brigitte Fossey; *D:* Robert Altman; *W:* Lionel Chetwynd, Patricia Resnick, Robert Altman, Frank Barhydt. *FOX*

Quiz Show 🎬🎬🎬🎬 1994 (PG-13)
Redford's intelligent, entertaining, and morally complex film about the TV game show scandals of the late '50s is his most accomplished work to date. At the center of the film is Charles Van Doren (Fiennes), an intellectual, golden boy who dethrones Herbert Stempel (Turturro), the reigning champion of the rigged "Twenty-One." The program's sponsor felt Stempel, a nerdy Jewish grad's everyman qualities were wearing thin and wanted a more polished image, which they found in handsome, sophisticated Van Doren. Federal investigator Goodwin (Morrow) suspects Van Doren's reign is a sham and sets out to expose him as a fraud. Acting is of the highest caliber with Fiennes, Turturro, and Morrow all giving beautiful performances. Notable among supporting cast is Scofield as Van Doren's Pulitzer prize-winning father. With strong script and gorgeous lensing, this modern Faust story is a brilliant reflection on corporate greed, class rivalry, and the powers of television. Based on the book "Remembering America: A Voice From the Sixties" by Richard N. Goodwin. *CW:* Some strong language. **133m/C VHS, LV, Closed Caption.** John Turturro, Rob Morrow, Ralph Fiennes, Paul Scofield, David Paymer, Hank Azaria, Christopher McDonald, Johann Carlo, Elizabeth Wilson, Mira Sorvino, Griffin

Dunne, Martin Scorsese, Barry Levinson; *D:* Robert Redford; *W:* Paul Attanasio; *C:* Michael Ballhaus; *M:* Mark Isham. British Academy Awards '94: Best Adapted Screenplay; New York Film Critics Awards '94: Best Film; Nominations: Academy Awards '94: Best Adapted Screenplay, Best Director (Redford), Best Picture, Best Supporting Actor (Scofield); Directors Guild of America Awards '94: Best Director (Redford); Golden Globe Awards '95: Best Director (Redford), Best Film—Drama, Best Screenplay, Best Supporting Actor (Turturro); Writers Guild of America '94: Best Adapted Screenplay. *HPH*

Quo Vadis 🎬🎬½ 1912
One of the first truly huge Italian silent epics. The initial adaptation of the Henryk Sienkiewicz novel about Nero and ancient Rome. Probably the cinema's first great financial success. **45m/B VHS, Beta.** *D:* Enrico Guazzoni. *FCT*

Quo Vadis 🎬🎬🎬 1951
Larger-than-life production about Nero and the Christian persecution. Done on a giant scale: features exciting fighting scenes, romance, and fabulous costumes. Definitive version of the classic novel by Henryk Siekiewicz. Remade for Italian television in 1985. **171m/C VHS, Beta, Closed Caption.** Robert Taylor, Deborah Kerr, Peter Ustinov, Patricia Laffan, Finlay Currie, Abraham Sofaer, Marina Berti, Buddy Baer, Felix Aylmer, Nora Swinburne; *Cameos:* Sophia Loren, Elizabeth Taylor; *D:* Mervyn LeRoy; *C:* Robert L. Surtees; *M:* Miklos Rozsa. Golden Globe Awards '52: Best Supporting Actor (Ustinov); Nominations: Academy Awards '51: Best Art Direction/Set Decoration (Color), Best Color Cinematography, Best Costume Design (Color), Best Film Editing, Best Picture, Best Supporting Actor (Genn, Ustinov), Original Dramatic/Comedy Score. *MGM, APD, IGP*

Quo Vadis 🎬🎬🎬 1985 (R)
Third screen version of Henryk Sienkiewicz's book. See the other two first. This one is slow and perfunctory. Brandauer is memorable as Nero; Quinn (in the lead) is the son of Anthony. **122m/C VHS, Beta, LV.** *IT* Klaus Maria Brandauer, Frederic Forrest, Christina Raines, Maria Therese Relin, Francesco Quinn, Barbara DeRossi, Phillippe LeRoy, Max von Sydow, Gabriele Ferzetti, Massimo Girotti, Leopoldo Trieste; *D:* Franco Rossi. *PSM, APD*

Rabbit Test 🎬½ 1978 (PG)
In Rivers' first directorial effort, a clumsy virginal guy becomes the world's first pregnant man. So irreverent it's almost never in good taste, and so poorly written it's almost never funny. **86m/C VHS, Beta, LV.** Billy Crystal, Roddy McDowall, Imogene Coca, Paul Lynde, Alex Rocco, George Gobel; *D:* Joan Rivers. *COL*

Rabid 🎬🎬½ *Rage* 1977 (R)
A young girl undergoes a radical plastic surgery technique and develops a strange and unexplained lesion in her armpit. She also finds she has an unusual craving for human blood. **90m/C VHS, Beta.** *CA* Marilyn Chambers, Frank Moore, Joe Silver; *D:* David Cronenberg; *W:* David Cronenberg. *WAR*

Rabid Grannies woof! 1989 (R)
Wicked satire about two aging sisters who receive a surprise birthday gift from their devilworshipping nephew. The gift turns their party into a gorefest as they rip into various family members—literally. Any humor will be lost on any but the most diehard Troma fans. Dubbed. **89m/C VHS, Beta, LV.** *BE* Catherine Aymerie, Caroline Brackman, Danielle Daven, Raymond Lescot, Anne Marie Fox, Richard Cotica, Patricia Davie; *D:* Emmanuel Kervyn; *W:* Emmanuel Kervyn. *MED, VTR*

Race for Glory 🎬½ 1989 (R)
A young motorcyclist builds a super-bike he hopes will help him win a world championship race. Will he win? Can you stand the suspense? Let's just say there's a happy ending. **102m/C VHS, Beta.** Alex McArthur, Peter Berg, Pamela Ludwig; *D:* Rocky Lang; *M:* Jay Michael Ferguson. *HBO*

Race for Life 🎬½ *Mask of Dust* 1955
A race car driver attempts to make a comeback despite objections from his wife. He races around Europe (great scenery); she leaves him; he tries to win her back and salvage his career. Standard, ungripping story. Car scenes are great. **69m/B VHS, Beta, LV.** *GB* Richard Conte, Mari Aldon, George Coulouris; *D:* Terence Fisher. *NO*

Race for Your Life, Charlie Brown 🎬🎬½ 1977 (G)
Another in the popular series of "Peanuts" character films. This one features Charlie Brown, Snoopy, and all the gang spending an exciting summer in the American wilderness. **76m/C VHS, Beta, LV.** *D:* Bill Melendez, Phil Roman; *W:* Charles M. Schulz; *M:* Ed Bogas; *V:* Gail Davis, Melanie Kohn, Duncan Watson, Gregory Felton, Stuart Brotman, Liam Martin, Ed Bogas. *PAR*

Race the Sun 🎬🎬 1996 (PG)
There's nothin' new under this sun. Tired story of a group of young losers who band together to beat the odds and compete in an unusual contest is trotted out once again for populist amusement. This time it's a Hawaiian high school solar car team traveling to Australia to go for the prize against the big shots and snobs. Based on true events, it features some nice scenery from Berry and the main locations, but not much else. Uninspired but basically harmless, this one's fine for the kids. **100m/C VHS, LV, Closed Caption.** Halle Berry, James Belushi, Casey Affleck, Eliza Dushku, Kevin Tighe, Anthony Michael Ruivivar, J. Moki Cho, Dion Basco, Sara Tanaka, Nadja Pionilla, Steve Zahn, Bill Hunter; *D:* Charles Kanganis; *W:* Barry Morrow; *C:* David Burr; *M:* Graeme Revell. *COL*

Race to Freedom: The Story of the Underground Railroad 🎬🎬½ 1994
Story of four fugitive slaves, in 1850, who struggle to get from North Carolina to the safety of Canada through a network of safe-houses and people willing to risk smuggling them to asylum. Made for cable TV. **90m/C VHS.** Courtney B. Vance, Janet Bailey, Glynn Turman, Michael Riley, Dawnn Lewis, Ron White; *Cameos:* Tim Reid; *D:* Don McBrearty; *W:* Nancy Trite Botkin, Diana Braithwaite. *XVC*

Race with the Devil 🎬½ 1975 (PG)
Vacationers are terrorized by devil worshippers after they witness a sacrificial killing. Heavy on car chases; light on plot and redeeming qualities. Don't waste your time. **88m/C VHS, Beta, Closed Caption.** Peter Fonda, Warren Oates, Loretta Swit, Lara Parker; *D:* Jack Starrett. *FOX, FCT*

The Racers 🎬🎬½ *Such Men are Dangerous* 1955
Douglas brings power to the role of a man determined to advance to the winners' circle. Exciting European location photography, but not much plot. **112m/C VHS, Closed Caption.** Gilbert Roland, Kirk Douglas, Lee J. Cobb, Cesar Romero, Bella Darvi; *D:* Henry Hathaway; *M:* Max Reich. *FOX, FCT*

Rachel and the Stranger 🎬🎬🎬 1948
A God-fearing farmer declares his love for his wife when a handsome stranger (Mitchum) nearly woos her away. Well-cast, well-paced, charming Western comedy-drama. **93m/B VHS, Beta, LV.** Loretta Young, Robert Mitchum, William Holden, Gary Gray; *D:* Norman Foster. *MED, TTC*

The Rachel Papers 🎬🎬🎬 1989 (R)
Based on the Martin Amis novel, this is the funny/sad tale of an Oxford youth who plots via his computer the seduction of a beautiful American girl. For anyone who has ever loved someone just out of their reach. **92m/C VHS, Beta, Closed Caption.** Dexter Fletcher, Ione Skye, James Spader, Jonathan Pryce, Bill Paterson, Michael Gambon, Lesley Sharp; *D:* Damian Harris; *W:* Damian Harris; *M:* Chaz Jankel. *FOX*

Rachel, Rachel 🎬🎬🎬½ 1968 (R)
Rachel teaches by day, wearing simple, practical dresses and her hair up. By night she caters to her domineering mother by preparing refreshments for her parties. This sexually repressed, spinster schoolteacher, however, gets one last chance at romance in her small Connecticut town. Woodward mixes just the right amounts of loneliness and sweetness in the leading role. A surprising award-winner that was an independent production of Newman. Based on Margaret Laurence's "A Jest of God." **102m/C VHS, Beta.** Joanne Woodward, James Olson, Estelle Parsons, Geraldine Fitzgerald, Donald Moffat; *D:* Paul Newman; *W:* Stewart Stern. Golden Globe Awards '69: Best Actress—Drama (Woodward), Best Director (Newman); National Board of Review Awards '68: 10 Best Films of the Year; New York Film Critics Awards '68: Best Actress (Woodward), Best Director (Newman); Nomi-

nations: Academy Awards '68: Best Actress (Woodward), Best Adapted Screenplay, Best Picture, Best Supporting Actress (Parsons). *WAR*

Rachel River 🎬🎬½ 1987 (PG-13) A divorced radio personality struggles to make something of her life in her small Minnesota town. 88m/C VHS, LV. Pamela Reed, Craig T. Nelson, Viveca Lindfors, James Olson, Zeljko Ivanek, Jo Henderson, Alan North, Jon DeVries; *D:* Sandy Smolan; *W:* Judith Guest; *M:* Arvo Part. *ACA*

Rachel's Man 🎬 1975 A big-screen version of the Biblical love story of Jacob and Rachel. 115m/C VHS, Beta. Mickey Rooney, Rita Tushingham, Leonard Whiting; *D:* Moshe Mizrahi. *LIV*

Racing Luck 🎬🎬 *Red Hot Tires* 1935 While working at a race track, a man is framed and forced to work for another stable. 56m/B VHS, Beta. William Boyd, Barbara Worth, George Ernest, Esther Muir, Dick Curtis; *D:* Sam Newfield. *GPV*

Racing with the Moon 🎬🎬🎬 1984 (PG) Sweet, nostalgic film about two buddies awaiting induction into the Marines in 1942. They have their last chance at summer romance. Benjamin makes the most of skillful young actors and conventional story. Great period detail. Keep your eyes peeled for glimpses of many rising young stars including Hannah and Carvey. 108m/C VHS, Beta, LV, Closed Caption. Sean Penn, Elizabeth McGovern, Nicolas Cage, John Karlen, Rutanya Alda, Max Casey Adams Showalter, Crispin Glover, Suzanne Adkinson, Page Hannah, Michael Madsen, Dana Carvey, Carol Kane, Michael Talbott; *D:* Richard Benjamin; *W:* Steven Kloves; *C:* John Bailey; *M:* Dave Grusin. *PAR*

The Racket 🎬🎬🎬 1951 Police captain Mitchum tries to break up mob racket of gangster Ryan. Internecine strife on both sides adds complexity. Mitchum and especially Ryan are super; fine, tense melodrama. 88m/B VHS, Beta, LV. Robert Ryan, Robert Mitchum, Lizabeth Scott, Ray Collins, William Conrad, Don Porter; *D:* John Cromwell. *MED, TTC*

The Racketeer 🎬🎬½ 1929 A racketeer falls in love with a pretty girl and attempts to win her over. As part of his plan, the gangster arranges to help the girl's boyfriend begin his musical career in exchange for the girl's promise to marry him. 68m/B VHS, Beta. Carole Lombard, Robert Armstrong, Hedda Hopper; *D:* Howard Higgin. *SNC, NOS, CAB*

Racketeers of the Range 🎬½ 1939 Cattlemen fights a crooked attorney who wants to sell his client's stock to a large meat packing company. 62m/B VHS, Beta. George O'Brien, Marjorie Reynolds, Chill Wills, Ray Whitley; *D:* David Ross Lederman. *MED*

Racquet 🎬 1979 Tennis pro Convy searches for true love and a tennis court or to call his own in Beverly Hills. Lame, sophomoric, and unfunny. 87m/C VHS, Beta. Bert Convy, Edie Adams, Lynda Day George, Phil Silvers, Bobby Riggs, Bjorn Borg, Tanya Roberts; *D:* David Winters. *NO*

Rad 🎬½ 1986 (PG) Teenage drama revolving around BMX racing and such dilemmas can the good guys beat the bad guys, who's got the fastest bike, must you cheat to win, and should our hero miss his SAT tests to compete in "the big race.." Directed by stunt-expert Needham. 94m/C VHS, Beta, LV, Closed Caption. Bill Allen, Bart Conner, Talia Shire, Jack Weston, Lori Loughlin; *D:* Hal Needham; *W:* Sam Bernard. *NLC*

Radar Men from the Moon *Retik, the Moon Menace* 1952 Commando Cody, with his jetpack, fights to defend the earth from invaders from the moon. Twelve-episode serial on two tapes. Silly sci-fi. 152m/B VHS, LV. George Wallace, Aline Towne, Roy Barcroft, William "Billy" Bakewell, Clayton Moore; *D:* Fred Brannon. *NOS, REP, SNC*

Radar Patrol vs. Spy King 1949 Special agent Alyn and his buxom Vargas girl Jean Dean battle the deadly Baroda and his ring of saboteurs, hell-bent on destroying America. 12 episodes of the serial edited onto two cassettes. 167m/B VHS. Kirk Alyn, Jeanne Dean. *REP, MLB*

Radar Secret Service 🎬½ 1950 Two servicemen witness the hijacking of a truck loaded with nuclear material. 59m/B VHS, Beta, LV. John Howard, Adele Jergens, Tom Neal, Ralph Byrd. *NO*

Radio Days 🎬🎬🎬 1987 (PG) A lovely, unpretentious remembrance of the pre-television radio culture. Allen tells his story in a series of vignettes centering around his youth in Brooklyn, his eccentric extended family, and the legends of radio they all followed. The ubiquitous Farrow is a young singer hoping to make it big. 96m/C VHS, Beta, LV. Mia Farrow, Dianne Wiest, Julie Kavner, Michael Tucker, Wallace Shawn, Josh Mostel, Tony Roberts, Jeff Daniels, Kenneth Mars, Seth Green, William Magerman, Diane Keaton, Renee Lippin, Gina DeAngelis, Kitty Carlisle Hart, Mercedes Ruehl, Tito Puente; *D:* Woody Allen; *W:* Woody Allen; *C:* Carlo DiPalma. Nominations: Academy Awards '87: Best Art Direction/Set Decoration, Best Original Screenplay. *HBO*

Radio Flyer 🎬🎬 1992 (PG-13) It's 1969 and Mike and Bobby have just moved to northern California with their divorced mom. Everything would be idyllic if only their mother hadn't decided to marry a drunken child abuser who beats Bobby whenever the mood strikes him. Mike decides to help Bobby escape by turning their Radio Flyer wagon into a magic rocketship that will carry Bobby to safety, but ultimately proves tragic. Appealing version of childhood dreams sans the child abuse angle (toned down though it was), which is abruptly and unsatisfactorily handled. 114m/C VHS, LV, Closed Caption. Elijah Wood, Joseph Mazzello, Lorraine Bracco, Adam Baldwin, John Heard, Ben Johnson; *D:* Richard Donner. *COL*

Radio Inside 🎬🎬½ 1994 Aimless Matthew (McNamara) comes to live with older brother Michael (Walsh) after their dad's death. Matthew needs someone to listen to him but, unfortunately, he picks his brother's neglected girlfriend Natalie (Shue). Aimless story, as well. Made for cable TV. 91m/C VHS, LV, Closed Caption. William McNamara, Dylan Walsh, Elisabeth Shue, Gil Goldstein; *D:* Jeffrey Bell; *W:* Jeffrey Bell. *MGM*

Radio Patrol 1937 Plenty of action and thrills abound in this 12-chapter serial. Pinky Adams, radio cop, is assisted by his trusty canine partner, Irish (Silverwolf). A cop's best friend is his dog. 235m/B VHS, Beta. Mickey Rentschler, Adrian Morris, Monte Montague, Jack Mulhall, Grant Withers, Catherine Hughes; *D:* Ford Beebe, Cliff Smith. *NOS, VDM, MLB*

Radioactive Dreams 🎬🎬 1986 (R) Surreal, practically senseless fantasy wherein two men, trapped in a bomb shelter for 15 years with nothing to read but mystery novels, emerge as detectives into a post-holocaust world looking for adventure. 94m/C VHS, Beta, LV. John Stockwell, Michael Dudikoff, Lisa Blount, George Kennedy, Don Murray, Michelle Little; *D:* Albert Pyun; *W:* Albert Pyun. *LIV, VES*

Radioland Murders 🎬½ 1994 (PG) Looks overwhelm weak plot in this mystery-comedy about 1939 Chicago radio station WBN. Lots of stock types (befuddled director, preening announcer, lusty vamp) with Masterson as Penny, the secretary holding everything together except for her marriage to head writer Roger (Benben). Then bodies start piling up during the live broadcast and everyone runs around frantically trying to solve the crimes and keep the broadcast going. Tiring and cliched. 112m/C VHS, LV, Closed Caption. Brian Benben, Mary Stuart Masterson, Ned Beatty, George Burns, Brion James, Michael Lerner, Michael McKean, Jeffrey Tambor, Scott Michael Campbell, Anita Morris, Stephen Tobolowsky, Christopher Lloyd, Larry Miller, Corbin Bensen; *Cameos:* Robert Klein, Harvey Korman, Peter MacNicol, Joey Lawrence, Bob(cat) Goldthwait; *D:* Mel Smith; *W:* Willard Huyck, Gloria Katz, Jeff Reno, Ron Osborn; *C:* David Tattersall; *M:* Joel McNeely. *USH*

Rafferty & the Gold Dust Twins 🎬½ *Rafferty and the Highway Hustlers* 1975 (R) Two women kidnap a motor vehicle inspector at gunpoint in Los Angeles and order him to drive to New Orleans. En route, they become pals. Wandering, pointless female buddy flick. 91m/C

VHS, Beta, Closed Caption. Alan Arkin, Sally Kellerman, MacKenzie Phillips, Charles Martin Smith, Harry Dean Stanton; *D:* Dick Richards; *M:* Artie Butler. *WAR*

The Raffle 🎬🎬½ 1994 (R) Frank and David travel the globe to find the world's most beautiful woman, who'll be the prize date of the lucky guy with the winning raffle ticket. *CW:* Some strong language; nudity. 100m/C VHS, LV. Nicholas Lea, Bobby Dawson, Jennifer Clement, Teri-Lynn Rutherford, Jay Underwood, Mark Hamill; *D:* Gavin Wilding; *W:* John Fairley; *M:* Robert O. Ragland. *APX*

Rage 🎬🎬 1972 (PG) Scott's directorial debut. A military helicopter sprays peace-loving rancher Scott and his son with nerve gas. The son's death is covered up; the rancher embarks on a vengeful rampage. Scott's sudden transformation to avenging killer is implausible and overwrought. 100m/C VHS, Beta. George C. Scott, Richard Basehart, Martin Sheen, Barnard Hughes, Kenneth Tobey, Ed Lauter, Nicholas Beauvy, Dabbs Greer; *D:* George C. Scott; *C:* Fred W. Koenekamp. *WAR*

Rage 🎬 1980 Well-acted, well-written, nerve-wracking drama about a convicted rapist who finds help through difficult therapy. Focuses on how the sex-offender discovers the "whys" behind his assaults. Made for television. 100m/C VHS, Beta. David Soul, James Whitmore, Yaphet Kotto, Caroline McWilliams, Vic Tayback, Sharon Farrell, Craig T. Nelson, Garry Walberg; *D:* William A. Graham; *C:* Allen Daviau. *WAR*

Rage 🎬½ 1995 (R) When Alex Gainer is kidnapped he becomes the target of a high-tech lab experiment. Injected with chemicals that induce blind and killing rages, Alex escapes and unwillingly goes on a murderous rampage. Now he must find the antidote and clear his name before it happens again. *CW:* Non-stop action/violence, language. 94m/C VHS, Closed Caption. Gary Daniels, Ken Tigar, Jillian McWhirter, Fiona Hutchinson. *PMH*

Rage and Honor 🎬🎬 1992 (R) Rothrock stars as Kris Fairfield, a high-school teacher who spends her spare time tutoring students in the martial-arts. Her present students are a group of cops, including Aussie visitor Preston Michaels. When Michaels witnesses a drug deal, he gets set-up by the dealers for a murder he didn't commit and only Kris can help him prove his innocence. *CW:* Language and violence. 93m/C VHS, LV, Closed Caption. Cynthia Rothrock, Richard Norton, Brian Thompson, Terri Treas, Catherine Bach, Alex Datcher; *D:* Terence H. Winkless; *W:* Terence H. Winkless. *COL, PMS*

Rage and Honor 2: Hostile Takeover 🎬🎬½ 1993 (R) Rothrock returns as black-belt CIA operative Kris Fairfield, whose latest assignment takes her to Jakarta where a banker is involved in a large-scale drug money laundering operation. She teams up with Preston Michaels (Norton), a renegade Australian cop, and winds up following a trail that leads to a fortune in diamonds and lots of trouble. 98m/C VHS. Cynthia Rothrock, Richard Norton, Patrick Muldoon, Frans Tumbuan, Ron Vreeken, Alex Tumundo; *D:* Guy Norris; *W:* Louis Sun, Steven Reich. *COL*

Rage at Dawn 🎬🎬½ *Seven Bad Men* 1955 An outlaw gang is tracked by a special agent who must "bend" the rules a little in order to get the bad guys. Not surprisingly, he gets his girl as well. A solid standard of the genre, with some clever plot twists. 87m/C VHS. Randolph Scott, Forrest Tucker, Mala Powers, J. Carrol Naish, Edgar Buchanan; *D:* Tim Whelan. *NOS, GHV, MRV*

A Rage in Harlem 🎬🎬🎬 1991 (R) The crime novels of Chester A. Himes were translated into the best movies of the early '70s blaxploitation era. Now, a Himes story gets the big budget Hollywood treatment with juice and aplomb. A voluptuous lady crook enters Harlem circa 1950 with a trunkful of stolen gold sought by competing crooks, and the chase is on, with one virtuous soul (Whitaker) who only wants the girl. Great cast and characters, much humor, but unsparing in its violence. *CW:* Language, violence, and sensuality. **108m/C VHS, LV, Closed Caption.** Forest Whitaker, Gregory Hines, Robin Givens, Zakes Mokae, Danny Glover, Tyler Collins, Ron Taylor, T.K. Carter, Willard Pugh, Samm-Art Williams, Jay Hawkins, Badja Djola, John Toles-Bey, Stack Pierce, George Wallace; *D:* Bill Duke; *M:* John Toles-Bey, Bobby Crawford; *M:* Elmer Bernstein. HBO, FCT

Rage of Angels ♂♂ 1983 Lengthy television miniseries adaptation of the Sidney Sheldon novel about an ambitious female attorney, her furs, and her men. Followed by "Rage of Angels: The Story Continues" (1986). **192m/C VHS, Beta.** Jaclyn Smith, Ken Howard, Armand Assante, Ronald Hunter, Kevin Conway, George Coe, Deborah May; *D:* Buzz Kulik; *M:* Billy Goldenberg. COL

Rage of Angels: The Story Continues ♂♂½ 1986 In this sequel to the Sidney Sheldon trash-with-flash television miniseries, Smith reprises her role as the beautiful lady lawyer who always gets involved with the wrong men. This time she tries to hide the fact of her illegitimate son from his father, who's about to become Vice President of the United States. **200m/C VHS.** Jaclyn Smith, Ken Howard, Michael Nouri, Susan Sullivan, Brad Dourif, Angela Lansbury, Mason Adams; *D:* Paul Wendkos; *C:* Jack Priestley; *M:* Billy Goldenberg. COL

Rage of Honor ♂ 1987 (R) A high-kicking undercover cop seeks vengeance on bad guys for his partner's murder. Standard of its type; why bother? **92m/C VHS, Beta.** Sho Kosugi, Lewis Van Bergen, Robin Evans, Gerry Gibson; *D:* Gordon Hessler; *W:* Wallace C. Bennett. MED, VTR

The Rage of Paris ♂♂♂ 1938 Scheming ex-actress and head waiter hope to gain by helping a beautiful French girl (Darrieux) snag a rich hubby. She comes to her senses, realizing that love, true love, matters more than wealth. Well-acted, quaint comedy. **78m/B VHS, Beta.** Danielle Darrieux, Douglas Fairbanks Jr., Mischa Auer, Helen Broderick; *D:* Henry Koster; *C:* Joseph Valentine. NOS, DVT, CAB

Rage of Wind ♂ 1982 Master boxer seeks revenge on a Japanese commandant who kidnaps his wife during WWII. **97m/C VHS, Beta.** Chen Hsing, Yasuka Kurata, Irene Ryder. WWE

Rage to Kill ♂½ 1988 (R) Jingoistic retelling of the 1982 Grenada invasion, complete with helpless American med students. Good-guy race car driver whips them into shape to fight the Soviet-supplied general (he's the bad guy). Guess who wins. **94m/C VHS, Beta.** Oliver Reed, James Ryan, Henry Cele, Cameron Mitchell; *D:* David Winters. AIP

Raggedy Ann and Andy: A Musical Adventure 1977 (G) Here are the fun-filled exploits of America's favorite fictional dolls, transformed into an enchanting animated musical. Includes 16 songs by Joe Raposo. **87m/C VHS, Beta, Closed Caption.** *D:* Richard Williams; *V:* Didi Conn, Joe Silver. FOX

Raggedy Man ♂♂♂ 1981 (PG) Spacek in her signature role as a lonely small-town woman. Here she's raising two sons alone in a small Texas town during WWII. Spacek's strong acting carries a weak-scripted story, unfortunately marred by an overwrought ending. **94m/C VHS, Beta, LV.** Sissy Spacek, Eric Roberts, Sam Shepard, Tracey Walter, William Sanderson, Henry Thomas; *D:* Jack Fisk; *W:* William D. Wittliff; *C:* Ralf Bode; *M:* Jerry Goldsmith. USH

The Raggedy Rawney ♂♂½ 1990 (R) A young Army deserter dresses in women's clothing and hides out as a mad woman with a band of gypsies. Good first directing effort by English actor Bob Hoskins. Unpretentious and engaging. **102m/C VHS.** Bob Hoskins, Dexter Fletcher, Zoe Nathenson, David Hill, Ian Dury, Zoe Wanamaker, J.G. Devlin, Perry Fenwick; *D:* Bob Hoskins; *W:* Bob Hoskins, Nicole De Wilde; *M:* Michael Kamen. CAN

Ragin' Cajun ♂ 1990 Retired kickboxer is forced into a death match to save his girlfriend. **91m/C VHS.** David Heavener, Charlene Tilton, Sam Bottoms, Samantha Eggar; *D:* William B. Hillman. AIP, HHE

Raging Angels ♂ 1995 (R) L.A. couple Chris (Flanery) and Lila (Mazur) are struggling rock 'n' rollers when Lila gets a job as a backup singer to star Colin (Pare), who's part of a cult called the Coalition for World Unity. Turns out they're a recruiting org for Satan and are looking for new souls. Our young duo are aided by flamboyant evangelist Sister Kate (Ladd) but it all comes down to a sky battle over downtown L.A. between a good angel and a satanic creature. Lots of unintentional laughs. The director wisely opted for the industry's Smithee pseudonym. *CW:* Language and some violence. **97m/C VHS, Closed Caption.** Sean Patrick Flanery, Monet Mazur, Michael Pare, Diane Ladd, Shelley Winters, Arielle Dombasle; *D:* Alan Smithee; *W:* Kevin Rock, David Markov, Chris Bittler; *C:* Bryan England; *M:* Terry Plumer. THV

Raging Bull ♂♂♂♂ 1980 (R) Scorsese's depressing but magnificent vision of the dying American Dream and suicidal macho codes in the form of the rise and fall of middleweight boxing champ Jake LaMotta, a brutish, dull-witted animal who can express himself only in the ring and through violence. A photographically expressive, brilliant drama, with easily the most intense and brutal boxing scenes ever filmed. De Niro provides a vintage performance, going from the young LaMotta to the aging has-been, and is ably accompanied by Moriarty as his girl and Pesci as his loyal, much beat-upon bro. **128m/B VHS, Beta, LV, 8mm, DVD.** Robert De Niro, Cathy Moriarty, Joe Pesci, Frank Vincent, Nicholas Colasanto, Theresa Saldana; *D:* Martin Scorsese; *W:* Paul Schrader, Mardik Martin; *C:* Michael Chapman. Academy Awards '80: Best Actor (De Niro), Best Film Editing; Golden Globe Awards '81: Best Actor—Drama (De Niro); Los Angeles Film Critics Association Awards '80: Best Actor (De Niro), Best Film; National Board of Review Awards '80: Best Actor (De Niro), Best Supporting Actor (Pesci); New York Film Critics Awards '80: Best Actor (De Niro), Best Actor (De Niro), Best Supporting Actor (Pesci), Best Supporting Actor (Pesci); National Society of Film Critics Awards '80: Best Cinematography, Best Director (Scorsese), Best Supporting Actor (Pesci); Nominations: Academy Awards '80: Best Cinematography, Best Director (Scorsese), Best Picture, Best Sound, Best Supporting Actor (Pesci), Best Supporting Actress (Moriarty). MGM, FOX, BTV

Rags to Riches ♂ 1987 A wealthy Beverly Hills entrepreneur decides to improve his public image by adopting six orphan girls. TV pilot. **96m/C VHS, Beta.** Joseph Bologna, Tisha Campbell. VTR, NWV

Ragtime ♂♂♂ 1981 (PG) The lives and passions of a middle class family weave into the scandals and events of 1906 America. A small, unthinking act represents all the racist attacks on one man, who refuses to back down this time. Wonderful period detail. From the E.L. Doctorow novel, but not nearly as complex. Features Cagney's last film performance. **156m/C VHS, Beta, LV.** Howard E. Rollins Jr., Kenneth McMillan, Brad Dourif, Mary Steenburgen, James Olson, Elizabeth McGovern, Pat O'Brien, James Cagney, Debbie Allen, Jeff Daniels, Moses Gunn, Donald O'Connor, Mandy Patinkin, Norman Mailer; *D:* Milos Forman; *W:* Michael Weller; *M:* Randy Newman. Nominations: Academy Awards '81: Best Adapted Screenplay, Best Art Direction/Set Decoration, Best Cinematography, Best Costume Design, Best Song ("One More Hour"), Best Supporting Actor (Rollins), Best Supporting Actress (McGovern), Best Original Score. PAR, FCT

Raid on Entebbe ♂♂♂ 1977 (R) Dramatization of the Israeli rescue of passengers held hostage by terrorists at Uganda's Entebbe Airport in 1976. A gripping actioner all the more compelling because true. Finch received an Emmy nomination in this, his last film. Made for television. **113m/C VHS, Beta.** Charles Bronson, Peter Finch, Horst Buchholz, John Saxon, Martin Balsam, Jack Warden, Yaphet Kotto, Sylvia Sidney; *D:* Irvin Kershner; *C:* Bill Butler; *M:* David Shire. NO

Raid on Rommel ♂½ 1971 (PG) A British soldier (Burton) poses as a Nazi and tries to infiltrate Rommel's team with his rag-tag brigade of misfits. Predictable drivel. Contains action footage from the 1967 film "Tobruk." **98m/C VHS, Beta.** Rich-

ard Burton, John Colicos, Clinton Greyn, Wolfgang Preiss; *D:* Henry Hathaway. USH

Raiders in Action ♂ 1971 Tale following the activities of a band of allied commandos in the closing days of the war. **89m/C VHS, Beta.** Paul Smith. TWE

Raiders of Atlantis ♂ *The Atlantis Interceptors* 1983 Battles break out when the lost continent surfaces in the Caribbean. The warriors in these apocalyptic frays deploy atomic arsenals. **100m/C VHS, Beta.** Christopher Connelly; *D:* Roger Franklin. PSM

Raiders of Ghost City ♂♂½ 1944 Serial in 13 chapters involves a Union Secret Service Agent after a ring of gold robbers who are posing as Confederate soldiers during the end of the Civil War. **?m/C VHS.** Dennis Moore, Lionel Atwill, Regis Toomey, Wanda McKay. MOV

Raiders of Red Gap ♂½ 1943 A cattle company tries running homesteaders off their land to get control of it. The Lone Rider saves the day. **56m/B VHS, Beta.** Al "Fuzzy" St. John, Bob Livingston. DVT, VYY, VCN

Raiders of Sunset Pass ♂♂ 1943 Wartime western quickie makes an interesting novelty today. With most cowboys off fighting the Axis, the ladies form the Women's Army of the Plains to watch out for 4-F rustlers. **57m/B VHS.** Eddie Dew, Smiley Burnette, Jennifer Holt, Roy Barcroft, Mozelle Cravens, Beverly Aadland, Nancy Worth, Kenne Duncan, Jack Rockwell, Budd Buster, Jack Ingram; *D:* John English. NOS, HEG

Raiders of the Border ♂ 1944 A white-hatted cowboy must prevent the takeover of a trading post. **55m/B VHS, Beta.** Johnny Mack Brown, Raymond Hatton, Ellen Hall. VDM

Raiders of the Lost Ark ♂♂♂♂ 1981 (PG) Classic '30s-style adventure reminiscent of early serials spawned two sequels and numerous rip-offs. Made Ford a household name as dashing hero and intrepid archeologist Indiana Jones. He battles mean Nazis, decodes hieroglyphics, fights his fear of snakes, and even has time for a little romance in his quest for the biblical Ark of the Covenant. Allen is perfectly cast as his feisty ex-flame, more than a little irritated with the smooth talker who dumped her years earlier. Asks viewers to suspend belief as every chase and stunt tops the last. Unrelated opening sequence does a great job of introducing the character. Followed by "Indiana Jones and the Temple of Doom." **115m/C VHS, Beta, LV, 8mm, Closed Caption.** Harrison Ford, Karen Allen, Wolf Kahler, Paul Freeman, John Rhys-Davies, Denholm Elliott, Ronald Lacey, Anthony Higgins, Alfred Molina; *D:* Steven Spielberg; *W:* George Lucas, Philip Kaufman; *M:* John Williams. Academy Awards '81: Best Art Direction/Set Decoration, Best Film Editing, Best Sound, Best Visual Effects; People's Choice Awards '82: Best Film; Nominations: Academy Awards '81: Best Cinematography, Best Director (Spielberg), Best Picture, Best Original Score. PAR

Raiders of the Sun ♂ 1992 (R) After the Earth has been ruined in a biological disaster, a futuristic warrior arrives to help restore world peace and order. Cheap "Mad Max" ripoff. *CW:* Language, war violence, and sensuality. **80m/C VHS, Closed Caption.** Richard Norton, Rick Dean, William Steis, Blake Boyd, Brigitta Stenberg; *D:* Cirio H. Santiago. NHO

Railroaded ♂♂ 1947 The police seek a demented criminal who kills his victims with perfumed-soaked bullets. Tense, excellent noir Anthony Mann crime drama. **72m/B VHS, Beta, LV.** John Ireland, Sheila Ryan, Hugh Beaumont, Ed Kelly; *D:* Anthony Mann. NOS, NWV, DVT

Railrodder ♂♂♂ 1965 Buster Keaton as the railroader in this slapstick short fumbles his way across Canada. As in the days of the silents, he speaks not a word. **25m/C VHS, Beta.** Buster Keaton. NFB

The Railway Children 🐾🐾🐾½ 1970 At the turn of the century in England, the father of three children is framed and sent to prison during Christmas. The trio and their mother must survive on a poverty stricken farm near the railroad tracks. They eventually meet a new friend who helps them prove their father's innocence. Wonderfully directed by Jeffries. From the classic Edith Nesbitt children's novel. 104m/C VHS, Beta. *GB* Jenny Agutter, William Mervyn, Bernard Cribbins, Dinah Sheridan, Iain Cuthbertson, Sally Thomsett, Peter Bromilow, Ann Lancaster, Gary Warren, Gordon Whiting, David Lodge; *D:* Lionel Jeffries. *NO*

The Railway Station Man 🐾🐾🐾 1992 Set in present-day Ireland. Christie plays a widowed artist struggling to put her life back together after her husband's death in a terrorist bombing. She meets a mysterious American (Sutherland) who's working on restoring the local railway station and finds herself falling in love. When she stumbles upon an IRA bombing plot she also finds out some unpleasant truths about her new lover. Wonderful performances, tragic story. Shot on location in County Donegal, Northern Ireland. Based on the novel by Jennifer Johnston. Made for cable television. 93m/C VHS, Beta, LV, **Closed Caption.** Julie Christie, Donald Sutherland, John Lynch, Mark Tandy, Frank McCusker, Niall Cusack; *D:* Michael Whyte; *W:* Shelagh Delaney. *TTC*

Rain 🐾🐾½ 1932 W. Somerset Maugham's tale of a puritanical minister's attempt to reclaim a "lost woman" on the island of Pago Pago. Crawford and Huston work up some static. Remake of the 1928 silent film "Sadie Thompson." Remade again in 1953 as "Miss Sadie Thompson." 92m/B VHS, Beta. Joan Crawford, Walter Huston, William Gargan, Guy Kibbee, Beulah Bondi, Walter Catlett; *D:* Lewis Milestone. *MON, NOS, CNG*

The Rain Killer 🐾 1990 (R) Big city cop and fed don goloshes to track serial killer who slays rich ladies during heavy precipitation. Soggy story. 94m/C VHS, LV. Ray Sharkey, David Beecroft, Maria Ford, Woody Brown, Tania Coleridge; *D:* Ken Stein; *W:* Ray Cunneff. *COL*

Rain Man 🐾🐾🐾½ 1988 (R) When his father dies, ambitious and self-centered Charlie Babbit finds he has an older autistic brother who's been institutionalized for years. Needing him to claim an inheritance, he liberates him from the institution and takes to the road, where both brothers undergo subtle changes. The Vegas montage is wonderful. Critically acclaimed drama and a labor of love for the entire cast. Cruise's best performance to date as he goes from cad to recognizing something wonderfully human in his brother and himself. Hoffman is exceptional. 128m/C VHS, Beta, LV, 8mm, **Closed Caption, DVD.** Dustin Hoffman, Tom Cruise, Valeria Golino, Jerry Molen, Jack Murdock, Michael D. Roberts, Ralph Seymour, Lucinda Jenney, Bonnie Hunt, Kim Robillard, Beth Grant; *D:* Barry Levinson; *W:* Ronald Bass, Barry Morrow; *C:* John Seale; *M:* Hans Zimmer. Academy Awards '88: Best Actor (Hoffman), Best Director (Levinson), Best Original Screenplay, Best Picture; Berlin International Film Festival '88: Golden Berlin Bear; Directors Guild of America Awards '88: Best Director (Levinson); Golden Globe Awards '89: Best Actor—Drama (Hoffman), Best Film—Drama; People's Choice Awards '89: Best Film—Drama; Nominations: Academy Awards '88: Best Art Direction/Set Decoration, Best Cinematography, Best Film Editing, Best Original Score. *MGM, BTV, HMV*

The Rain People 🐾🐾🐾 1969 (R) Pregnant housewife Knight takes to the road in desperation and boredom; along the way she meets retarded ex-football player Caan. Well directed by Coppola from his original script. Pensive drama. 102m/C VHS, Beta. Shirley Knight, James Caan, Robert Duvall; *D:* Francis Ford Coppola; *W:* Francis Ford Coppola; *C:* Bill Butler. *WAR*

Rain Without Thunder 🐾🐾½ 1993 (PG-13) Imagine the year 2042, a time when abortion is illegal and a fertilized egg has full Constitutional rights. Now imagine sitting through an 87 minute fake documentary that follows the story of a mother and daughter team who have been jailed for trying to go to Sweden so that the daughter can get an abortion. A one-sided, militant pro-choice effort that is neither entertaining nor informational. *CW:* Theme. 87m/C VHS. Betty Buckley, Jeff Daniels, Ali Thomas, Frederic Forrest, Carolyn McCormick, Linda Hunt, Robert Earl Jones, Graham Greene, Iona Morris, Austin Pendleton; *D:* Gary Bennett; *W:* Gary Bennett; *M:* Randall Lynch, Allen Lynch. *ORI*

Rainbow 🐾🐾 1978 Broadway's "Annie" is badly miscast as Judy Garland from her early years in vaudeville to her starring years at M.G.M. Based on the book by Christopher Finch. Made for television; directed by sometime Garland flame Jackie Cooper. 100m/C VHS, Beta, LV. Andrea McArdle, Jack Carter, Don Murray; *D:* Jackie Cooper; *M:* Charles Fox. *NO*

The Rainbow 🐾🐾🐾 1989 (R) Mature, literate rendering of the classic D.H. Lawrence novel about a young woman's sexual awakening. Beautiful cinematography. Companion/prequel to director Russell's earlier Lawrence adaptation, "Women in Love" (1969). 104m/C VHS, LV. *GB* Sammi Davis, Amanda Donohoe, Paul McGann, Christopher Gable, David Hemmings, Glenda Jackson, Kenneth Colley; *D:* Ken Russell; *W:* Vivian Russell, Ken Russell; *C:* Billy Williams; *M:* Carl Davis. *VES, IME*

Rainbow Bridge 🐾🐾 1971 (R) The adventures of a group of hippies searching for their consciousness in Hawaii. Features concert footage from Jimi Hendrix's final performance. 74m/C VHS, Beta. *D:* Chuck Wein. *RHI, FCT*

Rainbow Drive 🐾🐾½ 1990 (R) Made for cable tv cop thriller promises great things but fails to deliver. Weller is a good cop trapped in the political intrigues of Hollywood. He discovers five dead bodies; when the official count is four, he detects funny business. From the novel by Roderick Thorp. *CW:* Language, violence, and sensuality. 93m/C VHS. Peter Weller, Sela Ward, Bruce Weitz, David Caruso, James Laurenson, Chris Mulkey, Kathryn Harrold; *D:* Bobby Roth; *W:* Roderick Thorp, Bill Phillips, Bennett Cohen; *M:* Tangerine Dream. *BTV, THV*

The Rainbow Gang 🐾 1973 A trio of unlikely prospectors heads into a legendary mine in search of riches and fame. 90m/C VHS, Beta. Donald Pleasence, Don Calfa, Kate Reid. *NWV*

Rainbow Over Broadway 1933 A former Broadway star mother is set against having her son and daughter try their luck on Broadway. 52m/C VHS. Joan Marsh, Frank Albertson, Lucien Littlefield, Grace Hayes, Dell Henderson, Harry Myers, Gladys Blake, Glen Boles, Nat Carr; *D:* Richard Thorpe. *GPV*

Rainbow Ranch 🐾½ 1933 A Navy boxer returns home to his ranch to find murder and corruption. Needless to say, he rides off to seek revenge. 54m/B VHS. Rex Bell, Cecilia Parker, Robert F. (Bob) Kortman, Henry Hall, Gordon DeMain; *D:* Harry Fraser. *NOS, DVT, RGB*

Rainbow Warrior 🐾🐾½ 1994 (PG) True story of the bombing of the Greenpeace vessel and the two men who set out to solve the crime. 90m/C VHS. Sam Neill, Jon Voight, Kerry Fox, Bruno Lawrence; *D:* Michael Tuchner. *ABC*

Rainbow's End 🐾🐾 1935 Gibson must defend Gale, the female rancher, from an evil adversary who is trying to run Gale and her invalid father off of their land. Things get complicated when Gibson discovers that Stark works for his father! 54m/B VHS. Hoot Gibson, June Gale, Oscar Apfel, Ada Ince, Charles Hill, Warner Richmond; *D:* Norman Spencer. *NOS, DVT*

Raining Stones 🐾🐾 1993 A hard-up plumber becomes obsessed with buying an expensive first communion dress for his daughter and gets involved in numerous misadventures trying to get the money. Another of Loach's comedy-dramas about the British working class and their struggle to survive with dignity. 90m/C VHS. *GB* Bruce Jones, Julie Brown, Ricky Tomlinson, Tom Hickey, Gemma Phoenix, Jonathan James; *D:* Ken Loach; *W:* Jim Allen; *C:* Barry Ackroyd; *M:* Stewart Copeland. Cannes Film Festival '93: Special Jury Prize; Nominations: British Academy Awards '93: Best Film. *ORI*

The Rainmaker 🐾🐾🐾 1956 Reminiscent of "Elmer Gantry" in his masterful performance, Lancaster makes it all believable as a con man who comes to a small midwestern town and works miracles not only on the weather but on spinster Hepburn, although both were a little long in the tooth for their roles. Written by Nash from his own play. 121m/C VHS, LV, **Closed Caption.** Burt Lancaster, Katharine Hepburn, Wendell Corey, Lloyd Bridges, Earl Holliman, Cameron Prudhomme, Wallace Ford; *D:* Joseph Anthony; *W:* N. Richard Nash; *C:* Charles B(ryant) Lang; *M:* Alex North. Golden Globe Awards '57: Best Supporting Actor (Holliman); Nominations: Academy Awards '56: Best Actress (Hepburn), Original Dramatic/Comedy Score. *PAR, CCB*

The Rains Came 🐾🐾½ 1939 Living within a loveless marriage in the mythical Indian city of Ranchipur, English socialite Loy pursues extramarital love interests, including the compassionate doctor Power, potential heir to the maharajah's throne. When an earthquake hits and brings major destruction to the city, Loy aids the doctor in helping the injured. Hankies should be kept handy. Adapted from the Louis Bromfield novel. 104m/B VHS. Myrna Loy, Tyrone Power, George Brent, Brenda Joyce, Nigel Bruce, Maria Ouspenskaya, Joseph Schildkraut, Laura Hope Crews, Marilyn Nash, Jane Darwell, Marjorie Rambeau, Henry Travers, H.B. Warner, William Royle, Montague Shaw, Harry Hayden, Abner Biberman, George Regas; *D:* Clarence Brown; *W:* Philip Dunne, Julien Josephson; *C:* Arthur C. Miller; *M:* Alfred Newman. Academy Awards '40: Best Special Effects (Sersen); Nominations: Academy Awards '39: Best Black and White Cinematography, Best Film Editing, Best Sound, Best Original Score. *FXV*

Raintree County 🐾🐾½ 1957 A lavish, somewhat overdone epic about two lovers caught up in the national turmoil of the Civil War. An Indiana teacher (Clift) marries a southern belle (Taylor) just after the outbreak of war. The new wife battles mental illness. Producers had hoped this would be another "Gone With the Wind." Adapted from the novel by Ross Lockridge, Jr. Film was delayed in mid-production by Clift's near-fatal and disfiguring car crash. 175m/C VHS, Beta, LV. Elizabeth Taylor, Montgomery Clift, Eva Marie Saint, Lee Marvin, Nigel Patrick, Rod Taylor, Agnes Moorehead, Walter Abel; *D:* Edward Dmytryk; *C:* Robert L. Surtees. Nominations: Academy Awards '57: Best Actress (Taylor), Best Art Direction/Set Decoration, Best Costume Design, Best Score. *MGM*

Rainy Day 🐾🐾 1979 A successful actress' return home for her father's funeral brings back unpleasant childhood memories that force her to face the truth about herself. 35m/C VHS, Beta. Mariette Hartley. *LCA*

Raise the Red Lantern 🐾🐾🐾½ 1991 (PG) Set in 1920s China, Zhang explores its claustrophobic world of privilege and humiliation. Songlian, an educated 19-year-old beauty, is forced into marriage as the fourth wife of a wealthy and powerful old man. She discovers that the wives have their own separate quarters and servants, and spend most of their time battling to attract their husband's attention. Over the course of a year, Songlian's fury and resentment grow until self-defeating rebellion is all she has. Gong Li is exquisite as the young woman struggling for dignity in a portrayal which is both both haunting and tragic. 125m/C VHS, **Closed Caption.** *CH* Gong Li, Ma Jingwu, He Caifei, Cao Cuifeng, Jin Shuyuan, Kong Lin, Ding Weimin; *D:* Zhang Yimou. British Academy Awards '92: Best Foreign Film; Los Angeles Film Critics Association Awards '92: Best Cinematography; New York Film Critics Awards '92: Best Foreign Film; National Society of Film Critics Awards '92: Best Cinematography, Best Foreign Film; Nominations: Academy Awards '91: Best Foreign Language Film. *ORI, BTV*

Raise the Titanic woof! 1980 (PG) A disaster about a disaster. Horrible script cannot be redeemed by purported thrill of the ship's emergence from the deep after 70 years. It's a shame, because the free world's security hangs in the balance. Based on Clive Cussler's best seller. **112m/C VHS, Beta, LV.** Jason Robards Jr., Richard Jordan, Anne Archer, Alec Guinness, J.D. Cannon; *D:* Jerry Jameson; *M:* John Barry. *FOX*

A Raisin in the Sun 🎞🎞🎞🎞 1961

Outstanding story of a black family trying to make a better life for themselves in an all-white neighborhood in Chicago. The characters are played realistically and make for a moving story. Each person struggles with doing what he must while still maintaining his dignity and sense of self. Based on the Broadway play by Hansberry, who also wrote the screenplay. **128m/B VHS, Beta, LV.** Diana Sands, John Fiedler, Ivan Dixon, Louis Gossett Jr., Sidney Poitier, Claudia McNeil, Ruby Dee; *D:* Daniel Petrie; *W:* Lorraine Hansberry. National Board of Review Awards '61: 10 Best Films of the Year, Best Supporting Actress (Dee). *COL, HMV*

A Raisin in the Sun 🎞🎞🎞 1989

An "American Playhouse," made for television presentation of the Lorraine Hansberry play about a black family threatened with dissolution by the outside forces of racism and greed when they move into an all-white neighborhood in the 1950s. **171m/C VHS, Beta, Closed Caption.** Danny Glover, Esther Rolle, Starletta DuPois; *D:* Bill Duke. *MON, FRH*

Raising Arizona 🎞🎞🎞½ 1987 (PG-13)

Hi's an ex-con and the world's worst hold-up man. Ed's a policewoman. They meet, fall in love, marry, and kidnap a baby (one of a family of quints). Why not? Ed's infertile and the family they took the baby from has "more than enough," so who will notice? But unfinished furniture tycoon Nathan Arizona wants his baby back, even if he has to hire an axe-murderer on a motorcycle to do it. A brilliant, original comedy narrated in notorious loopy deadpan style by Cage. Innovative camerawork by Barry Sonnenfeld. Wild, surreal and hilarious. **94m/C VHS, Beta, LV, Closed Caption.** Nicolas Cage, Holly Hunter, John Goodman, William Forsythe, Randall "Tex" Cobb, Trey Wilson, M. Emmet Walsh, Frances McDormand; *D:* Joel Coen; *W:* Ethan Coen, Joel Coen; *M:* Carter Burwell. *FOX*

Raising Cain 🎞🎞 1992 (R)

Thriller evoking poor man's Hitchcock about a child psychiatrist who just happens to be nuts features Lithgow in five roles. Seems his supposedly dead Norwegian father has come to the United States and needs his son's help to steal babies for a child development experiment, so the son's alter ego, Cain, shows up to commit the nasty deed. Unfortunately Lithgow also catches his wife with another man, and that's when the bodies start piling up. *CW:* Language, terror violence, and sexuality. **95m/C VHS, Beta, LV, Closed Caption.** John Lithgow, Lolita Davidovich, Steven Bauer, Frances Sternhagen, Cindy Girard, Tom Bower, Mel Harris, Gabrielle Carteris, Barton Heyman; *D:* Brian DePalma; *W:* Brian DePalma; *C:* Stephen Burum; *M:* Pino Donaggio. *USH*

Rambling Rose 🎞🎞🎞 1991 (R)

Dern is Rose, a free-spirited, sexually liberated before her time young woman taken in by a Southern family in 1935. Rose immediately has an impact on the male members of the clan, father Duvall and son Haas, thanks to her insuppressible sexuality. This causes consternation with the strait-laced patriarch, who attempts to control his desire for the girl. Eventually Rose decides she must try to stick to one man, but this only causes further problems. Dern gives her best performance yet in this excellent period piece, and solid support is offered from the rest of the cast, in particular Duvall and Dern's real-life mother Ladd. **115m/C VHS, LV.** Laura Dern, Diane Ladd, Robert Duvall, Lukas Haas, John Heard, Kevin Conway, Robert John Burke, Lisa Jakub, Evan Lockwood; *D:* Martha Coolidge; *W:* Calder Willingham; *M:* Elmer Bernstein. Independent Spirit Awards '92: Best Director (Coolidge), Best Film, Best Supporting Actress (Ladd); National Board of Review Awards '91: 10 Best Films of the Year; Nominations: Academy Awards '91: Best Actress (Dern), Best Supporting Actress (Ladd). *LIV*

Rambo: First Blood, Part 2 🎞🎞

1985 (R) If anyone can save Our Boys still held prisoner in Asia it's John Rambo. Along the way he's tortured, flexes biceps, grunts, and then disposes of the bad guys by the dozen in one of filmdom's bigger dead body parades. Mindless action best enjoyed by testosterone-driven fans of the genre. Sequel to "First Blood" (1982); followed by "Rambo 3" (1988). **93m/C VHS, Beta, LV, Closed Caption.** Sylvester Stallone, Richard Crenna, Charles Napier, Steven Berkoff, Julia Nickson-Soul, Martin Kove; *D:* George P. Cosmatos; *W:* Sylvester Stallone, James Cameron; *C:* Jack Cardiff; *M:* Jerry Goldsmith. Golden Raspberry Awards '85: Worst Picture, Worst Actor (Stallone), Worst Screenplay, Worst Song ("Peace In Our Life"). *LIV*

Rambo 3 🎞½ 1988 (R)

John Rambo, the famous Vietnam vet turned Buddhist monk, this time invades Afghanistan to rescue his mentor. Meets up with orphan and fights his way around the country. Typically exploitative, kill now, ask questions later Rambo attack, lacking the sheer volume of no-brainer action of the first two Rambos. At the time, the most expensive film ever made, costing $58 million. Filmed in Israel. **102m/C VHS, Beta, LV.** Sylvester Stallone, Richard Crenna, Marc De Jonge, Kurtwood Smith, Spiros Focas; *D:* Peter MacDonald; *W:* Sylvester Stallone; *M:* Jerry Goldsmith. Golden Raspberry Awards '88: Worst Actor (Stallone). *LIV*

Rampage 🎞🎞 1987 (R)

Seemingly all-American guy Charles Reece (McArthur) goes on a murder spree, killing and then mutiliating his victims. Fraser (Biehn) is a liberal district attorney who questions his own views as he argues during the trial that Reece was sane when he committed the murders and deserves the death penalty. Director Friedkin makes no bones about his concerns that the criminal insanity defense often spares the perpetrator while denying justice to the victims. Adapted from the book by William P. Wood and loosely based on killer Richard Chase. Filmed in 1987, the movie wasn't released until 1992 due to the production company's financial difficulties. *CW:* Strong violence. **92m/C VHS, Beta, LV, Closed Caption.** Michael Biehn, Alex McArthur, Nicholas Campbell, Deborah Van Valkenburgh, John Harkins, Art LaFleur; *D:* William Friedkin; *W:* William Friedkin; *M:* Ennio Morricone. *PAR, BTV*

Ramparts of Clay 🎞🎞🎞 1971 (PG)

A young woman in Tunisia walks the line between her village's traditional way of life and the modern world just after her country's independence from France. Brilliantly shot on location; exquisitely poignant. In Arabic with English subtitles. **87m/C VHS, Beta.** *FR D:* Jean-Louis Bertucelli. *COL*

Ramrod 🎞🎞 1947

Lake is a tough ranch owner at odds with her father, who is being manipulated by a big-time cattleman into trying to put them out of business. She fights back, and McCrea is caught in the middle as the only good guy. Nothing special. **94m/B VHS.** Veronica Lake, Joel McCrea, Arleen Whelan, Don DeFore, Preston Foster, Charlie Ruggles, Donald Crisp, Lloyd Bridges; *D:* Andre de Toth. *REP*

The Ramrodder 🎞 Ramrodders 1969

An adult western spoof. **92m/C VHS, Beta.** *VDM, TPV*

Ran 🎞🎞🎞🎞 1985 (R)

The culmination of Kurosawa's career stands as his masterpiece. Loosely adapting Shakespeare's "King Lear," with plot elements from "Macbeth," he's fashioned an epic, heartbreaking statement about honor, ambition, and the futility of war. Aging medieval warlord Hidetora gives control of his empire to his oldest son, creating conflict with two other sons. Soon he's an outcast, as ambition and greed seize the two sons. Stunning battle scenes illuminate the full-blown tragedy of Kurosawa's vision. Superb acting with a scene-stealing Harada as the revenge-minded Lady Kaede; period costumes took three years to create. Japanese with English subtitles. **160m/C VHS, Beta, LV, Closed Caption.** *JP FR* Tatsuya Nakadai, Akira Terao, Jinpachi Nesu, Daisuke Ryu, Meiko Harada, Hisashi Igawa, Peter; *D:*

Akira Kurosawa; *W:* Akira Kurosawa, Hideo Oguni, Masato Ide; *M:* Toru Takemitsu. Academy Awards '85: Best Costume Design; British Academy Awards '86: Best Foreign Film; Los Angeles Film Critics Association Awards '85: Best Foreign Film; National Board of Review Awards '85: Best Director (Kurosawa); New York Film Critics Awards '85: Best Foreign Film; National Society of Film Critics Awards '85: Best Cinematography, Best Film; Nominations: Academy Awards '85: Best Art Direction/Set Decoration, Best Cinematography, Best Director (Kurosawa). *FOX, APD, HMV*

Rana: The Legend of Shadow Lake 🎞 1975

Gold at the bottom of a lake is guarded by a frog-monster, but treasure hunters try to retrieve it anyway. **96m/C VHS, Beta.** Alan Ross, Karen McDiarmid, Jerry Gregoris. *AHV*

The Ranch 🎞🎞 1988 (PG-13)

An executive who loses everything inherits a dilapidated ranch and renovates it into a health spa. **97m/C VHS, Beta.** Andrew Stevens, Gary Fjellgaard, Lou Ann Schmidt, Elizabeth Keefe; *D:* Stella Stevens. *HMD*

Rancho Deluxe 🎞🎞🎞 1975

Off-beat western spoof starring Bridges and Waterston as two carefree cowpokes. Cult favorite featuring music by Buffett, who also appears in the film. **93m/C VHS, Beta, Closed Caption.** Jeff Bridges, Sam Waterston, Elizabeth Ashley, Charlene Dallas, Clifton James, Slim Pickens, Harry Dean Stanton, Richard Bright, Jimmy Buffett; *D:* Frank Perry; *W:* Thomas McGuane; *M:* Jimmy Buffett. *MGM*

Rancho Notorious 🎞🎞🎞 1952

Kennedy, on the trail of his girlfriend's murderer, falls for dance hall girl Dietrich. Fine acting. A "period" sample of 50's westerns, but different. A must for Dietrich fans. **89m/C VHS, Beta, LV.** Marlene Dietrich, Arthur Kennedy, Mel Ferrer, William Frawley, Jack Elam, George Reeves; *D:* Fritz Lang; *W:* Daniel Taradash; *C:* Hal Mohr. *NO*

Random Harvest 🎞🎞🎞 1942

A masterful, tearjerking film based on the James Hilton novel. A shell-shocked WWI amnesiac meets and is made happy by a beautiful music hall dancer. He regains his memory and forgets about the dancer and their child. This is Garson's finest hour, and a shamelessly potent sobfest. **126m/B VHS, Beta.** Greer Garson, Ronald Colman, Reginald Owen, Philip Dorn, Susan Peters, Henry Travers, Margaret Wycherly, Bramwell Fletcher; *D:* Mervyn LeRoy; *C:* Joseph Ruttenberg. Academy Awards '42: Best Actor (Colman), Best Director (LeRoy), Best Interior Decoration, Best Picture, Best Screenplay, Best Supporting Actress (Peters), Original Dramatic/Comedy Score. *MGM*

Randy Rides Alone 🎞🎞 1934

Very young Wayne is good in this slappable but pleasant B effort. Wayne single-handedly cleans up the territory and rids the land of a passel o'bad guys. **53m/B VHS, Beta.** John Wayne, Alberta Vaughn, George "Gabby" Hayes; *D:* Harry Fraser. *COL, NOS, VCN*

Range Busters 🎞 1940

Range Busters are called in to find the identity of the phantom killer. **55m/B VHS, Beta.** Ray Corrigan, Max Terhune. *NOS, VCN, DVT*

Range Feud 🎞½ 1931

Wayne is a ranch owner's son falsely accused of murder. Just as he's about to hang, Jones, as the heroic sheriff, saves the day and reveals the real killer's identity. **58m/B VHS.** Buck Jones, John Wayne, Susan Fleming, William Walling, Wallace MacDonald, Harry Woods, Ed LeSaint; *D:* David Ross Lederman. *COL*

The Range Feud/Two Fisted Law 🎞🎞 1931

Two early, short Wayne oaters which reveal the Duke developing the drawl, gait and pleasingly profane style that would carry him to fame. In "Feud" he is a young rancher accused of murdering a cattle rustler. "Law" finds him playing a character named Duke who loses his land and girl to a neighboring land grabber. **112m/C VHS.** Buck Jones, Tim McCoy, John Wayne, Susan Fleming, Alice Faye, Walter Brennan; *D:* David Ross Lederman. *COL*

Range Law 🎞 1931

Another entry in the infamous Maynard series of horseplay, cliche, and repetitive plot elements. **60m/B VHS, Beta.** Ken Maynard, Charles "Blackie" King, Lafe McKee. *GPV, VCI, DVT*

Range Law 🎬½ **1944** Ranchers are being terrorized for their silver mine and its up to Brown and Hatton to catch the villains. **59m/B VHS.** Johnny Mack Brown, Raymond Hatton, Lloyd Ingraham, Sarah Padden, Ellen Hall, Steve Clark, Jack Ingram, Bud Osborne; **D:** Lambert Hillyer. *GPV*

Range Renegades 🎬½ **1948** Sheriff Wakely and his pals have their hands full when his deputy gets involved with the leader of a gang of outlaw women. Predictable B oater reflects the then developing trend of using wicked female characters in westerns. Paved the way for films like "Johnny Guitar" and "Rancho Notorious." **54m/B VHS.** Jimmy Wakely, Dub Taylor, Dennis Moore, Jennifer Holt, John James, Steve Clark, Frank LaRue; **D:** Lambert Hillyer; **W:** Ronald Davidson, William Lively. *MOV*

Range Rider **1952** Eight episodes of the series are on two tapes, including "Greed Rides the Range," "Silver Blade" and "Fatal Bullet." **60m/B VHS, Beta.** Jock Mahoney. *DVT*

Range Riders **1935** A gunman poses as a wimp and cleans out an outlaw gang. **46m/B VHS, Beta.** Buddy Roosevelt. *NO*

Rangeland Empire 🎬 **1950** Shamrock and Lucky are at it again, implicated as being members of a gang until that gang attacks them. **59m/B VHS, Beta, LV.** James Ellison, Russell Hayden, Stanley Price, John Cason. *NO*

Rangeland Racket 🎬½ **1941** The Lone Rider (Houston) has been wrongly accused of a crime. **60m/B VHS, Beta.** George Houston, Hillary Brooke, Al "Fuzzy" St. John. *VYY*

Ranger and the Lady 🎬½ **1940** Texas Ranger Rodgers romances the woman who is the leader of a wagon train. **54m/B VHS, Beta.** Roy Rogers, George (Gabby) Hayes; **D:** Joseph Kane. *NOS, DVT*

Ranger's Roundup 🎬 **1938** The Rangers prove their courage by rounding up an outlaw gang. **57m/B VHS, Beta.** Fred Scott, Al "Fuzzy" St. John. *NOS, DVT*

The Rangers Step In 🎬½ **1937** Allen leaves the Texas Rangers when a feud between his family and that of the girl he loves heats up again. Turns out rustlers are stirring things up in order to get some of the disputed land. **56m/B VHS.** Robert Allen, Eleanor Stewart, John Merton, Hal Taliaferro, Jack Ingram, Jack Rockwell, Lafe McKee, Robert F. (Bob) Kortman; **D:** Spencer Gordon Bennet. *GPV*

Rangers Take Over 🎬½ **1943** Gunlords are driven out by the Texas Rangers. **62m/B VHS, Beta.** Dave O'Brien, James Newill. *NOS, VYY, DVT*

Ransom 🎬🎬🎬 **1996 (R)** Tight and crafty thriller proves millionaire airline magnate Tom Mullen (Gibson) is a force to be reckoned with when son Sean (Nolte, son of actor Nick) is kidnapped. A vigilante Donald Trump (only gorgeous and brave), Mullen treats this like a high-stakes business deal and decides to get his kid back by announcing on TV that the $2 million ransom demand will instead become a bounty on the kidnappers. Wife Kate (Russo), predictably flips out but Mullen, after a few encounters with the heinous abductors, has sized them up and is convinced he's done the right thing. Lindo is a by-the-book fed with bad dialogue and Sinise is a bad cop playing for the other team. Gibson's emergency appendectomy delayed filming but he was soon leaping over cars for director Howard's well-staged action scenes. Based on the 1956 flick starring Glenn Ford. **CW:** Graphic bloody violence and strong language. **121m/C VHS, LV, Closed Caption.** Mel Gibson, Rene Russo, Gary Sinise, Delroy Lindo, Brawley Nolte, Lili Taylor, Liev Schreiber, Evan Handler, Dan Hedaya, Paul Guilfoyle, Jose Zuniga, Donnie Wahlberg, Michael Gaston; **Cameos:** Richard Price; **D:** Ron Howard; **W:** Richard Price, Alexander Ignon; **C:** Piotr Sobocinski; **M:** James Horner. Nominations: Golden Globe Awards '97: Best Actor—Drama (Gibson). *TOU*

Ransom Money 🎬½ **1988** A kidnapping scheme involving millions of dollars, in and around the Grand Canyon, backfires. **87m/C VHS, Beta.** Broderick Crawford, Rachel Romen, Gordon Jump, Randy Whipple; **D:** DeWitt Lee. *NO*

Ranson's Folly 🎬🎬½ **1926** Barthelmess makes a wager that he can impersonate a famous outlaw well enough to rob a stage with only a pair of scissors. When the army paymaster is killed, guess who gets caught with his swash unbuckled? **80m/B VHS, Beta.** Richard Barthelmess, Dorothy Mackaill, Anders Randolf, Pat Hartigan, Brooks Benedict; **D:** Sidney Olcott. *GPV*

Rapa Nui 🎬🎬½ **1993 (R)** The title refers to the Polynesian name for Easter Island, with the film set in the 17th-century (before Dutch explorers discovered the island). It depicts the annual rituals of the mysterious people who built the island's moai—the famous giant stone statues. Lee plays the heroic Noroinia, with Morales as his rival Make, and Holt as Ramana, the object of their desires. Faux primitive but with some great on-location filming. **CW:** Tribal violence and sexuality. **107m/C VHS, LV, Closed Caption.** Jason Scott Lee, Esai Morales, Sandrine Holt; **D:** Kevin Reynolds; **W:** Kevin Reynolds, Tim Rose Price; **M:** Stewart Copeland. *WAR*

Rape 🎬 **198?** Two guys investigate a third pal's mysterious death. They discover that his supernatural-power-imbued girlfriend is at the root of the matter. **90m/C VHS, Beta.** Rick Joss, Gil Vidal. *NO*

Rape and Marriage: The Rideout Case 🎬🎬½ **1980** The true story of an Oregon wife who accused her husband of rape. Thoughtfully explores the legal and moral questions raised by the case. Interpreted well enough, though not superbly, by a decent cast. although Rourke is a little too intense. Made for television. **96m/C VHS, Beta.** Mickey Rourke, Linda Hamilton, Rip Torn, Eugene Roche, Conchata Ferrell, Gail Strickland, Bonnie Bartlett, Alley Mills; **D:** Peter Levin. *LIV*

Rape of Love 🎬🎬½ **1979** The story begins with one of the most chilling rape scenes on film and then attempts to analyze the emotional impact of rape on its victim. Well-acted and directed. In French with English subtitles. **117m/C VHS, Beta.** **FR** Nathalie Nell, Alain Foures; **D:** Yannick Bellon. *COL*

The Rape of the Sabines woof! *El Rapto de las Sabinas; The Mating of the Sabine Women; Shame of the Sabine Women* **1961** The story of Romulus, king of Rome, and how he led the Romans to capture the women of Sabina. The battles rage, the women plot, and Romulus fights and lusts. Dubbed in English. **101m/C VHS, Beta.** **IT FR** Roger Moore, Mylene Demongeot, Jean Marais; **D:** Richard Pottier. *UNI*

Rapid Fire 🎬 **1989** Cheap, made-for-video quickie about a good guy U.S. agent who battles terrorists. Easy to skip. **90m/C VHS, Beta.** Joe Spinell, Michael Wayne, Ron Waldron; **D:** David A. Prior. *AIP*

Rapid Fire 🎬🎬½ **1992 (R)** Lee (son of martial arts cult film star Bruce Lee) is a Chinese-American art student who also happens to be a martial arts expert. He's tapped by the police to help stem the violence between the Asian and Italian gangs fighting for control over Chicago's drug trade. Typical martial arts movie is made better by uniquely choreographed action sequences and Lee's attractive presence. **CW:** Language, violence, and sexuality. **96m/C VHS, LV, Closed Caption.** Brandon Lee, Powers Boothe, Nick Mancuso, Raymond J. Barry, Kate Hodge, Tzi Ma, Tony Longo, Michael Paul Chan, Dustin Nguyen, John Vickery; **D:** Dwight Little; **W:** Alan B. McElroy, Cindy Cirile, Paul Attanasio; **M:** Christopher Young. *FXV*

Rappin' 🎬 **1985 (PG)** Ex-con Van Peebles gets into it with the landlord and a street gang leader. Forgettable action/music drivel. ♫*Rappin'; Two of a Kind; Call Me; Born to Love; Killer; Itching for a Scratch; Snack Attack; Dodge; Golly Gee.* **92m/C VHS, Beta.** Mario Van Peebles, Tasia Valenza, Harry Goz, Charles Flohe; **D:** Joel Silberg. *MGM*

The Rapture 🎬🎬 **1991 (R)** A beautiful telephone operator engages in indiscrimate sexual adventures to relieve the boredom of her job and life. She becomes curious by, and eventually converted to, evangelical Christianity, which leads her to a contented marriage and the birth of a daughter. When her husband is tragically killed she becomes convinced that she and her child will be taken by God into heaven if she only waits for the proper sign. **CW:** Some language, violence, and strong sensuality. **100m/C VHS, LV.** Mimi Rogers, David Duchovny, Patrick Bauchau, Will Patton; **D:** Michael Tolkin; **W:** Michael Tolkin; **C:** Bojan Bazelli. *COL*

Rapunzel **1982** A beautiful young woman locked in a tall tower is saved by the handsome prince who climbs her golden tresses. Part of Shelly Duvall's "Faerie Tale Theatre" series. **60m/C VHS, Beta, LV, Closed Caption.** Shelley Duvall, Gena Rowlands, Jeff Bridges. *KUI, FOX, FCT*

The Rare Breed 🎬🎬½ **1966** Plodding but pleasant Western. A no-strings ranch hand (Stewart) agrees to escort a Hereford Bull to Texas, where the widow of an English breeder plans to crossbreed the bull with longhorn cattle. The widow (O'Hara) insists that she and her daughter accompany Stewart on the trip, which features every kind of western calamity imaginable. When all others believe the attempt to crossbreed has failed, Stewart sets out to prove them wrong. **97m/C VHS, Beta, Closed Caption.** James Stewart, Maureen O'Hara, Brian Keith, Juliet Mills, Jack Elam, Ben Johnson; **D:** Andrew V. McLaglen; **C:** William Clothier; **M:** John Williams. *USH*

A Rare Breed 🎬½ **1981 (PG)** Real-life story of a kidnapped horse in Italy and a young girl's quest to retrieve it. Directed by David Nelson of television's "Ozzie and Harriet" fame, this movie is cute and old-fashioned. **94m/C VHS, Beta.** George Kennedy, Forrest Tucker, Tracy Vaccaro, Tom Hallick, Don DeFore; **D:** David Nelson. *VTR, LIV*

Rascal Dazzle **1981** Montage-like tribute to that best-loved group of children, the Our Gang kids. Narrated by Jerry Lewis. Includes scenes with Spanky, Alfalfa, Darla and the rest of the gang. **100m/B VHS, Beta, LV.**

The Rascals 🎬🎬½ **1981 (R)** An irrepressible youth at a rural Catholic boys' school comes of age. **93m/C VHS, Beta.** **FR** Thomas Chabrol; **D:** Bernard Revon.

Rashomon 🎬🎬🎬🎬 *In the Woods* **1951** In 12th century Japan, two travelers attempt to discover the truth about an ambush/rape/murder. They get four completely different versions of the incident from the three people involved in the crime and the single witness. An insightful masterpiece that established Kurosawa and Japanese cinema as major artistic forces. Fine performances, particularly Mifune as the bandit. Visually appealing and rhythmic. Remade as a western, "The Outrage," in 1964. In Japanese with English subtitles. **83m/B VHS, Beta, LV.** **JP** Machiko Kyo, Toshiro Mifune, Masayuki Mori, Takashi Shimura; **D:** Akira Kurosawa; **W:** Akira Kurosawa. Academy Awards '51: Best Foreign Language Film; National Board of Review Awards '51: 5 Best Foreign Films of the Year, Best Director (Kurosawa); Venice Film Festival '51: Best Film; Nominations: Academy Awards '52: Best Art Direction/Set Decoration (B & W). *CRC, NLC, PME*

Rasputin 🎬🎬🎬 *Agoniya* **1985** The long-censored and banned film of the story of the mad monk and his domination of the royal family before the Russian Revolution. Petrenko is superb. First released in the United States in 1988. In Russian with English subtitles. **104m/C VHS, Beta.** **RU** Alexei Petrenko, Anatoly Romashin, Velta Linne, Alice Freindlikh; **D:** Elem Klimov; **W:** Semyon Lunghin, Ilya Nusinov; **M:** Alfred Shnitke. *NO*

Rasputin and the Empress 🎬🎬🎬 *Rasputin: The Mad Monk* **1933** Lavish historical epic teamed the three Barrymore sibs for the first and only time, as they vied for scene-stealing honors. Ethel is Empress Alexandra of Russia, tied to the weak-willed Nicholas II (Morgan) and under the spell of Rasputin, played by Lionel. John is a nobleman who seeks to warn the Russian rulers of their perilous perch on the throne, made only worse by Rasputin's spreading power and corruption. Ethel's first talkie and Wyngard's first film role. Uncredited director Charles Brabin was replaced by Boleslawski due to his incompatability with the imperious Ethel. **123m/B VHS.** Ethel Barrymore, John Barrymore, Lionel Barrymore, Ralph Morgan, Diana Wynyard, Tad Alexander, C. Henry Gordon, Edward Arnold, Gustav von Seyffertitz, Anne Shirley, Jean Parker, Henry Kolker; **D:** Richard Boleslawski; **W:** Charles MacArthur; **C:** William H. Daniels. Nominations: Academy Awards '33: Best Story. *MGM, MOV*

Rasputin: Dark Servant of Destiny 🎬🎬🎬 1996 (R) Charismatic Russian peasant/mystic Grigori Rasputin (a mesmerizing Rickman), having received a vision of the Virgin Mary, comes to St. Petersburg in order to relieve the suffering of young hemophiliac, Prince Alexei (Findlay). Tsarina Alexandra (Scacchi) approves of anyone who can help her stricken son while Tsar Nicholas II (McKellen) tentatively agrees to accept the self-proclaimed holy man into the Russian court. Fine performances and beautiful photography make this one of the better made-for-cable efforts. Filmed in St. Petersburg. **120m/C VHS.** Alan Rickman, Ian McKellen, Greta Scacchi, Freddie Findlay, David Warner, John Wood, James Frain, Diana Quick, Ian Hogg, Peter Jeffrey, Ian McDiarmid, Julian Curry; **D:** Uli Edel; **W:** Peter Bruce; **C:** Elemer Ragaly; **M:** Brad Fiedel. *HBO*

Rasputin the Mad Monk 🎬🎬 1966 Hammer's version of Russian history of course emphasizes the evil powers of the mad Russian monk (Lee) who gains entry into the court of the czar. Poor script but Lee's good. **90m/B VHS.** *GB* Christopher Lee, Barbara Shelley, Richard Pasco, Francis Matthews, Suzan Farmer, Nicholas Pennell, Renee Asherson, Derek Francis; **D:** Don Sharp; **W:** John Elder; **C:** Michael Reed; **M:** Don Banks. *VTR*

Rat Pfink a Boo-Boo woof! 1966 Parody on "Batman" in which a bumbling superhero and his sidekick race around saving people. Notoriously inept. Title story is legendary—it was misspelled accidentally and Steckler didn't have the cash to fix it. **72m/B VHS, Beta.** Vin Saxon, Carolyn Brandt, Titus Moede, Mike Kannon; **D:** Ray Dennis Steckler. *NO*

The Rat Race 🎬🎬🎬 1960 A dancer and a musician venture to Manhattan to make it big, and end up sharing an apartment. Their relationship starts pleasantly and becomes romantic. Enjoyable farce. Well photographed and scripted, with the supporting characters stealing the show. **105m/C VHS.** Tony Curtis, Debbie Reynolds, Kay Medford, Don Rickles, Joe Bushkin; **D:** Robert Mulligan; **C:** Robert Burks; **M:** Elmer Bernstein. *PAR*

Ratboy 🎬🎬½ 1986 (PG-13) An unscrupulous woman attempts to transform a boy with a rat's face into a celebrity, with tragic results. First directorial effort by Locke that gradually loses steam. **105m/C VHS, Beta, Closed Caption.** Sondra Locke, Sharon Baird, Robert Townsend; **D:** Sondra Locke; **W:** Rob Thompson; **C:** Bruce Surtees; **M:** Lennie Niehaus. *WAR*

Rate It X 1986 (R) Sexism in a variety of national institutions, from pornography to consumerism, is revealed through the average man on the street via microphone interviews. **95m/C VHS, Beta.** **D:** Lucy Winer, Paula de Koenigsberg. *LIV*

Ratings Game 🎬🎬 *The Mogul* 1984 A bitter, out-of-work actor and a woman who works at the ratings service manage to mess up the television industry. Early directorial effort by DeVito is uneven but funny. Made for cable television. **102m/C VHS, Beta, LV, Closed Caption.** Danny DeVito, Rhea Perlman, Gerrit Graham, Kevin Macarthy, Jayne Meadows, Steve Allen, Ronny Graham, George Wenolt; **D:** Danny DeVito; **W:** Michael Barrie, Jim Mulholland. *PAR*

Rats 🎬🎬 1983 In 2225, the beleaguered survivors of a nuclear holocaust struggle with a mutant rodent problem. **100m/C VHS, Beta.** Richard Raymond, Richard Cross; **D:** Vincent Dawn. *NO*

The Rats are Coming! The Werewolves are Here! woof! 1972 (R) Low budget schlock revolves around a family of werewolves and the daughter who decides to put an end to the curse. Imaginative title promises much more than movie delivers. The killer rats were thrown in as an afterthought to increase the run time. **92m/C VHS, Beta.** Hope Stansbury, Jackie Skarvellis, Noel Collins, Joan Ogden, Douglas Phair, Bernard Kaler; **D:** Andy Milligan; **W:** Andy Milligan. *NO*

Rattle of a Simple Man 🎬🎬½ 1964 A naive, chaste, middle-aged bachelor (Corbett) who lives in London must spend the night with a waitress (Cilento) to win a bet. She knows of the bet and kindly obliges. Enjoyable sex comedy. **91m/B VHS, Beta.** *GB* Harry H. Corbett, Diane Cilento, Michael Medwin, Thora Hird; **D:** Muriel Box. *NO*

Rattled 🎬🎬½ 1996 (PG-13) Indiana Jones won't be the only snake-hater after seeing what hundreds of rattlesnakes can do. When their den is disturbed by construction on a new water project, hundreds of rattlers slither down the mountainside ready to attack anyone in their path. Based on the book "Rattlers" by Joseph Gilmore.**CW:** Terrifying snake attacks. **90m/C VHS, Closed Caption.** William Katt, Shanna Reed, Michael Galeota, Monica Creel, Clint Howard, Ian Abercrombie, Ed Lauter, Bibi Besch, Zack Eginton; **D:** Tony Randel; **W:** Jim Wheat, Ken Wheat. *USH*

Rattler Kid 🎬 197? Cavalry sergeant wrongly accused of murdering his commanding officer escapes from prison and finds the real killer. **86m/C VHS, Beta.** Richard Wyler, Brad Harris. *UNI*

Rattlers 🎬 1976 (PG) Made for television movie featuring poisonous rattlesnakes who attack at random. **82m/C VHS, Beta.** Sam Chew, Elizabeth Chauvet, Dan Priest; **D:** John McCauley. *NO*

Ravager 🎬½ 1997 (R) A biological entity, created as a weapon, stalks the passengers and crew of a space transport ship.**CW:** Sci-fi violence and gore. **92m/C VHS.** Bruce Payne, Yancy Butler, Juliet Landau, Salvator Xuereb; **D:** James D. Deck. *REP*

Rave Review 🎬🎬 1995 Desperate L.A. theatrical director wants to scare a powerful critic into giving his latest production a glowing review so that his small theater company can remain in business. Too bad he scares the critic to death. **91m/C VHS.** Jeff Seymour, Ed Begley Jr., Leo Rossi, Joe Spano, Bruce Kirby, James Handy; **D:** Jeff Seymour; **W:** Jeff Seymour. *HMD*

The Raven 🎬🎬 1915 An early, eccentric pseudo-biography of author Edgar Allan Poe. The film opens with a look at Poe's ancestors and follows the author to maturity when he turns to alcohol for solace. His drunken stupor produces hallucinations that lead to his tale of "The Raven." Silent with added music track. **80m/B VHS.** Henry B. Walthall, Wanda Howard; **D:** Charles Brabin. *GPV, HEG, GVV*

The Raven 🎬🎬🎬 1935 A lunatic surgeon (Lugosi), who has a dungeon full of torture gadgets inspired by Edgar Allan Poe's stories, is begged by a man to save his daughter's life. The surgeon does, and then falls in love with the girl. But when she rejects his love (she's already engaged), he plans revenge in his chamber of horrors. Karloff plays the criminal who winds up ruining the mad doctor's plans. Lugosi is at his prime in this role, and any inconsistencies in the somewhat shaky script can be overlooked because of his chilling performance. **62m/B VHS, LV.** Boris Karloff, Bela Lugosi, Irene Ware, Lester Matthews, Samuel S. Hinds; **D:** Lew (Louis Friedlander) Landers. *USH*

The Raven 🎬🎬🎬 1963 This could-have-been monumental teaming of horror greats Karloff, Lorre and Price is more of a satire than a true horror film. One of the more enjoyable of the Cor-

man/Poe adaptations, the movie takes only the title of the poem. As for the storyline: Price and Karloff play two rival sorcerers who battle for supremacy, with Lorre as the unfortunate associate turned into the bird of the title. **86m/C VHS, Beta, LV.** Vincent Price, Boris Karloff, Peter Lorre, Jack Nicholson, Hazel Court; **D:** Roger Corman; **W:** Richard Matheson; **C:** Floyd Crosby; **M:** Les Baxter. *MLB*

Ravenhawk 🎬🎬 1995 (R) Native American Ravenhawk (McLish) is falsely accused of murdering her parents and sent to a maximum security asylum. Twelve years later she returns to her home and learns that corporate slimeball Philip Thorne (Atherton) framed her. Now, he's built a nuclear waste plant on Shoshone land over the objections of the tribe and Ravenhawk is determined to even the score.**CW:** Violence; language; brief nudity. **88m/C VHS, LV.** Rachel McLish, John Enos, William Atherton, Ed Lauter, Mitch Pileggi; **D:** Albert Pyun; **W:** Kevin Elders; **C:** George Mooradian; **M:** Johnny Harris. *COL*

Ravishing Idiot 🎬🎬 *Agent 38-24-36; Adorable Idiot; The Warm-Blooded Spy; Bewitching Scatterbrain* 1964 An unemployed bank clerk becomes mixed up with Soviet spies. **99m/C VHS, Beta.** *FR* Brigitte Bardot, Anthony Perkins; **D:** Edouard Molinaro. *NO*

Raw Courage 🎬 *Courage* 1984 Three long-distance runners relax in New Mexico, but are kidnapped by vigilantes. Loosely based on a James Dickey novel. **90m/C VHS, Beta, LV.** Ronny Cox, Lois Chiles, Art Hindle, Tim Maier, M. Emmet Walsh; **D:** Robert L. Rosen. *NWV, VTR*

Raw Deal 🎬🎬🎬 1948 Sadistic Rick Coyle (Burr) framed one-time associate Joe Sullivan (O'Keefe), who wound up in prison. Joe's moll Pat (Trevor) helps him to escape and they take prison social worker Ann (Hunt), who's befriended Joe, as a hostage. They go after Coyle and Joe begins to fall for the demure dame, who finds the underworld life exciting and even saves Joe from one of Coyle's henchmen. No good guys here but it is fine film noir. **79m/B VHS.** Dennis O'Keefe, Claire Trevor, Raymond Burr, Marsha Hunt, John Ireland, Curt Conway, Whit Bissell; **D:** Anthony Mann; **W:** John C. Higgins, Leopold Atlas; **C:** John Alton; **M:** Paul Sawtell. *KIV*

Raw Deal 🎬½ 1986 (R) Don't ever give Schwarzenegger a raw deal! FBI agent Schwarzie infiltrates the mob and shoots lots of people. **106m/C VHS, Beta, LV, Closed Caption.** Arnold Schwarzenegger, Kathryn Harrold, Darren McGavin, Sam Wanamaker, Paul Shenar, Steven Hill; **D:** John Irvin; **W:** Gary De Vore, Patrick Edgeworth. *TLF*

Raw Force 🎬 *Shogun Island* 1981 (R) Three karate buffs visit an island inhabited by a sect of cannibalistic monks who have the power to raise the dead (it could happen). They fix the villains by kicking them all in the head. **90m/C VHS, Beta.** *PH* Cameron Mitchell, Geoffrey Binney, John Dresden, John Locke, Ralph Lombardi; **D:** Edward Murphy. *MED*

Raw Justice 🎬🎬 1993 (R) When the daughter of a powerful Southern mayor is murdered, tough ex-cop Mace (Keith) is hired to get the killer. Mace enlists the reluctant help of call girl Sarah (Anderson) to help him trap Mitch (Hayes), his prime suspect. Only things don't work out as Mace planned and the wary threesome must work together to save themselves from certain death. **92m/C VHS, LV, Closed Caption.** David Keith, Pamela Anderson Lee, Robert Hayes, Leo Rossi, Charles Napier, Stacy Keach; **D:** David A. Prior; **W:** David A. Prior. *REP*

Raw Nerve 🎬 1991 (R) A cast with possibilities can't overcome this poorly reasoned suspenser. A young man has visions of the local serial killer, but when he reports them to police he becomes the suspect. There are a few twists beyond that, none too thrilling.**CW:** Language and violence and drug content. **91m/C VHS, Beta, LV.** Glenn Ford, Traci Lords, Sandahl Bergman, Randall "Tex" Cobb, Ted Prior, Jan-Michael Vincent; **W:** David A. Prior. *AIP*

Raw Target ♫½ 1995 (R) Ex-kickboxer finds himself a police decoy in a drug bust and then learns that the drug gang's leader was also involved in his brother's death.*CW:* Bloody shootings and martial arts violence, a sex scene, and language. 92m/C VHS. Dale "Apollo" Cook, Ron Hall, Nick Hill, Mychelle Charters; *D:* Tim Spring; *W:* Larry Maddox; *C:* Bruce Dorfman; *M:* Jun Lupito. THV

Rawhead Rex ♫½ 1987 (R) An ancient demon is released from his underground prison in Ireland by a plowing farmer, and begins to decapitate and maim at will. Adapted by Clive Barker from his own short story. But Barker later disowned the film, so make your own judgment. 89m/C VHS, Beta, LV. David Dukes, Kelly Piper; *D:* George Pavlou; *W:* Clive Barker; *M:* Colin Towns. LIV, VES

Rawhide ♫ 1938 Rancher's Protection Association forces landowners to knuckle under resulting in friction. Lou Gehrig plays a rancher in a western released the year before he died. Bandleader Ballew could be more gripping in the lead. 60m/B VHS, Beta. Lou Gehrig, Smith Ballew, Evalyn Knapp; *D:* Ray Taylor. NOS, CCB, DVT

Rawhide ♫♫♫ *Desperate Siege* 1950 Four escaped convicts hijack a stagecoach way station and hold hostages while waiting for a shipment of gold. A suspenseful B-grade western with a bang-up ending. Well paced and cast with an abundance of good talent. A remake of "Show Them No Mercy" (1938). 86m/B VHS, Beta. Tyrone Power, Susan Hayward, Hugh Marlowe, Jack Elam, Dean Jagger, George Tobias, Edgar Buchanan, Jeff Corey; *D:* Henry Hathaway; *C:* Milton Krasner. FOX

Rawhide Romance ♫ 1934 Bill finds justice and love in this chap-slappin' opus, which finds him neglecting the thieves operating on the ranch as he romances his girl. Naturally he comes to his senses and goes after the crooks. 47m/B VHS, Beta, LV. Buffalo Bill Jr., Genee Boutell, Lafe McKee, Si Jenks; *D:* Victor Adamson. VYY

The Razor: Sword of Justice ♫♫ 1972 Reasonably honest cop Hanzo Itami knows he won't get a promotion under his corrupt boss Inspector Onishi unless he can blackmail him into it. And he finds a way when he discovers condemned prisoner Kanbei is actually living with his mistress Omino, who it turns out is busy with Onishi as well. A little knowledge could get Hanzo killed but he's willing to take the risk. Japanese with subtitles. 90m/C VHS, LV. *JP* Shintaro Katsu, Asaoka Yukiji, Atsumi Mari, Nishimura Akira; *D:* Kenji Misumi. ANI, MOV

Razorback ♫ 1984 (R) Young American travels to the Australian outback in search of his missing journalist wife. During his quest, he encounters a giant killer pig that has been terrorizing the area. Firmly establishes that pigs, with little sense of natural timing, make lousy movie villains. 95m/C VHS, Beta. *AU* Gregory Harrison, Bill Kerr, Arkie Whiteley, Judy Morris, Chris Haywood; *D:* Russell Mulcahy. WAR

The Razor's Edge ♫♫♫ 1946 Adaptation of the W. Somerset Maugham novel. A rich young man spends his time between WWI & WWII searching for essential truth, eventually landing in India. A satisfying cinematic version of a difficult novel, supported by an excellent cast. Remade in 1984 with Bill Murray in the lead role. 146m/B VHS, Beta, LV, Closed Caption. Tyrone Power, Gene Tierney, Anne Baxter, Clifton Webb, Herbert Marshall, John Payne, Elsa Lanchester; *D:* Edmund Goulding; *C:* Arthur C. Miller. Academy Awards '46: Best Supporting Actress (Baxter); Golden Globe Awards '47: Best Supporting Actor (Webb), Best Supporting Actress (Baxter); Nominations: Academy Awards '46: Best Interior Decoration, Best Picture, Best Supporting Actor (Webb). FXV, BTV

The Razor's Edge ♫♫½ 1984 (PG-13) A beautifully filmed but idiosyncratic version of the W. Somerset Maugham novel. WWI-ravaged Larry Darrell combs the world in search of the meaning of life. Murray is a little too old and sardonic to seem really tortured. Russell is great as the loser

he rescues. Subtly unique, with real shortcomings. 129m/C VHS, Beta, LV, Closed Caption. Bill Murray, Catherine Hicks, Theresa Russell, Denholm Elliott, James Keach, Peter Vaughan, Saeed Jaffrey, Brian Doyle-Murray; *D:* John Byrum; *W:* John Byrum; *M:* Jack Nitzsche. COL

Re-Animator ♫♫♫ 1984 Based on an H.P. Lovecraft story, this grisly film deals with a medical student who re-animates the dead. It has quickly turned into a black humor cult classic. Also available in an "R" rated version, and followed by "Bride of Re-Animator." 86m/C VHS, Beta, LV. Jeffrey Combs, Bruce Abbott, Barbara Crampton, David Gale, Robert Sampson; *D:* Stuart Gordon; *W:* Stuart Gordon, Dennis Paoli, William J. Norris; *C:* Mac Ahlberg; *M:* Richard Band. LIV, VES

Reach for the Sky ♫♫½ 1956 WW II flying ace loses both legs in an accident and learns to fly again. He becomes a hero during the Battle of Britain, then is shot down over France and held prisoner by the Germans. At war's end he returns to England to lead 3,000 planes over London in a victory flight. Inspirationally told true story. 136m/B VHS, Beta. *GB* Kenneth More, Alexander Knox, Nigel Green; *D:* John Addison. British Academy Awards '56: Best Film. NO

Reaching for the Moon ♫♫½ 1917 A day-dreaming department store employee finds himself in the unlikely position of ruling a kingdom. Vintage Fairbanks fun, based on a story by Anita Loos. Silent. 62m/B VHS, Beta. Douglas Fairbanks Sr., Eileen Percy, Millard Webb; *D:* John Emerson. VYY, GPV, GVV

Reaching for the Moon ♫♫½ 1931 Fairbanks is a businessman who falls for liquor and Daniels on a transatlantic cruise. Dull and cruel; not as light-hearted as it intends. One Irving Berlin song sung by Crosby. 62m/B VHS, Beta, 8mm. Douglas Fairbanks Sr., Bebe Daniels, Bing Crosby, Edward Everett Horton; *D:* Edmund Goulding. NOS, VYY, CAB

Reactor ♫ 1985 A low-budget sci-fi film about kidnapped scientists, alien ships and an activated nuclear reactor. 90m/C VHS, Beta. Yanti Somer, Melissa Long, James R. Stuart, Robert Barnes, Nick Jordan. NO

Ready to Wear ♫♫ *Pret-a-Porter* 1994 (R) Altman travels to Paris to take on the fashion industry with his trademark satire, ensemble cast, and cameo players in tow. The untimely death of a major industry player begins a swirl of random subplots involving a head-spinning array of fashion industry stereotypes. Loren and Mastroianni recreate their "Yesterday, Today and Tomorrow" boudoir striptease scene. Coterie of one-dimensional characters are set adrift with no discernable plot, which might make for interesting people watching, but results in a tedious movie. Altman did it better with "The Player" and "Short Cuts."*CW:* Contains profanity, sexual situations, and nudity. 132m/C VHS, LV, Closed Caption. Sophia Loren, Marcello Mastroianni, Julia Roberts, Tim Robbins, Kim Basinger, Stephen Rea, Anouk Aimee, Lauren Bacall, Lili Taylor, Sally Kellerman, Tracey Ullman, Linda Hunt, Rupert Everett, Forest Whitaker, Richard E. Grant, Danny Aiello, Teri Garr, Lyle Lovett, Jean Rochefort, Michel Blanc, Anne Canovas, Jean-Pierre Cassel, Francois Cluzet, Rossy de Palma, Kaisa Figura, Sam Robards; *Cameos:* Cher, Harry Belafonte, Issey Miyake, Sonia Rykiel, Jean-Paul Gaultier, Thierry Mugler; *D:* Robert Altman; *W:* Barbara Shulgasser, Robert Altman; *M:* Michel Legrand. Nominations: Golden Globe Awards '95: Best Film—Musical/Comedy, Best Supporting Actress (Loren). MAX

A Real American Hero ♫½ *Hard Stick* 1978 Made for television story of Tennessee sheriff Buford Pusser, the subject of three "Walking Tall" films. Here, he battles moonshiners, with the usual violence. 94m/C VHS, Beta. Brian Dennehy, Brian Kerwin, Forrest Tucker; *D:* Lou Antonio. VTR, PSM

Real Bruce Lee ♫ 1979 (R) Contains actual early films of Bruce Lee, once feared lost but recently discovered in the Chinese film archives, (the movies, not Bruce). 108m/C VHS, Beta. Bruce Lee. GEM, SUN, VTR

The Real Buddy Holly Story 1987 Documentary serves as a tribute to the rock 'n' roll legend who met an untimely death in 1959. 90m/C VHS, Beta, LV. SMV, IME, MVD

Real Bullets ♫ 1990 Stunt team performs the real thing when two members get imprisoned in a bad guy's desert castle. 86m/C VHS, Beta, LV. John Gazarian, Martin Landau; *D:* Lance Lindsay. THV

The Real Charlotte ♫♫½ 19?? When young, lovely, and flirtatious Francie Fitzpatrick (Roth) is romantically betrayed by a young English officer, she then sets her mind on the one man (Bergin) whom her plain and middle-aged cousin Charlotte (Crowley) has long loved. Set in Victorian-era Ireland; made for British TV. 240m/C VHS. *GB* Joanna Roth, Jeananne Crowley, Patrick Bergin. VTR

Real Genius ♫♫♫ 1985 (PG) Brainy kids in California work with lasers on a class project that is actually intended for use as an offensive military weapon. When they learn of the scheme, they use their brilliant minds to mount an amusingly elaborate strategic defense initiative of their own. Eccentric characters and an intelligent script provide a bevy of laughs for the family. 108m/C VHS, Beta, LV, Closed Caption. Val Kilmer, Gabe Jarret, Jonathan Gries, Michelle Meyrink, William Atherton, Patti D'Arbanville, Severn Darden; *D:* Martha Coolidge; *W:* Peter Torokvei, Neal Israel, Pat Proft; *M:* Thomas Newman. COL

The Real Glory ♫♫♫ 1939 After the U.S. capture of the Philippine islands during the Spanish-American war, an uprising of Moro tribesmen spreads terror. After most of the islands are evacuated only a small group of Army officers is left to lead the Filipino soldiers against the rebels. Cooper plays the heroic doctor, who is not afraid to fight, especially when he comes to the rescue of the beseiged Army fort. Great action sequences and paticularly good performances by Cooper and Niven. 95m/B VHS. Gary Cooper, Andrea Leeds, David Niven, Reginald Owen, Broderick Crawford; *D:* Henry Hathaway. MGM, WAR

Real Life ♫♫♫ 1979 (R) Writer/comedian Brooks's first feature sags in places, but holds its own as a vehicle for his peculiar talent. Brooks plays a pompous director whose ambition is to make a documentary of a "typical" American family. Good, intelligent comedy. 99m/C VHS, Beta. Charles Grodin, Frances Lee McCain, Albert Brooks; *D:* Albert Brooks; *W:* Monica Johnson, Harry Shearer, Albert Brooks. PAR

The Real McCoy ♫½ 1993 (PG-13) Generally awful crime-caper film about female bank robber Karen McCoy (Basinger). Just out of prison, all Karen wants to do is go straight and raise her young son but her plans are thwarted by former associates who kidnap the child to force her into one last heist. Kilmer is the small-time thief, with a crush on Karen, who tries to help her out. Dumb, slow-moving story with a vapid performance by Basinger. 104m/C VHS, LV, Closed Caption. Kim Basinger, Val Kilmer, Terence Stamp, Zach English, Gailard Sartain; *D:* Russell Mulcahy; *W:* William Davies, William Osborne. USH

Real Men ♫½ 1987 (PG-13) The junior Belushi brother is a spy forced to recruit ordinary guy Ritter to help him negotiate with aliens to save the world. Bizarre premise shows promise, but spy spoof doesn't fire on all comedic pistons. Nice try. 86m/C VHS, Beta, LV, Closed Caption. James Belushi, John Ritter, Barbara Barrie; *D:* Dennis Feldman; *C:* John A. Alonzo; *M:* Miles Goodman. FOX

Reality Bites ♫♫½ 1994 (PG-13) Humorous look at four recent college grads living, working, and slacking in Houston. Script by newcomer Childress is at its best when highlighting the trends: 7-Eleven Big Gulps, tacky '70s memorabilia, and games revolving around episodes of old TV shows like "Good Times," to name a few. Definite appeal for those in their early 20s, but anyone over 25 may encounter a "Generation X-er" gap, a noticeable problem since "Reality" claims to speak for the entire twentysomething generation. Decent directorial debut for Stiller; good cast, particularly Garofalo, in her film debut. **99m/C VHS, LV, Closed Caption.** Winona Ryder, Ethan Hawke, Ben Stiller, Janeane Garofalo, Steve Zahn, Swoosie Kurtz, Joe Don Baker, John Mahoney; *Cameos:* David Pirner, Anne Meara, Jeanne Tripplehorn, Karen Duffy, Evan Dando; *D:* Ben Stiller; *W:* Helen Childress; *M:* Karl Wallinger. Nominations: MTV Movie Awards '94: Best Kiss (Ethan Hawke/Winona Ryder). *USH*

Really Weird Tales 🎬🎬½ 1986 Several SCTV alumni highlight this three-story movie, which is science fiction with a satirical edge. **85m/C VHS, Beta.** John Candy, Martin Short, Joe Flaherty, Catherine O'Hara. *VTR*

Reap the Wild Wind 🎬🎬½ 1942 DeMille epic about salvagers off the Georgia coast in the 1840s featuring Wayne as the captain and Massey and a giant squid as the villains. Good cast, lesser story, fine underwater photography. **123m/C VHS, Beta.** Ray Milland, John Wayne, Paulette Goddard, Raymond Massey, Robert Preston, Lynne Overman, Susan Hayward, Charles Bickford, Walter Hampden, Louise Beavers, Martha O'Driscoll, Elisabeth Risdon, Hedda Hopper, Raymond Hatton, Barbara Britton; *D:* Cecil B. DeMille; *C:* Victor Milner. Academy Awards '42: Best Special Effects; Nominations: Academy Awards '42: Best Color Cinematography, Best Interior Decoration. *USH*

Rear Window 🎬🎬🎬🎬 1954 A newspaper photographer with a broken leg (Stewart) passes the time recuperating by observing his neighbors through the window. When he sees what he believes to be a murder, he decides to solve the crime himself. With help from his beautiful girlfriend and his nurse, he tries to catch the murderer without getting killed himself. Top-drawer Hitchcock blends exquisite suspense with occasional on-target laughs. Based on the story by Cornell Woolrich. **112m/C VHS, Beta, LV.** James Stewart, Grace Kelly, Thelma Ritter, Wendell Corey, Raymond Burr, Judith Evelyn; *D:* Alfred Hitchcock; *W:* John Michael Hayes; *C:* Robert Burks; *M:* Franz Waxman. Edgar Allan Poe Awards '54: Best Screenplay; Nominations: Academy Awards '54: Best Color Cinematography, Best Director (Hitchcock), Best Screenplay, Best Sound. *USH, TLF, HMV*

A Reason to Believe 🎬🎬 1995 (R) Campus date rape drama filmed at writer/director Tirola's alma mater, Miami University. Charlotte (Smith) goes to her boyfriend Wesley's (Quinn) big frat party, even though he's away and asked her not to. She drinks and flirts (a lot) with his best friend Jim (Underwood) and eventually leaves to collapse in a stupor on Wesley's bed. Jim follows and rapes her, though he'll tell his buddies Charlotte was a willing participant, which Wesley angrily believes. Meanwhile, the traumatized Charlotte is taken up by Linda (Emelin), the leader of the student feminist organization who wants the fraternities disbanded. Somewhat preachy and predicatable. *CW:* Strong sexuality, language, substance abuse, a rape. **109m/C VHS.** Allison Smith, Jay Underwood, Daniel Quinn, Georgia Emelin, Obba Babatunde; *D:* Douglas Tirola; *W:* Douglas Tirola; *C:* Sarah Cawley. *THV*

Reason to Die 🎬 1990 (R) Bounty hunter uses his own girlfriend as a decoy to trap a psychotic prostitute killer. **86m/C VHS, LV.** Liam Cundill, Wings Hauser, Anneline Kriel, Arnold Vosloo; *D:* Tim Spring. *THV*

A Reason to Live, A Reason to Die 🎬🎬 *Massacre at Fort Holman; Una Ragione Per Vivere e Una Per Morire* 1973 A bland Italian-French-German-Spanish western in which a group of condemned men attempt to take a Confederate fort. **90m/C VHS, Beta.** James Coburn, Telly Savalas, Bud Spencer, Robert Burton; *D:* Tonino Valerii. *NO*

Rebecca 🎬🎬🎬🎬 1940 Based on Daphne Du Maurier's best-selling novel about a young unsophisticated girl who marries a moody and prominent country gentleman haunted by the memory of his first wife. Fontaine and Olivier turn in fine performances as the unlikely couple. Suspenseful and surprising. Hitchcock's first American film and

only Best Picture Oscar. Laserdisc features: rare screen tests of Vivien Leigh, Anne Baxter, Loretta Young, and Joan Fontaine, footage from Rebecca's winning night at the Academy Awards, original radio broadcasts of film by Orson Welles and David O. Selznick, and commentary of film with interview excerpts with Hitchcock. **130m/B VHS, Beta, LV, Closed Caption.** Joan Fontaine, Laurence Olivier, Judith Anderson, George Sanders, Nigel Bruce, Florence Bates, Gladys Cooper, Reginald Denny, Leo G. Carroll, Sir C. Aubrey Smith, Melville Cooper; *W:* Joan Harrison, Robert Sherwood; *C:* George Barnes; *M:* Franz Waxman. Academy Awards '40: Best Black and White Cinematography, Best Picture; National Board of Review Awards '40: 10 Best Films of the Year; Nominations: Academy Awards '40: Best Actor (Olivier), Best Actress (Fontaine), Best Director (Hitchcock), Best Film Editing, Best Interior Decoration, Best Screenplay, Best Supporting Actress (Anderson), Best Original Score. *FOX, HMV, BTV*

Rebecca 🎬🎬🎬 1997 Daphne du Maurier's tale of marriage and jealousy makes its second TV incarnation. Worldly widower Maxim de Winter (Dance) takes his nameless, shy young bride (Fox) back to Manderley, the family estate. There she must compete with the ghost of the first Mrs. de Winter—the glamorous Rebecca—family secrets, and obsessive housekeeper, Mrs. Danvers (Rigg). The 1980 TV version (with Jeremy Brett as Maxim) starred Joanna David in the title role, coincidentally newcomer Fox's mother. **240m/C VHS.** *GB* Emilia Fox, Charles Dance, Diana Rigg, Faye Dunaway, Geraldine James, Jonathan Cake; *D:* Jim O'Brien; *W:* Arthur Hopcraft. *PBS, VIF, TVC*

Rebecca of Sunnybrook Farm 🎬🎬 1917 The original film version of the tale about an orphan who spreads sunshine and good cheer to all those around her. Silent with organ score. Based on the popular novel by Kate Douglas Wiggin; remade with Shirley Temple in 1938. **77m/B VHS, Beta, LV.** Mary Pickford, Eugene O'Brien, Marjorie Daw, Helen Jerome Eddy; *D:* Marshall Neilan; *M:* Gaylord Carter. *CCB*

Rebecca of Sunnybrook Farm 🎬🎬½ 1938 Temple becomes a radio star over her aunt's objections in this bouncy musical that has nothing to do with the famous Kate Douglas Wiggin novel. Temple sings a medley of her hits, and dances the finale with Bill "Bojangles" Robinson. 🎵On the Good Ship Lollipop/ When I'm With You/Animal Crackers medley; Crackly Corn Flakes; Alone With You; Happy Ending; Au Revoir; An Old Straw Hat; Come and Get Your Happiness; Parade of the Wooden Soldiers. **80m/B VHS, Beta, LV, Closed Caption.** Shirley Temple, Randolph Scott, Jack Haley, Phyllis Brooks, Gloria Stuart, Slim Summerville, Bill Robinson, Helen Westley, William Demarest; *D:* Allan Dwan; *C:* Arthur C. Miller. *FOX, MLB, MLT*

Rebel 🎬½ 1973 (PG) Mumbling student radical must decide between his love for a country girl and his loyalty to an underground terrorist organization. Notable (or not) for display of early Stallone. **80m/C VHS, Beta.** Sylvester Stallone, Anthony Page, Rebecca Grimes. *NO*

Rebel 🎬½ 1985 (R) A U.S. Marine falls in love with a Sydney nightclub singer and goes AWOL during WWII. Stylish but empty and badly cast. **93m/C VHS, Beta, LV, Closed Caption.** *AU* Matt Dillon, Debbie Byrne, Bryan Brown, Bill Hunter, Ray Barrett; *D:* Michael Jenkins. *LIV, VES*

Rebel High 🎬½ 1988 (R) Hijinks occur at a high school where youngsters study guerilla warfare and teachers wear bullet-proof vests. **92m/C VHS, Beta.** Harvey Berger, Stu Trivax, Larry Gimple, Shawn Goldwater; *D:* Harry Jacobs. *ACA*

Rebel Love 🎬 1985 Love grows between a northern widow and a Confederate spy. In better hands it might have been a good story. Here, it's overwrought and embarrassing historical melodrama. **84m/C VHS, Beta.** Terence Knox, Jamie Rose, Fred Ryan; *D:* Milton Bagby Jr.; *W:* Milton Bagby Jr. *LIV, VES*

Rebel Rousers 🎬🎬 1969 A motorcycle gang wreaks havoc in a small town where a drag-race is being held to see who will get the pregnant girlfriend of Dern's high-school buddy as the prize. Young Nicholson in striped pants steals the show. **81m/C VHS, Beta.** Jack Nicholson, Cameron Mitchell, Diane Ladd, Bruce Dern, Harry Dean Stanton; *D:* Martin B. Cohen. *MED*

The Rebel Set 🎬🎬½ *Beatsville* 1959 The owner of a beat generation coffeehouse plans an armed robbery with the help of some buddies. Genuinely suspenseful, competently directed. **72m/B VHS, Beta.** Gregg Palmer, Kathleen Crowley, Edward Platt, John Lupton, Ned Glass, Don Sullivan, Vicki Dougan, I. Stanford Jolley; *D:* Gene Fowler Jr.; *C:* Karl Struss. *SNC*

Rebel Storm 🎬 1990 (R) A group of freedom fighters team up to rescue America from the totalitarian rulers that are in charge in 2099 A.D. **99m/C VHS, Beta, LV.** Zach Galligan, Wayne Crawford, June Chadwick, Rod McCary, John Rhys-Davies, Elizabeth Kiefer; *D:* Francis Schaeffer. *ACA*

Rebel Vixens woof! 1985 Even though the war is over, ex-confederate soldiers continue looting and raping, until a brothel-full of prostitutes concoct a plan that has a lot to do with softcore sex. **94m/C VHS, Beta.** Maria Lease, Roda Spain. *MED*

Rebel Without a Cause 🎬🎬🎬🎬 1955 James Dean's most memorable screen appearance. In the second of his three films, he plays a troubled teenager from the right side of the tracks. Dean's portrayal of Jim Stark, a teen alienated from both his parents and peers, is excellent. He befriends outcasts Wood and Mineo in a police station and together they find a commonground. Superb young stars carry this in-the-gut story of adolescence. All three leads met with real-life tragic ends. **111m/C VHS, Beta, LV, Closed Caption.** James Dean, Natalie Wood, Sal Mineo, Jim Backus, Nick Adams, Dennis Hopper, Ann Doran, William Hopper, Rochelle Hudson, Corey Allen, Edward Platt; *D:* Nicholas Ray; *W:* Stewart Stern; *M:* Leonard Rosenman. Nominations: Academy Awards '55: Best Story, Best Supporting Actor (Mineo), Best Supporting Actress (Wood). *WAR*

The Rebels 🎬🎬 1979 In the sequel to the television mini series "The Bastard," Philip Kent (Stevens) continues his Revolutionary War battle on the side of American independence. He is assisted by Southerner Judson Fletcher (Johnson) in thwarting an assassination attempt on George Washington. In addition to Bosley's Ben Franklin, "The Rebels" offers Backus as John Hancock. Followed by "The Seekers;" based on the novel by John Jakes. **190m/C VHS, Closed Caption.** Andrew Stevens, Don Johnson, Doug McClure, Jim Backus, Richard Basehart, Joan Blondell, Tom Bosley, Rory Calhoun, MacDonald Carey, Kim Cattrall, William Daniels, Anne Francis, Peter Graves, Pamela Hensley, Wilfrid Hyde-White, Nehemiah Persoff, William Smith, Forrest Tucker, Tanya Tucker, Robert Vaughn, Deborah Richter; *D:* Russ Mayberry. *USH*

Reborn 🎬🎬 1978 A faith healer and a talent scout hire actors to be cured of fake ailments. **91m/C VHS, Beta.** Dennis Hopper, Michael Moriarty, Francesco Rabal, Antonella Murgia. *VES*

Rebound: The Legend of Earl "The Goat" Manigault 🎬🎬½ 1996 (R) Earl "The Goat" Manigault (Cheadle) was a '60s Harlem playground basketball phenom who was taken under the wing of parks director Holcomb Rucker (Whitaker), who tries to steer the young man towards college and a career in the NBA. Unfortunately, the easily influenced Manigault also attracts the attention of local drug dealer Legrand (Beach) and when Manigault's life starts to fall apart, he drops out of college and turns to heroin, eventually winding up in prison. Since this is an inspirational true story, Manigault does turn his life around to found his own basketball tournament in Harlem. Made for cable. *CW:* Graphic drug use, strong language, some sexuality and a scene of violence. **111m/C VHS.** Don Cheadle, Michael Beach, James Earl Jones, Loretta Devine, Glynn Turman,

Clarence Williams III, Forest Whitaker, Eriq LaSalle; **D:** Eriq LaSalle; **W:** Larry Golin, Alan Swyer; **C:** Alan Kivilo; **M:** Kevin Eubanks. *HBO*

Reckless ♂♂ **1935** Harlow, in a role originally intended for Joan Crawford, plays a showgirl coveted by a millionaire and secretly loved by her manager. Unfortunately, Harlow couldn't pull off the acting (much less the singing and dancing), although the plot strangely paralleled her own life. Songs include "Reckless," "Ev'rything's Been Done Before," "Trocadero," "Hear What My Heart Is Saying" and "Cyclone." **96m/B VHS, LV.** Jean Harlow, William Powell, Franchot Tone, May Robson, Ted Healy, Nat Pendleton, Rosalind Russell; **D:** Victor Fleming. *MGM*

Reckless ♂♂½ **1984 (R)** A sincere movie about a "good" girl who finds herself obsessed with a rebel from the wrong side of her small town. Differs from 1950s' wrong-side-of-the-track flicks only in updated sex and music. **93m/C VHS, Beta, LV.** Aidan Quinn, Daryl Hannah, Kenneth McMillan, Cliff DeYoung, Lois Smith, Adam Baldwin, Dan Hedaya, Jennifer Grey, Pamela Springsteen; **D:** James Foley; **W:** Chris Columbus; **C:** Michael Ballhaus; **M:** Thomas Newman. *MGM*

Reckless ♂♂ **1995 (PG-13)** Rachel (Farrow) thinks she has a happy marriage and family but her husband (Goldwyn) informs her that he's hired a hit man to kill her. This startling revelation sends her on a 15-year journey in which she meets many other people who are not what they seem. Rene and Lucas go for an ultra-stylized fable theme, exploring Rachel's (and America's) aversion to dealing with the world as it really is. Quirky characters and situations are at turns amusing and annoying. Adapted by Lucas from his own play. **CW:** Complex psychological themes and some disturbing images. **91m/C VHS, LV, Closed Caption.** Mia Farrow, Scott Glenn, Mary-Louise Parker, Tony Goldwyn, Stephen Dorff, Eileen Brennan, Giancarlo Esposito, Deborah Rush; **D:** Norman Rene; **W:** Craig Lucas; **C:** Frederick Elmes; **M:** Stephen Endelman. *HMK*

Reckless Disregard ♂½ **1984** A doctor whose career is ruined by a news report accusing him of involvement in a drug scam sues the newscaster. Made for television saga based on Dan Rather's "60 Minutes" story and ensuing lawsuit. **92m/C VHS, Beta.** Leslie Nielsen, Tess Harper, Ronny Cox, Kate Lynch; **D:** Harvey Hart. *LIV, VES*

Reckless Kelly ♂♂½ **1993 (PG)** Australian bank robber, pop culture hero, and local video store owner Kelly is upset when his gang's island retreat is about to be sold to a Japanese conglomerate, unless he can come up with a higher offer. So he prepares for a last-ditch defense of his home. Slapstick homage to legendary Australian outlaw Ned Kelly. **81m/C VHS, Closed Caption.** AU Yahoo Serious, Hugo Weaving, Melora Hardin, Alexei Sayle, Bob Maza, Kathleen Freeman; **D:** Yahoo Serious; **W:** Yahoo Serious. *WAR*

Reckless Moment ♂♂♂ **1949** A mother commits murder to save her daughter from an unsavory older man, and finds herself blackmailed. Gripping, intense thriller. **82m/B VHS, Beta.** James Mason, Joan Bennett, Geraldine Brooks; **D:** Max Ophuls; **C:** Burnett Guffey. *LCA*

The Reckless Way ♂½ **1936** A young woman struggles for her big break into the movies. **72m/B VHS, Beta.** Marion Nixon, Kane Richmond, Inez Courtney, Malcolm McGregor, Harry Harvey, Arthur Howard; **D:** Raymond K. Johnson. *GPV*

Record of a Tenement Gentleman ♂♂♂ **1947** An abandoned child picks a grumpy, middle-aged widow as a surrogate mother and she and her crazy neighbors come to love the little boy. Surprise ending. Japanese with subtitles. **72m/B VHS.** JP Choko Iida, Hohi Aoki, Chishu Ryu, Eitaro Ozawa; **D:** Yasujiro Ozu. *NYF*

Recruits ♂ **1986 (R)** Sophomoric gagfest about an inept Californian police force. Typical 80's-style mindless "comedy:" dumb gags ensue from perfunctory premise. **81m/C VHS, Beta, LV.** Alan Deveau, Annie McAuley, Lolita Davidovich; **D:** Rafal Zeilinski. *LIV, VES*

The Rector's Wife ♂♂ **1994** Anna Bouverie (Duncan) has spent 20 years as a clergyman's wife, scrimping and slaving to raise a family, serve God, and work for the parish on limited means. Tired of the financial strain she takes a job at a local supermarket causing additional disturbances in her already shaky marriage, disapproval of the parish, and the sudden interest of three different men. Based on the novel by Joanna Trollope; on four cassettes. **208m/C VHS.** GB Lindsay Duncan, Jonathan Coy, Simon Fenton, Lucy Dawson, Joyce Redman, Stephen Dillane, Ronald Pickup, Miles Anderson, Prunella Scales, Jonathan Cecil; **D:** Giles Foster; **W:** Hugh Whitemore; **M:** Richard Hartley. *SIG, AAE, NEW*

Red Alert ♂♂½ **1977** Good, suspenseful, topical made for televison thriller about nuclear meltdown. Will Minneapolis be saved? Usually Barbeau's name is in the credits is a red alert, but this one is better than most. **95m/C VHS, Beta.** William Devane, Ralph Waite, Michael Brandon, Adrienne Barbeau; **D:** Billy Hale. *PAR*

The Red and the Black ♂♂♂ *Le Rouge et le Noir* **1957** A big budgeted French adaptation of the classic Stendhal novel. A young man from the country seeks success, first in the Church and later in the employment and seduction of the gentry. In French with English subtitles. **134m/B VHS, Beta.** FR Danielle Darrieux, Gerard Philipe; **D:** Claude Autant-Lara. *IVY, MRV, FCT*

The Red and the White ♂♂♂ *Csillagosok, Katonak* **1968** Epic war drama about the civil war between the Red Army and the non-communist Whites in Russia in 1918. Told from the perspective of Hungarians who fought alongside the Reds. Little dialogue. In Hungarian with English subtitles. **92m/B VHS, LV.** HU **D:** Miklos Jancso. *KIV*

The Red Badge of Courage ♂♂♂½ **1951** John Huston's adaptation of the Stephen Crane Civil War novel is inspired, despite cutting room hatchet job by the studio. A classic study of courage and cowardice. Sweeping battle scenes and intense personal drama. **69m/B VHS, Beta.** Audie Murphy, Bill Mauldin, Douglas Dick, Royal Dano, Andy Devine; **D:** John Huston. National Board of Review Awards '51: 10 Best Films of the Year. *KUI, MGM, HMV*

Red Ball Express ♂♂½ **1952** Fast-paced action highlights this WWII story about the transportation corp that must supply the gas, food, and ammunition necessary for General Patton's tank assault on Nazi-held Paris. Tough company leader Lt. Campbell (Chandler) must get the cooperation of both his first sergeant (Nicol), who holds a pre-war grudge, and a black corporal (Poitier), who believes he's the target of racism, in order to accomplish his mission. **84m/B VHS, Closed Caption.** Jeff Chandler, Alex Nicol, Sidney Poitier, Charles Drake, Hugh O'Brian, Jack Kelly, Judith Braun, Jacqueline Duval; **D:** Budd Boetticher; **W:** John Michael Hayes; **C:** Maury Gertsman. *USH*

The Red Balloon ♂♂♂½ **1956** The story of Pascal, a lonely French boy who befriends a wondrous red balloon which follows him everywhere. Lovely, finely done parable of childhood, imagination and friendship. **34m/C VHS, Beta, LV, 8mm.** FR Pascal Lamorisse; **D:** Albert Lamorisse. Academy Awards '56: Best Original Screenplay; National Board of Review Awards '57: 5 Best Foreign Films of the Year. *HMV, HHT, DVT*

Red Balloon/Occurrence at Owl Creek Bridge ♂♂♂½ **1962** Two classic award-winning shorts have been combined on one tape: "The Red Balloon" (color, 1956) and "An Occurrence at Owl Creek Bridge." The former is a children's story about a balloon on the loose; the latter is a perfectly rendered adaptation of the Ambrose Bierce short story of the same

title, a taut narration of a Civil War hanging. **60m/C VHS, Beta.** FR Pascal Lamorisse, Roger Jacquet; **D:** Robert Enrico, Albert Lamorisse. *VYY, WFV, CAB*

Red Barry **1938** A comic strip detective tries to track down criminals who threaten the world. Thirteen episodes on one videotape. **?m/B VHS.** Buster Crabbe, Frances Robinson, Edna Sedgwick, Cyril Delevanti, Frank Lackteen; **D:** Ford Beebe, Alan James. *NOS, MLB*

Red Beard ♂♂♂ *Akahige* **1965** An uncharacteristic drama by Kurosawa, about a young doctor in Japan awakening to life and love under the tutelage of a compassionate old physician. Highly acclaimed; in Japanese with English subtitles. **185m/B VHS, Beta, LV.** JP Toshiro Mifune, Yuzo Kayama, Yoshio Tsuchiya, Reiko Dan; **D:** Akira Kurosawa. *CRC, FCT*

Red Blooded American Girl ♂ **1990 (R)** A scientist develops a virus that turns people into vampires. Those infected hit the streets in search of blood. **89m/C VHS, Beta, LV.** CA Christopher Plummer, Andrew Stevens, Heather Thomas, Kim Coates; **D:** David Blyth. *PSM*

Red Dawn ♂½ **1984 (PG-13)** During WWIII, Russian invaders overrun America's heartland and take over the country. Eight small-town teenagers, calling themselves the Wolverines, hide out in the rugged countryside and fight the Russians. Swayze and Grey met again in "Dirty Dancing." **114m/C VHS, Beta, LV.** Patrick Swayze, C. Thomas Howell, Harry Dean Stanton, Powers Boothe, Lea Thompson, Charlie Sheen, Ben Johnson, Jennifer Grey, Ron O'Neal, William Smith; **D:** John Milius; **W:** John Milius, Kevin Reynolds; **M:** Basil Poledouris. *MGM*

Red Desert ♂ **1950** The Pecos Kid is sent to track down the theft of a shipment of gold. **60m/B VHS, Beta, LV.** Jack Holt, Donald (Don "Red") Barry, Tom Neal, Joseph Crehan, Tom London; **D:** Charles Marquis Warren. *NO*

The Red Desert ♂♂♂ **1964** Antonioni's first color film, depicting an alienated Italian wife who searches for meaning in the industrial lunar landscape of northern Italy, to no avail. Highly acclaimed, and a masterpiece of visual form. Cinematography by Carlo di Palma. In Italian with English subtitles. **120m/C VHS, Beta.** IT Monica Vitti, Richard Harris, Carlos Chionetti; **D:** Michelangelo Antonioni; **W:** Michelangelo Antonioni, Tonino Guerra; **C:** Carlo DiPalma. Venice Film Festival '64: International Critics Award, Best Film. *FCT, CVC, TPV*

Red Desert Penitentiary **1983** A spoof of movie-making featuring caricatures of industry-types. **104m/C VHS, Beta.** James Michael Taylor, Cathryn Bissell, Will Rose; **D:** George Sluizer. *NO*

Red Dust ♂♂♂ **1932** The overseer of a rubber plantation in Indochina causes all kinds of trouble when he falls in love with a young engineer's wife. Filled with free-spirited humor and skillfully directed; remarkably original. Remade in 1940 as "Congo Maisie" and in 1954 as "Mogambo." **83m/B VHS, Beta.** Clark Gable, Jean Harlow, Mary Astor, Gene Raymond, Donald Crisp; **D:** Victor Fleming. *MGM*

Red Earth ♂♂ **19??** A satire about life under Hungarian socialism. Szanto is a bauxite mixer whose pigs have rooted out high quality bauxite from his backyard. Only the local bauxite prospectors don't want to believe in luck (and pigs) and credit, instead, careful planning. When Szanto's village is turned into a vast open mine, he's blamed. In Hungarian with English subtitles. **105m/C VHS.** HU Imre Nemeth, Sandor Kocsis, Kalman Toronyi, Ferenc Togh, Vilmos Gadori; **D:** Laszlo Vitezy; **W:** Istvan Darday. *FCT*

Red Firecracker, Green Firecracker ♂♂½ *Paoda Shuang Deng* **1993 (R)** Set in northern China before the 1911 revolution, this gorgeous saga focuses on the fortunes of the Cai family. The family, whose wealth depends on their fireworks business, has no male heirs and is headed by daughter Chun Zhi (Jing). To assume this lofty position, Chun Zhi must dress like a man and is forbidden to marry but that doesn't stop her from falling in love with bold young travelling artist Nie Bao (Gang). The household is thrown into a frenzy by their affair and it's decided that all Chun Zhi's potential suitors must undergo a firecracker ritual in order to win her hand. Mandarin Chinese with subtitles. **CW:** Language. 111m/C **VHS.** *HK CH* Ning Jing, Wu Gang, Zhao Xiaorui, Gai Yang; **D:** He Ping; **C:** Yang Lun. *HMK*

Red Flag: The Ultimate
Game 🐾🐾½ **1981** Pilots rival for success in battle simulation training with terrible consequences. Fine performances cover plot weaknesses. Well-written dialogue. Made for television. 100m/C **VHS, Beta.** Barry Bostwick, William Devane, Joan Van Ark, Fred McCarren, Debra Feuer, George Coe, Linden Chiles, Arlen Dean Snyder; **D:** Don Taylor. *LIV*

The Red Fury
🐾🐾 **197?** Young Indian boy struggles to overcome prejudice and caring for his horse shows him the way. Good family viewing. 105m/C **VHS.** William Jordan, Kathy Cannon. *TPV, HHE, BPG*

Red Garters
🐾🐾½ **1954** A musical parody of old-time westerns which doesn't quite come off. Mitchell palys the cowpoke who comes to town to avenge the death of his brother with Clooney as the saloon singer who uses him to make boyfriend Carson jealous. The adequate songs include "Red Garters," "Man and Woman," "A Dime and a Dollar," and "Vaquero." 91m/C **VHS, Closed Caption.** Guy Mitchell, Rosemary Clooney, Jack Carson, Gene Barry, Pat Crowley, Joanne Gilbert, Frank Faylen, Reginald Owen, Buddy Ebsen; **W:** Michael Fessier; **D:** George Marshall; **W:** Jay Livingston, Ray Evans. Nominations: Academy Awards '54: Best Art Direction/Set Decoration (Color). *PAR*

The Red Half-Breed
🐾½ **1970** A lonely half-breed Indian, wrongly accused of murder, discovers the real killer while running from the law. 103m/C **VHS, Beta.** Daniel Pilon, Genevieve Deloir; **D:** Gilles Carle. *NWV*

Red Headed Stranger
🐾½ **1987 (R)** Willie Nelson vehicle based on his 1975 album. Nelson is a gun-totin' preacher who kills his wife and is led to salvation by a good farm woman. But honestly: Morgan Fairchild as Willie Nelson's wife? Please. 108m/C **VHS, Beta, LV, Closed Caption.** Willie Nelson, Katharine Ross, Morgan Fairchild; **D:** William D. Wittliff; **W:** William D. Wittliff. *NLC*

Red Headed Woman
🐾🐾🐾 **1932** Harlow plays an unscrupulous woman who charms her way into the lives of influential men. She causes her boss to divorce his wife and marry her while she sleeps with the chauffeur (Boyer) and others. Audiences loved the scandalous material, but the Hays Office objected to the fact that the immoral woman goes unpunished. Boyer's small but important role salvaged his floundering American film career. Harlow is sultry and funny. 79m/B **VHS, Beta.** Jean Harlow, Chester Morris, Lewis Stone, Leila Hyams, Una Merkel, Henry Stephenson, May Robson, Charles Boyer, Harvey Clark; **D:** Jack Conway. *MGM, FCT*

Red Heat
🐾½ **1985** Blair is a tourist in East Germany mistakenly arrested and sent to a rough women's prison. Her fiance tries to free her. Meanwhile, she has to deal with tough-lady fellow jail bird Kristel. Familiar and marginal. 104m/C **VHS, Beta, LV.** Linda Blair, Sylvia Kristel, Sue Kiel, William Ostrander; **D:** Robert Collector. *LIV, VES*

Red Heat
🐾🐾 **1988 (R)** Two cops—one from the Soviet Union, one from Chicago—team up to catch the Eastern Bloc's biggest drug czar. Lots of action, but at times it seems too similar to Hill's earlier hit "48 Hours." Film claims to be the first major U.S. production shot in Red Square, Moscow. 106m/C **VHS, Beta, LV, DVD.** Arnold Schwarzenegger, James Belushi, Peter Boyle, Ed O'Ross, Laurence "Larry" Fishburne, Gina Gershon, Richard Bright; **D:** Walter Hill; **W:** Walter Hill; **M:** James Horner. *LIV, TLF*

Red Hot
🐾🐾½ **1995 (PG)** Alexi (Getty), a young Russian classical musician, is secretly smuggled American rock 'n' roll music (it's 1959) by his uncle. He immediately decides to form a band and plots the first underground Soviet rock concert. Too bad girlfriend Valentina's (Gugino) dad is a disapproving highly ranked Communist Party official and the KGB are giving Alexi the evil eye. 95m/C **VHS, LV.** Balthazar Getty, Carla Gugino, Donald Sutherland, Armin Mueller-Stahl; **D:** Paul Haggis; **W:** Paul Haggis, Michael Maurer. *COL*

The Red House
🐾🐾🐾 **1947** Robinson plays a crippled farmer who, after his daughter brings home a suitor, attempts to keep everyone from a mysterious red house located on his property. Madness and murder prevail. Strange film noir about tangled relationships and unsuccessful attempts to bury the horrid past. Based on the novel by George Agnew Chamberlain. 100m/B **VHS, Beta.** Edward G. Robinson, Lon McCallister, Judith Anderson, Allene Roberts, Rory Calhoun, Ona Munson, Julie London, Harry Shannon, Arthur Space, Walter Sande, Pat Flaherty; **D:** Delmer Daves; **W:** Delmer Daves; **C:** Bert Glennon; **M:** Miklos Rozsa. *CNG, NOS, SNC*

The Red Inn
🐾🐾 *L'Auberge Rouge* **1951** Yes, it is a comedy. An innkeeper and his wife have a second career involving the robbery and murder of stagecoach travellers staying at their isolated inn. And it's up to a monk (Fernandel) to stop the mayhem. French with subtitles. Yves Montand sings on the soundtrack. 95m/B **VHS.** *FR* Fernandel, Francoise Rosay, Julien Carette, Gregoire Aslan, Marie-Claire Olivia, Lud Germain; **D:** Claude Autant-Lara; **W:** Jean Aurenche, Pierre Bost; **C:** Andre Bac; **M:** Rene Cloerec. *FCT*

Red Kimono
🐾🐾 **1925** Exploitative silent melodrama about a young woman ditched by her husband. She becomes a prostitute, but is redeemed by true love. Interesting slice of this period. 95m/B **VHS, Beta.** Tyrone Power Sr., Priscilla Boner, Nellie Bly Baker, Mary Carr; **D:** Walter Lang. *NOS, VYY, DVT*

Red King, White Knight
🐾🐾½ **1989 (R)** An assassin tries to kill Mikhail Gorbachev during superpower peace talks. Ex-s pook Skerritt returns to duty to thwart him. Better than most "topical" thrill ers. Made for cable television. 106m/C **VHS, Beta.** Tom Skerritt, Max von Sydow, Helen Mirren; **D:** Geoff Murphy. *HBO*

Red Kiss
🐾🐾🐾 *Rouge Baiser* **1985** In 1952 Paris, Nadia, a 15-year-old French-Jewish Stalinist of Polish descent falls in love with Stephane, an older, apolitical photographer. She's torn between love and politics; he's worried (rightly) about her being under-age; and to make matters more complicated, her Polish mother has been reunited with her first love and Nadia's family may be split apart. The sensual Valandrey is a real find in her difficult coming-of-age role. In French with English subtitles. 110m/C **VHS, LV.** *FR* Charlotte Valandrey, Lambert Wilson, Marthe Keller, Gunter Lamprecht, Laurent Terzieff; **D:** Vera Belmont; **W:** Vera Belmont. Berlin International Film Festival '86: Best Actress (Valandrey). *FXL, FCT*

The Red Light Sting
🐾 **1984** A Justice Department rookie (Bridges) and a call girl (Fawcett) reluctantly team up to con the Mafia in order to convict a San Francisco rackets czar. Goes down easy, but also easily forgotten or skipped. 96m/C **VHS, Beta.** Farrah Fawcett, Beau Bridges, Harold Gould, Paul Burke, Sunny Johnson; **D:** Rod Holcomb. *USH*

Red Lights Ahead
1936 Grandpa tries to save the day as he fights against spiritualism and crystal balls to help a friend prove that he is not running a scam. 63m/C **VHS.** Andy Clyde, Paula Stone, Roger Imhof, Frank "Junior" Coghlan, Ben Alexander, Matty Kemp, Sam Flint, Addison Randall, Lucile Gleason, Dann Doran; **D:** Roland D. Reed. *GPV*

Red Line
🐾½ **1996 (R)** Race car driver (McQueen) loses his sponsorship, turns to petty crime to settle his debts, and winds up in trouble with the mob when he hooks up with a couple of hoods to steal some diamonds. 102m/C **VHS, LV.** Chad McQueen, Michael Madsen, Corey Feldman, Jan-Michael Vincent. *ORI*

Red Line 7000
🐾🐾 **1965** High stakes auto racers drive fast cars and date women. Excellent racing footage in otherwise routine four-wheel fest. 110m/C **VHS, LV, Closed Caption.** James Caan, Laura Devon, Gail Hire, Charlene Holt, John Crawford, Marianna Hill, George Takei; **D:** Howard Hawks; **C:** Milton Krasner. *PAR, FCT*

Red Lion
🐾🐾½ *Akage* **1969** A bumbling horse-tender in feudal Japan impersonates a military officer to impress his family, only to be swept into leading a liberating revolution. In Japanese with English subtitles. 115m/C **VHS, Beta.** *JP* Toshiro Mifune, Shima Iwashita; **D:** Kihachi Okamoto. *VDA*

The Red Menace
woof! 1949 Anti-Communist propaganda, made with unknown actors in documentary style has little to offer today's viewers other than unintentional laughs. Picture the Commies offering naive Americans money and sex to join the party, and you'll have an idea of the intellectual talent that went into this one. 87m/B **VHS, Beta.** Robert Rockwell, Hanne Axman, Shepard Menken, Betty Lou Gerson, Barbara Fuller; **D:** R.G. Springsteen. *REP, FCT*

Red Nightmare
🐾½ **1962** Anti-communist propaganda produced for the Department of Defense by Warner Brothers features the cast of "Dragnet." The story dramatizes the Red Menace, with communists conspiring to take over America, and shows what would happen to life in a small American town if the Commies took over. 30m/B **VHS, Beta.** Jack Webb, Jack Kelly, Jeanne Cooper, Peter Brown. *VYY, IHF*

Red Nights
🐾 **1987** A country boy goes to Hollywood seeking success and finds instead corruption, decadence, and dishonesty. Excellent soundtrack by Tangerine Dream. 90m/C **VHS, Beta.** Christopher Parker, Jack Carter, Brian Matthews; **D:** Izhak Hanooka. *TWE*

Red Planet Mars
🐾🐾 **1952** Anti-communist, pro-Christianity story about scientists discovering that the Voice of Radio Free Mars belongs to God. Incoherent film overburdened with messages about politics, religion, and science was ahead of its time. Based on the play "Red Planet" by John L. Balderson and John Hoare. 87m/B **VHS.** Peter Graves, Andrea King, Marvin Miller, Herbert Berghof, House Peters Jr., Vince Barnett; **D:** Harry Horner; **W:** Anthony Veiller, John Balderston. *MGM, FCT*

The Red Pony
🐾🐾🐾 **1949** A young boy escapes from his family's fighting through his love for a pet pony. Based on the novel by John Steinbeck. Remade for television in 1976. Timeless classic that the whole family can enjoy. 89m/C **VHS, LV.** Myrna Loy, Robert Mitchum, Peter Miles, Louis Calhern, Shepperd Strudwick, Margaret Hamilton, Beau Bridges; **D:** Lewis Milestone; **C:** Gaetano Antonio "Tony" Gaudio; **M:** Aaron Copland. *REP, KUI*

The Red Pony
🐾🐾🐾 **1976** Excellent TV remake of a classic 1949 adaptation of John Steinbeck. Fonda is superb as a troubled young boy's difficult father. 101m/C **VHS, Beta, LV.** Henry Fonda, Maureen O'Hara, Clint Howard, Jack Elam, Ben Johnson; **D:** Robert Totten. *BFA*

The Red Raven Kiss-Off
🐾 **1990 (R)** A seedy Hollywood detective becomes the key suspect in a movie-making murder. Based on the 1930s' Dan Turner mystery stories. Made for video. 93m/C **VHS, Beta.** Marc Singer, Tracy Scoggins, Nicholas Worth, Arte Johnson; **D:** Christopher Lewis. *FRH*

Red Riding Hood
🐾🐾½ **1988** Musical version of story of wolf who has little girl fetish. 81m/C **VHS, Beta.** Isabella Rossellini, Craig T. Nelson, Rocco Sisto. *MGM, CAN*

Red River
🐾🐾🐾🐾 **1948** The classic Hawks epic about a gruelling cattle drive and the battle of wills between father and son. Generally regarded as one of the best westerns ever made, and Wayne's shining moment as a reprehensible, obsessive man. Featuring Clift in his first film. Re-

stored version has eight minutes of previously edited material. Remade for television in 1988 with James Arness and Bruce Boxleitner. **133m/B VHS, Beta, LV, Closed Caption.** John Wayne, Montgomery Clift, Walter Brennan, Joanne Dru, John Ireland, Noah Beery Jr., Paul Fix, Coleen Gray, Harry Carey Jr., Harry Carey Sr., Chief Yowlachie, Hank Worden; **D:** Howard Hawks; **W:** Borden Chase, Charles Schnee; **M:** Dimitri Tiomkin. Nominations: Academy Awards '48: Best Film Editing, Best Story. *MGM, TLF, RDG*

Red River Valley ✔✔ *Man of the Frontier* 1936 Autry and partner Burnette go undercover to find out who's plaguing a dam construction site with explosions. Not to be confused with a 1941 Roy Rogers pic bearing the same title. **60m/B VHS.** Gene Autry, Smiley Burnette, Frances Grant, Boothe Howard, Sam Flint, George Chesebro, Charles "Blackie" King, Eugene Jackson, Frank LaRue, Lloyd Ingraham; **D:** B. Reeves Eason. *NOS, VDM, VCN*

Red Rock Outlaw ✔ 1947 A sleazy character tries to kill his twin brother and takes his place as an honest rancher. **56m/B VHS, Beta, LV.** Lee White. *NO*

Red Rock West ✔✔✔½ 1993 (R) Nothing is what it seems in this stylish and entertaining film noir set in a desolate Wyoming town. Perennial loser and nice guy Michael (Cage) is headed to a job at oil rig, but blows his chance by admitting he has a bad leg. Landing in the tiny burg of Red Rock, he's mistaken for the hit man hired by local barkeep Walsh to kill his pretty wife (Boyle). Then Boyle doubles Walsh's offer—what's a film noir boy to do? And Hopper, the real killer, strides into town. Full of twists, turns, and shades of "El Mariachi," this enjoyable, well-acted thriller is a real gem that escaped directly to cable before being rescued by a San Francisco exhibitor. **98m/C VHS, LV, Closed Caption.** Nicolas Cage, Dennis Hopper, Lara Flynn Boyle, J.T. Walsh, Timothy Carhart, Dan Shor, Dwight Yoakam, Bobby Joe McFadden, Craig Reay, Vance Johnson, Robert Apel, Dale Gibson, Ted Parks, Babs Bram, Robert Guajardo, Sarah Sullivan; **D:** John Dahl, Rick Dahl; **C:** Marc Reshovsky; **M:** William Olvis. Nominations: Independent Spirit Awards '95: Best Director (Dahl), Best Screenplay. *COL*

The Red Rope ✔½ 1937 A Western hero cuts his honeymoon short to track down some villains. **56m/B VHS.** Bob Steele, Lois January, Forrest Taylor, Charles "Blackie" King, Karl Hackett, Bobby Nelson; **D:** S. Roy Luby. *NOS, DVT*

Red Scorpion ✔ 1989 (R) A Soviet soldier journeys to Africa where he is to assassinate the leader of a rebel group. Will he succeed or switch allegiances? Poor acting and directing abound. **102m/C VHS, LV.** Dolph Lundgren, M. Emmet Walsh, Al White, T.P. McKenna, Carmen Argenziano, Brion James, Regopstaan; **D:** Joseph Zito; **W:** Arne Olsen, Jack Abramoff, Robert Abramoff; **C:** Joao Fernandes. *VTR*

Red Scorpion 2 ✔½ 1994 (R) Another "Dirty Dozen" rip-off finds your average ethnically-mixed good guys brought together by a government agency to be heroic. In this case the enemy is a neo-fascist businessman who uses skinheads to cause mayhem in minority communities.**CW:** Strong non-stop violence and some sexuality. **90m/C VHS, LV, Closed Caption.** Matt McColm, John Savage, Jennifer Rubin, Michael Ironside, Michael Covert, Real Andrews, George Touliatos; **D:** Michael Kennedy; **W:** Troy Bolotnick, Barry Victor; **M:** George Blondheim. *USH*

Red Shoe Diaries ✔✔ 1992 (R) After a woman's suicide her grieving lover discovers her diaries and finds out she led a secret erotic life, revolving around her shoe-salesman lover and a pair of sexy red shoes. Made for cable television; also available in an unrated version.**CW:** Language and strong sexuality. **105m/C VHS, LV, Closed Caption.** David Duchovny, Billy Wirth, Brigitte Bako; **D:** Zalman King. *REP*

Red Shoe Diaries 2: Double Dare ✔✔ 1992 (R) The erotic sequel to "Red Shoe Diaries" follows the libidinous fancies of three women. Severance begins a sexual affair with a stranger only to be torn between love and lust. Johnson gets naked to tease an office worker in the building next door. Crosby is a cop who is rejected by the man she desires—so she arrests and handcuffs him in order to play some kinky games. Also available in an unrated version.**CW:** Language and strong sexuality. **92m/C VHS, LV, Closed Caption.** Joan Severance, Laura Johnson, Denise Crosby, Steven Bauer, Arnold Vosloo, David Duchovny; **D:** Zalman King; Tibor Takacs. *REP, PMS*

Red Shoe Diaries 3: Another Woman's Lipstick ✔✔ 1993 (R) Another sexual anthology focusing on three stories of desire from the made for cable television series. In "Another Woman's Lipstick" Zoey finds out her husband is having an affair and follows him to his liaison—only to become intrigued with his lover herself. "Just Like That" finds the up-tight Trudie falling for two very opposite men. "Talk to Me Baby" finds Ida and her lover Bud caught up in a very obsessional relationship. Also available in an unrated version.**CW:** Language and erotic content. **90m/C VHS, LV, Closed Caption.** Nina Siemaszko, Matthew LeBlanc, Tcheky Karyo, Maryam D'Abo, Richard Tyson, Lydie Denier, Christina Fulton, Kevin Haley, David Duchovny; **D:** Ted Kotcheff, Rafael Eisenman, Zalman King; **W:** Zalman King, Chloe King. *REP*

Red Shoe Diaries 4: Auto Erotica ✔✔ 1993 (R) Yet another compilation of erotic tales courtesy of the Zalman King series. The first story finds a maid finding her employer's secret chamber and uncovering a very private fantasy. The second has an architect lured by a mystery woman into a game of seduction and the third finds a couple engaged in competitive obsessions. Also available in an unrated version. **83m/C VHS, Closed Caption.** Ally Sheedy, Scott Plank, David Duchovny, Sheryl Lee, Nicholas Chinlund; **D:** Zalman King. *REP*

Red Shoe Diaries 5: Weekend Pass ✔✔ 1995 (R) Yet another erotic saga from the cable series that features a model (Barbieri) hustling a pool hustler, a bounty hunter (Stansfield) becoming captivated by her prey, and an army recruit (Pouget) whose furlough involves a sexy drifter. **85m/C VHS, Closed Caption.** Paula Barbieri, Claire Stansfield, Ely Pouget, Francesco Quinn, Ron Marquette, Tony Addabbo; **D:** Ted Kotcheff. *REP*

Red Shoe Diaries 6: How I Met My Husband ✔✔ 1995 (R) Three more erotic vignettes from the cable series. "How I Met My Husband" finds Alice enrolling in a course on becoming a domanitrix and falling for Giuseppe, who's one of the training objects. Camille has inherited her father's vast fortune in "Naked in the Moonlight" on the condition that she take special care of his '57 Cadillac convertible—and the one mechanic allowed to work on the car. In "Midnight Bells," Claire reminisces about the mystery lover she meets on only one night of the year—New Year's Eve. **85m/C VHS, Closed Caption.** Luigi Amodeo, Neith Hunter, Raven Snow, Carsten Norgaard, John Enos, Charlotte Lewis, David Duchovny; **D:** Anne Goursaud, Philippe Angers, Bernard Auroux. *REP*

Red Shoe Diaries 7: Burning Up ✔✔ 1996 (R) Yet another trilogy of TV eroticism. "Burning Up" finds Lynn becoming obsessed with a handsome American, "Kidnap" features the workaholic Sara taken hostage during a bank robbery and finding out that her captor has decided to marry her, Alia is a top model in "Runway," who falls in lust with a cabby.**CW:** Strong sexuality and some language. **90m/C VHS.** Udo Kier, Ron Marquette, Jennifer Ciesar, Amber Smith, Anthony Guidera, Daniel Blasco, Alexandra Tydings, David Duchovny; **D:** Rafael Eisenman. *REP*

The Red Shoes ✔✔✔✔ 1948 British classic about a young ballerina torn between love and success. Inspired by the Hans Christian Andersen fairy tale. Noted for its lavish use of Technicolor. **136m/C VHS, Beta, LV, Closed Caption.** GB Anton Walbrook, Moira Shearer, Marius Goring, Leonide Massine, Robert Helpmann, Albert Basserman, Ludmila Tcherina, Esmond Knight; **D:** Emeric Pressburger, Michael Powell; **W:** Emeric Pressburger, Michael Powell; **C:** Jack Cardiff. Academy Awards '48: Best Art Direction/Set Decoration (Color), Original Dramatic/Comedy Score; Golden Globe Awards '49: Best Score; National Board of Review Awards '48: 10 Best Films of the Year; Nominations: Academy Awards '48: Best Film Editing, Best Picture, Best Story. *PAR, HMV*

Red Signals ✔✔ 1927 Mystery criminal makes trains collide. **70m/B VHS, Beta.** Wallace MacDonald, Earl Williams, Eva Novak, J.P. McGowan, Frank Rice; **D:** J.P. McGowan. *GPV, FCT*

Red Snow ✔ 1991 High in the Cascade Mountains, Kyle Lewis is the new snowboard instructor for the Hurricane Ridge Ski Resort. The job is fine in the beginning, until Kyle learns of the tragic fate of the last instructor. Before he knows it, Kyle is the next target and is framed for two murders. He secures the help of his fellow snowboard buddies in hopes of solving the mystery and getting the girl, too. High speed ski scenes and dangerous stunts are the film's only redeeming qualities. **86m/C VHS.** Carlo Scandiuzzi, Scott Galloway, Darla Slavens, Mitchell Cox, Tamar Tibbs, Brian Mahoney; **D:** Phillip J. Roth. *VHE*

Red Sonja ✔½ 1985 (PG-13) Two warriors join forces against an evil queen in this sword and sorcery saga. Big, beautiful bodies everywhere, with Bergman returning from her Conan adventures. Little humor, few special effects, and weak acting make this a poor outing. **89m/C VHS, Beta, LV, Closed Caption.** Arnold Schwarzenegger, Brigitte Nielsen, Sandahl Bergman, Paul Smith; **D:** Richard Fleischer; **M:** Ennio Morricone. Golden Raspberry Awards '85: Worst New Star (Nielsen). *MGM, FOX*

Red Sorghum ✔✔✔½ 1987 A stunning visual achievement, this new wave Chinese film (and Yimou's directorial debut) succeeds on many levels—as an ode to the color red, as dark comedy, and as a sweeping epic with fairy tale overtones. Set in rural China in the 1920s, during the period of the Japanese invasion. The sorghum plot nearby is a symbolic playing field in the movie's most stunning scenes. Here, people make love, murder, betray, and commit acts of bravery, all under the watchful eye of nature. In Mandarin with English subtitles. **91m/C VHS.** CH Gong Li, Jiang Wen, Ji Cun Hua; **D:** Zhang Yimou; **C:** Gu Changwei. *NYF*

The Red Squirrel ✔✔ *La Ardilla Roja* 1993 Former pop star Jota (Novo) is distraught over breaking up with his girlfriend and contemplating throwing himself off a bridge when he witnesses a motorcycle accident and rushes to help the young woman (Suarez) involved. After learning she's suffering from amnesia, Jota tells both the woman and the hospital that her name is Lisa and he's her lover. Then Jota invents a fictitious life for her, according to his own desires. Spanish with subtitles. **104m/C VHS.** SP Nancho Novo, Emma Suarez, Maria Barranco, Carmelo Gomez, Ana Garcia; **D:** Julio Medem; **W:** Julio Medem; **C:** Gonzalo F. Berridi; **M:** Alberto Iglesias. *NYF*

The Red Stallion ✔½ 1947 Good film for animal lovers, but it loses something when it comes to human relationships. A young boy raises his pony into an award-winning racehorse that saves the farm when it wins the big race. Good outdoor photography. **82m/B VHS.** Robert Paige, Noreen Nash, Ted Donaldson, Jane Darwell; **D:** Lesley Selander. *NOS, MOV, HEG*

Red Sun 1971 A gunfighter, a samurai, and a French bandit fight each other in various combinations in the 1860s. Ludicrous and boring. **115m/C VHS, Beta.** FR IT SP Charles Bronson, Toshiro Mifune, Alain Delon, Ursula Andress; **D:** Terence Young; **W:** William Roberts; **M:** Maurice Jarre. *GEM*

Red Sun Rising ✔½ 1994 (R) Kyoto cop Thomas Hoshino (Wilson) heads to L.A. in order to extradite a Japanese gangster, Yamata (Oh), and teams up with local detective Karen Ryder (Ferrell). Seems Yamata wants to start a turf war between two L.A. street gangs so he can sell guns to both sides. *CW:* Martial arts and gangster violence; brief language. **95m/C VHS.** Don "The Dragon" Wilson, Terry Farrell, Soon-Teck Oh, Mako, James Lew, Edward Albert, Michael Ironside; *D:* Francis Megahy; *C:* John Newby. *IMP*

Red Surf ♂♂ 1990 (R) Action abounds in this surfer film. A couple of hard-nosed wave-riders get involved with big money drug gangs and face danger far greater than the tide. **104m/C VHS, Beta, LV.** George Clooney, Doug Savant, Dedee Pfeiffer, Gene Simmons, Rick Najera, Philip McKeon; *D:* H. Gordon Boos. *ACA*

Red Tent ♂♂♂ *Krasnaya Palatka* 1969 (G) A robust, sweeping man-versus-nature epic based on the true story of the Arctic stranding of Italian explorer Umberto Nobile's expedition in 1928. A Russian-Italian co-production. **121m/C Beta, LV.** Sean Connery, Claudia Cardinale, Peter Finch, Hardy Kruger, Massimo Girotti, Luigi Vannucchi; *D:* Mikhail Kalatozov; *M:* Ennio Morricone. *PAR*

Red, White & Busted ♂ *Outside In* 1975 Amnesty or prison? That is the scorching, virtually unanswerable question asked by indictment of America. We follow three friends during the Vietnam War and see how they were affected by the events, whether or not they went. **85m/C VHS, Beta, LV.** Darrell Larson, Heather Menzies, Dennia Oliveri, John Bill. *NO*

Red Wind ♂♂ 1991 (R) Kris Morrow is a psychotherapist whose latest patient, Lila, has a number of disturbing sadomasochistic fantasies. When Kris feels she's getting too close to the situation, she refers Lila to another therapist. But Lila calls and tells Kris she's already acted out one of her fantasies by killing her husband. In order to stop Lila from killing again, Kris goes on a dangerous search for her deadly patient. *CW:* Violent scenes. **93m/C VHS, Closed Caption.** Lisa Hartman Black, Deanna Lund, Philip Casnoff, Christopher McDonald; *D:* Alan Metzger. *USH*

The Redeemer ♂ 1976 Group of adults at their high school reunion play the children's game of hide-and-seek, with deadly results. **80m/C VHS, Beta.** F.G. Finkbinder, Damien Knight, Jeanetta Arnetta; *D:* Constantine S. Gochis. *GHV*

The Redhead from Wyoming ♂♂½ 1953 Spirited sagebrush adventure with fiery-tempered O'Hara as a saloon proprietress with feelings for both a local cattle rustler and the town's sheriff. Based on a story by James. **81m/C VHS, Closed Caption.** Maureen O'Hara, Alex Nicol, William Bishop, Robert Strauss, Alexander Scourby, Jack Kelly, Jeanne Cooper, Dennis Weaver, Stacy Harris; *D:* Lee Sholem; *W:* Polly James, Herb Meadow. *USH*

Redneck ♂ 1973 Implausible, distasteful purported "thriller" about criminals on the run. **92m/C VHS, Beta.** *IT GB* Telly Savalas, Franco Nero, Mark Lester, Ely Galleani, Dulio Del Prete, Maria Michi; *D:* Silvio Narizzano. *NO*

Redneck Zombies ♂ 1988 (R) A bunch of backwoods rednecks become zombies after chug-a-lugging some radioactive beer. Eating local tourists becomes a hard habit to break. Betcha can't have just one! **83m/C VHS, Beta.** Floyd Piranha, Lisa DeHaven, W.E. Benson, William W. Decker, James Housely, Zoofoot, Tyrone Taylor, Perieles Lewnes. *TWE*

Reds ♂♂♂ 1981 (PG) The recreation of the life of author John Reed ("Ten Days that Shook the World"), his romance with Louise Bryant, his efforts to start an American Communist party, and his reporting of the Russian Revolution. A sweeping, melancholy epic using dozens of "witnesses" who reminisce about what they saw. See director Sergei Eisenstein's silent masterpiece "Ten Days that Shook the World," based on Reed's book, for the Russian view of some of the events depicted in Beatty's film. **195m/C VHS, Beta, LV, Closed Caption.** Warren Beatty, Diane Keaton, Jack Nicholson, Edward Herrmann, Maureen Stapleton, Gene Hackman, Jerzy Kosinski, George Plimpton, Paul Sorvino, William Daniels, M. Emmet Walsh, Dolph Sweet, Josef Sommer; *D:* Warren Beatty; *W:* Warren Beatty, Warren Beatty; *M:* Dave

Grusin, Stephen Sondheim. Academy Awards '81: Best Cinematography, Best Director (Beatty), Best Supporting Actress (Stapleton); British Academy Awards '82: Best Supporting Actor (Nicholson), Best Supporting Actress (Stapleton); Directors Guild of America Awards '81: Best Director (Beatty); Golden Globe Awards '82: Best Director (Beatty); Los Angeles Film Critics Association Awards '81: Best Cinematography, Best Director (Beatty), Best Supporting Actress (Stapleton); National Board of Review Awards '81: Best Director (Beatty), Best Supporting Actor (Nicholson); New York Film Critics Awards '81: Best Film; National Society of Film Critics Awards '81: Best Supporting Actress (Stapleton); Writers Guild of America '81: Best Original Screenplay; Nominations: Academy Awards '81: Best Actor (Beatty), Best Actress (Keaton), Best Art Direction/Set Decoration, Best Costume Design, Best Film Editing, Best Original Screenplay, Best Picture, Best Sound, Best Supporting Actor (Nicholson). *PAR, BTV*

Redwood Curtain ♂♂½ 1995 (PG) Geri Riordan (Salonga) is an Amerasian teenager, with a brilliant future as a concert pianist before her, until she becomes obsessed with learning about her past. Her wealthy adoptive father, Laird Riordan (Lithgow), provides understanding but no answers so she turns to her sympathetic Aunt Geneva (Monk), who lives in the redwood forest area of northern California. There Geri encounters homeless Vietnam vet Lyman Fellers (Daniels) and becomes convinced the troubled man is her birth father. Adapted from the play by Lanford Wilson; made for TV. **99m/C VHS, Closed Caption.** Lea Salonga, John Lithgow, Jeff Daniels, Debra Monk, Catherine Hicks; *D:* John Korty; *W:* Ed Namzug; *M:* Lawrence Shragge. *REP*

Redwood Forest Trail ♂♂ 1950 Environmental-themed oater about a camp for underprivileged city boys. The boys of the camp are blamed for the death of a landowner whose daughter then refuses to renew the camp's mortgage. Allen and Switzer set out to prove that the real culprits are sawmill workers out to control the area timber. Smokey the Bear also makes an appearance to lecture about careless forest fires and the need to preserve the woods. **67m/B VHS.** Rex Allen, Jeff Donnell, Carl "Alfalfa" Switzer, Jane Darwell, Marten Lamont, Pierre Watkin; *D:* Philip Ford; *W:* Bradford Ropes. *MOV*

Reefer Madness *Tell Your Children* 1938 (PG) Considered serious at the time of its release, this low-budget depiction of the horrors of marijuana has become an underground comedy favorite. Overwrought acting and lurid script contribute to the fun. **67m/B VHS, Beta.** Dave O'Brien, Dorothy Short, Warren McCollum, Lillian Miles, Thelma White, Carleton Young; *D:* Louis Gasnier. *SNC, NOS, HHT*

Reet, Petite and Gone ♂♂♂ 1947 All-Black musical featuring the music of neglected jive singer Louis Jordan, and his band, The Tympany Five. A girl's mother dies; sneaky lawyer tries to cheat her. Slick and enjoyable. **75m/B VHS, Beta.** Louis Jordan, June Richmond; *D:* William Forest Crouch. *MVD, NOS, VYY*

The Ref ♂♂♂ 1993 (R) The couple from hell turn the tables on Gus (Leary), a hard-nosed fugitive who takes Caroline (Davis) and her husband Lloyd (Spacey) hostage. Gus then finds himself trapped in the traditional Christmas ordeal of a family suffering from industrial-strength dysfunction. He plots his getaway while masquerading as the couple's marriage counselor, hence the film's title. This sometimes brutal, frequently hysterical satire of male-female relationships, family ties, and compulsory holiday rituals uses consistently sharp dialogue and superb acting to tell an absurd but convincing tale. *CW:* Strong language and crude sexual references. **97m/C VHS, LV, Closed Caption.** Denis Leary, Judy Davis, Kevin Spacey, Glynis Johns, Robert J. Steinmiller Jr., Christine Baranski; *D:* Ted Demme; *W:* Richard LaGravenese, Marie Weiss; *M:* David A. Stewart. *TOU*

The Reflecting Skin ♂♂ 1991 In a 1950s prairie town a small boy sees insanity, child-murder, and radiation sickness, leading him to fantasize that the tormented young widow next door is a vampire. The pretentious drama/freak show rationalizes its ghastly events as symbolizing the hero's loss of youthful innocence. But the Hound knows the score; this is "Faces of Death" for the arts crowd, a grotesque menagerie that dares you to watch. The exploding-frog opener is already notorious. Beautiful photography, with vistas inspired by the painting of Andrew Wyeth. **116m/C VHS, LV.** Viggo Mortensen, Lindsay Duncan, Jeremy Cooper; *D:* Philip Ridley; *W:* Philip Ridley; *M:* Nick Bicat. *NO*

A Reflection of Fear ♂♂ *Labyrinth* 1972 (PG) Lame psycho-thriller about a young girl's jealously of her father's girlfriend, with family members dying of supernatural causes. **90m/C VHS, Beta.** Robert Shaw, Sally Kellerman, Sondra Locke, Mary Ure; *D:* William A. Fraker; *W:* Lewis John Carlino. *COL*

Reflections in a Golden Eye ♂♂½ 1967 Huston's film adaptation of Carson McCullers novel about repressed homosexuality, madness, and murder at a Southern Army base in 1948. Star-studded cast cannot consistently pull off convoluted lives of warped characters; not for everyone, though it holds some interest. **109m/C VHS, Beta.** Elizabeth Taylor, Marlon Brando, Brian Keith, Julie Harris; *D:* John Huston; *C:* Oswald Morris. *WAR*

Reflections in the Dark ♂♂ *Reflections on a Crime* 1994 (R) Beautiful Regina (Rogers) is on death row for murdering her overbearing husband James (Terry). On execution-eve, she relates her tale to young guard Colin (Zane), dispatching hubby by a different method each time she varies her story. Takes itself too seriously though Rogers gives a star performance. *CW:* Adult situations, nudity, violence. **83m/C VHS, LV, Closed Caption.** Mimi Rogers, Billy Zane, John Terry, Kurt Fuller, Lee Garlington, Nancy Fish; *D:* Jon Purdy; *W:* Jon Purdy; *C:* Teresa Medina. *NHO*

Reflections of Murder ♂♂½ 1974 Evil schoolteacher's wife and mistress decide to kill him off and then are plagued by his phantom. Well done made for television remake of the French film "Diabolique." Suspenseful, with a great ending. **97m/C VHS.** Tuesday Weld, Joan Hackett, Sam Waterston, Lucille Benson, R.G. Armstrong, Michael Lerner, Ed Bernard, Lance Kerwin; *D:* John Badham; *M:* Billy Goldenberg. *REP*

Reform School Girl ♂ 1957 A young girl ends up behind bars when her boyfriend steals a car to go joy-riding and is involved in a hit-and-run murder. Extremely cheap production and incredulous story. Look for Kellerman in a bit part in her first screen appearance. **71m/B VHS, Closed Caption.** Gloria Castillo, Ross Ford, Edward Byrnes, Ralph Reed, Jack Kruschen, Sally Kellerman; *D:* Edward L. Bernds; *W:* Edward L. Bernds. *NLC*

Reform School Girls ♂ 1986 (R) Satiric raucous women's prison film, complete with tough lesbian wardens, brutal lesbian guards, sadistic lesbian inmates, and a single, newly convicted heterosexual heroine. Wendy O. Williams as a teenager? Come on. Overdone, over-campy, exploitative. **94m/C VHS, Beta, LV.** Linda Carol, Wendy O. Williams, Pat Ast, Sybil Danning, Charlotte McGinnis, Sherri Stoner; *D:* Tom De Simone. *VTR, NWV*

The Refrigerator ♂½ 1991 Filmed on a miniscule budget, this comic/horror flick tells the story of the innocent Batemans of Ohio who move into a grubby New York apartment where they discover their battered Norge refrigerator is actually a doorway to hell. The fridge has a taste for flesh and tends to eat the unwary visitor as well as defrosting blood (very messy). All the previous tenants disappeared without a trace—will the Batemans be next? Cartoon satire is too amateurish to be successful. **86m/C VHS.** David Simonds, Julia McNeal, Angel Caban, Nena Segal, Jaime Rojo, Michelle

DeCosta; *D:* Nicholas A.E. Jacobs; *W:* Nicholas A.E. Jacobs. *NO*

Regarding Henry 🎞🎞🎞 1991 (PG-13) A
cold-hearted lawyer gets shot in the head during a holdup and survives with memory and personality erased. During recovery the new Henry displays compassion and conscience the old one never had. Though too calculated in its yuppie-bashing ironies, the picture works thanks to splendid acting and low-key, on-target direction. 107m/C VHS, Beta, LV, Closed Caption. Harrison Ford, Annette Bening, Bill Nunn, Mikki Allen, Elizabeth Wilson, Robin Bartlett, John Leguizamo, Donald Moffat, Nancy Marchand; *D:* Mike Nichols; *W:* Jeffrey Abrams; *C:* Giuseppe Rotunno; *M:* Hans Zimmer. *PAR*

Regeneration 🎞🎞 1915 Irish hoodlum
Owen (Fellowes) is saved from his life of crime by social worker Mamie Rose (Nilsson). Walsh filmed on location in New York's Bowery district and used actual gangsters in roles. Also features the 10-minute 1910 short "The Police Force of New York City," produced by Thomas Edison. 72m/B VHS. Rockliffe Fellowes, Anna Q. Nilsson; *D:* Raoul Walsh. *KIV*

Reggie Mixes In 🎞🎞🎞 1916 Wealthy
man brawls in bar room and falls for barmaid. Taking a job to be near his beloved, he wipes out local thugs while tending to her welfare. Exhilarating fight scenes in which Fairbanks fists it out with real life boxers. 58m/B VHS, Beta. Douglas Fairbanks Sr., Bessie Love, Joseph Singleton, William E. Lowery, Wilbur Higby, Frank Bennett; *D:* Christy Cabanne. *GPV, FCT*

Regina 🎞🎞½ 1983 A woman controls all the
activities of her husband and son. At age 36, her son is ready to leave home and she refuses to let him. Fine performances in this strange and disturbing film. 86m/C VHS, Beta. *IT* Anthony Quinn, Ava Gardner, Ray Sharkey, Anna Karina; *D:* Jean-Yves Prate. *THV*

Reg'lar Fellers 🎞🎞 1941 A gang of kids
save the town and soften the heart of their grandmother, too. Production is sloppy. Based on a comic strip by Gene Byrnes. 66m/B VHS. Billy Lee, Carl "Alfalfa" Switzer, Buddy Boles, Janet Dempsey, Sarah Padden, Roscoe Ates; *D:* Arthur Dreifuss. *NOS, FMT, VYY*

Rehearsal for Murder 🎞🎞½ 1982 Movie star Redgrave is murdered on the night of her
Broadway debut. Seems it might have been someone in the cast. Brought to you by the creative team behind "Columbo." Challenging made for television whodunit a twist. Good cast. 96m/C VHS, Beta. Robert Preston, Lynn Redgrave, Patrick Macnee, Lawrence Pressman, Madolyn Smith, Jeff Goldblum, William Daniels; *D:* David Greene; *M:* Billy Goldenberg. *REP*

Reign of Terror 🎞🎞 *The Black Book* 1949
British-made adventure set during the French Revolution, with everyone after the black book that holds the names of those arch-fiend Robespierre plans to guillotine in his ruthless bid for power. Well-mounted, but historical personages and events are reduced to cartoon form. 89m/B VHS. Robert Cummings, Arlene Dahl, Richard Hart, Arnold Moss, Richard Basehart; *D:* Anthony Mann; *W:* Philip Yordan; *C:* John Alton. *NOS, MRV, CAB*

Reilly: Ace of Spies 🎞🎞🎞 1987 Covers the exploits of the real-life superspy and womanizer Sydney Reilly who uncovers Russian secrets in 1901, allowing the Japanese to sink the Russian fleet and invade China. After a lively spying career for the British, Reilly eventually plots against the Bolsheviks and comes close to overthrowing Lenin and installing himself as the new leader of the Russian government. Eleven episodes on four cassettes. 572m/C VHS, Beta, LV. GB Sam Neill, Sebastian Shaw, Jeananne Crowley; *D:* Jim Goddard. *SIG, HBO, FCT*

The Reincarnate 🎞 1971 (PG) Cult guarantees lawyer will live forever if he can find a new
body. Enter gullible sculptor; lawyer uses skill at persuasion. 89m/C VHS, Beta. *CA* Jack Creley, Jay Reynolds, Trudy Young, Terry Tweed; *D:* Don Haldane. *NO*

The Reincarnation of Golden
Lotus 🎞🎞🎞🎞 1989 In this highly erotic story of love and revenge, Wong escapes China for decadent Hong Kong by marrying a wealthy but foolish man. She has numerous sadomasochistic affairs and begins having flashbacks, revealing her to be the reincarnation of Golden Lotus, a courtesan of ancient China. In Mandarin Chinese with English subtitles. 99m/C VHS. *HK* Joi Wong, Eric Tsang, Lam Chen Yen; *D:* Clara Law. *CVC*

The Reincarnation of Peter
Proud 🎞🎞 1975 (R) A college professor has nightmares which lead him to believe the spirit of a murdered man is now possessing him. Kinda scary, but predictable. Screenplay by Ehrlich from his novel. 105m/C VHS, Beta, LV. Michael Sarrazin, Jennifer O'Neill, Margot Kidder, Cornelia Sharpe; *D:* J. Lee Thompson; *W:* Max Ehrlich; *M:* Jerry Goldsmith. *LIV, VES*

The Reivers 🎞🎞🎞½ 1969 (PG) Young boy
and two adult pals journey from small town Mississippi (circa 1905) to the big city of Memphis in a stolen car. Picaresque tale is delightful on-screen, as in William Faulkner's enjoyable last novel. 107m/C VHS, Beta. Steve McQueen, Sharon Farrell, Will Geer, Michael Constantine, Rupert Crosse; *D:* Mark Rydell; *W:* Harriet Frank Jr., Irving Ravetch; *M:* John Williams. Nominations: Academy Awards '69: Best Supporting Actor (Crosse), Best Original Score. *FOX*

The Rejuvenator 🎞🎞½ *Rejuvenatrix* 1988
(R) Also known as "Rejuvenatrix." An oft-told film story: an aging actress discovers a "youth" serum but finds out that the serum affects things other than her aging. Well-done. 90m/C VHS, LV. Marcus Powell, John MacKay, James Hogue, Vivian Lanko, Jessica Dublin; *D:* Brian Thomas Jones; *W:* Simon Nuchtern; *M:* Larry Juris. *NO*

Relative Fear 🎞½ 1995 (R) Little Adam has
bad luck with his friends and relatives—they keep getting murdered all around him. His mother begins to suspect something unnatural is going on, and discovers Adam is not her natural child, but the son of a homicidal madwoman. Has Adam inherited some deadly traits? *CW:* Violence involving psychological terror. 94m/C VHS, Closed Caption. Darlanne Fluegel, M. Emmet Walsh, James Brolin, Denise Crosby, Martin Neufeld, Linda Sorensen, Matthew Dupuis; *D:* George Mihalka; *W:* Kurt Wimmer. *REP*

Relentless 🎞🎞 1989 (R) Twisted psycho
Nelson, once rejected by the LAPD Academy on psychological grounds takes his revenge by murdering people and using his police training to cover his tracks. Good acting keeps sporadically powerful but cliched thriller afloat. 92m/C VHS, Beta, LV, Closed Caption. Judd Nelson, Robert Loggia, Meg Foster, Leo Rossi, Pat O'Bryan, Mindy Seeger, Angel Tompkins, Ken Lerner, George Flower; *D:* William Lustig. *COL*

Relentless 2: Dead On 🎞🎞 1991 (R)
Rossi, the detective from the first film, tracks yet another murderer whose occult-style mutilations mask an international political conspiracy. So-so slaughter with artsy camerawork. Honestly, how many "Relentless" fans can you name who've been waiting with anticipation? *CW:* Language and violence. 93m/C VHS, LV. Leo Rossi, Ray Sharkey, Meg Foster, Miles O'Keeffe; *D:* Michael Schroeder. *COL*

Relentless 3 🎞🎞 1993 (R) A serial killer
(Forsythe) likes to carve up his women victims and send various body parts to taunt the police. Then this sicko decides to really drive the cops crazy by stalking the beautiful girlfriend of the detective (Rossi) investigating the crimes. 84m/C VHS, Closed Caption. William Forsythe, Leo Rossi, Tom Bower, Robert Costanzo, Signy Coleman; *D:* James Lemmo; *W:* James Lemmo. *NLC*

Relentless 4 🎞½ 1994 (R) A psychiatrist
with a secret (Janssen) is the only clue Detective Sam Dietz (Rossi) has to a serial killer. Seems all the victims knew the shrink but what does she know? 91m/C VHS, LV, Closed Caption. Leo Rossi, Famke Janssen, Ken Lerner, Colleen Coffey; *D:* Oley Sassone; *W:* Mark Sevi, Terry Plumeri. *NLC*

The Relic 🎞🎞 1996 (R) Quiz time! Which is
more implausible: a huge reptilian creature from South American mythology who is crazy for decapitations running amok in a Chicago museum, or Miller as an evolutionary biologist? That's right! Both are equally implausible. But we're forced to accept both after a ship from Brazil arrives with crates for the museum and a completely headless crew (extra credit if you said it's implausible for people with no heads to pilot a ship). Superstitious police detective Vincent D'Agosto (Sizemore) decides to close down the museum's exhibit of...Superstition. That does not sit well with museum director Ann Cuthbert (Hunt), who decides she needs grant money (and the movie needs victims). The monster proceeds to suck brains until the sassy scientist decides she's had enough and takes off her high heels, which everyone knows means the end is near for the creature. Sound interesting? Only if you like Lifestyles of the Rich and Headless. *CW:* Monster violence and gore and for language. 110m/C VHS, Beta, Closed Caption. Penelope Ann Miller, Tom Sizemore, Linda Hunt, James Whitmore, Clayton Rohner, Thomas Ryan, Lewis Van Bergen, Chi Muoi Lo, Robert Lesser; *D:* Peter Hyams; *W:* Amy Holden Jones, John Raffo, Rick Jaffa, Amanda Silver; *C:* Peter Hyams; *M:* John Debney. *PAR*

The Reluctant Agent 🎞🎞 1995 Waitress Linda (Jackee) is persuaded to take the
place of injured twin sister Charlene, an FBI agent hot on the trail of shady-but-attractive businessman C. Gabriel Dash (Lawson). So, she goes undercover with the questionable assistance of agent John Fraser (Hedaya) to bring their criminal to justice. 94m/C VHS. Jackee, Richard Lawson, Dan Hedaya, Bill Fagerbakke, Harold Sylvester, Cynthia Stevenson, Sharon Barr, Eda Reiss Merin; *D:* Paul Lynch; *W:* Jeff Cohn, Kristi Kane; *M:* Tim Truman. *AEL*

The Reluctant Astronaut 🎞½ 1967
Roy Fleming (Knotts) is a carnival worker who operates the spaceship ride. Dad's upset the kid has no ambition and sends an application for Roy to NASA. Everyone's surprised when Roy gets accepted and he heads off to Florida but it turns out the job is janitorial. Still Roy does make friends with astronaut Red (Nielsen), who persuades NASA that Roy would be the perfect civilian to send up in an experimental capsule. Too bad Roy's terrified to fly in anything. 103m/C VHS, Closed Caption. Don Knotts, Leslie Nielsen, Joan Freeman, Arthur O'Connell, Jesse White, Jeanette Nolan, Joan Shawlee; *D:* Edward Montagne; *W:* James Fritzell, Everett Greenbaum; *C:* Rexford Wimpy; *M:* Vic Mizzy. *USH*

The Reluctant Debutante 🎞🎞🎞 1958
Harrison and Kendall are the urbane parents of Dee who are trying to find a suitable British husband for their girl. It seems their choices just won't do however, and Dee falls for American bad boy musician Saxon. A very lightweight yet extremely enjoyable romantic comedy thanks to Harrison and in particular his real-life wife Kendall, who unfortunately died the following year. 96m/C VHS, Beta, LV. Rex Harrison, Kay Kendall, John Saxon, Sandra Dee, Angela Lansbury, Diane Clare; *D:* Vincente Minnelli; *C:* Joseph Ruttenberg. *MGM*

The Reluctant Dragon 1941 Classic Disney short about a fun-loving dragon, based on the
Kenneth Grahame story; accompanied also by the Disney short "Morris, the Midget Moose." Not to be confused with the full-length 1941 Disney feature film. 28m/C VHS, Beta. *D:* Alfred Werker. *DIS, KUI*

The Remains of the Day 🎞🎞🎞 1993
(PG) If repression is your cup of tea then this is the film for you. Others may want to shake British butler par excellence Stevens (Hopkins) and tell him to express an emotion. In the 1930s, Stevens is the rigidly traditional butler to Lord Darlington (Fox). When Miss Kenton (Thompson) the almost vivacious new housekeeper expresses a quietly personal interest in Stevens his loyalty to an unworthy master prevents him from a chance at happiness. A quiet movie, told in flashback. Hop-

kins' impressive performance gets by strictly on nuance with Thompson at least allowed a small amount of natural charm. Based on the novel by Kazuo Ishiguro. **135m/C VHS, LV, 8mm, Closed Caption.** *GB* Anthony Hopkins, Emma Thompson, James Fox, Christopher Reeve, Peter Vaughan, Hugh Grant, Michael Lonsdale, Tim Pigott-Smith; *D:* James Ivory; *W:* Ruth Prawer Jhabvala; *C:* Tony Pierce-Roberts; *M:* Richard Robbins. British Academy Awards '93: Best Actor (Hopkins); Los Angeles Film Critics Association Awards '93: Best Actor (Hopkins); National Board of Review Awards '93: Best Actor (Hopkins); Nominations: Academy Awards '93: Best Actress (Thompson), Best Adapted Screenplay, Best Art Direction/Set Decoration, Best Costume Design, Best Director (Ivory), Best Picture, Best Original Score; British Academy Awards '94: Best Actress (Thompson), Best Adapted Screenplay, Best Director (Ivory), Best Film; Directors Guild of America Awards '93: Best Director (Ivory); Golden Globe Awards '94: Best Actor—Drama (Hopkins), Best Actress—Drama (Thompson), Best Director (Ivory), Best Film—Drama, Best Screenplay; Writers Guild of America '93: Best Adapted Screenplay. COL

Rembrandt 🐾🐾🐾 1936 Necessarily very visual biography of the great Dutch painter, Rembrandt. Superb acting by Laughton. **86m/B VHS, Beta, LV.** *GB* Charles Laughton, Elsa Lanchester, Gertrude Lawrence, Walter Hudd; *D:* Alexander Korda; *C:* Georges Perinal. National Board of Review Awards '36: 10 Best Films of the Year.

Rembrandt—1669 🐾🐾 1977 A recreation of the controversial artist's last year, with his egotism clashing with his artistic impulses. In Dutch with English subtitles. **114m/C VHS.** *NL* Frans Stelling, Tom de Koff, Aye Fil; *D:* Jos Stelling. CVC

Remedy for Riches 🐾🐾 1940 The fourth "Dr. Christian" comedy, has the small-town doctor trying to uncover a real estate fraud before it bankrupts his community. Mildly funny. **66m/B VHS, Beta, 8mm.** Jean Hersholt, Dorothy Lovett, Edgar Kennedy, Jed Prouty, Walter Catlett; *D:* Erle C. Kenton. NOS, VYY

Remember Me 🐾 1985 Just as a woman is starting to gain control of her life, her husband returns home from the mental hospital. **95m/C VHS, Beta.** Robert Grubb, Wendy Hughes, Richard Moir; *D:* Lex Marinos. NO

Remember the Night 🐾🐾🐾 1940 Another Sturges-scripted winner in which assistant D.A. MacMurray falls for sophisticated shoplifter Stanwyck, who has stolen a diamond bracelet amidst the Christmas holiday bustle. On a promise that she will return for the trial MacMurray postpones the trial and offers her a ride home for the holidays. Stanwyck is turned away by her mother and MacMurray brings her home for a real family Christmas, where love blooms. A sentimental, funny romance that boisters holiday cheer any time of year. **94m/B VHS, Closed Caption.** Barbara Stanwyck, Fred MacMurray, Beulah Bondi, Elizabeth Patterson, Willard Robertson, Sterling Holloway; *D:* Mitchell Leisen; *W:* Preston Sturges; *C:* Ted Tetzlaff; *M:* Friedrich Hollander. USH

Remington Steele, Vol. 1: License to Steele 1982 Pilot episode to the light-hearted detective TV series starring Zimbalist as Laura Holt, a female PI who sets up her agency under the name of her fictitious male boss. Then a mystery man appears claiming to be the real Remington Steele (Brosnan) and the two decide to join forces. Also in the first episode are Read as Laura's suspicious assistant, Murphy Michaels, and DeMay as Bernice Fox, the agency secretary. **60m/C VHS.** Stephanie Zimbalist, Pierce Brosnan, James Read, Janet DeMay. MOV, MTM

Remo Williams: The Adventure Begins 🐾🐾 1985 (PG-13) Adaptation of "The Destroyer" adventure novel series with a Bond-like hero who can walk on water and dodge bullets after being instructed by a Korean martial arts master. Funny and diverting, and Grey is excellent (if a bit over the top) as the wizened oriental. The title's assumption is that the adventure will continue. **121m/C VHS, Beta, LV.** Fred Ward, Joel Grey,

Wilford Brimley, Kate Mulgrew; *D:* Guy Hamilton. Nominations: Academy Awards '85: Best Makeup.NO

Remolina de Pasiones 🐾🐾 1987 A young woman is driven to suicide after succumbing to her mother's persistent lover. **89m/C VHS, Beta.** *SP* Amparo Rivelles, Carlos Pinar, Susana Dosamantes. MAD

Remote 🐾🐾½ 1993 (PG) Thirteen-year-old Randy is a whiz designing high-tech remote-control gadgets. When one of his toys wipes out a friend's science project, Randy's parents try to put a halt to his tinkering but the kid has other plans. Innocuous rip-off of "Honey, I Shrunk the Kids" with some "Home Alone" thrown in as well. **80m/C VHS, Beta, Closed Caption.** Chris Carrara, Jessica Bowman, John Diehl, Derya Ruggles, Tony Longo, Stuart Fratkin; *D:* Ted Nicolaou; *W:* Mike Farrow; *M:* Richard Band. PAR

Remote Control 🐾🐾½ 1988 (R) A circulating videotape of a 1950's sci-fi flick is turning people into murderous zombies, thanks to some entrepreneurial aliens. Silly, but performed by young actors with gusto. **88m/C VHS, Beta, LV.** Kevin Dillon, Deborah Goodrich, Christopher Wynne, Jennifer Tilly; *D:* Jeff Lieberman; *M:* Peter Bernstein. LIV, HHE

Remote Control 🐾🐾½ 1994 Quiet Axel lives with his mom, whose life revolves around the TV set, and his sister Maeja, who spends most of her time partying in a seedy club called Sodoma. Sodoma is run by three amateur gangsters who are anxious to get rid of a rival, Moli. Meanwhile, Axel falls in love with Moli's sister Unnur (who also happens to be Maeja's best friend). Then the gangsters kidnap Unnur and Axel sets out to rescue her. Icelandic with English subtitles. **85m/C VHS.** *IC* Bjorn Fridbjornsson, Margret H. Gustavsdottir, Helgi Bjornsson, Soley Eliasdottir; *D:* Oskar Jonasson; *W:* Oskar Jonasson. COL

Renaissance Man 🐾🐾½ 1994 (PG-13) Skeptical new teacher inspires a classroom of underachievers and finds his true calling. Based loosely on the experiences of screenwriter Burnstein at a base in Michigan. Civilian Bill Rago (DeVito) is an unemployed ad exec assigned to teach Shakespeare to a group of borderline Army recruits led by Hardison. Add half a bone for the recruits and their Hamlet rap, a breath of fresh air in an otherwise stale plot. Some funny moments, reminiscent of "Stripes," but not quite as wacky. On the other hand, Marshall does endearing well. Look for rapper Marky Mark with his shirt on (hard to recognize). Shot with the cooperation of the Army.*CW:* Language. **128m/C VHS, LV, Closed Caption.** Danny DeVito, Gregory Hines, James Remar, Stacey Dash, Ed Begley Jr., Mark Wahlberg, Lillo Brancato, Kadeem Hardison, Richard T. Jones, Khalil Kain, Peter Simmons, Jenifer Lewis; *Cameos:* Cliff Robertson; *D:* Penny Marshall; *W:* Jim Burnstein, Ned Mauldin; *M:* Hans Zimmer. TOU

Rendez-Moi Ma Peau 🐾🐾½ 1981 A modern-day witch transposes two people's personalities with comic results. In French with subtitles. **82m/C VHS, Beta.** *FR D:* Patrick Schulmann. FCT

Rendez-vous 🐾🐾🐾 1985 (R) A racy, dark film about the sensitive balance between sex and exploitation, the real world and the stage world. Some may be disturbed by chillingly explicit scenes. Impressive tour de force of imagination, direction, and cinematography. In French with English subtitles. **82m/C VHS, LV.** *FR* Juliette Binoche, Lambert Wilson, Wadeck Stanczak, Jean-Louis Trintignant; *D:* Andre Techine; *W:* Olivier Assayas; *C:* Philippe Angers. Cannes Film Festival '85: Best Director (Techine). CVC, TPV

Rendezvous in Paris 🐾🐾 *Les Rendez-vous de Paris* 1995 Three stories by Rohmer about the complications and disappointments of love. "Le Rendez-vous de 7 heures" finds Esther (Bellar) upset when boyfriend Horace (Basler) is spotted with another girl at a cafe. She decides to make him jealous by showing up at the same cafe with another man. A woman (Rauscher) decides

to leave her boring fiance in "Les Bancs de Paris" and tries to decide on a possible new romance with a provincial professor (Renko). In "Mere et Enfant 1907," a painter (Kraft) goes to an art gallery where he spots a woman (Loyen) admiring Picasso's painting "Mother and Child" and he decides to pursue her. French with subtitles. **100m/C VHS.** *FR* Clara Bellar, Antoine Basler, Mathias Megard, Judith Chancel, Aurore Rauscher, Serge Renko, Michael Kraft, Benedicte Loyen, Veronika Johansson; *D:* Eric Rohmer; *W:* Eric Rohmer; *C:* Diane Baratier; *M:* Sebastien Erms. NYF

Renegade Girl 🐾 1946 A special agent is sent west to capture the female head of a band of outlaws. **65m/B VHS, Beta, LV.** Alan Curtis, Ann Savage, Edward Brophy, Ray Corrigan, Jack Holt; *D:* William (Lester Williams) Berke. NOS, RXM, VYY

Renegade Monk 🐾🐾½ 1982 (R) Invincible warrior-monk dispenses his own brand of justice with his fists of aluminum foil. **90m/C VHS, Beta.** Liu Chang Liang, Huang Hsing Shaw, Ko Shou Liang, Lang Shih Chia, Hsu Chung Hsing. GEM

Renegade Ninja 🐾 1983 A man whose father was murdered kicks everyone within reach in his quest for revenge. **109m/C VHS, Beta.** Kensaku Marita; *D:* Sadao Nakajima. PSM

Renegade Ranger/Scarlet River 🐾🐾½ 1938 A western double feature: A Texas Ranger and his singing sidekick attempt to help out a woman accused of murder in the "The Renegade Ranger," and a cowboy tries to free his sweetheart from a band of cattle rustlers in "Scarlet River." **113m/B VHS, Beta.** Rita Hayworth, Tim Holt, George O'Brien, Ray Whitley, Tom Keene, Lon Chaney Jr., Myrna Loy, Bruce Cabot, Betty Furness; *D:* David Howard. TTC

Renegade Trail 🐾🐾 1939 Hopalong Cassidy helps a marshall and a pretty widow round up ex-cons and rustlers. The King's Men, radio singers of the era, perform a fistful of songs. **61m/B VHS.** William Boyd, George "Gabby" Hayes, Russell Hayden, Charlotte Wynters, Russell Hopton, Sonny Bupp, Jack Rockwell, Roy Barcroft, Eddie Dean; *D:* Lesley Selander. NOS

Renegades 🐾🐾 1989 (R) A young cop from Philadelphia and a Lakota Indian begrudgingly unite to track down a gang of ruthless crooks. Good action, and lots of it; not much story. **105m/C VHS, Beta, LV, Closed Caption.** Kiefer Sutherland, Lou Diamond Phillips, Rob Knepper, Jami Gertz, Bill Smitrovich; *D:* Jack Sholder; *C:* Phil Meheux; *M:* Michael Kamen. USH

Renfrew of the Royal Mounted 🐾🐾 1937 A Canadian Mountie goes after counterfeiters and sings a few songs in this mild adaptation of a popular kids' radio serial. Newill was a popular tenor of the day, but the Hound thinks Renfrew's dog "Lightning" should have been the star. **57m/B VHS, Beta.** Carol Hughes, James Newill, Kenneth Harlan; *D:* Al(bert) Herman. DVT, GPV, HEG

Renfrew on the Great White Trail 🐾½ *On the Great White Trail; Renfrew of the Royal Mounted on the Great White Trail* 1938 A frustrated fur trader takes off after a pack of thieves. **58m/B VHS.** James Newill, Terry Walker, Robert Frazer, Richard Alexander; *D:* Al(bert) Herman. NOS, DVT

Reno and the Doc 🐾🐾½ 1984 Enjoyable comedy about two endearingly cranky middle-aged men battling mid-life crises join together and test their mettle in the world of professional skiing. **88m/C VHS, Beta.** *CA* Ken Walsh, Henry Ramer, Linda Griffiths; *D:* Charles Dennis. NWV

Renoir Shorts 🐾🐾🐾 1927 Two early silent Renoir fantasies: "The Little Matchgirl," a lyrical adaptation of the Hans Christian Anderson fairy tale, and "Charleston," in which a space-traveling African and Parisian girl dance comically. **50m/B VHS, Beta.** Catherine Hessling; *D:* Jean Renoir. NOS, FCT

Rent-A-Cop 🐾🐾 1988 (R) A cop (Reynolds) is bounced from the force after he survives a drug-bust massacre under suspicious circumstances. He becomes a security guard and continues to track down the still-at-large killer with help from call girl Minnelli. **95m/C VHS, Beta, LV, Closed Caption.** Burt Reynolds, Liza Minnelli, James Remar, Richard Masur, Bernie Casey, John Stanton, John P. Ryan, Dionne Warwick, Robby Benson; **D:** Jerry London; **W:** Michael Blodgett; **M:** Jerry Goldsmith. Golden Raspberry Awards '88: Worst Actress (Minnelli). *HBO*

Rent-A-Kid 🎬🎬½ **1995 (G)** Businessman Harry Haber (Nielsen) is asked by his son to keep an eye out on the Mid-Valley Orphanage for a week. Then Harry meets a young couple who are unsure about having a family so, since Harry's business is renting all sorts of things, he decides to rent the couple three orphans so they can get a taste of parenting. **89m/C VHS, LV, Closed Caption.** Leslie Nielsen, Christopher Lloyd, Matt McCoy, Sherry Miller, Amos Crawley, Cody Jones, Tabitha Lupien, Tony Rosato; **D:** Fred Gerber; **W:** Paul Bernbaum; **C:** Rene Ohashi; **M:** Ron Ramin. *REP*

Rentadick 🎬🎬 **1972** A precursor to the Monty Python masterpieces, written by future members Chapman and Cleese. Private eye spoof isn't as funny as later Python efforts; but it is an indication of what was yet to come and fans should enjoy it. **94m/C VHS.** *GB* James Booth, Julie Ege, Ronald Fraser, Donald Sinden, Michael Bentine, Richard Briers, Spike Milligan; **D:** Jim Clark; **W:** Graham Chapman, John Cleese; **M:** Carl Davis. *NO*

Rented Lips 🎬 **1988 (R)** Two documentary film makers sell out, taking over the production of a porno film at the request of a public television producer who promises to help their careers. Mull and Shawn are well supported by an impressive cast, but everyone's effort is wasted in unfunny attempt at comedy. **82m/C VHS, Beta, LV.** Martin Mull, Dick Shawn, Jennifer Tilly, Kenneth Mars, Edy Williams, Robert Downey Jr., June Lockhart, Shelley Berman, Mel Welles, Pat McCormick, Eileen Brennan; **D:** Robert Downey. *NO*

Repentance 🎬🎬🎬 *Pokayaniye; Confession* **1987 (PG)** A popular, surreal satire of Soviet and Communist societies. A woman is arrested for repeatedly digging up a dead local despot, and put on trial. Wickedly funny and controversial; released under the auspices of glasnost. In Russian with English subtitles. **151m/C VHS, Beta, LV.** *RU* Avtandil Makharadze, Zeinab Botsvadze, Ia Ninidze, Edisher Giorgobiani, Ketevan Abuladze, Kakhi Kavsadze; **D:** Tengiz Abuladze. Cannes Film Festival '87: Grand Jury Prize. *MED*

Replikator: Cloned to Kill 🎬½ **1994 (R)** In the 21st century, a ruthless criminal gets hold of replication techology that can duplicate anything, including people. So it's up to a cop and two cyberpunks to stop the destruction. **CW:** Rated R for nudity and futuristic violence. **96m/C VHS, Closed Caption.** Michael St. Gerard, Brigitte Bako, Ned Beatty; **D:** G. Philip Jackson; **W:** Tony Johnston, Michelle Bellerose, John Dawson. *PSM*

Repo Jake 🎬½ **1990** Jake Baxter learns the myth of the carefree life of a repossession man in this action thriller. His illusion is destroyed by angry clients, pornography, a deadly underworld racetrack, and a sinister crime boss. **90m/C VHS.** Dan Haggerty, Robert Axelrod. *PMH*

Repo Man 🎬🎬🎬½ **1983 (R)** An inventive, perversely witty portrait of sick modern urbanity, following the adventures of a punk rocker taking a job as a car repossessor in a barren city. The landscape is filled with pointless violence, no-frills packaging, media hypnosis and aliens. Executive producer: none other than ex-Monkee Michael Nesmith. **93m/C VHS, Beta, LV.** Emilio Estevez, Harry Dean Stanton, Sy Richardson, Tracey Walter, Olivia Barash, Fox Harris, Jennifer Balgobin, Vonetta McGee, Angelique Pettyjohn; **D:** Alex Cox; **W:** Alex Cox. *USH*

The Report on the Party and the Guests 🎬🎬🎬🎬 **1966** A controversial, widely banned political allegory, considered a masterpiece from the Czech new wave. A picnic/lawn party deteriorates into brutality, fascist intolerance and persecution. Many Czech film makers, some banned at the time, appear. Based on a story by

Ester Krumbachova, who also co-wrote the screenplay. In Czech with English subtitles. **71m/B VHS, Beta.** *CZ* Jiri Nemec, Evald Schorm, Ivan Vyskocil, Jan Klusak, Zdena Skvorecka, Pavel Bosek; **D:** Jan Nemec; **W:** Jan Nemec. *FCT*

Report to the Commissioner 🎬🎬🎬 *Operation Undercover* **1974 (R)** A rough, energetic crime-in-the-streets cop thriller. A young detective accidentally kills an attractive woman who turns out to have been an undercover cop, then is dragged into the bureaucratic cover-up. **112m/C VHS, Beta.** Michael Moriarty, Yaphet Kotto, Susan Blakely, Hector Elizondo, Richard Gere, Tony King, Michael McGuire, Stephen Elliott; **D:** Milton Katselas; **W:** Abby Mann; **M:** Elmer Bernstein. *MGM*

Repossessed 🎬🎬 **1990 (PG-13)** A corny, occasionally funny takeoff on the human-possessed-by-the-devil films with Blair, as usual, as the afflicted victim. Nielsen, in another typecast role, plays the goofy man of the cloth who must save the day. Numerous actors appear in brief comedy sequences which lampoon current celebrities and constitute the film's highlights. For fans of "Airplane" and "The Naked Gun"; not necessarily for others. **89m/C VHS, LV, Closed Caption.** Linda Blair, Ned Beatty, Leslie Nielsen, Anthony Starke, Jesse Ventura; **D:** Bob Logan; **W:** Bob Logan; **M:** Charles Fox. Golden Raspberry Awards '90: Worst Song ("He's Comin' Back (The Devil)"). *LIV*

The Reptile 🎬🎬 **1966** The inhabitants of yet another Cornish village are turning up dead—mysteriously from snakebite. When Harry (Barrett) investigates his brother's death, he finds out Anna (Pearce) is the victim of a curse, which causes her to turn into a snake. Rather sympathetic characters for the horror genre. **90m/C VHS.** *GB* Jacqueline Pearce, Ray Barrett, Noel Willman, Jennifer Daniel, Michael Ripper, John Laurie; **D:** John Gilling; **W:** John Elder; **C:** Arthur Grant; **M:** Don Banks. *VTR*

Repulsion 🎬🎬🎬½ **1965** Character study of a young French girl who is repulsed and attracted by sex. Left alone when her sister goes on vacation, her facade of stability begins to crack, with violent and bizarre results. Polanski's first film in English and his first publicly accepted full-length feature. Suspenseful, disturbing and potent. **105m/B VHS, Beta, LV.** *GB* Catherine Deneuve, Yvonne Furneaux, Ian Hendry, John Fraser, Patrick Wymark, James Villiers, Renee Houston, Helen Fraser, Mike Pratt; **D:** Roman Polanski; **W:** Roman Polanski, Gerard Brach, David Stone. *VDM, VCN, MRV*

Requiem for a Heavyweight 🎬🎬🎬 **1956** The original television version of the story about an American Indian heavyweight boxer played by Palance who risks blindness in order to help his manager pay off bookies. Highly acclaimed teleplay written for "Playhouse 90." **90m/B VHS, Beta.** Jack Palance, Keenan Wynn, Ed Wynn, Kim Hunter, Ned Glass; **D:** Ralph Nelson; **W:** Rod Serling. *FUS, BTV, RHI*

Requiem for Dominic 🎬🎬🎬½ *Requiem fur Dominic* **1991 (R)** A Communist-bloc country in the midst of revolution accuses a man of terrorist activities. Can his friend, exiled for years, help him discover the truth? Interesting and timely premise matched with outstanding ensemble acting make for a superior thriller. Amnesty International receives partial proceeds from all sales of this video. In German with English subtitles. **CW:** Graphic views of a massacred corpse. **88m/C VHS, LV.** *GE* Felix Mitterer, Viktoria Schubert, August Schmolzer, Angelica Schutz; **D:** Robert Dornhelm. *HMD*

The Rescue 🎬½ **1988 (PG)** An elite team of U.S. Navy Seals is captured after destroying a disabled submarine. When the U.S. government writes off the men, their children decide to mount a rescue. Puerile, empty-headed trash for teens. **97m/C VHS, Beta, LV, Closed Caption.** Marc Price, Charles Haid, Kevin Dillon, Christina Harnos, Edward Albert; **D:** Ferdinand Fairfax; **W:** Jim Thomas, John Thomas; **C:** Russell Boyd; **M:** Bruce Broughton. *TOU, HHE*

Rescue Force 🎬🎬 **1990** A crack team of anti-terrorists, led by Lt. Col. Steel, takes on the kidnappers of an American ambassador. Action filled excitement. **85m/C VHS.** Richard Harrison. *NO*

Rescue Me 🎬🎬½ **1993 (PG-13)** Geek photographer Fraser carries a torch for high school honey Ginny and just happens to be on the scene (with camera) when she's kidnapped. So he persuades a scruffy Vietnam vet to help him rescue his damsel in distress. Likeable adventure with lots of chases. **CW:** Mild language and violence. **99m/C VHS, LV.** Michael Dudikoff, Stephen Dorff, Peter DeLuise, Ami Dolenz, William Lucking, Dee Wallace Stone; **D:** Arthur Seidelman; **W:** Michael Snyder; **C:** Hanania Baer; **M:** Al Kasha, Joel Hirschhorn, David Waters. *WAR*

The Rescuers 🎬🎬🎬 **1977 (G)** Bernard and Miss Bianca, two mice who are members of the Rescue Aid Society, attempt to rescue an orphan named Penny from the evil Madame Medusa, who's after the world's biggest diamond. They are aided by comic sidekick, Orville the albatross, and a group of lovable swamp creatures. Very charming in the best Disney tradition. Based on the stories of Margery Sharp. Followed by "The Rescuers Down Under." **76m/C VHS, LV, Closed Caption.** **D:** Wolfgang Reitherman, John Lounsbery; **M:** Artie Butler; **V:** Bob Newhart, Eva Gabor, Geraldine Page, Jim Jordan, Joe Flynn, Jeanette Nolan, Pat Buttram. Nominations: Academy Awards '77: Best Song ("Someone's Waiting for You"). *DIS, OM*

The Rescuers Down Under 🎬🎬½ **1990 (G)** "Crocodile" Dundee goes Disney; the followup to "The Rescuers" places its characters in Australia with only mild results for a Magic Kingdom product. Heroic mice Bernard and Bianca protect a young boy and a rare golden eagle from a poacher. The great bird closely resembles the logo of Republic Pictures. **77m/C VHS, Beta, LV, Closed Caption.** **D:** Hendel Butoy; **W:** Mike Gabriel; **W:** Jim Cox, Karey Kirkpatrick, Joe Ranft, Byron Simpson; **M:** Bruce Broughton; **V:** Bob Newhart, Eva Gabor, John Candy, Tristan Rogers, George C. Scott, Frank Welker, Adam Ryen. *DIS, OM*

Reservoir Dogs 🎬🎬🎬½ **1992 (R)** Ultraviolent tale of honor among thieves. Six professional criminals known by code names to protect their identities (Misters Pink, White, Orange, Blonde, Blue, and Brown) are assembled by Tierney to pull off a diamond heist. But two of the gang are killed in a police ambush. The survivors regroup in an empty warehouse and try to discover the informer in their midst. In probably the most stomach-churning scene (there is some competition here), a policeman is tortured just for the heck of it to the tune of the Stealers Wheel "Stuck in the Middle with You." Unrelenting; auspicious debut for Tarantino with strong ensemble cast anchored by Keitel as the very professional Mr. White. **CW:** Strong language and strong violence. **100m/C VHS, LV, Closed Caption, DVD.** Harvey Keitel, Tim Roth, Michael Madsen, Steve Buscemi, Christopher Penn, Lawrence Tierney, Kirk Baltz, Quentin Tarantino, Eddie Bunker, Randy Brooks; **D:** Quentin Tarantino; **W:** Quentin Tarantino; **C:** Andrzej Sekula. Independent Spirit Awards '93: Best Supporting Actor (Buscemi). *LIV, BTV*

The Respectful Prostitute 🎬🎬½ **1952** Sartre's tale of hooker who is cajoled into providing false testimony as a witness in the trial of a member of a prominent family. English language version of French drama. **75m/B VHS.** *FR* Ivan Desny, Barbara Laage, Walter Bryan; **D:** Marcel Pagliero, Charles Brabant; **W:** Jean-Paul Sartre. *XVC, FCT, TPV*

Rest In Pieces 🎬 **1987 (R)** A young woman inherits a Spanish mansion, and weird things begin to happen. It seems a cult of Satan worshippers is already living on the estate. As one might infer from the title, quite a bit of hacking and slashing ensues. **90m/C VHS, Beta.** Scott Thompson Baker, Lorin Jean, Dorothy Malone; **D:** Joseph Braunstein. *LIV*

Restless *The Beloved* 1972 A restless home-maker begins an affair with a childhood friend. Director Cosmatos later oversaw "Rambo." 75m/C VHS, Beta. **GR** Raquel Welch, Richard Johnson, Jack Hawkins, Flora Robson; **D:** George P. Cosmatos. THV

The Restless Breed 1958 Son is restless after dad, a secret service agent, is slain by gunrunners. Routine oater-revenge epic done in by listless script. 81m/C VHS, LV, **Closed Caption.** Scott Brady, Anne Bancroft, Jay C. Flippen, Rhys Williams, Jim Davis; **D:** Allan Dwan. FRH, IME

Restoration 1994 (R) Set in the 17th century after Charles II is restored to the British throne, the title may instead refer to the restoration of one man's values. After curing one of the king's dogs, physician Downey is elevated to courtier and falls into drunken debauchery. He is soon forced to marry (but not touch) the king's favorite mistress. Unfortunately, he is caught trespassing on his majesty's main squeeze and banished from the court. Cast among the common rabble, he encounters the plague and the Great Fire of London while trying to redeem himself. Strong cast and sumptuous set design help to propel Downey's performance. Adapted from Rose Tremain's 1989 novel. Release was delayed a year because no one could seem to come up with a marketing strategy.**CW:** Sexuality. 118m/C VHS, LV, **Closed Caption.** Robert Downey Jr., Meg Ryan, Sam Neill, Hugh Grant, David Thewlis, Polly Walker, Ian McKellen; **D:** Michael Hoffman; **W:** Rupert Walters; **C:** Oliver Stapleton; **M:** James Newton Howard. Academy Awards '95: Best Art Direction/Set Decoration, Best Costume Design. TOU

The Resurrected 1991 (R) One of the best recent H.P. Lovecraft horror adaptations, a fairly faithful try at "The Case of Charles Dexter Ward." Ward learns he has a satanic ancestor who possessed the secret of resurrection and eternal life—but, as the warlock says, it is very messy. Surprisingly tasteful even with occasional gore and truly ghastly monsters; in fact this pic could have used a bit more intensity.**CW:** Language and violence. 108m/C VHS. John Terry, Jane Sibbett, Chris Sarandon; **D:** Dan O'Bannon; **M:** Richard Band. LIV

Resurrection 1980 (PG) After a near-fatal car accident, a woman finds she has the power to heal others by touch. She denies that God is responsible, much to her Bible Belt community's dismay. Acclaimed and well-acted. 103m/C VHS, Beta. Ellen Burstyn, Sam Shepard, Roberts Blossom, Eva LeGallienne, Clifford David, Richard Farnsworth, Pamela Payton-Wright; **D:** Daniel Petrie; **W:** Lewis John Carlino; **M:** Maurice Jarre. National Board of Review Awards '80: 10 Best Films of the Year, Best Supporting Actress (LeGallienne); Nominations: Academy Awards '80: Best Actress (Burstyn), Best Supporting Actress (LeGallienne). USH

Resurrection of Zachary Wheeler 1971 (G) A presidential candidate, who narrowly escaped death in an auto crash, is brought to a mysterious clinic in New Mexico. A reporter sneaks into the clinic and discovers the horrors of cloning. 100m/C VHS, Beta. Angie Dickinson, Bradford Dillman, Leslie Nielsen, Jack Carter, James Daly; **D:** Bob Wynn. NO

Retreat, Hell! 1952 Korean War drama about the retreat from the Changjin Reservoir. Standard gun-ho military orientation with dismal results. 95m/B VHS. Frank Lovejoy, Richard Carlson, Russ Tamblyn, Anita Louise; **D:** Joseph H. Lewis. REP

Retribution 1988 (R) Struggling artist survives suicide attempt only to find himself possessed by the spirit of a criminal who was tortured to death. Seeing the hood's gruesome demise in his dreams, the survivor sets out to bring his murderers face-to-face with their maker. 106m/C VHS, Beta, LV. Dennis Lipscomb, Hoyt Axton, Leslie Wing, Suzanne Snyder; **D:** Guy Magar. NO

Retrievers 1982 Young man and a former CIA agent team up to expose the unsavory practices of the organization. 90m/C VHS, Beta. Max Thayer, Roselyn Royce. VES

The Return woof! *The Alien's Return* 1980 (PG) Vincent and Shepherd meet as adults and discover that they had both, as children, been visited by aliens who had given technology to a cattle-mutilating prospector. A mess with no idea of what sort of film it wants to be. 91m/C VHS, Beta. Cybill Shepherd, Raymond Burr, Jan-Michael Vincent, Martin Landau, Vincent Schiavelli, Zachary Vincent, Farah Bunch, Neville Brand, Susan Kiger; **D:** Greydon Clark. NO

Return 1988 (R) A woman believes that the man she loves is the reincarnation of her dead grandfather. Interesting concept, but overall, a disappointing mystery. 78m/C VHS, Beta, LV. Frederic Forrest, Anne Francis, Karlene Crockett, John Walcutt, Lisa Richards; **D:** Andrew Silver. ACA

Return Engagement 1978 A lonely middle-aged ancient history professor falls in love with one of her students. 76m/C VHS, Beta. Elizabeth Taylor, Joseph Bottoms, Peter Donat, James Ray; **D:** Joseph Hardy. NO

Return Fire 1991 (R) A former employee of the government finds that he must now fight the system if he wants to save his son. Trivial action fare. 97m/C VHS. Adam West, Ron Marchini. AIP

Return from Witch Mountain 1978 (G) A pair of evil masterminds use a boy's supernatural powers to place Los Angeles in nuclear jeopardy. Sequel to Disney's ever-popular "Escape to Witch Mountain." 93m/C VHS, Beta. Christopher Lee, Bette Davis, Ike Eisenmann, Kim Richards, Jack Soo; **D:** John Hough; **W:** Malcolm Marmorstein. DIS

The Return of a Man Called Horse 1976 (PG) Sequel to "A Man Called Horse" tells the story of an English aristocrat who was captured and raised by Sioux Indians, and then returned to his native homeland. Contains more of the torture scenes for which this series is famous, but not much of Harris. 125m/C VHS, Beta. Richard Harris, Gale Sondergaard, Geoffrey Lewis; **D:** Irvin Kershner; **W:** Jack DeWitt; **C:** Owen Roizman. FOX

The Return of Boston Blackie 1927 The oft-filmed crook/detective tries to retrieve an heiress's stolen jewels. Silent. 77m/B VHS, Beta. Raymond Glenn, Corliss Palmer, Strongheart, Rosemary Cooper, Coit Albertson; **D:** Harry Hoyt. VYY, GPV, FCT

Return of Captain Invincible 1983 (PG) Arkin is a derelict super-hero persuaded to fight crime again in this unique spoof. One liners fly faster than a speeding bullet. Lee gives one of his best performances as the mad scientist. Musical numbers by Rocky Horror's O'Brien and Hartley sporadically interrupt. Made on a shoe-string budget, offbeat film is entertaining but uneven. 90m/C VHS, Beta, LV. AU Alan Arkin, Christopher Lee, Kate Fitzpatrick, Bill Hunter, Graham Kennedy, Michael Pate, Hayes Gordon, Max Phipps, Noel Ferrier; **D:** Philippe Mora; **W:** Steven E. de Souza. NO

The Return of Casey Jones *Train 2419* 1934 Early adventure film featuring lots of great railroad action. 64m/B VHS. Charles Starrett, Ruth Hall, George "Gabby" Hayes, Robert Elliott, Margaret Seddon, Jackie Searl; **D:** John P. McCarthy. GPV

Return of Chandu 1934 This serial in 12 chapters features Bela Lugosi as Chandu, who exercises his magical powers to conquer a religious sect of cat worshippers inhabiting the island of Lemuria. In the process, he fights to save the Princess Nadji from being sacrificed by them. 156m/B VHS, Beta. Bela Lugosi, Maria Alba, Clara Kimball Young; **D:** Ray Taylor. DVT, NOS, SNC

The Return of Count Yorga 1971 (R) The vampire Count returns, taking up residence in a decrepit mansion nearby an orphanage. There he spies the toothsome Cynthia and Yorga decides to make her a vampiric bride. But the Count reckons without Cynthia's noble boyfriend who wants to keep his honey on this side of the grave. Preceded by "Count Yorga, Vampire."**CW:** Some horror violence. 97m/C VHS. Robert Quarry, Mariette Hartley, Roger Perry, Yvonne Wilder, Rudy DeLuca, George Macready, Walter Brooke; **D:** Bob Kelljan; **W:** Yvonne Wilder, Bob Kelljan. ORI

The Return of Dr. Mabuse Im Stahlnetz Des Dr. Mabuse; Phantom Fiend 1961 The evil doctor is back, this time sending his entranced slaves to attack a nuclear power plant. Frobe, the inspector, and Barker, the FBI man, team up to thwart him. Fun for fans of serial detective stories. 88m/B VHS, Beta. GE FR IT Gert Frobe, Lex Barker, Daliah Lavi, Wolfgang Preiss, Fausto Tozzi, Rudolph Forster; **D:** Harald Reinl. SNC

Return of Dracula *The Curse of Dracula* 1958 Low-budget film about the Count killing a Czech artist and assuming his identity as he makes his way to the States. Once there, he moves in with the dead man's family and begins acting rather strangely. Retitled "The Curse of Dracula" for TV. 77m/C VHS. Francis Lederer, Norma Eberhardt, Ray Stricklyn, Jimmie Baird; **D:** Paul Landres. MGM, FCT

Return of Draw Egan 1916 Vintage silent western wherein Hart is an outlaw-turned-greenhorn sheriff of a lawless town. Music score. 64m/B VHS, Beta, 8mm. William S. Hart, Louise Glaum; **D:** William S. Hart. VYY, GPV, GVV

The Return of Eliot Ness 1991 Ness comes out of retirement in 1947 Chicago to track down a friend's killer. And with Al Capone dead, Chicago mob bosses are fighting for their piece of illegal turf. Stack reprises his "The Untouchables" TV role from the early '60s in this made for TV movie. 94m/C VHS. Robert Stack, Charles Durning, Philip Bosco, Jack Coleman, Lisa Hartman Black, Anthony De Sando; **D:** James A. Contner. APX

Return of Frank Cannon 1980 Portly private eye Frank Cannon comes out of retirement to investigate the alleged suicide of an old friend. Made for television. 96m/C VHS, Beta. William Conrad, Diana Muldaur, Joanna Pettet, Allison Argo, Arthur Hill, Ed Nelson; **D:** Corey Allen; **M:** Bruce Broughton. WOV

Return of Frank James 1940 One of Lang's lesser Hollywood works, this is nonetheless an entertaining sequel to 1939's "Jesse James." Brother Frank tries to go straight, but eventually has to hunt down the culprits who murdered his infamous outlaw sibling. Tierney's first film. 92m/C VHS, Beta, LV, **Closed Caption.** Henry Fonda, Gene Tierney, Jackie Cooper, Henry Hull, John Carradine, Donald Meek, J. Edward Bromberg; **D:** Fritz Lang. FOX

The Return of Grey Wolf 1922 A wild dog must fight for survival in Northern Quebec and is befriended by a fur trapper. An intelligent hound, he repays the trapper's generosity by helping him put the moves on some fur thieves. Silent. 62m/B VHS, Beta, 8mm. Helen Lynch, Henry Pierce. VYY

The Return of Jafar 1994 (G) Clumsy thief Abis Mal inadvertently releases evil sorcerer Jafar from his lamp prison and now the powerful "genie Jafar" plots his revenge. So it's up to Aladdin and friends to save the Sultan's kingdom once again. Contains five new songs. ♫Just Forget About Love; Nothing In the World (Quite Like a Friend); I'm Looking Out for Me; You're Only Second Rate; Arabian Nights. 66m/C VHS, LV, **Closed Caption. W:** Kevin Campbell, Mirith J.S. Colao; **V:** Scott Weinger, Linda Larkin, Gilbert Gottfried, Val Bettin, Dan Castellaneta. DIS

Return of Jesse James 🎬🎬 1950
Look-alike of dead outlaw Jesse James joins in with some former members of the James Gang, leading townsfolk to believe the notorious bank robber never died. It's up to brother Frank James, now an upstanding citizen, to set the record straight. A little slow moving at times, but still worth viewing. **77m/B VHS, Beta.** John Ireland, Ann Dvorak, Reed Hadley, Henry Hull, Hugh O'Brian, Tommy Noonan, Peter Marshall; **D:** Arthur Hilton. *NO*

The Return of Josey Wales 🎬 1986
(R) No match for the original featuring Clint Eastwood, the title character is played woodenly by Parks. This installment finds Wales pitted against a bumbling lawman. Sequel to 1976's "The Outlaw Josey Wales." **90m/C VHS.** Michael Parks, Rafael Campos, Bob Magruder, Paco Vela, Everett Sifuentes, Charlie McCoy; **D:** Michael Parks. *HHE*

The Return of Martin Guerre 🎬🎬🎬½
Le Retour de Martin Guerre 1983 In this medieval tale, a dissolute village husband disappears soon after his marriage. Years later, someone who appears to be Martin Guerre returns, allegedly from war, and appears much kinder and more educated. Starring in a love story of second chances, Depardieu does not disappoint, nor does the rest of the cast. In French with English subtitles. Based on an actual court case. Remade in 1993 as "Sommersby." **111m/C VHS.** *FR* Gerard Depardieu, Roger Planchon, Maurice Jacquemont, Barnard Pierre Donnadieu, Nathalie Baye; **D:** Daniel Vigne; **W:** Daniel Vigne, Jean-Claude Carriere. Cesar Awards '83: Best Writing, Best Score; National Society of Film Critics Awards '83: Best Actor (Depardieu); Nominations: Academy Awards '83: Best Costume Design. *FXL, APD, HMV*

The Return of Our Gang 🎬½ 1925
Contains three vintage silent Pathe "Our Gang" shorts: "The School Play (Stage Fright)," "Summer Daze (The Cobbler)," and "Dog Days." **57m/B VHS, Beta, 8mm.** Joe Cobb, Ernie Morrison, Mickey Daniels, Farina Hoskins, Mary Kornman, Jackie Condon, Jack Davis, Jannie Hoskins, Andy Samuels, Eugene Jackson. *VYY*

The Return of Peter Grimm 🎬🎬½
1935 Man returns from death to try to tidy up the mess he left behind. Enjoyable if trite fantasy based on a play by David Belasco. **82m/B VHS.** Lionel Barrymore, Helen Mack, Edward Ellis, Donald Meek, George Breakston, James Bush; **D:** George Nicholls Jr. *TTC, FCT*

The Return of Spinal Tap 🎬🎬½
1992 Cult-fave mock rock group Spinal Tap is back with a feature-length video of performance and backstage footage from its recent reunion concert tour promoting their album "Break Like the Wind." Sequel to "This is Spinal Tap" features lots of heavy metal songs including the title track, "Majesty of Rock," "Bitch School," "Diva Fever," "Clam Caravan," and "Stinkin' Up the Great Outdoors." Not as great as the original satire, but will appeal to Spinal Tap fans. **110m/C VHS, LV.** Christopher Guest, Michael McKean, Harry Shearer, Rick Parnell, C.J. Vanston; **Cameos:** Paul Anka, Jeff Beck, Jamie Lee Curtis, Richard Lewis, Martha Quinn, Kenny Rogers, Martin Short, Mel Torme; **W:** Christopher Guest, Michael McKean, Harry Shearer. *MPI, MVD*

Return of Superfly 🎬 1990 **(R)** Man with
insect moniker pesters drug dealers and cops in Harlem. Long-awaited sequel to urban epic "Superfly," scored again by Mayfield. **94m/C VHS, Closed Caption.** Margaret Avery, Nathan Purdee, Sam Jackson; **M:** Ice-T, Curtis Mayfield. *THV*

The Return of Swamp Thing 🎬½
1989 **(PG-13)** The DC Comics creature rises again out of the muck to fight mutants and evil scientists. Tongue-in-cheek, and nothing at all like the literate, ecologically-oriented comic from which it was derived. **95m/C VHS, Beta, LV, Closed Caption.** Louis Jourdan, Heather Locklear, Sarah Douglas, Dick Durock; **D:** Jim Wynorski. *COL*

Return of the Aliens: The Deadly Spawn 🎬
The Deadly Spawn 1983 **(R)** Aliens infect the earth and violently destroy humans. Extremely violent and gory. Watch out for those officious offspring. **90m/C VHS.** Charles George Hildebrandt; **D:** Douglas McKeown. *NO*

Return of the Ape Man 🎬🎬 1944
Campy fun with Carradine and Lugosi. A mad scientist transplants Carradine's brain into the body of the "missing link." Hams galore. **51m/B VHS.** Bela Lugosi, John Carradine, George Zucco, Judith Gibson, Michael Ames, Frank Moran, Mary Currier; **D:** Phil Rosen. *MED*

Return of the Bad Men 🎬🎬 1948
Scott is a retired marshall who must fight against a gang of outlaws lead by the Sundance Kid. Sequel to "Badman's Territory." **90m/C VHS, Beta, Closed Caption.** Randolph Scott, Robert Ryan, Anne Jeffreys, George "Gabby" Hayes, Jason Robards Sr., Jacqueline White; **D:** Ray Enright; **W:** Charles "Blackie" O'Neal. *CCB, MED, TTC*

The Return of the Borrowers 🎬🎬🎬
1996 Sweet sequel to 1993's "The Borrowers" finds the six-inch Clock family—father Pod (Holm), mother Homily (Wilton), and teenaged daughter Arrietty (Callard)—having to find a new home. Lots of misadventures ensue as they must avoid nasty humans, a giant bee, a storm, and other dangers on their way to safety. Based on the novels by Mary Norton. **165m/C VHS.** *GB* Ian Holm, Penelope Wilton, Rebecca Callard, Sian Phillips, Tony Haygarth, Judy Parfitt, Ben Chaplin, Paul Cross, Pamela Cundell, Ross McCall, Richard Vernon, Danny Newman; **D:** John Henderson; **W:** Richard Carpenter; **C:** Clive Tucker; **M:** Howard Goodall. *TTC*

Return of the Chinese Boxer 🎬
1974 Samurai and ninja warriors fight, usually to the death. **93m/C VHS, Beta.** Jimmy Wang Yu, Lung Fei, Cheung Ying Chen, Chin Kang. *UNI*

Return of the Dragon 🎬🎬½ 1973 **(R)**
In Lee's last picture, a Chinese restaurant in Rome is menaced by gangsters who want to buy the property. On behalf of the owners, Lee duels an American karate champ in the Roman forum. The battle scenes between Lee and Norris are great and make this a must-see for martial arts fans. **91m/C VHS, Beta, LV, Closed Caption.** *CH* Bruce Lee, Nora Miao, Chuck Norris; **D:** Bruce Lee. *FOX, GEM*

Return of the Evil Dead 🎬
Return of the Blind Dead 1975 The sightless dead priests return to attack still more 1970s' Europeans in this second installment of the "blind dead" trilogy. Preceded by "Tombs of the Blind Dead" and followed by "Horror of the Zombies." Not to be confused with Raimi's "Evil Dead" slasher flicks. **85m/C VHS.** *SP PT* Tony Kendall, Esther Roy, Frank Blake; **D:** Armando de Ossorio. *JEF*

Return of the Family Man 🎬 1989 A
mass murderer seems unstoppable as he continues to slash whole families at a time...the family man is redefined in this bloody gore-fest. **90m/C VHS.** Ron Smerczak, Liam Cundill, Terence Reis, Michelle Constant; **D:** John Murlowski. *NO*

Return of the Fly 🎬🎬 1959 The son of
the scientist who discovered how to move matter through space decides to continue his father's work, but does so against his uncle's wishes. He soon duplicates his dad's experiments with similar results. This sequel to "The Fly" doesn't buzz like the original. Followed by "Curse of the Fly." **80m/B VHS, Beta, LV.** Vincent Price, Brett Halsey, John Sutton, Dan Seymour, David Frankham; **D:** Edward L. Bernds. *FOX, FCT*

Return of the Jedi 🎬🎬🎬½ 1983 **(PG)**
Third film in George Lucas' popular space saga. Against seemingly fearsome odds, Luke Skywalker battles such worthies as Jabba the Hut and heavy-breathing Darth Vader to save his comrades and triumph over the evil Galactic Empire. Han and Leia reaffirm their love and team with C3PO, R2-D2, Chewbacca, Calrissian, and a bunch of furry Ewoks to aid in the annihilation of the Dark Side. The special effects are still spectacular, even the third time around. Sequel to "Star Wars" (1977) and "The Empire Strikes Back" (1980). **132m/C VHS, Beta, LV, Closed Caption.** Mark Hamill, Carrie Fisher, Harrison Ford, Billy Dee Williams, David Prowse, James Earl Jones, Kenny Baker, Denis Lawson, Anthony Daniels, Peter Mayhew; **D:** Richard Marquand; **W:** George Lucas, Lawrence Kasdan; **M:** John Williams; **V:** Alec Guinness, Frank Oz. Academy Awards '83: Best Visual Effects; People's Choice Awards '84: Best Film; Nominations: Academy Awards '83: Best Art Direction/Set Decoration, Best Sound, Best Original Score. *FOX, RDG, HMV*

Return of the Killer Tomatoes! 🎬
1988 **(PG)** The man-eating plant-life from 1977's "Attack of the Killer Tomatoes" is back, able to turn into people due to the slightly larger budget. Astin is mad as the scientist. Not as bad as "Attack," representing a small hurdle in the history of filmdom. Followed by "Killer Tomatoes Strike Back." **98m/C VHS, Beta, LV, Closed Caption.** Anthony Starke, George Clooney, Karen Mistal, Steve Lundquist, John Astin, Charlie Jones, Rock Peace, Frank Davis, C.J. Dillon, Teri Weigel; **D:** John DeBello; **W:** John DeBello. *VTR, NWV*

The Return of the King 🎬🎬 1980 The third
and final animated episode of J.R.R Tolkien's Middle Earth Trilogy. This saga features Frodo, relative to Hobbit Bilbo Baggins, and his faithful servant, making middle Earth safe from Orcs, Gollums and other ooky creatures. **120m/C VHS. D:** Arthur Rankin Jr., Jules Bass; **V:** Orson Bean, Roddy McDowall, John Huston, Theodore Bikel, William Conrad, Glen Yarborough, Paul Frees, Casey Kasem, Sonny Melendrez. *XVC, VTR, FAF*

Return of the Lash 🎬 1947 Lash LaRue
once again defends settlers' rights from ruthless outlaws. **53m/B VHS, Beta.** Lash LaRue, Al "Fuzzy" St. John, Mary Maynard, George Chesebro; **D:** Ray Taylor. *COL*

Return of the Living Dead 🎬🎬½
1985 **(R)** Poisonous gas revives a cemetery and a morgue rendering an outrageous spoof on the living-dead sub-genre with fast-moving zombies, punk humor, and exaggerated gore. Its humor does not diminish the fear factor, however. Sequel follows. Directed by "Alien" writer O'Bannon. **90m/C VHS, Beta, LV.** Clu Gulager, James Karen, Linnea Quigley, Don Calfa, Jewel Shepard; **D:** Dan O'Bannon. *NO*

Return of the Living Dead 2 🎬½
1988 **(R)** An inevitable sequel to the original Dan O'Bannon satire about George Romero-esque brain-eating zombies attacking suburbia with zest and vigor. **89m/C VHS, Beta, LV, Closed Caption.** Dana Ashbrook, Marsha Dietlein, Philip Bruns, James Karen, Thom Mathews; **D:** Ken Wiederhorn; **C:** Robert Elswit. *ORI, WAR*

Return of the Living Dead 3 🎬½
1993 **(R)** When Curt's girlfriend Julie dies in a motorcycle accident you'd think that would be the end of romance. But not when your dad heads a secret project that involves reviving corpses. Only problem is now Julie's a zombie with long metal claws and glass spikes sticking out of various body parts. Hey, if it's true love Curt will get over it. Macabre special effects. Also available unrated.**CW:** Extreme violence. **97m/C VHS, LV, Closed Caption.** Mindy Clarke, J. Trevor Edmond, Kent McCord, Basil Wallace, Fabio Urena; **D:** Brian Yuzna; **W:** John Penney; **M:** Barry Goldberg. *THV*

Return of the Man from U.N.C.L.E. 🎬🎬 1983 Those dashing super
agents Napoleon Solo and Illya Kuryakin come out of retirement to settle an old score with their nemesis THRUSH. Made for television. **96m/C VHS, Beta.** Robert Vaughn, David McCallum, Patrick Macnee, Gayle Hunnicutt, Geoffrey Lewis; **D:** Ray Austin. *TWE*

The Return of the Musketeers 🎬🎬½ 1989 **(PG)** Lester's third
Musketeers film (after his successful double-act in the '70s) is a good-natured but average costume/comedy/buddy film. Twenty years after D'Artagnan, Athos, Porthos, and Aramis saved

the French queen from scandal it's time to do it all over again. Milady DeWinter, who hatched the first plot, is dead but her equally devious daughter Justine is more than able to take mama's scheming place. Just to add a little more excitement Athos' adopted son Raoul meets Justine and passions fly amidst the swordplay. Based on the Alexandre Dumas novel "Twenty Years After." **103m/C VHS, LV, Closed Caption.** *GB FR SP* Michael York, Oliver Reed, Frank Finlay, Richard Chamberlain, Kim Cattrall, C. Thomas Howell, Geraldine Chaplin, Roy Kinnear, Christopher Lee, Philippe Noiret, Jean-Pierre Cassel, Billy Connolly, Eusebio Lazaro; *D:* Richard Lester; *W:* George MacDonald Fraser. *USH, BTV, FCT*

The Return of the Native 🎬🎬½
1994 (PG) Wind-swept moors, a tempestuous heroine, two loves, and requisite tragedy all courtesy of Thomas Hardy's 1878 novel. Beautiful Eustacia Vye (Jones) longs to leave the boredom of Egdon Heath—even though she's involved with the roguish Damon Wildeve (Owen). Then businessman Clym Yeobright (Stevenson) returns from Paris and captures Eustacia's fancy. She marries him in the hope they'll return to the continent but she's bitterly disappointed when Clym wants to remain in Egdon. Meanwhile, Damon has married Clym's gentle cousin Thomasin (Skinner) but he and Eustacia can't seem to stay away from each other, leading to storms for all. **99m/C VHS, Closed Caption.** Catherine Zeta Jones, Clive Owen, Ray Stevenson, Claire Skinner, Joan Plowright, Steven Mackintosh, Celia Imrie, Paul Rogers; *D:* Jack Gold; *W:* Robert W. Lenski; *M:* Carl Davis. *REP*

Return of the Pink Panther 🎬🎬½
1974 (G) Bumbling Inspector Clouseau is called upon to rescue the Pink Panther diamond stolen from a museum. Sellers manages to produce mayhem with a vacuum cleaner and other devices that, in his hands, become instruments of terror. Clever opening credits. Fourth installment in the Pink Panther series but the first with Sellers since 1964's "A Shot In The Dark." **113m/C VHS, Beta, LV.** Peter Sellers, Christopher Plummer, Catherine Schell, Herbert Lom, Victor Spinetti; *D:* Blake Edwards; *W:* Frank Waldman, Blake Edwards; *C:* Geoffrey Unsworth; *M:* Henry Mancini. *FOX, FHE, FCT*

Return of the Rebels 🎬🎬
1981 Made for television fluff with Eden as a motorcycle matron whose campground is rid of riff-raff by the crow-lined participants in a 25-year reunion of a biker gang. **100m/C VHS.** Barbara Eden, Robert Mandan, Jamie Farr, Patrick Swayze, Don Murray, Christopher Connelly; *D:* Noel Nosseck. *NO*

Return of the Scorpion 🎬
1980 Big trouble abounds as that crazy kung fu guy, the "Scorpion," comes back to town. **90m/C VHS, Beta.** Yang Pan Pan, Lam Men Wei, Philip Ko. *NO*

Return of the Secaucus 7 🎬🎬🎬½
1980 Centers around a weekend reunion of seven friends who were activists during the Vietnam War in the turbulent '60s. Now turning 30, they evaluate their present lives and progress. Writer and director Sayles plays Howie in this excellent example of what a low-budget film can and should be. A less trendy predecessor of "The Big Chill" (1983) which, perhaps, was a few years ahead of its time. **110m/C VHS, Beta.** Mark Arnott, Gordon Clapp, Maggie Cousineau-Arndt, David Strathairn; *D:* John Sayles; *W:* John Sayles; *M:* Mason Daring. Los Angeles Film Critics Association Awards '80: Best Screenplay. *COL*

Return of the Seven 🎬🎬
Return of the Magnificent Seven **1966** The first sequel to "The Magnificent Seven" features the group liberating a compatriot who is held hostage. Yawn. **97m/C VHS, Beta.** Yul Brynner, Warren Oates, Robert Fuller, Claude Akins; *D:* Burt Kennedy; *W:* Larry Cohen; *C:* Paul Vogel; *M:* Elmer Bernstein. Nominations: Academy Awards '66: Best Adapted Score. *MGM*

Return of the Soldier 🎬🎬🎬
1982 A shell-shocked WWI veteran has no memory of his marriage, leaving his wife, his childhood flame, and an unrequited love to vie for his affections. Adapted from the novel by Rebecca West. **101m/C**

VHS, Beta. *GB* Glenda Jackson, Julie Christie, Ann-Margret, Alan Bates, Ian Holm, Frank Finlay; *D:* Alan Bridges; *M:* Richard Rodney Bennett. *NO*

Return of the Street Fighter 🎬½
197? Sequel to "The Street Fighter," finds Terry Tsuguri (Chiba) hired by a gang to silence a jailed informer. So, Terry gets arrested, practices his karate and does the guy in, and finds out the gang now wants to silence him. Big mistake! Notice a pattern yet? Followed by "The Street Fighter's Last Revenge" and "Sister Street Fighter." **88m/C VHS.** Sonny Chiba. *NLC*

Return of the Tall Blond Man With One Black Shoe 🎬🎬½
1974 Sequel to 1972's "The Tall Blond Man With One Black Shoe." Again a "klutz" is mistaken for a master spy and becomes unknowingly involved in the world of international intrigue. In French with English subtitles. Not quite as good as the original. **84m/C VHS, Beta.** *FR* Pierre Richard, Mireille Darc, Michael Duchaussoy, Jean Rochefort, Jean Carmet; *D:* Yves Robert; *W:* Francis Veber; *M:* Vladimir Cosma. *CVC, PSM*

Return of the Tiger 🎬½
1978 The Hoover Night Club in Bangkok fronts the operations of an international narcotics group headed by an American. When a rival Chinese gang tries to dominate the drug market, conflict and lots of kicking ensue. **95m/C VHS, Beta.** Bruce Li, Paul Smith, Chaing I, Angela Mao; *D:* Jimmy Shaw. *MED*

Return of the Vampire 🎬🎬
1943 A Hungarian vampire and his werewolf servant seek revenge on the family who drove a spike through his heart two decades earlier. **69m/B VHS, Beta, LV.** Bela Lugosi, Nina Foch, Miles Mander, Matt Willis, Frieda Inescort, Roland Varno; *D:* Lew (Louis Friedlander) Landers, Kurt Neumann. *GKK, MLB*

Return of Wildfire 🎬½
1948 Two sisters are left to run the family horse ranch when their brother is killed. A drifter aids the sisters in bringing the murderer to justice. **83m/B VHS, Beta.** Richard Arlen, Patricia Morison, Mary Beth Hughes. *NO*

Return to Africa 🎬🎬
1989 Rebels threaten the familial paradise of the tightknit Mallory clan. **95m/C VHS, Beta.** Stan Brock, Anne Collings, David Tors, Ivan Tors, Peter Tors, Steven Tors; *D:* Leslie Martinson. *PSM*

Return to Boggy Creek 🎬🎬
1977 (PG) Townspeople in a small fishing village learn from a photographer that a "killer" beast, whom they thought had disappeared, has returned and is living in Boggy Creek. Some curious children follow the shutterbug into the marsh, despite hurricane warnings, and the swamp monster reacts with unusual compassion. OK for the kiddies. Fictitious story unlike other "Boggy Creek" films, which are billed as semi-documentaries. Sequel to "Legend of Boggy Creek" and features Mary Ann from "Gilligan's Island." **87m/C VHS, Beta.** Dawn Wells, Dana Plato, Louise Belaire, John Hofeus; *D:* Tom Moore. *FOX*

Return to Earth 🎬🎬
1976 Made for television drama deals with the self-doubts faced by Apollo 11 astronaut Buzz Aldrin after his triumphant return to Earth. Based on Aldrin's own novel. **74m/C VHS, Beta.** Cliff Robertson, Shirley Knight, Ralph Bellamy, Stefanie Powers, Charles Cioffi; *D:* Jud Taylor. *TWE*

Return to Eden 🎬🎬
1989 A young woman falls in love with her philosophy tutor, but she can't return her affections. An interesting comparison between the passion of the primitive and the tangle of modern-day romance. **90m/C VHS.** Sam Bottoms, Edward Binns, Renee Coleman; *D:* William Olsen. *NO*

Return to Fantasy Island 🎬½
1977 Boss, boss, it's da plane! The second full-length television treatment of the once popular series wherein three couples get their most cherished fantasy fulfilled by Mr. Roarke. and company. **100m/C VHS, Beta.** Ricardo Montalban, Herve Villechaize, Adrienne Barbeau, Pat Crowley, Joseph Campanella, Karen Valentine, Laraine Day, George Maharis, Horst Buchholz,

France Nuyen, Joseph Cotten, Cameron Mitchell, George Chakiris; *D:* George McCowan. *PSM*

Return to Frogtown woof! 1992 (PG-13)
Sequel to "Hell Comes to Frogtown" finds Texas Rocket Ranger Ferrigno captured by mutant frogs. As unbelievably bad as it sounds. **90m/C VHS.** Lou Ferrigno, Charles Napier, Robert Z'Dar, Denice Duff, Don Stroud; *D:* Donald G. Jackson. *TPV, YHV*

Return to Horror High 🎬 1987 (R)
A horror movie producer makes a film in an abandoned and haunted high school, where a series of murders occurred years earlier. As in most "return" flicks, history repeats itself. **95m/C VHS, Beta.** Alex Rocco, Vince Edwards, Philip McKeon, Brendan Hughes, Lori Lethin, Scott Jacoby; *D:* Bill Froelich. *VTR, NWV*

Return to Lonesome Dove 🎬🎬½
1993 Routine sequel to successful western saga "Lonesome Dove" picks up after the burial of Gus McCrae in Texas by his friend, ex-Texas Ranger Woodrow F. Call (now played by Voight). The original dealt with a cattle drive, this one with horses. Along the way you'll run into the usual sidewinders as well as McCrae's lost love Clara (now Hershey) and Schroder, returning as Call's unacknowledged son Newt. Filmed on loction in Montana. TV production was already underway when author Larry McMurtry gave the producers his then unpublished sequel "Streets of Laredo" which differed from the script. Some changes were made but the book and miniseries don't match. **330m/C VHS, LV, Closed Caption.** Jon Voight, William L. Petersen, Rick Schroder, Barbara Hershey, Louis Gossett Jr., Oliver Reed, Reese Witherspoon, Nia Peeples, Dennis Haysbert, Timothy Scott, Barry Tubb, Chris Cooper, CCH Pounder, William Sanderson; *D:* Mike Robe; *W:* John Wilder. *CAF, FUS*

Return to Macon County 🎬🎬
1975 Tale of three young, reckless youths who become involved with drag racing and a sadistic law enforcement officer. Nolte turns in a good performance in his first film, as does Johnson, despite a mediocre script and dialogue. Sequel to 1974's "Macon County Line." **90m/C VHS, Beta.** Nick Nolte, Don Johnson, Robin Mattson; *D:* Richard Compton; *W:* Richard Compton. *LIV, VES*

Return to Mayberry 🎬🎬
1985 Andy Taylor returns to Mayberry after 20 years to obtain his old job as sheriff. Sixteen of the original actors reappeared for this nostalgia-fest. Made for television. **95m/C VHS, Beta.** Andy Griffith, Ron Howard, Don Knotts, Jim Nabors, Aneta Corsaut, Jack Dodson, George Lindsey, Betty Lynn; *D:* Bob Sweeney. *MCG*

Return to Oz 🎬🎬½
1985 (PG) Picking up where "The Wizard of Oz" left off, Auntie Em and Uncle Ed place Dorothy in the care of a therapist to cure her "delusions" of Oz. A natural disaster again lands her in the land of the yellow brick road, where the evil Nome King and Princess Mombi are spreading terror and squalor. Based on a later L. Frank Baum book. Enjoyable for the whole family although some scenes may frighten very small children. **109m/C VHS, Beta, LV.** Fairuza Balk, Piper Laurie, Matt Clark, Nicol Williamson, Jean Marsh; *D:* Walter Murch; *C:* David Watkin; *M:* David Shire. *DIS*

Return to Paradise 🎬🎬
1953 Cooper is a soldier of fortune wandering through the Polynesian islands in the late 1920s. On a remote atoll he comes across a crazy missionary intent upon subduing the native population. Cooper falls in love with a native beauty (Haynes in her screen debut) and leads the natives in a revolt against authority. Cliched but with nice scenery from the location shoot in Samoa. Loose adaptation of the short story "Mr. Morgan" by James Michener. **100m/C VHS, Beta.** Gary Cooper, Roberta Haynes, Barry Jones, John Hudson, Moira MacDonald; *D:* Mark Robson; *W:* Charles Kaufman. *MGM, FCT*

Return to Peyton Place ♂♂½ 1961 A young writer publishes novel exposing town as virtual Peyton Place, and the townsfolk turn against her and her family. Sequel to the scandalously popular '50s original and inspiration for the just-as-popular soap opera. Astor is excellent as the evil matriarch. 122m/C VHS, Closed Caption. Carol Lynley, Jeff Chandler, Eleanor Parker, Mary Astor, Robert Sterling, Luciana Paluzzi, Tuesday Weld, Brett Halsey, Bob Crane; D: Jose Ferrer. FOX, FCT

Return to Salem's Lot ♂♂ 1987 (R) Enjoyable camp sequel to the Stephen King tale, this time involving a cynical scientist and his son returning to the town only to find it completely run by vampires. 101m/C VHS, Beta, Closed Caption. Michael Moriarty, Ricky Addison Reed, Samuel Fuller, Andrew Duggan, Evelyn Keyes, Jill Gatsby, June Havoc, Ronee Blakley, James Dixon, David Holbrook; D: Larry Cohen; W: James Dixon, Larry Cohen. WAR

Return to Snowy River ♂♂♂ 1988 (PG) Continues the love story of the former ranch hand and the rancher's daughter in Australia's Victoria Alps that began in "The Man From Snowy River." Dennehy takes over from Kirk Douglas as the father who aims to keep the lovers apart. The photography of horses and the scenery is spectacular, making the whole film worthwhile. 99m/C VHS, Beta, LV. AU Tom Burlinson, Sigrid Thornton, Brian Dennehy, Nicholas Eadie, Mark Hembrow, Bryan Marshall; D: Geoff Burrowes; W: Geoff Burrowes. DIS, TVC

Return to the Blue Lagoon ♂ 1991 (PG-13) Neither the acting nor the premise has improved with age. Another photogenic adolescent couple experiences puberty on that island; for continuity, the young man is the son of the lovers in the first "Blue Lagoon." Breathtaking scenery—just turn down the sound. 102m/C VHS, LV, Closed Caption. Milla Jovovich, Brian Krause, Lisa Pelikan; D: William A. Graham; C: Robert Steadman. COL

Return to the Lost World ♂♂½ 1993 (PG) Rival scientists Challenger and Summerlee set out for the Lost World and find it threatened by oil prospectors. With a volcano about to explode the scientists set out to save their prehistoric paradise and its dinosaur inhabitants. Based on a story by Sir Arthur Conan Doyle. Sequel to "The Lost World." 99m/C VHS, Closed Caption. John Rhys-Davies, David Warner, Darren Peter Mercer, Geza Kovacs; D: Timothy Bond. WOV

Return to Two Moon Junction ♂½ 1993 (R) New York supermodel Savannah (Clarke) returns to her family's riverfront home in Georgia and promptly sheds her clothing for local sculptor Jake (Schafer). Must be something about the southern heat. This sequel should have the same video success as its predecessor since it keeps to the minimal plot/maximum teasing sex scenes outline. CW: Nudity. 96m/C VHS, LV, Closed Caption. Mindy Clarke, John Clayton Schafer, Louise Fletcher; D: Farhad Mann. THV

Reuben, Reuben ♂♂♂ 1983 (R) Brilliant, but drunken poet Conti turns himself around when he falls in love with earthy college girl McGillis in her film debut. The student's dog Reuben unwittingly alters Conti's progress, however, in the film's startling conclusion. Based on the writings of Peter DeVries. 100m/C VHS, Beta, Closed Caption. Tom Conti, Kelly McGillis, Roberts Blossom, E. Katherine Kerr, Cynthia Harris, Joel Fabiani, Kara Wilson, Lois Smith; D: Robert Ellis Miller; W: Julius J. Epstein; M: Billy Goldenberg. National Board of Review Awards '83: Best Actor (Conti); Writers Guild of America '83: Best Adapted Screenplay; Nominations: Academy Awards '83: Best Actor (Conti), Best Adapted Screenplay. FOX

Reunion ♂♂♂ 1988 (PG-13) Robards stars as a Jewish businessman, living in the U.S., who returns to his boyhood home of Stuttgart, Germany some 50 years after his leaving in 1933. He hopes to find out what happened to a boyhood school chum—the son of an aristocractic (and Aryan) German family. Film uses extensive flashbacks to show the the rise of anti-Semitism and how it affects the friendship of both youths. Thoughtful and well-acted though occasionally plodding drama based on Fred Uhlman's novel. 120m/C VHS, Beta, LV, Closed Caption. FR GE GB Jason Robards Jr., Christien Anholt, Sam West, Francoise Fabian, Maureen Kerwin, Barbara Jefford, Alexander Trauner; D: Jerry Schatzberg; W: Harold Pinter; C: Bruno de Keyzer. FRH, IME, FCT

Reunion in France ♂♂ Mademoiselle France; Reunion 1942 Parisian dress designer sacrifices her lifestyle to help an American flier flee France after the Nazis invade. Dated patriotic flag-waver. 104m/B VHS, Beta. Joan Crawford, John Wayne, Philip Dorn, Reginald Owen, Albert Basserman, John Carradine, Ann Ayars, J. Edward Bromberg, Henry Daniell, Moroni Olsen, Howard da Silva, Ava Gardner, John Considine; D: Jules Dassin. MGM

Revenge ♂½ Terror under the House; After Jenny Died; Inn of the Frightened People 1971 The parents of a girl who was brutally killed take the law into their own hands in this bloody, vengeful thriller. 89m/C VHS, Beta. GB Joan Collins, James Booth, Ray Barrett, Sinead Cusack, Kenneth Griffith; D: Sidney Hayers. MRV

Revenge woof! 1986 (R) Sequel to "Blood Cult" about a cult led by horror king Carradine. Seems these dog worshippers want McGowan's land and Senator Carradine will stop at nothing to get it. Woofer filled with gratuitous violence. 104m/C VHS, Beta. Patrick Wayne, John Carradine, Bennie Lee McGowan, Josef Hanet, Stephanie Kropke; D: Christopher Lewis. VCI

Revenge ♂♂ 1990 (R) Retired pilot Costner makes the mistake of falling in love with another man's wife. Quinn gives a first-rate performance as the Mexican crime lord who punishes his spouse and her lover, beginning a cycle of vengeance. Sometimes contrived, but artfully photographed with tantalizing love scenes. Based on the Jim Harrison novel. 123m/C VHS, Beta, LV, 8mm. Kevin Costner, Anthony Quinn, Madeleine Stowe, Sally Kirkland, Joe Santos, Miguel Ferrer, James Gammon, Tomas Milian; D: Tony Scott; W: Jim Harrison; M: Jack Nitzsche. COL

Revenge in the House of Usher ♂♂ 1982 House holds grudge. 90m/C VHS. Howard Vernon, Dan Villers; D: Jess (Jesus) Franco. MOV

Revenge of a Kabuki Actor ♂♂ 1963 When Kabuki actor Kazuo Hasegawa's parents are viciously murdered, he seeks their killer with a vengeance. In Japanese with English subtitles. 114m/C VHS. JP D: Kon Ichikawa. FST, FCT

Revenge of Doctor X woof! 198? A man/beast lies waiting for the pretty reporter who seeks her shipwrecked father in the jungles of an uncharted island. 90m/C VHS, Beta. John Ashley, Ronald Remy, Angelique Pettyjohn. NO

The Revenge of Frankenstein ♂♂½ 1958 Frankenstein (Cushing) is rescued from the guillotine by his dwarf servant and decides to relocate to Carlsbruck where he becomes the popular society physician, Dr. Stein. But the misunderstood doc just can't stop his ghoulish experiments and plans to transfer his servant's brain into another sewn together creature. Nicely macabre sequel to "The Curse of Frankenstein;" followed by "The Evil of Frankenstein." 89m/C VHS. GB Peter Cushing, Michael Gwynn, Francis Matthews, Oscar Quitak, Lionel Jeffries, Eunice Gayson, John Welsh; D: Terence Fisher; W: Jimmy Sangster. COL

Revenge of the Barbarians ♂ 1964 As the barbarians descend on Rome, Olympus must decide whether to save the empire or the beautiful Gallo, the woman he loves. Decisions, decisions. 99m/C Beta. Robert Alda, Anthony Steele. AIP

Revenge of the Barbarians ♂ 1985 A Scandinavian adventure about a young Celt seeking revenge against the Viking hordes that killed his family. 95m/C Beta. D: Hrafn Gunnlaugsson. NO

Revenge of the Cheerleaders ♂ 1976 (R) The cheerleaders pull out all the stops to save their school from a ruthless land developer. What spirit. 86m/C VHS, Beta. Jerii Woods, Cheryl "Rainbeaux" Smith, Helen Lang, Patrice Rohmer, Susie Elene, Eddra Gale, William Bramley, Carl Ballantine, David Hasselhoff; D: Richard Lerner. LIV

Revenge of the Creature ♂♂ 1955 In this follow up to "The Creature From the Black Lagoon," the Gill-man is captured in the Amazon and taken to a Florida marine park. There he is put on display for visitors and subjected to heartless experiments. Growing restless in his captive surroundings, the creature breaks free and makes for the ocean. Includes screen debut of Clint Eastwood as a lab technician. Originally shot in 3-D. Based on a story by William Alland. Available on laserdisc as part of a special Encore Edition Double Feature with "The Creature Walks Among Us." 82m/B VHS, LV, Closed Caption. John Agar, Lori Nelson, John Bromfield, John Wood, Nestor Paiva, Clint Eastwood; D: Jack Arnold; W: Martin Berkeley. USH, FCT

Revenge of the Dead ♂ 1984 (R) European archeological team discovers the existence of a powerful force that allows the dead to return to life. 100m/C VHS, Beta. IT Gabriele Lavia, Anne Canoras; D: Pupi Avati. LIV

Revenge of the Living Zombies ♂ 1988 (R) Teens on a Halloween hayride run headlong into flesh-craving zombies. Available in a slightly edited version. 85m/C VHS, Beta. Bill Hinzman, John Mowod, Leslie Ann Wick, Kevin Kindlan; D: Bill Hinzman. NO

Revenge of the Nerds ♂♂½ 1984 (R) When nerdy college freshmen are victimized by jocks, frat boys and the school's beauties, they start their own fraternity and seek revenge. Carradine and Edwards team well as the geeks in this better than average teenage sex comedy. Guess who gets the girls? Sequel was much worse. 89m/C VHS, Beta, LV, Closed Caption. Robert Carradine, Anthony Edwards, Timothy Busfield, Andrew Cassese, Curtis Armstrong, Larry B. Scott, Brian Tochi, Julia Montgomery, Michelle Meyrink, Ted McGinley, John Goodman, Bernie Casey; D: Jeff Kanew; W: Tim Metcalfe, Jeff Buhai; M: Thomas Newman. FOX

Revenge of the Nerds 2: Nerds in Paradise ♂ 1987 (PG-13) The nerd clan from the first film (minus Edwards who only makes a brief appearance) travels to Fort Lauderdale for a fraternity conference. They fend off loads of bullies and jocks with raunchy humor. Boy can Booger belch. Not as good as the first Nerds movie; a few laughs nonetheless. 89m/C VHS, Beta, LV, Closed Caption. Robert Carradine, Curtis Armstrong, Timothy Busfield, Andrew Cassese, Ed Lauter, Larry B. Scott, Courtney Thorne-Smith, Anthony Edwards, James Hong; D: Joe Roth. FOX

Revenge of the Nerds 3: The Next Generation ♂½ 1992 Adams College has nerd-loathing trustee Downey, Jr. mobilizing those frat boys against the bespectacled geeks, who turn to founding nerd Carradine to save them. Cookie-cutter characters and the gags won't hold your attention. Let's hope this is the last in the series. ?m/C VHS. Robert Carradine, Curtis Armstrong, Ted McGinley, Morton Downey Jr., Julia Montgomery. FXV

Revenge of the Nerds 4: Nerds in Love ♂♂½ 1994 Yes, even nerds deserve a little love. This time the gang get together for Booger's (Armstrong) wedding—complete with nerd bachelor party and wedding shower. Too bad Booger's future father-in-law is so reluctant to have a nerd in the family that he hires a sleazy detective to dig up some dirt. Made for TV. 90m/C VHS, Closed Caption. Curtis Armstrong, Robert Picardo, Ted McGinley, Larry B. Scott, Donald Gibb, Joseph Bologna, Julia Montgomery, Corinne Bohrer, Christina Pickles, Jessica Tuck, Robert Picardo; D: Steve Zacharias; W: Steve Zacharias, Steve Buhai. FXV

Revenge of the Ninja ♂♂½ 1983 (R)
Ninja Kosugi hopes to escape his past in Los Angeles. A drug trafficker, also ninja-trained, prevents him. The two polish off a slew of mobsters before their own inevitable showdown. Better-than the standard chop-socky fest from Cannon with amusing surreal touches like a battling grandma ninja. Sequel to "Enter the Ninja," followed by "Ninja III." **90m/C VHS, Beta.** Sho Kosugi, Arthur Roberts, Keith Vitali, Virgil Frye, Ashley Ferrare, Kane Kosugi, John Lamotta, Grace Oshita, Melvin C. Hampton, Mario Gallo; **D:** Sam Firstenberg; **W:** James R. Silke; **M:** Rob Walsh. *MGM*

Revenge of the Pink Panther ♂♂½ 1978 (PG) Inspector Clouseau survives his own assassination attempt, but allows the world to think he is dead in order to pursue an investigation of the culprits in his own unique, bumbling way. The last "Pink Panther" film before Sellers died, and perhaps the least funny. **99m/C VHS, Beta, LV.** Peter Sellers, Herbert Lom, Dyan Cannon, Robert Webber, Burt Kwouk, Robert Loggia; **D:** Blake Edwards; **W:** Blake Edwards, Ron Clark, Frank Waldman; **M:** Henry Mancini. *FOX, FCT*

Revenge of the Radioactive Reporter ♂♂ 1991 Nuclear plant honchos don't like journalist who's about to hang their dirty laundry, so they toss him into vat of nuclear waste. He returns as a reporter with a cosmetic peel. **90m/C VHS.** David Scammell, Kathryn Boese, Randy Pearlstein, Derrick Strange; **D:** Craig Pryce. *NO*

Revenge of the Red Baron ♂♂½ 1993 (PG-13) Jim Spencer (Rooney) is the WWI pilot who shot down Germany's fearsome Red Baron. Now aged and infirm he's tormented by what he thinks is his enemy's ghost. A vengeful ghost who takes after Spencer's family. **CW:** Language and violence. **90m/C VHS, LV.** Mickey Rooney, Toby Maguire, Laraine Newman, Cliff DeYoung; **D:** Robert Gordon; **W:** Michael James McDonald; **C:** Christian Sebaldt. *NHO*

Revenge of the Stepford Wives ♂½ 1980 Made for television sequel to the Ira Levin fantasy about suburban husbands who create obedient robot replicas of their wives. In this installment, the wives are not robots, but are simply made docile by drugs. Strange casting pairs Johnson and Kavner as husband and stepford wife. Begat "The Stepford Children." **95m/C VHS, Beta.** Sharon Gless, Julie Kavner, Don Johnson, Audra Lindley, Mason Adams, Arthur Hill; **D:** Robert Fuest. *NLC*

Revenge of the Teenage Vixens from Outer Space ♂♂ 1986 A low-budget film about three sex starved females from another planet who come to earth to find men. When the ones they meet do not live up to their expectations, the frustrated females turn the disappointing dudes are turned into vegetables. **84m/C VHS, Beta.** Lisa Schwedop, Howard Scott; **D:** Jeff Ferrell. *NO*

Revenge of the Virgins ♂ 1962 A tribe of topless 'Indian' women protect their sacred land from the white men. Exhumed exploitation for bad-film junkies, narrated by Kenne Duncan, an Ed Wood cohort. **53m/B VHS.** Jewell Morgan, Charles Veltman, Jodean Russo, Stanton Pritchard; **D:** Paul Perri. *NOS, SMW, VDM*

Revenge of the Zombies ♂½ 1943 In this sequel of sorts to "King of the Zombies," Carradine is creating an army of the undead for use by an evil foreign entity. **61m/B VHS.** John Carradine, Robert Lowery, Gale Storm, Veda Ann Borg, Mantan Moreland; **D:** Steve Sekely. *MLB*

Revenge of the Zombies ♂½ 1981 (R) Kung-fu exploitation film featuring man-eating alligators, zombies, mad magicians, and more. **?m/C VHS.** Ti Lung, Lily Tu. *LOO*

The Revenge Rider ♂♂ 1935 Orphan McCoy goes after the villains who killed his parents. Good performance from McCoy in an otherwise average film. **60m/B VHS.** Tim McCoy, Robert Allen, Billie Seward, Edward Earle, Jack Clifford, Lafe McKee; **D:** David Selman. *DVT, HEG*

The Revenger ♂ 1990 A framed man returns from prison and finds that a mobster has kidnapped his wife and wants $50,000 to give her back. **91m/C VHS, Beta.** Oliver Reed, Frank Zagarino; **D:** Cedric Sundstrom. *AIP*

Reversal of Fortune ♂♂♂½ 1990 (R) True tale of wealthy socialite Claus von Bulow (Irons) accused of deliberately giving his wife Sunny (Close) a near-lethal overdose of insulin. Comatose Close narrates history of the couple's courtship and married life, a saga of unhappiness and substance abuse, while Silver (as lawyer Dershowitz) et al prepare von Bulow's defense. An unflattering picture of the idle rich that never spells out what really happened. Irons is excellent as the eccentric and creepy defendant and richly deserved his Best Actor Oscar. From the novel by Dershowitz. **112m/C VHS, Beta, LV, 8mm, Closed Caption.** Jeremy Irons, Glenn Close, Ron Silver, Annabella Sciorra, Uta Hagen, Fisher Stevens, Julie Hagerty, Jack Gilpin, Christine Baranski; **D:** Barbet Schroeder; **W:** Nicholas Kazan. Academy Awards '90: Best Actor (Irons); Golden Globe Awards '91: Best Actor—Drama (Irons); Los Angeles Film Critics Association Awards '90: Best Actor (Irons), Best Screenplay; National Society of Film Critics Awards '90: Best Actor (Irons); Nominations: Academy Awards '90: Best Adapted Screenplay, Best Director (Schroeder). *WAR, FCT, BTV*

The Revolt of Job ♂♂♂ *Job Lazadasa* 1984 An elderly Jewish couple adopts an 8-year-old Gentile boy although it is illegal in WWII-torn Hungary and against the beliefs of the orthodox community. Moving story with fine performances. **98m/C VHS, Beta.** *GE HU* Fereno Zenthe, Hedi Tenessy; **D:** Imre Gyongyossy, Barna Kabay. *MGM, SWC*

Revolt of the Barbarians ♂ 1964 Ancient Rome is plagued by barbarian invasion and piracy. A consul travels to Gaul to try to put an end to their misdeeds. **?m/C VHS, Beta.** *IT* Roland Carey, Grazia Maria Spina, Mario Feliciani. *SNC*

Revolt of the Zombies ♂ 1936 A mad scientist learns the secret of bringing the dead to life and musters the zombies into an unique, gruesome military unit during WWI. Strange early zombie flick looks silly by today's standards. **65m/B VHS, Beta.** Dorothy Stone, Dean Jagger, Roy D'Arcy, Robert Noland, George Cleveland; **D:** Victor Halperin; **W:** Howard Higgin. *SNC, MLB, MRV*

Revolution ♂ 1985 (R) The American Revolution is the setting for this failed epic centering on an illiterate trapper and his son who find themselves caught up in the fighting. Long and dull, which is unfortunate, because the story had some potential. The cast is barely believable in their individual roles. Where did you get that accent, Al? **125m/C VHS, Beta, LV, Closed Caption.** *GB* Al Pacino, Donald Sutherland, Nastassia Kinski, Annie Lennox, Joan Plowright, Steven Berkoff, Dave King; **D:** Hugh Hudson; **W:** Robert Dillon. *WAR*

Revolution! A Red Comedy ♂♂♂ 1991 A group of students are lured away from their revolutionary tendencies by materialistic indulgences. This satirical comedy is in color and black and white. **84m/B VHS.** Kimberly Flynn, Christopher Renstrom, Georg Osterman; **D:** Jeff Kahn; **W:** Jeff Kahn. *NO*

Revolver ♂♂ 1992 (R) FBI agent Nick Sastro is paralyzed by an assassin's bullet when he tries to stop Aldo Testi, an arms and drug smuggler. But Nick decides to come out of retirement when a chance to nail Testi comes his way. **96m/C VHS, Closed Caption.** Robert Urich, Dakin Matthews, Steven Williams, Assumpta Serna; **D:** Gary Nelson. *COL*

Rhapsody ♂♂½ 1954 Taylor plays a wealthy woman torn between a famous young violinist and an equally talented pianist in this long and overdrawn soap opera. Although Taylor gives a superb performance, it's not enough to save this sugarcoated musical romance. Includes lush European scenery and sequences of classical music dubbed in by Claudio Arrau and Michael Rabin. Based on the adaptation of the Henry Handel Richardson novel "Maurice Guest." **115m/C VHS.** Elizabeth Taylor, Vittorio Gassman, John Ericson, Louis Calhern, Michael Chekhov, Barbara Bates, Celia Lovsky; **D:** Charles Vidor; **W:** Michael Kanin, Fay Kanin. *MGM*

Rhapsody in August ♂♂♂½ 1991 (PG) Talky family drama has four children spending the summer with their grandmother Kane in Nagasaki. They become obsessed with the memorials and bomb sites commemorating the dropping of the atomic bomb in 1945 and their grandmother's experiences. Then Kane's Eurasian nephew (Gere) comes for a visit, inciting more family discussions. Adapted from the novel "Nabe-no-Naka" by Kiyoko Murata. Minor Kurosawa; in Japanese with English subtitles. **98m/C VHS, LV.** *JP* Sachiko Murase, Narumi Kayashima, Hisashi Igawa, Richard Gere; **D:** Akira Kurosawa; **W:** Akira Kurosawa. *ORI*

Rhapsody in Blue ♂♂♂ 1945 Standard Hollywood biography of the great composer features whitewashed and non-existent characters to deal with the spottier aspects of Gershwin's life. Still, the music is the main attraction and it doesn't disappoint. ♫Rhapsody in Blue; Concerto in F; The Cuban Overture; Fascinatin' Rhythm; The Man I Love; Yankee Doodle Blues; Somebody Loves Me; Swanee; Mine. **139m/B VHS, LV.** Robert Alda, Joan Leslie, Alexis Smith, Charles Coburn, Julie Bishop, Albert Basserman, Morris Carnovsky, Rosemary De-Camp, Herbert Rudley, Charles Halton, Charles Shayne, Johnny Downs, Al Jolson; **D:** Irving Rapper; **W:** Howard Koch; **M:** George Gershwin, Max Steiner, Ira Gershwin. Nominations: Academy Awards '45: Best Sound, Scoring of a Musical. *MGM, FCT*

Rhinestone ♂ 1984 (PG) A country singer claims she can turn anyone, even a cabbie, into a singing sensation. Stuck with Stallone, Parton prepares her protege to sing at New York City's roughest country-western club, The Rhinestone. Only die-hard Dolly and Rocky fans need bother with this bunk. Some may enjoy watching the thick, New York accented Stallone learn how to properly pronounce dog ("dawg") in country lingo. Yee-haw. **111m/C VHS, Beta, LV, Closed Caption.** Sylvester Stallone, Dolly Parton, Ron Leibman, Richard Farnsworth, Tim Thomerson; **D:** Bob (Benjamin) Clark; **W:** Sylvester Stallone, Phil Alden Robinson. Golden Raspberry Awards '84: Worst Actor (Stallone), Worst Song ("Drinkenstein"). *FOX, OM*

Rhodes ♂♂½ *Rhodes of Africa* 1936 The story of Cecil Rhodes, a man who was instrumental in the Boer War in Africa and established the Rhodes Scholarships with $10 million, is told in this biography. Fine performance by Huston and Homolka. **91m/B VHS.** Walter Huston, Oscar Homolka, Basil Sydney, Frank Cellier, Peggy Ashcroft, Renne De Vaux, Percy Parsons, Bernard Lee, Ndanisa Kumalo; **D:** Berthold Viertel. *SNC, SNC*

Rhythm on the Range ♂♂½ 1936 Crosby stars as a singing cowboy who befriends freight car stowaway Farmer while transporting his prize steer back to his ranch in California. He invites her to his domicile and she falls in love with life on the range and with the rancher himself. Filled with lots of musical numbers, including an appearance from the Sons of the Pioneers featuring Roy Rogers. Comedy from Burns and Raye, who makes her feature film debut here, is as entertaining as always. Remade by Dean Martin and Jerry Lewis in 1956 as "Pardners." ♫I'm an Old Cowhand; Empty Saddles; I Can't Escape From You; The House That Jack Built for Jill; If You Can't Sing It You'll Have to Swing It; Round-up Lullaby; Drink It Down; Memories; Hang Up My Saddle. **88m/B VHS, Closed Caption.** Bing Crosby, Frances Farmer, Bob Burns, Martha Raye, Samuel S. Hinds, Warren Hymer, Lucile Watson; **D:** Norman Taurog; **W:** John Moffitt, Sidney Salkow, Walter DeLeon, Francis Martin; **C:** Karl Struss. *USH*

Rhythm on the River ♪♪½ 1940 Famous Broadway songwriter Rathbone has lost his magic touch so he hires melody maker Crosby to ghost for him while also hiring Martin to be the wordsmith. When the two fall in love they decide to strike off on their own but can't get their music heard since everyone assumes they've been co-pying Rathbone. Lots of backstage jokes with Rathbone terrific as an insecure egomaniac. ♪Rhythm on the River; When the Moon Comes Over Madison Square; Ain't It a Shame About Mame?; What Would Shakespeare Have Said?; Only Forever; That's for Me; I Don't Want to Cry Anymore. 94m/B VHS, Closed Caption. Bing Crosby, Mary Martin, Basil Rathbone, Oscar Levant, Oscar Shaw, Charley Grapewin, William Frawley, Charles Lane; D: Victor Schertzinger; W: Dwight Taylor; M: Victor Young. Nominations: Academy Awards '40: Best Song ("Only Forever"). USH

Rhythm Parade ♪♪ 1943 A woman takes off for Hawaii, leaving her infant in the care of an L.A. nightclub singer. A jealous rival of the singer takes the opportunity to cause problems. The thin plot serves as a vehicle for lots of singing. ♪Tootin' My Own Horn; Petticoat Army; Mimi From Tahiti; You're Drafted; Wait Till the Sun Shines Nellie; Sweet Sue; 'Neath the Yellow Moon In Old Tahiti. 68m/B VHS. Nils T. Granlund, Gale Storm, Robert Lowery, Margaret Dumont, Chick Chandler, Cliff Nazarro, Jan Wiley, Candy Candido, Yvonne De Carlo; D: Howard Bretherton. NOS, MLB

Rhythm Thief ♪♪ 1994 No-budget independent film finds alienated New York hustler Simon (Andrews) eking out a living selling tapes of local underground bands he has illegally recorded. He wants to be left alone but circumstances won't allow it. He's got one of the enraged bands after him, he's pestered by local "admirers," and his eccentric former girlfriend Marty (Daniels) suddenly turns up—severely shaking Simon's emotionally barren existence. Quirky character study gets lots of impact from tiny bucks. 88m/B VHS. Jason Andrews, Eddie Daniels, Kimberly Flynn, Kevin Corrigan, Sean Haggerty, Mark Alfred, Paul Rodriguez, Cynthia Sley; D: Matthew Harrison; W: Matthew Harrison, Christopher Grimm; C: Howard Krupa; M: Danny Brenner. Sundance Film Festival '95: Special Jury Prize; Nominations: Independent Spirit Awards '96: Debut Performance (Andrews). NYR

Ricco ♪♪ Summertime Killer 1974 (PG) A young man swears vengeance against the mobsters who killed his father. He kidnaps the daughter of a mafia kingpin and the battle begins. 90m/C VHS, Beta. FR IT SP Chris Mitchum, Karl Malden, Olivia Hussey, Raf Vallone, Claudine Auger, Gerard Tichy; D: Antonio Isasi. NO

Rich and Famous ♪♪ 1981 (R) The story of the 25-year friendship of two women, through college, marriage, and success. George Cukor's last film. 117m/C VHS, Beta, LV. Jacqueline Bisset, Candice Bergen, David Selby, Hart Bochner, Meg Ryan, Steven Hill, Michael Brandon, Matt Lattanzi; D: George Cukor; W: Gerald Ayres; M: Georges Delerue. Writers Guild of America '81: Best Adapted Screenplay. MGM

Rich and Strange ♪♪½ East of Shanghai 1932 Early Hitchcock movie is not in the same class as his later thrillers. A couple inherits a fortune and journeys around the world. Eventually the pair gets shipwrecked. 92m/B VHS, LV. GB Henry Kendall, Joan Barry, Betty Amann, Percy Marmont, Elsie Randolph; D: Alfred Hitchcock; W: Alfred Hitchcock, Alma Reville. REP, SNC, MLB

Rich Girl ♪ 1991 (R) A winsome, wealthy wench hides her millions by going to work in a rock'n'roll bar and falls in love with the local Bruce Springsteen wannabe. Despite the thick coating of music, sex, drugs and profanity, this consists of cliches that were old before talkies. Too earnestly-acted to be campy fun. Poor movie.CW: Language, drug content, and sensuality. 96m/C VHS, LV, Closed Caption. Jill Schoelen, Don Michael Paul, Ron Karabatsos, Sean Kanan, Willie Dixon, Paul Gleason; D: Joel Bender. COL

Rich Hall's Vanishing America 1986 Funnyman Hall travels across the country looking for the mail-order company that promised to give him a genuine Wilt Chamberlain basketball hoop. 50m/C VHS, Beta. Rich Hall, M. Emmet Walsh, Peter Isacksen, Harry Anderson, Wilt Chamberlain; D: Steve Rash. PAR

Rich in Love ♪♪½ 1993 (PG-13) Lighthearted look at the changes in a Southern family after matriarch Helen Odom leaves to pursue her own life, shattering the peaceful existence of those around her. Seen through the eyes of 17-year-old daughter Lucille who assumes the role of "mother" for her sister and father while trying to come to terms with her own confused feelings. Nice performances by newcomer Erbe and Finney can't overcome a mediocre script. Based on the novel by Josephine Humphreys.CW: Thematic elements. 105m/C VHS, LV, Closed Caption. Albert Finney, Jill Clayburgh, Kathryn Erbe, Kyle MacLachlan, Piper Laurie, Ethan Hawke, Suzy Amis, Alfre Woodard; D: Bruce Beresford; W: Alfred Uhry; M: Georges Delerue. MGM, BTV, FCT

Rich Kids ♪♪½ 1979 (PG) A young girl trying to cope with the divorce of her parents is aided by a boyfriend whose parents have already split. 97m/C VHS, Beta. John Lithgow, Kathryn Walker, Trini Alvarado, Paul Dooley, David Selby, Jill Eikenberry, Olympia Dukakis; D: Robert M. Young; C: Ralf Bode. MGM

Rich Man, Poor Man ♪♪ 1976 Classic television miniseries covers 20, sometimes bitter, years in the lives of the two Jordache brothers. It's 1945 in quiet Port Phillip, New York with embittered German baker Axel (Asner), his unfulfilled wife Mary (McGuire), and sons Tom (Nolte) and Rudy (Strauss). Tom is wild and irresponsible, Rudy is ambitious and college-bound, and Julie Prescott (Blakely), Rudy's girl, overshadows both their lives. Based on the novel by Irwin Shaw. The first series contained 12 episodes. A second series, of 21 episodes, primarily followed the tribulations of the next generation, although Strauss returned as Rudy. 720m/C VHS. Peter Strauss, Nick Nolte, Susan Blakely, Ed Asner, Dorothy McGuire, Bill Bixby, Robert Reed, Ray Milland, Kim Darby, Talia Shire, Lawrence Pressman, Kay Lenz; M: Alex North. CMB

The Rich Man's Wife ♪½ 1996 (R) Modern noir strands unhappy wife Josie (Berry) on Martha's Vineyard without her loathsome spouse (McDonald), where she makes the mistake of confiding her marital woes to sympathetic, yet obviously deranged stranger Cole (Greene). She tells Cole sometimes she wishes her husband was dead. Poof! Before you can say "foreshadowing," hubby's murdered and she's the prime suspect. Increasingly nutso Cole stalks our heroine, seemingly innocent, but possibly not as blameless as it appears. Failed mystery/thriller delivers little of either and the attempt at a "Strangers on a Train" premise and a "Usual Suspects" type ending fail miserably.CW: Strong violence and language. 95m/C VHS, Closed Caption. Halle Berry, Christopher McDonald, Clive Owen, Peter Greene, Charles Hallahan, Frankie Faison, Clea Lewis; D: Amy Holden Jones; W: Amy Holden Jones; C: Haskell Wexler; M: John Frizzell. TOU

Rich, Young and Pretty ♪♪½ 1951 Light-hearted, innocuous musical starring Powell as a Texas gal visiting Paris with her rancher father (Corey). Powell finds romance with Damone (in his screen debut) and a secret—the mother she has never known (Darrieux). Lamas (in his American screen debut) plays Darrieux's new heartthrob. ♪Dark is the Night; L'Amour Toujours; Tonight For Sure; Wonder Why; I Can See You; Paris; We Never Talk Much; How Do You Like Your Eggs in the Morning?; There's Danger in Your Eyes, Cherie; The Old Piano Roll Blues. 95m/C VHS. Jane Powell, Danielle Darrieux, Wendell Corey, Vic Damone, Fernando Lamas, Marcel Dalio, Una Merkel, Richard Anderson, Jean Murat, Hans Conried; D: Norman Taurog; W: Sidney Sheldon, Dorothy Cooper; M:

Sammy Cahn, Nicholas Brodszky. Nominations: Academy Awards '51: Best Song ("Wonder Why"). MGM, FCT

Richard III ♪♪♪½ 1955 This landmark film version of the Shakespearean play features an acclaimed performance by Laurence Olivier, who also directs. The plot follows the life of the mentally and physically twisted Richard of Gloucester and his schemes for the throne of England. 138m/C VHS, Beta, LV. GB Laurence Olivier, Cedric Hardwicke, Ralph Richardson, John Gielgud, Stanley Baker, Michael Gough, Claire Bloom; D: Laurence Olivier. British Academy Awards '55: Best Actor (Olivier), Best Director (Olivier), Best Film; Golden Globe Awards '57: Best Foreign Film; Nominations: Academy Awards '56: Best Actor (Olivier). COL, HMV, FUS

Richard III ♪♪♪½ 1995 (R) The Brits once again bring the Bard's most notorious monarch to the screen, this time in a new setting. McKellen stars in the title role of the deformed and ruthless English king, now in an imagined 1930s London of swanky Art Deco, Black Shirt thugs and modern media. Purists may resent major dialogue cuts, but famous speeches (such as the "winter of our discontent" opener) are amusingly staged in this modern take. Gorgeously polished visuals are perfect foil for the slimy, evil goings-on. Based on both Shakespeare's play and Richard Eyre's stage adaptation (in which McKellen also starred).CW: Violence and sexuality. 105m/C VHS, LV, Closed Caption. GB Ian McKellen, Annette Bening, Jim Broadbent, Robert Downey Jr., Nigel Hawthorne, Kristin Scott Thomas, Maggie Smith, John Wood; D: Richard Loncraine; W: Ian McKellen, Richard Loncraine; C: Peter Biziou; M: Trevor Jones. Nominations: Academy Awards '95: Best Art Direction/Set Decoration, Best Costume Design; British Academy Awards '96: Best Actor (McKellen), Best Adapted Screenplay; Golden Globe Awards '96: Best Actor—Drama (McKellen). MGM

Richard Petty Story ♪ 1972 (G) The biography of race car driver Petty, played by himself, and his various achievements on the track. 83m/C VHS, Beta. Richard Petty, Darren McGavin, Kathie Browne, Lynn Marta, Noah Beery Jr., L.Q. Jones. GEM

Richard's Things ♪♪ 1980 (R) A man's wife and his girlfriend find love and comfort in each other after his death. Screenplay by Frederic Raphael, from his novel. Very slow and dreary, with a weak performance from Ullman. 104m/C VHS, Beta. GB Liv Ullmann, Amanda Redman; D: Anthony Harvey; W: Frederic Raphael; C: Frederick A. (Freddie) Young; M: Georges Delerue.

Richie Rich ♪♪½ 1994 (PG) Yet another adaptation from the comics. Richie (Culkin), the world's richest boy, takes over the family business when his madcap parents Richard (Herrmann) and Regina (Ebersole) disappear thanks to the devious Laurence Van Dough (Larroquette). But there's kindly valet Cadbury (Hyde) and eccentric live-in inventor Keenbean (McShane) to help Richie save the day. Some silliness but Culkin has clearly outgrown this type of kid role. Biltmore, the 8,000 acre Vanderbilt estate in Asheville, North Carolina, serves as the Rich family home. 94m/C VHS, LV, Closed Caption. Macaulay Culkin, John Larroquette, Edward Herrmann, Christine Ebersole, Jonathan Hyde, Micheal McShane, Stephi Lineburg; Cameos: Reggie Jackson, Claudia Schiffer; D: Donald Petrie; W: Tom S. Parker, Jim Jennewein; C: Don Burgess; M: Alan Silvestri. Nominations: Golden Raspberry Awards '94: Worst Actor (Culkin). WAR

Ricky 1 ♪½ 1988 Mumbling pugilist spoof. Da Mob wants to make Ricky da fall guy, but uh, he's not as dumb as he looks. 90m/C VHS. Michael Michaud, Maggie Hughes, James Herbert, Lane Montano; D: Bill Naud; M: Joel Goldsmith. TPV, HHE

Ricochet ♪♪♪ 1991 (R) Rookie cop Washington causes a sensation when he singlehandedly captures notorious psychopath Lithgow. But this particular criminal is a twisted genius, and from his prison cell he comes up with a plan to destroy the young cop. Teaming up with old friend Ice-T, the rookie tries to outwit his evil arch-nemesis. Genuinely scary, tense and violent thriller. *CW:* Language, strong violence and drug content, and sensuality. **104m/C VHS, LV, 8mm, Closed Caption.** Denzel Washington, John Lithgow, Ice-T, Jesse Ventura, Kevin Pollak, Lindsay Wagner, Mary Ellen Trainor, Josh Evans, Victoria Dillard, John Amos, John Cothran Jr.; *D:* Russell Mulcahy; *W:* Steven E. de Souza; *M:* Alan Silvestri. *HBO, CCB*

Riddance *♫♫♫* 1973 The second of Meszaros' trilogy, about a Hungarian couple, an upper-class male student, and a factory-working young woman, and their difficulties in meshing their lives together. In Hungarian with English subtitles. **84m/B VHS, Beta.** *HU D:* Marta Meszaros. *KIV*

The Riddle of the Sands *♫♫½* 1979 Two English yachtsmen in 1903 inadvertently stumble upon a German plot to invade England by sea. British film based on the Erskine Childers spy novel. **99m/C VHS, Beta.** *GB* Michael York, Jenny Agutter, Simon MacCorkindale, Alan Badel; *D:* Tony Maylam; *M:* Howard Blake. *MOV, BMV*

Ride a Wild Pony *♫♫♫* 1975 (G) A poor Australian farmer's son is allowed to pick a horse of his own from a neighboring rancher's herd. After he trains and grows to love the pony, the rancher's daughter, a handicapped rich girl, decides to claim it for herself. Enjoyable Disney story is based on the tale "Sporting Proposition," by James Aldridge. **86m/C VHS, Beta.** *AU* John Meillon, Michael Craig, Robert Bettles, Eva Griffith, Graham Rouse; *D:* Don Chaffey; *C:* Jack Cardiff; *M:* John Addison. *DIS*

Ride 'Em Cowboy *♫♫½* 1942 Two peanut and hotdog vendors travel west to try their hand as cowpokes. Usual Abbott and Costello fare with a twist—there are lots of great musical numbers. ♫A Tisket, A Tasket; I'll Remember April; Wake Up Jacob; Beside the Rio Tonto; Rock 'n' Reelin'; Give Me My Saddle; Cow Boogie. **86m/B VHS.** Bud Abbott, Lou Costello, Anne Gwynne, Samuel S. Hinds, Dick Foran, Richard Lane, Johnny Mack Brown, Ella Fitzgerald, Douglass Dumbrille; *D:* Arthur Lubin. *USH*

Ride 'Em Cowgirl *♫♫* 1941 Singing cowgirl, Page, enters a horse race to expose the crook who cheated her father. **51m/B VHS.** Dorothy Page, Vince Barnett, Milton Frome; *D:* Samuel Diege. *VCN*

Ride Him, Cowboy *♫♫♫* 1932 Entertaining oater has Wayne saving horse Duke from being sentenced to death. This was the first of six series films Wayne made for Warner's, all of which costarred his white wonder horse, Duke. Remake of the 1926 Ken Maynard silent "The Unknown Cavalier." Based on the story by Kenneth Perkins. **55m/B VHS, Closed Caption.** John Wayne, Ruth Hall, Henry B. Walthall, Harry Gribbon, Otis Harlan, Charles Sellon; *D:* Fred Allen; *W:* Scott Mason. *MGM, GPV*

Ride in a Pink Car *♫* 1974 (R) When a Vietnam vet returns home, he discovers that his welcoming committee is really a lynch mob. **83m/C VHS, Beta.** Glenn Corbett, Morgan Woodward, Ivy Jones; *D:* Robert Emery. *ACA*

Ride in the Whirlwind *♫♫* 1967 Three cowboys are mistaken for members of a gang by a posse. Screenplay for the offbeat western by Nicholson. **83m/C Beta, LV.** Jack Nicholson, Cameron Mitchell, Millie Perkins, Katherine Squire, Harry Dean Stanton; *D:* Monte Hellman; *W:* Jack Nicholson. *MED, HHT, DVT*

Ride Lonesome *♫♫½* 1959 The heroic Scott is a bounty hunter looking for a killer (Best). It's not just the money, Scott hopes Best will lead him to the man who murdered Scott's wife. Along the trail he meets a pretty widow and two outlaws who hope if they capture Best, they'll get a pardon. A well-done example of a "B" western with good performances; Coburn's film debut. **73m/C VHS.** Randolph Scott, James Best, Karen Steele, Pernell Roberts, Lee Van Cleef, James Coburn; *D:* Budd Boetticher; *W:* Burt Kennedy. *MOV*

Ride, Ranger, Ride *♫♫½* 1936 Texas Ranger Autry is out to stop a group of Comanches from raiding a wagon train. **56m/B VHS, Beta.** Gene Autry, Smiley Burnette, Kay Hughes, Max Terhune, Monte Blue, Chief Thundercloud; *D:* Joseph Kane. *NOS, MED, VYY*

Ride the High Country *♫♫♫♫* Guns in the Afternoon 1962 The cult classic western about two old friends who have had careers on both sides of the law. One, Joel McCrea, is entrusted with a shipment of gold, and the other, Randolph Scott, rides along with him to steal the precious cargo. Although barely promoted by MGM, became a critics' favorite. Grimacing and long in the tooth, McCrea and Scott enact a fitting tribute and farewell to the myth of the grand ol' West. Wonderfully photographed by Lucien Ballard. The laserdisc edition carries the film in widescreen format along with the original movie trailer. **93m/C VHS, Beta, LV.** Randolph Scott, Joel McCrea, Mariette Hartley, Edgar Buchanan, R.G. Armstrong, Ronald Starr, John Anderson, James Drury, L.Q. Jones, Warren Oates; *D:* Sam Peckinpah; *C:* Lucien Ballard; *M:* George Bassman. *MGM*

Ride the Man Down *♫♫½* 1953 Story of a murderous land war between neighboring landowners tells the same old story: Greed knows no boundaries. **90m/C VHS.** Brian Donlevy, Chill Wills, Jack LaRue, Rod Cameron, Ella Raines, Barbara Britton; *D:* Joseph Kane. *REP*

Ride the Wild Surf *♫♫½* 1964 It's fun in the sun when surfers Fabian, Hunter, and Brown head to Hawaii in search of the ultimate waves. Throw in a little romance and a cool title song by Jan and Dean and you've got your better than average beach movie. The surfing footage is excellent. Cowabunga! **101m/C VHS, Closed Caption.** Fabian, Tab Hunter, Barbara Eden, Peter Brown, Susan Hart, Shelley Fabares, Jim Mitchum; *D:* Don Taylor. *COL*

Ride the Wind *♫♫* 1966 "Bonanza" gang goes to the aid of the Pony Express. **120m/C VHS, Beta.** Michael Landon, Lorne Greene, Dan Blocker. *REP*

Ride to Glory *♫♫* The Deserter; La Spina Dorsale del Diavolo 1971 In 1886, a cavalry officer deserts his troops to seek revenge on the Apaches that brutally killed his family. Hearing this, a general offers to pardon him if he will lead a dangerous group of men on a mission against the Apaches. Fast-paced and very bloody. **90m/C VHS.** Bekim Fehmiu, Richard Crenna, Chuck Connors, Ricardo Montalban, Ian Bannen, Slim Pickens, Woody Strode, Patrick Wayne, John Huston; *D:* Burt Kennedy. *SIM, PAR, HHE*

Rider from Tucson *♫♫* 1950 Two rodeo riders head out to Colorado for a friend's wedding. They find out the bride has been kidnapped by a bunch of claim jumpers after control of a gold mine. **60m/B VHS, Beta.** Tim Holt, Richard Martin, Elaine Riley, Douglas Fowley, Veda Ann Borg; *D:* Lesley Selander. *NO*

Rider of the Law *♫* 1935 A government agent poses as a greenhorn easterner to nab a gang of outlaws. **56m/B VHS, Beta.** Bob Steele. *NO*

Rider on the Rain *♫♫♫* Lepassager de la Pluie 1970 A young housewife is viciously raped by an escaped sex maniac. She kills him and disposes of his body, not knowing that he is being relentlessly pursued by mysterious American Bronson. Suspenseful, French-made thriller featuring one of Bronson's best performances. **115m/C VHS, Beta.** *FR* Marlene Jobert, Charles Bronson, Jill Ireland; *D:* Rene Clement. Golden Globe Awards '71: Best Foreign Film. *FCT*

Riders of Death Valley *♫♫½* 1941 Splendid western action serial in 15 episodes. Foran, Jones, and Carillo head a passel o'men watching for thieves and claim jumpers in a mining area. **320m/B VHS, Beta.** Dick Foran, Buck Jones, Leo Carrillo, Lon Chaney Jr.; *D:* Ford Beebe, Ray Taylor. *NOS, VCN, DVT*

Riders of Destiny *♫♫½* 1933 Wayne plays a government agent sent to find out who is stealing water from the local farmers. Very early Wayne has the Duke looking awfully young as an

agent securing water rights for ranchers. **59m/B VHS.** John Wayne, George "Gabby" Hayes, Cecilia Parker, Forrest Taylor, Al "Fuzzy" St. John; *D:* Robert North Bradbury. *COL, NOS, REP*

Riders of Pasco Basin *♫♫½* 1940 Outlaws are tricking ranchers out of their money by falsely promising to build a dam. So Brown and his cohorts come to set things right. **56m/B VHS.** Johnny Mack Brown, Fuzzy Knight, Bob Baker, Frances Robinson, Arthur Loft, Frank LaRue, Lafe McKee, Kermit Maynard; *D:* Ray Taylor; *W:* Ford Beebe. *GPV*

Riders of the Desert *♫♫½* 1932 Steele tracks down the loot from a stagecoach robbery. **57m/B VHS, Beta.** Bob Steele. *VYY, VCN*

Riders of the Purple Sage *♫♫½* 1925 When Texas Ranger Jim Lassiter's (Mix) sister and niece are kidnapped by the evil Walters (Oland), he devotes his life to finding them. While working on a ranch (and falling in love with the beautiful ranch owner), he learns Walters has changed his name and is passing himself off as a judge. Promptly shooting the skunk dead, Lassiter and his sweetie must run from a posse. Based on the Zane Grey novel. **63m/B VHS.** Tom Mix, Warner Oland, Mabel Ballin, Beatrice Burnham, Arthur Morrison, Fred Kohler Sr.; *D:* Lynn F. Reynolds; *W:* Edfrid Bingham. *GPV*

Riders of the Purple Sage *♫♫½* 1996 Legendary gunman (are there any other kind?) Lassiter (Harris) helps save Bern (Thomas) from a beating in a town run by a conservative religious sect, led by Deacon Tull (Weisser). Seems Bern's befriended ranch owner (and nonmember) Jane (Madigan) and the Deacon is not only after Jane but her considerable land and cattle holdings. Lassiter rides to the rescue. Properly brooding TV adaptation of the 1912 Zane Grey novel (the Grey novel specifies that the sect are Mormons but that caused considerable fuss). Filmed in Utah. **90m/C VHS.** Ed Harris, Amy Madigan, Henry Thomas, Norbert Weisser, Robin Tunney, G.D. Spradlin; *D:* Charles Haid; *W:* Gill Dennis; *C:* William Wages; *M:* Arthur Kempel. *TTC*

Riders of the Range *♫♫* 1924 Sheep invade the cattle range and a range war flares up between those who would herd and the ranchers. Silent flick of interest because of the stars. **62m/B VHS, Beta.** Edmund Cobb, Dolly Dale; *D:* Otis Thayer. *GPV*

Riders of the Range *♫♫* 1949 Cowboy rides into town just in time to save a girl's brother from gamblers. **60m/B VHS, Beta.** Tim Holt, Richard Martin. *NO*

Riders of the Range/Storm Over Wyoming *♫½* 1950 A double feature package of Tim Holt Westerns. **120m/B VHS, Beta.** Tim Holt, Richard Martin, Jacqueline Wells. *TTC*

Riders of the Rockies *♫♫½* 1937 An honest cowboy turns rustler in order to trap a border gang. One of Ritter's very best cowboy outings; good fun, and a very long fistfight with King. **60m/B VHS, Beta.** Tex Ritter, Yakima Canutt, Louise Stanley, Charles "Blackie" King, Snub Pollard; *D:* Robert North Bradbury. *NOS, VCI, VCN*

Riders of the Storm *♫½* The American Way 1988 (R) A motley crew of Vietnam vets runs a covert television broadcasting station from an inflight B-29, jamming America's legitimate airwaves. Interesting premise with boring result. **92m/C VHS, Beta, LV.** Dennis Hopper, Michael J. Pollard, Eugene Lipinski, James Aubrey, Nigel Pegram; *D:* Maurice Phillips; *W:* Scott Roberts. *NLC*

Riders of the Timberline *♫♫* 1941 Unusual for a Hopalong Cassidy programmer in that it puts him in timber country. Yes, he's a lumberjack and he's okay, as he fights against land-grabbing crooks all day. **59m/B VHS.** William Boyd, Brad King, Andy Clyde, J. Farrell MacDonald, Elaine Stewart, Anna Q. Nilsson, Hal Taliaferro, Tom Tyler, Victor Jory; *D:* Lesley Selander. *NOS*

Riders of the West ✗ **1942** An honest cowpoke fights off a band of rustlers. **58m/B VHS.** Buck Jones, Tim McCoy, Raymond Hatton, Sarah Padden, Harry Woods; **D:** Howard Bretherton. *NOS, DVT*

Riders of the Whistling Pines ✗✗ **1949** Our ever-so-bland hero solves a murder perpetrated by a passel of lumber thieves and saves the day for yet another damsel in distress. **70m/B VHS, Beta.** Gene Autry, Patricia White, Jimmy Lloyd; **D:** John English. *NOS, MED, DVT*

Riders of the Whistling Skull ✗✗½ *The Golden Trail* **1937** The Three Mesquiteers are guiding an expedition to an ancient Indian city. A gang of rustlers looting the city are holding an archeology professor hostage, and the Mesquiteers must rescue him. Swell cast; nifty, creepy plot; solid-as-usual leads. **58m/B VHS, Beta.** Bob Livingston, Ray Corrigan, Max Terhune, Yakima Canutt, Roland Winters; **D:** Mack V. Wright. *SNC, NOS, VCN*

Riders to the Sea ✗✗½ **1988** A mother envisions the death of her last son in the same manner her other sons died—by drowning. Based on the play by Irish dramatist John Millington Synge. **90m/C VHS, Beta.** Geraldine Page, Amanda Plummer, Sachi Parker, Barry McGovern; **D:** Ronan O'Leary. *NO*

Ridicule ✗✗✗½ **1996 (R)** Fish-out-of-water drama has minor country aristocrat Pondeludon (Berling) enter the depraved world of the 18th century court at Versailles. There, he hopes, the king will aid him in his quest to drain the disease-ridden swamps at his estate. The naive provincial finds he must master the weapons of choice for success within the court—wit, deadly ridicule, and impeccable lineage. After initial missteps due to lack of finesse, he quickly adapts, and finds some influential allies: the beautiful Madame de Blayac (Ardant) and sympathetic Marquis de Bellegarde (Rochefort). When the Marquis' spirited and attractive daughter, Mathilde (Godreche), shows up, the smitten Pondeludon must stir his loveless marriage of convenience. Perfectly cast, director Leconte's highly lauded period piece has all the emotional and technical elements of an engaging film. In French with subtitles.**CW:** Graphic nudity, some sexuality and brief violence. **102m/C VHS, LV, Closed Caption. FR** Charles Berling, Jean Rochefort, Fanny Ardant, Bernard Giraudeau, Judith Godreche, Bernard Dheran, Carlo Brandt, Jacques Mathou; **D:** Patrice Leconte; **W:** Remi Waterhouse, Michel Fessler, Eric Vicaut; **C:** Thierry Arbogast; **M:** Antoine Duhamel. British Academy Awards '96: Best Foreign Language Film; Cesar Awards '97: Best Director (Leconte), Best Film; Broadcast Film Critics Association Awards '96: Best Foreign Language Film; Nominations: Academy Awards '96: Best Foreign Language Film; Cesar Awards '97: Best Actor (Berling); Golden Globe Awards '97: Best Foreign Film. *TOU*

Ridin' Down the Canyon ✗✗½ **1942** Standard but entertaining entry in Rogers' popular series. It's Rogers to the rescue when a gang of outlaws are rustling cattle and selling to the government for wartime profits. Roy, along with the Sons of the Pioneers, also manages to croon a few tunes. Based on a story by Robert Williams and Norman Houston. **54m/B VHS.** Roy Rogers, George "Gabby" Hayes, Linda Hayes, Addison Richards, Adrian Booth, James Seay; **D:** Joseph Kane; **W:** Albert De Mond. *MOV*

Ridin' on a Rainbow ✗✗½ **1941** Has-been performer on a steamboat decides to rob a bank in the hopes of starting a new life for himself and his daughter. The money he robs had just been deposited by some cattlemen, one of whom joins the steamboat's crew, wins the daughter's heart, and gets to the father. Slow and dull, with too much singing, and too little plot and scenery. **79m/B VHS, Beta.** Gene Autry, Smiley Burnette, Mary Lee; **D:** Lew (Louis Friedlander) Landers. Nominations: Academy Awards '41: Best Song ("Be Honest With Me"). *REP, CCB, VCN*

Ridin' the California Trail ✗✗½ **1947** The Cisco Kid is wanted dead or alive in several states. **40m/B VHS, Beta.** Gilbert Roland. *DVT*

Ridin' the Lone Trail woof! **1937** Steele attempts to stop some criminals who've been harassing a stagecoach line. Republic was better than this weak western would lead us to believe. Steele, who went on to better things, is a bright spot in a film that sounds and looks bad. Keep your ears open for the sound of airplanes—apparently Newfield forgot they hadn't been invented in the time of the wild west. From a story by E.B. Mann. **56m/B VHS.** Bob Steele, Claire Rochelle, Charles "Blackie" King, Ernie Adams, Lew Meehan, Julian Rivero; **D:** Sam Newfield; **W:** Charles Francis Royal. *NOS, DVT*

Ridin' the Trail ✗ **1940** Scott stars as a cowboy out to rid the countryside of bad guys in this western. **60m/B VHS, Beta.** Fred Scott, Iris Lancaster, Harry Harvey, Jack Ingram, John Ward; **D:** Raymond K. Johnson. *NOS, DVT*

Ridin' Thru ✗✗ **1935** Another Tom Tyler western, in which the hero does battle with unscrupulous villains. **60m/B VHS, Beta.** Tom Tyler, Ruth Hiatt, Lafe McKee, Philo McCullough, Lew Meehan, Bud Osborne; **D:** Harry S. Webb. *NOS, DVT, HEG*

The Riding Avenger ✗✗½ **1936** To gain the love of a beautiful lady, a cowboy vows never to fight again, but is forced to break his promise when the town is terrorized. Aw, shucks. **56m/B VHS, Beta.** Hoot Gibson, Ruth Mix, Buzz Barton; **D:** Harry Fraser. *VCN*

Riding High ✗✗½ **1950** Capra remade his 1934 film "Broadway Bill" as this light-hearted musical. Horse trainer Crosby falls for the wealthy Gray who demands he choose between her and his horse. Bing chooses the horse who proves his loyalty by winning the big race and making Crosby a rich man. ♫ Someplace on Anywhere Road; Sunshine Cake; We've Got a Sure Thing; The Horse Told Me; The Whiffenpoof Song; De Camptown Races. **112m/B VHS, Beta, Closed Caption.** Bing Crosby, Coleen Gray, Charles Bickford, William Demarest, Frances Gifford, Raymond Walburn, James Gleason, Ward Bond, Percy Kilbride, Harry Davenport, Margaret Hamilton, Douglass Dumbrille, Gene Lockhart, Charles Lane, Frankie Darro, Paul Harvey, Marjorie Lord, Dub Taylor, Max Baer Sr., Oliver Hardy; **D:** Frank Capra; **W:** Robert Riskin, Melville Shavelson, Jack Rose; **C:** George Barnes. *USH*

Riding High ✗ **1978** It's a battle for supremacy between the kings of the motorcycle stunt world. Made for television movie's soundtrack includes songs from The Police, Dire Straits, Jerry Lee Lewis, and more. **92m/C VHS, Beta.** Murray Salem, Marella Oppenheim, Eddie Kidd, Irene Handl; **D:** Ross Cramer. *LIV*

Riding On ✗✗ **1937** Hayseed falls for the daughter of his father's arch rival. While his father battles it out over cattle, he pines for his enemy's daughter. Lots of action which is typical fare in mediocre western production. **59m/B VHS.** Tom Tyler, Germaine Greer, Rex Lease, John Elliott, Earl Dwire; **D:** Harry S. Webb. *NOS, DVT*

Riding on Air ✗✗ **1937** Small-town newspaper editor Brown discovers that his bumbling methods get him the right results. Smugglers and crazy inventions in a ho-hum Brown entry. **58m/B VHS, Beta.** Joe E. Brown; **D:** Edward Sedgwick. *NOS, BAR, FCT*

Riding Speed ✗ **1935** Our hero breaks up a gang of smugglers along the Mexican border. **50m/B VHS, Beta, LV.** Buffalo Bill Jr. *NO*

Riding the Sunset Trail ✗✗✗ **1941** Top-notch tale of Keene trying to stop a con from cashing in on his dead half-brother's fortune. Solid production values and an enthusiastic performance by Keene make this one of his best films after a string of flops. **56m/B VHS.** Tom Keene, Betty Miles, Frank Yaconelli, Sugar Dawn, Slim Andrews, Kenne Duncan; **D:** Robert Emmett Tansey; **W:** Robert Emmett, Frances Kavanaugh. *MOV*

The Riding Tornado ✗✗½ **1932** Bronc rider McCoy takes a job on Grey's ranch, promptly falling for her. Ranch foreman Oakman, who's really the leader of a gang of rustlers, kidnaps

Grey and McCoy goes after them. **63m/B VHS.** Tim McCoy, Shirley Grey, Wheeler Oakman, Wallace MacDonald, Russell Simpson, Montagu Love, Lafe McKee, Bud Osborne; **D:** David Ross Lederman. *GPV*

Riding with Death **1976** A man who can become invisible, thanks to a military experiment, uses his power to uncover a dastardly plot by a mad scientist. So-so TV pilot. **97m/C VHS, Beta.** Ben Murphy, Andrew Prine, Katherine Crawford, Richard Dysart; **D:** Alan J. Levi. *USH*

Riel ✗✗ **1979** The story of Louis Riel, a half-French, half-Indian visionary who challenged the Canadian army in his fight for equality and self-rule. **150m/C VHS, Beta.** Raymond Cloutier, Arthur Hill, William Shatner, Christopher Plummer, Leslie Nielsen; **D:** George Bloomfield. *PSM*

Riff Raff ✗✗ *Riffraff* **1935** Melodramatic story about the relationship of two waterfront workers in the tuna fishing business. Confusing script saddled with too many characters, but there is some good sharp dialogue between the leads. Also features the scenic California waterfront. **80m/B VHS, Closed Caption.** Jean Harlow, Spencer Tracy, Joseph Calleia, Una Merkel, Mickey Rooney, Victor Kilian, J. Farrell MacDonald, Roger Imhof; **D:** J. Walter Ruben. *MGM*

Riff-Raff ✗✗½ **1947** Various dramatic and comic complications arise when a dying man gives Panama City con man O'Brien a map to oil deposits. Interesting and quick-moving melodrama. **80m/B VHS, Beta.** Pat O'Brien, Walter Slezak, Anne Jeffreys, Jason Robards Sr., Percy Kilbride, Jerome Cowan; **D:** Ted Tetzlaff. *TTC*

Riff Raff ✗✗✗ **1992** Unsparing black comedy about the British working-class by director Loach. Ex-con Stevie comes to London from Scotland to look for work and escape his thieving past. He finds a nonunion job on a construction site, takes up squatter's rights in an abandoned apartment, and finds a girlfriend in equally struggling singer Susie, who turns out to be a junkie. Loach's characters deal with their unenviable lot in life through rough humor and honest sentiment. Regional accents are so thick that the film is subtitled. **96m/C VHS, LV. GB** Robert Carlyle, Emer McCourt, Jimmy Coleman, George Moss, Ricky Tomlinson, David Finch, Bill Jesse; **D:** Ken Loach; **W:** Bill Jesse; **M:** Stewart Copeland. *NLC, COL, IME*

Rififi ✗✗✗½ *Du Rififi Chez les Hommes* **1954** Perhaps the greatest of all "heist" movies. Four jewel thieves pull off a daring caper, only to fall prey to mutual distrust. The long scene of the actual theft, completely in silence, will have your heart in your throat. In French with English subtitles. **115m/B VHS, Beta. FR** Jean Servais, Carl Mohner, Robert Manuel, Jules Dassin; **D:** Jules Dassin; **W:** Jules Dassin. Cannes Film Festival '55: Best Director (Dassin); National Board of Review Awards '56: 5 Best Foreign Films of the Year. *VYY, NOS, HHT*

Rift ✗½ **1996** Bland romantic triangle set among Manhattan twentysomethings. Shy Tom (Sage) pines for Lisa (Bransford), the wife of his best friend, Bill (Cavanaugh). In fact, Tom begins having overwhelming nightmares, involving murder, about the situation. Not that you'll care since Tom is a mope, Lisa's a whiner, and Bill's a nasty-tempered bore. **87m/C VHS.** William Sage, Timothy Cavanaugh, Jennifer Bransford, Alan Davidson; **D:** Edward S. Barkin; **W:** Edward S. Barkin; **C:** Lee Daniel. *LEO*

The Right Hand Man ✗½ **1987 (R)** A brother and sister must deal with their crusty patriarch's demise in the Victorian-era Australian outback. Disappointing and overwrought. **101m/C VHS, Beta. AU** Rupert Everett, Hugo Weaving, Arthur Dignam; **D:** Di Drew. *VTR, NWV*

Right of Way ✗✗½ **1984** Stewart plays an elderly man who makes a suicide pact with his wife (Davis) when he learns of her terminal illness. Davis and Stewart's first film together is disappointing and stodgy, with an abrupt ending that looks like bad editing by a frightened studio. Made for TV. **102m/C VHS, Beta.** James Stewart, Bette Davis,

Priscilla Morrill, Melinda Dillon; **D:** George Schaefer; **M:** Brad Fiedel. *NO*

The Right Stuff ✓✓✓ 1983 (PG) A rambunctious adaptation of Tom Wolfe's nonfiction book about the beginnings of the U.S. space program, from Chuck Yeager's breaking of the sound barrier to the last of the Mercury missions. Featuring an all-star cast and an ambitious script. Rowdy, imaginative, and thrilling, though broadly painted and oddly uninvolving. Former astronaut John Glenn was running for president when this was out. **193m/C VHS, Beta, LV, Closed Caption, DVD.** Ed Harris, Dennis Quaid, Sam Shepard, Scott Glenn, Fred Ward, Charles Frank, William Russ, Kathy Baker, Barbara Hershey, Levon Helm, David Clennon, Kim Stanley, Mary Jo Deschanel, Veronica Cartwright, Pamela Reed, Jeff Goldblum, Harry Shearer, Donald Moffat, Scott Paulin, Lance Henriksen, Scott Wilson, John P. Ryan, Royal Dano; **D:** Philip Kaufman; **W:** Philip Kaufman; **C:** Caleb Deschanel; **M:** Bill Conti. Academy Awards '83: Best Film Editing, Best Sound, Best Original Score; Nominations: Academy Awards '83: Best Art Direction/Set Decoration, Best Cinematography, Best Picture, Best Supporting Actor (Shepard). *WAR*

The Right to Remain Silent ✓✓ 1995 (R) Rookie cop Christine Paley (Thompson) learns all about human foibles in her job processing incoming suspects. Based on a play by Brent Briscoe and Mark Fauser. **CW:** Language and brief violence. **96m/C VHS, Closed Caption.** Lea Thompson, Amanda Plummer, Christopher Lloyd, Laura San Giacomo, Judge Reinhold, Carl Reiner, L.L. Cool J., Patrick Dempsey, Fisher Stevens, Robert Loggia; **D:** Hubert de la Bouillerie. *REP*

Rikisha-Man ✓✓✓½ *Rickshaw Man; Muhomatsu no Issho* 1958 A tragic melodrama about a rickshaw puller who helps raise a young boy after his father has died, and loves the boy's mother from afar. Inagaki's remake of his original 1943 version. In Japanese with English subtitles. **105m/B VHS, Beta.** *JP* Toshiro Mifune; **D:** Hiroshi Inagaki. *FCT*

Rikky and Pete ✓✓½ 1988 (R) An engaging Australian comedy about a bizarre, precociously eccentric brother and sister. He's a Rube Goldberg-style mentor; she's a scientist-cum-country singer. They move together to the outback and meet a score of weird characters. A worthy follow-up to director Tass's "Malcolm." **103m/C VHS, Beta, LV, Closed Caption.** *AU* Nina Landis, Stephen Kearney, Tetchie Agbayani, Bruce Spence, Bruno Lawrence, Bill Hunter, Dorothy Allison, Don Reid, Lewis Fitz-gerald; **D:** Nadia Tass; **W:** David Parker; **M:** Phil Judd. *MGM, FOX*

Rikyu ✓✓✓ 1990 Set in 16th century Japan, Rikyu is a Buddhist priest who elevated the tea ceremony to an art form. To him it is a spiritual experience, to his master, Lord Hideyoshi Toilyotomi, the ruler of Japan, mastery of the ceremony is a matter of prestige. Conflict arises between Rikyu's ideal of profound simplicity, symbolized by the ceremony, and Toilyotomi's planned conquest of China, which Rikyu opposes. In Japanese with English subtitles. **116m/C VHS, LV.** *JP* Rentaro Mikuni, Tsutomu Yamazaki; **D:** Hiroshi Teshigahara. *CTL, LUM*

Rim of the Canyon ✓½ 1949 Autry has a dual role as a lawman tracking villains who were jailed by his father years before. **70m/B VHS, Beta.** Gene Autry, Nan Leslie, Thurston Hall, Clem Bevans, Walter Sande, Jock Mahoney, Alan Hale Jr., Denver Pyle; **D:** John English. *NOS, DVT, TIM*

Rimfire ✓✓½ 1949 An undercover agent tracks down some stolen U.S. Army gold, aided by the ghost of a wrongly-hanged gambler. Fun B western. **65m/B VHS, Beta, LV.** Mary Beth Hughes, Henry Hull, Fuzzy Knight, James Millican, Victor Kilian, Margia Dean, Jason Robards Sr., Reed Hadley; **D:** B. Reeves Eason. *NO*

Rin Tin Tin, Hero of the West ✓✓ 1955 In one of his last adventures, the famous German Shepherd proves his courage and hypercanine intelligence. Colorized. **75m/C VHS, Beta.** James Brown, Lee Aaker. *MON*

The Ring ✓✓½ 1927 Very early Hitchcock about boxer who marries carnival girl, loses carnival girl, and wins carnival girl back again. Standard romantic punch and roses yarn interesting as measure of young director's developing authority. **82m/B VHS.** *GB* Carl Brisson, Lillian Hall-Davis, Ian Hunter, Gordon Harker; **D:** Alfred Hitchcock; **W:** Alfred Hitchcock. *VEC, MLB*

The Ring ✓✓½ 1952 Poignant early fight movie that gives a lesson in prejudice against Chicanos. The main character feels that the only way to get respect from the world is to fight for it. Well-directed and perceptive. **79m/B VHS.** Gerald Mohr, Rita Moreno, Kiri Te Kanawa, Robert Arthur, Art Aragon, Jack Elam; **D:** Kurt Neumann. *MOV, DVT, HEG*

Ring of Bright Water ✓✓✓ 1969 (G) Well done story of a pet otter from Gavin Maxwell's autobiography. The film stars the couple that made the delightful "Born Free." Beautiful Scottish Highlands photography adds to this captivating and endearing tale of a civil servant who purchases an otter from a pet store and moves to the country. **107m/C VHS, Beta.** *GB* Bill Travers, Virginia McKenna, Peter Jeffrey, Archie Duncan; **D:** Jack Couffer. *FXV, FCT, SIG*

Ring of Death ✓½ 1972 A tough cop investigating a routine case becomes a hunted man after someone kills the man he is following. **93m/C VHS, Beta.** Franco Nero, Florinda Bolkan, Adolfo Celi. *CNG, MRV, GEM*

Ring of Fire ✓½ 1991 (R) Wilson is one of very few modern American kung-fu heroes of Asian descent, and he works messages against prejudice into this interracial Romeo-and-Juliet chopsocky tale. What foot through yonder window breaks? **100m/C VHS, LV, Closed Caption.** Don "The Dragon" Wilson, Maria Ford, Vince Murdocco, Dale Jacoby, Michael Delano, Eric Lee; **D:** Richard W. Munchkin. *IMP, HMV*

Ring of Fire 2: Blood and Steel ✓½ 1992 (R) Wilson returns as Dr. Johnny Wu in this martial-arts actioner which finds the good doctor the witness to a robbery. When one of the robbers is killed, the gang's leader kidnaps Johnny's fiance and holds her for ransom. He decides to bypass the police and use his own expertise to rescue her. **CW:** Language and martial arts violence. **94m/C VHS, Closed Caption.** Don "The Dragon" Wilson, Maria Ford, Sy Richardson, Michael Delano, Dale Jacoby, Vince Murdocco, Evan Lorie, Gary Robbins, Charlie Ganis, Ron Yuan; **D:** Richard W. Munchkin. *PMH*

Ring of Fire 3: Lion Strike ✓½ 1994 (R) Johnny Wu is supposed to be on vacation with his son and a beautiful forest ranger when they find themselves in the way of a violent group known as the Global Mafia. Seems Johnny has a computer disk that the gangsters want. **CW:** Violence; language. **90m/C VHS, LV, Closed Caption.** Don "The Dragon" Wilson, Bobbie Phillips, Robert Costanzo; **D:** Rick Jacobson. *PMH*

Ring of Steel ✓✓ 1994 (R) Alex, a one-time Olympic hopeful in fencing, is enticed into combat by the mysterious owner of a decadent nightclub where gladiator-type matches are staged for the thrill of the bored and jaded superrich. Unaware of the high stakes, Alex wins a duel and is showered with money and the attention of a beautiful, yet dangerous woman. When Alex discovers the club's dark secret, he no longer wants to fight, but blackmail draws him in even deeper. **94m/C VHS, LV, Closed Caption.** Joe Don Baker, Carol Alt, Robert Chapin, Gary Kasper, Darlene Vogel; **D:** David Frost; **W:** Robert Chapin; **M:** Jeff Beal. *USH*

Ring of Terror ✓ 1962 College boy who wants to join a fraternity must survive the initiation rights, which include stealing a ring from a corpse. Unfortunately, this seemingly invincible guy has a deadly terror of the dead. Cheaply made flop alledgedly based on a composite of actual hazing incidents. **72m/B VHS.** George Mather, Esther Furst, Austin Green, Joseph Conway; **D:** Clark Paylow. *NOS, SNC*

Ring of the Musketeers ✓✓½ 1993 (PG-13) Contemporary spoof of the Musketeers saga finds three descendants of the swashbuckling heroes carrying on the family tradition of protecting the weak and innocent. They even get stuck with a Musketeer-wannabe when they come to the rescue of a young boy who is kidnapped to prevent his dad from testifying against mobsters. **CW:** Action violence. **86m/C VHS, Closed Caption.** David Hasselhoff, Alison Doody, Thomas Gottschalk, Richard "Cheech" Marin, Corbin Bernsen, John Rhys-Davies; **D:** John Paragon; **W:** Joel Surnow. *COL*

Ringside ✓½ 1949 A concert pianist turns boxer to avenge his brother who was blinded in a fight. **64m/B VHS, Beta, LV.** Donald (Don "Red") Barry, Sheila Ryan, Tom Brown. *SNC*

The Rink ✓✓✓ 1916 Chaplin plays a waiter who spends his lunch hour on roller skates. Silent with musical soundtrack added. **20m/B VHS, Beta.** Charlie Chaplin; **D:** Charlie Chaplin. *CAB, GVV*

Rink/Immigrant 191? Two Chaplin shorts: "The Rink" (1916), in which Charlie defends his girlfriend's honor at a local roller skating rink; "The Immigrant" (1917), features Charlie as a newcomer to America. **56m/B VHS, Beta.** Charlie Chaplin, Mack Swain, Edna Purviance. *VYY*

Rio Bravo ✓✓✓½ 1959 The sheriff of a Texas border town (Wayne) takes a brutal murderer into custody and faces a blockade of hired gunmen determined to keep his prisoner from being brought to justice. Long, but continually entertaining. Generally regarded as an American film classic, with an all-star cast, didn't impress the critics at the time. Sequel: "El Dorado." Semi-remake was called "Assault on Precinct 13." **140m/C VHS, Beta.** John Wayne, Dean Martin, Angie Dickinson, Ricky Nelson, Walter Brennan, Ward Bond, Claude Akins, Bob Steele, John Russell; **D:** Howard Hawks. *WAR, TLF*

Rio Conchos ✓✓✓ 1964 Nifty nonstop action in this western set in Texas after the Civil War. Three Army buddies search for 2,000 stolen rifles. Boone is understated, O'Brien is good, and Brown memorable in his debut. **107m/C VHS, Beta.** Richard Boone, Stuart Whitman, Edmond O'Brien, Anthony (Tony) Franciosa, Jim Brown; **D:** Gordon Douglas; **M:** Jerry Goldsmith. *FOX*

Rio Diablo ✓✓½ 1993 Country Western singers abound in—what else—a made-for-TV Western movie. A bounty hunter (Rogers) and newlywed groom (Tritt) set off after a gang of thieving kidnappers who have snatched the young bride (Harring). Judd shows up as the owner of a desert hostelry, who happens to cross paths with the hunters. Watch out—this could be more fun than a Partridge Family reunion. **120m/C VHS.** Kenny Rogers, Travis Tritt, Naomi Judd, Stacy Keach, Brion James, Bruce Greenwood, Laura Harring; **M:** Larry Brown. *CAF, MVD*

Rio Grande ✓✓✓ 1950 The last entry in Ford's cavalry trilogy following "Fort Apache" and "She Wore a Yellow Ribbon." A U.S. cavalry unit on the Mexican border conducts an unsuccessful campaign against marauding Indians. The commander (Wayne) faces an unhappy wife and is estranged from his son, a new recruit. Featuring an excellent Victor Young score and several songs by the Sons of the Pioneers. **105m/B VHS, LV, Closed Caption.** John Wayne, Maureen O'Hara, Ben Johnson, Claude Jarman Jr., Harry Carey Jr., Victor McLaglen, Chill Wills, J. Carrol Naish; **D:** John Ford. *REP, TLF, RXM*

Rio Grande Raiders ✓ 1946 A stagecoach driver discovers that his kid brother is working for a crooked rival stage company. **54m/B VHS, Beta.** Sunset Carson, Linda Stirling, Bob Steele. *DVT, RXM*

Rio Lobo ✓✓½ 1970 (G) Hawks's final film takes place after the Civil War, when Union Colonel Wayne goes to Rio Lobo to take revenge on two traitors. Disappointing. The Duke has to carry weak supporting performances on his brawny shoulders—and nearly does. **114m/C VHS, Beta, LV, Closed Caption.** John Wayne, Jorge Rivero, Jennifer

O'Neill, Jack Elam, Chris Mitchum, David Huddleston, George Plimpton; **D:** Howard Hawks; **C:** William Clothier; **M:** Jerry Goldsmith. FOX

Rio Rattler 🐾½ 1935 Tyler takes the place of a murdered lawman in order to find his killer. **60m/B VHS, Beta.** Tom Tyler, Marion Shilling, Eddie Gribbon, William Gould, Tom London; **D:** Franklin Shamray. VCN, GPV

Rio Rita 🐾🐾½ 1942 Abbott & Costello are working on a ranch and somehow become involved with Nazi spies. Provides a few original comic bits for the duo but is otherwise mediocre. An updated remake of the 1929 Wheeler & Woolsey comedy. **91m/B VHS.** Bud Abbott, Lou Costello, Kathryn Grayson, John Carroll, Patricia Dane, Tom Conway, Peter Whitney; **D:** Sylvan Simon. MGM

Riot 🐾🐾½ 1969 (R) Men in cages throw tantrums until warden returns from vacation. Filmed in Arizona State Prison with real convicts as extras. Strong performances by fullback Brown and durable Hackman. Based on story by ex-con Frank Elli. Too oft-played theme song sung by Bill Medley of the Righteous Brothers. **97m/C VHS.** Gene Hackman, Jim Brown, Mike Kellin, Ben Carruthers, Frank Eyman; **D:** Buzz Kulik; **W:** James Poe. PAR

Riot 🐾 1996 (R) Dumb actioner set on Christmas Eve, 1999, amidst some L.A. riots. British Special Air Service officer Shane Alcott (Daniels) must rescue his kidnapped ex-girlfriend Anna-Lisa (Rowland), who just happens to be the British ambassador's daughter. She's being held by ghetto gangster Leon (Sanders), whose gang turn out to be pawns for IRA leader O'Flaherty (Kilpatrick), who has a score to settle. Predictable fights, lots of explosions. **95m/C VHS, Closed Caption.** Gary Daniels, Ray "Sugar Ray" Leonard, Patrick Kilpatrick, Paige Rowland, Dex Elliot Sanders, Charles Napier; **D:** Joseph Merhi; **W:** John Barmettler, William Applegate Jr.; **C:** Ken Blakey; **M:** Jim Halfpenny. PMH

Riot in Cell Block 11 🐾🐾🐾 1954 A convict leads four thousand prisoners in an uprising to improve prison conditions. Based on producer/ex-con Walter Wanger's own experience. Powerful and still timely. Filmed at Folsom Prison. **80m/B VHS, Beta.** Neville Brand, Leo Gordon, Emile Meyer, Frank Faylen; **D:** Donald Siegel. REP

Riot Squad 🐾🐾 1941 An intern poses as a doctor in order to find out who was responsible for putting a mob hit on a police captain. **55m/B VHS, Beta.** Richard Cromwell, Rita Quigley, John Miljan, Mary Ruth, Herbert Rawlinson, Mary Gordon, Arthur Space; **D:** Edward Finney. SNC, RXM

Rip-Off 🐾 1977 Two Greek wanderers enter the American way of life via sex, drugs, syndicated crime, and terrorism. **78m/C VHS, Beta.** Michael Benet, Michelle Simone, James Masters, Johnny Dark; **D:** Manolis Tsafos. UNI

The Rip Off 🐾 1978 (R) A colorful gang of hoodlums goes for the biggest heist of their lives—six million bucks in diamonds! **99m/C VHS, Beta.** Lee Van Cleef, Karen Black, Robert Alda, Edward Albert; **D:** Anthony (Antonio Margheriti) Dawson. WOV

Rip Roarin' Buckaroo 🐾 1936 A fighter sets out to avenge himself when he is framed in a dishonest fight. **51m/B VHS, Beta.** Tom Tyler, B.J. Quinn Jr., Beth Marion, Charles "Blackie" King; **D:** Robert F. "Bob" Hill. NOS, DVT, RXM

Rip van Winkle 🐾 1985 Sleepy Coppola adaptation of the Washington Irving story about a man who falls asleep for twenty years after a group of ghosts get him drunk. From the "Faerie Tale Theatre" series. **60m/C VHS, Beta, Closed Caption.** Harry Dean Stanton, Talia Shire; **D:** Francis Ford Coppola. KUI, FOX, FCT

The Ripper woof! 1986 The spirit of Jack-the-Ripper possesses a university professor's body. Ultra-violent. Shot on videotape for the video market. **90m/C VHS, Beta.** Wade Tower, Tom Schreier, Mona Van Pernis, Andrea Adams; **D:** Christopher Lewis. NO

Ripping Yarns 1975 Three episodes of the popular British comedy series written by Monty Python's Terry Jones and Michael Palin: "Tomkinson's Schooldays," "Escape from Stalag Luft 112B," and "Golden Gordon." The subsequent episodes are released as "More Ripping Yarns" and "Even More Ripping Yarns." **90m/C VHS, Beta, Closed Caption.** GB Michael Palin, Gwen Watford, Ian Ogilvy, Roy Kinnear, Bill Fraser; **D:** Terry Hughes, Jimmy Franklin, Alan Bell; **W:** Michael Palin, Terry Jones. FOX, VCO

Riptide 🐾🐾🐾 1934 Shearer is a carefree American married to stuffy English lord Marshall. He goes off to America on a business trip, she's bored and goes to a costume party (everyone dresses as insects!) where she meets old flame Montgomery. He gets drunk, follows her home in an effort to rekindle their passion, and winds up in the hospital after a drunken fall. The returning Marshall is appalled by the scandalous press and instigates divorce proceedings. Eventually, they come to their senses and decide they do love each other. Quality production with an entertaining cast. **90m/B VHS.** Norma Shearer, Herbert Marshall, Robert Montgomery, Richard "Skeets" Gallagher, Ralph Forbes, Lilyan Tashman; **D:** Edmund Goulding; **W:** Edmund Goulding. MGM

The Rise and Fall of Legs Diamond 🐾🐾½ 1960 Not quite historically accurate but fast-paced and entertaining gangster bio of legendary booze trafficker Legs Diamond. Danton's debut. **101m/B VHS, LV.** Ray Danton, Karen Steele, Jesse White, Simon Oakland, Robert Lowery, Elaine Stewart; **D:** Budd Boetticher. Nominations: Academy Awards '60: Best Costume Design (B & W). WAR, FCT

The Rise & Rise of Daniel Rocket 🐾🐾 1986 A exceptional young boy believes he can fly without the aid of a flying machine. From the "American Playhouse" series. **90m/C VHS, Beta.** Tom Hulce, Timothy Daly, Valerie Mahaffey; **D:** Emile Ardolino. ACA, PBS

The Rise of Louis XIV 🐾🐾🐾 La Prise de Pouvoir Par Louis XIV 1966 A masterful docudrama detailing the life and court intrigues of Louis XIV of France. Successfully captures the attitudes and mores of the royalty at the time. One of a series of historical films directed by Rossellini. Made for French television. In French with English subtitles. **100m/C VHS.** FR Jean-Marie Patte, Raymond Jourdan, Dominique Vincent, Silvagni, Pierre Barrat; **D:** Roberto Rossellini. HTV, FCT

Rising Son 🐾🐾🐾 1990 A family man who loves his job faces trauma when his factory closes at the same time his son informs he's quitting medical school. Solid family drama and parable of economic hard times of the early '80s, sustained by top-drawer performances by Dennehy, Damon, and Laurie. Well directed by Coles. Made for cable. **92m/C VHS, Beta, Closed Caption.** Brian Dennehy, Matt Damon, Piper Laurie, Graham Beckel, Ving Rhames, Jane Adams, Richard Jenkins, Emily Longstreth; **D:** John David Coles; **W:** Bill Phillips. TTC

Rising Sun 🐾🐾🐾 1993 (R) When a prostitute is found murdered in the boardroom of a powerful Japanese-owned corporation, seasoned cop (and Japanese expert) Connery and new partner Snipes are sent to investigate. Complicated yarn about business, prejudice, cops, and the differences between east and west. Filmed with stylized camera techniques, quick action, and good rapport between the two leads. Based on the book by Crichton, which offered ominous theories about international politics and business. These aspects had the film labeled as Japan-bashing, one of the reasons the script was rewritten to focus more on the murder mystery. **CW:** Language, some violence, and strong sexuality. **129m/C VHS, LV, Closed Caption.** Sean Connery, Wesley Snipes, Tia Carrere, Harvey Keitel, Kevin Anderson, Stan Egi, Mako, Cary-Hiroyuki Tagawa, Ray Wise, Tatjana Patitz; **D:** Philip Kaufman; **W:** Michael Backes, Michael Crichton, Philip Kaufman; **C:** Michael Chapman; **M:** Toru Takemitsu. FXV, BTV, FCT

Risk 🐾🐾🐾 1994 Maya (Sillas) is a struggling, emotionally distant, New York artist when she meets overly-friendly Joe (Ilku) on a bus. He follows her home and manages to entice Maya into letting him spend the night but Joe has some psychological problems, including criminal behavior, which manifests itself when he steals a car. Maya, nevertheless, agrees to drive with him to his older sister's home in rural Connecticut and finds bad blood and more mental anguish that she knows how to deal with. Terrifically honest performance by Sillas and an equally touching one by Ilku are highlights of this adult attempt at romance. **85m/C VHS.** Karen Sillas, David Ilku, Molly Price, Jack Gwaltney; **D:** Deirdre Fishel; **W:** Deirdre Fishel; **C:** Peter Pearce; **M:** John Paul Jones. LEO

Risky Business 🐾🐾 1928 Fortune-seeking mother disapproves of daughter's doctor fiance, and educates girl in marital woes. Video includes early Pollard short "Sold at Auction." **104m/B VHS, Beta, LV.** Vera Reynolds, ZaSu Pitts, Ethey Clayton; **D:** Alan Hale. GPV, FCT, WAR

Risky Business 🐾🐾🐾 1983 (R) With his parents out of town and awaiting word from the college boards, a teenager becomes involved in unexpected ways with a quick-thinking prostitute, her pimp, and assorted others. Cruise is likeable, especially when dancing in his underwear. Funny, well-paced, stylish prototypical '80s teen flick reintroduced Ray-Bans as the sunglasses for the wannabe hip. What a party! **99m/C VHS, Beta, LV, 8mm.** Tom Cruise, Rebecca DeMornay, Curtis Armstrong, Bronson Pinchot, Joe Pantoliano, Kevin Anderson, Richard Masur, Raphael Sbarge, Nicholas Pryor, Janet Carroll; **D:** Paul Brickman; **W:** Paul Brickman; **C:** Reynaldo Villalobos; **M:** Tangerine Dream. WAR

Rita Hayworth: The Love Goddess 🐾½ 1983 Made for television drama details the tragic life of the beautiful film star. Carter, lovely though she is, plays Rita weakly and without depth. **100m/C VHS, Beta.** Lynda Carter, Michael Lerner, Alejandro Rey, John Considine; **D:** James Goldstone. LIV

Rita, Sue & Bob Too 🐾🐾🐾 1987 (R) A middle-aged Englishman gets involved in a menage a trois with two promiscuous teenagers, until the whole town gets wind of it. A raunchy, amoral British comedy. **94m/C VHS, Beta, LV.** GB Michelle Holmes, George Costigan, Siobhan Finneran, Lesley Sharp, Willie Ross, Patti Nicholls, Kulvinder Ghir; **D:** Alan Clarke; **W:** Andrea Dunbar; **M:** Michael Kamen. ORI, WAR

The Rite 🐾🐾 The Ritual; Riten 1969 Members of a famous theatrical troupe are called before a judge to answer charges that a production is obscene. The judge's interrogation exposes their private and painful neuroses until the performers decide to turn on their accuser. Pessimistic even by Bergman standards and the first film the director made specifically for TV. Swedish with subtitles. **75m/B VHS.** SW Ingrid Thulin, Gunnar Bjornstrand, Erik Hell, Anders Ek; **D:** Ingmar Bergman; **W:** Ingmar Bergman; **C:** Sven Nykvist. HMV

Rituals 🐾½ The Creeper 1979 Group of five calm, rational men suddenly turn desperate after a chain of nightmarish events on a camping trip. Yet another low-budget "Deliverance" rip off. **100m/C VHS, Beta.** CA Hal Holbrook, Lawrence Dane; **D:** Peter Carter. VTR

The Ritz 🐾🐾🐾 1976 (R) Weston tries to get away from his gangster brother-in-law by hiding out in a gay bathhouse in New York. Moreno plays a talentless singer Googie Gomez, who performs in the bathhouse while waiting for her big break. Moreno is great reprising her Tony-winning stage role, and Lester's direction is spiffy. Written by Terence McNally from his play. **91m/C VHS, Beta, LV, Closed Caption.** Rita Moreno, Jack Weston, Jerry Stiller, Kaye Ballard, Treat Williams, F. Murray Abraham; **D:** Richard Lester. WAR

Rivals ✍½ *Deadly Rivals* **1972 (R)** Shallow, unconvincing drama about a stepfather challenged by his stepson, who wants to kill this new contender for his mother's love. Nice handling of cast credits, but other details—like acting, directing and photography—leave much to be desired. **103m/C VHS, Beta.** Robert Klein, Joan Hackett, Scott Jacoby; **D:** Krishna Shah. *TPI*

Rivals of the Silver Fox ✍½ **1980** Young kickers prove no match for their hoary, hard-chopping elder. **90m/C VHS, Beta.** Casanova Wong, Barry Lam, Chen Shao Ping, Lee Fat Yuen. *NO*

The River ✍✍✍✍ **1951** A massively lauded late film by Renoir about three British girls growing up in Bengal, India, all developing crushes on a one-legged American vet. Lyrical and heartwarming, with hailed cinematography by Claude Renoir. Rumer Godden wrote the novel, and co-scripted the screenplay with director Renoir. Satyajit Ray, one of India's greatest filmmakers, assisted Renoir. **99m/C VHS, Beta, LV.** *FR* Patricia Walters, Adrienne Corri, Nora Swinburne, Radha, Arthur Shields, Thomas E. Breen, Esmond Knight; **D:** Jean Renoir; **W:** Jean Renoir. National Board of Review Awards '51: 5 Best Foreign Films of the Year. *HMV, CRC*

The River ✍✍ **1984 (PG)** Farmers battle a river whose flood threatens their farm. Spacek, as always, is strong and believable as the wife and mother, but Gibson falters. Beautiful photography. The third in an onslaught of films in the early '80s that dramatized the plight of the small American farmer. "The River" isn't as strong as "Country" and "Places in the Heart" which managed to convey important messages less cloyingly. **124m/C VHS, Beta, LV, Closed Caption.** Mel Gibson, Sissy Spacek, Scott Glenn, Billy Green Bush; **D:** Mark Rydell; **W:** Julian Barry, Robert Dillon; **C:** Vilmos Zsigmond; **M:** John Williams. Nominations: Academy Awards '84: Best Actress (Spacek), Best Cinematography, Best Sound, Best Original Score. *USH*

River Beat ✍✍ **1954** A woman aboard an American freighter is unwittingly used as diamond smuggler, and is arrested when the ship docks in London. An inspector does his best to clear the hapless woman. **70m/B VHS, Beta.** Phyllis Kirk, John Bentley, Robert Ayres, Lenny White, Glyn Houston, Charles Lloyd Pack; **D:** Guy Green. *SNC*

The River Niger ✍✍½ **1976 (R)** Jones is riveting, and Tyson is good in an otherwise muddling adaptation of the Tony-award winning play about black ghetto life. Realistic emotions and believable characters. **105m/C VHS.** James Earl Jones, Cicely Tyson, Glynn Turman, Louis Gossett Jr., Roger E. Mosley, Jonelle Allen; **D:** Krishna Shah. *NO*

River of Death ✍½ **1990 (R)** Absurd adventure, based on an Alistair McLean novel, about a white man entering the Amazon jungle world of a forgotten tribe in search of wealth, tripping over Neo-Nazi scientists and war criminals. Too complex to be harmlessly enjoyable; too mindless for the complexity to be worth unraveling. **103m/C VHS, Beta, LV, Closed Caption.** Michael Dudikoff, Robert Vaughn, Donald Pleasence, Herbert Lom, L.Q. Jones, Cynthia Erland, Sarah Maur-Thorp; **D:** Steve Carver. *MGM, WAR*

River of Diamonds ✍ **1990** A daring adventurer with the standard beautiful woman at his side, battles evil curses and Nazis buried alive to find a fortune in diamonds. Yeah, sure. Another miserable "Indiana Jones" rip off. **88m/C VHS, Beta, Closed Caption.** Dack Rambo, Angela O'Neill, Ferdinand "Ferdy" Mayne, Graham Clark, David Sherwood, Tony Caprari, Dominique Tyawa; **D:** Robert J. Smawley. *TTC*

River of Evil ✍½ **1964** Action/adventure in which a young girl travels through the Amazon jungle searching for clues to her father's death. **?m/C VHS.** Barbara Rutting, Harald Leipnitz. *SNC*

River of Grass ✍½ **1994** No-budget noirish crime/romance set in the swampy, low-rent Florida area between Miami and the Everglades. Uncaring and frankly dumb housewife/mom Cozy (Bowman) hooks up with the boozing Lee Ray

(Fessenden) and the dim duo take an illegal dip in a private pool. Cozy manages to fire off Lee's gun and thinks she hit a man who suddenly appeared. Not bothering to find out if this is true, they decide to hold up in a motel until they can figure out what to do. You won't really care but director Reichardt does have a way with visuals so things aren't a total loss. **80m/C VHS.** Lisa Bowman, Larry Fessenden, Dick Russell; **D:** Kelly Reichardt; **W:** Jesse Hartman, Kelly Reichardt; **C:** Jim Denault. Nominations: Independent Spirit Awards '96: Best First Feature, Debut Performance (Bowman). *FCT*

River of No Return ✍✍½ **1954** During the gold rush, an itinerant farmer and his young son look for a heart-of-gold saloon singer search for her estranged husband. Rather crummy script is helped by the mere presence of Mitchum and Monroe. Marilyn sings the title song, "Down in the Meadow," and "I'm Going to File My Claim." **91m/C VHS, Beta, LV.** Robert Mitchum, Marilyn Monroe, Tommy Rettig, Rory Calhoun, Murvyn Vye, Douglas Spencer; **D:** Otto Preminger; **C:** Joseph LaShelle. *FOX*

River of Unrest ✍✍½ *Ourselves Alone* **1937** Remarkable visual expressiveness and emotional power mark this depiction of terrorism and open warfare during the Irish Rebellion. Based on a play, hence slow; but good acting pulls it up half a bone. **69m/B VHS, Beta.** John Lodge, John Loder, Antoinette Cellier. *VYY*

The River Pirates ✍✍½ **1994 (PG)** Mississippi boy discovers a lot about life over the summer of his 12th birthday in 1942. He finds the secret hiding place of a band of river thieves, endures a tornado, has some adventures with his friends, and finds out that his crush on the prettiest girl in town is reciprocated. Based on a novel by Willie Morris. **108m/C VHS, LV.** Ryan Francis, Richard Farnsworth, Gennie James, Doug Emerson, Anne Ramsey, Maureen O'Sullivan; **D:** Tom G. Robertson. *THV*

The River Rat ✍✍½ **1984 (PG)** Ex-con Jones is reunited with his daughter after spending thirteen years in prison. There's something in there about stashed loot that should have been jettisonned in favor of more getting-to-know-you father-daughter drama, which is good. **93m/C VHS, Beta, LV, Closed Caption.** Tommy Lee Jones, Brian Dennehy, Martha Plimpton, Shawn Smith, Melissa Davis; **D:** Tom Rickman. *PAR*

A River Runs Through It ✍✍✍½ **1992 (PG)** Contemplative exploration of family ties and coming of age with impact falling just short of the novel's is another well-crafted American tale directed by Redford. Set in Montana during the early part of the century, a Presbyterian minister teaches his two sons, one troubled and one on his way to success, about life and religion via fly-fishing. Based on the novel by Norman Maclean. The laser disc version includes commentary by Redford. **123m/C VHS, LV, 8mm, Closed Caption.** Craig Sheffer, Brad Pitt, Tom Skerritt, Brenda Blethyn, Emily Lloyd, Edie McClurg, Stephen Shellan, Susan Taylor; **D:** Robert Redford; **W:** Richard Friedenberg; **C:** Philippe Rousselot; **M:** Mark Isham. Academy Awards '92: Best Cinematography; Nominations: Academy Awards '92: Best Adapted Screenplay, Best Original Score. *COL, CRC, BTV*

The River Wild ✍✍½ **1994 (PG-13)** Dissatisfied wife Gail (Streep) plans a family whitewater rafting vacation with 10-year-old son Roarke (Mazzello) and workaholic husband Tom (Strathairn). A former guide (and white-water expert) Gail comes to the aid of river novices Wade (boyishly menacing Bacon) and Terry (Reilly), who quickly turn out to be violent criminals needing Gail's help with their escape. Slow start leads to nonstop thrills with Streep an adept action heroine, though undercut by the flic's need to do something with Strathairn's thankless role. Beautiful Montana and Oregon settings. **CW:** Some violence, threatening moments. **111m/C VHS, LV, Closed Caption.** Meryl Streep, David Strathairn, Joseph Mazzello, Kevin Bacon, John C. Reilly, Benjamin Bratt; **D:** Curtis Hanson; **W:** Raynold Gideon; **C:** Robert Elswit; **M:** Jerry Goldsmith. Nominations: Golden Globe Awards '95:

Best Actress—Drama (Streep), Best Supporting Actor (Bacon); Screen Actors Guild Award '94: Best Actress (Streep). *USH*

Riverbend ✍✍ **1989 (R)** A renegade black Army major escapes a rigged court martial only to be persecuted by racist whites in a small Southern town. Made for television. **106m/C VHS, Beta.** Steve James, Tony Frank, Julius Tennon, Margaret Avery; **D:** Sam Firstenberg. *PAR*

River's Edge ✍✍✍ **1987 (R)** Drug-addled high school student strangles his girlfriend and casually displays the corpse to his apathetic group of friends, who leave the murder unreported for days. Harrowing and gripping; based on a true story. Aging biker Hopper is splendid. **99m/C VHS, Beta, LV, 8mm, Closed Caption.** Keanu Reeves, Crispin Glover, Daniel Roebuck, Joshua Miller, Dennis Hopper, Ione Skye, Roxana Zal, Tom Bower, Constance Forslund, Leo Rossi, Jim Metzler; **D:** Tim Hunter; **W:** Neal Jimenez; **C:** Frederick Elmes; **M:** Jurgen Knieper. Independent Spirit Awards '88: Best Film, Best Screenplay; Sundance Film Festival '87: Special Jury Prize. *NLC*

Road Agent ✍½ *Texas Road Agent* **1926** Hoxie is the Kansas Kid, a fugitive hired by a crooked lawyer to pose as the long-lost heir to a ranching fortune. Only the Kid develops a soft spot for his "family" and may not be able to go through with the evil plot. **70m/B VHS, Beta.** Al Hoxie; **D:** J.P. McGowan. *NOS, DVT, MLB*

Road Games ✍✍ **1981 (PG)** Trucker Keach is drawn into a web of intrigue surrounding a series of highway "Jack the Ripper"-style murders. Curtis is a hitchhiker. Nothing special. Director Franklin later helmed "Psycho II." **100m/C VHS, Beta.** *AU* Stacy Keach, Jamie Lee Curtis; **D:** Richard Franklin; **M:** Brian May. *COL, NLC*

The Road Home ✍✍½ **1995 (PG)** Depression-era heart-tugger features two orphaned brothers who ride the rails from New York to Nebraska in search of a new home at Father Flanagan's Boys Town. **90m/C VHS, Closed Caption.** Keegan Macintosh, Will Estes, Kris Kristofferson, Charles Martin Smith, Danny Aiello, Dee Wallace Stone, Mickey Rooney; **D:** Dean Hamilton. *REP*

Road House ✍✍½ **1948** Nightclub singer Lupino inspires noir feelings between jealous road house owner Widmark and his partner Wilde. Widmark sets up Wilde to take the fall for a faked robbery, convinces the law to release him into his custody, then dares him to escape. **95m/B VHS, Beta.** Richard Widmark, Ida Lupino, Cornel Wilde, Celeste Holm, O.Z. Whitehead; **D:** Jean Negulesco. *FOX, FCT*

Road House ✍½ **1989 (R)** Bouncer Swayze is hired to do the impossible: clean up the toughest bar in Kansas City. When he lays down his rules he makes a lot of enemies, including exbar employees and local organized crime. Ample violence; an example of formula filmmaking at its most brain-numbing, with a rock soundtrack. **115m/C VHS, Beta, LV, 8mm.** Patrick Swayze, Sam Elliott, Kelly Lynch, Ben Gazzara, Kevin Tighe, Marshall Teague, Julie Michaels, Jeff Healey; **D:** Rowdy Herrington; **C:** Dean Cundey; **M:** Michael Kamen. *MGM*

Road Kill USA ✍✍½ **1993** Two sleazy drifters on a cross-country murder spree pick up a hitchhiking college student who joins in for the fun. When he refuses, he has two choices: kill or be killed. **98m/C VHS.** Andrew Porter, Sean Bridges, Deanna Perry; **D:** Tony Elwood. *AIP*

The Road Killers ✍✍ **1995 (R)** Sickening psycho Cliff (well-played by Sheffer) is head of a brutal quartet that terrorizes a family driving along a remote desert highway. Cliff kidnaps the family daughter and her mild-mannered dad (Lambert) must rescue her. **CW:** Violence; language. **89m/C VHS, LV, Closed Caption.** Christopher Lambert, Craig Sheffer, Adrienne Shelly; **D:** Deran Sarafian; **W:** Tedi Sarafian. *WEA, LIV*

Road Racers 🎬🎬 **1959** The roar of the engine, fast cars, and family ties combine in this movie about the thrill of speed. **73m/B VHS.** Joel Lawrence, Marian Collier, Skip Ward; **D:** Arthur Swerdloff; **W:** Stanley Kallis, Ed Lasko. COL

Road Show 🎬🎬½ **1941** Menjou stars as a young man wrongfully committed to an insane asylum. He escapes and joins a bankrupt carnival owned by Landis. Some really zany stuff keeps this from being just standard fare. Co-written by silent film comic Langdon. **87m/B VHS.** Adolphe Menjou, Carole Landis, John Hubbard, Charles Butterworth, Patsy Kelly, George E. Stone, Polly Ann Young, Edward Norris, Marjorie Woodworth, Florence Bates; **D:** Hal Roach; **W:** Harry Langdon. NOS

The Road to Bali 🎬🎬🎬 **1953** Sixth Bob-n-Bing road show, the only one in color, is a keeper. The boys are competing for the love of—that's right—Lamour. She must be some gal, cuz they chase her all the way to Bali, where they meet cannibals and other perils, including the actual Humphrey Bogart. Jones's debut, in a bit role. ♫Moonflowers; Chicago Style; Hoots Mon; To See You; The Merry-Go-Runaround; Chorale for Brass, Piano, and Bongo (instrumental). **90m/C VHS, Beta.** Bob Hope, Bing Crosby, Dorothy Lamour, Murvyn Vye, Ralph Moody, Jane Russell, Jerry Lewis, Dean Martin, Carolyn Jones; **D:** Hal Walker. UNI, DVT, MLB

The Road to Galveston 🎬🎬🎬 **1996** **(PG-13)** Texas widow Jordan Roosevelt (Tyson) needs to pay her mortgage so she turns her home into a residence for three Alzheimer patients. When her financial problems only worsen, Jordan decides to fulfill her lifetime goal and takes everyone on a trip to Galveston to see the ocean. Sentimental, fact-based TV movie cuts the saccharine through compelling performances.**CW:** Cicely Tyson, Piper Laurie, Tess Harper, Salle Ellis, Starletta DuPois, James McDaniel, Penny Johnson, Clarence Williams III, Stephen Root; **D:** Michael Toshiyuki Uno; **W:** Tony Lee; **M:** Stanley Clarke. PAR

The Road to Hong Kong 🎬🎬½ **1962** Last of the Crosby/Hope team-ups shows some wear, but still manages charm and humor. Lamour appears only briefly in this twisted comedy of hustlers caught in international espionage and cosmic goings-on. ♫Teamwork; Let's Not Be Sensible; It's The Only Way to Travel; We're On the Road to Hong Kong; Warmer Than a Whisper. **91m/B VHS, LV.** Bob Hope, Bing Crosby, Joan Collins, Dorothy Lamour, Peter Sellers; **D:** Norman Panama; **W:** Norman Panama; **C:** Jack Hildyard. MGM, BTV, FCT

The Road to Lebanon 🎬🎬 **1960** An original musical comedy featuring many stars, spoofing the famous Hope-Crosby "Road" films. **50m/B VHS, Beta.** Danny Thomas, Bing Crosby, Bob Hope, Hugh Downs, Claudine Auger, Sheldon Leonard. NOS, VYY, DVT

The Road to Life 🎬🎬 Putyovka V Zhizn **1931** In the turmoil caused by Russia's Revolutionary and Civil wars, thousands of orphans roam the countryside resorting to petty crime to survive. One group is sent to a collective as part of an experimental program where they can be reformed and learn a trade but their criminal pasts seem inescapable. Russian with subtitles. **100m/B VHS.** RU Nikolai Batalov, Maria Gonfa, Tsifan Kyria; **D:** Nicolai Ekk; **W:** Nicolai Ekk; **M:** Yakov Stollyar. FCT

The Road to Morocco 🎬🎬🎬½ **1942** The third in the road movie series finds Hope and Crosby in Morocco, stranded and broke. To get some money, Crosby sells Hope into slavery to be the princess's (Lamour) personal plaything. Feeling guilty, Crosby returns to the palace to rescue Hope, only to find that he and the princess are getting married because the royal astrologer said it was in the stars. Crosby then tries to woo Lamour and, when the astrologer discovers the stars are mistaken, those two decide to marry. Quinn, however, also wants her and hilarious scenes ensue when the boys rescue Lamour from

him. One of the funniest in the series. Watch for the camel at the end. ♫Constantly; Moonlight Becomes You; Ain't Got a Dime to My Name; Road to Morocco. **83m/C VHS, LV.** Bing Crosby, Bob Hope, Dorothy Lamour, Anthony Quinn, Dona Drake, Vladimir Sokoloff, Yvonne De Carlo; **D:** David Butler; **C:** William Mellor. Nominations: Academy Awards '42: Best Original Screenplay, Best Sound.USH

Road to Nashville 🎬🎬 **1967** **(G)** An agent travels to Nashville to enlist talent for a new musical. Why do so many of these semi-musicals insist on having a plot? Good music. **110m/C VHS, Beta.** Marty Robbins, Johnny Cash, Doodles Weaver, Connie Smith, Richard Arlen; **D:** Robert Patrick. NO

The Road to Rio 🎬🎬🎬½ **1947** The wisecracking duo travel to Rio De Janeiro to prevent Spanish beauty Lamour (there she is again) from going through with an arranged marriage. Topnotch entry; fifth in the "Road" series. ♫But Beautiful; You Don't Have To Know the Language; For What?; Experience; Apalachicola, Florida; Cavaquinho; Brazil. **100m/B VHS, Beta.** Bing Crosby, Bob Hope, Dorothy Lamour, Gale Sondergaard, Frank Faylen, The Andrews Sisters; **D:** Norman Z. McLeod; **W:** Jack Rose; **C:** Ernest Laszlo. Nominations: Academy Awards '47: Original Dramatic/Comedy Score. COL

The Road to Ruin 🎬🎬 **1928** The evils of smoking and drinking plummet a girl into a life of prostitution in this melodramatic, moralistic tale. An unintentional laugh-riot right up there with "Reefer Madness." Silent. **45m/B VHS, Beta.** Helen Foster, Grant Withers, Virginia Roye; **D:** Norton S. Parker; **W:** Erik Anjou. SNC, NOS, VYY

Road to Ruin 🎬🎬 **1991** **(R)** A rich playboy pretends to lose all his money to see if his girlfriend loves him for himself or for his wealth. But when his business partner embezzles his fortune, he must regain both his money and his girlfriend's trust.**CW:** Sexuality. **94m/C VHS.** Peter Weller, Carey Lowell, Michael Duchaussoy; **D:** Charlotte Brandstrom. LIV

Road to Salina 🎬🎬🎬 **1968** **(R)** A drifter is mistaken for (and might actually be) a desert-restaurant owner's long-lost son. He plays along, eventually seducing the man's daughter, who might be his sister. **97m/C VHS, Beta.** FR Robert Walker Jr., Rita Hayworth, Mimsy Farmer, Ed Begley Sr.; **D:** Georges Lautner. NLC

The Road to Singapore 🎬🎬½ **1940** This is the movie that started it all. Crosby and Hope decide to swear off women and escape to Singapore to enjoy the free life. There they meet Lamour, a showgirl who is abused by Quinn. The boys rescue Lamour, but soon find they are both falling for her. She's in love with one of them, but won't reveal her feelings. Who will get the girl? Not as funny as some of the other road movies, but it's great for a first try. ♫Captain Custard; The Moon and the Willow Tree; Sweet Potato Piper; Too Romantic; Kaigoon. **84m/C VHS, LV.** Bing Crosby, Bob Hope, Dorothy Lamour, Charles Coburn, Judith Barrett, Anthony Quinn, Jerry Colonna, Johnny Arthur, Pierre Watkin; **D:** Victor Schertzinger; **C:** William Mellor. USH

The Road to Utopia 🎬🎬🎬 **1946** Fourth of the "Road" films, wherein the boys wind up in Alaska posing as two famous escaped killers in order to locate a secret gold mine. One of the series' funniest and most spontaneous entries, abetted by Benchley's dry, upper-crust comments. ♫Put It There, Pal; Welcome to My Dreams; Would You?; Personality; Sunday, Monday, or Always?; Goodtime Charlie; It's Anybody's Spring. **90m/B VHS, Beta, LV.** Bing Crosby, Bob Hope, Dorothy Lamour, Jack LaRue, Robert Benchley, Douglass Dumbrille, Hillary Brooke; **D:** Hal Walker; **W:** Norman Panama; **C:** Lionel Lindon. Nominations: Academy Awards '46: Best Original Screenplay. USH

The Road to Wellville 🎬🎬 **1994** **(R)** Corn flake magnate John Harvey Kellogg takes good health to an intestine-invading extreme in this spa satire featuring Hopkins as the bucktoothed Kellogg. Broderick and Fonda portray a

wealthy couple who visit the turn-of-the-century sanitarium in search of Kellogg's cure, but receive only sexual frustration and anal humiliations. Bowel jokes and an essentially plotless scenario overshadow a gifted, but helpless cast. Adapted from T. Coraghessan Boyle's not-so-easily-adaptable novel.**CW:** Contains nudity, sexual situations, and incessant bathroom humor. **120m/C VHS, LV, Closed Caption.** Anthony Hopkins, Bridget Fonda, Matthew Broderick, John Cusack, Dana Carvey, Michael Lerner, Colm Meaney, John Neville, Lara Flynn Boyle, Traci Lind, Roy Brocksmith, Norbert Weisser; **D:** Alan Parker; **W:** Alan Parker; **C:** Peter Biziou; **M:** Rachel Portman. COL

The Road to Yesterday 🎬🎬½ **1925** Two couples thrown together on a crashing train are somehow thrown into the eighteenth century in roles parallel to their own lives. DeMille's first independent film; intriguing action/melodrama. Silent with musical soundtrack. **136m/B VHS, Beta.** Joseph Schildkraut, William Boyd, Jetta Goudal, Vera Reynolds, Iron Eyes Cody; **D:** Cecil B. DeMille. GPV, VYY

Road to Yesterday/The Yankee Clipper 🎬🎬½ **1927** Four train passengers are transported back to previous lives in "The Road to Yesterday." "The Yankee Clipper" races the British Lord of the Isles from China to New England to capture the tea trade. Both of these pictures are abridged versions. Silent. **56m/B VHS, Beta.** William Boyd, Elinor Fair, Joseph Schildkraut, Jetta Goudal, Vera Reynolds; **D:** Cecil B. DeMille. CCB

The Road to Zanzibar 🎬🎬 **1941** After selling a fake diamond mine to a criminal, Crosby and Hope flee to Zanzibar, where they meet up with Lamour and Merkel. The guys put up the money for a safari, supposedly to look for Lamour's brother, but they soon discover that they too have been tricked. Deciding to head back to Zanzibar, Crosby and Hope find themselves surrounded by hungry cannibals. Will they survive, or will they be someone's dinner? Not as funny as the other road movies, but amusing nonetheless. ♫It's Always You; You're Dangerous; On the Road to Zanzibar; You Lucky People You; Birds of a Feather; African Etude. **92m/C VHS, LV.** Bing Crosby, Bob Hope, Dorothy Lamour, Una Merkel, Eric Blore, Iris Adrian, Lionel Royce; **D:** Victor Schertzinger. USH

The Road Warrior 🎬🎬🎬½ **1982** **(R)** The first sequel to "Mad Max" takes place after nuclear war has destroyed Australia. Max helps a colony of oil-drilling survivors defend themselves from the roving murderous outback gangs and escape to the coast. The climactic chase scene is among the most exciting ever filmed; this film virtually created the "action-adventure" picture of the 1980s. **95m/C VHS, Beta, LV, DVD.** Mel Gibson, Bruce Spence, Emil Minty, Vernon Wells; **D:** George Miller; **W:** George Miller; **C:** Dean Semler; **M:** Brian May. Los Angeles Film Critics Association Awards '82: Best Foreign Film. WAR

Roadhouse Girl 🎬 Marilyn **1953** A sexy woman kindles a romance with one of her husband's employees and the result is murder. Reminiscent of "The Postman Always Rings Twice," but with poor production values and performances. **70m/B VHS, Beta.** GB Maxwell Reed, Sandra Dorne, Leslie Dwyer, Vida Hope, Ferdinand "Ferdy" Mayne; **D:** Wolf Rilla; **W:** Wolf Rilla. SNC

Roadhouse 66 🎬½ **1984** **(R)** Utterly unoriginal broke-down-in-a-hick-town nonsense. Snooty Reinhold and scruffy Dafoe go through the motions, and of course find a pair of female companions. Soundtrack features Los Lobos, the Pretenders, and Dave Edmunds. **90m/C VHS, Beta.** Willem Dafoe, Judge Reinhold, Karen Lee, Kate Vernon, Stephen Elliott; **D:** John Mark Robinson; **C:** Thomas Ackerman. FOX

Roadie 🎬½ **1980** **(PG)** Supposedly a look at the back-stage world of rock n' roll, but the performances and direction leave a lot to be desired. Meatloaf is a roadie who desperately wants to meet Alice Cooper, and spends the movie trying to do so. Features Art Carney, and musical names like Blondie, Roy Orbison, Hank Williams, Jr. and Don Cornelius (of "Soul Train" fame). **105m/C VHS.** Meat Loaf, Kaki Hunter, Art Carney, Art Carney, Gailard Sartain, Alice Cooper, Roy Orbison, Hank Williams Jr., Ramblin' Jack Elliot; *D:* Alan Rudolph; *W:* Alan Rudolph, Michael Ventura. *MVD, MGM*

Roadkill 🐾 1989 Cheap thriller about Ramona (Buhagiar), a concert promoter who tries to find a lost band, "The Children of Paradise," in the Canadian north woods. Along the way, she meets a would-be serial killer and other assorted weirdos. **85m/B VHS.** *CA* Valerie Buhagiar, Don McKellar, Bruce McDonald; *D:* Bruce McDonald; *W:* Don McKellar. Toronto-City Award '89: Best Canadian Feature Film. *NO*

Roads to the South 🐾🐾½ 1978 Onetime Spanish revolutionary turned screenwriter returns to his homeland to fight fascism, but finds himself attracted to his son's beautiful girlfriend. Much soul searching. In French with English subtitles. **100m/C VHS, LV.** *FR* Yves Montand, Miou-Miou, Laurent Malet; *D:* Joseph Losey; *W:* Jorge Semprun; *M:* Michel Legrand. *CVC, IME, FCT*

Roadside Prophets 🐾🐾 1992 (R) Counter-culture road trip, striving to be the '90s version of "Easy Rider," follows factory worker/biker Joe (Doe) on his mission to transport the ashes of a fellow biker to Nevada. He is accompanied by the pesky younger Sam (Horovitz), and together they meet up with lots of eccentrics and stay at lots of cheap motels. Interesting cast meanders through sentimental and slow-moving buddy flick from debut director Wool, who wrote "Sid and Nancy." Cusack completes the cameo hat trick, with appearances here and in 1992's "The Player" and "Shadows and Fog." *CW:* Language and drug use scene. **96m/C VHS, LV, Closed Caption.** John Doe, Adam Horovitz, David Carradine, Timothy Leary, Arlo Guthrie, Barton Heyman, Jennifer Balgobin; *Cameos:* John Cusack; *D:* Abbe Wool; *W:* Abbe Wool. *NLC*

The Roamin' Cowboy 🐾🐾 1937 In a town where the local ranchers are being threatened, a drifter comes to their rescue and wins both a girl and a job. **56m/B VHS.** Fred Scott, Al "Fuzzy" St. John, Lois January, Forrest Taylor, Roger Williams; *D:* Robert F. "Bob" Hill. *NOS, DVT*

Roamin' Wild 🐾🐾½ 1936 Exciting, action-packed early western with marshal Tyler saving a lady's stagecoach line from unsavory varmints. **60m/B VHS, Beta.** Tom Tyler, Carol Wyndham, Al Ferguson, George Chesebro, Max Davidson, Fred Parker; *D:* Bernard B. Ray. *NOS, DVT*

Roanoak 🐾🐾½ 1986 A dramatization in three parts of the mysterious fate of the early English settlement of Roanoak in North Carolina, which disappeared without a trace. Long, but intriguing. Made for PBS: "American Playhouse." **180m/C Beta.** Will Sampson, Victoria Racimo, Porky White, Adrian Sparks, Patrick Kilpatrick; *D:* Jan Egleson. *PBS*

Roarin' Lead 🐾½ 1937 Three Mesquiteers fight with a gang of rustlers while helping the orphans' and cattlemen's associations. **54m/B VHS, Beta.** Bob Livingston, Ray Corrigan, Max Terhune. *VCN*

Roaring City 🐾½ 1951 A hard-boiled detective searches for the person behind the murders of gangsters and prize fighters. **58m/B VHS, Beta, LV.** Hugh Beaumont, Edward Brophy, Richard Travis; *D:* William (Lester Williams) Berke. *NO*

Roaring Guns 🐾🐾½ 1936 An unflappable McCoy rides in to thwart a despicable landowner trying to drive all the small ranchers out of business. Low-budget fun. **66m/B VHS, Beta.** Tim McCoy, Rex Lease, Wheeler Oakman; *D:* Sam Newfield. *NOS, VCN, DVT*

Roaring Ranch 🐾½ 1930 Gibson is trying to protect his ranch from the evil Oakman while attempting to care for a baby as well. **65m/B VHS.** Hoot Gibson, Wheeler Oakman, Sally Eilers, Bobby Nelson, Frank Clark; *D:* B. Reeves Eason; *W:* B. Reeves Eason. *GPV*

The Roaring Road 🐾🐾½ 1919 Romantic comedy about a car salesman named Toodles, who drives for his company in a big race. Vintage racing footage; silent with original organ music. **57m/B VHS, Beta, 8mm.** Wallace Reid, Ann Little, Theodore Roberts; *D:* James Cruze. *VYY, GPV, GVV*

Roaring Roads 🐾 1935 An heir to a fortune acquires a lust for race car driving, and his family thinks a reckless death wish. **60m/B VHS, Beta, LV.** Gertrude Messinger, David Sharpe. *NO*

Roaring Six Guns 🐾½ 1937 Maynard protects his property against his crooked partner and his fiancee's father. **60m/B VHS, Beta.** Kermit Maynard, Mary Hayes, John Merton, Edward Cassidy. *NOS, DVT, DVT*

Roaring Speedboats 🐾 *Mile a Minute Love* 1937 Bakewell is a speedboat racer up against crooks who want to con him out of his money by tinkering with his invention. **62m/B VHS, Beta, 8mm.** William "Billy" Bakewell, Arletta Duncan, Renaldo Duncan, Vivien Oakland, Wilfrid Lucas; *D:* Elmer Clifton. *VYY*

The Roaring Twenties 🐾🐾🐾½ 1939 Three WWI buddies find their lives intersecting unexpectedly in Prohibition-era New York. Cagney becomes a bootlegger and vies with Bogart for status as crime boss. Lynn is the attorney working to prosecute them. Greatest of all gangster flicks. Cheesy script delivered with zest by top pros. **106m/B VHS, Beta, LV, Closed Caption.** James Cagney, Humphrey Bogart, Jeffrey Lynn, Priscilla Lane, Gladys George, Frank McHugh; *D:* Raoul Walsh. National Board of Review Awards '39: 10 Best Films of the Year. *MGM, FOX*

Rob Roy 🐾🐾🐾 1995 (R) Kilt-raising though overlong tale of legendary Scot Robert Roy MacGregor mixes love and honor with bloodlust and revenge. Neeson's rugged clan leader fends off a band of dastardly nobles led by Cunningham (Roth), a foppish twit with an evil bent. Misty highland scenery and intense romantic interplay between Neeson and Lange as the spirited Mary MacGregor lend a passionate twist to an otherwise earthy, robust adventure of lore capped by one of the best sword fights in years. Both Neeson and Lange provide a gutsy substance to their characters: Neeson's Celtic hero is sexy and steadfast (and generally sports an Irish accent), while Lange inhabits a soulful and tenacious Mary. Roth's delightfully hammy performance as MacGregor's loathsome, bewigged nemesis delivers zip amid the high-minded speeches, plot lulls, and separated body parts. Visually stunning, with on-location shooting in the Scottish Highlands. More ambience is provided by Buswell's evocative score. *CW:* Sexuality and violence, including a rape scene and a lot of bloody swordplay. **144m/C VHS, LV, Closed Caption.** Liam Neeson, Jessica Lange, Tim Roth, John Hurt, Eric Stoltz, Andrew Keir, Brian Cox, Brian McCardie, Gilbert Martin, Vicki Masson, David Hayman; *D:* Michael Caton-Jones; *W:* Alan Sharp; *C:* Karl Walter Lindenlaub. British Academy Awards '95: Best Supporting Actor (Roth); Nominations: Academy Awards '95: Best Supporting Actor (Roth); Golden Globe Awards '96: Best Supporting Actor (Roth). *MGM*

Rob Roy—The Highland Rogue 🐾½ *Rob Roy* 1953 In the early 18th century, Scottish Highlander Rob Roy must battle against the King of England's secretary, who would undermine the MacGregor clan to enact his evil deeds. Dull Disney drama. **84m/C VHS, Beta.** Richard Todd, Glynis Johns, James Robertson Justice, Michael Gough; *D:* Harold French. *DIS*

Robbers of the Sacred Mountain 🐾🐾 *Falcon's Gold* 1983 TV rip-off of "Raiders of the Lost Ark," loosely based on Arthur Conan Doyle's story "Challenger's Gold." Adventurers seek meteorites in the Mexican jungle. Billed as the first made for cable movie. **95m/C VHS, Beta.** John Marley, Simon MacCorkindale, Louise Vallance, George Touliatos; *D:* Bob Schulz. *PSM*

Robbery 🐾🐾½ 1967 Unoriginal but competent rendition of the hackneyed British Royal Mail robbery. Thieves plan and execute a heist of a late-night mail train carrying $10 million. **113m/C VHS, Beta.** *GB* Stanley Baker, James Booth, Joanna Pettet, Frank Finlay, Barry Foster; *D:* Peter Yates. *NLC*

Robbery 🐾 1985 A six-man platoon of Vietnam war veterans endeavors to assault and rob a mob of shiftless bookies. **91m/C VHS, Beta.** John Sheerin, Tony Rickards, Tim Hughes; *D:* Michael Thornhill. *LIV*

Robbery Under Arms 🐾🐾½ 1957 From Australia in the 1800s, similar to the American wild west, comes a tale of love and robbery. Finch is the leader of a band of outlaws. Rather dull story redeemed by excellent photography of beautiful landscape. **83m/C VHS.** *GB* Peter Finch, Ronald Lewis, Laurence Naismith, Maureen Swanson, David McCallum, Jill Ireland; *D:* Jack Lee. *IMP*

Robby 🐾🐾 1968 A young white boy and a young black boy shipwrecked on an island form a strong friendship that sees them through a series of adventures. **60m/C VHS, Beta.** Warren Raum, Ryp Siani, John Garces; *D:* Ralph Blumke. *FCT*

The Robe 🐾🐾🐾½ 1953 This moving, religious portrait follows the career and religious awakening of drunken and dissolute Roman tribune Marcellus (Burton), after he wins the robe of the just-crucified Christ in a dice game. Mature plays Burton's slave surprisingly well, and reprised the role in the sequel, "Demetrius and the Gladiators"; Burton is wooden. "The Robe" was the first movie to be filmed in CinemaScope. Based on the novel by Lloyd C. Douglas. **133m/C VHS, Beta, LV.** Richard Burton, Jean Simmons, Victor Mature, Michael Rennie, Richard Boone, Dean Jagger, Jeff Morrow, Jay Robinson, Dawn Addams, Ernest Thesiger; *D:* Henry Koster; *W:* Albert Maltz, Philip Dunne; *C:* Leon Shamroy. Academy Awards '53: Best Art Direction/Set Decoration (Color), Best Costume Design (Color); Golden Globe Awards '54: Best Film—Drama; National Board of Review Awards '53: 10 Best Films of the Year, Best Actress (Simmons); Nominations: Academy Awards '53: Best Actor (Burton), Best Color Cinematography, Best Picture. *FOX, IGP*

Robert et Robert 🐾🐾🐾 1978 Two 'ineligible' bachelors resort to using a computerized matrimonial agency to find the girls of their dreams. They become friends while they wait for their dates. Sensitive tale of loneliness and friendship. Warm and witty with fine performances throughout. French with English subtitles. **105m/C VHS, Beta.** *FR* Charles Denner, Jacques Villeret, Jean-Claude Brialy, Macha Meril, Germaine Montero, Regine; *D:* Claude Lelouch; *W:* Claude Lelouch; *C:* Jacques Lefrancois. Cesar Awards '79: Best Supporting Actor (Villeret). *COL*

Robert Kennedy and His Times 🐾🐾½ 1990 Another look at the Kennedy clan, this time from the Bobby angle. Good acting. Based on the book by Arthur Schlesinger. **309m/C VHS.** Brad Davis, Veronica Cartwright, Cliff DeYoung, Ned Beatty, Beatrice Straight, Jack Warden; *D:* Marvin J. Chomsky. *COL, PBS*

Roberta 🐾🐾🐾 1935 A football player inherits his aunt's Parisian dress shop and finds himself at odds with an incognito Russian princess. Dumb plot aside, this is one of the best Astaire-Rogers efforts. A later remake was titled "Lovely to Look At." ♫ Let's Begin; Yesterdays; Smoke Gets in Your Eyes; I'll Be Hard to Handle; I Won't Dance; Lovely to Look At; Back Home Again in Indiana; The Touch of Your Hand; You're Devasting. **85m/B VHS, Beta.** Fred Astaire, Ginger Rogers, Irene Dunne, Lucille Ball, Randolph Scott; *D:* William A. Seiter; *M:* Max Steiner. Nominations: Academy Awards '35: Best Song ("Lovely to Look At"). *MGM*

Robin and Marian 🐾🐾 1976 (PG) After a separation of twenty years, Robin Hood is reunited with Maid Marian, who is now a nun. Their dormant feelings for each other are reawakened as Robin spirits her to Sherwood Forest. In case you wanted to see Robin Hood robbed of all magic, spontaneity, and fun. Connery is dull, dull, dull, working with an uninspired script. 106m/C VHS, Beta, LV. *GB* Sean Connery, Audrey Hepburn, Robert Shaw, Richard Harris, Denholm Elliott, Ian Holm, Nicol Williamson, Ronnie Barker; *D:* Richard Lester; *C:* David Watkin; *M:* John Barry. COL, FOX

Robin and the 7 Hoods 🎭🎭½ 1964
Runyon-esque Rat Pack version of 1920s Chicago, with Frank and the boys as do-good gangsters in their last go-round. Fun if not unforgettable. ♫Bang! Bang!; Style; Mister Booze; Don't Be a Do-Badder; My Kind of Town. 124m/C VHS, Beta, LV. Frank Sinatra, Bing Crosby, Dean Martin, Sammy Davis Jr., Peter Falk, Barbara Rush, Allen Jenkins; *D:* Gordon Douglas. Awards: Academy Awards '64: Best Adapted Score, Best Song ("My Kind of Town"). WAR

Robin Hood 🎭🎭🎭½ 1922 Extravagant production casts Fairbanks as eponymous gymnastic swashbuckler who departs for Crusades as Earl of Huntington and returns as the hooded one to save King Richard's throne from the sinister Sheriff of Nottingham. Best ever silent swashbuckling. 110m/B VHS, Beta. Douglas Fairbanks Sr., Wallace Beery, Sam DeGrasse, Enid Bennett, Paul Dickey, William E. Lowery, Roy Coulson, Bill Bennett, Merrill McCormick, Wilson Benge, Willard Louis, Alan Hale, Maine Geary, Lloyd Talman; *D:* Allan Dwan. NOS, GPV, FCT

Robin Hood 🎭🎭🎭 1973 This time the Sherwood Forest crew are portrayed by appropriate cartoon animals, hence, Robin is a fox, Little John a bear, etc. Good family fare, but not as memorable as other Disney features. 83m/C VHS, Beta, LV, Closed Caption. *D:* Wolfgang Reitherman; *M:* George Bruns; *V:* Roger Miller, Brian Bedford, Monica Evans, Phil Harris, Andy Devine, Carol Shelley, Peter Ustinov, Terry-Thomas, Pat Buttram, George Lindsey, Ken Curtis. Nominations: Academy Awards '73: Best Song ("Love"). DIS, FCT, RDG

Robin Hood 🎭🎭🎭 1991 Dark version of the medieval tale. Bergin's Prince of Thieves is well developed and Thurman is a graceful Marion. Three studios announced plans to remake "Robin Hood" in 1990 and two were completed, including this one which was scaled down for cable television. 116m/C VHS, Beta, LV. Patrick Bergin, Uma Thurman, Juergen Prochnow, Edward Fox, Jeroen Krabbe, Jeff Nuttal, David Morrisey, Owen Teale; *D:* John Irvin; *M:* Geoffrey Burgon. FXV, FCT

Robin Hood: Men in Tights 🎭🎭½
Men in Tights 1993 (PG-13) Brooksian rendition of the classic legend inspires guffaws, but doesn't hit the bullseye on all it promises. Hood afficionados will appreciate the painstaking effort taken to spoof the 1938 Errol Flynn classic while leaving plenty of room to poke fun at the more recent Costner non-classic "Robin Hood: Prince of Thieves." Elwes, last seen swinging swords in "The Princess Bride," is well cast as the Flynn look-alike. Expect the usual off-color humor that's so prevalent in all Brooks outings.*CW:* Off-color humor. 105m/C VHS, Closed Caption. Cary Elwes, Richard Lewis, Roger Rees, Amy Yasbeck, Dave Chappelle, Isaac Hayes, Tracey Ullman, Mark Blankfield, Megan Cavanagh, Eric Allen Kramer, Tony Griffin, Dick Van Patten, Mel Brooks; *D:* Mel Brooks; *W:* Mel Brooks, J. David Shapiro, Evan Chandler; *M:* Hummie Mann. FXV

Robin Hood of Texas 🎭🎭½ 1947 Autry finds his calm life disturbed when he is falsely accused of robbing a bank. Pretty good plot for once, in Autry's last Republic western, and plenty of action. 71m/B VHS, Beta. Gene Autry, Lynn (Mary Hart) Roberts, Sterling Holloway, Adele Mara; *D:* Lesley Selander. NO

Robin Hood of the Pecos 🎭🎭½
1941 Ex-Confederate soldier takes on northern post-war politicians and carpetbaggers. Decent Rogers/Hayes outing. 56m/B VHS, Beta. Roy Rogers, George "Gabby" Hayes, Marjorie Reynolds, Jay Novello, Roscoe Ates; *D:* Joseph Kane. NOS, DVT, VYY

Robin Hood: Prince of Thieves 🎭🎭½ 1991 (PG-13) Costner is the politically correct Rebel with a Cause, but a thinker, not a doer—and therein lies the problem. His

quiet thoughtfulness doesn't add up to leadership and Rickman easily overpowers him as the wicked, crazed Sheriff of Nottingham. Freeman is excellent as a civilized Moor who finds England, and its people, inhospitable, dangerous, and not a little stupid. Mastrantonio, a last minute choice, excels as the lovely Lady Marian. Great action sequences, a gritty and morbid picture of the Middle Ages, and some fun scenes with the Merry Men. Revisionist in its ideas about the times and people, critics generally disapproved of the changes in the story and Costner's performance, though their comments about his lack of an English accent seem nitpicky in light of some basic plot problems. Still has lots of fun for lovers of action, romance and fairy tales. 144m/C VHS, LV, Closed Caption. Kevin Costner, Morgan Freeman, Mary Elizabeth Mastrantonio, Christian Slater, Alan Rickman, Geraldine McEwan, Micheal McShane, Brian Blessed, Michael Wincott, Nick Brimble, Jack Wild, Harold Innocent, Jack Wild; *Cameos:* Sean Connery; *D:* Kevin Reynolds; *W:* Pen Densham, John Watson; *M:* Michael Kamen. British Academy Awards '91: Best Supporting Actor (Rickman); MTV Movie Awards '92: Best Song ("(Everything I Do) I Do for You"); Golden Raspberry Awards '91: Worst Actor (Costner); Nominations: Academy Awards '91: Best Song ("(Everything I Do) I Do It for You"). WAR, RDG

Robin Hood: The Movie 1955 A colorized and re-mixed version of several episodes of the British television series adds up to a fine version of the classic tale. Excellent cast, clever editing and stunning colorization. 90m/C VHS. *GB* Richard Greene, Bernadette O'Farrell, Alan Wheatley; *D:* Ralph Smart, Daniel Birt, Terence Fisher. GKK

Robin Hood...The Legend: Herne's Son 🎭🎭½ 1985 When Robin Hood is killed by the Sheriff of Nottingham, he begs Robert of Huntington (Connery) to continue his work. Connery refuses, the band dissolves, Maid Marion is kidnapped, and they reunite to save her. Good entry in the BBC series. 101m/C VHS, Beta, Closed Caption. *GB* Jason Connery, Oliver Cotton, Michael Craig, Nickolas Grace, George Baker; *D:* Robert M. Young. FOX, FCT, TVC

Robin Hood...The Legend: Robin Hood and the Sorcerer 🎭🎭½ 1983 Robin Hood is chosen by the mystical Herne the Hunter to thwart the evil Sheriff of Nottingham and protect the English peasantry. He must defeat the supernatural powers of a sorcerer and gather together his men in this introduction to the made for British television series. 115m/C VHS, Closed Caption. *GB* Michael Praed, Anthony Valentine, Nickolas Grace, Clive Mantle, Peter Williams; *D:* Ian Sharp. FOX, FCT, TVC

Robin Hood...The Legend: The Swords of Wayland 🎭🎭½ 1983 A wicked sorceress provides a supernatural threat to Robin and his merry men. Second entry in the BBC series. Convoluted, breathless plot makes for swashbuckling fun and much derring-do. 115m/C VHS, Beta, Closed Caption. *GB* Michael Praed, Rula Lenska, Nickolas Grace; *D:* Robert M. Young. FOX, FCT

Robin Hood...The Legend: The Time of the Wolf 🎭🎭½ 1985 Robin Hood finds out that an old enemy is about to release his evil doings on the world and only he can stop him, while Maid Marian comes to a momentous decision. 105m/C VHS, Beta, Closed Caption. *GB* Jason Connery, Nickolas Grace, Richard O'Brien; *D:* Syd Roberson. FOX, FCT, TVC

Robin of Locksley 🎭🎭½ 1995 (PG) A modern-day, teenaged Robin Hood (Sawa) battles the bullies at his private boys school (thanks to his archery prowess), meets a girl named Marian, and takes on sinister FBI agent Nottingham. 97m/C VHS. Devon Sawa, Sarah Chalke, Joshua Jackson; *D:* Michael Kennedy. HMK

Robinson Crusoe 🎭🎭 1936 A real oddity: a British silent film originally made in 1927, re-edited ten years later. Music and sound effects were added, along with a narration by children's radio personality Carney. Follows the plot of the

famous adventure story by Daniel Defoe. 34m/B VHS, Beta. VYY

Robinson Crusoe & the Tiger 🎭½ 1972 (G) A tiger tells the famous story of how Robinson Crusoe became stranded on a desert island. 109m/C VHS, Beta, Closed Caption. Hugo Stiglitz, Ahui; *D:* Rene Cardona Jr.

Robinson Crusoe of Clipper Island 🎭🎭 1936 Fourteen-episodes serial featuring the investigative expertise of Mala, a Polynesian in the employ of the U.S. Intelligence Service. Each episode runs 16 minutes. Shortened version titled "Robinson Crusoe of Mystery Island." 256m/B VHS, LV. Mala, Rex, Buck, Kate Greenfield, John Ward, Tracy Lane, Robert F. (Bob) Kortman, Herbert Rawlinson; *D:* Mack V. Wright. SNC, NOS, REP

Robinson Crusoe of Mystery Island 🎭🎭 1936 A Polynesian employed by the U.S. Intelligence Service investigates saboteurs on a mysterious island. Would-be cliffhanger is a yawner; where are the chills and thrills? Edited from the serial "Robinson Crusoe of Clipper Island." 100m/B VHS, Beta. Mala, Rex, Buck, Herbert Rawlinson, Ray Taylor; *D:* Mack V. Wright. VCN

Robinson Crusoe on Mars 🎭 1964 Sci-fi interpretation of Defoe classic. West is one of two daring scientists who take a monkey with them on a mission to outer space. When a meteor strikes their ship, it hurtles out of control towards the red planet and only Mantee and Mona survive the wreckage. They meet Lundin, an escaped slave and teach him English until evil slave traders spoil the fun. 109m/C LV. Adam West, Vic Lundin, Paul Mantee; *D:* Byron Haskin; *W:* Ib Melchior, John C. Higgins; *C:* Winton C. Hoch; *M:* Nathan Van Cleave. IME

Robo-Chic *Cyber-Chic* 1989 A woman who is part cop, part machine, becomes a defender of justice. 90m/C VHS, Beta. Kathy Shower, Jack Carter, Burt Ward, Lyle Waggoner; *D:* Ed Hansen, Jeffrey Mandel. AIP

RoboCop 🎭🎭🎭 1987 (R) A nearly dead Detroit cop is used as the brain for a crime-fighting robot in this bleak vision of the future. Humor, satire, action, and violence keep this moving in spite of its underlying sadness. Slick animation techniques from Phil Tippet. Verhoeven's first American film. 103m/C VHS, Beta, LV, Closed Caption. Peter Weller, Nancy Allen, Ronny Cox, Kurtwood Smith, Ray Wise, Miguel Ferrer, Dan O'Herlihy, Robert DoQui, Felton Perry, Paul McCrane, Del Zamora; *D:* Paul Verhoeven; *W:* Michael Miner, Edward Neumeier; *C:* Jan De Bont; *M:* Basil Poledouris. Nominations: Academy Awards '87: Best Film Editing, Best Sound. ORI

RoboCop 2 🎭🎭 1990 (R) Grimer, more violent sequel to the initial fascinating look at the future, where police departments are run by corporations hungry for profit at any cost. A new and highly addictive drug has made Detroit more dangerous than ever. Robocop is replaced by a stronger cyborg with the brain of a brutal criminal. When the cyborg goes berserk, Robocop battles it and the drug lords for control of the city. Dark humor and graphic savagery, with little of the tenderness and emotion of the original. 117m/C VHS, Beta, LV, Closed Caption. Peter Weller, Nancy Allen, Belinda Bauer, Dan O'Herlihy, Tom Noonan, Gabriel Damon, Galyn Gorg, Felton Perry, Patricia Charbonneau; *D:* Irvin Kershner; *W:* Walon Green. ORI

RoboCop 3 🎭½ 1991 (PG-13) Robocop's new Japanese owners plan to build a huge, new, ultra-modern city (in place of the decrepit 21st-century Detroit) but first must evict thousands of people in this third installment of the "Robocop" films (which sat on the studio shelf before finally being released in 1993). There's an android Ninja warrior to do battle with Robo who's gone over to the rebel underground but the plot and action sequences are rehashed from better films. Watch the original. 104m/C VHS, LV, Closed Caption. Robert John Burke, Nancy Allen, John Castle, CCH Pounder, Bruce Locke, Rip Torn, Remi Ryan, Felton Perry; *D:* Fred Dekker; *W:* Fred Dekker, Frank Miller; *M:* Basil Poledouris. ORI

RoboCop the Series: The Future of Law Enforcement 1994
Premiere episode of the TV series, based on the movie about the unstoppable 21st-century Detroit robocop with the human touch. A murderous corporate creep and a mad doctor team up for nefarious corporate shenanigans. Helping out our hero is a murdered secretary who is merged into the city's central computer as Neuro-Brain. ?m/C VHS, LV. Richard Eden, Andrea Roth, Cliff DeYoung, John Rubinstein. ORI

Roboman 🐾🐾½ Who? 1975 (PG)
American scientist gets in car crash in Soviet Union. When he returns to the States as a cyborg, his friends seem to notice a change. 91m/C GB GE Elliott Gould, Trevor Howard, Joe Bova, Ed Grover, James Noble, John Lehne; D: Jack Gold. ACE, MTX

Robot Holocaust 🐾🐾 1987
Somewhere in the doomed future, after the Earth is laid waste by robots with superior intelligence, a human survivor dares to challenge them. If you're doomed to watch this, you just might survive; it's so so, unsurprisingly sci-fi. 79m/C VHS, Beta. Norris Culf, Nadine Hart, Joel von Ornsteiner, Jennifer Delora, Andrew Howarth, Angelika Jager, Rick Gianisi; D: Tim Kincaid; W: Tim Kincaid. NO

Robot in the Family 🐾🐾 1994
Slapstick comedy about Alex and his wacky but endearing robot who embark on a race against time through the streets of New York to track down a priceless antique that could save Alex's family from financial ruin. 92m/C VHS. Joe Pantoliano, John Rhys-Davies, Danny Gerard, Amy Wright, Tom Signorelli, Peter Maloney, John Wylie, David Shuman, Matthew Locricchio; D: Mark Richardson, Jack Shaoul; W: Jack Shaoul; M: Papo Gely, Ted Mason; V: Don Peoples. APX

Robot Jox 🐾½ 1990 (PG)
Two futuristic warriors battle to the finish in giant mechanical robots. Preteen fare. 84m/C VHS, LV, Closed Caption. Gary Graham, Anne-Marie Johnson, Paul Koslo, Robert Sampson, Danny Kamekona, Hilary Mason, Michael Alldredge; D: Stuart Gordon; W: Joe Haldeman; C: Mac Ahlberg. COL

Robot Monster 🐾🐾½ Monsters From the Moon 1953
Ludicrous cheapie is widely considered one of the worst films of all time, as a single alien dressed in a moth-eaten gorilla suit and diving helmet conspires to take over the Earth from his station in a small, bubble-filled California cave. Available in original 3-D format. 62m/B VHS, Beta, LV. George Nader, Claudia Barrett, Gregory Moffett, Selena Royle; D: Phil Tucker; M: Elmer Bernstein. RHI, FCT, COL

Robot Pilot 🐾 Emergency Landing 1941
Tucker stars as a WWII test pilot trying to promote a friend's invention. Along the way, he's involved in a subplot with enemy agents who steal a bomber. He also finds time to become romantically entangled with the boss' spoiled daughter. 68m/B VHS, Beta, 8mm. Forrest Tucker, Carol Hughes, Evelyn Brent, Emmett Vogan, William Halligan; D: William Beaudine. VYY, SNC

The Robot vs. the Aztec Mummy woof! El Robot Humano; La Momia Azteca Contra el Robot Humano 1959
Grade-Z Mexican horror film pits a jealous mummy who guards a tomb against tomb robbers and the robot they invent. Special effects are laughable today—the robot's ears are lightbulbs—but true mummy movie fans might want to watch this one. Everyone else will probably be better off skipping it. 65m/B VHS, Beta. MX Ramon Gay, Rosita Arenas, Crox Alvarado, Luis Aceves Cantaneda, Emma Rolden; D: Rafael Portillo; W: Alfredo Salazar. SNC, AOV, MRV

Robot Wars 🐾🐾 1993 (PG)
When what seems to be the last mega-robot on earth falls into enemy hands, a renegade pilot unearths another with the help of an engineer and archeologist to fight for the future of mankind. 106m/C VHS, Beta, LV, Closed Caption. Don Michael Paul, Barbara Crampton, James Staley, Lisa Rinna, Danny Kamekona, Yuji Okumoto, J. Downing, Peter Haskell; D: Albert Band. PAR

Rocco and His Brothers 🐾🐾🐾½
Rocco et Ses Freres 1960 A modern classic from top director Visconti, about four brothers who move with their mother from the Italian countryside to Milan. Very long, sometimes ponderous, but engrossing, complex drama. Available shortened to 90 minutes, but the unedited version is much more rewarding. In Italian with English subtitles. 175m/B VHS, LV. IT Alain Delon, Renato Salvatori, Annie Girardot, Katina Paxinou, Claudia Cardinale, Roger Hanin; D: Luchino Visconti; M: Nino Rota. VDM, CVC, TPV

The Rock 🐾🐾🐾 1996 (R)
Cage follows up his Oscar win with a big-budget action hero turn, with great results. In an attempt to get benefits for the families of soldiers killed in various covert operations, a decorated general (Harris) and his commando squad occupy Alcatraz island, taking hostages and threatening to unleash a deadly gas bomb on San Francisco. Biochemical weapons expert Stanley Goodspeed (Cage) is called in to disarm the rockets, aided by John Patrick Mason (Connery), only man to successfully escape from the island prison. Like most Simpson/Bruckheimer productions, credibility is stretched to the limit, but the action scenes and crisp pacing don't leave much time for pondering details, anyway. Connery, cool as ever, isn't lost a step. Cage effectively plays up his character's inexperience at being the hero. Co-producer Don Simpson died of drug overdose during production. CW: Strong violence, language and a sex scene. 136m/C VHS, LV, Closed Caption. Nicolas Cage, Sean Connery, Ed Harris, Michael Biehn, William Forsythe, David Morse, John Spencer, John C. McGinley, Tony Todd, Bokeem Woodbine, Danny Nucci, Vanessa Marcil, Claire Forlani, Gregory Sporleder; D: Michael Bay; W: Jonathan Hensleigh; C: John Schwartzman; M: Nick Glennie-Smith. MTV Movie Awards '97: Best On-Screen Duo (Sean Connery/Nicolas Cage); Nominations: Academy Awards '96: Best Sound; MTV Movie Awards '97: Best Film, Best Action Sequence. TOU

Rock-a-Doodle 🐾🐾½ 1992 (G)
Little Edmond is knocked out during a storm and has an Elvis-influenced vision. He sees Chanticleer, the sun-raising rooster, tricked into neglecting his duties by an evil barnyard owl. Humiliated and scorned, the earnest young fowl leaves the farm and winds up in a Las Vegas-like city as an Elvis-impersonating singer (complete with pompadour) where he meets with success and all its trappings. Mildly amusing, but bland by today's standards of animation, with music which is certainly nothing to crow about. 77m/C VHS, LV. D: Don Bluth; W: David A. Weiss; M: Robert Folk; V: Glen Campbell, Christopher Plummer, Phil Harris, Sandy Duncan, Ellen Greene, Charles Nelson Reilly, Eddie Deezen, Toby Scott Granger, Sorrell Booke. HBO, MVD

Rock All Night 🐾🐾 1957
Typically trashy Corman quickie (filmed in five days on one set) about some wild fifties teens and, in this case, a couple of murderers. Seems Cloud Nine, the local teen hangout, is invaded by a couple of murderers who hold the kids hostage. It's up to the hipster bartender, known as Shorty because he's five-foot-one, to save the day. Unrelated concert footage of The Platters and The Blockbusters opens the film. 62m/B VHS. Dick Miller, Abby Dalton, Russell Johnson, Jonathan Haze, Robin Morse; D: Roger Corman. COL, MOV, MVD

Rock & Roll Cowboys 🐾 1992
Set in the near-future. Mickey LaGrange is a roadie who has dreams of playing his own songs and becoming a rock and roll star himself. When he meets the mysterious Damien Shard he just may get the opportunity and a lot more besides. Shard is the inventor of an instrument that taps directly into the brain to transform thought into music. When Mickey uses the instrument he becomes an instant success—until he notices some horrifying side effects. 83m/C VHS. Peter Phelps, David Franklin, John Doyle; D: Robert Stewart. MOV

Rock & Rule 🐾🐾 1983
Animated sword & sorcery epic with a rock soundtrack. Voices are provided by Deborah Harry, Cheap Trick, Lou Reed, and Iggy Pop. 85m/C VHS, Beta, LV. D: Clive A. Smith; M: Deborah Harry, Lou Reed, Iggy Pop; V: Paul LeMat, Susan Roman, Don Francks, Dan Hennessey, Chris Wiggins, Catherine Gallant, Catherine O'Hara. MGM

Rock & the Money-Hungry Party Girls 🐾 1989
A struggling musician battles against Gabor-sister-worshiping bimbos in an effort to find unpublished songs by a '50s music legend. 90m/C VHS, Beta. Paul Sercu, Adam Small, Judi Durand, Mary Baldwin, Debra Lamb; D: Kurt MacCarley. NO

Rock, Baby, Rock It 🐾 1957
Weak and silly rock-and-roll crime drama about teens trying to fight the Mafia in Dallas in 1957. Features performances by many regional bands including Kay Wheeler, the Cell Block Seven, Johnny Carroll, Preacher Smith and the Deacons, and the Five Stars. If you grew up in Dallas in the '50s, the musical groups may bring back some fond memories; otherwise, this obscure film probably isn't worth your time. 84m/B VHS, Beta. Kay Wheeler, John Carroll; D: Murray Douglas Sporup. RHI

Rock House 🐾🐾 1992 (R)
When an L.A. narcotics officer's wife is murdered by drug runners he goes on an obsessive revenge mission to destroy the city's cocaine operations. 98m/C VHS. Joseph Jennings, Michael Robbin, Alan Shearer; D: Jack Vacek; W: Jack Vacek. HMD

Rock Hudson's Home Movies 1992
Farr re-creates the character of the late actor over numerous film clips used to suggest homoerotic themes in Hudson's movies. Low-budget and high camp. 93m/C VHS. Eric Farr; D: Mark Rappaport; W: Mark Rappaport. WBF, PPI

Rock 'n' Roll High School 🐾🐾🐾 1979 (PG)
The music of the Ramones highlights this non-stop high-energy cult classic about a high school out to thwart the principal at every turn. If it had been made in 1957, it would have been the ultimate rock 'n' roll teen movie. As it is, its 1970s' milieu works against it, but the performances are perfect for the material and the Ramones are great. Songs include "Teenage Lobotomy," "Blitzkrieg Bop," "I Wanna Be Sedated" and the title track, among others. Followed less successfully by "Rock 'n' Roll High School Forever." 94m/C VHS, Beta, Closed Caption. The Ramones, P.J. Soles, Vincent Van Patten, Clint Howard, Dey Young, Mary Woronov, Alix Elias, Dick Miller, Paul Bartel; D: Allan Arkush; C: Dean Cundey. NHO

Rock 'n' Roll High School Forever 🐾 1991 (PG-13)
Jesse Davis and his band just want to rock 'n' roll, but the new principal doesn't share their enthusiasm. Way late, way lame sequel to "Rock 'n' Roll High School" doesn't come close to the originality that made it a cult classic. Soundtrack includes music from The Divinyls, Dee Dee Ramone, Mojo Nixon, Will and the Bushmen, The Pursuit of Happiness, and more. 94m/C VHS, Beta, LV, Closed Caption. Corey Feldman, Mary Woronov, Mojo Nixon, Evan Richards, Michael Ceveris, Patrick Malone, Larry Linville, Sarah Buxton; D: Deborah Brock; W: Deborah Brock. LIV, IME

Rock 'n' Roll Nightmare 🐾½ The Edge of Hell 1985 (R)
A rock band is pursued by demons from another dimension. The usual lame garbage. 89m/C VHS, Beta. CA Jon Mikl Thor, Paula Francescatto, Rusty Hamilton; D: John Fasano. ACA

Rock, Pretty Baby 🐾 1956
Early rock-'n'-roll movie about a teenage band and high school riots. 89m/B VHS, Beta. Sal Mineo, John Saxon, Rod McKuen, Luana Patten, Fay Wray, Edward Platt, Alan Reed Jr.; D: Richard Bartlett; M: Henry Mancini. BAR

Rock River Renegades 🐾 1942
The Range Busters capture a band of renegades and restore peace to the territory once more. 59m/B VHS, Beta. Ray Corrigan, John "Dusty" King. NOS, DVT

Rock, Rock, Rock 🎞🎞½ **1956** A young girl tries to earn enough money for a prom gown after her father closes her charge account. Screen debut of Tuesday Weld. Ultra-low-budget, but a classic after a fashion. Includes classic musical numbers performed by Chuck Berry and other rock'n'roll pioneers. **78m/B VHS, Beta.** Alan Freed, Chuck Berry, Fats Domino, Tuesday Weld; **D:** Will Price. *MVD, MED, MRV*

Rocket Attack U.S.A. woof! **1958** Antiquated and ridiculous tale of nuclear warfare about the time of Sputnik, with Russia's first strike blowing up New York City and environs. Mercifully short, with time for a little romance. Everything about this movie is so bad it's good for a laugh. **70m/B VHS, Beta.** Monica Davis, John McKay, Dan Kern, Edward Czerniuk, Art Metrano; **D:** Barry Mahon. *NO*

Rocket Gibraltar 🎞🎞🎞 **1988 (PG)** On the occasion of a crusty patriarch's birthday, a large family unites on his remote estate to carry out his special birthday wish. Fine performance by Lancaster. Supported by a solid cast, overcomes a slim story, Culkin, later of "Home Alone," is loveable as the precocious five-year-old. Picturesque Long Island scenery. **92m/C VHS, Beta, Closed Caption.** Burt Lancaster, Bill Pullman, John Glover, Suzy Amis, Macaulay Culkin, Patricia Clarkson, Frances Conroy, Sinead Cusack, Bill Martin, Kevin Spacey; **D:** Daniel Petrie; **W:** Amos Poe; **M:** Andrew Powell. *COL*

Rocket to the Moon 🎞🎞 **1986** An adaptation of the Clifford Odets story about the mundane life of a 30-year-old Manhattan dentist and how he comes to terms with his life. From the PBS "American Playhouse" series. **118m/C VHS, Beta.** Judy Davis, John Malkovich, Eli Wallach; **D:** John Jacobs. *ACA, PBS*

The Rocketeer 🎞🎞🎞 **1991 (PG)** Lightheaded fun. A stunt flyer in the 1930s finds a prototype jet backpack sought by Nazi spies. Donning a mask, he becomes a flying superhero. Breezy family entertainment with stupendous effects; even better if you know movie trivia, as it brims with Hollywood references, like a great villain (Dalton) clearly based on Errol Flynn. **109m/C VHS, Beta, LV, Closed Caption.** Bill Campbell, Jennifer Connelly, Alan Arkin, Timothy Dalton, Paul Sorvino, Melora Hardin, Tiny Ron, Terry O'Quinn, Ed Lauter, James Handy; **D:** Joe Johnston; **W:** Danny Bilson, Paul DeMeo; **M:** James Horner. *DIS, CCB, IME*

Rocketship 🎞🎞 **1936** Flash Gordon battles sea monsters, ray guns, and robots in this sci-fi adventure, which is an edited version of a Flash serial. **?m/B VHS.** Buster Crabbe, Jean Rogers, Charles Middleton. *LOO, HEG*

Rocketship X-M 🎞🎞½ *Expedition Moon* **1950** A lunar mission goes awry and the crew lands on Mars, where they discover ancient ruins. Well acted and nicely photographed. Contains footage, a tinted sequence and previews of coming attractions from classis science fiction files. **77m/B VHS, Beta, LV.** Lloyd Bridges, Osa Massen, John Emery, Hugh O'Brian, Noah Beery Jr.; **D:** Kurt Neumann. *MED, RXM*

The Rockford Files: Backlash of the Hunter **1974** The two-part episode which launched the TV series about ex-con turned PI Jim Rockford, who lives (and works) in a beach trailer and only takes clients who have real trouble and real money. His first is a seemingly simple investigation into a man's death. His daughter wants to know if dad was murdered or really did commit suicide. **90m/C VHS.** James Garner, Lindsay Wagner, William Smith, Nita Talbot, Joe Santos; **D:** Richard T. Heffron; **W:** Stephen J. Cannell. *USH*

Rockin' Road Trip 🎞 **1985 (PG-13)** A guy meets a girl in a Boston bar, and finds himself on a drunken, slapstick road trip down the Eastern seaboard with a rock band. **101m/C VHS, Beta.** Garth McLean, Katherine Harrison, Margerie Currie, Steve Boles. *FOX*

The Rocking Horse Winner 🎞🎞½ **1949** Poignant tale of a young boy who discovers he can predict racehorse winners by riding his rocking horse. His spendthrift mother's greed leads to tragedy. Based on the short story by D.H. Lawrence. **91m/B VHS.** *GB* John Howard Davies, Valerie Hobson, Hugh Sinclair; **D:** Anthony Pelissier. *HMV*

Rocktober Blood 🎞½ **1985 (R)** A convicted and executed rock star comes back from the grave and starts killing people all over again. Yet another gorefest. **88m/C VHS, Beta.** Donna Scoggins, Tray Loren, Nigel Benjamin, Beverly Sebastian; **D:** Ferd Sebastian. *LIV, VES*

Rockula 🎞½ **1990 (PG-13)** Teen rock comedy about a young-yet-300-year-old vampire looking to lose his virginity. Recommended only for hardcore Diddley fans. **90m/C VHS, Beta, LV, Closed Caption.** Dean Cameron, Bo Diddley, Tawny Fere, Susan Tyrrell, Thomas Dolby, Toni Basil; **D:** Luca Bercovici; **W:** Luca Bercovici. *MGM, WAR*

Rockwell: A Legend of the Wild West 🎞🎞½ **1993** Black heroics in the wild west. U.S. Marshall Porter Rockwell and his posse of sharp shooters are after a vicious gang murdering supposed claim jumpers who just happen to be Rockwell's friends. **?m/C VHS, LV, Closed Caption.** Randy Gleave, Karl Malone, Michael Rudd, George Sullivan. *IMP*

Rocky 🎞🎞🎞½ **1976 (PG)** Box office smash about a young man from the slums of Philadelphia who dreams of becoming a boxing champion. Stallone plays Rocky, the underdog hoping to win fame and self-respect. Rags-to-riches story seems to parallel Stallone's life; he had been previously virtually unknown before this movie. Intense portrayal of the American Dream; loses strength in the subsequent (and numerous) sequels. **125m/C VHS, Beta, LV, 8mm, DVD.** Sylvester Stallone, Talia Shire, Burgess Meredith, Burt Young, Carl Weathers; **D:** John G. Avildsen; **W:** Sylvester Stallone; **M:** Bill Conti. Academy Awards '76: Best Director (Avildsen), Best Film Editing, Best Picture; Directors Guild of America Awards '76: Best Director (Avildsen); Golden Globe Awards '77: Best Film—Drama; Los Angeles Film Critics Association Awards '76: Best Film; National Board of Review Awards '76: 10 Best Films of the Year, Best Supporting Actress (Shire); New York Film Critics Awards '76: Best Supporting Actress (Shire); Nominations: Academy Awards '76: Best Actor (Stallone), Best Actress (Shire), Best Director, Best Original Screenplay, Best Song ("Gonna Fly Now"), Best Sound, Best Supporting Actor (Meredith, Young). *MGM, FOX, BTV*

Rocky 2 🎞🎞 **1979 (PG)** Time-marking sequel to the box office smash finds Rocky frustrated by the commercialism which followed his match to Apollo, but considering a return bout. Meanwhile, his wife fights for her life. The overall effect is to prepare you for the next sequel. **119m/C VHS, Beta, LV.** Sylvester Stallone, Talia Shire, Burt Young, Burgess Meredith, Carl Weathers; **D:** Sylvester Stallone; **W:** Sylvester Stallone; **C:** Bill Butler; **M:** Bill Conti. People's Choice Awards '80: Best Film. *MGM, FOX*

Rocky 3 🎞🎞½ **1982 (PG)** Rocky is beaten by big, mean Clubber Lang (played to a tee by Mr. T). He realizes success has made him soft, and has to dig deep to find the motivation to stay on top. Amazingly, Stallone regains his underdog persona here, looking puny next to Mr. T, who is the best thing about the second-best "Rocky" flick. **103m/C VHS, Beta, LV.** Sylvester Stallone, Talia Shire, Burgess Meredith, Carl Weathers, Mr. T, Leif Erickson, Burt Young; **D:** Sylvester Stallone; **W:** Sylvester Stallone; **C:** Bill Butler; **M:** Bill Conti. Nominations: Academy Awards '82: Best Song ("Eye of the Tiger"). *MGM, FOX*

Rocky 4 🎞½ **1985 (PG)** Rocky travels to Russia to fight the Soviet champ who killed his friend during a bout. Will Rocky knock the Russkie out? Will Rocky get hammered on the head a great many times and sag around the ring? Will Rocky ever learn? Lundgren isn't nearly as much fun as some of Rocky's former opponents, and Stallone overdoes the hyper-patriotism and relies too heavily on uplifting footage from earlier "Rocky" movies. **91m/C VHS, Beta, LV, Closed Caption.** Sylvester Stallone, Talia Shire, Dolph Lundgren, Brigitte Nielsen, Michael Pataki, Burt Young, Carl Weathers; **D:** Sylvester Stallone; **W:** Sylvester Stallone; **C:** Bill Butler. Golden Raspberry Awards '85: Worst Actor (Stallone), Worst Supporting Actress (Nielsen), Worst Director (Stallone), Worst Screenplay, Worst New Star (Nielsen). *MGM, FOX*

Rocky 5 🎞🎞 **1990 (PG)** Brain damaged and broke, Rocky finds himself back where he started on the streets of Philadelphia. Boxing still very much in his blood, Rocky takes in a protege, training him in the style that made him a champ (take a lickin' and keep on tickin'). However an unscrupulous promoter has designs on the young fighter and seeks to wrest the lad from under the former champ's wing. This eventually leads to a showdown between Rocky and the young boxer in a brutal streetfight. Supposedly the last "Rocky" film, it's clear the formula has run dry. **105m/C VHS, Beta, LV, 8mm, Closed Caption.** Sylvester Stallone, Talia Shire, Burt Young, Sage Stallone, Tom Morrison, Burgess Meredith; **D:** John G. Avildsen; **W:** Sylvester Stallone; **C:** Steven Poster; **M:** Bill Conti. *MGM*

The Rocky Horror Picture Show 🎞🎞🎞 **1975 (R)** When a young couple take refuge in a haunted castle, they find themselves the unwilling pawns in a warped scientist's experiment. Cult camp classic has been a midnight movie favorite for years and has developed an entire subculture built around audience participation. The tape includes a seven-minute short detailing the story behind the movie's popularity. May not be as much fun watching it on the little screen unless you bring the rice and squirt guns. 🎵The Time Warp; Science Fiction Double Feature; Wedding Song; Sweet Transvestite; The Sword of Damocles; Charles Atlas Song; Whatever Happened to Saturday Night; Touch-a Touch-a Touch-a Touch Me; Eddie's Teddy. **105m/C VHS, LV, Closed Caption.** Tim Curry, Susan Sarandon, Barry Bostwick, Meat Loaf, Little Nell, Richard O'Brien; **D:** Jim Sharman; **M:** John Barry. *FOX, FCT, PMS*

Rocky Jones, Space Ranger **1954** This syndicated space series followed the adventures of Rocky Jones, commander of the spaceship Orbit Jet, who worked for the United Worlds. The first three half-hour television episodes chronicle the story of how Rocky met his beautiful assistant Vena. Entitled "Beyond the Curtain of Space." Additional episodes available. **78m/B VHS, Beta.** Richard Crane, Sally Mansfield, Scotty Beckett. *MVC, MOV*

Rocky Jones, Space Ranger: Renegade Satellite 🎞½ **1954** Nostalgia freaks may embrace this revived edition of the infamous early live-TV space cadet show. Rocky squares off against enemies of the United Solar System like Dr. Reno and Rudy DeMarco. Really cheap. **69m/B VHS.** Richard Crane, Sally Mansfield, Maurice Cass. *VDM*

Rocky Mountain Rangers 🎞🎞 **1940** The Three Mesquiteers do what they do best: save a town from bad guys. **58m/B VHS.** Bob Livingston, Raymond Hatton, Duncan Renaldo, Leroy Mason, Dennis Moore, John St. Polis; **D:** George Sherman. *NOS*

Rodan 🎞🎞 *Radon; Radon the Flying Monster* **1956** A gigantic prehistoric bird is disturbed from his slumber by H-bomb tests. He awakens to wreak havoc on civilization. Big bugs also run amok. From the director of "Godzilla" and a host of other nuclear monster movies. **74m/C VHS, Beta, LV.** *JP* Kenji Sahara, Yumi Shirakawa; **D:** Inoshiro Honda. *PAR, MLB, VES*

Rodeo Girl 🎞🎞½ **1980** Ross is a restless housewife who joins the rodeo in this television drama based on the life of cowgirl Sue Pirtle. Particularly strong supporting cast of Hopkins, Clark, and Brimley. **100m/C VHS, Beta.** Katharine Ross, Bo Hopkins, Candy Clark, Jacqueline Brookes, Wilford Brimley, Parley Baer; **D:** Jackie Cooper. *LIV*

Rodrigo D.: No Future *♂♂* 1991 Gritty, realistic portrayal of the youth-killing culture of Medellin, Columbia. Minimal plot involves a young drummer and his drug-running friends. The actors used are actual untrained street kids, several of whom died before the film's completion. In Spanish with English subtitles. 92m/C VHS. Ramiro Meneses, Carlos Mario Resrepo; *D:* Victor Gaviria. *KIV*

Roe vs. Wade *♂♂♂* 1989 Hunter is excellent as the single woman from Texas who successfully challenged the nation's prohibitive abortion laws in a landmark Supreme Court case. Television drama based on the actual 1973 case of Norma McCorvey. 92m/C VHS, Beta, LV, **Closed Caption.** Holly Hunter, Amy Madigan, Terry O'Quinn, Stephen Tobolowsky, Dion Anderson, Kathy Bates, James Gammon, Chris Mulkey; *D:* Gregory Hoblit. *PAR*

Roger & Me *♂♂♂½* 1989 (R) Hilarious, controversial and atypical semi-documentary details Moore's protracted efforts to meet General Motors president Roger Smith and confront him with the poverty and despair afflicting Flint, Michigan, after GM closed its plants there. Includes some emotionally grabbing scenes: a Flint family is evicted just before Christmas; a woman makes a living by selling rabbits for food or pets; and a then soon-to-be Miss America addresses the socioeconomic impact of GM's decision. One of the highest-grossing non-fiction films ever released, and Moore's first. 91m/C VHS, Beta, LV, **Closed Caption.** Michael Moore, Bob Eubanks, Pat Boone, Anita Bryant; *D:* Michael Moore; *W:* Michael Moore. *WAR*

RoGoPaG *♂♂* 1962 Four episodic films by four European masters (the title refers to their last names), satirizing the human condition. Rossellini's "Virginity" finds an airline stewardess (Schiaffino) fending off an amorous passenger (Balabin). Godard's "The New World" features a post-nuclear Paris and its effect on romance. "La Ricotta" is Pasolini's controversial take on religion with Welles as the director of a religious epic. Gregoretti's "The Range Grown Chicken" finds Tognazzi the frazzled head of a family beset by consumerism. A mixed bag with Pasolini and Godard offering the most disturbing essays. 122m/B VHS. *IT* Orson Welles, Ugo Tognazzi, Rosanna Schiaffino, Alexandra Stewart, Jean-Mark Bory, Renato Salvatori, Lisa Gastoni, Bruce Balabin; *D:* Roberto Rossellini, Jean-Luc Godard, Pier Paolo Pasolini, Ugo Gregoretti; *W:* Roberto Rossellini, Jean-Luc Godard, Pier Paolo Pasolini, Ugo Gregoretti; *M:* Carlo Ristichelli. *KIV*

Rogue *♂* 1976 (R) The Rogue is a ruthless man who can make beautiful women do anything that he desires; so, of course, he does. 87m/C VHS, **Beta.** Milan Galvonic, Barbara Bouchet, Margaret Lee; *D:* Gregory Simpson. *NO*

Rogue Lion *♂½* 1975 A quasi-incompetent game warden more than meets his match when a voraciously carnivorous lion begins stalking an African community. 89m/C VHS, **Beta.** *VCI*

Rogue Male *♂♂½* 1976 TV movie finds '30s British aristocrat O'Toole plotting to assassinate Hitler. When his plan fails, he's on the run from both the Gestapo and the British police. Based on the novel by Geoffrey Household. 100m/C VHS. *GB* Peter O'Toole, Alastair Sim, John Standing, Cyd Hayman; *D:* Clive Donner; *W:* Frederic Raphael. *FCT*

Rogue of the Range *♂* 1936 A lawman pretends that he is a bandit in order to track down an outlaw gang. 60m/B VHS, **Beta.** Johnny Mack Brown. *NOS, DVT, RXM*

Rogue of the Rio Grande *♂½* 1930 Musical western in which the renowned bandit El Malo arrives in the peace-loving town of Sierra Blanca. One of Loy's earlier films. ♫Argentine Moon; Carmita; Song of the Bandoleros. 60m/B VHS, **Beta.** Myrna Loy, Jose Bohr, Raymond Hatton, Carmelita Geraghty. *VCN*

Rogue's Gallery *♂♂* 1944 A reporter and photographer covering the story of an inventor and his latest device are caught up in intrigue when he is found murdered. 60m/B VHS. Frank

Jenks, Robin Raymond, H.B. Warner, Ray Walker, Davison Clark, Robert E. Homans, Frank McGlynn, Pat Gleason, Edward Keane; *D:* Al(bert) Herman. *SNC, RXM*

Rogue's Tavern *♂♂* 1936 In this grade B curio, a blood-thirsty killer stalks the occupants of a country inn, bodies are found with their throats crushed, and a psycho psychic is on the loose. Surprise ending. 70m/B VHS, **Beta.** Wallace Ford, Joan Woodbury, Clara Kimball Young, Barbara Pepper, Jack Mulhall, John Elliott; *D:* Robert F. "Bob" Hill. *NOS, DVT, HEG*

Rogue's Yarn *♂♂* 1956 An investigator probes the death of a woman, ostensibly the result of a boating accident. Gradually he uncovers a plot involving the woman's husband and his mistress in this semi-entertaining British mystery. 80m/B VHS, **Beta.** *GB* Nicole Maurey, Derek Bond, Elwyn Brook-Jones, Hugh Latimer; *D:* Vernon Sewell. *SNC*

Roland the Mighty *♂½* 1958 Muscular, Herculeanesque hero takes on all comers in this sword and sandal epic set in the Asian steppes. ?m/C VHS, **Beta.** *IT* Rick Battaglia. *SNC*

Roll Along Cowboy *♂½* 1937 A vintage sagebrush saga about a cowboy caught by love. Based on Zane Grey's "The Dude Ranger." 55m/B VHS, **Beta.** Smith Ballew, Cecilia Parker; *D:* Gus Meins. *NOS, CCB, VDM*

Roll of Thunder, Hear My Cry *♂♂½* 1978 A black family struggles to survive in Depression-era Mississippi in this inspiring, if somewhat predictable, television production. Look for the always impressive Freeman in a supporting role. Set in the South of 1933 and based on the novels of Mildred Taylor. 110m/C VHS, **Beta.** Claudia McNeil, Janet MacLachlan, Morgan Freeman; *D:* Jack Smight. *LIV, LCA*

Roll on Texas Moon *♂* 1946 A cowpoke is hired to prevent a feud between the sheep men and the cattle ranchers. 68m/B VHS. Roy Rogers, George "Gabby" Hayes, Dale Evans, Dennis Hoey; *D:* William Witney. *NOS, DVT, MTX*

Roll, Wagons, Roll *♂½* 1939 Tex Ritter leads a wagon train to Oregon. 52m/B VHS, **Beta.** Tex Ritter; *D:* Al(bert) Herman. *NOS, VCN*

Roller Blade *♂* 1985 In a post-holocaust world a gang of Amazon-style nuns, who worship a "have a nice day" happy face, battle the forces of evil with martial arts and mysticism. Has to be seen to be believed. Extremely low-budget outing. 88m/C VHS, **Beta.** Suzanne Solari, Jeff Hutchinson, Shaun Mitchelle; *D:* Donald G. Jackson. *NWV*

Roller Blade Warriors: Taken By Force *♂♂* 1990 Roller babes battle evil mutant while balancing on big boots with small wheels. 90m/C VHS. Kathleen Kinmont, Rory Calhoun, Abby Dalton, Elizabeth Kaitan. *NO*

Roller Boogie woof! 1979 (PG) A truly awful film made at the time of the mercifully brief roller-disco craze. Blair runs away from home and winds up helping some friends thwart a businessman looking to close the local roller rink. Everything about this one reeks amateur. 103m/C VHS. Linda Blair, Jim Bray, Beverly Garland, Roger Perry, James Van Patten, Kimberly Beck, Mark Goddard, Stoney Jackson, Sean McClory; *D:* Mark L. Lester; *W:* Barry Schneider; *C:* Dean Cundey. *MGM*

Rollerball *♂♂* 1975 (R) Caan is utterly convincing in this futuristic tale in which a brutal sport assumes alarming importance to a sterile society. Flashy, violent, sometimes exhilirating. 123m/C VHS, **Beta, LV.** James Caan, John Houseman, Maud Adams, Moses Gunn, John Beck; *D:* Norman Jewison; *M:* Andre Previn. *MGM*

Rollercoaster *♂♂* 1977 (PG) A deranged extortionist threatens to sabotage an amusement park ride. Plucky Segal must stop him. Video renters will be spared the nauseating effects of film's original "Sensurround." 119m/C VHS, **Beta, LV.** George Segal, Richard Widmark, Timothy Bottoms, Henry Fonda, Susan Strasberg, Harry Guardino; *D:* James Goldstone; *W:* William Link; *M:* Lalo Schifrin. *USH*

Rollin' Plains *♂* 1938 A Texas Ranger tries to settle a feud between cattlemen and sheepmen over water rights. 60m/B VHS, **Beta.** Tex Ritter; *D:* Al(bert) Herman. *NOS, VCN, VCI*

Rolling Home *♂♂* 1948 Tame tale about aging cowpoke, his grandson, and a really swell horse. Saddle up and snooze. 71m/B VHS, **Beta, LV.** Jean Parker, Russell Hayden, Pamela Blake, Buss Henry, Raymond Hatton. *VYY*

Rolling Thunder *♂♂½* 1977 (R) Vietnam vet turns vigilante when he arrives home from POW camp and sees his family slaughtered. Graphically violent, potentially cathartic. Typical of screenwriter Paul Schrader. 99m/C VHS, **Beta, LV.** William Devane, Tommy Lee Jones, Linda Haynes; *D:* John Flynn; *W:* Paul Schrader, Heywood Gould; *C:* Jordan Cronenweth. *LIV, VES*

Rolling Vengeance *♂½* 1987 (R) Enterprising fellow constructs powerful truck to better facilitate the extermination of gang members who earlier slaughtered his family. Keep on truckin'. 90m/C VHS, **Beta, LV.** Don Michael Paul, Ned Beatty, Lawrence Dane, Lisa Howard; *D:* Steven Hilliard Stern. *NLC*

Rollover *♂½* 1981 (R) Turgid big-budget drama about Arab undermining of American economy. Kristofferson is lifeless, Fonda is humorless. Supporting players Sommer and Cronyn fare better. 117m/C VHS, **Beta.** Jane Fonda, Kris Kristofferson, Hume Cronyn, Bob Gunton, Josef Sommer, Martha Plimpton; *D:* Alan J. Pakula. *WAR*

Roman Holiday *♂♂♂½* 1953 Hepburn's first starring role is a charmer as a princess bored with her official visit to Rome who slips away and plays at being an "average Jane." A reporter discovers her little charade and decides to cash in with an exclusive story. Before they know it, love calls. Blacklisted screenwriter Trumbo was "fronted" by Ian McLellan Hunter, who accepted screen credit and the Best Story Oscar in Trumbo's stead. The Academy voted to posthumously award Trumbo his own Oscar in 1993. 118m/B VHS, **Beta, LV, 8mm.** Audrey Hepburn, Gregory Peck, Eddie Albert, Tullio Carminati; *D:* William Wyler; *W:* Dalton Trumbo. Academy Awards '53: Best Actress (Hepburn), Best Costume Design (B & W), Best Story; British Academy Awards '53: Best Actress (Hepburn); Golden Globe Awards '54: Best Actress—Drama (Hepburn); New York Film Critics Awards '53: Best Actress (Hepburn); Nominations: Academy Awards '53: Best Art Direction/Set Decoration (B & W), Best Black and White Cinematography, Best Director (Wyler), Best Film Editing, Best Picture, Best Screenplay, Best Supporting Actor (Albert). *PAR, BTV, HMV*

Roman Scandals *♂♂½* 1933 A penniless young man daydreams himself back to ancient Rome with uproarious results. Lucille Ball appears as one of the Goldwyn Girls. Dance sequences were choreographed by Busby Berkeley. ♫No More Love; Build A Little Home; Keep Young and Beautiful; Rome Wasn't Built in a Day; Put a Tax on Love. 91m/B VHS, **Beta.** Eddie Cantor, Ruth Etting, Gloria Stuart, Edward Arnold, Lucille Ball, Busby Berkeley; *D:* Frank Tuttle; *C:* Gregg Toland. *HBO*

Roman Spring of Mrs. Stone *♂♂♂*
The Widow and the Gigolo 1961 An aging actress determines to revive her career in Rome but finds romance with a gigolo instead in this adaptation of Tennessee Williams's novella. Leigh and Beatty are compelling, but Lenya nearly steals the show as Leigh's distinctly unappealing confidant. 104m/C VHS, **Beta.** Warren Beatty, Vivien Leigh, Lotte Lenya, Bessie Love, Jill St. John; *D:* Jose Quintero; *W:* Gavin Lambert. Nominations: Academy Awards '61: Best Supporting Actress (Lenya). *WAR, FHE*

Romance *♂♂* 1930 In only her second talkie, Garbo stars as an Italian opera star who seduces a young priest. Poor story and weak acting from everyone with the exception of Garbo. Even she can't save this one. Adapted from the play "Signora Cacllini." 77m/B VHS. Greta Garbo, Lewis Stone, Gavin Gordon, Elliott Nugent, Florence Lake, Clara Blandick; *D:* Clarence Brown; *C:* William H. Daniels. Nominations: Academy Awards '30: Best Actress (Garbo), Best Director (Brown). *MGM*

Romance in Manhattan 🐾🐾 1934 Recent immigrant to New York struggles to build new life, in spite of unemployment, language barriers, and loneliness. He meets Broadway chorine Rogers and song and dance ensues. America, ain't it a great place? 78m/B VHS. Ginger Rogers, Francis Lederer, J. Farrell MacDonald; *D:* Stephen Roberts; *M:* Max Steiner. *TTC, FCT*

Romance of a Horsethief 🐾🐾½ 1971 (PG) Brynner leads this entertaining but slow-paced "Fiddler on the Roof" comedic romp without the music. In 1904 Poland, a Cossack captain takes horses for the Russo-Japanese war. The residents of the town rise up, goaded on by Birkin. 100m/C VHS. *YU* Yul Brynner, Eli Wallach, Jane Birkin, Oliver Tobias, Lainie Kazan, David Opatoshu; *D:* Abraham Polonsky. *ACE, MOV*

Romance on the High Seas 🐾🐾🐾 1948 A woman is scheduled to take a cruise vacation but skips the boat when she believes her husband is cheating on her. Her husband believes she is taking the cruise to cheat on him and hires a private detective to follow her. Pleasant comedy features the film debut of Doris Day. 🎵It's Magic; It's You or No One; The Tourist Trade; Put 'Em in a Box, Tie 'Em with a Ribbon, and Throw 'Em in the Deep Blue Sea; Two Lovers Met in the Night; Run, Run, Run; I'm in Love; Cuban Rhapsody. 99m/C VHS, LV. Jack Carson, Janis Paige, Don DeFore, Doris Day, Oscar Levant, S.Z. Sakall, Eric Blore, Franklin Pangborn, Leslie Brooks, William "Billy" Bakewell; *D:* Michael Curtiz; *W:* Julius J. Epstein. Nominations: Academy Awards '48: Best Song ("It's Magic"), Scoring of a Musical. *FOX, FCT*

Romance on the Orient Express 🐾½ 1989 Sparks fly when former lovers meet again on the Orient Express. Don't expect any flesh, though, as film was made for television. 96m/C VHS, Beta. Cheryl Ladd, Stuart Wilson, John Gielgud; *D:* Lawrence Gordon Clark. *TTC*

Romance on the Range 🐾½ 1942 Rogers sets out to trap a gang of fur thieves and finds romance. 60m/B VHS. Roy Rogers, George "Gabby" Hayes, Sally Payne. *NOS, VCN, REP*

Romance with a Double Bass 🐾🐾🐾 1974 When a musician and a princess take a skinny dip in the royal lake and get their clothes stolen, comic complications arise. Reminiscent of Cleese's sojourn as a Monty Python member, with surreal, frequently raunchy humor. 40m/C VHS, Beta, LV. *GB* John Cleese, Connie Booth, Graham Crowden, Desmond Jones, Freddie Jones, Andrew Sachs; *D:* Robert M. Young. *FCT, SIG*

Romancing the Stone 🐾🐾🐾 1984 (PG) Uptight romance novelist lives out her fantasies after she receives a mysterious map from her murdered brother-in-law and her sister is kidnapped in South America—the ransom being the map. Out to rescue her sister, she's helped and hindered by an American soldier of fortune (Douglas) whose main concern is himself and the hidden treasure described in the map. Great chemistry between the stars and loads of clever dialogue in this appealing adventure comedy. First outing with Turner, Douglas, and DeVito. Followed by "The Jewel of the Nile." 106m/C VHS, Beta, LV, Closed Caption. Michael Douglas, Kathleen Turner, Danny DeVito, Zack Norman, Alfonso Arau, Ron Silver; *D:* Robert Zemeckis; *C:* Dean Cundey; *M:* Alan Silvestri. Golden Globe Awards '85: Best Actress—Musical/Comedy (Turner), Best Film—Musical/Comedy; Los Angeles Film Critics Association Awards '84: Best Actress (Turner); Nominations: Academy Awards '84: Best Film Editing. *FOX, HMV*

Romantic Comedy 🐾🐾 1983 (PG) Writing duo never seem to synchronize their desires for each other in this dull comedy. Engaging stars don't inspire each other much, and supporting cast can't make up the difference. Adapted from the Bernard Slade play. 102m/C VHS, Beta, Closed Caption. Dudley Moore, Mary Steenburgen, Frances Sternhagen, Ron Leibman; *D:* Arthur Hiller; *M:* Marvin Hamlisch. *MGM, FOX*

Romantic Englishwoman 🐾🐾🐾 1975 (R) Literate comedy-drama about the intertwined lives of several sophisticated and restrained Brits. Caine is a successful novelist with writer's block whose wife falls for another man while on a trip alone. He then invites his wife's lover to stay with them in order to generate ideas for his writing until his jealousy begins to surface. 117m/C VHS, Beta. *GB* Glenda Jackson, Michael Caine, Helmut Berger, Kate Nelligan; *D:* Joseph Losey; *W:* Tom Stoppard, Thomas Wiseman. *WAR, OM*

Rome Adventure 🐾🐾 *Lovers Must Learn* 1962 Spinster librarian Pleshette takes Roman vacation hoping to meet handsome prince. Donahue takes shine to her while girlfriend Dickinson is away, as does suave Roman Brazzi. Soapy, ill-paced romance. 119m/C VHS, LV, Closed Caption. Troy Donahue, Angie Dickinson, Suzanne Pleshette, Rossano Brazzi, Constance Ford, Al Hirt, Chad Everett; *D:* Delmer Daves; *W:* Delmer Daves; *M:* Max Steiner. *PAR, FCT, WAR*

Rome '78 🐾🐾½ 1978 Acclaimed underground film centered around Caligula and the Queen of Sheba in ancient Rome. 60m/C VHS. Eric Mitchell; *D:* James Nares. *MWF*

Romeo and Juliet 🐾🐾🐾½ 1936 One of MGM producer Irving Thalberg's pet projects (and starring Thalberg's wife, Norma Shearer), this Shakespeare classic was given the spare-no-expense MGM treatment. Physically too old to portray teen-age lovers, both Howard and Shearer let their acting ability supply all necessary illusions. Also notable is Barrymore's over-the-top portrayal of Mercutio. 126m/B VHS, LV. Leslie Howard, Norma Shearer, John Barrymore, Basil Rathbone, Edna May Oliver; *D:* George Cukor; *C:* William H. Daniels. Nominations: Academy Awards '36: Best Actress (Shearer), Best Interior Decoration, Best Picture, Best Supporting Actor (Rathbone). *MGM, CCB*

Romeo and Juliet 🐾🐾 1954 Unfulfilling adaptation of Shakespeare's timeless drama of young love cast against family antagonisms. Peculiar supporting cast features both Cabot and ubiquitous master Gielgud. 138m/C VHS, Beta. *IT* Laurence Harvey, Susan Shantall, Aldo Zollo, Sebastian Cabot, Flora Robson, Mervyn Johns, Bill Travers, John Gielgud; *D:* Renato Castellani; *C:* Robert Krasker. National Board of Review Awards '54: 5 Best Foreign Films of the Year, Best Director (Castellani). *LCA*

Romeo and Juliet 🐾🐾🐾½ 1968 (PG) Young couple share love despite prohibitive conflict between their families in this adaptation of Shakespeare's classic play. Director Zeffirelli succeeds in casting relative novices Whiting and Hussey in the leads, but is somewhat less proficient in lending air of free-wheeling sixties appeal to entire enterprise. Kudos, however, to cinematographer Pasquale de Santis and composer Nina Rota. Also available in a 45-minute edited version. 138m/C VHS, Beta, LV. *GB IT* Olivia Hussey, Leonard Whiting, Michael York, Milo O'Shea; *D:* Franco Zeffirelli; *C:* Pasquale De Santos; *M:* Nino Rota. Academy Awards '68: Best Cinematography, Best Costume Design; Golden Globe Awards '69: Best Foreign Film; National Board of Review Awards '68: 10 Best Films of the Year, Best Director (Zeffirelli); Nominations: Academy Awards '68: Best Director (Zeffirelli), Best Picture. *PAR, HMV, PBC*

Romeo Is Bleeding 🐾🐾½ 1993 (R) Jack (Oldman) is a police detective accepting mobster payoffs from boss Falcone (Scheider) for turning in federally protected witnesses. But the next target proves Jack's undoing—hitwoman Mona (Olin), who's more than a match for any man. Oldman's character is played for a patsy by everyone while Olin's is a kinky psycho-villainess with an enjoyment of violence, red lipstick, and a constant, maniacal laugh. Sciorra is generally wasted as Jack's unhappy wife while Lewis is annoying as his young and vacuous mistress. Part homage, part satire of film noir is overly stylized with intrusive narration but some effective shocks.*CW:* Strong language, strong violence, and strong sexuality. 110m/C VHS, LV, Closed

Caption. Gary Oldman, Lena Olin, Annabella Sciorra, Juliette Lewis, Roy Scheider, Michael Wincott, David Proval, Paul Butler, Will Patton, Larry Joshua, James Cromwell, Ron Perlman; *D:* Peter Medak; *W:* Hilary Henkin; *C:* Darius Wolski; *M:* Mark Isham. Nominations: MTV Movie Awards '94: Best Action Sequence. *PGV*

Romero 🐾🐾½ 1989 Julia is riveting as the Salvadoran archbishop who championed his destitute congregation despite considerable political opposition. A stirring biography financed by the United States Roman Catholic Church. 102m/C VHS, Beta, LV, Closed Caption. Raul Julia, Richard Jordan, Ana Alicia, Eddie Velez, Alejandro Bracho, Tony Plana, Lucy Reina, Harold Gould, Al Ruscio, Robert Viharo; *D:* John Duigan; *W:* John Sacret Young; *C:* Geoff Burton; *M:* Gabriel Yared. *THV*

Romola 🐾🐾½ 1925 Silent adventure. After Powell and his father are attacked by pirates, Powell escapes. But instead of rescuing his father, he opts for a life of corruption. Dad eventually escapes and returns to exact vengeance. A rather expensive film in its day, troubled by modern-day sights in what was supposed to be old Florence. Gish's drowning scene had to be re-shot because she wouldn't sink. Colman arranged for his then-wife Raye to have a bit part, but they were divorced soon after the film was finished. 120m/B VHS, Beta. Lillian Gish, Dorothy Gish, William Powell, Ronald Colman, Charles Lane, Herbert Grimwood, Bonaventure Ibanez, Frank Puglia, Thelma Raye; *D:* Henry King. *NO*

Romper Stomper 🐾🐾 1992 (R) Violent confrontations between Australian skinheads and the Vietnamese community mixed in with a disturbed love story. Suburban rich girl Gabe (McKenzie) is drawn to the charasmatic Hando (Crowe), the certifiably loony leader of a group of Melbourne's skinheads. Any romance takes a backseat to the carnage brought by the skinheads' attacks on the local Asian community, who fight back with equal force. Disquieting look at a brutal world which can't be ignored. Film caused a furor upon its Australian release with debates about whether the extreme violence was intended to titilate or explicate the plot. An unrated version at 89 minutes is also available. 85m/C VHS. *AU* Russell Crowe, Jacqueline McKenzie, Daniel Pollock; *D:* Geoffrey Wright; *W:* Geoffrey Wright. Australian Film Institute '92: Best Actor (Crowe), Best Sound, Best Score. *ACA, FCT*

Romy and Michele's High School Reunion 🐾½ 1997 (R) Two vacuous ditz queens, Romy (Sorvino) and Michele (Kudrow), best friends and roommates since high school, decide they must impress at their 10-year Tucson high school reunion by passing themselves off as wealthy and successful. Since they're barely bright enough to walk and chew gum at the same time, this proves to be a challenge, especially when the arrival of cynical Heather (Garofalo), who knows the truth, threatens their deception. Music's good, and there are a (very) few funny moments, but you'll concentration most on trying to ignore those annoying accents. You don't laugh with these would-be babes, you laugh at them. And even then, not all that much. Based on Schiff's play "The Ladies' Room." *CW:* Language. 91m/C VHS. Mira Sorvino, Lisa Kudrow, Janeane Garofalo, Alan Cumming, Julia Campbell, Elaine Hendrix, Jacob Vargas; *D:* David Mirkin; *W:* Robin Schiff; *C:* Reynaldo Villalobos; *M:* Steve Bartek. *NYR*

Ronnie and Julie 🐾🐾½ 1997 (PG) Yet another contemporary variation of "Romeo & Juliet" with high-school sweethearts Ronnie and Julie's relationship threatened by their respective parents political rivalry in a mayoral campaign. 99m/C VHS. Teri Garr, Joshua Jackson, Margot Finlay, Alexandra Purvis, Tom Butler, Garwin Sanford; *D:* Philip Spink. *HMK*

The Roof 🐾🐾 1956 Uninteresting outing about a young couple who married against their families' wishes and find that setting up a home of their own is more difficult than they thought. In Italian with English subtitles. 98m/B VHS, Beta. *IT*

Gabriella Pallotti, Giorgio Listuzzi; *D:* Vittorio De Sica. *NOS, HHT, APD*

Rooftops *♂♂½* **1989 (R)** Peculiar but predictable, centering on love between Hispanic girl and white youth who has mastered martial arts dancing. Director Wise is a long way from his earlier "West Side Story." See this one and be the only person you know who has. **108m/C VHS, Beta, LV.** Jason Gedrick, Troy Beyer, Eddie Velez, Tisha Campbell; *D:* Robert Wise; *W:* Allan Goldstein, Terrence (Terry) Brennan; *M:* Michael Kamen. *LIV*

The Rookie *♂♂* **1990 (R)** Routine cop drama has worldly veteran and wide-eyed newcomer team to crack stolen-car ring managed by Germans. Eastwood and Sheen are reliable, but Hispanics Julia and Braga, though miscast, nonetheless steal this one as the German villains. **121m/C VHS, Beta, LV, 8mm, Closed Caption.** Clint Eastwood, Charlie Sheen, Raul Julia, Sonia Braga, Lara Flynn Boyle, Pepe Serna, Marco Rodriguez, Tom Skerritt, Roberta Vasquez; *D:* Clint Eastwood. *WAR*

Rookie of the Year *♂♂½* **1993 (PG)** Kid's fluff fantasy come true. Twelve-year-old baseball fanatic Henry has dreams of making it to the big league. He falls, breaks his arm, and when it heals strangely he's blessed with a pitching arm so spectacular he finds himself not only playing for the Chicago Cubs, but leading them to the World Series. Enjoyable family outing for first-time director Stern (who also plays a seasoned and very incredulous ballplayer). Keep your eyes peeled for appearances by real-live sluggers Pedro Guerrero, Barry Bonds, and others. **103m/C VHS, LV, Closed Caption.** Thomas Ian Nicholas, Daniel Stern, Gary Busey, Dan Hedaya; *D:* Daniel Stern; *W:* Sam Harper; *C:* Jack N. Green; *M:* Bill Conti. Blockbuster Entertainment Awards '95: Family Movie, Video.*FXV*

The Room *♂♂* **1987** Altman takes on Pinter in this brooding mini-play about two young strangers who try to rent the room already occupied by a disconnected woman and her semi-catatonic husband. Made for television. **48m/C VHS, Beta.** Julian Sands, Linda Hunt, Annie Lennox, David Hemblen, Donald Pleasence; *D:* Robert Altman; *W:* Harold Pinter. *PSM*

Room at the Top *♂♂♂½* **1959** Ambitious factory man forsakes true love and marries boss's daughter instead in this grim drama set in industrial northern England. Cast excels, with Harvey and Sears as the worker and his wife. Signoret is also quite compelling as the abandoned woman. Adapted from John Braine's novel and followed by "Life at the Top" and "Man at the Top." **118m/B VHS.** *GB* Laurence Harvey, Simone Signoret, Heather Sears, Hermione Baddeley, Avril Ungar, Donald Wolfit, Wendy Craig, Ian Cuthbertson, Ian Hendry, Donald Houston, Raymond Huntley, Miriam Karlin, Wilfred Lawson, Richard Pasco, Mary Peach, Prunella Scales, Beatrice Varley, John Westbrook; *D:* Jack Clayton; *W:* Neil Paterson; *C:* Freddie Francis; *M:* Mario Nascimbene. Academy Awards '59: Best Actress (Signoret), Best Adapted Screenplay; British Academy Awards '58: Best Actress (Signoret), Best Film; Cannes Film Festival '59: Best Actress (Signoret); Nominations: Academy Awards '59: Best Actor (Harvey), Best Director (Clayton), Best Picture, Best Supporting Actress (Baddeley). *NO*

Room 43 *♂♂½* *Passport to Shame* **1958** Campy fable about a British cab driver who falls in love with a French girl, and stumbles onto a white-slavery ring when she falls victim to it. Features a young Caine and future novelist Collins in bit parts. **93m/B VHS, Beta.** Diana Dors, Herbert Lom, Eddie Constantine, Michael Caine, Jackie Collins; *D:* Alvin Rakoff. *VDM, TPV*

Room Service *♂♂½* **1938** The Marx Brothers provide less than the usual mayhem here with Groucho as penniless theatrical producer determined to remain in his hotel room until he can secure funds for his next play. Ball doesn't help matters much either. Not bad, but certainly not up to the zany Marx clan's usual stuff. **78m/B VHS, Beta, LV.** Groucho Marx, Harpo Marx, Chico Marx,

Lucille Ball, Ann Miller, Frank Albertson, Donald MacBride, Charles Halton; *D:* William A. Seiter. *CCB, MED, TTC*

Room to Let *♂♂* **1949** An elderly woman and her daughter take in boarders in Victorian England. They rent a room to a man who claims to be a doctor, but the two women eventually become prisoners of fear, believing the man is actually Jack the Ripper. Will there be a vacancy soon? Somewhat disturbing and suspenseful. **68m/B VHS, Beta.** Jimmy Hanley, Valentine Dyall, Christine Silver, Merle Tottenham, Charles Hawtrey, Connie Smith, Laurence Naismith; *D:* Godfrey Grayson. *NOS, SNC*

A Room with a View *♂♂♂♂* **1986** Engaging adaptation of E.M. Forster's novel of requited love. Carter stars as the feisty British idealist who rejects dashing Sands for supercilious Day Lewis, then repents and finds (presumably) eternal passion. A multi-Oscar nominee, with great music (courtesy of Puccini), great scenery (courtesy of Florence), and great performances (courtesy of practically everybody, but supporters Smith, Dench, Callow, and Elliott must be particularly distinguished). Truly romantic, and there's much humor too. **117m/C VHS, Beta, LV, Closed Caption.** *GB* Helena Bonham Carter, Julian Sands, Denholm Elliott, Maggie Smith, Judi Dench, Simon Callow, Daniel Day-Lewis, Rupert Graves, Rosemary Leach; *D:* James Ivory; *W:* Ruth Prawer Jhabvala; *C:* Tony Pierce-Roberts. Academy Awards '86: Best Adapted Screenplay, Best Art Direction/Set Decoration, Best Costume Design; British Academy Awards '86: Best Actress (Smith), Best Film, Best Supporting Actress (Dench); Golden Globe Awards '87: Best Supporting Actress (Smith); Independent Spirit Awards '87: Best Foreign Film; National Board of Review Awards '86: 10 Best Films of the Year, Best Supporting Actor (Day-Lewis); New York Film Critics Awards '86: Best Cinematography, Best Supporting Actor (Day-Lewis); Writers Guild of America '86: Best Adapted Screenplay; Nominations: Academy Awards '86: Best Cinematography, Best Director (Ivory), Best Picture, Best Supporting Actor (Elliott), Best Supporting Actress (Smith). *FOX, HMV*

Roommate **1984** A valedictorian church-goer and a rebellious iconoclast room together at Northwestern University in 1952, with the expected humorous results. Public television presentation based on a John Updike story. **96m/C VHS, Beta.** Lance Guest, Barry Miller, Elaine Wilkes, Melissa Ford, David Bachman; *D:* Neil Cox. *LIV, VES*

Roommates *♂♂½* **1995 (PG)** Rocky Holeczek (Falk) is a cantankerous coot who, at age 75, decides to care for orphaned 7-year-old grandson Michael. Over the 30 years they are together, they fight over Rocky's old school ways and a grown-up Michael's (Sweeney) attempt to have a family of his own. But despite their bickering, Michael soon realizes that his 107-years-old grandfather's words are truly pearls of wisdom when faced with tragedy. Film hits the right sentimental buttons without going overboard with the tissues and Falk's performance, underneath the layers of latex make-up, is charmingly irascible. Based on co-writer Apple's own grandfather. **108m/C VHS, LV, Closed Caption.** Peter Falk, D.B. Sweeney, Julianne Moore, Ellen Burstyn; *D:* Peter Yates; *W:* Max Apple, Stephen Metcalfe; *C:* Mike Southon; *M:* Elmer Bernstein. Nominations: Academy Awards '95: Best Makeup. *TOU*

Rooster Cogburn *♂♂½* **1975 (PG)** A Bible-thumping schoolmarm joins up with a hard-drinking, hard-fighting marshal in order to capture a gang of outlaws who killed her father. Tired sequel to "True Grit" but the chemistry between Wayne and Hepburn is right on target. **107m/C VHS, Beta, LV.** John Wayne, Katharine Hepburn, Richard Jordan, Anthony Zerbe, John McIntire, Strother Martin, Paul Koslo; *D:* Stuart Millar; *C:* Harry Stradling Jr. *USH, TLF*

Rooster: Spurs of Death! **woof!** **1983 (PG)** An expose on cock fighting, in which a young idealist tries to stop the thriving sport in a small southern town. Dog of a movie that (not surprisingly) went straight to video. **90m/C VHS, Beta.** Vincent Van Patten, Ty Hardin, Kristine DeBell, Ruta Lee. *NO*

Roosters *♂♂½* **1995 (R)** Gallo Morales (Olmos) is returning home, after serving seven years in prison for manslaughter, anxiously awaited by wife Juana (Braga), 20-year-old rebellious son Hector (Nucci), neglected adolescent daughter Angela (Lassez), and sexy sister Chata (Alonso). Gallo is a noted breeder of fighting cocks, which for him represent machismo and power but, to his resentment, it's Hector who owns a potential prize-winning bird, precipitating some explosive family conflicts. Adapted by Sanchez-Scott from her 1987 play. **93m/C VHS, Closed Caption.** Edward James Olmos, Sonia Braga, Maria Conchita Alonso, Danny Nucci, Sarah Lassez; *D:* Robert M. Young; *W:* Milcha Sanchez-Scott; *C:* Reynaldo Villalobos; *M:* David Kilay. *CAF*

Rootin' Tootin' Rhythm *♂* *Rhythm on the Ranch* **1938** All's not quiet on the range, but Autry comes along to sing things back to normal. Goofy, clumsy, ubiquitous sidekick Burnette is a symbol for this whole effort. **55m/B VHS, Beta.** Gene Autry, Smiley Burnette, Monte Blue; *D:* Mack V. Wright. *NOS, VYY, DVT*

Roots *♂♂♂♂* **1977** The complete version of Alex Haley's made for television saga following a black man's search for his heritage, revealing an epic panorama of America's past. Available on six tapes, complete at 570 minutes. **90m/C VHS, Beta.** Ed Asner, Lloyd Bridges, LeVar Burton, Chuck Connors, Lynda Day George, Lorne Greene, Burl Ives, O.J. Simpson, Cicely Tyson, Ben Vereen, Sandy Duncan; *D:* David Greene; *M:* Quincy Jones. *WAR, MOV, PBS*

Roots of Evil *♂½* **1991 (R)** This erotic thriller follows a cop on the trail of a murderer who specializes in killing Hollywood's most beautiful prostitutes. Also available in unrated and Spanish-language versions.*CW:* Language, strong violence, and strong sexuality. *?m/C VHS.* Alex Cord, Delia Sheppard, Charles Dierkop, Jillian Kesner; *D:* Gary Graver. *CAN*

Roots: The Gift *♂♂* **1988** It's Christmas, 1770, and Kunte Kinte (Burton) and Fiddler (Gossett) try to escape slavery via the Underground Railroad. In their attempt, they wind up giving the gift of freedom to several of their fellow slaves. A made for television movie based on the Alex Haley characters. **94m/C VHS.** Louis Gossett Jr., LeVar Burton, Michael Learned, Avery Brooks, Kate Mulgrew, Shaun Cassidy, John McMartin; *D:* Kevin Hooks; *C:* John A. Alonzo. *WAR, FCT*

Roots: The Next Generation *♂♂♂* **1979** Sequel to the landmark television miniseries continuing the story of author Alex Haley's ancestors from the Reconstruction era of the 1880s to 1967, culminating with Haley's visit to West Africa where he is told the story of Kunta Kinte. On seven tapes. **685m/C VHS.** Georg Stanford Brown, Lynne Moody, Henry Fonda, Richard Thomas, Marc Singer, Olivia de Havilland, Paul Koslo, Beah Richards, Stan Shaw, Harry (Henry) Morgan, Irene Cara, Dorian Harewood, Ruby Dee, Paul Winfield, James Earl Jones, Debbie Allen; *Cameos:* Al Freeman Jr., Marlon Brando. *MOV*

Rope *♂♂♂½* **1948 (PG)** In New York City, two gay college students murder a friend for kicks and store the body in a living room trunk. They further insult the dead by using the trunk as the buffet table and inviting his parents to the dinner party in his honor. Very dark humor is the theme in Hitchcock's first color film, which he innovatively shot in uncut ten-minute takes, with the illusion of a continuous scene maintained with tricky camera work. Based on the Patrick Hamilton play and on the Leopold-Laeb murder case. **81m/C VHS, Beta, LV.** James Stewart, John Dall, Farley Granger, Cedric Hardwicke, Constance Collier; *D:* Alfred Hitchcock; *W:* Arthur Laurents. *USH*

Rorret *♂♂* **1987** "Rorret" is "terror" spelled backwards—a good indication of the psychological and physical terror Mr. Rorret, the owner of the Peeping Tom Cinema, inflicts upon his female patrons. The Cinema is devoted to the horror film and Rorret himself dresses like Peter

Lorre in "M;" lives behind the movie screen, watching the films in mirror image; and enjoys the frightened reactions of his female patrons. He enjoys their reactions so much that he later stalks the women for real. Highlighted by recreated sequences from such psycho-terror classics as "Psycho," "Dial M for Murder," "Strangers on a Train," and "Peeping Tom." In Italian with English subtitles. **105m/C VHS.** *IT* Lou Castel, Anna Galiena, Massimo Venturiello; *D:* Fulvio Wetzl; *W:* Fulvio Wetzl. *NYF*

Rosa Luxemburg 🎭🎭 **1986** Based on the life of the Jewish political radical, murdered in 1919. Involving herself with the German Social Democratic Party, Luxemburg undergoes numerous imprisonments and maintains a tempestuous personal life. Based primarily on Luxemburg's letters and speeches; charismatic performance by Sukowa. In German with English subtitles. **122m/C VHS.** *GE* Barbara Sukowa, Daniel Olbrychski, Otto Sander, Adelheid Arndt; *D:* Margarethe von Trotta; *W:* Margarethe von Trotta. Cannes Film Festival '86: Best Actress (Sukowa). *NYF, FCT*

Rosalie 🎭🎭½ **1938** A gridiron great from West Point falls for a mysterious beauty from Vassar. He soon learns that her father reigns over a tiny Balkan nation. Expensive, massive, imperfect musical; exotic romantic pairing fails to conceal plot's blah-ness. Oh well, at least Porter's music is good. 🎵I've a Strange New Rhythm in My Heart; Why Should I Care?; Spring Love Is in the Air; Rosalie; It's All Over But the Shouting; Who Knows?; In the Still of the Night; To Love or Not to Love; Close (instrumental). **118m/B VHS, Beta.** Nelson Eddy, Eleanor Powell, Frank Morgan, Ray Bolger, Ilona Massey, Reginald Owen, Edna May Oliver, Jerry Colonna; *D:* Woodbridge S. Van Dyke; *M:* Cole Porter. *MGM*

Rosalie Goes Shopping 🎭🎭 **1989 (PG-13)** Satire about American consumerism hiding behind slapstick comedy, and it works, most of the time. Misplaced Bavarian (Sagebrecht) moves to Arkansas and begins spending wildly and acquiring "things." Twisty plot carried confidently by confident wackiness from Sagebrecht and supporters. **94m/C VHS, LV.** *GE* Marianne Saegebrecht, Brad Davis, Judge Reinhold, Willie Harlander, Alex Winter, Erika Blumberger, Patricia Zehentmayr; *D:* Percy Adlon; *W:* Eleonore Adlon, Percy Adlon; *M:* Bob Telson. *THV*

The Rosary Murders 🎭🎭 **1987 (R)** Based on the William X. Kienzle mystery about a serial killer preying on nuns and priests. Father Koesler (Sutherland) must betray the confessional to stop him. Interesting, though sometimes muddled and too rarely tense. Filmed on location in Detroit. **105m/C VHS, Beta, LV, Closed Caption.** Donald Sutherland, Charles Durning, Belinda Bauer, Josef Sommer, James Murtaugh, John Danelle, Addison Powell, Kathleen Tolan; *D:* Fred Walton; *W:* Fred Walton, Elmore Leonard. *VTR*

The Rose 🎭🎭🎭 **1979 (R)** Modeled after the life of Janis Joplin, Midler plays a young, talented and self-destructive blues/rock singer. Professional triumphs don't stop her lonely restlessness and confused love affairs. The best exhibition of the rock and roll world outside of documentaries. Electrifying film debut for Midler features an incredible collection of songs. 🎵Fire Down Below; I've Written A Letter to Daddy; Let Me Call You Sweetheart; The Rose; Stay With Me; Camellia; Sold My Soul To Rock 'n' Roll; Keep On Rockin'; When A Man Loves a Woman. **134m/C VHS, Beta, LV, Closed Caption.** Bette Midler, Alan Bates, Frederic Forrest, Harry Dean Stanton, David Keith; *C:* Vilmos Zsigmond. Golden Globe Awards '80: Best Actress—Musical/Comedy (Midler), Best Song ("The Rose"); National Society of Film Critics Awards '79: Best Supporting Actor (Forrest); Nominations: Academy Awards '79: Best Actress (Midler), Best Film Editing, Best Sound, Best Supporting Actor (Forrest). *FOX*

The Rose and the Jackal 🎭🎭 **1990** Fun, intriguing fictionalization about the founder of the Pinkerton detective agency. During the Civil War, bearded, Scottish Reeve tries to persuade a wealthy Southern lady to help save the Union. Made for cable television. **94m/C VHS, Beta, Closed Caption.** Christopher Reeve, Madolyn Smith, Granville Van Dusen, Carrie Snodgress, Kevin McCarthy; *D:* Jack Gold. *TTC*

The Rose Garden 🎭🎭½ **1989 (PG-13)** In modern Germany, a Holocaust survivor is put on trial for assaulting an elderly man. The victim, it turns out, was a Nazi guilty of heinous war crimes. Ullmann and Schell lend substance, though treatment of a powerful theme is inadequate. **112m/C VHS, Beta, LV.** Liv Ullmann, Maximilian Schell, Peter Fonda, Jan Niklas, Kurt Hubner; *D:* Fons Rademakers; *W:* Paul Hengge; *M:* Egisto Macchi. *CAN*

Rose Marie 🎭🎭🎭 *Indian Love Call* **1936** An opera star falls in love with the mountie who captured her escaped convict brother. Hollywood legend has it that when a British singer was presented with the first line in "Indian Love Song," which is "When I'm calling you-oo-oo-oo-oo-oo-oo," the confused performer sang, "When I'm calling you, double oh, double oh, double oh..." Maybe true, maybe not, but funny anyway. Classic MacDonald-Eddy operetta. Remade in 1954. 🎵Indian Love Call; Pardon Me, Madame; The Mounties; Rose Marie; Totem Tom Tom; Just for You; Tex Yeux; St. Louis Blues; Dinah. **112m/B VHS, Beta, LV.** Jeanette MacDonald, Nelson Eddy, James Stewart, Allan Jones, David Niven, Reginald Owen; *D:* Woodbridge S. Van Dyke; *C:* William H. Daniels; *M:* Rudolf Friml. *MGM*

Rose Marie 🎭🎭🎭 **1954 (G)** Blyth is a lonely Canadian woman wooed by a mean spirited fur trapper and a gallant mountie. Unremarkable remake of the Eddy/MacDonald musical is saved by spectular technicolor and CinemaScope photography. Choreography by Busby Berkeley. 🎵Rose Marie; Indian Love Call; Totem Tom Tom; The Mounties; I Have the Love; The Right Place For A Girl; Free to be Free; The Mountie Who Never Got His Man. **115m/C VHS, LV.** Ann Blyth, Howard Keel, Fernando Lamas, Bert Lahr, Marjorie Main, Joan Taylor, Chief Yowlachie, Abel Fernandez, Al Ferguson, Dabbs Greer, Lumsden Hare; *D:* Mervyn LeRoy; *C:* Paul Vogel. *MGM, MLB*

Rose of Rio Grande 🎭 **1938** A western musical about a Mexican gang that avenges the deaths of members of the upper strata. **60m/B VHS, Beta.** John Carroll, Movita, Antonio Moreno, Lena Basquette, Duncan Renaldo; *D:* William Nigh. *GPV*

Rose of Washington Square 🎭🎭½ **1939** Singer Faye gets involved with the no-account Power, much to the dismay of her friend Jolson. They marry, and she becomes a singing sensation in the Ziegfeld Follies while he becomes an embarassment, eventually winding up on the wrong side of the law. Jolson stole the movie, singing some of his best numbers. This thinly-disguised portrait of Fanny Brice caused the performer to sue for defamation of character; she eventually settled out of court. 🎵California, Here I Come; My Mammy; Pretty Baby; Toot Toot Tootsie Goodbye; Rock-A-Bye Your Baby with a Dixie Melody; My Man; I'm Just Wild About Harry; I Never Knew Heaven Could Speak; Rose of Washington Square. **86m/B VHS.** Alice Faye, Tyrone Power, Al Jolson, William Frawley, Joyce Compton, Hobart Cavanaugh, Moroni Olsen; *D:* Gregory Ratoff; *W:* Nunnally Johnson; *C:* Karl Freund. *FXV*

The Rose Tattoo 🎭🎭🎭½ **1955** Magnani, in her U.S. screen debut, is just right as a Southern widow who cherishes her husband's memory, but falls for virile trucker Lancaster. Williams wrote this play and screenplay specifically for Magnani, who was never as successful again. Interesting character studies, although Lancaster doesn't seem quite right as an Italian longshoreman. **117m/B VHS, Beta, LV, Closed Caption.** Anna Magnani, Burt Lancaster, Marisa Pavan, Ben Cooper, Virginia Grey, Jo Van Fleet; *D:* Daniel Mann; *W:* Tennessee Williams, Hal Kanter; *C:* James Wong Howe; *M:* Alex North. Academy Awards '55: Best Actress (Magnani), Best Art Direction/Set Decoration (B & W), Best Black and White Cinematography; British Academy Awards '56: Best Actress (Magnani); Golden Globe Awards '56: Best Actress—Drama (Magnani), Best Supporting Actress (Pavan); New York Film Critics Awards '55: Best Actress (Magnani); Nominations: Academy Awards '55: Best Costume Design (B & W), Best Film Editing, Best Picture, Best Supporting Actress (Pavan), Original Dramatic/Comedy Score. *PAR, FCT, BTV*

Roseanne: An Unauthorized Biography 🎭 **1994** Boring TV movie about the boorish (ex-)duo of Tom Arnold and Roseanne Barr Pentland Arnold. Recounts her troubled upbringing in Salt Lake City, her stormy marriage, and her long slog toward fame as a "domestic goddess" stand-up comedienne and TV series star. Miscasting of both leads hurts any chance this poor substitute had. **90m/C VHS.** Denny Dillon, David Graf, John Walcutt, John Karlen, Judith Scarpone, Danielle Harris. *PGV*

Rosebud 🎭 **1975 (PG)** Embarassingly dull film finds a group of PLO terrorists kidnapping five young women who were vacationing aboard O'Toole's yacht. He's supposedly a journalist but actually works for the CIA. Action ping-pongs between the plight of the victims and what's being done to rescue them but it's so boring you won't care. "Rosebud" is the name of the yacht. Based on a novel by Joan Hemingway and Paul Bonnecarrere. **126m/C VHS.** Peter O'Toole, Richard Attenborough, Kim Cattrall, Brigitte Ariel, Isabelle Huppert, Lalla Ward, Deborah Berger, Cliff Gorman, Claude Dauphin, Peter Lawford, Raf Vallone, Adrienne Corri; *D:* Otto Preminger; *W:* Eric Lee Preminger, Marjorie Kellogg. *MGM*

Rosebud Beach Hotel 🎭 *The Big Lobby; The No-Tell Hotel* **1985 (R)** Wimpy loser tries his hand at managing a run-down hotel in order to please his demanding girlfriend. Camp is okay, but this soft-porn excuse is horrible in every other way. **82m/C VHS, Beta, LV.** Colleen Camp, Peter Scolari, Christopher Lee, Fran Drescher, Eddie Deezen, Chuck McCann, Hank Garrett, Hamilton Camp, Cherie Currie; *D:* Harry Hurwitz; *C:* Joao Fernandes. *LIV, VES*

Roseland 🎭🎭🎭 **1977 (PG)** Three interlocking stories, set at New York's famous old Roseland Ballroom, about lonely people who live to dance. Not fully successful, but strong characters, especially in the second and third stories, make it worth watching, although it lacks energy. **103m/C VHS, Beta, LV.** Christopher Walken, Geraldine Chaplin, Joan Copeland, Teresa Wright, Lou Jacobi; *D:* James Ivory; *W:* Ruth Prawer Jhabvala. *VES, CVC*

Rosemary's Baby 🎭🎭🎭🎭 **1968 (R)** A young woman, innocent and religious, and her husband, ambitious and agnostic, move into a new apartment. Soon the woman is pregnant, but she begins to realize that she has fallen into a coven of witches and warlocks, and that they claim the child as the antichrist. Gripping and powerful, subtle yet utterly horrifying, with luminous performances by all. Polanski's first American film; from Levin's best-seller. **134m/C VHS, Beta, LV.** Mia Farrow, John Cassavetes, Ruth Gordon, Maurice Evans, Patsy Kelly, Elisha Cook Jr., Charles Grodin, Sidney Blackmer, William Castle, Ralph Bellamy; *D:* Roman Polanski; *W:* Roman Polanski; *C:* William A. Fraker; *M:* Krzysztof Komeda. Academy Awards '68: Best Supporting Actress (Gordon); Golden Globe Awards '69: Best Supporting Actress (Gordon); Nominations: Academy Awards '68: Best Adapted Screenplay. *PAR, MLB, BTV*

Rosencrantz & Guildenstern Are Dead 🎭🎭🎭 **1990 (PG)** Playwright Stoppard adapted his own absurdist 1967 play to film—which at first look makes as much sense as a "Swan Lake" ballet on radio. Patience is rewarded for those who stick with it. Two tragicomic minor characters in "Hamlet" squabble rhetorically and misperceive Shakespeare's plot tightening fatally around them. Uprooted from the stage environment, it's arcane but hilarious if you're paying attention. Roth and Oldman are superb as the doomed duo. **118m/C VHS, Beta, LV, Closed Caption.** Gary Oldman, Tim Roth, Richard Dreyfuss, Iain Glen; *D:* Tom Stoppard; *W:* Tom Stoppard; *C:* Peter Biziou. Venice Film Festival '91: Best Picture. *TOU, FCT*

Roses Bloom Twice ♂½ 1977 When a middle-aged widow decides to make up for some of the wild living that she missed during her marriage, she shocks her children. 87m/C VHS, Beta. Glynis McNicoll, Michael Craig, Diane Craig, John Allen, Jennifer West; **D:** David Stevens. NO

Rosewood ♂♂♂ 1996 (R) Based on the true story of the well-off African American community of Rosewood, Florida, which was destroyed by a white mob in 1923. Rhames is Mr. Mann, a war vet and Voight a white shopkeeper who, together, try to save innocent people from the tragic massacre that begins when a woman falsely accuses a black man of rape. Accurately shows the tensions present between blacks and whites of the time. Voight's character is not overly romanticized as the great white hope. The real hero is the reticent Rhames, a fictitious blend of real-life characters and Hollywood machismo. Both performances are strong and film succeeds as a detailed visual reminder of country's tragic history. Real-life survivors of the bloodshed finally won reparation from the Florida legislature in 1993. Singleton's location shoots in the Florida swamps caused problems for the crew, one of whom was sent to the hospital after a snake bite.**CW:** Violence and some sexuality. 142m/C VHS, LV, Closed Caption. Ving Rhames, Jon Voight, Don Cheadle, Michael Rooker, Bruce McGill, Loren Dean, Esther Rolle, Elise Neal, Catherine Kellner, Akosua Busia, Paul Benjamin, Mark Boone Jr., Muse Watson, Badja Djola, Kathryn Meisle, Jaimz Woolvett; **D:** John Singleton; **W:** Gregory Poirier; **C:** Johnny E. Jensen; **M:** John Williams. WAR

Rosie: The Rosemary Clooney Story ♂♂½ 1982 Above average biography of Clooney's up-and-down career. Locke lip-synches Clooney's voice in songs. Orlando doesn't help matters portraying Jose Ferrer. Made for television. 100m/C VHS, Beta. Sondra Locke, Tony Orlando, Penelope Milford, Katherine Helmond, Kevin McCarthy, John Karlen, Cheryl Anderson, Robert Ridgely, Joey Travolta; **D:** Jackie Cooper; **Performed by:** Rosemary Clooney. LIV

Roswell: The U.F.O. Cover-Up ♂♂½ 1994 (PG-13) Fact-based drama finds intelligence officer Major Jesse Marcel (McLachlan) investigating the wreckage of a craft near his Roswell, New Mexico air base in the summer of 1947. Marcel believes the craft is extraterrestrial—as are the strange bodies recovered from the wreckage. An Air Force press release announces a UFO but is quickly retracted and Marcel's suspicions ridiculed. A 30-year reunion still finds him obsessed and seeking to clear his name but this time Marcel's investigations may finally lead to the truth. Made for TV; based on the book "UFO Crash at Roswell" by Kevin D. Randle and Donald R. Schmitt.**CW:** Brief strong language. 91m/C VHS, LV, Closed Caption. Kyle MacLachlan, Dwight Yoakam, Kim Greist, Martin Sheen, Xander Berkeley, J.D. Daniels, Doug Wert, John M. Jackson, Peter MacNicol, Bob Gunton, Charles Martin Smith; **D:** Jeremy Paul Kagan; **W:** Jeremy Paul Kagan, Arthur Kopit, Paul Davids; **C:** Steven Poster; **M:** Elliot Goldenthal. REP

R.O.T.O.R. ♂ 1988 R.O.T.O.R. (Robotic Officer of Tactical Operations Research) is a law enforcement robot that is supposed to stop criminals. But watch out! It might go beserk and wreck your town. 90m/C VHS, LV. Richard Gesswein, Margaret Trigg, Jayne Smith; **D:** Cullen Blaine. IMP

Rough Cut ♂♂ 1980 (PG) American diamond thief Reynolds lives in London, pursued by an aging Scotland Yard detective who wants to end his career in a blaze of glory. A beautiful lady is the decoy. Good chemistry; lousy script. 112m/C VHS, Beta, LV. Burt Reynolds, Lesley-Anne Down, David Niven, Timothy West, Joss Ackland, Patrick Magee; **D:** Donald Siegel; **W:** Larry Gelbart; **C:** Frederick A. (Freddie) Young. PAR

Rough Justice ♂½ 1987 Spaghetti western about a lone gunfighter tracking down three killers. Kinski is a sexually aroused bad guy in this miserable excuse. What could he have been thinking? 95m/C VHS, Beta. IT Klaus Kinski, Steven Tedd; **D:** Mario Costa. TWE

Rough Magic ♂♂ Miss Shumway; Jette un Sort 1995 (PG-13) Fantasy-noir-romance-comedy-on-the-road-movie-nostalgia-fest can't decide what it wants to be when it grows up. Fonda is a magician's assistant, with latent powers of her own, who flees to Mexico after witnessing a murder. Her fiance (Moffett) turns out to be the culprit and he hires drifter Crowe to track her down. Along the way, they meet a quack doctor (Broadbent) trying to find a magic Mayan potion, a garage owner who becomes a sausage, and a shaman. Sure, it's confusing, but the performances are good, and you could always play "Name That Genre" afterwards. Adapted from the novel "Miss Shumway Waves a Wand" by James Hadley Chase.**CW:** Sex-related content and some violence. 104m/C VHS. GB FR Bridget Fonda, Russell Crowe, Jim Broadbent, D.W. Moffett, Paul Rodriguez, Euva Anderson; **D:** Clare Peploe; **W:** Clare Peploe, Robert Mundy, William Brookfield; **C:** John Campbell; **M:** Richard Hartley. NYR

Rough Night in Jericho ♂½ 1967 Martin plays unredeemable scum in this cliched western. He's an ex-lawman trying to take over the town of Jericho and all that's left to own is the stagecoach line run by Simmons and McIntire. Coming to Simmons aid is Peppard, a former deputy marshall turned gambler. Predicatably violent. 104m/C VHS, Closed Caption. Dean Martin, Jean Simmons, George Peppard, John McIntire, Slim Pickens, Don Galloway; **D:** Arnold Laven; **W:** Sydney Boehm, Marvin H. Albert. USH, FCT

Rough Riders of Cheyenne ♂½ 1945 Sunset Carson ends the feud between the Carsons and the Sterlings. 54m/B VHS, Beta. Sunset Carson, Peggy Stewart. MED

Rough Riders' Roundup ♂♂ 1939 Roy and the boys rid a mining town of its crooked manager; also better all around. 54m/B VHS, Beta. Roy Rogers, Raymond Hatton, Lynn (Mary Hart) Roberts, Dorothy Sebastian, Duncan Renaldo, George Montgomery; **D:** Joseph Kane. NOS, VDM, DVT

Rough Ridin' Rhythm ♂½ 1937 Wallace is kidnapped to care for the orphaned child of a bandit's sister with Maynard being accused of having murdered the woman. But he's innocent and fights the gang to clear his name. Based on the story "Getting a Start in Life" by James Oliver Curwood. 58m/B VHS. Kermit Maynard, Beryl Wallace, Ralph Peters, Betty Mack, Curly Dresden; **D:** J.P. McGowan. GPV

Rough Riding Rangers ♂½ The Secret Stranger 1935 Threatening letters plague a western ranch family. 57m/B VHS, Beta. Rex Lease, Janet Chandler. VCN

Roughnecks ♂½ 1980 A team of Texas oil drillers attempt to dig the deepest oil well in history and chase women on the side. Too long, and not particularly action-packed or gripping. Made for television. 240m/C VHS, Beta. Sam Melville, Cathy Lee Crosby, Vera Miles, Harry (Henry) Morgan, Steve Forrest, Stephen McHattie, Wilford Brimley; **D:** Bernard McEveety. PSM

Round Midnight ♂♂♂ 1986 (R) An aging, alcoholic black American jazz saxophonist comes to Paris in the late 1950s seeking an escape from his self-destructive existence. A devoted young French fan spurs him to one last burst of creative brilliance. A moody, heartfelt homage to such expatriate bebop musicians as Bud Powell and Lester Young. In English and French with English subtitles. Available in a Spanish-subtitled version. 132m/C VHS, Beta, LV, Closed Caption. FR Dexter Gordon, Lonette McKee, Francois Cluzet, Martin Scorsese, Herbie Hancock, Sandra Reaves-Phillips; **D:** Bertrand Tavernier; **W:** Bertrand Tavernier, David Rayfiel; **C:** Bruno de Keyzer; **M:** Herbie Hancock. Academy Awards '86: Best Original Score; Nominations: Academy Awards '86: Best Actor (Gordon). MVD, WAR, FCT

Round Numbers ♂½ 1991 (R) Judith Schweitzer believes her husband "Big Al the Muffler King" is having an affair with the gorgeous Muffler Mate of the Month, Mitzi (Playboy Playmate Hope Marie Carlton). Determined to get revenge, Judith books herself into the same health spa that Mitzi attends and the result is pure comedy.**CW:** Language. 98m/C VHS, Closed Caption. Kate Mulgrew, Samantha Eggar, Marty Ingels, Hope Marie Carlton, Shani Wallis, Natalie Barish, Debra Christofferson; **D:** Nancy Zala; **W:** Nancy Zala. HMD

Round Trip to Heaven ♂♂ 1992 (R) Party guy Larry (Feldman) and his innocent cousin (Galligan) take off in a borrowed Rolls Royce to go meet Larry's dream centerfold in a super model contest. Unfortunately, the Rolls' trunk is loaded with stolen money and Stoneface (Sharkey), the felon who stashed the cash, wants the money back. With Stoneface in pursuit these guys are in for the ride of their lives. For the teen set only. Also available with Spanish subtitles.**CW:** Langauge, nudity, violence, and some sexuality. 97m/C VHS, LV, Closed Caption. Corey Feldman, Zach Galligan, Julie McCullough, Rowanne Brewer, Ray Sharkey; **D:** Alan Roberts. PSM

The Round Up ♂♂½ Szegenylegenyek Nehezeletuck; The Hopeless Ones; The Poor Outlaws 1966 Brutal tale spins a realistic political web of fear. Set in 1868 in a prison camp, suspected Hungarian subversives, largely peasants and herdsmen, are thrown into jail and tortured. A direct and shocking exploration of life under dehumanizing, totalitarian rule. In Hungarian with English subtitles. 90m/B VHS. HU Janos Gorbe, Tibor Molnar, Andras Kozak; **D:** Miklos Jancso; **W:** Gyula Hernadi. FST, HTV

Round-Up Time in Texas ♂♂ 1937 Autry delivers a herd of horses to his diamond-prospector brother in South Africa and has to deal with bandits after the jewels. Typical early Autry entry, with singin' on the side. 54m/B VHS, Beta. Gene Autry, Smiley Burnette; **D:** Joseph Kane. NOS, VCN, VYY

The Rounders ♂♂½ 1965 Two aging, no-account cowboys (Ford and Fonda) dream of giving up their bronco-busting ways to open a bar in Tahiti where they can watch the world go by. But they have a habit of blowing all their money on women, whiskey, and bad bets. An ornery unbreakable horse may be the key to changing their luck. Mild-mannered comedy with beautiful Arizona scenery. 85m/C VHS, Closed Caption. Glenn Ford, Henry Fonda, Sue Ane Langdon, Hope Holiday, Chill Wills, Edgar Buchanan, Kathleen Freeman, Joan Freeman, Denver Pyle; **D:** Burt Kennedy; **W:** Burt Kennedy; **C:** Paul Vogel. MGM

Rounding Up the Law ♂♂½ 1922 Good guy dupes bad guy while organ plays. 62m/B VHS, Beta, 8mm. Russell Gordon, Chet Ryan, Patricia Palmer, William McCall, Guinn "Big Boy" Williams; **D:** Charles Seeling. VYY, GPV

Roustabout ♂♂½ 1964 A roving, reckless drifter joins a carnival and romances the owner's daughter. Elvis rides on good support from Stanwyck et al. Welch has a bit part in her film debut; look for Terri Garr as a dancer. ♫Roustabout; Poison Ivy League; One Track Heart; Little Egypt; Wheels on My Heels; It's a Wonderful World; It's Carnival Time; Hard Knocks; There's a Brand New Day on the Horizon. 101m/C VHS, Beta. Elvis Presley, Barbara Stanwyck, Joan Freeman, Leif Erickson, Sue Ane Langdon, Pat Buttram, Joan Staley, Dabbs Greer, Steve Brodie, Jack Albertson, Marianna Hill, Beverly Adams, Billy Barty, Richard Kiel, Raquel Welch; **D:** John Rich. FOX, MVD

The Rousters ♂♂½ 1990 (PG) Descendants of Wyatt Earp run a carnival in a small Western town. Comic misadventures arise when a modern varmint named Clayton comes looking for action. Cannell (of "The A-Team" and "Riptide" fame) co-wrote and produced—with his usual extraordinary mix of the absurd and the dangerous. Unusual vehicle for Rogers, but she keeps her style and humor. Made for TV. **72m/C VHS, LV.** Jim Varney, Mimi Rogers, Chad Everett, Maxine Stuart, Hoyt Axton; **D:** E.W. Swackhamer; **W:** E.W. Swackhamer, Stephen J. Cannell. THV

Rover Dangerfield ⅃⅃ **1991 (G)** Lovable Las Vegas hound Rover Dangerfield searches for respect but finds none. The results are hilarious. Quality animation from a project developed by Rodney Dangerfield and Harold Ramis. **78m/C VHS, LV, 8mm. D:** Jim George; **M:** Harold Ramis; **M:** David Newman; **V:** Rodney Dangerfield. WAR

Roxanne ⅃⅃⅃ **1987 (PG)** A modern comic retelling of "Cyrano de Bergerac." The romantic triangle between a big nosed, small town fire chief, a shy fireman and the lovely astronomer they both love. Martin gives his most sensitive and believable performance. Don't miss the bar scene where he gets back at a heckler. A wonderful adaptation for the modern age. **107m/C VHS, Beta, LV, 8mm, Closed Caption.** Steve Martin, Daryl Hannah, Rick Rossovich, Shelley Duvall, Michael J. Pollard, Fred Willard, John Kapelos, Max Alexander, Damon Wayans, Matt Lattanzi, Kevin Nealon; **D:** Fred Schepisi; **W:** Steve Martin; **C:** Ian Baker; **M:** Bruce Smeaton. Los Angeles Film Critics Association Awards '87: Best Actor (Martin); National Society of Film Critics Awards '87: Best Actor (Martin); Writers Guild of America '87: Best Adapted Screenplay. COL

Roxie Hart ⅃⅃½ **1942** Sassy '20s Chicago dance hall girl Roxie (Rogers) decides to take the fall when hubby (Chandler) murders a man. (She sees it as a publicity boost to her career). Slick lawyer Billy Flynn (Menjou) knows he can get the tootsie off if she justs flashes the jury her considerable sex appeal. Montgomery's a smitten reporter who catches Roxie's eye. Based on the play "Chicago" by Maurine Watkins and previously filmed in 1927. Bob Fosse later adapted the play for a Broadway musical. **75m/B VHS.** Ginger Rogers, Adolphe Menjou, George Montgomery, Lynne Overman, Nigel Bruce, Phil Silvers, Sara Allgood, William Frawley, Spring Byington, George Chandler; **D:** William A. Wellman; **W:** Nunnally Johnson; **C:** Leon Shamroy; **M:** Alfred Newman. FXV

The Royal Bed ⅃⅃½ *The Queen's Husband* **1931** King Eric's queen really wears the pants in the family, and when she leaves on a trip, he's left helpless and hapless. A revolution erupts, and his daughter announces she plans to marry a commoner. What's a king to do? **74m/B VHS, Beta.** Lowell Sherman, Nance O'Neil, Mary Astor, Anthony Bushell, Gilbert Emery, Robert Warwick, J. Carrol Naish; **D:** Lowell Sherman. VYY

Royal Flash ⅃⅃⅃ **1975 (PG)** Satirical adventure picture, witty and fast paced, with a few real life period characters thrown in for good measure. Cowardly swashbuckler Flashman, wanting to enter high society, is used to advance a political cause when he is forced to impersonate a Prussian nobleman and marry a duchess. Script by Fraser and based on his series of novels featuring the Flashman character. **98m/C VHS.** GB Malcolm McDowell, Alan Bates, Florinda Bolkan, Oliver Reed, Britt Ekland, Lionel Jeffries, Tom Bell, Alastair Sim, Michael Hordern, Joss Ackland, Christopher Cazenove, Bob Hoskins; **D:** Richard Lester; **W:** George MacDonald Fraser; **C:** Geoffrey Unsworth. NO

A Royal Scandal ⅃⅃½ **1996** And you thought Chuck and Di made a hash of their marriage. The British should be used to marital scandal as this saga on the disasters befalling Princess Caroline of Brunswick (Lynch) and Prince George (Grant), aptly demonstrates. The extravagant George is forced to marry through political and financial pressure but loathes the unrefined Caroline practically on sight. As soon as a royal heir is on the way, they cease to live together and George goes back to his mistresses. But although Caroline would agree to a settlement, she refuses a divorce and when George becomes King George IV, Caroline fully intends to be Queen. **60m/C VHS.** GB Richard E. Grant, Susan Lynch, Frances Barber, Michael Kitchen, Denis Lawson, Oliver Ford Davies, Irene

Richards; **D:** Sheree Folkson; **W:** Stanley Price; **C:** John Daly; **M:** John Altman. FOX

Royal Wedding ⅃⅃⅃ *Wedding Bells* **1951** Astaire and Powell play a brother-and-sister dance team who go to London during the royal wedding of Princess Elizabeth, and find their own romances. Notable for the inspired songs and Astaire's incredible dancing on the ceiling and walls; Lerner's first screenplay. The idea came from Adele Astaire's recent marriage to a British Lord. ♫Too Late Now; Sunday Jumps; How Can You Believe Me When I Said I Love You When You Know I've Been A Liar All My Life?; You're All the World to Me; The Happiest Day of My Life; Open Your Eyes; Ev'ry Night at Seven; I Left My Hat in Haiti; What A Lovely Day For A Wedding. **93m/C VHS, Beta, LV.** Fred Astaire, Jane Powell, Peter Lawford, Keenan Wynn, Sarah Churchill; **D:** Stanley Donen; **W:** Alan Jay Lerner. Nominations: Academy Awards '51: Best Song ("Too Late Now"). MGM, NOS, CAB

Royce ⅃⅃ **1993 (R)** After a successful mission, Royce's CIA team is disbanded. But some former agents aren't happy with early retirement and decide to go into business for themselves. **CW:** Language, topless dance scene, and violence. **98m/C VHS, Closed Caption.** James Belushi, Chelsea Field, Miguel Ferrer, Peter Boyle; **D:** Rod Holcomb; **W:** Paul Bernbaum. PAR

R.P.M.* (*Revolutions Per Minute) ⅃½ **1970 (R)** Another chance to relive the sixties. Student activists force the university hierarchy to appoint their favorite radical professor president. Hip prof-turned-prez Quinn is between a rock and a hard place, and allows police to crack down. Could have been intriguing, but loses steam; in any case, the script and direction both stink. **90m/C VHS, Beta.** Anthony Quinn, Paul Winfield, Gary Lockwood, Ann-Margret; **D:** Stanley Kramer; **W:** Erich Segal; **M:** Perry Botkin. COL

R.S.V.P. ⅃½ **1984 (R)** Hollywood party honoring a writer turns tragic when a body is found in the guest of honor's pool. Most interesting part is watching the porn stars who make up most of the cast fail at acting while dressed. **87m/C VHS, Beta, LV.** Harry Reems, Lynda Wiesmeier; **D:** Lem Amero. LIV, VES

Rubberface ⅃ **1981 (PG)** Tony Maroni (Carrey) is a very bad but very determined comedian. And he may just catch a break when he teams up with joke writer Janet (Glassbourg). Made for Canadian TV. **48m/C VHS, Closed Caption.** CA Jim Carrey, Adah Glassbourg; **D:** Glen Salzman, Rebecca Yates. THV

Rubdown ⅃⅃ **1993** An ex-baseball player, turned Beverly Hills masseur, finds himself the victim of a frame-up when one of his clients is murdered. **88m/C VHS, Beta, Closed Caption.** Jack Coleman, Michelle Phillips, Kent Williams, Alan Thicke, Catherine Oxenberg, William Devane; **D:** Stuart Cooper; **W:** Clyde Hayes; **M:** Gerald Gouriet. PAR

Rubin & Ed ⅃⅃ **1992 (PG-13)** Ed is a real estate groupie who bribes the eccentric Rubin to attend a get-rich-quick seminar. Rubin decides to cash in on the favor by taking Ed on the road in search of the perfect gravesite for Rubin's long-dead feline. If that sounds wacky, just wait—the fun really begins when the duo is stranded in Death Valley and begins to suffer from sunstroke and hallucinations. Those who dream of weirdos bonding in the desert may be enthused but other viewers may thirst for something more. **82m/C VHS, LV.** Crispin Glover, Howard Hesseman, Karen Black, Michael Greene, Brittney Lewis; **D:** Trent Harris; **W:** Trent Harris; **C:** Bryan Duggan. COL, FCT

Ruby ⅃⅃ **1977 (R)** A young woman, christened in blood and raised in sin, has a love affair with the supernatural and murders up a storm at a drive-in. Confused, uneven horror a step up from most similar flicks. **85m/C VHS, Beta.** Roger Davis, Janet Baldwin, Piper Laurie, Stuart Whitman; **D:** Curtis Harrington; **W:** Barry Schneider. NO

Ruby ⅃⅃½ **1992 (R)** Another in the increasing number of Kennedy assassination and conspiracy dramas—this one told from the viewpoint of Jack Ruby, Lee Harvey Oswald's killer. Confusing plot, somewhat redeemed by the performances of Aiello and Fenn. Combines actual footage of Ruby shooting Oswald with black-and-white filmed scenes. Based on the play "Love Field'" by Stephen Davis. **CW:** Language. **111m/C VHS, LV, Closed Caption.** Danny Aiello, Sherilyn Fenn, Arliss Howard, Tobin Bell, David Duchovny, Richard Sarafian, Joe Cortese, Marc Lawrence; **D:** John MacKenzie; **W:** Stephen Davis; **C:** Phil Meheux; **M:** John Scott. COL

Ruby Gentry ⅃⅃½ **1952** White-trash girl Jones, cast aside by man-she-loves Heston, marries wealthy Malden to spite him, then seeks revenge. Classic Southern theme of comeuppance, good direction and acting lift it a notch. **82m/B VHS, Beta.** Charlton Heston, Jennifer Jones, Karl Malden; **D:** King Vidor. FOX

Ruby in Paradise ⅃⅃⅃ **1993 (R)** Leaving her dead-end life in Tennessee, Gissing (Judd) moves to Panama City, Florida and lands a job selling souvenirs for no-nonsense Mildred Chambers (Lyman). Although pursued by two very different men, Ruby concentrates more on self-exploration, recording her thoughts in a journal. A seemingly effortless portrayal of Ruby Lee by Judd (daughter of Naomi and sister of Wynonna Judd) makes for a pleasurable character study of a young woman on her own. **CW:** Some language and some sexuality. **115m/C VHS, LV, Closed Caption.** Ashley Judd, Todd Field, Bentley Mitchum, Allison Dean, Dorothy Lyman, Betsy Dowds; **D:** Victor Nunez; **W:** Victor Nunez; **C:** Alex Vlacos; **M:** Charles Engstrom. Independent Spirit Awards '94: Best Actress (Judd); Sundance Film Festival '93: Grand Jury Prize; Nominations: Independent Spirit Awards '94: Best Cinematography, Best Director (Nunez), Best Film, Best Screenplay, Best Supporting Actor (Field). REP

Ruby Jean and Joe ⅃⅃ **1996 (PG-13)** Aging rodeo star Joe Wade (Selleck) doesn't want to leave the circuit even though it's obvious that his body can't take the punishment anymore. Joe gets more depressed until he picks up hitchhiker Ruby Jean (Johnson), a sarcastic teenager in search of a future. The unlikely duo form a friendship that may offer salvation to them both. Made for cable. **CW:** Brief nudity, sensuality and language. **100m/C VHS, LV, Closed Caption.** Tom Selleck, JoBeth Williams, Rebekah Johnson, Ben Johnson; **D:** Geoffrey Sax; **W:** James Lee Barrett; **C:** James L. Carter; **M:** Stephen Graziano. REP

Ruby's Dream ⅃⅃ **1992** A bowling alley and nightclub owner dreams of making it big in Las Vegas. After his dreams crash to the ground, however, he realizes what is truly important in life. **100m/C VHS.** Joe Pesci. QVD

Ruckus ⅃⅃ *The Loner* **1981 (PG)** A Vietnam vet uses his training to defend himself when he runs into trouble in a small Alabama town. Less obnoxious than "First Blood," (which came later), but basically the same movie. **91m/C VHS, Beta.** Dirk Benedict, Linda Blair, Ben Johnson, Richard Farnsworth, Matt Clark; **D:** Max Kleven; **C:** Don Burgess. NO

Ruddigore ⅃⅃ **197?** The Lords of Ruddigore have been bound for centuries by a terribly inconvenient curse; they must commit a crime every day or die a horribly painful death. When the Lord of Ruddigore passes his mantle on to the new heir, the young heir loses both his good reputation and his very proper fiancee. A new version of Gilbert and Sullivan's opera. **112m/C VHS, Beta.** Vincent Price, Keith Michell, Sandra Dugdale. FOX

Rude ⅃⅃ **1996 (R)** Rude's (Lewis) a Jamaican-Canadian pirate-radio DJ in Toronto, who narrates three stories about urban life: window dresser Maxine (Crawford) struggles to recover from an abortion after her lover leaves her; frightened boxer Jordan (Chevolleau) tries to deal with his own homosexuality after participating with friends in a gay bashing; and ex-con Luke (Wint) returns to his wife (now a police officer) and young son. He tries to resist returning to his drug dealing past and cope with a jealous younger brother (Johnson). Debut for director Virgo.**CW:** Strong graphic language, drug use, sexuality, and some violence. **90m/C VHS, LV. CA** Sharon M. Lewis, Richard Chevolleau, Rachael Crawford, Maurice Dean Wint, Stephen Ellen, Clark Johnson, Melanie Nicholls-King, Stephen Shellan; **D:** Clement Virgo; **W:** Clement Virgo; **C:** Barry Stone; **M:** Aaron David. *APX*

Rude Awakening 🎬🎬½ 1981 A real estate agent is tortured by bizarre nightmares which lead to an unusual series of events. Part of the "Thriller Video" series. **60m/C VHS, Beta.** Denholm Elliott, James Laurenson, Pat Heywood; **D:** Peter Sasdy. *LIV*

Rude Awakening 🎬🎬 1989 (R) Hippies Cheech and Roberts (where's Chong?) settled in a South American commune 20 years ago. Now they're back, and don't know what to make of old pals Carradine and Hagerty who have become - that's right - yuppies. Rip Van Winkle-ian farce draws a few yuks, but could have been much funnier. Points for trying. **100m/C VHS, Beta, LV.** Eric Roberts, Richard "Cheech" Marin, Julie Hagerty, Robert Carradine, Buck Henry, Louise Lasser, Cindy Williams, Andrea Martin, Cliff DeYoung; **D:** Aaron Russo, David Greenwalt; **W:** Richard LaGravenese; **M:** Jonathan Elias. *HBO*

Rudolph & Frosty's Christmas in July 1982 More animated adventures of Rudolph and friends. This time they are transported to a glittering, sunny seashore for a magical summer weekend that almost turns into tragedy. **97m/C VHS, Beta. V:** Red Buttons, Ethel Merman, Mickey Rooney, Jackie Vernon, Shelley Winters. *LIV, TLF*

Rudolph the Red-Nosed Reindeer 1964 The durable Christmas story of the nasally enhanced reindeer who saved the holiday; colorful stop-motion animation and character voices bring it to life, with a memorable guest visit from an abominable snowman. Made for television. **53m/C VHS, Beta, LV, 8mm, Closed Caption. D:** Larry Roemer. *FHE, LME*

Rudy 🎬🎬½ 1993 (PG) Likeable, true story about a little guy who triumphs over big odds. Daniel "Rudy" Ruettiger (Astin) dreams of playing football for Notre Dame, no matter how farfetched the dream. He's a mediocre student, physically unsuitable for big time college ball, but sheer determination helps him attain his dream. Astin delivers an engaging performance and is backed up by a good supporting cast. Sentimental story stretches the truth with typical shameless Hollywood manipulation, but is still entertaining. From the director and writer of another David beats Goliath sports film, "Hoosiers." **112m/C VHS, LV, 8mm, Closed Caption.** Sean Astin, Ned Beatty, Charles S. Dutton, Lili Taylor, Robert Prosky, Jason Miller, Ron Dean, Chelcie Ross, Jon Favreau, Greta Lind, Scott Benjaminson, Christopher Reed; **D:** David Anspaugh; **W:** Angelo Pizzo; **M:** Jerry Goldsmith. *COL*

Rudyard Kipling's The Jungle Book 🎬🎬½ *The Jungle Book* 1994 (PG) Respectable live-action version from Disney of the Rudyard Kipling tale of Mowgli (Lee), the boy who's raised by a wolf pack after getting lost in an Indian jungle. This time around Mowgli gets to grow up—enough to have a romantic interest in the lovely Kitty (Headey), the daughter of British officer, Major Brydon (Neill). His rival is the supercilious Captain Boone (Elwes), who learns Mowgli knows the location of a hidden jungle treasure. Now Mowgli must count on his friends, Grey Brother the wolf, Baloo the bear, and Bagheera the black panther, to defeat the greedy Boone and win Kitty. Filmed in India. **111m/C VHS, LV, Closed Caption.** Jason Scott Lee, Cary Elwes, Sam Neill, Lena Headey, John Cleese; **D:** Stephen Sommers; **W:** Stephen Sommers. *DIS*

Rudyard Kipling's the Second Jungle Book: Mowgli and Baloo 🎬🎬 *Jungle Book 2; Mowgli and Baloo: Jungle Book 2; The Second Jungle Book: Mowgli and Baloo* 1997 (PG) Actually a prequel to "Rudyard Kipling's The Jungle Book," the story centers on the ten-year-old Mowgli (Williams) and his efforts to stay among his animal friends in the jungle. After he is spotted by a scout for P.T. Barnum's circus (Campbell), he must elude the hastily organized group that's out to capture and exploit him. He must also dodge the Bandars, a group of funky monkeys who want to make Mowgli their unwilling leader. The special effects are nowhere near as good as its predecessor, with matte shots that make some of the animals look like they were added with magic markers. The story is a classic, however, and the performances (especially Williams') are good. **88m/C VHS, Closed Caption.** Jamie Williams, Bill Campbell, Roddy McDowall, Cornelia Hayes O'Herlihy, David Paul Francis, Gulsham Grover, B.J. Hogg, Amy Robbins, Hal Fowler; **D:** Duncan McLachlan; **W:** Bayard Johnson, Matthew Horton; **C:** Adolfo Bartoli; **M:** John Scott. *COL*

The Rue Morgue Massacres 🎬½ 1973 (R) A modern reprise of the Poe story with touches of Frankensteinia thrown in; plenty of gore. **90m/C VHS, Beta. SP** Paul Naschy, Rossana Yanni, Maria Perschy, Vic Winner, Mary Ellen Arpon; **D:** Javier Aguirre. *NO*

Ruggles of Red Gap 🎬🎬🎬🎬 1935 Classic comedy about an uptight British butler who is "won" by a barbarous American rancher in a poker game. Laughton as the nonplussed man-servant is hilarious; supporting cast excellent. Third and far superior filming of Harry Leon Wilson story. One of the all-time great comedies, the film was remade musically with Bob Hope and Lucille Ball as "Fancy Pants" (1950). **90m/B VHS, Beta.** Charles Laughton, Mary Boland, Charlie Ruggles, ZaSu Pitts, Roland Young, Leila Hyams, James Burke, Maude Eburne; **D:** Leo McCarey; **W:** Walter DeLeon; **M:** Ralph Rainger. National Board of Review Awards '35: 10 Best Films of the Year; New York Film Critics Awards '35: Best Actor (Laughton); Nominations: Academy Awards '35: Best Picture. *USH*

Rule #3 🎬🎬 1993 "Never believe everything you see." That's the rule con artist Travis West lives by. This time he's got two scams planned—a Las Vegas real estate swindle and a cash ripoff of a former nemesis. Double- and triple-crosses abound. Based on the true story of West, who swindled more than $9 million in 15 years. **93m/C VHS.** Mitchell Cox, Marcia Swayze; **D:** Mitchell Cox. *AVI*

Rulers of the City 🎬 1971 Young gangster avenges his father's death. **91m/C VHS, Beta.** Jack Palance, Edmund Purdom, Al Cliver, Harry Baer. *VDC*

The Rules of the Game 🎬🎬🎬🎬 *Le Regle du Jeu* 1939 Renoir's masterpiece, in which a group of French aristocrats, gathering for a weekend of decadence and self-indulgence just before WWII, becomes a metaphor for human folly under siege. The film was banned by the French government, pulled from distribution by the Nazis, and not restored to its original form until 1959, when it premiered at the Venice Film Festival. A great, subtle, ominous film landmark. In French with English subtitles. The laserdisc version includes a commentary by director Peter Bogdanovich. Heavily copied and poorly remade in 1989 as "Scenes from the Class Struggle in Beverly Hills." **110m/B VHS, Beta, LV, 8mm.** Marcel Dalio, Nora Gregor, Jean Renoir, Mila Parely, Julien Carette, Gaston Modot, Roland Toutain, Paulette Dubost, Odette Talazac; **D:** Jean Renoir; **W:** Jean Renoir. *NOS, HHT, VYY*

The Ruling Class 🎬🎬🎬½ 1972 (PG) The classic cult satire features O'Toole as the unbalanced 14th Earl of Gurney, who believes that he is either Jesus Christ or Jack the Ripper. Tongue-in-cheek look, complete with dance and music, at eccentric upper-class Brits and their institutions. Uneven, chaotic, surreal and noteworthy. **154m/C VHS, Beta, LV. GB** Peter O'Toole, Alastair Sim, Arthur Lowe, Harry Andrews, Coral Browne, Nigel Green; **D:** Peter Medak. National Board of Review Awards '72: 10 Best Films of the Year, Best Actor (O'Toole); Nominations: Academy Awards '72: Best Actor (O'Toole). *WBF*

Rumble Fish 🎬🎬🎬 1983 (R) A young street punk worships his gang-leading older brother, the only role model he's known. Crafted by Coppola into an important story of growing up on the wrong side of town, from the novel by S.E. Hinton. Ambitious and experimental, with an atmospheric music score; in black and white. **94m/B VHS, Beta, LV.** Matt Dillon, Mickey Rourke, Dennis Hopper, Diane Lane, Vincent Spano, Nicolas Cage, Diana Scarwid, Christopher Penn, Tom Waits; **D:** Francis Ford Coppola; **W:** Francis Ford Coppola; **C:** Stephen Burum; **M:** Stewart Copeland. *USH*

Rumble in the Bronx 🎬🎬½ 1996 (R) Singapore action star Chan plays a Hong Kong cop who comes to the South Bronx to attend his uncle's wedding and winds up caught in a crime war between the mob and a vicious motorcycle gang. Living special effect Chan choreographed and performed all of his own stunts, and they are remarkable (pay special attention to the hovercraft scene). Over-the-top cheesy dubbing and streets that are obviously not New York (filmed in Vancouver) add to the cartoonish fun. After several attempts to break into the American market, this is Chan's first release in the United States.**CW:** Some language and violent sequences. **91m/C VHS, LV, Closed Caption, DVD.** *HK* Jackie Chan, Anita Mui, Francoise Yip, Bill Tung, Morgan Lam, Marc Akerstream; **D:** Stanley Tong; **W:** Edward Tang, Fibe Ma; **C:** Jingle Ma; **M:** J. Peter Robinson. *NLC*

Rumble in the Streets 🎬½ 1996 (R) Street-smart young Rowe discovers that a psycho cop has decided to clean up the streets of Dallas by hunting down and killing kids like her and she must use her own toughness to survive. **74m/C VHS.** Kimberly Rowe, David Courtemarche, Patrick DeFazio; **D:** Bret McCormick. *NHO*

The Rumor Mill 🎬🎬½ *Malice in Wonderland* 1986 The careers and titanic rivalry of influential Hollywood gossip writer Hedda Hopper and Louella Parsons, played with verve by Taylor and Alexander. Fictionalized script based on the book "Hedda and Louella" by George Eels. Made for TV. **94m/C VHS, Beta, LV.** Elizabeth Taylor, Jane Alexander, Richard Dysart, Joyce Van Patten; **D:** Gus Trikonis; **W:** Jaqueline Feather, David Seidler; **M:** Charles Bernstein. *THV*

A Rumor of War 🎬🎬🎬½ 1980 The first big Vietnam drama for TV is a triumph, portraying the real-life experience of author Philip Caputo (based on his bestseller), from naive youth to seasoned soldier to bitter murder suspect at court martial. Succeeds where Stone's later, much-ballyhooed "Born on the Fourth of July" fails. Adapted by John Sacret Young. **195m/C VHS, Beta.** Brad Davis, Keith Carradine, Michael O'Keefe, Stacy Keach, Steve Forrest, Richard Bradford, Brian Dennehy, John Friedrich, Perry Lang, Chris Mitchum, Dan Shor, Jeff Daniels; **D:** Richard T. Heffron. *FRH*

Rumpelstiltskin 1982 From "Faerie Tale Theatre" comes the story of a woman who can spin straw into gold (Duvall) and the strange man who saves her life (Villechaize). Enjoyable for the whole family. **60m/C VHS, Beta, LV, Closed Caption.** Bud Cort, Ned Beatty, Shelley Duvall, Herve Villechaize, Paul Dooley. *FOX, FCT*

Rumpelstiltskin 🎬🎬 1986 (G) Musical retelling of the classic Brother Grimm fairy tale. Irving plays a young girl who says she can spin straw into gold. Barty is a dwarf who helps her. The catch: she must give up her first born to pay him. Lackluster direction and uninspired acting make this version a yawner. Irving's real-life mother (Pointer) and brother have roles too. **84m/C VHS, Beta, LV, Closed Caption.** Amy Irving, Billy Barty, Robert Symonds, Priscilla Pointer, Clive Revill, John Moulder-Brown; **D:** David Irving. *MED*

Rumpelstiltskin woof! 1996 (R) First director Jones inflicts "Leprechaun" upon us and now there's another warped dwarf on the loose. Single L.A. mom Shelly (Johnston-Ulrich) finds a wishing stone in a thrift shop and unwittingly summons up the little demon, who immediately tries to steal her young son. 91m/C VHS, Closed Caption. Kim Johnston-Ulrich, Tommy Blaze, Max Grodenchik, Allyce Beasley; **D:** Mark Jones. REP

Rumpole of the Bailey 198? John Mortimer's famed British barrister comes to life in McKern's portrait in two episodes taken from the television series. In "Rumpole and the Genuine Article," Rumpole is called on to defend an embittered artist in a forgery case. "Rumpole and the Old Boy Network" has the barrister drawn into blackmail and deception when a brothel is discovered in a respectable London neighborhood. Additional episodes available. 104m/C VHS. GB Leo McKern. MOV, SIG, TVC

Rumpole of the Bailey: Rumpole's Return 🐾🐾🐾 1990 A feature-length film based on the popular British television series. A middle aged barrister refuses to settle for less than justice. Based on the character created by John Mortimer. 106m/C VHS. GB Leo McKern. FCT

Run 🐾½ 1991 (R) A high energy action cartoon, with little plot but lots of stunts. Dempsey is a super-smart law student hired to drive a car to Atlantic City. A stop on the way starts trouble. Instant romance with a local girl balances mayhem from crime boss. Expect no more than physical feats and you'll be happy with this lightweight fare. 91m/C VHS, Beta, LV, Closed Caption. Patrick Dempsey, Kelly Preston, Ken Pogue, Alan C. Peterson, Sean McCann; **D:** Geoff Burrowes; **W:** Michael Blodgett; **C:** Bruce Surtees. HPH

Run, Angel, Run! 🐾½ 1969 (R) Ex-biker Angel is on the run from his former gang after he helps expose them in a magazine article. He settles on a sheep ranch with his girl and then the gang shows up with revenge in mind. Prime drive-in fare with title song sung by none other than Ms. Tammy Wynette. 90m/C VHS, Beta. William Smith, Margaret Markov, Valerie Starrett; **D:** Jack Starrett. NO

Run for the Dream: The Gail Devers Story 🐾🐾½ 1996 (PG-13) Inspirational made-for-cable biopic on U.S. track star Devers (Woodard) who won a gold medal in the 100m sprint in the 1992 Olympics. But 17 months before, Devers suffers complications from a debilitating thyroid condition, Graves' Disease, which could not only cost her her career but her life. 99m/C VHS, Closed Caption. Alfre Woodard, Louis Gossett Jr., Robert Guillaume. HMK

Run for the Roses 🐾½ Thoroughbred 1978 (PG) "National Velvet" clone about a young Puerto Rican boy and a champion race horse in Kentucky. Cheery family fare. 93m/C VHS, Beta. Lisa Eilbacher, Vera Miles, Stuart Whitman, Sam Groom; **D:** Henry Levin. LIV

Run If You Can 🐾 1987 (R) A woman sees a brutal murderer killing his victims on her television. Will she be next? 92m/C Beta. Martin Landau, Yvette Nipar, Jerry Van Dyke; **D:** Virginia Lively Stone. ALL

Run of the Arrow 🐾🐾 Hot Lead 1956 Rather than surrender to the North at the end of the Civil War, an ex-Confederate soldier (Steiger) joins the Sioux nation, engaged in war against the white man. Steiger's Irish brogue is weird and distracting, and the intriguing premise fails to satisfy, but the cast is competent and interesting. 85m/C VHS, Beta, LV. Rod Steiger, Brian Keith, Charles Bronson, Ralph Meeker, Tim McCoy; **D:** Samuel Fuller; **W:** Samuel Fuller. NO

The Run of the Country 🐾🐾🐾 1995 (R) Amid the scenic splendor of a small town south of the North Irish border in County Cavan, Danny (Keeslar) comes of age, sometimes the hard way. His relationship with his bullying dad

(Finney), the local Garda officer, begins to crumble after the tragic death of his mum. So he runs away to live with the town malcontent Prunty (Brophy) and falls in love with the beautiful Annagh (Smurfit), who lives north of the border. Life gets even more complicated when Annagh learns she's pregnant. Director Yates, reunited with Finney for the first time since they won Oscars for "The Dresser," sometimes digs too deep into a big crock of standard Irish stew, occasionally delivering Celtic melodrama instead of poignant slice of life. The usual themes of family dysfunction, religious rebellion and moral dilemma are augmented by the occasional appearance of the IRA. As the frustrated, violent father, Finney shines. In their debut, Keeslar and Smurfit are fine, but Brophy's Prunty is the one you'll remember. Adapted by Connaughton (who used similar geography for "The Playboys") from his novel. **CW:** Strong sex scene and some language. 109m/C VHS, LV, Closed Caption. Albert Finney, Matt Keeslar, Victoria Smurfit, Anthony Brophy, David Kelly; **D:** Peter Yates; **W:** Shane Connaughton; **C:** Mike Southon; **M:** Cynthia Millar. COL

Run, Rebecca, Run 🐾🐾½ 1981 Interesting family adventure yarn for the family about a South American refugee who tries to stop a young girl from leaving from an Australian island where they are both stranded. She eventually befriends him, and attempts to get permission for him to enter the country. 90m/C VHS, Beta. AU Simone Buchanan, Henri Szeps; **D:** Peter Maxwell. NO

Run Silent, Run Deep 🐾🐾🐾 1958 Submarine commander Gable battles his officers, especially the bitter Lancaster who vied for the same command, while stalking the Japanese destroyer that sunk his former command. Top-notch WWII sub action, scripted from Commander Edward L. Beach's novel. 93m/B VHS, Beta. Burt Lancaster, Clark Gable, Jack Warden, Don Rickles, Brad Dexter; **D:** Robert Wise; **W:** John Gay. MGM

Run, Stranger, Run 🐾🐾 Happy Mother's Day, Love, George 1973 (PG) The inhabitants of a seaside house in Nova Scotia are paralyzed with fear when a number of brutal murders occur. A couple of sicko slasher scenes, but hard to swallow. 110m/C VHS. Ron Howard, Patricia Neal, Cloris Leachman, Bobby Darin; **D:** Darren McGavin; **C:** Walter Lassally. COL

Runaway 🐾½ 1984 (PG-13) A cop and his sidekick track down a group of killer robots wreaking havoc. Self-serious, sorry sci-fi. Features Simmons of the rock group KISS. 100m/C VHS, Beta, LV, Closed Caption. Tom Selleck, Cynthia Rhodes, Gene Simmons, Stan Shaw, Kirstie Alley; **D:** Michael Crichton; **W:** Michael Crichton; **C:** John A. Alonzo; **M:** Jerry Goldsmith. COL

Runaway 1989 A boy blames himself for his friend's accidental death and runs away to live in the subway tunnels of New York City. After four months of life underground, a disabled veteran and a waitress lend the boy a hand. Adapted from the novel "Slake's Limbo" by Felice Holman. Made for PBS and aired as part of the "Wonderworks" series. 58m/C VHS, Closed Caption. Charles S. Dutton, Jasmine Guy, Gavin Allen; **D:** Gilbert Moses. PME, HMV, COL

The Runaway Barge 🐾🐾 1975 Tiresomely ordinary TV yarn about three adventurers earning their living on a riverboat. The usual cliches are present, including a gang of bad guys. 78m/C VHS. Bo Hopkins, Tim Matheson, Jim Davis, Nick Nolte, Devon Ericson, Christina Hart, James Best; **D:** Boris Sagal. LIV

The Runaway Bus 🐾🐾 1954 Filled with the requisite motley crew of passengers, including a gold-carrying thief and the ever-befuddled Margaret Rutherford, a bus gets lost between airports and ends up in a deserted village. Would-be wacky comedy. 78m/B VHS, Beta. GB Frankie Howerd, Margaret Rutherford, Petula Clark, George Coulouris; **D:** Val Guest. VYY, FCT

Runaway Father 🐾🐾½ 1991 Pat Bennett's husband fakes his own death in an attempt to abandon his family. When Bennett discovers he's alive she works to set a legal precedent—17 years worth of back child support. Based on a true story. Made for television. 94m/C VHS, Closed Caption. Donna Mills, Jack Scalia, Chris Mulkey, Jenny Lewis; **D:** John Nicolella. WOV

Runaway Nightmare 🐾 1984 Two western worm ranchers are kidnapped by a female gang whose members torture and initiate them, then talk about their plan to steal from organized criminals. Just another typical worm rancher flick. 104m/C VHS. Michael Cartel, Al Valletta; **D:** Michael Cartel. NO

Runaway Train 🐾🐾🐾 1985 (R) A tough jailbird and his sidekick break out of the hoosegow and find themselves trapped aboard a brakeless freight train heading for certain derailment in northwestern Canada. Harrowing existential action drama based on a screenplay by Akira Kurosawa. Voigt is superb. 112m/C VHS, Beta, LV, Closed Caption. Jon Voight, Eric Roberts, Rebecca DeMornay, John P. Ryan, T.K. Carter, Kenneth McMillan; **D:** Andrei Konchalovsky; **W:** Andrei Konchalovsky, Djordje Milicevic, Edward Bunker; **M:** Trevor Jones. Golden Globe Awards '86: Best Actor—Drama (Voight); Nominations: Academy Awards '85: Best Actor (Voight), Best Film Editing, Best Supporting Actor (Roberts). MGM

The Runaways 🐾🐾 1975 A boy runs away from an unhappy foster home situation and becomes friends with a leopard that has escaped from an animal park. Sentimental but well-done family fun. 76m/C VHS, Beta. Dorothy McGuire, John Randolph, Neva Patterson, Josh Albee; **D:** Harry Harris. NO

Runaways 🐾 1984 A corrupt politician's wife falls in love with the man who saved her when she attempted suicide. The two try to escape her husband's wrathful vengeance. 95m/C VHS, Beta. Steve Oliver, Sondra Currie, John Russell. NO

The Runestone 🐾🐾 1991 (R) After the eponymous viking relic is unearthed, an archaeologist's meddling frees a long-imprisoned wolf-beast that terrorizes New York. An adequate horror flick that taps the seldom-explored realm of Norse mythology. Based on a novel by Mark E. Rogers. 105m/C VHS, LV, Closed Caption. Peter Riegert, Joan Severance, William Hickey, Tim Ryan, Chris Young, Alexander Godunov; **D:** Willard Carroll; **W:** Willard Carroll; **M:** David Newman. LIV

The Runner Stumbles 🐾½ 1979 (R) Dated melodrama about a priest who goes on trial for murdering the nun with whom he fell in love in a mining town in the 1920s. Based on a true incident, from the play by Milan Stiff. Van Dyke in an unwanted serious role is miserably grim and wooden. 109m/C VHS, Beta, Closed Caption. Dick Van Dyke, Kathleen Quinlan, Maureen Stapleton, Ray Bolger, Beau Bridges, Tammy Grimes; **D:** Stanley Kramer; **M:** Ernest Gold. FOX

The Runnin' Kind 🐾🐾½ 1989 (R) A yuppie expecting to inherit his father's Ohio law firm goes on a wild spree with an all-girl rock band. Sexy drummer Howard shows him the sights of certain parts of L.A. Original, fun comedy. Independent. 89m/C VHS, Beta. David Packer, Pleasant Gehman, Brie Howard, Susan Strasberg; **D:** Max Tash. FOX

Running Against Time 🐾🐾½ 1990 (PG) A teacher tries to change history (and erase his brother's Vietnam War death) by time-warping back to 1963 and preventing JFK's murder. The made for cable TV movie takes an offhanded gee-whiz approach to a tantalizing premise, as temporal paradoxes multiply in "Back to the Future" style. No assassination-conspiracy theories, by the way, but Lyndon Johnson fans may not like his portrayal here. Based on the novel "A Time to Remember" by Stanley Shapiro. 93m/C VHS. Robert Hays, Catherine Hicks, Sam Wanamaker, James DiStefano, Brian Smiar; **D:** Bruce Seth Green; **W:** Robert Glass. USH

Running Away ♂♂ 1989 (PG-13) Bittersweet story of WWII romance, with a twist of adventure. Strong cast creates good chemistry, but somehow the story is not engaging. Loren and Penny are mother and daughter, leaving Rome for the hills and encountering dangers. 101m/C **VHS, LV, Closed Caption.** Sophia Loren, Sydney Penny, Robert Loggia, Andrea Occhipinti; **D:** Dino Risi. PSM, PAR, FCT

Running Blind ♂♂ 197? Espionage/adventure thriller has a double agent and a beautiful woman on the run in Iceland. 120m/C VHS. GB Stuart Wilson, Heidi Steindorsottir. FCT, VCO

Running Brave ♂♂ 1983 (PG) The true story of Billy Mills, a South Dakota Sioux Indian who won the Gold Medal in the 10,000 meter run at the 1964 Tokyo Olympics. Not bad, but hokey in the way of many of these plodding true-story flicks. 90m/C VHS, Beta, LV. Robby Benson, Claudia Cron, Pat Hingle, Denis Lacroix; **D:** D.S. Everett; **W:** Henry Bean. DIS, TPV

Running Cool ♂♂ 1993 (R) Two easy-going bikers join up with an old friend to protect his wetlands property from a lowlife developer and his stooges. Chicks (there's a romance with a local biker babe), motorcycles, fighting, and saving the environment—what more could you want? 106m/C VHS, Beta, **Closed Caption.** Andrew Divoff, Tracy Sebastian, Dedee Pfeiffer, James Gammon, Paul Gleason, Arlen Dean Snyder, Bubba Baker; **D:** Beverly Sebastian, Ferd Sebastian; **W:** Beverly Sebastian, Ferd Sebastian. PAR

Running Delilah ♂♂½ 1993 Delilah (Cattrall) is a secret agent who is apparently killed by a vicious arms dealer. Only her fellow agent (Zane) resurrects her and Delilah is transformed into a cybernetic super agent. And her assignment is to go after a terrorist who's building a nuclear weapon with plutonium supplied by Delilah's killer. 85m/C VHS, **Closed Caption.** Kim Cattrall, Billy Zane, Diana Rigg. ABC

Running Free ♂½ 1994 (PG) Sullen Garrett joins his naturalist mother in the Alaskan wilderness and establishes a friendship with a wolverine cub (who's smarter than the kid). 90m/C VHS, LV, **Closed Caption.** Jesse Montgomery Sythe, Jayme Lee Misfeldt, Michael Pena; **D:** Steve Kroschel. THV

Running Hot ♂♂½ Highway to Hell; Lucky 13 1983 (R) Seventeen-year-old convicted murderer Stoltz gets love letter in prison from older woman Carrico. When he escapes, they flee the law together. Quick-paced and entertaining. 88m/C VHS, Beta. Monica Carrico, Eric Stoltz, Stuart Margolin, Virgil Frye, Richard Bradford, Sorrels Pickard, Juliette Cummins; **D:** Mark Griffiths; **W:** Mark Griffiths. LIV, VES

The Running Man ♂♂½ 1987 (R) Special-effects-laden adaptation of the Stephen King novel about a futuristic television game show. Convicts are given a chance for pardon—all they have to do is survive an on going battle with specially-trained assassins in the bombed-out sections of Los Angeles. Sci-fi with an attitude. 101m/C VHS, Beta, LV. Arnold Schwarzenegger, Richard Dawson, Maria Conchita Alonso, Yaphet Kotto, Mick Fleetwood, Dweezil Zappa, Jesse Ventura; **D:** Paul Michael Glaser; **W:** Steven E. de Souza; **M:** Harold Faltermeyer. LIV, VES

Running Mates ♂♂♂ 1986 (PG-13) Occasionally intriguing drama of two teens who fall in love, but are kept apart by their fathers' local political rivalry. Could have been better, but cardboard characters abound. 90m/C VHS, Beta. Greg Webb, Barbara Howard, J. Don Ferguson, Clara Dunn; **D:** Thomas L. Neff. VTR, NWV

Running Mates ♂♂♂ 1992 (PG-13) Cynically amusing political satire about a bachelor politician and his too intelligent lady love. Harris is Hugh, a U.S. senator looking forward to the presidential primaries when he meets widowed children's novelist Aggie (Keaton). She hates politics and he's Mr. Slick, although decent enough behind the political expediency. Aggie, however, has a potentially damaging secret in her past which causes the scandal-scenting pack of press hounds to bay in salivating anticipation. Will Hugh stick by Aggie and will Aggie overcome her natural political distaste for everything to end happily? A well-played romp. Made for cable television.**CW:** Language and sensuality. 88m/C VHS, LV, **Closed Caption.** Ed Harris, Diane Keaton, Ed Begley Jr., Ben Masters, Robert Harper, Brandon Maggart, Russ Tamblyn; **D:** Michael Lindsay-Hogg; **W:** A.L. Appling. HBO

Running on Empty ♂♂♂ 1988 (PG-13) Two 1960s radicals are still on the run in 1988 for a politically motivated Vietnam War-era crime. Though they have managed to stay one step ahead of the law, their son wants a "normal" life, even if it means never seeing his family again. Well-performed, quiet, plausible drama. 116m/C VHS, Beta, LV, 8mm, **Closed Caption.** Christine Lahti, River Phoenix, Judd Hirsch, Martha Plimpton, Jonas Arby, Ed Crowley, L.M. Kit Carson, Steven Hill, Augusta Dabney, David Margulies, Sidney Lumet; **D:** Sidney Lumet; **W:** Naomi Foner; **M:** Tony Mottola. Golden Globe Awards '89: Best Screenplay; Los Angeles Film Critics Association Awards '88: Best Actress (Lahti); National Board of Review Awards '88: Best Supporting Actor (Phoenix); Nominations: Academy Awards '88: Best Original Screenplay, Best Supporting Actor (Phoenix). WAR

Running Out of Luck ♂½ 1986 (R) A light, song-packed story about a rock star very much like Jagger who is abandoned in South America and believed dead, until he returns to his world. Features songs from Jagger's solo album "She's the Boss". 88m/C VHS, Beta, LV. Mick Jagger, Dennis Hopper, Jerry Hall, Rae Dawn Chong; **D:** Julien Temple. MVD, FOX

Running Scared ♂♂ 1979 (PG) Two young men, returning from military service as stowaways aboard an Army cargo plane, are caught by an intelligence agent and thought to be spies, because Reinhold has unknowingly photographed a secret U.S. base with his stolen Army-issue camera. Not-bad spy thriller with a twist—the "spies" are hapless nobodies, now on the lam. 92m/C VHS, Beta, LV. Ken Wahl, Judge Reinhold, John Saxon, Annie McEnroe, Bradford Dillman, Pat Hingle; **D:** Paul Glickler. NO

Running Scared ♂♂½ 1986 (R) Hip, unorthodox Chicago cops Hines and Crystal have to handle an important drug arrest before taking an extended vacation in Key West. Not as relentless as "48 Hrs," but more enjoyable in some ways. Ever wonder what it's like to ride in a car at high speed on the tracks? Find out here. 107m/C VHS, Beta, LV, **Closed Caption.** Gregory Hines, Billy Crystal, Dan Hedaya, Jimmy Smits, Darlanne Fluegel, Joe Pantoliano, Steven Bauer; **D:** Peter Hyams; **W:** Gary De Vore. MGM

Running Wild ♂♂ 1927 Early silent comedy starring mustachioed Fields as an eternal coward who suddenly turns into a lion by hypnosis. Odd, often unfunny Fields entry sometimes hits the mark. He's awfully mean, though. 68m/B VHS, Beta. W.C. Fields, Mary Brian, Claud Buchanan; **D:** Gregory La Cava; **M:** Gaylord Carter. PAR

Running Wild ♂♂½ 1973 (G) A free-lance photographer becomes involved in a dispute to save a corral of wild mustang horses. The usual great Colorado scenery enhances a good, family-view story. 102m/C VHS, Beta. Lloyd Bridges, Dina Merrill, Pat Hingle, Gilbert Roland, Morgan Woodward; **D:** Robert McCahon; **W:** Robert McCahon. MED

Running Wild ♂ 1994 (R) Beautiful woman abandons her much older fiance to go on a wild road trip with his son that includes sex and crime.**CW:** Strong sexuality and language. 91m/C VHS, LV. Jennifer Barker, Daniel Dupont, Daniel Spector, Eliot Keener; **D:** Philippe Blot. APX

Rush ♂ 1984 A post-nuclear world war movie in which a rebel named Rush battles the rulers of a slave colony. 83m/C VHS. IT Conrad Nichols, Gordon Mitchell, Laura Trotter, Rita Furlan; **D:** Tonino Ricci. NO

Rush ♂♂♂ 1991 (R) Texas drug culture, circa 1975, is portrayed in this bleak cop drama. Rookie narcotics officer Kristen Cates (Leigh) goes undercover with the experienced Raynor (Patric) to catch a big-time dealer, menancingly played by Allman, and their bosses don't much care how they do it. Cates falls in love with Raynor and is drawn ever deeper into the drug-addicted world they are supposed to destroy. Fine performances and a great blues score by Clapton. The directorial debut of Zanuck. Based on ex-narcotics cop Kim Wozencraft's autobiographical novel.**CW:** Language, violence and graphic drug use, and sensuality. 120m/C VHS. Jason Patric, Jennifer Jason Leigh, Gregg Allman, Max Perlich, Sam Elliott, Tony Frank, William Sadler; **D:** Lili Fini Zanuck; **W:** Pete Dexter; **M:** Eric Clapton. MGM

Rush It ♂½ 1977 Scriptwriters ponder possible plots over capucino: "I've got it! 'Bike Messengers in Love'!" "Nah. The title's too obvious. Why don't we call it 'Rush It'?" Much hard work and many months later, the result is forgettable. 78m/C VHS, Beta. Tom Berenger, Jill Eikenberry. UNI

Rush Week ♂ 1988 (R) Dead coeds populate campus during frat week. Greg Allman has bit part and the Dickies perform two songs. 93m/C VHS, LV. Dean Hamilton, Gregg Allman, Kathleen Kinmont, Roy Thinnes, Pamela Ludwig; **D:** Bob Bravler. COL

The Russia House ♂♂½ 1990 (R) Russian scientist Brandauer attempts to publish book debunking Soviet Union's claims of military superiority by passing it through ex-lover Pfeiffer to British editor Connery, apparently unaware of impending glasnost. Star-studded spy thriller aspires to heights it never quite reaches. Adapted from John Le Carre's novel, Stoppard's screenplay is very fine, actually making some aspects of the novel work better.**CW:** Langauge. 122m/C VHS, LV, 8mm, **Closed Caption.** Sean Connery, Michelle Pfeiffer, Roy Scheider, James Fox, John Mahoney, Klaus Maria Brandauer, Ken Russell, J.T. Walsh, Michael Kitchen, David Threlfall, Ian McNeice, Christopher Lawford; **D:** Fred Schepisi; **W:** Tom Stoppard; **C:** Ian Baker; **M:** Jerry Goldsmith. MGM, FCT

Russian Roulette ♂♂ 1975 The Russian premier is visiting Vancouver in 1970, and the Mounties must prevent a dissident KGB terrorist from assassinating him. Un-thrilling spy yarn fails to deliver on intriguing premise. 100m/C VHS, Beta. George Segal, Christina Raines, Bo Brundin, Denholm Elliott, Louise Fletcher; **D:** Lou Lombardo. FOX

Russian Roulette ♂♂½ 1993 Routine story about an American woman on vacation in Russia who finds herself in the middle of a plot to locate a hidden Czarist artifact and smuggle it out of the country. Everyone on her tour group is suspect, an American businessman becomes involved, and a killer starts eliminating the number of players. Great location scenery. 89m/C VHS. Susan Blakely, Barry Bostwick, E.G. Marshall, Jeff Altman; **D:** Greydon Clark. MNC

The Russian Terminator ♂ 1990 (R) An FBI agent is up against a one-man "death squad." 90m/C VHS. Helena Michaelson, Frederick Offrein, Harley Melin, Tina Tjung; **D:** Mats Helge; **W:** Mats Helge. XVC, DMP

The Russians are Coming, the Russians are Coming ♂♂♂ 1966 Based on the comic novel "The Off-Islanders" by Nathaniel Benchley, this is the story of a Russian sub which accidentally runs aground off the New England coast. The residents falsely believe that the nine-man crew is the beginning of a Soviet invasion, though the men are only looking for help. A memorable set of silly events follows the landing, engineered by a gung-ho police chief and a town filled with overactive imaginations. 126m/C VHS, Beta, **Closed Caption.** Alan Arkin, Carl Reiner, Theodore Bikel, Eva Marie Saint, Brian Keith, Paul Ford, Jonathan Winters, Ben Blue, Tessie O'Shea, Doro Merande, John Phillip Law; **D:** Norman Jewison; **C:** Joseph Biroc. Golden Globe Awards '67: Best Actor—Musical/Comedy (Arkin), Best Film—Musical/Comedy; National Board of Review Awards '66: 10 Best Films of the Year; Nominations: Academy Awards '66: Best Actor (Arkin), Best Adapted Screenplay, Best Film Editing, Best Picture. *FOX, MLB*

Russkies ⅛½ **1987 (PG)** A jolly comedy about three adorable American kids who capture, and eventually grow to like, a stranded Russian sailor. Friendly and peace-loving, but dull. **98m/C VHS, Beta, LV, Closed Caption.** Joaquin Rafael (Leaf) Phoenix, Whip Hubley, Peter Billingsley, Stefan DeSalle, Susan Walters; *D:* Rick Rosenthal; *M:* James Newton Howard. *ORI, WAR*

Rustler's Hideout ⅛ *Rustler's Roundup* **1944** One of numerous westerns starring Crabbe as cowboy do-gooder Billy Carson, here plodding through standard histrionics against rustlers, a cardsharp, and a business fraud. **60m/C VHS, Beta.** Buster Crabbe, Al "Fuzzy" St. John, Charles "Blackie" King, John Merton, Lane Chandler, Hal Price, Edward Cassidy, Bud Osborne; *D:* Sam Newfield. *GPV*

Rustlers of Red Dog ⅛⅛½ **1935** A 12-chapter western serial about Indian wars and cattle rustlers. **235m/B VHS.** Johnny Mack Brown, Raymond Hatton, Joyce Compton, Walter Miller, Harry Woods, William Desmond, Wally Wales, Chief Thundercloud, Art Mix, Bill Patton, Bud Osborne, Lafe McKee; *D:* Lew (Louis Friedlander) Landers. *GPV*

Rustler's Paradise ⅛ **1935** Carey seeks revenge on the man who stole his wife and daughter. **59m/B VHS, Beta, LV.** Harry Carey Sr., Gertrude Messinger, Edmund Cobb; *D:* Harry Fraser. *NOS*

Rustler's Rhapsody ⅛⅛ **1985 (PG)** A singing cowboy rides into a small western town and encounters all kinds of desperados in this earnest would-be satire of '40s B-movie westerns. **89m/C VHS, Beta, LV, Closed Caption.** Tom Berenger, Patrick Wayne, G.W. Bailey, Andy Griffith, Marilu Henner; *D:* Hugh Wilson; *W:* Hugh Wilson; *C:* Jose Luis Alcaine; *M:* Stephen Dorff. *PAR*

Rustler's Roundup ⅛½ **1933** Mix rides to the rescue of Sinclair, whose daddy has been murdered by villains out to steal the ranch. **58m/B VHS.** Tom Mix, Diane Sinclair, Noah Beery Jr., Douglass Dumbrille, Roy Stewart, Nelson McDowell, William Desmond, Frank Lackteen, Pee Wee Holmes, Bud Osborne; *D:* Henry MacRae.

Rustler's Valley ⅛⅛ **1937** Hopalong Cassidy is a ranch foreman who tries to save his employer from the clutches of a crooked lawyer. Pretty fun ordinary range-ridin' saga. **59m/B VHS, Beta.** William Boyd, George "Gabby" Hayes, Lee J. Cobb; *D:* Nate Watt. *VYY*

Rusty's Birthday ⅛⅛½ **1949** Danny searches for the lost Rusty who's been taken in by a family of transient workers. When Danny discovers his pal, he finds the young son of the family doesn't want to give Rusty up. **61m/B VHS.** Ted Donaldson, John Litel, Ann Doran, Jimmy Hunt, Ray Teal; *D:* Seymour Friedman; *W:* Brenda Weisberg. *COL*

The Rutanga Tapes ⅛½ **1990 (R)** Soviet bloc country has representatives in Africa producing deadly chemicals used for war and a dissident has taped evidence of native deaths. Reporter babe Simpson wants an exclusive, Petersen wants the dissident, Libyan agents want the tapes, and you'll want to fast forward to the end. **CW:** Violence. **88m/C VHS.** Henry Cele, Arnold Vosloo, Wilson Dunster, David Dukes, Susan Anspach; *D:* David Lister. *NO*

The Rutherford County Line ⅛ **1987** A tough small-town sheriff searches for the killer of his deputies. **98m/C VHS, Beta.** Earl Owensby; *D:* Thom McIntyre. *USH*

The Ruthless Four ⅛⅛ *Every Man For Himself; Each One For Himself; Sam Cooper's Gold; Each Man For Himself* **1970** Quartet of unlikely mining partners match wills and wits and battle the elements. Not-so-hot spaghetti western, with good lead from Heflin. **97m/C VHS, Beta.** *IT* Van Heflin, Klaus Kinski, Gilbert Roland, George Hilton; *D:* Giorgio Capitani. *MON*

Ruthless People ⅛⅛⅛ **1986 (R)** DeVito and his mistress spend a romantic evening plotting his obnoxious wife's untimely demise. Before he can put his plan into action, he's delighted to discover she's been kidnapped by some very desperate people—who don't stand a chance with Bette. High farcical entertainment is a variation on the story "The Ransom of Red Chief," by O. Henry. **93m/C VHS, Beta, LV.** Bette Midler, Danny DeVito, Judge Reinhold, Helen Slater, Anita Morris, Bill Pullman; *D:* David Zucker, Jim Abrahams, Jerry Zucker; *W:* Dale Lanner; *C:* Jan De Bont; *M:* Michel Colombier. *TOU*

Ruyblas ⅛⅛ **1948** Revenge and romance beset the court of Charles II in this tale of mistaken identity (with Marais in a dual role). Based on the novel by Victor Hugo. **90m/B VHS.** *FR* Jean Marais, Danielle Darrieux; *D:* Pierre Billon; *W:* Jean Cocteau. *FCT*

Ryan's Daughter ⅛⅛½ **1970 (PG)** Irish woman (Miles) marries a man she does not love and then falls for a shell-shocked British major who arrives during the 1916 Irish uprising to keep the peace. Not surprisingly, she is accused of betraying the local IRA gunrunners to her British lover. Tasteful melodrama with lots of pretty scenery that goes on a bit too long. **194m/C VHS, Beta, LV.** *GB* Sarah Miles, Robert Mitchum, John Mills, Trevor Howard, Christopher Jones, Leo McKern; *D:* David Lean; *W:* Robert Bolt; *C:* Frederick A. (Freddie) Young; *M:* Maurice Jarre. Academy Awards '70: Best Cinematography, Best Supporting Actor (Mills); Golden Globe Awards '71: Best Supporting Actor (Mills); National Board of Review Awards '70: 10 Best Films of the Year; Nominations: Academy Awards '70: Best Actress (Miles), Best Sound. *MGM, BTV*

Ryder P.I. ⅛ **1988 (PG-13)** P.I Ryder and his sidekick fight crime and solve weird cases in the big city. **92m/C VHS, Beta.** Bob Nelson. *MOV, VTR*

Sabaka ⅛⅛ *The Hindu* **1955** Adventure set in India about a scary religious cult. Karloff and the cast of stalwart "B" movie performers have fun with this one, and you should, too. **81m/C VHS.** Boris Karloff, Reginald Denny, Victor Jory, Lisa Howard, Jeanne Bates, Jay Novello, June Foray; *D:* Frank Ferrin. *SNC*

Sabotage ⅛⅛⅛ *Woman Alone* **1936** Early Hitchcock thriller based on Conrad's "The Secret Agent." A woman who works at a movie theater (Sidney) suspects her quiet husband (Homolka) might be the terrorist planting bombs around London. Numerous sly touches of the Master's signature humor. **81m/B VHS, Beta, LV, 8mm.** Oscar Homolka, Sylvia Sidney, John Loder, Desmond Tester, Joyce Barbour, Matthew Boulton, S. J. Warmington, William Dewhurst, Austin Trevor, Torin Thatcher, Aubrey Mather, Peter Bull, Charles Hawtrey, Martita Hunt, Hal Walters, Frederick Piper; *D:* Alfred Hitchcock; *W:* Charles Bennett, Ian Hay, Alma Reville, E.V.H. Emmett, Helen Simpson. *SNC, NOS, HHT*

Saboteur ⅛⅛⅛ **1942** A man wrongly accused of sabotaging an American munitions plant during WWII sets out to find the traitor who framed him. Hitchcock uses his locations, including Boulder Dam, Radio City Music Hall, and the Statue of Liberty, to greatly intensify the action. Stunning resolution. **108m/B VHS, Beta, LV.** Priscilla Lane, Robert Cummings, Otto Kruger, Alan Baxter, Norman Lloyd, Charles Halton; *D:* Alfred Hitchcock; *W:* Alfred Hitchcock, Peter Viertel; *C:* Joseph Valentine. *USH*

Sabre Jet ⅛⅛ **1953** Run-of-the-mill wartime drama of hubbies flying combat missions in Korea and long-suffering spouses on the home front. **90m/C VHS, Beta.** Robert Stack, Amanda Blake, Louis King; *D:* Louis King. *NO*

Sabrina ⅛⅛⅛ *Sabrina Fair* **1954** Two wealthy brothers, one an aging businessman (Bogart) and the other a dissolute playboy (Holden), vie for the attention of their chauffeur's daughter (Hepburn), who has just returned from a French cooking school. Typically acerbic, in the Wilder manner, with Bogart and Holden cast interestingly against type (but it's Hepburn's picture anyway). Based on the play "Sabrina Fair" by Samuel Taylor. **113m/B VHS, Beta, LV.** Audrey Hepburn, Humphrey Bogart, William Holden, Walter Hampden, Francis X. Bush-

man, John Williams, Martha Hyer, Marcel Dalio; *D:* Billy Wilder; *W:* Billy Wilder, Ernest Lehman; *C:* Charles B(ryant) Lang. Academy Awards '54: Best Costume Design (B & W); Directors Guild of America Awards '54: Best Director (Wilder); Golden Globe Awards '55: Best Screenplay; National Board of Review Awards '54: 10 Best Films of the Year, Best Supporting Actor (Williams); Nominations: Academy Awards '54: Best Actress (Hepburn), Best Art Direction/Set Decoration (B & W), Best Black and White Cinematography, Best Director (Wilder), Best Screenplay. *PAR*

Sabrina ⅛⅛½ **1995 (PG)** Updated version of Billy Wilder's 1954 fairytale that starred a luminous Audrey Hepburn. This time around the pretty Ormond who gets closely involved with the wealthy Larrabees. And this time the emphasis is more on workaholic business mogul Linus (Ford), who plays a dangerous game when he decides to transfer Sabrina's affections from his feckless engaged brother David (Kinnear) to himself in order to protect a business merger. Ford's a little too stodgy (you'll wonder why Sabrina bothers except she's probably just too nice to say no) but Kinnear's suitably charming (in his film debut) and Marchand properly matriarchal. **127m/C VHS, Beta, Closed Caption.** Harrison Ford, Julia Ormond, Greg Kinnear, Nancy Marchand, John Wood, Richard Crenna, Angie Dickinson, Lauren Holly, Fanny Ardant, Dana Ivey, Patrick Bruel, Miriam Colon, Elizabeth Franz; *D:* Sydney Pollack; *W:* David Rayfiel, Barbara Benedek; *C:* Giuseppe Rotunno; *M:* John Williams. Nominations: Academy Awards '95: Best Song ("Moonlight"), Best Original Score; Golden Globe Awards '96: Best Actor—Musical/Comedy (Ford), Best Film—Musical/Comedy, Best Song ("Moonlight"). *PAR*

Sabrina the Teenage Witch ⅛⅛½ **1996 (PG)** Based on the Archie Comics, this lighthearted cable movie finds 16-year-old Sabrina (Hart) being told by her two eccentric aunts, Hilda (Miller) and Zelda (Fernetz), that she is a witch, descended from a long line of good witches and warlocks. Sabrina's having enough trouble fitting in at Riverdale High without this kind of news but she does find that her magical powers have their advantages. The pilot for the TV series. **90m/C VHS, Closed Caption.** Melissa Joan Hart, Charlene Fernetz, Sherry Miller, Michelle Beaudoin, Ryan Reynolds, Tobias Mehler, Lalainia Lindbjerg; *D:* Tibor Takacs; *W:* Barney Cohen, Kathryn Wallack, Nicholas Factor. *HMK*

Sacco & Vanzetti ⅛⅛ *Sacco e Vanzetti* **1971 (PG)** Two Italian immigrants and acknowledged anarchists are caught amidst communist witch-hunts and judicial negligence when they are tried and executed for murder in 1920s America. Based on the true-life case, considered by some a flagrant miscarriage of justice and political martyrdom, by others, honest American judicial-system proceedings. Well-made and acted. Joan Baez sings the title song "The Ballad of Sacco and Vanzetti." **120m/C VHS, Beta.** Gian Marie Volonte, Riccardo Cucciolla, Milo O'Shea, Cyril Cusack, Geoffrey Keen; *D:* Giuliano Montaldo; *M:* Ennio Morricone. Cannes Film Festival '71: Best Actor (Cucciolla). *NO*

The Sacketts ⅛⅛½ **1979** Follows the adventures of three Tennessee brothers who migrate to the West after the Civil War. Based on two Louis L'Amour novels. Made for television. **198m/C VHS, Beta.** Jeffery Osterhage, Tom Selleck, Sam Elliott, Glenn Ford, Ben Johnson, Mercedes McCambridge, Ruth Roman, Jack Elam, Gilbert Roland; *D:* Robert Totten. *WAR, HHE*

Sacred Ground ⅛⅛ **1983 (PG)** A trapper and his pregnant Apache wife unknowingly build shelter on the Paiute Indians' sacred burial ground. When the wife dies in childbirth, the pioneer is forced to kidnap a Paiute woman who has just buried her own deceased infant. Average western drama. **100m/C VHS, Beta, Closed Caption.** Tim McIntire, Jack Elam, L.Q. Jones, Mindi Miller; *D:* Charles B. Pierce; *W:* Charles B. Pierce. *FOX*

Sacred Mountain/White Flame ⅛ **1931** Two short films starring Riefenstahl, featuring mostly fluid dance sequences and Teutonic mountain boy/girl plots. Silent. **60m/B VHS, Beta.** *GE* Leni Riefenstahl. *FCT, GLV, MRV*

The Sacrifice 🎬🎬🎬 **1986 (PG)** Tarkovsky's enigmatic final film, released after his death. Deals with a retired intellectual's spiritually symbolic efforts at self-sacrifice in order to save his family on the eve of a nuclear holocaust. Stunning cinematography by Sven Nykvist. Acclaimed, but sometimes slow going; not everyone will appreciate Tarkovsky's visionary spiritualism. In Swedish with English subtitles. **145m/C VHS, Beta, LV.** *FR SW* Erland Josephson, Susan Fleetwood, Valerie Mairesse, Allan Edwall, Gudrun Gisladottir, Sven Wollter, Filippa Franzen; *D:* Andrei Tarkovsky; *C:* Sven Nykvist. British Academy Awards '87: Best Foreign Film. *TPV*

Sacrilege 🎬½ **1986** A nun and a nobleman engage in a hot love affair that fosters scandal, murder, and revenge. Cynical use of religious theme masks otherwise ordinary sex/romance flick. Controversial Italian-made erotic drama. **104m/C VHS, Beta.** *IT* Myriem Roussel, Alessandro Gassman; *D:* Luciano Odorisio. *PSM*

The Sad Sack 🎬🎬 **1957** A bumbling hero with a photographic memory winds up in Morocco as a member of the French Foreign Legion. Although a success at the box office, Lewis's second movie (without partner Dean Martin) seems jerky and out of sorts today. Based on the comic strip character by George Baker, but not effectively. **98m/B VHS.** Jerry Lewis, Phyllis Kirk, David Wayne, Peter Lorre, Gene Evans, Mary Treen; *D:* George Marshall; *C:* Loyal Griggs; *M:* Burt Bacharach, Hal David. *COL*

Sadat 🎬🎬½ **1983 (PG)** Gossett, Jr. well plays his title role of Egyptian leader and Nobel Peace Prize winner, Anwar el Sadat. But the controversial life and peace efforts of the president (assassinated in 1981) are given a quick overview in this average drama. Made for television. **195m/C VHS.** Louis Gossett Jr., John Rhys-Davies, Jeremy Kemp, Nehemiah Persoff, Madolyn Smith, Anne Heywood, Jeffrey Tambor, Barry Morse; *D:* Richard Michaels; *M:* Charles Bernstein. *COL*

Saddle Buster 🎬🎬 **1932** A rodeo cowboy loses his nerve after being thrown by a tough horse, but gets it back again by the end of the hour. Actual rodeo footage is incorporated in this low-budget bronco saga. **59m/B VHS.** Tom Keene, Helen Foster, Charles Quigley, Marie Quillen, Robert Frazer, Charles "Slim" Whitaker; *D:* Fred Allen. *NOS, HEG*

Saddle Mountain Round-Up 🎬 **1941** The Range Busters are on the trail again as they smoke out a murderer. **61m/B VHS, Beta.** Ray Corrigan, John "Dusty" King, Max Terhune. *NOS, DVT, RXM*

Sadie McKee 🎬🎬🎬 **1934** A melodrama with Crawford as a maid searching for love in the big city. She falls for a self-destructive ne'er-do-well, marries an alcoholic millionaire, and eventually finds true love with the wealthy Tone (who would become Crawford's third husband). Professional acting and directing elevate the story. **90m/B VHS.** Joan Crawford, Franchot Tone, Gene Raymond, Edward Arnold; *D:* Clarence Brown. *BTV*

Sadie Thompson 🎬🎬🎬 **1928** Swanson plays a harlot with a heart of gold, bawdy and good-natured, in the South Seas. A zealot missionary (Barrymore) arrives and falls in love with her. The last eight minutes of footage have been recreated by using stills and the original title cards, to replace the last reel which had decomposed. Remade as "Rain," "Dirty Gertie From Harlem," and "Miss Sadie Thompson." Based on W. Somerset Maugham's "Rain." **97m/B VHS, LV.** Gloria Swanson, Lionel Barrymore, Raoul Walsh, Blanche Frederici, Charles Lane, James Marcus; *D:* Raoul Walsh. Nominations: Academy Awards '28: Best Actress (Swanson), Best Cinematography. *KIV, MOV*

The Sadist 🎬🎬½ *The Profile of Terror* **1963** Three teachers on their way to Dodger Stadium find themselves stranded at a roadside garage and terrorized by a snivelling lunatic. Tense and plausible. Cinematography by Vilmos Zsigmond.

95m/B Beta. Arch Hall Jr., Helen Hovey, Richard Alden, Marilyn Manning; *D:* James Landis; *W:* James Landis. *SNC, RHI*

Safari 3000 🎬½ **1982 (PG)** "Playboy" writer is assigned to do a story on a three-day, 3,000 kilometer car race in Africa. Doesn't take itself too seriously, and neither should we. Dumb, dull, and disjointed. **91m/C VHS, Beta.** Stockard Channing, David Carradine, Christopher Lee; *D:* Harry Hurwitz; *M:* Ernest Gold. *MGM*

Safe 🎬🎬🎬 **1995 (R)** Surburban California housewife Carol (Moore) literally becomes allergic to her environment and winds up seeking relief in a holistic center in Albuquerque, where director Haynes takes a stab at the New Age and finds a link to the AIDS crisis. Serious, stylistically detached look at a near future riddled with environmental toxins is led by Moore's performance as the sunny suburbanite undone by the unseen. *CW:* Sex scene; brief language. **119m/C VHS, LV, Closed Caption.** Julianne Moore, Peter Friedman, Xander Berkeley, Susan Norman, James LeGros, Mary Carver, Kate McGregor Stewart, Jessica Harper, Brandon Cruz; *D:* Todd Haynes; *W:* Todd Haynes; *C:* Alex Nepomniaschy; *M:* Ed Tomney. Nominations: Independent Spirit Awards '96: Best Actress (Moore), Best Director (Haynes), Best Film, Best Screenplay. *COL*

Safe Passage 🎬🎬 **1994 (PG-13)** Grueling family drama with Sarandon and Shepherd portraying an unhappily married couple who are the parents of seven sons, one of whom is missing and presumed dead in the Sinai Desert war. One by one the grown boys arrive home to await any further news. They rehash memories, watch old videos, open old wounds, and generally affirm life. None of the performances, with the exception of Sarandon, are truly believable. She is the only one that brings any depth to her character as the tough matriarch that holds the family together. Feels like a TV movie, albeit one with classier names. Based on the novel by Ellyn Bache. *CW:* Profanity; scene of marijuana use. **98m/C VHS, LV, Closed Caption.** Susan Sarandon, Sam Shepard, Robert Sean Leonard, Sean Astin, Marcia Gay Harden, Nick Stahl, Jason London, Philip Bosco, Matt Keeslar; *D:* Robert Ackerman; *W:* Deena Goldstone; *C:* Ralf Bode; *M:* Mark Isham. *TTC, NLC*

Saga of Death Valley 🎬🎬½ **1939** Rogers battles a band of outlaws and discovers that their leader is his own brother. Exciting and likeable early Rogers western. **56m/B VHS, Beta.** Roy Rogers, George "Gabby" Hayes, Donald (Don "Red") Barry, Doris Day; *D:* Joseph Kane. *NOS, VDM, VCN*

The Saga of the Draculas 🎬 *Dracula Saga; Dracula: The Bloodline Continues...; The Saga of Dracula* **1972 (R)** An aging vampire wishes to continue his bloodline and seeks to convert his niece's baby to his bloodsucking ways. **90m/C VHS.** *SP* Narciso Ibanez Menta, Tina Sainz, Tony Isbert, Maria Koski, Cristina Suriani, Helga Line; *D:* Leon Klimovsky. *SNC*

Saga of the Vagabond 🎬🎬½ *Sengoku Gunto-Den* **1959** Arranged by master director Akira Kurosawa. A band of ruthless outlaws career across a civil war-torn countryside. With English subtitles. **115m/C VHS, Beta.** *JP* Toshiro Mifune, Michiyo Aratama; *D:* Toshio Sugie. *VDA*

Sagebrush Law 🎬½ **1943** Western yarn has Holt playing a young man trying to clear the name of his bank president father. Barclay serves as the love interest and "Ukulele Ike" Edwards provides needed comic and music relief. **56m/B VHS.** Tim Holt, Cliff Edwards, Joan Barclay, Edward Cassidy, Karl Hackett, Roy Barcroft, Ernie Adams; *D:* Sam Nelson; *W:* Bennett Cohen. *MOV*

Sagebrush Trail 🎬🎬🎬 **1933** Wayne's second-ever western, complete with all sorts of tumbleweed and white-hat cliches. Our hero is wrongly accused of killin' a man, and busts out of the hoosegow to clear his name. Interesting plot twists makes for fun, compelling viewing. **53m/B VHS, LV.** John Wayne, Yakima Canutt, Wally Wales; *D:* Armand Schaefer. *COL, REP, NOS*

Sahara 🎬🎬🎬 **1943** A British-American unit must fight the Germans for their survival in the Libyan desert during WWII. Plenty of action and suspense combined with good performances makes this one a step above the usual war movie. **97m/B VHS, Beta.** Humphrey Bogart, Dan Duryea, Bruce (Herman Brix) Bennett, Lloyd Bridges, Rex Ingram, J. Carrol Naish, Richard Nugent, Miklos Rozsa; *D:* Zoltan Korda. Nominations: Academy Awards '43: Best Black and White Cinematography, Best Sound, Best Supporting Actor (Naish). *COL*

Sahara woof! **1983 (PG)** Disappointing "Perils of Pauline" type adventure. Shields disguises herself as a man (sure) to complete a race across the desert in honor of her late father, and a sheik captures her. **111m/C VHS, Beta, LV.** Brooke Shields, Lambert Wilson, Horst Buchholz, John Rhys-Davies, Ronald Lacey, John Mills, Steve Forrest, Perry Lang, Cliff Potts; *D:* Andrew V. McLaglen; *W:* James R. Silke; *M:* Ennio Morricone. *MGM*

Saigon Commandos 🎬 **1988 (R)** Commandos, on the eve of the fall of Saigon in the 1970s, attempt to prevent heroin dealers from toppling the already-shaky government. So-so war/action flick. **84m/C VHS, Beta, LV.** Richard Young, P.J. Soles, John Allen Nelson, Jimi B Jr.; *D:* Clark Henderson. *MED*

Saigon: Year of the Cat 🎬 **1987** A made for British television drama about an American ambassador, a CIA operative, and a British bank clerk who try to leave Saigon in 1974 before the Vietcong enter the city. **106m/C VHS, Beta.** *GB* Frederic Forrest, E.G. Marshall, Judi Dench; *D:* Stephen Frears; *W:* David Hare; *M:* George Fenton. *HBO*

Sailing Along 🎬🎬 **1938** British musical about a young starlet who sacrifices her career for true love. **80m/B VHS.** *GB* Jessie Matthews, Barry Mackay, Jack Whiting, Roland Young, Noel Madison, Athene Seyler, Patrick Barr; *D:* Sonnie Hale. *FCT*

Sailor-Made Man/Grandma's Boy 🎬🎬🎬 **192?** Silent comedy shorts. In "A Sailor-Made Man" (1921) Lloyd joins the Navy. In "Grandma's Boy" (1922), he is given courage and good advice to win the hand of a girl and defeat a bully. **83m/B VHS, Beta.** Harold Lloyd. *TLF*

The Sailor Who Fell from Grace with the Sea 🎬🎬 **1976 (R)** Perverse tale of a disillusioned sailor who rejects the sea for the love of a lonely young widow and her troubled son. Graphic sexual scenes. Based on the novel by Yukio Mishima, the film suffers from the transition of Japanese culture to an English setting. **105m/C VHS, Beta, LV.** *GB* Sarah Miles, Kris Kristofferson, Jonathan Kahn, Margo Cunningham; *D:* Lewis John Carlino; *W:* Lewis John Carlino. *FOX*

The Saint **1967** Dashing and sophisticated Simon Templar (Moore), AKA "The Saint," is a gentlemanly hero/crook who takes on the causes of those who have been taken advantage of—and whose methods are often less than legal. Based on a popular series of mystery novels by Leslie Charteris, which debuted in the 1930s. Each volume from the British series contains two 50-minute episodes. **100m/C VHS.** *GB* Roger Moore, Ivor Dean. *PGV*

The Saint 🎬🎬 **1968** Moore is Simon Templar, Leslie Charteris' mysterious British detective/hero in this adventure tale that takes him to Naples. Revival and improvement on earlier movie series, and based on the very popular British television show. **98m/C VHS.** *GB* Roger Moore, Ian Hendry. *FOX*

The Saint 🎬🎬½ **1997 (PG-13)** The plot makes about as much sense as that of "Mission: Impossible," the villains are average ego-driven bad guys, and Shue's naive scientist/babe is totally unbelieveable (she's like a deer caught in a car's headlights). The only reason the movie works at all is due to the debonair, if angst-ridden, charms of Kilmer as super-thief and master of disguise Simon Templar. He's hired by Russian strongman Ivan Tretiak (Serbedzija) to steal the formula for cold fusion from scientist Emma Russell (Shue) so that Tretiak can save a freezing Moscow by delivering cheap energy and thus make Russia a formidable power once again (with himself as leader, natch). Only problem is Templar, who names all his alter egos after saints, falls for Emma and tries to get them out of harm's way by double-crossing Tretiak. At least the Moscow and Oxford settings are scenic. Templar's exploits are featured in a series of novels by Leslie Charteris, and previously appeared in earlier movies and on TV. *CW:* Action violence, brief strong language, some sensuality and drug content. 116m/C VHS. Val Kilmer, Elisabeth Shue, Rade Serbedzija, Valery Nikolaev, Henry Goodman, Alun Armstrong, Michael Byrne, Eugene Lazarev, Charlotte Cornwell, Irina Apeximova, Emily Mortimer; *D:* Phillip Noyce; *W:* Jonathan Hensleigh, Wesley Strick; *C:* Phil Meheux; *M:* Graeme Revell. *NYR*

St. Benny the Dip 🎬🎬½ *Escape If You Can* 1951 Three con-men evade police by posing as clergymen, and end up going straight after a series of adventures in a skid row mission. Funny in parts but extremely predictable. Still, good for a few laughs. 80m/B VHS. Dick Haymes, Nina Foch, Roland Young, Lionel Stander, Freddie Bartholomew; *D:* Edgar G. Ulmer. *NOS, FCT, HEG*

St. Elmo's Fire 🎬🎬½ 1985 (R) Seven Georgetown graduates confront adult problems during their first post-graduate year. Reminiscent of "The Big Chill," but a weak story wastes lots of talent and time. 110m/C VHS, Beta, LV, Closed Caption. Rob Lowe, Demi Moore, Andrew McCarthy, Judd Nelson, Ally Sheedy, Emilio Estevez, Mare Winningham, Martin Balsam, Jenny Wright, Joyce Van Patten, Andie MacDowell, Anna Maria Horsford; *D:* Joel Schumacher; *W:* Joel Schumacher; *C:* Stephen Burum; *M:* David Foster. Golden Raspberry Awards '85: Worst Supporting Actor (Lowe). *COL*

St. Helen's, Killer Volcano 🎬🎬½ 1982 A young man and an old man develop a deep friendship amid the devastation, fear, greed, and panic surrounding the eruption of the Mt. St. Helen's volcano. Based on the true story of Harry Truman (!), who refused to leave his home. Pretty good. 95m/C VHS, Beta. Art Carney, David Huffman, Cassie Yates, Bill McKinney, Ron O'Neal, Albert Salmi, Cesare Danova; *D:* Ernie Pintoff. *VES*

The Saint in London 🎬🎬 1939 The Saint investigates a gang trying to pass counterfeit banknotes. The third in "The Saint" series. 72m/B VHS, Beta. George Sanders, Sally Gray; *D:* John Paddy Carstairs. *MED*

The Saint in New York 🎬🎬 1938 The Saint, Simon Templar, turns Robin Hood to help the Civic Committee clean up a gang of desperados. First of "The Saint" series. 71m/B VHS, Beta. Louis Hayward, Kay Sutton, Jack Carson, Charles Halton; *D:* Ben Holmes. *MED*

St. Ives 🎬🎬 1976 (PG) Former police reporter Bronson agrees to recover some stolen ledgers and finds himself dealing with betrayal and murder. Bisset is sultry and the tale is slickly told, but dumb. Co-stars Travanti, later of TV's "Hill Street Blues." 94m/C VHS, Beta. Charles Bronson, Jacqueline Bisset, John Houseman, Harry Guardino, Maximilian Schell, Harris Yulin, Elisha Cook Jr., Daniel J. Travanti; *D:* J. Lee Thompson; *W:* Barry Beckerman; *M:* Lalo Schifrin. *WAR*

Saint Jack 🎬🎬 1979 (R) The story of a small-time pimp with big dreams working the pleasure palaces of late-night Singapore. Engrossing and pleasant. Based on Paul Theroux's novel. 112m/C VHS, Beta. Ben Gazzara, Denholm Elliott, Joss Ackland, George Lazenby; *D:* Peter Bogdanovich; *W:* Peter Bogdanovich. *LIV, VES*

Saint Joan 🎬🎬 1957 Film of the George Bernard Shaw play, adapted by Graham Greene, about the French Maid of Orleans at her trial. Otto Preminger went on a nationwide talent hunt for his leading actress and chose the inexperienced Seberg (her screen debut). A good thing for her career, but not for this ill-begotten, overambitious opus. Seberg doesn't fit. Also available colorized.

131m/B VHS, Beta. Jean Seberg, Anton Walbrook, Richard Widmark, John Gielgud, Harry Andrews, Felix Aylmer, Richard Todd; *D:* Otto Preminger; *C:* Georges Perinal. *WAR*

The Saint of Fort Washington 🎬🎬½ 1993 (R) Sweetly naive and schizophrenic Matthew (Dillon) is homeless and through government screw-ups is sent to the Fort Washington Armory, which houses more than 700 homeless men. Harassed by others, Matthew is befriended by Jerry, a kindly Vietnam vet, who tries to care for him. Subject is taken seriously but slips into mawkishness; good performances by the leads. *CW:* Langauge. 104m/C VHS, Beta, LV, Closed Caption. Danny Glover, Matt Dillon, Rick Aviles, Nina Siemaszko, Ving Rhames, Joe Seneca; *D:* Tim Hunter; *W:* Lyle Kessler; *C:* Frederick Elmes; *M:* James Newton Howard. *WAR*

The Saint Strikes Back 🎬🎬 1939 Sanders debuts as the mysterious Simon Templar in this competent series. On a trip to San Francisco, the Saint aims to clear the name of a murdered man. The second in the series. 67m/B VHS. George Sanders, Wendy Barrie, Jonathan Hale, Jerome Cowan, Neil Hamilton, Barry Fitzgerald, Edward Gargan, Robert Strange; *D:* John Farrow. *MOV*

The Saint Strikes Back: Criminal Court 🎬🎬 1946 A suspense double feature: The Saint helps a daughter clear the name of her murdered father, a San Francisco police commissioner in "The Saint Strikes Back," and a young lawyer becomes involved in murder in "Criminal Court." 127m/B VHS, Beta. George Sanders, Wendy Barrie, Barry Fitzgerald, Tom Conway, Steve Brodie; *D:* John Farrow. *TTC*

The Saint Takes Over 🎬🎬 1940 More adventures with the British mystery man; this time involving racetrack gambling. An original story that wasn't based on a Leslie Charteris novel as were the others. 69m/B VHS. George Sanders, Jonathan Hale, Wendy Barrie, Paul Guilfoyle, Morgan Conway, Cy Kendall; *D:* Jack Hively. *MOV*

The St. Tammany Miracle 🎬🎬½ 1994 Predictable, good-natured sports film about young coach Lootie Pfannder (Luner) who takes a job at a prep school and turns the losing girls basketball team into winners. Her broadcaster boyfriend Carl (Grosselaar) thinks she's crazy but aided by her assistant (Frye), Lootie is determined to prove everyone wrong. 90m/C VHS. Jamie Luner, Mark Paul Gosselaar, Soleil Moon Frye, Jeffrey Meek, Julie McCullough; *Cameos:* Steve Allen; *D:* Joy Houck Jr.; *W:* Jim McCullough Jr.; *M:* Jay Weigel. *VCI*

The St. Valentine's Day Massacre 🎬🎬½ 1967 Corman's big studio debut recreates the events leading to one of the most violent gangland shootouts in modern history: the bloodbath between Chicago's Capone and Moran gangs on February 14, 1929. Uninspired and unremittingly violent. Watch for Jack Nicholson's bit part. 100m/C VHS, Beta. Jason Robards Jr., Ralph Meeker, Jean Hale, Joseph Campanella, Bruce Dern, Clint Ritchie, Richard Bakalayan, George Segal; *D:* Roger Corman; *C:* Milton Krasner. *FOX, FCT*

Saints and Sinners 🎬½ 1995 (R) Streetsmart "Pooch" Puccia (Chapa) returns to his 'hood as an undercover cop to set up childhood buddy, drug dealer Big Boy Baynes (Plank), and winds up getting involved with seductive bad girl Eve (Rubin), who's also bedding Baynes. Then Pooch discovers his police contact is in the pay of the mob, so does he go through with the deal or not? Lots of macho posturing (attractive actors). *CW:* Strong violence, sexuality and language. 99m/C VHS, LV, Closed Caption. Damian Chapa, Scott Plank, Jennifer Rubin, Damon Whitaker, Panchito Gomez, William Atherton; *D:* Paul Mones; *W:* Paul Mones; *C:* Michael Bonvillain. *LIV*

The Saint's Double Trouble 🎬🎬 1940 Leslie Charteris' suave detective becomes embroiled in another mystery, this one involving jewel thieves. Sanders plays a dual role as the hero and the crook. The fourth in the series. 68m/B

VHS. George Sanders, Helene Whitney, Jonathan Hale, Bela Lugosi, Donald MacBride, John Hamilton; *D:* Jack Hively. *MED*

The Saint's Vacation/The Narrow Margin 1952 A mystery double feature. In "The Saint's Vacation," Simon Templar prevents a valuable secret from getting into the wrong hands, and in "The Narrow Margin," strange things happen to a detective when he takes a train ride with a witness to Chicago. Sinclair took over the sleuth's role from George Sanders in this series. 148m/B VHS, Beta. Hugh Sinclair, Sally Gray, Charles McGraw, Marie Windsor, Jacqueline White. *TTC*

Sakharov 🎬🎬🎬 1984 The true story of the Russian physicist who designed the H-bomb and then rose to lead the Soviet dissident movement and win the Nobel Peace Prize. Robards is excellent. Made for cable; topical and powerful. 120m/C VHS, Beta. Glenda Jackson, Jason Robards Jr., Michael Bryant; *D:* Jack Gold; *M:* Carl Davis. *PSM*

Sakura Killers 🎬 1986 Killer Ninjas steal a valuable gene-splicing formula and are hunted down by an American colonel. 87m/C VHS, Beta. Chuck Connors, Mike Kelly, Brian Wong, Thomas Lung; *D:* Richard Ward. *FOX*

Salaam Bombay! 🎬🎬🎬 1988 A gritty film about a child street beggar in the slums of Bombay trying to raise enough money to return to his mother's house in the country. The boy experiences every variety of gutter life imaginable, from humiliation to love. Moving and searing. Filmed on location, with actual homeless children; Nair's first feature. In Hindi with subtitles. 114m/C VHS, Beta, LV. *IN GB* Shafiq Syed, Hansa Vithal, Chanda Sharma, Nana Patekar, Aneeta Kanwar, Sarfuddin Quarassi, Raju Barnad, Raghubir Yadav; *D:* Mira Nair; *W:* Sooni Taraporevala; *C:* Sandi Sissel; *M:* L. Subramaniam. Nominations: Academy Awards '88: Best Foreign Language Film. *NO*

The Salamander 🎬½ 1982 (R) A French detective tries to find the assassin of the leaders of a neo-fascist underground movement in Italy and follows clues that lead back to WWII. Disappointing, overwrought adaptation of a Morris West novel. 101m/C VHS, Beta. *GB* Franco Nero, Anthony Quinn, Martin Balsam, Sybil Danning, Christopher Lee, Cleavon Little, Paul Smith, Claudia Cardinale, Eli Wallach; *D:* Peter Zinner; *M:* Jerry Goldsmith. *NLC*

Salammbo 🎬🎬½ 1914 An early silent epic in the grand Italian tradition. Loosely based on Flaubert's novel about ancient Carthage. 49m/B VHS, Beta. *IT* Ernesto Pagani; *D:* Giovanni Pastrone. *FCT*

Salem's Ghost *Witchcraft 8* 1995 (R) A 300-year-old warlock is awakened and causes terror for an innocent couple. *CW:* Some language; horror violence; strong sensuality. 90m/C VHS. Lee Grober, David Weilis, Tom Overmyer, Anthoni Stuart; *D:* Joseph John Barmettler Jr. *APX*

Salem's Lot 🎬🎬½ *Blood Thirst* 1979 (PG) Based on Stephen King's novel about a sleepy New England village which is infiltrated by evil. A mysterious antiques dealer takes up residence in a forbidding hilltop house—and it becomes apparent that a vampire is on the loose. Generally creepy; Mason is good, but Soul only takes up space in the lead as a novelist returning home. Also available in the original television miniseries version at 190 minutes on two cassettes. 112m/C VHS, Beta, LV. David Soul, James Mason, Lance Kerwin, Bonnie Bedelia, Lew Ayres, Ed Flanders, Elisha Cook Jr., Reggie Nalder, Fred Willard, Kenneth McMillan, Marie Windsor; *D:* Tobe Hooper. *WAR*

Sallah 🎬🎬🎬 1963 A North African Jew takes his family to Israel in 1949 in hopes of making his fortune. He finds himself in a transit camp and runs up against the local bureaucracy in a quest for permanent housing as well as the European work ethic. Amusing and enjoyable satire. In Hebrew with English subtitles. 105m/B VHS, Beta. *IS* Chaim Topol, Geula Noni, Gila Almagor, Arik Einstein, Shraga Friedman, Esther Greenberg; *D:* Ephraim Kishon; *C:* Floyd Crosby. Golden Globe Awards '65: Best Foreign Film;

Nominations: Academy Awards '64: Best Foreign Language Film. *MOV, ERG, NCJ*

Sally of the Sawdust 🎬🎬½ 1925 Fields' first silent feature; he is carnival barker Professor Eustace McGargle who's the guardian of orphaned Sally (Dempster). Then Sally's wealthy grandfather (Alderson), a stern judge, becomes determined to claim her from showbiz lowlifes. Fields gets to demonstrate his talent for juggling, conning customers, and car chasing. Interesting movie caught director Griffith on the decline and Fields on the verge of stardom. Remade as a talkie in 1936 entitled "Poppy." Includes musical score. 113m/B **VHS, Beta.** W.C. Fields, Carol Dempster, Erville Alderson; *D:* D.W. Griffith. *KIV, VYY, CCB*

Salmonberries 🎬½ 1991 (R) East German Roswitha (Zech) is devastated when her lover is killed trying to scale the Berlin Wall. She manages to escape and finds herself stuck in a remote Eskimo community in Alaska where she becomes involved with Kotzebue (lang in her film debut), who poses as a man to work on the Alaskan pipeline. The title has something to do with preserved berries—don't bother, it makes about as much sense as the entire movie. English and German with English subtitles. 94m/C **VHS.** *GE CA* Rosel Zech, k.d. lang, Chuck Connors; *D:* Percy Adlon; *W:* Percy Adlon, Felix Adlon. *FCT*

Salo, or the 120 Days of Sodom 🎬🎬 1975 Extremely graphic film follows sixteen children (eight boys and eight girls) who are kidnapped by a group of men in Fascist Italy. On reaching a secluded villa in the woods, the children are told to follow strict rules and then subjected to incredible acts of sadomasochism, rape, violence, and mutilation. This last film of Pasolini's was taken from a novel by the Marquis de Sade. Viewers are strongly recommended to use their utmost discretion when watching this controversial film. In Italian with English subtitles. 117m/C **VHS, LV.** *IT* Giorgio Cataldi, Umberto P. Quinavalle, Paolo Bonacelli; *D:* Pier Paolo Pasolini; *C:* Tonino Delli Colli; *M:* Ennio Morricone. *FCT, HHE, WBF*

Salome 🎬🎬½ 1922 Garish silent rendition of Oscar Wilde's scandalous tale. 54m/B **VHS, Beta.** Alla Nazimova, Rose Dione, Mitchell Lewis, Earl Schenck; *D:* Charles Bryant. *GPV, FCT, VYY*

Salome 🎬🎬 1953 An over-costumed version of Oscar Wilde's Biblical story about King Herod's lascivious stepdaughter who danced her way to stardom and tried to save the life of John the Baptist. Talented cast can't overcome hokey script. 103m/C **VHS, Beta.** Rita Hayworth, Stewart Granger, Charles Laughton, Judith Anderson, Cedric Hardwicke, Basil Sydney, Maurice Schwartz; *D:* William Dieterle; *C:* Charles B(ryant) Lang; *M:* George Duning. *COL, CCB*

Salome 🎬½ 1985 (R) An updated and graphic version of the Oscar Wilde historical fantasy about the temptress Salome who helped topple Herod's Biblical kingdom with her dance of the Seven Veils. Photographed by Pasqualino De Santis. Not really a remake of the 1953 film since this is set during the 1940s. 100m/C **VHS, Beta.** Jo Ciampa, Tomas Milian, Pamela Salem; *D:* Claude D'Anna. *MGM*

Salome/Queen Elizabeth 1923 Two famous silent shorts: "Salome," (1923), an atmospheric adaptation of Oscar Wilde's tale, with sets designed after Aubrey Beardsley; and "Queen Elizabeth," (1912), Bernhardt's famous, and famously stilted, singular film appearance. 91m/B **VHS, Beta, 8mm.** Alla Nazimova, Sarah Bernhardt, Lou Tellegen, Mitchell Lewis, Nigel de Brulier; *D:* Charles Bryant, Henri Desfontaines, Louis Mercanton. *VYY*

Salome, Where She Danced 🎬 1945 Set during the Franco-Prussian war. A European dancer helps an American reporter in a spy scheme. She eventually relocates to America and becomes the toast of San Francisco. Somehow, De Carlo managed to spring from this ridiculous camp outing to stardom. 90m/C **VHS, Beta.** Yvonne De Carlo, Rod Cameron, David Bruce, Walter Slezak; *D:*

Charles Lamont; *C:* William Howard Greene, Hal Mohr. *NOS, BAR, DVT*

Salome's Last Dance 🎬🎬 1988 (R) A theatrical, set-surreal adaptation of the Wilde story. Typically flamboyant Russell. 113m/C **VHS, Beta, LV.** Glenda Jackson, Stratford Johns, Nickolas Grace, Douglas Hodge, Imogen Millais Scott; *D:* Ken Russell; *W:* Ken Russell. *LIV, IME, VES*

Salsa 🎬🎬 1988 (PG) An auto repairman would rather dance in this "Dirty Dancing" clone. Rosa was formerly a member of the pop group Menudo. 97m/C **VHS, Beta, LV.** Robby Rosa, Rodney Harvey, Magali Alvarado, Miranda Garrison, Moon Orona; *D:* Boaz Davidson; *W:* Boaz Davidson, Tomas Benitez. *MGM, CAN*

Salt of the Earth 🎬🎬🎬½ 1954 Finally available in this country after being suppressed for thirty years, this controversial film was made by a group of blacklisted filmmakers during the McCarthy era. It was deemed anti-American, communist propaganda. The story deals with the anti-Hispanic racial strife that occurs in a New Mexico zinc mine when union workers organize a strike. 94m/B **VHS, Beta, LV, CD-I.** Rosaura Revueltas, Will Geer, David Wolfe; *D:* Herbert Biberman. *IHF, NOS, MPI*

Salty 🎬🎬 1973 A lovable but mischievous sea lion manages to complicate two brothers' lives when they volunteer to help a friend renovate a Florida marina, which is threatened by a mortgage foreclosure. Straightforward and inoffensive tale. 93m/C **VHS, Beta.** Clint Howard, Mark Slade, Nina Foch; *D:* Ricou Browning. *NO*

Salut l'Artiste 🎬🎬 1974 Two bad actors try to make it in the industry. Delightfully funny with an excellent cast, especially Mastroianni. Snide and irreverant, yet loving and comic look at the world of acting. In French with English subtitles. 96m/C **VHS.** *FR* Marcello Mastroianni, Jean Rochefort, Francoise Fabian, Carla Gravina; *D:* Yves Robert; *M:* Vladimir Cosma. *FCT, CVC*

Salute John Citizen 🎬🎬🎬 1942 The life of an average English family during the early days of WWII is depicted, focusing on the deprivation and horror of the Nazi blitzkrieg. 74m/B **VHS, Beta.** Peggy Cummins, Stanley Holloway, Dinah Sheridan, Jimmy Hanley. *VYY*

Salute to the "King of the Cowboys," Roy Rogers 197? Glimpses of Roy from song clips, home movies, trailers, out-takes, and other sources. 60m/B **VHS, Beta.** Roy Rogers. *DVT*

Salvador 🎬🎬🎬½ 1986 (R) Photo journalist Richard Boyle's unflinching and sordid adventures in war-torn El Salvador. Boyle (Woods) must face the realities of social injustice. Belushi and Woods are hard to like, but excellent. Early critical success for director Stone. 123m/C **VHS, Beta, LV, Closed Caption.** James Woods, James Belushi, John Savage, Michael Murphy, Elpidia Carrillo, Cynthia Gibb, Tony Plana, Colby Chester, Will MacMillan, Jose Carlos Ruiz, Jorge Luke, Juan Fernandez, Valerie Wildman; *D:* Oliver Stone; *W:* Oliver Stone, Richard Boyle; *C:* Robert Richardson; *M:* Georges Delerue. Independent Spirit Awards '87: Best Actor (Woods). Nominations: Academy Awards '86: Best Actor (Woods), Best Original Screenplay. *LIV, IME, VES*

Salvation! 🎬🎬½ *Salvation! Have You Said Your Prayers Today?* 1987 (R) A mean-tempered, timely satire about a money-hungry television evangelist beset by a family of fervent, equally money-hungry followers, who proceed to cheat, seduce and blackmail him. Occasionally quite funny, but sloppy and predictable. Underground director Beth B's first above-ground film. 80m/C **Beta.** Stephen McHattie, Exene Cervenka, Dominique Davalos, Viggo Mortensen, Rockets Redglare, Billy Bastiani; *D:* Beth B; *W:* Beth B. *NO*

The Salzburg Connection 🎬½ 1972 (PG) A list of Nazi collaborators is discovered in Austria. A vacationing American lawyer is caught up in the battle for its possession. Filmed on loca-

tion, it's still a poor, cheesy adaptation of the Helen MacInnes novel. 94m/C **VHS, Beta.** Barry Newman, Anna Karina, Klaus Maria Brandauer, Karen Jensen; *D:* Lee H. Katzin. *FOX*

Samantha 🎬🎬½ 1992 (PG) Twenty-one year-old Samantha discovers she was left on her parents' doorstep in a basket and decides to find out where she came from. Good cast and high charm quotient help this film along. 101m/C **VHS, Beta, Closed Caption.** Martha Plimpton, Dermot Mulroney, Hector Elizondo, Mary Kay Place, Ione Skye; *D:* Steven La Rocque; *W:* John Golden, Steven La Rocque. *ACA*

Samar 🎬🎬½ 1962 (PG) A liberal penal colony commandant rebels against his superiors by leading his prisoners through the Philippine jungles to freedom. Original action drama with an interesting premise. 89m/C **VHS, Beta.** George Montgomery, Gilbert Roland, Joan O'Brien, Ziva Rodann; *D:* George Montgomery. *NOS*

Samaritan: The Mitch Snyder Story 🎬🎬🎬 1986 Effective television drama based upon the true story of Vietnam vet Mitch Snyder (Sheen) who battles various government agencies and ultimately fasts to call national attention to his crusade against homelessness. Tyson appears as bag lady; Snyder eventually committed suicide. 90m/C **VHS, Beta, Closed Caption.** Martin Sheen, Roxanne Hart, Joe Seneca, Stan Shaw, Cicely Tyson; *D:* Richard T. Heffron. *FRH*

Same Time, Next Year 🎬🎬🎬 1978 A chance meeting between an accountant and a housewife results in a sometimes tragic, always sentimental 25-year affair in which they meet only one weekend each year. Well-cast leads carry warm, touching story based on the Broadway play by Bernard Slade. 119m/C **VHS, Beta, LV.** Ellen Burstyn, Alan Alda; *D:* Robert Mulligan; *C:* Robert L. Surtees; *M:* Marvin Hamlisch. Golden Globe Awards '79: Best Actress—Musical/Comedy (Burstyn); Nominations: Academy Awards '78: Best Actress (Burstyn), Best Adapted Screenplay, Best Cinematography, Best Song ("The Last Time I Felt Like This"). *USH*

Sammy & Rosie Get Laid 🎬🎬🎬 1987 An unusual social satire about a sexually liberated couple living in London whose lives are thrown into turmoil by the arrival of the man's father - a controversial politician in India. Provides a confusing look at sexual and class collisions. From the makers of "My Beautiful Launderette." 97m/C **VHS, Beta, LV.** *GB* Shashi Kapoor, Frances Barber, Claire Bloom, Ayub Khan Din, Roland Gift, Wendy Gazelle, Meera Syal; *D:* Stephen Frears; *W:* Hanif Kureishi; *M:* Stanley Myers. *ORI, WAR*

Sammy, the Way-Out Seal 🎬🎬 1962 Two young boys bring a mischievous seal to live in their beach house and try to keep it a secret from their parents. Disney in its early '60s phase. 89m/C **VHS, Beta.** Michael McGreevey, Billy Mumy, Patricia Barry, Robert Culp; *D:* Norman Tokar. *DIS*

Sam's Son 🎬🎬 1984 (PG) Sentimental, autobiographical tale about how a young man's athletic prowess opens the door for an acting career in Hollywood. Good performance by Wallach as the boy's father. Self-indulgent, though entertaining. 107m/C **VHS, Beta.** Eli Wallach, Anne Jackson, Timothy Patrick Murphy, Hallie Todd, James Karen, Allan Hayes, Joanna Lee, Michael Landon; *D:* Michael Landon; *W:* Michael Landon. *WOV*

Samson 🎬 1961 Samson attempts to keep wits and hair about him. 90m/C **VHS.** *IT* Brad Harris, Brigitte Corey, Alan Steel, Serge Gainsbourg, Mara Berni; *D:* Gianfranco Parolini. *SNC, MRV*

Samson Against the Sheik 1962 Samson survives long enough to battle a sheik in the Middle Ages. ?m/C **VHS, Beta.** *IT* Ed Fury. *SNC*

Samson and Delilah 🎬🎬🎬 1950 The biblical story of the vindictive Delilah, who after being rejected by the mighty Samson, robbed him of his strength by shearing his curls. Delivered in signature DeMille style. Wonderfully fun and engrossing. Mature is excellent. 128m/C **VHS, Beta, LV.** Victor Mature, Hedy Lamarr, Angela Lansbury, George

Sanders, Henry Wilcoxon, Olive Deering, Fay Holden; **D:** Cecil B. DeMille; **C:** George Barnes. Academy Awards '50: Best Art Direction/Set Decoration (Color), Best Costume Design (Color); Nominations: Academy Awards '50: Best Color Cinematography, Original Dramatic/Comedy Score. *PAR*

Samson and Delilah 🎬🎬 1984 A made for television version of the Biblical romance, semi-based on DeMille's 1950 version. Original Samson (Mature) plays Samson's father. Too long but inoffensive; see the DeMille version instead. 95m/C VHS, Beta. Antony Hamilton, Belinda Bauer, Max von Sydow, Jose Ferrer, Victor Mature, Maria Schell; **D:** Lee Philips; **M:** Maurice Jarre. *PSM*

Samson and Delilah 🎬🎬 1996 Another in TNT's biblical retellings, this time with Israelite shepherd Samson (Thal), who also the strongest man alive, falling for beautiful-but-treacherous Philistine Delilah (Hurley). Seems Samson is causing havoc with General Tariq's (Hopper) Philistine army and Delilah is to discover the secret of his strength. 180m/C VHS, Closed Caption. Eric Thal, Elizabeth Hurley, Dennis Hopper, Michael Gambon, Diana Rigg, Ben Becker, Paul Freeman, Daniel Massey, Pinkas Braun, Debora Caprioglio, Alessandro Gassman, Mark McGann, Jonathan Rhys Myers; **D:** Nicolas Roeg; **W:** Allan Scott; **C:** Raffaele Mertes. *TTC, VIF*

Samson and His Mighty Challenge 🎬½ 1964 In this rarely seen muscle epic, Hercules, Maciste, Samson and Ursus all take part in a battle royale. ?m/C VHS, Beta. *IT* Alan Steel. *SNC*

Samson and the 7 Miracles of the World 🎬🎬 *Maciste Alla Corte Del Gran Khan; Maciste at the Court of the Great Khan; Goliath and the Golden City* 1962 This time the hero known as Maciste (renamed Samson for Americans) is in the 13th century battling brutal Tartar warlords. The very Earth itself shakes when our hero goes into battle! 80m/C VHS, Beta. *FR IT* Gordon Scott, Yoko Tani, Gabriele Antonini, Leonardo Severini, Valeri Inkizhinov, Helene Chanel; **D:** Riccardo (Robert Hampton) Freda; **M:** Les Baxter. *SNC*

Samson in the Wax Museum 🎬½ *Santo en el Museo de Cera; Santo in the Wax Museum* 1963 Masked Mexican wrestling hero Santo (here called Samson) does battle with a scientist who has discovered a way to make wax monsters come to life. 92m/B VHS. *MX* Santo, Claudio Brook, Ruben Rojo, Norma Mora, Roxana Bellini; **D:** Alfonso Corona Blake. *SNC, HHT*

Samson vs. the Vampire Women 🎬½ 1961 Santo (here called Samson) the masked hero and athlete, battles the forces of darkness as a horde of female vampires attempt to make an unsuspecting girl their next queen. 89m/B VHS, Beta. *MX* Santo, Lorena Velasquez, Jaime Fernandez, Maria Duval; **D:** Alfonso Corona Blake. *SNC, HHT*

Samurai 🎬 1945 Truly bad spy-exploitation film about a Japanese orphan who was raised in America, turns traitor, and helps plot the invasion of California. *SNC, TPV* Paul Fung, Luke Chan, David Chow. *SNC, TPV*

Samurai 1: Musashi Miyamoto 🎬🎬🎬½ 1955 The first installment in the film version of Musashi Miyamoto's life, as he leaves his 17th century village as a warrior in a local civil war only to return beaten and disillusioned. Justly award-winning. In Japanese with English subtitles. 92m/C VHS, Beta, LV. *JP* Toshiro Mifune; **D:** Hiroshi Inagaki. Academy Awards '55: Best Foreign Language Film. *NLC, HMV*

Samurai 2: Duel at Ichijoji Temple 🎬🎬🎬½ 1955 Inagaki's second film depicting the life of Musashi Miyamoto, the 17th century warrior, who wandered the disheveled landscape of feudal Japan looking for glory and love. In Japanese with English subtitles. 102m/C VHS, Beta, LV. *JP* Toshiro Mifune; **D:** Hiroshi Inagaki. *NLC, HMV*

Samurai 3: Duel at Ganryu Island 🎬🎬🎬½ 1956 The final film of Inagaki's trilogy, in which Musashi Miyamoto confronts his lifelong enemy in a climactic battle. Depicts Miyamoto's spiritual awakening and realization that love and hatred exist in all of us. In Japanese with English subtitles. 102m/C VHS, Beta, LV. *JP* Toshiro Mifune, Koji Tsurata; **D:** Hiroshi Inagaki. *NLC, HMV*

Samurai Cowboy 🎬🎬 1993 Sato (Go) is a successful Japanese businessman who worships the American western ideal so he decides to give up the rat race by moving to Running Moose, Montana, and buying a cattle ranch. Talk about culture shock! Inoffensive fish-out-of-water comedy. Go is a popular singer in his native Japan. 101m/C VHS. Hiromi Go, Catherine Mary Stewart, Robert Conrad, Conchata Ferrell, Matt McCoy; **D:** Michael Keusch; **W:** Michael Keusch; **M:** Osamu Kitajima. *MNC*

Samurai Reincarnation 1981 After the Shogunate government kills 18,000 Christian rioters in the revolt of 1638, and brutally beheads the leader Shiro Amakusa, Shiro reincarnates during a monstrous thunderstorm. Consumed with hatred, he discards the teachings of Jesus Christ and seeks revenge. In Japanese with English subtitles. 122m/C VHS. *JP* **D:** Kinji Fukasaku. *FCT*

San Antonio 🎬🎬 1945 A bad girl working in a dance hall turns over a new leaf on meeting the good guy. Trite plot, but good production. 105m/C VHS, Beta, Closed Caption. Errol Flynn, Alexis Smith, S.Z. Sakall, Victor Francen, Florence Bates, John Litel, Paul Kelly; **D:** David Butler; **M:** Max Steiner. Nominations: Academy Awards '45: Best Interior Decoration, Best Song ("Some Sunday Morning"). *MGM, FCT, MLB*

San Demetrio, London 🎬🎬½ 1947 Set in 1940, the crew of a crippled tanker endures harrowing situations to reach port. A decent antiwar movie in its time, it's now showing its age. Based on a true story, the plot sags with unbelievable scenes and holes on the plot side. 76m/B VHS. Walter Fitzgerald, Mervyn Johns, Ralph Michael, Robert Beatty, Charles Victor, Frederick Piper; **D:** Charles Frend. *NOS*

San Fernando Valley 🎬🎬 1944 Also called "San Fernando". Another lawman-in-evil-town epic. Rogers received his first on-screen kiss in 1944's biggest western. Fairly typical, pleasant cowboy tale. 54m/B VHS, Beta. Roy Rogers, Dale Evans. *NOS, DVT*

San Francisco 🎬🎬🎬½ 1936 The San Francisco Earthquake of 1906 serves as the background for a romance between an opera singer and a Barbary Coast saloon owner. Somewhat overdone but gripping tale of passion and adventure in the West. Wonderful special effects. Finale consists of historic earthquake footage. Also available colorized. ♫San Francisco; A Heart That's Free; Would You?; Air des Bijoux; Sempre Libera. 116m/B VHS, Beta, LV. Jeanette MacDonald, Clark Gable, Spencer Tracy, Jack Holt, Jessie Ralph, Al Shear; **D:** Woodbridge S. Van Dyke; **W:** Anita Loos. Academy Awards '36: Best Sound; Nominations: Academy Awards '36: Best Actor (Tracy), Best Director (Van Dyke), Best Picture, Best Story. *MGM*

Sanctuary of Fear 🎬½ *Girl in the Park* 1979 A priest in New York City helps an actress subjected to a series of terrorizing incidents. Uninspired would-be TV pilot based on Chesterton's "Father Brown" series. 98m/C VHS, Beta. George Hearn, Barnard Hughes, Kay Lenz, Michael McGuire, Robert Schenkkan, David Rasche, Fred Gwynne, Elizabeth Wilson; **D:** John Llewellyn Moxey. *FOX*

Sand and Blood 🎬🎬½ *Blood and Sand; De Sable et de Sang* 1987 A young matador who wishes to escape poverty and a young, cultivated doctor, who despises bullfighting, meet and eventually become friends. A woman enters the picture and completes the love triangle. Widely praised by critics. Interesting and moving. In French with English subtitles. 101m/C VHS, Beta. *FR* Sami Frey, Andre Dussollier, Clementine Celarie, Patrick Catalifo, Maria Ca-

sares, Catherine Rouvel; **D:** Jeanne Labrune; **W:** Jeanne Labrune. *NYF, FCT*

The Sand Pebbles 🎬🎬🎬½ 1966 An American expatriate engineer, transferred to a gunboat on the Yangtze River in 1926, falls in love with a missionary teacher. As he becomes aware of the political climate of American imperialism, he finds himself at odds with his command structure; the treatment of this issue can be seen as commentary on the situation in Vietnam at the time of the film's release. Considered one of McQueen's best performances, blending action and romance. 193m/C VHS, Beta, LV. Steve McQueen, Richard Crenna, Richard Attenborough, Candice Bergen, Marayat Andriane, Gavin MacLeod, Larry Gates, Mako, Simon Oakland; **D:** Robert Wise; **W:** Robert Anderson; **M:** Jerry Goldsmith. Golden Globe Awards '67: Best Supporting Actor (Attenborough); Nominations: Academy Awards '66: Best Actor (McQueen), Best Art Direction/Set Decoration (Color), Best Color Cinematography, Best Film Editing, Best Picture, Best Sound, Best Supporting Actor (Mako), Best Original Score. *FOX, FCT*

Sandakan No. 8 🎬🎬🎬 *Brothel 8; Sandakan House 8* 1974 A Japanese woman working as a journalist befriends an old woman who was sold into prostitution in Borneo in the early 1900s. Justly acclaimed feminist story dramatizes the role of women in Japanese society. Japanese with English subtitles. 121m/C VHS, Beta. *JP* Kinuyo Tanaka, Yoko Takakashi, Komake Kurihara, Eitaro Ozawa; **D:** Kei Kumai. Berlin International Film Festival '75: Best Actress; Nominations: Academy Awards '75: Best Foreign Language Film. *FCT*

Sanders of the River 🎬🎬🎬 *Bosambo* 1935 A British officer in colonial Africa must work with the local chief to quell a rebellion. Tale of imperialism. Dated but still interesting and of value. Robeson is very good; superb location cinematography. 80m/B VHS, Beta. *GB* Paul Robeson, Leslie Banks, Robert Cochran; **D:** Zoltan Korda; **C:** Georges Perinal. *NOS, VYY, CAB*

Sandflow 🎬🎬½ 1937 Well-made Western with Jones playing a man whose father has cheated many ranchers. Jones is out to avenge all of his father's misdeeds and build a new life for himself in this above-average oater. 58m/B VHS. Buck Jones, Lita Chevret, Robert F. (Bob) Kortman, Arthur Aylesworth, Robert Terry, Enrique DeRosas; **D:** Lesley Selander. *GPV*

The Sandlot 🎬🎬🎬 1993 (PG) Young Scotty (Guiry) moves to a new neighborhood in California in 1962 and tries to make friends despite not knowing anything about playing baseball. His scrappy teammates include the friendly Benny (Vitar), a chubby loud-mouthed catcher named Ham (Renna), and Squints (Leopardi), a would-be Lothario before his time. Action revolves around Scotty's attempt to get baseball autographed by Babe Ruth out of the clutches of giant killer junkyard dog owned by Jones before dad Leary discovers it missing. Small wonder is nostalgic without being sentimental, and tells its tale with grace and humor, supported by a period soundtrack. 101m/C VHS, LV, Closed Caption. Tom Guiry, Mike Vitar, Patrick Renna, Chauncey Leopardi, Marty York, Brandon Adams, Karen Allen, James Earl Jones, Maury Wills, Art LaFleur, Marlee Shelton; **Cameos:** Denis Leary, Brooke Adams; **D:** David Mickey Evans; **W:** Robert Gunter, David Mickey Evans; **M:** David Newman; **V:** Arliss Howard. *FXV*

The Sandpiper 🎬🎬 1965 Free-spirited artist Taylor falls in love with Burton, the married headmaster of her son's boarding school. Muddled melodrama offers little besides starpower. Filmed at Big Sur, California. ♫The Shadow of Your Smile. 117m/C VHS, Beta. Elizabeth Taylor, Richard Burton, Charles Bronson, Eva Marie Saint, Robert Webber, Morgan Mason; **D:** Vincente Minnelli; **C:** Milton Krasner. Academy Awards '65: Best Song ("The Shadow of Your Smile"). *MGM*

Sandra of a Thousand Delights 🎬🎬 *Sandra; Of a Thousand Delights; Vaghe Stelle Dell'Orsa* 1965 Haunting drama with strong women (and weak men). Sandra returns to

Italy from her American home in order to attend a ceremony honoring her father—a Jewish scientist who died in a Nazi concentration camp. Back with her family, Sandra tries to deal with her past, including her mother's possible betrayal of her father and her brother's incestuous longings. Italian with subtitles. **100m/B VHS.** *IT* Claudia Cardinale, Jean Sorel, Marie Bell, Michael Craig, Renzo Ricci; *W:* Luchino Visconti, Suso Cecchi D'Amico; *W:* Luchino Visconti, Suso Cecchi D'Amico; *M:* Cesar Franck. *FCT*

Sands of Iwo Jima ♂♂♂½ 1949
Wayne earned his first Oscar nomination as a tough Marine sergeant, in one of his best roles. He trains a squad of rebellious recruits in New Zealand in 1943. Later they are responsible for the capture of Iwo Jima from the Japanese—one of the most difficult campaigns of the Pacific Theater. **109m/B VHS, LV, Closed Caption.** John Wayne, Forrest Tucker, John Agar, Richard Jaeckel; *D:* Allan Dwan. Nominations: Academy Awards '49: Best Actor (Wayne), Best Film Editing, Best Sound, Best Story. *REP, TLF, RDG*

Sands of Sacrifice ♂♂½ Tangled Trails 1921 Hart, a Northwest Mountie, seeks an unscrupulous promoter who's selling worthless mining stock. **56m/B VHS.** Neal Hart, Violet Palmer, Gladys Hampton, Jules Cowles, Jean Bary, Ed Roseman; *D:* Charles Bartlett. *GPV*

Sanjuro ♂♂♂ Tsubaki Sanjuro 1962 In this offbeat, satiric sequel to "Yojimbo," a talented but lazy samurai comes to the aid of a group of naive young warriors. The conventional ideas of good and evil are quickly tossed aside; much less earnest than other Kurosawa Samurai outings. In Japanese with English subtitles. **96m/B VHS, Beta, LV.** *JP* Toshiro Mifune, Tatsuya Nakadai; *D:* Akira Kurosawa. *NOS, HHT, HEG*

Sans Soleil ♂♂♂ Sunless 1982 A female narrator reads and comments on the letters she receives from a friend, a freelance cameraman traveling through Japan, West Africa, and Iceland. The cameraman meditates on the cultural dislocation he feels and the meaning of his work and of life itself. Both narrator and cameraman remain unseen while the visuals being the cameraman's work in progress. **100m/C VHS.** *FR D:* Chris Marker; *W:* Chris Marker. *NYF, BTV*

Sanshiro Sugata ♂♂♂ 1943 Kurosawa's first film. A young man learns discipline in martial arts from a patient master. Climactic fight scene is early signature Kurosawa. In Japanese with English subtitles. **82m/B VHS.** *JP* Denjiro Okochi, Yukiko Todoroki, Ranko Hanai, Ryonosuke Tsukigata, Sugisaku Aoyama, Kokuten Kodo, Susumo Fusuita, Takashi Shimura; *D:* Akira Kurosawa. *FCT, COL, NLC*

Sansho the Bailiff ♂♂♂♂ The Bailiff; Sansho Dayu 1954 A world masterpiece by Mizoguchi about feudal society in 11th century Japan. A woman and her children are sold into prostitution and slavery. As an adult, the son seeks to right the ills of his society. Powerful and tragic, and often more highly esteemed than "Ugetsu." In Japanese with English subtitles. **132m/B VHS, Beta, LV.** *JP* Kinuyo Tanaka, Yoshiaki Hanayagi, Kyoko Kagawa, Eitaro Shindo, Ichiro Sugai; *D:* Kenji Mizoguchi; *W:* Yoshikata Yoda; *M:* Fumio Hayasaka. *HMV*

Santa Claus woof! 1959 Santa Claus teams up with Merlin the Magician to fend off an evil spirit who would ruin everyone's Christmas. Mexican camp classic. **94m/C VHS, Beta.** *MX* Jose Elias Moreno, Cesareo Quezadas; *D:* Rene Cardona Sr. *SNC, MLB*

Santa Claus Conquers the Martians ♂ Santa Claus Defeats the Aliens 1964 A Martian spaceship comes to Earth and kidnaps Santa Claus and two children. Martian kids, it seems, are jealous that Earth tykes have Christmas. Features then-child star Pia Zadora. **80m/C VHS, Beta.** John Call, Pia Zadora, Leonard Hicks, Vincent Beck, Victor Stiles, Donna Conforti; *D:* Nicholas Webster. *COL, SNC, MRV*

Santa Claus Is Coming to Town 1970 Kris Kringle takes you along on his quest to give toys to the citizens of Sombertown. An animated classic. **53m/C VHS, Beta, LV, Closed Caption.** *D:* Arthur Rankin Jr.; Jules Bass; *V:* Mickey Rooney, Keenan Wynn, Paul Frees. *FHE, LME*

Santa Claus: The Movie ♂♂ 1985 (PG) A big-budgeted spectacle about an elf who falls prey to an evil toy maker and almost ruins Christmas and Santa Claus. Boring, 'tis-the-season fantasy-drama meant to warm our cockles. **112m/C VHS, Beta, LV, Closed Caption.** Dudley Moore, John Lithgow, David Huddleston, Judy Cornwell, Burgess Meredith; *D:* Jeannot Szwarc; *W:* David Newman; *M:* Henry Mancini. *MED*

The Santa Clause ♂♂½ 1994 (PG) If you like Allen, you'll enjoy this lightweight holiday comedy about divorced workaholic dad Scott Calvin and eight-year-old son Charlie (Lloyd). Seems Santa injures himself falling off the Calvin roof and dad winds up putting on Santa's suit. But as it turns out when you put on Santa's suit, you become Santa, including a noticeable weight gain, a fluffy beard, and all those reindeer and elves to deal with (but where's Mrs. Claus). **97m/C VHS, Closed Caption.** Tim Allen, Eric Lloyd, Judge Reinhold, Wendy Crewson, David Krumholtz, Mary Gross; *D:* John Pasquin; *W:* Leo Benvenuti, Steve Rudnick; *M:* Michael Convertino. Blockbuster Entertainment Awards '95: Male Newcomer, Theatrical (Allen); Nominations: MTV Movie Awards '95: Breakthrough Performance (Allen), Best Comedic Performance (Allen). *TOU*

Santa Fe ♂♂ 1951 Action-packed western with Scott playing a Confederate soldier who heads West to take a job with the Santa Fe Railroad. However, his brothers, with their wounded rebel pride, have different ideas for forgetting the defeat. Refusing to take money from Northern businesses, they become outlaws. Based on a story by Louis Stevens and the novel by James Marshall. **89m/C VHS, Beta.** Randolph Scott, Janis Carter, Jerome Courtland, Peter Thompson, John Archer, Warner Anderson, Roy Roberts, Billy House; *D:* Irving Pichel; *W:* Kenneth Gamet. *COL*

Santa Fe Bound ♂♂ 1937 Tyler must work to clear his name when he is falsely accused of having murdered a man. **58m/B VHS.** Tom Tyler, Jeanne Martel, Richard Cramer, Charles "Slim" Whitaker, Edward Cassidy, Lafe McKee, Dorothy Woods, Charles "Blackie" King; *D:* Harry S. Webb. *DVT, HEG, GPV*

Santa Fe Marshal ♂♂ 1940 The 27th Hopalong Cassidy movie, if anyone's counting. In the title job the Hopster goes undercover with a medicine show to smash a criminal gang. A little different than usual, right up to the surprise identity of the crooked mastermind. **66m/B VHS.** William Boyd, Russell Hayden, Marjorie Rambeau, Bernadene Hayes, Earle Hodgins, Kenneth Harlan, Eddie Dean; *D:* Lesley Selander. *NOS*

Santa Fe Stampede ♂♂½ 1938 The Three Mesquiteers join an old prospector in his claim but when he is killed, one of them (Wayne) is framed. The photography makes up for the weak story line and direction. **58m/B VHS.** John Wayne, Ray Corrigan, Max Terhune, William Farnum, June Martel, Leroy Mason, Yakima Canutt, Curly Dresden; *D:* George Sherman. *NOS*

Santa Fe Trail ♂♂½ 1940 Historically inaccurate but entertaining tale about the pre-Civil War fight for "bloody Kansas." The action-adventure depicts future Civil War Generals J.E.B. Stuart (Flynn) and George Armstrong Custer (Reagan!) as they begin their military career (although Custer was really just a youth at this time). Good action scenes. Also available colorized. **110m/B VHS, Beta.** Errol Flynn, Olivia de Havilland, Ronald Reagan, Van Heflin, Raymond Massey, Alan Hale; *D:* Michael Curtiz; *M:* Max Steiner. *MGM, NOS, PSM*

Santa Fe Uprising ♂♂½ 1946 Red Ryder has to save Little Beaver from kidnappers. Good first entry for Lane in the "Red Ryder" series. **54m/B VHS, Beta.** Allan "Rocky" Lane, Robert (Bobby) Blake. *MED*

Santa Sangre ♂♂♂ 1990 (R) A circus in Mexico City, a temple devoted to a saint without arms, and a son who faithfully dotes upon his armless mother are just a few of the bizarre things in this wildly fantastic film. Fenix acts as his mother's arms, plays the piano for her, and carries out any wish she desires—including murder. Visually intoxicating but strange outing may prove too graphic for some viewers. Not as rigorous as other Jodorowsky outings. Also available in an NC-17 version. **CW:** Bizarre violence/drug use and bizarre graphic sensuality. **123m/C VHS, LV, Closed Caption.** *IT MX* Axel Jodorowsky, Sabrina Dennison, Guy Stockwell, Blanca Guerra, Thelma Tixou, Adan Jodorowsky, Faviola Tapia, Jesus Juarez; *D:* Alejandro Jodorowsky; *W:* Robert Leoni, Claudio Argento, Alejandro Jodorowsky; *M:* Simon Boswell. *REP, FCT*

Santa with Muscles ♂½ 1996 (PG) Cartoonish holiday-themed comedy finds the Hulkster as Scrooge-like millionaire Blake Thorne. Through a series of stupid circumstances, Thorne winds up in a Santa suit in a shopping mall hiding from the cops. But a blow to the head makes him believe he's the Jolly-Old-Elf himself and he comes to the aid of a local orphanage, whose tykes are about to be evicted. Silly's the kindest thing to say. **97m/C VHS.** Hulk Hogan, Don Stark, Ed Begley Jr., Clint Howard, Robin Curtis, Garrett Morris, Adam Wylie; *D:* John Murlowski; *W:* Jonathan Bond, Fred Mata, Dorrie Krum Raymond; *C:* Michael Gfelner; *M:* James Covell. *CAF*

Santee ♂♂ 1973 (PG) A father-son relationship develops between a bounty hunter and the son of a man he killed. Good, but not great, Western. **93m/C VHS, Beta.** Glenn Ford, Dana Wynter, Jay Silverheels, John Larch; *D:* Gary Nelson. *PSM, HHE*

The Saphead ♂♂½ 1921 Keaton's first outing as the rich playboy has him playing the none-to-bright son of a Wall Street mogul. Some great moments provide a glimpse of cinematic greatness to come from the budding comedic genius. Based on the play "The New Henrietta" by Winchell Smith and Victor Mapes. Silent. **70m/B VHS.** William H. Crane, Buster Keaton, Carol Holloway, Edward Connelly, Irving Cummings; *D:* Herbert Blache. *NO*

Sapphire ♂♂♂ 1959 Two Scotland Yard detectives seek the killer of a beautiful black woman who was passing for white. Good mystery and topical social comment; remains interesting and engrossing. Superbly acted all around. **92m/C VHS, Beta.** *GB* Nigel Patrick, Yvonne Mitchell, Michael Craig, Paul Massie, Bernard Miles; *D:* Basil Dearden. British Academy Awards '59: Best Film. *NO*

Saps at Sea ♂♂½ 1940 A doctor advises Ollie to take a rest away from his job at a horn factory. He and Stan rent a boat, which they plan to keep tied to the dock, until an escaped criminal happens by and uses the boys (and their boat) for his getaway. Cramer is a good bad guy; Stan and Ollie cause too much trouble, as always. **57m/B VHS, Beta, LV.** Stan Laurel, Oliver Hardy, James Finlayson, Ben Turpin, Richard Cramer; *D:* Gordon Douglas. *CCB, MED, VTR*

Sara Dane ♂♂ 1981 A strong young woman in the 18th century rises in the world through marriage and business acumen. Interesting but imperfect and slow. **150m/C VHS, Beta.** *AU* Harold Hopkins, Brenton Whittle, Barry Quin, Sean Scully; *D:* Rod Hardy, Gary Conway. *PSM*

Sarafina! ♂♂♂ 1992 (PG-13) Part coming-of-age saga, part political drama, part musical, and all emotionally powerful. Sarafina is a young girl in a township school in Soweto, South Africa in the mid-'70s, gradually coming into a political awakening amid the Soweto riots. Khumalo recreates her stage role as the glowing and defiant Sarafina with both Goldberg and Makeba good in their roles as Sarafina's outspoken and inspirational teacher and her long-suffering mother, respectively. Adapted from Ngema's stage musical. **CW:** Apartheid-driven violence. **98m/C VHS, Beta, LV, Closed Caption.** Leleti Khumalo, Whoopi Gold-

berg, Miriam Makeba, John Kani, Mbongeni Ngema; **D:** Darrell Roodt; **W:** Mbongeni Ngema, William Nicholson; **M:** Stanley Myers. *TOU*

The Saragossa Manuscript &&½
Rekopis Znaleziony W Saragossie **1965** Ambitious fantasy based on the 1813 novel "Sanatorium under the Hourglass" by Bruno Schultz. A romantic Belgian army officer, travelling to Spain, meets two beautiful princesses who send him on a fantastic journey to prove himself worthy of their affections. Polish with subtitles. 174m/B VHS. **PL** Zbigniew Cybulski, Iga Cembrzynska, Joanna Jedryka, Slawomir Linder; **D:** Wojciech Has; **W:** Tadeusz Kwiatkowski; **M:** Krzysztof Penderecki. *FCT*

Sarah, Plain and Tall &&& **1991** (G)
New England school teacher (Close) travels to Kansas circa 1910 to care for the family of a widowed farmer who has advertised for a wife. Superior entertainment for the whole family. Adapted for television from Patricia MacLachlan's novel of the same name by MacLachlan and Carol Sobieski. Nominated for nine Emmy Awards. A "Hallmark Hall of Fame" presentation. 98m/C VHS, LV, **Closed Caption.** Glenn Close, Christopher Walken, Lexi Randall, Margaret Sophie Stein, Jon DeVries, Christopher Bell; **D:** Glenn Jordan. *REP*

Sarah's Child &&½ **1996** Sarah LaMere
is devastated to learn that she can never have children. While husband Michael tries to accept, Sarah's upbringing has lead her to believe that's her only purpose in life and she becomes increasingly unbalanced. Seemingly out of nowhere children's clothes and toys appear in their home and soon a strange young girl named Melissa appears, whom Sarah treats as her own child. When their landlady dies horribly after questioning Melissa, Michael is afraid the line between reality and fantasy has been breached but just how can he fight? 90m/C VHS. Mary Parker Williams, Michael Berger, Ruth Hale, Bryce Chamberlain; **D:** Ron Beckstrom; **W:** Muffy Mead Thomas; **C:** Gregg Stouffer; **M:** Jim Ball, Glenn Workman. *AEL*

Saratoga &&½ **1937** Gable plays a bookie
and Harlow the daughter of an impoverished horse breeder in this romantic comedy centered around the race tracks. This was the final film appearance for Harlow, who died before the film's completion. Mary Dees was chosen as her standin and had to finish many of the scenes. "Saratoga" was released just a month after Harlow's death and became one of the biggest moneymakers of the year. 94m/B VHS. Jean Harlow, Clark Gable, Lionel Barrymore, Walter Pidgeon, Frank Morgan, Una Merkel, Cliff Edwards, George Zucco, Hattie McDaniel, Jonathan Hale; **D:** Jack Conway; **W:** Anita Loos, Robert Hopkins. *MGM*

Saratoga Trunk &&½ **1945** Lavish, if
slow-moving, version of Edna Ferber's romance novel reteams Cooper and Bergman (who starred in "For Whom the Bell Tolls"). It's 1875 New Orleans and bitter Clio, the half-Creole illegitimate daughter of a local, is determined to marry rich. But first, she gets involved with Texas gambler Clint Maroon (Cooper). He's in a business deal with wealthy Van Steed (Warburton), about the Saratoga railroad line, and Clio decides to go after him. Of course, she really wants Clint and they go through lots of bother before ending up together. Filmed in 1943 but release was delayed because of WWII. 135m/B VHS, **Closed Caption.** Gary Cooper, Ingrid Bergman, John Warburton, Flora Robson, Florence Bates, Jerry Austin; **D:** Sam Wood; **W:** Casey Robinson; **C:** Ernest Haller; **M:** Max Steiner. Nominations: Academy Awards '46: Best Supporting Actress (Robson). *MGM*

Sardinia Kidnapped &&½ **1975** A
beautiful girl is trapped in a clash between two powerful families while on vacation in Sardinia, where the peasants' custom is to kidnap a member of a rival family and then exchange the victim for land. Former documentary maker Mingozzi creates a realistic and uncompromising look at culture and change. In Italian; dubbed. 95m/C VHS,

Beta. *IT* Charlotte Rampling, Franco Nero; **D:** Gianfranco Mingozzi. *AHV*

Sartana's Here...Trade Your Pistol for a Coffin & **1970** A soldier of fortune
searches for a missing shipment of gold in the Old West. 92m/C VHS, **Beta.** George Hilton, Charles Southwood, Erika Blanc, Linda Sini. *UNI*

S.A.S. San Salvador & **1984** A CIA
agent tries to prevent a psychotic from running amok in El Salvador. 95m/C VHS, **Beta.** Miles O'Keeffe, Dagmar Lassander, Catherine Jarrett. *LIV, VES*

Sasquatch woof! **1976** Purported "documentary" about the mythical creature Bigfoot. Includes pictures of the "actual" monster. For those real stupid moods. 94m/C VHS, **Beta.** George Lauris; **D:** Ed Ragozzini. *NO*

Satan in High Heels &½ **1962** Sordid
show-biz tale of a carnival dancer (Myles) who dreams of making it big on Broadway. First she finagles her way into a position as a nightclub singer and the mistress of a convenient millionaire. But she loses it all for love when she falls for the millionaire's misbehaving son. Flamboyant performance by Hall as the lesbian nightclub owner. 90m/C VHS. Meg Myles, Grayson Hall, Del Tenney; **D:** Jerald Intrator; **W:** John T. Chapman. *TPV*

The Satan Killer &½ **1993** A vicious serial killer is targeted by two tough police detectives. What makes it personal is Detective Stephen's fiance is one of the killer's victims and he's not going to let justice stand in the way of his revenge. 90m/C VHS. Steve Sayre, Billy Franklin, James Westbrook, Belinda Creason, Cindy Healy; **D:** Stephen Calamari. *AIP*

Satan Met a Lady && ½ **1936** A weak
adaptation of Dashiell Hammett's "Maltese Falcon." This version has Davis employing a private detective to track down a mysterious woman. The hunted woman is herself searching for a valuable collectible. 74m/B VHS. Bette Davis, Warren William, Alison Skipworth, Arthur Treacher, Marie Wilson, Porter Hall, Olin Howlin; **D:** William Dieterle. *MGM, FCT*

The Satanic Rites of Dracula &&
Count Dracula and His Vampire Bride **1973** Count Dracula is the leader of a satanic cult of prominent scientists and politicians who develop a gruesome plague virus capable of destroying the human race. Preceded by "Dracula A.D. 1972" and followed by "The 7 Brothers Meet Dracula." 88m/C VHS. *GB* Christopher Lee, Peter Cushing, Michael Coles, William Franklyn, Freddie Jones, Joanna Lumley, Richard Vernon, Patrick Barr, Barbara Yo Ling; **D:** Alan Gibson. *MLB*

Satanik & **1969** (R) A hideous old hag is
turned into a lovely young woman by a stolen potion, but it doesn't last long and she becomes a monster. 85m/C VHS. *IT SP* Magda Konopka, Julio Pena, Luigi Montini, Armando Calvo, Umberto Raho; **D:** Piero Vivarelli. *SNC*

Satan's Black Wedding & **1975** (R)
The ghouls arrive at a Monterey monastery in their Sunday best to celebrate devildom's most diabolical ritual, the "Black Wedding." 61m/C VHS, **Beta.** Greg Braddock, Ray Miles, Lisa Milano. *NO*

Satan's Brew && *Satansbraten* **1976** Aspiring poet (Raab) murders his mistress and assumes the identity of 19th-century symbolist poet Stefan George, including his idol's homosexual tastes. Fassbinder at his most excessive. German with subtitles. 100m/C VHS. *GE* Kurt Raab, Margit Carstensen, Volker Spengler, Ingrid Caven, Helen Vita; **D:** Rainer Werner Fassbinder; **W:** Rainer Werner Fassbinder; **C:** Michael Ballhaus; **M:** Peer Raben. *ORI*

Satan's Cheerleaders woof! **1977** (R) A
demonic high school janitor traps a bevy of buxom cheerleaders at his Satanic altar for sacrificial purposes. The gals use all of their endowments to escape the clutches of the evil sheriff and his fat wife. Is it ever campy! 92m/C VHS, **Beta.** John Carradine, John Ireland, Yvonne De Carlo, Kerry Sherman, Jacqulin Cole, Hilary Horan, Alisa Powell, Sherry Marks, Jack Kruschen, Sydney Chaplin; **D:** Greydon Clark. *VCI*

Satan's Harvest &½ **1965** American detective inherits estate in Johannesburg, only to find the place is being used by drug smugglers. Sidesteps the political climate and shows the beauty of the land. And a good thing: the story is virtually nonexistent. 88m/C VHS, **Beta.** George Montgomery, Tippi Hedren; **D:** Ferde Grofe Jr. *NO*

Satan's Princess & **1990** Satanic cult
with a female leader runs amuck. Sloppy and forgettable. 90m/C VHS, **Beta, Closed Caption.** Robert Forster, Caren Kaye, Lydie Denier; **D:** Bert I. Gordon. *PAR*

Satan's Sadists & **1969** (R) Tamblyn and
his biker gang terrorize folks in the Southern California desert, including a retired cop, a Vietnam vet and a trio of vacationing coeds. Violent film will probably be best appreciated by Adamson completists. 88m/C VHS. Russ Tamblyn, Regina Carrol, Gary Kent, Jackie Taylor, John Cardos, Kent Taylor, Robert Dix, Scott Brady, Evelyn Frank, Greydon Clark, Bill Bonner, Bobby Clark, Yvonne Stewart, Cheryl Anne, Randee Lynn, Bambi Allen, Breck Warwick; **D:** Al Adamson. *NO*

Satan's School for Girls &½ **1973**
When a young woman investigates the circumstances that caused her sister's suicide, it leads her to a satanic girl's academy. Dumb and puerile made for TV "horror." 74m/C VHS, **Beta.** Pamela Franklin, Roy Thinnes, Kate Jackson, Lloyd Bochner, Jamie Smith-Jackson, Jo Van Fleet, Cheryl Ladd; **D:** David Lowell Rich. *PSM, CNG*

Satan's Touch woof! **1984** (R) A simpleton worships the Devil and gets burned for his trouble. 86m/C VHS, **Beta.** James Lawless, Shirley Venard. *NO*

Satanwar woof! **1979** A fictional look at various forms of Satan worship. 95m/C VHS, **Beta.** Bart LaRue, Sally Schermerhorn, Jimmy Drankovitch. *NO*

Satisfaction & **1988** (PG-13) An all-girl, high
school rock band play out the summer before college. The Keatons should have sent Bateman to her room for this stunt. 93m/C VHS, Beta, LV, **Closed Caption.** Justine Bateman, Trini Alvarado, Britta Phillips, Julia Roberts, Scott Coffey, Liam Neeson, Deborah Harry; **D:** Joan Freeman; **W:** Charles Purpura; **M:** Michel Colombier. *FOX*

Saturday Night and Sunday Morning &&&½ **1960** This "kitchen sink"
drama finds the 23-year-old Finney in star form as working-class Arthur Seaton, who's devoted to good times, spending his weekends with boozing, brawling, and willing women. He's having an affair with the older, married Brenda (Roberts) and pursuing the strictly moral Doreen (Field), who refuses to sleep with him without a commitment. Arthur thinks he's falling in love and is (eventually) ready for marriage but not without complications and not before warning Doreen that he's unlikely to completely change his carefree ways. Reisz's first feature film; Sillitoe adapted from his novel. Finney was voted the most promising newcomer at the British Academy's (BAFTA) awards. 98m/B VHS. *GB* Albert Finney, Rachel Roberts, Shirley Anne Field, Bryan Pringle, Norman Rossington, Hylda Baker, Robert Cowdra, Elsie Wagstaff, Frank Pettitt; **D:** Karel Reisz; **W:** Alan Sillitoe; **C:** Freddie Francis; **M:** John Dankworth. British Academy Awards '60: Best Actress (Roberts), Best Film; National Board of Review Awards '61: Best Actor (Finney). *HMK*

Saturday Night Fever &&½ **1977** (R)
Brooklyn teenager (Travolta), bored with his daytime job, becomes the nighttime king of the local disco. Based on a story published in "New York Magazine" by Nik Cohn. Acclaimed for its disco dance sequences, memorable soundtrack by the Bee Gees, and carefree yet bleak script; extremely dated, although it made its mark on society in its time. Followed by the sequel "Staying Alive." Also available in a 112-minute "PG" rated version. ♫Staying Alive; Night Fever; More Than a Woman; How Deep Is Your Love?. 118m/C VHS, **Beta, LV.** John Travolta, Karen Gorney, Barry Miller, Donna Pescow; **D:** John Badham; **C:** Ralf Bode; **M:** David Shire. National Board of Review Awards '77: 10 Best Films of the

Year, Best Actor (Travolta); Nominations: Academy Awards '77: Best Actor (Travolta). *PAR*

Saturday Night Live 197? Premiere episode of the late night classic, SNL. Guests Steve Martin and Elliott Gould join in these "best of" skits which feature the Killer Bees, the Blues Brothers, and a parody of "Star Trek," among other bits. Additional episodes are available. **90m/C VHS, Beta.** Dan Aykroyd, John Belushi, Jane Curtin, Garrett Morris, Chevy Chase, Gilda Radner, Laraine Newman. *COL, MOV*

Saturday Night Serials 1940 A compilation of excerpts from four serials: "The Phantom Creeps," "The Phantom Empire," "Undersea Kingdom," and "Junior G-Men." **90m/B VHS, Beta.** Bela Lugosi, Gene Autry, Ray Corrigan, Lon Chaney Jr. *RHI*

Saturday Night Shockers 1950 Each volume in this series is comprised of two full-length horror flicks, featuring twisted twins, barbarous butchers and sinister snow creatures. Terror abounds. **150m/B VHS, Beta.** Daisy Hilton. *RHI*

Saturday Night Sleazies, Vol. 1 1966 Two sleazy films. "College Girl Confidential" (1968) and "Suburban Confidential" (1966) are each directed by the man who helmed "Orgy of the Dead." Also includes sleazy short subjects. **150m/B VHS, Beta.** Marsha Jordan, Harvey Shane; *D:* A.C. Stephen; *W:* A.C. Stephen. *RHI*

Saturday Night Special 💿½ 1992 (R) Country singer/songwriter Travis (played by Nashville stalwart Burnette) gets a job fronting the house band of Tennessee tavern owner T.J. (Dean). Travis also takes up with ambitious Darlene (Ford), who happens to be T.J.'s wife. But it's Darlene who has the brains in this unpleasant trio, she decides to get rid of hubby and sets Travis up to take the fall. It's all been done before (and better).*CW:* Language, some violence, and strong sexuality. **75m/C VHS.** Billy Burnette, Maria Ford, Rick Dean; *D:* Dan Golden; *W:* Jonathan Banks; *M:* Billy Burnette, Nicholas Rivera. *NHO*

Saturday the 14th 💿½ 1981 (PG) A parody of the popular axe-wielding-maniac genre, about a family inheriting a haunted mansion. Poorly made; not funny or scary. Followed by even worse sequel: "Saturday the 14th Strikes Back". **91m/C VHS, Beta.** Richard Benjamin, Paula Prentiss, Severn Darden; *D:* Howard R. Cohen; *W:* Howard R. Cohen, Jeff Begun.

Saturday the 14th Strikes Back 💿 1988 Pathetic sequel to the horror film spoof of the "Friday the 13th" series. **91m/C VHS, Beta.** Ray Walston, Avery Schreiber, Patty McCormack, Julianne McNamara, Jason Presson; *D:* Howard R. Cohen; *W:* Howard R. Cohen. *MGM*

Saturn 3 💿½ 1980 (R) Two research scientists create a futuristic Garden of Eden in an isolated sector of our solar system, but love story turns to horror story when a killer robot arrives. Sporadically promising, but ultimately lame; dumb ending. For Farrah fans only. **88m/C VHS, Beta, LV.** *GB* Farrah Fawcett, Kirk Douglas, Harvey Keitel, Ed Bishop; *D:* Stanley Donen; *W:* Martin Amis; *C:* Billy Williams; *M:* Elmer Bernstein. *FOX*

Saul and David *Saul e David* 1968 Beautifully filmed story of David's life with King Saul, the battle with Goliath, and the tragic end of Saul. From the "Bible" series. **120m/C VHS, Beta.** Norman Wooland, Gianni "John" Garko. *VCI, MOV, KEP*

Savage! woof! *Black Valor* 1973 (R) A savage foreign mess with ex-baseball star Iglehart killing people with grenades and guns, abetted by an army full of murderous models. **81m/C VHS, Beta.** *MX* James Iglehart, Lada Edmund, Carol Speed, Rossana Ortiz, Sally Jordan, Aura Aurea, Vic Diaz; *D:* Cirio H. Santiago. *NLC*

Savage 💿💿 1996 (R) Mad scientist discovers the gateway to a future world, which unleashes a powerful guardian known known as the Savage (Gruner). The Savage must prevent the doorway between the worlds from exploding and causing an apocalypse, even as he hunts his neme-

sis.*CW:* Continuous strong violence, a graphic sex scene and language. **103m/C VHS, Closed Caption.** Olivier Gruner, Kario Salem, Jennifer Grant, Sam McMurray, Kristin Minter; *D:* Avi Nesher; *W:* Patrick Highsmith, Peter Sagal; *C:* Peter Fernberger; *M:* Roger Neill. *REP*

Savage Abduction 💿 1973 (R) Two girls visiting Los Angeles are kidnapped by a bizarre man. **84m/C VHS, Beta.** Tom Drake, Stephen Oliver, Sean Kenney; *D:* John Lawrence. *GHV*

Savage Attraction 💿½ *Hostage: The Christine Maresch Story; Hostage* 1983 (R) True story of a 16-year-old girl forced to marry an ex-Nazi, and her hellish life thereafter. Frustrating because it could have been much better. **93m/C VHS, Beta.** *AU GE* Kerry Mack, Ralph Schicha; *D:* Frank Shields. *VTR*

Savage Beach 💿 1989 (R) A pair of well-endowed female federal agents battle assorted buccaneers on a remote Pacific isle over a rediscovered cache of gold from WWII. Exploitative, pornographic, and degrading to watch. Sequel to "Picasso Trigger." **90m/C VHS, Beta, LV.** Dona Speir, Hope Marie Carlton, Bruce Penhall, Rodrigo Obregon, John Aprea, Teri Weigel, Lisa London; *D:* Andy Sidaris. *COL*

The Savage Bees 💿💿 1976 A South American ship harbored at New Orleans during Mardi Gras unleashes killer bees into the celebratory crowds. Not bad, relatively exciting, TV thriller. **90m/C VHS, Beta.** Ben Johnson, Michael Parks, Paul Hecht, Horst Buchholz, Gretchen Corbett; *D:* Bruce Geller. *LIV*

Savage Capitalism 💿💿 *Capitalismo Salvaje* 1993 Melodramatic romance between a reporter and a mining company exec crumbles when the exec's presumed dead wife returns. Meanwhile, the reporter uncovers the truth behind the company's plans to mine in the interior of Brazil, which could cause ecological ruin. Portuguese with subtitles. **86m/C VHS.** *BR* Fernanda Torres, Jose Mayer, Marisa Orth, Marcelo Tass; *D:* Andre Klotzel; *W:* Andre Klotzel, Djalma Batista. *FCT*

Savage Dawn 💿½ 1984 (R) In yet another desert town, yet another pair of combat-hardened vets are confronted by yet another vicious motorcycle gang. Haven't we seen this one before? **102m/C VHS, Beta.** George Kennedy, Karen Black, Richard Lynch, Lance Henriksen, William Forsythe; *D:* Simon Nuchtern. *MED, VTR*

Savage Drums 💿½ 1951 Sabu returns to his South Seas island to help end tribal warfare there. Dated and dumb, but fun-to-watch melodrama/action. **70m/B VHS, Beta, LV.** Sabu, Lita Baron; *D:* William (Lester Williams) Berke. *NO*

Savage Fury 💿 *Call of the Savage* 1933 Feature-length version of the popular movie serial. **80m/B VHS, Beta.** Noah Beery Jr., Dorothy Short. *NOS, DVT, HEG*

The Savage Girl 💿 1932 A hunter journeys through the darkest jungle in search of prey. Instead, he stumbles across a beautiful white jungle girl, falls in love with her and attempts to take her back with him. **64m/B VHS.** Rochelle Hudson, Walter Byron, Harry Myers, Ted Adams, Adolph Milar, Floyd Schackleford; *D:* Harry Fraser. *SNC, NOS, DVT*

Savage Hearts 💿½ 1995 Terminally ill mob hitwoman Beatrice Baxter (D'Abo) has six months left to live and she wants her last days to be spent in style. So she steals $2 million from her mob employer Roger Focely (Harris)—who's determined to get the money back. **90m/C VHS.** Maryam D'Abo, Richard Harris, Miriam Cyr, Jerry Hall; *D:* Mark Ezra. *TRI*

Savage Hunger 💿 1984 Ten plane crash survivors struggle to survive in the Baja desert. **90m/C VHS, Beta.** Chris Makepeace, Scott Hylands, Anne Lockhart; *D:* Sparky Green. *VES*

Savage Instinct 💿💿 1991 A woman stumbles across a drug ring and becomes a target when they fear she could expose them. Only Mongo and his crew are even more surprised

when she decides to fight back. **95m/C VHS.** Debra Sweaney, Brian Oldfield. *AIP, MOV*

Savage Intruder 💿 1968 (R) A wandering opportunist worms his way into the heart and home of a rich ex-movie star. She soon discovers that he's a sexual deviant who mutilates and murders for fun. Twisted doings with Hopkins in her final role. **90m/C VHS.** John David Garfield, Miriam Hopkins, Gale Sondergaard, Florence Lake, Joe Besser, Minta Durfee; *D:* Donald Wolfe. *UNI*

Savage Is Loose woof! 1974 (R) Drivel about a scientist, his wife, and their son stranded on a deserted island for 20 years. Not surprisingly, as junior matures he realizes there isn't a woman for him—or is there? Completely lacking in redeeming qualities. Absurd pseudo-Freudian claptrap produced by Scott. **114m/C VHS, Beta.** George C. Scott, Trish Van Devere, John David Carson, Lee Montgomery; *D:* George C. Scott. *MLB*

Savage Island 💿½ 1985 (R) Women's prison in the tropics sets the scene for the usual exploitative goings-on. Blair is actually in the film only for a few minutes. Chopped-up, even worse version of "Escape From Hell." **74m/C VHS.** *SP IT* Nicholas Beardsley, Linda Blair, Anthony Steffen, Ajita Wilson, Christina Lai, Leon Askin; *D:* Edward Muller; *W:* Nicholas Beardsley. Golden Raspberry Awards '85: Worst Actress (Blair). *NO*

Savage Journey 💿½ 1983 (PG) A wagon train of pioneers has difficulty on its westward journey. Simple story with no real appeal. **99m/C VHS, Beta.** Richard Moll, Maurice Grandmaison, Faith Clift; *D:* Tom McGowan. *PSM*

Savage Justice 💿 1988 A young woman seeks revenge against leftist rebels (boo, hiss) in a Southeast Asian country who killed her parents and raped her. She hooks up with an ex-Green Beret, and they fight and love their way through the jungle. The usual nudity and violence; derivative and dumb. **90m/C Beta.** Julia Montgomery, Steven Memel. *VTR*

Savage Land 💿💿½ 1994 (PG) Family western finds a young brother and sister travelling by stage to meet up with their father. The stage is robbed by some bumbling bad guys, who then pursue the kids and two other passengers across the frontier. The kids, of course, are smarter than most of the adults, and manage to get the best of the bad hombres. **91m/C VHS, LV.** Graham Greene, Corbin Bernsen, Vivian Schilling, Mercedes McNab, Corey Carrier, Brion James, Bo Svenson, Charlotte Ross. *HMD*

Savage Messiah 💿💿💿 1972 (R) Bio of young French sculptor Henri Gaudier and his intense, though platonic, affair with a refined Polish woman 20 years his senior. Stylized drama is spared most of director Russell's noted excesses but he manages to believably show their magnetic attraction. Gaudier was killed in WWI at the age of 24. Based on the biography by H.S. Ede. **96m/C VHS.** *GB* Scott Antony, Dorothy Tutin, Helen Mirren, Lindsay Kemp, Peter Vaughan, Michael Gough; *D:* Ken Russell; *W:* Christopher Logue. *MGM*

Savage Run 💿💿💿 *Run, Simon, Run* 1970 Reynolds is Papago Indian framed and imprisoned for his brother's murder. Sprung from the pen, he heads back to the reservation to find the real killers and to avenge his brother's death. Convincing made for televisiondrama. Stevens' last role before her suicide. **73m/C VHS.** Burt Reynolds, Inger Stevens, James Best, Rodolfo Acosta, Don Dubbins, Joyce Jameson, Barney Phillips, Eddie Little Sky; *D:* George McCowan. *SIM*

Savage Sam 💿💿 1963 Intended as a sequel to "Old Yeller." Sam, the offspring of the heroic dog named Old Yeller, tracks down some children kidnapped by Indians. Fun, but not fully successful. **103m/C VHS, Beta.** Tommy Kirk, Kevin Corcoran, Brian Keith, Dewey Martin, Jeff York, Marta Kristen; *D:* Norman Tokar; *C:* Edward Colman. *DIS*

The Savage Seven 🎬🎬 1968 An underground classic where everyone loses. A motorcycle gang rides into an Indian town which is at the mercy of corrupt businessmen. The gang's leader becomes involved in the Indians' problems but the businessmen and the cops cause trouble for all concerned. Less than memorable. Produced by Dick Clark. 96m/C VHS. Larry Bishop, Joanna Frank, Adam Roarke, Robert Walker Jr.; **D:** Richard Rush. *NO*

Savage Streets 🎬½ 1983 (R) Blair seeks commando-style revenge on the street gang that raped her deaf sister. Extended rape scene betrays the exploitative intentions, though other bits are entertaining, in a trashy kind of way. 93m/C VHS, Beta, LV. Linda Blair, John Vernon, Sal Landi, Robert Dryer, Debra Blee, Linnea Quigley; **D:** Danny Steinmann; **M:** John D'Andrea. Golden Raspberry Awards '85: Worst Actress (Blair). *LIV, VES*

Savage Weekend woof! *The Killer Behind the Mask; The Upstate Murders* 1980 (R) A killer behind a ghoulish mask stalks human prey in the boonies, of couse. Astoundingly, there is one interesting role—William Sanderson's looney. Otherwise, throw this one no bones. 88m/C VHS, Beta. Christopher Allport. *NO*

Savage Wilderness 🎬🎬½ *The Last Frontier* 1955 When a trio of fur trappers lose a year's worth of skins to a band of marauding Indians, they decide to take scouting jobs at a cavalry outpost. But they find the new commander (Preston) hasn't gotten his nickname as the "Butcher of Shiloh" without reason. Adapted from the novel "The Gilded Rooster" by Richard Emery Roberts. 98m/C VHS. Victor Mature, Robert Preston, Guy Madison, James Whitmore, Anne Bancroft, Russell Collins, Peter Whitney, Pat Hogan, Manuel Donde, Guy Williams; **D:** Anthony Mann; **W:** Philip Yordan, Russell S. Hughes; **M:** Leigh Harline. *COL*

The Savage Woman 🎬🎬 1991 Marianna escapes from a desperate situation and is found unconscious in the woods by Elysee. He nurses her back to health, learns her terrible secret, and tries to help Marianna decides whether to turn herself into the police or keep running. In French with English subtitles. 100m/C VHS. CA Patricia Tulasne, Matthias Habich; **D:** Lea Pool. *WBF*

Savages 🎬🎬 1972 A group of savages descend on a palatial mansion, and after living there for some time, become refined ladies and gentlemen. The moral savages and "civilized" men are really the same. 106m/C VHS. Lewis J. Stadlen, Anne Francine, Thayer David, Salome Jens, Susan Blakely, Kathleen Widdoes, Sam Waterston; **D:** James Ivory; **C:** Walter Lassally. *CVC, FCT*

Savages 🎬🎬½ 1975 Griffith as a demented nut-case stalking another man in the desert? That's right, Opie. "The Most Dangerous Game" remade-sort of-for TV. 74m/C VHS, Beta. Andy Griffith, Sam Bottoms, Noah Beery Jr.; **D:** Lee H. Katzin. *NO*

Savages from Hell 🎬 *Big Enough and Old Enough* 1968 (R) Greasy biker dude beats up a young black guy because she was flirting with the biker's woman. The biker also tries to rape a migrant farmworker's daughter because he lusts after her. Trashy exploitation film. 79m/C VHS. Bobbie Byers, Cyril Poitier, Diwaldo Myers, Viola Lloyd, William P. Kelley; **D:** Joseph Prieto; **W:** Joseph Prieto. *SNC, TPV*

Savannah Smiles 🎬🎬½ 1982 (PG) Poor little rich girl Anderson runs away from home, into the clutches of two ham-handed crooks. She melts their hearts, and they change their ways. Decent, sentimental family drama. 104m/C VHS, Beta, LV. Bridgette Anderson, Mark Miller, Donovan Scott, Peter Graves, Chris Robinson, Michael Parks; **D:** Pierre De Moro. *NLC*

Save Me 🎬🎬 1993 (R) Jim Stevens' (Hamlin) wife has left him and his boss is involved in some dirty deals that could cost Jim his job. So things couldn't get worse, could they? Well, of course they could—and do. Because Jim meets Ellie (Anthony), a sexual adventuress just destined to bring trouble to a lonely guy. Also available in an unrated version. 89m/C VHS, LV, **Closed Caption.** Harry Hamlin, Lysette Anthony, Michael Ironside, Olivia Hussey, Bill Nunn, Steve Railsback; **D:** Alan Roberts; **W:** Neil Ronco; **M:** Rick Marvin. *COL*

Save the Lady 🎬🎬 1982 Plucky kids fight city hall to save an old ferry, the Lady Hope, from the scrap heap. Nothing offensive here—just a pleasant family flick. 76m/C VHS, Beta. Matthew Excell, Robert Clarkson, Miranda Cartledge, Kim Clifford; **D:** Leon Thau. *NO*

Save the Tiger 🎬🎬🎬 1973 (R) A basically honest middle-aged man sees no way out of his failing business except arson. The insurance settlement will let him pay off his creditors, and save face. David, as the arsonist, and Gilford, as Lemmon's business partner, are superb. Lemmon is also excellent throughout his performance. 100m/C VHS, Beta, LV. Jack Lemmon, Jack Gilford, Laurie Heineman, Patricia Smith, Norman Burton, Thayer David; **D:** John G. Avildsen; **M:** Marvin Hamlisch. Academy Awards '73: Best Actor (Lemmon); Writers Guild of America '73: Best Original Screenplay; Nominations: Academy Awards '73: Best Story & Screenplay, Best Supporting Actor (Gilford). *PAR, BTV*

Saving Grace 🎬🎬 1986 (PG) A tale of the fictional youngest Pope of modern times, Pope Leo XIV (Conti). Beset by duty, he decides to shed his robes and get in touch with the world's peasantry. Improbable, but that's okay; the mortal sin is that it's improbable and slow and boring. 112m/C VHS, Beta, LV, 8mm, Closed Caption. Tom Conti, Fernando Rey, Giancarlo Giannini, Erland Josephson, Donald Hewlett, Edward James Olmos; **D:** Robert M. Young; **W:** David S. Ward; **M:** William Goldstein. *NLC*

Sawbones 🎬 1995 (R) Medical school reject Harvey takes out his frustrations by murdering people and then performing gruesome surgeries on the bodies. Baldwin's the investigating cop. Made for cable.**CW:** Sadistic violence and gore; some language. 78m/C VHS. Don Harvey, Adam Baldwin, Barbara Carrera, Nina Siemaszko, Nicholas Sadler, Don Stroud; **D:** Catherine Cyran. *NHO*

Sawdust & Tinsel 🎬🎬🎬 *The Naked Night; Sunset of a Clown; Gycklarnas Afton* 1953 Early Bergman film detailing the grisly, humiliating experiences of a traveling circus rolling across the barren Swedish countryside. Lonely parable of human relationships. In Swedish with English subtitles. 87m/B VHS, Beta, LV. SW Harriet Andersson, Ake Gronberg; **D:** Ingmar Bergman; **W:** Ingmar Bergman. *HMV, NLC, FCT*

Sawmill/The Dome Doctor 🎬🎬½ 1922 Two silent comedies starring the inimitable klutz of the golden era, Larry Semon, whose name has been nearly forgotten today. 71m/B VHS, Beta. Larry Semon, Dorothy Dwan. *VYY*

Say Anything 🎬🎬🎬 1989 (PG-13) A semi-mature, successful teen romance about an offbeat loner interested in the martial arts (Cusack, in a winning performance) who goes after the beautiful class brain of his high school. Things are complicated when her father is suspected of embezzling by the IRS. Joan Cusack, John's real-life sister, also plays his sister in the film. Works well on the romantic level without getting too sticky. 100m/C VHS, Beta, LV, **Closed Caption.** John Cusack, Ione Skye, John Mahoney, Joan Cusack, Lili Taylor, Richard Portnow, Pamela Segall, Jason Gould, Loren Dean, Bebe Neuwirth, Aimee Brooks, Eric Stoltz, Chynna Phillips, Joanna Frank; **D:** Cameron Crowe; **W:** Cameron Crowe; **M:** Anne Dudley, Richard Gibbs, Nancy Wilson. *FOX*

Say Goodbye, Maggie Cole 🎬🎬½ 1972 A widow goes to work as a doctor in a Chicago street clinic and becomes emotionally involved with a dying child. Hayward's final role in moving made-for-TV drama. 78m/C VHS, Beta. Susan Hayward, Darren McGavin, Michael Constantine, Nichelle Nichols, Dane Clark; **D:** Jud Taylor. *THV*

Say Hello to Yesterday 🎬½ 1971 (PG) A May-December romance that takes place entirely in one day. An unhappy housewife meets an exciting young traveler while both are in London. Cast and director try hard but fail to get the point across to the audience. 91m/C VHS, Beta. GB Jean Simmons, Leonard Whiting, Evelyn Laye; **D:** Alvin Rakoff. *PSM*

Say Yes! 🎬½ 1986 (PG-13) A nutty millionaire (Winters) bets $250 million that his inept nephew cannot get married within 24 hours. Three times the length of usual wacky sitcom, alas. 87m/C VHS, Beta, LV. Jonathan Winters, Art Hindle, Logan Ramsey, Lissa Layng; **D:** Larry Yust. *NO*

Sayonara 🎬🎬🎬 1957 An Army major is assigned to a Japanese airbase during the Korean conflict at the behest of his future father-in-law. Dissatisfied with his impending marriage, he finds himself drawn to a Japanese dancer and becomes involved in the affairs of his buddy who, against official policy, marries a Japanese woman. Tragedy surrounds the themes of bigotry and interracial marriage. Based on the novel by James Michener. 147m/C VHS, Beta. Marlon Brando, James Garner, Ricardo Montalban, Patricia Owens, Red Buttons, Miyoshi Umeki, Martha Scott; **D:** Joshua Logan; **C:** Ellsworth Fredericks. Academy Awards '57: Best Art Direction/Set Decoration, Best Sound, Best Supporting Actor (Buttons), Best Supporting Actress (Umeki); Golden Globe Awards '58: Best Supporting Actor (Buttons); Nominations: Academy Awards '57: Best Actor (Brando), Best Adapted Screenplay, Best Cinematography, Best Director (Logan), Best Film Editing, Best Picture. *FOX, BTV*

The Scalawag Bunch 🎬 1975 Yet another retelling of Robin Hood and his Merry Men and their adventures in Sherwood Forest. 100m/C VHS, Beta. IT Mark Damon, Luis Davila, Silvia Dionisio; **D:** George Ferron. *MON, HHE*

Scalp Merchant 🎬 1977 Private investigator Cliff Rowan hunts for a missing payroll. Someone would rather see him dead than successful. 108m/C VHS, Beta. Cameron Mitchell, John Waters, Elizabeth Alexander, Margaret Nelson; **D:** Howard Rubie. *NO*

Scalpel 🎬🎬 *False Face* 1976 (R) After his daughter's death, a plastic surgeon creates her image on another woman to get an inheritance. Violent and graphic, with a surprise ending. Not too bad; interesting premise. 95m/C VHS, Beta. Robert Lansing, Judith Chapman, Arlen Dean Snyder; **D:** John Grissmer. *NLC*

The Scalphunters 🎬🎬½ 1968 Semi-successful, semi-funny western about an itinerant trapper (Lancaster) who is forced by Indians to trade his pelts for an educated black slave (Davis); many chases and brawls ensue. Good performances. 102m/C VHS, Beta. Burt Lancaster, Ossie Davis, Telly Savalas, Shelley Winters, Nick Cravat, Dabney Coleman, Paul Picerni; **D:** Sydney Pollack; **W:** William W. Norton Sr.; **M:** Elmer Bernstein. *MGM*

Scalps 🎬🎬 1983 (R) Hunted Indian princess and man whose family was killed by Indians form uneasy alliance in old West. 90m/C VHS, Beta. Karen Wood, Albert Farley, Benny Cardosa, Charlie Bravo, Vassili Garis; **D:** Werner Knox. *IMP, HHE*

Scam 🎬🎬½ 1993 (R) Maggie and her partner Barry are con artists making their living scamming high rollers in Miami Beach. Then Maggie tries to pull a con on the wrong man. Jack Shanks is an ex-FBI agent with a score to settle and he blackmails Maggie into helping him. 102m/C VHS. Christopher Walken, Lorraine Bracco, Miguel Ferrer; **D:** John Flynn. *FXV*

Scandal 🎬🎬 *Shuban* 1950 Handsome artist (Mifune) and beautiful concert singer (Yamaguchi) become the victims of a libelous article in a gossip magazine. The artist decides to sue but, being softhearted, chooses a questionable lawyer because the man's young daughter is dying. Then the unethical lawyer accepts a bribe to prejudice the case. Japanese with subtitles. 105m/B VHS. JP Toshiro Mifune, Takashi Shimura, Yoshiko Yamaguchi; **D:** Akira Kurosawa; **W:** Ryuzo Kikushima, Akira Kurosawa; **M:** Fumio Hayasaka. *FCT*

Scandal 🎬🎬🎬 1989 (R) A dramatization of Britain's Profumo government sex scandal of the 1960s. Hurt plays a society doctor who enjoys introducing pretty girls to his wealthy friends. One of the girls, Christine Keeler, takes as lovers both a Russian government official and a British Cabinet Minister. The resulting scandal eventually overturned an entire political party, and led to disgrace, prison, and death for some of those concerned. Also available in an unedited 115-minute version which contains more controversial language and nudity. Top-notch performances make either version well worth watching. **105m/C VHS, Beta, LV.** *GB* John Hurt, Joanne Whalley, Ian McKellen, Bridget Fonda, Jeroen Krabbe, Britt Ekland, Roland Gift, Daniel Massey, Leslie Phillips; *D:* Michael Caton-Jones; *W:* Michael Thomas; *M:* Carl Davis. HBO

Scandal in a Small Town 🎬🎬 1988 A cocktail waitress in a small town has to defend herself and her daughter from the town's critical eye and hateful actions. Self-righteous made for TV drama rehashes several earlier plots. **90m/C VHS, LV.** Raquel Welch, Christa Denton, Peter Van Norden, Ronny Cox; *D:* Anthony Page. THV

Scandal Man 🎬🎬½ 1967 A French photographer gets in over his head when he snaps the daughter of an American KKK leader embracing a black man in a nightclub. In French with English subtitles. **86m/C VHS, Beta.** Maurice Ronet; *D:* Richard Balducci. FCT

Scandalous 🎬½ 1984 (PG) A bumbling American television reporter becomes involved with a gang of British con artists. Starts well but peters out. Look for the scene where Gielgud attends a Bow Wow Wow concert. **93m/C VHS, Beta, LV.** Robert Hays, Pamela Stephenson, John Gielgud, Jim Dale, M. Emmet Walsh; *D:* Rob Cohen; *W:* Rob Cohen, Larry Cohen, John Byrum; *C:* Jack Cardiff; *M:* Dave Grusin. LIV, VES

Scandalous 🎬 1988 A duke and his uncle work together to find a secretary who disappeared after witnessing a murder. **90m/C VHS, Beta.** Albert Fortell, Lauren Hutton, Ursula Carven, Capucine; *D:* Robert W. Young. VTR, PSM

Scandalous John 🎬🎬 1971 (G) Comedy western about a last cattle drive devised by an aging cowboy (Keith) in order to save his ranch. Keith's shrewd acting as the ornery cattle man who won't sell to developers carries this one. **113m/C VHS, Beta.** Brian Keith, Alfonso Arau, Michele Carey, Rick Lenz, John Ritter, Harry (Henry) Morgan; *D:* Robert Butler. DIS

Scanner Cop 🎬½ 1994 (R) When deranged scientist Sigmund Glock escapes from prison, he's determined to take revenge on Peter Harrigan, the cop who put him behind bars. With the aid of an evil assistant and a mind-altering drug, Glock kidnaps and programs innocent citizens into cop-killing maniacs. Harrigan's only weapon is a rookie cop with the Scanner power to read minds—and then destroy them. **94m/C VHS, LV, Closed Caption.** Daniel Quinn, Darlanne Fluegel, Richard Lynch, Mark Rolston, Hilary Shepard, Gary Hudson, Cyndi Pass, Luca Bercovici, Brion James; *D:* Pierce David; *W:* John Bryant, George Saunders. REP

Scanner Cop 2: Volkin's Revenge 🎬🎬 1994 (R) Scanner cop Sam Staziak (Quinn) has become curious about his family, asking Carrie Goodart (Haje) to find out what she can. But Carrie's attacked by evil scanner Carl Volkin (Kilpatrick), whom Sam once sent to prison, and left in a coma. Then Sam discovers Volkin is draining the life force of other scanners in order to make himself invincible when he and Sam have their final showdown.*CW:* Language; sci-fi violence and gore. **95m/C VHS.** Daniel Quinn, Patrick Kilpatrick, Khrystyne Haje, Robert Forster, Stephen Mendel; *D:* Steve Barnett; *W:* Mark Sevi; *C:* Thomas Jewett. REP

Scanners 🎬🎬½ 1981 (R) "Scanners" are telepaths who can will people to explode. One scanner in particular harbors Hitlerian aspirations for his band of psychic gangsters. Gruesome but effective special effects. **102m/C VHS, Beta, LV.** *CA* Stephen Lack, Jennifer O'Neill, Patrick McGoohan, Lawrence Dane; *D:* David Cronenberg; *W:* David Cronenberg; *M:* Howard Shore. COL

Scanners 2: The New Order 🎬🎬½ 1991 (R) This not-bad sequel to the 1981 cult classic finds a power-mad police official out to build a psychic militia of captured Scanners. More story than last time, plus more and better special effects.*CW:* Strong violence and sci-fi action. **104m/C VHS, Beta, LV, Closed Caption.** *CA* David Hewlett, Deborah Raffin, Yvan Ponton, Isabelle Mejias, Valentin Trujillo, Tom Butler, Vlasta Vrana, Dorothee Berryman, Raoul Trujillo; *D:* Christian Duguay; *W:* B.J. Nelson; *M:* Marty Simon. MED, IME, VTR

Scanners 3: The Takeover 🎬½ 1992 (R) The third sequel in which Scanner siblings battle for control of the world. Lacks the creativity and storyline of the first two films.*CW:* Horror violence and sensuality. **101m/C VHS, Beta, LV, Closed Caption.** Steve Parrish, Liliana Komorowska, Valerie Valois; *D:* Christian Duguay. REP

Scanners: The Showdown 🎬½ 1994 (R) Carl Volkin (Kilpatrick), the "scanner" killer, has escaped jail and is stalking the streets of L.A. His ultimate target is Sam Staziak (Quinn), the scanner cop who sent him away. Since Volkin's powers grow with every kill, Staziak better get to Volkin in a hurry. **95m/C VHS, Closed Caption.** Patrick Kilpatrick, Daniel Quinn, Khrystyne Haje, Stephen Mendel, Brenda Swanson, Jewel Shepard, Robert Forster; *D:* Steve Barnett; *W:* Mark Sevi. REP

The Scar 🎬🎬½ *Hollow Triumph* 1948 A cunning criminal robs the mob, then hides by "stealing" the identity of a lookalike psychologist. But he's overlooked one thing...or two. Farfetched film noir showcases a rare villainous role for Henreid (who also produced). Based on a novel by Murray Forbes. **83m/B VHS.** Paul Henreid, Joan Bennett, Eduard Franz, Leslie Brooks, John Qualen, Mabel Paige, Herbert Rudley; *D:* Steve Sekely. REP, FCT, NOS

Scar of Shame 🎬🎬 1927 Explores the ill-fated romance between a successful black concert pianist and the lower-class woman he marries. Gives a look at the color caste system and divisions within the black community of the era. **90m/B VHS.** Harry Henderson, Lucia Lynn Moses, Ann Kennedy, Norman Johnstone; *D:* Frank Peregini. FCT, BTV

Scaramouche 🎬🎬🎬½ 1952 Thrilling swashbuckler about a nobleman (Granger, very well cast) searching for his family during the French Revolution. To avenge the death of a friend, he joins a theater troupe where he learns swordplay and becomes the character "Scaramouche." Features a rousing six-and-a-half-minute sword battle. **111m/C VHS, LV.** Stewart Granger, Eleanor Parker, Janet Leigh, Mel Ferrer, Henry Wilcoxon, Nina Foch, Richard Anderson, Robert Coote, Lewis Stone, Elisabeth Risdon, Howard Freeman; *D:* George Sidney; *C:* Charles Rosher. FCT

Scarecrow 🎬🎬½ 1973 (R) Two homeless drifters (Hackman and Pacino) walk across America, heading toward a car wash business they never mean to build. An oft-neglected example of the early 70s extra-realistic subgenre initiated by "Midnight Cowboy." Engrossing until the end, when it falls flat. Filmed on location in Detroit. **112m/C VHS, Beta.** Gene Hackman, Al Pacino, Ann Wedgeworth, Eileen Brennan, Richard Lynch; *D:* Jerry Schatzberg; *C:* Vilmos Zsigmond. Cannes Film Festival '73: Best Film. WAR

Scared Stiff 🎬🎬🎬 1953 Fleeing a murder charge, Martin and Lewis find gangsters and ghosts on a Caribbean island. Funny and scary, a good remake of "The Ghost Breakers," with cameos by Hope and Crosby. ♫San Domingo; Song of the Enchilada Man; Mama Yo Quiero; You Hit the Spot; I Don't Care If the Sun Don't Shine; I'm Your Pal; When Somebody Thinks You're Won-

derful. **108m/B VHS.** Dean Martin, Jerry Lewis, Lizabeth Scott, Carmen Miranda, Dorothy Malone; *Cameos:* Bob Hope, Bing Crosby; *D:* George Marshall. PAR, MLB, REP

Scared Stiff 🎬 1987 (R) Three people move into a mansion once owned by a sadistic slave trader. Once there, they become unwilling victims of a voodoo curse. Bad special effects and script, not redeemed by decent but unoriginal story. **85m/C VHS, LV.** Andrew Stevens, Mary Page Keller; *D:* Richard S. Friedman; *W:* Richard S. Friedman, Mark Frost, Daniel F. Bacaner. REP

Scared to Death 🎬½ 1947 Begins with a woman dying of fright when shown the death mask of the man she framed. Dead woman then proceeds to narrate remainder of the story, which focuses on events leading up to her unfortunate, untimely, and fairly uninteresting demise. Memorable as Lugosi's only color film. **70m/C VHS, Beta.** Bela Lugosi, George Zucco, Douglas Fowley, Nat Pendleton, Joyce Compton; *D:* Christy Cabanne. NOS, SNC, EEL

Scared to Death 🎬 1980 (R) A scientific experiment goes awry as a mutation begins killing off the residents of Los Angeles. **93m/C VHS, Beta.** John Stinson, Diana Davidson, David Moses, Kermit Eller; *D:* William Malone; *M:* Tom Chase. MED

Scared to Death/Dick Tracy's Dilemma 🎬🎬 1947 On one tape, two 40's programmers-Lugosi's only color film, about a psychotic magician who tortures a young girl, and a standard black-and-white Tracy entry. **125m/C VHS, Beta.** Bela Lugosi, George Zucco, Ralph Byrd, Kay Christopher, Ian Keith. AOV

Scarface 🎬🎬🎬 *Scarface: The Shame of a Nation* 1931 The violent rise and fall of a 1930s Chicago crime boss (based on the life of notorious gangster Al Capone). Release was held back by censors due to the amount of violence and its suggestion of incest between the title character and his sister. Producer Howard Hughes recut and filmed an alternate ending, without director Hawks' approval, to pacify the censors, and both versions of the film were released at the same time. Almost too violent and intense at the time. Remains brilliant and impressive. Remade in 1983. **93m/B VHS, Beta, LV.** Paul Muni, Ann Dvorak, Karen Morley, Osgood Perkins, George Raft, Boris Karloff; *D:* Howard Hawks; *C:* Lee Garmes. National Board of Review Awards '32: 10 Best Films of the Year. USH

Scarface 🎬🎬🎬 1983 (R) Al Pacino is a Cuban refugee who becomes powerful in the drug trade until the life gets the better of him. A remake of the 1932 classic gangster film of the same name, although the first film has more plot. Extremely violent, often unpleasant, but not easily forgotten. **170m/C VHS, Beta, LV.** Al Pacino, Steven Bauer, Michelle Pfeiffer, Robert Loggia, F. Murray Abraham, Mary Elizabeth Mastrantonio, Harris Yulin, Paul Shenar, Oliver Stone; *D:* Brian DePalma; *W:* Oliver Stone; *C:* John A. Alonzo. USH

Scarface Mob 🎬🎬 *Tueur de Ch icago* 1962 This is the original television pilot film for the popular series "The Untouchables," about Eliot Ness's band of good guys battling Chicago's crime lord, Al Capone. Still strong stuff. Narrated by Walter Winchell. **120m/B VHS, Beta.** Robert Stack, Neville Brand, Barbara Nichols; *D:* Phil Karlson; *W:* Paul Monash. PAR

The Scarlet & the Black 🎬🎬½ 1983 A priest clandestinely works within the shield of the Vatican's diplomatic immunity to shelter allied soldiers from the Nazis in occupied Rome. His efforts put him at odds with the Pope and target him for Gestapo assassination. Swashbuckling adventure at its second-best. Made for television. Based on the nonfiction book "The Scarlet Pimpernel of the Vatican" by J.P. Gallagher. **145m/C VHS, Beta, Closed Caption.** Gregory Peck, Christopher Plummer, John Gielgud, Raf Vallone; *D:* Jerry London; *M:* Ennio Morricone. FOX, FCT, IGP

The Scarlet Car ⬥⬥ 1917 Chaney is a bank cashier who discovers his boss has been embezzling funds. A fight causes Chaney to believe he has killed his employer and he hides out in a remote cabin where guilt preys on his mind. 50m/B VHS, Beta. Lon Chaney Sr., Franklyn Farnum, Edith Johnson, Sam DeGrasse; **D:** Joseph DeGrasse. SNC, GPV, FCT

Scarlet Claw ⬥⬥⬥ *Sherlock Holmes and the Scarlet Claw* 1944 Holmes and Watson solve the bloody murder of an old lady in the creepy Canadian village of Le Mort Rouge. The best and most authentic of the Sherlock Holmes series. 74m/B VHS, Beta, Closed Caption. Basil Rathbone, Nigel Bruce, Miles Mander, Gerald Hamer, Kay Harding; **D:** Roy William Neill. FOX

The Scarlet Clue ⬥⬥ 1945 A better script and faster pacing improved this Monogram entry in the Chan series. Charlie investigates a series of mysterious deaths which lead to a plot to steal secret government radar plans. 65m/B VHS. Sidney Toler, Benson Fong, Mantan Moreland, Robert E. Homans, Helen Devereaux; **D:** Phil Rosen. MGM

Scarlet Dawn ⬥⬥½ 1932 Lavish sets and costumes abound in this romantic drama starring Fairbanks as a Russian aristocrat and Carroll as his maid servant. Together they flee Russia during the Revolution, marry, and settle into the life of the common working class. Restless under his new status, Fairbanks pursues Tashman and tries his hand at swindling. A slow but interesting love story. Adapted from the novel "Revolt" by Mary McCall. 58m/B VHS. Douglas Fairbanks Jr., Nancy Carroll, Lilyan Tashman, Sheila Terry, Guy Kibbee, Richard Alexander, Frank Reicher; **D:** William Dieterle; **W:** Douglas Fairbanks Jr., Niven Busch, Erwin Gelsey. MGM

Scarlet Empress ⬥⬥⬥½ 1934 One of Von Sternberg's greatest films tells the story of Catherine the Great and her rise to power. Dietrich stars as the beautiful royal wife who outwits her maniacal husband to become empress of Russia. Incredibly rich decor is a visual feast for the eye, as perfectionist von Sternberg fussed over every detail. Dietrich is excellent as Catherine, and von Sternberg's mastery of lighting and camerawork makes for a highly extravagant film. Based on the diary of Catherine the Great. 110m/B VHS, Closed Caption. Marlene Dietrich, John Lodge, Sam Jaffe, Louise Dresser, Maria Sieber, Sir C. Aubrey Smith, Ruthelma Stevens, Olive Tell; **D:** Josef von Sternberg; **W:** Manuel Komroff. USH, FCT

The Scarlet Letter ⬥⬥ 1934 Unlikely comic relief provides only measure of redemption for this poorly rendered version of Hawthorne's classic novel about sin and Hester Prynne. 69m/B VHS, Beta. Colleen Moore, Hardie Albright, Henry B. Walthall, Alan Hale, Cora Sue Collins, Betty Blythe; **D:** Robert G. Vignola. NOS, BAR, VYY

The Scarlet Letter ⬥⬥⬥ 1973 A studied, thoughtful, international production of the Nathaniel Hawthorne classic about a woman's adultery which incites puritanical violence and hysteria in colonial America. Fine modernization by Wenders. In German with English subtitles. 90m/C VHS, Beta. SP GE Senta Berger, Lou Castel, Yella Rottlaender, William Layton, Yelena Samarina, Hans-Christian Blech; **D:** Wim Wenders. FCT, GLV

The Scarlet Letter woof! 1995 (R) Ewwwwww—ego-driven stinker of '95 ("Showgirls" not-withstanding). Feisty Hester Prynne (Moore) is condemned to wear the scarlet letter "A" of adultery by her 17-century Puritan neighbors because she bore a child out of wedlock. Oldman is the lusty Reverend Arthur Dimmesdale (her partner in illicit passion) while Duvall chews scenery as Hester's wronged hubby. This "freely adapted" version of the 1850 American classic should have set author Nathaniel Hawthorne spinning in his grave as his moral saga of sin and redemption meets 20th-century moviemaking by having the passion made explicit and a happy ending tacked on.**CW:** Violence and sexuality.

135m/C VHS, LV, Closed Caption. Demi Moore, Gary Oldman, Robert Duvall, Robert Prosky, Edward Hardwicke, Joan Plowright, Roy Dotrice, Dana Ivey, Sheldon Peters Wolfchild, Diane Salinger, Lisa Jolliff-Andoh, Amy Wright, Tim Woodward; **D:** Roland Joffe; **M:** John Barry. Golden Raspberry Awards '95: Worst Remake/Sequel. HPH

The Scarlet Pimpernel ⬥⬥⬥½ 1934 "The Scarlet Pimpernel," supposed dandy of the English court, assumes a dual identity to outwit the French Republicans and aid innocent aristocrats during the French Revolution. Classic rendering of Baroness Orczy's novel, full of exploits, 18th century costumes, intrigue, damsels, etc. Produced by Alexander Korda, who fired the initial director, Rowland Brown. Remade for television in 1982. Available in colorized version. 95m/B VHS, Beta. GB Leslie Howard, Joan Gardner, Merle Oberon, Raymond Massey, Anthony Bushell, Nigel Bruce, Bramwell Fletcher, Walter Rilla, O.B. Clarence, Ernest Milton, Edmund Breon, Melville Cooper, Gibb McLaughlin, Morland Graham, Allan Jeayes; **D:** Harold Young; **W:** Robert Sherwood, Arthur Wimperis, Lajos Biro. CNG, NOS, PSM

The Scarlet Pimpernel ⬥⬥⬥ 1982 Remake of the classic about a British dandy who saved French aristocrats from the Reign of Terror guillotines during the French Revolution. Made for British television version is almost as good as the original 1935 film, with beautiful costumes and sets and good performances from Seymour and Andrews. 142m/C VHS, Beta, LV. GB Anthony Andrews, Jane Seymour, Ian McKellen, James Villiers, Eleanor David; **D:** Clive Donner; **M:** Nick Bicat. LIV, VES, FUS

Scarlet Spear woof! 1954 Filmed in Nairobi National Park in Kenya. A great white hunter convinces a young African chief that the ancient practices of his people are uncivilized. Pathetically stated and culturally offensive by today's standards. 78m/C VHS, Beta. John Bentley, Martha Hyer, Morasi; **D:** George Breakston. MSP

Scarlet Street ⬥⬥⬥ 1945 A mild-mannered, middle-aged cashier becomes an embezzler when he gets involved with a predatory, manipulating woman. Lang remake of Jean Renoir's "La Chienne" (1931). Set apart from later attempts on the same theme by excellent direction by Lang and acting. Also available Colorized. 95m/B VHS, Beta. Edward G. Robinson, Joan Bennett, Dan Duryea, Samuel S. Hinds; **D:** Fritz Lang; **C:** Milton Krasner. CNG, NOS, HHT

Scarlett ⬥⬥½ 1994 (PG-13) Well, fiddle-dee-dee. While purists may object to any tampering of "Gone With the Wind," this epic TV miniseries, from the Alexandra Ripley novel, manages to be good if overlong fun for those willing to sit back and relax. Scarlett tries to get back Tara and Rhett (they divorce but still battle continuously); explores her Irish family ties and even moves to Ireland; then gets involved with the wrong man and is accused of murder so Rhett can save her and everything can turn out okay (there's lots more). The big budget is up on-screen with lavish costumes and sets and a big cast—although why two Brits got the leads in this Southern melodrama is anyone's guess (Whalley-Kilmer and Dalton try hard).**CW:** Violence including sexual abuse, sensuality and a childbirth. 360m/C VHS, Closed Caption. Joanne Whalley, Timothy Dalton, Ann-Margret, Barbara Barrie, Sean Bean, Brian Bedford, Stephen Collins, John Gielgud, Annabeth Gish, George Grizzard, Julie Harris, Tina Kellegher, Melissa Leo, Colm Meaney, Esther Rolle, Jean Smart, Elizabeth Wilson, Paul Winfield, Betsy Blair, Peter Eyre, Pippa Guard, Ronald Pickup, Gary Raymond, Dorothy Tutin; **D:** John Erman; **W:** William Hanley; **M:** John Morris. CAF

Scarred ⬥½ *Street Love; Red on Red* 1984 (R) Unwed teenage mother becomes prostitute to support baby. Predictable plot and acting pull this one down. 85m/C VHS, Beta. Jennifer Mayo, Jackie Berryman, David Dean; **D:** Rosemarie Turko; **W:** Rosemarie Turko. LIV, VES

The Scars of Dracula ⬥⬥½ 1970 (R) A young couple tangles with Dracula in their search for the man's missing brother. Gory, creepy, violent, sexy tale from the dark side. Don't see it late at night. Preceded by "Taste the Blood of Dracula" and followed by "Dracula A.D. 1972." Available on Laserdisc with "The Horror of Frankenstein." 96m/C VHS, Beta, LV. GB Christopher Lee, Jenny Hanley, Dennis Waterman, Wendy Hamilton, Patrick Troughton, Michael Gwynn, Anouska Hempel, Michael Ripper; **D:** Roy Ward Baker; **M:** James Bernard. REP, MLB

Scavenger Hunt ⬥ 1979 (PG) Action begins when a deceased millionaire's will states that his 15 would-be heirs must compete in a scavenger hunt, and whoever collects all the items first wins the entire fortune. Big cast wanders about aimlessly. 117m/C VHS, Beta. Richard Benjamin, James Coco, Ruth Buzzi, Cloris Leachman, Cleavon Little, Roddy McDowall, Scatman Crothers, Tony Randall, Robert Morley, Richard Mulligan, Dirk Benedict, Willie Aames, Vincent Price; **D:** Michael A. Schultz; **M:** Billy Goldenberg. FOX

Scavengers ⬥ 1987 (PG-13) A man and a woman become involved in a spy plot and wind up in all sorts of danger. Pathetic excuse for a "thriller." 94m/C VHS, Beta, LV. Kenneth Gilman, Brenda Bakke, Kem Gampu, Norman Anstey, Crispin De Nys; **D:** Duncan McLachlan. ACA

Scenario du Film Passion ⬥⬥⬥ 1982 A classically self-analyzing video piece by Godard, in which he recreates on tape the scenario for his film "Passion," resulting in a reflexive, experimental essay on the process of image-making and conceptualizing films, especially Godard's. In French with English subtitles. 54m/C VHS, Beta. **D:** Jean-Luc Godard, Anne-Marie Mieville, Barnard Menoud. EAI

Scene of the Crime ⬥⬥½ 1985 Three short mysteries, which the audience is asked to solve: "The Newlywed Murder," "Medium Is the Murder" and "Vote for Murder." Made for television. 74m/C VHS, Beta. Markie Post, Alan Thicke, Ben Piazza; **D:** Walter Grauman. USH

Scene of the Crime ⬥⬥⬥ 1987 Beautiful widow, trapped in small French town, is sexually awakened by escaped convict hiding out near her home. Acclaimed, but sometimes distracting camera technique and slow pace undermine the film. In French with English subtitles. 90m/C VHS. FR Catherine Deneuve, Danielle Darrieux, Wadeck Stanczak, Victor Lanoux, Nicolas Giraudi, Jean Bousquet, Claire Nebout; **D:** Andre Techine; **W:** Olivier Assayas. KIV, FCT

Scenes from a Mall ⬥⬥ 1991 (R) Conspicuous consumers spend sixteenth wedding anniversary waltzing in mall while marriage unravels with few laughs. Surprisingly superficial comedy given the depth of talent of Allen and Midler. 87m/C VHS, Beta, LV, Closed Caption. Woody Allen, Bette Midler, Bill Irwin, Daren Firestone, Rebecca Nickels; **Cameos:** Fabio Lanzoni; **D:** Paul Mazursky; **W:** Paul Mazursky; **C:** Fred Murphy. TOU, IME

Scenes from a Marriage ⬥⬥⬥⬥ 1973 (PG) Originally produced in six one-hour episodes for Swedish television, this bold and sensitive film excruciatingly portrays the painful, unpleasant, disintegration of a marriage. Ullmann is superb. Realistic and disturbing. Dubbed. 168m/C VHS, Beta. SW Liv Ullmann, Erland Josephson, Bibi Andersson, Jan Malmsjo, Anita Wall; **D:** Ingmar Bergman; **W:** Ingmar Bergman; **C:** Sven Nykvist. Golden Globe Awards '75: Best Foreign Film; National Board of Review Awards '74: 5 Best Foreign Films of the Year; New York Film Critics Awards '74: Best Actress (Ullmann), Best Screenplay; National Society of Film Critics Awards '74: Best Actress (Ullmann), Best Film, Best Screenplay, Best Supporting Actress (Andersson). HMV

Scenes from a Murder ⬥½ 1972 A killer (Savalas) stalks a beautiful actress (Heywood). Dull excuse for a suspense flick. 91m/C VHS, Beta. IT Telly Savalas, Anne Heywood, Giorgio Piazza; **D:** Alberto De Martino. NO

Scenes from the Class Struggle in Beverly Hills 🐾🐾½ **1989 (R)** Social satire about the wealthy, their servants, and their hangers-on in two Hollywood households. Two chauffeurs spend their spare time lusting after their lovely employers, and bet to see who can accomplish reality first. All kinds of erotic capers result. Usually funny and irreverent; occasionally misfires or takes itself too seriously. Reunites the trio from cult classic "Eating Raoul": Bartel, Woronov, and Beltran. Remake of Renoir's "The Rules of the Game." **103m/C VHS, Beta, LV.** Jacqueline Bisset, Ray Sharkey, Mary Woronov, Robert Beltran, Ed Begley Jr., Wallace Shawn, Paul Bartel, Paul Mazursky, Arnetia Walker, Rebecca Schaeffer, Edith Diaz; *Cameos:* Little Richard; *D:* Paul Bartel; *W:* Bruce Wagner; *M:* Stanley Myers. *NO*

Scenes from the Goldmine 🐾½ **1987 (R)** A young woman joins a rock band and falls in love with its lead singer. Realistic but bland; music not memorable (performed mostly by the actors themselves). **99m/C VHS, Beta, LV.** Catherine Mary Stewart, Cameron Dye, Joe Pantoliano, John Ford Coley, Steve Railsback, Timothy B. Schmit, Jewel Shepard, Alex Rocco, Lee Ving, Lesley-Anne Down; *D:* Marc Rocco. *NLC*

The Scent of a Woman 🐾🐾½ *Sweet Smell of Woman; Profumo di Donna* **1975** An acclaimed dark comedy that may be an acquired taste for some. A blinded military officer and his valet take a sensual tour of Italy, the sightless man seducing beautiful women on the way. But at the end of the journey awaits a shock, and the real point of the tale, based on a novel by Giovanni Arpino. In Italian with English subtitles. Remade in 1992 as "Scent of a Woman." **103m/C VHS.** *IT* Vittorio Gassman; *D:* Dino Risi. Nominations: Academy Awards '75: Best Adapted Screenplay, Best Foreign Language Film. *NO*

Scent of a Woman 🐾🐾🐾 **1992 (R)** Pacino is a powerhouse (verging on caricature) in a story that, with anyone else in the lead, would be your run-of-the-mill, overly sentimental coming of age/redemption flick. Blind, bitter, and semi-alcoholic Pacino is a retired army colonel under the care of his married niece. He's home alone over Thanksgiving, under the watchful eye of local prep school student Charlie (O'Donnell). Pacino's abrasive (though wonderfully intuitive and romantic) colonel makes an impact on viewers that lingers like a woman's scent long after the last tango. O'Donnell is competently understated in key supporting role, while the tango lesson between Pacino and Anwar dances to the tune of "classic." Box-office winner is a remake of 1975 Italian film "Profumo di Donna." The laserdisc version is available in letterbox format. *CW:* Language. **157m/C VHS, LV, Closed Caption.** Al Pacino, Chris O'Donnell, James Rebhorn, Gabrielle Anwar, Philip S. Hoffman, Richard Venture, Bradley Whitford, Rochelle Oliver, Margaret Eginton, Tom Riis Farrell, Frances Conroy; *D:* Martin Brest; *W:* Bo Goldman; *C:* Donald E. Thorin; *M:* Thomas Newman. Academy Awards '92: Best Actor (Pacino); Golden Globe Awards '93: Best Actor—Drama (Pacino), Best Film—Drama, Best Writing; Nominations: Academy Awards '92: Best Adapted Screenplay, Best Director (Brest), Best Picture; British Academy Awards '93: Best Adapted Screenplay. *USH, MOV, BTV*

The Scent of Green Papaya 🐾🐾🐾 **1993** Tranquil film, set in 1951 Vietnam, follows 10-year-old peasant girl Mui as she spends the next 10 years as a servant in a troubled family, gracefully accommodating herself to the small changes in her life. At 20, she finds a fairy-tale romance with her next employer, a young pianist. Presents a romanticized view of the stoicism of Vietnamese women but is visually beautiful. Directorial debut of Hung is based on his childhood memories of Vietnam, which he re-created on a soundstage outside Paris. In Vietnamese with English subtitles. **104m/C VHS, LV.** *VT* Tran Nu Yen-Khe, Lu Man San, Truong Thi Loc, Vuong Hoa Hoi; *D:* Tran Anh Hung; *W:* Tran Anh Hung, Patricia Petit. Nominations: Academy Awards '93: Best Foreign Language Film. *COL*

Scherzo **1939** One of McLaren's earliest films, an abstract meditation lost in 1939 and subsequently found and reconstructed in 1984. **2m/C VHS, Beta.** *D:* Norman McLaren. *NFB*

Schindler's List 🐾🐾🐾🐾 **1993 (R)** Spielberg's staggering evocation of the Holocaust finds its voice in Oscar Schindler (Neeson), womanizing German businessman and aspiring war profiteer, who cajoled, bribed, and bullied the Nazis into allowing him to employ Jews in his Polish factories during WWII. By doing so he saved over 1,000 lives. The atrocities are depicted matter of factly as a by-product of sheer Nazi evil. Shot in black and white and powered by splendid performances. Neeson uses his powerful physique as a protective buffer; Kingsley is watchful as his industrious Jewish accountant; and Fiennes personifies evil as Nazi Amon Goeth. Based on the novel by Thomas Keneally, which itself was based on survivor's memories. Filmed on location in Cracow, Poland; due to the sensitive nature of the story, sets of the Auschwitz concentration camp were reconstructed directly outside the camp after protests about filming on the actual site. A tour de force and labor of love for Spielberg, who finally garnered the attention and respect as a filmmaker he deserves. *CW:* Language, actuality violence, and some sexuality. **195m/B VHS, LV, Closed Caption.** Liam Neeson, Ben Kingsley, Ralph Fiennes, Embeth Davidtz, Caroline Goodall, Jonathan Sagalle, Mark Ivanir; *D:* Steven Spielberg; *W:* Steven Zaillian; *C:* Janusz Kaminski; *M:* John Williams. Academy Awards '93: Best Adapted Screenplay, Best Art Direction/Set Decoration, Best Cinematography, Best Director (Spielberg), Best Film Editing, Best Picture, Best Original Score; British Academy Awards '93: Best Adapted Screenplay, Best Director (Spielberg), Best Film, Best Supporting Actor (Fiennes); Directors Guild of America Awards '93: Best Director (Spielberg); Golden Globe Awards '94: Best Director (Spielberg), Best Film—Drama, Best Screenplay; Los Angeles Film Critics Association Awards '93: Best Cinematography, Best Film; National Board of Review Awards '93: Best Film; New York Film Critics Awards '93: Best Cinematography, Best Film, Best Supporting Actor (Fiennes); National Society of Film Critics Awards '93: Best Cinematography, Best Director (Spielberg), Best Film, Best Supporting Actor (Fiennes); Writers Guild of America '93: Best Adapted Screenplay; Nominations: Academy Awards '93: Best Actor (Neeson), Best Costume Design, Best Makeup, Best Sound, Best Supporting Actor (Fiennes); British Academy Awards '94: Best Actor (Neeson), Best Adapted Screenplay, Best Supporting Actor (Kingsley), Best Original Score; Golden Globe Awards '94: Best Actor—Drama (Neeson), Best Supporting Actor (Fiennes), Best Original Score; MTV Movie Awards '94: Best Film, Breakthrough Performance (Fiennes). *USH*

Schizo 🐾 *Amok; Blood of the Undead* **1977 (R)** Devious intentions abound as a middle-aged man is overcome by weird scenes and revelations, caused by the impending wedding of the figure skater he adores. Confusing tale of insanity, obsession, and skating. **109m/C VHS, Beta.** Lynne Frederick, John Layton; *D:* Pete Walker. *MED*

Schizoid 🐾 *Murder by Mail* **1980 (R)** Advice-to-the-lovelorn columnist Hill receives a series of threatening letters causing her to wonder whether psychiatrist Kinski is bumping off his own patients. Boring blood dripper that's difficult to follow. **91m/C VHS, Beta.** Klaus Kinski, Marianna Hill, Craig Wasson; *D:* David Paulsen. *USH*

Schlock 🐾🐾 *The Banana Monster* **1973 (PG)** Accurately titled horror parody is first directorial effort for Landis, who does double duty as a missing link who kills people and falls in love with blind girl. Look for cameo appearance by Forrest J. Ackerman; ape-makeup by Rick Baker. **78m/C VHS.** John Landis, Saul Kahan, Joseph Piantadosi, Eliza Garrett; *Cameos:* Forrest J. Ackerman; *D:* John Landis. *NO*

Schnelles Geld 🐾½ **1984** A mild-mannered guy gets involved with a prostitute, and is plunged into a world of crime and drugs. In German with English subtitles. **90m/C VHS, Beta.** *GE VCD, GLV*

School Daze 🐾🐾🐾 **1988 (R)** Director/writer/star Lee's second outing is a rambunctious comedy (with a message, of course) set at an African-American college in the South. Skimpy plot revolves around the college's homecoming weekend and conflict among frats and sororities and African-Americans who would lose their racial identity and others who assert it. Entertaining and thought provoking. A glimpse at Lee's "promise," fulfilled in "Do the Right Thing." **114m/C VHS, Beta, LV, Closed Caption.** Spike Lee, Laurence "Larry" Fishburne, Giancarlo Esposito, Tisha Campbell, Ossie Davis, Joe Seneca, Art Evans, Ellen Holly, Branford Marsalis, Bill Nunn, Kadeem Hardison, Darryl M. Bell, Joie Lee, Tyra Ferrell, Jasmine Guy, Gregg Burge, Kasi Lemmons, Samuel L. Jackson, Phyllis Hyman; *D:* Spike Lee; *W:* Spike Lee; *M:* Bill Lee. *COL, FCT*

School for Scandal 🐾🐾 **1965** British television adaptation of Richard Sheridan's comedic play of the morals and manners of 18th century England. **100m/B VHS, Beta.** *GB* Joan Plowright, Felix Aylmer. *VYY*

School Spirit 🐾 **1985 (R)** A hormonally motivated college student is killed during a date. He comes back as a ghost to haunt the campus, disrupt the stuffy president's affair, and fall in love. Forgettable, lame, low-grade teen sex flick. **90m/C VHS, Beta.** Tom Nolan, Elizabeth Foxx, Larry Linville; *D:* Allan Holleb; *W:* Geoffrey Baere; *M:* Tom Bruner. *MED*

School Ties 🐾🐾🐾 **1992 (PG-13)** Encino man Fraser does a dramatic turn as a talented 1950's quarterback who gets a scholarship to the elite St. Matthew prep school. To conform with the closed-mindedness of the McCarthy era, both his father and coach suggest that he hide his Jewish religion. Fraser's compliance results in his big-man-on-campus status, until his rival in football and his love interest both find out that he is Jewish, creating an ugly rift in the school. What easily could have been just another teen hunk flick looks at much more than just Fraser's pretty face in successful, unflinching treatment of anti-Semitism. **110m/C VHS, Beta, LV, Closed Caption.** Brendan Fraser, Matt Damon, Chris O'Donnell, Randall Batinkoff, Andrew Lowery, Cole Hauser, Ben Affleck, Anthony Rapp, Amy Locane, Peter Donat, Zeljko Ivanek, Kevin Tighe, Michael Higgins, Ed Lauter; *D:* Robert Mandel; *W:* Dick Wolf, Darryl Ponicsan; *M:* Maurice Jarre. *PAR*

Schtonk 🐾🐾 **1992** Hermann Willie is a down-and-out journalist who thinks he's come upon the find of the century when he's given what are supposedly Hitler's diaries. Based on the 1983 scandal when the German publication "Der Stern" paid $5 million and printed what turned out to be not-very-clever forgeries. Director Dietl mocks the greedy gullibility of the journal, the ingenuity of the forger, as well as the nostalgia of the ex- and neo-Nazis of the modern Germany. The title is a meaningless expletive uttered by Charlie Chaplin in "The Great Dictator." German with subtitles. **115m/C VHS.** *GE* Goetz George, Uwe Ochsenknecht, Rolf Hoppe; *D:* Helmut Dietl; *W:* Helmut Dietl. Berlin International Film Festival '92: Best Actor (George), Best Director (Dietl), Best Film; Nominations: Academy Awards '92: Best Foreign Language Film. *NYR*

Sci-Fighters 🐾🐾½ **1996 (R)** Renegade cop Cameron Grayson (Piper) is tracking rapist Adrian Dunn (Drago) in 2009 Boston and discovers that Dunn has been exposed to a deadly, mutating virus. It's actually changing the bad guy into an alien methane-breathing lifeform that, of course, wants to inhabit the earth. Appropriately gross alien makeup and some decent special effects. *CW:* Violence/gore and some strong sexuality. **94m/C VHS, LV.** Roddy Piper, Billy Drago, Jayne Heitmeyer; *D:* Peter Svatek. *TRI, ORI*

Science Crazed 🐾½ **1990** A scientist creates a monster who could conceivably destroy the world. **90m/C VHS, Beta.** *CA* Cameron Klein; *D:* Ron Switzer. *NO*

Scissors �✄½ 1991 (R) Yes, this Hitchock imitation needs trimming. An unstable young woman contends with a rapist, devious lookalikes, birds, and a prison-like apartment, not all of which are relevant to the plot. An unsharp stab at suspense from novelist/filmmaker DeFelitta. 105m/C **VHS, Beta, Closed Caption.** Sharon Stone, Steve Railsback, Michelle Phillips, Ronny Cox; **D:** Frank de Felitta; **W:** Frank de Felitta. *PAR*

Scorchers ✄✄ 1992 (R) Back in the bayou, Splendid (Lloyd), a newlywed who won't sleep with her husband, and her cousin Talbot (Tilly), a preacher's daughter whose husband prefers the town whore Thais (Dunaway), find their lives intertwined because of their marital and sexual problems. A real "scorcher."**CW:** Language and sexuality. 81m/C **VHS, Beta, LV.** Faye Dunaway, Denholm Elliott, James Earl Jones, Emily Lloyd, Jennifer Tilly, Leland Crooke, James Wilder, Anthony Geary; **D:** David Beaird; **W:** David Beaird. *FXV, VTR*

Scorchy ✄ 1976 (R) Low-budget female cop action flick about a narcotics agent (Stevens) on the trail of a drug kingpin. Blood and guts, guns, and violence. Poor casting. 100m/C **VHS, Beta.** Connie Stevens, William Smith, Cesare Danova, Marlene Schmidt; **D:** Howard (Hikmet) Avedis; **W:** Howard (Hikmet) Avedis. *LIV*

Scorned ✄✄ 1993 (R) Seductive Patricia Langley loves her husband Truman so much that she'll do anything to help him get that promotion, including seducing another man. Too bad Alex Weston gets the promotion instead. Really too bad, since Patricia decides Alex has ruined her life and she's going to get revenge by ruining his. Also available in an unrated version. 100m/C **VHS, LV.** Shannon Tweed, Andrew Stevens, Michael D. Arenz, Kim Morgan Greene, Stephen Young, Daniel McVicar; **D:** Andrew Stevens; **W:** Barry Avrich. *PSM*

Scorned 2 ✄✄½ 1996 (R) Amanda (McClure) seems happily married to psych prof Mark—even if she is having those bad dreams. But when her hubby is tempted by a pretty coed and Amanda finds out—well this is one woman that should never be scorned.**CW:** Strong sexuality, and for violence and gore. 105m/C **VHS.** Tane McClure, Wendy Schumacher, Myles O'Brien, John McCook, Andrew Stevens, Seth Jaffe; **D:** Rodney McDonald; **W:** Sean McGinley; **C:** Gary Graver; **M:** Patrick Seymour. *APX*

Scorpio ✄✄½ 1973 (PG) Okay cat-and-mouse espionage tale about a wily, veteran CIA agent (Lancaster) who may have turned traitor. He's set-up to be killed by a CIA boss but the assassin, code-name Scorpio (Delon), has some trouble fulfilling his assignment. Cross- and double-cross abound. 114m/C **VHS.** Burt Lancaster, Alain Delon, Paul Scofield, John Colicos, Gayle Hunnicutt, J.D. Cannon, Joanne Linville, Melvin Stewart, James B. Sikking, Vladek Sheybal, William Smithers, Celeste Yarnall; **D:** Michael Winner. *MGM*

The Scorpio Factor ✄✄ 1990 Murder and mayhem follow microchip heist. 87m/C **VHS.** Attila Bertalan, David Nerman, Wendy Dawn Wilson. *NO*

Scorpion ✄ 1986 (R) A karate-master and anti-terrorist expert defuses a skyjacking and infiltrates international assassination conspiracies. Ex-real life karate champ Tulleners is a ho-hum hero, and the story is warmed over. 98m/C **VHS, Beta, LV.** Tonny Tulleners, Allen Williams, Don Murray; **D:** William Reed. *COL, HHE*

Scorpion Spring ✄✄ 1996 (R) Drug runner Astor (Morales) is on the lam through the desert with a beautiful hostage (Aviles) when two unsuspecting travelers (Molina and McGaw) offer the stranded duo a ride. But drug lord El Rojo (McConaughey) wants Astor dead and doesn't care who gets in his way and there's also a border patrol officer (Blades) on their trail as well.**CW:** Violence, language and some nudity. 89m/C **VHS, LV, Closed Caption.** Esai Morales, Alfred Molina, Patrick McGaw, Matthew McConaughey, Angel Aviles, Ruben Blades, Miguel Sandoval, Richard Edson, John Doe; **D:** Brian Cox; **W:** Brian Cox; **C:** Nancy Schreiber; **M:** Lalo Schifrin. *NLC*

Scorpion with Two Tails ✄ 1982 In an underworld of terror, people die grotesque deaths that a woman dreams of. 99m/C **VHS.** John Saxon, Van Johnson. *NO*

The Scorpion Woman ✄✄ 1989 A female Viennese judge becomes entwined in an unusual case which partially parallels her own life. Her new young lover turns out to be bisexual. Not gripping. In German with English subtitles. 101m/C **VHS, Beta.** GE Angelica Domrose, Fritz Hammel; **D:** Susanne Zanke. *NO*

The Scorpion's Tail ✄ 1971 Graphic murder scenes rev up this early thriller by Martino filmed with plot twists and visual games. Dubbed in English. 90m/C **VHS.** IT SP Evelyn Stewart, Anita Strindberg, George Hilton, Luigi Pistilli, Janine Reynaud; **D:** Sergio Martino; **W:** Sauro Scavolini, Ernesto Gastaldi; **M:** Bruno Nicolai. *VSM*

Scotland Yard Inspector ✄✄ Lady in the Fog 1952 An American newspaperman (Romero) in London looks for a killer. Nothing special. 73m/B **VHS, Beta, LV.** GB Cesar Romero, Bernadette O'Farrell; **D:** Sam Newfield. *MLB*

Scott of the Antarctic ✄✄½ 1948 Drama of doomed British expedition of 1911 struggling to be the first group to reach the South Pole. Much of the stunning location filming was shot in the Swiss Alps. Story is authentic, but oddly uninvolving, as though seen from afar. 111m/C **VHS, Beta.** GB John Mills, Christopher Lee, Kenneth More, Derek Bond; **D:** Charles Frend; **C:** Geoffrey Unsworth. *REP, DVT, NOS*

Scott Turow's The Burden of Proof ✄✄½ The Burden of Proof 1992 Attorney Alejandro "Sandy" Stern (Elizondo) struggles to discover the reasons behind his wife's baffling suicide and deal with the problems caused by the federal investigation of his brother-in-law's commodities business. The character of Stern was also featured in the film "Presumed Innocent" (played by Raul Julia). TV movie; on 2 cassettes. 184m/C **VHS.** Hector Elizondo, Brian Dennehy, Mel Harris, Stefanie Powers, Victoria Principal, Adrienne Barbeau, Anne Bobby, Gail Strickland, Concetta Tomei, Jeffrey Tambor; **D:** Mike Robe; **C:** Kees Van Oostrum. *TVC*

Scoumoune ✄✄½ 1974 The local "fixer" and heavy gets into trouble and no one comes to help. A movie that searches for honesty. Dubbed in English. 87m/C **VHS, Beta.** FR Jean-Paul Belmondo, Claudia Cardinale. *NO*

The Scout ✄✄ 1994 (PG-13) Brooks is an about-to-be-canned scout for the New York Yankees who discovers a weird, though genuine, phenom pitcher (Fraser) on a trip to Mexico. He convinces the Yankees to take the phenom on, though he's not sure whether Fraser isn't a few innings shy of a complete game. But with a 100 mph fast ball and a bat that would have made Babe Ruth envious, who cares? Film straddles sports comedy and melodrama territories, satisfying in neither. Fraser plays variation on Encino Man. Brooks rewrote part of the script, adding much needed biting humor, but not enough. Bombastic real-life team owner Steinbrenner plays himself. 101m/C **VHS, Closed Caption.** Albert Brooks, Brendan Fraser, Dianne Wiest, Lane Smith, Michael Rapaport, Steve Garvey, Bob Costas, Roy Firestone, Anne Twomey, Tony Bennett; **D:** Michael Ritchie; **W:** Albert Brooks, Andrew Bergman, Monica Johnson; **M:** Bill Conti. *FXV*

Scout's Honor ✄✄ 1980 An orphan (Coleman) is determined to become the best Cub Scout ever when he joins a troop led by an executive who dislikes children. Harmless, enjoyable family tale includes several former child stars as Scout parents. Made for television. 96m/C **VHS, Beta.** Gary Coleman, Katherine Helmond, Wilfrid Hyde-White, Pat O'Brien, Joanna Moore, Meeno Peluce, Jay North, Harry (Henry) Morgan, Angela Cartwright; **D:** Henry Levin. *NO*

Scrambled Feet ✄✄½ 1983 An uninhibited satire of the world of show business. 100m/C **VHS, Beta.** Madeline Kahn. *TTC*

Scream ✄ 1983 (R) Vacationers on a raft trip down the Rio Grande are terrorized by a mysterious murderer. Hopelessly dull. 86m/C **VHS, Beta.** Pepper Martin, Hank Worden, Alvy Moore, Woody Strode, John Ethan Wayne; **D:** Byron Quisenberry. *LIV, VES*

Scream ✄✄✄ Scary Movie 1996 (R) Director Craven playfully tweaks the cliches of teen slasher pics (which he helped create with "Nightmare on Elm Street") with this tongue-in-cheek thriller. Yep, where there's a mad slasher on the loose, there must be a group of teenagers "just out for a good time." The difference is both the killer and the victims have been raised on 80s splatter movies and, therefore, know all the rules. Sexual activity and/or substance abuse? Start picking out coffins. The stalker uses his cellular phone to terrorize his victims. He also uses it to ask his prey trivia questions or offer critiques of low-grade horror movies. Campbell plays the virginal heroine in the tight sweater, with Ulrich playing opposite as the sexually frustrated boyfriend. More fun than a bucket full of Karo syrup with red dye #3.**CW:** Strong graphic horror violence and gore, and for language. 111m/C **VHS, LV, Closed Caption.** Drew Barrymore, Neve Campbell, Courteney Cox, David Arquette, Skeet Ulrich, Rose McGowan, Henry Winkler, Liev Schreiber, W. Earl Brown; Jamie Kennedy, Lawrence Hecht; **D:** Wes Craven; **W:** Kevin Williamson; **C:** Mark Irwin; **M:** Marco Beltrami. MTV Movie Awards '97: Best Film; Nominations: MTV Movie Awards '97: Best Female Performance (Campbell). *TOU*

Scream and Scream Again ✄✄½ 1970 (PG) Price is a sinister doctor who tries to create a super race of people devoid of emotions. Cushing is the mastermind behind the plot. Lee is the agent investigating a series of murders. Three great horror stars, a psychedelic disco, great '60s fashions; it's all here. 95m/C **VHS, Beta.** GB Vincent Price, Christopher Lee, Peter Cushing, Alfred Marks, Anthony Newlands, Uta Levka, Judi Bloom, Yutte Stensgaard; **D:** Gordon Hessler. *LIV, VES, ORI*

Scream, Baby, Scream ✄ Nightmare House 1969 An unsuccessful artist switches from sculpting clay to carving young models' faces into hideous deformed creatures. 86m/C **VHS, Beta.** Ross Harris, Eugenie Wingate, Chris Martell, Suzanne Stuart, Larry Swanson, Brad Grinter; **D:** Joseph Adler. *NO*

Scream Blacula Scream ✄✄ 1973 (R) Blacula returns from his dusty undoing in the original movie to once again suck the blood out of greater Los Angeles. A voodoo priestess (Grier) is the only person with the power to stop him. A weak follow up to the great "Blacula," but worth a look for Marshall and Grier. 96m/C **VHS.** William Marshall, Don Mitchell, Pam Grier, Michael Conrad, Richard Lawson, Lynne Moody, Janee Michelle, Barbara Rhoades, Bernie Hamilton; **D:** Bob Kelljan. *ORI, FCT*

Scream Bloody Murder woof! 1972 (R) A young boy grinds his father to death with a tractor but mangles his own hand trying to jump off. After receiving a steel claw and being released from a mental institution he continues his murderous ways in and around his home town. Inspiring. 90m/C **VHS, Beta.** Fred Holbert, Leigh Mitchell, Robert Knox, Suzette Hamilton; **D:** Robert Emery. *VCI*

Scream Dream ✄ 1989 (R) A beautiful rock star uses her supernatural powers to control her fans, turning them into revenge-seeking monsters when she wants to. Heavy on the blood and skin; heavily exploitative. 80m/C **VHS.** Melissa Moore, Carole Carr, Nikki Riggins, Jesse Ray; **D:** Donald Farmer; **W:** Donald Farmer. *NO*

Scream for Help ✄ 1986 (R) A young girl discovers that her cheating stepfather is plotting to murder her mother, but no one will believe her. Is she paranoid? So bad it's funny; otherwise, it's just bad, and far from suspenseful. 95m/C **VHS, Beta, LV.** Rachael Kelly, David Brooks, Marie Masters; **D:** Michael Winner; **W:** Tom Holland. *ORI, WAR*

Scream of Fear 🐾🐾🐾 *Taste of Fear* **1961** A wheelchair-bound young woman goes to visit her father and new stepmother only to find her father is away on business. But she believes she sees her father's corpse. Is someone trying to drive her mad? Abounds in plot twists and mistaken identities. A truly spooky film, suspenseful, and well-made. 81m/B VHS, Beta. *GB* Susan Strasberg, Ronald Lewis, Ann Todd, Christopher Lee; *D:* Seth Holt; *W:* Jimmy Sangster. *COL, MLB*

Scream of the Demon Lover woof! **1971** (R) A young biochemist has a busy day as she works for a reclusive Baron. She fantasizes about him, tries to track down a murderer, and eventually discovers a mutant in the cellar. About as bad as they come, but short! 75m/C VHS, Beta. Jennifer Hartley, Jeffrey Chase; *D:* J.L. Merino. *NLC*

Screamer 🐾 **1974** A woman wants revenge after she is viciously attacked and raped. Now every man she sees is her attacker as she becomes more and more unbalanced. 71m/C VHS, Beta. Pamela Franklin, Donal McCann. *NO*

Screamers 🐾 *L'Isola Degli Uomini Pesce; Island of the Fishmen; Something Waits in the Dark* **1980** (R) A mad scientist on a desert island gleefully turns escaped convicts into grotesque monstrosities. Gory and gratuitous. 83m/C VHS, Beta. Richard Johnson, Joseph Cotten, Barbara Bach; *D:* Dan T. Miller, Sergio Martino.

Screamers 🐾🐾 **1996** (R) In the year 2078 Colonel Joe Hendricksson (Weller) and a small band of survivors fight a civil war on the radiation contaminated planet Sirius 6B. They run up against the screamers—mechanical creatures with razor-sharp claws, originally designed to protect humans. The screamers are bent on destroying all life in the universe while somehow mutating and breeding on their own. Unfortunately, director Duguay doesn't give any indication how this is taking place. Some fine stunt work and special effects redeem standard action adventure. Based on the novella "Second Variety" by Philip K. Dick ("Blade Runner"). *CW:* Profanity, violence and gore. 107m/C VHS, LV, 8mm, Closed Caption. Peter Weller, Jennifer Rubin, Andrew Lauer, Charles Powell, Ron White, Michael Caloz; *D:* Christian Duguay; *W:* Dan O'Bannon, Miguel Tejada-Flores; *C:* Rodney Gibbons; *M:* Normand Corbeil. Nominations: Genie Awards '96: Best Art Direction/Set Decoration, Best Supporting Actor (White), Best Score. *COL*

The Screaming Dead 🐾 *Dracula vs. Frankenstein* **1972** Monsters rise from the tomb to do battle with planet Earth and each other. Not to be confused with the Al Adamson epic "Dracula vs. Frankenstein." 84m/C VHS. *SP* Dennis Price, Howard Vernon, Alberto Dalbes, Mary Francis, Genevieve Deloir, Josianne Gibert, Fernando Bilbao; *D:* Jess (Jesus) Franco. *NO*

The Screaming Skull 🐾½ **1958** Man redecorates house with skulls in attempt to drive already anxious wife insane. 68m/B VHS. William Hudson, Peggy Webber, Toni Johnson, Russ Conway, Alex Nicol; *D:* Alex Nicol; *M:* Ernest Gold. *NOS, SNC*

Screams of a Winter Night 🐾 **1979** (PG) Ghostly tale of an evil monster from the lake and the terror he causes. 92m/C VHS, Beta. Matt Borel, Gil Glasco. *NO*

Screamtime 🐾 **1983** (R) Two fiendish friends filch a trilogy of horror tapes for home viewing. After the show, real scary things happen. 89m/C VHS, Beta. Jean Anderson, Robin Bailey, Dora Bryan, David Van Day; *D:* Al Beresford. *LIV*

Screen Test woof! **1985** (R) Oversexed silly teenagers arrange fake screen tests in order to meet girls. 84m/C VHS, Beta, LV. Michael Allan Bloom, Robert Bundy, Paul Lueken, David Simpatico; *D:* Sam Auster; *W:* Sam Auster. *COL*

Screwball Academy 🐾½ **1986** (R) A beautiful female director makes a soft-core film on a secluded island, and gets trouble from thugs, evangelists, horny crew members and others. Former "SCTV" director John Blanchard understandably used a pseudonym to direct this lame effort. 90m/C VHS, Beta. Colleen Camp, Kenneth Welsh, Christine Cattall; *D:* Reuben Rose. *TWE*

Screwballs 🐾 **1983** (R) Freewheeling group of high school boys stirs up trouble for their snooty and virginal homecoming queen. Another inept teen sex comedy with no subtlety whatsoever. Sequel: "Loose Screws." 80m/C VHS, Beta. Peter Keleghan, Lynda Speciale; *D:* Rafal Zeilinski; *W:* Jim Wynorski. *WAR*

Scrooge 🐾🐾🐾 **1935** On Christmas Eve a miser changes his ways after receiving visits from the ghosts of Christmas past, present, and future. Co-scripter Hicks gives an interesting performance as Ebeneezer Scrooge. Based on the classic novel "A Christmas Carol" by Charles Dickens. 61m/B VHS, Beta. *GB* Seymour Hicks, Maurice Evans, Robert Cochran, Donald Calthrop, Mary Glynne, Oscar Asche; *D:* Henry Edwards; *W:* Seymour Hicks. *VYY, CCB, DVT*

Scrooge 🐾🐾½ **1970** (G) Well-done musical version of Charles Dickens' classic "A Christmas Carol," about a miserly old man who is faced with ghosts on Christmas Eve. Finney is memorable in the title role. ♫The Beautiful Day; Happiness; Thank You Very Much; A Christmas Carol; Christmas Children; I Hate People; Father Chris'mas; See the Phantoms; December the 25th. 86m/C VHS, Beta, LV, Closed Caption. *GB* Albert Finney, Alec Guinness, Edith Evans, Kenneth More; *D:* Ronald Neame; *W:* Leslie Bricusse; *C:* Oswald Morris; *M:* Leslie Bricusse. Golden Globe Awards '71: Best Actor—Musical/Comedy (Finney); Nominations: Academy Awards '70: Best Art Direction/Set Decoration, Best Costume Design, Best Song ("Thank You Very Much"), Original Song Score and/or Adaptation. *FOX, FUS*

Scrooged 🐾🐾 **1988** (PG-13) Somewhat disjointed big-budgeted version of the hallowed classic. A callous television executive staging "A Christmas Carol" is himself visited by the three ghosts and sees the light. Kane is terrific as one of the ghosts. Film is heavy-handed, Murray too sardonic to be believable. 101m/C VHS, Beta, LV, 8mm, Closed Caption. Bill Murray, Carol Kane, John Forsythe, David Johansen, Bob(cat) Goldthwait, Karen Allen, Michael J. Pollard, Brian Doyle-Murray, Alfre Woodard, John Glover, Robert Mitchum, Buddy Hackett, Robert Goulet, Jamie Farr, Mary Lou Retton, Lee Majors; *D:* Richard Donner; *W:* Mitch Glazer, Michael O'Donoghue; *C:* Michael Chapman; *M:* Danny Elfman. *PAR*

Scrubbers 🐾 **1982** (R) Young girl is sent to reform school where she's forced to survive in a cruel and brutal environment. Low-budget "reform school" movie with no point, but lots of lesbianism. 93m/C VHS, Beta. *GB* Amanda York, Chrissie Cotterill, Elizabeth Edmonds, Kate Ingram, Debbie Bishop, Dana Gillespie; *D:* Mai Zetterling. *NO*

Scruffy **1980** An orphan and his dog survive with the help of two crooks who are reformed through their love for the little boy. Animated. 72m/C VHS, Beta. *V:* Alan Young, June Foray, Hans Conried, Nancy McKeon. *WOV, GKK*

Scruples 🐾½ **1980** Set in the glamorous, jet-setting world of Beverly Hills, this top-rated miniseries follows the career of Billy Ikehorn (Wagner) as she weds a wealthy industrialist and opens a clothing boutique named "Scruples." She caters to high society's haute couture, and encounters unscrupulous individuals who threaten to dethrone her from her position of power and privilege. Based on the best-selling novel by Judith Krantz. 279m/C VHS, Beta, Closed Caption. Lindsay Wagner, Barry Bostwick, Kim Cattrall, Gavin MacLeod, Connie Stevens, Efrem Zimbalist Jr., Gene Tierney; *M:* Charles Bernstein. *WAR*

Scum 🐾🐾🐾 **1979** Adapted from Roy Minton's acclaimed play, this British production looks at the struggle among three young men in a British Borstal (a prison for young convicts). Portrays the physical, sexual, and psychological violence committed. Horrifying and powerful. 96m/C VHS, Beta. *GB* Phil Daniels, Mick Ford, Ray Winstone; *D:* Alan Clarke. *PSM*

Sea Chase 🐾🐾½ **1955** An odd post-war sea adventure, wherein a renegade German freighter captain is pursued by British and German navies as he leaves Australia at the outbreak of WWII. A Prussian Wayne rivaled only by his infamous Genghis Khan in "The Conqueror" for strange character selection. Turner is on board as Wayne's girlfriend. 117m/C VHS, Beta, LV. John Wayne, Lana Turner, Tab Hunter, James Arness, Lyle Bettger, David Farrar, Richard Davalos, Claude Akins, John Qualen; *D:* John Farrow; *C:* William Clothier. *WAR*

Sea Devils 🐾 **1931** Sentenced to prison for a crime he didn't commit, a man escapes and joins a boatload of treasure hunters, but mutiny is afoot. Don't get soaked by this cheapie. 77m/B VHS. Walter Long, Edmund Burns, Henry Otto, James Donnelly; *D:* Joseph Levering. *SNC, NOS*

Sea Devils 🐾🐾 **1937** The tale of a sea captain and his lovely daughter who have differing opinions on whom she should marry. While her father would like her to marry a tame gentlemen under his command, she has her heart set on another beau. Sound predictable? It is, but fun. 88m/B VHS. *GB* Victor McLaglen, Preston Foster, Ida Lupino, Donald Woods, Gordon Jones; *D:* Ben Stoloff. *MED*

Sea Devils 🐾🐾 **1953** A smuggler and a beautiful spy come together during the Napoleonic Wars in this sea romance filled with intrigue and adventure. 86m/C VHS, Beta. *GB* Rock Hudson, Yvonne De Carlo, Maxwell Reed; *D:* Raoul Walsh. *MED*

Sea Gypsies 🐾🐾 **1978** (G) A sailing crew of five is shipwrecked off the Aleutian Islands. They must escape before winter or learn to survive. Passable family drama. 101m/C VHS, Beta. Robert F. Logan, Mikki Jamison-Olsen, Heather Rattray, Cjon Damitri; *D:* Stewart Raffill; *W:* Stewart Raffill. *WAR*

The Sea Hawk 🐾🐾🐾½ **1940** An English privateer learns the Spanish are going to invade England with their Armada. After numerous adventures, he is able to aid his queen and help save his country, finding romance along the way. One of Flynn's swashbuckling best. Available colorized. 128m/B VHS, Beta, LV. Errol Flynn, Claude Rains, Donald Crisp, Alan Hale, Flora Robson, Brenda Marshall, Henry Daniell, Gilbert Roland, James Stephenson, Una O'Connor; *D:* Michael Curtiz; *W:* Howard Koch. Nominations: Academy Awards '40: Best Interior Decoration, Best Sound, Best Score. *MGM, TTC, FOX*

Sea Hound **1947** A 15-part series set in the late 1940s that charts the voyage of a group of pirates searching for buried treasure. Everything goes well until Crabbe emerges to wreck their hopes. ?m/B VHS. Buster Crabbe, Jimmy Lloyd, Pamela Blake, Ralph Hodges, Bob Barron; *D:* Walter B. Eason, Mack V. Wright. *MLB, GPV*

Sea Lion 🐾🐾 **1921** A vicious sea captain, embittered by a past romance, becomes sadistic and intolerable, until the truth emerges. Lots of action, but plodding, rehashed plot. Silent. 50m/B VHS, Beta. Hobart Bosworth. *VYY*

Sea of Dreams 🐾 **1990** Don't expect much in the way of a script from this soft-core production. 80m/C VHS, Beta. Jon Rodgers, Chad Scott, Jacky Peel, Renee O'Neil. *AHV, HHE*

Sea of Love 🐾🐾🐾½ **1989** (R) A tough, tightly wound thriller about an alcoholic cop with a mid-life crisis. While following the track of a serial killer, he begins a torrid relationship with one of his suspects. Pacino can't stand a chance when Barkin heats up the screen. 113m/C VHS, Beta, LV, Closed Caption. Al Pacino, Ellen Barkin, John Goodman, Michael Rooker, William Hickey, Richard Jenkins; *D:* Harold Becker; *W:* Richard Price; *M:* Trevor Jones. *USH*

Sea of Sand 🐾🐾½ *Desert Patrol* **1958** Typical actioner set in WWII finds a British desert patrol's latest mission is to blow up Rommel's fuel supply before the battle of El Alamein. Lots of heroics against the Nazis and stiff upper lips. 97m/B VHS. *GB* Richard Attenborough, John Gregson, Michael Craig, Vincent Ball, Ray McAnally; *D:* Guy Green; *W:* Robert Westerby; *C:* Wilkie Cooper; *M:* Clifton Parker. *FCT*

Sea Prince and the Fire Child 🎬🎬 1982 Japanese animated film follows two young lovers who set off on an adventure to escape the disapproval of their parents. **70m/C VHS, Beta.** *JP COL*

Sea Racketeers 🎬½ 1937 Soggy old tribute to the Coast Guard inadvertently makes them look like a bunch of bumblers, as they belatedly uncover a fur-smuggling racket working under their noses from a floating nightclub. **64m/B VHS, Beta.** Weldon Heyburn, Jeanne Madden, Warren Hymer, Dorothy McNulty, J. Carrol Naish, Joyce Compton, Charles Trowbridge, Syd Saylor, Lane Chandler, Benny Burt; *D:* Hamilton MacFadden. *SNC*

The Sea Serpent 🎬½ 1985 A young sea captain and a crusty scientist unite to search out a giant sea monster awakened by atomic tests. Not one of Milland's better films. **92m/C VHS, Beta.** *SP* Timothy Bottoms, Ray Milland, Jared Martin; *D:* Gregory Greens. *LIV*

The Sea Shall Not Have Them 🎬🎬½ 1955 A British bomber crashes into the North Sea during WWII. Film tells of the survivors' rescue by the Air-Sea Rescue Unit. Decent drama/adventure. **92m/B VHS.** Michael Redgrave, Dirk Bogarde; *D:* Lewis Gilbert; *M:* Malcolm Arnold. *REP*

The Sea Wolf 🎬🎬🎬½ 1941 Jack London's adventure novel about brutal, canny Captain Wolf Larsen (Robinson), his rebellious crew, and some unexpected passengers. Knox and Lupino are shipwreck survivors, picked up by Robinson and forced into working aboard his ship, the aptly named "Ghost." Crewman Garfield falls for Lupino and tries to rally his shipmates into resisting the meglomaniacal Robinson. Fine performances by all, especially Robinson as the personification of malevolent ego. Screen debut of Knox. Director Curtiz filmed entirely in studio tanks, sets, and pervasive fog machines. Previously filmed three times; later remade as "Barricade" and "Wolf Larsen." **90m/C VHS.** Edward G. Robinson, Alexander Knox, John Garfield, Ida Lupino, Gene Lockhart, Barry Fitzgerald, Stanley Ridges, Francis McDonald, David Bruce, Howard da Silva, Frank Lackteen, Ralf Harolde; *D:* Michael Curtiz; *W:* Robert Rossen. *MGM, MOV, BTV*

The Sea Wolf 🎬🎬 1993 Yet another adaptation of Jack London's classic battle of wills tale. Captain Wolf Larsen (Bronson) commands a surly ship of seal hunters through sheer ruthlessness and ego. He rescues snobbish theater critic Van Weyden (Reeve) and pretty scam artist Flaxen (Stewart) from a capsized ferry. The self-educated captain wants to test out his theories about survival of the fittest by making the rich Van Weyden his cabin boy (Flaxen gets leered at). Lots of teeth-gnashing and bellowing in this turgid TV remake, although Revill has fun as the sniveling Cookie. See the Edward G. Robinson version instead. **120m/C VHS.** Charles Bronson, Christopher Reeve, Catherine Mary Stewart, Clive Revill; *D:* Michael Anderson Sr.; *W:* Andrew J. Fenady; *M:* Charles Bernstein. *TTC*

Sea Wolves 🎬🎬½ 1981 **(PG)** True WWII story about a commando-style operation undertaken by a group of middle-aged, retired British cavalrymen in India in 1943. Decent acting, though Peck's British accent fades in and out, with Moore as Bond. **120m/C VHS, Beta, Closed Caption.** *GB* Gregory Peck, Roger Moore, David Niven, Trevor Howard, Patrick Macnee; *D:* Andrew V. McLaglen; *W:* Reginald Rose. *FOX, WAR*

The Seagull 🎬🎬🎬 1971 A pensive, sensitive adaptation of the famed Chekhov play about the depressed denizens of an isolated country estate. In Russian with English subtitles. **99m/B VHS, Beta.** Alla Demidova, Lyudmila Savelyeva, Yuri Yakovlev; *D:* Yuri Karasik. *FCT, MRV, AUD*

Seance on a Wet Afternoon 🎬🎬🎬½ 1964 Dark, thoughtful film about a crazed pseudo-psychic who coerces her husband into a kidnapping so she can gain recognition by divining the child's whereabouts. Directed splendidly by Forbes, and superb acting from Stanley and Attenborough, who co-produced with Forbes. **111m/B VHS, Beta.** *GB* Kim Stanley, Richard Attenborough, Margaret Lacey, Maria Kazan, Mark Eden, Patrick Magee; *D:* Bryan Forbes; *M:* John Barry. British Academy Awards '64: Best Actor (Attenborough); National Board of Review Awards '64: 10 Best Films of the Year, Best Actress (Stanley); New York Film Critics Awards '64: Best Actress (Stanley); Nominations: Academy Awards '64: Best Actress (Stanley). *HMV, BTV*

The Search 🎬🎬🎬½ 1948 Clift, an American solider stationed in post-WWII Berlin, befriends a homeless nine-year-old amnesiac boy (Jandl) and tries to find his family. Meanwhile, his mother has been searching the Displaced Persons camps for her son. Although Clift wants to adopt the boy, he steps aside, and mother and son are finally reunited. "The Search" was shot on location in the American Occupied Zone of Germany. Jandl won a special juvenile Oscar in his first (and only) film role. This was also Clift's first screen appearance, although this movie was actually filmed after his debut in "Red River," it was released first. **105m/B VHS.** Montgomery Clift, Aline MacMahon, Ivan Jandl, Jarmila Novotna, Wendell Corey; *D:* Fred Zinnemann. Academy Awards '48: Best Story; Golden Globe Awards '49: Best Actor (Clift); Nominations: Academy Awards '48: Best Actor (Clift), Best Director (Zinnemann), Best Screenplay. *MGM*

Search and Destroy 🎬 *Striking Back* 1981 **(PG)** Deadly vendetta is begun by a Vietnamese official during the war. It is continued in the U.S. as he hunts down the American soldiers he feels betrayed him. Sub-par, forgettable war/action flick. **93m/C VHS, Beta, LV.** Perry King, Don Stroud, Park Jong Soo, George Kennedy, Tisa Farrow; *D:* William Fruet. *VES*

Search and Destroy 🎬 1988 **(R)** Sci-fi action flick about the capture of a secret biological warfare research station. Lotsa action, that's for sure - where's the plot? **87m/C VHS, Beta.** Stuart Garrison Day, Dan Kuchuck, Peggy Jacobsen; *D:* J. Christian Ingvordsen. *MCG*

Search and Destroy 🎬🎬 1994 **(R)** Complex story finds bankrupt businessman Martin Mirkheim (Dunne) trying to overcome his financial woes by making a film based on a book by self-help guru, Dr. Luther Waxling (Hopper). Of course, since Martin's broke, he first has to find someone willing to invest in his venture, and the shady duo (Walken and Turturro) he does just leave him with more problems. Tediously stagy adaptation of Howard Korders' play. Directorial debut by artist Salle at least looks great and provides some quirky moments. *CW:* Strong language; some violence, nudity, and drug content. **91m/C VHS, LV, Closed Caption.** Griffin Dunne, Dennis Hopper, Rosanna Arquette, Christopher Walken, John Turturro, Illeana Douglas, Ethan Hawke; *Cameos:* Martin Scorsese; *D:* David Salle; *W:* Michael Almereyda; *C:* Michael Spiller, Bobby Bukowski; *M:* Elmer Bernstein. *HMK*

The Search for Bridey Murphy 🎬🎬 1956 Long before channelers, Ramtha and New-Age profiteers, there was a Colorado housewife who under hypnosis described a previous life as an Irish girl. Her famous claim was never proven—but that didn't stop this well-acted but dull dramatization. Neither sensationalist, nor likely to persuade skeptics. Based on the book by Morey Bernstein, hypnotist in the case. **84m/B VHS, Closed Caption.** Teresa Wright, Louis Hayward, Nancy Gates, Kenneth Tobey, Richard Anderson; *D:* Noel Langley; *W:* Noel Langley. *PAR, FCT*

The Search for One-Eyed Jimmy 🎬🎬 1996 **(R)** Good-natured slice-of-life comedy about lowlife friends in the Brooklyn neighborhood of Red Hook. Film school grad Les (McCallany) returns to his old stomping grounds to make a documentary and decides missing local character Jimmy (Rockwell) will be his topic. Only no one except Jimmy's parents seem really concerned and Les' friends are such dimwits that they couldn't find a hole in the ground anyway. *CW:* Language, adult situations. **86m/C VHS, Closed Caption.** Holt McCallany, Nicholas Turturro, Steve Buscemi, Michael Badalucco, Ray "Boom Boom" Mancini, Anne Meara, John Turturro, Samuel L. Jackson, Sam Rockwell; *D:* Sam Henry Kass; *W:* Sam Henry Kass; *C:* Charles Levey; *M:* William Bloom. *CAF*

Search for Signs of Intelligent Life in the Universe 🎬🎬🎬 1991 **(PG-13)** Tomlin's brilliant one-woman show has been expanded into a wonderful film. As Tomlin's cast of 12 female and male characters meet and interact, they show every viewer his/her own humanity. **120m/C VHS.** Lily Tomlin; *D:* John Bailey; *W:* Jane Wagner; *M:* Jerry Goodman. *WLF, BTV*

Search for the Gods 🎬½ 1975 A dig in the Southwest turns interesting when one of the archeologists comes across an exquisite ancient medallion that could answer questions about alien visitors. Pilot for a television series that didn't make it. **100m/C VHS.** Kurt Russell, Stephen McHattie, Ralph Bellamy, Victoria Racimo, Raymond St. Jacques; *D:* Jud Taylor. *UNI, HHE*

The Searchers 🎬🎬🎬🎬 1956 The classic Ford western, starring John Wayne as a hard-hearted frontiersman who spends years doggedly pursuing his niece, who was kidnapped by Indians. A simple western structure supports Ford's most moving, mysterious, complex film. Many feel this is the best western of all time. **119m/C VHS, Beta, LV.** John Wayne, Jeffrey Hunter, Vera Miles, Natalie Wood, Ward Bond, John Qualen, Harry Carey Jr., Olive Carey, Antonio Moreno, Henry Brandon, Hank Worden, Lana Wood, Dorothy Jordan, Patrick Wayne; *D:* John Ford; *W:* Frank Nugent; *C:* Winton C. Hoch; *M:* Max Steiner. *WAR, TLF*

Searching for Bobby Fischer 🎬🎬🎬½ 1993 **(PG)** 7-year-old Josh Waitzkin (Pomeranc, in his debut) shows an amazing gift for chess, stunning his parents, who must then try to strike the delicate balance of developing his abilities while also allowing him a "normal" childhood. Excellent cast features Mantegna and Allen as his parents, Kingsley as demanding chess teacher Pandolfini, and Fishburne as an adept speed-chess hustler. Pomeranc is great, and his knowledge of chess (he's a ranked player) brings authenticity to his role. Title comes from Pandolfini's belief that Josh may equal the abilities of chess whiz Bobby Fischer. Underrated little gem based on a true story and adapted from the book by Waitzkin's father. **111m/C VHS, Beta, LV, Closed Caption.** Joe Mantegna, Max Pomeranc, Joan Allen, Ben Kingsley, Laurence "Larry" Fishburne, Robert Stephens, David Paymer, William H. Macy; *D:* Steven Zaillian; *W:* Steven Zaillian; *C:* Conrad Hall; *M:* James Horner. MTV Movie Awards '94: Best New Filmmaker Award (Zaillian); Nominations: Academy Awards '93: Best Cinematography. *PAR*

Seaside Swingers 🎬½ *Every Day's a Holiday* 1965 A group of teenagers at a seaside resort work to win a talent competition on television. But where is the talent? Dumb teen romance comedy with accidental plot. 🎵All I Want Is You; A Girls Needs a Boy; Second Time Around; Indubitably Me; Love Me, Please; Now, Ain't That Somethin'—Caw Blimey; Romeo Jones; What's Cookin. **94m/C VHS, Beta.** *GB* Michael Sarne, Grazina Frame, John Leyton; *D:* James Hill. *NLC*

Season for Assassins 🎬½ 1971 Police commissioner Castroni is the only man who can stop a wave of violence enveloping Rome. **102m/C VHS, Beta.** Joe Dallesandro, Martin Balsam. *LIV*

Season of Change 🎬½ 1994 Tepid coming of age saga set in rural Montana, circa 1946. Thirteen-year-old Sally Mae (Tom) notices the tensions between her Bible-bound mother (Anderson) and war vet dad (Madsen), who's worried about finding a job to support his family. Sally

Mae tries to understand all these adult notions even as she herself becomes attracted to teen mechanic Bobby (Randall). Cliched script and awkward performances don't help. **93m/C VHS.** Nicholle Tom, Michael Madsen, Jo Anderson, Hoyt Axton, Ethan Randall; **D:** Robin Murray; **W:** Shirley Hillard. *MNC*

Season of Fear 🎬½ 1989 (R) A young man visits his estranged father's home. Abandoned as a child, he's embroiled in a murder scheme engineered by his father's beautiful young wife. Intriguing premise, forgettable execution. **89m/C VHS, Beta.** Michael Bowen, Clancy Brown, Clare Wren, Ray Wise, Michael J. Pollard; **D:** Douglas Campbell; **W:** Douglas Campbell. *FOX*

Season of the Witch 🎬½ *Hungry Wives; Jack's Wife* 1973 (R) A frustrated housewife becomes intrigued with a neighboring witch and begins to practice witchcraft herself, through murder and seduction. Meant to be suspenseful, thrilling, and topical, it is none of these. Poorly acted at best. Originally 130 minutes! **89m/C Beta.** Jan White, Ray Laine, Bill Thunhurst, Joedda McClain, Virginia Greenwald; **D:** George A. Romero; **W:** George A. Romero. *NO*

Sebastian 🎬🎬½ *Mr. Sebastian* 1968 Mathematics whiz is employed by the British to decipher codes. He falls in love with York, another code breaker, and becomes involved in international intrigue. A bit too fast-paced and busy, but enjoyable spy drama. Sutherland has a small role. **100m/C VHS.** *GB* Dirk Bogarde, Susannah York, Lilli Palmer, John Gielgud, Margaret Johnston, Nigel Davenport, Donald Sutherland; **D:** David Greene; **M:** Jerry Goldsmith. *MOV*

Sebastiane 🎬🎬🎬 1979 An audacious film version of the legend of St. Sebastian, packed with homoerotic imagery and ravishing visuals. Honest, faithful rendering of the Saint's life and refusal to obey Roman authorities. Jarman's first film, in Latin with English subtitles. **90m/C VHS, Beta.** Leonardo Treviglio, Barney James, Richard James, Neil Kennedy; **D:** Derek Jarman; **M:** Brian Eno. *CCN, FCT*

Second Best 🎬🎬🎬 1994 (PG-13) Quiet, intimate drama about a lonely Welsh postmaster (Hurt) who decides to adopt a son (Miles). James, the 11-year-old boy he considers adopting, comes from a troubled background and is prone to violent outbursts. Graham, the village postmaster, is dealing with emotional demons of his own, and his problems are interwoven with those of the deprived, temperamental James. Although Hurt seems miscast as a shy, middle-aged Welshman, he turns in one of the best performances of his career. Richly acted and flawlessly directed, Menges has created a convincing and effective father-son drama. Based on David Cook's novel.**CW:** Thematic elements. **105m/C VHS, LV, Closed Caption.** *GB* William Hurt, Chris Cleary Miles, Keith Allen, Prunella Scales, Jane Horrocks, Alan Cumming, John Hurt; **D:** Chris Menges; **W:** David Cook; **M:** Simon Boswell. *WAR*

Second Best Secret Agent in the Whole Wide World 🎬🎬½ *Licensed to Kill* 1965 A klutzy agent attempts to prevent a Swedish anti-gravity formula from falling into Russian hands. Surprisingly good early spoof of the James Bond genre. **93m/C VHS, Beta.** *GB* Tom Adams, Veronica Hurst, Peter Bull, Karel Stepanek, John Arnatt; **D:** Lindsay Shonteff. *NLC*

Second Chance 🎬🎬½ 1953 A former prizefighter (Mitchum) travels to Mexico where he protects a gangster's moll (Darnell) targeted for murder. But Palance is on their tail. Originally released theatrically on a wide screen in 3-D. Good melodrama. **82m/C VHS, Beta, LV.** Robert Mitchum, Linda Darnell, Jack Palance, Reginald Sheffield, Roy Roberts; **D:** Rudolph Mate. *MED*

Second Chance 🎬🎬 1980 When a woman finds her husband is in love with another, her marital happiness is shattered. She leaves her betrayer and struggles to adapt to life as a single mother. Made for British television. **270m/C VHS.** *GB* Susannah York, Ralph Bates; **D:** Gerry Mill, Richard Handford. *NO*

Second Chorus 🎬🎬½ 1940 Rivalry of two trumpet players for a girl and a job with Artie Shaw Orchestra. Music, dance, and romance. Nothing great, but pleasant. ♫Would You Like to Be the Love of My Life?; Poor Mr. Chisholm; (I Ain't Hep to That Step) But I'll Dig It; Swing Concerto; Sweet Sue; I'm Yours. **83m/B VHS, Beta, LV.** Fred Astaire, Paulette Goddard, Burgess Meredith, Artie Shaw, Charles Butterworth; **D:** H.C. Potter. Nominations: Academy Awards '40: Best Song ("Love of My Life"), Best Score. *NOS, HHT, CAB*

Second Coming of Suzanne 🎬🎬½ 1980 Young actress encounters a hypnotic film director. Her role: to star in a crucifixion—which may be more real than she imagines. Winner of two international film festivals. **90m/C VHS, Beta.** Sondra Locke, Richard Dreyfuss, Gene Barry, Paul Sand, Jared Martin; **D:** Michael Barry; **W:** Michael Barry; **C:** Isidore Mankofsky. *GEM*

Second Fiddle 🎬🎬½ *Irving Berlin's Second Fiddle* 1939 Power is a studio flack who's hired to mount a huge talent search for a girl to star in a new film epic (very clear parallels to the Scarlet O'Hara "Gone With the Wind" hunt). He's sent to smalltown Minnesota where he meets Henie, who lives with her forbidding aunt (Oliver), who doesn't want her niece to go to wicked Hollywood. Nevertheless, Henie gets the part, becomes a success, and falls for her co-star Vallee. But it's all a publicity stunt on his part and Power is the one who really loves the girl. Henie gets to do some skating. ♫Back to Back; I'm Sorry for Myself; I Poured My Heart Into Song; An Old-Fashioned Tune is Always New; When Winter Comes; Song of the Metronome. **86m/B VHS.** Sonja Henie, Tyrone Power, Rudy Vallee, Edna May Oliver, Mary Healy, Lyle Talbot, Alan Dinehart, Minna Gombell; **D:** Sidney Lanfield; **W:** Harry Tugend; **M:** Irving Berlin. Nominations: Academy Awards '39: Best Song ("I Poured My Heart Into Song"). *FXV*

Second Sight 🎬 1989 (PG) A detective (Larroquette) and a goofy psychic (Pinchot) set out to find a kidnapped priest. Flick is sidetracked along the way by such peculiarities as a pixieish nun for romantic, not religious, intrigue. Remember this one? No? That's because you blinked when it was released to theaters. Eminently missable. **84m/C VHS, Beta, LV, Closed Caption.** John Larroquette, Bronson Pinchot, Bess Armstrong, James Tolkan, Christine Estabrook, Cornelia Guest, Stuart Pankin, William Prince, John Schuck; **D:** Joel Zwick; **W:** Patricia Resnick, Tom Schulman. *WAR*

Second Thoughts 🎬 1983 (PG) Frustrated woman attorney divorces her stuffy husband and takes up with an aging hippie. She comes to regret her decision when it becomes obvious that her new man has his head firmly stuck in the 60s. Comedy-drama lacking real laughs or drama. **109m/C VHS, Beta.** Lucie Arnaz, Craig Wasson, Ken Howard, Joe Mantegna; **D:** Lawrence Turman; **W:** Steve Brown; **M:** Henry Mancini. *CNG*

Second Time Lucky 🎬 1984 The devil makes a bet with God that if the world began all over again Adam and Eve would repeat their mistake they made in the Garden of Eden. Bites off a lot, but has no teeth nor laughs. **98m/C VHS, Beta.** *AU NZ* Diane Franklin, Roger Wilson, Robert Morley, Jon Gadsby, Bill Ewens; **D:** Michael Anderson Sr. *ORI*

Second Victory 🎬🎬½ 1987 (PG) Major Mark Hanlon has been appointed an Occupation Officer in the winter of 1945. He expects this will be his chance to work for peace but when a good friend is brutally murdered all his thoughts turn to revenge. Based on the novel by Morris West. **95m/C VHS, LV, Closed Caption.** Anthony Andrews, Max von Sydow, Renee Soutendijk; **D:** Gerald Thomas. *AIP*

Second Wind 🎬🎬 1990 (PG) Wagner and Naughton are trying to settle into their new life together, but find they must make a variety of difficult choices. **93m/C VHS.** Lindsay Wagner, James Naughton. *NO*

Second Woman 🎬🎬½ *Here Lies Love; Twelve Miles Out* 1951 An architect, suffering from blackouts and depression, believes himself responsible for the death of his fiancee. Well-done psycho-drama. **91m/B VHS, Beta.** Robert Young, Betsy Drake, John Sutton; **D:** James V. Kern. *NOS, VDM, SNC*

Seconds 🎬🎬🎬 1966 (R) Aging banker Arthur Hamilton (Randolph) is frantic to escape his dead-end existence and accepts an invitation from a mysterious organization to give him a second chance at life. Through surgery, Arthur's transformed into handsome artist Tony Wilson (Hudson). Uncomfortably living in Malibu, he soons finds out all his new neighbors are also "seconds," who are afraid he'll betray their secrets. Wilson decides he wants out of his new arrangement and back to his former life but it comes at a very high price. Eerie film manages to (mostly) overcome its plot problems, with a fine performance by Hudson. Based on the novel by Donald Ely. **107m/B VHS, Beta, Closed Caption.** Rock Hudson, John Randolph, Salome Jens, Will Geer, Jeff Corey, Richard Anderson, Murray Hamilton, Karl Swenson, Khigh Deigh, Frances Reid, Wesley Addy; **D:** John Frankenheimer; **W:** Lewis John Carlino; **C:** James Wong Howe; **M:** Jerry Goldsmith. Nominations: Academy Awards '66: Best Black and White Cinematography. *PAR*

The Secret 🎬🎬½ 1993 Businessman and political candidate Mike Dunsmore (Douglas) comes to terms with his lifelong battle with dyslexia when his grandson begins to show signs of the same affliction. Set in picturesque New England fishing village. **92m/C VHS, Closed Caption.** Kirk Douglas, Bruce Boxleitner, Brock Peters, Laura Harrington; **D:** Karen Arthur. *CAF*

Secret Admirer 🎬🎬 1985 (R) A teenager's unsigned love letter keeps falling into the wrong hands. Intends to be funny, and sometimes is; too often, though, it surrenders to obviousness and predictability. **98m/C VHS, Beta, LV.** C. Thomas Howell, Cliff DeYoung, Kelly Preston, Dee Wallace Stone, Lori Loughlin, Fred Ward, Casey Siemaszko, Corey Haim, Leigh Taylor-Young; **D:** David Greenwalt. *NO*

The Secret Adversary 🎬🎬 1983 Set in 1920s London. Ace detectives Tommy and Tuppence Beresford must find a secret treaty before it falls into the wrong hands. Pilot for the "Partners in Crime" series. Based on the characters created by Agatha Christie. **120m/C VHS, Beta.** *GB* Francesca Annis, James Warwick. *TPV*

The Secret Agent 🎬🎬🎬 1936 Presumed dead, a British intelligence agent (Gielgud) reappears and receives a new assignment. Using his faked death to his advantage, he easily journeys to Switzerland where he is to eliminate an enemy agent. Strange Hitchcockian melange of comedy and intrigue; atypical, but worthy offering from the Master. **83m/B VHS, Beta, LV.** *GB* Madeleine Carroll, Peter Lorre, Robert Young, John Gielgud, Lilli Palmer; **D:** Alfred Hitchcock; **W:** Charles Bennett. *SNC, NOS, HHT*

Secret Agent 1964 Secret agent John Drake embarks upon dangerous and exciting assignments around the world in this mystery-adventure series, which ran during 1965 and 1966. All but two episodes are in black and white. **60m/B VHS, Beta.** Patrick McGoohan, Niall MacGinnis, Dawn Addams, Lelia Goldoni; **D:** Don Chaffey. *MOV*

The Secret Agent 🎬🎬 *Joseph Conrad's The Secret Agent* 1996 (R) Rain, rain go away. In this waterlogged adaptation of the Conrad novel, Hoskins plays Adolf Verloc, a cowardly agent provocateur who heads a group of anarchists in soggy Victorian England. His real mission, however, is to report the actions of the expatriates to the Russian government. After he is bullied into a terrorist attack on the Greenwich Observatory by his contact at the Russian embassy, the lives of Verloc, his wife Winnie (Arquette) and her mentally disabled brother Stevie (Bale) are blown to pieces (sometimes literally) by the consequences. The only spark in the otherwise dank and gloomy production is Williams (listed as George Spelvin) as the demented explosives expert known only as the Professor. Alfred Hitchcock also used a loose interpretation of Conrad's novel for "Sabotage." **CW:** Some moments of violence. **95m/C VHS, LV, Closed Caption.** *GB* Bob Hoskins, Patricia Arquette, Gerard Depardieu, Robin Williams, Jim Broadbent, Christian Bale, Elizabeth Spriggs, Peter Vaughan, Julian Wadham; **D:** Christopher Hampton; **W:** Christopher Hampton; **C:** Denis Lenoir; **M:** Philip Glass. *FXV*

Secret Agent 00 *🎞* *Operation Kid Brother*
1967 (R) A master criminal plans to blackmail the western world and only special Secret Agent 00 can stop him. Bad spy genre ripoff, interesting only as the screen debut of Sean Connery's brother. **97m/C VHS.** *IT* Neil Connery, Daniela Bianchi, Adolfo Celi; **D:** Alberto De Martino; **M:** Ennio Morricone. *NO*

The Secret Agent Club *🎞½* **1996 (PG)**
Secret agent Ray Chase (Hogan) steals a laser gun that evil Eve (Down) is determined to sell to the highest bidder. Ray returns home and, under the pretext of his job as a toy store owner, hides the gun in the store where his son Jeremy (McCurley) assumes it's a new toy. Eve's henchmen manage to capture Ray but not before Jeremy gets the gun and plans a rescue mission with his friends. **90m/C VHS.** Hulk Hogan, Richard Moll, Lesley-Anne Down, Mathew McCurley, Edward Albert, Lyman Ward, James Hong, Barry Bostwick, Jack Nance; **D:** John Murlowski; **W:** Rory Johnston; **C:** S. Douglas Smith. *CAF*

Secret Agent 00-Soul *🎞½* **1989** International spy decides to fulfill his dream of opening a detective agency in his old neighborhood. Release of this direct-to-video mishmash was delayed until '95. **71m/C VHS.** Billy Dee Williams, Amanda Le Flore, Marjean Holden, Tiny Lister; **D:** Julius Le Flore. *XVC*

Secret Agent Super Dragon *🎞* *Super Dragon* **1966** The CIA calls in the agent known as "Super Dragon" when it is discovered that a Venezuelan drug czar plans to spike U.S. gum and candy with an LSD-like drug. Less than competent production offers some unintended laughter. **95m/C VHS, Beta.** *FR IT GE* Ray Danton, Marisa Mell, Margaret Lee, Jess Hahn, Carlo D'Angelo, Adriana Ambesi; **D:** Calvin Jackson Padget. *SNC*

Secret Beyond the Door *🎞🎞* **1948** A wealthy heiress marries a widower and soon discovers that he murdered his first wife. Understandably, she wonders what plans he might have for her. Capably done chiller, but the plot is hackneyed pseudo-Hitchcock. **99m/B VHS.** Joan Bennett, Michael Redgrave, Barbara O'Neil, Anne Revere; **D:** Fritz Lang; **M:** Miklos Rozsa. *REP*

Secret Ceremony *🎞🎞½* **1969** An aging prostitute and a young, aimless waif resemble each other's dead mother and dead daughter, respectively, and the relationship goes on, strangely, from there. This original big-screen version is very good Freudian psycho-drama; 101-minute TV version is unfortunately greatly diluted. **109m/C VHS, Beta.** Elizabeth Taylor, Robert Mitchum, Mia Farrow, Pamela Brown, Peggy Ashcroft; **D:** Joseph Losey; **M:** Richard Rodney Bennett. *BAR*

The Secret Code **1942** A 15-chapter serial with the Black Commando (Kelly) thwarting the Nazis' attempts at sabotage. After each chapter's cliffhanger ending a new form of secret code is explained and decoded. **315m/B VHS.** Paul Kelly, Anne Nagel, Clancy Cooper, Trevor Bardette, Gregory Gay, Ludwig Donath, Ed Parker; **D:** Spencer Gordon Bennet. *GPV*

The Secret Diary of Sigmund Freud *🎞🎞* **1984** Spoofy look at the early years of Sigmund Freud, the father of modern psychoanalysis. Freud (Cort) has an affair with lisping nurse Kane while tending to patient Shawn and answering to mama Baker, who's carrying on with mad doctor Kinski. Talented cast falls asleep on couch. **129m/C VHS, Beta, Closed Caption.** Bud Cort, Carol Kane, Carroll Baker, Klaus Kinski, Marisa Beren-

son, Dick Shawn, Ferdinand "Ferdy" Mayne; **D:** Danford B. Greene. *FOX*

Secret File of Hollywood *🎞½* *Secret File: Hollywood* **1962** A down-and-out private eye gets a job taking photos for a sleazy Hollywood scandal sheet and finds himself in the midst of a blackmail plot masterminded by his editor. An often childish potboiler, perhaps inspired by the once-feared Confidential Magazine. **85m/B VHS.** Robert Clarke, Francine York, Syd Mason, Maralou Gray, John Warburton; **D:** Ralph Cushman. *NOS, LOO, TPV*

The Secret Four *🎞🎞* *The Four Just Men* **1940** Three young men seek to avenge the death of their friend at the hands of British traitors, and become involved in a plot to sabotage the Suez canal. Poorly adapted from the novel by Edgar Wallace. **79m/B VHS, Beta.** *GB* Hugh Sinclair, Griffith Jones, Francis L. Sullivan, Frank Lawton, Anna Lee, Alan Napier, Basil Sydney; **D:** Walter Forde. *SNC*

Secret Games *🎞½* **1992 (R)** An unhappily married woman (Brin) is searching for relief from her restrictive marriage. At the "Afternoon Demitasse," an exclusive brothel where women are paid for fulfilling their ultimate fantasies, she meets a man (Hewitt) who pushes her beyond her sexual limits and threatens to totally possess her. **90m/C VHS, Closed Caption.** Martin Hewitt, Michele Brin, Delia Sheppard, Billy Drago; **D:** Alexander Gregory Hippolyte. *IMP*

Secret Games 2: The Escort *🎞½* **1993 (R)** A performance artist (Hewitt) learns how to seduce women from a beautiful escort (Rochelle). However, he falls for his trainer despite being a star pupil who could have anyone he wanted. Plot conveniently lends itself to lots of steamy love scenes. Also available in an unrated version. **?m/C VHS, Closed Caption.** Martin Hewitt, Amy Rochelle, Sara Suzanne Brown, Marie Leroux; **D:** Alexander Gregory Hippolyte; **W:** Russell Lavalle; **M:** Ashley Irwin. *IMP*

Secret Games 3 *🎞½* **1994 (R)** A bored doctor's wife gets her kicks by visiting a club catering to women's fantasies. But then she meets a criminal who wants her all to himself. An unrated version is available at 91 minutes. **CW:** Strong sexuality. **82m/C VHS.** Woody Brown, Brenda Swanson, Rochelle Swanson; **D:** Alexander Gregory Hippolyte. *ACA*

The Secret Garden *🎞🎞🎞* **1949** The well-loved Frances Hodgson Burnett story has been remade and even revamped as a Broadway musical, but this is considered the definitive version. An orphan girl arrives at her uncle's somber Victorian estate. She starts tending a long-forgetten garden, and with its resurrection joy returns to the household. O'Brien leads an outstanding cast in one of her final juvenile roles. In black and white, with Technicolor for later garden scenes. **92m/B VHS, Beta, LV.** Margaret O'Brien, Herbert Marshall, Dean Stockwell, Gladys Cooper, Elsa Lanchester, Brian Roper; **D:** Fred M. Wilcox. *MGM*

The Secret Garden *🎞🎞½* **1984** Orphaned Mary Lennox is sent to live with her mysterious uncle after her parents die. Mary is willful and spoiled and her uncle's house holds a number of secrets, including a crippled cousin. When Mary discovers a mysteriously abandoned locked garden she makes it her mission to restore the garden to life. Based on the children's classic by Frances Hodgson Burnett. Made for British television. **107m/C VHS.** *GB* Sarah Hollis Andrews, David Patterson; **D:** Katrina Murray. *MOV, SIG, TVC*

The Secret Garden *🎞🎞🎞* **1987 (PG)** Lonely orphan Mary Lennox is sent to live with her uncle in England after her parent's deaths. Mary, who has grown up in India, is selfish and unhappy until she discovers two secrets on her uncle's estate. Class production of the children's classic by Frances Hodgson Burnett with wonderful performances; added prologue and afterword showing Mary as an adult are unnecessary, but don't detract either. Made for television as a "Hallmark Hall of Fame" special. **100m/C VHS, LV, Closed**

Caption. Gennie James, Barret Oliver, Jadrien Steele, Michael Hordern, Derek Jacobi, Billie Whitelaw, Lucy Gutteridge, Julian Glover, Colin Firth, Alan Grint. *REP*

The Secret Garden *🎞🎞🎞* **1993 (G)** Rekindled interest in Frances Hodgson Burnett's classic tale has prompted a Broadway musical, two TV movies, and this latest big screen version. Mary Lennox is an orphan sent to live in her reclusive uncle's forbidding mansion filled with secrets, including a crippled cousin she didn't know she had. She discovers a secret neglected garden and becomes determined to bring it back to life. Befitting director Holland's reputation this version is beautiful but dark, with children prey to very adult anxieties. **102m/C VHS, Beta, LV, Closed Caption.** Kate Maberly, Maggie Smith, Haydon Prowse, Andrew Knott, John Lynch; **D:** Agnieszka Holland; **W:** Caroline Thompson; **C:** Roger Deakins; **M:** Zbigniew Preisner. Los Angeles Film Critics Association Awards '93: Best Score; Nominations: British Academy Awards '93: Best Supporting Actress (Smith). *WAR, BTV*

Secret Honor *🎞🎞🎞* *Lords of Treason; Secret Honor: The Last Testament of Richard M. Nixon; Secret Honor: A Political Myth* **1985** Idiosyncratic, single-set, one-man film version adapted by Donald Freed and Arnold Stone from their stage play about Richard Nixon coping with the death of his presidency on the night he's decided to blow his brains out. Made with students at the University of Michigan, and carried by the ranting and raving of Hall as a tragic Shakespearean Nixon with plenty of darkly humorous lines. **90m/C VHS, Beta, LV.** Philip Baker Hall; **D:** Robert Altman; **M:** George Burt. *LIV, VES, CRC*

Secret Ingredient *🎞½* **1992** A legendary cognac recipe is the secret formula of the monks of St. Celare, whose monastery is located in the mountains of Yugoslavia. A wealthy American sends his flighty heiress daughter to pry the secret recipe from the monks but she runs into more than she bargains for when she falls for a handsome friar and gets caught up with a band of bumbling gypsies and the inept state police. **95m/C VHS.** Rick Rossovich, Catherine Hicks, Gary Kroeger, Jeff Corey, Brad Dexter, Sam Wanamaker; **D:** Slobodan Shijan. *HMD*

Secret Life of an American Wife *🎞🎞* **1968** A bored housewife (Jackson) tries to seduce a client of her husband's, with less than hilarious results. Too much dialogue, not enough genuine humor. Disappointing inversion of director Axelrod's "The Seven Year Itch." **97m/C VHS, Beta.** Walter Matthau, Anne Jackson, Patrick O'Neal, Edy Williams; **D:** George Axelrod; **W:** George Axelrod. *FOX*

The Secret Life of Walter Mitty *🎞🎞🎞* **1947** An entertaining adaptation of the James Thurber short story about a meek man (Kaye) who lives an unusual secret fantasy life. Henpecked by his fiancee and mother, oppressed at his job, he imagines himself in the midst of various heroic fantasies. While Thurber always professed to hate Kaye's characterization and the movie, it scored at the box office and today stands as a comedic romp for Kaye. Available with digitally remastered stereo and original movie trailer. **110m/C VHS, Beta, LV.** Danny Kaye, Virginia Mayo, Boris Karloff, Ann Rutherford, Fay Bainter, Florence Bates; **D:** Norman Z. McLeod; **C:** Lee Garmes. *HBO*

Secret Mission *🎞🎞½* **1942** Four British intelligence agents are sent into occupied France to assess the strength of Nazi forces. But after discovering the information, their cover is blown and it's a race to get the intelligence into the right hands before the Nazis get to them first. **94m/B VHS.** *GB* James Mason, Hugh Williams, Roland Culver, Michael Wilding, Carla Lehmann, Nancy Price, Percy Walsh, Karel Stepanek, Herbert Lom, Stewart Granger; **D:** Harold French; **W:** Anatole de Grunwald, Basil Bartlett; **C:** Bernard Knowles, Cyril Knowles; **M:** Mischa Spoliansky. *FCT*

Secret Obsession *⯁* 1988 (PG) A love tri-angle among a father, his illegitimate son, and the woman they both love, set in North Africa in 1955. Sounds intriguing, but don't be fooled. Slow, dull, and poorly acted. **82m/C VHS, Beta.** Julie Christie, Ben Gazzara, Patrick Bruel, Jean Carmet; **D:** Henri Vart. THV

The Secret of El Zorro *⯁½* 1957 Don Diego's friend, Don Ricardo, threatens to unmask Zorro's secret identity when he challenges the legendary swordsman to a duel. **75m/B VHS, Beta.** Guy Williams. DIS

The Secret of My Success *⯁⯁* 1987 (PG-13) Country bumpkin Fox goes to the Big Apple to make his mark. He becomes the corpo-rate mailboy who rises meteorically to the top of his company (by impersonating an executive) in order to win the love of an icy woman executive. He spends his days running frantically between his real job in the mailroom and his fantasy posi-tion, with various sexual shenanigans with the boss's wife thrown in to keep the viewer alert. Fox is charismatic while working with a cliche-ridden script that ties up everything very neatly at the end. **110m/C VHS, Beta, LV, Closed Caption.** Michael J. Fox, Helen Slater, Richard Jordan, Margaret Whitton; **D:** Herbert Ross; **W:** Jim Cash, Jack Epps Jr., A.J. Carothers; **C:** Carlo DiPalma; **M:** David Foster. USH

The Secret of Navajo Cave *⯁⯁* Leg-end of Cougar Canyon 1976 (G) Fair family adventure. Two young friends explore the mysterious Navajo cave, where one can be assured that a secret awaits. **84m/C VHS.** Holger Kasper, Steven Benally Jr., Johnny Guerro; **D:** James T. Flocker. XVC

The Secret of NIMH *⯁⯁⯁* 1982 (G) Animated tale, produced by a staff of Disney-trained artists led by "American Tail's" Bluth; con-cerns a newly widowed mouse who discovers a secret agency of superintelligent rats (they've es-caped from a science lab) who aid her in protect-ing her family. As is usually the case with Bluth films, the animation is superb while the socially aware plot struggles to keep pace. That aside, it's still an interesting treat for the youngsters. Adapt-ed from Robert C. O'Brien's "Mrs. Frisby and the Rats of N.I.M.H." **84m/C VHS, Beta, LV, 8mm, Closed Caption.** **D:** Don Bluth; **W:** Don Bluth; **M:** Jerry Goldsmith; **V:** John Carradine, Derek Jacobi, Dom DeLuise, Elizabeth Hartman, Peter Strauss, Aldo Ray, Edie McClurg, Wil Wheaton. MGM

The Secret of Roan Inish *⯁⯁⯁½* 1994 (PG) Irish myth comes to life in this fantasy about the importance of family and place, seen through the eyes of 10-year-old Fiona Coneelly (newcomer Courtney) who's sent to live with her grandparents in post-WWII County Donegal. Fio-na's drawn to her grandfather's stories about the family's ancestral home on the island of Roan In-ish and the loss of her baby brother Jamie, who was carried out to sea. Another family tale is about a Selkie—a beautiful seal/woman captured by a Coneelly fisherman who eventually returned to her ocean home. When Fiona visits Roan Inish she becomes convinced that Jamie is alive and being cared for by the island's seals. Director Sayles keeps a firm grip on the cuteness factor while cinematographer Wexler works his usual magic on the sea, sky, and land of Ireland. Based on the 1957 novel "Secret of the Ron Mor Skerry" by Rosalie K. Fry. **102m/C VHS, LV, Closed Caption.** Jeni Courtney, Michael Lally, Eileen Colgan, John Lynch, Richard Sheridan, Susan Lynch, Cillian Byrne; **D:** John Sayles; **W:** John Sayles; **C:** Haskell Wexler; **M:** Mason Dar-ing. Nominations: Independent Spirit Awards '96: Best Direc-tor (Sayles), Best Film, Best Screenplay. COL

Secret of the Black Trunk *⯁⯁½* 1962 Chilling Edgar Wallace story about a series of murders at a famed English hotel. Filmed in Great Britain. **96m/C VHS.** GE Joachim Hansen, Senta Berger, Hans Reiser, Leonard Steckel, Peter Carsten; **D:** Werner Klinger. SNC

The Secret of the Golden Eagle *⯁⯁* 1991 A boy and his new adventur-er friend are on a quest to find the strange "Gold-en Statue" that causes people to grow old before their time. They must take it from criminals who are using it for evil purposes. A good adventure/ fantasy for the entire family. **90m/C VHS.** Michael Ber-ryman, Brandon McKay; **D:** Cole McKay. WLA

Secret of the Ice Cave *⯁* 1989 (PG-13) A motley band of explorers, hijackers and mer-cenaries go after a secret treasure in the remote mountains. **106m/C VHS, Beta.** Michael Moriarty, Sally Kellerman, David Mendenhall, Virgil Frye, Gerald Anthony, Norbert Weisser; **D:** Radu Gabrea. MOV

The Secret of the Loch *⯁½* 1934 Scottish scientist claims to have seen the Loch Ness Monster but everyone thinks his bagpipe's blown a reed. **80m/B VHS.** GB Seymour Hicks, Nancy O'Neil, Gibson Gowland, Frederick Peisley; **D:** Milton Rosmer. NOS, SNC

The Secret of the Telegian *⯁⯁½* 1961 Rare Japanese sci-fi flick about a soldier who uses a teleportation device to kill fellow sol-diers who tried to kill him. He could find his victims wherever they hid. Also known as "The Telegian." **85m/C VHS.** JP Koji Tsurata, Yumi Shirakawa, Akihiko Hira-ta, Tadao Nakamura; **D:** Jun Fukuda. SNC

Secret of Yolanda *⯁* 1982 (R) Steamy romance about a young deaf-mute whose guard-ian and riding instructor both fall for her. **90m/C VHS, Beta.** Aviva Ger, Asher Zarfati, Shraga Harpaz. MGM

The Secret Passion of Robert Clayton *⯁⯁* 1992 (R) When Robert Clayton Jr. (Valentine) returns to his home town to take the position of D.A., he is forced to go head to head in a lurid murder trial with the defense attor-ney (Mahoney), who also happens to be his own father.**CW:** Violence and sexuality. **92m/C VHS.** John Mahoney, Scott Valentine, Eve Gordon, Kevin Conroy; **D:** E.W. Swackhamer; **W:** Brian Ross; **C:** Billy Dickson. PAR

Secret Passions *⯁½* 1978 A young cou-ple are haunted by a dark, romance-novel-type secret. Made for television. **99m/C VHS, Beta.** John James, Susan Lucci; **D:** Michael Pressman. NO

Secret Places *⯁⯁½* 1985 (PG) On the brink of WWII, a German girl in an English school finds friendship with a popular classmate. Touch-ing and involving, but somehow unsatisfying. **98m/C VHS, Beta, Closed Caption.** GB Maria Therese Relin, Tara MacGowran, Claudine Auger, Jenny Agutter; **D:** Zelda Barron; **W:** Zelda Barron. FOX

The Secret Policeman's Other Ball *⯁⯁⯁* 1982 (R) Engaging live perfor-mance by most of the Monty Python troupe and guest rock artists, staged for Amnesty Internation-al. Follows 1979's "The Secret Policeman's Ball," and followed by 1987's "The Secret Policeman's Third Ball." **101m/C VHS, Beta, LV.** GB John Cleese, Graham Chapman, Michael Palin, Terry Jones, Pete Town-shend, Sting, Billy Connolly, Bob Geldof; **D:** Julien Temple; **W:** Michael Palin. MGM

Secret Policeman's Private Parts *⯁⯁⯁* 1981 Various sketches and per-formances from the various Secret Policeman oc-casions, featuring classic Python sketches includ-ing "I'm a Lumberjack and I'm OK." Also featured are performances by Phil Collins, Pete Town-shend, Donovan, and Bob Geldof. Thank you very much. **77m/C VHS, Beta, LV.** GB John Cleese, Michael Palin, Terry Jones, Pete Townshend, Julien Temple; **D:** Roger Graef. MED

The Secret Rapture *⯁⯁* 1994 (R) Two sisters clash in this family drama, adapted by Hare from his 1988 play. The bohemian Isobel (Stevenson) and her estranged sister, the forbid-ding Marion (Wilton), are brought together by their father's death. While Isobel grieves, Marion seeks to gain advantage in the family business, and both must deal with their young, alcoholic, and volatile stepmother Katherine (Whalley-Kilmer). Emotional intensity with good performances but

abrupt shifts in tone.**CW:** Language; nudity; sexu-al situations. **96m/C VHS, LV.** GB Juliet Stevenson, Pe-nelope Wilton, Joanne Whalley, Alan Howard, Neil Pearson, Robert Stephens, Hilton McRae; **D:** Howard Davies; **W:** Da-vid Hare; **C:** Ian Wilson; **M:** Richard Hartley. FXV

A Secret Space *⯁⯁½* 1988 Story of a young man, born of secular parents, searching for the meaning of his Jewish roots as he nears his Bar Mitzvah. He is helped along by a group of Jews who are also searching for this meaning. **80m/C VHS, Beta.** Robert Klein, Phyllis Newman, John Matthews, Sam Schacht, Virginia Graham; **D:** Roberta Hodes. ERG

The Secret War of Harry Frigg *⯁½* 1968 (R) Non-conformist WWII Private Harry Frigg is promoted to general as part of a scheme to help five Allied generals escape from the custody of the Germans. Rare Newman bomb; dismal comedy. **123m/C VHS, Beta.** Paul Newman, Sylva Kosci-na, John Williams, Tom Bosley, Andrew Duggan; **D:** Jack Smight; **C:** Russell Metty. USH

Secret Weapon *⯁⯁* 1990 An Israeli tech-nician flees his country with atomic secrets and a beautiful government agent is sent to lure him to return. Based on the true case of Mordecai Vanunu. Slow-paced and not very suspenseful. Made for cable. **95m/C VHS, Beta, Closed Caption.** Griffin Dunne, Karen Allen, Stuart Wilson, Jeroen Krabbe, Brian Cox, John Rhys-Davies, Ian Mitchell; **D:** Ian Sharp. TTC

Secret Weapons *⯁½* Secrets of the Red Bedroom 1985 Sexy Russian babes are KGB-trained to get any secret from any man. Strains credibility as well as patience. Made for TV. **100m/C VHS.** Linda Hamilton, Sally Kellerman, Hunt Block, Vive-ca Lindfors, Christopher Atkins, Geena Davis, James Fran-ciscus; **D:** Don Taylor; **M:** Charles Bernstein. NO

The Secretary *⯁½* 1994 (R) Another bland variation of "The Temp." Career woman Ellen Bradford (Harris) has a new fast-track job and a highly efficient secretary in Deidre (Kelley). But it turns out Deidre's also lethally efficient in dispos-ing of co-workers through a series of inexplicable accidents and "suicides." So just what's Ellen go-ing to do to show Deidre who's boss?**CW:** Lan-guage; violence; some sexuality. **94m/C VHS, LV, Closed Caption.** Mel Harris, Sheila Kelley, Barry Bostwick, James Russo; **D:** Andrew Lane; **C:** Steve Bernstein; **M:** Louis Febre. REP

Secrets *⯁½* 1971 (R) A wife, her husband, and her daughter each have a sexual experience which they must keep secret. Bisset's nude love scene is an eye-opener. Fast forward through the rest of this dull, overwrought drama. **86m/C VHS.** Jacqueline Bisset, Per Oscarsson, Shirley Knight, Robert Powell, Tarka Kings, Martin C. Thurley; **D:** Philip Saville; **M:** Michael Gibbs. PSM

Secrets *⯁* 1977 An unhappy young bride starts having numerous affairs when her mother dies. Made for television. Hardly worth the effort. **100m/C VHS.** Susan Blakely, Roy Thinnes, Joanne Linville, John Randolph, Anthony Eisley, Andrew Stevens; **D:** Paul Wendkos. MGM

Secrets *⯁⯁* 1982 British drama about the confused life of an innocent schoolgirl who's the victim of a mess of authoritative misunderstand-ings. One of David Puttnam's "First Love" series. **79m/C VHS, Beta.** GB Helen Lindsay, Anna Campbell-Jones, Daisy Cockburn; **D:** Gavin Millar. MGM

Secrets and Lies *⯁⯁* 1995 (R) Too-long film focusing on family and identity. The adoptive parents of black Yuppie Londoner Hortense (Jean-Baptiste) have just died and she decides it's time to seek out her birth parents. She's warned about the emotional consequences, espe-cially upon discovering her biological mother is white—factory worker Cynthia (Blethyn), who has another daughter, Roxanne (Rushbrook), who doesn't get along with mum. Naturally, when Hor-tense is introduced to the rest of Cynthia's family, there's lots of dysfunction to explore. Good perfor-mances, although Hortense's character is bland, but pacing drags.**CW:** Language. **142m/C VHS.** *GB* Brenda Blethyn, Marianne Jean-Baptiste, Timothy Spall, Claire Rushbrook, Phyllis Logan, Lee Ross, Ron Cook, Leslie Manville, Irene Handl; **Cameos:** Alison Steadman; **D:** Mike Leigh; **W:** Mike Leigh; **C:** Dick Pope; **M:** Andrew Dickson. British Academy Awards '96: Best Actress (Blethyn), Best Original Screenplay; Cannes Film Festival '96: Best Actress (Blethyn), Best Film; Golden Globe Awards '97: Best Actress (Blethyn); Los Angeles Film Critics Association Awards '96: Best Actress (Blethyn), Best Director (Leigh), Best Film; Nominations: Academy Awards '96: Best Film, Best Actress (Blethyn), Best Director (Leigh), Best Picture, Best Supporting Actress (Jean-Baptiste), Best Writing; British Academy Awards '96: Best Actor (Spall), Best Director (Leigh), Best Film, Best Supporting Actress (Jean-Baptiste); Cesar Awards '97: Best Foreign Film; Directors Guild of America Awards '96: Best Director (Leigh); Golden Globe Awards '97: Best Film—Drama, Best Supporting Actress (Jean-Baptiste); Independent Spirit Awards '97: Best Foreign Film; Screen Actors Guild Award '96: Best Actress (Blethyn); Writers Guild of America '96: Best Original Screenplay. *FXV*

Secrets of a Married Man 🎬 1984 A married man's philandering ways are his ruination when he falls hard for a beautiful prostitute. Shatner and Shepherd contain their laughter as they make their way through this hyper-earnest family drama. **96m/C VHS, Beta.** William Shatner, Cybill Shepherd, Michelle Phillips, Glynn Turman; **D:** William A. Graham. *LIV*

Secrets of a Soul 🎬🎬½ 1925 A visually impressive presentation of Freudian psychoanalytic theory, in which a professor, wanting a child and jealous of his wife's childhood sweetheart, moves toward madness (we did say Freudian) and is cured through dream interpretation. Great dream sequences bring out the arm-chair psychoanalyst. Silent. **94m/B VHS, Beta.** *GE* Werner Krauss, Ruth Weyher, Jack Trevor; **D:** G.W. Pabst. *FCT*

Secrets of Sweet Sixteen woof! 1974 (R) Gag-fest about budding sexuality in high school. **84m/C VHS, Beta.** Suzie Atkins. *NO*

Secrets of Three Hungry Wives 🎬 1978 When a multi-millionaire is killed, the women with whom he was having affairs are suspected. Tacky made for television flick. **97m/C VHS, Beta.** Jessica Walter, Gretchen Corbett, Eve Plumb, Heather MacRae, James Franciscus, Craig Stevens; **D:** Gordon Hessler. *NO*

Secrets of Women 🎬🎬🎬 *Kvinnors Vantan; Waiting Women* 1952 A rare Bergman comedy about three sisters-in-law who tell about their affairs and marriages as they await their husbands at a lakeside resort. His first commercial success, though it waited nine years for release (1961). In Swedish with English subtitles. **114m/B VHS.** *SW* Anita Bjork, Karl Arne Homsten, Eva Dahlbeck, Maj-Britt Nilsson, Jarl Kulle; **D:** Ingmar Bergman; **W:** Ingmar Bergman. *HMV, NLC, FCT*

The Secrets of Wu Sin 🎬🎬 1932 A suicidal news writer in Chinatown is given a reason to live by a news editor who gives her a job. She starts investigating a ring smuggling Chinese workers, with the trail leading to, of course, Chinatown. Low-budget crime thriller. **65m/B VHS.** Lois Wilson, Grant Withers, Dorothy Revier, Robert Warwick, Toschia Mori; **D:** Richard Thorpe. *SNC, NOS, DVT*

Seduce Me: Pamela Principle 2 🎬½ *Pamela Principle 2* 1994 (R) Charles is a bored, married, architectural photographer who decides a change of pace is in order. So he starts shooting lingerie fashion spreads and gets seduced by model Pamela, who likes her men married. The only connection to the 1991 film is the married man/affair angle.**CW:** Nudity and sexual situations. **96m/C VHS.** Alina Thompson, Nick Rafter, India Allen; **D:** Edward Holzman. *APX*

Seduced 🎬 1985 When a rich businessman turns up dead, the ambitious politician who was involved with his wife must find the killer. Not memorable or exceptional, but not boring or offensive either. Made for television. **100m/C VHS.** Gregory Harrison, Cybill Shepherd, Jose Ferrer, Adrienne Barbeau, Michael C. Gwynne, Karmin Murcelo, Paul Stewart; **D:** Jerrold Freedman. *PSM*

Seduced and Abandoned 🎬🎬🎬 *Sedotta e Abbandonata* 1964 A lothario seduces his fiancee's young sister. When the girl becomes pregnant, he refuses to marry her. Family complications abound. A comic look at the Italian code of honor. In Italian with English subtitles. **118m/B VHS.** *IT* Saro Urzi, Stefania Sandrelli, Aldo Puglisi, Leopoldo Trieste; **D:** Pietro Germi; **W:** Pietro Germi. Cannes Film Festival '64: Best Actor (Urzi); National Board of Review Awards '64: 5 Best Foreign Films of the Year. *HTV, HHT, HEG*

Seduced by Evil 🎬🎬 1994 A journalist (Somers) is investigating a story in a small Southwest town when she encounters a sorcerer (Vargas) who decides he wants her for himself alone. Even if it means destroying everyone she holds dear. Adapted from the novel "Brujo" by Jann Arrington Wolcott. **88m/C VHS, Beta, Closed Caption.** Suzanne Somers, John Vargas, Julie Carmen, James B. Sikking, Mindy Spence, Nancy Moonves; **D:** Tony Wharmby; **W:** Bill Svanoe. *PAR*

The Seducer 🎬🎬 1982 (R) Things get dangerous when a playboy's goals turn from love to death. **72m/C VHS.** Christopher Mathews; **D:** Donovan Winters. *NO*

The Seducers 🎬 1970 An acid-dropping mother takes her shy, withdrawn son on a Mediterranean cruise and asks along some of her girlfriends in the hopes of stoking his libido. However, she finds it difficult to control her own impulses. The boy gets a chance when the ship runs aground on a remote island and he meets an innocent native girl. His mother, though, has designs of her own. Dubbed from Italian. **84m/C VHS.** *GE* Rosalba (Sara Bay) Neri, Edwige Fenech, Maud de Belleroche, Maurizio Bonuglia, Ruggero Miti, Ewa Thulin; **D:** Ottavio Alessi. *SMW, TPV*

Seducers 🎬 *Death Game* 1977 (R) Wealthy, middle-aged man unsuspectingly allows two young lesbians to use his telephone. A night of bizarre mayhem and brutal murder begins. They tease him, tear apart his house, and generally make him miserable. Why? Good question. **90m/C VHS, Beta.** Sondra Locke, Colleen Camp, Seymour Cassel, Beth Brickell; **D:** Peter S. Traynor. *GEM*

The Seduction 🎬 1982 (R) Superstar television anchorwoman is harassed by a psychotic male admirer. Usual run of the mill exploitive "B" thriller with no brains behind the camera. **104m/C VHS, Beta.** Morgan Fairchild, Michael Sarrazin, Vince Edwards, Andrew Stevens, Colleen Camp, Kevin Brophy; **D:** David Schmoeller; **W:** David Schmoeller; **C:** Mac Ahlberg; **M:** Lalo Schifrin. *MED, VTR*

The Seduction of Joe Tynan 🎬🎬½ 1979 (R) Political drama about a young senator (Alda) torn between his family, his political career, and his mistress (Streep). Alda also wrote the thin screenplay, which reportedly is loosely based on the remarkable life of Ted Kennedy. Relatively shallow treatment of the meaty themes of power, hypocrisy, sex, and corruption in our nation's capital. **107m/C VHS, Beta, LV.** Alan Alda, Meryl Streep, Melvyn Douglas, Barbara Harris, Rip Torn; **D:** Jerry Schatzberg; **W:** Alan Alda; **M:** Bill Conti. Los Angeles Film Critics Association Awards '79: Best Supporting Actor (Douglas), Best Supporting Actress (Streep); National Board of Review Awards '79: Best Supporting Actress (Streep); New York Film Critics Awards '79: Best Supporting Actress (Streep); National Society of Film Critics Awards '79: Best Supporting Actress (Streep). *USH*

Seduction of Mimi 🎬🎬🎬 1972 (R) Comic farce of politics and seduction about a Sicilian laborer's escapades with the Communists and the local Mafia. Giannini is wonderful as the stubborn immigrant to the big city who finds himself in trouble. One of the funniest love scenes on film. Basis for the later movie "Which Way is Up?" **92m/C VHS, Beta.** *IT* Giancarlo Giannini, Mariangela Melato; **D:** Lina Wertmuller; **W:** Lina Wertmuller. *FXL*

Seduction: The Cruel Woman 🎬🎬 1989 A curiously uninvolving look at sexual games and fantasies. Wanda is a dominatrix, who also owns a sado-masochistic gallery where her various friends and current and formers lovers act out

their basest desires. Stylized, with some graphic sex. Based on the novel "Venus in Furs" by Leopold Sacher-Masoch. In German with English subtitles. **84m/C VHS.** *GE* Mechthild Grossmann, Carola Regnier, Udo Kier, Sheila McLaughlin; **D:** Elfi Mikesch, Monika Treut; **W:** Elfi Mikesch, Monika Treut. *FRF*

See How She Runs 🎬🎬🎬 1978 Running becomes a central and redefining experience for a 40-year-old divorced schoolteacher (Woodward). Her training culminates with a run in the Boston marathon. Her loved ones, though concerned for her health and sanity, cheer her on. Excellent made for TV drama. Screen daughter Newman is also Woodward's real-life daughter. **92m/C VHS, Beta.** Joanne Woodward, John Considine, Lissy Newman, Barbara Manning; **D:** Richard T. Heffron. *NO*

See No Evil 🎬🎬🎬 *Blind Terror* 1971 (PG) A blind girl gradually discovers the murdered bodies of her uncle's family. Trapped in the family mansion, she finds herself pursued by the killer. Chilling and well crafted. **90m/C VHS, Beta, LV.** Mia Farrow, Dorothy Allison, Robin Bailey; **D:** Richard Fleischer; **W:** Brian Clemens; **M:** Elmer Bernstein. *COL*

See No Evil, Hear No Evil 🎬🎬 1989 (R) Another teaming for Pryor and Wilder, in which they portray a blind man and a deaf man both sought as murder suspects. Pryor and Wilder deserve better. **103m/C VHS, Beta, LV, 8mm, Closed Caption.** Gene Wilder, Richard Pryor, Joan Severance, Anthony Zerbe; **D:** Arthur Hiller; **W:** Gene Wilder, Andrew Kurtzman, Eliot Wald, Earl Barret, Arne Sultan; **M:** Stewart Copeland. *COL*

See You in the Morning 🎬½ 1989 (PG-13) Ill-conceived romantic comedy-drama about a divorced psychiatrist and a widow, both of whom had unhappy marriages, who meet and marry. They must cope with their respective children, family tragedies, and their own expectations, in order to make this second marriage work. **119m/C VHS, Beta, LV, Closed Caption.** Jeff Bridges, Alice Krige, Farrah Fawcett, Drew Barrymore, Lukas Haas, Macaulay Culkin, David Dukes, Frances Sternhagen, Theodore Bikel, George Hearn, Linda Lavin; **D:** Alan J. Pakula; **W:** Alan J. Pakula. *WAR*

Seedpeople 🎬🎬½ 1992 Mindless horror flick has bloodthirsty plants inhabiting peaceful Comet Valley after their seeds fall from outer space and germinate. These "seedpeople" possess tremendous powers and soon have the rural residents transformed into zombies. Bears an uncanny resemblance to "Invasion of the Bodysnatchers," and is so bad it's almost good. Also available with Spanish subtitles. **87m/C VHS, Beta, Closed Caption.** Sam Hennings, Andrea Roth, Dane Witherspoon, David Dunard, Holly Fields, Bernard Kates, Anne Betancourt, Sonny Carl Davis; **D:** Peter Manoogian; **W:** Jackson Barr; **M:** Bob Mithoff. *PAR*

Seeds of Evil 🎬🎬 *The Gardener* 1976 (R) Warhol alumnus Dallesandro is a strange gardener who grows flowers that can kill. He can also turn himself into a tree and figures to seduce rich and bored housewife Houghton (niece of Katharine Hepburn) after he finishes tending her garden. Strange, quirky horror flick. **97m/C VHS, Beta.** Katharine Houghton, Joe Dallesandro, Rita Gam; **D:** James H. Kay. *UNI*

The Seekers 🎬🎬 1979 The story of the Kent family continues, as Abraham Kent, his wife and young son are forced to leave the safety of Boston for the rugged, untamed Pacific Northwest. TV movie based on the novel by John Jakes; preceded by "The Bastard" and "The Rebels." **200m/C VHS, Closed Caption.** Randolph Mantooth, Edie Adams, Neville Brand, Delta Burke, John Carradine, George DeLoy, Julie Gregg, Roosevelt Grier, George Hamilton, Anne Keith, Brian Keith, Ross Martin, Gary Merrill, Martin Milner, Vic Morrow, Timothy Patrick Murphy, Hugh O'Brian, Robert Reed, Allen Rich, Barbara Rush, Sarah Rush, Stuart Whitman, Ed Harris, Jeremy Licht, Eric Stoltz; **D:** Sidney Hayers. *USH*

Seems Like Old Times 🎬🎬½ 1980 (PG) A sweet lawyer (Hawn) finds herself helping her ex-husband (Chase) when two robbers force him to hold up a bank. Grodin is the new spouse threatened by Chase's appearance and by the heavies he's trying to escape. Better-than-average script, with funny and appealing characters. 102m/C VHS, Beta, LV. Goldie Hawn, Chevy Chase, Charles Grodin, Robert Guillaume, Harold Gould, George Grizzard, T.K. Carter; **D:** Jay Sandrich; **W:** Neil Simon; **M:** Marvin Hamlisch. COL

Seize the Day 🎬🎬🎬 1986 A man approaching middle age (Williams) feels that he is a failure. Brilliant performances by all, plus a number of equally fine actors in small roles. Based on the short novel by Saul Bellow. 93m/C VHS, Beta, LV. Robin Williams, Joseph Wiseman, Jerry Stiller, Glenne Headly, Tony Roberts; **D:** Fielder Cook. MON

Seizure 🎬🎬 1974 (PG) Three demonic creatures from a writer's dreams come to life and terrorize him and his houseguests at a weekend party. Slick but disjointed; Stone's directorial debut. Interesting cast includes Tattoo from "Fantasy Island." 93m/C VHS, Beta. CA Jonathan Frid, Herve Villechaize, Christina Pickles; **D:** Oliver Stone; **W:** Oliver Stone. PSM

Seizure: The Story of Kathy Morris 🎬🎬 1982 The real-life anguish and struggle of a young music student who must have brain surgery and comes out of it unable to read or count. Workaday dramatization. 104m/C VHS, Beta. Leonard Nimoy, Penelope Milford; **D:** Gerald I. Isenberg. TLF

Selena 🎬🎬½ 1996 (PG) Lopez is appealing in the title role of the 23-year-old Tejano superstar singer who was just breaking into international prominence when she was murdered by the president of her fan club in 1995. Flashbacks show dad Abraham's (Olmos) dashed musical aspirations and he serves as a stage father to his children, recognizing his daughter Selena's exceptional voice. Film covers her marriage to guitarist Chris Perez (Seda) and her building success until the final tragedy (which isn't shown). Film concludes with concert footage of the real Selena. 127m/C VHS. Jennifer Lopez, Edward James Olmos, Jon Seda, Constance Marie, Jacob Vargas, Lupe Ontiveros, Jackie Guerra, Sal Lopez, Rebecca Lee Mezza; **D:** Gregory Nava; **W:** Gregory Nava; **C:** Edward Lachman; **M:** Dave Grusin. NYR

Self-Defense 🎬½ 1988 (R) When a city's police force goes on strike, the citizens band together into vigilante troops. 85m/C VHS, Beta, LV. Tom Nardini, Brenda Bazinet. MED

Sell Out 🎬🎬½ 1976 (PG) A former spy living in Jerusalem is called out of retirement; his protege, who defected to the Soviets, now wants out. 102m/C VHS, Beta. Richard Widmark, Oliver Reed, Gayle Hunnicutt, Sam Wanamaker; **D:** Peter Collinson. MED

Semi-Tough 🎬🎬½ 1977 (R) Likeable, still current social satire involving a couple of pro-football buddies and their mutual interest in their team owner's daughter. Romantic comedy, satire of the sports world, zany highjinks—it's all here, though not enough of any of these. Pleasant and enjoyable. Based on the novel by Dan Jenkins. 107m/C VHS, Beta, LV. Burt Reynolds, Kris Kristofferson, Jill Clayburgh, Lotte Lenya, Robert Preston, Bert Convy, Richard Masur, Carl Weathers, Brian Dennehy, John Matuszak, Ron Silver; **D:** Michael Ritchie; **W:** Walter Bernstein. MGM, FOX

The Senator was Indiscreet 🎬🎬🎬 Mr. Ashton was Indiscreet 1947 A farcical comedy concerning a slightly loony senator with presidential aspirations. He thinks he can win the nomination because he keeps a diary that would prove embarrassing to numerous colleagues. The diary then falls into the hands of a journalist. Powell is wonderful as the daffy politician. Playwright Kaufman's only directorial effort. 75m/B VHS. William Powell, Ella Raines, Hans Conried; **D:** George S. Kaufman; **C:** William Mellor. New York Film Critics Awards '47: Best Actor (Powell). REP

Send Me No Flowers 🎬🎬🎬 1964 Vintage Hudson-Day comedy. Hudson plays a hypochondriac who thinks his death is imminent. He decides to provide for his family's future by finding his wife a rich husband. She thinks he's feeling guilty for having an affair. 100m/C VHS, Beta. Rock Hudson, Doris Day, Tony Randall, Paul Lynde; **D:** Norman Jewison; **W:** Julius J. Epstein, Philip G. Epstein; **C:** Daniel F. Fapp. USH, CCB

The Sender 🎬🎬 1982 (R) An amnesiac young man is studied by a psychiatrist. She discovers that her patient is a "sender," who can transmit his nightmares to other patients at a hospital. 92m/C VHS, Beta, LV. GB Kathryn Harrold, Zeljko Ivanek, Shirley Knight, Paul Freeman, Sean Hewitt; **D:** Roger Christian; **W:** Thomas Baum; **M:** Trevor Jones. PAR

Senior Trip 🎬 1981 New York City will never be the same after a bunch of rowdy Midwestern high school seniors tear up the town on their graduation trip. Made for television. 96m/C VHS, Beta. Scott Baio, Mickey Rooney, Faye Grant, Vincent Spano, Jane Hoffman; **D:** Kenneth Johnson. WOV

Senior Week woof! 1988 A batch of girl-hungry teens have a wacky time on their Florida vacation just before graduation. 97m/C VHS, Beta. Michael St. Gerard, Devon Skye, Leesa Bryte; **D:** Stuart Goldman. LIV, VES

The Seniors 🎬🎬 1978 (R) A group of college students decide to open a phony sex clinic, but the joke is on them when the clinic becomes a success. Better than it sounds. Pretty good acting and much harmless goofiness. 87m/C VHS, Beta. Dennis Quaid, Priscilla Barnes, Jeffrey Byron, Gary Imhoff; **D:** Rod Amateau. VES

Senora Tentacion 🎬🎬 1949 Musical melodrama about a composer who fights to leave his mother, sister, and girlfriend in order to flee with Hortensia, a famous singer. In Spanish with English subtitles. 82m/B VHS, Beta. David Silva, Susana Guizar, Ninon Sevilla. VYY, APD

Sensation 🎬🎬 1994 (R) A college co-ed agrees to participate in a professor's paranormal experiments in order to test her psychic abilities. Unfortunately what she senses is her prof involved in the unsolved sex-murder of a former student. 102m/C VHS, LV, Closed Caption. Kari Wuhrer, Eric Roberts, Ron Perlman, Ed Begley Jr., Paul LeMat, Claire Stansfield, Kieran Mulroney, Tracey Needham; **D:** Brian Grant; **W:** Doug Wallace; **M:** Arthur Kempel. COL

Sensations 🎬🎬 1987 (R) A woman and a man who aren't exceptionally fond of one another share a lottery ticket and win. Vincent is best known as a former director of porno flicks, and he manages to work in sexual overtones. 91m/C VHS, Beta. Rebecca Lynn, Blake Bahner, Jennifer Delora, Rick Savage, Loretta Palma, Frank Stewart; **D:** Chuck Vincent. ACA

Sensations of 1945 🎬🎬½ Sensations 1944 A press agent turns his firm over to one of his clients, a dancer with some wild promotional ideas. Brings together numerous variety and musical acts. W. C. Fields has a cameo in his last film role. Mostly unremarkable, occasionally fun musical. 86m/B VHS, Beta. Eleanor Powell, Dennis O'Keefe, Sir C. Aubrey Smith, Eugene Pallette, Cab Calloway, Sophie Tucker, Woody Herman, Lyle Talbot, Marie Blake; **Cameos:** W.C. Fields; **D:** Andrew L. Stone. Nominations: Academy Awards '44: Scoring of a Musical. VDM

Sense & Sensibility 🎬🎬 1985 BBC miniseries adaptation of Jane Austen's first novel concerning two sisters striving for happiness in their well-ordered lives. 174m/C VHS, Beta, Closed Caption. GB Irene Richard, Tracey Childs; **D:** Rodney Bennett. FOX, TVC, HMV

Sense and Sensibility 🎬🎬🎬½ 1995 (PG) Thanks to the machinations of greedy relatives, the impecunious Dashwood family is forced to move to a country cottage when father dies. Sensible Elinor (Thompson) looks after the household while overly-romantic Marianne (Winslet) pines for passion—ignoring the noble attentions of middle-aged neighbor Brandon (Rickman) for the far more dashing Willoughby (Wise). Elinor has her own hopes for marriage with boyishly ineffectual Edward (Grant) but all three men have secrets that could crush romantic dreams (at least temporarily). Somewhat slow-paced but witty adaptation (by Thompson) of Jane Austen's first novel, well-acted and beautifully photographed (oh, to be in the English countryside). 135m/C VHS, LV, 8mm, Closed Caption. GB Emma Thompson, Kate Winslet, Hugh Grant, Alan Rickman, Greg Wise, Robert Hardy, Elizabeth Spriggs, Emile Francois, Gemma Jones, James Fleet, Harriet Walter, Imogen Stubbs, Imelda Staunton, Hugh Laurie, Richard Lumsden; **D:** Ang Lee; **W:** Emma Thompson; **C:** Michael Coulter; **M:** Patrick Doyle. Academy Awards '95: Best Adapted Screenplay; British Academy Awards '95: Best Actress (Thompson), Best Film, Best Supporting Actress (Winslet); Golden Globe Awards '96: Best Film—Drama, Best Screenplay; Los Angeles Film Critics Association Awards '95: Best Screenplay; National Board of Review Awards '95: Best Actress (Thompson), Best Director (Lee), Best Film; New York Film Critics Awards '95: Best Director (Lee); Screen Actors Guild Award '95: Best Supporting Actress (Winslet); Writers Guild of America '95: Best Adapted Screenplay; Broadcast Film Critics Association Awards '95: Best Film, Best Screenplay; Nominations: Academy Awards '95: Best Actress (Thompson), Best Cinematography, Best Costume Design, Best Picture, Best Supporting Actress (Winslet), Original Dramatic/Comedy Score; British Academy Awards '95: Best Adapted Screenplay, Best Cinematography, Best Director (Lee), Best Supporting Actor (Rickman), Best Supporting Actress (Spriggs), Best Score; Directors Guild of America Awards '95: Best Director (Lee); Golden Globe Awards '96: Best Actress—Drama (Thompson), Best Director (Lee), Best Supporting Actress (Winslet), Best Score; Screen Actors Guild Award '95: Best Actress (Thompson). Cast. COL

A Sense of Freedom 🎬🎬🎬 1978 (R) A hopeless racketeering criminal is thrust from institution to institution until the Scottish authorities decide on an innovative style of reform. Based on Jimmy Boyle's autobiographical book. Excellent and disturbing. 81m/C VHS, Beta. GB David Hayman, Alex Norton, Jake D'Arcy, Sean Scanlan, Fulton Mackay; **D:** John MacKenzie. NO

Senso 🎬🎬🎬 The Wanton Contessa 1954 Tragic story of romance and rebellion as Italian patriots battle the Austro-Hungarian empire for independence in 1866. An Italian noblewoman betrays her marriage, and almost her country, to be with a cynical Austrian soldier in this visually stunning piece of cinematography. In Italian with English subtitles or dubbed. 125m/C VHS. IT Alida Valli, Massimo Girotti, Heinz Moog, Farley Granger; **D:** Luchino Visconti; **C:** Robert Krasker. VCD, APD

The Sensual Man 🎬½ 1974 (R) Hot-blooded Italian falls in love and gets married only to find out that his wife cannot consummate their marriage. Exploitative, misogynistic, and unfunny. 90m/C VHS, Beta. Giancarlo Giannini, Rossana Podesta, Lionel Stander; **D:** Marco Vicario. COL

Sensual Partners woof! 1987 Young actresses are lured to Tangier by a fake movie producer and sold as sex slaves. Emphasis on soft-focus, soft-core flesh. 87m/C VHS, Beta. Gina Jansen, Eric Falk. MED

The Sensuous Nurse 🎬🎬 1976 (R) Italian comedy about a beautiful nurse hired by the greedy, treacherous relatives of a weak-hearted count in hopes that her voluptuousness will give him a heart attack. It doesn't, and she falls in love. Mindless, but fun and sexy. Dubbed in English. 79m/C VHS, Beta, Closed Caption. IT Ursula Andress, Mario Pisu, Dulio Del Prete, Jack Palance; **D:** Nello Rosatti. FOX

Sensuous Summer 🎬½ 1993 (R) When Bobby returns home to the town of Elk Lake he finds the family business, run by his brother Nick, is in deep trouble. It seems Alex, an unscrupulous banker, wants to foreclose. But business comes second to pleasure when Bobby is reunited with old flame Jill and Nick takes up again with ex-girlfriend Cindy. **CW:** Language and sexuality. 80m/C VHS. Tom Case, Christina Campbell, Brittany McGrea, Gina Jorand. CEL

The Sensuous Teenager woof! *Libido; Forbidden Passions* 1970 (R) Overwhelmingly erotic and uncontrollably seductive, a teenage girl aims to please by releasing all the sensuality within her. 80m/C VHS. Sandra Jullien, Janine Reynaud, Michel Lemoine; **D:** Max Pecas. *SUN*

The Sentinel 🎬🎬 1976 (R) A model, who has moved into a New York City brownstone, encounters an aging priest and some unusual neighbors. When she investigates strange noises she finds out that the apartment building houses the doorway to hell - and that she's intended to be the next doorkeeper. Modest suspense film with a good cast and enough shock and special effects to keep the viewer interested. 92m/C VHS, Beta. Chris Sarandon, Christina Raines, Ava Gardner, Jose Ferrer, Sylvia Miles, John Carradine, Burgess Meredith, Tom Berenger, Beverly D'Angelo, Jeff Goldblum; **D:** Michael Winner; **W:** Michael Winner. *USH*

Separate But Equal 🎬🎬🎬½ 1991 (PG) One of TV's greatest history lessons, a powerful dramatization of the 1954 Brown vs. The Board of Education case that wrung a landmark civil rights decision from the Supreme Court. Great care is taken to humanize all the participants, from the humblest schoolchild to NAACP lawyer Thurgood Marshall (Poitier). On two cassettes. 194m/C VHS, LV, Closed Caption. Sidney Poitier, Burt Lancaster, Richard Kiley, Cleavon Little, John McMartin, Graham Beckel, Lynne Thigpen, Albert Hall; **D:** George Stevens Jr.; **W:** George Stevens Jr. *REP, FCT, PTB*

Separate Lives 🎬½ 1994 (R) Psych prof Lauren Porter (Hamilton) is in need of some counseling herself. Seems she has a sexy alter ego calling herself Lena and Lauren fears she may have killed someone in her Lena persona. So she turns to her student Tom (Belushi), who happens to be an ex-cop, for help. Sketchy characters and a tired formula make this one a yawner. **CW:** Scenes of violence and sexuality; strong language. 101m/C VHS. Linda Hamilton, James Belushi, Vera Miles, Elissabeth Moss, Drew Snyder, Mark Lindsay Chapman, Marc Poppel, Elizabeth Arlen; **D:** David Madden; **W:** Steven Pressfield; **M:** William Olvis. *THV*

A Separate Peace 🎬🎬 1973 (PG) Two young men in a New England prep school during WWII come to grips with the war, coming of age, and a tragic accident. Cheap rendition of a not-so-great novel by John Knowles. 104m/C VHS, Beta. John Heyl, Parker Stevenson, William Roerick; **D:** Larry Peerce; **M:** Charles Fox. *PAR, HMV*

Separate Tables 🎬🎬🎬½ 1958 Adaptation of the Terence Rattigan play about a varied cast of characters living out their personal dramas in a British seaside hotel. Guests include a matriarch and her shy daughter, a divorced couple, a spinster, and a presumed war hero. Their secrets and loves are examined in grand style. Fine acting all around. 98m/B VHS, Beta. Burt Lancaster, David Niven, Rita Hayworth, Deborah Kerr, Wendy Hiller, Rod Taylor, Gladys Cooper, Felix Aylmer, Cathleen Nesbitt, Rod Taylor, Audrey Dalton, May Hallatt, Priscilla Morgan, Hilda Plowright; **D:** Delbert Mann; **W:** John Gay; **C:** Charles B(ryant) Lang; **M:** David Raksin. Academy Awards '58: Best Actor (Niven), Best Supporting Actress (Hiller); Golden Globe Awards '59: Best Actor—Drama (Niven); National Board of Review Awards '58: 10 Best Films of the Year; New York Film Critics Awards '58: Best Actor (Niven); Nominations: Academy Awards '58: Best Actress (Kerr), Best Adapted Screenplay, Best Black and White Cinematography, Best Picture, Original Dramatic/Comedy Score. *MGM, FOX, FCT*

Separate Tables 🎬🎬½ 1983 (PG) A remake of the 1958 film adapted from Terence Rattigan's play. Separated into two parts, "Table by the Window" and "Table Number Seven." The lives of the lonely inhabitants of a hotel are dramatized through wonderful acting by Christie and Bates. Made for cable television. 50m/C VHS, Beta. Julie Christie, Alan Bates, Claire Bloom, Irene Worth; **D:** John Schlesinger. *MGM*

Separate Vacations 🎬½ 1986 (R) A married man leaves his wife and kids to take a separate vacation, hoping he'll find exciting sex. Wife and kids end up at a ski resort, where romance comes her way. A lightweight, old story. 91m/C VHS, Beta. David Naughton, Jennifer Dale, Mark Keyloun; **D:** Michael Anderson Sr. *LIV*

Separate Ways 🎬½ 1982 (R) Unhappily married couple involved in various affairs split up in order to deal with themselves and their marriage. Good cast; bad script wandering down Maudlin Lane. 92m/C VHS, Beta, LV. Karen Black, Tony LoBianco, David-Naughton, Sybil Danning; **D:** Howard (Hikmet) Avedis; **C:** Dean Cundey. *VES*

The Separation 🎬🎬 1994 Emotions (and fine performances) rather than action move along this domestic drama. Anne (Huppert) and Pierre (Autueil) are living together in Paris with their toddler son when Anne suddenly announces that she's involved with another man. Anne doesn't see why this this should cause any rift in their domestic arrangements but Pierre slowly falls to pieces. Adapted from the novel by Dan Franck; French with subtitles. 85m/C VHS. FR Isabelle Huppert, Daniel Auteuil, Karin Viard, Jerome Deschamps; **D:** Christian Vincent; **W:** Christian Vincent, Dan Franck; **C:** Denis Lenoir. Nominations: Cesar Awards '94: Best Actor (Auteuil), Best Actress (Huppert). *NYR*

Sepia Cinderella 🎬🎬 1947 A songwriter, who finds himself with a hit, abandons his current life and love to try high society. He finds out it's not what he wants after all. 67m/B VHS, Beta. Sheila Guyse, Rubel Blakely, Freddie Bartholomew, Sid Catlett, Deke Wilson. *NOS, DVT, FCT*

September 🎬🎬 1988 (PG-13) Woody does Bergman again with a shuttered, claustrophobic drama about six unhappy people trying to verbalize their feelings in a dark summer house in Vermont. Well-acted throughout and interesting at first, but the whining and angst attacks eventually give way to boredom. Of course, the Woodman went on to "Crimes and Misdemeanors," blending his dark and comedic sides masterfully, so the best way to look at this is as a training film. 82m/C VHS, Beta, LV, Closed Caption. Mia Farrow, Dianne Wiest, Denholm Elliott, Sam Waterston, Elaine Stritch, Jack Warden; **D:** Woody Allen; **W:** Woody Allen; **C:** Carlo DiPalma; **M:** Art Tatum. *ORI*

September Affair 🎬🎬½ 1950 A married engineer and a classical pianist miss their plane from Naples. When the plane crashes, they're presumed dead, and they find themselves free to continue their illicit love affair. They find they cannot hide forever and must make peace with their pasts. Features the hit "September Song," recorded by Walter Huston. 104m/B VHS, LV. Joseph Cotten, Joan Fontaine, Francoise Rosay, Jessica Tandy, Robert Arthur; **D:** William Dieterle; **C:** Charles B(ryant) Lang. Golden Globe Awards '52: Best Score. *PAR*

September Gun 🎬🎬½ 1983 A nun hires an aging gunfighter to escort her and a group of Apache children to a church school two hundred miles away. Preston is excellent as the ornery varmint in this enjoyable, pleasant western comedy. Made for television. 94m/C VHS, Beta. Robert Preston, Patty Duke, Christopher Lloyd, Geoffrey Lewis, Sally Kellerman; **D:** Don Taylor. *WOV*

September 30, 1955 🎬🎬½ 1977 (PG) A college undergrad (Thomas) in a small Arkansas town is devastated when he learns of the death of his idol, James Dean. (The title refers to the day Dean died.) Jimmy gathers a group of friends together for a vigil which turns into a drinking-binge, resulting in police chases and, finally, tragedy. Film debut of Quaid. Also known as "9/30/55." 107m/C VHS, Closed Caption. Richard Thomas, Lisa Blount, Deborah Benson, Tom Hulce, Dennis Christopher, Dennis Quaid, Susan Tyrrell; **D:** James Bridges; **W:** James Bridges. *USH*

Sgt. Bilko 🎬½ 1995 (PG) Popular 50's sitcom doesn't march so much as limp to the big screen with Martin leading the troops as the wise-cracking title character, crafted so brilliantly by Phil Silvers on the small screen. Martin flims and flams with frenetic energy as he tries to save his base from Washington cutbacks and the film from utter disaster. Enter Major Thorn (Hartman), Bilko's old adversary, who's plotting revenge on the con artist sergeant. Aykroyd's Bilko's naive boss, Col. Hall, but has little to do. Director Lynn finds his usual comic flair on leave this time around—too few laughs, spread too thin. Sentimental stroke has Catherine Silvers, Phil's daughter, playing Lt. Monday. 95m/C VHS, LV, Closed Caption. Steve Martin, Dan Aykroyd, Phil Hartman, Glenne Headly, Daryl Mitchell, Max Casella, Brian Leckner, Pamela Segall, Eric Edwards, Dan Ferro, John Marshall Jones, Brian Ortiz; **D:** Jonathan Lynn; **W:** Andy Breckman; **C:** Peter Sova; **M:** Alan Silvestri. *USH*

Sergeant Matlovich vs. the U.S. Air Force 🎬🎬½ 1978 A serviceman fights to remain in the Air Force after admitting his homosexuality. Compelling theme (from a true story) and good lead performance from Dourif are not enough to carry a rather flat made for TV script. 100m/C VHS. Brad Dourif, Marc Singer, Frank Converse, William Daniels, Stephen Elliott, David Spielberg, Rue McClanahan, Mitchell Ryan, David Ogden Stiers; **D:** Paul Leaf. *LIV*

Sgt. Pepper's Lonely Hearts Club Band 🎬½ 1978 (PG) "Rip-off" would be putting it kindly. A classic album by one of the greatest rock bands of all time deserves the respect of not having a star-studded extravaganza "filmization" made of it. Gratuitous, weird casting, bad acting give it a surreal feel. And the Bee Gees? Please. A nadir of seventies popular entertainment. ♫ Sgt. Pepper's Lonely Hearts Club Band; With a Little Help From My Friends; Fixing a Hole; Getting Better; Here Comes the Sun; I Want You (She's So Heavy); Good Morning, Good Morning; Nowhere Man; Polythene Pam. 113m/C VHS, Beta, LV. Peter Frampton, The Bee Gees, Steve Martin, George Burns, Donald Pleasence; **D:** Michael A. Schultz. *USH*

Sergeant Rutledge 🎬🎬🎬 1960 The story of a court-martial, told in flashback, about a black cavalry officer on trial for rape and murder. A detailed look at overt and covert racism handled by master director Ford. It is always apparent Strode (as Rutledge) is a heroic, yet human, figure who refuses to be beaten down by circumstances. The courtroom setting is deliberately oppressive but does make the film somewhat static. Based on the novel "Captain Buffalo" by James Warner Bellah. 112m/C VHS. Woody Strode, Jeffrey Hunter, Constance Towers, Billie Burke, Juano Hernandez, Carleton Young, Charles Seel, Jan Styne, Mae Marsh; **D:** John Ford; **W:** Willis Goldbeck, James Warner Bellah; **M:** Howard Jackson. *WAR*

Sergeant Ryker 🎬🎬½ 1968 Confident lead acting from Marvin as a U.S. serviceman accused of treason during the Korean War carries this otherwise blah army/courtroom drama. Remake of 1963 TV film "The Case Against Sergeant Ryker." Dillman is good as Marvin's energetic lawyer. 85m/C VHS. Lee Marvin, Bradford Dillman, Vera Miles, Peter Graves, Lloyd Nolan, Murray Hamilton; **D:** Buzz Kulik; **M:** John Williams. *NO*

Sergeant York 🎬🎬🎬🎬 1941 Timely and enduring war movie based on the true story of Alvin York, the country boy from Tennessee drafted during WWI. At first a pacifist, Sergeant York (Cooper, well cast in an Oscar-winning role) finds justification for fighting and becomes one of the war's greatest heros. Gentle scenes of rural life contrast with horrific battlegrounds. York served as a consultant. 134m/B VHS, Beta. Gary Cooper, Joan Leslie, Walter Brennan, Dickie Moore, Ward Bond, George Tobias, Noah Beery Jr., June Lockhart, Stanley Ridges, Margaret Wycherly; **D:** Howard Hawks; **W:** Abem Finkel, Harry Chandlee, Howard Koch, John Huston; **M:** Max Steiner. Academy Awards '41: Best Actor (Cooper), Best Film

Editing; New York Film Critics Awards '41: Best Actor (Cooper); Nominations: Academy Awards '41: Best Black and White Cinematography, Best Director (Hawks), Best Interior Decoration, Best Original Screenplay, Best Picture, Best Sound, Best Supporting Actor (Brennan), Best Supporting Actress (Wycherly), Original Dramatic/Comedy Score. *MGM, FOX, BTV*

Serial *♂♂♂* **1980 (R)** Fun spoof of hyper-trendiness—open marriage, health foods, fad religions, navel-gazing—in Marin County, the really cool place to live across the Golden Gate from San Francisco. Mull in his first lead is the oddly normal guy surrounded by fruits and nuts. Based on Cyra McFadden's novel. **90m/C VHS, Beta, LV.** Martin Mull, Sally Kellerman, Tuesday Weld, Tom Smothers, Bill Macy, Peter Bonerz, Barbara Rhoades, Christopher Lee; *D:* Bill Persky; *W:* Rich Eustis, Michael Elias. *PAR*

Serial Killer *♂♂* **1995 (R)** Selby Younger (Delaney) is able to think like a killer in order to catch them. That's how the beautiful cop captured the serial killer (Bell) who has now escaped—Selby's his ultimate target but first he wants revenge. So he uses her friends as bait and leaves the bodies for Selby to discover. *CW:* Violence and terror; language. **94m/C VHS, Closed Caption.** Kim Delaney, Gary Hudson, Tobin Bell, Pam Grier, Marco Rodriguez, Lyman Ward, Cyndi Pass, Andrew Prine; *D:* Pierce David. *REP*

Serial Mom *♂♂♂* **1994 (R)** June Cleaver-like housewife Turner is nearly perfect, except when someone disrupts her orderly life. Didn't rewind your videotape? Chose the white shoes after Labor Day? Uh oh. Stardom reigns after she's caught and the murderer-as-celebrity phenomenon is exploited to the fullest. Darkly funny Waters satire tends toward the mainstream and isn't as perverse as earlier efforts, but still maintains a shocking edge (vital organs are good for an appearance or two). Turner's chameleonic performance as the perfect mom/crazed killer is right on target, recalling "The War of the Roses." Waterston, Lake, and Lillard are terrific as her generic suburban family. *CW:* Vulgar language, satirical presentation of violence, and sexual episodes. **93m/C VHS, LV, Closed Caption.** Kathleen Turner, Ricki Lake, Sam Waterston, Matthew Lillard, Mink Stole, Traci Lords; *Cameos:* Suzanne Somers, Joan Rivers, Patty Hearst; *D:* John Waters; *W:* John Waters; *M:* Basil Poledouris. *HBO*

The Serpent and the Rainbow woof! **1987 (R)** A good, interesting book (by Harvard ethnobotanist Wade Davis) offering serious speculation on the possible existence and origin of zombies in Haiti was hacked and slashed into a cheap Wes Craven-ized screen semblance of itself. And a shame it is: the result is racist, disrespectful, exploitative, and superficial. From the director of "Nightmare on Elm Street." **98m/C VHS, Beta, LV.** Bill Pullman, Cathy Tyson, Zakes Mokae, Paul Winfield, Conrad Roberts, Badja Djola, Theresa Merritt; *D:* Wes Craven; *W:* Richard Maxwell; *M:* Brad Fiedel. *USH*

Serpent Island *♂½* **1954** Two seamen fight over a Caribbean woman amid voodoo rituals, sea monsters and buried treasure. **63m/C VHS, Beta.** Sonny Tufts. *MED*

The Serpent's Egg *♂½* Das Schlangenei **1978 (R)** Big disappointment from the great Bergman in his second film in English. Ullmann is not sultry and Carradine is horrible. Big budget matched by big Bergman ego, making a big, bad parody of himself. The plot concerns a pair of Jewish trapeze artists surviving in Berlin during Hitler's rise by working in a grisly and mysterious medical clinic. **119m/C VHS, Beta.** *GE* David Carradine, Liv Ullmann, Gert Frobe, James Whitmore; *D:* Ingmar Bergman; *W:* Ingmar Bergman; *C:* Sven Nykvist. *LIV*

Serpent's Lair *♂♂* **1995 (R)** Tom (Fahey) and Alex (Medway) have just moved into what's supposed to be their dream apartment in L.A. Too bad there's lots of secrets and Tom's soon drawn into the web of sultry beauty Lillith (Lisa B.), who's not just your average femme fatale. *CW:* Sexuali-

ty, language and some violence. **90m/C VHS.** Jeff Fahey, Heather Medway, Lisa B, Anthony Palermo, Kathleen Noone, Taylor Nichols, Patrick Bauchau; *D:* Jeff Reiner; *W:* Marc Rosenberg; *C:* Feliks Parnell; *M:* Vinnie Golia. *REP*

Serpico *♂♂♂* **1973 (R)** Based on Peter Maas's book about the true-life exploits of Frank Serpico, a New York undercover policeman who exposed corruption in the police department. Known as much for his nonconformism as for his honesty, the real Serpico eventually retired from the force and moved to Europe. South Bronx-raised Pacino gives the character reality and strength. Excellent New York location photography. **130m/C VHS, Beta, LV.** Al Pacino, John Randolph, Jack Kehoe, Barbara Eda-Young, Cornelia Sharpe, F. Murray Abraham, Tony Roberts; *D:* Sidney Lumet. Golden Globe Awards '74: Best Actor—Drama (Pacino); National Board of Review Awards '73: Best Actor (Pacino); Writers Guild of America '73: Best Adapted Screenplay; Nominations: Academy Awards '73: Best Actor (Pacino), Best Adapted Screenplay. *PAR*

The Servant *♂♂♂½* **1963** A dark, intriguing examination of British class hypocrisy and the master-servant relationship. A rich, bored playboy is ruined by his socially inferior but crafty and ambitious manservant. Playwright Harold Pinter wrote the adaptation of Robin Maugham's novel in his first collaboration with director Losey. The best kind of British societal navel-gazing. **112m/B VHS, Beta.** *GB* Dirk Bogarde, James Fox, Sarah Miles, Wendy Craig; *D:* Joseph Losey; *W:* Harold Pinter. British Academy Awards '63: Best Actor (Bogarde); New York Film Critics Awards '64: Best Screenplay. *NO*

Servants of Twilight *♂♂* **1991 (R)** Religious zealots target a small boy for assassination because their cult leader says he's the anti-Christ. Adaptation of the Dean R. Koontz novel. Packed with action, its spell on the viewer hinges on a cruel shock ending that undercuts what came before. Made for cable television. **95m/C VHS, Closed Caption.** Bruce Greenwood, Belinda Bauer, Grace Zabriskie, Richard Bradford, Jarrett Lennon, Carel Struycken, Jack Kehoe, Kelli Maroney; *D:* Jeffrey Obrow; *W:* Stephen Carpenter. *THV*

Sesame Street Presents: Follow That Bird Follow That Bird **1985 (G)** Television's Big Bird suffers an identity crisis, and leaves Sesame Street to join a family of real birds. He soon misses his home, and returns, in a danger-filled journey. **92m/C VHS, Beta, LV, Closed Caption.** Sandra Bernhard, John Candy, Chevy Chase, Joe Flaherty, Dave Thomas, Waylon Jennings, Jim Henson's Muppets; *D:* Ken Kwapis; *M:* Lennie Niehaus. *WAR*

A Session with the Committee **1969** Collection of skits performed by a Los Angeles comedy troupe. **90m/C VHS.** Peter Bonerz, Barbara Bosson, Garry Goodrow, Carl Gottlieb, Jessica Myerson, Christopher Ross, Melvin Stewart, Melvin Sturdy; *D:* Jack Del. *NO*

Sessions *♂♂* **1983** Mentally exhausted by her roles as sister, single parent, lover, exercise enthusiast, and high-priced prostitute, Leigh Churchill (Hamel) seeks professional counselling. Hamel's first role after "Hill Street Blues" is only average in this made for TV drama. **96m/C VHS, Beta.** Veronica Hamel, Jeffrey DeMunn, Jill Eikenberry, David Marshall Grant, George Coe, Henderson Forsythe, Deborah Hedwall; *D:* Richard Pearce. *NO*

Set It Off *♂♂½* **1996 (R)** Lethal "Waiting to Exhale," finds four female friends in Los Angeles pushed over the edge and taking up bank robbery to escape poverty and strike a blow against "the man." The felonious, funky divas of crime include Stony (Pinkett, who seems to be having fun with this role) and Latifah (as Cleo, in a powerhouse performance). Butt-kicking action scenes are most entertaining combined with a soundtrack, including Seal, En Vogue, the Fugees and Brandy, to match. Melodramatic sequences, including Stony's romance with Keith (Underwood), drag. *CW:* Strong graphic violence, pervasive language, some sex and drug use. **121m/C VHS.** Jada Pinkett,

Queen Latifah, Vivica A. Fox, Kimberly Elise, Blair Underwood, John C. McGinley, Anna Maria Horsford, Ella Joyce, Charles Robinson, Chaz Lamas Shepard, Vincent Baum, Van Baum, Tom Byrd, Samantha MacLachlan; *D:* F. Gary Gray; *W:* Kate Lanier, Takashi Bufford; *C:* Marc Reshovsky; *M:* Christopher Young. Nominations: Independent Spirit Awards '97: Best Supporting Actress (Queen Latifah). *NLC*

The Set-Up *♂♂♂½* **1949** Excellent, original if somewhat overwrought morality tale about integrity set in the world of boxing. Filmed as a continuous narrative covering only 72 minutes in the life of an aging fighter (Ryan). Told to throw a fight, he must battle gangsters when he refuses. Powerful, with fine performances, especially from Ryan in the lead. Inspired by Joseph Moncure March's narrative poem. **72m/B VHS, Beta, LV.** Robert Ryan, Audrey Totter, George Tobias, Alan Baxter, James Edwards, Wallace Ford; *D:* Robert Wise; *C:* Milton Krasner. *CCB, MED*

The Set Up *♂♂* **1995 (R)** Electronic engineer-turned-cat burglar Charlie Thorpe (Zane) is now apparently reformed after a prison stint and works designing and installing security systems. His latest job is for Chairman Jeremiah Cole (Coburn) at Charter Trust bank where he begins romancing the beautiful Gina (Sara). But she becomes the hostage of Charlie's ex-prison buddy Kliff (Russo), who wants Charlie's help in breaking into the bank. However, there's a doublecross (or maybe even a triplecross) that has Charlie scrambling to save his life. Based on the book "My Laugh Comes Last" by James Hadley Chase. *CW:* Strong sexuality and violent action, and for language. **103m/C VHS, Closed Caption.** Billy Zane, Mia Sara, James Coburn, James Russo; *D:* Strathford Hamilton; *W:* Michael Thoma; *C:* David Lewis; *M:* Conrad Pope. *MGM*

Seven *♂♂½* **1979 (R)** Freelance desperado Smith takes $7 million of your tax dollars at work from the feds to get rid of Hawaiian gangsters. Might be tongue in cheek, though sometimes it's hard to tell. Fun action pic unfortunately characterized by bad camera work and over-earnest direction. Features the original of a gag made famous in "Raiders of the Lost Ark." **100m/C VHS, Beta.** William Smith, Barbara Leigh, Guich Koock, Art Metrano, Martin Kove, Paul Richards, Susan Kiger; *D:* Andy Sidaris. *LIV*

Seven *♂♂♂* **1995 (R)** If this grim thriller can't make you jump, you're dead, and you won't be the only one. Arrogant, ignorant detective David Mills (Pitt) is newly partnered with erudite old-timer William Somerset (Freeman) and they're stuck with the bizarre case of a morbidly obese man who was forced to eat himself to death. The weary Somerset is certain it's just the beginning and he's right—the non-buddy duo are on the trail of a serial killer who uses the seven deadly sins (gluttony, greed, sloth, pride, lust, envy, and wrath) as his modus operandi. Since most of the film is shot in dark, grimy, and unrelentingly rainy circumstances, much of the grotesqueness of the murders is left to the viewer's imagination—which will be in overdrive. *CW:* Grisly afterviews of horrific and bizarre killings, and for strong language. **127m/C VHS, LV, Closed Caption, DVD.** Brad Pitt, Morgan Freeman, Gwyneth Paltrow, Kevin Spacey, R. Lee Ermey, Richard Roundtree, John C. McGinley, Julie Araskog, Reg E. Cathey, Peter Crombie; *D:* David Fincher; *W:* Andrew Kevin Walker; *C:* Darius Khondji; *M:* Howard Shore. MTV Movie Awards '96: Best Film, Most Desirable Male (Pitt), Best Villain (Spacey); National Board of Review Awards '95: Best Supporting Actor (Spacey); New York Film Critics Awards '95: Best Supporting Actor (Spacey); Broadcast Film Critics Association Awards '95: Best Supporting Actor (Spacey); Nominations: Academy Awards '95: Best Film Editing; British Academy Awards '95: Best Original Screenplay; MTV Movie Awards '96: Best On-Screen Duo (Brad Pitt/Morgan Freeman). *NLC*

Seven Alone *♂♂½* House Without Windows **1975 (G)** Family adventure tale (based on Monroe Morrow's book "On to Oregon," based in turn on a true story) about seven siblings who undertake a treacherous 2000-mile journey from Missouri to

Oregon, after their parents die along the way. Inspiring and all that; good family movie. **85m/C VHS, Beta.** Dewey Martin, Aldo Ray, Anne Collins, Dean Smith, Stewart Peterson; **D:** Earl Bellamy. *NO*

Seven Beauties ♫♫♫♫ *Pasqualino Settebellezze; Pasqualino: Seven Beauties* 1976 Very dark war comedy about a small-time Italian crook in Naples with seven ugly sisters to support. He survives a German prison camp and much else; unforgettably, he seduces the ugly commandant of his camp to save his own life. Good acting and tight direction. **116m/C VHS, Beta, LV.** *IT* Giancarlo Giannini, Fernando Rey, Shirley Stoler, Elena Fiore, Enzo Vitale; **D:** Lina Wertmuller; **W:** Lina Wertmuller; **C:** Tonino Delli Colli. Nominations: Academy Awards '76: Best Actor (Giannini), Best Director (Wertmuller), Best Foreign Language Film, Best Original Screenplay. *COL, APD*

Seven Blows of the Dragon ♫♫½ 1973 (R) The Chinese novel, "All Men Are Brothers," is the basis for this spectacular martial arts epic. **81m/C VHS, Beta.** David Chiang. *WAR*

Seven Brides for Seven Brothers ♫♫♫½ 1954 The eldest of seven fur-trapping brothers in the Oregon Territory brings home a wife. She begins to civilize the other six, who realize the merits of women and begin to look for romances of their own. Thrilling choreography by Michael Kidd - don't miss "The Barn Raising." Charming performances by Powell and Keel, both in lovely voice. Based on Stephen Vincent Benet's story. Thrills, chills, singin', dancin'—a classic Hollywood good time. ♫ When You're In Love; Spring, Spring, Spring; Sobbin' Women; Bless Your Beautiful Hide; Goin' Co'tin; Wonderful, Wonderful Day; June Bride; Lonesome Polecat Lament. **103m/C VHS, Beta, LV, 8mm.** Howard Keel, Jane Powell, Russ Tamblyn, Julie Newmar, Jeff Richards, Tommy Rall, Virginia Gibson; **D:** Stanley Donen. Academy Awards '54: Scoring of a Musical; National Board of Review Awards '54: 10 Best Films of the Year; Nominations: Academy Awards '54: Best Color Cinematography, Best Film Editing, Best Picture, Best Screenplay. *MGM, HMV*

The 7 Brothers Meet Dracula ♫½ *Legend of the Seven Golden Vampires* 1973 Seven siblings meet guy with dental anomaly. **110m/C VHS.** *GB* Peter Cushing, David Chang, Robin Stewart, Julie Ege; **D:** Roy Ward Baker; **M:** James Bernard. *NO*

Seven Chances ♫♫♫½ 1925 Silent classic that Keaton almost didn't make, believing instead that it should go to Harold Lloyd. Lawyer Keaton finds that he can inherit $7 million if he marries by 7:00 p.m. After his girlfriend turns down his botched proposal, chaos breaks loose when he advertises for someone—anyone—to marry him and make him rich. Suddenly he finds what seems to be hundreds of women willing to make the sacrifice, setting up one of the great film pursuits. Memorable boulder sequence was added after preview audience indicated climax was lacking that certain something. **60m/B VHS.** Buster Keaton, T. Roy Barnes, Snitz Edwards, Ruth Dwyer, Frankie Raymond; **D:** Buster Keaton. *NO*

Seven Cities of Gold ♫♫ 1955 An expedition of Spanish conquistadors and missionaries descend on 18th-century California, looking for secret Indian caches of gold. Semi-lavish costume epic. **103m/C VHS, Beta.** Anthony Quinn, Michael Rennie, Richard Egan, Rita Moreno, Jeffrey Hunter, Eduardo Noriega, John Doucette; **D:** Robert D. Webb. *FOX*

Seven Days Ashore/Hurry, Charlie, Hurry 1944 A comedy double feature. In "Seven Days Ashore," three merchant marines on leave in San Francisco become romantically involved with three women. In "Hurry, Charlie, Hurry," a henpecked husband finds himself in a lot of trouble. **141m/B VHS, Beta.** Gordon Oliver, Virginia Mayo, Dooley Wilson, Margaret Dumont, Leon Errol, Mildred Coles. *TTC*

Seven Days in May ♫♫♫½ 1964 Topical but still gripping Cold War nuclear-peril thriller. An American general plans a military takeover because he considers the president's pacifism

traitorous. Highly suspenseful, with a breathtaking climax. Houseman's film debut in a small role. **117m/B VHS, Beta, LV.** Burt Lancaster, Kirk Douglas, Edmond O'Brien, Fredric March, Ava Gardner, John Houseman; **D:** John Frankenheimer; **W:** Rod Serling; **M:** Jerry Goldsmith. Golden Globe Awards '65: Best Supporting Actor (O'Brien); Nominations: Academy Awards '64: Best Art Direction/Set Decoration (B & W), Best Supporting Actor (O'Brien). *WAR*

Seven Days' Leave ♫♫ 1942 Radio star-crammed musical comedy about a soldier who must marry a certain already betrothed gal (Ball) within a week so he can inherit a fortune. Songs include "Can't Get Out of this Mood," "A Touch of Texas," and "Baby, You Speak My Language." Following the completion of the film, Mature joined the Coast Guard. Lively but not memorable. **87m/B VHS, Beta.** Victor Mature, Lucille Ball, Harold Peary, Mary Cortes, Ginny Simms, Marcy McGuire, Peter Lind Hayes, Walter Reed, Wallace Ford, Arnold Stang, Buddy Clark, Charles Victor; **D:** Tim Whelan. *TTC*

Seven Deadly Sins ♫♫♫ 1953 A collection of tales concerning destructive emotions and the downfalls they cause. Contains shorts from some of Europe's finest directors (five French and two Italian). Stories and their directors are "Avarice and Anger" (de Filippo), "Sloth" (Dreville), "Lust" (Allegret), "Envy" (Rossellini), "Gluttony" (Rim), "Pride" (Autant-Lara) and "The Eighth Sin" (Lacombe). **127m/B VHS.** *FR IT* Eduardo de Filippo, Isa Miranda, Jacqueline Plessis, Louis de Funes, Paolo Stoppa, Frank Villard, Jean Richard, Francoise Rosay, Jean Debucourt, Louis Seigner; **D:** Eduardo de Filippo, Jean Dreville, Yves Allegret, Roberto Rossellini, Carlo Rim, Claude Autant-Lara, Georges Lacombe. *IVY*

Seven Deaths in the Cat's Eye ♫♫ 1972 A ravenous beast slaughters people in a small Scottish village. This flick reveals a little-known fact about felines. **90m/C VHS, Beta.** *IT* Anton Diffring, Jane Birkin; **D:** Anthony (Antonio Margheriti) Dawson. *PSM*

Seven Doors of Death ♫♫ *The Beyond* 1982 (R) A young woman inherits a possessed hotel. Meanwhile, hellish zombies try to check out. Chilling Italian horror flick. **80m/C VHS, Beta.** *IT* Katherine MacColl, David Warbeck, Farah Keller, Tony St. John; **D:** Louis Fuller. *LIV*

Seven Doors to Death ♫ 1944 Young architect tries to solve a crime to avoid being placed under suspicion. The suspects are six shop owners in this low-budget attempt at a murder mystery. **70m/B VHS, Beta.** Chick Chandler, June Clyde, George Meeker, Gregory Gay, Edgar Dearing; **D:** Elmer Clifton. *VCI, MRV, SNC*

7 Faces of Dr. Lao ♫♫♫ 1963 Dr. Lao is the proprietor of a magical circus that changes the lives of the residents of a small western town. Marvelous special effects and makeup (Randall plays seven characters) highlight this charming family film in the Pal tradition. Charles Finney adapted from his novel. **101m/C VHS, Beta, LV.** Tony Randall, Barbara Eden, Arthur O'Connell, Lee Patrick, Noah Beery Jr., John Qualen, John Ericson; **D:** George Pal. *MGM*

The Seven Hills of Rome ♫♫½ 1958 Quiet story of a television star (Lanza) who follows his girlfriend (Castle) to Rome after a lovers' quarrel, and there falls in love with Allasio. Fantastic music makes up for a weak plot. Based on a story by Giuseppi Amato. ♫ Arrivederci Roma; Seven Hills of Rome; Never Till Now; Earthbound; Come Dance With Me; Lolita; There's Gonna Be a Party Tonight; Italian Calypso; Questa o Quella. **107m/C VHS.** Mario Lanza, Peggy Castle, Renato Rascel, Marisa Allasio, Clelia Matania, Rosella Como; **D:** Roy Rowland; **W:** Giorgio Prosperi, Art Cohn; **M:** Georgie Stoll. *MGM*

Seven Hours to Judgment ♫♫ 1988 (R) When the punks who murdered his wife go free, a psychotic man (Leibman) decides to take justice into his own hands. He kidnaps the wife of the judge in charge (Bridges, who also directed) and leads him on a wild goose chase. Leibman steals the film as the psycho. Ex-Springsteen

spouse Phillips plays the judge's wife. Ambitious but credulity-stretching revenge/crime drama. Screenplay written by de Souza under the pseudonym Elliot Stephens. **90m/C VHS, Beta, LV.** Beau Bridges, Ron Leibman, Julianne Phillips, Al Freeman Jr., Reggie Johnson; **D:** Beau Bridges; **W:** Steven E. de Souza, Walter Halsey Davis; **C:** Hanania Baer; **M:** John Debney. *MED, VTR*

Seven Keys to Baldplate 1917 Early version of the famous stage play by George M. Cohen in which George Washington Magee accepts a challenge that he can finish a novel in 24 hours while staying at the deserted Baldplate Inn. **66m/B VHS.** Hugh Ford, Anna Q. Nilsson, George M. Cohan, Elda Furry, Corene Uzzell, Joseph Smiley, Armand Cortes, C. Warren Cook; **D:** Mae Gaston. *GPV*

Seven Keys to Baldplate 1929 Early talkie version of the film which was based on the famous stage play of the same name by George M. Cohan which follows an author into a deserted Baldplate Inn on a bet that he can't finish a novel in 24 hours while in the Inn. **70m/B VHS.** Richard Dix, Miriam Seegar, Crauford Kent, Margaret Livingston, Lucien Littlefield; **D:** Reginald Barker. *GPV*

The Seven Little Foys ♫♫♫ 1955 Enjoyable musical biography of Eddie Foy (played ebulliantly by Hope) and his famed vaudevillian troupe. Cagney's appearance as George M. Cohan is brief, but long enough for a memorable dance duet with Hope. ♫ Mary's a Grand Old Name; I'm a Yankee Doodle Dandy; I'm the Greatest Father of Them All; Nobody; Comedy Ballet; I'm Tired; Chinatown, My Chinatown. **95m/C VHS, Beta.** Bob Hope, Milly Vitale, George Tobias, Angela Clark, James Cagney; **D:** Melville Shavelson; **W:** Jack Rose, Melville Shavelson. Nominations: Academy Awards '55: Best Story & Screenplay. *COL*

Seven Magnificent Gladiators ♫ 1984 (PG) Seven gladiators team up to save a peaceful Roman village from total annihilation. Dismal effort at a remake of "The Seven Samurai"—see the original instead, please. Ferrigno was "The Incredible Hulk" on TV. **86m/C VHS, Beta.** Lou Ferrigno, Sybil Danning, Brad Harris, Dan Vadis, Carla Ferrigno; **D:** Bruno Mattei. *MGM*

Seven Miles from Alcatraz/Flight from Glory ♫♫ 1943 Dramatic double feature: Two escaped convicts discover a hideout for Nazi spies in "Seven Miles From Alcatraz," and an evil man tries to recruit pilots to fly planes over the Andes Mountains in "Flight From Glory." **127m/B VHS, Beta.** James Craig, Bonita Granville, Chester Morris, Van Heflin, Onslow Stevens; **D:** Edward Dmytryk. *TTC*

Seven Minutes in Heaven ♫♫ 1986 (PG) Sensitive love story about a 15-year-old girl who invites her platonic male friend to live in her house, and finds it disturbs her boyfriend, as these things will. Ever so tasteful (unlike most other teen comedies), with gentle comedy—but forgettable. **90m/C VHS, Beta, Closed Caption.** Jennifer Connelly, Byron Thames, Maddie Corman, Lauren Holly; **D:** Linda Feferman; **W:** Jane Bernstein. *WAR*

The Seven-Per-Cent Solution ♫♫♫ 1976 (PG) Dr. Watson persuades Sherlock Holmes to meet with Sigmund Freud to cure his cocaine addiction. Holmes and Freud then find themselves teaming up to solve a supposed kidnapping. Adapted by Nicholas Meyer from his own novel. One of the most charming Holmes films; well-cast, intriguing blend of mystery, drama, and fun. **113m/C VHS, Beta, LV.** Alan Arkin, Nicol Williamson, Laurence Olivier, Robert Duvall, Vanessa Redgrave, Joel Grey, Samantha Eggar, Jeremy Kemp, Charles Gray, Regine; **D:** Herbert Ross; **W:** Nicholas Meyer; **C:** Oswald Morris; **M:** John Addison. National Board of Review Awards '76: 10 Best Films of the Year; Nominations: Academy Awards '76: Best Adapted Screenplay, Best Costume Design. *USH*

Seven Samurai ♫♫♫♫ *Shichinin No Samurai; The Magnificent Seven* 1954 Kurosawa's masterpiece, set in 16th-century Japan. A small farming village, beset by marauding bandits, hires seven professional soldiers to rid itself of the scourge. Wanna watch a samurai movie? This is the one. Sweeping, complex human drama with all the ingredients: action, suspense, comedy. Available in several versions of varying length, all long—and all too short. Splendid acting. In Japanese with English subtitles. **204m/B VHS, Beta, LV.** JP Toshiro Mifune, Takashi Shimura, Yoshio Inaba, Kuninori Kodo, Ko Kimura, Seiji Miyaguchi, Minoru Chiaki; **D:** Akira Kurosawa; **W:** Akira Kurosawa; **M:** Fumio Hayasaka. Venice Film Festival '54: Silver Prize; Nominations: Academy Awards '56: Best Art Direction/Set Decoration (B & W), Best Costume Design (B & W). *HMV, HHT, CAB*

Seven Sinners 🎬🎬🎬 *Cafe of the Seven Sinners* 1940 A South Seas cabaret singer (Dietrich) attracts sailors like flies, resulting in bar brawls, romance, and intrigue. Manly sailor Wayne falls for her. A good-natured, standard Hollywood adventure. Well cast; performed and directed with gusto. **83m/B VHS, Beta, LV.** Marlene Dietrich, John Wayne, Albert Dekker, Broderick Crawford, Mischa Auer, Billy Gilbert, Oscar Homolka; **D:** Tay Garnett. *USH, NOS, BAR*

Seven Thieves 🎬🎬🎬 1960 Charming performances and nice direction make this tale of the perfect crime especially watchable. Robinson, getting on in years, wants one last big heist. With the help of Collins and Steiger, he gets his chance. From the Max Catto novel "Lions at the Kill." Surprisingly witty and light-hearted for this subject matter, and good still comes out ahead of evil. **102m/C VHS, Closed Caption.** Joan Collins, Edward G. Robinson, Eli Wallach, Rod Steiger; **D:** Henry Hathaway; **C:** Sam Leavitt. Nominations: Academy Awards '60: Best Costume Design (B & W). *FOX, FCT*

The Seven-Ups 🎬½ 1973 (PG) An elite group of New York City detectives seeks to avenge the killing of a colleague and to bust crooks whose felonies are punishable by jail terms of seven years or more. Unoriginal premise portends ill; plotless cop action flick full of car chases. Scheider tries hard. Directed by the producer of "The French Connection." **109m/C VHS, Beta, LV, Closed Caption.** Roy Scheider, Tony LoBianco, Larry Haines, Jerry Leon; **D:** Phil D'Antoni. *FOX*

The Seven Year Itch 🎬🎬🎬 1955 Classic, sexy Monroe comedy. Stunning blonde model (who else?) moves upstairs just as happily married guy Ewell's wife leaves for a long vacation. Understandably, he gets itchy. Monroe's famous blown skirt scene is here, as well as funny situations and appealing performances. **105m/C VHS, Beta, LV.** Marilyn Monroe, Tom Ewell, Evelyn Keyes, Sonny Tufts, Victor Moore, Doro Merande, Robert Strauss, Oscar Homolka, Carolyn Jones; **D:** Billy Wilder; **W:** George Axelrod, Billy Wilder; **C:** Milton Krasner. Golden Globe Awards '56: Best Actor—Musical/Comedy (Ewell). *FOX, FUS, GVV*

Seven Years Bad Luck 🎬🎬🎬 1920 French comic Linder has the proverbial seven years' bad luck all in one day (!) after he breaks a mirror. Original and quite funny; full of fetching sophisticated sight gags. Silent with music score. **67m/B VHS, Beta.** Max Linder. *GPV, VYY*

1776 🎬🎬🎬 1972 (G) A musical comedy about America's first Continental Congress. The delegates battle the English and each other trying to establish a set of laws and the Declaration of Independence. Adapted from the Broadway hit with many members of the original cast. Available in widescreen format on laserdisc. ♫ The Lees of Old Virginia; He Plays the Violin; But, Mr. Adams; Sit Down John; Till Then; Piddle, Twiddle and Resolve; Yours, Yours, Yours; Mama, Look Sharp; The Egg. **141m/C VHS, Beta, LV.** William Daniels, Howard da Silva, Ken Howard, Donald Madden, Blythe Danner, Ronald Holgate, Virginia Vestoff, Stephen Nathan, Ralston Hill; **D:** Peter H. Hunt; **C:** Harry Stradling Jr. National Board of Review Awards '72: 10 Best Films of the Year; Nominations: Academy Awards '72: Best Cinematography. *COL, FCT*

The Seventeenth Bride 🎬🎬 1984 Set in a Czechoslovakian town; a strong-willed young woman is slowly destroyed by the insanity of war and racism. **92m/C VHS.** Lisa Hartman Black, Rosemary Leach; **D:** Israeli Nadav Levitan. *NO*

Seventh Cavalry 🎬🎬½ 1956 A somewhat different look at Custer's defeat at the Little Big Horn. A soldier who was branded a coward for not taking part in the festivities tries to assuage his guilt by heading up the burial detail. The muddled ending tries to tell us that the Indians were afraid of Custer's horse. **75m/C VHS.** Randolph Scott, Barbara Hale, Jay C. Flippen, Jeanette Nolan, Frank Faylen, Leo Gordon, Denver Pyle, Harry Carey Jr., Michael Pate, Donald Curtis, Frank Wilcox, Pat Hogan, Russell Hicks; **D:** Joseph H. Lewis; **C:** Ray Rennahan. *NOS*

The Seventh Coin 🎬🎬½ 1992 (PG-13) The legendary King Herod minted seven coins bearing his image which have become coin collector Emil Saber's (O'Toole) obsession. (He's a homicidal lunatic who thinks he's the reincarnation of Herod anyway.) Saber has found six of the coins but the seventh has fallen into the unsuspecting hands of Salim (Chowdhry), a pickpocket who has actually snatched it from the equally unsuspecting Ronnie (Powers), an American teenager visiting Jerusalem (good local color). The two become allies when Saber comes after them. They're an appealing couple; O'Toole camps it up shamelessly; and the movie is easygoing escapism.**CW:** One use of strong language, moment of nudity, and some violence. **92m/C VHS, LV.** Alexandra Powers, Navin Chowdhry, Peter O'Toole, John Rhys-Davies, Ally Walker; **D:** Dror Soref; **W:** Michael Lewis, Dror Soref; **C:** Avi Karpik. *HMD*

The 7th Commandment 🎬½ 1961 Unlikely melodrama about a man afflicted with amnesia following an auto accident. He becomes a successful evangelist only to be blackmailed by an old girlfriend. Don't you just hate when that happens? **82m/B VHS.** Jonathan Kidd, Lynn Statten; **D:** Irvin Berwick. *NOS, LOO*

The Seventh Cross 🎬🎬🎬 1944 Tracy stars as one of seven men who escape from a German concentration camp. When it is discovered they're gone, the commandant nails seven crosses to seven trees, intending them for the seven escapees. Watch for Tandy ("Driving Miss Daisy") in her first screen appearance. Effective war-time drama. **110m/B VHS.** Spencer Tracy, Signe Hasso, Hume Cronyn, Jessica Tandy, Agnes Moorehead, Herbert Rudley, Felix Bressart, Ray Collins, Alexander Granach, George Macready, Steve Geray, Karen Verne, George Zucco; **D:** Fred Zinnemann; **C:** Karl Freund. Nominations: Academy Awards '44: Best Supporting Actor (Cronyn). *MGM*

The Seventh Floor 🎬½ 1993 (R) Kate's computer-controlled apartment becomes her prison when a psycho takes charge of the system. **99m/C VHS.** Brooke Shields, Massaya Kato, Craig Pearce, Linda Cropper; **D:** Ian Barry. *APX*

The Seventh Seal 🎬🎬🎬🎬 *Det Sjunde Inseglet* 1956 As the plague sweeps through Europe a weary knight convinces "death" to play one game of chess with him. If the knight wins, he and his wife will be spared. The game leads to a discussion of religion and the existence of God. Considered by some Bergman's masterpiece. Von Sydow is stunning as the knight. In Swedish with English subtitles. Also available on laserdisc with a filmography of Bergman's work and commentary by film historian Peter Cowie. **96m/B VHS, Beta, LV, 8mm.** SW Gunnar Bjornstrand, Max von Sydow, Bibi Andersson, Bengt Ekerot, Nils Poppe, Gunnel Lindblom; **D:** Ingmar Bergman; **W:** Ingmar Bergman; **M:** Erik Nordgren. Cannes Film Festival '57: Grand Jury Prize. *VDM, CRC, DVT*

The Seventh Sign 🎬🎬 1988 (R) A pregnant woman realizes that the mysterious stranger boarding in her house and the bizarre events that accompany him are connected to Biblical prophesy and her unborn child. Tries hard, but it's diffi-

cult to get involved in the supernatural goings-on. **105m/C VHS, Beta, LV, Closed Caption.** Demi Moore, Juergen Prochnow, Michael Biehn, John Heard, Peter Friedman, Manny Jacobs, John Taylor, Lee Garlington, Akosua Busia; **D:** Carl Schultz; **M:** Jack Nitzsche. *COL*

The Seventh Veil 🎬🎬🎬½ 1946 A concert pianist loses the use of her hands in a fire, and with it her desire to live. Through the help of her friends and a hypnotizing doctor, she regains her love for life. Superb, dark psycho-drama. Todd as the pianist and Mason as her guardian are both unforgettable. Wonderful music and staging. **91m/B VHS, Beta.** GB James Mason, Ann Todd, Herbert Lom, Hugh McDermott, Albert Lieven; **D:** Compton Bennett. Academy Awards '46: Best Original Screenplay. *NO*

The Seventh Victim 🎬🎬🎬 1943 Another Val Lewton-produced low-budget exercise in shadowy suggestion, dealing with a woman searching for her lost sister, who'd gotten involved with Satanists. The Hays Office's squeamishness regarding subject matter makes the film's action a bit cloudy but it remains truly eerie. **71m/B VHS, Beta, LV.** Kim Hunter, Tom Conway, Jean Brooks, Hugh Beaumont, Erford Gage, Isabel Jewell, Evelyn Brent; **D:** Mark Robson; **W:** Charles "Blackie" O'Neal. *TTC*

The Seventh Voyage of Sinbad 🎬🎬🎬 1958 (G) Sinbad seeks to restore his fiancee from the midget size to which an evil magician (Thatcher) has reduced her. Ray Harryhausen works his animation magic around a well-developed plot and engaging performances by the real actors. Great score and fun, fast-moving plot. **94m/C VHS, Beta.** Kerwin Mathews, Kathryn Grant, Torin Thatcher, Richard Eyer; **D:** Nathan (Hertz) Juran; **W:** Kenneth Kolb; **M:** Bernard Herrmann. *COL, MLB, CCB*

Severance 🎬 1988 An ex-pilot attempts to save his daughter from the world of drugs and violence. **93m/C VHS, Beta.** Lou Liotta, Lisa Nicole Wolpe, Linda Christian-Jones; **D:** David Max Steinberg. *NO*

The Severed Arm woof! 1973 (R) Trapped in a cave, five men are compelled to cut off the arm of a companion in order to ward off starvation. Then as luck would have it, they're rescued. Years later, one-by-one they meet a bloody demise. Is it the one-armed man? **89m/C VHS, Beta.** Deborah Walley, Marvin Kaplan, Paul Carr, John Crawford, David Cannon; **D:** Thomas Alderman. *CNG, MRV, GEM*

Severed Ties 🎬½ 1992 (R) Brilliant genetic scientist experiments with human limb regeneration in order to re-grow his accidentally severed arm. His strange mixture of lizard and serial-killer genes results in a repulsive reptilian limb with a nasty habit of slithering out of his shoulder. His mother discovers his experiments and tries to sell his discovery to the Nazis but her son escapes into a bizarre subterranean society and vows revenge. So bad it's just bad.**CW:** Language and strong horror violence. **95m/C VHS.** Billy Morrissette, Elke Sommer, Oliver Reed, Garrett Morris; **D:** Damon Santostefano. *COL*

Sex 🎬🎬½ 1920 Interesting dated relic. Morality play about a Broadway star who uses her charms to destroy a marriage only to dump her lover for richer prospects. The businessman she lands then shamelessly betrays her. What a title, especially for its time! **87m/B VHS, Beta.** Adrienne Renault, Louise Glaum, Irving Cummings, Peggy Pearce, Myrtle Stedman; **D:** Fred Niblo. *CCB, GPV, GVV*

Sex Adventures of the Three Musketeers woof! 198? Soft-core spoof of the Dumas classic. Dubbed. **79m/C VHS, Beta.** Inga Steeger, Achim Hammer, Peter Graf, Jurg Coray. *MED*

Sex and Buttered Popcorn 1991 (R) Stylish and entertaining documentary of the Hollywood sexploitation moguls, and their films, from the 1920s through the 1950s. These films shamelessly catered to audience's prurient interests, but typically delivered saccharin-coated morality messages and stock footage of routine baby births or the horrible effects of sexually transmitted diseases. Hosted by Ned Beatty, and featuring clips from the actual films, plus an interview with the widow of Kroger Babb, the most notorious of the exploiteers. A real hoot. **70m/C VHS.** David Friedman; **D:** Sam Harrison. *CPM, FCT*

Sex and the College Girl 🐾 1964
Folks talk about their relationship problems while vacationing in Puerto Rico. Tame talkfest providing Grodin with his first role. Included as part of Joe Bob Brigg's "Sleaziest Movies in the History of the World" series, probably just for the title. **?m/C VHS.** Charles Grodin, Richard Arlen, Luana Anders; **D:** Joseph Adler. *VTR*

Sex and the Other Man 🐾🐾 Captive 1995 (R) Bill's (Eldard) having this little impotence problem, which girlfriend Jessica (Wuhrer) naturally finds frustrating. So much so that she succumbs to the charms of her married boss, Arthur (Tucci). But when Bill catches them together in bed, his reaction is something none of them expected. Based on the play "Captive" by Paul Weitz. **CW:** Strong sexuality and language. **89m/C VHS.** Ron Eldard, Kari Wuhrer, Stanley Tucci; **D:** Karl Slovin; **W:** Karl Slovin; **C:** Frank Prinzi; **M:** Anton Sanko. *APX*

Sex and the Single Girl 🐾 1964
Curtis is a reporter for a trashy magazine who intends to write an expose on "The International Institute of Advanced Marital and Pre-Marital Studies," an organization run by Wood. Curtis poses as a man having marital trouble, using his neighbor's name and marital problems, in order to get close to Wood. Things get sticky when Wood wants to meet Curtis' wife and three women show up claiming to be her. This confusing but amusing tale twists and turns until it reaches a happy ending. Loosely based on the book by Helen Gurley Brown. **114m/C VHS, LV, Closed Caption.** Tony Curtis, Natalie Wood, Henry Fonda, Lauren Bacall, Mel Ferrer, Fran Jeffries, Leslie Parrish, Edward Everett Horton, Larry Storch, Count Basie; **D:** Richard Quine; **C:** Charles B(ryant) Lang; **M:** Neal Hefti. *WAR*

Sex and the Single Parent 🐾½ 1982
St. James and Farrell, both divorced, both with kids, have a relationship. Complications set in—just how does one be a single parent and have a fulfilling sex life in this day and age? Some of these made for TV efforts are so formulaic! **98m/C VHS, Beta.** Susan St. James, Mike Farrell, Dori Brenner, Warren Berlinger, Julie Sommars, Barbara Rhoades; **D:** Jackie Cooper. *TLF*

Sex Crimes 🐾🐾 1992 A tough female judge is brutally raped and she keeps the attack a secret. However, she does ask a friendly police detective to teach her how to use a gun. He's suspicious of her reasons and decides to trail her as she sets out for revenge on her attacker. Predictable actioner. **90m/C VHS, Closed Caption.** Jeffery Osterhage, Maria Richwine, Fernando Garzon, Craig Alan, Grace Morley; **D:** David Garcia. *ATV*

Sex, Drugs, and Rock-n-Roll woof! 1984 Several girls frequent a rock club looking for all the action they can get their hands on. **90m/C VHS, Beta.** Jeanne Silver, Sharon Kane, Tish Ambrose, Josey Duval. *NO*

Sex, Drugs, Rock & Roll: Eric Bogosian 1991 (R) Bogosian's 1990 concert performance, taped live at the Wilur Theatre in Boston, exhibits the electricity and finely nuanced characters for which he is justly famous. The characters share a depressingly negative side, however, which keeps this film from being strictly belly-laugh territory. **CW:** Language; drug/sex related dialogue. **96m/C VHS.** Eric Bogosian; **D:** John McNaughton; **W:** Eric Bogosian. *MPI*

Sex Is Crazy 🐾 1979 A melange from Italian horror director Franco containing some epic, some horror, some sex, some sitcom, and some documentary. Little green aliens touch down and impregnate earth women in one skit. In another, a gambler's girlfriend demands two thugs ravage her for the sheer sexual thrill. And in a third, a

severed hand commands a heroine to martyr herself to the great god Cucufat. Spanish with English subtitles. **81m/C VHS.** SP Lina Romay, Anthony Mayans, Tony Skios; **D:** Jess (Jesus) Franco. *VSM*

sex, lies and videotape 🐾🐾🐾 1989 (R) Acclaimed, popular independent film by first-timer Soderbergh, detailing the complex relations among a childless married couple, the wife's adulterous sister, and a mysterious college friend of the husband's obsessed with videotaping women as they talk about their sex lives. Heavily awarded, including first prize at Cannes. Confidently uses much (too much?) dialogue and slow (too slow?) pace. Available on laserdisc with a deleted scene and interviews with the director; also includes two theatrical trailers and a short film by Soderbergh. **101m/C VHS, Beta, LV, 8mm, Closed Caption.** James Spader, Andie MacDowell, Peter Gallagher, Laura San Giacomo, Ron Vawter, Steven Brill; **D:** Steven Soderbergh; **W:** Steven Soderbergh; **C:** Walt Lloyd; **M:** Cliff Martinez. Cannes Film Festival '89: Best Actor (Spader), Best Film; Independent Spirit Awards '90: Best Actress (MacDowell), Best Director (Soderbergh), Best Film, Best Supporting Actress (San Giacomo); Los Angeles Film Critics Association Awards '89: Best Actress (MacDowell); Sundance Film Festival '89: Audience Award; Nominations: Academy Awards '89: Best Original Screenplay. *COL*

Sex, Love and Cold Hard Cash 🐾🐾½ 1993 (PG-13) Sarah (Williams) is a high-priced hooker whose life savings ($20 million in stocks and bonds) have just been stolen. She hires an ex-con (Denison) to help recover the money and the two partners find themselves on the wrong side of some Mob trouble as well. Enough twists to keep a viewer interested as well as the prerequisite amount of shootings and chase scenes. **86m/C VHS.** JoBeth Williams, Anthony John Denison; **D:** Harry S. Longstreet; **W:** Harry S. Longstreet. *USH*

The Sex Machine woof! 1976 (R) In the year 2037, a scientist finds two of the world's greatest lovers and unites them so he can transform their reciprocating motion into electricity. It worked on paper. **80m/C VHS, Beta.** Agostina Belli. *MED*

Sex on the Run woof! Cassanova and Co.; Some Like It Cool 1978 (R) Love-starved wife of an oil-rich sheik, stimulated by the idea of having Casanova for her lover, teases her master into delivering him, but Casanova finds peace in the arms of three convent lovelies. Disgusting, amateurish, and offensive. **88m/C VHS, Beta, LV.** Tony Curtis, Marisa Berenson, Britt Ekland; **D:** Francosis Legrand. *VES, MON*

Sex Through a Window 🐾 Extreme Close-Up 1972 (R) TV reporter becomes an obsessive voyeur after filing a report on high tech surveillance equipment. Flimsy premise is a yucky, lame excuse to show skin. **81m/C VHS, Beta.** James McMullan, James A. Watson Jr., Kate Woodville, Bara Byrnes, Al Checco, Antony Carbone; **D:** Jeannot Szwarc; **W:** Michael Crichton. *LIV, VES*

Sex with a Smile 🐾 1976 (R) Five slapstick episodes by five different directors with lots of sexual satire pointed at religion and politics in Italy. Don't know much about Italy? Then you'll be left out of the joke here. And really, only one episode is funny anyway (the one with Feldman of "Young Frankenstein" fame). **100m/C VHS, Beta.** IT Marty Feldman, Edwige Fenech, Alex Marino, Enrico Monterrano, Giovanna Ralli; **D:** Sergio Martino. *GEM*

Sexpot 🐾 1988 (R) A voluptuous woman's rich husbands mysteriously keep dying, but not before they leave their fortunes to her. **95m/C VHS, Beta.** Ruth Collins, Troy Donahue, Joyce Lyons, Gregory Patrick, Frank Stewart, Jack Carter; **D:** Chuck Vincent. *ACA*

Sextette woof! 1978 (PG) Lavish film about an elderly star who is constantly interrupted by former spouses and well-wishers while on a honeymoon with her sixth husband. West unwisely came out of retirement for this last film role, based on her own play. Exquisitely embarrassing to

watch. Interesting cast. **91m/C VHS, Beta.** Mae West, Timothy Dalton, Ringo Starr, George Hamilton, Dom DeLuise, Tony Curtis, Alice Cooper, Keith Moon, George Raft, Rona Barrett, Walter Pidgeon; **D:** Ken Hughes; **M:** Artie Butler. *MED, MLB*

Sexton Blake and the Hooded Terror 🐾🐾 1938 Sexton Blake a British private detective a la Holmes, is after "The Snake," a master criminal, and his gang The Hooded Terror. One of a series of melodramatic adventures interesting chiefly for Slaughter's performance as the gangleader. **70m/B VHS, Beta.** GB Tod Slaughter, Greta Gynt, George Curzon; **D:** George King. *VYY, SNC, MRV*

Sexual Intent 🐾🐾 1994 (R) Based on the true story of pathological liar John Walsome, known as "the Sweetheart Scammer," who seduced and robbed more than 40 women. This con artist transformed himself into whatever kind of Mr. Right his victim needed—until he picked on the wrong woman. **88m/C VHS.** Gary Hudson, Michele Brin, Sarah Hill; **D:** Kurt MacCarley; **W:** Kurt MacCarley. *COL*

The Sexual Life of the Belgians 🐾½ La Vie Sexuelle des Belges 1994 Autobiographical comedy of sexual manners covering 1950 to 1978. Jan Bucquoy (Compere) grows up with a grim mother and immediately takes an interest in sex and beautiful women, which only heightens as he winds up in Brussels during the hedonistic '60s. He has a short, disastrous marriage, lots of affairs, not much sense, and a mocking disregard for Belgian provincialism. French with subtitles. **80m/C VHS.** BE Jean-Henri Compere, Isabella Legros, Sophie Schneider, Michele Shor; **D:** Jan Bucquoy; **W:** Jan Bucquoy; **C:** Michel Baudour. *FRF*

Sexual Malice 🐾🐾 1993 (R) Another erotic thriller finds a bored wife involved in an obsessive affair with a mystery man who has murder on his mind. Also available in an unrated version. **96m/C VHS.** Diana Barton, John Laughlin, Chad McQueen, Edward Albert, Don Swayze, Kathy Shower, Samantha Phillips; **D:** Jag Mundhra; **W:** Carl Austin. *APX*

Sexual Response 🐾🐾 1992 (R) Eve, a radio talk show "sexologist," is ironically unhappy in her marriage but scoffs at her producer's suggestion of an affair. That is until she meets a brash sculptor and they begin a torrid, and increasingly obsessive, romance. Her lover suggests that her husband have an "accident" with his hunting rifle, but Eve refuses and throws him out. The sculptor, however, breaks into the husband's loft to steal the rifle and finds some news clippings about the man's past that could ruin the lives of many. Little more than an excuse for torrid love scenes. Also available in an unrated version. **CW:** Language, violence, and strong sex scenes. **87m/C VHS, LV, Closed Caption.** Shannon Tweed, Catherine Oxenberg, Vernon Wells, Emile Levisetti; **D:** Yaky Yosha. *COL*

Sexual Roulette 🐾 1996 (R) A distaff and decidedly raunchier "Indecent Proposal." Jed and Sally wind up in money trouble and get in deeper by trying to recoup their loses (and losing bigtime) in a Vegas horse race. Then a rich blonde with some kinky preferences makes Jed an offer he can't afford to refuse. The unrated version is six minutes longer. **CW:** Strong, pervasive sexuality, a scene of violence and some language. **90m/C VHS.** Tane McClure, Tim Abell, Gabriella Hall, Richard Gabai, Myles O'Brien, G. Gordon Brer; **D:** Gary Graver; **W:** Sean McGinly; **C:** Gary Graver. *APX*

S.F.W. 🐾🐾 1994 (R) Get out your cliche-o-meter for another look at Generation X. Suburban teen Cliff Spab (Dorff) unwillingly becomes a media sensation during a terrorist hostage crisis at a convenience store. The phrasemaking teen's apathetic words are adopted by his peers just as he realizes that there is something he actually cares about—fellow hostage Wendy Pfister (Witherspoon), a cheerleader who wouldn't have given him the time of day before. A somewhat heavy-handed commentary on fame in our tabloid-intensive society. Title acronym stands for "So F***ing What." Many reviewers had a similar reaction. Based on the novel by Andrew Wellman. *CW:* Pervasive strong language; scenes of brutal violence; constant drug and alcohol use; some sexuality. **92m/C VHS, Closed Caption.** Stephen Dorff, Reese Witherspoon, Jake Busey, Joey Lauren Adams, Pamela Gidley, David Barry Gray, Jack Noseworthy, Richard Portnow; *D:* Jefery Levy; *W:* Jefery Levy, James Foley. *PGV*

Shack Out on 101 🎬🎬🎬 1955 A waitress (Moore) in an isolated cafe on a busy highway notices suspicious doings among her customers. What could they be up to? Communist subversion, of course. Of-its-era anti-pinko propaganda, but with a twist: Moore uncovers commie plots, pleases her customers, and fends off unwelcome lecherous advances all in 80 minutes, on a single set! **80m/B VHS.** Lee Marvin, Terry Moore, Keenan Wynn, Frank Lovejoy, Whit Bissell; *D:* Edward Dein. *REP*

Shadey 🎬🎬½ 1987 (PG-13) The premise for this oddball comedy came to someone in the wee hours: I've got it! Mild-mannered mechanic can film people's thoughts; wants to use his gift only for good, but needs money for a sex-change operation. Assorted bad guys want to use him for evil purposes. Strange, but not bad; Helmond's character is memorable. **90m/C VHS, Beta, Closed Caption.** GB Anthony Sher, Billie Whitelaw, Patrick Macnee, Katherine Helmond, Leslie Ash, Larry Lamb, Bernard Hepton; *D:* Philip Saville; *W:* Snoo Wilson; *C:* Roger Deakins; *M:* Colin Towns. *FOX*

The Shadow 🎬🎬½ 1936 Scotland Yard pulls out all the stops to track down a murderous extortionist, enlisting the aid of a novelist in their efforts. Long on talk and short on action. **63m/B VHS, Beta.** GB Henry Kendall, Elizabeth Allan, Jeanne Stuart, Felix Aylmer, Cyril Raymond; *D:* George Cooper. *NOS, SNC*

The Shadow 🎬🎬½ 1994 (PG-13) Who knows what evil lurks in the hearts of men? Why "The Shadow" of course, as is shown in this highly-stylized big screen version of the '30s radio show that once starred Orson Welles. Billionaire playboy Lamont Cranston (Baldwin) is a master of illusion and defender of justice thanks to his alter ego. Aided by companion Margo Lane (Miller), da Shadow battles super-criminal Shiwan Khan (Lone), the deadliest descendant of Ghenghis Khan. Numerous and elaborate special effects provide icing on the cake for those in the mood for a journey back to the radio past or a quick superhero fix. *CW:* Fantasy action violence. **112m/C VHS, LV, Closed Caption.** Alec Baldwin, John Lone, Penelope Ann Miller, Peter Boyle, Ian McKellen, Tim Curry, Jonathan Winters; *D:* Russell Mulcahy; *W:* David Koepp; *C:* Stephen Burum. *USH*

The Shadow Box 🎬🎬🎬 1980 Three terminally ill people at a California hospice confront their destinies. Pulitzer Prize-winning play by Michael Cristofer is actually improved by director Newman and a superb, well-chosen cast. Powerful. **96m/C VHS, Beta.** Joanne Woodward, Christopher Plummer, Robert Urich, Valerie Harper, Sylvia Sidney, Melinda Dillon, Ben Masters, John Considine, James Broderick; *D:* Paul Newman; *M:* Henry Mancini. *KAR*

The Shadow Conspiracy 🎬 1996 (R) Laughable innocent-on-the-run tale of presidential advisor Bobby Bishop (Sheen), who finds himself smack in the middle of an assassination conspiracy against the Prez (Waterston). Accused of murder, Bishop hooks up with ex-gal pal, reporter Amanda Givens (Hamilton) to get to the truth before the police and the bad guys get to them. Hunting the duo is a pro known as "The Agent" (Lang). Lang's lethal Agent comes off as one of the only believable characters here, perhaps because he has absolutely no dialogue to sabotage him. Sutherland fares better than most as Chief of Staff Conrad Jacob. Ludicrous plot twists and unconvincing performances by leads Sheen and Hamilton. *CW:* Violence and language. **103m/C**

VHS. Charlie Sheen, Linda Hamilton, Stephen Lang, Donald Sutherland, Sam Waterston, Ben Gazzara, Nicholas Turturro, Charles Cioffi, Theodore Bikel, Stanley Anderson, Dey Young, Gore Vidal, Paul Gleason, Terry O'Quinn; *D:* George P. Cosmatos; *W:* Rick Gibbs, Wayne Beach; *C:* Buzz Feitshans IV; *M:* Bruce Broughton. *TOU*

Shadow Creature 🎬 1996 (R) Detective investigating a series of grisly murders finds a mad scientist and a mysterious formula that could unlock the secrets of immortality. The downside being the entire mutation of all life on earth into monsters. **?m/C VHS.** Shane Minor. *MTH, LEO*

Shadow Dancing 🎬🎬½ 1988 (PG) The proprietor of the auspicious Beaumont Theater of Dance is haunted by one of his former dancers who died unexpectedly during a performance of "Medusa." Now, over fifty years later, Jessica, the pick for the lead in a new production, begins to take on her predecessor's mannerisms and spirit as she faces her impending doom. Surprisingly believable and suspenseful—and scary! **100m/C VHS, Beta.** Nadine Van Der Velde, James Kee, John Colicos, Shirley Douglas, Christopher Plummer; *D:* John Furey; *M:* Jay Gruska. *NO*

Shadow Force 🎬½ 1992 Homicide detective Rick Kelly is investigating the murders of a district attorney and a police sergeant. With the help of Mary, the usual beautiful female journalist, he uncovers a plot to assassinate key law enforcement officers. **?m/C VHS, LV, Closed Caption.** Dirk Benedict, Lance LeGault, Lise Cutter, Jack Elam, Glenn Corbett, Bob Hastings; *D:* Darrell Davenport. *IMP*

Shadow Killers 🎬½ 1980 There's no time to fear your own shadow, for there is a far more terrifying darkness stalking the city. **90m/C VHS, Beta.** Chen Ching, Chang Wu Lang, Chen Chiang. *NO*

The Shadow Man 🎬🎬 *Street of Shadows* 1953 A casino operator in London (Romero) is accused of killing a former girlfriend and works to clear himself. Family conventional action mystery: nothing to write home about. **76m/B VHS, Beta.** GB Cesar Romero, Simone Silva, Kay Kendall, John Penrose, Edward Underdown; *D:* Richard Vernon. *NO*

Shadow Man 🎬 1975 (PG) A mysterious thief, a master of disguise, sets out to steal the Treasure of the Knights Templar and nothing will stand in his way. **89m/C VHS, Beta.** Josephine Chaplin, Gert Frobe, Gayle Hunnicutt. *MED*

Shadow of a Doubt 🎬🎬🎬½ 1943 Uncle Charlie has come to visit his relatives in Santa Rosa. Although he is handsome and charming, his young niece slowly comes to realize he is a wanted mass murderer - and he comes to recognize her suspicions. Hitchcock's personal favorite movie; a quietly creepy venture into Middle American menace. Good performances, especially by Cronyn. From the story by Gordon McConnell. **108m/B VHS, Beta, LV.** Teresa Wright, Joseph Cotten, Hume Cronyn, MacDonald Carey, Henry Travers, Wallace Ford; *D:* Alfred Hitchcock; *W:* Thorton Wilder, Sally Benson, Alma Reville; *C:* Joseph Valentine; *M:* Dimitri Tiomkin. Nominations: Academy Awards '43: Best Story. *COL*

Shadow of Angels 🎬🎬 *Schatten der Engel* 1976 Beautiful prostitute Lily Brest's (Caven) latest client, a wealthy real estate investor (Lowitsch), just wants to talk and Lily's a good listener. So good, that more and more of her clients tell her all their darkest secrets and fears, leaving Lily herself falling into such a deep depression that she wonders if she can go on. Based on Fassbinder's play "The Garbage, the City and Death;" Fassbinder himself appears as a pimp. German with subtitles. **103m/C VHS.** GE Ingrid Caven, Klaus Lowitsch; *Cameos:* Rainer Werner Fassbinder; *D:* Daniel Schmid; *W:* Rainer Werner Fassbinder, Daniel Schmid. *WBF*

Shadow of Chikara 🎬 *Thunder Mountain; The Curse of Demon Mountain* 1977 (PG) A Confederate Army Captain and an orphan girl encounter unexpected adventures as they search for a fortune in diamonds hidden in a river in northern Arkansas. **96m/C VHS, Beta, LV.** Joe Don Baker, Sondra Locke, Ted Neeley, Slim Pickens. *VTR, NWV*

Shadow of China 🎬🎬🎬 1991 (PG-13) A young man struggles for power and love in Hong Kong, while an English beauty and an Oriental activist hold the keys to his future and a past which could destroy him. Excellent acting, stunning location photography. Exotic and intense. Based on the Japanese best-seller "Snakehead." **100m/C VHS, LV.** John Lone, Sammi Davis, Vivian Wu; *D:* Mitsuo Yanagimachi; *W:* Mitsuo Yanagimachi, Richard Maxwell. *COL, NLC*

Shadow of Chinatown 🎬½ 1936 Mad scientist creates wave of murder and terror in Chinatown. Edited version of a 15-chapter serial. **70m/B VHS, Beta.** Bela Lugosi, Bruce (Herman Brix) Bennett, Joan Barclay. *NOS, SNC, VCN*

Shadow of the Eagle 1932 Former wartime flying ace Wayne is accused of being a criminal known as "The Eagle." He's using his flying skills (which include skywriting) to threaten a corporation which has stolen plans for a new invention. But can Wayne really be our villain? 12-chapter serial. **226m/B VHS.** John Wayne, Dorothy Gulliver, Walter Miller; *D:* Ford Beebe. *GPV, VYY, VCN*

Shadow of the Thin Man 🎬🎬🎬 1941 In the fourth "Thin Man" film, following "Another Thin Man," Nick and Nora stumble onto a murder at the racetrack. The rapport between Powell and Loy is still going strong, providing us with some wonderful entertainment. Followed by "The Thin Man Goes Home." **97m/B VHS, Beta.** William Powell, Myrna Loy, Barry Nelson, Donna Reed, Sam Levene, Alan Baxter, Dickie Hall, Loring Smith, Joseph Anthony, Henry O'Neill; *D:* Woodbridge S. Van Dyke. *MGM*

Shadow of the Wolf 🎬🎬 *Agaguk: Shadow of the Wolf* 1992 (PG-13) Phillips is Agaguk, the son of the village leader, in this epic saga of survival set against the wilderness of the Arctic. Agaguk decides he cannot accept the white man's intrusion, so he sets out on his own. His father believes his departure to be the ultimate betrayal and casts upon him the "curse of the white wolf." Now Agaguk and his companion (Tilly) must face the harsh tundra alone and struggle to stay alive in the Great White North. Based on the novel "A-gaguk" by Yves Theriault. *CW:* Violence and sensuality. **108m/C VHS, LV, Closed Caption.** CA Lou Diamond Phillips, Donald Sutherland, Jennifer Tilly, Toshiro Mifune; *D:* Jacques Dorfman; *W:* Rudy Wurlitzer, Evan Jones. Genie Awards '93: Best Art Direction/Set Decoration, Best Costume Design. *COL*

Shadow on the Sun 🎬½ 1988 The life of Beryl Markham, pioneer female aviator and adventurer of the 1930s. Way too long and boring made for TV answer to "Out of Africa." On two cassettes. **192m/C VHS.** Stefanie Powers, Claire Bloom, Frederic Forrest, James Fox, John Rubinstein, Jack Thompson; *D:* Tony Richardson. *VTR, NWV*

Shadow Play 🎬½ 1986 (R) A successful female playwright is haunted by visions of a past lover. Her life slowly falls apart, but not before this film does. **98m/C VHS, Beta.** Dee Wallace Stone, Cloris Leachman; *D:* Susan Shadburne; *W:* Susan Shadburne. *VTR, NWV*

The Shadow Riders 🎬🎬 *Louis L'Amour's "The Shadow Riders"* 1982 (PG) Two brothers who fought on opposite sides during the Civil War return home to find their brother's fiancee kidnapped by a renegade Confederate officer who plans to use her as ransom in a prisoner exchange, and they set out to rescue the woman. Preceded by "The Sacketts" and based on the works of Louis L'Amour. Made for television. **96m/C VHS.** Tom Selleck, Sam Elliott, Ben Johnson, Katharine Ross, Jeffery Osterhage, Gene Evans, R.G. Armstrong, Marshall Teague, Dominique Dunne, Jeanetta Arnetta; *D:* Andrew V. McLaglen. *THV*

The Shadow Strikes 🎬½ 1937 Adaptation of the radio serial. The sleuth pursues a killer and a gangster. Meanwhile, the police try to pin a robbery on the "Shadow." Who did it? The Shadow knows! **61m/B VHS, Beta.** Rod La Rocque, Lynn Anders. *GPV, NOS, CAB*

Shadow Warriors 🐾½ 1995 (R) Cyborg Lurie joins with his creators to stop a series of killings. **CW:** Non-stop violence. 80m/C VHS. Evan Lurie, Terry O'Quinn, Timothy Patrick Cavanaugh; **D:** Rick Jacobson. *NHO*

A Shadow You Soon Will Be 🐾🐾 *Una Sombra Ya Pronto Seras* 1994 An allegory of the emptiness of contemporary Argentinian society, following the end of military rule, and based on a 1990 novel by Soriano, who co-wrote the screenplay. A man known merely as "The Engineer" (Sola) returns from Europe where he's lived in exile during the military dictatorship. Without family or friends, he wanders through the southern pampas, briefly communicating with other eccentric travelers, and non-commitally watching the world go by. Spanish with subtitles. 105m/C VHS. *AR* Miguel Angel Sola, Eusebio Poncela, Pepe Soriano, Alicia Bruzzo, Luis Brandoni, Diego Torres, Gloria Carra; **D:** Hector Olivera; **W:** Hector Olivera, Osvaldo Soriano; **C:** Felix Monti; **M:** Osvaldo Montes. *NYF*

Shadowhunter 🐾🐾 1993 (R) Glenn stars as a burned-out big city detective who is sent to a Navajo reservation in Arizona to bring a murder suspect back to Los Angeles. When the alleged killer escapes custody Glenn must track him across forbidding desert territory and face his suspect's unusual mystical powers. 98m/C VHS, LV, **Closed Caption.** Scott Glenn; **D:** J.S. Cardone; **W:** J.S. Cardone. *REP*

Shadowlands 🐾🐾🐾 *C.S. Lewis Through the Shadowlands* 1985 A look at the later life of bachelor-scholar C.S. Lewis (also the author of the "Chronicles of Narnia"). A devout proponent of Christianity, the middle-aged Lewis fell in love and married Joy Gresham, a divorced American poet with two young sons. Joy was diagnosed with cancer and her illness provided Lewis with the clearest test of his faith. Wonderful performances by both Ackland and Bloom. 90m/C VHS. *GB* Joss Ackland, Claire Bloom, Rupert Baderman; **D:** Norman Stone. *FRV, KAR, GFV*

Shadowlands 🐾🐾🐾 1993 (PG) Touching, tragic story of the late-in-life romance between celebrated author and Christian theologian C.S. Lewis (Hopkins) and brash New York divorcee Joy Gresham (Winger). Attenborough's direction is rather stately and sweeping and Winger is really too young for her role but Hopkins is excellent as (another) repressed man who finds more emotions than he can handle. Critically acclaimed adaptation of Nicholson's play will require lots of kleenex. 130m/C VHS, LV, **Closed Caption.** *GB* Anthony Hopkins, Debra Winger, Edward Hardwicke, Joseph Mazzello, Michael Denison, John Wood, Peter Firth, Peter Howell; **D:** Richard Attenborough; **W:** William Nicholson; **M:** George Fenton. British Academy Awards '93: Best Film; Los Angeles Film Critics Association Awards '93: Best Actor (Hopkins); National Board of Review Awards '93: Best Actor (Hopkins); Nominations: Academy Awards '93: Best Actress (Winger), Best Adapted Screenplay; British Academy Awards '94: Best Actor (Hopkins), Best Actress (Winger), Best Adapted Screenplay, Best Director (Attenborough). *HBO*

Shadows 🐾🐾 1922 A Chinese laundryman (Chaney) lives with a group of his countrymen in a New England seacoast village. All is peaceful until the local minister decides to convert the "heathen" Chinese. Ludicrous but worth seeing for Chaney's fun performance. Silent with music score. 70m/B VHS. Lon Chaney Sr., Harrison Ford; **D:** Tom Forman. *KIV, NOS, CCB*

Shadows 🐾🐾🐾 1960 Director Cassavettes' first indie feature finds jazz player Hugh (Hurd) forced to play dives to support his brother Ben (Carruthers) and sister Lelia (Goldoni). Light-skinned enough to pass for white, Lelia takes on the uptown New York art crowd and gets involved with the white Tony (Ray), who leaves when he finds out her true heritage. Meanwhile, Ben drifts along with his friends who abandon him when trouble finds them. Script was improvised by cast. 87m/B VHS. Hugh Hurd, Lelia Goldoni, Ben Carruthers,

Anthony Ray, Rupert Crosse, Tom Allen; **D:** John Cassavetes; **C:** Erich Kollmar; **M:** Charles Mingus, Shifi Hadi. *FXL*

Shadows and Fog 🐾🐾 1992 (PG-13) Offbeat, unpredictable Allen film that is little more than an exercise in expressionistic visual stylings. The action centers around a haunted, alienated clerk (Allen) who is awakened in the middle of the night to join a vigilante group searching the streets for a killer. Although reminiscent of a silent film, Carlo Di Palma's black and white cinematography is stunning. Several stars appear briefly throughout this extremely unfocused comedy. 85m/B VHS, LV, **Closed Caption.** Woody Allen, Kathy Bates, John Cusack, Mia Farrow, Jodie Foster, Fred Gwynne, Julie Kavner, Madonna, John Malkovich, Kenneth Mars, Kate Nelligan, Donald Pleasence, Lily Tomlin, Philip Bosco, Robert Joy, Wallace Shawn, Kurtwood Smith, Josef Sommer, David Ogden Stiers, Michael Kirby, Anne Lange; **D:** Woody Allen; **W:** Woody Allen; **C:** Carlo DiPalma. *ORI*

Shadows in the Storm 🐾🐾 1988 (R) A librarian/poet retreats to a secluded forest after losing his job. There he meets an exotically beautiful young woman who becomes his lover. With her love, she brings blackmail, murder, and mystery. 90m/C VHS, LV. Ned Beatty, Mia Sara, Michael Madsen; **D:** Terrell Tannen. *THV*

Shadows of Death 🐾½ 1945 Crabbe is the hero who must track down a gang of outlaws who kill to grab the land along the path of a new railroad. One of the "Billy Carson" series. 60m/B VHS, Beta. Buster Crabbe, Al "Fuzzy" St. John. *VCN, VCI*

Shadows of Forgotten Ancestors 🐾🐾🐾 *Tini Zabutykh Predkiv; Shadows of Our Ancestors; Shadows of Our Forgotten Ancestors; Wild Horses of Fire* 1964 Set in rural Russia in the early 20th century. Brings to expressive life the story of a man whose entire life has been overtaken by tragedy. Folk drama about a peasant who falls in with the daughter of his father's killer, then marries another woman. Strange, resonant and powerful with distinctive camera work. In Ukrainian with English subtitles. 99m/C VHS, Beta. *RU* Ivan Micholaichuk, Larisa Kadochnikova; **D:** Sergei Paradjanov. *CVC, AUD, HMV*

Shadows of the Orient 🐾🐾 1937 Two detectives are out to smash a Chinese smuggling ring. 70m/B VHS. Regis Toomey, Esther Ralston. *SNC, NOS, DVT*

Shadows on the Stairs 🐾🐾 1941 A creepy boarding house is the scene of a number of mystery-drenched murders. A bizarre assortment of suspects make things even crazier. 63m/B VHS, Beta. Frieda Inescort, Paul Cavanagh, Heather Angel, Bruce Lester, Miles Mander, Lumsden Hare, Turhan Bey; **D:** David Ross Lederman. *SNC*

Shadows Over Shanghai 🐾½ 1938 This adventure relic was set during the Japanese invasion of China prior to WWII and uses much newsreel footage of that infamy. As for the plot, it's a groaner about good guys and bad skulking around the eponymous port in search of a treasure. 66m/B VHS. James Dunn, Ralph Morgan, Robert Barrat, Paul Sutton, Edward Woods; **D:** Charles Lamont. *NOS, LOO*

Shadows Run Black 🐾½ 1984 A police detective must save a college coed from the clutches of a maniac wielding a meat cleaver. Ordinary slash-em-up. Bet Costner's embarrassed now about this early role - like Stallone's porno role in "The Italian Stallion." 89m/C VHS, Beta. William J. Kulzer, Elizabeth Trosper, Kevin Costner; **D:** Howard Heard. *NO*

Shadowzone 🐾🐾 1989 (R) As a result of NASA experiments in dream travel, an interdimensional monster invades our world in search of victims. Begins well, with slightly interesting premise, but degenerates into typical monster flick. Good special effects. 88m/C VHS, Beta, LV, **Closed Caption.** Louise Fletcher, David Beecroft, James Hong, Shawn Weatherly, Lu Leonard; **D:** J.S. Cardone; **W:** J.S. Cardone. *PAR*

ShadowZone: The Undead Express 🐾🐾½ 1996 (PG-13) Teenaged Zach (Leopardi) winds up in New York's subway tunnels where he meets the vampire Valentine (Silver) and his fellow bloodsuckers. Based on the book by J.R. Black; made for cable. **CW:** Some horror violence and gore. 98m/C VHS, **Closed Caption.** Chauncey Leopardi, Ron Silver, Natanya Ross, Tony T. Johnson, Ron White; *Cameos:* Wes Craven; **D:** Stephen Williams; **W:** Roy Swallows; **C:** Curtis Petersen; **M:** Reg Powell. *EVE*

Shaft 🐾🐾🐾 1971 (R) A black private eye is hired to find a Harlem gangster's kidnapped daughter. Lotsa sex and violence; suspenseful and well directed. Great ending. Academy Award winning theme song by Isaac Hayes, the first music award from the Academy to an African American. Adapted from the novel by Ernest Tidyman. Followed by "Shaft's Big Score" and "Shaft in Africa." ♫Theme From Shaft. 98m/C VHS, Beta. Richard Roundtree, Moses Gunn, Charles Cioffi; **D:** Gordon Parks; **W:** John D.F. Black. Academy Awards '71: Best Song ("Theme from Shaft"); Golden Globe Awards '72: Best Score; Nominations: Academy Awards '71: Original Dramatic/Comedy Score. *MGM*

Shaft in Africa 🐾🐾½ 1973 (R) Violent actioner finds detective Shaft forced into helping an African nation stop some modern-day slave trading. Second sequel, following "Shaft's Big Score." 112m/C VHS. Richard Roundtree, Frank Finlay, Vonetta McGee, Neda Arneric, Jacques Marin; **D:** John Guillermin; **W:** Stirling Silliphant. *MGM*

Shaft's Big Score 🐾🐾½ 1972 (R) This first sequel to the extremely sucessful "Shaft" has Roundtree's detective trying to mediate between several mobsters while investigating a friend's murder. Lots of action and an exciting Brooklyn chase scene involving cars, helicopters, and boats but still routine when compared to the original. Followed by "Shaft in Africa." 105m/C VHS. Richard Roundtree, Moses Gunn, Joseph Macolo, Drew Bundi Brown, Wally Taylor, Kathy Imrie, Julius W. Harris, Rosalind Miles, Joe Santos; **D:** Gordon Parks; **W:** Ernest Tidyman; **M:** Gordon Parks. *MGM*

Shag: The Movie 🐾🐾🐾 1989 (PG) The time is 1963, the setting Myrtle Beach, South Carolina, the latest craze shaggin' when four friends hit the beach for one last weekend together. Carson (Cates) is getting ready to marry staid Harley (Power); Melaina (Fonda) wants to be discovered in Hollywood; and Pudge (Gish) and Luanne (Hannah) are off to college. They encounter lots of music, boys, and dancing in this delightful film. Not to be confused with other "teen" movies, this one boasts a good script and an above average cast. 96m/C VHS, Beta, LV. Phoebe Cates, Annabeth Gish, Bridget Fonda, Page Hannah, Scott Coffey, Robert Rusler, Tyrone Power Jr., Jeff Yagher, Carrie Hamilton, Shirley Anne Field, Leilani Sarelle Ferrer; **D:** Zelda Barron; **W:** Robin Swicord, Lanier Laney, Terry Sweeney. *HBO*

The Shaggy D.A. 🐾🐾 1976 (G) Wilby Daniels is getting a little worried about his canine alter ego as he is about to run for District Attorney. Fun sequel to "The Shaggy Dog." 90m/C VHS, Beta. Dean Jones, Tim Conway, Suzanne Pleshette, Keenan Wynn; **D:** Robert Stevenson; **M:** Buddy Baker. *DIS, OM*

The Shaggy Dog 🐾🐾🐾 1959 (G) When young Wilby Daniels utters some magical words from the inscription of an ancient ring he turns into a shaggy dog, causing havoc for family and neighbors. Disney slapstick is on target at times, though it drags in places. Followed by "The Shaggy D.A." and "Return of the Shaggy Dog." 101m/B VHS, Beta, LV. Fred MacMurray, Jean Hagen, Tommy Kirk, Annette Funicello, Tim Considine, Kevin Corcoran; **D:** Charles T. Barton; **C:** Edward Colman. *DIS, BTV*

Shaka Zulu 🐾🐾🐾 1983 British miniseries depicting the career of Shaka, king of the Zulus (Cele). Set in the early 19th century during British ascendency in Africa. Good, absorbing cross-cultural action drama would have been better with more inspired directing by Faure. 300m/C VHS, Beta. *GB* Edward Fox, Robert Powell, Trevor Howard,

Christopher Lee, Fiona Fullerton, Henry Cele; **D:** William C. Faure. *PSM, FCT*

Shake Hands with Murder 🎬🎬 1944 Three people spend their time bailing criminals out of jail for profit. One is murdered, and the other two become implicated in comedy. **63m/B VHS, Beta.** Iris Adrian, Frank Jenks, Douglas Fowley, Jack Raymond, Claire Rochelle, Herbert Rawlinson, Forrest Taylor; **D:** Al(bert) Herman. *SNC*

Shake Hands with the Devil 🎬🎬🎬 1959 It's the Irish Republican Army against the British Black and Tans as Ireland fights for independence in 1921. Cagney is a teaching surgeon who is secretly a militant, obsessed with the idea of gaining Irish freedom. He urges his students to join with him, which Irish-American Murray does. When Murray learns that Cagney is out to sabotage a peace treaty, he must decide whether to betray Cagney in order to stop further violence. Cagney is excellent as the hard-bitten revolutionary who can't see beyond his own ideals. Filmed on location in Dublin, which further heightens the film's tension. **110m/B VHS.** James Cagney, Don Murray, Dana Wynter, Glynis Johns, Michael Redgrave, Sybil Thorndike, Harry Brogan, Robert Brown; **D:** Michael Anderson Sr.; **W:** Ivan Goff. *MGM, FCT*

Shake, Rattle and Rock 🎬🎬½ 1957 A deejay wants to open a teen music club playing rock 'n' roll, which has all the conservative parents up in arms. A court case follows (which the kids win). Incidental plot to the great music by Fats Domino, Joe Turner, Annita Ray, and Tommy Charles. Songs include "Ain't It a Shame," "Honey Chile," "I'm in Love Again," "Feelin' Happy," and "Sweet Love on My Mind." **76m/C VHS.** Mike Connors, Lisa Gaye, Sterling Holloway, Margaret Dumont, Raymond Hatton, Douglass Dumbrille; **D:** Edward L. Cahn; **W:** Lou Rusoff. *COL, MOV, MVD*

Shakedown 🎬🎬½ 1988 (R) Power-packed action film. An overworked attorney and an undercover cop work together to stop corruption in the N.Y.P.D. Although lacking greatly in logic or plot, the sensational stunts make this an otherwise entertaining action flick. **96m/C VHS, Beta, LV.** Sam Elliott, Peter Weller, Patricia Charbonneau, Antonio Fargas, Blanche Baker, Richard Brooks, Jude Ciccolella, George Loros, Tom Waits, Shirley Stoler, Rockets Redglare, Kathryn Rossetter; **D:** James Glickenhaus; **W:** James Glickenhaus; **M:** Jonathan Elias. *USH*

Shaker Run 🎬½ 1985 A stunt car driver and his mechanic transport a mysterious package. They don't know what to do—they're carrying a deadly virus that every terrorist wants! Car chases galore, and not much else. However, if you like chase scenes... **91m/C VHS, Beta, LV.** *NZ* Leif Garrett, Cliff Robertson, Lisa Harrow; **D:** Bruce Morrison. *NLC*

Shakes the Clown 🎬 1992 (R) Chronicles the rise and fall of Shakes, an alcoholic clown wandering through the all-clown town of Palukaville. Framed for the murder of his boss by his archrival, Binky, Shakes takes it on the lam in order to prove his innocence, aided by his waitress girlfriend Judy, who dreams of becoming a professional bowler. Meant as a satire of substance-abuse recovery programs and the supposed tragedies of a performer's life, the film is sometimes zany, but more often merely unpleasant and unamusing. Williams has an uncredited role as a mime. **CW:** Language and drug use. **83m/C VHS, LV.** Bob(cat) Goldthwait, Julie Brown, Blake Clark, Adam Sandler, Tom Kenny, Sydney Lassick, Paul Dooley, Tim Kazurinsky, Florence Henderson, LaWanda Page; *Cameos:* Robin Williams; **D:** Bob(cat) Goldthwait; **W:** Bob(cat) Goldthwait. *COL*

Shakespeare Wallah 🎬🎬🎬½ 1965 Tender, plausible drama of romance and postcolonial relations in India. A troupe of traveling Shakespeareans quixotically tours India trying to make enough money to return to England. Wonderfully acted and exquisitely and sensitively directed by Ivory. **120m/B VHS, Beta.** Laura Liddell, Geoffrey Kendal, Felicity Kendal, Shashi Kapoor, Madhur Jaf-

frey; **D:** James Ivory; **W:** Ruth Prawer Jhabvala, James Ivory. *NLC*

The Shakiest Gun in the West 🎬🎬½ 1968 Remake of Bob Hope's "Paleface" has Philadelphia dentist Jesse W. Heywood (Knotts) heading off for a new practice in the wild west of Big Springs. There he unwittingly takes on bad guys and sultry Penny (Rhoades), an undercover government agent who ropes the nervous dentist into marriage for the sake of her job. **101m/C VHS, Closed Caption.** Don Knotts, Barbara Rhoades, Jackie Coogan, Donald (Don "Red") Barry, Ruth McDevitt, Dub Taylor, Noriyuki "Pat" Morita; **D:** Alan Rafkin; **W:** James Fritzell, Everett Greenbaum. *USH*

Shaking the Tree 🎬🎬½ 1992 (PG-13) Group of four high school buddies are still in quest of self-fulfillment ten years after high school as they grapple with problems in the real world of adulthood, seeking distraction in adventure, romance, friendship, and sex. **CW:** Language. **97m/C VHS.** Arye Gross, Gale Hansen, Doug Savant, Steven Wilde, Courteney Cox, Christina Haag, Michael Arabian, Nathan Davis; **D:** Duane Clark; **W:** Duane Clark; **M:** David E. Russo. *ACA*

Shakma 🎬½ 1989 A group of medical researchers involved with experiments on animal and human tendencies toward aggression take a night off to play a quiet game of "Dungeons and Dragons." The horror begins when their main experimental subject comes along and turns things nasty! **101m/C VHS.** Roddy McDowall, Christopher Atkins, Amanda Wyss, Ari Meyers; **D:** Hugh Parks. *HHE*

Shalako 🎬🎬 1968 Connery/Bardot pairing promises something special, but fails to deliver. European aristocrats on a hunting trip in New Mexico, circa 1880, are menaced by Apaches. U.S. Army scout tries to save captured countess Bardot. Strange British attempt at a Euro-western. Poorly directed and pointless. Based on a Louis L'Amour story. **113m/C VHS, Beta.** Brigitte Bardot, Sean Connery, Stephen Boyd, Honor Blackman, Woody Strode, Alexander Knox; **D:** Edward Dmytryk; **C:** Ted Moore. *FOX*

Shall We Dance 🎬🎬🎬 1937 And shall we ever! Seventh Astaire-Rogers pairing has a famous ballet dancer and a musical-comedy star embark on a promotional romance and marriage, to boost their careers, only to find themselves truly falling in love. Score by the Gershwins includes memorable songs. Thin, lame plot—but that's okay. For fans of good singing and dancing, and especially of this immortal pair. 🎵Slap That Bass; Beginner's Luck; Let's Call the Whole Thing Off; Walking the Dog; They All Laughed; They Can't Take That Away From Me; Shall We Dance. **116m/B VHS, Beta, LV.** Fred Astaire, Ginger Rogers, Edward Everett Horton, Eric Blore; **D:** Mark Sandrich; **M:** George Gershwin, Ira Gershwin. Nominations: Academy Awards '37: Best Song ("They Can't Take That Away From Me"). *TTC, CCB, MED*

Shallow Grave 🎬½ 1987 (R) Four coeds en route to Florida witness a murder in rural Georgia and then are pursued relentlessly by the killer, a local sheriff. Decent premise and talented cast could have offered something better, given a meatier script. **90m/C VHS, Beta.** Tony March, Lisa Stahl, Tom Law, Carol Cadby; **D:** Richard Styles. *PSM, PAR*

Shallow Grave 🎬🎬½ 1994 (R) Juliet (Fox), David (Eccleston), and Alex (McGregor), three completely unlikable housemates, face a moral dilemma when their new roomie, Hugo (Allen), turns up dead of a drug overdose, leaving behind a suitcase stuffed with cash. Their decision to chop up the body, bury the bits, and keep the loot leads to a well-deserved descent into paranoia, betrayal, and dementia. Interesting character study in which the veneer of civility is totally destroyed at the first hint of temptation. Style wins out over substance as the characters are never humanized before they're demonized. **CW:** Contains scenes of strong, grisly violence; some profanity and nudity. **91m/C VHS.** *GB* Kerry Fox, Christo-

pher Eccleston, Ewan McGregor, Keith Allen, Ken Stott, Colin McCredie, John Hodge; **D:** Danny Boyle; **W:** John Hodge; **C:** Brian Tufano; **M:** Simon Boswell. *PGV*

The Shaman 🎬½ 1987 (R) Members of a family succumb to the hypnotic spell of the Shaman as he searches for the perfect one to inherit his powers. **88m/C VHS, Beta.** Michael Conforti, Elvind Harum, James Farkas, Lynn Weaver; **D:** Michael Yakub. *IMP*

Shame 🎬🎬🎬½ *The Intruder; I Hate Your Guts; The Stranger* 1961 Strangely unsuccessful low-budget Corman effort, starring pre-"Star Trek" Shatner as a freelance bigot who travels around Missouri stirring up opposition to desegregation. Moralistic and topical but still powerful. Adapted from the equally excellent novel by Charles Beaumont. Uses location filming superbly to render a sense of everydayness and authenticity. **84m/B VHS, Beta, LV.** William Shatner, Frank Maxwell, Jeanne Cooper, Robert Emhardt, Leo Gordon; **D:** Roger Corman. *NOS, DVT, FCT*

The Shame 🎬🎬🎬½ 1968 (R) A Bergman masterpiece focusing on the struggle for dignity in the midst of war. Married concert musicians Ullmann and von Sydow flee a bloody civil war for a small island off their country's coast. Inevitably, the carnage reaches them and their lives become a struggle to endure and retain a small measure of civilized behavior as chaos overtakes them. Deeply despairing and brilliantly acted. In Swedish with English subtitles. **103m/C VHS.** *SW* Max von Sydow, Liv Ullmann, Gunnar Bjornstrand, Sigge Furst, Birgitta Valberg, Hans Alfredson, Ingvar Kjellson; **D:** Ingmar Bergman; **W:** Ingmar Bergman; **C:** Sven Nykvist. National Society of Film Critics Awards '68: Best Actress (Ullmann), Best Director (Bergman), Best Film. *MGM, BTV*

Shame 🎬🎬 1987 (R) Strange Australian revenge drama about a female lawyer/biker who rides into a small town and finds herself avenging the rape of a 16-year-old girl. Is it a genuinely feminist movie about justice and a strong woman taking charge? Or is it exploitative trash using a politically correct theme and "message" as a peg for much - very much - gratuitous violence? Hard to tell. Cultish for sure; made on a B budget. **95m/C VHS, LV.** *AU* Deborra-Lee Furness, Tony Barry, Simone Buchanan, Gillian Jones; **D:** Steve Jodrell; **W:** Beverly Blakenship, Michael Brindley. *REP*

Shame 🎬🎬 1992 In a small logging town a group of violent high school toughs get away with rape because the women are too terrified to go to the cops. Then lawyer Diana Cadell (Donohoe) gets stuck in town when her motorcycle breaks down. When she finds out what's been happening, she urges one victim (Balk) to speak out and suddenly they become the targets of both the vicious attackers and a town which would like to hush the entire mess up. Very strong performances by Donohoe and Balk. Made for cable U.S. version of the same-titled 1987 Australian movie. **91m/C VHS.** Amanda Donohoe, Fairuza Balk, Dean Stockwell, Dan Gauthier; **D:** Dan Lerner; **W:** Rebecca Soladay. *PSM*

Shame of the Jungle 1990 (R) Animated spoof on Tarzan featuring the voices of John Belushi, Bill Murray, and Johnny Weissmuller, Jr. **73m/C VHS.** **D:** Boris Szulzinger, Picha; **V:** Johnny Weissmuller Jr., John Belushi, Bill Murray, Brian Doyle-Murray, Christopher Guest, Andrew Duncan. *JEF*

Shame, Shame on the Bixby Boys 🎬½ 1982 Somewhere in the Old West, outside a small town, lives a band of misfits who persist in rustling cattle. The Bixby Boys and their Pa have made a bad habit into a family tradition. **90m/C VHS, Beta.** Monte Markham, Sammy Jackson; **D:** Anthony Bowers. *TLF*

Shameless 🎬🎬 *Mad Dogs and Englishmen* 1994 (R) Wealthy Antonia Dyer (Hurley) is the self-centered, drug addict daughter of aristocrat Sir Harry Dyer (Treves). Her dealer is upper-class Tony Vernon-Smith (Brett), who's involved with Sandy (Delamere), the daughter of corrupt narcotics cop Stringer (Ackland). Stringer discovers the two girls know each other and irrationally blames Antonia for his daughter's heroin habit. Meanwhile, American student Mike (Howell) has been trying to get girlfriend Antonia off the drugs. Hurley's properly snooty and manipulative while Howell seems out-of-place and uncomfortable.*CW:* Strong drug use and for violence, sexuality and language. 99m/C VHS. *GB* Elizabeth Hurley, C. Thomas Howell, Joss Ackland, Jeremy Brett, Frederick Treves, Claire Bloom, Louise Delamere, Chris Adamson; *D:* Henry Cole; *W:* Tim Sewell; *C:* John Peters; *M:* Barrie Guard. *BMG*

The Shaming 🐾🐾½ *The Sin; Good Luck, Miss Wyckoff* 1971 (R) Puritanical schoolteacher is raped by a janitor, then develops a voracious sexual appetite. Horrible script, offensive premise can't be saved by good cast. Based on a novel by William Inge. 90m/C VHS, Beta. Anne Heywood, Donald Pleasence, Robert Vaughn, Carolyn Jones; *D:* Marvin J. Chomsky. *NO*

Shampoo 🐾🐾½ 1975 (R) A satire of morals (and lack thereof) set in Southern California, concerning a successful hairdresser (Beatty) and the many women in his life. A notable scene with Julie Christie is set at a 1968 presidential election-night gathering. Fisher's screen debut, only one year before "Star Wars" made her famous. Has a healthy glow in places and a perky bounce, but too many split ends. 112m/C VHS, Beta, LV, Closed Caption. Warren Beatty, Julie Christie, Goldie Hawn, Jack Warden, Lee Grant, Tony Bill, Carrie Fisher, William Castle, Howard Hesseman; *D:* Hal Ashby; *W:* Warren Beatty, Robert Towne; *M:* John Barry. Academy Awards '75: Best Supporting Actress (Grant); National Society of Film Critics Awards '75: Best Screenplay; Writers Guild of America '75: Best Original Screenplay; Nominations: Academy Awards '75: Best Art Direction/Set Decoration, Best Original Screenplay, Best Supporting Actor (Warden). *COL, CRC*

Shamus 🐾🐾 1973 (PG) Private dick Reynolds investigates a smuggling ring, beds a sultry woman, gets in lotsa fights. Classic Burt vehicle meant as a send-up. Unoriginal but fun. 91m/C VHS, Beta, LV. Burt Reynolds, Dyan Cannon, John P. Ryan; *D:* Buzz Kulik; *W:* Barry Beckerman; *M:* Jerry Goldsmith. *GKK*

Shane 🐾🐾🐾🐾 1953 A retired gunfighter, now a drifter, comes to the aid of a homestead family threatened by a land baron and his hired gun. Ladd is the mystery man who becomes the idol of the family's young son. Classic, flawless western. Pulitzer prize-winning western novelist A.B. Guthrie, Jr. adapted from the novel by Jack Schaefer. Long and stately; worth savoring. 117m/C VHS, Beta, LV. Alan Ladd, Jean Arthur, Van Heflin, Brandon de Wilde, Jack Palance, Ben Johnson, Elisha Cook Jr., Edgar Buchanan, Emile Meyer; *D:* George Stevens; *W:* Jack Sher; *C:* Loyal Griggs; *M:* Victor Young. Academy Awards '53: Best Color Cinematography; National Board of Review Awards '53: 10 Best Films of the Year, Best Director (Stevens); Nominations: Academy Awards '53: Best Director (Stevens), Best Picture, Best Screenplay, Best Supporting Actor (de Wilde, Palance). *PAR, TLF*

The Shanghai Cobra 🐾½ 1945 Below-average mystery has Chan hired by the government to investigate several supposed cobra bite murders. All motives lead to stealing a supply of radium. 64m/B VHS. Sidney Toler, Benson Fong, Mantan Moreland, Walter Fenner, James B. Cardwell, Joan Barclay, James Flavin; *D:* Phil Karlson. *MGM*

Shanghai Express 🐾🐾🐾½ 1932 Dietrich is at her most alluring in this mystical and exotic story that made legends out of both star and director. Dietrich plays Shanghai Lily, a woman of objectionable reputation, who has a reunion of sorts with ex-lover Brooks aboard a slow-moving train through China. Remade as "Peking Express." 80m/B VHS. Marlene Dietrich, Clive Brook, Anna May Wong, Warner Oland, Eugene Pallette, Lawrence Grant, Louise Closser Hale; *D:* Josef von Sternberg; *W:* Jules Furthman; *C:* Lee Garmes. Academy Awards '32: Best Cinematography; Nominations: Academy Awards '32: Best Director (von Sternberg), Best Picture. *USH, FCT*

The Shanghai Gesture 🐾🐾½ 1942 A wildly baroque, subversive melodrama. An English financier tries to close a gambling den, only to be blackmailed by the female proprietor—who tells him not only is the man's daughter heavily indebted to her, but that she is the wife he abandoned long ago. Based on a notorious Broadway play. Von Sternberg had to make numerous changes to the script in order to get it past the Hays censors; the director's final Hollywood work, and worthy of his oeuvre, but oddly unsatisfying. 97m/B VHS, Beta, LV. Walter Huston, Gene Tierney, Victor Mature, Ona Munson, Albert Basserman, Eric Blore, Maria Ouspenskaya, Phyllis Brooks, Mike Mazurki; *D:* Josef von Sternberg. Nominations: Academy Awards '42: Best Interior Decoration, Original Dramatic/Comedy Score. *MFV*

Shanghai Surprise 🐾🐾½ 1986 (PG-13) Tie salesman Penn and missionary Madonna (yeah, right) are better than you'd think, and the story (of opium smuggling in China in the '30s) is intrepid and wildly fun, but indifferently directed and unsure of itself. Executive producer George Harrison wrote the songs and has a cameo. 90m/C VHS, Beta, LV. Sean Penn, Madonna, Paul Freeman, Richard Griffiths; *Cameos:* George Harrison; *D:* Robert Bentley; *M:* George Harrison, Michael Kamen. Golden Raspberry Awards '86: Worst Actress (Madonna). *LIV, VES*

Shanghai Triad 🐾🐾🐾½ 1995 (R) Seventh collaboration of director Yimou and star Li takes place in violent crime dynasty of 1930s Shanghai. Here, eight days are seen through the eyes of a young boy (Cuihua) initiated into the Triad to be the lackey of the mob boss's arrogant mistress (Li). The trio and some trusty associates flee to the country after things heat up with a rival mob. Yimou subtly distinguishes the dichotomy between the jaded criminals and the naive youth with the move from the city to the country and his use of color and tone while avoiding cliche. Plot twists are fresh and technical aspects impeccable. Chinese with subtitles.*CW:* Some language and images of violence. 108m/C VHS, LV. *FR CH* Gong Li, Li Bao-Tian, Li Xuejian, Shun Chun Shusheng, Wang Xiaoxiao Cuihua, Jiang Baoying; *D:* Zhang Yimou; *W:* Bi Feiyu; *C:* Lu Yue; *M:* Zhang Guangtain. Nominations: Academy Awards '95: Best Cinematography; Golden Globe Awards '96: Best Foreign Film. *COL*

Shanty Tramp 🐾 1967 Small-town tramp puts the moves on an evangelist, a motorcycle gang, and a young black man, who risks his life trying to save her from her loose morals. Another cheesy flick made for the drive-in crowd. 72m/B VHS. Lee Holland, Bill Rogers, Lawrence Tobin; *D:* Joseph Prieto. *SNC, TPV*

Shao Lin Popeye 🐾🐾 1994 A poor, but optimistic school boy has a crush on the principal's daughter. The girl's rich and rowdy boyfriend naturally begins to harass the lovesick lad. Much kicking, punching, and yelling ensues. m/C VHS. *CH* Ge-Ying Lin, Shao-Wen Haw, Shiao-Long She. *TPV*

Shaolin Ex-Monk 🐾 1982 Renegade Shaolin Monk is pursued by a Kung Fu master and his disciple. 94m/C VHS, Beta. John Liu, Ko Shou Liang, Huang Hsing Shaw. *WVE*

Shaolin Executioner 🐾 1987 Several generations of Shaolin defend the Shaolin Temple against all high-kicking odds. 104m/C Beta. Chen Kuan-Tai, Lo Lieh; *D:* Lu Chia-Liang. *NO*

Shaolin Kung Fu Mystagogue 🐾 1984 In this action-packed chop-fest, the mysterious "Floating in Blood" weapon enlivens the battle between the Ching Dynasty and Ming rebels. 90m/C VHS, Beta. *D:* Chang Peng-I. *NO*

Shaolin Temple Strikes Back 🐾 1972 The protective inhabitants of the Shaolin temple defend themselves against invading Manchu Barbarians. 90m/C VHS, Beta. Chen Chien Chang, Sho Kosugi, Chang Shan, Lung Fei; *D:* Joseph Kuo. *TWE*

Shaolin Traitor 🐾½ 1982 (R) Exotic weapons and dazzling martial-arts action are featured in this exciting tale of intrigue and mystery. 99m/C VHS, Beta. Carter Wong, Shangkuan Ling-Feng, Lung Chun-Eng, Chang Yi, Lung Fei. *GEM*

Shaolin Vengence 🐾½ 1982 Framed for murder and deceived into accepting guilt for the crime, a man does penance in a Shaolin temple. When he learns of the deception, he uses his newly learned Shaolin boxing skills to relentlessly pound the creeps who set him up. ?m/C VHS. Chen Sing. *MGI*

Shark! 🐾½ *Man-Eater; Un Arma de Dos Filos* 1968 (PG) American gun smuggler Reynolds, stranded in a tiny seaport in Africa, joins the crew of a marine biologist's boat. He soon discovers the boat's owner and his wife are trying to retrieve gold bullion that lies deep in shark-infested waters. Typical Reynoldsian action-infested dumbness. Like "Twilight Zone: The Movie", earned notoriety because of on-location tragedy: a stunt diver really was killed by a shark. Edited without the consent of Fuller, who disowned it. 92m/C VHS, Beta. Burt Reynolds, Barry Sullivan, Arthur Kennedy; *D:* Samuel Fuller; *W:* Samuel Fuller. *REP, MRV*

Shark Hunter 🐾 1984 (PG) Shark hunter gets ensnared in the mob's net off the Mexican coast as they race for a cache of sunken millions. The usual garden-variety B-grade adventure. 95m/C VHS, Beta. Franco Nero, Jorge Luke, Mike Forrest. *PSM, MRV*

Shark River 🐾½ 1953 A man attempts to get his brother, a Civil War veteran accused of murder, through the Everglades and send him to safety in Cuba. Good photography of the great swamp; disappointing story. 80m/C VHS, Beta. Steve Cochran, Carole Mathews, Warren Stevens; *D:* John Rawlins. *NO*

Sharks' Treasure 🐾½ 1975 (PG) A band of escaped convicts commandeer a boat filled with gold. Old fashioned sunken-treasure tale unexceptional except as a virtual one man show by writer/actor/director/producer/fitness nut Wilde. 96m/C VHS, Beta. Cornel Wilde, Yaphet Kotto, John Neilson, Cliff Osmond, David Canary, David Gilliam; *D:* Cornel Wilde. *MGM*

Sharky's Machine 🐾🐾½ 1981 (R) A tough undercover cop (Reynolds) is hot on the trail of a crooked crime czar. Meanwhile he falls for a high-priced hooker. Well done but overdone action, with much violence. Based on the William Diehl novel. 119m/C VHS, Beta, LV. Burt Reynolds, Rachel Ward, Vittorio Gassman, Brian Keith, Charles Durning, Bernie Casey, Richard Libertini, Henry Silva, John Fiedler, Earl Holliman; *D:* Burt Reynolds. *WAR*

Sharma & Beyond 🐾🐾½ 1984 A teenage would-be science fiction writer falls in love with the daughter of a famous sci-fi author. 85m/C VHS, Beta. Suzanne Burden, Robert Urquhart, Michael Maloney; *D:* Brian Gilbert; *M:* Rachel Portman. *MGM*

Sharon's Secret 🐾🐾½ 1995 (R) When the mutilated bodies of wealthy Richard Harly and his wife are discovered, investigating detective Thomas McGregor (Henry) looks to place the blame on their traumatized 16-year-old daughter Sharon (Cameron), who'll inherit a fortune. Psychiatrist Laurel O'Connor (Harris) is assigned to help Sharon recover and she's defended by family attorney Frank Bowdin (McArthur) but it seems everyone has something to hide. Made for cable.*CW:* Some strong violence. 91m/C VHS, Closed Caption. Candace Cameron, Mel Harris, Greg Henry, Alex McArthur, Paul Regina, Elaine Kagan, James Pickens Jr.; *D:* Michael Scott; *W:* Mark Homer. *USH*

Sharpe's Battle 🐾🐾 1994 Sharpe (Bean) must prepare the Royal Irish company, led by Lord Kiely (Durr) and used to only ceremonial duties, for their first battle. Meanwhile, Kiely's wife (Byrne) goes to Sharpe for help with a personal matter and there's more trouble with the French. Based on the novel by Bernard Cornwell; made for British TV. 100m/C VHS. *GB* Sean Bean, Daragh

O'Malley, Hugh Fraser, Jason Durr, Allie Byrne; **D:** Tom Clegg; **W:** Russell Lewis. *VCO*

Sharpe's Company 🎬🎬½ 1994 Sharpe (Bean) sets out to rescue Spanish lover Teresa (Serna) and his infant daughter, trapped in the French-held city of Badajoz, which is about to be stormed by British troops. To make matters worse, Sharpe must also deal with the machinations of underhanded madman Sergeant Obadiah Hakeswill (Postlethwaite), an old enemy with a grudge to settle. Based on the novel by Bernard Cornwell; made for British TV. **100m/C VHS.** *GB* Sean Bean, Assumpta Serna, Daragh O'Malley, Pete Postlethwaite, Hugh Fraser, Clive Francis, Louise Germaine; **D:** Tom Clegg; **W:** Charles Wood. *VCO*

Sharpe's Eagle 🎬🎬½ 1993 Sharpe (Bean) and his chosen band of sharpshooters are once again in the thick of battle against Napoleon's troops but this time they have the misfortune to be led by the imbecilic Sir Henry Simmerson (Cochrane). Thanks to Simmerson's cowardice, the regimental colors are captured and a heroic officer Sharpe admires is killed. Setting out for revenge, Sharpe is determined to capture the French mascot, a carved golden eagle carried into battle, and settle some personal scores. Based on the novel by Bernard Cornwell; made for British TV. **100m/C VHS.** *GB* Sean Bean, Assumpta Serna, Brian Cox, David Troughton, Michael Cochrane, Katia Caballero; **D:** Tom Clegg; **W:** Eoghan Harris. *VCO*

Sharpe's Enemy 🎬🎬½ 1994 Sharpe (Bean) is sent to a mountain stronghold, held by a band of deserters, to ransom Isabella (Hurley), the bride of English colonel, Sir Augustus Farthingdale (Child). But the evil Hakeswill (Postlethwaite) is leading the criminals and he refuses to make things easy for our hero—nor will the French troops leave the English soldiers in peace. Based on the novel by Bernard Cornwell; made for British TV. **100m/C VHS.** *GB* Sean Bean, Assumpta Serna, Pete Postlethwaite, Daragh O'Malley, Hugh Fraser, Elizabeth Hurley, Michael Byrne, Jeremy Child, Nicholas Rowe; **D:** Tom Clegg; **W:** Eoghan Harris. *VCO*

Sharpe's Gold 🎬🎬½ 1994 Circa 1813 and Richard Sharpe (Bean) has now been promoted to Major—still leading his band of renegade sharpshooters. This time they're assigned to trade rifles for deserters held by the partisans and search for hidden Aztec gold, as Wellington (Fraser) prepares to push on into France. Sharpe must also protect Wellington's cousin Bess (Linehan) and her daughter Ellie (Ashbourne) as they search for Bess' missing husband. Based on the novel by Bernard Cornwell; made for British TV. **100m/C VHS.** *GB* Sean Bean, Daragh O'Malley, Hugh Fraser, Rosaleen Linehan, Jayne Ashbourne, Abel Folk, Peter Eyre; **D:** Tom Clegg; **W:** Nigel Kneale. *VCO*

Sharpe's Honour 🎬🎬½ 1994 Sharpe (Bean) becomes a pawn of French spy Pierre Ducos when he's forced to cross enemy lines, disguised as a Spanish rebel, in order to defend himself against allegations of dishonor. Sharpe's also unable to resist the attractions of the Marquesa Dorada (Krige), who's also part of Ducos' plan. Based on the novel by Bernard Cornwell; made for British TV. **100m/C VHS.** *GB* Sean Bean, Daragh O'Malley, Alice Krige, Hugh Fraser, Michael Byrne, Ron Cook; **D:** Tom Clegg; **W:** Colin MacDonald. *VCO*

Sharpe's Mission 🎬🎬½ 1996 Sharpe (Bean) joins with Colonel Brand (Strong) and his men to blow up an ammunition depot as Wellington continues his invasion of France. But Brand arouses Sharpe's suspicions that the supposedly heroic Colonel is actually a French spy. Based on the novel by Bernard Cornwell. **100m/C VHS.** *GB* Sean Bean, Daragh O'Malley, Hugh Fraser, James Laurenson, Mark Strong, Abigail Cruttenden; **D:** Tom Clegg. *VCO*

Sharpe's Regiment 🎬🎬½ 1996 Wellington prepares for the invasion of France in June, 1813 but the South Essex batallion needs more men. So Sharpe (Bean) and Harper (O'Malley)

are sent back to London for recruits and uncover corruption in high places. Based on the novel by Bernard Cornwell. **100m/C VHS.** *GB* Sean Bean, Daragh O'Malley, Nicholas Farrell, Michael Cochrane, Abigail Cruttenden, Caroline Langrishe, James Laurenson; **D:** Tom Clegg. *VCO*

Sharpe's Rifles 🎬🎬½ 1993 Swashbuckling heroics dominate as the Duke of Wellington's British soldiers battle Napoleon's French forces in the 1809 Penisular War (fought in Spain and Portugal). Common soldier Richard Sharpe (Bean) has just been promoted and given the unenviable task of leading a group of malcontent sharpshooters on a secret mission to aid Britain's Spanish allies. But it's not all hard times for Sharpe since the Spanish commander happens to be a very lovely woman. Adapted from the novel by Bernard Cornwell; made for British TV. **100m/C VHS.** *GB* Sean Bean, Assumpta Serna, Brian Cox, David Troughton, Daragh O'Malley, Julian Fellowes, Timothy Bentinck, Simon Andreu, Michael Mears, John Tams, Jason Salkey, Paul Trussell; **D:** Tom Clegg; **W:** Eoghan Harris. *VCO*

Sharpe's Siege 🎬🎬½ 1996 In the winter of 1813, Napoleon Bonaparte sends his best spy, Major Ducos (Atkine), to find out where Wellington plans to invade France. The newly married Sharpe (Bean) is forced to leave his ill wife, Jane (Cruttenden), and capture a French fort while preventing Duclos' treachery. Based on the novel by Bernard Cornwell. **100m/C VHS.** *GB* Sean Bean, Daragh O'Malley, Hugh Fraser, Abigail Cruttenden, James Laurenson, Feodor Atkine; **D:** Tom Clegg. *VCO*

Sharpe's Sword 🎬🎬½ 1994 Sharpe's (Bean) sent to protect Wellington's top spy, El Mirador, and finds himself up against Napoleon's top swordsman Colonel Leroux (Fierry). When Sharpe's wounded, it's up to Lass (Mortimer), a young mute convent girl, to save our hero's life. Based on the novel by Bernard Cornwell; made for British TV. **100m/C VHS.** *GB* Sean Bean, Daragh O'Malley, Patrick Fierry, Emily Mortimer, John Kavanagh; **D:** Tom Clegg; **W:** Eoghan Harris. *VCO*

Shattered 🎬🎬🎬 *Scherben* 1921 Key film in Germany's kammerspiel (chamber play) movement, which emphasized naturalism with a minimum number of characters. A railway worker's daughter is seduced by her father's supervisor. When the man abandons her, the girl's father takes revenge. **62m/B VHS.** *GE* Werner Krauss, Edith Posca, Paul Otto; **D:** Lupu Pick; **W:** Carl Mayer. *FCT*

Shattered 🎬½ *Something to Hide* 1972 **(R)** Finch plays Harry, a man blamed for a failed marriage, held hostage in his home by his own paranoia, and driven to bouts of drinking. Slowly his tenuous grip on sanity slips and at any moment his fragile and crumbling life may be shattered. Tired, overwrought domestic drama. **100m/C VHS, Beta.** *GB* Peter Finch, Shelley Winters, Colin Blakely; **D:** Alastair Reid. *MED*

Shattered 🎬🎬 1991 **(R)** An architect recovering from a serious automobile accident tries to regain the memory that he has lost. As he begins to put together the pieces of his life, some parts of the puzzle don't quite fit. For example, he recalls his now loving wife's affair as well as his own. He remembers that he hired a private detective to follow his wife and shockingly, he remembers that he once believed his wife had planned to kill him. Are these memories the real thing, or are they all part of some mad, recuperative nightmare? Who knows.**CW:** Language, violence, and sensuality. **98m/C VHS, Beta, LV, 8mm, Closed Caption.** Tom Berenger, Bob Hoskins, Greta Scacchi, Joanne Whalley, Corbin Bernsen, Theodore Bikel; **D:** Wolfgang Petersen; **W:** Wolfgang Petersen. *MGM*

Shattered Dreams 🎬🎬½ 1994 TV movie about domestic violence finds Wagner as the battered wife of a prominent, high-profile government official. Based on a true story. **94m/C VHS.** Lindsay Wagner, Michael Nouri. *LIV*

Shattered Image 🎬🎬½ 1993 **(R)** Confusing thriller about the FBI's involvement in the kidnapping of the owner of a model agency, as well as plastic surgery, and a big money scam. Made for cable TV.**CW:** Language, violence, brief nudity, sex. **100m/C VHS, LV, Closed Caption.** Bo Derek, Jack Scalia, John Savage, Dorian Harewood, Ramon Franco, Carol Lawrence, Michael Harris, David McCallum; **D:** Fritz Kiersch. *THV*

Shattered Silence 🎬½ *When Michael Calls* 1971 A woman is tormented by phone calls that seem to be coming from her dead son as her life is torn apart by divorce. Leaves unanswered the question: Will there be any suspense? Made for TV. Worthless and dumb. **73m/C VHS.** Elizabeth Ashley, Ben Gazzara, Michael Douglas, Karen Pearson; **D:** Philip Leacock. *CCB*

Shattered Spirits 🎬½ 1991 **(PG-13)** Quiet family man cracks and goes on a rampage through his normally peaceful suburban neighborhood. Been done before and better. **93m/C VHS.** Martin Sheen, Melinda Dillon, Matthew Laborteaux, Roxana Zal, Lukas Haas. *THV*

Shattered Vows 🎬🎬 1984 A young nun struggles with her love for a priest and her desire for a child. Bertinelli is convincing as the confused teen in otherwise ordinary TV drama. Adapted from the true story of Dr. Mary Gilligan Wong as told in her book, "Nun: A Memoir." **95m/C VHS, Beta, Closed Caption.** Valerie Bertinelli, David Morse, Caroline McWilliams, Patricia Neal, Millie Perkins, Leslie Ackerman, Lisa Jane Persky; **D:** Jack Bender. *FRH*

The Shawshank Redemption 🎬🎬🎬½ 1994 **(R)** Bank veep Andy (Robbins) is convicted of the murder of his wife and her lover and sentenced to the "toughest prison in the Northeast." While there he forms a friendship with lifer Red (Freeman), experiences the brutality of prison life, adapts, offers financial advice to the guards, and helps the warden (Gunton) cook the prison books...all in a short 19 years. In his debut, director Darabont avoids belaboring most prison movie cliches while Robbins' talent for playing ambiguous characters is put to good use, and Freeman brings his usual grace to what could have been a thankless role. Adapted from the novella "Rita Hayworth and the Shawshank Redemption" by Stephen King.**CW:** Profanity; occasional violence. **142m/C VHS, LV, Closed Caption.** Tim Robbins, Morgan Freeman, Bob Gunton, William Sadler, Clancy Brown, Mark Rolston, Gil Bellows, James Whitmore; **D:** Frank Darabont; **W:** Frank Darabont; **C:** Roger Deakins. Nominations: Academy Awards '94: Best Actor (Freeman), Best Adapted Screenplay, Best Cinematography, Best Film Editing, Best Picture, Best Sound, Best Original Score; Directors Guild of America Awards '94: Best Director (Darabont); Golden Globe Awards '95: Best Actor—Drama (Freeman), Best Screenplay; Screen Actors Guild Award '94: Best Actor (Freeman), Best Actor (Robbins); Writers Guild of America '94: Best Adapted Screenplay. *COL*

She 🎬🎬½ 1921 H. Rider Haggard's famous story about the ageless Queen Ayesha, (Blythe), who renews her life force periodically by walking through a pillar of cold flame. Story and titles by Haggard. Blythe is a stirringly mean queen, and the story remains fresh and fun. Silent film with music score. **69m/B VHS, Beta.** Betty Blythe, Carlyle Blackwell, Mary Odette. *NOS, VYY, DVT*

She 🎬🎬½ 1935 First sound version of H. Rider Haggard's popular 1887 adventure tale, although the film's location was changed from Africa to the frozen Arctic. Explorers Scott and Bruce are searching for a fire that preserves rather than destroys life. They are captured by a mysterious tribe and discover a living goddess—She-Who-Must-Be-Obeyed (Gahagan)—who bathed in the Flame of Life and is now eternal. She falls for Scott, who doesn't return her love, and there's trouble. Fantastic Art Deco sets and special effects. **95m/B VHS.** Helen Gahagan, Randolph Scott, Nigel Bruce, Helen Mack, Gustav von Seyffertitz; **D:** Irving Pichel.

Lansing C. Holden; **W:** Dudley Nichols, Ruth Rose; **C:** J. Roy Hunt; **M:** Max Steiner. *KIV*

S*H*E 🎬🎬 **1979** A flashy made for TV spy thriller. The female agent S*H*E (Securities Hazards Expert) must save the world's oil; good locations, nifty plot and looker Sharpe as the she-Bond add up to a reasonably fun time. Scripted by "Bond"-writer Maibaum. **100m/C VHS, Beta.** Cornelia Sharpe, Robert Lansing, William Taylor, Isabella Rye, Anita Ekberg; *Cameos:* Omar Sharif; **D:** Robert Lewis; **W:** Richard Maibaum; **M:** Michael Kamen. *PSM*

She 🎬 **1983** A beautiful female warrior rules over the men in a post-holocaust world. She is kidnapped by a wealthy merchant who uses her to fight evil mutants. Utter rubbish vaguely based on the Haggard novel. **90m/C VHS, Beta.** Sandahl Bergman, Harrison Muller, Quin Kessler, David Goss; **D:** Avi Nesher. *LIV*

She and He 🎬🎬½ **1963** Hani's look at the oppression of women, marital and spiritual discontent, and class divisions. Naoko is a bored housewife, living in a sterile high-rise apartment with her equally dissatisfied husband, and yearning for something to express her inner feelings. She accidentally meets an old classmate of her husband's who has become a poor ragpicker and tries to aid him. But all her efforts only lead to further tragedies. In Japanese with English subtitles. **110m/C VHS.** *JP* Sachiko Hidari, Eiji Okada, Kikuji Yamashita; **D:** Susumu Hani. *FCT*

The She-Beast 🎬½ *Il Lago di Satana; The Revenge of the Blood Beast* **1965** Burned at the stake in 18th-century Transylvania, a witch returns in the body of a beautiful young English woman on her honeymoon (in Transylvania?!), and once again wreaks death and destruction. Caution, Barbara Steele fans: she appears for all of fifteen minutes. Sporadically funny. **74m/C VHS, Beta.** *IT YU* Barbara Steele, Ian Ogilvy, Mel Welles, Lucretia Love; **D:** Michael Reeves. *SNC, MPI*

She Came on the Bus woof! **1969** Young thugs break into a well-kept suburban home and terrorize the housewife through rape and torture. Then they kidnap a bus and pose as the drivers until they can find more victims. Contains scenes of graphic violence which would be considered offensive even by today's standards. **58m/C VHS.** **D:** Harry Vincent. *SMW, TPV*

She Came to the Valley 🎬 *Texas in Flames* **1977 (PG)** A tough pioneer woman becomes embroiled in political intrigue during the Spanish-American War. Based on Cleo Dawson's book. **90m/C VHS, Beta.** Ronee Blakley, Dean Stockwell, Scott Glenn, Freddy Fender. *MED, CNG*

She Couldn't Say No 🎬🎬 *Beautiful But Dangerous* **1952** A wealthy oil heiress (Simmons) with good intentions plans to give her money away to those friends who had helped her when she was struggling. Things don't go quite as planned; her philanthropy leads to unexpected mayhem in her Arkansas hometown. Passable, but not memorable comedy. Mitchum as a small-town doctor? **88m/B VHS, Beta.** Robert Mitchum, Jean Simmons, Arthur Hunnicutt, Edgar Buchanan, Wallace Ford; **D:** Lloyd Bacon. *CCB*

She Demons woof! **1958** Pleasure craft loaded with babes crashes into a remote island controlled by a mad ex-Nazi scientist who transforms pretty girls into rubber-faced Frankensteins. Incomprehensible, to say the least. **68m/B VHS, Beta.** Irish McCalla, Tod Griffin, Victor Sen Yung; **D:** Richard Cunha. *RHI, SNC, EEL*

She-Devil 🎬🎬½ **1989 (PG-13)** A comic book version of the acidic Fay Weldon novel "The Life and Loves of a She-Devil"; a fat, dowdy suburban wife (Arnold) becomes a vengeful beast when a smarmy romance novelist steals her husband. Uneven comedic reworking of a distinctly unforgiving feminist fiction. Arnold is given too much to handle (her role requires an actual range of emotions); Streep's role is too slight, though she does great things with it. **100m/C VHS, Beta, LV, Closed**

Caption. Meryl Streep, Roseanne, Ed Begley Jr., Linda Hunt, Elizabeth Peters, Bryan Larkin, A. Martinez, Sylvia Miles; **D:** Susan Seidelman; **W:** Mark Burns, Barry Strugatz; **M:** Howard Shore. *ORI*

She Devils in Chains 🎬🎬 **19?? (R)** A group of traveling female athletes are kidnapped by a groups of sadists who torture and beat them. In the end, however, the girls get their revenge, and it's bloody. **82m/C VHS, Beta.** Colleen Camp, Rosanne Katon, Sylvia Anderson, Ken Washington, Leo Martinez; **D:** Cirio H. Santiago. *SIM*

She-Devils on Wheels woof! **1968** Havoc erupts as an outlaw female motorcycle gang, known as "Maneaters on Motorbikes," terrorizes a town—especially the men. Really, really bad biker flick finely honed by Lewis. **83m/C VHS, Beta.** Betty Connell, Christie Wagner, Pat Poston, Nancy Lee Noble, Ruby Tuesday; **D:** Herschell Gordon Lewis. *VTR*

She Done Him Wrong 🎬🎬🎬 **1933** West stars as Lil, an 1890s saloon singer in the screen version of her Broadway hit "Diamond Lily," and imparts on the negligible plot her usual share of double entendres and racy comments. Grant is likeable as the hapless sap she beds. ♫Silver Threads Among the Gold; Masie, My Pretty Daisy; Easy Rider; I Like a Guy What Takes His Time; Frankie and Johnny. **65m/B VHS, Beta, LV.** Mae West, Cary Grant, Owen Moore, Noah Beery Sr., Gilbert Roland, Louise Beavers; **D:** Lowell Sherman; **C:** Charles B(ryant) Lang. National Board of Review Awards '33: 10 Best Films of the Year; Nominations: Academy Awards '33: Best Picture. *USH, MLB, BTV*

She-Freak 🎬 *Alley of Nightmares* **1967** Remake of Tod Browning's "Freaks." A cynical waitress burns everyone in a circus and gets mauled by the resident freaks. Pales beside its unacknowledged, classic original. **87m/C VHS, Beta.** Claire Brennan, Lynn Courtney, Bill McKinney, Lee Raymond, Madame Lee; **D:** Byron Mabe. *NO*

She Gods of Shark Reef 🎬 *Shark Reef* **1956** Typical no-budget Corman exploitation tale of two brothers shipwrecked on an island inhabited by beautiful pearl-diving women. Filmed in Hawaii. **63m/C VHS.** Bill Cord, Don Durant, Lisa Montell, Carol Lindsay, Jeanne Gerson; **D:** Roger Corman. *SNC, MRV, HEG*

She Goes to War 🎬🎬 **1929** King's first part-sound effort that takes place in the milieu of WWI. Boardman plays a spoiled rich girl who grows up fast when confronted with the horrors of the frontline while working in a canteen. **50m/B VHS, Beta, 8mm.** Eleanor Boardman, Alma Rubens, Al "Fuzzy" St. John; **D:** Henry King. *NOS, GVV, DVT*

She Likes You, Charlie Brown 1986 Romantic travails for Charlie Brown and the gang. Animated. **41m/C VHS, Beta.** *BAR*

She Must Be Seeing Things 🎬🎬 **1987** Filmmaker Jo (Weaver) is making a picture about a 17th-century woman who lived her life as a man. Jo's lover Agatha (Dabney) becomes disturbed when she reads Jo's diary, learns she's been having affairs with men, and begins to fantasize about Jo's unfaithfulness with the men in her film crew. Agatha's insecurities finally lead her to disguising herself as a man in order to spy on Jo—mirroring what's happening in Jo's film. **95m/C VHS.** Sheila Dabney, Lois Weaver, Kyle DiCamp, John Erdman; **D:** Sheila McLaughlin; **W:** Sheila McLaughlin. *TVC, FRF*

She Shall Have Music 🎬½ **1936** A magnate hires a dance band to broadcast from a cruise ship. Features music by Jack Hylton and his band, one of Britain's most popular orchestras of the 1930s. **76m/B VHS, Beta.** *GB* Jack Hylton, June Clyde, Claude Dampier, Bryan Lawrence, Gwen Farrar. *EEL*

She Waits 🎬🎬 **1971** When a newlywed couple moves into an old house, the bride becomes possessed by the spirit of her husband's first wife. Unoriginal and mediocre horror. Made for television. **74m/C VHS, Beta.** Dorothy McGuire, Patty Duke, David McCallum; **D:** Delbert Mann. *PSM*

She Wore a Yellow Ribbon 🎬🎬🎬½ **1949** An undermanned cavalry outpost makes a desperate attempt to repel invading Indians. Wayne shines as an officer who shuns retirement in order to help his comrades. Still fun and compelling. The second chapter in director Ford's noted cavalry trilogy, preceded by "Fort Apache" and followed by "Rio Grande." **93m/C VHS, Beta, LV.** John Wayne, Joanne Dru, John Agar, Ben Johnson, Harry Carey Jr., Victor McLaglen, Mildred Natwick, George O'Brien; **D:** John Ford; **C:** Winton C. Hoch. Academy Awards '49: Best Color Cinematography. *TTC, TLF*

Sheba, Baby 🎬🎬 **1975 (PG)** A female dick (Grier) heads to Louisville where someone is trying to threaten her rich father and his loan company. Oddly non-violent for action-flick vet Grier; poorly written and directed. **90m/C VHS, Beta.** Pam Grier, Rudy Challenger, Austin Stoker, D'Urville Martin, Charles Kissinger; **D:** William Girdler. *ORI, FCT*

Sheena woof! **1984 (PG)** Television sportscaster aids a jungle queen in defending her kingdom from being overthrown by an evil prince. Horrid bubble-gum "action" fantasy. **117m/C VHS, Beta, LV, Closed Caption.** Tanya Roberts, Ted Wass, Donovan Scott, Elizabeth Toro; **D:** John Guillermin; **W:** David Newman; **C:** Pasquale De Santos. *GKK*

The Sheep Has Five Legs 🎬🎬½ **1954** Quintuplet brothers return from around the world for a reunion in their small French village. Fernandel plays the father and all five sons; otherwise, comedy is only average-to-good. In French with English subtitles. **96m/B VHS, Beta, 8mm.** *FR* Fernandel, Edouard Delmont, Louis de Funes, Paulette Dubost; **D:** Henri Verneuil. Nominations: Academy Awards '55: Best Story. *NOS, DVT, VYY*

Sheer Madness 🎬🎬🎬 **1984** Focuses on the intense friendship between a college professor and a troubled artist, both women. Engrossing and subtle exposition of a relationship. Ambiguous ending underscores the general excellence. Subtitled. **105m/C VHS, Beta.** *GE FR* Hanna Schygulla, Angela Winkler; **D:** Margarethe von Trotta; **W:** Margarethe von Trotta; **C:** Michael Ballhaus. *MGM*

The Sheik 🎬🎬🎬 **1921** High camp Valentino has English woman fall hopelessly under the romantic spell of Arab sheik who flares his nostrils. Followed by "Son of the Sheik." **80m/B VHS, Beta.** Agnes Ayres, Rudolph Valentino, Adolphe Menjou, Walter Long, Lucien Littlefield, George Waggner, Patsy Ruth Miller; **D:** George Melford. *PAR, GPV*

She'll Be Wearing Pink Pajamas 🎬🎬 **1984** Eight women volunteer for a rugged survival course to test their mettle. The intense shared experience gives them all food for thought. Well acted from a pretty thin story. **90m/C VHS, Beta.** Julie Walters, Anthony Higgins; **D:** John Goldschmidt; **M:** John Du Prez. *ORI*

The Shell Seekers 🎬🎬½ **1989 (PG)** The widowed Penelope Keeling (Lansbury) is recovering from a heart attack and her three grown children want her to take things easy. But the scare has convinced Penelope to revisit her past and the happiness she once knew. So she returns to her childhood home in Cornwall to see what she can discover. Fine cast in a heart-tugger (with some lovely scenery from Cornwall, England and the island of Ibiza). Adapted from the novel by Rosamunde Pilcher. A Hallmark Hall of Fame presentation. **94m/C VHS, Closed Caption.** *GB* Angela Lansbury, Sam Wanamaker, Anna Carteret, Michael Gough, Christopher Bowen, Patricia Hodge, Denis Quilley, Sophie Ward, Irene Worth; **D:** Waris Hussein; **W:** John Pielmeier. *REP*

Shell Shock 🎬½ **198?** Four GI's fight off the Germans and the longings for home during WWII. **90m/C VHS, Beta.** **D:** John Hayes. *NO*

Shelley Duvall's Bedtime Stories 1992 A series of stories based on popular children's books, narrated by celebrities. Each tape is available individually and contains at least two stories. Nominated for cable's ACE award and an

Emmy award. Originally produced for cable television. **25m/C VHS, LV, Closed Caption.** *USH*

The Sheltering Sky 🐾🐾🐾 1990 (R)
American couple Winger and Malkovich flee the plasticity of their native land for a trip to the Sahara desert where they hope to renew their spirits and rekindle love. Accompanied by socialite acquaintance Scott with whom Winger soon has an affair, their personalities and belief systems deteriorate as they move through the grave poverty of North Africa in breathtaking heat. Based on the existential novel by American expatriate Paul Bowles who narrates and appears briefly in a bar scene. Overlong but visually stunning, with cinematography by Vittorio Storaro. **139m/C VHS, Beta, LV, Closed Caption.** Debra Winger, John Malkovich, Campbell Scott, Jill Bennett, Timothy Spall, Eric Vu-An, Sotigui Koyate, Amina Annabi, Paul Bowles; *D:* Bernardo Bertolucci; *W:* Mark Peploe, Bernardo Bertolucci; *C:* Vittorio Storaro; *M:* Ryuichi Sakamoto, Richard Horowitz. Golden Globe Awards '91: Best Score; New York Film Critics Awards '90: Best Cinematography. *WAR, FCT, CCB*

Shenandoah 🐾🐾🐾 1965
A Virginia farmer (Stewart, in a top-notch performance) who has raised six sons and a daughter, tries to remain neutral during the Civil War. War takes its toll as the daughter marries a Confederate soldier and his sons become involved in the fighting. Screen debut for Ross. **105m/C VHS, Beta, LV.** James Stewart, Doug McClure, Glenn Corbett, Patrick Wayne, Rosemary Forsyth, Katharine Ross, George Kennedy; *D:* Andrew V. McLaglen; *C:* William Clothier. Nominations: Academy Awards '65: Best Sound. *USH*

Shep Comes Home 🐾 1949
Shep the wonder canine accompanies an orphan through the Midwest where he nabs a band of bankrobbers. Sequel to "My Dog Shep." **62m/B VHS, Beta, LV.** Robert Lowery, Sheldon Leonard. *NO*

Sheriff of Tombstone 🐾🐾½ 1941
Trouble begins when a "judge" takes a sharpshooter in a poker game. **60m/B VHS, Beta.** Roy Rogers. *NOS, DVT, RXM*

Sherlock Holmes and the Deadly Necklace 🐾🐾½
Sherlock Holmes Und Das Halsband des Todes; Valley of Fear 1962 Once again, Holmes and Watson are up against their old nemesis Moriarty. This time, Moriarty wants to get his hands on a necklace stolen from Cleopatra's tomb. Not only does Scotland Yard not consider him a suspect, they seek his advice. Enter Holmes and Watson, and the game's afoot. The offbeat casting and direction help make this one of the odder versions of Conan Doyle's work. **84m/B VHS.** *GE* Christopher Lee, Senta Berger, Hans Sohnker, Hans Nielsen, Ivan Desny, Leon Askin, Thorley Walters; *D:* Terence Fisher. *NOS, SNC*

Sherlock Holmes and the Incident at Victoria Falls 🐾½
Incident at Victoria Falls 1991 A substandard Holmes excursion brings the Baker Street sleuth out of retirement to transport the world's largest diamond from Africa to London. The resulting mystery involves Teddy Roosevelt, the inventor of radio, and poor plotting. **120m/C VHS.** *GB* Christopher Lee, Patrick Macnee, Jenny Seagrove; *D:* Bill Corcoran. *VES*

Sherlock Holmes and the Secret Weapon 🐾🐾🐾
Secret Weapon 1942 Based on "The Dancing Men" by Sir Arthur Conan Doyle. Holmes battles the evil Moriarty in an effort to save the British war effort. Good Holmes mystery with gripping wartime setting. Hoey is fun as bumbling Inspector Lestrade. Available colorized. **68m/B VHS, LV, Closed Caption.** Basil Rathbone, Nigel Bruce, Karen Verne, William Post Jr., Dennis Hoey, Holmes Herbert, Mary Gordon, Henry Victor, Philip Van Zandt, George Eldridge, Leslie Denison, James Craven, Paul Fix, Hugh Herbert, Lionel Atwill; *D:* Roy William Neill. *REP, MED, AOV*

Sherlock Holmes Faces Death 🐾🐾🐾 1943
Dead bodies are accumulating in a mansion where the detecting duo are staying. Underground tunnels, life-size dress boards, and unanswered mysteries... Top-notch

Holmes. Peter Lawford appears briefly as a sailor. Also available with "Hound of the Baskervilles" on Laser Disc. **68m/B VHS, Beta, LV, Closed Caption.** Basil Rathbone, Nigel Bruce, Hillary Brooke, Milburn Stone, Halliwell Hobbes, Arthur Margetson, Gavin Muir; *D:* Roy William Neill. *FOX*

Sherlock Holmes in Washington 🐾🐾½ 1943
A top-secret agent is murdered; seems it's those blasted Nazis again! Holmes and Watson rush off to Washington, D.C. to solve the crime and to save some vitally important microfilm. Heavily flag-waving Rathbone-Bruce episode. Dr. Watson is dumbfounded by bubble gum. **71m/B VHS, Beta, Closed Caption.** Basil Rathbone, Nigel Bruce, Henry Daniell, George Zucco, Marjorie Lord, John Archer; *D:* Roy William Neill. *FOX*

Sherlock Holmes: The Master Blackmailer 1992
Brett returns as the supersleuth, along with sidekick Dr. Watson, in a tale which has the detective working against the evil scheming of London's most cunning and ruthless blackmailer. When Holmes disguises himself to enter the blackmailer's lair he even finds himself attracting the romantic attentions of a young lady. Based on the story "The Adventure of Charles Augustus Milverton" by Arthur Conan Doyle. Made for television. **120m/C VHS.** *GB* Jeremy Brett, Edward Hardwicke, Robert Hardy. *MPI, SIG*

Sherlock Holmes: The Sign of Four 🐾🐾 1984
Sherlock Holmes must find the man who murdered Bartholomew Sholto with a poison dart in the neck. **48m/C VHS, Beta.** *V:* Peter O'Toole. *PMS, PAR*

Sherlock Holmes: The Silver Blaze 🐾½ 1941
Sherlock Holmes mystery about the theft of a racehorse known as "The Silver Blaze." Remade in 1977. **70m/B VHS, Beta.** Arthur Wontner, Ian Fleming, Lyn Harding. *NOS, BAR, EEL*

Sherlock Holmes: The Voice of Terror 🐾🐾 1942
Holmes and Watson try to decode German radio messages during WWII. First Rathbone-as-Holmes effort for Universal, and first in which we are asked to believe the Victorian sleuth and his hairdo could have lived in this century. Patriotic and all that—and lots of fun. **65m/B VHS, Beta, LV, Closed Caption.** Basil Rathbone, Nigel Bruce, Hillary Brooke, Reginald Denny, Evelyn Ankers, Montagu Love; *D:* John Rawlins. *FOX*

Sherlock Hound: Tales of Mystery 1990
Sherlock, Watson and Moriarty are all pups in this animated children's adaptation of the popular Arthur Conan Doyle stories. Well worth a howl. **115m/C VHS, Beta.** *JFK*

Sherlock: Undercover Dog 🐾🐾½ 1994 (PG)
Billy (Eroen) arrives on Catalina island to spend the summer with his father, an eccentric inventor. He makes a human friend in Emma (Cameron) and a canine companion in Sherlock, a police dog who's able to talk but naturally only to the two kids. Seems Sherlock's policeman master has been kidnapped by bumbling smugglers and its up to the trio to come to the rescue. **80m/C VHS, Closed Caption.** Benjamin Eroen, Brynne Cameron, Anthony Simmons, Margy Moore, Barry Philips; *D:* Richard Harding Gardner; *W:* Richard Harding Gardner; *M:* Lou Forestieri. *COL*

Sherlock's Rivals & Where's My Wife 🐾½ 1927
Double feature includes a detective movie in which two used car dealers become amateur sleuths and a comedy in which a man has a hard time enjoying his weekend at a seashore resort. **53m/B VHS, Beta.** Milburn Morante, Monty Banks. *VYY*

Sherman's March: An Improbable Search for Love 1986
McElwee's "epic" which was originally planned as a historical documentary about General Sherman's catastrophic march through the South, ends up being about the filmmaker himself, and his disastrous quest for love. When his girlfriend dumps him, he puts

Sherman's story aside and films his own battle for romance, which includes help from his meddling family. The melodramatic women he meets and the neurotic energy of McElwee make this a very funny, uncensored film. **155m/C VHS.** *D:* Ross McElwee; *W:* Ross McElwee. *FRF*

She's a Good Skate, Charlie Brown 1980
Snoopy becomes Peppermint Patty's ice-skating coach, and he helps her train for the local competition. **30m/C VHS, Beta, Closed Caption.** *D:* Phil Roman. *VTR, HSE*

She's Back 🐾½ 1988 (R)
Murderee Fisher pesters hubby Joy from beyond the grave to avenge her death at the hands of a motorcycle gang. Uneven, but occasionally funny. **89m/C VHS, Beta, LV.** Carrie Fisher, Robert Joy; *D:* Tim Kincaid. *VES, LIV*

She's Dressed to Kill 🐾🐾
Someone's Killing the World's Greatest Models 1979 Beautiful models are turning up dead during a famous designer's comeback attempt at a mountain retreat. Who could be behind these grisly deeds? Suspenseful in a made for TV kind of way, but not memorable. **100m/C VHS.** Eleanor Parker, Jessica Walter, John Rubinstein, Connie Sellecca; *D:* Gus Trikonis. *LIV*

She's Gotta Have It 🐾🐾🐾 1986 (R)
Lee wrote, directed, edited, produced and starred in this romantic comedy about an independent-minded black girl in Brooklyn and the three men and one woman who compete for her attention. Full of rough edges, but vigorous, confident, and hip. Filmed entirely in black and white except for one memorable scene. Put Lee on the film-making map. **84m/B VHS, Beta, LV, Closed Caption.** Tracy C. Johns, Spike Lee, Tommy Redmond Hicks, Raye Dowell, John Canada Terrell, Joie Lee, Epatha Merkinson, Bill Lee, Cheryl Burr, Aaron Dugger, Stephanie Covington, Renata Cobbs, Cheryl Singleton, Monty Ross, Lewis Jordan, Erik Dellums, Reginald Hudlin, Eric Payne, Marcus Turner, Gerard Brown, Ernest R. Dickerson; *D:* Spike Lee; *W:* Spike Lee; *C:* Ernest R. Dickerson; *M:* Bill Lee. Independent Spirit Awards '87: Best First Feature. *FOX, FCT*

She's Having a Baby 🐾🐾½ 1988 (PG-13)
Newlyweds Bacon and McGovern tread the marital waters with some difficulty, when news of an impending baby further complicates their lives. Told from Bacon's viewpoint as the tortured young writer/husband, who wonders if the yuppie life they lead is trapping him. Hughes' first venture into the adult world isn't as satisfying as his teen angst flicks, although the charming leads help. Major drawbacks are the arguably sexist premise and dull resolution. Great soundtrack; observant viewers will notice the beemer's license plate is the title's acronym: "SHAB." **106m/C VHS, Beta, LV, 8mm, Closed Caption.** Kevin Bacon, Elizabeth McGovern, William Windom, Paul Gleason, Alec Baldwin, Cathryn Damon, Holland Taylor, James Ray, Isabel Lorca, Dennis Dugan, Edie McClurg, John Ashton; *D:* John Hughes; *W:* John Hughes; *M:* Stewart Copeland. *PAR*

She's in the Army Now 🐾 1981
Farce about military life. Two bubble-headed females undergo basic training. Made for TV "Private Benjamin" ripoff was meant as a series pilot. **97m/C VHS, Beta.** Jamie Lee Curtis, Kathleen Quinlan, Melanie Griffith, Susan Blanchard, Julie Carmen, Janet MacLachlan; *D:* Hy Averback; *M:* Artie Butler. *NLC*

She's Out of Control 🐾½ 1989
Dad Danza goes nuts when teen daughter Dolenz (real-life daughter of Monkee Mickey Dolenz) takes the advice of Dad's girlfriend on how to attract boys. Formulaic plot could almost be an episode of "Who's the Boss?" Danza is appealing, but not enough to keep this one afloat. **95m/C VHS, Beta, LV, 8mm, Closed Caption.** Tony Danza, Catherine Hicks, Wallace Shawn, Dick O'Neill; *D:* Stan Dragoti; *M:* Alan Silvestri. *COL*

She's So Lovely 🐾🐾½
She's De Lovely; Call It Love 1997 (R) Troubled young alcoholic Eddie (Penn) disappears for three days on his pregnant wife Maureen (Wright), and returns to discover that she has been brutalized by a neighbor. Retal-

iation costs him 10 years in a mental institution. Upon his release, Eddie decides to find his now ex-wife and the daughter he's never known. Maureen's moved on—she's happily married to Joey (Travolta), has two daughters by him, and is justifiable worried that Eddie's love (which is as strong as ever) will upset the balance of her new life. Somewhat unevenly directed by Nick Cassavetes from a screenplay written by his late father John, who had already cast Penn and was set to direct when he became ill. Film revels in the style that made the elder Cassavetes famous (or infamous), and is best appreciated as a tribute. Travolta and Penn play well off each other. **CW:** Strong language and some violence. **97m/C VHS.** Sean Penn, Robin Wright, John Travolta, Harry Dean Stanton, Debi Mazar, James Gandolfini, Gena Rowlands, Kelsey Mulrooney; **D:** Nick Cassavetes; **W:** John Cassavetes; **C:** Thierry Arbogast; **M:** Joseph Vitarelli. Cannes Film Festival '97: Best Actor (Penn). *NYR*

She's the One ♂♂½ **1996 (R)** Another Irish family saga from Burns covering lots of the same territory as "The Brothers McMullen." Semi-slacker taxi driver Mickey Fitzpatrick (Burns) impulsively marries passenger Hope (Bahns) and their romance is contrasted with the disintegrating marriage of Mickey's younger brother, buttoned-down stockbroker Francis (McGlone) and his frustrated wife Rene (Aniston). No wonder she's frustrated, Francis is having an affair with slutty Heather (Diaz), who turns out to be Mickey's former flame. Mahoney offers bad marital advice as the boys' father. Again the blustering men don't have a clue about the usually smarter women. **CW:** Language, including sex-related dialogue. **95m/C VHS, LV, Closed Caption.** Edward Burns, Mike McGlone, Jennifer Aniston, Cameron Diaz, Maxine Bahns, John Mahoney, Leslie Mann, George McCowan, Leslie Mann, Amanda Peet, Anita Gillette, Frank Vincent; **D:** Edward Burns; **W:** Edward Burns; **C:** Frank Prinzi; **M:** Tom Petty. *FXV*

Shifting Sands 1918 Compelling film tells the tale of a young girl looking to be a successful artist. Her landlord makes constant overtures towards her. She refuses, so he has her thrown in jail for prostitution as an act of revenge. She fears her past may prevent her from obtaining true love. **52m/B VHS, Beta, 8mm.** Gloria Swanson, Joe King, Lillian Langdon. *GPV, VYY, GVV*

Shiloh ♂♂½ **1997 (PG)** Schmaltzy but redeeming story about small town West Virginia 11-year-old Marty (Heron), who seeks to rescue and care for mistreated hunting dog Shiloh, who belongs to mean hermit Judd (Wilson). Goes beyond the typical "boy and his dog" theme with moral and ethical issues that Marty faces when he takes the dog from its owner. Frannie (who plays Shiloh) is a very cute and expressive beagle. Adapted from the Newberry award-winning novel by Phyllis Reynolds Naylor. **93m/C VHS, Closed Caption.** Blake Heron, Michael Moriarty, Scott Wilson, Rod Steiger, Ann Dowd, Bonnie Bartlett; **D:** Dale Rosenbloom; **W:** Dale Rosenbloom; **C:** Frank Byers; **M:** Joel Goldsmith. *WAR*

Shin Heike Monogatari ♂♂♂♂ **1955** Mizoguchi's second to last film, in which a deposed Japanese emperor in 1137 endeavors to win back the throne from the current despot, who cannot handle the feudal lawlessness. Acclaimed; his second film in color. In Japanese with English subtitles. Also called "New Tales of the Taira Clan." **106m/C VHS, Beta.** *JP* Raizo Ichikawa, Ichijiro Oya, Michiyo Kogure, Eijiro Yanagi, Tatsuya Ishiguro, Yoshiko Kuga; **D:** Kenji Mizoguchi. *FCT*

Shinbone Alley 1970 (G) Animated musical about Archy, a free-verse poet reincarnated as a cockroach, and Mehitabel, the alley cat with a zest for life. Based on the short stories by Don Marquis. **83m/C VHS, Beta.** *D:* John D. Wilson; *V:* Carol Channing, Eddie Bracken, John Carradine, Alan Reed. *GEM, KAR, HHE*

Shine ♂♂♂½ **1995 (PG-13)** Astonishing true portrayal of musical genius and its cost. Teenaged pianist David Helfgott (Taylor) is a prodigy in his native Australia but is pushed to the limit by his authoritarian father Peter (Mueller-Stahl). Eventually defying his father's strictures, David accepts a scholarship to London's Royal College of Music where he triumphs under the tutelege of professor Cecil Parkes (Gielgud), but then collapses from strain. For 15 years, he is confined to psychiatric hospitals, unable to play the piano, until the now-adult David (Rush) has a chance meeting with the loving Gillian (Redgrave), whose support enables him to resume his career. Helfgott himself plays piano for his screen counterparts. **CW:** Nudity/sensuality and intense thematic elements. **105m/C VHS, LV, Closed Caption, DVD.** *AU* Geoffrey Rush, Noah Taylor, Armin Mueller-Stahl, Lynn Redgrave, John Gielgud, Googie Withers, Chris Haywood, Sonia Todd, Alex Rafalowicz; **D:** Scott Hicks; **W:** Jan Sardi; **C:** Geoffrey Simpson; **M:** David Hirschfelder. Academy Awards '96: Best Actor (Rush); Australian Film Institute '96: Best Actor (Rush), Best Cinematography, Best Director (Hicks), Best Film, Best Film Editing, Best Screenplay, Best Sound, Best Supporting Actor (Mueller-Stahl), Best Score; British Academy Awards '96: Best Actor (Rush); Golden Globe Awards '97: Best Actor—Drama (Rush); Los Angeles Film Critics Association Awards '96: Best Actor (Rush); National Board of Review Awards '96: Best Film; New York Film Critics Awards '96: Best Actor (Rush); Screen Actors Guild Award '96: Best Actor (Rush); Broadcast Film Critics Association Awards '96: Best Actor (Rush); Nominations: Academy Awards '96: Best Director (Hicks), Best Film Editing, Best Picture, Best Supporting Actor (Mueller-Stahl), Best Writing, Original Dramatic/Comedy Score; Australian Film Institute '96: Best Actor (Taylor); British Academy Awards '96: Best Director (Hicks), Best Film, Best Original Screenplay, Best Supporting Actor (Gielgud), Best Supporting Actress (Redgrave); Directors Guild of America Awards '96: Best Director (Hicks); Golden Globe Awards '97: Best Director (Hicks), Best Film—Drama, Best Screenplay, Best Score; Screen Actors Guild Award '96: Best Supporting Actor (Taylor), Cast; Writers Guild of America '96: Best Original Screenplay. *NLC*

Shine on, Harvest Moon ♂♂ **1938** Rogers brings a band of outlaws to justice and clears an old man suspected of being their accomplice. Title bears no relation to storyline. **60m/B VHS, Beta.** Roy Rogers, Lynn (Mary Hart) Roberts, Stanley Andrews; **D:** Joseph Kane. *NOS, VYY, VDM*

The Shining ♂♂½ **1980 (R)** Very loose adaptation of the Stephen King horror novel about a writer and his family, snowbound in a huge hotel, who experience various hauntings caused by either the hotel itself or the writer's dementia. Technically stunning, and pretty dang scary, but too long, pretentious and implausible. Nicholson is excellent as the failed writer gone off the deep end. **143m/C VHS, Beta, LV, Closed Caption.** Jack Nicholson, Shelley Duvall, Scatman Crothers, Danny Lloyd, Joe Turkel, Barry Nelson, Philip Stone, Lia Beldam, Billie Gibson, Barry Dennan, David Baxt, Lisa Burns, Alison Coleridge, Kate Phelps, Anne Jackson, Tony Burton; **D:** Stanley Kubrick; **W:** Stanley Kubrick, Diane Johnson; **C:** John Alcott. *WAR*

The Shining Hour ♂♂½ **1938** A compelling melodrama in which Crawford portrays a New York night club dancer who is pursued by the rather conservative Douglas. His brother tries to persuade him from marrying Crawford, but then he soon finds himself attracted to her. A devastating fire wipes out all problems of family dissension in this intelligent soap opera. **76m/B VHS, Closed Caption.** Joan Crawford, Margaret Sullavan, Melvyn Douglas, Robert Young, Fay Bainter, Allyn Joslyn; **D:** Frank Borzage; **W:** Ogden Nash, Jane Murfin. *MGM*

A Shining Season ♂♂♂ **1979** Tearjerker about a potential-packed long-distance runner, John Baker, stricken with cancer. He spends his last year training a girls' track team to a championship. Earnest, well-performed and involving. Based on a true story. Made for TV. **100m/C VHS, Beta.** Timothy Bottoms, Rip Torn, Allyn Ann McLerie, Ed Begley Jr., Benjamin Bottoms, Mason Adams, Constance

Forslund, Ellen Geer; **D:** Stuart Margolin; **M:** Richard Bellis. *BTV*

Shining Star ♂½ *That's the Way of the World* **1975 (PG)** A recording company is run by the mob. Potentially interesting film is hampered by quality of sound and photography and general lack of purpose or direction. **100m/C VHS.** Harvey Keitel, Ed Nelson, Cynthia Bostick, Bert Parks; **D:** Sig Shore. *LIV*

Shining Through ♂♂½ **1992 (R)** Baby-voiced Griffith as a spy sent behind enemy lines without training? Douglas as a spy sent behind enemy lines without speaking German? Old-fashioned blend of romance, espionage, and derring-do where noble hero saves spunky heroine from nasty Nazis in WWII Germany works despite thin plot. Series of flash-forwards to an aged Griffith is annoying and tends to stop action cold, but everyone tries hard and period flavor is authentic. Adapted from best-selling Susan Isaacs novel, but bears little resemblance to book. **CW:** Sensual scene. **133m/C VHS, Closed Caption.** Michael Douglas, Melanie Griffith, Liam Neeson, Joely Richardson, John Gielgud, Francis Guinan, Patrick Winczewski, Sylvia Syms; **D:** David Seltzer; **W:** David Seltzer; **C:** Jan De Bont; **M:** Michael Kamen. Golden Raspberry Awards '92: Worst Picture, Worst Actress (Griffith), Worst Director (Seltzer). *FXV*

Shinobi Ninja ♂ **1984** Last-surviving member of Koga ninja clan returns to Japan from U.S. to save his homeland from enemy ninja clan. Mediocre pseudo ninja antics. Badly dubbed. **103m/C VHS, Beta.** *JP* Tadashi Yamashita, Eric Lee, Karen Lee Sheperd. *AHV*

Shiokari Pass ♂♂ **1977** A man has a divine revelation at the pass. In Japanese with English subtitles. **60m/C VHS.** *JP* **D:** Novuru Nakamuru. *REP, VBL*

Ship Ahoy ♂♂½ **1942** Songs, comedy, a spy spoof, and some patriotism thrown in for good measure. Powell plays a dancer who works with Tommy Dorsey and his orchestra. They're on their way to Puerto Rico, via ocean liner, along with her pulp fiction writer boyfriend (Skelton). Emery, posing as an FBI man, convinces Powell to smuggle a package for him but he's really a spy and the whole thing's a con which turns out to be based on one of Skelton's potboiler plots. An uncredited Frank Sinatra is the singer with the Dorsey band, along with drummer Buddy Rich and trumpeter Ziggy Elman who provide some great musical solos. ♪Last Call For Love; Poor You; On Moonlight Bay; Tampico; I'll Take Tallulah; Cape Dance; Ship Ahoy. **95m/B VHS.** Eleanor Powell, Red Skelton, Bert Lahr, Virginia O'Brien, John Emery, William Post Jr.; **D:** Edward Buzzell; **W:** Harry Kurnitz, Harry Clork, Irving Brecher. *MGM*

Ship of Fools ♂♂♂ **1965** A group of passengers sailing to Germany in the '30s find mutual needs and concerns, struggle with early evidence of Nazi racism, and discover love on their voyage. Twisted story and fine acting maintain interest. Appropriate tunes written by Ernest Gold. Based on the Katherine Ann Porter novel. Leigh's last film role; she died two years later. Kramer grapples with civil rights issues in much of his work. **149m/B VHS, Beta, LV, Closed Caption.** Vivien Leigh, Simone Signoret, Jose Ferrer, Lee Marvin, Oskar Werner, Michael Dunn, Elizabeth Ashley, George Segal, Jose Greco, Charles Korvin, Heinz Ruehmann; **D:** Stanley Kramer; **W:** Abby Mann; **C:** Ernest Laszlo; **M:** Ernest Gold. Academy Awards '65: Best Art Direction/Set Decoration (B & W), Best Black and White Cinematography; National Board of Review Awards '65: 10 Best Films of the Year, Best Actor (Marvin); New York Film Critics Awards '65: Best Actor (Werner); Nominations: Academy Awards '65: Best Actor (Werner), Best Actress (Signoret), Best Adapted Screenplay, Best Costume Design (B & W), Best Picture, Best Supporting Actor (Dunn). *COL, SWC*

Ships in the Night ♂ **1928** Logan is the plucky heroine who is searching for her missing brother who has been captured by pirates. She is aided in her search by handsome hero Mower. **86m/B VHS, Beta.** Frank Moran, Jacqueline Logan, Jack Mower, Andy Clyde. *GVV, FCT, GPV*

Shipwreck Island 🎬🎬 1961 Eight boys are shipwrecked on a deserted island, then make their way to another island where they must survive against wild animals and the elements for two years. 93m/C **VHS.** HTV, FCT

Shipwrecked 🎬🎬½ Haakon Haakonsen 1990 (PG) Kiddie swashbuckler based on the 1873 popular novel "Haakon Haakonsen." A cabin boy is marooned on an island where he defends the hidden pirate treasure he finds by boobytrapping the island. 93m/C **VHS, LV, Closed Caption.** NO Gabriel Byrne, Stian Smestad, Louisa Haigh, Trond Munch, Bjørn Sundquist, Eva Von Hanno, Kjell Stormoen; **D:** Nils Gaup; **W:** Nick Thiel, Nils Gaup; **M:** Patrick Doyle. TOU

Shirley Temple Festival 1933 A collection of four Shirley Temple short subjects from the 30s: "Dora's Dunkin Doughnuts," "Pardon My Pups," "War Babies" and "Kid N' Africa." 55m/B **VHS, Beta.** Shirley Temple, Andy Clyde. MRV

Shirley Valentine 🎬🎬🎬 1989 A lively middle-aged English housewife gets a new lease on life when she travels to Greece without her husband. Collins reprises her London and Broadway stage triumph. The character frequently addresses the audience directly to explain her thoughts and feelings; her energy and spunk carry the day. Good script by Russell from his play. From the people who brought us "Educating Rita." 108m/C **VHS, LV, 8mm, Closed Caption.** GB Pauline Collins, Tom Conti, Alison Steadman, Julia McKenzie, Joanna Lumley, Bernard Hill, Sylvia Syms; **D:** Lewis Gilbert; **W:** George Hadjinassios, Willy Russell; **M:** Willy Russell. British Academy Awards '89: Best Actress (Collins); Nominations: Academy Awards '89: Best Actress (Collins), Best Song ("The Girl Who Used to Be Me"). PAR, TVC, HMV

The Shock 🎬🎬½ 1923 Crippled low-life Chaney becomes restored spiritually by a small-town girl and rebels against his Chinese boss. This causes an unfortunate string of melodramatic tragedies, including the San Francisco earthquake of 1906. Silent. Odd, desultory tale with bad special effects is worth seeing for Chaney's good acting. 96m/B **VHS, Beta.** Lon Chaney Sr., Virginia Valli; **D:** Lambert Hillyer. SNC, NOS, HEG

Shock! 🎬🎬 1946 A psychiatrist is called on to treat a woman on the edge of a nervous breakdown. When he discovers she saw him murder his wife, and tries to keep her from remembering it. Interesting premise handled in trite B style. Price's first starring role. 70m/B **VHS, Beta.** Vincent Price, Lynn Bari, Frank Latimore, Anabel Shaw; **D:** Alfred Werker. SNC, NOS, BAR

Shock Corridor 🎬🎬🎬 1963 A reporter, dreaming of a Pulitzer Prize, fakes mental illness and gets admitted to an asylum, where he hopes to investigate a murder. He is subjected to disturbing experiences, including shock therapy, but does manage to solve the murder. However, he suffers a mental breakdown in the process and is admitted for real. Disturbing and lurid. 101m/B **VHS, LV.** Peter Breck, Constance Towers, Gene Evans, Hari Rhodes, James Best, Philip Ahn; **D:** Samuel Fuller; **W:** Samuel Fuller. HMV, CRC

Shock 'Em Dead 🎬🎬 1990 (R) A devil worshiper trades his life to Lucifer for a chance at rock and roll fame and beautiful Miss Lords. Sexy thriller, with a good share of violence and tension. Ironically, ex porn great Lords is one of the few starlets who doesn't disrobe in the film. 94m/C **VHS, LV.** Traci Lords, Aldo Ray, Troy Donahue, Stephen Quadros; **D:** Mark Freed; **W:** Andrew Cross. ACA

Shock! Shock! Shock! 🎬 1987 Another low-budget slasher flick, with a homicidal lunatic wielding a butcher knife. Space alien jewel thieves add an element, for what it's worth. Makes one ponder the cosmic question: What's the diff between a bad slasher flick and a spoof of a bad slasher flick? Whichever this one is, it's really bad! 60m/B **VHS, Beta.** Brad Issac, Cyndy McCrossen, Allen Rickman, Brian Fuorry; **D:** Todd Rutt, Arn McConnell. RHI, MWF

A Shock to the System 🎬🎬🎬 1990 (R) Business exec. Caine is passed over for a long-deserved promotion in favor of a younger man. When he accidentally pushes a panhandler in front of a subway in a fit of rage, he realizes how easy murder is and thinks it may be the answer to all his problems. Tries to be a satire take on corporate greed, etc., but somehow loses steam. Excellent cast makes the difference; Caine adds class. Based on the novel by Simon Brett. 88m/C **VHS, Beta, LV, Closed Caption.** Michael Caine, Elizabeth McGovern, Peter Riegert, Swoosie Kurtz, Will Patton, Jenny Wright, John McMartin, Barbara Baxley; **D:** Jan Egleson; **W:** Andrew Klavan; **M:** Gary Chang. HBO

Shock Treatment 🎬½ Traitement de Choc 1981 (PG) Seldom-seen mediocre semi-sequel to the cult classic, "The Rocky Horror Picture Show" (1975). Brad and Janet, now married and portrayed by different leads, find themselves trapped on a TV gameshow full of weirdos. Same writers, same director, and several original cast members do make an appearance. 94m/C **VHS, Beta, Closed Caption.** Richard O'Brien, Jessica Harper, Cliff DeYoung, Patricia Quinn, Charles Gray, Ruby Wax; **D:** Jim Sharman. FOX

Shock Waves 🎬🎬 Death Corps; Almost Human 1977 (PG) Group of mutant-underwater-zombie-Nazi-soldiers terrorizes stranded tourists staying at a deserted motel on a small island. Cushing is the mad scientist intent on recreating the Nazi glory days with the seaweed-attired zombies. Odd B-grade, more or less standard horror flick somehow rises (slightly) above badness. Halpin's name was erroneously listed as Halprin—even on the original movie poster! 90m/C **VHS, Beta.** Peter Cushing, Brooke Adams, John Carradine, Luke Halpin; **D:** Ken Wiederhorn; **M:** Richard Einhorn. PSM

Shocker 🎬🎬½ 1989 (R) Another Craven gore-fest. A condemned serial killer is transformed into a menacing electrical force after being fried in the chair. Practically a remake of Craven's original "Nightmare on Elm Street." Great special effects, a few enjoyable weird and sick moments. What's Dr. Timothy Leary doing here? 111m/C **VHS, Beta, LV, Closed Caption.** Michael Murphy, Peter Berg, Cami Cooper, Mitch Pileggi, Richard Price, Timothy Leary, Heather Langenkamp, Theodore (Ted) Raimi, Richard Brooks, Sam Scarber; **D:** Wes Craven; **W:** Wes Craven; **M:** William Goldstein. USH

Shocking Asia 🎬½ 1975 For the eye-covering delight of Western audiences, Mr. Fox compiles gruesome Asian oddities. 94m/C **VHS, Beta.** GE **D:** Emerson Fox. HHE

The Shoes of the Fisherman 🎬½ 1968 (G) Morris West's interesting, speculative best seller about Russian Pope brought to the big screen at much expense, but with little care or thought. Siberian prison-camp vet Quinn, elected Pope, tries to arrest nuclear war. Director Anderson wasted the prodigious talents of Olivier, Gielgud, et al. Sloppy use of good cast and promising plot. 160m/C **VHS, Beta, LV.** Anthony Quinn, Leo McKern, Laurence Olivier, John Gielgud, Vittorio De Sica, Oskar Werner, David Janssen; **D:** Michael Anderson Sr.; **M:** Alex North. Golden Globe Awards '69: Best Score; National Board of Review Awards '68: Best Supporting Actor (McKern); Nominations: Academy Awards '68: Best Art Direction/Set Decoration, Best Original Score. MGM, FCT

Shoeshine 🎬🎬🎬🎬 1947 Two shoeshine boys struggling to survive in post-war Italy become involved in the black market and are eventually caught and imprisoned. Prison scenes detail the sense of abandonment and tragedy that destroys their friendship. A rich, sad achievement in neo-realistic drama. In Italian with English subtitles. 90m/B **VHS, Beta.** IT Franco Interlenghi, Rinaldo Smordoni, Anniello Mele, Bruno Ortensi, Pacifico Astrologo; **D:** Vittorio De Sica; **W:** Cesare Zavattini, Sergio Amidei, Adolfo Franci, C.G. Viola. National Board of Review Awards '47: 10 Best Films of the Year; Nominations: Academy Awards '47: Best Original Screenplay. FCT

Shogun 🎬🎬🎬½ James Clavell's Shogun 1980 Television miniseries chronicling the saga of a shipwrecked English navigator who becomes the first Shogun, or Samurai warrior chief, from the Western world. Colorfully adapted from the James Clavell bestseller. Also released in a two-hour version, but this full-length version is infinitely better. 550m/C **VHS, Beta, LV.** Richard Chamberlain, Toshiro Mifune, Yoko Shimada, John Rhys-Davies, Damien Thomas; **D:** Jerry London; **M:** Maurice Jarre. PAR

Shogun Assassin 🎬🎬½ 1980 (R) Story of a proud samurai named Lone Wolf who served his Shogun master well as the Official Decapitator, until the fateful day when the aging Shogun turned against him. Extremely violent, with record-breaking body counts. Edited from two other movies in a Japanese series called "Sword of Vengeance"; a tour de force of the cutting room. The samurai pushes his son's stroller through much of the film-sets it aside to hack and slash. 89m/C **VHS, Beta, LV.** JP Tomisaburo Wakayama; **D:** Kenji Misumi, Robert Houston. USH, OM

Shogun's Ninja 🎬½ 1983 In 16th-century Japan, an age-old rivalry between two ninja clans sparks a search for a dagger which will lead to one clan's hidden gold. Martial arts performed and directed by Sonny Chiba. In Japanese with usual poor English dubbing. 115m/C **VHS, Beta.** Henry Sanada, Sue Shiomi, Sonny Chiba; **D:** Noribumi Suzuki. MED

Shoot 🎬 1985 (R) Five hunting buddies fall prey to a group of crazed killers after one man is shot by accident. What's the message: Anti-gun? Anti-hunting? Silly, unbelievable, irresponsibly moralistic, and gratuitously violent. 98m/C **VHS, Beta, LV.** CA Ernest Borgnine, Cliff Robertson, Henry Silva, Helen Shaver; **D:** Harvey Hart.

Shoot 🎬🎬 1992 (R) Photographer Katie Tracy goes undercover to expose an illegal gambling ring fronted by an exotic nightclub. The latest gambling stakes involve the Emperor's pearls, offered in a private auction which could turn deadly, especially when Katie gets involved with the group's handsome ringleader. 90m/C **VHS.** Dedee Pfeiffer, Miles O'Keeffe, Christopher Atkins; **D:** Hugh Parks. TRI, TPV

Shoot It Black, Shoot It Blue 🎬½ 1974 Rogue cop shoots a black purse snatcher and thinks he has gotten away with it. Unknown to him, a witness has filmed the incident and turns the evidence over to a lawyer. 93m/C **VHS, Beta.** Michael Moriarty. NO

Shoot Loud, Louder, I Don't Understand! 🎬½ Spara Forte, Piu Forte...Non Capisco 1966 A sculptor who has a hard time separating reality from dreams thinks he witnessed a murder. Shenanigans follow. Meant to be a black comedy, but when not dull, it is confusing. Welch looks good, as usual, but doesn't show acting talent here. In Italian with English subtitles. 101m/C **VHS, Beta.** IT Marcello Mastroianni, Raquel Welch; **D:** Eduardo de Filippo; **M:** Nino Rota. NLC

Shoot the Living, Pray for the Dead 🎬🎬 1973 While travelling through Mexico, the leader of a band of killers promises his guide half of a share in stolen gold if he can lead them to it. 90m/C **VHS, Beta.** Klaus Kinski. CNG

Shoot the Moon 🎬🎬½ 1982 (R) A successful writer, married and with four children, finds his life unrewarding and leaves his family to take up with a younger woman. The wife must learn to deal with her resentment, the fears of her children, and her own attempt at a new love. Fine acting but a worn-out story. 124m/C **VHS, Beta, LV.** Diane Keaton, Albert Finney, Karen Allen, Peter Weller, Dana Hill, Viveka Davis, Tracey Gold, Tina Yothers; **D:** Alan Parker; **W:** Bo Goldman. MGM

Shoot the Piano Player 🎬🎬🎬🎬 Tirez sur le Pianiste; Shoot the Pianist 1962 Former concert pianist (Aznavour, spendidly cast) changes his name and plays piano at a low-class Paris cafe. A convoluted plot ensues; he becomes involved with gangsters, though his girlfriend wants him to try a comeback. Lots of atmosphere, character development, humor, and romance. A Truffaut masterpiece based on a pulp novel by David Goodis. In French with English subtitles. **92m/B VHS, Beta, LV.** *FR* Charles Aznavour, Marie DuBois, Nicole Berger, Michele Mercier, Albert Remy; **D:** Francois Truffaut; **W:** Marcel Moussey, Francois Truffaut; **M:** Georges Delerue. *HMV, HHT, WFV*

Shoot the Sun Down 🎬½ **1981 (PG)** Four offbeat characters united in a search for gold turn against each other. "Gilligan's Island"-style assortment of characters (Indian; gunfighter; girl; sea captain) are cast away in a pointless plot from which they never escape. Too bad: talented cast could have done better. **102m/C VHS, Beta.** Christopher Walken, Margot Kidder, Geoffrey Lewis, Bo Brundin, Sacheen Little Feather; **D:** David Leeds. *NO*

Shoot to Kill 🎬🎬½ **1947** B-grade noir-esque mystery about a crooked D.A. and a gangster who bite the dust. Suspenseful, dark, street-level crime drama uncovered by ambitious journalist Ward. **64m/B VHS, Beta, LV.** Russell Wade, Susan Walters, Nestor Paiva, Edmund MacDonald, Vince Barnett; **D:** William (Lester Williams) Berke. *SNC, VYY*

Shoot to Kill 🎬🎬🎬 **1988 (R)** A city cop (Poitier, better than ever after 10 years off the screen) and a mountain guide (Berenger) reluctantly join forces to capture a killer who is part of a hunting party traversing the Pacific Northwest and which is being led by the guide's unsuspecting girlfriend (Alley). Poitier may be a bit old for the role, but he carries the implausible plot on the strength of his performance. Good action. **110m/C VHS, Closed Caption.** Sidney Poitier, Tom Berenger, Kirstie Alley, Clancy Brown, Richard Masur, Andrew (Andy) Robinson, Frederick Coffin, Andrew (Andy) Robinson, Kevin Scannell; **D:** Roger Spottiswoode; **W:** Michael Burton, Harv Zimmel, Dan Petrie Jr.; **C:** Michael Chapman; **M:** John Scott. *TOU*

Shoot to Kill 🎬🎬 *Disparan a Matar* **1990** An innocent young man is murdered during a police round-up while his mother watches helplessly. The police try a whitewash—proclaiming the victim a criminal—but she launches a long campaign for justice. Spanish with subtitles. **90m/C VHS.** *VZ* Carlos Azpurua. *FCT*

Shooters 🎬½ **1989** A wacky platoon of misfits is paired off against a group of vicious killers in a "war game" training session. Not completely unfunny or worthless. **84m/C VHS, Beta.** Ben Schick, Robin Sims, Aldo Ray. *AIP*

Shootfighter: Fight to the Death 🎬½ **1993 (R)** Two boys become experts in the martial arts and constant rivals. Now grown-up they take their rivalry to a deadly level in a "shootfight," a game which has no rules and is so brutal it's banned as a sport. Not that this stops them. An unrated version is also available. **CW:** Strong martial arts violence. **94m/C VHS, LV, Closed Caption.** Bolo Yeung, Martin Kove, William Zabka, Michael Bernardo, Maryam D'Abo, Edward Albert; **D:** Patrick Allen; **W:** Judd S. Lynn, Larry Feliz Jr., Peter Shaner. *COL*

Shootfighter 2: Kill or Be Killed! 🎬½ **1996 (R)** The Miami underworld is placed on alert when a police chief, seeking to avenge the death of his son, joins with a martial arts master to recruit and train a group of fighters. Then they'll infiltrate the illegal spectator games of to-the-death-combat and see what mayhem they can cause. **CW:** Non-stop violence, a sex scene and some language. **90m/C VHS, LV, Closed Caption.** Bolo Yeung, Michael Bernardo, William Zabka; **D:** Paul Ziller; **W:** Peter Shaner, Greg Mellott. *COL*

The Shooting 🎬🎬🎬 **1966** A mysterious woman, bent on revenge, persuades a former bounty hunter and his partner to escort her across the desert, with tragic results. Offbeat, small film filled strong by performances of Nicholson and Oates. Filmed concurrently with "Ride in the Whirlwind," with the same cast and director.

Bang-up surprise ending. **82m/C VHS, Beta, LV.** Warren Oates, Millie Perkins, Jack Nicholson, Will Hutchins; **D:** Monte Hellman. *MED, DVT, HHT*

Shooting 🎬 **1982** Three boys run away when they think they've killed a man in a hunting accident. **60m/C VHS, Beta.** Lynn Redgrave, Lance Kerwin, Barry Primus. *NO*

Shooting Elizabeth 🎬½ **1992 (PG-13)** A fed-up husband decides to shut his loudmouthed wife up—permanently. Only before he can kill her, she disappears. The police don't buy it and want to charge him with murder. Can he find his wife before things really get serious? **CW:** Brief nudity and drug use. **96m/C VHS, LV.** Jeff Goldblum, Mimi Rogers; **D:** Baz Taylor. *LIV*

The Shooting Party 🎬🎬½ **1977** Told in flashbacks, a story of a crime of passion, an innocent man, and guilty secrets. A magistrate cannot admit his love for a woodsman's daughter so she falls into a loveless marriage and a decadent affair. In a fit of passion, the magistrate kills her and then decides to prosecute her innocent husband for the crime. Based on a story by Chekhov. In Russian with English subtitles. **105m/C VHS.** *RU* Oleg Yankovsky, Galina Belyayeva; **D:** Emil Loteanu. *CVC, FCT*

The Shooting Party 🎬🎬🎬½ **1985** A group of English aristocrats assemble at a nobleman's house for a bird shoot on the eve of WWI. Splendid cast crowned Mason, in his last role. Fascinating crucible class anxieties, rich with social scheming, personality conflicts, and things left unsaid. Adapted from Isabel Colegate's novel. **97m/C VHS, Beta.** *GB* James Mason, Dorothy Tutin, Edward Fox, John Gielgud, Robert Hardy, Cheryl Campbell, Judi Bowker; **D:** Alan Bridges; **W:** Julian Bond. Los Angeles Film Critics Association Awards '85: Best Supporting Actor (Gielgud); National Society of Film Critics Awards '85: Best Supporting Actor (Gielgud). *NO*

Shooting Stars 🎬 **1985** Two actors who play private eyes on television are pushed out of their jobs by a jealous co-star. They take to the streets as "real" crime-fighting dicks. Interesting premise goes nowhere. Made for TV. **96m/C VHS, Beta.** Billy Dee Williams, Parker Stevenson, Efrem Zimbalist Jr., Edie Adams; **D:** Richard Lang. *AHV*

The Shootist 🎬🎬🎬½ **1976 (PG)** Wayne, in a supporting last role, plays a legendary gunslinger afflicted with cancer who seeks peace and solace in his final days. Town bad guys Boone and O'Brian aren't about to let him rest and are determined to gun him down to avenge past deeds. One of Wayne's best and most dignified performances about living up to a personal code of honor. Stewart and Bacall head excellent supporting cast. Based on Glendon Swarthout's novel. **100m/C VHS, Beta, LV.** John Wayne, Lauren Bacall, Ron Howard, James Stewart, Richard Boone, Hugh O'Brian, Bill McKinney, Harry (Henry) Morgan, John Carradine, Sheree North, Scatman Crothers; **D:** Donald Siegel; **C:** Bruce Surtees; **M:** Elmer Bernstein. National Board of Review Awards '76: 10 Best Films of the Year; Nominations: Academy Awards '76: Best Art Direction/Set Decoration. *PAR, TLF*

Shop Angel 🎬🎬 **1932** A department store dress designer encounters romance and scandal in this low-budget drama of intrigue and romance. She falls in love with the fiance of her boss's daughter, and schemes to blackmail him (the boss). Competently rendered if unexceptional tale. **66m/B VHS, Beta, 8mm.** Marion Shilling, Holmes Herbert, Creighton Hale; **D:** E. Mason Hopper. *VYY*

The Shop Around the Corner 🎬🎬🎬 **1940** A low-key romantic classic in which Stewart and Sullavan are feuding clerks in a small Budapest shop, who unknowingly fall in love via a lonely hearts club. Charming portrayal of romance in ordinary situations. Adapted from the Nikolaus Laszlo's play "Parfumerie." Later made into a musical called "In the Good Old Summertime" and, on Broadway, "She Loves Me." **99m/B VHS, LV, Closed Caption.** Margaret Sullavan, James Stewart, Frank Morgan, Joseph Schild-

kraut, Sara Haden, Felix Bressart, Charles Halton; **D:** Ernst Lubitsch; **C:** William H. Daniels. *MGM*

The Shop on Main Street 🎬🎬🎬🎬 *The Shop on High Street; Obch Od Na Korze* **1965** During WWII, a Slovak takes a job as an "Aryan comptroller" for a Jewish-owned button shop. The owner is an old deaf woman; they slowly build a friendship. Tragedy ensues when all of the town's Jews are to be deported. Sensitive and subtle. Surely among the most gutwrenching portrayals of human tragedy ever on screen. Exquisite plotting and direction. In Czechoslovakian with English subtitles. **111m/B VHS, Beta, LV.** *CZ* Ida Kaminska, Josef Kroner, Hana Slivkoua, Frantisek Holly, Martin Gregor; **D:** Jan Kadar, Elmar Klos. Academy Awards '65: Best Foreign Language Film; New York Film Critics Awards '66: Best Foreign Film; Nominations: Academy Awards '66: Best Actress (Kaminska). *COL, SWC, HMV*

Shopping 🎬🎬 **1993 (R)** A crumbling British industrial city (filmed at London's docklands) is the bleak setting for gangs of aimless youth who steal cars, crash into the windows of various shops, grab whatever comes to hand, and then lead the police on high-speed chases. Adrenaline junkie Billy (Law) is accompanied by thrill-seeking girlfriend Jo (Frost) on one such escapade while fending off rival Tommy (Pertwee), who doesn't like his burgeoning criminal empire disturbed. Tries too hard for that rebel youth feeling. **CW:** Violence/mayhem, pervasive language and some drug content. **86m/C VHS.** *GB* Jude Law, Sadie Frost, Sean Pertwee, Fraser James, Sean Bean, Marianne Faithfull, Jonathan Pryce, Danny Newman; **D:** Paul Anderson; **W:** Paul Anderson; **C:** Tony Imi; **M:** Barrington Pheloung. *NHO*

Shopworn Angel 🎬🎬🎬 **1938** Weepy melodrama about a sophisticated actress who leads on a naive Texas soldier who's in New York prior to being shipped out for WWI duty. Later, just before she goes on stage, she learns he's been killed at the front. She rallys to sing "Pack Up your Troubles in Your Old Kit Bag and Smile, Smile, Smile." Lots of tears. Adapted from the story "Private Pettigrew's Girl" by Dana Burnet. This remake of the same-titled 1929 film considerably softened the characters. Remade again in 1959 as "That Kind of Woman." **85m/B VHS.** Margaret Sullavan, James Stewart, Walter Pidgeon, Nat Pendleton, Alan Curtis, Sam Levene, Hattie McDaniel, Charley Grapewin, Charles D. Brown; **D:** H.C. Potter; **W:** Waldo Salt; **C:** Joseph Ruttenberg. *MGM, MOV*

Shore Leave 🎬🎬🎬 **1925** Dressmaker Mackaill isn't getting any younger. Tough-guy sailor Bilge Smith (Barthelmess, in top form) meets her on shore leave; little does he realize her plans for him! She owns a dry-docked ship, you see, and it (and she) will be ready for him when he comes ashore next. Lovely, fun (if rather plodding) romantic comedy. Later made into musicals twice, as "Hit the Deck" and "Follow the Fleet." **74m/B VHS.** Richard Barthelmess, Dorothy Mackaill; **D:** John S. Robertson. *GPV, GVV, VYY*

Short Circuit 🎬🎬 **1986 (PG)** A newly-developed robot designed for the military is hit by lightning and begins to think it's alive. Sheedy and Guttenberg help it hide from the mean people at the weapons lab who want to take it home. Followed two years later, save Sheedy and Guttenberg, by the lame "Short Circuit 2." **98m/C VHS, Beta, LV, Closed Caption.** Steve Guttenberg, Ally Sheedy, Austin Pendleton, Fisher Stevens, Brian McNamara; **D:** John Badham; **W:** S.S. Wilson, Brent Maddock; **M:** David Shire. *FOX*

Short Circuit 2 🎬½ **1988 (PG)** A sequel to the first adorable-robot-outwits-bad-guys tale. The robot, Number Five, makes his way through numerous plot turns without much human assistance or much purpose. Harmless (unless you have to spend time watching it), but pointless and juvenile. Very occasional genuinely funny moments. **95m/C VHS, Beta, LV, Closed Caption.** Fisher Stevens, Cynthia Gibb, Michael McKean, Jack Weston, David Hemblen; **D:** Kenneth Johnson; **W:** S.S. Wilson, Brent Maddock; **M:** Charles Fox. COL

Short Cuts 🎬🎬🎬½ 1993 **(R)** Multi-storied, fish-eyed look at American culture with some 22 characters intersecting—profoundly or fleetingly—through each other's lives. Running the emotional gamut from disturbing to humorous, Altman's portrait of the contemporary human condition is nevertheless fascinating. Based on nine stories and a prose poem by Raymond Carver. Available on laser disc in a movie-only edition or a special edition.**CW:** Graphic sexual language and nudity. 189m/C VHS, LV, **Closed Caption.** Annie Ross, Lori Singer, Jennifer Jason Leigh, Tim Robbins, Madeleine Stowe, Frances McDormand, Peter Gallagher, Lily Tomlin, Tom Waits, Bruce Davison, Andie MacDowell, Jack Lemmon, Lyle Lovett, Fred Ward, Buck Henry, Huey Lewis, Matthew Modine, Anne Archer, Julianne Moore, Lili Taylor, Christopher Penn, Robert Downey Jr., Jarrett Lennon, Zane Cassidy; **D:** Robert Altman; **W:** Frank Barhydt, Robert Altman; **C:** Walt Lloyd; **M:** Mark Isham. Independent Spirit Awards '94: Best Director (Altman), Best Film, Best Screenplay; National Society of Film Critics Awards '93: Best Supporting Actress (Stowe); Venice Film Festival '93: Best Film; Nominations: Academy Awards '93: Best Director (Altman); Golden Globe Awards '94: Best Screenplay; Independent Spirit Awards '94: Best Supporting Actress (Moore). COL

Short Eyes 🎬🎬🎬½ The Slammer 1979 **(R)** When a child molester (Davison) enters prison, the inmates act out their own form of revenge against him. Filmed on location at New York City's Men's House of Detention, nicknamed "The Tombs." Script by Manuel Pinero from his excellent play; he also acts in the film. Top-notch performances and respectful direction from Young bring unsparingly realistic prison drama to the screen. Title is prison jargon for child molester. 100m/C VHS, Beta. Bruce Davison, Miguel Pinero, Nathan George, Donald Blakely, Curtis Mayfield, Jose Perez, Shawn Elliott; **D:** Robert M. Young. LIV

Short Fuse 🎬½ Good to Go 1988 **(R)** A Washington, D.C. reporter uncovers the truth behind the rape and murder of a nurse. Interesting "go-go" music from the Washington D.C. ghetto aids an otherwise uninteresting film. 91m/C VHS, Beta. Art Garfunkel, Robert DoQui, Harris Yulin, Richard Brooks, Reginald Daughtry; **D:** Blaine Novak. THV

Short Time 🎬🎬🎬 1990 **(PG-13)** Somewhere between "Tango & Cash" and "Airplane" is where you'll find "Short Time." Non-stop action/comedy stars Dabney Coleman and Teri Garr as partners in crime and humor. Coleman is a cop days from retirement; wrongly told he is dying, he tries hard to get killed so his family will be provided for. Coleman is wonderful. Garr, no longer the long-suffering wife of "Oh, God" and "Close Encounters," is appealing here as the indulgent sidekick. 100m/C VHS, LV, **Closed Caption.** Dabney Coleman, Teri Garr, Matt Frewer, Barry Corbin, Joe Pantoliano, Xander Berkeley, Rob Roy, Jak-Erik Eriksen; **D:** Gregg Champion; **W:** John Blumenthal, Michael Berry; **M:** Ira Newborn. IME, LIV

The Shot 🎬🎬½ 1996 Shot in fourteen days for $40,000 dollars (and sometimes showing it), this independent release follows out-of-work actors Dern Reel (Bell) and Patrick St. Patrick (Rivkin) as they try to break into the movie business. The foil for the two sensitive artist-types is the shallow but successful director David Egoman. Offended by his brainless action movies, the duo decide to "kidnap" the only print of his latest epic. Although production values are low and the sound is a bit dicey, indie fans will probably like this depiction of Hollywood's shady side. Gained some publicity when ten reels of Kevin Spacey's "Albino Alligator" were swiped from an airport baggage claim shortly after its release. 84m/C VHS. Dan Bell, Michael Rivkin, Mo Gaffney, Michael DeLuise, Vincent Ward, Jack Kehler, Theodore (Ted) Raimi, Jude Horowitz; **Cameos:** Dana Carvey; **D:** Dan Bell; **W:** Dan Bell; **C:** Alan Caudillo; **M:** Dan Sonis.

A Shot in the Dark 🎬½ 1933 A minister suspects murder when a despised miser is thought to have committed suicide. He takes it on himself to investigate in this routine mystery. 53m/B VHS, Beta. GB Dorothy Boyd, O.B. Clarence, Jack Hawkins, Russell Thorndike, Michael Shepley; **D:** George Pearson. SNC

A Shot in the Dark 🎬🎬 1935 When his son is murdered at a New England college, a distraught dad takes it on himself to investigate. Movie cowboy Starrett plays the sleuthing pop in this undistinguished mystery. 69m/B VHS, Beta. Charles Starrett, Robert Warwick, Edward Van Sloan, Marion Shilling, Doris Lloyd, Helen Jerome Eddy, James Bush; **D:** Charles Lamont. NOS, SNC

A Shot in the Dark 🎬🎬🎬½ 1964 Second and possibly the best in the classic "Inspector Clouseau-Pink Panther" series of comedies. The bumbling Inspector Clouseau (Sellers, of course) investigates the case of a parlor maid (Sommer) accused of murdering her lover. Clouseau's libido convinces him she's innocent,even though all the clues point to her. Classic gags, wonderful music. After this film, Sellers as Clouseau disappears until 1975's "Return of the Pink Panther" (Alan Arkin played him in "Inspector Clouseau," made in 1968 by different folks). 101m/C VHS, Beta, LV. Peter Sellers, Elke Sommer, Herbert Lom, George Sanders, Bryan Forbes; **D:** Blake Edwards; **W:** William Peter Blatty, Blake Edwards; **M:** Henry Mancini. FOX, FCT

Shotgun 🎬🎬½ 1955 A sheriff on the trail of a killer is accompanied by a girl he's saved from Indians. Average western cowritten by western actor Rory Calhoun, who had hoped to star in the film, but was turned down by the studio. 81m/C VHS. Sterling Hayden, Zachary Scott, Yvonne De Carlo; **D:** Lesley Selander; **C:** Ellsworth Fredericks. PAR

The Shout 🎬🎬🎬 1978 **(R)** From a strange Robert Graves story, an even stranger film. A lunatic befriends a young couple, moves in with them, and gradually takes over their lives. The movie's title refers to the man's ability to kill by shouting, a power he learned from his Australian aboriginal past. 88m/C VHS, Beta. GB Alan Bates, Susannah York, John Hurt, Tim Curry; **D:** Jerzy Skolimowski; **W:** Michael Austin; **M:** Tony Banks. Cannes Film Festival '78: Grand Jury Prize. COL

Shout 🎬🎬 1991 **(PG-13)** Romance and rebellion set in a sleepy Texas town during the 1950s. Jesse Tucker's (Walters) rebellious ways land him in the Benedict Home for Boys and he seems lost until Jack Cabe (Travolta) enters town. Jack introduces Jesse and the gang to the exciting new sounds of rock 'n' roll. Been done before and better. 93m/C VHS, Beta, LV, **Closed Caption.** John Travolta, James Walters, Heather Graham, Richard Jordan, Linda Fiorentino, Scott Coffey; **D:** Jeffrey Hornaday; **C:** Robert Brinkmann; **M:** Randy Edelman. USH

Shout at the Devil 🎬½ 1976 **(PG)** English officer Moore and Irish-American adventurer Marvin seek to blow up a German battleship out for repairs in East Africa before the outbreak of WWI. There's also some intrigue about ivory smuggling. From the novel by Wilbur Smith and based on an actual incident, but that doesn't make the comedy adventure any more palatable. Marvin's hamming is ludicrous, Moore is unusually wooden, and the big budget permits any number of fairly pointless action-oriented excursions and explosions. 128m/C VHS, Beta, LV. GB Lee Marvin, Roger Moore, Barbara Parkins, Ian Holm; **D:** Peter Hunt; **M:** Maurice Jarre. LIV, VES

The Show 🎬🎬 1995 **(R)** Choppy and incoherent behind-the-scenes look at the attitude and people who make up the explosive hip-hop and rap scene. Mixes black and white concert footage and interviews with Russell Simmons, LL Cool J and Snoop Doggy Dogg, who discuss their music and fans. Will be a disappointment for those looking for a more in-depth study of the music, as this exercise merely scratches the surface. Includes an abundance of cameos from today's top hip hop

artists such as Notorious B.I.G., Naughty by Nature and Wu-Tang Clan.**CW:** Pervasive strong language and some drug content. 90m/B VHS, LV, **Closed Caption.** Craig Mack, Dr. Dre, Run DMC, Slick Rick, Warren G, Kurtis Blow; **D:** Brian Robbins; **C:** Larry Banks, Steven Consentino, Ericson Core, John Demps, Todd A. Dos Reis. COL

Show Boat 🎬🎬🎬🎬 1936 The second of three film versions of the Jerome Kern/Oscar Hammerstein musical (based on the Edna Ferber novel), filmed previously in 1929, about a Mississippi showboat and the life and loves of its denizens. Wonderful romance, unforgettable music. Director Whale also brought the world "Frankenstein." The laser edition includes a historical audio essay by Miles Kreuger, excerpts from the 1929 version, Ziegfeld's 1932 stage revival, "Life Aboard a Real Showboat" (a vintage short), radio broadcasts, and a 300-photo essay tracing the history of showboats. Remade 15 years later. 🎵Ol' Man River; Ah Still Suits Me; Bill; Can't Help Lovin' Dat Man; Only Make Believe; I Have the Room Above Her; You Are Love; Gallivantin' Around; Cotton Blossom. 110m/B VHS, Beta, LV. Irene Dunne, Allan Jones, Paul Robeson, Helen Morgan, Hattie McDaniel, Charles Winninger, Donald Cook, Bobs Watson; **D:** James Whale; **W:** Oscar Hammerstein; **M:** Oscar Hammerstein, Jerome Kern. MGM, CRC, MLB

Show Boat 🎬🎬½ 1951 Third movie version of the 1927 musical about the life and loves of a Mississippi riverboat theater troupe. Terrific musical numbers, with fun dance routines from Champion, who went on to great fame as a choreographer. Grayson is somewhat vapid, but lovely to look at and hear. Gardner didn't want to do the part of Julie, although she eventually received fabulous reviews—her singing was dubbed by Annette Warren. The 171-foot "Cotton Blossom" boat was built on the Tarzan lake on the MGM back lot at an astounding cost of $126,468.00. Warfield's film debut—his "Ole Man River"—was recorded in one take. Laserdisc version features the original motion picture trailer, excerpts from "Broadway," "Silent Film," and radio Version of "Show Boat," a documentary featuring life on a real show boat, and a commentary on the performers, the film, and the history of show boats. 🎵Make Believe; Can't Help Lovin' Dat Man; I Might Fall Back On You; Ol' Man River; You Are Love; Why Do I Love You?; Bill; Life Upon the Wicked Stage; After the Ball. 115m/C VHS, Beta, LV. Kathryn Grayson, Howard Keel, Ava Gardner, William Warfield, Joe E. Brown, Agnes Moorehead, Gower Champion; **D:** George Sidney; **C:** Charles Rosher; **M:** Jerome Kern, Oscar Hammerstein. Nominations: Academy Awards '51: Best Color Cinematography, Scoring of a Musical. MGM, TLF, CRC

Show Business 🎬🎬🎬 1944 Historically valuable film record of classic vaudeville acts, especially Cantor and Davis. A number of vaudevillians recreate their old acts for director Marin—unforgettable slapstick and songs. All this pegged on a plot that follows Cantor's rise to fame with the Ziegfeld Follies. 🎵Alabamy Bound; I Want a Girl (Just Like the Girl Who Married Dear Old Dad); It Had to Be You; Makin' Whoopee; Why Am I Blue; They're Wearing 'Em Higher in Hawaii; The Curse of an Aching Heart; While Strolling in the Park One Day; You May Not Remember. 92m/B VHS, Beta, LV. Eddie Cantor, Joan Davis, George Murphy; **D:** Edwin L. Marin. CCB, TTC

A Show of Force 🎬🎬 1990 **(R)** Reporter Irving investigates the coverup of a murder with political ramifications. Brazilian director Barreto cast (surprise!) his girlfriend in the lead; she doesn't exactly carry the day. Phillips is good, but you'll end up feeling cheated if you expect to see much of highly-billed Duvall or Garcia. Based on a real incident of 1978, but hardly believable as political realism or even moralism. 93m/C VHS, Beta, LV, **Closed Caption.** Amy Irving, Andy Garcia, Robert Duvall, Lou Diamond Phillips; **D:** Bruno Barreto; **W:** Evan Jones; **M:** Georges Delerue. PAR

The Show-Off 🐾½ 1946 Aubrey Piper (Skelton) has big dreams which far out weigh his modest talents. He tells outlandish tales to impress girlfriend Amy (Maxwell) and schemes to make them come true. Dated material which even gifted comedian Skelton can't rescue. Adapted from a play by George Kelly and previously filmed in 1926, 1929, and 1934. 83m/B VHS, Beta. Red Skelton, Marilyn Maxwell, Marjorie Main, Virginia O'Brien, Eddie Anderson, George Cleveland, Leon Ames, Marshall Thompson, Jacqueline White, Lila Leeds, Emory Parnell; *D:* Harry Beaumont; *W:* George Wells. MGM, FCT

Show People 🐾🐾🐾 1928 A pretty girl from the boonies tries to make it big in Tinseltown. But as a slapstick star?! She wanted to be a leading lady! Enjoyable, fun silent comedy shows Davies's true talents. Interesting star cameos, including director Vidor at the end. 82m/B VHS. Marion Davies, William Haines, Dell Henderson, Paul Ralli, William S. Hart, Rod La Rocque; *Cameos:* King Vidor; *D:* King Vidor. MGM

Show Them No Mercy 🐾🐾🐾 *Tainted Money* 1935 A couple and their baby out for a drive unwittingly stumble into a kidnapping that doesn't go as planned. Tense gangster drama reincarnated as the Western "Rawhide." 76m/B VHS. Rochelle Hudson, Cesar Romero, Bruce Cabot, Edward Norris, Edward Brophy, Warren Hymer, Herbert Rawlinson; *D:* George Marshall. FOX, FCT

The Showdown 🐾🐾 1940 The title actually refers to a tricky poker game, the highlight of yet another Hopalong Cassidy versus hoss thieves quickie epic. Kermit Maynard is the brother of cowboy hero Ken Maynard. 65m/B VHS. William Boyd, Russell Hayden, Britt Wood, Morris Ankrum, Jan Clayton, Roy Barcroft, Kermit Maynard; *D:* Howard Bretherton. NOS

The Showdown 🐾🐾½ 1950 Elliott plays trail boss Shad Jones who knows one of his fellow cowhands has murdered his brother. Jones is determined to find out who it is and even the score. Brennan is cast against type as a greedy cattle baron. Elliott's last film for Republic. 86m/B VHS. Wild Bill Elliott, Walter Brennan, Marie Windsor, Harry (Henry) Morgan, Rhys Williams, Jim Davis, Leif Erickson, Yakima Canutt; *D:* Stuart E. McGowan, Dorrell McGowan; *W:* Stuart E. McGowan, Dorrell McGowan. REP

Showdown 🐾🐾½ 1973 (PG) Billy Massey (Martin) and Chuck Garvis (Hudson) had been friends since childhood, until they fell out over the attentions of the pretty Kate (Clark), whom Chuck married. Chuck became the honest town sheriff while Billy took to train robbing. Now it's up to Chuck to bring Billy to justice. Director Seaton's final film. 99m/C VHS. Dean Martin, Rock Hudson, Susan Clark, Donald Moffat, John McLiam, Ed Begley Jr.; *D:* George Seaton; *W:* Theodore Taylor; *C:* Ernest Laszlo; *M:* David Shire. USH, FCT

Showdown 🐾½ 1993 (R) A small southern town is taken over by a motorcycle gang whose leader, Kincade, decides to set up his fencing and drug operations there. But the local law enforcement has other ideas, calling in a martial arts expert who wants revenge against Kincade for the death of his partner. *CW:* Language and martial arts violence. 92m/C VHS. Leo Fong, Werner Hoetzinger, Richard Lynch, Michelle McCormick, Frank Harth, Tom MacDowell, Troy Donahue; *D:* Leo Fong. AIP

Showdown 🐾½ 1993 (R) Ken, the new kid in a particularly nasty high school, gets picked on by the martial-arts expert school bully. After getting beaten up a lot Ken finds out the school janitor can help turn him into a high-kicking fighter. Lots of fast-paced fight scenes which is all the genre demands. An edited PG-13 version is also available. *CW:* Language and violence. 90m/C VHS, LV, Closed Caption. Ken Scott, Billy Blanks, Patrick Kilpatrick, Kenneth McLeod; *D:* Robert Radler. IMP

Showdown at Boot Hill 🐾🐾 1958 A U.S. Marshal (Bronson) kills a wanted murderer but cannot collect the reward because the townspeople will not identify the victim. 76m/B VHS. Charles Bronson, Robert Hutton, John Carradine; *D:* Gene Fowler Jr. REP

Showdown at the Equator 🐾 1983 (R) Chinese cops are trained to kill criminals with their feet, and they do. 95m/C VHS, Beta. Lo Lieh, Bruce Liang, Nora Miao, Lee Kan Kwun. GEM

Showdown at Williams Creek 🐾🐾½ *Kootenai Brown* 1991 (R) A graphic Canadian Western set in the old Montana territory, where an outcast settler goes on trial for killing an old man. Testimony recounts a shocking history of greed and betrayal. The dark side of the Gold Rush, generally well-acted. Inspired by an actual incident. *CW:* Language, violence, and sensuality. 97m/C VHS, Closed Caption. *CA* Tom Burlinson, Donnelly Rhodes, Raymond Burr, Michael Thrush, John Pyper-Ferguson, Alex Bruhanski; *D:* Allen Kroeker; *W:* John Gray; *M:* Michael Conway Baker. REP

Showdown in Little Tokyo 🐾🐾 1991 (R) Lundgren stars as a martial arts master/L.A. cop who was raised in Japan, and has all the respect in the world for his "ancestors" and heritage. Brandon Lee (son of Bruce) is Lundgren's partner, and he's a bona fide American-made, pop-culture, mall junkie. Together, they go after a crack-smuggling gang of "yakuza" (Japanese thugs). Lots of high-kicking action and the unique angle on stereotypes make this a fun martial arts film. *CW:* Language, strong violence and drug use, and sensuality. 78m/C VHS, Beta, LV, 8mm, Closed Caption. Dolph Lundgren, Brandon Lee, Tia Carrere, Cary-Hiroyuki Tagawa; *D:* Mark L. Lester; *W:* Caliope Brattlestreet. WAR

Showgirl Murders 🐾½ 1995 (R) Stripper Ford goes into management when she turns a failing Las Vegas bar into a money-maker but this femme fatale wants owner Douglas to stop sharing the wealth with his boozy wife Carter. Meanwhile, blackmailing DEA agent McFarland and hitman Alber cause problems. *CW:* Strong sexuality, including numerous erotic dance sequences, and for violence, language, and brief drug use. 84m/C VHS. Maria Ford, Jeff Douglas, Matt Preston, Kevin Alber, Samantha Carter, Bob McFarland; *D:* Gene Hertel. NHO

Showgirls woof! 1995 (NC-17) Long on ridiculous dialogue and bad acting and short on costumes, coming-of-age tale follows one young woman as she nakedly climbs the ladder of success as a Vegas showgirl. Oh, the things she must do to be headliner. Berkley makes the jump from television's "Saved by the Bell" to portray Nomi, the young lap dancer with the gift of pelvic thrust and the will to succeed. Whether cavorting clothed or nude, Berkley is uniformly wooden, a mass of lip gloss and mascara struggling to emote. Gershon, as her sly nemesis, brings some wit and splash to her role as the jaded headliner. Eszterhas script descends below its maker's usual standards, which are not particularly high. Titanic amount of female flesh on display fails to give film even a faint hint of sexuality, proof that there is a hell. Rent it, and be prepared to fast forward (to what, we're not sure, though there is a certain camp element that might have been amusing if not imprisoned here). Also available in "R" and unrated versions. *CW:* Nudity and erotic sexuality throughout, and for some graphic language and sexual violence. 131m/C VHS, Closed Caption. Elizabeth Berkley, Gina Gershon, Kyle MacLachlan, Glenn Plummer, Alan Rachins, Robert Davi, Gina Ravera; *D:* Paul Verhoeven; *W:* Joe Eszterhas; *C:* Jost Vacano; *M:* David A. Stewart. Golden Raspberry Awards '95: Worst Picture, Worst Actress (Berkley), Worst Director (Verhoeven), Worst Screenplay, Worst Song ("Walk into the Wind"), Worst New Star (Berkley); Nominations: Golden Raspberry Awards '95: Worst Actor (MacLachlan), Worst Supporting Actor (Davi), Worst Supporting Actress (Gershon). MGM

Shredder Orpheus 🐾 1989 Rock star Orpheus skateboards through hell to stop deadly television transmissions and rescue his wife. 93m/C VHS, Beta. Jesse Bernstein, Robert McGinley, Vera McCaughan, Megan Murphy, Carlo Scandiuzzi; *D:* Robert McGinley. AIP

Shriek in the Night 🐾🐾½ 1933 Two rival reporters (Rogers and Talbot, previously paired in "The Thirteenth Guest") turn detective to solve a string of apartment murders. Made on a proverbial shoestring, but not bad. 66m/B VHS, Beta. Ginger Rogers, Lyle Talbot, Harvey Clark; *D:* Albert Ray. SNC, NOS, BAR

Shriek of the Mutilated woof! 1974 (R) An anthropological expedition on a deserted island turns into a night of horror as a savage beast kills the members of the group one by one. 85m/C VHS, Beta. Alan Brock, Jennifer Stock, Michael Harris; *D:* Michael Findlay. LIV, SNC

The Shrieking 🐾 *Hex* 1973 (PG) Black magic women hang out with biker types in Nebraska in 1919. 93m/C VHS, Beta, LV. Keith Carradine, Christina Raines, Gary Busey, Robert Walker Jr., Dan Haggerty, John Carradine, Scott Glenn; *D:* Leo Garen; *M:* Charles Bernstein. PSM, IME

The Shrimp on the Barbie 🐾½ 1990 (R) When daddy refuses to bless her marriage to dim bulb boyfriend, Australian Samms hires L.A. low life Marin to pose as new beau. Another pseudonymous Smithee effort. *CW:* Sensuality. 86m/C VHS, Beta, LV, Closed Caption. Richard "Cheech" Marin, Emma Samms, Vernon Wells, Bruce Spence, Carole Davis; *D:* Alan Smithee. MED, VTR

Shrunken Heads 🐾🐾½ 1994 (R) Inspired by their comic book heroes three boys try to take on neighborhood thugs only to be gunned down. But along comes Mr. Sumatra, a retired voodoo specialist, who revives the three (in a somewhat smaller form) so they can fight the good fight once again. Title theme music by director Richard's brother, Danny Elfman. 86m/C VHS, Beta, LV. Aeryk Egan, Meg Foster, Julius W. Harris, Becky Herbst, A.J. Damato, Bo Sharon, Darris Love, Leigh-Allyn Baker, Troy Fromin; *D:* Richard Elfman; *W:* Matthew Bright; *M:* Richard Band. PAR

Shy People 🐾🐾🐾 1987 (R) An urbanized New York journalist and her spoiled daughter journey to the Louisiana bayou to visit long-lost relatives in order to produce an article for "Cosmopolitan." They find ignorance, madness, and ancestral secrets and are forced to examine their motives, their relationships and issues brought to light in the watery, murky, fantastic land of the bayous. Well-acted melodrama with an outstanding performance by Hershey as the cajun matriarch. Music by Tangerine Dream; cinematography by Chris Menges. 119m/C VHS, Beta, LV, Closed Caption. Jill Clayburgh, Barbara Hershey, Martha Plimpton, Mare Winningham, Merritt Butrick, John Philbin, Don Swayze, Pruitt Taylor Vince; *D:* Andrei Konchalovsky; *W:* Gerard Brach, Marjorie David; *C:* Chris Menges; *M:* Tangerine Dream. Cannes Film Festival '87: Best Actress (Hershey). WAR

Siberiade 🐾🐾🐾 1979 Depicts life in a Siberian village from 1909 to 1969 for a wealthy family and a peasant clan and how Soviet society affects them. Rambling narrative with strong characters. In Russian with subtitles. 190m/C VHS. *RU* Vladimir Samoilov, Vitaly Solomin, Nikita Mikhalkov, Ludmila Gurchenko, Nathalia Andretchenko; *D:* Andrei Konchalovsky; *W:* Valentin Yezhov, Andrei Konchalovsky; *M:* Eduard Artemyev. Cannes Film Festival '79: Grand Jury Prize. KIV

The Sibling 🐾🐾 *Psycho Sisters; So Evil, My Sister* 1972 (PG) Two sisters become involved in the accidental murder of a man who was a husband to one woman and lover to the other. Of course, one sister has just been released from the mental rehabilitation clinic. 85m/C VHS, Beta. Susan Strasberg, Faith Domergue, Sydney Chaplin, Steve Mitchell; *D:* Reginald LeBorg. PSM, HHE

Sibling Rivalry 🐾🐾 1990 (PG-13) Repressed doctor's wife (redundant) Alley rolls in hay with soon to be stiff stranger upon advice of footloose sister. Stranger expires from heart attack in hay and Alley discovers that the corpse is her long-lost brother-in-law. Slapstick cover-up ensues. **88m/C VHS, Beta, LV, 8mm, Closed Caption.** Kirstie Alley, Bill Pullman, Carrie Fisher, Sam Elliott, Jami Gertz, Ed O'Neill, Scott Bakula, Frances Sternhagen, Bill Macy; *D:* Carl Reiner. *COL, NLC*

The Sicilian *♂♂½* **1987** Adapted from the Mario Puzo novel and based on the life of Salvatore Giuliano. Chronicles the exploits of the men who took on the government, the Catholic Church, and the Mafia in an effort to make Sicily secede from Italy and become its own nation in the 1940s. Pretentious, overdone, and confused. This long, uncut version was unseen in America, but hailed by European critics; the 115-minute, R-rated American release is also available, but isn't as good. See "Salvatore Giuliano" (Francesco Rosi, 1962) instead of either version. **146m/C VHS, Beta, LV.** Christopher Lambert, John Turturro, Terence Stamp, Joss Ackland, Barbara Sukowa; *D:* Michael Cimino. *LIV, VES*

Sicilian Connection *♂½* **1974** A narcotics agent poses as a nightclub manager to bust a drug-smuggling organization. **100m/C VHS, Beta.** *IT* Ben Gazzara, Silvia Monti, Fausto Tozzi. *VCD*

The Sicilian Connection *♂* *The Pizza Connection* **1985 (R)** Two brothers in the mob serve out vendettas and generally create havoc wherever they go. **117m/C VHS, Beta.** Michele Placido, Mark Switzer, Simona Cavallari. *MGM*

Sid & Nancy *♂♂♂½* **1986 (R)** The tragic, brutal, true love story of The Sex Pistols' Sid Vicious and American groupie Nancy Spungen, from the director of "Repo Man." Remarkable lead performances in a very dark story that manages to be funny at times. Depressing but engrossing; no appreciation of punk music or sympathy for the self-destructive way of life is required. Oldman and Webb are superb. Music by Joe Strummer, the Pogues, and Pray for Rain. **111m/C VHS, Beta, LV, Closed Caption.** Gary Oldman, Chloe Webb, Debbie Bishop, David Hayman; *D:* Alex Cox; *W:* Alex Cox; *C:* Roger Deakins. National Society of Film Critics Awards '86: Best Actress (Webb). *MVD, NLC*

Side By Side *♂♂* **1988** In the same vein as "Cocoon," three senior citizens who aren't ready to retire decide to start their own business and launch a sportswear company designed for seniors. A witty portrayal of graceful aging that is uneven at times. **100m/C VHS, Beta, Closed Caption.** Milton Berle, Sid Caesar, Danny Thomas; *D:* Jack Bender. *TRI*

Side Out *♂½* **1990 (PG-13)** The first major film about volleyball!? What a claim! What a bore. Midwestern college guy spends summer in Southern Cal. working for slumlord uncle; instead enters "the ultimate" beach volleyball touring. Bogus. Don't see it, dude. **100m/C VHS, Beta, LV, Closed Caption.** C. Thomas Howell, Peter Horton, Kathy Ireland, Sinjin Smith, Randy Stoklos, Courtney Thorne-Smith, Harley Jane Kozak, Christopher Rydell; *D:* Peter Israelson. *COL*

Side Show *♂* **1984** A runaway teen joins the circus, witnesses a murder, and must use his wits to stay out of reach of the killer. Forced "suspense" and "drama" of the bad made for TV ilk. **98m/C VHS, Beta.** Lance Kerwin, Red Buttons, Anthony (Tony) Franciosa, Connie Stevens; *D:* William Conrad; *W:* Ralph Burns. *TWE*

Sideburns *♂♂* **1991** The Pushkin Club, a group of reactionaries who try to remove the western influence from Russia, attack first a rock band, then innocent civilians as they act as a social cleaning service. Uses humor to try and warn people against the rising fascism in Russia because of the battle between conservative and reformist forces. In Russian with English subtitles. **110m/C VHS.** *RU D:* Yuri Mamin. *FCT*

Sidekicks *♂♂* **1993 (PG)** Cutesy ego vehicle for executive producer Norris. (Brandis) is bullied by the kids at school and doesn't find much support at home from his well-meaning but ineffectual dad. He has a severe case of hero-worship for Norris, who appears as himself in a series of day-

dream karate sequences, saving the good guy and maiming the bad. Director Norris is actor Norris' brother. Predictable and sappy. **100m/C VHS, LV, 8mm, Closed Caption.** Chuck Norris, Jonathan Brandis, Beau Bridges, Mako, Julia Nickson-Soul, Danica McKellar, Richard Moll, Joe Piscopo; *D:* Aaron Norris; *W:* Donald W. Thompson, Lou Illar; *C:* Joao Fernandes; *M:* Alan Silvestri, David Shire. *COL*

Sidewalks of London *♂♂♂* *St. Martin's Lane* **1938** Laughton's a sidewalk entertainer who takes in homeless waif Leigh and puts her in his act and in his heart. Harrison steals her away and before long she's a star in the music halls. Meanwhile, Laughton has fallen on hard times. Memorable performances. **86m/B VHS, Beta.** *GB* Charles Laughton, Vivien Leigh, Rex Harrison, Larry Adler, Tyrone Guthrie, Gus McNaughton, Bart Cormack, Edward Lexy, Maire O'Neill, Basil Gill, Claire Greet, David Burns, Cyril Smith, Ronald Ward, Romilly Lunge, Helen Haye, Jerry Verno; *D:* Tim Whelan; *W:* Clemence Dane; *C:* Jules Kruger; *M:* Arthur Johnson. *KIV, HHT, CAB*

Sidewalks of New York *♂♂½* **1931** A hapless New York millionaire (Keaton) falls for tenement gal Page and tries to win her heart by saving her street urchin brother from joining the local gang of toughs. Keaton was a silent screen classic as a comedian but his talkie career was disappointing as he lost creative control and battled alcohol problems. **74m/B VHS, Beta.** Buster Keaton, Anita Page, Cliff Edwards, Frank LaRue, Frank Rowan, Norman Phillips Jr.; *D:* Jules White, Zion Myers. *MGM, FCT*

Sidewinder One *♂* **1977 (PG)** Motocross racing is the setting for a romance between a racer and an heiress. Good racing footage, but where's the plot? If you like cars a whole lot . . . **97m/C VHS, Beta.** Michael Parks, Marjoe Gortner, Susan Howard, Alex Cord, Charlotte Rae; *D:* Earl Bellamy; *W:* Nancy Voyles Crawford. *NLC*

Sidney Sheldon's Bloodline woof! *Bloodline* **1979 (R)** Wealthy businesswoman Hepburn finds she is marked for death by persons unknown. Exquisitely bad trash from another Sheldon bestseller. **116m/C VHS, Beta.** Audrey Hepburn, Ben Gazzara, James Mason, Michelle Phillips, Omar Sharif, Irene Papas, Romy Schneider, Gert Frobe, Maurice Ronet, Beatrice Straight; *D:* Terence Young; *C:* Frederick A. (Freddie) Young; *M:* Ennio Morricone. *PAR*

The Siege of Firebase Gloria *♂½* **1989** Story of the Marines who risked their lives defending an outpost against overwhelming odds during the 1968 Tet offensive in Vietnam. Purportedly patriotic war drama made by an Australian director; lead Hauser is a disgusting sadist, and plot is hopelessly hackneyed. **95m/C VHS, Beta, LV.** Wings Hauser, R. Lee Ermey; *D:* Brian Trenchard-Smith. *FRH*

Siegfried *♂♂♂♂* *Siegfrieds Tod; Siegfried's Death* **1924** Half of Lang's epic masterpiece "Der Niebelungen," based on German mythology. Title hero bathes in the blood of a dragon he has slain. He marries a princess, but wicked Queen Brumhilde has him killed. Part two, in which Siegfried's widow marries Attila the Hun, is titled "Kriemheld's Revenge." These dark, brooding, archetypal tours de force were patriotic tributes, and were loved by Hitler. Silent with music score. **100m/B VHS, LV.** *GE* Paul Richter, Margareta Schoen; *D:* Fritz Lang. *SNC, NOS, GPV*

Siesta *♂♂½* **1987 (R)** Barkin is a professional stunt woman who leaves her current lover/manager, played by Sheen, and returns to visit her former lover and trainer, Byrne, on the eve of his marriage to another woman. Her trip, marked by flashbacks and flights of seemingly paranoid fantasy, leads to the discovery of murder, but she cannot remember who, when, why, or where. The film distorts time, reality, and perception in a sometimes fascinating, sometimes frustrating psychological mystery. Attractively filmed by video director Lambert. Barkin and Byrne were married in real life a year after the film's release. **97m/C VHS, Beta, LV, Closed Caption.** Ellen Barkin, Gabriel Byrne, Jodie Foster, Julian Sands, Isabella Rossellini, Mar-

tin Sheen, Grace Jones, Alexei Sayle; *D:* Mary Lambert; *W:* Patricia Louisanna Knop; *M:* Miles Davis, Marcus Miller. *ORI, WAR*

The Sign of Four *♂♂½* **1983** Sherlock Holmes and the ever-faithful Watson are hired by a young woman who has been anonymously sent an enormous diamond. An inept production which looks good but that's all. **97m/C VHS, Beta, Closed Caption.** *GB* Ian Richardson, David Healy, Thorley Walters, Cherie Lunghi; *D:* Desmond Davis. *PAR*

The Sign of the Cross *♂♂½* **1933** Depraved Emperor Nero (Laughton) decides he wants a new city so he burns down Rome—blaming the fire on the Christians he also wants to get rid of (preferably by the lions in the arena). Meanwhile, Marcus (March), the Roman Prefect, has fallen for the virginal Christian Mercia (Landi) and risks his life to save her. Besides Laughton's overwhelmingly hammy performance, Colbert slinks seductively as the emperor's vixenish wife, Poppaea. Again, lots of crowd scenes (DeMille's specialty). Based on the play by Wilson Barrett. **125m/B VHS, Closed Caption.** Fredric March, Elissa Landi, Charles Laughton, Claudette Colbert, Ian Keith, Harry Beresford, Arthur Hohl, Nat Pendleton; *D:* Cecil B. DeMille; *W:* Waldemar Young, Sidney Buchman; *M:* Rudolph Kopp. Nominations: Academy Awards '33: Best Cinematography. *USH*

The Sign of Zorro *♂♂* **1960** Adventures of the masked swordsman as he champions the cause of the oppressed in early California. Full-length version of the popular late-50s Disney television series. **89m/C VHS, Beta.** Guy Williams, Henry Calvin, Gene Sheldon, Romney Brent, Britt Lomond, George Lewis, Lisa Gaye; *D:* Norman Foster, Lewis R. Foster. *DIS*

Signal 7 *♂♂* **1983** An improvised, neo-verite document of a night in the lives of two San Francisco taxi drivers. Nilsson's first major release and a notable example of his unique scriptless, tape-to-film narrative technique. **89m/C VHS, Beta.** Bill Ackridge, Dan Leegant; *D:* Rob Nilsson; *W:* Rob Nilsson. *WAR*

Signals Through the Flames *♂♂♂* **1983** A film by Sheldon Rochlin and Maxine Harris outlining the tumultuous history of the famous experimental group, The Living Theatre. **97m/C VHS, Beta.** Julian Beck, Judith Malina, Maxine Harris; *D:* Sheldon Rochlin. *MFV, TPV*

Signs of Life *♂♂* *Lebenszeichen* **1968** German soldier Stroszek (Brogle), injured during the occupation of Crete, is sent to recuperate on the remote island of Kos. With his Greek wife Nora, Stroszek has nothing to do but guard a deserted fortress and a store of abandoned ammunition. But soon the suspicious natives and the isolation begin to drive Stroszek to madness and he decides to blow up the ammunition dump (and the island along with it). German with subtitles. **90m/B VHS.** *GE* Peter Brogle, Wolfgang Reichmann, Athina Zacharopoulous, Wolfgang Stumpf; *D:* Werner Herzog; *W:* Werner Herzog; *C:* Thomas Mauch; *M:* Stavros Xarchakos. *NYF*

Signs of Life *♂♂½* *One for Sorrow, Two for Joy* **1989 (PG-13)** A boat-building company in Maine closes its doors after centuries in business; the employees and families whose lives have been defined by it for generations learn to cope. Wonderful performances compensate only partly for a week script. An episode on PBS's "American Playhouse." **95m/C VHS, Beta, LV.** Beau Bridges, Arthur Kennedy, Vincent D'Onofrio, Kevin J. O'Connor, Will Patton, Kate Reid, Michael Lewis, Kathy Bates, Mary-Louise Parker, Georgia Engel; *D:* John David Coles; *W:* Mark Malone; *C:* Elliot Davis; *M:* Howard Shore. *LIV*

Silas Marner *♂♂♂* **1985** Superb made for British television adaptation of the 1861 George Eliot classic about an itinerant weaver subjected to criminal accusation, poverty, and exile. Wonderful detail and splendid acting. Shot on location in the Cotswold district of England. **92m/C VHS, Beta, Closed Caption.** *GB* Ben Kingsley, Jenny Agutter,

Patrick Ryecart, Patsy Kensit; **D:** Giles Foster; **M:** Carl Davis. VCO, FOX, TVC

The Silence 🐾🐾🐾 *Tystnaden* 1963 A brutal, enigmatic allegory about two sisters, one a nymphomaniac, the other a violently frustrated lesbian, traveling with the former's young son to an unnamed country beset by war. Fascinating and memorable but frustrating and unsatisfying: What is it about? What is it an allegory of? Where is the narrative? The third in Bergman's crisis-of-faith trilogy following "Through a Glass Darkly" and "Winter Light." In Swedish with English subtitles or dubbed. **95m/B VHS, Beta, LV.** *SW* Ingrid Thulin, Gunnel Lindstrom, Birger Malmsten; **D:** Ingmar Bergman; **W:** Ingmar Bergman; **C:** Sven Nykvist. HMV, NLC

Silence 🐾🐾 *Crazy Jack and the Boy* 1973 (G) An autistic boy gets lost in the wilderness and faces an array of difficulties while his foster parents search for him. **82m/C VHS, Beta.** Will Geer, Ellen Geer, Richard Kelton, Ian Geer Flanders, Craig Kelly; **D:** John Korty. NO

Silence Like Glass 🐾🐾½ 1990 (R) Diagnosed with life-threatening illness, two young women struggle to overcome their anger at their fate. They find friendship and together, search for reasons to live. Fine performances, with pacing that keeps the melodrama to a minimum. **102m/C VHS, Beta, LV, Closed Caption.** Jami Gertz, Martha Plimpton, George Peppard, Rip Torn, James Remar; **D:** Carl Schenkel; **M:** Anne Dudley. MED, VTR

Silence of the Hams 🐾½ 1993 (R) Very feeble parody of "The Silence of the Lambs" and others in the thriller/horror genre. Director/writer Greggio also stars as the murder victim, stabbed in the shower, who narrates the story in flashback. There's an eager FBI recruit, a femme fatale, assorted cameo turns, and DeLuise, chewing more scenery than even Anthony Hopkins could swallow, as nutcase Dr. Animal Cannibal Pizza.**CW:** Language. **85m/C VHS, Closed Caption.** Ezio Greggio, Dom DeLuise, Billy Zane, Joanna Pacula, Charlene Tilton, Martin Balsam; *Cameos:* Stuart Pankin, John Astin, Phyllis Diller, Bubba Smith, Larry Storch, Rip Taylor, Shelley Winters, Mel Brooks, John Landis, John Carpenter, Joe Dante; **D:** Ezio Greggio; **W:** Ezio Greggio; **C:** Jacques Haitkin. CAF

Silence of the Heart 🐾🐾🐾 1984 Mother copes with aftermath of suicide of teenage son following their recent divorce. Hartley is captivating in this gripping drama. **100m/C VHS.** Mariette Hartley, Dana Hill, Howard Hesseman, Chad Lowe, Charlie Sheen; **D:** Richard Michaels; **W:** Phil Penningroth; **M:** Georges Delerue. PMH, HHE, VTR

The Silence of the Lambs 🐾🐾🐾½ 1991 (R) Foster is FBI cadet Clarice Starling, a woman with ambition, a cum laude degree in psychology, and a traumatic childhood. When a serial killer begins his ugly rounds, the FBI wants psychological profiles from other serial killers and she's sent to collect a profile from one who's exceptionally clever—psychiatrist Hannibal Lector, a vicious killer prone to dining on his victims. Brilliant performances from Foster and Hopkins, finely detailed supporting characterizations, and elegant pacing from Demme. Some brutal visual effects. Excellent portrayals of women who refuse to be victims. Based on the Thomas Harris novel. **118m/C VHS, Beta, LV, Closed Caption.** Jodie Foster, Anthony Hopkins, Scott Glenn, Ted Levine, Brooke Smith, Charles Napier, Roger Corman, Anthony Heald, Diane Baker, Chris Isaak; **D:** Jonathan Demme; **W:** Ted Tally; **C:** Tak Fujimoto; **M:** Howard Shore. Academy Awards '91: Best Actor (Hopkins), Best Actress (Foster), Best Adapted Screenplay, Best Director (Demme), Best Picture; British Academy Awards '91: Best Actor (Hopkins), Best Actress (Foster); Chicago Film Critics Awards '91: Best Actor (Hopkins), Best Actress (Foster), Best Director (Demme), Best Picture; Directors Guild of America Awards '91: Best Director (Demme); Golden Globe Awards '92: Best Actress—Drama (Foster); National Board of Review Awards '91: Best Director (Demme), Best Film, Best Supporting Actor (Hopkins); New York Film Critics Awards '91: Best Actor (Hopkins), Best Actress (Foster), Best Director (Demme), Best Film; People's Choice Awards '92: Best Film—Drama; Writ-

ers Guild of America '91: Best Adapted Screenplay; Nominations: Academy Awards '91: Best Film Editing, Best Sound. ORI, FCT, IME

Silence of the North 🐾🐾½ 1981 (PG) A widow (Burstyn) with three children struggles to survive under rugged pioneer conditions on the Canadian frontier. The scenery is, not surprisingly, stunning. Based on a true but generic story. **94m/C VHS, Beta.** *CA* Ellen Burstyn, Tom Skerritt; **D:** Allan Winton King; **M:** Michael Conway Baker. USH

The Silencer 🐾🐾 1992 (R) Walden stars as Harley-riding Angel who is out to stop a slavery and prostitution ring that abuses young runaways. Video-arcades hold the clues, and Angel must learn to kill without a conscience. Every time she kills, Angel seeks comfort in the arms of anonymous lovers. However, what she doesn't know is that her demented ex-boyfriend is watching.**CW:** Language, strong violence, and strong sexuality. **85m/C VHS, Closed Caption.** Lynette Walden, Chris Mulkey, Paul Ganus, Morton Downey Jr.; **D:** Amy Goldstein; **W:** Amy Goldstein, Scott Kraft. ACA

The Silencers 🐾🐾½ 1995 (R) Secret Service agent Chuck Rafferty (Scalia) discovers that his latest enemies, known as the Men In Black, are actually human-appearing aliens seeking to conquer Earth. Now Rafferty's only hope is to team up with inter-galactic peace officer Condor (Christopher) to defeat this evil.**CW:** Action violence. **103m/C VHS.** Jack Scalia, Dennis Christopher, Clarence Williams III, Carlos Lauchu, Lucinda Weist; **D:** Richard Pepin. PMH

The Silences of the Palace 🐾🐾🐾 *Les Silences du Palais* 1994 Set in 1950's Tunisia at the end of the ruling monarchy. Twenty-five-year-old Alia (Lacroix) returns to the run-down palace where she was born and grew up as the daughter of a lifelong servant, Khedija (Hedhili), who was also the sexual favorite of her master, Prince Sidi Ali (Fazaa). She remembers the limited, repressed existence they endured and realizes that, ten years after leaving the palace, she has traded one form of subjugation for another and has yet to find her own independence. Arabic with subtitles. **116m/C VHS.** *FR* Ghalia Lacroix, Amel Hedhili, Kamel Fazaa, Hend Sabri, Najia Overghi; **D:** Moufida Tlatli; **W:** Moufida Tlatli, Nouri Bouzid; **C:** Youssef Ben Youssef. CTL

Silent Assassins 🐾🐾 1988 Fists and bullets fly when a scientist is kidnapped in order to gain secrets to biological warfare. Chong and Rhee, real-life owners of a martial arts studio, produced and choreographed the film. Blair is here, but doesn't figure much. A notch up from most similar martial arts pics. **92m/C VHS.** Sam Jones, Linda Blair, Jun Chong, Phillip Rhee; **D:** Scott Thomas, Lee Doo-yong. MCG, VTR

Silent Code 🐾 1935 A Mountie is framed for the murder of a young miner. **55m/B VHS, Beta.** Tom Tyler. NO

The Silent Enemy 🐾🐾½ 1958 The true-life exploits of British frogmen battling Italian foes during WWII. Suspenseful and engrossing; good performances and good rendering of underwater action. Video release snips twenty minutes from the original and adds color. **91m/C VHS, Beta.** *GB* Laurence Harvey, John Clements, Michael Craig, Dawn Addams, Sidney James, Alec McCowen, Nigel Stock; **D:** William Fairchild. NO

Silent Fall 🐾½ 1994 (R) Grisly double murder of his parents is witnessed by autistic 9-year-old, Tim Warden (Faulkner), and his traumatized over-protective teenaged sister Sylvie (Tyler). Retired psychiatrist Jake Rainier (Dreyfuss) is reluctant to get involved, ever since an autistic child in his care died, but when authoritarian rival Dr. Harlinger (Lithgow) is called instead, Jake changes his mind. Second half of film takes a lurid turn as Jake probes Tim's damaged psyche to discover the killer. Trite, clueless whodunnit that generally wastes the talent involved; Tyler and Faulkner make their film debuts.**CW:** Strong language; violence. **101m/C VHS, LV, Closed Caption.** Richard Drey-

fuss, Ben Faulkner, John Lithgow, Liv Tyler, Linda Hamilton, J.T. Walsh; **D:** Bruce Beresford; **W:** Akiva Goldsman; **M:** Stewart Copeland. WAR

Silent Hunter 🐾½ 1994 (R) Undercover cop Jim Paradine (O'Keeffe) retreats to a remote mountains cabin when his family is killed by a gang of bank robbers. Naturally, the thugs just happen to crash land on Paradine's mountain top with their stolen loot and he goes off to hunt them down.**CW:** Language; sadistic violence; some sexuality. **97m/C VHS, LV, Closed Caption.** Miles O'Keeffe, Fred Williamson, Lynne Adams, Peter Colvey, Jason Cavalier, Sabine Karsenti; **D:** Fred Williamson. TTC, NLC

Silent Killers 🐾½ 19?? A scientist is responsible for the deaths of many people because of his research in germ warfare. He's haunted by the ghosts of his victims. Is he losing his mind or is it a sinister plot? **90m/C VHS.** Stephen Soul, Daniel Garfield. MOV

Silent Laugh Makers, No. 1 🐾🐾🐾 1915 Four hilarious short movies from the silent era: "Looking for Sally," about an immigrant in search of his best girlfriend; "Lucky Dog," with the young Laurel and Hardy; "His Night Out," about a wild evening with Charlie Chaplin and Ben Turpin; and "Hop-a-Long." Non-stop side-splitting fun. **50m/B VHS, Beta.** Charley Chase, Stan Laurel, Oliver Hardy, Charlie Chaplin, Ben Turpin, Arthur Lake. VYY

Silent Laugh Makers, No. 2 🐾🐾🐾 1917 Several short funny films of the silent picture era: "Fluttering Hearts," "Long Live the King," about a king who just can't get along with his nobles, starring Chase and Hardy; and "A Sea Dog Tale." All are unremittingly hilarious. **50m/B VHS, Beta.** Charley Chase, Oliver Hardy, Billy Bevan. VYY

Silent Laugh Makers, No. 3 🐾🐾🐾 1919 Four comedy shorts: "Picking Peaches" (1924), directed by Frank Capra, Langdon's first for Mack Sennett; "All Tied Up" (1925), featuring "A Ton of Fun"-four rotund comedians; "Don't Shove" (1919), featuring Harold Lloyd wooing Bebe Daniels; and "Some Baby" (1922), with Snub Pollard. **55m/B VHS, Beta.** Harry Langdon, Harold Lloyd, Bebe Daniels, Snub Pollard. VYY

Silent Madness 🐾 1984 (R) A psychiatrist must stop a deranged killer, escaped from an asylum, from slaughtering helpless college coeds in a sorority house. Meanwhile, hospital execs send orderlies to kill the patient, to conceal their mistake. Ludicrous. **93m/C VHS, Beta.** Belinda J. Montgomery, Viveca Lindfors, Sydney Lassick; **D:** Simon Nuchtern. MED

The Silent Mr. Sherlock Holmes 🐾🐾 1912 These two silent shorts are a rare treat for Holmes fans. "The Copper Beeches" was produced with the "personal supervision of Arthur Conan Doyle." In "The Man with the Twisted Lip," Holmes is hired to find out whether a banker was murdered. **68m/B VHS.** *GB* Ellie Norwood. VYY

Silent Motive 🐾🐾½ 1991 Laura is a Hollywood screenwriter who's shocked to discover that a killer is using her recent script as an outline for a series of film-industry murders. She's even more unnerved when a detective makes Laura his number one suspect. **90m/C VHS, Closed Caption.** Patricia Wettig, Mike Farrell, Ed Asner, Rick Springfield, David Packer; **D:** Lee Philips; **W:** William Bekkala. WOV

Silent Movie 🐾🐾½ 1976 (PG) A has-been movie director (Brooks) is determined to make a comeback and save his studio from being taken over by a conglomerate. Hilarious at times but uneven. An original idea; not as successful as it could have been. Has music and sound effects, but only one word of spoken dialogue by famous mime Marceau. **88m/C VHS, Beta, LV.** Mel Brooks, Marty Feldman, Dom DeLuise, Burt Reynolds, Anne Bancroft, James Caan, Liza Minnelli, Paul Newman, Sid Caesar, Bernadette Peters, Harry Ritz, Marcel Marceau; **D:** Mel Brooks; **W:** Mel Brooks, Ron Clark, Rudy DeLuca, Barry Levinson.

National Board of Review Awards '76: 10 Best Films of the Year. *FOX*

Silent Movies...Just For the Fun of It! 1926 Three short silent films: "The Iron Mule" (1925), "For Sadie's Sake" (1926), and "Hazel from Hollywood" (1918). 56m/B VHS, Beta, 8mm. Jimmie Adams, Dorothy Devore, Al "Fuzzy" St. John. *VYY*

Silent Night, Bloody Night 🎬🎬 *Night of the Dark Full Moon; Death House* 1973 (R) An escaped lunatic terrorizes a small New England town, particularly a mansion that was once an insane asylum. Not great, but well done by director Gershuny, with some nail-biting suspense and slick scene changes. 83m/C VHS. Patrick O'Neal, John Carradine, Walter Abel, Mary Woronov, Astrid Heeren, Candy Darling; D: Theodore Gershuny. *NO*

Silent Night, Deadly Night 🎬 1984 (R) A psycho ax-murders people while dressed as jolly old St. Nick. Violent and disturbing, to say the least. Caused quite a controversy when it was released to theaters. Santa gimmick sold some tickets at the time, but resist the urge to rent it: it's completely devoid of worth, whatever the killer's outfit. As if one were not enough, we've been blessed with four sequels. 92m/C VHS, Beta, LV. Lilyan Chauvin, Gilmer McCormick, Toni Nero; D: Charles E. Sellier; M: Perry Botkin. *LIV, IME*

Silent Night, Deadly Night 2 🎬 1987 (R) The psychotic little brother of the psychotic, Santa Claus-dressed killer from the first film exacts revenge, covering the same bloody ground as before. Almost half this sequel consists of scenes lifted whole from the original. 88m/C VHS, Beta, LV. Eric Freeman, James Newman, Elizabeth Cayton, Jean Miller; D: Lee Harry; M: Michael Armstrong. *LIV*

Silent Night, Deadly Night 3: Better Watch Out! 🎬½ 1989 (R) The now grown-up psycho goes up against a young blind woman. Santa is no longer the bad guy, thank goodness. The least bad of the lot, with black humor—though not enough to make it worth seeing. 90m/C VHS, Beta, LV. Richard Beymer, Bill Moseley, Samantha Scully, Eric Da Re, Laura Herring, Robert Culp; D: Monte Hellman. *LIV*

Silent Night, Deadly Night 4: Initiation 🎬 1990 (R) A secret L.A. cult of she-demons use the slasher Ricky for their own ends—making for more mayhem and horror. Has virtually nothing to do with its three "sequels"—which is not to say it's very good. 90m/C VHS, LV. Maud Adams, Allyce Beasley, Clint Howard, Reggie Bannister; D: Brian Yuzna. *MOV*

Silent Night, Deadly Night 5: The Toymaker 🎬 1991 (R) A young boy's Christmas is overrun by murderous Santas and vicious stuffed animals. Definitely for fans of the genre only.CW: Strong violence and strong sensuality. 90m/C VHS. Mickey Rooney, William Thorne, Jane Higginson. *LIV*

Silent Night, Lonely Night 🎬🎬 1969 Two lonely middle-aged people (Bridges and Jones) begin an affair at Christmas to stem the pain of their separately disintegrating marriages. Poignant but not successfully credible. Based on the play by Robert Anderson. Made for television. 98m/C VHS, Beta. Lloyd Bridges, Shirley Jones, Jeff Bridges, Cloris Leachman, Carrie Snodgress, Lynn Carlin; D: Daniel Petrie; M: Billy Goldenberg. *USH*

The Silent One 🎬½ 1986 Featuring underwater photography by Ron and Valerie Taylor, this is the odd story of a mysterious Polynesian boy who has a nautical relationship with a sea turtle. 96m/C VHS, Beta. NZ Telo Malese, George Henare; D: Yvonne Mackay. *NO*

The Silent Partner 🎬🎬🎬 1978 A bank teller (Gould) foils a robbery, but manages to take some money for himself. The unbalanced robber (Plummer) knows it and wants the money. Good script and well directed, with emphasis on suspense and detail. Unexpectedly violent at times. Early, non-comedic role for big guy Candy. 103m/C

VHS, Beta, LV. CA Elliott Gould, Christopher Plummer, Susannah York, John Candy; D: Daryl Duke; W: Curtis Hanson; C: Billy Williams. *FCT, VES*

The Silent Passenger 🎬🎬½ 1935 Amateur sleuth Lord Peter Wimsey makes cinematic debut investigating murder and blackmail on the British railway. Dorothy Sayer's character later inspired BBC mystery series. 75m/B VHS, Beta. GB John Loder, Peter Haddon, Mary Newland, Austin Trevor, Donald Wolfit, Leslie Perrins, Aubrey Mather, Ralph Truman; D: Reginald Denham. *NOS, SNC*

Silent Rage 🎬 1982 (R) Sheriff Norris of a small Texas town must destroy killer Libby who has been made indestructible through genetic engineering. Chuck Norris meets Frankenstein, sort of. Nice try, but still thoroughly stupid and boring. 100m/C VHS, Beta, LV, 8mm. Chuck Norris, Ron Silver, Steven Keats, Toni Kalem, Brian Libby; D: Michael Miller; M: Peter Bernstein. *COL*

Silent Raiders 🎬 1954 A commando unit is sent to France in 1943 to knock out a Nazi communications center. 72m/B VHS, Beta. Richard Bartlett, Earle Lyon, Jeanette Bordeau; M: Elmer Bernstein. *NO*

Silent Rebellion 🎬½ 1982 A Greek immigrant (Savalas) and his son return to Greece, where they reunite with mother and brother and re-discover their heritage and each other. Cross-cultural misunderstandings abound; could have been interesting, but the story is just too generic and uninspired. 90m/C VHS, Beta. Telly Savalas, Keith Gordon, Michael Constantine, Yula Gavala. *NO*

Silent Running 🎬🎬🎬 1971 (G) Members of a space station orbiting Saturn care for the last vegetation of a nuclear-devastated earth. When orders come to destroy the vegetation, Dern takes matters into his own hands. Speculative sci-fi at its best. Trumbull's directorial debut; he created special effects for "2001" and "Close Encounters." Strange music enhances the alien atmosphere. 90m/C VHS, Beta, LV. Bruce Dern, Cliff Potts, Ron Rifkin; D: Douglas Trumbull; W: Michael Cimino, Deric Washburn, Steven Bochco; M: Prof. Peter Schickele. *USH*

Silent Scream 🎬½ 1980 (R) College kids take up residence with the owners of an eerie mansion complete with obligatory murders. Obvious to the point of being gratuitous—and just plain uninteresting. 87m/C VHS, Beta. Rebecca Balding, Cameron Mitchell, Avery Schreiber, Barbara Steele, Steve Doubet, Brad Reardon, Yvonne De Carlo; D: Denny Harris; W: Wallace C. Bennett, Jim Wheat, Ken Wheat. *MED*

Silent Scream 🎬 1984 A former Nazi concentration camp commandant collects unusual animals and humans as a hobby. 60m/C VHS, Beta. GB Peter Cushing, Brian Cox, Elaine Donnelly; D: Alan Gibson. *NO*

Silent Tongue 🎬🎬 1992 (PG-13) Weird western finds the crazed Talbot Roe (Phoenix) alone in the wilderness, guarding the tree that is the burial place of his half-breed wife Awbonnie (Tousey). Roe's father (Harris) bought his son's bride from her greedy and abusive father McCree (Bates). In an effort to return Talbot to some semblance of normality, Roe offers to buy McCree's other daughter (Arredondo) for his son. But Talbot is haunted by his wife's angry ghost, who wants her spirit set free by ritual burning, and McCree himself fears the vengeance of his one-time Indian wife Silent Tongue (Cardinal). Messy, over-the-top plot with some poignant performances, especially Phoenix's.CW: Mildly violent. 101m/C VHS, LV, Closed Caption. River Phoenix, Sheila Tousey, Richard Harris, Alan Bates, Jeri Arredondo, Dermot Mulroney, Tantoo Cardinal; Cameos: Bill Irwin, David Shiner; D: Sam Shepard; W: Sam Shepard; C: Jack Conroy; M: Patrick O'Hearn. *THV*

The Silent Touch 🎬🎬½ 1994 (PG-13) Irascible, aged composer Henry Kesdi (Von Sydow), living in Denmark with his long-suffering wife Helena (Miles), hasn't written a note in 40 years. Music student Stefan (Blutheau) dreams of a composition he believes Henry started but nev-

er completed. So Stefan naturally sets out to help Henry finish his symphony by mystically healing his composer's block. Yes, it does sound hokey but the fluff is saved by Von Sydow's boyantly funny performance. 92m/C VHS. PL DK GB Max von Sydow, Lothaire Bluteau, Sarah Miles, Sofie Graboel, Aleksander Bardini, Peter Hesse Overgaard; D: Krzysztof Zanussi; W: Peter Morgan, Mark Wadlow; M: Wojciech Kilar. *ACA, FCT*

Silent Valley 🎬 1935 Adventure of the Old West with American cowboy star Tom Tyler. 60m/B VHS, Beta. Tom Tyler. *NOS, VCN, DVT*

Silent Victim 🎬🎬½ 1992 (R) Greene stars as Bonnie Jackson, a Georgia housewife whose marriage has not only gone wrong but turned violent. She takes a drug overdose in a suicide attempt but it results only in a miscarriage. Her furious husband sues her for the murder of their unborn child while an ambitious district attorney petitions the state to charge Bonnie with committing an illegal abortion. Bonnie's torment soon becomes a media circus as she goes on trial. Based on a true story.CW: Language, elements of domestic violence, and sexuality. 116m/C VHS, Closed Caption. Michelle Greene, Kyle Secor, Ely Pouget, Alex Hyde-White, Dori Brenner, Leann Hunley; D: Menahem Golan; W: Nelly Adnil, Jonathan Platnick; M: William T. Stromberg. *COL*

Silent Victory: The Kitty O'Neil Story 🎬🎬🎬 1979 Genuinely stirring real-life-overcoming-adversity story of the deaf woman who became a top stunt woman in Hollywood and holder of the land speed record for women. Channing is very good as O'Neil. Made for television. 96m/C Beta. Stockard Channing, Brian Dennehy, Colleen Dewhurst, Edward Albert, James Farentino; D: Lou Antonio. *NO*

Silent Witness 🎬 1985 (R) A woman (Bertinelli) witnesses her brother-in-law and his friend rape a young woman. She must decide whether to testify against them or keep the family secret. Exploitative and weakly plotted. Rip-off of the much-discussed Massachusetts barroom rape case. Made for television. 97m/C VHS, Beta. Valerie Bertinelli, John Savage, Chris Nash, Melissa Leo, Pat Corley, Steven Williams, Jacqueline Brookes, Alex McArthur, Katie McCombs; D: Michael Miller. *ACA*

Silhouette 🎬🎬 1991 (R) Detained in a small Texas town, a woman witnesses the murder of a local girl—but in silhouette, so the killer's identity takes a feature-length running time to resolve. A fair but contrived made for cable TV thriller that the leading lady co-produced.CW: Violence. 89m/C VHS. Faye Dunaway, David Rasche, John Terry, Carlos Gomez, Ron Campbell, Margaret Blye, Talisa Soto, Ritch Brinkley; D: Carl Schenkel; W: Victor Buell. *USH*

Silk 🎬 1986 (R) A beautiful and bloodthirsty detective cuts a swath through local heroin rings. 84m/C VHS, Beta. Cec Verrell, Bill McLaughlin, Fred Bailey; D: Cirio H. Santiago. *MGM*

Silk 2 🎬 1989 (R) A foreign-made sequel, in which a beautiful cop stops crime in Honolulu. Ludicrous plot, bad acting, lots of skin and violence—what more could you want? Dreadful. 85m/C VHS, Beta. Monique Gabrielle, Peter Nelson, Jan Merlin, Maria Clair; D: Cirio H. Santiago. *MGM*

Silk Degrees 🎬½ 1994 (R) Actress witnesses a murder and is targeted for elimination by the killer. She's supposed to be protected by a couple of federal agents but it seems there's a traitor around.CW: Violence and sexuality. 81m/C VHS, LV, Closed Caption. Deborah Shelton, Marc Singer, Mark Hamill, Michael Des Barres, Charles Napier, Gilbert Gottfried, Adrienne Barbeau; D: Armand Garabidian; W: Stuart Gibbs, Douglas J. Sloan, Robert Gottlieb; M: Larry Wolff. *IMP*

Silk n' Sabotage 🎬½ 1994 Serious-minded Jamie comes up with a program for a new computer game. When it's stolen by a con artist, Jamie and her frivolous roommates team up to retrieve it. Since the roomies operate a lingerie business there's lots of pulchritude on display.

Also available unrated. **70m/C VHS, Beta, LV.** Cherilyn Shea, Stephanie Champlin, Julie Skiru; **D:** Joe Cauley. *ACA*

The Silk Road 🐾🐾½ **1992 (PG-13)** In 11th-century China the ancient trading route leads to Dun Huang, a desert city that is the last Chinese outpost on the road. Zhao, a young scholar, travels in a caravan which is attacked by Chinese mercenaries. His life is spared and when his new home is attacked by a neighboring nation, he hides the city's treasures in nearby caves. Adapted from the novel by Yashushi Inoue, which was based on the Thousand Buddha Caves, where a treasure of Buddhist icons and scrolls were discovered in 1900. Billed as an epic, there's lots of pageantry and some impressive battle scenes but is too stately and overdone to be more than merely interesting. In Japanese with English subtitles. **99m/C VHS, LV.** *CH JP* Koichi Sato, Toshiyuki Nishida, Anna Nakagawa, Tsunehiko Watase, Daijiro Harada, Takahiro Tamura; **D:** Junya Sato; **M:** Masaru Sato. *THV*

Silk Stockings 🐾🐾🐾 **1957** Splendid musical comedy adaptation of "Ninotchka," with Astaire as a charming American movie man, and Charisse as the cold Soviet official whose commie heart he melts. Music and lyrics by Cole Porter highlight this film adapted from George S. Kaufman's hit Broadway play. Director Mamoulian's last film. ♪Too Bad; Paris Loves Lovers; Fated to Be Mated; The Ritz Roll 'n Rock; Silk Stockings; Red Blues; All of You; Stereophonic Sound; Josephine. **117m/C VHS, Beta, LV.** Fred Astaire, Cyd Charisse, Janis Paige, Peter Lorre, George Tobias; **D:** Rouben Mamoulian; **M:** Andre Previn. *MGM, TTC*

Silkwood 🐾🐾🐾 **1983 (R)** The story of Karen Silkwood, who died in a 1974 car crash under suspicious circumstances. She was a nuclear plant worker and activist who was investigating shoddy practices at the plant. Streep acts up a storm, disappearing completely into her character. Cher surprises with her fine portrayal of a lesbian co-worker, and Russell is also good. Nichols has a tough time since we already know the ending, but he brings top-notch performances from his excellent cast. **131m/C VHS, Beta, LV.** Meryl Streep, Kurt Russell, Cher, Diana Scarwid, Bruce McGill, Fred Ward, David Strathairn, Josef Sommer, Craig T. Nelson; **D:** Mike Nichols; **W:** Nora Ephron, Alice Arlen; **M:** Georges Delerue. Golden Globe Awards '84: Best Supporting Actress (Cher); Nominations: Academy Awards '83: Best Actress (Streep), Best Director (Nichols), Best Film Editing, Best Original Screenplay, Best Supporting Actress (Cher). *PAR*

Silver Bandit 🐾 **1947** A bookkeeper is sent to investigate a mine theft. Along the way he sings country and western songs. **54m/B VHS, Beta, LV.** Spade Cooley. *NOS*

Silver Bears 🐾🐾 **1978 (PG)** Caine is an unlikely mobster in this comedy. He's sent to Switzerland to buy a bank for laundering purposes and ends up being swindled himself. So-so entry adapted from the novel by Paul Erdman. **114m/C VHS, Beta.** Michael Caine, Cybill Shepherd, Louis Jourdan, Stephane Audran, David Warner, Tom Smothers, Martin Balsam, Jay Leno, Charles Gray, Joss Ackland; **D:** Ivan Passer; **M:** Claude Bolling. *NO*

The Silver Bullet **1934** Follows the adventures of Tom, the sheriff of a small gold mining town. **55m/C VHS.** Tom Tyler, Jayne Regan, Lafe McKee, Charles King, George Chesebro, Charles "Slim" Whitaker, Lew Meehan, Franklyn Farnum, Walt Williams; **D:** Bernard B. Ray. *GPV*

Silver Bullet 🐾🐾 *Stephen King's Silver Bullet* **1985 (R)** Adapted from Stephen King's "Cycle of the Werewolf," about a town whose inhabitants are being brutally murdered. It finally dawns on them the culprit is a werewolf. Action moves along at a good clip and the film has its share of suspense. **95m/C VHS, LV, Closed Caption.** Corey Haim, Gary Busey, Megan Follows, Everett McGill; **D:** Daniel Attias; **W:** Stephen King. *PAR*

The Silver Chalice 🐾 **1954** Newman's career somehow survived his movie debut in this bloated, turgid Biblical epic about the momentous events that befall a young Greek sculptor who fashions the cup that will be used at the Last Supper. Newman later took out an ad in Variety to apologize for the film, in which Greene also made his debut. Based on the novel by Thomas Costain. **135m/C VHS, Beta.** Paul Newman, Virginia Mayo, Pier Angeli, Jack Palance, Natalie Wood, Joseph Wiseman, Lorne Greene, E.G. Marshall; **D:** Victor Saville; **M:** Franz Waxman. Nominations: Academy Awards '54: Best Color Cinematography, Original Dramatic/Comedy Score. *WAR*

Silver City 🐾🐾 **1984 (PG)** A saga depicting the plight of Polish refugees in Australia in 1949. A pair of lovers find each other in a crowded refugee camp. He's married to her friend. Too-complex, slow but earnest effort. **110m/C VHS, Beta.** *AU* Gosia Dobrowolska, Ivar Kants; **D:** Sophia Turkiewicz. *ORI*

Silver City Bonanza 🐾🐾½ **1951** Lots of action in this outrageous oater that includes a haunted ranch and an undersea battle as plot devices. Singing cowboy Allen and sidekick Ebsen use a seeing-eye dog to track down the killer of a blind man. Since Roy Rogers and Republic parted company the year of this film's release, singing star Allen was groomed to become the new "King of the Cowboys." However, by this time, the singing-cowboy craze was almost old hat. **67m/B VHS, Closed Caption.** Rex Allen, Buddy Ebsen, Mary Ellen Kay, Billy Kimbley, Alix Ebsen, Bill Kennedy, Gregg Barton, Clem Bevans; **D:** George Blair; **W:** Bob Williams. *REP*

Silver City Kid 🐾 **1945** Two mine owners learn about a rich mineral vein under a rancher's land, kill him, and then try to steal the property from his sister. So it's up to ranch foreman Jack Adams (Lane) to expose the plot and bring the guilty to justice. **56m/B VHS, Closed Caption.** Allan "Rocky" Lane. *REP*

Silver Dream Racer 🐾½ **1983 (PG)** An English grease monkey wants to win the World Motorcycle Championship title away from an American biker. There's also after someone else's girlfriend. Boring, stilted, unoriginal "Big Race" flick. **103m/C VHS, Beta.** Beau Bridges, David Essex, Christina Raines, Diane Keen, Harry H. Corbett; **D:** David Wickes; **M:** David Essex. *LIV, VES*

The Silver Horde 🐾🐾½ **1930** Alaskan salmon fishery owner McCrea battles villainous competitor Gordon for both his livelihood and his ladyfriend—dancehall dame Brent. Arthur's the society gal who briefly catches McCrea's eye. Silent screen star Sweet ended her career with a brief role. Based on a novel by Rex Beach. **80m/B VHS.** Joel McCrea, Evelyn Brent, Jean Arthur, Gavin Gordon, Louis Wolheim, Raymond Hatton, Blanche Sweet; **D:** George Archainbaud. *FCT*

Silver Lode 🐾🐾½ **1954** A man accused of murder on his wedding day attempts to clear his name while the law launches an intensive manhunt for him. Ordinary story improved by good, energetic cast. **92m/C VHS, Beta.** John Payne, Dan Duryea, Lizabeth Scott, Stuart Whitman; **D:** Allan Dwan. *NO*

Silver Queen 🐾🐾 **1942** A woman finds out her father has gambled away a silver mine and left her with debts. She opens a saloon, only to have her fiance use the money to hunt for more silver. **81m/B VHS, Beta.** Priscilla Lane, George Brent, Bruce Cabot, Eugene Pallette; **D:** Lloyd Bacon. Nominations: Academy Awards '42: Best Interior Decoration, Original Dramatic/Comedy Score. *NO*

Silver River 🐾½ **1948** Average western that marked the final collaboration between director Walsh and star Flynn. It never even comes close to their previous works. Flynn plays a no-good, power-hungry cad who will stop at nothing to get what he wants. He happens to want Sheridan, who is married to Bennett, so Flynn schemes to get rid of him. Overall, Flynn acts as though he really isn't interested in the material and had to make a pact with Walsh that he would stay sober until five in the afternoon while filming. Based on

an unpublished novel by Stephen Longstreet. **108m/B VHS, Closed Caption.** Errol Flynn, Ann Sheridan, Thomas Mitchell, Bruce (Herman Brix) Bennett, Tom D'Andrea, Barton MacLane, Monte Blue, Jonathan Hale; **D:** Raoul Walsh; **W:** Stephen Longstreet, Harriet Frank Jr.; **M:** Max Steiner. *MGM*

Silver Spurs 🐾½ **1943** Villain tries to get some oil-rich property by murdering the ranch's owner. Ranch foreman Rogers saves the day. **60m/B VHS, Beta.** Roy Rogers, Jerome Cowan, John Carradine, Phyllis Brooks, Smiley Burnette, Joyce Compton; **D:** Joseph Kane. *NOS, VCN, DVT*

Silver Stallion 🐾½ **1941** Thunder the Wonder Horse plays the title character, who fights rattlesnakes, wild dogs and hoss thieves. Too bad he doesn't give acting lessons to the humans in the this frail family western with nice scenery and action scenes. **59m/C VHS, Beta.** David Sharpe, Carol Hughes, Leroy Mason, Walter Long; **D:** Edward Finney. *VYY, GPV*

The Silver Stallion: King of the Wild Brumbies 🐾🐾½ *The Silver Brumby* **1993 (G)** The adolescent Indi is enthralled as her writer-mother relates each new chapter in the saga of Thara, the amazing silver stallion. And she images each adventure as the horse triumphs over evil men, other horses, and the elements to become leader of the herd. Based on the Australian children's novel "The Silver Brumby" by Elyne Mitchell. **93m/C VHS, Beta, Closed Caption.** *AU* Caroline Goodall, Ami Daemion, Russell Crowe; **D:** John Tatoulis; **W:** John Tatoulis, Jon Stephens; **M:** Tassos Ioannides. *PAR*

Silver Star 🐾🐾 **1955** Man elected sheriff of a western town turns down the job because he is a pacifist. He changes his mind when his defeated opponent hires a trio of killers to come after him. **73m/B VHS, Beta.** Jimmy Wakely, Edgar Buchanan, Marie Windsor. *NO*

Silver Strand 🐾🐾½ **1995 (R)** Hunky Brian Del Piso (Bellows), a navel cadet in the S.E.A.L. training school, makes the big mistake of falling for sexy Michelle (Sheridan), who just happens to be an officer's wife. As if he didn't have enough challenges, should their affair be exposed Brian might just as well kiss his career goodbye. **CW:** Sexuality and strong language. **104m/C VHS, Closed Caption.** Gil Bellows, Nicolette Sheridan; **D:** George Miller; **W:** Douglas Day Stewart; **C:** David Connell; **M:** Joseph Conlan. *MGM*

The Silver Streak 🐾🐾 **1934** The sickly son of a diesel train designer needs an iron lung—pronto. A rival's super-fast locomotive is the only hope for the boy. Murders, runaway engines, and a crew that would rather walk enliven this race against time. **72m/B VHS, Beta.** Sally Blane, Charles Starrett, Arthur Lake, Edgar Kennedy, William Farnum; **D:** Thomas Atkins. *CCB*

Silver Streak 🐾🐾🐾 **1976 (PG)** Pooped exec Wilder rides a train from L.A. to Chicago, planning to enjoy a leisurely, relaxing trip. Instead he becomes involved with murder, intrigue, and a beautiful woman. Energetic Hitchcock parody features successful first pairing of Wilder and Pryor. **113m/C VHS, Beta, LV.** Gene Wilder, Richard Pryor, Jill Clayburgh, Patrick McGoohan, Ned Beatty, Ray Walston, Richard Kiel, Scatman Crothers; **D:** Arthur Hiller; **W:** Colin Higgins; **M:** Henry Mancini. Nominations: Academy Awards '76: Best Sound. *FOX*

Silverado 🐾🐾🐾 **1985 (PG-13)** Affectionate pastiche of western cliches has everything a viewer could ask for—except Indians. Straightforward plot has four virtuous cowboys rise up against a crooked lawman in a blaze of six guns. No subtlety from the first big Western in quite a while, but plenty of fun and laughs. Laserdisc edition features a wide screen film-to-tape transfer monitored by the photography director, set photos, release trailers, and other publicity hoohah as well as a special time-lapse sequence of the set construction, and interviews with the stars and director Kasdan. Letterboxed laserdisc version is available with dolby surround sound. 132m/C VHS, Beta, LV, **Closed Caption.** Kevin Kline, Scott Glenn, Kevin Costner, Danny Glover, Brian Dennehy, Linda Hunt, John Cleese, Jeff Goldblum, Rosanna Arquette, Jeff Fahey; **D:** Lawrence Kasdan; **W:** Lawrence Kasdan; **C:** John Bailey; **M:** Bruce Broughton. Nominations: Academy Awards '85: Best Sound, Best Original Score. COL, CRC

Simba 🎬🎬🎬 1955 A young Englishman arrives at his brother's Kenyan farm to find him murdered in a local skirmish between the Mau Maus and white settlers. Well made, thoughtful look at colonialism, racial animosity, and violence. 98m/C VHS, Beta, LV. GB Dirk Bogarde, Donald Sinden, Virginia McKenna, Orlando Martins; **D:** Brian Desmond Hurst; **C:** Geoffrey Unsworth. NO

Simon 🎬🎬½ 1980 (PG) A group of bored demented scientists brainwash a college professor into believing he is an alien from a distant galaxy, whereupon he begins trying to correct the evil in America. Screwball comedy, or semi-serious satire of some kind? Hard to tell. Some terrific set pieces but the movie as a whole doesn't quite hold together. Directorial debut of Brickman, who previously worked as a scriptwriter with Woody Allen ("Sleeper," etc.). 97m/C VHS, Beta. Alan Arkin, Madeline Kahn, Fred Gwynne, Adolph Green, Wallace Shawn, Austin Pendleton; **D:** Marshall Brickman; **W:** Marshall Brickman, Thomas Baum. WAR

Simon Bolivar 🎬🎬½ 1969 The title character leads the Venezuelan revolution in 1817. 110m/C VHS, Beta. Maximilian Schell, Rosanna Schiaffino. UNI

Simon, King of the Witches 🎬🎬½ 1971 (R) An L.A. warlock who lives in a sewer drain finds himself the center of attention when his spells actually work. This interesting hippie/witchcraft entry bogs down now and then but Prine's performance is droll and lively. 90m/C VHS, Beta. Andrew Prine, Brenda Scott, George Paulsin, Norman Burton, Ultra Violet; **D:** Bruce Kessler. UNI

Simon of the Desert 🎬🎬🎬½ 1966 Not Bunuel's very best, but worthy of the master satirist. An ascetic stands on a pillar in the desert for several decades—closer to God, farther from temptation. Pinal is a gorgeous devil that tempts Simon. Hilarious, irreverent, sophisticated. What's with the weird ending, though? In Spanish with English subtitles. 46m/B VHS, Beta. Claudio Brook, Silvia Pinal; **D:** Luis Bunuel; **W:** Luis Bunuel. HTV, HHT, DVT

Simple Justice 🎬½ 1989 (R) Mindless, justice-in-own-hands anti-liberal hogwash. Overwrought, smug, and violent story of a young couple beaten by robbers who remain at large. 91m/C VHS. Cesar Romero, John Spencer, Doris Roberts, Candy McClain; **D:** Deborah Del Prete. JTC

Simple Men 🎬🎬🎬 1992 (R) Odd-ball brothers Bill (a petty criminal) and Dennis (a shy college student) decide to track down their missing father in this fractured comedy. Dad, a former big-league baseball player who bombed the Pentagon in the '60s, is a long-time fugitive hiding out somewhere in the wilds of Long Island. Their search leads them to two equally opposite women, the wary Kate, whom Bill immediately falls for, and the sexy Elina, who turns out to know dear old dad quite well. Deliberately deadpan and cliched, Hartley's quirky style can either irritate or illuminate via the weird turnings of his characters' lives.**CW:** Language. 105m/C VHS, LV, **Closed Caption.** Robert John Burke, William Sage, Karen Sillas, Elina Lowensohn, Martin Donovan, Mark Bailey, John MacKay; **D:** Hal Hartley; **W:** Hal Hartley; **M:** Hal Hartley. COL, IME, NLC

A Simple Story 🎬🎬🎬 Une Histoire Simple 1979 A woman faces her 40th birthday with increasing uneasiness, though her life seems perfect from the outside. She evaluates her chances at love, child-bearing, and friendship, after having an abortion and breaking up with her lover. Schneider's performance is brilliant in this gentle, quiet drama. In French with English subtitles. 110m/C VHS, Beta. FR Romy Schneider, Bruno Cremer,

Claude Brasseur; **D:** Claude Sautet. Nominations: Academy Awards '79: Best Foreign Language Film; Cesar Awards '79: Best Actress (Schneider). FRF, COL

A Simple Twist of Fate 🎬🎬½ 1994 (PG-13) Comedy drama gives Martin chance to flex serious muscles with this update of George Eliot's "Silas Marner." Adoptive father Michael McMann wants to keep his daughter Mathilda (played by the prerequisite adorable twins) in the face of demands from her biological father (Byrne), who happens to be a local politician. Then revelations brought out at the custody hearing threaten the politician's career. Cuddly dad is hardly Martin's image (in spite of "Parenthood"), though strong cast limits the sugar.**CW:** A drug-related situation. 106m/C VHS, LV, **Closed Caption.** Steve Martin, Gabriel Byrne, Catherine O'Hara, Stephen Baldwin, Alana Austin, Alyssa Austin, Laura Linney, Anne Heche, Michael Des Barres, Byron Jennings; **D:** Gilles Mackinnon; **W:** Steve Martin; **M:** Cliff Eidelman. TOU

A Simple Wish 🎬🎬½ 1997 (PG) Equal employment opportunities now even extend to the fairy godmother realm. Anabel (Wilson) knows her dad (Pastorelli) wants to become a Broadway actor. So she wishes for a fairy godmother—and gets stuck with Murray (Short), the first affirmative-action male practitioner, who's really not very good at spellcasting. Both Anabel and Murray have bigger problems—evil fairy godmother Claudia (Turner) is after all the fairy godmothers' magic wands so she can rule the world's wishes. Short's brand of comic energy plays right into the kid audience, and Wilson lights up every scene she's in. ?m/C VHS. Mara Wilson, Martin Short, Kathleen Turner, Robert Pastorelli, Amanda Plummer, Teri Garr, Francis Capra; **D:** Michael Ritchie; **W:** Jeff Rothberg. NYR

Sin of Adam & Eve 🎬½ 1972 (R) The story of Adam and Eve in the Garden of Eden and their fall from grace. Voice-over narrator is only sound in this strange dialogue-less story of the Adam and Eve, how they got kicked out of the Garden of Eden, and how they lose and then find each other outside. Ancient plot, to say the least. 72m/C VHS, Beta. Candy Wilson, Jorge Rivero; **D:** Michael Zachary. VDM

The Sin of Harold Diddlebock 🎬🎬½ Mad Wednesday 1947 A man gets fired from his job, stumbles around drunk, and wins a fortune gambling. He then buys a circus and uses a lion to frighten investors into backing him. Inventive comedy, but missing the spark and timing of "The Freshman" (1925), of which it is a sequel. The final feature film for Lloyd (who did all his own stunts), made at the urging of director Sturges. 89m/B VHS, Beta. Harold Lloyd, Margaret Hamilton, Frances Ramsden, Edgar Kennedy, Lionel Stander, Rudy Vallee, Franklin Pangborn; **D:** Preston Sturges. NOS, BAR, AOV

The Sin of Madelon Claudet 🎬🎬🎬 The Lullaby 1931 Hayes plays common thief who works her way into upper crust of Parisian society only to tumble back into the street, all in the name of making a better life for her illegitimate son. Very sudsy stuff, with an outstanding performance by Hayes. 74m/B VHS. Helen Hayes, Lewis Stone, Neil Hamilton, Robert Young, Cliff Edwards, Jean Hersholt, Marie Prevost, Karen Morley, Charles Winninger, Alan Hale; **D:** Edgar Selwyn. Academy Awards '32: Best Actress (Hayes). MGM, FCT

Sin Takes a Holiday 🎬🎬½ 1930 A woman marries her boss to save him from his girl friend. On a trip to Paris, she is wooed by a refined European gentleman, but finds that she really does love her husband. By today's standards, it doesn't sound like much, but in the '30s, it was pretty sophisticated stuff. 81m/B VHS. Constance Bennett, Kenneth MacKenna, Basil Rathbone, Rita La Roy, ZaSu Pitts, Fred Walton, Richard Carle, Helen Johnson; **D:** Paul Stein. NOS, HEG

Sin You Sinners 🎬 1963 Aging stripper gets ahold of an amulet that allows her to look youthful and manipulate the lives of others. When she loses the amulet, however, bad things happen. Twisted ending. 73m/B VHS. June Colbourne, Dian Lloyd, Derek Murcott, Beverly Nazarow, Charles Clements; **D:** Anthony Farrar. SNC

Sinai Commandos 🎬🎬½ Sinai Commandos: The Story of the Six Day War; Ha'Matarah Tiran 1968 The story of a group of commandos in the Israeli Six-Day War in 1967 who are assigned to destroy important Arab radar installations. Includes actual combat footage. 99m/C VHS. Robert Fuller; **D:** Raphael Nussbaum. ATL, FCT

Sinatra 🎬🎬½ 1992 Made for television biopic chronicles the stormy life of crooner Frank Sinatra. Begins with his childhood in Hoboken, New Jersey and works its way through his big band tours, bobby soxer days, career skids, and triumphant comeback with his Oscar-winning performance in "From Here to Eternity," as well as his three marriages, "Rat Pack" friends, and mob connections. Executive Producer Tina Sinatra, Frank's daughter, doesn't gloss over her father's less savory character points and Casnoff does well with his leading role. Songs are lip-synched to classic Sinatra tunes with a few early recordings redone by actor Tom Burlinson and Frank Sinatra, Jr. 245m/C VHS, Beta, LV, **Closed Caption.** Philip Casnoff, Olympia Dukakis, Joe Santos, Gina Gershon, Nina Siemaszko, Marcia Gay Harden, Rod Steiger, Bob Gunton, David Raynr, James F. Kelly, Matthew Posey, Jay Robinson, Robin Gammell, Todd Waring, Joris Stuyck, Danny Gans, Jeff Corey; **D:** James Sadwith; **W:** William Mastrosimone; **C:** Reynaldo Villalobos. WAR

Sinbad 🎬🎬 1971 A sardonic portrait of an aging hedonist as he tries to hold onto the pleasures of drink, sex and gluttony. In Magyar (Hungarian), with English subtitles. 98m/C VHS, Beta. HU **D:** Zoltan Huszarik. KIV, FCT

Sinbad and the Eye of the Tiger 🎬🎬 1977 (G) The swashbuckling adventures of Sinbad the Sailor as he encounters the creations of Ray Harryhausen's special effects magic. Don't see this one for the plot, which almost doesn't exist. Otherwise, mildly fun. 113m/C VHS, Beta, LV. GB Patrick Wayne, Jane Seymour, Taryn Power, Margaret Whiting; **D:** Sam Wanamaker; **W:** Beverley Cross; **C:** Ted Moore. COL, CCB

Sinbad of the Seven Seas 🎬½ 1989 Italian muscle epic based on the ancient legends. Ferrigno isn't green, but he's still a hulk, and he still can't act. It's poorly dubbed, which makes little difference; it would be stupid regardless. 90m/C VHS, Beta, LV. IT Lou Ferrigno, John Steiner, Leo Gullotta, Teagan Clive; **D:** Enzo G. Castellari. WAR, OM

Sinbad, the Sailor 🎬🎬🎬 1947 Fairbanks fits well in his luminent father's swashbuckling shoes, as he searches for the treasure of Alexander the Great. Self-mocking but hamhanded, and confusing if you seek the hidden plot. Still, it's all in fun, and it is fun. 117m/C VHS, Beta, LV. Douglas Fairbanks Jr., Maureen O'Hara, Anthony Quinn, Walter Slezak, George Tobias, Jane Greer, Mike Mazurki, Sheldon Leonard; **D:** Richard Wallace; **C:** George Barnes. MED, TTC

Since You Went Away 🎬🎬🎬½ 1944 An American family copes with the tragedy, heartache and shortages of wartime in classic megatribute to the home front. Be warned: very long and bring your hankies. Colbert is superb, as is the photography. John Derek unobtrusively made his film debut, as an extra. 172m/B VHS, Beta, LV, **Closed Caption.** Claudette Colbert, Jennifer Jones, Shirley Temple, Joseph Cotten, Agnes Moorehead, Monty Woolley, Guy Madison, Lionel Barrymore, Robert Walker, Hattie McDaniel, Keenan Wynn, Craig Stevens, Albert Basserman, Alla Nazimova, Lloyd Corrigan, Terry Moore, Florence Bates, Ruth Roman, Andrew V. McLaglen, Dorothy Dandridge, Rhonda Fleming; **D:** John Cromwell; **W:** David O. Selznick; **M:** Max Steiner. Academy Awards '44: Original Dramatic/Comedy Score; Nominations: Academy Awards '44: Best Actress (Colbert), Best Black and White Cinematography, Best Film Editing, Best Interior Decoration, Best Picture, Best Supporting Actor (Woolley), Best Supporting Actress (Jones). FOX

Sincerely Charlotte �770 *Signe Charlotte* **1986** Huppert directs her sister in this film about a beautiful singer framed for her boyfriend's murder. She enlists an old lover to help her flee across the countryside. Love story/thriller is pleasingly odd and absorbing. In French with English subtitles. **92m/C VHS, Beta, LV, Closed Caption.** *FR* Isabelle Huppert, Niels Arestrup, Christine Pascal; **D:** Caroline Huppert; **C:** Bruno de Keyzer. COL

Sincerely Yours woof! **1956** Liberace wisely stayed away from acting after inauspiciously debuting in this horrible, maudlin remake of "The Man Who Played God." He plays a pianist who loses his hearing and decides to become a philanthropist to help those less fortunate than himself. Laughably cheesy. Thirty-one musical numbers, including Liberace's inimitable arrangement of "Chopsticks." **116m/C VHS, Beta, LV.** Liberace, Joanne Dru, Dorothy Malone, William Demarest; **D:** Gordon Douglas; **W:** Irving Wallace. WAR

A Sinful Life �770 **1989 (R)** A strained, offbeat, B-grade comedy about an odd, infantile mother fighting to keep her unusual child from being taken away. Definitely not a must-see; can be irritating and obnoxious, depending on viewer and mood. Morris is at her oddball comedic best as the mother and former show dancer. Adult Tefkin plays her little girl. Based on the play "Just Like the Pom Pom Girls." **112m/C VHS, Beta, LV.** Anita Morris, Rick Overton, Dennis Christopher, Blair Tefkin, Mark Rolston, Cynthia Szigeti; **D:** William Schreiner. COL

Sing ✓½ **1989 (PG-13)** The students in the real-life Brooklyn public school "Sing" program endure the trials of adolescence while putting together a musical revue. Hurtles over the edge into cheesiness from the start, with way too much (cheesy) music. From the creator of "Fame" and "Footloose." **111m/C VHS, Beta, LV.** Lorraine Bracco, Peter Dobson, Jessica Steen, Louise Lasser, George DiCenzo, Patti LaBelle; **D:** Richard Baskin; **M:** Jay Gruska. COL

Sing, Cowboy, Sing ✓✓ **1937** Decent adventure story about a wagon train heading west that runs into a band of outlaws doing outlaw stuff and must somehow get through. **60m/B VHS, Beta.** Tex Ritter. NOS, DVT

Sing Sing Nights ✓½ *Reprieved* **1935** A world-famous journalist is killed with three bullets. Three men have confessed, but only one could have actually done it. A professor sets out to solve the case. **60m/B VHS.** Conway Tearle, Mary Doran, Hardie Albright, Patricia "Boots" Mallory, Ferdinand Gottschalk, Berton Churchill, Jameson Thomas; **D:** Lewis D. Collins. SNC

Sing Your Worries Away ✓✓ **1942** Songwriter Ebsen inherits 3 million dollars and finds the money causes him nothing but trouble. Band of crooks cause the requisite wacky complications. Fun, harmless musical comedy. ♫ It Just Happened to Happen; Sally, My Dear Sally; Sing Your Worries Away; Cindy Lou McWilliams; How Do You Fall in Love. **71m/B VHS, Beta.** Buddy Ebsen, Bert Lahr, June Havoc, Patsy Kelly, Margaret Dumont; **D:** Edward Sutherland. CCB

Singapore ✓✓½ **1947** Rather boring romantic drama finds pearl smuggler Matt Gordon (MacMurray) returning to Singapore to resume his illegal trade at the end of WWII. He spots Linda (Gardner), the love of his life, but discovers she's suffering from amnesia and has married another man. Gangsters want Matt's hidden supply of pearls and kidnap Linda to get his cooperation. Remade with equal dullness in 1956 as "Istanbul." **80m/B VHS.** Fred MacMurray, Ava Gardner, Roland Culver, Richard Haydn, Thomas Gomez, Spring Byington, Porter Hall; **D:** John Brahm; **W:** Seton I. Miller, Robert Thoeren; **C:** Maury Gertsman; **M:** Daniele Amfitheatrof. USH

Singin' in the Rain ✓✓✓✓ **1952** One of the all-time great movie musicals—an affectionate spoof of the turmoil that afflicted the motion picture industry in the late 1920s during the changeover from silent films to sound. Co-director Kelly and Hagen lead a glorious cast. Music and lyrics by Arthur Freed and Nacio Herb Brown. Served as basis of story by Betty Comden and Adolph Green. Also available on laserdisc with the original trailer, outtakes, behind the scenes footage, and commentary by film historian Ronald Haver. Later a Broadway musical. ♫ All I Do is Dream of You; Should I?; Singin' in the Rain; Wedding of the Painted Doll; Broadway Melody; Would You; I've Got a Feelin' You're Foolin'; You Are My Lucky Star; Broadway Rhythm. **103m/C VHS, Beta, LV, Closed Caption, DVD.** Gene Kelly, Donald O'Connor, Jean Hagen, Debbie Reynolds, Rita Moreno, King Donovan, Millard Mitchell, Cyd Charisse, Douglas Fowley, Madge Blake, Joi Lansing; **D:** Gene Kelly, Stanley Donen; **W:** Adolph Green, Betty Comden. Golden Globe Awards '53: Best Actor—Musical/Comedy (O'Connor); National Board of Review Awards '52: 10 Best Films of the Year; Nominations: Academy Awards '52: Best Supporting Actress (Hagen), Scoring of a Musical. MGM, TLF, CRC

The Singing Blacksmith ✓✓½ **1938** A relic of American Yiddish cinema, adapting popular 1909 play by David Pinski. A married blacksmith is wooed by another woman and falls victim to alcoholism. Overlong, but Oysher and his rich baritone voice still shine. In Yiddish with English subtitles. **95m/B VHS.** *PL* Miriam Riselle, Florence Weiss, Moishe Oysher; **D:** Edgar G. Ulmer. ERG

Singing Buckaroo ✓✓ **1937** Dastardly bandits try to pilfer money from pretty blonde damsel and have to battle with yodelin' cowboy. B-level western good guy Scott belts out a few numbers and saves the day. Innocuously pleasant. **58m/B VHS, Beta.** Fred Scott, Victoria Vinton, Cliff Nazarro; **D:** Tom Gibson. NOS, VYY

Singing Cowboys, Vol. 2 **193?** Three films starring brave and talented singing cowboys. Rogers saves a young ranch heir from a couple of con artists in "Sunset Serenade." Tex Ritter plays a deputy sheriff trying to catch a gang of claim jumpers in his first singing western, "Song of the Gringo." Autry stars in "Public Cowboy No. 1," which has old fashioned cattle rustlers using airplanes, radios, and trucks to further their thieving ways. **175m/B VHS.** Gene Autry, Tex Ritter, Roy Rogers. BPG

The Singing Cowgirl ✓ **1939** Band of outlaws murder a ranch owner to get to a gold mine. Heroine Page rides in to save the day but gets shot down by western stereotypes. **60m/B VHS.** Dorothy Page, Dave O'Brien, Vince Barnett, Stanley Price; **D:** Samuel Diege; **W:** Arthur Hoerl. MOV

The Singing Nun ✓✓ **1966** The true story of a Belgian nun who takes a liking to a motherless little boy. She writes a song for him, and a kind-hearted priest talks to a record producer to see about getting the song to go somewhere. The song soon becomes an international hit, and the nun ends up on the "Ed Sullivan Show." Sentimental and sugary sweet, but a big box-office hit. **98m/C VHS.** Debbie Reynolds, Ricardo Montalban, Greer Garson, Agnes Moorehead, Chad Everett, Katharine Ross, Juanita Moore, Ricky Cordell, Michael Pate, Tom Drake; **D:** Henry Koster; **C:** Milton Krasner. Nominations: Academy Awards '66: Best Adapted Score. MGM

Singing the Blues in Red ✓✓✓ **1987** Dark, pessimistic character study of a protest singer/songwriter who leaves his native East Germany to escape repression and finds his loyalties divided. A moving personal story, as well as insightful, subtle social commentary. In English and German with subtitles. Cinematography by Chris Menges. **110m/C VHS, Beta.** GE Gerulf Pannach, Fabienne Babe, Cristine Rose, Trevor Griffiths; **D:** Ken Loach; **W:** Trevor Griffiths. NO

Single Bars, Single Women ✓½ **1984** Utterly formulaic made for TV comedy-drama based on Dolly Parton's song is not entirely without merit. Lonely people gather in a local pick-up joint and share their miseries and hopes. **96m/C VHS, Beta.** Shelley Hack, Christine Lahti, Tony Danza, Mare Winningham, Keith Gordon, Paul Michael Glaser; **D:** Harry Winer; **M:** Basil Poledouris. PSM, PAR, VTR

Single Room Furnished ✓½ **1968** The fall of a buxom blonde from uncorrupted innocence through pregnancies to desperate prostitution. Fails to demonstrate any range of talent in Mansfield, who died before it was completed. Exploitative and pathetic. **93m/C VHS, Beta.** Jayne Mansfield, Dorothy Keller; **D:** Matt Cimber, Matteo Ottaviano. VCI, HEG

The Single Standard ✓✓ **1929** San Francisco deb Garbo flings with artsy Asther and finds out the Hayes Code is just around the corner. **93m/B VHS.** Greta Garbo, Nils Asther, Johnny Mack Brown, Dorothy Sebastian, Lane Chandler, Zeffie Tilbury; **D:** John S. Robertson. MGM, FCT

Single White Female ✓✓½ **1992 (R)** Psycho thriller casts Fonda as chic Manhattan computer consultant Allison Jones, who advertises for a roommate after a falling out with her boyfriend. Leigh is the frumpy, shy, bookstore clerk Hedra who answers the ad and moves into Allie's great Upper West Side apartment. They hit it off, that is until Allie notices Hedra's beginning to look and sound very familiar. Hmm... Derivative, though bonus points for creative murder implements and interesting performances throughout, including Friedman as Allie's gay upstairs neighbor. Based on the novel "SWF Seeks Same" by John Lutz. **CW:** Language, violence, and strong sexuality. **107m/C VHS, Beta, LV, 8mm, Closed Caption.** Bridget Fonda, Jennifer Jason Leigh, Steven Weber, Peter Friedman, Stephen Tobolowsky, Francis Bay, Renee Estevez, Kenneth Tobey; **D:** Barbet Schroeder; **W:** Don Roos; **M:** Howard Shore. MTV Movie Awards '93: Best Villain (Leigh). COL, BTV

Singles ✓✓✓ **1992 (PG-13)** Seattle's music scene is the background for this lighthearted look at single twentysomethings in the '90s. Hits dead on thanks to Crowe's tight script and a talented cast, and speaks straight to its intended audience—the "Generation X" crowd. Real life band Pearl Jam plays alternative band Citizen Dick and sets the tone for a great soundtrack featuring the hot Seattle sounds of Alice in Chains, Soundgarden, and Mudhoney. The video contains six extra minutes of footage after the credits that was thankfully edited out of the final cut. Look for Horton, Stoltz (as a mime), Skerritt, and Burton in cameos. **100m/C VHS, Beta, LV, Closed Caption.** Matt Dillon, Bridget Fonda, Campbell Scott, Kyra Sedgwick, Sheila Kelley, Jim True, Bill Pullman, James LeGros, Ally Walker, Devon Raymond, Camillo Gallardo, Jeremy Piven; **Cameos:** Tom Skerritt, Peter Horton, Eric Stoltz, Tim Burton; **D:** Cameron Crowe; **W:** Cameron Crowe; **M:** Paul Westerberg. WAR, PMS

Singleton's Pluck ✓✓✓ *Laughterhouse* **1984** Touching British comedy about a determined farmer who must walk his 500 geese 100 miles to market because of a strike. He becomes a celebrity when the TV stations start covering his odyssey. **89m/C VHS, Beta.** GB Ian Holm, Penelope Wilton, Bill Owen, Richard Hope; **D:** Richard Eyre. VTR, NWV

The Sinister Invasion ✓ *Alien Terror; The Incredible Invasion* **1968** A turn-of-the-century scientist (Karloff) discovers a death ray. Aliens, who would like a closer peek at what makes it work, use a sex-fiend's body to do so. One of Karloff's last four films, made simultaneously in Mexico. The great horror master's final offering. Excruciating. **95m/C VHS, Beta.** MX Boris Karloff, Enrique Guzman, Jack Hill; **D:** Juan Ibanez. SNC

The Sinister Urge woof! *The Young and the Immortal; Hellborn* **1960** Vice cops Duncan and Moore search for the murderer of three women. Seems the disturbed slayer is unbalanced because he's been looking at pictures of naked ladies. Was this meant to be taken seriously at the time? The last film by camp director Wood, maker of the infamous "Plan 9 From Outer Space." A must see for Wood fans. **82m/B VHS, Beta.** Kenne Duncan, Duke Moore, Jean Fontaine; *D:* Edward D. Wood Jr. AOV, SNC

Sink the Bismarck 🎬🎬🎬 1960 British navy sets out to locate and sink infamous German battleship during WWII. Good special effects with stirring naval battles and stylish documentary-style direction. **97m/B VHS, Beta.** Kenneth More, Dana Wynter, Karel Stepanek, Carl Mohner, Laurence Naismith, Geoffrey Keen, Michael Hordern, Maurice Denham, Esmond Knight; *D:* Lewis Gilbert. FOX, HMV

Sinners 🎬 1989 Outrageous portrait of an Italian family in the Big Apple trying to come to terms with the violence that surrounds their neighborhood. **90m/C VHS, Beta.** Joey Travolta, Robert Gallo, Joe Palese, Lou Calvelli, Angie Daglas, Sabrina Ferrand; *D:* Charles Kanganis. PMH

Sinner's Blood WOOF! 1970 **(R)** Bikers terrorize and torture a small town. **81m/C VHS, Beta.** Stephen Jacques, Crusty Beal, Nancy Sheldon, Parker Herriott, Julie Connors; *D:* Neil Douglas. GHV

Sinners in Paradise 🎬🎬 1938 An assortment of trouble-plagued characters alternately hide and face up to their mysterious pasts when their plane crashes on a deserted island. Interesting "crucible" premise runs out of steam, but plucky, resourceful cast and competent direction keep it going. **64m/B VHS, Beta.** Madge Evans, John Boles, Bruce Cabot, Marion Martin, Gene Lockhart, Dwight Frye, Charlotte Wynters, Nana Bryant, Milburn Stone, Donald (Don "Red") Barry, Morgan Conway; *D:* James Whale. SNC, MLB

Sins 1985 On her way up the ladder of success in the fashion industry, Helene has stepped on a few toes. Those rivals and her ever-increasing acquisition of power and money make this film an exciting drama. **336m/C VHS, Beta.** Joan Collins, Timothy Dalton, Catherine Mary Stewart, Gene Kelly, James Farentino; *D:* Douglas Hickox. VTR, NWV, HHE

Sins of Desire 🎬🎬 1992 Highly erotic thriller with Roberts going undercover as a nurse in a sex therapy clinic. It seems her sister was a former patient at the clinic and has since died a mysterious death. Linking up with private eye Cassavetes, Roberts sets out to investigate the doctors who treated her sister, searching for clues to her untimely death. **90m/C VHS, Closed Caption.** Tanya Roberts, Jay Richardson, Delia Sheppard, Nick Cassavetes, Jan-Michael Vincent; *D:* Jim Wynorski; *W:* Mark Thomas McGee, Peter Paul Liapis. COL, THV, PMS

The Sins of Dorian Gray 🎬 1982 **(PG)** A modernized adaptation of "The Portrait of Dorian Grey" by Oscar Wilde, with Dorian as a beautiful woman who remains young for 30 years, while a video screen test ages, like the original character's mirror image. Might have been intriguing and stylish; instead, only disappointing and incompetent. Made for television. **95m/C VHS, Beta, Closed Caption.** Belinda Bauer, Joseph Bottoms, Anthony Perkins; *D:* Tony Maylam. FOX

Sins of Jezebel 🎬 1954 Biblical epic about Jezebel, who worships an evil god. She marries the king of Israel and brings the kingdom nothing but trouble. **74m/C VHS, Beta, LV.** Paulette Goddard, George Nader, John Hoyt, Eduard Franz; *D:* Reginald LeBorg. NO

Sins of Rome 🎬🎬 1954 Spartacus risks it all in a bold attempt to free his fellow slaves. Not nearly the equal of Kirk Douglas's "Spartacus," but much better than later Italian adventure epics. **75m/B VHS.** IT Ludmila Tcherina, Massimo Girotti, Gianna Maria Canale, Yves Vincent; *D:* Riccardo (Robert Hampton) Freda. SNC

Sins of the Night 🎬 1993 **(R)** An ex-con insurance investigator is hired to find a sultry exotic dancer. Also available in an unrated version. **82m/C VHS.** Nick Cassavetes, Deborah Shelton. ACA

Sinthia: The Devil's Doll 🎬🎬 1970 A little girl is thought to be possessed by a demon after she has horrible dreams about killing her father. **?m/C VHS.** Shula Roan, Diane Webber; *D:* Ray Dennis Steckler. SNC, TPV

Sioux City 🎬🎬½ 1994 **(PG-13)** Jesse Rainfeather Goldman (Phillips) is a Lakota Sioux adopted away from the reservation of his birth and raised in Beverly Hills by a Jewish family. Jesse's curious when his birth mother suddenly contacts him, but when he arrives at the Sioux City reservation, he discovers she's suddenly died under mysterious circumstances. So Jesse sticks around to find out what's going on and discovers his heritage along the way. Well-meaning but dull. **102m/C VHS, Closed Caption.** Lou Diamond Phillips, Salli Richardson, Melinda Dillon, Ralph Waite, Adam Roarke, Bill Allen, Gary Farmer; *D:* Lou Diamond Phillips; *W:* L. Virginia Browne; *M:* Christopher Lindsey. CAF

Sioux City Sue 🎬🎬 1946 Talent scouts looking to cast a western musical find Autry, then trick him into being the voice of a singing donkey in an animated production. But, the yodelin' cowboy belts out a number or two, and the poobahs give him the lead. Singin' and fancy ridin' abound in Autry's first post-WWII role. **69m/B VHS, Beta.** Gene Autry, Lynn (Mary Hart) Roberts, Sterling Holloway. NO

Sirens 🎬🎬½ 1994 **(R)** Staid minister takes Australian artist Norman Lindsay to task for submitting scandalous works to public exhibitions. Noted by one reviewer as "Enchanted April with nipples," comedy of manners is witty but lacks plot and looks remarkably like a centerfold layout. Ample displays of nudity as the models (including supermodel MacPherson in her acting debut) frolic in the buff. Grant is terrific as the seemingly enlightened but easily shocked minister, but Neill's Lindsay is poorly written and too often takes a back seat to the vamping models. Fictionalized account of a true incident from the 1930s; Lindsay's home and some of his artworks were used. Check out writer/director Duigan as a pompous village minister. *CW:* Language, abundant nudity, and sex-related scenes. **96m/C VHS, LV, Closed Caption.** AU GB Hugh Grant, Tara Fitzgerald, Sam Neill, Elle Macpherson, Kate Fischer, Portia de Rossi, Pamela Rabe, Ben Mendelsohn, John Polson, Mark Gerber, Julia Stone, Ellie MacCarthy, Vincent Ball; *Cameos:* John Duigan; *D:* John Duigan; *W:* Geoff Burton; *M:* Rachel Portman. Chicago Film Critics Awards '94: Most Promising Actor (Grant). MAX

Siringo 🎬🎬½ 1994 U.S. Deputy Marshal Charlie Siringo (Johnson) is out to capture escaped convict Wade Lewis (Macht). The two antagonists share a nasty history as Siringo, along with a young deputy, heads out to the ranch of former prostitute Kaitlin (Bernard) for a final showdown. **90m/C VHS.** Brad Johnson, Stephen Macht, Chad Lowe, Crystal Bernard; *D:* Kevin G. Cremin. AVE

Sirocco 🎬🎬½ 1951 An American gun-runner (Bogart) stuck in Syria in 1925 matches wits with a French intelligence officer amid civil war and intrigue. About the underbelly of human affairs. **111m/B VHS, Beta, LV.** Humphrey Bogart, Lee J. Cobb, Zero Mostel, Everett Sloane, Gerald Mohr; *D:* Curtis Bernhardt; *C:* Burnett Guffey. COL

Sister Act 🎬🎬½ 1992 **(PG)** Surprising box office hit casts Goldberg as a Reno lounge singer and inadvertent witness to a mob murder who hides out in a convent—where she's as comfortable in a habit as a fish is out of water. Much to the dismay of poker-faced Mother Superior Smith, she takes over the rag-tag choir and molds them into a swinging, religious version of a '60s girls group. Stock characters and situations are deflected by some genuinely funny moments and

good performances, especially by Najimy and Makkena. Coached by the very clever Shaiman, Whoopi handles her nun singing bits with gusto, highlight of which is "My God," sung to the tune of "My Guy." **100m/C VHS, Beta, LV, Closed Caption.** Whoopi Goldberg, Maggie Smith, Harvey Keitel, Bill Nunn, Kathy Najimy, Wendy Makkena, Mary Wickes, Robert Miranda, Richard Portnow, Joseph Maher; *D:* Emile Ardolino; *W:* Joseph Howard; *M:* Marc Shaiman. People's Choice Awards '93: Best Film—Musical/Comedy; NAACP Image Awards '33: Best Actress (Goldberg); NAACP Image Awards '93: Best Film. TOU, PMS

Sister Act 2: Back in the Habit 🎬🎬 1993 **(PG)** Mediocre retread finds Goldberg once again donning her nun's habit and getting a choir rocking. Deloris has established her singing career in Vegas, but she's persuaded by her nun friends to whip the incorrigible music students at a troubled inner-city high school into shape for an all-state choral competition. The musical numbers and singing are catchy and well-done but Goldberg seems to have phoned her work in; given her reported $7,000,000 salary, a little more life is expected. She's still sharp with the one-liners but it's all familiar ground. Geared directly towards young viewers. **107m/C VHS, LV, Closed Caption.** Whoopi Goldberg, Kathy Najimy, James Coburn, Maggie Smith, Wendy Makkena, Barnard Hughes, Mary Wickes, Sheryl Lee Ralph, Michael Jeter, Robert Pastorelli, Thomas Gottschalk, Lauryn Hill, Brad Sullivan; *D:* Bill Duke; *W:* James Orr, Jim Cruickshank, Judi Ann Mason; *M:* Miles Goodman. Blockbuster Entertainment Awards '95: Comedy Actress, Video (Goldberg); Nominations: MTV Movie Awards '94: Best Comedic Performance (Goldberg). TOU

Sister Dora 🎬🎬½ 1977 An idealistic young woman joins a nursing sisterhood in 19th century England but she questions her vocation when she falls in love. Adapted from a popular romance novel. **147m/C VHS.** GB Dorothy Tutin, James Grout, Peter Cellier; *D:* Mark Miller. NO

The Sister-in-Law 🎬🎬 1974 **(R)** Shady dealings, seduction, and adultery run rampant. Savage (who also wrote and sings the folk score) reluctantly agrees to deliver a package across the Canadian border for his brother. Intriguing. **80m/C VHS, Beta.** John Savage, Anne Saxon, W.G. McMillan, Meredith Baer; *D:* Joseph Rubin. PSM

The Sister-in-Law 🎬🎬½ 1995 **(PG-13)** Chilling cable suspenser finds the beautiful and evil Sarah Preston (Vernon) assuming the identity of the woman she's just killed—the widow of wealthy George Richards' (McCarthy) estranged son. George is dying and pathetically eager to accept Sarah at face value as is his vulnerable daughter Madlyn (Reed). But Sarah has not chosen the Richards family at random—she has a longtime grudge and plans to take her revenge slowly—so be prepared for a few more bodies to turn up. *CW:* Some violence and sensuality. **95m/C VHS, Beta, Closed Caption.** Kate Vernon, Kevin McCarthy, Shanna Reed, Craig Wasson; *D:* Noel Nosseck; *W:* David Callaway, Megan Marks. PAR

Sister Kenny 🎬🎬🎬 1946 Follows the story of a legendary Australian nurse crusading for the treatment of infantile paralysis. Stirring, well-made screen biography. Based on Elizabeth Kenny's memoir, "And They Shall Walk." **116m/B VHS, Beta, LV.** Rosalind Russell, Dean Jagger, Alexander Knox, Philip Merivale, Beulah Bondi, Charles Halton; *D:* Dudley Nichols; *C:* George Barnes. Golden Globe Awards '47: Best Actress—Drama (Russell); Nominations: Academy Awards '46: Best Actress (Russell). NOS, CCB, TTC

Sister My Sister 🎬🎬 1994 **(R)** True crime story that served as the inspiration for Jean Genet's play "The Maids." In a French provincial town lives the authoritarian Madame Danzard (Walters), who stifles daughter Isabelle (Thursfield), and subjects her two maids, sisters Christine (Richardson) and Lea (May), to an equally harsh discipline. The tension between the four women reaches a highstrung crescendo, leading to violence. Claustrophobic character study. *CW:* Sexuality and a brutal murder sequence. **89m/C VHS.** *GB* Julie Walters, Joely Richardson, Jodhi May, Sophie Thursfield; *D:* Nancy Meckler; *W:* Wendy Kellelman; *C:* Ashley Ropwe; *M:* Stephen Warbeck. *APX*

Sister, Sister 🐾🐾 **1987 (R)** A Congressional aide on vacation in Louisiana takes a room in an old mansion. He gradually discovers the secret of the house and its resident sisters. Dark Southern gothicism, full of plot surprises, with a twisted ending. **91m/C VHS, Beta, LV.** Eric Stoltz, Judith Ivey, Jennifer Jason Leigh, Dennis Lipscomb, Anne Pitoniak, Natalija Nogulich; *D:* Bill Condon; *W:* Bill Condon, Joel Cohen, Ginny Cerrella; *M:* Richard Einhorn. *VTR, NWV*

Sister Street Fighter 🐾 **1976** Action star Sonny Chiba takes a rest from his "Street Fighter" series in favor of protege Long, who's determined to deliver her own brand of deadly justice in this martial arts fest. **81m/C VHS.** Tina Long; *D:* Kazuhiko Yamaguchi. *NLC*

The Sisterhood 🐾 **1988 (R)** A pair of amazons fight for women's rights in a post-nuclear future. Cheap feminist theme laid over warmed-over sci-fi plot. **75m/C VHS, Beta, LV.** Rebecca Holden, Chuck Wagner, Lynn-Holly Johnson, Barbara Hooper; *D:* Cirio H. Santiago. *MED*

The Sisters 🐾🐾🐾 **1938** Lavish film of three sisters and their marital problems in turn of the century San Francisco. Davis gives a great performance as the oldest sister with the most trouble—notably in the form of unreliable sports reporter Flynn. Good for Susan Hayward in a bit role, as well as Bogart's wife, Mayo Methot. Based on the bestselling novel by Myron Brinig. **98m/B VHS, Closed Caption.** Bette Davis, Errol Flynn, Anita Louise, Jane Bryan, Ian Hunter, Henry Travers, Beulah Bondi, Donald Crisp, Dick Foran, Patric Knowles; *D:* Anatole Litvak; *M:* Max Steiner. *MGM*

Sisters 🐾🐾🐾 **1973 (R)** Siamese twins are separated surgically, but one doesn't survive the operation. The remaining sister is scarred physically and mentally with her personality split into bad and good. The bad side commits a murder, witnessed (or was it?) by an investigative reporter. And then things really get crazy. DePalma's first ode to Hitchcock, with great music by Hitchcock's favorite composer, Bernard Herrmann. Scary and suspenseful. **93m/C VHS, Beta.** Margot Kidder, Charles Durning, Barnard Hughes; *D:* Brian DePalma; *W:* Brian DePalma; *M:* Bernard Herrmann. *VCI*

Sisters of Death 🐾🐾 **1976 (PG)** Five members of a sorority gather together for a reunion in a remote California town. Little do they know, a psychopath is stalking them, one by one. Could it have something to do with the terrible secret they each keep? Good, cheap thrills and some Bicentennial fashions to boot. **87m/C VHS, Beta.** Arthur Franz, Claudia Jennings, Cheri Howell, Sherry Boucher, Paul Carr; *D:* Joseph Mazzuca. *VCI*

Sisters of Gion 🐾🐾🐾½ **1936** Mizoguchi's most famous and arguably best pre-war film. Two geisha sisters in Tokyo's red-light district reflect the tension in Japanese culture by waging a quiet battle of tradition vs. progressiveness. Highly acclaimed. In Japanese with English subtitles. **69m/B VHS, Beta.** *JP* Isuzu Yamada, Yoko Umemura; *D:* Kenji Mizoguchi. *FCT*

Sisters of Satan 🐾🐾½ **1975 (R)** The nuns of the infamous convent St. Archangelo choose to survive by trading God for the devil. **91m/C VHS, Beta.** *MX* Claudio Brook, David Silva, Tina Romero, Susana Kamini; *D:* Juan Lopez Moctezuma. *ACA, MPI*

Sitting Ducks 🐾🐾🐾 **1980 (R)** Mild-mannered accountant and lecherous pal rip off and then attempt to outrun the mob—all while swapping songs and confessions. Emil and Norman make it up as they go along; their hilarious repartee is largely improvised. They pick up a gorgeous lady (Townsend) and go about their way. **88m/C VHS, Beta.** Michael Emil, Zack Norman, Patrice Townsend, Richard Romanus, Irene Forrest, Henry Jaglom; *D:* Henry Jaglom; *W:* Henry Jaglom. *MED*

Six Degrees of Separation 🐾🐾½ **1993 (R)** Some believe that any two people, anywhere in the world, are connected by links to only six other people, hence the six degrees of separation. For the upper crust New Yorker Kittredges, Ouisa (Channing) and Flan (Sutherland), this becomes an issue when they encounter a charming young man (Smith) who claims to be Sidney Poitier's son and a friend of their children. The story unfolds as they realize they've been hustled—and don't understand why. Guare adapted his hit play, but what worked well there is almost too talky here. Channing, reprising her stage role, is very good as the stuffy Ouisa, with Sutherland delivering another interesting performance. Incredibly, the play was based on a true story. *CW:* Language and some sexuality. **112m/C VHS, LV, Closed Caption.** Stockard Channing, Will Smith, Donald Sutherland, Mary Beth Hurt, Bruce Davison, Ian McKellen, Richard Masur, Anthony Michael Hall, Heather Graham, Eric Thal, Anthony Rapp, Osgood Perkins, Kitty Carlisle Hart, Catherine Kellner; *D:* Fred Schepisi; *W:* John Guare; *C:* Ian Baker; *M:* Jerry Goldsmith. Nominations: Academy Awards '93: Best Actress (Channing); Golden Globe Awards '94: Best Actress—Musical/Comedy (Channing). *MGM*

Six Fois Deux/Sur et Sous la Communication 🐾🐾🐾 **1976** A six-part experimental series made for French television, in which Godard and Mieville analyze modern culture and socioeconomics via a free-form essay format, combining interviews, screened text, self-referential devices and news footage. In French with English voice-over. **100m/C VHS, Beta.** *FR D:* Jean-Luc Godard, Anne-Marie Mieville. *EAI*

Six Gun Gospel 🐾🐾 **1943** Hatton masquerades as a preacher to investigate some shady dealings. Laughs come when the women of the congregation prevail upon him to sing, and he croons a ballad about Jesse James! **59m/B VHS.** Johnny Mack Brown, Raymond Hatton, Inna Gest, Eddie Dew, Roy Barcroft, Kenneth MacDonald, Bud Osborne; *D:* Lambert Hillyer. *DVT, HEG*

Six Gun Rhythm 🐾½ **1939** Novelty western plot has football player traveling to Texas to avenge his father's murder. **59m/B VHS, Beta.** Tex Fletcher. *NOS, VDM, HEG*

633 Squadron 🐾🐾½ **1964** A skilled R.A.F. pilot attempts to lead his squadron on a mission deep into the fjords of Norway in search of a Nazi fuel plant. Robertson tries hard, as always, but is really not British officer material. Well-made war flick, based on a true story. **102m/C VHS, Beta.** Cliff Robertson, George Chakiris, Maria Perschy, Harry Andrews; *D:* Walter Grauman; *W:* James Clavell. *MGM*

Six in Paris 🐾🐾½ *Paris vu Par* **1968** Six short films by acclaimed French New Wave directors, each depicting a different Parisian neighborhood. "Saint-Germain-des-Pres" finds an American girl disillusioned by two French boys. "Gare du Nord" has a woman meeting a handsome stranger who announces he's going to kill himself. A shy dishwasher brings a prostitute to his room in the "Rue Saint-Denis." When a salesman is accosted by a derelict in the "Place de l'Etoile" he hits him with his umbrella and then thinks he's killed the man. "Montparnasse-Levallois" has a woman thinking she's mixed-up her meetings with her two lovers. "La Muette" finds a small boy buying earplugs to shut out the noise of his parents constant arguing. In French with English subtitles. **93m/C VHS.** *FR* Barbara Wilkin, Jean-Francois Chappey, Jean-Pierre Andreani, Nadine Ballot, Barbet Schroeder, Gilles Queant, Micheline Dax, Claude Melki, Jean-Michel Rouziere, Marcel Gallon, Joanna Shimkus, Philippe Hiquilly, Serge Davri, Stephane Audran, Gilles Chusseau, Dinah Saril, Claude Chabrol; *D:* Jean Douchet, Jean Rouch, Jean-Daniel Pollet, Eric Rohmer, Jean-Luc Godard, Claude Chabrol; *W:* Jean Douchet, George Keller, Jean Rouch, Jean-Daniel Pollet, Eric Rohmer, Jean-Luc Godard, Claude Chabrol; *C:* Nestor Almendros. *NYF, FCT*

Six of a Kind 🐾🐾🐾 **1934** When Flora (Boland) and J. Pinkham Whinney (Ruggles) decide to drive to California for a second honeymoon, they advertise for another couple to share expenses. Unfortunately, it's Burns and Allen and their exceptionally large Great Dane that answer the ad. There's numerous complications, including bank clerk Whinney's being suspected of embezzlement, prompting Sheriff "Honest John" Hoxley (Fields) to go after the supposed criminals. Veteran comedy performers make this one a delight. **63m/B VHS, Closed Caption.** Charlie Ruggles, Mary Boland, Gracie Allen, George Burns, W.C. Fields, Alison Skipworth; *D:* Leo McCarey; *W:* Walter DeLeon, Harry Ruskin; *C:* Henry Sharp; *M:* Ralph Rainger. *USH*

Six Pack 🐾½ **1982 (PG)** The Gambler goes auto racing. Rogers, in his theatrical debut, stars as Brewster Baker, a former stock car driver. He returns to the racing circuit with the help of six larcenous orphans (the six-pack, get it?) adept at stripping cars. Kinda cute if you're in the mood for sugar-powered race car story. **108m/C VHS, Beta.** Kenny Rogers, Diane Lane, Erin Gray, Barry Corbin, Anthony Michael Hall; *D:* Daniel Petrie; *M:* Charles Fox. *FOX*

Six Shootin' Sheriff 🐾🐾 **1938** A cowboy framed for bank robbery is released and seeks to rid his town of all evil. And he gets the girl! **59m/B VHS, Beta.** Ken Maynard, Marjorie Reynolds, Walter Long; *D:* Harry Fraser. *VYY, VCI, VCN*

Six Weeks 🐾🐾 **1982 (PG)** A young girl dying of leukemia brings together her work-driven mother and an aspiring married politician. Manipulative hanky-wringer has good acting from both Moores but oddly little substance. **107m/C VHS, Beta, LV.** Dudley Moore, Mary Tyler Moore, Katherine Healy; *D:* Tony Bill; *M:* Dudley Moore. *COL*

Six Wives of Henry VIII 🐾🐾🐾 **1971** Michell has been called the definitive Henry VIII, and this BBC Classic Television Series (shown as part of "Masterpiece Theatre" on PBS) was perhaps the most praised series on British TV. Henry's wives were: Catherine of Aragon, Anne Boleyn, Jane Seymour, Anne of Cleves, Catherine Howard, and Catherine Parr. Each episode tells of their, sometimes tragic, fates as pawns in Henry's quest for an heir, and his changes from an eager young man to aged, bitter monarch. The 90-minute videos are available individually or as a boxed set. **540m/C VHS.** *GB* Keith Michell, Annette Crosbie, Dorothy Tutin, Anne Stallybrass, Elvi Hale, Angela Pleasence, Rosalie Crutchley. *FCT, VCO, TVC*

Sixteen 🐾🐾 *Like a Crow on a June Bug* **1972 (R)** A naive country lass is attracted to the glitter and hum of the outside world. Her determination and optimism help her triumph. **84m/C VHS, Beta.** Mercedes McCambridge, Parley Baer, Ford Rainey, Beverly Powers, John Lozier, Simone Griffeth, Maidie Norman; *D:* Lawrence Dobkin. *NWV*

Sixteen Candles 🐾🐾🐾 **1984 (PG)** Over a decade after hitting the theaters, "Sixteen Candles" is still popular — reaching near cult status among generation X-ers. Hilarious comedy of errors features the pouty Ringwald as an awkard teen who's been dreaming of her sixteenth birthday. But the rush of her sister's wedding causes everyone to forget, turning her birthday into her worst nightmare. Hughes may not be critically acclaimed, but his movies are so popular they nearly take on a life of their own. Ringwald and Hall are especially charming as the angst ridden teens, encountering one trauma after another. Great soundtrack includes the title song by The Stray Cats. **93m/C VHS, Beta, LV.** Molly Ringwald, Justin Henry, Michael Schoeffling, Haviland Morris, Gedde Watanabe, Anthony Michael Hall, Paul Dooley, Carlin Glynn, Blanche Baker, Edward Andrews, Carole Cook, Max Casey Adams Showalter, Liane Curtis, John Cusack, Joan Cusack, Brian Doyle-Murray, Jami Gertz, Cinnamon Idles, Zelda Rubinstein; *D:* John Hughes; *W:* John Hughes; *M:* Ira Newborn. *USH*

Sixteen Fathoms Deep 🎬🎬 1934 A sponge fisherman risks it all, including his love, when a mean businessman threatens his operation. Good underwater photography, but otherwise undistinguished. **57m/B VHS.** Lon Chaney Jr., Sally O'Neil, George Regas, Maurice Black, Russell Simpson; **D:** Armand Schaefer. VYY, NOS, DVT

The Sixth Man 🎬½ 1997 (PG-13) College basketball star Antoine Tyler (Hardison) dies but returns as a ghost to help his brother (Wayans) lead their team to the NCAA finals. Basketball seems to be the sport of choice for Hollywood lately, so you'd think they'd be able to get one of these movies right. Once again, they blow the layup. The first half features the requisite flashback and tearjerker death scene, both of which are surprisingly effective. But then the focus turns to "hilarious" on-court hijinks and the all-time sports cliche champion: the second-half rally from an impossible deficit. Hardison and Wayans are the bright spots, displaying fine comic and dramatic chemistry. **CW:** Brief language and some innuendos. **107m/C VHS.** Kadeem Hardison, Marlon Wayans, David Paymer, Michael Michele, Kevin Dunn, Gary Jones, Vladimir Cuk, Chris Spencer, Kirk Baily, Saundra McClain, Lorenzo Orr, Travis Ford, Harold Sylvester; **D:** Randall Miller; **W:** Christopher Reed, Cynthia Carle; **C:** Michael Ozier; **M:** Marcus Miller. NYR

'68 🎬 1987 (R) A Hungarian family struggles with the generation gap in 1968 America. **99m/C VHS, Beta, LV.** Eric Larson, Terra Vandergaw, Neil Young; **D:** Steven Kovacks. VTR, NWV

Sizzle 🎬🎬 1981 When her boyfriend is murdered by the mob, nightclub singer Anderson, newly arrived from Hicksville in Roaring '20s Chicago, stops at nothing to get revenge. Bad-guy gangster Forsythe falls for her charms. Fun but unsophisticated. Made for TV. **100m/C VHS, Beta.** Loni Anderson, John Forsythe, Leslie Uggams, Roy Thinnes, Richard Lynch, Michael Goodwin; **D:** Don Medford; **M:** Artie Butler. PSM

Skag 🎬🎬🎬 1979 Disabled following a stroke, a Pittsburgh steel worker confronts a change in family roles and long-ignored family problems during his convalesence. Malden is exceptional and believable as a Joe Lunchbucket in this well-written, well-cast TV outing, pilot for the NBC series. **145m/C VHS, Beta.** Karl Malden, Piper Laurie, Craig Wasson, Leslie Ackerman, Peter Gallagher, Kathryn Holcomb, Powers Boothe; **D:** Frank Perry. NO

Skateboard 🎬 1977 (PG) A down-and-out Hollywood agent creates a pro skateboarding team and enters them in a race worth $20,000. Quickie premise executed lamely. **97m/C VHS, Beta.** Allen (Goorwitz) Garfield, Kathleen Lloyd, Chad McQueen, Leif Garrett, Richard Van Der Wyk, Tony Alva, Antony Carbone; **W:** Dick Wolf. NO

The Skateboard Kid 🎬½ 1993 (PG) When an outsider finds a magical talking skateboard, he suddenly becomes the envy of the in-group of skateboarding thrashers. **90m/C VHS.** Bess Armstrong, Timothy Busfield; **D:** Larry Swerdlove; **W:** Roger Corman; **V:** Dom DeLuise. NHO

Skeeter 🎬½ 1993 (R) Yes, it's the attack of the killer mosquito! Not just any mosquito of course, but a new gigantic species bred on toxic waste. They're invading the quiet desert town of Mesquite—and they're out for blood! **95m/C VHS, LV.** Tracy Griffith, Jim Youngs, Charles Napier, Michael J. Pollard; **D:** Clark Brandon; **W:** Clark Brandon, Lanny Horn; **M:** David Lawrence. COL

Skeezer 🎬🎬½ 1982 A dog becomes a key factor in a sympathetic doctor's efforts to communicate with emotionally unstable children. Based on reality, and a good cast makes it believable and moving. Quality family fare. **100m/C VHS.** Karen Valentine, Dee Wallace Stone, Tom Atkins, Mariclare Costello, Leighton Greer, Justine Lord; **D:** Peter H. Hunt. LIV

Skeleton Coast 🎬 1989 (R) Borgnine plays a retired U.S. Marine colonel who organizes a Magnificent Seven-like group of tough mercenaries to go into eastern Africa to save hostages held by Angolan terrorists. Cliches abound, including a token large-breasted woman, Mulford, getting her t-shirt ripped open. No plot and a bad script. Also called "Fair Trade." **94m/C VHS, LV.** Ernest Borgnine, Robert Vaughn, Oliver Reed, Herbert Lom, Daniel Greene, Nancy Mulford, Leon Isaac Kennedy; **D:** John Cardos. NLC

Sketch Artist 🎬🎬 1992 (R) Jack Whitfield (Fahey) is a police sketch artist whose latest rendering of a murder suspect looks suspiciously like his wife. Jack decides to keep this information to himself while he does some quiet investigating but he may not have any time. The police have a new murder suspect in mind—Jack! Made for cable television. **CW:** Language and sexuality. **89m/C VHS, Beta, LV, Closed Caption.** Jeff Fahey, Sean Young, Drew Barrymore, Frank McRae, Tcheky Karyo, James Tolkan, Charlotte Lewis; **D:** Phedon Papamichael; **W:** Michael Angeli. FXV, VTR

Sketch Artist 2: Hands That See 🎬🎬½ 1994 Fahey returns as police artist Jack Whitfield, who's asked to draw a sketch of a serial rapist/murderer. Near-victim Emmy (Cox) just happens to be blind but describes to Jack how the rapist looked as she felt his face. Emmy's hubby Glenn (Silverman) is concerned, especially when the creep warns Emmy about her trip to the cops. Solid characters build to good courtroom climax. **95m/C VHS, LV, Closed Caption.** Jeff Fahey, Courteney Cox, Jonathan Silverman, Michael Beach, Brion James, James Tolkan, Leilani Sarelle Ferrer, Michael Nicolosi, Scott Burkholder; **D:** Jack Sholder; **W:** Michael Angeli; **M:** Tim Truman. MGM

Sketches of a Strangler 🎬½ 1978 A psychotic art student sketches, then murders prostitutes. Interesting lead character but hardly chilling—just horrible to watch. Made for TV. **91m/C VHS, Beta.** Allen (Goorwitz) Garfield, Meredith MacRae; **D:** Paul Leder. MED

Ski Bum 🎬 1975 (R) A ski bum discovers corruption and violence at a Colorado Rockies resort. Eminently forgettable trash. Scantily based on a novel by Romain Gary. **94m/C VHS, Beta.** Charlotte Rampling, Zalman King, Dimitra Arliss, Anna Karina; **D:** Bruce Clark. NLC

Ski Patrol 🎬🎬 1989 (PG) Wacky ski groupies try to stop an evil developer. Good ski action in a surprisingly plotful effort from the crazy crew that brought the world "Police Academy." **85m/C VHS, Beta, LV, Closed Caption.** Roger Rose, Yvette Nipar, T.K. Carter, Leslie Jordan, Ray Walston, Martin Mull; **D:** Richard Correll. COL

Ski School 🎬 1991 (R) Rival ski instructors compete for jobs and babes. Brow lowering. **CW:** Language and sensuality. **89m/C VHS, LV, Closed Caption.** Ava Fabian, Dean Cameron, Tom Breznahan, Stuart Fratkin; **D:** Damian Lee. HBO

Ski School 2 🎬½ 1994 (R) Former ski instructor Dave finds that both his job and his ex-gal have been acquired by a jerk. So Dave decides to get them both back. **CW:** Nudity; language. **92m/C VHS.** Dean Cameron, Wendy Hamilton, Heather Campbell, Brent Sheppard, Bill Dwyer; **D:** David Mitchell; **W:** Jay Naples. MNC

Ski Troop Attack 🎬🎬 1960 During WWII, an American ski patrol is sent behind Nazi lines to blow up a German railway bridge. Unexceptional low-budget Corman outing; not among the greatest of war movies. **61m/B VHS, Beta.** Michael Forest, Frank Wolff, Sheila Carol. SNC, NOS, DVT

Skier's Dream 1988 This spectacular action-packed film focuses on a young executive in search of the ultimate run. Shot on the most exotic ski locations in the world; covers freestyle skiing, powder skiing, snowboarding, extreme skiing, cliff jumping, paragliding, and wave riding. **75m/C VHS, Closed Caption.** John Eaves, Ian Boyd; **M:** Jimi Hendrix, Tom Cochrane. COL, RAP

Skin 🎬½ Howard Beach: Making the Case for Murder 1989 (PG-13) Prosecutor seeks the truth after a black man is chased into highway traffic by a gang of white teenaged thugs from Queens. Based on the true story of the death of a young black man in Howards Beach, Queens. Made for TV. **95m/C VHS.** Daniel J. Travanti, Joe Morton, Dan Lauria, William Daniels; **C:** Ron Fortunato. NHO

Skin Art 🎬½ 1993 (R) Very offbeat character study focusing on Will, a tormented tattoo artist who specializes in decorating the backs of the young Asian prostitutes who work in a nearby brothel. Haunted by his memories as a Vietnam POW, Will decides to exorcise some demons on his latest female canvas. **CW:** Language, violence, and bizarre sexual situations. **90m/C VHS, LV, Closed Caption.** Kirk Baltz, Jake Weber, Nora Ariffin; **D:** W. Blake Herron; **W:** W. Blake Herron. FXV

Skin Deep 🎬½ 1989 (R) A boyish Don Juan tries everything to win back his ex-wife. Ritter whines about his mid-life crisis and seduces women; this substitutes for plot. A few funny slapstick scenes still don't make this worth watching. **102m/C VHS, Beta, LV.** John Ritter, Vincent Gardenia, Julianne Phillips, Alyson Reed, Nina Foch, Chelsea Field, Denise Crosby; **D:** Blake Edwards; **W:** Blake Edwards; **M:** Henry Mancini. CCB, MED, VTR

Skin Game 🎬½ 1931 Two British families feud over land rights. Not thrilling; not characteristic of working with Hitchcock. Way too much talking in excruciating, drawn-out scenes. Adapted from the play of the same name. **87m/B VHS, Beta.** GB Phyllis Konstam, Edmund Gwenn, Frank Lawton, C.V. France, Jill Esmond, Helen Haye; **D:** Alfred Hitchcock; **W:** Alfred Hitchcock. REP, NOS, MLB

Skin Game 🎬🎬🎬 1971 (PG) A fast talking con-artist (Garner) and his black partner (Gossett) travel throughout the antebellum South setting up scams—Gossett is sold to a new owner by Garner, who helps him escape. Garner and Gossett make a splendid comedy team in this different kind of buddy flick. All is well until Asner turns the tables on them. Finely acted comedy-drama. **102m/C VHS, Beta.** James Garner, Louis Gossett Jr., Susan Clark, Ed Asner, Andrew Duggan; **D:** Paul Bogart; **M:** David Shire. WAR

Skinheads: The Second Coming of Hate 🎬 1988 (R) Neo-fascists run rampant. Exploitative effort from schlock-doyen Clark. **93m/C VHS.** Chuck Connors, Barbara Bain, Brian Brophy, Jason Culp, Elizabeth Sagal; **D:** Greydon Clark; **W:** Greydon Clark. NO

Skinned Alive woof! 1989 A woman and her children travel cross-country to sell leather goods. When a detective discovers where the leather comes from he's hot on their trail. **90m/C VHS, Beta.** Mary Jackson, Scott Spiegel; **D:** Jon Killough; **W:** Jon Killough. NO

Skinner 🎬 1993 (R) Psychopath Dennis Skinner (Raimi) more than lives up to his grisly name with his penchant for stalking hookers with carving knives and cleavers. Now he's going after his innocent landlady (Lake) and it's up to Heidi (Lords), a victim who managed to get away, to find him before he can kill again. Lords in lingerie (and nasty scars) and some really disgusting skinning scenes. **CW:** Brutal bizarre violence and gore; some sexuality and language. **89m/C VHS, LV.** Theodore (Ted) Raimi, Traci Lords, Ricki Lake; **D:** Ivan Nagy. APX

Skinner's Dress Suit 🎬🎬½ 1926 Meek, hen-pecked office clerk tells domineering wife for a raise so she'll get off his back. She quickly insinuates them into upper crusty social circle, where the fib pays off big. Remake of the 1917 version based on Henry Irving Dodge's novel. **79m/B VHS, Beta.** Reginald Denny, Laura La Plante, Arthur Lake, Hedda Hopper; **D:** William A. Seiter. GPV

Skirts Ahoy! 🎬🎬 1952 Williams, Evans, and Blaine are three WAVES who have their eyes set on three handsome men. To get them, of course, they must sing and dance a lot, and Williams must perform one of her famous water ballets. ♫Oh By Jingo; Hold Me Close to You; What Makes a WAVE?; What Good is a Gal Without a Guy?; Skirts Ahoy!; Glad to Have You Aboard; The Navy Waltz; I Get a Funny Feeling; We Will

Fight. **109m/C VHS.** Esther Williams, Joan Evans, Vivian Blaine, Barry Sullivan, Keefe Brasselle, Billy Eckstine, Debbie Reynolds; **D:** Sidney Lanfield. *MGM*

The Skull 🎬🎬 **1965** Horror abounds when Cushing gets his hands on the skull of the Marquis de Sade but has mysterious, murderous powers. Based on a story by Robert Bloch. **83m/C VHS, Closed Caption.** Peter Cushing, Patrick Wymark, Christopher Lee, Nigel Green, Jill Bennett, Michael Gough, George Coulouris, Patrick Magee; **D:** Freddie Francis. *PAR*

Skull: A Night of Terror 🎬🎬 **1988 (R)** A cop vows not to use guns after a tragic accident, then single-handed and unarmed, takes on terrorists who kidnap his family. **80m/C VHS, Beta.** Nadia Capone, Robert Bideman, Robbie Fox, Paul Sanders; **D:** Robert Bergman; **W:** Robert Bergman, Gerard Ciccoritti. *ACA*

Skull & Crown 🎬🎬 **1935** Rin Tin Tin, Jr. helps the hero break up a group of smugglers. A favorite of Tin fans everywhere. **58m/B VHS, Beta.** Regis Toomey, Jack Mulhall, James Murray. *VYY, DVT, HEG*

Skullduggery 🎬½ **1970 (PG)** When a peaceful race of blond ape-people are discovered in New Guinea, a courtroom battle ensues to prevent their slaughter at the hands of developers. Interesting premise sadly flops. **105m/C VHS, Beta.** Burt Reynolds, Susan Clark, Roger C. Carmel, Chips Rafferty, Edward Fox, Wilfrid Hyde-White, Rhys Williams; **D:** Gordon Douglas. *MED*

Skullduggery woof! *Warlock* **1979 (PG)** Costume-store minion Haverstock carries a curse that makes him kill and mutilate. The usual unspeakable horror ensues for a group of medieval-game players. **95m/C VHS, Beta.** Thom Haverstock, Wendy Crewson, David Calderisi; **D:** Ota Richter. *MED*

The Sky Above, the Mud Below *Le Ciel et le Boue* **1961** An acclaimed documentary following a band of explorers transversing New Guinea in 1959, and their confrontations with native rituals, heretofore unknown cannibal tribes and physical calamities. In HiFi. **90m/C VHS, Beta.** **D:** Pierre-Dominique Gaisseau. Academy Awards '61: Best Feature Documentary. *ORI, WAR, FCT*

Sky Bandits 🎬½ **1940** Mounties uncover the mystery of a disappearing plane carrying gold from a Yukon mine. Last of the "Renfrew of the Mounties" pictures. **56m/B VHS, Beta, 8mm.** James Newill, Dave O'Brien, Louise Stanley. *NOS, SNC, VCN*

Sky Hei$t 🎬🎬 **1975** Criminals plan robbery of police helicopter carrying fortune in gold bullion. Made for television. **96m/C VHS.** Stefanie Powers, Joseph Campanella, Don Meredith, Larry Wilcox, Frank Gorshin, Shelley Fabares, Ken Swofford, Ray Vitte, Nancy Belle Fuller, Suzanne Somers; **D:** Lee H. Katzin. *UNI*

Sky High 🎬🎬½ **1922** Mix is an immigration agent after a gang smuggling Chinese laborers across the Mexican border. Thrills involve an airplane and mountaintop battles as well as some terrific location footage from the Grand Canyon. **58m/B VHS.** Tom Mix, Eva Novak, J. Farrell MacDonald, Sid Jordan; **D:** Lynn F. Reynolds; **W:** Lynn F. Reynolds. *GPV, GVV*

Sky High 🎬 **1951** A spy at an Air Force base is trying to get hold of the plans to a secret plane. A GI is recruited to catch him. **60m/B VHS, Beta, LV.** Sid Melton, Mara Lynn, Douglas Evans. *NO*

Sky High 🎬 **1984** Three college students become immersed in international intrigue when the C.I.A. and the K.G.B. pursue them through Greece looking for a secret Soviet tape. **103m/C VHS, Beta.** Daniel Hirsch, Clayton Norcross, Frank Schultz, Lauren Taylor; **D:** Nico Mastorakis. *LIV*

Sky Liner 🎬 **1949** An FBI agent is trailing a spy who has taken secret documents aboard a west-bound flight. **62m/B VHS, Beta, LV.** Richard Travis, Pamela Blake. *NO*

The Sky Pilot 🎬🎬½ **1921** Young clergyman sets up a parish on North Pacific coast and finds he must prove himself to the cowboys. He saves young woman from stampede, but her fa-

ther blames him for her maimed legs and sets the preacher's church on fire, providing girl with excuse to overcome handicap. **63m/B VHS, Beta.** John Bowers, Colleen Moore, David Butler, Donald Ian Macdonald; **D:** King Vidor. *GPV, FCT, GVV*

Sky Pirates woof! **1987** Space epic deals about pieces of ancient stone left by prehistoric extraterrestrials, now lost in a time warp. Bad stunts, bad script and notably bad acting make it a woofer in any era. **88m/C VHS, Beta, Closed Caption.** AU John Hargreaves, Max Phipps, Meredith Phillips; **D:** Colin Eggleston. *FOX*

Sky Riders 🎬🎬½ **1976 (PG)** Hang-gliders risk it all to take on a group of political kidnappers. Fine hang-gliding footage and glorious Greek locations make up for garden-variety plot. **93m/C VHS.** James Coburn, Susannah York, Robert Culp, Charles Aznavour, Harry Andrews, John Beck; **D:** Douglas Hickox; **W:** Jack DeWitt, Garry Michael White; **M:** Lalo Schifrin. *FOX*

Skylark 🎬🎬½ **1993 (G)** In a sequel to Hallmark Hall of Fame's hugely successful "Sarah, Plain and Tall," the whole Kansas crew shows up for more of their little-farm-on-the-prairie life. After two years in America's squarest state, mail-order bride Sarah (Close) loves Jacob (Walken), but not the scenery and still yearns for the lush greenery of Maine. When drought and fire threaten the farm, Jacob fears for the family's health and safety, and sends them back East for a visit. Close's "tough Yankee" expression grows a bit tiresome in a plot that is a tad predictable, yet the simplistic charm and nostalgia are unresistable and work to propel this quality Hallmark production. **98m/C VHS, Closed Caption.** Glenn Close, Christopher Walken, Lexi Randall, Christopher Bell, Tresa Hughes, Lois Smith, Lee Richardson, Elizabeth Wilson, Margaret Sophie Stein, Jon DeVries, James Rebhorn, Woody Watson; **D:** Joseph Sargent; **W:** Patricia MacLachlan. *REP, BTV*

Skyline 🎬🎬🎬 *La Linea Del Cielo* **1984 (R)** A Spanish photographer comes to New York City to work for a magazine and tries to adjust to his cultural dislocation. Quietly funny, with a startling ending. Partly in Spanish with English subtitles. **84m/C VHS, Beta, LV.** SP Antonio Resines, Beatriz Perez-Porro, Jaime Nos, Roy Hoffman; **D:** Fernando Colombo. *KIV, FCT, TPV*

The Sky's the Limit 🎬🎬½ **1943** Astaire spends his leave in Manhattan and falls in love with fetching journalist Leslie. He's in civvies, so little does she know he's a war hero. Nothing-special semi-musical, with Fred-Ginger spark missing. 🎵One For My Baby; My Shining Hour; I've Got a Lot in Common With You. **89m/B VHS, Beta.** Fred Astaire, Joan Leslie, Robert Benchley, Robert Ryan, Elizabeth Patterson; **D:** Edward H. Griffith. Nominations: Academy Awards '43: Best Song ("My Shining Hour"), Scoring of a Musical. *TTC, VYY, MED*

Skyscraper 🎬 **1995 (R)** Gun-wielding helicopter pilot/heroine Carrie Wink (Smith) must battle villainous mercenaries holding hostages in an LA skyscraper. But she stills manages to find time for lots of steamy showers (to best display the only assets the film has). **96m/C VHS, Closed Caption.** Anna Nicole Smith, Richard Steinmetz; **D:** Raymond Martino; **W:** William Applegate Jr.; **C:** Frank Harris; **M:** Jim Halfpenny. *PMH*

Skyscraper Souls 🎬🎬🎬 **1932** William stars as David Dwight, a ruthless businessman who manipulates stock prices and double-crosses lovers in order to have complete control of a 100-story office building. He sacrifices everything and everyone in this story of big business. Based on the novel "Skyscraper" by Faith Baldwin. **98m/B VHS, Closed Caption.** Warren William, Maureen O'Sullivan, Gregory Ratoff, Anita Page, Verree Teasdale, Norman Foster, Jean Hersholt, Wallace Ford; **D:** Edgar Selwyn. *MGM*

Slacker 🎬🎬🎬 **1991 (R)** Defines a new generation: Overwhelmed by the world and it's demands, "Slackers" react by retreating into lives of minimal expectations. Filmed as a series of improvisational stories about people living on the

fringes of the working world and their reactions (or lack thereof) to the life swirling around them. First feature for writer/director Linklater on a budget of $23,000; filmed on location in Austin, Texas with a cast of primarily non-professional actors.**CW:** Language. **97m/C VHS.** Richard Linklater, Rudy Basquez, Jean Caffeine, Jan Hockey, Stephan Hockey, Mark James, Samuel Dietert; **D:** Richard Linklater; **W:** Richard Linklater; **C:** Lee Daniel. *ORI*

Slam Dunk Ernest 🎬½ **1995 (PG-13)** Ernest (Varney) becomes a basketball star in a city league exhibition game when the Basketball Angel (Abdul-Jabbar) loans him his magic shoes.**CW:** Mild language. **93m/C VHS, LV, Closed Caption.** Jim Varney, Kareem Abdul-Jabbar, Jay Brazeau; **D:** John R. Cherry III; **W:** Daniel Butler, John R. Cherry III; **M:** Mark Adler. *TOU*

Slamdance 🎬½ **1987 (R)** A struggling cartoonist is framed for the murder of a beautiful young woman while being victimized by the real killer. A complicated murder mystery with a punk beat and visual flash. But the tale is unoriginal - and where's the slamdancing? **99m/C VHS, Beta, LV, Closed Caption.** Tom Hulce, Virginia Madsen, Mary Elizabeth Mastrantonio, Harry Dean Stanton, Adam Ant, John Doe; **D:** Wayne Wang. *FOX*

Slammer Girls 🎬 **1987 (R)** In this sex-drenched, unfunny spoof on women's prison films, the inmates of Loch Ness Penitentiary try to break out using their sexual wiles. The actresses are pseudonymous porn stars. **82m/C VHS, Beta, LV.** Tally Brittany, Jane Hamilton, Jeff Eagle, Devon Jenkin; **D:** Chuck Vincent. *LIV*

The Slap *La Gifle* **1976 (PG)** French teens learn about love the French way. **103m/C VHS.** FR Isabelle Adjani, Lino Ventura; **D:** Claude Pinoteau; **M:** Georges Delerue.

Slap Shot 🎬🎬🎬 **1977 (R)** A profane satire of the world of professional hockey. Over-the-hill player-coach Newman gathers an odd-ball mixture of has-beens and young players and reluctantly initiates them, using violence on the ice to make his team win. The strip-tease on ice needs to be seen to be believed. Charming in its own bone-crunching way. **123m/C VHS, Beta, LV.** Paul Newman, Michael Ontkean, Jennifer Warren, Lindsay Crouse, Jerry Houser, Melinda Dillon, Strother Martin; **D:** George Roy Hill; **M:** Elmer Bernstein. *USH*

Slapstick **193?** An anthology of great moments from Mack Sennett comedy shorts, featuring many great stars in some of their earliest film appearances. **76m/B VHS, Beta.** Charlie Chaplin, Harold Lloyd, Charley Chase, Buster Keaton, Ben Turpin, Stan Laurel. *REP*

Slapstick of Another Kind 🎬½ **1984 (PG)** Lewis and Kahn play dual roles as an alien brother and sister and their adoptive Earth parents, who are being pursued by U.S. agents. Rather miserable rendition of a Kurt Vonnegut novel. **85m/C VHS, Beta, LV.** Jerry Lewis, Madeline Kahn, Marty Feldman, Jim Backus, Noriyuki "Pat" Morita, Samuel Fuller, Orson Welles; **D:** Steven Paul. *LIV, VES*

Slash 🎬½ **1987** Each of four people caught in a political takeover harbors a secret that could harm one of the others. Extremely violent. **90m/C VHS, Beta.** Romano Kristoff, Michael Monty, Gwen Hung; **D:** John Gale. *NO*

Slashdance woof! **1989** A really pathetic thriller follows a lady cop undercover in a chorus line to find out who's been murdering the dancers. The acting is on the level of pro wrestling. Don't be fooled by the naked babes on the cassette box - there's no nudity. **83m/C VHS, Beta.** Cindy Maranne, James Carroll Jordan, Queen Kong, Joel von Ornsteiner, Jay Richardson; **D:** James Shyman; **W:** James Shyman. *NO*

Slashed Dreams 🎬🎬 *Sunburst* **1974 (R)** Hippie couple travels to California wilderness in search of a friend. A pair of woodsmen assault them and rape the woman, which really messes with their heads. Retitled and packaged as slasher movie. **74m/C VHS.** Peter Hooten, Katherine Baumann, Ric Carrott, Anne Lockhart, Robert Englund, Rudy Vallee, James Keach, David Pritchard, Peter Brown; **D:** James Polakof; **W:** James Keach, David Pritchard. **ACA**

The Slasher woof! **1974** A policeman must find the madman who has been killing off unfaithful married women. Miserably gory, pointless slasher (hence the title) interesting only as an early example of its kind. 88m/C VHS, Beta. Farley Granger, Sylva Koscina, Susan Scott. **NO**

Slate, Wyn & Me 🐾 **1987 (R)** Two bank-robbing, kidnapping brothers flee cross-country from the law, and fall in love with the girl they've snatched. Pointless, and pointlessly violent and vulgar. 90m/C VHS, Beta. Sigrid Thornton, Simon Burke, Martin Sacks; **D:** Don McLennan; **C:** David Connell. **NLC**

Slaughter 🐾 **1972 (R)** After his parents are murdered, a former Green Beret goes after their killers. Plenty of brutality. Followed by "Slaughter's Big Ripoff." 92m/C VHS, Beta, LV. Jim Brown, Stella Stevens, Rip Torn, Cameron Mitchell, Don Gordon, Marlene Clark; **D:** Jack Starrett. **FOX**

Slaughter High 🐾 **1986 (R)** A high school nerd is accidentally disfigured by a back-firing prank. Five years later, he returns to exact bloody revenge. Available in an unrated version. 90m/C VHS, Beta. Caroline Munro, Simon Scuddamore, Kelly Baker; **D:** George Dugdale. **LIV, VES**

Slaughter Hotel 🐾 *Asylum Erotica; La Bestia Uccide a Sangue Freddo* **1971 (R)** An asylum already inhabited by extremely bizarre characters is plagued by a series of gruesome murders. Lots of skin and lots of blood; Neri shines as a nymphomaniacal lesbian nurse. 72m/C VHS, Beta. Klaus Kinski, Rosalba (Sara Bay) Neri, Margaret Lee, John Ely; **D:** Fernando Di Leo. **MPI, GRG**

Slaughter in San Francisco 🐾 *Chuck Norris vs. the Karate Cop; Yellow Faced Tiger; Karate Cop* **1981 (R)** A Chinese-American cop leads a one-man fight against corruption in the department in Daly City, near San Francisco. Norris is the bad guy; made in 1973 but not released until he had an established following (and he still has only some 18 minutes of film footage). Plenty of kicking and karate chops. 92m/C VHS, Beta. **CH** Chuck Norris, Don Wong; **D:** William Lowe. **RHI**

Slaughter of the Innocents 🐾🐾 **1993 (R)** FBI agent Broderick (Glenn) is sent to Salt Lake City to investigate the murders of two children which are found to be connected to a series of bizarre killings that have occurred around Monument Valley. Unbeknownst to his associates, Broderick often uses his 11-year-old whiz-kid son Jesse's (Cameron-Glickenhaus) computer skills to aid his research. Only this time, his inquisitive son gets too close to a serial killer and unless Dad can figure things out on his own, Jesse will be the next victim. 104m/C VHS, LV, **Closed Caption.** Scott Glenn, Jesse Cameron-Glickenhaus, Sheila Tousey, Darlanne Fluegel, Zitto Kazann; **D:** James Glickenhaus; **W:** James Glickenhaus. **USH**

The Slaughter of the Vampires woof! *Curse of the Blood-Ghouls; Curses of the Ghouls* **1962** Newlyweds meet a bloodthirsty vampire in a Viennese chalet. Real, real bad horror flick, poorly dubbed. 81m/C VHS, Beta. **IT** Walter Brandi, Dieter Eppler, Graziella Granta; **D:** Robert Mauri; **W:** Robert Mauri. **SNC**

Slaughter Trail 🐾🐾 **1951** Rancher-turned-stage robber Young shoots two Indians and cavalry colonel Donlevy has to deal with the fallout. Peace returns when Young dies. Ordinary western with balladeer device helping the plot along, or trying to. 78m/C VHS, Beta. Brian Donlevy, Gig Young, Virginia Grey, Andy Devine, Robert Hutton; **D:** Irving Allen. **TTC**

Slaughterday 🐾½ **1977 (R)** An innocent woman is caught in the middle of an ex-con's elaborate scheme to commit the largest heist of his life. 87m/C VHS, Beta. Rita Tushingham, William Berger, Frederick Jaeger, Michael Hauserman, Gordon Mitchell; **D:** Peter Patzak. **GHV**

Slaughterhouse woof! **1987 (R)** A rotund, pig-loving country boy kills, maims, and eats numerous victims. Features the requisite dumb teens and plenty of blood. 87m/C VHS, Beta. Joe Barton, Sherry Bendorf, Don Barrett; **D:** Rick Roessler. **NLC**

Slaughterhouse Five 🐾🐾 **1972 (R)** A suburban optometrist becomes "unstuck" in time and flits randomly through the experiences of his life, from the Dresden bombing to an extraterrestrial zoo. Noticed at Cannes but not at theatres; ambitious failure to adapt Kurt Vonnegut's odd novel. 104m/C VHS, Beta, LV. Michael Sacks, Valerie Perrine, Ron Leibman, Eugene Roche, Perry King; **D:** George Roy Hill. Cannes Film Festival '72: Special Jury Prize. **USH**

Slaughterhouse Rock woof! **1988 (R)** The ghost of a sexy rock star draws a young man into a confrontation with a sadistic spirit that rules a deserted prison. There's also some cannibalism involved. Music group Devo did the score for this flick. 90m/C VHS, Beta. Nicholas Celozzi, Donna Denton, Toni Basil, Hope Marie Carlton; **D:** Dimitri Logothetis. **NO**

Slaughter's Big Ripoff 🐾½ **1973 (R)** Slaughter is back battling the Mob with guns, planes and martial arts. This undistinguished sequel features McMahon as a mob boss. 92m/C VHS, Beta. Jim Brown, Brock Peters, Don Stroud, Ed McMahon, Art Metrano, Gloria Hendry; **D:** Gordon Douglas. **FOX**

Slave Girls from Beyond Infinity 🐾🐾 **1987 (R)** In this B-movie spoof, two beautiful intergalactic slave girls escape their penal colony, land on a mysterious planet, and meet a cannibalistic despot. Fun spoof of '50s "B" sci-fi movies. 80m/C VHS, Beta, LV. Elizabeth Cayton, Cindy Beal, Brinke Stevens; **D:** Ken Dixon; **C:** Thomas Callaway. **AFE**

A Slave of Love 🐾🐾🐾 **1978** Poignant love story set in the Crimea as the Bolshevik Revolution rages around a film crew attempting to complete a project. Interesting as ideological cinema but also enjoyable romantic drama. In Russian with English subtitles. 94m/C VHS, Beta. **RU** Elena Solovei, Rodion Nakhapetov, Alexander Kalyagin; **D:** Nikita Mikhalkov; **M:** Eduard Artemyev. National Board of Review Awards '78: 5 Best Foreign Films of the Year. **COL, AUD**

Slave of the Cannibal God woof! *II Montagna di Dio Cannibale; Mountain of Cannibal Gods* **1979 (R)** Beautiful Andress is captured by "native" cannibals; Keach must save her. 86m/C VHS, Beta. **IT** Stacy Keach, Ursula Andress, Claudio Cassinelli; **D:** Sergio Martino. **VES**

Slave Trade in the World Today 🐾 **1964** Slavery practices in the modern world are shown, including actual scenes of a sheik's harem, slave auctions, and the kidnapping and selling of young women. 87m/C VHS, Beta. **D:** Roberto Malenotti. **VDC, TPV**

Slavers 🐾🐾 **1977 (R)** Detailed depiction of the 19th century African slave trade with a little romance thrown in. 102m/C VHS, Beta. **GE** Trevor Howard, Britt Ekland, Ron Ely, Cameron Mitchell, Ray Milland; **D:** Jurgen Goslar. **VCD**

Slaves in Bondage 🐾 **1937** Young, country girls are lured into the big city and initiated into a life of ill repute in this exploitation classic. A must for camp fans of the 30's. ?m/C VHS. Lona Andre, Wheeler Oakman. **SNC**

Slaves of New York 🐾½ **1989 (R)** Greenwich Village artists worry about life and love in the '80s and being artistic enough for New York. Adapted from the stories of Tama Janowitz, who also wrote the screenplay and appears as Abby. Disastrous adaptation of a popular novel. 115m/C VHS, Beta, LV. Bernadette Peters, Chris Sarandon, Mary Beth Hurt, Madeleine Potter, Adam Coleman Howard, Nick Corri, Mercedes Ruehl, Joe Leeway, Charles McCaughan, John Harkins, Anna Katarina, Tama Janowitz; **D:** James Ivory; **W:** Tama Janowitz. **COL**

The Slayer woof! *Nightmare Island* **1982 (R)** It's movies like this that give getting back to nature a bad name. That horrible monster is after those nice young people again! This time it's on an island off the coast of Georgia. 95m/C VHS, Beta. **D:** J.S. Cardone; **W:** J.S. Cardone; **M:** Robert Folk. **NO**

The Slayer/The Scalps 🐾 **1982 (R)** Double feature. "Scalps" is a slasher set in a Native American burial ground. "The Slayer" is about vacationing couples who run into more than they bargained for on their island retreat. 150m/C VHS, Beta. **D:** J.S. Cardone. **NO**

Slayground 🐾½ **1984 (R)** Man, distraught at the accidental death of his daughter, hires a hitman to exact revenge. Excruciating adaptation of the novel by Richard Stark (Donald E. Westlake). 85m/C VHS, Beta. **GB** Peter Coyote, Mel Smith, Billie Whitelaw, Philip Sayer, Kelli Maroney; **D:** Terry Bedford; **M:** Colin Towns. **REP**

Sleazemania **1985** Compilation of trailers 'n bits reviews some of the sleazier, sicker, and sexier selections of celluloid from the past 50 years. 60m/C VHS, Beta. **RHI**

Sleazemania III: The Good, the Bad & the Sleazy **1986** Another compilation of the cheapest, funniest and scurviest moments, from grade-Z horror films, including "Mondo Psycho" and "Smut Peddler Meets Emmanuel." 90m/B VHS, Beta. **RHI**

The Sleazy Uncle 🐾🐾 *Lo Zio Indegno* **1989** A successful but bored businessman is energized by an encounter with his vice-ridden uncle, a mooching, womanizing beatnik poet who knows how to enjoy life. An energetic but rather formulaic comedy. In Italian with English subtitles. 104m/C VHS, Beta. **IT** Giancarlo Giannini, Vittorio Gassman, Andrea Ferreol, Stefania Sandrelli; **D:** Franco Brusati. **TRI**

Sledgehammer woof! **1983** A madman is wreaking havoc on a small town, annihilating young women with a sledgehammer. 87m/C VHS, Beta. Ted Prior, Doug Matley, Steven Wright. **NO**

Sleep of Death 🐾½ **1979** Young Englishman's pursuit of a blue-blooded woman seems to set off a series of bizarre and mysterious murders. A gothic thriller based on Sheridan Le Fanu's short story. 90m/C VHS, Beta. Brendan Price, Marilu Tolo, Patrick Magee, Curt Jurgens, Per Oscarsson; **D:** Calvin Floyd. **PSM**

Sleep with Me 🐾🐾½ **1994 (R)** What happens when love comes between friendship? Sarah (Tilly), Joseph (Stoltz), and Frank (Sheffer) are soon to find out. Sarah and Joseph are about to get married when their best friend Frank realizes he's in love with Sarah. So he sets out to seduce her and when Joseph realizes what's going on, he not only questions Frank's friendship but wonders just what signals Sarah's been giving off (although Joseph's hardly blameless). Six writers each wrote one of the social scenes detailing their triangular troubles, including a party where Tarantino does a hilarious riff on the homoerotic subtext in "Top Gun." Kelly's directorial debut. **CW:** Language; nudity; sexuality; drug use. 117m/C VHS, LV. Craig Sheffer, Eric Stoltz, Meg Tilly, Todd Field, Adrienne Shelly, Lewis Arquette, Susan Traylor, Tegan West, Parker Posey, Dean Cameron, Thomas Gibson, June Lockhart, Quentin Tarantino, Joey Lauren Adams; **D:** Rory Kelly; **W:** Rory Kelly, Roger Hedden, Neal Jimenez, Michael Steinberg, Duane Dell'Amico, Joe Keenan; **M:** David Lawrence. **MGM**

Sleepaway Camp 🐾 **1983 (R)** Crazed killer hacks away at the inhabitants of a peaceful summer camp in this run-of-the-mill slasher. 88m/C VHS, Beta. Mike Kellin, Jonathan Tiersten, Felissa Rose, Christopher Collet. **MED**

Sleepaway Camp 2: Unhappy Campers 🐾½ **1988 (R)** A beautiful camp counselor is actually a blood-thirsty, murdering madwoman. Sequel to the 1983 slasher, "Sleepaway Camp." 82m/C VHS, Beta. Pamela Springsteen, Renee Estevez, Walter Gotell, Brian Patrick Clark; **D:** Michael A. Simpson. **NLC**

Sleepaway Camp 3: Teenage Wasteland woof! **1989 (R)** This second sequel is as bad as the first two movies. Another disturbed camper hacks up another bevy of teenagers. Better luck at the Motel Six. **80m/C VHS, Beta, LV.** Pamela Springsteen, Tracy Griffith, Michael J. Pollard; **D:** Michael A. Simpson. *NLC*

Sleeper 🎬🎬🎬½ **1973 (PG)** Hapless nerd Allen is revived two hundred years after an operation gone bad. Keaton portrays Allen's love interest in a futuristic land of robots and giant vegetables. He learns of the hitherto unknown health benefits of hot fudge sundaes; discovers the truth about the nation's dictator, known as The Leader; and gets involved with revolutionaries seeking to overthrow the government. Hilarious, fast-moving comedy, full of slapstick and satire. Don't miss the "orgasmatron." **88m/C VHS, Beta, LV, Closed Caption.** Woody Allen, Diane Keaton, John Beck, Howard Cosell; **D:** Woody Allen; **W:** Woody Allen, Marshall Brickman; **M:** Woody Allen. *MGM, FOX, FUS*

Sleepers 🎬🎬½ **1996 (R)** Tense, gritty drama based on Lorenzo Carcaterra's book about four teenaged friends from Hell's Kitchen who get into trouble and wind up being sent to a reform school, where they're brutalized by guards. John (Eldard) and Tommy (Crudup), who grow up to be hit men, recognize their chief abuser (Bacon) years later and kill him. Their trial is prosecuted by Michael (Pitt), another of the gang, who's now the assistant DA. It's supposed to be a true story (the book is published as non-fiction) but doubt has been cast on Carcaterra's veracity (his character is the fourth member, journalist Lorenzo, played by Patric). De Niro and Hoffman excel in relatively minor, but pivotal, roles. **CW:** Language, graphic violence and two scenes of strong sexual content. **150m/C VHS, LV, Closed Caption, DVD.** Brad Pitt, Jason Patric, Ron Eldard, Billy Crudup, Kevin Bacon, Robert De Niro, Dustin Hoffman, Vittorio Gassman, Minnie Driver, Terry Kinney, Brad Renfro, Jonathan Tucker, Joe Perrino, Geoff Wigdor, Bruno Kirby, Aida Turturro, Frank Medrano; **D:** Barry Levinson; **W:** Barry Levinson; **C:** Michael Ballhaus; **M:** John Williams. Academy Awards '96: Original Dramatic/Comedy Score. *WAR*

Sleeping Beauty 🎬🎬🎬 **1959 (G)** Classic Walt Disney version of the famous fairy tale is set to the music of Tchaikovsky's ballet. Lavishly produced. With the voices of Mary Costa, Bill Shirley, and Vera Vague. **75m/C VHS, Beta, LV, Closed Caption.** **D:** Clyde Geronomi, Eric Larson, Wolfgang Reitherman, Les Clark; **M:** George Bruns; **V:** Mary Costa, Bill Shirley, Barbara Luddy, Taylor Holmes, Verna Felton, Barbara Jo Allen, Pinto Colvig, Marvin Miller. Nominations: Academy Awards '59: Scoring of a Musical. *DIS*

Sleeping Beauty **1983** Peters is the princess put to sleep by the evil queen. Handsome prince Reeve comes to the rescue in this classy retelling of the Sleeping Beauty legend. Combines live action and animation. From Shelley Duvall's "Faerie Tale Theatre." **60m/C VHS, Beta, LV, Closed Caption.** Christopher Reeve, Bernadette Peters, Beverly D'Angelo. *FOX, FCT*

Sleeping Beauty 🎬½ **1989** Live action version of the beloved fairy tale, with Welch in the title role. **92m/C VHS.** Tahnee Welch, Morgan Fairchild, Nicholas Clay, Sylvia Miles, Kenny Baker. *MGM, PSM, CVC*

The Sleeping Car 🎬🎬 **1990** A vindictive ghost haunts a group of people living in an old railway car. Fairly fun, fairly competent horror. **87m/C VHS, LV.** David Naughton, Judie Aronson, Kevin McCarthy, Jeff Conaway, Dani Minnick, John Carl Buechler; **D:** Douglas Curtis. *THV*

Sleeping Car to Trieste 🎬🎬 **1945** Conspirators in the theft of a diplomat's diary ride the Orient Express, as a wily detective on board tries to piece together murder clues. Based on the story "Rome Express" by Clifford Grey. **95m/B VHS, Beta.** Jean Kent, Albert Lieven, David Tomlinson, Finlay Currie; **D:** John Paddy Carstairs. *FCT, LCA*

Sleeping Dogs 🎬🎬½ **1982** A man in near-future New Zealand finds it hard to remain neutral when he is caught between a repressive government and a violent resistance movement. The first New Zealand film ever to open in the U.S., and a fine debut for director Donaldson. **107m/C VHS, Beta.** *NZ* Sam Neill, Ian Mune, Nevan Rowe, Dona Akersten, Warren Oates; **D:** Roger Donaldson. *NO*

The Sleeping Tiger 🎬🎬 **1954** A thief breaks into the home of a psychiatrist, who captures him. In exchange for his freedom, the thief agrees to become a guinea pig for the doctor's rehabilitation theories with ultimately tragic results. Director Losey was originally compelled to release the film under a pseudonym, "Victor Hanbury," because he had been blacklisted by Hollywood during the 1950s red scare. First pairing of Losey and Bogarde, who collaborated on several later films, including "Modesty Blaise" (1966) and "Accident" (1967). **89m/B VHS.** Alexis Smith, Alexander Knox, Dirk Bogarde, Hugh Griffith; **D:** Joseph Losey; **M:** Malcolm Arnold. *NOS, SNC*

Sleeping with Strangers 🎬🎬½ **1994 (R)** Two hoteliers in a small British Columbia town find their rivalry increasing as one hotel gets a boost when a drunken rock star and his Hollywood starlet arrive with their entourage in tow. Of course, the media follows and so does the comedic hysteria. **CW:** Sexuality. **103m/C VHS, Closed Caption.** Adrienne Shelly, Neil Duncan, Shawn Thompson, Kymberley Huffman, Scott McNeil; **D:** William T. Bolson; **W:** Joan Carr-Wiggin. *PAR*

Sleeping with the Enemy 🎬🎬½ **1991 (R)** Roberts escapes from abusive husband by faking death, flees to Iowa, falls for drama professor, and, gasp, is found by psycho husband. Occasionally chilling but oft predictable thriller based on novel by Nancy Price. **CW:** Wife abuse terror and sex scene. **99m/C VHS, Beta, LV, Closed Caption.** Julia Roberts, Kevin Anderson, Patrick Bergin, Elizabeth Lawrence, Kyle Secor, Claudette Nevins; **D:** Joseph Ruben; **W:** Ronald Bass; **M:** Jerry Goldsmith. *FXV, IME, FCT*

Sleepless in Seattle 🎬🎬🎬½ **1993 (PG)** Witty, sweet romantic comedy explores the differences between men and women when it comes to love and romance. When widower Hanks talks about his wife on a national talk show, recently engaged Ryan responds. Writer/director Ephron's humorous screenplay is brought to life by a perfectly cast ensemble; it also breathed new life into the classic weepie "An Affair to Remember," comparing it to "The Dirty Dozen" in an unforgettable scene. A movie full of fine detail, from Sven Nykvist's camera work to the graphic layout of the opening credits to the great score. Captured millions at the box office, coming in as the fourth highest grossing movie of 1993. **105m/C VHS, LV, 8mm, Closed Caption, DVD.** Tom Hanks, Meg Ryan, Bill Pullman, Ross Malinger, Rosie O'Donnell, Gaby Hoffman, Victor Garber, Rita Wilson, Barbara Garrick, Carey Lowell, Rob Reiner, Sarah Trigger; **D:** Nora Ephron; **W:** Jeffrey Arch, Larry Atlas, David S. Ward, Nora Ephron; **C:** Sven Nykvist; **M:** Marc Shaiman. Nominations: Academy Awards '93: Best Original Screenplay, Best Song ("A Wink and a Smile"); British Academy Awards '93: Best Original Screenplay, Best Original Score; Golden Globe Awards '94: Best Actor—Musical/Comedy (Hanks), Best Actress—Musical/Comedy (Ryan), Best Film—Musical/Comedy; MTV Movie Awards '94: Best Actress (Ryan), Breakthrough Performance (Malinger), Best On-Screen Duo (Tom Hanks/Meg Ryan), Best Song ("When I Fall in Love"); Writers Guild of America '93: Best Original Screenplay. *COL, BTV, FCT*

Sleepstalker: The Sandman's Last Rites 🎬🎬 **1994 (R)** A serial killer known as the Sandman (Harris) is executed but returns as a shape-shifting horror who can strip the flesh off his victims with whirling sand. He haunts the nightmares of a reporter (Underwood), the only survivor of one of the killer's massacres, who teams up with a photographer (Morris) to learn the creature's origins and defeat him. Good special effects. **CW:** Some terror/violence and language. **101m/C VHS.** Jay Underwood, Michael Harris, Kathryn Morris; **D:** Turi Meyer. *PSM*

Sleepwalk 🎬🎬 **1988 (R)** Odd independent effort about a bored New York desk worker who is given an ancient text of Chinese fairy tales to translate, and finds they're manifesting themselves in dangerous ways in real life. Cinematography by Jim Jarmusch and Franz Prinzi. **78m/C VHS, Beta, LV.** Suzanne Fletcher, Ann Magnuson; **D:** Sara Driver. *NLC, ICA*

Sleepwalkers 🎬½ *Stephen King's Sleepwalkers* **1992 (R)** When Mary and her son Charles arrive in the small town of Travis, Indiana, ugly things begin to happen. And no wonder, it seems the deadly duo are sleepwalkers—fiendish, cat-like vampire creatures who can only survive by sucking the life force out of unsuspecting virgins. Gory but not without some humor, particularly in Krige's portrayal of the sexy and too-loving mother. Not nearly as good as some of King's other horror classics. **CW:** Language, strong violence, and strong sensuality. **91m/C VHS, LV, Closed Caption.** Brian Krause, Madchen Amick, Alice Krige, Jim Haynie, Cindy Pickett, Lyman Ward, Ron Perlman; **Cameos:** Dan Martin, Glenn Shadix, Joe Dante, John Landis, Clive Barker, Tobe Hooper, Stephen King, Mark Hamill; **D:** Mick Garris; **W:** Stephen King. *COL*

Sleepy Eyes of Death: The Chinese Jade 🎬🎬 **1963** Master swordsman Nemuri Kyoshiro slaughters six would-be ambushers and has the seductive Chisa trying to set him against her master's enemy, Chen Sun, all for the sake of discovering the secret of the Chinese Jade. Adapted from the novel by Shibata Renzaburo. Japanese with subtitles. **82m/C VHS, LV.** *JP* Raizo Ichikawa, Tamao Nakamura, Jo Kenzaburo; **D:** Tokuzo Tanaka. *ANI, MOV*

The Slender Thread 🎬🎬🎬 **1965** Based on a true story, Poitier plays a college student who volunteers at a crisis center and must keep would-be suicide Bancroft on the phone until the police can find her. Filmed on location in Seattle. First film for director Pollack. **98m/C VHS, Closed Caption.** Sidney Poitier, Anne Bancroft, Telly Savalas, Steven Hill; **D:** Sydney Pollack; **W:** Stirling Silliphant; **C:** Loyal Griggs; **M:** Quincy Jones. Nominations: Academy Awards '65: Best Art Direction/Set Decoration (B & W), Best Costume Design (B & W). *PAR*

Sleuth 🎬🎬🎬½ **1972 (PG)** A mystery novelist and his wife's lover face off in ever shifting, elaborate, and diabolical plots against each other, complete with red herrings, traps, and tricks. Playful, cerebral mystery thriller from top director Mankiewicz. Shaffer also scripted "Frenzy" for Hitchcock, from his play. **138m/C VHS, Beta, LV.** Laurence Olivier, Michael Caine; **D:** Joseph L. Mankiewicz; **W:** Anthony Shaffer; **C:** Oswald Morris; **M:** John Addison. Edgar Allan Poe Awards '72: Best Screenplay; New York Film Critics Awards '72: Best Actor (Olivier); Nominations: Academy Awards '72: Best Actor (Caine), Best Actor (Olivier), Best Director (Mankiewicz), Original Dramatic/Comedy Score. *MED, HMV, VTR*

Slightly Honorable 🎬🎬½ **1940** A lawyer gets involved in political scandals and becomes a murder suspect. Snappy comedy-drama with good performances but too many subplots. Based on the novel "Send Another Coffin" by F. G. Presnell. **75m/B VHS, Beta.** Pat O'Brien, Broderick Crawford, Edward Arnold, Eve Arden, Evelyn Keyes, Phyllis Brooks; **D:** Tay Garnett. *NOS, VYY, BAR*

A Slightly Pregnant Man 🎬🎬 **1979 (PG)** Comic complications abound as a construction worker becomes the world's first pregnant man. Surprise ending saves this simple and not very exciting film. **92m/C VHS, Beta.** Catherine Deneuve, Marcello Mastroianni; **D:** Jacques Demy. *NO*

Slightly Scarlet 🎬🎬½ **1956** Small-time hood Payne carries out an assignment from boss DeCorsia to smear a law-and-order politico running for mayor. He falls in love with the candidate's secretary, tries to go straight, and ends up running the mob when DeCorsia flees town. A spiffy, low-budget noir crime drama based on the James M. Cain novel "Love's Lovely Counterfeit." **99m/C VHS, Beta.** Rhonda Fleming, Arlene Dahl, John Payne, Kent Taylor, Ted de Corsia; *D:* Allan Dwan; *W:* Robert Blees. *NO*

Slime City *🎞* **1989** The widow of an alchemist poisons her tenants so they will join her husband in the hereafter. Very low-budget; occasionally funny. **90m/C VHS, Beta.** Robert C. Sabin, Mary Huner, T.J. Merrick, Dick Biel; *D:* Gregory Lamberson. *NO*

The Slime People woof! **1963** Huge prehistoric monsters are awakened from long hibernation by atomic testing in Los Angeles. They take over the city, creating the fog they need to live. Thank goodness for scientist Burton, who saves the day. Filmed in a butcher shop in Los Angeles. **76m/B VHS, Beta.** Robert Hutton, Robert Burton, Susan Hart, William Boyce, Les Tremayne; *D:* Robert Hutton. *NOS, GEM, RHI*

Sling Blade *🎞🎞🎞½* **1996 (R)** Mildly retarded killer Karl (Thornton, making his feature diectorial debut) is released from a mental hospital, where he was placed after killing his mother and her lover, after 25 years. Returning to his hometown, he befriends a boy (Black) with problems of his own. His mother is living with a mean, bullying drunkard (Yoakam, in a brilliant performance) who has no use for anyone, least of all mom's openly gay co-worker (Ritter). Thornton's excellent script moves at the slow pace of its hero, providing the superb cast plenty of opportunity to explore the rich characterization and dialogue. Filmed in Thornton's home state of Arkansas. **134m/C VHS.** Billy Bob Thornton, Dwight Yoakam, John Ritter, Lucas Black, Natalie Canerday, James Hampton, Robert Duvall, J.T. Walsh, Rick Dial, Brent Briscoe, Christy Ward, Col. Bruce Hampton, Vic Chesnutt, Mickey Jones, Jim Jarmusch, Ian Moore; *D:* Billy Bob Thornton; *W:* Billy Bob Thornton; *C:* Barry Markowitz; *M:* Daniel Lanois. Academy Awards '96: Best Adapted Screenplay; Independent Spirit Awards '97: Best First Feature; Writers Guild of America '96: Best Adapted Screenplay; Nominations: Academy Awards '96: Best Actor (Thornton); Screen Actors Guild Award '96: Best Actor (Thornton), Cast. *TOU*

The Slingshot *🎞🎞🎞* **1993 (R)** Quirky coming-of-age tale, set in 1920s Stockholm, finds 12-year-old Roland (Salen) trying to survive childhood dilemmas. His mother (Frydman) is a Russian Jew (who sells condoms illegally) and his father (Skarsgard) is a zealous socialist, so Roland is subjected to unceasing bullying and prejudice. But the resourceful Roland doesn't let society get him down—he uses the contraband condoms in an inventive slingshot design that brings him an unwarranted amount of attention. Based on the novel by Roland Schutt. Swedish with subtitles. **102m/C VHS, LV.** *SW* Jesper Salen, Stellan Skarsgard, Basia Frydman, Niclas Olund, Ernst-Hugo Jaregard, Jacob Leygraf; *D:* Ake Sandgren; *W:* Bjorn Isfalt, Ake Sandgren. *COL*

Slipping into Darkness *🎞½* **1988 (R)** Three spoiled, rich college girls are held responsible for a retarded local boy's death. Honest and overwrought. **86m/C VHS, Beta, LV.** Belle Mitchell, Laslo Papas, Rigg Kennedy, Beverly Ross, T.J. McFadden, Michelle Johnson, John DiAquino; *D:* Eleanor Gaver. *GHV, HHE*

Slipstream *🎞🎞* **1972** "Turgid" and "gloomy" are the words for this romantic drama set in remote Alberta. The minor plot concerns a young woman who teaches a lonely disc jockey a lesson about life and love. This film feels like a long Canadian winter. **93m/C VHS, Beta.** *CA* Julie Askew, Patti Oatman, Eli Rill. *TWE*

Slipstream *🎞🎞* **1989 (PG-13)** A sci-fi adventure set on a damaged Earthscape where people seek to escape a giant jetstream. While tracking down a bounty hunter gone bad, a futuristic cop follows his quarry into the dangerous river of wind. Ambitious "Blade Runner" clone with big names (Hamill is good) was never released theatrically in the US. **92m/C VHS, Beta, LV.** *GB* Mark Hamill, Bill Paxton, Bob Peck, Eleanor David, Kitty Aldridge,

Robbie Coltrane, Ben Kingsley, F. Murray Abraham; *D:* Steven Lisberger; *W:* Tony Kayden; *M:* Elmer Bernstein. *VTR*

Slither *🎞🎞🎞* **1973 (PG)** Caan and Boyle become wrapped up in a scheme to recover $300,000 in cash, stolen seven years previously. Along the way they pick up speed freak Kellerman, who assists them in a variety of loony ways. Frantic chase scenes are the highlight. **97m/C VHS, Beta.** James Caan, Peter Boyle, Sally Kellerman, Louise Lasser, Allen (Goorwitz) Garfield, Richard B. Shull, Alex Rocco; *D:* Howard Zieff; *W:* W.D. Richter. *MGM*

Slithis woof! **1978 (PG)** Slithis, the nuclear-waste creature, is the menace of Venice, California. Keep your pets (and yourself) indoors! **86m/C VHS, Beta.** Alan Blanchard, Judy Motulsky; *D:* Stephen Traxler; *W:* Stephen Traxler. *MED*

Sliver *🎞½* **1993 (R)** Another voyeuristic thriller starring Stone. She's Carly Norris, a lonely book editor who moves into one of Manhattan's toothpick thin buildings (the "sliver" of the title). She meets pulp novelist Jack (Berenger), whose libido is as overheated as his prose, but gets involved in a steamy affair with handsome neighbor Zeke (Baldwin), a computer whiz who also owns the building. Oh, by the way, he's installed video cameras in every unit that reveal many intimate secrets. Lots of sex and murders. Murky and underdeveloped and the ending, which was reshot, still leaves much to be desired. Lots of hype, little to recommend. *CW:* Language, violence, and strong sexuality. **106m/C VHS, Beta, LV, CD-I, Closed Caption.** Sharon Stone, William Baldwin, Tom Berenger, Martin Landau, Polly Walker, Colleen Camp, CCH Pounder, Nina Foch, Keene Curtis; *D:* Phillip Noyce; *W:* Joe Eszterhas; *C:* Vilmos Zsigmond; *M:* Howard Shore. MTV Movie Awards '94: Most Desirable Male (Baldwin); Nominations: MTV Movie Awards '94: Most Desirable Female (Stone), Best Song ("I Can't Help Falling in Love"). *PAR*

Sloane woof! **1984** Typical sleazy sex and violence flick. For the record: organized crime baddies kidnap good guy Resnick's girlfriend and he seeks revenge. **95m/C VHS, Beta.** Robert Resnick, Debra Blee, Paul Aragon; *D:* Dan Rosenthal. *LIV, VAE*

Slow Burn *🎞🎞* **1986** An ex-reporter tries some detective work in the seamy side of Palm Springs, and becomes embroiled in the standard drug, kidnapping, murder routine. Based on the novel "Castles Burning" by Arthur Lyons. Made for cable television. **92m/C VHS, Beta, Closed Caption.** Eric Roberts, Beverly D'Angelo, Dan Hedaya, Dennis Lipscomb; *D:* Matthew Chapman; *W:* Matthew Chapman; *M:* Loek Dikker. *USH*

Slow Burn *🎞* **1990 (R)** The Mafia and Chinese Triads are having troubles and a tired cop attempts to reach a peaceful solution. **90m/C VHS.** William Smith, Anthony James, Ivan Rogers. *XVC, DMP*

Slow Moves *🎞½* **1984** Slow story of slow people who meet slowly, have sluggish affair, and find tragedy eventually. **93m/C VHS, Beta.** Roxanne Rogers; *D:* Jon Jost. *FCT*

The Slugger's Wife *🎞½* Neil Simon's The Slugger's Wife **1985 (PG-13)** The marriage between an Atlanta Braves outfielder and a rock singer suddenly turns sour when their individual careers force them to make some tough choices. **105m/C VHS, Beta, LV, Closed Caption.** Michael O'Keefe, Rebecca DeMornay, Martin Ritt, Randy Quaid, Loudon Wainwright III, Cleavant Derricks, Lynn Whitfield; *D:* Hal Ashby; *W:* Neil Simon; *C:* Caleb Deschanel. *COL*

Slugs woof! **1987 (R)** A health inspector discovers that spilled toxic waste is being helpfully cleaned up by the slug population, saving Uncle Sam countless dollars. But wait! The slugs are mutating into blood-thirsty man-eaters. Is this the answer to military cut-backs? **90m/C VHS, Beta, LV.** Michael Garfield, Kim Terry, Philip Machale; *D:* J. Piquer Simon. *VTR, NWV*

Slumber Party '57 *🎞½* **1976 (R)** At a slumber party, six girls get together and exchange stories of how they lost their virginity. Lots of great music by the Platters, Big Bopper, Jerry Lee Lewis, the Crewcuts, and Paul and Paula but

complete schlock otherwise. **89m/C VHS, Beta, LV.** Noelle North, Bridget Hollman, Debra Winger, Mary Ann Appleseth, Cheryl "Rainbeaux" Smith, Janet Wood, R.L. Armstrong, Rafael Campos, Larry Gelman, Will Hutchins, Joyce Jillson, Victor Rogers, Joe E. Ross, Bill Thurman; *D:* William A. Levey; *M:* Miles Goodman. *MGM, VES*

The Slumber Party Massacre *🎞½* **1982 (R)** A psychotic killer with a power drill terrorizes a high school girls' slumber party. Contrived and forced, but not always unfunny. **84m/C VHS, Beta.** Michele Michaels, Robin Stille, Andre Honore, Michael Villela, Debra Deliso, Gina Mari, Brinke Stevens; *D:* Amy Holden Jones, Aaron Lipstadt; *W:* Rita Mae Brown. *NLC*

Slumber Party Massacre 2 woof! **1987** Drowsy babes in lingerie are drilled to death by a perverse madman. Another disappointing sequel. **75m/C VHS, Beta, LV, Closed Caption.** Crystal Bernard, Kimberly McArthur, Juliette Cummins, Patrick Lowe; *D:* Deborah Brock; *W:* Deborah Brock; *C:* Thomas Callaway. *NLC*

Slumber Party Massacre 3 woof! **1990 (R)** Parents: Don't let your daughters have any slumber parties! Yes, it's a drill—for the third time. **76m/C VHS, Beta.** Keely Christian, Brittain Frye, M.K. Harris, David Greenle, Hope Marie Carlton, Maria Ford; *D:* Sally Mattison; *W:* Catherine Cyran. *MGM*

The Small Back Room *🎞🎞🎞* Hour of Glory **1949** A crippled WWII munitions expert leads a tormented existence and laments government bureaucracy. Powerfully presented adult storyline. **106m/B VHS.** David Farrar, Jack Hawkins, Cyril Cusack, Kathleen Byron, Anthony Bushell, Michael Gough, Robert Morley; *D:* Michael Powell, Emeric Pressburger. *VYY, LOO, FCT*

Small Change *🎞🎞🎞🎞* **1976 (PG)** Pudgy, timid Desmouceaux and scruffy, neglected Goldman lead a whole pack of heartwarming tykes. A realistically and tenderly portrayed testament to the great director's belief in childhood as a "state of grace." Criticized for sentimentality, "Small Change" followed Truffaut's gloomy "The Story of Adele H." Steven Spielberg suggested the English translation of "L'Argent de Poche." In French with English subtitles. **104m/C VHS, Beta, LV.** *FR* Geory Desmouceaux, Philippe Goldman, Jean-Francois Stevenin, Chantal Mercier, Claudio Deluca, Frank Deluca, Richard Golfier, Laurent Devlaeminck, Francis Devlaeminck, Sylvie Grezel, Pascale Bruchon, Nicole Felix; *D:* Francois Truffaut; *W:* Francois Truffaut, Suzanne Schiffman; *C:* Pierre William Glenn; *M:* Maurice Jaubert. National Board of Review Awards '76: 5 Best Foreign Films of the Year. *MGM, FCT, WAR*

A Small Circle of Friends *🎞½* **1980 (R)** Three Harvard students struggle through their shifting relationships during their college years in the 1960s. **112m/C VHS, Beta.** Brad Davis, Jameson Parker, Karen Allen, Shelley Long; *D:* Rob Cohen. *FOX*

Small Faces *🎞🎞🎞* **1995 (R)** Semi-autobiographical account of three brothers growing up in a working class, gang-ridden section of Glasgow in 1968. Scottish lad Lex MacLean (Robertson) is at the crucial age of 13 and caught between two completely opposite brothers and two warring gangs. Sensitive brother Alan (McFadden) has the stigma of being an artist in a conscientiously macho society, while older brother Bobby (Duffy) has no such problem, being a gang member and all-around punk. When Lex unfortunately injures the eye of gang leader Malky (McKidd) with an air-gun, he unknowingly sets in motion a dangerous chain of events, forcing him to ally with both brothers. Writer/director MacKinnon makes sure even the most tense situations are offset with dark humor, and stages the violent scenes beautifully. Garnering comparisons with other Scottish youth fables like "Trainspotting," film follows somewhat the same storytelling formula, but is much more low-key. Character and plot are given equal attention and film greatly benefits from an outstanding performance by Robertson. CNT Violence and language. *CW:* Violence and language. **108m/C VHS.** *GB* Iain Robertson, Clare Higgins, Ian McElhinney, Kevin McKidd, Joseph McFadden, J.S. Duffy, Laura

Fraser, Garry Sweeney, Mark McConnochie, Steven Singleton, David Walker; **D:** Gilles Mackinnon; **W:** Gilles Mackinnon, Billy Mackinnon; **C:** John de Borman; **M:** John Keane. *EVE*

Small Hotel ✓✓ **1957** After discovering that he is to be replaced as headwaiter by a young woman, Harker plots to save his job through espionage, blackmail and cajolery. Average comedy, adapted from a popular British stage play as a star vehicle for Harker. **59m/B VHS.** Gordon Harker, Marie Lohr, John Loder, Irene Handl, Janet Munro, Billie Whitelaw, Francis Matthews, Dora Bryan; **D:** David MacDonald. *NOS*

Small Kill ✓½ **1993 (R)** Burghoff leaves his lovable MASH character far behind, testing his acting skills as a psycho who disguises himself as a female fortune teller to rob his victims of their life savings so he can become head druglord of his town (what a goal). Two cops try to stop him/her. **86m/C VHS.** Gary Burghoff, Rebecca Ferratti, Donnie Kehr, Jason Miller, Fred Carpenter; **D:** Robert M. Fresco; **W:** Fred Carpenter, James McTernan. *VCI*

A Small Killing ✓✓ **1981** An undercover cop and a college professor pose as a wino and a bag lady, when trying to put the tabs on a druglord. Made for TV mystery/romance based on "The Rag Bag Clan" by Richard Barth. **100m/C VHS, Beta.** Ed Asner, Jean Simmons, Sylvia Sidney, Andrew Prine, J. Pat O'Malley, Anne Ramsey; **D:** Steven Hilliard Stern. *LIV*

Small Sacrifices ✓✓½ **1989** The true story of Diane Downs, an Oregon woman who may have murdered her own three children in 1983. Fine performance from Fawcett, who seems to like made for TV tales of true-life domestic violence as an antidote to her earlier ditzy persona as a Charlie's Angel. Gripping, with a superb script. **159m/C VHS, Beta, LV.** Farrah Fawcett, Ryan O'Neal, John Shea, Emily Perkins, Gordon Clapp; **D:** David Greene; **W:** Joyce Eliason. *FRH*

Small Time ✓✓ **1991** Chronicles the downfall of a young, small-time Harlem thief. Vince knows nothing but the streets and peer pressure, indifference, and police abuse lead him inexorably to a fatal crime. Near documentary style only heightens the tensions. **88m/B VHS.** Richard Barboza, Carolyn Hinebrew, Keith Allen, Scott Ferguson, Jane Williams; **D:** Norman Loftis; **W:** Norman Loftis; **M:** Arnold Bieber. *XVC*

Small Town Boy ✓✓ **1937** The cast does what they can with the brief, hackneyed story of a guy whose personality changes for the worse when he finds a "fortune" (one thousand pre-inflationary dollars). **61m/B VHS.** Stuart Erwin, Joyce Compton, Jed Prouty, Clara Blandick, James "Doc" Blakely; **D:** Glenn Tryon; **W:** Glenn Tryon. *NOS, LOO, VYY*

Small Town Girl ✓✓½ *One Horse Town* **1953** Typical romantic musical of the era, as a city slicker picked up for speeding in a hick town is pursued by the sheriff's daughter. Several Busby Berkeley blockbuster musical numbers are shoehorned incongruously into the rural doings. ♫ Take Me To Broadway; I've Got To Hear That Beat; My Flaming Heart; Fine, Fine, Fine; The Fellow I'd Follow; Lullaby of the Lord; Small Towns Are Smile Towns; My Gaucho. **93m/C VHS, Beta.** Jane Powell, Farley Granger, Bobby Van, Ann Miller, Billie Burke, Robert Keith, S.Z. Sakall, Fay Wray, Nat King Cole, Chill Wills; **D:** Leslie Kardos; **M:** Andre Previn. Nominations: Academy Awards '53: Best Song ("My Flaming Heart"). *MGM*

A Small Town in Texas ✓✓ **1976 (PG)** An ex-con returns home looking for the sheriff who framed him on a drug charge, and who has stolen his woman. Not-too-violent, predictable revenge flick. **96m/C VHS, Beta.** Timothy Bottoms, Susan George, Bo Hopkins; **D:** Jack Starrett; **W:** William W. Norton Sr.; **C:** Charles Bernstein. *VES, LIV*

The Smallest Show on Earth ✓✓✓ *Big Time Operators* **1957** A couple inherit not only an old movie house, but the three people who work there as well. Very funny and charming, with a

wonderful cast. Sellers is delightful as the soused projectionist. **80m/B VHS.** *GB* Bill Travers, Virginia McKenna, Margaret Rutherford, Peter Sellers, Bernard Miles, Leslie Phillips, Stringer Davis, Francis De Wolff, Sidney James, June Cunningham; **D:** Basil Dearden; **W:** William Rose, John Eldridge. *NOS, FCT, VEC*

Smart-Aleck Kill **1985** An episode of the cable television-produced Phillip Marlowe series involving the drug-related murder of a Hollywood actor in the 20s. **53m/C VHS.** Powers Boothe, Michael J. Shannon, Liza Ross; **D:** Peter Hunt. *FOX*

Smart Alecks ✓½ **1942** The Bowery Boys get involved with gangsters when Jordan helps capture a crook. The usual wise-cracking from Hall and Gorcey helps keep things moving. **88m/B VHS.** Leo Gorcey, Huntz Hall, Gabriel Dell, Gale Storm, Roger Pryor Jr., Walter Woolf King, Herbert Rawlinson, Joe Kirk, Marie Windsor; **D:** Wallace Fox. *NOS*

Smart Money ✓✓½ **1988** A wrongly-jailed man enlists the help of his oddball pals to get revenge on the real thief who committed the computer fraud that put him behind bars. They get even while padding their pockets. **88m/C VHS.** Spencer Leigh, Alexandra Pigg, Ken Campbell. *NO*

Smash Palace ✓✓½ **1982** A compelling drama of a marriage jeopardized by his obsession with building a race car and her need for love and affection. Melodramatic, but worth watching. Robson as their young daughter is wonderful. **100m/C VHS, Beta, LV.** *NZ* Bruno Lawrence, Anna Jemison, Greer Robson, Keith Aberdein; **D:** Roger Donaldson; **W:** Bruno Lawrence. *LIV, VES*

Smash-Up: The Story of a Woman ✓✓✓ *A Woman Destroyed* **1947** A famous nightclub singer gives up her career for marriage and a family, only to become depressed when her husband's career soars. She turns to alcohol and her life falls apart. When her husband sues for divorce and custody of their child, she fights to recover from alcoholism. Hayward's first major role. **103m/B VHS, Beta.** Susan Hayward, Lee Bowman, Marsha Hunt, Eddie Albert; **D:** Stuart Heisler; **W:** John Howard Lawson. Nominations: Academy Awards '47: Best Actress (Hayward), Best Story. *NOS, PSM, DVT*

Smile ✓✓✓ **1975 (PG)** Barbed, merciless send-up of small-town America focusing on a group of naive California girls who compete for the "Young American Miss" crown amid rampant commercialism, exploitation and pure middle-class idiocy. Hilarious neglected '70s-style satire. Early role for Griffith. **113m/C VHS, Beta, LV.** Bruce Dern, Barbara Feldon, Michael Kidd, Nicholas Pryor, Geoffrey Lewis, Colleen Camp, Joan Prather, Annette O'Toole, Melanie Griffith, Denise Nickerson; **D:** Michael Ritchie; **W:** Jerry Belson; **C:** Conrad Hall. *MGM*

Smile, Jenny, You're Dead ✓✓ **1974** Janssen discovers that close friend's son-in-law has been murdered, and falls in love with the daughter, the main suspect. Pilot for Janssen's "Harry-O" detective series. **90m/C VHS.** David Janssen, John Anderson, Howard da Silva, Martin Gabel, Clu Gulager, Zalman King, Jodie Foster, Barbara Leigh; **D:** Jerry Thorpe. *UNI*

Smiles of a Summer Night ✓✓✓½ *Sommarnattens Leende* **1955** The best known of Bergman's rare comedies; sharp satire about eight Swedish aristocrats who become romantically and comically intertwined over a single weekend. Inspired Sondheim's successful Broadway musical "A Little Night Music," and Woody Allen's "A Midsummer Night's Sex Comedy." In Swedish with English subtitles. **110m/B VHS, Beta, LV.** *SW* Gunnar Björnstrand, Harriet Andersson, Ulla Jacobsson, Eva Dahlbeck, Jarl Kulle, Margit Carlqvist; **D:** Ingmar Bergman; **W:** Ingmar Bergman. *HMV, DVT, CRC*

Smilin' Through ✓✓✓ **1933** First sound version of this melodrama/romance which Franklin had directed as a silent in 1922. Shearer is set to marry Howard when jealous rival March shows up armed at the wedding and accidentally kills the bride. March escapes and Howard spends his years as a recluse until his young niece, the im-

age of his dead fiance (naturally, since she's also played by Shearer) arrives to live with him. She meets a young man who turns out to be March's son (played again by March) and they fall in love. Pure sentiment done with high gloss. Remade in 1941. **97m/B VHS.** Norma Shearer, Fredric March, Leslie Howard, O.P. Heggie, Ralph Forbes, Beryl Mercer, Margaret Seddon; **D:** Sidney Franklin; **C:** Lee Garmes. Nominations: Academy Awards '33: Best Picture. *FCT*

Smilin' Through ✓✓½ **1941** Third filming, second with sound, first in color, of a popular melodrama. An embittered man whose wife was murdered on their wedding day raises an orphaned niece, only to have her fall in love with the son of her aunt's murderer. Made MacDonald into a singing star. Songs include title tune and "A Little Love, a Little Kiss." **101m/C VHS, Beta.** Jeanette MacDonald, Brian Aherne, Gene Raymond, Ian Hunter, Frances Robinson; **D:** Frank Borzage. *MGM*

Smiling Madame Beudet/The Seashell and the Clergyman ✓✓✓½ **1928** Two famous shorts by Dulac; the second scripted by Artaud. Both are pioneering examples of surrealistic film. Silent. **62m/B VHS, Beta.** *FR* Alix Allin; **D:** Germaine Dulac; **W:** Antonin Artaud. *FCT*

Smilla's Sense of Snow ✓✓ **1996 (R)** Thriller starts off well but fails to sustain the suspense of the Peter Hoeg mystery on which it is based. Solitary scientist Smilla Jasperson (Ormond) is a half-Inuit, half-American (Danish in the book) resident of Copenhagen who's an expert on snow and ice. Born and raised in Greenland, Smilla is drawn back to her home when the body of six-year-old Isaiah (Miano), whom she's grudgingly befriended, is discovered at their apartment building. Smilla believes the boy was murdered and when she begins investigating it leads to the Greenland mining company where Isaiah's late father worked and which is run by the suspicious Tork (Harris). Location cinematography is particularly impressive. **CW:** Language, some violence and a sex scene. **121m/C VHS, LV, Closed Caption.** *GE DK SW* Julia Ormond, Gabriel Byrne, Richard Harris, Vanessa Redgrave, Robert Loggia, Jim Broadbent, Mario Adorf, Bob Peck, Tom Wilkinson, Peter Capaldi, Emma Croft, Clipper Miano; **D:** Bille August; **W:** Ann Biderman; **C:** Jorgen Persson; **M:** Hans Zimmer, Harry Gregson-Williams. *FXV*

Smith! ✓✓½ **1969 (G)** Naive but well intentioned look at present-day treatment of Native Americans. Rancher Ford becomes embroiled in the trial of murder suspect Ramirez. Based on Paul St. Pierre's novel "Breaking Smith's Quarter Horse." **101m/C VHS, Beta.** Glenn Ford, Frank Ramirez, Keenan Wynn; **D:** Michael O'Herlihy; **M:** Robert F. Brunner. *DIS*

Smithereens ✓✓½ **1982 (R)** Working-class girl leaves home for New York's music scene. Rugged, hip character study. Director Seidleman's first feature. **90m/C VHS, Beta, LV.** Susan Berman, Brad Rinn, Richard Hell, Christopher Noth; **D:** Susan Seidelman; **W:** Ron Nyswaner, Peter Askin. *FRF, TPV, FCT*

Smoke ✓✓½ **1970** A young boy nurses a lost German sheperd back to health with the help of his new stepfather, whom he learns to trust. Then he runs away with the dog when the original owners show up. Made for television Disney fare starring Opie/Richie (and later successful director) Howard. **89m/C VHS, Beta.** Earl Holliman, Ron Howard, Andy Devine; **D:** Vincent McEveety. *DIS*

Smoke ✓✓ **1993** Three days in the life of Michael, as he travels between fantasy and reality, past and present, searching for love with the perfect older man. **90m/C VHS. D:** Mark D'Auria; **M:** Arnold Bieber. *WBF*

Smoke ✓✓ **1995 (R)** Brooklyn slice of life centers around the local cigar store run by Auggie Wren (Keitel). An ensemble piece, divided into five chapters, which includes such characters as down-to-his luck novelist Paul (Hurt), troubled black teenager Rashid (Perrineau Jr.), Augie's ex-wife Ruby (Channing) and supposed daughter (Judd), and many more (some of whom get lost in the shuffle). Wonderfully acted but the stories tend to disappear in a wisp of smoke. Based on a story by Auster. Wang and Auster also made an impromptu companion film "Blue in the Face."*CW:* Language. **112m/C VHS, LV, Closed Caption.** Harvey Keitel, William Hurt, Stockard Channing, Forest Whitaker, Harold Perrineau Jr., Ashley Judd, Mary Ward, Victor Argo, Jared Harris, Giancarlo Esposito, Mel Gorham; *D:* Wayne Wang; *W:* Paul Auster; *C:* Adam Holender; *M:* Rachel Portman. Nominations: Independent Spirit Awards '96: Best Supporting Actor (Perrineau); Screen Actors Guild Award '95: Best Supporting Actress (Channing). *TOU*

Smoke in the Wind 🐾½ 1975 (PG) Subpar western about men accused of complicity with the Union in postbellum Arkansas. Minor role for Brennan was his last; also director Kane's last film. **93m/C VHS, Beta.** John Ashley, Walter Brennan, John Russell, Myron Healey; *D:* Joseph Kane. *PSM*

Smokescreen 🐾🐾½ 1990 (R) A young ad exec meets the girl of his dreams, and finds himself working for her gangster boyfriend. Competently made and acted, but phoney ending wrecks it. **91m/C VHS, LV, Closed Caption.** Kim Cattrall, Dean Stockwell, Matt Craven, Kim Coates, Brian George, Michael Hogan; *D:* Martin Lavut. *COL*

Smokey and the Bandit 🐾🐾½ 1977 (PG) If you don't know how to end a movie, you call for a car chase. The first and best of the horrible series about bootlegger Reynolds is one long car chase. Reynolds makes a wager that he can have a truck load of Coors beer—once unavailable east of Texas—delivered to Atlanta from Texas in 28 hours. Gleason is the "smokey" who tries to stop him. Field is the hitchhiker Reynolds picks up along the way. Great stunts; director Needham was a top stunt man. **96m/C VHS, Beta, LV.** Burt Reynolds, Sally Field, Jackie Gleason, Jerry Reed, Mike Henry, Paul Williams, Pat McCormick; *D:* Hal Needham; *W:* Charles Shyer. Nominations: Academy Awards '77: Best Film Editing. *USH*

Smokey and the Bandit, Part 2 🐾 *Smokey and the Bandit Ride Again* 1980 (PG) Pathetic sequel to "Smokey and the Bandit" proved a box-office winner, grossing $40 million. The Bandit is hired to transport a pregnant elephant from Miami to the Republican convention in Dallas. Sheriff Buford T. Justice and family are in hot pursuit. **101m/C VHS, Beta, LV.** Burt Reynolds, Sally Field, Jackie Gleason, Jerry Reed, Mike Henry, Dom DeLuise, Pat McCormick, Paul Williams; *D:* Hal Needham; *W:* Jerry Belson, Michael Kane. *USH*

Smokey and the Bandit, Part 3 🐾 1983 (PG) You thought the second one was bad? Another mega car chase, this time sans Reynolds and director Needham. **88m/C VHS, Beta, LV.** Jackie Gleason, Jerry Reed, Paul Williams, Pat McCormick, Mike Henry, Colleen Camp; *Cameos:* Burt Reynolds; *D:* Dick Lowry; *W:* Stuart Birnbaum, David Dashev. *USH*

Smokey & the Hotwire Gang 🐾½ 1979 (R) A convoy of truckers try to track down a beautiful woman driving a stolen car. **84m/C VHS, Beta.** James Keach, Stanley Livingston, Tony Lorea, Alvy Moore, George Barris. *NO*

Smokey & the Judge 🐾 1980 (PG) Police officer has his hands full with a trio of lovely ladies. **90m/C VHS.** Gene Price, Wayde Preston, Juanita Curiel. *SUN*

Smokey Bites the Dust 🐾 1981 (PG) Car-smashing gag-fest about a sheriff's daughter kidnapped by her smitten beau. Near-plotless and literally unoriginal: lifted footage from several other Corman-produced flicks, a technique that can aptly be called garbage picking. **87m/C VHS, Beta.** Janet Julian, Jimmy McNichol, Patrick Campbell, Kari Lizer, John Blythe Barrymore Jr.; *D:* Charles B. Griffith; *W:* Max Apple. *NLC*

Smokey Smith 🐾½ 1936 Ubiquitous Hayes and steely Steele hunt down the slayers of an elderly couple. Ordinary oater directed by Steele's father, Bradbury. **59m/B VHS, Beta.** Bob Steele, George "Gabby" Hayes; *D:* Robert North Bradbury. *VCN*

Smoking/No Smoking 🐾🐾 1994 Two linked films director Resnais adapted from writer Alan Ayckbourn's eight-play cycle "Intimate Exchanges" (although the screenwriters have only used six stories). Azema and Arditti play nine characters in various tableaux on marriage and affairs set at a Yorkshire school. The opening sequence of each episode provides the title tie-in, as faculty wife Celia goes onto the terrace, finds a pack of cigarettes, and decides whether or not to light up. A studio set provides all the frankly fake backdrops. Very slight and very long. French with subtitles. **285m/C VHS.** *FR* Sabine Azema, Pierre Arditti; *D:* Alain Resnais; *W:* Jean-Pierre Bacri, Agnes Jaoui. Cesar Awards '94: Best Actor (Arditti), Best Art Direction/Set Decoration, Best Director (Resnais), Best Film, Best Screenplay.

A Smoky Mountain Christmas 🐾🐾 1986 Dolly gets away from it all in a secluded cabin that has been appropriated by a gang of orphans, and sings a half dozen songs. Innocuous seasonal country fun. Winkler's TV directing debut. **94m/C VHS, Beta, Closed Caption.** Dolly Parton, Bo Hopkins, Dan Hedaya, Gennie James, David Ackroyd, Rene Auberjonois, John Ritter, Anita Morris, Lee Majors; *D:* Henry Winkler; *W:* Dolly Parton. *FOX*

Smooth Talk 🐾🐾🐾 1985 (PG-13) An innocent, flirtatious teenager catches the eye of a shady character, played by Williams. Disturbing and thought-provoking film that caused some controversy when it opened. Dern gives a brilliant performance as the shy, sheltered girl. Based on the Joyce Carol Oates story "Where Are You Going, Where Have You Been?" Made for PBS' "American Playhouse" series. **92m/C VHS, Beta, LV.** Laura Dern, Treat Williams, Mary Kay Place, Levon Helm; *D:* Joyce Chopra; *W:* Tom Cole. Sundance Film Festival '86: Grand Jury Prize. *LIV, VES*

Smooth Talker woof! 1990 (R) A serial killer stalks the women of a 976 party line. Bad acting, bad dialog, not a scare to be found.*CW:* Language and sex-related dialogue, violence, and sensuality. **89m/C VHS, Closed Caption.** Joe Guzaldo, Peter Crombie, Stuart Whitman, Burt Ward, Sydney Lassick, Blair Weickgenant; *D:* Tom Milo. *ACA*

Smouldering Fires 🐾🐾½ 1925 A tough businesswoman falls in love with an ambitious young employee, who is fifteen years her junior. After they marry, problems arise in the form of the wife's attractive younger sister. Surprisingly subtle melodrama, if that's not an oxymoron. **100m/B VHS, Beta.** Pauline Frederick, Laura La Plante, Tully Marshall, Malcolm McGregor, Wanda Hawley, Helen Lynch, George Cooper, Bert Roach; *D:* Clarence Brown. *VYY, GPV*

Smugglers 🐾 *Lover of the Great Bear* 1975 Opportunistic smugglers take advantage of the Russian Revolution to sack the land and make a bundle. **110m/C VHS, Beta.** *IT* Senta Berger, Giuliano Gemma; *D:* Valentino Orsini. *VCD*

Smugglers' Cove 🐾🐾🐾 1948 Gorcey wrongly believes he has inherited a mansion. He and the Bowery Boys move in, only to stumble across a smuggling ring. Plenty of slapstick; the boys at their best. **66m/B VHS.** Leo Gorcey, Huntz Hall, Gabriel Dell; *D:* William Beaudine. *NO*

Smuggler's Cove 🐾½ 1983 A young boy doggedly pursues a mysterious trawler captain despite warnings from his parents. **75m/C VHS, Beta.** *AU NO*

The Snake Hunter Strangler 🐾 1966 A young girl is rescued after fifteen years from an evil cult of snake people. **65m/C VHS, Beta.** Guy Madison, Ivan Desny; *D:* Luigi Capuano. *NO*

Snake in the Eagle's Shadow 2 🐾 1983 Three champions of self-defense mount a major offensive and win battle after battle. **89m/C VHS, Beta.** Wang Tao, Chen Shing, Lung Fei; *D:* Chang Shinn I. *TWE*

The Snake People 🐾 *Isle of the Snake People; Cult of the Dead; La Muerte Viviente; Isle of the Living Dead* 1968 A police captain investigates a small island littered with LSD-experimenting scientists, snake-worshippers, and voodoo. One of the infamous quartet of Karloff's final films, all made in Mexico. **90m/C VHS, Beta.** *MX* Boris Karloff, Julissa, Carlos East; *D:* Enrique Vergara. *SNC, MPI, HEG*

The Snake Pit 🐾🐾🐾½ 1948 One of the first films to compassionately explore mental illness and its treatment. Following an emotional collapse de Havilland is placed in a mental institution by her husband. The severity of her depression causes her sympathetic doctor to try such treatments as electric shock, hydrotherapy, and drugs, along with the psychoanalysis which gradually allows her to accept her fears and make her recovery. Tour-de-force performance by de Havilland. Based on the novel by Mary Jane Ward. **108m/B VHS.** Olivia de Havilland, Mark Stevens, Leo Genn, Celeste Holm, Glenn Langan, Helen Craig, Leif Erickson, Beulah Bondi; *D:* Anatole Litvak; *W:* Frank Partos, Millen Brand; *M:* Alfred Newman. Academy Awards '48: Best Sound; New York Film Critics Awards '48: Best Actress (de Havilland); Nominations: Academy Awards '48: Best Actress (de Havilland), Best Director (Litvak), Best Picture, Best Screenplay, Original Dramatic/Comedy Score. *FXV, MOV, BTV*

The Snake Woman 🐾 1961 A herpetologist working in a small English village during the 1890s is conducting strange experiments to try to cure his wife's madness. He tries injecting his pregnant wife with snake venom and she gives birth to a cold-blooded daughter, who, when she grows up, has the ability to change herself into a deadly snake. She promptly begins killing the local male populace until Scotland Yard is called in to investigate. The curvy Travers is appropriately snakey but this movie is dull. **68m/C VHS.** *GB* John P. McCarthy, Susan Travers, Arnold Marle; *D:* Sidney J. Furie. *CNM*

SnakeEater 🐾 1989 (R) Loner cop tracks down swine who killed his parents and kidnapped his sister. "Rambo" rip-off with little plot, but lots of action. Followed by two sequels. **89m/C VHS, Beta.** Lorenzo Lamas, Larry Csonka, Ron Palillo; *D:* George Erschbamer. *MED, VTR*

SnakeEater 2: The Drug Buster 🐾 1989 (R) A cop goes nuts and kills four drug dealers. As a result he is committed to an institution. Iron bars don't make a prison for this guy though, and he's soon back on the streets fighting crime with his pal "Speedboat." Silly sequel is quite bad; followed by yet another.*CW:* Language and some violence. **93m/C VHS, Beta, Closed Caption.** Lorenzo Lamas, Larry B. Scott, Michelle Scarabelli, Harvey Atkin, Jack Blum, Kathleen Kinmont; *D:* George Erschbamer. *PAR*

SnakeEater 3: His Law 🐾 1992 (R) Tough cop Jack Kelly (Lamas), aka SnakeEater, is out to avenge a woman's beating by a gang of thug bikers. Lots of action and violence, not much plot; based on W. Glenn Duncan's novel "Rafferty's Rules."*CW:* Language, strong violence, and sexuality. **109m/C VHS, Beta, Closed Caption.** Lorenzo Lamas, Minor Mustain, Tracy Cook, Holly Chester, Scott "Bam Bam" Bigelow; *D:* George Erschbamer; *W:* John Dunning. *PAR*

Snapdragon 🐾🐾 1993 (R) Police psychologist is led astray by his libido while investigating a luscious amnesiac. His sensible vice cop girlfriend then discovers the sexpot is actually a psycho serial killer calling herself the Snapdragon but will her boyfriend even care?*CW:* Strong language, strong violence, and strong sexuality. **96m/C VHS, Beta.** Steven Bauer, Pamela Anderson Lee, Chelsea Field; *D:* Worth Keeter; *W:* Gene Church. *PSM*

The Snapper ✶✶✶½ 1993 (R) Originally made for BBC television, Frears creates a small comic gem based on the second novel of Doyle's Barrytown trilogy. Set in Dublin, 20-year-old Sharon Curley (Kellegher) finds herself unexpectedly pregnant and refuses to name the father. Family and friends are understanding—until they discover the man's identity. Affecting performances, particularly from Meaney as Sharon's dad who takes a much greater interest in the birth of his grandchild than he ever did with his own children. Cheerful semi-sequel to "The Commitments" serves up domestic upheavals graced with humor and a strong sense of family loyalty. **CW:** Language and some sexuality. 95m/C VHS, LV, Closed Caption. *IR* Tina Kellegher, Colm Meaney, Ruth McCabe, Colm O'Byrne, Pat Laffan, Eanna MacLiam, Ciara Duffy; **D:** Stephen Frears; **W:** Roddy Doyle. Nominations: Golden Globe Awards '94: Best Actor—Musical/Comedy (Meaney). *TOU*

Snapshot ✶ 1977 (R) Typical grade Z sex comedy; a free-lance photographer ogles lots of variously dishabilled young women through his lens. 84m/C VHS, Beta. Jim Henshaw, Susan Petrie. *NO*

Snatched ✶✶ 1972 The wives of three wealthy men are held for ransom, but one man doesn't want to pay, while one of the victims needs insulin. Standard made for television fare. 73m/C VHS. Howard Duff, Leslie Nielsen, Sheree North, Barbara Parkins, Robert Reed, John Saxon, Tisha Sterling; **D:** Sutton Roley; **M:** Randy Edelman. *REP*

Sneakers ✶✶✶½ 1992 (PG-13) Competent thriller about five computer hackers with questionable pasts and an equally questionable government job. Of course, nothing is as it seems. Rather slow-going considering the talents and suspense involved but includes enough turns to keep a viewer's interest. 125m/C VHS, Beta, LV, Closed Caption. Robert Redford, Sidney Poitier, River Phoenix, Dan Aykroyd, Ben Kingsley, David Strathairn, Mary McDonnell, Timothy Busfield, George Hearn, Eddie Jones, James Earl Jones, Stephen Tobolowsky; **D:** Phil Alden Robinson; **W:** Lawrence Lasker, Walter F. Parkes, Phil Alden Robinson; **C:** John Lindley; **M:** James Horner, Branford Marsalis. *USH, PMS*

Sniper ✶✶✶ *The Deadly Tower* 1975 Suspenseful television drama based on true story of Charles Whitman, who shot at University of Texas students from Texas Tower on a summer day in 1966. Disney alumunus Russell breaks type as mass killer, with fine support by Yniguez as a police officer on the scene and Beatty as the passerby who lends a hand. Finely crafted recreation of disturbing, true event. 85m/C VHS. Kurt Russell, Richard Yniguez, John Forsythe, Ned Beatty, Pernell Roberts, Clifton James, Paul Carr, Alan Vint, Pepe Serna; **D:** Jerry Jameson. *XVC*

The Sniper ✶½ 1987 A law-abiding citizen becomes a vigilante killer after witnessing a violent crime. 90m/C VHS, Beta. Claudia Cardinale. *NO*

Sniper ✶½ 1992 (R) Less than compelling shoot-'em-up set in Panama. Lead characters include Sgt. Beckett (Berenger), a seasoned assassin who gets a rush from killing. Also assigned to the case is Richard Miller (Zane), a newcomer who knows his guns but not his jungles. Together they go in search of their target, a politician planning a coup with the help of a druglord. Action is poorly choreographed and plot is cursory at best. The laserdisc version is available letterboxed. **CW:** Language and strong violence. 99m/C VHS, LV, 8mm, Closed Caption. Tom Berenger, Billy Zane, J.T. Walsh, Aden Young, Ken Radley, Reinaldo Arenas, Carlos Alvarez, Roy Edmonds; **D:** Luis Llosa; **W:** Michael Frost Beckner, Crash Leyland; **C:** Bill Butler; **M:** Gary Chang. *COL*

Sno-Line ✶ 1985 (R) A New York gangster moves to Texas and begins to wipe out the competition on his way to building his drug and gambling dynasty. Bo-ring excuse for entertainment. No hope, no redemption, no titillation: just ultra-"realistic" depiction of organized crime, poorly acted. 89m/C VHS, Beta. Vince Edwards, Paul Smith, June Wilkinson; **D:** Douglas F. Oneans. *LIV*

Snoopy, Come Home ✶✶✶ 1972 (G) Snoopy leaves Charlie Brown to visit his former owner Lila in the hospital and returns with her to her apartment house. From Charles Schultz's popular comic strip "Peanuts." 80m/C VHS, Beta, LV, Closed Caption. **D:** Bill Melendez; **W:** Charles M. Schulz. *FXV*

Snoopy's Getting Married, Charlie Brown 1985 An animated Peanuts adventure wherein Snoopy prepares to get married. 30m/C VHS, Beta. *BAR*

Snow Country ✶✶½ 1957 Romantic drama of an unsuccessful, married artist from Tokyo who travels to a mountain resort to find himself. He requests a Geisha for the evening and, when none are available, the beautiful adopted daughter of the local music teacher is sent to him instead. Based on the novel by Nobel Prize winner Yasunari Kawabata. In Japanese with English subtitles. Remade in 1965. 104m/B VHS, Beta. *JP* Ryo Ikebe, Keiko Kishi, Akira Kubo, Kaoru Yachigusa, Hisaya Morishige, Mineko Yorozuyo, Etsuko Ichihara, Noriko Sengoku, Kumeko Urabe, Eiko Miyoshi, Akira Tan, Chieko Naniwa, Daisuke Kato, Haruo Tanaka; **D:** Shiro Toyoda. *CVC*

The Snow Creature woof! 1954 Stupid troop of explorers bring back a snow creature from the Himalayas. Critter escapes in L.A. and terrorizes all in its path before blending in with club crowd. Very bad monster epic (the first about a snow monster) that strains credibility frame by frame. Occasionally, depending upon camera angle, light, and viewer mood, monster appears to be something other than guy in bad suit sweating. Directed by Billy Wilder's brother and another argument against genetic consistency. 72m/B VHS, Beta. Paul Langton, Leslie Denison; **D:** W. Lee Wilder. *NOS, SNC*

Snow Kill ✶½ 1990 Five city-dwellers travel into the mountains for a fun survival training weekend, but the fun turns deadly when they accidentally come across a murderous drug gang. Pseudo - '30s suspense adventure fails to thrill or surprise. Made for cable. 90m/C VHS, Beta, Closed Caption. Terence Knox, Patti D'Arbanville, David Dukes; **D:** Thomas J. Wright; **W:** Harv Zimmel. *PAR, TTC*

The Snow Queen 1983 From "Fairie Tale Theatre" comes this adaptation of the Hans Christian Andersen tale. A boy and girl who grow up together are separated by evil when the boy is held captive in the icy palace of the Snow Queen. The girl sets out to rescue him. 60m/C VHS, Beta, Closed Caption. Lauren Hutton, Linda Manz, David Hemmings, Melissa Gilbert, Lee Remick, Lance Kerwin; **D:** Peter Medak. *FOX, FCT*

Snow: The Movie ✶ 1983 Rates creative zero for title, though there is snow, as well as skiing, growing up, romance, and good times among the young people involved. Filmed in Australia. 83m/C VHS, Beta. David Argue, Lance Curtis; **D:** Robert Gibson. *VCD*

Snow Treasure ✶ 1967 (G) With the help of an underground agent, Norwegian children smuggle gold out of the country right under the noses of the Nazis. Based on the novel by Marie McSwigan. 96m/C VHS, Beta. James Franciscus, Paul Anstad; **D:** Irving Jacoby. *LIV*

Snow White ✶✶ 1989 The incomparable Rigg stars in this witty retelling of the beautiful girl and her seven little friends. 85m/C VHS. Diana Rigg, Sarah Patterson, Billy Barty; **D:** Michael Berz. *WAR*

Snow White and the Seven Dwarfs ✶✶✶✶ 1937 (G) Classic adaptation of the Grimm Brothers fairy tale about the fairest of them all. Beautiful animation, memorable characters, and wonderful songs mark this as the definitive "Snow White." Set the stage for other animated features after Walt Disney took an unprecedented gamble by attempting the first animated feature-length film, a project which took over two years to create and $1.5 million to make, and made believers out of those who laughed at the concept. Lifelike animation was based on real stars; Margery Belcher (later Champion) posed for Snow, Louis Hightower was the Prince, and Lucille LaVerne gave the Queen her nasty look. ♪Some Day My Prince Will Come; One Song; With a Smile and a Song; Whistle While You Work; Bluddle-Uddle-Um-Dum; The Dwarfs' Yodel Song; Heigh Ho; I'm Wishing; Isn't This a Silly Song?. 83m/C VHS, LV, Closed Caption. **D:** David Hand; **W:** Ted Sears, Otto Englander, Earl Hurd, Dorothy Blank, Richard Creedon, Dick Richard, Merrill De Maris, Webb Smith; **M:** Frank Churchill, Paul Smith, Larry Morey, Leigh Harline; **V:** Adriana Caselotti, Harry Stockwell, Lucille LaVerne, Moroni Olsen, Billy Gilbert, Pinto Colvig, Otis Harlan, Scotty Matraw, Roy Atwell, Stuart Buchanan, Marion Darlington, Jim Macdonald. *DIS, OM*

Snow White and the Seven Dwarfs 1983 From cable television's "Faerie Tale Theatre" comes the story of a princess who befriends seven little men to protect her from the jealous evil queen. 60m/C VHS, Beta, LV, Closed Caption. Elizabeth McGovern, Rex Smith, Vincent Price, Vanessa Redgrave; **D:** Peter Medak. *FOX, FCT, HMV*

Snow White and the Three Stooges ✶ *Snow White and the Three Clowns* 1961 The Stooges fill in for the Seven Dwarfs when they go off prospecting in King Solomon's mines. Alas, see any Stooge movie but this one. 107m/C VHS, Beta, Closed Caption. Moe Howard, Curly Howard, Larry Fine, Carol Heiss, Patricia Medina; **D:** Walter Lang. *FOX, FCT*

Snowball Express ✶✶ 1972 (G) When a New York City accountant inherits a hotel in the Rocky Mountains, he decides to move his family west to attempt to make a go of the defunct ski resort, only to find that the place is falling apart. Run-of-the-mill Disney comedy, based on the novel "Chateau Bon Vivant" by Frankie and John O'Rear. 120m/C VHS, Beta. Dean Jones, Nancy Olson, Harry (Henry) Morgan, Keenan Wynn; **D:** Norman Tokar; **M:** Robert F. Brunner. *DIS*

Snowballin' ✶ 1985 A ski instructor gives private lessons to a bunch of snow bunnies. 90m/C VHS, Beta. Seline Lomez, Daniel Pilon. *JEF*

Snowballing ✶ 1985 (PG) Part of the polluted wave of teen-sex flicks of the 1980s, this is very mild for the genre but still no prize. Lusty high schoolers at a skiing competition look for action on and off the slopes, end up exposing a resort fraud. 96m/C VHS, Beta. Mary McDonough, Bob Hastings. *PSM*

Snowbeast ✶½ 1977 The residents of a ski resort are being terrorized by a half-human, half-animal beast leaving a path of dead bodies in its wake. "Jaws" hits the slopes. Not scary or even funny. Made for TV. 96m/C VHS, Beta. Bo Svenson, Yvette Mimieux, Sylvia Sidney, Clint Walker, Robert F. Logan; **D:** Herb Wallerstein. *WOV*

Snowblind ✶✶ *Ski Lift to Death* 1978 Two ski gondolas derail, placing the passengers in jeopardy. Among the passengers is a mobster being pursued by an assassin. 98m/C VHS. Deborah Raffin, Charles Frank, Howard Duff, Don Galloway, Gail Strickland, Don Johnson, Veronica Hamel, Clu Gulager, Lisa Reeves, Suzy Chaffee; **D:** William Wiard. *NO*

The Snows of Kilimanjaro ✶✶✶ 1952 Called by Hemingway "The Snows of Zanuck," in reference to the great producer, this film is actually an artful pastiche of several Hemingway short stories and novels. The main story, "The Snows of Kilimanjaro," acts as a framing device, in which the life of a successful writer is seen through his fevered flashbacks as he and his rich wife, while on safari, await a doctor to save his gangrenous leg. 117m/C Beta. Gregory Peck, Susan Hayward, Ava Gardner, Hildegarde Neff, Leo G. Carroll, Torin Thatcher, Ava Norring, Helene Stanley, Marcel Dalio, Vincente Gomez, Richard Allen, Leonard Carey; **D:** Henry King; **W:** Casey Robinson; **C:** Leon Shamroy. Nominations: Academy Awards '52: Best Art Direction/Set Decoration (Color), Best Color Cinematography. *NOS, GKK, SNC*

Snowy River, the MacGregor Saga: The Race 1993 A continuation of the "The Man from Snowy River" set in late 1800s Australia. Matt MacGregor (Clarke) is running a successful cattle ranch with his two grown sons and a teenage daughter. Naturally, there's some family strife as well as a horse race. Edited episodes from the TV series. 87m/C VHS. *AU* Andrew Clarke. *FHE*

Snuff-Bottle Connection *√* 1982 Russian envoy is spying for the government while delivering a gift to a Ching dynasty emperor. 96m/C VHS, Beta. Hwang Jang Lee, John Liu, Roy Horan. *WVE*

Snuffy Smith, Yard Bird *√√*½ *Private Snuffy Smith; Snuffy Smith* 1942 The pint-sized moonshiner finds himself in the Army, clashing with his sergeant. Followed by "Hillbilly Blitzkrieg" later the same year. Duncan is perfect for the part, and Kennedy is right on as his foil. 67m/B VHS. Bud Duncan, Edgar Kennedy, Sarah Padden, Doris Linden, J. Farrell MacDonald, Frank Austin, Jimmie Dodd; *D:* Eddie Cline. *NOS, VYY*

So Dear to My Heart *√√√*½ 1949 A farm boy and his misfit black sheep wreak havoc at the county fair. Several sequences combine live action with animation. Heartwarming and charming; straightforward and likeable but never sentimental. Wonderful, vintage Disney. ♫Sourwood Mountain; Billy Boy; So Dear To My Heart; County Fair; Stick-To-It-Ivity; Ol' Dan Patch; It's Whatcha Do With Watcha Got; Lavender Blue (Dilly Dilly). 82m/C VHS, Beta, LV. Bobby Driscoll, Burl Ives, Beulah Bondi, Harry Carey Sr., Luana Patten; *D:* Harold Schuster. Nominations: Academy Awards '49: Best Song ("Lavender Blue"). *DIS*

So Ends Our Night *√√√* 1941 German scorns Nazi ideology, flees Austria, and meets young Jewish couple seeking asylum. Fine adaptation of Erich Maria Remarque's novel "Flotsam," with splendid performances from Sullavan (on loan from Universal) and young Ford. 117m/B VHS. Fredric March, Margaret Sullavan, Frances Dee, Glenn Ford, Anna Sten, Erich von Stroheim; *D:* John Cromwell; *C:* William H. Daniels. Nominations: Academy Awards '41: Original Dramatic/Comedy Score. *IVY*

So Fine *√√*½ 1981 (R) Absent-minded English professor O'Neal tries to rescue his father's clothing business from going bottom-up. He accidentally invents peek-a-boo bottomed jeans, which become an immediate hit and make him rich. Comedy smorgasbord, setting outing from sometime novelist Bergman, hits and misses. O'Neal is memorable, as is the ubiquitous Warden and his sidekick. 91m/C VHS. Ryan O'Neal, Jack Warden, Mariangela Melato, Richard Kiel; *D:* Andrew Bergman; *W:* Andrew Bergman; *M:* Ennio Morricone. *WAR*

So I Married an Axe Murderer *√√*½ 1993 (PG-13) Combination comedy/romance/thriller. Charlie is a hip bookstore owner with a commitment problem. When he finally falls in love with a butcher, he comes to suspect she's a serial killer and he's in line as her next victim. "Saturday Night Live" star Myers has a dual role: as Charlie and as Scottish dad Stuart, allowing him to be fanatically Scottish as Stuart and somewhat more restrained as the angst-ridden Charlie. One-gag movie counted on Myers' "Wayne's World" popularity, which didn't pan out at the box office. Best appreciated by Myers' fans, this one is better on the small screen. *CW:* Language, nudity, and mock terror. 92m/C VHS, LV, 8mm, Closed Caption. Mike Myers, Nancy Travis, Anthony LaPaglia, Amanda Plummer, Brenda Fricker, Matt Doherty, Charles Grodin; *Cameos:* Phil Hartman, Steven Wright, Alan Arkin; *D:* Thomas Schlamme; *W:* Mike Myers, Robbie Fox; *M:* Bruce Broughton. *COL*

So Proudly We Hail *√√√* 1943 True story of the lives of three war-front nurses and their heroism under fire during WWII. Colbert is Lt. Davidson in charge of nine Red Cross Army nurses serving in the Pacific. Lake and Goddard play the other leads. With the popularity of its stars and the patriotic spirit of the film, the picture hit box office gold. Critics praised its authenticity, as the film never fell victim to the usual standards of Hollywood glamour. Fans of Lake beware: she has short hair in this film because the government requested that she not appear as a servicewoman with her famous peek-a-boo hair style because female factory workers were getting their long Lake-inspired hair caught in the machinery. 126m/B VHS, Closed Caption. Claudette Colbert, Paulette Goddard, Veronica Lake, George Reeves, Barbara Britton, Walter Abel, Sonny Tufts; *D:* Mark Sandrich; *W:* Allan Scott; *M:* Miklos Rozsa. Nominations: Academy Awards '43: Best Black and White Cinematography, Best Original Screenplay, Best Special Effects, Best Supporting Actress (Goddard). *USH*

So This Is Paris *√√√* 1926 Roguish pre-Hayes Code dancing duo seeks spice through alternative lovemates. Classic sophisticated Lubitsch, with outstanding camerawork and a bit of jazz. 68m/B VHS, Beta. Monte Blue, Patsy Ruth Miller, Lilyan Tashman, Andre de Beranger, Myrna Loy; *D:* Ernst Lubitsch. *GPV, FCT*

So This Is Washington *√√*½ 1943 The comedy team go to Washington with wacky inventions to help the war effort. Turns out there's too entirely too much nonsense going around, and the boys give 'em a piece of their mind. Fun, featherweight wartime comedy. 70m/B VHS, Beta. Lum & Abner, Alan Mowbray. Nominations: Academy Awards '43: Best Sound. *NOS, DVT*

Soapdish *√√√* 1991 (PG-13) The back stage lives of a daytime soap opera, "The Sun Also Sets," and its cast. When the soap's ratings fall, a character written out of series via decapitation is brought back to give things a lift. While the writer struggles to make the reincarnation believable, the cast juggles old and new romances, and professional jealousies abound. Some genuinely funny moments as film actors spoof the genre that gave many of them a start. 97m/C VHS, Beta, LV, 8mm, Closed Caption. Sally Field, Kevin Kline, Robert Downey Jr., Cathy Moriarty, Whoopi Goldberg, Elisabeth Shue, Carrie Fisher, Garry Marshall, Teri Hatcher, Paul Johansson, Costas Mandylor, Stephen Nichols, Kathy Najimy, Sheila Kelley; *Cameos:* Leeza Gibbons, John Tesh, Finola Hughes; *D:* Michael Hoffman; *W:* Andrew Bergman, Robert Harling; *M:* Alan Silvestri. *PAR*

S.O.B. *√√*½ 1981 (R) Blake Edwards' bitter farce about Hollywood and the film industry wheelers and dealers who inhabit it. When a multi-million dollar picture bombs at the box office, the director turns suicidal, until he envisions re-shooting it with a steamy, X-rated scene starring his wife, a star with a goody-two-shoes image. Edwards used his real-life wife, Julie ("Mary Poppins") Andrews, for the scene in which she bared her breasts. Oft-inspired, but oft-terrible. Zestfully vengeful. William Holden's last film. 121m/C VHS, Beta, LV. William Holden, Robert Preston, Richard Mulligan, Julie Andrews, Robert Webber, Shelley Winters, Robert Vaughn, Larry Hagman, Stuart Margolin, Loretta Swit, Craig Stevens, Larry Storch, Jennifer Edwards, Robert Loggia, Rosanna Arquette, Marisa Berenson; *D:* Blake Edwards; *W:* Blake Edwards; *C:* Harry Stradling Jr.; *M:* Henry Mancini. National Society of Film Critics Awards '81: Best Supporting Actor (Preston). *FOX, WAR*

Social Error *√√* 1935 An heiress mistakes her guards for a group of kidnappers. 60m/B VHS, Beta, LV. Gertrude Messinger, David Sharpe. *NOS, HEG*

The Social Secretary *√√*½ 1916 Driven from the rat race by lecherous men, Talmadge gets new job as rich woman's secretary, where she down-dresses to avoid further lewd encounters. She falls for her boss's son, but isn't considered marriage material until she proves herself. 56m/B VHS, Beta. Norma Talmadge, Kate Lester, Helen Weir, Gladden James, Herbert Frank; *D:* John Emerson. *GPV, FCT*

Society *√* 1992 (R) A teenager wonders if his visions are real or hallucinations when he believes his family, and everyone else around him, are flesh-eating predators. The puzzle isn't much but wait for the special-effects ladened ending to get your fill of gore.*CW:* Language, bizarre violence, and bizarre sexuality. 99m/C VHS, Closed Caption. Billy Warlock, Devin Devasquez, Evan Richards; *D:* Brian Yuzna. *REP*

Sodbusters *√√*½ 1994 (PG-13) Western spoof about homesteaders versus a greedy cattle baron and the railroad in 1875 Colorado. A lascivious farmer's wife and a mysterious gunslinger—as well as a couple of gay cowboys—are included for additional fun. 97m/C VHS, Closed Caption. Kris Kristofferson, John Vernon, Fred Willard, Wendel Meldrum, Max Gail, Steve Landesburg, Don Lake, James Pickens Jr., John Hemphill; *D:* Eugene Levy; *W:* John Hemphill, Eugene Levy. *REP*

Sodom and Gomorrah *√√* *Sodome et Gomorrhe; The Last Days of Sodom and Gomorrah* 1962 The Italian-made, internationally produced epic about Lot, the Hebrews and the destruction of the two sinful biblical cities. Moderately entertaining—but ponderous, to say the least, and very long. 154m/C VHS, Beta, LV, Closed Caption. *IT* Stewart Granger, Stanley Baker, Pier Angeli, Anouk Aimee, Rossana Podesta; *D:* Robert Aldrich; *M:* Miklos Rozsa. *FOX, IME*

Sofie *√√*½ 1992 Sweet family melodrama about a late 19th Jewish family in Denmark. Sofie (Mynster) is the unmarried 28-year-old daughter of loving, protective parents. She has fallen in love with a gentile artist (Christensen) but gives him up to marry within her faith. Unsuited, Sofie and Jonas (Zeller) lead melancholy lives, which Sofie redeems through her joy in her son. Self-effacing drama is Ullmann's directorial debut. Adapted from the novel "Mendel Philipsen & Son" by Henri Nathansen. In Swedish with English subtitles. 145m/C VHS. *SW* Karen-Lise Mynster, Ghita Norby, Erland Josephson, Jesper Christensen, Henning Moritzen, Torben Zeller, Stig Hoffmeyer, Kirsten Rolffes, Lotte Herman; *D:* Liv Ullmann; *W:* Liv Ullmann, Peter Poulsen. *FCT, ING*

Soft and Hard *√√*½ 1985 Made for English television, this video by Godard and Mieville intends to address the role of media and television in everyday life via a seemingly informal look at the couple's daily existence and the propensity for image production in it. In French with English subtitles. 48m/C VHS, Beta. *FR D:* Anne-Marie Mieville, Jean-Luc Godard. *EAI*

Soft Deceit *√√*½ 1994 (R) Master criminal Trent (Bergin) gets caught in the heist of $6 million in mob money. Then Anne (Vernon) shashays into prison offering Trent a deal—half the cash in exchange for breaking him out. She succeeds but maybe a doublecross is next on the agenda.*CW:* Some strong sexuality and language. 95m/C VHS, LV. Patrick Bergin, Kate Vernon, John Wesley Shipp, Gwynyth Walsh, Nigel Bennett, Damir Andrei; *D:* Jorge Montesi; *W:* Jorge Montesi. *TTC*

The Soft Kill *√√* 1994 (R) LA private eye Jack Ramsey (Bernsen) becomes the prime murder suspect when his girlfriend is strangled. Can he prove his innocence before more bodies pile up and the cops catch him?*CW:* Sexuality; language; violence. 95m/C VHS. Corbin Bernsen, Brion James, Matt McCoy, Michael Harris, Kim Morgan Greene, Carrie-Anne Moss; *D:* Eli Cohen. *TRI*

The Soft Skin *√√√* *Le Peau Douce; Silken Skin* 1964 A classic portrayal of marital infidelity by the master director. A writer and lecturer has an affair with a stewardess. After the affair ends, his wife confronts him, with tragic results. Cliche plot is forgivable; acted and directed to perfection. Frequent Truffaut star Jean-Pierre Leaud served here as an apprentice director. In French with English subtitles. 120m/B VHS, Beta, LV. *FR* Jean Desailly, Nelly Benedetti, Francoise Dorleac; *D:* Francois Truffaut; *M:* Georges Delerue. *HMV, FOX*

Soggy Bottom U.S.A. 🐾🐾 1984 (PG) A sheriff has his hands full trying to keep the law enforced in a small Southern town. Quite-good cast keeps the plot from disappearing altogether. **90m/C VHS, Beta.** Don Johnson, Ben Johnson, Dub Taylor, Ann Wedgeworth, Lois Nettleton, Anthony Zerbe; **D:** Theodore J. Flicker. *PSM, HHE*

Sois Belle et Tais-Toi 🐾🐾½ 1958 A police detective tracks jewel thieves and falls in love with a young waif. Several interesting and later famous actors have small parts. Light-hearted adventure. Subtitled in English. **110m/B VHS, Beta.** *FR* Henri Vidal, Mylene Demongeot, Jean-Paul Belmondo, Alain Delon; **D:** Marc Allegret. *BAR*

Solar Crisis 🐾🐾½ 1992 (PG-13) Eye-popping special effects highlight this Earth-on-the-edge-of-destruction sci-fier. In 2050 the sun has gone on self-destruct and begins throwing off giant solar flares which turn the Earth extra-crispy. A space team is sent to divert the flares but the mission may become a victim of sabotage. Director Sarafian actually forgoes credit for the standard Smithee pseudonym. **111m/C VHS, LV, Closed Caption.** Tim Matheson, Charlton Heston, Peter Boyle, Annabel Schofield, Jack Palance, Corin "Corky" Nemec; **D:** Richard Sarafian; **C:** Russell Carpenter; **M:** Maurice Jarre. *THV*

Solar Force 🐾🐾 1994 (R) Cop (Pare), stationed on the moon, is sent to earth to find a stolen chemical that is capable of restoring a destroyed environment. But there are secrets behind the assignment which could cost him his life. **91m/C VHS, LV, Closed Caption.** Michael Pare, Billy Drago, Walker Brandt; **D:** Boaz Davidson; **W:** Terrence Pare; **C:** Avi Karpik; **M:** Don Peake. *HMK*

Solarbabies 🐾 1986 (PG-13) Rollerskating youths in a drought-stricken future vie for a mysterious power that will replenish the Earth's water. Shades of every sci-fi movie you've ever seen, from "Mad Max" to "Ice Pirates." Pathetic. **95m/C VHS, Beta, LV, Closed Caption.** Richard Jordan, Sarah Douglas, Charles Durning, Lukas Haas, Jami Gertz, Jason Patric; **D:** Alan Johnson; **W:** Walon Green; **M:** Maurice Jarre. *MGM*

Solaris 🐾🐾 1972 With this the USSR tried to eclipse "2001: A Space Odyssey" in terms of cerebral science-fiction. Some critics thought they succeeded. You may disagree now that the lumbering effort is available on tape. Adapted from a Stanislaw Lem novel, it depicts a dilapidated space lab orbiting the planet Solaris, whose ocean, a vast fluid "brain," materializes the stir-crazy cosmonauts' obsessions—usually morose ex-girlfriends. Talk, talk, talk, minimal special effects. In Russian with English subtitles. In a two-cassette package, with a letterbox format preserving Tarkovsky's widescreen compositions. **167m/C VHS, LV.** *RU* Donatas Banionis, Natalya Bondarchuk; **D:** Andrei Tarkovsky; **W:** Eduard Artemyev. Cannes Film Festival '72: Grand Jury Prize. *FXL, FCT*

Soldat Duroc...Ca Va Etre Ta Fete! 🐾🐾 *Soldier Duroc* 196? Days after the 1944 liberation of Paris, a French soldier crosses back over the French lines to see his lover, and is caught as a German sympathizer by American troops. **105m/C VHS, Beta.** *FR* Pierre Tornade, Robert Webber, Michel Galabru, Roger Carel. *NO*

The Soldier 🐾 *Codename: The Soldier* 1982 (R) The Russians are holding the world at ransom with a pile of stolen plutonium, and a soldier finds himself in the position to carry out an unauthorized and dangerous plan to preserve the balance of world power. Wildly implausible, gratuitously violent spy trash. **90m/C VHS, Beta, Closed Caption.** Ken Wahl, Klaus Kinski; **D:** James Glickenhaus. *COL*

Soldier Blue 🐾🐾 1970 (R) Two survivors of an Indian attack make their way back to an army outpost. The cavalry then seeks revenge on the Cheyenne tribe accused of the attack. Gratuitously violent Vietnam-era western hits hard on racial themes. Based on the novel "Arrow in the Sun" by Theodore V. Olsen on the Sand Creek Indian massacre. **109m/C VHS, Beta.** Candice Bergen, Peter Strauss, Donald Pleasence, Dana Elcar, Jorge Rivero; **D:** Ralph Nelson; **W:** John Gay; **C:** Robert B. Hauser. *COL*

Soldier Boyz 🐾½ 1995 (R) Ex-Marine Major Howard Tolliver (Dudikoff), who now runs a high-security prison for youthful offenders, is called on to rescue a United Nations worker who's being held hostage by a group of revolutionaries in Vietnam. For help, he takes along six of his toughest prisoners. A variation of "The Dirty Dozen." **CW:** Strong non-stop violence and language. **91m/C VHS.** Michael Dudikoff, Cary-Hiroyuki Tagawa, Tyrin Turner, David Barry Gray, Channon Roe, Cedrick Terrell, Demetrius Navarro, Jacqueline Obradors; **D:** Louis Morneau; **W:** Darryl Quarles. *HBO*

Soldier in Love 🐾🐾 1967 Teleplay from "George Schaefer's Showcase Theatre" is based on the life of John Churchill, first Duke of Marlborough, and his wife Sarah. The ambitious young couple held the favor of Queen Anne for a time, until political intrigue brought about their downfall. **76m/C VHS, Beta.** Jean Simmons, Claire Bloom, Keith Michell; **D:** George Schaefer. *FHS*

Soldier in the Rain 🐾🐾½ 1963 An unusual friendship develops between career sergeant Gleason and wheeler-dealer McQueen. Gleason is in good form, but McQueen is listless, and the story (set in a Southern army camp) is unsatisfying. Weld is the comely teen who makes for an intriguing love triangle. From the novel by William Goldman. **88m/B VHS, Beta, Closed Caption.** Steve McQueen, Jackie Gleason, Tuesday Weld, Tony Bill, Tom Poston, Ed Nelson; **D:** Ralph Nelson; **W:** Blake Edwards; **M:** Henry Mancini. *FOX*

Soldier of Fortune 🐾🐾½ 1955 A woman (Hayward) enlists mercenaries to help find her lost husband in Red China. Late Gable vehicle with the formula beginning to feel the post-war strain and the star looking a trifle long in the tooth. Still, a fun adventure from a top star. Hayward had been among the myriad starlets vying for the Scarlett O'Hara roles nearly two decades earlier. **96m/C VHS, Beta, Closed Caption.** Clark Gable, Susan Hayward, Gene Barry, Alexander D'Arcy, Michael Rennie, Tom Tully, Anna Sten, Russell Collins, Leo Gordon, Jack Kruschen, Robert Quarry; **D:** Edward Dmytryk. *FOX*

Soldier of Orange 🐾🐾½ 1978 The lives of six Dutch students are forever changed by the WWII invasion of Holland by the Nazis. Based on the true-life exploits of Dutch resistance leader Erik Hazelhoff. Exciting and suspenseful; cerebral; carefully made and well acted. Made Rutger Hauer an international star. **144m/C VHS, Beta, LV.** *NL* Rutger Hauer, Jeroen Krabbe, Edward Fox, Susan Penhaligon; **D:** Paul Verhoeven; **W:** Paul Verhoeven; **C:** Jan De Bont. Los Angeles Film Critics Association Awards '79: Best Foreign Film. *MED*

Soldier of the Night 🐾½ 1984 Toy-store worker by day, vigilante killer by night. Israeli thriller set in Tel Aviv lacks vim and is badly dubbed. **89m/C VHS, Beta.** **D:** Dan Wolman. *MGM*

Soldier's Fortune 🐾½ 1991 (R) A traveling gun for hire leaves the combat of Central America for the jungles of Los Angeles, only to find out that his daughter had been taken hostage. That's the last thing these kidnappers will ever do when they are found by this tough guy looking for his child. **CW:** Language and violence. **96m/C VHS, Closed Caption.** Gil Gerard, Charles Napier, Dan Haggerty, P.J. Soles, Barbara Bingham, Janus Blythe; **D:** Arthur N. Mele. *REP*

Soldier's Revenge 🐾🐾 197? A Vietnam vet has a hard time adjusting to life at home. **92m/C VHS, Beta.** John Savage. *TWE*

A Soldier's Story 🐾🐾🐾 1984 (PG) A black army attorney is sent to a Southern base to investigate the murder of an unpopular sergeant. Features WWII, Louisiana, jazz and blues, and racism in and outside the corps. From the Pulitzer-prize winning play by Charles Fuller, with most of the Broadway cast. Fine performances from Washington and Caesar. **101m/C VHS, Beta, LV, Closed Caption.** Howard E. Rollins Jr., Adolph Caesar, Denzel Washington, Patti LaBelle, Robert Townsend, Scott Paulin, Wings Hauser, Art Evans, Larry Riley, David Alan Grier; **D:** Norman Jewison; **C:** Russell Boyd; **M:** Herbie Hancock. Edgar Allan Poe Awards '84: Best Screenplay; Los Angeles Film Critics Association Awards '84: Best Supporting Actor (Caesar); Nominations: Academy Awards '84: Best Adapted Screenplay, Best Picture, Best Supporting Actor (Caesar).*COL, FCT*

A Soldier's Tale 🐾🐾 1991 (R) During WWII, a menage-a-trois develops that can only lead to tragedy, yet the participants find themselves unable to resist. **96m/C VHS, Closed Caption.** Gabriel Byrne, Marianne Basler, Judge Reinhold, Paul Wyett; **D:** Larry Parr; **M:** John Charles. *REP*

Sole Survivor 🐾½ 1984 (R) A group of zombies are searching for a beautiful advertising executive who was the sole survivor of a plane crash. **85m/C VHS, Beta.** Anita Skinner, Kurt Johnson, Caren Larkey; **D:** Thom Eberhardt; **C:** Russell Carpenter. *LIV, VES*

Solid Gold Cadillac 🐾🐾🐾 1956 Holliday is a winning lead as Laura Patridge, an idealistic, small-time stockholder who discovers that the corporate board of directors are crooked. She makes waves at a stockholders meeting, gets noticed by the press, finds romance with former CEO Edward McKeever (Douglas), and works to oust the scalawags from power. The title comes from Laura's fervent desire to own a—you guessed it—solid gold cadillac. Based on the Broadway play by George S. Kaufman and Howard Teichmann. **99m/B VHS, Closed Caption.** Judy Holliday, Paul Douglas, Fred Clark, Neva Patterson, Arthur O'Connell, Ray Collins; **D:** Richard Quine; **W:** Abe Burrows; **C:** George B(ryant) Lang; **M:** Cyril Mockridge. Academy Awards '56: Best Costume Design (B & W); Nominations: Academy Awards '56: Best Art Direction/Set Decoration (B & W). *COL*

Solitaire for 2 🐾🐾½ 1994 (R) Sweet-natured romantic comedy about a rogue and a psychic. Handsome Daniel Becker (Frankel) is a behavioral psychologist who specializes in interpreting body language and using his expertise to bed as many beautiful women as happen his way. Uptight paleontologist Katie (Pays) has a problem with men—she can literally read their minds and gets angry at their lewd thoughts. So the path to true commitment is going to get a bit bumpy.**CW:** Some language and a sex scene. **105m/C VHS, Beta, Closed Caption.** GB Mark Frankel, Amanda Pays, Roshan Seth, Maryam D'Abo, Jason Isaacs, Annette Crosbie; **D:** Gary Sinyor; **W:** Gary Sinyor; **C:** Henry Braham; **M:** David A. Hughes, John Murphy. *PAR*

The Solitary Man 🐾🐾 1982 Glum look at a family breakup, from the husband's point of view. Holliman is good, but the exercise at large is regularly blues-inducing, and not especially inspiring or artful. Made for TV. **96m/C VHS, Beta.** Earl Holliman, Carrie Snodgress, Lara Parker, Lane Smith, Nicolas Coster, Michelle Pfeiffer; **D:** John Llewellyn Moxey. *TLF*

Solo 🐾🐾 1977 (PG) Young hitchhiker Peers enters the lives of fire patrol pilot Gil and his teenage son. A plotless friendship develops, headed nowhere—like this movie. Great New Zealand scenery might be worth the price of rental. **90m/C VHS, Beta.** Vincent Gil, Perry Armstrong, Martyn Sanderson, Lisa Peers; **D:** Tony Williams. *BPG, VES, HHE*

Solo 🐾🐾 1996 (PG-13) Fast-paced actioner stars Van Peebles as Solo, an android assassin with a heart of gold. It seems the muscle-bound, computerized killer is programmed with not only amazing fighting skills but the ability to think and learn. Solo who, being naughty in the sight of one-dimensional government bigwigs, is scheduled for replacement by a fighting machine that won't be so fickle when it comes to pulling the trigger. The chase is on when Solo learns of their plot and takes to the jungles of Central America, where together with the local peasants, the rebellious robot fights to preserve his humanity and his life. Poor man's "Terminator" is sprinkled with the kind of glib one-liners usually reserved for Schwarzenegger, although Van Peebles' performance hikes this rehashed premise up a notch. Adapted from Robert Mason's novel "Weapon." *CW:* Combat action violence and brief strong language. 106m/C VHS, LV, Closed Caption. Mario Van Peebles, William Sadler, Seidy Lopez, Barry Corbin, Adrien Brody, Abraham Verduzo, Jaime Gomez, Damian Bechir, Joaquin Garrido; *D:* Norberto Barba; *W:* David Corley; *C:* Chris Walling; *M:* Christopher Franke. COL

Solo Voyage: The Revenge 🎞🎞
1990 A Russian "Rambo" goes on a murderous rampage, the likes of which humanity has not yet seen. 91m/C VHS. *RU* Mikhail Nojkine, Alexandre Fatiouchine; *D:* Mikhail Toumanichulli. NO

Solomon and Sheba 🎞🎞 1959 King
Solomon's brother and the Egyptian Pharaoh send the Queen of Sheba to Israel to seduce King Solomon so they may gain his throne. Tyrone Power had filmed most of the lead role in this silly, overwrought epic when he died of a heart attack. The role was reshot, with Brynner (with a full head of hair) replacing him. Director Vidor's unfortunate last film. Shot on location in Spain. 139m/C VHS, Beta, LV. Yul Brynner, Gina Lollobrigida, Marisa Pavan, George Sanders, Alejandro Rey; *D:* King Vidor; *C:* Frederick A. (Freddie) Young; *M:* Malcolm Arnold. MGM, FOX

The Sombrero Kid 🎞🎞 1942 The Kid
unwittingly gets involved in a murder and is nearly hanged before his friends help him discover the real culprits. Plenty of action in this straight forward, fun western. 54m/B VHS, Beta. Donald (Don "Red") Barry, Lynn Merrick, Rand Brooks; *D:* George Sherman. VDM

Some Call It Loving 🎞 1973 (R) Bad,
pretentious modern version of Sleeping Beauty, set in L.A. King buys the sleeping girl (Farrow) from a carnival show, but she doesn't live up to his ideal. 103m/C VHS. Zalman King, Carol White, Tisa Farrow, Richard Pryor, Pat Priest; *D:* James B. Harris. NO

Some Came Running 🎞🎞🎞 1958
James Jones's follow-up novel to "From Here to Eternity" does not translate nearly as well to the screen. Overlong and with little plot, the action centers around a would-be writer, his floozy girl friend, and the holier-than-thou characters which populate the town in which he grew up and to which he has now returned. Strong performances by all. 136m/C VHS, Beta, LV. Frank Sinatra, Dean Martin, Shirley MacLaine, Martha Hyer, Arthur Kennedy, Nancy Gates; *D:* Vincente Minnelli; *C:* William H. Daniels; *M:* Elmer Bernstein. Nominations: Academy Awards '58: Best Actress (MacLaine), Best Costume Design, Best Song ("To Love and Be Loved"), Best Supporting Actor (Kennedy), Best Supporting Actress (Hyer). MGM

Some Girls 🎞🎞½ Sisters 1988 (R) A man
goes to Quebec to see his college girlfriend who informs him that she is not in love with him anymore. But she has two sisters ready to comfort him! Strange black comedy; Gregory as the girl's father elevates so-so story. 104m/C VHS, Beta. Patrick Dempsey, Andre Gregory, Lila Kedrova, Florinda Bolkan, Jennifer Connelly, Sheila Kelly; *D:* Michael Hoffman; *M:* James Newton Howard. PAR

Some Kind of Hero 🎞🎞 1982 (R) A
Vietnam prisoner of war returns home to a changed world. Pryor tries hard, but can't get above this poorly written, unevenly directed film. 97m/C VHS, Beta, LV. Richard Pryor, Margot Kidder, Ray Sharkey, Ronny Cox, Lynne Moody, Olivia Cole; *D:* Michael Pressman; *W:* Robert Boris. PAR

Some Kind of Wonderful 🎞🎞 1987
(PG-13) A high-school tomboy has a crush on a guy who also happens to be her best friend. Her feelings go unrequited as he falls for a rich girl with snobbish friends. In the end, true love wins out. Deutch also directed (and John Hughes also produced) the teen flick "Pretty in Pink," which had much the same plot, with the rich/outcast characters reversed by gender. OK, but completely predictable. 93m/C VHS, LV, Closed Caption. Eric Stoltz, Lea Thompson, Mary Stuart Masterson, Craig Sheffer, John Ashton, Elias Koteas, Molly Hagan; *D:* Howard Deutch; *W:* John Hughes. PAR

Some Like It Hot 🎞🎞🎞🎞 1959 Two un-
employed musicians witness the St. Valentine's Day massacre in Chicago. They disguise themselves as women and join an all-girl band headed for Miami to escape the gangsters' retaliation. Flawless cast includes a fetching Monroe at her best; hilarious script. Curtis does his Cary Grant impression. Classic scenes between Lemmon in drag and Joe E. Brown as a smitten suitor. Brown also has the film's famous closing punchline. Monroe sings "I Wanna Be Loved By You," "Running Wild," and "I'm Through With Love." One of the very funniest movies of all time. 120m/B VHS, Beta, LV, Closed Caption. Marilyn Monroe, Tony Curtis, Jack Lemmon, George Raft, Pat O'Brien, Nehemiah Persoff, Joe E. Brown, Joan Shawlee, Mike Mazurki; *D:* Billy Wilder; *W:* Billy Wilder, I.A.L. Diamond; *C:* Charles Lang Jr.; *M:* Adolph Deutsch. Academy Awards '59: Best Costume Design (B & W); British Academy Awards '59: Best Actor (Lemmon); Golden Globe Awards '60: Best Actor—Musical/Comedy (Lemmon), Best Actress—Musical/Comedy (Monroe), Best Film—Musical/Comedy; National Board of Review Awards '59: 10 Best Films of the Year; Nominations: Academy Awards '59: Best Actor (Lemmon), Best Adapted Screenplay, Best Art Direction/Set Decoration (B & W), Best Black and White Cinematography, Best Director (Wilder). MGM, FOX

Some Mother's Son 🎞🎞🎞 Sons and
Warriors 1996 (R) Young IRA members Gerard Quigley (Gillen) and Frank Higgins (O'Hara) are sentenced to long prison terms after an attack on the British army. Tough, politically active Annie Higgins (Flanagan) has already lost one son to "The Troubles" and is willing to support Frank in whatever he does. But her son Gerard's involvement takes apolitical schoolteacher Kathleen (Mirren) completely by surprise. When their sons join in a prison hunger strike, the two mothers must face the choice of supporting their sons' possible deaths by starvation or allowing the prison's officials to force-feed them. The leads give tough, terrific performances in a heartwrenching story. *CW:* Language and some political violence and suffering. 112m/C VHS. *IR GB* Helen Mirren, Fionnula Flanagan, Aidan Gillen, David O'Hara, John Lynch, Tim Woodward, Ciaran Hinds, Gerard McSorley, Geraldine O'Rawe; *D:* Terry George; *W:* Jim Sheridan, Terry George; *C:* Geoffrey Simpson; *M:* Bill Whelan. NYR

Somebody Has to Shoot the
Picture 🎞🎞🎞 **1990 (R)** Photographer Scheider is hired by a convicted man to take a picture of his execution. Hours before the event, Scheider uncovers evidence that leads him to believe the man is innocent. He then embarks in a race against time to save him. Adapted by Doug Magee from his book "Slow Coming Dark." Unpretentious, tough drama. Made for cable. *CW:* Language and violence. 104m/C VHS, Beta, LV, Closed Caption. Roy Scheider, Bonnie Bedelia, Robert Carradine, Andre Braugher, Arliss Howard; *D:* Frank Pierson; *W:* Doug Magee; *C:* Bojan Bazelli. USH

Somebody to Love 🎞🎞½ 1994 (R)
Spunky taxi dancer Mercedes (Perez) wants to be an actress despite the bad luck actor/boyfriend Harry (a subdued Keitel). One of her clients is the bumpious Ernesto (De Lorenzo), who quickly becomes infatuated with Mercedes and, to impress her, takes a job with local racketeer Emillio (Quinn). Ernesto even decides to take a contract hit to get the money Mercedes needs to help out Harry, leading to tragedy. Confusing look at the fringes of the L.A. showbiz scene, with lots of missed chances though Perez gets some flashy diva scenes. *CW:* Pervasive strong language, some violence and sexual content. 103m/C VHS. Rosie Perez, Harvey Keitel, Michael De Lorenzo, Anthony Quinn, Steve Buscemi, Stanley Tucci, Gerardo, Paul Herman; *Cameos:* Angelica Huston, Quentin Tarantino; *D:* Alexandre Rockwell; *W:* Alexandre Rockwell, Sergei Bodrov. CAF

Somebody Up There Likes
Me 🎞🎞🎞 **1956** Story of Rocky Graziano's gritty battle from his poor, street-wise childhood to his prison term and his eventual success as the

middleweight boxing champion of the world. Adapted from Graziano's autobiography. Superior performance by Newman (in his third screen role, after the miserable "The Silver Chalice" and forgettable "The Rack"); screen debuts for McQueen and Loggia. 113m/B VHS, Beta, Closed Caption. Paul Newman, Pier Angeli, Everett Sloane, Eileen Heckart, Sal Mineo, Robert Loggia, Steve McQueen; *D:* Robert Wise; *W:* Ernest Lehman; *C:* Joseph Ruttenberg. Academy Awards '56: Best Art Direction/Set Decoration (B & W), Best Black and White Cinematography; Nominations: Academy Awards '56: Best Film Editing. MGM

Someday You'll Find Her, Charlie
Brown **1981** Charlie Brown tries to find a beautiful girl he saw on tv. 24m/C VHS.

Someone at the Door 🎞🎞 1950 Re-
porter Medwin arranges to be suspected of killing his sister, thus providing him with a good story and advancing his career. His plan almost backfires, when he is almost executed. Remake of a 1936 film of the same name. 65m/B VHS, Beta. *GB* Michael Medwin, Garry Marsh, Yvonne Owen, Hugh Latimer; *D:* Francis Searle. SNC

Someone Behind the Door 🎞½ Two
Minds for Murder; Quelqu' Un Derriere la Porte 1971 (PG) Evil brain surgeon Perkins implants murderous suggestions into psychopathic amnesia victim Bronson's mind, then instructs him to kill his (the surgeon's) wife and her lover. 97m/C VHS, Beta, LV. Charles Bronson, Anthony Perkins, Jill Ireland, Henri Garcin; *D:* Nicolas Gessner. UNI, VTR

Someone Else's America 🎞🎞🎞 1996
(R) Euro-"Grumpy Old Men" explores friendship and the modern immigrant experience in Brooklyn. Bayo (Manojlovic) is a comical, sad-sack Serb who works at the bar of Alonso (Conti), a Spaniard who immigrated with his blind mother (Casares). Story follows Bayo's family as they illegally immigrate to chase the American dream and adapt to life once they arrive. Touchingly funny highlight involves a scheme by the men which enables Alonso's homesick mother to revisit her village in Spain. Filmed in Germany with sets built to resemble Brooklyn, picture has an appealingly unreal quality. Cast and crew together formed its own melting pot, with over 20 nationalities contributing. *CW:* Language and brief sexuality. 96m/C VHS. *FR GB GE* Tom Conti, Miki Manojlovic, Maria Casares, Zorka Manojlovic, Sergej Trifunovic, Chia-ching Niu, Andjela Stojkovic, Ananda Ellis; *D:* Goran Paskaljevic; *W:* Gordan Mihic; *C:* Yorgos Arvanitis; *M:* Andrew Dickson. NYF

Someone I Touched 🎞½ 1975 Way-
overdone melodrama starring Leachman as a finally-pregnant woman who learns her husband and a teenager she slept with have venereal disease. 74m/C VHS, Beta. Cloris Leachman, James Olson, Glynnis O'Connor, Andrew (Andy) Robinson, Allyn Ann McLerie; *D:* Lou Antonio. WOV

Someone to Die For 🎞🎞 1995 (R) Ac-
cused murderer (and cop) Bernsen is out to prove his innocence but learns that the real killer may be very close to home. *CW:* Violence, sexuality, and some language. 98m/C VHS. Corbin Bernsen, Ally Walker, Robert Stewart; *D:* Clay Borris. AVE

Someone to Love 🎞🎞 1987 (R) Rootless
filmmaker gathers all his single friends together and interviews them about their failed love lives. Welles's last film as an actor. Wildly uneven, interesting experiment. 110m/C VHS, Beta, LV, Closed Caption. Henry Jaglom, Orson Welles, Sally Kellerman, Andrea Marcovicci, Michael Emil, Oja Kodar, Stephen Bishop, Ronee Blakley, Kathryn Harrold, Monte Hellman; *D:* Henry Jaglom; *W:* Henry Jaglom; *C:* Hanania Baer. PAR

Someone to Watch Over Me 🎞🎞🎞
1987 (R) After witnessing the murder of a close friend, a beautiful and very wealthy woman must be protected from the killer. The working-class New York detective assigned the duty is more than taken with her, despite the fact that he has both a wife and son at home. A highly watchable, stylish romantic crime thriller. 106m/C VHS, Beta, LV,

Closed Caption. Tom Berenger, Mimi Rogers, Lorraine Bracco, Jerry Orbach, Andreas Katsulas, Tony DiBenedetto, James Moriarty, John Rubinstein; **D:** Ridley Scott; **W:** Howard Franklin; **C:** Steven Poster; **M:** Michael Kamen. *COL*

Something for Everyone ⬥⬥½ *The Rook; Black Flowers for the Bride* 1970 (R) A corrupt footman uses sex and murder in an attempt to take over the estate of an aristocratic Bavarian family in post-WWII Germany. He nearly succeeds in marrying the countess (Lansbury), but someone has been keeping tabs on him. Funny, ambitious black comedy. From the novel "The Code" by Harry Kressing. 112m/C VHS, Beta. Angela Lansbury, Michael York, Anthony Corlan, Heidelinde Weis; **D:** Harold Prince; **C:** Walter Lassally. *FOX*

Something in Common ⬥⬥½ 1986 A woman discovers her 22-year-old son is having an affair with a woman her own age. Nicely done comedy. Burstyn and Weld both make good use of a solid script. Made for TV. 94m/C VHS, Beta. Ellen Burstyn, Tuesday Weld, Don Murray, Patrick Cassidy, Eli Wallach; **D:** Glenn Jordan; **W:** Susan Rice; **M:** John Addison. *VTR, NWV*

Something of Value ⬥⬥⬥ 1957 Good ensemble performances in a serious colonial story about the Mau Mau rebellion in Kenya. Hudson and Poitier are torn between their friendship and their opposing loyalties. Drama solidly grounded in fact from the book by Robert Ruark. 113m/B VHS, Beta. Rock Hudson, Sidney Poitier, Wendy Hiller, Dana Wynter, Juano Hernandez; **D:** Richard Brooks; **W:** Richard Brooks; **M:** Miklos Rozsa. *MGM*

Something Short of Paradise ⬥½ 1979 (PG) The owner of a Manhattan movie theater has an on again/off again romance with a magazine writer. Would-be Allenesque romantic comedy is too talky and pretentious. 87m/C VHS, Beta. David Steinberg, Susan Sarandon, Jean-Pierre Aumont, Marilyn Sokol; **D:** David Helpern; **W:** Fred Barron. *LIV, VES*

Something Special ⬥⬥½ *Willy Milly; I Was a Teenage Boy* 1986 (PG-13) A fourteen-year-old girl has her wish come true when she is turned into a boy. Charming, original fantasy-comedy is fun for young and old. 93m/C VHS, LV. Pamela Segall, Patty Duke, Eric Gurry, John Glover, Seth Green; **D:** Paul Schneider; **W:** Walter Carbone. *NO*

Something to Sing About ⬥⬥ *Battling Hoofer* 1936 Musical melodrama about a New York bandleader's attempt to make it big in Hollywood. Allows Cagney the opportunity to demonstrate his dancing talents; he also sings. Rereleased in 1947. Also available colorized. Frawley was Fred on "I Love Lucy." ♫ *Any Old Love; Right or Wrong; Loving You; Out of the Blue; Something to Sing About.* 84m/B VHS, Beta, LV. James Cagney, William Frawley, Evelyn Daw, Gene Lockhart; **D:** Victor Schertzinger. Nominations: Academy Awards '37: Best Original Score. *NOS, VHE, CAB*

Something to Talk About ⬥⬥½ *Grace Under Pressure* 1995 (R) Romantic comedy/drama finds Grace (Roberts) running her overbearing father Wyly's (Duvall) horsebreeding operation and learning that her husband Eddie (the ever-charming Quaid) is tomcatting around. So Grace tosses him out and makes a temporary move with daughter Caroline (Aull) back home: Tart-tongued sister Emma Rae (Sedgwick) is sympathetic but long-suffering mama Georgia (Rowlands) thinks Grace should make the best of things (the way she's done). Naturally, Eddie wants his family back but the frazzled Grace is just coming to terms with what she wants out of life. Star appeal from both leads lends this familiar plot some spark.**CW:** Brief strong language. 106m/C VHS, LV, **Closed Caption.** Julia Roberts, Dennis Quaid, Robert Duvall, Gena Rowlands, Kyra Sedgwick, Brett Cullen, Haley Aull, Muse Watson, Anne Shropshire; **D:** Lasse Hallstrom; **W:** Callie Khouri; **C:** Sven Nykvist; **M:** Hans Zimmer. Nominations: Golden Globe Awards '96: Best Supporting Actress (Sedgwick). *WAR*

Something Weird woof! 1968 McCabe is disfigured horribly in an electrical accident. A seemingly beautiful witch fixes his face, on condition that he be her lover. The accident also gave him ESP—and it gets cheesier from there. 80m/C VHS, Beta. Tony McCabe, Elizabeth Lee; **D:** Herschell Gordon Lewis. *THV, VDM, TWE*

Something Wicked This Way Comes ⬥⬥ 1983 (PG) Two young boys discover the evil secret of a mysterious traveling carnival that visits their town. Bradbury wrote the screenplay for this much-anticipated, expensive adaptation of his own novel. Good special effects, but disappointing. 94m/C VHS, Beta, LV. Jason Robards Jr., Jonathan Pryce, Diane Ladd, Pam Grier, Richard Davalos, James Stacy; **D:** Jack Clayton; **W:** Ray Bradbury; **C:** Stephen Burum; **M:** James Horner. *DIS*

Something Wild ⬥⬥½ 1986 (R) Mild-mannered business exec Daniels is picked up by an impossibly free-living vamp with a Louise Brooks hairdo, and taken for the ride of his up-till-then staid life, eventually leading to explosive violence. A sharp-edged comedy with numerous changes of pace. Too-happy ending wrecks it, but it's great until then. Look for cameos from filmmakers John Waters and John Sayles. 113m/C VHS, Beta, LV, Closed Caption. Jeff Daniels, Melanie Griffith, Ray Liotta, Margaret Colin, Dana Peru, Jack Gilpin, Su Tissue, Kenneth Utt, Sister Carol East; *Cameos:* John Sayles, John Waters; **D:** Jonathan Demme; **W:** E. Max Frye; **C:** Tak Fujimoto; **M:** Laurie Anderson, Rosemary Paul, John Cale. Edgar Allan Poe Awards '86: Best Screenplay. *HBO*

Sometimes a Great Notion ⬥⬥⬥ *Never Give an Inch* 1971 (PG) Trouble erupts in a small Oregon town when a family of loggers decide to honor a contract when the other loggers go on strike. Newman's second stint in the director's chair; Fonda's first role as an old man. Based on the novel by Ken Kesey. 115m/C VHS, Beta. Paul Newman, Henry Fonda, Lee Remick, Richard Jaeckel, Michael Sarrazin; **D:** Paul Newman; **W:** John Gay; **M:** Henry Mancini. Nominations: Academy Awards '71: Best Song ("All His Children"), Best Supporting Actor (Jaeckel). *USH*

Sometimes They Come Back ⬥⬥ 1991 (R) Another Stephen King tale of terror. Matheson plays a man haunted by the tragedy in his past. A witness to his brother's death, he also witnesses the fiery crash of his brother's killers. Only now the killers have returned from the dead, to take their revenge on him. Made for television.**CW:** Terror violence. 97m/C VHS, LV, **Closed Caption.** Tim Matheson, Brooke Adams, Robert Rusler. *THV*

Sometimes They Come Back...Again ⬥½ 1996 (R) Psychologist John Porter (Gross) and his teenaged daughter (Swank) return to Porter's hometown after his mother's mysterious death. He should know you can never go home again since they're both soon threatened by a young man (Arquette) involved in the ritualistic murder of Porter's sister years before. Gruesome special effects are the highlight.**CW:** Strong horror violence and gore, some sexuality and language. 98m/C VHS. Michael Gross, Hilary Swank, Alexis Arquette, Jennifer Elise Cox; **D:** Adam Grossman. *THV*

Somewhere I'll Find You ⬥⬥⬥ 1942 Clark and Turner heat up the screen as correspondents running all over the war-torn world in their second film together. ("Honky Tonk" was their first.) Notable mainly because Gable's beloved wife, Carole Lombard, was killed in a plane crash only three days into production. Gable forced himself to finish the film and it became one of the studio's biggest hits. Although critics applauded his determination to complete the film, many felt his performance was subdued and strained. Film debut of Wynn. Based on a story by Charles Hoffman. 108m/B VHS. Clark Gable, Lana Turner, Robert Sterling, Reginald Owen, Lee Patrick, Charles Dingle, Tamara Shayne, Leonid Kinskey, Diana Lewis, Molly Lamont, Patricia Dane, Sara Haden, Keenan

Wynn; **D:** Wesley Ruggles; **W:** Walter Reisch, Marguerite Roberts. *MGM*

Somewhere in Sonora ⬥⬥ 1933 Early Wayne Western set in Old Mexico. Wayne plays a rodeo performer who joins an outlaw gang to save a friend and a silver mine. Like most of the other films of the series, this was a remake of a Ken Maynard silent. Based on a story and the novel "Somewhere South in Sonora" by Will Levington Comfort. 59m/B VHS, **Closed Caption.** John Wayne, Henry B. Walthall, Shirley Palmer, J.P. McGowan, Frank Rice, Billy Franey, Paul Fix, Ralph Lewis; **D:** Mack V. Wright; **W:** Joe Roach. *MGM*

Somewhere in Time ⬥½ 1980 (PG) Playwright Reeve (in his first post-Clark Kent role) falls in love with a beautiful woman in an old portrait. Through self-hypnosis he goes back in time to 1912 to discover what their relationship might have been. The film made a star of the Grand Hotel, located on Mackinac Island in Michigan, where it was shot. Drippy rip-off of the brilliant novel "Time and Again" by Jack Finney. Reeve is horrible; Seymour is underused. All in all, rather wretched. 103m/C VHS, Beta, LV. Christopher Reeve, Jane Seymour, Christopher Plummer, Teresa Wright; **D:** Jeannot Szwarc; **W:** Richard Matheson; **M:** John Barry. Nominations: Academy Awards '80: Best Costume Design. *USH*

Somewhere Tomorrow ⬥⬥½ 1985 (PG) A lonely, fatherless teenage girl is befriended by the ghost of a young man killed in a plane crash. Charming and moving, if not perfect. 91m/C VHS, Beta. Sarah Jessica Parker, Nancy Addison, Tom Shea; **D:** Robert Wiemer. *MED*

Sommersby ⬥⬥½ 1993 (PG-13) A too-good-to-be-true period romance based on the film "The Return of Martin Guerre." A Civil War veteran (Gere) returns to his wife's (Foster) less-than-open arms. She soon warms up to his kind, sensitive and caring manner, but can't quite believe the change that the war has wrought. Neither can the neighbors, especially the one (Pullman) who had his own eye on Laurel Sommersby. So is he really Jack Sommersby or an all too clever imposter? Lots of hankies needed for the tender-hearted. Strong performance by Foster. Filmed in Virginia (passing for the state of Tennessee.) The laserdisc version is available in letterbox format.**CW:** Sensuality. 114m/C VHS, Beta, LV, 8mm, **Closed Caption.** Richard Gere, Jodie Foster, Bill Pullman, James Earl Jones, William Windom, Brett Kelley, Richard Hamilton, Maury Chaykin, Lanny Flaherty, Frankie Faison, Wendell Wellman, Clarice Taylor, R. Lee Ermey; **D:** Jon Amiel; **W:** Nicholas Meyer, Sarah Kernochan; **M:** Danny Elfman. *WAR, FCT*

Son-in-Law ⬥½ 1993 (PG-13) Surfer-dude comic Shore's a laconic fish out of water as a city-boy rock 'n' roller who falls in love with a country beauty, marries her, and visits the family farm to meet the new in-laws. Once there, he weirds out family and neighbors before showing everyone how to live, Pauly style. Silly entertainment best appreciated by Shore fans.**CW:** Sexual situations. 95m/C VHS, Beta, LV, **Closed Caption.** Pauly Shore, Carla Gugino, Lane Smith, Cindy Pickett, Mason Adams, Patrick Renna, Dennis Burkley, Dan Gauthier, Tiffani-Amber Thiessen; **D:** Steve Rash; **W:** Shawn Schepps, Fax Bahr, Adam Small; **M:** Richard Gibbs. Nominations: MTV Movie Awards '94: Best Comedic Performance (Shore). *HPH*

Son of a Gun ⬥½ 1919 A loveable but ornery cowboy gets banished from the county for disturbing the peace. However, he wins the favor of the townspeople when he stands up to a gang of gambling swindlers. Silent. 68m/B VHS, Beta. "Broncho" Billy Anderson. *NOS, DVT, RXM*

Son of Ali Baba ⬥⬥ 1952 Kashma Baba, son of Ali Baba, enters the military academy to learn to withstand adversity. He has other ideas however, until he must suddenly fill his father's shoes and fight the evil Caliph. He fights bravely with the help of his childhood friend, a beautiful princess, in this swashbuckler. 85m/C VHS, **Closed Caption.** Tony Curtis, Piper Laurie, Susan

Cabot, Victor Jory, Hugh O'Brian, William Reynolds, Gerald Mohr; **D:** Ross Hunter. *USH, FCT*

Son of Blob 🐾🐾 *Beware! The Blob* 1972 (PG) A scientist brings home a piece of frozen blob from the North Pole; his wife accidentally revives the dormant gray mass. It begins a rampage of terror by digesting nearly everyone within its reach. A host of recognizable faces make for fun viewing. Post-Jeannie, pre-Dallas Hagman directed this exercise in zaniness. 87m/C VHS, Beta. Robert Walker Jr., Godfrey Cambridge, Carol Lynley, Shelley Berman, Larry Hagman, Burgess Meredith, Gerrit Graham, Dick Van Patten; **D:** Larry Hagman. *GEM*

Son of Captain Blood 🐾½ *Il Figlio del Capitano Blood* 1962 (G) The son of the famous pirate meets up with his father's enemies on the high seas. The son of the famous actor Errol Flynn—Sean—plays the son of the character the elder Flynn played in "Captain Blood." Let's just say the gimmick didn't work. 90m/C VHS, Beta. *IT SP* Sean Flynn, Ann Todd; **D:** Tulio Demicheli. *PSM, MLB*

Son of Dracula 🐾🐾🐾 *Young Dracula* 1943 In this late-coming sequel to the Universal classic, a stranger named Alucard is invited to America by a Southern belle obsessed with eternal life. It is actually Dracula himself, not his son, who wreaks havoc in this spine-tingling chiller. 80m/B VHS, Beta, LV. Lon Chaney Jr., Evelyn Ankers, Frank Craven, Robert Paige, Louise Allbritton, J. Edward Bromberg, Samuel S. Hinds; **D:** Robert Siodmak. *USH*

Son of Flubber 🐾🐾½ 1963 Sequel to "The Absent Minded Professor" finds Fred MacMurray still toying with his prodigious invention, Flubber, now in the form of Flubbergas, which causes those who inhale it to float away. Disney's first-ever sequel is high family wackiness. 96m/C VHS, Beta. Fred MacMurray, Nancy Olson, Tommy Kirk, Leon Ames, Joanna Moore, Keenan Wynn, Charlie Ruggles, Paul Lynde; **D:** Robert Stevenson; **M:** George Bruns. *DIS*

Son of Frankenstein 🐾🐾🐾 1939 The second sequel (after "The Bride of Frankenstein") to the 1931 version of the horror classic. The good doctor's skeptical son returns to the family manse and becomes obsessed with his father's work and with reviving the creature. Full of memorable characters and brooding ambience. Karloff's last appearance as the monster. 99m/C VHS, Beta, LV. Basil Rathbone, Bela Lugosi, Boris Karloff, Lionel Atwill, Josephine Hutchinson, Donnie Dunagan, Emma Dunn, Edgar Norton, Lawrence Grant; **D:** Rowland V. Lee. *USH*

Son of Fury 🐾🐾🐾 1942 Dashing Ben Blake (Power) is left penniless when his sinister uncle (Sanders) wrongfully takes the family fortune. Ben escapes to sea and then to an island paradise—all the while plotting his revenge. But he still finds time to fall for the beauteous Tierney. Fine 18th-century costumer done in grand style. Based on the novel "Benjamin Blake" by Edison Marshall. 98m/C VHS. Tyrone Power, Gene Tierney, George Sanders, Frances Farmer, Roddy McDowall, John Carradine, Elsa Lanchester, Harry Davenport, Kay Johnson, Dudley Digges, Halliwell Hobbes, Marten Lamont, Arthur Hohl, Pedro de Cordoba, Dennis Hoey, Heather Thatcher; **D:** John Cromwell; **W:** Philip Dunne; **M:** Alfred Newman. *FXV*

Son of God's Country 🐾½ 1948 Utterly hackneyed, near-comic attempt at a western. Good-guy U.S. Marshal poses as a crook to get the lowdown on the varmints. 60m/B VHS, Beta. Monte Hale, Pamela Blake, Adrian Booth. *DVT*

Son of Godzilla 🐾🐾 *Gojira no Musuko* 1966 Dad and junior protect beauty Maeda from giant spiders on a remote island ruled by a mad scientist. Fun monster flick with decent special effects. 86m/C VHS, Beta. *JP* Tadao Takashima, Akira Kubo; **D:** Jun Fukuda. *PSM, HHT, DVT*

Son of Ingagi 🐾½ 1940 Lonely ape-man kidnaps woman in search of romance. Early all-black horror film stars Williams of "Amos 'n' Andy." 70m/B VHS. Zack Williams, Laura Bowman, Alfred

Grant, Spencer Williams Jr.; **D:** Richard C. Kahn; **W:** Spencer Williams Jr. *NOS, SNC, MLB*

Son of Kong 🐾🐾½ 1933 King Kong's descendant is discovered on an island amid prehistoric creatures in this often humorous sequel to RKO's immensely popular "King Kong." Hoping to capitalize on the enormous success of its predecessor, director Schoedsack quickly threw this together. As a result, its success at the box office did not match the original's, and didn't deserve to, but it's fun. Nifty special effects from Willie O'Brien, the man who brought them to us the first time! 70m/B VHS, Beta, LV. Robert Armstrong, Helen Mack; **D:** Ernest B. Schoedsack; **M:** Max Steiner. *NOS, MED, FCT*

Son of Lassie 🐾🐾½ 1945 (G) It seems that Lassie's son Laddie just isn't quite as smart as his mother. After the dog sneaks onto his master's plane during WWII, the plane gets shot down, and Lawford parachutes out with Laddie in his arms. The dog goes to get help because Lawford is hurt, but he brings back two Nazis! A sequel to "Lassie Come Home." 102m/C VHS. Peter Lawford, Donald Crisp, June Lockhart, Nigel Bruce, William Severn, Leon Ames, Donald Curtis, Nils Asther, Robert Lewis; **D:** Sylvan Simon. *MGM*

The Son of Monte Cristo 🐾🐾½ 1941 Illegitimate offspring of the great swashbuckler with Robert Donat proves they made pathetic, pointless sequels even back then. 102m/B VHS, Beta, LV. Louis Hayward, Joan Bennett, George Sanders, Florence Bates, Montagu Love, Ralph Byrd, Clayton Moore; **D:** Rowland V. Lee. Nominations: Academy Awards '41: Best Interior Decoration. *DVT, BAR, CAB*

Son of Paleface 🐾🐾🐾½ 1952 Hilarious sequel to the original Hope gag-fest, with the Harvard-educated son of the original character (again played by Hope) heading west to claim an inheritance. Hope runs away with every cowboy cliche and even manages to wind up with the girl. Songs include "Buttons and Bows" (reprised from original), "There's a Cloud in My Valley of Sunshine," and "Four-legged Friend." 95m/C VHS, Beta, LV. Bob Hope, Jane Russell, Roy Rogers, Douglass Dumbrille, Iron Eyes Cody, Bill Williams, Harry von Zell; **D:** Frank Tashlin. Nominations: Academy Awards '52: Best Song ("Am I in Love"). *COL*

Son of Rusty 🐾🐾½ 1947 Danny and his friends are warned to stay away from the farm of suspicious Jed Barlow. But Rusty keeps running away to see Jed's dog Barb and Danny gets to know Jed. Then Danny must stand by his new friend when word of Jed's past turns folks against him. (Rusty and Barb have puppies too.) 70m/B VHS. Ted Donaldson. *COL*

Son of Samson 🐾½ *Le Geant de la Vallee Das Rois* 1962 Man with large pectoral muscles puts an end to the evil Queen of Egypt's reign of terror 89m/C VHS. *FR IT YU* Mark Forest, Chelo Alonso, Angelo Zanolli, Vira Silenti, Frederica Ranchi; **D:** Carlo Campogalliani. *SNC*

Son of Sinbad 🐾🐾 *Nights in a Harem* 1955 Sinbad, captured by the Khalif of Baghdad, must bring him the secret of Greek fire to gain his freedom and free the city from the forces of mighty Tamerlane. About three dozen nubile young women wear very little and gambol with our hero herein; much-anticipated skinfest caused a scandal, nurtured by Howard Hughes for profit. 88m/C VHS, Beta. Dale Robertson, Sally Forrest, Vincent Price, Lili St. Cyr, Mari Blanchard, Joi Lansing; **D:** Ted Tetzlaff. *NO*

Son of the Morning Star 🐾🐾🐾 1991 (PG-13) Lavish made for TV retelling of Custer's famed-butt kicking. Complex characterizations and unusual points of view, based on the book by Evan S. Connell. 186m/C VHS, LV, Closed Caption. Gary Cole, Rosanna Arquette, Dean Stockwell, Rodney Grant, Terry O'Quinn, David Strathairn, Stanley Anderson, George American Horse; **D:** Mike Robe. *REP, FCT*

Son of the Pink Panther 🐾½ *Blake Edwards' Son of the Pink Panther* 1993 (PG) Lame leftover from the formerly popular comedy series. Director Edwards has chosen not to resurrect Inspector Clouseau, instead opting for his son (Benigni), who turns out to be just as much of a bumbling idiot as his father. Commissioner Dreyfus (Lom), the twitching, mouth-foaming former supervisor of the original Clouseau is looking for a kidnapped princess (Farentino) along with Clouseau, Jr., who himself does not know he is the illegitimate son of his partner's dead nemesis. Many of the sketches have been recycled from previous series entrants. Rather than being funny, they seem used and shopworn like a threadbare rug. 115m/C VHS, LV, Closed Caption. Roberto Benigni, Herbert Lom, Robert Davi, Debrah Farentino, Claudia Cardinale, Burt Kwouk, Shabana Azmi; **D:** Blake Edwards; **W:** Blake Edwards; **M:** Henry Mancini. *MGM*

The Son of the Shark 🐾🐾 *Le Fils du Requin* 1993 Simon (Da Silva) and Martin Vanderhoes (Vandendaele) have been abandoned by their mother and prefer to live as homeless delinquents rather than with their drunken father. The boys commit petty crimes and vandalism to survive (always escaping from foster homes and institutions) while Martin dreams of running away to his true home in the ocean—proclaiming himself to be "the son of a female shark." Depressing and casually cruel; based on a true story. French with subtitles. 88m/C VHS. *FR* Ludovic Vandendaele, Erick Da Silva, Sandrine Blancke, Maxime LeRoux; **D:** Agnes Merlet; **W:** Agnes Merlet; **C:** Gerard Simon; **M:** Bruno Coulais. *FXL*

Son of the Sheik 🐾🐾🐾 1926 A desert sheik abducts an unfaithful dancing girl. Valentino's well-done, slightly self-mocking last film. Silent. Sequel to "The Sheik" (1921). 62m/B VHS, Beta, LV. Rudolph Valentino, Vilma Banky, Agnes Ayres; **D:** George Fitzmaurice; **C:** George Barnes. *NOS, CCB, VCN*

Son of Zorro 1947 Zorro takes the law into his own hands to protect ranchers from bandits. A serial in thirteen chapters. 164m/B VHS. George Turner, Peggy Stewart, Roy Barcroft, Edward Cassidy. *REP, VCN, MLB*

A Song is Born 🐾🐾🐾 1948 A group of music professors try to trace the history of music. Kaye is in charge of a U.S. music foundation whose research has led him up to ragtime. He is soon, however, thrust into the sometimes seedy world of jazz joints and night spots, all in the name of research. Enter love interest Mayo, a woman on the run from her gangster boyfriend who hides out at the foundation. Not one of Kaye's funniest or best, but if you enjoy big band music, you'll love this. Includes music by Louis Armstrong and his orchestra, Tommy Dorsey and his orchestra, and Charlie Barnet and his orchestra. This was Kaye's last film for Goldwyn. ♫ A Song is Born; Bach Boogie; Anitra's Dance; I'm Getting Sentimental Over You; Blind Barnabas; Mockin' Bird; Redskin Rhumba; The Goldwyn Stomp; Daddy-O. 113m/B VHS. Danny Kaye, Virginia Mayo, Benny Goodman, Hugh Herbert, Steve Cochran, J. Edward Bromberg, Felix Bressart; **D:** Howard Hawks; **C:** Gregg Toland. *GVV*

Song O' My Heart 🐾🐾🐾 1929 An early musical starring popular Irish tenor McCormack as a singer forced to abandon his career when he marries a woman he does not love. A tour de force for the lead in his movie debut. ♫ Little Boy Blue; Paddy Me Lad; I Hear You Calling Me; A Fair Story by the Fireside; Just For a Day; Kitty My Love; The Rose of Tralee; A Pair of Blue Eyes; I Feel You Near Me. 91m/B VHS, Beta. John McCormack, Maureen O'Sullivan, John Garrick, J.M. Kerrigan, Tommy Clifford, Alice Joyce; **D:** Frank Borzage. *VAI, FCT, TVC*

Song of Arizona 🐾🐾 1946 Rogers and the Sons of the Pioneers arrive to aid their pal Hayes against a gang of bank robbers in this modern-day oater. Eight songs perpetually punctuate the perfunctory plot, particularly "Will Ya Be My

Darling," "Half-a-Chance Ranch," and the title tune. **54m/B VHS, Beta.** Roy Rogers, Dale Evans, George "Gabby" Hayes, Lyle Talbot, Bob Nolan, The Pioneers; **D:** Frank McDonald. *NOS, VCN, HEG*

The Song of Bernadette 🎬🎬🎬 1943

Depicts the true story of a peasant girl who sees a vision of the Virgin Mary in a grotto at Lourdes in 1858. The girl is directed to dig at the grotto for water that will heal those who believe in its powers, much to the astonishment and concern of the townspeople. Based on Franz Werfel's novel. Directed with tenderness and carefully cast, and appealing to religious and sentimental susceptibilities, it was a box-office smash. **156m/B VHS, Beta, LV.** Charles Bickford, Lee J. Cobb, Jennifer Jones, Vincent Price, Anne Revere, Gladys Cooper; **D:** Henry King; **C:** Arthur C. Miller; **M:** Alfred Newman. Academy Awards '43: Best Actress (Jones), Best Black and White Cinematography, Best Interior Decoration, Original Dramatic/Comedy Score; Golden Globe Awards '44: Best Actress—Drama (Jones), Best Director (King), Best Film—Drama; Nominations: Academy Awards '43: Best Director (King), Best Film Editing, Best Picture, Best Screenplay, Best Sound, Best Supporting Actor (Bickford), Best Supporting Actress (Cooper, Revere). *FXV, KEP, IGP*

Song of Freedom 🎬🎬½ 1938

The story of a black dockworker whose gift of voice is discovered by an opera impresario. After realizing a career as a concert performer, Robeson ventures to Africa to investigate his ancestry and finds he has royal roots. Robeson turns in a fine performance in what is otherwise an average film. **70m/B VHS, Beta.** *GB* Paul Robeson, Elizabeth Welch, George Mozart; **D:** J. Elder Wills. *VYY, HHT, NOS*

Song of Nevada 🎬🎬½ 1944

Rogers woos the high-society daughter (Evans, of course) of a rancher (Hall). Quintessential Royn-Dale. 🎵 It's Love, Love, Love; New Moon Over Nevada; Hi Ho Little Dogies; The Harum Scarum Baron of the Harmonium; What Are We Going to Do?; A Cowboy Has to Yodel in the Morning. **60m/B VHS, Beta.** Roy Rogers, Dale Evans, Thurston Hall; **D:** Joseph Kane. *NOS, HHT, DVT*

Song of Norway 🎬🎬 1970 (G)

A dramatization of the early life of the beloved Norwegian Romantic composer Edvard Grieg. Filmed among the beautiful mountains, waterfalls, and forests of Norway and based on the popular '40s stage production. The scenery is the best thing because Grieg's life was dull—even with cinematic liberties taken. 🎵 Strange Music; The Song of Norway; The Little House; Be a Boy Again; Three There Were; A Rhyme and a Reason; Wrong to Dream; I Love You; The Solitary Wanderer. **143m/C VHS, Beta.** Toralv Maurstad, Florence Henderson, Edward G. Robinson, Christina Schollin, Frank Porretta, Oscar Homolka, Robert Morley, Harry Secombe; **D:** Andrew L. Stone. *FOX*

Song of Old Wyoming 🎬½ 1945

Three of those songs are presented in the course of an ordinary western about a spunky widow driving badmen out of Wyoming territory. La Rue plays the villainous Cheyanne Kid; this was before he got his own series as the heroic "Lash" La Rue. **65m/C VHS.** Eddie Dean, Sarah Padden, Lash La-Rue, Jennifer Holt, Emmett Lynn, John Carpenter, Ian Keith, Bob Barron; **D:** Robert Emmett Tansey. *NOS, HEG*

Song of Texas 🎬½ 1943

When a young woman journeys west to visit her father at "his" ranch, Roy and his pals must keep the father's secret that he is just another hired hand. Whenever possible, everyone breaks into song. **54m/B VHS, Beta.** Roy Rogers, Harry Shannon, Pat Brady, Barton MacLane, Arline Judge; **D:** Joseph Kane. *NOS, VYY, VCN*

Song of the Exile 🎬🎬½ 1990

A Chinese/Japanese student living in London in the early 1970s faces racial discrimination and decides to return to her native Hong Kong. But on the home front, she and her family clash emotionally until daughter and mother come to a gradual understanding of how the past affects the present. In Cantonese and Japanese with with English subtitles. **100m/C VHS.** *CH* Maggie Cheung, Shwu-Fen Chang; **D:** Ann Hui. *KIV, FCT*

Song of the Gringo 🎬🎬 *The Old Corral*

1936 Tex Ritter stars in his first singing western as a sheriff going after a gang of claim jumpers. **57m/B VHS, Beta.** Tex Ritter, Monte Blue, Joan Woodbury, Fuzzy Knight, Richard Adams, Warner Richmond; **D:** John P. McCarthy. *NOS, VCI, VCN*

Song of the Islands 🎬🎬½ 1942

Landing families in Hawaii feud over a beach, while the son of one (Mature) and the daughter of the other (Grable) fall in love. Plenty of songs, and dancing to display Grable's legs. Of course happiness and concord reign at the end. Songs include "O'Brien Has Gone Hawaiian," "Sing Me a Song of the Islands," and "What's Buzzin', Cousin?" **75m/C VHS, Beta, LV, Closed Caption.** Betty Grable, Victor Mature, Jack Oakie, Thomas Mitchell, Billy Gilbert; **D:** Walter Lang. *FOX, MLB*

Song of the Thin Man 🎬🎬½ 1947

The sixth and final "Thin Man" mystery. This time Nick and Nora Charles (Powell and Loy) investigate the murder of a bandleader. Somewhat more sophisticated than its predecessor, due in part to its setting in the jazz music world. Sequel to "The Thin Man Goes Home." **86m/B VHS, Beta.** William Powell, Myrna Loy, Keenan Wynn, Dean Stockwell, Philip Reed, Patricia Morison, Gloria Grahame, Jayne Meadows, Don Taylor, Leon Ames, Ralph Morgan, Warner Anderson; **D:** Edward Buzzell; **C:** Charles Rosher. *MGM*

Song of the Trail 🎬½ 1936

Our hero saves an old man hornswoggled at cards. **65m/B VHS, Beta.** Kermit Maynard, George "Gabby" Hayes, Fuzzy Knight, Wheeler Oakman, Evelyn Brent, Andrea Leeds; **D:** Russell Hopton. *NOS, VDM, VCN*

Song Spinner 🎬🎬½ 1995 (G)

In a mysterious land, a stranger gives a young girl the power of music, which she hopes to share with the king. But first she must get past the kingdom's noise police. **95m/C VHS, Closed Caption.** Meredith Henderson, Patti LuPone, John Neville; **D:** Randy Bradshaw. *HMK*

A Song to Remember 🎬🎬🎬 1945

With music performed by Jose Iturbi, this film depicts the last years of the great pianist and composer Frederic Chopin, including his affair with famous author George Sand, the most renowned French woman of her day. Typically mangled film biography. 🎵 Valse in D Flat (Minute Waltz); Mazurka In B Flat, Opus 7, No. 1; Fantasie Impromptu, Opus 66; Etude In A Flat, Opus 25, No. 1 (partial); Polonaise In A Flat, Opus 53 (partial); Scherzo In B Flat Minor; Etude In C Minor, Opus 10, No. 12; Nocturne In C Minor, Opus 48, No. 1; Nocturn In E Flat, Opus 9, No. 2. **112m/C VHS, Beta, LV.** Cornel Wilde, Paul Muni, Merle Oberon, Nina Foch, George Coulouris; **D:** Charles Vidor; **C:** Gaetano Antonio "Tony" Gaudio; **M:** Miklos Rozsa. Nominations: Academy Awards '45: Best Actor (Wilde), Best Color Cinematography, Best Film Editing, Best Sound, Best Story, Original Dramatic/Comedy Score. *COL, RDG, TVC*

Song Without End 🎬🎬½ 1960

This musical biography of 19th century Hungarian pianist/composer Franz Liszt is given the Hollywood treatment. The lavish production emphasizes Liszt's scandalous exploits with married women and his life among the royal courts of Europe rather than his musical talents. Features music from several composers including Handel, Beethoven, Bach and Schumann. This film marked the debut of Capucine. Director Vidor died during filming and Cukor stepped in, so there is a noticeable change in style. Although there is much to criticize in the story, the music is beautiful. 🎵 Mephisto Waltz; Spozalizio; Sonata In B Minor; Un Sospiro; Fantasy on Themes From "Rigoletto"; Consolation in D Flat; Liebestraum; Les Preludes; Piano Concerto No. 1. **130m/C VHS, LV.** Dirk Bogarde, Capucine, Genevieve Page, Patricia Morison, Ivan Desny, Martita Hunt, Lou Jacobi; **D:** Charles Vidor, George Cukor; **C:** James Wong Howe; **M:** Morris Stoloff, Harry Sukman. Academy Awards '60: Scoring of a Musical; Golden Globe Awards '61: Best Film—Musical/Comedy. *COL, TVC*

Songs and Bullets 🎬½ 1938

Simple zen-like title sums it up. The songs total five in number, the bullets somewhat more as hero cowboys battle rustlers in routine fashion. One of a handful of films (westerns and comedies) produced by funnyman Stan Laurel. **57m/B VHS.** Fred Scott, Al "Fuzzy" St. John, Alice Ardell, Charles "Blackie" King, Karl Hackett, Frank LaRue, Budd Buster; **D:** Sam Newfield. *NOS, HEG*

Songwriter 🎬🎬½ 1984 (R)

A high-falutin' look at the lives and music of two popular country singers with, aptly, plenty of country tunes written and performed by the stars. Singer-businessman Nelson needs Kristofferson's help keeping a greedy investor at bay. Never mind the plot; plenty of good music. 🎵 How Do You Feel About Foolin' Around?; Songwriter; Who'll Buy My Memories; Write Your Own Songs; Nobody Said It Was Going To Be Easy; Good Times; Eye of the Storm; Crossing the Border; Down to Her Socks. **94m/C VHS, Beta, LV, Closed Caption.** Willie Nelson, Kris Kristofferson, Rip Torn, Melinda Dillon, Lesley Ann Warren; **D:** Alan Rudolph. Nominations: Academy Awards '84: Original Song Score and/or Adaptation. *COL*

Sonny and Jed 🎬 *La Banda J.&S. Cronaca Criminale del Far West* 1973 (R)

An escaped convict and a free-spirited woman travel across Mexico pillaging freely, followed determinedly by shiny-headed lawman Savalas. Lame rip-off of the Bonnie and Clyde legend. **85m/C VHS, Beta.** *IT* Tomas Milian, Telly Savalas, Susan George, Rosanna Janni, Laura Betti; **D:** Sergio Corbucci; **M:** Ennio Morricone. *NO*

Sonny Boy woof! 1987 (R)

A transvestite and a psychopath adopt a young boy, training him to do their bidding, which includes murder. **96m/C VHS, Beta, LV.** *IT* David Carradine, Paul Smith, Brad Dourif, Conrad Janis, Sydney Lassick, Savina Gersak, Alexandra Powers, Steve Carlisle, Michael Griffin; **D:** Robert Martin Carroll; **W:** Graeme Whifler. *TWE, MED*

Sonora Stagecoach 🎬🎬 1944

Okay sagebrush saga with an interesting lineup; two cowboys, a heroic Indian and a tough gal pilot escort a murder suspect in the title conveyance and manage to clear him when the real bad guys attack. **61m/B VHS.** Hoot Gibson, Bob Steele, Chief Thundercloud, Rocky Camron, Betty Miles, Glenn Strange, George Eldridge, Karl Hackett; **D:** Robert Emmett Tansey. *NOS, HEG*

Sons 🎬🎬 1991

A Vietnam veteran's son joins the military, causing strains within the family. **?m/C VHS. D:** Alexandre Rockwell; **W:** Alexandre Rockwell, Brandon Cole. *LRP*

Sons of Hercules in the Land of Darkness 🎬 1955

Hercules' sons kill dragons, fight titans, and generally flex up a storm. **74m/B VHS, Beta.** Dan Vadis. *VYY*

Sons of Katie Elder 🎬🎬🎬 1965

After their mother's death, four brothers are reunited. Wayne is a gunman; Anderson is a college graduate; silent Holliman is a killer; and Martin is a gambler. When they learn that her death might have been murder, they come together to devise a way to seek revenge on the killer. The town bullies complicate matters; the sheriff tells them to lay off. Especially strong screen presence by Wayne, in his first role following cancer surgery. One of the Duke's most popular movies of the '60s. **122m/C VHS, Beta, LV.** John Wayne, Dean Martin, Earl Holliman, Michael Anderson Jr., Martha Hyer, Dennis Hopper, Paul Fix, James Gregory; **D:** Henry Hathaway; **M:** Elmer Bernstein. *PAR, TLF*

Sons of Steel 🎬🎬 1935

Two brothers, owners of a steel mill, lead vastly different lives. They raise their sons in their own images, causing problems. **65m/B VHS.** Charles Starrett, Polly Ann Young, William "Billy" Bakewell, Walter Walker, Aileen Pringle, Holmes Herbert, Florence Roberts, Adolf Millar, Lloyd Ingraham; **D:** Charles Lamont. *NOS*

Sons of the Desert 🎬🎬🎬 *Sons of the Legion; Convention City; Fraternally Yours* 1933

Laurel and Hardy in their best-written film. The boys try to fool their wives by pretending to go to Hawaii to cure Ollie of a bad cold when in fact, they are attending their lodge convention in Chicago. Also includes a 1935 Thelma Todd/Patsy Kelly short, "Top Flat." **73m/B VHS, Beta.** Stan Laurel, Oliver Hardy, Mae Busch, Charley Chase, Dorothy Christy; *D:* William A. Seiter. *MED, MLB, FAF*

Sons of the Pioneers ⁇⁇ 1942 Small town sheriff Hayes hires cowboy Roy to rid town of outlaws. **61m/B VHS.** Roy Rogers, George "Gabby" Hayes, Maris Wrixon, Forrest Taylor; *D:* Joseph Kane. *REP*

Sooner or Later ⁇½ 1978 13-year-old girl passes herself off as 16 with a local rock idol and must decide whether to go all the way. **100m/C VHS, Beta.** Rex Smith, Judd Hirsch, Denise Miller, Morey Amsterdam, Lynn Redgrave; *D:* Bruce Hart. *NWV*

Sophia Loren: Her Own Story ⁇⁇ 1980 Bio of Sophia Loren, watching her grow from a spindly child in working-class Naples to a world-renowned movie star, beauty queen, and mother. Loren plays herself and her mother in this tedious account. Based on the biography by A.E. Hotchner. Made for TV. **150m/C VHS, Beta.** Sophia Loren, Armand Assante, Ed Flanders, John Gavin; *D:* Mel Stuart; *W:* Joanna Crawford. *NO*

Sophie's Choice ⁇⁇⁇½ 1982 (R) A haunting modern tragedy about Sophie Zawistowska, a beautiful Polish Auschwitz survivor settled in Brooklyn after WWII. She has intense relationships with a schizophrenic genius and an aspiring Southern writer. An artful, immaculately performed and resonant drama, with an astonishing, commanding performance by the versatile Streep; a chilling portrayal of the banality of evil. From the best-selling, autobiographical novel by William Styron. **157m/C VHS, Beta, LV.** Meryl Streep, Kevin Kline, Peter MacNicol, Rita Karin, Stephen D. Newman, Josh Mostel; *D:* Alan J. Pakula; *W:* Alan J. Pakula; *C:* Nestor Almendros; *M:* Marvin Hamlisch. Academy Awards '82: Best Actress (Streep); Golden Globe Awards '83: Best Actress—Drama (Streep); Los Angeles Film Critics Association Awards '82: Best Actress (Streep); National Board of Review Awards '82: Best Actress (Streep); New York Film Critics Awards '82: Best Actress (Streep), Best Cinematography; National Society of Film Critics Awards '82: Best Actress (Streep); Nominations: Academy Awards '82: Best Adapted Screenplay, Best Cinematography, Best Costume Design, Best Original Score. *FOX, SWC*

Sophisticated Gents ⁇⁇⁇ 1981 Nine boyhood friends, members of a black athletic club, reunite after 25 years to honor their old coach and see how each of their lives has been affected by being black men in American society. Based on the novel "The Junior Bachelor Society" by John A. Williams. Originally made for television. **200m/C VHS.** Paul Winfield, Roosevelt Grier, Bernie Casey, Raymond St. Jacques, Thalmus Rasulala, Dick Anthony Williams, Ron O'Neal, Rosalind Cash, Denise Nicholas, Alfre Woodard, Melvin Van Peebles; *D:* Harry Falk; *W:* Melvin Van Peebles. *XVC*

Sorcerer ⁇⁇½ *Wages of Fear* 1977 (PG) To put out an oil fire, four men on the run in South America agree to try to buy their freedom by driving trucks loaded with nitroglycerin over dangerous terrain—with many natural and man-made obstacles to get in their way. Remake of "The Wages of Fear" is nowhere as good as the classic original, but has exciting moments. Puzzlingly retitled, which may have contributed to the box-office failure, and the near demise of Friedkin's directing career. **121m/C VHS, LV, Closed Caption.** Roy Scheider, Bruno Cremer, Francesco Rabal, Soudad Amidou, Ramon Bieri; *D:* William Friedkin; *W:* Walon Green; *M:* Tangerine Dream. Nominations: Academy Awards '77: Best Sound. *USH, FCT*

Sorceress woof! 1982 (R) The Harris girls are sisters who use their powers of sorcery and fighting skills to battle demons, dragons, and evil. Yeah, sure. Really, they're just a pair of babes parading for the camera. **83m/C VHS, Beta.** Leigh Anne Harris, Lynette Harris, Bob Nelson, David Milbern, Bruno Rey, Anna De Sade; *D:* Brian Stuart; *W:* Jim Wynorski. *NO*

Sorceress ⁇⁇⁇ 1988 A friar in medieval Europe feels insecure in his religious beliefs after encountering a woman who heals through ancient practices. Historically authentic and interestingly moody. Written, produced, and directed by two women: an art history professor and a collaborator of Francois Truffaut's. In French with English subtitles or dubbed. **98m/C VHS.** Tcheky Karyo, Christine Boisson, Jean Carmet; *D:* Suzanne Schiffman; *W:* Pamela Berger, Suzanne Schiffman. *MFV*

Sorceress ⁇½ 1994 (R) Larry Barnes (Poindexter) is on his way to a partnership at his law firm, especially since his wife Erica (Strain) eliminates his competition—permanently. But Erica goes after the wrong guy when she comes up against Howard Reynolds (Albert). Seems Howard's loving spouse Amelia (Blair) happens to be a witch and she has her own evil spells to cast. *CW:* Sexuality; violence. **93m/C VHS.** Julie Strain, Larry Poindexter, Linda Blair, Edward Albert; *D:* Jim Wynorski. *TRI*

Sorority Babes in the Slimeball Bowl-A-Rama ⁇⁇ 1987 (R) An ancient gremlin-type creature is released from a bowling alley, and the great-looking sorority babes have to battle it at the mall, with the help of a wacky crew of nerds. Horrible horror spoof shows plenty of skin. **80m/C Beta, LV.** Linnea Quigley, Brinke Stevens, Andras Jones, John Wildman; *D:* David DeCoteau; *M:* Guy Moon. *AFE*

Sorority Girl ⁇½ 1957 Camp classic in which beautiful co-ed Cabot is presented as a malicious rich kid involved in everything from petty fights to blackmail. Cheap production from the Corman factory. **60m/B VHS, Closed Caption.** Susan Cabot, Dick Miller, Barbara Crane, June Kennedy, Fay Baker, Jeanne Wood; *D:* Roger Corman. *NLC*

Sorority House Massacre woof! 1986 (R) A knife-wielding maniac stalks a sorority girl while her more elite sisters are away for the weekend. Yawn—haven't we seen this one before? Unfortunately for us we'll see it again because this one's followed by a sequel. **74m/C VHS, Beta.** Angela O'Neill, Wendy Martel, Pamela Ross, Nicole Rio; *D:* Carol Frank. *WAR*

Sorority House Massacre 2: Nighty Nightmare woof! 1992 Another no-brainer with a different cast and director. This time around three lingerie-clad lovelies are subjected to the terrors of a killer their first night in their new sorority house. College just keeps getting tougher all the time. **80m/C VHS.** Melissa Moore, Robin Harris, Stacia Zhivago, Dana Bentley; *D:* Jim Wynorski. *NHO*

Sorority House Party ⁇ 1992 (R) A famous rock guitarist is held against his will at the sexiest sorority house on campus. He definitely has mixed feelings about the experience considering the inhabitants saunter around in bikinis and "force" him to party with them. Anders and Attila are transplants from the modeling circuit. **95m/C VHS.** Attila, April Lerman, Kim Little, Avalon Anders, Joe Mundi, Rachel Latt, Mark Stulce, Michael Xavier; *D:* David Michael Latt; *W:* John Murdy, Steve Taylor. *APX*

Sorrento Beach ⁇⁇ *Hotel Sorrento* 1995 (R) A beachside community outside Melbourne, Australia, Sorrento is home to the Moynihans. The three Moynihan sisters—Meg (Goodall), Hillary (Gillmer), and Pippa (Morice)—are reunited after 10 years by their father's sudden death. Lots of tensions, rivalries, and jealousies come to the surface as well as old secrets regarding a family tragedy. Talky film hasn't quite cast off its stage origins (it's adapted from a play by Hannie Rayson) but the performances are noteworthy. *CW:* Language. **112m/C VHS.** Caroline Goodall, Caroline Gillmer, Tara Morice, Joan Plowright, Ray Barrett, Ben Thomas; *D:* Richard Franklin; *W:* Richard Franklin, Peter Fitzpatrick; *C:* Geoff Burton; *M:* Nerida Tyson-Chew. Australian Film Institute '95: Best Adapted Screenplay, Best Supporting Actor (Barrett); Nominations: Australian Film Institute '95: Best Actress (Gillmer), Best Actress (Goodall), Best Director (Franklin), Best Film. *THV*

The Sorrow and the Pity ⁇⁇⁇½ 1971 A classic documentary depicting the life of a small French town and its resistance during the Nazi occupation. Lengthy, but totally compelling. A great documentary that brings home the atrocities of war. In French with English narration. **265m/B VHS, Beta.** *FR D:* Marcel Ophuls. National Board of Review Awards '72: 5 Best Foreign Films of the Year. *COL, OM*

Sorrowful Jones ⁇⁇ 1949 A "Little Miss Marker" remake, in which bookie Hope inherits a little girl as collateral for an unpaid bet. Good for a few yuks, but the original is much better. **88m/B VHS, Beta.** Bob Hope, Lucille Ball, William Demarest, Bruce Cabot, Thomas Gomez, Mary Jane Saunders; *D:* Sidney Lanfield; *W:* Jack Rose, Melville Shavelson; *C:* Daniel F. Fapp. *USH*

Sorrows of Gin ⁇⁇½ 1979 Eight-year-old girl searches for a sense of family amid her parents' lives. Her efforts to deal with alienation and emotional isolation lead her to run away from home. From a short story by John Cheever. **60m/C VHS, Beta.** Edward Herrmann, Sigourney Weaver, Mara Hobel, Eileen Heckart, Rachel Roberts. *FLI*

The Sorrows of Satan ⁇⁇⁇ 1926 Dempster and Cortez star as writers in love with each other, but Cortez can't take his poverty and the rejection of publishers. As he is about to end it all, the devil appears to him in disguise and makes an offer he can hardly refuse. He is introduced to London society and winds up marrying a fortune hunter. When he discovers this he goes back to Dempster, who still loves him, and vows to give up everything for her. Menjou then reveals himself to be the devil but Dempster's faith is so strong that the evil is vanquished. **111m/B VHS, Beta.** Adolphe Menjou, Carol Dempster, Ricardo Cortez, Lya de Putti; *D:* D.W. Griffith. *GPV*

Sorry, Wrong Number ⁇⁇⁇½ 1948 A wealthy, bedridden wife overhears two men plotting a murder on a crossed telephone line, and begins to suspect that one of the voices is her husband's. A classic tale of paranoia and suspense. Based on a radio play by Louise Fletcher, who also wrote the screenplay. Remade for television in 1989. **89m/B VHS, Beta, LV.** Barbara Stanwyck, Burt Lancaster, Ann Richards, Wendell Corey, Harold Vermilyea, Ed Begley Sr.; *D:* Anatole Litvak. Nominations: Academy Awards '48: Best Actress (Stanwyck). *PAR*

Sorry, Wrong Number ⁇½ 1989 Cable remake of the 1948 Barbara Stanwyck thriller about a bed-ridden woman trying to get help after she realizes she's being stalked by a killer. Offers a new twist (drug dealing), but doesn't even approach the Stanwyck original. From the story by Lucille Fletcher. **90m/C VHS, Beta, LV, Closed Caption.** Loni Anderson, Hal Holbrook, Patrick Macnee, Miguel Fernandez, Carl Weintraub; *D:* Tony Wharmby; *W:* Ann Louise Bardach; *M:* Bruce Broughton. *PAR*

S.O.S. Coast Guard ⁇⁇½ 1937 A fiendish scientist creates a disintegrating gas and the U.S. Coast Guard must stop him from turning it over to unfriendly foreigners. Loads of action in this 12-part serial. **224m/B VHS, LV.** Ralph Byrd, Bela Lugosi, Maxine Doyle. *NOS, SNC, REP*

S.O.S. Pacific ⁇⁇ 1960 A seaplane crashes on a nuclear-test island and the survivors find that they have only five hours before they get nuked. Even though there is plenty of the usual action one would expect from such a film, the story really revolves around the characters. The British and U.S. versions have different endings. **91m/B VHS.** *GB* Eddie Constantine, Pier Angeli, Richard Attenborough, John Gregson, Eva Bartok; *D:* Guy Green. *NOS*

S.O.S. Titanic ⁇⁇½ 1979 The story of the Titanic disaster, recounted in flashback, in docudrama style. James Costigan's teleplay of the familiar story focuses on the courage that accompanied the horror and tragedy. Thoroughly professional, absorbing made-for-TV drama. **102m/C**

VHS, Beta. *GB* David Janssen, Cloris Leachman, Susan St. James, David Warner, Ian Holm, Helen Mirren, Harry Andrews, David Battley, Ed Bishop, Peter Bourke, Shevaun Briars, Nick Brimble, Jacob Brooke, Catherine Byrne, Tony Caunter, Warren Clarke, Nicholas Davies, Deborah Fallender; *D:* Billy Hale; *W:* James Costigan; *C:* Christopher Challis; *M:* Howard Blake. *QHV*

Sotto, Sotto 🐾🐾½ **1985 (R)** A minor Wertmuller comedy about an Italian businessman who is constantly suspicious of his wife's fidelity. As it happens, she's attracted to another woman (de Santis). Massimo Wertmuller is Lina's nephew. Entertaining. In Italian with English subtitles. 104m/C VHS, Beta. *IT* Enrico Montesano, Veronica Lario, Massimo Wertmuller, Luisa de Santis; *D:* Lina Wertmuller; *W:* Lina Wertmuller. *COL, APD*

Soul-Fire 🐾🐾 **1925** South Pacific high seas induce Cupid's arrow. Silent. 100m/B VHS, Beta. Richard Barthelmess, Bessie Love, Walter Long, Arthur Metcalfe; *D:* John S. Robertson. *GPV, FCT, GVV*

Soul Hustler woof! **1976 (PG)** A con man becomes rich and famous as a tent-show evangelist. Pathetic drivel. 81m/C VHS, Beta. Fabian, Casey Kasem, Larry Bishop, Nai Bonet; *D:* Burt Topper. *LIV*

Soul Man 🐾🐾 **1986 (PG-13)** Denied the funds he expected for his Harvard tuition, a young white student (Howell) masquerades as a black in order to get a minority scholarship. As a black student at Harvard, Howell learns about racism and bigotry. Pleasant lightweight comedy with romance thrown in (Chong is the black girl he falls for), and with pretensions to social satire that it never achieves. 101m/C VHS, Beta, LV, Closed Caption. C. Thomas Howell, Rae Dawn Chong, James Earl Jones, Leslie Nielsen, Arye Gross; *D:* Steve Miner; *W:* Carol Black. *NWV, VTR*

Soul of the Beast 🐾½ **1923** An elephant repeatedly saves Bellamy from the villainous Beery. Silent with original organ score. 77m/B VHS, Beta, 8mm. Madge Bellamy, Cullen Landis, Noah Beery Sr. *GPV, VYY*

Soul of the Game 🐾🐾🐾 **1996** TV movie follows the lives of three talented players in the Negro League during the 1945 season as they await the potential integration of baseball. Brooklyn Dodgers general manager Branch Rickey (Herrmann) has his scouts focusing on three men in particular: flashy, aging pitcher Satchel Paige (Lindo), mentally unstable catcher Josh Gibson (Williamson), and the young, college-educated Jackie Robinson (Underwood). Manages to resist melodrama through terrific performances. 105m/C VHS. Delroy Lindo, Mykel T. Williamson, Blair Underwood, Edward Herrmann, R. Lee Ermey, Gina Ravera, Salli Richardson, Obba Babatunde, Brent Jennings; *D:* Kevin Rodney Sullivan; *W:* David Himmelstein; *C:* Sandi Sissel; *M:* Lee Holdridge. *HBO*

Soul Patrol 🐾 **1980 (R)** Black newspaper reporter clashes with the all-white police department in a racist city. 90m/C VHS, Beta. Nigel Davenport, Ken Gampu, Peter Dyneley; *D:* Christopher Rowley. *SUN*

Soul Vengeance 🐾 *Welcome Home Brother Charles* **1975** Black man is jailed and brutalized for crime he didn't commit and wants revenge when he's released. Many afros and platform shoes. Vintage blaxploitation. 91m/C VHS. Marlo Monte, Reatha Grey, Stan Kamber, Tiffany Peters, Ven Bigelow, Jake Carter; *D:* Jamaa Fanaka; *W:* Jamaa Fanaka. *XVC*

Souls at Sea 🐾🐾½ **1937** Good buddy work by Cooper and Raft highlight this complicated seafaring yarn. In the 1840's sailor and abolitionist Nuggin Taylor (Cooper) is secretly sabotaging slave ships, working undercover for the British Navy. With loyal friend Powdah (Raft), Taylor tries to gather evidence against British officer Tarryton (Wilcoxon) even though he's fallen for Tarryton's sister Margaret (Dee). But after a sea disaster, Taylor's accused of murder and brought to trial. Will the truth come out in time to save him? 93m/B VHS, Closed Caption. Gary Cooper, George Raft, Henry Wilcoxon, Frances Dee, Olympe Bradna, George Zucco, Harry Carey Sr., Robert Cummings, Por-

ter Hall, Joseph Schildkraut; *D:* Henry Hathaway; *W:* Dale Van Every, Grover Jones; *C:* Charles Lang Jr. *USH*

Soultaker 🐾½ **1990 (R)** The title spirit is after a young couple's souls, and they have just an hour to reunite with their bodies after a car crash. Meanwhile, they're in limbo (literally) between heaven and earth. The ending's OK, if you can make it that far. *CW:* Drug content. 94m/C VHS, LV. Joe Estevez, Vivian Schilling, Gregg Thomsen, David Shark, Jean Reiner, Chuck Williams, Robert Z'Dar; *D:* Michael Rissi; *W:* Vivian Schilling. *AIP*

The Sound and the Silence 🐾🐾½ **1993** Bio of inventor Alexander Graham Bell (Bach). The Scottish Bell's father was a speech specialist and his beloved mother Eliza (Fricker) was severely hearing impaired. Bell himself trained to work with the deaf in Boston and experimented with transmitting speech electronically—a project which only grew when Bell married the deaf Mable Hubbard (Quinn). Bell's lifelong devotion lead to his development of the telephone as well as numerous other inventions (and his founding of "National Geographic" magazine). Bell was hardly a lively character but this made for television drama is lavishly done. In two parts. 93m/C VHS. John Bach, Elizabeth Quinn, Brenda Fricker, Ian Bannen; *D:* John Kent Harrison; *W:* Tony Foster, William Schmidt, John Kent Harrison; *M:* John Charles. *TTC*

Sound of Horror 🐾½ *El Sonido de la Muerte; Sound From a Million Years Ago; The Prehistoric Sound* **1964** The Hound usually admires creative efforts to keep budgets down, but this is too much (or too little). A dinosaur egg hatches, and out lashes an invisible predator. Yes, you'll have to use your imagination as archaeologists are slashed to bits by the no-show terror. 85m/B VHS. *SP* James Philbrook, Arturo Fernandez, Soledad Miranda, Ingrid Pitt; *D:* Jose Antonio Nieves-Conde. *NOS, LOO*

Sound of Love 🐾 **1977** The mutual attraction between a deaf female hustler and a deaf race car driver leads to a deep relationship where they both learn about their own fears and desires. 74m/C VHS, Beta. Celia de Burgh, John Jarratt.

Sound of Murder **1982** A successful children's book writer wants to exact revenge on his adulterous wife, but is himself murdered before he can "execute" his plan. 114m/C VHS, Beta. Michael Moriarty, Joanna Miles. *LIV*

The Sound of Music 🐾🐾🐾🐾 **1965** The classic film version of the Rodgers and Hammerstein musical based on the true story of the singing von Trapp family of Austria and their escape from the Nazis just before WWII. Beautiful Salzburg, Austria location photography and an excellent cast. Andrews, fresh from her Oscar for "Mary Poppins," is effervescent, in beautiful voice, but occasionally too good to be true. Not Rodgers & Hammerstein's most innovative score, but lovely to hear and see. Plummer's singing was dubbed by Bill Lee. Marni Nixon, behind-the-scenes songstress for "West Side Story" and "My Fair Lady," makes her on-screen debut as one of the nuns. ♫I Have Confidence In Me; Something Good; The Sound of Music; Preludium; Morning Hymn; Alleluia; How Do You Solve A Problem Like Maria?; Sixteen, Going on Seventeen; My Favorite Things. 174m/C VHS, Beta, LV, Closed Caption. Julie Andrews, Christopher Plummer, Eleanor Parker, Peggy Wood, Charmian Carr, Heather Menzies, Marni Nixon, Richard Haydn, Anna Lee, Norma Varden, Nicholas Hammond, Angela Cartwright, Portia Nelson, Duane Chase, Debbie Turner, Kym Karath; *D:* Robert Wise; *W:* Ernest Lehman; *M:* Richard Rodgers, Oscar Hammerstein. Academy Awards '65: Best Adapted Score, Best Director (Wise), Best Film Editing, Best Picture, Best Sound; Directors Guild of America Awards '65: Best Director (Wise); Golden Globe Awards '66: Best Film—Musical/Comedy (Andrews), Best Film—Musical/Comedy; National Board of Review Awards '65: 10 Best Films of the Year; Nominations: Academy Awards '65: Best Actress (Andrews), Best Art Direction/Set Decoration (Color), Best Color Cinematography, Best Costume Design (Color), Best Supporting Actress (Wood). *FOX, BTV, RDG*

Sounder 🐾🐾🐾🐾 **1972 (G)** The struggles of a family of black sharecroppers in rural Louisiana during the Depression. When the father is sentenced to jail for stealing in order to feed his family, they must pull together even more, and one son finds education to be his way out of poverty. Tyson brings strength and style to her role, with fine help from Winfield. Moving and well made, with little sentimentality and superb acting from a great cast. Adapted from the novel by William Armstrong. 105m/C VHS, Beta, LV, Closed Caption. Paul Winfield, Cicely Tyson, Kevin Hooks, Taj Mahal, Carmen Mathews, James Best, Janet MacLachlan; *D:* Martin Ritt; *W:* Lonne Elder III; *C:* John A. Alonzo; *M:* Taj Mahal. National Board of Review Awards '72: 10 Best Films of the Year, Best Actress (Tyson); National Society of Film Critics Awards '72: Best Actress (Tyson); Nominations: Academy Awards '72: Best Actor (Winfield), Best Actress (Tyson), Best Adapted Screenplay, Best Picture. *KUI, PAR, PTB*

Sounds of Silence 🐾🐾 **1991** A young deaf boy fears that a killer arsonist may be at large—but can he prove it? One of a number of obscure oddities featuring former youth idol Donahue. 108m/C VHS, Beta. Troy Donahue, Peter Nelson. *NO*

Soup for One 🐾🐾½ **1982 (R)** Writer-director Kaufer's first film is a solid entry in the Woody Allen-esque Manhattanite's angst genre. Young Jewish guy Rubinek pines for the woman of his dreams, finds her, is rejected, persists, gets her, wonders if she's what he wants after all. If you like Woody Allen, this is worth seeing. 84m/C VHS, Beta. Saul Rubinek, Marcia Strassman, Gerrit Graham, Richard Libertini, Andrea Martin; *D:* Jonathan Kaufer. *WAR*

Sourdough 🐾🐾 **1977** Fur trapper Perry escapes the hustle and bustle of modern life by fleeing to the Alaskan wilderness. Near-plotless travelog depends heavily on scenery—and there's plenty of that, for sure. 94m/C VHS, Beta, LV, Closed Caption. Gil Perry, Charles Brock, Slim Carlson, Carl Clark; *D:* Martin J. Spinelli. *IMP*

Sous Sol 🐾🐾 *Not Me* **1996** In 1967 Montreal, overly-sensitive 11-year-old Rene (Moffatt) spies on his parents while they make love and the next morning learns his father has died. Rene becomes certain that sex leads to death, which puts a crimp in his budding sexuality. As a matter of fact he literally refuses to grow up, remaining in his pre-adolescent state for several years while Mom Reine (Portal) eventually hooks up with a new boyfriend Roch (Godin), who moves in. This causes a few more problems for Rene. French with subtitles. 90m/C VHS. *CA* Louise Portal, Richard Moffatt, Isabelle Pasco, Patrice Godin; *D:* Pierre Gang; *W:* Pierre Gang; *C:* Pierre Mignot; *M:* Anne Bourne, Ken Myrh. Genie Awards '96: Best Original Screenplay; Nominations: Genie Awards '96: Best Actress (Portal). *NYR*

South Beach 🐾🐾 **1992 (R)** Two ex-football players turned private eyes are living the good life and partying it up in Miami Beach. However, their leisurely lifestyles are soon disrupted when they accept a mysterious challenge from the beautiful Vanity. *CW:* Strong violence and sexuality. 93m/C VHS. Fred Williamson, Gary Busey, Vanity, Peter Fonda; *D:* Fred Williamson; *W:* Mark Montgomery; *M:* Joe Renzetti. *PSM*

South Beach Academy 🐾 **1996 (R)** Eye candy focusing on a beach school that specializes in surfing, swimming, and volleyball rather than the usual academics. Maybe that's why the school's about to close—unless the lightly-clad student body can come up with a plan to save their alma mater. 91m/C VHS, Closed Caption. Corey Feldman, Al Lewis, James Hong, Elizabeth Kaitan; *D:* Joe Esposito. *LIV*

South Bronx Heroes 🐾½ *The Runaways; Revenge of the Innocents* **1985 (R)** A police officer helps two children when they discover their foster home is the headquarters for a pornography ring. 105m/C VHS, Beta. Brendan Ward, Mario Van Peebles, Megan Van Peebles, Melissa Esposito, Martin Zurla, Jordan Abeles; *D:* William Szarka. *NO*

South Central 🎬🎬 1992 (R) A low-budget urban drama set in a gang-infested L.A. neighborhood. Bobby is a young black man, and former gang leader, who has spent ten years in prison for murder. His wife has become a drug addict and his young son Jimmie has begun running with his dad's old gang. Now paroled, Bobby hopes to re-establish the bond with his son—enough to protect him from following in his nowhere-to-go-but-down footsteps. Worthy effort with an emotional ending. Feature debut of director Anderson. Based on the novel "Crips" by Donald Bakeer. **CW:** Language and gang violence and drug content. 99m/C VHS, Beta, LV, Closed Caption. Glenn Plummer, Carl Lumbly, Christian Coleman, LaRita Shelby, Byron Keith Minns; **D:** Steve Anderson; **W:** Steve Anderson. *WAR, PMS*

South of Hell Mountain 🎬½ 1970 (R) On the run from a gold mine robbery where they left 20 dead, the McHenry brothers meet a mother-daughter team that slows them down. 87m/C VHS, Beta. Ann Stewart, Sam Hall, Nicol Britton; **D:** William Sachs, Louis Leahman. *MGM*

South of Monterey 🎬½ 1947 Western adventure with the Cisco kid. 63m/B VHS, Beta. Gilbert Roland, Martin Garralaga, Frank Yaconelli, Marjorie Riordan; **D:** William Nigh. *VCN*

South of Pago Pago 🎬🎬½ 1940 The unsuspecting natives of a tropical isle are exploited by a gang of pirates searching for a seabed of rare pearls. A notch up from most similar adventure outings, with great violent action and excellent cinematography. Leading lady Farmer was thought to be a rising star, but retired at 29 in 1942 because of alcoholism and spent some time in mental institutions. "Frances" (1982), with Jessica Lange, is based on her life. 98m/B VHS, Beta. Victor McLaglen, Jon Hall, Frances Farmer, Gene Lockhart; **D:** Alfred E. Green. *NO*

South of Reno 🎬🎬½ 1987 (R) A man living a secluded life in the desert dreams of moving to Reno and learns his wife is cheating on him. Odd, minimal plot. Impressive first feature for Polish diretor Rezyka, who cut his teeth on music videos. 98m/C VHS, LV. Jeffery Osterhage, Lisa Blount, Joe Phelan, Lewis Van Bergen, Julia Montgomery, Brandis Kemp, Danitza Kingsley, Mary Grace Canfield, Bert Remsen; **D:** Mark Rezyka; **M:** Nigel Holton. *REP*

South of St. Louis 🎬🎬½ 1948 A peaceful cattle rancher turns renegade gunrunner during the Civil War when his stock is destroyed by Union guerrillas. Overplotted but exciting and action-packed western, with Smith dazzling in a plethora of costumes. 88m/C VHS. Joel McCrea, Zachary Scott, Victor Jory, Douglas Kennedy, Alexis Smith, Alan Hale, Dorothy Malone; **D:** Ray Enright; **C:** Karl Freund; **M:** Max Steiner. *REP*

South of Santa Fe 🎬🎬 1932 Mexican rebels give the hero a hard time in this standard Western. 60m/B VHS. Bob Steele, Janis Elliott, Chris-Pin Martin, Jack Clifford, Eddie Dunn, Robert Burns, Hank Bell, Allan Garcia; **D:** Bert Glennon. *NOS*

South of Santa Fe 🎬🎬 1942 Rogers and friends take on the mob—yes, the mob, armed with machine guns and airplanes—after they are falsely implicated in a crime. In lulls between the rootin' tootin' gunfights, Rogers belts out "We're Headin' for the Home Corral," "Down the Trail," and "Open Range Ahead." 60m/B VHS, Beta. Roy Rogers, George "Gabby" Hayes, Linda Hayes, Paul Fix, Judy Clark; **D:** Joseph Kane. *NOS, DVT, CAB*

South of the Border 🎬🎬 1939 Autry and Burnette are government agents sent to Mexico to investigate a possible revolution instigated by foreign agents. Propaganda-heavy singing western appeared just before the U.S. entered WWII; did well at the box office and boosted Autry's career. 70m/B VHS, Beta. Gene Autry, Smiley Burnette. *CCB, VCN*

South of the Rio Grande 🎬½ 1945 The Cisco Kid rides again as he comes to the aid of a rancher whose horses were stolen. Garden-variety law-and-order western. 60m/B VHS, Beta. Duncan Renaldo; **D:** Lambert Hillyer. *NO*

South Pacific 🎬🎬🎬½ 1958 A young American Navy nurse and a Frenchman fall in love during WWII. Expensive production included much location shooting in Hawaii. Based on Rodgers and Hammerstein's musical; not as good as the play, but pretty darn good still. The play in turn was based on James Michener's novel "Tales of the South Pacific." ♫My Girl Back Home; Dites-Moi; Bali Ha'i; Happy Talk; A Cockeyed Optimist; Soliloquies; Some Enchanted Evening; Bloody Mary; I'm Gonna Wash That Man Right Out of My Hair. 167m/C VHS, Beta, LV, Closed Caption. Mitzi Gaynor, Rossano Brazzi, Ray Walston, France Nuyen, John Kerr, Juanita Hall, Tom Laughlin; **D:** Joshua Logan; **C:** Leon Shamroy; **M:** Richard Rodgers, Oscar Hammerstein; **V:** Giorgio Tozzi. Academy Awards '58: Best Sound; Nominations: Academy Awards '58: Best Color Cinematography, Scoring of a Musical. *FOX, RDG, HMV*

South Riding 🎬🎬½ 1937 Estate owner Robert Carne (Richardson) lives with teenaged daughter Midge (Johns) and has money woes from keeping ill wife Madge (Todd) in a mental hospital. A city councilman as well, Carne's drawn into a plan that will supposedly built decent housing for the lower classes but is actually a scam (which he discovers). Adapted from the novel by Winifred Holtby. 85m/B VHS. *GB* Ralph Richardson, John Clements, Edna Best, Glynis Johns, Ann Todd, Edmund Gwenn, Marie Lohr, Milton Rosmer; **D:** Victor Saville; **W:** Ian Dalrymple; **C:** Harry Stradling; **M:** Richard Addinsell. *KIV*

South Seas Massacre woof! 19?? A cop and a prisoner, shackled together, try to survive modern-day pirates, natives, and each other. They may make it through, but viewers may wish they didn't. 60m/C VHS, Beta. Troy Donahue; **D:** Pablo Santiago. *PSM*

Southern Comfort 🎬🎬🎬 1981 (R) A group of National Guardsmen are on weekend maneuvers in the swamps of Louisiana. They run afoul of some of the local Cajuns, and are marked for death in this exciting and disturbing thriller. Boothe is excellent in a rare exploration of a little-understood way of life. Lots of blood. If you belong to the National Guard, this could make you queasy. 106m/C VHS, Beta, LV. Powers Boothe, Keith Carradine, Fred Ward, Franklyn Seales, Brion James, T.K. Carter, Peter Coyote; **D:** Walter Hill; **W:** Walter Hill, David Giler, Michael Kane; **M:** Ry Cooder. *HHE*

A Southern Yankee 🎬🎬½ *My Hero* 1948 Skelton plays a bumbling bellboy who ends up as a Union spy during the Civil War. Enjoyable comedy, thanks largely to the off-screen input of Buster Keaton. 90m/B VHS, Beta. Red Skelton, Brian Donlevy, Arlene Dahl, George Coulouris, Lloyd Gough, John Ireland, Minor Watson, Charles Dingle, Art Baker, Reed Hadley, Arthur Space, Addison Richards, Joyce Compton, Paul Harvey, Jeff Corey; **D:** Edward Sedgwick. *MGM*

The Southerner 🎬🎬🎬🎬 1945 A man used to working for others is given some land by an uncle and decides to pack up his family and try farming for himself. They find hardships as they struggle to support themselves. A superb, naturalistic celebration of a family's fight to survive amid all the elements. From the story "Hold Autumn in Your Hand," by George Sessions Perry. Novelist Faulkner had an uncredited hand in the script. He thought Renoir the best contemporary director, and later said "The Southerner" gave him more pleasure than any of his other Hollywood work (though this is faint praise; Faulkner is said to have hated Hollywood). 91m/B VHS, Beta, 8mm. Zachary Scott, Betty Field, Beulah Bondi, Norman Lloyd, Bunny Sunshine, Jay Gilpin, Estelle Taylor, Blanche Yurka, Percy Kilbride, J. Carrol Naish; **D:** Jean Renoir; **W:** Hugo Butler, William Faulkner, Jean Renoir. National Board of Review Awards '45: Best Director (Renoir); Venice Film Festival '46: Best Film; Nominations: Academy Awards '45: Best Director

(Renoir), Best Sound, Original Dramatic/Comedy Score. *NOS, PSM, VYY*

Southward Ho! 🎬🎬 1939 In the first western to team Rogers with sidekick Gabby Hayes, they portray ranchers investigating bloodshed in their valley, Roy meanwhile yodelin' four tunes. Fun outing. 56m/B VHS, Beta. Roy Rogers, George "Gabby" Hayes. *NOS, VCN, CAB*

Souvenir 🎬🎬 1988 (R) A German soldier returns to France after WWII to find the woman he left behind and the daughter he never saw. Might have been good, but too melodramatic and overwrought, with lukewarm acting. 93m/C VHS, Beta, LV, Closed Caption. Christopher Plummer, Catherine Hicks, Christopher Cazenove, Michael Lonsdale; **D:** Geoffrey Reeve. *PAR*

Soviet Spy 🎬🎬 1961 A French docu-drama written by Hans Otto Meissner, Chief of Protocol at the German Embassy in Tokyo during WWII, about the journalist Richard Sorge, a German hanged in 1944 for supplying information to the Soviets. In French with subtitles. 130m/B VHS, Beta. *FR FCT*

Soylent Green 🎬🎬½ 1973 (PG) In the 21st Century, hard-boiled police detective Heston investigates a murder and discovers what soylent green—the people's principal food—is made of. Robinson's final film is a disappointing end to a great career. Its view of the future and of human nature is relentlessly dark. Don't watch it with kids. 95m/C VHS, Beta, LV. Charlton Heston, Leigh Taylor-Young, Chuck Connors, Joseph Cotten, Edward G. Robinson, Brock Peters; **D:** Richard Fleischer. *MGM*

Space Jam 🎬🎬½ 1996 (PG) Expensive live action-animation combo finds basketball great Jordan forced to play ball against evil intergalatic invaders who are out to capture Bugs Bunny and the rest of the Looney Tunes characters. It's all fairly silly but the kids will enjoy it. 87m/C VHS, DVD. Michael Jordan, Bill Murray, Wayne Knight, Theresa Randle; **D:** Joe Pytka; **M:** Michael Chapman; **M:** James Newton Howard; **V:** Danny DeVito. Nominations: MTV Movie Awards '96: Best Song ("I Believe I Can Fly"). *WAR*

Space Marines 🎬½ 1996 (R) Cheesy cable thriller finds intergalactic marines battling 21st century space pirates who've stolen a nuclear cargo and taken hostages. 93m/C VHS, Closed Caption. Billy Wirth, John Pyper-Ferguson, Meg Foster, Edward Albert, James Shigeta, Cady Huffman; **D:** John Weidner; **C:** Garett Griffin. *REP*

Space Monster woof! *First Woman Into Space; Voyage Beyond the Sun* 1964 Really bad, low-budget flick with a rubber monster and a climactic crash into a "sea of monsters" which is really a fish tank full of crabs. Ultra cheap production with handed down cast and props. ?m/B VHS. *SMW*

Space Mutiny 🎬 1988 (PG) Spaceship falls under the attack of the mutinous Kalgan. To keep everyone from being sold into slavery, a small band of loyal passengers strike back. Will they be successful in thwarting the attack? Who cares? 93m/C VHS, Beta. Reb Brown, James Ryan, John Phillip Law, Cameron Mitchell; **D:** David Winters; **W:** Maria Dante. *AIP*

Space: 1999 1975 Landau and Bain star as the leaders of Moonbase Alpha, a scientific outpost which is hurled out of orbit by a nuclear explosion. In "Voyager's Return" the crew of Moonbase Alpha discover the original Voyager probe and excitedly prepare to extract its vast knowledge of the universe. To their horror, they discover that it has somehow been transformed into a planet-destroying monster. Bitter aliens are coming to exact their revenge on the machine and the crew is caught in the middle! Additional episodes available. 52m/C VHS, LV. *GB* Martin Landau, Barbara Bain, Barry Morse, Nick Tate, Jeremy Kemp, Barry Stokes, Alex Scott, Lawrence Trimble; **D:** Bob Kellett. *MOV*

Space: 1999—Alien Attack 🎬🎬🎬 1979 After an explosion on the moon, Moonbase Alpha loses contact with Earth forever. Pilot episode of the popular British sci-fi series. 109m/C

VHS, Beta. *GB* Martin Landau, Barbara Bain, Barry Morse, Nick Tate, Roy Dotrice, Philip Madoc, Lou Satton, Eric Carte; **D:** Lee H. Katzin. *LIV*

Space Ninja: Sword of the Space Ark ♂½ 1981
A young fighter pilot returns home to find his planet under siege and his family dead. He vows to seek revenge and sets out to destroy the evil emperor who is wreaking such havoc. 75m/C **VHS, Beta. D:** Bunker Jenkins. *LIV*

Space Patrol 1950
Buzz Corey, Commander-in-Chief of the Space Patrol, tries to maintain interplanetary peace and protect the people of Earth's neighboring planets. These episodes television series include previews of coming attractions from classic science fiction films. Additional episodes are available. 120m/B **VHS, Beta.** Edward Kemmer, Lyn Osborn. *MED, MOV*

Space Rage ♂ Trackers 1986 (R)
A criminal sentenced to life on a prison planet leads a revolt of the inmates. Lame, formula western set in outer space. 78m/C **VHS, Beta.** Michael Pare, Richard Farnsworth, John Laughlin, Lee Purcell; **D:** Conrad Palmisano. *LIV*

Space Raiders ♂♂ Star Child 1983 (PG)
A plucky 10-year-old blasts off into a futuristic world of intergalactic desperados, crafty alien mercenaries, starship battles and cliff-hanging dangers. Recycled special effects (from producer Corman's movie factory) and plot (lifted near-whole from "Star Wars"). 84m/C **VHS, Beta.** Vince Edwards, David Mendenhall; **D:** Howard R. Cohen; **W:** Howard R. Cohen. *WAR*

Space Riders woof! 1983 (PG)
Action-adventure about the world's championship motorcycle race, with a rock soundtrack featuring Duran Duran, Simple Minds and Melba Moore. 93m/C **VHS, Beta.** Barry Sheene, Gavan O'Herlihy, Toshiya Ito, Stephanie McLean, Sayo Inaba; **D:** Joe Massot. *NO*

Space Soldiers Conquer the Universe ♂♂ 1940
Edited version of the Flash Gordon serial "Flash Gordon Conquers the Universe." The evil Emperor Ming introduces a horrible plague from outer space called "The Purple Death." Dr. Zarkov, Dale, and Flash Gordon travel from the frozen wastes of Frigia to the palaces of Mongo and must take risk after risk. Twelve chapters at 20 minutes each. 240m/B **VHS, Beta.** Buster Crabbe, Charles Middleton, Carol Hughes. *NOS, CAB*

Spaceballs ♂♂½ 1987 (PG)
A humorous Brooks parody of recent science fiction pictures, mostly notably "Star Wars," with references to "Alien," the "Star Trek series," and "The Planet of the Apes." Disappointingly tame and tentative, but chuckle-laden enough for Brooks fans. The great man himself appears in two roles, including puny wise man/wise guy Yogurt. 96m/C **VHS, Beta, LV, Closed Caption.** Mel Brooks, Rick Moranis, John Candy, Bill Pullman, Daphne Zuniga, Dick Van Patten, John Hurt, George Wyner, Joan Rivers, Lorene Yarnell, Sal Viscuso, Stephen Tobolowsky, Dom DeLuise, Michael Winslow; **D:** Mel Brooks; **W:** Mel Brooks, Ronny Graham, Thomas Meehan; **M:** John Morris. *MGM*

Spaced Invaders ♂½ 1990 (PG)
Five ultra-cool aliens crash-land in a small midwestern town at Halloween. Local denizens mistake them for trick-or-treaters. Poorly made and a waste of time. 102m/C **VHS, Beta, LV, Closed Caption.** Douglas Barr, Royal Dano, Ariana Richards, Kevin Thompson, Jimmy Briscoe, Tony Cox, Debbie Lee Carrington, Tommy Madden; **D:** Patrick Read Johnson; **W:** Scott Lawrence Alexander; **C:** James L. Carter. *TOU*

Spaced Out woof! Outer Reach 1980 (R)
Naughty sci-fi sex comedy that parodies everything from "Star Wars" to "2001," though not very well. The sultry female aliens are visually pleasing, though. Watch this one with the sound turned off. 85m/C **VHS, Beta.** Barry Stokes, Glory Annen; **D:** Norman J. Warren. *NO*

Spacehunter: Adventures in the Forbidden Zone ♂½ 1983 (PG)
Galactic bounty hunter agrees to rescue three damsels held captive by a cyborg. Strauss ain't no Harrison Ford. Filmed in 3-D, but who cares? 90m/C **VHS, Beta, LV, Closed Caption.** *CA* Peter Strauss, Molly Ringwald, Michael Ironside, Ernie Hudson, Andrea Marcovicci; **D:** Lamont Johnson; **W:** Len Blum; **M:** Elmer Bernstein. *COL*

Spaceship ♂½ The Creature Wasn't Nice; Naked Space 1981 (PG)
Misguided attempt to spoof creature-features. Mad scientist tries to protect kindly monster from crazed crew. Not very funny, with the exception of the song-and-dance routine by the monster. 88m/C **VHS.** Cindy Williams, Bruce Kimmel, Leslie Nielsen, Gerrit Graham, Patrick Macnee, Ron Kurowski; **D:** Bruce Kimmel. *LIV*

Spaceways ♂½ 1953
Scientist Duff is beset by all sorts of troubles: his experimental rockets explode, his wife has an affair with an ambitious scientist, and when they disappear together, he's accused of killing them and placing their bodies in the exploded rocket. All in all, a pretty bad (and long) day for our hero. Why should we suffer through it with him? 76m/C **VHS, Beta, LV.** Howard Duff, Eva Bartok, Ceclie Cheyreau, Andrew Osborn; **D:** Terence Fisher. *MLB*

Spaghetti House ♂½ 1982
A handful of waiters are held hostage by ruthless killers in this innocuous but worthless Italian comedy. Dubbed. 103m/C **VHS, Beta.** *IT* Nino Manfredi, Rita Tushingham; **D:** Giullo Paradisi. *NO*

Spaghetti Western ♂½ 1969
A farmer and a publisher take on the vile oil baron who is taking over the town. A parody-or is it?—of Eastwoodian B-grade spaghetti westerns. No director credited. 90m/C **VHS, Beta.** Franco Nero, Martin Balsam, Sterling Hayden. *VDC*

Spalding Gray: Terrors of Pleasure 1988
The ultra-cool Gray tells the story of one man's dream to own land in his own inimitable way. HBO comedy special. 60m/C **VHS, Beta.** Spalding Gray; **D:** Thomas Schlamme. *HBO*

Spangles ♂ 1926
Silent circus drama. 58m/B **VHS, Beta.** Marion Nixon, Hobart Bosworth, Pat O'Malley, Gladys Brockwell; **D:** Frank O'Connor. *GPV*

The Spaniard's Curse ♂♂½ 1958
When a man is convicted for a murder he did not commit, he puts a curse on the judge and jury responsible. Mysteriously, the marked people begin dying. Is he responsible? Then he dies and the mystery thickens. Intriguing but sloppy murder mystery. 80m/B **VHS, Beta.** *GB* Tony Wright, Lee Patterson, Michael Hordern, Ralph Truman, Henry Oscar; **D:** Ralph Kemplen. *SNC*

The Spanish Gardener ♂♂♂ 1957
A boy in a prominent family spends more time with the gentle gardner than with the domineering father, so dad arranges for his rival to be framed and sent to prison. An affecting British adaptation of the A.J. Cronin novel, turned into a showcase for Bogarde in the title role. 95m/C **VHS.** Dirk Bogarde, Jon Whiteley, Michael Hordern, Cyril Cusack, Maureen Swanson, Lyndon Brook, Josephine Griffin, Bernard Lee; **D:** Philip Leacock. *VEC*

The Spanish Main ♂♂½ 1945
Typical, gusto-laden swashbuckler, RKO's first in Technicolor. Evil Spanish governor Slezak captures Dutch crew led by Henreid. They escape and kidnap his fiancee (O'Hara) off a ship coming from Mexico. Henreid forces her to marry him, but his crew uses the might of the armada and returns O'Hara to Slezak behind Henreid's back. Wow! 100m/C **LV.** Paul Henreid, Maureen O'Hara, Walter Slezak, Binnie Barnes, John Emery, Barton MacLane; **D:** Frank Borzage; **C:** George Barnes. Nominations: Academy Awards '45: Best Color Cinematography. *IME*

Spanking the Monkey ♂♂♂ 1994 (R)
"What'd ya do on your summer vacation?" Ray Aibelli (Davies) has an interesting answer in this dark comedy about family dysfunction, sexual politics, incest and masturbation, topics which guarantee it a special place on the video shelf. Returning from his freshman year at M.I.T., Ray learns he must give up a prestigious internship to care for his bedridden mother (Watson) while Dad goes on an extended "business" trip. Much sexual and emotional confusion follows. Mom, it seems, is rather attractive, controlling, and in need of hands-on assistance. Black comedy is understated and sensitive, focusing attention on the story and characters rather than the delicate subject matter, but you'll be aware of the delicate subject matter, nonetheless. Sharp directorial debut by Russell features fine performances by mostly unknown cast, elevating low-budget feel. See it with a relative. *CW:* mature themes, nudity, incest, sexual situations, minor violence 99m/C **VHS, LV.** Jeremy Davies, Alberta Watson, Benjamin Hendrickson, Carla Gallo, Matthew Puckett; **D:** David O. Russell; **W:** David O. Russell. Independent Spirit Awards '95: Best First Feature; Sundance Film Festival '94: Audience Award; Nominations: Independent Spirit Awards '95: Best Supporting Actress (Gallo), Debut Performance (Davies). *NLC, IME*

Spare Parts woof! 1985
Guests at a remote hotel discover that it is run by black marketeers who kill guests and sell the body parts. Of course, they don't bother signing out. 108m/C **VHS, Beta.** Judith Speidel, Wolf Roth. *THV*

Sparkle ♂♂½ 1976 (PG)
The saga of three singing sisters struggling to rise to the top of the charts in the 1950s. Sound familiar? Well done but cliched fictional version of the Supremes' career. McKee shines. Alcohol, drugs, and mobsters get in the way. Excellent musical score. 98m/C **VHS, Beta.** Irene Cara, Lonette McKee, Dwan Smith, Philip Michael Thomas, Mary Alice, Dorian Harewood, Tony King; **D:** Sam O'Steen; **W:** Joel Schumacher; **M:** Curtis Mayfield. *WAR*

Sparrows ♂♂♂ 1926
A woman cares for nine orphan children on an impoverished farm, warding off starvation and kidnappers. Silent melodrama features notable performance by Pickford, and a musical score. 81m/B **VHS, Beta, LV.** Mary Pickford, Roy Stewart, Gustav von Seyffertitz; **D:** William Beaudine; **C:** Charles Rosher; **M:** William Perry. *NOS, CCB, DVT*

Spartacus ♂♂♂♂ 1960 (PG-13)
The true story of a gladiator who leads other slaves in a rebellion against the power of Rome in 73 B.C. The rebellion is put down and the rebels are crucified. Douglas, whose political leanings are amply on display herein, also served as executive producer, surrounding himself with the best talent available. Magnificent climactic battle scene features 8,000 real, live Spanish soldiers to stunning effect. A version featuring Kubrick's "director's cut" is also available, featuring a restored, controversial homoerotic bath scene with Olivier and Curtis. Anthony Mann is uncredited as co-director. A box-office triumph that gave Kubrick much-desired financial independence. 196m/C **VHS, Beta, LV, Closed Caption.** Kirk Douglas, Laurence Olivier, Jean Simmons, Tony Curtis, Charles Laughton, Herbert Lom, Nina Foch, Woody Strode, Peter Ustinov, John Gavin, John Ireland, Charles McGraw, Joanna Barnes; **D:** Stanley Kubrick; **W:** Dalton Trumbo; **C:** Russell Metty; **M:** Alex North. Academy Awards '60: Best Art Direction/Set Decoration (Color), Best Color Cinematography, Best Costume Design (Color), Best Supporting Actor (Ustinov); Golden Globe Awards '61: Best Film—Drama; Nominations: Academy Awards '60: Best Film Editing, Original Dramatic/Comedy Score. *USH, APD, BTV*

Spasms woof! Death Bite 1982 (R)
Reed is the unfortunate big game hunter who encounters The Demon Serpent, known as N'Gana Simbu, the deadliest snake in the world. Lame-brained horror fantasy; the producers should have released the nifty Tangerine Dream soundtrack and chucked the movie. 92m/C **VHS, Beta.** *CA* Peter Fonda, Oliver Reed; **D:** William Fruet. *NO*

Spawn 1997 Todd McFarlane's comic book creation makes his cable TV animated debut. Hellspawn was once human CIA assassin Al Simmons, murdered in the line of duty, who sold his soul to see his wife one last time. When he comes back from the grave with superhuman powers it's again as a killer with attitude, who leaves a high body count. A PG-13 version clocks in at 90 minutes. 147m/C VHS. HBO

Spawn 🎬🎬🎬 1997 (PG-13) Government agent Al Simmons (White) returns to earth, six years after being murdered, in the form of Spawn, a hell-born creature with supernatural powers. He wants to avenge his death and also save his loved ones from the evil Violator (Leguizamo). With green eyes and a friendship with Satan, Spawn's more of a lethal weapon and way more sinister looking than the villain. An unrecognizable Leguizamo and sleazy Sheen team up as adequate adversaries. Extravagant special effects, and a complex, dark story put a unique spin on the over-exposed superhero premise. Adapted from the best-selling comic book. ?m/C VHS. Michael Jai White, John Leguizamo, Martin Sheen, Theresa Randle, D.B. Sweeney, Nicol Williamson, Alan B. McElroy; **D:** Mark Dippe; **W:** Todd McFarlane; **C:** Guillermo Navarro; **M:** Graeme Revell. NYR

The Spawning 🎬 1982 (R) The sequel to "Piranha." At Club Elysium the main course is the vacationers themselves. 88m/C VHS, Beta, LV. Steve Marachuk; **D:** James Cameron. NO

Speak Easily 🎬🎬½ 1932 Keaton is bored with his dull life as a college professor. Durante tries to spice things up with a phony inheritance letter, and Keaton decides to spend his supposed money backing a stage show. Keaton is the star, but Durante steals the show. Great supporting cast. 82m/B VHS. Buster Keaton, Jimmy Durante, Ruth Selwyn, Thelma Todd, Hedda Hopper, Sidney Toler, Lawrence Grant, Henry Armetta, Edward Brophy; **D:** Edward Sedgwick. MGM, GPV, NOS

Speak of the Devil 🎬 1990 A New Orleans evangelist who seduces his followers moves to Los Angeles and strikes a bargain with Satan. Exploitative, unthinking spoof of Swaggart/Bakker scandals of recent years. 99m/C VHS. Robert Elarton, Jean Miller, Bernice Tamara Goor, Louise Sherill, Walter Kay, Shawn Patrick Greenfield. AIP

Speaking Parts 🎬🎬🎬 1989 VCR-obsessed laundry worker and another woman battle for the attention of bit-part actor McManus who works in ritzy hotel. A telling picture of the inextricable nature of modern technology. 92m/C VHS, LV. **CA** Michael McManus, Arsinee Khanjian, David Hemblen, Gabrielle Rose, Tony Nardi, Patricia Collins, Gerard Parkes; **D:** Atom Egoyan; **W:** Atom Egoyan; **M:** Mychael Danna. FXL, FCT

Special Bulletin 🎬🎬🎬 1983 A pacifistic terrorist threatens to blow up Charleston, South Carolina with a nuclear warhead. Done quite well in docu-drama style as a TV news bulletin. Interesting examination of the media's treatment of dramatic events. Top-notch made-for-TV fare. 105m/C VHS, Beta. Ed Flanders, Christopher Allport, Kathryn Walker, Roxanne Hart; **D:** Edward Zwick; **W:** Marshall Herskovitz, Edward Zwick. BAR, ORI, WAR

A Special Day 🎬🎬🎬 Una Giornata Speciale; The Great Day 1977 The day of a huge rally celebrating Hitler's visit to Rome in 1939 serves as the backdrop for an affair between weary housewife Loren and lonely, unhappy homosexual radio announcer Mastroianni. Good performances from two thorough pros make a depressing film well worth watching. In Italian with English subtitles or dubbed. 105m/C VHS, Beta, LV. **CA** Sophia Loren, Marcello Mastroianni, John Vernon, Francoise Berd; **D:** Ettore Scola; **W:** Ettore Scola, Ruggero Maccari, Maurizio Costanzo; **C:** Pasquale De Santis; **M:** Armando Travaioli. Golden Globe Awards '78: Best Foreign Film; National Board of Review Awards '77: 5 Best Foreign Films of the Year; Nominations: Academy Awards '77: Best Actor (Mastroianni), Best Foreign Language Film. COL, APD

Special Delivery 🎬🎬½ 1976 (PG) Three unemployed Vietnam veterans decide to rob a bank but their getaway plans go awry. Svenson, the only robber who escapes, stashes the cash in a mailbox only to have it discovered by nutty artist, Shepherd, and crooked barkeep Gwynne. 99m/C VHS, Beta. Bo Svenson, Cybill Shepherd, Vic Tayback, Michael C. Gwynne, Tom Atkins, Sorrell Booke, Deidre Hall, Gerrit Graham, Jeff Goldblum; **D:** Paul Wendkos; **C:** Harry Stradling Jr.; **M:** Lalo Schifrin. LIV, VES

Special Effects 🎬🎬 1985 (R) A desperate movie director murders a young actress, then makes a movie about her death. Solid, creepy premise sinks in the mire of flawed execution; a good film about Hollywood ego trips and obsession is lurking inside overdone script. 103m/C VHS, Beta. Zoe Tamerlis, Eric Bogosian, Brad Rijn, Bill Oland, Richard Greene; **D:** Larry Cohen; **W:** Larry Cohen. NLC

Special Forces 🎬 Hell in Normandy 1968 Eight specially trained soldiers drop behind enemy lines to rescue prisoners of war in WWII. 90m/ C VHS, Beta. Peter Lee Lawrence, Guy Madison, Erika Blanc, Tony Norton. NO

Special Investigator 🎬🎬½ 1936 Dix is a criminal attorney who specializes in getting his mob clients freed. Then his FBI brother gets killed by the same criminals he's been defending. So Dix becomes a special agent and sets out to get the mob boss responsible for his brother's murder. Climax is the big shootout at the gang's hideaway. Based on the novel by Earle Stanley Gardner. 60m/B VHS. Richard Dix, J. Carrol Naish, Margaret Callahan, Erik Rhodes, Owen Davis Jr., Ray Mayer, Joseph Sawyer; **D:** Louis King. GPV

Special Olympics 1978 A father attempts to care for his three sons, one of whom is mentally retarded, following the death of his wife. Made for television. 104m/C VHS, Beta. Charles Durning, Philip Brown, George Parry, Irene Tedrow, Mare Winningham, Herb Edelman, Debra Winger, Constance McCashin; **D:** Lee Philips. GEM

Special Police 🎬🎬½ 1985 Police inspector protecting old friend's murder-witnessing sister learns that important politicians are involved with a seedy underground political movement. French thriller also available dubbed. 92m/C VHS. FR Richard Berry, Carole Bouquet, Fanny Cottencon; **D:** Michael Vianey; **W:** Michael Vianey. FRA, FCT

The Specialist 🎬½ 1975 (R) Lawyer West thinks he has seduced stunning Capri, but she has lured him into her clutches—she's been hired to kill him. Campy crud. It's old home week for '60s TV alums: West was Batman; bailiff Moore was Mr. Kimbell on Green Acres. 93m/C VHS, Beta. Adam West, John Anderson, Ahna Capri, Alvy Moore; **D:** Howard (Hikmet) Avedis. NO

The Specialist 🎬½ 1994 (R) Buffed bods do not a movie make—at least not in this mechanical actioner featuring Stone as the revenge-minded May Munro. Seems May's parents were killed by Cuban gangsters, led by father/son thugs Joe (Steiger) and Tomas Leon (Roberts), and she decides ex-CIA bomb specialist Ray Quick (Stallone) is just the man she needs to settle the score. But Quick has his own reasons for accepting—his ex-partner is nutball Ned Trent (Woods), who's now working for the Leons. Things blow up a lot, the two leads show off their toned flesh (but not much acting), and Woods gets to steal the movie with his amusing scenery chewing. **CW:** Violence; sexual scenes; strong language. 110m/C VHS, LV, Closed Caption. Sylvester Stallone, Sharon Stone, James Woods, Eric Roberts, Rod Steiger; **D:** Luis Llosa; **W:** Alexandra Seros; **M:** John Barry. Golden Raspberry Awards '94: Worst Actress (Stone); Nominations: MTV Movie Awards '95: Most Desirable Female (Stone); Golden Raspberry Awards '94: Worst Picture. WAR

Species 🎬🎬½ 1995 (R) A "friendly" galactic message containing a recipe on how to combine extraterrestrial DNA with human DNA is sent to scientists on Earth. The scientists, led by Fitch (Kingsley), whip up a batch of genetic material resulting in a sexy half alien, half human procreating/killing machine named Sil (model Henstridge's film debut). Naturally, Sil escapes from the lab, leaving the scientists with the unenviable task of catching her/it. All-star special effects team, including "Alien" designer H. R. Giger, create over-the-top, stomach-churning thrills. Dips liberally into the tricks of many sci-fi classics. For avid gore-meisters only. **CW:** Sci-fi violence; strong sexuality and some language. 108m/C VHS, LV, Closed Caption, DVD. Ben Kingsley, Michael Madsen, Alfred Molina, Forest Whitaker, Marg Helgenberger, Natasha Henstridge; **D:** Roger Donaldson; **W:** Dennis Feldman; **C:** Andrzej Bartkowiak; **M:** Christopher Young. MTV Movie Awards '96: Best Kiss (Natasha Henstridge/Anthony Guidera); Nominations: MTV Movie Awards '96: Breakthrough Performance (Henstridge). MGM

Specimen 🎬🎬½ 1995 (R) Twenty-four years ago, aliens impregnated Carol Hillary and she gave birth to a son, Mark. Now, the aliens have returned to claim him, only he doesn't want to go. 85m/C VHS, LV. Mark Paul Goesselaar, Doug O'Keefe, Michelle Johnson, Andrew Jackson; **D:** John Bradshaw; **W:** Damian Lee, Sheldon Inkol; **C:** Gerald R. Goozie; **M:** Terence Gowan. APX

The Speckled Band 🎬🎬🎬 1931 Set in 1930, this early talkie is a Sherlock Holmes adventure wherein the great detective must solve the mysterious death of a young woman. Massey makes his screen debut as Holmes, making the sleuth cynical, unhappy and pessimistic. Interesting prototypical Holmes case, faithful to the like-titled Conan Doyle story. 84m/B VHS, Beta, 8mm. Raymond Massey, Lyn Harding, Athole Stewart, Angela Baddeley, Nancy Price; **D:** Jack Raymond; **C:** Frederick A. (Freddie) Young. SNC, NOS, VYY

Specters 🎬 Spettri 1987 Archaeologists excavating the Roman catacombs break open the gates of hell. Hellishly confused plot is unoriginal, to boot; decent production values hardly compensate. 95m/C VHS, Beta. Donald Pleasence, John Pepper, Erna Schurer; **D:** Marcello Avallone. IMP

Spectre 🎬🎬 House of the Damned; Roger Corman Presents: House of the Damned 1996 (R) Maura South (Paul) is the heiress to a old mansion in Ireland and when she, husband Will (Evigan), and their young daughter Aubrey (played by Evigan's daughter Briana) move in they discover it's haunted by the vengeful spirit of a young girl. When they discover the girl's body, the family hope a proper burial will set her spirit to rest but the ghost has other ideas. Cable movie filmed in Ireland. **CW:** Scenes of strong terror, violence and sexuality. 82m/C VHS. Greg Evigan, Alexandra Paul, Briana Evigan, Eamon Draper, Dick Donaghue; **D:** Scott Levy; **W:** Brendan Broderick; **C:** Christopher Baffa; **M:** Christopher Lennertz. NHO

The Spectre of Edgar Allen Poe 🎬½ 1973 The horridly fictionalized writer of horror fiction visits the asylum where his love Lenore is being held, and discovers murder and torture. Based very loosely on Poe's own torments. Dorky, rip-off horror. 87m/C VHS, Beta. Cesar Romero, Robert Walker Jr., Tom Drake; **D:** Mohy Quandour. UNI

Spectre of the Rose 🎬🎬½ 1946 Strange film set in the world of ballet. An impressario contends with an over-the-hill ballerina and a young male dancer with a deadly affinity for knives. 90m/B VHS, LV. Judith Anderson, Michael Chekhov, Ivan Kirov, Viola Essen, Lionel Stander; **D:** Ben Hecht; **W:** Ben Hecht. REP

Speechless 🎬🎬½ 1994 (PG-13) Cute romantic comedy about sparring speechwriters who fall in love, and then briefly turn enemies when they discover they're working at professional odds. Davis is the idealistic liberal working for senatorial candidate Wannamaker, while Keaton is a TV sitcom writer doing a one-shot deal for a millionaire businessman, Republican Garvin. Both stars do a likable job; the supporting cast fares better with Reeve as an egotistical TV reporter, as well as Davis's fiance, and Bedelia as Keaton's ex-wife/campaign press secretary. Although the film parallels the real-life romance of rival Bush-Clinton spin doctors Mary Matalin and James Carville, it was written prior to the last presidential race. **CW:** Mild profanity, adult situations. **99m/C VHS, LV, Closed Caption.** Michael Keaton, Geena Davis, Christopher Reeve, Bonnie Bedelia, Ernie Hudson, Charles Martin Smith, Gailard Sartain, Ray Baker, Mitchell Ryan; **D:** Ron Underwood; **W:** Robert King; **M:** Marc Shaiman. Nominations: Golden Globe Awards '95: Best Actress—Musical/Comedy (Davis). **MGM**

Speed ♂♂♂½ **1994 (R)** Excellent dude Reeves has grown up (and bulked up) as Los Angeles SWAT cop Jack Traven, up against bomb expert Howard Payne (Hopper, more maniacal than usual), who's after major ransom money. First it's a rigged elevator in a very tall building. Then it's a rigged bus—if it slows, it will blow, bad enough any day, but a nightmare in LA traffic. And that's still not the end. Terrific directorial debut for cinematographer De Bont, who certainly knows how to keep the adrenaline pumping. Fine support work by Daniels, Bullock, and Morton and enough wit in Yost's script to keep you chuckling. Great nonstop actioner from the "Die Hard" school. **CW:** Language and violence. **115m/C VHS, LV, Closed Caption.** Keanu Reeves, Dennis Hopper, Sandra Bullock, Joe Morton, Jeff Daniels, Alan Ruck, Glenn Plummer, Richard Lineback, Beth Grant, Hawthorne James, David Kriegel, Carlos Carrasco, Natsuko Ohama, Daniel Villarreal; **D:** Jan De Bont; **W:** Graham Yost; **C:** Andrzej Bartkowiak; **M:** Mark Mancina. Academy Awards '94: Best Sound; MTV Movie Awards '95: Best Female Performance (Bullock), Most Desirable Female (Bullock), Best On-Screen Duo (Keanu Reeves/Sandra Bullock), Best Villain (Hopper), Best Action Sequence; Blockbuster Entertainment Awards '95: Movie, Video, Action Actress, Video (Bullock), Action Actress, Theatrical (Bullock); Nominations: Academy Awards '94: Best Film Editing; MTV Movie Awards '95: Best Film, Best Male Performance (Reeves), Most Desirable Male (Reeves), Best Kiss (Keanu Reeves/Sandra Bullock). **FXV**

Speed 2: Cruise Control ♂ **1997 (PG-13)** Bigger's certainly not better in this lame sequel. Annie's (Bullock) got a new beau, hotheaded cop Alex (Patric), and the twosome decide to go on a Caribbean cruise for a little romance. Annie's luck with transportation holds as the ship is taken over by villainous computer geek-with-a-grudge John Giger (a particularly wild-eyed Dafoe), who sends the liner on a collision course with an oil tanker. Since Alex is off performing heroics, there's not much togetherness and Annie's left to get taken hostage (again). De Bont spent $25 mil on the ship's endless crash into a Caribbean island, which still manages to look fake and only elicits "you've got to be kidding me" disappointment. Bullock's feisty but powerless to save the flick. Patric's bland, and Dafoe is never menacing enough to create any thrills. This sea disaster crashes against the rocks of high expectations and poor execution. **CW:** Frenetic disaster action and violence. **123m/C VHS.** Sandra Bullock, Jason Patric, Willem Dafoe, Temuera Morrison, Brian McCardie, Glenn Plummer, Royale Watkins, Colleen Camp, Lois Chiles, Michael G. Hagerty, Kimmy Robertson, Christine Firkins; **Cameos:** Tim Conway, Joe Morton; **D:** Jan De Bont; **W:** Jan De Bont, Jeff Nathanson, Randall McCormick; **C:** Jack N. Green; **M:** Mark Mancina. **NYR**

The Speed Lovers ♂ **1968** Stock car driver Lorenzen plays himself as an inspiration to a young man to join the auto racing circuit. More of a pat on the industry's back than a serious drama. Features footage from a number of race tracks around the country although shot principally in Atlanta. ♫Speed Lovers. **102m/C VHS.** Fred Lorenzen, William F. McGaha, Peggy O'Hara, David Marcus, Carol Street, Glenda Brunson; **D:** William F. McGaha; **W:** William F. McGaha, Elaine Wilkerson, Fred Tuch. **SMW, TPV**

Speed Reporter ♂ **1936** Talmadge is the intrepid reporter investigating a phony reform movement that's really a front for a gang of criminals. Mediocre drama with Talmadge's thick German accent a hindrance. **56m/B VHS.** Richard Talmadge, Luana Walters, Richard Cramer; **D:** Bernard B. Ray. **GPV**

The Speed Spook ♂ **1924** Silent ghost races car and steals documents. **85m/B VHS, Beta.** Johnny Hines, Warner Richmond; **D:** Charles Hines. **GPV**

Speed Zone ♂ **1988 (PG)** Comic celebrities take over a high speed auto race when a redneck cop locks up the real drivers. Unfunny sequel to "Cannonball Run." **96m/C VHS, Beta, LV.** Melody Anderson, Peter Boyle, Tim Matheson, Donna Dixon, John Candy, Eugene Levy, Joe Flaherty, Matt Frewer, Shari Belafonte, Tom Smothers, Dick Smothers, Brooke Shields, Lee Van Cleef, Jamie Farr, John Schneider, Michael Spinks; **D:** Jim Drake. Golden Raspberry Awards '89: Worst Supporting Actress (Shields). **MED, VTR**

Speeding Up Time ♂ **1971 (R)** An angry man wants to ice the dudes who torched his mother's tenement. **90m/C VHS, Beta.** Winston Thrash, Pamela Donegan. **NO**

Speedtrap ♂♂ **1978 (PG)** Typical chase scenes and cross-gender sparring characterize this tale of a private detective and a police officer pursuing car thieves. Good cast and fun chemistry between the leads; weak, typical script. **101m/C VHS, Beta.** Joe Don Baker, Tyne Daly, Richard Jaeckel, Robert Loggia, Morgan Woodward, Timothy Carey; **D:** Earl Bellamy. **MED**

Speedway ♂♂ **1968 (G)** Elvis the stock car driver finds himself being chased by Nancy the IRS agent during an important race. Will Sinatra keep to the business at hand? Or will the King melt her heart? Some cameos by real-life auto racers. Watch for a young Garr. Movie number 27 for Elvis. ♫Speedway; He's Your Uncle, Not Your Dad; There Ain't Nothing Like a Song. **90m/C VHS, Beta.** Elvis Presley, Nancy Sinatra, Bill Bixby, Gale Gordon, William Schallert, Carl Ballantine, Ross Hagen; **Cameos:** Richard Petty, Cale Yarborough, Teri Garr; **D:** Norman Taurog; **C:** Joseph Ruttenberg. **MGM**

Speedy ♂♂♂ **1928** Lloyd comes to the rescue when the last horse car in New York City, operated by his fiance's grandfather, is stolen by a gang. Thoroughly phoney, fun pursuit/action comedy shot on location. Look for a brief appearance by Babe Ruth. **72m/B VHS, Beta.** Harold Lloyd, Bert Woodruff, Ann Christy; **D:** Ted Wilde. Nominations: Academy Awards '28: Best Director (Wilde). **TLF**

The Spell ♂♂ **1977** An obese fifteen-year-old girl has the power to inflict illness and death on the people she hates. Necessarily mean-spirited, if we're being asked to sympathize with the main character. Therein lies the rub. Made for TV. **86m/C VHS, Beta.** Lee Grant, James Olson, Susan Myers, Barbara Bostock, Lelia Goldoni, Helen Hunt; **D:** Lee Philips. **GKK, WOV**

The Spellbinder ♂½ **1988 (R)** L.A. lawyer Daly falls in love with a woman he saves from an attacker, then discovers she's a fugitive from a satanic cult that wants her back. Unoriginal, but slickly made. **96m/C VHS, Beta, Closed Caption.** Timothy Daly, Kelly Preston, Rick Rossovich, Audra Lindley; **D:** Janet Greek; **W:** Tracy Torme; **M:** Basil Poledouris. **FOX**

Spellbound ♂♂ *The Spell of Amy Nugent* **1941** Broken-hearted over dead girlfriend, young college student attempts to contact her through spiritualism, succeeds, and suffers nervous breakdown. **75m/B VHS.** **GB** Derek Farr, Vera Lindsay, Frederick Leister, Hay Petrie, Felix Aylmer; **D:** John Harlow. **SNC**

Spellbound ♂♂♂½ **1945** Peck plays an amnesia victim accused of murder. Bergman plays the psychiatrist who uncovers his past through Freudian analysis and ends up falling in love with him. One of Hitchcock's finest films of the 1940s, with a riveting dream sequence designed by Salvador Dali. Full of classic Hitchcock plot twists and Freudian imagery. Based on Francis Beeding's novel "The House of Dr. Edwardes." **111m/B VHS, Beta, LV, Closed Caption.** Ingrid Bergman, Gregory Peck, Leo G. Carroll, Michael Chekhov, Wallace Ford, Rhonda Fleming, Regis Toomey; **D:** Alfred Hitchcock; **C:** George Barnes; **M:** Miklos Rozsa. Academy Awards '45: Original Dramatic/Comedy Score; New York Film Critics Awards '45: Best Actress (Bergman); Nominations: Academy Awards '45: Best Black and White Cinematography, Best Director (Hitchcock), Best Picture, Best Supporting Actor (Chekhov). **FOX, IME, TLF**

Spellbreaker: Secret of the Leprechauns ♂♂½ **1996 (G)** Youngster Mike Dennehy (Smith) is on summer vacation in Fairyhill, Ireland where he meets, what else, a band of leprechauns. He finds out the wee folk are battling sinister sorceress Nula, Queen of the Dead, who wants to seize the leprechauns power and destroy them. But not if Mike can stop her! **85m/C VHS, Beta, Closed Caption.** Gregory Edward Smith, Madeleine Potter, Godfrey James, Tina Martin, Sylvester McCoy, James Ellis; **D:** Ted Nicolaou; **W:** Ted Nicolaou; **C:** Adolfo Bartoli; **M:** Richard Kosinski. **PAR**

Spellcaster ♂ **1991 (R)** An evil wizard invites a DJ and a band of rock 'n roll fanatics to his thousand-year-old Italian castle for an evil and bloodcurdling treasure hunt. **83m/C VHS, LV, Closed Caption.** Richard Blade, Gail O'Grady, Harold Pruett, Bunty Bailey, Rafal Zeilinski, Adam Ant; **D:** Rafal Zeilinski. **COL**

Spencer's Mountain ♂♂½ **1963** Fonda plays the larger-than-life patriarch of 9 (with O'Hara as his wife), who's inherited the Wyoming mountain land claimed by his father. Fonda's dream is to build a new house large enough to contain his brood but something always gets in his way. This time it's eldest son MacArthur's dream of a college education. Sentimental family fare based on a novel by Earl Hamner, Jr., which also became the basis for the television series "The Waltons." **118m/C VHS.** Henry Fonda, Maureen O'Hara, James MacArthur, Donald Crisp, Wally Cox, Mimsy Farmer, Virginia Gregg, Lillian Bronson, Whit Bissell, Hayden Rorke, Dub Taylor, Victor French, Veronica Cartwright; **D:** Delmer Daves; **W:** Delmer Daves; **M:** Max Steiner. **WAR**

Spenser: Ceremony ♂♂½ **1993** Urich resumes his role as Robert B. Parker's Boston PI, which he played in the TV series "Spenser: For Hire." This time around Spenser is searching for a troubled runaway who's gotten involved in prostitution. But her suburban dad, who has political aspirations, seems reluctant to have her found. Brooks returns as Spenser's menacing associate Hawk. Toronto stands-in for Boston. Made for cable TV; based on Parker's novel "Ceremony." **?m/C VHS.** Robert Urich, Avery Brooks, Barbara Williams, Tanya Allen, David Nichols, Lynne Cormack; **D:** Paul Lynch; **W:** Joan H. Parker, Robert B. Parker. **PAR**

Spenser: Pale Kings & Princes ♂♂½ **1994** Spenser's (Urich) new case involves the murder of a reporter who was investigating a drug-ridden small New England town. But was the journalist killed for what he found out about a Colombian cocaine connection or did his womanizing have deadly consequences? Adapted from Robert B. Parker's novel; made for cable TV. **?m/C VHS.** Robert Urich, Avery Brooks, Barbara Williams. **PAR**

Spetters ♂♂½ **1980 (R)** Four Dutch teenagers follow the motorcycle racing circuit and motocross champ Hauer. Misdirected youth film with a spicy performance from Soutendijk. Plenty of violence, sex, and gripping photography. Verhoeven went on to direct "Robocop" and "Total Recall." **108m/C VHS, Beta, LV. NL** Rutger Hauer, Renee Soutendijk; **D:** Paul Verhoeven; **C:** Jan De Bont.

The Sphinx ♂♂½ **1933** A murderer causes havoc for his deaf-mute twin (Atwill, good in a dual role) when he frames him for his own crimes. Remade as "The Phantom Killer." **63m/B VHS.** Lionel Atwill, Theodore Newton, Sheila Terry, Paul Hurst, Luis Alberni, George "Gabby" Hayes; **D:** Phil Rosen. **SNC, VYY, GPV**

Sphinx WOOF! 1981 **(PG)** Woman archaeologist searches for hidden riches in the tomb of an Egyptian king. The scenery is impressive, but otherwise, don't bother. Based on the novel by Robin Cook. 117m/C VHS, Beta. Lesley-Anne Down, Frank Langella, John Gielgud, Maurice Ronet, John Rhys-Davies; *D:* Franklin J. Schaffner; *W:* John Byrum. *WAR*

Spices 🎬🎬🎬 1986 Poor woman Sonbai revolts against the sexist mores of rural colonial India in the 1940s. Features actress Patil in her final role. In Hindi with English subtitles. 98m/C VHS. *IN* Smita Patil; *D:* Ketan Mehta. *MFV, FCT*

The Spider and the Fly 🎬🎬½ 1994 **(PG-13)** Mystery writer Dianna Taylor (Harris) and her friends like to play a murder mystery charade known as "The Game." Their latest unsuspecting patsy is crime writer Michael Moore (Shackelford)—who falls for Dianna bigtime. Then their publisher is killed—in the same sort of murder scenario one of them devised. Made for cable television. 87m/C VHS, Beta, Closed Caption. Mel Harris, Ted Shackleford, Kim Coates, Colm Feore, Frankie Faison, Cynthia Belliveau, Kenneth Welsh, Peggy Lipton; *D:* Michael Katleman; *W:* Robert Pucci, Alanna Hamill; *M:* Richard Bellis. *PAR*

Spider Baby 🎬 *The Liver Eaters; Spider Baby, or the Maddest Story Ever Told; Cannibal Orgy, or the Maddest Story Ever Told* 1964 A tasteless horror-comedy about a chauffeur who takes care of a psychotic family. Theme song sung by Lon Chaney. 86m/B VHS, Beta. Lon Chaney Jr., Mantan Moreland, Carol Ohmart, Sid Haig, Beverly Washburn, Jill Banner; *D:* Jack Hill. *SNC, AOV, MLB*

Spider Woman 🎬🎬🎬 *Sherlock Holmes and the Spider Woman* 1944 A modernized Holmes and Watson adventure as the duo track down a woman responsible for a series of murders. His adversary uses poisonous spiders to do her work. Zestful, superior Holmes. 62m/B VHS, Beta, Closed Caption. Basil Rathbone, Nigel Bruce, Gale Sondergaard, Dennis Hoey; *D:* Roy William Neill. *FOX*

Spiderman: The Deadly Dust 1978 A live-action episode of Spiderman, from the TV seies, as he attempts to prevent a city-destroying plutonium accident. 93m/C VHS, Beta, Closed Caption. Nicholas Hammond, Robert F. Simon, Chip Fields; *D:* Ron Satlof. *FOX*

Spiders 🎬🎬🎬 1918 One of the earliest surviving films by director Lang, and it predates Indiana Jones by almost 60 years. In these first two chapters ("The Golden Lake" and "The Diamond Ship") an unfinished 4-part thriller, Carl deVogt battles with the evil Spider cult for a mystically powerful Incan diamond. Restored version has original color-tinted scenes. Silent with organ score. 137m/B VHS, Beta, LV. GE Lil Dagover; *D:* Fritz Lang; *M:* Gaylord Carter. *KIV, IME, GLV*

The Spider's Stratagem 🎬🎬🎬 1970 Thirty years after his father's murder by the facists, a young man returns to a small Italian town to learn why his father was killed. The locals resist his efforts, and he is trapped in a mysterious web where history and lies exert a stranglehold on the truth. Intriguing, high literate thriller; outrageously lovely color photography. Based on a short story by Jorge Luis Borges. In Italian with English subtitles. 97m/C VHS. IT Giulio Brogi, Alida Valli; *D:* Bernardo Bertolucci; *W:* Bernardo Bertolucci. *NYF, FCT, APD*

Spies 🎬🎬🎬½ *Spione* 1928 A sly criminal poses as a famous banker to steal government information and create chaos in the world in this silent Lang masterpiece. Excellent entertainment, tight plotting and pacing, fine performances. Absolutely relentless intrigue and tension. 88m/B VHS, Beta, LV. GE Rudolf Klein-Rogge, Lupu Pick, Fritz Rasp, Gerda Maurus, Willy Fritsch; *D:* Fritz Lang. *GPV, NOS, VYY*

Spies, Lies and Naked Thighs 🎬½ 1991 A pair of crackpot CIA agents find themselves in a whirlpool of comedic madness when they are assigned to track down a deadly assassin. The problem? The assassin happens to be the ex-wife of one of the guys. Can he go another round with her and this time come out on top? Who cares? 90m/C VHS, LV. Harry Anderson, Ed Begley Jr., Rachel Ticotin, Linda Purl, Wendy Crewson; *D:* James Frawley. *NLC*

Spies Like Us 🎬🎬½ 1985 **(PG)** Chase and Aykroyd meet while taking the CIA entry exam. Caught cheating on the test, they seem the perfect pair for a special mission. Pursued by the Soviet government, they nearly start WWIII. Silly, fun homage to the Bing Crosby-Bob Hope "Road" movies that doesn't capture those classics' quota of guffaws, but comes moderately close. Look for several cameos by film directors. 103m/C VHS, Beta, LV, Closed Caption. Chevy Chase, Dan Aykroyd, Steve Forrest, Bruce Davison, William Prince, Bernie Casey, Tom Hatton, Donna Dixon, Frank Oz; *Cameos:* Michael Apted, Constantin Costa-Gavras, Terry Gilliam, Ray Harryhausen, Joel Coen, Martin Brest, Bob Swaim; *D:* John Landis; *W:* Dan Aykroyd, Lowell Ganz, Babaloo Mandel; *M:* Elmer Bernstein. *WAR*

Spike of Bensonhurst 🎬🎬½ 1988 **(R)** A Brooklyn street kid dreams of becoming a championship boxer. He tries to gain the mob's help by courting the local Don's daughter. Hip-but-stereotyped Morrissey effort is helped by great cast. 101m/C VHS, Beta, LV. Sasha Mitchell, Ernest Borgnine, Maria Pitillo, Talisa Soto, Sylvia Miles, Anne DeSalvo, Geraldine Smith, Rick Aviles, Antonia Rey; *D:* Paul Morrissey; *W:* Alan Bowne, Paul Morrissey; *M:* Coati Mundi. *NO*

Spinout 🎬🎬 *California Holiday* 1966 A pouty traveling singer decides to drive an experimental race car in a rally. Usual Elvis fare with the King being pursued by an assortment of beauties. 🎵Adam and Eve; Stop, Look, Listen; All That I Am; Am I Ready; Smorgasbord; Never Say Yes; Beach Shack; I'll Be Back; Spinout. 93m/C VHS, Beta. Elvis Presley, Shelley Fabares, Carl Betz, Diane McBain, Cecil Kellaway, Jack Mullaney, Deborah Walley, Una Merkel, Warren Berlinger, Will Hutchins, Dodie Marshall; *D:* Norman Taurog. *MGM*

The Spiral Staircase 🎬🎬🎬 1946 A mute servant, working in a creepy Gothic mansion, may be the next victim of a murderer preying on women afflicted with deformities, especially when the next murder occurs in the mansion itself. Great performance by McGuire as the terrified victim. Remade for television in 1975. 83m/B VHS, LV. Dorothy McGuire, George Brent, Ethel Barrymore, Kent Smith, Rhonda Fleming, Gordon Oliver, Elsa Lanchester, Sara Allgood; *D:* Robert Siodmak. Nominations: Academy Awards '46: Best Supporting Actress (Barrymore). *FOX*

Spiral Staircase 🎬½ 1975 Mild TV remake of the 1946 classic about a mute servant who is menaced by a psychopathic killer. Why didn't they just show the original? 99m/C VHS, Beta. GB Jacqueline Bisset, Christopher Plummer, John Phillip Law, Mildred Dunnock, Sam Wanamaker, Gayle Hunnicutt; *D:* Peter Collinson; *W:* Allan Scott, Chris Bryant. *WAR*

Spirit Lost 🎬🎬 1996 **(R)** John (Leon) and wife Willy (Taylor) move to an old seaside home, where he hopes to find artistic inpiration. Instead, he finds an attractive ghost, Arabella (Williams), who has been hanging around for 200 years after her lover's betrayal. And the jealous Arabella wants to get her new lover's wife out of the way. Yes, ghosts CAN do it. Based on the book by Nancy Thayer. *CW:* Strong sexuality. 90m/C VHS, LV, Closed Caption. Leon, Regina Taylor, Cynda Williams, James Avery, Juanita Jennings; *D:* M. Neema Barnette; *W:* Joyce Renee Lewis; *C:* Yuri Neyman; *M:* Lionel Cole. *LIV*

Spirit of St. Louis 🎬🎬🎬 1957 A lavish Hollywood biography of famous aviator Charles Lindbergh and his historic transatlantic flight from Paris to New York in 1927, based on his autobiography. Intelligent; Stewart shines as the intrepid airman. Inexplicably, it flopped at the box office. 137m/C VHS, Beta. James Stewart, Patricia Smith, Murray Hamilton, Marc Connelly; *D:* Billy Wilder; *W:* Billy Wilder, Wendell Mayes; *M:* Franz Waxman. National Board of Review Awards '57: 10 Best Films of the Year. *WAR, HMV*

Spirit of '76 🎬½ 1991 **(PG-13)** In the 22nd century, the Earth faces certain disaster as a magnetic storm wipes out all of American culture. Now time travellers must return to 1776 to reacquire the Constitution to fix things up. But when their computer goes on the blink, the do-gooders land, not in 1776, but in 1976 at the beginning of disco fever! 82m/C VHS, LV, Closed Caption. David Cassidy, Olivia D'Abo, Leif Garrett, Geoff Hoyle, Jeff McDonald, Steve McDonald, Liam O'Brien, Barbara Bain, Julie Brown, Thomas Chong, Iron Eyes Cody, Don Novello, Carl Reiner, Rob Reiner, Moon Zappa; *D:* Lucas Reiner; *W:* Lucas Reiner. *NO*

Spirit of the Beehive 🎬🎬🎬 *El Espiritu de la Colmena* 1973 An acclaimed and haunting film about a young Spanish girl enthralled by the 1931 "Frankenstein," embarking on a journey to find the creature in the Spanish countryside. One of the best films about children's inner life; in Spanish with subtitles. 95m/C VHS, Beta, LV. SP Fernando Gomez, Teresa Gimpera, Ana Torrent, Isabel Telleria, Laly Soldevilla; *D:* Victor Erice; *W:* Victor Erice; *C:* Luis Cuadrado; *M:* Luis De Pablo. *HMV, CVC, TPV*

Spirit of the Eagle 🎬🎬 1990 **(PG)** Man and young son wander in mountains and make friends with feathered creature. Then boy is kidnapped, creating problems for dad. Somnolent family fare. 93m/C VHS, LV. Dan Haggerty, Bill Smith, Don Shanks, Jeri Arredondo, Trever Yarrish; *D:* Boon Collins; *W:* Boon Collins. *SGE, IME*

Spirit of the West 🎬½ 1932 Rodeo star Gibson and his ranch foreman brother work together to save a fair damsel's land from a gang of rustlers. Routine western of its era. 61m/B VHS, Beta. Hoot Gibson, Hooper Atchley; *D:* Otto Brower. *NOS, DVT, VCI*

The Spirit of West Point 🎬½ 1947 The true story of West Point's two All-American football greats, Doc Blanchard and Glenn Davis (who play themselves), while on leave after graduation from the title school. 77m/B VHS, Beta, LV. Felix "Doc" Blanchard, Glenn Davis, Tom Harmon, Alan Hale Jr., Anne Nagel, Robert Shayne; *D:* Ralph Murphy. *NWV*

The Spirit of Youth 🎬🎬 1937 Joe Louis supports his family with menial jobs until he shows his knack as a fighter. When he's knocked down, his gal appears at ringside to inspire him, and does. 70m/B VHS, Beta. Joe Louis, Mantan Moreland. *VYY, NOS, VCN*

Spirit Rider 🎬🎬🎬 1993 Jesse Threebears is a sullen 16-year-old Ojibway who has been shuttled from foster homes since the age of six. Repatriated to his family's Canadian reservation, he's left in the care of his grandfather, Joe Moon. The entire community works to make Jesse's return successful but there are Jesse's resentments and some family tragedies to be overcome first. Based on the novel "Winners" by Mary-Ellen Lang Collura. 120m/C VHS. CA Herbie Barnes, Adam Beach, Graham Greene, Tantoo Cardinal, Gordon Tootoosis, Tom Jackson, Michelle St. John. *PME, BTV*

Spiritism 🎬🎬 *Espiritismo* 1961 Mother uses one of her three wishes to bring back her dead son. Adapted from the "Monkey's Paw." 85m/B VHS. MX Nora Veyran, Jose Luis Jimenez, Jorge Mondragon, Rene Cardona Jr.; *D:* Benito Alazraki. *SNC*

Spirits 🎬½ 1990 **(R)** A priest tormented by his lust-filled dreams breaks his vows of chastity with a woman who turns out to be a murderer. Bad luck. *CW:* Language and sensuality. 88m/C VHS, Closed Caption. Erik Estrada, Carol Lynley, Robert Quarry, Brinke Stevens, Oliver Darrow, Kathrin Lautner; *D:* Fred Olen Ray. *THV*

Spirits of the Dead 🎬🎬🎬 *Histoires Extraordinaires* 1968 **(R)** Three Edgar Allan Poe stories adapted for the screen and directed by three of Europe's finest. "Metzengerstein," directed by Roger Vadim stars the Fonda siblings in a tale of incestuous lust. "William Wilson" finds Louis Malle directing Delon and Bardot in the story of a vicious Austrian army officer haunted by a murder victim. Finally, Fellini directs "Never Bet the Devil Your Head" or "Toby Dammit" in which Stamp plays a drunken British film star who has a gruesome date with destiny. Although Fellini's segment is generally considered the best (and was released on its own) all three provide an interesting, atmospheric vision of Poe. 117m/C VHS. **IT FR** Jane Fonda, Peter Fonda, Carla Marlier, Francoise Prevost, James Robertson Justice, Brigitte Bardot, Alain Delon, Katia Christine, Terence Stamp, Salvo Randone; **D:** Roger Vadim, Louis Malle, Federico Fellini; **M:** Nino Rota. *WBF, MLB, FRG*

Spite Marriage ✶✶✶ 1929 When Sebastian's lover dumps her like yesterday's garbage, she marries Keaton out of spite. Much postnuptial levity follows. Keaton's final silent. 82m/B VHS, Beta, LV. Buster Keaton, Dorothy Sebastian, Edward Earle, Leila Hyams, William Bechtel, Hank Mann; **D:** Edward Sedgwick. *MGM, FCT*

Spitfire ✶✶✶ 1934 Sentimental comedy drama starring Hepburn as a hillbilly faith healer from the Ozarks who falls into a love triangle. One in a string of early box-office flops for Hepburn. She wanted to play a role other than patrician Eastern Seaboard, and did, but audiences didn't buy it. 90m/B VHS, Beta, 8mm. Katharine Hepburn, Robert Young, Ralph Bellamy, Sidney Toler; **D:** John Cromwell; **M:** Max Steiner. *NO*

Spitfire ✶✶✶ *The First of the Few* 1942 True story of Reginald J. Mitchell, who designed "The Spitfire" fighter plane, which greatly assisted the Allies during WWII. Howard's last film. Heavily propagandist but enjoyable and uncomplicated biography, with a splendid score. 88m/B VHS, Beta. **GB** Leslie Howard, David Niven, Rosamund John, Roland Culver, David Horne, J.H. Roberts, Patricia Medina; **D:** Leslie Howard; **C:** Georges Perinal; **M:** William Walton. *CNG, NOS, HHT*

Spitfire ✶✶½ 1994 (R) Feisty gymnast Charlie Case (Phillips) has some super secret info slipped to her by her secret agent father (Henrikson) that is desired by evil Carla Davis (Douglas). With the help of reporter Rex Beacham (Thomerson), Charlie's gonna save the day. **CW:** Language; violence; some nudity. 95m/C VHS. Kristie Phillips, Sarah Douglas, Lance Henriksen, Tim Thomerson; **D:** Albert Pyun; **W:** Albert Pyun; **C:** George Mooradian; **M:** Tony Riparetti. *THV*

The Spitfire Grill ✶✶½ *Care of the Spitfire Grill* 1995 (PG-13) Newly released from prison, Perry Talbott (Elliott) moves to smalltown Gilead, Maine and gets a waitressing job at the Spitfire Grill, run by the cranky Hannah (Burstyn). Perry's upfront about her jail time, which doesn't endear her to the suspicious locals. Particularly censorious is businessman Nahum Goddard (Patton), who sends his downtrodden wife Shelby (Harden) to keep an eye on Perry. There are a number of personal dilemmas that take their toll in this familiar setting—redeemed by strong performances. **CW:** Thematic elements. 117m/C VHS, LV, Closed Caption. Alison Elliott, Ellen Burstyn, Marcia Gay Harden, Will Patton, Kiean Mulroney, Gailard Sartain, Louise De Cormier, John M. Jackson; **D:** Lee David Zlotoff; **W:** Lee David Zlotoff; **C:** Rob Draper; **M:** James Horner. Sundance Film Festival '96: Audience Award. *COL*

Spittin' Image ✶ 1983 After falling from her mean-spirited father's wagon, a young girl befriends a kind mountain man. She learns the ways of the wilderness and tobacco spitting. 92m/C VHS, Beta. Sunshine Parker, Trudi Cooper, Sharon Barr, Karen Barr; **D:** Russell Kern. *PSM*

Splash ✶✶½ 1984 (PG) A beautiful mermaid ventures into New York City in search of a man she's rescued twice when he's fallen overboard. Now it's her turn to fall—in love. Charming performances by Hanks and Hannah. Well-paced direction from Howard, with just enough slapstick. Don't miss the lobster scene. 109m/C VHS, Beta, LV, 8mm. Tom Hanks, Daryl Hannah, Eugene Levy, John Candy, Dody Goodman, Shecky Greene, Richard B. Shull, Bobby DiCicco, Howard Morris; **D:** Ron Howard; **W:** Babaloo Mandel, Lowell Ganz. National Society of Film Critics

Awards '84: Best Screenplay; Nominations: Academy Awards '84: Best Original Screenplay. *TOU*

Splatter University woof! 1984 A deranged killer escapes from an asylum and begins to slaughter and mutilate comely coeds at a local college. Abysmally motiveless killing and gratuitous sex. Also available in a 78-minute "R" rated version. 79m/C VHS, Beta. Francine Forbes, Dick Biel, Cathy Lacommaro, Ric Randing, Dan Eaton; **D:** Richard W. Haines; **M:** Chris Burke. *LIV*

Splendor in the Grass ✶✶✶ 1961 A drama set in rural Kansas in 1925, concerning a teenage couple who try to keep their love on a strictly intellectual plane and the sexual and family pressures that tear them apart. After suffering a mental breakdown and being institutionalized, the girl returns years later in order to settle her life. Film debuts of Beatty, Dennis, and Diller. Inge wrote the screenplay specifically with Beatty in mind, after the actor appeared in one of Inge's stage plays. Filmed not in Kansas, but on Staten Island and in upstate New York. 124m/C VHS, Beta, LV. Natalie Wood, Warren Beatty, Audrey Christie, Barbara Loden, Zohra Lampert, Phyllis Diller, Sandy Dennis; **D:** Elia Kazan; **W:** William Inge; **C:** Charles Durnham; **M:** David Amram. Academy Awards '61: Best Story & Screenplay; Nominations: Academy Awards '61: Best Actress (Wood). *WAR*

Split ✶ 1990 Humanoids from another dimension manipulate earth activity. 85m/C VHS. John Flynn, Timothy Dwight, Chris Shaw, Joan Bechtel; **D:** Chris Shaw. *AIP*

Split Decisions ✶✶ 1988 (R) An Irish family of boxers, dad and his two sons, slug it out emotionally and physically, as they come to terms with career choices and each other. Good scenes in the ring but the drama leans toward melodrama. Decent family drama, but somewhat of a "Rocky" rip-off. 95m/C VHS, LV, 8mm, Closed Caption. Gene Hackman, Craig Sheffer, Jeff Fahey, Jennifer Beals, John McLiam, Eddie Velez, Carmine Caridi, James Tolkan; **D:** David Drury; **W:** David Fallon; **M:** Basil Poledouris. *WAR*

Split Image ✶✶✶ 1982 (R) An all-American boy comes under the spell of a cult. His parents then hire a deprogrammer to bring the boy back to reality. Exceptional performances by Dennehy and Woods. This is a worthwhile film that spent far too little time in theatres. 113m/C VHS, Beta. Michael O'Keefe, Karen Allen, Peter Fonda, Brian Dennehy, James Woods; **D:** Ted Kotcheff; **W:** Robert Mark Kamen; **M:** Bill Conti.

Split Second ✶✶½ 1953 An escaped prisoner holds hostages in a Nevada atomic bomb testing area. McNally's excellent performance as the kidnapper, in addition to strong supporting performances, enhance a solid plot. Powell's directorial debut. 85m/B VHS, Beta. Paul Kelly, Richard Egan, Jan Sterling, Alexis Smith, Stephen McNally; **D:** Dick Powell; **W:** William Bowers, Irving Wallace. *TTC*

Split Second ✶½ 1992 (R) Hauer is a futuristic cop tracking down a vicious alien serial killer in London in the year 2008. The monster rips out the hearts of his victims and then eats them in what appears to be a satanic ritual in this bloodsoaked thriller wanna-be. Hauer gives a listless performance and overall, the action is quite dull. The music soundtrack also manages to annoy with the Moody Blues song "Nights in White Satin" playing at the most inappropriate times. A British/American co-production. **CW:** Language and gore. 91m/C VHS, Closed Caption. **GB** Rutger Hauer, Kim Cattrall, Neil Duncan, Michael J. Pollard, Alun Armstrong, Pete Postlethwaite, Ian Dury, Roberta Eaton; **D:** Tony Maylam. *HBO*

Splitting Heirs ✶✶½ 1993 (PG-13) Idle stars as the offspring of titled parents who is accidentally abandoned in a restaurant as an infant and raised by poor Pakistanis. (His mother winds up claiming the wrong abandoned baby.) When he discovers he's actually the 15th Duke of Bournemouth he plots, ineffectually, to kill off the

present unknowing imposter, a nitwit American (Moranis). Cleese pops in as a shabby lawyer hired by Idle to help him claim the title with Hershey as Idle's real mother, the addle-brained and sex-starved Duchess. Convoluted plot, bland comedy. **CW:** Sexual dialogue and nudity. 87m/C VHS, LV, Closed Caption. Eric Idle, Rick Moranis, Barbara Hershey, John Cleese, Catherine Zeta Jones, Sadie Frost, Stratford Johns, Brenda Bruce, William Franklyn, Jeremy Clyde; **D:** Robert M. Young; **W:** Eric Idle; **M:** Michael Kamen. *USH*

Splitz woof! 1984 (PG-13) An all-girl rock band agrees to help out a sorority house by participating in a series of sporting events. 89m/C VHS, Beta. Robin Johnson, Patti Lee, Shirley Stoler, Raymond Serra; **D:** Domonic Paris. *LIV, VES*

Spoiled Children ✶✶½ *Des Enfants Gates* 1977 A famous film director (Piccoli) tries to work on his new script at home but is too distracted by his family life. So he rents a high-rise apartment for peace and quiet but winds up involved in a tenant/landlord dispute and with a girl half his age. In French with English subtitles. 113m/B VHS. **FR** Michel Piccoli, Christine Pascal, Michel Aumont, Gerard Jugnot, Arlette Bonnard; **D:** Bertrand Tavernier; **W:** Christine Pascal, Charlotte Dubreuil, Bertrand Tavernier; **M:** Philippe Sarde. *FCT, CVC*

The Spoilers ✶✶½ 1914 Virtually unstaged account of gold hunting in the Alaskan wilderness enhanced by gritty film quality. Was a gold mine when released. 110m/B VHS, Beta. William Farnum, Thomas Santschi, Kathlyn Williams, Bessie Eyton, Frank Clark, Wheeler Oakman; **D:** Colin Campbell. *GPV*

The Spoilers ✶✶✶ 1942 Two adventurers in the Yukon are swindled out of their gold mine and set out to even the score. A trademark scene of all versions of the movie (and there are many) is the climactic fistfight, in this case between hero Wayne and bad-guy Scott. One of the better films adapted from the novel by Rex Beach. William Farnum, who starred in both the 1914 and the 1930 versions, has a small part. 88m/B VHS, Beta, LV. John Wayne, Randolph Scott, Marlene Dietrich, Margaret Lindsay, Harry Carey Sr., Richard Barthelmess, Charles Halton; **D:** Ray Enright; **C:** Milton Krasner. Nominations: Academy Awards '42: Best Interior Decoration. *USH, MLB, FCT*

Spontaneous Combustion ✶✶ 1989 (R) A grisly horror film detailing the travails of a hapless guy who has the power to inflict the title phenomenon on other people. 97m/C VHS, Beta, LV. Brad Dourif, Jon Cypher, Melinda Dillon, Cynthia Bain, William Prince; **D:** Tobe Hooper; **M:** Graeme Revell. *LIV, VTR*

Spook Busters ✶✶½ 1948 The Bowery Boys take jobs as exterminators, only to find themselves assigned the unenviable task of ridding a haunted house of ghosts. To make matters worse, the resident mad scientist wants to transplant Sach's brain into a gorilla. Essential viewing for anyone who thought "Ghostbusters" was an original story. 68m/B VHS. Leo Gorcey, Huntz Hall, Douglass Dumbrille, Bobby Jordan, Gabriel Dell, Billy Benedict, David Gorcey, Bernard Gorcey, Tanis Chandler, Maurice Cass, Charles Middleton; **D:** William Beaudine. *WAR, GPV*

The Spook Who Sat By the Door ✶½ 1973 (PG) A black CIA agent organizes an army of inner-city youths and launches a revolution. Based on the novel by Sam Greenlee. 95m/C VHS, Beta. Lawrence Cook, Paula Kelly, J.A. Preston; **D:** Ivan Dixon; **M:** Herbie Hancock. *VCD*

Spookies woof! 1985 (R) An old master sorcerer who lives in a run-down haunted house sacrifices humans to give eternal life to his unconscious bride. He needs only a few more victims when a group of teenagers come along to explore the house. 85m/C VHS, Beta, LV. Felix Ward, Dan Scott, Maria Pechukas, Brendan Faulkner, Eugine Joseph; **D:** Thomas Doran. *NO*

Spooks Run Wild 🎬🎬½ **1941** The East Side Kids seek refuge in a spooky mansion owned by the eerie Lugosi. A fun horror-comedy with the Kids' antics playing off Lugosi's scariness quite well. Co-scripter Carl Foreman later co-wrote "High-Noon," "The Bridge on the River Kwai," and "The Guns of Navarone." Not the same movie as "Ghosts on the Loose" which followed in '43 and also featured Lugosi and the Kids. **64m/B VHS, Beta.** Huntz Hall, Leo Gorcey, Bobby Jordan, Sammy Morrison, Dave O'Brien, Dennis Moore, Bela Lugosi; **D:** Phil Rosen; **W:** Carl Foreman. NOS, SNC, VYY

The Sporting Club woof! **1972 (R)** A semi-comic melodrama about a strict all men's club which, during a 100th anniversary party, reverts to savagery and primitive rites. **104m/C VHS, Beta.** Robert Fields, Margaret Blye, Nicolas Coster, Ralph Waite, Jack Warden, Linda Blair; **D:** Larry Peerce. NLC

Spotlight Scandals 🎬🎬 **1943** A barber and a vaudevillian team up and endure the ups and downs of showbiz life in this low-budget musical from prolific B-movie director Beaudine. ♫The Restless Age; Goodnight Now; The Lilac Tree; Tempo of the Trail; Oh Johnny. **79m/B VHS.** Billy Gilbert, Frank Fay, Bonnie Baker; **D:** William Beaudine. NOS, LOO

Spraggue 🎬🎬 **1984** A Boston professor and his eccentric aunt put the moves on a doctor who may have committed murder. Served as a TV pilot for a series that never materialized. **78m/C VHS.** Michael Nouri, Glynis Johns, James Cromwell, Mark Herrier, Patrick O'Neal, Andrea Marcovicci; **D:** Larry Elikann. LIV

The Spring 🎬½ **1989** Two archaeologists search Florida for the fountain of youth after they find new clues to its whereabouts. However, a greedy industrialist and an evil priest are both on their trail, fighting to keep the secret for themselves at any cost. **110m/C VHS.** Dack Rambo, Gedde Watanabe, Shari Shattuck, Steven Keats; **D:** John D. Patterson. NO

Spring Break 🎬 **1983 (R)** Four college students go to Fort Lauderdale on their spring vacation and have a wilder time than they bargained for, though viewer is deprived of excitement. **101m/C VHS, Beta.** Perry Lang, David Knell, Steve Bassett, Paul Land, Jayne Modean, Corinne Alphen; **D:** Sean S. Cunningham. COL

Spring Fever 🎬½ **1981** Heartaches of the junior tennis circuit are brought to the screen in this sports comedy. Previews promised a lot more than this film could ever hope to deliver. Even tennis fans will be disappointed. **93m/C VHS, Beta.** CA Susan Anton; **D:** Joseph L. Scanlan. LIV, VES

Spring Symphony 🎬🎬½ Fruhlingssinfonie **1986 (PG-13)** A moody, fairy-tale biography of composer Robert Schumann, concentrating on his rhapsodic love affair with pianist Clara Weick. Kinski is very good as the rebellious daughter, while the music is even better. Reasonably accurate in terms of history; dubbed. **102m/C VHS, Beta.** GE Nastassia Kinski, Rolf Hoppe, Herbert Gronemeyer; **D:** Peter Schamoni. LIV

Springfield Rifle 🎬🎬½ **1952** Based on the real-life story of Major Les Kearney, who joined forces with outlaws to catch the thief stealing government weapons. Average. **93m/C VHS.** Gary Cooper, Phyllis Thaxter, David Brian, Lon Chaney Jr., Paul Kelly, Phil Carey, Guinn "Big Boy" Williams; **D:** Andre de Toth; **M:** Max Steiner. WAR

Springtime in the Rockies 🎬🎬 **1937** Autry is a cattle-ranch foreman whose employer decides to try raising sheep. This doesn't set well with the other ranchers, but Autry manages to save the day and sing a little too. **60m/B VHS, Beta, Closed Caption.** Gene Autry, Polly Rowles, Smiley Burnette; **D:** Joseph Kane. NOS, VCN, DVT

Springtime in the Rockies 🎬🎬½ **1942** A Broadway duo just can't get along despite being in love with each other. Top-notch musical, with a touch of romantic tension and comedy. Beautifully filmed in the Canadian Rockies. ♫I Had the Craziest Dream; Run Little Rainrop Run; A Poem Set to Music; Pan American Jubilee; I Like to Be Love by You; Chattanooga Choo Choo; Tic Tac Do Meu Coracao. **91m/C VHS, LV.** Betty Grable, John Payne, Carmen Miranda, Cesar Romero, Charlotte Greenwood, Edward Everett Horton, Jackie Gleason; **D:** Irving Cummings; **C:** Ernest Palmer. FOX, MLB

Springtime in the Sierras 🎬🎬½ Song of the Sierra **1947** Rogers and Devine band together to fight a gang of poachers who prey on the wildlife of a game preserve. Features a number of songs by Rogers and The Sons of the Pioneers. **54m/B VHS, Beta.** Roy Rogers, Andy Devine, Jane Frazee, Stephanie Bachelor; **D:** William Witney. NOS, CAB, DVT

The Sprinter 🎬🎬½ **1984** A young homosexual, while trying to submerge his confusion in professional track and field, gets to know a homely shot-putter and is seduced by her. In German with English subtitles. **90m/C VHS, Beta.** VCD, GLV

Sprung 🎬🎬 **1996 (R)** The dating scene among four young African Americans is examined in this well-intended, yet unfocused romantic comedy. Couple A are Brandy (Campbell) and Montel (Cundieff) who realize that they have a chance at true love. Couple B are their friends Adina (Parker) and Clyde (Torry) who try to sabotage Brandy and Montel's happiness in order to save them from being "sprung" (in love) with each other. The camaraderie between the couples is funny, some of the time, but the humor often turns from vulgar to juvenile and scenes drag on a bit. Cundieff and Campbell are too bland to carry over the used plot but Torry is a comedic find who makes the film tolerable.**CW:** Some strong sexuality and language. **105m/C VHS.** Tisha Campbell, Paula Jai Parker, Rusty Cundieff, Joe Torry, John Witherspoon, Clarence Williams III; **D:** Rusty Cundieff; **W:** Rusty Cundieff, Darin Scott; **C:** Joao Fernandes; **M:** Stanley Clarke. THV

Spurs 🎬🎬 **1930** A rodeo star takes on a whole gang of rustlers and their imposing machine gun. This transitional western was made both with and without sound. **60m/B VHS.** Hoot Gibson, Robert E. Homans; **D:** B. Reeves Eason. NOS, DVT, HEG

Sputnik 🎬🎬 A Dog, a Mouse, and a Sputnik **1961** A Frenchman, amnesiac after a car crash, comes up against Russian scientists, space-bound dogs, and weightlessness. Pleasant and charming family fun though clearly dated. Another fine performance from Auer. Dubbed. **80m/B VHS, Beta.** FR Noelia Noel, Mischa Auer, Denise Grey; **D:** Jean Dreville. NO

Spy 🎬🎬 **1989** A former spy who knows too much becomes the target of a renegade agency. Made for television. **88m/C VHS, Beta, LV, Closed Caption.** Ned Beatty, Tim Choate, Bruce Greenwood, Catherine Hicks, Jameson Parker, Michael Tucker; **D:** Philip Frank Messina. PAR

Spy Hard 🎬 **1996 (PG-13)** Nielsen does yet another genre spoof—this time a combo of "Die Hard" meets James Bond. Agent Dick Steele aka WD40 (Nielsen) is brought out of retirement to thwart the plans of crazed General Rancor (Griffith) for world domination. Not much else plotwise, which ropes Nielsen along in domino fashion through the myriad of unimaginative spoofs on such films as "Speed" and "Pulp Fiction." Minus the charm and pace of parody pioneers Zucker/Abrahams/Zucker, this latest entry should retire the whole genre. Directorial debut of Friedberg.**CW:** Crude humor and sexual innuendo **80m/C VHS, LV, Closed Caption.** Leslie Nielsen, Nicollette Sheridan, Andy Griffith, Charles Durning, Marcia Gay Harden, Barry Bostwick; **D:** Rick Friedberg; **W:** Rick Friedberg, Dick Chudnow, Jason Friedberg, Aaron Seltzer; **C:** John R. Leonetti; **M:** Bill Conti. TOU

Spy in Black 🎬🎬🎬 **1939** A German submarine captain returns from duty at sea during WWI and is assigned to infiltrate one of the Orkney Islands and obtain confidential British information. Known in the U.S. as "U-Boat 29," this film is based on a J. Storer Clouston novel. This was the first teaming of director Powell and writer Pressburger, who followed with "Contraband" in 1940. **82m/B VHS, Beta, LV.** GB Conrad Veidt, Valerie Hobson, Sebastian Shaw, Marius Goring, June Duprez, Helen Haye, Cyril Raymond, Hay Petrie; **D:** Michael Powell; **M:** Miklos Rozsa. NOS, VYY, DVT

Spy of Napoleon 🎬🎬 **1936** A French aristocrat agrees to marry the illegitimate daughter of Emperor Napoleon III and finds himself working to uncover traitors to the throne. Based on Baroness Orczy's novel. **77m/B VHS, Beta.** GB Richard Barthelmess, Dolly Haas, Francis L. Sullivan. VYY

Spy Smasher **1942** A war reporter uses his supposed death (and a covenient twin brother) to go underground and fight Nazi counterfeiters trying to wreck the economy. 12-episode serial. "Spy Smasher Returns" is actually a condensed-version not a sequel. **185m/B VHS.** Kane Richmond, Marguerite Chapman, Sam Flint, Hans Schumm, Tristram Coffin; **D:** William Witney. REP

Spy Smasher Returns **1942** The exciting 12-part serial "Spy Smasher" was cut and edited into feature length and released under this title. The masked marvel and his twin brother battle enemy agents during WWII. This new version is just as exciting as the original cliffhanger. **185m/B VHS.** Kane Richmond, Marguerite Chapman, Sam Flint, Hans Schumm, Tristram Coffin; **D:** William Witney. REP, MLB

Spy Story 🎬🎬 **1986** A Cold War conflict, counter-intelligence, conspiracy, and a nuclear sub chase highlight this tale by Len Deighton. **105m/C VHS, Beta.** VCD, MOV

Spy Trap 🎬🎬½ **1992** Four junior-high school friends concoct bogus military plans using futuristic toys for blueprints. The "secret" plans get sold to the Russians and the kids find themselves chased by the unhappy KGB and the CIA. Family adventure. **96m/C VHS.** Elya Baskin, Danielle Du Clos, Jason Kristofer, Cameron Johann, Devin Ratray, Kimble Joyner; **D:** Arthur Sherman. HMD

The Spy Who Came in from the Cold 🎬🎬🎬½ **1965** The acclaimed adaptation of the John Le Carre novel about an aging British spy who attempts to infiltrate the East German agency. Prototypical Cold War thriller, with emphasis on de-glamorizing espionage. Gritty and superbly realistic with a documentary style which hampered it at the box office. **110m/B VHS, Beta, LV, Closed Caption.** Richard Burton, Oskar Werner, Claire Bloom, Sam Wanamaker, Peter Van Eyck, Cyril Cusack, Rupert Davies, Michael Hordern; **D:** Martin Ritt; **C:** Oswald Morris. British Academy Awards '66: Best Film; Edgar Allan Poe Awards '65: Best Screenplay; Golden Globe Awards '66: Best Supporting Actor (Werner); Nominations: Academy Awards '65: Best Actor (Burton), Best Art Direction/Set Decoration (B & W). PAR

The Spy Who Loved Me 🎬🎬 **1977 (PG)** James Bond teams up with female Russian Agent XXX to squash a villain's plan to use captured American and Russian atomic submarines in a plot to destroy the world. The villain's henchman, 7'2" Kiel, is the steel-toothed Jaws. Carly Simon sings the memorable, Marvin Hamlisch theme song, "Nobody Does It Better." **136m/C VHS, Beta, LV.** GB Roger Moore, Barbara Bach, Curt Jurgens, Richard Kiel, Caroline Munro, Walter Gotell, Geoffrey Keen, Valerie Leon, Bernard Lee, Lois Maxwell, Desmond Llewelyn; **D:** Lewis Gilbert; **M:** Marvin Hamlisch, Paul Buckmaster. Nominations: Academy Awards '77: Best Art Direction/Set Decoration, Best Song ("Nobody Does It Better"), Best Original Score. MGM, FOX, TLF

Spy with a Cold Nose 🎬🎬 **1966** A sporadically funny spy spoof about a bugged dog passed between British and Soviet intelligence. Hard-working cast keeps it from collapsing. **93m/C VHS, Beta.** GB Laurence Harvey, Daliah Lavi, Lionel Jeffries; **D:** Daniel Petrie. NLC

The Spy Within 🎬🎬 Flight of the Dove **1994 (R)** Spy Alex (Russell) is working undercover as a call girl and Will (Glenn) is an explosives expert on the run from his past. The two share more than a mutual attraction since a covert organization wants them both dead. Confusing plot but fast-paced action. Railsback's directorial debut. **CW:** Strong sexuality; violence and language. **92m/C VHS.** Theresa Russell, Scott Glenn, Lane Smith, Terence Knox, Katherine Helmond, Alex Rocco, Joe Pantoliano, Rudy Ramos; **D:** Steve Railsback; **W:** Lewis Green. NHO

Spymaker: The Secret Life of Ian Fleming ✓✓½ *Spymaker* 1990 Fictionalized account of the creator of the ultimate spy, James Bond, and his early days in the British Secret Service. Fans of the Bond movies will appreciate the numerous inside jokes. Connery is the son of Sean. Made for British television. **96m/C VHS, Closed Caption.** *GB* Jason Connery, Kristin Scott Thomas, Joss Ackland, Patricia Hodge, David Warner, Fiona Fullerton, Richard Johnson; **D:** Ferdinand Fairfax. TTC

S*P*Y*S ✓ 1974 (PG) An attempt to cash in on the success of "M*A*S*H," this unfunny spy spoof details the adventures of two bumbling CIA men who botch a Russian defection, and get both sides after them. Usually competent director Kershner had a bad day. **87m/C VHS, Beta.** Donald Sutherland, Elliott Gould, Joss Ackland, Zouzou, Shane Rimmer, Vladek Sheybal, Nigel Hawthorne; **D:** Irvin Kershner; **W:** Malcolm Marmorstein, Lawrence J. Cohen; **M:** Jerry Goldsmith. FOX

Squanto: A Warrior's Tale ✓✓✓ 1994 (PG) Family adventure tale about 17th-century Massachusetts brave Squanto (Beach), who's captured by English traders and taken to Plymouth, England for display as a "savage." He manages to escape, eventually hiding aboard a trading vessel bound for America, and on returning home even brings about a peace between fearful Pilgrims and a neighboring tribe (which culminates in the first Thanksgiving feast). It may be history lite but it's also a thoughtful, adventurous saga with good performances, and fine location filming in Nova Scotia and Cape Breton, Canada. **101m/C VHS, LV, Closed Caption.** Adam Beach, Mandy Patinkin, Michael Gambon, Nathaniel Parker, Eric Schweig, Donal Donnelly, Stuart Pankin, Alex Norton, Irene Bedard; **D:** Xavier Koller; **W:** Darlene Craviotto; **M:** Joel McNeely. DIS

Square Dance ✓✓½ *Home is Where the Heart Is* 1987 (PG-13) A Texas teenager leaves the farm where she's been raised by her grandfather to live in the city with her promiscuous mother (Alexander, cast against type) where she befriends a retarded young man (yes, it's Lowe, also cast against type). Too slow, but helped by good acting. **118m/C VHS, Beta, LV.** Jane Alexander, Jason Robards Jr., Rob Lowe, Winona Ryder, Deborah Richter, Guich Koock, Elbert Lewis; **D:** Daniel Petrie; **W:** Alan Hines; **M:** Bruce Broughton. NO

Square Dance Jubilee ✓½ 1951 Television scouts hit Prairie City in search of cowboy stars, and stumble onto cattle rustlers. Twenty-one C & W tunes support a near-invisible plot, suitable for fridge runs. **78m/B VHS, Beta, LV.** Mary Beth Hughes, Donald (Don "Red") Barry, Wally Vernon, John Eldridge; **D:** Paul Landres. NO

Square Shoulders ✓½ 1929 Adventures of young military school student with geometric anatomy (Coghlan). **58m/B VHS, Beta.** Frank "Junior" Coghlan, Louis Wolheim, Anita Louise, Montague Shaw; **D:** E. Mason Hopper. GPV, FCT

The Squeaker ✓✓½ *Murder on Diamond Row* 1937 Good Edgar Wallace mystery about a disgraced inspector trying to clear his name. **?m/C VHS.** Edmund Lowe, Sebastian Shaw; **M:** Miklos Rozsa. SNC

The Squeaker ✓✓½ 1965 Complicated but interesting thriller about the underworld goings-on after a big-time diamond heist. German remake of an early (1930) British talkie, also done in 1937, based on the Edgar Wallace novel. **95m/B VHS.** *GE* Heinz Drache, Eddi Arent, Klaus Kinski, Barbara Rutting; **D:** Alfred Vohrer. SNC

The Squeeze ✓✓ 1977 (R) Scotland Yard detective Keach, fired for drunkenness, gets a chance to reinstate himself when his ex-wife is caught up in a brutal kidnapping scheme. Slim script gives good cast uphill work. Ordinary thriller. Available with Spanish subtitles. **106m/C VHS, Beta, LV.** Stacy Keach, Carol White, David Hemmings, Edward Fox, Stephen Boyd; **D:** Michael Apted. WAR

The Squeeze ✓½ 1980 An aging safecracker is hired for a final job, but learns that his cohorts plan to kill him when the heist is finished. Blah revenge thriller. **93m/C VHS, Beta.** *IT* Lee Van Cleef, Karen Black, Edward Albert, Lionel Stander, Robert Alda; **D:** Anthony (Antonio Margheriti) Dawson. NO

The Squeeze woof! 1987 (PG-13) Keaton is wasted in this attempt at a comedy about a small-time con artist who discovers a Mafia plot to fix a lottery electromagnetically. **101m/C VHS, Beta, LV, Closed Caption.** Michael Keaton, Rae Dawn Chong, John Davidson, Ric Abernathy, Bobby Bass, Joe Pantoliano, Meat Loaf, Paul Herman; **D:** Roger Young; **C:** Arthur Albert; **M:** Miles Goodman. HBO

Squeeze Play woof! 1979 Group of young women start a softball team and challenge the boyfriends to a game. Standard battle of the sexes takes places, with a wet T-shirt contest thrown in for good measure. Cheap, plotless, offensive trash from Troma. **92m/C VHS, Beta, LV.** Al Corley, Jennifer Hetrick, Jim Metzler; **D:** Lloyd (Samuel Weil) Kaufman. NO

Squirm ✓✓ 1976 (R) Storm disrupts a highly charged power cable, electrifying a host of garden-variety worms. The worms then turn themselves into giant monsters that terrorize a small town in Georgia. The opening credits claim it's based on an actual 1975 incident. Yeah, right. Okay entry in the giant worm genre. **92m/C VHS, Beta, LV.** Don Scardino, Patricia Pearcy, Jean Sullivan; **D:** Jeff Lieberman; **W:** Jeff Lieberman. LIV, VES

Squizzy Taylor ✓✓ 1984 The rise and fall of real-life Australian mob boss Squizzy Taylor in the 1920s. Colorful period gangster drama loses steam about halfway through. **82m/C VHS, Beta.** *AU* Jacki Weaver, Alan Cassell, David Atkins; **D:** Kevin Dobson; **C:** Dan Burstall. NO

S.S. Experiment Camp 2 ✓ 1986 Hitler's elite corps of sadists get their kicks torturing and maiming prisoners during the dark days of WWII. **90m/C VHS, Beta.** John Braun, Macha Magal. NO

SS Girls woof! 1978 After the assassination attempt of July 1944, Hitler does not trust the Wehrmacht and extends the power of the SS over Germany. General Berger entrusts Hans Schillemberg to recruit a specially chosen group of prostitutes who must test the fighting spirit and loyalty of the generals. Seedy exploitation. **82m/C VHS, Beta.** Gabriele Carrara, Marina Daunia, Vassili Karis, Macha Magal, Thomas Rudy, Lucic Bogoljub Benny, Ivano Staccioli. MED

S.S. Love Camp No. 27 197? A beautiful young girl's life is torn to shreds when she is imprisoned in a Nazi brothel. **90m/C VHS, Beta.** VCD

Sssssss ✓✓ 1973 (PG-13) Campy, creepy story of snake expert Carl Stoner (Strother Martin) who's developed a serum from cobra venom that just happens to turn human beings into snakes. His latest unwitting guinea pig is research assistant David Blake (Benedict). Cool makeup effects. **99m/C VHS, Closed Caption.** Strother Martin, Dirk Benedict, Heather Menzies, Richard B. Shull, Tim O'Connor, Jack Ging; **D:** Bernard L. Kowalski; **W:** Hal Dresner; **C:** Gerald Perry Finnerman; **M:** Patrick Williams. USH

Stacey ✓½ *Stacey and Her Gangbusters* 1973 (R) Ex-Playmate Randall stars as Stacey Hansen, a beautiful, implausibly talented private detective. Hyper-convoluted plot, too much sex and violence detract from a potentially not-wretched whodunit. **87m/C VHS, Beta.** Anne Randall, Marjorie Bennett, Anitra Ford, Alan Landers, James Westmoreland, Christina Raines; **D:** Andy Sidaris. GEM

Stacking ✓✓ *Season of Dreams* 1987 (PG) In the 1950s, a Montana family is threatened with losing their farm. Typical, boring '80s farmland tragedy with coming of age tale. **95m/C VHS, Beta, LV.** Christine Lahti, Megan Follows, Frederic Forrest, Peter Coyote, Jason Gedrick; **D:** Martin Rosen; **W:** Victoria Jenkins; **C:** Richard Bowen, Paul Elliott, Richard Bowen; **M:** Patrick Gleeson. NLC

Stacy's Knights ✓✓ *Double Down* 1983 (PG) A seemingly shy girl happens to have an uncanny knack for blackjack. With the odds against her and an unlikely group of "knights" to aid her, she sets up an implausible "sting" operation. Blah TV fodder for the big screen. **95m/C VHS, Beta.** Kevin Costner, Andra Millian; **D:** Jim Wilson; **W:** Michael Blake. LIV, VES

Stage Door ✓✓✓½ 1937 An energetic ensemble peek at the women of the theater. A boarding house for potential actresses houses a wide variety of talents and dreams. Patrician Hepburn and wisecracking Rogers make a good team in a talent-packed ensemble. Realistic look at the sub-world of Broadway aspirations includes dialogue taken from idle chat among the actresses between takes. Based on the play by Edna Ferber and George S. Kaufman, who suggested in jest a title change to "Screen Door," since so much had been changed. Watch for young stars-to-be like Ball, Arden and Miller. **92m/B VHS, Beta.** Katharine Hepburn, Ginger Rogers, Lucille Ball, Eve Arden, Andrea Leeds, Jack Carson, Adolphe Menjou, Gail Patrick; **D:** Gregory La Cava. National Board of Review Awards '37: 10 Best Films of the Year; New York Film Critics Awards '37: Best Director (La Cava); Nominations: Academy Awards '37: Best Director (La Cava), Best Picture, Best Screenplay, Best Supporting Actress (Leeds). TTC, CCB, MED

Stage Door Canteen ✓✓½ 1943 The Stage Door Canteens were operated by the American Theatre Wing during WWII for servicemen on leave. They were staffed by some of the biggest stars of the day, 65 of whom are featured here. The slight, hokey plot concerns three soldiers who fall for canteen workers while on furlough in New York City. Many musical numbers, cameos, and walk-ons by a plethora of stars. ♫We Mustn't Say Goodbye; Bombshell From Brooklyn; The Machine Gun Song; Sleep, Baby, Sleep in Your Jeep; Quick Sands; You're Pretty Terrific Yourself; Don't Worry Island; We Meet in the Funniest Places; A Rookie and His Rhythm. **135m/B VHS, Beta, LV.** Cheryl Walker, William Terry, Marjorie Riordan, Lon McCallister, Sunset Carson, Tallulah Bankhead, Merle Oberon, Katharine Hepburn, Paul Muni, Ethel Waters, Judith Anderson, Ray Bolger; **Cameos:** Helen Hayes, Harpo Marx, Gertrude Lawrence, Ethel Merman, Edgar Bergen, George Raft, Benny Goodman, Peggy Lee, Count Basie, Kay Kyser, Guy Lombardo, Xavier Cugat, Johnny Weissmuller; **D:** Frank Borzage. Nominations: Academy Awards '43: Best Song ("We Mustn't Say Goodbye"), Scoring of a Musical. CNG, NOS, PSM

Stage Fright ✓✓✓ 1950 Wyman will stop at nothing to clear her old boyfriend, who has been accused of murdering the husband of his mistress, an actress (Dietrich). Disguised as a maid, she falls in love with the investigating detective, and discovers her friend's guilt. Dietrich sings "The Laziest Gal in Town." The Master's last film made in England until "Frenzy" (1971). **110m/B VHS, Beta, LV.** *GB* Jane Wyman, Marlene Dietrich, Alastair Sim, Sybil Thorndike, Michael Wilding, Kay Walsh; **D:** Alfred Hitchcock. National Board of Review Awards '50: 10 Best Films of the Year. WAR, MLB

Stage Fright ✓ 1983 Bashful actress is transformed into a homicidal killer after a latent psychosis in her becomes active. **82m/C VHS, Beta, LV.** Jenny Neumann, Gary Sweet; **M:** Brian May. NO

Stage Struck ✓✓½ 1957 Strasberg reprises the role made famous by Katharine Hepburn as a determined, would-be actress in this mediocre remake of "Morning Glory" (1933). Christopher Plummer's screen debut shows little of his later talent. **95m/B VHS, Beta, LV.** Henry Fonda,

Susan Strasberg, Christopher Plummer, Herbert Marshall, Joan Greenwood; **D:** Sidney Lumet; **M:** Alex North. *IME*

Stage to Mesa City ⚔️⚔️ 1948 Marshal LaRue must find out who is behind the pesky attacks on the stage line to Mesa City. Chesebro, as usual, is a good bad guy. A few chuckles between fist fights and shoot-em-ups. *52m/B VHS, Beta.* Lash LaRue, Al "Fuzzy" St. John, George Chesebro, Jennifer Holt, Russell Arms; **D:** Ray Taylor. *COL, GPV*

Stagecoach ⚔️⚔️⚔️⚔️ 1939 Varied group of characters with nothing in common are stuck together inside a coach besieged by bandits and Indians. Considered structurally perfect, with excellent direction by Ford, it's the film that made Wayne a star as the Ringo Kid, an outlaw looking to avenge the murder of his brother and father. The first pairing of Ford and Wayne changed the course of the modern western. Stunning photography by Bert Glennon and Ray Binger captured the mythical air of Monument Valley, a site that Ford was often to revisit. Based on the story "Stage to Lordsburg" by Ernest Haycox. Remade miserably with in 1966 and again—why?—as a TV movie in 1986. *100m/B VHS, Beta, LV.* John Wayne, Claire Trevor, Thomas Mitchell, George Bancroft, John Carradine, Andy Devine, Donald Meek, Louise Platt, Berton Churchill, Tim Holt, Tom Tyler, Chris-Pin Martin, Francis Ford, Jack Pennick; **D:** John Ford. Academy Awards '39: Best Supporting Actor (Mitchell), Best Score; National Board of Review Awards '39: 10 Best Films of the Year; New York Film Critics Awards '39: Best Director (Ford); Nominations: Academy Awards '39: Best Black and White Cinematography, Best Director (Ford), Best Film Editing, Best Interior Decoration, Best Picture. *WAR, VES, TLF*

Stagecoach ⚔️ 1986 A forgettable made-for-television remake of the classic 1939 western about a motley crew of characters in a cross-country coach beset by thieves and Indians. *95m/C VHS, Beta.* Willie Nelson, Waylon Jennings, Johnny Cash, Kris Kristofferson, John Schneider, Elizabeth Ashley, Mary Crosby, Anthony Newley, Anthony (Tony) Franciosa; **D:** Ted Post; **M:** Willie Nelson. *THV*

Stagecoach to Denver ⚔️⚔️ 1946 Lane as Red Ryder investigates a stagecoach wreck and uncovers a land-grabbing plot led by who else?—the pillar of the community (Barcroft). Well-directed "Red Ryder" episode. *53m/B VHS, Beta.* Allan "Rocky" Lane, Roy Barcroft, Robert (Bobby) Blake, Peggy Stewart, Martha Wentworth; **D:** R.G. Springsteen. *NOS, CAB, VCN*

Stagefright ⚔️ 1987 A maniacal serial killer tries to cover his trail by joining the cast of a play about mass murder. The other actors soon have more to worry about than remembering their lines. Typical low-grade horror. *95m/C VHS, Beta.* David Brandon, Barbara Cupisti, Robert Gligorov; **D:** Michele (Michael) Soavi. *IMP*

Stakeout ⚔️⚔️ 1962 An ex-con tries to start life anew, but every time he finds a good job, his past catches up with him. A return to the life of crime looks tempting. Predictable and familiar plot, but performances are sincere. *81m/B VHS.* Bing Russell, Billy Hughes, Bill Hale, Jack Harris; **D:** James Landis; **W:** James Landis. *SNC*

Stakeout ⚔️⚔️½ 1987 (R) A sometimes violent comedy-thriller about a pair of detectives who stake out a beautiful woman's apartment, hoping for a clue to the whereabouts of her psycho boyfriend who has broken out of prison. One of them (Dreyfuss) then begins to fall in love with her. Natural charm among Estevez, Dreyfuss, and Stowe that adds to the proceedings, which are palpably implausible and silly. Slapstick sequel "Another Stakeout" followed in 1993. *117m/C VHS, Beta, LV, 8mm, Closed Caption.* Richard Dreyfuss, Emilio Estevez, Madeleine Stowe, Aidan Quinn, Forest Whitaker, Dan Lauria, Earl Billings; **D:** John Badham; **W:** Jim Kouf; **M:** Arthur B. Rubinstein. Edgar Allan Poe Awards '87: Best Screenplay. *TOU*

Stalag 17 ⚔️⚔️⚔️⚔️ 1953 A group of American G.I.s in a German POW camp during WWII suspects the opportunistic Holden of being the spy in their midst. One of the very best American

movies of the 1950's, adapted from the play by Donald Bevan and Edmund Trzcinski. Wilder, so good at comedy, proved himself equally adept at drama, and brought a top-drawer performance out of Holden. Features superb photography from Ernest Laszlo, and a wonderful score. *120m/B VHS, Beta, LV.* William Holden, Don Taylor, Peter Graves, Otto Preminger, Harvey Lembeck, Robert Strauss, Sig Rumann, Richard Erdman, Neville Brand; **D:** Billy Wilder; **W:** Billy Wilder, Edwin Blum; **C:** Ernest Laszlo; **M:** Franz Waxman. Academy Awards '53: Best Actor (Holden); National Board of Review Awards '53: 10 Best Films of the Year; Nominations: Academy Awards '53: Best Director (Wilder), Best Supporting Actor (Strauss). *PAR, TLF, BTV*

Stalag Luft 19?? Senior British officer James Forrester (Fry) is regarded by fellow POWs as a first-class idiot, since he has a record 23 escapes and re-captures. But he's determined to break all 327 prisioners out of their Nazi camp while the nervous German Kommandant keeps one eye on the advancing Allied army and the other on his prisoners. *103m/C VHS.* **GB** Stephen Fry, Geoffrey Palmer, Nicholas Lyndhurst. *VCO*

Stalin ⚔️⚔️½ 1992 The story of the leader of the Soviet Union who ruled with an iron fist from 1924-1953. One of the most feared men of the 20th century, he wrenched the largest country in the world singlehandedly from a backward, pastoral farmland to an industrial landscape. He was also responsible for the feared purges of the late 1930s where more than a million people were executed. Also explored is the dictator's relationship with his family, including how marriage to a cunning, sadistic, paranoid tyrant affected his wife. Filmed at actual historical locations in Russia. Made for cable television. *173m/C VHS, LV, Closed Caption.* Robert Duvall, Julia Ormond, Jeroen Krabbe, Joan Plowright, Maximilian Schell, Frank Finlay, Roshan Seth, Daniel Massey, Miriam Margolyes, Jim Carter, Joanna Roth, Andras Balint; **D:** Ivan Passer; **W:** Paul Monash; **C:** Vilmos Zsigmond. *MGM, BTV*

Stalingrad ⚔️⚔️ 1994 Group of German stormtroopers fall victim to the brutal war of attrition over Stalingrad in 1942 and 1943. Realistic depiction of war is not for the fainthearted. Originally a TV miniseries; German with subtitles. *150m/C VHS.* **GE** Dominique Horwitz, Thomas Kretschmann, Jochen Nickel; **D:** Joseph Vilsmaier; **W:** Joseph Vilsmaier; **C:** Joseph Vilsmaier; **M:** Norbert J. Schneider. *FXL*

Stalk the Wild Child ⚔️½ 1976 Well-intentioned but unconvincing American remake of Truffaut's "The Wild Child," about a child psychologist's efforts to rehabilitate a boy raised by wolves. TV pilot inspired "Lucan," a short-lived series. *78m/C VHS.* David Janssen, Trish Van Devere, Benjamin Bottoms, Joseph Bottoms; **D:** William Hale. *WOV*

Stalked ⚔️½ 1994 (R) Daryl Gleeson (Underwood) saves the life of the widowed Brooke's (D'Abo) young son (Fennell). Naturally, she's grateful—only Daryl takes her gratitude for something more intimate and becomes fixated on her every move. **CW:** Violence; language; some nudity. *95m/C VHS, LV, Closed Caption.* Maryam D'Abo, Jay Underwood, Tod Fennell, Lisa Blount, Alex Karzis, Karen Robinson, Vivian Reis; **D:** Douglas Jackson. *REP*

Stalker ⚔️⚔️⚔️ 1979 A meteorite, crashing to Earth, has caused a wasteland area known as the Zone. The Zone is forbidden to anyone except special guides called Stalkers. Three Stalkers enter the region searching for its center, which contains a room that supposedly reveals fantasies. From the Soviet team that made "Solaris." Filmed with both color and black-and-white sequences. Suspenseful atmosphere due to the director's use of long takes, movement, and color. In Russian with English subtitles. *160m/C VHS.* **RU** Alexander Kaidanovsky, Nikolai Grinko, Anatoli Solonitzin, Alice Freindlikh; **D:** Andrei Tarkovsky; **M:** Eduard Artemyev. *FXL, FCT*

Stalking Danger ⚔️½ *C.A.T. Squad* 1986 (PG) A secret government group must terminate an assassination plot by a terrorist organization. *97m/C VHS, Beta, LV.* Joe Cortese, Steve James, Patricia

Charbonneau, Jack Youngblood; **D:** William Friedkin; **M:** Ennio Morricone. *THV*

Stalking Laura ⚔️½ *I Can Make You Love Me: The Stalking of Laura Black* 1993 Laura Black (Shields) has just landed her first job at a California engineering firm where she meets co-worker Richard Farley (Thomas). He asks her out—she turns him down—he starts harassing her. Laura reports it to the company, who eventually fire Farley, and obtains a restraining order. He goes on a murderous rampage. Fact-based TV movie with Thomas effective as the dangerous obsessive. *90m/C VHS.* Brooke Shields, Richard Thomas, Viveka Davis, William Allen Young, Richard Yniguez, Scott Bryce. *AEL*

The Stalking Moon ⚔️½ 1969 (G) Indian scout Peck, ready to retire, meets a woman and her half-breed son who have been captives of the Apaches for 10 years. He agrees to help them escape but learns that the woman's Indian husband is hunting them down. Skeletal plot with little meat on it; great scenery but you wouldn't know it. *109m/C VHS.* Gregory Peck, Eva Marie Saint, Robert Forster, Noland Clay; **D:** Robert Mulligan; **W:** Alvin Sargent. *ACE, WAR*

Stamp Day for Superman ⚔️⚔️ 1953 Based on the "Superman" television series, this program was made to promote defense savings stamps for kids. A "Superman" cartoon is also included. *25m/B VHS, Beta.* George Reeves, Jack Larson, Robert Shayne. *VDM*

Stamp of a Killer ⚔️ 1987 (PG) A tough cop tries to decipher the pattern of a rampaging serial killer. Made for television. *95m/C VHS.* Jimmy Smits, Judith Light, Audra Lindley, Michael Parks, Rhea Perlman; **D:** Larry Elikann. *VTR, NWV*

Stan without Ollie, Vol. 1 1923 Three silent comedy shorts featuring Laurel on his own, years before teaming with Ollie: "Kill or Cure," "Oranges & Lemons," and "The Noon Whistle." *53m/B VHS, Beta.* Stan Laurel. *VYY*

Stan without Ollie, Vol. 2 1923 Three silent shorts from Laurel before he met the big guy. *55m/B VHS, Beta.* Stan Laurel. *VYY*

Stan without Ollie, Vol. 3 1923 Three early Laurel shorts: "White Wings," "Man About Town," and "Smithy." *51m/B VHS, Beta.* Stan Laurel, James Finlayson. *VYY*

Stan without Ollie, Vol. 4 1925 Three classic pre-Hardy shorts featuring Laurel: "Half a Man," "Yes, Yes, Nanette," and "Save the Ship." *64m/B VHS, Beta, 8mm.* Stan Laurel, Blanche Payson, James Finlayson. *VYY*

Stand Alone ⚔️⚔️ 1985 (R) WWII vet Durning battles local dope dealers in his New York neighborhood. Self-serious anti-drug flick miscasts Durning (overweight and looking silly in fight scenes) and Grier. *94m/C VHS, Beta.* Charles Durning, Pam Grier, James Keach; **D:** Alan Beattie; **W:** Roy Carlson. *NWV, VTR*

Stand and Deliver ⚔️⚔️ 1928 War vet joins Greek ranks for the smell of gunpowder in the morning and meets woman of his dreams. Kidnapped by infamous outlaws, he pledges allegiance to them before turning them over to the authorities, and he's free to live happily ever after with heartthrob. *57m/B VHS, Beta.* Rod La Rocque, Lupe Velez, Warner Oland, James Dime, Frank Lanning, Donald Crisp; **D:** Donald Crisp. *GPV*

Stand and Deliver ⚔️⚔️ 1988 (PG) A tough teacher inspires students in an East L.A. barrio to take the Advanced Placement Test in calculus. A superb, inspirational true story, with a wonderful performance from Olmos. *105m/C VHS, LV, 8mm, Closed Caption.* Edward James Olmos, Lou Diamond Phillips, Rosana De Soto, Andy Garcia, Will Gotay, Ingrid Oliu, Virginia Paris, Mark Eliot, Eugene Glazer; **D:** Ramon Menendez; **W:** Ramon Menendez, Tom Musca; **C:** Tom Richmond; **M:** Craig Safan. Independent Spirit Awards '89: Best Actor (Olmos), Best Director (Menendez), Best Film, Best Screenplay, Best Supporting Actor (Phillips), Best Supporting Actress (De Soto); Nominations: Academy Awards '88: Best Actor (Olmos). *WAR, HMV*

Stand By Me 🎬🎬🎬 1986 (R) A sentimental, observant adaptation of the Stephen King novella "The Body." Four 12-year-olds trek into the Oregon wilderness to find the body of a missing boy, learning about death and personal courage. Told as a reminiscence by narrator "author" Dreyfuss with solid performances from all four child actors. Too much gratuitous obscenity, but a very good, gratifying film from can't-miss director Reiner. 87m/C VHS, Beta, LV, 8mm, Closed Caption. River Phoenix, Wil Wheaton, Jerry O'Connell, Corey Feldman, Kiefer Sutherland, Richard Dreyfuss, Casey Siemaszko, John Cusack; D: Rob Reiner; W: Raynold Gideon; M: Jack Nitzsche. Nominations: Academy Awards '86: Best Adapted Screenplay. COL

Stand-In 🎬🎬🎬 1937 When a Hollywood studio is threatened with bankruptcy, the bank sends in timid efficiency expert Howard to save it. Satire of studio executives and big-budget movie making. Bogart is interestingly cast and effective in his first comedy role, playing a drunken producer in love with star Shelton. 91m/B VHS, Beta. Humphrey Bogart, Joan Blondell, Leslie Howard, Alan Mowbray, Marla Shelton, Jack Carson; D: Tay Garnett. NO

Stand-In 🎬 1985 A strange comedy-action film that takes a behind-the-scenes look at sleaze films and organized crime. 87m/C VHS, Beta. Danny Glover; D: Robert Zagone. NO

Stand Off 🎬½ 1989 Two young hoodlums with guns take eighteen girls hostage in a dormitory. In Hungarian with English subtitles. 97m/C VHS. HU Ary Beri, Gabor Svidrony, Zbigniew Zapassiewicz, Istvan Szabo; D: Gyula Gazdag. EVD, FCT

Stand Off 🎬🎬½ April One 1993 (PG-13) Dramatization of a 14-hour hostage incident that took place at the Bahamanian High Commission in Ottawa on April Fools Day in 1986. Ex-con politely demands that an empty firehall become a shelter for women by taking the High Commissioner of the Bahamas as a hostage. Somewhat flawed but psychologically interesting. CW: Language, threat of violence. 90m/C VHS. CA Stephen Shellan, Djanet Sears, David Strathairn, Gordon Clapp, Pierre Curzi, Wayne Robson; D: Murray Battle; W: Murray Battle. MNC

Stand Up and Cheer 🎬🎬½ 1934 (PG) The new federal Secretary of Entertainment organizes a huge show to raise the country's depressed spirits. Near-invisible plot, fantastic premise are an excuse for lots of imagery, dancing, and comedy, including four-year-old Temple singing "Baby Take a Bow." Also available colorized. 🎵I'm Laughing; We're Out of the Red; Broadway's Gone Hillbilly; Baby Take a Bow; This Is Our Last Night Together; She's Way Up Thar; Stand Up and Cheer. 80m/B VHS, Beta, Closed Caption. Shirley Temple, Warner Baxter, Madge Evans, Nigel Bruce, Stepin Fetchit, Frank Melton, Lila Lee, James Dunn, John Boles, Scotty Beckett; D: Hamilton MacFadden; W: Will Rogers, Ralph Spence; C: Ernest Palmer. FOX

Standing Tall 🎬🎬 1978 A small-time cattle rancher takes on a high-class land baron in this average, made-for-TV western set during the Depression. Playing a "half-breed," Forster carries an otherwise mediocre effort. 100m/C VHS. Robert Forster, Linda Evans, Will Sampson, L.Q. Jones; D: Harvey Hart. WOV

Stanley 🎬½ 1972 (PG) Seminole Vietnam veteran Robinson uses rattlesnakes as his personal weapon of revenge against most of mankind. Thoroughly wretched effort in the gross-pets vein of "Willard" and "Ben." 108m/C VHS, Beta. Chris Robinson, Alex Rocco, Susan Carroll; D: William Grefe. NO

Stanley and Iris 🎬🎬½ 1990 (PG-13) Blue collar recent widow Fonda meets co-worker De Niro, whose illiteracy she helps remedy. Romance follows, inevitably but excruciatingly. Leads' strong presence helps along a very slow, underdeveloped plot. 107m/C VHS, Beta, LV, Closed Caption. Jane Fonda, Robert De Niro, Swoosie Kurtz, Martha Plimpton, Harley Cross, Jamey Sheridan, Feodor Chaliapin Jr, Zohra Lampert, Loretta Devine, Julie Garfield; D:

Martin Ritt; W: Harriet Frank Jr., Irving Ravetch; M: John Williams. MGM, FCT

Stanley and Livingstone 🎬🎬🎬 1939 The classic Hollywood kitsch version of the Victorian legend-based-on-fact. American journalist Tracy sets out into darkest Africa to locate a long lost Brisith explorer. Lavish, dramatically solid fictionalized history. (The real Stanley did not become a missionary—but hey, this is the movies). Tracy is excellent, as usual, and low-key. 101m/B VHS, Beta, Closed Caption. Spencer Tracy, Cedric Hardwicke, Nancy Kelly, Walter Brennan, Richard Greene, Charles Coburn, Henry Hull, Henry Travers, Miles Mander, Holmes Herbert, Paul Stanton, Brandon Hurst, Joseph Crehan, Russell Hicks; D: Henry King; C: George Barnes; M: Alfred Newman. FOX

Star! 🎬🎬 Those Were the Happy Times 1968 Campy showbiz extravaganza based on the life of famed musical comedy performer Gertrude Lawrence (Andrews), star of the London and Broadway stage. Film follows Lawrence's adventures from the British music halls to her fateful meeting with Noel Coward (Massey), who would not only become her dearest friend but perform with and write for her as well. A tumultuous private life is also on display. 17 lavishly staged musical numbers helped boost the cost of the film to $14 million—big bucks in '68. Movie was a colossal flop on opening and was recut, deleting 50 minutes, but still didn't recoup its losses. Has gained a cult following. 🎵Down at the Old Bull and Bush; Piccadilly; Star!; Oh, It's a Lovely War; In My Garden of Joy; Forbidden Fruit; Parisian Pierrot; Someday I'll Find You; Has Anybody Seen Our Ship?. 172m/C VHS, LV, Closed Caption. Julie Andrews, Daniel Massey, Richard Crenna, Michael Craig, Robert Reed, Bruce Forsyth, Beryl Reid, John Collin, Alan Oppenheimer, Anthony Eisley, Jenny Agutter, J. Pat O'Malley, Richard Karlan, Lynley Laurence, Harvey Jason, Elizabeth St. Clair; D: Robert Wise; W: William Fairchild; C: Ernest Laszlo. Nominations: Academy Awards '68: Best Adapted Score, Best Art Direction/Set Decoration, Best Cinematography, Best Costume Design, Best Song ("Star!"), Best Sound, Best Supporting Actor (Massey). FXV, BTV, FCT

The Star Chamber 🎬🎬 1983 (R) A conscientious judge (Douglas) sees criminals freed on legal technicalities and wonders if he should take justice into his own hands. He finds a secret society that administers justice extra-legally. Implausible yet predictable. 109m/C VHS, Beta, LV. Michael Douglas, Hal Holbrook, Yaphet Kotto, Sharon Gless, James B. Sikking; D: Peter Hyams; W: Peter Hyams, Roderick Taylor. FOX

Star Crash 🎬🎬½ Stella Star 1978 (PG) Trio of adventurers (woman, man, and robot) sent by emperor Plummer square off against interstellar evil (Spinell) by using their wits and technological wizardry. Semi-funny and cheesy sci-fi, done with style beyond its limited budget. 92m/C VHS, Beta, LV. IT Caroline Munro, Marjoe Gortner, Christopher Plummer, David Hasselhoff, Robert Tessier, Joe Spinell, Nadia Cassini, Judd Hamilton; D: Lewis (Luigi Cozzi) Coates; W: Lewis (Luigi Cozzi) Coates; M: John Barry. NLC

Star Crystal 🎬 1985 (R) Aboard a spaceship, an indestructible alien hunts down the human crew. Cheap imitation of "Alien." 93m/C VHS, Beta. C. Jutson Campbell, Faye Bolt, John W. Smith; D: Lance Lindsay. NWV, VTR, HHE

Star 80 🎬🎬 1983 (R) Based on the true-life tragedy of Playmate of the Year Dorothy Stratten and her manager-husband Paul Snider as they battle for control of her body, her mind, and her money, with gruesome results. Roberts is overpowering as the vile Snider, but the movie is generally unpleasant. Fosse's last film. 104m/C VHS, Beta, LV. Mariel Hemingway, Eric Roberts, Cliff Robertson, David Clennon, Josh Mostel, Roger Rees, Carroll Baker; D: Bob Fosse; C: Sven Nykvist; M: Ralph Burns. WAR

A Star is Born 🎬🎬🎬½ 1937 A movie star declining in popularity marries a shy girl and helps her become a star. Her fame eclipses his and tragic consequences follow. Shows Hollywood-behind-the-scenes machinations. Stunning

ending is based on the real-life tragedy of silent film star Wallace Reid, who died of a morphine overdose in 1923 at age 31. Remade twice, in 1954 and 1976. 111m/C VHS, Beta, LV. Janet Gaynor, Fredric March, Adolphe Menjou, May Robson, Andy Devine, Lionel Stander, Franklin Pangborn; D: William A. Wellman; W: William A. Wellman, David O. Selznick, Dorothy Parker; C: William Howard Greene; M: Max Steiner. Academy Awards '37: Best Story; National Board of Review Awards '37: 10 Best Films of the Year; Nominations: Academy Awards '37: Best Actor (March), Best Actress (Gaynor), Best Director (Wellman), Best Picture. CNG, NOS, VYY

A Star is Born 🎬🎬🎬½ 1954 (PG) Aging actor helps a young actress to fame. She becomes his wife, but alcoholism and failure are too much for him. She honors his memory. Remake of the 1937 classic was Garland's triumph, a superb and varied performance. Newly restored version reinstates over 20 minutes of long-missing footage, including three Garland musical numbers. 🎵I'll Get By; You Took Advantage of me; Black Bottom; Peanut Vendor; My Melancholy Baby; Swanee; It's A New World; Gotta Have Me Go With You; Somewhere There's Someone. 175m/C VHS, Beta, LV. Judy Garland, James Mason, Jack Carson, Tommy Noonan, Charles Bickford, Emerson Treacy, Charles Halton; D: George Cukor; C: Sam Leavitt. Golden Globe Awards '55: Best Actor—Musical/Comedy (Mason), Best Actress—Musical/Comedy (Garland); National Board of Review Awards '54: 10 Best Films of the Year; Nominations: Academy Awards '54: Best Actor (Mason), Best Actress (Garland), Best Art Direction/Set Decoration (Color), Best Costume Design (Color), Best Song ("The Man That Got Away"), Scoring of a Musical. WAR

A Star is Born 🎬🎬 1976 (R) Miserable update of the 1937 and 1954 classics permitting Ms. Streisand to showcase her hit song "Evergreen." The tragic story of one star (the relentlessly un-hip Streisand) on her way to the top and another (good old boy Kristofferson) whose career is in decline. Kristofferson is miscast, Streisand eventually numbing, but film may interest those looking into big-budget, big-star misfires. 🎵Watch Closely Now; Spanish Lies; Hellacious Acres; With One More Look At You; Woman in the Moon; Queen Bee; Everything; Crippled Cow; I Believe in Love. 140m/C VHS, Beta. Barbra Streisand, Kris Kristofferson, Paul Mazursky, Gary Busey, Sally Kirkland, Oliver Clark, Marta Heflin, Robert Englund; D: Frank Pierson; W: Frank Pierson, Joan Didion, John Gregory Dunne; C: Robert L. Surtees; M: Paul Williams. Academy Awards '76: Best Song ("Evergreen"); Golden Globe Awards '77: Best Actor—Musical/Comedy (Kristofferson), Best Actress—Musical/Comedy (Streisand), Best Film—Musical/Comedy, Best Song ("Evergreen"), Best Score; Nominations: Academy Awards '76: Best Cinematography, Best Sound, Original Song Score and/or Adaptation. WAR

Star Knight 🎬 Starknight 1985 (PG-13) Weird combo of sci fi and medieval romance. A spaceship lands near a European castle and the local princess falls for one of the visitors—much to her daddy's dismay. Very silly. 92m/C VHS, LV, Closed Caption. SP Harvey Keitel, Klaus Kinski, Fernando Rey; D: Fernando Colombo. THV

The Star Maker 🎬🎬 The Star Man; L'Uomo delle Stelle 1995 (R) Con man Joe Morelli (Castellitto) travels through the villages of 1950s Sicily claiming to be a movie talent scout. For a fee, he offers the locals a chance to shoot a screen test, which reveals various bits and pieces of their lives. There's a brief romance and Joe's scam eventually comes to light but the story's more nostalgia than narrative. Italian with subtitles. CW: Some strong sexuality, language and a brutal beating. 107m/C VHS, LV, Closed Caption. IT Sergio Castellitto, Tiziana Lodato; D: Giuseppe Tornatore; W: Giuseppe Tornatore, Fabio Rinaudo; C: Dante Spinotti; M: Ennio Morricone. Nominations: Academy Awards '95: Best Foreign Language Film. TOU

Star of Midnight 🎬🎬 1935 A lawyer/detective becomes involved in the disappearance of the leading lady in a Broadway show and the murder of a columnist. Powell and Rogers take on characters similar to Nick and Nora Charles, but the pizazz of the "Thin Man" series is missing. **90m/B VHS, Beta, LV.** Ginger Rogers, William Powell, Paul Kelly; **D:** Stephen Roberts. *TTC*

The Star Packer 🎬🎬 1934 Wayne puts on a marshal's badge, straightens out a gang of crooks, and still finds time for romance. Implausible and kind of dull early Wayne vehicle. **53m/B VHS, Beta.** John Wayne, George "Gabby" Hayes, Earl Dwire, Yakima Canutt; **D:** Robert North Bradbury. *COL, REP, NOS*

Star Quest 🎬 *Beyond the Rising Moon; Space 2074* 1989 A genetically engineered woman fights for freedom from her corporate creators. Mediocre effects and some pointless action; done much better by Ridley Scott in "Blade Runner." **90m/C VHS, Beta, LV.** Tracy Davis, Hans Bachman, Michael Mack; **D:** Phillip Cook. *NO*

Star Quest 🎬🎬½ 1994 (R) Eight astronauts, suspended in a cryogenic sleep for nearly 100 years, awaken to find the human race has been destroyed by a nuclear holocaust. **95m/C VHS, LV.** Steven Bauer, Emma Samms, Alan Rachins, Brenda Bakke, Ming-Na Wen, Gregory McKinney, Cliff DeYoung; **D:** Rick Jacobson. *NHO*

Star Reporter 🎬½ 1939 A son takes over his father's newspaper when dad is killed by gangsters. The son uses the paper in an attempt to destroy the underworld, but stumbles on some startling personal information that could drastically backfire on him. Generally interesting plot, but has some implausibility and too-broad characterization. **62m/B VHS, Beta.** Warren Hull, Marsha Hunt, Morgan Wallace, Clay Clement, Wallis Clark, Virginia Howell, Paul Fix, Joseph Crehan; **D:** Howard Bretherton. *SNC*

Star Slammer 🎬½ 1987 (R) A beautiful woman is unjustly sentenced to a brutal intergalactic prison ship. She leads the convicts to escape amid zany situations. Unevenly funny sci-fi comedy. **85m/C VHS, Beta, LV.** Ross Hagen, John Carradine, Sandy Brooke, Aldo Ray; **D:** Fred Olen Ray. *THV*

Star Spangled Girl 🎬½ 1971 (G) One of Neil Simon's lesser plays, one of his least movies. A pert, patriotic young lady captures the hearts of two left-wing alternative-newspaperguys next door; their political conflicts never rise above bland sitcom level. **94m/C VHS, Closed Caption.** Sandy Duncan, Tony Roberts, Todd Susman, Elizabeth Allen; **D:** Jerry Paris; **W:** Neil Simon; **C:** Sam Leavitt; **M:** Charles Fox. *PAR*

Star Spangled Rhythm 🎬🎬🎬 1942 Movie studio guard (Moore) has told his son (Bracken), a sailor, that he's actually the head of the studio in this WW2 musical/comedy. When he learns his son and his pals are coming for a visit, he enlists the aid of a friendly studio switchboard operator (Hutton) to pull a fast one. (Luckily, the real studio boss is out of town). Plot doesn't matter anyway since its just an excuse for a lot of studio stars to show up and perform. ♫A Sweater, a Sarong and a Peek-a-Boo Bang; That Old Black Magic; Hit the Road to Dreamland; Old Glory; On the Swing Shift; Doing It for Defense; Sharp as a Tack; He Loved Me Till the All-Clear Came. **99m/B VHS.** Betty Hutton, Eddie Bracken, Victor Moore, Bing Crosby, Ray Milland, Bob Hope, Veronica Lake, Dorothy Lamour, Susan Hayward, Dick Powell, Mary Martin, Alan Ladd, Paulette Goddard, Cecil B. DeMille, Arthur Treacher, Preston Sturges, Eddie Anderson, William Bendix; **D:** George Marshall. Nominations: Academy Awards '43: Best Song ("That Old Black Magic"), Scoring of a Musical. *USH*

Star Time 🎬½ 1992 Henry is a mentally ill loser who wants to be as happy and famous as his favorite TV stars. Deciding to kill himself, Henry is stopped by the mysterious Sam Bones, who offers him TV stardom—at a steep price. Henry achieves his 15 minutes of fame as a serial killer and his only link to reality is a female social worker. **85m/C VHS.** Michael St. Gerard, John P. Ryan, Maureen Teefy; **D:** Alexander Cassini; **W:** Alexander Cassini; **C:** Fernando Arguelles. *MNC*

Star Trek: The Motion Picture 🎬🎬½ 1980 (G) The Enterprise fights a strange alien force that threatens Earth in this first film adaptation of the famous television series. Very slow moving; followed by numerous sequels. Twelve additional minutes of previously unseen footage have been added to this home video version of the theatrical feature. The laserdisc edition offers the film in widescreen format. **143m/C VHS, Beta, LV, Closed Caption.** William Shatner, Leonard Nimoy, DeForest Kelley, James Doohan, Stephen Collins, Persis Khambatta, Nichelle Nichols, Walter Koenig, George Takei; **D:** Robert Wise; **M:** Jerry Goldsmith. Nominations: Academy Awards '79: Best Art Direction/Set Decoration, Best Original Score. *PAR*

Star Trek 2: The Wrath of Khan 🎬🎬🎬 1982 (PG) Picking up from the 1967 Star Trek episode "Space Seed," Admiral James T. Kirk and the crew of the Enterprise must battle Khan, an old foe out for revenge. Warm and comradly in the nostalgic mode of its successors. Introduced Kirk's former lover and unknown son to the series plot, as well as Mr. Spock's "death," which led to the next sequel (1984's "The Search for Spock"). Can be seen in widescreen format on laserdisc. **113m/C VHS, Beta, LV, 8mm, Closed Caption.** William Shatner, Leonard Nimoy, Ricardo Montalban, DeForest Kelley, Nichelle Nichols, James Doohan, George Takei, Walter Koenig, Kirstie Alley, Merritt Butrick, Paul Winfield; **D:** Nicholas Meyer; **M:** James Horner. *PAR*

Star Trek 3: The Search for Spock 🎬🎬½ 1984 (PG) Captain Kirk hijacks the USS Enterprise and commands the aging crew to go on a mission to the Genesis Planet to discover whether Mr. Spock still lives (supposedly he died in the last movie). Klingons threaten, as usual. Somewhat slow and humorless, but intriguing. Third in the series of six (so far) Star Trek movies. The laserdisc edition carries the film in widescreen format. **105m/C VHS, Beta, LV, 8mm, Closed Caption.** William Shatner, Leonard Nimoy, DeForest Kelley, James Doohan, George Takei, Walter Koenig, Mark Lenard, Robin Curtis, Merritt Butrick, Christopher Lloyd, Judith Anderson, John Larroquette, James B. Sikking, Nichelle Nichols, Cathie Shirriff, Miguel Ferrer, Grace Lee Whitney; **D:** Leonard Nimoy; **W:** Harve Bennett; **M:** James Horner. *PAR*

Star Trek 4: The Voyage Home 🎬🎬🎬 1986 (PG) Kirk and the gang go back in time (to the 1980s, conveniently) to save the Earth of the future from destruction. Filled with hilarious moments and exhilarating action; great special effects enhance the timely conservation theme. Watch for the stunning going-back-in-time sequence. Spock is particularly funny as he tries to fit in and learn the 80s lingo! Can be seen in widescreen format on laserdisc. Also available as part of Paramount's "director's series," in which Nimoy discusses various special effects aspects in the making of the film. The best in the six-part (so far) series. **119m/C VHS, Beta, LV, 8mm, Closed Caption.** William Shatner, DeForest Kelley, Catherine Hicks, James Doohan, Nichelle Nichols, George Takei, Walter Koenig, Mark Lenard, Leonard Nimoy; **D:** Leonard Nimoy; **W:** Nicholas Meyer, Harve Bennett. Nominations: Academy Awards '86: Best Cinematography, Best Sound, Best Original Score. *PAR*

Star Trek 5: The Final Frontier 🎬½ 1989 (PG) A renegade Vulcan kidnaps the Enterprise and takes it on a journey to the mythic center of the universe. Shatner's big-action directorial debut (he also co-wrote the script) is a poor follow-up to the Nimoy-directed fourth entry in the series. Heavy-handed and pretentiously pseudo-theological. Available in widescreen format on laserdisc. **107m/C VHS, Beta, LV, 8mm, Closed Caption.** William Shatner, Leonard Nimoy, DeForest Kelley, James Doohan, Laurence Luckinbill, Walter Koenig, George Takei, Nichelle Nichols, David Warner; **D:** William Shatner; **W:** William Shatner; **M:** Jerry Goldsmith. Golden Raspberry Awards '89: Worst Picture, Worst Actor (Shatner), Worst Director (Shatner). *PAR*

Star Trek 6: The Undiscovered Country 🎬🎬½ 1991 (PG) The final chapter in the long running Star Trek series is finally here. The Federation and the Klingon Empire are preparing a much-needed peace summit but Captain Kirk has his doubts about the true intentions of the Federation's longtime enemies. When a Klingon ship is attacked, Kirk and the crew of the Enterprise, who are accused of the misdeed, must try to find the real perpetrator. Has an exciting, climactic ending. As is typical of the series, the film highlights current events—glasnost—in its plotlines. Meyer also directed Star Trek movie 2 ("The Wrath of Khan") and wrote the screenplay for 4 ("The Voyage Home"). **110m/C VHS, Beta, CD-I, Closed Caption.** William Shatner, Leonard Nimoy, DeForest Kelley, James Doohan, George Takei, Walter Koenig, Nichelle Nichols, Christopher Plummer, Kim Cattrall, Iman, David Warner, Mark Lenard, Grace Lee Whitney, Brock Peters, Kurtwood Smith, Rosana De Soto, John Schuck, Michael Dorn; **D:** Nicholas Meyer; **W:** Nicholas Meyer, Denny Martin Flinn; **M:** Cliff Eidelman. Nominations: Academy Awards '91: Best Makeup. *PAR*

Star Trek Bloopers 1969 The television cast of "Star Trek" appears in these flubs and goofs that were edited out of the actual episodes. The blooper reels from all three seasons are included on this tape. **25m/C VHS, Beta.** William Shatner, Leonard Nimoy, DeForest Kelley, Nichelle Nichols, James Doohan, George Takei, Walter Koenig, Frank Gorshin. *MOV*

Star Trek Deep Space Nine: Emissary 1993 The second "Star Trek" spin-off, following "The Next Generation," finds Federation Commander Benjamin Sisko (Brooks) arriving at the space station, which orbits the planet Bajor. Bajor has just undergone a war of independence against the Cardassians, who have left both the planet and the station in a devastated condition. Sisko, naturally, must find a way to deal with a variety of unpleasant situations, crew, and station residents. The TV pilot is considered episodes one and two of the series; additional episodes are also available. **92m/C VHS, Beta.** Avery Brooks, Colm Meaney, Rene Auberjonois, Nana Visitor, Terry Farrell, Alexander Siddig, Armin Shimerman, Cirroc Lofton. *PAR*

Star Trek: First Contact 🎬🎬🎬 1996 (PG-13) The eighth big-screen Trek saga is firmly in the hands of the "Next Generation" cast as Picard and the Enterprise cross paths with the Borg and their sinister Queen. It's hard to tell whether the cry "Resistance is Futile" is coming from the Borg, or the Trek franchise itself, as this installment may well bring in new "Trekkers" with its "less techo-babble, more action" approach and the fact that this crew can act. The Borg attempt to change history by travelling back in time (to 2063) to prevent scientist Cromwell from inventing warp drive. While the less-interesting members of the crew stay on Earth to help out with the launch, the battle for the Enterprise rages on up in space. Trademark effects, humor, and idealism are in abundant supply and should please the long-time fan as well as the neophyte. **CW:** Some sci-fi adventure violence. **111m/C VHS, Beta, Closed Caption.** Patrick Stewart, Jonathon Frakes, Brent Spiner, LeVar Burton, Michael Dorn, Marina Sirtis, Gates McFadden, Alfre Woodard, James Cromwell, Alice Krige, Neal McDonough, Robert Picardo, Dwight Schultz; **D:** Jonathon Frakes; **W:** Brannon Braga, Ronald D. Moore; **C:** Matthew F. Leonetti; **M:** Jerry Goldsmith. Nominations: Academy Awards '96: Best Makeup. *PAR*

Star Trek Generations 🎬🎬🎬 1994 (PG) The sci-fi phenomena continues with the first film spun off from the recently departed "Star Trek: The Next Generation" TV series and the seventh following the adventures of the Enterprise crew. Captain Kirk is propelled into the future thanks to an explosion and manages to hook up with current starship captain, Picard. Of course, just in time to save the galaxy from the latest space loon, the villainous Dr. Soren (McDowell), renegade

Klingons, and your basic mysterious space entity. For comic relief, android Data gets an emotion chip. Terrific special effects (courtesy of Industrial Light and Magic) and yes, the heroic Kirk receives his mandatory grandiose death scene. Other original characters making a brief appearance are Scotty and Chekov. An entertaining romp through time and space. **117m/C VHS, Beta, Closed Caption.** William Shatner, Patrick Stewart, Malcolm McDowell, Whoopi Goldberg, Jonathon Frakes, Brent Spiner, LeVar Burton, Michael Dorn, Gates McFadden, Marina Sirtis, James Doohan, Walter Koenig, Alan Ruck; **D:** David Carson; **W:** Ronald D. Moore, Brannon Braga; **C:** John A. Alonzo; **M:** Dennis McCarthy. **PAR**

Star Trek: The Cage 1965 This cult series only ran from 1966-1969 but it's impact has been lasting. Join Captain Kirk and the crew of the starship Enterprise on its voyages of discovery. Additional episodes available. In this original pilot episode for the series Captain Chris Pike of the Enterprise faces the challenge of his life when he is captured by the telepathic aliens of Talos IV. Never telecast in its original form and later edited to form the flashback sequences of the two-part episode "Menagerie." Some portions are in black and white. Version was long believed to be lost, but was reconstituted from original color footage. **73m/C VHS, Beta, LV.** Jeffrey Hunter, Leonard Nimoy, Susan Oliver, Majel Barrett, Meg Wyllie, John Hoyt, Gene Roddenberry; **D:** Robert Butler. **PAR, MOV**

Star Trek the Next Generation: Encounter at Farpoint 1987 Roddenberry, the creator of the original "Star Trek" television series, spearheaded this episodic reincarnation for network syndication. Set 80 or so years beyond the original, with an entirely new crew and a modernized vessel, it places less emphasis on violent solutions to conflicts than the original TV series. In this first installment, a powerful life force named "Q" threatens the lives of Captain Picard and his crew as they attempt to figure out what's going on at Farpoint Station. Look for a cameo by Kelley, "Bones" from the original series, as a very old man waxing nostalgic about the old U.S.S. Enterprise. Excellent production values, including fine special effects. Additional episodes available. **96m/C VHS, LV, Closed Caption.** Patrick Stewart, Michael Dorn, Jonathon Frakes, Gates McFadden, Marina Sirtis, Denise Crosby, Brent Spiner, Wil Wheaton, LeVar Burton; **Cameos:** DeForest Kelley; **W:** Gene Roddenberry. **PAR, MOV**

Star Trek the Next Generation, the Final Episode: All Good Things... 1994 Since Q (de Lancie) was there to cause trouble in the first series episode, it seems only fitting that he's up to his usual tricks in the finale. A spatial anomaly has Picard time-traveling between past, present, and future with the very fate of humanity resting on his shoulders—and Q around to tell him that everyone's doomed. **92m/C VHS, Beta, Closed Caption.** Patrick Stewart, LeVar Burton, Brent Spiner, Marina Sirtis, Jonathon Frakes, Gates McFadden, Michael Dorn, John de Lancie, Denise Crosby, Colm Meaney, Brent Spiner, Wil Wheaton; **D:** Winrich Kolbe; **W:** Ronald D. Moore, Brannon Braga. **PAR**

Star Trek Voyager: Caretaker 1995 The third TV spinoff from the franchise sci-fi series features the 24th century adventures of Captain Kathryn Janeway (Mulgrew) and the USS Voyager. In the pilot episode, the crew is searching for Maquis rebels in an area of space known as the Badlands when the ship is mysteriously tossed 70,000 lightyears across the galaxy. The Voyager does find the Maquis ship, as well as an alien named Nelix (Phillips) and a planet run by a force called the Caretaker, whose inhabitants all live underground. This episode is currently available only as part of "The Captains Collection," a four-tape set. **92m/C VHS, Closed Caption.** Kate Mulgrew, Robert Beltran, Robert Picardo, Ethan Phillips, Roxann Biggs-Dawson, Robert Duncan McNeill, Tim Russ, Jennifer Lien, Garrett Wang; **D:** Winrich Kolbe. **PAR**

Star Wars 🎬🎬🎬🎬 1977 (PG) First entry Lucas's "Star Wars" trilogy proved to be one of the biggest box-office hits of all time. A young hero, a captured princess, a hot-shot pilot, cute robots, a vile villain, and a heroic and mysterious Jedi knight blend together with marvelous special effects in a fantasy tale about rebel forces engaged in a life or death struggle with the tyrant leaders of the Galactic Empire. Set a new cinematic standard for realistic special effects, making many pre-"Star Wars" effects seem almost laughable in retrospect. Followed by "The Empire Strikes Back" (1980) and "Return of the Jedi" (1983). **121m/C VHS, Beta, LV, Closed Caption.** Mark Hamill, Carrie Fisher, Harrison Ford, Alec Guinness, Peter Cushing, Kenny Baker, James Earl Jones, David Prowse, Anthony Daniels; **D:** George Lucas; **W:** George Lucas; **M:** John Williams. Academy Awards '77: Best Art Direction/Set Decoration, Best Costume Design, Best Film Editing, Best Sound, Best Visual Effects, Best Original Score; Golden Globe Awards '78: Best Score; Los Angeles Film Critics Association Awards '77: Best Film; National Board of Review Awards '77: 10 Best Films of the Year; People's Choice Awards '78: Best Film; Nominations: Academy Awards '77: Best Director (Lucas), Best Original Screenplay, Best Picture, Best Supporting Actor (Guinness). **FOX, RDG, HMV**

Starbird and Sweet William 🎬🎬 1973 (G) On a solo plane flight, a young Native American crashes in the wilderness. He must fight for survival in the harsh woods with his only friend, a bear cub. Good family fare. **95m/C VHS.** A. Martinez, Louise Fitch, Dan Haggerty, Skip Homeier; **D:** Jack B. Hively. **NO**

Starchaser: The Legend of Orin 🎬🎬½ 1985 (PG) Animated fantasy about a boy who must save the world of the future from malevolent hordes. **107m/C VHS, Beta, LV. D:** Steven Hahn; **M:** Andrew Belling. **PAR**

Stardust Memories 🎬🎬½ 1980 (PG) Allen's "8 1/2." A comic filmmaker is plagued with creative blocks, relationships, modern fears and fanatical fans. The last film in Allen's varying self-analysis, with explicit references to Fellini and Antonioni. **88m/B VHS, Beta, LV.** Woody Allen, Charlotte Rampling, Jessica Harper, Marie-Christine Barrault, Tony Roberts, Helen Hanft, Cynthia Gibb, Amy Wright, Daniel Stern; **D:** Woody Allen; **W:** Woody Allen; **C:** Gordon Willis. **MGM, FOX**

The Starfighters 🎬½ 1963 Air Force Lieutenant Dornan must prove his courage to his disapproving war hero Congressman father. Dornan flies his F-104 through a dangerous storm, thereby earning his father's respect, which leads them to form a bond. **84m/C VHS, Beta.** Robert Dornan, Richard Jordahl, Shirley Olmstead. **NO**

Starflight One 🎬🎬 1983 A space shuttle is called on to save the world's first hypersonic airliner trapped in an orbit above earth. Also called "Starflight: The Plane That Couldn't Land." The film features good special effects, but also a predictable "rescue-mission" plot. **155m/C VHS, Beta.** Ray Milland, Lee Majors, Hal Linden, Lauren Hutton, Robert Webber, Terry Kiser; **D:** Jerry Jameson. **LIV, VES**

Stargate 🎬🎬 1994 (PG-13) U.S. military probe of a ring-shaped ancient Egyptian artifact (your tax dollars at work) sends he-man colonel Russell and geeky Egyptologist Spader into a parallel universe. There they meet the builders of the pyramids who are enslaved by an evil despot (Davidson) posing as a sun god. Ambitious premise zapped from prepubescent imaginations gets an A for effort, but a silly plot that jumbles biblical epic panoramas and space odyssey special effects with otherworldly mysticism and needless emotional hang-ups trade shlock for style. Spader's shaggy scholar is neurotically fun, Russell's jarhead a bore, and Davidson's vampy villain an unintended hoot. **CW:** Sci-fi action violence. **119m/ C VHS, LV, Closed Caption, DVD.** Kurt Russell, James Spader, Jaye Davidson, Viveca Lindfors, Alexis Cruz, Leon Rippy, John Diehl, Erik Avari, Mili Avital; **D:** Roland Emmerich; **W:** Dean Devlin, Roland Emmerich; **C:** Jeff Okun. **LIV**

Starhops 🎬½ 1978 (R) A trio of buxom young women attract business to their drive-in restaurant by wearing skimpy outfits. Surprisingly inoffensive for an "R" rating. **92m/C VHS.** Dorothy Buhrman, Sterling Frazier, Jillian Kesner, Peter Paul Liapis, Paul Ryan, Anthony Mannino, Dick Miller; **D:** Barbara Peeters; **W:** Stephanie Rothman. **NO**

Stark 🎬½ 1985 Wichita detective journeys to Las Vegas in an effort to locate his missing sister. During his search, he finds himself taking on the mob. A television pilot for a series that never happened, and Tidyman's last screenplay. A sequel "Stark: Mirror Image," was made in 1986. **94m/C VHS, Beta, Closed Caption.** Nicolas Surovy, Dennis Hopper, Marilu Henner, Seth Jaffe; **D:** Rod Holcomb; **W:** Ernest Tidyman. **FOX**

Starlight Hotel 🎬🎬½ 1990 (PG) An unhappy teenage girl sets off to find her father, with the help of a shellshocked veteran wrongly accused of a crime. Set in New Zealand during the Depression. Lovely scenery and good acting highlight nice story of odd friendship. **90m/C VHS, LV. NZ** Greer Robson, Peter Phelps, Marshall Napier, Pat Smythe, Alice Fraser; **D:** Sam Pillsbury. **REP**

Starman 🎬🎬🎬 1984 (PG) An alien from an advanced civilization lands in Wisconsin. He hides beneath the guise of a grieving young widow's recently deceased husband. He then makes her drive him across country to rendezvous with his spacecraft so he can return home. Well-acted, interesting twist on the "Stranger in a Strange Land" theme. Bridges is fun as the likeable starman; Allen is lovely and earthy in her worthy follow-up to "Raiders of the Lost Ark." Available in widescreen format on laserdisc. **115m/C VHS, Beta, LV, Closed Caption.** Jeff Bridges, Karen Allen, Charles Martin Smith, Richard Jaeckel; **D:** John Carpenter; **W:** Bruce A. Evans, Raynold Gideon; **C:** Donald M. Morgan; **M:** Jack Nitzsche. Nominations: Academy Awards '84: Best Actor (Bridges). **COL**

Starring Bugs Bunny! 1948 Bug Bunny teams up with Yosemite Sam and others in some of these great hits. Friz Freleng's "Buccaneer Bunny" and "Hare Force," as well as Chuck Jones' "Hare Tonic." **54m/C VHS. D:** Isadore "Friz" Freleng, Chuck Jones, Robert McKimson. **MGM**

Stars and Bars 🎬🎬 1988 (R) O'Connor misfire strands Day-Lewis in the midst of hillbillies. A stuffy English art expert travels from New York to Georgia to price a Renoir, and happens on a bizarre backwoods family marginally run by Stanton. Stereotypical pursuit of humor teeters precariously on the edge of black comedy without actually being funny. Stinky script dooms fine cast to just acting weird in a "Deliverance" sort of way. Based on the novel by William Boyd. **95m/C VHS, Beta, LV, Closed Caption.** Daniel Day-Lewis, Harry Dean Stanton, John Cusack, Joan Cusack, Spalding Gray, Will Patton, Martha Plimpton, Glenne Headly, Laurie Metcalf, Maury Chaykin; **D:** Pat O'Connor; **W:** William Boyd. **COL**

Stars and Stripes Forever 🎬🎬🎬 Marching Along 1952 Sumptuous, Hollywoodized bio of composer John Phillip Sousa, based on his memoir "Marching Along," but more concerned with the romantic endeavors of young protege Wagner. Accuracy aside, it's solid entertainment even if you're not mad about march music. 🎵Stars and Stripes Forever; El Capitan; Washington Post; King Cotton; The Battle Hymn of the Republic; Dixie; Light Cavalry; Turkey in the Straw; Hail to the Chief. **89m/C VHS, Closed Caption.** Clifton Webb, Debra Paget, Robert Wagner, Ruth Hussey, Finlay Currie; **D:** Henry Koster. **FXV, FCT**

The Stars Fell on Henrietta 🎬🎬½ 1994 (PG) Down-on-his-luck wildcatter Mr. Cox (Duvall) searches for oil and redemption. He's looking for it on the failing farm of couple Don and Cora Day (Quinn and Fisher) in the middle of the 1930's Texas dustbowl with the reluctant backing of more successful oil man (Dennehy). Quiet character study of an obsessed wheeler-dealer playing with his last poker chip verges on the romantic in its quest for black gold, true to its message about never giving up hope. Directorial debut for Keach is led by typically excellent portrayals by Duvall and Dennehy, but Quinn and Fisher are given little to work with. Marks the first movie Clint Eastwood's Malpaso company has produced in which he didn't star or direct since "Ratboy." **110m/C VHS.** Robert Duvall, Aidan Quinn, Frances Fisher, Brian Dennehy, Lexi Randall, Kaytlyn Knowles, Francesca Ruth Eastwood; **D:** James Keach; **W:** Philip Railsback; **C:** Bruce Surtees; **M:** David Benoit. *WAR*

Stars in My Crown 🐾🐾🐾 1950 McCrea provides a moving performance as the pistol-wielding preacher who helps the residents of a 19th-century small town battle a typhoid epidemic and KKK terrorism. Adapted from the novel by Joe David Brown. **89m/B VHS, Closed Caption.** Joel McCrea, Ellen Drew, Dean Stockwell, Alan Hale, Lewis Stone, Amanda Blake, Juano Hernandez, Charles Kemper, Connie Gilchrist, Ed Begley Sr., James Arness, Jack Lambert, Arthur Hunnicutt; **D:** Jacques Tourneur; **W:** Margaret Fitts; **M:** Adolph Deutsch. *MGM*

The Stars Look Down 🐾🐾🐾 1939 A mine owner forces miners to work in unsafe conditions in a Welsh town and disaster strikes. Redgrave is a miner's son running for office, hoping to improve conditions, and to escape the hard life. Forceful, well-directed effort suffered at the box office, in competition with John Ford's similar classic "How Green Was My Valley." From the novel by A.J. Cronin. **96m/B VHS, Beta.** GB Michael Redgrave, Margaret Lockwood, Emlyn Williams, Cecil Parker; **D:** Carol Reed. National Board of Review Awards '41: 10 Best Films of the Year. *NOS, HHT, CAB*

Starship 🐾 *Lorca and the Outlaws* 1987 **(PG)** British sci-fi seems to be an oxymoron. To wit, this lame "Star Wars" ripoff is about human slaves on a planet run by evil robots. **91m/C VHS, Beta.** GB John Tarrant, Cassandra Webb, Donough Rees, Deep Roy, Ralph Cotterill; **D:** Roger Christian. *HHE*

Starship Invasions 🐾 1977 **(PG)** Lee leads a group of bad aliens seeking to take over the Earth. He's thwarted by UFO expert Vaughn, who is aided by a group of good aliens. Cheesy special effects have this one looking like a bad sci-fi serial from the '40s. **89m/C VHS.** CA Christopher Lee, Robert Vaughn, Daniel Pilon, Helen Shaver, Henry Ramer, Victoria (Vicki) Johnson; **D:** Edward Hunt; **W:** Edward Hunt. *WAR*

Starstruck 🐾🐾½ 1982 **(PG)** Fun-loving folly about a teen who tries to help his talented cousin make it as a singer. Playfully tweeks Hollywood musicals. Enjoyable and fun. **95m/C VHS.** AU Jo Kennedy, Ross O'Donovan, Pat Evison; **D:** Gillian Armstrong; **C:** Russell Boyd. *FXL*

Start the Revolution Without Me 🐾🐾🐾 1970 **(PG)** Hilarious, Moliere-esque farce about two sets of identical twins (Wilder and Sutherland) separated at birth, who meet 30 years later, just before the French Revolution. About as hammy as they come; Wilder is unforgettable. Neglected when released, but now deservedly a cult favorite. **91m/C VHS, Beta.** Gene Wilder, Donald Sutherland, Orson Welles, Hugh Griffith, Jack MacGowran, Billie Whitelaw, Victor Spinetti, Ewa Aulin; **D:** Bud Yorkin; **W:** Lawrence J. Cohen; **M:** John Addison. *WAR*

Starting Over 🐾🐾🐾 1979 **(R)** His life racked by divorce, Phil Potter learns what it's like to be single, self-sufficient, and lonely once again. When a blind date grows into a serious affair, the romance is temporarily halted by his hang-up for his ex-wife. Enjoyable love-triangle comedy loses direction after a while, but Reynolds is subtle and charming, and Bergen good as his ex, a very bad songwriter. Based on a novel by Dan Wakefield. **106m/C VHS, Beta, LV.** Burt Reynolds, Jill Clayburgh, Candice Bergen, Frances Sternhagen, Austin Pendleton, Mary Kay Place, Kevin Bacon, Daniel Stern; **D:** Alan J. Pakula; **W:** James L. Brooks; **C:** Sven Nykvist; **M:** Marvin Hamlisch. Nominations: Academy Awards '79: Best Actress (Clayburgh), Best Supporting Actress (Bergen). *PAR*

Starvengers 1982 Animated adventures with action and excitement meeting futuristic technology, resulting in the high-powered super-intelligence of the robot Starvenger. **105m/C VHS, Beta.** JP FUS, FHE, TPV

State Department File 649 🐾½ 1949 Insipid spy drama set in northern China. Mongolian rebels hold U.S. agent Lundigan captive; he hopes to capture a Chinese warlord. **87m/C VHS, Beta.** Virginia Bruce, William Lundigan; **D:** Sam Newfield. *SNC, NOS, DVT*

State Fair 🐾🐾🐾 *It Happened One Summer* 1945 The second version of the glossy slice of Americana about a family at the Iowa State Fair, featuring plenty of great songs by Rodgers and Hammerstein. Adapted from the 1933 screen version of Phil Stong's novel. Remade again in 1962. ♫It Might as Well Be Spring; It's a Grand Night for Singing; That's For Me; Isn't It Kinda Fun?; All I Owe Iowa; Our State Fair. **100m/C VHS, Beta.** Charles Winninger, Jeanne Crain, Dana Andrews, Vivian Blaine, Dick Haymes, Fay Bainter, Frank McHugh, Percy Kilbride, Donald Meek, William Marshall, Harry (Henry) Morgan; **D:** Walter Lang; **W:** Oscar Hammerstein; **C:** Leon Shamroy; **M:** Richard Rodgers, Oscar Hammerstein. Academy Awards '45: Best Song ("It Might as Well Be Spring"); Nominations: Academy Awards '45: Scoring of a Musical. *FOX*

State Fair 🐾🐾 1962 The third film version of the story of a farm family who travel to their yearly state fair and experience life. The original songs are still there, but otherwise this is a letdown. Texas setting required dropping the song "All I Owe Iowa." ♫Our State Fair; It's a Grand Night for Singing; That's for me; It Might as Well Be Spring; Isn't It Kinda Fun?; More Than Just a Friend; It's the Little Things in Texas; Willing and Eager; This Isn't Heaven. **118m/C VHS, Beta, Closed Caption.** Pat Boone, Ann-Margret, Bobby Darin, Tom Ewell, Alice Faye, Pamela Tiffin, Wally Cox; **D:** Jose Ferrer; **C:** William Mellor. *FOX*

State of Emergency 🐾🐾½ 1994 **(R)** John Novelli (Mantegna) is a cynical, overworked emergency-room doctor for an over-crowded, underequipped big-city hospital. His latest casualty is a head trauma case the hospital is ill-prepared to handle and as the patient's condition worsens both doctor and hospital are put at risk. Made for television.*CW:* Language; graphic depiction of emergency room traumas. **97m/C VHS, LV.** Joe Mantegna, Lynn Whitfield, Paul Dooley; **D:** Leslie Linka Glatter; **W:** Susan Black, Dr. Lance Gentile. *HBO*

State of Grace 🐾🐾🐾 1990 **(R)** Irish hood Penn returns to old NYC neighborhood as undercover cop and becomes involved in an Irish Westies mob in a fight for survival as urban renewal encroaches on their Hell's Kitchen turf. Shrinking client base for shakedown schemes and protection rackets forces them to become contract killers for the Italian mafia. Fine performances, with Penn tense but restrained, gang honcho Harris intense, and Oldman chewing up gritty urban scenery as psycho brother of Harris, but the story is long and meandering. Well-choreographed violence. **134m/C VHS, LV, Closed Caption.** Sean Penn, Ed Harris, Gary Oldman, Robin Wright, Joe Viterelli, John Turturro, Burgess Meredith, John C. Reilly; **D:** Phil Joanou; **W:** Dennis McIntyre; **C:** Jordan Cronenweth; **M:** Ennio Morricone. *ORI*

State of Siege 🐾🐾🐾 *Etat de Siege* 1973 Third pairing of Montand and Costa-Gavras, about the real-life death of USAID employee Daniel Mitrione, suspected to be involved in torture and murder in Uruguay in the '60s. Quietly suspenseful, with snazzy editing; conspiracy-theory premise is similar to Stone's "JFK," and similarly disturbing, whether you believe it or not. Dubbed. **119m/C VHS, Beta, LV.** FR Yves Montand, Renato Salvatori, O.E. Hasse, Jacques Perrin; **D:** Constantin Costa-Gavras. *COL*

State of the Union 🐾🐾🐾½ *The World and His Wife* 1948 Liberal multimillionaire Tracy is seeking the Republican presidential nomination. His estranged wife (Hepburn) is asked to return so they can masquerade as a loving couple for the sake of his political career. Hepburn tries to help Tracy, as the backstage political machinations erode his personal convictions. Adapted from a highly successful, topical Broadway play; the writers changed dialogue constantly to reflect the news. Capra and his partners at Liberty Pictures originally hoped to cast Gary Cooper and Claudette Colbert. Hepburn and Menjou were at odds politically (over communist witch hunts in Hollywood) but are fine together onscreen. **124m/B VHS, Beta, LV.** Spencer Tracy, Katharine Hepburn, Angela Lansbury, Van Johnson, Adolphe Menjou, Lewis Stone, Howard Smith; **D:** Frank Capra. *USH*

State of Things 🐾🐾🐾 1982 Ostensibly a mystery involving a film crew trying to remake a B-movie, "The Most Dangerous Man On Earth," but also an in-depth look at the process of filmmaking, a scathing look at nuclear warfare and an homage to Roger Corman and Hollywood at large. An enigmatic, complex film from Wenders prior to his American years. In German with English subtitles; some dialogue in English. **120m/B VHS, Beta, LV.** GE Patrick Bauchau, Allen (Goorwitz) Garfield, Isabelle Weingarten, Viva, Samuel Fuller, Paul Getty III, Roger Corman; **D:** Wim Wenders. Venice Film Festival '82: Best Film. *GLV*

Stateline Motel 🐾½ *Last Chance For a Born Loser* 1975 **(R)** Cheap Italian ripoff of "The Postman Always Rings Twice," with a surprise ending but little of great interest. **86m/C VHS, Beta.** IT Eli Wallach, Ursula Andress, Fabio Testi, Barbara Bach; **D:** Maurizio Lucidi. *NO*

State's Attorney 🐾🐾½ *Cardigan's Last Case* 1931 A burned-out attorney finds himself falling in love with the least likely person, a prostitute he is defending. Contrived, improbable story succumbs to star-quality lead acting from Barrymore. Remade in 1937 with Lee Tracy as "Criminal Lawyer." **79m/B VHS, Beta.** John Barrymore, Jill Esmond, William "Stage" Boyd, Helen Twelvetrees; **D:** George Archainbaud; **M:** Max Steiner. *TTC*

Static 🐾🐾½ 1987 **(PG-13)** A strange, disquieting independent film about an eccentric youth who claims to have built a machine through which one can see heaven. Uneven, with some dull stretches. **89m/C VHS, Beta, LV.** Keith Gordon, Amanda Plummer, Bob Gunton, Jane Hoffman, Barton Heyman, Lily Knight; **D:** Mark Romanek; **W:** Keith Gordon, Mark Romanek. *MCG*

Station 🐾🐾½ 1981 A Japanese detective's love affair is corrupted by his ruthless search for a bloodthirsty cop killer. With English subtitles. **130m/C VHS, Beta.** JP Ken Takakura, Chieko Baisho; **D:** Yasuo Furuhata. *NO*

The Station 🐾🐾 1992 A sophisticated woman, who has just abandoned her fiancee, waits in a tiny station for an early train. The only person around is the young and ordinary stationmaster. Gradually the two are drawn together in a number of charming and comic romantic fantasies. In Italian with English subtitles. **92m/C VHS.** IT Margherita Buy, Ennio Fantastichini; **D:** Sergio Rubini; **W:** Sergio Rubini. *FXL*

Station West 🐾🐾🐾 1948 A disguised Army officer is sent to uncover a mystery of hijackers and murderers. Along the way, he meets up with and falls for a beautiful woman who may be involved in the treachery. Good, solid western with a fine cast and plenty of fun action shot against the requisite beautiful western landscapes. Based on the Luke Short story. Also available colorized. **92m/B VHS, Beta.** Dick Powell, Jane Greer, Agnes Moorehead, Burl Ives, Tom Powers, Raymond Burr; **D:** Sidney Lanfield. *CCB, TTC*

The Stationmaster's Wife 🎬🎬½ 1977
In Germay's Weimar Republic a provincial sta-
tionmaster's wife expresses her boredom with her
pleasant ineffectual husband by having numerous
meaningless affairs. Meant to invoke postwar
German dread and the fake bourgeois morality
which covered political and social resentments.
Originally shown as a 200-minute miniseries for
German television. In German with English subti-
tles. 111m/C VHS. *GE* Elisabeth Trissenaar, Kurt Raab,
Gustal Bayrhammer, Bernard Helfrich, Udo Kier, Volker
Spengler; *D:* Rainer Werner Fassbinder; *W:* Rainer Werner
Fassbinder; *C:* Michael Ballhaus; *M:* Peer Raben. *NYF,
FCT*

The Statue 🎬 1971 (R) Famed sculptress
unveils a nude rendering of her Nobel Prize-winning husband. Much hilarity in the British vein is
meant to ensue, but doesn't. Niven is OK, but this
empty, plotless farce should have been much
shorter. 84m/C VHS, Beta. *GB* David Niven, Virna Lisi,
Robert Vaughn, Ann Bell, John Cleese; *D:* Rod Amateau.
PSM

Stavisky 🎬🎬🎬 1974 Sumptuously lensed
story of Serge Stavisky, a con-artist and bon-vivant whose machinations almost brought down
the French government when his corruption was
exposed in 1934. Belmondo makes as charismatic an antihero as you could find. Excellent score
complements the visuals. In French with English
subtitles. 117m/C VHS. Jean-Paul Belmondo, Anny Duperey, Charles Boyer, Francois Perier, Gerard Depardieu;
D: Alain Resnais; *C:* Sacha Vierny; *M:* Stephen Sondheim.
New York Film Critics Awards '74: Best Supporting Actor
(Boyer).*INT*

Stay As You Are 🎬½ 1978 Aging
French architect Mastroianni has designs on a
teenager who may be his illegitimate daughter
from an earlier affair. 95m/C VHS, Beta. *FR* Marcello
Mastroianni, Nastassia Kinski, Francesco Rabal; *D:* Alberto
Lattuada. *WAR, OM*

Stay Awake 🎬 1987 (R) A demon stalks,
haunts and tortures eight young girls sleeping together at a secluded Catholic school. Title might
be addressed to the viewer, who will be tempted
to snooze. 90m/C VHS, Beta, LV. *SA* Shirley Jane Harris,
Tanya Gordon, Jayne Hutton, Heath Kheater; *D:* John Bernard. *NLC*

Stay Away, Joe 🎬 1968 (PG) The King is
a singing half-breed rodeo star who returns to his
reservation where he finds love and trouble. Utterly cliche, embarrassing, and stupid even by Elvis-
movie standards. 98m/C VHS, Beta. Elvis Presley, Burgess Meredith, Joan Blondell, Thomas Gomez, L.Q. Jones,
Katy Jurado, Henry Jones; *D:* Peter Tewkesbury. *MGM*

Stay Hungry 🎬🎬🎬 1976 (R) A wealthy
southerner (Bridges) is involved in a real estate
deal which depends on the sale of a gym where a
number of body builders hang out. He becomes
immersed in their world and finds himself in love
with the working-class Field. Big Arnold's first
speaking role in his own inimitable accent (his first
role in "Hercules in New York" was dubbed.) Offbeat and occasionally uneven comedy-drama
based on a novel by Charles Gaines is a sleeper.
102m/C VHS, Beta, LV. Jeff Bridges, Sally Field, Arnold
Schwarzenegger, Robert Englund, Scatman Crothers; *D:*
Bob Rafelson; *W:* Bob Rafelson. *MGM, FOX*

Stay Tuned 🎬 1992 (PG-13) Suburban yuppie couple buys a large-screen TV and satellite
dish from Hellvision salesman, are sucked into
their dish, and wind up starring in hellish TV
shows such as "Wayne's Underworld," "Northern
Overexposure," "Sadistic Home Videos," and
"My Three Sons of Bitches." If they can survive
for 24 hours, they'll be able to return to their normal lives. Clever idea for a film is wasted as this
one never really gets off the ground; viewers may
not want to stay tuned to the low comedy and
frantic yucks. 90m/C VHS, LV, Closed Caption. John
Ritter, Pam Dawber, Jeffrey Jones, Eugene Levy, David
Tom, Heather McComb; *D:* Peter Hyams; *W:* Tom S. Parker; *M:* Bruce Broughton. *WAR*

Stay Tuned for Murder 🎬½ 1988 A
sexy news reporter gets caught in a web of financial wrongdoings and corruption. The financiers,
lawyers, and other sinister types she's investigating decide to give her a story she will never forget—if she ever gets the chance to tell it! 92m/C
VHS, Beta. Terry Reeves Wolf, Christopher Ginnaven; *D:*
Gary Jones. *IME*

Staying Alive 🎬½ 1983 (PG) "Saturday
Night Fever" was the ultimate cheesy 70's musical, hence likeable in a dorky way. This pathetic
sequel (directed by Stallone from a Rocky-esque
script about beating the odds, etc.) is utterly predictable and forgettable. Music mostly by Frank
Stallone, the great heir to Rodgers and Hammerstein. 🎵The Woman In You; I Love You Too
Much; Breakout; Someone Belonging to Someone; Life Goes On; Far From Over; Devils and
Seducers; (We Dance) So Close to the Fire; Hope
We Never Change. 96m/C VHS, Beta, LV, Closed
Caption. John Travolta, Cynthia Rhodes, Finola Hughes,
Norma Donaldson; *D:* Sylvester Stallone; *W:* Sylvester Stal-
lone; *M:* Frank Stallone. *PAR*

Staying On 🎬🎬½ 1980 Based on the Paul
Scott novel, this English drama follows the life of a
post-colonial British colonel and his wife who
chose to remain in India. 87m/C VHS, Beta. *GB* Trevor
Howard, Celia Johnson; *D:* Irene Shubik. *MTI*

Staying Together 🎬½ 1989 (R) Three
midwestern brothers go into a panic when their
father decides to sell the restaurant they've
worked at all their adult lives. Somehow they
manage the transition and learn about life. Sloppy
comedy-drama with way too many unresolved
subplots. 91m/C VHS, Beta, LV. Dermot Mulroney, Tim
Quill, Sean Astin, Stockard Channing, Melinda Dillon,
Daphne Zuniga; *D:* Lee Grant; *W:* Monte Merrick; *M:* Miles
Goodman. *HBO*

The Steagle 🎬 1971 (R) The threat of the
Cuban missile crisis lets a fantasizing professor
loose to enact his wildest dreams. Odd Mitty-esque fantasy comedy might have worked, but ends
up confusing and frustrating. 101m/C VHS, Beta.
Richard Benjamin, Cloris Leachman; *D:* Paul Sylbert. *NLC*

Steal Big, Steal Little 🎬🎬 1995 (PG-13)
Twins Robby and Reuben Martinez (Garcia) battle over the California ranch land left to Reuben by
their mother. Evil, manipulative Robby, all fancy
suits and slicked-back hair, wants to build condos
while gentle, less-fashionable Reuben must fight
to fulfill his dream of building a home for the migrant workers he employs. Yawn. Writer/director
Davis' flashy action movie technique doesn't fit
into the dramatic social commentary—it's too fast
and forced to work. Garcia's radical character.
changes are impressive though. Arkin provides
comic relief as the good-hearted used-car dealer
who tries to save the day, if not the film.*CW:*
Some strong language and a scene involving
marijuana use. 130m/C VHS, LV. Andy Garcia, Alan Arkin, Rachel Ticotin, Joe Pantoliano, David Ogden Stiers,
Charles Rocket, Holland Taylor; *D:* Andy Davis; *W:* Lee
Blessing, Jeanne Blake, Terry Kahn, Andy Davis; *C:* Frank
Tidy; *M:* William Olvis. *HBO*

Steal the Sky 🎬🎬 1988 Israeli agent
Hemingway seduces Iraqi pilot Cross and per-
suades him to steal a Soviet MIG jet and defect to
Israel. Unlikely plot but swell flying scenes. Hem-
ingway is poorly cast, as she often is. Made for
cable television. 110m/C VHS, Beta, LV, Closed
Caption. Mariel Hemingway, Ben Cross, Etta Ankri; *D:* John
Hancock. *HBO*

Stealing Beauty 🎬🎬½ 1996 (R) The film's
main asset, besides the beautiful Tuscan scenery, is the coltish charm of Tyler, who stars as
virginal teenager Lucy Harmon. An innocent
abroad, she's spending the summer with family
friends after her mother's suicide. Ostensibly artist Ian Grayson (McCann) is doing her portrait but
Lucy's more interested in finding romance with
neighbor lad Niccolo (Zibetti), who bestowed her
first kiss on a previous visit. Lucy's sunny appeal

doesn't go unnoticed by the villa's other inhabi-
tants, including dying playwright Alex (Irons), but
it seems Lucy's growing up won't be easy on any-
one (not even herself).*CW:* Strong sexuality, nu-
dity, some drug use and language. 118m/C VHS,
LV, Closed Caption. *IT GB FR* Liv Tyler, Jeremy Irons,
Donal McCann, Sinead Cusack, Jean Marais, D.W. Moffett,
Stefania Sandrelli, Carlo Cecchi, Roberto Zibetti, Joseph
Fiennes, Jason Flemyng, Leonardo Treviglio; *D:* Bernardo
Bertolucci; *W:* Susan Minot, Bernardo Bertolucci; *C:* Darius
Khondji; *M:* Richard Hartley. *FXV*

Stealing Heaven 🎬🎬½ 1988 (R) Based
on the lives of Abelard and Heloise. In 12th-centu-
ry Paris, a theologian and teacher falls in love with
a beautiful young woman, and the two must defend their bond from all comers, including her
righteous uncle. Steamy; trimmed to 108 minutes
after threatened X rating. Attractive and cerebral.
Available in a 115 minute-uncut, unrated version.
108m/C VHS, Beta, LV. *GB YU* Derek De Lint, Kim Thomson, Denholm Elliott, Mark Jax, Bernard Hepton, Kenneth
Cranham, Angela Pleasence, Rachel Kempson; *D:* Clive
Donner; *W:* Chris Bryant; *M:* Nick Bicat. *NO*

Stealing Home 🎬🎬½ 1988 (PG-13) A
washed-up baseball player learns his former babysitter (who was also his first love and inspiration), has committed suicide. Their bittersweet relationship is told through flashbacks. Foster's superb performance steals the show in this quiet
sleeper. 98m/C VHS, LV, Closed Caption. Mark Harmon,
Jodie Foster, William McNamara, Blair Brown, Harold
Ramis, Jonathan Silverman, John Shea, Helen Hunt, Richard Jenkins, Ted Ross, Thatcher Goodwin, Yvette Croskey;
D: Steven Kampmann, Will Aldis; *W:* Steven Kampmann,
Will Aldis; *M:* David Foster. *WAR*

Steamboat Bill, Jr. 🎬🎬🎬½ 1928 City-
educated student returns to his small home-town
and his father's Mississippi river boat, where he's
an embarrassment to dad. But bond they do, to
ward off the owner of a rival riverboat, whose
daughter Keaton falls for. Engaging look at small-
town life and the usual wonderful Keaton antics,
including braving the big tornado. 75m/B VHS, Beta,
LV. Buster Keaton, Ernest Torrence, Marion Byron, Tom
Lewis; *D:* Charles Riesner. *NOS, CCB, DVT*

Steaming 🎬 1986 (R) Six women get together in a London bathhouse and review their
various troubles with men. Unfortunate adaptation
of the good play by Nell Dunn. Where are the
laughs—and what happened to the dramatic tension? The last film of Dors and director Losey.
102m/C VHS, Beta, Closed Caption. *GB* Vanessa Redgrave, Sarah Miles, Diana Dors; *D:* Joseph Losey. *VTR,
NWV*

Steel 🎬🎬 *Look Down and Die; Men of Steel* 1980
(R) Construction workers on a mammoth sky-
scraper face insurmountable odds and strong op-
position. Will they finish their building? Worth
watching, if you don't have anything else to do.
100m/C VHS, Beta, LV. Lee Majors, Jennifer O'Neill, Art
Carney, George Kennedy, Harris Yulin, Terry Kiser, Richard
Lynch, Roger E. Mosley, Albert Salmi, R.G. Armstrong; *D:*
Steve Carver; *W:* Leigh Chapman; *M:* Michel Colombier.
VES

Steel 🎬🎬½ 1997 (PG-13) Metal specialist
John Henry Irons (O'Neal) has designed a top-secret military weapon that falls into the hands of a
street gang. Donning a suit of armor he designed,
he become super hero Steel and sets out to end
the reign of terror of former colleague turned super villian Burke (Nelson). Entertaining adaptation
of popular DC comic keeps target audience in
mind with lots of action and plenty of humor. Shaq
proves once again that as an actor he's a pretty
good basketball player, but he may have a slam-
dunk franchise here.*CW:* Some superhero action
violence. ?m/C VHS. Shaquille O'Neal, Judd Nelson, Annabeth Gish, Richard Roundtree, Irma P. Hall; *D:* Kenneth
Johnson; *W:* Kenneth Johnson. *NYR*

Steel and Lace 🎬½ 1990 (R) Davison is
the scientist brother of a classical pianist who
commits suicide after being raped. He revives her
as a cyborg, which promptly sets out to enact its

revenge. Depressing, morbid sci-fi. **92m/C VHS, Beta, LV, Closed Caption.** Bruce Davison, Clare Wren, Stacy Haiduk, David Naughton, David Lander; **D:** Ernest Farino; **W:** Joseph Dougherty, Dave Edison; **C:** Thomas Callaway. *FRH*

Steel Arena *🐾* **1972 (PG)** Several real life stunt-car drivers appear in this action-packed film, crammed with spins, jumps, explosions and world-record-breaking, life risking stunts. **99m/C VHS, Beta.** Dusty Russell, Gene Drew, Buddy Love; **D:** Mark L. Lester. *LIV, VES*

The Steel Claw *🐾🐾* **1961** One-handed ex-Marine Montgomery organizes guerilla forces against the Japanese in the Philippines in WWII. Good location shooting and plenty of action. **95m/C VHS, Beta.** George Montgomery, Charito Luna, Mario Barri; **D:** George Montgomery. *NO*

Steel Cowboy *🐾🐾* **1978** With his marriage, sanity, and livelihood on the line, an independent trucker agrees to haul a hot herd of stolen steers. Passable made-for-TV macho adventure. **100m/C VHS, Beta.** James Brolin, Rip Torn, Jennifer Warren, Strother Martin, Melanie Griffith, Lou Frizzell; **D:** Harvey Laidman; **M:** Charles Bernstein. *NO*

Steel Dawn *🐾½* **1987 (R)** Another "Mad Max" clone: A leather-clad warrior wields his sword over lots of presumably post-apocalyptic desert terrain. Swayze stars with his real-life wife Niemi in unfortunate follow-up to "Dirty Dancing." **90m/C VHS, Beta, LV.** Patrick Swayze, Lisa Niemi, Christopher Neame, Brett Hool, Brion James, Anthony Zerbe; **D:** Lance Hool. *LIV, VES*

Steel Fisted Dragon *🐾* **1982 (R)** Son seeks revenge on the gang who murdered his mother and burned her house to the ground. **85m/C VHS, Beta.** Stephen Lee, Johnny Kong Kong, Peter Chan. *NO*

Steel Frontier *🐾½* **1994 (R)** Post-apocalypse actioner finds a group of survivors trying to make a new life in a town they call New Hope. But then a group of bandit soldiers take over—until a lone hero comes along to save the day. **CW:** Nonstop action violence; language. **94m/C VHS, LV, Closed Caption.** Joe Lara, Brion James, Bo Svenson, Stacie Foster; **D:** Paul G. Volk, Jacobsen Hart; **W:** Jacobsen Hart. *PMH*

The Steel Helmet *🐾🐾🐾½* **1951** Hurriedly made Korean War drama stands as a top-notch war film. Brooding and dark, GIs don't save the world for democracy or rescue POWs; they simply do their best to survive a horrifying situation. Pointless death, confused loyalties and cynicism abound in writer-director Fuller's scathing comment on the madness of war. **84m/B VHS, Beta, LV.** Gene Evans, Robert Hutton, Steve Brodie, William Chun, James Edwards, Richard Loo, Sid Melton; **D:** Samuel Fuller; **W:** Samuel Fuller. *RXM*

Steel Magnolias *🐾🐾🐾* **1989 (PG)** Julia Roberts plays a young woman stricken with severe diabetes who chooses to live her life to the fullest despite her bad health. Much of the action centers around a Louisiana beauty shop where the women get together to discuss the goings-on of their lives. Screenplay by R. Harling, based on his partially autobiographical play. Sweet, poignant, and often hilarious, yet just as often overwrought. MacLaine is funny as a bitter divorcee; Parton is sexy and fun as the hairdresser. But Field and Roberts go off the deep end and make it all entirely too weepy. **118m/C VHS, Beta, LV, 8mm, Closed Caption.** Sally Field, Dolly Parton, Shirley MacLaine, Daryl Hannah, Olympia Dukakis, Julia Roberts, Tom Skerritt, Sam Shepard, Dylan McDermott, Kevin J. O'Connor, Bill McCutcheon, Ann Wedgeworth, Janine Turner; **D:** Herbert Ross; **W:** Robert Harling; **C:** John A. Alonzo; **M:** Georges Delerue. Golden Globe Awards '90: Best Supporting Actress (Roberts); People's Choice Awards '90: Best Film—Drama; Nominations: Academy Awards '89: Best Supporting Actress (Roberts). *COL*

Steele Justice *🐾* **1987 (R)** A tough 'Nam vet takes on the whole Vietnamese Mafia in Southern California after his friend is murdered. One of those head-scratchers: Should I laugh, or

be offended? **96m/C VHS, Beta, LV, Closed Caption.** Martin Kove, Sela Ward, Ronny Cox, Bernie Casey, Joseph Campanella, Sarah Douglas; **D:** Robert Boris; **W:** Robert Boris. *PAR*

Steele's Law *🐾🐾* **1991 (R)** A loner cop is forced to take the law into his own hands in order to track down an insane international assassin. **CW:** Language, violence, and sensuality. **90m/C VHS, LV.** Fred Williamson, Bo Svenson, Doran Inghram, Phyllis Cicero; **D:** Fred Williamson. *ACA*

Steelyard Blues *🐾🐾½* *The Final Crash* **1973 (PG)** A motley-crew comedy about a wacky gang that tries to steal an abandoned WW II airplane. Zany pranks abound. Technically flawed direction from Myerson mars a potentially hilarious story. **93m/C VHS, Beta.** Jane Fonda, Donald Sutherland, Peter Boyle, Howard Hesseman, John Savage, Garry Goodrow; **D:** Alan Myerson; **W:** David S. Ward; **M:** David Shire. *WAR*

Stella *🐾🐾½* **1955** Mercouri's film debut has her as a free-spirited bar singer who gets involved in a tragic romantic triangle with a middle-class writer and a local football hero. Melodramatic but Mercouri's earthy joie de vivre is already apparent. In Greek with English subtitles. **94m/B VHS.** *GR* Melina Mercouri, Yiorgo Fountas, Aiekos Alexandrikis, Sophia Vembo; **D:** Michael Cacoyannis; **M:** Manos Hadjidakis. *FCT*

Stella *🐾½* **1989 (PG-13)** Anachronistic remake update of "Stella Dallas" casts Midler as a single mother who sacrifices everything to give her daughter a better life. Barbara Stanwyck did it much better in 1937. Based on Olive Higgins Prouty's novel. **109m/C VHS, Beta, LV, Closed Caption.** Bette Midler, John Goodman, Stephen Collins, Eileen Brennan, Ben Stiller, Trini Alvarado, Marsha Mason; **D:** John Erman; **W:** Robert Getchell; **C:** Billy Williams. *TOU*

Stella Dallas *🐾🐾🐾* **1937** An uneducated woman lets go of the daughter she loves when she realizes that her ex-husband can give the girl more advantages. What could be sentimental turns out believable and worthwhile under Vidor's steady hand. Stanwyck never makes a wrong step. From a novel by Olive Higgins Prouty. Remade in 1989 as "Stella," starring Bette Midler. **106m/B VHS, Beta, LV.** Barbara Stanwyck, John Boles, Alan Hale, Marjorie Main; **D:** King Vidor. Nominations: Academy Awards '37: Best Actress (Stanwyck), Best Supporting Actress (Shirley). *COL*

Stella Maris *🐾🐾🐾* **1918** Pickford plays tattered waif who's a slave to an alcoholic who's married to the man she loves. But he's in love with Pickford playing a sheltered rich invalid. Brimming with the tragic consequences of love. **70m/B VHS, Beta.** Mary Pickford, Conway Tearle, Camille Ankewich, Ida Waterman; **D:** Marshall Neilan. *GPV, FCT*

Step Lively *🐾🐾½* **1944** A young playwright tries to recover the money he lent to a fast-talking Broadway producer and is forced to take the leading role in his play. Lively musical remake of "Room Service" (1938) was Sinatra's first starring role. Look for Dorothy Malone as a brunette switchboard operator. 🎵 *Some Other Time; As Long As There's Music; Where Does Love Begin?; Come Out, Come Out, Wherever You Are; Why Must There Be an Opening Song?; And Then You Kissed Me; Ask the Madame.* **88m/B VHS, Beta, LV.** Frank Sinatra, Gloria De Haven, George Murphy, Walter Slezak, Adolphe Menjou, Anne Jeffreys; **D:** Tim Whelan. Nominations: Academy Awards '44: Best Interior Decoration. *CCB*

The Stepfather *🐾🐾🐾* **1987 (R)** Creepy thriller about a seemingly ordinary stepfather who is actually a homicidal maniac searching for the "perfect family." An independently produced sleeper tightly directed and well written. Followed by two inferior sequels. **89m/C VHS, Beta, LV, Closed Caption.** Terry O'Quinn, Shelley Hack, Jill Schoelen, Stephen Shellan, Charles Lanyer; **D:** Joseph Ruben; **W:** Donald E. Westlake; **M:** Patrick Moraz. *COL*

Stepfather 2: Make Room for Daddy *🐾½* **1989 (R)** A poor sequel to the suspenseful sleeper, wherein the psychotic family man escapes from an asylum and woos another suburban family, murdering anyone who may suspect his true identity. Followed by yet another sequel. **93m/C VHS, Beta, LV.** Terry O'Quinn, Meg Foster, Caroline Williams, Jonathan Brandis; **D:** Jeff Burr; **W:** John P. Auerbach. *NO*

Stepfather 3: Father's Day *🐾* **1992 (R)** The father from Hell is back! Escaping from the loony bin with a surgically altered face, the stepfather settles in a small town and gets a job at a nursery (the plant kind, not the children kind). His favorite gardening tool fast becomes the mulch machine, and soon locals are fertilizing the garden. Well below the original, but it may please fans of this genre. **CW:** Violence and some sensuality. **110m/C VHS, LV, Closed Caption.** Robert Wightman, Priscilla Barnes, Season Hubley; **D:** Guy Magar; **C:** Alan Caso. *THV*

Stephano Quantestorie *🐾🐾* **1993** Walter Mitty-ish story about daydreaming cop Stephano (Nichetti) who falls for the prime suspect in a robbery he's investigating. He escapes his conflicting feelings by imagining himself living other lives—as a math professor, airline pilot, saxophone player, and thief, but soon all these alter ego are intruding into his work. Italian with subtitles. **90m/C VHS.** *IT* Maurizio Nichetti; **D:** Maurizio Nichetti; **W:** Maurizio Nichetti. *KIV*

Stephen King's Golden Years *🐾½* **1991** Stephen King creates a chilling vision of scientific progress gone awry in this shocking techno-thriller. After being accidentally exposed to exotic chemicals in a lab explosion, an aging janitor undergoes an extraordinary transformation and the government will sacrifice anything to learn more about it. Originally a made-for-television miniseries. **232m/C VHS, LV, Closed Caption.** Keith Szarabajka, Frances Sternhagen, Ed Lauter, R.D. Call. *WOV*

Stephen King's It *🐾🐾½* **1990** A group of small town children, who were terrorized by an evil force in their youth, are traumatized again some thirty years later, when they learn a new series of child murders occurred in their Eastern home town. The adults, who now all have successful and diverse careers, must come to terms with the terrible secret they share, as "IT" has returned to wreak havoc in their New England home town. Based on horror master King's bestselling novel of the same name. **193m/C VHS, Beta, LV.** Tim Reid, Richard Thomas, John Ritter, Annette O'Toole, Richard Masur, Dennis Christopher, Harry Anderson, Olivia Hussey, Tim Curry, Jonathan Brandis; **D:** Tommy Lee Wallace; **W:** Stephen King; **M:** Richard Bellis. *WAR*

Stephen King's The Langoliers *🐾½* *The Langoliers* **1995 (PG-13)** Bloated variation of "Ten Little Indians" finds 10 airline passengers dozing off on their L.A.-to-Boston flight and awakening to find their fellow passengers and the crew have vanished. Of course, one passenger (Morse) is a pilot and he gets them to Bangor, Maine (where the miniseries was filmed), only to discover the airport is deserted and very weird things are going on. Oh yeah, the "langoliers" look like flying cannonballs with piranha teeth and have something to do with neurotic Pinchot's character. Not that you'll care much. **CW:** Violence; some sci-fi terror. **180m/C VHS, LV, Closed Caption.** David Morse, Bronson Pinchot, Patricia Wettig, Dean Stockwell, Kate Maberly, Christopher Collet, Kimber Riddle, Mark Lindsay Chapman, Frankie Faison, Baxter Harris; **Cameos:** Stephen King, Tom Holland; **D:** Tom Holland; **W:** Tom Holland; **C:** Paul Maibaum; **M:** Vladimir Horunzhy. *REP*

Stephen King's The Stand *🐾🐾½* *The Stand* **1994** Ghoulish made for TV adaptation of the King novel about a superflu/plague that decimates the U.S. population. The few survivors are soon divided into two camps—those dreaming of a godly old black woman known as Mother Abigail and others of the satanic Randall Flagg, the Walkin' Dude. Boulder, Colorado (where King was living when he wrote the novel) serves as headquarters for Abigail's brood while Las Vegas (where else) is Flagg territory. It all comes down to a battle of good vs. evil, with the future of mankind at stake. Religious allegory can get tedious but it's a varied cast with some scenes not for those with queasy stomachs. On four cassettes. **360m/C VHS, LV, Closed Caption.** Jamey Sheridan, Ruby Dee, Gary Sinise, Molly Ringwald, Miguel Ferrer, Laura San Giacomo, Rob Lowe, Adam Storke, Matt Frewer, Corin "Corky" Nemec, Ray Walston, Bill Fagerbakke, Ossie Davis, Shawnee Smith, Kareem Abdul-Jabbar, Stephen King; *Cameos:* Ed Harris, Kathy Bates, Stephen King; **W:** Stephen King; **C:** Edward Pei. *REP*

Stephen King's The Tommyknockers 🎬🎬½ *The Tommyknockers* 1993 **(R)** Another of King's creepy tales, adapted for TV. Bobbi (Helgenberger) and Gard (Smits) live in the small town of Haven, Maine (actually filmed on New Zealand's North Island). She's an aspiring writer; he's a fading poet with a drinking problem and a metal plate in his head (this is important). Walking in the woods, Bobbi stumbles over a long-buried spaceship which begins to take possession of the townspeople—their eyes shine green, their teeth fall out, and they act out their (often violent) fantasies—all but Gard. The whole thing's more silly than scary. The title comes from an old children's rhyme. **CW:** Sci/fi terror/horror. **120m/C VHS, LV, Closed Caption.** Jimmy Smits, Marg Helgenberger, Joanna Cassidy, E.G. Marshall, Traci Lords, John Ashton, Allyce Beasley, Cliff DeYoung, Robert Carradine, Leon Woods, Paul McIver; **D:** John Power; **W:** Lawrence D. Cohen. *THV, TWV*

Stephen King's Thinner 🎬🎬 *Thinner* 1996 **(R)** Holland takes all the meat out of this supernatural horror by turning it into a formulaic pursuit-of-justice bore. Porcine lawyer Billy Halleck (Burke) accidentally hits a gypsy with his car and is cursed with a case of perpetual weight loss. Conveniently for Billy, the client he has just gotten an acquittal for is local mobster Richie "The Hammer" Ginelli (Mantegna) who is now determined to save him. Ponderous plot and lackluster-looking latex is redeemed by decent acting. King makes his requisite cameo as Dr. Bangor (get it, Maine?) Originally published in 1984 under King's pseudonym Richard Bachman. **CW:** Horror violence and gore, language and sexuality. **92m/C VHS, LV, Closed Caption.** Robert John Burke, Joe Mantegna, Lucinda Jenney, Michael Constantine, Kari Wuhrer, John Horton, Sam Freed, Daniel von Bargen, Elizabeth Franz, Joy Lentz, Jeff Ware; *Cameos:* Stephen King; **D:** Tom Holland; **W:** Michael McDowell, Tom Holland; **C:** Kees Van Oostrum; **M:** Daniel Licht. *REP*

Stepmonster 🎬½ 1992 **(PG-13)** A boy tries to convince his father that his new stepmother is a monster—literally. Doesn't work any better than "My Stepmother Is an Alien." **CW:** Horror elements. **?m/C VHS, Closed Caption.** Alan Thicke, Robin Riker, Corey Feldman, John Astin, Ami Dolenz, George Gaynes. *NHO*

The Stepmother 🎬½ 1971 Yet another Hitchcock ripoff story involving an evil stepmother. Rey is passable, but there's not much else to recommend this dredge. **100m/C VHS.** Alejandro Rey, John Anderson, Katherine Justice, John David Garfield, Marlene Schmidt, Claudia Jennings, Larry Linville; **D:** Howard (Hikmet) Avedis. Nominations: Academy Awards '72: Best Song ("Strange Are the Ways of Love"). *ACA*

Steppenwolf 🎬🎬½ 1974 **(PG)** Static, enigmatic film version of the famous Herman Hesse novel about a brooding writer searching for meaning and self-worth. Interesting to watch, but the offbeat novel doesn't translate to the screen; leaves you flat. **105m/C VHS, Beta, LV.** *SI* Max von Sydow, Dominique Sanda, Pierre Clementi, Carla Rominelli, Roy Bosier; **D:** Fred Haines; **W:** Fred Haines; **C:** Tomislav Pinter; **M:** George Gruntz. *THV, GLV*

Stepping Out 🎬🎬🎬 1991 **(PG)** Minnelli stars as a would-be Broadway dancer who gives tap dancing lessons in an old church to an assortment of offbeat and interesting characters. When the troupe is asked to perform for a local charity, they make the most of their opportunity. A warm and touching ensemble piece that avoids oversentimentalizing and utilizes its cast to best advantage. **113m/C VHS, Beta, LV, Closed Caption.** Liza Minnelli, Shelley Winters, Bill Irwin, Ellen Greene, Julie Walters, Robyn Stevan, Jane Krakowski, Sheila McCarthy, Andrea Martin, Carol Woods, Nora Dunn, Eugene Glazer; **D:** Lewis Gilbert; **W:** Richard Harris; **M:** Peter Matz. *PAR*

Steps from Hell 🎬 1992 Vald Tempest is an evil immortal in control of a cult of zombie women. He's stolen a sacred map that will lead to a gateway which, when opened, will unleash a supreme evil on the world. Unless the heroic John Clark can find a way to prevent it, of course. **90m/C VHS.** Bernardo Rosa, Rocky Tucker, Ron Odell, Philip Cable, Liz Stoeckel, Steve Quimby, Lisa Lund; **D:** James Tucker; **W:** James Tucker. *CTD*

Stepsisters **woof!** 1985 Murderous double-crosses occur among a pilot, his wife, and her sister. **75m/C VHS, Beta.** Hal Fletcher, Sharyn Talbert, Bond Gideon. *NO*

The Sterile Cuckoo 🎬🎬🎬 *Pookie* 1969 **(PG)** An aggressive co-ed pursues a shy freshman who seems to embody her romantic ideal. Minnelli's performance is outstanding; Burton as the naive young man is also fine. Pakula's splendid first directing job. **108m/C VHS, Beta, LV.** Liza Minnelli, Wendell Burton, Tim McIntire; **D:** Alan J. Pakula; **W:** Alvin Sargent; **C:** Milton Krasner. Nominations: Academy Awards '69: Best Actress (Minnelli), Best Song ("Come Saturday Morning"). *PAR*

Steve Martin Live 🎬🎬½ 1985 Martin shows veteran comedians his famous Universal Amphitheatre performance and his short "The Absent-Minded Waiter." **58m/C VHS, Beta, LV.** Steve Martin, Teri Garr, Buck Henry, David Letterman, Paul Simon. *LIV, VES*

Stevie 🎬🎬 1978 Jackson brings her flawless skill to the role of British poet Stevie Smith. Excellent performance from Washbourne as Stevie's spinster aunt. Wooden, lifeless screen rendition for the Hugh Whitemore stage play is redeemed greatly by good performances, but is too talky and, frankly, rather dull and self-absorbed. **102m/C VHS.** *GB* Glenda Jackson, Mona Washbourne, Alec McCowen, Trevor Howard; **D:** Robert Enders; **C:** Frederick A. (Freddie) Young. Los Angeles Film Critics Association Awards '78: Best Supporting Actress (Washbourne); Montreal World Film Festival '78: Best Actress (Jackson); New York Film Critics Awards '78: Best Supporting Actress (Washbourne). *UAV*

Stewardess School **woof!** 1986 **(R)** Airline spoof aims at wackiness, but misses the runway. Generic title betrays probable badness which turns out to be all too real. An utter woofer. **84m/C VHS, Beta, LV.** Sandahl Bergman, Wendie Jo Sperber, Judy Landers, Julia Montgomery, Corinne Bohrer; **D:** Ken Blancato; **W:** Ken Blancato; **M:** Robert Folk. *NO*

Stick 🎬½ 1985 **(R)** Ex-con Stick (Reynolds, directing himself) wants to start a new life for himself in Miami. Lots of drug dealers and guns don't help the interest level in this dull underworld tale. Based upon the Elmore Leonard novel. **109m/C VHS, Beta, LV, Closed Caption.** Burt Reynolds, Candice Bergen, George Segal, Charles Durning, Dar Robinson; **D:** Burt Reynolds; **W:** Elmore Leonard; **M:** Stephen Dorff. *USH*

The Stick-Up 🎬 *Mud* 1977 In 1935, a young American traveling in Great Britain is introduced to some rather illegal fun. Rather sorry attempt at romance/comedy/adventure. **101m/C VHS, Beta.** David Soul, Pamela McMyler; **D:** Jeffrey Bloom; **W:** Jeffrey Bloom. *HHE*

Stickfighter 🎬 1989 **(PG)** The oppressive reign of an evil Spanish ruler of the Philippines is challenged by the world's best stickfighter. **102m/C VHS.** *PH* Dean Stockwell, Nancy Kwan, Alejandro Rey, Roland Dantes; **D:** Luis Nepomuceno. *PSM*

Sticky Fingers 🎬 1988 **(PG-13)** Two female musicians, asked to watch nearly a million bucks in drug money, go on a mega shopping spree. Completely incredible, unlikeable and mean-spirited attempt at zany comedy. **89m/C VHS, Beta, LV.** Melanie Mayron, Helen Slater, Eileen Brennan, Carol Kane, Christopher Guest, Danitra Vance, Gwen Welles, Stephen McHattie; **D:** Catlin Adams; **W:** Melanie Mayron, Catlin Adams; **M:** Gary Chang. *MED*

Stigma 🎬½ 1973 "Miami Vice" star Thomas (then 23; later to restore his middle name, Michael) is a young doctor who treats a syphilis epidemic in a small town. He's indistinguishable, but better than anything else here. Ever seen close-ups of advanced syphilis? Here's your chance—but it's not pretty. **93m/C Beta.** Philip Michael Thomas, Harlan Cary Poe; **D:** David E. Durston. *NO*

Stiletto 🎬½ 1969 **(R)** Good cast is wasted in this mediocre depiction of the trouble encountered by a contract Mafia assassin when he decides to change careers. Based on the usual pulp cheese by Harold Robbins. **101m/C VHS, Beta.** Alex Cord, Britt Ekland, Patrick O'Neal, Joseph Wiseman, Barbara McNair, Roy Scheider, M. Emmet Walsh; *Cameos:* Raul Julia; **D:** Bernard L. Kowalski; **C:** Jack Priestley. *NO*

Still Life 🎬🎬 1992 **(PG-13)** The press has dubbed him "the Art Killer," a serial murderer who makes sculptures out of his victims. He's a sensation—and not ready to stop. This sicko's next "Still Life" may just be a struggling young musician. **83m/C VHS, Beta, LV.** Jason Gedrick, Jessica Steen, Stephen Shellan; **D:** Graeme Campbell; **M:** Mychael Danna. *PSM*

Still Not Quite Human 🎬🎬 1992 Teenage android Chip must do battle with unscrupulous industrialists and their robot weapon Spartacus to rescue his inventor father from their deadly clutches. **84m/C VHS, Beta, Closed Caption.** Alan Thicke, Christopher Neame, Betsy Palmer, Adam Philipson, Rosa Nevin, Ken Pogue, Jay Underwood; **D:** Eric Luke; **W:** Eric Luke. *DIS*

Still of the Night 🎬🎬 1982 **(PG)** A Hitchcock-style thriller about a psychiatrist infatuated with a mysterious woman who may or may not be a killer. **91m/C VHS, Beta, LV.** Meryl Streep, Roy Scheider, Jessica Tandy, Joe Grifasi, Sara Botsford, Josef Sommer; **D:** Robert Benton; **W:** Robert Benton, David Newman; **C:** Nestor Almendros. *MGM*

The Stilts 🎬🎬🎬 1984 From modern Spanish cinema's preeminent director, this is a study of sexual dynamics revolving around a doomed love triangle. Aging professor Gomez wants young Del Sol to commit to him, but she won't; she has another, younger lover. Overwrought at times, but well acted. In Spanish with English subtitles. **95m/C VHS, Beta.** *SP* Laura Del Sol, Francesco Rabal, Fernando Gomez; **D:** Carlos Saura. *XVC, MED*

The Sting 🎬🎬🎬½ 1973 **(PG)** Newman and Redford together again in this sparkling story of a pair of con artists in 1930s Chicago. They set out to fleece a big-time racketeer, pitting brain against brawn and pistol. Very inventive, excellent acting, Scott Joplin's wonderful ragtime music adapted by Marvin Hamlisch. The same directorial and acting team from "Butch Cassidy and the Sundance Kid" triumphs again. **129m/C VHS, Beta, LV, Closed Caption.** Paul Newman, Robert Redford, Robert Shaw, Charles Durning, Eileen Brennan, Harold Gould, Ray Walston; **D:** George Roy Hill; **W:** David S. Ward; **C:** Robert L. Surtees; **M:** Marvin Hamlisch. Academy Awards '73: Best Art Direction/Set Decoration, Best Costume Design, Best Director (Hill), Best Film Editing, Best Picture, Best Story & Screenplay, Original Song Score and/or Adaptation; Directors Guild of America Awards '73: Best Director (Hill); People's Choice Awards '75: Best Film; Nominations: Academy Awards '73: Best Actor (Redford), Best Cinematography, Best Sound. *USH, BTV*

The Sting 2 🎬½ 1983 **(PG)** Complicated comic plot concludes with the final con game, involving a fixed boxing match where the stakes top a million dollars and the payoff could be murder. Lame sequel to "The Sting" (1973). **102m/C VHS, Beta, LV.** Jackie Gleason, Mac Davis, Teri Garr, Karl Malden, Oliver Reed; **D:** Jeremy Paul Kagan; **W:** David S.

Ward; *C:* Bill Butler; *M:* Lalo Schifrin. Nominations: Academy Awards '83: Original Song Score and/or Adaptation. *USH*

Sting of the Dragon Masters 🎬
1974 (R) Martial arts adventure featuring Bruce Lee's female Kung-Fu counterpart, Angela Mao. **96m/C VHS, Beta.** Angela Mao, Thoon Rhee, Carter Huang; *D:* Huang Feng. *VCI*

Sting of the West 🎬
1976 (PG) Journeyman con artist swindles his way across the Wild West. **90m/C VHS, Beta.** Jack Palance, Timothy Brent, Lionel Stander. *MPI*

Stingray 🎬½
1978 (PG) Two guys buy a Corvette, not knowing it's loaded with stolen heroin. Gangsters with an interest in the dope come after them, and the chase is on. Very violent and not all that funny. **105m/C VHS, Beta.** Chris Mitchum, Sherry Jackson, Les Lannom; *D:* Richard Taylor. *COL*

Stir Crazy 🎬🎬½
1980 (R) Two down-on-their-luck losers find themselves convicted of a robbery they didn't commit and sentenced to 120 years behind bars with a mean assortment of inmates. Wilder and Pryor's second teaming isn't quite as successful as the first go-round, but still provides plenty of laughs. **111m/C VHS, Beta, LV.** Richard Pryor, Gene Wilder, Nicolas Coster, Lee Purcell, Craig T. Nelson, JoBeth Williams; *D:* Sidney Poitier. *COL*

Stitches 🎬
1985 (R) Adolescent comedy about med students playing practical jokes on the dean using laboratory specimens. So bad the director (actually Rod Holcomb) allegedly did not want his name associated with it. **92m/C VHS, Beta.** Eddie Albert, Parker Stevenson, Geoffrey Lewis, Brian Tochi; *D:* Alan Smithee; *W:* Michael Choquette. *MED*

The Stolen Children 🎬🎬🎬½
Il Ladro di Bambini **1992** Highly acclaimed Italian neo-realist film that tells the story of a shy carabiniere and two children who have been placed in his care. As they journey an emotionally battered 11-year-old girl who was forced into prostitution by her mother and her sullen 9-year-old brother. As they journey from Milan to Sicily and gradually get to know each other, all three of the characters undergo a slight transformation. Gracefully executed, this haunting masterpiece explores the overriding themes of guilt and innocence and keeps you thinking about them long after the movie's over. Italian with subtitles. **108m/C VHS.** *IT* Enrico Lo Verso, Valentina Scalici, Giuseppe Ieracitano, Florence Darel, Marina Golovine, Fabio Alessandrini; *D:* Gianni Amelio; *W:* Gianni Amelio, Sandro Petraglia, Stefano Rulli; *M:* Franco Piersanti. Cannes Film Festival '92: Grand Jury Prize. *NYR*

A Stolen Face 🎬🎬
1952 Creepy, implausible drama of a plastic surgeon, spurned by a beautiful concert pianist, who transforms a female convict to look just like her. The convict runs away, but perhaps there's hope in the future with the pianist. **71m/B VHS, Beta, LV.** *GB* Paul Henreid, Lizabeth Scott, Andre Morell, Susan Stephen; *D:* Terence Fisher; *M:* Malcolm Arnold. *MLB*

Stolen Hours 🎬🎬½
1963 Inferior remake of Bette Davis' "Dark Victory" casts Hayward as an oil-rich heiress who learns she has a fatal illness. Bring the tissues for this tearjerker. Based on the play "Dark Victory" by George Emerson Brewer, Jr. and Bertram Block. **100m/C VHS, Closed Caption.** Susan Hayward, Michael Craig, Diane Baker, Edward Judd, Paul Rogers; *D:* Daniel Petrie; *W:* Jessamyn West, Joseph Hayes. *MGM, FCT*

Stolen Identity 🎬½
1953 A Viennese cabbie sees his American dream dashed for lack of the proper papers. When an American businessman is murdered in his cab he is quick to seize the moment...and the dead man's identity. In no time at all he finds himself involved with the widow, entangled with the murderer and under suspicion for the killing. Predictable and sluggish, the story inches its way to the foregone conclusion. **81m/B VHS, Beta.** Francis Lederer, Donald Buka, Joan Camden, Adrienne Gessner; *D:* Gunther Fritsch. *SNC*

Stolen Kisses 🎬🎬🎬½
Baisers Voles **1968** Sequel to "The 400 Blows," the story of Antoine Doinel: his unsuccessful career prospects as a detective in Paris, and his initially awkward but finally successful adventures with women. Made during Truffaut's involvement in a political crisis involving the sack of Cinematique Francais director Henri Langlois. Truffaut dedicated the film to Langlois and the Cinematique, but it is a thoroughly apolitical, small-scale, charming (some say too charming) romantic comedy, Truffaut-style. Followed by "Bed and Board." **90m/C VHS, Beta.** *FR* Jean-Pierre Leaud, Delphine Seyrig; *D:* Francois Truffaut; *M:* Antoine Duhamel. National Board of Review Awards '69: 5 Best Foreign Films of the Year; National Society of Film Critics Awards '69: Best Director (Truffaut); Nominations: Academy Awards '68: Best Foreign Language Film. *COL*

A Stolen Life 🎬🎬
1946 Remake of 1939 film of the same title starring Elizabeth Bergner. Oddly, Davis chose this as her first and last producing effort. Implausible tale of an evil twin (Davis) who takes her sister's (Davis) place so she can have the man they both love. Davis pulls it off as both twins; Ford is good as the hapless hubby. **107m/B VHS, Beta.** Bette Davis, Glenn Ford, Dane Clark, Walter Brennan, Charlie Ruggles, Bruce (Herman Brix) Bennett, Esther Dale, Peggy Knudsen; *D:* Curtis Bernhardt; *M:* Max Steiner. *MGM*

Stolen Painting 🎬½
1979 A man's wife is kidnapped by an evil gang while having her portrait painted. Her husband rescues her, and they, in turn, are chased by the kidnappers. **11m/C VHS, Beta.** *BFA*

The Stone Boy 🎬🎬🎬
1984 (PG) A boy accidentally kills his older brother on their family's Montana farm. The family is torn apart by sadness and guilt. Sensitive look at variety of reactions during a crisis, with an excellent cast led by Duvall's crystal-clear performance. **93m/C VHS, Beta, Closed Caption.** Glenn Close, Robert Duvall, Jason Presson, Frederic Forrest, Wilford Brimley, Linda Hamilton; *D:* Christopher Cain; *W:* Gina Berriault; *C:* Juan Ruiz-Anchia; *M:* James Horner, John Beal. *FOX*

Stone Cold
woof! **1991 (R)** Flamboyant footballer Bosworth made his acting debut in this sensitive human document, playing the usual musclebound, one-punk-army terminator cop, out to infiltrate a sadistic band of fascist biker barbarians engaged in drug running and priest shooting. Profane, lewd, gory, self-deifying; a crash course (accent on crashes) in everything despicable about modern action pics. *CW:* Strong language, strong violence, and sensuality. **91m/C VHS, Beta, LV, 8mm, Closed Caption.** Brian Bosworth, Lance Henriksen, William Forsythe, Arabella Holzbog, Sam McMurray; *D:* Craig R. Baxley. *COL*

Stone Cold Dead 🎬½
1980 (R) Rugged cop Crenna battles crime lord Williams (Paul Williams? Yeah, sure) over a prostitution ring. Meanwhile, a sniper starts killing hookers. Unoriginal and thoroughly dull would-be thriller. **100m/C VHS, Beta.** Richard Crenna, Paul Williams, Linda Sorensen, Belinda J. Montgomery; *D:* George Mendeluk; *W:* George Mendeluk. *MED*

Stone Fox 🎬🎬
1987 Heartwarming family drama in which a young man must win a dogsled race to save the family farm. Based on John Reynolds Gardiner's popular children's book. **96m/C VHS.** Buddy Ebsen, Joey Cramer, Belinda J. Montgomery, Gordon Tootoosis; *D:* Harvey Hart. *WOV*

The Stone Killer 🎬🎬½
1973 (R) Bronson stars as a tough plainclothes cop in this action-packed death drama about a Mafia plot to use Vietnam vets in a mass killing. Violent but tense and action-packed revenge adventure set in the underworlds of New York and Los Angeles. **95m/C VHS, Beta, LV.** Charles Bronson, Martin Balsam, Norman Fell, Ralph Waite, John Ritter; *D:* Michael Winner. *COL*

The Stoned Age 🎬
1994 (R) Buddies look to get wasted and find some chicks. Set in the '70s. **90m/C VHS.** Michael Kopelow, China Kantner, Renee Griffen; *D:* James Melkonian. *THV*

Stones of Death 🎬
1988 (R) An aboriginal curse is invoked when a subdivision is built too close to an ancient burial site. Teenagers begin having all-too-real nightmares about death. **90m/C VHS, Beta.** Tom Jennings, Natalie McCurry, Zoe Carides, Eric Oldfield; *D:* James Bagle. *NO*

Stonewall 🎬🎬🎬
1995 (R) Fictional account of the June, 1969 police raid on Greenwich Village gay bar the Stonewall Inn, which is considered to have launched the modern gay rights movement. White-bread, midwestern activist Matty Dean (Weller) arrives in New York and gets thrown in jail for defending streetwise drag queen LaMiranda (Diaz) from harassing cops. They become lovers but Matty is also involved with conservative prepster Ethan (Corbalis), who thinks the flamboyant queens give the gay movement a bad name. Meanwhile, the drag queens at the mob-backed Stonewall are getting fed up with police raids and brutal treatment. Adapted from Martin Duberman's social history "Stonewall." Director Finch died during the final editing stages of the film. *CW:* Violence, sexuality, and language. **93m/C VHS.** Frederick Weller, Guillermo Díaz, Brendan Corbalis, Bruce MacVittie, Duane Boutte, Peter Ratray, Luis Guzman; *D:* Nigel Finch; *W:* Rikki Beadle Blair; *C:* Chris Seager; *M:* Michael Kamen. *BMG*

The Stooge 🎬🎬½
1951 Singer Bill Miller (Martin) asks the antic Ted Rogers (Lewis) to join him in his vaudeville act, where Rogers' clowning has them on the road to success. But then Miller decides he wants to go solo. Sounds more than a little autobiographical. ♫A Girl Named Mary and a Boy Named Bill; Who's Your Little Whozis?; Just One More Chance; With My Eyes Wide Open I'm Dreaming; Louise; I'm Yours. **100m/B VHS, Closed Caption.** Dean Martin, Jerry Lewis, Polly Bergen, Marion Marshall, Eddie Mayehoff, Richard Erdman, Frances Bavier; *D:* Norman Taurog; *W:* Martin Rackin, Fred Finklehoffe, Elwood Ullman; *C:* Daniel F. Fapp. *PAR*

Stoogemania 🎬
1985 A nerd becomes so obsessed with the Three Stooges that they begin to take over his life and ruin it. Harmless except as a waste of time. Includes actual Stooge footage including some colorized—but see an old Stooges movie instead. **95m/C VHS, Beta.** Josh Mostel, Melanie Chartoff, Sid Caesar; *D:* Chuck Workman; *M:* Hummie Mann. *PAR*

Stooges Shorts Festival 🎬
194? This collection of shorts includes "Disorder in the Court" (1936), "Sing a Song of Six Pants" (1947), and "Malice in the Palace" (1949). **55m/B VHS, Beta.** *HHT*

The Stooges Story 🎬🎬🎬
1990 "The Stooges Anthology" presents a history of the comedy team, from their vaudevillian beginnings to their television resurgence in the 60s. "Disorder in the Court" finds the trio making a mockery of the United States justice system, and in "Brideless Groom," Shemp must find a bride within forty-eight hours in order to collect an inheritance. **90m/B VHS.** Moe Howard, Larry Fine, Curly Howard, Shemp Howard. *SIM*

Stop! Look! and Laugh! 🎬🎬½
1960 Paul Winchell and his dummy Jerry Mahoney host a look at some of the Stooges funniest moments. Features the Marquis Chimps' interpretation of Cinderella for some reason. **78m/B VHS.** Moe Howard, Curly Howard, Shemp Howard, Larry Fine; *D:* Jules White. *COL*

Stop Making Sense 🎬🎬🎬½
1984 The Talking Heads perform eighteen of their best songs in this concert filmed in Los Angeles. Considered by many to be the best concert movie ever made. The band plays with incredible energy and imagination and Demme's direction and camera work is appropriately frenzied and original. Features such Talking Heads songs as

"Burning Down the House," "Psycho Killer," and "Once in a Lifetime." Band member Tina Weymouth's Tom Tom Club also performs for the audience. **99m/C VHS, Beta, LV. D:** Jonathan Demme; **C:** Jordan Cronenweth; **Performed by:** David Byrne, Tina Weymouth, Chris Franz, Jerry Harrison. *MVD, COL*

Stop! or My Mom Will Shoot 🎦

1992 (PG-13) Getty is an overbearing mother paying a visit to her cop son (Stallone) in Los Angeles. When mom witnesses a crime she has to stay in town longer than intended, which gives her time to meddle in her son's work and romantic lives. If Stallone wants to change his image this so-called comedy isn't the way to do it—because the joke is only on him. Viewers who rent this may find the joke is on them. **87m/C VHS, Beta, LV, Closed Caption.** Sylvester Stallone, Estelle Getty, JoBeth Williams, Roger Rees, Martin Ferrero, Gailard Sartain, Dennis Burkley; **D:** Roger Spottiswoode; **W:** William Osborne, William Davies, Blake Snyder; **M:** Alan Silvestri. Golden Raspberry Awards '92: Worst Actor (Stallone), Worst Supporting Actress (Getty), Worst Screenplay. *USH*

Stop That Cab 🎦½

1951 Sloppy crooks accidentally leave precious jewels in the back seat of a taxi, and pursue and torture the cabby who found and hid them. Rather mean-spirited, uninteresting comedy. **56m/B VHS, Beta, LV.** Sid Melton, Iris Adrian, Tom Neal. *NO*

Stopover Tokyo 🎦🎦

1957 An American intelligence agent uncovers a plot to assassinate the American ambassador while on leave in Japan. Nice location shooting and scenery; limp story and characters. Based on a novel by John P. Marquand. **100m/C VHS, Beta.** Robert Wagner, Joan Collins, Edmond O'Brien, Ken Scott; **D:** Richard L. Breen. *FOX*

The Stork Club 🎦🎦

1945 A little song, a little dance, will Betty Hutton find romance? The actors manage to rise above the script in this silly, overdone fable. Hutton stars as the poor but spunky hatcheck girl who unwittingly saves the life of a cynical billionaire. His expressions of gratitude are less than appreciated by her G.I. beau. Done mainly as a vehicle for Hutton's promotion, so Betty's die-hard fans may find it to their liking. 🎵Doctor, Lawyer, Indian Chief; Baltimore Oriole; I'm a Square in the Social Circle; If I Had a Dozen Hearts; Love Me; China Boy; In the Shade of the Old Apple Tree. **98m/B VHS.** Betty Hutton, Barry Fitzgerald, Don DeFore, Robert Benchley, Bill Goodwin, Iris Adrian, Noel Neill, Andy Russell; **D:** Hal Walker. *NOS*

Storm 🎦½

1987 (PG-13) Uneven thriller finds college students on a camping trip who must fight for their lives when they are confronted by killer thieves. Somewhat contrived, but interesting ending to this low-budget outing. **99m/C VHS, Closed Caption.** CA David Palfy, Stan Kane, Harry Freedman, Lawrence Elion, Tom Schioler; **D:** David Winning; **M:** Amin Bhatia. *WAR*

Storm and Sorrow 🎦🎦

1990 Molly Higgins is known as the "Spiderwoman of the Rockies" for her legendary mountain climbing abilities. Then she joins a team looking to scale the 24,000-foot peaks of Russia's Pamir Mountains. The group meets deadly hazards—both natural and those caused by the ego-driven rivalries of the group's members. A fact-based drama based on the novel by Richard Craig. **96m/C VHS, Closed Caption.** Lori Singer, Todd Allen, Steve Anderson, Jay Baker; **W:** Leigh Chapman. *WOV*

Storm in a Teacup 🎦🎦½

1937 A reporter starts a campaign to save a sheepdog that the town magistrate has ordered killed because the owner, an old woman, is unable to pay the license tax. As the dog's fate hangs in the balance, this often humorous film provides an interesting look at British society of the 1930s. **80m/B VHS, Beta.** GB Vivien Leigh, Rex Harrison, Cecil Parker, Sara Allgood; **D:** Victor Saville. *NOS, BAR, DVT*

Storm over Asia 🎦🎦🎦🎦

The Heir to Genghis Khan **1928** A Mongolian trapper is discovered to be descended from Genghis Khan and is made puppet emperor of a Soviet province. Beautiful and evocative. Silent masterpiece. **70m/B VHS, Beta.** RU I. Inkizhinov, Valeri Inkizhinov, A. Christiakov, A. Dedinstev, V. Tzoppi, Paulina Belinskaya; **D:** Vsevolod Pudovkin. National Board of Review Awards '30: 5 Best Foreign Films of the Year. *IHF, FST, VYY*

Storm over Wyoming 🎦🎦

1950 The old sheep-and-cattle battle again; Holt and Martin find themselves haplessly embroiled in a Wyoming range war. Action-packed but thin, ordinary western. **60m/B VHS, Beta.** Tim Holt, Richard Martin. *NO*

Storm Rider 🎦🎦

1957 A gunman hired to protect a group of ranchers from a powerful rancher falls in love with a local widow. After his job is done, however, he leaves her behind. Typical western fare. **70m/B VHS.** Scott Brady, Mala Powers, Bill Williams, Olin Howlin, William "Bill" Fawcett, John Goddard; **D:** Edward L. Bernds; **W:** Edward L. Bernds; **M:** Les Baxter. *NO*

The Storm Within 🎦🎦🎦½

Les Parents Terribles **1948** Based on Cocteau's play, many consider this domestic drama of a troubled family's tortured existence to be his finest work. De Bray plays the domineering mother, Marais plays the son, and Day is the woman he (and his father) love in this complex story of sexuality, parental rivalry and jealousy. With the film set in only two locations, Cocteau creates a claustrophobic intimacy within the walls of de Bray's family apartment and Day's apartment. An inferior remake, "Intimate Relations" was released in Britain in 1953. In French with English subtitles. **98m/B VHS.** FR Jean Marais, Yvonne de Bray, Gabrielle Dorziat, Marcel Andre, Josette Day; **D:** Jean Cocteau; **W:** Jean Cocteau. *WBF*

Stormquest woof!

1987 Deep in the jungle, a band of women warriors live without men. When it is discovered that one of the group has a male lover, she is sentenced to death. Her man tries to rescue her, and it turns into a war of the sexes—literally. In Spanish with subtitles. **90m/C VHS.** SP Kai Baker, Brent Huff; **D:** Alex Sessa. *MED*

Stormswept 🎦½

1995 Actress Brianna (Hughes) rents a haunted Louisiana mansion housing the spirit of a slave master. When a storm strands Brianna and friends, the spirit causes everyone to get up to all sorts of sexual escapades. **94m/C VHS.** Julie Hughes, Melissa Moore, Kathleen Kinmont; **D:** David Marsh. *MTH*

Stormy Monday 🎦🎦½

1988 (R) An American developer conspires to strike it rich in Newcastle, England real estate by resorting to violence and political manipulations. Sting plays the jazz club owner who opposes him. Slow plot, but acted and directed well; interesting photography. **108m/C VHS, Beta, LV, 8mm, Closed Caption.** GB Melanie Griffith, Tommy Lee Jones, Sting, Sean Bean, James Cosmo, Mark Long, Brian Lewis; **D:** Mike Figgis; **W:** Mike Figgis; **C:** Roger Deakins; **M:** Mike Figgis. *PAR, OM*

Stormy Trails 🎦🎦

1936 Bell battles bellicose bad guys who are after his property. At least all the gunfights should keep a viewer awake! **59m/B VHS, Beta.** Rex Bell. *VCN*

Stormy Waters 🎦🎦½

Remorques **1941** A romantic French drama about a sea captain falling in love with a woman he rescues from a storm. He goes back to his wife, however, when she becomes critically ill. Director Gremillon insisted on realistic footage of storms at sea; production was delayed because of the difficulties of the German occupation. Dubbed. **75m/B VHS, Beta.** FR Jean Gabin, Michele Morgan, Madeleine Renaud; **D:** Jean Gremillon. *VYY*

Stormy Weather 🎦🎦½

1943 In this cavalcade of black entertainment the plot takes a back seat to the nearly non-stop array of musical numbers, showcasing this stellar cast at their performing peak. 🎵There's No Two Ways About Love; Stormy Weather; Ain't Misbehavin'; Rhythm Cocktail; Rang Tang Tang; Dat, Dot, Dah; That Ain't Right; I Can't Give You Anything But Love, Baby; Digga Digga Doo. **77m/B VHS, Beta, LV, Closed Caption.** Lena Horne, Bill Robinson, Fats Waller, Dooley Wilson, Cab Calloway, Nicholas Brothers; **D:** Andrew L. Stone; **C:** Leon Shamroy. *FOX, PTB, FCT*

The Story Lady 🎦🎦½

1993 (G) A retiree uses her story-telling abilities as a hostess on a public-access children's program. She becomes so popular that two network execs want to exploit her as a spokesperson for a toy company. Only a young girl can help her find a way to resist going commercial. **93m/C VHS.** Jessica Tandy, Lisa Jakub, Ed Begley Jr., Charles Durning, Stephanie Zimbalist; **D:** Larry Elikann. *UNT*

The Story of a Cheat 🎦🎦🎦

1936 The hero of the film discovers at an early age that dishonesty is probably the best policy and he sets out to put his theory into use. Director/writer Guitry also turns in a great performance as the central character. Guitry was a major influence on such different directors as Welles, Resnais and Truffaut. Based on Guitry's novel "Memoires d'Un Tricheur." In French with English subtitles. **83m/B VHS.** FR Sacha Guitry; **D:** Sacha Guitry; **W:** Sacha Guitry. *INT, FCT*

Story of a Cowboy Angel 🎦

1981 On the Christmas Mountain Ranch, a cowboy angel descends to Earth to bestow various beneficences. **90m/C VHS, Beta.** Slim Pickens. *LIV, VES*

The Story of a Love Story 🎦🎦½

Impossible Object **1973** Bates plays a writer whose imagination gets the better of him when he attempts an extra-marital affair. Was he with her or not? Unusual concept doesn't stand up in the long run. Fine cast is under-utilized. **110m/C VHS.** FR Alan Bates, Dominique Sanda, Evans Evans, Lea Massari, Michel Auclair, Laurence De Monaghan; **D:** John Frankenheimer; **W:** Alan Bates. *NO*

The Story of a Three Day Pass 🎦🎦½

La Permission **1968** A black American GI falls in love with a white French girl he meets in peacetime Paris. Based on Van Peebles book "La Permission." With English subtitles. Made on a low budget and flawed, but poignant and impressive. **87m/B VHS.** Harry Baird, Nicole Berger, Pierre Doris; **D:** Melvin Van Peebles; **W:** Melvin Van Peebles. *XVC, FCT, HEG*

Story of Adele H. 🎦🎦🎦

L'Histoire d'Adele H **1975 (PG)** The story of Adele Hugo, daughter of Victor Hugo, whose love for an English soldier leads to obsession and finally to madness after he rejects her. Sensitive and gentle unfolding of characters and story. Beautiful photography. In French with English subtitles. **97m/C VHS, Beta, LV.** FR Isabelle Adjani, Bruce Robinson; **D:** Francois Truffaut; **W:** Suzanne Schiffman, Jean Gruault; **C:** Nestor Almendros. National Board of Review Awards '75: 5 Best Foreign Films of the Year, Best Actress (Adjani); New York Film Critics Awards '75: Best Actress (Adjani), Best Screenplay; National Society of Film Critics Awards '75: Best Actress (Adjani); Nominations: Academy Awards '75: Best Actress (Adjani). *MGM, FCT*

The Story of Alexander Graham Bell 🎦🎦🎦

1939 Lavish Fox biography on the inventor of the telephone provided Ameche with his most popular role. He's a serious Scot who comes to Boston to teach speech to the deaf and falls in love with the rich, beautiful and hearing impaired Young (whose three sisters, Georgianna, Polly Ann, and Sally are also in the film). Thanks to Young's rich daddy (Coburn), Bell gets the money to work on his invention, aided by enthusiastic assistant Watson (Fonda). No, it's not an entirely accurate retelling but it's well-done. **97m/B VHS.** Don Ameche, Loretta Young, Henry Fonda, Charles Coburn, Spring Byington, Gene Lockhart, Sally Blane, Polly Ann Young, Georgianna Young, Bobs Watson, Jonathan Hale, Harry Davenport; **D:** Irving Cummings; **W:** Lamar Trotti; **C:** Leon Shamroy. *FXV*

The Story of Boys & Girls 🎞🎞🎞
Storia de Ragazzi e di Ragazze 1991 Two very different families come together for the wedding feast of their children, during which family secrets are revealed and we come to know and care for everyone present. A twenty-course meal rivals the food scenes in "Babette's Feast" and is guaranteed to make your mouth water. Fine ensemble of actors, well directed, with a vivid evocation of 1930s Italy. In Italian with English subtitles. **92m/C VHS, LV. IT** Lucrezia Lante della Rovere, Massimo Bonetti, Davide Bechini, Enrica Maria Modugno, Valeria Bruni Tadeschi, Lina Bernardi, Anna Bonaiuto, Alessandro Haber; **D:** Pupi Avati; **W:** Pupi Avati; **M:** Riz Ortolani. *FXL*

The Story of David 🎞🎞🎞 1976 (PG)
Well-done Old Testament Bible drama about the shepherd boy who slew Goliath, overcame the Philistines, and united Israel. Then, as King David, he winds up involved in an illicit love affair with Bathsheba that threatens to destroy his kingdom. Fine acting and a literate script highlight this made for television production. On two cassettes. **192m/C VHS.** Timothy Bottoms, Anthony Quayle, Jane Seymour, Keith Michell, Susan Hampshire; **D:** Alex Segal; **W:** Ernest Kinoy. *COL, VIF*

The Story of Dr. Wassell 🎞🎞½ 1944
Courageous true story of Corydon M. Wassell (Cooper), who won the Navy Cross for humanitarianism in WWII. Stationed in Java when the Japanese overran the island, Wassell's placed in charge of evacuating the wounded. When he learns that stretcher cases must be left behind, he disobeys orders to rescue some badly wounded soldiers and get them to safety. (Naturally, there has to be some romance, so Cooper's paired with Day as a Red Cross nurse). Based on the book by James Hilton. **137m/C VHS, Closed Caption.** Gary Cooper, Laraine Day, Signe Hasso, Dennis O'Keefe, Carol Thurston, Carl Esmond, Stanley Ridges, Paul Kelly, Elliott Reid, Philip Ahn, Barbara Britton; **D:** Cecil B. DeMille; **W:** Charles Bennett, Alan LeMay; **C:** Victor Milner; **M:** Victor Young. *USH*

The Story of Esther Costello 🎞🎞½
Golden Virgin 1957 Rich American Margaret Landi (Crawford) is visiting her Irish homeland when she meets Esther (Sears), a young girl rendered deaf, mute, and blind by a childhood trauma. The childless Margaret is persuaded to take Esther in as a surrogate daughter and the waif gradually begins to respond to her care, sparking a media frenzy over the inspirational saga. This brings Carlo (Brazzi), Margaret's estranged and money-grubbing husband, out of the woodwork, with some get-rich-quick schemes. Well-done melodrama adapted from the book by Nicholas Monsarrat. **102m/B VHS. GB** Joan Crawford, Heather Sears, Rossano Brazzi, Lee Patterson, Ron Randell, Fay Compton, John Loder, Denis O'Dea; **D:** David Miller; **W:** Charles Kaufman; **C:** Robert Krasker; **M:** Georges Auric. *COL*

The Story of Fausta 🎞🎞½ *Romance da Empregada* 1988 (R)
An unhappily married cleaning woman in the slums of Rio entices all the money and gifts she can out of an elderly widower. Decidedly grim comedy-drama, well-done but unsparing in its depiction of overwhelming greed. In Portuguese with English subtitles. **90m/C VHS. BR** Betty Faria, Daniel Filho, Brandao Filho; **D:** Bruno Barreto; **M:** Ruben Blades. *FXL, FCT*

The Story of Jacob & Joseph 🎞🎞🎞 1974 (R)
Fine Biblical drama finds brothers Jacob and Esau fighting over their birthright, tearing apart their family for twenty years. When the brothers finally reconcile it's only to cast an envious eye on youngest brother Joseph, whom they sell into slavery. Taken to Egypt Joseph uses his talents to become the Pharoah's chief advisor but he can never forget his family or what was done to him. All-around good acting, directing and writing. Made for television. **96m/C VHS.** Keith Michell, Tony LoBianco, Julian Glover, Colleen Dewhurst, Herschel Bernardi, Harry Andrews; **D:** Michael Cacoyannis; **W:** Ernest Kinoy. *COL, VIF*

The Story of Louis Pasteur 🎞🎞🎞
1936 Formulaic Hollywood biopic raised a notch or two by Muni's superb portrayal of the famous scientist and his career leading up to his most famous discoveries. Acclaimed in its time; excellent despite low budget. **85m/B VHS, Beta.** Paul Muni, Josephine Hutchinson, Anita Louise, Fritz Leiber, Donald Woods, Porter Hall, Walter Kingsford; **D:** William Dieterle; **C:** Gaetano Antonio "Tony" Gaudio. Academy Awards '36: Best Actor (Muni), Best Story; National Board of Review Awards '36: 10 Best Films of the Year; Nominations: Academy Awards '36: Best Picture. *MGM, BTV*

The Story of O 🎞🎞 1975
A young woman's love for one man moves her to surrender herself to many men, in order to please him. Softcore porn with bondage and S&M beautified by camera work. Based on the classic Freudian-erotic novel by Pauline Reage. **97m/C VHS, Beta, LV.** Corinne Clery, Anthony Steel; **D:** Just Jaeckin. *HHE*

The Story of O, Part 2 🎞 1987
A sort-of sequel to the erotic classic, in which the somewhat soiled vixen takes over an American conglomerate by seducing everyone in it. **107m/C Beta, LV.** Sandra Wey, Carole James. *LIV, VES, HHE*

The Story of Qui Ju 🎞🎞🎞 *Qiu Ju Da Guansi* 1991 (PG)
A simple story, beautifully directed and acted, about a peasant woman's search for justice. The pregnant Qui Ju's husband is assaulted and injured by the head of their village. Outraged, Qui Ju slowly climbs the Chinese administrative ladder from official to higher official as she insistently seeks redress. Presents a close observance of daily life and customs with a strong female lead. Adapted from the novel "The Wan Family's Lawsuit" by Chen Yuan Bin. In Mandarin Chinese with English subtitles. **100m/C VHS, LV. CH** Gong Li, Lei Lao Sheng, Liu Pei Qu, Ge Zhi Jun, Ye Jun, Yang Liu Xia, Zhu Qanging, Cui Luowen, Yank Huiquin, Wang Jianfa, Lin Zi; **D:** Zhang Yimou; **W:** Liu Heng; **C:** Chi Xiaonin, Yu Xaioqun; **M:** Zhao Jiping. National Society of Film Critics Awards '93: Best Foreign Film; Venice Film Festival '92: Best Actress (Li), Best Film; Nominations: Independent Spirit Awards '94: Best Foreign Film. *COL*

The Story of Robin Hood & His Merrie Men 🎞🎞🎞 *The Story of Robin Hood*
1952 Well-made swashbuckler based on the English legend was Disney's second live action feature. Almost, but not quite, as memorable as the 1938 Michael Curtiz "Adventures of Robin Hood." Curtiz's version had Errol Flynn, after all. **83m/C VHS, Beta, Closed Caption.** Richard Todd, Joan Rice, Peter Finch, Martita Hunt; **D:** Ken Annakin. *DIS*

The Story of Ruth 🎞🎞 1960
Biblical saga of adventures of Ruth as she denounces her pagan gods and flees to Israel. Typically "epic" with overwrought performances. Alternately not too bad to downright boring. **132m/C VHS, Beta, Closed Caption.** Elana Eden, Viveca Lindfors, Peggy Wood, Tom Tryon, Stuart Whitman, Jeff Morrow, Thayer David, Eduard Franz; **D:** Henry Koster. *FOX, IGP*

The Story of Seabiscuit 🎞🎞½ *Pride of Kentucky* 1949
The famous racing winner Seabiscuit is featured in a fluffy story of a racetrack romance. Temple is in love with a jockey (McCallister) but wants him to give up racing. Her uncle (Fitzgerald), who is Seabiscuit's trainer, has other things in mind. **93m/C VHS.** Shirley Temple, Barry Fitzgerald, Lon McCallister, Rosemary DeCamp; **D:** David Butler. *MGM, BTV*

Story of the Dragon 🎞🎞 1982
How Bruce Lee developed the martial arts technique of Jeet Kune Do. **93m/C VHS, Beta.** Bruce Li, Hwang Jang Lee, Carter Wong, Roy Horan. *WVE*

The Story of the Late Chrysanthemum 🎞🎞½ 1939
Classic drama about the son of a Kabuki actor who falls in love with a servant girl against his father's wishes. Their doomed affair is the center of the plot. Acclaimed and sensitive drama, in Japanese with English subtitles. **115m/B VHS, Beta. JP** Shotaro Hanayagi, Kakuo Mori, Kokichi Takada, Gonjuro Kawarazaki, Yoko Umemura; **D:** Kenji Mizoguchi. *FCT*

The Story of Vernon and Irene Castle 🎞🎞🎞 1939
In this, their last film together for RKO, Astaire and Rogers portray the internationally successful ballroom dancers who achieved popularity in the early 1900s. Irene Castle served as technical advisor for the film and exasperated everyone on the set by insisting that Rogers be a brunette. Still fun, vintage Fred and Ginger. ♫Only When You're In My Arms; Missouri Waltz; Oh, You Beautiful Doll; Nights of Gladness; By the Beautiful Sea; Glow, Little Glow Worm; Destiny Waltz; Row, Row, Row; The Yama Yama Man. **93m/B VHS, Beta, LV.** Fred Astaire, Ginger Rogers, Edna May Oliver, Lew Fields, Jack Perrin, Walter Brennan; **D:** H.C. Potter. *TTC, MED*

Story of William S. Hart/Sad Clowns 192?
Features William S. Hart as a cowboy in "Hell's Hinges" and "Tumbleweeds" (1925). From "The History of the Motion Picture" series. **50m/B VHS, Beta.** William S. Hart, Buster Keaton, Harry Langdon. *CCB*

The Story of Women 🎞🎞🎞 *Une Affaire de Femmes* 1988
Riveting factual account of a woman (Huppert) who was guillotined for performing abortions in Nazi-occupied France. In French with English subtitles. **110m/C VHS. FR** Isabelle Huppert, Francois Cluzet, Marie Trintignant, Nils Tavernier, Louis Ducreux; **D:** Claude Chabrol; **W:** Claude Chabrol, Colo Tavernier O'Hagan; **M:** Matthieu Chabrol. Los Angeles Film Critics Association Awards '89: Best Foreign Film; New York Film Critics Awards '89: Best Foreign Film; Venice Film Festival '88: Best Actress (Huppert). *NYF*

Storybook 🎞🎞½ 1995 (G)
Eight-year-old Brandon finds a magic storybook and enters into a realm of fantasy. He discovers the only way to return home from Storyland is to save the kingdom from the rule of Queen Evilia and along with Woody the Woodsman, Pouch the Boxing Kangaroo, and Hoot the Wise Owl, Brandon just may succeed. **88m/C VHS, Closed Caption.** Sean Fitzgerald, William McNamara, Swoosie Kurtz, Robert Costanzo, James Doohan, Brenda Epperson, Gary Morgan, Richard Moll, Jack Scalia, Milton Berle; **D:** Lorenzo Doumani; **W:** Lorenzo Doumani, Susan Bowen. *REP*

Storyville 🎞½ 1974 (R)
Love and music overcome prostitution and poverty in this turn-of-the-century New Orleans jazz drama, but tragedy prevails. **96m/C VHS, Beta.** Tim Rooney, Jeannie Wilson, Butch Benit, Wayne Mack, Bond Gideon, Oley Sassone; **D:** Jack Weis. *NO*

Storyville 🎞🎞 1992 (R)
Southern Gothic tale set in New Orleans about a feckless young lawyer running for a local congressional seat. Neither Cray nor his family are strong candidates for the family values vote. Cray is separated from his wife and willingly indulges in an affair with a beautiful and mysterious young woman. This leads to a blackmail plot when he finds out his lover has been videotaping their antics. There's also a murder investigation and a host of family skeletons rattling around. Robards is fine as the crafty uncle but Spader's low-key attitude works against the story. Directorial debut of Frost. **CW:** Langauge, violent scene, and sensuality. **112m/C VHS, LV, Closed Caption.** James Spader, Joanne Whalley, Jason Robards Jr., Charlotte Lewis, Michael Warren, Piper Laurie, Michael Parks, Chuck McCann, Woody Strode, Charles Haid; **D:** Mark Frost; **W:** Mark Frost, Lee Reynolds; **M:** Carter Burwell. *COL*

Stowaway 🎞🎞🎞 1936 (G)
After her missionary parents are killed in a Chinese revolution, Shirley stows away on a San Francisco-bound liner and plays cupid to a bickering couple who adopt her. ♫Good Night, My Love; One Never Knows, Does One; You Gotta S-M-I-L-E to Be H-A-P-P-Y; I Wanna Go To the Zoo; That's What I Want For Christmas. **86m/B VHS, Beta, Closed Caption.** Shirley Temple, Robert Young, Alice Faye, Eugene Pallette, Helen Westley, Arthur Treacher, Astrid Allwyn; **D:** William A. Seiter; **C:** Arthur C. Miller. *FOX*

Straight for the Heart 🎬🎬 *A Corps Perdu* **1988** Photojournalist Pierre returns to Montreal after a harrowing assignment in Nicaragua. His homecoming is less than happy when he discovers both his lovers, David and Sarah, have deserted him. Pierre takes to wandering the Montreal streets, taking pictures, hoping they will help him make some sense of his life and help him reestablish a connection with beauty and humanity. In French with English subtitles. **92m/C VHS.** *CA* Matthias Habich, Johanne-Marie Tremblay; *D:* Lea Pool. *WBF*

Straight Line 🎬🎬 **1988** T.S. Turner is a private investigator who goes after street gangs in order to prevent further violence in this action-packed story. **95m/C VHS.** Mr. T, Sean Roberge, Ron Ryan. *CAF, MOV*

Straight Out of Brooklyn 🎬🎬 **1991** (R) A bleak, nearly hopeless look at a struggling black family in a Brooklyn housing project. The son seeks escape through crime, his father in booze. An up-close and raw look at part of society seldom shown in mainstream film, its undeniable power is sapped by ragged production values and a loose narrative prone to melodrama. Rich (seen in a supporting role) was only 19 years old when he completed this, funded partly by PBS-TV's "American Playhouse." *CW:* Language. **91m/C VHS.** George T. Odom, Ann D. Sanders, Lawrence Gilliard, Mark Malone, Larry Gilliard Jr., Reana E. Drummond, Barbara Sanon, Matty Rich; *D:* Matty Rich; *W:* Matty Rich; *C:* John Rosnell; *M:* Harold Wheeler. Independent Spirit Awards '92: Best First Feature; Sundance Film Festival '91: Special Jury Prize. *HBO, FCT, WAR*

Straight Shootin' 🎬🎬½ **1917** Ford's first major effort launched both Carey and Gibson to national fame. Prototypical western; great action, great scenery. Silent. **53m/B VHS, Beta.** Harry Carey Sr., Hoot Gibson, Mollie Malone; *D:* John Ford. *GPV, VCN, DVT*

Straight Talk 🎬🎬½ **1992** (PG) Shirlee (Parton), a down-home gal from Arkansas, heads for Chicago to start life anew. She finds a job as a receptionist at WNDY radio, but is mistaken for the new radio psychologist. Her homespun advice ("Get off the cross. Somebody needs the wood.") becomes hugely popular and soon "Dr." Shirlee is the toast of the town. Parton's advice is the funniest part of this flimsy movie, but she is helped immensely by Dunne and Orbach. Woods, however, is not in his element in a romantic comedy, and holds the movie down. **91m/C VHS, Beta, Closed Caption.** Dolly Parton, James Woods, Griffin Dunne, Michael Madsen, Deirdre O'Connell, John Sayles, Teri Hatcher, Spalding Gray, Jerry Orbach, Philip Bosco, Charles Fleischer, Jay Thomas; *D:* Barnet Kellman; *W:* Craig Bolotin, Patricia Resnick; *M:* Brad Fiedel. *HPH*

Straight Time 🎬🎬🎬 **1978** (R) Ex-con Hoffman hits the streets for the first time in six years and finds himself again falling into a life of crime. Well-told, sobering story flopped at the box office and has never received the recognition it deserved. Convincing, realistic portrayal of a criminal. Hoffman was the original director, but gave the reins to Grosbard. Based on the novel "No Beast So Fierce" by Edward Bunker. **114m/C VHS, Beta.** Dustin Hoffman, Harry Dean Stanton, Gary Busey, Theresa Russell, M. Emmet Walsh, Kathy Bates; *D:* Ulu Grosbard; *W:* Jeffrey Boam, Alvin Sargent, Edward Bunker; *C:* Owen Roizman; *M:* David Shire. *WAR*

Straight to Hell 🎬½ **1987** (R) A wildly senseless, anachronistic western spoof about a motley, inept gang of frontier thieves. An overplayed, indiscriminating punk spaghetti oat-opera. **86m/C VHS, Beta, Closed Caption.** Joe Strummer, Elvis Costello, Grace Jones, Jim Jarmusch, Dick Rude, Courtney Love, Sy Richardson; *D:* Alex Cox; *W:* Alex Cox. *FOX, OM*

Straight Up 🎬½ **1990** A musical f/x-ridden attempts to warn MTV-era children about drugs, but visual gimmicks often overwhelm the message. Gossett sings nicely as a cosmic sage of abstinence, who cautions a boy against substance abuse. The smartest segment lambasts cigarette and alcohol ads. **75m/C VHS, Beta.** Chad Allen, Louis Gossett Jr. *RHI*

Strait-Jacket 🎬🎬 **1964** After Crawford is released from an insane asylum where she was sent 20 years for axing her husband and his mistress, mysterious axe murders begin to occur in the neighborhood. Coincidence? Aging axist Crawford is the prime suspect, and even she cannot say for sure who's doing it. Daughter Baker is there to help her adjust. Moderately creepy grade B+ slasher is lifted somewhat by Crawford. Written by Robert Bloch ("Psycho"). Never one to miss a gimmick, director Castle arranged for the distribution of cardboard "bloody axes" to all theater patrons attending the movie. **89m/B VHS, Beta.** Joan Crawford, Leif Erickson, Diane Baker, George Kennedy; *D:* William Castle; *W:* Robert Bloch; *M:* Van Alexander. *COL*

Stranded 🎬🎬 **1987** (PG-13) A group of aliens escaping interplanetary persecution land on Earth and enlist the aid of an Earth family. Solid characters make it more than sci-fi; sort of a parable of intolerance, human (and alien) goodness, etc. **80m/C VHS, Beta, LV, Closed Caption.** Maureen O'Sullivan, Ione Skye, Cameron Dye; *D:* Tex Fuller; *W:* Alan Castle. *COL*

The Strange Affair of Uncle Harry 🎬🎬½ *Uncle Harry* **1945** Small-town gothic with fine acting by Sanders, an aging bachelor who plots murder when his romance is threatened by a jealous sister. A title card asks you not to reveal the 'surprise' ending—a hackneyed twist that appeased the censors but made producer Joan Harrison resign in protest. Based on a play by Robert Job. Tape suffers from poor film-video transfer. **80m/B VHS, LV.** George Sanders, Geraldine Fitzgerald, Ella Raines, Sara Allgood, Moyna MacGill, Samuel S. Hinds, Harry von Zell; *D:* Robert Siodmak. *REP, FCT*

A Strange and Deadly Occurence 🎬½ **1974** Strange things start to happen to a family when they move to a house in a remote area. Made-for-television. **74m/C VHS, Beta.** Robert Stack, Vera Miles, L.Q. Jones, Herb Edelman; *D:* John Llewellyn Moxey. *WOV*

Strange Awakening 🎬 **1958** Traveling in France while recuperating from amnesia, Barker is trapped in a cycle of fraud and theft. Confused and contrived. **75m/B VHS.** *GB* Lex Barker, Carole Mathews, Nora Swinburne, Richard Molinos, Peter Dyneley; *D:* Montgomery Tully. *SNC*

Strange Bedfellows 🎬🎬½ **1965** Within 24 hours of Carter Hudson (Hudson) arriving to work in London, he's met and married eccentric Italian Toni Vincenti (Lollobrigida). Complete opposites, the marriage is soon over and Carter returns to the States. Seven years later, he's back in London, ready to officially divorce Toni but learns from company PR whiz Dick Bramwell (Young) that his big promotion is contingent on his happy marriage. Carter courts Toni again, and tries to support her liberal causes and friends, but it turns out her latest stunt is aimed at his firm. Supposedly a check of the closing credits shows the film was shot on a Universal back lot and not on location. **104m/C VHS, Closed Caption.** Rock Hudson, Gina Lollobrigida, Gig Young, Edward Judd, Howard St. John, Nancy Kulp, Bernard Fox, Terry-Thomas; *D:* Melvin Frank; *W:* Melvin Frank, Michael Pertwee; *C:* Leo Tover; *M:* Leigh Harline. *USH*

Strange Behavior 🎬🎬 *Dead Kids; Small Town Massacre* **1981** (R) In a small Midwestern town, the police chief follows the clues from a series of murders to the experimental lab of the local college. Seems there's a mad scientist involved... Grisly and creepy, but unduly ballyhooed when it appeared. Shot on location in New Zealand. **105m/C Beta.** Michael Murphy, Louise Fletcher, Dan Shor, Fiona Lewis, Arthur Dignam, Marc McClure, Scott Brady; *D:* Michael Laughlin; *W:* Bill Condon. *COL, RHI*

Strange Brew 🎬🎬½ **1983** (PG) The screen debut of the SCTV alumni's characters Doug & Bob MacKenzie, the Great White North duo. They do battle with a powerful, megalomaniacal brew master over - what else? - a case of beer. Dumb, but what did you expect? Watch it, or be a hoser. **91m/C VHS, Beta, LV.** Rick Moranis, Dave Thomas, Max von Sydow, Paul Dooley; *D:* Rick Moranis, Dave Thomas; *W:* Rick Moranis, Dave Thomas, Steve DeJarnatt; *M:* Charles Fox. *MGM*

Strange Cargo 🎬🎬½ **1940** Convicts escaping from Devil's Island are mystically entranced by a Christ-like fugitive en route to freedom. An odd, pretentious Hollywood fable waiting for a cult following. Gable and Crawford's eighth and final pairing. Adapted by Anita Loos from the book "Not Too Narrow...Not Too Deep" by Richard Sale. **105m/B VHS, Beta.** Clark Gable, Joan Crawford, Ian Hunter, Peter Lorre, Paul Lukas, Albert Dekker, J. Edward Bromberg, Eduardo Ciannelli, Frederick Worlock; *D:* Frank Borzage. *MGM*

Strange Case of Dr. Jekyll & Mr. Hyde 🎬🎬 **1968** An adaptation of the classic Robert Louis Stevenson book about a scientist who conducts experiments on himself to separate good from evil. Palance is oddly but appealingly cast; Jarrott's bad direction wrecks it. Made for TV. **128m/C VHS, Beta.** Jack Palance, Leo Genn, Oscar Homolka, Billie Whitelaw, Denholm Elliott; *D:* Charles Jarrott. *LIV, MPI*

Strange Case of Dr. Jekyll & Mr. Hyde 🎬🎬½ **1989** The Robert Louis Stevenson classic, with Hyde portrayed as an icy, well-dressed sociopath. In Shelley Duvall's "Nightmare Classics" series. More psychological than special effect-y. Made for cable. **60m/C VHS, Beta.** Anthony Andrews, Laura Dern, George Murdock, Nicholas Guest; *D:* Michael Lindsay-Hogg. *WAR, OM*

The Strange Case of the End of Civilization as We Know It 🎬🎬½ **1993** Cleese stars as the detective grandson of Sherlock Holmes, who also has a reputation for making a mockery of police investigations. Nevertheless, the police commissioner summons him to capture that diabolical criminal Professor Moriarty. **55m/C VHS.** *GB* John Cleese, Stratford Johns, Connie Booth, Arthur Lowe. *KUL, FCT, SIG*

Strange Confession **1945** Contains one of the truly rare Inner Sanctum Mysteries from Universal. **62m/C VHS.** Lon Chaney Jr., Brenda Joyce, J. Carrol Naish, Milburn Stone, Lloyd Bridges; *D:* Jon Hoffman. *GPV*

The Strange Countess 🎬🎬 **1961** A girl is almost murdered and no apparent motive can be found until a 20-year old murder is uncovered in this Edgar Wallace story. **96m/C VHS.** *GE* Joachim Fuchsberger, Lil Dagover, Marianne Hoppe, Brigitte Grothum; *D:* Josef von Baky. *SNC*

Strange Days 🎬🎬🎬 **1995** (R) It's 1999 in volatile L.A. and vice cop-turned-street-hustler Lenny Nero (Fiennes) is plying his SQUID trade—discs that offer the wearer the chance to experience any vice. The seedily likeable Lenny draws the line at peddling snuff clips until one capturing the murder of his friend, hooker Iris (Bako), shows up. Lenny's in way over his head and turns to self-sufficient security agent Mace (Bassett) to save him. The phenomenal Bassett heats up the screen (and kicks major butt) while the generally cerebral Fiennes shows why someone could care about his desperate lowlife. Bigelow's an action expert and struts on the film's dark visuals while offering some emotional impact with her society-on-the-eve-of-destruction saga. *CW:* Intense disturbing violence, sexuality, nudity, and profanity. **145m/C VHS, Closed Caption.** Ralph Fiennes, Angela Bassett, Juliette Lewis, Tom Sizemore, Michael Wincott, Brigitte Bako, Vincent D'Onofrio, William Fichtner, Richard Edson, Glenn Plummer, Josef Sommer; *D:* Kathryn Bigelow; *W:* James Cameron, Jay Cocks; *C:* Matthew F. Leonetti; *M:* Graeme Revell. *FXV*

The Strange Door ⚉½ **1951** Laughton hams it up as the evil Alan de Maletroit (Laughton), who's imprisoned his brother Edmond (Cavanagh) for the crime of marrying Alan's one love. Now Maletroit wants to destroy his niece Blanche (Forrest) as well. But Edmond's faithful retainer Voltan (Karloff) is determined to stop the evil. Low-budget hokum adapted from the Robert Louis Stevenson story "The Sire de Maletroits's Door." 81m/B VHS, Closed Caption. Charles Laughton, Boris Karloff, Paul Cavanagh, Sally Forrest, Richard Stapley, Michael Pate, Alan Napier; *D:* Joseph Pevney; *W:* Jerry Sackheim; *C:* Irving Glassberg. USH

Strange Fruit ⚉⚉ **1979** Based on Lillian Smith's novel, this program tells the story of a black painter in Georgia, 1948, who faces racism. At first avoiding voter registration, he becomes involved and is killed. His death serves as an inspiration to his community. 33m/C VHS, Beta. LCA

Strange Illusion ⚉⚉½ *Out of the Night* **1945** Unbalanced teen Lydon believes his mother, about to remarry, was responsible for his father's death. He feigns insanity in a plan to catch her, but is sent to an asylum, where he nearly goes insane for real. Slow and implausible, but creepy enough to hold your interest. 87m/B VHS, Beta. Jimmy Lydon, Warren William, Sally Eilers, Regis Toomey, Charles Arnt, George Reed; *D:* Edgar G. Ulmer. SNC

Strange Interlude ⚉⚉⚉ *Strange Interval* **1932** Shearer is at her best in screen adaptation of talky Eugene O'Neill play in which she portrays a young wife who wants a child, but discovers that insanity runs in her husband's family. Doing the only sensible thing, she decides to have a child by another man (Gable). Interesting because the characters' thoughts are revealed to the audience through voice-overs. 110m/B VHS, Closed Caption. Norma Shearer, Clark Gable, May Robson, Ralph Morgan, Robert Young, Mary Alden, Maureen O'Sullivan, Henry B. Walthall; *D:* Robert Z. Leonard; *C:* Lee Garmes. MGM

Strange Interlude ⚉⚉½ **1990** Slow PBS production of Eugene O'Neill's famous drama covering two decades of the lives and loves of an upper-class family. Excellent performances help to make up for talkiness. On two cassettes. 190m/C VHS. Glenda Jackson, Jose Ferrer, David Dukes, Ken Howard, Edward Petherbridge; *D:* Herbert Wise. FRH, TVC

Strange Invaders ⚉⚉⚉ **1983** (PG) Bodysnatchers-from-space sci-fi with an attitude—fun spoof of '50s alien flicks. Space folks have taken over a midwestern town in the '50s, assuming the locals' appearance and attire before returning to their ship. Seems one of them married an earthling—but divorced and moved with her half-breed daughter to New York City. So the hicksters from space arrive in Gotham wearing overalls... 94m/C VHS, Beta, LV. Paul LeMat, Nancy Allen, Diana Scarwid, Michael Lerner, Louise Fletcher, Wallace Shawn, Fiona Lewis, Kenneth Tobey, June Lockhart, Charles Lane, Dey Young, Mark Goddard; *D:* Michael Laughlin; *W:* Bill Condon. VES

The Strange Love of Martha Ivers ⚉⚉⚉ **1946** Douglas is good in his screen debut as the wimpy spouse of unscrupulous Stanwyck. Stanwyck shines as the woman who must stay with Douglas because of a crime she committed long ago... Tough, dark melodrama; classic film noir. 117m/B VHS, Beta, LV. Barbara Stanwyck, Van Heflin, Kirk Douglas, Lizabeth Scott, Judith Anderson; *D:* Lewis Milestone; *C:* Victor Milner; *M:* Miklos Rozsa. Nominations: Academy Awards '46: Best Story. NOS, BAR, DVT

The Strange Love of Molly Louvain ⚉½ *Molly Louvain* **1932** Unwed mother Dvorak finds herself in hiding after her criminal beau fatally shoots a police officer. She falls in love with the unsuspecting newsman (Tracy) hot on her trail. Good performance from Dvorak but the film in general lacks sparkle. Adapted from the play "Tinsel Girl" by Maurine Watkins. 70m/B VHS. Ann Dvorak, Lee Tracy, Richard Cromwell, Guy Kibbee, Leslie Fenton, Frank McHugh, Evalyn Knapp, Charles Middleton, Mary Doran, C. Henry Gordon; *D:* Michael Curtiz; *W:* Erwin Gelsey, Brown Holmes. MGM

Strange New World ⚉½ **1975** Three astronauts awake from 188 years in the fridge to find cloning has arrived. Made for TV as a pilot for a hoped-for series that might have been even worse. 100m/C VHS. John Saxon, Kathleen Miller, Keene Curtis, Martine Beswick, James Olson, Catherine Bach, Richard Farnsworth, Ford Rainey; *D:* Robert Butler. UNI

Strange Shadows in an Empty Room ⚉ *Blazing Magnums; Shadows in an Empty Room* **1976** (R) Sleuth Whitman wants answers about the murder of his kid sis. He beats lots of people up, and the viewer leaves the empty living room to look at the inside of the fridge, which is more interesting. 97m/C VHS, Beta. Stuart Whitman, John Saxon, Martin Landau, Tisa Farrow, Carole Laure, Gayle Hunnicutt; *D:* Martin Herbert. VES

Strange Tales/Ray Bradbury Theatre ⚉⚉½ **1986** (R) An anthology of thrillers based on Bradbury stories: "Banshee," "The Screaming Woman," and "The Town Where No One Got Off." 86m/C VHS, Beta. Jeff Goldblum, Peter O'Toole, Drew Barrymore, Charles Martin Smith. CNG

The Strange Woman ⚉⚉ **1946** Uneventful Hollywood costume drama. Lamarr stalks man after man, but never creates much excitement in spite of Ulmer's fancy camera work and intense pace. 100m/B VHS. Hedy Lamarr, George Sanders, Louis Hayward, Gene Lockhart, Hillary Brooke, June Storey; *D:* Edgar G. Ulmer. NOS, FCT

Strange World of Coffin Joe ⚉ *o* *Estranho Mundo de Ze do Caixao* **1968** A collection of three shocking horror episodes about a truly disgusting dollmaker who becomes tempted by his human-like creations, a balloon seller's repulsive necrophiliac impulses, and a doctor (the disguised Coffin Joe) with a sadistic gift for excruciating torture. In Portugese with English subtitles. ?m/C VHS. BR Jose Mojica Marins; *D:* Jose Mojica Marins. SMW, FCT, TPV

The Strangeness woof! **1985** Miners in search of gold release a "strange" creature from far beneath the earth—eek! Made on a negative budget. 90m/C VHS, Beta. Dan Lunham, Terri Berland; *D:* David Michael Hillman. TWE

The Stranger ⚉⚉⚉½ **1946** Notably conventional for Welles, but swell entertainment nonetheless. War crimes tribunal sets Nazi thug Shayne free hoping he'll lead them to his superior, Welles. Robinson trails Shayne through Europe and South America to a small town in Connecticut. Tight suspense made on a tight budget saved Welles's directorial career. 95m/B VHS, Beta. Edward G. Robinson, Loretta Young, Martha Wentworth, Konstantin Shayne, Richard Long, Orson Welles; *D:* Orson Welles; *C:* Russell Metty. Nominations: Academy Awards '46: Best Story. CNG, NOS, PSM

The Stranger ⚉½ **1973** Corbett crashlands on a planet an awful lot like Earth - and must stay on the run. Uneven fugitive thriller in sci-fi drag. Made for TV. 100m/C VHS. Cameron Mitchell, Glenn Corbett, Sharon Acker, Lew Ayres, George Coulouris, Dean Jagger; *D:* Lee H. Katzin. NO

The Stranger ⚉⚉⚉ **1987** (R) Amnesiac car-wreck victim Bedelia begins regaining her memory, and realizes she witnessed several grisly murders. Is her shrink (Riegert) helping her remember, or keeping something from her? Good, neglected thriller. 93m/C VHS, Beta, 8mm, Closed Caption. AR Bonnie Bedelia, Peter Riegert, Barry Primus, David Spielberg, Julio de Grazia, Cecilia Roth, Marcus Woinski; *D:* Adolfo Aristarain; *W:* Dan Gurskis; *M:* Craig Safan. COL

The Stranger ⚉⚉½ **1992** Quiet comedy about family loyalties and devalued traditions. The upper-middle-class life of Sudhindra Bose is disturbed by the arrival of his wife Anila's long-lost uncle Manomohan. Although their young son is excited by the visit of this mysterious relative, Anila is bewildered and her husband suspicious—he thinks the man may be an imposter after their money. The independent Manomohan realizes the family's discomfort and slowly turns the tables on all their questions. Ray's last film. In Bengali with English subtitles. 100m/C VHS. IN Deepankar De, Mamata Shankar, Bikram Bhattacharya, Utpal Dutt, Dhritiman Chatterji, Rabi Ghosh, Subrata Chatterji; *D:* Satyajit Ray; *W:* Satyajit Ray. FRF

The Stranger ⚉⚉ **1995** (R) Mystery woman (Long) rides into small town and rids it of a vicious motorcycle gang. Femme version of the lone hero saga. *CW:* Action violence; strong sex scene; some language. 98m/C VHS, Closed Caption. Kathy Long, Andrew Divoff, Eric Pierpont, Robin Lynn Heath; *D:* Fritz Kiersch; *W:* Gregory Poirier. COL

A Stranger Among Us ⚉⚉ **1992** (PG-13) A missing jeweler turns up dead and more than $1 million in diamonds has disappeared. NYPD Detective Emily Eden (Griffith) is called in to solve the case, and she decides she must go undercover in a community of Hasidic Jews to find the perpetrator. She not only finds the criminal, but she also falls in love with one of the group's most devout residents. Griffith is out of her element as a tough cop with her baby voice and cutesy style, but other actors, including Thal (in his movie debut) and Sara, perform splendidly, even though they are held back by a cumbersome script that is similar in many respects to "Witness." 109m/C VHS, Beta, LV, Closed Caption. Melanie Griffith, Eric Thal, John Pankow, Tracy Pollan, Lee Richardson, Mia Sara, Jamey Sheridan; *D:* Sidney Lumet; *W:* Robert J. Avrech; *C:* Andrzej Bartkowiak; *M:* Jerry Bock. Golden Raspberry Awards '92: Worst Actress (Griffith). HPH

The Stranger and the Gunfighter ⚉⚉ **1976** The baddest spaghetti western of all time - or is it a kung fu movie? Alcoholic cowpoke Van Cleef and kung fu master Lieh pair up to find hidden treasure. There is a map, but parts are printed on the assorted fannies of various women. 106m/C VHS, Beta, LV, Closed Caption. Patty Shepard, Lee Van Cleef, Lo Lieh; *D:* Anthony (Antonio Margheriti) Dawson. COL

Stranger by Night ⚉⚉ **1994** (R) Detective Bobby Corcoran and his partner are hunting a mutilating serial killer. Since Corcoran suffers from black-outs and fits of rage the evidence begins pointing very close to home. 96m/C VHS. Steven Bauer, William Katt, Jennifer Rubin, Michael Parks, Michelle Greene, J.J. Johnston; *D:* Gregory Brown; *W:* Daryl Haney; *M:* Ashley Irwin. APX

The Stranger from Pecos ⚉⚉ **1945** Brown fights a cheater who swindles people at poker and then uses the money to buy their mortgages. Meanwhile, his pal Hatton finds a novel way to help a robbery victim buy back his property. 55m/B VHS. Johnny Mack Brown, Raymond Hatton, Kirby Grant, Christine McIntyre, Steve Clark, Kermit Maynard; *D:* Lambert Hillyer. DVT, HEG

The Stranger from Venus woof! *Immediate Disaster; The Venusian* **1954** "The Day the Earth Stood Still" warmed over. Venusian Dantine tells earth lady Neal he's worried about the future of her planet. Real low budget. Includes previews of coming attractions from classic sci-fi. 78m/C VHS, Beta. Patricia Neal, Helmut Dantine, Derek Bond. MED, MLB

Stranger in Paso Bravo ⚉ **1973** A distraught drifter returns to a strange Italian town to avenge the murders of his wife and daughter years before. Dubbed. 92m/C VHS, Beta. IT Anthony Steffen, Giulia Rubini, Eduardo Fajardo, Adriana Ambesi. UNI

Stranger in Town ⚉⚉ **1957** A young journalist looks into the murder of an American composer in a sleepy English village. He discovers blackmail and intrigue. So-so thriller. Based on the novel "The Uninvited" by Frank Chittenden. 73m/B VHS, Beta. GB Alex Nicol, Ann Page, Mary Laura Wood, Mona Washbourne, Charles Lloyd Pack; *D:* George Pollock. SNC

A Stranger is Watching ⚔️½ 1982 (R) Rapist-murderer Torn holds his victim's 10-year-old daughter hostage, along with a New York television anchorwoman. Complicated and distasteful. Made for TV. **92m/C VHS, Beta.** Rip Torn, Kate Mulgrew, James Naughton; **D:** Sean S. Cunningham. *MGM*

Stranger on the Third Floor ⚔️⚔️⚔️ 1940 Reporter McGuire's testimony helped convict cabbie Cook of murder, but he begins to have doubts. Odd, shadowy psycho-thriller considered by some the first film noir. The reporter comes to be suspected of the crime...and his fiancee pounds the pavement to prove him innocent. Average acting, but great camera work gives the whole a deliciously menacing feel. **64m/B VHS, Beta, LV.** Peter Lorre, John McGuire, Elisha Cook Jr., Margaret Tallichet, Charles Halton; **D:** Boris Ingster. *CCB, MED*

Stranger than Paradise ⚔️⚔️⚔️ 1984 (R) Regular guy, nerdy sidekick and Hungarian girl cousin traipse around America being bored and having fun and adventure. New York, then - on to Cleveland! The thinking person's mindless flick. Inventive, independent comedy made on quite a low budget was acclaimed at Cannes. **90m/B VHS, Beta, LV, Closed Caption.** *GE* Richard Edson, Eszter Balint, John Lurie; **D:** Jim Jarmusch; **W:** Jim Jarmusch; **M:** John Lurie. National Society of Film Critics Awards '84: Best Film. *FCT, FOX*

The Stranger Who Looks Like Me ⚔️⚔️ 1974 Adoptees Baxter and Bridges set out to find their real parents. Not-bad TV fare. Blake is Baxter's real-life mom. Look for a young Patrick Duffy. **74m/C VHS, Beta.** Meredith Baxter, Beau Bridges, Whitney Blake; **D:** Larry Peerce. *WOV*

The Stranger Within ⚔️½ 1974 Made-for-TV "Rosemary's Baby" rip-off. Eden is in a family way, though hubby Grizzard is impotent. The stranger within begins commanding her to do its bidding, just as if she were a genie. **74m/C VHS, Beta.** Barbara Eden, George Grizzard, Joyce Van Patten, Nehemiah Persoff; **D:** Lee Philips; **M:** Charles Fox. *LIV*

The Stranger Wore a Gun ⚔️⚔️ 1953 Hoping to remove a black mark against his name, Jeff Travis (Scott) goes to Arizona and ends up foiling a stagecoach robbery. Features a great action sequence in a burning saloon. Originally shot in 3-D, this is based on the novel "Yankee Gold" by John M. Cunningham. **83m/C VHS.** Randolph Scott, Claire Trevor, Joan Weldon, George Macready, Alfonso Bedoya, Lee Marvin, Ernest Borgnine, Pierre Watkin, Joseph Vitale; **D:** Andre de Toth. *COL*

Strangers ⚔️ 1990 Australian horror film revolves around a man in a troubled marriage who fools around with another woman, only to realize she is dead set on mating for life. When he hesitates, she vows to murder his wife. Very similar to the smash hit "Fatal Attraction." **83m/C VHS.** *AU* James Healey, Anne Looby; **D:** Craig Lahiff. *NO*

Strangers ⚔️⚔️ 1991 (R) Features three provocative vignettes that take place far from home. Fiorentino, Chen, and Hutton each star in an erotic story played out in a foreign land. **CW:** Language and sexuality. **85m/C VHS, LV, Closed Caption.** Linda Fiorentino, Joan Chen, Timothy Hutton; **D:** Joan Tewkesbury. *PSM*

Stranger's Gold ⚔️ 1971 A mysterious gunslinger eliminates corruption in a western mining town. **90m/C VHS, Beta.** Gianni "John" Garko, Antonio Vilar, Daniela Giordano. *GEM*

Strangers in Good Company ⚔️⚔️⚔️ *The Company of Strangers* 1991 (PG) A loving metaphor to growing older. Director Scott uses non-actors for every role in this quiet little film about a bus-load of elderly women lost in the Canadian wilderness. They wait for rescue without hystrionics, using the opportunity instead to get to know each other and nature. Beautifully made, intelligent, uncommon and worthwhile. **101m/C VHS, Beta, Closed Caption.** *CA* Alice Diabo, Mary Meigs, Cissy Meddings, Beth Webber, Winifred Holden, Constance Garneau, Catherine Roche, Michelle Sweeney; **D:** Cynthia

Scott; **W:** Cynthia Scott, David Wilson, Gloria Demers, Sally Bochner; **M:** Marie Bernard. *TOU*

Strangers in Paradise ⚔️½ 1986 A scientist who had cryogenically frozen himself to escape the Nazis is thawed out in the present, and his powers are used by a delinquent-obsessed sociopath. **81m/C VHS, Beta.** **D:** Ulli Lommel; **W:** Ulli Lommel. *LIV, VES*

Strangers in the City ⚔️⚔️ 1962 Puerto Ricans newly arrived in New York try to make their way. Serious but slightly overwrought immigrant-family melodrama. **80m/B VHS, Beta.** Robert Gentile, Camilo Delgado, Rosita De Triana; **D:** Rick Carrier. *NLC*

Strangers Kiss ⚔️⚔️½ 1983 (R) Circa 1955: Hollywood director encourages his two leads to have an off-screen romance to bring reality to his film. Conflict arises when the leading lady's boyfriend, the film's financier, gets wind of the scheme. Intriguing, fun, slightly off-center. Based on Stanley Kubrick's film "Killer Kiss." **93m/C VHS, Beta.** Peter Coyote, Victoria Tennant, Blaine Novak, Dan Shor, Richard Romanus, Linda Kerridge, Carlos Palomino; **D:** Matthew Chapman; **W:** Blaine Novak, Matthew Chapman; **M:** Gato Barbieri. *CNG*

Strangers of the Evening ⚔️⚔️ 1932 In its day this dark comedy/mystery caught flak for its gruesomeness. There's been a mixup at the undertaker's, and the wrong body was buried—possibly alive. Good photography and acting make the humor work, intentionally or not. Based on the novel "The Illustrious Corpse," by Tiffany Thayer. **70m/B VHS, Beta.** ZaSu Pitts, Eugene Pallette, Lucien Littlefield, Tully Marshall, Miriam Seegar, Theodore von Eltz; **D:** H. Bruce Humberstone. *SNC, NOS*

Strangers on a Train ⚔️⚔️⚔️⚔️ 1951 Long before there was "Throw Momma from the Train," there was this Hitchcock super-thriller about two passengers who accidentally meet and plan to "trade" murders. Amoral Walker wants the exchange and the money he'll inherit by his father's death; Granger would love to end his stifling marriage and wed Roman, a senator's daughter, but finds the idea ultimately sickening. What happens is pure Hitchcock. Screenplay co-written by murder-mystery great Chandler. Patricia Hitchcock, the director's only child, plays Roman's sister. The concluding "carousel" scene is a masterpiece. From the novel by Patricia Highsmith. **101m/B VHS, Beta, LV, DVD.** Farley Granger, Robert Walker, Ruth Roman, Leo G. Carroll, Patricia Hitchcock, Marion Lorne; **D:** Alfred Hitchcock; **W:** Raymond Chandler; **C:** Robert Burks; **M:** Dimitri Tiomkin. National Board of Review Awards '51: 10 Best Films of the Year; Nominations: Academy Awards '51: Best Black and White Cinematography. *WAR, MLB*

Strangers: The Story of a Mother and Daughter ⚔️⚔️⚔️ 1979 Rowlands is the long-estranged daughter of Davis, who won an Emmy for her portrayal of the embittered widow. The great actress truly is at her recent best in this made-for-TV tearjerker, and Rowlands keeps pace. **88m/C VHS, Beta.** Bette Davis, Gena Rowlands, Ford Rainey, Donald Moffat; **D:** Milton Katselas. *TLF*

Strangers When We Meet ⚔️⚔️½ 1960 A married architect and his equally married neighbor begin an affair. Their lives become a series of deceptions. Lavish but uninvolving soaper. Written by Evan Hunter and based on his novel. **117m/B VHS, Beta.** Kirk Douglas, Kim Novak, Ernie Kovacs, Walter Matthau, Barbara Rush, Virginia Bruce, Kent Smith; **D:** Richard Quine; **C:** Charles B(ryant) Lang. *COL*

Stranglehold ⚔️½ 1994 (R) Cooper (Trimble) is the executive assistant of Congresswoman Fillmore (McWhirter), who becomes the hostage of a nerve gas holding nutcase (Wells). Cooper manages to evade Fillmore's thugs while using his martial arts prowess to rescue his boss. **CW:** Commando and martial arts violence; language; some sexuality. **73m/C VHS.** *AU* Jerry Trim-

ble, Jillian McWhirter, Vernon Wells; **D:** Cirio H. Santiago. *NHO*

The Strangler ⚔️½ 1964 A confused, mother-fixated psychopath strangles young women. Made at the time the Boston Strangler was terrorizing Beantown. The film slayer strangles ten lasses before his love of dolls gives him away. **89m/B VHS, Beta.** Victor Buono, David McLean, Diane Sayer, Ellen Corby, Jeanne Bates, James B. Sikking; **D:** Burt Topper. *FXV, FOX, FCT*

Strangler of Blackmoor Castle ⚔️⚔️ 1963 Someone is murdering people at an old English castle and Scotland Yard sends an investigator to track down the killer. **?m/C VHS.** *GE* Karin Dor, Ingmar Zeisberg. *SNC*

Strangler of the Swamp ⚔️½ 1946 The ghost of an innocent man wrongly hanged for murder returns to terrorize the village where he was lynched. Decidedly B-grade horror features an out-of-focus ghost and Edwards—on the other side of the camera—as one of his would-be victims. **60m/B VHS, Beta.** Rosemary La Planche, Blake Edwards, Charles Middleton, Robert Barrat; **D:** Frank Wisbar. *COL*

Strapless ⚔️⚔️½ 1990 (R) Just-turned-40 American doctor Brown lives and works in London. She has just ended a long-term romance, and takes up with suave foreigner Ganz. Her young sister Fonda, arrives for a visit. Good, interesting if sometimes plodding story of adult relationships. **99m/C VHS, Beta, LV.** Blair Brown, Bridget Fonda, Bruno Ganz, Alan Howard, Michael Gough, Hugh Laurie, Suzanne Burden, Camille Coduri, Alexandra Pigg, Billy Roch, Gary O'Brien; **D:** David Hare; **W:** David Hare; **M:** Nick Bicat. *COL*

Strapped ⚔️⚔️½ 1993 Earnest urban drama about a young man who needs quick cash and turns to selling guns to get it. ("Strapped" in street lingo means both carrying a gun and needing money.) Diquan's (Woodbine) pregnant girlfriend is in jail for selling crack and he doesn't have the bail money. So he and a partner begin selling guns but it turns out Diquan has also cut a deal with the cops and the deal doesn't stay a secret for long. Whitaker's directorial debut. Made for cable television. **102m/C VHS, LV.** Bokeem Woodbine, Kia Joy Goodwin, Fred "Fredro" Scruggs, Michael Biehn, Craig Wasson; **D:** Forest Whitaker; **W:** Dena Kleiman. *HBO*

Strategic Air Command ⚔️⚔️½ 1955 A classic post-WWII chunk of Air Force patriotism. Veteran third baseman Stewart is recalled to flight duty at the hint of a nuclear war. He's already put in his time in the Big One and thinks he's being singled out now, but he answers his Uncle Sam's call. Allyson plays Stewart's wife for the third time. **114m/C VHS, Beta, LV.** James Stewart, June Allyson, Frank Lovejoy, Barry Sullivan; **D:** Anthony Mann; **C:** William H. Daniels. Nominations: Academy Awards '55: Best Story. *PAR*

The Stratton Story ⚔️⚔️⚔️ 1949 Stewart and Allyson teamed up for the first of the three pictures they'd make together in this true story of Monty Stratton, the Chicago White Sox pitcher. A baseball phenom, Stratton suffers a devastating hunting accident which leads to the amputation of one leg. Learning to walk with an artificial limb, Stratton also struggles to resume his baseball career. Stewart's fine as always, with Allyson lending noble support as the loving wife. Chisox manager Jimmy Dykes played himself as did pitcher Gene Bearden, lending further authenticity to an excellent production. **106m/B VHS, Beta.** James Stewart, June Allyson, Frank Morgan, Agnes Moorehead, Bill Williams, Bruce Cowling; **D:** Sam Wood; **W:** Guy Trosper, Douglas S. Morrow. Academy Awards '49: Best Story. *MGM, FCT, BTV*

Straw Dogs ⚔️⚔️⚔️ 1972 (R) An American mathematician, disturbed by the predominance of violence in American society, moves with his wife to an isolated Cornish village. He finds that primitive savagery exists beneath the most peaceful surface. After his wife is raped, Hoffman's character seeks revenge. Hoffman is good, a little too wimpy at times. A violent, frightening film reaction to the violence of the 1960s. **118m/C VHS, Beta, LV. GB** Dustin Hoffman, Susan George, Peter Vaughan, T.P. McKenna, David Warner; **D:** Sam Peckinpah; **W:** David Zelag Goodman. Nominations: Academy Awards '71: Original Dramatic/Comedy Score. **FOX**

Strawberry and Chocolate 🎬🎬🎬
Fresa y Chocolate **1993 (R)** Sex, politics, and friendship set in 1979 Havana. University student David (Cruz) is sitting morosely in a cafe eating chocolate ice cream when he's spotted by older, educated, gay, strawberry-eating Diego (Perugorria), who manages to persuade David to visit him at his apartment. Resolutely hetero (and communist), David is appalled not only by Diego's sexuality but his subversive politics. But gradually David's seduced by Diego's ideas and friendship into questioning the regime's harsh policies (and homophobia). Satiric and sympathetic—not only to the characters but to Cuba itself. Ill with cancer, Gutierrez Alea finished the film with the aid of Tabio. From the short story "The Wolf, the Forest and the New Man" by sceenwriter Paz. Spanish with subtitles. **CW:** Language; brief strong sexuality. **110m/C VHS. CU** Jorge Perugorria, Vladimir Cruz, Mirta Ibarra, Francisco Gattorno, Jorge Angelino, Marilyn Solaya; **D:** Tomas Gutierrez Alea, Juan Carlos Tabio; **W:** Tomas Gutierrez Alea, Senel Paz; **C:** Mario Garcia Joya; **M:** Jose Maria Vitier. Nominations: Academy Awards '94: Best Foreign Language Film. **TOU**

Strawberry Blonde 🎬🎬🎬 1941
A romantic comedy set in the 1890s, with Cagney as a would-be dentist infatuated with money-grubbing Hayworth (the strawberry blonde of the title), who wonders years later whether he married the right woman (chestnut brunette de Havilland). Attractive period piece remade from 1933's "One Sunday Afternoon," and revived yet again in 1948 by Raoul Walsh. **100m/B VHS, Beta.** James Cagney, Olivia de Havilland, Rita Hayworth, Alan Hale, George Tobias, Jack Carson, Una O'Connor, George Reeves; **D:** Raoul Walsh; **W:** Julius J. Epstein, Philip C. Epstein; **C:** James Wong Howe. Nominations: Academy Awards '41: Scoring of a Musical. **MGM**

Strawberry Roan 🎬🎬 1933
Maynard plays a stubborn rodeo cowboy, out to prove he ain't whipped yet. One of Maynard's most popular films. Gene Autry bought the story to help him out in later years; the 1948 Autry "remake" uses only the title. **59m/B VHS.** Ken Maynard, Ruth Hall; **D:** Ken Maynard. **NOS, DVT, HEG**

The Strawberry Statement 🎬🎬 1970 (R)
Dated message film about a campus radical who persuades a college student to take part in the student strikes on campus during the '60s. Ambitious anti-violence message is lost in too many subplots. Soundtrack features songs by Crosby, Stills, Nash and Young and John Lennon. **109m/C VHS, Beta.** Kim Darby, Bruce Davison, Bud Cort, James Coco, Kristina Holland, Bob Balaban, David Dukes, Jeannie Berlin; **D:** Stuart Hagmann; **W:** Israel Horovitz. Cannes Film Festival '70: Special Jury Prize. **MGM**

Stray Dog 🎬🎬🎬 1949
A tense, early genre piece by Kurosawa, about a police detective who has his revolver picked from his pocket on a bus, and realizes soon after it's being used in a series of murders. Technically somewhat flawed, but tense and intense. Mifune's pursuit of the criminal with his gun becomes metaphorically compelling. In Japanese with English subtitles. **122m/B VHS, Beta. JP** Toshiro Mifune, Takashi Shimura, Isao Kimura; **D:** Akira Kurosawa. **COL**

Strays 🎬🎬 1991 (R)
Here kitty kitty! A young couple move into their dream home, convinced it is the perfect place to raise their daughter. What they don't know is that the area is populated by a pack of wild cats. Before they can get rid of the kitties, one has marked their bedroom as his territory and they find themselves battling a swarm of mean kitties during a bad storm. **CW:** Violence and terror. **83m/C VHS, LV, Closed Caption.** Kathleen

Quinlan, Timothy Busfield, Claudia Christian; **D:** John McPherson; **W:** Shaun Cassidy. **USH**

Streamers 🎬🎬 1983 (R)
Six young soldiers in a claustrophobic army barracks tensely await the orders that will send them to Vietnam. Written by Rabe from his play. Well acted but downbeat and drawn out. **118m/C VHS, Beta, LV.** Matthew Modine, Michael Wright, Mitchell Lichtenstein, George Dzundza; **D:** Robert Altman; **W:** David Rabe. **MED, IME, FCT**

The Street 🎬🎬½ 1923
A dark classic of German Kammerspiel film, notable for its expressionist treatment of Paris street life. A middle-aged man decides to abandon his wife and job to see what excitement he can find. He is duped by a prostitute, accused of murder, imprisoned, and nearly commits suicide before being rescued. Silent. **87m/B VHS, Beta. GE D:** Karl Grune; **W:** Karl Grune. **VYY**

Street Asylum 🎬 1990 (R)
Real-life Watergate spook Liddy is pathetically bad as an evil genius who cooks up a scheme to rid the streets of deadbeats and scumbags by implanting cops with a gizmo that makes them kill. Also available in a 94-minute unrated version. **94m/C VHS, Beta, LV.** Wings Hauser, Alex Cord, Roberta Vasquez, G. Gordon Liddy, Marie Chambers, Sy Richardson, Jesse Doran, Jesse Aragon, Brion James; **D:** Gregory Brown. **NO**

Street Crimes 🎬🎬 1992 (R)
A street-wise cop convinces gang members to put down their weapons and settle their grudges in the boxing ring. But when a gang leader starts shooting down the police and civilians, the cop and his young partner must work together to keep the neighborhood safe. **CW:** Language and violence. **?m/C VHS, LV.** Dennis Farina, Max Gail, Mike Worth; **D:** Stephen Smoke; **W:** Stephen Smoke; **M:** John Gonzalez. **PMH**

The Street Fighter 🎬½ 1975
Fast-paced martial arts action finds freelance fighter Terry Tsuguri (Chiba) hired to spring a convicted killer from prison. But after he succeeds, his employers renege on their payment. Big mistake. Dubbed from Japanese. Three sequels: "Return of the Street Fighter," "The Street Fighter's Last Revenge," and "Sister Street Fighter." **91m/C VHS, LV.** Sonny Chiba; **D:** Sakae Ozawa. **NLC**

Street Fighter 🎬½ 1994 (PG-13)
Yes, it's a movie based on a popular video game (guess no one worried about the colossal flop of "Super Mario Bros"). Van Damme is action-minded Colonel Guile who is assigned to defeat crazed dictator General Bison (Julia in one of his last roles) in order to rescue kidnapped relief workers. Yes, there's lots of cartoon action but the game's more exciting (and even makes more sense). Shot on location in Australia and Bangkok. **CW:** Non-stop martial arts and action violence. **101m/C VHS, LV, Closed Caption.** Jean-Claude Van Damme, Raul Julia, Wes Studi, Ming-Na Wen, Damian Chapa, Simon Callow, Roshan Seth, Kylie Minogue, Byrun Mann; **D:** Steven E. de Souza; **W:** Steven E. de Souza; **M:** Graeme Revell. **USH**

The Street Fighter's Last Revenge 🎬 1979
Third in the martial arts series finds Terry Tsuguri (Chiba) hired by a mob boss to do some dirty work and then getting doublecrossed—resulting in the death of Terry's girl. So, Terry hunts the miscreants down one by one. Lots of action, not much acting. Followed by "Sister Street Fighter." **80m/C VHS.** Sonny Chiba, Sue Shiomi; **D:** Sakae Ozawa. **NLC**

Street Girls 🎬 1975 (R)
A father enters the world of urban drugs and prostitution to find his runaway daughter. **77m/C VHS, Beta.** Carol Case, Christine Souder, Paul Pompian; **D:** Michael Miller. **NLC**

Street Hawk 🎬 1984
A government agent operates an experimental, crime-fighting motorcycle in battling against a high-powered drug smuggling ring. **60m/C VHS, Beta.** Rex Smith, Jayne Modean, Richard Venture, Christopher Lloyd. **USH**

Street Hero woof! 1984
A young thug is torn between familial common sense and Mafia connections. **102m/C VHS, Beta.** Vince Colosimo, Sigrid Thornton, Sandy Gore. **LIV, VES**

Street Hitz 🎬½ 1992
Two brothers in the South Bronx find their family loyalties tested. Joey wants to finish college and get away from the violence in the streets while his brother Junior turns to the gangs to survive. **92m/C VHS.** Angelo Lopez, Melvin Muza, Lyota Ramirez; **D:** Joseph B. Vasquez. **AIP**

Street Hunter woof! 1990 (R)
Former cop turned freelance fighter quit the force when his integrity was questioned, but he still helps out now and then. Scumbag drug dealers line up a thug to waste him; epic kung fu battle ensues. **120m/C VHS, LV.** Steve James, Reb Brown, John Leguizamo, Valarie Pettiford, Frank Vincent, Richie Havens; **D:** John A. Gallagher; **C:** Phil Parmet. **COL**

Street Justice 🎬½ 1989 (R)
Over-complex tale of a CIA agent on the lam. Returning from years of Russian imprisonment, Ontkean finds his wife remarried, his daughter grown and both battling the corrupt town government. Good performances can't help the confusion of too many characters too flatly developed. **94m/C VHS, Beta.** Michael Ontkean, Joanna Kerns, Catherine Bach, J.D. Cannon, Jeanette Nolan, Richard Cox, William Windom; **D:** Richard Sarafian. **WAR**

Street Knight 🎬🎬 1993 (R)
Gang warfare in L.A. in a routine actioner. Jake is an ex-cop who gets drawn into a battle between two rival gangs when their truce is broken by mysterious murders on both sides. Seems there's an unsuspected third party involved—a para-military band of professional killers that want the gang violence to divert police interest from their own nefarious operations. **CW:** Language, strong violence, and sexuality. **88m/C VHS, Beta, LV, Closed Caption.** Jeff Speakman, Christopher Neame, Lewis Van Bergen, Bernie Casey, Jennifer Gatti, Richard Coca; **D:** Albert Magnoli. **WAR, CAN**

Street Law 🎬 1979 (R)
Vivid and violent study of one man's frustrated war on crime. **77m/C VHS, Beta.** Franco Nero, Barbara Bach, Reno Palmer. **NO**

Street Law 🎬🎬 1995 (R)
John Ryan (Wincott) is a down-on-his-luck trial lawyer whose childhood buddy Luis Calderone (Prieto) is willing to lend a helping hand. Too bad Luis is an ex-con who hasn't left his dangerous street ways behind him and now John is caught up in some unsavory action. **CW:** Violence, some strong sexuality, and language. **98m/C VHS.** Jeff Wincott, Paco Christian Prieto, Christina Cox. **TRI**

Street Music 🎬🎬½ 1981
The elderly people living in an old hotel join forces with a young couple to organize a protest that may save their building. Well-directed urban comedy-drama; good location shooting in San Francisco's Tenderloin. **88m/C VHS, Beta.** Larry Breeding, Elizabeth Daily, Ned Glass; **D:** Jenny Bowen; **C:** Richard Bowen. Sundance Film Festival '82: Grand Jury Prize. **LIV, VES**

Street of Forgotten Women 🎬 1925
Hollywood, in one of its periodic morality binges, came up with this purported expose on prostitution. An innocent girl is seduced and brutalized by a theatrical agent and eventually finds herself walking the pavement for less than moral purposes. Lots of shots of scantily clad showgirls and our heroine in her undies. **55m/B VHS.** **SNC, VYY**

Street of Shame 🎬🎬🎬½ Red-Light District; Akasen Chitai **1956** A portrayal of the abused lives of six Tokyo prostitutes. Typically sensitive to the roles and needs of women and critical of the society that exploits them, Mizoguchi creates a quiet, inclusive coda to his life's work in world cinema. Kyo is splendid as a hardened hooker and has a memorable scene with her father. Kogure is also good. The great director's last finished work was instrumental in the outlawing of prostitution in Japan. In Japanese with English subtitles. **88m/B VHS. JP** Machiko Kyo, Aiko Mimasu, Michiyo Kogure; **D:** Kenji Mizoguchi. **HMV, NLC**

Street People woof! 1976 (R) Gratuitous car chases and violence do not a movie make, as in this case in point. Utter woofer has Brit Moore cast as a mafiosa. Yeah, right. 92m/C VHS, Beta. Roger Moore, Stacy Keach, Ivo Garrani, Ettore Manni; *D:* Maurizio Lucidi. *LIV, VES*

Street Scene ✔✔✔ 1931 Life in a grimy New York tenement district, circa 1930. Audiences nationwide ate it up when Elmer Rice adapted his own Pulitzer Prize-winning play and top helmsman Vidor gave it direction. 80m/B VHS, Beta, 8mm. Sylvia Sidney, William Collier Jr., Estelle Taylor, Beulah Bondi, David Landau; *D:* King Vidor; *C:* George Barnes; *M:* Alfred Newman. *NOS, HHT, CAB*

Street Smart ✔✔½ 1987 (R) Reeve was blah as Superman (let's be frank), and he's blah here as a desperate New York freelance writer who fakes a dramatic story about prostitution. When his deception returns to haunt him, he's in trouble with pimps and murderers, as well as the D.A. Freeman and Baker are both superb. Based on screenwriter David Freeman's own experience with "New York" magazine. 97m/C VHS, Beta, LV, Closed Caption. Christopher Reeve, Morgan Freeman, Kathy Baker, Mimi Rogers, Andre Gregory, Jay Patterson, Anna Maria Horsford; *D:* Jerry Schatzberg; *W:* David Freeman; *C:* Adam Holender; *M:* Miles Davis. Independent Spirit Awards '88: Best Supporting Actor (Freeman); Los Angeles Film Critics Association Awards '87: Best Supporting Actor (Freeman); New York Film Critics Awards '87: Best Supporting Actor (Freeman); National Society of Film Critics Awards '87: Best Supporting Actor (Freeman), Best Supporting Actress (Baker); Nominations: Academy Awards '87: Best Supporting Actor (Freeman). *MED, IME*

Street Soldiers ✔½ 1991 (R) Martial artists are out to take back the streets from the punks and scum who now rule them. *CW:* Language and strong violence. 98m/C VHS, Beta, LV. Jun Chong, Jeff Rector, David Homb, Jonathan Gorman, Joon Kim, Katherine Armstrong, Joel Weiss; *D:* Lee Harry. *ACA*

Street Trash woof! 1987 In Brooklyn, a strange poisonous liquor is being sold cheap to bums, making them melt and explode. A gross, cheap, tongue-in-cheek shocker from the makers of "The Toxic Avenger." 91m/C VHS, Beta. R.L. Ryan, Vic Noto, Miriam Zucker, Bill Chepil, Mike Lackey; *D:* Jim Muro. *LIV*

Street War ✔ 197? A cop pursues the Mob in the name of revenge as well as duty. 90m/C VHS, Beta. James Mason, Cyril Cusack, Raymond Pellegrin. *NO*

Street Warriors woof! 1987 Ostensibly "serious" look at juvenile crime. Actually miserable, exploitative, offensive junk. 105m/C VHS, Beta. Christa Leem, Nadia Windell, Victor Petit, Francisco (Frank) Brana; *D:* Jose Antonio De La Loma. *NO*

Street Warriors, Part 2 woof! 1987 Even worse than its predecessor, and that's saying something. Horrible dubbing from Spanish would be laughable, if the rapes weren't so graphic. 105m/C VHS, Beta. Angel Fernandez, Paul Ramirez, Teresa Giminez, Veronica Miriel, Conrad Tortosa; *D:* Jose Antonio De La Loma. *NO*

Street Wars ✔½ 1991 (R) Violent low-budgeter about 17-year-old Sugarpop, who takes over older brother Frank's Los Angeles drug operation, after Frank is murdered, and finds himself battling a rival gang. 90m/C VHS, LV. Alan Joseph, Bryan O'Dell, Clifford Shegog, Jean Pace, Vaughn Cromwell, Cardella Demilo; *D:* Jamaa Fanaka; *W:* Jamaa Fanaka; *C:* John L. Demps Jr.; *M:* Michael Dunlap, Yves Chicha. *TRI*

The Street with No Name ✔✔✔ 1948 In follow-up to "Kiss of Death," Widmark confirms rep as one disturbed guy playing psychotic career criminal whose life is grisly trail of murder and brutality. 93m/B VHS. Mark Stevens, Richard Widmark, Lloyd Nolan, Barbara Lawrence, Ed Begley Sr., Donald Buka, Joseph Pevney; *D:* William Keighley. *FOX, FCT*

A Streetcar Named Desire ✔✔✔✔ 1951 (PG) Powerful film version of Tennessee Williams' play about a neurotic southern belle with a hidden past who comes to visit her sister and is abused and driven mad by her brutal brother-in-law. Grim New Orleans setting for terrific performances by all, with Malden, Leigh, and Hunter winning Oscars, and Brando making highest impact on audiences. Brando disliked the role, despite the great impact it had on his career. Remade for television in 1984. 122m/B VHS, Beta, LV, Closed Caption, DVD. Vivien Leigh, Marlon Brando, Kim Hunter, Karl Malden; *D:* Elia Kazan; *W:* Tennessee Williams; *C:* Harry Stradling; *M:* Alex North. Academy Awards '51: Best Actress (Leigh), Best Art Direction/Set Decoration (B & W), Best Supporting Actor (Malden), Best Supporting Actress (Hunter); British Academy Awards '52: Best Actress (Leigh); Golden Globe Awards '52: Best Supporting Actress (Hunter); National Board of Review Awards '51: 10 Best Films of the Year; New York Film Critics Awards '51: Best Actress (Leigh), Best Director (Kazan), Best Film; Nominations: Academy Awards '51: Best Actor (Brando), Best Black and White Cinematography, Best Costume Design (B & W), Best Director (Kazan), Best Picture, Best Screenplay, Best Sound, Original Dramatic/Comedy Score. *FOX, WAR, BTV*

A Streetcar Named Desire ✔✔✔ 1984 Excellent made for television adaptation of the Tennessee Williams drama about fading southern belle Blanche du Bois (Ann-Margret in a terrific performance). D'Angelo is her plain sister Stella who lives with brutish husband Stanley (Williams) in the seamy French Quarter of New Orleans. Can't surpass the original but this version does have the advantage of not having to soft-pedal the drama for the fifties censors. 94m/C VHS. Ann-Margret, Beverly D'Angelo, Treat Williams, Randy Quaid, Rafael Campos, Erica Yohn; *D:* John Erman; *C:* Bill Butler; *M:* Marvin Hamlisch. *FCT*

A Streetcar Named Desire ✔✔½ 1995 Baldwin and Lange recreate their 1992 stage roles of brutal Stanley Kowalski and fragile Southern belle Blanche DuBois in the Broadway revival of Tennessee Williams 1947 Pulitzer Prize-winning play. This TV version is truer to the dialogue and situations of the original production than the censored '51 film. 156m/C VHS, Closed Caption. Jessica Lange, Alec Baldwin, Diane Lane, John Goodman, Frederick Coffin; *D:* Glenn Jordan; *C:* Ralf Bode; *M:* David Mansfield. *TCF*

Streetfight ✔½ *Coonskin* 1975 (R) Semi-animated racist exploitation from the creator of "Fritz the Cat." Features some superb animation. 89m/C VHS, Beta. Philip Michael Thomas, Scatman Crothers; *D:* Ralph Bakshi; *W:* Ralph Bakshi. *ACA*

Streets ✔ 1990 (R) Applegate (of Fox TV's "Married...With Children") is believable as an illiterate runaway teen. Good drama set in Venice, California about life on the streets is flawed by near-gratuitous pairing with story of a crazy prostitute-killing cop. 90m/C VHS, Beta. Christina Applegate, David Mendenhall, Eb Lottimer; *D:* Katt Shea Ruben, Andy Ruben; *W:* Andy Ruben. *MGM*

Streets of Fire ✔✔½ 1984 A soldier of fortune rescues his ex-girlfriend, now a famous rock singer, after she's been kidnapped by a malicious motorcycle gang. Violently energetic in its insistent barrage of imagery. Director Hill's never-never land establishes a retro-futuristic feel and is beautifully photographed, however vacuous the ending may be. 93m/C VHS, Beta, LV, Closed Caption. Michael Pare, Diane Lane, Rick Moranis, Amy Madigan, Willem Dafoe, Deborah Van Valkenburgh, Richard Lawson, Rick Rossovich, Bill Paxton, Lee Ving, Stoney Jackson, Robert Townsend, Grand Bush, Mykel T. Williamson, Elizabeth Daily, Lynne Thigpen, Marine Jahan, Ed Begley Jr., John Dennis Johnston, Olivia Brown; *D:* Walter Hill; *W:* Walter Hill, Larry Gross; *M:* Ry Cooder. *USH*

Streets of Gold ✔✔½ 1986 (R) Brandauer is good as a Soviet boxer who defected and now washes dishes in Brooklyn. He trains a pair of street youngsters in the hope of beating his old coach in the Olympics. "Rocky"-like in the boxing, and in the rags-to-riches optimism. 94m/C VHS,

Beta, LV. Klaus Maria Brandauer, Adrian Pasdar, Wesley Snipes; *D:* Joe Roth; *W:* Richard Price, Heywood Gould, Tom Cole; *C:* Arthur Albert; *M:* Jack Nitzsche. *LIV, VES*

The Streets of L.A. ✔✔½ 1979 A frustrated middle-aged woman teaches some punks from an L.A. barrio a thing or two about pride and motivation when she demands reimbursement for the tires they slashed. Without thoroughly professional Woodward to carry it, there would not be much of a movie. Woodward's character is resourceful, and so is the actress. Made for TV. 94m/C VHS, Beta. Joanne Woodward, Robert Webber, Michael C. Gwynne; *D:* Jerrold Freedman; *C:* Allen Daviau. *NO*

The Streets of San Francisco ✔✔✔ 1972 The pilot that spawned the popular TV series. A streetwise old cop and his young college-boy partner (who else but Malden and Douglas as Stone and Keller) investigate the murder of a young woman. Adapted from "Poor, Poor Ophelia" by Carolyn Weston. 120m/C VHS, Beta. Karl Malden, Robert Wagner, Michael Douglas, Andrew Duggan, Tom Bosley, Kim Darby, Mako; *D:* Walter Grauman. *GKK*

Streets of Sin ✔✔½ *Not Wanted* 1949 Written and produced by movie star Lupino, this morality play tells the story of a naive girl's tribulations when she becomes infatuated with a musician and allows herself to become pregnant by him. Shunned by the musician, she enters a home for unwed mothers to sort out her life and feelings for a crippled veteran who wants to marry her. 91m/B VHS. Sally Forrest, Keefe Brasselle, Leonard Penn, Dorothy Adams, Rita Lupino; *D:* Elmer Clifton; *W:* Ida Lupino. *NOS*

Streetwalkin' ✔ 1985 (R) Life in the Big Apple isn't always rosy for a brother and sister who must contend with prostitutes, drug dealers, and tough cops. She turns to prostitution to get by. Miserable, exploitative trash. 86m/C VHS, Beta, LV. Melissa Leo, Dale Midkiff, Leon Robinson, Julie Newmar, Randall Batinkoff, Annie Golden, Antonio Fargas; *D:* Joan Freeman; *W:* Joan Freeman, Robert Alden. *LIV, VES*

Streetwise ✔✔✔½ 1984 Eye-opening and candid documentary inspired by a "Life" magazine article. Frank and honest look at homeless children making a living on the streets. Seattle provides the backdrop to the story as the filmmakers hang around with the kids, earning their trust, and receive the truth from them. Cruel, funny, enraging, but always sobering look into a population of homeless in America. A deservedly acclaimed, terrifying vision of urban America. 92m/C VHS, Beta, LV. *D:* Martin Bell; *M:* Tom Waits. *ORI, NWV*

Strictly Ballroom ✔✔✔½ 1992 (PG) Offbeat, cheerfully tacky dance/romance amusingly turns every movie cliche slightly askew. Scott (Mercurio) has been in training for the Pan-Pacific ballroom championships since the age of six. While talented, he also refuses to follow convention and scandalizes the stuffy dance establishment with his new steps. When his longtime partner leaves him, Scott takes up with a love-struck beginner (Morice), with some surprises of her own. Ballet dancer Mercurio (in his film debut) is appropriately arrogant yet vulnerable, with Morice as the plain Jane turned steel butterfly. Wonderful supporting cast; great debut for director Luhrmann. 94m/C VHS, LV, Closed Caption. *AU* Paul Mercurio, Tara Morice, Bill Hunter, Pat Thomsen, Barry Otto, Gia Carides, Peter Whitford, John Hannan, Sonia Kruger-Tayler, Kris McQuade, Pip Mushin, Leonie Page, Antonio Vargas, Armonia Benedito; *D:* Baz Luhrmann; *W:* Craig Pearce, Baz Luhrmann; *M:* David Hirshfelder. Australian Film Institute '92: Best Costume Design, Best Director (Luhrmann), Best Film, Best Film Editing, Best Supporting Actor (Otto), Best Supporting Actress (Thomsen), Best Writing; Nominations: Golden Globe Awards '94: Best Film—Musical/Comedy. *MAX, TOU, BTV*

Strictly Business ✔½ 1991 (PG-13) An upwardly mobile black broker has his career aspirations in order until he meets a beautiful club promoter who finds him square and boring. Wanting to impress her he asks the advice of a young man who works in the mail room for the proper way to dress and talk. A low-rent Pygmalion story. **83m/C VHS.** Halle Berry, Tommy Davidson, Joseph C. Phillips; **D:** Kevin Hooks; **M:** Michel Colombier. *WAR, FCT*

Strictly G.I. **1944** A collection of war-time patriotic shorts, including "All Star Bond Rally." The support and perception of WWII is historically intriguing. **45m/B VHS, Beta.** Bing Crosby, Frank Sinatra, Betty Grable, Judy Garland, Harpo Marx, Harry James, Bob Hope, Jerry Colonna. *NOS, DVT, HEG*

Strike *♂♂♂½* **1924** Eisenstein's debut, and a silent classic. Stirring look at a 1912 clash between striking factory workers and Czarist troops. **78m/B VHS, Beta.** *RU* **D:** Sergei Eisenstein. *NOS, KIV, IHF*

Strike a Pose *♂½* **1993 (R)** Erotic thriller finds international model-turned-fashion photographer Miranda Cross, her boyfriend LAPD detective Nick Carter, and Miranda's model friends stalked by a revenge-minded killer. Also available in an unrated version.**CW:** Violence and sexuality. **?m/C VHS, LV, Closed Caption.** Margie Peterson, Robert Eastwick, Michelle LaMothe; **D:** Dean Hamilton. *PMH*

Strike Back *♂♂* **1980** A convict escapes from prison to find the girl he loves, and is hounded by the police and the mob. **89m/C VHS, Beta.** Dave Balko, Brigette Wollner; **D:** Carl Schenkel. *LIV, VES*

Strike Commando woof! **1987 (R)** Cheap, exploitative ripoff of the expensive, exploitative mega-action thriller "Rambo." Sleepwalking actors; horrible, overwrought script. **92m/C VHS, Beta.** Reb Brown, Christopher Connelly, Locs Kamme; **D:** Vincent Dawn. *NO*

Strike Force *♂* *Crack* **1975** A New York City cop, a Federal agent and a state trooper work together to battle a large drug ring. Failed made-for-TV pilot. Early Gere appearance; not related to later Robert Stack film with the same title. **74m/C VHS, Beta.** Cliff Gorman, Richard Gere, Donald Blakely; **D:** Barry Shear. *THV*

Strike Force *♂♂* **1981** The jurors on an embezzlement case turn up bloody and headless around town, so a special criminal strike force is brought in to solve the murders. Why do the murders happen only on Tuesdays? Made for TV. **90m/C VHS, Beta.** Robert Stack, Dorian Harewood, Herb Edelman; **D:** Richard Lang. *AHV*

Strike It Rich *♂½* *Loser Take All* **1990 (PG)** A honeymooning couple find themselves resorting to the Monte Carlo gambling tables in order to raise money for the ride home. Lightweight fluff unfortunately adapted from Graham Greene's short novel "Loser Takes All." Only for hard-core Gielgudites. **86m/C VHS, Beta, LV.** Molly Ringwald, Robert Lindsay, John Gielgud, Max Wall, Simon de la Brosse; **D:** James Scott; **M:** Cliff Eidelman. *HBO*

Strike Up the Band *♂♂½* **1940** A high school band turns to hot swing music and enters a national radio contest. Rooney and Garland display their usual charm in this high-energy stroll down memory lane. ♫Over the Waves; The Light Cavalry Overture; Walkin Down Broadway; Five Foot Two, Eyes of Blue; After the Ball; Nobody; Strike Up the Band. **120m/B VHS, Beta, LV.** Judy Garland, Mickey Rooney, Paul Whiteman, William Tracy, June Preisser; **D:** Busby Berkeley. Academy Awards '40: Best Sound; Nominations: Academy Awards '40: Best Song ("Our Love Affair"), Best Score.*MGM*

Striker *♂♂* **1988 (R)** Mercenary John "Striker" Slade is sent to Nicaragua to free a captured American journalist, not knowing his superiors have betrayed him to the Contras and the Sandinistas. He battles it out with both groups while seeking revenge on the businessmen who set him up. **90m/C VHS, Beta.** Frank Zagarino, Melanie Rogers, Paul Werner; **D:** Stephen M. Andrews. *AIP*

Striker's Mountain *♂½* **1987** Story of a sports enthusiast who creates heliskiing and builds it into a business. Great ski scenes, but skip the rest. **99m/C VHS.** Bruce Greenwood, Mimi Kuzyk, Leslie Nielsen, August Schellenberg; **D:** Allen Simmonds. *VTR*

Striking Distance *♂♂½* **1993 (R)** Tom Hardy (Willis) is a hard-nosed fifth-generation Pittsburgh homicide cop whose police detective father (Mahoney) is killed, apparently by a serial killer. Hardy insists the perp was really a fellow cop and winds up on the River Rescue squad (at least his partner is the fetching Parker). When the serial killer starts striking at women with some connection to Hardy, he finds scant support from his fellow cops. High action quotient but the killer's identity won't be any surprise.**CW:** Strong language, violence, and one sex scene. **101m/C VHS, LV, 8mm, Closed Caption.** Bruce Willis, Sarah Jessica Parker, Dennis Farina, Tom Sizemore, Brion James, Robert Pastorelli, Timothy Busfield, John Mahoney, Andre Braugher; **D:** Rowdy Herrington; **W:** Marty Kaplan, Rowdy Herrington; **M:** Brad Fiedel. *COL*

Striking Point *♂½* **1994 (R)** Police detectives are determined to stop ex-KGB commandoes from smuggling high-tech weapons into the country.**CW:** Some language; sexuality; strong gangster violence. **96m/C VHS.** Chris Mitchum, Tracy Spaulding. *CAF*

Stripes *♂♂½* **1981 (R)** Feeling like losers and looking to straighten out their lives, two friends enlist in the Army under the mistaken impression that military life is something like a summer camp for grownups. A box-office success (despite a poorly written and directed script) due in large part to Murray's charm and his verbal and sometimes physical sparring with Oates, who is good as the gruff-tempered platoon sergeant. Features humorous stints from various "Second City" players, including Candy, whom Murray turns into a "lean, mean fighting machine." **105m/C VHS, Beta, LV, Closed Caption.** Bill Murray, Harold Ramis, P.J. Soles, Warren Oates, John Candy, John Larroquette, Judge Reinhold, Sean Young, Dave Thomas, Joe Flaherty; **D:** Ivan Reitman; **W:** Len Blum, Harold Ramis; **C:** Bill Butler; **M:** Elmer Bernstein. *COL*

Stripped to Kill *♂♂* **1987 (R)** A female cop goes undercover to lure a psycho killing strippers. Not-bad entry from Corman and cohorts. Followed by—you guessed it—"Stripped to Kill II." **88m/C VHS, Beta.** Kay Lenz, Greg Evigan, Norman Fell; **D:** Katt Shea Ruben; **W:** Katt Shea Ruben, Andy Ruben. *MGM*

Stripped to Kill II: Live Girls *♂* **1989** A young woman with extra-sensory powers dreams of murders which she discovers are all too real. A weak sequel, despite the interesting premise. **83m/C VHS, Beta.** Maria Ford, Eb Lottimer, Karen Mayo Chandler, Marjean Holden, Birke Tan, Debra Lamb; **D:** Katt Shea Ruben; **W:** Katt Shea Ruben. *MGM*

The Stripper *♂♂½* *Woman of Summer* **1963** A middle-aged stripper in a traveling show returns to the small Kansas town of her youth. Left stranded, she moves in with an old friend whose teenage son promptly falls in love with her. Based on the play "A Loss of Roses" by William Inge. **95m/B VHS, Beta.** Joanne Woodward, Richard Beymer, Claire Trevor, Carol Lynley, Robert Webber, Gypsy Rose Lee; **D:** Franklin J. Schaffner; **M:** Jerry Goldsmith. Nominations: Academy Awards '63: Best Costume Design (B & W). *FOX*

Stripper *♂♂½* **1986 (R)** A good undercovers glimpse of the life and work of several real-life strippers, culminating in the First Annual Stripper's Convention in 1984. **90m/C VHS, Beta.** Janette Boyd, Sara Costa, Kimberly Holcomb; **D:** Jerome Gary; **M:** Jack Nitzsche. *FOX*

Stripshow *♂* **1995 (R)** Veteran Vegas stripper shows the ropes to newcomer and then must vie with the upstart for her boyfriend's interest.**CW:** Strong sexuality and some language. **?m/C VHS.** Monique Parent, Tane McClure, Steven Tietsort; **D:** Gary Orona; **W:** Gary Orona. *MTH*

Striptease *♂♂½* **1996 (R)** Single mom Erin Grant (Moore) loses custody of her daughter Angela (Moore's real-life offspring, Rumer) to her lowlife ex, Darrell (Patrick). In order to raise the money for an appeal, she dances at a Miami strip club, where she runs across politician David Dilbeck (Reynolds), who has a thing for both vaseline and Erin. Unlike "Showgirls," this one's intentionally funny and features one fine script work and performances, which got overlooked amidst all the hype, including Moore's record-setting (for an actress) $12 million paycheck, 4 mil of which reportedly was for agreeing to dance nude. Based on the novel by Carl Hiaasen.**CW:** Nudity, erotic dancing and language. **115m/C VHS, LV, Closed Caption.** Demi Moore, Burt Reynolds, Ving Rhames, Armand Assante, Robert Patrick, Rumer Willis; **D:** Andrew Bergman; **W:** Andrew Bergman; **C:** Stephen Goldblatt; **M:** Howard Shore. Golden Raspberry Awards '96: Worst Picture, Worst Actress (Moore), Worst Director (Bergman), Worst Screenplay, Worst Song ("Pussy, Pussy, Pussy (Whose Kitty Cat Are You?)"); Nominations: Golden Raspberry Awards '96: Worst Supporting Actor (Reynolds). *COL*

Stripteaser *♂½* **1995 (R)** Sicko psycho Dean holds dancers and patrons hostage in an L.A. strip joint where he provides various humiliations for his captives. Ford's the beautiful ecdysiast whose been the object of the fellow's secret obsessions. Also available unrated. **82m/C VHS.** Rick Dean, Maria Ford, Lance August; **D:** Dan Golden. *NHO*

Stroke of Midnight *♂½* **1990 (PG)** Souped-up Cinderella with Lowe as egotistic high fashion designer, Grey as struggling shoe designer and a pumpkin-colored VW Bug. **102m/C VHS, Beta, LV.** Rob Lowe, Jennifer Grey, Andrea Ferreol; **D:** Tom Clegg. *MED, VTR*

Stroker Ace woof! **1983 (PG)** Flamboyant stock car driver tries to break an iron-clad promotional contract signed with a greedy fried-chicken magnate. Off duty, he ogles blondes as dopey as he is. One of the worst from Reynolds—and that's saying something. **96m/C VHS, Beta.** Burt Reynolds, Ned Beatty, Jim Nabors, Parker Stevenson, Loni Anderson, Bubba Smith; **D:** Hal Needham; **W:** Hal Needham, Hugh Wilson. Golden Raspberry Awards '83: Worst Supporting Actor (Nabors). *WAR*

Stromboli *♂♂½* **1950** Bergman is a Czech refugee who marries an Italian fisherman in order to escape from her displaced persons camp. He brings her to his home island of Stromboli where she finds the life bleak and isolated and her marriage a trial. In Italian with English subtitles. The melodrama was even greater off-screen than on; this is the movie which introduced Bergman and Rossellini and began their (then) scandalous affair. **81m/B VHS, Beta.** *IT* Ingrid Bergman, Mario Vitale, Renzo Cesana; **D:** Roberto Rossellini. *NO*

Strong Man **1926** A WWI veteran, passing himself off as an unlikely circus strongman, searches an American city for the girl whose letters gave him hope during the war. Perhaps Langdon's best full-length film. **78m/B VHS, Beta, LV.** Harry Langdon, Gertrude Astor, Tay Garnett; **D:** Frank Capra. *HBO, IME*

Strong Medicine *♂♂½* **1984** Strange, avant-garde film about a strange, off-written young woman. Cleverly directed experiment that's not for everyone. **84m/C VHS, Beta.** Carol Kane, Raul Julia, Wallace Shawn, Kate Manheim, David Warrilow; **D:** Guy Green. *NO*

Stroszek *♂♂♂* **1977** Three German misfits—a singer, a prostitute and an old man—tour the U.S. in search of their dreams. Touching, hilarious comedy-drama with a difference and an attitude. One of Herzog's easiest and also best films. In English and German with English subtitles. **108m/C VHS.** *GE* Eva Mattes, Bruno S, Clemens Scheitz; **D:** Werner Herzog; **M:** Chet Atkins. *NYF, FCT*

The Structure of Crystals *♂♂½* *Struktura Krysztalu* **1969** A member of the scientific elite meets with an old friend who has moved to a remote meteorological station and tries to persuade him to return to the city and resume his work. Zanussi's cerebral first feature was also the first of a series of films to explore the scientific community. In Polish with English subtitles. **76m/B VHS.** *PL* Andrzej Zamecki, Jan Myslowicz, Barbara Wrzesinska, Wladyslaw Jarema, Daniel Olbrychski; **D:** Krzysztof Zanussi; **W:** Edward Zebrowski, Krzysztof Zanussi. *FCT*

Struggle 🎬 **1931** Unfortunately, Griffith's final directorial effort is a ludicrous melodrama about the evils of alcohol. Because of Prohibition, working man Jimmie Wilson (Skelly) takes to illegal hootch, which turns out to be tainted, causing Jimmie to abuse his wife and daughter and destroy their formerly happy home. **87m/B VHS.** Hal Skelly, Zita Johann, Evelyn Baldwin, Charlotte Wynters, Helen Mack, Kate Bruce, Jackson Halliday, Edna Hagan, Claude Cooper, Arthur Lipson, Charles Richman, Dave Manley; **D:** D.W. Griffith; **W:** D.W. Griffith, Anita Loos, John Emerson; **C:** Joseph Ruttenberg; **M:** D.W. Griffith, Philip A. Scheib. *KIV*

Stryker woof! **1983 (R)** The ever-lovin' nuclear holocaust has occurred, and good guys and bad guys battle it out for scarce water. If you liked "Mad Max," go see it again; don't watch this miserable effort. **86m/C VHS, Beta.** *PH* Steve Sandor, Andria Fabio; **D:** Cirio H. Santiago; **W:** Howard R. Cohen. *VTR*

Stuart Saves His Family 🎬🎬 **1994 (PG-13)** Fired from his self-help television show on a Chicago public-access station, New-age advice guru Smalley (Franken) returns home to help his pathetically dysfunctional family sort out their problems and an inheritance, a nonplot that gives Smalley a chance to do his 12-step shtick. And that's...O.K. A tolerable installment in the endless parade of mediocre "Saturday Night Live" sketches stretched for the big screen that takes a few surprisingly maudlin turns. Based on Franken's book of Smalley's "daily affirmations," "I'm Good Enough, I'm Smart Enough, and Doggone It, People Like Me!" **CW:** Language; substance abuse. **97m/C VHS, Beta, Closed Caption.** Al Franken, Laura San Giacomo, Vincent D'Onofrio, Shirley Knight, Harris Yulin; **D:** Harold Ramis; **W:** Al Franken; **M:** Marc Shaiman. *PAR*

Stuck on You 🎬 **1984 (R)** Couple engaged in a palimony suit takes their case to a judge to work out their differences. Wing-clipped angel Gabriel (Corey) comes to earth to help them patch it up. Never mind. **90m/C VHS, Beta.** Prof. Irwin Corey, Virginia Penta, Mark Mikulski; **D:** Lloyd (Samuel Weil) Kaufman, Michael Herz.

Stuckey's Last Stand 🎬 **1978 (PG)** A group of camp counselors prepare to take 22 children on a nature hike they will never forget. Mindless teen fodder. **95m/C VHS, Beta.** Whit Reichert, Tom Murray, Rich Casentino. *NO*

The Stud woof! **1978 (R)** Owner of a fashionable "after hours" dance spot hires a young, handsome stud to manage the club and attend to her personal needs. Low-budget look and seemingly seedless. Faithfully adapted by sister Jackie Collins from her novel. **90m/C VHS, Beta.** *GB* Joan Collins, Oliver Tobias; **D:** Quentin Masters; **W:** Jackie Collins. *NO*

Student Affairs woof! **1988 (R)** A bunch of highschool misfits vie for roles in a movie about a bunch of high school misfits. **92m/C VHS, Beta.** Louie Bonanno, Jim Abele, Alan Fisler, Deborah Blaisdell; **D:** Chuck Vincent. *LIV, VES*

Student Bodies woof! **1981 (R)** A "Halloween"-style spoof of high-school horror films, except it's not funny. And what's so funny about bloody murder anyway? When the on-the-set problems and strife arose (which they did), why didn't everyone just cut their losses and go home? **86m/C VHS, Beta, LV.** Kristen Riter, Matthew Goldsby, Richard Brando, Joe Flood; **D:** Mickey Rose. *PAR*

Student Confidential 🎬 **1987 (R)** A Troma-produced spoof of seedy high school youth movies, new and old, involving four students who are led into the adult vices by a mysterious millionaire. Badly made and dull. Douglas and Jackson both have brothers named Michael. **99m/C VHS, Beta.** Eric Douglas, Marlon Jackson, Susan Scott, Ronee Blakley, Elizabeth Singer; **D:** Richard Horian. *MED*

The Student Nurses 🎬🎬 **1970 (R)** The adventures, amourous and otherwise, of four last-year nursing students. Followed by four sequels: "Private Duty Nurses," "Night Call Nurses," "The Young Nurses," and "Candy Stripe Nurses." Better than average exploitation fare. First release from Roger Corman's New World studios; it goes down hill from there. **89m/C VHS, Beta.** Elaine Giftos, Karen Carlson, Brioni Farrell, Barbara Leigh, Reni Santoni, Richard Rust, Lawrence Casey, Darrell Larson, Paul Camen, Richard Stahl, Scottie MacGregor, Pepe Serna; **D:** Stephanie Rothman. *NLC*

Student of Prague 🎬🎬🎬 **1913** Early silent classic based on the German Faust legend: a student makes a pact with the devil to win a beautiful woman. Poor fellow. With either German or English title cards. Music track. **60m/B VHS, Beta.** *GE* Lothar Koemer, Grete Berger, Paul Wegener; **D:** Paul Wegener, Stellan Rye. *DVT, GLV, GVV*

The Student Prince 🎬🎬🎬 **1954** Delightful rendition of Sigmund Romberg's famous operetta in which Purdom stars as the Prince of Heidelberg who falls for barmaid Blyth. Lanza recorded the soundtrack, but could not star in this film because of his weight problem. Previously filmed in 1919 and 1927 without music. 🎵Golden Days; Serenade; Deep in My Heart; To the Inn We're Marching; Drink, Drink, Drink; Come Boys, Let's All Be Gay, Boys; Summertime in Heidelberg; Beloved; I Walk With God. **107m/C VHS.** Ann Blyth, Edmund Purdom, John Ericson, Louis Calhern, Edmund Gwenn, S.Z. Sakall, Betta St. John; **D:** Richard Thorpe; **C:** Paul Vogel. *MGM*

The Student Prince in Old Heidelberg 🎬🎬½ *Old Heidelberg* **1927** Prince Karl Heinrich silently falls in love with lowly barmaid. **102m/B VHS.** Ramon Novarro, Norma Shearer; **D:** Ernst Lubitsch. *MGM, FCT*

The Student Teachers 🎬½ **1973** Yet another soft-core Corman product. Three student teachers sleep around, on screen. **79m/C VHS, Beta.** Susan Damante Shaw, Brooke Mills, Bob Harris, John Cramer, Chuck Norris; **D:** Jonathan Kaplan.

Studs Lonigan 🎬🎬 **1960** Drifting, too arty-sy rendering a James T. Farrell's trilogy about an Irish drifter growing up in Chicago in the twenties. Good period detail, but oddly off-kilter and implausible as history. **96m/B VHS, Beta.** Christopher Knight, Frank Gorshin, Jack Nicholson; **D:** Irving Lerner; **W:** Philip Yordan; **M:** Jerry Goldsmith. *MGM*

A Study in Scarlet 🎬🎬 **1933** Owen played Watson the previous year in "Sherlock Holmes;" here he's miscast as Holmes, and the plot differs from the Doyle story of the same title. **77m/B VHS, Beta.** Reginald Owen, Alan Mowbray, Anna May Wong, June Clyde, Alan Dinehart; **D:** Edwin L. Marin; **W:** Reginald Owen. *SNC, NOS, CAB*

A Study in Terror 🎬🎬🎬 *Sherlock Holmes Grosster Fall; Fog* **1966** A well-appointed Sherlock Holmes thriller. The second Holmes film in color. Premise has a young, athletic Holmes in pursuit of a well-educated Jack the Ripper in the atmosphere of London in the 1880s. **94m/C VHS, Beta, LV.** *GE GB* John Neville, Donald Houston, Judi Dench, Anthony Quayle, Robert Morley, Frank Finlay, Cecil Parker; **D:** James Hill. *COL*

The Stuff 🎬½ **1985 (R)** Surreal horror semi-spoof about an ice cream mogul and a hamburger king who discover that the new, fast-selling confection in town zombifies its partakers. Forced, lame satire from producer/director/writer Cohen. **93m/C VHS, Beta, Closed Caption.** Michael Moriarty, Andrea Marcovicci, Garrett Morris, Paul Sorvino, Danny Aiello, Brooke Adams; **D:** Larry Cohen; **W:** Larry Cohen. *NWV, VTR*

Stuff Stephanie in the Incinerator 🎬 **1989 (PG-13)** A Troma gagfest about wealthy cretins who torture and kill young women. "Funny" title betrays utter, exploitive mindlessness. **97m/C VHS, Beta, LV.** Catherine Dee, William Dame, M.R. Murphy, Dennis Cunningham; **D:** Don Nardo. *LIV*

The Stunt Man 🎬🎬🎬🎬 **1980 (R)** A marvelous and unique exercise in meta-cinematic manipulation. O'Toole, in one of his very best roles, is a power-crazed movie director; Railsback is a fugitive sheltered by him from sherrif Rocco. When a stunt man is killed in an accident, O'Toole prevails on Railsback to replace him, leading Railsback to wonder if O'Toole wants him dead. A labor of love for director-producer Rush, who spent nine years working on it, and waited two years to see it released, by Fox. Based on the novel by Paul Brodeur. **129m/C VHS, Beta, LV.** Peter O'Toole, Steve Railsback, Barbara Hershey, Chuck Bail, Alex Rocco, Allen (Goorwitz) Garfield, Adam Roarke, Sharon Farrell, Philip Bruns; **D:** Richard Rush; **W:** Lawrence B. Marcus, Richard Rush; **M:** Dominic Frontiere. Golden Globe Awards '81: Best Score; Montreal World Film Festival '80: Best Film; National Board of Review Awards '80: 10 Best Films of the Year; National Society of Film Critics Awards '80: Best Actor (O'Toole); Nominations: Academy Awards '80: Best Actor (O'Toole), Best Adapted Screenplay, Best Director (Rush). *FOX*

Stunt Pilot 🎬🎬 **1939** A young man takes a job at a film studio as a stunt pilot and finds mayhem and romance on and off the ground. One in the "Tailspin Tommy" series. Well-paced and fun to watch. **61m/C VHS.** John Trent, Marjorie Reynolds, Milburn Stone, Jason Robards Sr., Pat O'Malley; **D:** George Waggner. *NOS, MOV*

Stunts 🎬🎬 *Who Is Killing the Stuntman* **1977 (PG)** See "The Stunt Man" instead. OK script hides near-invisible plot; stunt man engages in derring-do. **90m/C VHS, Beta.** Robert Forster, Fiona Lewis, Joanna Cassidy, Darrell Fetty, Bruce Glover, James Luisi; **D:** Mark L. Lester; **M:** Michael Kamen. *NO*

Stuntwoman 🎬½ **1981** Welch plays a stuntwoman whose death-defying job interferes with her love life. What ever shall she do? **95m/C VHS.** Raquel Welch, Jean-Paul Belmondo; **D:** Claude Zidi. *NO*

The Stupids 🎬½ **1995 (PG)** In the tradition of "Dumb and Dumber," the aptly-named Stupids—dad Stanley (Arnold), mom Joan (Lundy), brother Buster (Hall), and sis Petunia (McKenna)—blunder unwittingly into and out of dangerous adventures involving their garbage. Landing Arnold for the lead seems like the casting coup of the decade but the movie itself is shaky and uninspired. Based on the children's best-selling books. Keep a lookout for Captain Kangaroo (Keeshan) and numerous other cameos. **93m/C VHS, LV, Closed Caption.** Tom Arnold, Jessica Lundy, Bug Hall, Alex McKenna, Mark Metcalf, Matt Keeslar, Frankie Faison, Christopher Lee, Bob Keeshan; **Cameos:** Robert Wise, Norman Jewison, Constantin Costa-Gavras, David Cronenberg, Atom Egoyan, Gillo Pontecorvo; **D:** John Landis; **W:** Brent Forrester; **C:** Manfred Guthe; **M:** Christopher Stone. Golden Raspberry Awards '96: Worst Actor (Arnold); Nominations: Golden Raspberry Awards '96: Worst Picture, Worst Director (Landis), Worst Screenplay. *NLC*

Submarine Seahawk 🎬🎬 **1959** When a group of Japanese warships mysteriously disappear, allied intelligence suspect a big battle is brewing. An inexperienced commander who has been tracking the movement of the Japanese ships is put in charge of the submarine Seahawk, even though the crew lacks faith in his command abilities. His own men may prove a bigger obstacle than any of the Japanese. Lots of action and stock WWII footage. **83m/B VHS.** John Bentley, Brett Halsey, Wayne Heffley, Steve Mitchell, Henry McCann, Frank Gerstle; **D:** Spencer Gordon Bennet. *COL*

Submission 🎬½ **1977 (R)** A pharmacist's sensuality is reawakened when she has a provocative affair with a clerk in her shop. **107m/C VHS, Beta.** *IT* Franco Nero, Lisa Gastoni; **D:** Salvatore Samperi. *PSM*

Subspecies 🎬½ **1990 (R)** New improved vampire demons descend on earth. The first full-length feature film shot on location in Transylvania. For horror buffs only. **CW:** Nudity and vampire violence. **90m/C VHS, LV, 8mm, Closed Caption.** Laura

Tate, Michael Watson, Anders Hove, Michelle McBride, Irina Movila, Angus Scrimm; **D:** Ted Nicolaou. *PAR, BTV*

The Substance of Fire 🐾🐾 1996 (R) Publisher Isaac Geldhart (Rifkin) is an autocrat in both his business and his personal life, which may be why he's having so much trouble with both. A Holocaust survivor, Geldhart's obsessive about publishing a lavish four-volume history of Nazi medical experiments that will bankrupt the family firm. So his children wind up ousting him from the company and Isaac slowly slips over the edge into madness. Very King Lear, with an astonishing performance by Rifkin who also played the character in Baitz's 1991 Off-Broadway play.**CW:** Language. 100m/C VHS, LV, Closed Caption. Ron Rifkin, Tony Goldwyn, Timothy Hutton, Sarah Jessica Parker, Ronny Graham, Elizabeth Franz; **D:** Daniel Sullivan; **W:** Jon Robin Baitz; **C:** Robert Yeoman; **M:** Joseph Vitarelli. *TOU*

The Substitute 🐾 1993 (R) Donohue plays a sexy high-school substitute teacher who turns out to have homicidal tendencies, which she decides to take out on her students. Film debut for rapper/underwear model Mark.**CW:** Terror/violence and some sexuality. 86m/C VHS, Beta, Closed Caption. Amanda Donohoe, Dalton James, Natasha Gregson Wagner, Eugene Glazer, Mark Wahlberg; **D:** Martin Donovan; **W:** Cynthia Verlaine; **M:** Gerald Gouriet. *PAR*

The Substitute 🐾 1996 (R) Berenger plays a Vietnam vet mercenary who poses as a substitute teacher to uncover a drug ring after his girlfriend (Venora) is roughed up by the gang. At one point, he displays his unique teaching style by throwing some unruly students out of the second floor window. Hmm...wonder if that was on the test. Being a concerned teacher, he decides to uncover the kingpin of the unruly drug gang. Being an unruly drug gang, they decide to shoot at him...a lot. Unless you're a fan of heavy weaponry, banal one liners or yelling at the screen in frustration, substitute another movie for this one.**CW:** Strong violence, language and brief nudity. 114m/C VHS, LV, Closed Caption, DVD. Tom Berenger, Ernie Hudson, Diane Venora, Mark Anthony, Glenn Plummer, Cliff DeYoung, William Forsythe, Raymond Cruz, Sharron Corley, Richard Brooks, Rodney Grant, Luis Guzman; **D:** Robert Mandel; **W:** Roy Frumkes, Rocco Simonelli, Alan Ormsby; **C:** Bruce Surtees; **M:** Gary Chang. *LIV*

The Substitute Wife 🐾🐾½ 1994 (PG-13) Dying Nebraska frontier woman Amy Hightower (Thompson) decides to find her husband Martin (Weller) a new wife to help on the farm and look after their four children. But women are so scarce (and the farm is so isolated) that the only one willing to give it a try is prostitute Pearl (Fawcett), who's fed up with her profession but isn't exactly the motherly time (at least not at first). Amusing relationships develop between the two women and the bewildered husband. Made for TV.**CW:** Some sexual themes and situations. 92m/C VHS. Farrah Fawcett, Lea Thompson, Peter Weller; **D:** Peter Werner; **W:** Stan Daniels; **C:** Neil Roach; **M:** Mark Snow. *THV*

Subterfuge 🐾🐾 1968 When a special American security agent goes to England for a "vacation," his presence causes speculation and poses several serious questions for both British Intelligence and the underworld. Nothing special, with the occasional suspenseful moment. 89m/C VHS, Beta. **GB** Joan Collins, Gene Barry, Richard Todd; **D:** Peter Graham Scott. *NO*

Suburban Commando 🐾🐾 1991 (PG) A goofy, muscular alien mistakenly lands on Earth while on vacation. He does his best to remain inconspicuous, resulting in numerous hilarious situations. Eventually he is forced to confront his arch, interstellar nemesis in order to defend the family who befriended him. A harmless, sometimes cute vehicle for wrestler Hogan, which will certainly entertain his younger fans. 88m/C VHS, LV, Closed Caption. Hulk Hogan, Christopher Lloyd, Shelley Duvall, Larry Miller, William Ball, JoAnn Dearing, Jack Elam, Roy Dotrice, Christopher Neame, Tony Longo; **D:** Burt Kennedy; **W:** Frank Cappello. *COL, NLC*

Suburban Roulette 🐾 1967 "Adults only" feature from splattermaster Lewis caters to the prurient. Groovy themes like wife swapping and other very daring subjects. Totally sixties. Presented as part of Joe Bob Brigg's "Sleaziest Movies in the History of the World" series. 91m/C VHS. **D:** Herschell Gordon Lewis. *VTR*

Suburbia 🐾 *The Wild Side* 1983 (R) When a group of punk rockers move into a condemned suburban development, they become the targets of a vigilante group. Low budget, needless violent remake of anyone of many '50s rebellion flicks that tries to have a "message." 99m/C VHS, Beta, LV. Chris Pederson, Bill Coyne, Jennifer Clay, Timothy Eric O'Brien, Aridrew Pece, Don Allen; **D:** Penelope Spheeris. *LIV, VES*

subUrbia 🐾🐾 1996 (R) Ensemble piece featuring three aimless post-high school friends, Jeff (Ribisi), Buff (Zahn), and Tim (Katt) who spend their time hanging out in the parking lot of a convenience store. What's different about this night is that they're joined by Jeff's girlfriend Sooze (Carey) and her friend Bee-Bee (Spybey), and they actually have a purpose for waiting around. The guys are expecting a visit from their old buddy Pony (Bartok), a rock musician just finding success. But when Pony does appear, the fact that he has done something to get out and succeed turns the meeting hostile. Based on the play by Eric Bogosian.**CW:** Strong language including sex and drug references, teen drinking and brief nudity. 121m/C VHS, Closed Caption. Giovanni Ribisi, Steve Zahn, Nicky Katt, Jayce Bartok, Amie Carey, Dina Spybey, Parker Posey, Ajay Naidu, Samia Shoaib; **D:** Richard Linklater; **W:** Eric Bogosian; **C:** Lee Daniel. *WAR*

Subway 🐾½ 1985 (R) Surreal, MTV-esque vision of French fringe life from the director of "Le Dernier Combat." A spike-haired renegade escapes the law by plunging into the Parisian subway system. Once there, he encounters a bizarre subculture living under the city. Plenty of angry-youth attitude, but where's the point? And frankly, too much bad New Wave music. 103m/C VHS, Beta, LV, Closed Caption. **FR** Christopher Lambert, Isabelle Adjani, Jean-Hugues Anglade, Jean Reno; **D:** Luc Besson; **W:** Luc Besson. Cesar Awards '86: Best Actor (Lambert), Best Art Direction/Set Decoration, Best Sound; Nominations: Cesar Awards '86: Best Supporting Actor (Anglade). *FOX*

Subway to the Stars 🐾🐾½ *Un Trem Para as Estrelas* 1987 Young saxophonist Fontes searches the back streets of Rio for his missing girlfriend. Realistic and sometimes depressing, if aimless at times. Overall, an intriguing "underworld" flick from Brazil. Portuguese with subtitles. 103m/C VHS. **BR** Guilherme Fontes, Milton Goncalves, Taumaturgo Ferreira, Ze Trindade, Ana Beatriz Wiltgen; **D:** Carlos Diegues. *FCT, NWV*

Success is the Best Revenge 🐾🐾½ 1984 A Polish film director living in London struggles with his rebellious teenage son. Both struggle with questions of exile and identity. Uneven but worthwhile and based on Skolimowski's own experiences. His better earlier film is "Moonlighting." 95m/C VHS, LV. **GB** Michael York, Michel Piccoli, Anouk Aimee, John Hurt, Jane Asher, Joanna Szerbic, Michael Lyndon, George Skolimowski; **D:** Jerzy Skolimowski; **M:** Hans Zimmer. *IME*

The Sucker 🐾🐾 *Le Corniauds* 1965 Antoine Marecchal (Bouvril) is on his way to an Italian vacation when his car is wrecked in an accident. The businessman who smashed his car offers Antoine a Cadillac to drive but this turns him into a smuggler. However, Antoine isn't as dumb as he may appear and he makes the most of his unusual situation. French with subtitles. 90m/C VHS. **FR** Bourvil, Louis de Funes; **D:** Gerard Oury. *FCT*

Sucker Money 🐾½ *Victims of the Beyond* 1934 Newspaper reporter works to expose phony spiritualist. Good title; little else. Boring. 59m/B VHS, Beta, LV. Mischa Auer, Phyliss Barrington, Earl McCarthy, Ralph Lewis, Mae Busch; **D:** Dorothy Davenport Reid. *NOS, SNC, VYY*

Sudden Death 🐾 1950 Shamrock and Lucky are back as cowboys posing as hired gunmen in order to foil a wealthy, homesteader-hating land baron. 55m/B VHS, Beta, LV. James Ellison, Russell Hayden, Stanley Price, Raymond Hatton, Julie Adams. *NO*

Sudden Death 🐾 1977 (R) Two professional violence merchants put themselves up for hire. 84m/C VHS, Beta. Robert Conrad, Felton Perry, Don Stroud, Bill Raymond, Ron Vawter, Harry Roskolenko; **D:** Richard Foreman. *MED*

Sudden Death 🐾 1985 (R) A beautiful businesswoman decides to kill every rapist she can find after she herself has been attacked. Exploitative in its own fashion; fueled and felled by rage. 95m/C VHS, Beta. Denise Coward, Frank Runyeon, Jamie Tirelli; **D:** Sig Shore. *LIV, VES*

Sudden Death 🐾 1995 (R) Terrorists invade a hockey arena where the Vice President and 17,000 fans, including Fire Marshal Jean-Claude and his kids, are watching the seventh game of the Stanley Cup Finals. The latest in the "Die Hard in a..." genre covers the territory with the now-standard lack of characterization, family member in peril, and ever-increasing body count. Boothe (playing Alan Rickman playing a bad guy) does most of the talking while Van Damme kicks people in the head and plays goalie. Producer Howard Baldwin owns the Pittsburgh Penguins, coincidentally one of the teams on the ice for the second pairing of "Timecop" vets Hyams and Van Damme.**CW:** Substantial amount of strong violence and language. 110m/C VHS, LV, Closed Caption. Jean-Claude Van Damme, Powers Boothe, Ross Malinger, Whittni Wright, Raymond J. Barry, Dorian Harewood, Kate McNeil, Audra Lindley; **D:** Peter Hyams; **W:** Gene Quintano; **C:** Peter Hyams; **M:** John Debney. *USH*

Sudden Fear 🐾🐾🐾 1952 Successful playwright/heiress Myra Hudson (Crawford) has a whirlwind romance, leading to marriage, with oh-so-charming actor Lester Blaine (Palance). But Les is more interested in Myra's money and gets together with former flame Irene (always the bad girl Grahame) to get rid of his new bride and inherit her fortune. But Myra finds out about the plot and puts her writing talent to work in coming up with a new scenario. Good suspenser with fine performances. Adapted from the book by Edna Sherry. 111m/B VHS. Joan Crawford, Jack Palance, Gloria Grahame, Bruce (Herman Brix) Bennett, Virginia Huston, Mike Connors; **D:** David Miller; **W:** Lenore Coffee, Robert Smith; **C:** Charles B(ryant) Lang; **M:** Elmer Bernstein. Nominations: Academy Awards '52: Best Actress (Crawford), Best Black and White Cinematography, Best Costume Design (B & W), Best Supporting Actor (Palance). *KIV*

Sudden Impact 🐾🐾½ 1983 (R) Eastwood directs himself in this formula thriller, the fourth "Dirty Harry" entry. This time "Dirty Harry" Callahan tracks down a revenge-obsessed murderess and finds he has more in common with her than he expected. Meanwhile, local mobsters come gunning for him. This is the one where he says, "Go ahead. Make my day." Followed by "The Dead Pool." 117m/C VHS, Beta, LV, 8mm, Closed Caption. Clint Eastwood, Sondra Locke, Pat Hingle, Bradford Dillman; **D:** Clint Eastwood; **W:** Charles B. Pierce; **C:** Bruce Surtees; **M:** Lalo Schifrin. *WAR, TLF*

Sudden Terror 🐾🐾 *Eyewitness* 1970 (PG) The murder of an African dignitary is witnessed by a young boy who has trouble convincing his parents and the police about the incident. Suspenseful but less than original. Shot on location in Malta. 95m/C VHS, Beta. **GB** Mark Lester, Lionel Jeffries, Susan George, Tony Bonner; **D:** John Hough. *FOX*

Suddenly 🐾🐾🐾½ 1954 Crazed gunman Sinatra holds a family hostage in the hick town of Suddenly, California, as part of a plot to kill the president, who's passing through town. Tense thriller is a good display for Sinatra's acting talent. Unfortunately hard to find because Sinatra forced United Artists to take it out of distribution after hearing that Kennedy assassin Lee Harvey Oswald had watched "Suddenly" only days before November 22, 1963. Really, Ol' Blue Eyes should have stuck with making top-notch thrillers like this one, instead of degenerating into the world's greatest lounge singer. **75m/B VHS, Beta.** Frank Sinatra, Sterling Hayden, James Gleason, Nancy Gates, Paul Frees; **D:** Lewis Allen. *SNC, NOS, VEC*

Suddenly, Last Summer 𝒵𝒵𝒵½ **1959** Brain surgeon is summoned to the mansion of a rich New Orleans matron who wishes him to perform a lobotomy on her niece, supposedly suffering from a mental breakdown. Based on the play by Tennessee Williams. Softened for the censors, though the themes of homosexuality, insanity, and murder, characterizations of evil, and unusual settings presage many movies of the next two decades. Extremely fine performances from Hepburn and Taylor. Clift never completely recovered from his auto accident two years before and does not come across with the strength of purpose really necessary in his character. Still, fine viewing. **114m/B VHS, Beta, LV.** Elizabeth Taylor, Katharine Hepburn, Montgomery Clift, Mercedes McCambridge, Albert Dekker; **D:** Joseph L. Mankiewicz; **W:** Gore Vidal; **C:** Jack Hildyard; **M:** Malcolm Arnold. Golden Globe Awards '60: Best Actress—Drama (Taylor); National Board of Review Awards '59: 10 Best Films of the Year; Nominations: Academy Awards '59: Best Actress (Hepburn), Best Actress (Taylor), Best Art Direction/Set Decoration (B & W). *COL*

Sudie & Simpson 𝒵𝒵𝒵 **1990** Heart-tugging tale of friendship set in rural 1940s Georgia. Twelve-year-old white Sudie's forbidden friendship with the adult black Simpson provides a lot of talk in their small town. Racial barriers finally cause Simpson to be accused of child molestation and the odds of his survival, despite his innocence, don't seem great. Based on Sara Flanigan Carter's autobiographical novel. Made for cable television. **95m/C VHS, Closed Caption.** Sara Gilbert, Louis Gossett Jr., Frances Fisher, John M. Jackson, Paige Danahy, Ken Strong; **D:** Joan Tewkesbury; **W:** Sara Flanigan Carter, Ken Koser. *WOV*

Suds 𝒵𝒵½ **1920** Pickford is tragic laundress with major crush on a guy who left his shirt at the laundry. **75m/B VHS, Beta, LV.** Mary Pickford, William Austin, Harold Goodwin, Rose Dione, Theodore Roberts; **D:** John Francis Dillon. *GPV*

Suffering Bastards 𝒵𝒵½ **1990** Buddy and Al have never worked a day in their lives—Mom's nightclub always gave them something to do and a regular paycheck. But when Mom's swindled out of the family business, they decide it's time to take charge. Soon they're caught between bullets, babes, and belly laughs in this action-filled comedy. **95m/C VHS.** Eric Bogosian, John C. McGinley, David Warshofsky. *AIP*

Sugar Cane Alley 𝒵𝒵𝒵 *Rue Cases Negres* **1983 (PG)** After the loss of his parents, an 11-year-old orphan boy goes to work with his grandmother on a sugar plantation. She realizes that her young ward's only hope is an education. Set in Martinique in the 1930s among black workers. Poignant and memorable. French with subtitles. **106m/C VHS, LV.** *FR* Garry Cadenat, Darling Legitimus, Douta Seck; **D:** Euzhan Palcy; **W:** Euzhan Palcy; **C:** Dominique Chapuis. *NYF, FCT*

Sugar Cookies woof! **1977 (R)** Erotic horror story in which young women are the pawns as a satanic satyr and an impassioned lesbian play out a bizarre game of vengeance, love, and death. **89m/C VHS, Beta.** Mary Woronov, Lynn Lowry, Monique Van Vooren; **D:** Michael Herz. *NO*

Sugar Hill 𝒵𝒵 **1994 (R)** Two brothers (Wright & Snipes) are heroin dealers who have built their own crime empire in the Sugar Hill section of Harlem. Snipes is moved to reconsider his career options when he falls for an aspiring actress (Randle). Jarring editing sequence recaps the seminal event in the brothers' upbringing and serves to explain how the wide-eyed boys became cold-blooded pushers. Good performances

by all, but formulaic plot will leave viewers asking themselves if they haven't seen it before and why it was they saw it then. Junkie dad Williams was Linc on "The Mod Squad" on television in the late 1960s and director of "Tales from the Hood." **123m/C VHS, LV, Closed Caption.** Wesley Snipes, Michael Wright, Theresa Randle, Clarence Williams III, Abe Vigoda, Ernie Hudson, Larry Joshua, Leslie Uggams, Khandi Alexander, Raymond Serra, Joe Dallesandro, Vondie Curtis-Hall; **D:** Leon Ichaso; **W:** Barry Michael Cooper; **C:** Bojan Bazelli; **M:** Terence Blanchard. *FXV*

Sugarbaby 𝒵𝒵𝒵 *Zuckerbaby* **1985 (R)** An acclaimed German film about a fat mortuary attendant living in Munich who transforms herself (but doesn't lose weight) in order to seduce a young, handsome subway conductor. Touching and warm film that introduced Sagebrecht to American audiences. A bit too cutting-edge cinematographically. In German with English subtitles. Remade as "Babycakes." Sagebrecht and director Adlon team up again for "Bagdad Cafe" and "Rosalie Goes Shopping." **103m/C VHS, Beta.** *GE* Marianne Saegebrecht, Eisi Gulp, Toni Berger, Will Spendler, Manuela Denz; **D:** Percy Adlon; **W:** Percy Adlon. *ORI, GLV, APD*

The Sugarland Express 𝒵𝒵𝒵 **1974 (PG)** To save her son from adoption, a young woman helps her husband break out of prison. In their flight to freedom, they hijack a police car, holding the policeman hostage. Speilberg's first feature film is a moving portrait of a couple's desperation. Based on a true story, adapted by Hal Barwood and Matthew Robbins. **109m/C VHS, Beta, LV.** Goldie Hawn, Ben Johnson, Michael Sacks, William Atherton; **D:** Steven Spielberg; **W:** Steven Spielberg, Matthew Robbins, Hal Barwood; **C:** Vilmos Zsigmond; **M:** John Williams. *USH*

Sugartime 𝒵𝒵½ **1995 (R)** Based on the true-life romance of '60s Chicago mobster Sam Giacana (Turturro) and song bird Phyllis Maguire (Parker), one of the wholesome Maguire Sisters. Naturally, getting involved with a crime boss did little for her image and Maguire's career hit the skids while Giacana's volatile jealousy brought unwanted attention from both fellow gangsters and the feds. (He was murdered in 1975 but had broken off with Phyllis before that). The real Maguire denounced the inaccuracy of the TV production. Suggested by William F. Roemer, Jr.'s book "Roemer: Man Against the Mob."**CW:** Violence, language, and sexuality. **108m/C VHS.** John Turturro, Mary-Louise Parker, Elias Koteas, Maury Chaykin, Louis Del Grande, Christopher Barry, Richard Blackburn; **D:** John N. Smith; **W:** Martyn Burke; **C:** Pierre Letarte. *HBO*

Suicide Battalion/Hell Squad 𝒵𝒵 **1958** A war movie double feature. In "Suicide Battalion," American troops must sneak through enemy territory to destroy a captured American command outpost in the Philippines during WWII. Five American soldiers are lost in the North African desert in "Hell Squad." After a series of fights with various enemies, one soldier survives, only to nearly be doublecrossed by a Nazi he meets in the desert. **150m/B VHS.** Mike Connors, John Ashley, Russ Bender, Jewell Lain, Bing Russell, Wally Campo, Brandon Carroll, Frederic Galvin; **D:** Edward L. Cahn, Burt Topper; **W:** Burt Topper. *COL*

Suicide Cult woof! **1977** A CIA employee predicts the second coming of Christ, and a battle ensues between the forces of good and evil for possession of the child. **82m/C VHS, Beta.** *NO*

Suicide Patrol 𝒵 **197?** A small band of saboteurs patrols a German-controlled Mediterranean island during WWII. **90m/C VHS, Beta.** Gordon Mitchell, Pierre Richard, Max Dean. *UNI, MOV*

Suite 16 𝒵𝒵 **1994 (R)** A penthouse suite in a French Riviera hotel is occupied by rich, manipulative, wheelchair-bound Glover (Postlethwaite). Young gigolo/thief Chris (Kamerling), who believes he's killed his latest trick, is given refuge by Glover in exchange for allowing the aging voyeur to watch Chris (via camera) perform with a suc-

cession of prostitutes. Finally, Chris wants to leave but Glover offers him a huge amount of money for one final vicarious—and deadly—thrill. Eurotrash, with corny dialogue, but Postlethwaite's chillingly creepy. Also available in an R-rated version.*CW:* Strong sexuality and language, and for some violence and drug use. **93m/C VHS.** *BE GB* Pete Postlethwaite, Antoine Kamerling, Geraldine Pailhas, Tom Jansen; **D:** Dominique Deruddere; **W:** Charles Higson, Lise Mayer; **C:** Jean-Francois Robin; **M:** Walter Hus. *APX*

The Suitors 𝒵 **1988** When a group of Iranians decide to sacrifice a lamb in their apartment, the New York police send in SWAT team assuming they're terrorists. First time effort by Ebrahimian, in Farsi with English subtitles. **106m/C VHS.** **D:** Ghasem Ebrahimian. *FCT*

Sullivan's Travels 𝒵𝒵𝒵 **1941** Sturges' masterpiece is a sardonic, whip-quick romp about a Hollywood director tired of making comedies who decides to make a serious, socially responsible film and hits the road masquerading as a hobo in order to know hardship and poverty. Beautifully sustained, inspired satire that mercilessly mocked the ambitions of Depression-era social cinema. Gets a little over-dark near the end before the happy ending; Sturges insisted on 20-year-old Lake as The Girl; her pregnancy forced him to rewrite scenes and design new costumes for her. As ever, she is stunning. **90m/B VHS, LV.** Joel McCrea, Veronica Lake, William Demarest, Robert Warwick, Franklin Pangborn, Porter Hall, Eric Blore, Byron Foulger, Robert Greig, Torben Meyer, Jimmy Conlin, Margaret Hayes, Chester Conklin, Alan Bridge; **D:** Preston Sturges; **W:** Preston Sturges. National Board of Review Awards '42: 10 Best Films of the Year. *USH*

The Sum of Us 𝒵𝒵𝒵 **1994 (R)** Sweet and faithful adaptation of David Stevens' stage play about a father and his gay son. Widowed Harry Mitchell (Thompson) shares his house with son Jeff (Crowe), who's never made a secret of his sexual orientation. Affable Harry only wants what's best for his boy, including his over-enthusiastic welcome to Jeff's potential new boyfriend (Polson). Too bad Harry's not so lucky in love—his new woman friend Joyce (Kennedy) has problems with Jeff's sexuality. Well, she just has to adjust. Pervasive feel-good message may leave less well-adjusted viewer addled. Sensitive performances, though the film's antecedents as a play are highlighted by having the main characters talk directly to the camera. Aussie slang provides a challenge.*CW:* Much sex-related dialogue; brief flash of nudity. **99m/C VHS.** *AU* Jack Thompson, Russell Crowe, John Polson, Deborah Kennedy, Mitch Mathews, Julie Herbert, Joss Moroney, Rebekah Elmaloglou; **D:** Kevin Dowling, Geoff Burton; **W:** David Stevens; **C:** Geoff Burton; **M:** Dave Faulkner. Australian Film Institute '94: Best Adapted Screenplay; Montreal World Film Festival '94: Best Screenplay; Nominations: Australian Film Institute '94: Best Film, Best Supporting Actor (Polson), Best Supporting Actress (Kennedy). *HMK*

Summer 𝒵𝒵𝒵½ *Le Rayon Vert; The Green Ray* **1986 (R)** The fifth and among the best of Rohmer's "Comedies and Proverbs" series. A romantic but glum young French girl finds herself stuck in Paris during the tourist season searching for true romantic love. Takes time and patience to seize the viewer; moving ending makes it all worthwhile. In French with English subtitles. **90m/C VHS, Beta, LV.** *FR* Marie Riviere, Lisa Heredia, Beatrice Romand, Eric Hamm, Rosette, Isabelle Riviere; **D:** Eric Rohmer; **W:** Eric Rohmer. *FCT, TPV*

Summer Affair 𝒵½ **1979** Two young lovers run away from their bickering parents and get shipwrecked on a desert island. **90m/C VHS, Beta.** *IT* Ornella Muti, Les Rannow; **D:** George S. Casorati. *NO*

Summer and Smoke 𝒵𝒵½ **1961** Repressed, unhappy belle falls for handsome doctor Harvey. A tour de force for Page, but that's all; adapted clumsily from the overwrought Tennessee Williams play. **118m/C VHS, Beta, LV, Closed Caption.** Laurence Harvey, Geraldine Page, Rita Moreno,

Una Merkel, John McIntire, Thomas Gomez, Pamela Tiffin, Lee Patrick, Max Casey Adams Showalter, Earl Holliman, Harry Shannon, Pattee Chapman; *D:* Peter Glenville; *C:* Charles B(ryant) Lang; *M:* Elmer Bernstein. Golden Globe Awards '62: Best Actress—Drama (Page); National Board of Review Awards '61: Best Actress (Page); Nominations: Academy Awards '61: Best Actress (Page), Best Art Direction/Set Decoration (Color), Best Supporting Actress (Merkel), Original Dramatic/Comedy Score. *PAR, FCT*

Summer Camp Nightmare 🎬½ *The Butterfly Revolution* 1986 (PG-13) See "Lord of the Flies" instead. A young fascist incites children at two summer camps to overthrow and imprison the adults. Barbarism rears its ugly head. Self-serious and anticlimatic. Based on the novel "The Butterfly Revolution" by William Butler. 89m/C VHS, Beta, LV, Closed Caption. Chuck Connors, Charles Stratton, Harold Pruett, Tom Fridley, Adam Carl; *D:* Bert L. Dragin; *C:* Don Burgess. *NLC*

Summer City 🎬½ *Coast of Terror* 1977 Fun-and-sun surfing movie complete with romance, hot rods, murder and great shots of the sea features Gibson in his debut. Ever wonder what Australian surf bums do on weekends? The same as their California counterparts—except they talk funny. 83m/C VHS, Beta. *AU* Mel Gibson, Phillip Avalon, John Jarratt, Christopher Fraser. *VCD*

Summer Fantasy 🎬 1984 Mindless TV surf saga about a curvy teen who would rather watch the beach hunks then go to medical school. 96m/C VHS, Beta. Julianne Phillips, Ted Shackleford, Michael Gross, Dorothy Lyman; *D:* Noel Nosseck; *M:* Peter Bernstein. *NO*

Summer Heat 🎬½ 1987 (R) In rural, mid-Depression North Carolina, a young, lonely wife and mother is seduced by a drifter and together they plot murder. Her husband neglects her, and you should neglect to see this utter yawner. Based on a Louise Shivers novel. 80m/C VHS, Beta, LV. Lori Singer, Anthony Edwards, Bruce Abbott, Kathy Bates; *D:* Michie Gleason; *C:* Elliot Davis. *PAR*

Summer Holiday 🎬🎬½ 1948 Rooney comes of age with a vengeance during summer vacation in musical rendition of "Ah, Wilderness." Undistinguished musical numbers, inferior to the original, but jazzy Technicolor cinematography. Ended up in the red by over $1.5 million, lotsa money back then. ♪It's Our Home Town; Afraid to Fall in Love; All Hail, Danville High; The Stanley Steamer; It's Independence Day; I Think You're the Sweetest Kid I've Ever Known; Weary Blues. 92m/C VHS. Mickey Rooney, Gloria De Haven, Walter Huston, Frank Morgan, Jackie "Butch" Jenkins, Marilyn Maxwell, Agnes Moorehead, Selena Royle, Anne Francis; *D:* Rouben Mamoulian. *MGM, TTC, FCT*

The Summer House 🎬🎬½ 1994 Comedy of manners set in 1959 England about the manipulations of three middle-aged women (Moreau, Plowright, Walters) over the impending marriage of one's dreamy young daughter (Headey) to a dolt (Threlfall). Moreau stirs things up as the spirited and skeptical friend of Walters, the deluded bride's mother whom she must interrupt from her busy nuptial preparations and somehow communicate the obvious. Plowright is perfectly cast as the gimlet-eyed groom's mother, well aware of her son's flaws, who achieves an odd alliance with polar opposite Moreau. Strong performances from all the veterans carry the day. Based on the novel by Alice Thomas Ellis. 85m/C VHS. *GB* Jeanne Moreau, Joan Plowright, Julie Walters, Lena Headey, David Threlfall, Padraig Casey, Britta Smith, John Wood; *D:* Waris Hussein; *W:* Martin Sherman; *M:* Stanley Myers. *HMK*

Summer Interlude 🎬🎬🎬½ *Illicit Interlude; Summerplay; Sommarlek* 1950 A ballerina recalls a romantic summer spent with an innocent boy, who was later tragically killed. Contains many earmarks and visual ideas of later Bergman masterpieces. In Swedish with English subtitles. 95m/B VHS, Beta. *SW* Maj-Britt Nilsson, Birger Malmsten, Alf Kjellin; *D:* Ingmar Bergman; *W:* Ingmar Bergman. *HMV, NLC*

Summer Lovers 🎬 1982 (R) Summer vacation finds young couple traveling to the exotic Greek island of Santorini. They meet up with a fun-loving woman and discover three-way sexual tension, but little in the way of plot, dialogue, or acting. From the director of "Grease" and "Blue Lagoon" and best watched late at night while half conscious. 98m/C VHS, Beta, LV. Peter Gallagher, Daryl Hannah, Valerie Quennessen; *D:* Randal Kleiser; *M:* Basil Poledouris. *COL*

Summer Magic 🎬🎬 1963 An impecunious recent widow is forced to leave Boston and settle her family in a small town in Maine. Typical, forgettable Disney drama; early Mills vehicle. A remake of "Mother Carey's Chickens." 116m/C VHS, Beta. Hayley Mills, Burl Ives, Dorothy McGuire, Deborah Walley, Una Merkel, Eddie Hodges; *D:* James Neilson; *M:* Buddy Baker. *DIS*

Summer Night 🎬🎬 1987 (R) A female tycoon who is concerned for the environment decides to strike out at the terrorists who are destroying it. This caper turns into one big comedy. In Italian with English subtitles. 94m/C VHS, Beta. *IT* Mariangela Melato, Michele Placido, Roberto Herlitzka, Massimo Wertmuller; *D:* Lina Wertmuller. *LIV*

Summer Night with Greek Profile, Almond Eyes & Scent of Basil 🎬🎬 1987 (R) A wealthy woman tycoon hires an ex-CIA man to kidnap a high-priced, professional terrorist and hold him for ransom. An ironic battle of the sexes follows. In Italian with English subtitles. 94m/C VHS, Beta. *IT* Mariangela Melato, Michele Placido, Roberto Herlitzka; *D:* Lina Wertmuller; *W:* Lina Wertmuller. *TPV*

The Summer of Aviya 🎬🎬 *Kayitz Shel Aviya* 1988 Ten-year-old Aviya has spent most of her life in orphanages as her partisan Jewish mother fought the Nazis. Now, Aviya faces the prospect of returning to a home and woman she doesn't really know, one who is also balanced on the edge of madness. Based on the memoirs of Almagor. Hebrew with subtitles. Followed by "Under the Domim Tree." ?m/C VHS. *IS* Kaipo Cohen, Gila Almagor; *D:* Eli Cohen; *W:* Gila Almagor. *FCT*

The Summer of Ben Tyler 🎬🎬½ 1996 (PG) Temple Rayburn (Woods) is an up-and-coming lawyer in a small southern town in 1942 and the protege of influential Spencer Maitland (Cariou). Before his family's black housekeeper dies, Rayburn agrees to take in her mentally handicapped teenaged son, Ben (Mattocks), to the dismay of the white community. Then Maitland insists Rayburn defend his son Junius (Isola) against a drunk driving charge where a woman was killed. TV movie. 134m/C VHS, Closed Caption. James Woods, Len Cariou, Elizabeth McGovern, Charles Mattocks, Kevin Isola, Julia McIlvaine, Clifton James; *D:* Arthur Allan Seidelman; *W:* Robert Inman; *C:* Neil Roach; *M:* Van Dyke Parks. *HMK*

Summer of Fear 🎬🎬 *Stranger in Our House; Stranger with My Face* 1978 A happy young woman must overcome evil forces when her cousin comes to live with her family. Based on a novel by Lois Duncan. Pretty scary if ordinary, dumb made-for-TV horror from later-famous Craven. 94m/C VHS, Beta. Linda Blair; *D:* Wes Craven. *NO*

Summer of '42 🎬🎬🎬 1971 (R) Touching if sentimental story about a 15-year-old boy's sexual coming of age during his summer vacation on an island off New England. While his friends are fumbling with girls their own age, he falls in love with a beautiful 22-year-old woman whose husband is off fighting in the war. 102m/C VHS, Beta, LV, Closed Caption. Jennifer O'Neill, Gary Grimes, Jerry Houser, Oliver Conant; *D:* Robert Mulligan; *C:* Robert L. Surtees. Academy Awards '71: Original Dramatic/Comedy Score; Nominations: Academy Awards '71: Best Cinematography, Best Film Editing, Best Story & Screenplay. *WAR*

The Summer of Miss Forbes 🎬🎬 *El Verano de la Senora Forbes* 1988 A governess rules over two young boys with an iron hand by day and cavorts nude and drunk by night. The boys fanta-

size about her murder, but fate has different plans. In Spanish with English subtitles. 85m/C VHS, LV. *SP* Hanna Schygulla, Alexis Castanares, Victor Cesar Villalobos, Guadalupe Sandoval, Fernando Balzaretti, Yuriria Munguia; *D:* Jaime Humberto Hermosillo. *FXL, FCT*

The Summer of My German Soldier 🎬🎬🎬 1978 A young Jewish girl befriends an escaped German prisoner of war in a small town in Georgia during WWII. Occasionally sentimental but more often genuinely moving made for TV drama. Rolle won a deserved Emmy. Adapted from Bette Green's novel. 98m/C VHS, Beta. Kristy McNichol, Esther Rolle, Bruce Davison; *D:* Michael Tuchner. *MTI*

A Summer Place 🎬🎬 1959 Melodrama about summer liaisons amid the young and middle-aged rich on an island off the coast of Maine. Too slick; romantic drama is little more than skin-deep, and dialogue is excruciating. Donahue's first starring role. Based on the novel by Sloan Wilson. Featuring "Theme from a Summer Place," which was a number-one hit in 1959. 130m/C VHS, Beta, LV. Troy Donahue, Richard Egan, Sandra Dee, Dorothy McGuire, Arthur Kennedy, Constance Ford, Beulah Bondi; *D:* Delmer Daves; *C:* Harry Stradling; *M:* Max Steiner. *WAR*

Summer Rental 🎬🎬 1985 (PG) That John Candy just can't win, can he? Here, as a hopeless, harried air traffic controller, he tries to have a few days to relax in sunny Florida. Enter mean rich guy Crenna. Candy can add something hefty to the limpest of plots, and does so here. Watch the first hour for yuks, then rewind. 87m/C VHS, Beta, LV, 8mm, Closed Caption. John Candy, Rip Torn, Richard Crenna, Karen Austin, Kerri Green, John Larroquette, Pierrino Mascarino; *D:* Carl Reiner; *M:* Alan Silvestri. *PAR*

Summer School 🎬 1977 (R) A teenaged boy's girlfriend will stop at nothing to prevent him from going out with the pretty new girl in town. 80m/C VHS, Beta. John McLaughlin, Steve Rose, Phoebe Schmidt. *AHV*

Summer School 🎬🎬½ 1987 (PG-13) A high-school teacher's vacation plans are ruined when he gets stuck teaching remedial English in summer school. It seems all these students are interested in is re-enacting scenes from "The Texas Chainsaw Massacre." Actually, one of the better films of this genre. 98m/C VHS, Beta, LV, Closed Caption. Mark Harmon, Kirstie Alley, Nels Van Patten, Courtney Thorne-Smith, Lucy Lee Flippin, Shawnee Smith, Robin Thomas, Dean Cameron; *D:* Carl Reiner; *W:* Jeff Franklin; *M:* Danny Elfman. *PAR*

Summer School Teachers woof! 1975 (R) Three sultry femmes bounce about Los Angeles high school and make the collective student body happy. Typical Corman doings; sequel to "The Students Teachers." 87m/C VHS, Beta. Candice Rialson, Pat Anderson, Rhonda Leigh Hopkins, Christopher Wales; *D:* Barbara Peeters. *NLC*

Summer Snow 🎬🎬 *Nuiyan, Seisap; Woman, Forty* 1994 Broad comedy mixed (not always successfully) with family drama. May (Siao) is forced to take in her father-in-law Sun (Chiao) after his wife dies. The old man immediately causes chaos with his habit of wandering off and bizarre behavior, which is finally diagnosed as being Alzheimer's disease. Working mother May tries to find a practical way to deal with her dilemmas but the strains are beginning to crack the family apart. Cantonese with subtitles. 106m/C VHS. *HK* Josephine Siao, Roy Chiao, Law Kar-ying, Allen Ting; *D:* Ann Hui; *W:* Chan Man-keung; *C:* Lee Ping-bing; *M:* Yoshihide Otomo. Berlin International Film Festival '94: Best Actress (Siao).*NYR*

Summer Solstice 🎬🎬½ 1981 Fonda and Loy are splendid as a couple married half a century who revisit the beach where they first met. Fonda especially shines, as a crusty old artist. Yes, it is an awful lot like "On Golden Pond." Made for

TV. 75m/C VHS, Beta. Henry Fonda, Myrna Loy, Lindsay Crouse, Stephen Collins; **D:** Ralph Rosenblum. *MTI*

Summer Stock 🎬🎬🎬 *If You Feel Like Singing* 1950 Garland plays a farm owner whose sister arrives with a summer stock troupe, led by Kelly, to rehearse a show in the family barn. Garland agrees, if the troupe will help her with the farm's harvest. When her sister decamps for New York, leaving the leading lady role open, guess who steps into the breach. Slim plot papered over with many fun song-and-dance numbers. Also features Garland's first MGM short, "Every Sunday," made in 1936 with Deanna Durbin. ♫Friendly Star; Mem'ry Island; Dig-Dig-Dig For Your Dinner; If You Feel Like Singing, Sing; Howdy Neighbor; Blue Jean Polka; Portland Fancy; You, Wonderful You; Get Happy. **109m/C VHS, Beta, LV.** Judy Garland, Gene Kelly, Gloria De Haven, Carleton Carpenter, Eddie Bracken, Phil Silvers, Hans Conried, Marjorie Main, Ray Collins, Deanna Durbin; **D:** Charles Walters. *MGM, TTC*

A Summer Story 🎬🎬🎬 1988 (PG-13) Superbly acted, typically British period drama about beautiful farm girl Stubbs and city lawyer Wilby, who fall in love. But can they overcome difference of social class? From the story "The Apple Tree" by John Galsworthy. **97m/C VHS, Beta, Closed Caption.** GB James Wilby, Imogen Stubbs, Susannah York, Sophie Ward, Kenneth Colley, Jerome Flynn; **D:** Piers Haggard; **W:** Penelope Mortimer; **M:** Georges Delerue. *MED*

A Summer to Remember 🎬🎬🎬 *Seryozha* 1961 A five-year-old boy spends a summer with his stepfather on a Soviet collective farm. The two become deeply attached. Scenes of collective life will be of more interest to Westerners than the near-sentimental story. Star Bondarchuk later directed the epic, award-winning "War and Peace." **80m/B VHS, Beta.** RU Borya Barkhazov, Sergei Bondarchuk, Irana Skobtseva. National Board of Review Awards '61: 5 Best Foreign Films of the Year. *NO*

A Summer to Remember 🎬🎬½ 1984 (PG) A deaf boy (played by Gerlis, himself deaf since birth) develops a friendship with an orangutan through sign language. Bad guys abduct the friendly ape - but all is right in the end. Nice, innocuous family viewing. Based on a story by Scott Swanton and Robert Lloyd Lewis. **93m/C VHS, Beta, Closed Caption.** Tess Harper, James Farentino, Burt Young, Louise Fletcher, Sean Gerlis, Bridgette Anderson; **D:** Robert Lewis; **M:** Charles Fox. *USH*

Summer Vacation: 1999 🎬🎬 *1999 - Nen No Natsu Yasumi* 1988 Four boys are left behind at boarding school during their summer vacation. They experience all the early pangs of adolescence from love to jealousy. Their summer is then disturbed by the arrival of another boy who appears to be the reincarnation of a dead friend. Romantic look at youth caught between innocence and awareness. In Japanese with English subtitles. **90m/C VHS, Beta.** JP Eri Miyagima, Miyuki Nakano, Tomoko Otakra, Rie Mizuhara; **D:** Shusuke Kaneko. *NYF, FCT*

Summer Wishes, Winter Dreams 🎬🎬 1973 (PG) Woodward and Balsam are a materially prosperous middle-aged couple with little but tedium in their lives—a tedium accurately replicated, in what feels like real life, in this slow, dull film. The two leads and Sidney—in her first screen role in 17 years—are all excellent, but the story of regret and present unhappiness wears the viewer down. **95m/C VHS, Beta.** Joanne Woodward, Martin Balsam, Sylvia Sidney, Dori Brenner, Ron Richards; **D:** Gilbert Cates; **W:** Stewart Stern. British Academy Awards '74: Best Actress (Woodward); National Board of Review Awards '73: Best Supporting Actress (Sidney); New York Film Critics Awards '73: Best Actress (Woodward); Nominations: Academy Awards '73: Best Actress (Woodward), Best Supporting Actress (Sidney). *COL*

Summerdog 🎬🎬 1978 (G) Harmless family tale about vacationers who rescue a cheerful, lovable mutt named Hobo. And a good thing they found him: He saves them from many perils.

Thanks, Hobo! **90m/C VHS, Beta.** James Congdon, Elizabeth Eisenman, Oliver Zabriskie, Tavia Zabriskie; **D:** John Clayton. *GEM*

Summer's Children 🎬 1984 Man who suffers from amnesia as a result of a car crash becomes the target of a mysterious killer. Forget about it. **90m/C VHS, Beta.** Tom Haoff, Pauly Jardine, Kate Lynch. *TWE*

Summertime 🎬🎬🎬½ *Summer Madness* 1955 Spinster Hepburn vacations in Venice and falls in love with Brazzi. She is hurt when inadvertently she learns he is married, but her life has been so bleak she is not about to end her one great romance. Moving, funny, richly photographed in a beautiful Old World city. From Arthur Laurents' play "The Time of the Cuckoo." **98m/C VHS, Beta, LV.** Katharine Hepburn, Rossano Brazzi; **D:** David Lean; **C:** Jack Hildyard. National Board of Review Awards '55: 10 Best Films of the Year; New York Film Critics Awards '55: Best Director (Lean); Nominations: Academy Awards '55: Best Actress (Hepburn), Best Director (Lean). *CRC, NLC, HMV*

Summertree 🎬🎬 1971 (PG) Douglas stars as a young musician in the 1960s trying to avoid the draft and the wrath of his parents. Contrived and heavy-handed. Produced by Douglas pere, Kirk. Adapted from the play by Ron Cower. **88m/C VHS, Beta.** Michael Douglas, Jack Warden, Brenda Vaccaro, Barbara Bel Geddes, Kirk Calloway, Bill Vint; **D:** Anthony Newley; **M:** David Shire. *WAR, OM*

The Sun Comes Up 🎬🎬 1949 MacDonald, in her last screen appearance, plays a bitter widow whose life is changed by an orphan's love for a collie. Songbird MacDonald manages to sing a number of songs, some of them backed by a chorus of "orphans." Based on short stories by Marjorie Kinnan Rawlings. **93m/C VHS, Beta.** Jeanette MacDonald, Lloyd Nolan, Claude Jarman Jr., Lewis Stone, Dwayne Hickman; **D:** Richard Thorpe; **W:** William Ludwig; **M:** Andre Previn. *MGM, FCT*

Sun Ra & His Intergalactic Solar Arkestra: Space Is the Place 🎬🎬 1974 Space age flick starring most appropriately Sun Ra, space-age prophet/jazz musician. Sun Ra returns from a space odyssey and embarks on saving black youth from the world's oppressive control by bringing them back into space with him. The shaman's philosophy on film. ♫Watusi; Outer Spaceways Inc.; The Satellites are Spinning. **63m/C VHS. D:** John Coney; **W:** Joshua Smith. *RHP*

The Sun Shines Bright 🎬🎬 1953 Heavily stereotyped, contrived tale of a Southern judge with a heart of gold who does so many good deeds (defending a black man accused of rape; helping a desperate prostitute) that he jeopardizes his re-election. Set during Reconstruction. An unfortunate remake of Ford's own 1934 "Judge Priest," starring Will Rogers. **92m/B VHS.** Charles Winninger, Arleen Whelan, John Russell, Stepin Fetchit, Milburn Stone, Russell Simpson; **D:** John Ford; **C:** Archie Stout. *REP*

Sun Valley Serenade 🎬🎬½ 1941 Wartime musical fluff about a band that adopts a Norwegian refugee waif as a publicity stunt. She turns out to be a full-grown man-chaser who stirs up things at a ski resort. Fun, but it ends abruptly—because, they say, Henie fell during the huge skating finale, and Darryl Zanuck wouldn't greenlight a reshoot. One of only two feature appearances by Glenn Miller and his Orchestra (the other was "Orchestra Wives"), on video with a soundtrack restored from original dual-track recordings. ♫Chattanooga Choo Choo; I Know Why and So Do You; It Happened In Sun Valley; The Kiss Polka; In the Mood. **86m/C VHS, Closed Caption.** Sonja Henie, John Payne, Glenn Miller, Milton Berle, Lynn Bari, Joan Davis, Dorothy Dandridge; **D:** H. Bruce Humberstone. Nominations: Academy Awards '41: Best Black and White Cinematography, Best Song ("Chattanooga Choo Choo"), Scoring of a Musical. *FXV, FCT, MLB*

Sunburn 🎬½ 1979 (PG) Insurance investigator Grodin hires model Fawcett to pretend to be his wife to get the scoop on a suicide/murder case of a rich guy in Acapulco. Made-for-TV drivel. **110m/C VHS, Beta.** Farrah Fawcett, Charles Grodin, Joan Collins, Art Carney, William Daniels; **D:** Richard Sarafian; **W:** James Booth. *PAR*

Sunchaser 🎬½ 1996 (R) Mishmash of medicine and mysticism focuses on yuppie UCLA oncologist Dr. Michael Reynolds (Harrelson) who's kidnapped by 16-year-old patient, Brandon "Blue" Monroe (Seda). Blue is a half-Navajo gangbanger whose cancer is inoperable and he needs the doc to drive him to a reservation in Arizona where he feels a medicine man and the waters of a supposedly magical lake can cure him. Reynolds naturally discovers some humanity on the trip and decides to help his truculent patient. Leads give sincere performances but film is half-baked at best. **CW:** Strong language and some violence. **123m/C VHS, Closed Caption.** Woody Harrelson, Jon Seda, Anne Bancroft, Alexandra Tydings, Matt Mulhern, Talisa Soto, Lawrence Pressman, Michael O'Neill, Harry Carey Jr.; **D:** Michael Cimino; **W:** Charles Leavitt; **C:** Doug Milsome; **M:** Maurice Jarre. *WAR*

Sundance and the Kid 🎬🎬 1976 (PG) Two brothers try to collect an inheritance against all odds. Originally known as "Sundance Cassidy and Butch the Kid." **84m/C VHS, Beta.** John Wade, Karen Blake; **D:** Arthur Pitt. *NO*

Sunday 🎬🎬 1996 Basically a two-character study of mistaken identity among lonely, middle-aged people. On a winter's Sunday morning in Queens, depressed Oliver (Suchet) is greeted by failing British actress Madeleine (Harrow), who mistakes him for a director she once met. She invites him to lunch and Oliver, who's actually a homeless former accountant, struggles to maintain the charade. The unstable Madeleine's bitter when she discovers his deception but is also unwillingly to let the connection between them die. **93m/C VHS.** David Suchet, Lisa Harrow, Larry Pine, Jared Harris, Joe Grifasi; **D:** Jonathan Nossiter; **W:** Jonathan Nossiter, James Lasdun; **C:** Michael Barrow, John Foster; **M:** Jonathan Nossiter. Sundance Film Festival '97: Best Screenplay, Grand Jury Prize. *NYR*

Sunday, Bloody Sunday 🎬🎬🎬 1971 (R) Adult drama centers around the intertwined love affairs of the homosexual Finch, the heterosexual Jackson, and self-centered bisexual artist Head, desired by both. Fully-drawn characters brought to life by excellent acting make this difficult story well worth watching—though Head's central character is sadly rather dull. Day-Lewis makes his first (brief) screen appearance as a car vandalizing teenager. Powerful, sincere and sensitive. **110m/C VHS, LV.** GB GB Glenda Jackson, Peter Finch, Murray Head, Daniel Day-Lewis; **D:** John Schlesinger. British Academy Awards '71: Best Actor (Finch), Best Actress (Jackson), Best Director (Schlesinger), Best Film; Golden Globe Awards '72: Best Foreign Film; New York Film Critics Awards '71: Best Screenplay; National Society of Film Critics Awards '71: Best Actor (Finch), Best Screenplay; Writers Guild of America '71: Best Original Screenplay; Nominations: Academy Awards '71: Best Actor (Finch), Best Actress (Jackson), Best Director (Schlesinger), Best Story & Screenplay. *FOX*

Sunday Daughters 🎬🎬🎬 1980 A teenage girl kept in a detention home constantly tries to escape and find some kind of familial love. Stronge performances mix with keen direction. In Hungarian with English subtitles. **100m/C VHS, Beta.** HU Julianna Nyako; **D:** Janosz Rozsa. *FCT*

A Sunday in the Country 🎬🎬🎬½ *Un Dimanche a la Campagne* 1984 (G) A lush, distinctively French affirmation of nature and family life. This character study with a minimal plot takes place during a single summer day in 1910 France. An elderly impressionist painter-patriarch is visited at his country home by his family. Highly acclaimed, though the pace may be too slow for some. Beautiful location photography. In French with English subtitles. **94m/C VHS, Beta.** FR Louis Ducreux, Sabine Azema, Michel Aumont; **D:** Bertrand Taverni-er; **W:** Bertrand Tavernier, Colo Tavernier O'Hagan; **C:** Bru-no de Keyzer. Cannes Film Festival '84: Best Director (Tav-ernier); Cesar Awards '85: Best Actress (Azema), Best Cin-ematography, Best Writing; National Board of Review Awards '84: Best Supporting Actress (Azema); New York Film Critics Awards '84: Best Foreign Film. *MGM*

Sunday in the Park with George 🎬🎬🎬 1986
Taped theatrical perfor-mance of the Tony, Grammy, and Pulitzer Prize-winning musical play, which is based upon im-pressionist Georges Seurat's painting "A Sunday Afternoon on the Island of Grande Jatte." Fea-tures a celebrated music score by Sondheim. 120m/C VHS, Beta, LV. Mandy Patinkin, Bernadette Pe-ters, Barbara Byrne, Charles Kimbrough; **D:** James Lapine; **M:** Stephen Sondheim. *ORI, WAR*

Sunday Too Far Away 🎬🎬🎬 1974
The rivalries between Australian sheep shearers and graziers leads to an ugly strike at a remote outback area in 1955. An uncomplicated story and a joy to watch. 100m/C VHS, Beta. *AU* Jack Thompson; **D:** Ken Hannam. Australian Film Institute '74: Best Actor (Thompson), Best Film.

Sundays & Cybele 🎬🎬🎬½ 1962
Les Di-manches de Ville d'Arvay; Cybele A ragged war veteran and an orphaned girl develop a strong emotional relationship, which is frowned upon by the townspeople. Warm and touching. In French with English subtitles. Also available in a letter-boxed edition. 110m/B VHS, Beta. *FR* Hardy Kruger, Nicole Courcel; **D:** Serge Bourguignon; **M:** Maurice Jarre. Academy Awards '62: Best Foreign Language Film; Nation-al Board of Review Awards '62: 5 Best Foreign Films of the Year; Nominations: Academy Awards '63: Best Adapted Score, Best Adapted Screenplay. *NYF, HHT, DVT*

Sunday's Children 🎬🎬🎬½ 1994
Lyrical exploration of childhood continues trilogy that in-cludes "Fanny and Alexander" and "Best Inten-tions." Wistful childhood memoir takes up the sto-ry of Ingmar Bergman's family eight years after the director was born. Many of the same familial issues surface, but story soon narrows its focus to the relationship between little Ingmar, whom ev-eryone calls Pu, and his stern father Henrik. Deeply emotional and intense, film represents the steps toward forgiveness that the elder Bergman is finally able to take regarding the painful rela-tionship he had with his own father. Father-son theme made more poignant with Ingmar's son Daniel making his feature debut as director. 118m/C VHS. *SW* Thommy Berggren, Lena Endre, Henrik Linn-ros, Jacob Leygraf, Maria Bolme, Bjorje Ahistedt, Per Myr-berg; **D:** Daniel Bergman; **W:** Ingmar Bergman. *FRF*

Sundown 🎬🎬½ 1941
In Africa at the begin-ning of WWII, a local girl aids the British against a German plot to run guns to the natives and start a rebellion. Engaging performances and efficient di-rection keep it above the usual cliches. Also avail-able in a colorized version. 91m/B VHS, Beta. Gene Tierney, Bruce Cabot, George Sanders, Harry Carey Sr., Cedric Hardwicke, Joseph Calleia, Dorothy Dandridge, Re-ginald Gardiner; **D:** Henry Hathaway; **C:** Charles B(ryant) Lang; **M:** Miklos Rozsa. Nominations: Academy Awards '41: Best Black and White Cinematography, Best Interior Deco-ration, Original Dramatic/Comedy Score. *NOS, VYY, DVT*

Sundown 🎬½ 1991 (R)
An ambitious shot at a vampire western fails because it drains almost all vampire lore and winds up resembling a stan-dard oater. Carradine plays a reformed vampire king (guess who) running a desert clinic that weans bloodsuckers away from preying on hu-mans. But undead renegades attack using six-guns and wooden bullets. The climax may out-rage horror purists. 104m/C VHS. David Carradine, Bruce Campbell, Deborah Foreman, Maxwell Caulfield, Morgan Brittany; **D:** Anthony Hickox. *VES*

Sundown Fury 🎬 1942
Young cowboy fights against a group of bandits to hold a tele-graph office. 56m/B VHS, Beta. Donald (Don "Red") Bar-ry. *VCN*

Sundown Kid 🎬½ 1943
A Pinkerton agent goes undercover to break up a counterfeiting op-eration. Routine western. 55m/B VHS, Beta. Donald (Don "Red") Barry. *DVT*

Sundown Riders 🎬 1948
Cowhands are victimized by noose-happy outlaws. Filmed in just over a week on a $30,000 budget and originally shot on 16mm to make it accessible to hospitals and schools with basic viewing equipment. The lesson here: it takes time and money to make a good western. 56m/B VHS, Beta, LV. Russell Wade, Andy Clyde, Jay Kirby; **D:** Lambert Hillyer. *NO*

Sundown Saunders 🎬 1936
A standard oater about a cowboy whose prize for winning a horse race is a ranch. Trouble is, an outlaw wants the homestead as well. 64m/B VHS, Beta. Bob Steele; **D:** Robert North Bradbury. *NOS, VYY, HEG*

The Sundowners 🎬🎬🎬½ 1960
Slow, beautiful, and often moving epic drama about a family of Irish sheepherders in Australia during the 1920s who must continually uproot them-selves and migrate. They struggle to save enough money to buy their own farm and wind up training a horse they hope will be a money-winner in rac-ing. Well-acted by all, with Johns and Ustinov pro-viding some humorous moments. Adapted from the novel by Jon Cleary. Filmed in Australia and London studios. 133m/C VHS, Beta, LV. Deborah Kerr, Robert Mitchum, Peter Ustinov, Glynis Johns, Dina Merrill, Chips Rafferty, Michael Anderson Jr., Lola Brooks, Wylie Watson; **D:** Fred Zinnemann; **C:** Jack Hildyard; **M:** Dimitri Tiomkin. National Board of Review Awards '60: 10 Best Films of the Year, Best Actor (Mitchum); New York Film Critics Awards '60: Best Actress (Kerr); Nominations: Acad-emy Awards '60: Best Actress (Kerr), Best Adapted Screen-play, Best Director (Zinnemann), Best Picture, Best Sup-porting Actress (Johns). *WAR, VTR, CCB*

Sunny 🎬🎬 1941
Another glossed-over, love-conquers-all musical with Neagle as a circus star who falls for a wealthy car maker's son. Dad and crew disapprove, putting a damper on the ro-mance. In spite of the weak storyline and flat di-rection, Kerns' music and Bolger's dancing make it enjoyable. 🎵Who?; D'ya Love Me?; Sunny; Two Little Bluebirds. 98m/B VHS. Anna Neagle, Ray Bolger, John Carroll, Edward Everett Horton, Frieda Inescort, Helen Westley, Benny Rubin, Richard Lane, Martha Tilton; **D:** Her-bert Wilcox. Nominations: Academy Awards '41: Scoring of a Musical.*NOS*

Sunny Side Up 🎬🎬½ 1928
As stress of pickle factory work takes toll on woman's friend, she makes heroic effort to help her to the country to recover. 66m/B VHS, Beta. Vera Reynolds, ZaSu Pitts, Edmund Burns, Sally Rand; **D:** Donald Crisp. *GPV*

Sunny Skies 🎬 1930
Bargain-basement retread has Lease donating a pint of blood. 🎵Sunny Days; I Must Have You; Wanna Find a Boy; Must Be Love. 98m/B VHS. Benny Rubin, Marce-line Day, Rex Lease, Marjorie Kane, Wesley Barry; **D:** Nor-man Taurog. *NOS*

Sunnyside woof! 1979 (R)
Travolta plays a street kid trying to bring an end to the local gang warfare so he can move to Manhattan. Features a host of pop tunes in an attempt to ride the coat-tails of brother John's successful "Saturday Night Fever." Laughably bad. 100m/C VHS. Joey Travolta, John Lansing, Stacey Pickren, Andrew Rubin, Michael Tuc-ci, Talia Balsam, Joan Darling; **D:** Timothy Galfas. *AIP, FOX*

Sunrise 🎬🎬🎬🎬 1927
Sunrise—A Song of Two Hu-mans Magnificent silent story of a simple country boy who, prodded by an alluring city woman, tries to murder his wife. Production val-ues wear their age well. Gaynor won an Oscar for her stunning performance. Remade in Germany as "The Journey to Tilsit." Based on a story by Hermann Suderman. 110m/B VHS. George O'Brien, Janet Gaynor, Bodil Rosing, Margaret Livingston, J. Farrell MacDonald, Carl Mayer; **D:** F.W. Murnau; **C:** Charles Rosh-er, Karl Struss. Academy Awards '28: Best Actress (Gay-nor), Best Cinematography; Nominations: Academy Awards '28: Best Interior Decoration. *GPV*

Sunrise at Campobello 🎬🎬🎬 1960
A successful adaptation (with Bellamy and Donehue repeating their roles) of the Tony award-winning play that chronicles Franklin D. Roosevelt's battle to conquer polio and ultimately receive the Demo-cratic presidential nomination in 1924. Garson gives an excellent performance as Eleanor Roo-sevelt. Screenplay by Schary, who adapted his own play, and also produced. 143m/C VHS, Beta. Ralph Bellamy, Greer Garson, Hume Cronyn, Jean Hagen, Jack Perrin, Lyle Talbot; **D:** Vincent J. Donehue; **W:** Dore Schary. Golden Globe Awards '61: Best Actress—Drama (Garson); National Board of Review Awards '60: 10 Best Films of the Year, Best Actress (Garson); Nominations: Academy Awards '60: Best Actress (Garson), Best Art Di-rection/Set Decoration (Color), Best Costume Design (Col-or), Best Sound. *WAR*

Sunrise Trail 🎬🎬½ 1931
Lots of action with Steele working undercover for the sheriff, try-ing to stop a rustler. He also finds the time to fall for barmaid Mehaffey. 65m/B VHS, Beta. Bob Steele, Blanche Mehaffey, Jack Clifford, Eddie Dunn; **D:** John P. McCarthy. *GPV*

The Sun's Burial 🎬🎬🎬 1960
Oshima's stylized and violent drama depicts life in Osaka's worst slum—a teeming underworld populated by teen gangs, prostitutes, and criminals. All want control of the area's most profitable business, an illegal blood-selling operation. In Japanese with English subtitles. 87m/C VHS. *JP* Kayoko Honoo, Koji Nakahara, Masahiko Tsugawa, Fumio Watanabe; **D:** Nagi-sa Oshima. *NYF*

Sunset 🎬🎬 1988 (R)
Edwards wanders the range in this soft-centered farce about a couple of Western legends out to solve a mystery. On the backlots of Hollywood, silent screen star Tom Mix (Willis) meets aging marshal Wyatt Earp (Garner) and participates in a time-warp western circa 1927. They encounter a series of misadventures while trying to finger a murderer. Garner ambles enjoyably, lifting him a level above the rest of the cast. 101m/C VHS, Beta, LV, Closed Caption. Bruce Wil-lis, James Garner, Mariel Hemingway, Darren McGavin, Jennifer Edwards, Malcolm McDowell, Kathleen Quinlan, M. Emmet Walsh, Patricia Hodge, Richard Bradford, Joe Dalle-sandro, Dermot Mulroney; **D:** Blake Edwards; **W:** Blake Ed-wards, Rod Amateau; **M:** Henry Mancini. Golden Raspberry Awards '88: Worst Director (Edwards); Nominations: Acade-my Awards '88: Best Costume Design. *COL*

Sunset Boulevard 🎬🎬🎬½ 1950
Famed tale of Norma Desmond (Swanson), aging silent film queen, who refuses to accept that stardom has ended and she hires a young down-on-his-luck screenwriter (Holden) to help engineer her movie comeback. The screenwriter, who be-comes the actress' kept man, assumes he can manipulate her, but finds out otherwise. Reality was almost too close for comfort, as Swanson, von Stroheim (as her major domo), and others very nearly play themselves. A darkly humorous look at the legacy and loss of fame with witty dia-log, stellar performances, and some now-classic scenes. Based on the story "A Can of Beans" by Brackett and Wilder. 100m/B VHS, Beta, LV. Gloria Swanson, William Holden, Erich von Stroheim, Nancy Ol-son, Buster Keaton, Jack Webb, Cecil B. DeMille, Fred Clark; **D:** Billy Wilder; **W:** Billy Wilder, Charles Brackett, D.M. Marshman Jr. Academy Awards '50: Best Art Direc-tion/Set Decoration (B & W), Best Story & Screenplay, Origi-nal Dramatic/Comedy Score; Golden Globe Awards '51: Best Actress—Drama (Swanson), Best Director (Wilder), Best Film—Drama, Best Score; Nominations: Academy Awards '50: Best Actor (Holden), Best Actress (Swanson), Best Black and White Cinematography, Best Director (Wild-er), Best Film Editing, Best Picture, Best Supporting Actor (von Stroheim), Best Supporting Actress (Olson). *PAR, HMV*

Sunset Grill 🎬🎬 1992 (R)
While investigat-ing his wife's murder, detective Ryder Hart (Wel-ler) discovers a pattern of grisly killings. Sexy singer Loren Duquesne (Singer) leads him south of the border to her boss and his bloody money-making scheme. Unrated version also avail-able.***CW:*** Language, violence, and sexuality.

103m/C VHS, **Closed Caption.** Peter Weller, Lori Singer, Alexandra Paul, John Rhys-Davies, Michael Anderson Jr., Stacy Keach; **D:** Kevin Connor. *NLC, PMS*

Sunset Heat ✓✓ *Midnight Heat* 1992 (R) Former drug dealer (Pare) returns to his home in Los Angeles with a legit job as a photojournalist. He stays with an old friend who turns out to be involved with the obsessed drug czar that Pare used to work for. Trouble comes along when the drug lord is robbed and blames Pare for the crime. Action-packed, with some good plot twists. An unrated version contains two additional minutes of footage.**CW:** Language, strong violence, and strong sensuality. 94m/C VHS, **Closed Caption.** Michael Pare, Dennis Hopper, Adam Ant, Daphne Ashbrook, Charlie Schlatter; **D:** John Nicolella. *NLC*

Sunset in El Dorado ✓✓½ 1945 Roy and Dale thwart a villainous scheme to defraud farmers of their land. 56m/B VHS, Beta. Roy Rogers, Dale Evans, George "Gabby" Hayes, Hardie Albright, Roy Barcroft, Tom London, Edmund Cobb; **D:** Frank McDonald. *GPV, VCN*

Sunset Limousine ✓✓½ 1983 An out-of-work stand-up comic gets thrown out by his girlfriend, then takes a job as a chauffeur. Standard vehicle with occasional bursts of speed. 92m/C VHS, Beta. John Ritter, Martin Short, Susan Dey, Paul Reiser, Audrie Neehan, Lainie Kazan; **D:** Terry Hughes. *LIV*

Sunset on the Desert ✓✓½ 1942 Rogers gets to wear a white hat and a black hat as both the leader of a gang of outlaws and the hero who brings them to justice. A poor man's Western omelette. 53m/B VHS, Beta. Roy Rogers, George "Gabby" Hayes, Lynne Carver, Frank M. Thomas Sr., Bob Nolan, Beryl Wallace, Glenn Strange, Douglas Fowley, Roy Barcroft, Pat Brady; **D:** Joseph Kane. *VYY*

Sunset Park ✓✓ 1996 (R) Brooklyn phys ed teacher Phyllis Saroka (Perlman) becomes the coach of a high school basketball team that, despite her total lack of knowledge about the game, makes it to the city championships. The cast's excellent performances hold interest, even though the predictable storyline gives away all of its moves before it gets near the hoop. Starr (of the rap group Onyx) is outstanding as the most talented (and most troubled) member of the team.**CW:** Some language and sexual references. 100m/C VHS, LV, **Closed Caption.** Rhea Perlman, Carol Kane, Terrence DaShon Howard, Camille Saviola, Fredro Starr, James Harris, Antwon Tanner, Shawn Michael Howard, De'Aundre Bonds; **D:** Steve Gomer; **W:** Seth Zvi Rosenfeld, Kathleen McGhee-Anderson; **C:** Robbie Greenberg; **M:** Kay Gee, Miles Goodman. *COL*

Sunset Range ✓✓½ 1935 The "World's All-Around Champion Cowboy" of 1912 stars in this chaps-slappin', bit-chompin', dust-raisin' saga of the plains. 59m/B VHS, Beta. Hoot Gibson. *NOS, VCN, VCI*

Sunset Serenade ✓✓ 1942 Roy and Gabby outwit murderous duo who plan to eliminate the new heir to a ranch. 60m/B VHS, Beta. Roy Rogers, George "Gabby" Hayes, Helen Parrish; **D:** Joseph Kane. *NOS, MED, HEG*

Sunset Strip ✓ 1985 A photographer investigates a friend's murder, and enters the seamy world of drugs and rock and roll in L.A. 83m/C VHS, Beta. Tom Elpin, Cheri Cameron Newell, John Mayall. *LIV, VES*

Sunset Strip woof! 1991 (R) A young dancer finds a job in a strip club and competes against the other women there to find the man of her dreams. The women take their jobs very seriously—even attending ballet classes to improve their performances. However, the viewer probably won't take this movie very seriously since it is just another excuse to show women in as little clothing as possible.**CW:** Nudity and sensuality. 95m/C VHS, LV. Jeff Conaway, Michelle Foreman, Shelley Michelle; **D:** Paul G. Volk; **M:** John Gonzalez. *PMH*

Sunset Trail ✓ 1932 Routine Maynard sagebrush saga with the hero protecting a woman rancher from outlaws. 60m/B VHS, Beta. Ken Maynard. *NOS, VCI, DVT*

The Sunshine Boys ✓✓✓ 1975 (PG) Two veteran vaudeville partners, who have shared a love-hate relationship for decades, reunite for a television special. Adapted by Neil Simon from his play. Matthau was a replacement for Jack Benny, who died before the start of filming. Burns, for his first starring role since "Honolulu" in 1939, won an Oscar. 111m/C VHS, Beta, LV. George Burns, Walter Matthau, Richard Benjamin, Lee Meredith, F. Murray Abraham, Carol Arthur, Howard Hesseman; **D:** Herbert Ross; **W:** Neil Simon. Academy Awards '75: Best Supporting Actor (Burns); Golden Globe Awards '76: Best Actor—Musical/Comedy (Matthau), Best Film—Musical/Comedy, Best Supporting Actor (Benjamin); Writers Guild of America '75: Best Adapted Screenplay; Nominations: Academy Awards '75: Best Actor (Matthau), Best Adapted Screenplay, Best Art Direction/Set Decoration. *MGM, BTV*

Sunshine Run ✓✓½ 1979 (PG) Two escaped slaves and a young widow search for Spanish treasure in the Everglades. Also on video as "Black Rage." 102m/C VHS, Beta. Chris Robinson, Ted Cassidy, David Legge, Phyllis Robinson; **D:** Chris Robinson. *NO*

Sunstroke ✓✓ 1992 (R) Seymour plays a desperate mother searching for her kidnapped child through the Arizona desert. Framed for murder, she cannot contact the police but must track the kidnappers herself, until she meets a drifter with secrets of his own.**CW:** Violence. 91m/C VHS, Beta, **Closed Caption.** Jane Seymour, Stephen Meadows, Steve Railsback, Ray Wise, Don Ameche; **D:** James Keach; **W:** Duane Poole. *PAR*

The Super ✓✓½ 1991 (R) Pesci stars as a slumlord who faces a prison sentence thanks to his terminal neglect. The option given to him is to live in his own rat hole until he provides reasonable living conditions. This he does, and predictably learns a thing or two about his own greed and the people who suffer as a result of it. Pesci as always gives an animated performance but poor scripting laden with stereotypes and cliches successfully restricts effort.**CW:** Language. 86m/C VHS. Joe Pesci, Vincent Gardenia, Madolyn Smith, Ruben Blades; **D:** Rod Daniel; **C:** Bruce Surtees. *FXV, CCB*

Super Bitch ✓✓½ *Mafia Junction* 1989 Nasty, cold, and uncaring woman uses men to keep up her expensive habits, then ruthlessly tosses them aside when she is done. She purposely entangles them in her drug trade and thinks nothing of their deaths. Proving once again that you get what you pay for. 90m/C VHS. Stephanie Beacham, Patricia Hayes, Gareth Thomas; **D:** Massimo Dallamano. *ATL*

Super Brother ✓ 1990 (R) The feared and respected leader of an oppressed people is imprisoned, much to everyone's regret. 90m/C VHS, Beta. Woody Strode. *ELE*

Super Force ✓✓ 1990 When astronaut Zach Stone (Olandt) returns from an assignment on Mars he finds his policeman brother has been murdered. He quits NASA and joins the force to get revenge, battling evil crime boss Tao Satori (Liddy). Stone also moonlights as a vigilante, complete with motorcycle and high-tech armoured suit. It's dumb but there's lots of action. 92m/C VHS, LV. Ken Olandt, G. Gordon Liddy, Larry B. Scott, Lisa Niemi, Marshall Teague; **Cameos:** Patrick Macnee; **D:** Richard Compton. *USH*

Super Fuzz ✓✓½ *Supersnooper* 1981 (PG) Rookie policeman develops super powers after being accidentally exposed to radiation. Somewhat ineptly, he uses his abilities to combat crime. Somewhat ineptly acted, written, and directed as well. 97m/C VHS, Beta. Terence Hill, Joanne Dru, Ernest Borgnine; **D:** Sergio Corbucci; **W:** Sergio Corbucci.

Super Mario Bros. ✓✓½ 1993 (PG) $42 million adventure fantasy based on the popular Nintendo video game. The brothers are in hot pursuit of the Princess Daisy who's been kidnapped by evil slimebucket Hopper and taken to Dinohattan, a fungi-infested, garbage-strewn, rat-hole version of Manhattan. Hopper will amuse the adults, doing a gleeful reptilian version of Frank Booth from "Blue Velvet." Hoskins and Leguizamo act gamely in broad Nintendo style, enthusiastically partaking in high-tech wizardry and the many gags. Hits bullseye of target audience—elementary and junior high kids—with frenetic pace, gaudy special effects, oversized sets, and animatronic monsters. 104m/C VHS, Beta, LV, **Closed Caption.** Bob Hoskins, John Leguizamo, Samantha Mathis, Fisher Stevens, Richard Edson, Dana Kaminsky, Dennis Hopper, Fiona Shaw, Mojo Nixon, Lance Henriksen; **D:** Rocky Morton, Annabel Jankel; **W:** Edward Solomon, Parker Bennett, Terry Runte; **M:** Alan Silvestri. *HPH, BTV, TOU*

Super Ninjas ✓ 198? A ninja battles evil hordes of like-trained ninja warriors, and wins over and over again. 104m/C VHS, Beta. Cheng Tien Chi, Lung Tien Hsiang, Chen Pei Hsi. *NO*

Super Seal ✓ 1977 (G) An injured seal pup disrupts a family's normal existence after the young daughter adopts him. 95m/C VHS, Beta. Foster Brooks, Sterling Holloway, Sarah Brown; **D:** Michael Dugan. *VCI*

Super Soul Brother 198? A lazy no-good-nik accidentally ingests a strange potion which turns him into a master thief. 80m/C VHS. Wildman Steve. *XVC*

Superargo ✓✓ *Il Re Dei Criminali; Superargo the Giant; The King of Criminals* 1967 A wrestler becomes a super-hero with psychic powers and a bullet-proof leotard. He fights against a madman who is turning athletes into robots. Successful Italian hero who wouldn't last two movies in the ring with Batman. 95m/C VHS, Beta. *IT SP* Guy Madison, Ken Wood, Liz Barrett, Diana Loris; **D:** Paul Maxwell. *SNC, MAD*

Superbug Super Agent ✓✓½ 1976 Dodo, the wonder car puts the brakes on crime in this silly action-adventure tale. A lemon in a lot full of Herbies. 90m/C VHS, Beta. Robert Mark, Heidi Hansen, George Goodman. *JEF*

Superchick woof! 1971 (R) Mild-mannered stewardess by day, sexy blonde with karate blackbelt by night. In addition to stopping a sky-jacking she regularly makes love to men around the world. A superbomb that never gets off the ground. 94m/C VHS, Beta. Joyce Jillson, Louis Quinn, Thomas Reardon; **D:** Ed Forsyth. *PSM*

Supercop ✓✓½ *Police Story 3: Supercop* 1992 (R) Super Hong Kong cop Kevin Chan (Chan) heads to China to assist the authorities in cracking an international drug ring. He's partnered with disciplined-but-beautiful Director Yang (Yeoh), who's also a terrific fighter, and the duo go undercover (as a married couple) to infiltrate the operation, which takes them to a Malaysian resort. Then Chan's girlfriend shows up, blowing their cover. Lots of action-packed fighting and wild chases. The 1996 American release loses about a half-hour of run time from the original. Dubbed from Cantonese.**CW:** Some violence. 93m/C VHS, LV, **Closed Caption.** *HK* Jackie Chan, Michelle Yeoh, Maggie Cheung, Kenneth Tsang, Andrew Kam Yeun Wah; **D:** Stanley Tong; **W:** Edward Tang, Fibe Ma, Lee Wai Yee; **C:** Ardy Lam; **M:** Joel McNeely. *TOU*

Superdad ✓ 1973 (G) A middle-aged parent is determined to bridge the generation gap by trying his hand at various teenage activities. Disney family fare that's about as complicated as a television commercial. The adolescents are two-dimensional throwbacks to the fun-loving fifties. 94m/C VHS, Beta. Bob Crane, Kurt Russell, Joe Flynn, Barbara Rush, Kathleen Cody, Dick Van Patten; **D:** Vincent McEveety; **M:** Buddy Baker. *DIS*

Superfly ✓✓½ 1972 (R) Controversial upon release, pioneering blaxploitation has Harlem dope dealer finding trouble with gangs and police as he attempts to establish retirement fund from one last deal. Excellent period tunes by Curtis Mayfield. Two lesser sequels. 98m/C VHS, Beta. Ron

O'Neal, Carl Lee, Sheila Frazier, Julius W. Harris; **D:** Gordon Parks Jr.; **M:** Curtis Mayfield. WAR

Superfly T.N.T. woof! *Super Fly T.N.T* 1973 (R) This confusing sequel to "Superfly" finds O'Neal returning as Youngblood Priest. The now ex-drug dealer has retired with his girlfriend to Rome where he is approached by an African gun-runner (Browne) for help in a revolution against an oppressive government. Cheap exploitation. 87m/C **Closed Caption.** Ron O'Neal, Roscoe Lee Browne, Sheila Frazier, Robert Guillaume, Jacques Sernas, William Berger; **D:** Ron O'Neal; **W:** Alex Haley. PAR

Supergirl ⍟½ 1984 (PG) Big-budget bomb in which Slater made her debut and nearly killed her career, with the help of Kryptonite. Unexciting and unsophisticated story of a young woman, cousin to Superman, with super powers, based on the comic book series. She's in pursuit of a magic paperweight, but an evil sorceress wants it too. Dunaway is a terrifically vile villainess with awesome black magic powers. Slater is great to look at, but is much better in almost any other film. 114m/C VHS, Beta, LV. *GB* Faye Dunaway, Helen Slater, Peter O'Toole, Mia Farrow, Brenda Vaccaro, Marc McClure, Simon Ward, Hart Bochner, Maureen Teefy, David Healy, Matt Frewer; **D:** Jeannot Szwarc; **M:** Jerry Goldsmith. LIV

Supergrass ⍟ 1987 (R) A low-brow British farce about a nebbish who poses as a drug smuggler to impress his girlfriend, and is then mistaken for a real one by the authorities. 105m/C VHS, Beta. *GB* Adrian Edmondson, Peter Richardson, Nigel Planer, Jennifer Saunders, Ronald Allen, Dawn French; **D:** Peter Richardson. NLC

Superman: The Movie ⍟⍟⍟½ 1978 (PG) The DC Comics legend comes alive in this wonderfully entertaining saga of Superman's life from a baby on the doomed planet Krypton to Earth's own Man of Steel. Hackman and Beatty pair marvelously as super criminal Lex Luthor and his bumbling sidekick. Award-winning special effects and a script that doesn't take itself too seriously make this great fun. Followed by three sequels. 144m/C VHS, Beta, LV. Christopher Reeve, Margot Kidder, Marlon Brando, Gene Hackman, Glenn Ford, Susannah York, Ned Beatty, Valerie Perrine, Jackie Cooper, Marc McClure, Trevor Howard, Sarah Douglas, Terence Stamp, Jack O'Halloran, Phyllis Thaxter; **D:** Richard Donner; **W:** Mario Puzo, Robert Benton, David Newman; **C:** Geoffrey Unsworth; **M:** John Williams. Academy Awards '78: Best Visual Effects; National Board of Review Awards '78: 10 Best Films of the Year; Nominations: Academy Awards '78: Best Film Editing, Best Sound, Best Original Score. WAR

Superman 2 ⍟⍟⍟ 1980 (PG) The sequel to "the movie" about the Man of Steel. This time, he has his hands full with three super-powered villains from his home planet of Krypton. The romance between reporter Lois Lane and our superhero is made believable and the storyline has more pace to it than the original. A sequel that often equals the first film—leave it to Superman to pull off the impossible. 127m/C VHS, Beta, LV. Christopher Reeve, Margot Kidder, Gene Hackman, Ned Beatty, Jackie Cooper, Sarah Douglas, Jack O'Halloran, Susannah York, Marc McClure, Terence Stamp, Valerie Perrine, E.G. Marshall; **D:** Richard Lester; **W:** Mario Puzo, David Newman; **M:** John Williams. WAR

Superman 3 ⍟⍟ 1983 (PG) Villainous businessman Vaughn tries to conquer Superman via the expertise of bumbling computer expert Pryor and the judicious use of an artifical form of Kryptonite. Superman explores his darker side after undergoing transformation into sleaze ball. Promising satiric start ultimately defeated by uneven story and direction and boring physical comedy. Notable is the absence of Lois Lane as a main character. Followed by "Superman 4." 123m/C VHS, Beta, LV. Christopher Reeve, Richard Pryor, Annette O'Toole, Jackie Cooper, Margot Kidder, Marc McClure, Annie Ross, Robert Vaughn; **D:** Richard Lester; **W:** David Newman; **M:** John Williams. WAR

Superman 4: The Quest for Peace ⍟⍟ 1987 (PG) The third sequel, in which the Man of Steel endeavors to rid the world of nuclear weapons, thereby pitting himself against nuclear-entrepreneur Lex Luthor and his superpowered creation, Nuclear Man. Special effects are dime-store quality and it appears that someone may have walked off with parts of the plot. Reeve deserves credit for remaining true to character through four films. 90m/C VHS, Beta, LV, **Closed Caption.** Christopher Reeve, Gene Hackman, Jon Cryer, Marc McClure, Margot Kidder, Mariel Hemingway, Sam Wanamaker; **D:** Sidney J. Furie; **W:** Mark Rosenthal; **M:** John Williams; **V:** Susannah York. WAR, APD

Superman & the Mole Men ⍟⍟½ *Superman and the Strange People* 1951 The cast of the popular 1950s' television show made this rarely seen feature as a "pilot" for the series. Superman faces the danger threatened by the invasion of radioactive mole-men who make their way to the surface world from the bowels of the earth through an oil-well shaft. Simple fun. 58m/C VHS, Beta. George Reeves, Phyllis Coates, Jeff Corey; **D:** Lee Sholem. WAR

Superman: The Serial, Vol. 1 1948 Superman was first seen in live action in this 15-part theatrical serial that has been rarely shown since its original release. 248m/B VHS, Beta. Kirk Alyn, Noel Neill, Pierre Watkin, Tommy "Butch" Bond, Thomas Carr; **D:** Spencer Gordon Bennet. WAR

Supernatural ⍟⍟½ 1933 Roma (Lombard) falls prey to a phony medium (Dinehart) who promises to call up the spirit of her recently murdered twin brother. At the same moment of the seance a murderess dies in the electric chair and her body is used in Dr. Houston's (Warner) life-after-death experiment. Too bad Roma becomes possessed by the woman's evil spirit. Now the doctor and Roma's fiance (Scott) must undo the curse. A hokey B-grade movie disliked by Lombard. 78m/B VHS, **Closed Caption.** Carole Lombard, Randolph Scott, H.B. Warner, Alan Dinehart, Vivienne Osborne, Beryl Mercer, William Farnum, Willard Robertson; **D:** Victor Halperin; **W:** Harvey Thew, Brian Marlow; **C:** Arthur Martinelli. USH

The Supernaturals ⍟½ 1986 (R) Confederate Civil War-era ghosts, bent on avenging their deaths, haunt a wooded area in which modern Yankee army maneuvers are practiced. Antebellum boredom. 85m/C VHS, Beta, **Closed Caption.** Maxwell Caulfield, LeVar Burton, Nichelle Nichols; **D:** Armand Mastroianni; **C:** Peter Collister. NLC

Supersonic Man woof! 1978 (PG) Incoherent shoestring-budget Superman spoof with a masked hero fighting to save the world from the evil intentions of a mad scientist. 85m/C VHS, Beta. *SP* Michael Coby, Cameron Mitchell, Diana Polakov; **D:** J. Piquer Simon. VCI

Superstar: The Life and Times of Andy Warhol ⍟⍟⍟ 1990 Even if you didn't grok Andy's 'pop' artwork and self-created celebrity persona, this ironic, kinetic, oft-rollicking documentary paints a vivid picture of the wild era he inspired and exploited. Interviewees range from Warhol cohorts like Dennis Hopper to proud executives at the Campbell Soup plant. One highlight: a Warhol guest shot on "The Love Boat." 87m/C VHS. Tom Wolfe, Sylvia Miles, David Hockney, Taylor Mead, Dennis Hopper; **D:** Chuck Workman. VES

Superstition ⍟½ *The Witch* 1982 A reverend and his family move into a vacant house despite warnings about a curse from the townsfolk. Some people never learn. 85m/C VHS, Beta. James Houghton, Albert Salmi, Lynn Carlin; **D:** James Robertson. LIV

Supervixens ⍟⍟ 1975 True to Meyer's low-rent exploitation film canon, this wild tale is filled with characteristic Amazons, sex and violence. A gas station attendant is framed for the grisly murder of his girlfriend and hustles out of town, meeting a succession of well-endowed women during his travels. As if it needed further problems, it's hampered by a tasteless storyline

and incoherent writing. 105m/C VHS. Shari Eubank, Charles Napier; **D:** Russ Meyer; **W:** Russ Meyer. RMF

Support Your Local Gunfighter ⍟⍟⍟ 1971 (G) Garner plays a western con man with his tongue firmly in his cheek. He comes to the small town of Purgatory and is thought to be a notorious gunfighter. He decides to go with the mistaken identity and use it to his profitable advantage. Elam is his bumbling sidekick and Pleshette the love interest. A delightful, deliberately cliche-filled western. A follow-up, not a sequel, to "Support Your Local Sheriff" (1969). 92m/C VHS, **Closed Caption.** James Garner, Jack Elam, Suzanne Pleshette, Harry (Henry) Morgan, Dub Taylor, John Dehner, Joan Blondell, Ellen Corby, Henry Jones; **D:** Burt Kennedy. MGM

Support Your Local Sheriff ⍟⍟⍟½ 1969 (G) Amiable, irreverent western spoof with more than its fair share of laughs. When a stranger stumbles into a gold rush town, he winds up becoming sheriff. Garner is perfect as the deadpan sheriff, particularly in the scene where he convinces Dern to remain in jail, in spite of the lack of bars. Neatly subverts every western cliche it encounters, yet keeps respect for formula western. Followed by "Support Your Local Gunfighter." 92m/C VHS, Beta, LV, **Closed Caption.** James Garner, Joan Hackett, Walter Brennan, Bruce Dern, Jack Elam, Harry (Henry) Morgan; **D:** Burt Kennedy; **W:** William Bowers; **C:** Harry Stradling Jr. National Board of Review Awards '69: 10 Best Films of the Year. FOX, MGM

Suppose They Gave a War and Nobody Came? ⍟⍟½ *War Games* 1970 (G) A small Southern town battles with a local army base in this entertaining but wandering satire. The different acting styles used as the producers wavered on making this a comedy or drama were more at war with one another than the characters involved. 113m/C VHS, LV. Tony Curtis, Brian Keith, Ernest Borgnine, Suzanne Pleshette, Ivan Dixon, Bradford Dillman, Don Ameche; **D:** Hy Averback; **W:** Don McGuire. FOX

Surabaya Conspiracy ⍟½ 1975 Mystery and intrigue surround a quest for gold in Africa. 90m/C VHS, Beta. Michael Rennie, Richard Jaeckel, Barbara Bouchet, Mike Preston; **D:** Roy Davis. NO

Sure Fire ⍟⍟ 1990 Wes (Blair) is a mercurial entrepreneur who thinks he has found the financial ticket to paradise with his vacation home scheme. Much to the chagrin of his wife Ellen (Dezina), he refuses to let anything stand in the way of his sure-fire fortune, even his family. Wes develops a little self-control as he realizes he's beginning to flake out, but it may be too late. Director Jost has put together a surprisingly unpretentious film with a virtually no-name cast, its plot speaking volumes on the American condition while unfolding in the bleak Utah desert. 86m/C VHS. Tom Blair, Kristi Hager, Robert Ernst, Kate Dezina, Phillip R. Brown; **D:** Jon Jost; **W:** Jon Jost. WAC

The Sure Thing ⍟⍟⍟ 1985 (PG-13) College students who don't like each other end up travelling to California together, and of course, falling in love. Charming performances make up for predictability. Can't-miss director (and ex-Meathead) Reiner's second direct hit at the box office. 94m/C VHS, Beta, LV, 8mm, **Closed Caption.** John Cusack, Daphne Zuniga, Anthony Edwards, Boyd Gaines, Lisa Jane Persky, Viveca Lindfors, Nicolette Sheridan, Tim Robbins; **D:** Rob Reiner; **W:** Jonathan Roberts, Steven L. Bloom; **C:** Robert Elswit. COL

Surf Nazis Must Die ⍟ 1987 A piece of deliberate camp in the Troma mold, about a group of psychotic neo-Nazi surfers taking over the beaches of California in the wake of a devastating earthquake. Tongue-in-cheek, tasteless and cheap, but intentionally so. 83m/C VHS, Beta, **Closed Caption.** Barry Brenner, Gail Neely, Michael Sonye, Dawn Wildsmith, Tom Shell, Bobbie Bresee; **D:** Peter George; **W:** John Ayre. MED, VTR

Surf Ninjas ✶✶½ *Surf Warriors* 1993 (PG) Action comedy for the kiddies finds two young surfer dudes who are actually the long-lost crown princes of the obscure nation of Patu San. The country's incompetent (what a surprise, it's Nielsen) warlord wants the boys to stay lost. Lame jokes and tame martial arts sequences. **87m/C VHS, LV, Closed Caption.** Ernie Reyes Jr., Nick Cowen, Leslie Nielsen, Tone Loc, Rob Schneider, John Karlen, Ernie Reyes Sr.; **D:** Neal Israel; **W:** Dan Gordon; **C:** Arthur Albert; **M:** David Kitay. *COL, NLC, IME*

Surf Party ✶½ 1964 Romance among the sands of Malibu with Vinton as the owner of a surf shop. Risque in 1964; utterly campy today. ♫If I Were an Artist; That's What Love Is; Pearly Shells. **68m/C VHS.** Bobby Vinton, Jackie De Shannon, Patricia Morrow, Kenny Miller; **D:** Maury Dexter. *MOV*

Surf 2 woof! *Surf 2: The End of the Trilogy* 1984 (R) A most excellent group of surfers get sick from drinking tainted Buzz Cola concocted by demented chemist Deezen in most heinous effort to obliterate surfer population from Southern California. Bogus, dude. No, you didn't miss "Surf 1" (there's not one), the title is the sort of in-joke this exercise in mental meltdown perpetuates as comedy. Ha. **91m/C VHS, Beta.** Morgan Paull, Cleavon Little, Lyle Waggoner, Ruth Buzzi, Linda Kerridge, Carol Wayne, Eddie Deezen, Eric Stoltz, Brandis Kemp, Terry Kiser; **D:** Randall Badat; **W:** Randall Badat; **M:** Peter Bernstein. *MVD, MED*

Surfacing woof! 1984 A girl braves the hostile northern wilderness to search for her missing father. This pseudo-psychological, sex-driven suspense flick makes little sense. **90m/C VHS, Beta.** Joseph Bottoms, Kathleen Beller, R.H. Thomson, Margaret Dragu; **D:** Claude Jutra. *NO*

The Surgeon ✶ *Exquisite Tenderness* 1994 (R) Routine hospital horror finds Dr. Theresa McCann (Glasser) caught up in murder when patients and doctors become poison victims. Aided by toxicologist Benjamin Hendricks (Remar), McCann finds a lollipop left behind and realizes the killer is ex-boyfriend/doctor Julian Matar (Haberle), whose unlawful experiments in tissue regeneration got him suspended. Now he's hiding out in the hospital and killing to get the pituitary glands necessary for his miracle serum. Film's original title "Exquisite Tenderness" is a term for the point when pain becomes so extreme it turns to pleasure—the film merely turns grisly. **CW:** Strong violence and gore, and for sexuality and language. **100m/C VHS.** GE Isabel Glasser, James Remar, Sean Haberle, Charles Dance, Peter Boyle, Malcolm McDowell, Charles Bailey-Gates, Gregory West, Mother Love; **D:** Carl Schenkel; **W:** Patrick Cirillo; **C:** Thomas Burstyn; **M:** Christopher Franke. *APX*

Surprise Attack ✶ 197? The Spanish Civil War forms the backdrop for this action opus. **124m/C VHS, Beta.** Simon Andrew, Danny Martin, Patty Shepard; **D:** Joseph Loman. *NO*

Surrender ✶½ 1987 (PG) A struggling woman-artist and a divorced author fall in love but won't admit it for fear of being hurt again. Jumbled plot, unfortunate casting. Available in a Spanish-subtitled version. **95m/C VHS, Beta, LV, Closed Caption.** Michael Caine, Sally Field, Steve Guttenberg, Peter Boyle, Jackie Cooper, Julie Kavner, Louise Lasser, Iman; **D:** Jerry Belson; **W:** Jerry Belson; **C:** Juan Ruiz-Anchia; **M:** Michel Colombier. *WAR, GVV*

Surrogate ✶✶ 1988 A young couple fights to keep their marriage afloat by turning to a sex surrogate. Strong cast helps carry odd, confusing script, with plenty of (you guessed it) sex, and a mystery to solve. **100m/C VHS, Beta.** CA Art Hindle, Shannon Tweed, Carole Laure, Michael Ironside, Marilyn Lightstone; **D:** Don Carmody. *MED*

Survival Game ✶ 1987 A young combat expert (Chuck Norris's son) gets involved with some ex-hippies in search of a $2 million cache. High-kickin' action. **91m/C VHS, Beta.** Mike Norris, Deborah Goodrich, Seymour Cassel; **D:** Herb Freed. *MED*

Survival of a Dragon ✶ 197? A medieval Chinese warrior is transported into the future, where he goes on a kicking rampage. **88m/C VHS, Beta.** Squall Hung, Jaguar Lee. *NO*

Survival of Spaceship Earth 1990 Man, his world and the protection of its ecology are discussed in this beautiful and fascinating film. Winner of numerous international awards due to the strength of its production values and writing. Nominated for 10 Emmy awards, winner of 2 Emmys. **63m/C VHS.** Rue McClanahan; **D:** Dirk Summers; **W:** Dirk Summers. *CPM, FCT, CRY*

Survival Quest ✶½ 1989 (R) Students in a Rocky Mountain survival course cross paths with a band of bloodthirsty mercenaries-in-training. A battle to the death ensues; you'll wish they'd all put each other out of their misery a lot sooner. **90m/C VHS, Beta, Closed Caption.** Lance Henriksen, Dermot Mulroney, Mark Rolston, Steve Antin, Paul Provenza, Ben Hammer, Traci Lind, Catherine Keener, Reggie Bannister; **D:** Don A. Coscarelli; **W:** Don A. Coscarelli. *FOX*

Survival Run ✶ 1980 (R) Six California teenagers become stranded in the Mexican desert, where they witness Graves and Milland making a shady deal. The chase is on, the story is lame, the gory parts aren't gory—so why bother? **90m/C VHS, Beta.** Peter Graves, Ray Milland, Vincent Van Patten; **D:** Larry Spiegel; **W:** Gerard M. Cahill. *MED*

Survival Zone woof! 1984 (R) Nuclear holocaust survivors battle a violent band of marauding motorcyclists on the barren ranches of the 21st century. Advice to director Rubens and cohorts: Next time, find a plot that's not growing mold. **90m/C VHS, Beta.** Gary Lockwood, Morgan Stevens, Camilla Sparv; **D:** Percival Rubens. *PSM*

The Survivalist ✶ 1987 (R) An arms-ready survivalist nut defends his family and supplies against a panicked society awaiting nuclear war. Poorly acted, little tension, and ineffective plotting make boredom seem a more critical issue than survival. **96m/C VHS, Beta, LV.** Steve Railsback, Susan Blakely, Marjoe Gortner, David Wayne, Cliff DeYoung; **D:** Sig Shore; **W:** Robert Dillon. *VES*

Surviving Desire ✶✶✶ 1991 Donovan plays Jude, a neurotic, romantic English professor who falls madly in love with an independently-minded student, Sophie. Unfortunately, Sophie is more interested in how the seduction will advance her writing than how it will affect her life. The lovers explore their brief affair by analyzing every emotion and motive in a series of quirky conversations. Intelligent, amusing, and stylized film from director Hartley. The tape also includes two Hartley shorts: "Theory of Achievement" and "Ambition." **86m/C VHS.** Martin Donovan, Mary B. Ward, Matt Malloy, Rebecca Nelson; **D:** Hal Hartley. *FXL*

Surviving Picasso ✶✶½ 1996 (R) Merchant-Ivory team takes time off from bodice-rippers to tear into the personal life of the Cubist legend, Pablo Picasso. Takes an unglamourous look at the mythically famous artist, focusing on the rocky ten-year affair with Francoise Gilot (newcomer McElhone), who met the artist in Nazi-occupied Paris when she was 22 and he was 62. Hopkins is well-cast as the insufferable senior and adds a strong dose of charm to soften his portrayal. Scores high tech credits, especially picture's sumptuous look, compliments of production designer and frequent collaborator Luciana Arrighi. Unfortunately adapted from the decidedly one-sided biography "Picasso: Creator and Destroyer" by controversial author Arianna Huffington. Denied use of the artist's works by his estate, the filmmakers settled for some "work in progress" replicas. **CW:** Scene of nudity and brief sex-related language. **126m/C VHS, LV, Closed Caption.** Anthony Hopkins, Natascha McElhone, Julianne Moore, Joss Ackland, Joan Plowright, Diane Venora, Peter Eyre, Jane Lapotaire, Joseph Maher, Bob Peck; **D:** James Ivory; **W:** Ruth Prawer Jhabvala; **C:** Tony Pierce-Roberts; **M:** Richard Robbins. *WAR*

Surviving the Game ✶ 1994 (R) Poorly made hunt-the-human story. Homeless Ice-T is hired by a group of men to assist them on their annual hunt. But wait, he's the prey. Unbelievable premise pits the streetwise, down and out Ice-T against the savvy and weapons rich group—and he beats them at their own game. Few high-impact action sequences. The violence, although there isn't as much as might be expected, is graphic. **94m/C VHS, LV, Closed Caption.** Rutger Hauer, Ice-T, F. Murray Abraham, Gary Busey, Charles S. Dutton, John C. McGinley, William McNamara, Jeff Corey; **D:** Ernest R. Dickerson; **W:** Eric Bernt; **C:** Bojan Bazelli; **M:** Stewart Copeland. *NLC*

Survivor ✶ 1980 A jetliner crashes, leaving but one survivor, the pilot, who is then plagued by visions, tragedies, and ghosts of dead passengers. Viewers also suffer. **91m/C VHS, Beta.** AU Robert Powell, Jenny Agutter, Joseph Cotten, Angela Punch McGregor; **D:** David Hemmings; **W:** David Ambrose; **M:** Brian May. *ORI, WAR*

Survivor ✶ 1987 A lone warrior on a post-nuclear holocaust wasteland battles a megalomaniac ruler. Moll as the evil villian is watchable, but overall the film is a wasteland, too. **92m/C VHS, Beta, LV.** Chip Mayer, Richard Moll, Sue Kiel; **D:** Michael Shackleton. *LIV, VES*

Survivors ✶✶ 1983 (R) Two unemployed men find themselves the target of a hit man, whom they have identified in a robbery attempt. One of the men goes gun-crazy protecting himself. Uneven comedy with wild Williams and laid-back Matthau. **102m/C VHS, Beta, LV, Closed Caption.** Robin Williams, Walter Matthau, Jerry Reed, John Goodman; **D:** Michael Ritchie; **W:** Michael Leeson; **C:** Billy Williams. *COL*

Susan and God ✶✶✶ *The Gay Mrs. Trexel* 1940 A selfish socialite returns from Europe and starts practicing a new religion, much to the dismay of her friends and family. Despite her preaching, her own domestic life is falling apart and she realizes that her preoccupation and selfish ways have caused a strain on her marriage and her relationship with her daughter. An excellent script and a fine performance from Crawford make this a highly satisfying film. **115m/B VHS, Closed Caption.** Joan Crawford, Fredric March, Ruth Hussey, John Carroll, Rita Hayworth, Nigel Bruce, Bruce Cabot, Rose Hobart, Rita Quigley, Marjorie Main, Gloria De Haven; **D:** George Cukor; **W:** Anita Loos. *MGM*

Susan Lenox: Her Fall and Rise ✶✶½ *The Rise of Helga; Rising to Fame* 1931 Garbo, the daughter of an abusive farmer, falls into the arms of the handsome Gable to escape an arranged marriage. Both stars are miscast, but the well-paced direction keeps the melodrama moving. **84m/B VHS, Beta.** Greta Garbo, Clark Gable, Jean Hersholt, John Miljan, Alan Hale, Hale Hamilton; **D:** Robert Z. Leonard; **C:** William H. Daniels. *MGM, FCT*

Susan Slept Here ✶✶½ 1954 While researching a movie on juvenile delinquents, a Hollywood script writer (Powell) is given custody of a spunky 18-year-old delinquent girl (Reynolds) during the Christmas holidays. Cute sex comedy. Based on the play "Susan," by Alex Gottlieb and Steve Fisher. **98m/C VHS, Beta, LV.** Dick Powell, Debbie Reynolds, Anne Francis; **D:** Frank Tashlin. Nominations: Academy Awards '54: Best Song ("Hold My Hand"), Best Sound. *NO*

Susana ✶✶✶ 1951 Minor though still interesting Bunuel, in which a sexy delinquent young girl is rescued from vagrancy by a Spanish family, and how she subsequently undermines the family's structure through sexual allurement and intimidation. In Spanish with English subtitles. **87m/B VHS, Beta.** MX Rosita Quintana, Fernando Soler, Victor Manuel Mendoza, Matilde Palou; **D:** Luis Bunuel. *XVC, APD*

Susanna Pass ✶ 1949 Oil deposits underneath a fish hatchery lake attract bad guys. They set off explosions to destroy the fishery, but game warden Rogers investigates. Minor outing for Roy. **67m/C VHS.** Roy Rogers, Dale Evans, Estelita

Rodriguez, Martin Garralaga, Robert Emmett Keane, Lucien Littlefield, Douglas Fowley; *D:* William Witney. *REP*

Susannah of the Mounties 🎬🎬½

1939 (PG) An adorable young girl is left orphaned after a wagon train massacre and is adopted by a Mountie. An Indian squabble gives Shirley a chance to play little peacemaker and teach Scott how to tap dance, too. Could she be any cuter? Available colorized. **78m/B VHS, Beta, Closed Caption.** Shirley Temple, Randolph Scott, Margaret Lockwood, J. Farrell MacDonald, Moroni Olsen, Victor Jory; *D:* William A. Seiter; *C:* Arthur C. Miller. *FXV*

Suspect 🎬🎬½

1987 (R) An overworked Washington, DC, public defender (Cher) is assigned to a controversial murder case in which her client is a deaf-mute, skid-row bum. A cynical lobbyist on the jury illegally researches the case himself. They work together to uncover a far-reaching conspiracy. Unrealistic plot, helped along by good performances and tight direction. **101m/C VHS, Beta, LV, 8mm.** Dennis Quaid, Cher, Liam Neeson, E. Katherine Kerr, Joe Mantegna, John Mahoney, Philip Bosco; *D:* Peter Yates; *W:* Eric Roth; *C:* Billy Williams; *M:* Michael Kamen. *COL*

Suspect Device 🎬½ *Roger Corman Presents:*

Suspect Device **1995 (R)** Nonsensical cable thriller finds government computer researcher Dan (Howell) mistakenly accessing a secret file and becoming an immediate assassination target. Then Dan discovers he isn't even human—he's really a genetically engineered cross between a robot and a nuclear bomb! Part "Terminator," part "Three Days of the Condor," and all silliness.*CW:* Strong violence, a sex scene and language. **90m/C VHS, Closed Caption.** C. Thomas Howell, Stacy Travis, Jed Allan, John Beck, Marcus Aurelius, Jonathan Fuller; *D:* Rick Jacobson; *W:* Alex Simon; *C:* John Aronson; *M:* Christopher Lennertz. *NHO*

Suspended Alibi 🎬½ *Suspected Alibi* 1956

British crime-drama about an adulterous man unjustly accused when his alibi is murdered. Overlook the convenient coincidence. **64m/B VHS.** *GB* Patrick Holt, Honor Blackman, Andrew Keir, Valentine Dyall; *D:* Alfred Shaughnessy. *NOS, SNC*

Suspicion 🎬🎬🎬½

1941 Alfred Hitchcock's suspense thriller about a woman who gradually realizes she is married to a killer and may be next on his list. An excellent production unravels at the end due to RKO's insistence that Grant retain his "attractive" image. This forced the writers to leave his guilt or innocence undetermined. Available colorized. **99m/B VHS, Beta, LV.** Cary Grant, Joan Fontaine, Cedric Hardwicke, Nigel Bruce, May Whitty, Leo G. Carroll, Heather Angel; *D:* Alfred Hitchcock; *C:* Harry Stradling. Academy Awards '41: Best Actress (Fontaine); New York Film Critics Awards '41: Best Actress (Fontaine); Nominations: Academy Awards '41: Best Picture, Original Dramatic/Comedy Score. *MED, MLB, BTV*

Suspicion 🎬🎬

1987 Remake of the chilling Hitchcock tale. Newlywed bride is consumed with fears about her wealthy new husband. The suspense builds as she comes to suspect that she is married to a cold-blooded killer. Curtin in way over her head. **97m/C VHS, Beta.** Jane Curtin, Anthony Andrews; *D:* Andrew Grieve. *MED*

Suspicious Agenda 🎬🎬½

1994 (R) Cop with a past is assigned to a task force that's hunting down a sadistic vigilante. **97m/C VHS.** Richard Grieco, Nick Mancuso, Jim Byrnes; *D:* Clay Borris; *W:* Kevin Rock. *AVE*

Suspiria 🎬🎬🎬

1977 (R) An American dancer enters a weird European ballet academy and finds they teach more than movement as bodies begin piling up. Sometimes weak plot is aided by great-but-gory special effects, fine photography, good music, and a chilling opening sequence. Also available in unrated version. **92m/C VHS, Beta, LV, Closed Caption.** *IT* Jessica Harper, Joan Bennett, Alida Valli, Udo Kier; *D:* Dario Argento; *W:* Dario Argento. *HHE, QVD*

Suture 🎬🎬

1993 Quirky thriller is a homage to late '50s melodramas with its strange tale of mistaken identity. Vincent wants to hide his unsavory past by assuming the identity of his estranged half-brother, Clay, which should be difficult since Vincent is white and Clay is black but the movie's premise is that everyone confuses the two. Vincent tries to kill Clay in an explosion but he survives—with amnesia and with everyone in the hospital assuming he's Vincent. Shifting points of view as he struggles to piece together his memory offer disorientation not just for Clay but the viewer as well. Feature film debut for the directors. **96m/B VHS.** Dennis Haysbert, Sab Shimono, Mel Harris, Michael Harris, Dina Merrill, David Graf, Fran Ryan; *D:* Scott McGehee, David Siegel; *W:* Scott McGehee, David Siegel; *C:* Greg Gardiner; *M:* Cary Berger. Sundance Film Festival '94: Best Cinematography; Nominations: Independent Spirit Awards '95: Best Cinematography, Best First Feature. *HMK*

Suzanne 🎬½

1980 (R) Set in 1950s Quebec, the story of a good woman whose criminal boyfriend leaves her pregnant when he is sent to prison. Ten years later, he returns, threatening her happy marriage. Confused script can't be saved by valiant cast. **90m/C VHS, Beta.** Sondra Locke, Richard Dreyfuss, Gene Barry. *VES*

Suzy 🎬🎬½

1936 Harlow's fourth film and her only one with Grant is a mixture of romance, action, and comedy set during WWI. Grant plays a French flier who falls in love with Harlow, although she is married to Tone. Excellent air footage and some good funny scenes keep this film moving right along. Even has Grant singing hit song, "Did I Remember?" **99m/B VHS, Closed Caption.** Jean Harlow, Franchot Tone, Cary Grant, Benita Hume, Lewis Stone, Inez Courtney; *D:* George Fitzmaurice. Nominations: Academy Awards '36: Best Song ("Did I Remember"). *MGM*

Svengali 🎬

1931 A music teacher uses his hypnotic abilities to manipulate one of his singing students and make her a star. Soon the young woman is singing for sell-out crowds, but only if her teacher is present. Barrymore in a hypnotic performance. Adapted from "Trilby" by George Du Maurier. Remade in 1955 and 1983. **76m/B VHS, Beta.** John Barrymore, Marian Marsh, Donald Crisp; *D:* Archie Mayo. Nominations: Academy Awards '31: Best Cinematography, Best Interior Decoration. *NOS, GPV, SNC*

Svengali 🎬🎬½

1955 Limp remake of the 1931 film about Trilby, an artist's model, falling under the mesmerizing spell of the title character, who is determined to make her into a famous singer. Chiefly notable for its visuals which were based on the illustrations from the original novel "Trilby" by George du Maurier. **82m/C VHS.** *GB* Hildegarde Neff, Donald Wolfit, Terence Morgan, Derek Bond, Paul Rogers, David Kossoff; *D:* Noel Langley; *W:* Noel Langley. *NO*

Svengali 🎬🎬½

1983 Flamboyant but faded music star O'Toole mentors Foster, a young pop singer looking for stardom. Boring, made for television remake of the Barrymore classic. **96m/C VHS.** Peter O'Toole, Jodie Foster, Elizabeth Ashley, Larry Joshua, Pamela Blair, Barbara Byrne, Holly Hunter; *D:* Anthony Harvey; *M:* John Barry. *NO*

Swamp Fire 🎬½

1946 Mississippi riverboat captain Weissmuller, wrestles alligators and battles with Crabbe for the woman he loves in this turgid drama. Look for Janssen in an early screen performance. **69m/B VHS, Beta.** Johnny Weissmuller, Virginia Grey, Buster Crabbe, Carol Thurston, Edwin Maxwell, Pedro de Cordoba, Pierre Watkin, David Janssen; *D:* William H. Pine. *NOS, SNC*

Swamp of the Lost Monster 🎬

1965 An incredible Mexican horror/western/musical that features a mouse-like monster that'll scare the cheese out of you. **88m/B VHS, Beta.** *MX* Gaston Santos, Sarah Cabrera, Manuel Donde; *D:* Rafael Baledon. *NOS, SNC, GHV*

Swamp Thing 🎬🎬½

1982 (PG) Overlooked camp drama about scientist accidentally turned into tragic half-vegetable, half-man swamp creature, with government agent Barbeau caught in the middle, occasionally while topless. A vegetarian nightmare or ecology propaganda? You be the judge. Adapted from the comic book by Craven. **91m/C VHS, Beta, LV.** Adrienne Barbeau, Louis Jourdan, Ray Wise, Dick Durock; *D:* Wes Craven; *W:* Wes Craven. *COL*

Swamp Women 🎬 *Swamp Diamonds; Cruel*

Swamp 1955 Four escaped women convicts, known as the "Nardo Gang," chase after a stash of diamonds in this super cheap, super bad action adventure from cult director Corman. **73m/C VHS.** Mike Connors, Marie Windsor, Beverly Garland, Carole Mathews, Susan Cummings; *D:* Roger Corman. *SNC*

The Swan 🎬🎬

1925 Princess' arranged marriage with a prince is complicated by a poor man also in love with her. Classic romantic comedy of the silent era. Remade in 1956. Based on a play by Ferenc Molnar. **50m/B VHS, Beta.** Adolphe Menjou, Ricardo Cortez, Frances Howard; *D:* Dimitri Buchowetzki. *NOS, DVT*

The Swan 🎬🎬🎬

1956 A twist on the Cinderella story with Kelly (in her last film before her marriage) as the charming beauty waiting for her prince. Both Guinness, as the crown prince, and Jourdan, as her poor tutor, want her hand (and the rest of her). Attractive cast, but story gets slow from time to time. Remake of a 1925 silent film. The laser disc version also includes "Wedding in Monaco," the news short showing Kelly's wedding to Prince Rainier. **112m/C VHS, LV.** Grace Kelly, Louis Jourdan, Alec Guinness, Jessie Royce Landis, Brian Aherne, Estelle Winwood; *D:* Charles Vidor; *C:* Joseph Ruttenberg, Robert L. Surtees. *MGM*

The Swan Princess 🎬🎬½

1994 (G) Formulaic prince-and-princess love story based loosely on "Swan Lake" takes a modern twist: Princess Odette, offended by the emphasis her intended, Prince Derek, places on her beauty, flees the kingdom. She's kidnapped by the evil Rothbart, an enchanter who turns her into a swan able to take human form only when touched by moonlight. A snappy trio of animal characters eventually helps Odette reunite with her newly P.C. love, with lots of zesty musical numbers and various Disney-inspired plot points along the way. Adults may yawn, but kiddies will be charmed just the same. **90m/C VHS, Closed Caption.** *D:* Richard Rich; *W:* Richard Rich, Brian Nissen; *M:* Lex de Azevedo; *V:* Jack Palance, Michelle Nicastro, Howard McGillin, Liz Callaway, John Cleese, Steven Wright, Steve Vinovich, Dakin Matthews, Sandy Duncan, Mark Harelik, James Arrington, Davis Gaines, Joel McKinnon Miller. Nominations: Golden Globe Awards '95: Best Song ("Far Longer than Forever"). *TTC*

Swann 🎬½

1996 Too many loose ends and weak direction from Benson Gyles (in her feature film debut) waste the efforts of a talented cast. Chicago-based writer Sarah Maloney (Richardson) is doing a biography of Mary Swann, wife/murder victim of a backwater Ontario farmer, who secretly wrote poetry (and gets compared to Emily Dickinson). Sarah heads to Nadeau to meet with Mary's friend Rose (Fricker) and discovers she may have altered some of the published poetry but there's not much there to really care about. Based on a novel by Carol Shields. **98m/C VHS.** *GB CA* Miranda Richardson, Brenda Fricker, Michael Ontkean, Sean McCann, John Neville, Sean Hewitt, Kyra Harper, David Cubitt, Geny Walter; *D:* Anna Benson Gyles; *W:* David Young; *C:* Gerald Packer; *M:* Richard Rodney Bennett. Nominations: Genie Awards '96: Best Actress (Fricker), Best Art Direction/Set Decoration, Best Costume Design, Best Supporting Actor (McCann), Best Score. *NYR*

Swann in Love 🎬🎬½ *Un Amour De Swann*

1984 (R) A handsome, wealthy French aristocrat makes a fool of himself over a beautiful courtesan who cares nothing for him. Elegant production lacks spark. Based upon a section of Marcel Proust's "Remembrance of Things Past." In

French with English subtitles or an English language version. 110m/C VHS, Beta. *FR GE* Jeremy Irons, Ornella Muti, Alain Delon, Fanny Ardant, Marie-Christine Barrault; *D:* Volker Schlondorff; *W:* Peter Brook, Jean-Claude Carriere; *C:* Sven Nykvist. Cesar Awards '85: Best Art Direction/Set Decoration, Best Costume Design. *XVC, MED*

The Swap *♂♂½* 1971 (R) Ex-con searches for his brother's killer. Muddled story uses clips from early De Niro film "Sam's Song." 120m/C VHS. Robert De Niro, Jered Mickey, Jennifer Warren, Terrayne Crawford, Martin Kelley; *D:* Jordan Leondopoulos. *MGM, CAN*

Swap Meet *♂* 1979 (R) Wacky teen sex comedy about shenanigans at a small town swap meet. Strictly bargain basement. 86m/C VHS. Ruth Cox, Deborah Richter, Danny Goldman, Cheryl Rixon, Jonathan Gries; *D:* Brice Mack. *NO*

The Swarm *♂* 1978 (PG) Low-brow insect contest as scientist Caine fends off a swarm of killer bees when they attack metro Houston. The bees are really just black spots painted on the film. And the acting is terrible. "B" movie on bees, but it's still better than "The Bees." 116m/C VHS, Beta. Michael Caine, Katharine Ross, Richard Widmark, Lee Grant, Richard Chamberlain, Olivia de Havilland, Henry Fonda, Fred MacMurray, Patty Duke, Ben Johnson, Jose Ferrer, Slim Pickens, Bradford Dillman, Cameron Mitchell; *D:* Irwin Allen; *W:* Stirling Silliphant; *C:* Fred W. Koenekamp; *M:* Jerry Goldsmith, John Williams. Nominations: Academy Awards '78: Best Costume Design. *WAR*

Swashbuckler *♂♂* *Scarlet Buccaneer* 1976 (PG) Jaunty pirate returns from sea to find his friends held captive by dastardly dictator for their political views. He rescues them, and helps them overthrow the erstwhile despot. 101m/C VHS, LV. Robert Shaw, James Earl Jones, Peter Boyle, Genevieve Bujold, Beau Bridges, Geoffrey Holder; *D:* James Goldstone; *W:* Jeffrey Bloom; *M:* John Addison. *USH*

Swashbuckler *♂♂½* *The Scarlet Buccaneer* 1984 Eighteenth-century pirate fracas that can't compete with Errol Flynn. 106m/C VHS. *FR* Jean-Paul Belmondo, Marlene Jobert, Laura Antonelli, Michel Auclair, Julien Guiomar; *D:* Jean-Paul Rappeneau. *USH*

Sweater Girls woof! 1978 (R) Sex comedy about two girls starting their own club called the "Sweater Girls." Terrible teen exploitaiton film. 90m/C VHS, Beta. Charlene Tilton, Harry Moses, Meegan King, Noelle North, Kate Sarchet, Carol Seflinger, Tamara Barkley, Julie Parsons; *D:* Donald M. Jones. *NO*

Swedenhielms *♂♂½* 1935 A poor Swedish scientist struggles to support his family while hoping to win a Nobel prize, while his two sons get involved in a moneylending scandal. Bergman is the rich fiance of one son, to whom poverty is a puzzlement. Fine performances by Ekman and the 20-year-old Bergman (in her third film). In Swedish with English subtitles. 92m/B VHS, LV. *SW* Gosta Ekman, Karin Swanstrom, Bjorn Berglund, Hakan Westergren, Tutta Rolf, Ingrid Bergman, Sigurd Wallen; *D:* Gustaf Molander. *WAC, LUM*

Sweeney Todd: The Demon Barber of Fleet Street 1984 A filmed performance of Sondheim's Tony-winning Broadway musical. Creepy thriller about a demon barber, his razor, and his wife's meatpies. 139m/C VHS, Beta, LV. *GB* Angela Lansbury, George Hearn; *D:* Harold Prince; *M:* Stephen Sondheim. *MVD, STS, TTC*

The Sweeper *♂♂½* 1995 (R) LA cop Mark Goddard (Howell) has a problem—his suspects have a bad habit of dying in his custody. Then he's recruited by a secret police organization whose aim is to dispense their own brand of deadly justice and Mark discovers a key to his troubled past and the murder of his cop father (Fahey). *CW:* Violence, some sexuality and language. 101m/C VHS. C. Thomas Howell, Ed Lauter, Cynda Williams, Jeff Fahey; *D:* Joseph Merhi. *PMH*

Sweet Adeline *♂♂* 1926 Smalltime hayseed makes it big in the music business while brother steals his girl back home. Not easily put off, young songster perseveres. 60m/B VHS, Beta.

Charles Ray, Gertrude Olmsted, Jack Clifford, Ida Lewis; *D:* Jerome Storm. *GPV, FCT*

Sweet Adeline *♂♂½* 1935 Dunne attracts all the men in her father's Hoboken beer garden but Woods plays the songwriter with whom she finds real love. Wonderful score. ♫ Play Us a Polka, Dot; Here Am I; We Were So Young; Why Was I Born?; Mollie O'Donahue; Lonely Feet; 'Twas Not So Long Ago; Don't Ever Leave Me. 87m/B VHS. Irene Dunne, Donald Woods, Hugh Herbert, Ned Sparks, Joseph Cawthorn, Louis Calhern; *D:* Mervyn LeRoy; *M:* Jerome Kern, Oscar Hammerstein. *MGM*

Sweet Beat *♂* *The Amorous Sex* 1962 A young woman gets a chance to become a singer when she reaches the finals of a British beauty contest. Pedestrian story enlivened by music from popular British bands of the time. 66m/B VHS, Beta. Julie Amber, Sheldon Lawrence, Irv Bauer, Billy Myles. *NOS, INC, TPV*

Sweet Bird of Youth *♂♂♂* 1962 An acclaimed adaptation of the Tennessee Williams play about Chance Wayne, a handsome drifter who travels with an aging movie queen to his small Florida hometown, hoping she'll get him started in a movie career. However, coming home turns into a big mistake, as the town boss wants revenge on Chance for seducing his daughter, Heavenly. Williams' original stage ending was cleaned up, providing a conventional "happy" movie ending for the censors. Remade for television in 1989 with Elizabeth Taylor and Mark Harmon in the lead roles. 120m/C VHS, Beta, LV. Paul Newman, Geraldine Page, Ed Begley Sr., Mildred Dunnock, Rip Torn, Shirley Knight, Madeline Sherwood; *D:* Richard Brooks; *W:* Richard Brooks; *C:* Milton Krasner. Academy Awards '62: Best Supporting Actor (Begley); Golden Globe Awards '63: Best Actress—Drama (Page); Nominations: Academy Awards '62: Best Actress (Page), Best Supporting Actress (Knight). *MGM, BTV, TRI*

Sweet Bird of Youth *♂♂* 1989 (R) Made for television remake of the Tennessee Williams' play, which was filmed for the big screen in 1962, with Harmon and Taylor having the unenviable task of following in the roles played by Paul Newman and Geraldine Page. She is an egotistical, has-been movie star and he is her ambitious gigolo who wants a movie career of his own. Unfortunately, the trouble that drove him from his Florida hometown is still there when he reappears, actress in tow. Things don't bode well. The television production uses Williams' original ending, which was cleaned up for a "happier" version in the '62 film. *CW:* Sexuality. 95m/C VHS. Elizabeth Taylor, Mark Harmon, Rip Torn, Valerie Perrine, Ruta Lee, Seymour Cassel, Kevin Geer, Michael Wilding Jr.; *D:* Nicolas Roeg; *W:* Gavin Lambert; *M:* Ralph Burns. *TRI*

Sweet Charity *♂♂♂* 1969 An ever-optimistic dime-a-dance girl has a hard time finding a classy guy to marry. MacLaine is appealing in this big-budget version of the popular Broadway musical by Neil Simon (derived from Fellini's "Notti di Cabiria"). Fosse's debut as film director. Watch for Cort as a flower child. ♫ My Personal Property; It's a Nice Face; Hey, Big Spender; Rich Man's Frug; If My Friends Could See Me Now; There's Gotta Be Something Better Than This; Rhythm of Life; Sweet Charity; I'm a Brass Band. 148m/C VHS, Beta, LV. Shirley MacLaine, Chita Rivera, John McMartin, Paula Kelly, Sammy Davis Jr., Ricardo Montalban, Bud Cort; *D:* Bob Fosse; *C:* Robert L. Surtees; *M:* Cy Coleman. Nominations: Academy Awards '69: Best Art Direction/Set Decoration, Best Costume Design, Scoring of a Musical. *USH*

Sweet Country *♂½* 1987 (R) During the overthrow of the Allende government in Chile, the lives of a Chilean family and an American couple intertwine. Heavy-going propaganda is a cross between tragedy and unintentional comedy. Made by the director of "Zorba the Greek." 147m/C VHS, Beta, LV. Jane Alexander, John Cullum, Carole Laure, Franco Nero, Joanna Pettet, Randy Quaid, Irene Papas, Jean-Pierre Aumont, Pierre Vaneck, Katia Dandoulaki; *D:* Michael Cacoyannis. *NO*

Sweet Country Road *♂½* 1981 A rock singer journeys to Nashville to try to cross over into country music. 95m/C VHS, Beta. Buddy Knox, Kary Lynn, Gordy Trapp, Johnny Paycheck, Jeanne Pruett. *NWV*

Sweet Creek County War *♂* 1982 Retired sheriff must leave his quiet ranch to battle a greedy businessman. 90m/C VHS, Beta. Richard Egan, Albert Salmi, Nita Talbot, Slim Pickens. *NO*

Sweet Dreams *♂♂½* 1985 (PG-13) Biography of country singer Patsy Cline, focusing mostly on her turbulent marriage. Her quick rise to stardom ended in an early death. Fine performances throughout. Cline's original recordings are used. ♫ Walking After Midnight; Crazy; Sweet Dreams; San Antonio Rose; Blue Moon of Kentucky; Lovesick Blues; Seven Lonely Days; Foolin' Around; Your Cheatin' Heart. 115m/C VHS, Beta, LV. Jessica Lange, Ed Harris, Ann Wedgeworth, David Clennon; *D:* Karel Reisz; *W:* Robert Getchell; *C:* Robbie Greenberg. Nominations: Academy Awards '85: Best Actress (Lange). *NO*

Sweet Ecstasy *♂½* *Douce Violence; Sweet Violence* 1962 Wealthy shenanigans on the French Riviera. Pezy is the upright young man who can't sleep with anyone unless he's in love, much to Sommer's dismay. 75m/B VHS. *FR* Elke Sommer, Pierre Brice, Christian Pezy, Claire Maurier; *D:* Max Pecas. *NO*

Sweet 15 1990 A young Hispanic girl learns that there is more to growing up than parties when she learns her father is an illegal alien. Originally aired on PBS as part of the "Wonderworks" family movie series. 120m/C VHS. Karla Montana, Panchito Gomez, Tony Plana, Jenny Gago, Susan Ruttan; *D:* Victoria Hochberg. *PME, HMV, FCT*

Sweet Georgia *♂* 1972 Soft-core star Jordan is a lusty wife whose husband is an alcoholic, so she has a roll in the hay with almost every other cast member. Lots of action, too, including a pitchfork fight. Ride 'em cowboy. 80m/C VHS. Marsha Jordan. *VDM*

Sweet Hearts Dance *♂♂* 1988 (R) Parallel love stories follow two long-time friends, one just falling in love, the other struggling to keep his marriage together. Charming performances from all, but a slow pace undermines the film. 95m/C VHS, Beta, LV, Closed Caption. Don Johnson, Jeff Daniels, Susan Sarandon, Elizabeth Perkins, Justin Henry, Holly Marie Combs; *D:* Robert Greenwald; *W:* Ernest Thompson; *M:* Richard Gibbs. *COL*

The Sweet Hereafter *♂♂♂* 1996 A schoolbus crash kills 14 children in the small town of Sam Dent, British Columbia. Big city lawyer Mitchell Stephens (Holm) arrives to persuade the townspeople to begin a class-action suit targeting city authorities and the bus manufacturer, while struggling to deal with his drug-addicted daughter Zoe (Banks). Teenaged survivor Nicole Burnell (Polley) tries to cope with the aftermath of the tragedy as does widower Billy Ansell (Greenwood), whose two children died in the crash. But the case soon begins to tear the reeling town apart as everyone struggles with loss and fate. Based on the novel by Russell Banks. 110m/C VHS. *CA* Ian Holm, Sarah Polley, Bruce Greenwood, Tom McCamus, Arsinee Khanjian, Alberta Watson, Gabrielle Rose, Maury Chaykin, David Hemblen, Earl Pastko, Peter Donaldson, Caerthan Banks; *D:* Atom Egoyan; *W:* Atom Egoyan; *C:* Paul Sarossy; *M:* Mychael Danna. Cannes Film Festival '97: Grand Jury Prize. *NYR*

Sweet Hostage *♂♂½* 1975 Escaped mental patient kidnaps uneducated farm girl and holds her captive in a remote cabin. Blair and Sheen turn in good performances. Adaptation of Nathaniel Benchley's "Welcome to Xanadu." Made-for-television. 93m/C VHS. Linda Blair, Martin Sheen, Jeanne Cooper, Lee DeBroux, Dehl Berti, Bert Remsen; *D:* Lee Philips. *IMP*

Sweet Justice *♂½* 1992 (R) This time its the women who get to be commandos, have all the adventures, and get revenge on various scum. The nominal plotline has Sunny Justice

(Carter) and her group of gal-warriors avenging the sadistic murder of a friend. Martial arts, weapons, and action galore. **CW:** Violence and sexuality. 92m/C VHS. Finn Carter, Kathleen Kinmont, Marc Singer, Frank Gorshin; *Cameos:* Mickey Rooney; *D:* Allen Plone; *W:* Allen Plone, Jim Tabilio. *TRI*

Sweet Killing 🎞🎞 1993 (R) A banker murders his shrewish wife to be with another woman. He thinks he has the perfect alibi, but then his fictitious excuse comes to life when a mysterious stranger begins stalking him. Based on the novel "Qualthrough" by Agnes Hall. **CW:** Language and sexuality. 87m/C VHS, Beta, **Closed Caption.** Anthony Higgins, F. Murray Abraham, Leslie Hope, Michael Ironside, Andrea Ferreol; *D:* Eddy Matalon; *W:* Eddy Matalon. *PAR*

Sweet Liberty 🎞🎞 1986 (PG) Alda's hometown is overwhelmed by Hollywood chaos during the filming of a movie version of his novel about the American Revolution. Pleasant but predictable. 107m/C VHS, Beta, LV, **Closed Caption.** Alan Alda, Michael Caine, Michelle Pfeiffer, Bob Hoskins, Lillian Gish; *D:* Alan Alda; *W:* Alan Alda; *M:* Bruce Broughton. *USH*

Sweet Lies 🎞½ 1988 (R) An insurance investigator tracking a scam artist in Paris is preyed upon by a group of single women betting one another that any man can be seduced. Slow comedy. 86m/C VHS, Beta, **Closed Caption.** Treat Williams, Joanna Pacula, Julianne Phillips, Laura Manszky, Norbert Weisser, Marilyn Dodd-Frank; *D:* Nathalie Delon; *M:* Trevor Jones. *FOX*

Sweet Light in a Dark Room 🎞🎞🎞 *Romeo, Julia a Tma; Romeo, Juliet and Darkness* 1960 A student in Prague during the Nazi Occupation hides a Jewish girl. He falls in love with her but becomes the suspect in the murder of a Nazi officer. Directed by the great Czech filmmaker Weiss who was himself forced to leave his country during Nazi occupation. In Czech with English subtitles. 93m/B VHS. *CZ* Ivan Mistrik, Dana Smutna; *D:* Jiri Weiss. *FCT, DVT, HEG*

Sweet Lorraine 🎞🎞🎞 1987 (PG-13) A bittersweet, nostalgic comedy about the staff and clientele of a deteriorating Catskills hotel on the eve of its closing. 91m/C VHS, Beta. Maureen Stapleton, Lee Richardson, Trini Alvarado, Freddie Roman, John Bedford Lloyd, Giancarlo Esposito, Edie Falco, Todd Graff, Evan Handler; *D:* Steve Gomer; *W:* Michael Zettler, Shelly Altman; *M:* Richard Robbins. *PAR*

Sweet Love, Bitter 🎞🎞½ *It Won't Rub Off, Baby; Black Love, White Love* 1967 The downfall of a black jazz saxophonist in the 1950's. The character is loosely based on the life of legendary musician Charlie "Bird" Parker. Alto sax man Charles McPherson dubs Gregory's solos. Adapted from the novel "Night Song" by John A. Williams. 92m/C VHS. Dick Gregory, Don Murray, Diane Varsi, Robert Hooks; *D:* Herbert Danska; *W:* Lewis Jacobs, Herbert Danska; *M:* Mal Waldron. *RHP, MVD, FCT*

Sweet Movie 🎞🎞 1975 A provocative cult classic concerning a South African tycoon who purchases a virgin bride and then exploits her sexually. In English and French with subtitles. 120m/C VHS, Beta. YU Carole Laure, Pierre Clementi, Sami Frey; *D:* Dusan Makavejev; *W:* Dusan Makavejev; *M:* Manos Hadjidakis. *FCT, MOV*

Sweet Murder woof! 1993 (R) "Single White Female" rip-off features Udy allowing Davidtz to share her apartment—with nasty consequences. **CW:** Language, stabbing scenes, and sexuality. 101m/C VHS. Helene Udy, Embeth Davidtz, Russell Todd; *D:* Percival Rubens. *THV*

Sweet Nothing 🎞🎞🎞 1996 (R) Wall Street up-and-comer Angel (Imperioli) is given some crack by a buddy (Calderon) to celebrate the birth of his child. This starts a downward spiral into addiction and dealing. At first, his wife Monika (Sorvino) goes along, but as Angel deteriorates, she learns not to trust him. Excellent performances by Imperioli and Sorvino avoid over-the-top theatrics. Script provides a realistic look at how addiction affects real people, and steers

clear of obvious cliches. Based on diaries found in a Bronx apartment building. Film's producers tracked down the author and paid for his rehab. **CW:** Mature themes, drug use, violence, language. 89m/C VHS, **Closed Caption.** Michael Imperioli, Mira Sorvino, Paul Calderone, Billie Neal; *D:* Gary Winick; *W:* Lee Drysdale. *WAR*

Sweet Perfection 🎞🎞 1990 (R) Jackson plans a big promotion for her beauty contest. Who will be voted the "Perfect Woman?" Tired premise, but it has its moments. 90m/C VHS. Stoney Jackson, Anthony Norman McKay, Catero Colbert, Liza Crusat, Reggie Theus, Tatiana Tumbtzen. *XVC, HHE*

Sweet Poison 🎞🎞 1991 (R) Bobby Stiles is a ruthless criminal who has just broken out of prison. He wants to get home and settle the score with his brother, who actually committed the crime Bobby was imprisoned for. Henry and Charlene Odell are traveling cross-country when Bobby crosses their path and forces them to drive him home. Bobby's not too busy eluding the police to notice that his captives' marriage is a little shaky—and that Charlene is attractive and sexy. As Bobby and Charlene get closer husband Henry just becomes another problem. **CW:** Strong violence and strong sexuality. 101m/C VHS, **Closed Caption.** Steven Bauer, Patricia Healy, Edward Herrmann; *D:* Brian Grant. *USH*

Sweet Revenge 🎞🎞 1987 (R) TV journalist kidnapped by a white slavery ring in the Asian jungles. After escaping, she returns for vengeance. Meek drama. 79m/C VHS, Beta. Ted Shackleford, Nancy Allen, Martin Landau; *D:* Mark Sobel. *MED*

Sweet Revenge 🎞🎞 1990 When a judge tells a divorced couple that the woman must pay the man alimony, she hires an actress to marry her ex. The tables are turned in this way-out marriage flick, reminiscent of the screwball comedies of the 1940s. 89m/C VHS, Beta, **Closed Caption.** Rosanna Arquette, Carrie Fisher, John Sessions; *D:* Charlotte Brandstrom; *W:* Janet Brownell; *M:* Hubert Bougis. *TTC*

Sweet Rosie O'Grady 🎞🎞½ 1943 Musical-comedy star Grable has returned to New York after success in England, where she caught the eye of nobleman Gardiner. Ex-boyfriend Young is a tabloid reporter who's expected by editor Menjou to get the scoop on her past. Seems she used to perform in Bowery saloons although that's not what Grable's been telling everyone. Slight story, charming performers, and lots of songs. Remade in 1948 as "That Wonderful Urge." ♫My Heart Tells Me; My Sam; Oh Where is the Groom?; The Wishing Waltz; Going to the Country Fair; Get Your Police Gazette; Battle Cry; Sweet Rosie O'Grady; Two Little Girls in Blue. 74m/C VHS. Betty Grable, Robert Young, Adolphe Menjou, Reginald Gardiner, Virginia Grey, Phil Regan, Sig Rumann, Alan Dinehart; *D:* Irving Cummings; *C:* Ernest Palmer. *RXM*

Sweet 16 🎞🎞 1981 (R) Serial killings in Texas town begin to set off muffled alarms in big head of sheriff Hopkins. Sixteen-year-old Melissa has recently moved into town. She's beautiful, mysterious, and promiscuous, and she has a big problem—all her boyfriends end up dead. No real puzzle. 90m/C VHS, Beta. Susan Strasberg, Bo Hopkins, Don Stroud, Dana Kimmell, Patrick Macnee, Larry Storch; *D:* Jim Sotos. *VES*

Sweet Smell of Success 🎞🎞🎞½ 1957 Evil New York City gossip columnist J.J. Hunsecker (Lancaster) and sleazy press agent (Curtis) cook up smear campaign to ruin career of jazz musician in love with J.J.'s sister. Engrossing performances, great dialogue. 96m/C VHS, LV. Burt Lancaster, Tony Curtis, Martin Milner, Barbara Nichols, Sam Levene; *D:* Alexander MacKendrick; *W:* Ernest Lehman, Clifford Odets; *C:* James Wong Howe; *M:* Elmer Bernstein. *MGM*

Sweet Spirits woof! 198? Soft-sell European fluff about a modern mannequin having a raucous affair with an artist. 87m/C VHS, Beta. Erika Blanc, Farley Granger. *MED*

Sweet Sugar 🎞½ *Chaingang Girls; Captive Women 3: Sweet Sugar* 1972 (R) Slave girls try to escape from a Costa Rican sugar cane plantation and its cruel owner. Needless to say, vulgar exploitation runs hither and yon in this film. 90m/C VHS. Phyllis E. Davis, Ella Edwards, Pamela Collins, Cliff Osmond, Timothy Brown; *D:* Michel Levesque. *NO*

Sweet Sweetback's Baadasssss Song 🎞🎞🎞 1971 A black pimp kills two policemen who beat up a black militant. He uses his street-wise survival skills to elude his pursuers and escape to Mexico. A thriller, but racist, sexist, and violent. 97m/C VHS, Beta. Melvin Van Peebles, Simon Chuckster, John Amos; *D:* Melvin Van Peebles; *W:* Melvin Van Peebles. *XVC*

Sweet Talker 🎞🎞½ 1991 (PG) Following his release from prison, a charming con man shows up in a small coastal village, thinking the townsfolk will be ripe for the picking. What he doesn't know is they can do some sweet talking of their own, and he soon finds himself caring for a pretty widow and her son. Enjoyable light comedy works thanks to likable leads. 91m/C VHS, LV, **Closed Caption.** AU Bryan Brown, Karen Allen, Chris Haywood, Bill Kerr, Bruce Spence, Bruce Myles, Paul Chubb, Peter Hehir, Justin Rosniak; *D:* Michael Jenkins; *W:* Tony Morphett; *M:* Richard Thompson, Peter Filleul. *LIV*

Sweet Trash woof! 1989 (R) A vice cop, having an affair with a 17-year-old prostitute, is blackmailed by an underworld figure. Lives up to its name. 80m/C VHS. Sebastian Gregory, Sharon Matt, Luke Perry, Bonnie Clark, Gene Blackey; *D:* John Hayes. *NO*

Sweet William 🎞🎞🎞 1979 (R) A philandering and seemingly irresistible young man finds that one sensitive woman hasn't the patience or time for his escapades. Adult comedy concerned with sex without displaying any on the screen. 88m/C VHS, Beta. GB Sam Waterston, Jenny Agutter, Anna Massey, Arthur Lowe; *D:* Claude Whatham; *W:* Beryl Bainbridge. *PSM*

Sweet Young Thing 19?? Young students at a French girls' school receive all sorts of attention from the male staff. 83m/C VHS, Beta. Jean Tolzac, Bernard Musson. *MED*

Sweetheart of the Navy 🎞½ 1937 Sailors help a cafe singer out of a jam, with one of them almost giving up his career for her. Standard fare, but Parker is well worth listening to. 63m/B VHS. Eric Linden, Cecilia Parker, Roger Imhof, Bernadene Hayes, Jason Robards Sr., Don Barclay; *D:* Duncan Mansfield. *NOS*

Sweethearts 🎞🎞🎞 1938 MacDonald and Eddy star as married stage actors trying to get some time off from their hectic schedule in this show-within-a-show. Trouble ensues when their conniving producer begs, pleads and tricks them into staying. Lots of well-staged musical numbers. ♫Wooden Shoes; Every Lover Must Meet His Fate; Sweethearts; Pretty as a Picture; Summer Serenade; On Parade. 114m/C VHS, LV. Jeanette MacDonald, Nelson Eddy, Frank Morgan, Florence Rice, Ray Bolger, Mischa Auer; *D:* Woodbridge S. Van Dyke. Nominations: Academy Awards '38: Best Sound, Best Score. *MGM*

Sweetie 🎞🎞🎞 1989 (R) Bizarre, expressive Australian tragicomedy about a pair of sisters—one a withdrawn, paranoid Plain Jane, the other a dangerously extroverted, overweight sociopath who re-enters her family's life and turns it upside down. Campion's first feature. 97m/C VHS, Beta, LV. AU Genevieve Lemon, Karen Colston, Tom Lycos, Jon Darling, Dorothy Barry, Michael Lake, Andre Pataczek; *D:* Jane Campion; *W:* Gerard Lee, Jane Campion; *M:* Martin Armiger. Nominations: Academy Awards '91: Best Foreign Language Film. *LIV*

Swept Away... 🎞🎞🎞 *Swept Away...By an Unusual Destiny in the Blue Sea of August* 1975 (R) A rich and beautiful Milanese woman is shipwrecked on a desolate island with a swarthy Sicilian deck hand, who also happens to be a dedicated communist. Isolated, the two switch roles, with the wealthy woman dominated by the crude proletarian. Sexy and provocative. Italian with subtitles. **116m/C VHS.** *IT* Giancarlo Giannini, Mariangela Melato; **D:** Lina Wertmuller; **W:** Lina Wertmuller; **C:** Julio Battiferri; **M:** Piero Piccioni. National Board of Review Awards '75: 5 Best Foreign Films of the Year.*FXL, APD*

Swift Justice ♫♫ 1988 Mayor of a small town thinks he's gotten away with murder after leaving a young girl for dead in a junk yard. However, the mayor and his violent pals are soon hunted by an ex-Green Beret with a penchant for justice. **81m/C VHS.** Jon Greene, Cindy Rome, Cameron Mitchell, Aldo Ray, Chuck "Porky" Mitchell, Wilson Dunster, Ted Leplat; **D:** Harry Hope. *TWE*

Swifty ♫½ 1936 A cowpoke is accused of murder but escapes to track down the real culprit and win the hand of the girl he loves. **60m/B VHS, Beta.** Hoot Gibson. *VCN*

Swim Team ♫ 1979 New coach for a terminally inept school swimming team whips them into shape. Doesn't hold much water. **81m/C VHS, Beta.** Stephen Furst, James Daughton, Jenny Neumann, Kim Day, Buster Crabbe; **D:** James Polakof. *PSM*

The Swimmer ♫♫♫½ 1968 (PG) A lonely suburbanite swims an existential swath through the pools of his neighborhood landscape in an effort at self-discovery. A surreal, strangely compelling work based on a story by John Cheever. **94m/C VHS, Beta, LV.** Burt Lancaster, Janice Rule, Janet Landgard, Marge Champion, Kim Hunter, Rose Gregorio, John David Garfield; **D:** Frank Perry; **M:** Marvin Hamlisch. *GKK*

Swimming Pool ♫♫½ 1970 (PG) Two men and two women spend a weekend in a villa on the French Riviera, manipulating each other, playing sexual games, and changing partners. Their escapades end in murder. Romantic melodrama is sensuous if slow-moving. French film dubbed in English. **85m/C VHS, Beta.** *FR* Romy Schneider, Alain Delon, Maurice Ronet, Jane Birkin; **D:** Jacques Deray. *NLC*

Swimming to Cambodia ♫♫♫ 1987 Gray tells the story of his bit part in "The Killing Fields," filmed in Cambodia, and makes ironic observations about modern life. It works. **87m/C VHS, Beta, LV, Closed Caption.** Spalding Gray; **D:** Jonathan Demme; **C:** John Bailey; **M:** Laurie Anderson. *ORI, WAR*

Swimming with Sharks ♫♫♫ *The Buddy Factor* 1994 (R) Budding screenwriter Guy (Whaley) goes to work for notoriously insulting movie producer Buddy (Spacey). Soon, Guy grows tired of his boss's demeaning treatment and cruel means of communication and devises a scheme which would even the score. Hollywood satire has more bite than "The Player," and a devious climax, but it's mostly an opportunity for Spacey to hang his hams, which he does with glee. Debut for director Huang, who based his script on his experience as a production assistant. See it with your boss.*CW:* Some scenes of psychological/physical torture; pervasive strong language. **93m/C VHS, LV, Closed Caption.** Kevin Spacey, Frank Whaley, Michelle Forbes, Benicio Del Toro; **D:** George Huang; **W:** George Huang; **C:** Steven Firestone. New York Film Critics Awards '95: Best Supporting Actor (Spacey); Nominations: Independent Spirit Awards '96: Best Actor (Spacey). *THV*

Swimsuit: The Movie ♫½ 1989 A young ad executive decides to revitalize a swimsuit company's failing business by sponsoring a contest for the perfect swimsuit model. Made-for-television fluff. **100m/C VHS.** William Katt, Catherine Oxenberg, Cyd Charisse, Nia Peeples, Tom Villard, Cheryl Pollak, Billy Warlock, Jack Wagner; **D:** Chris Thomson; **W:** Robert Schiff; **M:** John D'Andrea. *AIP*

The Swindle ♫♫ *Il Bidone* 1955 Three Italian conmen pull capers in Rome trying to make a better life for themselves. Dark overtones permeate one of Fellini's lesser efforts. Good cast can't bring up the level of this film. In Italian with English subtitles. **92m/C VHS, LV.** *IT* Broderick Crawford, Giulietta Masina, Richard Basehart, Franco Fabrizi; **D:**

Federico Fellini; **W:** Federico Fellini, Tullio Pinelli, Ennio Flaiano; **M:** Nino Rota. *IME, CVC, TPV*

Swindle ♫ 1992 Two life-long friends set up scam after scam in their quest for sex and money. Their latest con involves a phony marriage broker business, which provides the opportunity to meet a lot of lovely ladies. Only it turns out the hustlers may be the ones getting hustled. **85m/C VHS.** Robby West, Britt Houston, Elaina Dunn, Samantha Fong, Bobby Tess, Donna Thomas; **D:** Jason Holt. *CEL*

Swing High, Swing Low ♫♫½ 1937 A trumpet player fights the bottle and the dice to become a hit in the jazz world and marry the woman he loves. Solid drama. From the stage play "Burlesque." Made first as "The Dance of Life," then as "When My Baby Smiles At Me." **95m/B VHS, Beta.** Carole Lombard, Fred MacMurray, Charles Butterworth, Dorothy Lamour; **D:** Mitchell Leisen. *NOS, HHT, DVT*

Swing It, Professor ♫♫½ *Swing it Buddy* 1937 A stodgy music professor refuses to recognize jazz as a valid musical form and subsequently loses his job. During his unemployment, he wanders into a nightclub and discovers jazz isn't so bad after all. Nice camera work. ♫ I'm Sorta Kinda Glad I Met You; An Old-Fashioned Melody; Richer Than A Millionaire. **62m/B VHS.** Pinky Tomlin, Paula Stone, Mary Kornman, Milburn Stone, Pat Gleason; **D:** Marshall Neilan. *NOS, DVT, HEG*

Swing It, Sailor! ♫♫ 1937 Two footloose sailors go after the same woman while on shore leave. Decent screwball comedy. **61m/B VHS, Beta.** Wallace Ford, Ray Mayer, Isabel Jewell, Mary Treen; **D:** Raymond Cannon. *VYY, NOS*

Swing Kids ♫♫ 1993 (PG-13) In 1939 in Germany, big band or "swing" music is the instrument used by a group of young people to rebel against the conformity demanded by Hitler. Highlights the politics of the era, but concentrates mainly on three teenagers and the strains that Nazi power put on their friendship. Although the premise is based on historic fact, there is still something disturbingly silly about the entire production. Dance sequences are lively and well-choreographed. Branagh (in an uncredited role) plays a smooth-talking Gestapo chief. Filmed on location in Prague, Czechoslovakia (as a substitute for Hamburg, Germany). **114m/C VHS, Beta, LV, Closed Caption.** Robert Sean Leonard, Christian Bale, Frank Whaley, Barbara Hershey, Tushka Bergen, David Tom, Kenneth Branagh; **D:** Thomas Carter; **W:** Jonathan Marc Feldman; **M:** James Horner. *HPH*

Swing Parade of 1946 ♫½ 1946 One of the multitude of 1940s musicals. Young songwriter falls in love with club owner. Highlights include an appearance by the Three Stooges. ♫ Stormy Weather; Just a Little Fond Affection; Don't Worry About the Mule; A Tender Word Will Mend It All; On the Sunny Side of the Street; Oh, Brother; After All This Time; Caledonia. **74m/B VHS.** Gale Storm, Phil Regan, Moe Howard, Edward Brophy, Connee Boswell; **D:** Phil Karlson. *NO*

Swing Shift ♫♫½ 1984 (PG) When Hawn takes a job at an aircraft plant after her husband goes off to war, she learns more than riveting. Lahti steals the film as her friend and co-worker. A detailed reminiscence of the American home front during WWII that never seems to gel. Produced by Hawn. **100m/C VHS, Beta, LV.** Goldie Hawn, Kurt Russell, Ed Harris, Christine Lahti, Holly Hunter, Chris Lemmon, Belinda Carlisle, Fred Ward, Roger Corman, Lisa Pelikan; **D:** Jonathan Demme; **W:** Ron Nyswaner, Bo Goldman; **C:** Tak Fujimoto. New York Film Critics Awards '84: Best Supporting Actress (Lahti); Nominations: Academy Awards '84: Best Supporting Actress (Lahti). *WAR*

Swing Time ♫♫♫ 1936 Astaire, a dancer who can't resist gambling, is engaged to marry another woman, until he meets Ginger. One of the team's best efforts. Laserdisc version includes: production photos and stills, commentary on Fred Astaire and musical films, and excerpts from "Hooray for Love" featuring Bill "Bojangles" Rob-

inson and Fats Waller. ♫ The Way You Look Tonight; Waltz in Swing Time; Never Gonna Dance; Pick Yourself Up; A Fine Romance; Bojangles of Harlem. **103m/B VHS, Beta, LV.** Fred Astaire, Ginger Rogers, Helen Broderick, Betty Furness, Eric Blore, Victor Moore; **D:** George Stevens; **M:** Jerome Kern, Dorothy Fields. Academy Awards '36: Best Song ("The Way You Look Tonight").*TTC, MED, CRC*

Swingers ♫♫♫ 1996 (R) Hip, hilarious, and highly entertaining low-budget comedy features five young showbiz wannabes on the prowl for career breaks and beautiful "babies" in the Hollywood retro club scene. Mike (screenwriter Favreau) is a struggling actor/comedian from New York who's having trouble getting over his ex. His slick, handsome friend Trent (Vaughn, in a star-making turn) and the rest of his neo-Rat Pack buddies try to get him back in the game with nightly parties and lounge-hopping. Witty script and clever camera work make this one "money, baby, money!"*CW:* Language throughout. **96m/C VHS, LV, Closed Caption.** Jon Favreau, Vince Vaughn, Ron Livingston, Patrick Van Horn, Alex Desert, Brooke Langton, Heather Graham, Deena Martin, Katherine Kendall, Blake Lindsley; **D:** Doug Liman; **W:** Jon Favreau; **C:** Doug Liman; **M:** Justin Reinhardt. MTV Movie Awards '97: Best New Filmmaker Award (Liman). *TOU*

A Swingin' Summer ♫½ 1965 A bunch of groovy guys and gals go-go to the beach for a vacation of fun and sun and end up starting a rock 'n' roll concert series. Everybody gets part of the action...even the bespectacled Welch, who gets a chance to sing. Performances from the Righteous Brothers and rock semi-legends Donnie Brooks, Gary Lewis and the Playboys, and the Rip Chords. ♫ Red Hot Roadster; Justine; Penny the Poo; Out to Lunch; Nitro; Ready to Groove. **81m/C VHS.** James Stacy, William Wellman Jr., Quinn O'Hara, Martin West, Mary Mitchell, Allan Jones, Raquel Welch; **D:** Robert Sparr; **W:** Leigh Chapman. *NO*

The Swinging Cheerleaders 1974 (PG) A group of amorous cheerleaders turn on the entire campus in this typical sexploiter. **90m/C VHS, Beta.** Cheryl "Rainbeaux" Smith, Colleen Camp, Jo Johnston; **D:** Jack Hill. *MON*

Swinging Wives 1979 (R) Ribald humor for the discriminating viewer. **84m/C VHS, Beta.** Gale Mayberrie, Ron James. *NO*

Swiss Conspiracy ♫♫ 1977 (PG) Against the opulent background of the world's richest financial capital and playground of the wealthy, one man battles to stop a daring and sophisticated blackmailer preying on the secret bank account set. Fast-paced, if sometimes confusing. **92m/C VHS, Beta.** *GE* David Janssen, Senta Berger; **D:** Jack Arnold. *NO*

The Swiss Family Robinson ♫♫♫ 1960 A family, seeking to escape Napoleon's war in Europe, sets sail for New Guinea, but shipwrecks on a deserted tropical island. There they build an idyllic life, only to be confronted by a band of pirates. Lots of adventure for family viewing. Filmed on location on the island of Tobago. Based on the novel by Johann Wyss. **126m/C VHS, Beta, LV.** John Mills, Dorothy McGuire, James MacArthur, Tommy Kirk, Janet Munro, Sessue Hayakawa; **D:** Ken Annakin. *DIS, IGP*

Swiss Miss ♫♫½ 1938 Stan and Ollie are mousetrap salesmen on the job in Switzerland. Highlights include Stan's tuba serenade and the gorilla-on-the-bridge episode. Also included on this tape is a 1935 Thelma Todd/Patsy Kelly short, "Hot Money." **97m/B VHS, Beta.** Stan Laurel, Oliver Hardy, Della Lind, Walter Woolf King, Eric Blore, Thelma Todd, Patsy Kelly; **D:** John Blystone. *CCB, MED, FCT*

The Switch ♫♫ 1989 (R) An escaped convict takes the place of a talented conman and chaos ensues. **?m/C VHS.** Anthony Quinn, Adriano Celentano, Capucine, Corinne Clery. *NO*

Switch 🎬🎬🎬 1991 (R) A chauvinist louse, slain by the girlfriends he misused, is sent back to Earth as an alluring female to learn the other side's point of view. The plot may lack urgency, but this is a sparkling adult comedy that scores as it pursues the gimmicky concept to a logical, outrageous and touching conclusion. Barkin's act as swaggering male stuck in a woman's body is a masterwork of physical humor. **CW:** Language. 104m/C VHS, LV, **Closed Caption.** Ellen Barkin, Jimmy Smits, JoBeth Williams, Lorraine Bracco, Perry King, Bruce Martyn Payne, Tony Roberts; **D:** Blake Edwards; **W:** Blake Edwards; **M:** Henry Mancini. HBO, WAR

Switchblade Sisters woof! *The Jezebels; Playgirl Gang* 1975 Crime gang of female ex-cons wreaks pseudo-feminist havoc. Bruce is Lenny Bruce's daughter. 90m/C VHS. Robbie Lee, Joanne Nail, Monica Gayle, Kitty Bruce, Asher Brauner, Chase Newhart, Marlene Clark, Janice Karman, Don Stark, Kate Murtagh, Bill Adler; **D:** Jack Hill; **W:** F.X. Maier; **C:** Stephen M. Katz; **M:** Les Baxter, Medusa, Chuck Day, Richard Person. TOU, HHE

Switched at Birth 🎬🎬½ 1991 (PG) A fact-based made for television drama about two girls, switched in a hospital nursery at birth. Only when one girl dies, a decade later, do her parents discover that she could not have been their biological child. Their search for their daughter leads to an emotional conflict between the girl, the man that raised her, and the biological parents who seek to claim her. Beware of the sappy Hollywood ending, five years later the story of Kimberly Mays is still going through the U.S. judicial system. 200m/C VHS. Bonnie Bedelia, Brian Kerwin, Ed Asner, Caroline McWilliams, John M. Jackson, Lois Smith, Eve Gordon, Judith Hoag, Ariana Richards; **D:** Waris Hussein. COL, PMS

Switching Channels 🎬🎬½ 1988 (PG) A modernized remake of "His Girl Friday," and therefore the fourth version of "The Front Page." Beautiful television anchorwoman (Turner) wants to marry handsome tycoon (Reeve), but her scheming ex-husband (Reynolds) gets in the way. Weak performances from everyone but Beatty and lackluster direction render this oft-told story less funny than usual. 108m/C VHS, Beta, LV, **Closed Caption.** Burt Reynolds, Kathleen Turner, Christopher Reeve, Ned Beatty, Henry Gibson, George Newbern, Al Waxman, Ken James, Joe Silver, Charles Kimbrough, Tony Rosato; **D:** Ted Kotcheff; **W:** Jonathan Reynolds; **M:** Michel Legrand. COL

Swoon 🎬🎬🎬 1991 Kalin's directorial debut is a stylish rendering of the sensational 1924 kidnapping and murder of Bobby Franks by Richard Loeb and Nathan Leopold Jr. and their subsequent trial and imprisonment. Core elements of the case remain but Kalin imposes contemporary styles and morals on the past, particularly his protest against the homophobic attitudes influencing the trial while acknowledging the jaded and dispassionate behavior of the two young men. Previous cinematic versions of the murder case include "Rope" and "Compulsion" but Kalin graphically portrays the characters homosexuality, which was only hinted at in the earlier films. 95m/B VHS, LV, **Closed Caption.** Daniel Schlachet, Craig Chester, Ron Vawter, Michael Kirby, Michael Stumm, Valda Z. Drabla, Natalie Stanford; **D:** Tom Kalin; **W:** Tom Kalin; **C:** Ellen Kuras; **M:** James Bennett. Sundance Film Festival '92: Best Cinematography. NLC, IME

The Sword and the Cross 🎬½ 1958 A grade-B adventure about the life of Mary Magdelene. 93m/B VHS, Beta. Yvonne De Carlo, George Mistral; **D:** Carlo L. Bragaglia. NO

Sword & the Dragon 🎬🎬 *Ilya Mourometz* 1956 A young warrior must battle any number of giant mythical creatures. 81m/C VHS, Beta. RU Boris Andreyer, Andrei Abrikosov; **D:** Alexander Ptushko. VCI, SNC

The Sword & the Rose 🎬🎬½ *When Knighthood was in Flower* 1953 Mary Tudor, sister of King Henry VIII, shuns the advances of a nobleman for the love of a commoner. Johns is an obst-

inate princess; Justice, a fine king. Based on the book "When Knighthood Was in Flower." 91m/C VHS, Beta, LV. Richard Todd, Glynis Johns, Michael Gough, Jane Barrett, James Robertson Justice; **D:** Ken Annakin; **C:** Geoffrey Unsworth. DIS, HHE, BTV

Sword & the Sorcerer 🎬½ 1982 (R) Young prince strives to regain control of his kingdom, now ruled by an evil knight and a powerful magician. Mediocre script and acting is enhanced by decent special effects. 100m/C VHS, Beta, LV. Lee Horsley, Kathleen Beller, George Maharis, Simon MacCorkindale, Richard Lynch, Richard Moll, Robert Tessier, Nina Van Pallandt, Anna Bjorn, Jeff Corey; **D:** Albert Pyun; **W:** Albert Pyun. USH

The Sword in the Stone 🎬🎬🎬 1963 (G) The Disney version of the first volume of T.H. White's "The Once and Future King" wherein King Arthur, as a boy, is instructed in the ways of the world by Merlin and Archimedes the owl. Although not in the Disney masterpiece fold, boasts the usual superior animation and a gripping mythological tale. 79m/C VHS, Beta, LV, **Closed Caption.** **D:** Wolfgang Reitherman; **M:** George Bruns; **V:** Ricky Sorenson, Sebastian Cabot, Karl Swenson, Junius Matthews, Alan Napier, Norman Alden, Martha Wentworth, Barbara Jo Allen. Nominations: Academy Awards '63: Best Adapted Score. DIS, KUI, HMV

Sword of Doom 🎬🎬🎬 *Daibosatsu Toge* 1967 A rousing samurai epic detailing the training of an impulsive, bloodlusting warrior by an elder expert. In Japanese with English subtitles. 120m/B VHS, Beta. JP Tatsuya Nakadai, Toshiro Mifune; **D:** Kihachi Okamoto. NLC

The Sword of El Cid 🎬½ *La Spada del Cid* 1962 Not much dash and very little daring-do in this poorly plotted, overly dramatic saga of good vs. evil, Spanish style. Rightful heir to the crown threatens, challenges and enevitably crosses swords with the pretender to his throne. Costume mavens may find something to hold their interest. 86m/C VHS, Beta. SP IT Roland Carey, Sandro Moretti, Chantal Deberg, Iliana Grimaldi, Jose Luis Pellicena, Daniela Bianchi; **D:** Miguel Iglesias. SNC

Sword of Fury II 🎬½ 1973 The sequel. Two samurai fight to the death to determine who will become the premier swordsman of all Japan. With English subtitles. 77m/C VHS, Beta. JP Hideki Takahashi, Jiro Tamiya. NO

Sword of Gideon 🎬🎬½ 1986 An action packed and suspenseful made for television film about an elite commando group who set out to avenge the Munich Olympic killings of 1972. Adapted from "Vengeance" by George Jonas. 148m/C VHS, **Closed Caption.** Steven Bauer, Michael York, Rod Steiger, Colleen Dewhurst, Robert Joy, Laurent Malet, Lino Ventura, Leslie Hope; **D:** Michael Anderson Sr.; **W:** Chris Bryant; **M:** Georges Delerue. NO

Sword of Honor 🎬½ 1994 (R) Undercover cop and martial arts expert Johnny Lee (Leigh) investigates his partner's mysterious death amidst the tawdry glamor of Vegas. **CW:** Bloody shootings; martial arts violence; sexuality and language. ?m/C VHS, LV, **Closed Caption.** Steven Leigh, Sophia Crawford, Angelo Tiffe, Jerry Tiffe, Jeff Pruitt, Debbie Scofield; **D:** Robert Tiffe; **W:** Robert Tiffe, Clay Ayers; **M:** David Rubinstein. PMH

Sword of Lancelot 🎬🎬½ *Lancelot and Guinevere* 1963 A costume version of the Arthur-Lancelot-Guinevere triangle, with plenty of swordplay and a sincere respect for the old legend. 115m/C VHS, Beta. GB Cornel Wilde, Jean Wallace, Brian Aherne, George Baker; **D:** Cornel Wilde. USH

Sword of Monte Cristo 🎬½ 1951 Masked female avenger, seeking the liberty of the French people, discovers a valuable sword that holds the key to a vast fortune. But the sword is also desired by an evil government minister. 80m/C VHS, Beta. George Montgomery, Rita (Paula) Corday; **D:** Maurice Geraghty. VHE

Sword of Sherwood Forest 🎬🎬½ 1960 The Earl of Newark plots the murder of the Archbishop of Canterbury in yet another rendition of the Robin Hood legend. Cushing is truly evil as the villain. 80m/C VHS. GB Richard Greene, Peter Cushing, Niall MacGinnis, Richard Pasco, Jack Gwillim, Sarah Branch, Nigel Green, Oliver Reed; **D:** Terence Fisher. COL, MLB

Sword of the Valiant 🎬🎬 1983 (PG) The Green Knight arrives in Camelot to challenge Gawain. Remake of "Gawain And The Green Knight." Connery adds zest to a minor epic. 102m/C VHS, Beta. GB Sean Connery, Miles O'Keeffe, Cyrielle Claire, Leigh Lawson, Trevor Howard, Peter Cushing, Wilfrid Brambell, Lila Kedrova, John Rhys-Davies; **D:** Stephen Weeks; **W:** Philip M. Breen; **C:** Frederick A. (Freddie) Young. MGM

Sword of Venus 🎬 *Island of Monte Cristo* 1953 Uninspired production finds the son of the Count of Monte Cristo the victim in a scheme to deprive him of his wealth. 73m/B VHS. Robert Clarke, Catherine McLeod, Dan O'Herlihy, William Schallert; **D:** Harold Daniels. FCT

Swords of Death 🎬🎬 1971 Final film by Uchida, released posthumously, deals with the adventurous period exploits of the irrepressible Miyamoto Musashi. With English subtitles. 76m/C VHS, Beta. JP Kinnosuke Nakamura, Rentaro Mikuni; **D:** Tomu Uchida. VDA

The Swordsman 🎬🎬½ 1992 (R) The quest to return the stolen sword of the legendary Alexander the Great to a museum is muscular detective Lamas' assignment. Turns out the detective and his evil millionaire antagonist have been chasing each other through time in their endless quest for revenge and power. **CW:** Language and violence. 98m/C VHS, LV. Lorenzo Lamas, Claire Stansfield, Michael Champion; **D:** Michael Kennedy; **W:** Michael Kennedy. REP

Sworn Enemies 🎬🎬½ 1996 (R) Clifton Santier (Greene) goes on a killing spree in a small town where the local sheriff turns out to be his ex-partner, Pershing Quinn (Pare). Now the two enemies decide that only death will settle their old (and new) scores. 101m/C VHS, LV. Peter Greene, Michael Pare, Macha Grenon; **D:** Shimon Dotan; **W:** Rod Hewitt; **C:** Sylvain Brault; **M:** Walter Christian Rothe, Richard Anthony Boast. APX

Sybil 🎬🎬🎬 1976 Fact-based story of a woman who developed 16 distinct personalities, and the supportive psychiatrist who helped her put the pieces of her ego together. Excellent made-for-television production with Field's Emmy-winning performance. 122m/C VHS, Beta. Sally Field, Joanne Woodward, Brad Davis, Martine Bartlett, Jane Hoffman; **D:** Daniel Petrie. FOX

Sylvester 🎬🎬 1985 (PG) A 16-year-old girl and a cranky stockyard boss team up to train a battered horse named Sylvester for the National Equestrian trials. Nice riding sequences and good performances can't overcome familiar plot, but the kids will enjoy this one. 104m/C VHS, Beta, LV, **Closed Caption.** Melissa Gilbert, Richard Farnsworth, Michael Schoeffling, Constance Towers; **D:** Tim Hunter. COL

Sylvia 🎬🎬½ 1986 (PG) Biography of author/educator Sylvia Ashton-Warner, and her efforts to teach Maori children in New Zealand to read via unorthodox methods. David is a marvel. Based on Ashton-Warner's books "Teacher" and "I Passed This Way." 99m/C VHS, Beta, **Closed Caption.** NZ Eleanor David, Tom Wilkinson, Nigel Terry, Mary Regan; **D:** Michael Firth. FOX

Sylvia and the Phantom 🎬🎬🎬 *Sylvia and the Ghost* 1945 A charming French comedy about a lonely young girl who is befriended by the ghost of a man killed decades earlier in a duel over the girl's grandmother. Based on the play by Alfred Adam. In French with English subtitles. 88m/B VHS, Beta. FR Odette Joyeux, Jacques Tati, Francois Perier; **D:** Claude Autant-Lara. HMV, NLC

Sylvia Scarlett 🎬🎬½ **1935** An odd British comedy about a woman who masquerades as a boy while on the run with her father, who causes all kinds of instinctive confusion in the men she meets. **94m/B VHS, Beta, LV.** Katharine Hepburn, Cary Grant, Brian Aherne, Edmund Gwenn, Natalie Paley, Dennie Moore, Lennox Pawle, Daisy Belmore, Nola Luxford; **D:** George Cukor; **C:** Russell Metty. *FCT, TTC*

Sympathy for the Devil 🎬🎬 *One Plus One* **1970** Rolling Stones provide music for confused, revolutionary documentary. Episodic jumble is odd, sometimes fascinating. **110m/C VHS, Beta.** *FR* Mick Jagger, Rolling Stones; **D:** Jean-Luc Godard. *FOX, OM*

Symphony in the Mountains 🎬🎬½ **1935** An early German sound romance, where an Austrian singing teacher falls in love with the sister of one of his student's. Featuring choral work by the Vienna Boys' Choir. In German with English subtitles. **75m/B VHS, Beta.** *GE FCT, IHF, GLV*

Synapse 🎬🎬 **1995 (R)** Black-marketeer Andre (Makepeace) is doublecrossed by a partner and arrested by Life Corp., which runs this futuristic civilization. As an experimental punishment, his mind is implanted into the body of Celeste (Duffy), who manages to escape and join up with a band of revolutionaries determined to destroy the evil corporation. Fast-paced story and good special effects. **CW:** Strong violence, and for sexuality and language. **89m/C VHS.** Karen Duffy, Saul Rubinek, Matt McCoy, Chris Makepeace; **D:** Allan Goldstein. *AVE*

Syngenor 🎬½ **1990 (R)** Syngenor stands for Synthesized Genetic Organism, to differentiate it from all other organisms. Created by science, it escapes, and a crack team of scientists and gung-ho military types are mobilized to track it down. **96m/C VHS.** Starr Andreeff, Michael Laurence, David Gale, Charles Lucia, Riva Spier, Jeff Doucette, Bill Gratton, Lewis Arquette, Jon Korkes, Melanie Shatner; **D:** George Elanjian Jr.; **M:** Tom Chase, Steve Rucker. *HMD*

T-Bird Gang 🎬½ **1959** A high school student goes undercover to infiltrate a teen gang. When his cover is blown, things get hairy. Laughable sleazebag production. **75m/B VHS.** Ed Nelson, John Brinkley, Pat George, Beach Dickerson, Tony Miller; **D:** Richard Harbinger; **M:** Shelley Manne. *SNC*

T Bone N Weasel 🎬 **1992 (PG-13)** Hines and Lloyd play not-so-ex-cons who steal a car and try to lead a life of ease. Crime doesn't pay. Made for cable television. **94m/C VHS, LV.** Gregory Hines, Christopher Lloyd. *TTC*

T-Force 🎬🎬½ **1994 (R)** T-Force is a successful cybernetic law enforcement team set up in the year 2007. But when innocent people get caught in the T-Force crossfire, a team shutdown is ordered, causing the members to turn renegade and fight for their survival instead. The plot rarely gets in the way of the hard-hitting action. **CW:** Non-stop sci-fi violence; some sexuality. **101m/C VHS, LV, Closed Caption.** Jack Scalia, Erin Gray, Evan Lurie, Daron McBee; **D:** Richard Pepin. *PMH*

T-Men 🎬🎬🎬 **1947** Treasury Department agents Dennis O'Brien (O'Keefe) and Tony Genaro (Ryder) infiltrate a mob counterfeiting gang. Filmed in semi-documentary style, exciting tale serves also as an effective commentary on the similarities between the agents and those they pursue. Mann and cinematographer Alton do especially fine work here. **96m/B VHS, LV.** Alfred Ryder, Dennis O'Keefe, June Lockhart, Mary Meade, Wallace Ford, Charles McGraw; **D:** Anthony Mann; **C:** John Alton. Nominations: Academy Awards '47: Best Sound. *KIV, MED*

Table for Five 🎬🎬½ **1983 (PG)** A divorced father takes his children on a Mediterranean cruise and while sailing, he learns that his ex-wife has died. The father and his ex-wife's husband struggle over who should raise the children. Sentimental and well-acted. **120m/C VHS, LV.** Jon Voight, Millie Perkins, Richard Crenna, Robbie Kiger, Roxana Zal, Son Hoang Bui, Marie-Christine Barrault, Kevin Costner; **D:** Robert Liebmann; **W:** David Seltzer; **M:** Miles Goodman. *FOX*

Table Settings 🎬🎬 **1984** A taped performance of James Lapines' comedy about the lives of three generations of a Jewish family. **90m/C VHS, Beta.** Robert Klein, Stockard Channing, Dinah Manoff, Eileen Heckart. *NO*

Tabloid! 🎬½ **1988** Unorthodox woman prints and sells racy trash for enquiring minds. **99m/C VHS.** Scott Davis, Glen Cobum; **D:** Bret McCormick, Matt Shaffen. *HHE*

Tabu: A Story of the South Seas 🎬🎬🎬½ **1931** Fascinating docudrama about a young pearl diver's ill-fated romance. The gods have declared the young woman he desires "taboo" to all men. Filmed on location in Tahiti. Authored and produced by Murnau and Flaherty. Flaherty left in mid-production due to artistic differences with Murnau, who was later killed in an auto accident one week before the premiere of film. Oscar-winning cinematography by Floyd Crosby. **81m/B VHS, Beta.** *D:* Robert Flaherty, F.W. Murnau; **C:** Floyd Crosby. Academy Awards '31: Best Cinematography; National Board of Review Awards '31: 10 Best Films of the Year. *MIL, GVV, LUM*

Taffin 🎬½ **1988 (R)** An Irish bill collector battles a group of corrupt businessmen who want to replace the local soccer field with a hazardous chemical plant. Pretty dull fare, overall, with Brosnan much less charismatic than usual. **96m/C VHS, Beta, LV.** *GB* Pierce Brosnan, Ray McAnally, Alison Doody, Patrick Bergin; **D:** Francis Megahy; **W:** David Ambrose. *MGM*

Tag: The Assassination Game 🎬½ **1982 (PG)** An exciting new game has been discovered by a group of university students. Players act as spies and assassins, "killing" each other to make points. But a school newspaper sportswriter finds the game has become more real than make-believe. Timely topic in the early '80s when Dungeons and Dragons and other "war" games were popular on college campuses across the nation. **92m/C VHS, Beta.** Robert Carradine, Linda Hamilton, Michael Winslow, Kristine DeBell, Perry Lang; **D:** Nick Castle; **W:** Nick Castle.

Tagget 🎬 **1990 (PG-13)** A former CIA operative who has erased his nightmarish stint in Vietnam gradually begins to recall his past. When pieces of the puzzle begin to come together, he remembers a few things that the government would prefer he forget. Soon, CIA men are on his trail and their mission is to see that he forgets his past—permanently. Made for cable television. **89m/C VHS, Closed Caption.** Daniel J. Travanti, William Sadler, Roxanne Hart, Stephen Tobolowsky, Peter Michael Goetz, Sarah Douglas, Noel Harrison; **D:** Richard T. Heffron. *USH*

Tai Chi 2 🎬½ **19??** Young Tai Chi master (Wu) battles corrupt officials and English merchants who are flooding the country with opium. And then he turns around and battles a bunch of high-kicking rivals for the love of a beautiful revolutionary (Chung). Chinese with subtitles or dubbed. **95m/C VHS.** *HK* Jacky Wu, Christy Chung, Sibelle Hu; **D:** Yuen Woo Ping. *TAI*

Tai-Pan 🎬½ **1986 (R)** A 19th century Scottish trader and his beautiful Chinese mistress are the main characters in this confusing attempt to dramatize the story of Hong Kong's development into a thriving trading port. Too many subplots and characters are introduced in a short time to do justice to James Clavell's novel of the same name, the basis for the movie. The first American production completely filmed in China. **130m/C VHS, Beta, LV, Closed Caption.** Bryan Brown, Joan Chen, John Stanton, Kyra Sedgwick, Tim Guinee, Russell Wong, Bert Remsen; **D:** Daryl Duke; **W:** John Briley; **C:** Jack Cardiff; **M:** Maurice Jarre. *VES*

Tails You Live, Heads You're Dead 🎬🎬 **1995 (R)** Cable thriller features Bernsen as a psycho who kills at random—and tells a stranger, McGinley, whom he met at a bar that the man is his next victim. After several unsuccessful attempts on his life, McGinley turns to detective Matheson for help. Based on the short story "Liar's Dice" by Bill Pronzini. **CW:** Some violence. **91m/C VHS, Beta, Closed Caption.** Corbin Bernsen, Ted McGinley, Tim Matheson; **D:** Tim Matheson; **W:** Miguel Tejada-Flores. *PAR*

Tailspin: Behind the Korean Airline Tragedy 🎬🎬 **1989** Made-for-TV docudrama on the 1983 downing of Korean Aire flight 007 in Soviet airspace. Purports to show the U.S. government's reaction to what became a major international incident. **82m/C VHS, Beta, LV.** Michael Moriarty, Michael Murphy, Chris Sarandon, Harris Yulin, Gavan O'Herlihy, Ed O'Ross; **D:** David Darlow; **M:** David Ferguson. *PSM, PAR*

Tailspin Tommy **1934** Features twelve chapters of the great action serial. **?m/B VHS.** Maurice Murphy, Noah Beery Jr., Walter Miller, Patricia Farr, Grant Withers, John Davidson, William Desmond, Charles A. Browne; **D:** Lew (Louis Friedlander) Landers. *GPV*

Tainted 🎬½ **1988** Small-town woman tries to endure after being raped. Both her husband and the attacker are killed, and she is forced to conceal their deaths. Poorly scripted. **90m/C VHS, Beta.** Shari Shattuck, Park Overall, Gene Tootle, Magilla Schaus, Blaque Fowler; **D:** Orestes Matacena. *HMD*

Tainted Blood 🎬 **1993 (R)** Welch stars as an investigative reporter whose latest story has her attempting to find the teenage twin of a psychotic killer. **CW:** Violence. **86m/C VHS, Beta, Closed Caption.** Raquel Welch, Alley Mills, Kerri Green, Natasha Gregson Wagner, Joan Van Ark; **D:** Matthew Patrick; **W:** Kathleen Rowell, Ginny Cerrella; **C:** Billy Dickson. *PAR*

Tainted Image 🎬🎬 **1991** Artist woman starts to lose sanity with help of boyfriend, psycho neighbor and rash of bizarre deaths. She turns to canvas for solace and decides she needs secret ingredient that can't be found in art supply store to complete masterpiece. **95m/C VHS.** Tom Saunders, Sandra Frances, Annetta Arpin, Ken La Mothe, Heidi Emerich, Steve Kornacki. *HHT, DMP*

The Take 🎬🎬 **1990 (R)** Recovering alcoholic cop faces wrath of drug lord and marriage on the rocks. **91m/C VHS.** Ray Sharkey, R. Lee Ermey, Lisa Hartman Black, Larry Manetti, Joe Lala; **D:** Leon Ichaso; **W:** Edward Anhalt, Handel Glassberg; **M:** David Beal. *USH*

Take a Hard Ride 🎬½ **1975 (R)** Dull spaghetti western about a cowboy transporting money to Mexico, evading bandits and bounty hunters. **103m/C VHS, Beta.** Jim Brown, Lee Van Cleef, Fred Williamson, Jim Kelly, Barry Sullivan; **D:** Anthony (Antonio Margheriti) Dawson; **M:** Jerry Goldsmith. *FOX*

Take Down 🎬½ **1979 (PG)** Hermann is charming as a high school English teacher turned reluctant wrestling coach. **96m/C VHS, Beta.** Lorenzo Lamas, Kathleen Lloyd, Maureen McCormick, Edward Herrmann; **D:** Keith Merrill. *UNI*

Take It Big 🎬½ **1944** Uninspired B-musical starring the Tin Man from the "Wizard of Oz." Haley is an impoverished actor who inherits a ranch and saves it by—surprise—putting on a show. ♫ Sunday, Monday, and Always; Love and Learn; Life Can Be Beautiful; Take It Big; I'm a Big Success with You. **75m/B VHS, Beta.** Jack Haley, Harriet Hilliard Nelson, Mary Beth Hughes, Arline Judge, Nils T. Granlund, Fuzzy Knight, Ozzie Nelson; **D:** Frank McDonald. *NOS, VYY, DVT*

Take Me Back to Oklahoma 🎬 **1940** Musical western with comedy. **64m/B VHS, Beta.** Tex Ritter, Terry Walker, Karl Hackett, George Eldridge; **D:** Al(bert) Herman. *NOS, VCN, VYY*

Take Me Out to the Ball Game 🎬🎬½ *Everybody's Cheering* **1949** Williams manages a baseball team, locks horns with players Sinatra and Kelly, and wins them over with song. Naturally, there's a water ballet scene. Contrived and forced, but enjoyable. ♫ Take Me Out to the Ball Game; The Hat My Father Wore on St. Patrick's Day; O'Brien to Ryan to Goldberg; The Right Girl for Me; It's Fate, Baby, It's Fate; Yes, Indeedy; Strictly U.S.A. **93m/C VHS, Beta, LV.** Frank

Sinatra, Gene Kelly, Esther Williams, Jules Munshin, Betty Garrett, Edward Arnold, Tom Dugan, Richard Lane; **D:** Busby Berkeley. *MGM*

Take the Money and Run 🐾🐾🐾

1969 (PG) Allen's directing debut; he also co-wrote and starred. "Documentary" follows a timid, would-be bank robber who can't get his career off the ground and keeps landing in jail. Little plot, but who cares? Nonstop one-liners and slapstick. **85m/C VHS, Beta, LV.** Woody Allen, Janet Margolin, Marcel Hillaire, Louise Lasser; **D:** Woody Allen; **W:** Woody Allen; **M:** Marvin Hamlisch. *FOX*

Take This Job & Shove It 🐾🐾 1981

(PG) The Johnny Paycheck song inspired this story of a hot-shot efficiency expert who returns to his hometown to streamline the local brewery. Encounters with old pals inspire self-questioning. Alternately inspired and hackneyed. Cameos by Paycheck and other country stars. **100m/C VHS, Beta, Closed Caption.** Robert Hays, Art Carney, Barbara Hershey, David Keith, Martin Mull, Eddie Albert, Penelope Milford; **Cameos:** Johnny Paycheck, David Allen Coe, Charlie Rich, Lacy J. Dalton; **D:** Gus Trikonis; **W:** Barry Schneider. *COL*

Take Two 🐾 1987 (R)

A woman has an affair with her husband's twin brother. Interesting metaphysically: Are you my husband or my lover? But is an adultery/murder drama with Frank Stallone worth 101 minutes of your time? **101m/C VHS, Beta, LV.** Grant Goodeve, Robin Mattson, Frank Stallone, Warren Berlinger, Darwyn Swalve, Nita Talbot; **D:** Peter Rowe. *ACA*

Take Your Best Shot 🐾½ 1982

Standard TV fare about an out-of-work actor struggling with his low self-esteem and failing marriage. Made-for-television comedy. **96m/C VHS, Beta.** Robert Urich, Meredith Baxter, Jeffrey Tambor, Jack Bannon, Claudette Nevins; **D:** David Greene. *LIV*

Taken Away 🐾🐾½ 1989

Struggling young divorcee Stephanie Monroe waits tables during the day and studies to be a computer tech at night in order to provide her 8-year-old daughter Abby with a better life. Unable to afford child care, Stephanie leaves Abby alone in the afternoon until she can get home from work. But when the welfare system finds out Stephanie is accused of child neglect and must fight a bureaucratic nightmare in order to get her child back. Made for television. **94m/C VHS, LV, Closed Caption.** Valerie Bertinelli, Kevin Dunn, Joshua Maurer, Anna Maria Horsford, Juliet Sorcey, Nada Despotovich, Matthew Faison, James Arone; **D:** John D. Patterson; **W:** Robert Freedman, Selma Thomson. *USH*

The Takeover 🐾🐾 1994 (R)

East coast crime boss Danny Stein (Drago) decides to take over the L.A. operations of rival Tony Valachi (Mancuso). Lots of mayhem ensues. **CW:** Gangster violence, sexuality, and language. **91m/C VHS, LV, Closed Caption.** Billy Drago, Nick Mancuso, John Savage, Eric Da Re, Cali Timmins, David Amos, Gene Mitchell; **D:** Troy Cook; **W:** Gene Mitchell; **M:** Jimmy Lifton. *LIV*

Takin' It All Off

woof! **1987** In this sequel to "Takin' It Off," Kitten does it again with unbelievable bumps and grinds. **90m/C VHS.** Francesca "Kitten" Natividad; **D:** Ed Hansen. *LIV, VES*

Taking Care of Business 🐾½ Filofax

1990 (R) Too familiar tale of switched identity has crazed Cubs fan Belushi find Grodin's Filofax, allowing him to pose as businessman. Old jokes and a story full of holes. **108m/C VHS, Beta, LV, Closed Caption.** James Belushi, Charles Grodin, Anne DeSalvo, Loryn Locklin, Veronica Hamel, Hector Elizondo, Mako, Gates McFadden, Stephen Elliott; **D:** Arthur Hiller; **W:** Jeffrey Abrams. *HPH*

The Taking of Beverly Hills 🐾½

1991 (R) Deranged billionaire Bat Masterson designs a bogus toxic spill that leaves the wealth of Beverly Hills his for the taking. Football hero Boomer Hayes teams up with renegade cop Ed Kelvin to try and stop Masterson and save the city of Beverly Hills. **CW:** Language and some violence. **96m/C VHS, LV, Closed Caption.** Ken Wahl, Matt Frewer, Robert Davi, Harley Jane Kozak, Lee James, Bran-

scombe Richmond, Lyman Ward, Michael Bowen, William Prince, Ken Swofford, George Wyner; **D:** Sidney J. Furie; **W:** Sidney J. Furie, David Burke. *COL, NLC*

The Taking of Flight 847: The Uli Derickson Story 🐾🐾🐾 The Flight 1988

Wagner plays the stewardess who acted as a go-between for the passengers during a 1985 terrorist hijacking, saving all but one life. True-story drama is suspenseful and entertaining, nominated for several Emmys. Made-for-television drama. **100m/C VHS, LV.** Laurie Walters, Sandy McPeak, Ray Wise, Leslie Easterbrook, Lindsay Wagner, Eli Danker, Joseph Naser; **D:** Paul Wendkos; **W:** Norman Merrill. *IME*

The Taking of Pelham One Two Three 🐾🐾🐾 1974 (R)

A hijack team, lead by the ruthless Shaw, seizes a New York City subway car and holds the 17 passengers for one million dollars ransom. Fine pacing keeps things on the edge. New cinematic techniques used by cameraman Owen Roizman defines shadowy areas like never before. **105m/C VHS, Beta.** Robert Shaw, Walter Matthau, Martin Balsam, Hector Elizondo, James Broderick, Earl Hindman, Dick O'Neill, Jerry Stiller, Tony Roberts, James Broderick, Kenneth McMillan, Julius W. Harris, Sal Viscuso; **D:** Joseph Sargent; **C:** Owen Roizman; **M:** David Shire. *MGM, FOX*

Taking the Heat 🐾🐾½ 1993 (R)

When mobster Arkin kills a sporting-goods dealer with a golf club the murder is witnessed by yuppie Goldwyn. Whitfield is the ambitious cop who wants Goldwyn to testify against the gangster—if she can keep him alive long enough to get him to court. One long chase scene. Made for cable television. **91m/C VHS.** Lynn Whitfield, Tony Goldwyn, Alan Arkin, George Segal, Peter Boyle; **D:** Tom Mankiewicz; **W:** Dan Gordon. *FXV*

Tale of a Vampire 🐾🐾½ 1992 (R)

In present day London, ageless vampire Alex (Sands) still mourns his long-lost vampiric love, Virginia, when he meets Anne (Hamilton) who resembles Virginia. Alex doesn't know he's being stalked by Virginia's husband, Edgar (Cranham), also a vampire. Edgar decides to use Anne (with whom Alex has fallen in love) as bait, in a revenge plot. A tiny budget and slow pacing mar the film's fine visual style and good work by the two male leads. Film debut for director Sato. **CW:** Vampire violence and gore. **93m/C VHS.** GB Julian Sands, Kenneth Cranham, Suzanna Hamilton; **D:** Shimako Sato; **W:** Jane Corbett, Shimako Sato; **M:** Julian Joseph. *THV*

The Tale of Ruby Rose 🐾🐾🐾 1987

(PG) Living in the mountains of Tasmania, Ruby Rose, her husband Henry, and their adopted son Gem, struggle to survive the '30s depression by hunting and trapping. Having spent all her life in the mountains, Ruby Rose has a very superstitious view of life and a terror of nightfall. But after an argument with her husband, Ruby Rose sets out on a cross-country journey to find her grandmother and discover the secrets of her past. **101m/C VHS.** AU Melita Jurisic, Chris Haywood; **D:** Roger Sholes; **W:** Roger Sholes; **M:** Paul Schutze. *NO*

A Tale of Springtime 🐾🐾½ 1992 (PG)

Comedy-romance is the first film in Rohmer's planned new series, the "Tales of the Four Seasons," not to be confused with his "Six Moral Tales" or his "Comedies and Proverbs." Centers around Jeanne, a high school philosophy teacher; Natacha, a young student; and Igor, Natacha's father. As characteristic of Rohmer films, texture and character largely overshadow linear plots and social messages. However, the efficiency and directness of his camerawork make it a pleasure to watch. **107m/C VHS, Closed Caption.** FR Anne Teyssedre, Hugues Quester, Florence Darel, Eloise Bennett, Sophie Robin; **D:** Eric Rohmer; **W:** Eric Rohmer. *ORI*

The Tale of the Frog Prince 🐾🐾🐾½ 1983

Superb edition of Shelley Duvall's "Faerie Tale Theatre" finds Williams the victim of an angry fairy godmother's spell. Garr to the rescue as the self-centered princess who saves him with a kiss. Directed and written

by Idle of Monty Python fame. **60m/C VHS, Beta, LV, Closed Caption.** Robin Williams, Teri Garr; **D:** Eric Idle; **W:** Eric Idle. *FOX*

A Tale of Two Cities 🐾🐾🐾🐾 1936

Lavish production of the Dickens' classic set during the French Revolution, about two men who bear a remarkable resemblance to each other, both in love with the same girl. Carefree lawyer Sydney Carton (Colman) roused to responsibility, makes the ultimate sacrifice. A memorable Madame DeFarge from stage star Yurka in her film debut, with assistance from other Dickens' film stars Rathbone, Oliver and Walthall. **128m/B VHS, Beta.** Ronald Colman, Elizabeth Allan, Edna May Oliver, Reginald Owen, Isabel Jewell, Walter Catlett, H.B. Warner, Donald Woods, Basil Rathbone, Blanche Yurka, Henry B. Walthall; **D:** Jack Conway; **W:** W.P. Lipscomb, S.N. Behrman; **M:** Herbert Stothart. **Nominations:** Academy Awards '36: Best Film Editing, Best Picture. *MGM, KUI, IGP*

A Tale of Two Cities 🐾🐾🐾 1958 A

well-done British version of the Dickens' classic about a lawyer who sacrifices himself to save another man from the guillotine during the French Reign of Terror. The sixth remake of the tale. **117m/B VHS, Beta.** GB Dirk Bogarde, Dorothy Tutin, Christopher Lee, Donald Pleasence, Ian Bannen, Cecil Parker; **D:** Ralph Thomas. *LCA, FHS*

A Tale of Two Cities 🐾🐾½ 1980

Impressive looking but bloodless adaptation of the Dickens novel set in the French Revolution. Saradon takes on the dual role of sacrificing English lawyer Carton and French nobleman Darnay, with Krige as the lovely woman caught between the two. Made for television. **156m/C VHS.** Chris Sarandon, Alice Krige, Peter Cushing, Kenneth More, Barry Morse, Flora Robson, Billie Whitelaw; **D:** Jim Goddard; **W:** John Gay. *LIV, FUS*

A Tale of Two Cities 🐾🐾🐾 1991

Masterpiece Theatre production of the classic Dickens tale. The French revolution was a time of revenge and brutality, but also provided the proving ground for a love greater than life. Terrific cast and perfectly detailed production. On two cassettes. **240m/C VHS, Closed Caption.** James Wilby, Serena Gordon, John Mills, Jean-Pierre Aumont, Anna Massey. *PBS, VIF, TVC*

Tale of Two Cities/In the Switch Tower 🐾½ 1915

A package of two medium-length silent films, the latter featuring a rare acting appearance by director Borzage. **70m/B VHS, Beta, 8mm.** Walter Edwards, Maurice Costello, Florence Turner, Frank Borzage, Norma Talmadge, Leo Delaney. *VYY*

Tale of Two Sisters 🐾½ 1989

Sheen narrates sensual drama about two beautiful, ambitious sisters. **90m/C VHS.** Valerie Breiman, Claudia Christian, Sydney Lassick, Jeff Conaway. *NO*

A Tale of Winter 🐾🐾½ Conte D'Hiver 1992

Portrays the romantic trials of a young French woman who cannot choose between her two smitten lovers and her one true love, the long disappeared father of her child. Felicie (Very) hopelessly loves Charles (Van Den Driessche), whom she met five years before, but mistakenly gave the wrong address. Rohmer's trademark conversation-filled scenes find her brooding over her predicament, running from one lover and back again, until a revelation during a viewing of Shakespeare's "The Winter's Tale." A charming cast carries the story to a surprise twist of an ending. Second in the series "Tales of the Four Seasons." In French with English subtitles. **114m/C VHS.** FR Charlotte Very, Frederic Van Dren Driessche, Michel Voletti, Herve Furic, Ava Loraschi, Jean-Luc Revol, Haydee Caillot, Jean-Claude Biette, Rosette, Marie Riviere; **D:** Eric Rohmer; **W:** Eric Rohmer; **C:** Luc Pages; **M:** Sebastien Erms. *NYF*

Talent for the Game 🐾🐾½ 1991 (PG)

A slight but handsomely produced baseball pleasantry about a talent scout who recruits a phenomenonal young pitcher, then sees the kid exploited by the team owner. More like an anecdote than a story, with an ending that aims a little too hard to please. Good for sports fans and family audiences. **91m/C VHS, Beta, LV, Closed Caption.** Edward James Olmos, Lorraine Bracco, Jeff Corbett, Jamey Sheridan, Terry Kinney; **D:** Robert M. Young; **W:** David Himmelstein, Tom Donnelly, Larry Ferguson; **M:** David Newman. *PAR*

Tales from Avonlea, Vol. 1: The Journey Begins *Road to Avonlea; Avonlea* 1990
From the producer of the popular "Anne of Green Gables" movie and its sequel comes this weekly TV series, a collaboration of the Disney channel and CBC Television. In "The Journey Begins," Sara meets the stuffy Aunt Hetty and her cousins Felix and Felicity. Unhappy with her life, she decides whether to stay or run away. "The Proof of the Pudding" finds the grownups away and Felicity in charge of her siblings and Sara for the weekend. The same attention to detail, particularly in scenic views of lovely Prince Edward Island and the costumes, is shown in the series. Based on the writings of Lucy Maud Montgomery. **106m/C VHS, Beta, Closed Caption.** CA Sarah Polley, Jackie Burroughs, Gema Zamprogna. *DIS, DVD*

Tales from the Crypt ⚔⚔⚔ 1972 (PG)
A collection of five scary stories from the classic EC comics that bear the movie's title. Richardson tells the future to each of five people gathered in a cave, each tale involving misfortune and, of course, gore. **92m/C VHS, Beta.** GB Ralph Richardson, Joan Collins, Peter Cushing, Richard Greene, Ian Hendry; **D:** Freddie Francis. *PSM*

Tales from the Crypt 1989
Three contemporary tales of the macabre, "The Man Who Was Death," "'Twas the Night Before," and "Dig That Cat...He's Real Gone," linked together by a special-effects host. Ry Cooder provides the musical score for the second episode. Based on stories published by William M. Gaines in EC Comics; made-for-cable-television. **81m/C VHS, Beta, LV.** William Sadler, Mary Ellen Trainor, Larry Drake, Joe Pantoliano, Robert Wuhl, Gustav Vintas; **D:** Walter Hill, Robert Zemeckis, Richard Donner; **M:** Ry Cooder, Alan Silvestri. *HBO*

Tales from the Crypt Presents Bordello of Blood ⚔⚔ *Bordello of Blood* 1996 (R)
Detective Rafe Guttman (Miller) is on the case of a Bible thumper's (Eleniak) missing brother (Feldman). The trail leads him to a unique establishment, a brothel presided over by vampire queen Lilith (Everhart), whose clients all wind up dead (but probably with smiles on their faces), and the strange Reverend Current (Sarandon, who made a time vampire himself in "Fright Night"). Crypt Keeper's second big screen outing showcases Miller's slant on the leading man gig and serves up campy fun with the blood. **CW:** Horror violence and gore, sexuality, nudity, and strong language. **87m/C VHS, LV, Closed Caption.** Dennis Miller, Angie Everhart, Chris Sarandon, Corey Feldman, Erika Eleniak; **D:** Gilbert Adler; **W:** Gilbert Adler, A.L. Katz; **C:** Tom Priestley; **M:** Chris Boardman. *USH*

Tales from the Crypt Presents Demon Knight ⚔⚔ *Demon Knight; Demon Keeper* 1994 (R)
Gruesomely garish big-screen version of the TV series that was inspired by the lurid 1950s E.C. comics. Horrormeister Crypt Keeper offers his usual pun-filled introduction to a tale set in a seedy boarding-house. Brayker (Sadler) is the guardian of an ancient key that keeps the forces of darkness from overwhelming mankind, a key desired by the charismatic Collector (Zane), who unleashes a disgusting mix of demons against the house's inhabitants. Curious hybrid of spoof/splatter pic that doesn't quite work in either. **CW:** Violence; gore; nudity; strong language. **93m/C VHS, LV, Closed Caption.** Billy Zane, William Sadler, Jada Pinkett, Brenda Bakke, CCH Pounder, Dick Miller, Thomas Haden Church, John Schuck, Gary Farmer, Charles Fleischer; **D:** Ernest R. Dickerson; **W:** Ethan Reiff, Cyrus Voris, Mark Bishop; **C:** Rick Bota; **M:** Ed Shearmur; **V:** John Kassir. *USH, NHO*

Tales from the Crypt, Vol. 3 1990
Three more tales of terror from the made-for-cable-television series. "Dead Right" has Moore as a golddigger who takes a fortuneteller's advice and marries a penniless slob. "Cutting Cards" has Tighe and Hendricksen involved in a very high stakes game. "The Switch" features Hickey as a wealthy old man bartering for a new body to woo the beautiful Preston. **80m/C VHS, Beta, Closed Caption.** Demi Moore, William Hickey, Kelly Preston, Jeffrey Tambor, Rick Rossovich, Lance Henriksen, Kevin Tighe; **D:** Arnold Schwarzenegger, Walter Hill, Howard Deutch. *WAR, MOV*

Tales from the Darkside 1985
Each episode of this series features several short Twilight Zone-esque stories of fantasy and suspense. Additional tapes available. **70m/C VHS, Beta, LV.** *LIV, MOV*

Tales from the Darkside: The Movie 1990 (R)
Three short stories in the tradition of the ghoulish TV show are brought to the big screen, with mixed results. The plot centers around a boy who is being held captive by a cannibal. In order to prolong his life, he tells her horror stories. The tales were written by Sir Arthur Conan Doyle, Stephen King, and Michael McDowell. **93m/C VHS, Beta, LV, Closed Caption.** Deborah Harry, Christian Slater, David Johansen, William Hickey, James Remar, Rae Dawn Chong, Julianne Moore, Robert Klein; **D:** John Harrison; **W:** Stephen King, Michael McDowell, Sir Arthur Conan Doyle. *PAR*

Tales from the Gimli Hospital ⚔⚔ 1988
A smallpox outbreak at the turn of the century finds Einar and Gunnar sharing a hospital room. They begin telling each other increasingly bizarre personal secrets and develop a serious rivalry. Sharp dialogue with some equally grotesque imagery. Director Maddin first feature film. **72m/B VHS, Closed Caption.** Kyle McCulloch, Michael Gottli; **D:** Guy Maddin. *KIV, FCT*

Tales from the Hood ⚔⚔ 1995 (R)
Horror anthology with that urban twist. Three young thugs search for lost drugs inside a funeral parlor run by creepy Mr. Simms (Williams III) and instead walk into a world of four chilling and funny stories of fright dealing with racism and black on black crime. Tales aren't very original and are often too preachy for true enjoyment, but its nice to see someone attempt to breath life into an old and familiar genre. Williams III, with his pop-eyed stares and Don King coif, is fitting as the eerie storyteller. **CW:** Graphic brutal violence and strong language. **97m/C VHS.** Clarence Williams III, Corbin Bernsen, David Alan Grier, Wings Hauser, Rosalind Cash, Rusty Cundieff, Joe Torry, Anthony Griffith; **D:** Rusty Cundieff; **W:** Rusty Cundieff, Darin Scott; **C:** Anthony B. Richmond; **M:** Christopher Young. *HBO*

Tales from the Snow Zone 1991
"Tales from the Snow Zone" is the latest feature length ski film from RAP producers Jon Long and James Angrove. Filmed entirely in the 1991 ski season, this film captures the essence of the sport and lifestyle. "Tales" covers true extreme skiing, radical free skiing, moguls, downhill ski racing, telemarking, snowboarding, and monoskiing. Filmed in Europe and North America, "Tales" features skiers from the United States, Canada, France, Sweden, and Australia. **70m/C VHS.** *RAP*

Tales of Beatrix Potter ⚔⚔⚔½ *Peter Rabbit and Tales of Beatrix Potter* 1971 (G)
The Royal Ballet Company of England performs in this adaptation of the adventures of Beatrix Potter's colorful and memorable creatures. Beautifully done. **90m/C VHS.** GB D: Reginald Mills. *REP, HMV*

The Tales of Hoffmann ⚔⚔½ 1951
A ballet-opera consisting of three stories by Jacques Offenbach covering romance, magic and mystery arising out of a poet's misadventures in love. Lavishly designed and highly stylized. **138m/C VHS, LV.** Robert Rounseville, Robert Helpmann, Moira Shearer; **D:** Michael Powell, Emeric Pressburger. Nomina-tions: Academy Awards '51: Best Art Direction/Set Decoration (Color), Best Costume Design (Color). *HMV, PME*

Tales of Manhattan ⚔⚔⚔ 1942
Star-studded anthology about a tailor who curses a tailcoat that then travels, with varying degrees of good and bad fortune, from owner to owner. There's a love triangle, a love match, a concert appearance, a down-on-his-luck lawyer, a swanky party, a crook, and a windfall for some sharecroppers. Fields' party episode (he wears the coat to give a lecture and winds up wrecking havoc) was cut out of the original theatrical release. **118m/C VHS, Closed Caption.** Charles Boyer, Rita Hayworth, Thomas Mitchell, Ginger Rogers, Henry Fonda, Cesar Romero, Elsa Lanchester, Charles Laughton, Edward G. Robinson, George Sanders, Jackie Gleason, J. Carrol Naish, Paul Robeson, Ethel Waters, Eddie Anderson, W.C. Fields, Margaret Dumont; **D:** Julien Duvivier; **W:** Ben Hecht, Donald Ogden Stewart, Samuel Hoffenstein, Ferenc Molnar, Alan Campbell; **C:** Joseph Walker; **M:** Sol Kaplan. *TCF*

Tales of Ordinary Madness ⚔ 1983
Gazzara as a poet who drinks and sleeps with assorted women. Based on the stories of Charles Bukowski. Pretentious and dull. **107m/C VHS, Beta.** Ben Gazzara, Ornella Muti, Susan Tyrrell, Tanya Lopert, Roy Brocksmith, Katya Berger; **D:** Marco Ferreri; **C:** Tonino Delli Colli. *LIV, VES*

Tales of Robin Hood ⚔½ 1952
A low-budget depiction of the Robin Hood legend. **59m/B VHS, Beta, LV.** Robert Clarke, Mary Hatcher; **D:** James Tinling. *NO*

Tales of Terror ⚔⚔ *Poe's Tales of Terror* 1962
Three tales of terror based on stories by Edgar Allan Poe: "Morella," "The Black Cat," and the "The Case of M. Valdemar." Price stars in all three segments and is excellent as the bitter and resentful husband in "Morella." **90m/C VHS, Beta.** Vincent Price, Peter Lorre, Basil Rathbone, Debra Paget, Joyce Jameson; **D:** Roger Corman; **W:** Richard Matheson; **C:** Floyd Crosby; **M:** Les Baxter. *MLB, ORI*

Tales of the Klondike: In a Far Country ⚔⚔ 1987
An adaptation of Jack London's story exploring the fears, dangers, and joys experienced by prospectors in the harsh wilderness of northwest Canadian gold country. **60m/C VHS, Beta.** Robert Carradine, Scott Hylands; **D:** Janine Manatis. *AHV*

Tales of the Klondike: Race for Number One ⚔⚔ 1987
Two men compete in a highly contested dog-sled race—the goal of which is to be the first to reach a tract of gold-laden land. Adapted from a story by Jack London. **60m/C VHS, Beta.** David Ferry, John Ireland; **D:** David Cobham. *AHV*

Tales of the Klondike: The Scorn of Women ⚔⚔ 1987
An available man is enthusiastically courted by every single woman in Dawson City, Alaska. From a story by Jack London. **60m/C VHS, Beta.** Tom Butler, Eva Gabor; **D:** Claude Fournier. *AHV*

Tales of the Klondike: The Unexpected ⚔⚔ 1987
Five gold prospectors grow rich, but lose all that is most valuable through overwhelming greed. Adapted from a story by Jack London. **60m/C VHS, Beta.** John Candy, Cherie Lunghi; **D:** Peter Pearson. *AHV*

Tales of the Unexpected ⚔⚔½ 1991
Four tales designed to startle the senses and provoke the imagination. Episodes include "People Don't Do Such Things," about a marriage gone awry, "Youth from Vienna," about a weird fountain of youth, "Skeleton in the Cupboard," which tells of a man desperately trying to hide some strange secret and finally, "Bird of Prey," in which a pet parrot leaves its owners an enormous egg before dying. **101m/C VHS, Beta, LV.** Arthur Hill, Samantha Eggar, Don Johnson, Dick Smothers, Sharon Gless, James Carroll Jordan, Charles Dance, Zoe Wanamaker, Sondra Locke, Frank Converse; **D:** Gordon Hessler, Norman Lloyd; Paul Annett, Ray Danton. *PSM, IME*

Tales That Witness Madness 🎬🎬½ 1973 (R) An asylum is the setting for four tales of horror, as a doctor tells a visitor how four patients ended up in his clinic. Stories are "Mr. Tiger," "Penny Farthing," "Mel" and "Luau." At the time this was Novak's first film appearance in four years. 90m/C VHS, Closed Caption. *GB* Jack Hawkins, Donald Pleasence, Suzy Kendall, Joan Collins, Kim Novak, Mary Tamm, Georgia Brown, Donald Houston, David Wood, Peter McEnery; *D:* Freddie Francis. *PAR*

Talion 🎬🎬 *An Eye for an Eye* 1966 (PG) A western revenge movie that features two disabled men, a rancher and a bounty hunter, who team up to find the gang that slaughtered the rancher's family. 92m/C VHS, Beta. Robert Lansing, Slim Pickens, Patrick Wayne; *D:* Michael Moore. *COL, NLC*

Talk 🎬🎬 1994 Sharp conversation between two thirtysomething women as they wander around the streets of Sydney. Stephanie (Milliken) and Julia (Longley) are collaborators on graphic novels-Stephanie's single and adventurous while Julia is seemingly settled in the country with her lover and child. As they talk, the women learn that both their lives have conflicts. Fantasy sequences, which slow the story down, find the women stepping into their own comic-book adventures. 86m/C VHS. *AU* Victoria Longley, Angie Milliken, Richard Roxburgh, Jacqueline McKenzie, John Jarratt; *D:* Susan Lambert; *W:* Jan Cornall; *C:* Ron Hagen; *M:* John Clifford White. *NYR*

Talk of the Town 🎬🎬🎬 1942 A brilliantly cast, strange mixture of screwball comedy and lynch-mob melodramatics. An accused arsonist, a Supreme Court judge and the girl they both love try to clear the former's name and evade the cops. 118m/B VHS, Beta, LV. Ronald Colman, Cary Grant, Jean Arthur, Edgar Buchanan, Glenda Farrell, Rex Ingram, Emma Dunn; *D:* George Stevens. Nominations: Academy Awards '42: Best Black and White Cinematography, Best Film Editing, Best Interior Decoration, Best Picture, Best Screenplay, Best Story, Original Dramatic/Comedy Score. *COL*

Talk Radio 🎬🎬🎬 1988 (R) Riveting Stone adaptation of Bogosian's one-man play. An acidic talk radio host confronts America's evil side and his own past over the airwaves. The main character is loosely based on the life of Alan Berg, a Denver talk show host who was murdered by white supremacists. 110m/C VHS, Beta, LV. Eric Bogosian, Alec Baldwin, Ellen Greene, John Pankow, John C. McGinley, Michael Wincott, Leslie Hope; *D:* Oliver Stone; *W:* Eric Bogosian, Oliver Stone; *C:* Robert Richardson; *M:* Stewart Copeland. *USH*

Talk to Me 🎬½ 1982 A successful New York accountant checks into the Hollins Communication Institute to cure his stuttering. While there, he meets and falls in love with a squirrel-hunting stuttering woman from Arkansas. 90m/C VHS, Beta, Closed Caption. Austin Pendleton, Michael Murphy, Louise Fletcher, Brian Backer, Clifton James. *FOX*

Talkin' Dirty After Dark 🎬🎬 1991 (R) Sexy comedy starring Lawrence as a suave comedian who will do anything to get a late-night spot at Dukie's comedy club. *CW:* Strong language and sexual dialogue and sex scenes. 89m/C VHS, Closed Caption. Martin Lawrence, Jedda Jones, Phyllis Stickney, Darryl Sivad; *D:* Topper Carew; *W:* Topper Carew. *NLC, FCT*

Talking About Sex 🎬🎬½ 1994 Publishing party for a shrink's self-help manual sparks many conversations about sex and romance among a group of fashionable Los Angelenos. The breezy party chatter is broken up by B&W pseudo-documentary interludes of women exchanging confidences. 83m/C VHS. Kim Wayans, Marcy Walker, Daniel Beer, Randy Powell, Kerry Ruff, Joe Richards, Daria Lynn; *D:* Aaron Speiser; *W:* Aaron Speiser, Carl Nelson; *M:* Tim Landers. *LEO*

Talking Walls 🎬½ *Motel Vacancy* 1985 A college sociology student uses high-tech surveillance equipment to spy on the clients of a seedy motel, in order to complete his thesis on human sexuality. 85m/C VHS, Beta. Stephen Shellan, Marie Laurin, Barry Primus, Sally Kirkland; *D:* Stephen Verona. *VTR, NWV*

The Tall Blond Man with One Black Shoe 🎬🎬🎬 *Le Grand Blond Avec Une Chassure Noire* 1972 (PG) A violinist is completely unaware that rival spies mistakenly think he is also a spy, and that he is the center of a plot to booby-trap an overly ambitious agent at the French Secret Service. A sequel followed called "Return of the Tall Blond Man with One Black Shoe" which was followed by a disappointing American remake, "The Man with One Red Shoe." In French with English subtitles or dubbed. 90m/C VHS, Beta, 8mm. *FR* Pierre Richard, Bernard Blier, Jean Rochefort, Mireille Darc, Jean Carmet; *D:* Yves Robert; *W:* Francis Veber; *M:* Vladimir Cosma. *CVC, COL, VYY*

Tall, Dark and Deadly 🎬🎬½ 1995 (R) TV cable movie finds Roy (Scalia) romancing Maggie (Delaney), a young woman he's met in a bar. The viewer's already clued in that Roy's a bad 'un (seein' as how he's killed one woman) and when he chains Maggie to a sink, she picks up on the idea that he's a wacko. Basic damsel-in-distress with a cast that manages to keep straight faces in the most preposterous of circumstances. *CW:* Violence, terror, and sexuality. 88m/C VHS, Closed Caption. Jack Scalia, Kim Delaney, Todd Allen, Gina Mastrogiacomo, Ely Pouget; *D:* Kenneth Fink; *W:* MaryAnne Kasica, Michael Scheff; *M:* Joseph Vitarelli. *PAR*

The Tall Guy 🎬🎬🎬 1989 (R) Goldblum is a too-tall actor who tries the scene in London and lands the lead in a musical version of 'The Elephant Man,' becoming an overnight success. Not consistently funny, but good British comedy, including an interesting sex scene. 92m/C VHS, LV. Jeff Goldblum, Emma Thompson, Rowan Atkinson, Geraldine James, Kim Thomson, Anna Massey; *D:* Mel Smith; *W:* Richard Curtis; *M:* Peter Brewis. *COL, FCT*

Tall in the Saddle 🎬🎬½ 1944 A misogynist foreman (Wayne) finds himself accused of murder. Meanwhile, he falls in love with his female boss's niece. An inoffensive and memorable western. 79m/B VHS, Beta, LV. John Wayne, Ella Raines, George "Gabby" Hayes, Ward Bond; *D:* Edwin L. Marin. *MED, TTC*

Tall Lie 🎬🎬 *For Men Only* 1953 A student quits a fraternity hazing exercise. He's pursued by a psychotic bunch of his fraternity brothers and is killed in a smash-up. A local doctor goes onto an anti-hazing campaign in the aftermath. 93m/B VHS, Beta, LV. Paul Henreid, Robert Sherman; *D:* Paul Henreid. *NO*

The Tall Men 🎬🎬 1955 Standard western features frontier hands on a rough cattle drive confronting Indians, outlaws, and the wilderness while vying with each other for the love of Russell. 122m/C VHS, Beta. Clark Gable, Jane Russell, Robert Ryan, Cameron Mitchell, Mae Marsh; *D:* Raoul Walsh. *FOX*

Tall Story 🎬🎬 1960 Perkins is a star basketball player who must pass a crucial test in order to continue to play the game. In addition to the pressure of the exam, he is being pressured by gamblers to throw a game against the Russians. Fonda makes her screen debut as a cheerleader who is so awe-struck by Perkins that she takes the same classes just to be close to him. Based on the play by Howard Lindsay and Russel Crouse, and the novel "The Homecoming Game" by Howard Nemerov. 91m/C VHS, LV. Anthony Perkins, Jane Fonda, Ray Walston, Marc Connelly, Anne Jackson, Tom Laughlin; *D:* Joshua Logan; *W:* Julius J. Epstein, Philip C. Epstein; *C:* Ellsworth Fredericks. *WEA*

The Tall T 1957 A veteran rancher (Pat) stumbles onto big trouble when by chance he catches a stage coach that is eventually overrun by an evil band of cut-throats. After killing everyone on the coach except Pat and the daughter of a wealthy copper mine owner (Doretta), the renegades decide to leave the scene with the unfortunate two as hostages. Pat and Doretta, although in dire straits, find time to fall in love and devise an intricate plan for their escape. Regarded in certain western-lover circles as a cult classic. 77m/B VHS. Randolph Scott, Richard Boone, Maureen O'Sullivan, Arthur Hunnicutt, Skip Homeier, Henry Silva, Robert Burton, Robert Anderson; *D:* Budd Boetticher; *W:* Burt Kennedy. *GKK*

Tall Tale: The Unbelievable Adventures of Pecos Bill 🎬 1995 (PG) Having trouble with greedy land owners out for his pa's land, Daniel Hackett (Stahl) summons the help of three Old West legends: Pecos Bill (Swayze), John Henry (Brown), and Paul Bunyan (Platt) to face off with the evil industrialist J.P. Stiles (Glenn). Disney's variation on the "Wizard of Oz" is riddled with cartoonish characters and sleep-inducing dialogue. It would truly be a tall tale if it were said that this movie was any good. 98m/C VHS, LV, Closed Caption. Patrick Swayze, Oliver Platt, Roger Brown, Nick Stahl, Scott Glenn, Stephen Lang, Jared Harris, Catherine O'Hara; *D:* Jeremiah S. Chechik; *W:* Steven L. Bloom, Robert Rodat; *C:* Janusz Kaminski. *DIS*

Tall, Tan and Terrific 1946 Things really go crazy when the owner of a nightclub in Harlem is accused of murder. 40m/C VHS, Beta. Mantan Moreland, Monte Hawley, Francine Everett, Dots Johnson; *D:* Bud Pollard. *NOS*

Tall Texan 🎬🎬½ 1953 A motley crew seeks gold in an Indian burial ground in the desert. Flawed but interesting and suspenseful. Greed, lust, Indians and desert heat. 82m/B VHS, Beta, LV. Lloyd Bridges, Lee J. Cobb, Marie Windsor, George Steele; *D:* Elmo Williams; *C:* Joseph Biroc. *RXM*

Talons of the Eagle 🎬🎬 1992 (R) Martial arts adventure centers around three undercover agents who go up against crimelord Mr. Li (Hong). To impress Li, martial arts champion Tyler Wilson (Blanks) and vice detective Michael Reeds (Merhi) enter a deadly martial arts tournament. They later hook up with beautiful agent Cassandra Hubbard (Barnes), who has already investigated Li's drug, gambling, and prostitution rings. Features the most advanced fighting techniques ever filmed. *CW:* Martial arts violence and sexuality. 96m/C VHS, LV, Closed Caption. Billy Blanks, Jalal Merhi, James Hong, Priscilla Barnes, Matthias Hues; *D:* Michael Kennedy; *W:* J. Stephen Maunder. *USH, SGE*

Tamango 🎬🎬 1959 A confusing drama set on a slave ship travelling from Africa to Cuba in 1830. Jurgens is the ship's captain who takes the black Dandridge as his mistress. Meanwhile, the slaves are plotting a revolt, with Dandridge as a conspirator. The interracial romance does takes a secondary role to the racial conflicts. The title refers to the leader of the slave revolt, played by Cressan. Filmed in both English- and French-language versions. 98m/C VHS. *FR* Curt Jurgens, Dorothy Dandridge, Jean Servais, Alex Cressan; *D:* John Berry. *IVY*

The Tamarind Seed 🎬½ 1974 Andrews and Sharif are star-crossed lovers kept apart by Cold War espionage. Dated, dull and desultory. 123m/C VHS, Beta. Julie Andrews, Omar Sharif, Anthony Quayle, Dan O'Herlihy, Sylvia Syms; *D:* Blake Edwards; *W:* Blake Edwards; *C:* Frederick A. (Freddie) Young; *M:* John Barry.

The Taming of the Shrew 🎬🎬½ 1929 Historically interesting early talkie featuring sole (if perhaps unfortunate) pairing of Pickford and Fairbanks. Features the legendary credit line "By William Shakespeare, with additional dialogue by Sam Taylor." Re-edited in 1966; 1967 Zeffirelli remake featured Taylor and Burton. 66m/B VHS, Beta, LV. Mary Pickford, Douglas Fairbanks Sr., Edwin Maxwell, Joseph Cawthorn; *D:* Sam Taylor; *C:* Karl Struss. *NOS, CCB*

The Taming of the Shrew 🎬🎬🎬½ 1967 A lavish screen version of the classic Shakespearean comedy. Burton and Taylor are violently physical and perfectly cast as the battling Katherine and Petruchio. At the time the film was made, Burton and Taylor were having their own marital problems, which not only added an inner fire to their performances, but sent the interested movie-goers to the theatres in droves. **122m/C VHS, Beta, LV.** *IT* Elizabeth Taylor, Richard Burton, Michael York, Michael Hordern, Cyril Cusack; *D:* Franco Zeffirelli; *W:* Franco Zeffirelli; *C:* Oswald Morris; *M:* Nino Rota. National Board of Review Awards '67: 10 Best Films of the Year; Nominations: Academy Awards '67: Best Art Direction/Set Decoration, Best Costume Design. **COL, TVC, PBS**

The Taming of the Shrew 🎬🎬 1981
The classic Shakespearean comedy about the battle of the sexes where Petruchio attempts to tame his fiery, free-spirited wife, Kate. **152m/C VHS, Beta.** *D:* Peter Dews.

Tammy and the Bachelor 🎬🎬½ 1957
A backwoods Southern girl becomes involved with a romantic pilot and his snobbish family. They don't quite know what to make of her but she wins them over with her down-home philosophy. Features the hit tune, "Tammy." Charming performance by Reynolds. **89m/C VHS, Beta.** Debbie Reynolds, Leslie Nielsen, Walter Brennan, Fay Wray, Sidney Blackmer, Mildred Natwick, Louise Beavers; *D:* Joseph Pevney; *W:* Oscar Brodney. Nominations: Academy Awards '57: Best Song ("Tammy").*USH*

Tammy and the Doctor 🎬🎬 1963
Sandra Dee reprises Debbie Reynolds's backwoods gal ("Tammy and the Bachelor"). Dee becomes a nurse's aide and is wooed by doctor Fonda, in his film debut. **88m/C VHS, Beta.** Sandra Dee, Peter Fonda, MacDonald Carey; *D:* Harry Keller; *W:* Oscar Brodney. *USH*

Tammy and the T-Rex 🎬🎬½ 1994
(PG-13) All Michael (Walker) wanted was a date with the lovely Denise (Richards)—he didn't expect to almost die for her. Nor did he expect a mad scientist to transplant his brain into a mechanical three-ton dinosaur. Part teen angst—part camp horror—all good-natured hooey.*CW:* Comic monster violence and some sex-related scenes. **82m/C VHS, LV, Closed Caption.** Paul Walker, Denise Richards, Terry Kiser, John Franklin; *D:* Stewart Raffill. *IMP*

Tampopo 🎬🎬🎬 1986
A hilarious, episodic Japanese comedy. A widowed noodle shop owner is coached by a ten-gallon-hatted stranger in how to make the perfect noodle. Popular, free-form hit that established Itami in the West. In Japanese with English subtitles. **114m/C VHS, LV.** *JP* Ken Watanabe, Tsutomu Yamazaki, Nobuko Miyamoto, Koji Yakusho, Rikiya Yasuoka, Kinzo Sakura, Shoji Otake; *D:* Juzo Itami. *REP*

Tangiers 🎬 1983
The disappearance of a British intelligence agent in Gibraltar sets off a chain-reaction of violent incidents. **82m/C VHS.** Ronny Cox. *WAR*

Tangled Destinies 🎬🎬½ 1932
Old dark house thriller involving a deserted mansion, murder, and faux diamonds. Good acting and a decent storyline make it one of the few successful independently made films of its time. **64m/B VHS.** Lloyd Whitlock, Glenn Tryon, Vera Reynolds, Doris Hill, Sidney Bracy; *D:* Frank Strayer; *W:* Edward T. Lowe. *SNC*

Tango 🎬½ 1936
An early melodrama follows the ups and down of a chorus girl and the guy who sticks with her through thick and thin and poorly-filmed dance routines. Based on a novel by Vida Hurst. **66m/B VHS.** Marion Nixon, Chick Chandler, Matty Kemp, Marie Prevost, Warren Hymer, Herman Bing, Franklin Pangborn, George Meeker; *D:* Phil Rosen. *NOS, LOO*

Tango and Cash 🎬🎬 1989
(R) Stallone and Russell are L.A. cops with something in common: they both think they are the best in the city. Forced to work together to beat drug lord Palance, they flex their muscles a lot. Directing completed by Albert Magnoli, after Andrei Konchalovsky left in a huff. **104m/C VHS, Beta, LV, 8mm, Closed Caption.** Sylvester Stallone, Kurt Russell, Jack Palance, Brion James, Teri Hatcher, Michael J. Pollard, James Hong, Marc Alaimo, Robert Z'Dar; *D:* Andrei Konchalovsky; *W:* Randy Feldman; *M:* Harold Faltermeyer. *WAR*

Tango Bar 🎬🎬½ 1988
A romantic triangle between a tango dancer who leaves Argentina during a time of political unrest, his former partner, and his wife, who both stay behind. They are reunited after years of separation. Gives the viewer a detailed vision of the historical and cultural significance of the tango. Charming, interesting and very watchable. In Spanish with English subtitles. **90m/C VHS, Beta.** AR Raul Julia, Valeria Lynch, Ruben Juarez; *D:* Marcos Zurinaga. *WAR*

Tank 🎬½ 1983
(PG) Retired Army officer Garner's son is thrown into jail on a trumped-up charge by a small town sheriff. Dad comes to the rescue with his restored Sherman tank. Trite and unrealistic portrayal of good versus bad made palatable by Garner's performance. **113m/C VHS, Beta, LV, Closed Caption.** James Garner, Shirley Jones, C. Thomas Howell, Mark Herrier, Sandy Ward, Jenilee Harrison, Dorian Harewood, G.D. Spradlin; *D:* Marvin J. Chomsky; *M:* Lalo Schifrin. *USH*

Tank Commando 🎬½ 1959
Mediocre WWII actioner, set in Italy, about a demolition squad of battle-hardened Americans trying to locate a secret German crossing point. It turns out to be an underwater bridge and an Italian orphan is the only one, besides the Germans, to know its location. Can the Americans persuade the kid to talk? **79m/B VHS.** Bob Baron, Wally Campo, Maggie Lawrence, Donato Farretta, Leo V. Metranga, Jack Sowards, Anthony Rich, Larry Hudson; *D:* Burt Topper; ~~*W:* Burt Topper~~. *COL*

Tank Girl 🎬½ 1994
(R) Big-budget adaption of the underground British comic book about a brash punker chick (Petty), her mutant friends, and the evil establishment in the post-apocalyptic future. The heavily-armed pixie battles the tyrannical Department of Water and Power, run by evil Dr. Kesslee (McDowell), for control of the world's water supply in the year 2033. Straying a bit too far from the source comic, the plot (such as it is) is crammed into a rigid action-movie structure that lacks excitement. Plays like a cheap Gen-X marketing ploy with its bizarre mixture of pop culture references and a hipper-than-thou soundtrack coordinated by Courtney Love.*CW:* Contains violence, profanity, brief nudity, and adult themes. **104m/C VHS, LV, Closed Caption.** Lori Petty, Malcolm McDowell, Ice-T, Naomi Watts, Jeff Kober, Reg E. Cathey, Scott Coffey, Ann Cusack, Don Harvey, Brian Wimmer, Staci Linn Ramsower; *Cameos:* Iggy Pop, Ann Magnuson; *D:* Rachel Talalay; *W:* Tedi Sarafian; *M:* Graeme Revell. *MGM*

Tanks a Million 🎬🎬 1941
Despite the title, tanks aren't even mentioned in this. Tracy stars as a wacky genius who gets drafted. His excellent memory keeps getting him into one predicament after another. Though he gets promoted quickly, he shows himself no leader. Lots of time-worn gags, but they still work. **50m/B VHS.** William Tracy, James Gleason, Noah Beery Jr., Joseph Sawyer, Elyse Knox, Douglas Fowley, Frank Faylen, Dick Wessel, Frank Melton, Harold Goodwin, William Gould, Norman Kerry; *D:* Fred Guiol. Nominations: Academy Awards '41: Original Dramatic/Comedy Score. *NOS*

Tanner '88 *Tanner: A Political Fable* 1988
Murphy is excellent as a longshot politician on the trail of the Democratic presidential nomination. Story by Gary Trudeau of Doonesbury fame. A precise political satire made for cable. **120m/C VHS, LV.** Michael Murphy, Pamela Reed, Cynthia Nixon; *D:* Robert Altman. *PBS, BTV*

Tanya's Island 🎬🎬½ 1981
(R) Abused girlfriend fantasizes about life on deserted island and romance with an ape. Vanity billed as D.D. Winters. **100m/C VHS, Beta.** Vanity, Dick Sargent, Mariette Levesque, Don McCleod; *D:* Alfred Sole. *NO*

Tap 🎬🎬½ 1989
(PG-13) The son of a famous tap dancer, a dancer himself, decides to try to get away from his former life of crime by helping an aging hoofer revitalize the art of tap dancing. Fun to watch for the wonderful dancing scenes. Davis' last big screen appearance. Hines is sincere in this old-fashioned story, and dances up a storm.

Captures some never-before filmed old hoofers. **106m/C VHS, Beta, LV, Closed Caption.** Gregory Hines, Sammy Davis Jr., Suzanne Douglas, Joe Morton, Terrance McNally, Steve Condos, Jimmy Slyde, Harold Nicholas, Etta James, Savion Glover, Dick Anthony Williams, Sandman Sims, Bunny Briggs, Pat Rico, Arthur Duncan; *D:* Nick Castle; *W:* Nick Castle; *M:* James Newton Howard. **COL, MVD**

Tapeheads 🎬🎬½ 1989
(R) Silly, sophomonic, sexy comedy starring Cusack and Robbins as young wannabe rock-video producers who strike it big. Many big-name cameos; good soundtrack; laughs. **93m/C VHS, LV.** John Cusack, Tim Robbins, Mary Crosby, Connie Stevens, Susan Tyrrell, Lyle Alzado, Don Cornelius, Katy Boyer, Doug McClure, Clu Gulager, Jessica Walter; *Cameos:* Stiv Bators, Sam Moore, Junior Walker, Martha Quinn, Ted Nugent, Weird Al Yankovic; *D:* Bill Fishman; *C:* Bojan Bazelli. *NO*

Taps 🎬🎬½ 1981
(PG) Military academy students led by Hutton are so true to their school they lay siege to it to keep it from being closed. An antiwar morality play about excesses of zeal and patriotism. Predictable but impressive. **126m/C VHS, Beta.** Timothy Hutton, George C. Scott, Ronny Cox, Sean Penn, Tom Cruise; *D:* Harold Becker; *W:* Darryl Ponicsan, Robert Mark Kamen; *M:* Maurice Jarre. *FOX*

Tarantula 🎬🎬 1955
If you're into gigantic killer insect movies this is one of the best with nifty special effects and some good action. Carroll plays a scientist working on a growth formula which he's testing on a spider when it accidentally gets loose. This eight-legged horror grows to 100 feet high and causes havoc in the Arizona desert until the Air Force napalms the sucker. Look for Eastwood in the final sequence as an Air Force pilot. **81m/B VHS, Closed Caption.** Leo G. Carroll, John Agar, Mara Corday, Nestor Paiva, Ross Elliott, Clint Eastwood; *D:* Jack Arnold; *W:* Robert M. Fresco, Martin Berkeley. *USH*

Tarantulas: The Deadly Cargo 🎬 1977
Eek! Hairy spiders terrizing our sleepy town and destroying our orange crop! Made-for-TV cheapie not creepy; will make you sleepy. **100m/C VHS.** Claude Akins, Charles Frank, Deborah Winters, Pat Hingle, Sandy McPeak, Bert Remsen, Howard Hesseman, Tom Atkins, Charles Siebert; *D:* Stuart Hagmann. *LIV*

Taras Bulba 🎬🎬½ 1962
Well-photographed costume epic on the 16th century Polish revolution. Brynner as the fabled Cossack; Curtis plays his vengeful son. Good score. Shot on location in Argentina. Based on the novel by Nikolai Gogol. **122m/C VHS, LV.** Tony Curtis, Yul Brynner, Christine Kaufmann, Sam Wanamaker, George Macready, Vladimir Sokoloff, Perry Lopez; *D:* J. Lee Thompson. Nominations: Academy Awards '62: Best Original Score. *MGM*

Target 🎬🎬 1985
(R) Normal dad/hubby Hackman slips into a figurative phone booth and emerges as former CIA when his better half is kidnapped in Paris. Good action scenes, but poorly scripted and too long. **117m/C VHS, Beta, LV, Closed Caption.** Gene Hackman, Matt Dillon, Gayle Hunnicutt, Josef Sommer; *D:* Arthur Penn; *W:* Howard Berk. *FOX*

Target Eagle 🎬🎬 1984
Spanish police chief von Sydow hires mercenary Rivero to infiltrate drug ring. Good performances; ho-hum story. **99m/C VHS, Beta.** SP MX Max von Sydow, George Peppard, Maud Adams, Chuck Connors, George Rivero, Susana Dosamantes; *D:* J. Anthony Loma. *NO*

Target: Favorite Son 🎬🎬 1987
(R) An attractive, ammunition-laden woman sharpshoots her way to power in this made-for-TV movie.*CW:* Violence and sensuality. **115m/C VHS, Closed Caption.** Linda Kozlowski, Harry Hamlin, Robert Loggia, Ronny Cox, James Whitmore. *THV*

Target for Killing 🎬 1966
Mediocre thriller about a secret agent who must protect a young heiress from a Lebanese syndicate that's out to kill her. **93m/C VHS.** Stewart Granger, Curt Jurgens, Molly Peters, Adolfo Celi, Klaus Kinski, Rupert Davies; *D:* Manfred Kohler. *SNC*

Targets 🎬🎬🎬 1968 (PG) Bogdanovich's suspenseful directorial debut. An aging horror film star plans his retirement, convinced that real life is too scary for his films to have an audience. A mad sniper at a drive-in movie seems to prove he's right. Some prints still have anti-gun prologue, which was added after Robert Kennedy's assassination. 90m/C VHS, Beta. Boris Karloff, James Brown, Tim O'Kelly; *D:* Peter Bogdanovich; *W:* Peter Bogdanovich. PAR

Tarka the Otter 198? The story of Tarka the Otter who encounters many dangers as he pursues his favorite eel meals. 91m/C VHS, Beta. TWE

Tarnished Angels 🎬🎬🎬 1957 Reporter Burke Devlin (Hudson) is writing a story for the local New Orleans paper about a tormented trio of air circus barnstormers. A former WWI ace, Roger Shumann (Stack) cares more about flying than he does his sizzling wife Laverne (Malone), who's loved-from-afar by loyal mechanic Jiggs (Carson). When Roger's plane cracks up, he uses his wife to obtain use of an experimental aircraft in order to win a race—and brings disaster crashing around them all. Good action, fine cast. Based on William Faulkner's 1930 novel "Pylon." 91m/B VHS, Closed Caption. Rock Hudson, Robert Stack, Dorothy Malone, Jack Carson, Robert Middleton, Troy Donahue, Alan Reed, Robert J. Wilke, William Schallert; *D:* Douglas Sirk; *W:* George Zuckerman; *M:* Irving Glassberg; *M:* Frank Skinner. USH

Tartuffe 🎬🎬½ 1984 Popular French leading man Depardieu makes directorial debut with Moliere classic about religious hypocrisy and an imposter taking advantage of a wealthy merchant and his family. In French with English subtitles. 140m/C VHS, LV. *FR* Gerard Depardieu, Francois Perier, Elisabeth Depardieu; *D:* Gerard Depardieu. CVC, FCT, APD

Tartuffe 🎬🎬½ 1990 Moliere's famous comedy has Tartuffe posing as a holy man who has attracted the incredulous merchant Orgon. Orgon is willing to give Tartuffe anything—money, social position, even his daughter—and Tartuffe is more than happy to accept. 110m/C VHS, Beta. Anthony Sher, Nigel Hawthorne, Alison Steadman; *D:* Bill Alexander. TTC

Tarzan and His Mate 🎬🎬🎬 1934 Second entry in the lavishly produced MGM Tarzan series. Weissmuller and O'Sullivan cohabit in unmarried bliss before the Hays Code moved them to a tree house with twin beds. Many angry elephants, nasty white hunters, and hungry lions. Laserdisc includes the original trailer. 93m/B VHS, LV. Johnny Weissmuller, Maureen O'Sullivan, Neil Hamilton, Paul Cavanagh; *D:* Jack Conway; *C:* Clyde De Vinna. MGM, FCT

Tarzan and the Green Goddess 🎬½ *New Adventures of Tarzan* 1938 Tarzan searches for a statue that could prove dangerous if in the wrong hands. 72m/B VHS, Beta. Bruce (Herman Brix) Bennett, Ula Holt, Frank Baker; *D:* Edward Kull. HHT, SNC, VYY

Tarzan and the Trappers 🎬½ 1958 Bad-guy trappers and would-be treasure-seekers wish they hadn't messed with the ape man. 74m/B VHS, Beta. Gordon Scott, Eve Brent, Ricky Sorenson, Maurice Marsac; *D:* H. Bruce Humberstone. SNC, NOS, VYY

Tarzan Escapes 🎬🎬🎬 1936 Jane is tricked by evil hunters into abandoning her fairy tale life with Tarzan, so the Ape Man sets out to reunite with his one true love. The third entry in MGM's Weissmuller/O'Sullivan series is still among the better Tarzan movies thanks to the leads, but the Hays Office made sure Jane was wearing a lot more clothes this time around. 95m/B VHS. Johnny Weissmuller, Maureen O'Sullivan, John Buckler, Benita Hume, William Henry; *D:* Richard Thorpe. FOX, FCT

Tarzan Finds a Son 🎬🎬🎬 1939 Weissmuller and O'Sullivan returned to their roles after three years with the addition of the five-year-old Sheffield as Boy. He's an orphan whose awful relatives hope he stays lost so they can collect an inheritance. Jane and Tarzan fight to adopt the tyke and when the new family are captured by a wicked tribe only an elephant stampede can save them! 90m/B VHS. Johnny Weissmuller, Maureen O'Sullivan, Johnny Sheffield, Ian Hunter, Henry Stephenson, Frieda Inescort, Henry Wilcoxon; *D:* Richard Thorpe. MGM

Tarzan of the Apes 🎬🎬 1917 Brawny Lincoln is the original screen Tarzan. Silent film well done and more faithful to the book than later versions. 63m/B VHS, Beta. Elmo Lincoln, Enid Markey; *D:* Scott Sidney. GPV, VYY, WFV

Tarzan, the Ape Man 🎬🎬🎬 1932 The definitive Tarzan movie; the first Tarzan talkie; the original of the long series starring Weissmuller. Dubiously faithful to the Edgar Rice Burroughs story, but recent attempts to remake, update or improve it (notably the pretentious 1984 Greystoke) have failed to have the original's entertainment value or even its technical quality. O'Sullivan as Jane and Weissmuller bring style and wit to their classic roles. 99m/B VHS, Beta, LV. Johnny Weissmuller, Maureen O'Sullivan, Neil Hamilton; *D:* Woodbridge S. Van Dyke; *C:* Clyde De Vinna. MGM, FCT

Tarzan, the Ape Man woof! 1981 (R) Plodding, perverted excuse to see Derek cavort nude in jungle. So bad not even hard-core Tarzan fans should bother. 112m/C VHS, Beta, LV. Bo Derek, Richard Harris, John Phillip Law, Miles O'Keeffe; *D:* John Derek; *M:* Perry Botkin. Golden Raspberry Awards '81: Worst Actress (Derek). MGM

Tarzan the Fearless 🎬½ 1933 Tarzan (Crabbe) helps a young girl find her missing father. 84m/B VHS, Beta. Buster Crabbe, Jacqueline Wells, E. Alyn Warren, Edward Woods, Philo McCullough, Matthew Betz; *D:* Robert F. "Bob" Hill. SNC, NOS, CAB

Tarzan the Tiger 1929 Series of 15 chapters is loosely based on the Edgar Rice Burroughs novel entitled "Tarzan and the Jewels of Opar." These chapters were filmed as silent pieces, and were later released with a musical score and synchronized sound effects. Here Merrill is the first to sound the cry of the bull ape, Tarzan's trademark. ?m/B VHS. Frank Merrill, Natalie Kingston, Lilian Worth, Al Ferguson; *D:* Henry MacRae. NOS, FCT, MOV

Tarzana, the Wild Girl 🎬 1972 Jungle cheapie about an expedition that finds a beautiful, scantily clad girl living wildly in the jungle. 87m/C VHS. Kenneth Clark, Franca Polesello, Frank Ressel, Andrew Ray, James Reed; *D:* Philip Shaw. SNC

Tarzan's New York Adventure 🎬🎬½ 1942 O'Sullivan's final appearance as Jane is a so-so adventure with some humorous moments when Tarzan meets the big city. When Boy is kidnapped by an evil circus owner, Tarzan, Jane, and Cheta head out to rescue him. Tarzan shows off his jungle prowess by climbing skyscrapers and diving off the Brooklyn Bridge into the Hudson River. Lincoln, the screen's first Tarzan, has a cameo. 70m/B VHS. Johnny Weissmuller, Maureen O'Sullivan, Johnny Sheffield, Virginia Grey, Charles Bickford, Paul Kelly, Chill Wills, Russell Hicks, Cy Kendall; *Cameos:* Elmo Lincoln; *D:* Richard Thorpe. MGM

Tarzan's Revenge 🎬 1938 Morris is a better Olympic runner than actor; Holm is horrible. Only for serious Tarzan fans. 70m/B VHS, Beta. Glenn Morris, Eleanor Holm, Hedda Hopper; *D:* David Ross Lederman. SNC, NOS, VYY

Tarzan's Secret Treasure 🎬🎬½ 1941 Tarzan saves an expedition from a savage tribe only to be repaid by having the greedy hunters hold Jane and Boy hostage. They want Tarzan's help in finding a secret cache of gold. But Tarzan doesn't take kindly to threats to his family and teaches those evil-doers a lesson! 81m/B VHS.

Johnny Weissmuller, Maureen O'Sullivan, Johnny Sheffield, Reginald Owen, Barry Fitzgerald, Tom Conway, Philip Dorn; *D:* Richard Thorpe. MGM

Task Force 🎬🎬½ 1949 History of naval aviation and the development of the aircraft carrier highlighted by actual WWII combat footage (in color). Cooper and his naval buddies try to convince the brass that planes can be landed on the decks of ships. Slowly the Navy goes ahead and when Pearl Harbor is attacked, Cooper is given command of his own aircraft carrier. The use of the carriers proved very effective in Pacific battles and Cooper is finally vindicated. 116m/B VHS, Beta. Gary Cooper, Jane Wyatt, Wayne Morris, Walter Brennan, Julie London, Bruce (Herman Brix) Bennett, Jack Holt, Stanley Ridges, John Ridgely, Richard Rober, Art Baker, Moroni Olsen; *D:* Delmer Daves; *W:* Delmer Daves. MGM, FCT

A Taste for Flesh and Blood 1990 (R) A monster from outer space comes to earth and is delighted with the easy pickings for his insatiable appetite. A brave boy and girl, and a NASA commander must join forces to take the alien out. This one is billed as a campy salute to '50s B movies. 84m/C VHS. Rubin Santiago, Lori Karz, Tim Ferrante. NO

A Taste for Killing 🎬 1992 (R) Two boys, both from well-to-do families, decide to take summer jobs on an offshore Texas oil rig. The best friends think a summer of adventure awaits them; however, their lives are made miserable by their blue-collar boss, who is resentful of their high society background. Then they meet Bo Landry, who befriends them and helps them survive. Unfortunately, Bo turns out to be anything but a friend as he reveals himself as a deadly con-artist in this intense psychological thriller. 87m/C VHS, LV, Closed Caption. Jason Bateman, Henry Thomas, Michael Biehn, Blue Deckert, Helen Cates; *D:* Lou Antonio; *W:* Dan Bronson. USH

Taste of Death 🎬 1977 A youth discovers his courage within when he stands up to the bandits invading his village. 90m/C VHS, Beta. John Ireland. NO

A Taste of Hell 🎬 1973 (PG) Two American soldiers fight a guerilla outfit in the Pacific during WWII. A low-budget film with few redeeming characteristics. 90m/C VHS, Beta. William Smith, John Garwood. NWV, VTR

A Taste of Honey 🎬🎬🎬 1961 A plain working-class girl falls in love with a black sailor. When she becomes pregnant, a homosexual friend helps her out. A moving film with strong, powerful performances. Based on the London and Broadway hit play by Shelagh Delaney. 100m/B VHS. *GB* Rita Tushingham, Robert Stephens, Dora Bryan, Murray Melvin, Paul Danquah; *D:* Tony Richardson; *W:* Tony Richardson, Shelagh Delaney; *C:* Walter Lassally; *M:* John Addison. British Academy Awards '61: Best Film, Best Supporting Actress (Bryan); British Academy Awards '62: Best Screenplay; Cannes Film Festival '62: Best Actor (Melvin), Best Actress (Tushingham). NO

The Taste of the Cherry 🎬🎬 Ta'm e Guilass; *Taste of Cherries* 1996 Despairing, middle-aged Mr. Badii (Ershadi) is contemplating suicide and looking for someone who will bury his corpse discreetly. (He's already dug his own shallow grave in the countryside.) He drives through the streets and picks up several different men—all of whom remind him that suicide goes against the teachings of Islam. Finally, one old Turkish man relates his own story of attempted suicide and seemingly persuades Badii to rethink his actions. 95m/C VHS. Homayon Ershadi, Abdolrahma Bagheri; *D:* Abbas Kiarostami; *W:* Abbas Kiarostami; *C:* Homayun Payvar. Cannes Film Festival '97: Best Film. NYR

Taste the Blood of Dracula 🎬🎬½ 1970 (PG) Lee's Dracula only makes a brief appearance in this Hammer horror film which has three children taking over from the bloodsucker. Three Victorian dandies have killed the wizard who revived Dracula and he seeks their deaths by using their own children as the means of his revenge. Not enough Lee but still creepy. Preceded by "Dracula Has Risen from the Grave" and followed by "Scars of Dracula." **91m/C VHS.** *GB* Christopher Lee, Ralph Bates, Geoffrey Keen, Gwen Watford, Linda Hayden, John Carson, Peter Sallis, Isla Blair, Martin Jarvis, Roy Kinnear; *D:* Peter Sasdy; *M:* James Bernard. *WAR*

Tatie Danielle ✍✍✍ 1991 Pitch-black comedy from the director of "Life Is a Long Quiet River" sees a bitter, elderly widow moving in with her young nephew and making his life a hell. In French with yellow English subtitles. **114m/C VHS, LV.** *FR* Tsilla Chelton, Catherine Jacob, Isabelle Nanty, Neige Dolsky, Eric Prat, Laurence Fevrier; *D:* Etienne Chatiliez; *W:* Etienne Chatiliez. *LIV*

The Tattered Web ✍✍ 1971 A police sergeant confronts and accidently kills the woman with whom his son-in-law has been cheating. He's then assigned the case. When he tries to frame a wino for the murder, things get more and more messy. Fine performances aid this made-for-television story. **74m/C VHS, Beta.** Lloyd Bridges, Frank Converse, Broderick Crawford, Murray Hamilton, Sallie Shockley; *D:* Paul Wendkos. *ORI*

Tattle Tale ✍½ 1992 (PG) Vindictive ex-wife writes book accusing her actor ex of abusing her and he loses out on his career-breaking role. So he decides to disguise himself and seduce her into telling the truth. Even dumber than it sounds. **96m/C VHS, LV.** C. Thomas Howell, Ally Sheedy; *D:* Baz Taylor. *LIV*

Tattoo ✍✍ 1981 (R) A model becomes the object of obsession for a crazy tattoo artist. He relentlessly pursues her, leaving behind all his other more illustrated clients. Starts out fine, but deteriorates rapidly. Controversial love scene between Dern and Adams. **103m/C VHS, Beta.** Bruce Dern, Maud Adams, Leonard Frey, Rikke Borge, John Getz; *D:* Bob Brooks; *W:* Joyce Bunuel. *FOX*

Tattoo Connection ✍ 1978 (R) A gang of lethal Oriental diamond thieves is pursued with whip-snapping flamboyance by a taciturn kung-fu investigator. **95m/C VHS, Beta.** Jim Kelly; *D:* Luk Pak Sang. *ORI*

Tattooed Hit Man ✍ 1976 Japanese gangster violence in a revenge-doesn't-pay action story. **81m/C VHS, Beta.** *JP* Mayumi Nagisa, Bunta Sugawara, Tsunehiko Watase. *MED*

Tax Season ✍ 1990 (PG-13) A small-time businessman buys a Hollywood tax service sight-unseen, and finds it employing a hooker, a bookie and a variety of other unconventional types. **93m/C VHS, Beta.** Fritz Bronner, James Hong, Jana Grant, Toru Tanaka, Dorie Krum, Kathryn Knotts, Arte Johnson, Rob Slyker; *D:* Tom Law. *PAR*

Taxi Blues ✍✍✍½ 1990 A political allegory with the two protagonists representing the new and old Soviet Union. A hard-working, narrow-minded cabdriver keeps the saxophone of a westernized, Jewish, jazz-loving musician who doesn't have his fare. The two strike up a wary friendship as each tries to explain his view of life to the other. Good look at the street life of Moscow populated by drunks, punks, and black marketeers. Directorial debut of Lounguine. In Russian with English subtitles. **110m/C VHS.** *RU* Piotr Mamonov, Piotr Zaitchenko, Natalia Koliakanova, Vladimir Kachpour; *D:* Pavel Lounguine; *W:* Pavel Lounguine. Cannes Film Festival '90: Best Director (Lounguine). *NYF*

Taxi Dancers ✍½ 1993 Smalltown Billie arrives in Hollywood with dreams of becoming an actress. Naturally, her dreams turn to despair and she resorts to "dancing" at the Shark Club where she becomes involved with a gambler who owes money to the wrong people. **97m/C VHS, LV.** Sonny Landham, Robert Miano, Brittany McCrena, Tina Fite, Mirage Micheaux, Michele Hess, Randall Irwin; *D:* Norman Thaddeus Vane; *W:* Norman Thaddeus Vane; *M:* Larry Blank. *AIP*

Taxi Driver ✍✍✍ 1976 (R) A psychotic New York City taxi driver tries to save a child prostitute and becomes infatuated with an educated political campaigner. He goes on a violent rampage when his dreams don't work out. Repellant, frightening vision of alienation and urban catharsis. On-target performances from Foster and De Niro. The laserdisc version is slightly longer, with commentary by Scorsese and screenwriter Paul Schrader, storyboards, complete screenplay, and Scorsese's production photos. **112m/C VHS, Beta, LV, 8mm, DVD.** Robert De Niro, Jodie Foster, Harvey Keitel, Cybill Shepherd, Peter Boyle, Albert Brooks; *D:* Martin Scorsese; *W:* Paul Schrader; *C:* Michael Chapman. British Academy Awards '76: Best Supporting Actress (Foster); Cannes Film Festival '76: Best Film; Los Angeles Film Critics Association Awards '76: Best Actor (De Niro); New York Film Critics Awards '76: Best Actor (De Niro); National Society of Film Critics Awards '76: Best Actor (De Niro), Best Director (Scorsese), Best Supporting Actress (Foster); Nominations: Academy Awards '76: Best Actor (De Niro), Best Picture, Best Supporting Actress (Foster), Best Original Score. *COL*

The Taxi Mystery ✍ 1926 Guy saves Broadway starlet from band of ne'er-do-wells thanks to deserted taxi, then tries to figure out who she is, unaware that her sinister understudy plans to do her in. **50m/B VHS, Beta.** Edith Roberts, Robert Agnew, Virginia Pearson, Phillips Smalley; *D:* Fred Windermere. *GPV*

Taxi zum Klo ✍✍✍ 1981 An autobiographical semi-documentary about the filmmaker's aimless existence and attempts at homosexual affairs after being fired from his job as a teacher. Explicit. In German with English subtitles. Sordid sexual situations. **98m/C VHS, Beta.** *GE* Bernd Broaderup, Frank Ripploh; *D:* Frank Ripploh. *FCT, GLV, CCN*

A Taxing Woman ✍✍✍½ *Marusa No Onna* 1987 Satiric Japanese comedy about a woman tax collector in pursuit of a crafty millionaire tax cheater. Followed by the equally hilarious "A Taxing Woman's Return." In Japanese with English subtitles. **127m/C VHS, Beta, LV.** *JP* Nobuko Miyamoto, Tsutomu Yamazaki; *D:* Juzo Itami; *W:* Juzo Itami. *FXL, LUM, FCT*

A Taxing Woman's Return ✍✍✍ *Marusa No Onna II* 1988 Funny, sophisticated, action-packed. Miyamoto returns as the dedicated tax investigator to fight industrialists, politicians, and other big swindlers, who have contrived to inflate Tokyo's real estate values. Sequel to "A Taxing Woman." In Japanese with English subtitles. **127m/C VHS, LV.** *JP* Nobuko Miyamoto, Rentaro Mikuni, Masahiko Tsugawa, Tetsuro Tamba, Toru Masuoka, Takeya Nakamura, Hosei Komatsu, Mihoko Shibata; *D:* Juzo Itami; *W:* Juzo Itami. *NYF*

TC 2000 ✍½ 1993 (R) Jason Storm and Zoey Kinsella are cops working for The Controller, who has the unenviable task of protecting the community from roving gangs of vicious punks. When Zoey is killed, The Controller converts her into a super-cybernetic killing machine unleashed on the gangs. Meanwhile Jason is considered a liability and must battle the gangs, The Controller, and cyber-Zoey to save himself. Oh, there's also something about saving the Earth's atmosphere from nuclear destruction. Lots of action.**CW:** Some language and continuous violence. **92m/C VHS, LV, Closed Caption.** Billy Blanks, Bobbie Philips, Jalal Merhi, Bolo Yeung, Matthias Hues; *D:* T.J. Scott; *W:* T.J. Scott. *USH, SGE*

Tchaikovsky ✍✍½ 1971 The glorious music is all that saves this pedestrian biography of the 19th century Russian composer, which ignores his homosexuality and glosses over the dissolution of his marriage. Lead performance by Smoktunovsky does manage to rise above the moribund script. Originally released at 191 minutes. In Russian with English subtitles. **153m/C VHS.** *RU* Innokenti Smoktunovsky, Antonina Shuranova, Yevgeny Leonov, Maya Plisetskaya, Vladislav Strzelztldh, Alla Demidova, Kirill Lavrov; *D:* Igor Talankin. Nominations: Academy Awards '71: Best Foreign Language Film, Original Song Score and/or Adaptation. *KIV, FCT*

Tchao Pantin ✍✍✍ 1984 An acclaimed French film noir about an ex-cop being drawn into drug smuggling underground via a young Arab. English subtitles. Finely drawn characters skillfully portrayed make this a winner. **100m/C VHS, Beta.** *FR* Coluche, Richard Anconina, Agnes Soral; *D:* Claude Berri. Cesar Awards '84: Best Actor (Coluche), Best Cinematography, Best Sound, Best Supporting Actor (Anconina). *FCT*

Tea and Sympathy ✍✍✍ 1956 A young prep school student, confused about his sexuality, has an affair with an older woman, his teacher's wife. The three leads recreate their Broadway roles in this tame adaption of the Robert Anderson play which dealt more openly with the story's homosexual elements. **122m/C VHS, LV, Closed Caption.** Deborah Kerr, John Kerr, Leif Erickson, Edward Andrews, Darryl Hickman, Norma Crane, Dean Jones; *D:* Vincente Minnelli; *W:* Robert Anderson; *C:* John Alton. *MGM, FCT*

Tea For Three ✍✍ 1984 (R) Sexual trio develops and seeks therapy after a fledgling doctor has been having sexual relationships with two women, and the females finally meet. **89m/C VHS, Beta.** Iris Berben, Mascha Gonska, Heinz Marecek; *D:* Gerhard Janda. *MED*

Tea for Two ✍✍✍ 1950 This take-off on the Broadway play "No, No, Nanette" features Day as an actress who takes a bet that she can answer "no" to every question for twenty-four hours (life was less complex back then). If she can, she gets to finance and star in her own Broadway musical. ♫ I Know That You Know; Crazy Rhythm; Charleston; I Only Have Eyes For You; Tea For Two; I Want to be Happy; Oh Me, Oh My; The Call of the Sea; Do Do Do. **98m/C VHS.** Doris Day, Gordon MacRae, Gene Nelson, Patrice Wymore, Eve Arden, Billy DeWolfe, S.Z. Sakall, Bill Goodwin, Virginia Gibson, Crauford Kent, Harry Harvey; *D:* David Butler. *WAR, CCB, MVD*

The Teacher ✍✍ *The Seductress* 1974 (R) TV's "Dennis the Menace" (North) has an affair with his high school teacher; the pair is menaced by a deranged killer. Cheap but enjoyable. **97m/C VHS, Beta, LV.** Angel Tompkins, Jay North, Anthony James; *D:* Howard (Hikmet) Avedis. *NO*

Teachers ✍✍ 1984 (R) A lawsuit is brought against a high school for awarding a diploma to an illiterate student. Comedy-drama starts slowly and seems to condemn the school system, never picking up strength or resolving any issues, though Nolte is fairly intense. Shot in Columbus, Ohio. **106m/C VHS, Beta, LV, Closed Caption.** Nick Nolte, JoBeth Williams, Lee Grant, Judd Hirsch, Ralph Macchio, Richard Mulligan, Royal Dano, Morgan Freeman, Laura Dern, Crispin Glover, Madeline Sherwood, Zohra Lampert; *D:* Arthur Hiller. *MGM, FOX*

Teacher's Pet ✍✍✍ 1958 This charming comedy features a cynical newspaper editor who enrolls in a night college journalism course, believing that it won't teach anything of substance. He later becomes enamored of his instructor. Well written script and superb performance by Young as Gable's rival for Day. **120m/B VHS, Beta.** Clark Gable, Doris Day, Mamie Van Doren, Gig Young, Nick Adams; *D:* George Seaton; *W:* Michael Kanin. Nominations: Academy Awards '58: Best Story & Screenplay, Best Supporting Actor (Young).*PAR, BAR*

The Teahouse of the August Moon ✍✍½ 1956 An adaptation of the John Patrick play. Post-war American troops are assigned to bring civilization to a small village in Okinawa and instead fall for Okinawan culture and romance. Lively cast keeps it generally working, but assessments of Brando's comedic performance vary widely. **123m/C VHS, Beta, LV.** Glenn Ford, Marlon Brando, Eddie Albert, Paul Ford, Machiko Kyo, Harry (Henry) Morgan; *D:* Daniel Mann; *C:* John Alton. *MGM*

Teamster Boss: The Jackie Presser Story ✍✍✍ 1992 (R) A well-done made-for-cable-television movie powered by a riveting performance by Dennehy. Presser followed

Jimmy Hoffa as president of the Teamsters and was equally caught between the mob and the government as he tried to do what he considered best for the union.*CW:* Strong language and some violence. 111m/C VHS, LV, Closed Caption. Brian Dennehy, Jeff Daniels, Maria Conchita Alonso, Eli Wallach, Robert Prosky, Donald Moffat, Tony LoBianco, Kate Reid, Henderson Forsythe, Al Waxman; *D:* Alastair Reid. HBO, PMS

Tearaway 🎬½ 1987 (R) Australian story of a street punk with an alcoholic father. Story has potential, but ends up going nowhere. 100m/C VHS, Beta. *NZ AU* Matthew Hunter, Mark Pilisi, Peter Bland, Kim Willoughby, Rebecca Saunders; *D:* Bruce Morrison. ORI, WAR

Tears in the Rain 🎬🎬 1988 Casey Cantrell (Stone) travels to London to deliver a deathbed letter from her mother to Lord Richard Bredon. While in England, she is pursued by two men, an heir to the Bredon fortune, and his wealthy friend. After she finds a love which is forbidden, she makes a bizarre discovery that changes her life forever. Made for British television. 100m/C VHS. *GB* Sharon Stone, Christopher Cazenove, Leigh Lawson, Paul Daneman; *D:* Don Sharp. VCO

Tecumseh: The Last Warrior 🎬🎬½ 1995 Oh-so-noble TV biography of the Shawnee leader (1768-1813) and his refusal to give up the battle against white settlement of the Indiana Territory. North Carolina substitutes for Ohio and Indiana. Based on the book "Panther in the Sky" by James Alexander Thom. 90m/C VHS. Jesse Borrego, David Clennon, Tantoo Cardinal, David Morse, Holt McCallany, August Schellenberg, Jimmie F. Skaggs, Jeri Arredondo; *D:* Larry Elikann; *W:* Paul F. Edwards; *M:* David Shire. TTC

Ted & Venus 🎬🎬½ 1993 (R) Cort plays Ted, an oddball cult poet in love with Linda, a beach beauty who finds him repulsive. The more she rejects him, the more obsessed about her Ted gets, especially when his equally oddball friends offer him romantic advice.*CW:* Strong language and sexual dialogue, some drug content, and sensuality. 100m/C VHS. Bud Cort, Kim Adams, Rhea Perlman, James Brolin, Carol Kane; *Cameos:* Gena Rowlands, Martin Mull, Woody Harrelson, Andrea Martin, Timothy Leary, Cassandra Peterson; *D:* Bud Cort, Paul Ciotti. COL

Teddy at the Throttle 🎬🎬 1916 Teddy, the Great Dane, must rescue Gloria Swanson from a villain who has tied up her boyfriend. Silent. 20m/B VHS, Beta. Bobby Vernon, Gloria Swanson, Wallace Beery; *D:* Clarence Badger. CCB

Teddy at the Throttle/Speeding Along 🎬🎬 1917 A silent comedy about stealing fortunes from innocent heroines and another about racing cars in a farm area. 54m/B VHS, Beta. Gloria Swanson, Wallace Beery, Bobby Vernon. VYY

Teen Alien 🎬 *The Varrow Mission* 1988 (PG) On Halloween, a young boy and his friends run into a hostile alien. It could happen. 88m/C VHS. Vern Adix; *D:* Peter Senelka. PSM

Teen Vamp 🎬 1988 Dorky high schooler is bitten by a prostitute; becomes a cool vampire. Mindless "comedy." 87m/C VHS, Beta. Clu Gulager, Karen Carlson, Angela Brown; *D:* Samuel Bradford. VTR, NWV

Teen Witch 🎬🎬 1989 (PG-13) A demure high schooler uses black magic to woo the most popular guy in school. 94m/C VHS, Beta. Robin Lively, Zelda Rubinstein, Dan Gauthier, Joshua Miller, Dick Sargent; *D:* Dorian Walker; *W:* Robin Menken. MED, VTR

Teen Wolf 🎬🎬½ 1985 (PG) A nice, average teenage basketball player begins to show werewolf tendencies which suddenly make him popular at school when he leads the team to victory. The underlying message is to be yourself, regardless of how much hair you have on your body. Lighthearted comedy carried by the Fox charm; followed by subpar "Teen Wolf Too." 92m/C VHS, Beta, LV, 8mm, Closed Caption. Michael J. Fox, James

Hampton, Scott Paulin, Susan Ursitti, *D:* Rod Daniel; *M:* Miles Goodman. PAR

Teen Wolf Too 🎬🎬 1987 (PG) The sequel to "Teen Wolf" in which the Teen Wolf's cousin goes to college on a boxing scholarship. More evidence that the sequel is rarely as good as the original. 95m/C VHS, Beta, Closed Caption. Jason Bateman, Kim Darby, John Astin, Paul Sand; *D:* Christopher Leitch. PAR

Teenage 🎬 1944 Low budget juvenile schlock film that tries to figure out what's wrong with modern youth. Pure camp. ?m/C VHS. Herbert Heyes, Wheeler Oakman. SNC

Teenage Bad Girl 🎬🎬½ *Bad Girl; My Teenage Daughter* 1959 A woman who edits a magazine for teenagers can't control her own daughter. The kid does time in the pen after staying out all night and generally running around with the wrong crowd. Syms first lead performance is memorable in an otherwise routine teensploitation flick. 100m/B VHS, Beta. Anna Neagle, Sylvia Syms, Norman Wooland, Wilfrid Hyde-White, Kenneth Haigh, Julia Lockwood; *D:* Herbert Wilcox. SNC, DVT

Teenage Bonnie & Klepto Clyde 🎬½ 1993 (R) Like their early 30s namesakes Clyde Barrow and Bonnie Parker are just two high-spirited kids who let their need for excitement get in the way of their better judgement (ha!). Bonnie and Clyde meet in a fast-food joint, become shoplifting buddies, fall in love, graduate to armed robbery, try to run for the border, and die. 90m/C VHS. Maureen Flannigan, Scott Wolf; *Cameos:* Don Novello. THV

Teenage Caveman 🎬🎬 *Out of the Darkness; Prehistoric World* 1958 A teenage boy living in a post-apocalyptic yet prehistoric world journeys across the river, even though he was warned against it, and finds an old man who owns a book about past civilizations in the 20th Century. Schlocky, and one of the better bad films around. The dinosaur shots were picked up from the film "One Million B.C." 66m/B VHS. Robert Vaughn, Darrah Marshall, Leslie Bradley, Frank De Kova; *D:* Roger Corman. COL

Teenage Crime Wave 🎬 1955 Route 66 provides thrills for a couple of teen punks, but things get out of hand when they blow a sheriff's head off. They scoop up a couple of babes and hightail it with the police close behind, ultimately confronting their destiny at a mountain top observatory. 77m/B VHS. Tommy Cook, Mollie McCart, Sue England, Frank Griffin, James Bell, Kay Riehl; *D:* Fred F. Sears. SNC, AOV

Teenage Devil Dolls 🎬 1953 A cheap exploitation teenage flick wherein an innocent girl is turned on to reefer and goofballs, and eventually ends up on the street. 70m/C VHS, Beta. Barbara Marks, Bramlef L. Price Jr.; *D:* B. Lawrence Price. RHI

Teenage Exorcist 🎬½ 1993 Tired horror spoof finds the prim Diane (Stevens) renting a creepy house from an equally creepy real estate agent (Berryman). After she moves in, Diane begins having horrible nightmares and calls her family for help. When they arrive Diane has turned into a chainsaw-wielding seductress. The family is so distressed that they misdial the phone and wind up with a pizza delivery geek (Deezen) instead of the exorcist they need. 90m/C VHS, LV. Brinke Stevens, Eddie Deezen, Michael Berryman, Robert Quarry, Jay Richardson, Tom Shell, Elena Sahagun; *D:* Grant Austin Waldman; *W:* Brinke Stevens. AIP

Teenage Frankenstein 🎬½ 1958 A descendent of Dr. Frankenstein makes his own scramble-faced monster out of a teenage boy. Lurid '50s drive-in fare (companion to "I Was a Teenage Werewolf") is campy fun in small doses only. 72m/B VHS. Whit Bissell, Phyllis Coates, Robert Burton, Gary Conway, George Lynn, John Cliff; *D:* Herbert L. Strock. COL

Teenage Gang Debs 🎬 1966 These chicks throw a sleazy coming out party the likes of which defy description. Simply the most important social function of 1966. 77m/B VHS. Diana Conti, Linda Gale, Eileen Scott, Sandra Kane, Robin Nolan, Linda Cambi, Sue McManus, Geri Tyler, Joey Naudic, John Batis, Tom Yourk, Thomas Andrisano, George Winship, Doug Mitchell, Tom Eldred, Frank Spinella, Alec Primrose, Gene Marrin, Lyn Kennedy, Janet Banzet; *D:* Sande N. Johnson; *W:* Hy Cahl. SMW, TPV

Teenage Mother woof! 1967 A Swedish sex education teacher comes to town and poisons the minds of the local high school kids. Naturally one becomes pregnant and has to try to trick the father into marrying her. More awful stuff from the director of "Girl on a Chain Gang." 78m/C VHS, Beta. Arlene Sue Farber, Frederick Riccio, Julie Ange, Howard Le May, George Peters; *D:* Jerry Gross. SNC, TPV

Teenage Mutant Ninja Turtles: The Movie 🎬🎬½ 1990 (PG) Four sewer-dwelling turtles that have turned into warrior ninja mutants due to radiation exposure take it upon themselves to rid the city of crime and pizza. Aided by a television reporter and their ninja master, Splinter the Rat, the turtles encounter several obstacles, including the evil warlord Shredder. A most excellent live-action version of the popular comic book characters which will hold the kids' interest. Much head-kicking and rib-crunching action as Leonardo, Donatello, Raphael, and Michelangelo fight for the rights of pre-adolescents everywhere. Combines real actors with Jim Henson creatures. 95m/C VHS, Beta, LV, 8mm, Closed Caption. Judith Hoag, Elias Koteas; *D:* Steven Barron; *W:* Todd W. Langen; *C:* John Fenner; *M:* John Du Prez; *V:* Robbie Rist, Corey Feldman, Brian Tochi, Kevin Clash, David McCharen. FHE, LIV

Teenage Mutant Ninja Turtles 2: The Secret of the Ooze 🎬🎬 1991 (PG) Amphibious pizza-devouring mutants search for the toxic waste that turned them into marketable martial artist ecologically correct kid idols. Same formula as the first go-round with some new characters tossed in. Animatronic characters from the laboratory of Jim Henson, first screen appearance by rapper Vanilla Ice. Marked end of pre-teen turtle craze. 88m/C VHS, Beta, Closed Caption. Francois Chau, David Warner, Paige Turco, Ernie Reyes Jr., Vanilla Ice; *D:* Michael Pressman. COL, NLC

Teenage Mutant Ninja Turtles 3 🎬🎬 1993 (PG) Check it out dudes; the Teenage Mutant Ninja Turtles hit 17th century Japan to rescue loyal friend, reporter April O'Neil. Plenty of smoothly executed, blood-free martial arts moves keep the pace rolling, while the turtles battle an evil lord and English pirates. Seeing the TMNT's use a little more of their reptilian grey matter, and snarf a little less pizza should contribute to a relatively high adult tolerance level (considering the genre), and loads of good clean fun for the kiddies. 95m/C VHS, LV. Elias Koteas, Paige Turco, Stuart Wilson, Sab Shimono, Vivian Wu; *D:* Stuart Gillard; *W:* Stuart Gillard; *M:* John Du Prez; *V:* Randi Mayem Singer, Matt Hill, Jim Raposa, David Fraser. NLC, COL, IME

Teenage Strangler woof! 1964 A homicidal teen terrorizes his school. Cheap film features drag races, rumbles, dances, babes, rock 'n' roll and more. One for the "bad enough to be fun" category. 61m/C VHS, Beta. Bill A. Bloom, Jo Canterbury, John Ensign; *D:* Bill Posner. SNC, SMW

Teenage Wolfpack 🎬½ 1957 Boring film about German juvenile delinquents, robbery, violence, and murder. 90m/C VHS. *GE* Horst Buchholz, Karin Baal, Christian Doermer; *D:* Georg Tressler. SNC

Teenage Zombies woof! 1958 Mad scientist on remote island kidnaps teenagers and uses her secret chemical formula to turn them into zombies as part of her plan to enslave the world. Not as good as it sounds. 71m/B VHS, Beta. Don Sullivan, Katherine Victor, Chuck Niles; *D:* Jerry Warren; *W:* Jacques LeCotier. NOS, SNC, VYY

Teenager 🎬 1974 (R) Three desperate, reckless individuals, all caught up in making a low budget movie, interact and eventually self-destruct. 91m/C VHS, Beta. Andrea Cagan, Reid Smith, Susan Bernard; **D:** Gerald Seth Sindell. NWV

Teenagers from Outer Space woof!
The Gargon Terror 1959 Low-budget sci-fi effort finds extraterrestrial youngsters visiting earth to conquer it and find food for their "monstrous pets" (they're really lobster shadows.) So cheaply made and melodramatic that it just may be good for a laugh. 86m/B VHS. Tom Graeff, Dawn Anderson, Harvey B. Dunn, Bryant Grant, Tom Lockyear; **D:** Tom Graeff. SNC

TekWar 🎬🎬½ 1994 It's 2044 and society is plagued by "Tek," an illegal, addictive drug-like computer disk that creates powerful but destructive virtual-reality fantasies. Jake Cardigan (Evigan) is an cop framed on drug and murder charges, fresh out of prison, who's trying to both clear his name and find out what happened to his now ex-wife and son. Shatner, who wrote the Tek novels, guests as Walter Bascom, the head of a detective agency who promises to help Cardigan if Jake helps find a missing scientist. Made for TV. 92m/C VHS. Greg Evigan, Eugene C. Clark, Torri Higginson, William Shatner; **D:** William Shatner. USH

Telefon 🎬🎬 1977 (PG) Suspenseful, slick spy tale. Soviet agents battle a lunatic comrade who tries to use hypnotized Americans to commit sabotage. Daly, later of TV's "Cagney and Lacey," is memorable. 102m/C VHS, Beta. Charles Bronson, Lee Remick, Donald Pleasence, Tyne Daly, Patrick Magee, Sheree North; **D:** Donald Siegel; **W:** Stirling Silliphant, Peter Hyams; **M:** Lalo Schifrin. MGM

Telegraph Trail 🎬½ 1933 Weak Wayne entry about an Army scout who helps some workers complete the first transcontinental wire line. Of course, Wayne ends up getting tough with some Indians. Cheaply made, with most of the action footage lifted from the 1926 silent, "The Red Raiders." 60m/B VHS, Closed Caption. John Wayne, Marceline Day, Frank McHugh, Otis Harlan, Yakima Canutt, Lafe McKee; **D:** Tenny Wright; **W:** Kurt Kempler. MGM

The Telephone woof! 1987 (R) A neurotic out-of-work actress begins a comedic chain of events via a few prank phone calls. Goldberg has managed to salvage some bad material with the strength of her comedic performances, but not so here. In fact, she sued to prevent this version from ever seeing the light of day. Too bad she didn't have a better lawyer. Torn's directorial debut. 96m/C VHS, Beta, LV, Closed Caption. Whoopi Goldberg, Elliott Gould, John Heard, Amy Wright; **D:** Rip Torn; **W:** Terry Southern. VTR, NWV

Tell It to the Judge 🎬🎬½ 1949 Russell plays the exuberant ex-wife of lawyer Cummings. They repeatedly try reconciling but ditzy blonde McDonald always manages to catch Cummings' eye. Fed up Russell takes off for a holiday in the mountains where she meets Young. When her ex-hubby follows her, she decides to try and make him jealous using Young as the bait. 87m/B VHS. Rosalind Russell, Robert Cummings, Gig Young, Marie McDonald, Harry Davenport, Louise Beavers; **D:** Norman Foster. FCT

Tell Me a Riddle 🎬🎬½ 1980 (PG) A dying woman attempts to reconcile with her family in this poignant drama about an elderly couple rediscovering their mutual love after 47 years of marriage. Fine acting; Grant's directorial debut. 94m/C VHS, Beta, LV. Melvyn Douglas, Lila Kedrova, Brooke Adams, Peter Coyote; **D:** Lee Grant; **W:** Joyce Eliason. MED

Tell Me That You Love Me 🎬½ 1984 (R) A tear-jerking portrait of a disintegrating modern marriage. 88m/C VHS, Beta. Nick Mancuso, Barbara Williams, Belinda J. Montgomery; **D:** Tzipi Trope. LIV, VES

Tell Me Where It Hurts 🎬🎬 1974 A middle-aged housewife changes her life when she forms a women's consciousness-raising group with her friends. The script won an Emmy. Stapleton's performance is redeeming in this otherwise slow movie. 78m/C VHS, Beta. Maureen Stapleton, Paul Sorvino; **D:** Paul Bogart; **M:** David Shire. LCA

The Tell-Tale Heart 🎬🎬½ The Hidden Room of 1,000 Horrors 1962 Daydreaming author fantasizes about falling for major babe and killing his best friend for her. Adapted Poe tale. 78m/B VHS. GB Laurence Payne, Adrienne Corri, Dermot Walsh, Selma Vaz Dias, John Scott, John Martin, Annette Carell, David Lander; **D:** Ernest Morris; **W:** Brian Clemens. NOS, SNC, LOO

Tell Them Willie Boy Is Here 🎬🎬🎬 1969 (PG) Western drama set in 1909 California about a Paiute Indian named Willie Boy and his white bride. They become the objects of a manhunt (led by the reluctant local sheriff, Redford) after Willie kills his wife's father in self-defense. This was once-blacklisted Polonsky's first film in 21 years. 98m/C VHS, Beta, LV. Robert Redford, Katharine Ross, Robert (Bobby) Blake, Susan Clark, Barry Sullivan, John Vernon, Charles McGraw; **D:** Abraham Polonsky; **W:** Abraham Polonsky; **C:** Conrad Hall; **M:** Dave Grusin. USH

The Temp woof! 1993 (R) Unbelievably bad attempt at office horror. Beautiful, mysterious Kris temps for Hutton, a junior exec at the Mrs. Appleby baked goods company. She's almost too good to be true with unbelievable organizational skills and her dead serious ambition to climb the corporate ladder. Pyscho-drama has pyscho, but lacks drama, direction, plot development, intelligent dialogue, and anything resembling motive. While Hutton is tolerable, we nominate ex-Twin Peaker Boyle for the bad acting hall of shame as the conniving psycho. CW: Language and violent scenes. 99m/C VHS, Beta, LV, Closed Caption. Timothy Hutton, Lara Flynn Boyle, Faye Dunaway, Dwight Schultz, Oliver Platt, Steven Weber, Scott Coffey, Colleen Flynn, Dakin Matthews, Maura Tierney; **D:** Tom Holland; **W:** Kevin Falls. Golden Raspberry Awards '93: Worst Supporting Actress (Dunaway). PAR

The Tempest 🎬🎬🎬 1928 A Russian peasant soldier rises through the ranks to become an officer, only to be undone by his love for the daughter of his commanding officer. Silent with musical score. 105m/B VHS, Beta. John Barrymore, Louis Wolheim; **D:** Sam Taylor; **C:** Charles Rosher. Academy Awards '28: Best Interior Decoration; Nominations: Academy Awards '28: Best Cinematography. NOS, CCB, VYY

The Tempest 🎬🎬½ 1963 Shakespeare's classic tale of the fantasy world of spirits, sorcerers, maidens, monsters, and scheming noblemen is brought to life in George Schaefer's ethereal production. 76m/C VHS, Beta. Maurice Evans, Richard Burton, Roddy McDowall, Lee Remick, Tom Poston; **D:** George Schaefer. TVC, FHS

The Tempest 🎬🎬🎬 1982 (PG) A New York architect, fed up with city living, chucks it all and brings his daughter to live with him on a barren Greek island. Based on Shakespeare's play of the same name. Well-written, thoughtfully acted, and beautifully realized. 140m/C VHS, Beta, LV. John Cassavetes, Gena Rowlands, Susan Sarandon, Vittorio Gassman, Molly Ringwald, Paul Stewart, Sam Robards, Raul Julia; **D:** Paul Mazursky; **W:** Paul Mazursky, Leon Capetanos. COL

The Tempest/The Eagle 🎬🎬 1927 A Russian soldier during the Revolution is betrayed and humiliated by the woman he loves in "The Tempest." In "The Eagle," an outcast guardsman becomes the Russian version of Robin Hood. 56m/B VHS, Beta. John Barrymore, Camilla Horn, Rudolph Valentino, Louise Dresser; **D:** Sam Taylor, Clarence Brown. CCB

Temptation 🎬🎬 1994 (R) Ex-con Eddie (Fahey) gets hired to work on a luxury yacht, which helps him keep track of his double-crossing former partner. Too bad for Eddie that the guy's wife is such a distraction. 91m/C VHS, LV, Closed Caption. Jeff Fahey, Alison Doody, Philip Casnoff, David Keith, Patricia Durham, W. Paul Bodie; **D:** Strathford Hamilton. LIV

Temptation of a Monk 🎬🎬 1994 Costume drama about China's seventh-century Tang Dynasty finds General Shi (Hsin-kuo) duped into an assassination plot against the crown prince. After a massacre, the General flees and finds sanctuary with a group of Buddhist monks at a remote temple. There's also the General's sometime lover and a mystery woman (both played by Chen). Sometimes slow-moving and confusing but with exotic visuals. Based on a novel by Lilian Lee; Mandarin with subtitles. 118m/C VHS. CH Wu Hsin-kuo, Joan Chen, Zhang Fengyi, Michael Lee; **D:** Clara Law; **C:** Andrew Lesnie. FXL

The Tempter 🎬 L'Anticristo; The Antichrist 1974 (R) Mirrors the gruesomeness of "The Exorcist," with story following an invalid's adventures with witchcraft, bestiality, and Satanism. 96m/C VHS, Beta. IT Mel Ferrer, Carla Gravina, Arthur Kennedy, Alida Valli, Anita Strindberg, George Coulouris; **D:** Alberto De Martino; **M:** Ennio Morricone.

The Temptress 🎬🎬½ 1949 A doctor attempting to find a cure for polio is coerced by an irresistible woman into murder and blackmail. Well-told story, if somewhat grim. 85m/B VHS, Beta. GB Joan Maude, Arnold Bell, Don Stannard, Shirley Quentin, John Stuart, Ferdinand "Ferdy" Mayne; **D:** Oswald Mitchell. SNC

Temptress 🎬🎬 1995 (R) Photographer Karin Swann (Delaney) returns from a spiritual retreat in India obsessed with the deadly goddess Kali. Karin's new overtly sexual personality startles lover Matthew (Sarandon) while her work has also undergone some changes. When a friend is murdered, Matthew begins to wonder if Kali's evil powers have overtaken Karin. 93m/C VHS, Beta, Closed Caption. Kim Delaney, Chris Sarandon, Corbin Bernsen, Dee Wallace Stone, Jessica Walter, Ben Cross; **D:** Lawrence Lanoff; **W:** Melissa Mitchell; **M:** Michael Stearns. PAR

Temptress Moon 🎬🎬 Feng Yue 1996 (R) 1920's Shanghai is displayed in all its decadence with opium-addicted Ruyi (Li) forced to officially head the Pang family after the death of her father. Power actually lies with distant male cousin Duanwen (Lin), who manages the household and is drawn to his cold relative. Ruyi's childhood playmate and fellow addict, Zhongliang (Cheung), is now a professional gigolo and blackmailer, working for a gangster (Tian) who wants him to seduce Ruyi and steal the Pang fortune. What happens is an obsessive affair between two beautiful manipulators. Chilly high style soap opera. Mandarin with subtitles. CW: Some intense images of sexuality and opium use. 113m/C VHS. HK Gong Li, Leslie Cheung, Kevin Lin, Xie Tian, Zhou Jie, He Saifei; **D:** Chen Kaige; **W:** Shu Kei; **C:** Christopher Doyle; **M:** Zhao Jiping. NYR

10 🎬🎬½ 1979 (R) A successful songwriter who has everything finds his life is incomplete without the woman of his dreams, the 10 on his girl-watching scale. His pursuit brings surprising results. Also popularizes Ravel's "Bolero." 121m/C VHS, Beta, LV, DVD. Dudley Moore, Julie Andrews, Bo Derek, Dee Wallace Stone, Brian Dennehy, Robert Webber; **D:** Blake Edwards; **W:** Blake Edwards; **M:** Henry Mancini. Nominations: Academy Awards '79: Best Song ("Song from 10 (It's Easy to Say)"), Best Original Score. WAR, FCT

Ten Brothers of Shao-lin 🎬 198? Martial arts adventure from the days of warlords and warriors, when men were fierce and strong and struggles to the death occurred several times a day. 90m/C VHS, Beta. Chia Ling, Wang Tao, Chang Yi. NO

The Ten Commandments 🎬🎬½ 1923 The silent epic that established DeMille as a popular directorial force and which he remade 35 years later as an even bigger epic with sound. Follows Moses' adventures in Egypt, plus a modern story of brotherly love and corruption. Features a new musical score by Gaylord Carter. Remade in 1956. 146m/B VHS, Beta. Theodore Roberts, Richard Dix, Rod La Rocque, Edythe Chapman, Nita Naldi;

D: Cecil B. DeMille; *C:* Archie Stout; *M:* Gaylord Carter. *PAR*

The Ten Commandments 🎬🎬🎬

1956 (G) DeMille's remake of his 1923 silent classic (and his last film) is a lavish Biblical epic that tells the life story of Moses, who turned his back on a privileged life to lead his people to freedom outside of Egypt. Exceptional cast, with Fraser Heston (son of Charlton) as the baby Moses. Parting of Red Sea rivals any modern special effects. Available in widescreen on laserdisc. A 35th Anniversary Collector's Edition is available uncut at 245 minutes, in widescreen format and Dolby Surround stereo, and 1,000 copies of an Autographed Limited Edition that includes an engraved bronze plaque and an imprinted card written and personally signed by Charlton Heston are also available. **219m/C VHS, Beta, LV.** Charlton Heston, Yul Brynner, Anne Baxter, Yvonne De Carlo, Nina Foch, John Derek, H.B. Warner, Henry Wilcoxon, Judith Anderson, John Carradine, Douglass Dumbrille, Cedric Hardwicke, Martha Scott, Vincent Price, Debra Paget; *D:* Cecil B. DeMille; *C:* Loyal Griggs; *M:* Elmer Bernstein. Academy Awards '56: Best Special Effects; Nominations: Academy Awards '56: Best Art Direction/Set Decoration (Color), Best Color Cinematography (Color), Best Costume Design (Color), Best Film Editing, Best Picture, Best Sound. *PAR, FUS, IGP*

Ten Days That Shook the World 🎬🎬🎬½

October 1927 Silent masterpiece based on American author John Reed's book of the same name. Eisenstein, commissioned by the Soviet government, spared no expense to chronicle the Bolshevik Revolution of 1917 (in a flattering Communist light, of course). He was later forced to cut his portrayal of Leon Trotsky, who was then an enemy of the state. Includes rare footage of the Czar's Winter Palace in Leningrad. Haunting score, combined with some of Eisenstein's most striking work. See Warren Beatty's "Reds" for a fictional look at Reed and the Russian Revolution. **104m/B VHS, Beta, LV.** *RU* Nikandrov, N. Popov, Boris Livanov; *D:* Grigori Alexandrov, Sergei Eisenstein; *M:* Dimitri Shostakovich. *VYY, IHF, WFV*

Ten Days Wonder 🎬🎬½

1972 (PG) Mystery/drama focuses on the patriarch of a wealthy family (Welles), his young wife, and his adopted son (Perkins), who is having an affair with his stepmother. It also turns out that Perkins is certifiable and is trying to break all of the Ten Commandments, which he succeeds in doing before killing himself (gruesomely). Based on the mystery novel by Ellery Queen. **101m/C VHS.** *FR* Orson Welles, Anthony Perkins, Marlene Jobert, Michel Piccoli, Guido Alberti; *D:* Claude Chabrol. *MOV, CVC, TPV*

Ten Little Indians 🎬🎬½

And Then There Were None **1975 (PG)** Ten people are gathered in an isolated inn under mysterious circumstances. One by one they are murdered, each according to a verse from a children's nursery rhyme. British adaptation of the novel and stage play by Agatha Christie. **98m/C VHS, Beta.** *GB* Herbert Lom, Richard Attenborough, Oliver Reed, Elke Sommer, Charles Aznavour, Stephane Audran, Gert Frobe, Adolfo Celi, Orson Welles; *D:* Peter Collinson. *NLC*

Ten Little Indians 🎬🎬

Agatha Christie's Ten Little Indians **1989 (PG)** A group of prize-winning vacationers find themselves embarking on an African adventure. They all wind up at the same camp, and realize that they are being murdered one by one. Based on the work of Agatha Christie. **100m/C VHS, Beta, LV.** Donald Pleasence, Brenda Vaccaro, Frank Stallone, Herbert Lom, Sarah Maur-Thorp; *D:* Alan Birkinshaw. *CAN*

The Ten Million Dollar Getaway 🎬🎬

1991 (PG-13) True story of the 1978 Lufthansa robbery at Kennedy Airport in which the criminals were forced to leave ten of their twenty-million-dollar heist behind when a pick-up van didn't show. Standard made-for-cable fare produced to cash in on the same scenario played out in "Goodfellas." **93m/C VHS, Beta, Closed Caption.** John Mahoney, Karen Young, Tony LoBianco,

Gerry Bamman, Joseph Carberry, Terrence Mann, Kenneth John McGregor, Christopher Murney; *D:* James A. Contner; *W:* Christopher Canaan. *PAR*

Ten Nights in a Bar Room 🎬🎬

1913 The evils of alcohol are dramatized when they ruin a man's life. One of many propaganda films about alcohol and the problems that it caused that were made during the prohibition era. Silent, with a musical score. Remade in 1931. **68m/B VHS, Beta.** Robert Lawrence, Marie Trado. *VCN*

Ten Nights in a Bar-Room 🎬🎬

1931 A turn-of-the-century mill owner succumbs to alcoholism and ruins his life and family. Later, he sees the error of his ways and gives up drinking. This was one of many films made during this era that chronicled the evils of alcohol and fanned the flames of the prohibition debate. Remake of the 1913 silent film. **60m/B VHS, Beta.** William Farnum, Thomas Santschi, John Darrow, Robert Frazer; *D:* William O'Connor. *VYY, GPV*

Ten North Frederick 🎬🎬½

1958 A shrewish wife (Fitzgerald) forces her gentle lawyer husband (Cooper) into cut-throat politics. He consoles himself in the arms of a much younger woman. Good performances, hokey script, based on the John O'Hara novel. **102m/B VHS, Beta.** Gary Cooper, Diane Varsi, Suzy Parker, Geraldine Fitzgerald, Tom Tully, Stuart Whitman; *D:* Philip Dunne; *W:* Philip Dunne. *TCF*

10 Rillington Place 🎬🎬🎬

1971 (PG) A grimy, upsetting British film about the famed serial killer John Christie and the man wrongly hanged for his crimes, the incident that led to the end of capital punishment in England. Impeccably acted. One of Hurt's earliest films. **111m/C VHS, Beta, LV.** *GB* Richard Attenborough, John Hurt, Judy Geeson, Gabrielle Daye, Andre Morell; *D:* Richard Fleischer. *MOV*

Ten Speed 🎬🎬

1976 Two advertising executives compete in a 400-mile bicycle race from San Francisco to Malibu. **89m/C VHS, Beta.** William Woodbridge, Patricia Hume, David Clover. *LIV*

Ten to Midnight 🎬🎬

1983 (R) Vigilante Bronson is on the prowl again, this time as a police officer after a kinky serial murderer. The psychotic killer stalks his daughter and Dad's gonna stop him at any cost. **101m/C VHS, Beta, LV.** Charles Bronson, Wilford Brimley, Lisa Eilbacher, Andrew Stevens; *D:* J. Lee Thompson; *W:* William Roberts. *MGM*

10 Violent Women

woof! **1979 (R)** Ten women who take part in a million dollar jewelry heist are tossed into a women's prison where brutal lesbian guards subject them to degradation and brutality. **97m/C VHS, Beta.** Sherri Vernon, Dixie Lauren, Sally Gamble; *D:* Ted V. Mikels. *NO*

Ten Wanted Men 🎬

1954 A successful cattle baron is confronted by a pistol-wielding landowner determined to ruin him. Standard fare, with better than average performances from Scott and Boone. **80m/C VHS, Beta, LV.** Randolph Scott, Jocelyn Brando, Richard Boone, Skip Homeier, Leo Gordon, Jack Perrin, Donna Martell; *D:* H. Bruce Humberstone; *W:* Harriet Frank Jr., Irving Ravetch. *COL*

Ten Who Dared 🎬🎬

1960 Ten Civil War heroes brave the Colorado River in an effort to chart its course. Although it's based on an actual historic event, the film is poorly paced and lacks suspense. **92m/C VHS, Beta.** Brian Keith, John Beal, James Drury; *D:* William Beaudine. *DIS*

The Tenant 🎬🎬🎬½

Le Locataire **1976 (R)** Disturbing story of a hapless office worker who moves into a spooky Paris apartment house. Once lodged inside its walls, he becomes obsessed with the previous occupant, who committed suicide, and the belief that his neighbors are trying to kill him. Based on a novel by Roland Topor. **126m/C VHS, Beta.** *FR* Roman Polanski, Isabelle Adjani, Melvyn Douglas, Jo Van Fleet, Bernard Fresson, Shelley Winters; *D:* Roman Polanski; *W:* Roman Polanski, Gerard Brach; *C:* Sven Nykvist. *PAR*

The Tender Age 🎬🎬

The Little Sister **1984** Troubled 18-year-old girl gets out of a detention home and is put on probation. She captivates her idealistic probation officer, whose interest may extend beyond professional concern. Fine idea, but under-played. **103m/C VHS, Beta.** John Savage, Tracy Pollan, Roxanne Hart, Richard Jenkins; *D:* Jan Egleson; *W:* Jan Egleson. *LIV*

Tender Comrade 🎬🎬

1943 Flag-waving violin-accompanied tearjerker about five women who live together to make ends meet while their men do manly things during WWII. Intended to puff your heart up with patriotic gusto. Ironically, thanks to the girls' communal living arrangement, director Dmytryk was later accused of un-American activities. **101m/B VHS.** Ginger Rogers, Robert Ryan, Ruth Hussey, Patricia Collinge, Mady Christians, Kim Hunter, Jane Darwell, Mary Forbes, Richard Martin; *D:* Edward Dmytryk. *TTC, FCT*

Tender Is the Night 🎬🎬½

1955 A television-special adaptation of the F. Scott Fitzgerald classic, set in the roaring '20s, in which a psychiatrist marries one of his patients and then heads down the road to ruin, driven by his marriage and the times in which he lives. An entry from the "Front Row Center" series. **60m/B VHS, Beta.** Mercedes McCambridge, James Daly. *NOS, DVT*

Tender Loving Care 🎬

1973 Three nurses dispense hefty doses of T.L.C. in their hospital, and the patients aren't the only ones on the receiving end. **72m/C VHS, Beta.** Donna Desmond, Leah Simon, Anita King; *D:* Don Edmunds.

Tender Mercies 🎬🎬🎬

1983 (PG) A down-and-out country western singer finds his life redeemed by the love of a good woman. Aided by Horton Foote's script, Duvall, Harper and Barkin keep this from being simplistic and sentimental. Duvall wrote as well as performed the songs in his Oscar-winning performance. Wonderful, life-affirming flick. **88m/C VHS, Beta, LV.** Robert Duvall, Tess Harper, Betty Buckley, Ellen Barkin, Wilford Brimley; *D:* Bruce Beresford; *W:* Horton Foote; *C:* Russell Boyd; *M:* George Dreyfus. Academy Awards '83: Best Actor (Duvall), Best Original Screenplay; Golden Globe Awards '83: Best Actor—Drama (Duvall); Los Angeles Film Critics Association Awards '83: Best Actor (Duvall); New York Film Critics Awards '83: Best Actor (Duvall); Writers Guild of America '83: Best Original Screenplay; Nominations: Academy Awards '83: Best Director (Beresford), Best Picture, Best Song ("Over You"). *REP, BTV, HMV*

The Tender Trap 🎬🎬½

1955 Charlie Reader (Sinatra) is a bachelor not content with the many women in his life. He meets the innocent Julie Gillis (Reynolds) and falls head over heels for her. He then torments himself over a marriage proposal, unwilling to let go of his freedom. **111m/C VHS, LV.** Frank Sinatra, Debbie Reynolds, Celeste Holm, David Wayne, Carolyn Jones, Lola Albright, Tom Helmore, Howard St. John, Willard Sage, James Drury, Benny Rubin, Frank Sully, David White; *D:* Charles Walters; *W:* Julius J. Epstein; *C:* Paul Vogel. Nominations: Academy Awards '55: Best Song ("(Love Is) The Tender Trap"). *MGM, MOV*

The Tender Warrior 🎬🎬

1971 (G) A beautifully photographed animal adventure with Haggerty as the woodsman. **85m/C VHS, Beta.** Dan Haggerty, Charles Lee, Liston Elkins; *D:* Stewart Raffill. *VCD*

The Tender Years 🎬🎬

1947 Sentimental drama of a minister trying to outlaw dog fighting, spurred on by his son's fondness for a particular dog. **81m/B VHS, Beta.** Joe E. Brown, Richard Lyon, Noreen Nash, Charles Drake, Josephine Hutchinson; *D:* Harold Schuster. *TCF*

Tennessee Stallion 🎬

1978 A low-class horse-trainer breaks into the world of aristocratic thoroughbred racing. **87m/C VHS, Beta.** Audrey Landers, Judy Landers, James Van Patten. *LIV, VES*

Tennessee's Partner 🎬

1955 Enjoyable, unexceptional buddy Western. Reagan intervenes in an argument and becomes Payne's pal. Adapted from a story by Bret Harte. **87m/C**

VHS, Beta. Ronald Reagan, Rhonda Fleming, John Payne; *D:* Allan Dwan. *NO*

Tension at Table Rock 🎬🎬 1956 Accused of cowardice, a lone gunman must prove he killed in self-defense. Well-cast serious Western. 93m/C VHS, Beta. Richard Egan, Dorothy Malone, Cameron Mitchell; *D:* Charles Marquis Warren. *NO*

Tentacles woof! 1977 (PG) Cheesy Italian version of "Jaws" lacking only the suspense and cogent storytelling. Huston slums as the investigator charged with finding the octopus gone mad, while Fonda collects check and makes a quick exit. Hopkins is in charge of the killer whales that save the day. You'll cheer when Winters is devoured by sea pest. From the director of an "Exorcist" rip-off, "Beyond the Door" (that's not a recommendation). 90m/C VHS, Beta. *IT* John Huston, Shelley Winters, Bo Hopkins, Henry Fonda, Cesare Danova; *D:* Oliver Hellman; *W:* Steven W. Carabatsos. *LIV, VES*

Tentacles of the North 🎬🎬½ 1926 Two ships are trapped in the ice of the Arctic with the only survivor of one ship being a fearful young girl. Tinted print. 54m/B VHS. Gaston Glass, Alice Calhoun, Al Ferguson, Joseph Girard; *D:* Louis Chaudet. *GPV*

The Tenth Man 🎬🎬½ 1988 Hopkins stars as a wealthy French lawyer, captured by the Nazis and sentenced to death. He discovers a fellow prisoner who is willing to take his place in exchange for Hopkins' wealth going to support the man's family. After his release, Hopkins returns to his old home, now occupied by the dead man's family, but doesn't reveal his true identity. When an imposter appears, claiming to be Hopkins, another twist is added. Slow-going but the usual excellent performances by Hopkins and Jacobi. Based on a novella by Graham Greene. Made for television. 99m/C VHS, LV, Closed Caption. Anthony Hopkins, Kristin Scott Thomas, Derek Jacobi, Cyril Cusack, Brenda Bruce, Paul Rogers; *D:* Jack Gold. *MGM*

Tenth Month 🎬🎬 1979 Carol Burnett plays a divorced, middle-aged woman who becomes pregnant by a married man. She refuses help, choosing instead to live alone and keep an ever hopeful vigil for the birth of her child. Sappy but touching made-for-TV drama. 123m/C VHS, Beta. Carol Burnett, Keith Michell, Dina Merrill; *D:* Joan Tewkesbury. *TLF*

10th Victim 🎬🎬🎬 *La Decima Vittima; La Dixieme Victime* 1965 Sci-fi cult film set in the 21st century has Mastroianni and Andress pursuing one another in a futuristic society where legalized murder is used as the means of population control. Intriguing movie where Andress kills with a double-barreled bra, the characters hang out at the Club Masoch, and comic books are considered literature. Based on "The Seventh Victim" by Robert Sheckley. 92m/C VHS, Beta. *IT* Ursula Andress, Marcello Mastroianni, Elsa Martinelli, Salvo Randone, Massimo Serato; *D:* Elio Petri; *W:* Tonino Guerra. *NLC*

Teorema 🎬🎬 1968 Scathing condemnation of bourgeois complacency. Stamp, either a devil or a god, mysteriously appears and enters into the life of a well-to-do Milanese family and raises each member's spirituality by sleeping with them. Ultimately, the experience leads to tragedy. In Italian with English subtitles. 98m/C VHS. *IT* Terence Stamp, Silvana Mangano, Massimo Girotti, Anna Wiazemsky, Laura Betti, Andres Jose Cruz; *D:* Pier Paolo Pasolini; *M:* Ennio Morricone. *TPV, CVC*

Tequila Sunrise 🎬🎬½ 1988 (R) Towne's twisting film about two lifelong friends and a beautiful woman. Gibson is a (supposedly) retired drug dealer afraid of losing custody of his son to his nagging ex-wife. Russell is the cop and old friend who's trying to get the lowdown on a drug shipment coming in from Mexico. Pfeiffer runs the poshest restaurant on the coast and is actively pursued by both men. Questions cloud the plot and confuse the viewer; loaded with doublecrosses, intrigue and surprises around every corner, still the photogenic leads are pleasant to watch. Steamy love scene between Pfeiffer and

Gibson. 116m/C VHS, Beta, LV, 8mm, Closed Caption. Mel Gibson, Kurt Russell, Michelle Pfeiffer, Raul Julia, Arliss Howard, Arye Gross, J.T. Walsh, Ann Magnuson; *D:* Robert Towne; *W:* Robert Towne; *C:* Conrad Hall; *M:* Dave Grusin. Nominations: Academy Awards '88: Best Cinematography. *WAR*

Teresa Venerdi 🎬🎬🎬 1941 An unusual Italian comedy about a man and his financial difficulties. His mistress, his fiance and a young girl make his troubles more confusing. Unusually sweet and humorous DeSica. 90m/B VHS, Beta. *IT D:* Vittorio De Sica. *CIG*

Teresa's Tattoo 🎬 1994 A bimbo (Shelly) with a Chinese dragon tattoo somehow obtains a pair of earrings containing details of the U.S. space program. She's kidnapped by inept thugs and dies in a freak accident. Now the kidnappers need a look-alike for their extortion scheme so they kidnap another girl (Shelly again) and drug and tattoo her. Naturally, when she wakes up she manages to escape. Thin farce striving too hard to be madcap and whimsical. 88m/C VHS. Adrienne Shelly, C. Thomas Howell, Nancy McKeon, Lou Diamond Phillips, Casey Siemaszko, Jonathan Silverman; *Cameos:* Majel Barrett, Anthony Clark, Nanette Fabray, Tippi Hedren, k.d. lang, Joe Pantoliano, Mary Kay Place, Mare Winningham, Kiefer Sutherland; *D:* Julie Cypher; *W:* Georgie Huntington; *M:* Melissa Etheridge. *THV*

Tereza 🎬🎬🎬 1961 In politically chaotic Czechoslovakia, a female police detective tries to solve an intricate murder mystery. In Czech with English subtitles. 91m/B VHS, Beta. *CZ* Jirina Svorcova; *D:* Pavel Blumenfeld. *FCT, IHF*

Terminal Bliss 🎬½ 1991 (R) Teen heartthrob Perry stars as a spoiled rich druggie in this "Less Than Zero" knock-off. Perry and childhood pal Owen grow up sharing everything—lacrosse, girlfriends, and drugs. However, their friendship is really put to the test when a beautiful new girl (Chandler) moves to town just before graduation. Release was delayed, but obviously wants to capitalize on Perry's popularity. *CW:* Language, violence and drug use, and sexuality. 94m/C VHS, LV, Closed Caption. Luke Perry, Timothy Owen, Estee Chandler, Sonia Curtis, Micah Grant, Alexis Arquette; *D:* Jordan Alan; *W:* Jordan Alan; *C:* Greg Smith; *M:* Frank Becker. *WAR, CAN*

Terminal Choice 🎬½ 1985 (R) Staff at a hospital conduct a betting pool on patients' life expectancies. Someone decides he should win more often and uses a computer to help hedge his bets. Wasted cast on this unsuspenseful and bloody film. 98m/C VHS, Beta. Joe Spano, Diane Venora, David McCallum, Ellen Barkin; *D:* Sheldon Larry; *W:* Neal Bell. *VES*

Terminal Entry 🎬½ 1987 (R) Teen computer geeks accidentally find a terrorist online network, and inadvertently begin transmitting instructions to destroy U.S. targets. The premise is intriguing but poorly done. 95m/C VHS, Beta. Edward Albert, Yaphet Kotto, Kabir Bedi; *D:* John Kincade; *C:* James L. Carter. *CEL*

Terminal Exposure 🎬🎬 1989 (R) Predictable but likeable comedy-mystery. A pair of Venice, CA, beach denizens capture a murder on film and try to solve it. 105m/C VHS, Beta, LV. Steve Donmyer, John Vernon, Ted Lange, Joe Phelan, Hope Marie Carlton, Mark Hennessy, Scott King; *D:* Nico Mastorakis. *LIV, VES*

Terminal Force 🎬 1988 (R) Stupid, poorly executed story of kidnapping and the mob. So bad it never saw the inside of a theater; went straight to video. 83m/C VHS, LV. Troy Donahue, Richard Harrison, Dawn Wildsmith; *D:* Fred Olen Ray. *VTR, NWV*

Terminal Impact 🎬🎬 1995 (R) Two independent federal marshals find themselves battling indestructible, hi-tech soldiers when they investigate the disappearance of a television news reporter. 94m/C VHS, LV, Closed Caption. Bryan Genesse, Frank Zagarino, Jennifer Miller. *NLC*

Terminal Island 🎬½ 1973 (R) Tough southern California penal colony is crowded with inmates from death row. When prison becomes coed, violence breaks out. Exploitative and unappealing. 88m/C VHS, Beta. Phyllis E. Davis, Tom Selleck, Don Marshall, Ena Hartman, Marta Kristen; *D:* Stephanie Rothman. *NO*

The Terminal Man 🎬🎬½ 1974 (R) A slick, visually compelling adaptation of the Michael Crichton novel. A scientist plagued by violent mental disorders has a computer-controlled regulator implanted in his brain. The computer malfunctions and he starts a murdering spree. Futuristic vision of man-machine symbiosis gone awry. Well acted, but still falls short of the novel. 107m/C VHS, Beta. George Segal, Joan Hackett, Jill Clayburgh, Richard Dysart, James B. Sikking, Norman Burton; *D:* Mike Hodges; *W:* Mike Hodges. *WAR*

Terminal Velocity 🎬🎬 1994 (PG-13) Skydiving instructor Ditch Brodie (Sheen) thinks he sees student Chris Morrow (Kinski) plummet to her death, only it turns out she's not dead and certainly not a beginner. Upon further investigation, he finds the usual web of international intrigue descending upon him, and that the KGB definitely wants him to mind his own business. Still, he pushes on. Another no-brainer actioner with few surprises satisfies the guilty pleasures of action addicts only. *CW:* Scenes of strong action/violence; brief strong language. 132m/C VHS, LV, Closed Caption. Charlie Sheen, Nastassia Kinski, James Gandolfini, Christopher McDonald, Melvin Van Peebles; *D:* Deran Sarafian; *W:* David N. Twohy; *M:* Joel McNeely. *HPH*

Terminal Virus 🎬🎬 1996 (R) A deadly sexually trasmitted disease has made reproduction impossible, so humanity is on the verge of extinction. It's up to an outlaw and a scientist to convince a suspicious population that a new serum is the cure everyone's been waiting for. *CW:* Violence, some sexuality and language. 74m/C VHS. James Brolin, Richard Lynch, Bryan Genesse. *NHO*

The Terminator 🎬🎬🎬 1984 (R) Futuristic cyborg is sent to present-day Earth. His job: kill the woman who will conceive the child destined to become the great liberator and arch-enemy of the Earth's future rulers. The cyborg is also pursued by another futuristic visitor, who falls in love with the intended victim. Cameron's pacing is just right in this exhilarating, explosive thriller which displays Arnie as one cold-blooded villain who utters a now famous line: "I'll be back." Followed by "Terminator 2: Judgment Day." 108m/C VHS, Beta, LV. Arnold Schwarzenegger, Michael Biehn, Linda Hamilton, Paul Winfield, Lance Henriksen, Bill Paxton, Rick Rossovich, Dick Miller, Earl Boen; *D:* James Cameron; *W:* James Cameron; *M:* Brad Fiedel. *NO*

Terminator 2: Judgment Day 🎬🎬🎬½ 1991 (R) He said he'd be back and he is, programmed to protect the boy who will be mankind's post-nuke resistance leader. But the T-1000, a shape-changing, ultimate killing machine, is also on the boy's trail. Twice the mayhem, five times the special effects, ten times the budget of the first, but without Arnold it'd be half the movie. The word hasn't been invented to describe the special effects, particularly THE scariest nuclear holocaust scene yet. Worldwide megahit, but the $100 million budget nearly ruined the studio; Arnold accepted his $12 million in the form of a jet. Laserdisc features include pan and scan, widescreen and a "Making of T-2" short. *CW:* Language and strong sci-fi action and violence. 139m/C VHS, LV, 8mm, Closed Caption, DVD. Arnold Schwarzenegger, Linda Hamilton, Edward Furlong, Robert Patrick, Earl Boen, Joe Morton; *D:* James Cameron; *W:* James Cameron; *M:* Brad Fiedel. Academy Awards '91: Best Makeup, Best Sound, Best Sound Effects Editing, Best Visual Effects; MTV Movie Awards '92: Best Film, Best Male Performance (Schwarzenegger), Best Female Performance (Hamilton), Breakthrough Performance (Furlong), Most Desirable Female (Hamilton), Best Action Sequence; People's Choice Awards '92: Best Film; Nominations: Academy Awards '91: Best Cinematography, Best Film Editing. *LIV*

Termini Station 🎬🎬½ **1989** Dewhurst gives an excellent performance as the alcoholic matriarch of a small-town Canadian family. She drinks all day and dreams of traveling to Italy, while her children work and believe there is something more to life than their mundane existence. When they finally do leave, they discover an intriguing new world. Dewhurst and Follows also appear together in "Anne of Green Gables" and "Anne of Avonlea." **105m/C VHS, Closed Caption.** *CA* Colleen Dewhurst, Megan Follows, Gordon Clapp, Hannah Lee, Leon Pownall, Debra McGrath, Elliott Smith, Norma Dell'Agnese; *D:* Allen King; *M:* Mychael Danna. *FXL, FCT*

Terms of Endearment 🎬🎬🎬 **1983 (PG)** A weeper following the changing relationship between a young woman and her mother, over a thirty-year period. Beginning as a comedy, turning serious as the years go by, this was Brooks' debut as screenwriter and director. Superb supporting cast headed by Nicholson's slyly charming neighbor/astronaut, with stunning performances by Winger and MacLaine as the two women who often know and love each other too well. Adapted from Larry McMurtry's novel. **132m/C VHS, Beta, LV, Closed Caption.** Shirley MacLaine, Jack Nicholson, Debra Winger, John Lithgow, Jeff Daniels, Danny DeVito; *D:* James L. Brooks; *W:* James L. Brooks; *C:* Andrzej Bartkowiak; *M:* Michael Gore. Academy Awards '83: Best Actress (MacLaine), Best Adapted Screenplay, Best Director (Brooks), Best Picture, Best Supporting Actor (Nicholson); Directors Guild of America Awards '83: Best Director (Brooks); Golden Globe Awards '84: Best Actress—Drama (MacLaine), Best Film—Drama, Best Screenplay, Best Supporting Actor (Nicholson); Los Angeles Film Critics Association Awards '83: Best Actress (MacLaine), Best Director (Brooks), Best Film, Best Screenplay, Best Supporting Actor (Nicholson); National Board of Review Awards '83: Best Actress (MacLaine), Best Director (Brooks), Best Supporting Actor (Nicholson); New York Film Critics Awards '83: Best Actress (MacLaine), Best Film, Best Supporting Actor (Nicholson); National Society of Film Critics Awards '83: Best Actress (Winger), Best Supporting Actor (Nicholson); Writers Guild of America '83: Best Adapted Screenplay; Nominations: Academy Awards '83: Best Actress (Winger), Best Art Direction/Set Decoration, Best Film Editing, Best Sound, Best Supporting Actor (Lithgow), Best Original Score. *PAR, BTV, HMV*

Terraces 🎬🎬½ **1977** TV series pilot about high-rise tenants whose balconies are their only common ground. Good performances. **90m/C VHS, Beta.** Lloyd Bochner, Eliza Garrett, Julie Newmar, Tim Thomerson; *D:* Lila Garrett. *WOV*

Terranova 🎬🎬 **1991** Six characters in search of themselves, with the profound changes in their lives coming through an unlikely friendship. Rosetta is the poor matriarch of an Italian immigrant family while wealthy Noemi is an aristocratic landowner. But they share similiar frustrations and the desire to change their lives. Set in a rural Venezuelan town in the 1950's. Spanish with subtitles. **96m/C VHS.** *IT* Marisa Laurito, Mimi Lazo, Antonio Banderas, Patrick Bauchau, Massimo Bonetti, Nathalia Martinez; *D:* Calogero Salvo. *CCN*

Terrified 🎬🎬½ **1994 (R)** Erotic thriller about a nympho being stalked by a mystery assailant. Genuinely creepy. *CW:* Some strong violence and sexuality, and for language. **90m/C VHS.** Heather Graham, Lisa Zane, Rustam Branaman, Tom Breznahan; *Cameos:* Max Perlich, Balthazar Getty, Richard Lynch, Don Calfa; *D:* James Merendino. *APX*

The Terror 🎬🎬 **1938** A hostelry is the scene of a number of brutal murders. Remake of a 1928 film and based on a play by Edgar Wallace. Good story, but weak version of it. **63m/B VHS, Beta.** *GB* Wilfred Lawson, Bernard Lee, Arthur Wontner, Linden Travers, Henry Oscar, Alastair Sim; *D:* Richard Bird. *SNC*

The Terror 🎬🎬 *Lady of the Shadows* **1963** A lieutenant in Napoleon's army chases a lovely maiden and finds himself trapped in a creepy castle by a mad baron. Movie legend has it Corman directed the movie in 3 days as the sets (from his previous movie "The Raven") were being torn down around him. **81m/C VHS, Beta.** Boris Karloff,

Jack Nicholson, Sandra Knight; *D:* Roger Corman. *NOS, SNC, PSM*

The Terror woof! **1979 (R)** After 100 years, a man reveals in a film that his family killed a witch. Friends who see the film are attacked by supernatural forces. Originally double-billed with "Dracula's Dog." **86m/C VHS, Beta.** John Nolan, Carolyn Courage, James Aubrey; *D:* Norman J. Warren. *VCI, VCD, HHE*

Terror at London Bridge 🎬🎬 *Bridge Across Time; Arizona Ripper* **1985** London Bridge is transported brick by brick to Arizona. It carries its history with it, including the havoc-wreaking spirit of Jack the Ripper. Campy made-for-TV effort. **96m/C VHS, Beta.** David Hasselhoff, Stephanie Kramer, Adrienne Barbeau, Randolph Mantooth; *D:* E.W. Swackhamer; *C:* Gil Hubbs. *FRH*

Terror at Red Wolf Inn 🎬🎬 *Club Dead; Terror House; The Folks at Red Wolf Inn* **1972 (R)** Young woman wins a vacation; finds she's been invited for dinner, so to speak. Made campy enough to overcome stupidity. **90m/C VHS, Beta.** Linda Gillin, Arthur Space, John Neilson, Mary Jackson, Janet Wood, Margaret Avery; *D:* Bud Townsend. *ACA*

Terror at Tenkiller 🎬 **1986** Two girls vacationing in the mountains are seemingly surrounded by a rash of mysterious murders. Made for video. **87m/C VHS, Beta.** Mike Wiles, Stacey Logan. *VCI*

Terror at the Opera 🎬½ **1988 (R)** A bizarre staging of Verdi's "Macbeth" is plagued by depraved gore murders. But the show must go on, as one character chirps in badly-dubbed English. Italian horrormeister Argento's ever-fluid camera achieves spectacular shots, but the lurid, ludicrous script make this one for connoisseurs only. The operatic scenes employ the voice of Maria Callas. Available in an edited "R" rated version. *CW:* Terror and violence and sensual scene. **107m/C VHS.** Christina Marsillach, Ian Charleson, Urbano Barberini, William McNamara, Antonella Vitale, Barbara Cupisti, Coralina Cataldi Tassoni, Daria Nicolodi; *D:* Dario Argento; *W:* Dario Argento. *FCT*

Terror Beach 🎬 **198?** A doctor and his bride move to a coastal village, only to find it enmeshed in witchcraft and devil worship. **90m/C VHS, Beta.** Victor Petit, Julie James, Mary Costi, Sandra Mozar. *NO*

Terror Beneath the Sea 🎬🎬½ *Kaitei Daisenso; Water Cyborgs* **1966** A mad scientist wants to rule the world with his cyborgs. American and Japanese scientists unite to fight him. Fine special effects, especially the transformation from human to monster. **85m/C VHS, Beta.** *JP* Sonny Chiba, Peggy Neal, Franz Gruber, Gunther Braun, Andrew Hughes, Mike Daneen; *D:* Hajime Sato. *DVT*

Terror by Night 🎬🎬½ **1946** Holmes and Watson attempt to solve the murder of the owner of a gigantic, beautiful jewel. Their investigation must be completed before their train arrives at its destination, where the murderer can escape. **60m/B VHS, Closed Caption.** Basil Rathbone, Nigel Bruce; *D:* Roy William Neill. *CNG, REP, FOX*

Terror by Night/Meeting at Midnight 🎬🎬 **1946** In "Terror by Night" (1946), Sherlock Holmes and Dr. Watson board a train to protect a fabulous diamond. In "Meeting at Midnight" (1944), Charlie Chan becomes involved in magic and murder. **122m/B VHS, Beta.** Basil Rathbone, Nigel Bruce, Sidney Toler; *D:* Roy William Neill. *MED*

Terror Creatures from the Grave 🎬 **1966** Husband summons medieval plague victims to rise from the grave to drop in on his unfaithful wife. Should've been better. **85m/C VHS.** *IT* Barbara Steele, Riccardo Garrone, Walter Brandi; *D:* Ralph Zucker. *SNC*

Terror Eyes 🎬½ **1987 (PG-13)** Spoof-thriller revolves around an "agent from Hell," sent to Earth to recruit writers for a horror film. **90m/C VHS, Beta.** Daniel Roebuck, Vivian Schilling, Dan Bell, Lance August. *AIP*

Terror in a Texas Town 🎬🎬½ **1958** George Hansen (Hayden) is a Swedish seaman who returns home to discover his farmer father has been gunned down by the greedy Johnny Crale (Young), who's after the land so he can drill for oil. So Hansen's out for revenge. There's a final showdown that not only includes six-shooters but a harpoon. **120m/B VHS.** Sterling Hayden, Nedrick Young, Sebastian Cabot, Victor Millan; *D:* Joseph H. Lewis; *W:* Ben L. Perry; *C:* Ray Rennahan; *M:* Gerald Fried. *MGM*

Terror in Beverly Hills woof! **1990** When the President's daughter is kidnapped, it's up to an ex-marine to save her. The trouble is, the head terrorist hates the marine's guts as he blames him for the deaths of his wife and children. So incredibly bad it's campy and fun. **88m/C VHS, Beta, LV.** Frank Stallone, Cameron Mitchell, William Smith; *D:* John Myhers; *W:* John Myhers. *AIP*

Terror in Paradise 🎬½ **1990 (R)** Jason and Vickie think they're going to have a romantic holiday on a beautiful island paradise. But they've picked the wrong spot to vacation. It seems the island harbors a terrorist group and when they see more than they should the lovers become the next targets. **?m/C VHS.** Joanna Pettet, Gary Lockwood, David Anthony Smith, Leslie Ryan; *D:* Peer J. Oppenheimer. *NHO*

Terror in the Haunted House 🎬🎬½ **1958** Newlyweds move into an old house. The bride remembers it from her nightmares. First release featured the first use of Psychorama, a technique in which scary words or advertising messages were flashed on the screen for a fraction of a second—just long enough to cause subliminal response. The technique was banned later in the year. **90m/C VHS, Beta.** Gerald Mohr, Cathy O'Donnell, William Ching; *D:* Harold Daniels. *RHI, MLB, CCB*

Terror in the Jungle 🎬 **1968 (PG)** Plane crashes in Peruvian wilds and young boy survivor meets Jivaro Indians who think he's a god. Much struggling to survive and battling with horrible script. **95m/C VHS.** Jimmy Angle, Robert Burns, Fawn Silver; *D:* Tom De Simone; *M:* Les Baxter. *ACA*

Terror in the Swamp 🎬 **1985 (PG)** When not hanging out in the local murky waters, a swamp creature terrorizes the residents of a small town. **89m/C VHS, Beta, LV.** Billy Holliday; *D:* Joe Catalanotto. *NWV, VTR*

Terror in the Wax Museum woof! **1973 (PG)** The owner of a wax museum is killed while mulling over the sale of the museum. The new owner has little better luck as the bodies continue to pile up. Production uses every out-of-work horror film actor of the time. The most suspenseful part of this low-budget flick is waiting to see how long the "wax dummies" can hold their breath. **94m/C VHS, Beta.** Ray Milland, Broderick Crawford, Elsa Lanchester, Louis Hayward, Maurice Evans, John Carradine; *D:* Georg Fenady; *W:* Jameson Brewer; *M:* George Duning. *LIV*

Terror in Toyland 🎬½ *Christmas Evil; You Better Watch Out* **1985** Once again a knife-wielding lunatic dresses as Santa Claus to strike terror and death into the hearts of children. **90m/C VHS, Beta.** Brandon Maggart, Jeffrey DeMunn; *D:* Lewis Jackson. *ACA*

Terror Is a Man 🎬 *Blood Creature* **1959** A mad scientist attempts to turn a panther into a man on a secluded island. Early Filipino horror attempt inspired by H.G. Wells' "The Island of Doctor Moreau." **89m/B VHS.** *PH* Francis Lederer, Greta Thyssen, Richard Derr, Oscar Keesee; *D:* Gerardo (Gerry) De Leon. *SNC*

Terror of Mechagodzilla 🎬½ *Monsters from the Unknown Planet; The Escape of Megagodzilla; Mekagojira No Gyakushu* **1978 (G)** It's monster vs. machine in the heavyweight battle of the universe as a huge mechanical Godzilla built by aliens is pitted against the real thing. The last Godzilla movie made until "Godzilla 1985." **79m/C VHS, Beta.** *JP* Katsuhiko Sasaki, Tomoko Ai. *PAR*

Terror of Rome Against the Son of Hercules 🎬 1964 Muscle-bound gladiators battle it out in this low-budget Italian action flick. Dubbed. **100m/C VHS, Beta.** *FR IT* Mark Forest, Marilu Tolo; **D:** Mario Ciano. *SNC, NLC*

Terror of the Bloodhunters 🎬 1962 A French author is sentenced to Devil's Island for a crime he didn't commit. The warden's daughter takes a liking to him and arranges for him and a friend to escape, but numerous perils await them in the jungle. **60m/B VHS, Beta.** Robert Clarke, Steve Conte, Dorothy Haney; **D:** Jerry Warren; **W:** Jerry Warren. *SNC*

Terror of the Steppes 🎬 1964 Yet another sword and sandal extravaganza in which a musclebound hero conquers all. **?m/C VHS, Beta.** *IT* Kirk Morris. *SNC*

Terror of Tiny Town 🎬🎬 1938 Main characteristic of this musical/western is its entire midget cast, all members of Jed Buell's Midgets. Otherwise the plot is fairly average and features a bad guy and the good guy who finally teaches him a lesson. Newfield plays up the cast's short stature—they walk under saloon doors and ride Shetland ponies. **65m/B VHS, Beta.** Bill Curtis, Yvonne Moray; **D:** Sam Newfield. *SNC, NOS, DVT*

Terror on Alcatraz 🎬 1986 The only prisoner to successfully escape from Alcatraz Island returns to retrieve the safety deposit box key he needs to get his stolen loot. And anyone who gets in his way is in for trouble. **96m/C VHS.** Veronica Porsche Ali, Sandy Brooke, Aldo Ray, Scott Ryder; **D:** Philip Marcus. *TWE, HHE*

Terror on the 40th Floor 🎬 1974 Seven people make an attempt to escape from the 40th floor of an inflamed skyscraper. Poorly done re-hash of "Towering Inferno." Uninspired. **98m/C VHS, Beta.** John Forsythe, Anjanette Comer, Don Meredith, Joseph Campanella; **D:** Jerry Jameson. *PSM*

Terror on Tour woof! 1983 The Clowns, a rock group on their way up, center their stage performance around sadistic, mutilating theatrics. When real murders begin, they become prime suspects. Exploitive, bloody, disgusting. **90m/C VHS, Beta.** Dave Galluzzo, Richard Styles, Rick Pemberton; **D:** Don Edmunds. *MED*

Terror Out of the Sky 🎬½ 1978 A scientist must disguise himself as one of the insects to divert the attention of a horde of killing bees from a busload of elementary children. Sub-par sequel to "The Savage Bees." **95m/C VHS, Beta.** Efrem Zimbalist Jr., Dan Haggerty; **D:** Lee H. Katzin; **M:** William Goldstein. *LIV*

Terror Ship 🎬🎬 1954 Three people find an abandoned yacht which they believe was used for smuggling. While searching it, they find that it was used to transport stolen uranium. Before the police can arrive, the thieves show up. Not a very good handling of what was actually an interesting idea. Released as "Dangerous Voyage" in Great Britain. **72m/B VHS.** *GB* William Lundigan, Naomi Chance, Vincent Ball, Jean Lodge, Richard Stewart; **D:** Vernon Sewell. *NOS*

Terror Squad 🎬🎬 1987 An unsuspecting high school population is put under siege by Libyan terrorists. The students get a hands-on lesson in revolution and guerrilla war tactics. **95m/C VHS.** Kerry Brennan, Bill Calvert, Chuck Connors, Greer Brodie; **D:** Peter Maris. *MCG, VTR*

Terror Stalks the Class Reunion 🎬🎬½ 1993 (PG-13) Kay (Nelligan) is a teacher who disappears at a class reunion. Police dismiss the case as a runaway wife, except for Virginia, a young detective (Beals) who doesn't accept that theory. And she's right—Kay is held hostage in a remote cabin by an obsessed former student (Davies). Kay needs all her wits to fend off her deranged and possibly deadly suitor while Virginia races to find her. Based on the novel by Mary Higgins Clark. **CW:** Some violence and terror. **95m/C VHS, Closed Caption.** Kate Nelligan, Jennifer Beals, Geraint Wyn Davies. *REP*

Terror Street 🎬 1954 An Air Force pilot's wife is murdered. He has 36 hours to clear his name and find the killer. **84m/B VHS, Beta, LV.** Dan Duryea, Elsy Albiin, Ann Gudrun, Eric Pohlmann. *NO*

Terror Trail 🎬½ 1933 As usual, Mix uses guns and fists to bring bad guys to justice, and gets the girl in the bargain. **62m/B VHS.** Tom Mix, Naomi Judge, Arthur Rankin, Raymond Hatton, Francis McDonald, Robert F. (Bob) Kortman, John St. Polis, Lafe McKee, Buffalo Bill Jr.; **D:** Armand Schaefer. *GPV, HEG, DVT*

Terror Train 🎬🎬 *Train of Terror* 1980 (R) A masquerade party is held on a chartered train. But someone has more than mask-wearing in mind as a series of dead bodies begin to appear. Copperfield provides magic, Curtis provides screams in this semi-scary slasher movie. **97m/C VHS, Beta, LV.** Jamie Lee Curtis, Ben Johnson, Hart Bochner, David Copperfield, Vanity; **D:** Roger Spottiswoode. *FOX*

The Terror Within 🎬 1988 (R) Reptilian mutants hit the streets searching for human women to breed with. Have the Teenage Mutant Ninja Turtles grown up? **82m/C VHS, Beta.** George Kennedy, Andrew Stevens, Starr Andreeff, Terri Treas; **D:** Thierry Notz; **W:** Thomas McKelvey Cleaver; **M:** Rick Conrad. *MGM*

The Terror Within 2 🎬½ 1991 (R) In a world destroyed by biological warfare, a warrior and the woman he rescued traverse the badlands occupied by hideous mutants. What they don't know is that the real terror comes from within. How can they possibly survive? Not without decent dialogue, that's for sure. **CW:** Language, strong violence and gore, and sensuality. **90m/C VHS.** Andrew Stevens, Stella Stevens, Chick Vennera, R. Lee Ermey; **D:** Andrew Stevens. *VES, LIV*

Terrorgram 🎬 1990 (R) Not a very special delivery. An offscreen James Earl Jones introduces three lesser tales of terror. Best seg: a sleazy filmmaker gets trapped in the world of his own exploitation scripts. The other two are bloody but negligible revenge-from-the-grave yarns. All start off with the receipt of a sinister package, hence a postal motif. **CW:** Language, horror violence and drug content, and sensuality. **88m/C VHS.** Michael Hartson, J.T. Wallace. *NO*

The Terrorists 🎬½ 1974 (PG) Just as later he was a Scottish Lithuanian sub-commander in "The Hunt for Red October" (1990), here Connery is a Scottish Norwegian security chief. Good cinematography and premise are wasted; generic title betrays sloppy screenplay. **89m/C VHS, Beta, Closed Caption.** Sean Connery, Ian McShane, John Quentin; **D:** Caspar Wrede; **M:** Jerry Goldsmith. *FOX*

Terrorists 🎬 1983 An Army investigator discovers a plot to assassinate the President. It's up to him to move quickly enough to stop it. Brutal action. **61m/C VHS, Beta.** Marland Proctor, Irmgard Millard. *NO*

The Terrornauts woof! 1967 When man begins space exploration, Earth is attacked by aliens. The defenders are taken to an out-dated fortress where they learn that their forebears were similarly attacked. Juvenile, lackluster, contrived, and really dumb. **77m/C VHS, Beta.** *GB* Simon Oates, Zena Marshall, Charles Hawtrey, Stanley Meadows; **D:** Montgomery Tully. *NLC*

Terrorvision woof! 1986 (R) OUR TV GAVE BIRTH TO SPACE ALIENS! It's amazing what modern technology can do: Suburban family buys a fancy satellite dish; bad black comedy and gory special effects result. **84m/C VHS, Beta.** Gerrit Graham, Mary Woronov, Diane Franklin, Bert Remsen, Alejandro Rey; **D:** Ted Nicolaou; **W:** Ted Nicolaou; **M:** Richard Band. *LIV*

The Terry Fox Story 🎬🎬🎬 1983 In the spring of 1980, a young man who had lost his right leg to cancer dipped his artificial limb into the Atlantic Ocean and set off on a fund-raising "Marathon of Hope" across Canada, drawing national attention. Inspiring made-for-TV true story is well-scripted and avoids corniness. Good acting from real-life amputee Fryer and, as usual, from Duvall. **96m/C VHS, Beta.** Eric Fryer, Robert Duvall, Chris Makepeace, Michael Zelniker, Rosalind Chao; **D:** Ralph L. Thomas; **M:** Bill Conti. Genie Awards '84: Best Actor (Fryer), Best Film, Best Supporting Actor (Zelniker). *VES*

Tess 🎬🎬🎬 1980 (PG) Sumptuous adaptation of the Thomas Hardy novel "Tess of the D'Ubervilles." Kinski is wonderful as an innocent farm girl who is seduced by the young aristocrat she works for and then finds marriage to a man of her own class only brings more grief. Polanski's direction is faithful and artful. Nearly three hours long, but worth every minute. **170m/C VHS, Beta, LV.** *GB FR* Nastassia Kinski, Peter Firth, Leigh Lawson, John Collin; **D:** Roman Polanski; **W:** Roman Polanski, Gerard Brach; **C:** Ghislan Cloquet, Geoffrey Unsworth. Academy Awards '80: Best Art Direction/Set Decoration, Best Cinematography, Best Costume Design; Cesar Awards '80: Best Cinematography, Best Director (Polanski), Best Film; Golden Globe Awards '81: Best Foreign Film; Los Angeles Film Critics Association Awards '80: Best Cinematography, Best Director (Polanski); National Board of Review Awards '80: 10 Best Films of the Year; New York Film Critics Awards '80: Best Cinematography; Nominations: Academy Awards '80: Best Director (Polanski), Best Picture, Best Original Score. *COL*

Test of Donald Norton 🎬🎬½ 1926 Good early Western. A young man raised by Indians finds work with the Hudson's Bay Company and does well, but is haunted by suspicions that he is a half-breed. **68m/B VHS, Beta, 8mm.** George Walsh, Tyrone Power Sr., Eugenia Gilbert, Robert Graves, Virginia True Boardman; **D:** B. Reeves Eason. *GPV, VYY*

A Test of Love *Annie's Coming Out* 1984 (PG) Incorrectly diagnosed as retarded, a young woman with cerebral palsy struggles to adjust to life outside an institution. Predictable but touching and well-acted. **93m/C VHS, Beta.** *AU* Angela Punch McGregor, Drew Forsythe, Tina Arhondis; **D:** Gil Brealey; **W:** Chris Borthwick. Australian Film Institute '84: Best Film. *USH*

Test Pilot 🎬🎬🎬½ 1938 Gable and Spencer star as daring test pilot and devoted mechanic respectively. When Gable has to land his experimental craft in a Kansas cornfield, he meets and falls in love with farm girl Loy. The two marry and raise a family, all the while she worries over his dangerous profession. When the Air Force asks him to test their new B-17 bomber, she refuses to watch, thinking the test will end in tragedy. Superb aviation drama featuring excellent cast. **118m/B VHS, Beta.** Clark Gable, Myrna Loy, Spencer Tracy, Lionel Barrymore, Samuel S. Hinds; **D:** Victor Fleming. Nominations: Academy Awards '38: Best Film Editing, Best Picture, Best Story. *MGM, TLF, CCB*

Test Tube Babies woof! 1948 A married couple's morals begin to deteriorate as they mourn the fact they can't have a child. The day is saved, however, when they learn about the new artificial insemination process. Amusing, campy propaganda in the vein of "Reefer Madness." Rereleased in 1967 as "The Pill" with extra scenes featuring Monica Davis and John Maitland. **83m/B VHS, Beta.** Dorothy Dube, Timothy Farrell, William Thompson; **D:** W. Merle Connell. *GVV, SNC, DVT*

Test Tube Teens from the Year 2000 🎬 *Virgin Hunters* 1993 (R) When sex is banned in the year 2000, horny teenagers are left with no choice but to travel through time for some action. **CW:** Strong sexuality. **74m/C VHS, Beta, LV, Closed Caption.** Morgan Fairchild, Ian Abercrombie, Brian Bremer, Christopher Wolf, Michelle Matheson, Sara Suzanne Brown, Don Dowe; **D:** Ellen Cabot; **W:** Kenneth J. Hall; **M:** Reg Powell. *PAR*

Testament 🎬🎬🎬 1983 (PG) Well-made and thought-provoking story of the residents of a small California town struggling to survive after a nuclear bombing. Focuses on one family who tries to accept the reality of post-holocaust life. We see the devastation but it never sinks into sensationalism. An exceptional performance from Alexander.

90m/C VHS, Beta, LV, Closed Caption. Jane Alexander, William Devane, Ross Harris, Roxana Zal, Kevin Costner, Rebecca DeMornay; *D:* Lynne Littman; *W:* John Sacret Young; *M:* James Horner. Nominations: Academy Awards '83: Best Actress (Alexander). *PAR*

The Testament of Dr. Cordelier 🐾🐾🐾 1959 A strange, experimental fantasy about a Jekyll and Hyde-type lunatic stalking the streets and alleys of Paris. Originally conceived as a television play, Renoir attempted to create a new mise-en-scene, using multiple cameras covering the sequences as they were performed whole. In French with English subtitles. 95m/C VHS, Beta. *FR* Jean-Louis Barrault; *D:* Jean Renoir. *FCT*

Testament of Dr. Mabuse 🐾🐾½ *The Crimes of Dr. Mabuse; The Last Will of Dr. Mabuse* 1962 The director of an asylum is controlled by the evil genius, Dr. Mabuse, who hypnotizes him in this well-done remake of Lang's 1933 classic. **?m/C VHS.** Gert Frobe, Wolfgang Preiss, Senta Berger. *SNC, LSV*

The Testament of Orpheus 🐾🐾🐾½ 1959 Superb, personal surrealism; writer-director Cocteau's last film. Hallucinogenic, autobiographical dream-journey through time. Difficult to follow, but rewarding final installment in a trilogy including "The Blood of the Poet" and "Orpheus." In French with English subtitles. 80m/B VHS, Beta. *FR* Jean Cocteau, Edouard Dermithe, Maria Casares, Francois Perier, Yul Brynner, Jean-Pierre Leaud, Daniel Gelin, Jean Marais, Pablo Picasso, Charles Aznavour; *D:* Jean Cocteau. *HMV, FCT, HEG*

Tetsuo: The Iron Man 🐾🐾 1992 A weird live-action science-fiction cartoon about a white-collar Japanese worker who finds himself being gradually transformed into a walking metal collection of cables, drills, wires, and gears. The newly-formed metal creature then faces off with an equally bizarre metals fetishist (played by the director) in Japanese with English subtitles. 67m/B VHS. *JP* Tomoroh Taguchi, Kei Fujiwara, Shinya Tsukamoto; *D:* Shinya Tsukamoto; *W:* Shinya Tsukamoto. *FXL*

Tevye 🐾🐾½ *Tevye der Milkhiker* 1939 Sholom Aleichem's story of Jewish family life, intermarriage, and turmoil in Poland. When Khave, the daughter of Tevye the dairyman, seeks to marry a Ukrainian peasant, Tevye must come to terms with his love for his daughter and his faith and loyalty to tradition. Also the basis for the musical "Fiddler on the Roof." In Yiddish with English subtitles. 96m/B VHS, Beta. Maurice Schwartz, Miriam Riselle; *D:* Maurice Schwartz. *ERG, NCJ, TPV*

Tex 🐾🐾½ 1982 (PG) Fatherless brothers in Oklahoma come of age. Dillon is excellent. Based on the novel by S.E. Hinton. 103m/C VHS, Beta, LV. Matt Dillon, Jim Metzler, Meg Tilly, Bill McKinney, Frances Lee McCain, Ben Johnson, Emilio Estevez; *D:* Tim Hunter; *M:* Pino Donaggio. *DIS, OM*

Tex Rides with the Boy Scouts 🐾½ 1937 Scouts aid Ritter in capturing gold bandits with a little bit of singing thrown in for good measure. 60m/B VHS, Beta. Tex Ritter. *NOS, DVT*

The Texans 🐾🐾½ 1938 Ex-Confederate soldier Kirk Jordan (Scott) struggles to make a new life for himself as a trail boss, aiming to get 10,000 head of cattle to the railroad in Abilene. But there's temptation in the form of Ivy Preston (Bennett) and a scheme to reignite the war. Remake of 1924 silent "North of '36." 93m/B VHS, Closed Caption. Randolph Scott, Joan Bennett, Walter Brennan, May Robson, Robert Cummings, Raymond Hatton, Robert Barrat, Harvey Stephens, Chris-Pin Martin, Francis Ford; *D:* James Hogan; *W:* Bertram Millhauser, Paul Sloane, William Haines. *USH*

Texas 🐾🐾🐾 1941 Two friends wander through the West after the Civil War getting into scrapes with the law and eventually drifting apart. Ford takes a job on a cattle ranch run by Trevor and discovers Holden has joined a gang of rustlers aiming to steal her herd. The two men vie for

Trevor's affections. Although friends, a professional rivalry also existed between the two leading actors and they competed against each other, doing their own stunts during filming. Well-acted, funny, and enthusiastic Western. 94m/B VHS, Beta. William Holden, Glenn Ford, Claire Trevor, Edgar Buchanan, George Bancroft; *D:* George Marshall. *COL*

Texas 🐾🐾½ *James A. Michener's Texas* 1994 Stephen Austin (Duffy) sets up a colony in 1821 Texas, with Mexican law requiring the settlers to become Mexican citizens. Eventually, calls for statehood begin and Austin's initial resistance is overturned by rebellion and prodding from Sam Houston (Keach) and Jim Bowie (Keith). Lots of action amidst the history, including the battle for the Alamo, but it's a routine extravaganza. Made for TV miniseries adapted from Michener's novel. Filmed on location in Del Rio, Texas. 180m/C VHS, LV, Closed Caption. Patrick Duffy, Stacy Keach, David Keith, Maria Conchita Alonso, Anthony Michael Hall, Rick Schroder, Benjamin Bratt, Chelsea Field, John Schneider, Grant Show, Randy Travis, Woody Watson; *D:* Richard Lang; *W:* Sean Meredith; *M:* Lee Holdridge. *REP*

Texas Across the River 🐾🐾½ 1966 Sam Hollis (Martin) is a wise-cracking gun runner who, along with Indian sidekick Kronk (Bishop), is recruiting men to help him ship guns through hostile Comanche territory. Don Andrea, a Spanish nobleman (played by Frenchman Delon) wrongly accused of murder, joins up and much comic misadventure ensues. 101m/C VHS, LV. Dean Martin, Alain Delon, Joey Bishop, Rosemary Forsyth, Tina Aumont, Peter Graves, Michael Ansara, Linden Chiles, Andrew Prine, Richard Farnsworth; *D:* Michael Gordon; *W:* Ben Starr, Wells Root, Harold Greene; *C:* Russell Metty. *USH, BTV, FCT*

Texas Bad Man 🐾½ 1932 Sheriff Mix goes undercover to get in with Kohler's gang of outlaws and bring them to justice. 60m/B VHS. Tom Mix, Fred Kohler Sr., Lucille Powers, Ed LeSaint, Richard Alexander; *D:* Edward Laemmle. *GPV*

Texas Buddies 🐾½ 1932 Steele plays a former military pilot who uses his trusty monoplane to round up outlaws. Interesting twist on standard oater, but suffers from poor execution. 57m/B VHS. Bob Steele, Nancy Drexel, George "Gabby" Hayes, Francis McDonald, Harry Semels; *D:* Robert North Bradbury; *W:* Robert North Bradbury. *MOV, GPV*

Texas Carnival 🐾🐾 1951 Williams and Skelton star as carnival performers who operate the dunk tank. When Skelton is mistaken for an oil tycoon, he lives high on the hog until the mistake is discovered. Believe it or not, this musical has only one water ballet sequence. Songs include "It's Dynamite," "Whoa! Emma," and "Young Folks Should Get Married." 77m/C VHS. Esther Williams, Red Skelton, Howard Keel, Ann Miller, Paula Raymond, Keenan Wynn, Tom Tully; *D:* Charles Walters. *MGM*

The Texas Chainsaw Massacre 🐾🐾½ 1974 (R) The movie that put the "power" in power tools. An idyllic summer afternoon drive becomes a nightmare for a group of young people pursued by a chainsaw-wielding maniac. Made with tongue firmly in cheek, this is nevertheless a mesmerizing saga of gore, flesh, mayhem, and violence. 86m/C VHS, LV, Closed Caption. Marilyn Burns, Allen Danzinger, Paul A. Partain, William Vail, Teri McMinn, Edwin Neal, Jim Siedow, Gunnar Hansen, John Dugan, Jerry Lorenz; *D:* Tobe Hooper; *W:* Ken Henkel, Tobe Hooper; *M:* Wayne Bell. *MPI*

Texas Chainsaw Massacre, Part 2 woof! 1986 (R) A tasteless, magnified sequel to the notorious blood-bucket extravaganza, about a certain family in southern Texas who kill and eat passing travelers. Followed by "Leatherface: Texas Chainsaw Massacre III." 90m/C VHS, Beta, LV, Closed Caption. Dennis Hopper, Caroline Williams, Bill Johnson, Jim Siedow; *D:* Tobe Hooper; *W:* L.M. Kit Carson. *MED, VTR*

Texas Cyclone 🐾🐾 1932 A stranger rides into a town that turns out to be incredibly friendly. Later he realizes the entire town thinks he is a prominent citizen who disappeared years ago.

58m/B VHS. Tim McCoy, Wheeler Oakman, Shirley Grey, Walter Brennan, John Wayne, Wallace MacDonald, Vernon Dent, Mary Gordon; *D:* David Ross Lederman. *COL, DVT, NOS*

Texas Detour 🐾 1977 On a trip across country, a trio of young Californians have their van stolen. They decide to take the law into their own hands when the redneck sheriff gives them no help. Dull, undistinguished "action" flick. 90m/C VHS, Beta. Cameron Mitchell, Priscilla Barnes, Patrick Wayne, Mitch Vogel, Lindsay Bloom, R.G. Armstrong; *D:* Howard (Hikmet) Avedis. *PSM*

Texas Gunfighter 🐾🐾 1932 Your basic western from the Maynard series, with everything a western could have. 60m/B VHS, Beta. Ken Maynard. *NOS, VCI, DVT*

Texas Guns 🐾🐾 *Once Upon a Texas Train* 1990 (PG) A gritty western about an old-time gunman (Nelson) and his quest for one last robbery, killing those who stand in his way and some just for fun. Also watch for Cassidy's comeback. 96m/C VHS, LV. Willie Nelson, Richard Widmark, Shaun Cassidy, Angie Dickinson, Kevin McCarthy, Royal Dano, Chuck Connors, Ken Curtis, Dub Taylor. *THV*

Texas Jack 🐾½ 1935 The head of a medicine show tries to trace the disappearance of his sister. 55m/B VHS. Jack Perrin, Jayne Regan, Nelson McDowell, Budd Buster, Lew Meehan; *D:* Bernard B. Ray. *GPV*

Texas John Slaughter: Geronimo's Revenge 🐾🐾 1960 An Indian-loving rancher frets and fights when Geronimo attacks innocent settlers. Compiled fom Walt Disney television episodes. 77m/C VHS, Beta. Tom Tryon, Darryl Hickman, Betty Lynn; *D:* Harry Keller. *DIS*

Texas John Slaughter: Stampede at Bitter Creek 🐾🐾 1962 Good guy Texas John Slaughter meets a variety of threatening obstacles when he tries to move his cattle herd into New Mexico. Originally from the "Walt Disney Presents" television series. 90m/C VHS, Beta. Tom Tryon; *D:* Harry Keller. *DIS*

Texas Justice 🐾½ 1942 The "Lone Rider" cavorts around in the desert, dispensing justice in the guise of a monk. 60m/B VHS, Beta. George Houston, Al "Fuzzy" St. John, Dennis Moore, Wanda McKay, Claire Rochelle; *D:* Sam Newfield. *NOS, DVT*

Texas Kid 🐾½ 1943 A typical western. Hero helps a vengeance-minded kid catch the robbergang who robbed and killed his father. Yee-Haw. 53m/B VHS, Beta. Johnny Mack Brown, Kermit Maynard, Raymond Hatton, Shirley Patterson, Edmund Cobb, Charles "Blackie" King; *D:* Lambert Hillyer. *VDM, GPV*

Texas Lady 🐾🐾 1956 When a woman wins $50,000 gambling, she buys a Texas newspaper on the stipulation that she can edit it in this standard fare western. Good vehicle for Colbert to look beautiful, but the plot and script are average and uninspired. 86m/C VHS. Claudette Colbert, Barry Sullivan, Gregory Walcott; *D:* Tim Whelan. *REP*

Texas Layover woof! 1975 Impossible-to-describe western/exploitation entry from trashmeister Adamson involving multiple stewardesses and the remnants of the Ritz Brothers. 88m/C VHS. Yvonne De Carlo, Bob Livingston, Donald (Don "Red") Barry, Connie Hoffman, Regina Carrol, Jimmy Ritz, Harry Ritz; *D:* Al Adamson. *NO*

Texas Legionnaires 🐾🐾 *Man from Music Mountain* 1943 Roy comes back to his home town and gets caught between feuding cattle and sheep herders. 71m/B VHS. Roy Rogers, Ruth Terry, Paul Kelly, Ann Gillis, George Cleveland, Pat Brady; *D:* Joseph Kane. *NOS, DVT*

Texas Lightning 🐾½ 1981 (R) Innocuous B-grade touching movie about a father and son and their family woes. 93m/C VHS, Beta. Cameron Mitchell, Channing Mitchell, Maureen McCormick, Peter Jason. *MED*

Texas Masquerade 🎬🎬 1944 Standard good cowboys versus land-grabbers action filler. William Boyd plays Hopalong Cassidy. Andy Clyde plays California Carson. Jimmy Rogers plays...Jimmy Rogers. 59m/B VHS. William Boyd, Andy Clyde, Jimmy Rogers, Mady Correll, Don Costello, Russell Simpson, Nelson Leigh, Francis McDonald, J. Farrell MacDonald; *D:* George Archainbaud. *NOS, RXM*

Texas Payback 🎬🎬 1995 (R) Convicted killer busts out of prison in order to get revenge on the now-retired-and-working-in-Vegas Texas Ranger who put him away.*CW:* Violence and nudity. 96m/C VHS, Closed Caption. Sam Jones, Gary Hudson, Kathleen Kinmont, Bo Hopkins; *D:* Richard W. Munchkin; *W:* Brian Page; *C:* Mark Morris; *M:* Jim Halfpenny. *CAF*

Texas Pioneers 🎬½ *The Blood Brother* 1932 A frontier scout is sent to an outpost town besieged by crooks. 54m/B VHS, Beta. Bill Cody. *VDM*

The Texas Rangers 🎬🎬½ 1936 Banditos Jim Hawkins (MacMurray) and Wahoo Jones (Oakie) roam the Texas frontier until the Rangers come in, establishing order. So, they switch over to the good guys but are then told to bring in their old partner-in-crime Sam McGee (Nolan). Lots of confronting villains and battling varmints. Based on the book by Walter Prescott Webb. Followed by "The Texas Rangers Ride Again" and remade as "The Streets of Laredo" (1949). 99m/B VHS, Closed Caption. Fred MacMurray, Jack Oakie, Lloyd Nolan, Jean Parker, Edward Ellis, Fred Kohler Sr., George "Gabby" Hayes; *D:* King Vidor; *W:* Louis Stevens. Nominations: Academy Awards '36: Best Sound. *USH*

The Texas Rangers 🎬🎬 1951 A prisoner is given the opportunity to capture the notorious Sam Bass gang in exchange for freedom. Good B Western; lotsa shootin'. 68m/C VHS, Beta. George Montgomery, Gale Storm, Jerome Courtland, Noah Beery Jr.; *D:* Phil Karlson. *GKK*

The Texas Rangers Ride Again 🎬🎬½ 1940 When cattle keep disappearing from the Dangerfield ranch, owner Robson secretly calls in the Texas Rangers to find out what's going on. Howard and Crawford work undercover to root out the criminals while Howard also finds the time to make goo-goo eyes at Robson's granddaughter Drew. 68m/B VHS, Closed Caption. John Howard, Broderick Crawford, May Robson, Ellen Drew, Anthony Quinn, Akim Tamiroff, Charley Grapewin, Harvey Stephens; *D:* James Hogan; *W:* William R. Lipman, Horace McCoy. *USH*

Texas Terror 🎬🎬 1935 Young Wayne resigns his badge when he mistakenly believes he has shot and killed his friend. He later rescues his friend's sister, learns the truth, and (naturally) finds true love. 50m/B VHS. John Wayne, George "Gabby" Hayes, Lucille Browne. *COL, CNG, NOS*

Texas to Bataan 🎬½ 1942 The Range Busters ship horses to the Philippines and encounter enemy spies. Part of the "Range Busters" series. 56m/B VHS, Beta. John "Dusty" King, David Sharpe, Max Terhune; *D:* Robert Emmett Tansey. *VYY*

Texas Trouble 🎬½ 193? Standard matinee fare with cowboy Bob Steele. 0m/B VHS, Beta. Bob Steele. *VCN*

Texas Wildcats 🎬½ 1939 A cowboy helps make sure that sinister adversaries are brought to justice on the American Frontier. 60m/B VHS, Beta. Tim McCoy. *NOS, DVT, MOV*

Texasville 🎬🎬½ 1990 (R) Sequel to "The Last Picture Show" finds the characters still struggling after 30 years, with financial woes from the energy crisis, mental illness inspired by the Korean War, and various personal tragedies. Lacks the melancholy sensitivity of its predecessor, but has some of the wit and wisdom that comes with age. Based again on a Larry McMurtry novel. Not well received during its theatrical release. 120m/C VHS, LV, Closed Caption. Timothy Bottoms, Jeff Bridges, Annie Potts, Cloris Leachman, Eileen Brennan, Randy Quaid, Cybill Shepherd, William McNamara; *D:* Peter Bogdanovich; *W:* Peter Bogdanovich. *COL, THV*

The Texican 🎬½ 1966 Former sheriff Jess Carlin (Murphy) is living in Mexico but must return to the Texas town of Rim Rock when his newspaperman brother is murdered. Town boss Luke Starr (Crawford) is behind the crime but the townspeople are too scared to help Carlin out—except for saloon gal Kit (Lorys). 86m/C VHS. Audie Murphy, Broderick Crawford, Diana Lorys, Aldo Sambrel, Antonio Casas; *D:* Lesley Selander; *W:* John C. Champion; *C:* Francis Marin. *COL*

Thank God It's Friday 🎬½ 1978 (PG) Episodic and desultory disco-dancing vehicle which won the Best Song Oscar for Donna Summer's rendition. Life is irony. Co-produced by Motown. ♫Last Dance; After Dark; Find My Way; It's Serious; Let's Make A Deal; Romeo and Juliet; You're the Reason I Feel Like Dancing; From Here to Eternity; Dance All Night. 100m/C VHS, Beta. Valerie Landsburg, Teri Nunn, Chick Vennera, Jeff Goldblum, Debra Winger; *D:* Robert Klane; *W:* Armyan Bernstein. Academy Awards '78: Best Song ("Last Dance"). *COL*

Thank You & Good Night 1991 Director Oxenberg gathers members of her own family around a purple armchair of grandma's to talk about life, love, and family memories, including grandma's illness and recent death. 81m/C VHS. *D:* Jan Oxenberg; *W:* Jan Oxenberg; *C:* Claudia Rashke. *ORI, BTV, FXL*

Thank Your Lucky Stars 🎬🎬🎬 1943 A lavish, slap-dash wartime musical that emptied out the Warner's lot for an array of uncharacteristic celebrity turns. Features Shore in her movie debut. ♫They're Either Too Young or Too Old; Blues in the Night; Hotcha Cornia; Ridin' For A Fall; We're Staying Home Tonight; Goin' North; Love Isn't Born, It's Made; No You, No Me; Ice Cold Katie. 127m/B VHS, Beta, LV. Eddie Cantor, Dinah Shore, Joan Leslie, Errol Flynn, Bette Davis, Edward Everett Horton, Humphrey Bogart, John Garfield, Alan Hale, Ann Sheridan, Ida Lupino, Jack Carson, Dennis (Stanley Morner) Morgan, Olivia de Havilland; *D:* David Butler; *W:* Norman Panama. Nominations: Academy Awards '43: Best Song ("They're Either Too Young or Too Old"). *MGM*

Tharus Son of Attila 🎬 1987 A couple of sword-wielding barbarians battle each other and an evil emperor. 89m/C VHS, Beta. Jerome Courtland, Rik von Nutter, Lisa Gastoni; *D:* Robert Montero. *TWE*

That Brennan Girl 🎬½ 1946 A maudlin soap opera about how a girl's upbringing by an inconsiderate mother makes her a devious little wench. Fortunately her second husband had a better mom, and redemption is at hand. 95m/B VHS. James Dunn, Mona Freeman, William Marshall, June Duprez, Frank Jenks, Charles Arnt; *D:* Alfred Santell. *NOS*

That Certain Age 🎬🎬½ 1938 Alice (Durbin) is charmed by her newspaper-owning father's houseguest, older and sophisticated journalist Vincent Bullitt (Douglas). She gets a big crush and dumps boyfriend Ken (Cooper), causing much consternation to all. ♫That Certain Age; You're as Pretty as a Picture; Be a Good Scout; Has Anybody Ever Told You Before?; My Own. 101m/B VHS, Closed Caption. Deanna Durbin, Melvyn Douglas, Jackie Cooper, John Halliday, Irene Rich, Nancy Carroll, Jackie Searl, Charles Coleman; *D:* Edward Ludwig; *W:* Bruce Manning; *C:* Joseph Valentine. Nominations: Academy Awards '36: Best Song ("My Own"); Academy Awards '38: Best Sound. *USH*

That Certain Thing 🎬🎬½ 1928 Very early silent Capra comedy about a bachelor with a silver spoon in his mouth who loses his inheritance when he marries for love. It's got that certain Capra screwball feeling. 65m/B VHS, Beta. Viola Dana, Ralph Graves, Burr McIntosh, Aggie Herring, Syd Crossley; *D:* Frank Capra. *GPV*

That Certain Woman 🎬🎬½ 1937 Sentimental drama with Davis portraying a gangster's widow who wants to make a new life for herself. Fonda plays the rich playboy with whom she falls in love. Because of Davis' star power, she demanded that Fonda play opposite her. It seems Davis had a real life crush on him when they were

both players in a stock company several years earlier. Remake of Goulding's "The Trespasser" which starred Gloria Swanson. 91m/B VHS, Closed Caption. Bette Davis, Henry Fonda, Ian Hunter, Anita Louise, Donald Crisp, Katherine Alexander, Minor Watson; *D:* Edmund Goulding; *W:* Edmund Goulding; *M:* Max Steiner. *MGM*

That Championship Season 🎬🎬 1982 (R) Long-dormant animosities surface at the reunion of a championship basketball team. Unfortunate remake of Miller's Pulitzer-prize winning play, with none of the fire which made it a Broadway hit. 110m/C VHS, Beta. Martin Sheen, Bruce Dern, Stacy Keach, Robert Mitchum, Paul Sorvino, Jason Miller; *D:* Jason Miller; *C:* John Bailey; *M:* Bill Conti. *MGM*

That Cold Day in the Park 🎬🎬½ 1969 (R) Early Altman. An unhappy woman takes in a homeless young man from the park near her home. The woman (Dennis) is obsessive and odd; so is the film. Dennis is excellent. Reminiscent of "The Collector." 91m/C VHS, Beta. Sandy Dennis, Michael Burns, Susanne Benton, Michael Murphy, John David Garfield; *D:* Robert Altman. *REP, FCT*

That Darn Cat 🎬🎬½ 1965 (G) Vintage Disney comedy about a Siamese cat that helps FBI Agent Jones thwart kidnappers. Could be shorter, but suspenseful and funny with characteristic Disney slapstick. Based on the book "Undercover Cat" by The Gordons. 115m/C VHS, Beta. Hayley Mills, Dean Jones, Dorothy Provine, Neville Brand, Elsa Lanchester, Frank Gorshin, Roddy McDowall; *D:* Robert Stevenson; *C:* Edward Colman; *M:* Robert F. Brunner. *DIS*

That Darn Cat 🎬🎬½ 1996 (PG) Innocuous Disney remake of the 1965 Disney comedy falls into the "why bother" category. Bored 16-year-old Patti (Ricci) finds some unexpected excitement when her alley-wandering cat D.C. (for Darned Cat) returns home from a prowl with a wristwatch around his neck. Turns out it's a clue in a bungled kidnapping and Patti manages to convince rookie FBI agent Zeke (Doug) to investigate. Jones, who played the FBI agent in the original, is the wealthy husband of would-be-kidnap victim Cannon. Ricci's appealing as the sarcastic teen and Elvis the cat has a certain scrappy charm as well. Based on the novel "Undercover Cat" by Mildred and Gordon Gordon. 89m/C VHS, LV, Closed Caption. Christina Ricci, Doug E. Doug, Dean Jones, George Dzundza, Peter Boyle, Michael McKean, Bess Armstrong, Dyan Cannon, John Ratzenberger, Estelle Parsons, Rebecca Schull, Tom Wilson, Brian Haley, Mark Christopher Lawrence; *D:* Bob Spiers; *W:* Scott Alexander, Larry Karaszewski; *C:* Jerzy Zielinski; *M:* Richard Kendall Gibbs. *DIS*

That Darn Sorceress 🎬 1988 A child witch has grown up, and so has her power. To keep her disciples, she must perform increasingly horrible feats. 89m/C VHS, Beta. Pauline Adams, Betty Page; *D:* Whitney Bain. *NO*

That Eye, The Sky 🎬🎬 1994 Alice (Harrow) and Sam (Fairall) Flack live on a small farm with their two children and senile grandmother. Sam's in a serious car crash and is eventually returned home still in a deep coma. Alice, who's having trouble coping, is grateful when wandering evangelist Harry Warburton (Coyote) shows up on her doorstep offering his help. But is this mystery man offering a miracle or more heartache? Based on the book by Tim Winton. 105m/C VHS. AU Lisa Harrow, Peter Coyote, Mark Fairall, Jamie Croft, Amanda Douge, Alethea McGrath; *D:* John Ruane; *W:* John Ruane, Jim Barton; *C:* Ellery Ryan; *M:* David Bridie. Australian Film Institute '95: Best Supporting Actress (Douge); Nominations: Australian Film Institute '95: Best Actress (Harrow), Best Director (Ruane), Best Film. *NYR*

That Forsyte Woman 🎬🎬 *The Forsyte Saga* 1950 Based on the novel "A Man of Property" by John Galsworthy, a married Victorian woman falls for an architect engaged to be wed. Remade later, and better for BBC-television as "The Forsythe Saga." 112m/C VHS. Errol Flynn, Greer Garson, Walter Pidgeon, Robert Young, Janet Leigh, Harry Davenport, Stanley Logan, Lumsden Hare, Aubrey Mather, Matt Moore; **D:** Compton Bennett; **C:** Joseph Ruttenberg. Nominations: Academy Awards '50: Best Costume Design (Color). *MGM, CCB*

That Gang of Mine 🐾🐾 1940 "East Side Kids" episode about gang member Mugg's ambition to be a jockey. Good racing scenes. **62m/ B VHS, Beta.** Bobby Jordan, Leo Gorcey, Clarence Muse, Dave O'Brien; **D:** Joseph H. Lewis. *NOS, DVT, HEG*

That Girl from Paris 🐾🐾½ 1936 An opera singer from Paris stows away on an ocean liner to be near the swing bandleader she has fallen in love with. An entertaining film with many songs; remade as "Four Jacks and a Jill." ♫*Una Voce Poco Fa; The Blue Danube; Love and Learn; The Call to Arms; Seal It With A Kiss; My Nephew From Nice; Moon Face; Tarantella.* **105m/ B VHS, Beta.** Lily Pons, Gene Raymond, Jack Oakie, Herman Bing, Lucille Ball, Mischa Auer, Frank Jenks; **D:** Leigh Jason. Nominations: Academy Awards '36: Best Sound. *TTC*

That Hamilton Woman 🐾🐾🐾 *Lady Hamilton* 1941 Screen biography of the tragic 18th-century love affair between British naval hero Lord Nelson and Lady Hamilton. Korda exaggerated the film's historical distortions in order to pass the censor's production code about adultery. Winston Churchill's favorite film which paralleled Britain's heroic struggles in WWII. **125m/B VHS, Beta, LV.** Laurence Olivier, Vivien Leigh, Gladys Cooper, Alan Mowbray, Sara Allgood, Henry Wilcoxon; **D:** Alexander Korda; **M:** Miklos Rozsa. Academy Awards '41: Best Sound; Nominations: Academy Awards '41: Best Black and White Cinematography, Best Interior Decoration. *HBO*

That Long Night in '43 🐾🐾½ 1960 A gripping story of fascist terror during WWII. **110m/ B VHS.** Florestano Vancini. *CIG*

That Lucky Touch 1975 York is a reporter covering NATO games; Moore is Bond warmed over as an arms dealer. Sexual and professional tension becomes unlikely romance. Slight and dull. Cobb's last film. **92m/C VHS, Beta.** Roger Moore, Susannah York, Shelley Winters, Lee J. Cobb, Jean-Pierre Cassel, Raf Vallone, Sydne Rome; **D:** Christopher Miles; **W:** John Briley. *TWE*

That Man from Rio 🐾🐾½ *L'Homme de Rio; L'Uomo di Rio* 1964 Engaging adventure spoof with Belmondo as a pilot whose girlfriend (Dorleac) has just been kidnapped. Her father led an expedition to South America in search of an Amazon treasure and the kidnappers think she knows how to find it. So of course Belmondo does some international adventuring in order to rescue her. In French with English subtitles. **114m/C VHS.** *FR IT* Jean-Paul Belmondo, Francoise Dorleac, Jean Servais, Simone Renant; **D:** Philippe de Broca; **W:** Philippe de Broca, Jean-Paul Rappeneau; **M:** Georges Delerue. New York Film Critics Awards '64: Best Foreign Film; Nominations: Academy Awards '64: Best Story & Screenplay. *MGM*

That Midnight Kiss 🐾🐾½ 1949 Glossy production of a musical romance featuring Lanza in his film debut. Thin plot has Lanza starring as a singing truck driver who is discovered by opera diva Grayson. ♫*They Didn't Believe Me; I Know, I Know, I Know; Three O'Clock in the Morning; Santa Lucia; Down Among the Sheltering Palms; Revolutionary Etude; Cara Nome; Celeste Aida; Una Furtiva Lacrima.* **96m/C VHS.** Kathryn Grayson, Jose Iturbi, Ethel Barrymore, Mario Lanza, Keenan Wynn, J. Carrol Naish, Jules Munshin; **D:** Norman Taurog; **C:** Robert L. Surtees. *MGM*

That Naughty Girl 🐾🐾 1958 The bored daughter of a nightclub owner decides to experience all life has to offer. **77m/C VHS, Beta.** *FR* Brigitte Bardot, Jean Bretonniere, Francoise Fabian; **D:** Michel Boisrond. *JEF*

That Night 🐾🐾½ 1993 (PG-13) A view of romance through the eyes of a young girl, circa 1961. Ten-year-old Alice (Dushku) is the confidant of rebellious 17-year-old neighbor Cheryl (Lewis), who enlists the young girl's aid as a go-between with her wrong-side-of-the-tracks boy-

friend Rick (Howell). 21 soundtrack oldies are featured. Directorial debut for screenwriter Bolotin. Based on a novel by Alice McDermott. **89m/C VHS, Beta, LV, Closed Caption.** C. Thomas Howell, Juliette Lewis, Eliza Dushku, Helen Shaver, John Dossett; **D:** Craig Bolotin; **W:** Craig Bolotin. *WAR*

That Obscure Object of Desire 🐾🐾🐾½ *Cet Obscur Objet Du Desir* 1977 (R) Bunuel's last film, a comic nightmare of sexual frustration. A rich Spaniard obtains a beautiful girlfriend who, while changing physical identities, refuses to sleep with him. Based on a novel by Pierre Louys, which has been used as the premise for several other films, including "The Devil is a Woman," "La Femme et le Pantin," and "The Female." Available with subtitles or dubbed. **100m/ C VHS, Beta, LV.** *SP* Fernando Rey, Carole Bouquet, Angela Molina; **D:** Luis Bunuel; **W:** Luis Bunuel, Jean-Claude Carriere. Los Angeles Film Critics Association Awards '77: Best Foreign Film; National Board of Review Awards '77: 5 Best Foreign Films of the Year, Best Director (Bunuel); National Society of Film Critics Awards '77: Best Director (Bunuel); Nominations: Academy Awards '77: Best Adapted Screenplay, Best Foreign Language Film. *COL, APD*

That Old Feeling 🐾🐾 1996 (PG-13) Bitter ex-spouses Lilly (Midler) and Dan (Farina) are reunited at the wedding of their daughter and things turn ugly. They cause a scene and are sent out of the reception to cool down. Instead, their old passion flares up and they're found reeling in that old feeling in the back seat of a Porshe. After leaving to see where their whirlwind of romance takes them, they are trailed by their daughter (Marshall), her weenie husband (Denton), and their respective current spousal units Rowena (O'Grady) and Alan (Rasche). Fluffy romantic comedy carried mostly by the performances of Midler and Farina.**CW:** Language and sex-related material. **105m/C VHS.** Bette Midler, Dennis Farina, Danny Nucci, Paula Marshall, Gail O'Grady, David Rasche, Jayne Eastwood; **D:** Carl Reiner; **W:** Leslie Dixon; **C:** Steve Mason; **M:** Patrick Williams. *USH*

That Sinking Feeling 🐾🐾🐾 1979 (PG) A group of bored Scot teenagers decide to steal 90 sinks from a plumber's warehouse. Well received early film from Forsyth is genuinely funny as the boys try to get rid of the sinks and turn a profit. **82m/C VHS, Beta, LV.** *GB* Robert Buchanan, John Hughes, Billy Greenlees, Alan Love; **D:** Bill Forsyth; **W:** Bill Forsyth; **C:** Michael Coulter.

That Summer of White Roses 🐾🐾½ 1990 (R) Compelling action drama about a lifeguard working at a resort in Nazi-occupied Yugoslavia and his love for a woman resistance fighter and her child. **98m/C VHS, Beta, LV, Closed Caption.** Tom Conti, Susan George, Rod Steiger; **D:** Rajko Grlic. *MED, IME, VTR*

That Thing You Do! 🐾🐾🐾 1996 (PG) The Wonders, a small-town foursome, hit the big time in 1964 after a substitute drummer (like that could ever happen) adds some kick to the band's new song and sets the local kids a-fruggin'. Developed by freshman director/screenwriter Hanks (who also plays the band's Svengali-like record exec) as a diversion from Oscar hype, it's nostalgic and uncomplicated to a fault, but engaging nonetheless. Hanks clone Scott puts the beat into the charmingly wholesome quartet, while the underused Tyler is disarming as the put-upon girlfriend. Look quick or you'll miss bosom buddy Scolari as a TV host. Can't-get-it-out-of-your-head title track (played 11 times in the film) was selected from over 300 submissions after Hanks put out the call to music publishers. **110m/C VHS, LV, Closed Caption.** Tom Everett Scott, Johnathon Schaech, Liv Tyler, Steve Zahn, Ethan Embry, Tom Hanks, Charlize Theron, Obba Babatunde, Peter Scolari, Alex Rocco, Bill Cobbs, Rita Wilson, Chris Isaak, Kevin Pollak; **D:** Tom Hanks; **W:** Tom Hanks; **C:** Tak Fujimoto; **M:** Howard Shore. Nominations: Academy Awards '96: Best Song ("That Thing You Do!"); Golden Globe Awards '97: Best Song ("That Thing You Do!"). *TCF*

That Touch of Mink 🐾🐾½ 1962 In New York City, an unemployed secretary finds herself involved with a business tycoon. On a trip to Bermuda, both parties get an education as they play their game of "cat and mouse." Enjoyable romantic comedy. **99m/C VHS, LV.** Cary Grant, Doris Day, Gig Young, Audrey Meadows, John Astin, Dick Sargent; **D:** Delbert Mann; **C:** Russell Metty. Golden Globe Awards '63: Best Film—Musical/Comedy; Nominations: Academy Awards '62: Best Art Direction/Set Decoration (Color), Best Sound, Best Story & Screenplay. *REP, MLB*

That Uncertain Feeling 🐾🐾½ 1941 Light comedy about a couple's marital problems increasing when she develops the hiccups and a friendship with a flaky piano player. A remake of the earlier Lubitsch silent film, "Kiss Me Again." Available colorized. **86m/B VHS, Beta.** Merle Oberon, Melvyn Douglas, Burgess Meredith, Alan Mowbray, Eve Arden, Sig Rumann, Harry Davenport; **D:** Ernst Lubitsch; **C:** George Barnes. Nominations: Academy Awards '41: Original Dramatic/Comedy Score.*NOS, VYY, DVT*

That Was Then...This Is Now 🐾🐾 1985 (R) Lame adaptation of S.E. Hinton teen novel about a surly kid who is attached to his adoptive brother and becomes jealous when the brother gets a girlfriend. **102m/C VHS, LV, Closed Caption.** Emilio Estevez, Craig Sheffer, Kim Delaney, Jill Schoelen, Barbara Babcock, Frank Howard, Larry B. Scott, Morgan Freeman; **D:** Christopher Cain; **W:** Emilio Estevez. *PAR*

That'll Be the Day 🐾🐾½ 1973 (PG) The early rock 'n' roll of the 1950s is the only outlet for a frustrated young working-class Brit. Prequel to "Stardust." Good, meticulous realism; engrossing story. **91m/C VHS, Beta, LV.** Ringo Starr, Keith Moon, David Essex, Rosemary Leach, James Booth, Billy Fury, Rosalind Ayres, Robert Lindsay, Brenda Bruce, Verna Harvey, James Ottoway, Deborah Watling, Beth Morris, Daphne Oxenford, Kim Braden, Ron Hackett, Johnny Shannon, Susan Holderness, The Debonairs; **D:** Claude Whatham; **W:** Ray Connolly; **C:** Peter Suschitzky. *REP, TVC, CNG*

That's Adequate 🐾🐾 1990 (R) Mock documentary about a fictional film studio. Lampoons just about every movie made in the last 60 years. Premise might have been adequate for a sketch, but hardly for a feature-length film. Zaniness gets old quickly. **82m/C VHS.** Tony Randall, Robert Downey, Rocky Aoki, Bruce Willis, Robert Townsend, James Coco, Jerry Stiller, Peter Riegert, Susan Dey, Richard Lewis, Robert Vaughn, Renee Taylor, Stuart Pankin, Brother Theodore, Anne Bloom, Chuck McCann, Anne Meara; **D:** Harry Hurwitz; **W:** Harry Hurwitz. *HMD*

That's Dancing! 1985 (G) This anthology features some of film's finest moments in dance from classical ballet to break-dancing. **104m/C VHS, Beta, LV.** Fred Astaire, Ginger Rogers, Ruby Keeler, Cyd Charisse, Gene Kelly, Shirley MacLaine, Liza Minnelli, Sammy Davis Jr., Mikhail Baryshnikov, Ray Bolger, Jennifer Beals, Dean Martin; **D:** Jack Haley Jr.; **M:** Henry Mancini. *MGM*

That's Entertainment 1974 (G) A compilation of scenes from the classic MGM musicals beginning with "The Broadway Melody" (1929) and ending with "Gigi" (1958). Great fun, especially for movie buffs. **132m/C VHS, Beta, LV.** Judy Garland, Fred Astaire, Frank Sinatra, Gene Kelly, Esther Williams, Bing Crosby; **D:** Jack Haley Jr.; **M:** Henry Mancini. *MGM*

That's Entertainment, Part 2 1976 (G) A cavalcade of great musical and comedy sequences from MGM movies of the past. Also stars Jeanette MacDonald, Nelson Eddy, the Marx Brothers, Laurel and Hardy, Jack Buchanan, Ann Miller, Mickey Rooney, Louis Armstrong, Oscar Levant, Cyd Charisse, Elizabeth Taylor, Maurice Chevalier, Bing Crosby, Jimmy Durante, Clark Gable, and the Barrymores. Not as unified as its predecessor, but priceless nonetheless. **129m/C VHS, Beta, LV.** Fred Astaire, Gene Kelly. *MGM*

That's Entertainment, Part 3 1993 (G)

Third volume contains 62 MGM musical numbers from over 100 films, hosted by nine of the original stars, and is based on outtakes and unfinished numbers from studio archives. One new technique used here is a split-screen showing both the actual film with a behind-the-scenes shot that includes cameramen, set designers, and dancers scurrying around. Although it has its moments, TE3 doesn't generate the same reverence for Hollywood's Golden Age that its predecessors managed to do. That 18-year gap between sequels may say something about what the studio execs thought of their film vault's remainders. 113m/C VHS, Beta, LV, Closed Caption. *D:* Bud Friedgen, Michael J. Sheridan; *W:* Bud Friedgen, Michael J. Sheridan; *M:* Marc Shaiman. MGM

That's Life! 🐾🐾 1986 (PG-13)

A lackluster semi-home movie starring Edwards' family and friends. A single weekend in the lives of a writer who's turning sixty, his singer wife who has been diagnosed with cancer, and their family. 102m/C VHS, Beta, LV, Closed Caption. Jack Lemmon, Julie Andrews, Sally Kellerman, Chris Lemmon, Emma Walton, Rob Knepper, Robert Loggia, Jennifer Edwards; *D:* Blake Edwards; *W:* Blake Edwards; *M:* Henry Mancini. Nominations: Academy Awards '86: Best Song ("Life in a Looking Glass"). CCB, LIV, VES

That's My Baby! 🐾 1988 (PG-13)

A man wants his girlfriend to have their baby, but the only thing she wants is a career. War between the sexes poorly done. 97m/C VHS, Beta. Sonja Smits, Timothy Webber; *D:* Edie Yolles, John Bradshaw. TWE

That's Singing: The Best of Broadway 1984

A tribute to the American musical theatre featuring performances of memorable songs from twenty Broadway shows. 111m/C VHS, Beta, LV. ORI, WAR

Theatre of Blood 🐾🐾🐾 1973 (R)

Critics are unkind to Shakespearian ham Price, and he eliminates them by various Bard-inspired methods with the assistance of his lovely daughter. Top drawer comedy noir. 104m/C VHS, LV. GB Vincent Price, Diana Rigg, Ian Hendry, Robert Morley, Dennis Price, Diana Dors, Milo O'Shea; *D:* Douglas Hickox. MGM

Theatre of Death 🐾🐾½ Blood Fiend 1967

Horror master Lee is back, this time as a theatre director in Paris. Meanwhile, police are baffled by a series of mysterious murders, each bearing a trace of vampirism. Well-plotted suspense. A racy voodoo dance sequence, often cut, is available on some video versions. 90m/C VHS, Beta. Christopher Lee, Lelia Goldoni, Julian Glover, Evelyn Laye, Jenny Till, Ivor Dean; *D:* Samuel Gallu. REP, SNC

Thelma & Louise 🐾🐾🐾 1991 (R)

Hailed as the first "feminist-buddy" movie, Sarandon and Davis bust out as best friends who head directly into one of the better movies of the year. Davis is the ditzy Thelma, a housewife rebelling against her dominating, unfaithful, abusive husband (who, rather than being disturbing, provides some of the best comic relief in the film). Sarandon is Louise, a hardened and world-weary waitress in the midst of an unsatisfactory relationship. They hit the road for a respite from their mundane lives, only to find violence and a part of themselves they never knew existed. Outstanding performances from Davis and especially Sarandon, with Pitt notable as the stud who gets Davis' motor revved. Director Scott has a fine eye for set details. *CW:* Strong language, some violence, and sensuality. 130m/C VHS, Beta, LV, 8mm, Closed Caption. Susan Sarandon, Geena Davis, Harvey Keitel, Christopher McDonald, Michael Madsen, Brad Pitt, Timothy Carhart, Stephen Tobolowsky, Lucinda Jenney; *D:* Ridley Scott; *W:* Callie Khouri; *M:* Hans Zimmer. Academy Awards '91: Best Original Screenplay; National Board of Review Awards '91: 10 Best Films of the Year, Best Actress (Sarandon, Davis); National Society of Film Critics Awards '91: Best Supporting Actor (Keitel); Writers Guild of America '91: Best Original Screenplay; Nominations: Academy Awards '91: Best Actress (Davis), Best Actress (Sarandon), Best Cinematography, Best Director (Scott), Best Film Editing. MGM, OM

Them! 🐾🐾🐾 1954

A group of mutated giant ants wreak havoc on a southwestern town. The first of the big-bug movies, and far surpassing the rest, this is a classic fun flick. See how many names you can spot among the supporting cast. 93m/B VHS, Beta, LV. James Whitmore, Edmund Gwenn, Fess Parker, James Arness, Onslow Stevens, Jack Perrin; *D:* Gordon Douglas. WAR

The Theme 🐾🐾🐾 Tema 1979

Esenin is a mediocre middle-aged playwright who knows his success comes from kow-towing to the party line. Trying to find inspiration he visits his native village where he meets the young Sasa, an artist who has refused to compromise. Although Esenin falls for her, Sasa has only contempt for his lack of principles and stays with her poet/lover, who is reduced to digging graves and has decided to emigrate to Israel. The film went unreleased for 8 years because of its themes of artistic freedom and emigration. In Russian with English subtitles. 100m/C VHS. *RU* Mikhail Ulyanov, Inna Churikova, Stanislav Lyubshin, Evgeny Vesnik, Sergei Nikonenko, Natalya Selezneva; *D:* Gleb Panfilov. Berlin International Film Festival '79: Golden Berlin Bear. KIV, FCT

Theodora Goes Wild 🐾🐾🐾 1936

Tiny, priggish Lynnfield, Connecticut is shocked to discover that a scandalous best seller about small-town life has been written pseudonymously by their very own Theodora Lynn (Dunne). When Theodora gets a chance to meet sophisticated New Yorker Michael Grant (Douglas), who did the illustrations for her book, she falls for him. But both must throw aside their own (and everyone else's) expectations and limitations for them to be happy. Dunne's first comedic lead role. 94m/B VHS. Irene Dunne, Melvyn Douglas, Thomas Mitchell, Thurston Hall, Rosalind Keith, Spring Byington, Elisabeth Risdon, Margaret McWade; *D:* Richard Boleslawski; *W:* Sidney Buchman; *C:* Joseph Walker; *M:* Morris Stoloff. Nominations: Academy Awards '36: Best Actress (Dunne), Best Film Editing. COL

Theodore Rex 🐾🐾½ 1995 (PG)

Futuristic comedy finds cynical, seasoned cop Katie Coltrane (Goldberg) furious at being teamed with Teddy, who just happens to be an eight-foot-tall, three-ton, returned-from-extinction Tyrannosaurus Rex (who has a taste for cookies). And Teddy's not exactly the brightest dinosaur on the block, which makes Katie's job all the harder when they stumble across a major crime caper. 92m/C VHS, LV, Closed Caption. Whoopi Goldberg, Armin Mueller-Stahl, Richard Roundtree, Juliet Landau; *D:* Jonathan Betuel; *W:* Jonathan Betuel; *C:* David Tattersall; *M:* Robert Folk. Nominations: Golden Raspberry Awards '96: Worst Actress (Goldberg). NLC

There Goes Barder 🐾🐾 1964

Constantine plays a con-man who's hired by a crooked ship owner to be a security agent. ?m/C VHS. FR Eddie Constantine, May Britt. SNC, VYY

There Goes Kelly 🐾½ 1945

Moran and Miller are page boys at a radio station who try to get the station receptionist a singing job. When the vocalist on a popular show is murdered, the duo not only get their protege a break but get themselves a mystery to solve as well. 62m/B VHS. Jackie Moran, Sidney Miller, Wanda McKay, Ralph Sanford, Jan Wiley, Anthony Warde; *D:* Phil Karlson. GPV

There Goes My Baby 🐾🐾½ 1992 (R)

Eight California high school grads confront their futures on two nights in '65 (as the Watts riots ignite). There are Vietnam protests, flower children, would-be rock stars, friendships, and romantic complications. Yes, it sounds a lot like "American Graffiti" but the cast are winning and there's a good deal of affection without sinking to mawkishness. 99m/C VHS, LV, Closed Caption. Dermot Mulroney, Rick Schroder, Kelli Williams, Jill Schoelen, Noah Wyle, Kristin Minter, Lucy Deakins, Kenny Ransom, Seymour Cassel, Paul Gleason, Frederick Coffin, Andrew (Andy) Robinson, Shon Greenblatt, J.E. Freeman; *D:* Floyd Mutrux; *W:* Floyd Mutrux. ORI

There Goes the Neighborhood 🐾🐾½ 1992 (PG-13)

A dying convict tells prison psychiatrist Daniels where he has buried 8.5 million dollars—under the home of neighbor O'Hara. Daniels and O'Hara try to discreetly dig up the fortune but when the neighborhood finds out everyone wants a chance at the cash. 88m/C VHS, Beta, Closed Caption. Jeff Daniels, Catherine O'Hara, Dabney Coleman, Hector Elizondo, Judith Ivey, Rhea Perlman, Harris Yulin, Jonathan Banks, Chazz Palminteri, Mary Gross; *D:* Bill Phillips; *M:* David Bell. PAR

There was a Crooked Man 🐾🐾🐾½ 1970 (R)

An Arizona town gets some new ideas about law and order when an incorruptible and innovative warden takes over the town's prison. The warden finds he's got his hands full with one inmate determined to escape. Offbeat western black comedy supported by an excellent and entertaining production, with fine acting all around. 123m/C VHS, Beta. Kirk Douglas, Henry Fonda, Warren Oates, Hume Cronyn, Burgess Meredith, John Randolph, Arthur O'Connell, Alan Hale Jr., Lee Grant; *D:* Joseph L. Mankiewicz; *W:* Robert Benton, David Newman; *C:* Harry Stradling Jr. WAR

Theremin: An Electronic Odyssey 🐾🐾🐾 1995 (PG)

Profiles the life of Russian scientist Leon Theremin (who died in 1993), founder of electronic music, and his revolutionary musical invention, the Theremin. Martin located the 95-year old Thermin in Moscow in 1991, interviewed him on camera, then brought him back to the U.S. to film reunions with friends and colleages he hadn't seen in 50 years. Martin's focus is on the impact of the Theremin on Hollywood movie scores heard in 50s sci-fi and thriller classics ("The Day the Earth Stood Still") and in popular music (The Beach Boys' "Good Vibrations" is commented on by Brian Wilson). Theremin's life proves as curious as his instrument, with his controversial interracial marriage to a ballet star, abduction by Russian agents, and imprisonment in a Soviet mental hospital. "Theremin" provides a fascinating and heartfelt tribute to the man's work and life. 84m/C VHS, LV, Closed Caption. *D:* Steven M. Martin; *W:* Steven M. Martin; *C:* Robert Stone, Edward Lachman, Chris Lombardi; *M:* Hal Wilner. ORI

There's a Girl in My Soup 🐾🐾 1970 (R)

Sellers is a gourmet who moonlights as a self-styled Casanova. Early post "Laugh-In" Hawn is the young girl who takes refuge at his London love nest when her boyfriend dumps her. Lust ensues. Has its funny parts, but not a highlight of anyone's career. Based on the hit play. 95m/C VHS, Beta. GB Peter Sellers, Goldie Hawn, Diana Dors; *D:* Roy Boulting. GKK

There's No Business Like Show Business 1954

A top husband and wife vaudevillian act make it a family affair. Filmed in CinemaScope, allowing for full and lavish musical numbers. Good performances and Berlin's music make this an enjoyable film. ♫When the Midnight Choo-Choo Leaves for Alabam; Let's Have Another Cup of Coffee; Play a Simple Melody; After You Get What You Want You Don't Want It; You'd Be Surprised; A Sailor's Not a Sailor; A Pretty Girl is Like a Melody; A Man Chases a Girl Until She Catches Him. 117m/C VHS, Beta, LV, Closed Caption. Ethel Merman, Donald O'Connor, Marilyn Monroe, Dan Dailey, Johnny Ray, Mitzi Gaynor, Frank McHugh, Hugh O'Brian; *D:* Walter Lang. Nominations: Academy Awards '54: Best Costume Design (Color), Best Story, Scoring of a Musical. FOX, FCT

There's No Time for Love, Charlie Brown 1987

An animated adventure with the Peanuts gang as they travel to a museum on a class trip. 30m/C VHS, Beta. BAR

There's Nothing Out There 🐾🐾 1990

A group of seven teenagers spends Spring Break at a secluded mountain cabin. It sounds wonderful, but one of the boys (who claims to have seen every horror movie on video) knows the signs of a horror movie just waiting to happen. **91m/C VHS, Beta, LV.** Craig Peck, Wendy Bednarz, Mark Collver, Bonnie Bowers, John Carhart III, Claudia Flores, Jeff Dachis; **D:** Rolfe Kanefsky; **W:** Rolfe Kanefsky. **PSM**

Therese 🎬🎬🎬 1986 Stylish biography of a young French nun and her devotion to Christ bordering on romantic love. Explores convent life. Real-life Therese died of TB and was made a saint. A directorial tour de force for Cavalier. In French with English subtitles. **90m/C VHS, Beta. FR** Catherine Mouchet, Aurore Prieto, Sylvie Habault, Ghislaine Mona; **D:** Alain Cavalier; **W:** Alain Cavalier. Cannes Film Festival '86: Special Jury Prize; Cesar Awards '87: Best Cinematography, Best Director (Cavalier), Best Film, Best Writing. **APD, MED, TPV**

Therese & Isabelle 🎬🎬½ *Therese Und Isabell* 1968 Story of growing love and physical attraction between two French schoolgirls. On holiday together, they confront their mutual desires. Richly photographed soft porn. Not vulgar, but certainly for adults. **102m/C VHS, Beta. GE** Essy Persson, Anna Gael, Barbara Laage, Anne Vernon; **D:** Radley Metzger. **NO**

These Girls Won't Talk 192? Three female stars of early silent pictures are featured separately in: "Her Bridal Nightmare," "Campus Carmen," and "As Luck Would Have It." **50m/B VHS, Beta.** Colleen Moore, Carole Lombard, Betty Compson. **VYY**

These Three 🎬🎬🎬½ 1936 A teenaged girl ruins the lives of two teachers by telling a malicious lie. Excellent cast. Script by Lillian Hellman, based on her play "The Children's Hour." Remade by the same director as "The Children's Hour" in 1961. **92m/B VHS, Beta, LV.** Miriam Hopkins, Merle Oberon, Joel McCrea, Bonita Granville, Marcia Mae Jones, Walter Brennan, Margaret Hamilton; **D:** William Wyler; **C:** Gregg Toland. Nominations: Academy Awards '36: Best Supporting Actress (Granville).

They 🎬 *Invasion from Inner Earth; Hell Fire* 1977 Beings from beneath the earth's crust take their first trip to the surface. **88m/C VHS, Beta.** Paul Dentzer, Debbie Pick, Nick Holt; **D:** Ito Rebane. **NO**

They All Kissed the Bride 🎬🎬½ 1942 Tough cookie Margaret Drew (Crawford) must take over the family's trucking business when dad dies and support her ditzy mother (Burke) and younger sister Vivian (Parrish). Crusading newspaperman Michael Holmes (Douglas) blasts Margaret's business practices in print but when they finally meet, the sparks fly. Crawford manages the physical comedy well and Douglas is suitably charming. **87m/B VHS.** Joan Crawford, Melvyn Douglas, Billie Burke, Helen Parrish, Roland Young, Allen Jenkins, Emory Parnell; **D:** Alexander Hall; **W:** Andrew Solt, P.J. Wolfson; **C:** Joseph Walker; **M:** Werner R. Heymann. **COL**

They All Laughed 🎬🎬 1981 (PG) Three detectives become romantically involved with the women they were hired to investigate. Essentially light-hearted fluff with little or no script. Further undermined by the real-life murder of Stratten before the film's release. **115m/C VHS, Beta, LV.** Ben Gazzara, John Ritter, Audrey Hepburn, Colleen Camp, Patti Hansen, Dorothy Stratten, Elizabeth Pena; **D:** Peter Bogdanovich; **W:** Peter Bogdanovich. **VES**

They Bite woof! 1995 (R) A pornographic filmmaker's latest epic about lustful gill-men is filming at the same Florida beach where a zoologist is investigating reports of man-like fish monsters killing swimmers. Just a coincidence? Ultra- (and deliberately) cheesy; an unrated version is also available. **CW:** Nudity, language, mild violence. **96m/C VHS.** Donna Frotscher, Nick Baldasare, Charlie Barnett; **D:** Bret Piper. **MTH**

They Call It Sin 🎬🎬 *The Way of Life* 1932 Often told story of a young country girl heading to the Big Apple in search of her big break and "Mr. Right." Young is a chorus line girl romantically involved with her married producer (Calhern) while faithful admirer Brent waits nearby. Predict-

able plot adapted from the novel by Alberta Stedman Eagan. **68m/B VHS.** Loretta Young, George Brent, David Manners, Louis Calhern, Una Merkel, Joseph Cawthorn, Helen Vinson; **D:** Thornton Freeland; **W:** Lillie Hayward, Howard J. Green. **MGM**

They Call Me Bruce? 🎬🎬 *A Fist Full of Chopsticks* 1982 (PG) A bumbling Bruce Lee lookalike meets a karate-chopping Mafia moll in this farce. Silly premise creates lots of laughs. Followed by a sequel, "They Still Call Me Bruce." **88m/C VHS, Beta.** Johnny Yune, Margaux Hemingway; **D:** Elliot Hong; **W:** Tim Clawson. **VES**

They Call Me Mr. Tibbs! 🎬🎬 1970 (R) Lieutenant Virgil Tibbs (Poitier) investigates the murder of a prostitute. The prime suspect is his friend, the Reverend Logan Sharpe (Landau). He is torn between his duty as a policeman, his concern for the reverend, and the turmoil of his domestic life. Less tense, less compelling sequel to "In the Heat of the Night." **CW:** Violent scene with nudity. **108m/C VHS, Beta.** Sidney Poitier, Barbara McNair, Martin Landau, Juano Hernandez, Anthony Zerbe, Ed Asner, Norma Crane, Jeff Corey; **D:** Gordon Douglas; **W:** Alan R. Trustman; **M:** Quincy Jones. **MGM, FOX**

They Call Me Trinity 🎬🎬½ *Lo Chiamavano Trinita* 1972 (G) Lazy drifter-gunslinger and his outlaw brother join forces with Mormon farmers to rout bullying outlaws. Spoofs every western cliche with relentless comedy, parodying "The Magnificent Seven" and gibing the spaghetti western. Followed by "Trinity is Still My Name." Dubbed. **110m/C VHS, Beta. IT** Terence Hill, Bud Spencer, Farley Granger, Steffen Zacharias; **D:** E.B. Clucher. **CCB, HHE**

They Came from Beyond Space 🎬 1967 Aliens invade the earth and possess the brains of humans. They only want a few slaves to help them repair their ship which crashed on the moon. The only person able to stop them is a scientist with a steel plate in his head. Silly and forgettable. **86m/C VHS, Beta. GB** Robert Hutton, Michael Gough; **D:** Freddie Francis.

They Came from Within 🎬🎬½ *Shivers; The Parasite Murders* 1975 (R) The occupants of a high-rise building go on a sex and violence spree when stricken by an aphrodisiac parasite. Queasy, sleazy and weird. First major film by Cronenberg. **87m/C VHS, Beta. CA** Paul Hampton, Joe Silver, Lynn Lowry, Barbara Steele; **D:** David Cronenberg; **W:** David Cronenberg. **LIV, VES**

They Came to Cordura 🎬🎬½ 1959 Mexico, 1916: a woman and six American soldiers—five heroes and one who has been branded a coward—begin a journey to the military headquarters in Cordura. Slow journey brings out personalities. Look for "Bewitched" hubby Dick York. Based on Glendon Swarthout's best-seller. **123m/C VHS, Beta, LV.** Gary Cooper, Rita Hayworth, Van Heflin, Tab Hunter, Dick York, Richard Conte; **D:** Robert Rossen. **COL**

They Died with Their Boots On 🎬🎬🎬 1941 The Battle of Little Big Horn is recreated Hollywood style. Takes liberties with historical fact, but still an exciting portrayal of General Custer's last stand. The movie also marks the last time de Havilland worked with Flynn. Also available colorized. **141m/B VHS, Beta.** Errol Flynn, Sydney Greenstreet, Anthony Quinn, Hattie McDaniel, Arthur Kennedy, Gene Lockhart, Regis Toomey, Olivia de Havilland, Charley Grapewin; **D:** Raoul Walsh; **M:** Max Steiner. **MGM, MLB, FOX**

They Drive by Night 🎬🎬🎬½ *The Road to Frisco* 1940 Two truck-driving brothers break away from a large company and begin independent operations. After an accident to Bogart, Raft is forced to go back to the company where Lupino, the boss's wife, becomes obsessed with him and kills her husband to gain the company and win Raft. When he rejects her, she accuses him of the murder. Well-plotted film with great dialogue. Excellent cast gives it their all. **97m/B VHS, Beta.** Humphrey Bogart, Ann Sheridan, George Raft, Ida Lupino,

Alan Hale, Gale Page, Roscoe Karns, Charles Halton; **D:** Raoul Walsh. **FOX, FCT**

They Got Me Covered 🎬🎬 1943 Two WWII-era journalists get involved in a comic web of murder, kidnapping and romance. Hope is very funny and carries the rest of the cast. Look for Doris Day in a bit part and listen for Bing Crosby singing whenever Hope opens his cigarette case. **95m/B VHS, Beta, LV.** Bob Hope, Dorothy Lamour, Otto Preminger, Eduardo Ciannelli, Donald Meek, Walter Catlett; **D:** David Butler.

They Knew What They Wanted 🎬🎬🎬 1940 A lonely San Francisco waitress begins a correspondence romance with a grape grower and agrees to marry him after he sends her a photo which shows him as being young and handsome. She arrives to discover Laughton had sent her a picture of another man. An accident, an affair, and a pregnancy provide further complications before a satisfactory ending is suggested. Flawed adaptation of Sidney Howard's play still has strong performances from Lombard and Laughton. **96m/B VHS, Beta.** Charles Laughton, Carole Lombard, Harry Carey Sr., Karl Malden, William Gargan; **D:** Garson Kanin; **C:** Harry Stradling. Nominations: Academy Awards '40: Best Supporting Actor (Gargan). **NO**

They Live 🎬🎬½ 1988 (R) A semi-serious science-fiction spoof about a drifter who discovers an alien conspiracy. They're taking over the country under the guise of Reaganism, capitalism and yuppiedom. Screenplay written by Carpenter under a pseudonym. Starts out fun, deteriorates into cliches and bad special effects makeup. **88m/C VHS, Beta, LV.** Roddy Piper, Keith David, Meg Foster, George Flower, Peter Jason, Raymond St. Jacques, John Lawrence, Sy Richardson, Jason Robards III, Larry Franco; **D:** John Carpenter; **W:** John Carpenter; **M:** Alan Howarth, John Carpenter. **USH**

They Live by Night 🎬🎬🎬½ *The Twisted Road; Your Red Wagon* 1949 A young fugitive sinks deeper into a life of crime thanks to his association with two hardened criminals. Classic film noir was Ray's first attempt at directing. Based on Edward Anderson's novel "Thieves Like Us," under which title it was remade in 1974. Compelling and suspenseful. **95m/B VHS, Beta, LV.** Cathy O'Donnell, Farley Granger, Howard da Silva, Jay C. Flippen, Helen Craig; **D:** Nicholas Ray. **HHT**

They Made Me a Criminal 🎬🎬½ *I Became a Criminal; They Made Me a Fugitive* 1939 A champion prizefighter, believing he murdered a man in a drunken brawl, runs away. He finds refuge in the West with the Dead End Kids. Remake of "The Life of Jimmy Dolan." Berkeley was best-known for directing and choreographing musicals and surprisingly did very well with this movie. **92m/B VHS, Beta, LV.** John Garfield, Ann Sheridan, Claude Rains, Leo Gorcey; **D:** Busby Berkeley; **C:** James Wong Howe; **M:** Max Steiner. **NOS, PSM, VHE**

They Meet Again 🎬🎬 1941 The final segment of the Dr. Christian series. The country doctor sets out to prove the innocence of a man who has been wrongly accused of stealing money. Slow moving and not particularly exciting. **68m/B VHS, Beta, 8mm.** Jean Hersholt, Dorothy Lovett; **D:** Erle C. Kenton. **NOS, VYY, VYY**

They Met in Bombay 🎬🎬½ 1941 Two jewel thieves team up in this romantic action-comedy, complete with exotic locations and two big box-office stars. A Japanese invasion makes Russell reconsider her life of crime and gives Gable a chance to play hero. Look for Alan Ladd in a bit part in his pre-"This Gun for Hire" days. Based on a story by John Kafka. **86m/B VHS.** Clark Gable, Rosalind Russell, Peter Lorre, Jessie Ralph, Reginald Owen, Eduardo Ciannelli, Alan Ladd; **D:** Clarence Brown; **W:** Anita Loos, Edwin Justus Mayer, Leon Gordon. **MGM**

They Might Be Giants 🎬🎬🎬 1971 (G) Woodward is a woman shrink named Watson who treats retired judge Scott for delusions that he is Sherlock Holmes. Scott's brother wants him committed so the family loot will come to him. Very funny in places; Woodward and Scott highlight a solid cast. **98m/C VHS, Beta.** George C. Scott, Joanne Woodward, Jack Gilford, Eugene Roche, Kitty Winn, F. Murray Abraham, M. Emmet Walsh; **D:** Anthony Harvey; **M:** John Barry. *USH*

They Never Come Back 𝒅𝒅½ 1932 A
boxer is thrown in jail and then stages a comeback. **62m/B VHS, Beta, LV.** Regis Toomey, Dorothy Sebastian. *SNC*

They Only Kill Their Masters 𝒅𝒅𝒅½
1972 (PG) Garner plays a California police chief investigating the death of a wild beach town resident, supposedly killed by her doberman pinscher. He discovers the woman was actually drowned and there are any number of secrets to uncover. Mild whodunit. **98m/C VHS.** James Garner, Katharine Ross, June Allyson, Hal Holbrook, Harry Guardino, Christopher Connelly, Tom Ewell, Peter Lawford, Edmond O'Brien, Arthur O'Connell, Ann Rutherford, Art Metrano; **D:** James Goldstone; **M:** Perry Botkin. *MGM*

They Paid with Bullets: Chicago 1929 𝒅½ 197? The story of one man's rise to
power, and eventual downfall as a Mafia consigliatore. **88m/C VHS, Beta.** Peter Lee Lawrence, Ingrid Schoeller. *CNG*

They Saved Hitler's Brain woof!
Madmen of Mandoras; The Return of Mr. H **1964** Fanatical survivors of the Nazi holocaust gave eternal life to the brain of their leader in the last hours of the war. Now it's on a Caribbean island giving orders again. One of the truly great "bad" movies. Shot in pieces in the U.S., the Philippines, and elsewhere, with chunks of other films stuck in to hold the "story" together. **91m/B VHS, Beta, 8mm.** Walter Stocker, Audrey Caire; **D:** David Bradley. *VYY*

They Shall Have Music 𝒅𝒅 *Melody of
Youth; Ragged Angels* **1939** A poverty-stricken child hears a concert by violinist Heifetz and decides to become a musician. He joins Brennan's nearly bankrupt music school and persuades Heifetz to play at a benefit concert. Hokey but enjoyable Goldwyn effort to bring classical music to the big screen. ♫Rondo Capriccioso; Hora Staccato; Estrellita; Melody; Concerto in E Minor for Violin and Orchestra; Waltz in D Flat, Opus 64, No. 1; Cara Nome; Casta Diva. **101m/B VHS, Beta.** Walter Brennan, Joel McCrea, Gene Reynolds, Jascha Heifetz, Marjorie Main, Porter Hall, Andrea Leeds, Terence Kilburn; **D:** Archie Mayo. Nominations: Academy Awards '39: Best Score. *HBO*

They Shoot Horses, Don't They? 𝒅𝒅𝒅½ 1969 (R) Powerful period
piece depicting the desperation of the Depression Era. Contestants enter a dance marathon in the hopes of winning a cash prize, not realizing that they will be driven to exhaustion. Fascinating and tragic. **121m/C VHS, LV.** Jane Fonda, Michael Sarrazin, Susannah York, Gig Young, Red Buttons, Bonnie Bedelia, Bruce Dern, Allyn Ann McLerie, Chaing I; **D:** Sydney Pollack. Academy Awards '69: Best Supporting Actor (Young); British Academy Awards '70: Best Supporting Actress (York); Golden Globe Awards '70: Best Supporting Actor (Young); New York Film Critics Awards '69: Best Actress (Fonda); Nominations: Academy Awards '69: Best Actress (Fonda), Best Adapted Screenplay, Best Art Direction/Set Decoration, Best Costume Design, Best Director (Pollack), Best Film Editing, Best Supporting Actress (York), Scoring of a Musical. *ABC, TCF, FOX*

They Still Call Me Bruce 𝒅 1986 (PG)
A Korean searches for the American who saved his life when he was young and instead becomes big brother to an orphan. Supposedly a sequel to "They Call Me Bruce," but has little in common with it. Poorly done and not particularly entertaining. **91m/C VHS, Beta.** Johnny Yune, Robert Guillaume, Pat Paulsen; **D:** Johnny Yune. *NWV, VTR*

They Watch 𝒅𝒅½ *They* 1993 (PG-13) Wor-
kaholic Bergin neglects his family and suffers the consequences when his young daughter dies in an auto accident. In fact, he's so distressed that he relies on blind psychic Redgrave to get in

touch with his little girl's spirit. Based on the story "They" by Rudyard Kipling. Made for television. **100m/C VHS.** Patrick Bergin, Vanessa Redgrave, Valerie Mahaffey; **D:** John Korty; **W:** Edithe Swenson; **M:** Gerald Gouriet. *COL*

They Went That-a-Way & That-a-Way woof! 1978 (PG) Two bumbling deputies
pose as convicts in this madcap prison caper. Terrible re-hash of Laurel-and-Hardy has nothing going for it. **96m/C VHS, Beta.** Tim Conway, Richard Kiel, Chuck McCann; **D:** Edward Montagne; **W:** Tim Conway. *COL*

They Were Expendable 𝒅𝒅𝒅 1945
Two American captains pit their PT boats against the Japanese fleet. Based on the true story of a PT boat squadron based in the Philippines during the early days of WWII. One of the best (and most underrated) WWII films. Also available in a colorized version. **135m/B VHS, Beta.** Robert Montgomery, John Wayne, Donna Reed, Jack Holt, Ward Bond, Cameron Mitchell, Leon Ames, Marshall Thompson; **D:** John Ford. Nominations: Academy Awards '45: Best Sound. *MGM*

They Were So Young 𝒅𝒅½ 1955 Eu-
ropean models become the pawns of wealthy Brazilian magnates when they are sent to South America. They are threatened with death if they do not cooperate. The scenes were shot in Italy and Berlin. Well acted and believable, although rather grim story. **78m/B VHS, Beta, LV.** *GE* Scott Brady, Johanna Matz, Raymond Burr; **D:** Kurt Neumann. *NO*

They Were Ten 𝒅𝒅½ 1961 Ten Soviet
Jews make Palestine their home in the 1800s despite Arab and Turkish persecution and pressures among themselves. In Hebrew with English subtitles. **105m/B VHS, Beta.** *IS* Ninette, Oded Teomi, Leo Filer, Yosef Safra; **D:** Baruch Dienar. *ERG, FCT*

They Won't Believe Me 𝒅𝒅𝒅 1947 A
man plots to kill his wife, but before he does, she commits suicide. He ends up on trial for her "murder." Interesting acting by Young and Hayward against type. Surprising, ironic ending. **95m/ B VHS, Beta, LV.** Robert Young, Susan Hayward, Rita Johnson, Jane Greer; **D:** Irving Pichel. *MED, TTC*

They Won't Forget 𝒅𝒅𝒅½ 1937 When
a young girl is murdered in a southern town, personal interests take precedence over justice. Turner is excellent in her first billed role, as are the other actors. Superb script, and expert direction by LeRoy pulls it all together. Based on Ward Greene's "Death in the Deep South." **95m/B VHS.** Claude Rains, Otto Kruger, Lana Turner, Allyn Joslyn, Elisha Cook Jr., Edward Norris; **D:** Mervyn LeRoy; **W:** Robert Rossen, Aben Kandel. *WAR, OM*

They're Playing with Fire woof! 1984
(R) An English teacher seduces a student and gets him involved in a murder plot to gain an inheritance. Turns out someone else is beating them to the punch. Sleazy semi-pornographic slasher. **96m/C VHS, Beta.** Sybil Danning, Eric Brown, Andrew Prine, Paul Clemens, K.T. Stevens, Alvy Moore; **D:** Howard (Hikmet) Avedis; **W:** Howard (Hikmet) Avedis. *VTR*

Thicker Than Water 𝒅𝒅 1993 Eerie
psychological thriller exploring the relationship between identical twins. Sam Crawford (Pryce) is a successful doctor, happily married to Jo (Russell), whose sister Debbie (Russell again) is completely different in temperament. The two share a strong psychic bond, however, and when Jo dies in a suspicious hit-and-run accident Debbie feels compelled to make Sam her own. Based on the novel by Dylan Jones. **150m/C VHS.** *GB* Theresa Russell, Jonathan Pryce, Robert Pugh; **D:** Marc Evans; **W:** Trevor Preston. *TVC*

The Thief 𝒅𝒅 1952 An American commits
treason and is overcome by guilt. Novel because there is not one word of dialogue, though the gimmmick can't sustain the ordinary story. A product of the Communist scare of the 1950s, it tends to be pretentious and melodramatic. **84m/C VHS, Beta, LV.** Ray Milland, Rita Gam, Martin Gabel, Harry Bronson, John McKutcheon; **D:** Russel Rouse; **C:** Sam Leavitt. Nominations: Academy Awards '52: Original Dramatic/Comedy Score. *VCI*

Thief 1971 A successful businessman (Crenna)
attempts to put his criminal past behind him. He's trapped when looking for a quick way to get some money to pay off a gambling debt. Made for television drama that's well-written and directed with tepid acting. **74m/C VHS, Beta.** Richard Crenna, Angie Dickinson, Cameron Mitchell, Hurd Hatfield, Robert Webber; **D:** William A. Graham. *ORI*

Thief 𝒅𝒅𝒅 *Violent Streets* 1981 (R) A big-time
professional thief likes working solo, but decides to sign up with the mob in order to make one more big score and retire. He finds out it's not that easy. Taut and atmospheric thriller is director Mann's feature film debut. **126m/C VHS, Beta, LV.** James Caan, Tuesday Weld, Willie Nelson, James Belushi, Elizabeth Pena, Robert Prosky; **D:** Michael Mann; **W:** Michael Mann; **C:** Donald E. Thorin. *MGM, FOX*

The Thief and the Cobbler 𝒅𝒅𝒅½
1996 (G) Musically animated fairy tale about Tack, a humble cobbler (Broderick) who aids the clever and beautiful Princess Yum Yum (Beals) when their town's golden treasures are stolen. Legendary villain Price lends his voice as the evil Zig Zag. Three time Oscar winning director Williams (of "Who Framed Roger Rabbit?" fame), and a team of animators led by Harris (part of the team that created Bugs Bunny) created sophisticated optical illusions that the team dubbed "two and a half dimensional." Incorporating intricate lighting, shadows and smooth motion, the project took almost three decades to complete. Soundtrack performed by the London Symphony Orchestra. **72m/ C VHS, Closed Caption. D:** Richard Williams; **W:** Richard Williams; **C:** John Leatherbarrow; **M:** Robert Folk; **V:** Vincent Price, Matthew Broderick, Jennifer Beals, Eric Bogosian, Toni Collette, Jonathan Winters, Clive Revill, Kenneth Williams, Clinton Sundberg, Thick Wilson. *TOU*

The Thief of Bagdad 𝒅𝒅𝒅½ 1940 A
wily young thief enlists the aid of a powerful genie to outwit the Grand Vizier of Baghdad. An Arabian Nights spectacular with lush photography, fine special effects, and striking score. Outstanding performance by Ingram as the genie. **106m/C VHS, Beta, LV.** Sabu, Conrad Veidt, June Duprez, Rex Ingram; **D:** Tim Whelan, Michael Powell, Ludwig Berger; **C:** Georges Perinal; **M:** Miklos Rozsa. Academy Awards '40: Best Color Cinematography; Nominations: Academy Awards '40: Best Original Score. *MLB, FUS*

The Thief of Baghdad 𝒅𝒅𝒅 1924
The classic silent crowd-pleaser, about a roguish thief who uses a genie's magic to outwit Baghdad's evil Caliph. With famous special effects in a newly struck print, and a new score by Davis based on Rimsky-Korsakov's "Scheherezade." Remade many times. **153m/B VHS, Beta, LV.** Douglas Fairbanks Sr., Snitz Edwards, Charles Belcher, Anna May Wong, Etta Lee, Brandon Hurst, Sojin, Julanne Johnston; **D:** Raoul Walsh; **M:** Carl Davis. *SNC, NOS, CCB*

Thief of Baghdad 𝒅𝒅 *Il Ladro Di Bagdad;
Le Voleur De Bagdad* **1961** An Arabian Nights fantasy about a thief in love with a Sultan's daughter who has been poisoned. He seeks out the magical blue rose which is the antidote. Not as lavish as the previous two productions by this title, nor as much fun. **89m/C VHS, Beta.** *IT* Georgia Moll, Steve Reeves; **D:** Arthur Lubin.

The Thief of Baghdad 𝒅𝒅½ 1978 (G)
A fantasy-adventure about a genie, a prince, beautiful maidens, a happy-go-lucky thief, and magic. Easy to take, but not an extraordinary version of this oft-told tale. Ustinov is fun as he tries to marry off his daughter. Made for television. **101m/C VHS, Beta.** Peter Ustinov, Roddy McDowall, Terence Stamp, Frank Finlay, Ian Holm; **D:** Clive Donner. *GEM*

Thief of Hearts 𝒅𝒅 1984 (R) A thief
steals a woman's diary when he's ransacking her house. He then pursues the woman, using his secret knowledge. Slick, but too creepy. Re-edited with soft porn scenes in some video versions. Stewart's first film. **101m/C VHS, Beta, LV, Closed Caption.** Steven Bauer, Barbara Williams, John Getz, Christine Ebersole, George Wendt; **D:** Douglas Day Stewart; **M:** Harold Faltermeyer. *PAR*

The Thief Who Came to Dinner 🎬🎬 1973 (PG) A computer analyst and a wealthy socialite team up to become jewel thieves and turn the tables on Houston's high society set. Comedy plot gets complex, though O'Neal and Bisset are likeable. Early Clayburgh role as O'Neal's ex. Based on a novel by Terence Lore Smith. 103m/C VHS, Beta. Ryan O'Neal, Jacqueline Bisset, Warren Oates, Jill Clayburgh, Ned Beatty, Gregory Sierra, Michael Murphy, Austin Pendleton, John Hillerman, Charles Cioffi; **D:** Bud Yorkin; **W:** Walter Hill; **M:** Henry Mancini. *WAR*

Thieves Like Us 🎬🎬🎬½ 1974 (R) Story of doomed lovers during the Depression is thoughtfully told by Altman. Older criminals Remsen and Schuck escape from jail with young killer Carradine. They only know one way to make a living—robbing banks—and it isn't long before they're once more working at their trade. They get a lot of press but they have a distinct problem. They're not really very good at what they do. Cops on their trail, the gang tries, unsuccessfully, to survive. Fletcher's film debut as Remsen's sister-in-law. Good period atmosphere and strong characters. Based on the novel by Edward Anderson and previously filmed as "They Live by Night." 123m/C VHS. Keith Carradine, Shelley Duvall, Bert Remsen, John Schuck, Louise Fletcher, Anne Latham, Tom Skerritt; **D:** Robert Altman; **W:** Joan Tewkesbury, Calder Willingham, Robert Altman. *MGM*

Thieves of Fortune woof! 1989 (R) Former Miss Universe stars as a contestant in a high stakes fortune hunt that spans half the globe. She meets with more than her share of action-packed encounters among the ruffians who compete for the $28 million purse. Implausible; horrible script; cliched. 100m/C VHS, Beta, LV. Michael Nouri, Lee Van Cleef, Shawn Weatherly. *ACA*

The Thin Blue Line 🎬🎬🎬½ 1988 The acclaimed docudrama about the 1977 shooting of a cop in Dallas County, and the incorrect conviction of Randall Adams for the crime. A riveting, spellbinding experience. Due to the film's impact and continued lobbying by Morris, Adams is now free. 101m/C VHS, Beta, LV, Closed Caption. **D:** Errol Morris; **M:** Philip Glass. Edgar Allan Poe Awards '88: Best Screenplay. *HBO, CCB*

Thin Ice 🎬🎬🎬 1937 Successful musical romance featuring European prince Power falling for commoner Henie. A fine score, solid script, and Henie's excellent ice skating routines make this her best film. Based on the play "Der Komet" by Attila Obok. ♫I'm Olga from the Volga; My Swiss Hillbilly; My Secret Love Affair; Over Night. 78m/B VHS. Sonja Henie, Tyrone Power, Arthur Treacher, Raymond Walburn, Joan Davis, Alan Hale, Sig Rumann, Melville Cooper, Maurice Cass, George Givot, Torben Meyer; **D:** Sidney Lanfield; **W:** Boris Ingster, Milton Sperling. *FXV*

A Thin Line Between Love and Hate 🎬 1996 (R) Writer/director/star Lawrence shows that there's no line between a crude, foulmouthed ego trip and an unfunny, unsuspenseful film. Darnell Wright is a smooth talker constantly on the lookout for women to conquer and discard. Eventually, he meets the wrong lady (Whitfield), a classic movie psycho who turns his life upside down. Drawing heavily from "Fatal Attraction," this halfhearted effort offers bad pacing, a weak script, and totally unsympathetic characters, which could almost be overlooked if it was at all funny. Whitfield holds the flick's only redeeming value as the femme fatale.**CW:** Violence, profanity and nudity. 106m/C VHS, LV, Closed Caption. Martin Lawrence, Lynn Whitfield, Regina King, Bobby Brown, Della Reese, Roger E. Mosley, Malinda Williams, Daryl Mitchell, Simbi Khali; **D:** Martin Lawrence; **W:** Martin Lawrence, Bentley Kyle Evans, Kenny Buford, Kim Bass; **C:** Francis Kenny; **M:** Roger Troutman. *TTC*

The Thin Man 🎬🎬🎬½ 1934 Married sleuths Nick and Nora Charles investigate the mysterious disappearance of a wealthy inventor. Charming and sophisticated, this was the model for all husband-and-wife detective teams that followed. Don't miss Asta, their wire-hair terrier. Based on the novel by Dashiell Hammett. Its enormous popularity triggered five sequels, starting with "After the Thin Man." 90m/B VHS, Beta, LV. William Powell, Myrna Loy, Maureen O'Sullivan, Cesar Romero, Porter Hall, Nat Pendleton, Minna Gombell, Natalie Moorhead, Edward Ellis; **D:** Woodbridge S. Van Dyke; **C:** James Wong Howe. Nominations: Academy Awards '34: Best Actor (Powell), Best Adapted Screenplay, Best Director (Van Dyke), Best Picture. *MGM, HMV*

The Thin Man Goes Home 🎬🎬½ 1944 Married sleuths Nick and Nora Charles solve a mystery with Nick's disapproving parents looking on in the fifth film from the "Thin Man" series. Despite a three-year gap and slightly less chemistry between Powell and Loy, audiences welcomed the skinny guy. Sequel to "Shadow of the Thin Man;" followed by "Song of the Thin Man." 100m/B VHS, Beta. William Powell, Myrna Loy, Lucile Watson, Gloria De Haven, Anne Revere, Harry Davenport, Helen Vinson, Lloyd Corrigan, Donald Meek, Edward Brophy, Charles Halton; **D:** Richard Thorpe. *MGM*

The Thing 🎬🎬🎬½ *The Thing From Another World* 1951 One of the best of the Cold War allegories and a potent lesson to those who won't eat their vegetables. Sci fi classic about an alien craft and creature (Arness in monster drag), discovered by an Arctic research team. The critter is accidentally thawed and then wreaks havoc, sucking the blood from sled dog and scientist alike. It's a giant seed-dispersing vegetable run amuck, unaffected by missing body parts, bullets, or cold. In other words, Big Trouble. Excellent direction, assisted substantially by producer Hawks, and supported by strong performances. Available colorized; remade in 1982. Loosely based on "Who Goes There?" by John Campbell. 87m/B VHS, Beta, LV. James Arness, Kenneth Tobey, Margaret Sheridan, Dewey Martin; **D:** Christian Nyby, Howard Hawks; **W:** Charles Lederer; **M:** Dimitri Tiomkin. *MED, TTC, MLB*

The Thing 🎬🎬½ 1982 (R) A team of scientists at a remote Antarctic outpost discover a buried spaceship with an unwelcome alien survivor still alive. Bombastic special effects overwhelm the suspense and the solid cast. Less a remake of the 1951 science fiction classic than a more faithful version of John Campbell's short story "Who Goes There?," since the seeds/spores take on human shapes. 127m/C VHS, Beta, LV. Kurt Russell, Wilford Brimley, T.K. Carter, Richard Masur, Keith David, Richard Dysart, David Clennon, Donald Moffat, Thomas G. Waites, Charles Hallahan; **D:** John Carpenter; **C:** Dean Cundey; **M:** Ennio Morricone. *USH*

The Thing Called Love 🎬🎬½ 1993 (PG-13) Take last year's surprise hit "Singles" and replace grunge rock and Seattle with Country/Western and Nashville for this unsentimental tale of four twentysomething singles trying to make their mark in the world of country music. The idea for the plot comes from the real-life Bluebird Cafe—the place where all aspiring singers and songwriters want to perform. Phoenix, Mathis, Mulroney, and Bullock bled their own singing; look for Oslin as the Cafe owner. Phoenix's last completed film role.**CW:** Some language. 116m/C VHS, Beta, LV, Closed Caption. River Phoenix, Samantha Mathis, Sandra Bullock, Dermot Mulroney, K.T. Oslin, Anthony Clark, Webb Wilder; **Cameos:** Trisha Yearwood; **D:** Peter Bogdanovich; **W:** Allan Moyle, Carol Heikkinen. *PAR*

Things 🎬 198? A man creates a monster during his freakish experiments with artificial insemination. The monster returns to his house seeking revenge, and the man's visiting brother and a friend disappear, probably a clever move given their lackluster circumstances. 90m/C VHS, Beta. Barry Gillis, Amber Lynn, Doug Bunston, Bruce Roach; **D:** Andrew Jordan. *NO*

Things 🎬🎬½ 1993 Two horror tales told by a jilted wife who's holding her husband's mistress hostage. "The Box" finds evil Mayor Black (Delama) incensed about a newly-opened brothel in his hick Nevada town. So he decides to teach the hookers a lesson with the help of a bizarre, boxed creature that's with him at all times. "Thing in a Jar" finds an abusive husband and his mistress plotting to kill his mousy wife. Only the murder victim comes back to haunt the deadly duo—at least parts of her do. Nicely grotesque special effects courtesy of Mike Tristano. 90m/C VHS. Neil Delama, Trey Howard, Debra Stevens, Courtney Lercara, Kinder Hunt; **Cameos:** Jeff Burr; **D:** Dennis Devine, Jay Woelfel; **W:** Dennis Devine, Steve Jarvis, Mike Bowler. *VSE*

Things Change 🎬🎬🎬 1988 (PG) An old Italian shoeshine guy agrees, for a fee, to be a fall guy for the Mafia. A lower-echelon mob hood, assigned to watch over him, decides to give the old guy a weekend of fun in Vegas before going to jail. Director Mamet co-wrote the screenplay with Silverstein, best-known for his children's books ("Where the Sidewalk Ends," "The Giving Tree"). Combines charm and menace with terrific performances, especially from Ameche and Mantegna. 114m/C VHS, Beta, LV, Closed Caption. Joe Mantegna, Don Ameche, Robert Prosky, J.J. Johnston, Ricky Jay, Mike Nussbaum, Jack Wallace, Dan Conway, J.T. Walsh; **D:** David Mamet; **W:** Shel Silverstein, David Mamet; **M:** Alaric Jans. Venice Film Festival '80: Best Actor (Ameche); Venice Film Festival '88: Best Actor (Mantegna). *COL*

Things Happen at Night 🎬 1948 Scientist and insurance investigator determine that friendly ghost has possessed a family's youngest daughter. Not much happens. 79m/B VHS, Beta. GB Gordon Harker, Alfred Drayton, Robertson Hare, Olga Lindo, Wylie Watson; **D:** Francis Searle. *NOS, SNC*

Things in Their Season 🎬🎬½ 1974 Made for TV melodrama about the imminent death of the mother of a Wisconsin farm family who makes those around her realize the value of happiness. Neal is excellent, rest of cast better than average in a well-told and sincere film. 79m/C VHS, Beta. Patricia Neal, Ed Flanders, Marc Singer, Meg Foster; **D:** James Goldstone. *LCA*

The Things of Life 🎬🎬🎬 *Les Choses De La Vie* 1970 A car crash makes a man re-evaluate his life, goals, and loves. In the end he must choose the course of his future and decide between his wife and mistress. In French with English subtitles. 90m/C VHS, Beta, LV. FR Romy Schneider, Michel Piccoli, Lea Massari; **D:** Claude Sautet. *CVC*

Things to Come 🎬🎬🎬½ 1936 Using technology, scientists aim to rebuild the world after a lengthy war, followed by a plague and other unfortunate events. Massey and Scott each play two roles, in different generations. Startling picture of the world to come, with fine sets and good acting. Based on an H.G. Wells story, "The Shape of Things to Come." 92m/B VHS, Beta. GB Raymond Massey, Margaretta Scott, Ralph Richardson, Cedric Hardwicke, Derrick DeMarney; **D:** William Cameron Menzies; **C:** Georges Perinal. *NOS, PSM, SNC*

Things to Do In Denver When You're Dead 🎬🎬🎬 1995 (R) Jimmy the Saint (Garcia) is an ex-mobster gone straight who is called upon by his former boss, the Man With the Plan (Walken), to do one last easy-money job. Jimmy agrees and rounds up his old gang, a colorfully off-color group which includes Pieces (Lloyd), a porn movie projectionist and Critical Bill (Williams), a hair-trigger psycho who works in a funeral parlor. The job goes awry and the group becomes a target of hitman Mr. Shhh (Buscemi). Hipster dialogue, crime-gone-wrong formula, and the presence of Buscemi instantly scream Tarantino rip-off, but the performances make it a worthwhile genre entry.**CW:** Strong graphic violence and language, and for brief images of a sex film. 115m/C VHS, LV, Closed Caption. Andy Garcia, Christopher Lloyd, William Forsythe, Bill Nunn, Treat Williams, Jack Warden, Steve Buscemi, Fairuza Balk, Gabrielle Anwar, Christopher Walken; **D:** Gary Fleder; **W:** Scott Rosenberg; **C:** Elliot Davis; **M:** Michael Convertino. *TOU*

Think Big ✂✂½ 1990 (PG-13) Former professional wrestlers, the Pauls are truck drivers in this silly, enjoyable comedy. They pick up a brilliant teenager running from bad guys. Mayhem ensues. 86m/C VHS, Beta, LV. Peter Paul, David Paul, Martin Mull, Ari Meyers, Richard Kiel, David Carradine, Richard Moll, Peter Lupus; **W:** Jim Wynorski, R.J. Robertson. *LIV, VTR*

Think Dirty ✂✂ *Every Home Should Have One* 1970 (R) Lascivious comedy about advertising executive Feldman's attempt to develop a series of sexy commercials to sell cereal. At the same time his wife forms a "clean up television" group. Not very interesting or funny. 93m/C VHS, Beta. Marty Feldman, Judy Cornwell, Shelley Berman; **D:** Jim Clark. *COL*

Thinkin' Big ✂ 1987 (R) Guys and gals cavort on the Texas coast, except for one lonely fat guy who tries to increase his sexual prowess. The usual teen sex frenzy. 96m/C VHS, Beta. Bruce Anderson, Kenny Sargent, Randy Jandt, Nancy Buechler, Darla Ralston; **D:** S.F. Brownrigg. *VTR, PSM*

Third Degree Burn ✂✂ 1989 A made-for-cable-television mystery about a small-time detective hired by a businessman to follow a woman, only to become a suspect when the woman's real husband is killed. 97m/C VHS, Beta, LV, Closed Caption. Treat Williams, Virginia Madsen, Richard Masur; **D:** Roger Spottiswoode. *PAR*

The Third Key ✂✂½ *The Long Arm* 1957 A solid British crime drama follows a dogged detective as he probes serial safe-crackings, with a climax set at London's Festival Hall. Based on the book by Robert Barr, who co-scripted. 96m/B VHS. Jack Hawkins, Dorothy Allison, Geoffrey Keen, Richard Leech, Ian Bannen; **D:** Charles Frend. *NOS*

The Third Man ✂✂✂✂ 1949 An American writer of pulp westerns (Cotten) arrives in post-war Vienna to take a job with an old friend, but discovers he has been murdered. Or has he? Based on Graham Greene's mystery, this classic film noir thriller plays on national loyalties during the Cold War. Welles is top-notch as the manipulative Harry Lime, blackmarket drugdealer extraordinare. The underground sewer sequence is not to be missed. With a haunting (sometimes irritating) theme by Anton Karas on unaccompanied zither. Special edition features trailer. 104m/B VHS, Beta, LV, 8mm. Joseph Cotten, Orson Welles, Alida Valli, Trevor Howard, Bernard Lee, Wilfrid Hyde-White, Ernst Deutsch, Erich Ponto, Siegfried Breuer, Hedwig Bleibtreu, Paul Hoerbiger, Frederick Sehreicker, Herbert Halbik, Jenny Werner, Nelly Arno, Alexis Chesnakov, Leo Bieber, Paul Hardtmuth; **D:** Carol Reed; **W:** Graham Greene; **C:** Robert Krasker; **M:** Anton Karas. Academy Awards '50: Best Black and White Cinematography; British Academy Awards '49: Best Film; Cannes Film Festival '49: Best Film; Directors Guild of America Awards '49: Best Director (Reed); National Board of Review Awards '50: 5 Best Foreign Films of the Year; Nominations: Academy Awards '50: Best Director (Reed), Best Film Editing. *SNC, REP, MED*

Third Man on the Mountain ✂✂✂½ *Banner in the Sky* 1959 (G) A family epic about mountain climbing, shot in Switzerland and based on James Ramsey Ullman's "Banner in the Sky." A young man is determined to climb the "Citadel" as his ancestors have. He finds there's more to climbing than he imagined. Look for Helen Hayes (MacArthur's mother) in a cameo. Standard Disney adventure drama. 106m/C VHS, Beta. James MacArthur, Michael Rennie, Janet Munro, James Donald, Herbert Lom, Laurence Naismith; **Cameos:** Helen Hayes; **D:** Ken Annakin. *DIS*

The Third Sex ✂ 1959 One of the first films to deal with homosexuality in which parents try to "straighten out" their gay son. ?m/C VHS. Paul Dahlke, Paula Wesley. *SNC*

Third Solution ✂✂ *Russicum* 1989 (R) An Italian-made film about the discovery of a secret pact made between the Kremlin and the Vatican that may start WWIII. Well-cast, but poorly conceived spook drama, with music by Vangelis. 93m/C VHS, Beta, LV. *IT* Treat Williams, F. Murray Abraham,

Danny Aiello, Nigel Court, Rita Rusic, Rossano Brazzi; **D:** Pasquale Squitieri; **M:** Vangelis. *COL*

Third Walker ✂✂✂ 1979 A desperate woman sacrifices her marriage to immerse herself in efforts to reunite her twin sons, who were inadvertently separated at birth. An original and intriguing directorial debut by McLuhan. 85m/C VHS, Beta. William Shatner, Colleen Dewhurst; **D:** Marshall McLuhan. *NO*

Thirst ✂✂ 1987 (R) A girl is abducted by a secret society that wants her to become their new leader. There is just one catch: she has to learn to like the taste of human blood. Chilling but weakly plotted. 96m/C VHS, Beta. David Hemmings, Henry Silva, Chantal Contouri; **D:** Rod Hardy. *MED*

The Thirsty Dead woof! *The Blood Cult of Shangri-La* 1974 (PG) Maybe they could learn to like Gatorade. An eternally young jungle king is looking for a wife. She can be young forever too, if she's not above vampirism and sacrificing virgins. In spite of the jungle vampire slant, this Filipino-made movie is a woofer. Also released on video, as "Blood Hunt." 90m/C VHS, Beta. *PH* John Considine, Jennifer Billingsley, Judith McConnell, Fredricka Meyers, Tani Phelps Guthrie; **D:** Terry Becker. *NO*

13 Ghosts ✂✂½ 1960 A dozen ghosts need another member to round out their ranks. They have four likely candidates to choose from when a family moves into the house inhabited by the ghoulish group. Originally viewed with "Illusion-O," a technology much like 3-D, which allowed the viewing of the ghosts only through a special pair of glasses. 88m/C VHS, Beta. Charles Herbert, Jo Morrow, Martin Milner, Rosemary DeCamp, Donald Woods, Margaret Hamilton; **D:** William Castle. *GKK*

13 Rue Madeleine ✂✂✂ 1946 Cagney plays a WWII spy who infiltrates Gestapo headquarters in Paris in order to find the location of a German missile site. Actual OSS footage is used in this fast-paced early postwar espionage propaganda piece. Rex Harrison rejected the part taken by Cagney. 95m/B VHS, Beta. James Cagney, Annabella, Richard Conte, Frank Latimore, Walter Abel, Sam Jaffe, Melville Cooper, E.G. Marshall, Karl Malden, Red Buttons; **D:** Henry Hathaway. *FOX, FCT*

Thirteenth Day of Christmas 1985 A made-for-British-television yarn about a psychotic boy left alone by his parents on Christmas night. 60m/C VHS, Beta. *GB* Patrick Allen, Elizabeth Spiggs. *PSM*

The 13th Floor ✂½ 1988 (R) A young girl fuses with the spirit of a young boy her father ruthlessly killed years before, and together they wreak havoc. 86m/C VHS, Beta. Lisa Hensley, Tim McKenzie, Miranda Otto; **D:** Chris Roach. *PAR*

13th Guest ✂✂ *Lady Beware* 1932 Two people try to solve a murder that occurred at a dinner party. An incredibly creaky early talkie melodrama that created some of the cliches of the genre. 70m/B VHS, Beta. Ginger Rogers, Lyle Talbot, J. Farrell MacDonald, Paul Hurst; **D:** Albert Ray. *SNC, NOS, VYY*

The Thirteenth Man ✂✂½ 1937 When a journalist investigating the murder of a district attorney is also killed, the paper's gossip columnist takes the case. Entertaining, fast-paced mystery. 70m/B VHS, Beta. Weldon Heyburn, Inez Courtney, Selmer Jackson, Milburn Stone, Matty Fain; **D:** William Nigh. *NOS, SNC, MLB*

The 13th Mission ✂½ 1991 A low-budget overseas combat adventure, no better than the first twelve. 95m/C VHS. Robert Marius, Jeff Griffith, Michael Monty, David Morisson, Paul Home, John Falch, Albert Bronski, Chantal Manz; **D:** Antonio Perez. *VTR*

Thirteenth Reunion ✂ 1981 A newspaperwoman uncovers a bizarre secret society when she does a routine story on a health spa. 60m/C VHS, Beta. Julia Foster, Dinah Sheridan, Richard Pearson; **D:** Peter Sasdy. *LIV*

The 30-Foot Bride of Candy Rock ✂ 1959 A junk dealer invents a robot, catapults into space and causes his girlfriend to grow to 30 feet in height. Lightweight, whimsical

fantasy was Costello's only solo starring film, and his last before his untimely death. 73m/B VHS, Beta. Lou Costello, Dorothy Provine, Gale Gordon; **D:** Sidney Miller. *GKK*

30 Is a Dangerous Age, Cynthia ✂✂½ 1968 Dudley Moore stars as a nightclub pianist who spends a lot of his time daydreaming about being rich, famous and married to a beautiful woman. Moore determines to attain all these dreams before his thirtieth birthday, which is only six weeks away. 85m/C VHS, Beta. *GB* Dudley Moore, Suzy Kendall, Eddie Foy Jr.; **D:** Joseph McGrath; **W:** Dudley Moore; **M:** Dudley Moore. *NO*

Thirty Seconds Over Tokyo ✂✂✂ 1944 Dated but still interesting classic wartime flagwaver details the conception and execution of the first bombing raids on Tokyo by Lt. Col. James Doolittle and his men. Look for Blake Edwards, as well as Steve Brodie in his first screen appearance. Based on a true story. 138m/B VHS, Beta. Spencer Tracy, Van Johnson, Robert Walker, Robert Mitchum, Phyllis Thaxter, Scott McKay, Stephen McNally, Louis Jean Heydt, Leon Ames, Paul Langton; **D:** Mervyn LeRoy; **W:** Dalton Trumbo; **C:** Robert L. Surtees. Academy Awards '44: Best Special Effects; Nominations: Academy Awards '44: Best Black and White Cinematography. *MGM, FCT, TLF*

32 Short Films about Glenn Gould ✂✂✂ 1993 Perceptive docudrama about the iconoclastic Canadian classical pianist who secluded himself in the studio, forsaking live performances for much of his career. A combination of dramatic recreation, archival material, and interviews depict the biographical details of the driven artist who died at the age of 50. Feore is memorable in the title role, especially since he's never actually playing the piano. Title and film structure refer to Bach's "Goldberg" Variations, a recording which made Gould's reputation. 94m/C VHS, LV. *CA* Colm Feore, Gale Garnett, David Hughes, Katya Ladan, Gerry Quigley, Carlo Rota, Peter Millard, Yehudi Menuhin, Bruno Monsaingeon; **D:** Francois Girard; **W:** Don McKellar, Francois Girard; **C:** Alan Dostie. Genie Awards '93: Best Cinematography, Best Director (Girard), Best Film, Best Film Editing; Nominations: Independent Spirit Awards '95: Best Foreign Film. *COL*

36 Fillete ✂✂✂ 1988 Lili, an intellectually precocious 14-year old French girl who's literally bursting out of her children's dress size 36 fillete, discovers her sexuality. So while on vacation with her family she becomes determined to see if she can seduce a middle-aged playboy. In French with English subtitles. 88m/C VHS. *FR* Delphine Zentout, Etienne Chicot, Oliver Parniere, Jean-Pierre Leaud; **D:** Catherine Breillat. *FXL*

Thirty-Six Hours of Hell ✂½ 1977 A troop of Marines battle Japanese forces in the South Pacific during WWII. Dubbed. 95m/C VHS, Beta. Richard Harrison, Pamela Tudor; **D:** Roberto Marrtero. *UNI*

'38: Vienna Before the Fall ✂✂½ 1988 Wartime Vienna explodes with love and politics. Academy Award Nominee for best foreign language film. In German with English subtitles. 97m/C VHS, LV. *GE* Tobias Engel, Sunnyi Melles; **D:** Wolfgang Gluck. *LUM*

The 39 Steps ✂✂✂✂ 1935 The classic Hitchcock mistaken-man-caught-in-intrigue thriller, featuring some of his most often copied setpieces and the surest visual flair of his pre-war British period. The laserdisc version includes a twenty-minute documentary tracing the director's British period. Remade twice, in 1959 and 1979. 81m/B VHS, Beta, LV, 8mm. *GB* Robert Donat, Madeleine Carroll, Godfrey Tearle, Lucie Mannheim, Peggy Ashcroft, John Laurie, Wylie Watson, Helen Haye, Frank Cellier, Gus McNaughton, Jerry Verno, Peggy Simpson, Hilda Trevelyan, John Turnbull, Elizabeth Inglis, Wilfrid Brambell; **D:** Alfred Hitchcock; **W:** Charles Bennett, Alma Reville, Ian Hay; **M:** Louis Levy. *CNG, NOS, VHE*

The Thirty-Nine Steps 🎬🎬½ 1979 Hitchcock remake is a visually interesting, but mostly uninvolving, mystery. Powell is the man suspected of stealing plans to begin WWI. Above average, but not by much. **98m/C VHS, Beta.** *GB* Robert Powell, David Warner, Eric Porter, Karen Dotrice, John Mills, Andrew Keir; *D:* Don Sharp. *MED, VYY, CNG*

This Boy's Life 🎬🎬🎬 1993 (R) Carolyn and her teenage son are in search of a new life, far from her abusive ex-boyfriend. In the town of Concrete, just outside Seattle, she meets ex-military man Dwight (De Niro), a slick but none too suave mechanic who might be the answer to her dreams, but then again, he might not. Nicely crafted performances from all, but keep your eye on DiCaprio (great in his first major role) as the confused and abused teen divided between dreams of prep school and the allure of the going-nowhere crowd. Based on the memoirs of Tobias Wolff; director Caton-Jones sensitively illustrates the skewed understanding of masculinity in the 1950s. Vintage soundtrack takes you back.*CW:* Strong language and strong sexuality. **115m/C VHS, Beta, LV, Closed Caption.** Robert De Niro, Ellen Barkin, Leonardo DiCaprio, Jonah Blechman, Eliza Dushku, Chris Cooper, Carla Gugino, Zachary Ansley, Tracey Ellis, Kathy Kinney, Gerrit Graham; *D:* Michael Caton-Jones; *W:* Robert Getchell; *C:* David Watkin; *M:* Carter Burwell. *WAR, FCT, BTV*

This Could Be the Night 🎬🎬½ 1957 Rocco and Tony are two small-fry gangsters who run a nightclub. Anne is a prim schoolteacher who takes a part-time job as their secretary. She falls for the handsome Tony much to the dismay of Rocco who knows his partner's less-than-sterling character. Sweet but minor comedy. Franciosa's first film. ♫This Could Be The Night; Hustlin' News Gal; I Got It Bad; I'm Gonna Live Till I Die; Taking a Chance on Love; Trumpet Boogie; Mamba Combo; Blue Moon; Dream Dancing. **105m/B VHS, LV.** Jean Simmons, Paul Douglas, Anthony (Tony) Franciosa, Joan Blondell, Julie Wilson, Neile Adams, J. Carrol Naish, Rafael Campos, ZaSu Pitts, Tom Helmore; *D:* Robert Wise. *MGM, MOV*

This England 🎬½ 1942 Patriotic morale booster is a rather dull jog through Britain's fight for freedom as an American journalist, visiting England, learns a village's history from a country squire, including surviving the Norman conquest, Spanish Armada, Napoleonic Wars, WWI, and the 1940 air attacks. **84m/B VHS.** *GB* Emlyn Williams, John Clements, Constance Cummings; *D:* David MacDonald. *FCT*

This Gun for Hire 🎬🎬🎬½ 1942 In his first major film role, Ladd plays a hired gun seeking retribution from a client who betrays him. Preston is the cop pursuing him and hostage Lake. Ladd's performance as the cold-blooded killer with a soft spot for cats is stunning; his train-yard scene is an emotional powerhouse. Based on Graham Greene's novel "A Gun for Sale." Remade as "Short Cut to Hell." The first of several films using the Ladd-Lake team, but the only one in which Ladd played a villain. **81m/B VHS, Beta, LV.** Alan Ladd, Veronica Lake, Robert Preston, Laird Cregar; *D:* Frank Tuttle; *W:* Albert Maltz, W.R. Burnett. *USH, FCT*

This Gun for Hire 🎬🎬 1990 (R) A professional assassin finds that he has been duped into killing a powerful political figure, whom he was told was a New Orleans mobster. Now on the run, he takes a nightclub performer hostage, unaware that she is the fiance of the FBI agent who is after him. All odds are against him, but the special relationship he forms with the woman may just be his ticket out. Adapted from novel by Graham Greene.*CW:* Violence and sensuality. **89m/C VHS.** Robert Wagner, Nancy Everhard, Frederic Lehne, John Harkins; *D:* Lou Antonio. *USH*

This Happy Breed 🎬🎬🎬½ 1947 A celebrated film version of Noel Coward's classic play depicts the changing fortunes of a large family in England between the world wars. Happiness,

hardships, triumph and tragedy mix a series of memorable episodes, including some of the most cherished moments in popular British cinema, though its appeal is universal. Narrated by Laurence Olivier. **114m/C VHS.** *GB* Robert Newton, Celia Johnson, John Mills, Kay Walsh, Stanley Holloway, Amy Veness, Alison Leggatt, Eileen Erskine, John Blythe, Guy Verney, Betty Fleetwood, Merle Tottenham; *D:* David Lean; *W:* David Lean, Ronald Neame; *M:* Noel Coward, Muir Mathieson. *HMV, FCT*

This Happy Feeling 🎬🎬½ 1958 Reynolds is a young woman who is romantically attracted to both Jurgens, a sophisticated retired actor, and Saxon, a younger suitor who is Jurgens' neighbor. Good acting all around. Charming telling of old tale. **83m/C VHS, Beta.** Curt Jurgens, Debbie Reynolds, John Saxon, Alexis Smith, Mary Astor, Estelle Winwood; *D:* Blake Edwards; *W:* Blake Edwards. *BAR, FCT*

This Is a Hijack 🎬 1975 (PG) Gambler hijacks the plane carrying his wealthy boss to help pay his debts. What it lacks in suspense, it lacks in performance and direction as well. **90m/C VHS, Beta.** Adam Roarke, Neville Brand, Jay Robinson, Lynn Borden, Dub Taylor. *NO*

This Is Elvis 🎬🎬 1981 (PG) The life of Elvis, combining documentary footage with dramatizations of events in his life. Includes more than three dozen songs. Generally seen as an attempt to cash in on the myth, but was well-received by his fans. **144m/C VHS, Beta.** Elvis Presley; *D:* Malcolm Leo, Andrew Solt; *W:* Malcolm Leo, Andrew Solt; *C:* Gil Hubbs. *MVD, WAR*

This Is My Life 🎬🎬 1992 (PG-13) The story of a working mother torn between her skyrocketing career as a stand-up comic and her two daughters. Kavner plays the divorced mom who is determined to chuck her cosmetic sales job for comic success. Her career starts to really take off; she hires an agent and makes appearances on talk shows. As offers pour in, she eventually realizes that her girls are suffering as a result of her success. Good performances highlight an otherwise average drama. **105m/C VHS, Closed Caption.** Julie Kavner, Samantha Mathis, Carrie Fisher, Dan Aykroyd, Gaby Hoffman; *D:* Nora Ephron; *W:* Nora Ephron, Delia Ephron. *FXV*

This Is Not a Test 🎬🎬 1962 When news comes of an impending nuclear attack, a state trooper at a roadblock offers sanctuary to passing travellers. The effectiveness of the film's social commentary is hindered by its small budget. **72m/B VHS, Beta.** Seamon Glass, Mary Morlass, Thayer Roberts, Aubrey Martin; *D:* Frederic Gadette. *SNC*

This Is Spinal Tap 🎬🎬🎬½ *Spinal Tap* 1984 (R) Pseudo-rockumentary about heavy-metal band Spinal Tap, profiling their career from "England's loudest band" to an entry in the "where are they now file." Hilarious satire, featuring music performed by Guest, McKean, Shearer, and others. Included are Spinal Tap's music video "Hell Hole," and an ad for their greatest hits album, "Heavy Metal Memories." Features great cameos, particularly David Letterman's Paul Schaefer as a record promoter and Billy Crystal as a surly mime. First feature for Reiner (Meathead on "All in the Family"). Followed by "The Return of Spinal Tap." **82m/C VHS, Beta, LV, 8mm.** Michael Keen, Christopher Guest, Harry Shearer, Tony Hendra, Bruno Kirby, Rob Reiner, June Chadwick, Howard Hesseman, Dana Carvey, Ed Begley Jr., Patrick Macnee, Fran Drescher; *Cameos:* Billy Crystal, Paul Shaffer, Anjelica Huston; *D:* Rob Reiner; *W:* Christopher Guest. *MVD, NLC*

This Is the Army 🎬🎬½ 1943 A robust tribute to the American soldier of WWII based on the hit play by Irving Berlin. Murphy, who later was a senator from California, played Reagan's father. ♫Your Country and My Country; My Sweetie; Poor Little Me, I'm on K.P.; We're On Our Way to France; What Does He Look Like?; This is the Army, Mr. Jones; I'm Gettin' Tired So I Can Sleep; Mandy; Ladies of the Chorus. **105m/C VHS, Beta.**

George Murphy, Joan Leslie, Ronald Reagan, Alan Hale, Kate Smith, George Tobias, Irving Berlin, Joe Louis; *D:* Michael Curtiz; *M:* Max Steiner. Academy Awards '43: Scoring of a Musical; Nominations: Academy Awards '43: Best Interior Decoration, Best Sound. *NOS, DVT, CAB*

This Island Earth 🎬🎬½ 1955 The planet Metaluna is in desperate need of uranium to power its defense against enemy invaders. A nuclear scientist and a nuclear fission expert from Earth are kidnapped to help out. The first serious movie about interplanetary escapades. Bud Westmore created pulsating cranium special effects makeup. **86m/C VHS, Beta, LV.** Jeff Morrow, Faith Domergue, Rex Reason, Russell Johnson; *D:* Joseph M. Newman; *M:* Herman Stein. *USH, MLB*

This Land is Mine 🎬🎬🎬 1943 A timid French schoolteacher gathers enough courage to defy the Nazis when they attempt to occupy his town. Laughton's characterization is effective as the meek fellow who discovers the hero within himself in this patriotic wartime flick. **103m/B VHS, Beta, LV.** Charles Laughton, Maureen O'Hara, George Sanders, Walter Slezak, George Coulouris, Una O'Connor; *D:* Jean Renoir. Academy Awards '43: Best Sound. *TTC*

This Lightning Always Strikes Twice 1985 An elegant murder mystery made for British television. **60m/C VHS, Beta.** *GB* Claire Bloom, Trevor Howard, Charles Dance. *PSM*

This Man Must Die 🎬🎬🎬🎬 *Que La Bete Meure; Uccidero Un Uomo* 1970 (PG) A man searches relentlessly for the driver who killed his young son in a hit-and-run. When found, the driver engages him in a complex cat-and-mouse chase. Another stunning crime and punishment tale from Chabrol. **112m/C VHS, Beta.** *FR* Michael Duchaussoy, Caroline Cellier, Jean Yanne; *D:* Claude Chabrol. National Board of Review Awards '70: 5 Best Foreign Films of the Year. *FOX*

This Property is Condemned 🎬🎬 1966 It's a hot time down south once again in this adaptation of the Tennessee Williams play. Wood is the overly-flirtatious southern charmer who takes a shine to the latest tenant of her loathsome mama's boardinghouse. And since it's Redford, who can blame her. Things steam up when he returns her interest but there's trouble a'brewin'. Both leads are lovely but the film itself is overly southern-fried. Williams was reportedly unhappy with the script and wanted his name removed from the film. **109m/C VHS, Beta, LV, Closed Caption.** Robert Redford, Natalie Wood, Charles Bronson, Kate Reid, Mary Badham, Jon Provost, Robert (Bobby) Blake, John Harding; *D:* Sydney Pollack; *W:* Francis Ford Coppola, Edith Sommer, Fred Coe. *PAR*

This Special Friendship 🎬🎬½ *Les Amities Particulieres* 1967 Powerful, if overdone French drama about an emotionally sensitive young man at a Catholic boarding school. His sexual relationship with another boy leads to tragedy. Based on the novel by Roger Peyrefitte. **99m/B VHS, Beta.** *FR* Francis Lacombrade, Didier Haudepin, Lucien Nat, Louis Seigner, Michel Bouquet, Francois Leccia; *D:* Jean Delannoy. *FCT*

This Sporting Life 🎬🎬🎬 1963 A gritty, depressing portrait of a former coal miner who breaks into the violent world of professional rugby, and whose inability to handle social differences causes problems. He begins an affair with the widow from whom he rents a room but finds they are capable of only a physical attachment. One of the best of the British early '60s working-class angry young man melodramas. **134m/B VHS, Beta.** *GB* Richard Harris, Rachel Roberts, Alan Badel, William Hartnell, Colin Blakely, Vanda Godsell, Arthur Lowe; *D:* Lindsay Anderson; *W:* David Storey. British Academy Awards '63: Best Actress (Roberts); Cannes Film Festival '63: Best Actor (Harris); National Board of Review Awards '63: 10 Best Films of the Year; Nominations: Academy Awards '63: Best Actor (Harris), Best Actress (Roberts). *PAR*

This Stuff'll Kill Ya! woof! 1971 (PG) A backwoods preacher who believes in free love and moonshining runs into trouble with the locals when a series of gruesome religious murders are committed. Southern drive-in material from one of the genre's masters. Holt's last film. **100m/C VHS.** Jeffrey Allen, Tim Holt, Gloria King, Ray Sager, Eric Bradly, Terence McCarthy; **W:** Herschell Gordon Lewis; **W:** Herschell Gordon Lewis. *TWE, FRG, TPV*

This Sweet Sickness 🐾🐾½ *Dites-Lui Que Je L'Aime* **1977** Destructive passion and sexual delusion is explored in this adaptation of the Patricia Highsmith novel. David seems to be a hardworking loner who is loved by the sweet Juliette. Rejected by him, Juliette then discovers that David has built a remote mountain chalet for the woman he does love, Lise, who's married and unaware of David's obsessional devotions. Extravagant emotions lead to tragedy. In French with English subtitles. **107m/C VHS.** *FR* Gerard Depardieu, Miou-Miou, Dominique Laffin, Claude Pieplu, Christian Clavier, Jacques Denis, Josiane Balasko, Veronique Silver, Jacqueline Jeanne, Michel Such; **D:** Claude Miller; **W:** Claude Miller, Luc Beraud. *WAC, FCT*

This Time I'll Make You Rich 🐾 **1975 (PG)** Two American hoodlums work out a drug-ring heist in the Far East. **97m/C VHS, Beta.** Tony Sabato, Robin McDavid; **D:** Frank Kramer. *NLC*

The Thomas Crown Affair 🐾🐾🐾 *Thomas Crown and Company; The Crown Caper* **1968 (R)** A multi-millionaire (McQueen) decides to plot and execute the perfect theft, a daring daylight robbery of a bank. Dunaway is the gorgeous and efficient insurance investigator determined to nab him. One of the best visual scenes is the chess match between the two as they begin to fall in love. Strong production with Oscar-winning theme "The Windmills of Your Mind." ♫The Windmills of Your Mind. **102m/C VHS, Beta.** Steve McQueen, Faye Dunaway, Jack Weston, Yaphet Kotto; **D:** Norman Jewison; **W:** Alan R. Trustman; **C:** Haskell Wexler. Academy Awards '68: Best Song ("The Windmills of Your Mind"); Golden Globe Awards '69: Best Song ("The Windmills of Your Mind"); Nominations: Academy Awards '68: Best Original Score. *MGM, FCT, FOX*

Thomas Graal's Best Film 🐾🐾🐾 **1917** The famous comical adventures of a film scriptwriter wooing his secretary, followed by "Thomas Graal's First Child." Silent. **70m/B VHS, Beta.** *SW* Victor Sjostrom, Karin Molander; **D:** Mauritz Stiller. *FCT, GPV*

Thomas Graal's First Child 🐾🐾🐾 **1918** The sequel to "Thomas Graal's Best Film." The comical screenwriter and actress couple attempt to raise a baby. Silent. **70m/B VHS, Beta.** Victor Sjostrom, Karin Molander; **D:** Mauritz Stiller. *FCT*

Thompson's Last Run 🐾½ **1990** Boyhood friends grow up on either side of the law. They come face-to-face, though, when one is assigned to transport the other to prison. Made for television. **95m/C VHS, Beta, LV.** Robert Mitchum, Wilford Brimley, Kathleen York, Susan Tyrrell; **D:** Jerrold Freedman; **M:** Miles Goodman. *NO*

Thor and the Amazon Women 🐾 **1960** The mighty Thor leads his enslaved men on an attack against the evil Queen Nera and her female-dominated Amazon society. **85m/C VHS.** Joe Robinson, Susy Anderson. *AIP*

The Thorn 🐾½ **1973 (R)** The Virgin Mary and Joseph try to raise Jesus Christ in the modern world. **90m/C VHS, Beta.** Bette Midler, John Bassberger. *NO*

The Thorn Birds 🐾🐾🐾 **1983** Pioneers find danger and romance in the Australian outback as they struggle to begin a dynasty. Charismatic priest sometimes hurts, sometimes helps them. One of Stanwyck's last performances; Ward's American television debut. Originally a ten-hour television epic based on Colleen McCullough novel. Emmy nominations for Actor Chamberlain, Supporting Actor(s) Brown and Plummer, Supporting Actress Laurie, direction, photography, music, costume design, and editing. On four cassettes. **486m/C VHS, Beta, Closed Caption.** Rachel Ward, Richard Chamberlain, Jean Simmons, Ken Howard, Mare Winningham, Richard Kiley, Piper Laurie, Bryan

Brown, Christopher Plummer, Barbara Stanwyck; **D:** Daryl Duke; **C:** Bill Butler; **M:** Henry Mancini. *WAR, MOV, TVC*

Thoroughbreds Don't Cry 🐾🐾½ **1937** Rooney plays a jockey who throws a race so his no-good father can win enough money to pay for his supposed medical problems. The owner of the horse then drops dead from a heart attack. Rooney feels guilty, so he asks his father to loan the owner's grandson $1,000 to run in another race. His father says no, so Rooney steals the money from him, and when the father finds out he tells the track officials that Rooney threw the race. Garland is Rooney's best friend and moral support, and she sings a few songs too! A fairly good horse racing story. **80m/B VHS.** Judy Garland, Mickey Rooney, Sophie Tucker, Sir C. Aubrey Smith, Ronald Sinclair, Forrester Harvey; **D:** Alfred E. Green. *MGM, MVD*

Thoroughly Modern Millie 🐾🐾½ **1967 (G)** Andrews is a young woman who comes to New York in the early 1920s where she meets another newcomer, the innocent Moore. Andrews decides to upgrade her image to that of a "modern" woman, a flapper, and sets out to realize her ambition, to become a stenographer and marry the boss. Meanwhile, Moore has become an object of interest to Lillie, who just happens to run a white-slavery ring. Lots of frantic moments and big production numbers in this campy film. Channing and Lillie are exceptional fun. ♫Thoroughly Modern Millie; The Tapioca; Jimmy; The Jewish Wedding Song; Baby Face; Do It Again; Poor Butterfly; Rose of Washington Square; I Can't Believe That You're In Love With Me. **138m/C VHS, Beta, LV.** Julie Andrews, Carol Channing, Mary Tyler Moore, John Gavin, Beatrice Lillie, James Fox, Noriyuki "Pat" Morita; **D:** George Roy Hill; **W:** Richard Morris; **C:** Russell Metty; **M:** Elmer Bernstein. Academy Awards '67: Best Original Score; Golden Globe Awards '68: Best Supporting Actress (Channing); Nominations: Academy Awards '67: Best Art Direction/Set Decoration, Best Costume Design, Best Song ("Thoroughly Modern Millie"), Best Sound, Best Supporting Actress (Channing), Best Original Score. *USH*

Those Calloways 🐾🐾½ **1965 (PG)** A small town family attempts to establish a sanctuary for the flocks of wild geese who fly over the woods of Swiftwater, Maine. Fine Disney family fare, with good cast. Based on Paul Annixter's novel "Swiftwater." **131m/C VHS, Beta.** Brian Keith, Vera Miles, Brandon de Wilde, Walter Brennan, Ed Wynn, John Qualen, Linda Evans; **D:** Norman Tokar; **C:** Edward Colman; **M:** Max Steiner. *DIS*

Those Daring Young Men in Their Jaunty Jalopies 🐾🐾 *Monte Carlo or Bust; Quei Temerari Sulle Loro Pazze, Scatenate, Scalcinate Carriole* **1969 (G)** Daring young men in noisy slow cars trek 1500 miles across country in the 1920s and call it a race. **125m/C VHS, LV, Closed Caption.** *GB* Tony Curtis, Susan Hampshire, Terry-Thomas, Eric Sykes, Gert Frobe, Peter Cook, Dudley Moore, Jack Hawkins; **D:** Ken Annakin; **W:** Ken Annakin, Jack Davies. *PAR, FCT*

Those Endearing Young Charms 🐾🐾 **1945** Romance develops between a young Air Corps mechanic and a salesgirl. Complications arise when another man enters the scene. Light romantic comedy. Based on the play by Edward Chodorov. **82m/B VHS, Beta.** Robert Young, Laraine Day, Anne Jeffreys, Lawrence Tierney; **D:** Lewis Allen. *CCB*

Those Fantastic Flying Fools 🐾🐾½ *Blast-Off; Jules Verne's Rocket to the Moon* **1967** A mad race to be the first on the moon brings hilarious results. Loosely based on a Jules Verne story. **95m/C VHS.** *GB* Burl Ives, Troy Donahue, Gert Frobe, Terry-Thomas, Hermione Gingold, Daliah Lavi, Lionel Jeffries; **D:** Don Sharp. *NO*

Those Glory, Glory Days 🐾½ **1983** An English woman, secure in her position as a sports journalist, reminisces about the days when she and her friends idolized the boys on the soccer team. Nothing extraordinary, but nicely made. **92m/C VHS, Beta.** *GB* Zoe Nathenson,

Liz Campion, Cathy Murphy; **D:** Philip Saville; **M:** Trevor Jones. *MGM*

Those Lips, Those Eyes 🐾🐾½ **1980 (R)** A pre-med student takes a job as a prop boy in a summer stock company and winds up falling in love with the company's lead dancer. Sub-plot about aging actor is more interesting, better played by Langella. O'Connor is appropriately lovely. Nicely made, charming sleeper of a film. **106m/C VHS, Beta.** Frank Langella, Tom Hulce, Glynnis O'Connor, Jerry Stiller, Kevin McCarthy; **D:** Michael Pressman. *MGM*

Those Magnificent Men in Their Flying Machines 🐾🐾🐾 **1965** In 1910, a wealthy British newspaper publisher is persuaded to sponsor an air race from London to Paris. Contestants come from all over the world and shenanigans, hijinks, double-crosses, and romance are found along the route. Skelton has fun in prologue, while Terry-Thomas is great as the villain. Fun from start to finish. **138m/C VHS, Beta, LV.** *GB* Stuart Whitman, Sarah Miles, Robert Morley, Alberto Sordi, James Fox, Gert Frobe, Jean-Pierre Cassel, Flora Robson, Sam Wanamaker, Terry-Thomas, Irina Demick, Benny Hill, Gordon Jackson, Millicent Martin, Red Skelton; **D:** Ken Annakin; **W:** Ken Annakin, Jack Davies. Nominations: Academy Awards '65: Best Story & Screenplay. *FOX*

Thou Shalt Not Kill...Except 🐾 **1987** A Vietnam vet seeks revenge on the violent cult who kidnapped his girlfriend. **84m/C VHS, Beta.** Brian Schulz, Robert Rickman, John Manfredi, Tim Quill, Cheryl Hansen, Sam Raimi, Cheryl Hansen, Perry Mallette, Theodore (Ted) Raimi, Glenn Barr; **D:** Josh Becker; **W:** Josh Becker, Glenn Barr; **M:** Joseph Loduca. *PSM*

Thoughts are Free 🐾🐾🐾½ **1984 (PG)** A young soldier, wounded in WWII, escapes from the train that is transporting him and his comrades to a Soviet labor camp and rejoins his family. Under the repressive communist regime, he plots his family's escape to the West but his plans are thwarted when the Berlin Wall is erected, leaving him in the West and his wife and daughter in the East. As the years go by, they can get together only by outwitting the bureaucrats. The film's title is taken from an old German folk song "Die Gedanken sind frei." **93m/C VHS, Beta.** Herbert Ludwig, Kathrin Kratzer; **D:** Josef Sommer. *NO*

A Thousand and One Nights 🐾🐾½ **1945** Handsome Aladdin (Wilde) falls in love with beautiful Princess Armina (Jergens) but fate steps in and Aladdin and sidekick Abdullah (Silvers) are off in search of a magic lamp. This time around the genie is a beautiful woman (Keyes), who falls for Aladdin herself and tries to thwart his would-be romance. Clever fun. **92m/C VHS.** Cornel Wilde, Evelyn Keyes, Adele Jergens, Phil Silvers, Rex Ingram, Dennis Hoey, Philip Van Zandt, Gus Schilling; **D:** Alfred E. Green; **W:** Jack Henley, Richard English; **C:** Ray Rennahan; **M:** Marlin Skiles. *COL*

A Thousand Clowns 🐾🐾🐾 **1965** A nonconformist has resigned from his job as chief writer for an obnoxious kiddie show in order to enjoy life. But his independence comes under fire when he becomes guardian for his young nephew and social workers take a dim view of his lifestyle. Balsam won an Oscar for his role as Robard's agent brother. Adapted from Herb Gardner's Broadway comedy. **118m/B VHS, Beta.** Jason Robards Jr., Barry Gordon, William Daniels, Barbara Harris, Gene Saks, Martin Balsam; **D:** Fred Coe; **W:** Herb Gardner. Academy Awards '65: Best Supporting Actor (Balsam); National Board of Review Awards '65: 10 Best Films of the Year; Nominations: Academy Awards '65: Best Adapted Score, Best Adapted Screenplay, Best Picture. *MGM, FOX, BTV*

The Thousand Eyes of Dr. Mabuse 🐾🐾½ *The Secret of Dr. Mabuse; The Diabolical Dr. Mabuse; The Shadow Versus the Thousand Eyes of Dr. Mabuse* **1960** Lang's last film is a return to his pre-war German character, the evil Dr. Mabuse. A series of strange murders occur in a Berlin hotel and police believe the killer thinks he's a reincarnation of the doctor. Disorienting chiller.

103m/B VHS. *GE* Dawn Addams, Peter Van Eyck, Gert Frobe, Wolfgang Preiss; **D:** Fritz Lang. *FCT, GPV*

A Thousand Heroes 🐾🐾½ 1994 (PG) Based on the true story of United Airlines Flight 232 which took off on a flight from Denver to Chicago and then suffered engine explosions over Iowa. The jumbo jet crashed in a fiery explosion but some 200 people survived. 95m/C VHS, LV. Richard Thomas, Charlton Heston, James Coburn. *NHO*

Thousand Pieces of Gold 🐾🐾🐾 1991 (PG-13) A young Chinese woman is sold by her father to a marriage broker, but instead of a respectable marriage she is shipped to America and expected to work as a prostitute in an Idaho mining town. Instead she works taking in laundry as she tries to make her way in a man's world, finding a sweet romance of opposites along the way. Based on a true story. Excellent performances by Chao and Cooper. 105m/C VHS, LV, **Closed Caption.** Rosalind Chao, Dennis Dun, Michael Paul Chan, Chris Cooper, Jimmie F. Skaggs, William Oldham, David Hayward, Beth Broderick; **D:** Nancy Kelly; **W:** Anne Makepeace; **C:** Bobby Bukowski; **M:** Gary Remal Malkin. *HMD*

Thousands Cheer 🐾🐾½ 1943 A flag-waving wartime musical about a tap-dancing Army private who falls in love with the colonel's daughter, culminating with an all-star (MGM) USO show. Songs include "Honeysuckle Rose," sung by Horne, and "The Joint Is Really Jumping Down at Carnegie Hall," sung by Garland. 126m/C VHS, **Beta, LV.** Gene Kelly, Kathryn Grayson, Judy Garland, Mickey Rooney, Mary Astor, John Boles, Lucille Ball, Eleanor Powell, Virginia O'Brien, Margaret O'Brien, Red Skelton, Lionel Barrymore, June Allyson, Frank Morgan, Kay Kyser, Bob Crosby, Lena Horne, Donna Reed; **D:** George Sidney. Nominations: Academy Awards '43: Best Color Cinematography, Best Interior Decoration, Scoring of a Musical. *MGM*

Thrashin' 🐾 1986 (PG-13) A new-to-L.A. teen must prove himself to a tough gang on skateboards by skateboarding a certain treacherous race. For skateboarding fans only. 93m/C VHS, **Beta.** Josh Brolin, Pamela Gidley, Robert Rusler, Chuck McCann; **D:** David Winters; **W:** Paul Brown; **M:** Barry Goldberg. *NO*

Threads 🐾🐾🐾 1985 The famed dramatic recreation of the effects of nuclear war on a British city and two of its families. A disturbing, uncompromising, and somewhat plausible drama. Made for British television. 110m/C VHS, Beta. *GB* Karen Meagher, Rita May, David Brierly, Reece Dinsdale, Harry Beety; **D:** Mick Jackson. *NO*

Threat 🐾🐾½ 1949 A killer escapes from jail and returns to settle the score with those who convicted him. Tense, fast-moving thriller. 66m/B **VHS, Beta.** Michael O'Shea, Virginia Grey, Charles McGraw; **D:** Felix Feist. *NO*

Three Ages 🐾🐾🐾 1923 A parody of D.W. Griffith's 1916 film "Intolerance." Keaton's first feature film casts him in prehistoric days, ancient Rome, and in modern times. Silent with musical score. 59m/B VHS, Beta. Wallace Beery, Oliver Hardy, Buster Keaton; **D:** Buster Keaton, Eddie Cline. *NOS, VDM, DVT*

Three Amigos 🐾🐾 1986 (PG) Three out-of-work silent screen stars are asked to defend a Mexican town from bandits; they think it's a public appearance stint. Spoof of Three Stooges and Mexican bandito movies that at times falls short, given the enormous amount of comedic talent involved. Generally enjoyable with some very funny scenes. Co-written by former "Saturday Night Live" producer Michaels. Short's first major film appearance. 105m/C VHS, Beta, LV, **Closed Caption.** Chevy Chase, Steve Martin, Martin Short, Joe Mantegna, Patrice Martinez, Jon Lovitz, Alfonso Arau, Randy Newman; **D:** John Landis; **W:** Steve Martin, Randy Newman, Lorne Michaels; **M:** Elmer Bernstein. *HBO*

The Three Avengers 🐾🐾½ 1980 (R) Hung Tack (Lee) is the master of a kung fu school in a town plagued by two evil businessmen, who force Hung to take on the local gangs. During a

fight, he's spotted by a talent scout and starts a career in the movies but is around to rescue a friend who's gotten into trouble. Hey, the fighting's the important part anyway. 93m/C VHS. Bruce Lee. *FCT*

Three Broadway Girls 🐾🐾🐾 *The Greeks Had a Word for Them* 1932 Three gold-diggers go husband-hunting. Well-paced, very funny telling of this old story. Remade many times, including "How to Marry a Millionaire," "Three Blind Mice," "Moon Over Miami," and "Three Little Girls in Blue." 78m/B VHS, Beta. Joan Blondell, Ina Claire, Madge Evans, David Manners, Lowell Sherman; **D:** Lowell Sherman. *NOS, CAB, BAR*

Three Brothers 🐾🐾🐾 1980 (PG) An acclaimed Italian film by veteran Rosi about three brothers summoned to their small Italian village by a telegram saying their mother is dead. Sensitive and compassionate. In Italian with English subtitles. Adapted from Platonov's story "The Third Son." 113m/C VHS, Beta. *IT* Philippe Noiret, Charles Vanel, Michele Placido, Vittorio Mezzogiorno, Andrea Ferreol; **D:** Francesco Rosi; **W:** Francesco Rosi; **C:** Pasquale De Santos. Nominations: Academy Awards '81: Best Foreign Language Film. *APD*

Three Bullets for a Long Gun 🐾½ 1973 (PG) Two prairie renegades battle bandits as they search for an inherited gold mine. 89m/C VHS, Beta. Keith Van Der Wat, Beau Brummel, Patrick Munhardt; **D:** Peter Henkel; **W:** Keith Van Der Wat. *COL, NLC, SIM*

Three by Hitchcock 🐾🐾 1928 Condensed versions of three of Hitchcock's early films (1927-28). Consists of "The Ring," "Champagne," and "The Manxman," his last silent film. 90m/B VHS, Beta. **D:** Alfred Hitchcock. *GVV*

The Three Caballeros 🐾🐾½ 1945 Donald Duck stars in this journey through Latin America. Full of music, variety, and live-action/animation segments. Stories include "Pablo the Penguin," "Little Gauchito," and adventures with Joe Carioca, who was first introduced in Disney's "Saludos Amigos." Today this film stands as one of the very best pieces of animation ever created. Great family fare. "Saludos Amigos" is available on the laserdisc version. 🎵The Three Caballeros; Baia. 71m/C VHS, Beta, LV. **D:** Norman Ferguson; **V:** Sterling Holloway, Aurora Miranda. Nominations: Academy Awards '45: Best Sound, Scoring of a Musical. *DIS, APD*

Three Came Home 🐾🐾🐾 1950 Colbert is an American married to a British administrator in the Far East during WWII. Conquering Japanese throw the whole family into a brutal POW concentration camp, and their confinement is recounted in harrowing and unsparing detail. Superior drama, also laudable for a fairly even-handed portrayal of the enemy captors. Based on an autobiographical book by Agnes Newton-Keith. 106m/B VHS. Claudette Colbert, Patric Knowles, Sessue Hayakawa; **D:** Jean Negulesco. *NOS, HEG*

Three Cases of Murder 🐾🐾🐾 1955 Three fast-paced tales of mayhem. "In the Picture" features a deranged taxidermist, a creepy house, and a hapless museum guide. From a story by Roderick Wilkinson. Two friends are in love with the same girl in "You Killed Elizabeth" and when she turns up dead it's clear one of them is guilty. From a story by Brett Halliday. The best features Welles as "Lord Mountdrago," who destroys the career of a fellow Parliament Member and is haunted by fears of retaliation. Based on a story by W. Somerset Maugham. 99m/B VHS. *GB* Alan Badel, John Gregson, Orson Welles, Elizabeth Sellars, Hugh Pryse, Jack Lambert; **D:** Wendy Toye, David Eady, George More O'Ferrell; **W:** Donald Wilson, Sidney Carroll, Ian Dalrymple; **C:** Georges Perinal; **M:** Doreen Carwithen. *HMV*

Three Charlies and One Phoney! 1918 Three of Charlie Chaplin's best comedy shorts, plus one featuring his best-known imitator—Billy West. Included are "Recreation" ("Fun is Fun") ("Spring Fever"), "His Musical Career" ("The Piano Movers") ("Musical Tramps"), "The

Bond" (featuring Charlie in a Liberty Bond appeal) and "His Day Out" with Billy West imitating Chaplin. All but "His Day Out" were written and directed by Chaplin. 69m/B VHS, Beta, 8mm. Charlie Chaplin, Mack Swain, Charley Chase, Edna Purviance, Sydney Chaplin, Albert Austin; **D:** Charlie Chaplin; **W:** Charlie Chaplin. *VYY*

Three Coins in the Fountain 🐾🐾½ 1954 Three women throw money into fountain and get romantically involved with Italian men. Outstanding CinemaScope photography captures beauty of Italian setting. Sammy Cahn theme song sung by Frank Sinatra. 🎵Three Coins in the Fountain. 102m/C VHS, Beta. Clifton Webb, Dorothy McGuire, Jean Peters, Louis Jourdan, Maggie McNamara, Rossano Brazzi; **D:** Jean Negulesco; **C:** Milton Krasner. Academy Awards '54: Best Color Cinematography, Best Song ("Three Coins in the Fountain"); Nominations: Academy Awards '54: Best Picture. *FOX*

Three Comrades 🐾🐾🐾 1938 Taylor, Tone, and Young are three friends, reunited in bleak, post-WWI Germany, who meet and befriend Sullavan, a tubercular beauty. Reluctant to marry because of her health, she's finally persuaded to wed Taylor, amidst the country's increasing unrest. Tragedy strikes Sullavan and the politicized Young and the two remaining comrades face an uncertain future. Bleak but forceful and passionate drama. Sullavan's performance is superb. Based on the novel by Erich Maria Remarque. Fitzgerald's script was heavily re-written because both Sullavan and producer Mankiewicz found his approach too literary with unspeakable dialogue. 99m/B VHS. Robert Taylor, Margaret Sullavan, Robert Young, Franchot Tone, Lionel Atwill, Guy Kibbee, Henry Hull, George Zucco, Monty Woolley, Charley Grapewin, Spencer Charters, Sarah Padden; **D:** Frank Borzage; **W:** F. Scott Fitzgerald, Edward Paramore; **C:** Joseph Ruttenberg; **M:** Franz Waxman. New York Film Critics Awards '38: Best Actress (Sullavan); Nominations: Academy Awards '38: Best Actress (Sullavan). *MGM, MOV, BTV*

Three Daring Daughters 🐾🐾½ 1948 When her husband leaves her and she almost misses her daughter's graduation due to a fainting spell, MacDonald takes hiatus on a cruise ship where she meets and marries pianist Iturbi. Unknowing, the three daughters at home conspire to get Dad back in the family. Enraged when Mom returns with newfound hubby, the threesome do all in their power to make the newlyweds as miserable as possible. Happily-ended musical-comedy is chock full of memorable tunes. Based on the play "The Bees and the Flowers" by Kohner and Albert Manning. 🎵Route 66; The Dickey Bird Song; Alma Mater; Fleurette; Passepied; Where There's Love; Ritual Fire Dance; You Made Me Love You; Happy Birthday. 115m/C VHS, **Closed Caption.** Jeanette MacDonald, Jose Iturbi, Jane Powell, Edward Arnold, Harry Davenport, Moyna MacGill, Elinor Donahue, Ann Todd; **D:** Fred M. Wilcox; **W:** Sonya Levien, John Meehan, Albert Mannheimer, Frederick Kohner. *MGM*

Three Days in Beirut 🐾 1983 (PG) A soldier of fortune and a beautiful interpreter join forces against a backdrop of Middle Eastern politics, espionage, and violence. 94m/C VHS, Beta. Diana Sands, Calvin Lockhart; **D:** Michael A. Schultz. *PSM*

Three Days of the Condor 🐾🐾🐾 1975 (R) CIA researcher Redford finds himself on the run from unknown killers when he is left the only survivor of the mass murder of his office staff. Good performance by Dunaway as the photographer who shelters him. Excellent suspense tale. Based on "Six Days of the Condor" by James Grady. 118m/C VHS, Beta, LV, Closed Caption. Robert Redford, Faye Dunaway, Cliff Robertson, Max von Sydow, John Houseman; **D:** Sydney Pollack; **W:** David Rayfiel; **C:** Owen Roizman; **M:** Dave Grusin. Edgar Allan Poe Awards '75: Best Screenplay; Nominations: Academy Awards '75: Best Film Editing. *PAR*

Three Days to a Kill 🐾🐾 1991 (R) Calvin Sims is a mercenary hired to rescue a kidnapped ambassador—by any means necessary.**CW:** Language, violence, and some sexuality. **90m/C VHS, LV, Closed Caption.** Fred Williamson, Bo Svenson, Henry Silva, Chuck Connors, Van Johnson, Sonny Landham; **D:** Fred Williamson. *HBO*

Three Desperate Men ♂♂ 1950 Three brothers accused of murder become outlaws. Not innovative, but satisfactory tale of the Old West. **71m/B VHS, Beta.** Preston Foster, Virginia Grey, Jim Davis; **D:** Sam Newfield. *NO*

The Three Faces of Eve ♂♂♂½ 1957 An emotionally disturbed woman seeks the help of a psychiatrist, who discovers she has three distinct personalities. Powerful performances highlight this fascinating study based on a true story. **91m/B VHS, LV.** Joanne Woodward, David Wayne, Lee J. Cobb, Nancy Kulp, Vince Edwards; **D:** Nunnally Johnson. Academy Awards '57: Best Actress (Woodward); Golden Globe Awards '58: Best Actress—Drama (Woodward). *FXV, BTV*

Three Faces West ♂♂ *The Refugee* 1940 A dust bowl community is helped by a Viennese doctor who left Europe to avoid Nazi capture. He's aided by the Duke in this odd combination of Western frontier saga and anti-Nazi propaganda. Works only part of the time. **79m/B VHS.** John Wayne, Charles Coburn, Sigrid Gurie, Sonny Bupp, Russell Simpson; **D:** Bernard Vorhaus. *REP*

3:15—The Moment of Truth ♂♂ 1986 (R) A vicious high school gang is confronted by an angry ex-member in this so-so teen delinquent film. **86m/C VHS, Beta.** Adam Baldwin, Deborah Foreman, Rene Auberjonois, Danny De La Paz; **D:** Larry Gross; **W:** Sam Bernard; **M:** Gary Chang. *MED*

Three for Bedroom C ♂♂ 1952 A movie star and a scientist make romance on a train bound for Los Angeles. Swanson's follow-up to "Sunset Boulevard." **74m/C VHS, Beta.** Gloria Swanson, Fred Clark, Steve Brodie, Hans Conried, Margaret Dumont; **D:** Milton Bren. *LIV*

Three for the Road ♂♂ 1987 (PG) A young aspiring political aide and his roommate must escort a Senator's ill-mannered and spoiled daughter to a reform institution. On the road, they run into more than a few obstacles. Good performances elevate a bland script. Sheen made this movie before his riveting performance as a young GI in "Platoon." **98m/C Beta, LV.** Charlie Sheen, Kerri Green, Alan Ruck, Sally Kellerman; **D:** Bill W.L. Norton; **W:** Tim Metcalfe; **M:** Barry Goldberg. *NO*

Three Fugitives ♂♂ 1989 (PG-13) An ex-con holdup man determined to go straight is taken hostage by a bungling first-time bank robber, who is only attempting the holdup in order to support his withdrawn young daughter. Ex-con Nolte winds up on the lam with the would-be robber and his daughter. The comedy is fun, the sentimental moments too sweet and slow. Remake of French "Les Fugitifs." **96m/C VHS, Beta, LV, Closed Caption.** Nick Nolte, Martin Short, James Earl Jones, Kenneth McMillan, Sarah Rowland Doroff, Alan Ruck; **D:** Francis Veber; **W:** Francis Veber; **C:** Haskell Wexler. *TOU*

Three Godfathers ♂♂♂ 1948 A sweet and sentimental western has three half-hearted outlaws on the run, taking with them an infant they find in the desert. Dedicated to western star and Ford alumni Harry Carey, Sr. (whose son is one of the outlaws in the film), who died of cancer the year before. Ford had first filmed the tale with Carey Sr. as "Marked Men" in 1919. **82m/C VHS, Beta.** John Wayne, Pedro Armendariz Sr., Harry Carey Jr., Ward Bond, Mae Marsh, Jane Darwell, Ben Johnson, Mildred Natwick, Guy Kibbee; **D:** John Ford; **C:** Winton C. Hoch. *MGM*

Three Guys Named Mike ♂♂ 1951 Wyman plays an overly enthusiastic airline stewardess who finds herself the object of affection from three guys named Mike, including an airline pilot, an advertising man, and a scientist. A cute comedy. **89m/B VHS.** Jane Wyman, Van Johnson, Barry Sullivan, Howard Keel, Phyllis Kirk, Jeff Donnell; **D:** Charles Walters; **W:** Sidney Sheldon. *VDM*

The 317th Platoon ♂♂♂ 1965 An emotionally gripping war drama of the French-Vietnamese War in which the 317th Platoon of the French Army, consisting of 4 French commanders and 41 Laotians, is ordered to retreat to camp Dien Bien Phu. The men begin their march and slowly succomb to the elements and ambushes. Days later, when what is left of the platoon finally reaches Dien Bien Phu, the camp is in enemy hands and the remnants of the 317th Platoon are killed in cold blood. Director Shoendorffer portrays this struggle, conflict, and the quiet haunting tension of war with great skill. In French with English subtitles. **100m/B VHS, LV.** *FR* Jacques Perrin, Bruno Cremer, Pierre Fabre, Manuel Zarzo; **D:** Pierre Schoendoerffer; **W:** Pierre Schoendoerffer. *INT, IME, FCT*

357 Magnum ♂ 1977 Jonathan Hightower, the CIA's special investigator in the Far East, speaks softly and carries a very big gun. **91m/C VHS, Beta.** Marland T. Stewart, James Whitworth, Kathryn Hayes. *NO*

Three Husbands ♂♂½ 1950 A deceased playboy leaves letters for the title characters incriminating their wives in extramarital affairs. The men's reactions are pure farce—even though this same concept was played straight with a sex change in the earlier "A Letter to Three Wives." **79m/B VHS.** Eve Arden, Ruth Warrick, Vanessa Brown, Howard da Silva, Shepperd Strudwick, Jane Darwell; **D:** Irving Reis. *NOS, VDM*

Three in the Attic ♂♂½ 1968 (R) A college student juggles three girlfriends at the same time. When the girls find out they are being two-timed, they lock their boyfriend in an attic and exhaust him with forced sexual escapades. Then they talk. Limited trashy and foolish appeal. **92m/C VHS, Beta.** Christopher Jones, Yvette Mimieux, John Beck; **D:** Richard Wilson. *MLB*

Three in the Cellar ♂♂ *Up in the Cellar* 1970 (R) A disgruntled college student seeks revenge on the school president by seducing his wife, daughter and mistress. Good screenplay helps carry it off. **92m/C VHS.** Wes Stern, Joan Collins, Larry Hagman, Judy Pace; **D:** Theodore J. Flicker. *HBO*

Three in the Saddle ♂½ 1945 Ritter and the Texas Rangers fight for law and order. **61m/B VHS, Beta.** Tex Ritter, Dave O'Brien, Charles "Blackie" King; **D:** Harry Fraser. *NOS, VCN*

Three Kinds of Heat ♂ 1987 (R) Three Interpol agents track down a warring Oriental crime lord. Alternately tongue-in-cheek and silly. Never released in theaters, it found a home on video. Stevens created "The Outer Limits" for television. **88m/C VHS, Beta, Closed Caption.** Robert Ginty, Victoria Barrett, Shakti; **D:** Leslie Stevens. *WAR*

Three Legionnaires ♂♂½ *Three Crazy Legionnaires* 1937 Three soldiers cavort in a post-WWI Siberian tank town. **67m/B VHS, Beta, LV.** Robert Armstrong, Lyle Talbot, Fifi d'Orsay, Anne Nagel, Donald Meek. *VYY*

The Three Little Pigs 1984 From "Faerie Tale Theatre" comes the story of three little pigs, the houses they lived in and the wolf that tried to do them in. **60m/C VHS, Beta, Closed Caption.** Billy Crystal, Jeff Goldblum, Valerie Perrine; **D:** Howard Storm. *KUI, FOX, FCT*

Three Little Words ♂♂½ 1950 A musical biography of songwriting team Harry Ruby and Bert Kalmar, filled with Kalmar-Ruby numbers. Helen Kane (famous for her boop-boop-de-boops) dubbed "I Wanna Be Loved By You" for Reynolds. A musical in the best MGM tradition. ♫ I Wanna Be Loved By You; Who's Sorry Now?; Three Little Words; I Love You So Much; She's Mine, All Mine; So-Long, Oo-Long; Hooray for Captain Spaulding; Up In the Clouds; All Alone Monday. **102m/C VHS, Beta.** Fred Astaire, Red Skelton, Vera-Ellen, Arlene Dahl, Keenan Wynn, Gloria De Haven, Debbie Reynolds, Gale Robbins; **D:** Richard Thorpe; **M:** Andre Previn. Golden Globe Awards '51: Best Actor—Musical/Comedy (Astaire); Nominations: Academy Awards '50: Scoring of a Musical. *MGM*

The Three Lives of Thomasina ♂♂♂ 1963 (PG) In turn-of-the-century Scotland, a veterinarian orders his daughter's beloved cat destroyed when the pet is diagnosed with tetanus. After the cat's death (with scenes of kitty heaven), a beautiful and mysterious healer from the woods is able to bring the animal back to life and restore the animal to the little girl. Lovely Disney fairy tale with good performances by all. **95m/C VHS, Beta, Closed Caption.** Patrick McGoohan, Susan Hampshire, Karen Dotrice, Matthew Garber; **D:** Don Chaffey. *DIS, TVC*

Three Men and a Baby ♂♂♂ 1987 (PG) The arrival of a young baby forever changes the lives of three sworn bachelors living in New York. Well-paced, charming and fun, with good acting from all. A remake of the French movie "Three Men and a Cradle." **102m/C VHS, Beta, LV, 8mm, Closed Caption.** Tom Selleck, Steve Guttenberg, Ted Danson, Margaret Colin, Nancy Travis, Philip Bosco, Celeste Holm, Derek De Lint, Cynthia Harris, Lisa Blair, Michelle Blair; **D:** Leonard Nimoy; **W:** James Orr, Jim Cruickshank; **M:** Marvin Hamlisch. People's Choice Awards '88: Best Film—Musical/Comedy. *TOU*

Three Men and a Cradle ♂♂♂½ *Trois Hommes et un Couffin* 1985 (PG-13) Remade in the U.S. in 1987 as "Three Men and a Baby," this French film is about three bachelors living together who suddenly find themselves the guardians of a baby girl. After the initial shock of learning how to take care of a child, they fall in love with her and won't let her go. Fans of the American version may find themselves liking the original even more. In French with English subtitles. **100m/C VHS, LV.** *FR* Roland Giraud, Michel Boujenah, Andre Dussollier; **D:** Coline Serreau; **W:** Coline Serreau. Cesar Awards '86: Best Film, Best Supporting Actor (Boujenah), Best Writing; Nominations: Academy Awards '85: Best Foreign Language Film. *LIV, MGM*

Three Men and a Little Lady ♂♂½ 1990 (PG) In this sequel to "Three Men and a Baby," the mother of the once abandoned infant decides that her child needs a father. Although she wants Selleck, he doesn't get the message and so she chooses a snooty British director. The rest of the movie features various semi-comic attempts to rectify the situation. **100m/C VHS, Beta, LV, Closed Caption.** Tom Selleck, Steve Guttenberg, Ted Danson, Nancy Travis, Robin Weisman, Christopher Cazenove, Fiona Shaw, Sheila Hancock, John Boswall, Jonathan Lynn, Sydney Walsh; **D:** Emile Ardolino; **W:** Charlie Peters, Sara Parriott, Josann McGibbon; **M:** James Newton Howard. *TOU*

Three Men on a Horse ♂♂♂ 1936 Comedy classic about mild-mannered McHugh's ability to predict horse races and the bettors that try to take advantage of him. Blondell is great as the Brooklynese girlfriend of one of the bettors. Lots of laughs, but don't watch for the horse-racing scenes, because there aren't many. **88m/B VHS, Closed Caption.** Frank McHugh, Joan Blondell, Carol Hughes, Allen Jenkins, Guy Kibbee, Sam Levene; **D:** Mervyn LeRoy. *MGM*

The Three Musketeers ♂♂ *D'Artagnan* 1916 One of the many movie adaptation of Alexandre Dumas' adventure, but this one comes from the hand of famed movie pioneer Ince. D'Artagnan joins the title characters in saving France's Queen Anne from a nefarious plot. Silent with the original organ score. **74m/B VHS, Beta, 8mm.** Orin Johnson, Dorothy Dalton, Louise Glaum, Walt Whitman; **D:** Charles Swickard. *VYY, GPV, DVT*

The Three Musketeers ♂♂♂½ 1921 D'Artagnan swashbuckles silently amid stylish sets, scores of extras and exquisite costumes. Relatively faithful adaptation of Alexandre Dumas novel, slightly altered in favor of D'Artagnan's lover. Classic Fairbanks, who also produced. **120m/B VHS, Beta, LV.** Douglas Fairbanks Sr., Leon Barry, George Siegmann, Eugene Pallette, Boyd Irwin, Thomas Holding, Sidney Franklin, Charles Stevens, Nigel de Brulier, Willis Robards; **D:** Fred Niblo. *GPV, FCT, KIV*

The Three Musketeers 1933 Modern adaptation of the classic tale by Alexander Dumas depicts the three friends as members of the Foreign Legion. Weakest of Wayne serials, in 12 parts. **215m/B VHS, Beta.** John Wayne, Raymond Hatton, Lon Chaney Jr. *NOS, VCN, VDM*

The Three Musketeers 🎬🎬 1935 Three swordsmen, loyal to each other, must battle the corrupt Cardinal Richelieu. Generally regarded as the least exciting adaptation of Alexander Dumas' classic tale. The first talking version. **95m/B VHS, Beta, LV.** Walter Abel, Paul Lukas, Moroni Olsen, Ian Keith, Margot Grahame, Heather Angel, Onslow Stevens, Miles Mander; **D:** Rowland V. Lee; **M:** Max Steiner. *IME, TTC*

The Three Musketeers 🎬🎬½ *The Singing Musketeer* 1939 Musical-comedy version of the famed Alexandre Dumas swashbuckling saga. Ameche is a singing D'Artagnan and the three Ritz brothers are the inept and cowardly Musketeers (who turn out to be phonies, after all). Silly fun. 🎵My Lady; Song of the Musketeers; Voila; Chicken Soup. **73m/B VHS.** Don Ameche, The Ritz Brothers, Binnie Barnes, Lionel Atwill, Miles Mander, Gloria Stuart, Pauline Moore, Joseph Schildkraut, John Carradine, Douglass Dumbrille; **D:** Allan Dwan; **W:** M.M. Musselman, William A. Drake, Sam Hellman. *FXV*

The Three Musketeers 🎬🎬½ 1948 The three musketeers who are "all for one and one for all" join forces with D'Artagnan to battle the evil Cardinal Richelieu in this rambunctious adaptation of the classic tale by Alexander Dumas. Good performances by the cast, who combined drama and comedy well. Turner's first color film. **126m/C VHS, Beta, LV.** Lana Turner, Gene Kelly, June Allyson, Gig Young, Angela Lansbury, Van Heflin, Keenan Wynn, Robert Coote, Reginald Owen, Frank Morgan, Vincent Price, Patricia Medina; **D:** George Sidney. Nominations: Academy Awards '48: Best Color Cinematography. *MGM, CCB*

The Three Musketeers 🎬🎬🎬½ 1974 **(PG)** Extravagant and funny version of the Dumas classic. Three swashbucklers and their country cohort, who wishes to join the Musketeers, set out to save the honor of the French Queen. To do so they must oppose the evil cardinal who has his eyes on the power behind the throne. A strong cast leads this winning combination of slapstick and high adventure. Followed by "The Four Musketeers" and "The Return of the Musketeers." **105m/C VHS, Beta.** Richard Chamberlain, Oliver Reed, Michael York, Raquel Welch, Frank Finlay, Christopher Lee, Faye Dunaway, Charlton Heston, Geraldine Chaplin, Simon Ward, Jean-Pierre Cassel; **D:** Richard Lester; **C:** David Watkin. Golden Globe Awards '75: Best Actress—Musical/Comedy (Welch). *COL*

The Three Musketeers 🎬🎬½ 1993 **(PG)** Yet another version of the classic swashbuckler with Porthos, Athos, Aramis, and the innocent D'Artanan banding together against the evil Cardinal Richelieu and the tempting Milady DeWinter to save France. Cute stars, a little swordplay, a few jokes, and cartoon bad guys. Okay for the younger crowd. **105m/C VHS, LV, Closed Caption.** Kiefer Sutherland, Charlie Sheen, Chris O'Donnell, Oliver Platt, Rebecca DeMornay, Tim Curry, Gabrielle Anwar, Julie Delpy, Michael Wincott; **D:** Stephen Herek; **W:** David Loughery; **M:** Michael Kamen. Nominations: MTV Movie Awards '94: Best Song ("All for Love"). *DIS*

3 Ninjas 🎬🎬½ 1992 **(PG)** Lively kid's actioner about three brothers who are trained as ninjas by their grandpa. When a group of bad guys tries to kidnap the boys, they're in for trouble. Sort of a cross between "The Karate Kid" and "Home Alone" that is suitable for family viewing. Followed by "3 Ninjas Kick Back." **84m/C VHS, Beta, LV, Closed Caption.** Victor Wong, Michael Treanor, Max Elliott Slade, Chad Power, Rand Kingsley, Alan McRae, Margarita Franco, Toru Tanaka, Patrick Laborteaux; **D:** Jon Turteltaub; **W:** Edward Emanuel; **M:** Rick Marvin. *TOU, PMS*

3 Ninjas Kick Back 🎬🎬½ 1994 **(PG)** Sequel to the popular "3 Ninjas." Three brothers help their grandfather protect a ceremonial knife won in a ninja tournament in Japan 50 years earlier. Gramps' ancient adversary in that tournament, now an evil tycoon, wants the sword back and he's willing to enlist the aid of his three American grandchildren, members of garage band Teenage Vomit, to get it. The showdown eventually heads to Japan, where "Kick Back," unlike predecessors, dispenses with the Japan-bashing. High-spirited action fare that kids will enjoy. **95m/C VHS, LV, Closed Caption.** Victor Wong, Max Elliott Slade, Sean Fox, Evan Bonifant, Sab Shimono, Dustin Nguyen, Jason Schombing, Caroline Junko King, Angelo Tiffe; **D:** Charles Kanganis; **W:** Mark Saltzman; **M:** Rick Marvin. *COL*

3 Ninjas Knuckle Up 🎬🎬½ 1992 **(PG-13)** Brothers Rocky (Treanor), Tum Tum (Power), and Colt (Slade) spend their vacation with ever-wise Grandpa Mori (Wong) and get to practice their martial arts skills on a variety of villains. Seems a waste management company has been illegally dumping toxins onto the nearby Indian reservation where the boys' friend Jo (Lightning) lives and have even kidnapped her dad (Shanks) to keep him silent. So it's our pint-sized heroes to the rescue. Filmed in '92 but released after "3 Ninjas Kick Back," which explains why Treanor and Power are missing from the second film. **CW:** Non-stop ninja action. **94m/C VHS, LV.** Victor Wong, Michael Treanor, Chad Power, Max Elliott Slade, Crystle Lightning, Patrick Kilpatrick, Don Shanks, Charles Napier, Nick Ramus, Vincent Schiavelli; **D:** Simon S. Sheen; **W:** Alex S. Kim; **C:** Eugene Shlugleit; **M:** Gary Stevan Scott. *COL*

Three Nuts in Search of a Bolt 🎬½ 1964 **(R)** Three neurotics send a surrogate to a comely psychiatrist for help, but the shrink thinks the surrogate's a three-way multiple personality. Raunchy monkey-shines ensue. Includes Van Doren's infamous beer bath scene. **78m/C VHS, Beta.** Mamie Van Doren, Tommy Noonan, Paul Gilbert, Alvy Moore; **D:** Tommy Noonan. *NO*

301, 302 🎬 1994 Confusing horror story told in flashbacks focuses on two women in neighboring high-rise apartments. A young policeman is investigating the disappearance of the woman from apartment 302 (Hwang). He questions the tenant across the hall in 301 (Pang), an obsessive cook who tries to share her culinary results with Hwang, who happens to be an anorexic writer. Both have dark secrets in their pasts, which they share, leading to a grotesque resolution of their friendship. **99m/C VHS.** Eun-Jin Pang, Sin-Hye Hwang; **D:** Chul-Soo Park; **W:** Suh-Goon Lee. *NYR*

Three O'Clock High 🎬🎬½ 1987 **(PG)** A nerdy high school journalist is assigned a profile of the new kid in school, who turns out to be the biggest bully, too. He approaches his task with great unease. Silly teen-age farce is given souped-up direction by Spielberg protege Joanou. Features decent work by the young cast. **97m/C VHS, Beta, LV.** Casey Siemaszko, Anne Ryan, Stacey Glick, Jonathan Wise, Richard Tyson, Jeffrey Tambor, Philip Baker Hall, John P. Ryan; **D:** Phil Joanou; **W:** Richard Christian Matheson, Thomas Szollosi; **M:** Tangerine Dream. *USH*

Three of Hearts 🎬½ 1993 **(R)** Slick look at love in contemporary downtown New York. The triangle consists of Connie (Lynch), just dumped by bisexual girlfriend Ellen (Fenn), who is in turn seduced by hired escort Joe (Baldwin), who will break her heart, causing her to turn back to the sympathetic Connie. But guess what happens. Hiply superficial plot is transparent although the three leads are likeable, especially Lynch as the lanky lovelorn Connie. Don't read further if you don't want to know what happens since the film was shot with two endings. The U.S. release pairs Joe and Ellen for a typically American happy ending; the European release doesn't. **CW:** Strong language and strong sexuality. **102m/C VHS, LV.** Kelly Lynch, William Baldwin, Sherilyn Fenn, Joe Pantoli-

ano, Gail Strickland, Cec Verrell, Claire Callaway, Tony Amendola; **D:** Yurek Bogayevicz; **W:** Philip C. Epstein, Adam Greenman; **M:** Richard Gibbs. *COL, IME, FCT*

Three on a Match 🎬🎬🎬 1932 An actress, a stenographer and a society woman get together for a tenth year reunion. They become embroiled in a world of crime when Blondell's gangster boyfriend takes a liking to Dvorak. She leaves her husband and takes up with the crook. The results are tragic. Bogart's first gangster role. **64m/B VHS, Beta.** Joan Blondell, Warren William, Ann Dvorak, Bette Davis, Lyle Talbot, Humphrey Bogart, Patricia Ellis, Grant Mitchell; **D:** Mervyn LeRoy. *MGM, FCT*

Three on a Meathook woof! 1972 When a young man and his father living on an isolated farm receive female visitors, bloodshed is quick to follow. Essentially a remake of "Psycho," and very loosely based on the crimes of Ed Gein. Filmed in Louisville, Kentucky. **85m/C VHS, Beta.** Charles Kissinger, James Pickett, Sherry Steiner, Carolyn Thompson; **D:** William Girdler; **W:** William Girdler. *NO*

The Three Penny Opera 🎬🎬🎬 *Die Dreigroschenoper* 1962 Mack the Knife presides over an exciting world of thieves, murderers, beggars, prostitutes and corrupt officials in a seedy section of London. Based on the opera by Kurt Weill and Bertold Brecht, which was based on "The Beggar's Opera" by John Gay. Remake of "The Threepenny Opera" (1931). **124m/C VHS, Beta, LV.** GE Curt Jurgens, Hildegarde Neff, Gert Frobe, June Ritchie, Lino Ventura, Sammy Davis Jr. *MVD, FCT*

Three Secrets 🎬🎬½ 1950 A plane crashes and the only survivor is a five-year-old boy. Three women, each with a secret, seek to claim him as the child each gave up for adoption five years before. Tearjerker with good cast. **98m/B VHS.** Eleanor Parker, Patricia Neal, Ruth Roman, Frank Lovejoy, Leif Erickson; **D:** Robert Wise. *REP*

The Three Sisters 🎬🎬½ 1965 A stage production from the Actor's Studio of Chekhov's play about unhappy siblings in turn-of-the-century Russia. The three sisters believe all their problems are caused by living in the provinces and would be solved if they could return to their childhood home in Moscow. **167m/B VHS.** Shelley Winters, Sandy Dennis, Geraldine Page, Kevin McCarthy, Kim Stanley, Luther Adler, Robert Loggia, James Olson, Gerald Hiken; **D:** Paul Bogart. *HTV, FCT*

Three Smart Girls 🎬🎬🎬½ 1936 Fast-moving musical features three high-spirited sisters who attempt to bring their divorced parents back together. Their plan is thwarted when they learn of their father's plan to marry a gold digger. 15-year-old singing sensation Durbin made her debut in this film. Based on a story by Commandini. Followed by "Three Smart Girls Grow Up." 🎵My Heart is Singing; Someone to Care for Me. **84m/B VHS.** Deanna Durbin, Binnie Barnes, Alice Brady, Ray Milland, Charles Winninger, Mischa Auer, Nan Grey, Barbara Read; **D:** Henry Koster; **W:** Adele Comandini, Austin Parker; **C:** Joseph Valentine. Nominations: Academy Awards '36: Best Picture, Best Sound, Best Story. *USH*

Three Smart Girls Grow Up 🎬🎬🎬 1939 Durbin once again plays matchmaker, this time for her two older sisters and their fellas. A delightful mix of comedy and song, this lighthearted sequel turned out to be one of the top-grossing films of the year. Durbin sings "Because," which became one of her biggest hits. **88m/B VHS.** Deanna Durbin, Charles Winninger, Nan Grey, Helen Parrish, Robert Cummings, William Lundigan, Ernest Cossart; **D:** Henry Koster; **W:** Felix Jackson, Bruce Manning. *USH*

Three Sovereigns for Sarah 🎬🎬½ 1985 Witch-hunters tortured and toasted Sarah's two sisters for practicing witchcraft in the past. Now, accused of witchery herself, she struggles to prove the family's innocence. Excellent, made-for-PBS. Fine performances from all, especially Redgrave. **152m/C VHS, Beta.** Vanessa Redgrave, Phyllis Thaxter, Patrick McGoohan; **D:** Philip Leacock. *PSM, PBS*

Three Stooges Comedy Capers: Vol. 1
194? Compilation includes: "Disorder in the Court" (1936), "Malice in the Palace" (1949), "Sing a Song of Six Pants" (1947), and "The Brideless Groom" (1947). **80m/B VHS, Beta.** Moe Howard, Larry Fine, Curly Howard, Shemp Howard. *NOS, MED*

Three Stooges Comedy Classics
1949 The antics of the Stooges are featured in this collection of five original shorts, along with an early Ted Healy comedy that features all four Stooges: "Hollywood on Parade," "Disorder in the Court," "Malice in the Palace," "Brideless Groom," and "Sing a Song of Six Pants." **79m/B VHS.** Moe Howard, Larry Fine, Curly Howard, Shemp Howard, Ted Healy. *REP*

Three Stooges: Cookoo Cavaliers and Other Nyuks
1940 The boys star in "Cookoo Cavaliers," "Busy Buddies," and "Booby Dupes." **55m/B VHS.** Moe Howard, Curly Howard, Larry Fine. *COL*

Three Stooges Festival
1949 Three original shorts by the comedy trio, including: "Disorder in the Court" (1936-Curly), "Sing a Song of Six Pants" (1949-Shemp) and "Malice in the Palace" (1949-Shemp). **60m/B VHS, Beta.** Moe Howard, Larry Fine, Shemp Howard, Curly Howard. *AOV, VYY*

Three Stooges: From Nurse to Worse and Other Nyuks
1945 The irrepressible Stooges star in "From Nurse to Worse," "Crash Goes the Hash," and "G.I. Wanna Go Home." **55m/B VHS.** Moe Howard, Larry Fine, Curly Howard. *COL*

The Three Stooges: Half-Wit's Holiday and Other Nyuks
1935 Includes, "Half-Wit's Holiday," "Horse Collars," and "How High Is Up?" **55m/B VHS.** Moe Howard, Curly Howard, Larry Fine. *COL*

The Three Stooges: Idiots Deluxe and Other Nyuks
1940 Curly, Larry and Moe star in, "Idiots Deluxe," "I Can Hardly Wait," and "Idle Roomers." **55m/B VHS.** Moe Howard, Curly Howard, Larry Fine. *COL*

Three Stooges in Orbit
ÆÆ½ 1962 Three television performers (you know who) looking for a schtick and a place to live, encounter a crazy scientist with a rocket-like invention. In a shocking plot twist, the boys accidently launch the rocket and must battle Martians to save the world and their TV career. **87m/B VHS.** Moe Howard, Larry Fine, Joe DeRita, Emil Sitka, Carol Christensen, Edson Stroll; *D:* Edward L. Bernds. *COL*

The Three Stooges Meet Hercules
ÆÆ½ 1961 The Three Stooges are transported back to ancient Ithaca by a time machine with a young scientist and his girlfriend. When the girl is captured, they enlist the help of Hercules to rescue her. **80m/B VHS, Beta.** Moe Howard, Larry Fine, Joe DeRita, Vicki Trickett, Quinn Redeker; *D:* Edward L. Bernds. *GKK, COL*

The Three Stooges: Nutty but Nice and Other Nyuks
1936 The boys star in "Nutty but Nice," "The Sitter-Downers," and "Slippery Silks." **55m/B VHS.** Moe Howard, Curly Howard, Larry Fine. *COL*

The Three Stooges: They Stooge to Conga and Other Nyuks
1940 WWII madness from the Stooges in "They Stooge to Conga," "You Natzy Spy!" and "I'll Never Heil Again." **55m/B VHS.** Moe Howard, Curly Howard, Larry Fine. *COL*

Three Stops to Murder
Æ 1953 An FBI agent investigates the murder of a beautiful model in this early, unspectacular Hammer production. **76m/B VHS, Beta.** *GB* Tom Conway, Mila Parely, Naomi Chance, Eric Pohlmann, Andrew Osborn, Richard Wattis, Eileen Way, Delphi Lawrence; *D:* Terence Fisher. *SNC, MLB*

Three Strange Loves
ÆÆÆ *Thirst* 1949 Men and women struggle with loneliness, old age, and sterility. Sometimes disjointed, but for the most part, well-made. Finely acted. In Swedish with English subtitles. **88m/B VHS, Beta.** *SW* Eva Henning, Brigit Tengroth, Birger Malmsten; *D:* Ingmar Bergman. *NOS, HHT, NLC*

3:10 to Yuma
ÆÆÆ½ 1957 In order to collect $200 he desperately needs, a poor farmer has to hold a dangerous killer at bay while waiting to turn the outlaw over to the authorities arriving on the 3:10 train to Yuma. Stuck in a hotel room with the outlaw's gang gathering outside, the question arises as to who is the prisoner. Farmer Heflin is continually worked on by the outlaw Ford, in a movie with more than its share of great dialogue. Suspenseful, well-made action western adapted from an Elmore Leonard story. **92m/B VHS, Beta, LV.** Glenn Ford, Van Heflin, Felicia Farr, Richard Jaeckel; *D:* Delmer Daves; *M:* George Duning. *GKK*

Three Texas Steers
Æ½ *Danger Rides the Range* 1939 A circus owner inherits some land that the government wants for a water project and her manager tries to get it for himself. Enter the terrific trio to set things right. Last of the series for Terhune. The scenes of the circus fire were taken from "Circus Girl" (1937). **59m/B VHS.** John Wayne, Ray Corrigan, Max Terhune, Carole Landis, Ralph Graves, Roscoe Ates; *D:* George Sherman. *NOS*

Three the Hard Way
ÆÆ½ 1974 (R) An insane white supremacist has a plan to eliminate blacks by contaminating water supplies. A big blaxploitation money maker and the first to team Brown, Williamson, and Kelly, who would go on to make several more pictures together. **93m/C VHS.** Jim Brown, Fred Williamson, Jim Kelly, Sheila Frazier, Jay Robinson, Alex Rocco; *D:* Gordon Parks. *XVC*

Three Violent People
ÆÆ 1957 Family feud set in post-Civil War Old West features Heston and Baxter impulsively marrying and returning to run the family ranch. Heston's brother (Tryon) wants to sell the ranch in order to get his share of the inheritance and then Heston finds out Baxter was once a prostitute. In this case family squabbles don't make for an exciting film. **100m/C VHS, Closed Caption.** Charlton Heston, Anne Baxter, Gilbert Roland, Tom Tryon, Forrest Tucker, Elaine Stritch, Bruce (Herman Brix) Bennett, Barton MacLane; *D:* Rudolph Mate; *W:* James Edward Grant; *C:* Loyal Griggs; *M:* Walter Scharf. *PAR*

Three Warriors
Æ½ 1977 Young Native American boy is forced to leave the city and return to the reservation, where his contempt for the traditions of his ancestors slowly turns to appreciation and love. **100m/C VHS, Beta.** Charles White Eagle, Lois Red Elk, McKee "Kiko" Red Wing, Christopher Lloyd, Randy Quaid. *NO*

Three Way Weekend
Æ 1981 (R) Two young girls set off on a back-packing trip through the mountains of Southern California to enjoy camping and romance. **78m/C VHS, Beta.** Dan Diego, Jody Lee Olhava, Richard Blye, Blake Parrish; *D:* Emmett Alston. *ACA*

The Three Weird Sisters
ÆÆ 1948 The three weird sisters from "Macbeth" strive to maintain their life of luxury by plotting to kill their half-brother for the inheritance. Not a bad effort for Birt's first time out as director; script co-written by his wife, Louise and poet Thomas. **82m/B VHS.** *GB* Nancy Price, Mary Clare; *D:* Daniel Birt; *W:* Dylan Thomas, Louise Birt. *VDM, SNC, THV*

Three Wishes
ÆÆ 1995 (PG) Mysterious—and perhaps mystical—stranger Jack (Swayze) moves into the lives of a 1950s suburban widow (Mastrantonio) and her kids (Mazzello and Mumy) after she hits him with her car. Jack proceeds to use Zen philosophy, stories of a genie disguised as a dog, and nude sunbathing to help the kids' Little League team win, make a boy fly, and scandalize the neighborhood. Adults will recognize the beatnik, Kerouac-influenced philosophy of nonconformity. They'll also recognize the sellout of that ideal with the sickeningly sappy ending. Mumy is the son of former "Lost in Space" child star Billy Mumy. **115m/C VHS, LV, Closed Caption.** Patrick Swayze, Mary Elizabeth Mastrantonio, Joseph Mazzello, David Marshall Grant, Michael O'Keefe, John Diehl, Jay O. Sanders, Diane Venora, Seth Mumy; *D:* Martha Coolidge; *W:* Elizabeth Anderson; *C:* Johnny E. Jensen; *M:* Cynthia Millar. *HBO*

Three Word Brand
ÆÆ 1921 Hart plays three roles in this film, a homesteader who is killed by Indians and his twin sons, who are separated after their father's death and reunited many years later. Silent with musical score. **75m/B VHS, Beta.** William S. Hart, Jane Novak, S.J. Bingham; *D:* Lambert Hillyer. *GPV, VYY*

The Three Worlds of Gulliver
ÆÆ½ *The Worlds of Gulliver* 1959 A colorful family version of the Jonathan Swift classic about an Englishman who discovers a fantasy land of small and giant people. Visual effects by Ray Harryhausen. **100m/C VHS, Beta, LV.** Kerwin Mathews, Jo Morrow, Basil Sydney, Mary Ellis; *D:* Jack Sher; *W:* Arthur Ross, Jack Sher; *M:* Bernard Herrmann. *COL, MLB, CCB*

The Threepenny Opera
ÆÆ *Die Dreigroschenoper; L'Opera De Quat'Sous; Beggars' Opera* 1931 A musical about the exploits of gangster Mack the Knife. Adapted from Bertolt Brecht's play and John Gay's "The Beggar's Opera." In German with English subtitles. **107m/B VHS.** Rudolph Forster, Lotte Lenya, Carola Neher, Reinhold Schunzel, Fritz Rasp, Valeska Gert; *D:* G.W. Pabst. *VDM, AUD, HEG*

Three's Trouble
Æ 1985 A middle-class family erupts when a young male babysitter enters to care for its three mischievous sons. **93m/C VHS, Beta.** *AU* John Waters, Jacki Weaver, Steven Vidler; *D:* Chris Thomson. *NWV*

Threesome
woof! 1994 (R) Another Generation X movie that tries hard to be hip, but fails miserably. Due to a college administrative error, Alex (Boyle) winds up sharing a suite with two male roommates, Eddy (Charles) and Stuart (Baldwin). Despite having completely different personalities, they soon become best friends and form one cozy little group, with cozy being the key word. Sexual tension abounds—Alex wants Eddy who wants Stuart who wants Alex. Filled with pathetic dialogue (most of it relating to bodily functions and body parts) and shallow, obnoxious characters, this menage a trois film is a flop. **93m/C VHS, LV, 8mm, Closed Caption.** Lara Flynn Boyle, Stephen Baldwin, Josh Charles, Alexis Arquette, Mark Arnold, Martha Gehman, Michelle Matheson; *D:* Andrew Fleming; *W:* Andrew Fleming; *M:* Thomas Newman. *COL*

Threshold
ÆÆ½ 1983 (PG) An internationally-acclaimed research biologist is frustrated by his inability to save a dying 20-year-old woman born with a defective heart. She becomes the recipient of the first artificial heart. Solid performances. **97m/C VHS, Beta.** *CA* Donald Sutherland, Jeff Goldblum, John Marley, Mare Winningham; *D:* Richard Pearce. Genie Awards '83: Best Actor (Sutherland). *FOX*

The Thrill Killers
woof! *The Monsters Are Loose; The Maniacs Are Loose* 1965 Young murderous thugs rampage through Los Angeles suburbs, killing indiscriminately. Pretentious and exploitative. Sometimes shown with Hallucinogenic Hypo-Vision—a prologue announcing the special effect would be shown before the film, and on cue, hooded ushers would run through the theatre with cardboard axes. Weird. **82m/C VHS, Beta.** Cash Flagg, Liz Renay, Brick Bardo, Carolyn Brandt, Atlas King; *D:* Ray Dennis Steckler. *NO*

Thrill of a Romance
ÆÆ 1945 Johnson, an Army hero, meets Williams, a swimming instructor of all things, at a resort in the Sierra Nevadas. The only problem is that she's married. Typical swim-romance vehicle. ♫Please Don't Say No, Say Maybe; I Should Care; Lonely Night; Vive L'Amour; Schubert's Serenade; The Thrill of a Romance. **105m/C VHS.** Esther Williams, Van Johnson, Frances Gifford, Henry Travers, Spring Byington, Lauritz Melchior; *D:* Richard Thorpe. *MGM*

The Thrill of It All! 🎬🎬½ 1963 An average housewife becomes a star of television commercials, to the dismay of her chauvinist husband, a gynecologist. Fast and funny, with numerous acidic jokes about television sponsors and programs. 108m/C VHS, Beta. James Garner, Doris Day, Arlene Francis, Edward Andrews, Carl Reiner, Elliott Reid, Reginald Owen, ZaSu Pitts; *D:* Norman Jewison; *W:* Carl Reiner; *C:* Russell Metty. *USH*

Thrilled to Death 🎬½ 1988 (R) An utterly naive husband and wife get caught in the middle of a lethal game when they befriend a scheming couple. 90m/C VHS. Blake Bahner, Rebecca Lynn, Richard Maris, Christine Moore; *D:* Chuck Vincent. *REP*

Thrillkill 🎬 1984 A young girl is enmeshed in a multi-million-dollar burglary scheme after her computer-whiz/embezzler sister disappears. 88m/C VHS, Beta. Robin Ward, Gina Massey, Anthony Kramroither; *D:* Anthony D'Andrea. *MED*

Throne of Blood 🎬🎬🎬🎬 *Kumonosujo, Kumonosu-djo; Cobweb Castle; The Castle of the Spider's Web* 1957 Kurosawa's masterful adaptation of "Macbeth" transports the story to medieval Japan and the world of the samurai. Mifune and Chiaki are warriors who have put down a rebellion and are to be rewarded by their overlord. On their way to his castle they meet a mysterious old woman who prophesizes that Mifune will soon rule—but his reign will be short. She is dismissed as crazy but her prophesies come to pass. So steeped in Japanese style that it bears little resemblance to the Shakespearean original, this film is an incredibly detailed vision in its own right. In Japanese with English subtitles. 105m/B VHS, Beta, LV. *JP* Toshiro Mifune, Isuzu Yamada, Takashi Shimura, Minoru Chiaki, Akira Kubo; *D:* Akira Kurosawa; *W:* Hideo Oguni, Shinobu Hashimoto, Ryuzo Kikushima, Akira Kurosawa; *M:* Masaru Sato. *HMV, CRC, IHF*

Throne of Fire woof! 1982 A mighty hero battles the forces of evil to gain control of the powerful Throne of Fire. Dubbed. 91m/C VHS, Beta. *IT* Peter McCoy, Sabrina Siani; *D:* Franco Prosperi. *MGM*

Through a Glass Darkly 🎬🎬🎬 1961 Oppressive interactions within a family sharing a holiday on a secluded island: a woman recovering from schizophrenia, her husband, younger brother, and her psychologist father. One of Bergman's most mysterious, upsetting and powerful films. In Swedish with English subtitles. Part of Bergman's Silence-of-God trilogy followed by "Winter Light" and "The Silence." 91m/B VHS, Beta. *SW* Harriet Andersson, Max von Sydow, Gunnar Bjornstrand, Lars Passgard; *D:* Ingmar Bergman; *W:* Ingmar Bergman; *C:* Sven Nykvist. Academy Awards '61: Best Foreign Language Film; National Board of Review Awards '62: 5 Best Foreign Films of the Year; Nominations: Academy Awards '62: Best Story & Screenplay. *NOS, NLC*

Through Naked Eyes 🎬🎬½ 1987 Made-for-television thriller about two people who spy on each other. They witness a murder and realize that someone else is watching them. What a coincidence. 91m/C VHS, Beta. David Soul, Pam Dawber; *D:* John Llewellyn Moxey. *MED*

Through the Breakers 🎬½ 1928 Heartbroken woman suffers silently on South Pacific isle. 55m/B VHS, Beta. Margaret Livingston, Holmes Herbert, Clyde Cook, Natalie Joyce. *GPV, FCT*

Through the Eyes of a Killer 🎬🎬½ 1992 (R) Laurie Fisher (Helgenberger) has dumped cheating boyfriend Jerry (Pantoliano) and has declared her independence by finding a spacious but crummy New York apartment in desperate need of renovation. Enter handsome handyman Ray Bellano (Anderson), who's happy to work on the apartment—and Laurie as well. But where Laurie sees a fling, Ray sees true love, and since brooding Ray's got the prerequisite mystery past, you know Laurie's in for the shock of her life. Long-time nice guy Anderson does a credible turn as an obsessive psycho. Based on the short story "The Master Builder" by Christopher Fowler; made for TV. *CW:* Terror/violence and some sexu-

ality. 94m/C VHS, Beta, Closed Caption. Richard Dean Anderson, Marg Helgenberger, Joe Pantoliano, David Marshall Grant, Melinda Culea, Tippi Hedren; *D:* Peter Markle; *W:* John Pielmeier; *M:* George S. Clinton. *PAR*

Through the Olive Trees 🎬🎬🎬 *Under the Olive Trees; Zire Darakhtan Zeyton* 1994 (G) Film-within-a-film is the last of a trilogy concerned with Persian village life, following "Where Is My Friend's House?" and "And Life Goes On." Director, filming in an earthquake-ravaged village, discovers that the young bricklayer playing the bridegroom in his film is actually in love with the local girl who's playing the bride. However, she's turned down his real-life marriage proposal, feeling that the uneducated man is beneath her. Farsi with subtitles. It may be rated G but considering the subject matter and the fact that the film is subtitled, don't consider this one for the kiddies. 104m/C VHS. Zarifeh Shivah, Hossein Rezai, Mohamad Ali Keshavarz, Taherek Ladania; *D:* Abbas Kiarostami; *W:* Abbas Kiarostami; *C:* Hossein Jafarian, Farhad Saba. Nominations: Independent Spirit Awards '96: Best Foreign Film. *NYR*

Throw Momma from the Train 🎬🎬🎬 1987 (PG-13) DeVito plays a man, henpecked by his horrific mother, who tries to persuade his writing professor (Crystal) to exchange murders. DeVito will kill Crystal's ex-wife and Crystal will kill DeVito's mother. Only mama isn't going to be that easy to get rid of. Fast-paced and entertaining black comedy. Ramsey steals the film. Inspired by Hitchcock's "Strangers on a Train." 88m/C VHS, Beta, LV, Closed Caption. Danny DeVito, Billy Crystal, Anne Ramsey, Kate Mulgrew, Kim Greist, Branford Marsalis, Rob Reiner, Bruce Kirby; *D:* Danny DeVito; *W:* Stu Silver; *M:* David Newman. Nominations: Academy Awards '87: Best Supporting Actress (Ramsey). *ORI*

The Throwback 🎬½ 1935 When Jones was a lad the townspeople accused his father of cattle rustling. When he returns as an adult he sets out to clear his father's name. 61m/B VHS. Buck Jones, Muriel Evans, Eddie Phillips, George "Gabby" Hayes, Bryant Washburn, Paul Fix, Frank LaRue; *D:* Ray Taylor. *GPV*

Thumb Tripping 🎬🎬 1972 (R) A dated sixties/hippie film. Two flower children hitchhike and encounter all kinds of other strange people in their travels on the far-out roads. 94m/C VHS, Beta. Meg Foster, Michael Burns, Bruce Dern, Marianna Hill, Michael Conrad, Joyce Van Patten; *D:* Quentin Masters. *NLC*

Thumbelina 1982 From "Faerie Tale Theatre" comes the story of a tiny girl who gets kidnapped by a toad and a mole, but meets the man of her dreams in the nick of time. Adapted from the classic tale by Hans Christian Andersen. Made for television. 60m/C VHS, Beta, LV, Closed Caption. Carrie Fisher, William Katt, Burgess Meredith; *D:* Michael Lindsay-Hogg. *KUI, FOX, FCT*

Thumbelina 🎬🎬½ *Hans Christian Andersen's Thumbelina* 1994 (G) Ornery little girl named Mia gets magically sucked into the pages of the "Thumbelina" storybook she's reading and finds all sorts of adventures. Loose adaptation of Hans Christian Andersen fairy tale from Bluth is lackluster, with acceptable songs. Not up to the level of recent Disney animated features, but pleasant enough for the kids. 86m/C VHS, Beta, LV, Closed Caption. *D:* Don Bluth, Gary Goldman; *W:* Don Bluth; *M:* William Ross, Barry Manilow, Barry Manilow, Jack Feldman, Bruce Sussman; *V:* Jodi Benson, Gary Imhoff, Charo, Gilbert Gottfried, Carol Channing, John Hurt, Will Ryan, June Foray, Kenneth Mars. Golden Raspberry Awards '94: Worst Song ("Marry the Mole"). *WAR*

Thunder Alley 🎬½ 1985 In middle America, two friends and their rock group struggle for success. One of the friends dies after an accidental overdose and the other's grief propels him to stardom. ♫Can't Look Back; Just Another Pretty Boy; Sometimes in the Night; Heart to Heart; Can You Feel My Heart Beat; Do You Feel Alright?; Danger, Danger; Surrender; Gimme Back My

Heart. 102m/C VHS, Beta. Roger Wilson, Leif Garrett, Jill Schoelen; *D:* J.S. Cardone; *W:* J.S. Cardone. *MGM*

Thunder and Lightning 🎬🎬 1977 (PG) A mismatched young couple chase a truckload of poisoned moonshine. Action-packed chases ensue. Nice chemistry between Carradine and Jackson. 94m/C VHS, Beta, Closed Caption. David Carradine, Kate Jackson, Roger C. Carmel, Sterling Holloway, Eddie Barth; *D:* Corey Allen. *FOX*

Thunder & Mud 1989 Female mud wrestlers battle over their favorite rock band. Hahn's attempt to cash in on her notoriety after the Bakker scandal. 90m/C VHS, Beta, LV. Jessica Hahn; *D:* Penelope Spheeris. *COL*

Thunder Bay 🎬🎬🎬 1953 Stewart and Duryea are a pair of Louisiana wildcat oil drillers who believe there is oil at the bottom of the Gulf of Mexico off the coast of the town of Port Felicity. They decide to construct an oil platform which the shrimp fisherman of the town believe will interfere with their livelihoods. Tensions rise between the two groups and violence seems likely. Action packed, with timely storyline as modern oil drillers fight to drill in waters that have historically been off-limits. 82m/C VHS, Beta. James Stewart, Joanne Dru, Dan Duryea, Gilbert Roland, Marcia Henderson; *D:* Anthony Mann; *W:* John Michael Hayes; *C:* William H. Daniels. *USH*

Thunder County 🎬½ 1974 Federal agents and drug runners are after a group of four convicts who have just escaped from prison. 78m/C VHS, Beta. Mickey Rooney, Ted Cassidy, Chris Robinson. *PSM*

Thunder in God's Country 🎬 1951 A dishonest gambler eyes a peaceful western town as the next Vegas-like gambling capital. Before this occurs he is exposed as a cheat. 67m/B VHS, Beta. Rex Allen, Mary Ellen Kay. *DVT*

Thunder in Paradise 🎬🎬½ 1993 (PG-13) R.J. Hurricane Spencer (Hogan) is a soldier of fortune who heads into Cuba to help a woman and child escape political imprisonment, using his high-tech, weapon-filled speedboat. He has to fight off a small army and manages to find a buried treasure as well. Simple-minded TV pilot. *CW:* Language, some action, and sensuality. 104m/C VHS, LV. Hulk Hogan, Robin Weisman, Chris Lemmon, Carol Alt, Patrick Macnee, Sam Jones, Charlotte Rae; *D:* Douglas Schwartz. *THV*

Thunder in Paradise 2 🎬½ 1994 (PG) Damsel sends up a distress signal and it's the Hulkster and his pal to the rescue. Unfortunately, their commando radial fails and now they need an escape plan. From the syndicated TV series. 90m/C VHS, Closed Caption. Hulk Hogan, Chris Lemmon, Carol Alt, Patrick Macnee; *D:* Douglas Schwartz. *THV*

Thunder in Paradise 3 🎬½ 1994 (PG-13) Hogan is on a top secret mission to capture a drug lord who's holding his daughter hostage. 88m/C VHS. Hulk Hogan. *THV*

Thunder in the City 🎬🎬🎬 1937 Robinson is an intense American promoter in the sales game who is sent to London by his employers to learn a more subdued way of doing business. Instead, he meets a pair of down-on-their-luck aristocrats whose only asset is an apparently worthless Rhodesian mine. Robinson, however, comes up with a way to promote the mine and get enough capital together to make it profitable. Good satire with Robinson well cast. Robinson wasn't taken with the script in its original form and persuaded his friend, playwright Robert Sherwood, to re-write it. 85m/B VHS, Beta. *GB* Edward G. Robinson, Nigel Bruce, Ralph Richardson, Constance Collier; *D:* Marion Gering; *M:* Miklos Rozsa. *NOS, DVT, BAR*

Thunder in the Desert 🎬 1938 A cowhand joins an outlaw gang in order to catch his uncle's killer. 56m/C VHS, Beta. Bob Steele, Louise Stanley, Don Barclay, Charles "Blackie" King, Lew Meehan, Budd Buster; *D:* Sam Newfield. *NOS, DVT, GPV*

Thunder in the Pines ⬥ 1949 Two lumberjack buddies send for the same French girl to marry, unbeknownst to each other. When she arrives, the dismayed men agree to a contest to see who will marry her. Meanwhile the French girl falls for the local saloon owner and his jilted girlfriend vows to get even. She does, with the help of the lumberjacks. **61m/B VHS, Beta, LV.** Denise Darcel, George Reeves, Ralph Byrd, Lyle Talbot, Michael Whalen, Roscoe Ates, Vince Barnett; **D:** Robert Edwards. *NO*

Thunder Mountain ⬥½ 1935 Zane Grey's novel about two prospectors who are bushwhacked on their way to file a claim comes to life on the screen. **56m/B VHS, Beta.** George O'Brien. *DVT, HHE, MLB*

Thunder Over Texas ⬥ 1934 The cowboy hero gets embroiled in a railroad scandal that involves a kidnapping. Directed by Edgar G. Ulmer, who used the alias John Warner because he was moonlighting. His first western; previously he was best known for "The Black Cat." **52m/B Beta.** Marion Shilling, Helen Westcott, Victor Potel, Tiny Skelton; **D:** Edgar G. Ulmer. *VDM*

Thunder Pass ⬥⬥ 1937 Gold and greed are the motives for murder as two young brothers become separated when their wagon train is attacked and their family is slaughtered. One brother searches for the other and finds him several years later. Based on the novel "Arizona Ames" by Zane Grey. Also released as "Thunder Trail." **58m/B VHS.** Charles Bickford, Marsha Hunt, Gilbert Roland, Monte Blue; **D:** Charles T. Barton. *NOS, VDM, DVT*

Thunder Pass ⬥⬥ 1954 Routine story about a wagon train threatened by hostile Indians and the Army officer who leads them to safety. Based on a story by George Van Marter. **76m/B VHS.** Dane Clark, Dorothy Patrick, Andy Devine, Raymond Burr, John Carradine, Mary Ellen Kay; **D:** Frank McDonald; **W:** Tom Hubbard, Fred Eggers. *MOV*

Thunder River Feud ⬥⬥ 1942 The Rangebusters help two ranchers avoid a range war. Part of "The Rangebusters" series. **58m/B VHS, Beta.** Ray Corrigan, John "Dusty" King, Max Terhune. *NOS, VCN, DVT*

Thunder Road ⬥⬥⬥ 1958 (PG) Mitchum comes home to Tennessee from Korea and takes over the family moonshine business, fighting both mobsters and federal agents. An exciting chase between Mitchum and the feds ends the movie with the appropriate bang. Robert Mitchum not only produced, wrote and starred in this best of the moonshine-running films, but also wrote the theme song "Whippoorwill" (which later became a radio hit). Mitchum's son, James, made his film debut, and later starred in a similar movie "Moonrunners." A cult favorite, still shown in many drive-ins around the country. **92m/B VHS, Beta.** Robert Mitchum, Jacques Aubuchon, Gene Barry, Keely Smith, Trevor Bardette, Sandra Knight, Jim Mitchum, Betsy Holt, Frances Koon; **D:** Arthur Ripley; **W:** Robert Mitchum. *MGM*

Thunder Run ⬥ 1986 (PG-13) When a load of uranium needs to be transferred across Nevada, a retired trucker takes on the job. The trip is made more difficult since terrorists are trying to hijack the shipment to use for a bomb. **84m/C VHS, Beta.** Forrest Tucker, John Ireland, John Shepherd, Jill Whitlow, Wally Ward, Cheryl Lynn; **D:** Gary Hudson; **W:** Charles Davis. *MED*

Thunder Trail 1937 Set of twins, separated by a wagon trail massacre, meet up years later on opposite sides of the law. **58m/C VHS.** Gilbert Roland, Charles Bickford, Marsha Hunt, J. Carrol Naish, James Craig, Monte Blue; **D:** Charles T. Barton. *GPV*

Thunder Warrior ⬥ *Thunder* 1985 (R) A young Indian turns into a one-man army determined to punish the local authorities who are abusing his fellow tribe members. **84m/C VHS, Beta.** Raymond Harmstorf, Bo Svenson, Mark Gregory; **D:** Larry Ludman. *TWE*

Thunder Warrior 2 ⬥ 1985 (PG-13) A tough Native American is provoked to violence by small-town prejudice. **114m/C VHS, Beta.** *IT* Mark Gregory, Karen Reel, Bo Svenson; **D:** Larry Ludman. *TWE*

Thunder Warrior 3 ⬥ 1988 The Indian Thunder has vowed to live in peace, but forswears the oath when his wife is kidnapped and family is terrorized. Revenge is the top priority as he torments the bad guys. **90m/C VHS.** Mark Gregory, John Phillip Law, Ingrid Lawrence, Werner Pochat, Horts Schon; **D:** Larry Ludman. *IMP*

Thunderball ⬥⬥½ 1965 (PG) The fourth installment in Ian Fleming's James Bond series finds 007 on a mission to thwart SPECTRE, which has threatened to blow up Miami by atomic bomb if 100 million pounds in ransom is not paid. One of the more tedious Bond entries but a big box-office success. Tom Jones sang the title song. Remade as "Never Say Never Again" in 1983 with Connery reprising his role as Bond after a 12-year absence. **125m/C VHS, Beta, LV.** *GB* Sean Connery, Claudine Auger, Adolfo Celi, Luciana Paluzzi, Rik von Nutter, Martine Beswick, Molly Peters, Guy Doleman, Bernard Lee, Lois Maxwell, Desmond Llewelyn; **D:** Terence Young; **W:** John Hopkins, Richard Maibaum; **C:** Ted Moore; **M:** John Barry. Academy Awards '65: Best Visual Effects. *MGM, TLF*

Thunderbolt & Lightfoot ⬥⬥⬥ 1974 (R) Eastwood is an ex-thief on the run from his former partners (Kennedy and Lewis) who believe he's made off with the loot from their last job, the robbery of a government vault. He joins up with drifter Bridges, who helps him to escape. Later, Eastwood manages to convince Kennedy he doesn't know where the money is. Bridges then persuades the men that they should plan the same heist and rob the same government vault all over again, which they do. But their getaway doesn't go exactly as planned. All-around fine acting; notable is Bridges' scene dressed in drag. First film for director Cimino. **115m/C VHS, Beta, LV.** Clint Eastwood, Jeff Bridges, George Kennedy, Geoffrey Lewis, Gary Busey; **D:** Michael Cimino; **W:** Michael Cimino; **M:** Dee Barton. Nominations: Academy Awards '74: Best Supporting Actor (Bridges). *MGM*

Thunderground ⬥ 1989 (R) A beautiful con artist teams with a fighter and together they travel to New Orleans to arrange a bout with the king of bare-knuckled fighting. **92m/C VHS, LV.** Paul Coufos, Margaret Langrick, Jesse Ventura, M. Emmet Walsh; **D:** David Mitchell. *IME*

Thunderheart ⬥⬥⬥ 1992 (R) Young FBI agent Kilmer is sent to an Oglala Sioux reservation to investigate a murder. He is himself part Sioux, but resents being chosen for the assignment because of it. Aided by a veteran partner (Shepard), Ray learns, professionally and personally, from a shrewd tribal police officer (well played by Greene). Set in the late 70's the film is loosely based on actual events plaguing the violence-torn Native American community at that time. Great cinematography by Roger Deakins. Filmed on the Pine Ridge Reservation in South Dakota. Director Apted deals with the actual incidents this film is based on in his documentary about Leonard Peltier, "Incident at Oglala." **CW:** Language and some areas of violence. **118m/C VHS, LV.** Val Kilmer, Sam Shepard, Graham Greene, Fred Ward, Fred Dalton Thompson, Sheila Tousey, Chief Ted Thin Elk, John Trudell, Dennis Banks, David Crosby; **D:** Michael Apted; **W:** John Fusco; **C:** Roger Deakins; **M:** James Horner. *COL, FCT, BTV*

Thundering Forest ⬥⬥ 1941 Australian actioneer pitting loggers against saboteurs. **?m/C VHS.** *AU* Frank Leighton. *LOO*

Thundering Gunslingers ⬥ 1940 A group of gunmen terrorizing townspeople finally meet their match in this Western. **61m/B VHS, Beta.** Buster Crabbe. *NOS, DVT*

Thundering Ninja ⬥½ 198? Three secret agents fight off an army of ninjas. Plenty of heel-to-head antics. **89m/C VHS, Beta.** Bernard Geurts, Joe Redner, Klaus Mutter, Ken Kerr, Jimmy Wang Yu; **D:** Joseph Kong. *TWE*

Thundering Trail ⬥ *Thunder on the Trail* 1951 Two cowboys encounter plenty of trouble before they take the President's newly appointed territorial governor to his office. **55m/B VHS, Beta.** Lash LaRue, Al "Fuzzy" St. John, Sally Anglim, Archie Twitchell, Ray Bennett. *NOS, DVT*

Thundersquad ⬥ 1985 Mercenaries help a South American rebel leader rescue his kidnapped son. **90m/C VHS, Beta.** Sal Borgese, Julia Fursich, Antonio Sabato. *NO*

Thursday's Child ⬥⬥ 1943 A child's success in films causes trouble for her family. Melodramatic and sappy, but Howes, as the kid, is excellent. One of Granger's early supporting roles. **95m/B VHS, Beta.** *GB* Stewart Granger, Sally Ann Howes, Wilfred Lawson, Kathleen O'Regan, Eileen Bennett, Marianne Davis, Gerhard Kempinski, Felix Aylmer, Margaret Yarde, Vera Bogetti, Percy Walsh, Ronald Shiner; **D:** Rodney Ackland; **W:** Rodney Ackland. *NOS, DVT, HEG*

Thursday's Game ⬥⬥⬥ 1974 (PG) Two crisis-besieged businessmen meet every Thursday, using poker as a ruse to work on their business and marital problems. Wonderful cast; intelligently written. Made for television. **99m/C VHS, Beta, LV.** Gene Wilder, Ellen Burstyn, Bob Newhart, Cloris Leachman, Nancy Walker, Valerie Harper, Rob Reiner; **D:** James L. Brooks; **W:** James L. Brooks. *THV*

THX 1138 ⬥⬥⬥ 1971 (PG) In the dehumanized world of the future, people live in underground cities run by computer, are force-fed drugs to keep them passive, and no longer have names—just letter/number combinations (Duvall is THX 1138). Emotion is also outlawed and when the computer-matched couple THX 1138 and LUH 3417 discover love, they must battle the computer system to escape. George Lucas' first film, which was inspired by a student film he did at USC. The laserdisc format carries the film in widescreen. **88m/C VHS, Beta, LV.** Robert Duvall, Donald Pleasence, Maggie McOmie; **D:** George Lucas; **W:** George Lucas; **M:** Lalo Schifrin. *WAR, FUS*

Tiara Tahiti ⬥⬥ 1962 Intrigue, double-cross, romance, and violence ensue when two old army acquaintances clash in Tahiti. Very fine performances from the two leading men. **100m/C VHS, Beta.** James Mason, John Mills, Claude Dauphin, Rosenda Monteros, Herbert Lom; **D:** Ted Kotcheff.

Ticket of Leave Man ⬥⬥ 1937 London's most dangerous killer fronts a charitable organization designed to help reform criminals. It actually steers them into a crime syndicate that cheats philanthropists out of their fortunes. **71m/B VHS, Beta.** *GB* Tod Slaughter, John Warwick, Marjorie Taylor. *VYY, SNC*

Ticket to Heaven ⬥⬥⬥ 1981 (PG) A young man, trying to deal with the painful breakup of a love affair, falls under the spell of a quasi-religious order. His friends and family, worried about the cult's influence, have him kidnapped in order for him to be de-programmed. Mancuso is excellent, as are his supporting players Rubinek and Thomson. **109m/C VHS, Beta.** *CA* Nick Mancuso, Meg Foster, Kim Cattrall, Saul Rubinek, R.H. Thomson, Jennifer Dale, Guy Boyd; **D:** Ralph L. Thomas; **W:** Anne Cameron. Genie Awards '82: Best Actor (Mancuso), Best Film, Best Supporting Actor (Rubinek). *MGM*

Ticket to Tomahawk ⬥⬥½ 1950 A gunslinger is hired by a stagecoach company to sabotage a railroad. Look for Marilyn Monroe as a chorus girl in a musical number. **90m/C VHS.** Anne Baxter, Rory Calhoun, Walter Brennan, Charles Kemper, Connie Gilchrist, Arthur Hunnicutt, Victor Sen Yung; **D:** Richard Sale. *TCF*

Tickle Me ⬥½ 1965 An unemployed rodeo star finds work at an all-girl health spa and dude ranch. He falls in love with a young lady who has a treasure map and keeps her safe from the evil men who want her fortune. For die-hard Elvis fans only. ♫(It's a) Long, Lonely Highway; Night Rider; It Feels So Right; Dirty, Dirty Feeling; (Such an) Easy Question; Put the Blame on Me; I'm Yours; I Feel That I've Known You Forever; Slowly but Surely. **90m/C VHS, Beta.** Elvis Presley, Julie Adams, Jack Mullaney; **D:** Norman Taurog. *FOX, MVD*

Ticks 🗡½ *Infested* 1993 **(R)** Mammoth mutant killer insects terrorize a Northern California campground! The predatory woodticks are the victims of steroids dumped in the water supply and a group of unwary teen campers fall prey to their deadly venom! And if that's not bad enough, a forest fire breaks out, trapping the teens! **85m/C VHS, LV, Closed Caption.** Ami Dolenz, Rosalind Allen, Alfonso Ribeiro, Peter Scolari; **D:** Tony Randel. *REP*

Tidal Wave 🗡½ *Nippon Chiubotsu; The Submersion of Japan; Japan Sinks* 1975 **(PG)** Scientists discover that Japan is slowly sinking and order the island to be evacuated. Originally a popular Japanese production, the American version is a poorly dubbed, re-edited mess. **82m/C VHS.** *JP* Lorne Greene, Keiju Kobayashi, Rhonda Leigh Hopkins, Hiroshi Fujioka, Shiro Moriana; **D:** Andrew Meyer. *NWV*

Tides of War 🗡🗡 1990 In the twilight of the second world war, a German officer begins to question his role in a proposed missile attack on Washington in light of the S.S. brutality he witnesses. **90m/C VHS.** Yvette Heyden, Rodrigo Obregon, David Soul, Bo Svenson; **D:** Neil Rossati. *NO*

Tidy Endings 🗡½ 1988 A man who died from AIDS leaves behind his male lover and his ex-wife. The two form a friendship as they both try to cope with the man's death. Based on the play by Fierstein. **54m/C VHS, Beta.** Harvey Fierstein, Stockard Channing; **D:** Gavin Millar; **W:** Harvey Fierstein. *PSM*

Tie Me Up! Tie Me Down! 🗡🗡½ *Atame* 1990 **(NC-17)** A young psychiatric patient kidnaps a former porno actress he has always had a crush on, and holds her captive, certain that he can convince her to love him. Black comedy features a fine cast and is well directed. At least one fairly explicit sex scene and the bondage theme caused the film to be X-rated, although it was originally released unrated by the distributor. In Spanish with English subtitles.**CW:** Adult situations; substance abuse, nudity, violence, and sexual situations. **105m/C VHS, LV.** *SP* Victoria Abril, Antonio Banderas, Loles Leon, Francesco Rabal, Julieta Serrano, Maria Barranco, Rossy de Palma; **D:** Pedro Almodovar; **W:** Pedro Almodovar; **C:** Jose Luis Alcaine; **M:** Ennio Morricone. *COL*

The Tie that Binds 🗡 1995 **(R)** Insipid thriller is a cheap imitation of its cousin, "The Hand that Rocks the Cradle" (made by the same producers), but what the former movie did to the nanny business, this flick does to a whole genre. Leanne and John Netherwood (Hannah and Carradine) are psycho parents out to reclaim their daughter from the lame-brain yuppie couple (Spano and Kelly) who adopted her. Out of all the children there, they choose the one who likes to sleep with a butcher knife under her pillow. Duh! Every "family in danger from psychotic" cliche is employed in a vain attempt to build suspense for the silly conclusion. Dismal directorial debut of screenwriter Strick.**CW:** Strong terror/violence; language; scene of sexuality. **98m/C VHS, LV, Closed Caption.** Daryl Hannah, Keith Carradine, Moira Kelly, Vincent Spano, Julia Devin, Ray Reinhardt, Cynda Williams; **D:** Wesley Strick; **W:** Michael Auerbach; **C:** Bobby Bukowski; **M:** Graeme Revell. *MAX*

Tiefland 🗡🗡½ 1944 Melodrama based on the libretto for D'Abert's opera about a gypsy dancer and her loves. Unreleased until 1954, this film is the last of Riefenstahl's career; she subsequently turned to still photography. In German with English subtitles. **98m/B VHS, Beta.** *GE* Leni Riefenstahl, Franz Eichberger, Bernard Minetti, Maria Koppenhofer, Luise Rainer; **D:** Leni Riefenstahl. *NOS, FCT, GLV*

Tiffany Jones 🗡 1975 **(R)** Tiffany Jones is a secret agent who has information that presidents and revolutionaries are willing to kill for. **90m/C VHS, Beta.** Anouska Hempel, Ray Brooks, Eric Pohlmann, Martin Benson, Susan Sneers; **D:** Pete Walker. *MON*

Tiger and the Pussycat 🗡🗡½ *Il Tigre* 1967 **(R)** A successful Italian businessman's infatuation with an attractive American art student leads him to marital and financial woes. **110m/C VHS, Beta.** Ann-Margret, Vittorio Gassman, Eleanor Parker; **D:** Dino Risi. *HHE*

Tiger Bay 🗡🗡🗡 1959 A young Polish sailor, on leave in Cardiff, murders his unfaithful girlfriend. Lonely ten-year-old Gillie sees the crime and takes the murder weapon, thinking it will make her more popular with her peers. Confronted by a police detective, she convincingly lies but eventually the sailor finds Gillie and kidnaps her, hoping to keep her quiet until he can get aboard his ship. A delicate relationship evolves between the child and the killer as she tries to help him escape and the police close in. Marks Hayley Mills' first film role and one of her finest performances. **107m/B VHS, Beta.** *GB* John Mills, Horst Buchholz, Hayley Mills, Yvonne Mitchell, Megs Jenkins, Anthony Dawson, Kenneth Griffith, Michael Anderson Jr.; **D:** J. Lee Thompson; **W:** John Hawkesworth; **C:** John Hawkesworth; **M:** Laurie Johnson. *PAR*

Tiger Claws 🗡½ 1991 **(R)** The pretty, petite Rothrock has been called the female Bruce Lee. Perhaps, but at least he got a good script every once in a while. This time Rothrock's a kung-fu cop investigating the strange ritual-murders of martial-arts champions.**CW:** Language and violence. **93m/C VHS, Beta, LV, Closed Caption.** Cynthia Rothrock, Bolo Yeung, Jalal Merhi; **D:** Kelly Markin. *USH*

Tiger Fangs 🗡½ 1943 When Nazis threaten the Far East rubber production with man-eating tigers, real-life big game hunter Frank Buck comes to the rescue. **57m/B VHS.** Frank Buck, June Duprez, Duncan Renaldo; **D:** Sam Newfield. *SNC, NOS, DVT*

Tiger Heart 🗡🗡½ 1996 **(PG-13)** Teenaged karate champ Eric Chase (Roberts) is looking forward to a lazy summer with girlfriend Stephanie (Lyons) before heading off to college. But when his neighborhood comes under attack from an unscrupulous developer and Stephanie runs afoul of his goons, Eric decides to take action.**CW:** Martial arts violence and menace. **90m/C VHS, Closed Caption.** Ted Jan Roberts, Jennifer Lyons, Robert LaSardo, Carol Potter, Timothy Williams; **D:** Georges Chamchoum; **W:** William Applegate Jr.; **M:** John Gonzalez. *PMH*

Tiger Joe 🗡 1985 There's trouble in Southeast Asia, and the U.S. military confuses things even more. **96m/C VHS.** Alan Collins, David Warbeck; **D:** Anthony (Antonio Margheriti) Dawson. *LIV*

Tiger of the Seven Seas 🗡🗡 1962 A female pirate takes over her father's command and embarks on adventures on the high seas. Generous portions of action, intrigue, and romance. Sequel to "Queen of the Pirates." **90m/C VHS.** *IT FR* Gianna Maria Canale, Anthony Steel, Grazia Maria Spina, Ernesto Calindri; **D:** Luigi Capuano. *NO*

Tiger Town 🗡🗡½ 1983 **(G)** A baseball player, ending an illustrious career with the Detroit Tigers, sees his chance of winning a pennant slipping away. A young fan, however, proves helpful in chasing that elusive championship. Made for the Disney cable station. **76m/C VHS, Beta.** Roy Scheider, Justin Henry, Ron McLarty, Bethany Carpenter, Noah Moazezi; **D:** Alan Shapiro; **C:** Robert Elswit. *DIS*

A Tiger Walks 🗡🗡½ 1964 A savage tiger escapes from a circus and local children start a nationwide campaign to save its life. Notable for its unflattering portrayal of America's heartland and small town dynamics. Radical departure from most Disney films of the period. **88m/C VHS, Beta.** Sabu, Pamela Franklin, Brian Keith, Vera Miles, Kevin Corcoran, Peter Brown, Una Merkel, Frank McHugh, Edward Andrews; **D:** Norman Tokar; **M:** Buddy Baker. *DIS*

Tiger Warsaw 🗡½ *The Tiger* 1987 **(R)** A young man returns to the town where he once lived, before he shot his father. He hopes to sort out his life and repair family problems. Muddled and sappy. **92m/C VHS, Beta.** Patrick Swayze, Barbara Williams, Piper Laurie, Bobby DiCicco, Kaye Ballard, Lee Richardson, Mary McDonnell; **D:** Amin Q. Chaudhri. *COL*

Tigers in Lipstick 🗡½ *Wild Beds* 1980 **(R)** Seven short vignettes featuring the beautiful actresses as aggressive women and the men that they influence. **88m/C VHS, Beta.** *IT* Laura Antonelli, Monica Vitti, Ursula Andress, Sylvia Kristel; **D:** Luigi Zampa. *MON*

A Tiger's Tale 🗡½ 1987 **(R)** A middle-aged divorced nurse begins an affair with her daughters's ex-boyfriend. **97m/C VHS, Beta, LV, Closed Caption.** Ann-Margret, C. Thomas Howell, Charles Durning, Kelly Preston, Ann Wedgeworth, Tim Thomerson, Steven Kampmann, Traci Lind, Angel Tompkins; **D:** Peter Douglas; **C:** Tony Pierce-Roberts. *NO*

Tigershark 🗡 1987 **(R)** A martial arts expert goes to Southeast Asia to rescue his girlfriend, who has been kidnapped by communist forces and held captive for arms and ammunition. Strictly for fans of the martial arts. **97m/C VHS, Beta.** Mike Stone, John Quade, Pamela Bryant; **D:** Emmett Alston; **W:** Ivan Rogers. *NO*

Tightrope 🗡🗡🗡 1984 **(R)** Police inspector Wes Block pursues a killer of prostitutes in New Orleans' French Quarter. The film is notable both as a thriller and as a fascinating vehicle for Eastwood, who experiments with a disturbing portrait of a cop with some peculiarities of his own. **115m/C VHS, Beta, LV, Closed Caption.** Clint Eastwood, Genevieve Bujold, Dan Hedaya, Jennifer Beck, Alison Eastwood, Randi Brooks, Regina Richardson, Jamie Rose; **D:** Richard Tuggle; **C:** Bruce Surtees; **M:** Lennie Niehaus. *WAR, TLF*

The Tigress 🗡½ 1993 **(R)** In 1920s Berlin two con artists set out to scam a rich American using sex as a lure. Things don't go as planned. Also available in an unrated version.**CW:** Language and sexuality. **89m/C VHS, LV, Closed Caption.** Valentina Vargas, James Remar, George Peppard. *THV*

Til There Was You 🗡½ 1996 **(PG-13)** You know what most great romance movies have in common? The couples actually meet each other before the end of the movie. Not here. That's one of the reasons this one isn't even good. Ghostwriter Gwen (Tripplehorn) and architect Nick (McDermott), although seemingly destined for one another, have more near-misses than a drunken, near-sighted airline pilot. They're shown in the same room, in adjoining rooms, leaving a room as soon as the other enters, etc., etc. Meanwhile, minor characters appear, speak some ham-fisted dialogue and then disappear. This happens for twenty years. Then they meet and the movie is (thankfully) over. Parker, however, does an excellent job as a rehab-addicted former child star who has ties to both characters. Feature directorial debut for Winant.**CW:** Sensuality, language and drug references. **113m/C VHS.** Dylan McDermott, Sarah Jessica Parker, Jeanne Tripplehorn, Jennifer Aniston, Ken Olin, Craig Bierko, Nina Foch, Alice Drummond, Christine Ebersole, Michael Tucker, Patrick Malahide; **D:** Scott Winant; **W:** Winnie Holzman; **C:** Bobby Bukowski; **M:** Miles Goodman, Terence Blanchard. *NYR*

Tilai 🗡🗡 *The Law* 1990 When Saga returns to his African village after a long absence, it's to discover that his young fiancee, Nogma, has been forced into marriage with his own father. According to his tribe's code of honor Saga can do nothing but love won't be denied and they begin an affair, which is deemed incestuous by the village. So Saga and Nogma flee, hoping to live out of the reach of tribal law. **81m/C VHS.** **D:** Idrissa Ouedraogo. Cannes Film Festival '90: Grand Jury Prize. *NYF*

Till Death Do Us Part 🎬½ 1972 (PG)
Three married couples spend a weekend at a counseling retreat, unaware that the proprietor is a murderous maniac. **77m/C VHS, Beta.** James Keach, Claude Jutra, Matt Craven; **D:** Timothy Brand. **VES**

Till Death Do Us Part 🎬🎬 1992 (R)
An ex-cop turns into an evil killer who seduces unsuspecting women and murders them for their insurance money. Contains footage not seen in the TV movie. Based on a true story and the book by Vincent Bugliosi. **CW:** Violence and sexual scene. **93m/C VHS, Beta.** Treat Williams, Arliss Howard, Rebecca Jenkins; **D:** Yves Simoneau. **TRI**

Till Marriage Do Us Part 🎬🎬½ Dio Mio, Come Sono Caduta in Basso; How Long Can You Fall?
1974 (R) An innocent couple discovers on their wedding night that they are really brother and sister. Since they can't in good conscience get a divorce or consummate their marriage, they must seek sexual gratification elsewhere. Antonelli is deliciously tantalizing in this silly satire. In Italian with English subtitles. **97m/C VHS, Beta, LV.** IT Laura Antonelli, Alberto Lionello, Jean Rochefort, Michele Placido, Karin Schubert; **D:** Luigi Comencini. **VES**

Till Murder Do Us Part 🎬🎬½ A Woman Scorned: The Betty Broderick Story 1992 (PG-13)
Based on the true story of Betty Broderick, an obsessively devoted wife and mother whose husband leaves her for another woman. Even after a bitter divorce, Betty refuses to let go. Until she commits murder. Made for television. **95m/C VHS.** Meredith Baxter, Stephen Collins, Michelle Johnson, Kelli Williams, Stephen Root; **D:** Dick Lowry. **NHO**

Till the Clouds Roll By 🎬🎬½ 1946
An all-star, high-gloss musical biography of songwriter Jerome Kern, that, in typical Hollywood fashion, bears little resemblance to the composer's life. Filled with wonderful songs from his Broadway hit. ♫ Showboat Medley; Till the Clouds Roll By; Howja Like to Spoon with Me?; The Last Time I Saw Paris; They Didn't Believe Me; I Won't Dance; Why Was I Born?; Who?; Sunny. **137m/C VHS, Beta, LV.** Robert Walker, Van Heflin, Judy Garland, Frank Sinatra, Lucille Bremer, Kathryn Grayson, June Allyson, Dinah Shore, Lena Horne, Virginia O'Brien, Tony Martin; **D:** Richard Whorf; **C:** Harry Stradling. **CNG, NOS, MGM**

Till the Clouds Roll By/A Star Is Born 🎬🎬🎬 1946
Ostensibly concerns the life and career of songwriter Jerome Kern. Highlighted by stellar performances from a number of musical stars of the day. Maudlin and unconcerned with factual accuracy, the film nonetheless is an exuberant celebration of Kern's talent. **249m/C VHS, Beta.** Judy Garland, Frank Sinatra, Robert Walker, Fredric March, Janet Gaynor, Andy Devine, Lionel Stander, Franklin Pangborn, Van Heflin, Lucille Bremer, Kathryn Grayson, Lena Horne, Tony Martin, Angela Lansbury, Dinah Shore, Virginia O'Brien, Cyd Charisse, Adolphe Menjou; **D:** William A. Wellman, Richard Whorf. **DVT**

Till the End of the Night 🎬½ 1994 (R)
D'arcy (Enos) is an ex-con who will do anything to get back his ex-wife Diana Davenport (Lang) and it doesn't matter that she has a new husband, John (Valentine) and two kids. D'arcy manages to kidnap Diana and it's up to John to save his wife. **90m/C VHS.** John Enos, Katherine Kelly Lang, Scott Valentine, David Keith; **D:** Larry Brand; **W:** Larry Brand. **COL**

Till the End of Time 🎬🎬½ 1946
Three GIs have trouble adjusting to civilian life in their home town after WWII. Fine performances and excellent pacing. Popular title song. Adapted from "They Dream of Home" by Niven Busch. **105m/C VHS, Beta, LV.** Robert Mitchum, Guy Madison, Bill Williams, Dorothy McGuire, William Gargan, Tom Tully; **D:** Edward Dmytryk. **TTC**

Till There was You 🎬 1991 (PG-13)
A struggling musician travels to a faraway tropical isle to solve the mystery of his brother's death. **94m/C VHS, Closed Caption.** Mark Harmon, Deborah Unger, Jeroen Krabbe, Shane Briant; **D:** John Seale; **M:** Graeme Revell. **USH**

Tillie Wakes Up 🎬🎬½ 1917
Third in the Tillie series, following "Tillie's Punctured Romance" and "Tillie's Tomato Surprise." Tillie (Dressler) decides she needs a little fun in her life so she asks her hen-pecked neighbor Mr. Pipkin (Hines) to spend the day with her on Coney Island. **48m/B VHS.** Marie Dressler, Johnny Hines, Frank Beamish, Ruby de Remer; **D:** Harry Davenport; **W:** Frances Marion. **GPV**

Tillie's Punctured Romance 🎬🎬 1914
The silent comedy which established Chaplin and Dressler as comedians. Chaplin, out of his Tramp character, is the city slicker trying to put one over on farm girl Dressler, who pursues revenge. First feature length comedy film. Followed by "Tillie's Tomato Surprise" and "Tillie Wakes Up," which starred Dressler but not Chaplin. **73m/B VHS, Beta, LV.** Charlie Chaplin, Marie Dressler, Mabel Normand, Mack Swain, Chester Conklin; **D:** Mack Sennett. **NOS, CCB, HHT**

Tilt 🎬 1978 (PG)
Flimsy storyline concerns a young runaway's adventures with an aspiring rock star. Shields' pinball expertise eventually leads her to a match against pinball champ Durning. **111m/C VHS.** Charles Durning, Ken Marshall, Brooke Shields, Gregory Lewis; **D:** Rudy Durand; **W:** Rudy Durand, Donald Cammell. **NO**

Tim 🎬🎬½ 1979
Follows the relationship between a handsome, mentally retarded young man and an attractive older businesswoman. Sappy storyline is redeemed by Gibson's fine debut performance. Based on Colleen McCullough's first novel. **94m/C VHS, Beta.** AU Mel Gibson, Piper Laurie, Peter Gwynne, Alwyn Kurts, Pat Evison; **D:** Michael Pate. Australian Film Institute '79: Best Actor (Gibson). **MED, OM**

Tim Tyler's Luck 1937
Lost but not forgotten serial in its twelve-chapter entirety. The fearless Tim Tyler uses whatever he can to do battle with the sinister Spider Web gang. **235m/B VHS.** Frankie Thomas Jr., Frances Robinson, Al Shear, Norman Willis, Earl Douglas, Jack Mulhall, Frank Mayo, Pat O'Brien; **D:** Ford Beebe, Wyndham Gittens. **NOS, GPV, FCT**

Timber Queen 🎬🎬 1944
A WWII flier comes home and aids his best friend's widow, who must make a quota of timber or lose her sawmill to gangsters. Old-fashioned. **66m/B VHS.** Richard Arlen, Mary Beth Hughes, June Havoc, Sheldon Leonard, George E. Stone, Dick Purcell; **D:** Frank McDonald. **NOS, LOO**

Time After Time 🎬🎬🎬 1979 (PG)
In Victorian London, circa 1893, H.G. Wells is experimenting with his time machine. He discovers the machine has been used by an associate, who turns out to be Jack the Ripper, to travel to San Francisco in 1979. Wells follows to stop any further murders and the ensuing battle of wits is both entertaining and imaginative. McDowell is charming as Wells and Steenburgen is equally fine as Well's modern American love interest. **112m/C VHS, Beta, LV.** Malcolm McDowell, David Warner, Mary Steenburgen, Patti D'Arbanville, Charles Cioffi; **D:** Nicholas Meyer; **W:** Nicholas Meyer; **M:** Miklos Rozsa. National Board of Review Awards '79: 10 Best Films of the Year. **WAR**

Time Bandits 🎬🎬½ 1981 (PG)
A group of dwarves help a young boy to travel through time and space with the likes of Robin Hood, Napoleon, Agamemnon, and other time-warp playmates. Epic fantasy from Monty Python alumni. **110m/C VHS, Beta, LV, Closed Caption.** GB John Cleese, Sean Connery, Shelley Duvall, Katherine Helmond, Ian Holm, Michael Palin, Ralph Richardson, Kenny Baker, Peter Vaughan, David Warner; **D:** Terry Gilliam; **W:** Michael Palin, Terry Gilliam; **C:** Peter Biziou. **PAR**

Time Chasers 🎬🎬 1995
Nick Miller (Burch) invents a device that permits his airplane to travel through time. But, after selling his invention, he soon discovers that it has turned the future into a desolate wasteland. Now Nick must try to regain control and put things back to normal. **90m/C VHS.** Matthew Burch, Bonnie Pritchard, Peter Harrington; **D:** David Giancola. **SDE**

Time Fighters 🎬½ 1985
A time machine has the ability to travel at the speed of light from prehistoric times to the distant future. This is a great help to the Time fighters. **60m/C VHS, Beta.**

Time Flies When You're Alive 1989
A made-for-cable-television presentation of actor Linke's performance monologue detailing the traumas and experiences he and his family underwent as his wife Francesca slowly died of cancer. **79m/C VHS, Beta.** Paul Linke; **D:** Roger Spottiswoode. **HBO**

A Time for Miracles 🎬½ 1980
Dramatic biography of the first native-born American saint, Elizabeth Bayley Seton, who was canonized in 1975. Made for television. **97m/C VHS, Beta.** Kate Mulgrew, Lorne Greene, Rossano Brazzi, John Forsythe, Jean-Pierre Aumont, Milo O'Shea; **D:** Michael O'Herlihy. **NLC**

Time for Revenge 🎬🎬½ 1982
A demolitions worker attempts to blackmail his corrupt employer by claiming a workplace explosion made him speechless. He finds himself in a contest of silence and wits. In Spanish with English subtitles. **112m/C VHS, Beta.** AR Federico Luppi, Haydee Padilla, Julio de Grazia, Ulises Dumont; **D:** Adolfo Aristarain. Montreal World Film Festival '82: Best Film. **XVC, MED, AUD**

The Time Guardian 🎬½ 1987 (PG)
Time-travelers of the future arrive in the Australian desert in 1988, intent on warning the local populace of the impending arrival of killer cyborgs from the 40th century. Muddled and confusing. **89m/C VHS, Beta, LV, 8mm.** Tom Burlinson, Carrie Fisher, Dean Stockwell, Nikki Coghill; **D:** Brian Hannant; **W:** Brian Hannant, John Baxter; **C:** Geoff Burton. **COL, NLC**

Time Indefinite 🎬🎬 1993
Cinema verite effort once again follows filmmaker McElwee who returns to his Southern roots to confront personal tragedy by recording every moment on film. It is an emotional journey in which he discovers that his camera may not be enough to protect him from his own feelings. Moving, with occasional lapses into self-absorption. Companion film to McElwee's "Sherman's March." **117m/C VHS.** **D:** Ross McElwee; **W:** Ross McElwee. **FRF**

Time is Running Out 🎬🎬 1952
A man races against the clock in this taut thriller. **?m/C VHS.** Dave Clark, Mike Smith, Lenny Davidson. **SNC**

Time Lock 🎬🎬 1957
An expert safecracker races against time to save a child who is trapped inside a bank's pre-set time-locked vault. Canada is the setting, although the film was actually made in England. Based on a play by Arthur Hailey. **73m/B VHS, Beta.** GB Sean Connery, Robert Beatty, Lee Patterson, Betty McDowall, Vincent Winter; **D:** Gerald Thomas. **NO**

The Time Machine 🎬🎬🎬 1960
English scientist living near the end of the 19th century invents time travel machine and uses it to travel into various periods of the future. Rollicking version of H.G. Wells' classic cautionary tale boasts Oscar-winning special effects. Remade in 1978. **103m/C VHS, Beta, LV.** Rod Taylor, Yvette Mimieux, Whit Bissell, Sebastian Cabot, Alan Young; **D:** George Pal; **C:** Paul Vogel. Academy Awards '60: Best Special Effects. **MGM, MLB**

Time Machine 🎬½ 1978 (G)
Yet another adaptation of H.G. Wells' classic novel about a scientist who invents a machine that enables him to travel through time. Inferior remake of the 1960 version. **99m/C VHS, Beta.** John Beck, Priscilla Barnes, Andrew Duggan; **D:** Henning Schellerup. **NO**

A Time of Destiny 🎬🎬 1988 (PG-13)
During WWII, an American soldier vows to kill his brother-in-law, who he believes caused his father's death. Meanwhile, the two men have become good friends in the army, never realizing their connection. A strange, overblown family saga from the director of "El Norte." Beautiful photography, terrific editing. **118m/C VHS, Beta, LV, 8mm.** William Hurt, Timothy Hutton, Melissa Leo, Stockard Channing, Megan Follows, Francesco Rabal; **D:** Gregory

Nava; **W:** Gregory Nava, Anna Thomas; **M:** Ennio Morricone. COL

Time of Indifference 🎬🎬 Gli Indifferenti; Les Deux Rivales 1964
Based on the novel by Alberto Moravia. Tale of the disintegration of values in 1920s Italy is unable to take full advantage of its fine cast or potentially thought-provoking themes. **84m/B VHS.** IT Rod Steiger, Shelley Winters, Claudia Cardinale, Paulette Goddard, Tomas Milian; **D:** Francesco Maselli. GKK

Time of the Apes 🎬 1987
A Japanese-made horror film about a woman and two kids thrust into an underground world ruled by intelligent gorillas. **98m/C VHS, Beta.** JP CEL

Time of the Gypsies 🎬🎬🎬 Dom Za Vesanje 1990 (R)
Acclaimed Yugoslavian saga about a homely, unlucky Gypsy boy who sets out to steal his way to a dowry large enough to marry the girl of his dreams. Beautifully filmed, magical, and very long. In the Gypsy language, Romany, it's the first feature film made in the Gypsy tongue. **136m/C VHS, Beta, LV.** YU Davor Dujmovic, Sinolicka Trpkova, Ljubica Adzovic, Hunsija Hasimovic, Bora Todorovic; **D:** Emir Kusturica. Cannes Film Festival '89: Best Director (Kusturica). COL

The Time of Their Lives 🎬🎬½ The Ghost Steps Out 1946
A pair of Revolutionary War-era ghosts haunt a modern country estate. One of the best A & C comedies. **82m/B VHS, Beta.** Bud Abbott, Lou Costello, Marjorie Reynolds, Binnie Barnes, Gale Sondergaard, John Shelton; **D:** Charles T. Barton. USH

The Time of Your Life 🎬🎬½ 1948
The only Cagney film that ever lost money. A simple but engaging story of people trying to live their dreams. Cagney is delightful as a barroom philosopher who controls the world around him from his seat in the tavern. Although it was not very popular with audiences at the time, the critics hailed it as an artistic achievement. Based on William Saroyan's play. **109m/B VHS.** James Cagney, William Bendix, Jeanne Cagney, Broderick Crawford, Ward Bond, James Barton, Paul Draper, Natalie Schafer; **D:** H.C. Potter. NOS, VEC, HEG

Time Out for Love 🎬🎬½ Les Grandes Personnes; The Five Day Lover 1961
An American girl travels to Paris in search of romance, but discovers more than she bargained for. In French with English subtitles. **91m/B VHS.** IT FR Jean Seberg, Micheline Presle, Maurice Ronet, Francoise Prevost, Annabelle Ninchi, Fernando Bruno; **D:** Jean Valere; **M:** Georges Delerue. DVT, HEG

Time Runner 🎬🎬 1992 (R)
It's 2022 and the Earth is being used as target practice by alien invaders. Space captain Hamill manages to find a hole in time and slip back to 1992 where he can battle the first of the alien infiltrators and maybe change Earth's destiny. The time-travel theme (including Hamill watching his own birth) is fun and the special effects are well done. **CW:** Language and violence. **90m/C VHS, LV, Closed Caption.** Mark Hamill, Brion James, Rae Dawn Chong; **D:** Michael Mazo. NLC, COL

Time Stands Still 🎬🎬🎬 1982
Two brothers experience troubled youth in Budapest. Artful, somberly executed, with American pop soundtrack. Subtitled in English. **99m/C VHS, Beta.** HU Istvan Znamenak, Henrik Pauer, Aniko Ivan, Sander Soth, Peter Galfy; **D:** Peter Gothar. New York Film Critics Awards '82: Best Foreign Film. COL

Time to Die 🎬½ Seven Graves for Rogan 1983 (R)
WWII victim of heinous war crimes, obsessed with revenge, stalks his prey for a final confrontation, while eluding U.S. intelligence. Disappointing despite good cast working with Mario Puzo story. **89m/C VHS, Beta.** Edward Albert, Rex Harrison, Rod Taylor, Raf Vallone; **D:** Matt Cimber; **M:** Ennio Morricone. MED

A Time to Die 🎬½ 1991 (R)
Lords plays a police photographer who, well, photographs the police. But her camera catches one in the act of murder. Routine crime thriller. **CW:** Violence and drug content and sensuality. **93m/C VHS, LV.** Traci Lords, Jeff Conaway, Richard Roundtree, Bradford Bancroft, Nitchie Barrett; **D:** Charles Kanganis; **W:** Charles Kanganis; **M:** Ennio Morricone. PMH

Time to Kill Tempo di Uccidere 1989 (R)
A young soldier in Africa wanders away from his camp and meets a woman whom he rapes and kills. But when he returns to his outfit he finds he can't escape his tormenting conscience. **CW:** Occasional strong language and one scene of brute sexuality. **110m/C VHS, LV, Closed Caption.** Nicolas Cage, Giancarlo Giannini, Robert Liensol; **D:** Giuliano Montaldo; **W:** Furio Scarpelli; **M:** Ennio Morricone. REP

A Time to Kill 🎬🎬🎬½ 1996 (R)
Powerful story of revenge, racism, and the question of justice in the "new south." John Grisham had a lot of clout when he finally sold his first and favorite novel to the movies, including veto power over the leading man—director Schumacher was for Woody Harrelson, Grisham was opposed but both finally agreed on newcomer McConaughey. He's outstanding as idealistic smalltown Mississippi lawyer Jake Brigance, called to defend anguished father Carl Lee Hailey (Jackson), who's accused of killing the rednecks who raped his young daughter. Jake's assisted by former mentor Lucien Wilbanks (Sutherland) and ambitious northern law student Ellen Roark (Bullock) against ruthless prosecutor Rufus Buckley (Spacey). Is it emotionally manipulative? You betcha. But Grisham's done well on screen and Schumacher (who also did "The Client") knows how to get the most from his cast and script. **CW:** Violence and some graphic language. **150m/C VHS, LV, Closed Caption, DVD.** Matthew McConaughey, Samuel L. Jackson, Sandra Bullock, Kevin Spacey, Donald Sutherland, Brenda Fricker, Oliver Platt, Charles S. Dutton, Kiefer Sutherland, Chris Cooper, Ashley Judd, Patrick McGoohan, Rae'ven Kelly, John Diehl, Tonea Stewart, M. Emmet Walsh, Anthony Heald, Kurtwood Smith; **D:** Joel Schumacher; **W:** Akiva Goldsman; **C:** Peter Menzies Jr.; **M:** Elliot Goldenthal. MTV Movie Awards '97: Breakthrough Performance (McConaughey); Nominations: Golden Globe Awards '97: Best Supporting Actor (Jackson); MTV Movie Awards '97: Best Female Performance (Bullock), Best Villain (Sutherland). MGM

A Time to Live 🎬½ 1985
Made-for-television adaptation of Mary Lou Weisman's "Intensive Care" about a family's adjustment to a young boy's fight with Muscular Dystrophy. Minnelli's first appearance in a television movie. **97m/C Beta.** Liza Minnelli, Jeffrey DeMunn, Swoosie Kurtz, Corey Haim, Scott Schwartz; **D:** Rick Wallace; **M:** Georges Delerue. NO

A Time to Live and a Time to Die 🎬🎬 Tong Nien Wang Shi 1985
Family from southern mainland China emigrate to Taiwan in the '40s to escape from hardship and are unable to return after the communist takeover. They find themselves cut off from their cultural heritage, and though the years pass, everyone still thinks of the mainland as home. Taiwanese with subtitles. **137m/C VHS.** CH D: Hou Hsaio-hsien. FCT

A Time to Love & a Time to Die 🎬🎬½ 1958
Lush adaptation of Erich Maria Remarque novel about a young WWII German soldier who falls in love with a young girl during furlough. The two are married, only to be separated when he is forced to return to the Russian front. Sympathetic treatment of Germans opposed to Hitler's policies. Hutton's first film, credited to his real name, Dana J. Hutton. **133m/C VHS, Beta.** John Gavin, Lilo (Liselotte) Pulver, Jock Mahoney, Keenan Wynn, Klaus Kinski, Jim Hutton; **D:** Douglas Sirk; **M:** Miklos Rozsa. Nominations: Academy Awards '58: Best Sound. BAR

A Time to Remember 🎬½ 1990
Sticky with sentiment, this family film tells of a boy with a gift for singing, encouraged by a priest, discouraged by his father. At one point the kid loses his voice—he probably choked on the pathos. **90m/C VHS.** Donald O'Connor, Morgana King. IGP

Time Trackers 🎬🎬 1988 (PG)
A Roger Corman cheapie about a race through time, from present-day New York to medieval England, to recover a time machine before it alters the course

of history. **87m/C VHS, Beta.** Kathleen Beller, Ned Beatty, Will Shriner; **D:** Howard R. Cohen. MGM

The Time Travelers 🎬🎬 Time Trap 1964
Scientists discover and pass through a porthole leading to earth's post-armageddon future where they encounter unfriendly mutants. Frightened, they make a serious effort to return to the past. Remade as "Journey to the Center of Time." **82m/C VHS, Beta.** Preston Foster, Phil Carey, Merry Anders, John Hoyt, Joan Woodbury, Dolores Wells, Dennis Patrick; **D:** Ib Melchior. NO

Time Troopers 🎬 Morgen Grauen; Morning Terror 1989 (R)
In another post-nuke society, special police must execute anyone who has misused their allotted "energy clips" for illicit behavior. Dime-store budget sci-fi. **90m/C VHS, Beta.** AT Albert Fortell, Hannelore Elsner; **D:** L.E. Neiman. PSM

Time Walker 🎬 1982 (PG)
An archaeologist unearths King Tut's coffin in California. An alien living inside is unleashed and terrorizes the public. **86m/C VHS, Beta.** Ben Murphy; **D:** Tom Kennedy; **M:** Richard Band. NLC

Time Without Pity 🎬🎬½ 1957
Anti-capital punishment plea finds desperate alcoholic David Graham (Redgrave) discovering that his son Alec (McCowen) is about to be executed for murder. But David doesn't believe in the boy's guilt and has 24 hours to find the real killer. The audience knows Alec is innocent from the get-go, making for a certain suspense. Based on the play "Someone Waiting" by Emlyn Williams. **88m/B VHS.** GB Michael Redgrave, Alec McCowen, Ann Todd, Leo McKern, Peter Cushing, Renee Houston, Paul Daneman, Lois Maxwell, Richard Wordsworth, George Devine, Joan Plowright; **D:** Joseph Losey; **W:** Ben Barzman; **C:** Freddie Francis; **M:** Tristram Cary. HMV, TVC

Timebomb 🎬🎬½ 1991 (R)
When someone attempts to kill Biehn, he turns to a beautiful psychiatrist for help. She triggers flashbacks that send her hunted patient on a dangerous, perhaps deadly, journey into his past. **CW:** Occasional strong language, graphic violence, and strong sensuality. **96m/C VHS, Beta, LV, Closed Caption.** Michael Biehn, Patsy Kensit, Tracy Scoggins, Robert Culp, Richard Jordan, Raymond St. Jacques, Jim Maniaci, Billy Blanks, Ray "Boom Boom" Mancini, Steven J. Oliver; **D:** Avi Nesher; **W:** Avi Nesher; **M:** Patrick Leonard. MGM

Timecop 🎬🎬½ 1994 (R)
"Terminator" rip-off is fodder for Van Damme followers with lots of action and special effects (you weren't expecting acting too). 2004 policeman Max Walker (Van Damme) must travel back in time to prevent corrupt politician Aaron McComb (Silver) from altering history for personal gain. It's also Walker's chance to alter his personal history since his wife Melissa (Sara) was killed in an explosion he can now prevent. Futuristic thriller based on a Dark Horse comic. **98m/C VHS, LV, Closed Caption.** Jean-Claude Van Damme, Ron Silver, Mia Sara, Bruce McGill, Scott Lawrence, Kenneth Welsh, Gabrielle Rose, Duncan Fraser, Ian Tracey, Gloria Reuben, Scott Bellis, Jason Schombing, Kevin McNulty, Sean O'Byrne, Malcolm Stewart, Alfonso Quijada, Glen Roald, Theodore Thomas; **D:** Peter Hyams; **W:** Mark Verheiden, Gary De Vore. USH

Timemaster 🎬🎬½ 1995 (PG-13)
The orphaned 12-year-old Jesse (Cameron-Glickenhaus) dreams his parents are alive in another time, so he asks inventor Isaiah (Morita) for help. The duo discover Jesse's parents are being held hostage by a galactic dictator (Dorn), who's using them in sinister virtual-reality games and Jesse must time-travel to rescue them. **CW:** Some strong action-adventure violence. **100m/C VHS, LV, Closed Caption.** Jesse Cameron-Glickenhaus, Noriyuki "Pat" Morita, Joanna Pacula, Michael Dorn, Duncan Regehr, Michelle Williams; **D:** James Glickenhaus; **W:** James Glickenhaus. USH

Timepiece 🎬🎬 1965
This tape features one of Jim Henson's earlier films about an overworked, young executive. **10m/C VHS, Beta.** Jim Henson. FLL

Timerider 🎬½ *The Adventure of Lyle Swan* **1983 (PG)** Motorcyclist riding through the California desert is accidentally thrown back in time to 1877, the result of a scientific experiment that went awry. There he finds no gas stations and lots of cowboys. Co-written and co-produced by Michael Nesmith, best known for his days with the rock group "The Monkees." **93m/C VHS, Beta, LV.** Fred Ward, Belinda Bauer, Peter Coyote, Richard Masur, Ed Lauter, L.Q. Jones, Tracey Walter; *D:* William Dear; *W:* William Dear. *NO*

Times of Harvey Milk 1983 A powerful and moving documentary about the life and career of San Francisco supervisor and gay activist Harvey Milk. The film documents the assassination of Milk and Mayor George Moscone by Milk's fellow supervisor, Dan White. Highly acclaimed by both critics and audiences, the film gives an honest and direct look at the murder and people's reactions. News footage of the murders and White's trial is included. **90m/C VHS, Beta, LV.** *D:* Robert Epstein. Academy Awards '83: Best Feature Documentary. *TPV*

Times Square 1980 (R) A 13-year-old girl learns about life on her own when she teams up with a defiant, anti-social child of the streets. Unappealing and unrealistic, the film features a New Wave music score. **111m/C VHS, Beta.** Tim Curry, Trini Alvarado, Robin Johnson, Peter Coffield, Elizabeth Pena, Anna Maria Horsford; *D:* Allan Moyle; *W:* Jacob Brackman. *NO*

Times to Come 🎬🎬🎬 *Lo Que Vendra* **1981** Taut thriller reminiscent of bleak futuristic movies like "Clockwork Orange." Three people try to survive in a desolate, aggressive, and unstable future. In Spanish with English subtitles. **98m/C VHS.** *AR* Hugo Soto, Juan Leyrado, Charly Garcia; *D:* Gustavo Mosquera. *CCN, FCT, TPV*

Timestalkers 🎬🎬½ **1987** A college professor's infatuation with a young woman is complicated by their pursuit of a criminal from the 26th century into the past. Mildly entertaining adventure. Tucker's last film. Made for television. **100m/C VHS.** William Devane, Lauren Hutton, Klaus Kinski, John Ratzenberger, Forrest Tucker, Gail Youngs; *D:* Michael A. Schultz. *FRH*

Tin Cup 🎬🎬🎬 **1996 (R)** You've got your romantic triangle, you've got your sports, you've got Costner reteamed with Shelton—"Bull Durham" on a golf course? Can lightening strike twice? Ron "Tin Cup" McAvoy (Costner) is a West Texas golf hustler who has the ability but not the steadiness to be on the pro tour. When McAvoy decides on a last-ditch effort to qualify for the U.S. Open, he turns to psychologist Dr. Molly Griswold (Russo) to get his game together. And the fact that Molly is the girlfriend of McAvoy's longtime rival—and successful PGA player—Don Simms (Johnson), well Tin Cup isn't adverse to playing for the lady's affections either. The U.S. Open scenes were filmed at Houston's Kingwood Country Club and the actors do hit their own shots. *CW:* Language and brief nudity. **133m/C VHS, LV, Closed Caption.** Kevin Costner, Don Johnson, Rene Russo, Richard "Cheech" Marin, Linda Hart, Dennis Burkley, Rex Linn, Lou Myers, Richard Lineback, Mickey Jones; *D:* Ron Shelton; *W:* Ron Shelton, John Norville; *C:* Russell Boyd; *M:* William Ross. Nominations: Golden Globe Awards '97: Best Actor—Musical/Comedy (Costner). *MGM*

The Tin Drum 🎬🎬🎬🎬 *Die Blechtrommel* **1979 (R)** German child in the 1920s wills himself to stop growing in response to the increasing Nazi presence in Germany. He communicates his anger and fear by pounding on a tin drum. Memorable scenes, excellent cast. In German with English subtitles. Adapted from the novel by Gunter Grass. **141m/C VHS, Beta.** *GE* David Bennent, Mario Adorf, Angela Winkler, Daniel Olbrychski, Katharina Thalbach, Heinz Bennent, Andrea Ferreol, Charles Aznavour; *D:* Rainer Werner Fassbinder, Volker Schlondorff; *W:* Jean-Claude Carriere, Volker Schlondorff; *M:* Maurice Jarre. Academy Awards '79: Best Foreign Language Film; Cannes Film Festival '79: Best Film; Los Angeles Film Critics Association Awards '80: Best Foreign Film; National Board of Review Awards '80: 5 Best Foreign Films of the Year. *KIV, APD, GLV*

Tin Man 🎬🎬½ **1983** Garage mechanic born totally deaf designs and builds a computer that can both hear and speak for him. His world is complicated, however, when a young speech therapist introduces him to new and wonderful sounds and unscrupulous and exploitative computer salesmen. Interesting premise and nice performances. **95m/C VHS, Beta.** Timothy Bottoms, Deana Jurgens, Troy Donahue; *D:* John G. Thomas. *MED*

Tin Men 🎬🎬½ **1987 (R)** Set in Baltimore in the 1960s, this bitter comedy begins with two aluminum-siding salesmen colliding in a minor car accident. They play increasingly savage pranks on each other until one seduces the wife of the other, ruining his marriage. Like "Diner," the movie is full of Levinson's idiosyncratic local Baltimore color. **112m/C VHS, Beta, LV, Closed Caption.** Richard Dreyfuss, Danny DeVito, Barbara Hershey, John Mahoney, Jackie Gayle, Stan Brock, Seymour Cassel, Bruno Kirby, J.T. Walsh, Michael Tucker; *D:* Barry Levinson; *W:* Barry Levinson; *C:* Peter Sova; *M:* David Steele. *TOU*

Tin Pan Alley 🎬🎬½ **1940** Tin Pan Alley songwriters Oakie and Payne meet singing sisters Faye and Grable, who agree to plug their material. At first their music business thrives but when the women head off to sing in a hit London show, the business goes downhill. Since WWI has been declared, the boys enlist and wind up in England, where they get a second chance to see their gals. The first teaming of Faye and Payne, who would star together in three more films. Remade as "I'll Get By." ♫The Sheik of Araby; You Say the Sweetest Things, Baby; America I Love You; Goodbye Broadway, Hello France; K-K-K-Katy; Moonlight Bay; Honeysuckle Rose; Moonlight and Roses. **92m/B VHS.** Alice Faye, John Payne, Betty Grable, Jack Oakie, Allen Jenkins, Esther Ralston, John Loder, Elisha Cook Jr., Fred Keating, Billy Gilbert; *D:* Walter Lang; *W:* Robert Ellis, Helen Logan; *C:* Leon Shamroy; *M:* Alfred Newman. Academy Awards '40: Best Score. *FXV*

The Tin Soldier 🎬🎬½ **1995 (PG)** Updated version of the Hans Christian Andersen story finds 12-year-old Billy (Knight) moving with his widowed mom (Sheedy) to a tough L.A. neighborhood. He's intimidated by the school bully to join a gang and smitten by a pretty girl who doesn't like his new friends. What's a guy to do? Why meet a mysterious toy shop owner (DeLuise), who gives Billy a tin soldier that magically transforms into a very real medieval knight named Yarik (Voight). Good intentions—no subtlety. Voight's directorial debut; made for cable TV. **99m/C VHS, Closed Caption.** Trenton Knight, Ally Sheedy, Dom DeLuise, Jon Voight; *D:* Jon Voight. *REP*

The Tin Star 🎬🎬🎬 **1957** Perkins is the young sheriff who persuades veteran bounty hunter Fonda to help him rid the town of outlaws. Excellent Mann western balances humor and suspense. **93m/B VHS, Beta.** Henry Fonda, Anthony Perkins, Betsy Palmer, Neville Brand, Lee Van Cleef, John McIntire, Michel Ray; *D:* Anthony Mann; *C:* Loyal Griggs; *M:* Elmer Bernstein. Nominations: Academy Awards '57: Best Story & Screenplay. *PAR, BAR*

The Tingler 🎬🎬🎬 **1959** Coroner Price discovers that a creepy creature is capable of growing on the human spine and increasing in size through fear. The only way to get rid of it is through constant screaming. Price takes what is probably the screen's first LSD trip and a partial color sequence fights nice red blood pouring from a faucet. One of Castle's cheesy best that originally wowed movie audiences in "Percepto" format, which consisted of installing electric buzzers under the seats for that true tingling sensation. **82m/B VHS.** Vincent Price, Darryl Hickman, Judith Evelyn, Philip Coolidge, Patricia Cutts; *D:* William Castle; *W:* Robb White. *COL*

Tintorera...Tiger Shark woof! *Tintorera; Tintorera...Bloody Waters* **1978 (R)** Three shark hunters attempt to discover why buxom swimmers are disappearing. Phony takeoff of "Jaws." **91m/C VHS, Beta.** *GB MX* Susan George, Fiona Lewis, Jennifer Ashley; *D:* Rene Cardona Jr. *MED*

Tiny Toon Adventures: How I Spent My Vacation 🎬🎬🎬 **1991** How the tiny toons of Acme Acres spend their summer vacation in this animated adventure that spoofs several popular films and amusements. Plucky Duck and Hampton Pig journey to "Happy World Land" (a takeoff on Walt Disney World), Babs and Buster Bunny's water adventure parodies "Deliverance," there's a spoof of "The Little Mermaid," and the Road Runner even makes a cameo appearance. Parents will be equally entertained by the level of humor and the fast-paced action. Based on the Steven Spielberg TV cartoon series, this is the first made-for-home-video animated feature ever released in the United States. **80m/C VHS, Beta, LV, 8mm, Closed Caption.** *WAR*

The Tioga Kid 🎬½ **1948** Dean takes on two roles here, that of a Texas Ranger and an outlaw who goes by the name of "The Tioga Kid." Andy Parker and the Plainsmen provide the cowboy tunes. **54m/B VHS.** Eddie Dean, Roscoe Ates, Jennifer Holt, Dennis Moore, William "Bill" Fawcett; *D:* Ray Taylor; *W:* Ed Earl Repp. *MOV*

The Tip-Off 🎬🎬½ **1931** Lovable boxer (Armstrong) and vivacious girlfriend (Rogers) save less-than-bright friend from getting involved with mean mobster's girlfriend. Major chemistry between Rogers and Armstrong. **75m/B VHS.** Eddie Quillan, Robert Armstrong, Ginger Rogers, Joan Peers, Ernie Adams; *D:* Albert Rogell. *TTC, FCT*

'Tis a Pity She's a Whore 🎬🎬½ *Addio, Fratello, Crudele* **1973 (R)** A brother and sister engage in an incestuous affair. She becomes pregnant and is married off. Her husband, however, becomes infuriated when he learns of his wife's pregnancy. Photography is by Vittorio Storaro in this highly stylized drama set in Renaissance Italy. **102m/C VHS, Beta.** *IT* Charlotte Rampling, Oliver Tobias, Fabio Testi, Antonio Falsi, Rick Battaglia, Angela Luce, Rino Imperio; *D:* Giuseppe Patroni Griffi; *M:* Ennio Morricone. *ACA*

Titanic 🎬🎬🎬 **1953** Hollywoodized version of the 1912 sinking of the famous luxury liner sets the scene for the personal drama of a mother (Stanwyck) who wants to flee her husband (Webb) for a new life in America. Story gets a little too melodramatic, but it's not a bad retelling of the sea tragedy. Film is quite effective in conveying the panic and the calm of the actual sinking. A 20-foot-long model of the ship was built for the re-creation of that fateful moment when the "Titanic" hit the inevitable iceberg. **98m/B VHS.** Clifton Webb, Barbara Stanwyck, Robert Wagner, Richard Basehart, Audrey Dalton, Thelma Ritter, Brian Aherne; *D:* Jean Negulesco; *W:* Charles Brackett, Walter Reisch, Richard L. Breen. Academy Awards '53: Best Story & Screenplay; Nominations: Academy Awards '53: Best Art Direction/Set Decoration (B & W), Best Screenplay, Best Story. *FXV*

Titanic 🎬½ **1996 (PG-13)** Dull and draggy TV version of the 1912 tragedy between the luxury liner and an iceberg that resulted in the deaths of more than 1000 passengers. There are the usual romantic subplots, villains, and heroes, and Scott is properly noble as the veteran captain making his last voyage before retirement. Otherwise you've seen this many times before. *CW:* Scene of sexual assault and other violent elements. **?m/C VHS.** George C. Scott, Peter Gallagher, Catherine Zeta Jones, Eva Marie Saint, Tim Curry, Roger Rees, Harley Jane Kozak, Marilu Henner, Felicity Waterman, Scott Hylands, Kevin McNulty, Malcolm Stewart; *D:* Robert Lieberman; *W:* Ross LaManna, Joyce Eliason; *C:* David Hennings; *M:* Lennie Niehaus. *EVE*

Title Shot *&* 1981 (R) A crafty manager convinces a millionaire to bet heavily on the guaranteed loss of his heavyweight contender in an upcoming fight. He doesn't realize the boxer is too stupid to throw the fight. 88m/C VHS, Beta. Tony Curtis, Richard Gabourie, Susan Hogan, Robert Delbert; *D:* Les Rose. LIV

Tito and Me *&&&* 1992 Ten-year-old Zoran lives in 1954 Belgrade and is fascinated by Yugoslavian leader Marshall Tito. Crowded into a flat with his extended family, Zoran learns about volatility firsthand. Then there's romance—he has a crush on a classmate who breaks up with him when she is chosen as one of Tito's Young Pioneers, which means a two-week trip to the country. Political indoctrination means nothing but love—ahh. Debut role for the young Vojnov, who carries the weight of the movie with perfect aplomb. In Serbo-Croation with English subtitles. 104m/C VHS. *YU* Dimitrie Vojnov, Lazar Ristovski, Anica Dobra, Predrag Manojlovic, Olivera Markovic; *D:* Goran Markovic; *W:* Goran Markovic. FXL, FCT

TNT Jackson woof! 1975 (R) A kung fu mama searches for her brother while everyone in Hong Kong tries to kick her out of town. 73m/C VHS, Beta. Jeanne Bell; *D:* Cirio H. Santiago. NLC

To All a Goodnight woof! 1980 (R) Five young girls and their boyfriends are planning an exciting Christmas holiday until a mad Santa Claus puts a damper on things. Total gorefest, with few, if any, redeeming virtues. 90m/C VHS, Beta. Jennifer Runyon, Forrest Swanson, Linda Gentile, William Lover; *D:* David Hess. MED

To All My Friends on Shore *&&&* 1971 A made-for-television story about a father dealing with his young son's sickle cell anemia. Fine performances, realistic script make this an excellent outing. 74m/C VHS, Beta. Bill Cosby, Gloria Foster, Dennis Hines; *D:* Gilbert Cates. NO

To Be or Not to Be *&&&½* 1942 Sophisticated black comedy set in wartime Poland. Lombard and Benny are Maria and Josef Tura, the Barrymores of the Polish stage, who use the talents of their acting troupe against the invading Nazis. The opening sequence is regarded as a cinema classic. One of Benny's finest film performances, the movie marks Lombard's final screen appearance. Classic Lubitsch. Remade in 1983. 102m/B VHS, Beta. Carole Lombard, Jack Benny, Robert Stack, Sig Rumann, Lionel Atwill, Felix Bressart, Helmut Dantine, Tom Dugan, Charles Halton; *D:* Ernst Lubitsch. Nominations: Academy Awards '42: Original Dramatic/Comedy Score. VES, WAR

To Be or Not to Be *&&½* 1983 (PG) In this remake of the 1942 film, Bancroft and Brooks are actors in Poland during WWII. They accidently become involved with the Polish Resistance and work to thwart the Nazis. Lots of laughs, although at times there's a little too much slapstick. 108m/C VHS, Beta, LV, Closed Caption. Mel Brooks, Anne Bancroft, Charles Durning, Jose Ferrer, Tim Matheson, Christopher Lloyd; *D:* Alan Johnson; *W:* Ronny Graham. Nominations: Academy Awards '83: Best Supporting Actor (Durning). FOX

To Be the Best *&½* 1993 (R) Eric, a member of the U.S. Kickboxing Team, lets his love for the beautiful Cheryl and his hot temper get the best of him. When a ruthless gambler threatens to kill Cheryl if Eric doesn't throw his big match, he joins with his family, fellow teammates, and most feared opponent, to set things right. 99m/C VHS, Closed Caption. Mike Worth, Martin Kove, Phillip Troy, Brittney Powell, Alex Cord, Steven Leigh; *D:* Joseph Merhi; *W:* Michael January. PMH

To Catch a Killer *&&&* 1992 A chilling performance by Dennehy highlights this true-crime tale of a detective's relentless pursuit of serial killer John Wayne Gacy, who preyed on young men and hid the bodies in his home. Made for television. 95m/C VHS, LV. Brian Dennehy, Michael Riley, Margot Kidder, Meg Foster; *D:* Eric Till. WOV

To Catch a King *&&* 1984 Garr is a singer working in Wagner's nightclub in 1940s' Lisbon. The pair becomes involved in trying to foil the Nazi plot to kidnap the vacationing Duke and Duchess of Windsor. Average made-for-cable fare. 120m/C VHS, Beta. Robert Wagner, Teri Garr, Horst Janson, Barbara Parkins, John Standing; *D:* Clive Donner; *M:* Nick Bicat. PSM

To Catch a Thief *&&&* 1955 On the French Riviera, a reformed jewel thief falls for a wealthy American woman, who suspects he's up to his old tricks when a rash of jewel thefts occur. Oscar-winning photography by Robert Burks, a notable fireworks scene, and snappy dialogue. A change of pace for Hitchcock, this charming comedy-thriller proved to be as popular as his other efforts. Kelly met future husband Prince Rainier during shooting in Monaco. Based on the novel by David Dodge. 103m/C VHS, Beta, LV. Cary Grant, Grace Kelly, Jessie Royce Landis, John Williams, Charles Vanel, Brigitte Auber; *D:* Alfred Hitchcock; *W:* John Michael Hayes; *C:* Robert Burks. Academy Awards '55: Best Color Cinematography; Nominations: Academy Awards '55: Best Art Direction/Set Decoration (Color), Best Costume Design (Color). PAR, MLB, HMV

To Cross the Rubicon *&&½* 1991 Romantic comedy finds Kendall (Royce) getting dumped by David (Souther), her boyfriend of eight years, who then reconciles with former flame, Claire (Devon). Meanwhile, Kendall involves herself with James (Burke), a young musician, and becomes new best friends with—you guessed it—Claire. But will David and Kendall's previous relationship cause friction? 120m/C VHS. Patricia Royce, J.D. Souther, Lorraine Devon, Billy Burke; *D:* Barry Caillier; *W:* Patricia Royce, Lorraine Devon. MTH

To Dance with the White Dog *&&&* 1993 (PG) Robert Samuel Peek (Cronyn) is a pecan-tree grower from rural Georgia who has been married to Cora (Tandy) for 57 years. Then she dies and their fussing daughters (Baranski and Wright) wonder how their father will survive. But Sam's increasing loneliness is checked when he befriends a stray white dog that it seems no one else can see. Based on the novel by Terry Kay. Made for television. 98m/C VHS, Closed Caption. Hume Cronyn, Jessica Tandy, Christine Baranski, Amy Wright, Esther Rolle, Harley Cross, Frank Whaley, Terry Beaver, Dan Albright, David Dwyer; *D:* Glenn Jordan; *W:* Susan Cooper; *C:* Neil Roach. REP

To Die for *&½* 1989 (R) A vampire stalks, woos, and snacks on a young real estate woman. 99m/C VHS, Beta, LV. Brendan Hughes, Scott Jacoby, Duane Jones, Steve Bond, Sydney Walsh, Amanda Wyss, Ava Fabian; *D:* Deran Sarafian; *W:* Cliff Eidelman. ACA

To Die For *&&&* 1995 (R) Beauteous, manipulative Suzanne Stone (Kidman) wants to be somebody—preferably a big TV personality—and nothing will stop her. She recruits a scruffy threesome to help her ice sweet-but-dim hubby, Larry (Dillon), even if it does mean seducing aimless teenager Jimmy (Phoenix). Black comedy, loosely based on the Pamela Smart murder case and adapted from the novel by Joyce Maynard, takes on the media-obsessed culture with a wicked grin. Van Sant retains his fresh and hip storytelling in his first film for a major studio. Backed by Henry's zesty script, all the actors shine—with standout performances from Kidman as the monstrous Suzanne and Phoenix (River's younger brother) as the lost/horny Jimmy. Shot entirely in Canada. *CW:* Strong sexual content; language. 103m/C VHS, LV, 8mm, Closed Caption. Nicole Kidman, Matt Dillon, Joaquin Rafael (Leaf) Phoenix, Casey Affleck, Alison Folland, Illeana Douglas, Dan Hedaya, Wayne Knight, Kurtwood Smith, Holland Taylor, Maria Tucci, Susan Traylor; *Cameos:* George Segal, Buck Henry; *D:* Gus Van Sant; *W:* Buck Henry, Danny Elfman; *M:* Danny Elfman. Golden Globe Awards '96: Best Actress—Musical/Comedy (Kidman); Broadcast Film Critics Association Awards '95: Best Actress (Kidman); Nominations: British Academy Awards '95: Best Actress (Kidman); MTV Movie Awards '96: Most Desirable Female (Kidman). COL

To Die for 2: Son of Darkness *&½* 1991 (R) This far outclasses part one in terms of acting and production values, but the plot still isn't back from the grave. Strange, because all the vampires are; despite their fiery deaths last time they flock around the adoptive mother of a baby secretly sired by a bloodsucker. 95m/C VHS, Closed Caption. Rosalind Allen, Steve Bond, Scott Jacoby, Michael Praed, Jay Underwood, Amanda Wyss, Remy O'Neill; *D:* David F. Price. THV

To Die Standing *&½* 1991 (R) Two mavericks team up to do what the D.E.A. and cops simply cannot... capture a dangerous international drug lord. High action. 87m/C VHS, LV. Cliff DeYoung, Robert Beltran, Jamie Rose, Gerald Anthony, Orlando Sacha, Michael Ford; *D:* Louis Morneau; *W:* Ross Bell, Daryl Haney. COL

To Forget Venice *&&½* 1979 Portrays the sensitive relationships among four homosexuals, and their shared fears of growing older. Dubbed in English. 90m/C VHS, Beta. *IT* Erland Josephson, Mariangela Melato, David Pontremoli, Elenora Giorgi; *D:* Franco Brusati. Nominations: Academy Awards '79: Best Foreign Language Film. COL

To Gillian on Her 37th Birthday *&&* 1996 (PG-13) Overly sentimental weeper explores the effects of a mother's death on the ones she's left behind. Gillian's been dead for two years but widower David Lewis (Gallagher) hasn't been able to let her spirit go and daughter Rachel (Danes) is having trouble growing up with a father who spends more time on the beach with his dead wife's ghost than with her. Enter nosy sister-in-law Esther (Baker) and annoying husband (Altman) who try to set him up on the anniversary of Gillian's death and you've got a mental family breakdown coming. Pfeiffer appears as Gillian in this script by husband Kelley, based on the play by Michael Brady. *CW:* Scene involving strong language, and for some sensuality and teen drinking. 92m/C VHS, LV, Closed Caption. Peter Gallagher, Claire Danes, Kathy Baker, Wendy Crewson, Bruce Altman; *Cameos:* Michelle Pfeiffer; *D:* Michael Pressman; *W:* David E. Kelley; *C:* Tim Suhrstedt; *M:* James Horner. COL

To Grandmother's House We Go *&&½* 1994 The Olsen twins want to give mom a restful Christmas vacation so they decide to visit Grandma (on their own) and wind up in the hands of a pair of bumbling kidnappers. Made for TV movie. 89m/C VHS, Closed Caption. Ashley Olsen, Mary-Kate Olsen, Cynthia Geary, Rhea Perlman, J. Eddie Peck, Stuart Margolin; *Cameos:* Bob Saget, Lori Loughlin; *D:* Jeff Franklin; *W:* Jeff Franklin. WAR

To Have & Have Not *&&&½* 1944 Martinique charter boat operator gets mixed up with beautiful woman and French resistance fighters during WWII. Top-notch production in every respect. Classic dialogue and fiery romantic bouts between Bogart and Bacall. Bacall's first film. Based on a story by Ernest Hemingway. Remade in 1950 as "The Breaking Point" and in 1958 as "The Gun Runners." 100m/B VHS, Beta, LV. Humphrey Bogart, Lauren Bacall, Walter Brennan, Hoagy Carmichael, Marcel Dalio, Dolores Moran, Sheldon Leonard, Dan Seymour; *D:* Howard Hawks. MGM

To Heal a Nation *&&½* 1988 The story of veteran Jan Scruggs, who spearheaded the movement to build the Vietnam Veterans memorial. The then little-known Ross Perot provided major financial support for Scruggs' dream. Made for television. 100m/C VHS. Eric Roberts, Conrad Bachmann, Glynnis O'Connor, Marshall Colt, Scott Paulin, Lee Purcell, Laurence Luckinbill, Linden Chiles, Brock Peters; *D:* Michael Pressman; *W:* Lionel Chetwynd. TTC

To Hell and Back *&&½* 1955 Adaptation of Audie Murphy's autobiography. Murphy plays himself, from his upbringing to WWII, where he was the most-decorated American soldier. Features realistic battle sequences punctuated with grand heroics. 106m/C VHS, Beta. Audie Murphy, Marshall Thompson, Jack Kelly; *D:* Jesse Hibbs. USH, TLF

To Joy 🎬🎬🎬 1950 The rocky marriage of a violinist and his wife illuminate the problems of the young in Swedish society. Early Bergman. In Swedish with English subtitles or dubbed. 90m/B VHS, Beta, LV. *SW* **D:** Ingmar Bergman. NO

To Kill a Clown 🎬🎬 1972 (R) Painter and his wife working to save their marriage are trapped on an isolated island and terrorized by a crazed Vietnam veteran. This helps pull them together. Some holes in the plot, but generally effective. 82m/C VHS, Beta. Alan Alda, Blythe Danner, Heath Lamberts; **D:** George Bloomfield. MED

To Kill a Mockingbird 🎬🎬🎬🎬 1962 Faithful adaptation of powerful Harper Lee novel, both an evocative portrayal of childhood innocence and a denunciation of bigotry. Peck's performance as southern lawyer defending a black man accused of raping a white woman is flawless. Duvall debuted as the dim-witted Boo Radley. Lee based her characterization of "Dill" on Truman Capote, a childhood friend. 129m/B VHS, Beta, LV. Gregory Peck, Brock Peters, Phillip Alford, Mary Badham, Robert Duvall, Rosemary Murphy, William Windom, Alice Ghostley, John Megna, Frank Overton, Paul Fix, Collin Wilcox; **D:** Robert Mulligan; **W:** Horton Foote; **M:** Elmer Bernstein. Academy Awards '62: Best Actor (Peck), Best Adapted Screenplay, Best Art Direction/Set Decoration (B & W); Golden Globe Awards '63: Best Actor—Drama (Peck), Best Score; Nominations: Academy Awards '62: Best Black and White Cinematography, Best Director (Mulligan), Best Picture, Best Supporting Actress (Badham), Best Original Score. KUI, USH, BTV

To Kill a Priest 🎬🎬 1989 (R) Based on the true story of Father Jerzy Popieluszko, a young priest in 1984 Poland who defies his church and speaks out publicly on Solidarity. He is killed by the government as a result. Harris is good as the menacing police official. 110m/C VHS, Beta, LV, Closed Caption. Christopher Lambert, Ed Harris, David Suchet, Tim Roth, Joanne Whalley, Pete Postlethwaite, Cherie Lunghi, Joss Ackland; **D:** Agnieszka Holland; **W:** Agnieszka Holland; **C:** Adam Holender; **M:** Georges Delerue. COL

To Kill a Stranger 🎬🎬 1984 A beautiful pop singer is stranded in a storm, and then victimized by a mad rapist/murderer. 100m/C VHS, Beta. Donald Pleasence, Dean Stockwell, Angelica Maria, Aldo Ray, Sergio Aragones. NO

To Live 🎬🎬🎬🎬 Huozhe 1994 Superb drama follows the lives of one family—weak but adaptable Fugui (You), his strong-willed wife Jiazhen (Li), and their young daughter and son—from prerevolutionary China in the 1940s through the '60s Cultural Revolution. Fugui loses the family fortune in the gambling houses, actually a blessing when the Communists come to power, and the family must struggle to survive financial and increasingly difficult political changes, where fate can change on a whim. Subtle saga about ordinary human lives reacting to terrifying conditions boasts extraordinary performances and evocative imagery. Adapted from the novel "Lifetimes" by Yu Hua. Chinese with subtitles. 130m/C VHS, LV. *CH* Ge You, Gong Li, Niu Ben, Guo Tao, Jiang Wu; **D:** Zhang Yimou; **W:** Lu Wei, Yu Hua; **M:** Zhao Jiping. British Academy Awards '94: Best Foreign Film; Cannes Film Festival '94: Best Actor (You), Grand Jury Prize; Nominations: Golden Globe Awards '95: Best Foreign Film. HMK, IME

To Live and Die in Hong Kong 🎬½ 1989 Two sailors arrive in Hong Kong for a little R & R, until they are mistaken for spies by both the Hong Kong police and the Chinese mob. Action-packed tale. 98m/C VHS. Rowena Cortes, Lawrence Jan, Mike Kelly, Laurens C. Postma; **D:** Lau Shing Hon. ELV

To Live & Die in L.A. 🎬🎬 1985 (R) Fast-paced, morally ambivalent tale of cops and counterfeiters in L.A. After his partner is killed shortly before his retirement, a secret service agent sets out to track down his ruthless killer. Lots of violence; some nudity. Notable both for a riveting car chase and its dearth of sympathetic characters. 114m/C VHS, Beta, LV, Closed Caption.

William L. Petersen, Willem Dafoe, John Pankow, Dean Stockwell, Debra Feuer, John Turturro, Darlanne Fluegel, Robert Downey; **D:** William Friedkin; **W:** William Friedkin. LIV, VES

To Love Again 🎬½ 1980 A middle-aged love story about a reclusive college professor and the campus handyman. 96m/C VHS, Beta. Lynn Redgrave, Brian Dennehy, Conchata Ferrell; **D:** Joseph Hardy. NLC

To Paris with Love 🎬🎬½ 1955 A British man and his son fall in love with a shop girl and her boss while on vacation in Paris. Charming and humorous, with a witty performance from Guinness. 75m/C VHS, Beta. Alec Guinness, Odile Versois, Vernon Gray; **D:** Robert Hamer; **M:** Edwin Astley. NO

To Play or To Die 🎬🎬 1991 The introverted Kees attends an all-boy school where powerful bullies and sadomasochistic games are the rule. Kees is fascinated by the handsome Charel, the bullies leader. He invites Charel to his home, intending to turn the tables on his tormentor, but nothing goes as planned. Intense and controversial look at gay teens. Directorial debut of Krom. In Dutch with English subtitles. 150m/C VHS. *NL* Geert Hunaerts, Tjebbo Gerritsma; **D:** Frank Krom; **W:** Anne Van De Putte, Frank Krom. WBF

To Play the King 🎬🎬 1993 Sequel to "The House of Cards" finds Francis Urquhart (Richardson), having murdered his way to the Prime Ministery, now bored with his political situation. But things may be changing—the Queen has been succeeded by her liberal son (Kitchen) and Francis, goaded by his equally vicious wife (Fletcher), plots treachery to bring down the monarchy. Followed by "The Final Cut;" adapted from the novel by Michael Dobbs. 212m/C VHS, Closed Caption. *GB* Ian Richardson, Michael Kitchen, Diane Fletcher, Kitty Aldridge, Bernice Stegers, Colin Jeavons, Rowena King, Erika Hoffman, Nicholas Farrell; **D:** Paul Seed; **W:** Andrew Davies. FOX, TVC

To Please a Lady 🎬🎬½ Red Hot Wheels 1950 Romantic comedy-drama about race car driver Gable and reporter Stanwyck. Although leads do their best with the script, they're unable to generate any sparks. However, race track scenes are excellent. Filmed at the Indianapolis Speedway, the spectacular racing footage makes up for overall average film. 91m/B VHS. Clark Gable, Barbara Stanwyck, Adolphe Menjou, Will Geer, Roland Winters; **D:** Clarence Brown; **W:** Barre Lyndon, Marge Decker. MGM

To Protect and Serve 🎬🎬 1992 (R) When crooked cops start getting killed, two young cops are assigned to investigate. Suspicion points to a rookie (Howell), who just may have decided to clean things up his own way. **CW:** Language, violence and drug use, and sexuality. 93m/C VHS. C. Thomas Howell, Leslie Deane, Richard Romanus, Joe Cortese; **D:** Eric Weston. LIV

To Race the Wind 🎬🎬 1980 Blind man wants to be treated like a normal person as he struggles through Harvard Law School. Based upon Harold Krents' autobiography "Butterflies Are Free." Made for television. 97m/C VHS, Beta. Steve Guttenberg, Lisa Eilbacher, Randy Quaid, Barbara Barrie; **D:** Walter Grauman. UNI

To See Paris and Die 🎬🎬 1993 Elena Orekhova (Vasilyeva) is a Russian stage mother who will do absolutely anything to ensure pianist son Yuri gets chosen for a prestigious competition in Paris—even though she knows secrets from her past could place a blight on his career. Russian with subtitles. 100m/C VHS. *RU* Tatyana Vasilyeva; **D:** Alexander Proshkin. NYF

To See Such Fun 1981 Hilarious excerpts from 80 years of the greatest British movie comedies. 90m/C VHS, Beta. *GB* Peter Sellers, Marty Feldman, Benny Hill, Eric Idle, Alec Guinness, Margaret Rutherford, Dirk Bogarde, Spike Milligan. NO

To Sir, with Love 🎬🎬 1967 Teacher in London's tough East End tosses books in the wastebasket and proceeds to teach his class about life. Skillful and warm performance by Poiti-

er as idealistic teacher; supporting cast also performs nicely. Based on the novel by E.R. Braithwaite. LuLu's title song was a big hit in 1967-68. 105m/C VHS, Beta. *GB* Sidney Poitier, Lulu, Judy Geeson, Christian Roberts, Suzy Kendall, Faith Brook; **D:** James Clavell; **W:** James Clavell. COL

To Sleep with a Vampire 🎬🎬 1992 (R) A Los Angeles bloodsucker is tired of his violent existence and craves the one thing he can't have—daylight. As he stalks his latest victim, a stripper, he decides to take her home and have her tell him about living in daytime. When she realizes what's going on, the intended victim decides to fight for her life. Action and eroticism raises this one above the norm. Remake of "Dance of the Damned." **CW:** Language, violence, and sexuality. 90m/C VHS. Scott Valentine, Charlie Spradling, Richard Zobel, Ingrid Vold, Stephanie Hardy; **D:** Adam Friedman. NHO

To Sleep with Anger 🎬🎬🎬½ 1990 (PG) At first a comic, introspective look at a black middle-class family going about their business in the heart of Los Angeles. Sly charmer Glover shows up and enthralls the entire family with his slightly sinister storytelling and a gnawing doom gradually permeates the household. Insightful look into the conflicting values of Black America. Glover's best performance. 105m/C VHS, Beta, Closed Caption. Danny Glover, Mary Alice, Paul Butler, Richard Brooks, Carl Lumbly, Vonetta McGee, Sheryl Lee Ralph; **D:** Charles Burnett; **W:** Charles Burnett; **C:** Walt Lloyd. Independent Spirit Awards '91: Best Actor (Glover), Best Director (Burnett), Best Screenplay, Best Supporting Actress (Ralph); National Society of Film Critics Awards '90: Best Screenplay; Sundance Film Festival '90: Special Jury Prize. COL, FCT, IME

To the Death 🎬½ 1993 (R) A kickboxer wants to retire from the boxing tournaments but the corrupt promoters refuse to let him go unless he manages to kill his rivals in the ring. 90m/C VHS, LV, Closed Caption. John Barrett, Michael Quissi; **D:** Darrell Roodt. CAN

To the Devil, A Daughter 🎬🎬 Child of Satan 1976 (R) A nun is put under a spell by a priest who has been possessed by Satan. She is to bear his child. A writer on the occult intervenes. Based on the novel by Dennis Wheatley. One of Kinski's early films. 93m/C VHS, Beta. Richard Widmark, Christopher Lee, Nastassia Kinski, Honor Blackman, Denholm Elliott, Michael Goodliffe; **D:** Peter Sykes; **C:** David Watkin. REP, MLB

To the Last Man 🎬 1933 An early Scott sagebrush epic, about two feuding families. Temple is seen in a small role. Based on Zane Grey's novel of the same name. 70m/B VHS, Beta. Randolph Scott, Esther Ralston, Jack LaRue, Noah Beery Sr., Buster Crabbe, Gail Patrick, Barton MacLane, Fuzzy Knight, John Carradine, Jay Ward, Shirley Temple; **D:** Henry Hathaway. NOS, DVT, MLB

To the Lighthouse 🎬🎬 1983 A proper British holiday turns into a summer of disillusionment in this adaptation of the Virginia Woolf novel. 115m/C VHS, Beta. Rosemary Harris, Michael Clough, Suzanne Bertish, Lynsey Baxter. NO

To the Limit 🎬 1995 (R) Actioner finds the pulchritudinous Colette (Smith) revealing to mobster Frank (Travolta) that she's a CIA agent (and if you believe that I have a bridge in Brooklyn to sell you) and that they are the targets of a rogue agent (Richmond). No, Smith can't act but since she takes lots of showers and is supported by some professionals who can, this gets by on trash value alone. **CW:** Strong sexuality, violence and language. 96m/C VHS. Anna Nicole Smith, Joey Travolta, Michael Nouri, Branscombe Richmond, John Aprea, Kathy Shower, Rebecca Ferratti, David Proval; **D:** Raymond Martino; **W:** Joey Travolta, Raymond Martino; **M:** Jim Halfpenny. PMH

To the Shores of Hell 🎬🎬 1965 Leaving his sweetheart behind, Major Greg Donahue attacks Da Nang and plots to rescue his brother from the Viet Cong. 82m/C VHS, Beta. Marshall Thompson, Kiva Lawrence, Richard Jordahl. NO

To the Shores of Tripoli 🎬🎬 1942 Wartime propaganda in the guise of drama, in which a smarmy playboy is transformed into a Marine in boot camp. 82m/C VHS, Beta. John Payne, Maureen O'Hara, Randolph Scott, Nancy Kelly, Harry (Henry) Morgan, Maxie "Slapsie" Rosenbloom, William Tracy, Minor Watson, Alan Hale Jr., Hugh Beaumont, Hillary Brooke; **D:** H. Bruce Humberstone. Nominations: Academy Awards '42: Best Color Cinematography. FOX, MLB

To Wong Foo, Thanks for Everything, Julie Newmar 🎬🎬½ 1995 (PG-13) Hot on the high heels of "The Adventures of Priscilla, Queen of the Desert," comes the sanitized for your protection Yankee version. And its all about hanging on to your dreams and how we're all the same inside, with politically correct gay drag queens doing the sermonizing. Yes, this is the feel-good drag road movie for the 90s. Den mother Vida (Swayze), tough beauty queen Noxeema (Snipes), and hot-blooded Chi Chi (Leguizamo doing his best Rosie Perez) head to Hollywood in a 1967 Cadillac convertible that inconveniently breaks down in a tiny Nebraska town. The "girls" work their magic, and presumably the people of this uncultured, anachronistic backwater will never be the same. One-dimensional characters, flat direction, and inconsistent script undercut exceptional efforts by Swayze and Leguizamo.**CW:** Subject matter involving men living in drag; brief scene of spousal abuse; some language. 108m/C VHS, LV, Closed Caption. Wesley Snipes, Patrick Swayze, John Leguizamo, Stockard Channing, Blythe Danner, Melinda Dillon, Arliss Howard, Jason London, Christopher Penn; **Cameos:** Julie Newmar, Robin Williams; **D:** Beeban Kidron; **W:** Douglas Carter Beane; **M:** Rachel Portman. Nominations: Golden Globe Awards '96: Best Actor—Musical/Comedy (Swayze), Best Supporting Actor (Leguizamo).USH

The Toast of New Orleans 🎬🎬½ 1950 A poor fisherman rises to stardom as an opera singer. Likable, though fluffy production features a plethora of musical numbers. 🎵Be My Love; Tina Lina; I'll Never Love You; The Toast of New Orleans; Song of the Bayou; Boom Biddy Boom Boom. 97m/C VHS, Beta. Kathryn Grayson, Mario Lanza, David Niven, Rita Moreno, J. Carrol Naish; **D:** Norman Taurog. Nominations: Academy Awards '50: Best Song ("Be My Love"). MGM

Toast of New York 🎬🎬🎬 1937 Arnold plays Jim Fisk, a New England peddler who rises to become one of the first Wall Street giants of industry. Atypical Grant performance. 109m/B VHS, Beta, LV. Edward Arnold, Cary Grant, Frances Farmer, Jack Oakie, Donald Meek, Billy Gilbert; **D:** Rowland V. Lee. TTC

Tobor the Great 🎬½ 1954 Sentimental and poorly executed, this film tells the tale of a boy, his grandfather, and Tobor the robot. Villainous communists attempt to make evil use of Tobor, only to be thwarted in the end. 77m/B VHS, LV. Charles Drake, Billy Chapin, Karin Booth, Taylor Holmes, Joan Gerber, Steve Geray; **D:** Lee Sholem. REP

Tobruk 🎬🎬 1966 American GI's endeavor to knock out the guns of Tobruk, to clear the way for a bombing attack on German fuel supply depots of North Africa in this WWII actioner. 110m/C VHS, Beta. Rock Hudson, George Peppard, Guy Stockwell, Nigel Green; **D:** Arthur Hiller. USH

Toby McTeague 🎬🎬 1987 (PG) A story about an Alaskan family that breeds Siberian Huskies. When his father is injured, the youngest son tries to replace him in the regional dog-sled race. 94m/C VHS, Beta, LV. Winston Rekert, Wannick Bisson, Timothy Webber; **D:** Jean-Claude Lord; **W:** Djordje Milicevic, Jamie Brown. COL, NLC

Toby Tyler 🎬🎬🎬 1959 (G) A boy runs off to join the circus, and teams up with a chimpanzee. A timeless and enjoyable Disney film that still appeals to youngsters. Good family-fare. 93m/C VHS, Beta. Kevin Corcoran, Henry Calvin, Gene Sheldon, Bob Sweeney; **D:** Charles T. Barton. DIS

Today I Hang 🎬🎬 1942 A man is framed for murder and sentenced to hang. His buddies on the outside do their best to prove his innocence. Meanwhile, in prison, the accused encounters any number of interesting characters. 67m/B VHS, Beta. Walter Woolf King, Mona Barrie, William Farnum, Harry Woods, James Craven; **D:** Oliver Drake. SNC

Today We Kill, Tomorrow We Die 🎬 1971 (PG) A rancher is unjustly sent to prison; when his sentence is over he hires a gang to relentlessly track down the culprit who framed him. 95m/C VHS, Beta. Montgomery Ford, Bud Spencer, William Berger, Tatsuya Nakadai, Wayde Preston; **D:** Tonino Cervi. PSM

Today We Live 🎬🎬½ 1933 Triangle love story set in WWI. Crawford is a hedonistic Brit having a fling with her naval brother's (Tone) friend (Young). When American flyer Cooper appears she sets her sights on him but soon he's off to combat in France where he's reported killed. Crawford returns to Young but, naturally, reports of Cooper's death have been greatly exaggerated and the two eventually reunite. Faulkner co-scripted from his story "Turn About" which had no female character and concerned the rivalry between naval officers and fly boys. 113m/B VHS, Beta. Gary Cooper, Joan Crawford, Franchot Tone, Robert Young, Roscoe Karns, Louise Closser Hale; **D:** Howard Hawks; **W:** Dwight Taylor, William Faulkner, Edith Fitzgerald. MGM, FCT

The Todd Killings 🎬½ A Dangerous Friend; Skipper 1971 (R) A psychotic young man commits a series of murders involving young women. Sleazy, forgettable picture wastes a talented cast. 93m/C VHS. Robert F. Lyons, Richard Thomas, Barbara Bel Geddes, Ed Asner, Sherry Miles, Gloria Grahame, Belinda J. Montgomery; **D:** Barry Shear; **W:** Joel Oliansky. WAR

Toga Party 🎬 1979 (R) Fraternity house throws a wild toga party in this raunchy low-rent depiction of college life. 82m/C VHS, Beta. Bobby H. Charles, Mary Mitchell. NO

Together? 🎬½ 1979 (R) Divorced woman and a male chauvinist test the limits of their sexual liberation as well as viewer patience. 91m/C VHS, Beta. IT Maximilian Schell, Jacqueline Bisset, Terence Stamp, Monica Guerritore; **D:** Armenia Balducci; **M:** Burt Bacharach.

Togetherness 🎬½ 1970 Two wealthy, good-for-nothing playboys chase after the same blonde, a Communist, in Greece. 101m/C VHS, Beta, LV. George Hamilton, Peter Lawford, Olinka Berova, John Banner, Jesse White; **D:** Arthur Marks. NO

Tokyo Decadence 🎬½ 1991 (NC-17) Ai is a high-paid prostitute working in Tokyo for an agency that specializes in sado-masochism. Film follows her various sexual escapades in humiliating detail as well as her drug-addled search for a client Ai thinks she's in love with. Since Ai remains a cipher, the film also remains unfocused except for its creepy and explicit sex scenes. Adaptation of director Murakami's novel "Topaz." In Japanese with English subtitles or dubbed.**CW:** Sexually explicit. 92m/C VHS, LV. JP Miho Nikaido, Tenmei Kano, Yayoi Kusama, Sayoko Amano; **D:** Ryu Murakami; **W:** Ryu Murakami; **M:** Ryuichi Sakamoto. TRI, FCT

Tokyo-Ga 🎬🎬🎬½ 1985 Impelled by his love for the films of Yasujiro Ozu, Wenders traveled to Tokyo and fashioned a caring document of both the city and of Ozu's career, using images that recall and comment on Ozu's visual motifs. 92m/C VHS, Beta. **D:** Wim Wenders; **W:** Wim Wenders. TPV

Tokyo Joe 🎬½ 1949 A war hero/nightclub owner returns to Tokyo and becomes ensnared in blackmail and smuggling while searching for his missing wife and child. Slow-moving tale has never been considered one of Bogart's better movies. 88m/B VHS, Beta, LV. Humphrey Bogart, Florence Marly, Alexander Knox, Sessue Hayakawa, Jerome Courtland, Lore Lee Michel; **D:** Stuart Heisler. COL

Tokyo Olympiad 1966 A monumental sports documentary about the 1964 Olympic Games in its entirety. Never before available for home viewing. Letterboxed with digital sound. In Japanese with English subtitles. 170m/C VHS, Beta, LV. JP **D:** Kon Ichikawa. TPV, WFV, CRC

Tokyo Pop 🎬🎬½ 1988 (R) A punk rocker travels to Japan to find stardom and experiences a series of misadventures. Enjoyable in its own lightweight way. Hamilton is the daughter of Carol Burnett. 99m/C VHS, LV, Closed Caption. Carrie Hamilton, Yutaka Tadokoro, Tetsuro Tamba, Taiji Tonoyama, Masumi Harukawa; **D:** Fran Rubel Kazui; **W:** Lynn Grossman, Fran Rubel Kazui; **M:** Alan Brewer. WAR

Tokyo Story 🎬🎬🎬🎬 1953 Poignant story of elderly couple's journey to Tokyo where they receive little time and less respect from their grown children. Masterful cinematography, and sensitive treatment of universally appealing story. In Japanese with English subtitles. 134m/B VHS. JP Chishu Ryu, Chieko Higashiyama, So Yamamura, Haruko Sugimura, Setsuko Hara; **D:** Yasujiro Ozu; **W:** Yasujiro Ozu. NYF, FCT

Tol'able David 🎬🎬 1921 A simple tale of mountain folk, done in the tradition of Mark Twain stories. A family of hillbillies is embroiled in a feud with a clan of outlaws. When the community's mail is stolen by the troublesome ruffians, the family's youngest member, who harbors dreams of becoming a mail driver, comes to the rescue. Silent film. 79m/B VHS, Beta. Richard Barthelmess, Gladys Hulette, Ernest Torrence; **D:** Henry King. NOS, VYY, CCB

Toll Gate 🎬🎬½ 1920 Quick on the draw outlaw Hart risks capture to rescue drowning child, and consequently gets involved with the boy's mother. Silent classic. 55m/B VHS, Beta. William S. Hart, Anna Q. Nilsson, Jack Richardson, Joseph Singleton; **D:** Lambert Hillyer. GPV, VCN

Toll of the Desert 🎬 1935 A lawman learns that his father is a ruthless, back-stabbing renegade. Now he must try and catch him. 58m/B VHS, Beta, LV. Roger Williams, Ted Adams, Edward Cassidy, Tom London, Earl Dwire, Betty Mack, Fred Kohler Jr.; **D:** William (Lester Williams) Berke. NOS, DVT

Tollbooth 🎬🎬 1994 (R) Romantic dreamer Jack (Von Dohlen) mans a tollbooth on a stretch of Florida Keys highway while his equally longing honey Doris (Balk) works at a nearby gas station and has a thing going on the side with bait salesman Dash (Patton). The return of Doris' longgone daddy Leon (Cassel) causes some family problems while Jack's new associate Vic (Wilder) has a scam that's drawing interest from the state police. Thin plot but lots of charm from the two leads helps hold interest in Breziner's first film.**CW:** Scene of strong sexuality and for language and some gore. 108m/C VHS, LV, Closed Caption. Fairuza Balk, Lenny Von Dohlen, Will Patton, Seymour Cassel, James Wilder, Louise Fletcher, William Katt; **D:** Salome Breziner; **W:** Salome Breziner; **C:** Henry Vargas; **M:** Adam Gorgoni. NLC

Tom and Huck 🎬🎬🎬 1995 (PG) Tom Sawyer and pal Huck Finn are the only witnesses to a murder. Tom's friend Muff is framed for the crime and the boys are being tracked by the real killer, Injun Joe. They must decide to come forward, expose the true fiend, and risk their own hides or run away and let an innocent man hang. True to the Twain story, Thomas plays a mischievous Tom to Renfro's troublemaking Huck. Film was shot in Mooresville, Alabama, population 69, just down the road a piece from the Hannibal, Missouri of Twain fame. 91m/C VHS, Closed Caption. Jonathan Taylor Thomas, Brad Renfro, Eric Schweig, Charles Rocket, Amy Wright, Micheal McShane, Marian Seldes, Rachel Leigh Cook, Lanny Flaherty, Courtland Mead, Peter M. MacKenzie, Heath Lamberts; **D:** Pete Hewitt; **W:** Stephen Sommers, David Loughery; **C:** Bobby Bukowski; **M:** Stephen Endelman. TOU

Tom and Jerry: The Movie 🎬🎬 1993 (G)
Everybody's favorite animated cat/mouse duo (who began life in a 1940 MGM short "Puss Gets the Boot") hit the big screen, this time talking (unlike their animated shorts). Rather than cartoon mayhem our two protagonists are goody-two-shoes (with songs yet!) but still retain their charm. Kids will like it, but true "Tom and Jerry" fans should probably stick to the original cartoons. **84m/C VHS, Closed Caption. D:** Phil Roman; **W:** Dennis Marks; **M:** Henry Mancini, Leslie Bricusse; **V:** Richard Kind, Dana Hill, Charlotte Rae, Henry Gibson, Rip Taylor, Howard Morris, Edmund Gilbert, David Lander. *FHE*

Tom & Viv 🎬🎬🎬 1994 (PG-13)
American T.S. Eliot (Dafoe) is an Oxford student in 1914 when he meets the moody, monied Vivien Haigh-Wood (Richardson). After a whirlwind courtship, they marry—disastrously. Eliot begins to establish himself as a poet, while Vivien serves as muse/typist and unsuccessfully battles her misdiagnosed illnesses with too much drinking and drugs, as well as embarrassing public scenes. As Eliot gains success, he increasingly distances himself from the unhappy Viv, until finally committing her to an asylum. Dafoe is fine as the chilly, withdrawn poet but Richardson steals the film as his flamboyant, lost wife. Based on the play by Michael Hastings, who co-wrote the screenplay.**CW:** Mature thematic elements. **115m/C VHS, LV, Closed Caption. C:** Willem Dafoe, Miranda Richardson, Rosemary Harris, Tim Dutton, Nickolas Grace, Philip Locke, Clare Holman, Joanna McCallum; **D:** Brian Gilbert; **W:** Michael Hastings, Adrian Hodges; **M:** Debbie Wiseman. National Board of Review Awards '94: Best Actress (Richardson), Best Supporting Actress (Harris); Nominations: Academy Awards '94: Best Actress (Richardson), Best Supporting Actress (Harris); British Academy Awards '93: Best Actress (Richardson), Best Film; Golden Globe Awards '95: Best Actress—Drama (Richardson).*TOU*

Tom Brown's School Days 🎬🎬½
Adventures at Rugby **1940** Depicts life among the boys in an English school during the Victorian era. Based on the classic novel by Thomas Hughes. Remade in 1951. **86m/B VHS, Beta. GB** Cedric Hardwicke, Jimmy Lydon, Freddie Bartholomew; **D:** Robert Stevenson. *NOS, HHT, PSM*

Tom Brown's School Days 🎬🎬🎬
1951 Tom enrolls at Rugby and is beset by bullies in classic tale of English school life. British remake of the 1940 version. Based on the novel by Thomas Hughes. **93m/B VHS, Beta. GB** Robert Newton, John Howard Davies, James Hayter; **D:** Gordon Parry. *VCI*

Tom, Dick, and Harry 🎬🎬½ 1941
Dreamy girl is engaged to three men and unable to decide which to marry. It all depends on a kiss. Remade as "The Girl Most Likely." **86m/B VHS, Beta, LV.** Ginger Rogers, George Murphy, Burgess Meredith, Alan Marshal, Phil Silvers; **D:** Garson Kanin. National Board of Review Awards '41: 10 Best Films of the Year; Nominations: Academy Awards '41: Best Story. *CCB, TTC, FCT*

Tom Horn 🎬🎬 1980 (R)
The final days of one of the Old West's legends. Gunman Tom Horn, hired by Wyoming ranchers to stop cattle rustlers, goes about his job with a zeal that soon proves embarrassing to his employers. Beautifully photographed and authentic in its attention to details of the period, the film nonetheless takes liberties with the facts of Horn's life and is lacking in other aspects of production. **98m/C VHS, Beta.** Steve McQueen, Linda Evans, Richard Farnsworth, Billy Green Bush, Slim Pickens; **D:** William Wiard; **W:** Thomas McGuane; **C:** John A. Alonzo; **M:** Ernest Gold. *WAR*

Tom Jones 🎬🎬🎬🎬 1963
Bawdy comedy based on Henry Fielding's novel about a rustic playboy's wild life in 18th century England. Hilarious and clever with a grand performance by Finney. One of the sexiest eating scenes ever. Redgrave's debut. Theatrically released at 129 minutes, the film was recut by the director, who decided it needed tightening before its 1992 re-release on video. **121m/C VHS, Beta, LV. GB** Albert Finney, Susannah York, Hugh Griffith, Edith Evans, Joan Greenwood, Diane Cilento, George Devine, David Tomlinson, Joyce Redman, Lynn Redgrave, Julian Glover, Peter Bull, David Warner; **D:** Tony Richardson; **W:** John Osborne; **C:** Walter Lassally; **M:** John Addison. Academy Awards '63: Best Adapted Screenplay, Best Director (Richardson), Best Picture, Best Original Score; British Academy Awards '63: Best Film, Best Screenplay; Directors Guild of America Awards '63: Best Director (Richardson); Golden Globe Awards '64: Best Film—Musical/Comedy, Best Foreign Film; National Board of Review Awards '63: Best Director (Richardson); New York Film Critics Awards '63: Best Actor (Finney), Best Director (Richardson), Best Film; Nominations: Academy Awards '63: Best Actor (Finney), Best Art Direction/Set Decoration (Color), Best Supporting Actor (Griffith), Best Supporting Actress (Cilento, Evans, Redman). *HBO, FOX, BTV*

Tom Mix Compilation 1 1916
This compilation of six "Great American Cowboy" films from Tom Mix's early period includes: "Jimmy Hayes and Muriel," "The Stagecoach Driver and the Girl," "Sagebrush Tom," "An Arizona Wooing," "Roping a Bride" and "Local Color." **60m/B VHS, Beta.** Tom Mix. *GVV*

Tom Mix Compilation 2 1916
Five films from Tom Mix's early period include "Never Again," "An Angelic Attitude," "A Western Masquerade," "A $5,000 Elopement," and "Local Color." **60m/B VHS, Beta.** Tom Mix. *GVV*

Tom Sawyer 🎬🎬🎬 1930
Winning adaptation of Mark Twain's oft told tale of boyhood in Hannibal, Missouri. Cast reprised their roles the following year in "Huckleberry Finn." **86m/B VHS, Beta.** Jackie Coogan, Mitzie Green, Lucien Littlefield, Tully Marshall; **D:** John Cromwell; **C:** Charles B(ryant) Lang. *MGM*

Tom Sawyer 🎬🎬½ 1973 (G)
Musical version of the Mark Twain tale of the boisterous Tom, his friend Becky Thatcher, and various adventures, including the fence whitewashing. Amusing kid fare shot on location in Missouri. ♫River Song; Gratification; Tom Sawyer; Freebootin'; Aunt Polly's Soliloquy; If'n I Was God; A Man's Gotta Be What He's Born To Be; How Come?; Hannibal, Mo. **104m/C VHS, LV.** Johnny Whitaker, Jodie Foster, Celeste Holm, Warren Oates, Jeff East; **D:** Don Taylor; **M:** John Williams. Nominations: Academy Awards '73: Best Art Direction/Set Decoration, Best Costume Design, Original Song Score and/or Adaptation. *MGM*

Tom Thumb 🎬🎬🎬 1958
Diminutive boy saves village treasury from bad guys. Adapted from classic Grimm fairy tale. Special effects combine live actors, animation, and puppets. **92m/C VHS, Beta, LV. GB** Russ Tamblyn, Peter Sellers, Terry-Thomas; **D:** George Pal; **C:** Georges Perinal. Academy Awards '58: Best Special Effects. *MGM*

Tomb 🎬🎬 1986
Fortune seekers disturb the slumber of a magical, sadistic princess much to their everlasting regret. Adapted from a Bram Stoker novel. **106m/C VHS, Beta.** Cameron Mitchell, John Carradine, Sybil Danning, Richard Hench, Michelle (McClellan) Bauer; **D:** Fred Olen Ray; **C:** Paul Elliott. *TWE*

Tomb of Ligeia 🎬🎬 *Tomb of the Cat* 1964
The ghost of a man's first wife expresses her displeasure when groom and new little missus return to manor. One of the better Corman adaptations of Poe. Also available with "The Conqueror Worm" on Laser Disc. **82m/C VHS, Beta, LV. GB** Vincent Price, Elizabeth Shepherd, John Westbrook, Oliver Johnston, Richard Johnson; **D:** Roger Corman; **W:** Robert Towne. *MLB*

Tomb of the Undead 🎬½ 1972
The sadistic guards of a prison camp are rudely awakened by the prisoners they tortured to death when they return as flesh-eating zombies looking to settle the score. **60m/C VHS, Beta. GB** Duncan McLeod, Lee Frost, John Dennis; **D:** John Hayes. *NOS, INC*

Tomb of Torture woof! *Metempsycose*
1965 Murdered countess is reincarnated in the body of a newspaperman's mistress. Together they investigate monster reports in a murder-ridden castle. The butler may have something to do with it. Filmed in Sepiatone and dubbed. **88m/B VHS, Beta.** Annie Albert, Thony Maky, Mark Marian; **D:** William Grace. *MSP*

The Tomboy 🎬½ 1924
A young woman behaves boyishly in Colonial America. **64m/B VHS, Beta.** Dorothy Devore, Lotta Williams, Herbert Rawlinson, Harry Gribbon, Lee Moran; **D:** David Kirkland. *GPV, FCT*

Tomboy 🎬 1940
Shy country boy and a not-so-shy city girl meet, fall in love, and overcome obstacles that stand in their path. **70m/B VHS, Beta.** Jackie Moran, Marcia Mae Jones. *VYY*

Tomboy woof! 1985 (R)
A pretty auto mechanic is determined to win not only the race but the love and respect of a superstar auto racer. **91m/C VHS, Beta.** Betsy Russell, Eric Douglas, Jerry Dinome, Kristi Somers, Richard Erdman, Toby Iland; **D:** Herb Freed. *LIV, VES*

Tomboy & the Champ 🎬🎬 1958
Despite many obstacles, a music-loving calf becomes a prize winner with the help of its loving owner. Kids will love it, but adults will think this one a little sugary. **82m/C VHS, Beta.** Candy Moore, Ben Johnson, Jesse White; **D:** Francis D. Lyon. *VCI*

Tombs of the Blind Dead 🎬🎬½
The Blind Dead; La Noche dell Terror Ciego **1972 (PG)** Blinded by crows for using human sacrifice in the thirteenth century, zombies rise from the grave to wreak havoc upon 20th-century Spaniards. Atmospheric chiller was extremely popular in Europe and spawned three sequels. Originally titled "The Blind Dead." The sequels, also on video, are "Return of the Evil Dead" and "Horror of the Zombies." **86m/C VHS, Beta.** SP PT Caesar Burner, Lone Fleming, Helen Harp; **D:** Armando de Ossorio. *NO*

Tombstone 🎬🎬🎬 1993 (R)
Saga of Wyatt Earp and his band of law-abiding large moustaches beat the Kasdan/Costner vehicle to the big screen by several months. Legendary lawman Wyatt (Russell) moves to Tombstone, AZ aiming to start a new life with his brothers, but alas, that's not to be. The infamous gunfight at the OK Corral is here, and so is best buddy Doc Holliday, gunslinger and philosopher, a role designed for scenery chewing (Kilmer excels). Romance is supplied by actress Josephine, though Delany lacks the necessary romantic spark. Russell spends a lot of time looking troubled by the violence while adding to the body count. Too self-conscious, suffers from '90s western revisionism, but blessed with a high energy level thanks to despicable villains Lang, Biehn, and Boothe.**CW:** Strong western violence. **130m/C VHS, LV, Closed Caption.** Kurt Russell, Val Kilmer, Michael Biehn, Sam Elliott, Dana Delany, Bill Paxton, Powers Boothe, Stephen Lang, Jason Priestley, Dana Wheeler-Nicholson, Billy Zane, Thomas Haden Church, Joanna Pacula, Michael Rooker, Harry Carey Jr., Billy Bob Thornton, Charlton Heston, Robert John Burke, John Corbett, Buck Taylor, Terry O'Quinn, Pedro Armendariz Jr., Chris Mitchum, Jon Tenney; **D:** George P. Cosmatos; **W:** Kevin Jarre; **M:** Bruce Broughton. Nominations: MTV Movie Awards '94: Best Actor (Kilmer), Most Desirable Male (Kilmer). *HPH*

Tombstone Canyon 🎬½ 1935
Death rides the range until Maynard and his horse Tarzan put a halt to it. **60m/B VHS, Beta.** Ken Maynard, Sheldon Lewis, Cecilia Parker. *SNC, NOS, RXM*

Tombstone Terror 🎬 1934
A cowboy is beleaguered by a case of mistaken identity. **55m/B VHS, Beta.** Bob Steele. *NO*

Tomcat: Dangerous Desires 🎬🎬
1993 (R) Tom (Grieco) suffers from a rare degenerative condition and agrees to become a guinea pig in a secret, genetic imprinting experiment that has him injected with feline RNA. Tom's health is restored but the side effects give him the predatory instincts of a cat and the need to kill to stay alive. **96m/C VHS, LV, Closed Caption.** Richard Grieco, Maryam D'Abo, Natalie Radford. *REP*

Tommy 🎬🎬 1975 (PG)
Peter Townsend's rock opera as visualized in the usual hyper-Russell style about the deaf, dumb, and blind boy who becomes a celebrity due to his amazing skill at the pinball machines. A parade of rock musicians

perform throughout the affair, with varying degrees of success. Despite some good moments, the film ultimately falls prey to ill-conceived production concepts and miscasting. ♫Undertue; Captain Walker Didn't Come Home; It's A Boy; '51 is Going to Be A Good Year; What About the Boy?; The Amazing Journey; Christmas; See Me, Feel Me; Eyesight to the Blind. **108m/C VHS, Beta, LV.** Ann-Margret, Elton John, Oliver Reed, Tina Turner, Roger Daltrey, Eric Clapton, Keith Moon, Pete Townshend, Jack Nicholson, Robert Powell, Paul Nicholas, Barry Winch, Victoria Russell, Ben Aris, Mary Holland, Jennifer Baker, Susan Baker, Arthur Brown, John Entwhistle; **D:** Ken Russell; **W:** Ken Russell, Keith Moon, John Entwhistle; **C:** Dick Bush; **M:** The Who, Pete Townshend. Golden Globe Awards '76: Best Actress—Musical/Comedy (Ann-Margret); Nominations: Academy Awards '75: Best Actress (Ann-Margret), Original Song Score and/or Adaptation. COL, MVD, WME

Tommy Boy 🎬🎬 1995 (PG-13) Not-too-bright rich kid Tommy (Farley) teams up with snide, officious accountant Richard (Spade) to save the family auto parts business after dad (Dennehy) buys the farm. Tommy and Richard must deal with a conniving stepmom and stepbrother (Derek and Lowe), a ruthless rival (Aykroyd), and a road trip from hell to drum up some new business. Not as bad as it sounds, but suffers from connection with the currently unfunny "Saturday Night Live." Inconsistent direction and too-familiar characters offset the amusing chemistry between Farley and Spade, who show promise as a possible "Abbott and Costello"-type comedy team for the 90's. **CW:** Sex-related humor; some drug content and nudity. **98m/C VHS, Beta, Closed Caption.** Chris Farley, David Spade, Brian Dennehy, Bo Derek, Dan Aykroyd, Julie Warner, Rob Lowe; **D:** Peter Segal; **W:** Bonnie Turner, Terry Turner; **M:** David Newman. MTV Movie Awards '96: Best On-Screen Duo (Chris Farley/David Spade); Nominations: MTV Movie Awards '96: Best Comedic Performance (Farley). PAR

Tomorrow 🎬🎬🎬 1972 (PG) Powerful tale of the love of two lonely people. Outstanding performance by Duvall as lumber mill worker who falls for a pregnant woman. Based on the neglected Faulkner story. **102m/B VHS, Beta.** Robert Duvall, Olga Bellin, Sudie Bond; **D:** Joseph Anthony; **W:** Horton Foote. MON

Tomorrow at Seven 🎬🎬½ 1933 A mystery writer is determined to discover the identity of the Ace of Spades, a killer who always warns his intended victim, then leaves an ace of spades on the corpse as his calling card. **62m/B VHS, Beta.** Chester Morris, Vivienne Osborne, Frank McHugh, Allen Jenkins, Henry Stephenson; **D:** Ray Enright. SNC, NOS, VYY

Tomorrow Is Forever 🎬🎬½ 1946 Welles and Colbert marry shortly before he goes off to fight in WWI. Badly wounded and disfigured, he decides to stay in Europe while Colbert, believing Welles dead, eventually marries Brent. Fast forward to WWII when Brent, a chemical manufacturer, hires a new scientist to work for him in the war effort (guess who). This slow-moving melodrama wastes a good cast. Six-year-old Wood debuts as Colbert's daughter. **105m/B VHS.** Claudette Colbert, Orson Welles, George Brent, Lucile Watson, Richard Long, Natalie Wood; **D:** Irving Pichel; **C:** Joseph Valentine; **M:** Max Steiner. MGM

Tomorrow Never Comes 🎬½ 1977 When he discovers his girlfriend has been unfaithful, a guy goes berserk and eventually finds himself in a stand-off with the police. Violent. **109m/C VHS, Beta.** Oliver Reed, Susan George, Raymond Burr, John Ireland, Stephen McHattie, Donald Pleasence; **D:** Peter Collinson. UNI, HHE

Tomorrow's Child 🎬🎬 1982 Made-for-television drama about in vitro fertilization (test-tube babies) and surrogate motherhood. **100m/C VHS, Beta, Closed Caption.** Stephanie Zimbalist, William Atherton, Bruce Davison, Ed Flanders, Salome Jens, James Shigeta, Susan Oliver, Arthur Hill; **D:** Joseph Sargent. FOX

Tomorrow's Children 🎬 1934 An alarmist melodrama warning against the threat of government-induced female sterilization asks the question: if a woman's family is weird, should her tubes be tied? **55m/B VHS, Beta.** Sterling Holloway, Diana Sinclair, Sarah Padden, Don Douglas; **D:** Crane Wilbur. SNC, NOS, VYY

The Tong Man 🎬🎬½ 1919 Robbins owes the tong money and Hayakawa, as the tong's executioner, is sent to kill him when he won't pay up. Only it turns out Hayakawa is in love with Eddy, Robbins daughter, and refuses. Then the tong decide to kill him for disobeying their orders. **58m/B VHS.** Sessue Hayakawa, Helen Jerome Eddy, Marc Robbins, Toyo Fujita; **D:** William Worthington. GPV

Tongs: An American Nightmare 🎬 1988 (R) Chinese-American street gangs in Chinatown battle over turf and drug shipments. **80m/C VHS, Beta.** Ian Anthony Leung, Christopher O'Conner, Simon Yam; **D:** Philip Chan. ACA

Toni 🎬🎬🎬½ 1934 An Italian worker falls for his landlady and they make plans to marry. A grim turn of events, however, brings tragic consequences. Based on the lives of several townsfolk in the village of Les Martiques, the film was shot in the town and members of the local populace were used as characters. In French with English subtitles. **90m/B VHS, Beta.** FR Charles Blavette, Jenny Helia, Edouard Delmont, Celia Montalvan; **D:** Jean Renoir. DVT

Tonight and Every Night 🎬🎬½ 1945 Cabaret singer and RAF pilot fall in love during WWII. Her music hall post puts her in the midst of Nazi bombing, and her dedication to her song and dance career puts a strain on the romance. Imaginative production numbers outweigh pedestrian storyline. ♫Cry and You Cry Alone; What Does an English Girl Think of a Yank; Anywhere; The Boy I Left Behind; You Excite Me; Tonight and Every Night. **92m/C VHS, Beta.** Rita Hayworth, Lee Bowman, Janet Blair, Marc Platt, Leslie Brooks; **D:** Victor Saville. Nominations: Academy Awards '45: Best Song ("Anywhere"), Scoring of a Musical. COL

Tonight for Sure 🎬½ 1961 Coppola made this nudie, his first film, as a student at UCLA. Two men, one who spies on women and the other who imagines nude women everywhere, plan an escapade. **66m/B VHS, Beta.** **D:** Francis Ford Coppola; **W:** Francis Ford Coppola; **M:** Carmine Coppola. VYY, TPV

Tonio Kroger 🎬🎬 1965 A young writer travels through Europe in search of intellectual and sensual relationships and a home that will suit him. He must balance freedom and responsibility. Works best if one is familiar with the Thomas Mann novel on which film is based. In German with English subtitles. **92m/B VHS, Beta.** GE Jean-Claude Brialy, Nadja Tiller, Gert Frobe; **D:** Rolf Thiele. VYY, APD, GLV

Tonka 🎬🎬½ A Horse Named Comanche 1958 A children's story about a wild horse tamed by a young Indian, only to have it recruited for the Battle of Little Bighorn. Mineo is fine as the Indian brave determined to be reunited with his steed. The film also makes a laudable effort to portray the Indians as a dignified race. The movie, however, stumbles at its conclusion and is contrived throughout. **97m/C VHS, Beta.** Sal Mineo, Phil Carey, Jerome Courtland; **D:** Lewis R. Foster. DIS

Tonto Basin Outlaws 🎬🎬 1941 The Range Busters team up with Teddy Roosevelt's Rough Riders in order to stop a gang of cattle rustlers. Standard oater material. Based on the story by Earle Snell. **60m/B VHS.** Ray Corrigan, John "Dusty" King, Max Terhune, Jan Wiley, Tristram Coffin, Edmund Cobb; **D:** S. Roy Luby; **W:** John Vlahos. MOV

The Tonto Kid 🎬 1935 Action-packed western featuring Rex Bell. **56m/B VHS, Beta.** Rex Bell, Ruth Mix, Buzz Barton, Joseph Girard, Jack Rockwell, Murdock McQuarrie; **D:** Harry Fraser. NOS, DVT, VDM

Tony Draws a Horse 🎬🎬½ 1951 An eight-year old draws an anatomically correct horse on the door of his father's office, leading to a rift between the parents as they argue how to handle the heartbreak of precociousness. Somewhat uneven but engaging comedy, based on a play by Lesley Storm. **90m/B VHS.** Cecil Parker, Anne Crawford, Derek Bond, Barbara Murray, Mervyn Johns, Barbara Everest, David Hurst; **D:** John Paddy Carstairs. NOS

Tony Rome 🎬🎬½ 1967 The Marvin H. Albert private eye agency investigates a millionaire's daughter's disappearance and her involvement in organized crime. Entertaining and complex plot, although the cast is a numbingly large one. **110m/C VHS, Beta.** Frank Sinatra, Jill St. John, Simon Oakland, Gena Rowlands, Richard Conte, Lloyd Bochner, Jeffrey Lynn, Sue Lyon; **D:** Gordon Douglas. FOX

Too Beautiful for You 🎬🎬 Trop Belle Pour Toi 1988 (R) A successful car salesman, married for years to an extraordinarily beautiful woman, finds himself head over heels for his frumpy secretary. Depardieu plays the regular guy who finds he's never believed in the love and fidelity of a woman he thinks is too beautiful for him. In French with English subtitles. **91m/C VHS.** FR Gerard Depardieu, Josiane Balasko, Carole Bouquet, Roland Blanche; **D:** Bertrand Blier; **W:** Bertrand Blier. Cannes Film Festival '89: Grand Jury Prize; Cesar Awards '90: Best Actress (Bouquet), Best Director (Blier), Best Film, Best Writing. ORI, FXL, FCT

Too Far to Go 🎬🎬🎬 1979 Terrific TV adaptation of a series of John Updike stories focusing on the rocky longtime marriage of not-so-proper New Englanders Danner and Moriarty. **98m/C VHS.** Blythe Danner, Michael Moriarty, Glenn Close, Ken Kercheval; **W:** William Hanley. MON

Too Hot to Handle 🎬🎬🎬 1938 Two rival photographers searching for a beautiful ladypilot's missing brother wind up in Brazil, where they encounter a dangerous tribe of voodoo types. Amusing, if exaggerated, picture of the lengths to which reporters will go to for a story. Classic Gable. **105m/B VHS, Closed Caption.** Clark Gable, Myrna Loy, Walter Pidgeon, Walter Connolly, Leo Carrillo, Virginia Weidler; **D:** Jack Conway. MGM, FCT

Too Hot to Handle 🎬 1976 Voluptuous lady contract killer fights against the mob with all the weapons at her disposal. Filmed on location in Manila. **88m/C VHS, Beta.** Cheri Caffaro, Aharon Ipale, Vic Diaz, Corinne Calvet; **D:** Don Schain. WAR

Too Late for Tears 🎬🎬🎬 Killer Bait 1949 An honest husband and his not so honest wife stumble on a load of mob-stolen cash and become entangled in a web of deceit and murder as the wife resorts to increasingly desperate measures to keep her newfound fortune. Atmospheric and entertaining film noir albeit sometimes confusing. **99m/B VHS, Beta.** Lizabeth Scott, Don DeFore, Dan Duryea, Arthur Kennedy, Kristine Miller, Barry Kelley, Denver Pyle, Jimmy Ames, Billy Halop, Jimmie Dodd; **D:** Byron Haskin; **W:** Roy Huggins; **C:** William Mellor; **M:** Dale Butts. SNC, VDM, NOS

Too Late the Hero 🎬🎬🎬 Suicide Run 1970 (PG) Unlikely band of allied soldiers battle Japanese force entrenched in the Pacific during WWII. Rousing adventure, fine cast. **133m/C VHS, Beta.** Michael Caine, Cliff Robertson, Henry Fonda, Ian Bannen, Harry Andrews, Denholm Elliott; **D:** Robert Aldrich; **C:** Joseph Biroc. FOX

Too Many Crooks 🎬🎬 1959 A British spoof of crime syndicate films. Crooks try to extort, but bungle the job. Terry-Thomas is fun, as always. **85m/B VHS, Beta.** GB Terry-Thomas, Brenda de Banzie, George Cole; **D:** Mario Zampi. NO

Too Many Girls 🎬🎬½ 1940 Beautiful heiress goes to a small New Mexico college to escape from a cadre of gold-digging suitors. Passable adaptation of the successful Rodgers and Hart Broadway show, with many original cast members and the original stage director. Lucy and Desi met while making this film, and married shortly after. ♫Spic and Spanish; Heroes in the

Fall; Pottawatomie; 'Cause We All Got Cake; Love Never Went to College; Look Out; I Didn't Know What Time It Was; The Conga; You're Nearer. **85m/B VHS, Beta, LV.** Lucille Ball, Richard Carlson, Eddie Bracken, Ann Miller, Desi Arnaz Sr., Hal LeRoy, Libby Bennett, Frances Langford, Van Johnson; **D:** George Abbott; **M:** George Bassman, Richard Rodgers, Lorenz Hart. *TTC*

Too Much Sun 🐾½ 1990 (R)
A dying man can prevent his fortune from falling into the hands of a corrupt priest simply by having one of his two children produce an heir. The problem is, they're both gay! **97m/C VHS, LV.** Robert Downey Jr., Ralph Macchio, Eric Idle, Andrea Martin, Laura Ernst, Jim Haynie; **D:** Robert Downey. *COL*

Too Pretty to Be Honest 🐾🐾 Trop Jolie pour Etre Honette 1972
Four women sharing an apartment witness a robbery and begin to suspect that their neighbor is the culprit. So they decide to steal the money from him. In French with subtitles. **95m/C VHS, Beta.** FR Jane Birkin, Bernadette LaFont, Serge Gainsbourg; **D:** Richard Balducci; **M:** Serge Gainsbourg. *FCT*

Too Scared to Scream 🐾🐾½ 1985 (R)
Policeman and an undercover agent team up to solve a bizarre series of murders at a Manhattan apartment house. **104m/C VHS, Beta.** Mike Connors, Anne Archer, Leon Isaac Kennedy, John Heard, Ian McShane, Maureen O'Sullivan, Murray Hamilton; **D:** Tony LoBianco; **W:** Neal Barbera. *LIV, VES*

Too Shy to Try 🐾🐾 1982 (PG)
A incredibly shy man meets his dream girl, and enrolls in a psychology course to overcome his ineptitude. A ribald, slapstick French comedy. **89m/C VHS, Beta.** FR Pierre Richard, Aldo Maccione; **D:** Pierre Richard.

Too Wise Wives 🐾🐾 1921
A story of would-be marital infidelity and misunderstandings. Silent. **90m/C VHS, Beta.** Louis Calhern, Claire Windsor; **D:** Lois Weber. *GVV*

Too Young to Die 🐾🐾 1990 (R)
Teenager Amanda (Lewis) hooks up with the wrong guy in sleazy Billy (Pitt), who hooks her on drugs and turns her into a prostitute. She meets nice guy Mike (O'Keefe), who briefly takes her away from the life but when their relationship falls apart, Amanda goes back to Billy. Billy eggs her on to get revenge for being dumped and Amanda winds up on trial for murder. Fact-based TV movie. **CW:** Intense plot material involving a minor. **92m/C VHS, Closed Caption.** Juliette Lewis, Brad Pitt, Michael Tucker, Michael O'Keefe, Emily Longstreth, Alan Fudge; **D:** Robert Markowitz; **W:** David Hill; **C:** Eric Van Haren Noman; **M:** Charles Bernstein. *REP*

The Toolbox Murders 🐾 1978 (R)
Unknown psychotic murderer brutally claims victims one at a time, leaving police mystified and townsfolk terrified. Sick and exploitative, with predictably poor production values. **93m/C VHS, Beta.** Cameron Mitchell, Pamelyn Ferdin, Wesley Eure, Nicholas Beauvy, Aneta Corsaut, Tim Donnelly, Evelyn Guerrero; **D:** Dennis Donnelly. *VCI, VTR*

Tootsie 🐾🐾🐾🐾 1982 (PG)
A stubborn, unemployed actor disguises himself as a woman to secure a part on a soap opera. As his popularity on television mounts, his love life becomes increasingly soap operatic. Hoffman is delightful, as is the rest of the stellar cast. Debut of Davis; Murray's performance unbilled. Laserdisc version features audio commentary by director Sidney Pollack, behind the scenes footage and photographs, and complete coverage of Tootsie's production. **110m/C VHS, Beta, LV, Closed Caption.** Dustin Hoffman, Jessica Lange, Teri Garr, Dabney Coleman, Bill Murray, Charles Durning, Geena Davis, George Gaynes, Estelle Getty, Christine Ebersole, Sydney Pollack; **D:** Sydney Pollack; **W:** Larry Gelbart, Murray Schisgal, Don McGuire; **C:** Owen Roizman; **M:** Dave Grusin. Academy Awards '82: Best Supporting Actress (Lange); British Academy Awards '83: Best Actor (Hoffman); Golden Globe Awards '83: Best Actor—Musical/Comedy (Hoffman), Best Film—Musical/Comedy, Best Supporting Actress (Lange); Los Angeles Film Critics Association Awards '82: Best Screenplay; New York Film Critics Awards '82: Best Director (Pollack), Best

Screenplay, Best Supporting Actress (Lange); National Society of Film Critics Awards '82: Best Actor (Hoffman), Best Film, Best Screenplay, Best Supporting Actress (Lange); Writers Guild of America '82: Best Original Screenplay; Nominations: Academy Awards '82: Best Actor (Hoffman), Best Cinematography, Best Director (Pollack), Best Film Editing, Best Original Screenplay, Best Picture, Best Song ("It Might Be You"), Best Sound, Best Supporting Actress (Garr). *COL, CRC, BTV*

Top Dog 🐾½ 1995 (PG-13)
Another cop-and-dog-team-up-to-get-the-bad-guys flick. This one, however, is meant to appeal to the kids who liked "Sidekicks." That raises a problem with the unfortunately topical right-wing-hate group-bombing plot. Jake Wilder (Norris), a beer-swillin' karate-choppin' loner cop, teams up with canine Reno, whose ex-partner was killed by the neo-Nazi terrorists. Weak script and erratic storyline can't find a comfortable balance between the too-cute pooch scenes and the (admittedly toned-down) violence. Reno steals every scene he's in, and provides the flick's few redeeming moments. **CW:** Shootings and martial arts violence; strong language. **93m/C VHS, LV, Closed Caption.** Chuck Norris, Clyde Kusatsu, Michele Lamar Richards, Carmine Caridi, Peter Savard Moore, Erik von Detten, Herta Ware, Kai Wulff, Francesco Quinn, Timothy Bottoms; **D:** Aaron Norris; **W:** Ron Swanson; **C:** Joao Fernandes. *LIV*

Top Gun 🐾🐾½ 1986 (PG)
Young Navy pilots compete against one another on the ground and in the air at the elite Fighter Weapons School. Cruise isn't bad as a maverick who comes of age in Ray Bans, but Edwards shines as his buddy. Awesome aerial photography and high-cal beefcake divert from the contrived plot and stock characters. The Navy subsequently noticed an increased interest in fighter pilots. Features Berlin's Oscar-winning song "Take My Breath Away." ♫Take My Breath Away; Danger Zone; Destination Unknown; Heaven in Your Eyes; Hot Summer Nights; Mighty Wings; Playing with the Boys; Through the Fire; Top Gun Anthem. **109m/C VHS, Beta, LV, 8mm, Closed Caption.** Tom Cruise, Kelly McGillis, Val Kilmer, Tom Skerritt, Anthony Edwards, Meg Ryan, Rick Rossovich, Michael Ironside, Barry Tubb, Whip Hubley, John Stockwell, Tim Robbins, Adrian Pasdar; **D:** Tony Scott; **W:** Jim Cash, Jack Epps Jr.; **M:** Harold Faltermeyer. Academy Awards '86: Best Song ("Take My Breath Away"); Golden Globe Awards '87: Best Song ("Take My Breath Away"); People's Choice Awards '87: Best Film; Nominations: Academy Awards '86: Best Film Editing, Best Sound. *PAR*

Top Hat 🐾🐾🐾🐾 1935
Ginger isn't impressed by Fred's amorous attentions since she's mistaken him for a friend's other half. Many believe it to be the duo's best film together. Choreography by Astaire and score by Berlin makes this one a classic Hollywood musical. Look for a young Lucille Ball as a clerk in a flower shop. ♫Cheek to Cheek; Top Hat, White Tie and Tails; Isn't This A Lovely Day; The Piccolino; No Strings. **97m/B VHS, Beta, LV, 8mm.** Fred Astaire, Ginger Rogers, Erik Rhodes, Helen Broderick, Edward Everett Horton, Eric Blore, Lucille Ball; **D:** Mark Sandrich; **W:** Dwight Taylor, Allan Scott; **M:** Irving Berlin, Max Steiner. Nominations: Academy Awards '35: Best Interior Decoration, Best Picture, Best Song ("Cheek to Cheek"). *TTC, HMV*

Top of the Heap 🐾 1972 (R)
A cop is denied a promotion and gets angry. Deciding to chuck the laws of due process, he goes on a criminal-killing rampage. **91m/C VHS, Beta.** Christopher St. John, Paula Kelly, Patrick McVey; **D:** Christopher St. John. *NO*

Top Secret! 🐾🐾🐾 1984 (PG)
Unlikely musical farce parodies spy movies and Elvis Presley films. Young American rock star Nick Rivers goes to Europe on goodwill tour and becomes involved with Nazis, the French Resistance, an American refugee, and more. Sophisticated it isn't. From the creators of "Airplane!" **90m/C VHS, Beta, LV, Closed Caption.** Val Kilmer, Lucy Gutteridge, Christopher Villiers, Omar Sharif, Peter Cushing, Jeremy Kemp, Michael Gough; **D:** Jim Abrahams, Jerry Zucker, David Zucker; **W:** Jim Abra-

hams, Jerry Zucker, David Zucker, Martyn Burke; **M:** Maurice Jarre. *PAR*

Topaz 🐾🐾🐾 1969 (PG)
American CIA agent and French intelligence agent combine forces to find information about Russian espionage in Cuba. Cerebral and intriguing, but not classic Hitchcock. Based on the novel by Leon Uris. Laser disc video release includes two alternate endings. **126m/C VHS, Beta, LV.** John Forsythe, Frederick Stafford, Philippe Noiret, Karin Dor, Michel Piccoli; **D:** Alfred Hitchcock; **C:** Jack Hildyard; **M:** Maurice Jarre. National Board of Review Awards '69: 10 Best Films of the Year, Best Director (Hitchcock), Best Supporting Actor (Noiret). *USH*

Topaze 🐾🐾🐾 1933
A shy, depressed teacher is fired from his job at a private school and takes a new job, unaware that his boss is using him in a business scam. From the French play by Marcel Pagnol. An American version was also filmed in 1933; Pagnol produced his own version in '51. In French with English subtitles. **92m/B VHS, Beta, Closed Caption.** FR Louis Jouvet, Edwige Feuillere, Marcel Vallee; **D:** Louis Gasnier; **W:** Marcel Pagnol; **M:** Max Steiner. *INT, FOX, HEG*

Topaze 🐾🐾🐾 1933
American adaptation of the Marcel Pagnol play, about an innocent, doltish schoolmaster who becomes the unknowing front for a baron's illegal business scam. Remade in two French versions, in 1933, and in 1951 by Pagnol. **127m/B VHS, Beta, Closed Caption.** John Barrymore, Myrna Loy, Jobyna Howland, Jackie Searl; **D:** Harry D'Abbadie D'Arrast. *FOX*

Topaze 🐾🐾🐾½ 1951
After losing his job, a pathetic school teacher gets involved with the mob and winds up a powerful businessman. Remake of two earlier versions, one French and one American. Based on the play by director Pagnol. In French with English subtitles. **95m/B VHS, Closed Caption.** FR Fernandel, Helen Perdriere, Pierre Larquey; **D:** Marcel Pagnol. *DVT, APD*

The Topeka Terror 🐾🐾 1945
Lane stars as a federal agent who joins forces with a frontier lawyer to stop greedy land-grabber Barcroft from ripping off a group of homesteaders. Based on a story by Patricia Harper. **55m/B VHS.** Allan "Rocky" Lane, Linda Stirling, Roy Barcroft, Earle Hodgins, Bud Geary; **D:** Howard Bretherton; **W:** Patricia Harper, Norman S. Hall. *MOV*

Topkapi 🐾🐾🐾 1964
An international bevy of thieves can't resist the treasures of the famed Topkapi Palace Museum, an impregnable fortress filled with wealth and splendor. Comic thriller based on Erie Ambler's "The Light of Day." **122m/C VHS, Beta.** Melina Mercouri, Maximilian Schell, Peter Ustinov, Robert Morley, Akim Tamiroff; **D:** Jules Dassin; **M:** Manos Hadjidakis. Academy Awards '64: Best Supporting Actor (Ustinov); National Board of Review Awards '64: 10 Best Films of the Year. *FOX*

Topper 🐾🐾🐾½ 1937
George and Marion Kerby return as ghosts after a fatal car accident, determined to assist their pal Cosmo Topper. Immensely popular at the box office, followed by "Topper Takes a Trip" and "Topper Returns." The series uses trick photography and special effects to complement the comedic scripts. Inspired a television series and remade in 1979 as television movie. Also available colorized. **97m/B VHS, Beta.** Cary Grant, Roland Young, Constance Bennett, Billie Burke, Eugene Pallette, Hoagy Carmichael; **D:** Norman Z. McLeod. Nominations: Academy Awards '37: Best Sound, Best Supporting Actor (Young). *MED, CCB, VTR*

Topper Returns 🐾🐾🐾 1941
Cosmo Topper helps ghost find the man who mistakenly murdered her and warns her friend, the intended victim. Humorous conclusion to the trilogy preceded by "Topper" and "Topper Takes a Trip." Followed by a television series. Also available colorized. **87m/B VHS, Beta, LV.** Roland Young, Joan Blondell, Dennis O'Keefe, Carole Landis, Eddie Anderson, H.B. Warner, Billie Burke; **D:** Roy Del Ruth. Nominations: Academy Awards '41: Best Sound. *SNC, NOS, CAB*

Topper Takes a Trip 🎭🎭🎭 1939 Cosmo Topper and his wife have falling out and ghosts Kerby help them get back together. The special effects sequences are especially funny. Followed by "Topper Returns." Also available colorized. **85m/B VHS, Beta.** Constance Bennett, Roland Young, Billie Burke, Franklin Pangborn, Alan Mowbray; *D:* Norman Z. McLeod. Nominations: Academy Awards '39: Best Special Effects. *MED, VTR*

Topsy Turvy 🎭½ 1984 (R) A comedy about reckless romance and not much else. **90m/C VHS, Beta.** Lisbet Dahl, Ebbe Rode; *D:* Edward Fleming. *LIV, VES*

Tor 🎭½ 1964 Medieval barbarian endeavors to free an enslaved village from a band of murderous hoodlums. **94m/C VHS, Beta.** Joe Robinson, Bella Cortez, Harry Baird; *D:* Antonio Leonuiola. *TWE*

Tora! Tora! Tora! 🎭🎭 1970 (G) The story of events leading up to December 7, 1941, is retold by three directors from both Japanese and American viewpoints in this tense, large-scale production. Well-documented and realistic treatment of the Japanese attack on Pearl Harbor that brought the US into WWII; notable for its good photography but lacks a storyline equal to its epic intentions. **144m/C VHS, Beta, LV.** Martin Balsam, Soh Yomamura, Joseph Cotten, E.G. Marshall, Tatsuya Mihashi, Wesley Addy, Jason Robards Jr., James Whitmore, Leon Ames, George Macready; *D:* Richard Fleischer, Toshio Masuda, Kinji Fukasaku; *M:* Jerry Goldsmith. Academy Awards '70: Best Visual Effects; National Board of Review Awards '70: 10 Best Films of the Year; Nominations: Academy Awards '70: Best Art Direction/Set Decoration, Best Cinematography, Best Film Editing, Best Sound. *FOX, TLF, HMV*

The Torch 🎭🎭½ 1950 Mexican revolutionary restores law and order when he captures a small town but then finds himself in turmoil as he falls for an aristocratic young woman. **90m/C VHS.** MX Gilbert Roland, Paulette Goddard, Pedro Armendariz Sr., Walter Reed; *D:* Emilio Fernandez. *FCT*

Torch Song 🎭🎭 1953 In this muddled melodrama, a tough, demanding Broadway actress meets her match when she is offered true love by a blind pianist. Contains a couple of notoriously inept musical numbers. Made to show off Crawford's figure at age 50. Crawford's singing in the movie is dubbed. **90m/C VHS, LV.** Joan Crawford, Michael Wilding, Marjorie Rambeau, Gig Young, Harry (Henry) Morgan, Dorothy Patrick, Benny Rubin, Nancy Gates; *D:* Charles Walters. Nominations: Academy Awards '53: Best Supporting Actress (Rambeau). *MGM*

Torch Song Trilogy 🎭🎭½ 1988 (R) Adapted from Fierstein's hit Broadway play about a gay man who "just wants to be loved." Still effective, but the rewritten material loses something in the translation to the screen. Bancroft heads a strong cast with a finely shaded performance as Fierstein's mother. **126m/C VHS, Beta, LV, Closed Caption.** Anne Bancroft, Matthew Broderick, Harvey Fierstein, Brian Kerwin, Karen Young, Charles Pierce; *D:* Paul Bogart; *W:* Harvey Fierstein; *C:* Mikael Salomon; *M:* Peter Matz. *COL*

Torchlight 🎭 1985 (R) A young couple's life begins to crumble when a wealthy art dealer teaches them how to free base cocaine. Heavy-handed treatment of a subject that's been tackled with more skill elsewhere. **90m/C VHS, Beta, LV.** Pamela Sue Martin, Steve Railsback, Ian McShane, Al Corley, Rita Taggart; *D:* Thomas J. Wright.

Torero 🎭 1956 A young man becomes a bullfighter to overcome his fear of bulls. **89m/B VHS, Beta.** MX Luis Procuna, Manolete, Dolores Del Rio, Carlos Arruza; *D:* Carlos Velo; *W:* Carlos Velo, Hugo Butler. *MAD*

Torment 🎭🎭🎭 *Hets; Frenzy* 1944 Tragic triangle has young woman in love with fellow student and murdered by sadistic teacher. Atmospheric tale hailed by many as Sjoberg's finest film. Ingmar Bergman's first filmed script. In Swedish with English subtitles. **90m/B VHS, Beta.** SW *D:* Alf Sjoberg; *W:* Ingmar Bergman. *HMV, NLC*

Torment 🎭 1985 (R) A mild-mannered fellow is secretly a mass murderer specializing in young lovers. He struggles to hide his secret as his daughter approaches dating age and a relentless detective gets closer to the truth. A low-budget slasher. **85m/C VHS, Beta.** Taylor Gilbert, William Witt, Eve Brenner; *D:* Samson Aslanian, John Hopkins; *W:* Samson Aslanian, John Hopkins. *VTR, NWV*

Tormented 🎭½ 1960 Man pushes his mistress out of a lighthouse, killing her. Her ethereal body parts return to haunt him. **75m/B VHS.** Richard Carlson, Susan Gordon, Juli Reding; *D:* Bert I. Gordon. *SNC*

The Tormentors woof! 198? (R) Vaguely neo-Nazi gangs rape and murder a man's family, and he kills them all in revenge. **78m/C VHS, Beta.** James Craig, Anthony Eisley, Chris Nole; *D:* Boris Eagle. *NO*

Torn Apart 🎭🎭 1989 (R) Traditional Middle East hatreds undermine the love affair between two young people. Excellent performances from the principals highlight this drama. Adapted from the Chayin Zeldis novel "A Forbidden Love." **95m/C VHS, Beta.** Adrian Pasdar, Cecilia Peck, Machram Huri, Arnon Zadok, Barry Primus; *D:* Jack Fisher; *M:* Peter Arnow. *WAR, BTV*

Torn Between Two Lovers 🎭🎭 1979 A beautiful married woman has an affair with an architect while on a trip. Remick is enjoyable to watch, but it's a fairly predictable yarn. Made for television. **100m/C VHS, Beta, LV.** Lee Remick, Joseph Bologna, George Peppard, Giorgio Tozzi; *D:* Delbert Mann. *LIV*

Torn Curtain 🎭🎭½ 1966 American scientist poses as a defector to East Germany in order to uncover details of the Soviet missile program. He and his fiancee, who follows him behind the Iron Curtain, attempt to escape to freedom. Derivative and uninvolving. **125m/C VHS, Beta, LV.** Paul Newman, Julie Andrews, Lila Kedrova, David Opatoshu; *D:* Alfred Hitchcock; *W:* Brian Moore; *M:* John Addison. *USH*

Tornado 🎭 1983 An army sergeant revolts against his superiors and the enemy when his captain leaves him stranded in Vietnam. **90m/C VHS, Beta.** Timothy Brent, Tony Marsina, Alan Collins; *D:* Anthony (Antonio Margheriti) Dawson. *LIV*

Tornado! 🎭½ 1996 (PG) TV movie with cheesy special effects chronicles a week with tornado chaser Campbell, meteorologist Hudson, and government accountant Sturges who wants to stop funding for Hudson's new storm-warning device. Lame attempt to capture some of the "Twister" audience fails miserably. **90m/C VHS, LV.** Bruce Campbell, Ernie Hudson, Shannon Sturges, L.Q. Jones, Beau Eason; *D:* Noel Nosseck; *W:* John Logan; *C:* Paul Maibaum; *M:* Garry Schyman. *HMK*

Torpedo Alley 🎭🎭 1953 A guilt-ridden WWII Navy pilot feels responsible for the deaths of his crew. After the war, he joins a submarine crew and gradually learns to deal with his guilt. Average drama with plenty of submarine footage. **84m/B VHS.** Dorothy Malone, Mark Stevens, Charles Winninger, Bill Williams; *D:* Lew (Louis Friedlander) Landers. *REP*

Torpedo Attack 🎭 1972 Greek sailors, in an outdated submarine, bravely but hopelessly attack Mussolini's Italy during WWII. **88m/C VHS, Beta.** GR John Ferris, Sidney Kazan; *D:* George Law. *LIV*

Torpedo Run 🎭🎭 1958 Standard submarine melodramatics, about a U.S. sub that must torpedo a Japanese aircraft carrier which holds some of the crew's family members. Sometimes slow, generally worthwhile. **98m/C VHS, Beta.** Glenn Ford, Ernest Borgnine, Dean Jones, Diane Brewster, L.Q. Jones; *D:* Joseph Pevney. *MGM*

Torrents of Spring 🎭🎭 1990 (PG-13) Based on an Ivan Turgenev story, this lavishly filmed and costumed drama concerns a young Russian aristocrat circa 1840 who is torn between two women. Predictably, one is a good-hearted innocent, the other a scheming seductress. **102m/C VHS, Beta, LV.** Timothy Hutton, Nastassia Kinski, Valeria

Golino, William Forsythe, Urbano Barberini, Francesca De Sapio, Jacques Herlin; *D:* Jerzy Skolimowski. *NO*

Torso woof! *I Corpi Presentano Tracce Di Violenza Carnale* 1973 (R) Crazed psychosexual killer stalks beautiful women and dismembers them. Fairly bloodless and uninteresting, in spite of lovely Kendall. Italian title translates: The Bodies Showed Signs of Carnal Violence—quite an understatement for people missing arms and legs. **91m/C VHS, Beta.** IT Suzy Kendall, Tina Aumont, John Richardson; *D:* Sergio Martino; *W:* Ernesto Gastaldi, Sergio Martino. *PSM*

Tortilla Flat 🎭🎭🎭 1942 Based on the John Steinbeck novel of the same name, two buddies, Tracy and Garfield, struggle to make their way on the wrong side of the tracks in California. Garfield gets a break by inheriting a couple of houses, Tracy schemes to rip-off a rich, but eccentric, dog owner. In the meantime, both fall for the same girl, Lamarr, in perhaps the finest role of her career. Great performances from all, especially Morgan. **105m/B VHS.** Spencer Tracy, Hedy Lamarr, John Garfield, Frank Morgan, Akim Tamiroff, Sheldon Leonard, John Qualen, Donald Meek, Connie Gilchrist; *D:* Victor Fleming; *C:* Karl Freund. Nominations: Academy Awards '42: Best Supporting Actor (Morgan). *MGM, CCB*

Torture Chamber of Baron Blood 🎭🎭½ *Baron Blood* 1972 (PG) Baron with gorgeous thirst for the red stuff is reanimated and lots of innocent bystanders meet a grisly fate in this spaghetti gorefest. Familiar story has that certain Bava feel. **90m/C VHS, Beta.** IT Joseph Cotten, Elke Sommer, Massimo Girotti, Rada Rassimov; *D:* Mario Bava; *M:* Les Baxter. *NO*

The Torture Chamber of Dr. Sadism 🎭🎭½ *Blood Demon; Castle of the Walking Dead; Die Schlangengrube und das Pendel* 1969 Decapitated and drawn and quartered for sacrificing twelve virgins, the evil Count Regula is pieced together forty years later to continue his wicked ways. Great fun, terrific art direction. Very loosely based on Poe's "The Pit and the Pendulum." Beware of the heavily edited video version. **120m/C VHS, Beta.** GE Christopher Lee, Karin Dor, Lex Barker, Carl Lange, Vladimir Medar, Christiane Rucker, Dieter Eppler; *D:* Harald Reinl. *NO*

Torture Dungeon 🎭 1970 (R) Director Milligan tortures audience with more mindless medieval pain infliction from Staten Island. **80m/C VHS.** Jeremy Brooks, Susan Cassidy; *D:* Andy Milligan. *NO*

Torture Garden 🎭🎭 1967 A sinister man presides over an unusual sideshow where people can see what is in store if they allow the evil side of their personalities to take over. Written by Bloch ("Psycho") and based on four of his short stories. **93m/C VHS, Beta, LV.** GB Jack Palance, Burgess Meredith, Peter Cushing, Beverly Adams; *D:* Freddie Francis; *W:* Robert Bloch; *M:* Don Banks, James Bernard. *COL*

The Torture of Silence 🎭🎭½ *Master Dolorosa* 1917 A simple little drama about a doctor's neglected wife seeking out the doctor's best friend for love, remade by Gance again in 1932; both originally titled "Mater Dolorosa." Silent. **55m/B VHS, Beta.** *D:* Abel Gance. *FCT*

Torture Ship 🎭½ 1939 Director Halperin, who earlier made the minor horror classic "White Zombie," was all at sea in this becalmed thriller about a mad doctor who uses convicts for glandular experiment in his shipboard laboratory. Based on the short story "A Thousand Deaths" by Jack London. **57m/B VHS.** Lyle Talbot, Irving Pichel, Jacqueline Wells, Sheila Bromley; *D:* Victor Halperin. *NOS, LOO*

Torture Train 🎭½ 1983 (R) Mayhem, murder and knife-wielding psychosis occurs on board a train. **78m/C VHS, Beta.** Patty Edwards, Kay Beal. *JEF*

Total Eclipse 🎭 1995 (R) Unfortunate look at the mutually destructive relationship between 19th-century French poets Arthur Rimbaud (DiCaprio) and Paul Verlaine (Thewlis). Rimbaud was a 16-year-old Parisian sensation for his iconoclastic work but what's presented is an obnoxious showoff, while the older, married Verlaine is a drunken lout who abuses his teenaged wife Mathilde (Bohringer). There's lots of dissolute, violent behavior and absolutely no insight into their work (which is the only reason to care). Ugly film wastes a lot of talent.**CW:** Strong sexuality and nudity, language, and some startling violence. 111m/C VHS, Closed Caption. Leonardo DiCaprio, David Thewlis, Romane Bohringer, Dominique Blanc; **D:** Agnieszka Holland; **W:** Christopher Hampton; **C:** Yorgos Arvanitis. NLC

Total Exposure 🎞 1991 (R) Total idiocy involving unclad babes and hormonally imbalanced men in blackmail and murder. 1990 Playboy Playmate Deborah Driggs proves there is life of sorts after playmatedom.**CW:** Some language, violence, and sensuality. 96m/C VHS, LV, Closed Caption. Michael Nouri, Season Hubley, Christian Bocher, Robert Prentiss, Deborah Driggs, Jeff Conaway; **D:** John Quinn. REP

Total Recall 🎞🎞🎞 1990 (R) Mind-bending sci-fi movie set in the 21st century. Construction worker Quaid (Schwarzenegger) dreams every night about the colonization of Mars, so he decides to visit a travel service that specializes in implanting vacation memories into its clients' brains and buy a memory trip to the planet. Only during the implant, Quaid discovers his memories have been artificially altered and he must find out just what's real and what's not. Intriguing plot and spectacular special effects. Laced with graphic violence. Based on Phillip K. Dick's "We Can Remember It For You Wholesale."**CW:** Adult situations; language, nudity, gore effects, and sexual situations. 113m/C VHS, Beta, LV, 8mm, Closed Caption, DVD. Arnold Schwarzenegger, Rachel Ticotin, Sharon Stone, Michael Ironside, Ronny Cox, Roy Brocksmith, Marshall Bell, Mel Johnson Jr.; **D:** Paul Verhoeven; **W:** Gary Goldman, Dan O'Bannon; **C:** Jan De Bont; **M:** Jerry Goldsmith. Academy Awards '90: Best Visual Effects; Nominations: Academy Awards '90: Best Sound. IME, FUS, LIV

Totally F*ed Up** 🎞🎞 1994 The first of director Araki's teen trilogy, followed by "The Doom Generation" and "Nowhere," concerns itself with the teen angst experienced by a loose group of friends—four gays and a lesbian couple. In short chapters, they meet, talk, and wander through a soulless L.A. as one of their group, film school student Steven (Luna), makes a video documentary about their situation (footage of which is intercut throughout the film). 80m/C VHS. James Duval, Gilbert Luna, Lance May, Roko Belic, Susan Behshid, Jenee Gill, Alan Boyce; **D:** Gregg Araki; **W:** Gregg Araki; **C:** Gregg Araki. FCT, SHV

Toto le Heros 🎞🎞🎞 Toto the Hero 1991 (PG-13) Bitter old man, who as a child fantasized that he was a secret agent named Toto, harbors deep resentment over not living the life he's convinced he should have had. He maintains a childhood fantasy that he and his rich neighbor were switched at birth in the confusion of a fire at the hospital. Series of flashbacks and fast forwards show glimpses of his life, not necessarily as it was, but how he perceived it. Sounds complex, but it's actually very clear and fluid. Mix of comedy and tragedy, with lots of ironic twists, and precise visuals. In French with English subtitles. 90m/C VHS, Beta, LV, Closed Caption. **FR** Michel Bouquet, Jo De Backer, Thomas Godet, Mireille Perrier, Sandrine Blancke, Didier Ferney, Hugo Harold Harrisson, Gisela Uhlen, Peter Bohlke; **D:** Jaco Van Dormael; **W:** Jaco Van Dormael. Cesar Awards '91: Best Foreign Film. PAR, BTV

The Touch 🎞½ Be Roringen 1971 (R) Straightforward story of a woman who is satisfied with her husband until the arrival of a stranger. The stranger soon has her yearning for a life she has never known. Bergman's first English film lacks the sophistication of his earlier work. 112m/C VHS, Beta. **SW** Bibi Andersson, Elliott Gould, Max von Sydow; **D:** Ingmar Bergman; **W:** Ingmar Bergman; **C:** Sven Nykvist. FOX

Touch 🎞🎞½ 1996 (R) Sleazebags, fundamentalists, and a maybe saint would seem to make for a surefire success in this easygoing adaptation of the offbeat Elmore Leonard novel. And while individual scenes and performances shine, the film doesn't completely hang together. Young Juvenal (Ulrich) is a former monk, now working at an L.A. alcohol rehab center, who possesses the stigmata and seems to have an authentic gift for healing. Naturally, this brings the crazies and the scammers out of the woodwork, including former preacher Bill Hill (Walken), whose partner (Fonda) falls for the lad, and paramilitary religious fanatic August Murray (Arnold).**CW:** Some sexuality, language and a scene of violence. 96m/C VHS, Closed Caption. Skeet Ulrich, Bridget Fonda, Christopher Walken, Tom Arnold, Gina Gershon, Lolita Davidovich, Paul Mazursky, Janeane Garofalo, John Doe, Conchata Ferrell, Mason Adams, Breckin Meyer, Anthony Zerbe; **D:** Paul Schrader; **W:** Paul Schrader; **C:** Edward Lachman; **M:** David Grohl. MGM

Touch & Go 🎞🎞 1980 (PG) Three beautiful women commit grand larceny in order to raise funds for underprivileged children. 92m/C VHS, Beta. **AU** Wendy Hughes; **D:** Peter Maxwell; **W:** Alan Ormsby. NO

Touch and Go 🎞½ 1986 (R) Sentimental drama about a self-interested hockey pro who learns about love and giving through a young delinquent and his attractive mother. 101m/C VHS, Beta, LV, Closed Caption. Michael Keaton, Maria Conchita Alonso, Ajay Naidu, Maria Tucci, Max Wright, John C. Reilly; **D:** Robert Mandel; **W:** Harry Colomby. NO

Touch Me Not 🎞🎞 The Hunted 1974 (PG) A neurotic secretary is used by an industrial spy to gain information on her boss. Weak thriller. 84m/C VHS. **GB** Lee Remick, Michael Hinz, Ivan Desny, Ingrid Garbo; **D:** Douglas Fifthian. NO

A Touch of Class 🎞🎞🎞 1973 (PG) Married American insurance adjustor working in London plans quick and uncommitted affair but finds his heart doesn't obey the rules. Jackson and Segal create sparkling record of a growing relationship. 105m/C VHS, Beta. George Segal, Glenda Jackson, Paul Sorvino, Hildegarde Neil, K. Callan, Mary Barclay, Cec Linder; **D:** Melvin Frank; **W:** Jack Rose. Academy Awards '73: Best Actress (Jackson); Golden Globe Awards '74: Best Actor—Musical/Comedy (Segal), Best Actress—Musical/Comedy (Jackson); Writers Guild of America '73: Best Original Screenplay; Nominations: Academy Awards '73: Best Picture, Best Song ("All That Love Went to Waste"), Best Story & Screenplay, Original Dramatic/Comedy Score. MED

Touch of Evil 🎞🎞🎞🎞 1958 Stark, perverse story of murder, kidnapping and police corruption in Mexican border town. Welles portrays a police chief who invents evidence to convict the guilty. Filled with innovative photography reminiscent of "Citizen Kane," as filmed by Russell Metty. 108m/B VHS, Beta, LV. Charlton Heston, Orson Welles, Janet Leigh, Joseph Calleia, Akim Tamiroff, Marlene Dietrich, Valentin de Vargas, Dennis Weaver, Zsa Zsa Gabor, Mort Mills, Victor Milian, Joanna Moore, Joi Lansing; **Cameos:** Ray Collins, Mercedes McCambridge, Joseph Cotten; **D:** Orson Welles; **W:** Orson Welles; **C:** Russell Metty; **M:** Henry Mancini. USH

The Touch of Satan 🎞 The Touch of Melissa; Night of the Demon; Curse of Melissa 1970 (PG) Lost on the road, a young man meets a lovely young woman and is persuaded to stay at her nearby farmhouse. Things there are not as they seem, including the young woman—who turns out to be a very old witch. 90m/C VHS, Beta. Michael Berry, Emby Mallay, Lee Amber, Yvonne Wilson, Jeanne Gerson; **D:** Don Henderson. NO

Touched 🎞🎞 1982 (R) Two young people struggle with the outside world after their escape from a mental institution. Although melodramatic and poorly scripted, the film is saved by fine performances by Hays and Beller. 89m/C VHS, Beta. Robert Hays, Kathleen Beller, Ned Beatty, Gilbert Lewis; **D:** John Flynn. MED

Touched by Love 🎞🎞½ To Elvis, With Love 1980 (PG) The true story of a handicapped child who begins to communicate when her teacher suggests she write to Elvis Presley. Sincere and well performed. 95m/C VHS, Beta. Deborah Raffin, Diane Lane, Christina Raines, Clu Gulager, John Amos; **D:** Gus Trikonis; **W:** Hesper Anderson; **M:** John Barry. COL

Tough and Deadly 🎞½ 1994 (R) CIA agent teams up with bounty hunter to stop a drug ring.**CW:** Non-stop acts of violence; strong language; drug use. 92m/C VHS. Billy Blanks, Roddy Piper. USH

Tough Assignment 🎞 1949 A reporter in the West discovers and infiltrates a gang of organized rustlers who are forcing butchers to buy inferior meat. 64m/B VHS, Beta, LV. Donald (Don "Red") Barry, Marjorie Steele, Steve Brodie. NO

Tough Enough 🎞🎞 1983 (PG) A country-western singer and songwriter decides to finance his fledgling singing career by entering amateur boxing matches. Insipid and predictable, with fine cast wasted. 107m/C VHS, Beta. Dennis Quaid, Charlene Watkins, Warren Oates, Pam Grier, Stan Shaw, Bruce McGill, Wilford Brimley, Bob Watson; **D:** Richard Fleischer. FOX

Tough Guy 🎞 1953 Based on the play by Bruce Walker, a London hood carouses, mugs, breaks hearts and personifies his generation's anxiety. 73m/B VHS, Beta. **GB** James Kenney, Hermione Gingold, Joan Collins; **D:** Lewis Gilbert. UNI

Tough Guy 🎞 197? Two undercover policemen battle local gangsters in a bid to smash their crime ring. 90m/C VHS, Beta. Chen Ying, Charlie Chiang; **D:** Chieng Hung. NO

Tough Guys 🎞🎞½ 1986 (PG) Two aging ex-cons, who staged America's last train robbery in 1961, try to come to terms with modern life after many years in prison. Amazed and hurt by the treatment of the elderly in the 1980s, frustrated with their inability to find something worthwhile to do, they begin to plan one last heist. Tailor-made for Lancaster and Douglas, who are wonderful. Script becomes cliched at end. 103m/C VHS, Beta, LV. Burt Lancaster, Kirk Douglas, Charles Durning, Eli Wallach, Jake Steinfeld, Dana Carvey, Alexis Smith, Darlanne Fluegel, Billy Barty, Monty Ash; **D:** Jeff Kanew; **W:** James Orr, Jim Cruickshank; **M:** James Newton Howard. TOU

Tough Guys Don't Dance 🎞🎞½ 1987 (R) Mailer directed this self-satiric mystery thriller from his own novel. A writer may have committed murder—but he can't remember. So he searches for the truth among various friends, enemies, lovers, and cohorts. 110m/C VHS, Beta, LV, Closed Caption. Ryan O'Neal, Isabella Rossellini, Wings Hauser, Debra Sandlund, John Bedford Lloyd, Lawrence Tierney, Clarence Williams III, Penn Jillette, Frances Fisher; **D:** Norman Mailer; **W:** Norman Mailer; **C:** John Bailey; **M:** Angelo Badalamenti. Golden Raspberry Awards '87: Worst Director (Mailer). MED, CDV, VTR

Tough Kid 🎞 1939 A bad kid with gang connections attempts to shield his boxer brother from corruption at the hands of the same gang. Poor production all around. 61m/B VHS, Beta. Frankie Darro, Dick Purcell, Judith Allen, Lillian Elliot; **D:** Howard Bretherton. SNC

Tough to Handle 🎞½ 1937 ...And no picnic to watch, either. A reporter cracks a criminal racket that rips off lottery sweepstakes winners. A laughably inept production. 58m/B VHS. Frankie Darro, Kane Richmond, Phyllis Fraser, Harry Worth; **D:** S. Roy Luby. NOS, LOO

Tougher than Leather 🎞 1988 (R) The rap triumvirate battles criminals, vigilante-style, in their home neighborhood. Poorly executed and exploitative fare. 92m/C VHS, Beta. Run DMC, The Beastie Boys, Slick Rick, Richard Edson, Jenny Lumet; **D:** Rick Rubin. COL

Toughlove 🎞🎞 1985 The parents of a juvenile delinquent organize a tough parental philosophy and a support group for other parents having a difficult time with their teens. Made for television. 100m/C VHS, Beta. Lee Remick, Bruce Dern, Piper

Laurie, Louise Latham, Dana Elcar, Jason Patric, Eric Schiff, Dedee Pfeiffer; **D:** Glenn Jordan. *FRH*

Touki Bouki ♂♂ *Journey of the Hyena* 1973 Feeling alienated from their African society, Mory and Anta see freedom in the flashy consumerism of European culture and embark on a quest to meet happiness in Paris. A Bonnie & Clyde-like story symbolizing Africa's advancement toward a technological civilization. In Wolof with English subtitles. 85m/C VHS. **D:** Djibril Diop Mambety. *KIV*

Tour of Duty ♂♂½ 1987 Follows the trials that the members of an American platoon face daily during the Vietnam war. The pilot movie for a television series. 93m/C VHS, Beta, LV. Terence Knox, Stephen Caffrey, Joshua Maurer, Ramon Franco; **D:** Bill W.L. Norton. *NWV, HHE*

Tourist Trap ♂ 1979 (PG) While traveling through the desert, a couple's car has a flat. A woman's voice lures the man into an abandoned gas station, where he discovers that the voice belongs to a mannequin. Or is it? Not very interesting or suspenseful. 90m/C VHS, Beta, LV, **Closed Caption.** Tanya Roberts, Chuck Connors, Robin Sherwood, Jocelyn Jones; **D:** David Schmoeller; **W:** David Schmoeller; **M:** Pino Donaggio. *PAR*

Tournament ♂♂½ 1929 Renoir's second-to-last silent film, in which Protestants and Catholics joust out their differences in era of Catherine de Medici. French title: "Le Tournoi dans la Cite." 90m/B VHS, Beta. **FR** Aldo Nadi; **D:** Jean Renoir. *FCT*

Tous les Matins du Monde ♂♂♂
All the Mornings of the World 1992 Haunting tale of two 17th century French baroque composers and their relationship with each other and their music. Gerard Depardieu plays Marin Marais who eventually becomes a court composer at Versailles. As a young man, he studies under Sainte Colombe, a private and soulful musician, about whom little is known even today. Depardieu's son Guillaume (in his film debut) plays the young Marais, who startles the quiet Sainte Colombe home and has an affair with one of his daughters (Brochet). Filmmaker Corneau lends a quiet austere tone which parallels the life and music of Sainte Colombe. In French with English subtitles. 114m/C VHS, LV. **FR** Gerard Depardieu, Guillaume Depardieu, Jean-Pierre Marielle, Anne Brochet, Caroline Sihol, Carole Richert, Violaine Lacroix, Nadege Teron, Miriam Boyer, Michel Bouquet; **D:** Alain Corneau; **W:** Pascal Quignard, Alain Corneau; **C:** Yves Angelo; **M:** Jordi Savall. Cesar Awards '92: Best Cinematography, Best Director (Corneau), Best Film, Best Supporting Actress (Brochet), Best Score. *FCT*

Toute Une Nuit ♂♂♂ *All Night Long* 1982 Assorted people stumble melodramatically in and out of one another's lives on steamy summer night in Brussels. Fine combination of avant-garde technique and narrative. In French with English subtitles. 90m/C VHS. **BE FR** Aurore Clement, Tcheky Karyo, Veronique Silver, Angelo Abazoglou, Natalia Ackerman; **D:** Chantal Akerman; **W:** Andra Akers. *WAC, FCT*

Toward the Terra ♂♂ 1980 In the distant future mankind is forced to evacuate Earth and settles on the planet Atarakusha. Society ruthlessly suppresses anything which could destabilize it in an effort to prevent the mistakes which destroyed the Earth. The most destabilizing presence is the MU, a new race with incredible mental powers, who are ruthlessly hunted and eliminated. But the leader of the MU reaches out to a human with his own inexplicable powers to aid in establishing a new world. In Japanese with subtitles. 112m/C VHS. **JP** *CPM*

Tower of Evil woof! *Horror on Snape Island; Beyond the Fog* 1972 (R) Anthropologists and treasure hunters unite in search of Phoenician hoard on Snape Island. Suddenly, inanimate bodies materialize. Seems the island's single inhabitant liked it quiet. Cult favorite despite uneven performances. So bad it's not bad. 86m/C VHS, Beta. **GB** Bryant Halliday, Jill Haworth, Jack Watson, Mark Edwards, George Coulouris; **D:** James O'Connolly. *NO*

The Tower of London ♂♂½ 1939 Tells the story of Richard III (Rathbone), the English monarch who brutally executed the people who tried to get in his way to the throne. This melodrama was considered extremely graphic for its time, and some of the torture scenes had to be cut before it was released. 93m/B VHS. Basil Rathbone, Boris Karloff, Barbara O'Neil, Ian Hunter, Vincent Price, Nan Grey, John Sutton, Leo G. Carroll, Miles Mander; **D:** Rowland V. Lee. *USH*

Tower of London ♂♂ 1962 A deranged lord (Price) murdering his way to the throne of England is eventually crowned Richard III. Sophisticated and well-made Poe-like thriller. More interesting as historic melodrama than as horror film. A remake of the 1939 version starring Basil Rathbone, in which Price played a supporting role. 79m/B VHS, Beta. Vincent Price, Michael Pate, Joan Freeman, Robert Brown; **D:** Roger Corman. *MGM, FCT*

Tower of Screaming Virgins ♂ 1968 The Queen of France maintains a tower in which she has her lovers killed—after she makes love to them. An extremely loose adaptation of a Dumas novel; with English subtitles. 89m/C VHS, Beta, 8mm. **GE** Terry Torday, Jean Piat. *VYY, VDM, SNC*

Tower of Terror ♂½ 1942 (NC-17) Woman escapes from a German concentration camp and takes refuge in a lighthouse. The proprietor sees in her an uncanny resemblance to his late wife, whom he killed, and soon plots to do away with her. Story hampered by poor acting. 62m/B VHS, Beta. **GB** Wilfred Lawson, Movita, Michael Rennie, Morland Graham, John Longden, George Woodbridge; **D:** Lawrence Huntington. *NOS, SNC*

The Towering Inferno ♂♂ 1974 (PG) Raging blaze engulfs the world's tallest skyscraper on the night of its glamorous dedication ceremonies. Allen had invented the disaster du jour genre two years earlier with "The Poseidon Adventure." Features a new but equally noteworthy cast. ♫We May Never Love Like This Again. 165m/C VHS, Beta, LV, **Closed Caption.** Steve McQueen, Paul Newman, William Holden, Faye Dunaway, Fred Astaire, Jennifer Jones, Richard Chamberlain, Susan Blakely, O.J. Simpson, Robert Vaughn, Robert Wagner; **D:** John Guillermin, Irwin Allen; **W:** Stirling Silliphant; **C:** Joseph Biroc, Fred W. Koenekamp; **M:** John Williams. Academy Awards '74: Best Cinematography, Best Film Editing, Best Song ("We May Never Love Like This Again"); British Academy Awards '75: Best Supporting Actor (Astaire); Golden Globe Awards '75: Best Supporting Actor (Astaire); Nominations: Academy Awards '74: Best Art Direction/Set Decoration, Best Picture, Best Sound, Best Supporting Actor (Astaire), Original Dramatic/Comedy Score. *FOX*

A Town Called Hell ♂ *A Town Called Bastard* 1972 (R) Two men hold an entire town hostage while looking for "Aguila," the Mexican revolutionary. Greed, evil, and violence take over. Shot in Spain. Whatever you call it, just stay out of it. 95m/C VHS, Beta. **GB SP** Robert Shaw, Stella Stevens, Martin Landau, Telly Savalas, Fernando Rey; **D:** Robert Parrish. *GEM*

A Town Like Alice ♂♂½ 1985 An Australian miniseries based on a novel by Nevil Shute. The story follows women prisoners of war during WWII. Jean Paget is a British prisoner in the camps of Malaya when she meets and falls in love with a fellow prisoner, the rugged Australian, Joe. Separated by their captors, they reunite years later and try to see if their love has survived. Remake of a 1951 film of the same name that is also known as "Rape of Malaya." 301m/C VHS, Beta. **AU** Bryan Brown, Helen Morse, Gordon Jackson; **D:** David Stevens. *SIG, NWV, IME*

Town that Dreaded Sundown ♂♂½ 1976 (R) A mad killer is on the loose in a small Arkansas town. Based on a true story, this famous 1946 murder spree remains an unsolved mystery. 90m/C VHS, Beta. Ben Johnson, Andrew Prine, Dawn Wells; **D:** Charles B. Pierce. *WAR, OM*

The Toxic Avenger ♂½ 1986 (R) Tongue-in-cheek, cult fave has 98-pound weakling fall into barrel of toxic waste to emerge as a lumbering, bloodthirsty hulk of sludge and mire. He falls for a blind babe and sets out to do good (and get revenge). Billed as "The first Super-Hero from New Jersey." Two sequels followed: "Toxic Avenger Part II" and "Toxic Avenger Part III: The Last Temptation of Toxie." 90m/C VHS, Beta, LV. Mitchell Cohen, Andree Maranda, Jennifer Baptist, Robert Prichard, Cindy Manion; **D:** Michael Herz, Lloyd (Samuel Weil) Kaufman; **W:** Joe Ritter. *VES, LIV*

The Toxic Avenger, Part 2 ♂½ 1989 (R) Sequel to "Toxic Avenger." Hulky slimer targets Japanese corporations that built toxic chemical dump in Tromaville. Followed by "Toxic Avenger Part III: The Last Temptation of Toxie." 90m/C VHS, Beta, LV, **Closed Caption.** Ron Fazio, Phoebe Legere, Rick Collins, John Altamura; **D:** Michael Herz, Lloyd (Samuel Weil) Kaufman; **W:** Lloyd (Samuel Weil) Kaufman, Gay Partington Terry. *WAR*

The Toxic Avenger, Part 3: The Last Temptation of Toxie ♂½ 1989 (R) Unemployed superhero is tempted to sell out to greedy capitalists when his cutie Claire needs an eye operation. Also available in an unrated version. 102m/C VHS, Beta, LV. Ron Fazio, Phoebe Legere, John Altamura, Rick Collins, Lisa Gaye, Jessica Dublin; **D:** Michael Herz, Lloyd (Samuel Weil) Kaufman; **W:** Lloyd (Samuel Weil) Kaufman, Gay Partington Terry. *VES, LIV*

The Toy ♂½ 1982 (PG) Penniless reporter finds himself the new "toy" of the spoiled son of a multimillionaire old man. Unfortunate casting of Pryor as the toy owned by Gleason, with heavy-handed lecturing about earning friends. Slow and terrible remake of the Pierre Richard comedy "Le Jouet." 99m/C VHS, Beta, LV, 8mm. Richard Pryor, Jackie Gleason, Ned Beatty, Wilfrid Hyde-White; **D:** Richard Donner. *COL*

Toy Soldiers ♂½ 1984 (R) A group of college students are held for ransom in a war-torn Central American country. When they escape, they join forces with a seasoned mercenary who leads them as a vigilante force. 85m/C VHS, Beta, LV. Cleavon Little, Jason Miller, Tim Robbins, Tracy Scoggins; **D:** David Fisher. *NWV, VTR*

Toy Soldiers ♂♂ 1991 (R) This unlikely action tale stops short of being laughable but still has a fair share of silliness. South American narco-terrorists seize an exclusive boys' school. The mischievous students turn their talent for practical jokes to resistance-fighting. Orbach has an uncredited cameo. Based on a novel by William P. Kennedy. **CW:** Language and violence. 104m/C VHS, Beta, LV, 8mm, **Closed Caption.** Sean Astin, Wil Wheaton, Keith Coogan, Andrew Divoff, Denholm Elliott, Louis Gossett Jr.; **Cameos:** Jerry Orbach; **D:** Dan Petrie Jr.; **W:** Dan Petrie Jr.; **C:** Thomas Burstyn; **M:** Robert Folk. *COL*

Toy Story ♂♂♂♂ 1995 (G) First feature length, wholly computer animated film confirms what we suspected all along—toys do have lives of their own when we're not around. Pull-string cowboy Woody (Hanks), as favorite toy, presides over his fellow playthings in Andy's room. Enter new toy on the block, Buzz Lightyear (Allen), a space ranger action figure who thinks he's real. Jealous Woody and his delusional, high-tech companion soon find themselves in the outside world, where they must join forces to survive. Funny, intelligent script and voice characterizations that rival many live-action movies in depth and emotion. All this, and Don Rickles berating an actual hockey puck. 84m/C VHS, LV, **Closed Caption.** **D:** John Lasseter; **W:** Joss Whedon, Joel Cohen, Alec Sokolow; **M:** Randy Newman; **V:** Tom Hanks, Tim Allen, Annie Potts, John Ratzenberger, Wallace Shawn, Jim Varney, Don Rickles, John Morris, R. Lee Ermey, Laurie Metcalf, Erik von Detten. Nominations: Academy Awards '95: Best Screenplay, Best Song ("You've Got a Friend"), Best Original Score; Golden Globe Awards '96: Best Film—Musical/Comedy, Best Song ("You Got a Friend in Me"); MTV Movie Awards '96: Best On-Screen Duo (Tom Hanks/Tim Allen). *TOU*

Toys ♫½ 1992 (PG-13) Disappointingly earnest comedy about Leslie (Williams), the whimsical son of a toy manufacturer who must fight to keep the playful spirit of the factory alive after it passes into the hands of his deranged uncle (Gambon). This uncle is a general who attempts to transform the factory into an armaments plant. Leslie receives assistance in this battle from his sister Alsatia (Cusack) and his cousin Patrick (L.L. Cool J). Flat characters; generally falls short by trying too hard to send a message to viewers about the folly of war. Does have extremely vivid and intriguing visuals and special effects. 121m/C VHS. Robin Williams, Joan Cusack, Michael Gambon, L.L. Cool J., Robin Wright; *Cameos:* Donald O'Connor; **D:** Barry Levinson; **W:** Valerie Curtin, Barry Levinson. Nominations: Academy Awards '92: Best Art Direction/Set Decoration, Best Costume Design. FXV

Toys in the Attic ♫♫½ 1963 A man returns to his home in New Orleans with his child bride, where they will live with his two impoverished, spinster sisters. Toned-down version of the Lillian Hellman play. 88m/B VHS, Closed Caption. Dean Martin, Geraldine Page, Yvette Mimieux, Wendy Hiller, Gene Tierney, Nan Martin, Larry Gates, Frank Silvera; **D:** George Roy Hill; **W:** James Poe; **C:** Joseph Biroc. Nominations: Academy Awards '63: Best Costume Design (B & W). MGM

Traces of Red ♫♫ 1992 (R) Set in affluent Palm Beach, and filled with dead bodies, colorful suspects, and red herrings. The complex plot, often so serious it's funny, leads viewers through a convoluted series of events. Cop Jack Dobson (Belushi) is found dead in the opening scene; in homage to "Sunset Boulevard," his corpse acts as the narrator, a vehicle which unfortunately doesn't work as well here. He promises to recount the events leading up to his death which circle around a series of murders, and the people in his life who are possible suspects. Although Belushi's performance is average, Goldwyn, as Dobson's partner, shows off the talent he displayed in "Ghost."*CW:* Language, violence, and sexuality. 105m/C VHS, LV, Closed Caption. James Belushi, Lorraine Bracco, Tony Goldwyn, William Russ, Michelle Joyner, Joe Lisi, Jim Piddock; **D:** Andy Wolk; **M:** Graeme Revell. HBO

Track of the Moonbeast ♫♫ 1976 An American Indian uses mythology to capture the Moonbeast, a lizard-like creature that is roaming the deserts of New Mexico. 90m/C VHS, Beta. Chase Cordell, Donna Leigh Drake; **D:** Richard Ashe. PSM

Track of the Vampire ♫½ *Blood Bath* 1966 Half an hour of leftover footage from a Yugoslavian vampire movie stuck into the story of a California painter who kills his models. Gripping and atmospheric, but disjointed. 80m/B VHS. YU William Campbell, Jonathan Haze, Sid Haig, Marissa Mathes, Lori Saunders, Sandra Knight; **D:** Stephanie Rothman, Jack Hill. SNC, GNS

Track 29 ♫½ 1988 (R) A confusing black comedy about a lonely woman, her husband who has a model train fetish, and a stranger who claims to be her son. Filmed in North Carolina. 90m/C VHS. Theresa Russell, Gary Oldman, Christopher Lloyd, Colleen Camp, Sandra Bernhard, Seymour Cassel, Leon Rippy, Vance Colvig; **D:** Nicolas Roeg; **W:** Dennis Potter. MGM, CAN

The Tracker ♫♫½ *Dead or Alive* 1988 HBO western about a retired gunman/tracker who must again take up arms. His college-educated son joins him as he searches for a murdering religious fanatic. Fairly decent for the genre. Made for cable television. 102m/C VHS, Beta, Closed Caption. Kris Kristofferson, Scott Wilson, Mark Moses, David Huddleston, John Quade, Don Swayze, Brynn Thayer; **D:** John Guillermin. HBO, WAR

The Trackers ♫½ 1971 A frontier man searches for the people who kidnapped his daughter and killed his son. He is joined by a cocky black tracker. Borgnine brings strength to his character as the rancher seeking revenge. Made for television. 73m/C VHS, Beta. Sammy Davis Jr., Ernest Borgnine, Julie Adams, Connie Kreski, Jim Davis; **D:** Earl Bellamy. FOX

Tracks ♫½ 1976 (R) Vietnam veteran accompanies the body of a buddy on a long train ride home. He starts suffering flashbacks from the war and begins to think some of the passengers are out to get him. 90m/C VHS, Beta, Closed Caption. Dennis Hopper, Dean Stockwell, Taryn Power, Zack Norman, Michael Emil, Barbara Flood; **D:** Henry Jaglom; **W:** Henry Jaglom; **C:** Paul Glickman. PAR

Tracks of a Killer ♫♫ 1995 (R) David and Clair Hawker are vacationing at an isolated winter retreat that's invaded by a killer.*CW:* Sadistic violence, a sex scene and language. 100m/C VHS, LV, Closed Caption. Kelly Le Brock, James Brolin, Wolf Larson, Courtney Taylor, George Touliatos; **D:** Harvey Frost; **W:** Michael Cooney; **C:** Bruce Worrall; **M:** Barron Abramovitch. LIV

Trade Off ♫♫ 1995 (R) Beautiful, unhappily married Jackie (Russell) seduces equally miserable married businessman Thomas (Baldwin) and jokes about getting rid of their respective spouses. Then Thomas' wife is killed in a car crash and Thomas learns Jackie caused the "accident." He should have watched "Strangers on a Train" to see where trading murders can get you.*CW:* Sexuality; language; some violence. 92m/C VHS, LV, Closed Caption. Theresa Russell, Adam Baldwin, Megan Gallagher, Barry Primus, Pat Skipper; **D:** Andrew Lane. REP

Trade Secrets ♫♫ 199? Special investigator Jerry Morrison is assigned to probe the mysterious death of an heiress to a wine fortune. His investigation leads to the secrets and private fantasies of the woman's family and friends. 91m/C VHS. Sam Waterston, Marisa Berenson, Lauren Hutton, Arielle Dombasle; **D:** Claude Feraldo; **W:** Claude Feraldo. TRI

Trader Horn ♫♫½ 1931 Early talkie was the first Hollywood picture to be filmed in Africa. Carey and Renaldo are traders who tangle with a native tribe while searching for the long-lost daughter of a missionary, who turns out to be a tribal goddess. Based on a novel by Alfred Aloysius Horn and Ethelreda Lewis. Boring remake in 1973. 105m/B VHS. Harry Carey Sr., Duncan Renaldo, Edwina Booth, Sir C. Aubrey Smith, Mutia Omoolu, Olive Golden Carey; **D:** Woodbridge S. Van Dyke; **W:** Cyril Hume, Richard Schayer, Dale Van Every, John Thomas Neville; **C:** Clyde De Vinna. Nominations: Academy Awards '31: Best Picture. MGM

Trader Tom of the China Seas 1954 A young island trader and a shipwrecked beauty get involved in espionage while helping the UN to safeguard the Asian corridor. A 12-part serial on two cassettes. 167m/B VHS. Harry Lauter, Aline Towne, Lyle Talbot, Fred Graham. REP

Trading Hearts ♫♫ 1987 (PG) Over-the-hill baseball player falls for an unsuccessful singer and single mom at a Florida training camp set in the 1950s. 88m/C VHS, Beta, LV. Beverly D'Angelo, Raul Julia, Jerry Lewis, Parris Buckner, Robert Gwaltney; **D:** Neil Leifer; **W:** Frank Deford. LIV

Trading Mom ♫♫½ 1994 (PG) Harried single parent Spacek is erased from the lives of her three kids, who decide they want a parent who's more fun. So, thanks to some magic, they head off to the Mommy Mart to try out a trio of bizarre choices. This gives Spacek a chance at three more roles before the kids come to their senses. Based on "The Mommy Market" by Nancy Brelis; directorial debut for daughter Tia. 82m/C VHS, LV, Closed Caption. Sissy Spacek, Anna Chlumsky, Aaron Michael Metchik, Asher Metchik, Maureen Stapleton; **D:** Tia Brelis; **W:** Tia Brelis; **M:** David Kitay. THV

Trading Places ♫♫½ 1983 (R) Two elderly businessmen wager that environment is more important than heredity in creating a successful life, using a rich nephew and an unemployed street hustler as guinea pigs. Curtis is winning as a hooker-with-a-heart-of-gold who helps the hapless Aykroyd. Oft-told tale succeeds thanks to strong cast. Murphy's second screen appearance.

118m/C VHS, Beta, LV, 8mm, Closed Caption. Eddie Murphy, Dan Aykroyd, Jamie Lee Curtis, Ralph Bellamy, Don Ameche, Denholm Elliott, Paul Gleason, James Belushi; **D:** John Landis; **W:** Herschel Weingrod, Timothy Harris; **M:** Elmer Bernstein. British Academy Awards '83: Best Supporting Actor (Elliott), Best Supporting Actress (Curtis); Nominations: Academy Awards '83: Original Song Score and/or Adaptation. PAR

Traenen in Florenz ♫ *Tears in Florence* 1984 A woman involved in a car accident winds up falling in love with the man who injured her, only to discover later that they are actually brother and sister, long separated. In German with English subtitles. 90m/C VHS, Beta. GE **D:** Marianne Schafer. VCD, APD, GLV

Traffic ♫♫½ 1971 Eccentric auto designer Monsieur Hulot tries to transport his latest contraption from Paris to Amsterdam for an international auto show. As usual, everything goes wrong. Tati's last feature film and his fifth to feature Hulot. French with subtitles. 89m/C VHS. FR Jacques Tati, Maria Kimberly, Marcel Fraval; **D:** Jacques Tati. HMV

Traffic in Souls ♫♫♫ 1913 A silent melodrama dealing with white slavery. Immigrants and gullible country girls are lured into brothels where they are trapped with no hope of escape until, in a hail of bullets, the police raid the dens of vice and rescue them. 74m/B VHS, Beta. Matt Moore, Jane Gail, William Welsh; **D:** George Tucker. GPV, KIV

Traffic Jam ♫♫½ *Jutai* 1991 A light comedy about a Japanese family's attempt to travel on a holiday weekend. Tokyo couple and their two young children decide to visit the husband's family who happen to live on a distant island. Naturally, traffic's horrendous, they have very little time, and things continuously go wrong. Japanese with subtitles. 108m/C VHS. JP Kenichi Hagiwara, Hitomi Kuroki, Ayako Takarada, Shingo Yazawa, Eiji Okada; **D:** Mitsuo Kurotsuchi. WBF

Traffik ♫♫♫ 1990 A tense, unnerving look at the international world of heroin smuggling. The British drama follows the lives of three men involved in the drug trade — a farmer in the poppy fields of Pakistan, a drug smuggler in Hamburg, and a Tory cabinet minister who heads his government's anti-drug cabinet and then comes to realize his own daughter is an addict. On three cassettes. Made for British television. 360m/C VHS. GB Lindsay Duncan, Bill Paterson, Jamal Shah, Talat Hussain, Fritz Muller-Scherz, Julia Ormond; **D:** Alastair Reid. SIG, TVC, PBS

The Tragedy of a Ridiculous Man ♫♫ *La Tragedia di un Uomo Ridicolo* 1981 (PG) The missing son of an Italian cheese manufacturer may or may not have been kidnapped by terrorists. Lesser Bertolucci effort may or may not have a point. In Italian with English subtitles. 116m/C VHS. IT Ugo Tognazzi, Anouk Aimee, Victor Cavallo, Ricardo Tognazzi, Laura Morante; **D:** Bernardo Bertolucci; **W:** Bernardo Bertolucci; **C:** Carlo DiPalma; **M:** Ennio Morricone. Cannes Film Festival '81: Best Actor (Tognazzi). WAR, FCT

Tragedy of Flight 103: The Inside Story ♫♫♫ 1991 (PG) Dramatization of the events surrounding the destruction of Pan Am flight 103 over Lockerbie, Scotland, due to a terrorist-planted bomb. 89m/C VHS. Ned Beatty, Peter Boyle, Vincent Gardenia, Timothy West, Michael Wincott, Harry Ditson, Aharon Ipale, John Shrapnel; **D:** Leslie Woodhead. MGM

Trahir ♫♫♫ *Betrayal* 1993 In 1948 Romania journalist George Vlaicu (Leysen) writes a controversial article on the death of democracy in his country and is imprisoned for 11 years. In 1959 he's offered a deal, go free as long as he talks weekly to a police inspector (Repan). He begins a new career as a poet and marries his former typist, Laura (Perrier), but after a tragedy learns that his meetings with the inspector aren't as innocuous as they've seemed. Excellent performances and a cold look at how a police state is able to control its artists and writers. Filmed primarily in Romania. Director Mihaileanu's first feature film. French with subtitles. **104m/C VHS. FR SI SP RO** Johan Leysen, Mireille Perrier, Alexandru Repan, Razvan Vasilescu, Maia Morgenstern, Radu Beligan; **D:** Radu Mihaileanu; **W:** Laurent Moussard, Radu Mihaileanu; **M:** Temistocle Popa. Montreal World Film Festival '93: Best Actor (Leysen), Best Film. **NYR**

Trail Beyond 🎬½ **1934** A cowboy and his sidekick go on the trek to the northwest to find a girl and a gold mine. **57m/B VHS.** John Wayne, Noah Beery Sr., Verna Hillie; **D:** Robert North Bradbury. **COL, REP, NOS**

Trail Drive 🎬 **1935** Adventures of a cowboy during a big cattle drive. **63m/B VHS, Beta.** Ken Maynard. **NOS, VCN, CAB**

Trail of Robin Hood 🎬🎬½ **1950** Rogers sees to it that poor families get Christmas trees, in spite of the fact that a big business wants to raise the prices. Features a number of western stars, including Holt playing himself. **67m/C VHS.** Roy Rogers, Penny Edwards, Gordon Jones, Jack Holt, Emory Parnell, Rex Allen, Allan "Rocky" Lane, Clifton Young, Monte Hale, Kermit Maynard, Tom Keene, Ray Corrigan, William Farnum; **D:** William Witney. **REP**

Trail of Terror 🎬 **1935** G-Man poses as an escaped convict to get the goods on a gang. **60m/B VHS, Beta, LV.** Bob Steele, Beth Marion, Forrest Taylor, Charles "Blackie" King, Lloyd Ingraham, Charles French; **D:** Robert North Bradbury. **GPV**

Trail of the Hawk 🎬 **1937** Saga of frontier justice and love on the plains. **50m/B VHS, Beta.** Yancey Lane, Betty Jordan, Dick Jones; **D:** Edward Dmytryk. **NOS, DVT, RXM**

Trail of the Mounties 🎬 **1947** A Mountie gallops smack into a murdering slew of fur thieves. **41m/B VHS, Beta, LV.** Donald (Don "Red") Barry, Robert Lowery, Tom Neal, Russell Hayden. **NO**

Trail of the Pink Panther 🎬🎬 **1982** **(PG)** The sixth in Sellers' "Pink Panther" series. Inspector Clouseau disappears while he is searching for the diamond known as the Pink Panther. Notable because it was released after Sellers' death, using clips from previous movies to fill in gaps. Followed by "Curse of the Pink Panther." **97m/C VHS, Beta, LV, Closed Caption.** Peter Sellers, David Niven, Herbert Lom, Capucine, Burt Kwouk, Robert Wagner, Robert Loggia; **D:** Blake Edwards; **W:** Blake Edwards, Frank Waldman; **M:** Henry Mancini. **MGM**

Trail of the Silver Spurs 🎬½ **1941** A lone man remaining in a ghost town discovers gold and becomes rich. Part of the "Range Busters" series. **57m/B VHS.** Ray Corrigan, John "Dusty" King, Max Terhune, I. Stanford Jolley, Dorothy Short; **D:** S. Roy Luby. **NOS, DVT**

Trail Riders 🎬½ **1942** The Range Busters set a trap to capture a gang of outlaws who killed the son of the town marshal during a bank robbery. Part of the "Range Busters" series. **55m/B VHS, Beta.** John "Dusty" King, David Sharpe, Max Terhune, Evelyn Finley, Forrest Taylor, Charles "Blackie" King. **NOS, VYY, DVT**

Trail Street 🎬½ **1947** Scott is Bat Masterson, the western hero. He aids the struggle of Kansans as they conquer the land and local ranchers. **84m/B VHS, Beta.** Randolph Scott, Robert Ryan, Anne Jeffreys, George "Gabby" Hayes, Madge Meredith, Jason Robards Sr.; **D:** Ray Enright. **CCB, MED**

Trailin' 🎬🎬½ **1921** Mix stars as a cowboy in search of his parentage. Based on the Max Brand story. **58m/B VHS.** Tom Mix, Eva Novak, James Gordon; **D:** Lynn F. Reynolds. **GPV**

Trailing Double Trouble 🎬½ **1940** A corrupt attorney murders a rancher to pursue a business scheme. Three ranch hands kidnap the rancher's orphaned baby to keep her safe from the attorney. The second entry in the "Range Busters" series. **56m/B VHS, Beta.** Ray Corrigan, John "Dusty" King, Max Terhune. **NOS, VDM, VYY**

Trailing Trouble 🎬½ **1930** Gibson is a cowpoke who gets robbed of the money he received for a cattle sale. When he rescues a Chinese girl from danger he helps her recover the money. He also has to battle a rival for his girlfriend's affections. He should have battled for a better script. **58m/B VHS.** Hoot Gibson, Margaret Quimby, Peter Morrison, Olive Young, William McCall; **D:** Arthur Rosson. **GPV, VYY, DVT**

The Train 🎬🎬🎬🎬 **Le Train; Il Treno 1965** During the German occupation of Paris in 1944, a German colonel (Scofield) is ordered to ransack the city of its art treasures and put them on a train bound for Germany. Word gets to the French Resistance who then persuade the train inspector (Lancaster) to sabotage the train. A battle of wills ensues between Scofield and Lancaster as each becomes increasingly obsessed in outwitting the other—though the cost to all turns out to be as irreplaceable as the art itself. Filmed on location in France. Frankenheimer used real locomotives, rather than models, throughout the film, even in the spectacular crash sequences. **133m/C VHS, LV.** Burt Lancaster, Paul Scofield, Jeanne Moreau, Michel Simon, Suzanne Flon, Wolfgang Preiss, Albert Remy; **D:** John Frankenheimer; **W:** Frank Davis, Walter Bernstein; **M:** Maurice Jarre. Nominations: Academy Awards '65: Best Story & Screenplay. **MGM**

The Train Killer 🎬 **1983** A mad Hungarian is bent on destroying the Orient Express. **90m/C VHS, Beta.** Michael Sarrazin; **D:** Sandor Simo. **VES**

Train of Events 🎬🎬½ **1949** An interesting look at lives affected by a train wreck just outside London, taking the form of four short episodes. Three are frankly somber, depressing tales of the ill-fated train driver, a murderer and an escaped prisoner-of-war. The fourth segment is a refreshingly lighthearted piece about romantic jealousies in a traveling orchestra. A precursor to the later swarm of cross disaster films, except here emphasis is on character over special effects. **89m/B VHS.** Jack Warner, Gladys Henson, Susan Shaw, Patric Doonan, Miles Malleson, Leslie Phillips, Joan Dowling, Laurence Payne, Valerie Hobson, John Clements, Peter Finch, Mary Morris, Laurence Naismith, Michael Hordern; **D:** Sidney Cole, Basil Dearden, Charles Crichton. **NOS, FCT**

Train Robbers 🎬🎬 **1973 (PG)** A widow employs the services of three cowboys to help her recover some stolen gold in order to clear her late husband's name. At least that's what she says. **92m/C VHS, Beta, LV.** John Wayne, Ann-Margret, Rod Taylor, Ben Johnson, Christopher George, Ricardo Montalban, Bobby Vinton, Jerry Gatlin; **D:** Burt Kennedy; **W:** Burt Kennedy; **C:** William Clothier. **WAR**

Train Station Pickups 🎬 **197?** Trashy film about young girls who hook at a local train depot, until something goes wrong. **96m/C VHS.** Marco Knoger, Katja Carrol, Ingeborg Steinbach, Benjamin Carwath; **D:** Walter Boos. **ACN**

Train to Hollywood 🎬🎬🎬 **1986** Marilyn Monroe-obsessed young Polish girl daydreams incessantly as she works on dining car. Funny and surreal. Polish dialogue with English subtitles. **96m/C VHS. PL D:** Radoslaw Piwowarski. **FCT**

Train to Tombstone 🎬 **1950** A train running from Albuquerque to Tombstone carries a motley mob of the usual characters. **60m/B VHS, Beta, LV.** Donald (Don "Red") Barry, Judith Allen, Robert Lowery, Tom Neal; **D:** Charles F. Reisner. **NO**

Trained to Kill 🎬½ **1988** Two brothers seek revenge on the mean streets of L.A. **94m/C VHS, LV.** Frank Zagarino, Glen Eaton, Lisa Aliff, Marshall Teague, Robert Z'Dar, Henry Silva, Arlene Golonka, Ron O'Neal, Harold Diamond, Chuck Connors; **D:** H. Kaye Dyal; **W:** H. Kaye Dyal, Arthur Webb. **PSM**

Trained to Kill, U.S.A. 🎬½ **1983 (R)** Vietnam veteran relives his war experiences when a gang of terrorists threaten his hometown. **88m/C VHS, Beta.** Stephen Sander, Heidi Vaughn, Rockne Tarkington. **NO**

Trainspotting 🎬🎬🎬 **1995 (R)** From the same team who offered the violently comedic "Shallow Grave," comes an equally destructive look at a group of Edinburgh junkies and losers. Heroin-user Mark Renton (McGregor) once again decides to get off junk but to do so he has to get away from his friends: knife-wielding psycho Begbie (Carlyle), Sick Boy (Miller), Spud (Bremner), and Tommy (McKidd). He heads for a semi-respectable life in London but Begbie and Spud wind up involving him in a serious money drug deal that spells trouble. Strong fantasy visuals depict drug highs and lows while heavy Scottish accents (and humor) may prove difficult. Based on the 1993 cult novel by Irvine Welsh. Film drew much controversy for supposedly being pro-heroin but the junkie's life is hardly portrayed as being attractive in any way. **CW:** Graphic heroin use and resulting depravity, strong language, sex, nudity, and some violence. **94m/C VHS, LV, Closed Caption.** GB Ewan McGregor, Ewen Bremner, Jonny Lee Miller, Robert Carlyle, Kevin McKidd, Kelly Macdonald, Shirley Henderson, Pauline Lynch; **D:** Danny Boyle; **W:** John Hodge; **C:** Brian Tufano. British Academy Awards '95: Best Adapted Screenplay; Nominations: Academy Awards '96: Best Adapted Screenplay; Australian Film Institute '96: Best Foreign Film; British Academy Awards '95: Best Film; Independent Spirit Awards '97: Best Foreign Film; MTV Movie Awards '97: Breakthrough Performance (McGregor); Writers Guild of America '96: Best Adapted Screenplay. **TOU**

The Traitor 🎬½ **1936** Undercover man joins a gang of bandits. **57m/B VHS, Beta.** Tim McCoy; **D:** Sam Newfield. **NOS, VCI, VCN**

Tramp & a Woman 🎬🎬 **1915** Two shorts made for the Essanay Company in 1915 which offer the Little Tramp wooing Purviance in typical Chaplin fashion. Silent with musical score. **45m/B VHS, Beta.** Charlie Chaplin, Edna Purviance. **VYY**

Tramp at the Door 🎬🎬½ **1987** Delightful drama about a wandering, magical man who enters the lives of an embittered family. He helps them sort the skeletons in their closets, and works wonders on their relationships. **81m/C VHS, Beta.** Ed McNamara, August Schellenberg, Monique Mercure, Eric Peterson; **D:** Allen Kroeker. **NO**

Tramplers 🎬 **1966** A rebel father and son split over the hanging of a Yankee during the Civil War. Italian made spaghetti western without much plot and lots of gratuitous gunplay. **103m/C VHS, Beta.** IT Joseph Cotten, Gordon Scott; **D:** Albert Band, Mario Sequi. **COL, HHE**

Trancers 🎬🎬 **Future Cop 1984 (PG-13)** A time-traveling cult from the future goes back in time to 1985 to meddle with fate. Only Jack Deth, defender of justice, can save mankind. Low-budget "Blade Runner." Followed by two sequels. **76m/C VHS, Beta, LV, Closed Caption.** Tim Thomerson, Michael Stefoni, Helen Hunt, Art LaFleur, Telma Hopkins; **D:** Charles Band; **W:** Danny Bilson. **LIV, VES**

Trancers 2: The Return of Jack Deth 🎬🎬 **1990 (R)** Retro cop is back from the future again, but seems to have lost his wit and nerve in between sequels. Ward is miscast and the pacing undermines whatever suspense that might have been. **CW:** Violence. **85m/C VHS, Beta, LV, Closed Caption.** Tim Thomerson, Helen Hunt, Megan Ward, Biff Manard, Martine Beswick, Jeffrey Combs, Barbara Crampton, Richard Lynch; **D:** Charles Band. **PAR**

Trancers 3: Deth Lives 🎬🎬½ **1992 (R)** In the third film of the "Trancers" series, time-traveling cop Jack Deth fights the deadliest form of government-sponsored Trancer yet—it has a brain. **CW:** Language, strong violence, and sexuality. **83m/C VHS, Beta, LV, Closed Caption.** Tim Thomerson, Melanie Smith, Andrew (Andy) Robinson, Tony Pierce, Dawn Ann Billings, Helen Hunt, Megan Ward, Stephen Macht, Telma Hopkins; **D:** C. Courtney Joyner; **M:** Richard Band. **PAR**

Trancers 4: Jack of Swords 🎬🎬½ **1993 (R)** Time-traveling cop Jack Deth finds himself in a mystical new dimension where the blooksucking Trancers have enslaved the local population as feeders. If Jack expects to conquer he'll first need to survive an ancient wizard's prophecy of death. Filmed on location in Romania. **74m/C VHS, Beta, Closed Caption.** Tim Thomerson, Stacie Randall, Ty Miller, Terri Ivens, Mark Arnold, Clare Hartley, Alan Oppenheimer, Stephen Macht, David Nutter; **W:** Peter David; **M:** Gary Fry. *PAR*

Trancers 5: Sudden Deth 🎬🎬½
1994 (R) Irreverant time-travelling cop Jack Deth (Thomerson) returns to help the Tunnel Rats occupy the castle of Caliban. But the evil Lord Caliban is resurrected and his only desire is to destroy Jack. This is supposedly the final chapter of Deth's saga.**CW:** Language. **73m/C VHS, Beta, Closed Caption.** Tim Thomerson, Stacie Randall, Ty Miller, Terri Ivens, Mark Arnold, Clare Hartley, Alan Oppenheimer, Jeff Moldovan, Lochlyn Munro, Stephen Macht; **D:** David Nutter; **W:** Peter David; **M:** Gary Fry. *PAR*

Transatlantic Merry-Go-Round 🎬🎬
1934 An early semi-musical mystery about an eclectic assortment of passengers aboard a luxury liner. ♫It Was Sweet of You; Rock and Roll; Moon Over Monte Carlo; Oh Leo, It's Love; If I Had a Million Dollars. **90m/B VHS, Beta, Beta.** Jack Benny, Gene Raymond, Nancy Carroll, Boswell Sisters, Ralph Morgan, Sidney Blackmer; **D:** Ben Stoloff. *NO*

Transatlantic Tunnel 🎬🎬½ *The Tunnel*
1935 An undersea tunnel from England to America is attempted, despite financial trickery and undersea disasters. Made with futuristic sets which were advanced for their time. **94m/B VHS, Beta.** *GB* Richard Dix, Leslie Banks, Madge Evans, Helen Vinson, Sir C. Aubrey Smith, George Arliss, Walter Huston; **D:** Maurice Elvey. *VYY, SNC, HHT*

Transformations 🎬½ **1988 (R)** An interplanetary pilot battles a deadly virus that threatens life throughout the universe. Obscure space jetsam.**CW:** Language, violence, and sensuality. **84m/C VHS, LV.** Rex Smith, Patrick Macnee, Lisa Langlois, Christopher Neame; **D:** Jay Kamen. *VTR*

Transformers: The Movie 🎬 **1986 (G)**
A full-length animated film featuring the universe-defending robots fighting the powers of evil. These robots began life as real toys, so there's some marketing going on. **85m/C VHS, Beta.** **D:** Nelson Shin; **V:** Orson Welles, Eric Idle, Judd Nelson, Leonard Nimoy, Robert Stack. *FHE*

Transmutations 🎬 *Underworld* **1985 (R)** Mad scientist Elliott develops a mind-altering drug which is tested by a group of young people. They find out too late that the drug causes horrible facial disfigurement, as well as leaving them hopelessly addicted, and they hide out underground, plotting their revenge. Cowper, a young hooker in the group, turns out to be immune to the side effects and works with her ex-mobster boss to get help. Confusing. Barker co-scripted from one of his stories but later disowned the film. **103m/C VHS, Beta, LV.** *GB* Denholm Elliott, Steven Berkoff, Miranda Richardson, Nicola Cowper, Larry Lamb, Art Malik, Ingrid Pitt, Irina Brook, Paul Brown; **D:** George Pavlou; **W:** James Caplin, Clive Barker. *LIV, VES*

Transport from Paradise 🎬🎬½ *Transport Z Raje* **1965** Follows the story of Jewish life in the Terezin ghetto before the inhabitants are imprisoned and shipped off to Auschwitz as part of Hitler's final solution. Based on a novel by Arnold Lustig. In Czech with English subtitles. **93m/B VHS, Beta.** *CZ* Zbynek Brynych. *FCT*

Transylvania 6-5000 🎬½ **1985 (PG)** Agreeably stupid horror spoof about two klutzy reporters who stumble into modern-day Transylvania and encounter an array of comedic creatures. Shot in Yugoslavia. **93m/C VHS, Beta, LV, Closed Caption.** Jeff Goldblum, Joseph Bologna, Ed Begley Jr., Carol Kane, John Byner, Geena Davis, Jeffrey Jones, Norman Fell; **D:** Rudy DeLuca; **W:** Rudy DeLuca. *VTR, NWV*

Transylvania Twist 🎬½ **1989 (PG-13)** Moronic comedy about vampires, teenage vampire hunters and half-naked babes. **90m/C VHS, Beta.** Robert Vaughn, Teri Copley, Steve Altman, Ace Mask,

Angus Scrimm, Jay Robinson, Brinke Stevens; **D:** Jim Wynorski; **W:** R.J. Robertson. *MGM*

The Trap 🎬 **1922** Chaney kidnaps the son of a man he's sent to prison on false charges. Rather than give up the kid when the man is released, he plans a trap. **?m/C VHS.** Lon Chaney Sr., Alan Hale, Irene Rich. *SNC, GVV*

The Trap 🎬🎬½ *The Baited Trap* **1959** In trying to escape justice, a ruthless crime syndicate boss holds a small desert town in a grip of fear. **84m/C VHS, Beta.** Richard Widmark, Tina Louise, Lee J. Cobb, Earl Holliman, Lorne Greene, Carl Benton Reid; **D:** Norman Panama; **W:** Norman Panama. *BAR*

Trap 🎬🎬 *L'Aventure Sauvage* **1966** A trapper buys a mute girl as his wife. Together they try to make a life for themselves in the Canadian wilderness. Fine telling of interesting western tale. Unusual and realistic. **106m/C VHS, Beta.** *GB CA* Rita Tushingham, Oliver Reed, Rex Sevenoaks; **C:** Robert Krasker. *NO*

Trap on Cougar Mountain 🎬 **1972 (G)** A young boy begins a crusade to save his animal friends from the traps and bullets of hunters. **97m/C VHS, Beta, LV.** Erik Larsen, Keith Larsen, Karen Steele; **D:** Keith Larsen. *NWV, VTR*

Trap Them & Kill Them 🎬 **1984** American group traveling through the Amazon jungle encounter a terrifying aborigine tribe. Point of trip undergoes considerable reexamination. **90m/C VHS, Beta.** Gabriele Tinti, Susan Scott, Donald O'Brien. *TWE*

Trapeze 🎬🎬🎬 **1956** Lancaster is a former trapeze artist, now lame from a triple somersault accident. Curtis, the son of an old friend, wants Lancaster to teach him the routine. Lollobrigida, an aerial acrobat, is interested in both men. Exquisite European locations, fine camera work. The actors perform their own stunts. **105m/C VHS, Beta, LV.** Burt Lancaster, Tony Curtis, Gina Lollobrigida, Katy Jurado, Thomas Gomez; **D:** Carol Reed; **C:** Robert Krasker; **M:** Malcolm Arnold. *MGM, FOX*

Trapped 🎬🎬½ **1949** Semi-documentary crime drama shows in semi-documentary style how the feds hunt down a gang of counterfeiters by springing one of their comrades from prison. Well-paced, suspenseful and believable. **78m/B VHS.** Lloyd Bridges, Barbara Payton, John Hoyt, James Todd; **D:** Richard Fleischer. *NOS, DVT, HEG*

Trapped 🎬½ **1989 (R)** A woman working late in her high-rise office is stalked by a killer and must rely on her ingenuity to outwit him. Made-for-cable-television thriller. **93m/C VHS, Beta.** Kathleen Quinlan, Bruce Abbott, Katy Boyer, Ben Loggins; **D:** Fred Walton; **W:** Fred Walton. *USH*

Trapped Alive 🎬½ **1993** Robin and Monica are abducted by three escaped convicts who want their car as a getaway vehicle. Trying to avoid a police roadblock the car crashes through the cover of a long-abandoned mine. When the group try to find their way out of the maze of tunnels they realize they're not down there alone. **92m/C VHS, Beta.** Alex Kubik, Elizabeth Kent, Michael Nash, Randolph Powell, Mark Witsken, Sullivan Hester, Laura Kallison, Cameron Mitchell; **D:** Leszek Burzynski; **W:** Leszek Burzynski. *AIP*

Trapped by the Mormons 🎬🎬 *The Mormon Peril* **1922** Mormons seduce innocent young girls to add to their harems. An interesting piece of paranoid propaganda. Silent with original organ music. **97m/B VHS, Beta, 8mm.** Evelyn Brent, Lewis Willoughby. *GPV, VYY, NOS*

Trapped In Paradise 🎬½ **1994 (PG-13)** Three bungling brothers make off with a bundle of cash from the Paradise—the town not the afterlife—bank on Christmas Eve. The locals, naive refugees from a Rockwell painting, don't recognize the buffoons as criminals, and reward their crime with hospitality that would make Frank Capra proud. Chase scenes and subplots abound as the boys spend what seems an eternity trying to make their getaway. Routine, humdrum comedy is hampered by an obvious plot. Watchable only

because of Carvey, Lovitz, and Cage.**CW:** Contains mild profanity. **111m/C VHS, LV, Closed Caption.** Nicolas Cage, Jon Lovitz, Dana Carvey, John Ashton, Madchen Amick, Donald Moffat, Richard Jenkins, Florence Stanley, Angela Paton, Vic Manni, Frank Pesce, Sean McCann, Paul Lazar, Richard B. Shull; **D:** George Gallo; **W:** George Gallo; **M:** Robert Folk. *FXV*

Trapped in Silence 🎬🎬 **1986** Young Sutherland, abused since childhood, stops speaking to protect himself mentally and physically. Psychologist Mason is determined to break down the walls to help him confront his pain. Interesting cameo by Silver as a gay counselor forced out of his job when his sexual preference is discovered. Mildly melodramatic made-for-TV message drama. **94m/C VHS.** Marsha Mason, Kiefer Sutherland, John Mahoney, Amy Wright; **Cameos:** Ron Silver; **D:** Michael Tuchner. *TTC*

Trapped in Space 🎬🎬½ **1994 (PG-13)** On a mission to Venus a space shuttle is damaged by a meteor strike, leaving only enough oxygen for one person. So, what's everyone else suppose to do? Based on a short story by Arthur C. Clarke. **87m/C VHS, Beta, Closed Caption.** Jack Wagner, Jack Coleman, Craig Wasson, Sigrid Thornton, Kay Lenz; **D:** Arthur Seidelman; **W:** John Vincent Curtis, Melinda M. Snodgrass; **M:** Jay Gruska. *PAR*

Trapper County War 🎬 **1989 (R)** A city boy and a Vietnam vet band together to rescue a young woman held captive by a backwoods clan. **98m/C VHS, LV.** Robert Estes, Bo Hopkins, Ernie Hudson, Betsy Russell, Don Swayze; **D:** Worth Keeter. *REP*

Traps 🎬🎬½ **1993 (R)** Australian journalist Michael Duffield (Reynolds) and his English photographer wife Louise (Reeves) arrive for an assignment in 1950 French Indochina. Michael is to write about life on a French-owned rubber plantation, managed by Daniel (Frey), who lives with his rather peculiar daughter Viola (McKenzie). The plantation is troubled by the increasingly militant Viet-Minh rebels and it becomes clear that the four characters all have their own emotional difficulties to deal with, as well. Loosely adapted from the novel "Dreamhouse" by Kate Grenville. Feature film directing debut for Chan.**CW:** Strong sexuality, nudity, and some violence. **95m/C VHS.** *AU* Saskia Reeves, Robert Reynolds, Sami Frei, Jacqueline McKenzie; **D:** Pauline Chan; **W:** Pauline Chan, Robert Carter; **C:** Kevin Hayward; **M:** Douglas Stephen Rae. *NYR*

Trash 🎬🎬 **1970** Andy Warhol's profile of a depraved couple (Warhol-veteran Dallesandro and female impersonater Woodlawn) living in a lower east side basement and scouting the streets for food and drugs. Not for those easily offended by nymphomaniacs, junkies, lice, and the like; a must for fans of underground film and the cinema verite style. **110m/C VHS, Beta.** Joe Dallesandro, Holly Woodlawn, Jane Forth, Micael Sklar, Geri Miller, Bruce Pecheur; **D:** Paul Morrissey. *PAR*

Trauma 🎬½ **1962** A girl suffers amnesia after the trauma of witnessing her aunt's murder. She returns to the mansion years later to piece together what happened. A sometimes tedious psychological thriller. **93m/C VHS, Beta.** John Conte, Lynn Bari, Lorrie Richards, David Garner, Warren Kemmerling, William Bissell, Bond Blackman, William Justine; **D:** Robert M. Young. *VES*

Traveling Man 🎬🎬 **1989** A made-for-cable-television drama about a veteran traveling salesman who's assigned an eager young apprentice when his sales go down. Lithgow gives a great performance as the burnt-out traveling salesman. **105m/C VHS, Beta.** John Lithgow, Jonathan Silverman, Margaret Colin, John Glover; **D:** Irvin Kershner; **M:** Miles Goodman. *HBO*

Traveller 🎬🎬🎬 **1996 (R)** Deriving its name from the real-life group of wily Irish-American con men who prowl the Southeast, this view into the lives and clannish ways of its members may have you checking that brand-spankin' new driveway sealant. Their basic philosophy is: if you're not one of us, we're allowed to take all of your money.

Bokky (Paxton) is the jack-of-all-tricks who takes the younger Pat (Wahlberg) under his wing after the boy is shunned by the rest of the group. Pat's father married outside the clan, and that's not allowed. Bokky falls into the same trap, however, when a beautiful bartender (Margulies), who he has just fleeced, steals his heart. Rather violent ending dims the good feeling that builds and may leave you feeling...well, cheated. Directorial debut of long-time Clint Eastwood cinematographer Jack Green, who also shot "Twister" with Paxton. **CW:** Strong language and violence **100m/C VHS.** Bill Paxton, Mark Wahlberg, Julianna Margulies, James Gammon, Luke Askew, Michael Shaner, Nikki Deloach, Danielle Wiener; **D:** Jack N. Green; **W:** Jim McGlynn; **C:** Jack N. Green; **M:** Andy Paley. *EVE*

Travelling North 🎬🎬 1987 (PG-13) A belligerent retiree falls in love with a divorcee and they move together to a rustic retreat. They have an idyllic existence until the man discovers he has a serious heart condition. Adaptation of David Williamson's play has fine performances. **97m/C VHS, Beta.** *AU* Leo McKern, Julia Blake; **D:** Carl Schultz; **W:** David Williamson. Australian Film Institute '87: Best Actor (McKern); Montreal World Film Festival '87: Best Actor (McKern). *NO*

Travels with My Aunt 🎬🎬½ 1972 (PG) A banker leading a mundane life is taken on a wild, whirlwind tour of Europe by an eccentric woman claiming to be his aunt. Based on Graham Greene's best-selling novel. **109m/C LV.** Maggie Smith, Alec McCowen, Louis Gossett Jr., Robert Stephens, Cindy Williams; **D:** George Cukor; **W:** Jay Presson Allen. Academy Awards '72: Best Costume Design; Nominations: Academy Awards '72: Best Actress (Smith), Best Art Direction/Set Decoration, Best Cinematography. *MGM*

Traxx 🎬 1987 (R) Satire about an ex-cop soldier of fortune. Not surprisingly, Stevens doesn't do much with this lame script. **84m/C VHS, Beta.** Shadoe Stevens, Priscilla Barnes, William E. Pugh, John Hancock, Robert Davi, Rick Overton; **D:** Jerome Gary; **W:** Gary De Vore; **M:** Jay Gruska. *HBO*

Treacherous Crossing 🎬🎬 1992 (PG) When her husband disappears on their honeymoon cruise heiress Wagner tries to get the ship's crew to help her. They think she's crazy, but aided by new friend Dickinson, Wagner intends to find out just what's going on. Based on the radio play "Cabin B-13" by John Dickson Carr. **88m/C VHS, Beta, Closed Caption.** Lindsay Wagner, Angie Dickinson, Grant Show, Joseph Bottoms, Karen Medak, Charles Napier, Jeffrey DeMunn; **D:** Tony Wharmby; **W:** Elisa Bell. *PAR, PMS*

Treasure Island 🎬🎬🎬½ 1934 Fleming's adaptation of Robert Louis Stevenson's eighteenth century English pirate tale of Long John Silver is a classic. Beery is great as the pirate; Cooper has trouble playing the boy. Also available colorized. Multitudinous remakes. **102m/B VHS, Beta, LV.** Wallace Beery, Jackie Cooper, Lionel Barrymore, Lewis Stone, Otto Kruger, Douglass Dumbrille, Chic Sale, Nigel Bruce; **D:** Victor Fleming; **C:** Clyde De Vinna. *MGM, TLF, HMV*

Treasure Island 🎬🎬🎬½ 1950 (PG) Spine-tingling Robert Louis Stevenson tale of pirates and buried treasure, in which young cabin boy Jim Hawkins matches wits with Long John Silver. Some editions excise extra violence. Stevenson's ending is revised. Full Disney treatment, excellent casting. **96m/C VHS, Beta, LV, Closed Caption.** Bobby Driscoll, Robert Newton, Basil Sydney, Walter Fitzgerald, Denis O'Dea, Ralph Truman, Finlay Currie; **D:** Byron Haskin; **C:** Frederick A. (Freddie) Young. *DIS, IGP*

Treasure Island 🎬🎬 *La Isla Del Tersoro* 1972 (G) Unexceptional British reheat of familiar pirate tale. Welles' interpretation of Long John Silver may be truer to Stevenson, but it's one heckuva blustering binge. **94m/C VHS.** *GB* Orson Welles, Kim Burfield, Walter Slezak, Lionel Stander; **D:** John Hough; **W:** Orson Welles. *BTV*

Treasure Island 🎬🎬 1989 Excellent made for cable version of the classic Robert Louis Stevenson pirate tale with Heston as Long John Silver. Written, produced and directed by Fraser Heston, son of Charlton. **131m/C VHS, Closed Caption.** Charlton Heston, Christian Bale, Julian Glover, Richard Johnson, Oliver Reed, Christopher Lee, Clive Wood, Nicholas Amer, Michael Halsey; **D:** Fraser Heston; **W:** Fraser Heston. *TTC*

Treasure of Arne 🎬🎬½ 1919 A 16th century Scottish mercenary kills and loots the estate of rich, well-to-do property owner Sir Arne. Famous early Swedish silent that established Stiller as a director. **78m/B VHS, Beta.** *SW* **D:** Mauritz Stiller. *FCT*

The Treasure of Bengal 🎬½ 1953 Sabu attempts to stop his chief from trading the village's precious gem (the largest ruby in the world) for firearms. **72m/C VHS.** Sabu. *NO*

Treasure of Fear 🎬½ *Scared Stiff* 1945 A bungling newspaper reporter gets involved with four jade chessmen once owned by Kubla Khan. A few laughs in this contrived haunted house story. **66m/B VHS, Beta.** Jack Haley, Barton MacLane, Ann Savage, Veda Ann Borg; **D:** Frank McDonald. *SNC, NOS, FCT*

The Treasure of Jamaica Reef 🎬½ 1974 (PG) Adventurers battle sharks and other nasty fish as they seek a sunken Spanish galleon and its cache of golden treasure. **96m/C VHS, Beta.** Cheryl Ladd, Stephen Boyd, Roosevelt Grier, David Ladd, Darby Hinton; **D:** Virginia Lively Stone. *NO*

The Treasure of Matecumbe 🎬🎬 1976 (G) A motley crew of adventurers led by a young boy search for buried treasure as they are pursued by Indians and other foes. Filmed in the Florida Key Islands. **107m/C VHS, Beta.** Billy Attmore, Robert Foxworth, Joan Hackett, Peter Ustinov, Vic Morrow; **D:** Vincent McEveety; **M:** Buddy Baker. *DIS*

Treasure of Monte Cristo 🎬🎬 1950 A woman marries a seaman said to be an ancestor of the Count for his inheritance. Instead, she finds love and mystery. **78m/B VHS, Beta, LV.** *GB* Adele Jergens, Steve Brodie, Glenn Langan; **D:** William (Lester Williams) Berke. *NO*

Treasure of Pancho Villa 🎬½ 1955 An American adventurer plots a gold heist to help Villa's revolution. He encounters every obstacle in the West while on his way to help the Mexican rebel. **96m/C VHS, Beta.** Rory Calhoun, Shelley Winters, Gilbert Roland; **D:** George Sherman. *NO*

The Treasure of the Amazon 🎬½ *El Tesoro del Amazones* 1984 Three fortune hunters embark on a perilous search for wealth in the South American jungles. Silly and unnecessarily violent. **105m/C VHS, Beta.** *MX* Stuart Whitman, Donald Pleasence, Ann Sydney, Bradford Dillman, John Ireland; **D:** Rene Cardona Jr. *LIV, VES*

Treasure of the Four Crowns 🎬 1982 (PG) Aging history professor hires a team of tough commandos to recover four legendary crowns containing the source of mystical powers. The crowns are being held under heavy guard by a crazed cult leader. **97m/C VHS, Beta.** *SP* Tony Anthony, Anna Obregon, Gene Quintano; **D:** Ferdinando Baldi; **W:** Lloyd Battista, James Bryce; **M:** Ennio Morricone. *MGM*

Treasure of the Golden Condor 🎬🎬½ 1953 A swashbuckler heads to the jungles of 18th-century Guatemala in search of ancient treasure. Contains interesting footage of Mayan ruins, but otherwise ordinary. A remake of "Son of Fury." **93m/C VHS.** Cornel Wilde, Constance Smith, Fay Wray, Anne Bancroft, Leo G. Carroll, Robert (Bobby) Blake; **D:** Delmer Daves. *TCF*

Treasure of the Lost Desert 🎬½ 1983 A Green Beret crushes a terrorist operation in the Middle East. **93m/C VHS, Beta.** Bruce Miller, Susan West, Larry Finch; **D:** Tony Zarindast. *LIV*

Treasure of the Moon Goddess WOOF! 1988 (R) A dizzy nightclub singer is mistaken by Central American pirates and natives for the earthly manifestation of their Moon Goddess. **90m/C VHS, Beta.** Don Calfa, Joann Ayres, Asher Brauner; **D:** Joseph Louis Agraz. *THV*

Treasure of the Sierra Madre 🎬🎬🎬🎬 1948 Three prospectors in search of gold in Mexico find suspicion, treachery and greed. Bogart is superbly believable as the paranoid, and ultimately homicidal, Fred C. Dobbs. Huston directed his father and wrote the screenplay, based on a B. Traven story. **126m/B VHS, Beta, LV.** Humphrey Bogart, Walter Huston, Tim Holt, Bruce (Herman Brix) Bennett, Barton MacLane, Robert (Bobby) Blake, Alfonso Bedoya; **D:** John Huston; **W:** John Huston; **M:** Max Steiner. Academy Awards '48: Best Director (Huston), Best Screenplay, Best Supporting Actor (Huston); Golden Globe Awards '49: Best Director (Huston), Best Film—Drama, Best Supporting Actor (Huston); National Board of Review Awards '48: 10 Best Films of the Year, Best Actor (Huston); New York Film Critics Awards '48: Best Director (Huston), Best Film; Nominations: Academy Awards '48: Best Picture. *MGM, FOX, TLF*

Treasure of the Yankee Zephyr 🎬🎬 *Race for the Yankee Zephyr* 1983 (PG) Trio joins in the quest for a plane that has been missing for 40 years...with a cargo of $50 million. They have competition in the form of Peppard and cronies. Decent cast muddles through the predictable plotting. **108m/C VHS, Beta.** *AU NZ* Ken Wahl, George Peppard, Donald Pleasence, Lesley Ann Warren, Bruno Lawrence, Grant Tilly; **D:** David Hemmings; **M:** Brian May. *LIV, VES*

The Treasure Seekers 🎬 1979 Four rival divers set off on a perilous Caribbean expedition in search of the legendary treasure of Morgan the Pirate. **88m/C VHS, Beta.** Rod Taylor, Stuart Whitman, Elke Sommer, Keenan Wynn, Jeremy Kemp. *MGM*

A Tree Grows in Brooklyn 🎬🎬🎬 1945 (PG) Sensitive young Irish lass growing up in turn-of-the-century Brooklyn tries to rise above her tenement existence. Based on the novel by Betty Smith. Kazan's directorial debut. **128m/B VHS, Beta, LV, Closed Caption.** Peggy Ann Garner, James Dunn, Dorothy McGuire, Joan Blondell, Lloyd Nolan, Ted Donaldson, James Gleason, John Alexander, Charles Halton; **D:** Elia Kazan; **C:** Leon Shamroy; **M:** Alfred Newman. Academy Awards '45: Best Supporting Actor (Dunn); National Board of Review Awards '45: 10 Best Films of the Year; Nominations: Academy Awards '45: Best Screenplay.*FXV, BTV, HMV*

The Tree of Wooden Clogs 🎬🎬🎬½ *L'Albero Degli Zoccoli* 1978 Epic view of the lives of four peasant families working on an estate in turn of the century Northern Italy. The title comes from the shoes the peasants wear. When a young boy breaks a shoe, his father risks punishment by cutting down one of his landlord's trees to make a new pair of clogs. Slow moving and beautiful, from former industrial filmmaker Olmi. In Italian with English subtitles. **185m/C VHS, Beta, LV.** *IT* Luigi Omaghi, Francesca Moriggi, Omar Brignoli, Antonio Ferrari; **D:** Ermanno Olmi; **W:** Ermanno Olmi. Cannes Film Festival '78: Best Film; New York Film Critics Awards '79: Best Foreign Film.*FXL, APD*

Tree's Lounge 🎬🎬½ 1996 (R) First time director/writer Buscemi takes a look at the downward spiraling life of Tommy Basilio (Buscemi), a working-class misfit who loses his job and then spends most of his time hanging out at the dreary local bar. He finally winds up driving an ice cream truck, only leading to more trouble when his teenaged helper, Debbie (Sevigny), develops a crush on him—a situation her hot-headed father Jerry (Baldwin) takes exception to. And the irresponsible Tommy is finally forced to realize that his ill-concerned actions have consequences.**CW:** Plentiful strong language and some drug content. **94m/C VHS.** Steve Buscemi, Chloe Sevigny, Daniel Baldwin, Elizabeth Bracco, Anthony LaPaglia, Debi Mazar, Carol Kane, Seymour Cassel, Mark Boone, Eszter Balint, Mimi Rogers, Kevin Corrigan, Samuel L. Jackson; **D:** Steve

Buscemi; *W:* Steve Buscemi; *C:* Lisa Rinzler; *M:* Evan Lurie. Nominations: Independent Spirit Awards '97: Best First Feature. *LIV*

Tremors 🎬🎬½ **1989 (PG-13)** A tiny desert town is attacked by giant man-eating worm-creatures. Bacon and Ward are the handymen trying to save the town. Amusing, with good special effects. **96m/C VHS, Beta, LV, Closed Caption.** Kevin Bacon, Fred Ward, Finn Carter, Michael Gross, Reba McEntire, Bibi Besch, Bobby Jacoby, Charlotte Stewart, Victor Wong, Tony Genaros; *D:* Ron Underwood; *W:* S.S. Wilson, Brent Maddock; *M:* Ernest Troost. *USH*

Tremors 2: Aftershocks 🎬🎬½ **1996 (PG-13)** They're baaaaack! The Graboids have resurfaced to eat their way through Mexican oil fields and it's up to tough guys Earl Bassett (Ward) and Burt Gummer (Gross) to get rid of the toothy worms once and for all. Same mix of tongue-in-cheek humor and special effects as the first film.*CW:* Sci-fi creature violence and gore. **100m/C VHS, LV, Closed Caption.** Fred Ward, Michael Gross, Helen Shaver, Christopher Gartin, Marcelo Tubert; *D:* S.S. Wilson; *W:* S.S. Wilson, Brent Maddock. *USH*

Trenchcoat 🎬½ **1983** Aspiring mystery writer travels to Malta to research her new novel and is drawn into a real-life conspiracy. Silly and contrived spoof of the detective genre. **95m/C VHS, Beta.** Margot Kidder, Robert Hays; *D:* Michael Tuchner; *W:* Jeffrey Price, Peter S. Seaman; *M:* Charles Fox. *DIS, OM*

Trespass 🎬🎬 *Looters* **1992 (R)** Violent crime tale set in East St. Louis, Illinois. Two redneck firemen learn about stolen gold artifacts supposedly hidden in an abandoned building and go on a treasure hunt. When they witness a murder they also get involved in a battle between two crime lords—who want these interlopers dead. What follows is a deadly game of cat-and-mouse. Lots of action but it's all fairly routine. Original release date of summer 1992 was delayed until the winter because of unfortunate similarities to the L.A. riots.*CW:* Language and violence. **104m/C VHS, Beta, LV.** Ice Cube, Ice-T, William Sadler, Bill Paxton, Art Evans; *D:* Walter Hill; *W:* Robert Zemeckis, Bob Gale; *C:* Lloyd Ahern; *M:* Ry Cooder. *USH*

Trespasser 🎬🎬 **1985** A painter has an affair with a young woman. He comes to regret destroying his family and their life together. Based on a D.H. Lawrence novel. **90m/C VHS, Beta.** Alan Bates, Dinah Stabb, Pauline Morgan, Margaret Whiting. *NO*

Trespasses 🎬 **1986 (R)** A rape victim and a cattleman get involved and become the target of her husband's revenge. Murder and lust in a small Texas town in this tedious film. **90m/C VHS, Beta.** Lou Diamond Phillips, Robert Kuhn, Ben Johnson, Adam Roarke, Mary Pillot, Van Brooks; *D:* Lauren Bivens. *ACA, MTX, VTR*

The Trial 🎬🎬🎬 *Le Proces; Der Prozess; Il Processo* **1963** Expressionistic Welles adaptation of classic Kafka novella about an innocent man accused, tried, and convicted of an unknown crime in an unnnamed exaggeratedly bureaucratic country. Another Welles project that met with constant disaster in production, with many lapses in continuity. **118m/B VHS, Beta.** *FR* Anthony Perkins, Jeanne Moreau, Orson Welles, Romy Schneider, Akim Tamiroff, Elsa Martinelli; *D:* Orson Welles. *CVC, NOS, HHT*

The Trial 🎬🎬 **1993** Spare adaptation of Franz Kafka's novel finds Prague bank clerk Joseph K (MacLachlan) arrested on unknown charges. His increasing guilt and paranoia fit well into a world where the most illogical things happen in the most matter of fact way. Good visuals. **120m/C VHS, LV.** Kyle MacLachlan, Anthony Hopkins, Jason Robards Jr., Polly Walker, Juliet Stevenson, Alfred Molina; *D:* David Jones; *W:* Harold Pinter. *ORI*

Trial & Error 🎬🎬½ *The Dock Brief* **1962** Comedic satire, based on the play by John Mortimer, finds hapless lawyer Morgenhall (Sellers) thinking he's finally got his big chance when he defends wife murderer Fowle (Attenborough). Fowle wants to plead guilty but Morgenhall dreams of being a court star and insists on pleading his client innocent. It's a disaster just waiting to happen. **78m/B VHS.** *GB* Peter Sellers, Richard Attenborough, Beryl Reid, David Lodge, Frank Pettingell, Eric Woodburn; *D:* James Hill; *W:* Pierre Rouve; *C:* Edward Scaife; *M:* Ron Grainer. *FXL*

Trial and Error 🎬🎬½ **1992** Peter Hudson (Matheson) is an overly-zealous prosecutor who successfully convicts a small time criminal of murder, sending him to death row. This launches Hudson's political career and five years later he's about to be nominated for Lieutenant Governor, just as the felon's execution draws near. Suddenly, new evidence points to the man's innocence, but if Hudson investigates it could ruin his political future. But he's got a bigger problem—the real killer decides to make Hudson's wife his next victim. **91m/C VHS, Beta, Closed Caption.** Tim Matheson, Helen Shaver, Sean McCann, Eugene C. Clark; *D:* Mark Sobel. *USH*

Trial and Error 🎬🎬½ **1996 (PG-13)** Courtroom comedy may remind you of another law oriented movie. No, not "Kramer vs. Kramer." It's "My Cousin Vinny," also directed by Lynn. Both feature smalltown lawyers defending hopeless clients in small towns. In this case, lawyer Charles Tuttle (Daniels) is too messed up from his bachelor party to make it to court for a case in which the defendent Benny (Torn), a relative of Chuck's bigwig future father-in-law, is accused of selling mailorder "commemorative copper Lincoln engravings" which are actually pennies. His best bud Richard (Richards), an actor, decides to stand in for him, and the legal slip-and-pratfalls ensue. Richards as the physical comedian and Daniels as the white bread straight man have great comic chemistry, but the plot won't surprise you much.*CW:* Some sexual content. **98m/C VHS.** Michael Richards, Jeff Daniels, Rip Torn, Charlize Theron, Jessica Steen, Austin Pendleton, Alexandra Wentworth, Lawrence Pressman, Dale Dye, Max Casella, Jennifer Coolidge; *D:* Jonathan Lynn; *W:* Sarah Bernstein, Gregory Bernstein; *C:* Gabriel Beristain; *M:* Phil Marshall. *NYR*

Trial by Jury 🎬🎬½ **1994 (R)** Strong cast, lame script. Idealistic single mother Valerie Alston (Whalley-Kilmer) winds up on the jury trying notorious mobster Rusty Pirone (Assante). Rusty's henchman, Tommy Vesey (Hurt), lets Valerie know that her son is in mortal danger if she doesn't find his boss innocent. Of course DA Daniel Graham (Byrne) is equally adamant about a conviction and is willing to use Valerie any way he has to.*CW:* Language and violence. **107m/C VHS, LV, Closed Caption.** Joanne Whalley, William Hurt, Gabriel Byrne, Armand Assante, Kathleen Quinlan, Stuart Whitman, Margaret Whitton, Ed Lauter, Joe Santos, Richard Portnow; *D:* Heywood Gould; *W:* Heywood Gould; *C:* Frederick Elmes; *M:* Terence Blanchard. *WAR*

The Trial of Billy Jack WOOF! **1974 (PG)** Billy Jack takes on the feds and beats the hell out of a lot of people to prove that the world can live in peace. Awful, pretentious film. **175m/C VHS.** Tom Laughlin, Delores Taylor, Victor Izay, Teresa Laughlin, William Wellman Jr.; *D:* Frank Laughlin; *M:* Elmer Bernstein. *NO*

The Trial of Lee Harvey Oswald 🎬🎬 **1977** What would've happened if Jack Ruby had not shot Oswald. Oswald's trial and its likely results are painstakingly created. In 2 volumes. Made for television. **192m/C VHS, Beta.** Ben Gazzara, Lorne Greene, John Pleshette, Lawrence Pressman; *D:* Gordon Davidson. *WOV*

Trial of the Catonsville Nine 🎬🎬½ **1972 (PG)** Riveting political drama that focuses on the trial of nine anti-war activists, including Father Daniel Berrigan, during the Vietnam War days of the late 1960s. Imperfect, but involving. **85m/C VHS, Beta.** Ed Flanders, Douglas Watson, William Schallert, Peter Strauss, Richard Jordan; *D:* Gordon Davidson. *COL*

The Trial of the Incredible Hulk 🎬🎬 **1989** The Hulk returns to battle organized crime and is aided by his blind superhero/lawyer friend Daredevil. Followed by "The Death of the Incredible Hulk." Made for television. **96m/C VHS.** Bill Bixby, Lou Ferrigno, Rex Smith, John Rhys-Davies, Marta DuBois, Nancy Everhard, Nicholas Hormann; *D:* Bill Bixby. *VTR*

The Trials of Oscar Wilde 🎬🎬🎬 *The Man with the Green Carnation; The Green Carnation* **1960** Finch is the highlight as playwright/wit Wilde, who ill-advisedly sues the Marquis of Queensbury (Jeffries) for libel when the peer accuses him of being a sodomite. Wilde is, in fact, having an affair with the Marquis' son, Lord Alfred Douglas (Fraser), which eventually leads to Wilde's imprisonment and the destruction of his life. Based on the play "The Stringed Lute" by John Furnell and the book "The Trials of Oscar Wilde" by Montgomery Hyde. **123m/C VHS.** *GB* Peter Finch, John Fraser, Lionel Jeffries, Nigel Patrick, James Mason, Yvonne Mitchell, Maxine Audley, James Booth, Paul Rogers, Ian Fleming, Laurence Naismith; *D:* Ken Hughes; *W:* Ken Hughes; *C:* Ted Moore; *M:* Ron Goodwin. *FCT*

The Triangle Factory Fire Scandal 🎬🎬 **1979** Based on the true-life Triangle factory fire at the turn of the century. The fire killed 145 garment workers and drastically changed industrial fire and safety codes. Made for television. **100m/C VHS.** Tom Bosley, David Dukes, Tovah Feldshuh, Janet Margolin, Stephanie Zimbalist, Lauren Front, Stacey Nelkin, Ted Wass, Charlotte Rae, Milton Selzer, Valerie Landsburg; *D:* Mel Stuart. *LIV*

Tribes 🎬🎬½ *The Soldier Who Declared Peace* **1970** A made-for-television movie about a hippie drafted into the Marines. Despite the furious efforts of his drill sergeant, he refuses to conform to military life. Soon his boot-camp mates are trying his methods of defiance and survival. Well-made mix of comedy and social commentary. **90m/C VHS, Beta.** Jan-Michael Vincent, Darren McGavin, Earl Holliman; *D:* Joseph Sargent. *MGM, FOX*

Tribute 🎬🎬 **1980 (PG)** A dying man is determined to achieve a reconciliation with his estranged son. Adapted by Bernard Slade from his play. **125m/C VHS.** *CA* Jack Lemmon, Robby Benson, Lee Remick, Kim Cattrall; *D:* Bob (Benjamin) Clark. Nominations: Academy Awards '80: Best Actor (Lemmon). *VES, FCT*

Tribute to a Bad Man 🎬🎬🎬 **1956** Hard-nosed rancher Cagney will stop at nothing to retain his worldly possessions in this 1870's Colorado territory western. His ruthless behavior drives girlfriend Papas into the arms of hired hand Dubbins. Spencer Tracy and Grace Kelly were originally cast for the roles of Jeremy Rodock and Jocasta Constantine, but Kelly backed out and Tracy was fired due to differences with director Wise. Based on the short story by Jack Schaefer. **95m/C VHS, Closed Caption.** James Cagney, Don Dubbins, Stephen McNally, Irene Papas, Vic Morrow, Royal Dano, Lee Van Cleef, James Griffith, Onslow Stevens, James Bell, Jeanette Nolan, Bud Osborne, Tom London, Dennis Moore, Buddy Roosevelt, Carl Pitti; *D:* Robert Wise; *W:* Michael Blankfort; *M:* Miklos Rozsa. *MGM*

A Tribute to the Boys 🎬🎬 **1992** An all-star salute to the comedy of Laurel & Hardy featuring clips from more than 30 of their comedies, including scenes from their silent film days. Guests include Johnny Carson, Steve Allen, Walter Matthau, Rich Little, Henny Youngman, Robert Klein, Bronson Pinchot, and The Smothers Brothers. **85m/C VHS.** *CAF*

Tricheurs 🎬🎬 *Cheaters* **1984** Scam artists hit largest casino in the world and look forward to golden years of retirement. From the director of "Reversal of Fortune." In French with English subtitles. **95m/C VHS, Beta.** *FR* Jacques Dutronc, Bulle Ogier, Kurt Raab, Virgilio Teixeira, Steve Baes; *D:* Barbet Schroeder. *WAR, BTV, FCT*

Trick or Treat 🎬½ 1986 (R) A high school student is helped to exact violent revenge against his bullying contemporaries. His helper is the spirit of a violent heavy metal rock star who he raises from the dead. Sometimes clever, not terribly scary. **97m/C VHS, Beta, Closed Caption.** Tony Fields, Marc Price, Ozzy Osbourne, Gene Simmons; **D:** Charles Martin Smith; **C:** Robert Elswit. *ORI, WAR*

Trick or Treats woof! 1982 (R) Young boy's pranks on his terrified babysitter backfire on Halloween night. His deranged father, escaped from an asylum, shows up to help him "scare" her. Giroux doesn't look very frightened in this extremely tedious film from Welles' best camera man. **90m/C VHS, Beta.** Carrie Snodgress, David Carradine, Jackie Giroux, Steve Railsback; **D:** Gary Graver. *LIV, VES*

Tricks of the Trade 🎬🎬 1988 (R) Goody-two-shoe housewife and hooker accomplice search for husband's murderer. Racy made-for-television fodder. **100m/C VHS, LV.** Cindy Williams, Markie Post, Chris Mulkey, James Whitmore Jr., Scott Paulin, John Ritter, Apollonia; **D:** Jack Bender. *ACA*

Trident Force 1988 International counter-terrorism team is ordered to destroy the Palestinian Revolutionary Legion by any means possible. **90m/C VHS, Beta.** Anthony Alonzo, Mark Gil, Nanna Anderson, Steve Rogers, Eddie M. Gaerlan; **D:** Richard Smith. *NO*

The Trigger Effect 🎬½ 1996 (R) Nightmare in yuppiedom when a suspicious electromagnetic pulse knocks out all electrical power, telephone, and broadcast signals for hundreds of miles around a tranquil southern California community, which becomes increasingly unsettled. Matt (MacLachlan), wife Annie (Shue), and friend Joe (Mulroney) hang out together during the mystery power outage with lots of mounting tension both within and without. Film, however dread-producing, doesn't really make that much sense.**CW:** Language and some violence. **103m/C VHS, LV, Closed Caption.** Kyle MacLachlan, Elisabeth Shue, Dermot Mulroney, Michael Rooker, Richard T. Jones, Bill Smitrovich, William Lucking, Molly Morgan, Richard Schiff; **D:** David Koepp; **W:** David Koepp; **C:** Newton Thomas Sigel; **M:** James Newton Howard. *USH*

Trigger Happy 🎬½ *Mad Dog Time* 1996 (R) Director Bishop (son of Rat-Packer Joey, who's in the film) tells a tale of crime lord Vic (Dreyfuss) and various gangsters in what should be a knowingly cool story but isn't. Vic's about to get out of the loony bin and has informed his enforcer, Ben London (Byrne), to get rid of his rivals and disloyal fellow mobsters in time for his return. Meanwhile, his chief of staff, Mickey (Goldblum), has been romancing both Vic's gal Grace (Lane) and her jealous older sister, Rita (Barkin). This situation does not make Vic happy. The movie won't make you happy either.**CW:** Violence, language, and sexuality. **93m/C VHS, Closed Caption.** Richard Dreyfuss, Gabriel Byrne, Jeff Goldblum, Diane Lane, Ellen Barkin, Gregory Hines, Kyle MacLachlan, Larry Bishop, Burt Reynolds, Henry Silva; **Cameos:** Joey Bishop, Angie Everhart, Michael J. Pollard, Richard Pryor, Rob Reiner, Billy Idol; **D:** Larry Bishop; **W:** Larry Bishop; **C:** Frank Byers; **M:** Earl Rose. *MGM*

Trigger, Jr. 🎬🎬½ 1950 Rogers and his Western Show find themselves in the middle of a dispute between intimidated ranchers and an evil local range patrol office. When Trigger is injured by a killer stallion, Roy turns to two unlikely allies—a 10-year-old boy who's scared of horses and frisky Trigger, Jr. **67m/B VHS, Closed Caption.** Roy Rogers, Dale Evans, Grant Withers, Pat Brady, Gordon Jones, Peter Miles, George Cleveland; **D:** William Witney; **W:** Gerald Geraghty. *REP*

Trigger Men 🎬½ *Billy the Kid's Fighting Pals* 1941 Steele, Young, and St. John find a dying U.S. marshal who has been ambushed by the villainous Peil. Seems Peil and his gang have taken over a small border town in order to set up a smuggling operation with Mexico. So the trio

avenge the marshal by putting a stop to the nefarious doings. Newfield directed under the pseudonym Sherman Scott. **59m/B VHS.** Bob Steele, Al "Fuzzy" St. John, Carleton Young, Edward Peil Sr., Phyllis Adair, Charles "Blackie" King, Curly Dresden, Hal Price, George Chesebro, Forrest Taylor, Budd Buster; **D:** Sam Newfield. *GPV, DVT*

Trigger Pals 🎬½ 1939 Jarrett stars in this basic oater about bringing a gang of rustlers to justice. Besides the usual gunplay, he also attempts to sing a few songs. **58m/B VHS.** Art Jarrett, Lee Powell, Al "Fuzzy" St. John, Dorothy Fay, Charles "Blackie" King, Frank LaRue; **D:** Sam Newfield. *GPV, VCN, DVT*

Trigger Tricks 🎬½ 1930 Gibson's brother becomes the victim of a vicious cattleman and Hoot is out for revenge. **60m/B VHS.** Hoot Gibson, Sally Eilers, Neal Hart, Monte Montague, Peter Morrison, Robert E. Homans, Jack Richardson; **D:** B. Reeves Eason. *GPV, DVT*

The Trigger Trio 🎬½ 1937 Rancher with diseased cattle kills a ranch inspector. The Three Mesquiteers are called in to crack the case. **54m/B VHS, Beta.** Ray Corrigan, Max Terhune, Ralph Byrd, Robert Warwick, Cornelius Keefe, Wally Wales; **D:** William Witney. *VCN, DVT, GPV*

Trilby 🎬🎬🎬 1917 Original screen production of Du Maurier's classic tale of Svengali. **59m/B VHS, Beta.** Clara Kimball Young, Wilton Lackaye, Chester Barnett; **D:** Maurice Tourneur. *GPV, FCT*

Trilogy of Terror 🎬🎬½ 1975 Black shows her versatility as she plays a tempting seductress, a mousy schoolteacher and the terrified victim of an African Zuni fetish doll in three horror shorts. Made for television. **78m/C VHS, Beta.** Karen Black, Robert Burton, John Karlen, Gregory Harrison; **D:** Dan Curtis; **W:** Richard Matheson. *NO*

Trilogy of Terror 2 🎬🎬 1996 (R) Curtis follows up his 1975 TV movie with an okay sequel headed by Anthony. "Graveyard Rats" features flesh-eating, cemetery-dwelling rodents and a greedy wife who bumped off her wealthy husband, a mother strikes a fiendish bargain to bring her drowned son back to life in "Bobby," and the deadly African Zuni fetish doll returns in "He Who Kills."**CW:** Violence and terror. **90m/C VHS, Beta, Closed Caption.** Lysette Anthony, Richard Fitzpatrick, Geraint Wyn Davies, Matt Clark, Geoffrey Lewis, Blake Heron; **D:** Dan Curtis; **W:** William F. Nolan, Dan Curtis, Richard Matheson; **M:** Robert Cobert. *PAR*

Trinity is Still My Name 🎬🎬½ *Continuavamo A Chiamarlo Trinita* 1975 (G) Sequel to "They Call Me Trinity." Insouciant bumbling brothers Trinity and Bambino, oblivious to danger and hopeless odds, endure mishaps and adventures as they try to right wrongs. A funny parody of Western cliches that never becomes stale. **117m/C VHS, Beta, LV.** *IT* Bud Spencer, Terence Hill, Harry Carey Jr.; **D:** E.B. Clucher. *CCB, HHE*

Trio 🎬🎬🎬 1950 Sequel to "Quartet," featuring the W. Somerset Maugham stories "The Verger," "Mr. Knowall" and "Sanatorium Acclaimed." Cinematography by Geoffrey Unsworth and Reg Wyer. **88m/B VHS, Beta.** Jean Simmons, Michael Rennie, Bill Travers, James Hayter, Kathleen Harrison, Felix Aylmer, Nigel Patrick, Finlay Currie, John Laurie; **D:** Ken Annakin, Harold French. Nominations: Academy Awards '50: Best Sound.*NO*

The Trip 🎬🎬 1967 A psychedelic journey to the world of inner consciousness, via drugs. A television director, unsure where his life is going, decides to try a "trip" to expand his understanding. Hopper is the drug salesman, Dern, the tour guide for Fonda's trip through sex, witches, torture chambers and more. Great period music. **85m/C VHS, Beta.** Peter Fonda, Dennis Hopper, Susan Strasberg, Dick Miller, Peter Bogdanovich, Bruce Dern; **D:** Roger Corman; **W:** Jack Nicholson; **M:** Barry Goldberg. *LIV, VES*

The Trip to Bountiful 🎬🎬🎬 1985 (PG) An elderly widow, unhappy living in her son's fancy modern home, makes a pilgrimage back to her childhood home in Bountiful, Texas. Based on the Horton Foote play. Fine acting with Oscar-winning performance from Page. **102m/C VHS, Beta, LV, 8mm, Closed Caption.** Geraldine Page, Rebecca DeMornay, John Heard, Carlin Glynn, Richard Bradford; **D:** Peter Masterson; **W:** Horton Foote; **C:** Fred Murphy. Academy Awards '85: Best Actress (Page); Independent Spirit Awards '86: Best Actress (Page), Best Screenplay; National Media Owl Awards '87: First Prize; Nominations: Academy Awards '85: Best Adapted Screenplay.*COL, BTV, NLC*

Triple Cross 🎬🎬🎬 1967 Plummer is a British safecracker imprisoned on the channel islands at the outbreak of WWII. When the Germans move in, he offers to work for them if they set him free. The Germans buy his story and send him to England, but once there he offers his services to the British as a double agent. Based on the exploits of Eddie Chapman, adapted from his book, "The Eddie Chapman Story." **91m/C VHS, Beta.** *FR GB* Christopher Plummer, Romy Schneider, Trevor Howard, Gert Frobe, Yul Brynner, Claudine Auger, Georges Lycan, Jess Hahn, Howard Vernon; **D:** Terence Young. *ACE, MOV, HHE*

Triple Echo 🎬🎬½ *Soldier in Skirts* 1977 (R) A young woman falls for an army deserter who is hiding from the military police by dressing as a woman. Mistrust and deception get the best of some of the involved parties. **90m/C VHS, Beta.** *GB* Glenda Jackson, Oliver Reed, Brian Deacon; **D:** Michael Apted; **W:** Robin Chapman. *NO*

Triple Impact 🎬 1992 Hall, Cook, and Riley are three martial-arts experts who join forces against illegal gambling syndicates who are staging full-contact bloodmatches. Their alliance leads them to Asia where the prize is death—or a fortune in gold. **97m/C VHS, LV.** Dale "Apollo" Cook, Ron Hall, Bridgett "Baby Doll" Riley, Robert Marius, Steve Rogers, Nick Nicholson, Ned Hourani, Mike "Cobra" Cole; **D:** David Hunt; **W:** Steve Rogers. *AIP*

Triple Trouble/Easy Street 1918 Two of Chaplin's classic two-reel silent comedy shorts are shown on video. **60m/B VHS, Beta, 8mm.** Charlie Chaplin, Edna Purviance, Eric Campbell. *VYY*

TripleCross 🎬½ 1985 Three former cops strike it rich and although they love the money, they miss the game, so they get involved in a murder case. These wealthy detectives encounter high-level gangsters, a baseball scandal, and a hit man in their race to solve the perfect crime. **97m/C VHS, Beta, Closed Caption.** Ted Wass, Markie Post, Gary Swanson; **D:** David Greene. *PSM*

Triplecross 🎬🎬½ 1995 (R) Jewel thief Jimmy Ray (Bergin) is after a fortune in diamonds and obsessive FBI agent Oscar (Williams) is looking to bring him down. Oscar decides to use Jimmy Ray's ex-cell mate Teddy (Pare) but Teddy gets involved with J.R.'s girlfriend Julia (Laurence) instead of tending to business. Wooden crime caper made for cable TV.**CW:** Strong violence, language, and a scene of sexuality. **95m/C VHS.** Patrick Bergin, Billy Dee Williams, Michael Pare, Ashley Laurence; **D:** Jeno Hodl. *HMK*

Tripods: The White Mountains 🎬½ 1984 Sci-fi thriller about the takeover of earth by alien tripods. The conquerors start controlling human minds, but not until after they are sixteen years old. Two boys seek to end the terror. **150m/C VHS, Beta.** John Shackley, Jim Baker, Cari Seel; **D:** Graham Theakston. *IME*

Tripwire 🎬½ 1989 (R) A vengeance-crazed government agent tracks down the terrorist who murdered his wife. **120m/C VHS, Beta, LV.** Terence Knox, David Warner, Charlotte Lewis, Isabella Hoffman, Yaphet Kotto, Thomas Chong, Meg Foster; **D:** James Lemmo. *COL*

Tristana 🎬🎬🎬🎬 1970 (PG) Allegorical tale of a beautiful girl (Deneuve) who moves in with a hypocritical benefactor following the death of her mother. She is quickly exploited and seduced by the one who would protect her, but runs away with an artist in pursuit of love. Searing in its commentary on Catholicism, death, lust, and the woebegone place of humanity in the world, the movie is also widely seen as a depiction of fascist Spain's attempt to find its place in the twentieth century. Based on the novel by Benito Perez Galdos. In Spanish with English subtitles. 98m/C VHS. *SP IT FR* Catherine Deneuve, Fernando Rey, Franco Nero, Lola Gaos, Antonio Casas, Jesus Fernandez, Vincent Solder; **D:** Luis Bunuel; **W:** Luis Bunuel. Nominations: Academy Awards '70: Best Foreign Language Film. *HTV*

The Triumph of Sherlock Holmes 🐾🐾½ 1935
Wontner and Fleming teamed for an early series of Holmesian romps. In one of their best outings, Sherlock Holmes comes out of retirement as a series of bizarre murders of Pennsylvania coal miners lure him back into action. From "The Valley of Fear" by Sir Arthur Conan Doyle. 84m/B VHS, Beta. *GB* Arthur Wontner, Ian Fleming; **D:** Leslie Hiscott. *SNC, NOS, CAB*

Triumph of the Son of Hercules 1963
All other victories pale when compared to this, the Son of Hercules' greatest! ?m/C VHS, Beta. *IT* Kirk Morris, Cathia Caro. *SNC*

Triumph of the Spirit 🐾🐾🐾 1989 (R)
Gritty account of boxer Salamo Arouch's experiences in Auschwitz. The boxer became champion in matches between prisoners conducted for the amusement of Nazi officers. Filmed on location in Auschwitz. 115m/C VHS, Beta, LV. Willem Dafoe, Robert Loggia, Edward James Olmos, Wendy Gazelle, Kelly Wolf, Costas Mandylor, Kario Salem; **D:** Robert M. Young; **W:** Andrzej Krakowski, Laurence Heath, Arthur Coburn, Millard Lampell, Robert M. Young, Shimon Arama; **M:** Cliff Eidelman. *COL*

Triumph of the Will 1934
Director Riefenstahl's formidable, stunning film, documenting Hitler and the Sixth Nazi Party Congress in 1934 in Nuernberg, Germany. The greatest and most artful propaganda piece ever produced. German dialogue. Includes English translation of the speeches. 115m/B VHS, Beta. *GE* **D:** Leni Riefenstahl. *NOS, VYY, BAR*

Triumphs of a Man Called Horse 🐾🐾 1983 (R)
An Indian must save his people from prospectors in order to keep his title as Peace, Chief of the Yellow Hand Sioux. Inadequate sequel to two previous films: "A Man Called Horse" and "The Return of a Man Called Horse." 91m/C VHS, Beta. *MX* Richard Harris; **D:** John Hough; **W:** Carlos Aured, Jack DeWitt, Kenneth G. Blackwell. *NO*

Trois Couleurs: Blanc 🐾🐾🐾 *White; Three Colors: White* 1994 (R)
Bittersweet comedic rags-to-riches tale spiced with revenge and lasting love. "White" focuses on equality and begins when a bewildered Polish hairdresser is divorced by his disdainful French wife, who takes him for everything he has. Returning to his family in Poland, Karol doggedly works his way into wealth. Then he decides to fake his death and leave his fortune to the ex he still loves—or does he? In Polish and French with English subtitles. Part 2 of Kieslowski's trilogy, following "Trois Couleurs: Bleu" and followed by "Trois Couleurs: Rouge." **CW:** Language and sexuality. 92m/C VHS. *FR SI PL* Zbigniew Zamachowski, Julie Delpy, Janusz Gajos, Jerzy Stuhr, Aleksander Bardini, Grzegorz Warchol, Cezary Harasimowicz, Jerzy Nowak, Jerzy Trela, Cezary Pazura, Michel Lisowski, Philippe Morier-Genoud; **Cameos:** Juliette Binoche, Florence Pernel; **D:** Krzysztof Kieslowski; **W:** Krzysztof Kieslowski, Krzysztof Piesiewicz; **C:** Edward Klosinski; **M:** Zbigniew Preisner. Berlin International Film Festival '94: Best Director (Kieslowski). *MAX*

Trois Couleurs: Bleu 🐾🐾🐾 *Three Colors: Blue; Blue* 1993 (R)
First installment of director Kieslowski's trilogy inspired by the French tricolor flag. "Blue" stands for liberty—here freedom is based on tragedy as Julie (Binoche) reshapes her life after surviving an accident which killed her famous composer husband and their young daughter. Excellent performance by Binoche,

which relies on the internalized grief and brief emotion which flits across her face rather than overwhelming displays for expression. In French with English subtitles. 98m/C VHS, LV. *FR* Juliette Binoche, Benoit Regent, Florence Pernel, Charlotte Very, Helene Vincent, Phillipe Volter, Claude Duneton, Hugues Quester, Florence Vignon, Isabelle Sadoyan, Yann Tregouet, Jacek Ostaszewski; **Cameos:** Emmanuelle Riva; **D:** Krzysztof Kieslowski; **W:** Krzysztof Kieslowski, Krzysztof Piesiewicz, Slawomir Idziak, Agnieszka Holland, Edward Zebrowski; **C:** Slawomir Idziak. Cesar Awards '94: Best Actress (Binoche), Best Film Editing, Best Sound; Los Angeles Film Critics Association Awards '93: Best Score; Venice Film Festival '93: Best Actress (Binoche), Best Film; Nominations: Golden Globe Awards '94: Best Actress—Drama (Binoche), Best Foreign Film, Best Original Score. *TOU*

Trois Couleurs: Rouge 🐾🐾🐾½ *Three Colors: Red; Red* 1994 (R)
"Red" is for fraternity in the French tricolor flag and, in director Kieslowski's last film in his trilogy, emotional connections are made between unlikely couples. There's law student Auguste and his girlfriend Karin, young fashion model Valentine, and a nameless retired judge, brought together by circumstance and destined to change each other's lives. Subtle details make for careful viewing but it's a rewarding watch and a visual treat (keep an eye on cinematographer Sobocinski's use of the color red). Binoche and Delpy, who starred in the earlier films, also make an appearance, as Kieslowski uses the finale to tie up loose ends. In French with English subtitles. **CW:** Brief but strong sex scene. 99m/C VHS, LV. *FR PL SI* Irene Jacob, Jean-Louis Trintignant, Frederique Feder, Jean-Pierre Lorit, Samuel Lebihan, Marion Stalens, Teco Celio, Bernard Escalon, Jean Schlegel, Elzbieta Jasinska; **Cameos:** Juliette Binoche, Julie Delpy, Benoit Regent, Zbigniew Zamachowski; **D:** Krzysztof Kieslowski; **W:** Krzysztof Kieslowski, Krzysztof Piesiewicz; **C:** Piotr Sobocinski; **M:** Zbigniew Preisner. Cesar Awards '94: Best Score; Independent Spirit Awards '95: Best Foreign Film; Los Angeles Film Critics Association Awards '94: Best Foreign Film; New York Film Critics Awards '94: Best Foreign Film; National Society of Film Critics Awards '94: Best Foreign Film; Nominations: Academy Awards '94: Best Cinematography, Best Director (Kieslowski), Best Original Screenplay; Cesar Awards '94: Best Actor (Trintignant), Best Actress (Jacob), Best Director (Kieslowski), Best Film; Golden Globe Awards '95: Best Foreign Film. *MAX*

Trojan Women 🐾🐾 1971 (G)
Euripides' tragedy on the fate of the women of Troy after the Greeks storm the famous city. The play does not translate well to the screen, in spite of tour-de-force acting. 105m/C VHS, Beta. Katharine Hepburn, Vanessa Redgrave, Irene Papas, Genevieve Bujold, Brian Blessed, Patrick Magee; **D:** Michael Cacoyannis. National Board of Review Awards '71: Best Actress (Papas). *FHS*

Troll 🐾½ 1986 (PG-13)
A malevolent troll haunts an apartment building and possesses a young girl in hopes of turning all humans into trolls. Sometimes imaginative, sometimes embarrassing. Followed by a sequel. 86m/C VHS, Beta, LV. Noah Hathaway, Gary Sandy, Anne Lockhart, Sonny Bono, Shelley Hack, June Lockhart, Michael Moriarty; **D:** John Carl Buechler; **M:** Richard Band. *LIV, VES*

Troll 2 🐾½ 1992 (PG-13)
A young boy can only rely on his faith in himself when no one believes his warnings about an evil coming to destroy his family. Entering into a nightmare world, Joshua must battle witches' spells and the evil trolls who carry out their bidding. 95m/C VHS, Closed Caption. Michael Stephenson, Connie McFarland; **D:** Drago Floyd; **W:** Clyde Anderson. *COL*

A Troll in Central Park 🐾🐾½ 1994 (G)
Animated fantasy about Stanley the troll, who is cast out of his kingdom (because he's a good guy) and winds up in New York's Central Park. There, Stanley brings happiness to a little girl and her skeptical brother, all the while battling the evil troll queen. Strictly average family fare. 76m/C VHS, LV, Closed Caption. **D:** Don Bluth, Gary Goldman; **W:** Stu Krieger; **M:** Robert Folk; **V:** Dom DeLuise, Cloris Leachman, Jonathan Pryce, Hayley Mills, Charles Nelson Reilly, Phillip Glasser, Robert Morley, Sy Goraleb, Tawney Sunshine Glover, Jordan Metzner. *WAR*

Troma's War WOOF! 1988 (R)
The survivors of an air crash find themselves amid a tropical terrorist-run civil war. Also available in a 105-minute, unrated version. Devotees of trash films shouldn't miss this one. 90m/C VHS. Ara Romanoff, Michael Ryder, Carolyn Beauchamp, Sean Bowen; **D:** Michael Herz, Lloyd (Samuel Weil) Kaufman. *TTV*

Tromba, the Tiger Man 🐾🐾½ *Tromba* 1952
A circus tiger tamer uses a special drug that hypnotizes the critters into obeying his every whim. When he tries the same drug on women, things get out of hand. 62m/B VHS, Beta. *GE* Rene Deltgen, Angelika Hauff, Gustav Knuth, Hilde Weissner, Grethe Weiser, Gardy Granass, Adrian Hoven; **D:** Helmut Weiss. *SNC*

Tromeo & Juliet 🐾🐾 1995 (R)
There've been many versions of Shakespeare but the Bard may never recover from being "Tromatized." On the outskirts of New York City, teenaged Tromeo Que (Keenan) falls in lust with babe Juliet Capulet (Jensen) but the family feud is still around to cause major disharmony. There's lots of profanity, perversity, and gore to keep your interest. As the movie's tagline says "Body Piercing. Kinky Sex. Dismemberment. The things that made Shakespeare great." The unrated version is 105 minutes. **CW:** Strong sexuality, violence/gore, language and some drug content. 95m/C VHS. Will Keenan, Jane Jensen, Debbie Rochon, Lemmy; **D:** Lloyd (Samuel Weil) Kaufman; **W:** James Gunn; **C:** Brendan Flynt. *TTV*

Tron 🐾🐾 1982 (PG)
A video game designer enters into his computer, where he battles the computer games he created and seeks revenge on other designers who have stolen his creations. Sounds better than it plays. Terrific special effects, with lots of computer-created graphics. 96m/C VHS, Beta, LV. Jeff Bridges, Bruce Boxleitner, David Warner, Cindy Morgan, Barnard Hughes, Dan Shor; **D:** Steven Lisberger. Nominations: Academy Awards '82: Best Costume Design, Best Sound. *DIS*

Troop Beverly Hills 🐾 1989 (PG)
Spoiled housewife Long isn't really spoiled, just misunderstood. She takes over leadership of her daughter's Wilderness Girls troop and finds the opportunity to redeem herself by offering her own unique survival tips to the uncooperative little brats who make up the troop. Everyone learns meaningful life lessons, Long is finally understood, and everyone lives happily ever after in posh Beverly Hills. Sheer silliness makes this one almost painful to watch, a shame since it boasts a good cast whose talent is totally wasted. 105m/C VHS, Beta, LV, 8mm, Closed Caption. Shelley Long, Craig T. Nelson, Betty Thomas, Mary Gross, Stephanie Beacham, Audra Lindley, Edd Byrnes, Ami Foster, Jenny Lewis, Kellie Martin; **D:** Jeff Kanew; **W:** Pamela Norris, Margaret Grieco Oberman; **M:** Randy Edelman. *COL*

Tropic of Cancer 🐾🐾🐾 1970 (NC-17)
Based on Henry Miller's once-banned, now classic novel, this film portrays the sexual escapades of the expatriate author living in 1920's Paris. Torn stars as the carefree, loose-living writer and Burstyn plays his disgusted wife. 87m/C VHS. Rip Torn, James Callahan, Ellen Burstyn, David Bauer, Phil Brown; **D:** Joseph Strick. *PAR, FCT*

Tropical Heat 🐾🐾 1993 (R)
When the Maharajah is killed on safari, his grieving widow (D'Abo) files a five-million-dollar insurance claim before returning to India. She's followed by an investigator (Rossovich) who becomes infatuated with the lovely D'Abo. Through palaces, primitive villages, and ancient jungle temples, they are drawn into a mystery involving blackmail and murder. Based on a story by Jag Mundhra, Michael W. Potts and Simon Levy. **CW:** Some violence and sexuality. 86m/C VHS. Rick Rossovich, Maryam D'Abo, L'ee Ann Beaman, Asha Siewkumar; **D:** Jag Mundhra; **W:** Michael W. Potts; **M:** Del Casher. *PSM*

Tropical Snow 🎬 1988 (R) A pair of lovers living poorly in Colombia decide to enter the drug trade in exchange for passage to the U.S. offered to them by drug kingpin Carradine. Unfortunately, they get more than they bargained for. Shot on location. 87m/C VHS, Beta, LV, Closed Caption. David Carradine, Madeleine Stowe, Nick Corri, Argermiro Catiblanco; *D:* Ciro Duran. PAR

Trouble Along the Way 🎬🎬½ 1953 Wayne is a once big-time college football coach who takes a coaching job at a small, financially strapped Catholic college in an effort to retain custody of his young daughter. His underhanded recruiting methods result in his firing—and the probable loss of his daughter. Unusual and sentimental role for Wayne proves he can handle comedy as well as action. 110m/B VHS. John Wayne, Donna Reed, Charles Coburn, Tom Tully, Sherry Jackson, Marie Windsor, Tom Helmore, Dabbs Greer, Leif Erickson, Douglas Spencer; *D:* Michael Curtiz; *W:* Jack Rose, Melville Shavelson; *M:* Max Steiner. WAR

Trouble Bound 🎬🎬 1992 (R) Madsen is Harry, a guy just out of prison, on his way to Nevada with trouble dogging him every step. He's got a dead body in the car trunk, drug dealers after him, and when he offers a lift to a pretty cocktail waitress (Arquette) his luck only gets worse. She plans to kill a Mob boss and it's no secret. Chases and violence.*CW:* Language, violence, and sexuality. 90m/C VHS, LV, Closed Caption. Michael Madsen, Patricia Arquette, Florence Stanley, Seymour Cassel, Sal Jenco; *D:* Jeff Reiner; *W:* Darrell Fetty, Francis Delia; *M:* Vinnie Golia. FXV

Trouble Busters 🎬 1933 Troubled locals worry about who to call when oil is discovered in their town, bringing evil profiteers with it. The Trouble Busters come into town to set things straight. 51m/B VHS, Beta. Jack Hoxie, Lane Chandler; *D:* Lewis D. Collins. NOS, DVT

Trouble in Mind 🎬🎬🎬 1986 (R) Stylized romance is set in the near future in a rundown diner. Kristofferson is an ex-cop who gets involved in the lives of a young couple looking for a better life. Look for Divine in one of her/his rare appearances outside of John Waters' works. 111m/C VHS, Beta, LV, 8mm, Closed Caption. Kris Kristofferson, Keith Carradine, Genevieve Bujold, Lori Singer, Divine, Joe Morton, George Kirby, John Considine, Dirk Blocker, Gailard Sartain, Tracy Kristofferson; *D:* Alan Rudolph; *W:* Alan Rudolph; *C:* Toyomichi Kurita; *M:* Mark Isham. Independent Spirit Awards '86: Best Cinematography. COL, NLC

Trouble in Paradise 🎬🎬 1988 Welch stars as a widow stranded in a tropical island paradise with an Australian sailor. The two must struggle as they are stalked by a gang of drug smugglers, hence the title. Made for television. 92m/C VHS. Raquel Welch, Jack Thompson, Nicholas Hammond, John Gregg; *D:* Di Drew. CAF

Trouble in Store 🎬🎬½ 1953 A bumbling department store employee stumbles on a gangster's plot. Fun gags and a good cast. 85m/B VHS. *GB* Margaret Rutherford, Norman Wisdom, Moira Lister, Megs Jenkins; *D:* John Paddy Carstairs. REP

Trouble in Texas 🎬🎬 1937 Outlaws go to a rodeo and try to steal the prize money. Tex wants to find out who killed his brother and in his spare time, sings and tries to stop the crooks. Notable because it is the last film Hayworth made under her original stage name (Rita Cansino). 65m/B VHS, Beta. Tex Ritter, Rita Hayworth, Earl Dwire, Yakima Canutt; *D:* Robert North Bradbury. NOS, DVT, VCI

Trouble in the Glen 🎬🎬½ 1954 A Scottish-American soldier returns to his ancestral home and becomes involved in a dispute between the town residents and a lord over a closed road. Uneven script undermines comic idea. 91m/C VHS. *GB* Orson Welles, Victor McLaglen, Forrest Tucker, Margaret Lockwood; *D:* Herbert Wilcox. REP

The Trouble with Angels 🎬🎬½ 1966 (PG) Two young girls turn a convent upside down with their endless practical jokes. Russell is everything a Mother Superior should be: understanding, wise, and beautiful. 112m/C VHS, Beta, LV. Hayley Mills, June Harding, Rosalind Russell, Gypsy Rose Lee, Binnie Barnes; *D:* Ida Lupino; *C:* Lionel Lindon; *M:* Jerry Goldsmith. COL

The Trouble with Dick 🎬 1988 (R) An ambitious young science fiction writer's personal troubles begin to appear in his writing. Although the box cover displays a "Festival Winner" announcement, don't be fooled! Story becomes tedious after first five minutes. 86m/C VHS, Beta. Tom Villard, Susan Dey; *D:* Gary Walkow; *M:* Roger Bourland. Sundance Film Festival '87: Grand Jury Prize. ACA

The Trouble with Father*The Stu Erwin Show* 1950 Erwin starred in the classic comedy series about a bumbling father which aired from 1950–1955. Two episodes per tape. On this tape: "Yvette," a 1954 episode in which Stu tries to surprise June with a lifelike female mannequin as an anniversary gift and the 1952 episode "What Paper Do you Read" when June enrolls in Stu's evening government classes. 50m/B VHS, Beta. Stuart Erwin, June Collyer Erwin, Sheila James, Ann Todd, Martin Milner, Willie Best. NOS, MOV, DVT

The Trouble with Girls (and How To Get Into It) 🎬🎬🎬 *The Chautauqua* 1969 (G) A 1920s traveling show manager tries to solve a local murder. Not as much singing as his earlier films, but good attention is paid to details. This is definitely one of the better Elvis vehicles. ♫Almost; Clean Up Your Own Back Yard. 99m/C VHS, Beta. Elvis Presley, Marlyn Mason, Nicole Jaffe, Sheree North, Edward Andrews, John Carradine, Vincent Price, Joyce Van Patten, Dabney Coleman, John Rubinstein, Anthony Teague; *D:* Peter Tewkesbury. MGM

The Trouble with Harry 🎬🎬🎬 1955 (PG) When a little boy finds a dead body in a Vermont town, it causes all kinds of problems for the community. No one is sure who killed Harry and what to do with the body. MacLaine's film debut and Herrmann's first musical score for Hitchcock. 90m/C VHS, Beta, LV. John Forsythe, Shirley MacLaine, Edmund Gwenn, Jerry Mathers, Mildred Dunnock, Mildred Natwick, Royal Dano; *D:* Alfred Hitchcock; *W:* John Michael Hayes; *C:* Robert Burks; *M:* Bernard Herrmann. USH, HMV

The Trouble with Spies 🎬 1987 (PG-13) A bumbling British spy goes to Ibizia to locate a Russian agent, makes a million mistakes and wins anyway. A loser of a film, wasted a fine cast. Made in 1984; no one bothered to release it for 3 years. 91m/C VHS, Beta. Donald Sutherland, Malcolm Morley, Lucy Gutteridge, Ruth Gordon, Ned Beatty, Michael Hordern, Robert Morley; *D:* Burt Kennedy; *W:* Burt Kennedy. HBO

Troublemakers 🎬½ 1994 (PG) Travis (Hill) is the fastest gun in the west—too bad his brother Moses (Spencer) is the country's meanest bounty hunter. But their mother loves them, and wants both her boys home for Christmas. So she leaves it up to Travis to lure Moses back to the homestead. 98m/C VHS. Terence Hill, Bud Spencer. TRI

Truck Stop 🎬 19?? This truck stop has all a trucker needs—including the owner, voluptuous Pamela. 80m/C VHS. Nikki Gentile, Elizabeth Turner; *D:* Jean Marie Pallardy. MED

Truck Stop Women 🎬🎬 1974 (R) Female truckers become involved in smuggling and prostitution at a truck stop. The mob wants a cut of the business and will do anything to get their way. Better than it sounds. 88m/C VHS, Beta. Claudia Jennings, Lieux Dressler, John Martino, Dennis Fimple, Dolores Dorn, Gene Drew, Paul Carr, Jennifer Burton; *D:* Mark L. Lester. VES

Truck Turner 🎬½ 1974 (R) He's a bounty hunter, he's black and he's up against a threadbare plot. Hayes methodically eliminates everyone involved in his partner's murder while providing groovy soundtrack. Quintessential blaxploi-

tation. 91m/C VHS. Isaac Hayes, Yaphet Kotto, Annazette Chase, Nichelle Nichols, Scatman Crothers, Dick Miller; *D:* Jonathan Kaplan; *W:* Leigh Chapman; *M:* Isaac Hayes. ORI, FCT

Trucker's Woman 🎬 1983 (R) Man takes a job driving an 18-wheel truck in order to find the murderers of his father. 90m/C VHS, Beta. Michael Hawkins, Mary Cannon; *D:* Will Zens. NO

True Believer 🎬🎬½ 1989 (R) Cynical lawyer, once a '60s radical, now defends rich drug dealers. Spurred on by a young protege, he takes on the hopeless case of imprisoned Asian-American accused of gang-slaying. Tense thriller with good cast. 103m/C VHS, Beta, LV, Closed Caption. James Woods, Robert Downey Jr., Yuji Okumoto, Margaret Colin, Kurtwood Smith, Tom Bower, Miguel Fernandez, Charles Hallahan; *D:* Joseph Ruben; *W:* Wesley Strick; *M:* Brad Fiedel. COL

True Blood 🎬🎬 1989 (R) A man returns to his home turf to save his brother from the same ruthless gang who set him up for a cop's murder. 100m/C VHS, Beta, LV. Chad Lowe, Jeff Fahey, Sherilyn Fenn; *D:* Peter Maris. FRH, IME

True Colors 🎬🎬½ 1987 (PG-13) A woman fights for her homeland of France in order to save the country from being taken over by Hitler. 160m/C VHS, Beta. Noni Hazlehurst, John Waters, Patrick Ryecart, Shane Briant, Alan Andrews; *D:* Pino Amenta. ACA

True Colors 🎬🎬 1991 (R) Law school buddies take divergent paths in post grad real world. Straight and narrow Spader works for Justice Department while dropout Cusack manipulates friends and acquaintances to further his position as Senator's aid. Typecast, predictable and, moralizing.*CW:* Language and sensuality. 111m/C VHS, Beta, LV, Closed Caption. John Cusack, James Spader, Imogen Stubbs, Mandy Patinkin, Richard Widmark; *D:* Herbert Ross. PAR

True Confessions 🎬🎬🎬 1981 (R) Tale of corruption pits two brothers, one a priest and the other a detective, against each other. Nice 1940s period look, with excellent performances from De Niro and Duvall. Based on a true case from the Gregory Dunne novel. 110m/C VHS, Beta, LV. Robert De Niro, Robert Duvall, Kenneth McMillan, Charles Durning, Cyril Cusack, Ed Flanders, Burgess Meredith, Louisa Moritz; *D:* Ulu Grosbard; *W:* John Gregory Dunne, Joan Didion; *C:* Owen Roizman; *M:* Georges Delerue. MGM

True Crime 🎬🎬½ *Dangerous Kiss* 1995 (R) High school student turns detective when a classmate is killed, hooks up with a police cadet, and finds herself on the trail of a serial killer.*CW:* Psychopathic violence; strong sexuality; language. 94m/C VHS. Alicia Silverstone, Kevin Dillon; *D:* Pat Verducci. THV

The True Game of Death 197? A story of the circumstances behind the death of superstar Bruce Lee. 90m/C VHS, Beta. Shou Lung. NO

True Grit 🎬🎬🎬 1969 (G) Hard-drinking U.S. Marshal Rooster Cogburn (Wayne) is hired by a young girl (Darby) to find her father's killer. Won Wayne his only Oscar. Based on the Charles Portis novel. Prompted sequel, "Rooster Cogburn." 128m/C VHS, Beta, LV. John Wayne, Glen Campbell, Kim Darby, Robert Duvall; *D:* Henry Hathaway; *M:* Elmer Bernstein. Academy Awards '69: Best Actor (Wayne); Golden Globe Awards '70: Best Actor—Drama (Wayne); National Board of Review Awards '69: 10 Best Films of the Year; Nominations: Academy Awards '69: Best Song ("True Grit"). PAR, HHE, TLF

True Heart Susie 🎬🎬½ 1919 A simple, moving story about a girl who is in love with a man who marries another girl from the city. Silent. 87m/B VHS, Beta. Lillian Gish, Robert "Bobbie" Harron; *D:* D.W. Griffith. NOS, VYY, DVT

True Identity 🎬🎬 1991 (R) Henry, a comic superstar in England, stars as an innocent black man marked for death by the Mafia. He hides by disguising himself as white and gets a taste of life on the other side of the color line. The interesting premise was based on a classic Eddie Murphy sketch on "Saturday Night Live," but isn't treated with sufficient imagination or humor here.*CW:* Language. **94m/C VHS, Beta, Closed Caption.** Lenny Henry, Frank Langella, Anne-Marie Johnson, Charles Lane; *D:* Charles Lane; *W:* Andy Breckman. *TOU, FCT*

True Lies 🐾🐾½ 1994 (R) Brain candy with a bang offers eye popping special effects and a large dose of unbelievability. Sort of like a big screen "Scarecrow and Mrs. King" as supposed computer salesman Ah-nuld keeps his spy work secret from mousy, neglected wife Curtis, who has a few secrets of her own and inadvertantly ends up right in the thick of things. Raunchy and extremely sexist, but not without charm; the stupidity is part of the fun. Perfectly cast sidekick Arnold holds his own as a pig, but Heston is wasted as the head honcho. Tons of special effects culminate in a smashing finish. Very loosely adapted from the 1991 French comedy "La Total."*CW:* Some language and a lot of action/violence. **114m/C VHS, LV, Closed Caption.** Arnold Schwarzenegger, Jamie Lee Curtis, Tom Arnold, Bill Paxton, Tia Carrere, Art Malik, Eliza Dushku, Charlton Heston, Grant Heslov; *D:* James Cameron; *W:* James Cameron; *C:* Russell Carpenter. Golden Globe Awards '95: Best Actress—Musical/Comedy (Curtis); Blockbuster Entertainment Awards '96: Action Actress, Video (Curtis); Nominations: Academy Awards '94: Best Visual Effects; MTV Movie Awards '95: Best Female Performance (Curtis), Best Comedic Performance (Arnold), Best Kiss (Arnold Schwarzenegger/Jamie Lee Curtis), Best Action Sequence, Best Dance Sequence (Arnold Schwarzenegger/Tia Carrere). *FXV*

True Love 🐾🐾🐾 1989 (R) Low-budget, savagely observed comedy follows the family and community events leading up to a Bronx Italian wedding. Authentic slice-of-life about two young people with very different ideas about what marriage and commitment mean. Acclaimed script and performances. **104m/C VHS, Beta, LV, Closed Caption.** Annabella Sciorra, Ron Eldard, Aida Turturro, Roger Rignack, Michael J. Wolfe, Star Jasper, Kelly Cinnante, Rick Shapiro, Suzanne Costallos, Vinny Pastore; *D:* Nancy Savoca; *W:* Nancy Savoca, Richard Guay; *C:* Lisa Rinzler. Sundance Film Festival '89: Grand Jury Prize.*MGM*

True Romance 🐾🐾½ 1993 (R) Geeky Clarence (Slater) and wide-eyed whore Alabama (Arquette) meet and fall instantly in love (and marriage). The inept duo skips town after an accidental murder and hit the road to L.A. with the mob in pursuit. Gem performances in small roles include Walken's debonair mafioso who's not adverse to torture; Clarence's dad (Hopper), an ex-cop who runs afoul of Walken; Pitt's space-case druggie; and the ghost of Elvis (Kilmer), whom Clarence talks to in times of stress. Horrific violence mixed with very black humor (courtesy of a script by pre "Reservoir Dogs" Tarantino and "Last Boy Scout" director Scott). An unrated version is also available.*CW:* Strong language, strong violence and drug use, and sexuality. **116m/C VHS, Beta, LV, Closed Caption.** Christian Slater, Patricia Arquette, Gary Oldman, Brad Pitt, Val Kilmer, Dennis Hopper, Christopher Walken, Samuel L. Jackson, Christopher Penn, Bronson Pinchot, Michael Rapaport, Saul Rubinek, Conchata Ferrell, James Gandolfini, Tom Sizemore, Ed Lauter; *D:* Tony Scott; *W:* Quentin Tarantino; *M:* Hans Zimmer. Nominations: MTV Movie Awards '94: Best Kiss (Christian Slater/Patricia Arquette). *WAR, BTV*

True Stories 🐾🐾🐾½ 1986 (PG) Quirky, amusing look at the eccentric denizens of a fictional, off-center Texas town celebrating its 150th anniversary. Notable are Kurtz as the Laziest Woman in America and Goodman as a blushing suitor. Directorial debut of Byrne. Worth a look. **89m/C VHS, Beta, LV, Closed Caption.** David Byrne, John Goodman, Swoosie Kurtz, Spalding Gray, Annie McEnroe, Pops Staples, Tito Larriva; *D:* David Byrne; *W:* David Byrne, Beth Henley, Stephen Tobolowsky; *M:* David Byrne. MVD, WAR

True West 🐾🐾🐾 1986 Filmed performance of the acclaimed Sam Shepard play about two mismatched brothers. Made for Television. **110m/C VHS, Beta.** John Malkovich, Gary Sinise; *D:* Allan Goldstein. *ACA*

Truly, Madly, Deeply 🐾🐾🐾 1991 (PG) The recent death of her lover drives a young woman into despair and anger, until he turns up at her apartment one day. Tender and well written tale of love and the supernatural, with believable characters and plot-line. Playwright Minghella's directorial debut. **107m/C VHS.** Juliet Stevenson, Alan Rickman, Bill Paterson, Michael Maloney, Christopher Rozycki, Keith Bartlett, David Ryall, Stella Maris; *D:* Anthony Minghella; *W:* Anthony Minghella; *C:* Remi Adefarasin. Australian Film Institute '92: Best Foreign Film; British Academy Awards '91: Best Original Screenplay.*TOU*

Truman 🐾🐾½ 1995 (PG) Cable bio follows "Give 'em Hell" Harry (Sinise) from 1917 to 1968. The 33rd U.S. President, derided as a political hack, was determined to prove himself against the odds and by making the tough decisions, including authorizing use of the A-bomb on Japan. Sinise gives the appropriate no-nonsense performance, matched by Scarwid as ever-loyal wife Bess. Based on David McCullough's Pulitzer Prize-winning book. ?m/C VHS. Gary Sinise, Diana Scarwid, Colm Feore, Richard Dysart, James Gammon, Tony Goldwyn, Pat Hingle, Harris Yulin, Leo Burmester, Zeljko Ivanek, David Lansbury, Marian Seldes, Lois Smith, Richard Venture, Daniel von Bargen; *D:* Frank Pierson; *W:* Tom Rickman; *C:* Paul Elliott; *M:* David Mansfield. *HBO*

Trumps 🐾🐾 *Enormous Changes at the Last Minute* 1983 (R) Three dramas about women and contemporary relationships in New York City. Based on three stories—"Faith's Story," "Virginia's Story," and "Alexandra's Story"—by Grace Paley. **90m/C VHS.** Ellen Barkin, Kevin Bacon, Maria Tucci, Ron McLarty, Zvee Scooler, David Strathairn, Jeffrey DeMunn, Sudie Bond; *D:* Mira Bank, Ellen Hovde; *W:* John Sayles, Susan Rice. *HHE*

Trust 🐾🐾 1991 (R) An obnoxious girl, tossed out by her family after becoming pregnant, forms a loving bond with a strange, possibly deranged guy from an abusive household. Similar in style and theme to Hartley's "The Unbelievable Truth" - a peculiar sardonic comedy/drama not for every taste. **107m/C VHS, LV, Closed Caption.** Adrienne Shelly, Martin Donovan, Merritt Nelson, Edie Falco, John MacKay, Marko Hunt; *D:* Hal Hartley; *W:* Hal Hartley; *C:* Mark Spiller; *M:* Phil Reed. Sundance Film Festival '91: Best Screenplay. *REP*

Trust Me 🐾🐾 1989 (R) A cynical L.A. art dealer decides to promote a young artist's work and then kill him off to increase the value of his paintings. Satirical view of the Los Angeles art crowd. **94m/C VHS, Beta, LV.** Adam Ant, Talia Balsam, David Packer, Barbara Bain, Joyce Van Patten, William DeAcutis; *D:* Bobby Houston. *LEO*

Trusting Beatrice 🐾½ 1992 (PG) Lame comedy finds feckless landscaper Claude (Jacobs) the bewildered caretaker of Beatrice (Jacob), a Frenchwoman stranded in America without a green card and with a young Cambodian refugee girl. So Claude decides to take Beatrice home to his determinedly eccentric family. Tries for quirky but fails miserably. **86m/C VHS.** Irene Jacob, Mark Evan Jacobs, Leonardo Cimino, Charlotte Moore, Steve Buscemi, Pat McNamara; *D:* Cindy Lou Johnson; *W:* Cindy Lou Johnson. *FRF*

The Truth About Cats and Dogs 🐾🐾🐾 1996 (PG-13) Funny, intelligent Abby (Garofalo) hosts a popular radio call-in show for pet lovers. When a handsome Brit photographer (Chaplin) phones in with a Great Dane problem, he becomes intrigued by her voice, and asks for a date. Insecure about her looks, Abby asks her beautiful-but-dim girlfriend Noelle (Thurman) to fill in. Naturally, both women fall for the shy Englishman. Charming, updated version of "Cyrano de Bergerac" theme works because of strong lead performances, especially Garofalo, who steals the show with her dry, self-effacing wit. En-

tertaining romantic comedy features some nice scenes of Santa Monica, too.*CW:* Sex-related scene and brief strong language. **97m/C VHS, LV, Closed Caption.** Janeane Garofalo, Uma Thurman, Ben Chaplin, Jamie Foxx, Richard Coca, Stanley DeSantis; *D:* Michael Lehmann. Nominations: MTV Movie Awards '97: Best Comedic Performance (Garofalo). *TCF*

Truth About Women 🐾🐾 1958 An old aristocrat recounts his youthful adventures to his son-in-law. A pale British comedy of manners. **107m/C VHS, Beta.** *GB* Laurence Harvey, Julie Harris, Mai Zetterling, Eva Gabor, Wilfrid Hyde-White, Derek Farr; *D:* Muriel Box. *NOS*

Truth or Consequences, N.M. 🐾 1997 (R) Yes, the name of the town is real. No, Bob Barker is not the mayor. Dim parolee Raymond (Gallo) and his even dimmer girlfriend Addy (Dickens) are reunited and just want to settle down, to tell the truth. Instead, they fall immediately back into a life of crime. Along with their accomplices Marcus (Williamson) and Curtis (Sutherland), they plan to rip off a drug dealer for big bucks (no whammies!). The heist, of course, goes bad; they steal an RV and kidnap its owners Gordon (Pollack) and Donna (Phillips). An attempt to unload the drugs on a powerful Mafia boss (Steiger) also goes awry, and that starts a real family feud. As the mob hit man (Sheen), the cops, and the crooks all converge on the eponymous New Mexico town, everyone is in jeopardy. Not logical, not original and not good. Directorial debut for Sutherland, who should really quit playing coked-up psychopathic murderers.*CW:* Substantial amount of strong violence, and for sex, language, and drug use. **106m/C VHS.** Vincent Gallo, Kim Dickens, Kiefer Sutherland, Mykel T. Williamson, Grace Phillips, Kevin Pollak, Martin Sheen, Rod Steiger; *D:* Kiefer Sutherland; *W:* Brad Mirman; *C:* Ric Waite. *NYR*

Truth or Dare? 🐾 1986 The childhood game of truth or dare turns deadly in this violent thriller. **87m/C VHS, Beta.** John Brace, Mary Fanaro, Geoffrey Lewis Miller; *D:* Yale Wilson. *HHE*

Truth or Dare 🐾🐾½ *In Bed with Madonna; Madonna Truth or Dare* 1991 (R) A quasi-concert-documentary—here is music superstar Madonna tarted up in fact, fiction, and fantasy—exhibitionism to the nth power. Tacky, self-conscious and ultimately, if you are a Madonna fan, moving. On camera Madonna stings ex-boyfriend Warren Beatty, disses admirer Kevin Costner, quarrels with her father, reminisces, and does sexy things with a bottle. Oh yes, she occasionally sings and dances. Both those who worship and dislike the Material Girl will find much to pick apart here. Available in Widescreen format on laserdisc.*CW:* Strong sexual dialogue and strong sexual situations. **118m/C VHS, LV, Closed Caption, DVD.** Madonna; *D:* Alek Keshishian. *LIV, FCT*

Truth or Die 🐾🐾 *Doing Life* 1986 (PG-13) This trite, cliched TV movie chronicles the life of convict Jerry Rosenberg, the first prisoner to earn a law degree from his cell. Still, an uncharacteristic role for sitcom guy Danza. Based on Rosenberg's book "Doing Life." **96m/C VHS, LV, Closed Caption.** Tony Danza, Jon DeVries, Lisa Langlois, Rocco Sisto; *D:* Gene Reynolds. *THV*

Try and Get Me 🐾🐾 *Sound of Fury* 1950 A small town is incited into a manhunt for kidnappers who murdered their victim. Suspenseful melodrama analyzes mob rule and the criminal mind. **91m/B VHS.** Lloyd Bridges, Kathleen Ryan, Richard Carlson, Frank Lovejoy, Katherine Locke; *D:* Cy Endfield. *REP*

Tryst 🐾½ 1994 (R) Julia plots to kill her husband with the help of a detective, but when her housekeeper's son arrives, Julia decides another pawn is just what her deceitful plan needs. **101m/C VHS, Closed Caption.** Barbara Carrera, Louise Fletcher, David Warner, Steve Bond, Andy Romano, Johnny LaSpada; *D:* Peter Foldy; *W:* Peter Foldy; *M:* Tom Howard. *PAR*

The Tsar's Bride 🎬🎬🎬 *Tsarskaya Nevesta* 1966 A lovely young woman is chosen to be the bride of the horrible Tsar Glebov but when the Tsar's bodyguard falls for her, romantic difficulties ensue. A hybrid of the 1899 Rimsky-Korsakov opera and an 1849 play. 95m/B **VHS.** *RU* Raisa Nedashkovskaya, Natalya Rudnaya, Otar Koberidze; *D:* Vladimir Gorikker. *KUL, MVD, PME*

Tucker: The Man and His Dream 🎬🎬🎬 1988 (PG) Portrait of Preston Tucker, entrepreneur and industrial idealist, who in 1946 tried to build the car of the future and was effectively run out of business by the powers-that-were. Ravishing, ultra-nostalgic lullaby to the American Dream. Watch for Jeff's dad, Lloyd, in a bit role. 111m/C **VHS, Beta, LV, 8mm, Closed Caption.** Jeff Bridges, Martin Landau, Dean Stockwell, Frederic Forrest, Mako, Joan Allen, Christian Slater, Lloyd Bridges, Elias Koteas, Nina Siemaszko, Corin "Corky" Nemec, Marshall Bell, Don Novello, Peter Donat, Dean Goodman, Patti Austin; *D:* Francis Ford Coppola; *W:* Arnold Schulman, David Seidler; *M:* Joe Jackson, Carmine Coppola. Golden Globe Awards '89: Best Supporting Actor (Landau); New York Film Critics Awards '88: Best Supporting Actor (Stockwell); Nominations: Academy Awards '88: Best Art Direction/Set Decoration, Best Costume Design, Best Supporting Actor (Landau). *PAR*

Tuff Turf 🎬🎬 1985 (R) The new kid in town must adjust to a different social lifestyle and a new set of rules when his family is forced to move to a low-class section of Los Angeles. He makes enemies immediately when he courts the girlfriend of one of the local toughs. Fast-paced with a bright young cast. Music by Jim Carroll, Lene Lovich, and Southside Johnny. 113m/C **VHS, Beta, LV, Closed Caption.** James Spader, Kim Richards, Paul Mones, Matt Clark, Olivia Barash, Robert Downey Jr., Catya Sassoon; *D:* Fritz Kiersch; *M:* Jonathan Elias. *NWV, VTR*

Tulips 🎬½ 1981 (PG) Would-be suicide takes a contract out on himself, and then meets a woman who makes life worth living again. Together they attempt to evade the gangland hit man. Limp comedy. 91m/C **VHS, Beta.** *CA* Gabe Kaplan, Bernadette Peters, Henry Gibson; *D:* Stan Ferris.

Tulsa 🎬🎬🎬 1949 High-spirited rancher's daughter begins crusade to save her father's oil empire when he's killed. Having become ruthless and determined to succeed at any cost, she eventually sees the error of her ways. Classic Hayward. 96m/C **VHS, Beta.** Susan Hayward, Robert Preston, Chill Wills, Ed Begley Sr., Pedro Armendariz Sr.; *D:* Stuart Heisler; *C:* Winton C. Hoch. *NOS, BPG, MED*

Tumbledown Ranch in Arizona 🎬 1941 After a rodeo accident, an unconscious college student dreams of adventure out west. Part of the "Range Busters" series. 60m/B **VHS.** Ray Corrigan, John "Dusty" King, Max Terhune, Sheila Darcy, Marian Kerby; *D:* S. Roy Luby. *NOS, DVT*

Tumbleweed Trail 🎬½ 1942 Action-packed thundering western. 57m/B **VHS, Beta.** William Boyd, Art Davis, Lee Powell, Jack Rockwell; *D:* Sam Newfield. *VCN*

Tumbleweeds 🎬🎬🎬 1925 William S. Hart's last western. Portrays the last great land rush in America, the opening of the Cherokee Strip in the Oklahoma Territory to homesteaders. Preceded by a sound prologue, made in 1939, in which Hart speaks for the only time on screen, to introduce the story. Silent, with musical score. 114m/B **VHS, Beta, LV.** William S. Hart, Lucien Littlefield, Barbara Bedford; *D:* King Baggot. *GPV, CCB, VYY*

Tundra 🎬🎬½ *The Mighty Thunder* 1936 Quasi adventure-drama/documentary set in the Alaskan tundra. A young man, known only as the "Flying Doctor," tends to the sick in small villages throughout the wilderness. But his own survival is at stake when his small plane crashes. Filmed on location. 72m/B **VHS.** Del Cambre; *D:* Norman Dawn. *VYY*

The Tune 🎬🎬 1992 30,000 ink and water-color drawings make up this animated gem which tells the story of Del (Neiden), a failed songwriter who gets a fresh start when he makes a wrong turn on the freeway and winds up in Flooby Nooby. The strange inhabitants of this town teach Del to throw out his rhyming dictionary and write about his experiences. Plympton's first full-length animated feature. Also includes "The Making of The Tune" and the animated short "Draw." 80m/C **VHS.** *D:* Bill Plympton; *W:* Maureen McElheron, Bill Plympton; *V:* Daniel Neiden, Maureen McElheron, Marty Nelson, Emily Bindiger, Chris Hoffman. *TRI*

Tune in Tomorrow 🎬🎬 1990 (PG-13) Lovesick young Martin (Reeves) wants to woo divorced older babe aunt-by-marriage Julia (Hershey) and is romantically counseled by wacky soap opera writer Pedro (Falk). Seems even soap operas draw on real life, and Martin's story is immortalized on the airwaves, circa 1951 New Orleans. The story-within-a-story also features Pedro's radio characters coming to hammy life. Sometimes funny, sometimes not (the Albanian jokes are tiresome). Adapted from the novel "Aunt Julia and the Scriptwriter" by Mario Vargas Llosa. 90m/C **VHS, LV, Closed Caption.** Barbara Hershey, Keanu Reeves, Peter Falk, Bill McCutcheon, Patricia Clarkson, Peter Gallagher, Dan Hedaya, Buck Henry, Hope Lange, John Larroquette, Elizabeth McGovern, Robert Sedgwick, Henry Gibson; *D:* Jon Amiel; *W:* William Boyd; *M:* Wynton Marsalis. *HBO*

Tunes of Glory 🎬🎬🎬½ 1960 Guinness and Mills are wonderful in this well made film about a brutal, sometimes lazy colonel and a disciplined and educated man moving up through the ranks of the British military. York's film debut. From the novel by James Kennaway, who adapted it for the screen. Laserdisc version contains interview with director Neame. 107m/C **VHS, Beta, LV.** *GB* Alec Guinness, John Mills, Dennis Price, Kay Walsh, Susannah York; *D:* Ronald Neame; *M:* Malcolm Arnold. Nominations: Academy Awards '60: Best Adapted Screenplay. *TVC, NLC*

Tunes of Glory/Horse's Mouth 1960 Guinness double feature. First, "Tunes of Glory" looks at the relationship between good and bad soldiers vying for the same rank. "Horse's Mouth" takes a much lighter tone. Guinness plays a truly obsessed painter who creates his work on public property. Wildly humorous. 305m/C **VHS, Beta.** Alec Guinness, Kay Walsh, Renee Houston, John Mills, Robert Coote; *D:* James Kennaway, Ronald Neame. *CRC*

The Tunnel 🎬🎬½ 1989 (R) Obsessive romance film with a trace of suspense. Artist sees the woman in his dreams at a showing of his work. Her marriage, and her trepidation, don't keep his obsession from consuming him. 99m/C **VHS, Beta, LV.** Jane Seymour, Peter Weller, Fernando Rey; *D:* Antonio Drove. *VES, IME*

The Tunnel of Love 🎬🎬½ 1958 Day and Widmark are a married couple who find themselves over their heads in red tape when they try to adopt a baby. A beautiful, disapproving adoption investigator also causes more problems for the couple when she believes Widmark is less than ideal father material. Widmark is not in his element at comedy but Day and Young (as their next-door neighbor) are fine in this lightweight adaptation of the Joseph Fields-Peter DeVries play. 98m/B **VHS, LV.** Doris Day, Richard Widmark, Gig Young, Gia Scala, Elisabeth Fraser, Elizabeth Wilson; *D:* Gene Kelly. *MGM, MOV*

Tunnel Vision 🎬½ 1995 (R) Detective Kelly Wheatstone (Kensit) and her partner Frank Yanovitch (Reynolds) are after a serial killer whose victims are all beautiful women killed in a ritualistic fashion. But all the clues begin to point to Yanovitch as the one committing the crimes. *CW:* Sexuality, nudity, violence and brief language. 100m/C **VHS.** *AU* Patsy Kensit, Robert Reynolds, Rebecca Rigg; *D:* Clive Fleury. *TRI*

Tunnelvision 🎬🎬½ 1976 (R) A spoof of television comprised of irreverent sketches. Fun to watch because of the appearances of several now-popular stars. 70m/C **VHS, Beta.** Chevy Chase, John Candy, Laraine Newman, Joe Flaherty, Howard Hesseman, Gerrit Graham, Al Franken, Tom Davis, Ron Silver; *D:* Neal Israel. *NO*

Turbo: A Power Rangers Movie 🎬 1996 (PG) The Power Rangers must battle the evil Divatox (Turner), who's kidnapped the wizard Lerigot so she can use his power to free her even more evil boyfriend Maligore. It's all around cheesy but if you're a five-year-old you may still enjoy the action. 99m/C **VHS, Closed Caption.** Jason David Frank, Stephen Antonio Cardenas, John Yong Bosch, Catherine Sutherland, Nakia Burrise, Blake Foster, Paul Schrier, Jason Narvy, Amy Jo Johnson, Austin St. John, Hilary Shepard Turner, Jon Simanton; *D:* David Winning, Shuki Levy; *W:* Shuki Levy, Shell Danielson; *C:* Ilan Rosenberg; *M:* Shuki Levy. *TCF*

Turbulence 🎬½ 1996 (R) When you fly, it's usually the turbulence that makes you throw up. Well, this movie isn't that bad, but you may experience a touch of nausea. Flight attendant Teri (Holly) is pushing the drink cart on a strangely vacant New York to L.A. Christmas Eve run. Among the passengers are convicted felons Ryan (Liotta) and Stubbs (Gleeson), who are either on their way to a more secure prison or fulfilling the "consumption of airline food" portion of their sentence. The prisoners seize a gun from the marshals and accidentally rub out the cockpit crew. With all the passengers locked away, Teri must battle the serial rapist/killer Ryan as well as learn to fly the plane through a horrible storm. Passengers on the left of the screen may look out and see "Passenger 57," while those on the right can see the ancient monument of "Airport 75." *CW:* Terror, strong violence and language. 103m/C **VHS, DVD.** Ray Liotta, Lauren Holly, Hector Elizondo, Brendan Gleeson, Ben Cross, Rachel Ticotin, Jeffrey DeMunn, John Finn, Catherine Hicks; *D:* Robert Butler; *W:* Jonathan Brett; *C:* Lloyd Ahern; *M:* Shirley Walker. *HBO*

Turf Boy 🎬🎬 *Mr. Celebrity* 1942 Desperate for cash, a boy and his uncle try to get an old horse into prime condition for racing. A minor equine melodrama, just the right length for an old-time matinee double-feature. 68m/B **VHS.** Robert "Buzzy" Henry, James Seay, Doris Day, William Halligan, Gavin Gordon; *D:* William Beaudine. *NOS, LOO*

Turk 182! 🎬½ 1985 (PG-13) The angry brother of a disabled fireman takes on City Hall in order to win back the pension that he deserves. He attacks through his graffiti art. Hutton is too heavy for the over-all comic feel of this mostly silly film. 96m/C **VHS, Beta, Closed Caption.** Timothy Hutton, Robert Culp, Robert Urich, Kim Cattrall, Peter Boyle, Darren McGavin, Paul Sorvino; *D:* Bob (Benjamin) Clark. *FOX*

Turkish Delights 🎬🎬½ 1973 Free spirit sculptor falls in love with free spirit gal from bourgeois family and artsy soft porn ensues. That is until a brain tumor puts an end to their fun, and he's left to wallow in flashbacks and more artsy soft porn. Dubbed. Verhoeven later became big box office in the U.S. with "Total Recall." 100m/C **VHS.** *NL* Monique Van De Ven, Rutger Hauer, Tonny Huurdeman, Wim Van Den Brink; *D:* Paul Verhoeven; *C:* Jan De Bont. Nominations: Academy Awards '73: Best Foreign Language Film. *NO*

The Turn of the Screw 🎬🎬 1974 Supernatural powers vie with a young governess for control of the souls of the two children in her charge. Redgrave does well in this chilling film adapted from the Henry James story. Remade in 1989. 120m/C **VHS, Beta, LV.** Lynn Redgrave, Jasper Jacobs, Eva Griffith; *D:* Dan Curtis. *LIV*

The Turn of the Screw 🎬🎬 1989 (R) The young charges of an English nanny are sought for their souls by a dark, unimaginable evil in the mansion. Another version of the Henry James classic. 60m/C **VHS, Beta, LV.** Amy Irving, David Hemmings; *D:* Graeme Clifford. *CAN*

The Turn of the Screw 🐾🐾 1992 (R) Yet another version of the Henry James classic as a young governess struggles with sexual obsession and the two children in her care who are possessed by evil. **CW:** Images of terror and sexual images. 95m/C VHS, LV, **Closed Caption.** Julian Sands, Patsy Kensit, Stephane Audran, Marianne Faithfull; **D:** Rusty Lemorande; **M:** Simon Boswell. *LIV*

Turnaround 1987 (R) Unusual action/suspense film set in a small town. Relentless gang rampages the citizens. Finally, a man decides he's had enough, and turns on the heathens with his knowledge of magic. 97m/C VHS, **Beta.** Doug McKeon, Tim Maier, Eddie Albert, Gayle Hunnicutt; **D:** Ola Solum. *NO*

Turner and Hooch 🐾🐾 1989 (PG) A dog witnesses a murder, and a fussy cop is partnered with the drooling mutt and a weak script in his search for the culprit. Drool as a joke will only go so far, but Hanks is his usual entertaining self. 99m/C VHS, **Beta, LV.** Tom Hanks, Mare Winningham, Craig T. Nelson, Scott Paulin, J.C. Quinn; **D:** Roger Spottiswoode; **W:** Jim Cash, Jack Epps Jr., Michael Blodgett. *TOU*

The Turning 🐾½ 1992 Twenty-two-year-old Cliff Harnish (Dolan) returns home after a four-year absence to shock his family with his strident Neo-Nazi beliefs. May be of curiosity value to Anderson's "X-Files" fans, since she appears (relatively briefly and partially nude) as the guy's girlfriend in a kitchen sex scene. Based on the play by Ceraso. 92m/C VHS. Michael Dolan, Raymond J. Barry, Karen Allen, Tess Harper, Gillian Anderson; **D:** L.A. Puopolo; **W:** L.A. Puopolo, Chris Ceraso; **C:** J. Michael McClary. *LEO*

The Turning Point 🐾🐾½ 1977 (PG) A woman who gave up ballet for motherhood must come to terms as her daughter launches a ballet career and falls for the lead male dancer. The mother finds herself threatened by her daughter's affection toward an old friend who sacrificed a family life for the life of a ballerina. Baryshnikov's film debut. Melodramatic ending and problems due to lengthy ballet sequences. 119m/C VHS, **Beta.** Shirley MacLaine, Anne Bancroft, Tom Skerritt, Leslie Browne, Martha Scott, Marshall Thompson, Mikhail Baryshnikov; **D:** Herbert Ross; **W:** Arthur Laurents; **C:** Robert L. Surtees. Golden Globe Awards '78: Best Director (Ross), Best Film—Drama; Los Angeles Film Critics Association Awards '77: Best Director (Ross); National Board of Review Awards '77: 10 Best Films of the Year, Best Actress (Bancroft), Best Supporting Actor (Skerritt); Writers Guild of America '77: Best Original Screenplay; Nominations: Academy Awards '77: Best Actress (Bancroft), Best Actress (MacLaine), Best Art Direction/Set Decoration, Best Cinematography, Best Director (Ross), Best Film Editing, Best Original Screenplay, Best Picture, Best Sound, Best Supporting Actor (Baryshnikov), Best Supporting Actress (Browne). *FOX*

Turtle Diary 🐾🐾🐾 1986 (PG) Two lonely Londoners collaborate to free giant turtles from the city aquarium with the aid of a zoo-keeper, and the turtles' freedom somehow frees them as well. Jackson and Kingsley are stunning. Adapted by Harold Pinter from the Russell Hoban book. 90m/C VHS, **Beta, LV, Closed Caption.** *GB* Ben Kingsley, Glenda Jackson, Richard Johnson, Michael Gambon, Rosemary Leach, Jeroen Krabbe, Eleanor Bron; **D:** John Irvin; **W:** Harold Pinter; **M:** Geoffrey Burgon. *LIV, VES*

Turumba 🐾🐾🐾 1984 A quiet satire about a family of papier-mache animal makers in a Philippine village who get a gargantuan order in time for the Turumba holiday, and desperately try to fill it. In Tagalog with English subtitles. 94m/C VHS, **Beta.** *PH* **D:** Kidlat Tahimik. *FFM, FCT*

The Tuskegee Airmen 🐾🐾🐾 1995 (PG-13) Cable drama based on the formation and WWII achievements of the U.S. Army Air Corps' first squadron of black combat fighter pilots, the "Fighting 99th" of the 332nd Fighter Group. They were nicknamed after the segregated military outpost where they trained in Tuskegee, Alabama and distinguished themselves in combat, never losing a single bomber, and receiving more than 800 medals. Cast all do a fine job in what turns out to essentially be a standard action/war movie. Based on a story by former Tuskegee airman, Robert W. Williams. **CW:** Strong language, thematic elements, and brief strong war violence. 107m/C VHS. Laurence "Larry" Fishburne, Cuba Gooding Jr., Allen Payne, Malcolm Jamal Warner, Courtney B. Vance, Andre Braugher, John Lithgow, Rosemary Murphy, Christopher McDonald; **D:** Robert Markowitz; **W:** Paris Qualles, Ron Hutchinson, Trey Ellis; **C:** Ronald Orieux; **M:** Lee Holdridge. *HBO*

Tusks 🐾½ *Fire in Eden* 1989 (R) A ruthless hunter tries to kill elephants. 99m/C VHS, **Beta, LV.** Andrew Stevens, John Rhys-Davies, Lucy Gutteridge, Julian Glover; **D:** Tara Hawkins Moore. *NO*

Tut & Tuttle 🐾½ 1982 Young dabbler in magic is transported to ancient Egypt where he is able to demonstrate courage and wits against the evil Horemheb, who has kidnapped Prince Tut. 97m/C VHS, **Beta.** Christopher Barnes, Eric Greene, Hans Conried, Vic Tayback. *NO*

The Tuttles of Tahiti 🐾🐾🐾 1942 The Tuttles lead a life of leisure in the South Seas. Laughton's child becomes enamoured of his rival's offspring, causing problems between the two families. More interesting than it sounds. 91m/C VHS, **Beta, LV.** Charles Laughton, Jon Hall, Peggy Drake, Victor Francen, Gene Reynolds, Florence Bates, Mala, Alma Ross, Curt Bois; **D:** Charles Vidor. *HHT*

Tuxedo Warrior 🐾½ 1982 Set in South Africa, this film involves the adventures of a well-dressed mercenary who is caught between the police, diamond thieves, and an old girlfriend's bank robbing. 93m/C VHS, **Beta.** John Wyman, Carol Royle, Holly Palance; **D:** Andrew Sinclair. *VTR, NWV*

TV's Best Adventures of Superman 1951 This first package of episodes from the original television series, which ran from 1951-1957, contains "Superman on Earth," the black & white series pilot about the Man of Steel's childhood on Krypton and Earth, and "All That Glitters," the series' final episode, wherein Lois Lane and Jimmy Olsen acquire super powers. Also includes the 1941 animated cartoon "Superman," the first-ever screen appearance of the superhero. Additional episodes available. 62m/C VHS, **Beta.** George Reeves, Phyllis Coates, Noel Neill, Jack Larson, John Hamilton, Robert Shayne. *WAR, MOV*

Twelfth Night 🐾🐾½ 1996 (PG) Director Nunn's take on Shakespeare's gender-bending, romantic-comedy, which is now set in the 1890s. Shipwrecked on an unfriendly Illyrian shore, Viola (Stubbs), believing twin brother Sebastian (Mackintosh) to be dead, disguises herself in male attire and joins the retinue of the lovesick Duke Orsino (Stephens). He's pining for the Countess Olivia (Bonham Carter) and decides to use Viola-turned-Cesario as a surrogate wooer. Too bad Olivia's becoming more interested in her effeminate pseudo-suitor and that Orsino's having a few sexual quandries of his own. 133m/C VHS, LV, **Closed Caption.** *GB* Imogen Stubbs, Helena Bonham Carter, Toby Stephens, Steven Mackintosh, Richard E. Grant, Nigel Hawthorne, Ben Kingsley, Imelda Staunton, Mel Smith, Nicholas Farrell; **D:** Trevor Nunn; **W:** Trevor Nunn; **C:** Clive Tickner; **M:** Shaun Davey. *NLC*

Twelve Angry Men 🐾🐾🐾🐾 1957 Fonda sounds the voice of reason as a jury inclines toward a quick-and-dirty verdict against a boy on trial. Excellent ensemble work. Lumet's feature film debut, based on a television play by Reginald Rose. 95m/B VHS, **Beta, LV, Closed Caption.** Henry Fonda, Martin Balsam, Lee J. Cobb, E.G. Marshall, Jack Klugman, Robert Webber, Ed Begley Sr., John Fiedler, Jack Warden, George Voskovec, Edward Binns, Joseph Sweeney; **D:** Sidney Lumet; **W:** Reginald Rose; **C:** Boris Kaufman. Berlin International Film Festival '57: Golden Berlin Bear; British Academy Awards '57: Best Actor (Fonda); Edgar Allan Poe Awards '57: Best Screenplay; National Board of Review Awards '57: 10 Best Films of the Year; Nominations: Academy Awards '57: Best Adapted Screenplay, Best Director (Lumet), Best Picture. *MGM, FOX*

Twelve Chairs 🐾🐾🐾 1970 (PG) Take-off on Russian folktale first filmed in Yugoslavia in 1927. A rich matron admits on her deathbed that she has hidden her jewels in the upholstery of one of twelve chairs that are no longer in her home. A Brooksian treasure hunt ensues. 94m/C VHS, **Beta, LV.** Mel Brooks, Dom DeLuise, Frank Langella, Ron Moody, Bridget Brice; **D:** Mel Brooks; **W:** Mel Brooks. *MED*

12 Monkeys 🐾🐾🐾 1995 (R) Forty years after a plague wipes out 99 percent of the human population and sends the survivors underground, scientists send prisoner James Cole (Willis) to the 1990s to investigate the connection between the virus and seriously deranged fanatic Jeffrey Goines (Pitt), whose father happens to be a renowned virologist. Director Gilliam's demented vision is a bit tougher and less capricious than usual, and the convoluted plot and accumulated detail require a keen attention span, but as each piece of the puzzle falls into place the story becomes a fascinating sci-fi spectacle. Pitt drops the pretty-boy image with a nutzoid performance that'll make revelers stop swooning in a heartbeat. Inspired by the 1962 French short "La Jetee." **CW:** Contains some nudity and sadistic violence. 131m/C VHS, LV, **Closed Caption.** Bruce Willis, Madeleine Stowe, Brad Pitt, Christopher Plummer, David Morse, Frank Gorshin, Jon Seda; **D:** Terry Gilliam; **W:** David Peoples, Janet Peoples; **M:** Paul Buckmaster. Golden Globe Awards '96: Best Supporting Actor (Pitt); Nominations: Academy Awards '95: Best Costume Design, Best Supporting Actor (Pitt); MTV Movie Awards '96: Best Male Performance (Pitt). *USH*

Twelve O'Clock High 🐾🐾🐾½ 1949 Epic drama about the heroic 8th Air Force, with Peck as bomber-group commander sent to shape up a hard-luck group, forced to drive himself and his men to the breaking point. Compelling dramatization of the strain of military command. Includes impressive footage of actual WWII battles. Best-ever flying fortress movie. 132m/B VHS, **Beta, LV.** Gregory Peck, Hugh Marlowe, Gary Merrill, Millard Mitchell, Dean Jagger, Paul Stewart; **D:** Henry King; **C:** Leon Shamroy. Academy Awards '49: Best Sound, Best Supporting Actor (Jagger); Nominations: Academy Awards '49: Best Actor (Peck), Best Picture; New York Film Critics Awards '50: Best Actor (Peck). *FXV, FCT, BTV*

12:01 🐾🐾½ 1993 (PG-13) It's the "Groundhog Day" premise played for thrills. Barry Thompson (Silverman) is an employee at a scientific research firm who finds himself reliving the same twenty-four hour period over and over again. And what a day it is—he discovers a secret project is causing the mysterious time warp, falls in love with beauteous scientist Lisa (Slater) and watches as she gets murdered. Can Barry figure out how to stop what's going on and change things enough to save her? Adaptation of the short story "12:01" by Richard Lupoff, which was previously made into a short film. Made for television. 92m/C VHS, LV, **Closed Caption.** Jonathan Silverman, Helen Slater, Martin Landau, Nicolas Surovy, Jeremy Piven; **D:** Jack Sholder. *NLC, IME*

12 Plus 1 🐾🐾🐾 *The Thirteen Chairs* 1970 (R) A man sells 13 chairs left to him by his aunt, only to find that one of them contained a hidden fortune. He chases across Europe in search of each of them. Some good cameos help move this remake of a Russian folk-tale along, but it remains lightweight. Tate's last movie, before her death at the hands of Manson and his "family." 94m/C VHS, **Beta.** *FR* *IT* Sharon Tate, Orson Welles, Vittorio Gassman, Mylene Demongeot, Terry-Thomas, Tim Brooke; *Cameos:* Vittorio De Sica; **D:** Nicolas Gessner. *NO*

Twentieth Century 🐾🐾🐾🐾 1934 Maniacal Broadway director Barrymore transforms shop girl Lombard into a smashing success adored by public and press. Tired of Barrymore's manic-excessive ways, she heads for the Hollywood hills, pursued by the Profile in fine form. 91m/B **Beta.** Carole Lombard, John Barrymore, Walter Connolly, Roscoe Karns, Edgar Kennedy, Ralph Forbes,

Charles Lane, Etienne Girardot, Snow Flake; **D:** Howard Hawks; **W:** Charles MacArthur, Ben Hecht. COL

Twenty Bucks ♂♂♂ 1993 (R) Whimsical film follows a $20 dollar bill from its "birth" at a cash machine to its "death" as it is returned to the bank, tattered and torn, for shredding. The bill is passed from owner to owner, sometimes simply and briefly, sometimes altering fate. The original screenplay is nearly 60 years old: Endre Bohem originally drafted it in 1935, and his son revised and updated it. Clever transitions allow the various stories and characters to blend almost seamlessly. The strongest character is Shue's, a young waitress and aspiring writer. Rosenfeld's directorial debut is worth a look. Filmed in Minneapolis.**CW:** Language and brief violence. **91m/C VHS, Closed Caption.** Linda Hunt, David Rasche, George Morfogen, Brendan Fraser, Gladys Knight, Elisabeth Shue, Steve Buscemi, Christopher Lloyd, Sam Jenkins, Kamal Holloway, Melora Walters, William H. Macy, Diane Baker, Spalding Gray, Matt Frewer, Concetta Tomei, Nina Siemaszko; **D:** Keva Rosenfeld; **W:** Leslie Bohem, Endre Bohem; **C:** Emmanuel Lubezki; **M:** David Robbins. Independent Spirit Awards '94: Best Supporting Actor (Lloyd). COL

Twenty Dollar Star ♂♂½ 1991 (R) Steamy thriller about an prominent actress who leads a double life as a cheap hooker, and consequent occupational hazards. The title may as well refer to the budget.**CW:** Sex-related violence and sensuality. **92m/C VHS, Closed Caption.** Rebecca Holden, Bernie White, Eddie Barth, Marilyn Hassett, Dick Sargent; **D:** Paul Leder. PAR

20 Million Miles to Earth ♂♂½ 1957 A spaceship returning from an expedition to Venus crashes on Earth, releasing a fast-growing reptilian beast that rampages throughout Athens. Another entertaining example of stop-motion animation master Ray Harryhausen's work, offering a classic battle between the monster and an elephant. **82m/B LV.** William Hopper, Joan Taylor, Frank Puglia, John Zaremba; **D:** Nathan (Hertz) Juran. COL

20,000 Leagues Under the Sea ♂♂♂ 1916 Outstanding silent adaptation of Jules Verne's "20,000 Leagues Under the Sea" and "The Mysterious Island" filmed with a then revolutionary underwater camera. Much octopus fighting. Look for newly mastered edition. **105m/B VHS, Beta.** Matt Moore, Allen Holubar, June Gail, William Welsh, Chris Benton, Dan Hamlon; **D:** Stuart Paton; **W:** Stuart Paton. KIV, GPV, DVT

20,000 Leagues Under the Sea ♂♂♂½ 1954 From a futuristic submarine, Captain Nemo wages war on the surface world. A shipwrecked scientist and sailor do their best to thwart Nemo's dastardly schemes. Buoyant Disney version of the Jules Verne fantasy. **127m/C VHS, Beta, LV, Closed Caption.** Kirk Douglas, James Mason, Peter Lorre, Paul Lukas, Robert J. Wilke, Carleton Young; **D:** Richard Fleischer. Academy Awards '54: Best Art Direction/Set Decoration (Color), Best Special Effects; National Board of Review Awards '54: 10 Best Films of the Year; Nominations: Academy Awards '54: Best Film Editing. DIS

Twenty-One ♂♂½ 1991 (R) Modern morality tale of a young English woman who moves to the U.S. to make a new start, but falls into the same old habits. Kensit is frank and charming, in spite of difficulties with her drug addict boyfriend and the illegal alien she marries. Director Boyd leaves it to the viewer to decide between right and wrong and where Kensit fits. **92m/C VHS, LV.** Patsy Kensit, Jack Shepherd, Patrick Ryecart, Maynard Eziashi, Rufus Sewell, Sophie Thompson, Susan Wooldridge, Julia Goodman; **D:** Don Boyd; **W:** Don Boyd; **M:** Michael Berkeley. NO

21 Days ♂♂½ Twenty-One Days Together; The First and the Last 1937 Dull film somewhat redeemed by its stars. Leigh is a married woman carrying on with Olivier. When her husband confronts them, Olivier accidentally kills him in a fight. They keep quiet but then a mentally deranged man is taken into custody for the crime. Since he will be held 21 days before coming to trial, the lovers decide to

spend the time together before Olivier confesses. Based on the play "The First and the Last" by John Galsworthy. **75m/C VHS.** GB Vivien Leigh, Laurence Olivier, Leslie Banks, Francis L. Sullivan, Hay Petrie, Esme Percy, Robert Newton; **D:** Basil Dean; **W:** Graham Greene, Basil Dean. FCT

21 Hours at Munich ♂♂♂ 1976 Made-for-TV treatment of the massacre of Israeli athletes by Arab terrorists at the 1972 Olympics. Well-done. The film was produced using the actual Munich locations. **100m/C VHS.** William Holden, Shirley Knight, Franco Nero, Anthony Quayle, Noel Willman; **D:** William A. Graham. MOV

23 1/2 Hours Leave ♂♂ 1937 Amusing WWI service comedy as a barracks wiseacre bets that by the following morning he'll be breakfasting with a general. It's a song-filled remake of a 1919 film, whose star Douglas MacLean later produced this. **73m/B VHS.** James Ellison, Terry Walker, Morgan Hill, Arthur Lake, Paul Harvey; **D:** John Blystone. NOS, LOO

Twenty-Four Eyes ♂♂♂ Nijushi No Hitomi 1954 Miss Oishi (Takamine), a teacher on a remote Japanese island in the 1920's, attempts to transmit peaceful values to her 12 pupils amidst the clamor of a nation gearing up for war. As she watches them grow up, many of them doomed to an early death, she remains a pillar of quiet strength. In Japanese with English subtitles. **158m/B VHS, Beta.** JP Hideko Takamine, Chishu Ryu, Toshiko Kobayashi; **D:** Keisuke Kinoshita. NO

24 Hours in a Woman's Life ♂♂ 1961 A girl in love with an irresponsible guy hears a cautionary tale from grandma Bergman, who once had a whirlwind romance with a young gambler and naively thought she could reform him. A static TV adaptation of an oft-filmed Stefan Zweig novel, unusually lavish for its time but on the dull side. **90m/C VHS.** Ingrid Bergman, Rip Torn, John Williams, Lili Darvas, Jerry Orbach; **D:** Silvio Narizzano; **W:** John Mortimer. FCT

24 Hours to Midnight ♂½ 1992 A widow uses her ninja skills to wipe out the crime bosses and henchmen who killed her husband. **91m/C VHS, Closed Caption.** Cynthia Rothrock, Stack Pierce; **D:** Leo Fong. AIP

25 Fireman's Street ♂♂♂ Almok a hazrol 1973 An evocative drama about the residents of an old house in Hungary which is about to be torn down, and their evening of remembrances of life before, during and after WWII. In Hungarian with English subtitles. **97m/C VHS, Beta.** HU Rita Bekes, Peter Muller, Lucyna Winnicka; **D:** Istvan Szabo; **C:** Sandor Sara. KIV

29th Street ♂♂½ 1991 (R) Compelling comedy-drama based on the true story of Frank Pesce, a New York actor who won six million dollars in that state's first lottery. Great performance from Aiello, as usual, but the direction falters in the dramatic sequences. Based on the book by Frank Pesce and James Franciscus. **101m/C VHS, Closed Caption.** Danny Aiello, Anthony LaPaglia, Lainie Kazan, Frank Pesce, Donna Magnani, Rick Aiello, Vic Manni, Ron Karabatsos, Robert Forster, Joe Franklin, Pete Antico; **D:** George Gallo; **W:** George Gallo; **M:** William Olvis. FXV, CCB

The 27 Day ♂♂½ 1957 Temperate cold war allegory has aliens deliver five mysterious capsules to five Earthlings from different countries. Each capsule, if opened, is capable of decimating the population of the entire planet, but is rendered ineffective after 27 days or upon the death of the holder. Wild ending. Based on John Mantley novel. **75m/B VHS.** Gene Barry, Valerie French, George Voskovec, Arnold Moss, Stefan Schnabel, Ralph Clanton, Friedrich Ledebur, Mari Tsien. MOV, MLB

Twice a Judas ♂ 196? An amnesiac is swindled and has his family killed by a ruthless renegade. He wants to get even, even though he can't remember who anyone is. **90m/C VHS, Beta.** Klaus Kinski. UNI, MOV

Twice a Woman ♂ 1979 Man and woman divorce, and then both fall in love with the same provocative young woman. It's complicated. **90m/C VHS, Beta.** Bibi Andersson, Anthony Perkins, Sandra Dumas. PSM

Twice Dead woof! 1988 A family moves into a ramshackle mansion haunted by a stage actor's angry ghost. The ghost helps them battle some attacking delinquent boys. Uninteresting story, poorly done. Never released in theaters. **94m/C VHS, Beta, LV.** Tom Breznahan, Jill Whitlow, Sam Melville, Brooke Bundy, Todd Bridges, Jonathan Chapin, Christopher Burgard; **D:** Bert L. Dragin; **M:** David Bergeaud. NLC

Twice in a Lifetime ♂♂♂ 1985 (R) Middle-aged man takes stock of his life when he's attracted to Ann-Margret. Realizing he's married in name only, he moves in with his new love while his former wife and children struggle with shock, disbelief, and anger. Well-acted, realistic, and unsentimental. **117m/C VHS, Beta, LV, Closed Caption.** Gene Hackman, Ellen Burstyn, Amy Madigan, Ann-Margret, Brian Dennehy, Ally Sheedy; **D:** Bud Yorkin; **W:** Colin Welland. Nominations: Academy Awards '85: Best Supporting Actress (Madigan).LIV, VES

Twice-Told Tales ♂♂♂ Nathaniel Hawthorne's "Twice Told Tales" 1963 Horror trilogy based loosely on three Nathaniel Hawthorne tales, "Dr. Heidegger's Experiment," "Rappaccini's Daughter," and "The House of Seven Gables." Price is great in all three of these well-told tales. **120m/C VHS, Beta.** Vincent Price, Sebastian Cabot, Brett Halsey; **D:** Sidney Salkow. MGM, MLB

Twilight in the Sierras ♂♂½ 1950 Lots of heroics and music in this action-packed western. An ex-outlaw gone straight is kidnapped for his notorious criminal finesse. Rogers must come to rescue. **67m/C VHS.** Roy Rogers, Dale Evans, Estelita Rodriguez, Pat Brady, Russ Vincent, George Meeker; **D:** William Witney. REP

Twilight Man ♂♂½ 1996 (R) University professor and novelist Jordan Cooper (Matheson) finds his great life turned upside down when a brief altercation with a stranger turns into a nightmare. Turns out the stranger is very strange indeed—computer hacker Hollis Dietz (Stockwell) has made Cooper his own deadly obsession. Suddenly his medical records say he's schizophrenic and even a killer and Cooper must elude police to clear his name.**CW:** Language and violence. **99m/C VHS, LV, Closed Caption.** Tim Matheson, Dean Stockwell, L. Scott Caldwell, Yvette Nipar, Georgann Johnson; **D:** Craig R. Baxley; **W:** Pablo F. Fenjves, Jim Korris. USH

Twilight of the Cockroaches ♂½ Gokiburi 1990 Mr. Saito is a slovenly bachelor who winds up leaving the remains of his meals for the anthropomorphic cockroaches that infest his apartment. The cockroaches have had it so good for so long that they don't know about insecticides and fearing humans. That is, until Mr. Saito's fastidious new girlfriend makes her appearance and declares war on the vermin. A lifelessly animated tale too dumb for both children and adults and with decidedly unpleasant subject matter, despite the singing, dancing insects. In Japanese with English subtitles. **105m/C VHS, LV.** JP D: Hiroaki Yoshida; **V:** Kaoru Kobayashi, Setsuko Karamsumarau. FCT, STP, LUM

The Twilight of the Golds ♂♂½ 1997 The upper-middle class Jewish Gold family seem conventional if fretful: there's doctor dad Walter (Marshall), concerned mom Phyllis (Dunaway), married daughter Suzanne (Beals), and aspiring theatrical producer son David (Fraser), who's gay. It seems everyone's dealt with David's homosexuality until Suzanne's geneticist husband, Rob Stein (Tenney), informs his pregnant wife that tests on their unborn son show genes statistically link to him being gay. (The theory is unproven.) Suzanne considers abortion and David is understandably upset when no one tries to talk her out of it, beginning a family estrangement. Cable movie based on the play by Tolins. **95m/C VHS.** Garry Marshall, Faye Dunaway, Jennifer Beals, Brendan Fraser, Jon Tenney, Jack Klugman, Sean O'Bryan, Rosie O'Donnell; **D:** Ross Kagen Marks; **W:** Jonathan Tolins, Seth Bass; **C:** Tom Richmond; **M:** Lee Holdridge. *NYR*

Twilight on the Rio Grande 🐶 1941
Autry runs into a female knife thrower and some jewel smugglers in this far-fetched western. **54m/C VHS, Beta.** Gene Autry, Sterling Holloway, Adele Mara, Bob Steele; **D:** Frank McDonald. *VCN*

Twilight on the Trail 🐶🐶 1941 Cattle
rustlers disappear and Hopalong Cassidy and his sidekicks become "dude" detectives to solve the crime. **54m/B VHS, Beta.** William Boyd, Brad King, Andy Clyde, Jack Rockwell, Wanda McKay, Howard Bretherton. *GVV*

Twilight People woof! Beasts 1972 (PG)
When a mad scientist's creations turn on him for revenge, he runs for his life. Boring, gory, with bad make-up and even poorer acting. This one should fade away into the night. **84m/C VHS, Beta.** **PH** John Ashley, Pat Woodell, Jan Merlin, Pam Grier; **D:** Eddie Romero. *VCI*

The Twilight Zone 1961 Travel through
another dimension in Rod Serling's classic science fiction series. Two episodes per tape. On this tape: "The Invaders," written by Richard Matheson, sees a farm house inhabited by a mute woman become the destination of strange, miniature space travellers. In "Nothing in the Dark," written by George Clayton Johnson, an elderly woman is given an interesting lesson regarding her fear of death. **50m/B VHS, Beta, LV.** Agnes Moorehead, Douglas Heyes, Gladys Cooper, Robert Redford, R.G. Armstrong; **D:** Lamont Johnson; **W:** Richard Matheson, George Clayton Johnson. *FXV, FOX, MOV*

Twilight Zone: The Movie 🐶🐶½
1983 (PG) Four short horrific tales are anthologized in this film as a tribute to Rod Sterling and his popular television series. Three of the episodes, "Kick the Can," "It's a Good Life" and "Nightmare at 20,000 Feet," are based on original "Twilight Zone" scripts. Morrow was killed in a helicopter crash during filming. **101m/C VHS, Beta, LV.** Dan Aykroyd, Albert Brooks, Vic Morrow, Kathleen Quinlan, John Lithgow, Billy Mumy, Scatman Crothers, Kevin McCarthy, Bill Quinn, Selma Diamond, Abbe Lane, John Larroquette, Jeremy Licht, Patricia Barry, William Schallert, Burgess Meredith, Cherie Currie; **D:** John Landis, Steven Spielberg, George Miller, Joe Dante; **W:** John Landis; **C:** Allen Daviau; **M:** Jerry Goldsmith. *WAR*

Twilight's Last Gleaming 🐶🐶½ 1977
(R) A maverick general takes a SAC missile base hostage, threatening to start WWIII if the U.S. government doesn't confess to its Vietnam policies and crimes. Gripping film, with good performances. Based on a novel by Walter Wager. "Viper Three." **144m/C VHS, Beta, LV.** Burt Lancaster, Charles Durning, Richard Widmark, Melvyn Douglas, Joseph Cotten, Paul Winfield, Burt Young, Roscoe Lee Browne, Richard Jaeckel, William Marshall, Vera Miles, Leif Erickson, Charles McGraw, William Smith, John Ratzenberger; **D:** Robert Aldrich; **W:** Ronald M. Cohen; **C:** Robert B. Hauser; **M:** Jerry Goldsmith. *FOX*

Twin Peaks 🐶🐶 1990 Sketchy home video
distillation of the eccentric TV series. It preserves much of the setup episode (the murder of teen-queen Laura Palmer and nest of small-town weirdness it reveals), then rushes piecemeal through the rest of the season. There's an altered quasi-solution to the enigma and a bizarre backward sequence not broadcast in the US. In this compressed form it's best for initiates of the TP cult; others won't be converted. **113m/C VHS, LV, Closed Caption.** Kyle MacLachlan, Michael Ontkean, Sherilyn Fenn, Lara Flynn Boyle, Joan Chen, Peggy Lipton, Piper Laurie, Michael Horse, Russ Tamblyn, Richard Beymer, Madchen Amick, Catherine Coulson, Warren Frost, Everett McGill, Jack Nance, Ray Wise, Eric Da Re, Harry Goaz, Sheryl Lee; **D:** David Lynch; **M:** Angelo Badalamenti. *WAR, FCT*

Twin Peaks 1990 Premiere episode of David
Lynch's bizarre TV drama. In this episode, Agent Cooper and Sheriff Truman begin the investigation into the death of prom queen, Laura Palmer. All seven episodes are available in a boxed set. **50m/C VHS.** Michael Ontkean, Kyle MacLachlan, Joan Chen, Piper Laurie, Sherilyn Fenn, Peggy Lipton, Madchen Amick, Lara Flynn Boyle, Michael Horse, Russ Tamblyn, Richard Beymer, Dana Ashbrook, Warren Frost, Everett McGill, Jack Nance, Ray Wise, Eric Da Re, Catherine Coulson, Harry Goaz, Sheryl Lee; **D:** David Lynch; **M:** Angelo Badalamenti. *WOV, MOV*

Twin Peaks: Fire Walk with
Me 🐶🐶 1992 (R) Prequel to the cult TV series is weird and frustrating, chronicling the week before Laura Palmer's death. Suspense is lacking since we know the outcome, but Lynch manages to intrigue with dream-like sequences and interestingly offbeat characters. On the other hand, it's exploitative and violent enough to alienate series fans. Includes extremely brief and baffling cameos by Bowie as an FBI agent and Stanton as the manager of a trailer park. Several of the show's regulars are missing, and others appear and disappear very quickly. On the plus side are the strains of Badalamenti's famous theme music and Isaak as an FBI agent with amazingly acute powers of observation. **CW:** Language, strong violence and drug content, and strong sexuality. **135m/C VHS, LV, Closed Caption.** Kyle MacLachlan, Sheryl Lee, Moira Kelly, Chris Isaak, Ray Wise, Kiefer Sutherland, Peggy Lipton, Dana Ashbrook, James Marshall, David Lynch; **Cameos:** David Bowie, Harry Dean Stanton; **D:** David Lynch; **W:** David Lynch; **M:** Angelo Badalamenti. *NLC*

Twin Sisters 🐶½ 1991 Woman discovers
her missing twin sister was a high-priced prostitute and a detective tries to protect her from the lowlifes sis was involved with. **92m/C VHS, Closed Caption.** Stephanie Kramer, Susan Almgren, Frederic Forrest, James Brolin; **D:** Tom Berry; **M:** Lou Forestieri. *THV*

Twin Town 🐶🐶½ 1997 Dark comedy about
class warfare, escalating revenge, and drug abuse in a small seaside Welsh town features sharp, profane, and very funny dialogue, well-developed and played characters, and uneven direction. Brothers Julian (Evans) and Jeremy (Ifans) like to steal expensive cars and get high on any substance they can find and control. They live with their handyman dad Fatty (Ceredig) and massage parlor receptionist sister (Scorgie) on the wrong side of the tracks. Dad falls off a roof while working for the local contractor/drug kingpin (Thomas) and is not fairly compensated. This starts a cycle of revenge that begins with public urination and gets nasty from there. Sort of a Welsh "Trainspotting," which featured a cameo by "Twin" writer/director Allen. Some scenes may be too much for some viewers (especially animal lovers). **95m/C VHS.** **GB** Llyr Evans, Rhys Ifans, Huw Ceredig, Dorien Thomas, Dougray Scott; **D:** Kevin Allen; **W:** Kevin Allen, Paul Durden; **C:** John Mathieson; **M:** Mark Thomas. *NYR*

Twins 🐶🐶½ 1988 (PG) A genetics experi-
ment gone awry produces twins rather than a single child. One is a genetically-engineered superman, the other a short, lecherous petty criminal. Schwarzenegger learns he has a brother, and becomes determined to find him, despite their having been raised separately. The two meet and are immediately involved in a contraband scandal. Amusing pairing of Schwarzenegger and DeVito. **107m/C VHS, Beta, LV.** Arnold Schwarzenegger, Danny DeVito, Kelly Preston, Hugh O'Brian, Chloe Webb, Bonnie Bartlett, Marshall Bell, Trey Wilson, Nehemiah Persoff; **D:** Ivan Reitman; **W:** William Davies, William Osborne, Timothy Harris, Herschel Weingrod; **C:** Andrzej Bartkowiak; **M:** Georges Delerue, Randy Edelman. People's Choice Awards '89: Best Film—Musical/Comedy. *USH*

Twins of Evil 🐶½ 1971 Beautiful female
twins fall victim to the local vampire, and their God-fearing uncle is out to save/destroy them. Hammer sex and blood-sucking epic starring the Collinsons, who were featured in the October

1970 issue of Playboy as the first twin Playmates. **86m/C VHS, Beta.** **GB** Madeleine Collinson, Mary Collinson, Peter Cushing, Kathleen Byron, Dennis Price, Damien Thomas, David Warbeck, Katya Wyeth, Maggie Wright, Luan Peters, Kristen Lindholm, Judy Matheson; **D:** John Hough. *MLB*

Twinsanity 🐶 Goodbye Gemini 1970 (R) Evil
twins are charged with the murder of a man who attempted to blackmail them. **91m/C VHS, Beta.** **GB** Judy Geeson, Martin Potter, Alexis Kanner, Michael Redgrave, Freddie Jones, Peter Jeffrey; **D:** Alan Gibson; **W:** Edmund Ward; **M:** Christopher Gunning. *PSM*

Twinsitters 🐶🐶½ 1995 (PG-13) Twins Peter
and David Falcone (Peter and David Paul) find themselves unexpectedly saving the life of corrupt businessman Frank Hillhurst (Martin). Hillhurst is turning state's evidence on his crooked operations and his disturbed partners have threatened both his life and the lives of his twin 10-year-old nephews. So Hillhurst hires the Falcones to protect his hellacious pint-sized relatives—who manage to get themselves kidnapped. **93m/C VHS, Closed Caption.** Peter Paul, David Paul, Christian Cousins, Joseph Cousins, Jared Martin, George Lazenby, Rena Sofa, Mother Love; **D:** John Paragon; **W:** John Paragon. *COL*

Twirl 🐶🐶 1981 Satirical look at the cutthroat
world of baton twirling. Parents apply relentless pressure on their daughters to win a contest. Decent made-for-TV movie. **100m/C VHS, Beta.** Stella Stevens, Charles Haid, Lisa Whelchel, Erin Moran, Edd Byrnes, Sharon Spelman, Matthew Tobin, Donna McKechnie, Rosalind Chao, Heather Locklear, Deborah Richter, Jamie Rose, Tracy Scoggins; **D:** Gus Trikonis. *LIV*

Twist 🐶½ Folies Bourgeoises 1976 A tepid
French drama chronicling the infidelities of various wealthy aristocrats. The aristocrats are boring, as is the film. In French with English subtitles or dubbed. **105m/C VHS, Beta.** **FR** Bruce Dern, Stephane Audran, Ann-Margret, Sydne Rome, Jean-Pierre Cassel, Curt Jurgens, Maria Schell, Charles Aznavour; **D:** Claude Chabrol; **M:** Manuel De Sica. *LIV*

Twist & Shout 🐶🐶🐶 Hab Og Karlighed
1984 (R) Sequel to the popular Danish import "Zappa," in which two teenage lovers discover sex and rock and roll. Transcends the teens discovering sex genre. Danish with English subtitles. Profanity, nudity, and sex. **107m/C VHS, Beta.** **DK** Lars Simonsen, Adam Tonsberg, Ulrikke Juul Bondo, Camilla Soeberg; **D:** Bille August; **W:** Bille August. *NO*

Twisted 🐶🐶 1986 (R) This curio from Slater's
early career came out on tape to take advantage of his rising stardom. He's properly creepy as a brilliant but evil teen using electronics, psychology, and swordplay to terrorize victims. The suspense isn't too bad when direction doesn't go overboard, which unfortunately is half the time. Based on the play "Children! Children!" by Jack Horrigan **87m/C VHS.** Lois Smith, Christian Slater, Tandy Cronyn, Brooke Tracy, Dina Merrill, Dan Ziskie, Karl Taylor, Noelle Parker, John Cunningham, J.C. Quinn; **D:** Adam Holender. *NO*

Twisted Brain 🐶 Horror High 1974 (R) An
honor student develops a serum that makes him half man and half beast. Now he can exact revenge on all the jocks and cheerleaders who have humiliated him in the past. Cardi is okay, the rest of the cast is awful. Silly, horrific teen monster epic. **89m/C VHS, Beta.** Pat Cardi, Austin Stoker, Rosie Holotik, John Niland, Joyce Hash, Jeff Alexander, Joe "Mean Joe" Greene; **D:** Larry N. Stouffer. *NO*

Twisted Justice 🐶½ 1989 Set in 2020,
Heavener is a cop determined to stop a ruthless killer. Matters become complicated, however, when his gun is taken away. Now he's forced to rely on his cunning to outwit his sadistic opponent. **90m/C VHS.** David Heavener, Erik Estrada, Jim Brown, Shannon Tweed, James Van Patten, Don Stroud, Karen Black, Lori Warren; **D:** David Heavener; **W:** David Heavener. *NO*

Twisted Love ♂️½ 1995 (R) Wallflower becomes obsessed with the most popular guy in school. He has a motorcycle accident-that-was-no-accident and winds up in her tender care. Sounds like "Misery" to me.*CW:* Violence, sexuality, and some language. 80m/C VHS. Lisa Dean Ryan, Mark Paul Gosselaar, Soleil Moon Frye; *D:* Eb Lottimer. NHO

Twisted Nightmare ♂️ 1987 (R) The people responsible for a young retarded boy's death are hunted by a strange figure lurking in the shadows. 95m/C Beta. Rhonda Gray, Cleve Hall, Brad Bartrum, Robert Padilla; *D:* Paul Hunt. TWE

Twisted Obsession ♂️♂️ 1990 (R) A man becomes passionately obsessed with a woman, and it leads to murder. 109m/C VHS, Beta, LV. Jeff Goldblum, Miranda Richardson, Anemone, Dexter Fletcher, Daniel Ceccaldi, Liza Walker, Jerome Natali, Arielle Dombasle; *D:* Fernando Trueba; *C:* Jose Luis Alcaine; *M:* Antoine Duhamel. LIV

Twister ♂️♂️ 1989 (PG-13) An intriguing independent feature about a bizarre midwestern family, its feverish eccentricities and eventual collapse. Awaiting a cult following. 93m/C VHS, Beta, LV. Dylan McDermott, Crispin Glover, Harry Dean Stanton, Suzy Amis, Jenny Wright, Lindsay Christman, Lois Chiles; *D:* Michael Almereyda; *W:* Michael Almereyda; *C:* Renato Berta; *M:* Hans Zimmer. LIV, VES

Twister ♂️♂️½ 1996 (PG-13) Director De Bont's sophomore directorial effort is another non-stop adrenaline drive, but instead of a mad bomber, nature is the bad guy. Hunt leads a collegiate team of storm chasing scientists though Oklahoma in hopes of placing a robotic mechanism inside a tornado which, in turn, will help them predict and prepare for future funnel forces. There's also the matter of Hunt's soon-to-be ex-husband Paxton, and a competitor (Elwes) who's in charge of a slick group of rival scientists. There's a lot of things flying around, including trucks, houses, cows and the plausibility of the plot. But a contrived plot didn't keep from making $100 million dollars in its first two weeks of release. Some nice chemistry between Hunt and Paxton, apparently the only people who can still look attractive in high winds and blowing debris.*CW:* Intense depiction of very bad weather. 105m/C VHS, LV, Closed Caption, DVD. Bill Paxton, Helen Hunt, Cary Elwes, Jami Gertz, Alan Ruck, Lois Smith, Sean Whalen, Gregory Sporleder, Abraham Benrubi, Jake Busey; *D:* Jan De Bont; *W:* Michael Crichton, Anne-Marie Martin; *C:* Jack N. Green; *M:* Mark Mancina. MTV Movie Awards '97: Best Action Sequence; Nominations: Academy Awards '96: Best Sound, Best Visual Effects; MTV Movie Awards '97: Best Female Performance (Hunt); Golden Raspberry Awards '96: Worst Supporting Actress (Gertz). WAR

Twister Kicker ♂️ 1985 When the woman he loves is in jeopardy, an invincible man battles the best of fighters from three continents. Despite all this action, it's pretty ho-hum. 93m/C VHS. Wang Hoi, Yeung Oi Wa, Po Pei. NO

Twitch of the Death Nerve ♂️♂️ *Bay of Blood; Last House on the Left, Part 2; Carnage* 1971 (R) Four vacationers are relentlessly pursued by a homicidal maniac armed with a sickle, bent on decapitation. Supposedly the inspiration for the "Friday the 13th" series. 87m/C VHS, Beta. IT Claudine Auger, Chris Avran, Isa Miranda, Claudio Volonte, Luigi Pistilli; *D:* Mario Bava. NO

Two Assassins in the Dark ♂️ 198? Martial arts adventure about a pair of kung-fu killers who fight in the dark. 90m/C VHS, Beta. Wang Tao, Chang Yi, Lung Chun-Eng. NO

Two Bits ♂️♂️½ *A Day to Remember* 1996 (PG-13) Depression-era drama tells the story of a 12-year-old boy and his emotional coming of age. Title refers to a quarter Gennaro (Barone, in his film debut) seeks in order to attend the grand opening of a glamorous, air-conditioned movie palace. A heavily made-up Pacino (looking suspiciously like Marlon Brando in the garden scene of

"The Godfather"), co-stars as the boy's grandfather, who leaves him his last quarter. Gramps promises that he can collect later that day, when, he says, he will die. Fine performances all around and some powerful scenes go a long way toward masking the fact that the material is a bit too thin to stretch over an entire feature film.*CW:* Mature themes. 85m/C VHS, LV, Closed Caption. Al Pacino, Gerlando Barone, Mary Elizabeth Mastrantonio, Joe Grifasi, Joanna Merlin, Andy Romano, Ron McLarty, Donna Mitchell, Patrick Borriello, Mary Lou Rosato, Rosemary DeAngelis; *D:* James Foley; *W:* Joseph Stefano; *C:* Juan Ruiz-Anchia; *M:* Jane Musky; *V:* Alec Baldwin. TOU

Two Bits & Pepper ♂️♂️½ 1995 (PG) Bumbling criminals (both played by Piscopo) still manage to kidnap a young girl and her friend and it's up to the title characters, a pet horse and a pony, to attempt a daring rescue. 90m/C VHS, Closed Caption. Joe Piscopo, Lauren Eckstrom, Rachel Crane, Perry Stephens, Kathrin Lautner, Dennis Weaver; *D:* Corey Michael Eubanks; *W:* Corey Michael Eubanks; *C:* Jacques Haitkin; *M:* Louis Febre. REP

Two by Forsyth ♂️♂️ 1986 Two short films based on stories by Frederick Forsyth, one dealing with a dying millionaire's clever efforts to prevent his fortune from being inherited by greedy relatives, the other about a mild-mannered stamp dealer who avenges himself on a nasty gossip columnist. 60m/C VHS, Beta. Dan O'Herlihy, Cyril Cusack, Milo O'Shea, Shirley Anne Field. PSM

Two Daughters ♂️♂️♂️ *Teen Kanya* 1961 Director Ray wrote the scripts for two stories based on the writings of Nobel Prize winner Rabindranath Tagore, one about the relationship between an orphan and a postman, the other about a young man who declines to marry the girl arranged to be his intended. In Hindi with English subtitles. 114m/B VHS, Beta. IN D: Satyajit Ray; *W:* Satyajit Ray. NLC

Two Days in the Valley ♂️♂️ 1996 (R) Film adds two days with ten characters in one locale and one half dozen separate plots and tries to come up with a dark comedy/thriller and winning debut for Herzfeld. It almost succeeds. San Fernando Valley is the backdrop, with a diverse ensemble of disturbed characters thrown together by the murder of a philandering spouse. Too disjointed to really work, there are some fine comic moments and interesting character development, especially Aiello's culinary hitman, Dosmo Pizzo. Theron's Helga adds eye candy. For those too young to remember "Dynasty," you may want to check out the intense cat-fight between Hatcher's Becky Foxx and Helga.*CW:* Violence, sexuality and language. 105m/C VHS, Closed Caption. Danny Aiello, Jeff Daniels, Marsha Mason, Teri Hatcher, Glenne Headly, James Spader, Eric Stoltz, Greg Cruttwell, Peter Horton, Charlize Theron, Keith Carradine, Louise Fletcher, Austin Pendleton, Paul Mazursky, Kathleen Luong; *D:* John Herzfeld; *W:* John Herzfeld; *C:* Oliver Wood; *M:* Anthony Marinelli. Nominations: Golden Raspberry Awards '96: Worst Supporting Actress (Hatcher). HBO

Two Deaths ♂️♂️ 1994 (R) Sex, brutality, power, madness, death, revolution—sounds like a Roeg concoction. In 1989 Romania, the Ceaucescu government is under siege and a civil war rages outside. But inside the opulent apartment of cynical Dr. Daniel Pavenic (Gambon) calmness prevails, as three longtime friends join him for their annual reunion dinner. Dinner is served by Pavenic's housekeeper Ana (Braga), who has a strange, disturbing relationship with the possessive doctor that he relates to his friends. His candor leads to similar revelations by his companions. Based on the novel "The Two Deaths of Senora Puccini" by Stephen Dobyns.*CW:* Strong violence, including a graphic abortion scene, nudity/sexuality and related dialogue. 102m/C VHS. GB Michael Gambon, Sonia Braga, Patrick Malahide, Nickolas Grace, John Shrapnel, Ion Caramitru; *D:* Nicolas Roeg; *W:* Allan Scott; *C:* Witold Stok; *M:* Hans Zimmer. FXL

Two English Girls ♂️♂️♂️½ *Les Deux Anglaises et le Continent* 1972 (R) A pre-WWI French lad, with a possessive mother, loves two English sisters, one an impassioned, reckless artist, the other a repressed spinster. Tenderly delineates the triangle's interrelating love and friendship over seven years. Based on the novel "Les Deux Anglaises et le Continent" by Henri-Pierre Roche. In French with English subtitles. 108m/C VHS, Beta, LV. FR Jean-Pierre Leaud, Kika Markham, Stacey Tendeter, Sylvia Marriott, Marie Mansert, Philippe Leotard; *D:* Francois Truffaut; *C:* Nestor Almendros; *M:* Georges Delerue. HMV, FOX, APD

Two Evil Eyes ♂️♂️ *Due Occhi Diabolici* 1990 (R) Horror kings Romero and Argento each direct an Edgar Allan Poe tale in this release, hence the title. Barbeau, the scheming younger wife of a millionaire, hypnotizes her husband with the help of her lover in "The Facts in the Case of M. Valdemar." When hubby dies too soon to validate changes made in his will, the lovers decide to freeze him for two weeks in order that death can be recorded at the correct time. In "Black Cat" a crime photographer used to photographing gore adopts a feline friend and starts getting sick on the job. 121m/C VHS, Beta, LV. IT Adrienne Barbeau, Ramy Zada, Harvey Keitel, Madeleine Potter; *D:* George A. Romero, Dario Argento; *W:* Dario Argento; *M:* Pino Donaggio. FXV, VTR

Two-Faced Woman ♂️♂️♂️ 1941 Garbo, in her last film, attempts a ruse when she finds her husband may be interested in an old flame. Pretending to be her twin sister in an attempt to lure Douglas away from the other woman, she's fooled a little herself. Romantic comedy unfortunately miscasts Garbo as an Americanized ski bunny. 90m/B VHS, Beta. Greta Garbo, Melvyn Douglas, Constance Bennett, Roland Young, Ruth Gordon, Robert Sterling, George Cleveland, Frances Carson; *D:* George Cukor; *C:* Joseph Ruttenberg. MGM

The Two Faces of Dr. Jekyll ♂️♂️½ *House of Fright; Jekyll's Inferno* 1960 Henry Jekyll's (Massie) experiments lead to the release of his suave alter ego Edward Hyde. When Hyde discovers that Jekyll's long-suffering wife has taken up with his best friend, Hyde pits everyone against each other, while Jekyll struggles to retain control over his invidious other half. 87m/C VHS, Closed Caption. GB Paul Massie, Dawn Addams, Christopher Lee, David Kossoff; *D:* Terence Fisher. COL

The Two Faces of Evil ♂️ 1982 A family's vacation turns into a night of unbearable terror when they pick up a sinister hitchhiker. 60m/C VHS, Beta. Anna Calder-Marshall, Gary Raymond, Denholm Elliott, Pauline Delany, Philip Latham; *D:* Peter Sasdy, Alan Gibson. LIV

Two Fathers' Justice 1985 Two dads, one tough and one a wimp, seek revenge on the men who killed their kids. Made for television. 100m/C VHS. Robert Conrad, George Hamilton, Brooke Bundy, Catherine Corkill, Whitney Kershaw, Greg Terrell; *D:* Rod Holcomb. MCG

Two Fisted Justice ♂️ 1931 A cowboy protects a town against a daring and deadly Indian attack. 45m/B VHS, Beta. Tom Tyler. VDM

Two-Fisted Justice ♂️ 1943 The Range Busters do their part to maintain law and order in the old West. 55m/B VHS, Beta. John "Dusty" King, David Sharpe, Max Terhune. NOS, DVT

Two-Fisted Law ♂️½ 1932 McCoy plays a rancher who borrows big bucks from the corrupt Oakman, who's actually a land grabber. McCoy then teams up with a posse to bring the evildoer to justice. Early (and small) screen roles for Wayne and Brennan. 58m/B VHS. Tim McCoy, Tully Marshall, Wheeler Oakman, Alice Day, Wallace MacDonald, John Wayne, Walter Brennan; *D:* David Ross Lederman. COL

Two for the Road ♂️♂️♂️½ 1967 After over a decade of marriage, Finney and Hepburn look back and find only fragments of their relationship. Mancini score adds poignancy to the couple's reflections on their stormy life. Touching and well-acted. 112m/C VHS, LV. *GB* Audrey Hepburn, Albert Finney, Eleanor Bron, William Daniels, Claude Dauphin, Nadia Gray, Jacqueline Bisset, Georges Descrieres, Gabrielle Middleton, Judy Cornwell, Irene Hilda, Roger Dann, Libby Morris, Yves Barsac; *D:* Stanley Donen; *W:* Frederic Raphael; *C:* Christopher Challis; *M:* Henry Mancini. Nominations: Academy Awards '67: Best Story & Screenplay. *FXV, BTV, FUS*

Two for the Seesaw 🎭🎭🎭 1962
Mitchum stars as a Nebraska attorney who comes to New York and gets involved with MacLaine. Humorous and touching comedy-drama worked better on stage, because the large screen magnified the talkiness of Gibson's play. Unusual casting of Mitchum as a Midwest lawyer and MacLaine as a New York Jewish bohemian. 119m/B VHS, LV, **Closed Caption.** Robert Mitchum, Shirley MacLaine, Edmon Ryan, Elisabeth Fraser, Eddie Firestone, Billy Gray, Vic Lundin; *D:* Robert Wise; *W:* Isobel Lennart; *M:* Andre Previn. Nominations: Academy Awards '62: Best Black and White Cinematography, Best Song ("Song fromm Two for the Seesaw (Second Chance)"). *MGM*

Two Girls and a Sailor 🎭🎭🎭 1944
Wartime musical revue loosely structured around a love triangle involving a sailor on leave. Vintage hokum with lots of songs. 🎵Paper Doll; The Young Man with a Horn; Concerto for Index Finger; Take it Easy; Ritual Fire Dance; Inka Dinka Doo; My Mother Told Me; A Love Like Ours; In A Moment of Madness. 124m/B VHS, Beta, LV. June Allyson, Gloria De Haven, Van Johnson, Xavier Cugat, Jimmy Durante, Tom Drake, Lena Horne, Harry James, Gracie Allen, Virginia O'Brien, Jose Iturbi, Carlos Ramirez, Donald Meek, Ben Blue; *Cameos:* Buster Keaton; *D:* Richard Thorpe; *W:* Robert L. Surtees. Nominations: Academy Awards '44: Best Original Screenplay. *MGM*

Two Graves to Kung-Fu 🎭 1982 (R)
Young kung-fu student is framed for murder. When the real murderers kill his teacher, he escapes from prison to seek revenge. 95m/C VHS, Beta. Liu Chia-Yung, Shek Kin, Chen Hung-Lieh. *GEM*

The Two Great Cavaliers 🎭 1973
A Ming warrior has a hard time with the Manchurian army, fending it off as he must with only his bare instep, heel, and wrist. 95m/C VHS, Beta. Chen Shing, Mao Ying; *D:* Yeung Ching Chen. *UNI*

Two Gun Man 🎭½ 1931
America's first singing cowboy, Ken Maynard, performs hair-raising stunts in this old oater. One of the first "talkies!" 60m/B VHS, Beta. Ken Maynard, Lafe McKee, Charles "Blackie" King, Tom London, Lucille Powers; *D:* Phil Rosen. *GPV, VCN, DVT*

Two-Gun Man from Harlem 1938
Big city guy travels to the wild West in search of a little truth. 60m/B VHS. Herbert Jeffries, Marguerite Whitten, Mantan Moreland, Matthew "Stymie" Beard; *D:* Richard C. Kahn. *NOS, TPV*

Two-Gun Troubador 🎭 *The Lone Troubador* 1937
A masked singing cowboy struggles to uncovers his father's murderer. 59m/B VHS, Beta. Fred Scott, Claire Rochelle, John Merton. *NOS, BAR, HEG*

200 Motels 🎭½ 1971 (R)
Rambling, non-narrative self-indulgent video album by and about Frank Zappa and the Mothers of Invention, as they document a long and especially grueling road tour. For fans only. 99m/C VHS, Beta. Frank Zappa, Ringo Starr; *D:* Frank Zappa. *MGM, MVD*

Two If by Sea 🎭½ *Stolen Hearts* 1995 (R)
Small-time hood Frank (Leary) and his girlfriend Roz (Bullock) hole up in a New England mansion after Frank steals a valuable Matisse painting. Between verbal sparring matches, the two try to mingle with the upper crusty residents with predictable results. Pursuing the pair are the FBI, led by the deluded O'Malley (Kotto), and Frank's bonehead cousin Beano (Robson) and his trio of dim henchmen. Tries to be a caper/romantic comedy but fails to deliver on all fronts. The usually caustic Leary takes some of the edge off of his trademark bitter humor, and the alleged witty repartee is just plain annoying as a result. Nova Scotia

turns in a fine performance as New England.*CW:* Language. 96m/C VHS, LV, **Closed Caption.** Sandra Bullock, Denis Leary, Stephen Dillane, Yaphet Kotto, Wayne Robson, Jonathan Tucker, Mike Starr, Michael Badalucco, Lenny Clarke, John Friesen; *D:* Bill Bennett; *W:* Denis Leary, Michael Armstrong; *C:* Andrew Lesnie. *WAR*

The Two Jakes 🎭🎭 1990 (R)
Ten years have passed and Jake Gittes is still a private investigator in this sequel to 1974's "Chinatown." When a murder occurs while he's digging up dirt on an affair between the wife of a real estate executive and the executive's partner, Jake must return to Chinatown to uncover the killer and face the painful memories buried there. Despite solid dialogue and effective performances, it's unreasonably difficult to follow if you haven't seen "Chinatown." Outstanding photography by Vilmos Zsigmond. 137m/C VHS, Beta, LV, **Closed Caption.** Jack Nicholson, Harvey Keitel, Meg Tilly, Madeleine Stowe, Eli Wallach, Ruben Blades, Frederic Forrest, David Keith, Richard Farnsworth, Tracey Walter; *D:* Jack Nicholson; *W:* Robert Towne; *C:* Vilmos Zsigmond; *M:* Van Dyke Parks. *PAR, FCT*

Two Kinds of Love 🎭🎭 1985
Adapted from Peggy Mann's novel "There Are Two Kinds of Terrible" this is the story of a young boy who learns to love his distant, workaholic father after his protective mother suddenly dies. Made for television. 94m/C VHS, Beta, **Closed Caption.** Rick Schroder, Lindsay Wagner, Peter Weller; *D:* Jack Bender. *FOX*

Two Lost Worlds woof! 1950
A young hero battles monstrous dinosaurs, pirates, and more in this cheaply when he and his shipmates are shipwrecked on an uncharted island. Don't miss the footage from "Captain Fury," "One Billion B.C. ," and "Captain Caution" and Arness long before his Sheriff Dillon fame, and his "big" role in "The Thing." 63m/B VHS, Beta. James Arness, Laura Elliott, Bill Kennedy; *D:* Norman Dawn. *NO*

Two Men & a Wardrobe 1958
Polanski's project while a student at the Polish Film Institute. Consideration of modern man's lack of privacy and made without dialogue. Two men emerge from the sea carrying nothing but a piece of furniture. Absurd and funny. 19m/B VHS, Beta. *D:* Roman Polanski. *IHF, GVV*

Two Minute Warning 🎭 1976 (R)
A sniper plans to take out the president of the United States at an NFL playoff game in this boring, pointless, disaster film that goes on forever. Features all the ready-made characters inherent in the genre but, until its too late, precious little of the mayhem. To get caught watching the TV version, which features more characters and an additional subplot, would be truly disastrous. 116m/C VHS, LV. Charlton Heston, John Cassavetes, Martin Balsam, Beau Bridges, Marilyn Hassett, David Janssen, Jack Klugman, Walter Pidgeon, Gena Rowlands; *D:* Larry Peerce; *M:* Charles Fox. Nominations: Academy Awards '76: Best Film Editing. *USH*

The Two Mrs. Carrolls 🎭🎭½ 1947
Bogart is a psycho-killer/artist who paints portraits of his wives as the Angel of Death—and then kills them. The married Bogart falls for Stanwyck, poisons his current wife, and the two marry. After a few years, Bogart falls for Smith and decides to rid himself of Stanwyck in the same manner as his first killing. Stanwyck, however, becomes increasingly suspicious and calls on an old beau for help. Melodrama cast Bogart against type (not always successfully). Filmed in 1945, but was unreleased until 1947. 99m/B VHS. Humphrey Bogart, Barbara Stanwyck, Alexis Smith, Nigel Bruce, Pat O'Moore, Ann Carter; *D:* Peter Godfrey. *MGM*

Two Moon Junction 🎭½ 1988 (R)
A soon-to-be-wed Southern debutante enters into a wild love affair with a rough-edged carnival worker. Poorly acted, wildly directed, with many unintentional laughs. 104m/C VHS, Beta, LV. Sherilyn Fenn, Richard Tyson, Louise Fletcher, Burl Ives, Kristy McNichol, Millie Perkins, Don Galloway, Herve Villechaize, Dabbs Greer, Jay Hawkins; *D:* Zalman King; *W:* Zalman King; *M:*

Jonathan Elias. Golden Raspberry Awards '88: Worst Supporting Actress (McNichol). *COL*

Two Much 🎭½ 1996 (PG-13)
Banderas does double duty as a con man pretending to be twins in order to romance two sisters (Griffith and Hannah). Embarrassingly light comedy suffers from a complicated plot (which still manages to leave holes), weak or non-existent characterization, and a general lack of humor. About the only thing it has going for it is Cusack as a wisecracking secretary. It was on the set of this film that Banderas and Griffith started their real-life romance. While that may have helped the box office and gossip columns in Banderas's homeland, the fireworks didn't find their way to the screen.*CW:* Sexual situations and language. 118m/C VHS, LV, **Closed Caption.** Melanie Griffith, Antonio Banderas, Daryl Hannah, Joan Cusack, Danny Aiello, Eli Wallach, Vincent Schiavelli; *D:* Fernando Trueba; *W:* Fernando Trueba, David Trueba; *C:* Jose Luis Alcaine; *M:* Michel Camilo. Nominations: Golden Raspberry Awards '96: Worst Actress (Griffith), Worst Supporting Actress (Hannah). *TOU*

Two Mules for Sister Sara 🎭🎭🎭 1970 (PG)
American mercenary in 19th century Mexico gets mixed up with a cigar-smoking nun and the two make plans to capture a French garrison. MacLaine and Eastwood are great together. Based on a Boetticher story. 105m/C VHS, Beta. Clint Eastwood, Shirley MacLaine; *D:* Donald Siegel; *W:* Albert Maltz; *M:* Ennio Morricone. *USH*

Two Nights with Cleopatra 🎭½ *Due Notti Con Cleopatra* 1954
A piece of Italian pizza involving Cleopatra's double (also played by Loren) falling in love with one of the guards. Notable only for the 19-year-old Sophia's brief nudity. 77m/C VHS, Beta. *IT* Sophia Loren, Ettore Manni, Alberto Sordi, Paul Muller, Alberto Talegalli, Rolf Tasna, Gianni Cavalieri, Fernando Bruno, Riccardo Garrone, Carlo Dale; *D:* Mario Mattoli; *W:* Nino Maccari, Ettore Scola. *VDM*

Two of a Kind 🎭🎭½ 1982
In his television movie debut, Burns plays an elderly man whose mentally handicapped grandson helps him put the starch back in his shirt. Sensitively produced and performed. 102m/C VHS, Beta, **Closed Caption.** George Burns, Robby Benson, Cliff Robertson, Barbara Barrie, Frances Lee McCain, Geri Jewell, Ronny Cox; *D:* Roger Young. *FOX*

Two of a Kind 🎭🎭 1983 (PG)
Angels make a bet with God—two selfish people will redeem themselves or God can blow up the Earth. Bad acting, awful direction, and the script needs divine intervention. 88m/C VHS, Beta, LV, **Closed Caption.** John Travolta, Olivia Newton-John, Charles Durning, Beatrice Straight, Scatman Crothers, Oliver Reed; *D:* John Herzfeld; *C:* Fred W. Koenekamp. *FOX*

The Two of Us 🎭🎭🎭½ *Le Vieil Homme Et L'Enfant; Claude; The Old Man and the Boy* 1968
Young Jewish boy flees Nazi-occupied Paris to live in the country with an irritable, bigoted guardian. Sensitive, eloquent movie about racial prejudice and anti-Semitism. In French with English subtitles. 86m/B VHS. *FR* Michel Simon, Alain Cohen, Luce Fabiole, Roger Carel, Paul Preboist, Charles Denner; *D:* Claude Berri; *M:* Georges Delerue. *NO*

Two or Three Things I Know About Her 🎭🎭 *Deux ou Trois Choses Que Je Sais d'Elle* 1966
Inspired by a magazine article about housewife-prostitutes, Godard takes on the bourgeoise. Juliette (Vlady) is a wife and mother who lives in the suburbs of Paris and goes into the city once a week to work as a prostitute in order to buy consumer goods. French with subtitles. 95m/C VHS. *FR* Marina Vlady, Anny Duperey, Roger Montsoret, Jean Narboni, Raoul Levy; *D:* Jean-Luc Godard; *W:* Jean-Luc Godard; *C:* Raoul Coutard. *NYF*

Two Rode Together 🎭🎭½ 1961
A Texas marshal and an army lieutenant negotiate with the Comanches for the return of captives, but complications ensue. 109m/C VHS, Beta, LV. James Stewart, Richard Widmark, Shirley Jones, Linda Cristal, Andy Devine, John McIntire; *D:* John Ford. *COL*

The Two Sisters 1937 Goldstein, in her only film role, plays an older sister who sacrifices everything for the younger. The younger thanks her by stealing her fiance. In Yiddish with English subtitles. 70m/B VHS. Jenney Goldstein, Michael Rosenberg. ALD

Two Small Bodies 🎬🎬 1993 Police detective Brann investigates the disappearance of two young children, suspecting their mother Eileen may have murdered them. Two character study set in Eileen's home with both verbally recreating versions of the possible crime. Based on the play by Neal Bell. 85m/C VHS. Fred Ward, Suzy Amis; **D:** Beth B; **W:** Beth B, Neal Bell. ORI

2000 Maniacs 🎬🎬½ 1964 One of cult director Lewis' most enjoyably watchable films. A literal Civil War "ghost town" takes its revenge 100 years after being slaughtered by renegade Union soldiers by luring unwitting "yankee" tourists to their centennial festival. The hapless Northerners are then chopped, crushed, ripped apart etc. while the ghostly rebels party. Quite fun in a cartoonishly gruesome sort of way. Filmed in St. Cloud, FL. 75m/C VHS, Beta. Thomas Wood, Connie Mason, Jeffrey Allen, Ben Moore, Gary Bakeman, Jerome Eden, Shelby Livingston, Michael Korb, Yvonne Gilbert, Mark Douglas, Linda Cochran, Vincent Santo, Andy Wilson; **D:** Herschell Gordon Lewis; **W:** Herschell Gordon Lewis. NO

2001: A Space Odyssey 🎬🎬🎬🎬 1968 Space voyage to Jupiter turns chaotic when a computer, HAL 9000, takes over. Seen by some as a mirror of man's historical use of machinery and by others as a grim vision of the future, the special effects and music are still stunning. Critically acclaimed and well accepted by some, simply confusing to others. Martin Balsam originally recorded the voice of HAL, but was replaced by Rain. From Arthur C. Clarke's novel "The Sentinel." Followed by a sequel "2010: The Year We Make Contact." Laserdisc edition is presented in letterbox format and features a special supplementary section on the making of "2001," a montage of images from the film, production documents, memos and photos. Also included on the disc is a NASA film entitled "Art and Reality," which offers footage from the Voyager I and II flybys of Jupiter. 139m/C VHS, Beta, LV. **GB** Keir Dullea, Gary Lockwood, William Sylvester, Dan Richter; **D:** Stanley Kubrick; **W:** Arthur C. Clarke, Stanley Kubrick; **C:** Geoffrey Unsworth; **V:** Douglas Rains. Academy Awards '68: Best Visual Effects; National Board of Review Awards '68: 10 Best Films of the Year; Nominations: Academy Awards '68: Best Art Direction/Set Decoration, Best Director (Kubrick), Best Story & Screenplay. MGM, CRC, FCT

2010: The Year We Make Contact 🎬🎬🎬 1984 (PG) The film version of Arthur C. Clarke's "The Sentinel" continues in this sequel to "2001: A Space Odyssey." Americans and Russians unite to investigate the abandoned starship Discovery's decaying orbit around Jupiter and try to determine why the HAL 9000 computer sabotaged its mission years before, while signs of cosmic change are detected on and around the giant planet. 116m/C VHS, Beta, LV, Closed Caption. Roy Scheider, John Lithgow, Helen Mirren, Bob Balaban, Keir Dullea, Madolyn Smith, Mary Jo Deschanel; **D:** Peter Hyams; **W:** Peter Hyams; **M:** David Shire; **V:** Douglas Rains. Nominations: Academy Awards '84: Best Art Direction/Set Decoration, Best Costume Design, Best Makeup, Best Sound. MGM

2020 Texas Gladiators WOOF! 1985 (R) In the post-nuclear holocaust world, two groups, one good, one evil, battle for supremacy. 91m/C VHS, Beta. **IT** Harrison Muller, Al Cliver, Daniel Stephen, Peter Hooten, Al Yamanouchi, Sabrina Santi; **D:** Kevin Mancuso. MED

2069: A Sex Odyssey 🎬½ 1978 (R) Team of beautiful, sensuous astronauts are sent to Earth to obtain male sperm which they must bring back to Venus. Tongue-in-cheek soft core sci-fi spoof. 73m/C VHS, Beta. Alena Penz, Nina Fredric,

Gerti Sneider, Raul Retzer, Catherine Conti, Heidi Hammer, Michael Mein, Herb Heesel; **D:** George Keil. ACA, HHE

Two Tickets to Broadway 🎬🎬½ 1951 A small-town singer and a crooner arrange a hoax to get themselves on Bob Crosby's television show. Appealing but lightweight. 🎵Let the Worry Bird Worry For You; Pagliacci; There's No Tomorrow; Manhattan; Big Chief Hole in the Ground; The Closer You Are; Baby, You'll Never Be Sorry; Pelican Falls High; It Began In Yucatan. 106m/C VHS, Beta. Tony Martin, Janet Leigh, Gloria De Haven, Joi Lansing; **D:** James V. Kern; **M:** Leo Robin, Jule Styne; **Performed by:** Smith & Dale. Nominations: Academy Awards '51: Best Sound. TTC

Two to Tango 🎬½ 1988 (R) A hired assassin goes to Buenos Aires to kill a crime boss, and falls in love with his tango-dancing mistress. Based on the novel by J.P. Feiman. 87m/C VHS, Beta. **AR** Don Stroud, Adrienne Sachs; **D:** Hector Olivera. NO

Two-Way Stretch 🎬🎬½ 1960 Three prison inmates in a progressive jail plan to break out, pull a diamond heist, and break back in, all in the same night. Fast-paced slapstick farce. 84m/B VHS, Beta. **GB** Peter Sellers, Wilfrid Hyde-White, Liz Fraser, David Lodge; **D:** Robert Day. NO

Two Weeks in Another Town 🎬🎬 1962 Douglas and Robinson are a couple of Hollywood has-beens who set out to make a comeback picture but meet with adversity at every turn. Extremely sappy melodrama is based on Irwin Shaw's trashy novel and represents one of director Minnelli's poorer efforts. Laserdisc features a letterboxed screen and the original movie trailer. 107m/C VHS, LV, Closed Caption. Kirk Douglas, Edward G. Robinson, Cyd Charisse, George Hamilton, Daliah Lavi, Claire Trevor, James Gregory, Rosanna Schiaffino, George Macready, Stefan Schnabel, Vito Scotti, Leslie Uggams; **D:** Vincente Minnelli; **C:** Milton Krasner. MGM

Two Weeks to Live 🎬½ 1943 The comedy team inherits a railroad line, only to find it's a pile of junk. 60m/B VHS, Beta. Lum & Abner, Franklin Pangborn. NOS, DVT

Two Weeks with Love 🎬🎬 1950 Reynolds and family wear funny bathing suits in the Catskills in the early 1900s while the Debster sings songs and blushes into young adulthood. 🎵Aba Daba Honeymoon; The Oceana Roll; A Heart That's Free; By the Light of the Silvery Moon; My Hero; Row, Row, Row; That's How I Need You; Beautiful Lady. 92m/C VHS. Debbie Reynolds, Jane Powell, Ricardo Montalban, Louis Calhern, Ann Harding, Phyllis Kirk, Carleton Carpenter, Clinton Sundberg, Gary Gray; **D:** Roy Rowland. MGM, FCT

Two Women 🎬🎬🎬🎬 La Ciociara 1961 A mother and her 13-year-old daughter travel war-torn Italy during WWII and must survive lack of food, crazed monks and brutal soldiers. Tragic, moving, well-directed. Loren received well-deserved Oscar. In Italian with English subtitles or dubbed. 99m/B VHS, Beta. **IT** Sophia Loren, Raf Vallone, Eleonora Brown, Jean-Paul Belmondo; **D:** Vittorio De Sica; **W:** Cesare Zavattini, Vittorio De Sica; **M:** Armando Trovajoli. Academy Awards '61: Best Actress (Loren); British Academy Awards '61: Best Actress (Loren); Cannes Film Festival '61: Best Actress (Loren); Golden Globe Awards '62: Best Foreign Film; National Board of Review Awards '61: 5 Best Foreign Films of the Year; New York Film Critics Awards '61: Best Actress (Loren).COL, APD, BTV

Two Wondrous Tigers 🎬 1979 Awesome Kung-fu gang terrorizes a small town until a local dares to out-chop the bullies. 87m/C VHS, Beta. John Chang; **D:** Wilson Tong. TWE

The Two Worlds of Jenny Logan 🎬🎬½ 1979 A woman travels back and forth in time whenever she dons a 19th century dress she finds in her old house. She is also able to fall in love twice, in different centuries. Made for television and adapted from "Second Sight," a novel by David Williams. Stylish and well made. 97m/C VHS, Beta. Lindsay Wagner, Marc Singer, Alan Feinstein, Linda Gray, Constance McCashin, Henry Wilcox-

on, Irene Tedrow, Joan Darling, Allen Williams, Pat Corley, Gloria Stuart; **D:** Frank de Felitta. FRH, LIV

Two Wrongs Make a Right 🎬 1989 A quiet nightclub owner beats and clubs his way through his tough neighborhood to protect himself and his woman. 85m/C VHS, Beta. Ivan Rogers, Ron Blackstone, Rich Komenich; **D:** Robert Brown. UNI

Twogether 🎬🎬½ 1994 (R) Struggling artist John (Cassavettes) and environmentalist Allison (Bakke) have this lust thing going on. It leads to a drunken Las Vegas wedding and a quickie divorce but they still don't keep their hands off of each other (or any other body parts) and Allison gets pregnant. They decide to become partners in raising the baby but first they'll have to do some growing up of their own. Also available unrated. 108m/C VHS, Closed Caption. Brenda Bakke, Nick Cassavetes, Jeremy Piven, Jim Beaver; **D:** Andrew Chiaramonte; **W:** Andrew Chiaramonte; **C:** Eugene Shlugleit; **M:** Nigel Holton. COL

Tycoon 🎬🎬½ 1947 Wayne goes to Latin America to build a road for an American industrialist. When the industrialist insists on a shorter but more dangerous route, Wayne must satisfy his own sense of honor. Meanwhile, he's found romance with the industrialist's half-Spanish daughter. Long, but well-acted. 129m/C VHS, Beta, LV. John Wayne, Laraine Day, Cedric Hardwicke, Judith Anderson, James Gleason, Anthony Quinn; **D:** Richard Wallace. CCB, TTC

Typhoon Treasure 🎬 1939 Whilst recovering his sunken treasure, the hero battles bad guys, savage natives and a crocodile, all of whom could probably have made a more sophisticated film. 68m/B VHS. **AU** Campbell Copelin, Gwen Munro, Joe Valli, Douglas Herald; **D:** Noel Monkman. NOS, LOO

Tyrant of Lydia Against the Son of Hercules 🎬 1963 Hercules' son takes on a wicked king in this startling adventure. ?m/C VHS, Beta. **IT** Gordon Scott, Massimo Serato. SNC

Tyson 🎬 1995 Based on the life of former World Heavyweight Champion, Mike Tyson (White) who rose from the streets of Brownsville to a million dollar lifestyle and a spectacular fall to a rape conviction and a prison term (which are handled in voiceover). Story begins with trainer Cus D'Amato (Scott) finding unpolished and troubled young Tyson and training him for the Junior Olympics. When promoter Don King (Winfield) enters the picture, Tyson's career really takes off. Pulls no punches about Tyson's short fuse and brutal abilities. Based on the book "Fire and Fear: The Inside Story of Mike Tyson" by Jose Torres. 90m/C VHS. Michael Jai White, Paul Winfield, George C. Scott, Malcolm Jamal Warner, Tony LoBianco, James B. Sikking, Clark Gregg, Kristen Wilson, Sheila Wills, Holt McCallany, Lilyan Chauvin, Georg Stanford Brown, Joe Santos, Charles Napier; **D:** Uli Edel; **W:** Robert Johnson; **M:** Stewart Copeland. HBO

U-Boat Prisoner 🎬 1944 Bennett is an American sailor who's captured by a Nazi U-boat. He promptly defeats the crew, leaving the U-boat to the mercy of a U.S. destroyer. Silly, silly, silly. 65m/B VHS. Bruce (Herman Brix) Bennett, John Abbott, John Wood, Kenneth MacDonald, Erik Rolf, John Wengraf; **D:** Lew (Louis Friedlander) Landers. GPV

UFO: Target Earth 🎬 1974 (G) Scientist attempts to fish flying saucer out of lake and costs studio $70,000. 80m/C VHS. Nick Plakias, Cynthia Cline, Phil Erickson; **D:** Michael de Gaetano. MOV

Uforia 🎬🎬 1981 Two rival evangelists meet up with a UFO-infatuated girl. Under her guidance, they wait for UFO encounters they intend to use to milk their revivalist audiences. Sometimes clumsy, but more often fun. 92m/C VHS, Beta. Cindy Williams, Harry Dean Stanton, Fred Ward; **D:** John Binder; **W:** John Binder; **M:** Richard Baskin. COL

Ugetsu 🎬🎬🎬🎬 Ugetsu Monogatari 1953 The classic film that established Mizoguchi's reputation outside of Japan. Two 16th century Japanese peasants venture from their homes in pursuit of dreams, and encounter little more than their own hapless folly and a bit of the supernatural. A wonderful mix of comedy and action with nifty camera movement. Based on the stories of Akinara Ueda. In Japanese with English subtitles. **96m/B VHS, Beta, LV, 8mm.** JP Machiko Kyo, Masayuki Mori, Kinuyo Tanaka, Sakae Ozawa; **D:** Kenji Mizoguchi. Venice Film Festival '53: Silver Prize; Nominations: Academy Awards '55: Best Costume Design (B & W). *HMV, WFV, DVT*

The Ugly American 🎬🎬½ 1963
A naive American ambassador to a small, civil-war-torn Asian country fights a miniature Cold War against northern communist influence. Too preachy, and the "Red Menace" aspects are now very dated, but Brando's performance is worth watching. Based on the William J. Lederer novel. **120m/C VHS, Beta.** Marlon Brando, Sandra Church, Eiji Okada, Pat Hingle, Arthur Hill; **D:** George Englund; **W:** Stewart Stern. *USH*

The Ugly Dachshund 🎬🎬½ 1965
Jones and Pleshette are married dog lovers who raise Dachshunds. When Ruggles convinces them to take a Great Dane puppy, the fun begins! The Great Dane thinks he is a Dachshund because he has been raised with them—just imagine what happens when such a large dog acts as if he is small! Kids will love this wacky Disney film. **93m/C VHS, Beta.** Dean Jones, Suzanne Pleshette, Charlie Ruggles, Kelly Thordsen, Parley Baer; **D:** Norman Tokar; **C:** Edward Colman. *DIS, OM*

UHF 🎬🎬 1989 (PG-13)
A loser is appointed manager of a bargain-basement UHF television station. He turns it around via bizarre programming ideas. Some fun parodies of TV enhance this minimal story. Developed solely as a vehicle for Yankovic. **97m/C VHS, Beta, LV, Closed Caption.** Weird Al Yankovic, Kevin McCarthy, Victoria Jackson, Michael Richards, David Bowie, Anthony Geary; **D:** Jay Levey; **M:** John Du Prez. *ORI*

Ulee's Gold 🎬🎬🎬 1997 (R)
Slow-paced, deliberate character study, set in the Florida panhandle. Ulysses "Ulee" Jackson (Fonda) is a widowed, middleaged Vietnam vet who puts most of his energies into his work as a beekeeper, much to the detriment of his family. Son Jimmy (Wood) is in prison and druggie daughter-in-law Helen (Dunford) has disappeared, leaving the taciturn Ulee to care for his troubled granddaughters, teenaged Casey (Biel) and 9-year-old Penny (Zima). But their ordinary lives change when Helen turns up in Orlando with two violent hoods from Jimmy's past and Ulee must not only rescue her but find the emotional release to make them all a home. Splendidly moving performance from Fonda. **CW:** Language. **111m/C VHS.** Peter Fonda, Tom Wood, Vanessa Zima, Jessica Biel, Christine Dunford, Patricia Richardson, Steve Flynn, Dewey Weber, J. Kenneth Campbell; **D:** Victor Nunez; **W:** Victor Nunez; **C:** Virgil Marcus Mirano; **M:** Charles Engstrom. *NYR*

Ulterior Motives 🎬½ 1992 (R)
P.I. Jack Blaylock agrees to protect a pretty reporter from Japanese gangsters. He finds himself caught up in deception and betrayal and uses all his considerable, and violent, skills to make certain he does his job. **CW:** Some strong violence. **90m/C VHS, Closed Caption.** Thomas Ian Griffith, Mary Page Keller, Joe Yamanaka, Ellen Crawford, Ken Howard, Tyra Ferrell; **D:** James Becket. *IMP*

Ultimate Desires 🎬🎬 1991 (R)
When a high class hooker is brutally killed, beautiful Scoggins puts on what there is of the victim's clothes in order to solve the mystery. But trouble lies in wait as she actually begins to enjoy her funky new double life. Can she solve the crime before becoming lost in her own hot fantasy world? **CW:** Language, strong violence and drug content, and strong sexuality. **93m/C VHS, Beta, Closed Caption.** Tracy Scoggins, Brion James, Marc Singer, Marc Baur, Marc Bennett, Suzy Joachim, Jason Scott, John Wood; **D:** Lloyd A. Simanol. *PSM*

The Ultimate Imposter 🎬 1979
A secret agent acquires voluminous knowledge through a computer brain linkup, but can only retain the knowledge for 72 hours. In that timespan he has

to rescue a defecting Russian from hordes of assassins. Made for television. **97m/C VHS, Beta.** Keith Andes, Erin Gray, Joseph Hacker, Macon McCalman; **D:** Paul Stanley. *USH*

The Ultimate Thrill 🎬½ The Ultimate Chase 1974 (PG)
Businessman's paranoia about his wife's affairs leads him to follow her to Colorado on a ski holiday and stalk her lovers. Well-filmed skiing scenes and not much else. **84m/C VHS, Beta.** Britt Ekland, Barry Brown, Michael Blodgett, John Davis Chandler, Eric (Hans Gudegast) Braeden; **D:** Robert Butler. *GEM, CNG*

The Ultimate Warrior 🎬🎬½ 1975 (R)
Yul Brynner must defend the plants and seeds of a pioneer scientist to help replenish the world's food supply in this thriller set in 2012. **92m/C VHS, Beta.** Yul Brynner, Max von Sydow, Joanna Miles, Richard Kelton, Lane Bradbury, William Smith; **D:** Robert Clouse; **W:** Robert Clouse. *WAR*

Ultra Warrior 🎬½ Welcome to Oblivion 1992 (R)
A basic post-apocalyptic adventure tale of a radioactive earth, mutants, and various battles by the good guys to save the planet. **CW:** Violence and sexuality. **80m/C VHS.** Dack Rambo, Meshach Taylor, Clare Beresford. *NHO*

Ultraviolet 🎬½ 1991 (R)
Another warning against playing the good samaritan. Young couple on vacation in Death Valley try to help a stranded stranger only to have him turn on them. **CW:** Language, violence, and sensuality. **80m/C VHS, Closed Caption.** Esai Morales, Stephen Meadows, Patricia Healy; **D:** Mark Griffiths. *NHO*

Ulysses 🎬🎬½ Ulisse 1955
An Italian made version of the epic poem by Homer, as the warrior returns to his homeland and the ever-faithful Penelope after the Trojan war. Ambitious effort provides for the ultimate mixed review. Douglas is good in the role and his stops along the ten-year way are well visualized. Sometimes sluggish with poor dubbing. Seven writers helped bring Homer to the big screen. **104m/C VHS, Beta.** IT Kirk Douglas, Silvana Mangano, Anthony Quinn, Rossana Podesta; **D:** Mario Camerini. *WAR, OM*

Ulysses 🎬🎬½ 1967
James Joyce's probably unfilmable novel was given a noble effort in this flawed film covering a day in the life of Leopold Bloom as he wanders through Dublin. Shot in Ireland with a primarily Irish cast. **140m/B VHS, LV.** Milo O'Shea, Maurice Roeves, T.P. McKenna, Martin Dempsey, Sheila O'Sullivan, Barbara Jefford; **D:** Joseph Strick. Nominations: Academy Awards '67: Best Adapted Screenplay. *MFV*

Ulysses' Gaze 🎬🎬 The Look of Ulysses; To Vlemma Tou Odyssea; The Gaze of Ulysses 1995
Nameless Greek-American filmmaker (Keitel) journeys across the Balkans from Athens to Sarajevo while making a documentary on pioneer filmmakers, the Manakia brothers, who ignored national and ethnic strife in order to record the lives of ordinary people. Keitel has heard that some undeveloped film shot by the brothers has turned up in Sarajevo and he's determined to see it despite the turmoil in Bosnia. Moving and pessimistic depiction of the Balkan conflict seen through a filmmaker's eyes. English and Balkan dialogue. **177m/C VHS.** GR FR IT Harvey Keitel, Maia Morgenstern, Erland Josephson, Thanassis Vengos, Yorgos Michalokopoulos, Dora Volonaki; **D:** Theo Angelopoulos; **W:** Theo Angelopoulos, Tonino Guerra, Petros Markaris; **C:** Yorgos Arvanitis; **M:** Eleni Karaindrou. Cannes Film Festival '95: Grand Jury Prize. *NYR*

Ulzana's Raid 🎬🎬🎬 1972 (R)
An aging scout and an idealistic Cavalry lieutenant lock horns on their way to battling a vicious Apache chieftain. A violent, gritty western that enjoyed critical re-evaluation years after its first release. **103m/C VHS, Beta, LV, Closed Caption.** Burt Lancaster, Bruce Davison, Richard Jaeckel, Lloyd Bochner, Jorge Luke; **D:** Robert Aldrich; **C:** Joseph Biroc. *USH*

Umberto D 🎬🎬🎬🎬 1955
A government pensioner, living alone with his beloved dog, struggles to keep up a semblance of dignity on his inadequate pension. De Sica considered this his masterpiece. A sincere, tender treatment of the struggles involved with the inevitability of aging. In Italian with English subtitles. Laser edition features letterboxed print. **89m/B VHS, Beta, LV, 8mm.** IT Carlo Battista, Maria Pia Casilio, Lina Gennari; **D:** Vittorio De Sica; **W:** Cesare Zavattini, Vittorio De Sica. New York Film Critics Awards '55: Best Foreign Film; Nominations: Academy Awards '56: Best Story. *HMV, HHT, DVT*

Umbrellas of Cherbourg 🎬🎬🎬½ Les Parapluies De Cherbourg; Die Regenschirme Von Cherbourg 1964
A bittersweet film operetta with no spoken dialog. Deneuve is the teenaged daughter of a widow who owns an umbrella shop. She and her equally young boyfriend are separated by his military duty in Algeria. Finding she is pregnant, the girl marries a wealthy man, and when her former lover returns, he too marries someone else. But when they meet once again will their love be rekindled? Lovely photography and an evocative score enhance the story. In French with subtitles; also available dubbed in English (not with the same effectiveness). Oscar nominee for cinematography and story. **90m/C VHS, Beta.** FR Catherine Deneuve, Nino Castelnuovo, Anne Vernon, Ellen Farner, Marc Michel, Mireille Perrey, Jean Champion, Alfred Wolff, Dorothee Blanck; **D:** Jacques Demy; **W:** Jacques Demy; **M:** Michel Legrand. Cannes Film Festival '64: Best Film; Nominations: Academy Awards '65: Best Foreign Language Film, Best Song ("I Will Wait for You"), Best Story & Screenplay, Best Original Score. *FXL, APD, LIV*

Un Air de Famille 🎬🎬 1996
Comedy, adapted from a play, about a dysfunctional family. They're meeting at the family's rundown bar to celebrate the birthday of son Philippe's (Yordanoff) silly wife, Yolande (Frot). The bar is run by his brother Henri (Bacri), whose wife calls to say she's left him, while their tactless mother (Maurier) frets over their sister, Betty (Jaoui), who's 30 and still single. What no one knows is that Betty has been secretly seeing Denis (Darroussin), the bartender, whom everyone thinks is simple but is actually the only one with any clue to the family's hypocrisy. French with subtitles. **107m/C VHS.** FR Jean-Pierre Bacri, Agnes Jaoui, Jean-Pierre Darroussin, Catherine Frot, Claire Maurier, Wladimir Yordanoff; **D:** Cedric Klapisch; **W:** Jean-Pierre Bacri, Agnes Jaoui, Cedric Klapisch; **C:** Benoit Delhomme. Nominations: Cesar Awards '97: Best Director (Klapisch), Best Film. *NYR*

Un Chien Andalou 🎬🎬🎬🎬 1928
Masterful surrealist short features a host of classic sequences, including a razor across an eye, a severed hand lying in the street, ants crawling from a hole in a man's hand, priests, dead horses, and a piano dragged across a room. A classic. Score features both Wagner and tango. **20m/B VHS, Beta.** FR Pierre Batcheff, Simone Mareuil, Jaime Miravilles; **D:** Luis Bunuel, Salvador Dali. *HHT, GVV, APD*

Un Coeur en Hiver 🎬🎬½ A Heart in Winter 1993
An anti-romance romantic drama where passion is frozen and real emotion is reserved for the inanimate. Serious Stephane (Auteuil) is a master craftsman at repairing violins; his partner Maxime (Dussollier) runs the business side and deals with the musicians, including beautiful violinist Camille (Beart) with whom he has fallen in love. Camille is single-mindedly fixated on her career and she recognizes a kindred spirit in Stephane but their calculated emotional seduction causes problems for all. Can be frustrating since the smooth surface of the characters is rarely cracked. In French with English titles. **100m/C VHS, LV.** FR Emmanuelle Beart, Daniel Auteuil, Andre Dussollier, Elisabeth Bourgine, Brigitte Catillon, Maurice Garrel, Miriam Boyer; **D:** Claude Sautet; **W:** Yves Ulmann, Jacques Fieschi, Jerome Tonnerre. Cesar Awards '93: Best Director (Sautet), Best Supporting Actor (Dussollier); Nominations: British Academy Awards '93: Best Foreign Film. *REP*

Un Singe en Hiver 🎬🎬½ *A Monkey in Winter; It's Hot in Hell* 1962 A young wanderer (Belmondo) befriends a crusty old alcoholic (Gabin) who has kept his vow to abstain since his village survived the German bombing of WWII. Moving tale of regret and the passage of time. In French with English subtitles. 105m/B VHS, Beta. Jean-Paul Belmondo, Jean Gabin, Suzanne Flon, Paul Frankeur; **D:** Henri Verneuil. *BAR*

The Unapproachable 🎬🎬½ 1982 A rendition of the Polish director's two one-act plays concerning a reclusive aging stage star being manipulated by her hangers-on. 92m/C VHS, Beta. PL Leslie Caron, Daniel Webb, Leslie Malton; **D:** Krzysztof Zanussi. *MGM*

The Unbearable Lightness of Being 🎬🎬🎬½ 1988 (R) Tomas (Day Lewis), a young Czech doctor in the late 1960s, leads a sexually and emotionally carefree existence with a number of women, including provocative artist Olin. When he meets the fragile Binoche, he may be falling in love for the first time. On the eve of the 1968 Russian invasion of Czechoslovakia the two flee to Switzerland, but Binoche can't reconcile herself to exile and returns, followed by the reluctant Tomas who has lost his position because of his new-found political idealism. They lead an increasingly simple life, drawn ever closer together. The haunting ending caps off superb performances. Based on the novel by Milan Kundera. 172m/C VHS, Beta, LV, Closed Caption. Daniel Day-Lewis, Juliette Binoche, Lena Olin, Derek De Lint, Erland Josephson, Pavel Landovsky, Donald Moffat, Daniel Olbrychski, Stellan Skarsgard, Tomek Bork, Bruce Myers, Pavel Slaby, Pascale Kalensky, Jacques Ciron, Anne Lonnberg, Laszlo Szabo, Vladimir Valenta, Clovis Cornillac, Leon Lissek, Consuelo de Havilland; **D:** Philip Kaufman; **W:** Jean-Claude Carriere, Philip Kaufman; **C:** Sven Nykvist; **M:** Mark Adler, Ernie Fosselius, Leos Janacek. British Academy Awards '88: Best Adapted Screenplay; Independent Spirit Awards '89: Best Cinematography; National Society of Film Critics Awards '88: Best Director (Kaufman), Best Film; Nominations: Academy Awards '88: Best Adapted Screenplay, Best Cinematography. *ORI*

The Unbeaten 28 🎬 198? A group of kung fu masters is forced to fight for their lives against evil criminals. 90m/C VHS, Beta. Lisa Chiao, Meng Fei, Lung Sikar; **D:** Joseph Kuo. *MPI*

The Unbelievable Truth 🎬🎬½ 1990 (R) Ex-con Robocop-to-be Burke meets armageddon-obsessed model and sparks fly until bizarre murder occurs. Quirky black comedy shot in less than two weeks.**CW:** Adult situations; language, mild violence, and sexual situations. 100m/C VHS, LV. Adrienne Shelly, Robert John Burke, Christopher Cooke, Julia Mueller, Julia McNeal, Mark Bailey, Gary Sauer, Kathrine Mayfield; **D:** Hal Hartley; **W:** Hal Hartley; **M:** Jim Coleman. *THV*

The Unborn 🎬½ 1991 (R) An infertile wife gets inseminated at unorthodox clinic. But once pregnant she suspects that her unborn baby is a monstrous being. Tasteless B-movie with an A-performance from Adams; if the rest had been up to her standard this could have been another "Stepford Wives." Instead it cops out with cheap gore.**CW:** Some language, violence and gore, and sensuality. 85m/C VHS, LV. Brooke Adams, Jeff Hayenga, James Karen, K. Callan, Jane Cameron; **D:** Rodman Flender. *COL*

The Unborn 2 🎬 1994 (R) Greene's blood-craving baby thinks nothing of feasting off the babysitter until a gun-wielding avenger comes to the rescue. Some notably gross scenes.**CW:** Some language and violence and gore. 84m/C VHS, LV. Michelle Greene, Scott Valentine, Robin Curtis; **D:** Rick Jacobson. *NHO*

The Unbreakable Alibi 🎬🎬 1983 A wealthy young man asks Tommy and Tuppence Beresford to help him prove that one of two alibis an Australian journalist created is false. Based on the mysteries by Agatha Christie. Made for television. 51m/C VHS, Beta. GB Francesca Annis, James Warwick. *TPV*

Uncaged 🎬 *Angel in Red* 1991 (R) Five beautiful young prostitutes hit Sunset Strip, each of them dreaming of a better life. When a crazy pimp brutally murders one of their friends, they set out to avenge that girl, and her broken dreams.**CW:** Strong sensuality, strong violence, and strong language. 78m/C VHS, LV. Leslie Bega, Jeffrey Dean Morgan, Pamella O'Pella, Gregory Millar, Henry Brown, Jason Oliver, Elena Sahagun; **D:** William Duprey; **W:** Robert Alden, Joan Freeman, Catherine Cyran. *COL*

The Uncanny WOOF! 1978 Horror anthology of three tales concerned with feline attempts to control the world. Waste of good cast and cats on silly stories. Not released in the U.S. 85m/C VHS, Beta. GB Peter Cushing, Ray Milland, Samantha Eggar, Donald Pleasence; **D:** Denis Heroux. *MED*

Uncensored 🎬½ 1985 This fast-paced comedy special features dozens of hilarious skits and sketches. 60m/C VHS, Beta. Murray Langston, Cassandra Peterson, John Paragon, Ben Powers. *NO*

Uncertain Glory 🎬🎬 1944 Errol plays a French thief who's willing to pretend to be a saboteur and die for his country. Based on a story by Joe May and Laszlo Vadnay. 102m/B VHS, Beta. Errol Flynn, Paul Lukas, Jean Sullivan, Lucile Watson, Faye Emerson, James Flavin, Douglass Dumbrille, Dennis Hoey, Sheldon Leonard; **D:** Raoul Walsh; **W:** Laszlo Vadnay, Max Brand. *MGM*

The Unchastened Woman 🎬🎬 1925 A married couple is torn apart by infidelity despite their impending parenthood, and wife Bara heads overseas to run wild and have the baby. She returns with a foreign flame, whom she dumps when erstwhile husband finds fatherly feelings in his heart. One of Bara's last films. 52m/B VHS, Beta. Theda Bara, Wyndham Standing, Dale Fuller, John Miljan; **D:** James Young. *GPV, FCT*

Uncivilized 🎬🎬 1994 Young couple, on a vacation in the mountains, run into a gang of drug runners who don't want their whereabouts revealed. So, the duo have to play a deadly game of hide-and-seek to survive. 90m/C VHS. Martin Kove, Rick Aiello. *SWI*

Uncle Buck 🎬🎬🎬 1989 (PG) When Mom and Dad have to go away suddenly, the only babysitter they can find is good ol' Uncle Buck, a lovable lout who spends much of his time smoking cigars, trying to make up with his girlfriend, and enforcing the teenage daughter's chastity. More intelligent than the average slob/teen comedy with a heart, due in large part to Candy's dandy performance. Memorable pancake scene. 100m/C VHS, Beta, LV. John Candy, Amy Madigan, Jean Kelly, Macaulay Culkin, Jay Underwood, Gaby Hoffman, Laurie Metcalf, Elaine Bromka, Garrett M. Brown; **D:** John Hughes; **W:** John Hughes; **C:** Ralf Bode; **M:** Ira Newborn. *USH*

Uncle Moses 🎬🎬½ 1932 The clash of old-world values and new-world culture in a story of East European Jewish immigrants transplanted to turn of the century New York's Lower East Side. Patriarch Uncle Moses struggles to keep traditional family values as romantic difficulties and labor union struggles intrude. Based on the novel by Sholem Asch. In Yiddish with English subtitles. 87m/B VHS. Maurice Schwartz, Rubin Goldberg, Judith Abarbanel, Zvee Scooler; **D:** Sidney Goldin, Aubrey Scotto. *ERG, NCJ*

Uncle Tom's Cabin 🎬🎬 1914 Satisfying version of Harriet Beecher Stowe's tale from the view of a founder of the underground railroad. Lucas was the first black actor to garner a lead role. 54m/C VHS, Beta. Mary Eline, Irving Cummings, Sam Lucas; **D:** William Robert Daly. *GPV, FCT, DVT*

Uncle Tom's Cabin 🎬½ *Onkel Toms Hutte; La Case de L'Oncle Tom; Cento Dollari D'Odio; Cica Tomina Koliba* 1969 (G) Ambitious adaptation of Harriet Beecher Stowe's stirring book about the Southern slavery and the famous underground railroad devised to aid those most determined to reach freedom. The film has the habit of drifting away from the facts. Though set in Kentucky, the picture was filmed in Yugoslavia with an international cast. 120m/C VHS, Beta. FR IT YU GE Herbert Lom, John Kitzmiller, O.W. Fischer, Eleanora Rossi-Drago, Mylene Demongeot, Juliette Greco; **D:** Geza von Radvanyi; **V:** Ella Fitzgerald. *XVC, AFR*

Uncle Tom's Cabin 🎬🎬½ 1987 The first American sound version of this film. Excellent cast and interestingly adapted script are perfect for a message that is still socially relevant today. Based on the novel by Harriet Beecher Stowe. Made for television. 110m/C VHS. Avery Brooks, Kate Burton, Bruce Dern, Paula Kelly, Phylicia Rashad, Kathryn Walker, Edward Woodward, Frank Converse, George Coe, Albert Hall; **D:** Stan Lathan. *FCT, WOV*

Uncle Was a Vampire 🎬🎬 1959 Lee stars as Count Dracula in this vampire story. ?m/C VHS. Christopher Lee, Kay Fisher. *SNC*

Uncommon Valor 🎬🎬½ 1983 (R) After useless appeals to the government for information on his son listed as "missing in action" in Vietnam, Colonel Rhodes takes matters into his own hands. Hackman is solid and believable as always, surrounded with good cast in generally well-paced film. 105m/C VHS, Beta, LV, 8mm, Closed Caption. Gene Hackman, Fred Ward, Reb Brown, Randall "Tex" Cobb, Robert Stack, Patrick Swayze, Harold Sylvester, Tim Thomerson; **D:** Ted Kotcheff; **C:** Stephen Burum; **M:** James Horner. *PAR*

Unconquered 🎬🎬½ 1947 Silly epic about America finds indentured servant Abby (Goddard), meeting Virginia militia man Christopher Holden (Cooper). He nobly buys her contract and frees her but scurvy trader Martin Garth (da Silva) manages to get Abby working in his saloon. Garth also illegally sells guns to the local Seneca Indian tribe and persuades their chief, Guyasuta (Karloff), to attack the colonists. Cooper has to save rescuing Goodard throughout the movie, as well as battling da Silva and helping the settlers fight Indians. Based on the novel "The Judas Tree" by Neil H. Swanson. 147m/C VHS, Closed Caption. Gary Cooper, Paulette Goddard, Howard da Silva, Boris Karloff, Cecil Kellaway, Ward Bond, Katherine DeMille, Henry Wilcoxon, Sir C. Aubrey Smith, Victor Varconi, Virginia Grey, Mike Mazurki, Porter Hall; **D:** Cecil B. DeMille; **W:** Charles Bennett, Jesse Lasky Jr., Frederic M. Frank; **C:** Ray Rennahan; **M:** Victor Young. *USH*

The Undead 🎬🎬 1957 A prostitute is accidentally sent back to the Middle Ages as the result of a scientific experiment and finds herself condemned to die for witchcraft. Early Corman script filled with convoluted storylines, laughable characters, violence, and heaving bosoms. 75m/B VHS. Pamela Duncan, Richard Garland, Allison Hayes, Mel Welles, Billy Barty; **D:** Roger Corman. *NOS, AIP, MLB*

Undeclared War 🎬🎬 1991 (R) Suspenseful espionage thriller that takes you behind the scenes of an international terrorist plot, which has been cleverly disguised as a bloody global revolution. Intense action heightened by conflicts between worldwide intelligence networks, the news media and terrorist organizations.**CW:** Strong action violence. 103m/C VHS, LV, Closed Caption. Vernon Wells, David Hedison, Olivia Hussey, Peter Lapis; **D:** Ringo Lam. *IMP*

Undefeatable 🎬½ 1994 (R) Rothrock is out to avenge the murder of her sister at the hands of a serial killer, who, coincidentally, happens to be a martial arts expert. You watch for Cynthia to kick butt not for plot anyway.**CW:** Violence, nudity, language. 88m/C VHS. Cynthia Rothrock, Don Niam, John Miller, Donna Jason; **D:** Godfrey Hall. *FXV*

The Undefeated 🎬🎬 1969 (G) A Confederate and Yankee find they must team up on the Rio Grande. They attempt to build new lives in the Spanish held Mexico territory, but are caught in the battle for Mexican independence. Standard fare made palatable this way by Wayne and Hudson. 119m/C VHS, Beta, LV, Closed Caption. John Wayne, Rock Hudson, Lee Meriwether, Merlin Olsen, Bruce Cabot, Ben Johnson, Jan-Michael Vincent, Harry Carey Jr., Antonio Aguilar, Roman Gabriel; **D:** Andrew V. McLaglen; **C:** William Clothier. *FOX*

Under California Stars 🖤🖤 *Under California Skies* 1948 Shady gang making a living rounding up wild horses decides they can make more money by capturing Rogers' horse, Trigger. 71m/C **VHS, Beta.** Roy Rogers, Andy Devine, Jane Frazee, The Pioneers; **D:** William Witney. NOS, VYY, DVT

Under Capricorn 🖤🖤½ 1949 Bergman is an Irish lass who follows her convict husband Cotten out to 1830s Australia where he makes a fortune. She turns to drink, perhaps because of his neglect, and has her position usurped by a housekeeper with designs on her husband. When Bergman's cousin (Wilding) arrives, Cotten may have cause for his violent jealousy. There's a plot twist involving old family skeletons, but this is definitely lesser Hitchcock. Adapted from the Helen Simpson novel. Remade in 1982. 117m/C **VHS, Beta, LV. GB** Ingrid Bergman, Joseph Cotten, Michael Wilding, Margaret Leighton, Jack Watling, Cecil Parker, Denis O'Dea; **D:** Alfred Hitchcock; **C:** Jack Cardiff. VES

Under Capricorn 🖤🖤 1982 An Australian remake of the 1949 Hitchcock film about family secrets, an unhappy marriage, and violence set in 1830's Australia. 120m/C **VHS, Beta. AU** Lisa Harrow, John Hallam, Peter Cousens, Julia Blake, Catherine Lynch; **D:** Rod Hardy. PSM

Under Colorado Skies 🖤½ 1947 Medical student Hale is accused of robbery and escapes the law to clear his name. 65m/C **VHS, Closed Caption.** Monte Hale, Adrian Booth, Paul Hurst, Tom London; **D:** R.G. Springsteen; **W:** Louise Rousseau; **C:** Alfred S. Keller. REP

Under Fire 🖤🖤🖤½ 1983 (R) Three foreign correspondents, old friends from the past working together, find themselves in Managua, witnessing the 1979 Nicaraguan revolution. In a job requiring objectivity, but a situation requiring taking sides, they battle with their ethics to do the job right. Fine performances, including Camp as a mercenary. Interesting view of American media and its political necessities. 128m/C **VHS, Beta, LV.** Gene Hackman, Nick Nolte, Joanna Cassidy, Ed Harris, Richard Masur, Hamilton Camp, Jean-Louis Trintignant; **D:** Roger Spottiswoode; **W:** Ron Shelton, Clayton Frohman; **M:** Jerry Goldsmith. Nominations: Academy Awards '83: Best Original Score. VES

Under Investigation 🖤🖤½ 1993 (R) Burned out cop Hamlin is after a crazed killer. His cool lover Pacula turns out to be the prime suspect. Who's deceiving who?**CW:** Murders and sex scenes. 94m/C **VHS.** Harry Hamlin, Joanna Pacula, Ed Lauter, Richard Beymer, Lydie Denier; **D:** Kevin Meyer; **W:** Kevin Meyer. NLC

Under Milk Wood 🖤🖤½ 1973 (PG) An adaptation of the Dylan Thomas play about the lives of the residents of a village in Wales. Burton and O'Toole are wonderful in this uneven, but sometimes engrossing film. 90m/C **VHS, Beta. GB** Richard Burton, Elizabeth Taylor, Peter O'Toole, Glynis Johns, Vivien Merchant; **D:** Andrew Sinclair. FOX

Under Montana Skies 🖤½ 1930 An early talkie western features music and comedy in abundance, relegating the action to second place. A singing cowboy protects a travelling burlesque show from evildoers. 55m/B **VHS, Beta.** Kenneth Harlan, Dorothy Gulliver, Lafe McKee, Ethel Wales, Slim Summerville; **D:** Richard Thorpe. GPV

Under Nevada Skies 🖤🖤½ 1946 Fairly good matinee-era western centers on a missing map to a uranium deposit, climaxing with Rogers heading a posse of Indian allies to the rescue. The Sons of the Pioneers contribute songs. 69m/B **VHS.** Roy Rogers, George "Gabby" Hayes, Dale Evans, Douglass Dumbrille, Tristram Coffin, Rudolph Anders, Iron Eyes Cody; **D:** Frank McDonald. NOS, HEG

Under Satan's Sun 🖤🖤🖤 *Under the Sun of Satan; Sous le Soleil de Satan* 1987 A rural priest is tortured by what he sees as his sins and failings to his parishioners. He is further tempted from the straight path by a beautiful murderess, a worldly priest, and, perhaps by Satan in disguise. Stylized film is not easily accessible, but Depardieu's performance is worth the effort. Based on the Georges Bernanos book "Diary of a Country Priest." In French with English subtitles. 97m/C **VHS. FR** Gerard Depardieu, Sandrine Bonnaire, Yann Dedet, Alain Artur, Maurice Pialat; **D:** Maurice Pialat; **W:** Maurice Pialat. Cannes Film Festival '87: Best Film. NYF, FCT, CVC

Under Siege 🖤🖤 1992 (R) The USS Missouri becomes the battleground for good-guy-with-a-secret-past Seagal. He's up against the deranged Jones, as an ex-Special Forces leader, and Busey, a corrupt naval officer looking to steal the battleship's nuclear arsenal. May be predictable (especially the graphic violence) but the action is fast, the villains swaggering, and Seagal efficient at dispatching the enemy. Work for "Die Hard 3" was reportedly scrapped after Warner announced this film because DH's John McClane was supposed to save the passengers of a boat from terrorists. Sound familiar?**CW:** Language, strong violence, and strong sensuality. 100m/C **VHS, Beta, LV, 8mm, Closed Caption.** Steven Seagal, Tommy Lee Jones, Gary Busey, Patrick O'Neal, Erika Eleniak; **D:** Andrew Davis; **W:** J.F. Lawton; **M:** Gary Chang. Nominations: Academy Awards '92: Best Sound, Best Sound Effects Editing. WAR

Under Siege 2: Dark Territory 🖤🖤 1995 (R) Kicking terrorists' butts and slinging hash have worn out ex-Navy SEAL and gourmet chef Casey Ryback (Seagal), so he takes a little vacation to the Rocky Mountains. By coincidence, the train he boards is command central for psychotic computer expert Dane's (Bogosian) scheme to control the world's deadliest satellite. Pretty familiar territory for Seagal, who's acting technique consists of "look mad and hurt poeple." Bigger budget means bigger, and more frequent, explosions. Bogosian takes over the Jones/Busey role of evil villain-talented actor.**CW:** Strong violence and language. 100m/C **VHS, LV, Closed Caption.** Steven Seagal, Eric Bogosian, Katherine Heigl, Morris Chestnut, Everett McGill, Andy Romano, Nick Mancuso, Brenda Bakke; **D:** Geoff Murphy; **W:** Richard Hatem; **C:** Robbie Greenberg; **M:** Basil Poledouris. WAR

Under Suspicion 🖤🖤½ 1992 (R) Christmas 1959 in Brighton finds seedy private eye Tony Aaron and his wife faking adultery cases for those desperate to get around England's strict divorce laws. Sordid tale takes a turn when Tony bursts in to snap incriminating photos and finds both his wife and their client, a famous artist, murdered. Dark who-dunnit has some interesting twists that could have made it exceptional rather than the conventional melodrama it turned out to be. Neeson is very good as the charmingly sleazy Tony but nobody else stands out, except the unfortunately miscast San Giacomo. Theatrical feature debut for director Moore. 99m/C **VHS, LV, Closed Caption. GB** Liam Neeson, Laura San Giacomo, Alphonsia Emmanuel, Kenneth Cranham, Maggie O'Neill, Martin Grace, Stephen Moore; **D:** Simon Moore; **W:** Simon Moore; **M:** Christopher Gunning. COL

Under the Biltmore Clock 🖤🖤 1985 F. Scott Fitzgerald's story, "Myra Meets His Family," is the basis for this American Playhouse installment for PBS television. It is outwit or be outwitted in this tale of a fortune-hunting '20s flapper who is outsmarted by the man she has set her sights on when he hires actors to play his eccentric "family." 70m/C **VHS, Beta, LV, 8mm.** Sean Young, Lenny Von Dohlen, Barnard Hughes; **D:** Neal Miller. NLC

Under the Boardwalk 🖤½ 1989 (R) A pair of star-crossed teenage lovers struggle through familial and societal differences in 1980s California. 102m/C **VHS, Beta, LV.** Keith Coogan, Danielle von Zerneck, Richard Joseph Paul, Hunter von Leer, Tracey Walter, Roxana Zal, Dick Miller, Sonny Bono, Corky Carroll; **D:** Fritz Kiersch; **C:** Don Burgess. VTR, NWV

Under the Cherry Moon 🖤½ 1986 (PG-13) Prince portrays a fictional musician of the 1940s who travels to the French Riviera, seeking love and money. Songs include "Under the Cherry Moon," "Kiss," "Anotherloverholeinyourhead," "Sometimes It Snows in April," and "Mountains." A vanity flick down to its being filmed in black and white. 100m/B **VHS, Beta, LV, Closed Caption.** Prince, Jerome Benton, Francesca Annis, Kristin Scott Thomas; **D:** Prince; **C:** Michael Ballhaus. Golden Raspberry Awards '86: Worst Picture, Worst Actor (Prince), Worst Supporting Actor (Benton), Worst Director (Prince), Worst Song ("Love or Money"). MVD, WAR, FCT

Under the Domim Tree 🖤🖤½ *Etz Hadomim Tafus* 1995 Sequel to "The Summer of Aviya," set in 1953, finds 15-year-old Aviya (Cohen) living in an Israeli community with other teenagers who were scarred by the Holocaust. As they get to know one another, each must deal with their own tormented memories. Based on a memoir by Almagor, who plays Aviya's institutionalized mother. Hebrew with subtitles. 102m/C **VHS, LV. IS** Kaipo Cohen, Julino Mer, Ohad Knoller, Orli Perl, Riki Blich, Gila Almagor; **D:** Eli Cohen; **W:** Gila Almagor, Eyal Sher; **C:** David Gurfinkel; **M:** Benny Nagari. FXL

Under the Earth 🖤🖤🖤 *Debajo del Mundo* 1986 (R) An Argentine-Czech co-production, depicting the plight of a family of Polish Jews forced to live underground for two years to avoid the Nazis. Harrowing and critically well-received. In Spanish with subtitles. 100m/C **VHS, Beta, LV. SP** Victor Laplace; **D:** Beda Ocampo Feijoo, Juan Bautista Stagnaro. NWV, SWC

Under the Gun 🖤🖤 1988 (R) A cop recruits a lawyer to help him find the man who murdered his brother. Action drives this formulaic plot along. 89m/C **VHS, LV.** Sam Jones, Vanessa Williams, John Russell, Michael Halsey; **D:** James Sbardellati; **W:** James Sbardellati, Almer John Davis. IME

Under the Gun 🖤½ 1995 (R) Debt-ridden club owner Frank Torrance (Norton) is in trouble with everyone he knows. But he can't clear his debts just by quitting the business, so he decides to fight back.**CW:** Strong violence, language and some drug content. 90m/C **VHS, LV.** Richard Norton, Kathy Long; **D:** Matthew George. TRI

Under the Hula Moon 🖤🖤½ 1995 (R) Buzzard (Baldwin) and Betty (Lloyd) Wall are living unhappily in the charmless desert town of Cactus Gulch. Their trailer home is festooned in faux-Hawaiian finery and the duo dream of the day they can actually move to their island paradise. Buzz's invented an ultraprotective sunscreen that may be their ticket out, if his prison-escapee, trigger-happy half-brother Turk (Penn), who's also kidnapped Betty, doesn't get them all killed first. Charming lead performances—very lightweight story.**CW:** Violence, language, some sexuality. 94m/C **VHS.** Stephen Baldwin, Emily Lloyd, Christopher Penn, Musetta Vander, Edie McClurg, Pruitt Taylor Vince, Bill Campbell, Carel Struycken; **D:** Jeff Celentano; **W:** Jeff Celentano; **C:** Phil Parmet. TTC

Under the Rainbow woof! 1981 (PG) Comic situations encountered by a talent scout and a secret service agent in a hotel filled with Munchkins during filming of "The Wizard of Oz." Features midgets, spies, and a prevailing lack of taste. International intrigue adds to the strange attempt at humor. 97m/C **VHS, Beta.** Chevy Chase, Carrie Fisher, Eve Arden, Joseph Maher, Robert Donner, Mako, Pat McCormick, Billy Barty, Zelda Rubinstein; **D:** Steve Rash; **W:** Pat McCormick, Martin Smith, Harry Hurwitz, Fred Bauer, Pat Bradley. WAR

Under the Red Robe 🖤🖤½ 1936 A French soldier of fortune is trapped into aiding Cardinal Richelieu in his persecution of the Huguenots and winds up falling in love with the sister of his intended victim. Good costume adventure-drama. Sjostrom's last film as a director. 82m/B **VHS, Beta. GB** Raymond Massey, Conrad Veidt, Annabella, Romney Brent; **D:** Victor Sjostrom; **C:** James Wong Howe. NOS, HHT, WFV

Under the Roofs of Paris 🖤🖤🖤½ *Sous les Toits de Paris* 1929 An early French sound film about the lives of young Parisian lovers. A gentle, highly acclaimed melodrama. In French with English subtitles. 95m/B **VHS, Beta. FR** Albert

Prejean, Pola Illery, Gaston Modot; **D:** Rene Clair; **C:** Georges Perinal. National Board of Review Awards '31: 5 Best Foreign Films of the Year. *VYY, NOS, CAB*

Under the Volcano 🎬🎬🎬 1984 An alco-holic British ex-consul finds his life further deterio-rating during the Mexican Day of the Dead in 1939. His half-brother and ex-wife try to save him from himself, but their affair sends him ever-deep-er into his personal hell. Finney's performance is pathetic and haunting. Adapted from the novel by Malcolm Lowry. **112m/C VHS, Beta, LV.** Albert Finney, Jacqueline Bisset, Anthony Andrews, Katy Jurado; **D:** John Huston; **M:** John Beal, Alex North. Los Angeles Film Critics Association Awards '84: Best Actor (Finney); Nominations: Academy Awards '84: Best Actor (Finney), Best Original Score. *USH*

Under the Yum-Yum Tree 🎬🎬½ 1963 When womanizing landlord Hogan's (Lem-mon) ex-fiance Irene (Adams) moves out, he doesn't pine. Instead he plots to romance her niece Robin (Lynley) who's just moved into his building. But his romantic shenanigans are thwarted by the presence of fiance David (Jones), who's living platonically with Robin to test their compatibility. Silly sex comedy based on the play by Roman. **110m/C VHS.** Jack Lemmon, Carol Lynley, Dean Jones, Edie Adams, Imogene Coca, Paul Lynde, Rob-ert Lansing, Bill Bixby; **D:** David Swift; **W:** David Swift, Law-rence Roman; **C:** Joseph Biroc; **M:** Frank De Vol. *COL*

Under Western Stars 🎬 1945 Roy's first starring vehicle. A newly elected congressman goes to Washington and fights battles for his con-stituents, caught in the middle of the Dust Bowl and drought. **83m/B VHS, Beta.** Roy Rogers, Smiley Burnette; **D:** Jean Yarbrough. *NOS, DVT, VCN*

The Underachievers 🎬 1988 (R) A night school is the scene for typical libido-oriented gags, but this time instead of teenagers it's adult education providing the plot. Only a few real laughs in this one. **90m/C VHS, Beta.** Barbara Carrera, Edward Albert, Michael Pataki, Vic Tayback, Garrett Morris, Susan Tyrrell; **D:** Jackie Kong. *LIV, VES*

Undercover 🎬½ 1987 (R) Routine cop ac-tion film in which an eastern detective finds him-self undercover in a southern high school in search of a cop-murdering drug ring. Plagued with cliches. Director Stockwell is appropriately better known for his role as "Cougar" in "Top Gun." **92m/ C VHS, Closed Caption.** David Neidorf, Jennifer Jason Leigh, Barry Corbin, David Harris, Kathleen Wilhoite; **D:** John Stockwell; **M:** Bruce Smeaton. *WAR*

Undercover 🎬½ 1994 (R) Police detective (and hot babe) Cindy Hanen (Massey) gets an undercover assignment to capture a murderer who's targeted an upscale brothel. It's an excuse for interesting undies (or less). **CW:** Sexuality, nu-dity. **93m/C VHS.** Athena Massey, Tom Tayback, Anthony Guidera, Rena Riffel, Jeffrey Dean Morgan, Meg Foster; **D:** Alexander Gregory Hippolyte; **W:** Lalo Wolf, Oola Bloome. *APX*

Undercover Blues 🎬🎬½ 1993 (PG-13) Comedy-thriller starring Turner and Quaid as married spies Jane and Jeff Blue, on parental leave from the espionage biz, who are on vaca-tion with their 11-month-old daughter in New Orle-ans. But the holiday is interrupted when they're recruited by their boss to stop an old adversary from selling stolen weapons. The leads play cute together and the baby is adorable but this is strict-ly routine escapism. Stick with "The Thin Man" instead. **CW:** One use of strong language and mock violence. **90m/C VHS, LV, Closed Caption.** Kath-leen Turner, Dennis Quaid, Fiona Shaw, Stanley Tucci, Lar-ry Miller, Obba Babatunde, Park Overall, Tom Arnold, Saul Rubinek, Michelle Schuelke; **D:** Herbert Ross; **W:** Ian Abrams; **M:** David Newman. *MGM*

Undercover Cop 🎬 1994 True story of Sergeant George Aguilar and the high-speed chase that left one dead and the police dealing their revenge on all the offenders. **90m/C VHS.** Dan-ny Trejo, Kevin Anthony Cole; **D:** Martin Greene; **W:** Glenn A. Bruce; **M:** Randall Kent Heddon. *AIP*

Undercover Man 🎬½ 1936 A Wells Fargo agent goes undercover to expose a crooked sher-iff. **57m/B VHS.** Johnny Mack Brown, Suzanne Kaaren, Ted Adams, Lloyd Ingraham, Horace Murphy; **D:** Albert Ray. *NOS, DVT, RXM*

The Underdog 🎬½ 1943 After the bank forecloses, a farm family must move to the city. The family's young son has only his loyal dog to turn to for friendship, but the gallant animal proves his mettle by rounding up a gang of spies plotting some WWII sabotage. Believe it if you dare. **65m/B VHS, Beta, 8mm.** Barton MacLane, Bobby Larson, Jan Wiley; **D:** William Nigh. *VYY*

Undergrads 🎬🎬🎬 1985 A bright genera-tional Disney comedy with Carney, estranged from his stick-in-the-mud son, deciding to attend college with his free-thinking grandson. Made for television. **102m/C VHS, Beta.** Art Carney, Chris Makep-eace, Jackie Burroughs, Len Birman; **D:** Steven Hilliard Stern. *DIS*

Underground 🎬🎬🎬 *Once Upon a Time There Was a Country* 1995 Exhausting black comedy, set in Yugoslavia from 1941 to 1992, follows the adven-tures of Marko (Manojlovic) and his best friend Blacky (Ristovski). They run a black-market oper-ation and lead Communist Party meetings while trying to avoid the Gestapo in WWII Belgrade. Hiding out in a cellar, where refugees have put together a munitions factory, the treacherous Marko manages to convince everyone that the war is still going on—20 years later in fact—until the truth unexpectedly comes out (thanks to a pet monkey). The final section sees Marko unscrupu-lously dealing arms and drugs amidst the breakup of Yugoslavia in a civil war and the violence on all sides. **192m/C VHS.** FR GE HU Miki Manojlovic, Lazar Ristovski, Mirjana Jokovic, Slavko Stimac, Ernst Stotzner, Srdan Todorovic, Mirjana Karanovic; **Cameos:** Emir Kustu-rica; **D:** Emir Kusturica; **W:** Emir Kusturica, Dusan Kovacev-ic; **C:** Vilko Filac; **M:** Goran Bregovic. Cannes Film Festival '95: Best Film. *NYR*

Underground Aces woof! 1980 (PG) A group of parking lot attendants transforms a sheik into an attendant in order to help him meet the girl of his dreams. A bad "Car Wash" spinoff. **93m/C VHS, Beta.** Dirk Benedict, Melanie Griffith, Frank Gorshin, Jerry Orbach, Robert Hegyes, Audrey Landers; **D:** Robert Butler; **W:** Jim Carabatsos. *LIV, VES*

Underground Rustlers 🎬 1941 The Range Busters are commissioned by the govern-ment to stop unscrupulous gold-marketeers. **58m/ B VHS, Beta.** Ray Corrigan, Max Terhune, John "Dusty" King; **D:** S. Roy Luby. *VDM*

Underground Terror 🎬 1988 A gang of murderers, organized by a psychopath, rampages through the New York City subway system. One cop enthusiastically tries to snuff out each one. **91m/C VHS.** Doc Dougherty, Lenny Y. Loftin; **D:** James McCalmont. *NO*

Underground U.S.A. 🎬 1984 Street hust-ler picks up a has-been underground movie star at the chic New York new wave disco, The Mudd Club. **85m/C VHS, Beta.** Patti Astor, Eric Mitchell; **D:** Eric Mitchell. *NO*

The Underneath 🎬🎬🎬 1995 (R) Recover-ing gambling addict Michael Chambers (Gallagh-er) returns home after skipping out on his debts and his wife Rachel (sultry newcomer Elliott) sev-eral years before. Old passions ignite in more ways than one, and Michael's lust for his ex, now married to a hot-tempered hoodlum, leads him to risk it all for a final big score. Moody and tense study of the complexities of emotion is capped by smart lead performances but style wins out over substance and the finale definitely leaves more questions than answers. Remake of the 1949 film noir classic "Criss Cross," based on Don Tracy's novel of the same name. **CW:** Some violence, lan-guage and a discreet sex scene. **99m/C VHS.** Shel-ley Duvall, Richard Linklater, Dennis Hill, Peter Gallagher, Alison Elliott, William Fichtner, Elisabeth Shue, Adam Trese, Paul Dooley, Joe Don Baker, Anjanette Comer, Har-

ry Goaz, Vincent Gaskins, Tony Perenski, Helen Cates, John Martin, David Jensen, Joseph Chrest; **D:** Steven So-derbergh; **W:** Daniel Fuchs, Sam Lowry; **C:** Elliot Davis; **M:** Cliff Martinez. Nominations: Independent Spirit Awards '96: Best Cinematography. *USH*

Undersea Kingdom 1936 Adventure be-neath the ocean floor. In twelve chapters of thir-teen minutes each; the first chapter runs twenty minutes. Later re-edited into one film, "Sharad of Atlantis." **226m/B VHS, LV.** Ray Corrigan, Lon Chaney Jr.; **D:** B. Reeves Eason. *NOS, SNC, VCN*

Understudy: The Graveyard Shift 2 🎬½ 1988 (R) Vampire survives poorly direct-ed cliche-riddled original to be cast as a vampire cast as a vampire in a horror movie within a horri-ble sequel. **88m/C VHS, Beta, LV.** Wendy Gazelle, Mark Soper, Silvio Oliviero; **D:** Gerard Ciccoritti. *NO*

The Undertaker and His Pals 🎬🎬 1967 Undertaker teams up with diner owners in murder scheme to improve mortician's business and expand restaurateurs' menu. Pretty violent stuff, with some good laughs and a campy flare, but not for every one's palate. **70m/C VHS.** Ray Dan-nis, Brad Fulton, Larrene Ott, Robert Lowery, Sally Frei; **D:** David C. Graham. *MTH*

Undertow 🎬🎬 1995 (R) Drifter Jack Ketch-um (Phillips) loses control of his car in a storm and wakes up in the secluded cabin of paranoid Lyle Yates (Dance) and his terrified wife, Willie (Sara). Since the storm's worse, Jack can't leave—too bad for him that Willie's so darn attrac-tive and Lyle's so crazy. Cable thriller. **CW:** Vio-lence, language and some sexuality. **90m/C VHS, Closed Caption.** Lou Diamond Phillips, Mia Sara, Charles Dance; **D:** Eric Red; **W:** Kathryn Bigelow, Eric Red; **C:** Geza Sinkovics; **M:** John Frizzell. *REP*

Underwater! 🎬🎬 1955 A team of skin div-ers faces danger when they try to retrieve trea-sure from a Spanish galleon. The second film af-ter "The Outlaw" masterminded by Howard Hughes, primarily to show off Russell's figure. **99m/C VHS, Beta, LV.** Jane Russell, Richard Egan, Gilbert Roland, Jayne Mansfield; **D:** John Sturges. *MED, TTC*

Underworld 🎬🎬🎬 1927 Inspired gangster saga finds bank robber Bull Weed (Bancroft) be-friending a genteel bum, known as Rolls Royce (Brook), and taking him into his gang. The bum has brains and soon makes Weed king of the underworld but there's jealousy when Weed's moll Feathers (Brent) falls for Royce. Climactic shootout set a standard for the genre. **85m/B VHS.** George Bancroft, Clive Brook, Evelyn Brent, Larry Semon, Fred Kohler Sr.; **D:** Josef von Sternberg. Academy Awards '28: Best Story. *GPV*

Underworld 🎬🎬 1996 (R) Considering the on-screen talent, this crime comedy/thriller is a disappointment. Ex-wiseguy Johnny Crown (Leary) studied psychotherapy in the joint and, when he's released, decides to put his new knowledge to work on bossman Frank Gavilan (Mantegna), who may be behind the hit on John-ny's old man. Contrived dialogue and story but a sleek-looking production. **CW:** Pervasive strong language and violence, and for sexuality. **95m/C VHS, LV, Closed Caption.** Denis Leary, Joe Mantegna, Annabella Sciorra, Larry Bishop, Abe Vigoda, James Toi-kan, Robert Costanzo; **D:** Roger Christian; **W:** Larry Bishop; **C:** Steve Bernstein; **M:** Anthony Marinelli. *THV*

Underworld Scandal 🎬🎬 1947 An edi-tor attempts to break up a ring of basketball game fixers. **?m/C VHS.** Philip Reed, Hillary Brooke. *SNC*

The Underworld Story 🎬🎬½ 1950 Big city journalist at large moves to smalltown New England after losing job for unethical reporting and uncovers scheme to frame innocent man for murder. Solid performances. **90m/B VHS.** Dan Du-ryea, Herbert Marshall, Gale Storm, Howard da Silva, Mi-chael O'Shea, Mary Anderson, Gar Moore, Melville Cooper, Frieda Inescort, Art Baker, Harry Shannon, Alan Hale Jr., Steve Dunne, Roland Winters; **D:** Cy Endfield. *FOX, FCT*

Underworld, U.S.A. 🎬🎬🎬 1960 A man infiltrates a tough crime syndicate to avenge his father's murder, which winds up with him caught between the mob and the feds. A well-acted and directed look at the criminal underworld. 99m/B **VHS, Beta.** Cliff Robertson, Dolores Dorn, Beatrice Kay, Robert Emhardt, Larry Gates, Paul Dubov; **D:** Samuel Fuller; **W:** Samuel Fuller; **C:** Hal Mohr. COL

The Undying Monster 🎬🎬½ The Hammond Mystery 1942 Upper crusty Brit is werewolf with insatiable appetite. Familiar story with lots of atmosphere and style. Photography by Lucien Ballard. 63m/B **VHS.** James Ellison, Heather Angel, John Howard, Bramwell Fletcher, Heather Thatcher, Aubrey Mather, Halliwell Hobbes, Heather Wilde; **D:** John Brahm. MOV

The Unearthing 🎬 1993 (R) An unwanted pregnancy seems to find a happy solution when a woman decides to marry the heir to a wealthy estate and pass off her child as his. Only the family has some very strange tastes, including a taste for the blood of the unborn. Based on a Filipino vampire legend (!) 83m/C **VHS, LV.** Norman Moses, Tina Ona Paukstelis; **D:** Wyre Martin, Barry Poltermann; **W:** Wyre Martin, Barry Poltermann. PSM

The Unearthly 🎬½ 1957 A mad scientist is trying to achieve immortality through his strange experiments, but all he winds up with is a basement full of mutants. When his two latest about-to-be victims fall in love, the doctor's mutant assistant decides enough is enough and things come to an unpleasant end. Carradine is typecast. Absurd, but fun. 76m/B **VHS, Beta.** John Carradine, Tor Johnson, Allison Hayes, Myron Healey; **D:** Brooke L. Peters. SNC, DVT, MLB

The Unearthly Stranger 🎬🎬½ 1964 Earth scientist marries woman and decides she's from another planet. Not a nineties style gender drama; seems she's part of an invading alien force, but really does love her earth man. Surprisingly good low-budget sci-fi. 75m/B **VHS.** GB John Neville, Gabriella Licudi, Philip Stone, Patrick Newell, Jean Marsh, Warren Mitchell; **D:** John Krish. MOV

Uneasy Terms 🎬 1948 Rennie is a detective investigating the murder of one of his own clients. Evidence points to stepchildren and inheritance money but things may not be as they seem. Written for the screen by Peter Cheyney, adapted from his own novel. 91m/B **VHS, Beta.** GB Michael Rennie, Moira Lister, Faith Brook, Joy Shelton, Patricia Goddard, Barry Jones, Nigel Patrick, Paul Carpenter, Marie Ney, Sydney Tafler, J.H. Roberts, John Robinson; **D:** Vernon Sewell; **W:** Peter Cheyney. SNC

An Unexpected Family 🎬🎬½ 1996 (PG) Barbara Whitney (Channing) is a Manhattan career woman who is unwillingly thrust into the role of surrogate mom when her irresponsible sister, Ruth (Ebersole), dumps her two children at Barbara's door. Along with her friend Sam (Collins), Barbara and the children slowly make a new family but, after a year, Ruth returns, demanding her children back. Predictable made for cable fare is redeemed by good performances from Channing and Ebersole. 93m/C **VHS, Closed Caption.** Stockard Channing, Stephen Collins, Christine Ebersole, Noah Fleiss, Chelsea Russo; **D:** Larry Elikann; **W:** Lee Rose; **C:** Eric Van Haren Noman; **M:** Tom Scott. USH

Unexplained Laughter 🎬🎬 1989 A cynical journalist vacations in Wales with her timid vegetarian friend and stumbles across a mystery in this darkly comic British TV-movie. 85m/C **VHS.** GB Diana Rigg, Elaine Page, Jon Finch. FCT, VCO

Unfaithfully Yours 🎬🎬🎬½ 1948 A conductor suspects his wife is cheating on him and considers his course of action. He imagines punishment scenarios while directing three classical works. Well-acted by all, but particularly by Harrison as the egotistical and jealous husband. Another of Sturges' comedic gems. Remade in 1984. 105m/B **VHS, Beta, LV, Closed Caption.** Rex Harrison, Linda Darnell, Kurt Kreuger, Rudy Vallee, Lionel Stander, Edgar Kennedy; **D:** Preston Sturges; **C:** Victor Milner. FOX

Unfaithfully Yours 🎬🎬 1984 (PG) A symphony conductor suspects his wife of fooling around with a musician; in retaliation, he plots an elaborate scheme to murder her with comic results. No match for the 1948 Preston Sturges film it's based on. 96m/C **VHS, Beta, LV, Closed Caption.** Dudley Moore, Nastassia Kinski, Armand Assante, Albert Brooks, Cassie Yates, Richard Libertini, Richard B. Shull; **D:** Howard Zieff; **W:** Valerie Curtin, Barry Levinson, Robert Klane; **M:** Bill Conti. FOX

Unfinished Business 🎬🎬½ 1989 A 17 year-old girl leads a troubled adolescent life with her divorced parents. She decides running away will ease her problems—not a smart move. Sequel to "Nobody Waved Goodbye." 88m/C **VHS, Beta.** CA Isabelle Mejias, Peter Kastner, Leslie Toth, Peter Spence, Chuck Shamata, Julie Biggs; **D:** Don Owen. JEF

An Unfinished Piece for a Player Piano 🎬🎬🎬½ 1977 A general's widow invites family and friends to a weekend house party in 1910 Russia. Romantic and familial entanglements begin to intrude in a lyrical adaptation of Chekov's play "Platonov." In Russian with English subtitles. 100m/C **VHS, Beta.** RU Alexander Kalyagin, Elena Solovei, Antonina Shuranova, Oleg Tabakov, Yuri Bogatyrev, Nikita Mikhalkov; **D:** Nikita Mikhalkov. FCT, CVC

Unforgettable 🎬🎬 1996 (R) Unfortunately, the film doesn't live up to its title. On-the-edge medical examiner David Krane (Liotta) has barely escaped conviction for his wife's brutal murder. Living under a cloud of suspicion, he turns to university researcher Martha Briggs (Fiorentino, wasted as a nerdy scientist), whose experiments in memory transference lead David to believe he can uncover the killer. But, like a Chinese puzzle box, one discovery only leads to a further complication. Too many, in fact, for the story to stay focused (and the ending is less than satisfying).**CW:** Strong violence, language and nudity. 116m/C **VHS, LV, Closed Caption.** Ray Liotta, Linda Fiorentino, Peter Coyote, Christopher McDonald, Kim Cattrall, David Paymer, Kim Coates, Duncan Fraser, Garwin Sanford; **D:** John Dahl; **W:** Bill Geddie; **C:** Jeffrey Jur; **M:** Christopher Young. MGM

An Unforgettable Summer 🎬🎬½ 1994 The elegant Marie-Therese Dumitriu (Scott Thomas) has married Army officer Petre (Bleont) and tried to focus on maintaining a serene life, following the Communist takeover of Romania. When Petre is transferred to an isolated border town, he and his family are caught between what the Army demands and what is just. The local Bulgarian peasants are accused of attrocities against the soldiers and Petre is ordered to execute a group of them as an example—guilty or not. Set in 1925 and based on the short story "La Salade" by Petru Dumitriu. English, French, and Romanian with subtitles. 82m/C **VHS.** RO Kristin Scott Thomas, Claudiu Bleont, Olga Tudorache, George Constantin; **D:** Lucian Pintilie; **W:** Lucian Pintilie; **C:** Calin Ghibu; **M:** Anton Suteu. NYF

The Unforgiven 🎬🎬🎬 1960 A western family is torn asunder when it is suspected that the eldest daughter is of Indian birth. Film takes place in 1850s' Texas. One of Huston's weakest ventures, but viewed in terms of 1950s' prejudices it has more resonance. Fine acting from all the cast, especially Gish. Watch for the stunning Indian attack scene. 123m/C **VHS, Beta, LV.** Burt Lancaster, Audrey Hepburn, Lillian Gish, Audie Murphy, John Saxon, Charles Bickford, Doug McClure, Joseph Wiseman, Albert Salmi; **D:** John Huston. MGM, BTV

Unforgiven 🎬🎬🎬½ 1992 (R) Will Munny (Eastwood) lives a quiet life with his stepchildren on his failing pig farm, but his desperado past catches up with him when the Schofield Kid invites him to a bounty hunt. Munny reluctantly agrees, mistakenly believing that once the killing is through he can take up his peaceful ways again. Enter sadistic sheriff Little Bill Daggett (Hackman), who doesn't want any gunmen messing up his town. Eastwood uses his own status as a screen legend to full advantage as the aging gunman who realizes too late that his past can never be forgotten. Director Eastwood is also in top form with his well-seasoned cast and myth-defying Old West realism. Surprising critical and box office hit. The laserdisc version is available in letterbox format.**CW:** Language, violence, and sexual scene. 131m/C **VHS, Beta, LV, Closed Caption, DVD.** Clint Eastwood, Gene Hackman, Morgan Freeman, Richard Harris, Jaimz Woolvett, Saul Rubinek, Frances Fisher, Anna Thomson, David Mucci, Rob Campbell, Anthony James; **D:** Clint Eastwood; **W:** David Peoples; **C:** Jack N. Green; **M:** Lennie Niehaus. Academy Awards '92: Best Director (Eastwood), Best Film Editing, Best Picture, Best Supporting Actor (Hackman); British Academy Awards '92: Best Director (Eastwood), Best Film, Best Supporting Actor (Hackman); Directors Guild of America Awards '92: Best Director (Eastwood); Golden Globe Awards '93: Best Director (Eastwood), Best Supporting Actor (Hackman); Los Angeles Film Critics Association Awards '92: Best Actor (Eastwood), Best Director (Eastwood), Best Film, Best Screenplay, Best Supporting Actor (Hackman); New York Film Critics Awards '92: Best Supporting Actor (Hackman); National Society of Film Critics Awards '92: Best Director (Eastwood), Best Film, Best Screenplay, Best Supporting Actor (Hackman); Nominations: Academy Awards '92: Best Actor (Eastwood), Best Art Direction/Set Decoration, Best Cinematography, Best Original Screenplay, Best Sound. WAR, MOV, BTV

The Unholy 🎬½ 1988 (R) A New Orleans priest battles a demon that's killing innocent parishioners. Confusing and heavy-handed. 100m/C **VHS, Beta, LV.** Ben Cross, Hal Holbrook, Trevor Howard, Ned Beatty, William Russ, Jim Carroll; **D:** Camilo Vila; **W:** Philip Yordan; **M:** Roger Bellon. LIV, VES, HHE

Unholy Four 🎬½ 1954 An amnesiac returns home after three years to attempt to find out which of his three fishing buddies left him for dead. Confusing at times, but has some suspenseful moments. British title was "A Stranger Came Home." 80m/B **VHS, Beta, LV.** GB Paulette Goddard, Paul Carpenter, William Sylvester, Patrick Holt, Russell Napier; **D:** Terence Fisher; **W:** Michael Carreras. NO

Unholy Rollers 🎬 Leader of the Pack 1972 (R) Jennings stars as a factory worker who makes it big as a tough, violent roller derby star. Typical "Babes-on-Wheels" film that promises nothing and delivers even less. 88m/C **VHS.** Claudia Jennings, Louis Quinn, Betty Anne Rees, Roberta Collins, Alan Vint, Candice Roman; **D:** Vernon Zimmerman. HBO

The Unholy Three 🎬🎬🎬½ 1925 Ventriloquist Chaney, working with other carnival cohorts, uses his talent to gain entrance to homes which he later robs. Things go awry when two of the gang strike out on their own and the victim is killed. When the wrong man is accused, his girl, one of Chaney's gang, begs Chaney to get him free, which he does by using his vocal talents. Chaney decides being a criminal is just too hard and goes back to his ventriloquism. 70m/B **VHS.** Lon Chaney Sr., Harry Earles, Victor McLaglen, Mae Busch, Matt Moore, Matthew Betz, William Humphreys; **D:** Tod Browning. NO

The Unholy Three 🎬🎬🎬 1930 Chaney remade his silent hit of 1925 for his first and only talking picture (he died before the film was released). The story is essentially the same. Chaney is a ventriloquist who, with his circus friends, work as scam artists and thieves. When an innocent man is accused of their crimes Chaney tries his ventriloquist tricks to come to his aid, only in this version Chaney is exposed as a fraud and is sent to prison. Rumors that Chaney was a mute had him agreeing to appear in a "talkie" and he actually used five different voices for his various roles. 75m/B **VHS, LV.** Lon Chaney Sr., Lila Lee, Elliott Nugent, Harry Earles, John Miljan; **D:** Jack Conway. FCT

Unholy Wife 𝒜½ 1957 A young woman plans to murder her wealthy husband, but her plan goes awry when she accidentally kills someone else. Muddled and heavy-handed, with Steiger chewing scenery. **94m/C VHS, Beta.** Rod Steiger, Diana Dors, Tom Tryon, Marie Windsor, Beulah Bondi; **D:** John Farrow. *HHE*

Unhook the Stars 𝒜𝒜½ 1996 (R) Director Cassavetes does mom Rowlands proud (and she him) with the lead role of widowed Mildred, who discovers there's life after the kids leave the nest. At loose ends, Mildred befriends her wild young neighbor Monica (Tomei), who conveniently needs a babysitter for her solemn six-year-old son, J.J. (Lloyd). Monica also tries to get Mildred to loosen up by taking her to a local joint, where French-Canadian trucker Tommy (Depardieu) knows a good woman when he sees one. Mildred makes some tentative steps towards independence and we get to enjoy the stellar Rowlands once again. **CW:** Strong language. **105m/C VHS, LV, Closed Caption.** Gena Rowlands, Marisa Tomei, Gerard Depardieu, Moira Kelly, Jake Lloyd, David Sherrill; **D:** Nick Cassavetes; **W:** Helen Caldwell, Nick Cassavetes; **C:** Phedon Papamichael; **M:** Steven Hufsteter. Nominations: Screen Actors Guild Award '96: Best Actress (Rowlands), Best Supporting Actress (Tomei). *TOU*

Unicorn 𝒜𝒜 1983 A small boy hears the legend that if one rubs the horn of a Unicorn his wishes will come true. Mistakenly he buys a one-horned goat and sets out to fulfill his dreams. **29m/C VHS, Beta.** *GB* Diana Dors, David Kossoff, Celia Johnson; **D:** Carol Reed. *NLC*

Unidentified Flying Oddball 𝒜𝒜½ 1979 (G) An astronaut and his robotic buddy find their spaceship turning into a time machine that throws them back into Arthurian times and at the mercy of Merlin the magician. Futuristic version of Twain's "A Connecticut Yankee at King Arthur's Court." **92m/C VHS, Beta.** Dennis Dugan, Jim Dale, Ron Moody, Kenneth More, Rodney Bewes; **D:** Russ Mayberry. *DIS*

The Uninvited 𝒜𝒜𝒜 1944 A brother and sister buy a house in England, only to find it is haunted. Doors open and close by themselves, strange scents fill the air, and they hear sobbing during the night. Soon they are visited by a woman with an odd link to the house—her mother is the spirit who haunts the house. Chilling and unforgettable, this is one of the first films to deal seriously with ghosts. **99m/B VHS, LV.** Ray Milland, Ruth Hussey, Donald Crisp, Cornelia Otis Skinner, Gail Russell; **D:** Lewis Allen; **C:** Charles B(ryant) Lang. Nominations: Academy Awards '44: Best Black and White Cinematography. *USH*

The Uninvited woof! 1988 A mutant cat goes berserk onboard a luxury yacht, killing the passengers one by one with big, nasty, pointy teeth. **89m/C VHS, Beta, LV.** George Kennedy, Alex Cord, Clu Gulager, Toni Hudson, Eric Larson, Shari Shattuck, Austin Stoker; **D:** Greydon Clark. *NO*

Uninvited 𝒜𝒜½ 1993 (R) Grady is a mysterious old man who leads eight misfits to the top of a sacred mountain with the promise of finding gold. But the fortune hunters have trespassed on a sacred Indian burial ground and find their nightmares becoming a violent reality. **CW:** Violence and sexuality. **?m/C VHS, Closed Caption.** Jack Elam, Christopher Boyer, Erin Noble, Bari Buckner, Jerry Rector, Zane Paolo, Dennis Gibbs, Ted Haler, Eno Brutto; **D:** Michael Derek Bohusz; **W:** Michael Derek Bohusz. *IMP, IME*

Union City 𝒜𝒜 1981 (R) Deborah "Blondie" Harry's husband gets a little edgy when someone steals the milk. Murder ensues, and they're on the run from the law. Intended as a film noir spoof, and not without some good moments. **82m/C VHS, Beta, LV.** Deborah Harry, Everett McGill, Dennis Lipscomb, Pat Benatar; **D:** Mark Reichart. *COL*

Union Pacific 𝒜𝒜𝒜 1939 Full DeMille treatment highlights this saga about the building of America's first transcontinental railroad. Jeff Butler (McCrea) is the construction overseer who must battle saboteurs and Indians (although the U.S. Cavalry does arrive to save the day). He also gets to fall for self-sufficient postmistress Mollie Monahan (Stanwyck). DeMille borrowed the actual golden spike used to drive in the last rail in 1869 for his reenactment of the completion celebration. Based on the book "Trouble Shooters" by Ernest Haycox. **136m/B VHS, Closed Caption.** Joel McCrea, Barbara Stanwyck, Robert Preston, Brian Donlevy, Akim Tamiroff, Lynne Overman, Robert Barrat, Anthony Quinn, Stanley Ridges, Henry Kolker, Evelyn Keyes, Regis Toomey; **D:** Cecil B. DeMille; **W:** Walter DeLeon, Jesse Lasky Jr., C. Gardner Sullivan; **C:** Victor Milner. *USH*

Union Station 𝒜𝒜 1950 Holden plays the chief of the railway police for Chicago's Union Station. He learns the station is to be used as a ransom drop in a kidnapping; but for all his security, the main thug gets away with the money, and the hunt is on. Good acting raises this film above the ordinary. **80m/B VHS, Beta.** William Holden, Barry Fitzgerald, Nancy Olson, Jan Sterling, Lee Marvin, Allene Roberts, Lyle Bettger; **D:** Rudolph Mate; **C:** Daniel F. Fapp. *BAR*

Universal Soldier 𝒜𝒜 1992 (R) A reporter discovers a secret government project to design perfect robo-soldiers by using the bodies of dead GIs, including tough guys Lundgren and Van Damme who were killed in Vietnam. But the knowledge is going to get her killed until Van Damme has flashbacks of his past (the soldier's memories have supposedly been erased) and agrees to help her. Lundgren doesn't have the same compassion and goes after them both. Big-budget thriller with some good action sequences and a lot of violence. **CW:** Strong language and strong graphic violence. **98m/C VHS, LV, Closed Caption.** Jean-Claude Van Damme, Dolph Lundgren, Ally Walker, Ed O'Ross, Jerry Orbach; **D:** Roland Emmerich. *LIV*

The Unkissed Bride 𝒜 *Mother Goose A Go-Go* 1966 (PG) A young newlywed couple are driven to distraction by the husband's inexplicable fainting spells and his strange obsession with Mother Goose. **82m/C VHS, Beta.** Tommy Kirk, Anne Helm, Danica D'Hondt, Henny Youngman; **D:** Jack H. Harris. *NWV*

The Unknown 𝒜𝒜𝒜½ 1927 Typically morbid Chaney fare has him working as a circus freak while trying to win the heart of his assistant. After drastic romancing he's still rejected by her, so he plots to kill the object of her intentions. Ghoulish as it is, the picture is really top-notch. **60m/B VHS.** Lon Chaney Sr., Norman Kerry, Joan Crawford, Nick De Ruiz, Frank Lanning, John St. Polis; **D:** Tod Browning. *FCT*

Unknown Island 𝒜½ 1948 Scientists travel to a legendary island where dinosaurs supposedly still exist. Bogus dinosaurs and cliche script. **76m/C VHS.** Virginia Grey, Philip Reed, Richard Denning, Barton MacLane; **D:** Jack Bernhard. *NOS, MOV, HEG*

Unknown Origin 𝒜 *The Alien Within; Roger Corman Presents: The Alien Within* 1995 (R) Scientific crew is stuck in an underwater installation with a deadly parasite. It's "Aliens" under the sea but a few twists will tweak your interest. Made for cable. **CW:** Violence; nudity; brief language. **75m/C VHS.** Roddy McDowall, Melanie Shatner, Alex Hyde-White, Don Stroud; **D:** Scott Levy. *NHO*

Unknown Powers woof! 1980 (PG) Science and drama are combined to examine ESP and magic. Are they gifts or curses, and how are peoples' lives affected by them? Members of the cast introduce various sections of this totally inept film. **97m/C VHS, Beta.** Samantha Eggar, Jack Palance, Will Geer, Roscoe Lee Browne; **D:** Don Como. *GEM*

The Unknown Ranger 𝒜½ 1936 Allen's first cowboy role has him foiling a gang of rustlers. The real highlight turns out to be the battle between his horse and a wild stallion. Eat your heart

out, Trigger! **57m/B VHS.** Robert Allen, Harry Woods, Martha Tibbetts, Hal Taliaferro, Robert "Buzzy" Henry; **D:** Spencer Gordon Bennet. *GPV*

Unknown World 𝒜 1951 A group of scientists tunnel to the center of the Earth to find a refuge from the dangers of the atomic world. Big start winds down fast. Director Terry Morse sometimes credited as Terrell O. Morse. **73m/B VHS, Beta.** Bruce Kellogg, Marilyn Nash, Victor Kilian, Jim Bannon; **D:** Terry Morse; **M:** Ernest Gold. *NOS, PSM, SNC*

Unlawful Entry 𝒜𝒜 1992 (R) After a break-in, Karen and Michael Carr naturally call the cops. Handsome, polite policeman Pete Davis responds to the call and agrees to help burglar-proof their home. But Pete has some definite quirks—he falls for the beauteous Karen and begins stalking the couple, deciding to get rid of Michael in order to have his wife. A lurid combination of the worst moments of "Internal Affairs" and "Fatal Attraction" undermines this usually-talented cast. **CW:** Language, terror and violence, and sexuality. **107m/C VHS, LV, Closed Caption.** Kurt Russell, Ray Liotta, Madeleine Stowe, Roger E. Mosley, Ken Lerner, Deborah Offner, Carmen Argenziano, Andy Romano, Barry W. Blaustein, Dick Miller; **D:** Jonathan Kaplan; **W:** Lewis Colick; **C:** Jamie Anderson; **M:** James Horner. *FXV*

Unlawful Passage 1994 (R) Vacation turns into a nightmare when a man's wife is kidnapped. **?m/C VHS.** Lee Horsley. *YHV*

An Unmarried Woman 𝒜𝒜𝒜 1978 (R) Suddenly divorced by her husband of 17 years, a woman deals with change. She enters the singles scene, copes with her daughter's growing sexuality, and encounters a new self-awareness. Mazursky puts real people on screen from start to finish. **124m/C VHS, Beta.** Jill Clayburgh, Alan Bates, Cliff Gorman, Michael Murphy; **D:** Paul Mazursky; **W:** Paul Mazursky; **M:** Bill Conti. Cannes Film Festival '78: Best Actress (Clayburgh); Los Angeles Film Critics Association Awards '78: Best Screenplay; National Board of Review Awards '78: 10 Best Films of the Year; New York Film Critics Awards '78: Best Screenplay; National Society of Film Critics Awards '78: Best Screenplay; Nominations: Academy Awards '78: Best Actress (Clayburgh), Best Original Screenplay, Best Picture. *FOX*

Unmasked Part 25 𝒜½ 1988 A second-generation serial killer takes up where dad left off. This one is intended to be a parody of slasher films, but it's still very bloody. **85m/C VHS, Beta.** *GB* Gregory Cox, Fiona Evans, Edward Brayshaw, Debbie Lee London; **D:** Anders Palm. *ACA*

Unmasking the Idol 𝒜 1986 A suave hero with tongue firmly in check battles Ninja warlords. Sequel to "Order of the Black Eagle." **90m/C VHS, Beta.** *GB* Ian Hunter, William T. Hicks, Charles K. Bibby; **D:** Worth Keeter. *CEL*

The Unnamable 𝒜 1988 The adaptation of the H.P. Lovecraft story about a particular New England ancestral home haunted by a typically Lovecraftian bloodthirsty demon borne of a woman hundreds of years before. College students, between trysts, investigate the myths about it. Uncut version, unseen in theaters, available only on video good for a few giggles and thrills. **87m/C VHS, Beta, LV.** Mark Kinsey Stephenson, Alexandra Durrell; **D:** Jean-Paul Ouellette. *VTR, THV*

The Unnamable 2: The Statement of Randolph Carter 𝒜½ 1992 (R) Randolph Carter is investigating a series of murders at Miskatonic University. Evidence leads Carter back to a 17th-century warlock who had the misfortune to summon an evil creature known as Alyda. The half-demon, half-woman now wants to permanently return to the mortal plane and every new victim just helps her evil purpose along. Based on a story by H.P. Lovecraft. **CW:** Nudity and horror violence. **104m/C VHS, LV, Closed Caption.** Mark Kinsey Stephenson, John Rhys-Davies, David Warner, Julie Strain, Maria Ford; **D:** Jean-Paul Ouellette. *PSM*

Unnatural 🎬🎬½ 1952 A mad scientist creates a souless child from the genes of a murderer and a prostitute. The child grows up to be the beautiful Neff, who makes a habit of seducing and destroying men. Dark, arresting film from a very popular German story. **90m/B VHS.** Hildegarde Neff, Erich von Stroheim, Karl-Heinz Boehm, Harry Meyen, Harry Helm, Denise Vernac, Julia Koschka; **D:** Arthur Maria Rabenalt. **SNC**

Unnatural Causes 🎬🎬🎬 1986 A dying Vietnam vet believes that his illness is the result of exposure to Agent Orange. With the help of a VA counselor, they lobby for national programs to assist other veterans who have been exposed to the chemical and together bring publicity to the issue. A made-for-television drama that is exceptionally well-acted. **96m/C VHS, Beta, LV.** John Ritter, Patti LaBelle, Alfre Woodard, John Sayles, Sean McCann, John Vargas, Gwen E. Davis; **D:** Lamont Johnson; **W:** John Sayles; **C:** Charles Fox. **NO**

Unnatural Pursuits 🎬🎬 1991 Playwright Simon Gray's black comic look at a British playwright's sojourn from London to L.A., Dallas, and New York and the Broadway debut of his new work. Alcoholic Hamish Partt (Bates), in the throes of a midlife crisis, is plagued by ego, indignities, and hostile actors, audiences, and critics as he tries desperately to work. Made for British TV. **60m/C VHS.** *GB* Alan Bates, Keith Szarabajka, Deborah Rush, John Mahoney, Tom Hickey, Richard Wilson, David Healy, Jack Gilpin, Paul Zimet, Bob Balaban; **W:** Simon Gray. **TVC**

An Unremarkable Life 🎬🎬 1989 (PG) Two aging sisters live symbiotically together, until one views the other's romantic attachment to a charming widower as destructive to her own life. **97m/C VHS, Beta.** Shelley Winters, Patricia Neal, Mako, Rochelle Oliver, Charles S. Dutton, Lily Knight; **D:** Amin Q. Chaudhri. **IME, COL**

Unsane 🎬🎬½ *Tenebrae* 1982 A mystery novelist realizes that a series of bizarre murders strangely resembles the plot of his latest book. Bloody fun from Argento. **91m/C VHS.** *IT* Anthony (Tony) Franciosa, John Saxon, Daria Nicolodi, Giuliano Gemma, Christian Borromeo, Mirella D'Angelo, Veronica Lario; **D:** Dario Argento; **W:** Dario Argento. **MED**

The Unseen 🎬½ 1980 Three young women from a television station are covering a story in a remote area of California. Before nightfall, two are horribly killed, leaving the third to come face to face with the terror. **91m/C VHS, Beta.** Barbara Bach, Sydney Lassick, Stephen Furst; **D:** Peter Foleg. **NO**

Unsettled Land 🎬🎬 1988 (PG) Young Israeli settlers try to survive the elements and Bedouin attackers in Palestine during the 1920s. **109m/C VHS, Beta, LV, 8mm.** *IS* Kelly McGillis, John Shea, Arnon Zadok, Christine Boisson; **D:** Uri Barbash. **NLC**

The Unsinkable Molly Brown 🎬🎬🎬 1964 A spunky backwoods girl is determined to break into the upper crust of Denver's high society and along the way survives the sinking of the Titanic. This energetic version of the Broadway musical contains many Meredith Willson ("Music Man") songs and lots of hokey, good-natured fun. 🎵Colorado Is My Home; Leadville Johnny Brown (Soliloquy); I Ain't Down Yet; Belly Up to the Bar, Boys; He's My Friend; I've Already Started; The Beautiful People of Denver; I May Never Fall in Love with You; Up Where the People Are. **128m/C VHS, Beta, LV.** Debbie Reynolds, Harve Presnell, Ed Begley Sr., Martita Hunt, Hermione Baddeley; **D:** Charles Walters; **C:** Daniel F. Fapp; **M:** Meredith Willson. Nominations: Academy Awards '64: Best Actress (Reynolds), Best Adapted Score, Best Art Direction/Set Decoration (Color), Best Color Cinematography, Best Costume Design (Color), Best Sound. **MGM**

The Unstoppable Man 🎬½ 1959 The son of an American businessman is kidnapped while they are in London. No pushover he, dad develops his own plan to destroy the criminals, eventually pursuing him with a flame thrower. **68m/B VHS, Beta.** *GB* Cameron Mitchell, Marius Goring,

Harry H. Corbett, Lois Maxwell, Denis Gilmore; **D:** Terry Bishop. **NOS, SNC**

Unstrung Heroes 🎬🎬½ 1995 (PG) Semi-autobiographical tale of Steven Lidz (Watt), growing up in 1960s California with a mother who is dying of cancer (MacDowell) and a nutty professor-type father (Turturro) who refuses to accept her illness. A desperate Steven goes to live with his two oddball uncles (Richards and Chaykin) who provide understanding and insight for the youngster, as well as a new name, Franz. Moving and quirky without being sappy, Keaton's feature debut avoids what would've been easy stereotypes. Based on the autobiography by Franz Lidz. **93m/C VHS, LV, Closed Caption.** Andie MacDowell, John Turturro, Michael Richards, Maury Chaykin, Nathan Watt, Kendra Krull; **D:** Diane Keaton; **W:** Richard LaGravenese; **C:** Phedon Papamichael; **M:** Thomas Newman. Nominations: Academy Awards '95: Best Original Score. **HPH**

Unsuitable Job for a Woman 🎬🎬½ 1982 Independent Cordelia Gray, following the death of her boss, takes over his detective agency and gets involved with murder. Based on the novel by P.D. James. **94m/C VHS, Beta.** *GB* Pippa Guard, Paul Freeman, Billie Whitelaw; **D:** Christopher Petit. **NO**

The Untamable 🎬🎬 1923 Unusual silent about volatile woman suffering from schizophrenia. **65m/B VHS, Beta.** Gladys Walton, Malcolm McGregor, John St. Polis, Etta Lee; **D:** Herbert Blache. **GPV, FCT**

Untamed Heart 🎬🎬½ 1993 (PG-13) Adam (Slater), the painfully shy busboy with a heart condition, loves Caroline (Tomei), the bubbly waitress, from afar. She doesn't notice him until he saves her from some would-be rapists and their love blooms in the coffee shop where they both work. Tomei and Slater are both strong in the leads and Perez, as Caroline's best buddy Cindy, hurls comic barbs with ease. Charmingly familiar surroundings help set this formulaic romance apart. Filmed on location in Minneapolis. Laserdisc version is in letterbox format. **CW:** Strong language, strong violence, and sensuality. **102m/C VHS, Beta, LV, Closed Caption.** Christian Slater, Marisa Tomei, Rosie Perez, Kyle Secor, Willie Garson; **D:** Tony Bill; **W:** Tom Sierchio; **M:** Cliff Eidelman. MTV Movie Awards '93: Most Desirable Male (Slater), Best Kiss (Christian Slater/Marisa Tomei). **MGM**

Until September 🎬🎬 1984 (R) An American tourist becomes stranded in Paris. She meets and falls in love with a married banker while she is stuck in her hotel. Routine romance. **96m/C VHS, Beta, Closed Caption.** Karen Allen, Thierry Lhermitte, Christopher Cazenove, Johanna Pavlis; **D:** Richard Marquand; **M:** John Barry. **MGM**

Until The End of The World 🎬🎬🎬½ 1991 (R) Convoluted road movie set in 1999 follows the travails of Sam Farber (Hurt) through 15 cities in 8 countries on 4 continents as he is chased by Dommartin, her lover (Neill), a bounty hunter, a private detective, and bank robbers, until all wind up in the Australian outback. And this is only the first half of the movie. For true cinematic satisfaction, don't expect logic—just go with the flow. Visually stunning, unexpectedly humorous, with excellent performances from an international cast. Footage created with high definition (HDTV) video technology is a technological first. The soundtrack features Lou Reed, David Byrne, U2, and others. **CW:** Language and sensuality. **158m/C VHS, Beta, LV, Closed Caption.** William Hurt, Solveig Dommartin, Sam Neill, Max von Sydow, Ruediger Vogler, Ernie Dingo, Jeanne Moreau; **D:** Wim Wenders; **W:** Wim Wenders, Peter Carey; **M:** Graeme Revell. **WAR**

Until They Get Me 🎬½ 1918 Northern Mountie rides horse in silence as he tracks criminal to the edge of the earth. **58m/B VHS, Beta.** Pauline Starke, Joe King. **GPV, FCT**

Until They Sail 🎬🎬½ 1957 Soap opera set in New Zealand during WWII. Plot centers around the lives of four sisters involved in love and murder. Dee's film debut. Based on a story by James Michener. **95m/B VHS, Closed Caption.** Jean Simmons, Joan Fontaine, Paul Newman, Piper Laurie, Charles Drake, Sandra Dee, Wally Cassell, Alan Napier; **D:** Robert Wise; **W:** Robert Anderson. **MGM**

The Untold Story 🎬🎬 1993 New restaurant owner Wong discovers that the previous owner and his family mysteriously disappeared. Then the police detective (Lee) on the case makes a very shocking discovery. Modern cult classic includes footage cut from the original Hong Kong release and its violence is not for the squeamish. Cantonese with subtitles. **95m/C VHS, LV.** *HK* Anthony Wong, Danny Lee; **D:** Herman Yau. **TAI**

The Untouchables 🎬🎬🎬½ 1987 (R) Big-budget, fast-paced and exciting re-evaluation of the popular TV series about the real-life battle between Treasury officer Eliot Ness and crime boss Al Capone in 1920s' Chicago. History sometimes takes a back seat to Hollywood's imagination in the screenplay, but it doesn't really matter since there are splendid performances by De Niro as Capone and Connery as Ness' mentor to help it look realistic. Costner does a fine job showing the change in Ness from naive idealism to steely conviction. Beautifully filmed with excellent special effects. **119m/C VHS, Beta, LV, 8mm, Closed Caption.** Kevin Costner, Sean Connery, Robert De Niro, Andy Garcia, Charles Martin Smith, Billy Drago, Richard Bradford, Jack Kehoe; **D:** Brian DePalma; **W:** David Mamet; **C:** Stephen Burum; **M:** Ennio Morricone. Academy Awards '87: Best Supporting Actor (Connery); Golden Globe Awards '88: Best Supporting Actor (Connery); National Board of Review Awards '87: 10 Best Films of the Year, Best Supporting Actor (Connery); Nominations: Academy Awards '87: Best Art Direction/Set Decoration, Best Costume Design, Best Original Score. **PAR, BTV**

Unveiled 🎬🎬½ 1994 (R) Stephanie Montgomery's (Zane) friend falls victim to a killer in Marrakesh. So Steph sets out to trap the killer, with the help of government offficial Peter (Hubley). **CW:** Language, brief nudity, and sexual situations. **103m/C VHS, LV, Closed Caption.** Lisa Zane, Whip Hubley, Nicholas Chinlund, Martha Gehman; **D:** William Cole; **M:** Michael Diamond, Roger Kumble; **M:** Christopher Tyng. **FXV**

Unzipped 🎬🎬🎬 1994 (R) Witty, behind-the-scenes look at whiz-kid fashion designer Isaac Mizrahi as he prepares for the showing of his 1994 collection. Alternately filmed in black-and-white and color in a variety of film stocks, Keeve (Mizrahi's former lover) captures Mizrahi's varying moods, from his creative struggles to his unique sense of humor and gift for mimicry. Highlights include scenes with Mizrahi's doting mother. Fashionphiles will love every minute, and strictly off-the-rack viewers can enjoy the supermodels on parade. **CW:** Some language. **76m/C VHS, LV, Closed Caption. D:** Douglas Keeve. Sundance Film Festival '95: Audience Award. **WAR**

Up Against the Wall 🎬🎬 1991 (PG-13) A black kid from the Chicago projects attends school in the affluent suburbs, but there too he must resist temptation, crime and violence. A well-intentioned but didactic cautionary drama, adapted from the book by African-American author/commentator Dr. Jawanza Kunjufu. **103m/C VHS.** Marla Gibbs, Stoney Jackson, Catero Colbert, Ron O'Neal, Salli Richardson; **D:** Ron O'Neal. **BMG**

Up Close and Personal 🎬🎬🎬 1996 (PG-13) Ambitious Reno card dealer Tally Atwater (Pfeiffer) wants to get into broadcasting and finds her chance at a Miami TV station where she's mentored by successful veteran-reporter-turned-producer Warren Justice (Redford). They fall in love but find their careers clashing as Tally climbs the media success ladder. Originally inspired by the tragic life of NBC reporter Jessica Savitch, whose problems with drugs and abusive relationships led to a sad ending, film turned into a star-powered romance with media trappings and another variation of "A Star is Born." It's now "suggested" by Alanna Nash's book "Golden Girl." **CW:** Brief strong language, some sensuality and depictions of violence. **124m/C VHS, LV, Closed Caption.** Michelle Pfeiffer, Robert Redford, Kate Nelligan, Stockard Channing, Joe Mantegna, Glenn Plummer, James Rebhorn, Noble Willingham, Scott Bryce, Raymond Cruz, Dedee Pfeiffer, Miguel Sandoval, James Karen; **D:** Jon Avnet; **W:** Joan Didion, John Gregory Dunne; **C:** Karl Walter Lindenlaub; **M:** Thomas Newman. Nominations: Academy Awards '96: Best Song ("Because You Loved Me"); Golden Globe Awards '97: Best Song ("Because You Loved Me"). *TOU*

Up from the Depths 🐾½ 1979 (R)
Something from beneath the ocean is turning the paradise of Hawaii into a nightmare. Prehistoric fish are returning to the surface with one thing on their minds—lunch. "Jaws" rip-off played for humor. **85m/C VHS, Beta.** Sam Bottoms, Suzanne Reed, Virgil Frye; **D:** Charles B. Griffith; **W:** Alfred Sweeney; **M:** James Horner. *LIV, VES*

Up in Arms 🐾🐾 1944 Danny Kaye's first film presents a typical Kaye scenario: he plays a twitching hypochondriac who is drafted into the Army and sneaks his girlfriend aboard the troopship bound for the Pacific. Features an appearance by the Goldwyn Girls. Remake of the film "The Nervous Wreck." ♫Theatre Lobby Number; Now I Know; All Out for Freedom; Tess's Torch Song; Melody in 4-F. **105m/C VHS, Beta, LV.** Danny Kaye, Dinah Shore, Constance Dowling, Dana Andrews, Margaret Dumont, Goldwyn Girls, Lyle Talbot, Louis Calhern, Charles Halton; **D:** Elliott Nugent; **C:** Ray Rennahan. Nominations: Academy Awards '44: Best Song ("Now I Know"), Scoring of a Musical.

Up in the Air 🐾🐾 1940 Darro and Moreland have ambitions as radio comedians, and their friend Reynolds wants to be a singer. Their break comes when other performers are murdered on the air. First, though, they must solve the killings. **62m/B VHS.** Frankie Darro, Marjorie Reynolds, Mantan Moreland, Gordon Jones, Tristram Coffin, John Holland, Carleton Young; **D:** Howard Bretherton. *NOS*

Up Periscope 🐾🐾½ 1959 Garner is a demolitions expert unwillingly assigned to a submarine commanded by O'Brien. His mission: to sneak onto a Japanese-held island and steal a top-secret code book. Trouble is, O'Brien may not wait for Garner to complete his mission before taking the sub back underwater. A routine submarine film. **111m/C VHS, LV.** James Garner, Edmond O'Brien, Andra Martin, Alan Hale Jr., Carleton Carpenter, Frank Gifford, Richard Bakalayan; **D:** Gordon Douglas. *WAR*

Up River 🐾 1979 Wealthy land baron rapes and murders the wife of a simple pioneer, who is beaten and whose homestead is burned by the baron as well. The pioneer lives to seek terrible vengeance. **90m/C VHS.** Jeff Corey, Morgan Stevens, Debbie AuLuce; **D:** Carl Kitt. *NO*

Up the Academy 🐾 *Mad Magazine's Up the Academy; The Brave Young Men of Weinberg* 1980 (R)
Four teenaged delinquents are sent to an academy for wayward boys where they encounter a sadistic headmaster and a gay dance instructor. Sometimes inventive, often tasteless fare from "Mad" magazine. **88m/C VHS, Beta.** Ron Leibman, Ralph Macchio, Barbara Bach, Tom Poston, Stacey Nelkin, Wendell Brown, Tom Citera; **D:** Robert Downey. *WAR*

Up the Creek 🐾🐾 1958 Crazy antics abound in this tale of an old British destroyer, a black-market scheme run by the crew, and the new skipper whose hobby is rocket building. Followed by "Further Up the River." **83m/B VHS, Beta.** GB David Tomlinson, Wilfrid Hyde-White, Peter Sellers, Vera Day, Michael Goodliffe, Lionel Jeffries; **D:** Val Guest. *MON*

Up the Creek 🐾½ 1984 (R) Four college losers enter a whitewater raft race to gain some respect for their school. The soundtrack features songs by Heart, Cheap Trick and The Beach Boys. Routine. **95m/C VHS, Beta, LV.** Tim Matheson,

Jennifer Runyon, Stephen Furst, John Hillerman, James B. Sikking, Julia Montgomery, Jeana Tomasina; **D:** Robert Butler; **M:** William Goldstein. *LIV, VES*

Up the Down Staircase 🐾🐾🐾 1967 A naive, newly trained New York public school teacher is determined to teach the finer points of English literature to a group of poor students. She almost gives up until one student actually begins to learn. Good production and acting. Based on Bel Kaufman's novel. **124m/C VHS.** Sandy Dennis, Patrick Bedford, Eileen Heckart, Ruth White, Jean Stapleton, Sorrell Booke; **D:** Robert Mulligan. *WAR, OM*

Up the Sandbox 🐾🐾 1972 (R) A bored housewife fantasizes about her life in order to avoid facing her mundane existence. Fine acting from Streisand, with real problems of young mothers accurately shown. **98m/C VHS, Beta.** Barbra Streisand, David Selby, Jane Hoffman, Barbara Rhoades; **D:** Irvin Kershner; **C:** Gordon Willis; **M:** Billy Goldenberg. *WAR*

Up to a Certain Point 🐾🐾 *Up to a Point; Hasta Cierto Punto* 1983 Writer Oscar believes he has a liberal attitude (to go along with Cuban political ideology) but his belief is shaken when he interviews workers on the Havana docks about their notions of machismo. Seems when Oscar falls for a sexy dockworker his ideas of maleness and a woman's place are more traditional than he imagines. Spanish with subtitles. **70m/C VHS.** CU Oscar Alvarez, Mirta Ibarra, Omar Valdes, Coralia Veloz, Rogelio Blain, Ana Vina; **D:** Tomas Gutierrez Alea; **W:** Tomas Gutierrez Alea; **M:** Leo Brower. *NYF*

Up Your Alley 🐾🐾 1989 (R) A female reporter, pursuing a story on homelessness, and a skidrow bum find romance. Langston, who produced and co-wrote the film, is better known as "The Unknown Comic." **90m/C VHS, Beta, LV.** Linda Blair, Murray Langston, Ruth Buzzi, Johnny Dark, Bob Zany, Yakov Smirnoff; **D:** Bob Logan. *LIV*

Uphill All the Way 🐾🐾 1985 A couple of card-cheatin' good old boys are pursued by posses and cavalry alike, and end up killing real outlaws. Made for television. **91m/C VHS, Beta.** Roy Clark, Mel Tillis, Glen Campbell, Trish Van Devere, Burl Ives, Burt Reynolds; **D:** Frank Q. Dobbs. *NWV, VTR*

Upper Crust 🐾½ 1988 Boring tale of corruption and greed that takes place at the highest levels of American business and government. **95m/C VHS, Beta.** Frank Gorshin, Broderick Crawford, Nigel Davenport. *NO*

The Uprising 🐾🐾🐾 1981 A Nicaraguan drama filmed just months after the 1979 Sandinista revolution, wherein a young guard of Somoza retains his job for the money, while his father is active in the revolutionary forces. In Spanish with English subtitles. **96m/C VHS, Beta.** SP **D:** Peter Lilienthal. *KIV*

Uptown Angel 🐾🐾 1990 (R) A young woman is determined to work her way out of her home on the wrong side of town. Black cast brings new life to old premise. **90m/C VHS.** Caron Tate, Cliff McMullen, Gloria Davis Hill, Tracy Hill; **D:** Joy Shannon; **W:** Joy Shannon. *XVC*

Uptown New York 🐾🐾 1932 A young man pressured by his family marries a rich girl instead of the woman he loves, who in turn marries a man she does not love. Routine melodrama. **81m/B VHS, Beta.** Jack Oakie, Shirley Green, Leon Ames, Shirley Grey, George Cooper, Raymond Hatton; **D:** Victor Schertzinger. *NOS, FCT, DVT*

Uptown Saturday Night 🐾🐾½ 1974 (PG) Two working men attempt to recover a stolen lottery ticket from the black underworld after being ripped off at an illegal gambling place. Good fun, with nice performances from both leads and from Belafonte doing a black "Godfather" parody of Brando. Followed by "Let's Do It Again." **104m/C VHS, Beta.** Sidney Poitier, Bill Cosby, Harry Belafonte, Flip Wilson, Richard Pryor, Calvin Lockhart; **D:** Sidney Poitier; **W:** Richard Wesley; **C:** Fred W. Koenekamp. *WAR*

The Uranium Conspiracy 🐾½ 1978 (PG) A secret agent and a mercenary soldier try to stop a shipment of uranium out of Zaire from falling into enemy hands. It won't be easy. **100m/C VHS, Beta.** Fabio Testi, Janet Agren, Assaf Dayan. *NO*

Uranus 🐾🐾🐾 1991 (R) After WWII a French provincial town has been liberated from Nazi invaders—but not its own suspicions, as citizens try to rebuild knowing some of them collaborated with the enemy. An important subject is heavily talked over in static fashion, with a robust Depardieu either a standout or a ham as the earthy saloonkeeper. Based on a novel by Marcel Ayme, himself accused of pro-Vichy leanings during the era. In French with English subtitles. **100m/C VHS, LV.** FR Gerard Depardieu, Michel Blanc, Jean-Pierre Marielle, Philippe Noiret, Gerard Desarthe, Michel Galabru, Fabrice Luchini, Daniel Prevost; **D:** Claude Berri; **W:** Claude Berri; **M:** Jean-Claude Petit. *NO*

Urban Cowboy 🐾🐾½ 1980 (PG) A young Texas farmer comes to Houston to work in a refinery. After work he hangs out at Gilley's, a roadhouse bar. Here he and his friends, dressed in their cowboy gear, drink, fight, and prove their manhood by riding a mechanical bull. Film made Winger a star, was an up in Travolta's roller coaster career, and began the craze for country western apparel and dance and them there mechanical bulls. Ride 'em, cowboy! **135m/C VHS, Beta, LV.** John Travolta, Debra Winger, Scott Glenn, Madolyn Smith, Barry Corbin; **D:** James Bridges; **W:** James Bridges, Aaron Latham; **C:** Reynaldo Villalobos; **M:** Ralph Burns. *PAR*

Urban Crossfire 🐾🐾½ 1994 (PG-13) Two veteran white Brooklyn detectives investigating gang violence are aided by a young black patrolman whose partner was killed by a gang leader. Solid cast, fast paced action. **CW:** Profanity, brief nudity, and violence, drug abuse. **95m/C VHS, LV.** Mario Van Peebles, Ray Sharkey, Peter Boyle, Michael Boatman; **D:** Dick Lowry. *NHO*

Urban Warriors 🐾 1975 Savage barbarians roam and pillage a post-nuclear war Earth, but one invincible warrior ushers them out. **90m/C VHS, Beta.** Karl Landgren, Alex Vitale, Deborah Keith; **D:** Joseph Warren. *CAN*

Urge to Kill 🐾 1984 (PG) A man returning from a mental hospital after pleading temporary insanity to the murder of his girlfriend returns to her town and tries to uncover the truth, with the help of her younger sister. Made for television. **96m/C VHS, Beta.** Karl Malden, Holly Hunter, William Devane, Alex McArthur; **D:** Mike Robe. *FOX, VTR*

Urotsukidoji 1: Legend of the Overfiend 🐾🐾 *The Wandering Kid* 1993 (NC-17) Legend has it that the world is made up of Humans, Man-Beasts, and Monster-Demons. Every 3000 years superfiend Chojin is supposed to unite the three into a single Land of Eternity. However, the heroic Amano discovers this land will be a nightmare world and unless he can successfully battle Chojin humanity may not survive. Ultra-violent and sexually explicit. Animated; dubbed into English. **108m/C VHS.** JP CPM, MOV

Urotsukidoji 2: Legend of the Demon Womb 🐾🐾 1993 The fiendish Dr. Munhihausen's life work has been to render the dimensional boundaries between the World of Man-Beasts and the World of Monster Demons and to conjure the dreaded Overfiend. Years later, his son seeks to find a way to conquer the Overfiend and his cohorts from Hell and assume its powers for himself. Munhihausen's efforts may soon be rewarded when his hapless cousin, who accidentally received the demon's blood, begins developing monstrous powers. Animated; dubbed from Japanese. **88m/C VHS.** JP CPM, MOV

Ursus in the Valley of the Lions 🐾½ *The Mighty Ursus; Ursus* 1962 Ursus attempts to rescue his love from druids but is dismayed to find that she has taken up homicide in her free time. **92m/C VHS.** IT SP Ed Fury, Luis Prendes,

Moira Orfei, Cristina Gajoni, Maria Luisa Merlo; **D:** Carlo Campogalliani. *SNC*

Urusei Yatsura Movie 1: Only You

198? Lum is a Princess of the Oni, an alien race who have come to repossess Earth. The planet's one chance is for an earthling to beat Lum in the Oni's national sport—tag. When unlucky teenager Ataru Moroboshi is chosen he actually beats Lum. Which means he has to marry her. In Japanese with English subtitles. 100m/C VHS. *JP ANI*

Urusei Yatsura Movie 2: Beautiful Dreamer

1992 Unlucky teenager Ataru Moroboshi and his classmates at Tomobiki High School find themselves reliving the day before the School Festival over and over again. Funny and dreamlike. In Japanese with English subtitles. 90m/C VHS, LV. *JP* **D:** Oshii Mamoru. *CPM, ANI*

Urusei Yatsura Movie 3: Remember My Love

1985 A magician family friend of Princess Lum put a curse on her at birth when she wasn't invited to Lum's christening—that Lum would never be happy with her true love. But Ataru is the real victim. When the magician happens upon him in the new amusement park she turns him into a pink hippotamus to spite Lum. In Japanese with English subtitles. 93m/C VHS, LV. *JP ANI*

Urusei Yatsura Movie 4: Lum the Forever

1986 When a great cherry tree is cut down near where Lum and friends are making a movie she mysteriously loses her horns, and with them her powers. In Japanese with English subtitles. 94m/C VHS, LV. *JP ANI, ING*

Urusei Yatsura Movie 5: The Final Chapter

19?? Boy meets girl with Japanimation twist. Lum's fiance, Lupa, is introduced and the fate of the Earth is in Ataru's hands. Japanese with English subtitles. 90m/C VHS, LV. *JP*

Urusei Yatsura Movie 6: Always My Darling

1991 Space princess Lupica abducts Aturu in order to get the greatest love potion in the galaxy. Lum wants him back. In Japanese with English subtitles. 77m/C VHS. *JP ANI, ING*

Used Cars 🐾🐾🐾 1980 (R) A car dealer is

desperate to put his jalopy shop competitors out of business. The owners go to great lengths to stay afloat. Sometimes too obnoxious, but often funny. 113m/C VHS, Beta, LV, 8mm. Kurt Russell, Jack Warden, Deborah Harmon, Gerrit Graham, Joe Flaherty, Michael McKean; **D:** Robert Zemeckis; **W:** Robert Zemeckis. *COL*

Used People 🐾🐾½ 1992 (PG-13) A study in

ethnicity and characterization, three Oscar-winning actresses lead a talented cast playing a Jewish family living in Queens in 1969. When the father dies, Joe (Mastroianni), an old friend with an old torch for the widow, Pearl (MacLaine), shows up at the funeral and manages to charm her into a date for coffee. Pearl's new relationship with her Italian suitor affects each of the somewhat off-balance family members and washes the whole clan with a sense of hope and renewal. Adapted from screenwriter Graff's play "The Grandma Plays" that was based on memories of his grandmother. Director Kidron's American debut. 116m/C VHS, LV, **Closed Caption.** Shirley MacLaine, Marcello Mastroianni, Kathy Bates, Marcia Gay Harden, Jessica Tandy, Sylvia Sidney, Bob Dishy, Joe Pantoliano, Matthew Branton, Louis Guff, Charles Cioffi, Doris Roberts, Helen Hanft; **D:** Beeban Kidron; **W:** Todd Graff; **M:** Rachel Portman. *FXV*

Users 🐾🐾 1978 Small-town girl who worked

as a prostitute meets a faded film star and becomes involved in the movie business. Ode to decadent Hollywood. Based on the Joyce Haber novel. Made for television. 125m/C VHS, Beta. Jaclyn Smith, Tony Curtis, John Forsythe, Red Buttons, George Hamilton; **D:** Joseph Hardy; **M:** Maurice Jarre. *PSM*

The Usual Suspects 🐾🐾🐾½ 1995 (R)

Twisted noir-thriller about some crooks, a $91 million heist, and mysterious crime lord Keyser Soze. Customs agent Kujan (Palminteri) tries to get a

straight story out of small-time con man "Verbal" Kint (Spacey) about a burning tanker in the San Pedro harbor, 27 dead bodies, and the other four tempermental criminals involved: ex-cop-turned thief Keaton (Byrne), explosives expert Hockney (Pollak), and hot-headed partners McManus (Baldwin) and Fenster (Del Toro). Nothing is as it seems, and the ending keeps everyone guessing, right up to the final credits. Terrific performances from all complement the intelligent, humorous script. And yes, the title does come from the famous line in "Casablanca." **CW:** Violence; substantial amount of strong language. 105m/C VHS, LV, Closed Caption, DVD. Kevin Spacey, Gabriel Byrne, Chazz Palminteri, Kevin Pollak, Stephen Baldwin, Benicio Del Toro, Giancarlo Esposito, Pete Postlethwaite, Dan Hedaya, Suzy Amis, Paul Bartel, Peter Greene; **D:** Bryan Singer; **W:** Christopher McQuarrie; **C:** Newton Thomas Sigel; **M:** John Ottman. Academy Awards '95: Best Original Screenplay, Best Supporting Actor (Spacey); British Academy Awards '95: Best Original Screenplay; Independent Spirit Awards '96: Best Screenplay, Best Supporting Actor (Del Toro); National Board of Review Awards '95: Best Supporting Actor (Spacey); New York Film Critics Awards '95: Best Supporting Actor (Spacey); Broadcast Film Critics Association Awards '95: Best Supporting Actor (Spacey); Nominations: British Academy Awards '95: Best Film; Golden Globe Awards '96: Best Supporting Actor (Spacey); Independent Spirit Awards '96: Best Cinematography; Screen Actors Guild Award '95: Best Supporting Actor (Spacey). *PGV*

Utah 🐾🐾 1945 A musical comedy star who

inherits a ranch wishes to sell it to finance one of her shows. She is persuaded not to by Rogers, the ranch foreman. 54m/B VHS, Beta. Roy Rogers, Dale Evans, George "Gabby" Hayes; **D:** John English. *NOS, VDM, VCN*

Utah Trail 🐾 1938 Lawman Ritter is hired to

stop a gang of cattle rustlers. Cheapie oater made for Grand National, which went bankrupt soon after. 57m/B VHS, Beta. Tex Ritter; **D:** Al(bert) Herman. *NOS, VCN, DVT*

Utamaro and His Five Women 🐾🐾½

Five Women Around Utamaro; Utamaro O Meguru Gonin No Onna 1946 Utamaro is a legendary 19th-century Edo artist who gained inspiration from Tokyo's "floating world," of courtesans, brothels, drinking parties, and violent passions. His gorgeous portraits worship women but he dislikes the complications that flesh-and-blood females bring. Heavily stylized look at the artistic impulse. In Japanese with English subtitles. 89m/B VHS. *JP* Minnosuke Bando, Kinuyo Tanaka, Kotaro Bando, Hisato Osawa, Tamezo Mochizuki, Hiroko Kawasaki; **D:** Kenji Mizoguchi; **W:** Yoshikata Yoda. *NYF, FCT*

Utilities 🐾½ *Getting Even* 1983 (PG) A frustrat-

ed social worker enlists the help of his friends in his efforts to impress an attractive policewoman by taking on a large corporate utility. 94m/C VHS, Beta, LV. **CA** Robert Hays, Brooke Adams, John Marley, Ben Gordon, Helen Burns; **D:** Harvey Hart. *LIV, VES*

Utopia 🐾🐾 *Atoll K; Robinson Crusoeland; Esca-*

pade 1951 Laurel and Hardy inherit a paradisaical island, but their peace is disturbed when uranium is discovered. Final screen appearance of the team is diminished by poor direction and script. 82m/B VHS, Beta. **FR** Stan Laurel, Oliver Hardy, Suzy Delair, Max Elloy; **D:** Leo Joannon. *CNG, MRV, VYY*

Utu 🐾🐾🐾 1983 (R) A Maori tribesman serving

with the colonizing British army in 1870 explodes into ritual revenge when his home village is slaughtered. Filmed in New Zealand. 104m/C VHS, Beta, **Closed Caption. NZ** Anzac Wallace, Kelly Johnson, Tim Elliot, Bruno Lawrence; **D:** Geoff Murphy; **M:** John Charles. *FOX*

Utz 🐾🐾½ 1993 The Baron von Utz (Mueller-

Stahl) collects both women and priceless porcelain figures. When his friend, art dealer Marius Fischer (Riegert), travels to Prague for a visit he finds that both Utz's housekeeper (Fricker), who has suffered from unrequited love, and the porcelain have disappeared. So Marius teams up with the Baron's old friend Dr. Orlick (Scofield) to find out what's going on. Based on the novel by Bruce

Chatwin. 95m/C VHS. **GB GE IT** Armin Mueller-Stahl, Peter Riegert, Brenda Fricker, Paul Scofield; **D:** George Sluizer. *FRF, BTV, FCT*

V 🐾🐾🐾 1983 Very creepy sci-fi miniseries that

spawned a short-lived TV show. Advanced aliens, known as the Visitors, come to Earth on a seemingly friendly quest. But their human-like appearance is a facade—as is their mission. Fake skin masks a repitilian hide and what they want is complete planetary control. Naturally, some earthlings don't fall for their smooth talk and a resistance movement is born. Followed by miniseries conclusion "V: The Final Battle." 190m/C VHS. Marc Singer, Jane Badler, Faye Grant, Robert Englund, Michael Durrell, Peter Nelson, Neva Patterson, Andrew Prine, Richard Herd, Rafael Campos; **D:** Kenneth Johnson; **W:** Kenneth Johnson. *WAR, MOV*

V: The Final Battle 🐾🐾½ 1984 It's four-

months since the Visitors appeared on earth, proclaiming their false friendship. But a resistance movement knows these reptiles, who hide behind a human appearance, are only interested in harvesting earth's inhabitants as a new food source. Continuation of the TV miniseries "V." 285m/C VHS, **Closed Caption.** Marc Singer, Robert Englund, Michael Ironside; **D:** Richard T. Heffron. *WAR*

The Vacillations of Poppy Carew 🐾🐾½

1994 Free-spirited Poppy is just trying to make funeral arrangements for her father when she becomes involved in a series of unexpected and complicated romances. Based on a novel by Mary Wesley. 109m/C VHS. **GB** Tara Fitzgerald, Sian Phillips, Charlotte Coleman; **D:** James Cellan Jones. *VTR, CCB*

The Vagabond 1916 The Little Tramp is a

pathetic fiddler making a scanty living who rescues a damsel in distress. Silent with musical soundtrack added. 20m/B VHS, Beta. Charlie Chaplin, Edna Purviance, Eric Campbell, Albert Austin; **D:** Charlie Chaplin. *CAB, GVV, VYY*

Vagabond 🐾🐾🐾 *Sans Toit Ni Loi* 1985

Bleak, emotionally shattering, powerful and compelling, this film traces the peripatetic life of an amoral and selfish young French woman who has no regard for social rules and tremendous fear of responsibility in her drifting yet inexorable journey into death. Told via flashbacks from the moment when she is found dead, alone, and unaccounted for by the roadside, this film will not leave you unscathed. Written by New Wave director Varda. In French with English subtitles. 105m/C VHS, Beta, LV. **FR** Sandrine Bonnaire, Macha Meril, Stephane Freiss, Elaine Cortadellas, Marthe Jarnias, Yolanda Moreau; **D:** Agnes Varda; **W:** Agnes Varda; **C:** Patrick Blossier. Cesar Awards '86: Best Actress (Bonnaire); Los Angeles Film Critics Association Awards '86: Best Actress (Bonnaire), Best Foreign Film. *TPV*

Vagabond Lover 🐾🐾½ 1929 The amus-

ing tale of the loves, hopes, and dreams of an aspiring saxophone player. Rudy croons through his megaphone in his movie debut. Appealing, with Dressler sparkling in the role of the wealthy aunt. ♫If You Were the Only Girl in the World; A Little Kiss Each Morning; Heigh Ho Everybody; Piccolo Pete; I Love You; I'll Be Reminded of You; I'm Just a Vagabond Lover. 66m/B VHS, Beta. Rudy Vallee, Sally Blane, Marie Dressler; **D:** Marshall Neilan. *VYY, RXM, DVT*

The Vagrant 🐾 1992 (R) Run-of-the-mill

creeper with a mind-game playing derelict inhabiting the home of a young exec. A series of murders has this wimp yuppie wondering how to get rid of his unwelcome intruder. **CW:** Some violence and some sensuality. 91m/C VHS, **Closed Caption.** Bill Paxton, Michael Ironside, Marshall Bell, Stuart Pankin; **D:** Chris Walas. *MGM*

Valdez is Coming 🐾🐾½ 1971 (PG)

Though not a world-class western, this filmed-in-Spain saga does feature a probing script (based on an Elmore Leonard novel) on the nature of race relations. Fine performance by Lancaster as a Mexican-American who ignites the passions of a town, and ultimately confronts the local land baron. **90m/C VHS, Closed Caption.** Burt Lancaster, Susan Clark, Jon Cypher, Barton Heyman, Richard Jordan, Frank Silvera, Hector Elizondo; **D:** Edwin Sherin; **W:** David Rayfiel. *MGM*

Valentino 🎬🎬 1977 (R) Another one of director Russell's flamboyantly excessive screen biographies, this time of silent screen idol Rudolph Valentino (Nureyev). The details hardly matter but the movie is told in flashback from Valentino's funeral to his beginnings as a dance instructor and his eventual success as a screen lover. Nureyev is noticeably stiff in his screen debut but at least he possesses some charisma. **127m/C VHS.** **GB** Rudolf Nureyev, Leslie Caron, Michelle Phillips, Carol Kane, Felicity Kendal, Seymour Cassel, Peter Vaughan, William Hootkins, Huntz Hall, David DeKeyser, Alfred Marks, Anton Diffring; **D:** Ken Russell; **W:** Mardik Martin, Ken Russell, John Byrum. *MGM*

Valentino Returns 🎬🎬 1988 (R) A kid in 1955 California buys a pink Cadillac he nicknames "Valentino Returns," thinking it will help him meet girls, as his parents undergo a stormy divorce. Weak script fades fast from fine premise, good start. Nice period feel. **97m/C VHS, Beta, LV.** Frederic Forrest, Veronica Cartwright, Jenny Wright, Barry Tubb; **D:** Peter Hoffman. *THV*

Valley Girl 🎬🎬½ *Bad Boyz* 1983 (R) Slight but surprisingly likeable teen romantic-comedy inspired by Frank Zappa novelty tune. Title stereotype falls for a leather-jacketed rebel. Really. It may look like a music video, but the story is straight from "Romeo and Juliet" via Southern California. Helped launch Cage's career. Music by Men at Work, Culture Club, and others. **95m/C VHS, Beta, LV.** Nicolas Cage, Deborah Foreman, Colleen Camp, Frederic Forrest; **D:** Martha Coolidge; **W:** Wayne Crawford; **C:** Frederick Elmes. *VES*

The Valley Obscured by the Clouds 🎬🎬 1972 A group of dropouts and seekers search for the valley of the gods in the wilds of New Guinea, and experience a sexual and spiritual metamorphosis. In French with English subtitles. **106m/C VHS.** **FR D:** Barbet Schroeder; **C:** Nestor Almendros; **M:** Pink Floyd. *FCT, WAR, BTV*

The Valley of Decision 🎬🎬🎬 1945 Entertaining poor-girl-meets-rich-boy story with Peck as a wealthy mill owner who falls in love with beautiful housemaid Garson (the Queen of MGM at the time). Set in 1870 Pittsburgh; based on Marcia Davenport's novel. **111m/B VHS.** Gregory Peck, Greer Garson, Donald Crisp, Lionel Barrymore, Preston Foster, Gladys Cooper, Marsha Hunt, Reginald Owen, Dan Duryea, Jessica Tandy, Barbara Everest; **D:** Tay Garnett; **W:** John Meehan, Sonya Levien; **C:** Joseph Ruttenberg. Nominations: Academy Awards '45: Best Actress (Garson), Original Dramatic/Comedy Score. *MGM*

Valley of Fire 🎬🎬 1951 Autry is the mayor of a boom town that suffers from a lack of women. He decides to import a caravan of brides for the men in town but villains attempt to kidnap the women. **63m/B VHS, Beta.** Gene Autry, Gail Davis, Pat Buttram; **D:** John English. *CCB*

The Valley of Gwangi 🎬🎬🎬 1969 (G) One of the best prehistoric-monster-westerns out there. Cowboys discover a lost valley of dinosaurs and try to capture a vicious, carnivorous allosaurus. Bad move, kemosabe! The creatures move via the stop-motion model animation by f/x maestro Ray Harryhausen, here at his finest. **95m/C VHS, Beta, LV.** James Franciscus, Gila Golan, Richard Carlson, Laurence Naismith, Freda Jackson; **D:** James O'Connolly; **W:** Nicolas Cage, Deborah Foreman. *WAR*

Valley of Terror 🎬½ 1938 Maynard is framed for cattle rustling. Can he prove his innocence? **59m/B VHS.** Kermit Maynard, Harley Wood, John Merton, Jack Ingram, Dick Curtis, Roger Williams; **D:** Al(bert) Herman. *NOS, CCB, DVT*

Valley of the Dolls 🎬🎬 1967 (PG) Camp/trash classic was rated as a bomb by many critics but is really of the so-bad-it's-good variety. Three beauties, Tate, Duke, and Parkins, dream

of Hollywood stardom but fall victim to Hollywood excess, including drug dependency (the "dolls" of the title). There's unhappy love affairs, porno parts, health risks, and hysterics of various kinds—all designed to have you dropping your jaw in disbelief. The bathroom scene between Duke and Hayward involving a wig is not to be missed. Based on the novel by Jacqueline Susann who has a bit part as a reporter. Remade for television as "Jacqueline Susann's Valley of the Dolls" in 1981. **123m/C VHS.** Barbara Parkins, Patty Duke, Sharon Tate, Paul Burke, Tony Scotti, Martin Milner, Susan Hayward, Charles Drake, Lee Grant, Alex Davion, Robert Harris, Robert Viharo, Joey Bishop, George Jessel; *Cameos:* Jacqueline Susann; **D:** Mark Robson; **W:** Dorothy Kingsley, Helen Deutsch; **C:** William H. Daniels; **M:** John Williams. Nominations: Academy Awards '67: Best Adapted Score. *FXV, BTV*

Valley of the Eagles 🎬½ 1951 When his wife and partner take off into the Lapland wilderness with his new invention, a scientist leads the police across the tundra in pursuit. Setting is at least a plus. **83m/B VHS, Beta.** **GB** Jack Warner, Nadia Gray, John McCallum, Martin Boddey, Christopher Lee; **D:** Terence Young; **M:** Nino Rota. *MSP*

Valley of the Lawless 🎬 1936 A cowboy rides into trouble aplenty while out searching for treasure. A routine western for Brown fans only. **59m/B VHS, Beta, LV.** Johnny Mack Brown; **D:** Robert North Bradbury; **W:** Robert North Bradbury. *NO*

Valley of the Sun 🎬🎬 1942 A government agent tracks a crooked Indian liaison to prevent an Indian uprising in Arizona. Ball, well before her "Lucy" days, plays the restaurant owner both men romance. Better than average, with good cast, some laughs, and lots of excitement. **84m/B VHS, Beta.** Lucille Ball, James Craig, Cedric Hardwicke, Dean Jagger, Peter Whitney, Billy Gilbert, Tom Tyler, Antonio Moreno, George Cleveland, Hank Bell; **D:** George Marshall. *TTC*

Valley of Wanted Men 🎬½ 1935 Three cons escape during a jailbreak and one uses his wits and nerve to prove another was framed. **56m/B VHS, Beta, 8mm.** Frankie Darro. *VYY*

Valmont 🎬🎬🎬 1989 (R) Another adaptation of the Choderlos de Laclos novel "Les Liaisons Dangereuses." Various members of the French aristocracy in 1782 mercilessly play each other for fools in a complex game of lust and deception. Firth and Bening are at first playfully sensual, then the stakes get too high. They share an interesting bathtub scene. Well-acted, the 1988 Frears version, "Dangerous Liaisons," is edgier. Seeing the two films together makes for interesting comparisons of characters and styles. **137m/C VHS, Beta, LV, Closed Caption.** Colin Firth, Meg Tilly, Annette Bening, Fairuza Balk, Sian Phillips, Jeffrey Jones, Fabia Drake, Henry Thomas, Vincent Schiavelli, T.P. McKenna, Ian McNeice; **D:** Milos Forman; **W:** Jean-Claude Carriere; **M:** Christopher Palmer. Cesar Awards '90: Best Art Direction/Set Decoration, Best Costume Design; Nominations: Academy Awards '89: Best Costume Design. *ORI*

The Vals 🎬½ 1985 (R) The glibly hip lethargy which is characteristic of four southern California teenaged girls turns to socially conscious resolve when a local orphanage is threatened. Like, for sure. **100m/C VHS, Beta.** Jill Carroll, Elana Stratheros, Gina Calabrese, Michelle Laurita, Chuck Connors, Sonny Bono, John Carradine, Michael Leon; **D:** James Polakof. *LIV, VES*

Vamp 🎬½ 1986 (R) Two college freshmen encounter a slew of weird, semi-vampiric people in a seamy red-light district nightclub. Starts cute but goes kinky. Jones is great as the stripping vampire. **93m/C VHS, Beta, LV, Closed Caption.** Grace Jones, Chris Makepeace, Robert Rusler, Gedde Watanabe; **D:** Richard Wenk; **C:** Elliot Davis; **M:** Jonathan Elias. *NWV, VTR*

Vamping 🎬½ 1984 (PG) Struggling musician plans to burglarize a wealthy widow's home. Once inside, he finds himself attracted to his proposed victim. Tedious going. **110m/C VHS, Beta.** Patrick Duf-

fy, Catherine Hyland, Rod Arrants, Fred A. Keller; **D:** Frederick King Keller. *FOX*

The Vampire 🎬🎬 *Mark of the Vampire* 1957 Pale man with big teeth attempts to swindle a beautiful babe out of fortune. Followed by "The Vampire's Coffin." **95m/B VHS.** **MX** Abel Salazar, Ariadne Welter, German Robles, Carmen Montejo, Jose Luis Jimenez; **D:** Fernando Mendez. *SNC*

Vampire at Midnight 🎬½ 1988 Fairly stupid homicide detective stalks a rampaging vampire in Los Angeles. Occasional moments of gratuitous sex thrown in for good measure. **93m/C VHS, Beta, Closed Caption.** Jason Williams, Gustav Vintas, Jeanie Moore, Christina Whitaker, Leslie Milne; **D:** Gregory McClatchy. *FOX*

The Vampire Bat 🎬🎬½ 1932 A mad scientist and a vampire bat and its supernatural demands set the stage for murders in a small town. Sets and actors borrowed from Universal Studios in this low-budget flick that looks and plays better than it should. Weird and very exploitative for 1932, now seems dated. **69m/B VHS, Beta.** Lionel Atwill, Fay Wray, Melvyn Douglas, Dwight Frye, Maude Eburne, George E. Stone; **D:** Frank Strayer. *VYY, SNC, WFV*

Vampire Circus 🎬🎬½ 1971 (R) A circus appears in an isolated Serbian village in the 19th century but instead of bringing joy and happiness, this circus brings only death, mutilation and misery. It seems all the members are vampires who have the unique ability to transform themselves into animals. They intend to take revenge on the small town, whose inhabitants killed their evil ancestor 100 years previously. Excellent Hammer production. **84m/C VHS.** **GB** Adrienne Corri, Laurence Payne, Thorley Walters, John Moulder-Brown, Lynne Frederick, Elizabeth Seal, Anthony Corlan, Richard Owens, Domini Blythe, David Prowse; **D:** Robert W. Young. *FRG, MLB*

Vampire Cop 🎬½ 1990 (R) A vampire cop (not to be confused with zombie, maniac, midnight, psycho, future or Robo) teams up with a beautiful reporter to 'collar' a drug kingpin. **CW:** Language, strong violence, and strong sensuality. **89m/C VHS.** Melissa Moore, Ed Cannon, Terence Jenkins. *ATL*

The Vampire Happening 🎬½ 1971 (R) An actress discovers to her chagrin that her ancestors were vampires and so is she. **90m/C VHS, Beta.** **GE** Ferdinand "Ferdy" Mayne; **D:** Freddie Francis. *NO*

The Vampire Hookers 🎬 *Cemetary Girls; Sensuous Vampires; Night of the Bloodsuckers; Twice Bitten* 1978 (R) Man in makeup recruits bevy of beautiful bloodsuckers to lure warm blooded victims to his castle. High ham performance by Carradine. Alternate titles: "Cemetery Girls," "Sensuous Vampires," "Night of the Bloodsuckers." **82m/C VHS, Beta.** **PH** John Carradine, Bruce Fairbairn, Trey Wilson, Karen Stride, Lenka Novak, Katie Dolan, Lex Winter; **D:** Cirio H. Santiago. *NO*

Vampire in Brooklyn 🎬 1995 (R) Murphy switches gears to play a Carribean vampire traveling to New York in search of his vampiric lady love—who turns out to be half-vamp-half-cop Bassett. As in "Coming to America," Murphy plays multiple characters, but that's three times the disappointment. Stale humor and cheap horror effects do little to break the zombie curse plaguing Murphy's career. Three days into filming, a stunt double for Bassett was killed after doing a routine jump on the set, providing a bad omen Murphy should have heeded. **CW:** Strong language and vampire violence. **103m/C VHS.** Eddie Murphy, Angela Bassett, Kadeem Hardison, Allen Payne, Zakes Mokae, John Witherspoon; **D:** Wes Craven; **W:** Charles Murphy, Christopher Parker, Michael Lucker; **C:** Mark Irwin; **M:** J. Peter Robinson. *PAR*

Vampire Journals 🎬🎬 1996 (R) Revenge-minded Zachary (Gunn) vows to destroy Ash (Morris), the ancient vampire who created him centuries before, especially when they both become interested in the same mortal woman, Sofia (Cerre). Shot on location in Transylvania. **CW:** Nudity, sexual situations, violence. 82m/C VHS. David Gunn, Jonathan Morris, Kirsten Cerre, Starr Andreeff; **D:** Ted Nicolaou. FLL

The Vampire Lovers ☊☊½ 1970 (R) An angry father goes after a lesbian vampire who has ravished his daughter and other young girls in a peaceful European village. Innovative story was soon used in countless other vampire vehicles. Hammer Studio's first horror film with nudity, another addition to the genre which spread rapidly. Based on the story "Carmilla" by Sheridan Le Fanu. Followed by "Lust for a Vampire." 91m/C VHS, Beta. **GB** Ingrid Pitt, Pippa Steele, Madeleine Smith, Peter Cushing, George Cole, Dawn Addams, Kate O'Mara, Ferdinand "Ferdy" Mayne; **D:** Roy Ward Baker. ORI, MLB

The Vampire People ☊½ *The Blood Drinkers* 1966 (PG) A dwarf-assisted vampire attempts to save the life of his true love by transplanting her sister's heart. Typical Filipino vampire movie. In color and sepia-tone. 79m/C VHS, Beta. **PH** Ronald Remy, Amalia Fuentes, Eddie Fernandez, Eva Montez; **D:** Gerardo (Gerry) De Leon. SNC

Vampire Raiders—Ninja Queen woof! 1989 The white ninjas versus the black ninjas. The evil black ninjas are plotting to infiltrate the hotel industry. The white ninjas come to the rescue. 90m/C VHS. Agnes Chan, Chris Petersen; **D:** Bruce Lambert. TWE

Vampire Vixens from Venus ☊ 1994 Three hideous drug smuggling aliens transform themselves into bodacious babes on earth so they can get what they came for. Seems their drug fix is derived from the life essence of men and they plan to drain every last drop they can. 90m/C VHS. Michelle (McClellan) Bauer, Charlie Callas. SHR

The Vampire's Coffin ☊½ *El Ataud Del Vampiro; El Ataud Del Coffin* 1958 Count Lavud is relieved when faithful servant removes stake implanted in his heart. 86m/B VHS. **MX** Abel Salazar, Ariadne Welter, German Robles; **D:** Fernando Mendez. SNC

The Vampire's Ghost ☊ 1945 A 400-hundred-year-old vampire/zombie, doomed to walk the earth forever, heads the African underworld. He can't be killed and can even go out during the day if he wears sunglasses. His future's so bright he's just gotta wear shades. 59m/B VHS. John Abbott, Peggy Stewart; **D:** Lesley Selander. NOS, DVT, HEG

Vampire's Kiss ☊☊☊ 1988 (R) Cage makes this one worthwhile; his twisted transformation from pretentious post-val dude to psychotic yuppie from hell is inspired. If his demented torment of his secretary (Alonso) doesn't give you the creeps, his scene with the cockroach will. Cage fans will enjoy his facial aerobics; Beals fans will appreciate her extensive sucking scenes (she's the vamp of his dreams). More for psych majors than horror buffs. 103m/C VHS, Beta, LV. Nicolas Cage, Elizabeth Ashley, Jennifer Beals, Maria Conchita Alonso, Kasi Lemmons, Bob Lujan, Jennifer Lundy; **D:** Robert Bierman; **C:** Stefan Czapsky; **M:** Colin Towns. HBO

Vampyr ☊☊ *Vampyr, Ou L'Etrange Aventure de David Gray; Vampyr, Der Traum des David Gray; Not Against the Flesh; Castle of Doom; The Strange Adventure of David Gray; The Vampire* 1931 Dreyer's classic portrays a hazy, dreamlike world full of chilling visions from the point of view of a young man who believes himself surrounded by vampires and who dreams of his own burial in a most disturbing way. Evil lurks around every corner as camera angles, light and shadow sometimes overwhelm plot. A high point in horror films based on a collection of horror stories by Sheridan le Fanu. In German with English subtitles. 75m/B VHS, Beta. **GE** Julien West, Sybille Schmitz, Harriet Gerard, Maurice Schutz; **D:** Carl Theodor Dreyer; **W:** Carl Theodor Dreyer; **M:** Wolfgang Zeller. VYY, NOS, SNC

The Vampyr ☊☊ 1992 Uncut version of the BBC musical production about a lustful vampire. Text sets present-day lyrics to the 1827 opera by Heinrich Marschner. Vampire Ripley (Ebrahim) has just been set free in London after having been trapped in an underground tomb for 200 years. Unless he puts the bite on three lovely ladies within three days he will be condemned to eternal damnation. Everyone gets to sing in the nude. Surreally amusing. 115m/C VHS. **GB** Omar Ebrahim, Willemijn Van Gent, Fiona O'Neill, Sally-Ann Shepherdson. FOX

Vampyres ☊☊½ *Vampyres, Daughters of Dracula; Blood Hunger; Satan's Daughters* 1974 (R) Alluring female vampires coerce unsuspecting motorists to their castle for a good time, which ends in death. Anulka was the centerfold girl in Playboy's May 1973 issue. Originally titled "Vampyres, Daughters of Dracula." 90m/C VHS, Beta. **GB** Marianne Morris, Anulka, Murray Brown, Brian Deacon, Sally Faulkner; **D:** Joseph Larraz. NO

The Van ☊ *Chevy Van* 1977 (R) A recent high school graduate passes on the college scene so he can spend more time picking up girls in his van. A lame sex (and sexist) comedy. 92m/C VHS, Beta. Stuart Getz, Deborah White, Danny DeVito, Harry Moses, Maurice Barkin; **D:** Sam Grossman. NO

The Van ☊☊☊ 1995 (R) The last of writer Roddy Doyle's Barrytown trilogy (following "The Commitments" and "The Snapper") is set in 1989-90, in Dublin, where baker Bimbo (O'Kelly) has just lost his job. Tired of sitting around the pub, he takes his redundancy money and buys a filthy, dilapidated fish 'n' chips van, which he decides to run with best friend Larry (Meany), with their families helping out. The months pass quickly and their venture turns out to be a big success but the close quarters puts a strain on the mens' friendship until Bimbo has another idea. **CW:** Strong language. 105m/C VHS. **GB** Donal O'Kelly, Colm Meaney, Ger Ryan, Caroline Rotwell, Neili Conroy, Ruaidhri Conroy; **D:** Stephen Frears; **W:** Roddy Doyle; **C:** Oliver Stapleton; **M:** Eric Clapton, Richard Hartley. NYR

Van Gogh ☊☊☊ 1992 (R) "One doesn't produce 100 masterpieces in a state of depression—Van Gogh died from having had a glimpse of happiness." This is the way director Pialat sums up his approach to the last 67 days in the life of Vincent Van Gogh. Dutronc is skillful in portraying Van Gogh as a man with no excuses, and even a sense of humor. Not a psychological portrait and offers no answers—it's simply one artist's view of another. In French with English subtitles. **CW:** Nudity and sexuality. 155m/C VHS. **FR** Jacques Dutronc, Alexandra London, Gerard Sety, Bernard LeCoq, Corinne Bourdon; **D:** Maurice Pialat; **W:** Maurice Pialat; **M:** Edith Vesperini. Cesar Awards '92: Best Actor (Dutronc). COL, FCT

Van Nuys Blvd. ☊½ 1979 (R) The popular boulevard is the scene where the cool southern California guys converge for cruising and girl watching, so naturally it's where a country hick comes to test his drag racing skills and check out the action. 93m/C VHS, Beta. Bill Adler, Cynthia Wood, Dennis Bowen, Melissa Prophet; **D:** William Sachs. NO

Vanina Vanini ☊☊☊½ 1961 An acclaimed Rossellini historical drama about the daughter of an Italian aristocrat in 1824 who nurses and falls in love with a wounded patriot hiding in her house. Based on a Stendhal short story. In Italian with English subtitles. 113m/B VHS, Beta. **IT** Sandra Milo, Laurent Terzieff; **D:** Roberto Rossellini. FCT

The Vanishing ☊☊☊ *Spoorloos* 1988 When his wife suddenly disappears, a young husband finds himself becoming increasingly obsessed with finding her. Three years down the road, his world has become one big, mad nightmare. Then, just as suddenly, the answer confronts him, but the reality of it may be too horrible to face. Well-made dark thriller based on "The Golden Egg" by Tim Krabbe. In French and Dutch with English subtitles. Remade by Sluizer in 1992. 107m/C VHS. NL FR Barnard Pierre Donnadieu, Johanna Ter Steege, Gene Bervoets; **D:** George Sluizer. FXL

The Vanishing ☊☊½ 1993 (R) Director Sluizer remakes his own 1988 Dutch film "Spoorloos" to lesser effect. Tense thriller about the disappearance of a woman (Bullock) at a highway rest stop. Her boyfriend (Sutherland) becomes obsessed with locating her, searching for some three years as he is haunted by her memory. Unlike the Dutch original, the remake resorts to a clumsy ending designed for feel-good appeal. Based on the novel "The Golden Egg" by Tim Krabbe. **CW:** Language and terror and violence. 110m/C VHS, Closed Caption. Jeff Bridges, Kiefer Sutherland, Nancy Travis, Sandra Bullock, Park Overall, Lisa Eichhorn, George Hearn, Maggie Linderman, Lynn Hamilton; **D:** George Sluizer; **W:** Todd Graff; **M:** Jerry Goldsmith. FXV

Vanishing Act ☊☊½ 1988 (PG) While on his honeymoon, Harry Kenyon reports his wife missing to the local police. Within a short period of time his wife is found, but Harry says the woman is an impostor. This thriller follows Harry's desperate attempt to get to the truth. Made for television. 94m/C VHS, Beta. Mike Farrell, Margot Kidder, Elliott Gould, Fred Gwynne, Graham Jarvis; **D:** David Greene; **W:** Richard Levinson, William Link. THV

Vanishing American ☊☊ 1926 The mistreatment of the American Indian is depicted in this sweeping Western epic. Musical score. 114m/B VHS, Beta. Richard Dix, Noah Beery Sr.; **D:** George B. Seitz. GPV, VYY

Vanishing Legion 1931 Western serial with outdoor action and gunplay. Twelve chapters, 13 minutes each. 156m/B VHS, Beta. Frankie Darro, Harry Carey Sr.; **D:** B. Reeves Eason. GPV, NOS, VCN

Vanishing Point ☊☊ 1971 (PG) An ex-racer makes a bet to deliver a souped-up car from Denver to San Francisco in 15 hours. Taking pep pills along the way, he eludes police, meets up with a number of characters, and finally crashes into a roadblock. Rock score helps attract this film's cult following. 98m/C VHS, Beta, LV. Barry Newman, Cleavon Little, Gilda Texler, Dean Jagger, Paul Koslo, Robert Donner, Severn Darden, Victoria Medlin; **D:** Richard Sarafian; **C:** John A. Alonzo. FOX

Vanishing Prairie ☊☊☊ 1954 This documentary examines the wonders of nature that abound in the American prairie. From the "True-Life Adventures" series. 60m/C VHS, Beta. **D:** James Algar. Academy Awards '54: Best Feature Documentary. DIS

The Vanishing Westerner ☊☊ 1950 A cowboy, falsely accused of murder, works to vindicate himself and uncovers a series of robberies. This one has enough plot twists to take it out of the routine. 60m/B VHS, Beta. Monte Hale, Arthur Space, Aline Towne, Paul Hurst, Roy Barcroft, Richard Anderson, William Phipps, Rand Brooks; **D:** Philip Ford. DVT

Vanishing Wilderness ☊☊ 1973 (G) This documentary looks at the wild animals roaming across North America. 90m/C VHS, Beta. **D:** Arthur Dubs. MED, VTR

Vanity Fair ☊☊ 1932 Loy stars in this tale of a wily and manipulative woman looking for the perfect marriage. This was the 58th film for the 27-year-old Loy, but even she couldn't save it. Of course, none of the three films based on the story by Thackeray have done it justice. 67m/B VHS. Myrna Loy, Conway Tearle, Barbara Kent, Walter Byron, Anthony Bushell, Billy Bevan, Montagu Love, Mary Forbes; **D:** Chester M. Franklin. NOS, HEG

Vanity Fair ☊☊½ 1967 BBC TV adaptation of William Makepeace Thackeray's satire on human folly in 19th-century England. Amoral governess (and anti-heroine) Becky Sharp (Hampshire) will stop at nothing to climb the social ladder, aided by a wealthy marriage and her own audacity, which ultimately leads to scandal. 250m/C VHS. **GB** Susan Hampshire, Robert Flemyng, Richard Caldicot, Barbara Couper, Roy Marsden, Bryan Marshall; **D:** David Giles. FCT, TVC

Vanya on 42nd Street 🎬🎬🎬½ 1994
(PG) Group of actors in street clothes rehearse a workshop production of Chekhov's play, "Uncle Vanya" in New York's dilapidated New Amsterdam Theater. Theatrical director Gregory first gets his group together in 1989, with Mamet's contemporary adaptation, and they continue to work in private until Malle films their production some four years later before a small, select audience. Shawn, best known for "My Dinner with Andre" portrays Vanya with depth and complexity. The other actors shine as well, often against type, in this complex Russian drama of desperation. 119m/C VHS, LV. Wallace Shawn, Julianne Moore, Brooke Smith, Larry Pine, George Gaynes, Lynn Cohen, Madhur Jaffrey, Phoebe Brand, Jerry Mayer, Andre Gregory; **D:** Louis Malle; **W:** Andre Gregory, David Mamet; **C:** Declan Quinn; **M:** Joshua Redman. Nominations: Independent Spirit Awards '95: Best Supporting Actor (Pine), Best Supporting Actress (Smith). COL

Varan the Unbelievable 🎬 Daikaiju Baran; The Monster Baran 1961 A chemical experiment near a small island in the Japanese archipelago disturbs a prehistoric monster beneath the water. The awakened monster spreads terror on the island. Most difficult part of this movie is deciding what the rubber monster model is supposed to represent. 70m/B VHS, Beta. **JP** Myron Healey, Tsuruko Kobayashi; **D:** Inoshiro Honda. NOS, VCI

Varieties on Parade 🎬 1952 A vaudeville show on film, featuring an array of second-rate comics and musical personalities. Sad to watch its demise. 55m/B VHS, Beta, LV. Jackie Coogan, Eddie Garr, Tom Neal, Iris Adrian. NO

Variety 🎬🎬🎬 1925 Simple and tragic tale of a scheming young girl and the two men of whom she takes advantage. The European circus in all its beautiful sadness is the setting. Extraordinary cast and superb cinematography. Silent. 104m/B VHS, Beta. **GE** Emil Jannings, Lya de Putti, Warwick Ward, Werner Krauss; **D:** E.A. Dupont. VYY, NOS, DVT

Variety 🎬🎬½ 1983 A girl takes a job selling tickets in a Times Square porn theater. Her initial loathing for the genre gives way to a fascination with its clients, one of whom is a gangster, and she becomes drawn to the seamy world inside. An independently made feature. 101m/C VHS, Beta. Sandy McLeod, Will Patton, Richard Davidson; **D:** Bette Gordon. MED

Variety Lights 🎬🎬🎬½ Luci Del Varieta; Lights of Variety 1951 Fellini's first (albeit joint) directorial effort, wherein a young girl runs away with a travelling vaudeville troupe and soon becomes its main attraction as a dancer. Filled with Fellini's now-familiar delight in the bizarre and sawdust/tinsel entertainment. In Italian with English subtitles. 93m/B VHS, Beta. **IT** Giulietta Masina, Peppino de Filippo, Carla Del Poggio, Folco Lulli; **D:** Federico Fellini, Alberto Lattuada; **W:** Federico Fellini, Tullio Pinelli, Ennio Flaiano, Alberto Lattuada. HMV, APD, CVC

Vasectomy: A Delicate Matter woof! Vasectomy 1986 (PG-13) A mother of eight issues a final decree to her husband about their sex life. He must get a vasectomy or there won't be any. As good as it sounds. 92m/C VHS, Beta. Paul Sorvino, Abe Vigoda, Cassandra Edwards, Lorne Greene, Ina Balin, June Wilkinson, William Marshall; **D:** Robert Burge; **W:** Robert Burge. WOV

Vatican Conspiracy 🎬½ 1981 The members of the Vatican's College of Cardinals do everything in their power to discredit a newly-appointed radical pontiff. 90m/C VHS, Beta. Terence Stamp; **D:** Marcello Aliprandi. NO

Vault of Horror 🎬🎬½ Tales from the Crypt II 1973 (R) A collection of five terrifying tales based on original stories from the E.C. comic books of the 1950s. Stories include, "Midnight Mess," "Bargain in Death," "This Trick'll Kill You," "The Neat Job" and "Drawn and Quartered." 86m/C VHS, Beta. **GB** Terry-Thomas, Curt Jurgens, Glynis Johns, Dawn Addams, Daniel Massey, Tom Baker, Michael Craig,

Anna Massey, Denholm Elliott; **D:** Roy Ward Baker; **W:** Milton Subotsky. MED

Vegas 🎬 1978 A private detective, with Las Vegas beauties as assistants and pursuers, solves the murder of a teenage runaway girl. Pilot for television series. Scriptwriter Mann went on to do "Miami Vice." 74m/C VHS, Beta. Robert Urich, June Allyson, Tony Curtis, Will Sampson, Greg Morris; **D:** Richard Lang; **W:** Michael Mann. PSM

Vegas in Space woof! 1994 Four male astronauts take a secret mission to the planet Clitoris, the all-female pleasure plant where men are forbidden to trod. To capture a heinous villainous, they swallow gender-reversal pills in order to infiltrate the resort as show-girls. Typical Troma trash. Boasts an all-transvestite cast. 85m/C VHS. Doris Fish, Miss X, Ginger Quest, Ramona Fischer, Lori Naslund, Timmy Spence, Silvana Nova, Sandelle Kincaid, Tommy Pace, Arturo Galster, Jennifer Blowdryer, Freida Lay, Tippi; **D:** Phillip R. Ford; **W:** Phillip R. Ford, Doris Fish, Miss X; **C:** Robin Clark; **M:** Ramona Fischer, Timmy Spence. TTV

The Vegas Strip Wars 🎬🎬 Las Vegas Strip War 1984 Rival casino owners battle it out in the land of lady luck. Unmemorable except for Jones's Don King impersonation and the fact that it was Hudson's last TV movie. 100m/C VHS, Beta. Rock Hudson, James Earl Jones, Noriyuki "Pat" Morita, Sharon Stone, Robert Costanzo; **D:** George Englund. LIV

Vegas Vacation 🎬 1996 (PG) It may not have come out under the "National Lampoon" banner but you'll recognize both the characters and the situations. The innocent Griswold clan head from their Chicago home to the bright lights and gambling temptations of Las Vegas. Clark (Chase) blows all their money, Ellen (D'Angelo) reveals a hidden passion for Wayne Newton, daughter Audrey (Nichols) decides to become a go-go dancer, and son Rusty (Embry) turns into a high roller who draws the attention of the mob. Oh yeah, dimwit cousin Eddie (Quaid) also tries to supply a few yucks. 98m/C VHS, LV, Closed Caption. Chevy Chase, Beverly D'Angelo, Randy Quaid, Ethan Embry, Miriam Flynn, Marisol Nichols, Shae D'Lyn, Wallace Shawn, Wayne Newton; **Cameos:** Sid Caesar, Julia Sweeney, Christie Brinkley; **D:** Stephen Kessler; **W:** Elisa Bell; **C:** William A. Fraker; **M:** Joel McNeely. WAR

Velnio Nuotaka 🎬🎬½ The Devil's Bride 1975 A popular Lithuanian musical based on the play "Baltargio Malunas" by K. Boruta. English subtitles. 78m/C VHS, Beta. LI IHF

Velvet Smooth 🎬 1976 (R) A protection agency's sultry boss, Velvet Smooth, gets involved solving the problems of a numbers racket. 89m/C VHS. Johnnie Hill; **D:** Janace Fink. NO

Velvet Touch 🎬🎬🎬 1948 Well-engineered thriller about an actress who craftily murders her producer. A theater-loving police detective winds up accusing the wrong woman—sending the overwrought murderess into a moral tailspin. Things don't work out as you may expect. Fine acting. 97m/B VHS, Beta. Rosalind Russell, Leo Genn, Claire Trevor, Sydney Greenstreet, Leon Ames, Frank McHugh, Walter Kingsford, Dan Tobin, Lex Barker, Nydia Westman; **D:** George Sherman; **W:** Leo Rosten. TTC

The Velvet Vampire 🎬🎬 Cemetary Girls; Through the Looking Glass 1971 (R) Yarnall is a sexy, sun-loving, dune buggy-riding vampiress who seduces a young, sexy, swinging, Southern California couple in her desert home. Lots of atmosphere to go along with the blood and nudity. 82m/C VHS, Beta, LV. Michael Blodgett, Sherry Miles, Celeste Yarnall, Gene Shane, Jerry Daniels, Sandy Ward, Paul Prokop, Chris Woodley, Robert Tessier; **D:** Stephanie Rothman.

Vendetta 🎬½ 1985 A woman gets herself arrested and sent to the penitentiary in order to exact revenge there for her sister's death. Acting and pacing make this better than the average sexploitation flick. 89m/C VHS, Beta. Karen Chase, Sandy Martin, Durga McBroom, Kin Shriner, Eugene Glazer; **D:** Bruce Logan; **W:** David Newman. LIV, VES

Vendetta for the Saint 🎬 1968 A feature-length episode of the television series "The Saint," in which Simon Templar pursues a Sicilian mobster on a personal vendetta. 98m/C VHS, Beta. **GB** Roger Moore; **D:** James O'Connolly. FOX

Vengeance 🎬🎬 1937 A police officer resigns in shame after failing to thwart a holdup. He attempts to redeem himself by working on his own to infiltrate the same gang. 61m/B VHS. Lyle Talbot, Wendy Barrie, Wally Albright, Marc Lawrence; **D:** Del Lord. VYY, MOV

Vengeance 🎬 1980 Four burglars take hostages after their robbery is bungled, but they won't get away—especially after the hostages die. 92m/C VHS, Beta. Sally Lockett, Nicholas Jacquez, Bob Elliott; **D:** Bob Blizz. NO

Vengeance 🎬 1986 A low-budget film about rebels fighting off an authoritarian government. 114m/C VHS, Beta. Jason Miller, Lea Massari; **D:** Antonio Isasi. TWE

Vengeance 🎬🎬 Vengeance: The Story of Tony Cimo 1989 (R) A bereaved young man strikes out against the injustice of his parents' murder. His revenge against the killers takes him several steps beyond the law, and he's not so sure it was the right idea. Made for television. 90m/C VHS, LV. Brad Davis, Roxanne Hart, Brad Dourif, William Conrad; **D:** Marc Daniels. IME

Vengeance Is Mine 🎬🎬🎬 1979 Told in flashbacks, the film focuses on the life of a habitual criminal whose life of deprivation leads to murder. Contains violence and nudity. Based on a true story. In Japanese with English subtitles. 129m/C VHS, LV. **JP** Ken Ogata; **D:** Shohei Imamura. FCT

Vengeance Is Mine woof! 1984 (R) A demented farmer captures three criminals and tortures them in horrifyingly sadistic ways. Gratuitously grisly. 90m/C VHS, Beta, LV. Ernest Borgnine, Michael J. Pollard, Hollis McLaren; **D:** John Trent. VTR, GEM

Vengeance of the Snowmaid 🎬½ 197? Some Kung Fu creepies raped her mom. Now nobody can get a sword in edgewise on the Snow Maid as she seeks revenge. 82m/C VHS, Beta. Mo Ka Kei, Chen Chen. NO

Vengeance of the Zombies 🎬½ 1972 A madman seeks revenge by setting an army of walking corpses to stalk the streets of London. 90m/C VHS, Beta. **SP** Paul Naschy; **D:** Leon Klimovsky. SNC

Vengeance Valley 🎬🎬 1951 Lancaster and Walker are foster brothers with Walker being an envious weasel who always expects Lancaster to get him out of scrapes. Lancaster is even accused of a crime committed by Walker and must work to clear himself. Good cast is let down by uneven direction. 83m/C VHS, Beta. Burt Lancaster, Joanne Dru, Robert Walker, Sally Forrest, John Ireland, Hugh O'Brian; **D:** Richard Thorpe. NOS, DVT, CAB

Venice, Venice 🎬🎬½ 1992 (R) Alternately earnest and satirical, Jaglom pokes fun at himself and movie-making in a movie about, well, himself and movie-making. Consciously straddling the genre fence, he uses real people and events, but adopts a pseudonym, Dean. In Venice, Italy, young filmmaker Alard decides to make a film about Dean/Jaglom, a plot which creates the effect of two mirrors reflecting each other into infinity. Dean/Jaglom and Alard return to Venice, California, where he conducts auditions for a movie in which he will star and direct. Art imitating life or life imitating art? More importantly, does it really matter? **CW:** Language. 108m/C VHS. Nelly Alard, Henry Jaglom, Suzanne Bertish, Melissa Leo, Daphna Kastner, David Duchovny, Diane Salinger, Zack Norman, Marshall Barer, John Landis, Pierre Cottrell, Edna Fainaru, Klaus Hellwig; **D:** Henry Jaglom; **W:** Henry Jaglom; **C:** Hanania Baer. FXL

Venom woof! **1982 (R)** Deadly black mamba is loose in an elegant townhouse, terrorizing big-name cast. The snake continually terrorizes an evil kidnapper, his accomplices and his kidnapped victim. Participants walk through tired cliches with that far-away look in their eyes—like they wish they were anywhere else. Original director Tobe Hooper was replaced. **92m/C VHS, Beta.** *GB* Sterling Hayden, Klaus Kinski, Sarah Miles, Nicol Williamson, Cornelia Sharpe, Susan George, Michael Gough, Oliver Reed; **D:** Piers Haggard; **W:** Robert B. Carrington; **M:** Michael Kamen. *VES*

Venus Against the Son of Hercules **1962** Our hero must use all his genetically procured musculature in his battle against the lovely but deadly Venus. **?m/C VHS, Beta.** *IT* Roger Brown, Jackie Lane. *SNC*

Venus in Furs *♂½* *Paroxismus; Puo Una Morta Rivivere Per Amore?; Venus in Peltz* **1970 (R)** Jazz musician working in Rio de Janeiro becomes obsessed with a mysterious woman; she resembles a murder victim whose body he discovered months earlier. Weird mix of horror, sadism, black magic, and soft porn. **90m/C VHS, Beta.** *GB* James Darren, Klaus Kinski, Barbara McNair, Dennis Price, Maria Rohm; **D:** Jess (Jesus) Franco. *REP, TPV*

Venus Rising *♂♂* **1995 (R)** In the year 2000, Eve and August manage to escape from the island prison on which they were raised. They discover that the mainland world features emotions that are controlled by drugs and love is only a game on the virtual reality network. Hunted, the fugitives try to fit in and figure out what's real and what's fantasy. Be forewarned—Fairchild's role is very small. **CW:** Violence, sexuality, and some language. **91m/C VHS, Closed Caption.** Audie England, Costas Mandylor, Billy Wirth, Morgan Fairchild; **D:** Leora Barish; **W:** Leora Barish. *COL*

Venus the Ninja *♂* **198?** A comely female Ninja battles an evil warlord. **90m/C VHS, Beta.** Pearl Cheung, Meng Fei; **D:** Sze Ma Peng. *TWE*

Vera Cruz *♂♂½* **1953** Two soldiers of fortune become involved in the Mexican Revolution of 1866, a stolen shipment of gold, divided loyalties, and gun battles. Less than innovative plot is made into an exciting action flick. **94m/C VHS, LV.** Gary Cooper, Burt Lancaster, Denise Darcel, Cesar Romero, George Macready, Ernest Borgnine, Charles Bronson, Jack Elam; **D:** Robert Aldrich; **C:** Ernest Laszlo. *MGM, FOX, FCT*

Verboten! *♂♂½* **1959** In post-war occupied Berlin, an American G.I. falls in love with a German girl. Good direction maintains a steady pace. **93m/B VHS.** James Best, Susan Cummings, Tom Pittman, Paul Dubov; **D:** Samuel Fuller. *IME*

Verdi *♂♂* **1953** The story of the Italian operatic composer and the loves of his life. Dubbed in English. **80m/C VHS.** *IT* Pierre Cressoy. *FCT*

The Verdict *♂♂♂* **1982 (R)** Newman plays an alcoholic failed attorney reduced to ambulance chasing. A friend gives him a supposedly easy malpractice case which turns out to be a last chance at redeeming himself and his career. Adapted from the novel by Barry Reed. One of Newman's finest performances. **122m/C VHS, Beta, LV.** Paul Newman, James Mason, Charlotte Rampling, Jack Warden, Milo O'Shea, Lindsay Crouse; **D:** Sidney Lumet; **W:** David Mamet; **C:** Andrzej Bartkowiak. National Board of Review Awards '82: Best Director (Lumet); Nominations: Academy Awards '82: Best Actor (Newman), Best Adapted Screenplay, Best Director (Lumet), Best Picture, Best Supporting Actor (Mason). *FOX*

Vermont Is for Lovers *♂½* **1992** Pre-wedding jitters consume stressed-out Manhattanites Marya (Cohn) and George (Thrush) when they travel to bucolic Tunbridge, Vermont to get married on Marya's Aunt Ann's farm. After continuously arguing, they decide to spend the day before the wedding apart and George wanders around the community asking marriage advice from various old-timers. The Yuppie leads aren't terribly compelling and neither is the improvised

dialogue. **86m/C VHS.** George Thrush, Marya Cohn, Ann O'Brien; **D:** John O'Brien; **C:** John O'Brien; **M:** Tony Silbert. *FCT, KIV*

Verne Miller *♂♂* **1988 (R)** A film of the true story of Verne Miller, Al Capone's hit man. After rescuing a friend from the Feds, Miller is hunted down by both the cops and the mob. **95m/C VHS, Beta, LV.** Scott Glenn, Barbara Stock, Thomas G. Waites, Lucinda Jenney, Sonny Carl Davis; **D:** Rod Hewitt. *NLC*

The Vernonia Incident *♂½* **1989** Urban guerillas invade a small town, killing the police chief. The townspeople gather up their shotguns and fight back. That's entertainment. **95m/C VHS, Beta.** David Jackson, Shawn Stevens, Floyd Ragner, Ed Justice, Robert Louis Jakson; **D:** Ray Etheridge; **W:** Ray Etheridge. *NO*

Veronico Cruz *♂♂½* *La Dueda Interna; The Debt* **1987** Despite its sincerity, Pereira's feature debut offers muddled response to the human waste incurred by the Falklands War. Set in a tiny remote village in the Argentinean mountains, the film's narrative is derived from the growing friendship between a shepherd boy and a teacher from the city. Well-meaning anti-war movie. In Spanish with English subtitles. **96m/C VHS.** *AR GB* Juan Jose Camero, Gonzalo Morales, Rene Olaguivel, Guillermo Delgado; **D:** Miguel Pereira. *CCN, TPV*

Veronika Voss *♂♂♂* *Die Sehns Ucht Der Veronika Voss* **1982 (R)** Highlights the real life of fallen film star Sybille Schmitz who finally took her own life out of despair. Played by Zech, Voss is exploited by her physician to turn over all of her personal belongings for morphine. A lover discovers the corruption and reveals it to the authorities. This causes great upheaval resulting in Voss' suicide. Highly metaphoric and experimental in its treatment of its subject. In German with English subtitles. **105m/C VHS.** *GE* Rosel Zech, Hilmar Thate, Conny Froboess, Anna Marie Duringer, Volker Spengler; **D:** Rainer Werner Fassbinder; **M:** Peer Raben. *APD, FCT*

Vertigo *♂♂♂♂* **1958 (PG)** Hitchcock's romantic story of obsession, manipulation and fear. Stewart plays a detective forced to retire after his fear of heights causes the death of a fellow policeman and, perhaps, the death of a woman he'd been hired to follow. The appearance of her double (Novak), whom he compulsively transforms into the dead girl's image, leads to a mesmerizing cycle of madness and lies. Features Herrmann's haunting music. **126m/C VHS, LV, Closed Caption.** James Stewart, Kim Novak, Barbara Bel Geddes, Tom Helmore, Ellen Corby, Henry Jones, Raymond Bailey, Lee Patrick; **D:** Alfred Hitchcock; **W:** Sam Taylor; **C:** Robert Burks; **M:** Bernard Herrmann. Nominations: Academy Awards '58: Best Art Direction/Set Decoration, Best Sound. *USH, TLF*

A Very Brady Christmas *♂♂* **1988** Many of the original Bradys returned for this yuletide special. After Mike and Carol's vacation plans go awry, they decide to invite the whole bunch home for a family reunion. This was the highest rated television movie in 1989. Spawned yet another unsuccessful "Brady" series sequel. **94m/C VHS, Closed Caption.** Florence Henderson, Robert Reed, Ann B. Davis, Maureen McCormick, Eve Plumb, Jennifer Runyon, Barry Williams, Christopher Knight, Michael Lookinland, Jerry Houser, Caryn Richman; **D:** Peter Baldwin. *PAR*

A Very Brady Sequel *♂♂½* **1996 (PG-13)** They're back! The cast from the surprise hit "The Brady Bunch Movie" returns and Brady mom Carol (Long) is shocked when her presumed dead first husband Roy Martin (Matheson) suddenly appears on their doorstep. The Bradys must travel to Hawaii to attempt to save the family (based on a three-part episode from the original TV series). The stuck-in-the-'70s gang is still too far-out for the '90s, but in Hawaii it's always a sunshine day. Not as good as the first, but still worth a few laughs. **CW:** Sex-related humor and drug content. Watch out for innuendos about Greg and Marcia. **90m/C VHS, Beta, Closed Caption.** Shelley Long, Gary Cole, Tim Matheson, Christopher Daniel Barnes, Christine Taylor, Paul Sutera, Jennifer Elise Cox,

Henriette Mantel, Olivia Hack, Jesse Lee; **D:** Arlene Sanford; **W:** Harry Elfont, Deborah Kaplan, Stan Zimmerman, James Berg; **C:** Mac Ahlberg; **M:** Guy Moon. Nominations: MTV Movie Awards '97: Best Kiss (Christopher Daniel Barnes/Christine Taylor). *PAR*

A Very British Coup *♂♂♂* **199?** McAnally plays Harry Perkins, a former steelworker who gets involved in British politics. Although a left-wing radical, the charismatic Perkins is actually elected Prime Minister. However, his radical policies cause the entrenched government officials to conspire to bring him down. And you thought American politics were dirty! Made for British television. **180m/C VHS.** *GB* Ray McAnally. *SIG, TVC, FUS*

Very Close Quarters *♂* **1984** Thirty people face many trials and tribulations as they share an apartment in Moscow. Interesting cast is wasted in this mostly un-funny flick. **97m/C VHS, Beta.** Shelley Winters, Paul Sorvino, Theodore Bikel, Farley Granger; **D:** Vladmir Rif. *LIV, VES*

A Very Curious Girl *♂♂½* *La Fiancee du Pirate; Dirty Mary; Pirate's Fiancee* **1969 (R)** A peasant girl realizes she is being used by the male population of her village, and decides to charge them for sex, creating havoc. In French with English subtitles. **105m/C VHS, Beta.** *FR* Bernadette LaFont, Georges Geret; **D:** Nelly Kaplan. *NO*

The Very Edge *♂♂½* **1963** A pregnant woman suffers a miscarriage after being brutally attacked. The repercussions nearly destroy her marriage until her attacker is caught. A disturbing psycho-drama. **90m/B VHS, Beta.** *GB* Anne Heywood, Richard Todd, Jeremy Brett, Jack Hedley, Barbara Mullen, Maurice Denham, William Lucas, Gwen Watford, Patrick Magee; **D:** Cyril Frankel; **W:** Elizabeth Jane Howard. *NO*

A Very Natural Thing *♂♂* **1973** Twenty-six-year-old Jason leaves the priesthood to pursue a gay lifestyle in New York. He becomes a teacher, meets ad exec David, and finds love. Considered to be the first film to explore homosexuality in a realistic manner, made by a gay director, and given national, commercial distribution. **85m/C VHS.** Robert Joel, Curt Gareth, Bo White; **D:** Christopher Larkin; **W:** Christopher Larkin, Joseph Coencas. *WBF*

A Very Old Man with Enormous Wings *♂♂* *Un Senor Muy Viejo Con Unas Alas Enormes* **1988** An angel, battered during a hurricane, seeks refuge on a tiny Caribbean island. There, two men keep him and charge an increasingly curious world admission to view the creature. A colorful, musical expose of human failings based on a story by Gabriel Garcia Marquez. In Spanish with English subtitles. **90m/C VHS, LV.** *SP IT* Daisy Granados, Asdrubal Melendez, Luis Alberto Ramirez, Fernando Birri; **D:** Fernando Birri. *FXL, FCT*

A Very Private Affair *♂♂½* *La Vie Privee; Vita Privata* **1962** A movie star finds that she has no privacy from the hordes of fans and paparazzi who flock to her side. The glare of publicity helps to destroy her relationship with a married director, and to fuel her desire for privacy, a desire that ends tragically. An appealing, better-than-average Bardot vehicle, it is nonetheless below-average (early) Malle. In French with English subtitles. **95m/C VHS, Beta.** *FR* Marcello Mastroianni, Brigitte Bardot; **D:** Louis Malle. *MGM*

V.I. Warshawski *♂♂* **1991 (R)** The filmmakers seem to think they can slum with the oldest cliches in detective shows just as long as the tough gumshoe is a woman. They're wrong. Turner is terrific as the leggy shamus of the title (from a popular series of books by Sara Paretsky), but the plot is nothing special, featuring stock characters in the killing of a pro athlete and a real-estate deal. **CW:** Language and moments of violence. **89m/C VHS, Beta, LV, Closed Caption.** Kathleen Turner, Jay O. Sanders, Angela Goethals, Charles Durning; **D:** Jeff Kanew; **W:** Nick Thiel, David Aaron Cohen; **M:** Randy Edelman. *HPH*

Via Appia 🗡🗡 1992 Fictional documentary about Frank, a German airline steward who brings a film crew with him when travels back to Rio de Janeiro in search of the street hustler who gave him AIDS. Grim guided tour of the city's gay subculture along the "Via Appia," the Rio district where the male prostitutes hang out. Film is firmly unapologetic for its sexual explicitness and lack of moralizing. In German and Portuguese with English subtitles. 90m/C VHS. GE BR Peter Senner, Guilherme de Padua, Yves Jansen, Margarita Schmidt, Luiz Kleber; *D:* Jochen Hick; *W:* Jochen Hick. MOV, FCT

Vibes 🗡 1988 (PG) Two screwball psychics are sent on a wild goose chase through the Ecuadorean Andes in search of cosmic power and, of course, fall in love. Flat offering from the usually successful team of writers, Lowell Ganz and Babaloo Mandel ("Splash" and "Night Shift"). Lauper's first starring role (and so far, her last). 99m/C VHS, Beta, Closed Caption. Jeff Goldblum, Cyndi Lauper, Julian Sands, Googy Gress, Peter Falk, Elizabeth Pena; *D:* Ken Kwapis; *W:* Babaloo Mandel, Lowell Ganz; *C:* John Bailey; *M:* James Horner. COL

Vibrations 🗡🗡½ 1994 (R) Anamika (Applegate), a dance club manager, befriends TJ (Marshall), a homeless, alcoholic, once-promising musician who lost his hands in a brutal attack. The duo find romance as Anamika encourages TJ to try again.*CW:* Language; some sexuality. 104m/C VHS, LV, Closed Caption. James Marshall, Christina Applegate, Faye Grant, Paige Turco, Bruce Altman, David Burke, Scott Cohen, Shane Butterworth; *D:* Michael Paseornek; *W:* Michael Paseornek; *M:* Bob Christianson. TOU

Vice Academy 🗡½ 1988 (R) Two females join the Hollywood vice squad. Allen was a former porn queen. 90m/C VHS, Beta, LV. Linnea Quigley, Ginger Lynn Allen, Karen Russell, Jayne Hamil, Ken Abraham, Stephen Steward, Jeannie Carol; *D:* Rick Sloane. PSM

Vice Academy 2 🗡 1990 (R) Two vice cop babes try to stop a female crime boss from dumping aphrodisiacs in the city's water supply. 90m/C VHS, Beta. Linnea Quigley, Ginger Lynn Allen, Jayne Hamil, Scott Layne, Jay Richardson, Joe Brewer, Marina Benvenga, Teagan Clive; *D:* Rick Sloane. PSM

Vice Academy 3 woof! 1991 (R) The worst of the series, and not just because cult actress Linnea Quigley is absent. Wit, pacing and even sets are nonexistent as the girls battle a toxic villainess called Malathion.*CW:* Nudity. 88m/C VHS, Beta. Ginger Lynn Allen, Elizabeth Kaitan, Julia Parton, Jay Richardson, Johanna Grika, Steve Mateo; *D:* Rick Sloane; *W:* Rick Sloane. PSM

Vice Squad 🗡🗡 1931 Lukas is forced to turn police informer to save his own neck, which almost ruins him. Just when he thinks he's free of the cops they come back threatening the woman he loves unless he plays stoolie again. Rather flat, but the different cop/criminal angle makes for some unusual twists. 80m/B VHS, Beta, LV. Paul Lukas, Kay Francis, Helen Johnson, William B. Davidson, Esther Howard; *D:* John Cromwell; *C:* Charles B(ryant) Lang.

Vice Squad woof! 1982 (R) Violent and twisted killer-pimp goes on a murderous rampage, and a hooker helps a vice squad plainclothesman trap him. Sleazy and disturbing, with little to recommend it. 97m/C VHS, Beta, LV. Wings Hauser, Season Hubley, Gary Swanson, Cheryl "Rainbeaux" Smith; *D:* Gary Sherman; *W:* Robert Vincent O'Neil. NLC

Vice Versa 🗡🗡🗡 1988 (PG) Another 80s comedy about a workaholic father and his 11-year-old son who switch bodies, with predictable slapstick results. Reinhold and Savage carry this, appearing to have a great time in spite of overdone story. 97m/C VHS, Beta, LV, Closed Caption. Judge Reinhold, Fred Savage, Swoosie Kurtz, David Proval, Corinne Bohrer, Jane Kaczmarek, William Prince, Gloria Gifford; *D:* Brian Gilbert; *W:* Dick Clement, Ian LaFrenais; *M:* David Shire. COL

Vicious 🗡 1988 A bored young woman falls in with people your mother warned you about and soon their high school hi-jinks turn into murder. Graphic violence. 88m/C VHS. Tamblyn Lord, Craig Pearce, Tiffany Dowe; *D:* Karl Zwicky. NO

The Vicious Circle 🗡🗡½ *The Circle* 1957 A prominent London physician becomes involved in murder and an international crime ring when he agrees to perform an errand for a friend. Good performances and tight pacing. 84m/B VHS, Beta. GB John Mills, Wilfrid Hyde-White, Rene Ray, Lionel Jeffries, Noelle Middleton; *D:* Gerald Thomas. NO

Victim 🗡🗡🗡½ 1961 A successful married English barrister (Bogarde) with a hidden history of homosexuality is threatened by blackmail after the death of his ex-lover. When the blackmailers, who are responsible for his lover's suicide, are caught, Bogarde decides to prosecute them himself, even though it means revealing his hidden past. One of the first films to deal straightforwardly with homosexuality. Fine performances. 100m/C VHS, Beta. GB Dirk Bogarde, Sylvia Syms, Dennis Price, Peter McEnery, Nigel Stock, Donald Churchill, Anthony Nicholls, Hilton Edwards, Norman Bird, Derren Nesbitt, Alan McNaughton, Noel Howlett, Charles Lloyd Pack, John Barrie, John Bennett; *D:* Basil Dearden; *W:* John McCormick, Janet Green.

Victim of Beauty 🗡🗡 1991 A small-town girl comes to the big city and becomes a successful model. However, she then becomes the victim of a fatal attraction killer as all her would-be suitors get killed off one by one. Made for cable television. 90m/C VHS, Closed Caption. Jennifer Rubin, Sally Kellerman, Stephen Shellan, Peter Outerbridge; *Cameos:* Michael Ironside; *D:* Paul Lynch. WOV, PMS

Victim of Desire 🗡½ 1994 (R) Mysterious death of an embezzler is investigated, only the investigator falls for the sexy widow and begins to doubt her innocence. Also available in an unrated version.*CW:* Sexuality; violence; some language. 85m/C VHS. Shannon Tweed, Julie Strain. NHO

Victim of Love 🗡🗡 1991 (PG-13) A therapist doesn't know whom to believe when she finds out she and one of her more neurotic patients are sharing the same boyfriend. Only the patient claims the man murdered his wife to be with his lover. Who will be the next victim? Made for television. 92m/C VHS, Beta, LV. Pierce Brosnan, JoBeth Williams, Virginia Madsen, Georgia Brown; *D:* Jerry London. ACA

Victimless Crimes 1990 (R) The seemingly victimless crime of robbing art galleries turns deadly when betrayal and murder enter the picture.*CW:* Language and violence. 85m/C VHS. Debra Sandlund, Craig Bierko, Larry Brandenburg, Peggy Dunne, Richard Redlin, Cheryl Lynn Bruce; *D:* Peter Hawley. NO

Victor/Victoria 🗡🗡🗡 1982 (PG) An unsuccessful actress in Depression-era Paris impersonates a man impersonating a woman and becomes a star. Luscious music and sets. Warren as femme fatale and Preston as Andrews' gay mentor are right on target; Garner is charming as the gangster who falls for the woman he thinks she is. ♪You and Me; The Shady Dame from Seville; Le Jazz Hot; Crazy World; Chicago Illinois; Gay Peree. 133m/C VHS, Beta, LV. Julie Andrews, James Garner, Robert Preston, Lesley Ann Warren, Alex Karras, John Rhys-Davies; *D:* Blake Edwards; *W:* Blake Edwards; *M:* Henry Mancini. Academy Awards '82: Original Song Score and/or Adaptation; Cesar Awards '83: Best Foreign Film; Golden Globe Awards '83: Best Actress—Musical/Comedy (Andrews); National Board of Review Awards '82: Best Supporting Actor (Preston); Writers Guild of America '82: Best Adapted Screenplay; Nominations: Academy Awards '82: Best Actress (Andrews), Best Adapted Screenplay, Best Art Direction/Set Decoration, Best Costume Design, Best Supporting Actor (Preston), Best Supporting Actress (Warren). MGM

Victoria Regina 🗡🗡 1961 In a succession of vignettes, the life of Queen Victoria is viewed, from her ascension to the throne of England in 1837 through the celebration of her Diamond Jubilee. A presentation from "George Schaefer's Showcase Theatre." Made for television. 76m/C VHS, Beta. Julie Harris, James Donald, Felix Aylmer, Pamela Brown, Basil Rathbone; *D:* George Schaefer. FHS

Victory 🗡🗡½ 1981 (PG) Soccer match between WWII American prisoners of war and a German team is set up so that the players can escape through the sewer tunnels of Paris. Of course they want to finish the game first. Not particularly believable as either a soccer flick (even with Pele and other soccer stars) or a great escape, but watchable. 116m/C VHS, Beta, Closed Caption. Sylvester Stallone, Michael Caine, Max von Sydow, Pele, Carole Laure, Bobby Moore, Daniel Massey; *D:* John Huston; *W:* Jeff Maguire, Djordje Milicevic; *M:* Bill Conti. FOX, WAR

The Victory 🗡🗡 1988 (PG) In 1967 Montreal, an American college exchange student falls in love with a French-Canadian co-ed. Can love survive their different cultures? 95m/C VHS, Beta. Vincent Van Patten, Cloris Leachman, Eddie Albert, Claire Pimpare, Nicholas Campbell, Jack Wetherall, Jacques Godin, Marthe Mercure; *D:* Larry Kent. POF

The Video Dead woof! 1987 (R) Gore-farce in which murderous zombies emerge from a possessed television and wreak havoc. 90m/C VHS, Beta. Roxanna Augesen, Rocky Duvall, Michael St. Michaels; *D:* Robert Scott. NLC

Video Murders 🗡 1987 A police detective tracks down a rapist/murderer who tapes all his own crimes. 90m/C VHS, Beta. Eric Brown, Virginia Loridans, John Ferita. TWE

Video Violence 🗡 1987 A gory spoof about a video store owner who discovers that his customers have grown bored with the usual Hollywood horror movies and decide to shoot some flicks of their own. Followed by a sequel. 90m/C VHS, Beta. Art Neill, Jackie Neill, William Toddie, Bart Sumner; *D:* Gary P. Cohen. NO

Video Violence Part 2...The Exploitation! 🗡 1987 Two sickos named Howard and Eli run a cable television network where talk show guests are spindled and mutilated. 90m/C VHS, Beta. Uke, Bart Sumner, Lee Miller; *D:* Gary P. Cohen. NO

Video Wars woof! 1984 Video games explode randomly. A wicked computer whiz is behind it all in a blackmail scheme. 90m/C VHS. George Diamond. BFV

Videodrome 🗡🗡 1983 Woods is a cable TV programmer with a secret yen for sex and violence, which he satisfies by watching a pirated TV show. "Videodrome" appears to show actual torture and murder, and also seems to control the thoughts of its viewers—turning them into human VCRs. Cronenberg's usual sick fantasies are definitely love 'em or leave 'em. Special effects by Rick Baker. 87m/C VHS, Beta, LV. CA James Woods, Deborah Harry, Sonja Smits, Peter Dvorsky; *D:* David Cronenberg; *W:* David Cronenberg; *M:* Howard Shore. Genie Awards '84: Best Director (Cronenberg). USH

Vietnam, Texas 🗡 1990 (R) Vietnam vet leaves his past to become a priest. But he returns to violence when he discovers his Vietnamese daughter is in the hands of Houston's most relentless gangster. 101m/C VHS, Beta, LV. Robert Ginty, Haing S. Ngor, Tamlyn Tomita, Tim Thomerson; *D:* Robert Ginty; *W:* C. Courtney Joyner, Tom Badal. COL

Vietnam War Story 1 1988 Three hard-hitting Vietnam War stories on tape. "The Mine," "Home," and "The Pass." Each is an intimate account straight from the men who lived them. Poignant and action-packed. Made for television. 87m/C VHS, Closed Caption. Eriq La Salle, Nicholas Cascone, David Harris, Tom Fridley. NO

Vietnam War Story 2 1988 Three short, made-for-television war stories set in Vietnam: "An Old Ghost Walks the Earth," "R & R," and "The Fragging." 90m/C VHS, Beta, Closed Caption. Tim Guinee, Tate Donovan, Cynthia Bain, Wesley Snipes, David Niedorf. NO

Vietnam War Story 3 1989 Three episodes of the television series: "Separated," "Dusk to Dawn" and "The Promise." 90m/C VHS, **Beta.** Tom Hodges, Todd Graff, Gregory Cooke, Francois Chau, Stacy Edwards, Laura Harrington, Raymond Cruz. *NO*

A View to a Kill ✗✗ 1985 (PG) This James Bond mission takes him to the United States, where he must stop the evil Max Zorin from destroying California's Silicon Valley. Feeble and unexciting plot with unscary villain. Duran Duran performs the catchy title tune. Moore's last appearance as 007. 131m/C VHS, Beta, LV, **Closed Caption.** GB Roger Moore, Christopher Walken, Tanya Roberts, Grace Jones, Patrick Macnee, Lois Maxwell, Dolph Lundgren, Desmond Llewelyn; **D:** John Glen; **W:** Michael G. Wilson; **M:** John Barry. *FOX, TLF*

Vigil ✗✗✗ 1984 A stark, dreamy parable about a young girl, living on a primitive farm in a remote New Zealand valley, who watches her family collapse after a stranger enters their territory. Visually ravishing and grim; Ward's first American import. Predecessor to "The Navigator." 90m/C VHS. NZ Penelope Stewart, Bill Kerr, Fiona Kay, Gordon Shields, Frank Whitten; **D:** Vincent Ward; **W:** Vincent Ward. *FXL*

Vigilante woof! *Street Gang* 1983 (R) Frustrated ex-cop, tired of seeing criminals returned to the street, joins a vigilante squad dedicated to law and order. Often ridiculous and heavy handed. 91m/C VHS, Beta. Carol Lynley, Robert Forster, Rutanya Alda; **D:** William Lustig. *LIV, VES*

The Vigilantes are Coming ✗✗ 1936 "The Eagle" sets out to avenge his family and upsets a would-be dictator's plot to establish an empire in California. In twelve chapters; the first is 32 minutes, and additional chapters are 18 minutes each. 230m/B VHS, Beta. Bob Livingston, Kay Hughes, Guinn "Big Boy" Williams, Raymond Hatton, William Farnum; **D:** Mack V. Wright, Ray Taylor. *NOS, VCN, MED*

Vigilantes of Boom Town ✗½ 1946 A championship prize fight is the cover for a bank robbery which must be foiled by Red Ryder. 54m/C VHS, Beta. Allan "Rocky" Lane, Robert (Bobby) Blake, Peggy Stewart, Martha Wentworth, Roscoe Karns, Roy Barcroft, George Turner, John Dehner; **D:** R.G. Springsteen. *NOS, VCN, MED*

Viking Massacre ✗½ *Knives of the Avenger; I Coltelli Del Vendicatore* 1965 Brutal ax-bearing Vikings ruin the days of hundreds in this primitive story of courage and desperation. John Hold is the pseudonym for director Mario Bava. 90m/C VHS, Beta. IT Cameron Mitchell; **D:** John Hold. *NO*

The Viking Sagas ✗½ 1995 (R) Moeller is the warrior who must avenge his father's execution, defend his people, and fight for his country's survival against evil oppressors. At least there's a beautiful babe around to offer him some comfort. The Icelandic scenery is the best thing about the movie.**CW:** Brutal and bloody Viking combat; some sexuality. 83m/C VHS, LV, **Closed Caption.** Ralph Moeller, Ingibjorg Stefansdottir, Sven-Ole Thorsen; **D:** Michael Chapman; **W:** Dale Herd, Paul R. Gurian; **M:** George S. Clinton. *NLC*

The Vikings ✗✗½ 1958 A Viking king and his son kidnap a Welsh princess and hold her for ransom. Depicts the Vikings' invasion of England. Great location footage of both Norway and Britanny. Basic costume epic with good action scenes. Narrated by Welles. 116m/C VHS, Beta, LV. Kirk Douglas, Ernest Borgnine, Janet Leigh, Tony Curtis, James Donald, Alexander Knox; **D:** Richard Fleischer; **W:** Calder Willingham; **C:** Jack Cardiff. *MGM*

Villa Rides ✗✗ 1968 A flying gun-runner aids Francisco "Pancho" Villa's revolutionary Mexican campaign. Considering the talent involved, this one is a disappointment. Check out Brynner's hair. 125m/C VHS, Beta, LV. Yul Brynner, Robert Mitchum, Charles Bronson, Herbert Lom, Jill Ireland, Robert Towne; **D:** Buzz Kulik; **W:** Robert Towne, Sam Peckinpah; **C:** Jack Hildyard; **M:** Maurice Jarre. *BAR*

A Village Affair ✗✗½ 1995 Ward is a young wife and mother, living what appears to be a perfect life in a quiet English village, when she meets a neighbor's daughter (Fox) who's just returned from America. Fox makes her interests clear and soon the two women are having an affair that shatters the peacefulness around them. Based on a novel by Joanna Trollope. 108m/C VHS. GB Sophie Ward, Kerry Fox, Nathaniel Parker, Claire Bloom, Michael Gough, Barbara Jefford, Jeremy Northam, Rosalie Crutchley; **D:** Moira Armstrong; **W:** Alma Cullen; **C:** John Else. *VTR, VIF*

Village of the Damned ✗✗✗ 1960 A group of unusual children are born in a small English village. They avoid their fathers and other men, except for the one who is their teacher. He discovers they are the vanguard of an alien invasion and leads the counter-attack. Exciting and bone-chilling low-budget thriller. From the novel, "The Midwich Cuckoos," by John Wyndham. The sequel, "The Children of the Damned" (1964) is even better. 78m/B VHS, Beta, LV. GB George Sanders, Barbara Shelley, Martin Stephens, Laurence Naismith, Michael C. Goetz, Michael Gwynn, John Phillips, Richard Vernon, Jenny Laird, Richard Warner, Thomas Heathcote, Charlotte Mitchell, John Stuart, Bernard Archard; **D:** Wolf Rilla; **W:** Wolf Rilla, Stirling Silliphant, George Harley. *MGM, MLB*

Village of the Damned ✗½ 1995 The quiet town of Midwich, California has been enveloped by a strange force that seems to have impregnated the local women. The albino children born of this incident have disturbing telepathic powers that they display through their bright orange and red eyes— supposedly precipitating a plot to take control. A pale remake of the 1960 British horror classic, which was based on John Wyndham's novel "The Midwich Cuckoos." Fails to capture the eeriness of it's predecessor and is bogged down with awkward casting, absurd dialogue and a brood of children with glowing eyes that make them less like a threat and more like Nintendo addicts.**CW:** Some sci-fi terror and violence. 98m/C VHS, LV, **Closed Caption.** Christopher Reeve, Kirstie Alley, Linda Kozlowski, Mark Hamill, Meredith Salenger, Michael Pare, Peter Jason, Constance Forslund; **D:** John Carpenter, David Himmelstein; **C:** Gary B. Kibbe; **M:** John Carpenter, Dave Davies. *USH*

Village of the Giants ✗ 1965 A group of beer-guzzling teenagers become giants after eating a mysterious substance invented by a twelve-year-old genius. Fun to pick out all the soon-to-be stars. Totally silly premise with bad special effects and minimal plot follow-through. Based on an H.G. Wells story. 82m/C VHS, Beta. Ron Howard, Johnny Crawford, Tommy Kirk, Beau Bridges, Freddy Cannon, Beau Brummel; **D:** Bert I. Gordon; **M:** Jack Nitzsche. *NLC, MLB*

The Villain ✗½ *Cactus Jack* 1979 (PG) An unfunny spoof of "B" westerns that is almost like a live-action "Roadrunner" cartoon. Douglas plays Cactus Jack, a highwayman who keeps trying to kidnap fair damsel Ann-Margret. Hero Schwarzenegger keeps rescuing her. Lynde is amusing as the uptight Indian chief Nervous Elk. 93m/C VHS. Kirk Douglas, Ann-Margret, Arnold Schwarzenegger, Paul Lynde, Foster Brooks, Ruth Buzzi, Jack Elam, Strother Martin, Robert Tessier, Mel Tillis; **D:** Hal Needham. *COL*

The Villain Still Pursued Her ✗✗ 1941 A poor hero and rich villain vie for the sweet heroine in this satire of old-fashioned temperance melodrama. Keaton manages to shine as the hero's sidekick. 67m/B VHS, Beta. Anita Louise, Alan Mowbray, Buster Keaton, Hugh Herbert; **D:** Eddie Cline. *NOS, VYY, DVT*

Vincent & Theo ✗✗✗½ 1990 (PG-13) The story of Impressionist painter Vincent van Gogh, and his brother Theo, a gallery owner who loved his brother's work, yet could not get the public to buy it. Increasing despair and mental illness traps both men, as each struggles to create beauty in a world where it has no value. Altman has created a stunning portrait of "the artist" and his needs. The exquisite cinematography will make you feel as if you stepped into van Gogh's work. 138m/C VHS, Beta, LV. Tim Roth, Paul Rhys, Johanna Ter Steege, Wladimir Yordanoff; **D:** Robert Altman. *TVC*

Vincent, Francois, Paul and the Others ✗✗✗ 1976 Three middle-aged Frenchmen rely on their friendships to endure a host of mid-life crises. In French with English subtitles. 113m/C VHS, Beta, LV. FR Yves Montand, Gerard Depardieu, Michel Piccoli, Stephane Audran; **D:** Claude Sautet. *FCT, CVC, TPV*

Vincent: The Life and Death of Vincent van Gogh ✗✗✗ 1987 Van Gogh's work and creativity is examined in a documentary manner through his life and his letters. Thoughtful and intriguing production. Narrated by John Hurt as van Gogh. 99m/C VHS, LV, AU D: Paul Cox; **W:** Paul Cox; **M:** Norman Kaye; **V:** John Hurt. *FCT, CRY, SIG*

The Vindicator ✗✗ *Frankenstein '88* 1985 (R) A scientist killed in a lab accident is transformed into a cyborg who runs amok and murders indiscriminately. A modernized Frankenstein, with interesting special effects and well drawn characters. 92m/C VHS, Beta, **Closed Caption.** CA Terri Austin, Richard Cox, David McIlwraith, Pam Grier; **D:** Jean-Claude Lord. *FOX*

The Vineyard ✗ 1989 (R) Hapless victims are lured to a Japanese madman's island, where he drinks their blood and maintains a questionable immortality. 95m/C VHS, Beta, LV. James Hong, Karen Witter, Michael Wong; **D:** James Hong, Bill Rice. *VTR, NWV*

Violated ✗ 1953 Pathetic production about New York police attempting to track down a sex-maniac murderer who slays his victims and then gives them a haircut. Unbelievably bad. 78m/B VHS. Wim Holland, Lili Dawn, Mitchell Kowal, Vicki Carlson, William Martell; **D:** Walter Strate. *SNC*

Violated woof! 1984 A detective endeavors to implicate a local businessman in the rapes of two beautiful women. Exploitative and dreary. 88m/C VHS, Beta. John Heard, J.C. Quinn, April Daisy White, Samantha Fox; **D:** Richard Cannistraro. *LIV, VES*

Violence at Noon ✗✗✗ 1966 Highly disturbing film in which two women protect a brutal sex murderer from the law. Living among a quiet community of intellectuals, this conspiracy ends in a shocking finale in Oshima's stylized masterpiece. In Japanese with English subtitles. 99m/B VHS, **Closed Caption.** JP Saeda Kawaguchi, Akiko Koyama; **D:** Nagisa Oshima. *KIV*

Violent Breed ✗ 1983 A CIA operative is sent on a mission to put a black marketeer out of business. 91m/C VHS, Beta. IT Henry Silva, Harrison Muller, Woody Strode; **D:** Fernando Di Leo. *MGM*

The Violent Men ✗✗½ *Rough Company* 1955 Big-time land baron Robinson is trying to push out all other landowners in the valley, including Ford. At first Ford refuses to fight back, but after one of Robinson's henchmen kills one of his hired hands, he starts an all-out war against Robinson to save his land. Stanwyck as Robinson's wife and Keith as his brother are wicked as the two urging him on and having an affair behind his back. Based on the novel "Rough Company" by Donald Hamilton. 95m/C VHS, LV. Glenn Ford, Barbara Stanwyck, Edward G. Robinson, Dianne Foster, Brian Keith, May Wynn; **D:** Rudolph Mate; **C:** Burnett Guffey. *COL*

Violent Ones woof! 1968 Three men who are suspected of raping a young girl are threatened with lynching by an angry mob of townspeople. Badly acted, poorly directed, uneven and feeble. 96m/C VHS, Beta. Fernando Lamas, David Carradine; **D:** Fernando Lamas. *REP*

Violent Professionals ✗½ *La Polizia vuole Giustizia* 1973 Suspended cop runs into resistance inside and outside the force when he infiltrates the mob to get the goods on a crime boss.

100m/C VHS, **Beta.** *IT* Richard Conte, Luc Merenda; **D:** Sergio Martino. *NO*

Violent Women 🎞 1959 Five female convicts escape and embark on a bloody journey through the countryside, pursued by the authorities. Shows women can be just as brutal as any man. 61m/C VHS, **Beta.** Jennifer Slater, Jo Ann Kelly, Sandy Lyn, Eleanor Blair, Pati Magee; **D:** Barry Mahon. *THV*

The Violent Years woof! *Female* 1956 Spoiled high-school debutantes form a vicious all-girl gang and embark on a spree that includes murder, robbery, and male rape. Justice wins out in the end. Exploitive trash written by Wood, who directed the infamous "Plan 9 from Outer Space." 60m/B VHS, **Beta.** Jean Moorehead, Barbara Weeks, Glenn Corbett; **D:** Edward D. Wood Jr., Franz Eichhorn; **W:** Edward D. Wood Jr. *SNC, RHI, AOV*

Violent Zone 🎞 1989 Mercenaries go on a supposed rescue mission in the wilderness. 92m/C VHS. John Douglas, Chad Hayward, Christopher Weeks; **D:** John Garwood; **W:** David Pritchard, John Bushelman. *HMD*

Violets Are Blue 🎞🎞½ 1986 (PG-13) Two high-school sweethearts are reunited in their hometown years later and try to rekindle their romance—even though the man is married. 86m/C VHS, Beta, LV, **Closed Caption.** Kevin Kline, Sissy Spacek, Bonnie Bedelia, John Kellogg, Augusta Dabney, Jim Standford; **D:** Jack Fisk; **W:** Naomi Foner; **C:** Ralf Bode; **M:** Patrick Williams. *COL*

Violette 🎞🎞🎞 *Violette Noziere* 1978 (R) Fascinating true-life account of a nineteen-year-old French girl in the 1930s who, bored with her life and wanting to be with her lover, decides to poison her parents so she can receive her inheritance. Her mother survives but her father dies, and the girl is sent to prison for murder. Extraordinary performance by Huppert and the film is visually stunning. 122m/C VHS. *FR* Isabelle Huppert, Stephane Audran, Jean Carmet, Jean Francoise, Bernadette LaFont; **D:** Claude Chabrol. Cannes Film Festival '78: Best Actress (Huppert); Cesar Awards '79: Best Supporting Actress (Audran). *NYF*

VIP, My Brother Superman 1990 The Vips are modern-day descendants of superbeings about to become legends in their own times. SuperVip is broad of chest and pure in spirit while his brother MiniVip possesses only limited powers. From the creator of "Allegro Non Troppo" comes this enticing, amusing piece of animation. 90m/C VHS. **D:** Bruno Bozzetto. *EXP, TPV*

Viper 🎞 1988 A woman battles a cryptic anti-terrorist band to avenge the murder of her husband. 96m/C VHS. Linda Purl, Chris Robinson, James Tolkan; **D:** Peter Maris. *FRH*

The V.I.P.'s 🎞🎞🎞 1963 Slick, sophisticated drama set in the V.I.P. lounge of a British airport. Trapped by fog, several of the passengers get acquainted and are forced to face their problems as they spend the night in the airport lounge. Taylor stars as Frances Andros, a wealthy young woman leaving her husband (Burton) for life in the U.S. with her lover, Jourdan. A movie tycoon, an Australian entrepreneur, his secretary, and a duchess are among the other passengers grounded by the fog. Both Rutherford and Smith give excellent performances and it was a tossup as to which actress would be nominated for the Oscar. 119m/C VHS. *GB* Elizabeth Taylor, Richard Burton, Louis Jourdan, Elsa Martinelli, Margaret Rutherford, Maggie Smith, Rod Taylor, Orson Welles, Linda Christian, Dennis Price; **D:** Anthony Asquith; **W:** Terence Rattigan; **C:** Jack Hildyard; **M:** Miklos Rozsa. Academy Awards '63: Best Supporting Actress (Rutherford); Golden Globe Awards '64: Best Supporting Actress (Rutherford); National Board of Review Awards '63: Best Supporting Actress (Rutherford). *MGM*

Virgin Among the Living Dead 🎞 1971 (R) Young woman travels to remote castle when she hears of relative's death. Once there, she finds the residents a tad weird and has bad dreams in which zombies chase her. Bizarre even

for Franco, who seems to have been going through a "Pasolini" phase while making this one. 90m/C VHS, **Beta.** *SP* Christina von Blanc, Britt Nichols, Howard Vernon, Anne Libert, Rose Kiekens, Paul Muller; **D:** Jess (Jesus) Franco. *NO*

The Virgin and the Gypsy 🎞🎞½ 1970 (R) An English girl brought up in a repressive household in 1920s England falls in love with a gypsy. Based on the novel by D.H. Lawrence. Directorial debut of Miles. 92m/C VHS. *GB* Joanna Shimkus, Franco Nero, Honor Blackman, Mark Burns; **D:** Christopher Miles; **W:** Alan Plater. *NO*

Virgin High 🎞 1990 (R) Three young men sneak into an all-girls Catholic boarding school with hilarious consequences. Ward (TV's Robin, from "Batman") makes a special appearance in bondage in this sex farce. 90m/C VHS, LV. Burt Ward, Linnea Quigley, Tracy Dali, Richard Gabai, Catherine McGuiness, Chris Dempsey; **D:** Richard Gabai; **W:** Richard Gabai, Jeff Neal. *COL*

Virgin Machine 🎞🎞 *Jungfrauenmaschine* 1988 Lesbian journalist Dorothy Muller (Blum) is unhappy in her native Hamburg and decides to move to California to pursue her idea of romantic love. English and German with English subtitles. 91m/B VHS. *GE* Ina Blum, Susie Bright, Marianne Enserink, Gad Klein, Dominique Gaspar; **D:** Monika Treut; **W:** Monika Treut; **C:** Elfi Mikesch. *FRF*

The Virgin of Nuremberg 🎞½ *Horror Castle; Terror Castle; Castle of Terror; La Vergine de Norimberga* 1965 A young woman enters her new husband's ancestral castle and is stalked by the specter of a legendary sadist. 82m/C VHS, **Beta.** *IT* Rossana Podesta, George Riviere, Christopher Lee, Jim Dolen; **D:** Anthony (Antonio Margheriti) Dawson. *MOV*

The Virgin Queen 🎞🎞🎞 1955 Davis stars in this historical drama, which focuses on the stormy relationship between the aging Queen and Sir Walter Raleigh. Collins is the lady-in-waiting who is the secret object of Raleigh's true affections. Previously, Davis played Queen Elizabeth I in "Elizabeth and Essex." Davis holds things together. 92m/C VHS, Beta, **Closed Caption.** Bette Davis, Richard Todd, Joan Collins, Herbert Marshall, Dan O'Herlihy, Jay Robinson, Romney Brent; **D:** Henry Koster. Nominations: Academy Awards '55: Best Costume Design (Color). *FOX*

Virgin Queen of St. Francis High 🎞 1988 (PG) Two high school foes make a bet that one of them can take the "virgin" title away from gorgeous Christensen by summer's end. She has to fight off their advances, but grows to like Straface. 89m/C VHS, Beta, LV. *CA* Joseph R. Straface, Stacy Christensen, J.T. Wotton; **D:** Francesco Lucente. *MED*

Virgin Sacrifice 🎞 1959 A great white hunter looking for zoo-bound jaguars confronts the virgin-sacrificing, Tiger God-revering natives of Guatemala. 67m/C VHS, Beta, LV. David Dalie, Antonio Gutierrez, Angelica Morales, Fernando Wagner; **D:** Fernando Wagner. *NO*

The Virgin Soldiers 🎞🎞½ 1969 (R) A British comedy about greenhorn military recruits stationed in Singapore, innocent of women as well as battle, and their struggles to overcome both situations. A good cast raises this above the usual low-brow sex farce. Based on the novel by Leslie Thomas. Followed by "Stand Up Virgin Soldiers." 96m/C VHS, **Beta.** *GB* Hywel Bennett, Nigel Davenport, Lynn Redgrave, Nigel Patrick, Rachel Kempson, Jack Shepherd, Tsai Chin; **D:** John Dexter; **W:** John Hopkins. *COL*

The Virgin Spring 🎞🎞🎞½ *Jungfrukallan* 1959 Based on a medieval ballad and set in 14th-century Sweden. The rape and murder of a young innocent spurs her father to vengeance and he kills her attackers. Over the girl's dead body, the father questions how God could have let any of it happen, but he comes to find solace and forgiveness. Stunning Bergman compositions. In Swedish with English subtitles; also available in dubbed version. 88m/B VHS, **Beta.** *SW* Max von Sy-

dow, Birgitta Valberg, Gunnel Lindblom, Brigitta Pattersson, Axel Duborg; **D:** Ingmar Bergman; **C:** Sven Nykvist. Academy Awards '60: Best Foreign Language Film; Golden Globe Awards '61: Best Foreign Film; Nominations: Academy Awards '60: Best Costume Design (B & W). *HMV*

The Virgin Witch 🎞½ *Lesbian Twins* 1970 (R) Two beautiful sisters are sent to the British countryside, ostensibly for a modeling job. They soon find themselves in the midst of a witches' coven however, and discover one of them is to be sacrificed. The Michelles were "Playboy" magazine's first sister centerfolds. 89m/C VHS, Beta. *GB* Anne Michelle, Vicki Michelle, Patricia Haines, Keith Buckley, James Chase, Neil Hallett; **D:** Ray Austin. *PSM*

Virginia City 🎞🎞🎞 1940 Action-packed western drama set during the Civil War. Flynn is a Union soldier who escapes from a Confederate prison run by Scott, after learning of a gold shipment being sent by Southern sympathizers to aid the Confederacy. He ends up in Virginia City (where the gold-laden wagon train is to leave from) and falls for a dance-hall girl (Hopkins) who turns out to be a Southern spy working for Scott but who falls for Flynn anyway. Bogart is miscast as a half-breed outlaw who aids Scott but wants the gold for himself. Considered a follow-up to "Dodge City." 121m/C VHS. Errol Flynn, Miriam Hopkins, Randolph Scott, Humphrey Bogart, Frank McHugh, Alan Hale, Guinn "Big Boy" Williams, Douglass Dumbrille, Charles Halton; **D:** Michael Curtiz; **M:** Max Steiner. *MGM*

The Virginia Hill Story 🎞½ 1976 Fictionalized biography of mobster Bugsy Siegel's girlfriend who, in the mid-fifties, was subpoenaed to appear before the Kefauver investigation on crime in the U.S. As the examining lawyer presents questions regarding her background and connections with the underworld, we see the story of her life. Made for television. 90m/C VHS, Beta. Dyan Cannon, Harvey Keitel, Robby Benson, Allen (Goorwitz) Garfield, John Vernon; **D:** Joel Schumacher. *NO*

The Virginian 🎞🎞½ 1923 The second silent version of Owen Wister's classic western novel, inferior to both the 1914 Cecil B. DeMille silent and the 1929 Victor Fleming talkie. Harlan plays the title role as the cowpoke who leads a posse against cattle rustlers and falls in love with a schoolteacher. 79m/B VHS. Kenneth Harlan, Florence Vidor, Russell Simpson, Pat O'Malley, Raymond Hatton; **D:** Tom Forman. *GPV*

The Virginian 🎞🎞🎞 1929 A classic early-talkie western about a ranch-hand defeating the local bad guys. One line of dialogue has become, with modification, a standard western cliche: "If you want to call me that, smile." Based on the novel by Owen Wister. With this starring role, Cooper broke away from the juvenile lovers he had been playing to the laconic, rugged male leads he would be known for. Huston is perfectly cast as the outlaw leader. 95m/B VHS, Beta. Gary Cooper, Walter Huston, Richard Arlen, Chester Conklin, Eugene Pallette; **D:** Victor Fleming. *BAR*

The Virginian 🎞🎞½ 1946 Cowboy good guy, known as the Virginian (McCrea), and his best pal Steve (Tufts) both fall for Molly (Britton), the Eastern-bred schoolmarm who's come to their Wyoming town. Steve wants to make some quick money and joins up with leader Trampas' (Donlevy) cattle rustling gang. So the Virginian is forced to chose between friendship and the code of the west and Molly wonders if she can accepts the country's harsh ways. Based on Owen Wister's 1902 novel. 87m/C VHS, **Closed Caption.** Joel McCrea, Sonny Tufts, Barbara Britton, Brian Donlevy, Fay Bainter, Tom Tully, Henry O'Neill, William Frawley; **D:** Stuart Gilmore; **W:** Frances Goodrich, Albert Hackett; **C:** Harry Hallenberger; **M:** Daniele Amfitheatrof. *USH*

Viridiana 🎞🎞🎞🎞 1961 Innocent girl, with strong ideas about goodness, visits her worldly uncle's home before she takes her vows as a nun. He has developed a sick obsession for her, but after drugging the girl he finds he cannot violate her purity. He tells her, however, she is no longer chaste so she will not join the church. After her uncle's suicide, Viridiana learns she and his illegitimate son Jorge have inherited her uncle's run-down estate. Viridiana opens the house to all sorts of beggars, who take shameless advantage, while Jorge works slowly to restore the estate and improve the lives of those around him. Considered to be one of Bunuel's masterpieces and a bitter allegory of Spanish idealism versus pragmatism and the state of the world. In Spanish with English subtitles. **90m/B VHS, Beta.** *SP MX* Silvia Pinal, Francesco Rabal, Fernando Rey, Margarita Lozano, Victoria Zinny; *D:* Luis Bunuel; *W:* Luis Bunuel. Cannes Film Festival '61: Best Film. *NOS, HHT, DVT*

Virtual Assassin 🎬🎬 *Cyberjack* 1995 (R) 21st century sci-fi actioner finds the crooked Zef (James) leading his band of thugs into a research lab to steal a powerful computer virus. Naturally, the janitor (Dudikoff) just happens to be an ex-cop with a score to settle with Zef. Predictable but with decent special effects. *CW:* Language, violence, brief nudity. **99m/C VHS, LV.** *CA JP* Michael Dudikoff, Brion James, Jon Cuthbert, Suki Kaiser, James Thom; *D:* Robert Lee; *W:* Eric Poppen. *TTC*

Virtual Combat 🎬🎬 1995 (R) Ex-cop Quarry (Wilson) teams up with some cyber-girls to stop a madman who's able to manipulate virtual reality programs into living beings and releases a killer who wants to lead a destructive virtual army. **97m/C VHS.** Don "The Dragon" Wilson, Athena Massey, Loren Avedon, Kenneth McLeod, Turhan Bey, Stella Stevens; *D:* Andrew Stevens. *APX*

Virtual Desire 🎬½ 1995 (R) Brad Collins is bored with his marriage and finds some excitement via sexual games on the Internet. But someone is taking a very close interest in Brad's virtual amours and when his wife is murdered, Brad becomes the prime suspect. *CW:* Strong sexuality. **92m/C VHS, LV.** Michael Meyer, Julie Strain, Gail Harris. *TRI*

Virtual Seduction 🎬🎬 1996 (R) Liam's (Fahey) taken a job testing a virtual reality pod that can interpret what the user wants—and Liam wants to see his dead girlfriend Paris (Genzel). Only he spends so much time with the virtual Paris, that his real-life gal Laura (Dolenz) is worried about his health and sanity—too bad project developer Grant (Novak) isn't so concerned. *CW:* Some strong sexuality, violence and language. **84m/C VHS.** Jeff Fahey, Ami Dolenz, Carrie Genzel, Frank Novak, Meshach Taylor; *D:* Paul Ziller. *NHO*

Virtue's Revolt 🎬½ 1924 A small-town girl is corrupted by the sleazy world of showbiz. Silent. **51m/B VHS, Beta.** Edith Thornton, Crawford Kent. *NO*

Virtuosity 🎬½ 1995 (R) Ex-cop-with-a-tragic-past Parker Barnes (Washington) is sprung from prison to help capture computer-generated killer Sid 6.7 (Crowe), who escapes from cyberspace and goes on a rampage in 1997 Los Angeles. Seems this virtual reality bad guy has a personality composed of some 200 serial killers and criminal minds so Parker's got his work cut out for him. But criminal-behavior psychologist Madison Carter (Lynch) is around to lend her expert advice. Both the charismatically evil Crowe and the sufferingly noble Washington are wasted in this effects-laden thriller that sacrifices character for flash. *CW:* Strong futuristic violence, some brutal beatings, some language. **105m/C VHS, Beta, Closed Caption.** Denzel Washington, Russell Crowe, Kelly Lynch, Stephen Spinella, William Forsythe, Louise Fletcher, William Fichtner, Costas Mandylor, Kevin J. O'Connor; *D:* Brett Leonard; *W:* Eric Bernt; *C:* Gale Tattersall; *M:* Christopher Young. *PAR*

Virus 🎬🎬 *Fukkatsu no Hi* 1982 (PG) After nuclear war and plague destroy civilization, a small group of people gather in Antarctica and struggle with determination to carry on life. A look at man's genius for self-destruction and his endless hope. **102m/C VHS, Beta.** *JP* George Kennedy, Sonny Chiba, Glenn Ford, Robert Vaughn, Stuart Gillard, Stephanie Faulkner, Ken Ogata, Bo Svenson, Olivia Hussey, Chuck Connors, Edward James Olmos; *D:* Kinji Fukasaku. *VTR, MED*

Virus 🎬½ 1996 (PG-13) Secret Service agent Ken Fairchild (Bosworth) finds out that biological-warfare chemicals have been spilt in a national park that's the site for an ecological summit between the president and world leaders. It's up to Fairchild and a park ranger (Pinsent) to battle the minions of the chemical's manufacturer who wants to keep the whole thing quiet. *CW:* Violence, language. **90m/C VHS.** Brian Bosworth, Leah K. Pinsent; *D:* Allan Goldstein. *THV*

The Vision 🎬🎬 1987 Suspenseful British production about televangelists who attempt to control their viewers' minds through worldwide satellite broadcasting. **103m/C VHS, Beta.** *GB* Lee Remick, Dirk Bogarde, Helena Bonham Carter, Eileen Atkins; *D:* Norman Stone. *NO*

Vision Quest 🎬🎬½ *Crazy for You* 1985 (R) A high school student wants to win the Washington State wrestling championship and the affections of a beautiful older artist. He gives it his all as he trains for the meet and goes after his "visionquest." A winning performance by Modine raises this above the usual teen coming-of-age movie. Madonna sings "Crazy for You" in a nightclub. Based on novel by Terry Davis. **107m/C VHS, Beta, LV, Closed Caption.** Matthew Modine, Linda Fiorentino, Ronny Cox, Roberts Blossom, Daphne Zuniga, Charles Hallahan, Michael Schoeffling; *D:* Harold Becker; *W:* Darryl Ponicsan; *Performed by:* Madonna. *WAR*

Visions 🎬½ 1990 A man's ability to "see" murders before they happen leads police to suspect him of committing them, and he must clear himself. **90m/C VHS.** Joe Balogh, Alice Villarreal, Tom Taylor, A.R. Newman, J.R. Pella; *D:* Stephen E. Miller. *NO*

Visions of Evil 🎬 1973 A young woman, recently released from a mental institution, is plagued by a series of terrifying visions when she moves into a house where a brutal axe murder took place. **85m/C VHS, Beta.** Lori Sanders, Dean Jagger. *PSM*

Visions of Light: The Art of Cinematography 🎬🎬🎬 1993 Excellent documentary on the way films look and how the art of photographing movies can contribute as much, if not more, than cast, director, and script. Scenes from 125 films, from "Birth of a Nation" to "GoodFellas" are shown, with commentary from a number of cinematographers, including Gordon Willis, William A. Fraker, Conrad Hall, Ernest Dickerson, Vilmos Zsigmond, and Michael Chapman, on how they achieved certain effects and their collaborations with the director of the film. **95m/C VHS, LV.** *D:* Arnold Glassman, Stuart Samuels, Todd McCarthy; *W:* Todd McCarthy. New York Film Critics Awards '93: Best Feature Documentary; National Society of Film Critics Awards '93: Best Feature Documentary. *FXV*

Visitants 🎬 1987 Aliens descend irreverently on a small town in the 1950s, with unexpected comedic results. **93m/C VHS, Beta.** Marcus Vaughter, Johanna Grika, Joel Hile, Nicole Rio; *D:* Rick Sloane. *TWE*

Visiting Hours 🎬 *The Fright; Get Well Soon* 1982 (R) Psycho-killer slashes his female victims and photographs his handiwork. Grant is one of his victims who doesn't die, so the killer decides to visit the hospital and finish the job. Fairly graphic and generally unpleasant. **101m/C VHS, Beta.** *CA* Lee Grant, William Shatner, Linda Purl, Michael Ironside; *D:* Jean-Claude Lord; *W:* Brian Taggert. *FOX*

The Visitor 🎬½ 1980 (R) Affluent handsome doctor and mate conspire with grisly devil worshippers to conceive devil child. **90m/C VHS.** Mel Ferrer, Glenn Ford, Lance Henriksen, John Huston, Shelley Winters, Joanne Nail, Sam Peckinpah; *D:* Giulio Paradisi. *UAV, HHE*

Visitor from the Grave 🎬 1981 When an American heiress and her boyfriend dispose of a dead man's body, his spirit comes back to haunt them. This annoys them. **60m/C VHS, Beta.** Simon MacCorkindale, Kathryn Leigh Scott, Gareth Thomas, Mia Nadasi. *LIV*

The Visitors 🎬½ 1989 (R) Ghosts come to stay at a young family's dream house in Sweden. Not exactly a novel treatment or a novel premise. **102m/C VHS, Beta, LV.** *SW* Keith Berkeley, Lena Endre, John Force, John Olsen, Joanna Berg, Brent Landiss, Patrick Ersgard; *D:* Joakim Ersgard. *THV*

The Visitors 🎬🎬 *Les Visiteurs* 1995 (R) Time travel comedy features 12th-century knight Godefroy (Reno) and his vassal Jacquasse (Clavier) crossing paths with a powerful witch (and evidently pissing her off) since she casts a spell causing Godefroy to accidentally kill his father-in-law. So Godefroy contacts a wizard to give him a time travel potion so he can go back and stop the shooting. Too bad the potion hurls knight and vassal forward into present-day France. French with subtitles. *CW:* Language. **106m/C VHS, LV, Closed Caption.** *FR* Jean Reno, Christian Clavier, Mariann Chazel, Valerie Lemercier, Christian Bujeau; *D:* Jean-Marie Poire; *W:* Christian Clavier, Jean-Marie Poire; *C:* Jean-Yves Le Mener; *M:* Eric Levi. *TOU*

Vital Signs 🎬 1990 (R) Hackneyed drama about six medical students enduring the tribulations of their profession. **102m/C VHS, Beta, LV, Closed Caption.** Adrian Pasdar, Diane Lane, Jack Gwaltney, Laura San Giacomo, Jane Adams, Tim Ransom, Bradley Whitford, Lisa Jane Persky, William Devane, Norma Aleandro, Jimmy Smits, James Karen, Telma Hopkins; *D:* Marisa Silver; *W:* Jeb Stuart; *M:* Miles Goodman. *FOX*

Viva Knievel woof! *Seconds to Live* 1977 (PG) Crooks plan to sabotage Knievel's daredevil jump in Mexico and then smuggle cocaine back into the States in his coffin. Unintentionally campy. **106m/C VHS, Beta.** Evel Knievel, Gene Kelly, Lauren Hutton, Red Buttons, Leslie Nielsen, Cameron Mitchell, Marjoe Gortner, Albert Salmi, Dabney Coleman; *D:* Gordon Douglas; *M:* Charles Bernstein. *WAR*

Viva Las Vegas 🎬🎬½ *Love in Las Vegas* 1963 Race care driver Elvis needs money to compete against rival Danova in the upcoming Las Vegas Grand Prix. He takes a job in a casino and romances fellow employee Ann-Margret, who turns out to be his rival for the grand prize in the local talent competition. Good pairing between the two leads, and the King does particularly well with the title song. 🎵The Lady Loves Me; Viva Las Vegas; What'd I Say; I Need Somebody to Lean On; Come On, Everybody; Today, Tomorrow and Forever; If You Think I Don't Need You; Appreciation; My Rival. **85m/C VHS, Beta, LV.** Elvis Presley, Ann-Margret, William Demarest, Jack Carter, Cesare Danova, Nicky Blair, Larry Kent; *D:* George Sidney; *C:* Joseph Biroc. *MGM*

Viva Maria! 🎬🎬½ 1965 (R) Tongue-in-cheek comedy with Bardot and Moreau as two dancers (both named Maria) in a show traveling through Mexico. The two become incensed by the poverty of the peasants and decide to turn revolutionary (especially after Moreau has an affair with revolutionary leader Hamilton, who promptly gets killed). The two French sex symbols are a fine match. **119m/C VHS.** *FR IT* Jeanne Moreau, Brigitte Bardot, George Hamilton, Paulette Dubost, Claudio Brook; *D:* Louis Malle; *W:* Louis Malle, Jean-Claude Carriere; *M:* Georges Delerue. *MGM*

Viva Max 🎬🎬½ 1969 A blundering modern-day Mexican general and his men recapture the Alamo, and an equally inept American force, headed by Winters, is sent to rout them out. Mostly works, with some very funny scenes. Ustinov is great. **93m/C VHS, Beta.** Peter Ustinov, Jonathan Winters, John Astin, Pamela Tiffin, Keenan Wynn; *D:* Jerry Paris. *REP*

Viva Villa! 🎬🎬🎬 1934 Exciting action biography of Mexican revolutionary Pancho Villa, well-portrayed by the exuberant Beery. The film follows the early Robin Hood-like exploits of Villa and his men who soon join Walthall and his peasant army in overthrowing the government. But Villa's bandito instincts and ego cause problems and a power struggle ensues. Director Howard Hawks went uncredited for his work on the film, being fired by the studio after an incident while on location in Mexico. **115m/B VHS, LV.** Wallace Beery, Fay

Wray, Stuart Erwin, Leo Carrillo, Donald Cook, George E. Stone, Joseph Schildkraut, Henry B. Walthall, Katherine DeMille, David Durand, Frank Puglia; **D:** Jack Conway; **W:** Ben Hecht. Nominations: Academy Awards '34: Best Adapted Screenplay, Best Picture, Best Sound. *MGM, MOV, BTV*

Viva Zapata! ✓✓✓✓ **1952** Chronicles the life of Mexican revolutionary Emiliano Zapata. Brando is powerful as he leads the peasant revolt in the early 1900s, only to be corrupted by power and greed. Quinn well deserved his Best Supporting Actor Oscar for his performance as Zapata's brother. Based on the novel "Zapata the Unconquered" by Edgcumb Pinchon. 112m/B VHS, Beta, LV. Marlon Brando, Anthony Quinn, Jean Peters, Margo, Arnold Moss, Joseph Wiseman, Mildred Dunnock; **D:** Elia Kazan; **W:** John Steinbeck; **M:** Alex North. Academy Awards '52: Best Supporting Actor (Quinn); British Academy Awards '52: Best Actor (Brando); Cannes Film Festival '52: Best Actor (Brando); Nominations: Academy Awards '52: Best Actor (Brando), Best Art Direction/Set Decoration (B & W), Best Story & Screenplay, Original Dramatic/Comedy Score. *FOX, BTV*

Vivacious Lady ✓✓✓ **1938** Romantic comedy about a mild-mannered college professor who marries a chorus girl. Problems arise when he must let his conservative family and his former fiancee in on the marriage news. Good performances. Appealing. 90m/B VHS, Beta. Ginger Rogers, James Stewart, James Ellison, Beulah Bondi, Charles Coburn, Jack Carson, Franklin Pangborn; **D:** George Stevens. Nominations: Academy Awards '38: Best Cinematography, Best Sound. *CCB, MED*

Vive L'Amour ✓✓ *Aiqing Wansui* **1994** A furnished Taipei luxury apartment is the setting for three characters who make use of the space but have little connection to each other. Guimei is the real estate agent who's trying to sell the apartment and uses it for casual sex, including an encounter with street vendor Zhaorong. The third part of the triangle is young salesman Kangsheng, who's broken into the place to commit suicide but is forestalled by Zhaorong, with whom Kangsheng then becomes sexually intrigued. The trio come and go, mostly alone, so dialogue is at a minimum. Taiwanese with subtitles. 118m/C VHS. *TW* Yang Guimei, Chen Zhaorong, Li Kangsheng; **D:** Tsai Ming-Liang. *FXL*

Vogues of 1938 ✓✓ *All This and Glamour Too; Vogues* **1937** As a lark, a rich girl takes a job as a fashion model and incurs the displeasure of Baxter, the owner of the chic fashion house where she works. An early Technicolor fashion extravaganza. ♫That Old Feeling; Lovely One; Turn On the Red Hot Heat (Burn the Blues Away); King of Jam. 110m/C VHS, Beta. Joan Bennett, Warner Baxter, Helen Vinson, Mischa Auer, Hedda Hopper, Penny Singleton, Alan Mowbray; **D:** Irving Cummings. Nominations: Academy Awards '37: Best Interior Decoration, Best Song ("That Old Feeling"). *NO*

Volcano ✓✓ **1997 (PG-13)** L.A. has already had to deal with earthquakes, mudslides, raging fires, riots and the acting career of Anna Nicole Smith. Now it's completely roasted by millions of gallons of molten lava. This overblown Rescue 911 has Mike Roark (Jones), the standard take-charge guy, trying to avert total destruction while being assisted by the brainy-but-beautiful seismologist Dr. Amy Barnes (Heche). Many tongue-in-cheek jokes about the general state of chaos in L.A. even on the best of days; but aside from these, the dialogue is cheesy beyond belief. The special effects are very impressive, however. Wilshire Blvd. was actually recreated on a 17-acre set (believed to be the biggest ever) in order to meet its fiery doom.**CW:** Intense depiction of urban disaster and related injuries. 120m/C VHS. Tommy Lee Jones, Anne Heche, Gaby Hoffman, Don Cheadle, Keith David, John Corbett, Michael Rispoli, John Carroll Lynch, Jacqueline Kim; **D:** Mick Jackson; **W:** Billy Ray, Jerome Armstrong; **C:** Theo van de Sande; **M:** Alan Silvestri. *NYR*

Volere Volare ✓✓½ **1992 (R)** Shy sound engineer Nichetti shares a studio with his brother. The brother employs a bevy of beauties to dub sound effects onto soft-core porn films while Nichetti works on dubbing classic cartoons. He becomes so involved in his work he actually turns into a cartoon figure, which does nothing for his love life. Then he meets Martina, who's strangely attracted to this cartoon figure. Quirky comedy mixes animation and live action with too many gimmicks and not enough heart. In Italian with English subtitles.**CW:** Nudity. 92m/C VHS, LV. *IT* Maurizio Nichetti, Angela Finocchiaro, Mariella Valentini, Patrizio Roversi, Remo Remotti, Renato Scarpa; **D:** Maurizio Nichetti, Guido Manuli; **W:** Maurizio Nichetti, Guido Manuli. Montreal World Film Festival '92: Best Director (Nichetti). *COL, FCT*

Volpone ✓✓✓ **1939** A classic adaptation of Ben Jonson's famous tale. A greedy merchant pretends he is dying, leaving a fortune behind, in order see what his family will do to become his heir. In French with English subtitles. 95m/B VHS, Beta. *FR* Harry Baur, Louis Jouvet, Fernand Ledoux; **D:** Maurice Tourneur. *NOS, HHT, APD*

Volunteers ✓✓ **1985 (R)** Ivy League playboy joins the newly formed Peace Corps to escape gambling debts and finds himself on a bridge-building mission in Thailand. Has its comedic moments, especially with Candy. 107m/C VHS, Beta, LV. Tom Hanks, John Candy, Rita Wilson, Tim Thomerson, Gedde Watanabe, George Plimpton, Ernest Harada; **D:** Nicholas Meyer; **M:** James Horner. *NO*

Von Ryan's Express ✓✓✓ **1965** An American Air Force colonel leads a group of prisoners-of-war in taking control of a freight train in order to make their exciting escape from a WWII P.O.W. camp in Italy. Strong cast. 117m/C VHS, Beta, LV. Frank Sinatra, Trevor Howard, Brad Dexter, Raffaella Carra, Sergio Fantoni, John Leyton, Vito Scotti, Edward Mulhare, Adolfo Celi, James Brolin, James B. Sikking; **D:** Mark Robson; **W:** Wendell Mayes; **C:** William H. Daniels; **M:** Jerry Goldsmith. *FOX, FCT*

Voodoo ✓✓ **1995 (R)** College student Andy (Feldman) must battle a fraternity, lead by an evil voodoo priest, when they decide to make his girlfriend their next human sacrifice.**CW:** Violence/gore; some nudity. 91m/C VHS, LV, Closed Caption. Corey Feldman, Sarah Douglas, Jack Nance; **D:** Rene Eram; **W:** Brian DiMuccio, Dino Vindeni; **M:** Keith Bilderbeck. *APX*

Voodoo Black Exorcist ✓ **1989** Some 3000 years ago, a black prince was buried alive for messin' with another man's woman. Now he's back...and he's mad—real mad. He's prepared to kill just about everyone. Can he be stopped before all in the modern world are dead?? ?m/C VHS. Aldo Sambrel, Tenyeka Stadle, Fernando Sancho. *HHE*

Voodoo Dawn ✓✓ **1989 (R)** Two New Yorkers travel to the Deep South to visit a friend who, it turns out, is the latest victim in a series of really gross voodoo murders. A beautiful girl is written into the plot, and the New York guys have an excuse to stay in voodooville, even though bimbolina's southern accent comes and goes for no discernable reason. Filmed near Charleston, South Carolina and co-written by Russo of "Night of the Living Dead" fame. 83m/C VHS. Raymond St. Jacques, Theresa Merritt, Gina Gershon, Kirk Baily, Billy "Sly" Williams, J. Grant Albrecht, Tony Todd; **D:** Steven Fierberg; **W:** John Russo, Jeffrey Delman. *ACA*

Voodoo Woman ✓ **1957** An innocent girl is lured into the jungle by an evil scientist who is trying to create the perfect woman to commit murders. He turns the girl into an ugly monster in an attempt to get her to obey his telepathic commands. A campy classic that's as bad as it sounds. 77m/B VHS. Marla English, Tom Conway, Mike Connors, Lance Fuller; **D:** Edward L. Cahn. *COL, PAR*

Vortex ✓½ **1981** Punk/film noir style in which a female private eye becomes immersed in corporate paranoia and political corruption. 87m/C VHS. Lydia Lunch, James Russo, Bill Rice, Richard France, Ann

Magnuson, Haoui Montaug, Adele Bertei, Bill Landis; **D:** Scott B, Beth B; **W:** Scott B, Beth B; **M:** Lydia Lunch, Adele Bertei. *ICA*

Voulez-Vous Danser Avec Moi? ✓✓ *Come Dance with Me; Do You Want to Dance with Me?* **1959** A young bride endeavors to clear her husband of murder charges and find the real killer. In French with English subtitles. 90m/C VHS, Beta. *FR* Brigitte Bardot, Henri Vidal; **D:** Michel Boisrond. *BAR*

A Vow to Kill ✓✓½ **1994 (PG-13)** Predictable made for cable thriller finds the wealthy Phillips marrying the charming Grieco after a whirlwind courtship. Then, on their honeymoon, she accidentally learns that her new husband has contacted her family and is masquerading as a kidnapper—demanding a large ransom for her safe release. But maybe it's not such a masquerade after all.**CW:** Some terror/violence. 91m/C VHS, Beta, Closed Caption. Julianne Phillips, Richard Grieco, Gordon Pinsent, Peter MacNeill, Tom Cavanagh, Nicole Oliver; **D:** Harry S. Longstreet; **W:** Harry S. Longstreet, Sean Silas. *PAR*

Voyage ✓½ **1993 (R)** Boring rip-off of "Dead Calm" and other couple-in-peril-from-psycho-on-boat films. Hauer and Allen are having marital problems and decide to sail away from their troubles with new-found friends Roberts and Nielson. Only their guests are sociopaths. Hauer takes a breather from his psycho roles for a turn as the good guy while Roberts could do his patented crazy act in his sleep. Made for cable television. ?m/C VHS. Rutger Hauer, Karen Allen, Eric Roberts, Connie Nielson; **D:** John MacKenzie. *ITC*

Voyage en Balloon ✓✓½ **1959** This is the delightful story of a young boy (played by the star of "The Red Balloon") who stows away on his grandfather's hot air balloon for an adventurous trip across France. 82m/C VHS, Beta. *FR* Pascal Lamorisse, Andre Gille, Maurice Baquet; **D:** Albert Lamorisse; **W:** Albert Lamorisse. *COL*

Voyage en Douce ✓✓ **1981** Helene and Lucie have been friends since childhood. Helene wants to rent a summer house, and Lucie, fed up with her marriage, agrees to join her on a leisurely journey through the south of France. Thoughtful look at friendship among women. French with subtitles. 95m/C VHS. *FR* Dominique Sanda, Geraldine Chaplin; **D:** Michel DeVille. *NYF*

The Voyage of Tanai ✓✓ **1975 (G)** A young Polynesian battles nature's snarls on his quest to save his village. 90m/C VHS, Beta. **D:** John Latos. *NO*

Voyage of Terror: The Achille Lauro Affair ✓✓½ **1990** Recounting of the 1985 Italian cruise-ship hijacking by four Palestinians. Lancaster is the wheelchair-bound Leon Klinghoffer and Saint is wife Marilyn. Shot on the actual ship and route where the tragedy occurred. Originally a made-for-television miniseries. 120m/C VHS, Closed Caption. Burt Lancaster, Eva Marie Saint, Robert Culp, Brian Bloom, Dominique Sanda, Rebecca Schaeffer, Joseph Nasser, Gabriele Ferzetti, Renzo Montagnani; **D:** Alberto Negrin. *PSM*

Voyage of the Damned ✓✓✓ **1976 (G)** The story of one of the most tragic incidents of WWII. In 1939, 1,937 German-Jewish refugees fleeing Nazi Germany are bound for Cuba aboard the Hamburg-America liner S.S. St. Louis. They are refused permission to land in Cuba (and everywhere else) and must sail back to Germany and certain death. Based on the novel by Gordon Thomas and Max Morgan-Witts. 134m/C VHS, Beta. Faye Dunaway, Max von Sydow, Oskar Werner, Malcolm McDowell, Orson Welles, James Mason, Lee Grant, Katharine Ross, Ben Gazzara, Lynne Frederick, Wendy Hiller, Jose Ferrer, Luther Adler, Sam Wanamaker, Denholm Elliott, Nehemiah Persoff, Julie Harris, Maria Schell, Janet Suzman; **D:** Stuart Rosenberg; **C:** Billy Williams; **M:** Lalo Schifrin. Golden Globe Awards '77: Best Supporting Actress (Ross); Nominations: Academy Awards '76: Best Adapted Screenplay, Best Supporting Actress (Grant), Best Original Score. *FOX*

Voyage of the Heart 🦴🦴 1990 An aging fisherman meets up with a sexy college girl and the passion begins. 88m/C VHS. Bill Aldrij, Dunja Djordjenic. *AIP*

Voyage of the Rock Aliens 🦴 1987 A quasi-satiric space farce about competing alien rock stars. 97m/C VHS, Beta. Pia Zadora, Tom Nolan, Craig Sheffer, Rhema, Ruth Gordon, Michael Berryman, Jermaine Jackson; *D:* James Fargo. *PSM*

The Voyage of the Yes 🦴🦴 1972 (PG) Two teenagers, one white and one black, in a small sailboat hit rough weather and battle the elements while learning about themselves. Average made-for-television movie. 100m/C VHS. Desi Arnaz Jr., Mike Evans, Beverly Garland, Skip Homeier, Della Reese, Scoey Mitchell; *D:* Lee H. Katzin. *NO*

A Voyage' Round My Father 🦴🦴🦴 1989 John Mortimer's adaptation of his semi-autobiographical stage play. Olivier is the eccentric, opinionated blind barrister-father and Bates the exasperated son as both try to come to terms with their stormy family relationship. Well-acted and directed. Made for television. 85m/C VHS, Beta. *GB* Laurence Olivier, Alan Bates, Jane Asher, Elizabeth Sellars; *D:* Alvin Rakoff. *HBO*

Voyage-Suprise 🦴🦴🦴 1946 A slapstick comedy about a crazy old man who runs a mystery tour from a dilapidated bus as he takes an unknowing mob of tourists on a cross-country escapade through a brothel, a wedding, criminals, police, terrorists and the Haute-Provence. In French with English subtitles. 108m/B VHS, Beta. *FR* Martine Carol, Sioel; *D:* Pierre Prevert; *C:* Jean Bourgoin. *FCT, FST*

Voyage to Italy 🦴🦴½ 1953 An unhappy couple, on the verge of divorce, inherit a house in Italy and make a trip to see it. In Italy, they dally with other people but realize their attachment to each other demands they attempt to salvage their marriage. Not the best of the Rossellini-Bergman collaborations. Poor editing and directing undermine weak script. Sanders and Bergman do their best. 87m/B VHS, Beta. Ingrid Bergman, George Sanders; *D:* Roberto Rossellini. *NOS, FCT*

Voyage to the Bottom of the Sea 🦴🦴🦴 1961 The crew of an atomic submarine must destroy a deadly radiation belt which has set the polar ice cap ablaze. Fun stuff, with good special effects and photography. Later became a television show. 106m/C VHS, Beta, LV, Closed Caption. Walter Pidgeon, Joan Fontaine, Barbara Eden, Peter Lorre, Robert Sterling, Michael Ansara, Frankie Avalon; *D:* Irwin Allen; *W:* Irwin Allen, Charles Bennett; *C:* Winton C. Hoch. *FOX, FCT*

Voyage to the Planet of Prehistoric Women WOOF! *Gill Woman; Gill Women of Venus* 1968 Astronauts journey to Venus, where they discover a race of gorgeous, sea-shell clad women led by Van Doren, as well as a few monsters. Incomprehensible but fun. The third film incorporating the Russian "Planeta Burg" footage. Directed (and narrated) by Bogdanovich under the pseudonym Derek Thomas. 78m/C VHS. Mamie Van Doren, Mary Mark, Paige Lee; *D:* Peter Bogdanovich. *SNC*

Voyage to the Prehistoric Planet 🦴½ *Voyage to a Prehistoric Planet* 1965 In the year 2020, an expedition to Venus is forced to deal with dinosaurs and other perils. In the making of this movie, Roger Corman edited in special effects and additional footage from a recently acquired Russian film, "Planeta Burg," and his own "Queen of Blood." 80m/C VHS. Basil Rathbone, Faith Domergue, Marc Shannon, Christopher Brand; *D:* Curtis Harrington. *NOS, SNC*

Voyager 🦴🦴🦴 1991 (PG-13) Restless, middle-aged engineer Walter Faber (Shepherd) tells his life story in a series of flashbacks. Twenty years before (the film starts in 1957) he abandons his pregnant girlfriend who promises to get an abortion. He laters hears she married, had a child, and divorced. While sailing to New York from France Walter falls in love with a young student and accompanies her to Greece to visit her mother. Only then does he realize her true identity, leading to a tragic conclusion. Shepherd's is a glum, repressed performance (in keeping with the character) while Delpy personifies youthful sweetness. Based on the novel "Homo Faber" by Max Frisch. 110m/C VHS, LV. *FR GE* Sam Shepard, Julie Delpy, Barbara Sukowa, Dieter Kirchlechner, Traci Lind, Deborra-Lee Furness, August Zirner, Thomas Heinze; *D:* Volker Schlondorff; *W:* Volker Schlondorff, Rudy Wurlitzer. *ACA*

The Voyeur 🦴 1994 After ten years of marriage, a couple tries to ignite those sexual fires by spending a weekend in Napa Valley and indulging in erotic sexual games. Based on Lonnie Barbach's book "Erotic Edge". 80m/C VHS. Al Sapienza, Kim Dawson; *D:* Deborah Shames; *W:* Udana Power. *TPV*

Vukovar 🦴 1994 Vukovar is a Croat town just across the Danube river from Serbia, in the former Yugoslavia, where different ethnic groups had managed to coexist peacefully. When Croatian Anna (Jokovic) marries her childhood sweetheart, the Serbian Toma (Isakovic), however, their celebration is marred by nationalist demonstrations. Soon Anna's pregnant, Toma has been drafted, and the town comes under siege, with Tomas' parents fleeing, Anna's family killed in a bombing, and Ann herself struggling to survive. Film was condemned by the Croatian government as pro-Serbian propaganda though director Draskovic, a Serbian whose parents are Croatian and Bosnian, strove to be nonpartisan. Serbo-Croatian with subtitles. 94m/C VHS. *YU* Mirjana Jokovic, Boris Isakovic, Monica Romic; *D:* Boro Draskovic; *W:* Boro Draskovic, Maja Draskovic; *C:* Aleksandar Petkovic. *NYF*

Vulcan God of Fire WOOF! *Vulcan, Son of Jupiter* 1962 Flash is a muscle-bound Vulcan fighting off cheesy monsters in an effort to win the hand of Venus. 76m/C VHS, Beta. *IT* Rob Flash, Gordon Mitchell, Bella Cortez; *D:* Emmimo Salvi. *TWE*

Vulture 🦴 1967 In an attempt to carry out a curse on the descendants of the man who killed his forefather, a scientist tries an atomic transmutation experiment and winds up combining himself with a bird. 91m/C VHS, Beta. Robert Hutton, Akim Tamiroff, Broderick Crawford, Diane Clare, Philip Friend, Patrick Holt, Annette Carell; *D:* Lawrence Huntington. *NO*

Vultures 🦴 1984 A dying patriarch summons his predatory family to his home in order to straighten out the distribution of inheritance. One by one, they fall victim to a mysterious murderer. 101m/C VHS, Beta. Yvonne De Carlo, Stuart Whitman, Jim Bailey, Meredith MacRae, Aldo Ray; *D:* Paul Leder. *PSM*

W 🦴½ *I Want Her Dead* 1974 (PG) A woman and her husband are terrorized and must find out why. A single letter "W" is found at the scene of the crimes. Notable only as model Twiggy's first film. 95m/C VHS, Beta. Twiggy, Dirk Benedict, John Vernon, Eugene Roche; *D:* Richard Quine. *LIV, VES*

Wackiest Ship in the Army 🦴🦴½ 1961 A completely undisciplined warship crew must smuggle an Australian spy through Japanese waters during WWII. Odd, enjoyable mixture of action and laughs. Became a TV series. In the middle of the war effort, Nelson straps on a guitar and sings "Do You Know What It Means to Miss New Orleans." 99m/C VHS, Beta, LV. Jack Lemmon, Ricky Nelson, Chips Rafferty, John Lund, Mike Kellin, Patricia Driscoll; *D:* Richard Murphy. *COL*

Wackiest Wagon Train in the West 🦴 1977 (G) Hapless wagon master is saddled with a dummy assistant as they guide a party of five characters across the West. Based on the minor TV sitcom "Dusty's Trail." Produced by the same folks who delivered the similarly premised TV series "Gilligan's Island" and "The Brady Bunch." 86m/C VHS, Beta. Bob Denver, Forrest Tucker, Jeannine Riley. *MED*

Wacko WOOF! 1983 (PG) Group of nymphettes and tough guys get caught up in a wild Halloween-pumpkin-lawnmower murder. This spoof of the "Halloween" series works too hard for as few laughs as it gets. 84m/C VHS, Beta, LV. Stella Stevens, George Kennedy, Joe Don Baker, Andrew Dice Clay; *D:* Greydon Clark. *VES*

The Wacky World of Wills & Burke 🦴🦴 1985 Comedy based on the adventures of Wills and Burke, the two 19th-century explorers who led the first unsuccessful expedition across the outback—the Lewis and Clark of Australia, if you will. In real life they died during the adventure, a less than wacky finale. "Burke and Wills," out the same year, was a serious treatment of the same story. 102m/C VHS, Beta. *AU* Garry McDonald, Kim Gyngell, Peter Collingwood, Jonathon Hardy, Mark Little; *D:* Bob Weis. *NO*

Wager of Love 🦴🦴 1990 While vacationing on their annual pleasure cruise, four women bet on their individual power of seduction. They find themselves competing for passion as each woman's erotic adventure unravels in this exciting and sensual tale. 75m/C VHS, Closed Caption. Steve Landers, Shelly Johnson, Elliot Silverman, Lisa Cook; *D:* Jason Holt. *CEL*

Wages of Fear 🦴🦴🦴🦴 *Le Salaire De La Peur* 1955 American oil company controls a desolate Central American town whose citizens desperately want out—so desperately that four are willing to try a suicide mission to deliver nitroglycerine to put out a well-fire raging 300 miles away. The company's cynical head has offered $2,000 to each man, enough to finance escape from the hell-hole they live in. Complex, multi-dimensional drama concentrates on character development for the first half—crucial to the film's greatness. This is the restored version. Remade by William Friedkin as "Sorcerer" in 1977. Based on a novel by Georges Arnaud. In French with English subtitles. 138m/B VHS, Beta, LV. *FR* Yves Montand, Charles Vanel, Peter Van Eyck, Vera Clouzot, Folco Lulli, William Tubbs; *D:* Henri-Georges Clouzot; *W:* Henri-Georges Clouzot; *M:* Georges Auric. British Academy Awards '54: Best Film; Cannes Film Festival '53: Best Actor (Vanel), Best Film. *HHT, SNC, VYY*

Wagner: The Complete Epic 🦴🦴 1985 The unedited version of the epic made-for-television miniseries dramatizing the life of German composer Richard Wagner. The excellent photography does justice to the elaborate production, shot on some 200 different locations. The actors cringe in the presence of the subject's grandeur; Burton, a shell of his former cinematic self, is painful to watch in his last released film. Frankly, this is way too long. 540m/C VHS, Beta. *GB* HU Richard Burton, Vanessa Redgrave, Ralph Richardson, John Gielgud, Laurence Olivier; *D:* Tony Palmer. *MVD, KUL*

Wagner: The Movie 🦴½ 1985 Slightly half it's original length, the world's biggest biopic is still huge, sweeping, and long. Incoherent and over-acted. Wagner's music is conducted by Sir Georg Solti. Made for television. 300m/C VHS, Beta. *GB HU* Richard Burton, Vanessa Redgrave, John Gielgud, Franco Nero, Laurence Olivier; *D:* Tony Palmer. *MVD, GLV*

Wagon Master 🦴🦴 1950 Two cowboys are persuaded to guide a group of Mormons, led by Bond, in their trek across the western frontier. They run into a variety of troubles, including a band of killers who joins the wagon train to escape a posse. Sensitively directed, realistic and worthwhile. Inspired the TV series "Wagon Train." Also available colorized. 85m/B VHS, Beta, LV, Closed Caption. Ben Johnson, Joanne Dru, Harry Carey Jr., Ward Bond, Jane Darwell, James Arness; *D:* John Ford. *MED, TTC*

Wagon Tracks 🦴🦴½ 1919 Hart searches for the man responsible for his brother's death. 64m/B VHS. William S. Hart, Jane Novak, Robert McKim, Lloyd Bacon; *D:* Lambert Hillyer. *GPV*

Wagon Trail ✰✰½ **1935** The sheriff's son is blackmailed into helping a gang of robbers, with terrible consequences for himself and his father (Carey), who is fired from his job after the son breaks jail. The new sheriff is secretly chief of the outlaw band. Carey rides back into town and eventually virtue triumphs. Good, tense—but not too tense—western. **59m/B VHS, Beta.** Harry Carey Sr.; **D:** Harry Fraser. *VCN*

Wagon Wheels ✰✰ *Caravans West* **1934** Recycling was in vogue in '34, when unused footage from "Fighting Caravans" (1931) with Gary Cooper was used to remake the very same plot. The result is biodegradable. Settlers heading to Oregon are ambushed by bad guy Blue, employed by fur traders. Blue sics Injuns on them too, but don't worry, they make it. Adapted from Zane Grey's novel "Fighting Caravans." **54m/B VHS, Beta.** Randolph Scott, Monte Blue, Gail Patrick, Billy Lee; **D:** Charles T. Barton. *NOS, DVT*

Wagons East ✰ **1994 (PG-13)** Fed up with prairie hardships, pioneers decide to hitch up to a wagon train and head east. Candy (who died during filming) plays the drunken former wagonmaster hired to get them back home, with Lewis (out of his depth) as a neurotic ex-doctor, and McGinley stuck in the role of a gay bookseller that reeks of stereotypical mannerisms. Script is desperate for humor, which it never finds, and it's hard to watch Candy's performance knowing this mess was his last role. **CW:** Off-color humor. **100m/C VHS, LV, Closed Caption.** John Candy, Richard Lewis, Ellen Greene, John C. McGinley, Robert Picardo, William Sanderson, Thomas F. Duffy, Russell Means, Rodney Grant, Michael Horse, Gailard Sartain, Lochlyn Munro, Stuart Proud Eagle Grant; **D:** Peter Markle; **W:** Matthew Carlson, Jerry Abrahamson. *LIV*

Wagon's Westward ✰½ **1940** Good government agent Morris assumes identity of bad twin brother, who's in jail, in order to catch some outlaws. **53m/B VHS.** Chester Morris, Buck Jones, Guinn "Big Boy" Williams, Douglas Fowley, George "Gabby" Hayes, Anita Louise, Ona Munson; **D:** Lew (Louis Friedlander) Landers. *GPV*

Waikiki ✰½ **1980** Two private eyes set out to prove that their friend is not the "cane field murderer" who is terrorizing the Hawaiian island of Oahu. Harmless but pointless TV pilot. **96m/C VHS, Beta.** Dack Rambo, Steve Marachuk, Donna Mills, Cal Bellini, Darren McGavin; **D:** Ron Satlof. *ORI*

Waikiki Wedding ✰✰✰ **1937** Enjoyable musical about a scheming pineapple promoter (Crosby) who meets the woman of his dreams in a contest he concocted. Contest winner Ross dislikes Hawaii and wants to go home and Crosby must keep her from going...first for business reasons and later, for love. Supporting cast includes Hawaiian Prince Leilani and a pig. Lots of song and dance and Hawaiian sunsets, along with Burns and Raye, the other couple destined for love on the islands, keep the story moving. ♫Sweet Leilani; Sweet Is the Word for You; In a Little Hula Heaven; Blue Hawaii; Okolehao; Nani Ona Pua. **89m/B VHS, Closed Caption.** Bing Crosby, Bob Burns, Martha Raye, Shirley Ross, George Barbier, Leif Erickson, Grady Sutton, Granville Bates, Anthony Quinn; **D:** Frank Tuttle; **W:** Frank Butler, Don Hartman, Walter DeLeon, Francis Martin; **C:** Karl Struss; **M:** Leo Robin, Ralph Rainger. Academy Awards '37: Best Song ("Sweet Leilani"). *USH*

Wait Till Your Mother Gets Home ✰✰ **1983** "Mr. Mom"—like zaniness abounds as a football coach cares for the kids and does chores while his wife takes her first job in 15 years. Almost too darn cute, but well written. Made for television. **97m/C VHS, Beta.** Paul Michael Glaser, Dee Wallace Stone, Peggy McKay, David Doyle, Raymond Buktenica, James Gregory, Joey Lawrence, Lynne Moody; **D:** Bill Persky. *PSM*

Wait Until Dark ✰✰✰ **1967** A photographer unwittingly smuggles a drug-filled doll into New York, and his blind wife, alone in their apartment, is terrorized by murderous crooks in search

of it. A compelling thriller based on the Broadway hit by Frederick Knott, who also wrote "Dial M for Murder." The individual actors' performances were universally acclaimed in this spinetingler. **105m/C VHS, Beta, LV.** Audrey Hepburn, Alan Arkin, Richard Crenna, Efrem Zimbalist Jr., Jack Weston; **D:** Terence Young; **W:** Robert B. Carrington; **C:** Charles B(ryant) Lang; **M:** Henry Mancini. Nominations: Academy Awards '67: Best Actress (Hepburn). *WAR*

Wait Until Spring, Bandini ✰✰½ **1990 (PG-13)** A flavorful immigrant tale about a transplanted Italian family weathering the winter in 1925 Colorado, as seen through the eyes of a young son. Alternately funny and moving, with one of Dunaway's scenery-chewing performances as a local temptation for the father. Based on the autobiographical novel by John Fante, co-produced by Francis Ford Coppola. **104m/C VHS, Closed Caption.** Joe Mantegna, Faye Dunaway, Burt Young, Ornella Muti, Alex Vincent, Renata Vanni, Michael Bacall, Daniel Wilson; **D:** Dominique Deruddere; **M:** Angelo Badalamenti. *WAR*

Waiting for Guffman ✰✰ **1996 (R)** The eccentric citizens of Blaine, Missouri plan an original musical ("Red, White, and Blaine") to celebrate the town's 150th anniversary with the aid of former New Yorker and semi-hysteric Corky St. Claire (Guest) as their director. Everyone's very game—and almost completely talentless. The Guffman of the title is the Broadway producer Corky knows and whom he's invited to see their disaster-in-the-making. A little too deliberately quirky for its own good.**CW:** Brief strong language. **84m/C VHS, Closed Caption.** Christopher Guest, Eugene Levy, Catherine O'Hara, Parker Posey, Fred Willard, Lewis Arquette, Matt Keeslar; **D:** Christopher Guest; **W:** Christopher Guest, Eugene Levy; **C:** Roberto Schaefer; **M:** Michael McKean, Harry Shearer, Christopher Guest. *WAR*

Waiting for the Light ✰✰½ **1990 (PG)** When a woman takes over a small-town diner, she gets the surprise of her life. Seems an angel has made his home there and now the townsfolk are flocking to see him. MacLaine is wonderful and Garr is fetching and likeable. Set during the Cuban missile crisis. Enjoyable, tame comedy. **94m/C VHS, LV, 8mm, Closed Caption.** Shirley MacLaine, Teri Garr, Vincent Schiavelli, John Bedford Lloyd; **D:** Christopher Monger; **W:** Christopher Monger. *COL*

Waiting for the Moon ✰½ **1987 (PG)** Hunt as Alice B. Toklas is a relative treat in this ponderous, frustrating biopic about Toklas and Gertrude Stein, her lover. Made for "American Playhouse" on PBS. **88m/C VHS, Beta, Closed Caption.** Linda Hunt, Linda Bassett, Andrew McCarthy, Bruce McGill, Jacques Boudet, Bernadette LaFont; **D:** Jill Godmilow. Sundance Film Festival '87: Grand Jury Prize. *FOX*

Waiting to Exhale ✰✰✰ **1995 (R)** Adaptation of Terry McMillan's novel about four African-American women hoping to reach the point in their love lives when they can relax and stop waiting for the right man. After the string of dogs and users they choose, you want to tell them not to hold their breath. The women are supposed to be close friends, but all of their stories are broken up into vignettes. This erodes the ensemble feeling of the movie, but performances are strong all around. Retaining the book's feel of just-between-friends girl talk, it may be a little harsh for those who are, shall we say, estrogen-challenged. A lush R&B soundtrack is the perfect backdrop for the ladies' soulful yearning for real love.**CW:** Language and some strong sexuality. **120m/C VHS.** Whitney Houston, Angela Bassett, Loretta Devine, Lela Rochon, Gregory Hines, Dennis Haysbert, Mykel T. Williamson, Michael Beach, Leon, Wendell Pierce, Donald A. Faison, Jeffrey D. Sams, Toyomichi Kurita; **Cameos:** Wesley Snipes; **D:** Forest Whitaker; **W:** Ronald Bass; **M:** Babyface. MTV Movie Awards '96: Best Song ("Sittin' Up in My Room"); Nominations: MTV Movie Awards '96: Breakthrough Performance (Rochon), Best Song ("Exhale (Shoop Shoop)"). *TCF*

Waitress woof! *Soup to Nuts* **1981 (R)** Three beautiful girls are waitresses in a crazy restaurant where the chef gets drunk, the kitchen explodes, and the customers riot. Awful premise, worse production. **89m/C VHS, Beta.** Jim Harris, Carol Drake, Carol Bever; **D:** Lloyd (Samuel Weil) Kaufman. *NO*

Wake Island ✰✰✰ **1942** After Pearl Harbor, a small group of Marines face the onslaught of the Japanese fleet on a small Pacific island. Although doomed, they hold their ground for 16 days. Exciting, realistic, and moving. The first film to capitalize on early "last stands" of WWII; also among the most popular war movies. Shown to soldiers in training camps with great morale-raising success. **88m/B VHS, Beta.** Robert Preston, Brian Donlevy, William Bendix, MacDonald Carey, Albert Dekker, Walter Abel, Rod Cameron, Barbara Britton; **D:** John Farrow. New York Film Critics Awards '42: Best Director (Farrow); Nominations: Academy Awards '42: Best Director (Farrow), Best Original Screenplay, Best Picture, Best Supporting Actor (Bendix). *USH, TLF*

Wake of the Red Witch ✰✰½ **1949** Wayne captains the ship of the title and battles shipping tycoon Adler for a fortune in pearls and the love of a beautiful woman (Russell). Wayne shows impressive range in a non-gun-totin' role. **106m/B VHS, Beta.** John Wayne, Gail Russell, Gig Young, Luther Adler, Henry Daniell; **D:** Edward Ludwig. *REP*

Walk, Don't Run ✰✰½ **1966** Romantic comedy involving a British businessman (Grant) unable to find a hotel room in Tokyo due to the crowds staying for the 1964 summer Olympic Games. He winds up renting a room from an Embassy secretary (Eggar) and then meets and invites Hutton, a member of the U.S. Olympic walking team, also without a place to stay, to share it with him. Grant then proceeds to play matchmaker, despite the fact that Eggar has a fiance. Grant's last film. Innocuous, unnecessary remake of "The More the Merrier." **114m/C VHS, Beta.** Cary Grant, Samantha Eggar, Jim Hutton, John Standing, Miiko Taka; **D:** Charles Walters; **M:** Quincy Jones. *COL*

A Walk in the Clouds ✰✰½ **1995 (PG-13)** Gorgeously photographed, if sappy, romantic fantasy finds WWII vet Paul Sutton (Reeves), returning to his unhappy marriage and salesman job. So when the good-hearted Paul meets beautiful Victoria (Sanchez-Gijon), the pregnant and unmarried daughter of a possessive Napa vineyard owner (Giannini), he's more than happy to help by posing as her husband. Naturally, dad is livid at their "marriage" and Paul falls in love with his sham bride. Quinn gets to do his part as wise family patriarch and yes, there's even a grape harvest (and some grape stomping) to put everyone in the proper romantic mood. Based on the 1942 Italian film "Four Steps in the Clouds."**CW:** Moments of sensuality and war action. **103m/C VHS, Closed Caption.** Keanu Reeves, Aitana Sanchez-Gijon, Giancarlo Giannini, Anthony Quinn, Angelica Aragon, Evangelina Elizondo, Freddy Rodriguez, Debra Messing; **D:** Alfonso Arau; **W:** Robert Mark Kamen; **C:** Emmanuel Lubezki; **M:** Leo Brower. Golden Globe Awards '96: Best Score; Nominations: MTV Movie Awards '96: Most Desirable Male (Reeves), Best Kiss (Keanu Reeves/Aitana Sanchez-Gijon). *FXV*

Walk in the Spring Rain ✰✰½ **1970 (PG)** The bored wife of a college professor follows him to rural Tennessee when he goes on sabbatical, where she meets the married Quinn and the two begin an affair. When Quinn's disturbed son learns of the affair, he attacks the woman, with tragic results. Fine cast should have had better effect on low-key script. **98m/C VHS, Beta.** Ingrid Bergman, Anthony Quinn, Fritz Weaver, Katherine Crawford, Tom Fielding, Virginia Gregg; **D:** Guy Green; **W:** Stirling Silliphant; **C:** Charles B(ryant) Lang; **M:** Elmer Bernstein. *NO*

A Walk in the Sun ✰✰✰½ *Salerno Beachhead* **1946** The trials of a group of infantrymen in WWII from the time they land in Italy to the time they capture their objective, a farmhouse occupied by the Germans. Excellent ensemble acting shows well the variety of civilians who make up any fighting force and explores their fears, motivations, and weaknesses. Producer and director Milestone also made "All Quiet on the Western Front" and the Korean War masterpiece "Pork Chop Hill." Released in the final days of the war, almost concurrently with two other WWII films of the first echelon, "The Story of G.I. Joe" and "They Were Expendable." **117m/B VHS, Beta, LV, 8mm.** Dana Andrews, Richard Conte, John Ireland, Lloyd Bridges, Sterling Holloway; **D:** Lewis Milestone; **W:** Robert Rossen. *LUM, NOS, DVT*

Walk into Hell 🐾🐾 1957 A mining engineer and his assistant searching for oil meet the primitive natives of New Guinea. Tedious at times and dated, but pleasant enough. **91m/C VHS, Beta.** *AU* Chips Rafferty, Francoise Christophe, Reg Lye; **D:** Lee Robinson. *VYY, NLC*

Walk Like a Man 🐾½ 1987 (PG) In a take-off of Tarzan movies, Mandel plays a man raised by wolves. Comic problems arise when he is found by his mother and the family attempts to civilize him. Juvenile script wastes fine cast. **86m/C VHS, Beta.** Howie Mandel, Christopher Lloyd, Cloris Leachman, Colleen Camp, Amy Steel, George DiCenzo; **D:** Melvin Frank. *MGM*

Walk on the Wild Side 🐾🐾 1962 In 1930s New Orleans, a man searches for his long-lost love, finds her working in a whorehouse and fights to save her from the lesbian madame Stanwyck. Melodrama, based only loosely on the Nelson Algren novel and adapted by cult novelist John Fante, with Edmund Morris. Much-troubled on the set, and it shows. **114m/B VHS, Beta.** Jane Fonda, Laurence Harvey, Barbara Stanwyck, Capucine, Anne Baxter; **D:** Edward Dmytryk; **M:** Elmer Bernstein. Nominations: Academy Awards '62: Best Song ("Walk on the Wild Side"). *COL*

Walk Softly, Stranger 🐾🐾 1950 Two-bit crook is reformed by the love of an innocent peasant girl. If you can stand the cliche masquerading as a plot, the performances are good. **81m/B VHS, Beta.** Alida Valli, Joseph Cotten, Spring Byington, Paul Stewart, Jack Paar, Jeff Donnell, John McIntire; **D:** Robert Stevenson. *TTC*

Walk the Proud Land 🐾🐾½ 1956 Story of Indian agent John Clum (Murphy), who fights for the rights of the Apache in 1870's Arizona and who convinces their leader Geronimo (Silverheels) to surrender to the authorities. Adapted from the biography "Apache Agent" by Woodworth Clum. **88m/C VHS.** Audie Murphy, Jay Silverheels, Anne Bancroft, Pat Crowley, Charles Drake; **D:** Jesse Hibbs; **W:** Jack Sher, Gil Doud; **C:** Harold Lipstein. *USH*

Walkabout 🐾🐾🐾½ 1971 (PG) Beautifully told and filmed story (by Roeg in his debut) about a nameless young brother (John, Roeg's six-year-old son) and sister (Agutter), who are abandoned in the Australian outback when their father kills himself. The children wander, with little chance of survival, until a young aborigine (Gumpilil) finds them. He interrupts his own "walkabout," a rite of passage, to teach them to survive, leading to betrayal and tragedy. Based on a novel by James Vance Marshall. **100m/C VHS.** *AU* Jenny Agutter, Lucien John, David Gumpilil, John Meillon; **D:** Nicolas Roeg; **W:** Edward Bond; **C:** Nicolas Roeg; **M:** John Barry. *HMV*

Walker 🐾🐾 1987 (R) Slapdash, tongue-in-cheek historical pastiche about the real-life American William Walker (played previously in "Burn!" by Marlon Brando), and how he led a revolution in Nicaragua in 1855 and became its self-declared president. A bitter, revisionist farce never for a moment attempting to be accurate. Matlin's unfortunate, though fortunately brief, follow-up to her Oscar-winning performance. **95m/C VHS, Beta.** Ed Harris, Richard Masur, Peter Boyle, Rene Auberjonois, Marlee Matlin, Miguel Sandoval; **D:** Alex Cox; **W:** Rudy Wurlitzer; **M:** Joe Strummer. *USH*

Walker: Texas Ranger: Deadly Reunion 🐾🐾½ 1994 Feature-length version of the TV series finds Walker (Norris) trying to protect a senator, with presidential leanings and big enemies, who's been targeted by a killer posing as a cop. In addition to the usual good guys, Walker is assisted by veteran ex-Ranger Laredo (Whitman), who has his own reasons for going after the bad guy. **92m/C VHS, Beta, LV, Closed Caption.** Chuck Norris, Clarence Gilyard Jr., Sheree J. Wilson, Noble Willingham, Stuart Whitman, Jonathan Banks. *WAR*

Walker: Texas Ranger: One Riot, One Ranger 🐾🐾½ 1993 (PG-13) Norris sticks with the action-adventure mode with this tv pilot movie about Cordell Walker, a good guy with a code and some martial arts skills, who teams up with an ex-gridiron star and a female district attorney to go after lawbreakers. This time its bank robbers and three hoods after a teenaged girl. **96m/C VHS, LV, Closed Caption.** Chuck Norris, Sheree J. Wilson, Clarence Gilyard Jr., Gailard Sartain, Floyd "Red Crow" Westerman, James Drury; **D:** Virgil W. Vogel; **W:** Louise McCarn. *CAN, MOV*

Walking and Talking 🐾🐾½ 1996 (R) Low-budget, lighthearted estrogen romp through the lives of two best friends in New York, Amelia (Keener) and Laura (Heche), going through commitment crises. Freshman writer/director Holofcener scores by making a lackluster story imminently watchable. Likable cast of mostly unknowns (Heche was deemed a rising star at a recent Cannes Festival) deliver Holofcener's clever and humorous exchanges. Corrigan's video store clerk and all-around "ugly guy" is a highlight. Brit Bragg brings in a worthy score. **CW:** Sexuality, language and brief drug use. **86m/C VHS, LV, Closed Caption.** Anne Heche, Catherine Keener, Liev Schreiber, Todd Field, Kevin Corrigan, Randall Batinkoff, Joseph Siravo, Vinny Pastore, Lynn Cohen, Andrew Holofcener; **D:** Nicole Holofcener; **W:** Nicole Holofcener; **C:** Michael Spiller; **M:** Billy Bragg. Nominations: Independent Spirit Awards '97: Best Actress (Keener), Best Supporting Actor (Corrigan). *MAX*

Walking Back 🐾🐾 1926 Troubled teens go for joyride and bash mirthmobile to smithereens. The body shop agrees to give them a different car, but they find themselves in the middle of a heist at a plant belonging to the father of one of the boys. **53m/B VHS, Beta.** Sue Carol, Richard Walling, Ivan Lebedeff, Robert Edeson, Florence Turner, Arthur Rankin; **D:** Rupert Julian. *GPV, FCT*

The Walking Dead 🐾🐾 1994 (R) Depicts the Vietnam War from the perspectives of four black and one white Marine assigned to rescue POWs from a North Vietnam camp in 1972. Fairly routine story with stock characters (by-the-book sergeant, family man, naive youngster, cynical hustler) and flashbacks to depict their back home struggles. Cast tries but is defeated by a one-dimensional script. **CW:** Graphic war violence; strong language; brief sexuality. **89m/C VHS.** Joe Morton, Eddie Griffin, Allen Payne, Vonte Sweet, Roger Floyd; **D:** Preston A. Whitmore II; **W:** Preston A. Whitmore II; **C:** John L. Demps Jr.; **M:** Gary Chang. *HBO*

Walking on Air 1987 Ray Bradbury's story comes to life as a handicapped boy dreams of completing a real space walk. Originally aired on PBS as part of the "Wonderworks" series. **60m/C VHS.** Lynn Redgrave, Jordan Marder, James Treuer, Katheryn Trainor; **D:** Ed Kaplan. *PME, FCT, BTV*

Walking Tall 🐾🐾½ 1973 (R) A Tennessee sheriff takes a stand against syndicate-run gambling and his wife is murdered in response. Ultraviolent crime saga wowed the movie going public and spawned several sequels and a TV series. Based on the true story of folk-hero Buford Pusser, admirably rendered by Baker. **126m/C VHS, Beta, LV.** Joe Don Baker, Elizabeth Hartman, Noah Beery Jr., Gene Evans, Rosemary Murphy, Felton Perry; **D:** Phil Karlson; **W:** Mort Briskin. *LIV*

Walking Tall: Part 2 🐾🐾 1975 (PG) Club-wielding Tennessee sheriff Buford Pusser, this time played less memorably by Svenson, attempts to find the man who killed his wife. Even more violent than the original. **109m/C VHS, Beta, LV.** Bo Svenson, Noah Beery Jr., Angel Tompkins, Richard Jaeckel; **D:** Earl Bellamy. *LIV, VES*

Walking Tall: The Final Chapter 🐾½ 1977 (PG) The final months in the life of Tennessee sheriff Buford Pusser and the mystery surrounding his death. It wasn't the final chapter. Still to come: a TV flick and series. **112m/C VHS, Beta, LV.** Bo Svenson, Forrest Tucker, Leif Garrett, Morgan Woodward; **D:** Jack Starrett; **C:** Robert B. Hauser. *LIV*

Walking the Edge 🐾½ 1983 (R) A widow hires a taxi driver to help her seek vengeance against the men who killed her husband and her son. Forster does what he can with the lousy story and script. **94m/C VHS, Beta.** Robert Forster, Nancy Kwan, Joe Spinell, Aarika Wells; **D:** Norbert Meisel; **W:** Curt Allen. *LIV*

Walking Through the Fire 🐾🐾½ 1980 A young woman's real-life struggle with Hodgkin's disease. Her fight for her own and her unborn baby's survival is a stirring testament to the power of faith. Absorbing made-for-television drama. **143m/C VHS, Beta.** Bess Armstrong, Tom Mason, Bonnie Bedelia, Richard Masur, Swoosie Kurtz, J.D. Cannon, June Lockhart; **D:** Robert Day. *TLF*

The Wall 🐾🐾🐾½ *Guney's The Wall; Le Mur; Duvar* 1983 The last film by Guney, author of "Yol," about orphaned boys in prison in the Turkish capitol of Ankara trying to escape and/or rebel after ceaseless rapings, beatings and injustice. An acclaimed, disturbing film made from Guney's own experience. He died in 1984, three years after escaping from prison. Brutal and horrifying. In Turkish with English subtitles. **117m/C VHS, Beta.** *TU* Ayse Emel Mesci, Saban, Sisko; **D:** Yilmaz Guney; **W:** Yilmaz Guney. *NO*

Wall Street 🐾🐾🐾 1987 (R) Stone's energetic, high-minded big business treatise in which naive, neophyte stockbroker Sheen is seduced into insider trading by sleek entrepreneur Douglas, much to his blue-collar father's chagrin. A fast-moving drama of 80's-style materialism with a mesmerizing, award-winning performance by Douglas as greed personified. Expert direction by Stone, who co-wrote the not-very-subtle script. His father, to whom this film is dedicated, was a broker. Look for Stone in a cameo. **126m/C VHS, Beta, LV, Closed Caption.** Michael Douglas, Charlie Sheen, Martin Sheen, Daryl Hannah, Sean Young, James Spader, Hal Holbrook, Terence Stamp, Richard Dysart, John C. McGinley, Saul Rubinek, James Karen, Josh Mostel, Millie Perkins, Cecilia Peck, Grant Shaud, Franklin Cover; *Cameos:* Oliver Stone; **D:** Oliver Stone; **W:** Oliver Stone, Stanley Weiser; **C:** Robert Richardson; **M:** Stewart Copeland. Academy Awards '87: Best Actor (Douglas); Golden Globe Awards '88: Best Actor—Drama (Douglas); National Board of Review Awards '87: Best Actor (Douglas); Golden Raspberry Awards '87: Worst Supporting Actress (Hannah). *FOX, BTV*

Wall Street Cowboy 🐾 1939 When his land is threatened, a cowboy fights big business in the big city. **54m/B VHS, Beta.** Roy Rogers. *NOS, DVT, TIM*

Wallaby Jim of the Islands 🐾🐾 1937 The singing captain of a pearl fishing boat must protect his treasure from marauding pirates. Pleasant enough musical adventure. **61m/B VHS.** George Houston, Douglas Walton; **D:** Charles Lamont. *NOS, DVT, HEG*

The Walloping Kid 🐾½ 1926 A B-western with photography done in Monument Valley. Silent with original organ music. **67m/B VHS, Beta, 8mm.** Kit Carson, Pauline Curley; **D:** Robert J. Horner. *VYY*

Walls of Glass 🐾🐾½ 1985 (R) An aging New York cabby tries to make it as an actor. Effective performances by all override the thin plot. Slow and uneven, but involving. Also called "Flan-again." **85m/C VHS, Beta.** Geraldine Page, Philip Bosco, William Hickey, Olympia Dukakis, Brian Bloom, Linda Thorson; *D:* Scott Goldstein. *MED*

The Walls of Malapaga 🎬🎬 *Au-Dela des Grilles; Le Mura di Malapaga* 1949 Frenchman Gabin, who's killed his mistress, stows away aboard a ship to Italy. He arrives in Genoa only to have all his money and papers stolen. Gabin then meets Miranda, a lonely waitress with a young daughter, and the two fall in love. But it's only temporary as the authorities come closing in. French with subtitles. **91m/C VHS.** *FR IT* Jean Gabin, Isa Miranda, Vera Talchi, Andrea Checchi, Robert Dalban; *D:* Rene Clement; *W:* Jean Aurenche, Pierre Bost; *M:* Roman Vlad. Academy Awards '50: Best Foreign Language Film. *FCT*

Walpurgis Night 🎬🎬🎬 *Valborgmassoafton* 1941 Soapy Swedish drama about abortion was racy for its time. Office gal Bergman secretly loves her boss (Hanson). His wife refuses to have children and goes through an abortion. An unscrupulous fellow blackmails her with this knowledge. Bergman bides her time. Stay tuned... Interesting document on the mores of another time. In Swedish with English subtitles. **82m/B VHS, Beta.** *SW* Lars Hanson, Karin Carlsson, Victor Sjostrom, Ingrid Bergman, Erik Berglund, Sture Lagerwall, Georg Rydeberg, Georg Blickingberg; *D:* Gustaf Edgren. *WAC*

The Waltons: A Thanksgiving Story 1973 As the Walton family anticipates the Thanksgiving holiday, John-Boy prepares for college entrance exams and Jenny Pendleton's visit. John-Boy suffers a head injury and is faced with a risky operation that may either help him or leave him permanently disabled. A holiday special from the television series. **100m/C VHS.** Richard Thomas, Ralph Waite, Michael Learned, Will Geer, Ellen Corby, Judy Norton-Taylor, Kami Cotler, Jon Walmsley, Mary McDonough, Eric Scott, David W. Harper; *D:* Philip Leacock. *IGP*

The Waltons: The Christmas Carol 🎬🎬 1980 The winter solstice brings no special joy to Walton's mountain; WWII has taken many men, with short wave reports indicating the Nazi terror spreading across Europe. But huddled in the glow of Walton's barn, the children rediscover the true meaning of Christmas. **94m/C VHS, Beta, Closed Caption.** Judy Norton-Taylor, Jon Walmsley, Mary McDonough, Eric Scott, Kami Cotler, Joe Conley, Ronnie Clare, Leslie Winston, Peggy Rea; *D:* Lawrence Dobkin. *ORI*

Waltz Across Texas 🎬🎬½ 1983 Young oil man Jastrow and good-lookin' rock scientist Archer at first don't take to each other, but there's something in the air, and romance blossoms. Jastrow and Archer cowrote and coproduced, and cohabitated as spouses in real-life. **100m/C VHS, Beta.** Terry Jastrow, Anne Archer, Mary Kay Place, Richard Farnsworth; *D:* Ernest Day; *C:* Robert Elswit. *VES*

Waltz King 🎬🎬 1963 Typically hokey Disney biography of the young composer Johann Strauss during his Old Viennese heyday. Fine music, pretty German locations. Well-made family fare. **94m/C VHS, Beta.** Kerwin Mathews, Senta Berger, Brian Aherne; *D:* Steve Previn. *DIS*

Waltz of the Toreadors 🎬🎬🎬 *The Amorous General* 1962 Retired general Sellers doesn't care for his wealthy, shrewish wife and tries to rekindle a 17-year-old romance with a French woman. It doesn't work out (seems his illegitimate son also has a soft spot for the lady), but the general decides to keep his eyes open for other possibilities. Interestingly cast adaptation of Jean Anouilh's play. Sellers is hilarious, as usual. **105m/C VHS, Beta.** *GB* Peter Sellers, Dany Robin, Margaret Leighton, Cyril Cusack; *D:* John Guillermin. *NO*

A Waltz Through the Hills 1988 Two orphans head into the Australian outback and experience many adventures en route to the coast where they can set sail for England and their grandparents. Aired on PBS as part of the "Wonderworks" series. **116m/C VHS, Closed Caption.** Tina Kemp, Andre Jansen, Ernie Dingo, Dan O'Herlihy; *D:* Frank Arnold. *PME, HMV, FCT*

Wanda Nevada 🎬½ 1979 (PG) Gambler Fonda wins nubile young Shields in a poker game, so he drags her with him to the Grand Canyon to look for gold. Director/star Fonda sure picked a lemon for his only screen appearance with dad Henry (a grizzled old varmint appearing briefly). Shields is in her usual form—stellar for a shampoo commercial. **105m/C VHS, Beta.** Peter Fonda, Brooke Shields, Henry Fonda, Fiona Lewis, Luke Askew, Ted Markland, Severn Darden, Paul Fix; *D:* Peter Fonda. *NO*

Wanda, The Sadistic Hypnotist 🎬 1967 A comely vixen hypnotizes an innocent pedestrian, ties him up and whips him to indulge her whims. Despite the "victim's" protests, she unleashes a gang of sexually playful women on him, and he is subjected to a multitude of "tortures." **70m/C VHS.** Katharine Shubeck, Janice Sweet, Dick Dangerfield, Daryl Cobinot; *D:* Gregory Corarito. *SMW, TPV*

The Wanderer 🎬🎬 *Le Grand Meaulnes* 1967 Two friends fall in love—Frantz with Valentine and his friend Augustin with Frantz's sister, Yvonne. When the two women disappear on Frantz's wedding day, the two men begin a search to find both the women and the reasons for their disappearance. In French with English subtitles. **108m/C VHS.** *FR* Brigitte Fossey, Jean Blaise, Alain Noury, Juliette Villard; *D:* Jean-Gabriel Albicocco. *CVC*

Wanderers 🎬🎬🎬½ 1979 (R) Richard Price's acclaimed novel about youth gangs coming of age in the Bronx in 1963. The "Wanderers," named after the Dion song, are a gang of Italian-American teenagers about to graduate high school, who prowl the Bronx with the feeling that something is slipping away from them. Fascinating, funny and touching. Manz is unforgettable as a scrappy gal. A wonderful 60s soundtrack (Dion, the Four Seasons) colors this "coming of age the hard way" film. **113m/C VHS, Beta.** Ken Wahl, John Friedrich, Karen Allen, Linda Manz; *Cameos:* Richard Price; *D:* Philip Kaufman; *W:* Philip Kaufman; *C:* Michael Chapman. *WAR*

Wandering Jew 🎬🎬½ 1920 An excellent print of the rare Austrian film version of the classic legend, one of at least three silent versions. A Jew is condemned to wander the earth for eternity. **65m/B VHS, Beta.** *AT* Rudolf Schildkraut, Joseph Schildkraut. *GVV*

The Wannsee Conference 🎬🎬🎬½ *Wannseekonferenz* 1984 A startling, important film depicting, in real time, the conference held at the Wannsee on January 20, 1942, during which 14 members of the Nazi hierarchy decided in 85 minutes the means and logistics of effecting the Final Solution. Recreated from the original secretary's notes. Horrifying and chilling. Along with "Shoah," a must-see for understanding the Holocaust and the psychology of genocide. In German with English subtitles. **87m/C VHS, Beta, LV.** *GE* Dietrich Mattausch, Gerd Brockmann, Peter Beckhaus; *D:* Heinz Schirk. *HMV, APD, GLV*

Wanted: Babysitter woof! 1975 A young student accidentally becomes involved by her roommate in a plot to kidnap the child she is babysitting. Schneider is truly awful; Italian comic Pazzetto is at sea in a bad role as her boyfriend. Also released as "The Babysitter." **90m/C VHS.** Robert Vaughn, Vic Morrow, Maria Schneider, Renato Pozzetto, Nadja Tiller, Carl Mohner, Sydne Rome; *D:* Rene Clement. *AHV*

Wanted: Dead or Alive 1959 This western series, which ran from 1958-1961, launched the career of McQueen who starred as bounty hunter Josh Randall. In this episode, "Reunion for Revenge," Randall must protect the man in his custody from escaped criminals with vengeance on their mind. Also available colorized. Additional episodes available. **22m/B VHS, Beta.** Steve McQueen, Wright King, Jane Burns, James Coburn, Cloris Leachman, John Baer, Ralph Meeker; *D:* Thomas Carr, Richard Donner. *MOV*

Wanted Dead or Alive 🎬½ 1986 (R) Ex-CIA agent Hauer is now a high-tech bounty hunter assigned to bring in an international terrorist. When the terrorist kills Hauer's friend and girlfriend, he forgets the $50,000 bonus for bringing him in alive. Official "sequel" to the Steve McQueen television series with Hauer as the McQueen character's great-grandson. The link is meaningless, and the plot is a thin excuse for much violence and anti-terrorist flag-waving. **104m/C VHS, Beta, LV, Closed Caption.** Rutger Hauer, Gene Simmons, Robert Guillaume, William Russ, Jerry Hardin, Mel Harris; *D:* Gary Sherman; *W:* Brian Taggert. *NWV, VTR*

Wanted: The Perfect Guy 🎬🎬½ 1990 Danny and Melanie try to find Mister Right for their divorced Mom (Kahn). An Emmy Award winner about single parents and their children. **45m/C VHS.** Madeline Kahn, Melanie Mayron. *AIM*

The War 🎬🎬½ 1994 (PG-13) Post-Vietnam war drama, set in 1970 Mississippi, centers on a children's battle over a treehouse but becomes a sermon on love, death, family values, pacifism, and the physical and spiritual wounds of war. After helping son Stu (Wood) and daughter Lidia (Randall) build their treehouse, troubled Vietnam vet Stephen Simmons (Costner) tries to coax Stu to make peace with the bullies trying to take it over. However cliched, director Avnet allows a talented cast of kids to thoughtfully express a child's view of the world but gosh-darn-it the preachy tone can get down-right annoying. **126m/C VHS, LV, Closed Caption.** Elijah Wood, Kevin Costner, Lexi Randall, Mare Winningham, Christine Baranski, Bruce A. Young, Gary Basaraba, Raynor Scheine, Nick Searcy; *D:* Jon Avnet; *W:* Kathy McWorter. *USH*

War & Love 🎬🎬 1984 (PG-13) Two Jewish teenagers in Warsaw are torn apart by WWII and Nazi persecution. After the war they search for each other. Sincere, but not adequately developed, drama based on the book "The Survivors" by film's producer Jack Eisner. **112m/C VHS, Beta.** Sebastian Keneas, Kyra Sedgwick; *D:* Moshe Mizrahi. *MGM, SWC*

War and Peace 🎬🎬½ 1956 Lengthy adaptation of Tolstoy's great (and likewise lengthy) novel about three families caught up in Russia's Napoleonic Wars from 1805 to 1812; filmed in Rome. Bad casting and confused script (by six writers) are somewhat overcome by awesome battle scenes and Hepburn. Remade in 1968. **208m/C VHS, Beta, LV.** Audrey Hepburn, Mel Ferrer, Henry Fonda, Anita Ekberg, Vittorio Gassman, John Mills, Oscar Homolka, Herbert Lom, Vittorio Gassman; *M:* Nino Rota. Golden Globe Awards '57: Best Foreign Film; National Board of Review Awards '56: 5 Best Foreign Films of the Year; Nominations: Academy Awards '56: Best Color Cinematography, Best Costume Design (Color), Best Director (Vidor). *PAR*

War and Peace 🎬🎬🎬 1968 The massive Russian production of Leo Tolstoy's masterpiece, adapting the classic tome practically scene by scene. All of the production took place in the Soviet Union. So painstaking that it took more than five years to finish, no other adaptation can touch it. Hugely expensive ($100 million, claimed the Russians), wildly uneven production. Great scenes of battle and aristocratic life. Though this version is far from perfect, one asks: Is it humanly possible to do screen justice to such a novel? In Russian with English subtitles. On four tapes. (Beware the two-part, poorly dubbed version that was also released.) **373m/C VHS, Beta, LV.** *RU* Lyudmila Savelyeva, Sergei Bondarchuk, Vyacheslav Tihonor, Hira Ivanov-Golarko, Irina Gubanova, Antonina Shuranova; *D:* Sergei Bondarchuk; *C:* Jack Cardiff. Academy Awards '68: Best Foreign Language Film; Golden Globe Awards '69: Best Foreign Film; National Board of Review Awards '68: 5 Best Foreign Films of the Year; New York Film Critics Awards '68: Best Foreign Film; Nominations: Academy Awards '68: Best Art Direction/Set Decoration. *KUL, TVC, TPV*

War & Remembrance, Part 1 🎞️½
1988 Tedious sequel to the epic television mini-series "The Winds of War," based on the novel by Herman Wouk. Historical fiction is created around the events of WWII, including Nazi persecution and naval battles in the Pacific. Seven cassette series. Followed by "War and Remembrance: The Final Chapter." 120m/C VHS, Beta. Robert Mitchum, Jane Seymour, Hart Bochner, Victoria Tennant, Barry Bostwick, Polly Bergen, David Dukes, Michael Woods, Sharon Stone, Robert Morley, Sami Frey, Chaim Topol, John Rhys-Davies, Ian McShane, William Schallert, Jeremy Kemp, Steven Berkoff, Robert Hardy, Ralph Bellamy, John Gielgud; *D:* Dan Curtis. *MPI, MOV*

War & Remembrance, Part 2 🎞️½
1989 The final installments of the excruciatingly boring and long mini-series. Herman Wouk's historical fiction concerning the last years of WWII. Six cassettes, in Hi-Fi stereo. 120m/C VHS, Beta. Robert Mitchum, Jane Seymour, Hart Bochner, Ralph Bellamy, Victoria Tennant, Barry Bostwick, John Gielgud, Polly Bergen, David Dukes, Michael Woods; *D:* Dan Curtis. *MPI*

War & Remembrance, Part 3 **1988** A
brief glimmer of hope appears in this volume involving the lovers' reunion in Hawaii and the military power's changing of hands due to command of the Americans following the infamous Midway battle. 120m/C VHS, Beta. Robert Mitchum, Jane Seymour, Hart Bochner, Victoria Tennant, Polly Bergen, David Dukes, Michael Woods; *D:* Dan Curtis. *MPI*

War & Remembrance, Part 4 **1988**
The middle part of 1942 sees its way through the American infiltration of Guadacanal, the treacherous stranglehold of Nazi Germany on Europe and other parts of the world, and the defiance toward defeat of the Russian Army. 120m/C VHS, Beta. Robert Mitchum, Jane Seymour, Hart Bochner, Victoria Tennant, Polly Bergen, David Dukes, Michael Woods; *D:* Dan Curtis. *MPI*

War & Remembrance, Part 5 **1988** As
1942 draws to a close, Wouk's well-known character, Pug, finds himself heading for a new assignment. North Africa welcomes the Allies in lieu of the Nazis. Stalingrad is mortified by an ever-strong Nazi invasion. 120m/C VHS, Beta. Robert Mitchum, Jane Seymour, Hart Bochner, Victoria Tennant, Polly Bergen, David Dukes, Michael Woods; *D:* Dan Curtis. *MPI*

War & Remembrance, Part 6 **1988**
After leaving his dear cruiser behind, Pug says hello to Russia. The Ally leaders meet with much to discuss. Hitler is getting stronger and shrewder. 120m/C VHS, Beta. Robert Mitchum, Jane Seymour, Hart Bochner, Victoria Tennant, Polly Bergen, David Dukes, Michael Woods; *D:* Dan Curtis. *MPI*

War & Remembrance, Part 7 **1988**
The Sicilian win by Patton brings about the devestation of Mussolini. Hitler's henchman are getting nervous and tired of battle. Germany succumbs to Allied troops in North Africa. 120m/C VHS, Beta. Robert Mitchum, Jane Seymour, Hart Bochner, Victoria Tennant, Polly Bergen, David Dukes, Michael Woods; *D:* Dan Curtis. *MPI*

War & Remembrance: The Final Chapter, Part 8 **1989** The final episodes of
Herman Wouk's sweeping saga, following "The Winds of War" and "War and Remembrance," deal with the struggle of a Jewish family in war-torn Europe. Natalie and her son, Louis, are trapped in a ghetto under the reign of a vicious Nazi, who considers a bribe for the sake of the mother and son. On 5 cassettes. 120m/C VHS, Beta. Robert Mitchum, Jane Seymour, Hart Bochner, Victoria Tennant, Polly Bergen, David Dukes, Michael Woods, Sharon Stone, Robert Morley, Sami Frey, Chaim Topol, John Rhys-Davies, Ian McShane, William Schallert, Jeremy Kemp, Steven Berkoff, Robert Hardy, Ralph Bellamy, John Gielgud; *D:* Dan Curtis. *MPI, MOV*

War & Remembrance: The Final Chapter, Part 9 **1989** Both D-Day and an
assassination of Hitler are in the works. Natalie and Louis are still in a desperate situation with the tyrannical Nazi endangering them constantly. 120m/C VHS, Beta. Robert Mitchum, Jane Seymour, Hart

Bochner, Victoria Tennant, Polly Bergen, David Dukes, Michael Woods; *D:* Dan Curtis. *MPI*

War & Remembrance: The Final Chapter, Part 10 **1989** Though Louis be-
comes gravely ill, Natalie and Aaron are shipped to Auschwitz. Hitler lives in spite of the botched assasination threat, but the allies are closing in rapidly. 120m/C VHS, Beta. Robert Mitchum, Jane Seymour, Hart Bochner, Victoria Tennant, Polly Bergen, David Dukes, Michael Woods; *D:* Dan Curtis. *MPI*

War & Remembrance: The Final Chapter, Part 11 **1989** The infamous Battle
of the Bulge takes place. Louis is taken away in the Nazi retreat. Natalie and Aaron continue to defy death in Auschwitz. 120m/C VHS, Beta. Robert Mitchum, Jane Seymour, Hart Bochner, Victoria Tennant, Polly Bergen, David Dukes, Michael Woods; *D:* Dan Curtis. *MPI*

War & Remembrance: The Final Chapter, Part 12 **1989** The climax culmi-
nates into the death of both FDR and Hitler, whose suicide shocked and relieved an entire world. The Nazi reign of terror crumbles, and the allies are victorious. But this series ends on the note of displacement and the effort of rebuilding what has so quickly and deftly been destroyed. 120m/C VHS, Beta. Robert Mitchum, Jane Seymour, Hart Bochner, Victoria Tennant, Polly Bergen, David Dukes, Michael Woods; *D:* Dan Curtis. *MPI*

War Arrow 🎞️🎞️ **1953** Army Major Howell
Brady (Chandler) is sent by Washington to end the Kiowa uprisings in Texas in this cavalry vs. Indians western. Along the way, he tries to win the heart of O'Hara. 79m/C VHS, Closed Caption. Maureen O'Hara, Jeff Chandler, Suzan Ball, John McIntire, Noah Beery Jr., Henry Brandon, Dennis Weaver, Jay Silverheels; *D:* George Sherman; *W:* John Michael Hayes. *USH*

The War at Home 🎞️½ **1996 (R)** In 1972
Vietnam vet Jeremy Collier (Estevez) has been home in the Dallas suburbs for a year but the war and its effects still linger. Mom Maureen (Bates) is a conservative control freak and dad Bob (Sheen) just can't connect, while teenaged sis Karen (Williams) is going through her own rebellion. The tense situation comes to a bitter head over a Thanksgiving weekend. Based on the 1984 play "Home Front" by James Duff. *CW:* War-related shooting, an intense sequence of violent threat, and for language. 124m/C VHS. Kathy Bates, Martin Sheen, Emilio Estevez, Kimberly Williams, Carla Gugino, Geoffrey Barish, Corin "Corky" Nemec, Ann Hearn; *D:* Emilio Estevez; *W:* James Duff; *C:* Peter Levy; *M:* Basil Poledouris. *NYR*

War Between the Tates 🎞️🎞️ **1976** A
college professor's affair with a female student is the basis for a tension filled stand-off with his wife. Mediocre made for television adaptation of the Allison Lurie novel, somewhat redeemed by Ashley's performance. 90m/C VHS, Beta. Richard Crenna, Elizabeth Ashley, Granville Van Dusen; *D:* Lee Philips; *M:* John Barry. *TLF*

The War Boy 🎞️🎞️½ **1985 (R)** Difficulties
encountered by a young Canadian boy as he grows up in Central Europe during WWII. Not to be compared with "Empire of the Sun" or "Hope and Glory," both of which were released later; successful in its modest ambitions. Beautiful performance from 12-year-old star Hopely. 86m/C VHS. *CA* Helen Shaver, Kenneth Welsh, Jason Hopely; *D:* Allan Eastman. *HHE*

War Brides 🎞️ **198?** Civil War brides con-
front life after the war. Low-budget drama. 100m/C VHS, Beta. Elizabeth Richardson, Sharry Fleet, Sonja Smits. *TWE*

War Bus Commando 🎞️ **1989** A fully
loaded bus is the only way out when soldiers are caught behind enemy lines in Afghanistan. A case of the spoof coming first: The plot is almost exactly the same as "Stripes"—only this one isn't funny. In Hi-Fi. 90m/C VHS. *IT* Savina Gersak, Mark Gregory, John Vernon; *D:* Frank Valenti. *NO*

War in Space 🎞️ **1977** Powerful U.N.
Space Bureau Starships and UFOs band together to battle alien invaders among the volcanoes and deserts of Venus. 91m/C VHS, Beta. *JP* Kensaku Marita, Yuko Asano, Ryo Ikebe. *VDA*

War in the Sky 🎞️🎞️🎞️ **1982** Director Wil-
liam Wyler's documentary account of the Army Air Corps in action. Extraordinary footage of the Thunderbolt, the P47 Fighter, and the B17 Bomber. 90m/C VHS, Beta. *D:* William Wyler. *GEM*

The War Lord 🎞️🎞️🎞️ **1965** Set in the 11th
century, Heston stars as Chrysagon, a Norman knight and war lord who commands a peasant village. While battling his enemies, he becomes enamored of a peasant girl named Bronwyn (Forsyth), who is unfortunately engaged to someone else. Pulling rank, Chrysagon uses an ancient law that allows noblemen the first night with a bride and the two fall in love. The two vow to never part, but that sets the stage for even more bloody battles. Fine acting and great production values make this a well-adapted version of the play "The Lovers" by Leslie Stevens. 121m/C VHS, Beta, LV. Charlton Heston, Richard Boone, Rosemary Forsyth, Guy Stockwell, Niall MacGinnis, Henry Wilcoxon, James Farentino, Maurice Evans, Michael Conrad; *D:* Franklin J. Schaffner; *W:* John Collier, Millard Kaufman; *C:* Russell Metty. *USH*

War Lover 🎞️🎞️½ **1962** An American dare-
devil flying captain and his co-pilot find themselves vying for the affections of a woman during WWII in England. Seeks human frailty beneath surface heroism. McQueen is impressive, no thanks to mediocre script. Excellent aerial photography, and featuring one of only a very few serviceable WWII B-17s then remaining. Based on John Hersey's novel. 105m/B VHS, Beta, LV. *GB* Steve McQueen, Robert Wagner, Shirley Anne Field, Bill Edwards, Gary Cockrell; *D:* Philip Leacock; *W:* Howard Koch. *GKK*

War of the Buttons 🎞️🎞️½ **1995 (PG)**
Two sleepy Irish fishing villages provide childish battle grounds for two groups of local lads. The Ballys (Ballydowse village), lead by Fergus (Fitzgerald), and the Carricks (Carrickdowse), with leader Geronimo (Coffey), have an intense rivalry and capture by the other gang leads to the removal of every clothing button for the unfortunate captive. When Fergus becomes a Carrick victim, he organizes a retaliatory strike, and emotions threaten to overwhelm all concerned. Based on the French novel "La Guerre des Boutons" by Louis Pergaud. Filmed on location in West Cork, Ireland. 94m/C VHS. Gregg Fitzgerald, John Coffey, Liam Cunningham, Paul Batt, Eveanna Ryan, Colm Meaney, Johnny Murphy; *D:* John Roberts; *W:* Colin Welland; *C:* Bruno de Keyzer; *M:* Rachel Portman. *WAR*

The War of the Colossal Beast 🎞️½ *The Terror Strikes* **1958** This sequel to
"The Amazing Colossal Man" finds the seventy-foot Colonel Manning even angrier at the attempts to kill him than he was in the first film. So he wreaks more havoc until scolded by his sister into committing suicide for being such a troublemaker. Cheesy special effects but good for a laugh. 68m/B VHS. Dean Parkin, Sally Fraser, Russ Bender, Roger Pace, Charles Stewart; *D:* Bert I. Gordon. *COL*

War of the Gargantuas 🎞️ *Furankenshu-
tain No Kaijusanda Tai Gailah; Sanda Tai Gailah; Duel of the Gargantuas* **1970 (G)** Tokyo is once again the boxing ring for giant monsters. This time it's a good gargantua (half human, half monster) against a bad gargantua. This is a strange one. 92m/C VHS, LV, Closed Caption. *JP* Russ Tamblyn, Kumi Mizuno, Kipp Hamilton, Yu Fujiki. *PAR*

War of the Robots 🎞️ **1978** A dying alien
civilization kidnaps two brilliant Earth scientists in the hope that they'll help it survive. 99m/C VHS, Beta, LV. Antonio Sabato, Melissa Long, James R. Stuart. *VCI*

The War of the Roses 🎬🎬🎬 1989 (R)
Acidic black comedy about a well-to-do suburban couple who can't agree on a property settlement in their divorce so they wage unreserved and ever-escalating combat on each other, using their palatial home as a battleground. Expertly and lovingly (if that's the word) directed by DeVito, who plays the lawyer. Turner and Douglas are splendid. Adapted from the novel by Warren Adler. Laserdisc version includes previously deleted scenes and commentary from DeVito. 116m/C VHS, **Beta, LV, Closed Caption.** Michael Douglas, Kathleen Turner, Danny DeVito, Marianne Saegebrecht, Sean Astin, G.D. Spradlin, Peter Donat, Heather Fairfield, Dan Castellaneta, Danitra Vance, Tony Crane; *D:* Danny DeVito; *W:* Michael Leeson; *C:* Stephen Burum; *M:* David Newman. *FOX, IME*

War of the Wildcats 🎬🎬½ *In Old Oklahoma* 1943 Fast-moving western with Wayne as a tough cowboy battling a powerful land baron. They fight over land, oil and a woman. Unusual because Wayne's character acts on behalf of the Indians to drill and transport oil. 102m/B VHS. John Wayne, Martha Scott, Albert Dekker, George "Gabby" Hayes, Sidney Blackmer; *D:* Albert Rogell. Nominations: Academy Awards '43: Best Sound, Original Dramatic/Comedy Score. *REP*

War of the Wizards 🎬½ *The Phoenix* 1981 (PG) Low-budget sci-fi thriller about an alien woman with supernatural powers who comes to take over the Earth. But, lucky for all earthlings, she's challenged by a hero-type just in the nick of time. 90m/C VHS, Beta. Richard Kiel; *D:* Richard Caan. *NO*

The War of the Worlds 🎬🎬🎬½ 1953
H.G. Wells's classic novel of the invasion of Earth by Martians, updated to 1950s California, with spectacular special effects of destruction caused by the Martian war machines. Pretty scary and tense; based more on Orson Welles's radio broadcast than on the book. Still very popular; hit the top 20 in sales when released on video. Classic thriller later made into a TV series. Produced by George Pal, who brought the world much sci-fi, including "The Time Machine," "Destination Moon," and "When Worlds Collide," and who appears here as a street person. 85m/C VHS, Beta, LV. Gene Barry, Ann Robinson, Les Tremayne, Lewis Martin, Robert Cornthwaite, Sandro Giglio; *C:* George Barnes. Academy Awards '53: Best Special Effects; Nominations: Academy Awards '53: Best Film Editing, Best Sound. *PAR*

War Party 🎬🎬 1989 (R) During a 100-year commemoration of an Indian massacre in the Midwest, a murder occurs and a lynch mob chases a pack of young Blackfeet into the mountains before the inevitable showdown. A feeble attempt at portraying the unfair treatment of Native Americans. Un-subtle, Hollywood style, this time in favor of the Indians, and therefore un-serious. Too bad; the premise had potential. 99m/C VHS, Beta, LV, Closed Caption. Kevin Dillon, Billy Wirth, Tim Sampson, M. Emmet Walsh; *D:* Franc Roddam; *C:* Brian Tufano. *HBO*

The War Room 🎬🎬🎬 1993 (PG) Eye opening, sometimes disturbing documentary presents a behind the scenes peek at what really goes on during a Presidential campaign. When filming began in June '92 Bill Clinton was an unknown political quantity and advisors George Stephanopoulous and James Carville were masterminding his campaign. The "War Room" refers to the building in Little Rock where they struggled to organize a small army of volunteers into a winning team. Highlights include the Democratic National Convention, the North Carolina leg of Clinton's campaign bus tour, three Presidential debates, and the week leading up to election night. 93m/C VHS, LV, Closed Caption. *D:* Chris Hegedus, D.A. Pennebaker. National Board of Review Awards '93: Best Feature Documentary; Nominations: Academy Awards '93: Best Feature Documentary. *THV*

The War Wagon 🎬🎬🎬 1967 The Duke plans revenge on Cabot, the greedy mine owner who stole his gold claim and framed him for murder for which he spent years in prison. He assembles a gang to aid him, including a wise-cracking Indian (Keel) and the man sent by Cabot to kill him (Douglas). Wayne's plan is to steal the gold being shipped in Cabot's armor-plated stagecoach, the "war wagon." Well-written, good performances, lots of action. Based on the book "Badman" by Clair Huffaker. The laserdisc version is available in letterbox format. 101m/C VHS, Beta, LV. John Wayne, Kirk Douglas, Howard Keel, Robert Walker Jr., Keenan Wynn, Bruce Dern, Bruce Cabot, Joanna Barnes; *D:* Burt Kennedy; *C:* William Clothier. *USH*

Warbirds 🎬🎬 1988 (R) American pilots are off to quell a revolution in a Middle East country. Too little action fails to support mediocre plot and characters. 88m/C VHS, Beta. Jim Eldert, Cully Holland, Bill Brinsfield; *D:* Ulli Lommel; *W:* Ulli Lommel. *VTR, THV*

Warbus 🎬🎬 1985 (R) Marines lead a school bus load of Americans through war-torn Vietnam to safety. Decent action and surprisingly enjoyable characters. Otherwise mediocre. 90m/C VHS, Beta. Daniel Stephen, Romano Kristoff, Urs Althaus; *D:* Ted Kaplan. *NLC*

WarCat 🎬 *Angel of Vengeance* 1988 The daughter of a green beret fights for her life against a blood-thirsty gang. 78m/C VHS. Macka Foley, Jannina Poynter, David O'Hara, Carl Erwin; *D:* Ted V. Mikels. *TWE*

Ward Six 🎬🎬 19?? An insane asylum is the setting for various analogies regarding the perception of reality as defined by societal values. When it is felt that the residing physician is no more sane than his patients, he is placed among them, in Ward Six. Adapted from a story by Anton Chekhov. In Serbian with English subtitles. 93m/C VHS, Beta. *YU D:* Lucian Pintilie. *FCT*

Wardogs 🎬½ *The Assassination Team* 1987 A man tries to rescue his brother from becoming one of an elite, brainwashed group of ex-Vietnam vets trained by the government as professional assassins. Might not have been quite so bad; promising inversion of many 'Nam cliches wrecked by unnecessary violence and bad acting. 95m/C Beta. *SW* Tim Earle, Bill Redvers, Daniel Hubenbecker; *D:* Daniel Hubenbecker. *NO*

WarGames 🎬🎬½ 1983 (PG) A young computer whiz, thinking that he's sneaking an advance look at a new line of video games, breaks into the country's NORAD missile-defense system and challenges it to a game of Global Thermonuclear Warfare. The game might just turn out to be the real thing. Slick look at the possibilities of an accidental start to WWIII. Entertaining and engrossing, but with a B-grade ending. 110m/C VHS, Beta, LV, Closed Caption. Matthew Broderick, Dabney Coleman, John Wood, Ally Sheedy; *D:* John Badham; *W:* Walter F. Parkes, Lawrence Lasker. Nominations: Academy Awards '83: Best Cinematography, Best Original Screenplay, Best Sound. *FOX*

Warhead 🎬½ 1996 (R) Special Forces Ranger Tannen (Zagarino) has to stop a renegade military group, led by his former compatriot Craft (Lara), that have stolen a nuclear warhead and are threatening Washington. *CW:* Strong violence and some language. 97m/C VHS. Frank Zagarino, Joe Lara; *D:* Mark Roper. *THV*

Warkill 🎬🎬½ 1965 WWII action set in the jungles of the Philippines. Journalist who idolizes violent, hard-edged colonel, loses his illusions, but gains a more genuine respect for his men. Not-bad war flick. 99m/C VHS, Beta. George Montgomery, Tom Drake, Eddie Infante; *D:* Ferde Grofe Jr.; *W:* Ferde Grofe Jr. *AHV*

Warlock 🎬🎬🎬 1959 Claustrophic, resonant town-bound tale of a marshal (Fonda) and his adoring sidekick (Quinn) who clean up a town which then turns against him. Unusual story, fine performances carry this well beyond the run-of-the-mill cow flick. Fonda re-established himself at the box office as a western star, after "Stage Struck" and "Twelve Angry Men." From the novel by Oakley Hall. Look for "Bones" McCoy from "Star Trek" in a bit part. 122m/C VHS, Beta. Henry Fonda, Anthony Quinn, Richard Widmark, Dorothy Malone, Wallace Ford, Richard Arlen, Regis Toomey, DeForest Kelley; *D:* Edward Dmytryk; *W:* Robert Alan Aurthur. *VTR, FOX*

Warlock 🎬🎬½ 1991 (R) It's 1691 and the most powerful warlock (Sands) in the New World is only hours away from execution. Luckily, his pal, Satan, whisks him (and witchhunter Grant, by mistake) three hundred years in the future to present-day Los Angeles, where he crash-lands in Singer's house. Surprisingly witty dialogue and neat plot twists outshine occasionally cheesy special effects. 103m/C VHS, Closed Caption. Richard E. Grant, Julian Sands, Lori Singer, Mary Woronov, Richard Kuss, Kevin O'Brien, Anna Levine, Allan Miller, David Carpenter; *D:* Steve Miner; *W:* David N. Twohy; *C:* David Eggby; *M:* Jerry Goldsmith. *THV*

Warlock Moon 🎬½ 1973 Young woman is lured to a secluded spa and falls prey to a coven of witches. 75m/C VHS, Beta. *MX* Laurie Walters, Joe Spano; *D:* Bill Herbert. *UNI*

Warlock: The Armageddon 🎬🎬½ 1993 (R) Sequel finds Sands back again as the sinister Warlock. This time he's out to gather six Druidic rune stones which have the power to summon Satan's emissary (in the wrong hands) or to stop his nefarious activities (in the right ones). A sect in a small California town serves as the keeper of the stones, only their designated champions are two unprepared teenagers. Sands has all the fun, gleefully dispatching his would-be opponents with some good special effects. *CW:* Violence. 93m/C VHS. Julian Sands, Chris Young, Paula Marshall, Steve Kahan, Charles Hallahan, R.G. Armstrong, Bruce Glover, Zach Galligan, Dawn Ann Billings, Joanna Pacula; *D:* Anthony Hickox; *W:* Kevin Rock, Sam Bernard. *THV*

Warlords 🎬½ 1988 (R) Lone soldier Carradine battles mutant hordes in a post-apocalyptic desert. Amateurish futuristic drivel. 87m/C VHS, Beta, LV. David Carradine, Sid Haig, Ross Hagen, Fox Harris, Robert Quarry, Victoria Sellers, Brinke Stevens, Dawn Wildsmith; *D:* Fred Olen Ray. *THV*

Warlords from Hell woof! 1987 (R) Two young men motorcycling through Mexico are captured by a bloodthirsty gang and forced to do hard labor in the marijuana fields. We can only hope that they just learn to say no. 76m/C VHS, Beta. Brad Henson, Jeffrey Rice; *D:* Clark Henderson. *WAR*

Warlords of the 21st Century 🎬½ *Battletruck* 1982 Bandit gang speed around the galaxy in an indestructible battle cruiser. Then the boys are challenged by a space lawman. Gratuitously violent action pic lacking real action. Filmed on planet New Zealand. 91m/C VHS, Beta. Michael Beck, Annie McEnroe, James Wainwright; *D:* Harley Cokliss; *W:* Harley Cokliss, Irving Austin, John Beech; *C:* Chris Menges.

Warlords 3000 🎬½ 1993 (R) In the future, Earth is a barren wasteland ravaged by raging electrical storms. Deadly cancers are rampant and the few people who have survived take their comfort in a hallucinogenic drug that provides a temporary pleasure and a permanent madness. Drug lords control the planet but one man is out to eliminate the scum and save the future. 92m/C VHS. Jay Roberts Jr., Denise Marie Duff, Steve Blanchard, Wayne Duvall; *D:* Faruque Ahmed; *W:* Ron Herbst, Faruque Ahmed. *COL*

Warm Nights on a Slow-Moving Train 🎬🎬 1987 (R) A hot-blooded schoolteacher turns tricks for cash to support her brother on the Sunday-night train to Melbourne, until she meets a stranger who has a deadly masquerade of his own. Interestingly different; much sex, as you can imagine. Australian-made. 90m/C VHS, Beta, LV. *AU* Wendy Hughes, Colin Friels, Norman Kaye, John Clayton, Peter Whitford; *D:* Bob Ellis; *W:* Bob Ellis, Denny Lawrence. *PSM, PAR*

Warm Summer Rain *√½* 1989 (R) A young couple meet under unusual circumstances and develop a relationship in a desert cabin as they reflect on their unfulfilled pasts. Lust, self-doubt and longing for something to hold onto draw them together as the days pass. Thoroughly self-indulgent romantic comedy that's oddly self-pitying and poorly directed. **85m/C VHS, Beta, LV.** Kelly Lynch, Barry Tubb; **D:** Joe Gayton. *COL*

The Warning *√* 1980 A pair of proverbial honest cops investigate ties between the mob and the police department. Hard to follow. **101m/C VHS, Beta.** *IT* Martin Balsam, Giuliano Gemma, Giancarlo Zanetti; **D:** Damiano Damiani. *MED*

Warning from Space *√½* *The Mysterious Satellite; The Cosmic Man Appears in Tokyo; Space Men Appear in Tokyo; Unknown Satellite Over Tokyo; Uchujin Tokyo Ni Arawaru* 1956 Aliens visit Earth to warn of impending cosmic doom. When it becomes apparent that the one-eyed starfish look is off-putting, they assume human form. Japanese sci fi. **87m/B VHS.** *JP* Toyomi Karita, Keizo Kawasaki, Isao Yamagata, Shozo Nanbu, Buntaro Miake, Mieko Nagai, Kiyoko Hirai; **D:** Koji Shima. *NOS, SMW, SNC*

Warning Shadows *√√√* 1923 Classic example of interior German Expressionism. Brilliantly portrays a jealous husband's emotions and obsessions through shadows. Innocent events seem to reek of sin. A seldom-seen study of the oft-precarious distinction between love and obsession; directly influenced by the classic "The Cabinet of Dr. Caligari." Silent with German and English titles. **93m/B VHS, Beta, 8mm.** *GE* Fritz Kortner; **D:** Arthur Robison. *GPV, FCT, GLV*

Warning Sign *√½* 1985 (R) A high-tech thriller in which a small town is terrorized by the accidental release of an experimental virus at a research facility. Shades of "The Andromeda Strain" and "The China Syndrome," though less originality and quality. **99m/C VHS, Beta, Closed Caption.** Sam Waterston, Kathleen Quinlan, Yaphet Kotto, Richard Dysart, Rick Rossovich; **D:** Hal Barwood; **W:** Hal Barwood, Matthew Robbins; **C:** Dean Cundey. *FOX*

The Warrior & the Sorceress *√½* 1984 (R) Mercenary Carradine offers his services to rival factions fighting for control of a water well in an impoverished desert village located on a planet with two suns. He attempts to aggravate the conflicts between the factions, playing the shifty go-between. The sorceress is topless throughout. "A Fistful of Dollars" goes to outer space. Inoffensive, except that better judgment is expected of Carradine. **81m/C VHS, Beta, LV.** David Carradine, Luke Askew, Maria Socas, Harry Townes; **D:** John Broderick; **W:** John Broderick. *LIV, VES*

Warrior of Justice *√* 1996 Karate instructor has one of his students disappear after competing in a secret tournament. He then uncovers a black market ring specializing in selling human organs that's run by a former opponent. **90m/C VHS.** Richard Lynch, Jorge Rivero, Nick Hill, Ian Jacklin, Jorgo Ognenovski; **D:** Jorgo Ognenovski, Mike Tristano. *HVF*

Warrior of the Lost World woof! 1984 A warrior must destroy the evil Omega Force who tyrannically rules the world in the distant future, etcetera, etcetera. One-size-fits-all premise; horrible special effects; miserably directed. Only for really hard-core Pleasence fans. **90m/C VHS, Beta.** Robert Ginty, Persis Khambatta, Donald Pleasence; **D:** David Worth. *NO*

Warrior Queen *√* 1987 (R) Long ago in ancient Rome, overly histrionic mayor Pleasence married porn queen with a wandering eye Fox, and much gratuitous sex and erupting volcanoes resulted. Even the score blows. Also available in an "Unrated" version. Brit pop star Fox is billed as Stasia Micula. **69m/C VHS, LV.** Sybil Danning, Donald Pleasence, Richard Hill, Josephine Jacqueline Jones, Tally Chanel, Samantha Fox. *LIV, VES*

Warrior Spirit *√√½* 1994 (PG-13) After getting kicked out of their prep school, two boys decide to head for the Yukon and search for gold. **CW:** Adventure violence. **94m/C VHS.** Lukas Haas, Jimmy Herman, Allan Musy; **D:** Rene Manzor. *THV*

The Warriors *√√½* *The Dark Avenger* 1955 Swashbuckling adventure about Prince Edward's valiant rescue of Lady Joan and her children from the clutches of the evil Count De Ville. Flynn looks old and pudgy, but buckles his way gallantly through intrepid adventure. Also the last Flynn to see: fun, but more or less completely derivative and familiar. Filmed in England. **85m/C VHS, Beta.** *GB* Errol Flynn, Peter Finch, Joanne Dru, Yvonne Furneaux, Noel Willman, Michael Hordern; **D:** Henry Levin. *FOX, MLB*

The Warriors *√√½* 1979 (R) Action story about a turf battle between New York City street gangs that rages from Coney Island to the Bronx. Silly plot works because of fine performances and direction, excellent use of action and color, and nonstop pace. Fight scenes are very carefully, even obviously, choreographed. **94m/C VHS, Beta, LV.** Michael Beck, James Remar, Deborah Van Valkenburgh, Thomas G. Waites, David Patrick Kelly; **D:** Walter Hill; **W:** Walter Hill. *PAR*

Warriors *√√* 1994 (R) Col. Frank Vail (Busey) is the leader of a top secret government anti-terrorist hit squad, considered so deadly that its members are confined behind the walls of a military prison. But when Vail escapes, it's up to his lethal protege Colin Newl (Pare) to hunt him down. **100m/C VHS, LV, Closed Caption.** Gary Busey, Michael Pare; **D:** Shimon Dotan. *REP*

Warriors from Hell *√½* 1990 (R) Western forces in a small African country battle rebel fighters who threaten the hapless native villagers. **CW:** Language and violence. **90m/C VHS.** Deon Stewardson, Shayne Leith, Adrienne Pierce, Glen Gabela, Hector Manthanda, Ivan Dean, Connie Chume; **D:** Ronnie Isaacs; **W:** Ronnie Isaacs. *COL*

Warriors of the Apocalypse woof! *Searchers of the Voodoo Mountain; Time Raiders* 1985 (R) After a nuclear holocaust, heavily sworded and loin-clothed men search for the secret of eternal life and instead find an Amazon realm in the jungle. A terrible waste of post-apocalyptic scenery. **96m/C VHS, Beta.** Michael James, Debrah Moore, Ken Metcalfe, Franco Guerrero; **D:** Bobby Suarez. *LIV*

Warriors of the Wasteland woof! *The New Barbarians; I Nuovi Barbari* 1983 (R) It's the year 2019, and the world has been devastated by a nuclear war. The few survivors try to reach a distant land which emits radio signals indicating the presence of human life. They are hindered by attacks from the fierce homosexual Templars, led by a self-proclaimed priest called One. Mindless rip-off of "Road Warrior" and obviously made on the proverbial shoestring budget. Dubbed. **92m/C VHS, Beta.** *IT* Fred Williamson, Timothy Brent, Anna Kanakis; **D:** Enzo G. Castellari. *NO*

Warriors of Virtue *√√½* 1997 (PG) Teenaged Ryan Jefers (Yedidia) is transported to the land of Tao where he learns the five virtues (righteousness, benevolence, integrity, wisdom, and loyalty) from the kangaroo-like Warmblood warriors, who live in harmony with humans. Then he must use his knowledge to fight the evil Komodo (MacFadyen), who wishes to steal the energy from Tao to make himself immortal. Nice message for the kids, with enough action to keep them interested, but the Warmbloods are dorky-looking. **101m/C VHS.** Mario Yedidia, Angus MacFadyen, Marlee Shelton, Chao-Li Chi; **D:** Ronny Yu; **W:** Michael Vickerman, Hugh Kelley; **C:** Peter Pau; **M:** Don Davis. *NYR*

The Wash *√√√* 1988 Quiet domestic drama about a couple who drift apart after 40 years of marriage. Set interestingly among Japanese-Americans in California; treats social and cultural factors with intelligence. Superb cast takes it a notch higher. **94m/C VHS, Beta, LV.** Mako, Nobu McCarthy, Sab Shimono; **D:** Michael Toshiyuki Uno; **W:** Philip Kan Kotanda; **C:** Walt Lloyd. *ACA*

Washington Affair *√√* 1977 (PG) A tale of intrigue in the nation's capital. Sullivan is a businessman who uses women and blackmail to capture government contracts. Selleck is the hapless bureaucrat he preys on. Remake of Stoloff's own "Intimacy" was not released until "Magnum P.I." became a hit. **90m/C VHS, Beta.** Tom Selleck, Carol Lynley, Barry Sullivan; **D:** Victor Stoloff.

Washington Mistress *√½* 1981 Eminently ordinary made-for-TV grist about Capitol Hill aide Arnaz, politician Jordan, and their affair. Listless performances. **96m/C VHS.** Lucie Arnaz, Richard Jordan, Tony Bill; **D:** Peter Levin. *NO*

The Wasp Woman *√* 1959 In her quest for eternal beauty, a woman uses a potion made from wasp enzymes. Naturally, she turns into a wasp monster at night. Good fun, courtesy of Corman. **84m/B VHS.** Susan Cabot, Anthony Eisley, Barboura Morris, Michael Marks, William Roerick, Frank Gerstle, Bruno Ve Sota, Frank Wolff; **D:** Roger Corman. *NOS, RHI, SNC*

Wasp Woman *√√* 1996 (R) Equally campy cable remake of the 1959 flick finds ex-supermodel-turned-cosmetics company exec Janice Starlin (Rubin) discovering that her fading beauty is causing problems both with her company and her love life. So she turns to a mysterious doctor for help and injects herself with his untested serum, an experimental wasp hormone. She's hoping to discover a fountain of youth and is instead transformed into a nasty-tempered giant insect. Cool, disgusting makeup/costuming. **CW:** Monster violence and sexuality. **81m/C VHS.** Jennifer Rubin, Daniel J. Travanti, Maria Ford; **D:** Jim Wynorski. *NHO*

Watch It *√√√* 1993 (R) Four self-absorbed twenty-something guys share a house in Chicago for the summer. They pursue a post-adolescent game, consisting of increasingly complicated practical jokes, where the unsuspecting victim is set up for a "watch it" gag. The rivalry escalates, and turns increasingly unpleasant, when cousins John and Michael vie for the affections of Anne, who's wary of involvement because of male selfishness. A first-rate cast with recognizable situations and emotions. **CW:** Language and sexual scene. **102m/C VHS.** Jon Tenney, Peter Gallagher, Suzy Amis, John C. McGinley, Tom Sizemore, Lili Taylor, Cynthia Stevenson, Terri Hawkes, Jordanna Capra; **D:** Tom Flynn; **W:** Tom Flynn; **M:** Stanley Clarke. *PAR*

Watch Me When I Kill *√* 1981 (R) We'd rather not. A young nightclub dancer stops by a drugstore seconds after the owner was killed. She doesn't see the killer's face, but his rasping voice remains to torment her and the viewer. Dubbed. **95m/C VHS, Beta.** *IT* Richard Stewart, Sylvia Kramer, Anthony Bido. *NO*

Watch on the Rhine *√√√½* 1943 Couple involved with the anti-Nazi underground has escaped the country, but is pursued and harassed by Nazi agents. Adapted by Hammett and Hellman from her play. Performed on stage before the U.S. entered the war, it was the first American play and movie to portray the ugliness of fascism as an ideology, as opposed to the more devious evil of its practical side. The Production Code at the time required that a killer always be punished; the murderer (whose screen motives had been noble) refused to film the offending scene, which explains the tacked-on ending. Superb drama from a pair of highly gifted writers and a great cast. Shumlin also directed the play. **114m/B VHS, Beta.** Bette Davis, Paul Lukas, Donald Woods, Beulah Bondi, Geraldine Fitzgerald, George Coulouris, Henry Daniell, Helmut Dantine; **D:** Herman Shumlin; **W:** Lillian Hellman, Dashiell Hammett; **C:** Hal Mohr; **M:** Max Steiner. **Academy Awards '43:** Best Actor (Lukas); **Golden Globe Awards '44:** Best Actor—Drama (Lukas); **National Board of Review Awards '43:** 10 Best Films of the Year; **New York Film Critics Awards '43:** Best Actor (Lukas), Best Film; Nominations: **Academy Awards '43:** Best Picture, Best Screenplay, Best Supporting Actress (Watson). *FOX, MGM, FCT*

Watch the Birdie 🎬🎬½ **1950** It's Skelton three times over as cameraman, father, and grandfather! First, he accidentally films a scam that would send the lovely Miss Dahl filing for bankruptcy. Later a crazy chase scene unfolds, that will have viewers rolling, as Skelton the cameraman nabs the bad guys and turns them over to the cops. Light fun that will charm Skelton fans. **70m/B VHS, Beta.** Red Skelton, Arlene Dahl, Ann Miller, Leon Ames; *D:* Jack Donohue. *MGM*

Watched 🎬🎬 **1973** A former U.S. attorney, gone underground, has a nervous breakdown and kills the narcotics agent who has him under surveillance. Self-important, too serious social/political conspiracy drama of the Watergate era. Keach and Yulin are good, but not good enough to save it. **95m/C VHS, Beta.** Stacy Keach, Harris Yulin, Bridgit Polk; *D:* John Parsons. *LIV, VES*

The Watcher in the Woods 🎬🎬 **1981 (PG)** When an American family rents an English country house, the children are haunted by the spirit of a long-missing young girl. A very bland attempt at a ghost story. **83m/C VHS, Beta.** Bette Davis, Carroll Baker, David McCallum, Ian Bannen, Lynn-Holly Johnson; *D:* John Hough; *W:* Brian Clemens. *DIS*

Watchers 🎬🎬 **1988 (R)** From the suspense novel by Dean R. Koontz, a secret experiment goes wrong, creating half-human monsters. A boy and his extremely intelligent dog are soon pursued. Low-budget, Corman-influenced production is tacky but effective. **99m/C VHS, Beta, LV.** Barbara Williams, Michael Ironside, Corey Haim; *D:* Jon Hess; *M:* Joel Goldsmith. *LIV*

Watchers 2 🎬🎬 **1990 (R)** Sequel to "Watchers" follows the further adventures of a super-intelligent golden retriever who leads a Marine to an animal psychologist and then attempts to warn them both of a mutant killer. The dog says woof, but this movie doesn't quite. Fun for lovers of hounds or horror flicks. **101m/C VHS, Beta, LV.** Marc Singer, Tracy Scoggins; *D:* Thierry Notz; *M:* Rick Conrad. *LIV*

Watchers 3 🎬½ **1994 (R)** A secret military outpost in the South American jungles is attacked by a carnivorous predator. Ex-military convicts are sent to rescue the remaining survivors and to make certain the government experiment that started the terror never comes to light.*CW:* Language; violence; gore. **95m/C VHS.** Wings Hauser, Gregory Scott Cummins, Daryl Roach, John K. Linton, Lolita Ronalds, Frank Novak; *D:* Jeremy Stanford. *NHO*

Water 🎬 **1985 (PG-13)** The resident governor of a Caribbean British colony juggles various predatory interests when a valuable mineral water resource is found. The good cast is wasted in this all-too-silly effort. **89m/C VHS, Beta.** *GB* Michael Caine, Brenda Vaccaro, Leonard Rossiter, Valerie Perrine, Jimmie Walker; *Cameos:* Eric Clapton, George Harrison, Fred Gwynne, Ringo Starr; *D:* Dick Clement; *W:* Dick Clement, Ian LaFrenais, Bill Persky. *PAR*

Water Babies 🎬🎬 *Slip Slide Adventures* **1979 (G)** When a chimney sweep's 12-year-old apprentice is wrongly accused of stealing silver, the boy and his dog fall into a pond and eventually rescue some of the characters they find there. Combination of live-action and animated fairy-tale story set in nineteenth-century London. Boring, unless you're a young child with equivalent standards. Based on the book by Charles Kingsley. **93m/C VHS, Beta.** *GB* James Mason, Billie Whitelaw, David Tomlinson, Paul Luty, Sammantha Coates; *D:* Lionel Jeffries.

The Water Engine 🎬🎬½ **1992** Charles Lang (Macy) is a luckless machinist struggling to survive in Depression-era Chicago. Lang invents a remarkable engine, that runs on water, and holds the promise of limitless, cheap power. To protect his invention he finds a seedy patent attorney (Mahoney), which leads to the sinister Oberman (Mantegna), a mysterious and powerful figure who wants Lang's invention—at any cost. Based on the play by David Mamet; made for cable TV. **110m/C VHS.** Charles Durning, Patti LuPone, William H. Macy, John Mahoney, Joe Mantegna, Joanna Miles, Mike Nussbaum, Treat Williams, Andrea Marcovicci, Peter Michael Goetz, David Mamet; *D:* Steven Schachter; *W:* David Mamet; *C:* Bryan England. *TTC*

Water Rustlers 🎬½ **1939** Unscrupulous land baron builds a dam on his side of the creek with the intention of drying out the cattle pastures. Heroine Page, whose pop has been rubbed out by varmints, and good guy/lover O'Brien save her property and avenge her father. Second of three Page westerns. **55m/B VHS, Beta.** Dorothy Page, Dave O'Brien; *D:* Samuel Diege. *VCN, VDM*

The Waterdance 🎬🎬🎬 **1991 (R)** Autobiographical film based on the experiences of writer/co-director Jimenez. When writer Joel Garcia (Stoltz) is paralyzed in a hiking accident he finds himself dealing with not only the rehab process itself but his feelings, the feelings of his married lover, and those of his fellow patients. Deals unsentimentally with all the physical adjustments, including the sexual ones. Resolutions may be predictable but the performances rise above any script weaknesses. The title refers to Hill's dream of dancing on water—and the fear of drowning if he stops.*CW:* Language and sensuality. **106m/C VHS, LV, Closed Caption.** Eric Stoltz, Wesley Snipes, William Forsythe, Helen Hunt, Elizabeth Pena, Grace Zabriskie; *D:* Neal Jimenez, Michael Steinberg; *W:* Neal Jimenez; *C:* Mark Plummer; *M:* Michael Convertino. Independent Spirit Awards '93: Best First Feature, Best Screenplay; Sundance Film Festival '92: Best Screenplay, Audience Award. *COL, PMS, BTV*

Waterfront 🎬½ **1939** Dreary dockside melodrama, with drinking and brawling longshoreman Jim (Morgan) avenging his brother's death. Based on the play "Blindspot" by Kenyon Nicholson. **59m/B VHS.** Dennis (Stanley Morner) Morgan, Gloria Dickson, Marie Wilson, Larry Williams, Sheila Bromley, Ward Bond, Frank Faylen; *D:* Terry Morse; *W:* Arthur Ripley, Lee Katz. *GPV*

Waterfront 🎬🎬 **1944** Nazis coerce German-Americans into helping them in WWII-era San Francisco. Credulity defying spy doings, but that's okay. Fairly entertaining wartime drama about paranoia on the home front. **68m/B VHS, Beta.** John Carradine, J. Carrol Naish, Terry Frost, Maris Wrixon, Edwin Maxwell; *D:* Steve Sekely. *SNC, VCI*

Waterfront 🎬🎬½ **1983** Effective romantic drama set in Melbourne, Australia. Australian workers strike after taking forced pay cuts. As a result, Italian immigrants are hired as scabs to keep the docks going. Despite the tension, an Italian woman and an Australian man fall deeply in love, only to find that they must struggle to keep that love alive. **294m/C VHS, Beta.** *AU* Jack Thompson, Greta Scacchi, Frank Gallacher, Tony Rickards, Mark Little, Jay Mannering, Ray Barrett, Chris Haywood, Warren Mitchell, Noni Hazlehurst, John Karlsen, Elin Jenkins; *D:* Chris Thomson. *PSM, PAR*

Waterhole #3 🎬🎬½ **1967 (PG)** Three Confederate army buddies steal a fortune in gold bullion from the Union Army and hide it in a waterhole in the desert. One of the funnier entries in the Western comedy genre. **95m/C VHS.** James Coburn, Carroll O'Connor, Margaret Blye, Claude Akins, Bruce Dern, Joan Blondell, James Whitmore; *D:* William A. Graham; *C:* Robert Burks; *M:* Dave Grusin. *PAR*

Waterland 🎬🎬 **1992 (R)** Meandering drama about a history teacher who tries to solve a personal crisis by using his class as a sounding board to describe his troubled past in England. Dark secrets abound, including incest, madness, murder, and the terrifying love between the teacher and his childhood bride. Melancholy, overwrought but partially redeemed by the lead performances of Irons and his (real-life and cinematic) wife, Cusack. The film's setting has been unfortunately moved from London to Pittsburgh, destroying story links. Based on the novel by Graham Swift.*CW:* Language and sexuality and an abortion scene. **95m/C VHS, LV.** Jeremy Irons, Ethan Hawke, Sinead Cusack, John Heard, Grant Warnock, Lena Headey,

Pete Postlethwaite, Cara Buono; *D:* Stephen Gyllenhaal; *W:* Peter Prince; *C:* Robert Elswit; *M:* Carter Burwell. *NLC, COL*

Waterloo 🎬🎬 **1971 (G)** Massive chronicle of Napoleon's European conquests and eventual defeat at the hands of Wellington. Filmed on location in Italy and the Ukraine, it bombed due largely to Steiger's bizarre rendition of Napoleon. **122m/C VHS, Closed Caption.** *IT RU* Rod Steiger, Orson Welles, Virginia McKenna, Michael Wilding, Donal Donnelly, Christopher Plummer, Jack Hawkins, Dan O'Herlihy, Terence Alexander, Rupert Davies, Ivo Garrani, Gianni "John" Garko; *D:* Sergei Bondarchuk; *W:* H.A.L. Craig, Sergei Bondarchuk; *M:* Nino Rota. *PAR, FCT, FUS*

Waterloo Bridge 🎬🎬🎬 **1940** In London during WWI, a soldier from an aristocratic family and a ballet dancer begin a tragic romance when they meet by chance on the foggy Waterloo Bridge. When he's listed as dead, her despair turns her to prostitution. But then he returns from POW camp, they once again meet by accident on Waterloo Bridge, and their romance resumes. Four-hanky drama with fine performances by Leigh (her first after "Gone with the Wind") and Taylor. **109m/B VHS, Beta, LV, Closed Caption.** Vivien Leigh, Robert Taylor, Lucile Watson, Sir C. Aubrey Smith, Maria Ouspenskaya, Virginia Field; *D:* Mervyn LeRoy; *C:* Joseph Ruttenberg. Nominations: Academy Awards '40: Best Black and White Cinematography, Best Original Score. *MGM*

Watermelon Man 🎬🎬 **1970 (R)** The tables are turned for a bigoted white guy when he wakes up one morning to discover he has become a black man. Broad comedy with not much place to go is still engaging. Cambridge takes on both roles, appearing in unconvincing white makeup. **97m/C VHS, Beta, LV.** Godfrey Cambridge, Erin Moran, Estelle Parsons, Howard Caine; *D:* Melvin Van Peebles. *COL, FCT*

Watership Down 🎬🎬½ **1978 (PG)** Wonderfully animated story based on Richard Adams's allegorical novel about how a group of rabbits escape fear and overcome oppression while searching for a new and better home. It's really an adult theme with sufficient violence to the poor with wabbits to scare the kiddies. **92m/C VHS, Beta, LV, 8mm.** *GB D:* Martin Rosen; *W:* Martin Rosen; *V:* Ralph Richardson, Zero Mostel, John Hurt, Denholm Elliott, Harry Andrews, Michael Hordern, Joss Ackland. *WAR, TVC*

Waterworld 🎬🎬½ **1995 (PG-13)** "The Man From Atlantis" meets "Mad Max." Industry knives sharpened with glee before release, with some insiders calling this luck-impaired project "Fishtar" and "Kevin's Gate." With an estimated $150 million budget, the film must look to overseas sales and secondary markets to make any money. Most of said budget seems to have ended up on screen, which makes for a visually striking, and at times daunting, film. Costner, who did just about everything but cater the meals, stars as Mariner, a mutant man-fish who reluctantly helps human survivors search for the mythical Dryland since the polar ice caps melted, flooding the earth. The bad guys are the Smokers, led by the evil Hopper, who can play these roles in his sleep. Entertaining, but not riveting, as the budget and PR hype leads one to expect. The floating set was anchored (not very well, apparently) off the Hawaiian coast and was lost once during a tropical storm. Costner bet the boat on this one and stands to lose more than just money. With rumors of internal production battles, out of control budgets, and his other recent box office disappointments, his star power is in question.*CW:* Some intense scenes of action violence, brief nudity and language. **135m/C VHS, LV, Closed Caption.** Kevin Costner, Dennis Hopper, Jeanne Tripplehorn, Tina Majorino, Michael Jeter, R.D. Call, Robert Joy; *D:* Kevin Reynolds; *W:* Peter Rader, Marc Norman, David N. Twohy; *C:* Dean Semler; *M:* James Newton Howard. Golden Raspberry Awards '95: Worst Supporting Actor (Hopper); Nominations:

Academy Awards '95: Best Sound; Golden Raspberry Awards '95: Worst Picture, Worst Actor (Costner). *USH*

Wavelength 🎬🎬½ 1983 (PG) A rock star living in the Hollywood Hills with his girlfriend stumbles on an ultra-secret government project involving friendly aliens from outer space recovered from a recent UFO crash site. Fun, enthusiastically unoriginal cheap sci-fi. Soundtrack by Tangerine Dream. **87m/C VHS, Beta, LV.** Robert Carradine, Cherie Currie, Keenan Wynn; **D:** Mike Gray; **W:** Mike Gray; **M:** Tangerine Dream. *VTR*

Wavelength 🎬½ 1996 (R) Physicist and Oxford professor Paul Higgins (Piven) has a few problems—a wife, Claire (Williams), a girlfriend, Lucy (Walker), Lucy's father who just happens to be the head of the physics department, and a mysterious presence (Attenborough) who's trying to help Paul with his research on nuclear fission. Piven's character is so selfish you'll wonder why either woman wants him and the happy ending feels contrived. **94m/C VHS, Closed Caption.** *GB* Jeremy Piven, Kelli Williams, Liza Walker, James Villiers, James Faulkner, Richard Attenborough, Byrne Piven, Nicholas Marco, Dominic West; **D:** Benjamin Fry; **W:** Benjamin Fry; **C:** Chris Middleton; **M:** Michael Storey. *PAR*

Wax, or the Discovery of Television Among the Bees 🎬🎬 1993 Intricate and eccentric fable dealing with alternate realities and perceptions. Jacob Maker (Blair) keeps a hive of very unusual bees, a family legacy passed down from his grandfather. Jacob begins experiencing a eerie communication with his bees and suffering mysterious blackouts, which cause him to perceive the world through blurred bee vision. New Mexico desert setting provides a surreal and desolate landscape. **85m/C VHS.** David Blair, Meg Savlov, Florence Ormezzano, William S. Burroughs; **D:** David Blair; **W:** David Blair; **M:** Beo Morales, Brooks Williams. *FRF*

Waxwork 🎬½ 1988 (R) A wax museum opens up, and it is soon evident that the dummies are not what they seem. Garbled nonthriller. Available in a 100-minute unrated version. **97m/C VHS, Beta, LV.** Zach Galligan, Deborah Foreman, Michelle Johnson, Dana Ashbrook, Miles O'Keeffe, Patrick Macnee, David Warner; **D:** Anthony Hickox; **M:** Roger Bellon. *LIV, VES*

Waxwork 2: Lost in Time 🎬🎬½ 1991 (R) A young couple (Galligan and Schnarre) barely escape with their lives when the infamous waxworks museum burns down. A severed hand also gets loose and follows Schnarre home and murders her stepfather, leaving her to take the blame. In order to prove her innocence, the couple must travel through a bizarre time machine. Extraordinary special effects, strange plot twists, and recreations of scenes from past horror movies make this a highly entertaining sequel. **CW:** Language and comic horror violence. **104m/C VHS, Closed Caption.** Zach Galligan, Alexander Godunov, Bruce Campbell, Michael Des Barres, Monika Schnarre; **D:** Anthony Hickox. *LIV*

Waxworks 🎬🎬🎬 1924 A major achievement in German Expressionism, in which a poet imagines scenarios in a wax museum fairground that involve Jack the Ripper, Ivan the Terrible and Haroun al-Rashid. Influential and considered ahead of its time. Silent. **63m/B VHS, Beta.** *GE* William Dieterle, Emil Jannings, Conrad Veidt, Werner Krauss, John Gottowt, Olga Belajeff; **D:** Paul Leni; **W:** Henrik Galeen. *SNC, NOS, LIV*

Way Back Home 🎬🎬 *Old Greatheart; Other People's Business* 1932 Man wants to adopt a boy to release him from the clutches of his cruel guardian. Minor role for the then unknown Davis. **81m/B VHS, Beta.** Phillips Lord, Frank Albertson, Bette Davis; **D:** William A. Seiter; **M:** Max Steiner. *TTC, FCT*

Way Down East 🎬🎬🎬 1920 Melodramatic silent drama of a country girl who is tricked into a fake marriage by a scheming playboy. The famous final scene of Gish adrift on the ice floes is in color. One of Griffith's last critical and popular successes. This tape includes the original Griffith-approved musical score. Remade in 1935 with Henry Fonda. **107m/B VHS, Beta, LV.** Lillian Gish, Richard Barthelmess, Lowell Sherman, Creighton Hale; **D:** D.W. Griffith. *NOS, BAR, VYY*

Way Down South 🎬½ 1939 The orphan son of a plantation owner tries to take over his father's estate, only to find out that the place has been run into the ground by a corrupt lawyer and a cruel slave driver. Black poet Hughes and actor Muse collaborated on the screenplay. German-born director Vorhaus was in his second year in Hollywood, after making his mark in Britain directing talkies. 🎵Good Ground; Louisiana; Nobody Know De Trouble I See; Sometimes I Feel Like a Motherless Child; Lord I You Can't Come Send One Angel Down. **62m/B VHS.** Bobby Breen, Alan Mowbray, Ralph Morgan, Clarence Muse, Steffi Duna, Sally Blane, Edwin Maxwell; **D:** Bernard Vorhaus; **W:** Clarence Muse, Langston Hughes. Nominations: Academy Awards '39: Best Score. *NOS*

Way He Was 🎬🎬 1976 (R) A satirical reenactment of the events that led up to the Watergate burglary and the coverup that followed. **87m/C VHS, Beta.** Steve Friedman, Al Lewis, Merrie Lynn Ross, Doodles Weaver. *VCI*

Way of the Black Dragon 🎬 1981 When slave-trading drug traffickers threaten the moral fiber of our nation, two commandoes join forces to halt their extension. **88m/C VHS, Beta.** Ron Van Cliff, Carter Wang, Charles Bonet; **D:** Chan Wui Ngai. *TWE*

Way of the West 🎬½ 1935 Them durn pesky sheepherders are up to it again! Okay, so the cow/sheep thing is a classic western plot, but here it's offered perfunctorily. **52m/B VHS, Beta.** Wally Wales, William Desmond, Art Mix, Jim Sheridan, Bobby Nelson; **D:** Robert Emmett Tansey. *NOS, DVT, RXM*

The Way Out 🎬🎬 *Dial 999* 1956 Average crime drama starring Nelson as a fugitive accused of killing a bookie. **90m/C VHS.** *GB* Gene Nelson, Mona Freeman, John Bentley, Michael Goodliffe, Sydney Tafler; **D:** Montgomery Tully. *SNC*

Way Out West 🎬🎬🎬 1937 The classic twosome journey way out west to deliver the deed to a gold mine to the daughter of their late prospector pal. The obligatory romance is missing, but you'll be laughing so hard you won't notice. One of Stan and Ollie's best. Score includes the song "Trail of the Lonesome Pine." Also included on this tape is a 1932 Todd and Pitts short, "Red Noses." Available colorized. **86m/B VHS, Beta, Closed Caption.** Stan Laurel, Oliver Hardy, Rosina Lawrence, James Finlayson, Sharon Lynne, ZaSu Pitts, Thelma Todd, William Haines; **D:** James W. Horne. Nominations: Academy Awards '37: Best Original Score. *CCB, MED, MLB*

The Way We Were 🎬🎬🎬 1973 (PG) Big box-office hit follows a love story between opposites from the 1930s to the 1950s. Streisand is a Jewish political radical who meets the handsome WASP Redford at college. They're immediately attracted to one another, but it takes years before they act on it and eventually marry. They move to Hollywood where Redford is a screenwriter and left-wing Streisand becomes involved in the Red scare and the blacklist, much to Redford's dismay. Though always in love, their differences are too great to keep them together. An old-fashioned and sweet romance, with much gloss. Hit title song sung by Streisand. Adapted by Arthur Laurents from his novel. 🎵The Way We Were. **118m/C VHS, Beta, LV, 8mm.** Barbra Streisand, Robert Redford, Bradford Dillman, Viveca Lindfors, Herb Edelman, Murray Hamilton, Patrick O'Neal, James Woods, Sally Kirkland; **D:** Sydney Pollack; **W:** Arthur Laurents; **C:** Harry Stradling Jr.; **M:** Marvin Hamlisch. Academy Awards '73: Best Song ("The Way We Were"), Original Dramatic/Comedy Score; Golden Globe Awards '74: Best Song ("The Way We Were"); National Board of Review Awards '73: 10 Best Films of the Year; Nominations: Academy Awards '73: Best Actress (Streisand), Best Art Direction/Set Decoration, Best Cinematography, Best Costume Design. *COL*

The Way West 🎬½ 1967 A wagon train heads to Oregon. A poor and muddled attempt at recreating the style of a John Ford western. What really galls is that it's based on the Pulitzer-winning novel by A.B. Guthrie, Jr. Boy, is the book better than the movie. Field's first film. **122m/C VHS.** Kirk Douglas, Robert Mitchum, Richard Widmark, Lola Albright, Michael Witney, Stubby Kaye, Sally Field, Jack Elam; **D:** Andrew V. McLaglen; **C:** William Clothier. *MGM*

Wayne Murder Case 🎬🎬🎬 *Strange Adventure* 1938 A fast-moving, cleverly constructed murder mystery. A rich old man dies just as he is about to sign a new will. Though no one was standing near him, a knife is found stuck in his back. **61m/B VHS, Beta.** June Clyde, Regis Toomey, Jason Robards Sr. *SNC, VYY*

Wayne's World 🎬🎬🎬 1992 (PG-13) Destined to become one of the top movies of all time—Not! This "Saturday Night Live" skit proved to be so popular that it got its own movie, not unlike the plot, which has slimy producer Lowe take the public access "Wayne's World" into the world of commercial television. The zany duo of Wayne and Garth are as much fun on the big screen as they are on SNL and there are many funny moments, several of which are destined to become comedy classics. A huge box office hit that spawned a sequel. **93m/C VHS, LV.** Mike Myers, Dana Carvey, Rob Lowe, Tia Carrere, Brian Doyle-Murray, Lara Flynn Boyle, Kurt Fuller, Colleen Camp, Donna Dixon, Ed O'Neill; **Cameos:** Alice Cooper, Meat Loaf; **D:** Penelope Spheeris; **W:** Mike Myers, Bonnie Turner, Terry Turner; **M:** J. Peter Robinson. MTV Movie Awards '92: Best On-Screen Duo (Mike Myers/Dana Carvey). *PAR, FCT*

Wayne's World 2 🎬🎬 1993 (PG-13) Good-natured rerun of the original has plenty of sophomoric gags, but feels tired. Wayne and Garth are on their own, planning a major concert, Waynestock. "If you book them they will come," Jim Morrison says in a dream. Meanwhile, Wayne's girlfriend (Carrere) is falling for slimeball record promoter Walken. Offers a few brilliantly funny segments. If you liked the "Bohemian Rhapsody" spot in the original, get ready for the Village People here. Heston has a funny cameo, and Walken and Basinger push the limits without going over the top. Feature film debut for director Surjik. **CW:** Ribald humor. **94m/C VHS, Beta, LV, Closed Caption.** Mike Myers, Dana Carvey, Tia Carrere, Christopher Walken, Ralph Brown, Kim Basinger, James Hong, Chris Farley, Ed O'Neill, Olivia D'Abo, Kevin Pollak, Drew Barrymore; **Cameos:** Charlton Heston, Rip Taylor; **D:** Stephen Surjik; **W:** Mike Myers, Bonnie Turner, Terry Turner; **M:** Carter Burwell. Nominations: MTV Movie Awards '94: Best On-Screen Duo (Mike Myers/Dana Carvey), Best Kiss (Dana Carvey/Kim Basinger). *PAR*

The Wayward Wife 🎬🎬 *La Provinciale* 1952 Young woman, married to a university professor, is blackmailed over her less-than-respectable past. Based on the novel by Alberto Moravia. Italian with subtitles. **92m/B VHS.** *IT* Gina Lollobrigida, Gabriele Ferzetti, Franco Interlenghi, Renaldo Baldini; **D:** Mario Soldati. *FCT*

W.C. Fields Comedy Bag 1933 Compilation of three classic Fields shorts: "The Golf Specialist" (1930), "The Dentist" (1932) and "The Fatal Glass of Beer" (1933). **56m/B VHS, Beta.** W.C. Fields, Babe Kane, Dorothy Granger, George Chandler. *BAR*

W.C. Fields: Flask of Fields 1930 Three classic Fields shorts: "The Golf Specialist" (1930), in which J. Effington Bellweather finds himself teaching a lovely young lady how to play the game; "The Fatal Glass of Beer" (1933); and "The Dentist" (1932), in which Fields tackles a room filled with patients. **61m/B VHS, Beta, 8mm.** W.C. Fields, Babe Kane, Elise Cavanna, Bud Jamison, Rosemary Theby. *VYY*

We All Loved Each Other So Much 🎬🎬🎬½ 1977 Sensitive comedy follows three friends over 30 years, beginning at the end of WWII. All three have loved the same woman, an actress. Homage to friendship and to postwar Italian cinema. Includes a full-scale recreation of the fountain scene in "La Dolce Vita." In Italian with English subtitles. **124m/C VHS, Beta, LV.** *IT* Vittorio Gassman, Nino Manfredi, Stefano Satta Flores, Stefania Sandrelli, Marcello Mastroianni, Federico Fellini; *D:* Ettore Scola. *COL, APD*

We are the Children 🎬🎬 1987 Cynical reporter covering the famine in Ethiopia meets an idealistic nurse who's been living there for years. Romance blossoms among the starving in made-for-TV drama co-produced by Danson. **92m/C VHS, Beta.** *D:* Robert M. Young. *PSM*

We Dive at Dawn 🎬🎬🎬 1943 Interesting, tense British submarine drama. The "Sea Tiger" attempts to sink the German battleship "Brandenburg" off Denmark. Good cast. Mills prepared for the role by riding an actual submarine, turning "a pale shade of pea-green" when it crash-dived. **98m/B VHS, Beta.** *GB* Eric Portman, John Mills; *D:* Anthony Asquith. *NOS, DVT, MED*

We of the Never Never 🎬🎬🎬 1982 (G) In turn-of-the-century Australia a city-bred woman marries a cattle rancher and moves from civilized Melbourne to the barren outback of the Northern Territory. Based on the autobiographical story written by Jeannie Gunn, the first white woman to travel in the aboriginal wilderness. She finds herself fighting for her own rights as well as for those of the aborigines in this sincere, well-done film. **136m/C VHS, Beta.** *AU* Angela Punch McGregor, Arthur Dignam, Tony Barry; *D:* Igor Auzins. *COL*

We the Living 🎬🎬½ 1942 The torpid long-lost and restored Italian version of Ayn Rand's unique political tome. Deals with a young Soviet woman in revolutionary Petrograd who is slowly ruined by the system and her affair with a romantic counter-revolutionary. Made under the Fascists' nose during WWII. A fascinating dialectic between utopian melodrama and Rand dogma. In Italian with subtitles. **174m/B VHS, Beta.** *IT* Alida Valli, Rossano Brazzi, Fosco Giachetti; *D:* Goffredo Alessandrini. *LUM*

We Think the World of You 🎬🎬🎬 1988 (PG) When bisexual Oldman goes to prison, his lover Bates, whose feelings are unresolved and complex, finds friendship with Oldman's dog. Odd, oft-bitter comedy-drama of love and loyalty characterized by excellent acting and respectful, gentle direction. From the novel by Joseph R. Ackerly. **94m/C VHS, Beta, LV.** *GB* Alan Bates, Gary Oldman, Frances Barber, Liz Smith, Max Wall, Kerry Wise; *D:* Colin Gregg. *NLC*

We Will Not Enter the Forest 🎬🎬🎬 1979 Moral dilemmas afflict a group of French Resistance fighters during WWII when they must decide what to do with four German deserters they've captured. In French with subtitles. **88m/C VHS, Beta.** *FR* Marie-France Pisier; *D:* Georges Dumoulin. *FCT*

The Weaker Sex 🎬🎬½ 1949 Typical patriotic British weepie finds a British widow and her daughters trying to hold on to hope as D-Day approaches. **89m/B VHS.** *GB* Ursula Jeans, Cecil Parker, Joan Hopkins, Derek Bond, Lana Morris; *D:* Roy Ward Baker. *FCT*

Weapons of Death 🎬 1983 Kung Fu expert Lee splatters his enemies all over San Francisco's Chinatown. **90m/C VHS, Beta.** Eric Lee, Bob Ramos, Ralph Castellanos. *NO*

Weather in the Streets 🎬½ 1984 (PG) A young woman enters into an ill-fated love affair after spending a few moments with an aristocratic married man. Cliched drama set in England between the two world wars. **108m/C VHS, Beta.** Michael York, Joanna Lumley, Lisa Eichhorn, Isabel Dean, Norman Pitt; *M:* Carl Davis. *NO*

Web of Deceit 🎬🎬½ 1990 (PG-13) Defense lawyer Purl returns to her Southern hometown to defend an unjustly accused teenager. She falls in love with the prosecutor, but could he be

the killer? Shades of "Jagged Edge." Good, suspenseful made-for-TV movie. **93m/C VHS, Beta, Closed Caption.** Linda Purl, James Read, Paul DeSouza, Larry Black, Len Birman, Barbara Rush; *D:* Sandor Stern; *W:* Sandor Stern. *PAR*

Web of Deception 🎬 1971 (R) A jewel thief disappears with five million dollars worth of jewels. When the case turns to murder, a private detective becomes the prime suspect. **90m/C VHS, Beta.** *SP* Thomas Hunter, Aelina Nathaniel, Gabriele Tinti, Marilia Branco. *NO*

Web of the Spider 🎬🎬 *Nella Stretta M Orsa Del Ragno; In the Grip of the Spider; Dracula in the Castle of Blood; And Comes the Dawn...But Colored Red* 1970 Kinski as Poe is really the only good thing about this run-of-the-mill horror outing. A man stays the night in a spooky house to prove it's not haunted. Remake of "Castle of Blood." **94m/C VHS.** *GE FR IT* Anthony (Tony) Franciosa, Klaus Kinski, Michele Mercier, Peter Carsten, Karin Field; *D:* Anthony (Antonio Margheriti) Dawson. *SNC*

A Wedding 🎬½ 1978 (PG) The occasion of a wedding leads to complications galore for the relatives and guests on the happy day. Silent film legend Gish's 100th screen role. Miserable, self-indulgent outing for Altman, who went through quite a dry spell after "Nashville." **125m/C VHS, Beta.** Mia Farrow, Carol Burnett, Lillian Gish, Lauren Hutton, Viveca Lindfors, Geraldine Chaplin, Paul Dooley, Howard Duff, Dennis Christopher, Peggy Ann Garner, John Considine, Nina Van Pallandt, Dina Merrill, Pat McCormick, Vittorio Gassman, Desi Arnaz Jr.; *D:* Robert Altman; *W:* John Considine, Allan Nicholls, Patricia Resnick, Robert Altman. *FOX*

Wedding Band 🎬🎬 1989 Episodic comedy about a rock 'n roll band that plays all sorts of weddings. Thin and lame but inoffensive. **95m/C VHS, Beta, LV.** William Katt, Joyce Hyser, Tino Insana, Fran Drescher, David Rasche, Joe Flaherty, Tim Kazurinsky, James Belushi; *D:* Daniel Raskov. *COL*

The Wedding Banquet 🎬🎬🎬 *Xiyan; Hsi Yen* 1993 (R) Charming story about a clash of customs and secrets. Naturalized American Wai Tung (Chao, in his debut) lives comfortably with his lover Simon (Lichtenstein) while hiding the fact that he's gay from his Chinese parents. To appease his parents and get his "wife" a green card, he marries for convenience and watches as the deception snowballs. Comedy of errors was shot on a small budget ($750,000) and examines small details with as much care as the larger ones. A fine effort from director Lee that's solidly humorous, but also poignant. In English and Chinese with English subtitles. *CW:* Language. **111m/C VHS, LV, Closed Caption.** *TW* Winston Chao, May Chin, Mitchell Lichtenstein, Sihung Lung, Ah-Leh Gua; *D:* Ang Lee; *W:* Ang Lee, Neil Peng, James Schamus. Nominations: Academy Awards '93: Best Foreign Language Film; Golden Globe Awards '94: Best Foreign Film; Independent Spirit Awards '94: Best Actor (Lichtenstein), Best Actress (Chin), Best Director (Lee), Best Film, Best Screenplay, Best Supporting Actress (Gua). *FXV*

Wedding Bell Blues 🎬🎬 1996 (R) Three thirtyish single friends/roommates cope with a variety of crises. Pregnant Tanya (Porikova) learns that her boyfriend Tom (Edson) has no intention of marrying her, Micki's (Warner) fiance has just called off their wedding, and Jasmine's (Douglas) conservative parents are upset by their promiscuous daughter's approach to life. Stressed, the women decide to seek their fortunes in Vegas—preferably through some quickie marriages and even quickier divorces. Looks like it was shot on a shoestring budget and the lighting could be better, but the dialogue rings true and the actors do a decent job. Look for Seinfeld's TV mom as Micki's overbearing mother and Jackson as a disgruntled shopper. Reynolds plays herself. *CW:* Sex-related content. **100m/C VHS.** Illeana Douglas, Paulina Porizkova, Julie Warner, John Corbett, Jonathan Penner, Richard Edson, Charles Martin Smith, Stephanie Beacham, Carla Gugino, Leo Rossi, John Capodice, Richard Edson, Victoria Jackson, Jeff Seymour; *Cameos:* Debbie Reynolds; *D:*

Dana Lustig; *W:* Annette Goliti Gutierrez; *C:* Kent Wakeford; *M:* Paul Christian Gordon, Tal Bergman. *BMG*

The Wedding Gift 🎬🎬🎬 *Wide-Eyed and Legless* 1993 (PG-13) Offbeat charm and humor go a long way to overcome the inherent tragedy in this true story made for British TV. Longtime happily marrieds Diana (Walters) and Deric (Broadbent) Longden are struggling to cope with Diana's mysterious and increasingly debilitating illness, which causes blackouts, pain, and the inability to use her limbs. Diana comes to accept the fact that she's going to die and decides to find her hubby a new wife, aided by Deric's friendship with a blind novelist (Thomas). Terrific performances keep the mawkishness at bay. Based on Deric Longden's books "Diana's Story" and "Lost for Words." **87m/C VHS, LV, Closed Caption.** *GB* Julie Walters, Jim Broadbent, Sian Thomas, Thora Hird, Andrew Lancel, Anastasia Mulrooney; *D:* Richard Loncraine; *W:* Jack Rosenthal; *C:* Remi Adefarasin. *MAX*

Wedding in Blood 🎬🎬🎬 1974 (PG) Two French lovers plot to kill their respective spouses, and proceed to do so amid calamity and much table-turning. Sharp social satire and suspenseful mystery. Based on a true story. In French with English subtitles. **98m/C VHS, Beta.** *FR IT* Claude Pieplu, Stephane Audran, Michel Piccoli; *D:* Claude Chabrol. *COL*

A Wedding in Galilee 🎬🎬🎬 *Noce In Galilee* 1987 The elder of a Palestinian village is given permission to have a traditional wedding ceremony for his son if Israeli military officers can attend as the guests of honor. As the event approaches, conflicts arise among the villagers, the family, and the Israelis. Long but fascinating treatment of traditional culture in the modern world amidst political tension. In Arabic and Hebrew, with English subtitles. **113m/C VHS, LV.** *BE FR* Ali M. El Aleili, Nazih Akleh, Anna Achdian; *D:* Michel Khleifi. *KIV*

Wedding in White 🎬🎬 1972 (R) A rape and out-of-wedlock pregnancy trouble a poor British clan living in Canada during WWII. Sad, glum way to spend an evening. Kane is good in a non-comic role. Her screen father cares more for honor than he does for her. **103m/C VHS, Beta.** *CA* Donald Pleasence, Carol Kane, Leo Phillips; *D:* William Fruet.

The Wedding March 🎬🎬🎬🎬 1928 Von Stroheim's famous silent film about romantic couplings in pre-WWI Vienna. The director also stars as a prince preparing to marry for money, who falls in love with a beautiful, but poor woman. Romance and irony, with a memorable finale. Like many of his other great films, it was taken from him and re-edited. Initially the first of two halves; the second, "The Honeymoon," has been lost. Next to "Greed," the most successful film. **113m/B VHS, Beta.** Erich von Stroheim, Fay Wray, ZaSu Pitts, George Fawcett, Maude George, Matthew Betz, George Nicholls, Cesare Gravina; *D:* Erich von Stroheim; *C:* Hal Mohr; *M:* Gaylord Carter. *PAR*

The Wedding Party 🎬½ 1969 Apprehensive groom is overwhelmed by his too-eager bride and her inquisitive relatives at a prenuptial celebration. Hokey, dull, would-be comedy. First screen appearances of both Clayburgh and De Niro (spelled DeNero in the credits). **90m/C VHS, Beta.** Jill Clayburgh, Robert De Niro, William Finley; *D:* Brian DePalma, Cynthia Munroe, Wilford Leach; *W:* Brian DePalma. *NO*

Wedding Rehearsal 🎬🎬½ 1932 A young nobleman thwarts his grandmother's plans to marry him off by finding suitors for all the young ladies offered to him until he finally succumbs to the charms of his mother's secretary. Enjoyable, fun comedy. First featured roles for actresses Oberon, Barrie, and Gardner. **84m/B VHS, Beta, LV.** Merle Oberon, Roland Young, John Loder, Wendy Barrie, Maurice Evans, Joan Gardner; *D:* Alexander Korda.

Wee Willie Winkie 🎬🎬🎬 1937 (PG) A precocious little girl is taken in by a British regiment in India. Sugar-coated. If you're a cinematic diabetic, be warned. If you're a Temple fan, you've probably already seen it. If not, you're in for a treat. Inspired by the Rudyard Kipling story. **99m/B VHS, Beta, Closed Caption.** Shirley Temple, Victor McLaglen, Sir C. Aubrey Smith, June Lang, Michael Whalen, Cesar Romero, Constance Collier; **D:** John Ford; **C:** Arthur C. Miller. Nominations: Academy Awards '37: Best Interior Decoration. *FOX*

Weeds 🎬🎬🎬 1987 (R) A highly fictionalized account of the career of Rick Cluchey, who, as a lifer in San Quentin federal prison, wrote a play. He was eventually paroled and went on to form a theater group made up of ex-cons. Original and often enjoyable with a tight ensemble performance. Filmed on location at Stateville Correctional Center in Illinois, with inmates serving as extras. **115m/C VHS, Beta, LV.** Nick Nolte, Rita Taggart, William Forsythe, Lane Smith, Joe Mantegna, Ernie Hudson, John Toles-Bey, Mark Rolston, Anne Ramsey, Charlie Rich; **D:** John Hancock; **W:** John Hancock, Dorothy Tristan; **M:** Angelo Badalamenti. *HBO*

Week-End In Havana 🎬🎬½ 1941 Set in pre-revolution Cuba, this frothy musical finds salesgirl Faye on a long-awaited cruise when her ship gets stranded in Havana. She's escorted around town by shipping-official Payne and catches the eye of gambler-lothario Romero, who has a jealous girlfriend in Miranda. Fun fluff. ♫Romance and Rhumba; Tropical Magic; The Nango; A Weekend in Havana; When I Love, I Love; Maria Inez; Rebola a Bola. **80m/C VHS.** Alice Faye, John Payne, Cesar Romero, Carmen Miranda, Cobina Wright Jr., George Barbier, Sheldon Leonard, Billy Gilbert; **D:** Walter Lang; **W:** Karl Tunberg; **M:** Alfred Newman. *FXV*

Weekend 🎬🎬🎬 1967 A Parisian couple embark on a drive to the country. On the way they witness and are involved in horrifying highway wrecks. Leaving the road they find a different, equally grotesque kind of carnage. Godard's brilliant, surreal, hyper-paranoiac view of modern life was greatly influenced by the fact that his mother was killed in an auto accident in 1954 (he himself suffered a serious motorcycle mishap in 1975). In French with English subtitles. **105m/C VHS.** *FR IT* Mireille Darc, Jean Yanne, Jean-Pierre Kalfon, Valerie Lagrange, Jean-Pierre Leaud, Yves Beneyton; **D:** Jean-Luc Godard; **W:** Jean-Luc Godard; **M:** Antoine Duhamel. *NYF, FCT*

Weekend at Bernie's 🎬🎬½ *Hot and Cold* 1989 (PG-13) Two computer nerds discover embezzlement at their workplace after being invited to their boss's beach house for a weekend party. They find their host murdered. They endeavor to keep up appearances by (you guessed it) dressing and strategically posing the corpse during the party. Kiser as the dead man is memorable, and the two losers gamely keep the silliness flowing. Lots of fun. **101m/C VHS, VHS, Beta.** Andrew McCarthy, Jonathan Silverman, Catherine Mary Stewart, Terry Kiser, Don Calfa, Louis Giambalvo; **D:** Ted Kotcheff; **W:** Robert Klane; **M:** Andy Summers. *LIV*

Weekend at Bernie's 2 🎬½ 1993 (PG) Unlikely but routine sequel to the original's cavorting cadaver slapstick, except now McCarthy and Silverman are frantically hunting for Bernie's (Kiser) cash stash, a quest that takes them and poor dead Bernie to the Caribbean. See Bernie get stuffed in a suitcase, see Bernie hang glide, see Bernie tango, see Bernie attract the opposite sex. Thin script with one-joke premise done to death but fun for those in the mood for the postmortem antics of a comedic stiff. Plenty of well-executed gags involving the well-preserved corpse (particularly one that's been dead for two films now) should lure back fans of the 1989 original. **89m/C VHS, LV, Closed Caption.** Andrew McCarthy, Jonathan Silverman, Terry Kiser, Tom Wright, Steve James, Troy Beyer, Barry Bostwick; **D:** Robert Klane; **W:** Robert Klane; **M:** Peter Wolf. *COL*

Weekend at the Waldorf 🎬🎬🎬 1945 Glossy, americanized remake of "Grand Hotel" set at the famous Park Avenue hotel, the Waldorf-Astoria, in New York City. Turner and Rogers star in the roles originated by Joan Crawford and Greta Garbo. Johnson and Pidgeon play their love interests. Combining drawing room comedy with slapstick and a touch of romance proved to be a hit, as this film was one of the top grossers of 1945 and was just what war-weary moviegoers wanted to see. Based on the play "Grand Hotel" by Vicki Baum. **130m/B VHS.** Ginger Rogers, Walter Pidgeon, Van Johnson, Lana Turner, Robert Benchley, Edward Arnold, Leon Ames, Warner Anderson, Phyllis Thaxter, Keenan Wynn, Porter Hall, Samuel S. Hinds; **D:** Robert Z. Leonard; **W:** Samuel Spewack, Bella Spewack, Guy Bolton. *MGM*

A Weekend in the Country 🎬🎬½ 1996 (R) Ensemble comedy finds a varied group of couples and would-be couples traveling to California's wine country for a weekend of relaxation at a bed and breakfast inn. Nothing quite works out as planned but Cupid's arrow does strike. Made for cable movie filmed on location in Temecula, CA.**CW:** Some language. **94m/C VHS, Closed Caption.** Rita Rudner, Faith Ford, Christine Lahti, Jack Lemmon, Richard Lewis, Dudley Moore, Betty White, Dan Cortese, Jennifer Elise Cox; **D:** Martin Bergman; **W:** Rita Rudner, Martin Bergman; **M:** Patrick Williams. *HMK*

Weekend of Shadows 🎬🎬🎬 1977 Confident, moralistic murder drama about a posse after an innocent immigrant they believe has killed a woman. Police sergeant Roberts is interested only in his reputation, not in justice. Posse member Waters begins to sympathize with the hunted man and defends his innocence. Intelligent, well-conceived, and professionally directed. **94m/C VHS, Beta.** John Waters, Melissa Jaffer, Graeme Blundell, Wyn Roberts, Barbara West, Graham Rouse; **D:** Tom Jeffrey.

Weekend Pass 🎬 1984 (R) Moronic rookie sailors who have just completed basic training are out on a weekend pass, determined to forget everything they have learned. They find this surprisingly easy to do. **92m/C VHS, Beta, LV.** D.W. Brown, Peter Ellenstein, Phil Hartman, Patrick Hauser, Chip McAllister; **D:** Lawrence Bassoff; **W:** Lawrence Bassoff; **C:** Bryan England. *LIV, VES*

Weekend War 🎬🎬½ 1988 (PG-13) A group of National Guardsmen are sent to the Honduras for their annual tour of duty. But when a guerilla war between Honduras and Nicaragua breaks out, the Guardsmen are forced to fight for their lives. The "Bridge on the River Kwai" finale features the dilemma over a bridge linking the two countries. Made for television.**CW:** War violence. **96m/C VHS.** Daniel Stern, Stephen Collins, Charles Haid, Evan Mirand, Michael Beach, Scott Paulin, James Tolkan; **D:** Steven Hilliard Stern; **M:** Brad Fiedel. *COL*

Weekend Warriors 🎬½ 1986 (R) Young film-studio employees evade the draft in 1961 by enlisting for National Guard weekend duty. Grade "C" dumb comedy from professional celebrity and first-time director Convy. **88m/C VHS, Beta.** Chris Lemmon, Lloyd Bridges, Daniel Greene, Tom Villard, Vic Tayback; **D:** Bert Convy; **W:** Bruce Belland; **M:** Perry Botkin. *LIV*

Weekend with the Babysitter woof! *Weekend Babysitter* 1970 (R) Sordid teen drama about a weekend babysitter who goes to a film director's house and babysits everyone but the kids, running into a heroin-smuggling ring along the way. Casting-couch story with a twist. **93m/C VHS, Beta.** Susan Roman, George E. Carey, James Almanzar, Luanne Roberts; **D:** Don Henderson. *PSM*

Weep No More My Lady 🎬🎬 1993 (PG-13) Suspense-filled whodunit about a wealthy businessman who comes between two sisters and a sibling rivalry that turns into a deadly game of murder. Based on the best-selling book by Mary Higgins Clark. **92m/C VHS, Closed Caption.** Daniel J. Travanti, Shelley Winters, Kristin Scott Thomas. *REP*

Weird Science 🎬🎬 1985 (PG-13) Hall is appealing, and Hughes can write dialogue for teens with the best of them. However, many of the jokes are in poor taste, and the movie seems to go on forever. Hall and his nerdy cohort Mitchell-Smith use a very special kind of software to create the ideal woman who wreaks zany havoc in their lives from the outset. **94m/C VHS, Beta, LV, Closed Caption.** Kelly Le Brock, Anthony Michael Hall, Ilan Mitchell-Smith, Robert Downey Jr., Bill Paxton; **D:** John Hughes; **W:** John Hughes; **C:** Matthew F. Leonetti; **M:** Ira Newborn. *USH*

Weird Woman/Frozen Ghost 194? In 1944's "Weird Woman" professor Chaney and his South Seas bride suffer the wrath of a jealous woman. In 1945's "The Frozen Ghost" hypnotist Chaney is ruined when a volunteer dies on stage. He relaxes at a friend's (who happens to own a wax museum) where he comes under a diabolical plot to drive him mad. Based on radio's "The Inner Sanctum Mysteries." **?m/C VHS.** Lon Chaney Jr., Evelyn Ankers, Ralph Morgan, Lois Collier, Douglass Dumbrille, Elena Verdugo. *USH*

Weird World of LSD 🎬½ 1967 Cheap exploitation film featuring the evil effects of LSD. **?m/C VHS.** Terry Tessem, Ann Lindsay, Yolanda Morino. *SNC, TPV*

The Weirdo 🎬 1989 "The Jerk" meets Freddie Krueger. This film is absolutely wretched, even by horror movie standards. **91m/C VHS, Beta.** Steve Burlington, Jessica Straus; **D:** Andy Milligan. *NO*

Welcome Back Mr. Fox 1983 An award-winning science fiction short wherein an obnoxious movie producer cheats death by being cryogenically frozen, and then wakes up years later no wiser for the experience. Suitably, he receives his comeuppance. **21m/C VHS, Beta.** E.D. Phillips, Gustav Vintas; **D:** Walter W. Pitt III. *NO*

Welcome Home 🎬🎬 1989 (R) A missing-in-action Vietnam vet (Kristofferson) leaves his wife and children in Cambodia to return to America more than 15 years after he was reported dead. He finds his first wife remarried and discovers a teen-aged son he unknowingly fathered. This plotless, sporadically-moving film was Schaffner's last. Made for cable television. **92m/C VHS, Beta, LV.** Kris Kristofferson, JoBeth Williams, Sam Waterston, Brian Keith, Trey Wilson, Thomas Wilson Brown; **D:** Franklin J. Schaffner; **C:** Fred W. Koenekamp; **M:** Henry Mancini. *VES, LIV*

Welcome Home, Roxy Carmichael 🎬🎬 1990 (PG-13) Ryder, as a young misfit, is the bright spot in this deadpan, would-be satire. Hollywood star Roxy Charmichael returns to her small Ohio hometown and begins fantasizing that she is really her mother. It is obvious why this deadpan, hard-to-follow movie was a box-office flop. **98m/C VHS, Beta, LV, 8mm, Closed Caption.** Winona Ryder, Jeff Daniels, Laila Robins, Dinah Manoff, Ava Fabian, Robbie Kiger, Sachi Parker; **D:** Jim Abrahams; **C:** Paul Elliott. *PAR*

Welcome Stranger 🎬🎬½ 1947 New doctor's ideas clash with the old doctor's ways in a small town until the younger saves the live of the elder. Crosby and Fitzgerald star as the two clashing medics in this reunion of the cast of "Going My Way." He wins the heart of the town and the heart of local teacher Caulfield in the meantime. Sheekman's script calls for Marx Brothers'-like comedy and director Nugent appears in a cameo as another doctor. **107m/B VHS, Closed Caption.** Bing Crosby, Barry Fitzgerald, Joan Caulfield, Wanda Hendrix, Frank Faylen, Elizabeth Patterson, Robert Shayne, Don Beddoe, Percy Kilbride, Larry Young; **Cameos:** Elliott Nugent; **D:** Elliott Nugent; **W:** Arthur Sheekman; **C:** Lionel Lindon; **M:** Johnny Burke, James Van Heusen. *USH*

Welcome to Blood City 🎬½ 1977 An anonymous totalitarian organization kidnaps a man and transports him electronically to a fantasy western town where the person who murders the most people becomes the town's "kill master."

Amateurish and low-budget. **96m/C VHS, Beta.** Jack Palance, Keir Dullea, Samantha Eggar, Barry Morse. *LIV*

Welcome to 18 🐾 1987 (PG-13) Three girls, just out of high school, take summer jobs at a dude ranch, work a local casino, flirt, tease and get in trouble. The movie isn't funny in the least, and is filled with utter nonsense. Hargitay is the daughter of actress Jayne Mansfield. **91m/C VHS, Beta.** Courtney Thorne-Smith, Mariska Hargitay, Jo Ann Willette, Christine Kaufmann; **D:** Terry Carr. *LIV*

Welcome to L.A. 🐾🐾🐾 1977 (R) Rudolph's ambitious directorial debut focuses on the sexual escapades of a group of Southern Californians. Based on the music suite "City of the One Night Stands" by Baskin, which also (unfortunately) serves as the soundtrack. Rudolph improved greatly after this initial effort. **106m/C VHS, Beta, Closed Caption.** Sissy Spacek, Sally Kellerman, Keith Carradine, Geraldine Chaplin, Lauren Hutton, Viveca Lindfors, Harvey Keitel, John Considine; **D:** Alan Rudolph; **W:** Alan Rudolph; **M:** Richard Baskin. *FOX*

Welcome to Spring Break 🐾½ 1988 (R) College co-eds are stalked by a killer on the beaches of Florida. **92m/C VHS, Beta, LV.** John Saxon, Michael Parks. *NO*

Welcome to the Dollhouse 🐾🐾½ 1995 (R) Eleven-year-old, glasses-wearing Dawn Wiener (Matarazzo) is the middle child of a middle-class family in an average New Jersey town. It's her first year in junior high and Dawn's bewildered—by school, by family, by life in general and where she fits in. Puberty sucks.**CW:** Language. **87m/C VHS, LV, Closed Caption.** Heather Matarazzo, Brendan Sexton III, Daria Kalinina, Matthew Faber, Angela Pietropinto, Eric Mabius; **D:** Todd Solondz; **W:** Todd Solondz; **C:** Randy Drummond; **M:** Jill Wisoff. Independent Spirit Awards '97: Debut Performance (Matarazzo); Sundance Film Festival '96: Grand Jury Prize; Nominations: Independent Spirit Awards '97: Best Director (Solondz), Best Film, Best Supporting Actor (Faber), Debut Performance (Sexton). *COL*

The Well 🐾🐾🐾 1951 A young black girl disappears and a white man (Morgan) is accused of kidnapping her. When it is discovered that the girl is trapped in a deep well, Morgan's expertise is needed to help free her. **85m/B VHS, Beta.** Richard Rober, Harry (Henry) Morgan, Barry Kelley, Christine Larson; **D:** Leo Popkin, Russel Rouse; **C:** Ernest Laszlo. Nominations: Academy Awards '51: Best Film Editing, Best Story & Screenplay. *VCI*

Well-Digger's Daughter 🐾🐾🐾 *La Fille Du Puisatier* 1946 As her lover goes off to war, a well-digger's daughter discovers that she is pregnant causing both sets of parents to feud over who's to blame. This is the first film made in France after the end of WWII and marks the return of the French film industry. In French with English subtitles. **142m/B VHS, Beta.** Raimu, Josette Day, Fernandel, Charpin; **D:** Marcel Pagnol. *NOS, DVT, APD*

Wend Kuuni 🐾🐾 *God's Gift* 1982 A fable for modern times set in Burkina Faso before the coming of Islam or Christianity. A mute, memoryless child is found by a peddler and adopted by the peddler's village. One day the boy finds a body hanging from a tree. Shocked, he recovers his speech and tells the story of his tragic past, when he and his mother were cast out of their own village. When his mother dies, the boy is bereft of family and tradition. Without these ties to his history he loses both speech and memory. In More with English subtitles. **70m/C VHS.** **D:** Gaston Kabore. *KIV*

We're Back! A Dinosaur's Story 🐾🐾½ 1993 (G) Animated adventures of a pack of revived dinosaurs who return to their old stomping grounds—which are now modern-day New York City. Smart-mouth human boy Louie and his girlfriend Cecilia take the dinos under their wing (so to speak), wise them up to modern life, and try to prevent their capture by the evil Professor Screweyes. Slow-moving with some violence.

Adapted from the book by Hudson Talbott. **78m/C VHS, LV.** **D:** Dick Zondag, Ralph Zondag, Phil Nibbelink, Simon Wells; **W:** John Patrick Shanley; **V:** John Goodman, Felicity Kendal, Walter Cronkite, Joey Shea, Jay Leno, Julia Child, Kenneth Mars, Martin Short, Rhea Perlman, Rene LeVant, Blaze Berdahl, Charles Fleischer, Yeardley Smith. *USH*

We're in the Legion Now 🐾½ 1937 Denny and Barnett star as a couple of American gangsters who join the French Foreign Legion to escape rival hoods from back home. **56m/B VHS, Beta, 8mm.** Reginald Denny, Vince Barnett, Esther Ralston. *VYY*

We're in the Navy Now 1927 The famed comedy duo is back again with another armed forces farce. A mild successor to "Behind the Front." **60m/B VHS, Beta.** Wallace Beery, Raymond Hatton. *GPV, FCT*

We're No Angels 🐾🐾½ 1955 Three escapees from Devil's Island hide out with the family of a kindly French storekeeper. One of Bogart's few comedies. From the French stage play of the same name. Claustrophobic and talky. Later remade with De Niro and Penn. **103m/C VHS, Beta.** Humphrey Bogart, Aldo Ray, Joan Bennett, Peter Ustinov, Basil Rathbone, Leo G. Carroll; **D:** Michael Curtiz; **C:** Loyal Griggs. *PAR*

We're No Angels 🐾🐾½ 1989 (R) Two escaped cons disguise themselves as priests and get in the appropriate series of jams. De Niro and Penn play off each other well, turning in fine comic performances. Distantly related to the 1955 film of the same name and the David Mamet play. **110m/C VHS, Beta, LV, Closed Caption.** Robert De Niro, Sean Penn, Demi Moore, Hoyt Axton, Bruno Kirby, James Russo, John C. Reilly, Ray McAnally, Wallace Shawn; **D:** Neil Jordan; **W:** David Mamet; **C:** Philippe Rousselot; **M:** George Fenton. *PAR*

We're Not Dressing 🐾🐾🐾 1934 Loose musical adaptation of J.M. Barrie's "The Admirable Crichton" with the butler transformed into singing sailor Crosby. Fabulously wealthy heiress Lombard invites her pals for a South Seas yachting adventure. Only the ship gets wrecked and everyone winds up on a small island where the practical Crosby whips everyone into shape (and romances Lombard). Burns and Allen supply additional comedy as a pair of botanists who just happen to be studying the local fauna. ♫Good Night Lovely Little Lady; I'll Sing About the Birds and the Bees; It's Just a New Spanish Custom; Let's Play House; Love Thy Neighbor; May I?; Once in a Blue Moon; She Reminds Me of You. **74m/B VHS, LV, Closed Caption.** Bing Crosby, Carole Lombard, George Burns, Gracie Allen, Ethel Merman, Leon Errol, Ray Milland; **D:** Norman Taurog; **W:** Horace Jackson, Francis Martin; **M:** Harry Revel, Mack Gordon. *USH*

We're Not Married 🐾🐾🐾 1952 Five couples learn that they are not legally married when a judge realizes his license expired before he performed the ceremonies. The story revolves around this quintet of couples who now must cope with whether or not they really do want to be married. Although the episodes vary in quality, the Allen-Rogers sequence is excellent. Overall, the cast performs well in this lightweight comedy. **85m/B VHS, Closed Caption.** Ginger Rogers, Fred Allen, Victor Moore, Marilyn Monroe, Paul Douglas, David Wayne, Eve Arden, Louis Calhern, Zsa Zsa Gabor, James Gleason, Jane Darwell, Eddie Bracken, Mitzi Gaynor; **D:** Edmund Goulding; **W:** Nunnally Johnson, Dwight Taylor. *FXV*

We're Talkin' Serious Money 🐾🐾½ 1992 (PG-13) Sal and Charlie are a couple of loser scam-artists always after the elusive big score. They borrow $10,000 from the mob for another get-rich-quick scheme and wind up over their heads with both the mob and the FBI out to get them. **92m/C VHS, LV.** Dennis Farina, Leo Rossi, Fran Drescher, John Lamotta; **D:** James Lemmo; **W:** Leo Rossi, James Lemmo; **M:** Scott Grusin. *COL*

Werewolf 🐾 1995 (R) A remote desert town is stricken by an ancient curse that turns its occupants into werewolves at the full moon. This doesn't help the tourism industry.**CW:** Sex scene. **99m/C VHS, LV.** George Rivero, Fred Cavalli, Adrianna Miles, Richard Lynch, Joe Estevez, R.C. Bates, Heidi Bjorn, Randall Oliver, Nena Belini, Tony Zarindast; **D:** Tony Zarindast; **W:** Tony Zarindast; **C:** Robert Hayes, Dan Gilman. *APX*

Werewolf in a Girl's Dormitory 🐾 *Lycanthropus; The Ghoul in School* 1961 Girls' school headmaster undergoes dental transformation at night. Atrocious dubbing, with equally atrocious theme song "The Ghoul in School." **82m/B VHS.** *IT* Barbara Lass, Carl Schell, Curt Lowens, Maurice Marsac; **D:** Richard Benson. *SMW, SNC*

Werewolf of London 🐾🐾½ 1935 A scientist searching for a rare Tibetan flower is attacked by a werewolf. He scoffs at the legend, but once he's back in London, he goes on a murderous rampage every time the moon is full. Dated but worth watching as the first werewolf movie made. **75m/B VHS.** Henry Hull, Warner Oland, Valerie Hobson, Lester Matthews, Spring Byington; **D:** Stuart Walker. *USH*

Werewolf of Washington 🐾🐾 1973 (PG) Stockwell is a White House press secretary with a problem—he turns into a werewolf. And bites the President, among others. Sub-plot involves a short mad scientist who operates a secret monster-making lab in a White House bathroom. Occasionally engaging horror spoof and political satire made during Watergate era. **90m/C VHS, Beta.** Dean Stockwell, Biff Maguire, Clifton James; **D:** Milton Moses Ginsberg. *NO*

The Werewolf vs. the Vampire Woman 🐾½ *Blood Moon* 1970 (R) Hirsute Spanish wolfman teams with two female students in search of witch's tomb. One is possessed by the witch, and eponymous title results. **82m/C VHS.** *SP GE* Paul Naschy, Gaby Fuchs, Barbara Capell, Patty Shepard, Valerie Samarine, Julio Pena, Andres Resino; **D:** Leon Klimovsky. *SNC, HEG*

Werewolves on Wheels woof! 1971 (R) A group of bikers are turned into werewolves due to a Satanic spell. A serious attempt at a biker/werewolf movie, however, too violent and grim, not at all funny, and painful to sit through. McGuire had a hit with "Eve of Destruction." **85m/C VHS, Beta.** Stephen Oliver, Severn Darden, Donna Anderson, Duece Barry, Billy Gray, Barry McGuire; **D:** Michel Levesque. *UNI*

Wes Craven Presents Mind Ripper 🐾🐾 *Mind Ripper* 1995 (R) A top secret government experiment, intended to produce a superhuman, goes wrong and traps the scientists in a remote desert outpost with their deadly, pissed-off creation.**CW:** Sci-fi gore; some language. **90m/C VHS.** Lance Henriksen, John Diehl, Natasha Gregson Wagner, Dan Blom, Claire Stansfield; **D:** Joe Gayton; **W:** Jonathan Craven, Phil Mittleman; **C:** Fernando Arguelles; **M:** J. Peter Robinson. *AVE*

Wes Craven's New Nightmare 🐾🐾🐾 1994 (R) Seems the six previous conjurings of Freddy's tortured but fictional soul have inadvertently created a real supernatural force bent on tormenting the lives of retired scream queen Langenkamp, her son (Hughes), writer-director Craven, and surprisingly mild alter-ego Englund. Craven's solution is to write a script that reunites series principals for a final showdown with the slashmaster in Hell. Clever and original in a genre known for neither trait, this movie-in-a-movie-about-a-movie is equal parts playful gimmick and inspired terror that will give even the most seasoned Kruegerphile the heebie-jeebies.**CW:** explicit horror, violence, and gore; language **112m/C VHS, LV, Closed Caption.** Robert Englund, Heather Langenkamp, Miko Hughes, David Newsom, Tracy Middendorf, Fran Bennett, John Saxon, Wes Craven, Robert Shaye, Sara Risher, Marianne Maddalena; **D:** Wes Craven; **W:** Wes Craven; **C:** Mark Irwin; **M:**

J. Peter Robinson. Nominations: Independent Spirit Awards '95: Best Film. *NLC*

West-Bound Limited 🎬🎬½ 1923 A Romantic adventurer rescues a girl from certain death as a train is about to hit her, and the two fall in love. Lucky for him, she happens to be the boss' daughter. This film is a good example of classic silent melodrama with music score. **70m/B VHS, Beta.** John Harron, Ella Hall, Claire McDowell. *VYY*

West of Nevada 🎬🎬 1936 A rare film, featuring the former Lieutenant Governor of Nevada (and Clara Bow's husband) in a fast-moving adventure about a band of Indians who must protect their gold from thieves. Bell is the good guy who aids the Indians. **59m/B VHS, Beta.** Rex Bell, Joan Barclay, Al "Fuzzy" St. John, Steve Clark. *GVV*

West of Pinto Basin 🎬🎬 1940 The Range Busters are riding around checking the territory for badmen in this tale of the old west. The music score includes "That Little Prairie Gal of Mine," "Rhythm of the Saddle," and "Ridin' the Trail Tonight." **60m/B VHS, Beta.** Ray Corrigan, Max Terhune, John "Dusty" King, Jack Perrin. *NOS*

West of the Divide 🎬🎬½ 1934 A young cowboy (Wayne) impersonates an outlaw in order to hunt down his father's killer and find his missing younger brother. He saves a proud rancher and his feisty daughter along the way. A remake of "Partners of the Trail," and a solid early Wayne oater. **53m/B VHS, Beta.** John Wayne, George "Gabby" Hayes, Lloyd Whitlock, Yakima Canutt; **D:** Robert North Bradbury. *COL, REP, NOS*

West of the Law 🎬🎬 1942 A group of ranchers turn to lawmen for protection from a band of outlaws. Part of the Rough Riders series. **60m/B VHS, Beta.** Buck Jones, Tim McCoy, Raymond Hatton; **D:** Howard Bretherton. *NOS, VCN, DVT*

West of the Pecos 🎬🎬½ 1945 Rill (Hale) is a society gal on her way to the family ranch in Texas. She's disguised as a boy for safety, which turns out to be a smart idea when outlaws attack the stagecoach. Fortunately, Pecos Smith (Mitchum) is also around to lend a hand. Based on the novel by Zane Grey; first filmed in 1935. **66m/B VHS.** Robert Mitchum, Barbara Hale, Richard Martin, Thurston Hall, Rita (Paula) Corday, Russell Hopton, Harry Woods; **D:** Edward Killy; **C:** Russell Metty. *GPV*

West of Zanzibar 🎬🎬½ 1928 Chaney plays an ivory trader, ruling a jungle kingdom, who lives for revenge on the man who left him a cripple. He decides to ruin the man's daughter and turn her into a prostitute but his plan backfires. Chaney and director Browning offer a steamy atmosphere amidst a number of script flaws. **63m/B VHS, LV.** Lon Chaney Sr., Lionel Barrymore, Warner Baxter, Mary Nolan; **D:** Tod Browning. *FCT*

The West Point Story 🎬🎬½ Fine and Dandy 1950 Cagney stars as an on-the-skids Broadway director offered a job staging a show at West Point. Seems cadet MacRae has written a musical and his uncle happens to be a producer. Cagney, with girlfriend Mayo, finds all the rules and regulations getting the better of his temper, so much so that he's told unless he can conform to academy standards the show won't go on! Day is the showgirl MacRae falls for. Cagney's energy and charm carry the too-long film but it's not one of his better musical efforts. 🎵Ten Thousand Sheep; You Love Me; By the Kissing Rock; Long Before I Knew You; Brooklyn; It Could Only Happen in Brooklyn; Military Polka. **107m/B VHS.** James Cagney, Virginia Mayo, Gordon MacRae, Doris Day, Roland Winters, Gene Nelson, Alan Hale Jr., Wilton Graff, Jerome Cowan; **D:** Roy Del Ruth; **W:** John Monks Jr., Charles Hoffman, Irving Wallace; **M:** Sammy Cahn, Jule Styne. Nominations: Academy Awards '50: Scoring of a Musical. *WAR, MVD*

West Side Story 🎬🎬🎬½ 1961 Gang rivalry and ethnic tension on New York's West Side erupts in a ground-breaking musical. Loosely based on Shakespeare's "Romeo and Juliet," the story follows the Jets and the Sharks as they fight for their turf while Tony and Maria fight for love. Features frenetic and brilliant choreography by co-director Robbins, who also directed the original Broadway show, and a high-caliber score by Bernstein and Sondheim. Wood's voice was dubbed by Marni Nixon and Jimmy Bryant dubbed Beymer's. The laserdisc version includes the complete storyboards, production sketches, re-issue trailer, and an interview with Wise in a letterbox format with digital stereo surround sound. 🎵Prologue; Jet Song; Something's Coming; Dance at the Gym; Maria; America; Tonight; One Hand, One Heart; Gee, Officer Krupke. **151m/C VHS, Beta, LV, Closed Caption.** Natalie Wood, Richard Beymer, Russ Tamblyn, Rita Moreno, George Chakiris, Simon Oakland, Ned Glass; **D:** Robert Wise, Jerome Robbins; **W:** Ernest Lehman; **C:** Daniel F. Fapp; **M:** Leonard Bernstein, Stephen Sondheim. Academy Awards '61: Best Art Direction/Set Decoration (Color), Best Color Cinematography, Best Costume Design (Color), Best Director (Wise), Best Film Editing, Best Picture, Best Sound, Best Supporting Actor (Chakiris), Best Supporting Actress (Moreno), Scoring of a Musical; Directors Guild of America Awards '61: Best Director (Wise), Best Director (Robbins); Golden Globe Awards '62: Best Film—Musical/Comedy, Best Supporting Actor (Chakiris), Best Supporting Actress (Moreno); New York Film Critics Awards '61: Best Film; Nominations: Academy Awards '61: Best Adapted Screenplay. *MGM, OM*

West to Glory 🎬½ 1947 Glory isn't necessarily exciting, as the hero helps a Mexican rancher save his gold and jewels from evildoers in this slow-paced oater. **61m/B VHS, Beta.** Eddie Dean, Roscoe Ates, Dolores Castle, Gregg Barton, Alex Montoya, Harry Vejar; **D:** Ray Taylor. *NOS*

Western 🎬🎬 1996 Spaniard Paco (Lopez), a traveling rep for a shoe manufacturer in France, picks up hitchhiking Russian emigre Nino (Bourdo) and soon finds himself minus car, shoe samples, and luggage. He's rescued by local beauty Marinette (Vitali) and, since he's been fired, decides to hang around the town where she lives. But when Paco spots Nino again, he promptly beats him up, sending the Russian to the hospital. Oddly, this serves as a bond for the two men and they decide to do a little traveling through Brittany together, with Paco trying to teach the naive Nino how to pick up pretty girls. Funny, if extended, French road trip. French with subtitles. **136m/C VHS.** **FR** Sergei Lopez, Sacha Bourdo, Elisabeth Vitali, Marie Matheron, Basile Siekoua; **D:** Manuel Poirier; **W:** Jean-Francois Goyet, Manuel Poirier; **C:** Nara Keo Kosal; **M:** Bernardo Sandoval. Cannes Film Festival '97: Special Jury Prize. *NYR*

Western Double Feature 1 1938 In "Utah" (1945, 55 minutes), Rogers foils a land swindle and helps a lady ranch owner; in "Man from Music Mountain" (1938, 60 minutes), Autry foils a worthless gold mining stock swindle. **115m/B VHS, Beta.** Roy Rogers, Dale Evans, George "Gabby" Hayes, Gene Autry, Smiley Burnette; **D:** Joseph Kane. *HHT*

Western Double Feature 1: Wild Bill & Sunset Carson 194? Double feature: in "Calling Wild Bill Elliott" (1943), Wild Bill comes to the aid of homesteaders; in "Santa Fe Saddlemates" (1945), Carson breaks up a diamond smuggling ring. **120m/B VHS, Beta.** Wild Bill Elliott, Sunset Carson; **D:** Spencer Gordon Bennet. *MED*

Western Double Feature 2 1933 Wayne and Hayes are teamed together in two hour-long B-westerns: "Star Packer" (1934) and "West of the Divide" (1933). **120m/B VHS, Beta.** John Wayne, George "Gabby" Hayes; **D:** Robert North Bradbury. *HHT*

Western Double Feature 2: Wayne & Hale Nightriders; Home on the Range 198? Double feature; in "Night Riders" (1939), Wayne battles injustice; in "Home on the Range" (1946, color), Hale protects a wild animal refuge. **120m/B VHS, Beta.** John Wayne, Monte Hale; **D:** George Sherman. *MED*

Western Double Feature 3 1936 Two Wayne westerns are on this tape: "Helltown" (1938, 59 minutes), in which Wayne catches a cattle rustler; and "Winds of the Wasteland" (1936, 54 minutes), where he plays an out-of-work Pony Express rider. **113m/B VHS, Beta.** John Wayne, Johnny Mack Brown, Marsha Hunt, Phyllis Fraser; **D:** Charles T. Barton, Mack V. Wright. *HHT*

Western Double Feature 3: Rogers & Allen 1950 Double feature. In "Twilight in the Sierras" (1950), Rogers catches a gang of crooks; in "Under Mexicali Stars" (1950), Allen is a cowboy who uncovers a counterfeiting ring. **134m/C VHS, Beta.** Roy Rogers, Dale Evans, Rex Allen; **D:** William Witney. *MED*

Western Double Feature 4 1937 Rogers plays a dual role in a case of mistaken identity in "Billy the Kid Returns" (1938, 56 minutes); in "Round Up Time in Texas" (1937, 56 minutes), Autry is framed on a charge of diamond smuggling. **112m/B VHS, Beta.** Roy Rogers, Gene Autry, Smiley Burnette; **D:** Joseph Kane. *HHT*

Western Double Feature 4: Rogers & Evans Don't Fence Me In; Sheriff of Wichita 194? In "Don't Fence Me In" (1945), Rogers helps out a woman reporter; in "Sheriff of Wichita" (1948), a frontier investigator solves a crime. **120m/B VHS, Beta.** Roy Rogers, Dale Evans, George "Gabby" Hayes, Allan "Rocky" Lane. *MED*

Western Double Feature 5 1935 Wayne stars in both halves of this double feature: in "Desert Trail" (1935, 54 minutes), he plays a rodeo star; in "Man from Utah" (1934, 55 minutes), he brings a gang of murderers to justice. **109m/B VHS, Beta.** John Wayne, Polly Ann Young; **D:** Robert North Bradbury. *HHT*

Western Double Feature 5: Rogers & Autry 1937 "The Big Show" (1937) features songs, action, and horses; in "Home in Oklahoma" (1946), Roger tracks down a murderer. **108m/B VHS, Beta.** Gene Autry, Roy Rogers, Smiley Burnette; **D:** Mack V. Wright, William Witney. *MED*

Western Double Feature 6: Rogers & Trigger Trigger, Jr.; Gangs of Sonora 1950 "Trigger Jr." (1950) is the story of Trigger's colt; "Gangs of Sonora" (1941, black and white) deals with a fight to save a small frontier newspaper. **120m/C VHS, Beta.** Roy Rogers, Dale Evans, Bob Livingston, Bob Steele; **D:** William Witney. *MED*

Western Double Feature 7: Wild Bill & Crabbe Phantom of the Plains; Prairie Rustlers 1945 "Phantom of the Plains" deals with a plan to save a woman from a gigolo; "Prairie Rustlers" tells of the problems of a man who is the identical double of Billy the Kid. **120m/B VHS, Beta.** Wild Bill Elliott, Buster Crabbe. *MED*

Western Double Feature 8: Hale & Carradine 194? In "Silver Spurs" (1943), ranchers wanting to get the right-of-way through oil land run into an ambitious resort owner; in "Out California Way" (1946), Hale is a young cowboy looking for work in Hollywood. **121m/B VHS, Beta.** Roy Rogers, Monte Hale, John Carradine. *MED*

Western Double Feature 9: LaRue & Beery 194? In "Cheyenne Takes Over" (1947), LaRue battles outlaws; in "Tulsa Kid" (1940), a young man must face a gunfighter. **120m/B VHS, Beta.** Lash LaRue, Donald (Don "Red") Barry, Noah Beery Sr. *MED*

Western Double Feature 10: Roy, Dale, & Trigger 198? In "Bells of Coronado" (1950), Rogers must solve a murder and uranium ore theft; in "King of the Cowboys" (1943, black and white), Roy investigates a band of saboteurs. **120m/C VHS, Beta.** Roy Rogers, Dale Evans; **D:** William Witney. *MED*

Western Double Feature 11 1950 Roy and Trigger act as modern day Robin Hoods to end crooked dealing in the West; Roy hides behind a smile and a song to capture murderers of a deputy and a ranch owner. **121m/B VHS, Beta.** Roy Rogers, Penny Edwards, Gordon Jones, George "Gabby" Hayes. *MED*

Western Double Feature 12 1944 Red Ryder learns of a plot to scare ranchers into selling out before an oil strike is discovered; the Three Musketeers are sent to the Caribbean as U.S. envoys to sell Army horses. 108m/B VHS, Beta. Bob Livingston, Wild Bill Elliott, Duncan Renaldo, Robert (Bobby) Blake. MED

Western Double Feature 13 194? Red Ryder foils outlaws trying to swindle the Duchess' stage line in a small isolated town in "Wagon Wheels Westward" (1945). "Rocky Mountain Rangers" (1940), features the Three Mesquiteers pursuing the deadly Barton Gang. 108m/B VHS, Beta. Red Ryder, Bob Livingston, Robert (Bobby) Blake. MED

Western Double Feature 14 1952 Outlaws, good guys, and romance on the old frontier. Amateur Robin Hoods steal back money wrongfully taken. 123m/C VHS, Beta. Tim Holt, Jack Holt, Nan Leslie, Noreen Nash. MED

Western Double Feature 15 1950 Rogers breaks up a cattle rustling ring; the good guys try to bring law and order to a vast Wyoming territory plagued by a crooked political boss. 122m/B VHS, Beta. Roy Rogers, Penny Edwards, Donald (Don "Red") Barry, Lynn Merrick. MED

Western Double Feature 16 1946 Autry is sent to quell a revolution in Mexico; Rogers's horse Lady and Hayes's horse Golden Sovereign are the focal points of the second part of this double feature. 108m/B VHS, Beta. Gene Autry, Smiley Burnette, Roy Rogers, George "Gabby" Hayes. MED

Western Double Feature 17 194? Rogers stars in "The Golden Stallion" (1949). Roy battles diamond smugglers who use wild horses to transport the goods. "The Cherokee Flash" (1945), starring Carson, deals with a respectable citizen's outlaw past catching up to him. 121m/C VHS, Beta. Roy Rogers, Sunset Carson; D: William Witney. MED

Western Double Feature 18 194? A Rogers double feature: in "Eyes of Texas" (1948), a westerner turns his ranch into a camp for war-orphaned boys; in "Helldorado" (1946), Roy travels to Las Vegas. 108m/B VHS, Beta. Roy Rogers, Andy Devine, Dale Evans; D: William Witney. MED

Western Double Feature 19 1945 Rogers helps a young woman foil a plot by crooks to swindle her inheritance. Roy appears in his first starring role (1938) and fights an outlaw gang. 108m/B VHS, Beta. Roy Rogers, Dale Evans, Pat Brady. MED

Western Double Feature 21 194? Roy battles crooks in "Susanna Pass" (1949). In "Sheriff of Las Vegas" (1944), Red must find the murderer of Judge Blackwell. 121m/C VHS, Beta. Roy Rogers, Red Ryder, Dale Evans, Robert (Bobby) Blake; D: William Witney. MED

Western Double Feature 22 194? A Rogers double feature: "Under California Stars" (1948), Roy rounds up a gang of wild horse rustlers; "San Fernando Valley" (1944), Roy brings law and order to the valley. 108m/B VHS, Beta. Roy Rogers; D: William Witney. MED

Western Double Feature 24 194? In "Cowboy and the Senorita" (1944), Roy solves the mystery of a missing girl. "Colorado Serenade" (1946) is a musical western in Cinecolor starring Dean. 122m/C VHS, Beta. Roy Rogers, Dale Evans, Eddie Dean. MED

Western Frontier 🐾🐾 1935 Ordinary cowpoke Maynard is called on to lead the fight against a band of outlaws led by the Indian-raised sister he never knew he had. Action-packed, fast, and fun. Maynard's first outing for Columbia. 56m/B VHS, Beta. Ken Maynard, Lucille Browne, Nora Lane, Robert "Buzzy" Henry, Frank Yaconelli; D: Al(bert) Herman. NOS, DVT

Western Gold 1937 Western set during the Civil War in which the character played by Smith Ballew is sent west to stop thieves who are stealing gold from the Union. 57m/C VHS. Smith Ballew, Heather Angel, Leroy Mason, Howard Hickman, Ben Alexander, Frank McGlynn, Otis Harlan, Tom London, Bud Osborne; D: Howard Bretherton. GPV

Western Justice 🐾🐾 1935 Good Guy Steele brings western-style justice to a lawless town. Ordinary oater with horses, etc., and a few chuckles on the side. 56m/B VHS, Beta. Bob Steele; D: Robert North Bradbury. VTR, NOS

Western Mail 🐾🐾 1942 Yet another western in which the hero goes undercover so he can bring the bad guys to justice. Yaconelli plays a guitar tune, accompanied by his monkey. 54m/B VHS. Tom Keene, Frank Yaconelli, Leroy Mason, Jean Trent, Fred Kohler Jr.; D: Robert Emmett Tansey. NOS, DVT, HEG

Western Pacific Agent 🐾🐾 1951 A Western Pacific agent chases an outlaw who has committed robbery and murder. The agent falls in love with the victim's sister and, of course, prevails. Rather violent. 62m/B VHS, Beta, LV. Kent Taylor, Sheila Ryan, Mickey Knox, Robert Lowery; D: Sam Newfield. NO

Western Trails 🐾 1938 Forgettable western about the clean-up of a Wild West town terrorized by outlaws. Thin script, bad acting, and a little singin' and funnin' around. 59m/B VHS, Beta. Bob Baker, Marjorie Reynolds, Robert Burns; D: George Waggner. NOS, DVT, HEG

Western Union 🐾🐾🐾½ 1941 A lavish, vintage epic romantically detailing the political machinations, Indian warfare and frontier adventure that accompanied the construction of the Western Union telegraph line from Omaha, Nebraska, to Salt Lake City, Utah, during the Civil War. A thoroughly entertaining film in rich Technicolor. This was Lang's second western, following his personal favorite, "The Return of Frank James." Writer Carson utilized the title, but not the storyline, of a Zane Grey book. The German Lang showed himself a master of the most American of genres, yet made only one more western, "Rancho Notorious" (1952), another masterpiece. 94m/C VHS, Beta, Closed Caption. Randolph Scott, Robert Young, Dean Jagger, Slim Summerville, Virginia Gilmore, John Carradine, Chill Wills, Barton MacLane, Minor Watson, Charles Middleton, Irving Bacon; D: Fritz Lang. FOX, MLB

The Westerner 🐾🐾🐾½ 1940 A sly, soft-spoken drifter champions Texas border homesteaders in a land war with the legendary Judge Roy Bean. "The Law West of the Pecos" sentences drifter Cooper to hang, but Cooper breaks out of jail. He falls for damsel Davenport and stays in the area, advocating the rights of homesteaders to Brennan. Brennan's Bean is unforgettable and steals the show from Cooper. Film debuts of actors Tucker and Andrews. Amazing cinematography; Brennan's Oscar was his third, making him the first performer to pull a hat trick. 100m/B VHS, Beta, LV. Gary Cooper, Walter Brennan, Doris Davenport, Dana Andrews, Forrest Tucker, Charles Halton; D: William Wyler; C: Gregg Toland. Academy Awards '40: Best Supporting Actor (Brennan); Nominations: Academy Awards '40: Best Interior Decoration, Best Story. HBO, BTV

Westfront 1918 🐾🐾🐾 1930 A dogmatic anti-war film by the German master (his first talkie), about German and French soldiers on the fields of WWI, dying together without victory. Stunning in its portrayal of war's futility, with excellent photography that achieves a palpable realism. In German with English subtitles. 90m/B VHS, Beta. GE Gustav Diesl, Fritz Kampers, Claus Clausen, Hans Joachim Moebis; D: G.W. Pabst. GLV, NLC

Westward Ho 🐾½ 1935 Wayne is determined to bring to justice his parents' slayer. Haven't we seen this one before? Seems the bad guys have corrupted his brother. Wayne's group

of vigilantes is called "The Singing Riders," so naturally he sings—or is made to appear to. He looks and sounds ridiculous. 55m/B VHS. John Wayne, Sheila Mannors; D: Robert North Bradbury. REP, VCN, NOS

Westward Ho, the Wagons! 🐾½ 1956 The promised land lies in the west, but to get there these pioneers must pass unfriendly savages, thieves, villains, and scoundrels galore. Suitable for family viewing, but why bother? Well, the cast does include four Mouseketeers. 94m/B VHS, Beta. Fess Parker, Kathleen Crowley, Jeff York, Sebastian Cabot, George Reeves; D: William Beaudine; M: George Bruns. DIS

Westward the Women 🐾🐾🐾 1951 Taylor is Buck Wyatt, a scout hired to wagon-train 150 mail-order brides from Chicago to California. When his lustful hired hands turn out to be all hands, Taylor and the ladies must fight off attacking Indians on their own. Notable film allowing women to be as tough as men is not your typical western. Based on the Frank Capra story. 116m/C VHS, Closed Caption. Robert Taylor, Denise Darcel, Hope Emerson, John McIntire, Beverly Dennis, Lenore Lonergan, Marilyn Erskine, Julie Bishop, Renata Vanni, Frankie Darro, George Chandler; D: William A. Wellman; W: Charles Schnee; C: William Mellor; M: Jeff Alexander. MGM

Westworld 🐾🐾🐾 1973 (PG) Crichton wrote and directed this story of an adult vacation resort of the future which offers the opportunity to live in various fantasy worlds serviced by lifelike robots. Brolin and Benjamin are businessmen who choose a western fantasy world. When an electrical malfunction occurs, the robots begin to go berserk. Brynner is perfect as a western gunslinging robot whose skills are all too real. 90m/C VHS, Beta, LV. Yul Brynner, Richard Benjamin, James Brolin, Dick Van Patten, Majel Barrett; D: Michael Crichton; W: Michael Crichton. MGM

Wet and Wild Summer WOOF! 1992 (R) Topless beach resort is the playground for stud lifeguards and sexy resort owners. 95m/C VHS, LV. Christopher Atkins, Elliott Gould, Julian McMahon, Rebecca Cross; D: Maurice Murphy. THV

Wet Gold 🐾 1984 A beautiful young woman and three men journey to retrieve a sunken treasure. Nice scenery. Proves that it is possible to make "The Treasure of the Sierra Madre" without making a classic. John Huston, where are you? Made for television. 90m/C VHS, Beta. Brooke Shields, Brian Kerwin, Burgess Meredith, Tom Byrd; D: Dick Lowry. NO

Wetherby 🐾🐾🐾 1985 (R) Playwright David Hare's first directorial effort, which he also wrote, about a Yorkshire schoolteacher whose life is shattered when a young, brooding stranger comes uninvited to a dinner party, and then shoots himself in her living room. Compelling but oh, so dark. Richardson, who plays a young Redgrave, is actually Redgrave's daughter. 97m/C VHS, Beta, Closed Caption. GB Vanessa Redgrave, Ian Holm, Judi Dench, Joely Richardson, Tim McInnery, Suzanna Hamilton; D: David Hare; W: David Hare; M: Nick Bicat. Berlin International Film Festival '85: Golden Berlin Bear; National Society of Film Critics Awards '85: Best Actress (Redgrave). MGM

Whale for the Killing 🐾🐾½ 1981 An ecologist stranded in a remote Alaskan fishing village battles to save a beached humpbacked whale from a malicious Russian fisherman. Platitudinous and self-congratulatory, if well-meaning. Made for television from a book by Farley Mowat. 145m/C VHS, Beta, Closed Caption. Richard Widmark, Peter Strauss, Dee Wallace Stone, Bruce McGill, Kathryn Walker; D: Richard T. Heffron; M: Basil Poledouris. FOX

Whale Music 🐾🐾 1994 Off-beat saga of a burned-out rock star and the runaway who invades his life. Desmond Howl (Chaykin) has retreated to a tumbledown estate in the Pacific Northwest, tired of the music grind, and wanting to devote himself to his masterwork—a symphony for whales. Runaway Claire (Preston) provides a surprisingly welcome presence in contrast to

Howl's other visitors—ex-wife Fay (Dale), who wants him to sell the estate, rapacious recording exec Kenneth (Welsh), and Howl's brother, singer Daniel (Gross), who happens to be dead and haunting his sibling. Haphazard direction helps dissipate powerful lead performances. Adapted from the novel by Paul Quarrington. **100m/C VHS.** *CA* Maury Chaykin, Cyndy Preston, Jennifer Dale, Kenneth Welsh, Paul Gross; *D:* Richard J. Lewis; *W:* Paul Quarrington, Richard J. Lewis; *C:* Vic Sarin; *M:* George Blondheim. Genie Awards '94: Best Actor (Chaykin), Best Song ("Claire"), Best Sound; Nominations: Genie Awards '94: Best Director (Lewis), Best Film. *NYR*

Whale of a Tale ♂ 1976 (G) A young boy trains a killer whale to appear in the big show in the main tank at "Marineland." **90m/C VHS, Beta.** William Shatner, Marty Allen, Abby Dalton, Andy Devine, Nancy O'Conner; *D:* Ewing Miles Brown. *VCI*

The Whales of August ♂♂♂½ 1987 Based on the David Berry play, the story of two elderly sisters—one caring, the other cantankerous, blind, and possibly senile—who decide during a summer in Maine whether or not they should give up their ancestral house and enter a nursing home. Gish and Davis are exquisite to watch, and the all-star supporting cast is superb—especially Price as a suave Russian. Lovingly directed by Anderson in his first US outing. **91m/C VHS, Beta, LV, 8mm.** Lillian Gish, Bette Davis, Vincent Price, Ann Sothern, Mary Steenburgen, Harry Carey Jr., Tisha Sterling, Margaret Ladd; *D:* Lindsay Anderson; *W:* David Berry. National Board of Review Awards '87: Best Actress (Gish); National Media Owl Awards '88: First Prize; Nominations: Academy Awards '87: Best Supporting Actress (Sothern). *NLC*

The Wharf Rat ♂♂ 1995 (R) Waterfront con man Petey Martin (Phillips) teams up with a journalist (Ticotin) to avenge the murder of his policeman brother by a group of corrupt cops lead by the crazy Doc (Reinhold). Made for cable. *CW:* Violence and language. **88m/C VHS, Closed Caption.** Lou Diamond Phillips, Rachel Ticotin, Judge Reinhold, Rita Moreno, Scott Cohen; *D:* Jimmy Huston; *W:* Jimmy Huston; *C:* Levie Isaacks; *M:* Mervyn Warren. *PAR*

What a Carve-Up! ♂♂ *No Place Like Homicide* 1962 A group of relatives gather in an old, spooky mansion to hear the reading of a will. Tries too hard. Remake of "The Ghoul". **87m/B VHS.** *GB* Kenneth Connor, Sidney James, Shirley Eaton, Donald Pleasence, Dennis Price, Michael Gough; *D:* Pat Jackson. *SNC*

What a Way to Die ♂½ 1970 (R) An evil assassin plots dispatching with a difference. **87m/ C VHS, Beta.** William Berger, Anthony Baker, Helga Anders, Georgia Moll; *D:* Helmut Foernbacher. *NO*

What About Bob? ♂♂♂ 1991 (PG) Bob, a ridiculously neurotic patient, follows his psychiatrist on vacation, turning his life upside down. The psychiatrist's family find Bob entertaining and endearing. Murray is at his comedic best; Dreyfuss's overly excitable characterization occasionally wears thin. **99m/C VHS, Beta, LV.** Richard Dreyfuss, Bill Murray, Julie Hagerty, Charlie Korsmo, Tom Aldredge, Roger Bowen, Fran Brill, Kathryn Erbe, Doris Belack, Susan Willis; *D:* Frank Oz; *W:* Tom Schulman, Alvin Sargent; *C:* Michael Ballhaus; *M:* Miles Goodman. *TOU*

What Comes Around ♂♂ 1985 (PG) A good-ole-boy drama about a doped-up country singer who is kidnapped by his brother for his own good. The singer's evil manager sends his stooges out to find him. Might have been funny, but isn't. But is it meant to be? Good Reed songs; mildly interesting plot. **92m/C VHS, Beta, LV, Closed Caption.** Jerry Reed, Bo Hopkins, Arte Johnson, Barry Corbin; *D:* Jerry Reed. *NLC*

What Did You Do in the War, Daddy? ♂½ 1966 Unfunny comedy set in WWII about a group of weary American soldiers trying to get a small town in Sicily to surrender. Things don't go smoothly thanks to a combination soccer festival/wine, not to mention the Germans deciding to attack. Director Edwards comedic verve deserted him. **119m/C VHS.** Dick

Shawn, James Coburn, Sergio Fantoni, Giovanna Ralli, Aldo Ray, Harry (Henry) Morgan, Carroll O'Connor, Jay Novello, Vito Scotti; *D:* Blake Edwards; *W:* William Peter Blatty, Blake Edwards; *M:* Henry Mancini. *MGM*

What Do You Say to a Naked Lady? ♂♂½ 1970 Funt takes his Candid Camera to the streets to find out how people react when confronted by nude members of the opposite sex. Sporadically hilarious. **92m/C VHS, Beta.** *D:* Allen Funt. *FOX*

What Ever Happened To... ♂♂½ 1993 Sisters play sisters as the Redgraves (in their first film together) tackle this remake of "What Ever Happened to Baby Jane" in all its demented glory. Former actress Blanche (Vanessa) and former child star "Baby Jane" (Lynn) are living in a decaying mansion, which Blanche, confined to a wheelchair, is talking about selling. "Baby" snaps (not that she was ever very stable) and proceeds to torment her sis (more than usual). **94m/C VHS.** Vanessa Redgrave, Lynn Redgrave, Bruce A. Young, Amy Steel, John Scott Clough, John Glover; *D:* David Greene; *W:* Brian Taggert. *AEL, FCT*

What Ever Happened to Baby Jane? ♂♂♂½ 1962 Davis and Crawford portray aging sisters and former child stars living together in a decaying mansion. When the demented Jane (Davis) learns of her now-crippled sister's (Crawford) plan to institutionalize her, she tortures the wheelchair-bound sis. Davis plays her part to the hilt, unafraid of Aldrich's unsympathetic camera, and the viciousness of her character. She received her tenth Oscar nomination for the role. **132m/B VHS, Beta, LV, Closed Caption.** Bette Davis, Joan Crawford, Victor Buono, Anna Lee, B.D. Merrill; *D:* Robert Aldrich. Nominations: Academy Awards '62: Best Actress (Davis), Best Black and White Cinematography, Best Costume Design (B & W), Best Sound, Best Supporting Actor (Buono). *WAR*

What Happened to Rosa? ♂♂♂ 1921 This early Goldwyn release, a whimsical Cinderella story, casts Normand as an endearing shop girl duped by a gypsy's bogus predictions. Believing herself to be the reincarnation of a Castillian noblewoman she dons a fancy gown, attends a fancy shipboard ball and captures the heart of the fancy doctor of her dreams. But fearing his rejection of her true identity she slips away during the chaos of a brawl, leading the good doctor to believe that she is dead. A comedy of errors unfolds before they meet again and live happily ever after. No doubt it jerked a few tears in its day. **42m/B VHS.** Mabel Normand, Hugh Thompson, Doris Pawn, Tully Marshall, Eugenie Besserer, Buster Trow; *D:* Victor Schertzinger. *NOS, FHV*

What Happened Was... ♂♂ 1994 (R) Two-character study about a weirdly nightmarish first date. Law secretary Jackie (Sillas) has been eyeing bookish paralegal Michael (Noonan) and finally invites him for dinner at her loft. The two struggle to relax and make small talk that turns into some unexpected soul baring. Emotionally distant Michael is unexpectedly hostile about his job and claims to be writing an expose of their law firm while overly-friendly Jackie is writing a children's book, which turns out to be jarringly violent and apparently autobiographical. Provides an idiosyncratic, if limited, appeal thanks to a compelling performance by Sillas. *CW:* Some language; verbal description of child abuse. **92m/C VHS.** Tom Noonan, Karen Sillas; *D:* Tom Noonan; *W:* Tom Noonan; *C:* Joe DeSalvo; *M:* Lodovico Sorret. Sundance Film Festival '94: Best Screenplay, Grand Jury Prize; Nominations: Independent Spirit Awards '95: Best Actress (Sillas), First Screenplay. *HMK*

What Have I Done to Deserve This? ♂♂♂ *Que He Hecho Yo Para Merecer Esto!* 1985 A savage parody on Spanish mores, about a speed-addicted housewife who ends up selling her son and killing her husband with a ham bone. Black, black comedy, perverse and funny as only Almodovar can be. In Spanish with subtitles. Nudity and profanity. **100m/C VHS, Beta, LV.** Carmen Maura, Chus Lampreave; *D:* Pedro Almodovar; *W:* Pedro Almodovar. *CCN, TPV*

What! No Beer? ♂♂ 1933 Two dim-bulb friends decide to put their money into a defunct brewery hoping for the end of Prohibition. They start up operations too soon and wind up attracting the unwelcome attentions of gangster bootleggers and the cops. Mediocre comedy and Keaton's last starring role as his own problems with alcohol affected his work. **66m/B VHS.** Buster Keaton, Jimmy Durante, Phyllis Barry, Roscoe Ates, John Miljan, Henry Armetta, Edward Brophy; *D:* Edward Sedgwick. *MGM*

What Price Glory? ♂♂♂ 1952 Remake of the 1926 silent classic about a pair of comradely rivals for the affections of women in WWI France. Strange to have Ford directing an offbeat comedy, but it works: masterful direction, good acting. Demarest broke both legs in a motorcycle accident during shooting. **111m/C VHS, Beta.** James Cagney, Dan Dailey, Corinne Calvet, William Demarest, James Gleason, Robert Wagner, Max Casey Adams Showalter, Craig Hill, Marisa Pavan; *D:* John Ford. *FOX, FCT*

What Price Hollywood? ♂♂♂ 1932 Aspiring young starlet decides to crash film world by using an alcoholic director as her stepping stone. Bennett is lovely; Sherman is superb as an aging, dissolute man who watches her potential slip away. From a story by Adela Rogers St. Johns. Remade three times as "A Star is Born." **88m/B VHS, Beta, LV.** Constance Bennett, Lowell Sherman, Neil Hamilton; *D:* George Cukor; *C:* Charles Rosher; *M:* Max Steiner. Nominations: Academy Awards '32: Best Story. *CCB, TTC, FCT*

What the Moon Saw ♂♂½ 1990 When a young boy is confronted by a less than friendly theater owner, he uses favorite scenes from "Sinbad" to deal with the aggressor. **86m/C VHS, Closed Caption.** Pat Evison; *D:* Pino Amenta. *FHE, BTV*

What the Peeper Saw ♂♂ *Night Hair Child; Child of the Night* 1972 The wife of a wealthy author finds her comfortable life turning into a terrifying nightmare when her young stepson starts acting funny. Juicy and terrifying. **97m/C VHS, Beta.** Britt Ekland, Mark Lester, Hardy Kruger, Lilli Palmer. *VCI*

What Waits Below ♂½ 1983 (PG) A scientific expedition encounters a lost race living in caves in South America. Good cast, bad acting, and lousy script. Might have been much better. **88m/C VHS, Beta.** Timothy Bottoms, Robert Powell, Lisa Blount; *D:* Don Sharp. *LIV*

Whatever Happened to Aunt Alice? ♂♂♂ 1969 (PG) After murdering her husband to inherit his estate, a poor, eccentric widow develops an awful habit: she hires maids, only to murder them and steal their savings. The only evidence is a growing number of trees by the drive. Sleuth Ruth Gordon (of "Harold and Maude" fame, acting here just as odd) takes the job in hopes of solving the mystery. Thoroughly amusing. **101m/C VHS, Beta.** Geraldine Page, Ruth Gordon, Rosemary Forsyth, Robert Fuller, Mildred Dunnock; *D:* Lee H. Katzin; *C:* Joseph Biroc. *FOX, MLB*

Whatever Happened to Susan Jane? ♂½ 1984 A bored housewife searches for an off-beat college friend, and enters into the seamy, strange world of San Francisco's lunatic fringe. Music by Tuxedo Moon, Indoor Life and other punk groups. **90m/C VHS, Beta.** *NO*

What's Eating Gilbert Grape ♂♂♂ *Gilbert Grape* 1993 (PG-13) Offbeat is mildly descriptive. Depp stars as Gilbert Grape, the titular head of a very dysfunctional family living in a big house in a small Iowa town. His Momma (Cates) weighs more than 500 pounds and hasn't left the house in 7 years, he has two squabbling teenage sisters, and 17-year-old brother Arnie (DiCaprio) is mentally retarded and requires constant supervision. What's a good-hearted grocery clerk to do? Well, when free-spirited Becky (Lewis) is momentarily marooned in town, Gilbert may have found a true soulmate. Performances, especially DiCaprio's, save this from the oddball/cute factor although flick would have benefitted from streamlining, particularly the scenes involving Depp and bad-haircut Lewis. Based on the novel by Hedges. 118m/C VHS, Beta, LV, **Closed Caption.** Johnny Depp, Leonardo DiCaprio, Juliette Lewis, Mary Steenburgen, Darlene Cates, Laura Harrington, Mary Kate Schellhardt, Kevin Tighe, John C. Reilly, Crispin Glover, Penelope Branning; **D:** Lasse Hallstrom; **W:** Peter Hedges; **M:** Alan Parker, Bjorn Isfalt. National Board of Review Awards '93: Best Supporting Actor (DiCaprio); Nominations: Academy Awards '93: Best Supporting Actor (DiCaprio); Golden Globe Awards '94: Best Supporting Actor (DiCaprio).PAR

What's Good for the Goose 🐾🐾½

1969 Stuffy, married financial institution executive's lifestyle receives a major overhaul when he attends a banking conference and meets a beautiful and free-spirited young woman whom he takes as a lover. Unfortunately, he perpetually finds her in bed with other men, and then his wife gets in on the act, too. Classic British humor. 104m/C VHS. **GB** Norman Wisdom, Sally Geeson, Sarah Atkinson, Sally Bazely; **D:** Menaham Golan; **W:** Norman Wisdom, Menaham Golan; **M:** Reg Tilsley. NMD

What's Love Got to Do with It? 🐾🐾½

1993 (R) Energetic biopic of powerhouse songstress Tina Turner. Short sequences cover her early life before moving into her abusive relationship with Ike and solo comeback success. Bassett may not look like Tina, but her exceptionally strong performance leaves no question as to who she's supposed to be, even during on-stage Tina sequences. Some credibility is lost when Turner is shown in the final concert sequence—Gibson would have been wise to let Bassett finish what she started. Fishburne is a sympathetic but still chilling Ike, rising to the challenge of showing both Ike's initial charm and longtime cruelty. Based on "I, Tina" by Turner and Kurt Loder.**CW:** Strong language, domestic violence and drug use, and some sexuality. 118m/C VHS, LV, **Closed Caption.** Angela Bassett, Laurence "Larry" Fishburne, Vanessa Bell Calloway, Jenifer Lewis, Phyllis Stickney, Khandi Alexander, Pamela Tyson, Penny Johnson, Rae'ven Kelly, Robert Miranda, Chi; **D:** Brian Gibson; **W:** Kate Lanier; **C:** Jamie Anderson; **M:** Stanley Clarke. Golden Globe Awards '94: Best Actress—Musical/Comedy (Bassett); Blockbuster Entertainment Awards '95: Female Newcomer, Video (Bassett); Nominations: Academy Awards '93: Best Actor (Fishburne), Best Actress (Bassett); MTV Movie Awards '94: Best Actress (Bassett). TOU

What's the Matter with Helen? 🐾🐾½

1971 (PG) Two women, the mothers of murderous sons, move to Hollywood to escape their past and start a new life. They open a school for talented children, and seem to be adjusting to their new lives until strange things start happening. It is soon revealed that one of the mothers is a psychotic killer, and the other mother becomes part of an eerie finale. A fine starring vehicle for two aging actresses. Great score. 101m/C VHS. Debbie Reynolds, Shelley Winters, Dennis Weaver, Agnes Moorehead, Michael MacLiammoir; **D:** Curtis Harrington. Nominations: Academy Awards '71: Best Costume Design. MGM

What's Up, Doc? 🐾🐾🐾

1972 (G) A shy musicologist from Iowa (Ryan) travels to San Francisco with his fiance (Kahn) for a convention. He meets the eccentric Streisand at his hotel and becomes involved in a chase to recover four identical flight bags containing top secret documents,

a wealthy woman's jewels, the professor's musical rocks, and Streisand's clothing. Bogdanovich's homage to the screwball comedies of the '30s. Kahn's feature film debut. 94m/C VHS, Beta. Barbra Streisand, Ryan O'Neal, Kenneth Mars, Austin Pendleton, Randy Quaid, Madeline Kahn; **D:** Peter Bogdanovich; **W:** David Newman, Buck Henry, Robert Benton; **M:** Artie Butler. Writers Guild of America '72: Best Original Screenplay. WAR

What's Up Front 🐾½ *The Fall Guy; A Fourth for Marriage*

1963 Occasionally funny '60s gag-fest about an ogle-eyed bra salesman who decides to sell door-to-door in order to save a failing brassiere company. Filmed in "Girl-O-Rama" by the young Vilmos Zsigmond. Dated and weird, with camp value. No nudity. Costumes were done by Frederick's of Hollywood. 90m/C VHS, Beta. Tommy Holden, Marilyn Manning, Carolyn Walker, William Watters; **D:** Bob Wehling. RHI

What's Up, Tiger Lily? 🐾🐾🐾

1966 This legitimate Japanese spy movie—"Kagi No Kag" (Key of Keys), a 1964 Bond imitation—was re-edited by Woody Allen, who added a new dialogue track, with hysterical results. Characters Terri and Suki Yaki are involved in an international plot to secure egg salad recipe; Allen's brand of Hollywood parody and clever wit sustain the joke. Music by the Lovin' Spoonful, who make a brief appearance. 90m/C VHS, Beta, LV. **JP** Woody Allen, Tatsuya Mihashi, Mie Hama, Akiko Wakabayashi; **D:** Woody Allen, Senkichi Taniguhi; **M:** Jack Lewis. VES

Wheel of Fortune 🐾🐾 *A Man Betrayed; Citadel of Crime*

1941 A shrewd small-town lawyer, working on a case in the big city, is forced to expose his girlfriend's father as a crooked politician. Strange to see the Duke here in the lead, but what the hey. Not great, but interesting. 83m/B VHS. John Wayne, Frances Dee, Edward Ellis, Ward Bond, Wallace Ford; **D:** John H. Auer. REP

The Wheeler Dealers 🐾🐾🐾 *Separate Beds*

1963 Garner plays a supposedly penniless investor (actually a Texas millionaire) who comes to New York stock analyst Remick for investment advice. Her shyster boss (Backus) tells her to sell the aw-shucks cowboy worthless stock which turns out to be worth a fortune. Zany spoof of Wall Street ethics. 100m/C VHS. James Garner, Lee Remick, Jim Backus, Phil Harris, Shelley Berman, Chill Wills, John Astin, Louis Nye; **D:** Arthur Hiller. MGM

Wheels of Fire 🐾 *Vindicator*

1984 (R) The earth is a wasteland controlled by sadistic highway hoodlums. When they kidnap the hero's sister, he fights back in a flame-throwing car. Horrible "Road Warrior" rip-off. 81m/C VHS, Beta, LV. Gary Watkins, Lynda Wiesmeier; **D:** Cirio H. Santiago. LIV, VES

Wheels of Terror 🐾

1990 (R) Possessed black car stalks children in isolated village. Bus driver Cassidy gets behind the wheel of B-8 super-charged school bus to initiate most interminable chase scene in screen history. 86m/C VHS, Beta. Joanna Cassidy, Marcie Leeds, Carlos Cervantes, Arlen Dean Snyder; **D:** Christopher Cain; **C:** Rick Bota; **M:** Jay Gruska. PAR

When a Man Loves a Woman 🐾🐾½ *To Have and to Hold; Significant Other*

1994 (R) Time to get suspicious when song titles become hit titles. Alice Green (Ryan) is the mother in a perfect little family, with a loving husband (Garcia), two little girls, and a satisfying career. She's also a closet alcoholic. Less about her alcoholism than the effect on her family and her hubby in particular, shown as a '90s sort of guy who allows Alice to keep her secret. Ryan's detox treatments and struggle back to sobriety are fertile ground for psycho-babble and 12-step cliches, but solid performances save this picture from drying out.**CW:** Language. 126m/C VHS, LV, **Closed Caption.** Meg Ryan, Andy Garcia, Lauren Tom, Philip S. Hoffman, Tina Majorino, Mae Whitman, Ellen Burstyn, Eugene Roche, Latanya Richardson; **D:** Luis Mandoki; **W:** Ronald Bass, Al Franken; **M:** Zbigniew Preisner. Blockbus-

ter Entertainment Awards '95: Drama Actress, Video (Ryan); Nominations: MTV Movie Awards '95: Best Female Performance (Ryan), Most Desirable Male (Garcia); Screen Actors Guild Award '94: Best Actress (Ryan). TOU

When a Man Rides Alone 🐾🐾

1933 Tyler relieves trains of their gold shipments in order to reimburse swindled investors. Lovely Lacey frowns on his initiative, so he kidnaps her to keep her quiet. The two fall in love, and the man who rides alone works beside his beloved. 60m/B VHS. Tom Tyler, Adele Lacey, Alan Bridge, Robert Burns, Frank Ball, Alma Chester, Bud Osborne; **D:** J.P. McGowan. NOS, GPV

When a Man Sees Red 🐾½

1934 Jones is a ranch foreman whose new boss is Campbell (she inherited the property). The two argue constantly but then come to realize all the fighting is just hiding true love. 60m/B VHS. Buck Jones, Peggy Campbell, Dorothy Revier, Syd Saylor, Leroy Mason, Charles French, Robert F. (Bob) Kortman; **D:** Alan James. GPV

When a Stranger Calls 🐾½

1979 (R) Babysitter is terrorized by threatening phone calls and soon realizes that the calls are coming from within the house. Story was expanded from director Walton's short film "The Sitter." Distasteful and unlikely, though the first half or so is tight and terrifying. 97m/C VHS, Beta, LV. Carol Kane, Charles Durning, Colleen Dewhurst, Rachel Roberts; **D:** Fred Walton. COL

When a Stranger Calls Back 🐾🐾½

1993 (R) Sequel to "When a Stranger Calls" finds college student Julia Jenz (Schoelen) still trying to put her life together five years after a terrifying ordeal with a stalker. She turns to her advisor Jill (Kane), who went through a similar fate, but once Jill becomes involved she again becomes the pawn of a psychopath. It's up to retired detective John Clifford (Durning), who saved Jill before, to do his heroics once again. Scary opening sequence but suspense peters out toward the end. Made for cable television. 94m/C VHS, **Closed Caption.** Carol Kane, Charles Durning, Jill Schoelen, Gene Lythgow, Karen Austin; **D:** Fred Walton; **W:** Fred Walton. USH

When a Woman Ascends the Stairs 🐾🐾 *Onna Ga Kaidan O Agaru Toki*

1960 A young widow with an elderly mother and a useless brother supports them all by working as a Ginza bar hostess. As she approaches the perilous professional age of 30, Keiko must decide whether to open her own bar or marry once again. In Japanese with English subtitles. 110m/B VHS. **JP** Hideko Takamine, Tatsuya Nakadai, Masayuki Mori; **D:** Mikio Naruse. WAC

When Angels Fly 🐾

1982 In this emotional tale of love and murder, a young woman sets out to find the exact circumstances surrounding the mysterious death of her sister. 96m/C VHS, Beta. Jennifer Dale, Robin Ward. UNI, MOV

When Comedy was King 🐾

1959 A compilation of the greatest silent screen comedians, including Keaton, Chaplin, Langdon, and Turpin. 81m/C VHS, Beta, LV. Buster Keaton, Charlie Chaplin, Harry Langdon, Ben Turpin; **D:** Robert Youngson. NO

When Dinosaurs Ruled the Earth 🐾🐾

1970 (G) When "One Million Years B.C." ruled the box office the Brits cranked out a few more lively prehistoric fantasies. A sexy cavegirl, exiled because of her blond hair, acquires a cave-beau and a dinosaur guardian. Stop-motion animation from Jim Danforth, story by J.G. Ballard. Under the name Angela Dorian, Vetri was Playmate of the Year in 1968 (A.D.). 96m/C VHS, Beta, LV. **GB** Victoria Vetri, Robin Hawdon, Patrick Allen, Drewe Henley, Sean Caffrey, Magda Konopka, Imogen Hassall, Patrick Holt, Jan Rossini; **D:** Val Guest; **W:** Val Guest. WAR, FCT, MLB

When Every Day was the Fourth of July 🐾🐾½

1978 A nine-year-old girl asks her father, a lawyer, to defend a mute handyman accused of murder, knowing this will bring on him the contempt of the community. Well handled, but see "To Kill a Mockingbird" first. Based on producer/director Curtis's childhood. Sequel: "The Long Days of Summer." Made for television. **100m/C VHS, Beta.** Katy Kurtzman, Dean Jones, Louise Sorel, Harris Yulin, Chris Petersen, Geoffrey Lewis, Scott Brady, Henry Wilcoxon, Michael Pataki; **D:** Dan Curtis. *LIV*

When Father was Away on Business ♂♂♂½ 1985 (R)
Set in 1950s Yugoslavia. A family must take care of itself when the father is sent to jail for philandering with a woman desired by a Communist Party offical. The moving story of the family's day-to-day survival is seen largely through the eyes of the father's six-year-old son, who believes dad is "away on business." In Yugoslavian with English subtitles. **144m/C VHS.** *YU* Moreno D'E Bartoli, Miki Manojlovic, Mirjana Karanovic; **D:** Emir Kusturica. Cannes Film Festival '85: Best Film; Nominations: Academy Awards '85: Best Foreign Language Film. *FXL*

When Gangland Strikes ♂♂ 1956
A country lawyer, blackmailed by the mob, tries to protect his family without caving in. Unexceptional remake of "Main Street Lawyer." **70m/B VHS.** Raymond Greenleaf, Marjie Millar, Anthony Caruso, Jack Perrin, John Hudson; **D:** R.G. Springsteen; **M:** Van Alexander. *REP*

When Harry Met Sally... ♂♂♂ 1989
(R) Romantic comedy follows the long relationship between two adults who try throughout the changes in their lives (and their mates) to remain platonic friends—and what happens when they don't. Wry and enjoyable script is enhanced by wonderful performances. Another directional direct hit for "Meathead" Reiner, and a tour de force of comic screenwriting for Ephron, with improvisational help from Crystal. Great songs by Sinatra sound-alike Connick. **96m/C VHS, Beta, LV, 8mm, Closed Caption.** Billy Crystal, Meg Ryan, Carrie Fisher, Bruno Kirby, Steven Ford, Lisa Jane Persky, Michelle Nicastro, Harley Jane Kozak; **D:** Rob Reiner; **W:** Nora Ephron; **M:** Harry Connick Jr., Marc Shaiman. British Academy Awards '89: Best Original Screenplay; Nominations: Academy Awards '89: Best Original Screenplay. *NLC*

When Hell Broke Loose ♂½ 1958
Routine WWII actioner about a small-time crook (Bronson) who joins the Army, changes his ways because of the love of a good woman, and gets a chance to be a hero when he stumbles upon a Nazi assassination plot against General Eisenhower. **78m/B VHS.** Charles Bronson, Violet Rensing, Richard Jaeckel, Arvid Nelson, Robert Easton; **D:** Kenneth Crane; **W:** Oscar Brodney. *PAR*

When Hell Was in Session ♂♂♂ 1982
In more than seven years as a prisoner of the Viet Cong, Holbrook is subjected to torture, starvation, and psychological warfare to break his will. Based on the true story of Navy Commander Jeremiah Denton. Painful and violent. Made for TV. **98m/C VHS, Beta.** Hal Holbrook, Eva Marie Saint, Ronny Cox; **D:** Paul Krasny. *TLF*

When He's Not a Stranger ♂♂♂ 1989
Date rape is the subject of this made-for-television drama. Lyn is a college freshman who goes to a campus party hosted by the football team. When Ron, the star quarterback, invites Lyn to his dorm room, the situation gets out of hand. Only Lyn calls it rape and Ron calls her a liar. Intense performances are a highlight of this well-done story. **100m/C VHS.** Annabeth Gish, John Terlesky, Kevin Dillon, Paul Dooley, Kim Meyers; **D:** John Gray. *TRI*

When Knights were Bold ♂♂½ 1936
An English nobleman living in India inherits a castle in his native land. Returning home, he is knocked unconscious by a falling suit of armor while trying to impress a young lady and dreams himself back to medieval days. Enjoyable comedy about that ubiquitous British class hierarchy. **55m/B VHS, Beta.** Fay Wray, Jack Buchanan, Martita Hunt; **C:** Frederick A. (Freddie) Young. *VYY*

When Ladies Meet ♂♂½ 1941
Entertaining story of a love quadrangle that features several of MGM's top stars of the '40s. In this remake of the 1933 film, Crawford plays a novelist and an early proponent of the women's liberation movement. She falls in love with her publisher (Marshall), who just happens to be married to Garson. Meanwhile, Taylor, who is in love with Crawford, attempts to show her that he isa more suitable match for her than Marshall, but Crawford has yet to catch on.The lengthy dialogue on women's rights is badly dated, but the real-life rivalry between Crawford and Garson adds a certain bite to their witty exchanges. Also known as "Strange Skirts." **105m/B VHS, Closed Caption.** Joan Crawford, Robert Taylor, Greer Garson, Herbert Marshall, Spring Byington; **D:** Robert Z. Leonard; **W:** Anita Loos, S.K. Lauren. Nominations: Academy Awards '41: Best Interior Decoration. *MGM*

When Lightning Strikes woof! 1934
Lightning the Wonder Dog prevents the owner of a rival lumber company from stealing his master's land. He gets to use his talents of running, swimming, barking, and smoking cigars. Proves that real woofers were made way back when, even though in 1934 they didn't feature scantily clad babes. Part of Video Yesteryear's Golden Turkey series. **51m/B VHS, Beta.** Francis X. Bushman. *VYY*

When Nature Calls woof! 1985 (R)
A city family "gets back to nature" in this collection of mostly ineffective gags and poor satirical ideas. Probably your first and last chance to see Liddy and Mays on screen together. **76m/C VHS, Beta, LV.** Davie Orange, Barbara Marineau, Nicky Beim, Tina Marie Staiano, Willie Mays, G. Gordon Liddy; **D:** Charles Kaufman. *MED*

When Night is Falling ♂♂♂ 1995 (R)
Camille (Bussieres) is a professor of mythology at a Calvinist college in Toronto and engaged to theologian Martin (Czerny). Vaguely unsatisfied, Camille meets Petra (Crawford), a trapeze artist in a traveling circus, gets drawn into her world, falls in love, and must decide what she wants from her life. Lots of yearning, romance, and fantasy. Lesbian lovemaking scenes caused a ratings problem (the MPAA originally deemed them worthy of NC-17).**CW:** Strong sexuality and some language. **96m/C VHS.** *CA* Pascale Bussieres, Rachael Crawford, Henry Czerny, David Fox, Don McKellar, Tracy Wright; **D:** Patricia Rozema; **W:** Patricia Rozema; **C:** Douglas Koch; **M:** Lesley Barber. *EVE*

When Taekwondo Strikes ♂ 1983 (R)
One brave Taekwondo master leads the Korean freedom fighters against the occupying army of WWII Japan. **95m/C VHS, Beta.** Jhoon Rhee, Ann Winton, Angela Mao, Huang Ing Sik; **D:** Raymond Chow.

When the Bough Breaks ♂♂ 1986
A psychologist helps the police with the case of a murder-suicide witnessed by a child. He finds one sick secret society at work in this unkinder, ungentler TV thriller, based on the novel by Jonathan Kellerman. Danson co-produced. **100m/C VHS.** Ted Danson, Richard Masur, Rachel Ticotin, David Huddleston, James Noble, Kim Miyori, Merritt Butrick; **D:** Waris Hussein. *WOV*

When the Bough Breaks ♂♂ 1993 (R)
A Texas police chief (Sheen) discovers seven severed hands and turns to a forensic expert (Walker) for help. But then the specialist discovers a psychic link between a mentally disturbed child and the serial killer.**CW:** Violence; mature themes; language. **103m/C VHS, Closed Caption.** Ally Walker, Martin Sheen, Ron Perlman; **D:** Michael Cohn; **W:** Michael Cohn; **C:** Michael Bonvillain. *TTC*

When the Bullet Hits the Bone ♂ 1996 (R)
Particularly nasty vigilante flick as EMS doc Jack Davies (Wincott) decides to get even with a drug cartel, after being seriously wounded while merely being an innocent bystander.**CW:** Strong action violence and language. **82m/C VHS.** Jeff Wincott, Michelle Johnson, Doug O'Keefe, Richard Fitzpatrick; **D:** Damian Lee. *NHO*

When the Clouds Roll By ♂♂♂½ 1919
Psycho-satire pits demented doctor against Fairbanks in experiment to make him suicidal basket case. Fairbanks seems to contract ferocious nightmares, passionate superstitions, a spurning lover, and a warrant for his arrest, none of which suppresses his penchant for acrobatics. **77m/B VHS, Beta.** Douglas Fairbanks Sr., Herbert Grimwood, Kathleen Clifford, Frank Campeau, Ralph Lewis, Daisy Robinson, Albert MacQuarrie; **D:** Victor Fleming. *GPV, FCT*

When the Dark Man Calls ♂♂½ 1995 (R)
Shock ending and a strong lead performance by Van Ark enhance this cable TV mystery. Call-in radio shrink Julianne Kaiser (Van Ark) is stalked by ex-con Parmenter (Lewis). Twenty-five years ago she testified that he murdered her parents although the bitter man's always proclaimed his innocence. Now Kaiser is having grisly flashbacks to her childhood but can she figure out the truth before Parmenter kills her? Based on a novel by Stuart M. Kaminsky.**CW:** Violence and terror. **89m/C VHS, Closed Caption.** Joan Van Ark, Geoffrey Lewis, Chris Sarandon, James Read, Frances Hyland, Janet-Laine Green; **D:** Nathaniel Gutman; **W:** Pablo F. Fenjves. *PAR*

When the Greeks ♂♂ Ton Kero Ton Hellinon 1981
At the turn of the century, a rich young landowner is kidnapped by a group of nationalist bandits who demand a hefty ransom. But soon the young man realizes he's seeing his true Greek heritage for the first time and begins to identify with his captors. Greek with subtitles. **100m/C VHS.** *GR* Alexis Damianos, Kostas Arzoglou, George Sampanis, Stavros Mermighis; **D:** Lakis Papastathis; **W:** Lakis Papastathis; **M:** George Papadakis. *FCT*

When the Legends Die ♂♂ 1972
(PG) A Ute Indian strives to preserve his heritage in an often harsh modern world. Recorded in hi-fi. **105m/C VHS, Beta.** Richard Widmark, Frederic Forrest; **D:** Stuart Millar. *FOX*

When the Line Goes Through ♂ 1971
A drifter arrives in a small West Virginia town and changes the lives of two pretty sisters. **90m/C VHS, Beta.** Martin Sheen, Davey Davidson, Beverly Washburn. *NO*

When the North Wind Blows ♂♂ 1974 (G)
An old, lone trapper hunts for and later befriends the majestic snow tiger of Siberia in the Alaskan wilderness. A good family film. **113m/C VHS, Beta.** Henry Brandon, Herbert Nelson, Dan Haggerty; **D:** Stewart Raffill. *VCI*

When the Party's Over ♂♂½ 1991 (R)
Twenty-somethings share a southern California house and a hip—but ultimately empty— lifestyle. **114m/C VHS.** Rae Dawn Chong, Fisher Stevens, Elizabeth Berridge, Sandra Bullock, Brian McNamara, Kris Kramm; **D:** Matthew Irmas. *LIV*

When the Screaming Stops ♂ 1973
(R) A hunter is hired to find out who has been cutting the hearts out of young women who reside in a small village near the Rhine River. Turns out it's a she-monster who rules a kingdom beneath the river. Bad effects; gory gore; outlandish plot. All the ingredients, in other words, of a classic dog. **86m/C VHS, Beta.** *SP* Tony Kendall, Helga Line, Sylvia Tortosa; **D:** Armando de Ossorio. *NHO*

When the Time Comes ♂♂ 1991
(PG-13) A woman dying of cancer wants to take her own life, but when her husband refuses, she seeks the help of a male friend. Excellent acting doesn't provide the needed depth. Less a disease-of-the-week TV movie, more of an ethical-dilemma-of-the-week, and just as trivial. **94m/C VHS, Closed Caption.** Bonnie Bedelia, Brad Davis, Terry O'Quinn, Karen Austin, Donald Moffat, Wendy Schaal; **D:** John Erman; **M:** Marvin Hamlisch. *REP*

When the West Was Young ♂½ 1932
An outdoor adventure about rounding up horses in the Old West. Based on a novel by Zane Grey; also titled "Wild Horse Mesa." **58m/B**

VHS, **Beta.** Randolph Scott, Sally Blane, Guinn "Big Boy" Williams; **D:** Henry Hathaway. NOS, DVT, VYY

When the Whales Came 🐾🐾½ 1989

(PG) A conservationist fable about two children and a grizzled old codger living on a remote British isle during WWI. They try to avert disaster as mysterious narwhal whales descend on the island. Moralistic and uninvolving; poorly acted; slumber-inducing. Adapted from the novel by Morpugo. 100m/C VHS, Beta, LV, Closed Caption. **GB** Paul Scofield, Helen Mirren, David Threlfall, David Suchet, Jeremy Kemp, Max Rennie, Helen Pearce, Barbara Jefford; **D:** Clive Rees; **W:** Michael Morpugo; **M:** Christopher Gunning, Ruth Rennie. FOX

When the Wind Blows 🐾🐾🐾 1986 An

animated feature about a retired British couple when their peaceful—and naive—life in the country is destroyed by nuclear war. Poignant, sad, and thought-provoking, and just a little scary. Features the voices of Ashcroft and Mills; Roger Waters, David Bowie, Squeeze, Genesis, Hugh Cornell, and Paul Hardcastle all contribute to the soundtrack. Based on the novel by Raymond Briggs. 80m/C VHS, Beta, LV. **GB D:** Jimmy T. Murakami; **V:** Peggy Ashcroft, John Mills. LIV

When Thief Meets Thief 🐾½ 1937 A

cat burglar finds his world turned upside down when he begins to fall in love with one of his victims. Not much happening except a few nice stunts by Fairbanks. 85m/B VHS, Beta. **GB** Douglas Fairbanks Jr., Valerie Hobson, Alan Hale, Jack Melford, Leo Genn, Ian Fleming; **D:** Raoul Walsh. NOS, SNC

When Time Ran Out 🐾 1980 (PG) A vol-

cano erupts on a remote Polynesian island covered with expensive hotels and tourists with no way to escape. Contains scenes not seen in the theatrically released print of the film. A very good cast is wasted in this compilation of disaster film cliches. 144m/C VHS, Beta. Paul Newman, Jacqueline Bisset, William Holden, Ernest Borgnine, Edward Albert, Barbara Carrera, Valentina Cortese, Burgess Meredith, Noriyuki "Pat" Morita, Red Buttons; **D:** James Goldstone; **W:** Stirling Silliphant; **C:** Fred W. Koenekamp; **M:** Lalo Schifrin. Nominations: Academy Awards '80: Best Costume Design. WAR

When We Were Kings 1996 (PG) Chroni-

cles the 1974 heavyweight championship fight, held in Zaire, between underdog Muhammad Ali and George Foreman. Gast uses original footage of the prefight hype as well as current interviews from George Plimpton and Norman Mailer (who covered the fight at the time) and Spike Lee. 94m/C VHS, LV. **D:** Leon Gast. Academy Awards '96: Best Feature Documentary. PGV

When Wolves Cry 🐾½ The Christmas Tree

1969 (G) Tearjerker about an estranged father and young son reunited on a Corsican vacation. Their newfound joy sours when the lad is diagnosed with a fatal illness. Hardly one of Holden's best films. 108m/C VHS, Beta. William Holden, Virna Lisi, Brook Fuller, Andre Bourvil; **D:** Terence Young. GEM, VCI

When Women Had Tails 🐾½ Quando

De Donne Avevando La Coda **1970 (R)** A primitive comedy about prehistoric man's discovery of sex. And boy, did they ever discover it. Harmless (more or less), though not exactly cerebral. Followed by "When Women Lost Their Tails." 99m/C VHS, Beta. **IT** Senta Berger, Frank Wolff; **D:** Pasquale Festa Campanile; **M:** Ennio Morricone. SNC

When Women Lost Their Tails 🐾

1975 (R) Ostensible sequel to "When Women Had Tails" about prehistoric cavemen and their sexual habits. 94m/C VHS, Beta. **IT** Senta Berger; **D:** Pasquale Festa Campanile; **M:** Ennio Morricone. NO

When Worlds Collide 🐾🐾½ 1951 (G)

Another planet is found to be rushing inevitably towards earth, but a select group of people attempt to escape in a spaceship; others try to maneuver their way on board. Oscar-quality special effects and plot make up for cheesy acting and bad writing. 81m/C VHS, Beta, LV. Richard Derr, Barbara Rush, Larry Keating, Peter Hanson; **D:** Rudolph Mate; **C:**

William Howard Greene. Academy Awards '51: Best Special Effects; Nominations: Academy Awards '51: Best Color Cinematography. PAR

When Your Lover Leaves 🐾 1983 Al-

leged comedy about a woman, dumped by her married boyfriend, who gets involved in a short-lived relationship with a neighbor. When that also doesn't work out, she decides she must first do something to please herself. Here endeth the lesson. Produced by Fonzie and Richie of "Happy Days." Made for television. 100m/C VHS. Valerie Perrine, Betty Thomas, David Ackroyd, Ed O'Neill, Dwight Schultz, Shannon Wilcox; **D:** Jeff Bleckner; **M:** Randy Edelman. NWV, VTR

When's Your Birthday? 🐾🐾½ 1937

Brown stars in this comedy about a prize-fighter who is working his way through astrology school with his fighting skills. The stars, in turn, tell him when to fight. Lame zaniness (what other kind is there?) meant as a vehicle for Brown, though Kennedy is funnier. The opening sequence, an animated cartoon showing the influence of the moon over the planets, was filmed in Technicolor. 77m/B VHS, Beta. Joe E. Brown, Marian Marsh, Edgar Kennedy; **D:** Harry Beaumont. NOS, VYY, JEF

Where 🐾🐾 1994 Young man living in Buda-

pest begins a psycho-sexual relationship with a young woman that explores the nature of domination and submission. After moving to Los Angeles, he subjects himself to the whims of a student. In English and Hungarian with subtitles. ?m/C VHS. HU **D:** Gabor Zabo. WAC

Where Angels Fear to Tread 🐾🐾🐾

1991 (PG) Another turn-of-the-century tale of the English in Italy from the pen of E.M. Forster. Widowed, fortyish Lilia (Mirren) is urged by her stuffy in-laws to spend some time in Italy. Much to everyone's dismay she impulsively marries a 21-year-old Italian—with disastrous consequences. Based on Forster's first novel, the characters are more stereotypical and the story less defined than his later works and the movies made from them. Impressive performances and beautiful settings make up for a somewhat lackluster direction that isn't up to the standards set by the team of Merchant Ivory, responsible for the Forster films "A Room with a View" and "Howard's End." 112m/C VHS, LV, Closed Caption. **GB** Rupert Graves, Helena Bonham Carter, Judy Davis, Helen Mirren, Giovanni Guidelli, Barbara Jefford, Thomas Wheatley, Sophie Kullman; **D:** Charles Sturridge; **M:** Rachel Portman. NLC

Where Angels Go, Trouble Follows 🐾🐾½ 1968 Follow-up to "The Trou-

ble with Angels," with Russell reprising her role as the wise Mother Superior challenged by her mischief loving students. Younger, modern nun Stevens tries to convince Russell to update her old-fashioned ways and persuades her to take the convent students on a bus trip to a California peace rally. A very young Saint James is one of the convent's irrepressible troublemakers. Very dated but still mildly amusing. 94m/C VHS, Closed Caption. Rosalind Russell, Stella Stevens, Binnie Barnes, Mary Wickes, Susan St. James, Dolores Sutton, Alice Rawlings; **Cameos:** Milton Berle, Arthur Godfrey, Van Johnson, Robert Taylor; **D:** James Neilson; **W:** Blanche Hanalis. COL

Where Are the Children? 🐾½ 1985

(R) Based on Mary Higgins Clark's bestseller. A woman who was cleared of murdering the children from her first marriage remarries. Then the children from her second marriage are kidnapped. Sustains suspense completely, until it falls apart. 92m/C VHS, Beta, Closed Caption. Jill Clayburgh, Max Gail, Barnard Hughes, Clifton James, Harley Cross, Elisabeth Harnois, Elizabeth Wilson, Frederic Forrest; **D:** Bruce Malmuth. COL

Where Eagles Dare 🐾🐾🐾 1968 (PG)

During WWII, a small group of Allied commandos must rescue an American general held by the Nazis in a castle in the Bavarian Alps. Relentless plot twists and action keep you breathless. Well-made suspense/adventure. Alistair MacLean

adapted his original screenplay into a successful novel. 158m/C VHS, Beta, LV. Clint Eastwood, Richard Burton, Mary Ure, Michael Hordern, Anton Diffring, Ingrid Pitt, Patrick Wymark, Robert Beatty; **D:** Brian G. Hutton. MGM, TLF

Where East Is East 🐾🐾½ 1929 In In-

dochina a badly scarred trapper (Chaney) lives with his daughter (Velez) and sells wild animals to circuses. Velez falls in love with a circus owner's son but finds out her own mother, seeking revenge on her ex-husband, trying to seduce the young man. A gorilla figures in the plot as well. Chaney's makeup, which contributed to his "Man of a Thousand Faces" nickname, highlights a contrived movie. 140m/B VHS. Lon Chaney Sr., Lupe Velez, Estelle Taylor, Lloyd Hughes. FCT

Where Have All the People Gone? 🐾 1974 Solar explosion turns most of

Earth's inhabitants to dust while the Anders family vacations in a cave. The family tries to return home amid the devastation. Bad timing, bad acting, bad script. Made for television. 74m/C VHS, Beta. Peter Graves, Kathleen Quinlan, Michael-James Wixted, George O'Hanlon Jr., Verna Bloom; **D:** John Llewellyn Moxey. ORI

Where Is My Child? 🐾🐾½ 1937 Immi-

gration to the New World brings only misfortune and betrayal in this tale of Jews in Eastern Europe between 1911 and 1937, as many experience the loss of family ties and religion. In Yiddish with English subtitles. 92m/B VHS. Celia Adler, Anna Lillian, Morris Strassberg; **D:** Abraham Leff, Harry Lynn. NCJ

Where is My Friend's House? 🐾🐾🐾

Where is the Friend's Home?; Khaneh-Je Doost Kojast? **1987** At the village school, Mohamed is told by his teacher that he'll be expelled if he doesn't do his homework in the required exercise book. But that evening schoolmate Ahmed realizes he's taken Mohamed's book by mistake so he sets off to find his friend's house in a neighboring village. However, Ahmed gets lost and none of the adults he meets will help him. Farsi with subtitles. Followed by "Life and Nothing More..." and "Through the Olive Trees." 90m/C VHS. Babek Ahmed Poor, Ahmed Ahmed Poor, Kheda Barech Defai; **D:** Abbas Kiarostami; **W:** Abbas Kiarostami; **C:** Farhad Saba. FCT

Where Love Has Gone 🐾🐾½ 1964 A

soaper about a teenage daughter who kills her nympho mother's current boyfriend. Her divorced parents end up dragging the ordeal out in a murder trial/custody battle and a lot of family skeletons come out of their closets. Davis is the manipulative grand dame grandmother. Based on the novel by Harold Robbins. 114m/C VHS, Closed Caption. Bette Davis, Susan Hayward, Joey Heatherton, Jane Greer, George Macready; **D:** Edward Dmytryk; **W:** John Michael Hayes. Nominations: Academy Awards '64: Best Song ("Where Love Has Gone"). PAR, FCT

Where Sleeping Dogs Lie 🐾🐾 1991

(R) A struggling writer moves into an abandoned California home five years after a wealthy family was murdered there. While doing research for his novel on their brutal killings, he revives their ghosts as well as the very real presence of their killer. CW: Language. 92m/C VHS, Closed Caption. Dylan McDermott, Tom Sizemore, Sharon Stone; **D:** Charles Finch. COL

Where the Boys Are 🐾🐾½ 1960 Four

college girls go to Fort Lauderdale to have fun and meet boys during their Easter vacation. Features the film debuts of Francis, who had a hit single with the film's title song, and Prentiss. Head and shoulders above the ludicrous '84 remake. 99m/C VHS, Beta, LV. George Hamilton, Jim Hutton, Yvette Mimieux, Connie Francis, Paula Prentiss, Dolores Hart; **D:** Henry Levin. MGM

Where the Boys Are '84 woof! 1984

(R) Horrible remake of the 1960 comedy still features girls searching for boys during spring break in Fort Lauderdale. Telling about its era: charm gives way to prurience. 95m/C VHS, Beta, Closed Caption. Lisa Hartman Black, Wendy Schaal, Lorna Luft,

Lynn-Holly Johnson; *D:* Hy Averback; *W:* Jeff Burkhart. Golden Raspberry Awards '84: Worst Supporting Actress (Johnson). *FOX*

Where the Buffalo Roam *♂♂½* 1980 (R)
Early starring role for Murray as the legendary "gonzo" journalist Hunter S. Thompson. Meandering satire based on Thompson's books "Fear and Loathing in Las Vegas" and "Fear and Loathing on the Campaign Trail '72." Either confusing or offensively sloppy, depending on whether you've read Thompson. Music by Neil Young, thank goodness, or this might be a woof. 98m/C VHS, Beta. Bill Murray, Peter Boyle, Susan Kellerman; *D:* Art Linson; *M:* Neil Young. *USH*

Where the Bullets Fly *♂♂* 1966 Fast-paced Bond spoof. A British spy takes on the intelligence forces of several governments in his search for a new fuel elixir. Fun, if not scintillating. 88m/C VHS. *GB* Tom Adams, Dawn Addams, Michael Ripper, Tim Barrett; *D:* John Gilling. *FOX*

Where the Day Takes You *♂♂½*
1992 (R) Runaways on Hollywood Boulevard are depicted in an unfortunately heavy-handed drama. King (Mulroney) is the slightly older leader of a group of street kids who tries to discourage his friends from getting involved in the violence and drugs they see all around them. He falls in love with new runaway Heather (Boyle) but their love is blighted by the relentless bleakness of their lives. Among the other members of King's "family" are Astin, as a young druggie in thrall to his older dealer (MacLachlan) and Getty, as a young hustler drawn to violence. The story's predictability undercuts some convincing acting. *CW:* Language and violence and drug use. 105m/C VHS, LV, Closed Caption. Dermot Mulroney, Lara Flynn Boyle, Balthazar Getty, Sean Astin, James LeGros, Ricki Lake, Kyle MacLachlan, Rob Knepper, Peter Dobson, Stephen Tobolowsky, Will Smith, Adam Baldwin, Christian Slater, Nancy McKeon, Alyssa Milano, David Arquette, Leo Rossi, Rachel Ticotin; *D:* Marc Rocco; *W:* Michael Hitchcock, Kurt Voss, Marc Rocco; *M:* Mark Morgan; *V:* Laura San Giacomo. *COL*

Where the Eagle Flies *♂♂* Pickup on 101 1972 (PG) Ersatz sixties rock'n'roll road movie shuffles together free spirited college coed, hobo with heart of gold, and rock and roller who's making a lane change out of the fast track. 93m/C VHS. Jack Albertson, Lesley Ann Warren, Martin Sheen, Michael Ontkean; *D:* John Florea. *NO*

Where the Green Ants Dream *♂♂½* Wo Die Grunen Ameisen Traumen 1984 A mining excavation in the Outback is halted by Aborigines who declare ownership of the sacred place where the mythical green ants are buried. A minor entry in the Herzog vision of modern-versus-primal civilization. Too obvious and somehow unsure of itself artistically. 99m/C VHS, Beta. *GE* Bruce Spence, Wandjuk Marika, Roy Marika, Ray Barrett, Norman Kaye, Colleen Clifford; *D:* Werner Herzog. *XVC, MED*

Where the Heart Is *♂♂* 1990 (R) Wealthy dad Coleman kicks his spoiled kids out on the streets to teach them the value of money. Meant as farce with a message. Flops in a big way; one senses it should have been much better. 111m/C VHS, LV, Closed Caption. Dabney Coleman, Uma Thurman, Joanna Cassidy, Suzy Amis, Crispin Glover, Christopher Plummer; *D:* John Boorman; *W:* John Boorman, Telsche Boorman. National Society of Film Critics Awards '90: Best Cinematography. *TOU*

Where the Hot Wind Blows *♂♂* La Legge; La Loi; The Law 1959 The sexual scene in Sicily is sadly not succinctly summarized in this so-so cinematic soap. Cross-generational and cross-class couplings are constant. Think of it as "The Last Picture Show" in a similarly sorry setting, except boring. 120m/C VHS, Beta. *FR IT* Gina Lollobrigida, Marcello Mastroianni, Yves Montand, Melina Mercouri, Paolo Stoppa; *D:* Jules Dassin; *W:* Jules Dassin. *VYY, NOS, FCT*

Where the Lilies Bloom *♂♂♂* 1974
(G) The touching story of four backwoods children who are left orphans when their father dies. They don't report his death to authorities, because they are afraid the family will be separated and sent to an orphanage. Stanton is great as the crusty landlord the children gradually accept as a friend. Based on the book by Vera and Bill Cleaver. 96m/C VHS. Julie Gholson, Jan Smithers, Matthew Burrill, Helen Harmon, Harry Dean Stanton, Rance Howard, Sudie Bond, Tom Spratley, Helen Bragdon, Alice Beardsley; *D:* William A. Graham. *MGM*

Where the North Begins *♂* 1947 A Mountie ransacks the Canadian countryside in search of crime. 41m/B VHS, Beta, LV. Russell Hayden, Jennifer Holt. *NO*

Where the Red Fern Grows *♂♂½*
1974 (G) A young boy in Dust Bowl-era Oklahoma learns maturity from his love and responsibility for two Redbone hounds. Well produced, but tends to be hokey; good family fare. Followed by a sequel nearly twenty years later. 97m/C VHS, Beta. James Whitmore, Beverly Garland, Jack Ging, Lonny Chapman, Stewart Peterson; *D:* Norman Tokar; *C:* Dean Cundey. *FHE, VES, HHE*

Where the Red Fern Grows: Part 2 *♂♂½* 1992 (G) Sequel to one of the most popular family movies of all time starring Brimley as Grandpa Coleman. Set deep in the Louisiana woods, this magical coming of age tale will touch the hearts of young and old viewers alike. 105m/C VHS, Closed Caption. Wilford Brimley, Doug McKeon, Lisa Whelchel, Chad McQueen; *D:* Jim McCullough. *VCI*

Where the River Runs Black *♂♂*
1986 (PG) An orphaned Indian child is raised in the Brazilian jungles by river dolphins. He is eventually befriended by a kindly priest who brings him into the modern world of violence and corruption. Slow pace is okay until the boy arrives at the orphanage, at which point the dolphin premise sadly falls by the wayside. 96m/C VHS, Beta, Closed Caption. Charles Durning, Peter Horton, Ajay Naidu, Concha Ferrell, Alessandro Rabelo, Castulo Guerra; *D:* Christopher Cain; *C:* Juan Ruiz-Anchia; *M:* James Horner. *FOX*

Where the Rivers Flow North *♂♂½*
1994 (PG-13) Vermont logger Noel Lord (Torn) has lived on the land all his life and doesn't want to sell out to the power company. His blunt-talking Indian housekeeper/lover Bangor (Cardinal) knows it's best to take the money and move on. Set in 1927 and adapted from the novella by Howard Frank Mosher. Flat storytelling with a good performance by Cardinal. *CW:* One sexual reference. 104m/C VHS. Rip Torn, Tantoo Cardinal, Bill Raymond, Mark Margolis, John Griesemer, Amy Wright, Dennis Mientka, Jusef Bulos; *Cameos:* Michael J. Fox, Treat Williams; *D:* Jay Craven; *W:* Jay Craven, Don Bredos. *APX*

Where the Sky Begins 1984 From the director of "Black Orpheus," this is a seven-part recreated history of turn-of-the-century aviation. 420m/C VHS, Beta. *FR D:* Marcel Camus. *VCD*

Where the Spirit Lives *♂♂½* 1989 (PG) Native children kidnapped by Canadian government agents are forced to live in dreadful boarding schools where they are abused emotionally and physically. St. John is a new arrival who refuses to put up with it and tries to escape. Engrossing and moving. 97m/C *CA* Michelle St. John; *D:* Bruce Pittman. *BTV, HHE, UWA*

Where There's Life *♂♂½* 1947 Wisecracking Hope is a New York DJ about to be married to Marshe when he discovers he's the heir to the kingdom of Borovia (whose last king was assassinated). Hasso works her feminine wiles as the general who's guarding Hope when the assassins come after him. Oh, and Marshe and her cop brother Bendix are tracking him down to go through with the wedding ceremony. Frantic antics. 75m/B VHS. Bob Hope, Signe Hasso, William Bendix, Vera Marshe, George Coulouris, George Zucco, Dennis Hoey, John Alexander; *D:* Sidney Lanfield; *W:* Melville Shavelson, Allen Boretz. *USH*

Where Time Began *♂♂* 1977 (G) The discovery of a strange manuscript of a scientist's journey to the center of the earth leads to the decision to recreate the dangerous mission. Based on Jules Verne's classic novel "Journey to the Center of the Earth," but not anywhere near as fun or stirring. 87m/C VHS, Beta. Kenneth More, Pep Munne, Jack Taylor; *D:* J. Piquer Simon.

Where Trails Divide *♂½* 1937 Keene is a U.S. Marshal who poses as a lawyer to bring a gang of thieves to justice. Lacks action. 54m/B VHS. Tom Keene, Eleanor Stewart, Warner Richmond, David Sharpe, Charles French, Hal Price, Bud Osborne; *D:* Robert North Bradbury. *GPV*

Where Trails End *♂♂* 1942 Novel sci-fi western set during WWII with just about everything, including phosphorescent-clothed good guys, Nazis, scoundrels, literate horses, and Gallic sidekicks. Interestingly different. 54m/B VHS, Beta. Tom Keene, Joan Curtis, Charles "Blackie" King; *D:* Robert Emmett Tansey. *VDM, VYY*

Where Truth Lies *♂♂* 1996 (R) After a severe breakdown, troubled psychiatrist Ian Lazarre (Savage) is sent to a clinic run by the sinister Dr. Renquist (McDowell). Lazarre's given an experimental drug that causes him to have visions of executed serial killer Jonas Keller (Forrest) and also to develop ESP. The plot doesn't make much sense in any case. 92m/C VHS. John Savage, Kim Cattrall, Malcolm McDowell, Sam Jones, Eric Pierpont, Candice Daly, Dennis Forrest; *D:* William H. Molina; *W:* Ted Perkins; *C:* William H. Molina; *M:* David Wurst, Eric Wurst. *PAR*

Where Were You When the Lights Went Out? *♂½* 1968 (PG) A complicated, unsuccessful farce about a retiring Broadway actress, her jealous, possibly philandering husband, her greedy agent, an embezzler, and a citywide blackout. Film was actually not based on the 1965 New York City blackout but on a French play, "Monsieur Masure" by Claude Magnier, which was written nine years before. 94m/C VHS. Doris Day, Patrick O'Neal, Robert Morse, Terry-Thomas, Lola Albright, Steve Allen, Jim Backus, Ben Blue, Pat Paulsen; *D:* Hy Averback. *MGM, MOV*

Where's Piccone *♂♂♂* 1984 A woman attempts, with the assistance of a two-bit hustler, to locate her missing husband, only to discover that he has led a double life in the Neapolitan underworld. Giannini as the sleazy hubby is perfectly cast. On-target social and political satire. In Italian with English subtitles. 110m/C VHS, Beta. *IT* Giancarlo Giannini, Lina Sastri, Aldo Guiffre, Clelia Rondinelli; *D:* Nanni Loy. *FCT, WBF, TPV*

Where's Poppa? *♂♂♂* Going Ape 1970 A Jewish lawyer's senile mother constantly ruins his love life, and he considers various means of getting rid of her, including dressing up as an ape to scare her to death. Filled with outlandish and often tasteless humor, befitting its reign as a black comedy cult classic. Adapted by Robert Klane from his novel. 84m/C VHS, Beta, LV, Closed Caption. George Segal, Ruth Gordon, Ron Leibman, Vincent Gardenia, Rob Reiner, Trish Van Devere; *D:* Carl Reiner; *C:* Jack Priestley. *FOX*

Where's the Money, Noreen? *♂♂½*
1995 (PG-13) Noreen's (Phillips) out on parole and trailed by the police who believe she knows the whereabouts of the $3 million she helped to steal 12 years before. Made for cable. *CW:* Scene of sensuality and some violence. 93m/C VHS, Beta, Closed Caption. Julianne Phillips, A. Martinez, Nigel Bennett, Colm Feore. *PAR*

Where's Willie? 1977 (G) Willie is a very bright boy; perhaps a little too bright. When he reveals his latest invention to the folks in his small town, everyone is out to get him. 91m/C VHS, Beta. Guy Madison, Henry Darrow, Kate Woodville, Marc Gilpin; *D:* John Florea. *NO*

Which Way Home 🎬🎬 1990 A Red Cross nurse attempts to flee Cambodia with four young orphans. An Australian smuggler befriends and helps her. Way too long and wandering, though like many a TV movie, it means well. 141m/C VHS, Beta, Closed Caption. Cybill Shepherd, John Waters, Peta Toppano, John Ewart, Ruben Santiago-Hudson, Marc Gray; *D:* Carl Schultz; *W:* Michael Laurence. *TTC*

Which Way Is Up? 🎬🎬½ 1977 (R) Pryor plays three roles in this story of an orange picker who accidentally becomes a union hero. He leaves his wife and family at home while he seeks work in Los Angeles. There he finds himself a new woman, starts a new family, and sells out to the capitalists. American version of the Italian comedy "The Seduction of Mimi" tries with mixed success for laughs. Pryor as a dirty old man is the high point. 94m/C VHS, Beta. Richard Pryor, Lonette McKee, Margaret Avery, Morgan Woodward, Marilyn Coleman; *D:* Michael A. Schultz; *W:* Carl Gottlieb; *C:* John A. Alonzo. *USH*

Which Way to the Front? 🎬½ 1970 (G) Assorted Army rejects form a guerilla band and wage their own small-scale war during WWII. 96m/C VHS, Beta. Jerry Lewis, Jan Murray, George L. Baxt, Steve Franken; *D:* Jerry Lewis; *W:* Dee Caruso. *WAR*

Whiffs 🎬 1975 (PG) A gullible man plays guinea pig in an Army experiment on germ warfare which leaves him with the intellect of a chimpanzee. Naturally, he then devises a plan to use the volatile gas in a chain of bank robberies. The title is appropriate—this movie is a stinker. 91m/C VHS. Elliott Gould, Eddie Albert, Harry Guardino, Godfrey Cambridge, Jennifer O'Neill, Alan Manson; *D:* Ted Post; *W:* Malcolm Marmorstein. Nominations: Academy Awards '75: Best Song ("Now That We're in Love"). *MED*

While I Live 🎬½ 1947 Woman meets female pianist with uncanny resemblance to sister who's been dead 25 years and rethinks her position on reincarnation. 88m/B VHS, Beta. *GB* Tom Walls, Clifford Evans, Carole Raye, Patricia Burke, Sonia Dresdel, John Warwick; *D:* John Harlow; *C:* Frederick A. (Freddie) Young. *SNC*

While the City Sleeps 🎬🎬🎬 1956 Three newspaper reporters vie to crack the case of a sex murderer known as "The Lipstick Killer" with the editorship of their paper the prize. Good thriller-plus with the emphasis on the reporters' ruthless methods of gaining information rather than on the killer's motivations. Lang's last big success. Based on "The Bloody Spur" by Charles Einstein. 100m/B VHS, Beta, LV, VCI. Dana Andrews, Rhonda Fleming, George Sanders, Howard Duff, Thomas Mitchell, Ida Lupino, Vincent Price, Mae Marsh; *D:* Fritz Lang; *C:* Ernest Laszlo. *VCI*

While You Were Sleeping 🎬🎬🎬 1995 (PG) Feel-good romantic comedy finds lonely Lucy Moderatz (Bullock) collecting tokens for the Chicago train system and admiring Yuppie lawyer Peter Callaghan (Gallagher) as he commutes to and fro. Fate conspires to throw them together when Lucy rescues Peter after a mugging. Trouble is, he's not conscious so Lucy goes to the hospital with him, where she's mistaken for his fiancee. She continues the charade and is warmly welcomed by the Callaghan family, with the exception of Peter's brother, Jack (Pullman), who smells a rat even as he falls under the token collector's spell. Meanwhile, Peter remains in a coma, allowing Jack and Lucy to supply romantic comedy. Gallagher brings a serenity to his role as the unconscious Peter, while Bullock and Pullman take the predictable plot and deliver performances that earn them another notch on the climb to stardom. 103m/C VHS, LV, Closed Caption. Sandra Bullock, Bill Pullman, Peter Gallagher, Jack Warden, Peter Boyle, Glynis Johns, Micole Mercurio, Jason Bernard, Michael Rispoli, Ally Walker, Monica Keena; *D:* Jon Turteltaub; *W:* Fred Lebow, Daniel G. Sullivan; *C:* Phedon Papamichael; *M:* Randy Edelman. Blockbuster Entertainment Awards '96: Comedy Actress, Video (Bullock), Comedy Actress, Theatrical (Bullock); Nominations: Golden Globe Awards '96: Best Actress—Musical/Comedy (Bullock); MTV Movie Awards '96: Best Female Performance (Bullock), Most Desirable Female (Bullock). *TOU*

Whirlwind Horseman 🎬 1938 Substandard horse opera. Maynard's search for a gold prospector friend leads him to a rancher and his pretty daughter. He beats up some bad guys, etcetera. 60m/B VHS, Beta. Ken Maynard, Joan Barclay, Bill Griffith; *D:* Robert F. "Bob" Hill. *NOS, DVT, VCN*

Whiskey Galore 🎬🎬🎬½ *Tight Little Island* 1948 During WWII, a whiskey-less Scottish island gets a lift when a ship, carrying 50,000 cases of spirits, wrecks off the coast. A full-scale rescue operation and the evasion of both local and British government authorities ensue. The classic Ealing studio comedy is based on the actual wreck of a cargo ship off the Isle of Eriskay in 1941. 81m/B VHS, Beta. *GB* Basil Radford, Joan Greenwood, Gordon Jackson, James Robertson Justice; *D:* Alexander MacKendrick. *HMV*

Whiskey Mountain 🎬 1977 (PG) Two couples go on a treasure hunt to Whiskey Mountain but instead find terror. 95m/C VHS, Beta. Christopher George, Preston Pierce, Linda Borgeson, Roberta Collins, Robert Leslie; *D:* William Grefe. *BFV*

A Whisper to a Scream 🎬 1988 (R) An actress, in researching a film part, takes a job at a telephone sex service, creating different personas as she talks to keep herself interested. Soon, women resembling the personas are being murdered. Great premise fails to deliver fully, though there is some suspense. 96m/C VHS, Beta, LV. *CA* Nadia Capone, Yaphet Kotto, Lawrence Bayne, Silvio Oliviero; *D:* Robert Bergman; *W:* Robert Bergman, Gerard Ciccoritti. *NO*

The Whispering 🎬🎬 1994 (R) Scary little low-budget tale about an insurance investigator who's checking out several suicides and meets up with the Grim Reaper (who just happens to be female).*CW:* Sexuality, language and violence/gore. 88m/C VHS, Beta. Leif Garrett, Leslie Danon, Tom Patton, Maxwell Rutherford, Mette Holt; *D:* Gregory Gieras; *W:* Leslie Danon. *APX*

Whispering City 🎬🎬🎬 1947 A female reporter receives an inside tip incriminating a prominent attorney in a murder committed several years earlier. She tries to get the evidence she needs before she becomes his latest victim. Highly suspenseful, thanks to competent scripting and directing. 89m/B VHS, Beta. *CA* Helmut Dantine, Mary Anderson, Paul Lukas; *D:* Fedor Ozep. *NOS, SNC*

Whispering Shadow 1933 Serial starring the master criminal known as the "faceless whisperer." Twelve chapters, 13 minutes each. 156m/B VHS, Beta. Bela Lugosi, Robert Warwick; *D:* Al(bert) Herman, Colbert Clark. *NOS, SNC, VCN*

Whispers 🎬🎬 1989 (R) Psycho Le Clerc repeatedly bothers writer Tennant even though she seems to have killed him. This dismays police guy Sarandon. Based on the novel by Dean R. Koontz. 96m/C VHS, LV. Victoria Tennant, Chris Sarandon, Jean LeClerc; *D:* Douglas Jackson; *W:* Anita Doohan, Don Carmody. *LIV*

Whispers in the Dark 🎬🎬 1992 (R) A psychiatrist counsels two odd patients—one is an ex-con turned painter with a violent streak, the other is a woman who reveals her kinky sexual experiences with a mystery man. Things get interesting when the doctor finds out her new lover is her patient's mystery man, and the patient turns up murdered. Confusing thriller seems forced but the experienced cast is worth watching.*CW:* Language, strong violence, and strong sexuality. 103m/C VHS, Beta, LV, Closed Caption. Annabella Sciorra, Jamey Sheridan, Anthony LaPaglia, Jill Clayburgh, John Leguizamo, Deborah Unger, Alan Alda, Anthony Heald; *D:* Christopher Crowe; *W:* Christopher Crowe; *C:* Michael Chapman; *M:* Thomas Newman. *PAR, PMS*

Whispers of White 🎬½ 1993 (R) Bridgetown's mayor has been trying for years to put a stop to the drug dealing going on in his fair community. Finally, his new Chief of Police decides to deploy a special task force to clean-up the streets—using whatever methods are necessary (and they're all violent). 98m/C VHS. Nicholette Goulet, Anthony De Sardo, Tony Craig, April Bransome, Ron Gorton Sr.; *D:* Ron Gorton Sr.; *W:* Ron Gorton Sr. *AIP*

The Whistle Blower 🎬🎬🎬 1987 A young government worker in England with a high-security position mysteriously dies. His father, a former intelligence agent, begins investigating his son's death and discovers sinister Soviet-related conspiracies. A lucid, complex British espionage thriller. Adapted from the John Hale novel by Julian Bond. 98m/C VHS, Beta, LV, Closed Caption. *GB* Michael Caine, Nigel Havers, John Gielgud, James Fox, Felicity Dean, Gordon Jackson, Barry Foster, David Langton; *D:* Simon Langton; *W:* Julian Bond; *M:* John Scott. *NLC*

Whistle Down the Wind 🎬🎬🎬½ 1962 Three children of strict religious upbringing find a murderer hiding in their family's barn and believe him to be Jesus Christ. A well done and hardly grim or dull allegory of childhood innocence based on a novel by Mills's mother, Mary Hayley Bell. For a film relying heavily on child characters, it's important to portray childhood well and realistically. That is done here, as in "To Kill a Mockingbird." Mills is perfect. The film is Forbes's directorial debut and Richard Attenborough's second production. 98m/B VHS, Beta. *GB* Hayley Mills, Bernard Lee, Alan Bates; *D:* Bryan Forbes; *M:* Malcolm Arnold. National Board of Review Awards '62: 10 Best Films of the Year. *NLC*

Whistle Stop 🎬🎬 1946 A small-town girl divides her attentions between low-life gambler Raft, and villainous nightclub owner McLaglen, who plans a robbery-murder to get rid of any rivals. A forgettable gangster drama. 85m/B VHS, Beta. George Raft, Ava Gardner, Victor McLaglen; *D:* Leonide Moguy; *W:* Philip Yordan. *NOS, DVT, FCT*

Whistlin' Dan 🎬🎬 1932 Yet another lead cowpoke sets out to avenge the murder of a close relative. Maynard whistles while he walks (and rides) woodenly through this one. 60m/B VHS, Beta. Ken Maynard, Joyzelle Joyner, Lew Meehan, Georges Renevant, Dan Terry, Harlan E. Knight, Bud McClure, Hank Bell, Iron Eyes Cody, Frank Ellis; *D:* Phil Rosen. *NOS, VCI, GPV*

Whistling Bullets 🎬🎬½ 1936 Action galore in the story of an undercover Texas Ranger infiltrating a gang of thieves. The low budget doesn't detract from an exciting script and tight direction. 58m/B VHS, Beta. Kermit Maynard, Jack Ingram; *D:* John English. *NOS, DVT, RXM*

Whistling in Brooklyn 🎬🎬½ 1943 Skelton again plays radio crime-solver Wally Benton in this third and last entry following "Whistling in the Dark" and "Whistling in Dixie." A cop-killer and the Brooklyn Dodgers baseball team figure in the mystery, which finds Skelton a suspect in the crimes. 87m/B VHS. Red Skelton, Ann Rutherford, Jean Rogers, Rags Ragland, Ray Collins, Henry O'Neill, William Frawley, Sam Levene; *D:* Sylvan Simon; *M:* George Bassman. *MGM*

Whistling in Dixie 🎬🎬½ 1942 The second appearance of Skelton as radio sleuth Wally "The Fox" Benton (following "Whistling in the Dark") finds him traveling to Georgia with girlfriend Carol (Rutherford). She's worried about an ex-sorority sister who knows the secret of a hidden Civil War treasure. When Wally gets involved, humorous trouble follows. Followed by "Whistling in Brooklyn." 73m/B VHS, Beta. Red Skelton, Ann Rutherford, George Bancroft, Guy Kibbee, Diana Lewis, Peter Whitney, Rags Ragland; *D:* Sylvan Simon; *W:* Nat Perrin. *MGM, FCT*

Whistling in the Dark 🎬🎬🎬 1941 Skelton plays Wally Benton, a radio sleuth nicknamed "The Fox," in the first of a three-film series. Veidt (an always excellent villain) is the leader of a phony religious cult, after the money of one of his followers. He decides to kidnap Skelton and have him come up with a plan for the perfect murder but of course there are all sorts of comic complications. Skelton's first starring role is a clever comic mystery and a remake of the 1933 film. Followed by "Whistling in Dixie" and "Whistling in Brooklyn." **78m/B VHS.** Red Skelton, Ann Rutherford, Conrad Veidt, Virginia Grey, Rags Ragland, Eve Arden, Don Douglas, Don Costello, Paul Stanton, William Tannen, Reed Hadley; **D:** Sylvan Simon. *MGM*

Whitcomb's War 🎬½ 1987 Small town becomes a battleground among a host of comic characters who are unaware who really is in charge. **67m/C VHS.** Patrick Pankhurst, Leon Charles, Bill Morey, Robert Denison, Garnett Smith; **D:** Russell S. Doughten Jr.

The White Balloon 🎬🎬🎬½ Badkonake Sefid 1995 Beautifully told story from the viewpoint of determined 7-year-old Tehranian Razieh (Mohammadkhani), who wants to properly celebrate the Islamic New Year by buying a particularly plump goldfish (a symbol of harmony) from the pet shop. She manages to beg the money from her mother and sets off but, distracted by the street sights, Reziah loses the banknote, which falls into a street grate. Various characters seek to help her out but it's Reziah's resourceful brother Ali (Kafili) who gets a balloon seller to finally retrieve the money. Farsi with subtitles. **85m/C VHS.** Aida Mohammadkhani, Mohsen Kalifi, Fereshteh Sadr Ofrani, Anna Bourkowska, Mohammad Shahani, Mohammad Bahktiari; **D:** Jafar Panahi; **W:** Abbas Kiarostami; **C:** Farzad Jowdat. New York Film Critics Awards '96: Best Foreign Film. *HMK*

The White Buffalo 🎬🎬 Hunt to Kill 1977 (PG) A strange, semi-surreal western parable about the last days of Wild Bill Hickok (Bronson) and his obsession with a mythical white buffalo that represents his fear of mortality. Something of a "Moby Dick" theme set in the Wild West. Clumsy but intriguing. **97m/C VHS, Beta.** Charles Bronson, Jack Warden, Will Sampson, Kim Novak, Clint Walker, Stuart Whitman, John Carradine, Slim Pickens, Cara Williams, Douglas Fowley; **D:** J. Lee Thompson; **M:** John Barry. *MGM*

White Cargo 🎬🎬½ 1942 Lamarr holds the corny story together with one of her best-known roles as sultry native girl Tondelayo. Pidgeon is a cynical African rubber planter who advises new assistant Carlson against Lamarr's sarong-clad charms. But hormones speak louder than warnings and Pidgeon has to take some strong action to save Carlson from this femme fatale. Based on the novel "Hell's Playground" by Ida Vera Simonton and adapted for both stage and screen by Gordon. **90m/B VHS.** Hedy Lamarr, Walter Pidgeon, Richard Carlson, Frank Morgan, Reginald Owen, Bramwell Fletcher, Henry O'Neill, Clyde Cook, Richard Ainley; **D:** Richard Thorpe; **W:** Leon Gordon; **M:** Bronislau Kaper. *MGM*

White Cargo 🎬½ 1996 Detective Joe Hargatay is investigating a series of fashion model murders that lead him to Chinatown gangsters, corrupt cops, and the crazy world of model agencies. **92m/C VHS.** David Bradley, Shannon Tweed, Lydie Denier, Tiny Lister, David Groh; **D:** Daniel Reardon. *TCE*

White Christmas 🎬🎬🎬 1954 Two exarmy buddies become a popular comedy team and play at a financially unstable Vermont inn at Christmas for charity's sake. Many swell Irving Berlin songs rendered with zest. Paramount's first Vista Vision film. Presented in widescreen on laserdisc. 🎵The Best Things Happen While You're Dancing; Love, You Didn't Do Right By Me; Choreography; What Can You Do With a General; Mandy; The Minstrel Show; Sisters; Heat Wave. **120m/ C VHS, Beta, LV, 8mm, Closed Caption.** Bing Crosby, Danny Kaye, Rosemary Clooney, Vera-Ellen, Dean Jagger; **D:** Michael Curtiz; **W:** Norman Panama; **C:** Loyal Griggs. Nominations: Academy Awards '54: Best Song ("Count Your Blessings Instead of Sheep"). *PAR, FUS*

The White Cliffs of Dover 🎬🎬🎬 1944 Prime example of a successful 40s "women's weepie." American Dunne goes to England in 1914, falls in love, and marries the British Marshal. He joins the WWI troops and is killed, without knowing he had a son. Dunne raises the boy

in England as a new threat looms with the rise of Hitler. Now grown, he goes off to do his duty and she joins the Red Cross, where she sees him again among the wounded, another victim of the ravages of war. Dunne is fine in her noble, sacrificing role. McDowall is the young son with Taylor (with whom he'd already worked in "Lassie Come Home") as a childhood friend. Based on the poem by Alice Duer Miller. Bring the hankies. **126m/B VHS.** Irene Dunne, Alan Marshal, Frank Morgan, Peter Lawford, Gladys Cooper, May Whitty, Sir C. Aubrey Smith, Roddy McDowall, Van Johnson, Elizabeth Taylor, June Lockhart, John Warburton, Jill Esmond, Norma Varden, Tom Drake, Arthur Shields; **D:** Clarence Brown. Nominations: Academy Awards '44: Best Black and White Cinematography. *MGM, MOV*

White Comanche 🎬½ 1967 Half-breed twins battle themselves and each other to a rugged climax. **90m/C VHS, Beta.** William Shatner, Joseph Cotten, Perla Cristal, Rossana Yanni; **D:** Gilbert Kay. *NOS, VCI, VTR*

The White Dawn 🎬🎬½ 1975 (PG) Three whalers are stranded in the Arctic in the 1890s and are taken in by an Eskimo vilage. They teach the villagers about booze, gambling, and other modern amenities. Resentment grows until a clash ensues. All three leads are excellent, especially Oates. Much of the dialogue is in an Eskimo language, subtitled in English, as in "Dances with Wolves." **110m/C VHS, Beta, LV.** Warren Oates, Timothy Bottoms, Louis Gossett Jr., Simonie Kopapik, Joanasie Salomonie; **D:** Philip Kaufman; **C:** Michael Chapman; **M:** Henry Mancini. *PAR*

White Dwarf 🎬½ 1995 Confusing sci-fi adventure finds edgy Manhattan internist Driscoll Rampart (McDonough) serving his residency on Rusta, a war-torn planet located in a white-dwarf star system. The planet is divided into two hemispheres, one in perpetual darkness and the other in constant light. Rampart learns the ropes from mystical doc Akada (Winfield), who's also involved in a peace accord between Rusta's warring leaders. Visually striking but overly-ambiguous—probably because it was intended as the pilot for a weekly series. **91m/C VHS, Closed Caption.** Paul Winfield, Neal McDonough, CCH Pounder, Ele Keats, Michael McGrady, Katy Boyer; **D:** Peter Markle; **W:** Bruce Wagner; **M:** Stewart Copeland. *CAF*

White Eagle 🎬🎬 1932 A white man who believes himself to be an Indian gets a job as a Pony Express rider and gets mixed up with horse rustlers. When he finds out who he really is, he is free to marry the white woman he's had his eye on. Interesting plot twist caused by the narrowmindedness of the Hays Office. **64m/B VHS.** Buck Jones, Barbara Weeks, Robert Ellis, Jason Robards Sr., Robert Elliott, Jim Thorpe, Ward Bond; **D:** Lambert Hillyer. *DVT, HEG*

White Fang 🎬🎬🎬 1991 (PG) Boy befriends canine with big teeth and both struggle to survive in third celluloid rendition of Alaska during the Gold Rush. Beautiful cinematography. Fun for the entire family based on Jack London's book. Followed by "White Fang 2: The Myth of the White Wolf." **109m/C VHS, LV, Closed Caption.** Klaus Maria Brandauer, Ethan Hawke, Seymour Cassel, James Remar, Susan Hogan; **D:** Randal Kleiser; **W:** Jeanne Rosenberg, Nick Thiel, David Fallon; **C:** Tony Pierce-Roberts; **M:** Basil Poledouris. *TOU, DIS, TVC*

White Fang 2: The Myth of the White Wolf 🎬🎬 1994 (PG) White boy and his wolf-dog lead starving Native American tribe to caribou during the Alaskan Gold Rush. Simplistic story with obvious heroes and villains, yes, but this is also wholesome (and politically correct) family fare compliments of Disney. Focuses less on the wolf, a flaw, and more on Bairstow and his love interest Craig, a Haida Indian princess, while exploring Native American mythology and dreams in sequences that tend to stop the action cold. Still, kids will love it, and there are plenty of puppies to achieve required awwww factor. Beautiful scenery filmed on location in Colorado and British

Columbia. **106m/C VHS, LV, Closed Caption.** Scott Bairstow, Alfred Molina, Geoffrey Lewis, Charmaine Craig, Victoria Racimo, Paul Coeur, Anthony Michael Ruivivar, Al Harrington; **Cameos:** Ethan Hawke; **D:** Ken Olin; **W:** David Fallon; **M:** John Debney. *TOU*

White Fang and the Hunter 🎬🎬 1985 (G) The adventures of a boy and his dog who survive an attack from wild wolves and then help to solve a murder mystery. Loosely based on the novel by Jack London. **87m/C VHS, Beta.** Pedro Sanchez, Robert Wood; **D:** Alfonso Brescia. *VTR, HHE*

White Fire 🎬🎬 Three Steps to the Gallows 1953 Brady, in search of his lost brother, gets involved in a smuggling ring. Seems the brother is falsely accused of murder and about to hang. Brady and bar singer Castle solve the case. Good photography; bad script. **82m/C VHS, Beta.** GB Scott Brady, Mary Castle, Ferdinand "Ferdy" Mayne; **D:** John Gilling. *NOS, SNC, VYY*

White Fire 🎬 1983 Two jewel thieves will stop at nothing to own White Fire, a two hundred-carat diamond. **90m/C VHS, Beta.** Robert Ginty, Fred Williamson. *TWE*

White Fury 1990 Couples on a campout are victimized by sleazy hoodlums during a snowstorm. **89m/C VHS.** Deke Anderson, Sean Holton, Douglas Hartier, Christine Shinn, Chastity Hammons; **D:** David A. Prior. *AIP*

White Ghost 🎬 1988 (R) An Intelligence Officer who disappeared in the jungles of Asia 18 years ago is ready to come back to the United States, but not everyone wants to see him again. **90m/C VHS, Beta.** William Katt, Rosalind Chao, Martin Hewitt, Wayne Crawford, Reb Brown; **D:** B.J. Davis. *TWE*

White Gold 🎬🎬🎬 1928 Shepherd's son weds Mexican woman and his disgruntled father contrives apparent rendezvous between the wife and a ranch-hand, who's found dead in her bedroom. Seems no one believes the wife's story. Unprecedented, dark, silent drama. **73m/B VHS, Beta.** Jetta Goudal, Kenneth Thomson, George Bancroft, George Nicholls Jr., Clyde Cook; **D:** William K. Howard. *GPV*

White Gorilla woof! 1947 A great white hunter sets out to kill a gigantic white gorilla that is terrorizing the black natives. Imperialist trash. On any informed person's list of all-time worst movies. **62m/B VHS, Beta, LV.** Ray Corrigan, Lorraine Miller. *NO*

White Heat 🎬🎬🎬½ 1949 A classic gangster film with one of Cagney's best roles as a psychopathic robber/killer with a mother complex. The famous finale—perhaps Cagney's best-known scene—has Cagney trapped on top of a burning oil tank shouting "Made it, Ma! Top of the world!" before the tank explodes. Cagney's character is allegedly based on Arthur "Doc" Barker and his "Ma," and his portrayal is breathtaking. Also available colorized. **114m/B VHS, Beta, LV, Closed Caption.** James Cagney, Virginia Mayo, Edmond O'Brien, Margaret Wycherly, Steve Cochran; **D:** Raoul Walsh; **M:** Max Steiner. Nominations: Academy Awards '49: Best Story. *MGM, FOX*

White Hot 🎬½ 1988 (R) A young businessman loses his prestigious Wall Street job, and in order to live the good life, he resorts to selling drugs. Benson stars and directs. **95m/C VHS, Beta, LV.** Robby Benson, Tawny Kitaen, Danny Aiello, Sally Kirkland, Judy Tenuta; **D:** Robby Benson. *ACA*

White Hot: The Mysterious Murder of Thelma Todd 🎬🎬 1991 Thelma Todd was a Hollywood starlet found dead under strange circumstances in 1935. Buffs have sought a solution to the maybe-murder ever since; this treatment (based on the book "Hot Toddy" by Andy Edmunds) leaves too many loose ends for purists and isn't sufficiently gripping for the uninitiated. **95m/C VHS.** Loni Anderson, Robert Davi, Paul Dooley, Lawrence Pressman; **D:** Paul Wendkos. *NO*

White Hunter, Black Heart ✓✓✓ **1990 (PG)** Eastwood casts himself against type as Hustonesque director who is more interested in hunting large tusked creatures than shooting the film he came to Africa to produce. Based on Peter Viertel's 1953 account of his experiences working on James Agee's script for Huston's "African Queen." Eastwood's Huston impression is a highlight, though the story occasionally wanders off with the elephants. **112m/C VHS, Beta, LV, 8mm, Closed Caption.** Clint Eastwood, Marisa Berenson, George Dzundza, Jeff Fahey, Timothy Spall, Charlotte Cornwell, Mel Martin, Alun Armstrong, Richard Vanstone; **D:** Clint Eastwood; **W:** Peter Viertel, James Bridges, Burt Kennedy; **C:** Jack N. Green; **M:** Lennie Niehaus. *MGM, FCT, WAR*

White Huntress ✓½ *Golden Ivory* **1957** Two brothers venturing into the jungle encounter a beautiful young woman, the daughter of a settlement leader. Meanwhile, a killer is on the loose. **86m/C VHS, Beta.** *GB* Robert Urquhart, John Bentley, Susan Stephen; **D:** George Breakston. *SNC*

The White Legion ✓½ **1936** Workers and engineers push their way through steaming jungles and reeking swamps while building the Panama Canal. Many fall victim to yellow fever. Physician Keith does some medical sleuthing and saves the day. Plodding, predictable drama. **81m/B VHS, Beta.** Ian Keith, Tala Birell, Snub Pollard; **D:** Karl Brown. *VYY*

White Lie ✓✓½ **1991 (PG-13)** Len Madison, Jr. (Hines), a press secretary for the mayor of New York, receives an old photo of a lynched black man who he learns is his father, hung for raping a white woman. Madison returns to his Southern hometown to find out the truth behind his father's death, assisted by a white doctor (O'Toole) whose mother was a rape victim. They fall in love, adding to an already complicated situation, and incur the wrath of locals who are trying to keep the truth hidden. Based on the novel "Louisiana Black" by Samuel Charters. **93m/C VHS, Closed Caption.** Gregory Hines, Annette O'Toole, Bill Nunn; **D:** Bill Condon. *USH*

White Light ✓✓ **1990 (R)** "Flatliners" with a flatfoot; after a near-death experience a cop returns with memories of a beautiful woman. He tries to find out who she is/was in plodding fashion. The voyage to the afterlife is represented by a jog through a storm sewer. **CW:** Language, violence, and sensuality. **96m/C VHS, LV.** Martin Kove, Allison Hossack, Martha Henry, Heidi von Palleske, James Purcell, Bruce Boa; **D:** Al Waxman. *ACA*

White Lightning ✓✓½ *McKlusky* **1973 (PG)** Good ol' boy Reynolds plays a moonshiner going after the crooked sheriff who murdered his brother. Good stunt-driving chases enliven the formula. The inferior sequel is "Gator." **101m/C VHS, Beta.** Burt Reynolds, Ned Beatty, Bo Hopkins, Jennifer Billingsley, Louise Latham; **D:** Joseph Sargent; **W:** William W. Norton Sr.; **M:** Charles Bernstein. *MGM*

White Line Fever ✓✓½ **1975 (PG)** A young trucker's search for a happy life with his childhood sweetheart is complicated by a corrupt group in control of the long-haul trucking business. Well-done action film of good triumphing over evil. **89m/C VHS, Beta, LV.** Jan-Michael Vincent, Kay Lenz, Slim Pickens, L.Q. Jones, John David Garfield; **D:** Jonathan Kaplan; **W:** Jonathan Kaplan, Ken Friedman; **C:** Fred W. Koenekamp. *COL*

White Mama ✓✓✓ **1980** A poor widow (Davis, in a splendid role) takes in a street-wise black kid (Harden) in return for protection from the neighborhood's dangers, and they discover friendship. Poignant drama, capably directed by Cooper, featuring sterling performances all around Made-for-TV drama at its best. **96m/C VHS, Beta.** Bette Davis, Ernest Harden, Eileen Heckart, Virginia Capers, Lurene Tuttle, Anne Ramsey; **D:** Jackie Cooper. *LIV*

White Mane ✓✓✓ **1952** The poignant, poetic story of a proud and fierce white stallion that continually eludes attempts by ranchers to capture it. In French with English subtitles. **38m/B VHS, Beta, LV.** Alain Emery, Frank Silvera; **D:** Albert Lamorisse. Cannes Film Festival '52: Best Film. *NLC, HMV*

White Man's Burden ✓✓ **1995 (R)** In a world where blacks have all the wealth and power, and whites comprise the struggling underclasses, Caucasian factory worker Louis Pinnock (John Travolta) is fired by his bigoted black CEO (Belafonte) due to a misunderstanding. Driven by poverty-level financial strain, Louis kidnaps his wealthy boss to show him how the other half lives. Gimmicky premise is full of reversed stereotypes, such as black cops beating a white guy, and skinheads taking over as inner-city gangsters. Treads too lightly, and rehashes too many familiar stories, to make any real impact. Travolta had to be talked into this role by "Pulp Fiction" producer Lawrence Bender. **CW:** Strong language; some violence. **89m/C VHS, Closed Caption.** John Travolta, Harry Belafonte, Kelly Lynch, Margaret Avery, Tom Bower, Carrie Snodgrass, Sheryl Lee Ralph; **D:** Desmond Nakano; **W:** Desmond Nakano; **C:** Willy Kurant; **M:** Howard Shore. *HBO*

White Men Can't Jump ✓✓ **1992 (R)** Sometimes they can't act either. Small-time con man Harrelson stands around looking like a big nerd until someone dares him to play basketball and he proves to be more adept than he looks. After he beats Snipes, they become friends and start hustling together. Harrelson lays to rest the rumor that he can't act; here, he proves it. Fast-paced, obscenity-laced dialogue does not cover up for the fact that the story hovers between dull and dismal, redeemed only by the surreal "Jeopardy" game show sequence and the convincing b-ball action. Snipes manages to rise above the material as well as the rim, while Perez, as wooden Woody's spitfire Hispanic girlfriend, is appropriately energetic. **CW:** Language and sensuality. **115m/C VHS.** Wesley Snipes, Woody Harrelson, Rosie Perez, Tyra Ferrell, Cylk Cozart, Kadeem Hardison, Ernest Harden, John Jones; **D:** Ron Shelton; **W:** Ron Shelton; **C:** Russell Boyd. *FXV*

White Mile ✓✓½ **1994 (R)** Abusive L.A. advertising exec Dan Cutler (Alda) invites his top execs and important clients on a white-water rafting expedition along the Chilko River in the Canadian Rockies (filmed at Northern California's Russian River). But competition and arrogance causes the deaths of several participants and the widow of one sues the agency for damages. Alda excels in arrogant, self-serving nastiness. Fact-based TV movie based on court transcripts. **CW:** Language. **97m/C VHS, LV.** Alan Alda, Peter Gallagher, Robert Loggia, Fionnula Flanagan, Dakin Matthews, Bruce Altman, Robert Picardo, Max Wright, Jack Gilpin, Ken Jenkins; **D:** Robert Butler; **W:** Michael Butler. *HBO*

White Mischief ✓✓✓ **1988 (R)** An alternately ghastly and hilarious indictment of the English upper class between the World Wars, and the decadence the British colonists perpetrated in Kenya, which came to world attention with the murder of the philandering Earl of Errol in 1941. Exquisitely directed and photographed. Acclaimed and grandly acted, especially by Scacchi; Howard's last appearance. **108m/C VHS, Beta, LV, 8mm.** Greta Scacchi, Charles Dance, Joss Ackland, Sarah Miles, John Hurt, Hugh Grant, Geraldine Chaplin, Trevor Howard, Murray Head, Susan Fleetwood, Alan Dobie, Jacqueline Pearce; **D:** Michael Radford; **W:** Michael Radford; **C:** Roger Deakins; **M:** George Fenton. *NLC*

White Nights ✓✓✓ **1957** Based on a love story by Dostoyevski. A young woman pines for the return of her sailor while a mild-mannered clerk is smitten by her. Both of their romantic fantasies are explored in the dance-hall cadence is mixed with dreamy, fantastic flashbacks. Equally good Soviet version made in 1959. **107m/C VHS.** *IT* Maria Schell, Jean Marais, Marcello Mastroianni; **D:** Luchino Visconti; **M:** Nino Rota. *FCT*

White Nights ✓✓½ **1985 (PG-13)** A Russian ballet dancer who defected to the U.S. (Baryshnikov) is a passenger on a jet that crashes in the Soviet Union. With the aid of a disillusioned expatriate tap dancer (Hines), he plots to escape again. The excellent dance sequences elevate the rather lame story. ♫Say You, Say Me. **135m/C VHS, Beta, LV, Closed Caption.** Mikhail Baryshnikov, Gregory Hines, Isabella Rossellini, Helen Mirren, Jerzy Skolimowski, Geraldine Page; **D:** Taylor Hackford; **C:** David Watkin; **M:** Michel Colombier. Academy Awards '85: Best Song ("Say You, Say Me"); Golden Globe Awards '86: Best Song ("Say You, Say Me"); Nominations: Academy Awards '85: Best Song ("Separate Lives (Love Theme from White Nights)"). *COL, MOV*

White of the Eye ✓✓✓ **1988 (R)** A murdering lunatic is on the loose in Arizona, and an innocent man must find him to acquit himself of the murders. A tense, effective thriller; dazzling technique recalls the experimental films of the 1960s. **111m/C VHS, Beta, Closed Caption.** David Keith, Cathy Moriarty, Art Evans, Alan Rosenberg, Michael Greene, Alberta Watson, Marc Hayashi; **D:** Donald Cammell; **W:** China Cammell, Donald Cammell; **M:** Nick Mason, Rick Fenn, George Fenton. *PAR*

The White Orchid ✓✓ **1954** Romantic triangle ventures into the wilds of Mexico in search of Toltec ruins. Exceptional sets. **81m/C VHS, Beta.** William Lundigan, Peggy Castle, Armando Silvestre, Rosenda Monteros; **D:** Reginald LeBorg. *SNC, DVT, HEG*

White Palace ✓✓½ **1990 (R)** Successful widowed Jewish lawyer Spader is attracted to older, less educated hamburger waitress Sarandon, and ethnic/cultural strife ensues, as does hot sex. Adapted from the Glenn Savan novel, it starts out with promise but fizzles toward the end. **103m/C VHS, LV, Closed Caption.** Susan Sarandon, James Spader, Jason Alexander, Eileen Brennan, Griffin Dunne, Kathy Bates, Steven Hill, Rachel Levin, Corey Parker, Spiros Focas, Renee Taylor, Kim Myers; **D:** Luis Mandoki; **W:** Alvin Sargent, Ted Tally; **C:** Lajos Koltai; **M:** George Fenton. *USH, FCT, CCB*

White Phantom: Enemy of Darkness ✓ **1987** Ninja warriors in modern day society battling against other evil ninjas. **89m/C VHS, Beta.** Page Leong, Jay Roberts Jr., Bo Svenson; **D:** Dusty Nelson; **W:** David Hamilton, Chris Gallagher. *THV*

White Pongo woof! **1945** A policeman goes undercover with a group of British biologists to capture a mythic white gorilla believed to be the missing link. A camp jungle classic with silly, cheap special effects. **73m/B VHS, Beta.** Richard Fraser, Maris Wrixon, Lionel Royce; **D:** Sam Newfield. *SNC, NOS, HHT*

The White Rose ✓✓✓ **1923** An aspiring minister travels to see the world he intends to save, and winds up falling from grace. Complicated menage a trois is finally sorted out at the end. Silent. **120m/B VHS, Beta.** Mae Marsh, Carol Dempster, Ivor Novello, Neil Hamilton, Lucille LaVerne; **D:** D.W. Griffith. *GPV*

The White Rose ✓✓✓ **1983** The true story of a group of dissident students in Munich in 1942, who put their lives in danger by distributing leaflets telling the truth of what was going on in the concentration camps. Hans Scholl was an Army officer who discovered the truth and told the others. In the end, most of the students were captured by the Gestapo and executed. "The White Rose" was the name of the group, but none survived to tell where the name came from. Verhoeven's film telling is engrossing and compelling, with excellent acting from the young cast. In German with English subtitles. **108m/C VHS, Beta.** *GE* Lena Stolze, Wulf Kessler, Oliver Siebert, Ulrich Tucker; **D:** Michael Verhoeven. *MGM, GLV, SWC*

White Sands ✓✓½ **1992 (R)** When a dead man's body is found at a remote Indian reservation clutching a gun and a briefcase filled with $500,000, the local sheriff (Dafoe) takes his identity to see where the money leads. Using a phone number found on a piece of paper in the dead man's stomach, the sheriff follows clues until he finds himself mixed up with an rich woman (Mastrantonio) who sells black market weapons and uses the money to support "worthy" causes, and an FBI man (Jackson) who uses him as bait to lure a CIA turncoat/arms dealer (Rourke). Sound confusing? It is, and despite the strong cast and vivid scenery of the southwest United States, this film just doesn't cut it. **CW:** Language, violence, and sensual scene. **101m/C VHS, Beta, LV, Closed Caption.** Willem Dafoe, Mary Elizabeth Mastrantonio, Mickey Rourke, Mimi Rogers, Samuel L. Jackson, M. Emmet Walsh, James Rebhorn, Maura Tierney, Beth Grant, Miguel Sandoval, John Lafayette; **Cameos:** Fred Dalton Thompson, John P. Ryan; **D:** Roger Donaldson; **W:** Daniel Pyne; **C:** Peter Menzies Jr.; **M:** Patrick O'Hearn. *WAR, FCT*

The White Shadow, Vol. 1 1978 After an injury curtails his career with the Chicago Bulls, Ken Reeves (Howard) becomes the basketball coach at Carver High School in Los Angeles, an inner-city school with a team of wisecracking players. The pilot episode finds Reeves trying to adjust to his new life and help his students. **60m/C VHS.** Ken Howard, Ed Bernard, Kevin Hooks, Byron Stewart, Thomas Carter, Timothy Van Patten, Ira Angustain, Joan Pringle, Eric Kilpatrick, Nathan Cook, Ken Michelman. *MOV, MTM*

White Shadows in the South Seas 🐾🐾½ 1929 Alcohol, drugs, and prostitution take their toll on the native population of Tahiti in this early talkie. Blue plays a western doctor who marries the daughter of a native chief. However, he finds greed for the island's pearl treasures drawing other unscrupulous westerners to destroy the unspoiled paradise. **88m/B VHS.** Monte Blue, Robert Anderson, Raquel Torres; **D:** Woodbridge S. Van Dyke; **C:** Clyde De Vinna. Academy Awards '29: Best Cinematography. *FCT*

The White Sheik 🐾🐾🐾 *Lo Sceicco Bianco* 1952 Fellini's first solo effort. A newly wed bride meets her idol from the comic pages (made with photos, not cartoons; called fumetti) and runs off with him. She soon finds he's as ordinary as her husband. Brilliant satire in charming garb. Remade as "The World's Greatest Lover." Woody Allen's "The Purple Rose of Cairo" is in a similar spirit. In Italian with subtitles. **86m/B VHS.** *JP* Alberto Sordi, Giulietta Masina, Brunella Bova, Leopoldo Trieste; **D:** Federico Fellini; **W:** Federico Fellini, Tullio Pinelli, Ennio Flaiano; **M:** Nino Rota. *HMV, APD, VDM*

The White Sin 🐾🐾 1924 An innocent country girl hires on as maid of a rich woman and is seduced and abandoned by the woman's profligate son, but everything turns out all right by the end of the third handkerchief. Silent with original organ music. **93m/B VHS, Beta, 8mm.** Madge Bellamy, John Bowers, Billy Bevan; **D:** William A. Seiter. *VYY*

The White Sister 🐾🐾🐾½ 1923 Gish is an Italian aristocrat driven from her home by a conniving sister. When her true love (Colman) is reported killed she decides to become a nun and enters a convent. When her lover does return he tricks her into leaving the convent but before he can persuade her to renounce her vows Vesuvius erupts and he goes off to warn the villagers, dying for his efforts. Gish then re-dedicates herself to her faith. Colman's first leading role, which made him a romantic star. Filmed on location in Italy. **108m/B VHS, Beta.** Lillian Gish, Ronald Colman, Gail Kane, J. Barney Sherry, Charles Lane; **D:** Henry King. *DVT, HEG*

White Slave 🐾 *Amazonia: The Catherine Miles Story* 1986 **(R)** An Englishwoman is captured by bloodthirsty cannibals and, rather than being eaten, is tormented and made a slave. **90m/C VHS, Beta.** Elvire Avoray, Will Gonzales, Andrew Louis Coppola; **D:** Roy Garrett. *NO*

White Squall 🐾🐾½ 1996 **(PG-13)** Based on the 1960 true story of 13 young men who become students at Ocean Academy, a year-long adventure spent aboard the brigantine Albatross. Bridges plays the ship's captain and surrogate

dad. The boys agonize over their various crises, making the first half of the movie into a veritable "Dead Poets Yachting Society." However, a sudden storm overtakes the ship in the Caribbean and several crew members are killed. There's a shift to a "Caine Mutiny" type trial in which Bridges must prove the tragedy was not his fault while the survivors rally to his defense. Director Scott excels at showing the fury of nature in the prolonged storm scene, but takes his time getting there. **CW:** Some sexuality and a traumatic shipwreck. **128m/C VHS, LV, Closed Caption.** Jeff Bridges, Scott Wolf, Caroline Goodall, Balthazar Getty, John Savage, Jeremy Sisto, Jason Marsden, David Selby, Zeljko Ivanek, Ryan Phillippe, David Lascher, Eric Michael Cole, Julio Mechoso, Ethan Embry; **D:** Ridley Scott; **W:** Todd Robinson; **C:** Hugh Johnson; **M:** Jeff Rona. *TOU*

White Tiger 🐾🐾½ 1923 Three crooks pull off a major heist and hide out in a mountain cabin where their mistrust of each other grows. **81m/C VHS.** Priscilla Dean, Matt Moore, Raymond Griffith, Wallace Beery; **D:** Tod Browning. *GPV, FCT*

White Tiger 🐾½ 1995 **(R)** DEA agent decides to take the law into his own fists when his partner is murdered by a Chinese gang leader. **CW:** Non-stop violence and language, and for sexuality and drug content. **93m/C VHS, Closed Caption.** Gary Daniels, Matt Craven, Cary-Hiroyuki Tagawa, Julia Nickson-Soul; **D:** Richard Martin; **W:** Gordon Melbourne; **M:** Graeme Coleman. *HMK*

The White Tower 🐾🐾🐾 1950 Five men and a woman set out to scale the infamous White Tower in the Alps. Each person's true nature is revealed as he or she scales the peak, which has defied all previous attempts. Slightly overwrought, but exciting. Filmed in Technicolor on location in the Swiss Alps. **98m/C VHS, Beta.** Glenn Ford, Claude Rains, Cedric Hardwicke, Oscar Homolka, Lloyd Bridges; **D:** Ted Tetzlaff. *HHT, TTC*

White Water Summer 🐾½ *Rites of Summer* 1987 **(PG)** A group of young adventurers trek into the Sierras, and find themselves struggling against nature and each other to survive. Bacon is the rugged outdoorsman (yeah, sure) who shows them what's what. Chances are it was never at a theater near you, and with good reason. **90m/C VHS, Beta, LV.** Kevin Bacon, Sean Astin, Jonathan Ward, Matt Adler; **D:** Jeff Bleckner; **M:** Michael Boddicker. *COL*

White Wolves 2: Legend of the Wild 🐾🐾½ 1994 **(PG)** Troubled teens are on a school assignment involving a conservation foundation's rescue of a pair of young wolves. They must overcome lots of obstacles, including the fact that they can't stand each other. Average teens-in-the-woods adventure. **95m/C VHS.** Corin "Corky" Nemec, Justin Whalin, Jeremy London, Elizabeth Berkley, Ernie Reyes Jr., Ele Keats; **D:** Terence H. Winkless. *NHO*

The White Zombie 🐾🐾🐾 1932 Lugosi followed his success in "Dracula" with the title role in this low-budget horror classic about the leader of a band of zombies who wants to steal a beautiful young woman from her new husband. Set in Haiti; the first zombie movie. Rich and dark, though ludicrous. Based on the novel "The Magic Island" by William Seabrook. **73m/B VHS, Beta.** Bela Lugosi, Madge Bellamy, John Harron; **D:** Victor Halperin; **M:** Xavier Cugat. *NOS, PSM, CAB*

WhiteForce 🐾 1988 **(R)** A secret agent tracks an enemy. His government tracks him. He runs around with a big machine gun and a couple of hand grenades. He fires the gun and throws the grenades. **90m/C Beta.** Sam Jones, Kimberly Pistone; **D:** Eddie Romero. *NO*

Whitewater Sam 🐾🐾½ 1978 **(G)** Whitewater Sam and his Siberian Husky, Sybar, embark on an exciting trip through the uncharted wilds of the Great Northwest. The likeable, intelligent hound steals the show. Good family adventure. **87m/C VHS, Beta.** Keith Larsen; **D:** Keith Larsen; **W:** Keith Larsen. *MON*

Who Am I This Time? 🐾🐾🐾 1982 Two shy people can express their love for each other only through their roles in a local theater production of "A Streetcar Named Desire." Good cast responds well to competent direction from Demme; poignant, touching and memorable. Based on a story by Kurt Vonnegut, Jr. Made for television. **60m/C VHS, Beta, LV.** Susan Sarandon, Christopher Walken, Robert Ridgely; **D:** Jonathan Demme. *MON, BTV*

Who Done It? 🐾🐾 1942 Average Abbott and Costello comedy about two would-be radio mystery writers, working as soda-jerks, who play detective after the radio station's president is murdered. **77m/B VHS, Beta.** Bud Abbott, Lou Costello, William Gargan, Patric Knowles, Louise Allbritton, Don Porter, Jerome Cowan, William Bendix, Mary Wickes; **D:** Erle C. Kenton. *USH*

Who Done It? 🐾🐾½ 1956 Film debut of the rakish Hill as ice-rink sweeper, Hugo Dill. When Dill comes into some money and a dog, he launches a private investigating firm. A woman enters the picture and Hugo discovers his sleuthing has gotten him in over his head. Lots of typical gags and car chases. **79m/B VHS, Closed Caption.** *GB* Benny Hill, Belinda Lee, David Kossoff, Ernest Thesiger; **D:** Basil Dearden. *REP*

Who Framed Roger Rabbit 🐾🐾🐾½ 1988 **(PG)** Technically marvelous, cinematically hilarious, eye-popping combination of cartoon and live action create a Hollywood of the 1940s where cartoon characters are real and a repressed minority working in films. A 'toon-hating detective is hired to uncover the unfaithful wife of 2-D star Roger, and instead uncovers a conspiracy to wipe out all 'toons. Special appearances by many cartoon characters from the past. Coproduced by Touchstone (Disney) and Amblin (Spielberg). Adapted from "Who Censored Roger Rabbit?" by Gary K. Wold. **104m/C VHS, Beta, LV.** Bob Hoskins, Christopher Lloyd, Joanna Cassidy, Alan Tilvern, Stubby Kaye; **D:** Robert Zemeckis; **W:** Jeffrey Price, Peter S. Seaman; **C:** Dean Cundey; **M:** Alan Silvestri; **V:** Charles Fleischer, Mae Questel, Kathleen Turner, Amy Irving, Mel Blanc, June Foray, Frank Sinatra. Academy Awards '88: Best Film Editing, Best Visual Effects; National Board of Review Awards '88: 10 Best Films of the Year; Nominations: Academy Awards '88: Best Art Direction/Set Decoration, Best Cinematography, Best Sound. *TOU*

Who Has Seen the Wind? 🐾🐾 1977 Two boys grow up in Saskatchewan during the Depression. So-so family viewing drama. Ferrer as a bootlegger steals the otherwise small-paced show. **102m/C VHS, Beta, Closed Caption.** Jose Ferrer, Brian Painchaud, Charmion King, Helen Shaver.

Who Is Killing the Great Chefs of Europe? 🐾🐾🐾 *Too Many Chefs; Someone is Killing the Great Chefs of Europe* 1978 **(PG)** A fast-paced, lightly handled black comedy. When a gourmand, well-played by Morley, learns he must lose weight to live, a number of Europe's best chefs are murdered according to their cooking specialty. A witty, crisp, international mystery based on Ivan and Nan Lyon's novel. **112m/C VHS, Closed Caption.** George Segal, Jacqueline Bisset, Robert Morley, Jean-Pierre Cassel, Philippe Noiret, Jean Rochefort, Joss Ackland, Nigel Havers; **D:** Ted Kotcheff; **M:** Henry Mancini. Los Angeles Film Critics Association Awards '78: Best Supporting Actor (Morley). *WAR*

Who Is the Black Dahlia? 🐾🐾🐾 1975 In L.A. in 1947, a detective tries to find out who murdered a star-struck 22-year-old woman nicknamed "The Black Dahlia" (Arnaz). Based on a famous unsolved murder case which was later the basis for "True Confessions." Made for TV. **96m/C VHS, Beta.** Efrem Zimbalist Jr., Lucie Arnaz, Ronny Cox, MacDonald Carey, Linden Chiles; **D:** Joseph Pevney; **W:** Robert W. Lenski. *WOV*

Who Killed Baby Azaria? 🐾🐾 1983 Parents are arrested for infanticide after they claim their baby was stolen by a wild dog while vacationing on a supposedly haunted Australian mountain, or was it an aboriginal spirit that absconded with the tyke? Less compelling than the American remake, "A Cry in the Dark." Made for Australian TV. **96m/C VHS, Beta.** *AU* Elaine Hudson, John Hamblin, Peter Carroll; *D:* Judy Rymer. *PSM*

Who Killed Doc Robbin? *Sinister House; Curley and His Gang in the Haunted Mansion* 1948 A group of youngsters try to clear their friend, Dan, the town handyman, when the sinister Dr. Robbin is murdered. The follow-up to "The Adventures of Curly and His Gang;" intended as part of a Roach kid-comedy series in the manner of "Our Gang." Fast pace and lots of slapstick give a first impression of spirited juvenile hijinks, but not much is genuinely funny. And the names of the two black kids—"Dis" and "Dat"—aren't funny either. **50m/C VHS, Beta.** Larry Olsen, Don Castle, Bernard Carr, Virginia Grey. *SNC, NOS, HHT*

Who Killed Mary What's 'Er Name? 🐾🐾 *Death of a Hooker* 1971 (PG) A diabetic ex-fighter tracks a prostitute's killer through Greenwich Village. Illogical, incredible and disjointed attempt at comedy/mystery. Odd, unsatisfying ending, with the boxer going into a coma. Good supporting cast. **90m/C VHS, Beta.** Red Buttons, Sylvia Miles, Conrad Bain, Ron Carey, David Doyle, Sam Waterston; *D:* Ernie Pintoff. *GEM, PSM*

Who Shot Pat? 🐾🐾½ *Who Shot Patakango?* 1992 (R) Funny, nostalgic, coming of age story set in fifties Brooklyn. Knight stars as Bic Bickham, the leader of a clean-living "gang" of seniors at a Brooklyn vocational school. Memorable vintage soundtrack features hits by legendary artists Chuck Berry and Bo Diddly. *CW:* Language. **102m/C VHS, Closed Caption.** David Knight, Sandra Bullock, Kevin Otto, Aaron Ingram, Brad Randall; *D:* Robert Brooks; *W:* Halle Brooks, Robert Brooks. *WAR*

Who Slew Auntie Roo? 🐾🐾½ *Whoever Slew Auntie Roo?; Gingerbread House* 1971 (PG) An updated twist on the Hansel and Gretel fairy tale. Features Winters as an odd, reclusive widow mistaken for the fairy tale's children-eating witch by one of the orphans at her annual Christmas party—with dire consequences. **90m/C VHS, Beta.** Shelley Winters, Ralph Richardson, Mark Lester, Lionel Jeffries, Hugh Griffith; *D:* Curtis Harrington; *W:* Robert Blees. *VES*

Whodunit 🐾 1982 (R) The bad horror flicks always seem to have (usually young) characters murdered one at a time, often on a remote island. This loser is no exception. **82m/C VHS, Beta.** Rick Bean, Gary Phillips; *D:* Bill Naud; *W:* Anthony Shaffer. *LIV, VES*

The Whole Shootin' Match 🐾🐾🐾 1979 Two thirty something Texas nobodies chase the American Dream via a sure-fire invention called the Kitchen Wizard, after failing in the small-animal business and polyurethane. Offbeat, very low-budget independent feature shot interestingly in sepia tones. Sympathetic and human. **108m/C VHS.** Matthew L. Perry, Sonny Carl Davis, Doris Hargrave; *D:* Eagle Pennell. *NO*

The Whole Wide World 🐾🐾🐾 1996 (PG) Adaptation of Novalyne Price Ellis' memoirs about her friendship with "Conan the Barbarian" pulp writer Robert E. Howard. In 1933, proper young Cross Plains, Texas schoolteacher (and aspiring writer) Price (Zellweger) arranges an introduction to local eccentric Howard (D'Onofrio), who lives with his overprotective, dying mother (Wedgeworth) and respected doctor father (Presnell) while churning out his bloody tales. Howard has few, if any, social skills but his unpredictability appeals to the sensible Price and the two have a turbulent emotional relationship that never blooms into a full romance. Howard committed suicide in 1936 at the age of 30. **120m/C VHS.** Renee Zellweger, Vincent D'Onofrio, Ann Wedgeworth, Harve Presnell, Helen Cates, Benjamin Mouton, Michael Corbett, Marion Eaten, Leslie Berger, Chris Shearer, Sandy Walper, Dell Aldrich, Libby Villari, Antonia Bogdanovich, Elizabeth D'Onofrio, Stephen Marshall; *D:* Dan Ireland; *W:* Michael Scott Myers, Novalyne Price Ellis; *C:* Claudio Rocha; *M:* Hans Zimmer,

Harry Gregson-Williams. Nominations: Independent Spirit Awards '97: Best Actress (Zellweger). *NYR*

Who'll Save Our Children? 🐾🐾🐾 1982 Two children are abandoned and left on the doorstep of a middle-aged, childless couple. Years later the natural parents, now reformed, attempt to reclaim their children. Well cast and topical. Made for TV. **96m/C VHS, Beta.** Shirley Jones, Len Cariou, Conchata Ferrell, Frances Sternhagen, Cassie Yates, David Hayward; *D:* George Schaefer. *TLF*

Who'll Stop the Rain? 🐾🐾🐾½ *Dog Soldiers* 1978 (R) A temperamental Vietnam vet (Nolte) is enlisted in a smuggling scheme to transport a large amount of heroin into California. An excellent blend of drama, comedy, action, suspense, and tragedy. Based on Robert Stone's novel "Dog Soldiers." Outstanding period soundtrack by Creedence Clearwater Revival, including title song. Violent and compelling tale of late-'60s disillusionment. **126m/C VHS, Beta, LV.** Nick Nolte, Tuesday Weld, Michael Moriarty, Anthony Zerbe, Richard Masur, Ray Sharkey, David Opatoshu, Charles Haid, Gail Strickland; *D:* Karel Reisz; *W:* Judith Rascoe. *MGM*

Wholly Moses! woof! 1980 (PG) Set in biblical times, this alleged comedy concerns a phony religious prophet who begins to believe that his mission is to lead the chosen. Horrible ripoff of "Life of Brian," released the previous year. What a cast—what a waste! **125m/C VHS, Beta, LV.** Dudley Moore, Laraine Newman, James Coco, Paul Sand, Dom DeLuise, Jack Gilford, John Houseman, Madeline Kahn, Richard Pryor, John Ritter; *D:* Gary Weis. *COL*

Whoopee! 🐾🐾 1930 Cantor stars in his first sound picture as a rich hypochondriac sent out west for his health, where he encounters rugged cowboys and Indians. Filmed in two-color Technicolor and based on Ziegfeld's 1928 Broadway production with the same cast. Dances supervised by Busby Berkeley. ♫The Song of the Setting Sun; Mission Number; Makin' Whoopee; A Girlfriend of a Boyfriend of Mine; My Baby Just Cares for Me; I'll Still Belong to You; Stetson. **93m/C VHS, Beta.** Eddie Cantor, Ethel Shutta, Paul Gregory, Eleanor Hunt, Betty Grable; *D:* Thornton Freeland. Nominations: Academy Awards '31: Best Interior Decoration. *HBO*

The Whoopee Boys 🐾 1986 (R) A New York lowlife in Palm Beach tries to reform himself by saving a school for needy children so his rich girlfriend will marry him. Full of unfunny jokes and very bad taste, with no redeeming qualities whatever. **89m/C VHS, Beta, LV.** Michael O'Keefe, Paul Rodriguez; *D:* John Byrum; *W:* Jeff Buhai; *C:* Ralf Bode; *M:* Jack Nitzsche. *PAR*

Whoops Apocalypse 🐾🐾½ 1983 Satiric account of events leading up to WWIII. Invasion in South America leads British prime minister to suggest nuclear retaliation. Uneven, lacking in the Strangelovian element, but funny in spots. Based on the British hit television series and scripted by series writers Marshall and Renwick. **137m/C VHS, Beta.** *GB* John Cleese, John Barron, Richard Griffiths, Peter Jones, Bruce Montague, Barry Morse, Rik Mayall, Ian Richardson, Alexei Sayle, Herbert Lom, Joanne Pearce; *D:* Tom Bussmann; *W:* Andrew Marshall, David Renwick. *NO*

Whoops Apocalypse 🐾🐾 1988 (R) America's first female president Swit, recently ensconced after the untimely death of the ex-circus clown previous president, is forced to contend with hotheaded superpowers who want to kick off WWIII with a bang. Uneven black comedic satire of holocaust genre. Based on the BBC TV series. **93m/C VHS, Beta.** Loretta Swit, Peter Cook, Michael Richards. *MGM*

Whore 🐾🐾 *If You Can't Say It, Just See It* 1991 (R) Ken Russell's gritty night in the life of cynical prostitute Theresa Russell is strong medicine, a powerful antidote to sappy Hollywood films that glorify streetwalking. Also available in the 92-minute original uncut version, an 85-minute NC-17 version, and an alternate R-Rated version. *CW:* Strong sexual dialogue, some violence, and

strong sexual situations. **80m/C VHS, Closed Caption.** Theresa Russell, Antonio Vargas; *D:* Ken Russell; *W:* Ken Russell, Deborah Dalton. *THV*

Whore 2 🐾½ *Bad Girls* 1994 (R) Jack is a middle-aged writer who moves into Hell's Kitchen in order to do research for a book about prostitutes. Then Jack gets involved with two of the girls—the tough, jealous Lori and childlike Mary Lou. *CW:* Strong sexuality and language; violence; drug use. **85m/C VHS, LV.** Amos Kollek, Marla Sucharetza, Mari Nelson; *D:* Amos Kollek; *W:* Amos Kollek. *THV*

Who's Afraid of Virginia Woolf? 🐾🐾🐾 1966 Nichols debuts as a director in this biting Edward Albee play. A teacher and his wife (Segal and Dennis) are invited to the home of a burned-out professor and his foulmouthed, bitter, yet seductive wife (Burton and Taylor). The guests get more than dinner, as the evening deteriorates into brutal verbal battles between the hosts. Taylor and Dennis won Oscars; Burton's Oscar-nominated portrait of the tortured husband is magnificent. Richard and Liz's best film together. **127m/B VHS, Beta, LV.** Richard Burton, Elizabeth Taylor, George Segal, Sandy Dennis; *D:* Mike Nichols; *W:* Ernest Lehman; *M:* Alex North. Academy Awards '66: Best Actress (Taylor), Best Art Direction/Set Decoration (B & W), Best Black and White Cinematography, Best Costume Design (B & W), Best Supporting Actress (Dennis); British Academy Awards '66: Best Actor (Burton), Best Actress (Taylor), Best Film; National Board of Review Awards '66: 10 Best Films of the Year, Best Actress (Taylor); New York Film Critics Awards '66: Best Actress (Taylor); Nominations: Academy Awards '66: Best Actor (Burton), Best Adapted Screenplay, Best Director (Nichols), Best Film Editing, Best Picture, Best Sound, Best Supporting Actor (Segal), Best Original Score. *WAR, BTV*

Who's Got the Action? 🐾½ 1963 Martin and Turner are a husband and wife divided by his love of playing the ponies. In order to keep his gambling under control Turner schemes to become his new bookie. But when Martin suddenly goes on a winning streak, the new bookie is in trouble with her former competition, who just happen to be the Mob. Strained, flat comedy with Turner especially miscast. **93m/C VHS.** Lana Turner, Dean Martin, Walter Matthau, Eddie Albert, Nita Talbot, Margo, Paul Ford, John McGiver, Jack Albertson; *D:* Daniel Mann; *W:* Jack Rose. *PAR*

Who's Harry Crumb? 🐾½ 1989 (PG-13) Bumbling detective Candy can't even investigate a routine kidnapping! His incompetence is catching: the viewer can't detect a single genuinely funny moment. Candy is the only likeable thing in this all-around bad, mindless farce. **95m/C VHS, Beta, LV, Closed Caption.** John Candy, Jeffrey Jones, Annie Potts, Tim Thomerson, Barry Corbin, Shawnee Smith, Valri Bromfield, Renee Coleman, Joe Flaherty, Lyle Alzado, James Belushi, Stephen Young; *D:* Paul Flaherty; *W:* Robert Conte; *M:* Michel Colombier. *COL*

Who's Minding the Mint? 🐾🐾🐾 1967 A money checker at the U.S. Mint must replace $50,000 he accidentally destroyed. He enlists a retired money printer and an inept gang to infiltrate the mint and replace the lost cash, with predictable chaos resulting. Non-stop zaniness in this wonderful comedy that never got its due when released. Thieves who befriend Hutton include Denver of "Gilligan's Island" and Farr, later of "M*A*S*H." **97m/C VHS, Beta.** Jim Hutton, Dorothy Provine, Milton Berle, Joey Bishop, Bob Denver, Walter Brennan, Jamie Farr; *D:* Howard Morris; *C:* Joseph Biroc. *GKK*

Who's That Girl? 🐾 1987 (PG) A flighty, wrongly-convicted parolee kidnaps her uptight lawyer and they have wacky adventures as she goes in search of the crumb that landed her in the pokey. Plenty of Madonna tunes, if that's what you like; they briefly keep you from wondering why you're not laughing. Kind of a remake (a bad one) of "Bringing Up Baby" (1938). **94m/C VHS, Beta, LV, 8mm, Closed Caption.** Madonna, Griffin Dunne, John Mills, Haviland Morris; *D:* James Foley; *C:* Jan De

Bont. Golden Raspberry Awards '87: Worst Actress (Madonna). **WAR**

Who's That Knocking at My Door? ♦♦♦ *J.R.; I Call First* 1968 Interesting debut for Scorsese, in which he exercises many of the themes and techniques that he polished for later films. An autobiographical drama about an Italian-American youth growing up in New York City, focusing on street life, Catholicism and adolescent bonding. Begun as a student film called "I Call First"; later developed into a feature. Keitel's film debut. **90m/B VHS, Beta.** Harvey Keitel, Zena Bethune; **D:** Martin Scorsese. **FCT, WAR**

Who's the Man? ♦♦ 1993 (R) Two clowning companions who work in a barbershop in Harlem get recruited into the police force to investigate a murder. Doctor Dre and Ed Lover (themselves) make use of their hip-hop music connections and full-throttle slapstick humor to enliven the search. Salt of "Salt 'n' Pepa," is the female lead and Ice-T plays a gangster. First-time director Demme works his star duo for both foolish and vulgar humor. Filming done mostly on location in Harlem. Includes a lengthy list of cameo appearances by several hip-hop performers. For fans; based on a story by Dre, Lover, and Seth Greenland. **124m/C VHS, Closed Caption.** Ed Lover, Cheryl "Salt" James, Ice-T, Jim Moody, Colin Quinn, Kim Chan, Rozwill Young, Badja Djola, Richard Bright, Denis Leary, Andre B. Blake, Bill Bellamy; **D:** Ted Demme; **W:** Seth Greenland; **M:** Michael Wolff. **NLC, IME, COL**

Who's Who ♦♦ 1978 In a satire on climbing the British social ladder, workers in a London brokerage firm struggle with class issues and find the higher you climb, the more you find greed, pettiness, and stupidity. Made for British television. **75m/C VHS.** *GB* Bridget Kane, Simon Chandler, Adam Norton, Philip Davis, Joolia Cappleman; **D:** Mike Leigh; **W:** Mike Leigh. **WBF, BTV, FCT**

Whose Child Am I? ♦ 1975 (R) A woman so desperately wants a child of her own that she doesn't mind who the father is. Ludicrous and vulgar. **90m/C VHS.** Kate O'Mara, Paul Freeman, Edward Judd, Felicity Devonshire; **D:** Lawrence Britten. **ATL**

Whose Life Is It Anyway? ♦♦♦½ 1981 (R) Black humor abounds. Sculptor Dreyfuss is paralyzed from the neck down in an auto accident. What follows is his struggle to persuade the hospital authorities to let him die. Excellent cast headed impressively by Dreyfuss; Lahti as his doctor and hospital head Cassavetes also are superb. From Brian Clark's successful Broadway play. **118m/C VHS, Beta.** Richard Dreyfuss, John Cassavetes, Christine Lahti, Bob Balaban, Kenneth McMillan, Kaki Hunter, Thomas Carter; **D:** John Badham; **W:** Reginald Rose, Brian Clark. **MGM**

Why Change Your Wife? ♦♦½ 1920 A rare, recently re-discovered silent comedy. Swanson and Meighan play married couple Beth and Robert who find themselves drifting apart after ten years of marriage. Robert becomes involved with someone else and Beth demands a divorce. After Robert remarries, Beth decides she wants him back and the real fun begins as she tries every trick in the book to regain her ex-husband. Piano scored. **100m/B VHS, Beta.** Gloria Swanson, Thomas Meighan, Bebe Daniels; **D:** Cecil B. DeMille. **GPV**

Why Does Herr R. Run Amok? ♦♦ *Warum Lauft Herr R Amok?* 1969 Notorious Fassbinder black comedy about a middle-class man, unable to cope with the increasing problems of modern life, who suddenly murders his family. The characters are called by the actors' names to heighten the sense of reality. Film is based on a case history. In German with English subtitles. **88m/C VHS.** *GE* Kurt Raab, Lilith Unger, Amadeus Fengler, Hanna Schygulla, Franz Maron; **D:** Rainer Werner Fassbinder, Michael Fengler; **W:** Rainer Werner Fassbinder, Michael Fengler. **NYF, FCT, ING**

Why Has Bodhi-Darma Left for the East ♦♦ 1989 Set in a remote monastery in the Korean mountains, film follows an old master, close to death, who must lead his disciples in their search for spiritual freedom. The film's title is a Zen koan—an unanswerable riddle that serves as an aid on the path to enlightenment. Korean with subtitles. **135m/C VHS.** **D:** Bae Young-kyun; **W:** Bae Young-kyun; **C:** Bae Young-kyun. **MIL**

Why Me? ♦♦ 1990 (R) Two jewel thieves unknowingly steal an enormously valuable ruby ring and are in over their heads trying to evade the cops and everyone else. In the same vein as the much-funnier "Nuns on the Run," this caper is done in by bad acting and too much ill-conceived slapstick. Adapted by Donald E. Westlake from his own novel. **96m/C VHS, LV, Closed Caption.** Christopher Lambert, Christopher Lloyd, Kim Greist, J.T. Walsh, Michael J. Pollard, Tony Plana, John Hancock, Lawrence Tierney; **D:** Gene Quintano; **W:** Donald E. Westlake. **COL**

Why Shoot the Teacher ♦♦♦ 1979 A young teacher sent to a one-room schoolhouse in a small prairie town in Saskatchewan during the Depression gets a cold reception on the cold prairie. One of the more popular films at the Canadian box office. Cort was Harold in "Harold and Maude." Based on the novel by Max Braithwaite. **101m/C VHS, Beta.** *CA* Bud Cort, Samantha Eggar, Chris Wiggins; **D:** Silvio Narizzano; **W:** James DeFelice.

The Wicked ♦ 1989 Though packaged as serious horror, this is a cheap, tacky spoof with folks stranded at the country residence of a vampire family. Sole point of interest: these Transylvanian cliches take place in the Australian outback. Kids might actually like this (gore isn't severe), if they can surmount the thick Down Under accents. **87m/C VHS.** Brett Cumo, Richard Morgan, Angela Kennedy, Maggie Blinco, John Doyle; **D:** Colin Eggleston. **HMD**

Wicked City ♦♦ 1992 Humans are uneasily coexisting with Reptoids (creatures that can assume human shape) in this sci-fi tale based on a Japanese comic strip. Then Hong Kong police discover a plot by the Reptoids to destroy mankind and rule the world (what else is new). Nifty special effects. Available dubbed or in Cantonese with subtitles. **88m/C VHS.** *HK* Jacky Cheung, Leon Lai, Michelle Li; **D:** Peter Mak. **FXL**

The Wicked Lady ♦♦ 1945 Posh but lame costume drama about a bored 17th century noblewoman who takes to highway robbery to spice up her life. Credulity-stretcher extraordinaire. Based on "The Life and Death of Wicked Lady Skelton" by Magdalen King-Hall. Mason is cheeky as a fellow highwayman. Remade in 1983 with Faye Dunaway. **103m/B VHS, Beta.** *GB* James Mason, Margaret Lockwood, Patricia Roc, Michael Rennie, Felix Aylmer, Enid Stamp-Taylor, Griffith Jones; **D:** Leslie Arliss. **NO**

The Wicked Lady ♦½ 1983 (R) Remake of the 1945 costumer about a 17th-century noblewoman trying her hand at highway robbery. More noted for its low-cut costumes and racy humor than any talent involved. **99m/C VHS, Beta.** *GB* Faye Dunaway, John Gielgud, Denholm Elliott, Alan Bates, Glynis Barber, Oliver Tobias, Prunella Scales; **D:** Michael Winner; **W:** Michael Winner; **C:** Jack Cardiff; **M:** Tony Banks. **MGM**

Wicked Stepmother ♦ 1989 (PG-13) A family discovers that an aged stepmother is actually a witch. Davis walked off the film shortly before she died, and was replaced by Carrera. Davis's move was wise; the result is dismal, and would have been had she stayed. As it is the viewer wonders: How come the stepmother isn't Davis anymore? Davis's unfortunate last role. **90m/C VHS, Beta.** Bette Davis, Barbara Carrera, Colleen Camp, Lionel Stander, David Rasche, Tom Bosley, Seymour Cassel, Evelyn Keyes, Richard Moll, Laurene Landon; **D:** Larry Cohen; **W:** Larry Cohen; **C:** Bryan England; **M:** Robert Folk. **MGM**

The Wicker Man ♦♦♦½ 1975 The disappearance of a young girl leads a devoutly religious Scottish policeman to an island whose denizens practice bizarre pagan sexual rituals. An example of occult horror that achieves its mounting terror without gratuitous gore. The first original screenplay by playwright Shaffer. Beware shortened versions that may still lurk out there; the 103-minute restored director's cut is definitive. **103m/C VHS, Beta.** Edward Woodward, Christopher Lee, Britt Ekland, Diane Cilento, Ingrid Pitt; **D:** Robin Hardy; **W:** Anthony Shaffer. **REP**

Wide Open Faces ♦♦ 1938 Every crook in town is looking for some missing stolen loot. Soda jerk Brown outwits them all in his own inimitable way. The story may be predictable, but Brown's physical humor keeps things interesting. **67m/B VHS.** Joe E. Brown, Jane Wyman, Alison Skipworth, Alan Baxter, Lucien Littlefield, Sidney Toler, Berton Churchill, Barbara Pepper, Stanley Fields, Horace Murphy; **D:** Kurt Neumann; **C:** Paul Vogel. **NOS**

Wide Sargasso Sea ♦♦ 1992 (NC-17) Jamaica in the 1840's is a seething, mysterious paradise—a former British slave colony with a mix of powerful voodoo culture, beauty, and eroticism providing a very potent brew, a perfect setting for this soaper. Based on the novel by Jean Rhys, which is something of a prequel to Charlotte Bronte's "Jane Eyre." Properly English Edward Rochester meets and marries the tragic Antoinette—the same mad wife locked in the attic in the Bronte novel. Explicit nudity and sex earn the NC-17, but the film is tragic without being sensationalized. Also available in an edited R-rated and unrated versions. **CW:** Strong sexuality. **98m/C VHS, LV, Closed Caption.** *AU* Karina Lombard, Nathaniel Parker, Rachel Ward, Michael York, Martine Beswick, Claudia Robinson, Rowena King, Huw Christie Williams; **D:** John Duigan; **W:** Jan Sharp, Carole Angier, John Duigan; **C:** Geoff Burton; **M:** Stewart Copeland. **NLC, IME, BTV**

The Widow ♦♦ 1976 A story about a woman slowly learning to deal with her own grief, her children's traumas and monetary worries after the death of her husband. Straightforward, passable made for TV domestic drama based on Lynn Caine's best-selling novel. **99m/C VHS, Beta.** Michael Learned, Farley Granger, Bradford Dillman, Robert Lansing; **D:** J. Lee Thompson. **TLF**

Widow Couderc ♦♦♦ 1974 A provincial widow unknowingly includes an escaped murderer among her liaisons. Based on a novel by Georges Simenon. In French with English subtitles. **92m/C VHS, Beta.** *FR* Simone Signoret, Alain Delon; **D:** Pierre Granier-Deferre. **FCT**

Widow's Kiss ♦♦ 1994 (R) Young man is suspicious when his dad dies in the arms of his sexy, younger bride and he hires a detective who learns that the widow has left a number of dead husbands behind. So, the grieving son decides to get close to his new stepmommy to find out what's going on. Rather dull cable drama wastes its talented cast. **CW:** Some strong sexuality, language and some violence. **103m/C VHS.** Beverly D'Angelo, Bruce Davison, MacKenzie Astin, Dennis Haysbert, Michael Des Barres, Anna Maria Horsford; **D:** Peter Foldy; **W:** Peter Foldy, Mark Donnelly; **C:** Doyle Smith; **M:** Robert Sprayberry. **HBO**

Widow's Nest ♦♦ 1977 Three widowed sisters live in a bizarre fantasy world when they lock themselves in a dingy mansion in Cuba of the 1930s. Filmed in Spain. **90m/C VHS, Beta.** Patricia Neal, Susan Oliver, Lila Kedrova, Valentina Cortese; **D:** Tony Navarro. **NO**

Widow's Peak ♦♦½ 1994 (PG) 1920's Irish community is run by a dictatorship of well-to-do widows with Mrs. Doyle-Counihan (Plowright) at the helm. Troubles begin for the town non-widow (Farrow) upon the arrival of recently widowed Broome (Richardson), who attracts Dunbar, the nitwit son of Plowright. Entertaining performances (Farrow shows that success is possible after the Wood-man) and beautiful scenery help boost a

script that seems torn between whimsical comedy and dark drama. 98m/C VHS, LV. Mia Farrow, Joan Plowright, Natasha Richardson, Adrian Dunbar, Jim Broadbent, John Kavanagh, Gerard McSorley, Anne Kent, Rynagh O'Grady, Michael James Ford, Garrett Keogh; **D:** John Irvin; **W:** Hugh Leonard; **M:** Carl Davis. NLC

The Wife 🐾🐾 1995 (R) The routine of married psychotherapists Jack (Noonan) and Rita (Hagerty), who live in an isolated Vermont farmhouse, is disrupted by the unexpected (and unwelcome) appearance of Jack's patient Cosmo (Shawn), who's in crisis, and his wife Arlie (Young). Everyone's got secrets and marital dilemmas that come spilling out over too much wine. A variation on "Who's Afraid of Virginia Woolf?" **CW:** Language, some nudity. 101m/C VHS. Tom Noonan, Julie Hagerty, Karen Young, Wallace Shawn; **D:** Tom Noonan; **W:** Tom Noonan; **C:** Joe DeSalvo; **M:** Lodovico Sorret. FXL

Wife Versus Secretary 🐾🐾🐾½ 1936 Excellent acting against type creates a near-perfect picture of romantic relationships. Harlow and Gable play a secretary and her boss who have a wonderful professional relationship, but Loy worries something else is afoot. Could have been a heavy-handed soap opera, but the witty dialogue and Brown's fine pacing make it much more. Stewart later claimed that he purposely messed up his romantic scenes with Harlow in order to spend more time in her arms. 89m/B VHS. Clark Gable, Jean Harlow, Myrna Loy, May Robson, Hobart Cavanaugh, James Stewart, George Barbier, Gilbert Emery; **D:** Clarence Brown. MGM

Wifemistress 🐾🐾½ Mogliamante; Lover, Wife 1979 (R) In the early 1900s, an invalid wife resents her neglectful husband. When he goes into hiding because of a murder he didn't commit, she begins to drift into a world of sexual fantasies. Fine performances. Italian dialogue with English subtitles. 101m/C VHS, Beta. IT Marcello Mastroianni, Laura Antonelli; **D:** Marco Vicario. COL

Wigstock: The Movie 🐾🐾½ 1995 (R) Documentary of the eponymous annual Labor Day event in Manhattan, billed as the Superbowl of drag. Shils intercuts stage numbers with interviews from a variety of the talented, witty festival performers, such as Lypsinka, Mistress Formika, and RuPaul. One of the best numbers is performed by the Dueling Bankheads (as in Tallulah) singing "Born to Be Wild." Like the event itself, documentary is more a celebration than a probing, psychological look at drag. Won't appeal to everyone, but a lot of fun for those who can appreciate high hair and high fashion. **CW:** Sex-related material and language. 92m/C VHS. **D:** Barry Shils. HMK

The Wilby Conspiracy 🐾🐾🐾 1975 (PG) A political activist and an Englishman on the wrong side of the law team up to escape the clutches of a prejudiced cop in apartheid Africa. The focus of the film is on the chase, not the political uprising taking place around it. Well-done chase film with fine performances throughout. 101m/C VHS, Closed Caption. Sidney Poitier, Michael Caine, Nicol Williamson, Prunella Gee, Persis Khambatta, Saeed Jaffrey, Rutger Hauer, Helmut Dantine; **D:** Ralph Nelson; **W:** Rod Amateau. MGM, FCT

The Wild Aces 🐾½ 1985 A relentless action flick with real documentary footage of the aerial war above Vietnam. 58m/C VHS, Beta. BMV, FGF

Wild America 🐾🐾🐾 1997 (G) Warner Bros. invades Disney's well-marked territory of family-friendly real-life adventure with this bio of famed nature documentarians Mark, Marty, and Marshall Stouffer. Pic focuses on the origins of the boys' fascination with animals, which started when their parents gave them a used 16mm camera to mess around with. After getting some footage of backyard wildlife, they're hooked, and hit the road to find more dangerous (and endangered) beasts to shoot (in the good way). As you

would expect, the scenery and camera work are splendid, and any expected wild animal gore and violence has been toned way down. There's plenty to hold the interest of adults as well as children, with a big assist going to the clever script. Title is taken from Marty Stouffer's long-running PBS nature series. 105m/C VHS. Jonathan Taylor Thomas, Devon Sawa, Scott Bairstow, Jamey Sheridan, Frances Fisher; **D:** William Dear; **W:** David Michael Wieger; **C:** David Burr. NYR

The Wild and the Free 🐾🐾 1980 Light-hearted comedy about research chimps. The lab-raised bunch become the instruments for radioactive experimenting. Scheming scientists return the chimps to their home to save them from their demise. Made for TV. 100m/C VHS, Beta. Granville Van Dusen, Linda Gray, Bill Gribble; **D:** James Hill. LIV

Wild & Wooly 🐾½ 1978 In 1903, a tough cowgirl and her friends must prevent the assassination of the President. Made for television. 120m/C VHS, Beta. Chris DeLisle, Susan Bigelow, Elyssa Davalos, Jessica Walter, Doug McClure, David Doyle, Ross Martin, Vic Morrow, Charles Seibert, Sherry Bain, Paul Burke; **D:** Philip Leacock; **M:** Charles Bernstein. PSM

The Wild Angels 🐾🐾½ 1966 (PG) Excessively violent film but B-movie classic about an outlaw biker gang and the local townspeople. Typical Corman fodder was one of AIP's most successful productions. 124m/C VHS. Peter Fonda, Nancy Sinatra, Bruce Dern, Diane Ladd, Michael J. Pollard, Gayle Hunnicutt; **D:** Roger Corman; **W:** Charles B. Griffith, Peter Bogdanovich. ORI

Wild at Heart 🐾🐾🐾½ 1990 (R) Dern and Cage are on the lam, going across country to escape her mother, his parole officer, and life. Humorous and frightening, sensual and evocative as only Lynch can be. Sweet love story of Sailor and Lula is juxtaposed with the violent and bizarre, obsessive brand of love of the people they encounter. Unmistakable Wizard of Oz imagery sprinkled throughout, as are some scenes of graphic violence. Ladd is unnerving as Dern's on-screen mother (she also has the role off-screen). 125m/C VHS, Beta, LV, Closed Caption. Nicolas Cage, Laura Dern, Diane Ladd, Willem Dafoe, Isabella Rossellini, Harry Dean Stanton, Crispin Glover, Grace Zabriskie, J.E. Freeman, Freddie Jones, Sherilyn Fenn, Sheryl Lee; **D:** David Lynch; **W:** David Lynch; **C:** Frederick Elmes; **M:** Angelo Badalamenti. Cannes Film Festival '90: Best Film; Independent Spirit Awards '91: Best Cinematography; Nominations: Academy Awards '90: Best Supporting Actress (Ladd). CCB, MED, IME

The Wild Beasts woof! Savage Beasts 1985 Children and animals clash violently after drinking water tainted with PCP. Disgusting premise; unredeemably violent. 92m/C VHS, Beta. John Aldrich, Lorraine De Selle; **D:** Franco Prosperi. LIV

Wild Bill 🐾🐾½ 1995 (R) Realistic, un-heroic portrait of Wild Bill Hickok (Bridges), seen mostly in flashback. From trapper and lawman to his last days in Deadwood, South Dakota, focus is on the events haunting the glaucoma-stricken, opium-addicted legend in his later years, such as twice deserting his true love (Lane). Action packed first twenty minutes mellows along with the aging Hickok and the rest gets a bit talky for a Western, albeit an arty one. Bridges's Hickok is brilliant, but Barkin is given a somewhat tedious Calamity Jane. Based on the novel "Deadwood" by Pete Dexter and the play "Fathers and Sons" by Thomas Babe. **CW:** Western violence; sex scene. 97m/C VHS, Closed Caption. Jeff Bridges, Ellen Barkin, John Hurt, Diane Lane, Keith Carradine, Christina Applegate, Bruce Dern, James Gammon, David Arquette, Marjoe Gortner; **D:** Walter Hill; **W:** Walter Hill; **C:** Lloyd Ahern; **M:** Van Dyke Parks. MGM

The Wild Bunch 🐾🐾🐾🐾 1969 (R) Acclaimed western about a group of aging outlaws on their final rampage, realizing time is passing them by. Highly influential in dialogue, editing style, and lyrical slow-motion photography of violence; Peckinpah's main claim to posterity. Holden and Ryan create especially memorable char-

acters. Arguably the greatest western and one of the greatest American films of all times. Beware of shortened versions; after a pre-release showing to the East Coast critics, producer Feldman cut key scenes without Peckinpah's knowledge or consent. 145m/C VHS, Beta, LV, DVD. William Holden, Ernest Borgnine, Robert Ryan, Warren Oates, Strother Martin, L.Q. Jones, Albert Dekker, Bo Hopkins, Edmond O'Brien, Ben Johnson, Jaime Sanchez, Emilio Fernandez, Dub Taylor; **D:** Sam Peckinpah; **W:** Walon Green, Sam Peckinpah; **C:** Lucien Ballard. National Society of Film Critics Awards '69: Best Cinematography; Nominations: Academy Awards '69: Best Story & Screenplay, Best Original Score. WAR

Wild Cactus 🐾🐾 1992 (R) Philip and Alexandria Marcus decide to take a romantic vacation at a desert resort where they meet up with a homicidal ex-con and his seductive girlfriend. The two couples find themselves entangled in some violent and kinky games. An unrated version is also available. **CW:** Language, strong violence, and strong language. 92m/C VHS, Closed Caption. David Naughton, India Allen, Gary Hudson, Michelle Moffett, Kathy Shower, Robert Z'Dar, Paul Gleason, Anna Karin, David Wells; **D:** Jag Mundhra; **W:** Carl Austin. IMP

The Wild Child 🐾🐾🐾½ L'Enfant Sauvage 1970 (G) The brilliant film based on the journal of a 19th century physician who attempts to educate and civilize a young boy who has been found living in the wilderness, without any comprehension of human life. Tenderly told coming of age tale, with surprising sensitivity for its subject. In French with English subtitles. 85m/B VHS. FR **D:** Francois Truffaut; **W:** Jean Gruault; **C:** Nestor Almendros; **M:** Antoine Duhamel. National Board of Review Awards '70: Best Director (Truffaut); National Society of Film Critics Awards '70: Best Cinematography. MGM, FCT

Wild Country 🐾½ 1947 Tame western. A U.S. Marshal races to stop the bad guy from killing the late sheriff's daughter and snatching her ranch. 57m/B VHS. Eddie Dean, Roscoe Ates, Peggy Wynn, Douglas Fowley, I. Stanford Jolley, William "Bill" Fawcett; **D:** Ray Taylor. NOS, HEG

The Wild Country 🐾🐾½ The Newcomers 1971 (G) Children's fare detailing the trials and tribulations of a Pittsburgh family moving into an inhospitable Wyoming ranch in the 1880s. Based on the novel "Little Britches" by Ralph Moody. 92m/C VHS, Beta. Steve Forrest, Ron Howard, Rance Howard; **D:** Robert Totten; **M:** Robert F. Brunner. DIS

The Wild Duck 🐾½ 1984 (PG) A father discovers that his beloved daughter is illegitimate and turns against her. To regain his love, she plans to sacrifice her most prized possession. Irons overacts; Ullmann almost disappears into the woodwork. Child star Jones is insufferable, and the whole family squeaks with "literary" pomposity. A horrid adaptation of the classic Ibsen play. 96m/C VHS, Beta. AU Jeremy Irons, Liv Ullmann, Lucinda Jones, Arthur Dignam; **D:** Henri Safran. LIV, VES

Wild Engine/Mistaken Orders 🐾🐾 1923 The early screen daredevil Holmes stars in two railroad-and-betrayal epics. 48m/B VHS, Beta. Helen Holmes, Jack Hoxie, Hoot Gibson. CCB

Wild Frontier 🐾🐾½ 1948 A rugged old lawman and his sons team up to rid a town of outlaws. Lane, playing a character with his own name for first time, takes over from his murdered father and roots out the evildoer (Holt). Decent, enjoyable, good-guys-win western. 59m/B VHS, Beta. Allan "Rocky" Lane, Jack Holt. DVT

Wild Geese 🐾🐾 1978 (R) The adventure begins when a veteran band of mercenaries land deep inside Africa to rescue the imprisoned leader of an emerging African nation, in the interest of protecting British commercial interest. Their mission meets an unexpected turn when they are betrayed by their financial backers. Too much training in the early part; too long; too much dialogue. Where's the action? 132m/C VHS, Beta, LV. GB Richard Burton, Roger Moore, Richard Harris, Hardy

Kruger, Stewart Granger, Frank Finlay, Jeff Corey; **D:** Andrew V. McLaglen; **W:** Reginald Rose. *FOX*

Wild Geese 2 🦢½ **1985 (R)** Lame sequel to the flamed and overlong "Wild Geese," which depended on its name stars. More of the same, this time sans Burton, Harris and Moore. Sure, it's got Olivier, but it still stinks. **124m/C VHS, Beta.** *GB* Laurence Olivier, Edward Fox, Scott Glenn, Barbara Carrera, Robert Webber; **D:** Peter Hunt; **W:** Reginald Rose. *MGM*

Wild Guitar woof! **1962** A swinging youth cycles into Hollywood and, improbably, becomes an instant teenidol. Considered a top contender for "Worst Picture of All Time" honors. **92m/B VHS, Beta.** Arch Hall Jr.; **D:** Ray Dennis Steckler. *RHI*

Wild Gypsies 🦢 **1969** A band of gypsies seek revenge against a renegade member who returned to rape and pillage. Without merit except for the good photography of Steven Burum, who has become respected doing cinematographically intriguing films like "Rumblefish." **85m/C VHS, LV.** Todd Grange, Gayle Clark, Laurel Welcome. *NWV*

Wild Hearts Can't Be Broken 🦢🦢🦢 **1991 (G)** Depicts the true-life story of Sonora Webster, a small town Georgia girl who runs away from a foster home to join a carnival in the early 1930s, hoping to become a stunt rider. She becomes a horse-diver (a Depression-era sideshow phenomena) and is blinded in a diving accident, but returns to find romance and ride again. Storyline has little screen tension, but it doesn't detract from this fresh family film with a feisty heroine, a sweet romance, and horses. Nice U.S. screen debut for British actress Anwar. **89m/C VHS, Beta, Closed Caption.** Gabrielle Anwar, Cliff Robertson, Dylan Kussman, Michael Schoeffling, Kathleen York, Frank Renzulli; **D:** Steve Miner; **W:** Oley Sassone; **M:** Mason Daring. *DIS*

Wild Horse 🦢½ *Silver Devil* **1931** Gibson is the lead (in his favorite talking role), but his magnificent mount Mut commands most of the attention. Interesting historically as an example of stars' (Gibson's in this case) difficulty adjusting to talking pictures. **68m/B VHS, Beta.** Hoot Gibson, Stepin Fetchit, Edmund Cobb, Alberta Vaughn; **D:** Richard Thorpe, Sidney Algier. *NOS, GPV, VYY*

Wild Horse Canyon 🦢🦢 **1925** Yakima Canutt, the man credited with creating the profession of stunt man, stars in this tale about a lady rancher who requires saving from her evil foreman. The climactic stampede scene gives Yakima a chance to demonstrate a high dive off a cliff and a somersault onto his horse. Silent, with musical score. **68m/B VHS, Beta.** Yakima Canutt, Edward Cecil, Helene Rosson, Jay Talbet. *NOS, GPV, VYY*

Wild Horse Canyon 🦢½ **1939** One of those westerns designed to run as half of a double-feature, this one's shorter than most, but hardly notable. The hero goes after a rustler who shot his brother. **57m/B VHS.** Jack Randall, Dorothy Short, Frank Yaconelli, Dennis Moore, Warner Richmond, Charles "Blackie" King, Sherry Tansey; **D:** Robert F. "Bob" Hill. *NOS, GPV*

Wild Horse Hank 🦢🦢 **1979** A young woman risks everything to save a herd of wild mustangs from being slaughtered for use as dog food. Creena is good; otherwise, it's sentimental family fare. Based on the novel "The Wild Horse Killers" by Mel Ellis. **94m/C VHS, Beta.** *CA* Linda Blair, Richard Crenna, Michael Wincott, Al Waxman; **D:** Eric Till. *LIV, VES*

Wild Horse Phantom 🦢🦢 **1944** A Wild West banker plans to fake a robbery in a diabolical deception to part honest ranchers from their lands. Surely this man's not a member of the F.D.I.C. Okay sagebrush saga. **56m/B VHS, Beta.** Buster Crabbe, Al "Fuzzy" St. John, Charles "Blackie" King, John Merton, Lane Chandler, Edward Cassidy, Bud Osborne; **D:** Sam Newfield. *GPV*

Wild Horse Rodeo 🦢½ **1937** When a gunman appears at a rodeo, trouble starts. Part of "The Three Mesquiteers" series. Ordinary action-packed western, the good guys win. Actor Dick Weston, who sings, later gained fame as singing cowboy Roy Rogers. **53m/B VHS, Beta.** Ray Corrigan. *NOS, DVT*

Wild Horses 🦢🦢 **1982** A man attempts to make a living by capturing and selling wild horses. Adventure fans will love this film which deals with the common theme of man against nature. **88m/C VHS, Beta.** *NZ* Keith Aberdein, John Bach, Robyn Gibbes; **D:** Derek Morton. *VES*

Wild Horses 🦢🦢 **1984** Ex-rodeo champ Rogers is hankering to escape his dull life. He joins a roundup of wild horses and with Dawber's help exposes a bureaucrat's scheme for them. Rogers is likable and sings, but the supporting cast carries this one. Made for TV. **90m/C VHS, Beta.** Kenny Rogers, Pam Dawber, Ben Johnson, Richard Masur, David Andrews, Karen Carlson; **D:** Dick Lowry. *NO*

Wild in the Country 🦢🦢½ **1961** Backwoods delinquent Presley is aided in his literary aspirations by woman psychiatrist Lange. Okay, so that's fairly novel. Strange plot lines but in general Elvis is going to college and reading and writing and singing and playing his guitar. Meanwhile Weld wanders around seductively to provide that hint of Tennessee Williams ambience as interpreted by Odet but hey, who cares? Interesting if convoluted Elvis dramatic turn. ♫ Wild in the Country; In My Way; I Slipped, I Stumbled, I Fell; Lonely Man. **114m/C VHS, Beta.** Elvis Presley, Hope Lange, Tuesday Weld, Millie Perkins, John Ireland, Gary Lockwood, Alan Napier; **D:** Philip Dunne; **W:** Clifford Odets; **C:** William Mellor. *FOX, MVD*

Wild in the Streets 🦢🦢½ **1968** Satire set in the future, where a malcontent rock star becomes president after the voting age is lowered to 14. Adults over 30 are imprisoned and fed a daily dose of LSD. The president gets his comeuppance when challenged by even younger youths. Very groovy, very political in its own way, very funny. **97m/C VHS, Beta, LV.** Shelley Winters, Christopher Jones, Hal Holbrook, Richard Pryor, Diane Varsi, Millie Perkins, Ed Begley Sr.; **D:** Barry Shear; **M:** Les Baxter. Nominations: Academy Awards '68: Best Film Editing. *HBO*

The Wild Life 🦢 **1984 (R)** A recent high school graduate takes on a wild and crazy wrestler as his roommate in a swinging singles apartment complex. The same writer and producer as "Fast Times at Ridgemont High" but lacks that film's commercial success. Just as adolescent, though. **96m/C VHS, Beta, LV, Closed Caption.** Christopher Penn, Randy Quaid, Rick Moranis, Hart Bochner, Eric Stoltz, Jenny Wright, Lea Thompson, Sherilyn Fenn, Lee Ving, Ashley St. John, Francesca "Kitten" Natividad; **D:** Art Linson; **W:** Cameron Crowe. *USH*

Wild Man 🦢 **1989** A Las Vegas gambling magnate with supernatural powers decides to avenge the murder of his friend and sets out on an adventure to find the killer. Crummy acting in yet another "ex-agent called back for one more mission" yarn. **106m/C VHS, Beta.** Ginger Lynn Allen, Michelle (McClellan) Bauer, Don Scribner, Kathleen Middleton; **D:** Fred J. Lincoln. *CEL*

Wild Mustang 🦢🦢½ **1935** Sheriff's son (Gordon) joins some outlaws to help father (Carey) spring a trap. The plan is sidetracked, and Gordon is captured and nearly branded by the baddies. Don't worry, though; everything turns out all right. Good western. **62m/B VHS, Beta.** Harry Carey Sr., Del Gordon; **D:** Harry Fraser. *NOS, VCN, DVT*

The Wild One 🦢🦢🦢½ **1954** The original biker flick: two motorcycle gangs descend upon a quiet midwestern town and each other. Brando is the leader of one, struggling against social prejudices and his own gang's lawlessness to find love and a normal life. The classic tribute to 1950s rebelliousness. Based vaguely on a real incident in California. Quaint after nearly 40 years, but still the touchstone for much that has come since, and still a central role in Brando's now-long career. Brando himself believes it failed to explore Motivations for youth gangs and violence, only depicting them. Banked in Britain until 1967. **79m/B VHS, Beta, LV, Closed Caption.** Marlon Brando, Lee Marvin, Mary Murphy, Robert Keith, Jerry Paris, Alvy Moore, Jay C. Flippen; **D:** Laslo Benedek; **C:** Hal Mohr. *COL*

Wild Ones on Wheels woof! *Drivers to Hell* **1962** A gang of teenage hot-rod punks meet an ex-con in the Mojave desert who is searching for the half-a-million bucks he buried there years earlier. Before they find out where the money is, they kill him. In an attempt to find the stash, they kidnap the dead con's wife, hoping she'll sing like a bird. Plenty of unintended laughter. **92m/B VHS, Beta.** Francine York, Edmund Tontini, Robert Blair; **D:** Rudolph Cusumano. *SNC*

Wild Orchid 🦢 **1990 (R)** One of the most controversial theatrical releases of 1990. Rourke is a mystery millionaire involved with two beautiful women in lovely Rio de Janeiro. Bisset is strange as an international real estate developer with unusual sexual mores. Very explicit sex scenes, but otherwise mostly boring and unbelievable. Rourke allegedly took his method-acting technique to the limit in the last love scene with Otis. Available in an unrated version as well. From the producers of "9 1/2 Weeks." Followed by an unrelated sequel. **107m/C VHS, Beta, LV, Closed Caption.** Mickey Rourke, Jacqueline Bisset, Carre Otis, Assumpta Serna, Bruce Greenwood; **D:** Zalman King; **W:** Zalman King. *COL, FCT*

Wild Orchid 2: Two Shades of Blue woof! **1992 (R)** Blue's jazz-musician, heroin-addict dad dies after a bad fix and she's sold into prostitution, until she runs away to find her true love and live a "normal" life. Effort from soft-core expert King has nothing to do with the first "Wild Orchid" and is almost laughably bad. Siemaszko is whiny, the plot is unbelievable, and the dialogue is unintentionally funny. Yes, you get sex, lots of it, but rather than passionate, it merely looks staged. Also available in an unrated version at 111 minutes. **CW:** Language, drug content, and strong sensuality. **105m/C VHS, Closed Caption.** Nina Siemaszko, Wendy Hughes, Brent Fraser, Robert Davi, Tom Skerritt, Joe Dallesandro, Christopher McDonald, Liane Curtis; **D:** Zalman King; **W:** Zalman King. *COL*

Wild Orchids 🦢🦢½ **1928** A husband suspects his wife of infidelity while they take a business cruise to Java. One of Garbo's earliest silent films. Garbo is lushly surrounded with great scenery, costumes and sets, making the best of her as she makes the best of a cheery tale. **119m/B VHS, Beta.** Greta Garbo, Lewis Stone, Nils Asther; **D:** Sidney Franklin; **C:** William H. Daniels. *MGM, FCT*

The Wild Pair 🦢½ *Hollow Point; Devil's Odds* **1987 (R)** Two cops track down a cocaine smuggling ring and uncover a private army planning to conquer the United States. Lloyd Bridges is memorable as a rabid right-winger, and the wild pairing of Bubba and Beau inspires head-scatching. Otherwise, what we have here is a typical action pic, complete with car chases. Beau Bridges' inauspicious feature directing debut. **89m/C VHS, Beta, LV.** Beau Bridges, Bubba Smith, Lloyd Bridges, Gary Lockwood, Raymond St. Jacques; **D:** Beau Bridges; **M:** John Debney. *MED, VTR*

Wild Palms 🦢🦢 **1993** In 2007 Los Angeles, Harry (Belushi) takes a job at a TV station that offers virtual reality programming to viewers, only this isn't benign technology. Delany is stuck in a thankless role as his wife, Cattrall is his former lover, but Dickinson has the most fun as Harry's power-mad mother-in-law who's also a sadistic co-conspirator of a nasty senator (Loggia). Lesson in weird style over substance really doesn't make much sense, but unlike "Twin Peaks" (to which this TV miniseries was heavily compared) it at least has an ending. Executive producer Stone has a cameo which concerns the JFK conspiracy. Based on the comic strip by Wagner. In two parts.

300m/C VHS, Closed Caption. James Belushi, Robert Loggia, Dana Delany, Kim Cattrall, Angie Dickinson, Ernie Hudson, Bebe Neuwirth, Nick Mancuso, Charles Hallahan, Robert Morse, David Warner, Ben Savage, Bob Gunton, Brad Dourif, Charles Rocket; *Cameos:* Oliver Stone; *D:* Phil Joanou, Kathryn Bigelow, Keith Gordon, Pete Hewitt; *W:* Bruce Wagner; *C:* Phedon Papamichael; *M:* Ryuichi Sakamoto. ABC, FCT

Wild Party 🐾🐾½ 1974 (R) It's 1929, a year of much frivolity in Hollywood. Drinking, dancing, maneuvering and almost every sort of romance are the rule of the night at silent film comic Jolly Grimm's sumptuous, star-studded party that climaxes with, among other things, a murder. Well performed but somehow hollow; ambitious Ivory effort unfortunately falls short. Based on Joseph Moncure March's poem, and loosely on the Fatty Arbuckle scandal. 90m/C VHS, Beta. Raquel Welch, James Coco, Perry King, David Dukes, Royal Dano, Tiffany Bolling; *D:* James Ivory; *C:* Walter Lassally.

Wild Pony 🐾 1983 A young boy spurns his new stepfather, preferring to live with his pony instead. Reversal of the evil-stepmother-and-girl-loves-horse theme. 87m/C VHS, Beta. Marilyn Lightstone, Art Hindle, Josh Byrne; *D:* Kevin Sullivan; *M:* Hagood Hardy. FHE, VES, LIV

Wild Rapture 🐾 1950 The hunting and dissecting of an elephant and gorilla, a look at a tribe that practices lip-splitting, and other gruesome events abound in this shock-fest. Banned for 18 years. 68m/B VHS, Beta. NOS, HEG

Wild Rebels 🐾 1971 (R) A two-faced member of a ruthless motorcycle gang informs the police of the gang's plans to rob a bank. Lots of bullet-flying action. Dumb, ordinary biker flick; star Pastrano was a former boxing champ in real life. 90m/C VHS, Beta. Steve Alaimo, Willie Pastrano, John Vella, Bobbie Byers; *D:* William Grefe. ACA

Wild Reeds 🐾🐾🐾 *Les Roseaux Sauvages* 1994 Emotional coming of age tale set in 1962 (at the end of the French war in Algeria) and focusing on three classmates at a French boarding school. Sensitive Francois (Morel) is just coming to the realization that he likes boys, and especially working-class Serge (Rideau) who's attracted to Francois's confidante Maite (Bouchez). The provocateur is Algerian-born Henri (Gorny), a bitter political militant who enjoys his battles with classmates and teachers alike. Politics and youthful passions are forced into crises. French historical/political context may prove a barrier. French with subtitles. 110m/C VHS. FR Gael Morel, Stephane Rideau, Elodie Bouchez, Frederic Gorny, Michele Moretti; *D:* Andre Techine; *W:* Gilles Taurand, Olivier Massart, Andre Techine; *C:* Jeanne Lapoirie. Cesar Awards '95: Best Director (Techine), Best Film, Best Screenplay; Los Angeles Film Critics Association Awards '95: Best Foreign Film; National Society of Film Critics Awards '95: Best Foreign Film. FXL

The Wild Ride 🐾🐾 1960 Nicholson, in an early starring role, portrays a rebellious punk of the Beat generation who hotrods his way into trouble and tragedy. He kidnaps now-straight ex-buddy Bean's squeeze (Carter); kills a few cops; then is killed. Interesting only if you're interested in Nicholson. 59m/B VHS, Beta. Jack Nicholson, Georgianna Carter, Robert Bean; *D:* Harvey Berman. SNC, NOS, VYY

Wild Riders woof! *Angels for Kicks* 1971 (R) Two ruthless, amoral bikers molest, kidnap, rape, and beat two beautiful, naive young society ladies. Despicable story, with deplorable acting, but the ending, in which a husband slays a biker with a cello, surely is unique. 91m/C VHS, Beta. Alex Rocco, Elizabeth Knowles, Sherry Bain, Arell Blanton; *D:* Richard Kanter. ACA

Wild Rovers 🐾🐾 1971 (PG) An aging cowboy and his younger colleague turn to bank robbing and are pursued by a posse in a wacky comedy-adventure from director Edwards. Uneven script and too much referential baggage (faint shades of "Butch Cassidy") doom this valiant effort, with the two stars hanging right in there all

the way. 138m/C VHS, Beta, LV. William Holden, Ryan O'Neal, Karl Malden, Lynn Carlin, Tom Skerritt, Joe Don Baker, Rachel Roberts, Moses Gunn; *D:* Blake Edwards; *W:* Blake Edwards; *M:* Jerry Goldsmith. MGM

Wild Side 🐾🐾 1995 (R) Bank employee Alex (Heche) moonlights as a hooker and gets caught in a federal sting operation. Forced to inform on one of her clients, Bruno (Walken), who's involved in a money-laundering scheme, Alex complicates matters by falling in love with Bruno's mistress, Victoria (Chen). The unrated version is 96 minutes. Original director Cammell (who retained his screenwriter's credit) removed his name from the film after disagreeing with cuts made by the production company.*CW:* Strong sexuality, language, and violence, including a rape. 90m/C VHS, Closed Caption. Anne Heche, Christopher Walken, Joan Chen, Steven Bauer; *D:* Franklyn Brauner; *W:* Donald Cammell, China Cammell. EVE

Wild Strawberries 🐾🐾🐾🐾 *Smultronstallet* 1957 Bergman's landmark film of fantasy, dreams and nightmares. An aging professor, on the road to accept an award, must come to terms with his anxieties and guilt. Brilliant performance by Sjostrom, Sweden's first film director and star. Excellent use of flashbacks and film editing. An intellectual and emotional masterpiece. In Swedish with English subtitles. 90m/B VHS, Beta, LV, 8mm. SW Victor Sjostrom, Bibi Andersson, Max von Sydow, Ingrid Thulin, Gunnar Bjornstrand, Folke Sundquist, Bjorn Bjelvenstam; *D:* Ingmar Bergman; *W:* Ingmar Bergman. Golden Globe Awards '60: Best Foreign Film; National Board of Review Awards '59: 5 Best Foreign Films of the Year; Nominations: Academy Awards '59: Best Story & Screenplay. VYY, HMV, FOX

Wild Style 🐾🐾 1983 Zoro, a mild-mannered Bronx teenager, spends his evenings spray-painting subway cars. Intended as a depiction of urban street life, including graffiti, break-dancing and rap music. Mildly interesting social comment, but unconvincing as cinema. Too "realistic," with too little vision. 82m/C VHS, Beta. Lee George Quinones, Fredrick Braithwaite, Dondi White; *D:* Charlie Ahearn; *M:* Fred Brathwaite. FCT

Wild Thing 🐾½ 1987 (PG-13) A modern variation on the Wild Child/Tarzan myth, as a feral kid stalks a crime-ridden ghetto. Sayles, a usually imaginative writer and director, really takes a dive here. And of course, the Troggs' overplayed title hit is abused as the theme. 92m/C VHS, Beta, LV. Kathleen Quinlan, Rob Knepper, Robert Davi, Betty Buckley, Maury Chaykin; *D:* Max Reid, Ken Cameron; *W:* John Sayles; *M:* George S. Clinton, Guy Moon. NO

Wild Times 🐾🐾 1979 Too long but pleasant rendition of the life of High Candill, early Wild West showman. Based on the novel by Brian Garfield. Made for TV, originally in two parts. 200m/C VHS, Beta. Sam Elliott, Trish Stewart, Ben Johnson, Dennis Hopper, Pat Hingle; *D:* Richard Compton. PSM

Wild Weed 🐾 *The Devil's Weed; She Shoulda Said No; Marijuana the Devil's Weed* 1949 Funny smelling cigarettes ruin the lives of all who inhale. Viewers' advice: just say no. Leed's actual drug bust with Robert Mitchum got her the lead. 70m/B VHS. Lila Leeds, Alan Baxter, Lyle Talbot, Jack Elam, David Gorcey; *D:* Sam Newfield. SNC, AOV, TPV

Wild West 🐾🐾 *Prairie Outlaws* 1946 The hero and loyal companions (with names like Skinny, Stormy and Soapy) tackle desperadoes trying to stop telegraph line construction. More mild than wild, it was later trimmed and released under its alternate title, but here you're getting the original. 73m/C VHS. Eddie Dean, Roscoe Ates, Lash LaRue, Robert "Buzzy" Henry, Sarah Padden, Louise Currie, Warner Richmond, Chief Yowlachie, Bud Osborne; *D:* Robert Emmett Tansey. NOS, HEG

Wild West 1987 A compilation of scenes from dozens of western films. 90m/C VHS, Beta. John Wayne, Clint Eastwood, Steve McQueen, Charles Bronson. NO

Wild West 🐾🐾 1993 Three Pakistani brothers, living in London, decide to form an American-style country and western band they call the Honky Tonk Cowboys and dream of making it big in Nashville. A little romance, lots of energy, but too many gags leave the film unfocused. 83m/C VHS. GB Naveen Andrews, Sarita Choudhury, Ronny Jhutti, Ravi Kapoor; *D:* David Attwood; *W:* Harwant Bains. THV

Wild Wheels woof! 1975 (PG) A group of dune-buggy enthusiasts seek revenge against a gang of motorcyclists who have ravaged a small California beach town. 81m/C VHS, Beta. Casey Kasem, Dovie Beams, Terry Stafford, Robert Dix. GEM

Wild, Wild Planet 🐾½ 1965 Alien beings from a distant planet are miniaturizing Earth's leaders in a bid to destroy our planet, and a dubbed, wooden hero comes to the rescue. A rarely seen Italian SF entry, great fun for genre fans. A must for "robot girls in skin tight leather outfits" completists. 93m/C VHS. IT Tony Russell, Lisa Gastoni, Massimo Serato, Franco Nero; *D:* Anthony (Antonio Margheriti) Dawson. SMW

Wild, Wild West Revisited 🐾🐾½ 1979 A feature-length reprise of the tongue-in-cheek western series. Irreverent and fun, in the spirit of its admirable predecessor-though it's probably just as well the proposed new series didn't see fruition. Made for television. 95m/C VHS, Beta. Robert Conrad, Ross Martin, Harry (Henry) Morgan, Rene Auberjonois; *D:* Burt Kennedy. FOX

Wild, Wild World of Jayne Mansfield 🐾🐾 1968 The life and times of Mansfield are explored in this unique documentary, which was unfinished at the time of her death. Jayne takes the viewer on a worldwide examination of sexual mores, from prostitution, nudist colonies, and the racy strip clubs of Europe, to the transvestite and topless bars of America. Perverse (did you expect otherwise?), footage of her fatal car crash was included. 89m/C VHS, Beta. Jayne Mansfield. VDM, DVT, TPV

Wild Women 🐾 1953 Extremely hilarious schlocker about a safari of white men captured by a savage tribe of jungle women. Total camp. ?m/C VHS. Lewis Wilson, Frances Dubay, Dana Wilson. SNC, HEG

Wild Women 🐾½ 1970 Five female convicts are released during the Texas/Mexico dispute to help smuggle arms to American forces. Innocuous western, original in a made-for-TV kind of way. 90m/C VHS, Beta. Hugh O'Brian, Anne Francis, Marilyn Maxwell, Marie Windsor; *D:* Don Taylor. FOX

Wild Women of Wongo 🐾½ 1959 The denizens of a primitive isle, essentially beautiful women and ugly men, meet the natives of a neighboring island, handsome men and ugly women. Not quite bad enough to be true camp fun, but stupidly silly in a low-budget way. 73m/C VHS, Beta. Pat Crowley, Ed Fury, Adrienne Bourbeau, Jean Hawkshaw, Johnny Walsh; *D:* James L. Wolcott. DVT, MED, NEG

The Wild World of Batwoman 🐾🐾 1966 A campy cult film in which Batwoman and a bevy of Bat Girls are pitted against an evil doctor in order to find the prototype of an atomic hearing aid/nuclear bomb. Also released theatrically as "She Was a Hippy Vampire." 70m/C VHS, Beta. Katherine Victor, George Andre, Steve Brodie, Lloyd Nelson; *D:* Jerry Warren. RHI, SNC, DVT

Wild Zone 🐾 1989 (R) An American ex-soldier combats mercenaries in Africa in order to rescue his kidnapped father. 100m/C VHS, Beta, LV. Edward Albert, Philip Brown, Carla Herd; *D:* Percival Rubens. COL

Wildcard 🐾½ 1992 (PG-13) When a veteran pilot is killed in a helicopter crash, a friend suspects foul play. He calls in Preacher, a special forces veteran, to investigate and what he discovers is murder, greed, and corruption. 86m/C VHS, LV. Powers Boothe, Cindy Pickett, Rene Auberjonois, Terry O'Quinn, M. Emmet Walsh, John Lacy; *D:* Mel Damski; *W:* Scobie Richardson. USH

Wildcat ✗✗ **1942** Crabbe, famous as the serials' Flash Gordon, is a villain in this petrochemical adventure. The hero overextends his credit when he buys an oil well and must produce a gusher or else. **73m/B VHS.** Richard Arlen, Arline Judge, Buster Crabbe, William Frawley, Arthur Hunnicutt, Elisha Cook Jr., Billy Benedict; **D:** Frank McDonald. *NOS*

Wildcats ✗✗ **1986 (R)** A naive female physed teacher (Hawn) is saddled with the job of coach for a completely undisciplined, inner city, high school football team. Formulaic, connect-the-dots comedy; moderately funny, and of course Hawn triumphs in adversity, but at nearly two hours a very long sitcom episode. **106m/C VHS, Beta, LV, Closed Caption.** Goldie Hawn, James Keach, Swoosie Kurtz, Bruce McGill, M. Emmet Walsh, Woody Harrelson, Wesley Snipes, Tab Thacker; **D:** Michael Ritchie; **M:** James Newton Howard. *WAR*

Wilder Napalm ✗½ **1993 (PG-13)** Lame comedy about two at-odds brothers, the woman they both love, and their dangerous pyrokinetic abilities. Wilder (Howard) and Wallace (Quaid) Foudroyant have been feuding for years—and not just over the fact that Wallace is in love with Wilder's wife Vida (Winger). Wallace wants to use their family "gift" to become rich and famous but Wilder doesn't want them to exploit their fiery powers. They finally decide on an incendiary showdown to settle the score once and for all. Good actors lost in witless characters and a incoherent plot. **109m/C VHS, LV, Closed Caption.** Dennis Quaid, Arliss Howard, Debra Winger, M. Emmet Walsh, Jim Varney, Mimi Lieber, Marvin J. McIntyre; **D:** Glenn Gordon Caron; **W:** Vince Gilligan; **M:** Michael Kamen. *COL*

Wildest Dreams ✗½ *Bikini Genie* **1990 (R)** Released from its bottle by a lovely nebbish, a genie puts a love spell on one beautiful girl after another in order to find him the right one, resulting in a bevy of women clamoring for our hero's attention. **84m/C VHS, Beta, LV.** James Davies, Heidi Paine, Deborah Blaisdell, Ruth Collins, Jane Hamilton, Jill Johnson; **D:** Chuck Vincent. *LIV, VES*

Wildfire ✗½ **1945** Two horse traders come to the aid of ranchers beset by horse thieves. Early color outing for Steele. Harmless, ordinary oater. **60m/C VHS, Beta, LV.** Bob Steele, Sterling Holloway, John Miljan, William Farnum, Eddie Dean, Sarah Padden, Frank Ellis; **D:** Robert Emmett Tansey. *NOS, VDM, HEG*

Wildfire ✗✗ **1988 (PG)** As teenagers, Frank and Kay run away to get married but Frank is sent to prison for robbing a bank and Kay winds up making a new life for herself. Released from prison after eight years, Frank discovers Kay is married with two children and doesn't want anything further to do with him. But when Frank violates his parole, Kay discovers she can't leave him again and the two go on the run together. **98m/C VHS, Closed Caption.** Steven Bauer, Linda Fiorentino, Will Patton, Marshall Bell; **D:** Zalman King; **W:** Zalman King, Matthew Bright; **C:** Bill Butler; **M:** Maurice Jarre. *USH*

Wildflower ✗✗✗ **1991** Set in the Depression-era South, Alice is a 17 year-old partially deaf girl who also suffers from epilepsy. Her stepfather believes she's possessed and confines her to a shed. Growing up ignorant and abused Alice is befriended by a neighboring brother and sister who decide to rescue her. A three-hankie family picture with moving performances and inspirational themes. Based on the novel "Alice" by Sara Flanigan. Made for cable television. **94m/C VHS, Closed Caption.** Patricia Arquette, Beau Bridges, Susan Blakely, William McNamara, Reese Witherspoon, Collin Wilcox Paxton; **D:** Diane Keaton. National Academy of Cable Programming ACE Awards '93: Best Actress (Arquette). *WOV*

Wilding ✗½ **1990** A pair of cops are on the trail of a gang of kids who go "wilding," which involves sprees of killing, raping and looting. Exploitive fare based on horrible, recent events in New York. The filmmakers skirt controversy by making the criminals rich suburban kids. **92m/C VHS, Beta.** Wings Hauser, Joey Travolta, Karen Russell, Steven Cooke; **D:** Eric Louzil. *AIP*

Wildrose ✗✗✗ **1985** Eichhorn is memorable as a recent divorcee who must assert herself among her otherwise all-male co-workers at a Minnesota strip mine. She finds a new love, and tries to put her life back together. Filmed on location. **96m/C VHS, Beta.** Lisa Eichhorn, Tom Bower, James Cada; **D:** John Hanson; **W:** John Hanson, Eugene Corr. *LIV*

Will: G. Gordon Liddy ✗✗½ **1982** The life of the Watergate conspirator, based on his autobiography. Made for TV. Producer/star Conrad reportedly objected strongly to cuts from the original three-hour length, apparently with cause: the first half is superficial pap. The portrayal of Liddy's time in prison, though, is fascinating, and Conrad is excellent. **100m/C VHS.** Robert Conrad, Kathy Cannon, Gary Bayer, Peter Ratray, James Rebhorn, Red West, Maurice Woods, Danny Lloyd; **D:** Robert Liebmann. *LIV*

Will Penny ✗✗✗½ **1967** Just back from a cattle drive, a range-wandering loner looks for work in the wrong place and offends a family of outlaws who come after him. His escape from them leads to another kind of trap—one set by a love-hungry woman (Hackett, in a strong performance). Heston considers this film his personal best, and he's probably right. Superbly directed western, with excellent cinematography and professional, realistic portrayals, flopped in theaters, moviegoers preferring simultaneous Heston outing "Planet of the Apes." Photography by Lucien Ballard. **109m/C VHS, Beta, LV, Closed Caption.** Charlton Heston, Joan Hackett, Donald Pleasence, Lee Majors, Bruce Dern, Anthony Zerbe, Ben Johnson, Clifton James; **D:** Tom Gries; **M:** Elmer Bernstein. *PAR*

Will Success Spoil Rock Hunter? ✗✗½ **1957** Dated advertising satire finds ad man Hunter (Randall) hoping to get the key to the executive washroom but he may instead find himself on the unemployment line unless he can convince the profitable Stay-Put lipstick account not to change agencies. One day Rock see movie star Rita Marlowe (Mansfield), and her kissable lips, on TV and tries to convince her to endorse the product but she'll only agree if he'll pose as her new boyfriend to make ex-beau Bobo (Mansfield's real-life hubby Hargitay) jealous. Naturally, the lipstick ads take off bigtime but success does indeed spoil Rock (at least temporarily). Very slightly based on the play by George Axelrod. **94m/C VHS.** Tony Randall, Jayne Mansfield, Betsy Drake, Mickey Hargitay, John Williams, Henry Jones, Joan Blondell; **Cameos:** Groucho Marx; **D:** Frank Tashlin; **W:** Frank Tashlin; **C:** Joe MacDonald; **M:** Cyril Mockridge. *FXV*

Willa ✗✗ **1979** Raffin, a hash-joint waitress with two kids and one in the pipeline, is deserted by her husband and determines to get ahead by becoming a trucker. Okay made-for-TV drama. **95m/C VHS, Beta.** Cloris Leachman, Deborah Raffin, Clu Gulager, John Amos, Diane Ladd; **D:** Claudio Guzman, Joan Darling; **M:** John Barry. *PSM*

Willard ✗✗ **1971 (PG)** Willard is a lonely, psychotic youngster who trains a group of rats, his only friends, to attack his enemies. Not as disgusting as it might have been (rated PG), but pretty weird and not redeemed by any sense of style or humor. Popular at the box office; followed by inferior "Ben." Based on by Stephen Gilbert's novel "Ratman's Notebooks." **95m/C VHS, Beta, LV.** Bruce Davison, Ernest Borgnine, Elsa Lanchester, Sondra Locke; **D:** Daniel Mann; **C:** Robert B. Hauser; **M:** Alex North. *PSM, PAR*

William Faulkner's Old Man ✗✗½ *Old Man* **1997 (PG)** TV adaptation of a part of Faulkner's 1939 novel "The Wild Palms" that is set in the '20s. The "Old Man" in question is the mighty Mississippi, which has flooded leaving a pregnant Tripplehorn, abandoned by her husband, stranded and about to give birth. But prison-farm inmate Howard is sent by the warden to row to her rescue, becoming a surrogate father when the baby is born, and traveling the river to New Orleans to get mother and child to safety. **98m/C VHS.** Jeanne Tripplehorn, Arliss Howard, Leo Burmester; **D:** John Kent Harrison; **W:** Horton Foote. *HMK*

William Shakespeare's Romeo and Juliet ✗✗✗ *Romeo and Juliet* **1996 (PG-13)** Bright, loud update of Shakespeare's tragedy of feuding families and first love. Contemporary fantasy setting, Verona Beach, and attitude (the Montagues and the Capulets are business rivals), with the 16th-century Elizabethan language intact, although Luhrmann's said to have cut half the text. Hot-blooded Romeo (DiCaprio) takes one look at angelic Juliet (Danes) and falls immediately in love/lust. This doesn't please Juliet's family, including quick-tempered cousin Tybalt (Leguizamo) who goes after Romeo with far-reaching consequences. DiCaprio's remarkable and the young duo look wonderful together. A big hit with the teens. Filmed in Mexico City. **CW:** Scenes of contemporary violence and some sensuality. **120m/C VHS, LV, Closed Caption.** Leonardo DiCaprio, Claire Danes, John Leguizamo, Paul Sorvino, Brian Dennehy, Diane Venora, Pete Postlethwaite, Paul Rudd, Harold Perrineau Jr., Jesse Bradford, Miriam Margolyes, Vondie Curtis-Hall, Christina Pickles, M. Emmet Walsh; **D:** Baz Luhrmann; **W:** Baz Luhrmann, Craig Pearce; **C:** Donald McAlpine; **M:** Nellee Hooper. MTV Movie Awards '97: Best Female Performance (Danes); Nominations: Academy Awards '96: Best Art Direction/Set Decoration; MTV Movie Awards '97: Best Film, Best Male Performance (DiCaprio), Best On-Screen Duo (Leonardo DiCaprio/Clare Danes), Best Song ("#1 Crush"), Best Kiss (Leonardo DiCaprio/Claire Danes). *FXV*

Willie & Phil ✗✗½ **1980 (R)** At the start of the '70s, two buddies (Ontkean and Sharkey) fall for the same girl (Kidder). They become a threesome and are entangled in each other's lives for the rest of the decade. Insightful comedy-drama. **111m/C VHS, LV.** Michael Ontkean, Margot Kidder, Ray Sharkey, Jan Miner, Julie Bovasso, Natalie Wood, Laurence "Larry" Fishburne, Louis Guss, Kaki Hunter, Kristine DeBell; **D:** Paul Mazursky; **W:** Paul Mazursky; **C:** Sven Nykvist; **M:** Claude Bolling. *FXV*

The Willies ✗✗ **1990 (PG-13)** Three youngsters gross each other out with juvenile tales of horror and scariness while camping out in the backyard. Pointless but not without a few yuks (in both senses of the term). **120m/C VHS, LV.** James Karen, Sean Astin, Kathleen Freeman, Jeremy Miller; **D:** Brian Peck. *PSM*

Willow ✗✗½ **1988 (PG)** Blockbuster fantasy epic combines the story of Moses with "Snow White," dwarves and all. Willow is the little Nelwyn who finds the lost baby Daikini and is assigned the task of returning her safely to her people. Willow discovers that the girl is actually a sacred infant who is destined to overthrow the evil queen Bavmorda and rule the land. As you might expect from executive producer George Lucas, there is much action and plenty of clever, high-quality special effects. But the "Star Wars"-esque story (by Lucas) is strangely predictable, and a bit too action-packed. Not really for children. **118m/C VHS, Beta, LV, 8mm, Closed Caption.** Warwick Davis, Val Kilmer, Jean Marsh, Joanne Whalley, Billy Barty, Pat Roach, Ruth Greenfield, Patricia Hayes, Gavan O'Herlihy, Kevin Pollak; **D:** Ron Howard; **W:** Bob Dolman; **M:** James Horner. *COL*

Willy Wonka & the Chocolate Factory ✗✗✗½ **1971 (G)** When the last of five coveted "golden tickets" falls into the hands of sweet but very poor Charlie, he and his Grandpa Joe get a tour of the most wonderfully strange chocolate factory in the world. The owner is the most curious hermit ever to hit the big screen. He leads the five young "winners" on a thrilling and often dangerous tour of his fabulous factory. Adapted from Roald Dahl's "Charlie and the Chocolate Factory." Without a doubt one of the best "kid's" movies ever made; a family classic worth watching again and again. ♫ Willy Wonka, the Candy Man; Cheer Up, Charlie; I've Got a Golden Ticket; Oompa-Loompa-Doompa-Dee-Doo; Pure Imagination. **100m/C VHS, Beta, LV,**

Closed Caption. Gene Wilder, Jack Albertson, Denise Nickerson, Peter Ostrum, Roy Kinnear, Aubrey Woods, Michael Bollner, Ursula Reit, Leonard Stone, Dodo Denney; **D:** Mel Stuart; **M:** Leslie Bricusse. Nominations: Academy Awards '71: Original Song Score and/or Adaptation. *WAR, APD, HMV*

Wilma 🐾🐾 1977 Based on the true story of Wilma Rudolph, a young black woman who overcame childhood illness to win three gold medals at the 1960 Olympics. Plodding made-for-TV biography suffers from sub-par script and acting. 100m/C VHS, Beta. Joe Seneca, Cicely Tyson, Shirley Jo Finney; **D:** Bud Greenspan; **M:** Irwin Bazelon. *COL, FCT*

Wilson 🐾🐾🐾 1944 Biography of Woodrow Wilson from his days as the head of Princeton University, to the governorship of New York, and as U.S. President during WWI. After the war, Wilson conceives of the League of Nations but is unable to sell it to a U.S. still bent on isolationism. This lavish film won critical plaudits but was a major money-loser. 154m/C VHS. Alexander Knox, Charles Coburn, Geraldine Fitzgerald, Thomas Mitchell, Ruth Nelson, Cedric Hardwicke, Vincent Price, William Eythe, Mary Anderson, Sidney Blackmer, Stanley Ridges, Eddie Foy Jr., Charles Halton; **D:** Henry King; **W:** Lamar Trotti; **C:** Leon Shamroy; **M:** Alfred Newman. Academy Awards '44: Best Color Cinematography, Best Film Editing, Best Interior Decoration, Best Original Screenplay, Best Sound; Golden Globe Awards '45: Best Actor—Drama (Knox); Nominations: Academy Awards '44: Best Actor (Knox), Best Director (King), Best Picture, Original Dramatic/Comedy Score. *FXV, MOV, BTV*

Wimps 🐾 1987 (R) A collegiate wimp is subjected to a brutal fraternity initiation, but eventually gets the girl. Cheap ripoff of Cyrano de Bergerac, turned into a teen sex flick. 94m/C VHS, Beta. Louie Bonanno, Jim Abele, Deborah Blaisdell; **D:** Chuck Vincent. *LIV*

Win, Place, or Steal 🐾½ *The Big Payoff; Three For the Money; Just Another Day at the Races* 1972 (PG) Lame comedy set at the racetrack about three grown men and their adolescent schemes to win big. Better you should scratch. 88m/C VHS, Beta. McLean Stevenson, Alex Karras, Dean Stockwell; **D:** Richard Bailey. *LIV, VES*

Winchester '73 🐾🐾🐾½ 1950 Superb acting and photography characterize this classic, landmark western. Simple plot—cowboy Stewart pursues his stolen state-of-the-art rifle as it changes hands—speeds along and carries the viewer with it, ending with an engrossing and unforgettable shoot-out. Almost singlehandedly breathed new life into the whole genre. Laser videodisc version contains a special narration track provided by Stewart. Mann's and Stewart's first teaming. 82m/C VHS, Beta, LV. James Stewart, Shelley Winters, Stephen McNally, Dan Duryea, Millard Mitchell, John McIntire, Will Geer, Jay C. Flippen, Rock Hudson, Tony Curtis, Charles Drake; **D:** Anthony Mann; **C:** William H. Daniels. *USH*

The Wind 🐾🐾🐾🐾 1928 One of the last great silents still stands as a magnificent entertainment. Gish, in possibly her best role, is an innocent Easterner who finds herself married to a rough cowpoke and raped by a married man in a bleak frontier town. Director Sjostrom has a splendid feel for landscape, and the drama—climaxing with a tumultuous desert storm—is intense yet fully believable. Based on the novel by Dorothy Scarborough. 74m/B VHS, Beta. Lillian Gish, Lars Hanson, Montagu Love, Dorothy Cumming, Edward Earle, William Orlamond; **D:** Victor Sjostrom; **W:** Frances Marion. *MGM*

The Wind 🐾 1987 Foster is terrorized by Hauser while attempting to write her next thriller in Greece. Let's hope her book is more exciting than this movie. Shot on location in Greece. 92m/C VHS, Beta. Meg Foster, Wings Hauser, Steve Railsback, David McCallum, Robert Morley; **D:** Nico Mastorakis. *LIV*

Wind 🐾🐾½ 1992 (PG-13) Sailor Will Parker (Modine) chooses the opportunity to be on the America's Cup team over girlfriend Grey and then has the dubious honor of making a technical error that causes their loss. Undaunted, he locates Grey and her new engineer boyfriend (Skarsgard) and convinces them to design the ultimate boat for the next set of races. ESPN carried extensive coverage of the America's Cup races for the first time in the summer of '92 and viewers discovered that a little goes a long way. The same holds true for "Wind" which has stunning race footage, but little else. The script lacks substance and was written as filming progressed, and it shows.*CW:* Some sensuality. 123m/C VHS, LV, 8mm, Closed Caption. Matthew Modine, Jennifer Grey, Cliff Robertson, Jack Thompson, Stellan Skarsgard, Rebecca Miller, Ned Vaughn; **D:** Carroll Ballard; **W:** Yuri Wurlitzer, Mac Gudgeon; **C:** John Toll; **M:** Basil Poledouris. *COL*

The Wind and the Lion 🐾🐾🐾 1975 (PG) In turn-of-the-century Morocco, a sheik (Connery) kidnaps a feisty American woman (Bergen) and her children and holds her as a political hostage. President Teddy Roosevelt (Keith) sends in the Marines to free the captives, who are eventually released by their captor. Directed with venue and style by Milius. Highly entertaining, if heavily fictionalized. Based very loosely on a historical incident. 120m/C VHS, Beta, LV. Sean Connery, Candice Bergen, Brian Keith, John Huston, Geoffrey Lewis; **D:** John Milius; **W:** John Milius; **C:** Billy Williams; **M:** Jerry Goldsmith. Nominations: Academy Awards '75: Best Sound, Best Original Score. *MGM*

A Wind Named Amnesia 1993 A strange amnesia wind sweeps away all of mankind's knowledge and human civilization vanishes. Then a mysterious young man is miraculously re-educated and searches for those who destroyed man's memories. In Japanese with English subtitles. 80m/C VHS. *JP D:* Kazuo Yamazaki; **W:** Hideyuki Kikuchi. *CPM*

The Wind That Walks 1985 Two girls trek into the New Jersey wilds after an unknown animal called by the Indians "the wind that walks." 30m/C Beta. *NJN*

Windjammer 🐾🐾 1937 Western star O'Brien took a break from the lone prairie to make this seafaring rescue drama. He is a deputy state's attorney who signs up for a yacht race in order to serve a subpoena. Bad guys arrive on the scene, and the initially moody yacht denizens rely on our trusty hero to save them. Decent adventure. 75m/B VHS. George O'Brien, Constance Worth; **D:** Sam Newfield. *NOS, DVT, HEG*

Windmills of the Gods 🐾🐾½ *Sidney Sheldon's Windmills of the Gods* 1988 Glamor, romance, intrigue, and politics all mixed together in eastern Europe. Smith is named ambassador to Romania, finds the suave Wagner in residence, and becomes the target of assassins. Based on the novel by Sidney Sheldon. Made for television. 95m/C VHS. Jaclyn Smith, Robert Wagner, Franco Nero, Christopher Cazenove, David Ackroyd, Jean-Pierre Aumont, Ruby Dee, Jeffrey DeMunn, Michael Moriarty, Ian McKellen, Susan Tyrrell; **D:** Lee Philips; **W:** John Gay; **M:** Perry Botkin. *LIV*

Windom's Way 🐾🐾🐾 1957 Finch, in a strong role in this intriguing political drama, is an idealistic doctor in a remote village in Malaysia. He juggles a failing marriage and a budding romance, then finds himself caught in a local labor dispute. He works for a peaceful solution, but is captured by an insurgent army. Disillusioned, he plans to leave the country, but his wife persuades him to stay and tend the wounded. Based on a novel by James Ramsey Ullman. 90m/B VHS, Beta. *GB* Peter Finch, Mary Ure; **D:** Ronald Neame. *NO*

The Window 🐾🐾🐾½ 1949 A little boy (Disney star Driscoll, intriguingly cast by director, Tetzlaff) has a reputation for telling lies, so no one believes him when he says he witnessed a murder...except the killers. Almost unbearably tense, claustrophobic thriller about the helplessness of childhood. Tetzlaff clearly learned more than a thing or two from the master, Hitchcock, for whom he photographed "Notorious." Based on the novella "The Boy Who Cried Murder" by Cornell Woolrich. Driscoll was awarded a special miniature Oscar as Outstanding Juvenile for his performance. 73m/B VHS, Beta, LV. Bobby Driscoll, Barbara Hale, Arthur Kennedy, Ruth Roman; **D:** Ted Tetzlaff. Edgar Allan Poe Awards '49: Best Screenplay; Nominations: Academy Awards '49: Best Film Editing. *MED*

Window Shopping 🐾🐾½ 1986 Multiple, confusing romances occur at the "Toison d' Or" shopping mall in Paris. A modern, French homage to the classic Hollywood musical. In French with English subtitles. 96m/C VHS. *FR* Delphine Seyrig, Charles Denner, Fanny Cottencon, Miriam Boyer, Lio, Pascale Salkin, Jean-Francois Balmer; **D:** Chantal Akerman; **W:** Chantal Akerman. *WAC, FCT*

Window to Paris 🐾🐾 1995 (PG-13) East and West meet unexpectedly when a young music teacher (Dontsov) rents a room in St. Petersburg with a secret window that opens onto a Paris rooftop. Loony adventures ensue as Dontsov and his friends escape their dreary existence to exploit the bounties of Western capitalism in this sharp satire of Russian social ills. Relentless humor based on cross-cultural stereotypes wears thin (the Russians are cantankerous drunks; the Parisians, self-important snobs), but it keeps a sunny cast upon what could have been a scathing commentary. Russian and French with subtitles.*CW:* Contains momentary nudity. 92m/C VHS, LV. *RU FR* Serguej Dontsov, Agnes Soral, Viktor Michailov, Nina Oussatova; **D:** Yuri Mamin; **W:** Arkadi Tigai, Yuri Mamin; **M:** Aleksei Zalivalov, Yuri Mamin. *COL*

Windows 🐾 1980 (R) A lonely lesbian (Ashley) becomes obsessed with her quiet neighbor (Shire) and concocts a plot to get close to her. Director Willis is known for his unbeatable cinematography, most notably for Woody Allen in "Manhattan." His debut in the chair is a miserable, offensive flop. 93m/C VHS. Talia Shire, Joe Cortese, Elizabeth Ashley, Kay Medford, Linda Gillin; **D:** Gordon Willis; **C:** Gordon Willis; **M:** Ennio Morricone. *NO*

Windrider 🐾½ 1986 Simple love story made in Australia. A wind surfer and a rock star become lovers. Self-indulgent overwrought garbage with rare moments of promise. 83m/C VHS. *AU* Tom Burlinson, Nicole Kidman, Charles Tingwell, Jill Perryman, Simon Chilvers; **D:** Vincent Monton. *MGM*

Windrunner 🐾🐾½ 1994 (PG) Angry at his football-star dad and rejected by the local high school team, Greg Cima (Wiles) finds an unlikely ally in the spirit of Native American Olympic hero Jim Thorpe (Means). Seems Thorpe needs some aid to return to the spirit world and, by coaching Cima, he'll also get the help he needs. Believable performances and an exploration of the power of Native American mysticism help the unlikely premise along. 110m/C VHS. Russell Means, Jason Wiles, Amanda Peterson, Margot Kidder, Jake Busey, Max Casella, Bruce Weitz; **D:** William Clark; **M:** Arthur Kempel. *AVE*

The Winds of Jarrah 🐾½ 1983 English woman runs from broken heart to Australia to become nanny for misogynist, and Harlequin code prevails. Based on a Harlequin romance novel. 78m/C VHS, Beta. *AU* Terence Donovan, Susan Lyons; **D:** Mark Egerton; **M:** Bruce Smeaton. *NO*

The Winds of Kitty Hawk 🐾🐾 1978 Visually interesting but talky account of the Wright brothers attempt to beat their rival Glenn Curtiss and his backer, phone man Alexander Graham Bell. Rule of thumb: Fast-forward through the parts when they are on the ground, or see Stacy Keach's public-TV version instead. 96m/C VHS, Beta. Michael Moriarty, David Huffman, Kathryn Walker, Eugene Roche, John Randolph, Scott Hylands; **D:** E.W. Swackhamer; **M:** Charles Bernstein. *FRH*

Winds of the Wasteland 🐾🐾½ 1936 Would-be Pony Express contractors, Wayne and Chandler, race rivals to land government work. Competent western that put Wayne on the Hollywood map. 54m/B VHS. John Wayne, Phyllis Fraser,

Lane Chandler, Yakima Canutt; **D:** Mack V. Wright. REP, NOS, VCN

The Winds of War 🎬🎬 1983 On seven tapes, the excruciatingly long and dull television mini-series based on Herman Wouk's bestseller about WWII. The book was much better; Mitchum appears to be fighting sleep unsuccessfully for much of the show. Two follow-ups were produced: "War and Remembrance" and "War and Remembrance: The Final Chapter." **900m/C VHS, Beta, Closed Caption.** Robert Mitchum, Ali MacGraw, Ralph Bellamy, Polly Bergen, Jan-Michael Vincent, David Dukes, John Houseman, Victoria Tennant, Peter Graves, Chaim Topol, Ben Murphy, Jeremy Kemp, Anton Diffring, Lawrence Pressman, Andrew Duggan, Barbara Steele; **D:** Dan Curtis. PAR, MOV

Windwalker 🎬🎬🎬 1981 Howard, the only cast member who is not a Native American, is an aged chief who shares the memories of his life with his grandchildren. Filmed in the Crow and Cheyenne Indian languages and subtitled in English throughout. A beautifully photographed, intelligent independent project. **108m/C VHS, Beta.** Trevor Howard, James Remar, Dusty Iron Wing McCrea; **D:** Keith Merrill. FOX

Windy City 🎬🎬 1984 (R) A group of seven childhood friends must come to terms with the harsh realities of their failed ambitions when they meet for a weekend in Chicago. Told from the point of view of one of the group, recounting the sorts of memories we all prefer to forget. Typical and overwrought '80s yuppie reunion/regret drama. Aren't these people too young to be unhappy? **103m/C VHS, Beta, LV, Closed Caption.** John Shea, Kate Capshaw, Josh Mostel, Jeffrey DeMunn, Lewis J. Stadlen, James Sutorius; **W:** Armyan Bernstein; **M:** Jack Nitzsche. FOX

A Wing and a Prayer 🎬🎬🎬 1944 Better-than-average WWII Air Force action flick. Battles rage throughout the Pacific theater and the men aboard the aircraft carrier struggle to do their part to save the world for freedom. Fine cast receives Hathaway's excellent unsentimental direction. **97m/B VHS.** Don Ameche, Dana Andrews, William Eythe, Charles Bickford, Cedric Hardwicke, Kevin O'Shea, Richard Jaeckel, Harry (Henry) Morgan; **D:** Henry Hathaway. Nominations: Academy Awards '44: Best Original Screenplay. FXV

Wing Chun 🎬🎬 1994 Wing Chun (Yeoh) battles horse stealing bandits and the male chauvinists around her that don't think a woman can be strong and independent (as well as a fighting expert). Chinese with subtitles or dubbed. **93m/C VHS, LV.** HK Michelle Yeoh, Donnie Yan, Waise Lee; **D:** Yuen Woo Ping. TAI

Wings 🎬🎬½ 1927 The silent classic about friends, Rogers and Arlen, their adventures in the Air Corps during WWI, and their rivalry for the hand of a woman. Contains actual footage of combat flying from the Great War. Won the very first Best Picture Oscar. Too-thin plot hangs on (barely) to the stirring, intrepid dogfight scenes. **139m/B VHS, Beta, LV.** Clara Bow, Charles "Buddy" Rogers, Richard Arlen, Gary Cooper; **D:** William A. Wellman. Academy Awards '27: Best Picture. BTV, PAR

Wings of Danger 🎬 Dead on Course 1952 A pilot tries to save his friend from blackmailing gold smugglers. **72m/B VHS, Beta, LV.** GB Zachary Scott, Kay Kendall, Robert Beatty, Naomi Chance; **M:** Malcolm Arnold. MLB, RXM

Wings of Desire 🎬🎬🎬½ Der Himmel Uber Berlin 1988 (PG-13) An ethereal, haunting modern fable about one of many angels observing human life in and above the broken existence of Berlin, and how he begins to long to experience life as humans do. A moving, unequivocable masterpiece, with as many beautiful things to say about spiritual need as about the schizophrenic emptiness of contemporary Germany; Wenders' magnum opus. In German with English subtitles, and with black-and-white sequences. Magnificent cinematography by Henri Alekan. **130m/C VHS, Beta,**

LV. GE Bruno Ganz, Peter Falk, Solveig Dommartin, Otto Sander, Curt Bois; **D:** Wim Wenders; **W:** Wim Wenders, Peter Handke; **C:** Henri Alekan; **M:** Jurgen Knieper. Independent Spirit Awards '89: Best Foreign Film; Los Angeles Film Critics Association Awards '88: Best Cinematography, Best Foreign Film; New York Film Critics Awards '88: Best Cinematography; National Society of Film Critics Awards '88: Best Cinematography. ORI, GLV, MOV

Wings of Eagles 🎬🎬½ 1957 Hollywood biography of Frank 'Spig' Wead, a famous WWI aviation pioneer turned screenwriter. Veers wildly from comedy to stolid drama, though Bond's lampoon of Ford as "John Dodge" is justly famous. **110m/C VHS, Beta.** John Wayne, Ward Bond, Maureen O'Hara, Dan Dailey, Edmund Lowe, Ken Curtis, Kenneth Tobey, Sig Rumann, Veda Ann Borg; **D:** John Ford; **C:** Paul Vogel. MGM

Wings of Fame 🎬🎬½ 1993 (R) Comic afterlife fantasy skewering celebrity status. Recently departed celebs check into a posh hotel, but as their fame on earth declines so do their afterlife accomodations, until they reach the state of oblivion. The latest hotel arrivals are a renowned, arrogant actor (O'Toole) and the frustrated writer (Firth) whose claim to fame has come from murdering him. **109m/C VHS, Beta, Closed Caption.** Peter O'Toole, Colin Firth; **D:** Otakar Votocek; **W:** Herman Koch, Otakar Votocek. PAR

Wings of the Morning 🎬🎬½ 1937 Maria (Annabella), a descendant of Spanish gypsies, comes to Ireland with her grandmother (Vanbrugh) who's entering a horse in the Epsom Downs Derby. Maria disguises herself as a boy so she can ride in the race but is discovered by Canadian horse-trainer Kerry (Fonda), who promptly falls in love with her. Legendary tenor John McCormack sings several songs. The first British movie to be filmed in Technicolor. **89m/C VHS.** GB Annabella, Henry Fonda, Edward Underdown, Irene Vanbrugh, Leslie Banks, Stewart Rome; **D:** Harold Schuster; **W:** Tom Geraghty; **C:** Jack Cardiff, Henry Imus, Ray Rennahan; **M:** Arthur Benjamin. KIV

Wings Over the Pacific 🎬½ 1943 Love and his daughter Cooper are living quietly on a Pacific island when a pair of pilots, American Norris and the Nazi Guttman, crash-land after a dogfight. The island is strategic because of its oil supply but Norris manages to prevent the Nazis from taking control and wins Cooper's love in the process. Veteran actor Love died shortly before the film's release. **60m/B VHS.** Montagu Love, Inez Cooper, Edward Norris, Henry Guttman, Robert Armstrong, Ernie Adams; **D:** Phil Rosen; **W:** George Wallace Sayre. GPV

A Winner Never Quits 🎬🎬½ 1986 (PG) A true story based on the life of 1940s baseball player Pete Gray. As a boy Gray lost his right arm above the elbow in an accident. He's determined to prove himself as a baseball player and during WWII is given a tryout, although his teammates consider him a sideshow freak. A Memphis sportswriter takes an interest in Pete's career and Gray's success on the field leads to a career with the St. Louis Browns. Along the way he becomes the inspiration to a young fan, who's also lost an arm. Made for television. **96m/C VHS.** Keith Carradine, Mare Winningham, Huckleberry Fox, Dennis Weaver, Dana Delany, G.W. Bailey, Charles Hallahan, Fionnula Flanagan, Jack Kehoe; **D:** Mel Damski; **W:** Burt Prelutsky. COL

Winner Takes All 🎬🎬 1986 (R) A young college student during the Vietnam War comes to grips with maturity and growing pains. **94m/C VHS, Beta, Closed Caption.** GB Jason Connery, Diane Cilento. ACA

Winners of the West 1940 A landowner schemes to prevent a railroad from running through his property. The railroad's chief engineer leads the good guys in an attempt to prevent sabotage. A fun serial in thirteen chapters, full of shooting, blown-up bridges, locomotives afire, etc.; and of course, the requisite damsel in distress. **250m/B VHS.** Anne Nagel, Dick Foran, James

Craig, Harry Woods; **D:** Ray Taylor, Ford Beebe. GPV, VCN, NOS

Winners Take All 🎬🎬 1987 (PG-13) A handful of friends compete in Supercross races. Spirited but thoroughly cliche sports flick. **103m/C VHS, Beta, LV, Closed Caption.** Don Michael Paul, Kathleen York, Robert Krantz; **D:** Fritz Kiersch. NLC

Winning 🎬🎬🎬 1969 (PG) A race car driver (Newman) will let nothing, including his new wife (Woodward), keep him from winning the Indianapolis 500. Newman does his own driving. Thomas' film debut. **123m/C VHS, Beta, LV.** Paul Newman, Joanne Woodward, Robert Wagner, Clu Gulager; **D:** James Goldstone; **M:** Dave Grusin. USH

Winning of the West 🎬🎬 1953 Yodelin' ranger Autry vows to protect a crusading publisher from unscrupulous crooks, including his own dog-gone brothers. The brothers see the light, and the two corral the varmints. Autry tunes include "Cowboy Blues," "Cowpoke Poking Along," and "Find Me My 45." **57m/B VHS, Beta.** Gene Autry, Smiley Burnette, Gail Davis, Richard Crane; **D:** George Archainbaud. CCB

The Winning Team 🎬🎬½ 1952 Reagan stars in this biography of baseball legend Grover Cleveland Alexander and Day plays his dedicated wife. Some controversial issues were glossed over in the film, such as Alexander's real-life drinking problem and the fact that he had epilepsy. Although this was one of Reagan's favorite roles, he was upset by the studio's avoidance of all-too-human problems. Nonetheless, it's an entertaining enough movie about a very talented ballplayer. **98m/B VHS, LV, Closed Caption.** Doris Day, Ronald Reagan, Frank Lovejoy, Eve Miller, James Millican, Russ Tamblyn; **D:** Lewis Seiler. WAR

The Winslow Boy 🎬🎬🎬½ 1948 A cadet at the Royal Naval College is wrongly accused of theft and expelled. Donat as the boy's lawyer leads a splendid cast. Despite consequences for his family, the boy's father (Hardwicke) sues the government and fights his son's battle, as the case makes the papers and he approaches bankruptcy. Plot would seem far-fetched if it weren't based on fact. Absorbing. Based on a play by Rattigan, who co-wrote the script. **112m/B VHS, Beta.** GB Robert Donat, Cedric Hardwicke, Margaret Leighton, Frank Lawton, Kathleen Harrison, Basil Radford; **D:** Anthony Asquith; **W:** Terence Rattigan; **C:** Frederick A. (Freddie) Young. HEG

Winter Flight 🎬🎬 1984 A small, gentle British drama about an RAF recruit and a barmaid who quickly become lovers, and then are confronted with her pregnancy. **105m/C VHS, Beta.** GB Reece Dinsdale, Nicola Cowper, Gary Olsen; **D:** Roy Battersby. MGM

Winter Kills 🎬🎬🎬 1979 (R) Distinctive political black comedy suffers a hilariously paranoid version of American public life. Bridges, the younger brother of a U.S. president assassinated 15 years earlier, uncovers the plot. Huston is delightful as Bridges' horny old father. Uneven, but well worth seeing; flopped at the box office, but was re-released in 1983. Taylor was not billed. **97m/C VHS, Beta, LV.** Jeff Bridges, John Huston, Anthony Perkins, Richard Boone, Sterling Hayden, Eli Wallach, Ralph Meeker, Belinda Bauer, Dorothy Malone, Toshiro Mifune, Elizabeth Taylor, Donald Moffat, Tisa Farrow, Brad Dexter, Joe Spinell; **D:** William Richert; **M:** Maurice Jarre. COL

The Winter Light 🎬🎬🎬½ Nattvardsgaesterna 1962 The second film in Bergman's famous trilogy on the silence of God, preceded by "Through a Glass Darkly" and followed by "The Silence." Bleak and disturbing view of a tortured priest who searches for the faith and guidance he is unable to give his congregation. Hard to swallow for neophyte Bergmanites, but challenging, deeply serious and rewarding for those accustomed to the Swede's angst. Polished and personal. In Swedish with English subtitles. **80m/B VHS, Beta, LV.** SW Gunnar Bjornstrand, Ingrid Thulin, Max von Sydow; **D:** Ingmar Bergman; **W:** Ingmar Bergman; **C:**

Sven Nykvist. National Board of Review Awards '63: 5 Best Foreign Films of the Year. *NLC*

Winter Meeting 🐾🐾 1948 Overwrought drama with Bette Davis starring as a spinster poetess who falls in love with a war hero who wants to be a priest. Very talky script, of interest only as the sole romantic lead for James Davis, whose claim to fame was westerns and the TV series "Dallas." **104m/B VHS, Closed Caption.** Bette Davis, Janis Paige, James Davis, John Hoyt, Florence Bates, Walter Baldwin, Ransom Sherman; *D:* Bretaigne Windust; *M:* Max Steiner. *MGM*

The Winter of Our Dreams 🐾🐾½ 1982 Down Under slice of seamy life as a heroin-addicted prostitute becomes involved with an unhappy bookshop owner. Davis shines in otherwise slow and confusing drama. **89m/C VHS, Beta.** *AU* Judy Davis, Bryan Brown, Cathy Downes, Baz Luhrmann, Peter Mochrie, Mervyn Drak, Margie McCrae, Marcie Deane-Johns; *D:* John Duigan. Australian Film Institute '81: Best Actress (Davis). *LIV*

Winter People 🐾🐾½ 1989 (PG-13) A clock-making widower and a woman living alone with her illegitimate son experience tough times together with feuding families in a Depression-era Appalachian community. Silly, rehashed premise doesn't deter McGillis, who gamely gives a fine performance. Based on the novel by John Ehle. **109m/C VHS, Beta, LV, 8mm, Closed Caption.** Kurt Russell, Kelly McGillis, Lloyd Bridges, Mitchell Ryan, Jeffrey Meek, Eileen Ryan, Amelia Burnette; *D:* Ted Kotcheff; *W:* Carol Sobieski; *M:* John Scott. *NLC*

Winterbeast 🐾 1992 Winter resort community dwellers begin mysteriously disappearing until somebody remembers that the resort was built over a sacred Indian burial ground. Sgt. Bill Whitman, the valiant park ranger and his Barney Fife-like assistant Stillman, question the town's wise old sage, Sheldon, who's sitting on a secret that could threaten the entire community. **77m/C VHS.** Tim R. Morgan, Mike Magri. *TEM, MOV*

Winterset 🐾🐾½ 1936 A son seeks to clear his father's name of a falsely accused crime 15 years after his electrocution. Powerful at the time, though time has lessened its impact. Loosely based on the trial of Sacco and Vanzetti and adapted from Maxwell Anderson's Broadway play, with stars in the same roles. Meredith's film debut. **85m/B VHS, Beta.** Burgess Meredith, Margo, John Carradine; *D:* Alfred Santell. Nominations: Academy Awards '36: Best Interior Decoration, Best Original Score. *MON, HHT, CAB*

Wintertime 🐾½ 1943 Forgettable and mindless Henie musical. Plot revolves around Henie travelling in Canada with her wealthy uncle, and saving an old, run-down hotel. An appearance by Woody Herman and his Orchestra give the film a much-needed boost. Based on a story by Arthur Kober. **82m/B VHS.** Sonja Henie, Jack Oakie, Cesar Romero, Carole Landis, S.Z. Sakall, Cornel Wilde, Woody Herman; *D:* John Brahm; *W:* E. Edwin Moran, Jack Jevne, Lynn Starling. *FXV*

Wired 🐾 1989 (R) A justly lambasted, unintentionally hilarious biography of comic genius and overdose victim John Belushi, very loosely based on Bob Woodward's bestselling muckraking book. The chronicle of addiction and tragedy is tried here as a weird sort of comedy; was it meant as a tribute to its off-kilter subject? If so, it misses by a mile. And, we're sorry, but Chiklis doesn't cut it as Belushi—who would?! **112m/C VHS, Beta, LV.** Michael Chiklis, Ray Sharkey, Patti D'Arbanville, J.T. Walsh, Gary Groomes, Lucinda Jenney, Alex Rocco, Jere Burns, Billy Preston; *D:* Larry Peerce; *M:* Basil Poledouris. *LIV*

Wired to Kill woof! 1986 (R) In a futuristic world, two teenagers seek justice for their parents' murder by building a remote-controlled erector set programmed for revenge. Laughably porous plot drops any pretence of credibility. Dizzyingly bad. **96m/C VHS, Beta.** Merritt Butrick, Emily Longstreth, Devin Hoelscher, Frank Collison; *D:* Francis Schaeffer. *LIV*

Wisdom 🐾½ 1987 (R) Unemployed young guy (Estevez) becomes a bank robber with Robin Hood aspirations, coming to the aid of American farmers by destroying mortgage records. Estevez became the youngest person to star in, write, and direct a major motion picture. And, my goodness, it shows. **109m/C VHS, Beta, LV, Closed Caption.** Emilio Estevez, Demi Moore, Tom Skerritt, Veronica Cartwright; *D:* Emilio Estevez; *M:* Danny Elfman. *WAR*

Wise Blood 🐾🐾🐾½ 1979 (PG) Gothic drama about a drifter who searches for sin and becomes a preacher for a new religion, The Church Without Christ. Excellent cast in achingly realistic portrayal of ersatz religion, southern style. Many laughs are more painful than funny. Superb, very dark comedy from Huston. Adapted from the Flannery O'Connor novel. **106m/C VHS, Beta.** Brad Dourif, John Huston, Ned Beatty, Amy Wright, Harry Dean Stanton; *D:* John Huston; *M:* Alex North. *USH*

Wise Guys 🐾½ 1986 (R) Two small-time hoods decide to rip off the mob. When their boss figures out their plan he decides to set them up instead. Lame black comedy that has too few moments. **100m/C VHS, Beta, Closed Caption.** Joe Piscopo, Danny DeVito, Ray Sharkey, Captain Lou Albano, Dan Hedaya, Julie Bovasso, Patti LuPone; *D:* Brian DePalma; *M:* Ira Newborn. *FOX, FCT*

Wisecracks 🐾🐾🐾 1993 Women comics perform and talk about their work in this documentary directed by Gail Singer. The comics featured have, in some cases, little more in common than their work, but all share interesting perspectives on what they do. Interesting mix of performance clips and interviews sometimes includes banal comments about the nature of comedy, but is more often insightful, especially remarks by seasoned vet Phyllis Diller. Although there exists here the potential for an angry feminist diatribe on gender-based humor, the focus is more towards talented women who are just plain funny. **93m/C VHS.** *D:* Gail Singer; *Performed by:* Whoopi Goldberg, Paula Poundstone, Ellen DeGeneres, Kim Wayans, Pam Stone, Joy Behar, Maxine Lapidus, Phyllis Diller, Jenny Jones. *MNC*

Wish Me Luck 🐾½ 1995 A babe genie (Avalon) has a dilemma—unless she can make a man of a geek college student (Gesner) in 48 hours, she'll become the property of an evil sorcerer for a thousand years. She gets three equally bodacious college cheerleaders to help her out. Also available in an edited version that cuts six minutes worth of fleshy fantasies. **91m/C VHS.** Avalon Anders, Zen Gesner; *D:* Philip Jones. *SDE*

Wish You Were Here 🐾🐾🐾 1987 Poignant yet funny slice of British postwar life roughly based on the childhood memoirs of famous madame, Cynthia Payne. A troubled and freedom-loving teenager expresses her rebellion in sexual experimentation. Mum is dead and Dad just doesn't understand, so what's a girl to do, but get the boys excited? Lloyd, in her first film, plays the main character with exceptional strength and feistiness. Payne's later life was dramatized in the Leland-scripted "Personal Services." **92m/C VHS, Beta, LV.** *GB* Emily Lloyd, Tom Bell, Clare Clifford, Barbara Durkin, Geoffrey Hutchings, Charlotte Barker, Chloe Leland, Trudy Cavanagh, Jesse Birdsall, Geoffrey Durham, Pat Heywood; *D:* David Leland; *W:* David Leland; *M:* Stanley Myers. British Academy Awards '87: Best Original Screenplay; National Society of Film Critics Awards '87: Best Actress (Lloyd). *FRH, TVC*

Wishful Thinking 🐾🐾 1992 A lovelorn screenwriter rescues a peculiar man from mysterious assassins and receives a magical writing pad for his efforts. It seems that whatever Michael writes on the paper will come true, so he decides to write himself into the life of the luscious Diane. **94m/C VHS.** Murray Langston, Michelle Johnson, Ruth Buzzi, Billy Barty, Johnny Dark, Ray "Boom Boom" Mancini, Vic Dunlop, Kip Addotta; *D:* Murray Langston. *HMD*

The Wishing Ring 🐾🐾🐾 1914 Light and charming romance, beautifully filmed by Tourneur, based on Owen Davis' play. The son of an earl in Old England is expelled from college and told by his father he must earn half a crown on his own before the family will take him back. With the help of a minister's daughter, he sets things right. **50m/B VHS, Beta.** Vivian March, Alec B. Francis, Chester Barnett, Simeon Wiltsie, Walter Morton; *D:* Maurice Tourneur; *W:* Maurice Tourneur. *GPV*

The Wishmaker 1985 A young man squanders the three wishes granted to him for helping a strange old woman and her timid daughter. **54m/C VHS, Beta.** *GEM*

Wishman 🐾🐾½ 1993 Hollywood hustler Basie Banks (Le Mat) meets Hitch (Lewis), a two million year old genie whose magic bottle has been stolen. In exchange for Banks' help in recovering his home, Hitch agrees to help Banks get the girl of his dreams. **89m/C VHS.** Paul LeMat, Geoffrey Lewis, Paul Gleason, Quin Kessler, Nancy Parsons, Gailard Sartain, Brion James; *D:* Mike Marvin; *M:* Mike Marvin. *MNC*

The Wistful Widow of Wagon Gap 🐾🐾 The Wistful Widow 1947 Lou, a traveling salesman, accidentally kills a man, and according to the law of the west he has to take care of the dead man's widow and children—all seven of them. Because the family is so unsavory, Lou knows that no other man will kill him, so he allows himself to be appointed sheriff and clears the town of lowlifes. Usual Abbott & Costello fare is highlighted with their zany antics. **78m/B VHS.** Bud Abbott, Lou Costello, Marjorie Main, George Cleveland, Gordon Jones, William Ching, Peter Thompson, Glenn Strange, Olin Howlin; *D:* Charles T. Barton. *USH*

The Witch 🐾½ La Strega in Amore; Aura 1966 Historian hired by family to assemble the late father's works falls in love with beautiful daughter. Seems she's no angel. **103m/B VHS.** *IT* Rosanna Schiaffino, Richard Johnson, Sarah Ferrati, Gian Marie Volonte, Margherita Guzzinati; *D:* Damiano Damiani. *SNC*

Witch Hunt 🐾🐾½ 1994 (R) Mock fantasy/mystery set in 1953 Hollywood. Private eye H. Phillip Lovecraft (Hopper) is hired by actress Kim Hudson (Miller) to shadow her philandering studio hubby Gottlieb (Rosenberg), who dies in an untimely fashion. The kicker is that witchcraft is commonplace, with the studio hiring witches and warlocks to cast spells. Also, a blowhard senator (Bogosian) is heading a McCarthy-like campaign to ban magic and Lovecraft fears his sorceress friend (Ralph) is going to be the scapegoat for Gottlieb's murder. Great special effects; fuzzy plot.*CW:* Some strong language; scene of nudity. **101m/C VHS.** Dennis Hopper, Penelope Ann Miller, Eric Bogosian, Sheryl Lee Ralph, Julian Sands, Alan Rosenberg, Valerie Mahaffey, Debi Mazar; *D:* Paul Schrader; *W:* Joseph Dougherty; *M:* Angelo Badalamenti. *HBO*

Witch Who Came from the Sea 🐾½ 1976 (R) Witch terrorizes all the ships at sea, but doesn't exactly haunt the viewer. **98m/C VHS, Beta.** Millie Perkins, Lonny Chapman, Vanessa Brown, Peggy Feury, Rick Jason; *D:* Matt Cimber. *UNI*

A Witch Without a Broom 🐾½ Una Bruja Sin Escoba 1968 Shoestring time travel fantasy. When an American professor catches the eye of a 15th century apprentice witch, the trip begins. Since the witch is only learning the ropes, they end up visiting a number of periods other than their own before the professor gets home. **78m/C VHS.** *SP* Jeffrey Hunter, Maria Perschy, Perla Cristal, Gustavo Rojo; *D:* Joe Lacy. *NO*

Witchboard 🐾🐾½ 1987 (R) During a college party, a group of friends bring out the Ouija board and play with it for laughs. One of the girls discovers she can use the board to communicate with a small boy who died years before. In her effort to talk with him she unwittingly releases the evil spirit of an ax murderer who haunts and murders members of the group. An entertaining, relatively inoffensive member of its genre that displays some attention to characterization and plot. **98m/C VHS, Beta, LV.** Todd Allen, Tawny Kitaen, Stephen Nichols, Kathleen Wilhoite, Burke Byrnes, Rose Marie, James W. Quinn, Judy Tatum, Gloria Hayes, J.P. Luebsen, Susan Nickerson; **D:** Kevin S. Tenney; **W:** Kevin S. Tenney; **C:** Roy Wagner; **M:** Dennis Michael Tenney. **HHE**

Witchboard 2: The Devil's Doorway 🐾🐾½ 1993 (R) There seem to be a lot of doorways to hell because someone is always finding a new one (and making a movie about it). This time it's the innocent Paige Benedict (Dolenz), who moves into an artist's loft and finds an old Ouija board in a closet. Through the board, Paige is contacted by a former tenant who claims to be a murder victim. Soon her fellow tenants are dying in violent and mysterious ways and Paige's dreams are haunted by evil. What hath she wrought—and can she get it back in the closet where it belongs. **98m/C VHS, LV, Closed Caption.** Ami Dolenz, Laraine Newman, Timothy Gibbs, John Gatins; **D:** Kevin S. Tenney; **W:** Kevin S. Tenney; **M:** Dennis Michael Tenney. **REP**

Witchboard 3: The Possession 🐾🐾½ 1995 (R) A Ouija board opens the gates to hell (yet again or we wouldn't have a movie) and the board's spirit steals Brian's soul and takes control of his body—much to the bewilderment of his girlfriend Julie.**CW:** Strong sexuality and violence; language. **93m/C VHS, Closed Caption.** David Nerman, Locky Lambert, Cedric Smith, Donna Sarrasin; **D:** Peter Svatek; **W:** Kevin S. Tenney, Jon Ezrine; **C:** Barry Gravelle. **REP**

Witchcraft woof! 1988 (R) A young mother meets a couple killed three centuries ago for performing witchcraft. They want her baby, of course, to be the son of the devil. "Rosemary's Baby" ripoff, that is thoroughly predictable. **90m/C VHS, Beta, LV.** Anat 'Topol' Barzilai, Gary Sloan, Lee Kisman, Deborah Scott; **D:** Robert Spera. **ACA**

Witchcraft 2: The Temptress 🐾 1990 (R) A sensuous woman seduces an innocent young man into the rituals of witchcraft and the occult. Sequel to "Witchcraft" does not succeed where original failed, but does have a fair share of sex and violence. **88m/C VHS, Beta, LV.** Charles Solomon, Mia Ruiz, Delia Sheppard; **D:** Mark Woods. **ACA**

Witchcraft 3: The Kiss of Death 🐾🐾 1990 (R) Once a master of the occult, William Spanner now seeks only to live a normal life. His plans are changed, however, when a sensual creature from Hell is sent to seduce him. More sex and violence, with an emphasis on sex. The best of the "Witchcraft" trio, for those trying to plan a festive evening.**CW:** Language, violence, and strong sensuality. **85m/C VHS.** Charles Solomon, Lisa Toothman, William L. Baker, Lena Hall; **D:** R.L. Tillmanns. **ACA**

Witchcraft 4: Virgin Heart 🐾 1992 (R) Supernatural horror continues as attorney Will Spanner sinks even deeper into his enemy's satanic trap in this shocking sequel to the popular series. His only hope is to use his own black magic powers and to enlist the help of a seductive stripper (Penthouse Pet Strain).**CW:** Language, horror violence, and sexuality. **92m/C VHS, LV, Closed Caption.** Charles Solomon, Julie Strain, Clive Pearson, Jason O'Gulihar, Lisa Jay Harrington, Barbara Dow; **D:** James Merendino. **ACA**

Witchcraft 5: Dance with the Devil 🐾 1992 (R) This undistinguished horror series continues with several successful people finding the unpleasant loopholes in their satanic contracts. A demon named Cain is behind all the trouble. The horror special effects are cheap but there are several soft-core sex scenes (pointless to the plot) which provide a minimal interest. An unrated version is also available.**CW:** Language, violence, and strong sexuality.`94m/C VHS.` Marklen Kennedy, Carolyn Taye-Loren, Nicole Sassaman, Aysha Hauer; **D:** Talun Hsu. **ACA**

Witchcraft 6: The Devil's Mistress 🐾 1994 (R) Police detectives Lutz and Garner's new case involves young women turning up naked and dead. Turns out satanic disciple Savanti is expected to impress the boss with a virgin sacrifice before an impending eclipse. But since virgins are scarce, he's having a real tough time. Practically no gore but lots of skin, along with hit-or-miss humor. **86m/C VHS.** Kurt Alan, John E. Holiday, Bryan Nutter, Jerry Spicer, Shannon Lead; **D:** Julie Davis; **W:** Julie Davis. **NO**

Witchcraft 7: Judgement Hour 🐾 1995 (R) Modern-day warlock must sacrifice his earthly existence to kill an evil vampire.**CW:** Strong sexuality and language. **91m/C VHS.** David Byrnes, April Breneman, Alisa Christensen, John Cragen, Loren Schmalle; **D:** Michael Paul Girard; **W:** Peter Fleming; **C:** Denis Maloney; **M:** Miriam Cutler. **APX**

Witchcraft 9: Bitter Flesh 🐾 1996 Yet another sequel to the endless erotic horror series finds the LAPD investigating a series of murders. They get a tip from a strange call girl who claims to be chanelling the spirit of a warlock, who's about to open the gates to hell. **90m/C VHS.** Landon Hall, David Byrnes, Stephanie Beaton, Mikul Robins; **D:** Michael Paul Girard; **W:** Stephen J. Downing; **C:** Jeff Gateman; **M:** Michael Paul Girard. **VSE**

Witchcraft Through the Ages 🐾🐾🐾 *Haxan* 1922 The demonic Swedish masterpiece in which witches and victims suffer against various historical backgrounds. Nightmarish and profane, especially the appearance of the Devil as played under much make-up by Christiansen himself. Silent. **74m/B VHS, Beta.** *SW* Maren Pedersen, Clara Pontoppidan; **D:** Benjamin Christiansen. **GPV, MPI, WFV**

Witchery 🐾 1988 A photographer and his girlfriend vacation at a New England hotel where they discover a horrifying, satanic secret. One by one (as always, in this kind of bad flick, in the interest of "suspense"), people are killed off. Seems it's a witch, bent on revenge. Forget room service and bar the door. **96m/C VHS, Beta.** David Hasselhoff, Linda Blair, Catherine Hickland, Hildegarde Knef, Leslie Cumming, Bob Champagne, Richard Farnsworth, Michael Manches; **D:** Fabrizio Laurenti. **THV**

The Witches 🐾🐾🐾 1990 (PG) Nine-year-old boy on vacation finds himself in the midst of a witch convention, and grand high witch Huston plans to turn all children into furry little creatures. The boy, with the help of his good witch grandmother, attempts to prevent the mass transmutation of children into mice. Top-notch fantasy probably too spooky for the training wheel set. Wonderful special effects; the final project of executive producer Jim Henson. Based on Roald Dahl's story. **92m/C VHS, Beta, LV, 8mm, Closed Caption.** Anjelica Huston, Mai Zetterling, Jasen Fisher, Rowan Atkinson, Charlie Potter, Bill Paterson, Brenda Blethyn, Jane Horrocks; **D:** Nicolas Roeg; **W:** Allan Scott; **M:** Stanley Myers. Los Angeles Film Critics Association Awards '90: Best Actress (Huston); National Society of Film Critics Awards '90: Best Actress (Huston). **WAR, FCT, ORI**

Witches' Brew 🐾🐾 1979 (PG) Three young women try to use their undeveloped skills in witchcraft and black magic to help Garr's husband get a prestigious position at a university, with calamitous results. Oft-funny spoof is silly and oft-predictable. Turner's role is small as an older, experienced witch. **98m/C VHS, Beta.** Teri Garr, Richard Benjamin, Lana Turner, Kathryn Leigh Scott; **D:** Richard Shorr, Herbert L. Strock.

Witches' Mountain 🐾 1971 A troubled couple is captured by a coven of witches in the Pyrenees. Dull and pointless. **98m/C VHS, Beta.** *MX* Patty Shepard, John Caffari, Monica Randall; **D:** Raul Artigot. **UNI, HEG**

The Witches of Eastwick 🐾🐾½ 1987 (R) "Mad Max" director Miller meets Hollywood in this unrestrained, vomit-filled treatment of John Updike's novel about three lonely small-town New England women and their sexual liberation. A strange, rich, overweight and balding, but none-theless charming man knows their deepest desires and makes them come true with decadent excess. Raunchy fun, with Nicholson over-acting wildly as the Mephisto. Miller lends a bombastic violent edge to the effort, sometimes at the expense of the story. Filmed on location in Cohasset, Massachusetts. **118m/C VHS, Beta, LV, 8mm, Closed Caption.** Jack Nicholson, Cher, Susan Sarandon, Michelle Pfeiffer, Veronica Cartwright, Richard Jenkins, Keith Joakum, Carel Struycken; **D:** George Miller; **W:** Michael Cristofer; **C:** Vilmos Zsigmond; **M:** John Williams. Los Angeles Film Critics Association Awards '87: Best Actor (Nicholson); New York Film Critics Awards '87: Best Actor (Nicholson); Nominations: Academy Awards '87: Best Sound, Best Original Score. **WAR**

Witchfire 🐾 1986 (R) After their pyschiatrist dies in an automobile accident, three maniacal women escape from an asylum and hide out in the woods. Winters then holds seances to contact the dead doctor, but instead captures a young, very much alive hunter. For dedicated fans of Winters. **92m/C VHS, Beta.** Shelley Winters, Gary Swanson, David Mendenhall, Corinne Chateau; **D:** Vincent J. Privitera; **W:** Vincent J. Privitera. **LIV**

The Witching woof! *Necromancy* 1972 Poorly made story of man's continuing quest for supernatural power. Welles slums as the high priest out to get victim Franklin. **90m/C VHS, Beta.** Orson Welles, Pamela Franklin, Michael Ontkean, Lee Purcell; **D:** Bert I. Gordon; **C:** Winton C. Hoch. **NO**

The Witching of Ben Wagner 🐾🐾½ 1995 (G) Strange occurrences have Ben believing his friend Regina and her grandmother may be witches. But, if so, they're friendly ones as they help Ben adjust to a new home and neighborhood. **96m/C VHS, Closed Caption.** Justin Gocke, Harriet Hall, Sam Bottoms; **D:** Paul Annett. **AVE**

Witching Time 🐾½ 1984 Elvira presents this film, in which a young composer is visited by a horny 17th-century witch while his wife is away from home. When the wife returns, both women fight to possess him. **60m/C VHS, Beta.** Jon Finch, Prunella Gee, Patricia Quinn, Ian McCulloch; **D:** Don Leaver. **LIV**

The Witchmaker 🐾 *Legend of Witch Hollow; Witchkill* 1969 Remote, crocodile-infested bayou in Louisiana is the scene of witchcraft and the occult as young girls are murdered in order for a group of witches to become youthful again. **101m/C VHS, Beta.** John Lodge, Alvy Moore, Thordis Brandt, Anthony Eisley, Shelby Grant, Robyn Millan; **D:** William O. Brown; **W:** William O. Brown. **NO**

The Witch's Mirror 🐾🐾 1960 A sorceress plots to destroy the murderer of her goddaughter. The murderer, a surgeon, begins a project to restore the disfigured face and hands of his burned second wife, and he doesn't care how he gets the materials. For true fans of good bad horror flicks. Badly dubbed (which adds to the charm); dark (of course); and offbeat (naturally). **75m/B VHS, Beta.** *MX* Rosita Arenas, Armando Calvo, Isabela Corona, Dina De Marco; **D:** Chano Urueto. **SNC, HHT**

WitchTrap 🐾 1989 (R) Lame sequel to "Witchboard." A mansion's new owner hires psychics to exorcise the disturbed ghost of his predecessor. **87m/C VHS, Beta, LV.** James W. Quinn, Kathleen Bailey, Linnea Quigley; **D:** Kevin S. Tenney. **IME**

With Honors 🐾🐾½ 1994 (PG-13) Pesci is a bum who finds desperate Harvard student Fraser's Honors thesis, and, like any quick-witted bum with a yen for literature, holds it for ransom. Desperate to salvage his future gold card, Fraser and his roommates agree to fix Joe's homeless state. Self-involved students learn something about love and life while Madonna drones in the background. Fraser is believable as the ambitious student about to endure Pesci's enlightenment. Pesci is Pesci, doing his best to overcome numerous script difficulties. **100m/C VHS, LV.** Joe Pesci, Brendan Fraser, Moira Kelly, Patrick Dempsey, Josh Hamilton, Gore Vidal; **D:** Alek Keshishian; **W:** William Mastrosimone; **M:** Patrick Leonard. Nominations: Golden Globe

Awards '95: Best Song ("I'll Remember"); MTV Movie Awards '95: Best Song ("I'll Remember").*WAR*

With Kit Carson Over the Great Divide 🐾🐾½ 1925 A large-scale silent western about a doctor's family gone asunder and then reunited during the Fremont expeditions out of St. Louis in the 1840s. Snow's final screen appearance. Recently refound. Fun cinematic history (in two senses of the phrase). Beautiful landscape. 72m/B VHS, Beta, 8mm. Roy Stewart, Frank S. Walthall, Marguerite Snow, Sheldon Lewis, Earl Metcalfe; *D:* Frank S. Mattison. *VYY*

With Six You Get Eggroll 🐾🐾 *A Man in Mommy's Bed* 1968 (G) A widow with three sons and a widower with a daughter elope and then must deal with the antagonism of their children and even their dogs. Brady Bunch-esque family comedy means well, but doesn't cut it. Hershey's debut. Jamie Farr, William Christopher, and Vic Tayback have small parts. To date, Day's last big-screen appearance. 95m/C VHS, Beta. Doris Day, Brian Keith, Pat Carroll, Alice Ghostley, Vic Tayback, Jamie Farr, William Christopher, Barbara Hershey; *D:* Howard Morris; *C:* Harry Stradling Jr. *FOX*

Within the Rock 🐾🐾 1996 (R) Space crew must shift a wandering moon before it collides with earth but beyond that problem they've got an alien predator that's escaped.*CW:* Some sci-fi violence and gore. 91m/C VHS. Xander Berkeley, Bradford Tatum, Brian Krause, Caroline Barclay, Calvin Levels, Earl Boen, Dale Dye; *D:* Gary J. Tunnicliffe. *APX*

Withnail and I 🐾🐾🐾½ 1987 (R) A biting and original black comedy about a pair of unemployed, nearly starving English actors during the late 1960s. They decide to retreat to a country house owned by Withnail's uncle, for a vacation and are beset by comic misadventures, particularly when the uncle, who is gay, starts to hit on his nephew's friend. Robinson, who scripted "The Killing Fields", makes his successful directorial debut, in addition to drafting the screenplay from his own novel. Co-produced by George Harrison and Richard Starkey (Ringo Starr). 108m/C VHS, Beta, LV. *GB* Richard E. Grant, Paul McGann, Richard Griffiths, Ralph Brown, Michael Elphick; *D:* Bruce Robinson; *W:* Bruce Robinson; *M:* David Dundas. *FCT*

Without a Clue 🐾🐾½ 1988 (PG) Spoof of the Sherlock Holmes legend, in which Holmes is actually portrayed by a bumbling, skirt-chasing actor, and Watson is the sole crime-solving mastermind, hiring the actor to impersonate the character made famous by the doctor's published exploits. The leads have some fun and so do we; but laughs are widely spaced. 107m/C VHS, Beta, LV, Closed Caption. *GB* Michael Caine, Ben Kingsley, Jeffrey Jones, Lysette Anthony, Paul Freeman, Nigel Davenport, Peter Cook, Pat Keen; *D:* Thom Eberhardt; *W:* Gary Murphy, Larry Strawther; *M:* Henry Mancini. *ORI*

Without a Trace 🐾🐾 1983 (PG) One morning, a six-year-old boy is sent off to school by his loving mother, never to return. The story of the mother's relentless search for her son. Cardboard characters, wildly unrealistic ending that is different from the real-life incident on which it's based. Scripted by Gutcheon from her book "Still Missing." Jaffe's directorial debut. 119m/C VHS, Beta. Kate Nelligan, Judd Hirsch, Stockard Channing, David Dukes; *D:* Stanley R. Jaffe; *C:* John Bailey; *M:* Jack Nitzsche. *FOX*

Without Anesthesia 🐾🐾 *Rough Treatment; Bez Znieczulenia* 1978 Journalist Jerzy returns from a trip abroad to discover his wife has left him for an obnoxious young writer. Against advice, Jerzy fights the divorce and searches for an explanation. Meanwhile, he has mysteriously fallen out of political favor and finds his career falling apart as well. Polish with English subtitles. 111m/C VHS. *PL* Zbigniew Zapasiewicz, Ewa Dalkowska, Krystyna Janda, Andrzej Seweryn; *D:* Andrzej Wajda; *W:* Agnieszka Holland, Andrzej Wajda. *NYF*

Without Evidence 🐾🐾 1996 When Oregon correctional director Michael Francke (Garrett) is visiting younger brother Kevin (Plank) in Florida, he mentions his suspicions about an operation within his department involving drugs in prison. Then the next phone call Kevin gets is that Michael's been murdered. When he heads to Oregon, Kevin seems to be getting the official runaround and becomes increasingly suspicious about a coverup. A tension-building true story that remains unsolved. 132m/C VHS. Scott Plank, Anna Gunn, Andrew Prine, Angelina Jolie, Paul Perri, Alan Nause, Ernie Garrett; *D:* Gill Dennis; *W:* Gill Dennis, Phil Stanford; *C:* Victor Nunez; *M:* Franco Piersanti. *NYR*

Without Honors 🐾🐾 1932 A man seeks to restore the reputation of his dead brother, accused of murder and theft. He joins the Texas Rangers and brings the real criminals to justice. Excellent location shooting lifts ordinary early western. 62m/B VHS, Beta, LV. Harry Carey Sr., Mae Busch, Gibson Gowland, George "Gabby" Hayes; *D:* William Nigh. *NO*

Without Love 🐾🐾½ 1945 Tracy is a scientist, Hepburn, a woman with an empty basement for his laboratory. Since the neighbors would be scandalized by the idea of unmarried people living together, however platonically, they decide to get married, although each has sworn off romance. Snappy dialogue, expertly rendered by the Tracy/Hepburn team. Terrific supporting cast makes this minimally plotted outing afloat. Adapted from the play of the same name by Philip Barry. 113m/B VHS, Beta. Spencer Tracy, Katharine Hepburn, Lucille Ball, Keenan Wynn, Carl Esmond, Patricia Morison, Felix Bressart; *D:* Harold Bucquet; *W:* Donald Ogden Stewart; *C:* Karl Freund. *MGM*

Without Love 🐾🐾 1980 Ambitious young journalist experiences resentment from her peers because of her aggressive methods, and they decide to teach her a lesson by drawing her into a situation destined for disaster. In Polish with English subtitles. 104m/C VHS. *PL D:* Barbara Sass. *FCT*

Without Mercy 🐾½ 1995 (R) Marine platoon is shafted by the government when they're left to die while on a U.N. peacekeeping mission in Africa. Survivor Zagarino then winds up in a deadly martial arts contest, only to find himself set up by corrupt promoters.*CW:* Strong violence, and for some sexuality and language. 88m/C VHS, LV, Closed Caption. Frank Zagarino, Martin Kove, Ayu Azhari, Frans Tumbuan; *D:* Robert Anthony; *W:* Robert Anthony; *C:* Gerry Lively. *LIV*

Without Reservations 🐾🐾½ 1946 Hollywood-bound novelist Colbert encounters Marine flyer Wayne and his pal (DeFore) aboard a train. She decides he would be perfect for her newest movie. They both dislike her famous book and don't realize they're traveling with the renowned author. Misadventures and misunderstandings abound as this trio make their way to Tinseltown. Of course, Colbert and Wayne fall in love. Box-office success with a tired script and too few real laughs. The Duke is interesting but miscast. Based on the novel "Thanks, God, I'll Take It From Here" by Jane Allen. 101m/B VHS, Beta, LV. Claudette Colbert, John Wayne, Don DeFore, Phil Brown, Frank Puglia; *Cameos:* Louella Parsons, Cary Grant, Jack Benny; *D:* Mervyn LeRoy; *C:* Milton Krasner. *VCI, VCN, TTC*

Without Warning 🐾🐾½ *The Story Without A Name* 1952 Inexperienced director and actors pull out a minor success in this fairly ordinary murder mystery, about a serial killer of beautiful blondes. 75m/C VHS. *FR* Maurice Ronet, Adam Williams, Gloria Franklin, Edward Binns; *D:* Arnold Laven. *NO*

Without Warning: The James Brady Story 🐾🐾🐾 1991 (R) White House Press Secretary Brady took a bullet in the brain during the 1981 shooting of President Reagan, and made a slow, grueling recovery. This fine made for cable TV film spares none of it, concentrating on the stricken man and his family, and opting out of disease-of-the-week cliches (though the pic's politics won't please the gun-adorers). Based on Mollie Dickinson's biography "Thumbs Up."*CW:* Language. 120m/C VHS. Beau Bridges, Joan Allen, David Strathairn, Christopher Bell, Gary Grubbs, Bryan Clark, Steve Flynn, Christine Healy, Susan Brown; *D:* Michael Toshiyuki Uno; *W:* Robert Bolt. *HBO*

Witness 🐾🐾🐾½ 1985 (R) A young Amish boy traveling from his father's funeral witnesses a murder in a Philadelphia bus station. The investigating detective (Ford, in one of his best roles) soon discovers the killing is part of a conspiracy involving corruption in his department. He follows the child and his young widowed mother to their home in the country. A thriller with a difference, about the encounter of alien worlds, with a poignant love story. McGillis, in her first major role, is luminous as the Amish mother, while Ford is believable as both a cop and a sensitive man. An artfully crafted drama, richly focusing on the often misunderstood Amish lifestyle. 112m/C VHS, Beta, LV, 8mm, Closed Caption. Harrison Ford, Kelly McGillis, Alexander Godunov, Lukas Haas, Josef Sommer, Danny Glover, Patti LuPone; *D:* Peter Weir; *C:* John Seale; *M:* Maurice Jarre. Academy Awards '85: Best Film Editing, Best Original Screenplay; Edgar Allan Poe Awards '85: Best Screenplay; Writers Guild of America '85: Best Original Screenplay; Nominations: Academy Awards '85: Best Actor (Ford), Best Art Direction/Set Decoration, Best Cinematography, Best Director (Weir), Best Picture, Best Original Score. *PAR, HMV*

Witness for the Prosecution 🐾🐾🐾½ 1957 An unemployed man is accused of murdering a wealthy widow whom he befriended. Ailing defense attorney Laughton can't resist taking an intriguing murder case, and a straitforward court case becomes increasingly complicated in this energetic adaptation of an Agatha Christie story and stage play. Outstanding performances by Laughton, with excellent support by real life wife, Lanchester, as his patient nurse. Power, as the alleged killer, and Dietrich as a tragic woman are top-notch (see if you can detect Dietrich in an unbilled second role). 116m/B VHS, Beta, LV. Charles Laughton, Tyrone Power, Marlene Dietrich, Elsa Lanchester, John Williams, Henry Daniell, Una O'Connor; *D:* Billy Wilder; *W:* Harry Kurnitz, Billy Wilder. Golden Globe Awards '58: Best Supporting Actress (Lanchester); Nominations: Academy Awards '57: Best Actor (Laughton), Best Director (Wilder), Best Film Editing, Best Picture, Best Sound, Best Supporting Actress (Lanchester). *MGM, FOX, MLB*

Witness to the Execution 🐾🐾 1994 (PG-13) It's 1999 and Tycom Entertainment, a pay-per-view network, is looking for some hot entertainment. Top exec Jessica (Young) decides to televise the electric chair execution of convicted criminal Dennis Casterline (Daly). But Casterline claims to be innocent and as the execution date nears Jessica is unsettled by new evidence that may supports his claim. The cutthroat TV execs provide amusement but this TV movie fare quickly becomes muddled.*CW:* Thematic elements and violence. 92m/C VHS. Sean Young, Timothy Daly, Len Cariou, George Newbern; *D:* Tommy Lee Wallace; *W:* Thomas Baum. *THV*

Wittgenstein 🐾🐾 1993 Complicated, experimental portrait of Viennese-born philosopher Ludwig Wittgenstein (Johnson), executed as a series of blackout sketches (that feature a green Martian dwarf and such friends as Bertrand Russell and Ottoline Morrell). Assumes a familiarity with the eccentric Wittgenstein's ideas but does manage to convey some emotion and wit. 75m/C VHS. *GB* Karl Johnson, Michael Gough, Tilda Swinton, John Quentin, Nabil Shaban; *D:* Derek Jarman; *W:* Derek Jarman, Terry Eagleton, Ken Butler. *KIV*

Wives Under Suspicion 🐾🐾½ 1938 While prosecuting a man who murdered his wife out of jealousy, a district attorney finds his own home life filled with similar tension. Director Whale's unnecessary remake of his own earlier film, "The Kiss Before the Mirror." He is best known for

"Frankenstein." **75m/B VHS, Beta.** Warren William, Gail Patrick, Constance Moore, William Lundigan; **D:** James Whale. *NOS, DVT, HEG*

The Wiz 🐾🐾 **1978 (G)** Black version of the long-time favorite "The Wizard of Oz," based on the Broadway musical. Ross plays a Harlem schoolteacher who is whisked away to a fantasy version of New York City in a search for her identity. Some good character performances and musical numbers, but generally an overblown and garish effort with Ross too old for her role. Pryor is poorly cast, but Jackson is memorable as the Scarecrow. High-budget ($24 million) production with a ton of name stars, lost $11 million, and cooled studios on black films. Horne's number as the good witch is the best reason to sit through this one. ♫The Feeling That We Have; Can I Go On Not Knowing; Glinda's Theme; He's the Wizard; Soon as I Get Home; You Can't Win; Ease on Down the Road; What Would I Do If I Could Feel?; Slide Some Oil to Me. **133m/C VHS, Beta, LV.** Diana Ross, Michael Jackson, Nipsey Russell, Ted Ross, Mabel King, Thelma Carpenter, Richard Pryor, Lena Horne; **D:** Sidney Lumet; **W:** Joel Schumacher; **C:** Oswald Morris; **M:** Quincy Jones. Nominations: Academy Awards '78: Best Art Direction/Set Decoration, Best Cinematography, Best Costume Design, Original Song Score and/or Adaptation. *USH, FCT*

The Wizard 🐾½ **1989 (PG)** Facing the dissolution of his dysfunctional family, a youngster decides to whisk his autistic, video game-playing little brother across the country to a national video competition. Way too much plot in pretentious, blatantly commercial feature-length Nintendo ad, featuring the kid from "The Wonder Years." For teen video addicts only. **99m/C VHS, Beta, LV, Closed Caption.** Fred Savage, Beau Bridges, Christian Slater, Luke Edwards, Jenny Lewis; **D:** Todd Holland; **W:** David Chisholm. *USH*

The Wizard of Gore 🐾 **1970 (R)** The prototypical Lewis splatter party, about a magician whose on-stage mutilations turn out to be messily real. High camp and barrels of bright movie blood. **96m/C VHS, Beta.** Ray Sager, Judy Cler, Wayne Ratay, Phil Lauenson, Jim Rau, Don Alexander, Monika Blackwell, Corinne Kirkin; **D:** Herschell Gordon Lewis. *NO*

The Wizard of Loneliness 🐾🐾½ **1988 (PG-13)** A disturbed young boy goes to live with his grandparents during WWII, and slowly discovers family secrets centering on his aunt. Excellent performances barely save an aimless plot with an overdone denouement. Based on the novel by John Nichols. **110m/C VHS, Beta, LV, Closed Caption.** Lukas Haas, Lea Thompson, John Randolph, Lance Guest, Anne Pitoniak, Jeremiah Warner, Dylan Baker; **D:** Jenny Bowen; **W:** Nancy Larson; **C:** Richard Bowen; **M:** Michel Colombier. *NO*

The Wizard of Oz 🐾🐾½ **1925** An early silent version of the L. Frank Baum fantasy, with notable plot departures from the book and later 1939 adaptation, starring long-forgotten comedian Semon as the Scarecrow, supported by a pre-Laurel Hardy as the Tin Woodman. With music score. **93m/B VHS, Beta, 8mm.** Larry Semon, Dorothy Dwan, Bryant Washburn, Charles Murray, Oliver Hardy, Josef Swickard, Virginia Pearson; **D:** Larry Semon. *NOS, VYY, MLB*

The Wizard of Oz 🐾🐾🐾🐾 **1939** From the book by L. Frank Baum. Fantasy about a Kansas farm girl (Garland, in her immortal role) who rides a tornado to a brightly colored world over the rainbow, full of talking scarecrows, munchkins and a wizard who bears a strange resemblance to a Kansas fortune-teller. She must outwit the Wicked Witch if she is ever to go home. Delightful performances from Lahr, Bolger, and Hamilton; King Vidor is uncredited as co-director. Director Fleming originally wanted Deanna Durbin or Shirley Temple for the role of Dorothy, but settled for Garland who made the song "Over the Rainbow" her own. She received a special Academy Award for her performance. For the 50th anniversary of

its release, "The Wizard of Oz" was restored and includes rare film clips of Bolger's "Scarecrow Dance" and the cut "Jitterbug" number, and shots by Buddy Ebsen as the Tin Man before he became ill and left the production. Laserdisc edition includes digital sound, commentary by film historian Ronald Haver, and test footage, trailers and stills, as well as Jerry Maren talking about his experiences as a Munchkin. Yet another special release of the film, "The Ultimate Oz," contains a documentary on the making of the film, a reproduction of the original script, still photos, and liner notes. ♫Munchkinland; Ding Dong the Witch is Dead; Follow the Yellow Brick Road; If I Only Had a Brain/a Heart/the Nerve; If I Were the King of the Forest; The Merry Old Land of Oz; Threatening Witch; Into the Forest of the Wild Beast; The City Gates are Open. **101m/C VHS, Beta, LV, Closed Caption, DVD.** Judy Garland, Margaret Hamilton, Ray Bolger, Jack Haley, Bert Lahr, Frank Morgan, Charley Grapewin, Clara Blandick, Mitchell Lewis, Billie Burke; **D:** Victor Fleming; **W:** Noel Langley; **M:** Herbert Stothart. Academy Awards '39: Best Song ("Over the Rainbow"), Best Original Score; Nominations: Academy Awards '39: Best Color Cinematography, Best Interior Decoration, Best Picture, Best Special Effects. *MGM, TLF*

The Wizard of Speed and Time 🐾🐾½ **1988 (PG)** A special-effects wizard gets the break of his life when he's hired by a movie studio, but there's more to this particular studio than he realizes. Jittlov, a real special-effects expert, plays himself in this personally financed production. Although brimming with inside jokes and references, this self-indulgence succeeds with its enthusiasm and ambition, despite being rather obviously self-produced. Unique special effects make it memorable. **95m/C VHS, LV, Closed Caption.** Mike Jittlov, Richard Kaye, Page Moore, David Conrad, Steve Brodie, John Massari, Frank Laloggia, Philip Michael Thomas, Angelique Pettyjohn, Arnetia Walker, Paulette Breen; **D:** Mike Jittlov; **W:** Mike Jittlov, Richard Kaye, Deven Chierighino; **C:** Russell Carpenter; **M:** John Massari.

Wizards 🐾🐾½ **1977 (PG)** A good, bumbling sorcerer battles for the sake of a magic kingdom and its princess against his evil brother who uses Nazi propaganda films to inspire his army of mutants. Profane, crude, & typically Bakshian fantasy with great graphics. Animated. **81m/C VHS, Beta, LV, Closed Caption.** **D:** Ralph Bakshi; **W:** Ralph Bakshi; **M:** Andrew Belling; **V:** Bob Holt, Jesse Wells, Richard Romanus, David Proval. *FOX*

Wizards of the Demon Sword 🐾 **1994 (R)** Group of warriors battle over a sword with the power to control the world. **CW:** Some nudity and violence. **90m/C VHS.** Lawrence Tierney, Michael Berryman, Russ Tamblyn, Lyle Waggoner, Blake Bahner, Heidi Paine, Dan Speaker, Jay Richardson, Dawn Wildsmith; **D:** Fred Olen Ray; **W:** Dan Golden, Ernest Farino. *TTV*

Wizards of the Lost Kingdom 🐾½ **1985 (PG)** A boy magician, aided by various ogres and swordster Svenson battles an all-powerful wizard for control of his kingdom. Family fare a bit too clean and harmless. **76m/C VHS, Beta.** Bo Svenson, Vidal Peterson, Thom Christopher; **D:** Hector Olivera. *MED*

Wizards of the Lost Kingdom 2 🐾 **1989 (PG)** A boy wizard is charged with vanquishing the evil tyrants from three kingdoms. Barely a sequel; no plot continuation or cast from earlier kiddie sword epic. **80m/C VHS, Beta.** David Carradine, Bobby Jacoby, Lana Clarkson, Mel Welles, Susan Lee Hoffman, Sid Haig; **D:** Charles B. Griffith. *MED*

WKRP in Cincinnati, Vol. 1 **1978** In the pilot episode for the TV sitcom, WKRP is a failing radio station with the cautious Arthur Carlson as the station manager (the station is owned by his mother). Andy Travis is hired as the new program director to turn things around and promptly turns WKRP towards rock and roll. Other regulars included newsman Les Nesman, sales manager Herb Tarlek, DJs Dr. Johnny Fever and Venus Flytrap, as well as ever-efficient secretary

Jennifer Marlowe. **50m/C VHS.** Gary Sandy, Gordon Jump, Loni Anderson, Richard Sanders, Frank Bonner, Jan Smithers, Howard Hesseman, Tim Reid. *MTM*

Wolf 🐾 **1986** To everyone's lasting regret, an ex-Vietnam POW strives to rescue an American ambassador kidnapped by Central American rebels. **95m/C VHS, Beta.** J. Antonio Carreon, Ron Marchini; **D:** Charlie Ordonez. *TWE*

Wolf 🐾🐾½ **1994 (R)** Harrison's original script is massaged by Nichols into an upscale new age men's movement horror spectacle lacking a suitable climax. Stressed out Manhattan book editor Will Randall's (Nicholson) car hits a wolf on a country road and he's bitten when he tries to help the animal. Normally a wishy-washy guy, he notices some distinctly hairy changes to both his body and personality, leading him to make some drastic changes at work by knocking off his firm's greedy honchos and taking over. Talk about being ruthless in business. Boss' daughter Pfeiffer takes a shine to Randall's new animal magnetism, but is just visual candy. Walks a fine line between black comedy, camp, romance, and horror, though Jack baying at the moon seems sort of campy. **CW:** Language and werewolf attacks. **125m/C VHS, Beta, LV, 8mm, Closed Caption.** Jack Nicholson, Michelle Pfeiffer, James Spader, Kate Nelligan, Christopher Plummer, Richard Jenkins, Om Puri, Eileen Atkins, David Hyde Pierce, Ron Rifkin, Prunella Scales; **D:** Mike Nichols; **W:** Wesley Strick, Jim Harrison; **C:** Giuseppe Rotunno; **M:** Ennio Morricone. *COL*

The Wolf at the Door 🐾🐾½ **1987 (R)** A well-appointed, sincere biography of impressionist Paul Gauguin in the middle period of life, during his transition from the petty demands of his Parisian life to the freedom of Tahiti. Not definitive or compelling, but serves the purpose of a biography—arousing interest in the subject's life and art. **90m/C VHS, Beta, Closed Caption.** DK FR Donald Sutherland, Jean Yanne, Sofie Graboel, Ghita Norby, Max von Sydow, Merete Voldstedlund, Fanny Bastien, Valerie Morea; **D:** Henning Carlsen; **W:** Christopher Hampton; **M:** Roger Bourland. *FOX*

Wolf Blood 🐾🐾½ **1925** When Dick (Chesebro) is hurt in an accident, Dr. Horton uses wolf's blood for a transfusion. Soon there are unexplained deaths and Dick fears he's becoming a man-beast. Early precursor to the wolfman films. **68m/B VHS.** George Chesebro, Marguerite Clayton, Ray Hanford, Roy Watson, Milburn Morante; **D:** George Chesebro, George Mitchell. *GPV*

Wolf Call 🐾½ **1939** Carroll plays the son of a miner who travels with his devoted hound to see his father's old mine and start it working again. Gangsters and a beautiful Indian maiden get in his way. Master and pooch both find romance, and both sing. From the Jack London novel. **62m/B VHS, Beta, 8mm.** John Carroll, Movita, Wheeler Oakman, Peter George Lynn; **D:** George Waggner. *VYY, FCT*

Wolf Dog **1933** A boy and his dog. Outdoor action and adventure. Twelve chapters, 13 minutes each. **156m/B VHS, Beta.** Frankie Darro, Patricia "Boots" Mallory; **D:** Harry Fraser, Colbert Clark. *SNC, VCN, MLB*

Wolf Lake 🐾½ **1979** WWII veteran, whose son was killed in Vietnam, and a Vietnam army deserter clash with tragic consequences during their stay at a Canadian hunting lodge. Steiger gives it a go, but overwrought revenge pic resists quality upgrade. **90m/C VHS, Beta.** Rod Steiger, David Hoffman, Robin Mattson, Jerry Hardin, Richard Herd, Paul Mantu; **D:** Burt Kennedy. *PSM*

The Wolf Man 🐾🐾🐾½ **1941** Fun, absorbing classic horror with Chaney as a man bitten by werewolf Lugosi. His dad thinks he's gone nuts, his screaming gal pal just doesn't understand, and plants on the Universal lot have no roots. Ouspenskaya's finest hour as the prophetic gypsy woman. Ow-ooo! Chilling and thrilling. **70m/B VHS, Beta, LV.** Lon Chaney Jr., Claude Rains, Maria Ouspenskaya, Ralph Bellamy, Bela Lugosi, Warren William, Patric Knowles, Evelyn Ankers; **D:** George Waggner; **C:** Joseph Valentine. *USH*

Wolf Trap 🐾🐾 1957 Trapped indeed—small town veterinarian is suffocating in a marriage to an older, domineering and needy wife. The two adopt an orphaned teenager, which turns out to be a big mistake as the unhappy husband gradually falls in love with the girl. Czech with subtitles. 95m/C VHS. *CZ D:* Jiri Weiss. *FCT*

Wolfen 🐾🐾🐾 1981 (R) Surrealistic menace darkens this original and underrated tale of super-intelligent wolf creatures terrorizing New York City. Police detective Finney tries to track down the beasts before they kill again. Notable special effects in this thriller, which covers environmental and Native American concerns while maintaining the tension. Feature film debuts of Hines and Venora. Based on the novel by Whitley Strieber. Available in widescreen on laserdisc. 115m/C VHS, Beta, LV. Albert Finney, Gregory Hines, Tom Noonan, Diane Venora, Edward James Olmos; *D:* Michael Wadleigh; *M:* James Horner. *WAR*

Wolfheart's Revenge 1925 An honest cowboy, helped by Wolfheart the Wonder Dog, steps in when a sheep rancher is murdered. Silent film with original organ score. 64m/B VHS, Beta, 8mm. Guinn "Big Boy" Williams. *VYY, GPV*

The Wolfman 🐾 1982 In 1910, a young man learns that his family is heir to the curse of the Werewolf. Same old stuff. 91m/C VHS, Beta. Earl Owensby, Kristina Reynolds; *D:* Worth Keeter. *NO*

The Wolves 🐾🐾🐾 1982 Gosha shows the world of the yakuza (gangster) during the 1920s. Reminiscent of the samurai, the movie combines ancient Japanese culture with the rapidly changing world of 20th Century Japan. In Japanese with English subtitles. 131m/C VHS, LV. *JP* Tatsuya Nakadai; *D:* Hideo Gosha. *NO*

A Woman and a Woman 🐾🐾 1980 Covers a ten-year period in the friendship of Barbara and Irena and how it survives their professional and personal conflicts. In Polish with English subtitles. 99m/C VHS. *PL* Halina Labonarska, Anna Romantowska; *D:* Richard Bugajski. *FCT*

A Woman at Her Window 🐾🐾½ *Une Femme a sa Fentre* 1977 Aristocratic, jaded Margot (Schneider), the wife of dissolute nobleman Rico (Orsini), is pursued by capitalistic businessman Raoul (Noiret). But Margot herself is taken by idealistic Michel (Lanoux), a communist evading the secret police in 1936 Greece, and has a daughter from their brief and ultimately tragic union. Years later, Margot's now-grown daughter returns to Greece to learn more about her parents. Adapted from the novel by Pierre Drieu La Rochelle. French with subtitles. 110m/C VHS. *FR* Romy Schneider, Philippe Noiret, Victor Lanoux, Umberto Orsini, Delia Boccardo, Gastone Moschin, Carl Mohner; *D:* Pierre Granier-Deferre; *W:* Pierre Granier-Deferre, Jorge Semprun. *FCT*

A Woman at War 🐾🐾½ 1994 (PG-13) True-story of a young woman's heroic fight against the Nazis. Nineteen-year-old Helene Moskiewicz (Plimpton) has had her parents arrested by the Gestapo in occupied Brussels, Belgium. She joins the resistance and falls for Franz Boehler (Stoltz), a young businessman who is not above lining his pockets with Nazi profits. When persecution of the Jews intensifies, Helene risks infiltrating Gestapo headquarters in order to save lives. *CW:* Some acts of violence. 115m/C VHS, Closed Caption. Martha Plimpton, Eric Stoltz; *D:* Edward Bennett; *W:* Edward Bennett. *REP*

A Woman Called Golda 🐾🐾🐾 1982 Political drama following the life and career of Golda Meir, the Israeli Prime Minister and one of the most powerful political figures of the 20th century. Davis portrays the young Golda, Bergman taking over as she ages. Superior made-for-television bio-epic. 192m/C VHS, Beta. Ingrid Bergman, Leonard Nimoy, Anne Jackson, Ned Beatty, Robert Loggia, Judy Davis; *D:* Alan Gibson; *W:* Steven Gethers, Howard Gast. *PAR*

A Woman Called Moses 🐾🐾½ 1978 The story of Harriet Ross Tubman, who bought her freedom from slavery, founded the underground railroad, and helped lead hundreds of slaves to freedom before the Civil War. Wonderful performance by Tyson but the made-for-television film is bogged down by a so-so script. Based on the novel by Marcy Heldish. 200m/C VHS. Cicely Tyson, Dick Anthony Williams, Will Geer, Robert Hooks, Hari Rhodes, James Wainwright; *D:* Paul Wendkos; *W:* Lonne Elder III. *XVC, FCT, CCP*

Woman Condemned 🐾½ 1933 A reporter tries to clear a woman's name of murder. 58m/B VHS, Beta, LV. Mischa Auer, Lola Lane, Claudia Dell, Richard Hemingway. *NO*

Woman Hater 🐾🐾 1949 Delightful farce about the belief in the single life. Confirmed bachelor plays games with a single woman. They eventually disregard their solitary ways in favor of romance. 101m/B VHS. Stewart Granger, Edwige Feuillere, Ronald Squire, Mary Jerrold; *D:* Terence Young. *HMK*

The Woman He Loved 🐾🐾½ 1988 The infamous romance of Edward VIII, who gave up the throne of England for American divorcee, Wallis Warfield Simpson. Seymour and Andrews are fine in their roles but the made-for-television drama is slow-going. 100m/C VHS. Anthony Andrews, Jane Seymour, Olivia de Havilland, Lucy Gutteridge, Julie Harris, Robert Hardy, Phyllis Calvert; *D:* Charles Jarrott. *VTR*

A Woman, Her Men and Her Futon 🐾🐾 1992 (R) A beautiful woman tries to find her identity by having a number of lovers but none can satisfy her every need. *CW:* Language and strong sexuality. 90m/C VHS, Closed Caption. Jennifer Rubin, Lance Edwards, Grant Show, Michael Ceveris, Delaune Michel, Robert Lipton; *D:* Mussef Sibay; *W:* Mussef Sibay; *M:* Joel Goldsmith. *REP*

Woman Hunt woof! *The Highest Bidder* 1972 (R) Men kidnap women, then hunt them in the jungle for fun. So deeply offensive, we would give it negative bones if we could. "Hee Haw" bimbo Todd plays a sadistic lesbian. 81m/C VHS, Beta. John Ashley, Lisa Todd, Eddie Garcia, Laurie Rose; *D:* Eddie Romero. *NLC*

The Woman Hunter 🐾½ 1972 A wealthy woman recovering from a traffic accident in Mexico believes someone is after her for her jewels and possibly her life. Eden dressed well, if nothing else; suspense builds ploddingly to a "Yeah, sure" climax. Made for television. 73m/C VHS, Beta. Barbara Eden, Robert Vaughn, Stuart Whitman, Sydney Chaplin, Larry Storch, Enrique Lucero; *D:* Bernard L. Kowalski. *NO*

Woman in Black 🐾🐾½ 1989 Chilling ghost story set in 1925 and adapted from the novel by Susan Hill. Soliciter Arthur Kidd is sent to a remote house to settle the estate of a client. He's haunted by the mysterious figure of a woman in black, who according to the locals, has put a curse on the village. Arthur's driven close to the edge of sanity by the ghostly figure and the tragedy that haunts the past. Made for television. 100m/C VHS. *GB* Adrian Rawlins; *D:* Herbert Wise. *VCO, FCT, TVC*

Woman in Brown 🐾🐾½ *The Vicious Circle; The Circle* 1948 It's Hungary, 1882, and five Jewish men are on trial for the murder of a man who actually committed suicide. Despite the prejudice and hatred from the locals, their lawyer believes in and fights for their innocence. 77m/B VHS, Beta. Conrad Nagel, Fritz Kortner, Reinhold Schunzel, Philip Van Zandt, Eddie LeRoy, Edwin Maxwell; *D:* W. Lee Wilder. *SNC*

A Woman in Flames 🐾🐾🐾 *Die Flambierte Frau* 1984 (R) A bored middle-class housewife leaves her overbearing husband and becomes a high-priced prostitute. She has a passionless affair with an aging bisexual gigolo. Dark and dreary tale of human relationships and the role of sex in people's lives. Interesting but depressing. 106m/C VHS, Beta. *GE* Gudrun Landgrebe, Robert Van Ackeren,

Matthieu Carriere, Gabriele Lafari, Hanns Zischler; *D:* Robert Van Ackeren. *GLV*

The Woman in Green 🐾🐾 *Sherlock Holmes and the Woman in Green* 1945 Murder victims are found with missing index fingers, and it's up to Holmes and Watson to try to solve this apparently motiveless crime. Available colorized. 68m/B VHS, LV, Closed Caption. Basil Rathbone, Nigel Bruce, Hillary Brooke, Henry Daniell, Paul Cavanagh, Frederick Worlock, Mary Gordon, Billy Bevan; *D:* Roy William Neill. *SNC, REP, VYY*

Woman in Grey 🐾🐾 1919 A man and a woman battle wits when they attempt to locate and unravel the Army Code while staying one step ahead of J. Haviland Hunter, a suave villain after the same fortune. Silent. 205m/B VHS, Beta. Arline Pretty, Henry Sell. *NOS, CCB, MLB*

The Woman in Question 🐾🐾½ *Five Angles on Murder* 1950 When carnival fortune teller Astra (Kent) is murdered, Police Inspector Lodge (MacRae) finds that all her acquaintances have differing views about her character, making his investigation even more difficult. 82m/B VHS. *GB* Jean Kent, Dirk Bogarde, Susan Shaw, Duncan MacRae, John McCallum, Hermione Baddeley, Charles Victor, Lana Morris, Vida Hope, Joe Linnane, Duncan Lament, Bobbie Scroggins, Anthony Dawson, John Boxer, Julian D'Albie, Josephine Middleton, Everley Gregg, Albert Chevalier, Richard Pearson; *D:* Anthony Asquith; *W:* John Cresswell; *C:* Desmond Dickinson; *M:* John Wooldridge. *HMV*

The Woman in Red 🐾🐾½ 1984 (PG-13) Executive Wilder's life unravels when he falls hard for stunning Le Brock. Inferior Hollywood-ized remake of the ebulliant "Pardon Mon Affaire." Somehow the French seem to do the sexual force thing with more verve, but this one has its moments, and Wilder is likeable. Music by Stevie Wonder. ♫I Just Called to Say I Love You; Don't Drive Drunk; It's More Than You; It's You; Love Light in Flight; Moments Aren't Moments; Weakness; Woman in Red. 87m/C VHS, Beta, LV. Gene Wilder, Charles Grodin, Kelly Le Brock, Gilda Radner, Judith Ivey, Joseph Bologna; *D:* Gene Wilder; *W:* Gene Wilder; *M:* John Morris. Academy Awards '84: Best Song ("I Just Called to Say I Love You"); Golden Globe Awards '85: Best Song ("I Just Called to Say I Love You"). *LIV, VES*

Woman in the Dunes 🐾🐾🐾🐾 *Suna No Onna; Woman of the Dunes* 1964 Splendid, resonant allegorical drama. A scientist studying insects in the Japanese sand dunes finds himself trapped with a woman in a hut at the bottom of a pit. Superbly directed and photographed (by Hiroshi Segawa). Scripted by Kobo Abe from his acclaimed novel. In Japanese with English subtitles. 123m/B VHS. *JP* Eiji Okada, Kyoko Kishida, Koji Mitsui, Hiroko Ito, Sen Yano; *D:* Hiroshi Teshigahara; *M:* Toru Takemitsu. Cannes Film Festival '64: Grand Jury Prize; Nominations: Academy Awards '65: Best Director (Teshigahara), Best Foreign Language Film. *CVC, NYF, VDM*

Woman in the Moon 🐾🐾½ *By Rocket to the Moon; Girl in the Moon* 1929 Assorted people embark on a trip to the moon and discover water, and an atmosphere, as well as gold. Lang's last silent outing is nothing next to "Metropolis," with a rather lame plot (greedy trip bashers seek gold), but interesting as a vision of the future. Lang's predictions about space travel often hit the mark. Silent with music. 115m/B VHS, Beta. *GE* Klaus Pohl, Willy Fritsch, Gustav von Wagenheim, Gerda Maurus; *D:* Fritz Lang. *VYY, IHF, LSV*

Woman in the Shadows 🐾🐾 1934 A ex-con retreats to the woods for serenity and peace, but is assaulted by mysterious women, jealous lovers, and gun-slinging drunks, until he explodes. A man can only take so much. From a Dashiell Hammett story. 70m/B VHS, Beta. Fay Wray, Ralph Bellamy, Melvyn Douglas, Roscoe Ates, Joe King. *VYY*

Woman in the Window 🐾🐾🐾 1944 Psycho-melodrama finds staid college professor Richard Wanley straying off the straight and narrow into a world of trouble—thanks to beautiful model Alice (Bennett). She invites him over but when her jealous boyfriend Claude (Loft) arrives unexpectedly, he attacks them both and Richard kills Claude in self-defense. Thinking no one will believe them, and afraid of scandal, the inept duo bury the body in the woods. Too bad Richard's best friend Frank (Massey) is the D.A. and there's a blackmailer around. Or is there? Surprise ending. Based on the novel "Once Off Guard" by J.H. Wallis. **99m/B VHS, Closed Caption.** Edward G. Robinson, Joan Bennett, Raymond Massey, Arthur Loft, Dan Duryea, Edmund Breon, Dorothy Peterson, Robert (Bobby) Blake; **D:** Fritz Lang; **W:** Nunnally Johnson; **C:** Milton Krasner; **M:** Arthur Lange. Nominations: Academy Awards '45: Original Dramatic/Comedy Score. *MGM*

The Woman Inside 🐾½ 1983 (R) Low-budget gender-bender depicts the troubled life of a Vietnam veteran who decides on a sex-change operation to satisfy his inner yearnings. Blondell's unfortunate last role as his/her aunt. Cheesy like Limburger; almost too weird and boring even for camp buffs. **94m/C VHS, Beta.** CA Gloria Manon, Dave Clark, Joan Blondell; **D:** Joseph Van Winkle. *NO*

A Woman is a Woman 🐾🐾🐾 Une Femme Est Une Femme; La Donna E Donna 1960 Godard's affectionate sendup of Hollywood musicals is a hilarious comedy about a nightclub dancer (Karina) who desperately wants a baby. When boyfriend Belmondo balks, she asks his best friend Brialy. Much ado is had, with the three leads all splendid. Godard's first film shot in color and cinemascope, with great music. In French with English subtitles. **88m/C VHS.** *FR* Jean-Claude Briary, Jean-Paul Belmondo, Anna Karina, Marie DuBois; **D:** Jean-Luc Godard; **M:** Michel Legrand. *INT*

A Woman Named Jackie 🐾🐾½ 1991 (PG) Three-part TV miniseries covering the life of Jacqueline Bouvier Kennedy Onassis. Downey offers a pretty picture as the enigmatic and beleaguered heroine but this version is simplistic at best. Based on the book by C. David Heymann. On three cassettes. **246m/C VHS, LV.** Roma Downey, Stephen Collins, William Devane, Joss Ackland, Rosemary Murphy, Wendy Hughes, Josef Sommer; **D:** Larry Peerce; **W:** Roger O. Hirson. *NHO, IME*

The Woman Next Door 🐾🐾🐾 La Femme d'a Cote 1981 (R) One of Truffaut's last films before his sudden death in 1984. The domestic drama involves a suburban husband who resumes an affair with a tempestuous now-married woman after she moves next door, with domestic complications all around. An insightful, humanistic paean to passion and fidelity by the great artist, though one of his lesser works. Supported by strong outings from the two leads. In French with English subtitles. **106m/C VHS, Beta, LV.** *FR* Gerard Depardieu, Fanny Ardant, Michele Baumgartner, Veronique Silver, Roger Van Hool; **D:** Francois Truffaut; **W:** Suzanne Schiffman; **M:** Georges Delerue. *HMV, FOX*

A Woman Obsessed 🐾 1988 (R) Pathetic, over-cooked drama about a woman obsessed with her long-lost son. "Ruth Raymond" is really porn-flick vet Georgina Spelvin. Soon-to-be camp classic takes itself with utter seriousness. **105m/C VHS, VHS, Beta.** Ruth Raymond, Gregory Patrick, Troy Donahue, Linda Blair; **D:** Chuck Vincent. *ACA*

A Woman of Affairs 🐾🐾 1928 Garbo, who can't have the guy she really loves (Gilbert), marries scoundrel. When she finds out husband's true profession, he kills himself and Gilbert comes back. In order to preclude happy ending, she decides the affair wasn't meant to be and expires. Tragically. Silent. **90m/B VHS.** Greta Garbo, John Gilbert, Lewis Stone, Johnny Mack Brown, Douglas Fairbanks Jr., Hobart Bosworth, Dorothy Sebastian; **D:** Clarence Brown. *MGM, FCT*

Woman of Desire 🐾 1993 (R) Christina Ford (Derek) is a femme fatale who is yachting with rich boyfriend Ted when there is a terrible storm. Christina, Ted, and yacht captain Jack are washed overboard and Jack is found washed ashore with no memory. When Christina turns up she claims Jack killed Ted. So Jack gets a lawyer,

Walter J. Hill (played by the redoubtable Mitchum) but is he wily enough to discredit the deceitful Christina? Bo's body is once again on display. Also available in an unrated version. **97m/C VHS, LV, Closed Caption.** Bo Derek, Jeff Fahey, Steven Bauer, Robert Mitchum. *THV*

A Woman of Distinction 🐾🐾🐾 1950 Slapstick comedy with potential to be ordinary is taken over the top by a good, vivacious cast. Russell, the stuffy Dean of a women's college, is driven to distraction by a reporter linking her romantically to Milland, a visiting professor. **85m/C VHS, Beta, LV.** Ray Milland, Rosalind Russell, Edmund Gwenn, Francis Lederer; **Cameos:** Lucille Ball; **D:** Edward Buzzell. *COL*

Woman of Paris/Sunnyside 🐾🐾🐾½ 1923 This double feature highlights the talents of Charlie Chaplin. "A Woman of Paris" is the tragic story of a French country girl who winds up a kept woman. Chaplin's only dramatic directional outing; he makes only a cameo appearance. Straightforward but hip story of sex and society. In "Sunnyside," an example of high Chaplin highjinks, the comic plays a hotel handyman who can't win. **111m/B VHS, Beta.** Adolphe Menjou, Edna Purviance, Carl Miller, Lydia Knott; **Cameos:** Charlie Chaplin; **D:** Charlie Chaplin. *FOX*

A Woman of Rome 🐾🐾 La Romana 1956 Standard Italian star vehicle, with Lollobrigida portraying a successful prostitute in Rome who decides to change her life. Dubbed. **93m/B VHS, Beta.** *IT* Gina Lollobrigida, Daniel Gelin, Franco Fabrizi, Raymond Pellegrin; **D:** Luigi Zampa. *NOS, FCT*

A Woman of Substance, Episode 1: Nest of Vipers 🐾🐾½ 1984 The woman of the title, Emma Harte, rises from poverty to wealth and power through self-discipline. First episode of three. Made for TV saga has our heroine working as a servant for the snooty Fairley family. **100m/C VHS, Beta.** Jenny Seagrove, Barry Bostwick, Deborah Kerr; **D:** Don Sharp. *LIV*

A Woman of Substance, Episode 2: The Secret is Revealed 🐾🐾½ 1984 Emma Harte struggles to rise from a life of poverty to wealth and social acceptance. Second miniseries episode has Emma fighting to get by in the big city. Fun TV drama. **100m/C VHS, Beta.** Jenny Seagrove, Barry Bostwick, Deborah Kerr; **D:** Don Sharp. *LIV*

A Woman of Substance, Episode 3: Fighting for the Dream 🐾🐾½ 1984 Third installment is pretty good romantic TV saga. Rags-to-riches Emma finds love and happiness—at last! **100m/C VHS, Beta.** Jenny Seagrove, Barry Bostwick, Deborah Kerr; **D:** Don Sharp. *LIV*

The Woman of the Town 🐾🐾½ 1944 Frontier marshal and newspaperman Bat Masterson is portrayed convincingly by Dekker as a very human hero who seeks justice when the woman he loves, a dance hall girl who works in the town for social causes, is killed by an unscrupulous rancher. Fictionalized but realistic western shows "heroes" as good, ordinary people. **90m/B VHS, Beta.** Claire Trevor, Albert Dekker, Barry Sullivan, Henry Hull, Porter Hall, Percy Kilbride; **D:** George Archainbaud; **M:** Miklos Rozsa. Nominations: Academy Awards '44: Original Dramatic/Comedy Score. *NOS, HEG, FCT*

Woman of the Year 🐾🐾🐾🐾 1942 First classic Tracy/Hepburn pairing concerns the rocky marriage of a renowned political columnist and a lowly sportswriter. Baseball scene with Hepburn at her first game is delightful. Hilarious, rich entertainment that tries to answer the question "What really matters in life?" Tracy and Hepburn began a close friendship that paralleled their quarter-century celluloid partnership. Hepburn shepherded Kamin and Lardner's Oscar-winning script past studio chief Louis B. Mayer, wearing four-inch heels to press her demands. Mayer caved in, Tracy was freed from making "The Yearling," and the rest is history. **114m/B VHS, Beta, LV.** Spencer Tracy, Katharine Hepburn, Fay Bainter, Dan Tobin, Reginald

Owen, Roscoe Karns, William Bendix, Minor Watson; **D:** George Stevens; **W:** Ring Lardner Jr., Michael Kanin; **C:** Joseph Ruttenberg; **M:** Franz Waxman. Academy Awards '42: Best Original Screenplay; Nominations: Academy Awards '42: Best Actress (Hepburn). *MGM*

A Woman Rebels 🐾🐾½ 1936 A young Victorian woman challenges Victorian society by fighting for women's rights. Excellent performance from Hepburn lifts what might have been a forgettable drama. Screen debut of Van Heflin. Based on Netta Syrett's "Portrait of a Rebel." **88m/B VHS, Beta.** Katharine Hepburn, Herbert Marshall, Elizabeth Allan, Donald Crisp, Van Heflin; **D:** Mark Sandrich. *CCB*

Woman Times Seven 🐾🐾½ Sept Fois Femme; Sette Volte Donna 1967 (PG) Italian sexual comedy: seven sketches, each starring MacLaine with a different leading man. Stellar cast and good director should have delivered more, but what they have provided has its comedic moments. **99m/C VHS, Beta.** *IT FR* Shirley MacLaine, Peter Sellers, Rossano Brazzi, Vittorio Gassman, Lex Barker, Elsa Martinelli, Robert Morley, Alan Arkin, Michael Caine, Patrick Wymark, Anita Ekberg, Philippe Noiret; **D:** Vittorio De Sica. *COL, NLC*

A Woman Under the Influence 🐾🐾🐾 1974 (R) Strong performances highlight this overlong drama about a family's disintegration. Rowlands is the lonely, middle-aged housewife who's having a breakdown and Falk is her blue-collar husband who can't handle what's going on. **147m/C VHS, Beta, Closed Caption.** Gena Rowlands, Peter Falk, Matthew Cassel, Matthew Laborteaux, Christina Grisanti; **D:** John Cassavetes; **W:** John Cassavetes. Golden Globe Awards '75: Best Actress—Drama (Rowlands); National Board of Review Awards '74: Best Actress (Rowlands); Nominations: Academy Awards '74: Best Actress (Rowlands), Best Director (Cassavetes). *TOU, FCT*

Woman Undone 🐾🐾½ 1995 (R) Husband Allen Hansen (Quaid) and wife Terri (McDonnell) are involved in a car crash on a lonely stretch of desert highway. He dies, she's thrown clear, but an autopsy reveals he was actually shot in the head before the accident. Then attorney Ross Bishop (Elliott) gets involved and in a California courtroom Terri must prove that her unhappy marriage wasn't ended by murder. **CW:** Strong sexuality, language and some domestic abuse. **91m/C VHS, LV, Closed Caption.** Mary McDonnell, Randy Quaid, Sam Elliott, Benjamin Bratt; **D:** Evelyn Purcell; **W:** William Mickelberry; **C:** Toyomichi Kurita; **M:** Daniel Licht. *REP*

The Woman Who Came Back 🐾🐾 1945 A young woman who believes she suffers from a witch's curse returns to her small hometown with unhappy results. Good cast; bad script. Indifference inducing. **69m/B VHS, Beta.** Nancy Kelly, Otto Kruger, John Loder, Ruth Ford, Jeanne Gail; **D:** Walter Colmes. *COL*

The Woman Who Willed a Miracle 🐾🐾 1983 Made-for-television drama has a devoted mother encouraging her mentally retarded son to pursue his interest in the piano. **72m/C VHS, Beta.** Cloris Leachman, James Noble; **D:** Sharron Miller. *NO*

Woman With a Past 🐾🐾½ 1992 (PG-13) Reed gets out of an abusive marriage only to have her ex kidnap their kids. Since the law's no help she hires a bounty hunter to find them—committing armed robbery to pay the fees. Caught and imprisoned, Reed escapes, changes her identity, remarries, and even is reunited with her sons. Then she's suddenly arrested when her fugitive status comes to light 10 years later. Based on a true story; made for TV melodrama. **CW:** Thematic elements and scenes of abusive behavior. **95m/C VHS.** Pamela Reed, Dwight Schultz, Paul LeMat, Carrie Snodgress, Richard Lineback; **D:** Mimi Leder. *NHO*

A Woman Without Love 🐾🐾🐾 1951 A rarely seen film from Bunuel's Mexican period based on a classic Guy de Maupassant tale about a forbidden romance. Family tragedy results later when the husband "misbequeaths" his fortune. Minor but fascinating bug-the-bourgeoisie Bunuel. In Spanish with English subtitles. **91m/C VHS, Beta.** *MX* Rosario Granados, Julio Villareal, Tito Junco; *D:* Luis Bunuel. *XVC, MED*

A Woman's Face 🎬🎬🎬 *En Kvinnas Ansikte* 1938 An unpleasant, bitter woman with a hideous scar on her face blackmails illicit lovers as a form of revenge for a happiness she doesn't know. She even plots to murder a child for his inheritance. But after plastic surgery, she becomes a nicer person and doubts her plan. Lean, tight suspense with a bang-up finale. In Swedish with English subtitles. Remade in Hollywood in 1941. **100m/B VHS, Beta.** *SW* Ingrid Bergman, Anders Henrikson, Karin Carlsson, Georg Rydeberg, Goran Bernhard, Tore Svennberg; *D:* Gustaf Molander. *WAC*

A Woman's Face 🎬🎬🎬 1941 A physically and emotionally scarred woman becomes part of a blackmail ring. Plastic surgery restores her looks and her attitude. Begins with a murder trial and told in flashbacks; tight, suspenseful remake of the 1938 Swedish Ingrid Bergman vehicle. Climax will knock you out of your chair. **107m/B VHS.** Joan Crawford, Conrad Veidt, Melvyn Douglas, Osa Massen, Reginald Owen, Albert Basserman, Marjorie Main, Donald Meek, Charles Quigley, Henry Daniell, George Zucco, Robert Warwick; *D:* George Cukor. *MGM*

A Woman's Guide to Adultery 🎬🎬½ 1993 Four female friends, living and working in London, find their lives turned upside down by their passions for unavailable men. Political advisor Jo (Donohoe) is involved with married politician Martin (McElhinney) while art tutor Jennifer (Gillies) wants her student David (Morrissey), despite his having a live-in girlfriend. Ad execs Helen (Lacey) and Michael (Dunbar) find their marriage in tatters when Helen admits to an affair with their boss and photographer Rose (Russell) breaks her own rule about adultery by getting involved with married university instructor Paul (Bean). Based on the novel by Carol Clewlow. Made for TV. **145m/C VHS.** *GB* Theresa Russell, Amanda Donohoe, Sean Bean, Adrian Dunbar, Ingrid Lacey, Fiona Gillies, Neil Morrissey, Danny Webb, Ian McElhinney, Julie Peasgood, Caroline Lee-Johnson; *D:* David Hayman; *W:* Frank Cottrell Boyce; *C:* Graham Frake; *M:* Daemion Barry. *VCO*

A Woman's Secret 🎬🎬 1949 O'Hara admits to murder she didn't commit. Why? It's as indiscernible as why the plot should be muddled by flashbacks. RKO lost big bucks on this one. **85m/B VHS, Beta.** Maureen O'Hara, Melvyn Douglas, Gloria Grahame, Bill Williams, Victor Jory, Jay C. Flippen; *D:* Nicholas Ray; *W:* Herman J. Mankiewicz. *TTC, FCT*

A Woman's Tale 🎬🎬🎬 1992 (PG-13) The superlative performance of Florence highlights this look at aging and death. Martha, 78, has been diagnosed with terminal lung cancer. She is looked after by a much-younger nurse and in turn looks after the older friends who share her apartment house. This gentle story quietly depicts the feisty, joyous Martha's last days and the simple pleasures she derives from her remaining time. Florence herself died from cancer not long after completing the film. **94m/C VHS, LV, Closed Caption.** *AU* Sheila Florence, Gosia Dobrowolska, Norman Kaye, Chris Haywood, Myrtle Woods, Ernest Gray, Monica Maughan, Bruce Myles, Alex Menglet; *D:* Paul Cox; *W:* Paul Cox. Australian Film Institute '91: Best Actress (Florence). *ORI, BTV*

A Woman's World 🎬🎬🎬 1954 Slick, sophisticated look at big business in the '50s, with Webb as the boss who chooses his next general manager based on the suitability of the executive's wives. Beautiful costumes, witty dialogue, and good acting make this worthwhile viewing. Plus, film offers a nostalgic look at New York in the '50s, with several shots of Fifth Avenue, Macy's, Park Avenue, and the long-gone Stork Club. Based on a story by Mona Williams. **94m/C VHS.** Clifton Webb, June Allyson, Van Heflin, Lauren Bacall, Fred MacMurray, Arlene Dahl, Cornel Wilde, Elliott Reid,

Margalo Gillmore, Alan Reed, David Hoffman, George Melford; *D:* Jean Negulesco; *W:* Claude Binyon, Richard Sale, Mary Loos, Howard Lindsay, Russel Crouse. *FXV*

Wombling Free 🎬🎬 1977 An English girl makes friends with a race of tiny, litter-hating furry creatures called Wombles. The creatures are visible only to the little girl because she is the only one who believes. Together they try to clean up a dirty world. British society is less cutting-edge about social roles, etc. than our enlightened one; be prepared for retrograde characterizations. Fun scene with Kelly/Astaire-style dance number. **86m/C VHS, Beta, Closed Caption.** *GB* Bonnie Langford, David Tomlinson; *D:* Lionel Jeffries; *M:* George Bassman. *COL*

The Women 🎬🎬🎬½ 1939 A brilliant adaptation of the Clare Boothe Luce stage comedy about a group of women who destroy their best friends' reputations at various social gatherings. Crawford's portrayal of the nasty husband-stealer is classic, and the fashion-show scene in Technicolor is one not to miss. Hilarious bitchiness all around. Remade semi-musically as "The Opposite Sex." Another in that long list of stellar 1939 pics. **133m/B VHS, Beta, LV.** Norma Shearer, Joan Crawford, Rosalind Russell, Joan Fontaine, Mary Boland, Lucile Watson, Margaret Dumont, Paulette Goddard, Ruth Hussey, Marjorie Main; *D:* George Cukor; *W:* Anita Loos; *C:* Joseph Ruttenberg. *MGM*

Women & Men: In Love There Are No Rules 🎬🎬½ 1991 (R) Made for cable extravaganza chronicling the relationships of three couples, each adapted from the short story of a renowned author. Irwin Shaw's "Return to Kansas City" tells of a young boxer who is prematurely pushed into a match by his ambitious wife. In Carson McCullers' "A Domestic Dilemma," a marriage begins to crumble thanks to an alcoholic wife. Finally, Henry Miller's "Mara" has an aging man and a young Parisian prostitute spending a revealing evening together. *CW:* Some language. **90m/C VHS, LV, Closed Caption.** Matt Dillon, Kyra Sedgwick, Ray Liotta, Andie MacDowell, Scott Glenn, Juliette Binoche, Jerry Stiller; *D:* Kristi Zea, Walter Bernstein, Mike Figgis. *HBO*

Women & Men: Stories of Seduction 🎬🎬½ 1990 Three famous short stories are brought to the screen in this made for TV collection. Mary McCarthy's "The Man in the Brooks Brothers Shirt," Dorothy Parker's "Dusk Before Fireworks," and Hemingway's "Hills Like White Elephants" between them cover every aspect of male-female relationships. Since there are three casts and three directors, there is little to join the stories in style, calling attention to some flaws in pacing and acting ability; still, worth watching. **90m/C VHS, LV, Closed Caption.** James Woods, Melanie Griffith, Peter Weller, Elizabeth McGovern, Beau Bridges, Molly Ringwald; *D:* Ken Russell, Tony Richardson, Frederic Raphael. *HBO, FCT*

Women From the Lake of Scented Souls 🎬🎬 1994 Mournful film, set in a rural Chinese village, focuses on matriarchal businesswoman Xiang (Gaowa), who runs the local sesame oil making factory that has just attracted the attention of Japanese investors. Seems the water of the nearby lotus-covered lake, scene of local tragedies, is Xiang's special ingredient. With her new-found wealth, Xiang is able to purchase a very reluctant bride, Huanhuan (Yujuan), for her mentally-retarded son—a disaster in the making. Rich detail and nuanced performances; Chinese with subtitles. **105m/C VHS.** *CH* Siqin Gaowa, Wu Yujuan, Lei Luosheng, Chen Baoguo; *D:* Xie Fei; *W:* Xie Fei; *C:* Bao Xianran; *M:* Wang Liping. *AVI*

Women in Cell Block 7 woof! *Diario Segreto Di Un Carcere Femminele* 1977 (R) Exploitative skinfest about women in prison suffering abuse from their jailers and each other. Seems that one of the prisoners knows the location of massive heroin stash. Badly dubbed. **100m/C VHS, Beta.** *IT* Anita Strindberg, Eve Czemeys, Olga Bisera, Jane Avril, Valeria Fabrizi, Jenny Tamburi; *D:* Rino Di Silvestro. *NO*

Women in Fury woof! 1984 A woman is sentenced to imprisonment in a mostly lesbian Brazilian jail, and subsequently leads a breakout. **94m/C VHS, Beta.** *BR* Suzanne Carvalno, Gloria Cristal, Zeni Pereira, Leonardo Jose. *LIV*

Women in Love 🎬🎬🎬 1970 (R) Drama of two steamy affairs, based on D.H. Lawrence's classic novel. Deservedly Oscar-winning performance by Jackson; controversial nude wrestling scene with Bates and Reed is hard to forget. Plot is dumped on in favor of atmosphere. Followed nearly two decades later (1989) by a "prequel": "The Rainbow," also from Lawrence, also directed by Russell and starring Jackson. **129m/C VHS, Beta, LV.** *GB* Glenda Jackson, Jennie Linden, Alan Bates, Oliver Reed, Michael Gough, Eleanor Bron; *D:* Ken Russell; *C:* Billy Williams; *M:* Georges Delerue. Academy Awards '70: Best Actress (Jackson); Golden Globe Awards '71: Best Foreign Film; National Board of Review Awards '70: 10 Best Films of the Year, Best Actress (Jackson); New York Film Critics Awards '70: Best Actress (Jackson); National Society of Film Critics Awards '70: Best Actress (Jackson); Nominations: Academy Awards '70: Best Adapted Screenplay, Best Cinematography, Best Director (Russell). *MGM, FOX, BTV*

Women in Prison 🎬🎬 *Women without Names* 1949 A pseudo-documentary style expose of the hardships endured by women in Italian detention camps following WWII. Controversial for its examination of such themes as human rights, abortion, lesbianism, and sexuality. English, French, Italian, with English subtitles. **94m/C VHS.** *IT* Simone Simon; *D:* Geza Radvanyi; *W:* Geza Radvanyi. *FCT*

The Women of Brewster Place 🎬🎬🎬 1989 Seven black women living in a tenement fight to gain control of their lives. (Men in general don't come out too well.) Excellent, complex script gives each actress in a fine ensemble headed by Winfrey (in her TV dramatic debut) time in the limelight. Pilot for the series "Brewster Place." Based on the novel by Gloria Naylor. Winfrey was executive producer. **180m/C VHS, Beta.** Oprah Winfrey, Mary Alice, Olivia Cole, Robin Givens, Moses Gunn, Jackee, Paula Kelly, Lonette McKee, Paul Winfield, Cicely Tyson; *D:* Donna Deitch; *W:* Karen Hall; *M:* David Shire. *JTC, FCT*

Women of the Prehistoric Planet woof! 1966 On a strange planet, the members of a space rescue mission face deadly perils. Typical bad sci-fi of its era, with horrid special effects, including "giant" lizards. Get this: there's one woman, and she's not of the planet in question. See if you can last long enough to catch the amazing plot twist at the end. **87m/C VHS, Beta.** Wendell Corey, Irene Tsu, Robert Ito, Stuart Margolin, Lyle Waggoner, Adam Roarke, Merry Anders; *D:* Arthur C. Pierce. *NO*

Women of Valor 🎬½ 1986 During WWII, a band of American nurses stationed in the Philippines are captured by the Japanese and struggle to survive in a brutal POW camp. TV feature was made 40 years too late, adding up to a surreal experience. **95m/C VHS, Beta.** Susan Sarandon, Kristy McNichol, Alberta Watson, Valerie Mahaffey, Suzanne Lederer, Pat Bishop, Terry O'Quinn, Neva Patterson; *D:* Buzz Kulik; *M:* Georges Delerue. *NO, PSM*

Women on the Verge of a Nervous Breakdown 🎬🎬🎬½ *Mujeres al Borde de un Ataque de Nervios* 1988 (R) Surreal and hilarious romp through the lives of film dubber Maura, her ex-lover, his crazed ex-mistress, his new lover, his son, and his son's girlfriend. There's also Maura's friend Barranco, who inadvertently lent her apartment to Shiite terrorists and now believes the police are after her as an accomplice in an airline hijacking. They meet in a comedy of errors, missed phone calls, and rental notices, while discovering the truth and necessity of love. Fast-paced and full of black humor, with loaded gazpacho serving as a key element. Introduced Almodovar to American audiences. In Spanish with English subtitles. **88m/C VHS, Beta, LV.** *SP* Carmen Maura, Fernando Guillen, Julieta Serrano,

Maria Barranco, Rossy de Palma, Antonio Banderas; **D:** Pedro Almodovar; **W:** Pedro Almodovar; **C:** Jose Luis Alcaine; **M:** Bernardo Bonazzi. National Board of Review Awards '88: 5 Best Foreign Films of the Year; New York Film Critics Awards '88: Best Foreign Film; Nominations: Academy Awards '88: Best Foreign Language Film. *ORI*

Women Unchained woof! 197? (R) Five women escape from a maximum security prison and make a run for the Mexican border, shunning civilized behavior along the way. Much less-than-honorable entry in desperate women genre. 82m/C **VHS, Beta.** Carolyn Judd, Teri Guzman, Darlene Mattingly, Angel Colbert, Bonita Kalem; **D:** Kent Osborne; **W:** Kent Osborne. *GEM*

Women's Club 🎞️½ 1987 (R) Table-turning sex comedy about a wealthy matron who patronizes a talented (?) young movie writer, but really wants—you know what. She begins lending his services to friends—and does he ever get worn out! This excuse may be intended to be uproarious, but it's hard to tell. And all that sex gets very perfunctory after awhile. 89m/C **VHS, Beta.** Michael Pare, Maud Adams, Eddie Velez; **D:** Sandra Weintraub; **M:** Paul Antonelli. *LIV, VES*

Women's Prison Escape 🎞️½ *Cell Block Girls* 19?? Four tough broads blow the pen and are forced to high-tail it through the Everglades. They can't decide which is worse, the snakes and 'gators, or the corrupt and sleazy life they left behind. Only cinematic pairing of Rooney and Lurch. 90m/C **VHS.** Ted Cassidy, Chris Robinson, Mickey Rooney; **D:** Chris Robinson. *QVD*

Women's Prison Massacre woof! 1985 Four male convicts temporarily detained at a woman's prison (why?) violently take hostages and generally make trouble for the authorities and the women. Horribly dubbed. 89m/C **VHS, Beta.** IT Laura Gemser, Lorraine De Selle, Francoise Perrot, Ursula Flores, Gabriele Truti; **D:** Gilbert Roussel. *LIV, VES*

Wonder Man 🎞️🎞️½ 1945 When a brash nightclub entertainer (Kaye) is killed by gangsters, his mild-mannered twin brother (Kaye) takes his place to smoke out the killers. One of Kaye's better early films. The film debuts of Vera-Ellen and Cochran. Look for Mrs. Howell of "Gilligan's Island." ♫So In Love; Bali Boogie; Ortchi Chornya; Opera Number. 98m/C **VHS, Beta, LV.** Danny Kaye, Virginia Mayo, Vera-Ellen, Steve Cochran, S.Z. Sakall, Otto Kruger; **D:** H. Bruce Humberstone; **C:** Victor Milner. Academy Awards '45: Best Special Effects; Nominations: Academy Awards '45: Best Song ("So in Love"), Best Sound, Scoring of a Musical.

The Wonderful, Horrible Life of Leni Riefenstahl 1993 Documentary portrait of Hitler's favorite filmmaker. At 91, Riefenstahl tells of her start as an actress, her first directorial effort "The Blue Light" (1932), and the two infamous propaganda films; "Triumph of the Will" (1935) and "Olympia" (1938), which still provoke. She discusses her relationship with Hitler and Joseph Goebbels and the accusations that have continued to haunt her film. Still active, Riefenstahl's current work documents the Nuba tribes of Africa and underwater filming of rare aquatic life in the Seychelles Islands. German with English subtitles. 180m/C VHS. **GE** *D:* Ray Muller. *KIV*

The Wonderful World of the Brothers Grimm 🎞️🎞️½ 1962 Big-budget fantasy based very loosely on the Grimm Brothers' lives and three of their stories: "The Dancing Princesses," "The Cobbler and the Elves," and "The Singing Bone." Good, fun Puppetoon scenes, but leaves much else to be desired. A megawatt cast and the ubiquitous hand of producer-director Pal are not enough to cover the flaws. The biographical parts are hokey, and the tales used are the wrong ones. Disappointing but historically interesting. The second-ever story line done in Cinerama. ♫The Theme From the Wonderful World of the Brothers Grimm; Gypsy Rhapsody; Christmas Land; Ah-Oom; Above the Stars; Dee-Are-A-Gee-O-En (Dragon). 134m/C **VHS, Beta,**

LV. Laurence Harvey, Karl-Heinz Boehm, Claire Bloom, Buddy Hackett, Terry-Thomas, Russ Tamblyn, Yvette Mimieux, Oscar Homolka, Walter Slezak, Beulah Bondi, Martita Hunt, Otto Kruger, Barbara Eden, Jim Backus, Arnold Stang; **D:** Henry Levin, George Pal; **W:** William Roberts; **C:** Paul Vogel. Academy Awards '62: Best Costume Design (Color); Nominations: Academy Awards '62: Best Adapted Score, Best Art Direction/Set Decoration (Color), Best Color Cinematography. *MGM*

Wonderland 🎞️🎞️🎞️ *The Fruit Machine* 1988 Campy thriller follows two young gay boys in England, inadvertent witnesses to a murder, who find themselves on the run. Fast paced, dreamy atmosphere makes up for the sometimes confusing plot. Often overlooked British import. 103m/C **VHS, LV.** *GB* Emile Charles, Tony Forsyth, Robert Stephens, Clare Higgins, Bruce Payne, Robbie Coltrane; **D:** Philip Saville; **W:** Frank Clarke; **M:** Hans Zimmer. *LIV, VES*

Wonderland Cove 🎞️ 1975 Seafaring adventurer adopts five orphan children and embarks on journeys to exotic locales. 78m/C **Beta.** Clu Gulager, Sean Marshall, Randi Kiger, Lori Walsh; **D:** Jerry Thorpe. *PSM*

The Wonders of Aladdin 🎞️½ *Les Mille Et Une Nuits; Le Meraviglie Di Aladino* 1961 Slapstick comedy based on the ancient rubbed-lamp-and-genie chestnut. Kids'll love it; adults will yawn. 93m/C **VHS, Beta.** IT FR Donald O'Connor, Vittorio De Sica; **D:** Henry Levin, Mario Bava. *NLC*

Wonderwall: The Movie 🎞️½ 1969 Bizarre characters trip over themselves in love while groovy music plays in background. 82m/C **VHS, Beta.** *GB* Jack MacGowran, Jane Birkin, Irene Handl; **D:** Joe Massot; **M:** George Harrison, Eric Clapton, Ravi Shankar. *FCT, MVD*

Wonsan Operation 🎞️ 1978 U.N. soldiers plunge into the muddy depths of enemy territory in search of secret information that would end the Korean War. Dubbed. 100m/C **VHS, Beta.** Lew Montania, Frederick Hill; **D:** Terrence Sul. *VDA*

Woodchipper Massacre woof! 1989 Aunt Tess is frozen in the freezer, waiting to be turned into whatever the fleshy equivalent of woodchips is by her three unloving relations, and her totally evil son has just broken out of prison looking to retrieve his inheritance. You think you have problems? You'll have one less if you leave this one on the shelf. 90m/C **VHS, Beta.** Jon McBride, Patricia McBride; **D:** Jon McBride. *DMP*

The Wooden Gun 🎞️🎞️½ 1979 Conflicts arise between two teenage factions in 1950's Tel Aviv: native Israelis, and the children of Jews arrived from Europe since WWII. In Hebrew with English subtitles. 91m/C **VHS, Beta.** IS **D:** Han Moshenson. *ERG, FCT*

Wooden Horse 🎞️🎞️🎞️ 1950 Lean thriller of British POWs escaping a Nazi camp through a tunnel beneath their exercise horse. Based on a true incident in 1943 and on "The Tunnel Escape" by Eric Williams; set the tone for all British prison-camp movies to follow: stiff upper lip and all that, and adolescent-style trickery reminiscent of English boarding schools. 98m/C **VHS, Beta.** Anthony Steel, Leo Genn, David Tomlinson, Bryan Forbes, Peter Finch; **D:** Jack Lee. *NO*

The Wooden Man's Bride 🎞️🎞️ 1994 The inhabitants of this austere 1920s, northwest Chinese community live in stone fortresses, fearful of being attacked by roving armed bandits. Which is what happens to the bridal party of Young Mistress (Lan), who's kidnapped by bandit leader Tang (Mingjun). She's released unharmed when her servant Kui (Shih) impresses Tang with his bravery but her bridegroom has been killed in a freak accident and formidable Madame Liu (Yumei), who runs the fortress, forces her to marry a wooden likeness of the deceased. Despairing Young Mistress begins an affair with Kui, which can only end badly. Mandarin with subtitles. 114m/C VHS. CH Wang Lan, Chang Shih, Wang Yu-mei, Kao Mingjun; **D:** Huang Jianxin; **W:** Yang Zhengguang; **C:** Zhang Xiaoguang; **M:** Zhang Dalong. *HMK*

Woodstock 🎞️🎞️🎞️ 1970 (R) Step into the way-back machine and return to the times of luv, peace, and understanding. Powerful chronicle of the great 1969 Woodstock rock concert celebrates the music and lifestyle of the late '60s. More than 400,000 spectators withstood lack of privacy, bathrooms, parking, and food while wallowing in the mud for four days to catch classic performances by a number of popular performers and groups. Martin Scorcese helped edit the documentary, trail-blazing in its use of split-screen montage. A director's cut is available at 225 minutes. 180m/C **VHS, Beta, LV, Closed Caption. D:** Michael Wadleigh. Academy Awards '70: Best Feature Documentary; Nominations: Academy Awards '70: Best Film Editing, Best Sound. *MVD, WAR*

Woodstock '94 1994 The 25th anniversary of the original festival was celebrated with a three-day music explosion (complete with mud). Includes backstage footage and interviews with some of the 30 acts, including Aerosmith, Peter Gabriel, Blind Melon, Metallica, and the Red Hot Chili Peppers. 165m/C VHS. *PGV, MVD*

Woof! 🎞️🎞️½ 1990 Follows the misadventures of a boy who metamorphosed into a dog. 82m/C **VHS, Closed Caption. D:** David Cobham. *FHE, UND, BTV*

The Word 🎞️🎞️½ 1978 Intriguing premise has an archeologist finding a perviously unknown text purporting to be written by the younger brother of Jesus. If authentic and publicized, it would wreak theological havoc. Janssen is off to Italy to check up; he finds murder and skullduggery. Well-acted, interesting story. 300m/C **VHS, Beta, LV.** David Janssen, James Whitmore, Florinda Bolkan, Eddie Albert, Geraldine Chaplin, Hurd Hatfield, John Huston, Kate Mulgrew, Janice Rule, Nicol Williamson; **D:** Richard Lang; **M:** Alex North. *FRH*

Words and Music 🎞️🎞️½ 1948 Plot based on the careers of Rodgers and Hart is little more than a peg on which to hang lots of classic songs, sung by a parade of MGM stars. Also includes Kelly's dance recreation of "Slaughter on Tenth Avenue." Good advice: if no one's singing or dancing, fast forward. 122m/C **VHS, Beta.** Mickey Rooney, Tom Drake, Judy Garland, Gene Kelly, Lena Horne, Mel Torme, Cyd Charisse, Marshall Thompson, Janet Leigh, Betty Garrett, June Allyson, Perry Como, Vera-Ellen, Ann Sothern; **D:** Norman Taurog; **M:** Richard Rodgers, Lorenz Hart. *MGM*

Words by Heart 1984 An African American family in turn of the century Missouri faces issues of discrimination and prejudice. Twelve-year-old Lena wins a speech contest and begins to question their place in the community and their aspirations for a better life. Based on a book by Ouida Sebestyen. Aired by PBS as part of the "Wonderworks" family movie series. 116m/C **VHS, Closed Caption.** Charlotte Rae, Robert Hooks, Alfre Woodard; **D:** Robert Thompson. *PME, FCT, HMV*

Work/Police 🎞️🎞️🎞️½ 1916 Two Chaplin two-reelers. In "Work (The Paper Hanger)" (1915), a family hires Charlie and cohorts Armstrong and Purviance to re-paper a house. Little did they know! In "Police" (1916), Charlie plays an ex-con released into the cruel world. Unremittingly hilarious. Silent with music score. 54m/B **VHS, Beta.** Charlie Chaplin, Billy Armstrong, Charles Insley, Marta Golden, Edna Purviance; **D:** Charlie Chaplin. *VYY*

Workin' for Peanuts 1985 A young man who sells beer at a baseball stadium falls in love with the stadium owner's daughter. 52m/C **VHS, Beta, Closed Caption.** Carl Marotte, Jessica Steer. *NO*

Working Girl 🎞️🎞️🎞️ 1988 (R) Romantic comedy set in the Big Apple has secretary Griffith working her way to the top in spite of her manipulative boss (Weaver in a powerful parody). Griffith gets her chance to shine when Weaver breaks a leg. She meets Ford for business that turns to romance. A 1980s Cinderella story that's sexy, funny, and sharply written and directed. Nice work by Ford, but this is definitely Griffith's movie. And keep an eye on gal pal Cusack. ♫Let the River

Run. 115m/C VHS, Beta, LV, Closed Caption. Melanie Griffith, Harrison Ford, Sigourney Weaver, Joan Cusack, Alec Baldwin, Philip Bosco, Ricki Lake, Nora Dunn, Olympia Dukakis, Oliver Platt, James Lally, Kevin Spacey, Robert Easton; **D:** Mike Nichols; **W:** Kevin Wade; **C:** Michael Ballhaus; **M:** Carly Simon, Rob Mounsey. Academy Awards '88: Best Song ("Let the River Run"); Golden Globe Awards '89: Best Actress—Musical/Comedy (Griffith), Best Film—Musical/Comedy, Best Song ("Let the River Run"), Best Supporting Actress (Weaver); Nominations: Academy Awards '88: Best Actress (Griffith), Best Director (Nichols), Best Picture, Best Supporting Actress (Cusack, Weaver). FOX

Working Girls ⅊ 1975 (R) Three girls who share an apartment in Los Angeles are willing to do anything for money. And they do. For lack of anything else to recommend, watch for the striptease by Peterson, better known as Elvira on TV. 80m/C VHS, Beta. Sarah Kennedy, Laurie Rose, Mark Thomas, Cassandra Peterson; **D:** Stephanie Rothman. VCI

Working Girls ⅊⅊⅊ 1987 An acclaimed, controversial look by independent filmmaker Borden into lives of modern brothel prostitutes over the period of one day. The sex is realistically candid and perfunctory; the docudrama centers on a prostitute who is a Yale graduate and aspiring photographer living with a female lover. Compelling, touching, and lasting, with sexually candid language and scenery. 93m/C VHS, Beta. Amanda Goodwin, Louise Smith, Ellen McElduff, Maurisia Zach, Janne Peters, Helen Nicholas; **D:** Lizzie Borden; **W:** Lizzie Borden, Sandra Kay; **M:** David Van Tiegham. COL, NLC, HHE

Working Winnie/Oh So Simple 1922 Two rare, second-echelon short silent comedies. 61m/B VHS, Beta, 8mm. Ethlyn Gibson, Bobby Ray. VYY

The World According to Garp ⅊⅊⅊ 1982 (R) Comedy turns to tragedy in this relatively faithful version of John Irving's popular (and highly symbolic) novel, adapted by Steve Tesich. Chronicles the life of T.S. Garp, a struggling everyman beset by the destructive forces of modern society. Nevertheless, Garp maintains his optimism even as his life unravels around him. At the core of the film is a subplot involving a group of extreme feminists inspired in part by Garp's mother, the author of "A Sexual Suspect." Close and Lithgow (as a giant transsexual) are spectacular, while Williams is low-key and tender as the beleaguered Garp. Ultimately pointless, perhaps, but effectively and intelligently so. 136m/C VHS, Beta, LV, Closed Caption. Robin Williams, Mary Beth Hurt, John Lithgow, Glenn Close, Hume Cronyn, Jessica Tandy, Swoosie Kurtz, Amanda Plummer, Warren Berlinger, Brandon Maggart; **Cameos:** George Roy Hill; **D:** George Roy Hill; **W:** Steve Tesich; **M:** David Shire. Los Angeles Film Critics Association Awards '82: Best Supporting Actor (Lithgow), Best Supporting Actress (Close); National Board of Review Awards '82: Best Supporting Actor (Lithgow); New York Film Critics Awards '82: Best Supporting Actor (Lithgow); Nominations: Academy Awards '82: Best Supporting Actor (Lithgow), Best Supporting Actress (Close). WAR

The World Accuses ⅊½ 1935 A woman takes a job in a nursery, unaware that one child is her own, put up for adoption after her wealthy husband died. Then, her ex-lover shows up in her attic after escaping from prison and takes her hostage. Whew! Everything works out, except that the viewer is left confused and incredulous. 62m/B VHS. Vivian Tobin, Dickie Moore, Russell Hopton, Cora Sue Collins, Mary Carr; **D:** Charles Lamont. NOS, DVT

World and Time Enough ⅊½ 1995 Sculptor Mark's (Guidry) father compulsively designed Gothic cathedrals and after his death Mark decides to build his own version in a field belonging to a sympathetic cleric. Meanwhile, his equally eccentric lover, garbage-collector Joey (Giles), goes on a search for his birth parents. Lots of symbols, not much sense. 90m/C VHS. Matt Guidry, Gregory G. Giles, Kraig Swartz, Peter Macon; **D:** Eric Mueller; **W:** Eric Mueller; **C:** Kyle Bergersen; **M:** Eugene Huddleston. FCT

A World Apart ⅊⅊⅊½ 1988 (PG) Cinematographer Menges' first directoral effort is a blistering, insightful drama told from the point of view of a 13-year-old white girl living in South Africa, oblivious to apartheid until her crusading journalist mother is arrested under the 90-Day Detention Act, under which she might remain in prison permanently. Political morality tale is also a look at the family-vs-cause choices activists must make. Heavily lauded, with good reason; the autobiographical script is based on Slovo's parents, persecuted South African journalists Joe Slovo and Ruth First. 114m/C VHS, Beta, LV, Closed Caption. GB Barbara Hershey, Jodhi May, Linda Mvusi, David Suchet, Jeroen Krabbe, Paul Freeman, Tim Roth; **D:** Chris Menges; **W:** Shawn Slovo; **C:** Peter Biziou; **M:** Hans Zimmer. British Academy Awards '88: Best Original Screenplay; Cannes Film Festival '88: Best Actress (Hershey), Best Actress (May, Mvusi), Grand Jury Prize; New York Film Critics Awards '88: Best Director (Menges). MED

The World Gone Mad ⅊⅊½ *The Public Be Hanged; Public Be Damned* 1933 During Prohibition, a tough reporter discovers the district attorney is the intended victim of a murder plot involving crooked Wall Street types. Full circle: this interesting drama of white-collar crime is again topical, though dialogue heavy and desultory. 70m/B VHS, Beta. Pat O'Brien, Louis Calhern, J. Carrol Naish; **D:** Christy Cabanne. NOS, CAB, DVT

World Gone Wild ⅊½ 1988 (R) Action yarn about a post-apocalyptic world of the future where an evil cult leader brainwashes his disciples. Together they battle a small band of eccentrics for the world's last water source. Stale rehash (with ineffective satiric elements) of the Mad Max genre, served with Ant for campy appeal. 95m/C VHS, Beta, LV. Bruce Dern, Michael Pare, Adam Ant, Catherine Mary Stewart, Rick Podell; **D:** Lee H. Katzin; **C:** Don Burgess. MED, VTR

The World in His Arms ⅊⅊½ 1952 Action and romance, circa 1850. Seal hunter Jonathan Clark (Peck) and his crew are in San Francisco when he meets beautiful Countess Marina Selanova (Blyth), who's fleeing an arranged marriage and is anxious to join her Uncle (Rumann), who happens to be the Governor General of Alaska (which is under Russian control). The twosome fall quickly in love but Marina's kidnapped by her would-be fiance, Prince Semyon (Esmond), who takes off for Alaska and Clark must go to rescue his love. Based on the book by Rex Beach. 104m/C VHS. Gregory Peck, Ann Blyth, Anthony Quinn, Carl Esmond, Sig Rumann, John McIntire, Hans Conried, Andrea King; **D:** Raoul Walsh; **W:** Borden Chase; **C:** Russell Metty; **M:** Frank Skinner. USH

The World is Full of Married Men WOOF! 1980 (R) A philandering ad exec gets involved with a reckless model, inspiring his fed-up wife also to look for extramarital sex. Promiscuously raunchy melodrama was written by the queen of sleaze, Jackie Collins, based on her novel. 106m/C VHS, Beta. GB Anthony (Tony) Franciosa, Carroll Baker, Sherrie Croon, Gareth Hunt, Paul Nicholas; **D:** Robert W. Young; **W:** Jackie Collins. FOX

The World of Abbott & Costello 1964 Compilation of the duo's most famous routines from their 18 films, including the frog in the soup sketch from "The Wistful Widow of Wagon Gap," the cobra skit from "Abbott & Costello Meet the Mummy," and their legendary baseball routine "Who's on First?" from "The Naughty Nineties." 75m/B VHS, Closed Caption. Bud Abbott, Lou Costello. USH

The World of Apu ⅊⅊⅊⅊ *Apu Sansat; Apur Sansar* 1959 Finale of director Ray's acclaimed Apu trilogy (following "Pather Panchali" and "Aparajito"). Aspiring writer Apu drops out of the university for want of money and takes up with an old chum. An odd circumstance leads him to marry his friend's cousin, whom he comes to love. She dies in childbirth (though her baby boy lives); Apu is deeply distraught, destroys the novel he

was working on, and becomes a wanderer. His friend finds him five years later and helps him begin again with his young son. Wonderfully human, hopeful story told by a world-class director. From the novel "Aparajito" by B. Bandopadhaya. In Bengali with English subtitles. 103m/B VHS, Beta. IN Soumitra Chatterjee, Sharmila Tagore, Alok Charkravarty, Swapan Makerji; **D:** Satyajit Ray; **W:** Satyajit Ray; **M:** Ravi Shankar. National Board of Review Awards '60: 5 Best Foreign Films of the Year. HHT, VYY, DVT

The World of Henry Orient ⅊⅊⅊½ 1964 Charming, eccentric comedy about two 15-year-old girls who, madly in love with an egotistical concert pianist, pursue him all around New York City. Sellers is hilarious, Walker and Spaeth are adorable as his teen groupies; Bosley and Lansbury are great as Walker's indulgent parents. For anyone who has ever been uncontrollably infatuated. Screenplay by the father/daughter team, Nora and Nunnally Johnson, based on Nora Johnson's novel. 106m/C VHS, Beta, LV, Closed Caption. Peter Sellers, Tippy Walker, Merrie Spaeth, Tom Bosley, Angela Lansbury, Paula Prentiss, Phyllis Thaxter, Bibi Osterwald; **D:** George Roy Hill; **W:** Nunnally Johnson, Nora Johnson; **C:** Boris Kaufman; **M:** Elmer Bernstein. National Board of Review Awards '64: 10 Best Films of the Year. MGM, FCT

A World of Strangers ⅊⅊⅊ 1962 A harsh look at apartheid through the eyes of an Englishman who has traveled to South Africa to manage a publishing house. Filmed in strict secrecy in Johannesburg due to the film's aggressive condemnation of the practice. Based on a novel by Nadine Gordimer. 89m/B VHS. DK Ivan Jackson, Zakes Mokae; **D:** Henning Carlsen. CVC

The World of Suzie Wong ⅊⅊ 1960 Asian prostitute Kwan plays cat-and-mouse with American painter Holden. She lies to him about her profession, her family, and herself. His association with her ruins relationships in his life. Why, then, does he not get a clue? Good question, not answered by this soap opera that would be a serious drama. Offensively sanitized picture of the world of prostitution in an Asian metropolis. On the other hand, it's all nicely shot, much of it on location in Hong Kong. Based on Paul Osborn's play which was taken from Richard Mason's novel. 129m/C VHS, Beta, LV. GB William Holden, Nancy Kwan, Sylvia Syms, Michael Wilding, Laurence Naismith, Jacqueline "Jackie" Chan; **D:** Richard Quine; **C:** Geoffrey Unsworth. PAR

World of the Depraved ⅊ 1967 Tango (Storm) runs an exercise club for young lovelies that are systematically being stalked by the mysterious full moon sex killer. Enter police detectives Riley and Hamilton (Decker, Reed), joking types who peep on their charges through keyholes, etc. When the plot finally gets around to the issue of the killer, the point of the movie has already been made clear. Silly, trivial, sophomoric humor lacking a trace of sincerity. Volume 6 of Frank Henenlotter's Sexy Shockers series. 73m/C VHS. Tempest Storm, Johnnie Decker, Larry Reed; **D:** Herbert Jeffries; **W:** Herbert Jeffries. SMW

The World Owes Me a Living ⅊⅊ 1947 Melodrama about pilot Farrar losing his memory in a plane crash and Campbell trying to spark his recollection of the past. 91m/B VHS. GB David Farrar, Judy Campbell, Jack Livesey, John Laurie; **D:** Vernon Sewell; **W:** Vernon Sewell. LOO

World War II: When Lions Roared ⅊⅊½ 1994 The "Lions" are Franklin Delano Roosevelt, Winston Churchill, and Joseph Stalin. The three Allied leaders formed an uneasy alliance to crush Hitler and Mussolini, all against much internal treachery. Uses lots of WWII newsreel footage. Made for television; on two cassettes. 186m/C VHS. John Lithgow, Bob Hoskins, Michael Caine, Ed Begley Jr., Jan Tiska; **D:** Joseph Sargent; **W:** David W. Rintels; **C:** John A. Alonzo. MPI

World War III 🐾🐾½ 1986 How's that for a title? A Russian plot is afoot to seize and destroy the Alaskan pipeline. When the plot is discovered, negotiation is needed to prevent world war. Executive branch showdown ensues between U.S. prez Hudson and Soviet chief Keith. Director Boris Sagal was killed on location, whereupon Greene took over, and shooting was moved indoors with dramatic tension lost in the transition. Made for TV. **186m/C VHS, Beta, Closed Caption.** Brian Keith, David Soul, Rock Hudson, Cathy Lee Crosby, Katherine Helmond, Robert Prosky, James Hampton, Richard Yniguez, Herbert Jefferson Jr.; **D:** David Greene; **W:** Robert L. Joseph. FOX

The Worldly Madonna 🐾🐾½ 1922 Young plays two roles as Janet, a convent novitiate, and her cabaret dancer sister, Lucy. Lucy thinks she's killed a man and Janet agrees to change places with her. **47m/B VHS.** Clara Kimball Young, Richard Tucker, George Hackathorne, William P. Carleton, Jean De Limur, William Marion, Milla Davenport; **D:** Harry Garson. GPV, FCT

The World's Greatest Athlete 🐾🐾 1973 (G) Lame Disney comedy about a Tarzan-like jungle-man (Vincent) recruited by an unsuccessful American college coach (Amos) and his bumbling assistant (Conway). Fun special effects, weak script add up to mediocre family fare. Cameo by Howard Cosell as—who else?—himself. **89m/C VHS, Beta.** Jan-Michael Vincent, Tim Conway, John Amos, Roscoe Lee Browne, Dayle Haddon; **Cameos:** Howard Cosell; **D:** Robert Scheerer; **W:** Dee Caruso; **M:** Marvin Hamlisch. DIS, OM

World's Greatest Lover 🐾🐾½ 1977 (PG) Milwaukee baker Rudi Valentine, played oft-hilariously by Wilder, tries to make it big in 1920s Hollywood. He has a screen test as a Hollywood movie sheik, but his wife (Kane) leaves him for the real McCoy. Episodic and uneven, it's alternately uproarious, touching and downright raunchy. **89m/C VHS, LV.** Gene Wilder, Carol Kane, Dom DeLuise, Fritz Feld, Carl Ballantine, Michael Huddleston, Matt Collins, Ronny Graham; **D:** Gene Wilder; **W:** Gene Wilder. FOX

The World's Oldest Living Bridesmaid 🐾🐾½ 1992 Hokey romantic comedy about a successful woman attorney who just can't find Mr. Right. Brenda feels even worse when she attends yet another friend's wedding. However, when she hires a younger, male secretary (former model Wimmer) the romantic sparks fly. An appealing and attractive cast helps this made-for-television fare. **100m/C VHS.** Donna Mills, Brian Wimmer, Beverly Garland, Winston Reckert, Art Hindle, Laura Press; **D:** Joseph L. Scanlan. AIP

The Worm Eaters woof! 1977 (PG) Mean developers want to take over a reclusive worm farmer's land. He unleashes his livestock on them. The bad guys turn into—eeck!—"worm people." A truck runs over our hero nearly 75 minutes too late to save the viewer. **75m/C VHS, Beta.** Herb Robins, Barry Hostetler, Lindsay Armstrong Black; **D:** Herb Robins; **W:** Herb Robins. NO

The Worst of Hollywood: Vol. 1 1990 Two really bad movies for your viewing displeasure. "Maniac" is a mad-scientist fest and "Protect Your Daughter" warns of the perils of the Flapper era. **115m/B VHS, Beta.** Bill Woods, Horace Carpenter, Phyllis Diller; **D:** Dwain Esper. INC

The Worst of Hollywood: Vol. 2 1990 A von Stroheim-fest of mediocrity. In "Fugitive Road" Erich plays an Austrian officer of the First World War. "The Crime of Dr. Crespi" has him portray a mad scientist. **131m/B VHS, Beta.** Erich von Stroheim, Dwight Frye; **D:** Erich von Stroheim. INC

The Worst of Hollywood: Vol. 3 1990 Two more awful, exploitive docudramas. "Nation Aflame" features many silent screen stars who teach the virtues of living in racial harmony. "Probation" boasts the first screen appearance of Grable, as a promiscuous woman who ends up in prison. **140m/B VHS, Beta.** Betty Grable. INC

The Worst Witch 🐾🐾½ 1986 (G) Fantasy about a school for young witches where the educational lessons never go quite as planned. Adapted from the children's book "The Worst Witch" by Jill Murphy. **70m/C VHS, Beta, LV.** Diana Rigg, Charlotte Rae, Tim Curry, Fairuza Balk; **D:** Robert M. Young. PSM, IME

Worth Winning 🐾½ 1989 (PG-13) A notoriously eligible Philadelphia bachelor takes a bet to become engaged to three women within three months, and finds himself in hot water. A critically dead-in-the-water chucklefest. **103m/C VHS, Beta, LV, Closed Caption.** Mark Harmon, Lesley Ann Warren, Madeleine Stowe, Maria Holvoe, Mark Blum, Andrea Martin, Alan Blumenfeld, Brad Hall, Tony Longo; **D:** Will MacKenzie; **W:** Sara Parriott, Josann McGibbon. FOX

The Would-Be Gentleman 🐾🐾½ 1958 The Comedie Francaise troupe performs Moliere's famous farce-comedy. Valuable as a record of the famous troupe on stage. When they're long gone, our grandkids can enjoy this. We can too (if we can't afford the trip to France), though it's less a film than a filming of a play. In French with English subtitles. **93m/C VHS, Beta.** FR Louis Seigner, Jean Meyer, Jean Piat. DVT

Woyzeck 🐾🐾 1978 Chilling portrayal of a man plunging into insanity. Mired in the ranks of the German Army, Woyzeck is harassed by his superiors and tortured in scientific experiments, gradually devolving into homicidal maniac. Based on Georg Buchner play. In German with English subtitles. **82m/C VHS.** GE Klaus Kinski, Eva Mattes, Wolfgang Reichmann, Josef Bierbichler; **D:** Werner Herzog; **W:** Werner Herzog. NYF

WR: Mysteries of the Organism 🐾🐾🐾 1971 Makavejev's breakthrough film, a surreal, essayist exploration of the conflict/union between sexuality and politics—namely, Wilheim Reich and Stalin. A raunchy, bitterly satiric non-narrative that established the rule-breaking Yugoslav internationally. In Serbian with English subtitles. **84m/C VHS, Beta.** Milena Dravic, Jagoda Kaloper, Tuli Kupferberg, Jackie Curtis; **D:** Dusan Makavejev; **W:** Dusan Makavejev. FCT

The Wraith 🐾½ 1987 (PG-13) Drag-racing Arizona teens find themselves challenged by a mysterious, otherworldly stranger. Hot cars; cool music; little else to recommend it. Lousy script; ludicrous excuse for a premise. Most of the stars herein are related to somebody famous. **92m/C VHS, Beta, LV.** Charlie Sheen, Nick Cassavetes, Sherilyn Fenn, Randy Quaid, Matthew Barry, Clint Howard, Griffin O'Neal; **D:** Mike Marvin. LIV

Wrangler 🐾🐾½ 1988 When an Australian rancher dies his daughter tries to hang on to the family ranch from a ruthless creditor. She also has to deal with the attentions of two men—one a businessman and the other a cattleman, both equally dashing and handsome. Beautiful scenery of the Australian Outback as well as romance and adventure. **93m/C VHS, LV.** Jeff Fahey, Tushka Bergen, Steven Vidler, Richard Moir, Shane Briant, Drew Forsythe, Cornelia Frances, Sandy Gore, Frederick Parslow; **D:** Ian Barry; **W:** John Sexton; **M:** Mario Millo. NO

The Wreck of the Mary Deare 🐾🐾½ 1959 Slow-moving adventure drama focusing on the wreck of the freighter called the Mary Deare. Heston plays a ship salvager who comes upon a seemingly empty ship one night and Cooper is the only crew member on board. Special effects are the main attraction in this interesting sea drama. Film originally was to be directed by Hitchcock, but he turned down the offer to do "North by Northwest." **105m/C VHS, LV, Closed Caption.** GB Gary Cooper, Charlton Heston, Michael Redgrave, Emlyn Williams, Cecil Parker, Alexander Knox, Virginia McKenna, Richard Harris; **D:** Michael Anderson Sr. MGM

The Wrestler 🐾 1973 All-star wrestling, which is fictional anyway, gets said treatment in the appropriate way. Honest promoter (yeah, sure) bumps heads with bad-guy crooks who want in on the action. Made-for-TV opportunity for Asner to slum. **103m/C VHS, Beta.** Ed Asner, Elaine Giftos, Verne Gagne, Harold Sakata. NWV

Wrestling Ernest Hemingway 🐾🐾 1993 (PG-13) A shy barber and a rollicking sea captain, both 75 and retired, form an unlikely companionship in a Florida retirement mecca. Duvall is the persnickety introvert who quietly follows routine and Harris is the would-be ladies' man whose endless tall tales include having tangled with Papa Hemingway in his youth. They share walks in the park, little league baseball from the bleachers, and coffee klatches that reveal the emptiness of their lives. Director Haines's focus on the principals' emotional baggage considerably dampens the proceedings. Depression in the elderly may be a topic that is not quite ready to come out of Hollywood's closet. **CW:** Language. **123m/C VHS, Closed Caption.** Robert Duvall, Richard Harris, Piper Laurie, Shirley MacLaine, Sandra Bullock; **D:** Randa Haines; **W:** Steve Conrad; **C:** Lajos Koltai; **M:** Michael Convertino. WAR

Wrestling Women vs. the Aztec Ape woof! Doctor of Doom 1962 An unclassifiable epic wherein female wrestlers battle a mad doctor and his Aztec robot gorilla. Dubbed badly, of course. Much anticipated follow-up to "Wrestling Women vs. the Aztec Mummy." **75m/C VHS, Beta.** MX Elizabeth Campbell, Lorena Velasquez, Armando Silvestre, Roberto Canedo; **D:** Rene Cardona Sr. RHI, HHT, SNC

Wrestling Women vs. the Aztec Mummy woof! 1959 Women, broad of shoulder, wrestle an ancient Aztec wrestler who comes to life. Furnished with a new rock soundtrack. **88m/C VHS, Beta.** MX Lorena Velasquez, Armando Silvestre; **D:** Rene Cardona Sr. SNC, RHI, HHT

Write to Kill 🐾½ 1991 (R) A young mystery writer seeks revenge when his brother is murdered by a ring of counterfeiters. **CW:** Language, violence, and sensuality. **120m/C VHS, LV.** Scott Valentine, Chris Mulkey, Joan Severance, G.W. Bailey, Ray Wise; **D:** Ruben Preuss. COL

Writer's Block 🐾🐾 1991 (R) Fairchild is a successful thriller writer whose latest books feature a serial killer. She decides to kill the character off and is soon stalked by a psycho who is using her plots for some copy-cat killings. Tepid made for cable television movie with San Diego locations the only highlight. **90m/C VHS, Beta, Closed Caption.** Morgan Fairchild, Joe Regalbuto, Michael Praed, Cheryl Anderson, Mary Ann Pascal, Douglas Rowe, Ned Bellamy; **D:** Charles Correll; **W:** Elisa Bell. PAR

Written on the Wind 🐾🐾🐾 1956 Sirk's frenzied, melodrama-as-high-art dissection of both the American Dream and American movies follows a Texas oil family's self-destruction through wealth, greed and unbridled lust. Exaggerated depiction of and comment on American ambition and pretension, adapted from Robert Wilder's novel. **99m/C VHS, Beta.** Lauren Bacall, Rock Hudson, Dorothy Malone, Robert Stack, Robert Keith, Grant Williams, Edward Platt, Harry Shannon; **D:** Douglas Sirk; **W:** George Zuckerman; **C:** Russell Metty. Academy Awards '56: Best Supporting Actress (Malone); Nominations: Academy Awards '56: Best Song ("Written on the Wind"), Best Supporting Actor (Stack). USH, BTV

The Wrong Arm of the Law 🐾🐾🐾 1963 Loopy gangster yarn about a trio of Aussie gangsters who arrive in London and upset the local crime balance when they dress up as cops and confiscate loot from apprehended robbers. General confusion erupts among the police, the local crooks, and the imposters. Riotous and hilarious, with Sellers leading a host of familiar faces. **94m/B VHS, Beta.** GB Peter Sellers, Lionel Jeffries, Nanette Newman, Bernard Cribbins, Dennis Price; **D:** Cliff Owen; **M:** Richard Rodney Bennett. MON

The Wrong Box 🐾🐾🐾 1966 Two elderly Victorian brothers try to kill each other so that one of them may collect the large inheritance left to them. Based on a Robert Louis Stevenson novel.

Well-cast black comedy replete with sight gags, many of which flop. **105m/C VHS, Beta.** *GB* Peter Sellers, Dudley Moore, Peter Cook, Michael Caine, Ralph Richardson, John Mills; *D:* Bryan Forbes; *W:* Larry Gelbart; *M:* John Barry. *COL*

The Wrong Guys 🐾 **1988 (PG)** Five giants of stand-up comedy star as a group of men who reunite their old boy scout pack and go camping. A crazed convict mistakes them for FBI agents. It's supposed to get zany after that, but succeeds only in being clumsy and embarrassing. **86m/C VHS, Beta, LV, Closed Caption.** Richard Lewis, Richard Belzer, Louie Anderson, Tim Thomerson, Franklin Ajaye, John Goodman, Ernie Hudson, Timothy Van Patten; *D:* Danny Bilson; *W:* Danny Bilson, Paul DeMeo. *VTR, NWV*

Wrong is Right 🐾 *The Man With The Deadly Lens* **1982 (R)** A black action comedy about international terrorism, news reporting and the CIA. Connery is terrific, as usual, as a TV reporter in a head-scratching attempt at satire of our TV-influenced society. **117m/C VHS, Beta, LV.** Sean Connery, Katharine Ross, Robert Conrad, George Grizzard, Henry Silva, G.D. Spradlin, John Saxon, Leslie Nielsen, Robert Webber, Rosalind Cash, Hardy Kruger, Dean Stockwell, Ron Moody, Jennifer Jason Leigh; *D:* Richard Brooks; *W:* Richard Brooks; *C:* Fred W. Koenekamp. *COL*

The Wrong Man 🐾🐾🐾½ **1956** Nightclub musician Fonda is falsely accused of a robbery and his life is destroyed. Taken almost entirely from the real-life case of mild-mannered bass player "Manny" Balestrero; probes his anguish at being wrongly accused; and showcases Miles (later to appear in "Psycho") and her character's agony. Harrowing, especially following more lighthearted Hitchcock fare such as "The Trouble with Harry." Part of the "A Night at the Movies" series, this tape simulates a 1956 movie evening with a color Bugs Bunny cartoon, "A Star Is Bored," a newsreel and coming attractions for "Toward the Unknown." **126m/B VHS, Beta, LV, Closed Caption.** Henry Fonda, Vera Miles, Anthony Quayle, Nehemiah Persoff; *D:* Alfred Hitchcock; *C:* Robert Burks. *WAR, MLB*

The Wrong Man 🐾🐾½ **1993 (R)** American sailor Alex Walker (Anderson) is framed for the murder of a Mexican smuggler. He eludes the police and winds up hitching a ride from wacko couple Phillip (Lithgow) and Missy Mills (Arquette). Missy does topless table dancing and is very interested in their fugitive passenger. Alex may be better off with the police. Made for cable television.*CW:* Nudity. **98m/C VHS, LV, Closed Caption.** Kevin Anderson, John Lithgow, Rosanna Arquette, Robert Harper; *D:* Jim McBride; *C:* Alfonso Beato. *REP*

The Wrong Move 🐾🐾½ **1978** A loose adaptation of Goethe's "Sorrows of Young Werther" by screenwriter Peter Handke. Justly acclaimed and engrossing, though slow. Kinski's first film. A young poet, searching for life's meaning, wanders aimlessly through Germany. In German with English subtitles. **103m/C VHS, Beta.** *GE* Nastassia Kinski, Hanna Schygulla, Ruediger Vogler, Hans-Christian Blech; *D:* Wim Wenders. *FCT, GLV, TPV*

The Wrong Road 🐾½ **1937** A young couple embark on a robbery spree, and subsequently end up in prison. On their release, they search for the loot they had previously hidden, but find the man who was holding it for them has died. Will they ever recover their ill-gotten stash? **62m/B VHS, Beta.** Richard Cromwell, Helen Mack, Lionel Atwill, Horace McMahon, Russ Powell, Billy Bevan, Marjorie Main, Rex Evans; *D:* James Cruze. *SNC*

The Wrong Woman 🐾🐾½ **1995 (PG-13)** When Melanie Brooke's (McKeon) boss is murdered, she's framed to take by rap by the company's sleazy comptroller (Field). Melanie begins a desperate hunt for the real culprit with the killer and the cops both after her.*CW:* Scenes of violence. **90m/C VHS, Closed Caption.** Nancy McKeon, Chelsea Field. *REP*

Wuthering Heights 🐾🐾🐾🐾 **1939** The first screen adaptation of Emily Bronte's romantic novel about the doomed love between Heathcliff and Cathy on the Yorkshire moors. This film dynamically captures the madness and ferocity of the classic novel, remaining possibly the greatest romance ever filmed. Excellent performances from Wyler's sure direction, particularly Olivier's, which made him a star, and Oberon in her finest hour as the exquisite but selfish Cathy. Remade twice, in 1953 (by Luis Bunuel) and in 1970. **104m/B VHS, Beta, LV.** Laurence Olivier, Merle Oberon, David Niven, Geraldine Fitzgerald, Flora Robson, Donald Crisp, Cecil Kellaway, Leo G. Carroll, Miles Mander, Hugh Williams; *D:* William Wyler; *W:* Ben Hecht, Charles MacArthur; *C:* Gregg Toland; *M:* Alfred Newman. Academy Awards '39: Best Black and White Cinematography; National Board of Review Awards '39: 10 Best Films of the Year; New York Film Critics Awards '39: Best Film; Nominations: Academy Awards '39: Best Actor (Olivier), Best Director (Wyler), Best Interior Decoration, Best Picture, Best Screenplay, Best Supporting Actress (Fitzgerald), Best Original Score. *HBO, HMV*

Wuthering Heights 🐾🐾½ *Abismos de Pasion* **1953** Bunuel tackles the Bronte classic during his Mexican period, and comes up with a film containing little passion, but much of the customary Bunuel manic cynicism. The 1939 version is far superior, but fans of Bunuel will probably enjoy this one. Loosely adapted; in Spanish with English subtitles. Remade in another English-language version in 1970. **90m/B VHS, Beta.** *MX* Irasema Dilian, Jorge Mistral, Lilia Prado, Ernesto Alonso; *D:* Luis Bunuel. *XVC, MED, APD*

Wuthering Heights 🐾🐾½ **1970 (G)** The third screening of the classic Emily Bronte romance about two doomed lovers. Fuest's version features excellent photography, and Calder-Marshall's and Dalton's performances are effective, but fail even to approach the intensity and pathos of the 1939 film original (or of the book). Filmed on location in Yorkshire, England. **105m/C VHS, Beta.** *GB* Anna Calder-Marshall, Timothy Dalton, Harry Andrews, Pamela Brown, Judy Cornwell, James Cossins, Rosalie Crutchley, Hilary Dwyer, Hugh Griffith, Ian Ogilvy; *D:* Robert Fuest. *CNG, KAR, TVC*

Wyatt Earp 🐾🐾½ **1994 (PG-13)** Revisionist epic suffers from bad timing as it follows "Tombstone" in telling the story of tarnished badge Earp (Costner), his brothers, and tubercular friend Doc Holliday (Quaid). Costner is barely believable as a twentysomething lad, but fares better as he ages. 40 pounds lighter and likely delusional from lack of food, Quaid is unrecognizable but terrific, hacking his way to supporting Oscar territory. 'Course, Val Kilmer got there first. Huge cast finds screen time precious, even though film is some 40 minutes too long, due to prolonged intro to early Wyatt life. Originally envisioned as a TV miniseries till sheriff Costner took a hankering to bring tall tale to the big screen. Filmed on location in Sante Fe, New Mexico. For the full Earp effect, see it with "Tombstone" and relive the legend.*CW:* Some language, strong gunfights, and some sensuality. **191m/C VHS, LV, Closed Caption.** Kevin Costner, Dennis Quaid, Gene Hackman, Jeff Fahey, Mark Harmon, Michael Madsen, Catherine O'Hara, Bill Pullman, Isabella Rossellini, Tom Sizemore, JoBeth Williams, Mare Winningham, Betty Buckley, Adam Baldwin, Rex Linn, Todd Allen, David Andrews, Linden Ashby, Annabeth Gish, Joanna Going, Martin Kove, Tea Leoni, James Caviezel, Karen Grassle; *D:* Lawrence Kasdan; *W:* Dan Gordon, Lawrence Kasdan; *C:* Owen Roizman; *M:* James Newton Howard. Golden Raspberry Awards '94: Worst Remake/Sequel, Worst Actor (Costner); Nominations: Academy Awards '94: Best Cinematography; Golden Raspberry Awards '94: Worst Picture. *WAR*

Wyatt Earp: Return to Tombstone 🐾🐾½ **1994** O'Brian, who starred in TV's "The Life and Legend of Wyatt Earp" from 1955 to 1961, returns to Tombstone in 1914. Colorized clips from the series are used for flashbacks. Filmed on location in Tombstone, Arizona. **94m/C VHS, LV.** Hugh O'Brian, Bruce Boxleitner,

Paul Brinegar, Harry Carey Jr., Bo Hopkins, Martin Kove, Don Meredith, Alex Hyde-White, Jay Underwood. *ORI*

Wyoming Outlaw 🐾 **1939** Based on an actual incident, the story revolves around a small-town man who kills an outlaw. Barry, in the role that made him a western star, is forced into crime after a corrupt politician extorts money from him in exchange for a job. Lincoln, the screen's first Tarzan, appears in a supporting role. **62m/B VHS.** John Wayne, Ray Corrigan, Raymond Hatton, Donald (Don "Red") Barry, Adele Pearce, Leroy Mason, Charles Middleton, Elmo Lincoln, Jack Ingram, Yakima Canutt, Curly Dresden; *D:* George Sherman. *NOS, MLB*

The X-Files: Pilot Episode/Deep Throat **1993** By-the-book FBI agent Dana Scully (Anderson) is first paired with maverick Fox Mulder (Duchovny), who's devoted to the study of unexplained phenomena and works only on cases outside the mainstream. In the pilot episode they investigate the mysterious deaths of Oregon high school students. "Deep Throat" finds Mulder investigating the disappearance of a test pilot—the sixth at the same air force base. Mulder's given encouragement and information from a government contact known only by his code name. Additional episodes available. **90m/C VHS, Closed Caption.** David Duchovny, Gillian Anderson, Charles Cioffi, Cliff DeYoung, Zachary Ansley, Jerry Hardin; *D:* Robert Mandel, Daniel Sackheim; *W:* Chris Carter. *FXV, MOV*

X from Outer Space 🐾 **1967 (PG)** A space voyage to Mars brings back a giant rampaging creature. Badly dubbed. **85m/C VHS, Beta.** *JP* Eiji Okada, Peggy Neal, Toshiya Wazaki, Itoko Harada, Shinichi Yanagisawa, Franz Gruber, Keisuke Sonoi, Mike Daning, Torahiko Hamada; *D:* Nazui Nihonmatsu. *ORI*

X Marks the Spot 🐾🐾 **1942** When a police sergeant is killed, his detective son investigates his murder. He's drawn into a crime ring which smuggles rubber (a scarce commodity during WWII). Quick pacing enlivens standard cliches. **55m/B VHS, Beta.** Damian O'Flynn, Helen Parrish, Dick Purcell, Jack LaRue, Neil Hamilton, Robert E. Homans, Anne Jeffreys, Dick Wessel, Vince Barnett; *D:* George Sherman. *SNC*

X: The Man with X-Ray Eyes 🐾🐾🐾 *The Man With the X-Ray Eyes; X* **1963** First-rate Corman has Milland gain power to see through solid materials. Predates Little Caesars campaign. **79m/C VHS, Beta, LV.** Ray Milland, Diana Van Der Vlis, Harold J. Stone, John Hoyt, Don Rickles, Dick Miller, Jonathan Haze; *D:* Roger Corman; *W:* Ray Russell, Robert Dillon; *C:* Floyd Crosby; *M:* Les Baxter. *WAR*

X, Y & Zee 🐾½ *Zee & Co* **1972 (R)** A brassy, harsh version of the menage a trois theme, wherein the vicious wife (Taylor) of a philandering (Caine) decides to avenge herself by seducing his mistress. An embarrassment for everyone involved. **110m/C VHS, Beta.** Michael Caine, Elizabeth Taylor, Susannah York, Margaret Leighton; *D:* Brian G. Hutton; *W:* Edna O'Brien; *C:* Billy Williams. *COL*

Xanadu WOOF! **1980 (PG)** Dorky star-vehicle remake (of 1947's "Down to Earth") eminently of its era, which is now better forgotten. Newton-John is a muse who descends to Earth to help two friends open a roller disco. In the process she proves that as an actor, she's a singer. Kelly attempts to soft shoe some grace into the proceedings, though he seems mystified as anyone as to why he's in the movie. Don Bluth adds an animated sequence. ♫I'm Alive; The Fall; Don't Walk Away; All Over the World; Xanadu; Magic; Suddenly; Dancing; Suspended in Time. **96m/C VHS, Beta, LV.** Olivia Newton-John, Michael Beck, Gene Kelly, Sandahl Bergman; *D:* Robert Greenwald; *W:* Richard Danus. Golden Raspberry Awards '80: Worst Director (Greenwald). *USH*

Xica 🐾 **1976** A diamond rush in 18th century Brazil transformed that country's interior into a place of undreamed wealth and excess. Black slave Xica uses her sexual allure to rise out of poverty and capture the attentions of Joao, the governor of the diamond-mining town. She gleefully wields her increasing wealth and power, becoming the unofficial Empress of Brazil. Reportedly based on a real-life character. In Portuguese with English subtitles. **109m/C VHS.** *BR* Zeze Motta, Walmor Chagas, Altair Lima, Jose Wilker, Marcus Vinicius, Elke Maravilha; *D:* Carlos Diegues; *W:* Joao Felicio. *NYF, BTV, FCT*

Xtro WOOF! **1983 (R)** An Englishman, abducted by aliens three years before, returns to his family with a deadly, transforming disease. Slime-bucket splatter flick notable for the scene where a woman gives birth to a full-grown man, and various sex slashings. **80m/C VHS, Beta, LV.** *GB* Philip Sayer, Bernice Stegers, Danny Brainin, Simon Nash, Maryam D'Abo, David Cardy, Anna Wing, Peter Mandell, Robert Fyfe; *D:* Harry Bromley Davenport. *NLC*

Xtro 2: The Second Encounter 🎬🎬 **1991 (R)** Research facility conducts an experiment to transfer people to a parallel dimension. Out of the three researchers sent to the other side, only one returns, unconscious. Turns out that he is playing host to a biohazardous creature brought over from the other dimension who escapes into the air shafts and threatens to kill everyone in the building. One more problem: if the creature isn't killed, the computer system will fill the building with radiation. Sound familiar? It should, because this is a low-budget remake of "Alien." Good photography, adequate acting, but Vincent just isn't credible as a brilliant scientist. A sequel to "Xtro" in name only. *CW:* Language and sci-fi/horror violence. **92m/C VHS, LV.** *CA* Jan-Michael Vincent, Paul Koslo, Tara Buckman, Jano Frandsen, Nicholas Lea, W.F. Wadden, Rolf Reynolds, Nic Amoroso, Tracy Westerholm; *D:* Harry Bromley Davenport. *NLC*

Xtro 3: Watch the Skies 🎬🎬 **1995 (R)** Military unit arrives at a remote island where the government has covered up a UFO landing. However, the island is now inhabited by a pissed-off alien whose mate has been killed. *CW:* Sci-fi violence and gore, strong language. **90m/C VHS, LV.** Sal Landi, Jim Hanks, Robert Culp, Andrew Divoff, Karen Moncrieff; *D:* Harry Bromley Davenport. *TRI*

The Yakuza 🎬🎬½ *Brotherhood of the Yakuza* **1975 (R)** An ex G.I. (Mitchum) returns to Japan to help an old army buddy find his kidnapped daughter. He learns the daughter has been kidnapped by the Japanese version of the Mafia (the Yakuza) and he must call on old acquaintances to help free her. A westernized oriental gangster drama with a nice blend of buddy moments, action, ancient ritual, and modern Japanese locations. **112m/C VHS, Beta, LV.** Robert Mitchum, Richard Jordan, Ken Takakura, Brian Keith, Herb Edelman; *D:* Sydney Pollack; *W:* Paul Schrader, Leonard Schrader, Robert Towne; *M:* Dave Grusin. *WAR*

Yanco 🎬🎬 **1964** A young Mexican boy makes visits to an island where he plays his homemade violin. Unfortunately, no one can understand or tolerate his love for music, save for an elderly violinist, who gives him lessons on an instrument known as "Yanco." No dialogue. Not exactly riveting, but sensitively played. **95m/B VHS, Beta.** *MX* Ricardo Ancona, Jesus Medina, Maria Bustamante. *WFV, DVT*

A Yank in Australia 🎬🎬 **1943** Australian farce/war mystery/romance/documentary tells the story of two WWII newspaper reporters whose ship gets torpedoed, stranding them in the Australian outback, where they manage to foil a Japanese invasion. **56m/B VHS, Beta, 8mm.** *AU VYY*

Yank in Libya 🎬½ **1942** No, not the American bombing raid of Khadafy, rather a low-budget WWII adventure pitting an American man and an English girl against Libyan Arabs and Nazis. **65m/B VHS, Beta.** Walter Woolf King, Joan Woodbury, H.B. Warner, Parkyakarkus. *VCI*

A Yank in the R.A.F. 🎬🎬½ **1941** Power's enthusiastic performance as a brash American pilot boosts this dated WWII adventure. He and his British allies seem more concerned over who gets showgirl Betty Grable than in the Nazis,

but climactic air attacks retain excitement. Produced by Darryl F. Zanuck to drum up American support for embattled Britain and France. **98m/B VHS, Beta.** Tyrone Power, Betty Grable, John Sutton, Reginald Gardiner; *D:* Henry King. *FOX, FCT*

Yankee Clipper 🎬🎬½ **1927** Deceit, treachery, and romance are combined in this depiction of a fierce race from China to New England between the American ship Yankee Clipper, and the English ship Lord of the Isles. Silent. **68m/B VHS, Beta.** William Boyd, Elinor Fair, Frank "Junior" Coghlan, John Miljan, Walter Long; *D:* Rupert Julian. *GPV, VYY, CCB*

Yankee Doodle Dandy 🎬🎬🎬🎬 **1942** Nostalgic view of the Golden Era of show business and the man who made it glitter—George M. Cohan. His early days, triumphs, songs, musicals and romances are brought to life by the inexhaustible Cagney in a rare and wonderful song-and-dance performance. Told in flashback, covering the Irishman's struggling days as a young song writer and performer to his salad days as the toast of Broadway. Cagney, never more charismatic, dances up a storm, reportedly inventing most of the steps on the day. 🎵Give My Regards to Broadway; Yankee Doodle Dandy; You're a Grand Old Flag; Over There; I Was Born in Virginia; Off the Record; You're a Wonderful Girl; Blue Skies, Grey Skies; Oh You Wonderful Girl. **126m/B VHS, Beta, LV, Closed Caption.** James Cagney, Joan Leslie, Walter Huston, Richard Whorf, Irene Manning, Rosemary DeCamp, Jeanne Cagney, S.Z. Sakall, Walter Catlett, Frances Langford, Eddie Foy Jr., George Tobias, Michael Curtiz; *D:* Michael Curtiz; *W:* Robert Buckner; *C:* James Wong Howe. Academy Awards '42: Best Actor (Cagney), Best Sound, Scoring of a Musical; New York Film Critics Awards '42: Best Actor (Cagney); Nominations: Academy Awards '42: Best Director (Curtiz), Best Film Editing, Best Picture, Best Story, Best Supporting Actor (Huston). *MGM, FOX, FCT*

Yankee Doodle in Berlin 🎬🎬½ **1919** A spoof of WWI dramas, with the hero dressing up as a woman and seducing the Kaiser into giving up his war plans. Typical Sennett slapstick with a music and effects score added to the silent film. **60m/B VHS, Beta.** Ford Sterling, Ben Turpin, Marie Prevost, Bothwell Browne. *GPV, CCB*

Yankee Zulu 🎬🎬 **1995 (PG)** A young black boy, Zulu, and a young white boy, Rhino, begin a friendship in their South African homeland that is torn apart by apartheid. Twenty-five years later, they are reunited by chance and forced into race-reversal roles that lead to a number of comedic disasters and a renewal of their boyhood friendship. **89m/C VHS, Closed Caption.** *SA* Leon Schuster, John Matshikiza, Wilson Dunster, Terri Treas; *D:* Gray Hofmeyr; *W:* Leon Schuster, Gray Hofmeyr. *COL*

Yanks 🎬🎬 **1979** An epic-scale but uneventful drama depicts the legions of American soldiers billeted in England during WWII, and their impact—mostly sexual—on the staid Britons. No big story, no big deal, despite a meticulous recreation of the era. **139m/C VHS, LV, Closed Caption.** Richard Gere, Vanessa Redgrave, William Devane, Lisa Eichhorn, Rachel Roberts, Chick Vennera, Arlen Dean Snyder, Annie Ross; *D:* John Schlesinger; *W:* Colin Welland, Walter Bernstein; *M:* Richard Rodney Bennett. British Academy Awards '79: Best Supporting Actress (Roberts); National Board of Review Awards '79: Best Director (Schlesinger). *USH*

A Year in Provence 🎬🎬🎬 **1989** Retired London executive Peter Mayle and his wife Annie decide to leave England to live in the south of France. They buy a 200-year-old farmhouse and experience all the trials and amusements of forging a new life in a different country, complete with different language and customs. They hoped for tranquility and what they got were eccentric neighbors, endless renovations, lots of company, and a taste for good food and drink. Based on Mayle's autobiographical novels "A Year in Provence" and "Tonjours Provence" and filmed on location. Made for British television. On four cassettes, each depicting one season of the year.

360m/C VHS. *GB* John Thaw, Lindsay Duncan, Bernard Spiegel, Jean-Pierre Delage, Maryse Kuster, Louis Lyonnet; *D:* David Tucker; *W:* Michael Sadler. *AAE, SIG, BTV*

The Year My Voice Broke 🎬🎬🎬 **1987 (PG-13)** Above average adolescent drama: a girl breaks a boy's heart by getting pregnant by a tougher, older boy; then leaves town. Blues-inducing, explicit, and not pleasant; but good acting from newcomers carries the day. Followed by "Flirting." **103m/C VHS, Beta, LV.** *AU* Noah Taylor, Leone Carmen, Ben Mendelsohn, Graeme Blundell, Lynette Curran, Malcolm Robertson, Judi Farr; *D:* John Duigan; *W:* John Duigan; *C:* Geoff Burton; *M:* Christine Woodruff. Australian Film Institute '87: Best Film. *LIV*

The Year of Living Dangerously 🎬🎬🎬½ **1982 (PG)** Political thriller features Gibson as an Australian journalist covering a political story in Indonesia, circa 1965. During the coup against President Sukarno, he becomes involved with a British attache (Weaver) at the height of the bloody fighting and rioting in Jakarta. Hunt is excellent as male photographer Billy Swan, central to the action as the moral center. Rumored to be based on the activities of CNN's Peter Arnett, although the original source is a novel by C.J. Koch, who reportedly collaborated/battled with Weir on the screenplay. Fascinating, suspenseful film, set up brilliantly by Weir. Shot on location in the Philippines (then moved to Sydney after cast and crew were threatened). First Australian movie financed by a U.S. studio. **114m/C VHS, Beta, LV, Closed Caption.** *AU* Mel Gibson, Sigourney Weaver, Linda Hunt, Michael Murphy; *D:* Peter Weir; *W:* Peter Weir, David Williamson; *C:* Russell Boyd; *M:* Maurice Jarre. Academy Awards '83: Best Supporting Actress (Hunt); Los Angeles Film Critics Association Awards '83: Best Supporting Actress (Hunt); National Board of Review Awards '83: Best Supporting Actress (Hunt); New York Film Critics Awards '83: Best Supporting Actress (Hunt). *MGM, BTV*

Year of the Comet 🎬🎬 **1992 (PG-13)** Amusing adventure/romantic comedy throws straightlaced Maggie (Miller) together with carefree Oliver (Daly) in a quest for a rare bottle of wine. Fine wine is Maggie's passion, and snagging this particular bottle will boost her status in the family business. Oliver is a pretzels and beer kind of guy, but his boss wants this bottle and will pay a lot to get it. Wants to be another "Romancing the Stone," but plot and characters are too thin. Nice chemistry between Miller and Daly sort of saves this one despite a disappointing script. Beautiful location shots of Scotland. **135m/C VHS, LV, Closed Caption.** Penelope Ann Miller, Timothy Daly, Louis Jourdan, Art Malik, Ian Richardson, Ian McNeice, Timothy Bentinck, Julia McCarthy, Jacques Mathou; *D:* Peter Yates; *W:* William Goldman; *M:* Hummie Mann. *NLC*

Year of the Dragon 🎬🎬½ **1985 (R)** Polish police Captain Stanley White of the NYPD vows to neutralize the crime lords running New York's Chinatown. Brilliant cinematography, well-done action scenes with maximum violence, a racist hero you don't want to root for, murky script, and semi-effective direction are the highlights of this tour through the black market's underbelly and hierarchy. Based on Robert Daley's novel. **136m/C VHS, Beta, LV, Closed Caption.** Mickey Rourke, John Lone, Ariane, Leonard Termo, Raymond J. Barry; *D:* Michael Cimino; *W:* Oliver Stone, Michael Cimino. *MGM*

Year of the Gun 🎬🎬½ **1991 (R)** McCarthy is an American journalist in Rome who begins a novel based on the political instability around him, using the names of real people in his first draft. Soon, ambitious photojournalist Stone wants to collaborate with him, and the Red Brigade terrorist group wants to "remove" anyone associated with the book. Although failing on occasion to balance the thin line it establishes between reality and perception, "Gun" aspires to powerful drama, offering a realistic look at the lives and priorities of political terrorists. Love scenes between Stone and McCarthy are torrid. **111m/C VHS, LV, 8mm.** Andrew McCarthy, Sharon Stone,

Valeria Golino, John Pankow, Mattia Sbragia, George Murcell; *D:* John Frankenheimer; *W:* David Ambrose, Jay Presson Allen; *M:* Bill Conti. COL

Year of the Quiet Sun 🐾🐾🐾½ 1984
(PG) A poignant, acclaimed love story about a Polish widow and an American soldier who find each other in the war-torn landscape of 1946 Europe. Beautifully rendered, with a confident sense of time and place, making this much more than a simple love story. In Polish with English subtitles. 106m/C VHS, Beta, LV. PL GE Scott Wilson, Maja Komorowska; *D:* Krzysztof Zanussi. Venice Film Festival '84: Best Film. BAR, WAR

The Yearling 🐾🐾🐾½ 1946 This family classic is a tear-jerking adaptation of the Marjorie Kinnan Rawlings novel about a young boy's love for a yearling fawn during the post civil-war era. His father's encouragement and his mother's bitterness play against the story of unqualified love amid poverty and the boy's coming of age. Wonderful footage of Florida. Jarman was awarded a special Oscar as outstanding child actor. 128m/C VHS, Beta, LV. Gregory Peck, Jane Wyman, Claude Jarman Jr., Chill Wills, Henry Travers, Jeff York, Forrest Tucker, June Lockhart, Margaret Wycherly; *D:* Clarence Brown; *C:* Charles Rosher. Academy Awards '46: Best Color Cinematography, Best Interior Decoration; Golden Globe Awards '47: Best Actor—Drama (Peck); Nominations: Academy Awards '46: Best Actor (Peck), Best Actress (Wyman), Best Director (Brown), Best Film Editing, Best Picture. KUI, MGM, TLF

The Yearling 🐾🐾½ 1994 TV remake of the classic Marjorie Kinnan Rawlings novel about a boy and his orphaned fawn. The Baxters are struggling in '30s Florida: Pa Penny (Strauss) is a hardscrabble farmer and severe Ma Ora (Smart) has lost three of her four children. Surviving son, 12-year-old Jody (Horneff), gets more than his share of life's hard lessons—with even his adored pet causing problems. On the cloying side, the 1946 big-screen version is still the one to watch. Filmed in South Carolina. 98m/C VHS. Peter Strauss, Jean Smart, Wil Horneff, Brad Greenquist, Jarred Blanchard, Philip S. Hoffman, Nancy Moore Atchison; *D:* Rod Hardy; *W:* Joe Wiesenfeld; *M:* Lee Holdridge. CAF

The Yellow Cab Man 🐾🐾½ 1950 Skelton plays a cab driver who is also an inventor of safety gadgets. When he invents unbreakable elastic glass he finds various crooks after him for the formula. Skelton's wacky inventions are amusing and the movie culminates in a breakneck chase through a home show exposition. 85m/B VHS. Red Skelton, Gloria De Haven, Walter Slezak, Edward Arnold, James Gleason, Jay C. Flippen, Paul Harvey; *D:* Jack Donohue. MGM

Yellow Cargo 🐾🐾 1936 Ingenious "B" movie about a pair of undercover agents who blow the lid off a smuggling scam. It seems that the smugglers have been masquerading as a movie crew, and use disguised Chinese "extras" to transport their goods. The agents pose as actors to infiltrate the gang. 70m/B VHS, Beta. Conrad Nagel, Eleanor Hunt, Vince Barnett, Jack LaRue, Claudia Dell; *D:* Crane Wilbur; *W:* Crane Wilbur. SNC, DVT

Yellow Dust 🐾½ 1936 Dull story of a gold miner (Dix) who hits a big strike but before he can make good on it he's accused of a series of stagecoach robberies. So he goes undercover to clear his name. Based on the play "Mother Lode" by Dan Totheroh and George O'Neil. 68m/B VHS. Richard Dix, Leila Hyams, Andy Clyde, Onslow Stevens, Moroni Olsen, Jessie Ralph; *D:* Wallace Fox. GPV

Yellow Earth 🐾🐾½ *Huang Tudi* 1989 In 1939 a soldier arrives in a small Chinese village to research folk songs. He becomes involved in the lives of a local peasant family, including a 14-year-old girl who wishes to escape from a pre-arranged marriage. Mixture of poetry, dance, music, and drama set against the barren landscape of the title. In Mandarin Chinese with English subtitles. 89m/C VHS. CH Xue Bai, Wang Xueqi, Tan Tuo, Liu Qiang; *D:* Chen Kaige; *W:* Zhang Ziliang. FXL, FCT, BTV

Yellow Hair & the Fortress of Gold 🐾½ *Yellow Hair and the Pecos Kid* 1984 (R) Princess who's part Indian and her sidekick fight bad guys and seek gold. Well-meaning, self-conscious parody. 102m/C VHS, Beta. SP Laurene Landon, Ken Robertson; *D:* Matt Cimber; *M:* Matt Cimber. LIV

The Yellow Rose of Texas 🐾🐾 1944 Rogers works as an undercover insurance agent (he's singing on a river boat) to clear the name of an old man falsely accused of a stagecoach robbery. The usual melodious Rogers lead. 55m/B VHS, Beta. Roy Rogers, Dale Evans, Grant Withers, Harry Shannon; *D:* Joseph Kane. NOS, VCN, CAB

Yellow Submarine 🐾🐾🐾½ 1968 (G) The acclaimed animated fantasy based on a plethora of mid-career Beatles songs, sees the Fab Four battle the Blue Meanies for the sake of Sgt. Pepper, the Nowhere Man, Strawberry Fields, and Pepperland. The first full-length British animated feature in 14 years features a host of talented cartoonists. Fascinating LSD-esque animation and imagery. Speaking voices provided by John Clive (John), Geoff Hughes (Paul), Peter Batten (George), and Paul Angelis (Ringo). The Beatles themselves do appear in a short scene at the end of the film. Martin fills in as music director, and Segal of "Love Story" fame co-scripts. 🎵Yellow Submarine; All You Need is Love; Hey, Bulldog; When I'm Sixty Four; Nowhere Man; Lucy in the Sky With Diamonds; Sgt. Pepper's Lonely Hearts Club Band; A Day in the Life; All Together Now. 87m/C VHS, Beta, LV. GB D: George Duning, Dick Emery; *W:* Erich Segal; *M:* George Martin. MVD, MGM

Yellowbeard 🐾🐾 1983 (PG) An alleged comedy with a great cast who wander about with little direction. Follows the efforts of an infamous pirate (Chapman) to locate a buried treasure using the map tattooed on the back of his son's head. Final role for Feldman, who died during production. 97m/C VHS, Beta, LV. Graham Chapman, Peter Boyle, Richard "Cheech" Marin, Thomas Chong, Peter Cook, Marty Feldman, Martin Hewitt, Michael Hordern, Eric Idle, Madeline Kahn, James Mason, John Cleese, Susannah York, David Bowie; *D:* Mel Damski; *W:* Graham Chapman, Peter Cook, Bernard McKenna. VES

Yellowneck 🐾🐾 1955 A handful of Confederate Army soldiers desert, hoping to cross the Florida Everglades and eventually reach Cuba. The swamp takes its toll, however, and one by one the men fall by the wayside. A sole survivor reaches the coast. Will the escape boat be waiting for him? 83m/C VHS. Lin McCarthy, Stephen Courtleigh, Berry Kroeger, Harold Gordon, Bill Mason; *D:* R. John Hugh. FCT

Yellowstone 🐾🐾 1936 An ex-con is murdered at Yellowstone National Park, at the site of a hidden cache of money, of which assorted folks are in search. Uncomplicated, well-meaning mystery. 65m/B VHS, Beta, 8mm. Andy Devine, Ralph Morgan, Judith Barrett; *D:* Arthur Lubin. NOS, DVT, VYY

Yentl 🐾🐾½ 1983 (PG) The famous Barbra adaptation of Isaac Bashevis Singer's story set in 1900s Eastern Europe about a Jewish girl who masquerades as a boy in order to study the Talmud, and who becomes enmeshed in romantic miscues. Lushly photographed, with a repetitive score that nevertheless won an Oscar. Singer was reportedly appalled by the results of Streisand's hyper-controlled project. 🎵A Piece of Sky; No Matter What Happens; This Is One of Those Moments; Tomorrow Night; Where Is It Written; No Wonder; The Way He Makes Me Feel; Papa, Can You Hear Me; Will Someone Ever Look at Me That Way?. 134m/C VHS, Beta, LV, Closed Caption. Barbra Streisand, Mandy Patinkin, Amy Irving, Nehemiah Persoff, Steven Hill, Allan Corduner, Ruth Goring, David DeKeyser, Bernard Spear; *D:* Barbra Streisand; *C:* David Watkin; *M:* Michel Legrand, Alan Bergman, Marilyn Bergman. Academy Awards '83: Original Song Score and/or Adaptation; Golden Globe Awards '84: Best Director (Streisand), Best Film—Musical/Comedy; Nominations: Academy Awards '83: Best Art Direction/Set Decoration, Best Song ("Papa, Can You Hear Me?", "The Way He

Makes Me Feel"), Best Supporting Actress (Irving). MGM, IME

Yes, Giorgio 🐾🐾 1982 (PG) Opera singer Pavarotti in his big-screen debut. He has an advantage over other non-actors trapped in similar situations (e.g., Hulk Hogan): He can sing (but of course, not wrestle). Lame plot (famous opera star falls for lady doctor) is the merest excuse for the maestro to belt out "If We Were in Love," "I Left My Heart in San Francisco," and arias by Verdi, Donizetti, and Puccini. 111m/C VHS, Beta, LV. Luciano Pavarotti, Kathryn Harrold, Eddie Albert, James Hong; *D:* Franklin J. Schaffner; *W:* Norman Steinberg; *M:* John Williams. Nominations: Academy Awards '82: Best Song ("If We Were in Love"). MGM

Yes, Sir, Mr. Bones 🐾½ 1951 Entertaining but dated musical about a boy who wanders into a rest home and inspires the old folks there to reminisce about their days as riverboat minstrels. 🎵I Want to Be a Minstrel Man; Stay Out of the Kitchen; Is Your Rent Paid Up in Heaven?; Flying Saucers; Memphis Bill; Southland. 60m/B VHS, Beta. Pete Daily, Jimmy O'Brien, Sally Anglim, Cotton Watts, Chick Watts, Chet Davis, F.E. Miller, Scatman Crothers; *D:* Ron Ormond; *W:* Ron Ormond. NO

The Yesterday Machine woof! 1963 Camp sci-fi: A mad doctor tries to bring back Hitler. Don't worry, though: the good guys win. Predictable, dumb drivel. 85m/B VHS, Beta. Tim Holt, James Britton, Jack Herman; *D:* Russ Marker. SNC, VCD

Yesterday, Today and Tomorrow 🐾🐾🐾½ *Ieri, Oggi E Domani; She Got What She Asked For* 1964 Trilogy of comic sexual vignettes featuring Loren and her many charms. She plays a black marketeer, a wealthy matron, and a prostitute. Funny, and still rather racy. Loren at her best, in all senses; includes her famous striptease for Mastroianni. 119m/C VHS. IT FR Sophia Loren, Marcello Mastroianni, Tony Pica, Giovanni Ridolfi; *D:* Vittorio De Sica. Academy Awards '64: Best Foreign Language Film; British Academy Awards '64: Best Actor (Mastroianni). JEF, HHE

Yesterday's Hero 🐾½ 1979 A fading soccer star finds his career and love-life on the upswing. Poor production with equally lame pop music score. 95m/C VHS, Beta. GB Ian McShane, Suzanne Somers, Adam Faith, Paul Nicholas, Glynis Barber, Sandy Ratcliff; *D:* Neil Leifer; *W:* Jackie Collins. HHE

Yesterday's Target 🐾🐾 1996 (R) Paul (Baldwin), Jessica (Haiduk), and Carter (Carter) all possess special psychic powers in their future society, which is on the verge of destruction. They're sent back in time to rescue a young boy who may hold the key to saving their world but a glitch leaves them with collective amnesia and ruthless hunter Holden (McDowell) on their trail. 80m/C VHS, Closed Caption. Daniel Baldwin, Stacy Haiduk, T.K. Carter, LeVar Burton, Malcolm McDowell, Trevor Goddard; *D:* Barry Samson. REP

Yidl Mitn Fidl 🐾🐾 *Yiddle with a Fiddle; Castle in the Sky* 1936 Disguised as a man, a young woman travels about the countryside with a group of musicians, revealing their female identity only after falling for a man. One of Picon's finest roles and Green's biggest successes. Vaudevillian fare in Yiddish with English subtitles. 🎵Yiddle With His Fiddle; Arye With His Bass. 92m/B VHS, Beta. PL Molly Picon, Simche Fostel, Max Bozyk, Leon Liebgold; *D:* Joseph Green. ERG, DVT, TPV

Yin & Yang of Mr. Go 🐾 1971 (R) A CIA operative must retrieve the stolen plans of an awesome weapons system. Set in Hong Kong, features a strong cast in a tangled tale of no particular merit. Unworthy spoof of Oriental intrigue flicks. 89m/C VHS, Beta. Jeff Bridges, James Mason, Broderick Crawford, Burgess Meredith; *D:* Burgess Meredith; *W:* Burgess Meredith. NO

Yodelin' Kid From Pine Ridge 🐾½ *The Hero of Pine Ridge* 1937 Autry tries to stop a war between cattlemen and woodsmen in Georgia. Standard horse opera notable for its location. 59m/B VHS, Beta. Gene Autry, Smiley Burnette, Betty Bronson,

Charles Middleton, Art Mix; **D:** Joseph Kane. *NOS, VCN, DVT*

Yog, Monster from Space 🎦 *The Space Amoeba* 1971 (G)

When a spaceship crashes somewhere near Japan, the aliens in it create monsters out of ordinary critters in order to destroy all the cities. A promoter gets a gleam in his eye and sees the potential for a vacation spot featuring the viscious creatures. Standard Japanese monster flick utilizing the usual out-of-synch dub machine. Dubbed. 105m/C VHS, Beta. *JP* Akira Kubo, Yoshio Tsuchiya; **D:** Inoshiro Honda. *SNC*

Yojimbo 🎦🎦🎦🎦 1961

Two clans vying for political power bid on the services of a samurai (Mifune) who comes to town. The samurai sells his services to both parties, with devastating results for all. In Japanese with English subtitles or dubbed. Re-made by Sergio Leone as the western "A Fist Full of Dollars." 110m/B VHS, Beta, LV, 8mm. *JP* Toshiro Mifune, Eijiro Tono, Suuzu Yamda, Seizaburo Kawazu, Isuzu Yamada; **D:** Akira Kurosawa; **W:** Hideo Oguni, Shinobu Hashimoto, Akira Kurosawa; **M:** Masaru Sato. Nominations: Academy Awards '61: Best Costume Design (B & W). *VYY, HHT, NOS*

Yol 🎦🎦🎦½ 1982 (PG)

Five Turkish prisoners are granted temporary leave to visit their families. An acclaimed, heartfelt film, written by Guney while he himself was in prison. A potent protest against totalitarianism. In Turkish with English subtitles. 126m/C VHS, Beta. *TU* Tarik Akan, Serif Sezer; **D:** Serif Goren; **W:** Yilmaz Guney; **M:** Sebastian Argol. Cannes Film Festival '82: Best Film. *COL, AUD*

Yolanda and the Thief 🎦🎦½ 1945

A charming, forgotten effort from the Arthur Freed unit about a con man who convinces a virginal South American heiress that he is her guardian angel. Songs include a lengthy Dali-esque ballet built around "Will You Marry Me?" 🎵This is the Day for Love; Angel; Yolanda; Coffee Time; Will You Marry Me. 109m/C VHS, Beta. Fred Astaire, Lucille Bremer, Leon Ames, Mildred Natwick; **D:** Vincente Minnelli; **C:** Charles Rosher; **M:** Arthur Freed, Harry Warren. *MGM*

Yongkari Monster of the Deep 🎦 *Dai Koesu Yongkari; Monster Yongkari; Great Monster Yongkari* 1967 (PG)

A giant burrowing creature is causing earthquakes and generally ruining scores of Japanese models. Dubbed. 79m/C VHS, Beta. Oh Young Il, Nam Chung-Im; **D:** Kim Ki-dak. *ORI*

Yor, the Hunter from the Future 🎦 *Il Mondo Di Yor; The World of Yor* 1983 (PG)

Lost in a time warp where the past and the future mysteriously collide, Yor sets out on a search for his real identity, with his only clue a golden medallion around his neck. 88m/C VHS, Beta, LV. *IT* Reb Brown, Corinne Clery, John Steiner; **D:** Anthony (Antonio Margheriti) Dawson; **W:** Anthony (Antonio Margheriti) Dawson, Robert Bailey. *COL*

You Can't Cheat an Honest Man 🎦🎦🎦 1939

The owner of a misfit circus suffers a variety of headaches including the wisecracks of Charlie McCarthy. Contains Field's classic ping-pong battle and some of his other best work. 79m/B VHS, Beta. W.C. Fields, Edgar Bergen, Constance Moore, Eddie Anderson, Mary Forbes, Thurston Hall; **D:** George Marshall; **C:** Milton Krasner. *BAR*

You Can't Fool Your Wife 🎦🎦 1940

Ball in two roles gives zip to this otherwise ordinary marital comedy. Previously blah hubby has a fling; previously blah better half wins him back with glamour. 69m/C VHS, Beta. Lucille Ball, James Ellison, Robert Coote, Emma Dunn, Nita Naldi; **D:** Ray McCarey. *TTC*

You Can't Hurry Love 🎦 1988 (R)

A jilted-at-the-altar Ohio bachelor moves to Los Angeles and flounders in the city's fast-moving fast lane. A dull film with Fonda, daughter of "Easy Rider" Peter, playing a minor role. 92m/C VHS, Beta, LV. David Leisure, Scott McGinnis, Sally Kellerman, Kristy McNichol, Charles Grodin, Anthony Geary, Bridget Fonda, David Packer, Frank Bonner; **D:** Richard Martini; **C:** Peter Collister. *LIV, VES*

You Can't Take It with You 🎦🎦🎦½ 1938

The Capra version of the Kaufman-Hart play about an eccentric New York family and their nonconformist houseguests. Alice Sycamore (Arthur), the stable family member of an offbeat clan of free spirits, falls for Tony Kirby (Stewart), the down-to-earth son of a snooty, wealthy and not always quite honest family. Amidst the confusion over this love affair, the two families rediscover the simple joys of life. 127m/B VHS, Beta, LV, **Closed Caption.** James Stewart, Jean Arthur, Lionel Barrymore, Spring Byington, Edward Arnold, Mischa Auer, Donald Meek, Samuel S. Hinds, Ann Miller, H.B. Warner, Halliwell Hobbes, Dub Taylor, Mary Forbes, Eddie Anderson, Harry Davenport, Lillian Yarbo; **D:** Frank Capra; **W:** Robert Riskin. Academy Awards '38: Best Director (Capra), Best Picture; Nominations: Academy Awards '38: Best Cinematography, Best Film Editing, Best Screenplay, Best Sound, Best Supporting Actress (Byington). *COL, BTV*

You Can't Take It with You 🎦🎦🎦 1984

Taped performance of the Kaufman and Hart comedy about the strange pastimes of the Sycamore family who must behave themselves to impress their daughter's boyfriend's stuffy family. 116m/C VHS, Beta, LV. Colleen Dewhurst, James Coco, Jason Robards Jr., Elizabeth Wilson, George Rose; **D:** Ellis Raab. *COL, VES, LIV*

You Light Up My Life woof! 1977 (PG)

Sappy sentimental story of a young singer trying to break into the music business. Debbie Boone's version of the title song was a radio smash, the constant playing of which drove many people over the edge. 🎵You Light Up My Life. 91m/C VHS, Beta. Didi Conn, Michael Zaslow, Melanie Mayron; **D:** Joseph Brooks; **W:** Joseph Brooks; **M:** Joseph Brooks. Academy Awards '77: Best Song ("You Light Up My Life"); Golden Globe Awards '78: Best Song ("You Light Up My Life") *COL*

You Must Remember This 199? When

Uncle Buddy (Guillaume) receives a mysterious trunk, Ella's curiosity gets the best of her. She opens the trunk to discover a number of old movies made by W.B. Jackson—Uncle Buddy. Ella takes the films to a movie archive to find out about her uncle's past as an independent black filmmaker. After researching the history of black cinema, Ella convinces her uncle to be proud of his contribution to the film world. Includes a viewers' guide. Part of the "Wonderworks" series. 110m/C VHS. Robert Guillaume, Tim Reid, Daphne Maxwell Reid, Vonetta McGee. *PME, HMV, BTV*

You Only Live Once 🎦🎦½ 1937

Ex-con Fonda wants to mend his ways and tries to cross into Canada with his girlfriend in tow. Impressively scripted, but a glum and dated Depression-era tale. 86m/B VHS, Beta. Henry Fonda, Sylvia Sidney, Ward Bond, William Gargan, Barton MacLane, Margaret Hamilton, Jean Dixon, Warren Hymer, Chic Sale, Guinn "Big Boy" Williams, Jerome Cowan, John Wray, Jonathan Hale, Ben Hall, Jean Stoddard, Wade Boteler, Henry Taylor, Walter DePalma; **D:** Fritz Lang. *NO*

You Only Live Twice 🎦🎦½ 1967 (PG)

007 travels to Japan to take on arch-nemesis Blofeld, who has been capturing Russian and American spacecraft in an attempt to start WWIII. Great location photography; theme sung by Nancy Sinatra. Implausible plot, however, is a handicap, even though this is Bond. 125m/C VHS, Beta, LV. *GB* Sean Connery, Mie Hama, Akiko Wakabayashi, Tetsuro Tamba, Karin Dor, Charles Gray, Donald Pleasence, Tsai Chin, Bernard Lee, Lois Maxwell, Desmond Llewelyn; **D:** Lewis Gilbert; **C:** Frederick A. (Freddie) Young; **M:** John Barry. *MGM, TLF*

You So Crazy 🎦½ *Martin Lawrence You So Crazy* 1994

Scandalous star of television show "Martin" and host of HBO's "Def Comedy Jam" follows in the footsteps of raunchy humorists Richard Pryor and Eddie Murphy. Threatened with an NC-17 rating, Lawrence refused to edit and Miramax, the original distributor, dropped it. It was picked up by Samuel Goldwyn, who released the original version, uncut and unrated. Filmed live at the Brooklyn Academy of Music, Lawrence

displays too little of his considerable talent, and too much vulgarity and poor taste. 85m/C VHS. Martin Lawrence; **D:** Thomas Schlamme; **C:** Arthur Albert. *HBO*

You Talkin' to Me? 🎦 1987 (R)

Fledgling actor who idolizes De Niro moves to the West Coast for his big break. He fails, so he dyes his hair blond and digs the California lifestyle. Embarrassingly bad. 97m/C VHS, Beta. Chris Winkler, Jim Youngs, Faith Ford; **D:** Charles Winkler; **W:** Charles Winkler. *MGM*

You Were Never Lovelier 🎦🎦🎦½ 1942

Charming tale of a father who creates a phony Romeo to try to interest his daughter in marriage. Astaire appears and woos Hayworth in the flesh. The dancing, of course, is superb, and Hayworth is stunning. 🎵Dearly Beloved; I'm Old Fashioned; Shorty George; Wedding in the Spring; You Were Never Lovelier. 98m/B VHS, Beta, LV. Fred Astaire, Rita Hayworth, Leslie Brooks, Xavier Cugat, Adolphe Menjou, Larry Parks; **D:** William A. Seiter; **M:** Jerome Kern, Johnny Mercer. Nominations: Academy Awards '42: Best Song ("Dearly Beloved"), Best Sound, Scoring of a Musical. *COL*

You'll Find Out 🎦🎦 1940

A comic mix of music and mystery as Kay Kyser and his Band, along with a debutante in distress, are terrorized by Lugosi, Karloff, and Lorre. 🎵The Bad Humor; I'd Know You Anywhere; You've Got Me This Way; Like the Fella Once Said; I've Got a One-Track Mind; Don't Think it Ain't Been Charming. 97m/B VHS, Beta. Kay Kyser, Boris Karloff, Bela Lugosi, Dennis O'Keefe, Helen Parrish; **D:** David Butler. Nominations: Academy Awards '40: Best Song ("I'd Know You Anywhere"). *HHT, MLB*

You'll Never Get Rich 🎦🎦🎦 1941

A Broadway dance director is drafted into the Army, where his romantic troubles cause him to wind up in the guardhouse more than once. He of course gets the girl. Exquisitely funny. 🎵Since I Kissed My Baby Goodbye; The A-stairable Rag; Shootin' the Works for Uncle Sam; Wedding Cake Walk; Dream Dancing; Boogie Barcarolle; So Near and Yet So Far. 88m/B VHS, Beta, LV. Fred Astaire, Rita Hayworth, Robert Benchley; **D:** Sidney Lanfield. Nominations: Academy Awards '41: Best Song ("Since I Kissed My Baby Goodbye"), Scoring of a Musical, Best Original Score. *COL*

The Young Americans 🎦🎦 1993 (R)

Tough New York cop John Harris (Keitel) is sent to London to aid the police with their investigations into a series of killings related to a drug smuggling operation working out of the club scene. Harris wants to tie everything to the sleazeball gangster Carl Frazer (Mortensen) that he's been trailing. Slick formula with hard-working cast. Debut for 25-year-old director Cannon. 108m/C VHS, LV. *GB* Harvey Keitel, Viggo Mortensen, Iain Glen, John Wood, Keith Allen, Craig Kelly, Thandie Newton, Terence Rigby; **D:** Danny Cannon; **M:** Danny Cannon, David Hilton; **M:** David Arnold. *LIV*

Young & Free 🎦½ 1978

Following the death of his parents, a young man must learn to face the perils of an unchartered wilderness alone. Ultimately he must choose between returning to civilization, or remain with his beloved wife and life in the wild. 87m/C VHS, Beta. Erik Larsen; **D:** Keith Larsen. *MON*

Young and Innocent 🎦🎦🎦 *The Girl Was Young* 1937

Somewhat uneven thriller about a police constable's daughter who helps a fugitive prove he didn't strangle a film star. 80m/B VHS, Beta, LV. *GB* Derrick DeMarney, Nova Pilbeam, Percy Marmont, Edward Rigby, Mary Clare, John Longden, George Curzon, Basil Radford, Pamela Carme, George Merritt, J.H. Roberts, Jerry Verno, H.F. Maltby, John Miller, Beatrice Varley, Syd Crossley, Frank Atkinson, Torin Thatcher; **D:** Alfred Hitchcock; **W:** Charles Bennett, Alma Reville, Gerald Savory, Antony Armstrong, Edwin Greenwood. *SNC, NOS, VDM*

The Young and the Guilty 🎦🎦 1958

Two star-crossed teenagers are frustrated in their romance when their parents find one of their love letters and hit the ceiling. Told not to see each other again, the two take to sneaking around, which adds an edge to their relationship. Moving performances by the two young leads. **65m/B VHS.** Phyllis Calvert, Andrew Ray, Edward Chapman, Janet Munro, Campbell Singer; *D:* Peter Cotes. *NOS*

Young & Willing 🐾🐾½ 1942 A group of struggling actors gets hold of a terrific play and tries various schemes to get it produced. Based on the Broadway Play "Out of the Frying Pan" by Francis Swann. Unexceptional but enjoyable comedy. **83m/B VHS, Beta.** William Holden, Susan Hayward, Eddie Bracken, Robert Benchley, Martha O'Driscoll, Barbara Britton; *D:* Edward H. Griffith; *W:* Virginia Van Upp. *NO*

Young Aphrodites 🐾🐾½ *Mikres Aphrodites* 1963 Two young teenagers of a primitive Greek tribe discover sexuality. An acclaimed film retelling the myth of Daphnis and Chloe. Narrated in English. **87m/B VHS, Beta.** *GR D:* Nikos Koundouros. Berlin International Film Festival '63: Best Director (Koundouros). *NLC*

Young at Heart 🐾🐾½ 1954 Fanny Hurst's lighthearted tale of a cynical hard-luck musician who finds happiness when he falls for a small town girl. A remake of the 1938 "Four Daughters." ♫Young at Heart; Someone to Watch Over Me; One for My Baby; Hold Me in Your Arms; Ready, Willing and Able; Till My Love Comes Back to Me; There's a Rising Moon For Every Falling Star; You, My Love. **117m/C VHS.** Frank Sinatra, Doris Day, Gig Young, Ethel Barrymore, Dorothy Malone, Robert Keith, Elisabeth Fraser, Alan Hale Jr.; *D:* Gordon Douglas; *W:* Julius J. Epstein, Liam O'Brien. *REP*

Young Bess 🐾🐾🐾½ 1953 Simmons and real-life husband Granger star in this splashy costume drama about 16th century England's young Queen. Features outstanding performances by Simmons as Elizabeth I and Laughton (repeating his most famous role) as Henry VIII. Based on the novel by Margaret Irwin. **112m/C VHS.** Jean Simmons, Stewart Granger, Deborah Kerr, Charles Laughton, Kay Walsh, Guy Rolfe, Kathleen Byron, Cecil Kellaway, Rex Thompson; *D:* George Sidney; *W:* Jan Lustig, Arthur Wimperis; *C:* Charles Rosher; *M:* Miklos Rozsa. Nominations: Academy Awards '53: Best Art Direction/Set Decoration (Color), Best Costume Design (Color). *MGM*

Young Bill Hickok 🐾🐾 1940 A Rogers vehicle in the form of a very fictionalized biography of the famous gunfighter. **54m/B VHS, Beta.** Roy Rogers, George "Gabby" Hayes. *NOS, DVT, TIM*

Young Blood 🐾🐾 1933 A cowboy robs from the rich to help the poor. He's also interested in a foreign actress having trouble bonding with the townfolk. Lots of old fashioned western violence. **61m/B VHS, Beta.** Bob Steele, Charles "Blackie" King, Helen Foster; *D:* Phil Rosen. *NOS, DVT*

The Young Bruce Lee 19?? Bruce learns and uses the deadly skills that made him famous while only knee-high to a grasshopper. **90m/C VHS, Beta.** Han Kwok Choi. *MGI*

Young Buffalo Bill 🐾🐾 1940 Buffalo Bill battles the Spanish land-grant patrons. **54m/B VHS, Beta.** Roy Rogers, George "Gabby" Hayes, Pauline Moore; *D:* Joseph Kane. *NOS, DVT*

Young Caruso 🐾 1951 Dramatic biography of legendary tenor Enrico Caruso, following his life from childhood poverty in Naples to the beginning of his rise to fame. Dubbed in English. **78m/B VHS, Beta.** Gina Lollobrigida, Ermanno Randi, Mario del Monaco. *VYY, NOS, MVD*

Young Catherine 🐾🐾🐾 1991 Made-for-TV account of Russia's strongest female ruler, the girl who would be Catherine the Great. Star-studded cast and excellent production values. Script and strong cast make Ormond look like a lightweight. Filmed in Leningrad. Also available in 186-minute version. **150m/C VHS, Beta, Closed Caption.** Vanessa Redgrave, Christopher Plummer, Marthe Keller, Franco Nero, Julia Ormond, Maximilian Schell, Reece Dinsdale, Mark Frankel; *D:* Michael Anderson Sr.; *W:* Chris Bryant. *TTC*

Young Charlie Chaplin 🐾🐾 1988 A British-made TV biography of the legendary silent screen comic. **160m/C VHS, Beta.** Ian McShane, Twiggy; *M:* Rachel Portman. *NO*

A Young Connecticut Yankee in King Arthur's Court 🐾🐾½ 1995 A modern-day teenager timetravels back to the court of King Arthur and Camelot. Based on the book by Mark Twain. **93m/C VHS.** Michael York, Theresa Russell, Nick Mancuso, Philippe Ross, Jack Langedijk, Polly Shannon, Paul Hopkins; *D:* R.L. Thomas; *W:* R.L. Thomas, Frank Encarnacao; *C:* John Berrie; *M:* Alan Reeves. *CAF*

Young Doctors in Love 🐾🐾 1982 (R) Spoof of medical soap operas features a chaotic scenario at City Hospital, where the young men and women on the staff have better things to do than attend to their patients. Good cast keeps this one alive, though many laughs are forced. Includes cameos by real soap star, including then-General Hospital star Moore. **95m/C VHS, Beta, LV.** Dabney Coleman, Sean Young, Michael McKean, Harry Dean Stanton, Hector Elizondo, Patrick Macnee, Pamela Reed, Saul Rubinek; *Cameos:* Demi Moore, Janine Turner; *D:* Garry Marshall; *W:* Michael Elias, Rich Eustis; *M:* Maurice Jarre. *PAR, VES*

Young Dragon 🐾½ 1977 (R) The Young Dragon's girlfriend is kidnapped by the underworld society, and he sets out to rescue her single-handedly. **90m/C VHS.** Yang Sze, Lo Lai, Yuen Man Chi, Wong Ching, Nora Miao. *SUN*

Young Einstein 🐾🐾 1989 (PG) A goofy, irreverent Australian farce starring, directed, co-scripted and co-produced by Serious, depicting Einstein as a young Outback clod who splits beer atoms and invents rock and roll. Winner of several Aussie awards. Fun for the kids. **91m/C VHS, Beta, LV, Closed Caption.** *AU* Yahoo Serious, Odile Le Clezio, John Howard, Pee Wee Wilson, Su Cruickshank; *D:* Yahoo Serious; *W:* Yahoo Serious; *M:* Martin Armiger. *WAR*

Young Frankenstein 🐾🐾🐾🐾 1974 (PG) Young Dr. Frankenstein (Wilder), a brain surgeon, inherits the family castle back in Transylvania. He's skittish about the family business, but when he learns his grandfather's secrets, he becomes obsessed with making his own monster. Wilder and monster Boyle make a memorable song-and-dance team to Irving Berlin's "Puttin' on the Ritz," and Hackman's cameo as a blind man is inspired. Garr ("What knockers!" "Oh, sank you!") is adorable as a fraulein, and Leachman ("He's vass my—boyfriend!") is wonderfully scary. Wilder saves the creature with a switcheroo, in which the doctor ends up with a certain monster-sized body part. Hilarious parody. **108m/B VHS, Beta, LV, Closed Caption.** Peter Boyle, Gene Wilder, Marty Feldman, Madeline Kahn, Cloris Leachman, Teri Garr, Kenneth Mars, Richard Haydn; *Cameos:* Gene Hackman; *D:* Mel Brooks; *W:* Gene Wilder, Mel Brooks; *M:* John Morris. Nominations: Academy Awards '74: Best Adapted Screenplay, Best Sound.*FOX, HMV*

The Young Graduates 🐾 1971 (PG) Hormonally imbalanced teens come of age in spite of meandering plot. Features "Breaking Away" star Christopher in big screen debut. **99m/C VHS.** Patricia Wymer, Steven Stewart, Gary Rist, Bruce Kirby, Jennifer Ritt, Dennis Christopher; *D:* Robert Anderson. *ACA*

Young Guns 🐾🐾½ 1988 (R) A sophomoric Wild Bunch look-alike that ends up resembling a western version of the Bowery Boys. Provides a portrait of Billy the Kid and his gang as they move from prairie trash to demi-legends. Features several fine performances by a popular group of today's young stars. **107m/C VHS, Beta, LV, Closed Caption.** Emilio Estevez, Kiefer Sutherland, Lou Diamond Phillips, Charlie Sheen, Casey Siemaszko, Dermot Mulroney, Terence Stamp, Terry O'Quinn, Jack Palance, Brian Keith, Patrick Wayne, Sharon Thomas; *D:* Christopher Cain; *W:* John Fusco; *M:* Anthony Marinelli, Brian Backus, Brian Banks. *LIV, VES*

Young Guns 2 🐾🐾 1990 (PG-13) Brat Pack vehicle neo-Western sequel about Billy the Kid (Estevez) and his gang. This time they're making a run for the border with the law on their trail. **105m/C VHS, LV, Closed Caption.** Emilio Estevez, Kiefer Sutherland, Lou Diamond Phillips, Christian Slater, William L. Petersen, Alan Ruck, R.D. Call, James Coburn, Balthazar Getty, Jack Kehoe, Rob Knepper, Jenny Wright, Tracey Walter, Ginger Lynn Allen, Jon Bon Jovi; *D:* Geoff Murphy; *W:* John Fusco; *M:* Alan Silvestri. Golden Globe Awards '91: Best Song ("Blaze of Glory"); Nominations: Academy Awards '90: Best Song ("Blaze of Glory"). *FXV, BTV, CCB*

The Young in Heart 🐾🐾🐾 1938 A lonely, old woman allows a family of con-artists into her life for companionship. Impressed by her sweet nature, the parasitic brood reforms. The cute comedy was a real crowd-pleaser in its day, especially after the bittersweet ending was replaced with a happier variety. Based on the novel "The Gay Banditti" by I.A.R. Wylie. **90m/C VHS.** Janet Gaynor, Douglas Fairbanks Jr., Paulette Goddard, Roland Young, Billie Burke, Minnie Dupree, Richard Carlson, Charles Halton; *D:* Richard Wallace; *W:* Charles Bennett, Paul Osborn. Nominations: Academy Awards '38: Best Cinematography, Best Original Score. *NO*

Young Ivanhoe 🐾🐾½ 1995 Ivanhoe learns how to be a warrior, with some help from Robin Hood and the Black Knight, inspiring others to follow him into battle to save their land from seizure by the Norman invaders. **96m/C VHS.** Stacy Keach, Nick Mancuso, Margot Kidder, Kris Holdenried, Rachel Blanchard, Matthew Daniels; *D:* R.L. Thomas; *W:* R.L. Thomas, Frank Encarnacao; *C:* John Berry; *M:* Alan Reeves. *CAF*

Young Lady Chatterly 2 🐾½ 1985 A poor sequel to the popular MacBride film, with only the name of the Lawrence classic. Chatterly inherits the family mansion and fools around with the servants and any one else who comes along. Unrated version with 13 minutes of deleted footage is also available. **87m/C VHS, Beta, LV.** Sybil Danning, Adam West, Harlee MacBride; *D:* Alan Roberts. *LIV*

The Young Land 🐾½ 1959 Less-than-inspiring western does feature a good performance by Hopper as malcontent bully Hatfield Carnes. Carnes kills a respected Mexican in a barroom gunfight in 1848 California and sheriff Jim Ellison (Wayne) is quick to call territorial judge Isham (O'Herlihy) to insure a fair trial—with the rest of the Spanish-speaking town looking on in skepticism. Based on the story "Frontier Frenzy" by John Reese. **88m/C VHS.** Dennis Hopper, Patrick Wayne, Dan O'Herlihy, Yvonne Craig, Ken Curtis, Pedro Gonzalez-Gonzalez; *D:* Ted Tetzlaff; *W:* Norman S. Hall; *C:* Winton C. Hoch, Henry Sharp; *M:* Dimitri Tiomkin. Nominations: Academy Awards '59: Best Song ("Strange Are the Ways of Love"). *HTV*

The Young Lions 🐾🐾🐾 1958 A cynical WWII epic following the experiences of a young American officer and a disillusioned Nazi in the war's last days. Martin does fine in his first dramatic role. As the Nazi, Brando sensitively considers the belief that Hitler would save Germany. A realistic anti-war film. **167m/B VHS, Beta, LV.** Marlon Brando, Montgomery Clift, Dean Martin, Hope Lange, Barbara Rush, Lee Van Cleef, Maximilian Schell; *D:* Edward Dmytryk; *W:* Edward Anhalt. Nominations: Academy Awards '58: Best Black and White Cinematography, Best Sound, Original Dramatic/Comedy Score. *FOX*

Young Love, First Love 🐾½ 1979 A made-for-television movie about a young woman who must decide whether to have sex with her boyfriend. Sound familiar? Pretty blah, earnest story, though well cast. **100m/C VHS, Beta.** Valerie Bertinelli, Leslie Ackerman, Timothy Hutton, Arlen Dean Snyder, Fionnula Flanagan; *D:* Steven Hilliard Stern. *LIV*

Young Love—Lemon Popsicle 7 🐾 1987 (R) Three hunks stalk the beaches in search of babes. **91m/C VHS, Beta.** Yftach Katzur, Zachi Noy, Jonathan Segall, Sonja Martin; *D:* Walter Bennett. *WAR*

Young Man with a Horn ♂♂♂ 1950 Dorothy Baker's novel, which was loosely based on the life of jazz immortal Bix Beiderbecke, was even more loosely adapted for this film, featuring Kirk as an angst-ridden trumpeter who can't seem to hit that mystical "high note." ♫The Very Thought of You; I May be Wrong; The Man I Love; Too Marvelous for Words; With a Song in My Heart; Pretty Baby; I Only Have Eyes for You; Limehouse Blues; Melancholy Rhapsody. 112m/B VHS, Beta, LV. Kirk Douglas, Doris Day, Lauren Bacall, Hoagy Carmichael; **D:** Michael Curtiz. WAR

Young Master ♂♂ 1980 Chan, searching for his missing brother, is mistaken for a fugitive and has to save himself from bounty hunters and police. Oh, and get the real bad guys so he can clear his name. Chinese with subtitles or dubbed. 90m/C VHS, LV. HK Jackie Chan; **D:** Jackie Chan. TAI

Young Mr. Lincoln ♂♂♂½ 1939 A classy Hollywood biography of Lincoln in his younger years from log-cabin country boy to idealistic Springfield lawyer. A splendid drama, and one endlessly explicated as an American masterpiece by the French auteur critics in "Cahiers du Cinema." 100m/B VHS, Beta, LV, Closed Caption. Henry Fonda, Alice Brady, Marjorie Weaver, Arleen Whelan, Eddie Collins, Ward Bond, Donald Meek, Richard Cromwell, Eddie Quillan, Charles Halton; **D:** John Ford; **W:** Lamar Trotti. National Board of Review Awards '39: 10 Best Films of the Year; Nominations: Academy Awards '39: Best Story. FOX

The Young Nurses ♂♂ Nightingale 1973 (R) The fourth entry in the Roger Corman produced "nurses" series. Three sexy nurses uncover a drug ring run from their hospital, headed by none other than director Fuller. Also present is Moreland, in his last role. Preceded by "The Student Nurses," "Private Duty Nurses," "Night Call Nurses," followed by "Candy Stripe Nurses." Also on video as "Young L.A. Nurses 3." 77m/C VHS, Beta. Jean Manson, Ashley Porter, Angela Gibbs, Zack Taylor, Dick Miller, Jack LaRue, William Joyce, Sally Kirkland, Allan Arbus, Mary Doyle, Don Keefer, Nan Martin, Mantan Moreland, Samuel Fuller; **D:** Clinton Kimbrough. NLC

Young Nurses in Love ♂ 1989 (R) Low-budget sex farce in which a foreign spy poses as a nurse to steal sperm from a sperm bank donated by world leaders, celebrities and geniuses. 82m/C VHS, Beta, LV. Jeanne Marie, Alan Fisher, Barbra Robb, James Davies; **D:** Chuck Vincent. LIV, VES

The Young One ♂♂½ La Joven; Island of Shame 1961 Traver (Hamilton) is a black jazz musician who escapes from his southern town when he's wrongly accused of raping a white woman. He hides out on a small island which is used as a private hunting ground for rich sportsmen, overseen by Miller (Scott), the game keeper. Hamilton gets work as the new handyman and becomes close to the young Evalyn (Meersman). When Miller rapes Evalyn, it's Traver who's once again accused until things can be put right. Racist elements are heavy-handed; one of Bunuel's lesser efforts. Based on the story "Travelin' Man" by Peter Matthiessen. 94m/C VHS. MX Bernie Hamilton, Zachary Scott, Kay Meersman, Claudio Brook, Graham Denton; **D:** Luis Bunuel; **W:** Hugo Butler, Luis Bunuel. CVC, FCT

The Young Ones 1988 Three episodes from the hilarious, offbeat British television sitcom about four violently eccentric college roommates. Episodes included are "Oil," "Boring," and "Flood." 96m/C VHS, Beta. GB Rik Mayall, Ade Edmondson, Nigel Planer, Christopher Ryan, Alexei Sayle; **D:** Geoffrey Posner. FOX

Young People ♂♂½ 1940 (G) Temple's 12 in this lesser vehicle and almost-adolescence doesn't serve her well with this tired plot. She's an orphan adopted by showbiz team Oakie and Greenwood who've decided to retire to rural life. They even get to put on a show to prove to the small-minded small-towners what a swell trio they are. Temple's last film for 20th-Century Fox does include nostalgic clips from earlier Shirley hits, including "Stand Up and Cheer" and "Curly Top," to explain her character's background. ♫Tra-La-La; Fifth Avenue; I Wouldn't Take a Million; The Mason-Dixon Line; Young People. 78m/C VHS, Closed Caption. Shirley Temple, Jack Oakie, Charlotte Greenwood, Arleen Whelan, George Montgomery, Kathleen Howard; **D:** Allan Dwan; **W:** Edwin Blum, Don Ettlinger. FXV

The Young Philadelphians ♂♂♂ The City Jungle 1959 Ambitious young lawyer Newman works hard at making an impression on the snobbish Philadelphia upper crust. As he schemes and scrambles, he woos debutante Rush and defends buddy Vaughn on a murder charge. Long, but worth it. Part of the "A Night at the Movies" series, this package simulates a 1959 movie evening with a Bugs Bunny cartoon, "People Are Bunny," a newsreel and coming attractions for "The Nun's Story" and "The Hanging Tree." 136m/B VHS, Beta. Paul Newman, Barbara Rush, Alexis Smith, Billie Burke, Brian Keith, John Williams, Otto Kruger, Robert Vaughn; **D:** Vincent Sherman; **C:** Harry Stradling; **M:** Ernest Gold. Nominations: Academy Awards '59: Best Black and White Cinematography, Best Costume Design (B & W), Best Supporting Actor (Vaughn). WAR

The Young Poisoner's Handbook ♂♂♂ 1994 (R) Based on the true story of London teenager Graham (O'Conor), who's obsessed with chemistry and at odds with his stepmother. So, he poisons her chocolates and she dies. Sent to Broadmoor prison for the criminally insane, Graham comes under the care of Dr. Ziegler (Sher), who, eight years later, recommends Graham for parole. Now working in a photographic lab, Graham decides to experiment with doctoring his co-workers tea—which results in eight more deaths before Graham is caught. Locked up again, Graham spends his time writing a poisoner's handbook for Dr. Ziegler. Be warned that the sufferings of the poisoned victims are gruesome.**CW:** Murders by poisoning, language and some nude photos. 99m/C VHS, Closed Caption. GB Hugh O'Conor, Anthony Sher, Ruth Sheen, Charlotte Coleman, Roger Lloyd Pack, Paul Stacey, Samantha Edmonds, Charlie Creed-Miles; **D:** Benjamin Ross; **W:** Benjamin Ross, Jeff Rawle; **C:** Hubert Taczanowski; **M:** Robert Lane, Frank Strobel. CAF

Young Sherlock Holmes ♂♂ 1985 (PG-13) Holmes and Watson meet as schoolboys. They work together on their first case, solving a series of bizarre murders gripping London. Watch through the credits for an interesting plot twist. Promising "what if" sleuth tale crashes and burns, becoming a typical high-tech Spielberg film. Second half bears too strong a resemblance to "Indiana Jones and the Temple of Doom." 109m/C VHS, Beta, LV, 8mm, Closed Caption. Nicholas Rowe, Alan Cox, Sophie Ward, Freddie Jones, Michael Hordern; **D:** Barry Levinson; **W:** Chris Columbus; **M:** Bruce Broughton. PAR

Young Tiger ♂♂ 1980 (R) First a ninety-minute movie never before seen in the U.S. featuring an expert in martial arts who is accused of murder. Next is a twelve-minute documentary featuring Jackie Chan, kung-fu sensation, demonstrating his skills. What an evening. 102m/C VHS, Beta. Jackie Chan. GEM

Young Tom Edison ♂♂½ 1940 Two teenaged years in the life of Thomas Alva Edison, as he drives his family crazy with his endless experiments on his way to becoming the famed inventor. Rooney manages to be enthusiastic without being overwhelming. Followed by "Edison the Man," with Spencer Tracy in the adult role. 82m/B VHS, Beta. Mickey Rooney, Fay Bainter, George Bancroft, Virginia Weidler, Eugene Pallette, Victor Kilian, Bobby Jordan, Lloyd Corrigan; **D:** Norman Taurog; **W:** Dore Schary, Bradbury Foote, Hugo Butler. MGM, FCT, BTV

Young Warlord ♂♂ 1975 Arthur roams western England in 500 AD, leading a band of guerrilla cavalrymen. When the Saxons invade, Arthur unites the tribe, holds off the attack and becomes king. 97m/C VHS, Beta. Oliver Tobias, Michael Gothard, Jack Watson, Brian Blessed; **D:** Peter Sasdy. NO

Young Warriors ♂½ 1983 (R) Frat boys turn vigilante to avenge a street gang murder. Weird mix of teen sex comedy, insufferable self-righteous preachiness, and violence. 104m/C VHS, Beta. Ernest Borgnine, James Van Patten, Richard Roundtree, Lynda Day George, Dick Shawn; **D:** Lawrence Foldes; **W:** Lawrence Foldes, Richard Matheson, Russell W. Colgin; **C:** Mac Ahlberg. MGM

Young Winston ♂♂♂ 1972 (PG) Based on Sir Winston Churchill's autobiography "My Early Life: A Roving Commission." Follows him through his school days, journalistic career in Africa, early military career, and his election to Parliament at the age of 26. Ward is tremendous as the prime minister-to-be. 145m/C VHS, Beta. GB Simon Ward, Robert Shaw, Anne Bancroft, John Mills, Jack Hawkins, Ian Holm, Anthony Hopkins, Patrick Magee, Edward Woodward, Jane Seymour; **D:** Richard Attenborough. Golden Globe Awards '73: Best Foreign Film; Nominations: Academy Awards '72: Best Art Direction/Set Decoration, Best Costume Design, Best Story & Screenplay. COL, TVC

Youngblood ♂♂ 1986 (R) An underdog beats the seemingly insurmountable odds and becomes a hockey champion. Some enjoyable hockey scenes although the success storyline is predictable. 111m/C VHS, Beta, LV. Rob Lowe, Patrick Swayze, Cynthia Gibb, Ed Lauter, George Finn, Fionnula Flanagan, Keanu Reeves; **D:** Peter Markle. MGM

Younger & Younger ♂♂½ 1994 (R) Jonathan Younger (Sutherland) is forced to run the family storage business after his long-suffering wife Penny (Davidovich) dies. The business starts to fail, even after Jonathan's son (Fraser) arrives to help out, and the widower begins having visions of the woman he mistreated. And each time he sees her she looks younger and more beautiful than ever. 97m/C VHS, LV, Closed Caption. Donald Sutherland, Brendan Fraser, Lolita Davidovich, Sally Kellerman, Julie Delpy, Linda Hunt; **D:** Percy Adlon; **W:** Percy Adlon, Felix Adlon; **C:** Bernd Heinl; **M:** Hans Zimmer. PAR

Your Place or Mine ♂½ 1983 Self-indulgent made-for-television yuppie pap about middle-aged singles trying to find the right mate. 100m/C VHS, Beta. Bonnie Franklin, Robert Klein, Peter Bonerz, Tyne Daly, Penny Fuller; **D:** Robert Day; **M:** Gerald Alters. LIV

Your Ticket Is No Longer Valid ♂ 1984 (R) Prurient excuse for a serious drama. Impotent failed businessman has disturbing erotic dreams about his girlfriend. Adapted from a novel by Romain Gary. 96m/C VHS, Beta. CA Richard Harris, George Peppard, Jeanne Moreau; **D:** George Kaczender. VES

Your Turn Darling ♂♂ A Toi De Faire; Mignonne 1963 French espionage thriller with Constantine once again playing Lemmy Caution, a U.S. secret agent involved with a gang of spies. 93m/C VHS. FR Eddie Constantine, Gaia Germani, Elga Andersen; **D:** Bernard Borderie. SNC

You're a Big Boy Now ♂♂♂ 1966 Kastner, a virginal young man working in the New York Public Library, is told by his father to move out of his house and grow up. On his own, he soon becomes involved with man-hating actress Hartman and a discotheque dancer. A wild and weird comedy. Coppola's commercial directorial debut. 96m/C VHS, Beta. Elizabeth Hartman, Geraldine Page, Peter Kastner, Julie Harris, Rip Torn, Michael Dunn, Tony Bill, Karen Black; **D:** Francis Ford Coppola; **W:** Francis Ford Coppola. Nominations: Academy Awards '66: Best Supporting Actress (Page). WAR

You're a Good Man, Charlie Brown 1987 A filmed version of Charles Schulz's Broadway musical, based on his famous characters. 60m/C VHS, Beta. BAR, KAR

You're in Love, Charlie Brown 1967 The animated Peanuts gang in a new adventure about Charlie Brown and the proverbial little red-haired girl. 30m/C VHS, Beta. BAR

You're Jinxed, Friend, You've Met Sacramento 🎗🎗 1970 The tongue-in-cheek adventures of a cool-headed cowboy as he passes from town to colorful town. Great title, too. 99m/C VHS, Beta. Ty Hardin, Christian Hay, Jenny Atkins; *D:* George Cristallini. UNI

Yours, Mine & Ours 🎗🎗½ 1968 Bigger, better, big screen version of "The Brady Bunch." It's the story of a lovely lady (Ball) with eight kids who marries a a widower (Fonda) who has ten. Imagine the zany shenanigans! Family comedy manages to be both wholesome and funny. Based on a true story. 114m/C VHS, Beta, LV, Closed Caption. Lucille Ball, Henry Fonda, Van Johnson, Tim Matheson, Tom Bosley, Tracy Nelson; *D:* Melville Shavelson; *W:* Melville Shavelson. MGM

Youth Aflame woof! *Hoodlum Girls* 1959 Trash film that tells the tale of two sisters—one good, one bad. Poor dialogue and weak performances do, however, make for some great camp. Based on a story by Helen Kiedy. 61m/B VHS. Joy Reese, Warren Burr, Kay Morley, Michael Owen, Rod Rogers; *D:* Elmer Clifton; *W:* Elmer Clifton. SNC

Youth on Parole 🎗½ 1937 Same old story: Boy gets paroled. Girl gets paroled. Parolee meets parolette and romance blossoms as they beat a further rap. 60m/B VHS. Marian Marsh, Gordon Oliver. LOO, VYY

You've Got to Have Heart 🎗 1977 (R) A young bridegroom's life gets complicated after he does not sexually satisfy his bride on their wedding night. 98m/C VHS, Beta. Carroll Baker, Edwige French. PSM

You've Ruined Me, Eddie 🎗 1958 A spoiled rich girl gets knocked up and her boyfriend will never know peace again. Meanwhile, their once quiet town is outraged. m/B VHS. SMW, TPV

Yukon Flight 🎗🎗 1940 A Renfrew of the Mounties adventure. The hero finds illegal gold mining operations and murder in the Yukon. 57m/B VHS, Beta. James Newill, Dave O'Brien. NOS, VCN

The Yum-Yum Girls 🎗½ 1978 (R) Pair of innocent girls arrive in New York City to pursue their dreams. Gives an inside looks at the fashion industry. Not as funny or as cute as it wants to be. 89m/C VHS, Beta. Judy Landers, Tanya Roberts, Barbara Tully, Michelle Daw; *D:* Barry Rosen. USH

Yuma 🎗🎗 1970 An old-style made-for-television Western about a sheriff (Walker) who rides into town, cleans it up, and saves his own reputation from a plot to discredit him. Dull in places, but action-packed ending saves the day. 73m/C VHS, Beta. Clint Walker, Barry Sullivan, Edgar Buchanan; *D:* Ted Post; *M:* George Duning. FOX, VTR

Yuri Nosenko, KGB 🎗🎗½ 1986 Fact-based account of a KGB defector and the CIA agent who must determine if he's on the up-and-up. Made for British television. 85m/C VHS. GB Tommy Lee Jones, Oleg Rudnik, Josef Sommer, Ed Lauter, George Morfogen, Stephen D. Newman; *D:* Mick Jackson. CNG

Z 🎗🎗🎗🎗 1969 The assassination of a Greek nationalist in the 1960s and its aftermath are portrayed by the notorious political director as a gripping detective thriller. Excellent performances, adequate cinematic techniques, and important politics in this highly acclaimed film. 128m/C VHS, Beta, LV. Yves Montand, Jean-Louis Trintignant, Irene Papas, Charles Denner, Georges Geret, Jacques Perrin, Francois Perier, Marcel Bozzuffi; *D:* Constantin Costa-Gavras; *W:* Constantin Costa-Gavras. Academy Awards '69: Best Film Editing, Best Foreign Language Film; Cannes Film Festival '69: Special Jury Prize, Best Actor (Trintignant); Edgar Allan Poe Awards '69: Best Screenplay; Golden Globe Awards '70: Best Foreign Film; New York Film Critics Awards '69: Best Director (Costa-Gavras), Best Film; National Society of Film Critics Awards '69: Best Film; Nominations: Academy Awards '69: Best Adapted Screenplay, Best Director (Costa-Gavras), Best Picture; Cannes Film Festival '69: Best Film. FXL

Zabriskie Point 🎗🎗🎗 1970 (R) Antonioni's first U.S. feature. A desultory, surreal examination of the American way of life. Worthy but difficult. Climaxes with a stylized orgy in Death Valley. 112m/C VHS, Beta, LV. Mark Frechette, Daria Halprin, Paul Fix, Rod Taylor, Harrison Ford, G.D. Spradlin; *D:* Michelangelo Antonioni; *W:* Michelangelo Antonioni, Sam Shepard, Fred Gardner, Tonino Guerra, Clare Peploe. MGM, MLB

Zachariah 🎗🎗½ 1970 (PG) A semi-spoof '60s rock western, wherein two gunfighters given to pursuing wealth-laden bands of outlaws separate and experience quixotic journeys through the cliched landscape. Scripted by members of The Firesign Theater and featuring appearances by Country Joe and The Fish, The New York Rock Ensemble and The James Gang. 93m/C VHS, Beta. Don Johnson, John Rubinstein, Pat Quinn, Dick Van Patten; *D:* George Englund. FOX

Zalmen or the Madness of God 🎗🎗½ 1975 Elie Wiesel's mystical story about a rabbi's struggle against religious persecution in post-Stalin Russia. 120m/C VHS, Beta. Joseph Wiseman. WNE

Zandalee woof! 1991 (R) The sexual adventures of a bored sexy young woman who has a fling with her husband's friend. Bad script, graphic sex. Also available in an unrated version. *CW:* Sexual dialogue and language and strong sensuality. 100m/C VHS, LV, Closed Caption. Nicolas Cage, Judge Reinhold, Erika Anderson, Viveca Lindfors, Aaron Neville, Joe Pantoliano, Ian Abercrombie, Marisa Tomei, Zach Galligan; *D:* Sam Pillsbury; *W:* Mari Kornhauser. LIV

Zandy's Bride 🎗½ 1974 (PG) Basic story about a rancher who sents for a mail-order bride. She's shocked by his ill-treatment of her and stands up to his bullying, thus winning his respect and love. Beautiful scenery, courtesy of Big Sur, California, but predictable all-around and essentially a waste of an experienced cast. Based on the novel "The Stranger" by Lillian Bos Ross. 97m/C VHS. Gene Hackman, Liv Ullmann, Eileen Heckart, Harry Dean Stanton, Joe Santos, Sam Bottoms, Susan Tyrrell, Frank Cady; *D:* Jan Troell; *W:* Marc Norman; *C:* Jordan Cronenweth; *M:* Michael Franks. WAR

The Zany Adventures of Robin Hood 🎗 1984 Hackneyed spoof of the Robin Hood legend. Medieval man robs from the rich to help the poor. Not nearly as funny as Mel Brooks' TV series that spoofed "Robin Hood." 95m/C VHS, Beta. George Segal, Morgan Fairchild, Roddy McDowall, Roy Kinnear, Janet Suzman, Tom Baker; *D:* Ray Austin. MED

Zapped! 🎗 1982 (R) Teen genius discovers he possesses telekinetic powers. He does the natural thing, using his talent to remove clothing from nearby females. A teen boy's dream come true. 98m/C VHS, Beta, LV. Scott Baio, Willie Aames, Robert Mandan, Felice Schachter, Scatman Crothers, Roger Bowen, Marya Small, Greg Bradford, Hilary Beane, Sue Ane Langdon, Heather Thomas, Merritt Butrick, LaWanda Page, Rosanne Katon; *D:* Robert J. Rosenthal; *M:* Charles Fox. NLC

Zapped Again 🎗 1989 (R) The lamebrained sequel to 1982's "Zapped" about a high schooler who has telekinetic powers and lust on his mind. 93m/C VHS, Beta, LV, 8mm. Todd Eric Andrews, Kelli Williams, Reed Rudy, Linda Blair, Karen Black, Lyle Alzado; *D:* Douglas Campbell. COL

Zardoz 🎗🎗 1973 A surreal parable of the far future, when Earth society is broken into strict classes: a society of intellectuals, a society of savages, and an elite unit of killers who keep the order. Connery is the man who destroys the old order of things. Visually interesting but pretentious. 105m/C VHS, Beta, LV. Sean Connery, Charlotte Rampling, John Alderton, Sara Kestelman; *D:* John Boorman; *W:* John Boorman. FOX

Zarkorr! The Invader 🎗 1996 (PG) Aliens studying earth decide humans need a challenge (like we don't have enough problems of our own) so they send a 185-foot tall, laser-eyed monster to crush (American) cities and cause general terror in the population. And who's our hero? A postal worker—aided by a five-inch tall alien girl. Low-budget spoof has its moments, but eventually wears thin. 80m/C VHS, LV. Rhys Pugh, Deprise Grossman, Mark Hamilton, Charles Schneider, Eileen Wesson; *D:* Aaron Osborne; *W:* Benjamin Carr; *C:* Joe C. Maxwell; *M:* Richard Band. AFE

Zatoichi: Master Ichi and a Chest of Gold 🎗🎗 1964 A violent thriller about a blind gambler and former samurai who tries to clear his name after being framed for a gold robbery. Adapted from a novel by Kazuo Miyagawa. In Japanese with English subtitles. 83m/C VHS. JP Shintaro Katsu; *D:* Kazuo Ikehiro. FCT

Zatoichi: The Blind Swordsman and the Chess Expert 🎗🎗 1965 Zatoichi, the blind gambler and former samurai, befriends a master chess player and gets involved with Japanese gangsters. In Japanese with English subtitles. 87m/C VHS. JP Shintaro Katsu; *D:* Kenji Misumi. FCT

Zatoichi: The Blind Swordsman and the Fugitives 🎗🎗 1968 This time Zatoichi, the blind masseur and master swordsman, is pitted against a band of outlaws. When the local bandits brutalize the countryside Zatoichi steps in to defend the weak and faces a showdown with outlaw leader Genpachiro. In Japanese with English subtitles. 82m/C VHS. JP Shintaro Katsu, Yumiko Nogawa, Kayo Mikimoto, Kyosuke Machida; *D:* Kimiyoshi Yasuda. FCT

Zatoichi: The Blind Swordsman's Vengeance 🎗🎗 1966 Zatoichi defends a dying man against a group of gangsters who have taken over an isolated village. In Japanese with English subtitles. 83m/C VHS. JP Shintaro Katsu, Shigeru Amachi, Kei Sato, Mayumi Ogawa; *D:* Tokuzo Tanaka. FCT

Zatoichi: The Life and Opinion of Masseur Ichi 🎗🎗 1962 The first film in the action series about the Zen-like blind masseur, gambler, and swordsman. Zatoichi is drawn into a revenge match between two ruthless gangs. When one gang tries to hire him the other hires a savage killer. This sets in motion a war between the yakuza gangs and mercenary samurai. In Japanese with English subtitles. 96m/C VHS. JP Shintaro Katsu, Masayo Mari, Ryuzo Shimada, Gen Mitamura, Shigeru Amachi; *D:* Kenji Misumi. FCT

Zatoichi vs. Yojimbo 🎗🎗🎗½ *Zatoichi Meets Yojimbo; Zato Ichi To Yojimbo* 1970 The legendary blind warrior-samurai, Zatoichi, wants to retire, but his village is being held captive by outlaws. He is forced to fight Yojimbo, the crude wandering samurai without a master, and the sparks really fly! This was a comic send-up of Akiro Kurosawa's "Yojimbo" with Mifune recreating his role here and playing it for laughs. Subtitled. 90m/C VHS. JP Toshiro Mifune, Shintaro Katsu, Osamu Takizawa; *D:* Kihachi Okamoto. VDA

Zatoichi: Zatoichi's Flashing Sword 🎗🎗 1964 Blind swordsman Zatoichi gets caught up in a feud between two competing yakuza bosses. When Zatoichi declares his alliegence to Tsumugi, the unhappy Yasu tries to get his revenge. In Japanese with English subtitles. 82m/C VHS. JP Shintaro Katsu, Mayumi Nagisa, Naoko Kubo, Ryutaro Gami, Yutaka Nakamura; *D:* Kazuo Ikehiro. FCT

Zazie dans le Metro 🎗🎗🎗½ *Zazie in the Underground; Zazie in the Subway* 1961 One of Malle's early movies, this is one of the best of the French New Wave comedies. A young girl, wise beyond her years, visits her drag queen uncle in Paris. She wants to ride the subway, but the ensuing hilarious adventures keep her from her goal. In French with English subtitles. 92m/C VHS. FR Catherine Demonget, Philippe Noiret, Carla Marlier; *W:* Louis Malle. NYF

Zebra Force 🕮 1976 (R) Group of army veterans embark on a personal battle against organized crime, using their military training with deadly precision. Non-distinguished substandard action-adventure. 81m/C VHS, Beta. Mike Lane, Richard X. Slattery, Rockne Tarkington, Glenn Wilder, Anthony Caruso; *D:* Joe Tornatore. *MED*

Zebra in the Kitchen 🕮🕮½ 1965 A 12-year-old boy living in a small town is upset when he sees the run-down condition of the local zoo. So he decides to set all the animals free, which causes pandemonium in the town. Pleasant family fare. 92m/C VHS. Jay North, Martin Milner, Andy Devine, Joyce Meadows, Jim Davis; *D:* Ivan Tors. *MGM, BTV*

Zebrahead 🕮🕮🕮 1992 (R) Zack and Nikki are two high schoolers in love—which would be okay except Zack's white and Nikki's black. Writer/director Drazan's expressive debut features one of last appearances by Sharkey as Zack's dad. Outstanding performances by the young and largely unknown cast, particularly Rapaport and Wright, and a great musical score enrich the action. Filmed on location in Detroit, with plenty of authentic Motown scenery to chew on, including Cody High School and a shootout at the eastside Skateland. Developed with assistance by the Sundance Institute.*CW:* Strong language. 102m/C VHS, LV, 8mm, Closed Caption. Michael Rapaport, N'Bushe Wright, Ray Sharkey, DeShonn Castle, Ron Johnson, Marsha Florence, Paul Butler, Abdul Hassan Sharif, Dan Ziskie, Candy Ann Brown, Helen Shaver, Luke Reilly, Martin Priest, Kevin Corrigan; *D:* Tony Drazan; *W:* Tony Drazan; *C:* Maryse Alberti; *M:* Taj Mahal. Sundance Film Festival '92: Filmmakers Trophy. *COL*

A Zed & Two Noughts 🕮🕮🕮 1988 A serio-comic essay by the acclaimed British filmmaker. Twin zoologists, after their wives are killed in an accident, explore their notions of death by, among other things, filming the decay of animal bodies absconded from the zoo. Heavily textured and experimental; Greenaway's second feature film. 115m/C VHS, Beta. *GB* Eric Deacon, Brian Deacon, Joss Ackland, Andrea Ferreol, Frances Barber; *D:* Peter Greenaway; *W:* Peter Greenaway; *C:* Sacha Vierny; *M:* Michael Nyman. *TPV*

Zelig 🕮🕮🕮½ 1983 (PG) Documentary spoof stars Allen as Leonard Zelig, the famous "Chameleon Man" of the 1920s, whose personality was so vague he would assume the characteristics of those with whom he came into contact, and who had a habit of showing up among celebrities and at historic events. Filmed in black-and-white; intersperses bits of newsreel and photographs with live action. Allen-style filmmaking at its best. 79m/B VHS, Beta, LV, 8mm. Woody Allen, Mia Farrow, Susan Sontag, Saul Bellow, Irving Howe; *D:* Woody Allen; *W:* Woody Allen; *C:* Gordon Willis. New York Film Critics Awards '83: Best Cinematography; Nominations: Academy Awards '83: Best Cinematography, Best Costume Design. *WAR*

Zelly & Me 🕮🕮🕮 *Phoebe* 1988 (PG) A strange little drama about a young orphan living with her maniacally possessive grandmother, who forces the child into her own interior life through humiliation and isolation from anyone she cares for. Well-acted and interesting film that suffers from an overly introspective plot and confusing gaps in the narrative. Look for director Lynch on the other side of the camera. 87m/C VHS, Beta, LV, Closed Caption. Isabella Rossellini, Alexandra Johnes, David Lynch, Glynis Johns, Kaiulani Lee, Joe Morton; *D:* Tina Rathborne; *W:* Tina Rathborne; *C:* Mikael Salomon; *M:* Pino Donaggio. *COL*

Zentropa 🕮🕮 1992 (R) Clever cinematic allusions and visuals aside, this is essentially a conventional thriller. German-American pacifist Leopold travels to Germany in 1945 to help in the postwar rebuilding. He finds work as a sleeping-car conductor for a giant railway system called Zentropa and finds himself romancing the mysterious Katharina, who draws the hapless Leopold into an intrigue involving Nazi sympathizers. Director von Trier uses the voice of Von Sydow as an omniscient narrator to address the audience and move the story along. Filmed primarily in black-and-white with bursts of color denoting dramatic moments. In English and German with English subtitles.*CW:* Violent scenes. 112m/C VHS, Beta, LV, Closed Caption. *GE* Jean-Marc Barr, Barbara Sukowa, Udo Kier, Eddie Constantine; *D:* Lars von Trier; *W:* Niels Vorsel, Lars von Trier. *TOU*

Zeppelin 🕮🕮½ 1971 (G) During WWI, the British enlist the aid of York as a double agent. His mission is to steal Germany's plans for a super-dirigible. Accompanying the Germans on the craft's maiden voyage, York discovers they are actually on a mission to steal British treasures. Although the script is poor, the battle scenes and the blimp itself are very impressive. 102m/C VHS, Beta, LV, Closed Caption. *GB* Michael York, Elke Sommer, Peter Carsten, Marius Goring, Anton Diffring, Andrew Keir, Rupert Davies, Alexandra Stewart; *D:* Etienne Perier. *WAR, FCT*

Zeram 🕮🕮 1991 Zeram is a giant renegade space alien lured to earth by a female bounty hunter. How does she expect to capture it? Why with a warp machine, space bazooka, electric shield, and a computer named Bob, of course. Dubbed. 92m/C VHS. *JP* Yuko Moriyama, Yukihiro Hotaru, Kunihiko Ida; *D:* Keita Amemiya; *W:* Hajime Matsumoto. *FXL, FCT*

Zero 1984 WWII story about the building of the zero fighter that was used to devastating effect in the invasion of Pearl Harbor. 128m/C VHS, Beta. Yuzo Kayama, Tetsuro Tamba; *D:* Toshio Masuda. *NO*

Zero Boys woof! 1986 (R) Teenage survivalists in the Californian wilderness are stalked by a murderous lunatic. Exploitative and mean-spirited. 89m/C VHS, Beta. Daniel Hirsch, Kelli Maroney, Nicole Rio, Joe Phelan; *D:* Nico Mastorakis. *LIV*

Zero Degrees Kelvin 🕮🕮½ *Zero Degrees Kelvin; Kjaerlighetens Kjotere* 1995 Brrrr! Get the ice scraper ready, because you may have to clear off your TV screen in this chilly tale of trappers in 1920's Greenland. Henrik Larsen (Eidsvold), a poet living in Oslo, decides to join the band of trappers after his girlfriend Gertrude (Martens) spurns his marriage proposal. On his arrival in the stark and frozen landscape, he is forced to share a cabin with the stoic, silent Holm (Sundquist) and the lewd, violent Randbaek (Skarsgard). Randbaek holds the newcomer and his city-boy ways in disdain, creating an air of tension and menace that inevitably results in a clash between the two. Instead of dwelling on the action aspect, director Moland uses the minimalist landscape to echo the psychological battles the men must face with the frigid terrain and between themselves. Norwegian with subtitles. 113m/C VHS. *NO* Garb B. Eidsvold, Stellan Skarsgard, Bjorn Sundquist, Camilla Martens; *D:* Hans Petter Moland; *W:* Hans Petter Moland, Lars Bill Lundheim; *C:* Philip Ogaard; *M:* Terje Rypdal. *NYR*

Zero for Conduct 🕮🕮🕮🕮 *Zero de Conduit* 1933 Vigo's classic French fantasy about an outrageous rebellion of schoolboys against bureaucratic adults. More of a visual poem than a drama, it inspired Lindsay Anderson's "If...." One of only four films created by Vigo before his early death. Banned across Europe at release. In French with English subtitles. 49m/B VHS, Beta. *FR* Jean Daste, Robert Le Flon, Louis Lef'evre, Constantin Kelber, Gerard de Bedarieux; *D:* Jean Vigo; *W:* Jean Vigo; *C:* Boris Kaufman. *VYY, NOS, HHT*

Zero for Conduct/Taris/A Propos de Nice 1991 Three short films by the famed Jean Vigo. "Zero for Conduct" is a fascinating and fluid surrealist film about rebellion in a boy's prep school. "Taris" consists of underwater footage of the swimmer Jean Taris, and "A Propos de Nice" is a documentary that focuses on the great economic schism of the rich and the poor in the popular French vacation spot, Nice. 75m/B VHS. *FR* *D:* Jean Renoir. *NO*

Zero Patience 🕮🕮 1994 Yes, it's an audacious film musical about AIDS myths and ghosts and Victorian explorers—among other things. Infamous Patient Zero (Fauteux) is the Canadian flight attendant reputed to have carried the virus to North America. Ghostly Zero pleads for someone to tell his story and his cause is taken up by Victorian explorer Sir Richard Francis Burton (Robinson), who happens to have achieved eternal life after an encounter with the Fountain of Youth, and who is also preparing an exhibit on contagious diseases. Sharp mix of politics, humor, and fantasy. 100m/C VHS. *CA* John Robinson, Normand Fauteux, Dianne Heatherington, Ricardo Keens-Douglas; *D:* John Greyson; *W:* John Greyson; *M:* Glenn Schellenberg. *CCN*

Zero Population Growth 🕮½ *Z.P.G.* 1972 In the 21st century the government has decreed that no babies may be born for a 30-year span in order to control the population. But Chaplin and Reed secretly have a child and when they are discovered are sent to be executed. Can they escape? Maudlin and simplistic. 95m/C VHS. Oliver Reed, Geraldine Chaplin, Diane Cilento, Don Gordon; *D:* Michael Campus; *W:* Frank de Felitta, Max Ehrlich. *PAR*

Zero to Sixty 🕮 1978 (PG) Newly divorced man finds his car has been repossessed for non-payment. Seeking out the manager of the finance company, he gets a job as a repo man with a sassy 16-year-old girl as his assistant. Repartee develops, stuff happens, and the movie ends. 96m/C VHS, Beta. Darren McGavin, Sylvia Miles, Denise Nickerson, Joan Collins; *D:* Don Weis; *M:* John Beal.

Zero Tolerance 🕮🕮½ 1993 (R) FBI agent Jeff Douglas (Patrick) is assigned to travel to Mexico and pick up a drug-runner who works for the White Hand cartel, whose latest product is liquid heroin. When they are ambushed Douglas is forced to carry a shipment of drugs across the border—the lives of his wife and child hang in the balance. But after the dirty deed is done, Douglas finds his family has been murdered anyway. So he sets out to execute the cartel druglords.*CW:* Language and violence and drug-related scenes. 92m/C VHS, LV, Closed Caption. Robert Patrick, Miles O'Keeffe, Mick Fleetwood, Titus Welliver, Jeffrey Anderson-Gunter, Gustav Nintas, Michael Gregory, Maurice Lamont; *D:* Joseph Merhi; *W:* Jacobsen Hart. *PMH, WEA*

Zertigo Diamond Caper 🕮 1982 Utilizing his heightened senses, a blind boy solves a diamond caper and proves his mother's innocence. 50m/C VHS, Beta. Adam Rich, David Groh, Jane Elliot. *GEM*

Zeus and Roxanne 🕮🕮 1996 (PG) Hey, I know! Let's combine "Flipper" and "Benji" with "The Parent Trap!" You know, for the kids! Marine biologist and single mom Mary Beth (Quinlan) meets her unconventional (and conveniently widowed) new neighbor Terry (Guttenberg) and his dog Zeus. Cuteness ensues. Mary Beth's daughters and Terry's young son go about getting the two adults together. Meanwhile, Zeus and Roxanne, Mary Beth's dolphin, strike up a unique friendship of their own. Showing up to provide drama is evil guy Claude (Vosloo), who is vying for the same grant as Mary Beth. Unlikely animal couple steals the show, and the story would have benefitted from focusing on the entertaining bond between those two and less on the human romance. Not much appeal for anyone over the age of nine. 98m/C VHS, Closed Caption, DVD. Kathleen Quinlan, Steve Guttenberg, Arnold Vosloo, Miko Hughes, Dawn McMillan, Majandra Delfino, Jennifer Howell; *D:* George Miller; *W:* Tom Benedek; *C:* David Connell; *M:* Bruce Rowland. *HBO*

Ziegfeld Follies 🕮🕮½ 1946 A lavish revue of musical numbers and comedy sketches featuring many MGM stars of the WWII era. Highlights include Astaire and Kelly's only duet and a Astaire-Bremer ballet number. ♫Bring on Those Wonderful Men; Bring on Those Beautiful Girls; The Drinking Song; La Traviata; This Heart is

Mine; Love; When Television Comes; There's Beauty Everywhere; The Babbitt and the Bromide. **115m/C VHS, Beta, LV.** Fred Astaire, Judy Garland, Gene Kelly, Red Skelton, Fanny Brice, William Powell, Jimmy Durante, Edward Arnold, Lucille Bremer, Hume Cronyn, Victor Moore, Lena Horne, Lucille Ball, Esther Williams; **D:** Vincente Minnelli; **C:** Charles Rosher. *MGM, MLB*

Ziegfeld Girl 🎬🎬🎬 1941 Three star-struck girls are chosen for the Ziegfeld follies and move on to success and heartbreak. Lavish costumes and production numbers in the MGM style. 🎵You Stepped Out of a Dream; I'm Always Chasing Rainbows; Minnie from Trinidad; Mr. Gallagher & Mr. Shean; You Never Looked So Beautiful. **131m/B VHS, Beta, LV.** James Stewart, Judy Garland, Hedy Lamarr, Lana Turner, Tony Martin, Jackie Cooper, Ian Hunter, Charles Winninger, Al Shean, Edward Everett Horton, Philip Dorn, Paul Kelly, Eve Arden, Dan Dailey, Fay Holden, Felix Bressart, Mae Busch, Reed Hadley; **D:** Robert Z. Leonard. *MGM*

Zipperface 🎬 1992 A Palm Beach serial killer is making mincemeat of the local prostitutes. In order to capture the scum, the prerequisite beautiful police detective goes undercover only to find herself the killer's biggest threat. **90m/C VHS, LV.** Dona Adams, David Clover, John Dagnen; **D:** Mansour Pourmand. *AIP*

Zis Boom Bah 🎬½ 1942 Musical-comedy star buys a cafe for his college son. He and his friends transform the place into a restaurant-theater with predictable results. 🎵Annabella; It Makes No Difference When You're In the Army; Put Your Trust in the Moon; Zis Boom Bah; Good News Tomorrow; I've Learned to Smile Again. **61m/B VHS, Beta.** Peter Lind Hayes, Mary Healy, Grace Hayes, Huntz Hall, Benny Rubin. *NOS, HEG, DVT*

The Zodiac Killer 🎬½ 1971 (R) Based on a true story, this tells the violent tale of the San Francisco murders that occurred in the late 1960s. Doesn't have the suspense it should. **87m/C VHS, Beta.** Tom Pittman, Hal Reed, Bob Jones, Ray Lynch; **D:** Tom Hanson. *ACA*

Zoltan...Hound of Dracula 🎬½ *Dracula's Dog* 1978 The vampire and his bloodthirsty dog go to Los Angeles to find the last of Count Dracula's living descendants. Campy and just original enough to make it almost worth watching. **85m/C VHS, Beta.** Michael Pataki, Reggie Nalder, Jose Ferrer; **D:** Albert Band; **W:** Frank Ray Perilli; **M:** Andrew Belling. *REP, VCI, FCT*

Zombie 🎬 *Zombie Flesh Eaters* 1980 Italianmade white-men-in-the-Caribbean-with-flesh-eating-zombies cheapie. **91m/C VHS, Beta, LV.** Tisa Farrow, Ian McCulloch, Richard Johnson, Al Cliver, Arnette Gay, Olga Karlatos, Stefania Dafmario; **D:** Lucio Fulci. *VES*

Zombie and the Ghost Train 🎬 *Zombie ja Kummitusjuna* 1991 Absurdist punk comedy about the vicissitudes of a down-and-out bass player. Finnish with subtitles. **88m/C VHS.** **FI D:** Mika Kaurismaki; **W:** Mika Kaurismaki; **C:** Olli Varja; **M:** Mauri Sumen. *FRF*

The Zombie Army 🎬 1993 Tough drill sergeant tries to whip a bunch of raw female recruits up to muster for a special mission. Toward that end, the government has conveniently bought a defunct lunatic asylum as a training ground. Only problem is that a few of the former inmates have been left behind and are able to menace the troops with their penchant for psychotic weirdness. **80m/C VHS.** Eileen Saddow. *TEM, MOV*

Zombie High 🎬 *The School That Ate My Brain* 1987 (R) Students at a secluded academy are being lobotomized by the school president. Mindless, in two senses of the word. **91m/C VHS, Beta.** Virginia Madsen, Richard Cox, Kay E. Kuter, James Wilder, Sherilyn Fenn, Paul Williams, Scott Coffey; **D:** Ron Link. *VTR*

Zombie Island Massacre 🎬 1984 (R) In this trying film, tourists travel to see a voodoo ritual, and then are systematically butchered by the rite-inspired zombies. Featuring former con-

gressional wife and Playboy Magazine model Jenrette. **89m/C VHS, Beta.** Rita Jenrette, David Broadnax; **D:** John N. Carter. *TTV, MED*

Zombie Lake 🎬 1984 Killed in an ambush by villagers during WWII, a group of Nazi soldiers turned zombies reside in the town's lake, preying on unsuspecting swimmers, especially dog paddling nude young women. Laughable FX, almost bad enough to be good. From the team that produced "Oasis of the Zombies." **90m/C VHS.** **FR SP** Howard Vernon, Pierre Escourrou, Anouchka, Anthony Mayans, Nadine Pascale, Jean Rollin; **D:** J.A. Laser. *VCI*

Zombie Nightmare woof! 1986 (R) A murdered teenager is revived by a voodoo queen and slaughters his punk-teen assailants. Cheap and stupid just about sums this one up. Music by Motorhead, Death Mask, Girlschool and Thor. **89m/C VHS, Beta.** Adam West, Jon Mikl Thor, Tia Carrere, Frank Dietz, Linda Singer, Mandn E. Turbride, Hamibh McEwen; **D:** John Bravman. *NWV*

Zombies of Moratau woof! 1957 A diver and his girlfriend seek to retrieve an undersea treasure of diamonds protected by zombies. So boring you'll want to die. **70m/B VHS, Beta.** Gregg Palmer, Allison Hayes, Jeff Clark, Autumn Russel, Joel Ashley; **D:** Edward L. Cahn. *COL, MLB*

Zombies of the Stratosphere *Satan's Satellites* 1952 A serial in twelve chapters in which a cosmic policeman fights Zombies attempting to blow the Earth out of orbit. Also available in a 93 minute, colorized version. **152m/B VHS, Beta, LV.** Judd Holdren, Aline Towne, Leonard Nimoy, John Crawford, Ray Boyle; **D:** Fred Brannon. *REP, VCN, MLB*

Zombies on Broadway 🎬🎬½ *Loonies On Broadway* 1944 Two press agents travel to the Caribbean in search of new talent, but find Lugosi performing experiments on people and turning them into sequel material. RKO hoped this would be equally successful follow-up to "I Walked with a Zombie." **68m/B VHS, LV.** Wally Brown, Alan Carney, Bela Lugosi, Anne Jeffreys, Sheldon Leonard, Frank Jenks, Russell Hopton, Joseph Vitale, Ian Wolfe, Louis Jean Heydt, Darby Jones, Sir Lancelot; **D:** Gordon Douglas. *TTC, FCT, IME*

Zombiethon 🎬½ 1986 A campy compilation of clips from cheapo zombie films, such as "Space Zombies," "Zombie Lake," and "The Invisible Dead." **90m/C VHS, Beta.** Dominique Singleton, Janelle Lewis, Tracy Burton. *NO*

Zone of the Dead 🎬 1978 A mortician is using his morgue for other than embalming—and it isn't pretty! **81m/C VHS, Beta.** John Ericson, Ivor Francis, Charles Aidman, Bernard Fox. *NO*

Zone Troopers 🎬½ 1984 (PG) Five American G.I.'s in WWII-ravaged Europe stumble upon a wrecked alien spacecraft and enlist the extraterrestrial's help in fending off the Nazis. **86m/C VHS, Beta.** Timothy Van Patten, Tim Thomerson, Art LaFleur, Biff Manard; **D:** Danny Bilson; **W:** Danny Bilson, Paul DeMeo; **C:** Mac Ahlberg; **M:** Richard Band. *LIV*

Zontar, the Thing from Venus 🎬 1966 Scientist is taken over by alien batlike thing from Venus, and attempts to take over the Earth. A parody of itself. **68m/C VHS.** John Agar, Anthony Huston, Susan Bjorman, Pat Delaney, Warren Hammack; **D:** Larry Buchanan; **W:** Larry Buchanan; **C:** John Alcott. *SNC, VDM*

The Zoo Gang 🎬½ 1985 (PG-13) A group of teens want to open a nightclub. Will they bring their dream to fruition, or will the mean rival gang foil their plans? **96m/C VHS, Beta.** Jackie Earle Haley, Tiffany Helm, Ben Vereen, Jason Gedrick, Eric Gurry; **D:** John Watson, Pen Densham; **W:** John Watson, Pen Densham; **M:** Patrick Gleeson. *NWV, VTR*

Zooman 🎬🎬🎬 1995 (R) Hard-hitting message on violence and responsibility. Gang member Zooman (Kain) spots members of a rival gang in a Brooklyn neighborhood, whips out his gun, and begins firing. When the shooting stops, a little girl sitting on her stoop is dead—what's even worse for her estranged parents is the fact that obvious witnesses refuse to identify the gunman

for fear of their own safety. So father Reuben (Gossett Jr.) puts up a sign about their plight, attracting lots of media attention, and neighborhood hostility. Based on Fuller's 1978 play "Zooman and the Sign." Made for cable TV.**CW:** Strong language; some violent content. **95m/C VHS, Closed Caption.** Louis Gossett Jr., Charles S. Dutton, Khalil Kain, Cynthia Martells, CCH Pounder, Vondie Curtis-Hall, Hill Harper; **D:** Leon Ichaso; **W:** Charles Fuller. *REP*

Zoot Suit 🎬🎬🎬 1981 (R) Based on Luis Valdez' play, this murder mystery/musical is rooted in the historical Sleepy Lagoon murder in the 1940s. Valdez plays a Mexican-American accused of the crime. His friends (and defense lawyers) rally around him to fight this travesty of justice. Lots o'music and dancing. **104m/C VHS, LV.** Edward James Olmos, Daniel Valdez, Tyne Daly, Charles Aidman, John Anderson; **D:** Luis Valdez; **W:** Luis Valdez. *USH, FCT*

Zora Is My Name! 🎬🎬½ 1990 The funny, moving story of Zora Neal Hurston, a Black writer known for her stories and folklore of the rural South of the '30s and '40s. From PBS's American Playhouse. **90m/C VHS, LV.** Ruby Dee, Louis Gossett Jr. *PBS, KAR, FCT*

Zorba the Greek 🎬🎬🎬½ *Zormba* 1964 A young British writer (Bates) comes to Crete to find himself by working his father's mine. He meets Zorba, an itinerant Greek laborer (Quinn), and they take lodgings together with an aging courtesan, who Zorba soon romances. The writer, on the other hand, is attracted to a lovely young widow. When she responds to him, the townsmen jealously attack her. Zorba teaches the young man the necessary response to life and its tragedies. Based on a novel by Nikos Kazantzakis. Masterpiece performance from Quinn. Beautifully photographed, somewhat overlong. Film later written for stage production. **142m/B VHS, Beta, LV.** Anthony Quinn, Alan Bates, Irene Papas, Lila Kedrova; **D:** Michael Cacoyannis; **C:** Walter Lassally. Academy Awards '64: Best Art Direction/Set Decoration (B & W), Best Black and White Cinematography, Best Supporting Actress (Kedrova); National Board of Review Awards '64: 10 Best Films of the Year, Best Actor (Quinn); Nominations: Academy Awards '64: Best Actor (Quinn), Best Adapted Screenplay, Best Director (Cacoyannis), Best Picture. *FXV, BTV, FUS*

Zorro Rides Again 1937 Zorro risks his life to outwit enemy agents endeavoring to secure ancestor's property. In twelve chapters, the first runs 30 minutes, the rest 17. **215m/B VHS, Beta.** John Carroll, Helen Christian, Noah Beery Sr., Duncan Renaldo; **D:** William Witney, John English. *NOS, VCN, MED*

Zorro, the Gay Blade 🎬🎬½ 1981 (PG) Tongue-in-cheek sword play with Hamilton portraying the swashbuckling crusader and his long-lost brother, Bunny Wigglesworth, in this spoof of the Zorro legend. The fashion-conscious hero looks his best in plum. Leibman is fun to watch. **96m/C VHS, Beta, Closed Caption.** George Hamilton, Lauren Hutton, Brenda Vaccaro, Ron Leibman; **D:** Peter Medak; **W:** Greg Alt; **C:** John A. Alonzo. *FOX*

Zorro's Black Whip 1944 A young girl dons the mask of her murdered brother (Zorro) to fight outlaws in the old West. Serial in twelve episodes. **182m/B VHS, LV.** George Lewis, Linda Stirling, Lucien Littlefield, Francis McDonald, Tom London; **D:** Spencer Gordon Bennet; **W:** Wallace Grissell. *NOS, GPV, MED*

Zorro's Fighting Legion 1939 Zorro forms a legion to help the president of Mexico fight a band of outlaws endeavoring to steal gold shipments. A serial in 12 chapters. **215m/B VHS, LV.** Reed Hadley, Sheila Darcy; **D:** William Witney, John English. *NOS, VCN, VDM*

Zotz! 🎬🎬 1962 The holder of a magic coin can will people dead by uttering "zotz"; spies pursue the mild-mannered professor who possesses the talisman. Adapted from a Walter Karig novel. Typical William Castle fare; his gimic in the theatrical release of the movie was to distribute plastic "zotz" coins to the theatre patrons. **87m/B VHS,**

Beta. Tom Poston, Julia Meade, Jim Backus, Fred Clark, Cecil Kellaway; **D:** Ray Russell; **W:** Ray Russell. COL

Zou Zou ♬♬½ **1934** Lavish backstage musical/drama of a laundress who fills in for the leading lady on opening night and becomes a hit. Baker's talking picture debut. In French with English subtitles. **92m/B VHS, LV.** FR Josephine Baker, Jean Gabin; **D:** Marc Allegret. MVD, KIV, APD

Zulu ♬♬½ **1964** In 1879, a small group of British soldiers try to defend their African outpost from attack by thousands of Zulu warriors. Amazingly, the British win. Dated colonial epic based on an actual incident; battle scenes are magnificent. Prequel "Zulu Dawn" (1979) depicts British mishandling of the situation that led to the battle. **139m/C VHS, Beta, LV, Closed Caption.** Michael Caine, Jack Hawkins, Stanley Baker, Nigel Green; **D:** Cy Endfield; **M:** John Barry. NLC

Zulu Dawn ♬♬♬ **1979 (PG)** An historical epic about British troops fighting the Zulus at Ulandi in 1878. Shows the increasing tensions between the British colonial government and the Zulus. Stunning landscapes unfortunately don't translate to the small screen. Good but unoriginal colonial-style battle drama. **117m/C VHS, Beta, LV.** Burt Lancaster, Peter O'Toole, Denholm Elliott, Nigel Davenport, John Mills, Simon Ward, Bob Hoskins, Freddie Jones; **D:** Douglas Hickox; **M:** Elmer Bernstein. TWE

Zvenigora ♬♬♬♬ **1928** Dovzhenko's first major film, and a lyrical revelation in the face of Soviet formality: a passionate, funny fantasy tableaux of 1,000 years of Ukrainian history, encompassing wild folk myths, poetic drama, propaganda and social satire. Silent. **73m/B VHS, Beta.** RU Mikola Nademsy, Alexander Podorozhny, Semyon Svashenko; **D:** Alexander Dovzhenko. FCT

Category List

The **Category Index** contains genre, sub-genre, thematic, or significant scene classifications, ranging from the very general terms (comedy, drama) to the fairly particular (phone terror, killer cars, exploding fish tanks). The terms are defined (more or less) below. We've done our best to provide serious subject references while also including fun categories and lists to make your video viewing experience a little more enjoyable. No one list is all-inclusive. We are continuously reclassifying, adding, and subtracting movies. Many of the categories in this list are new, and therefore represent only a beginning. We're also trying to pare down some of the bigger categories, like **Romance**, by creating more focused subject categories, such as **Lovers on the Lam** or **Romantic Triangles**. *VideoHound* invites readers to participate in this pastime by sending in suggestions for new categories and adding movies to existing ones. **An asterisk (*) denotes a new category for this edition.**

ABBA-ca-da-bra: Australian films pay homage to the kitschy '70s pop icons, reviving 'Dancing Queen' and 'Waterloo'

Action-Adventure: Adrenaline testers for those weary of the conventions of plot think Stallone, think Snipes, and quit thinking

Adoption & Orphans: Cute kids lacking permanent authority figures, ranging from *Annie* to *Wild Hearts Can't Be Broken*

Adventure Drama: Action with more attention to dramatic content *Apocalypse Now* to *Robin Hood, Prince of Thieves*

Advertising: Corporate shenanigans at the agency *How to Get Ahead in Advertising* to *The Horse in the Gray Flannel Suit*

Africa: Banana Republic franchise; *Out of Africa* to *Zulu Dawn*

African America: Dominant African American themes

AIDS: Someone usually dies; *An Early Frost* to *Longtime Companion*

Air Disasters: Contraptions up in the sky, but not for long

Airborne: Contraptions up in the sky

Alien Beings Benign: Friendly space visitors, including *Howard the Duck* and little buddy *E.T.*

*Alcatraz: Prison island off San Francisco, aka *The Rock*

*Alien Babes: Women who possess otherworldly beauty (and appetites)

Alien Beings Vicious: Not-so-friendly space visitors, notably the multi-jawed *Alien* continually harassing Sigourney Weaver

*Aliens Are People, Too: Space visitors pretend to be human, or just take over the bodies—*Invasion of the Body Snatchers* kinda stuff

American South: Theatrics amid much brow mopping and drawling; *A Streetcar Named Desire* rattling down *Flamingo Road*

America's Heartland: Generally heartwarming small-town sagas

Amnesia: Phone call for *Anastasia*

Amusement Parks: Cotton candy, ferris wheels, Coney Island, *Godzilla on Monster Island, Rollercoaster*

Angels: Benevolent winged visitors from above: *Wings of Desire*

Animated Musicals: Boys, girls, dogs, ducks, birds, mice, and monkeys croon; many of Disney vintage, including *Aladdin* and *Sleeping Beauty*

Animation & Cartoons: Antics of Daffy, Donald, Bugs, Mickey, Chip, Dale, Tom, Jerry, Fred, Wilma, Charlie, and the rest of the gang

Anthology: More than one story to a cassette

Anti-Heroes: From *Billy Jack* to *Dirty Harry* to *Thelma & Louise*

Anti-War War Movies: Recognizes that war really is hell from *All Quiet on the Western Front* to *Glory* to *M*A*S*H*

Apartheid: Afrikaans term for racial segregation in South Africa

Art & Artists: They paint, pause, and propagate with equal passion

Asia: *China White, Red Dust, Sand Pebbles*

Asian America: Asian experience in the US *The Joy Luck Club, Come See the Paradise*

Assassinations: Lincoln, *JFK, La Femme Nikita, Times of Harvey Milk,* and more

*At the Drive-In: Scenes in which people watch movies...at the drive-in.

At the Movies: The movie within a movie or movies about watching the movies, from *The Purple Rose of Cairo* to *Last Action Hero* to *Matinee*

Avant-garde: Ahead of its time or completely bewildering to most in the audience

Babysitting: Supervision of small-fry pranksters not your own; *Uncle Buck* to *The Hand that Rocks the Cradle*

Bad Dads: Daddy-Os with unpredictable mean streak: *The Shining, Kiss Daddy Goodbye*

*Bad Hair Days: Oddly coiffed characters

Ballet: On your toes *The Turning Point*

Ballooning: Up, up and away, or *Around the World in 80 Days*

Baltimore: Take a look at the Maryland city, hometown of director Barry Levinson and favorite digs of John Waters

*Bar & Grill: Most, if not all, of the action takes place in a drinking establishment.

Baseball: Action on the diamond, ranging from *Bull Durham* to *A League of Their Own* to *Rookie of the Year*

Basketball: Roundball thrillers, including the memorable *The Fish that Saved Pittsburgh* and *White Men Can't Jump*

Bathroom Scenes: Encompassing bathtubs, hottubs, showers, sinks and toilets, including *Psycho, Fatal Attraction* and that poor fellow in *Jurassic Park*

Beach Blanket Bingo: Annette, Frankie, sand, surf, bikinis

*Beach Driving: Enjoy the feel of sand between your treads

*Beatniks: Jazz beards, bongos, poetry that doesn't rhyme, berets

Beauty Pageants: From the heartless to the hilarious, beauty is a big business *Smile* girls!

Behind the Scenes: Peek behind show business curtain, from *A Chorus Line* to *Truth or Dare*

Berlin: City in Germany divided after WWII, now it's one big happy city again

Bicycling: Two wheels, no motor, much leg action and sweating

Big Battles: Big-budget (or at least illusion of such) clash of large, opposing military forces, from *Cromwell* to *Ran*

Big Budget Stinkers: Millions spent for no apparent reason

Big Daddies: Usually troublesome, with Freudian overtones

Big Digs: Anthropology and archaeology, from Indiana Jones to various mummy on-the-loose stories

Big Ideas: Philosophy, ideology and other semi-mental pursuits somehow translated to film

Big Rigs: *Smokey and the Bandit* speed down *Thieves' Highway* in a *Convoy*

Bigfoot/Yeti: Large, hairy, seldom-seen beast with really big feet

Bikers: Usually with a mean streak and traveling in leather-clad packs

Category List

Birds: Beaks, feathers, talons, bird #%!; *The Birds, Beaks: The Movie, Howard the Duck*

Bisexuality: Going both ways *Basic Instinct, Three of Hearts*

Black Comedy: Funny in a biting or despairing sort of way, from *The Addams Family* to *The Hospital*

Black Gold: Oil, that is; aka *Oklahoma Crude*

Blackmail: I'm gonna tell, unless... *The Last Seduction, Letter to My Killer*

Blaxploitation: '70s remakes of horror classics with black casts: *Blacula, Blackenstein, Dr. Black, Mr. Hyde*

Blindness: Can't see or sight impaired; *Afraid of the Dark*

Bloody Mayhem: Expanded scenes of arterial explosions, including *Blood Bride, Blood Cult, Blood Diner, Blood Feast, Blood Lake, Blood Legacy, Blood Mania,* and *Bloodbath in Psycho Town*

Bloody Messages: Cryptic warnings to the living written in the blood of the poor slob who was just killed–Redrum

Bodyguards: Costner looks after Whitney's personal business

Books: As a major plot device: *La Lectrice* to *Crossing Delancey*

Boom!: Really big explosions, bombs, and other noisy or fiery messes popular in big budget action flicks

Boomer Reunions: thirtysomethings gather and reminisce: *The Big Chill*

Boston: Beantown, where everybody knows your name.

*Bounty Hunters: Bring 'em back dead or alive–for a price

Bowling: Heavy round ball is thrown down waxed alley toward club-like pins; all fall down

Boxing: Yo, Adrian!

Bringing Up Baby: *Look Who's Talking* to *Raising Arizona*, plus infants with that little something different *Alien 3, Enemy Mine, Basket Case 3: The Progeny*

Buddies: Butch and Sundance, Bill and Ted, Rubin and Ed, *Thelma and Louise*

Buddy Cops: Couple of police hanging together, usually practicing limited repartee at a donut shop; *Lethal Weapon, Tango and Cash*

Buses: Large truck-like passenger vehicles *Speed, The Big Bus, The Trip to Bountiful*

*Cabbies: Where to, Mac?

Calcutta: Big, overpopulated city in India

Camelot (New): The exploits of JFK, Jackie, and various relatives and hangers-on

Camelot (Old): The exploits of King Arthur and his *Knights of the Round Table*

Campus Capers: What really goes on at college *Assault of the Party Nerds*

Canada: Renfrew of the Mounties plus lots of wilderness and the occasional hockey puck

Canine Cops: He's a cop, he's got a badge, he's a dog *K-9, Turner & Hooch*

Cannibalism: People who eat people are the luckiest people; *Alive, Rabid Grannies, Cannibal Women in the Avocado Jungle of Death, The Cook, the Thief, His Wife & Her Lover*

Capitol Capers: Hollywood versions of hijinks in Washington, D.C. *Dave, Mr. Smith Goes to Washington, All the President's Men*

Carnivals & Circuses: Big top, little top, domes: *Shakes the Clown* to *Rollercoaster*, plus *Big Top Pee Wee, State Fair,* and metaphoric circuses: *Brewster McCloud, La Strada*

Cats: Lesser vertebrate nonetheless much beloved by Hollywood

Cave People: From the most primitive (*The Clan of the Cave Bear*) to the fairly modernized (*The Flintstones*)

Central America: Mostly Latin warfare, with at least three sides to every conflict

Chases: Who are those guys? Someone's after someone else, usually at high-speed with transportation ranging from horses to autos to bikes to trains to trucks

Cheerleaders: Give me an A! *The Positively True Adventures of the Alleged Texas Cheerleader-Murdering Mom* meets *Revenge of the Cheerleaders*

Chicago: City in Illinois, right at the bottom of Lake Michigan

Child Abuse: Not very funny at all *Mommie Dearest, Fallen Angel*

Childhood Visions: Stories dominated by the kid point of view, or by an adult flashbacking to childhood; *Au Revoir Les Enfants, Home Alone*

China: *The Last Emperor* to *Red Sorghum* to *The World of Suzie Wong*

Christmas: Reindeer, Santa, children make appearance amid much sentimentality

Cinderella Stories: Gal down on her luck meets fairy godmother (or father) and finds true love *Pretty Woman, Flashdance, Cinderella*

Civil Rights: Fighting for equality *The Autobiography of Miss Jane Pittman, Mississippi Burning*

Civil War: The Yankees against the Confederates; aka *The Blue and the Gray*

Classic Horror: Boris Karloff, Vincent Price, piercing screams

*Cloning Around: Makin' copies–of people or animals. *Multiplicity* to *Jurassic Park*

Clowns: Big red noses, huge feet, painted smiles frighten many

*Cockroaches: Creepy crawlies signifying the work of the supernatural, or a lack of housekeeping skills

Cold Spots: Set in a frostbitten locale with lots of shivering; *Ice Station Zebra, Never Cry Wolf, Quest for Fire*

Comedy: Yuk fests not listed in other comedy categories *Fletch, I Wanna Hold Your Hand, Tampopo*

Comedy Anthologies: More than one yuk fest on a cassette

Comedy Drama: Drama with a comedic touch or comedy underwired with drama *Avalon, The Big Chill, Fried Green Tomatoes, One Flew Over the Cuckoo's Nest, Tootsie*

Comedy Mystery: Wacky whodunits like *Murder by Death, Clue*

Comedy Sci-Fi: Laughs in space! *Spaceballs*

Comic Adventure: Adventurous romps liberally laced with humor: *Romancing theStone* to *Bird on a Wire* to *Crocodile Dundee*

Coming of Age: Hard-fought adolescent battle for adulthood, led by *American Graffiti, The Apprenticeship of Duddy Kravitz, The Karate Kid*

Computers: Bits and bytes play major role

Concert Films: Rock or comedy concerts from *Woodstock* to *Divine Madness* to *Eddie Murphy: Raw*

Contemporary Musicals: Thematically modern and made during last 20 years; *All That Jazz*

Contemporary Noir: Dark and moody or tributes to dark and moody that pay homage to the original Film Noir genre *Blue Velvet, 9- Weeks, sex, lies, and videotape, Wild Orchid*

Cops: Police and pseudo-police work, including *Action Jackson, Blue Steel, The Choirboys, RoboCop, Lethal Weapon, National Lampoon's Loaded Weapon 1*

Corporate Shenanigans: Big Business runs amuck *Barbarians at the Gate, Wall Street*

Credits Chaos!: Don't rewind, 'cuz it's not over till it's over

Creepy Houses: Scary dwellings *Amityville Horror* 1 through 33

Crime & Criminals: Bad guys and gals, including *Avenging Disco Godfather, TheGrifters, In Cold Blood*

Crime Sprees: Bad guy, gal or couple goes on a crime binge and other tales of obsessional criminal activity, including *Bonnie & Clyde, The Boys Next Door*

Crimes of Passion: Love, sex, and death

Crop Dusters: Down on the farm: *Bitter Harvest, Pelle the Conqueror, Jean de Florette, The River*

Cult Items: Recognized for that something different by a relatively small group (at least initially) of boomer-type people: *Basket Case, Blood Simple, Harold and Maude, Mad Max,* and the greatest cult of them all *The Rocky Horror Picture Show*

Cult Items New: Revered by a relatively large group of Generation X-type people: *Bill & Ted's Excellent Adventure, Grease, Sixteen Candles, The Sure Thing*

Cults: Something like a gang but more intense and usually governed by a state of mind similar to irrationality *Helter Skelter*

Cyberpunk: Dark, moody, futuristic flicks *Blade Runner, Freejack, Tank Girl*

Dads: Fathers play a major role

Dance Fever: Whole lotta foot-tapping going on, including *An American in Paris, Daddy Long Legs,* and *Dirty Dancing*

Dates from Hell: Fun evening for two singles turns into a nightmare for one of them *Bye Bye Love, Singles, Something Wild*

*A Day In The Life: All the action takes place within a 24-hour period

Deafness: Can't hear or hearing impaired; *Bridge to Silence, The Miracle Worker*

Death & The Afterlife: Could be ghosts, could be voices from the beyond, could be any number of post-dead things *Beetlejuice, Carnival of Souls, Flatliners, Poltergeist, Weekend at Bernie's*

Death Row: Waitin' for a call from the Governor; *Dead Man Walking, Angels with Dirty Faces*

Dedicated Teachers: From *The Dead Poet's Society* to *The Blackboard Jungle* to *The Miracle Worker*

Deep Blue: The sea around us, including *ffolkes* and *Splash*

Demons & Wizards: Swords, sorcery and wrinkled old men with wands *The Alchemist, The Hobbit, The Sword & the Sorcerer*

Dental Mayhem: Tooth-pickin' uproars; *Marathon Man, The Dentist*

Desert War/Foreign Legion: Big battles among the dunes

Deserts: Endless beach minus the water *Ishtar, Lawrence of Arabia*

Detective Spoofs: Putting together clues in humorous fashion *The Adventures of Sherlock Holmes' Smarter Brother, The Naked Gun*

Detectives: Clue happy but often grizzled and cynical *The Drowning Pool, V.I .Warshawski*

Devils: Some may meet on *Judgment Day*

*Devil's Island: French Island prison in the South Atlantic

Dinosaurs: *Jurassic Park* and other less animated thundering lizards

Disaster Flicks: Natural and man-made, including 47 *Airport* sequels

Disco Musicals: '70s tackiness reigns supreme, from *Saturday Night Fever* to *Xanadu*

Disease of the Week: Bulimia, anorexia, polio, cancer, and so on

Disorganized Crime: Stupid crime, including *Amos and Andrew, Dog Day Afternoon, Home Alone, Quick Change*

Divorce: Breaking up is hard to do; *Accidental Tourist, Heartburn, Kramer vs. Kramer*

Doctors & Nurses: Men and women in scrubs concerned about health of complete strangers for profit, often to the dismay of the patient *Autopsy, Candy Stripe Nurses, Dead Ringers*

Docudrama: *The Thin Blue Line* between documentaries and drama

Documentary: Real life manipulated on film *A Brief History of Time, The Last Waltz, Paris Is Burning, Roger and Me*

Down Under: Australian, New Zealand settings *The Rescuers Down Under, Gallipoli, The Man from Snowy River, The Thorn Birds*

Dragons: Legendary medieval lizards, usually with fiery dispositions; *Dragonheart, Pete's Dragon*

Drama: Conflict, tension, climax, resolution

Dream Girls: Product of male mid-life crisis; *Battling Amazons, Cycle Vixens, The Doll Squad, The Woman in Red*

Earthquakes: Common occurrence in California

Eco-Vengeance!: Nature wreaks havoc on man watch out for *Alligators, Frogs* and *Piranhas*

Edibles: Something's cooking *Babette's Feast, Like Water for Chocolate*

*Elephants: Pachyderms play a BIG part in the plot–*Dumbo, Larger Than Life*

Elevators: Sometimes the oddest things happen in them...

Emerging Viruses: Deadly virus spreads like wildfire as frantic medical personnel search for a cure; think ebola

The Empire State Building: Used to be the tallest building in NYC, still the most famous

Erotic Thrillers: Hot sex and murder, including *Basic Instinct, Body of Evidence*

Ethics & Morals: Examination of values (or lack of) *Crimes & Misdemeanors, Judgment at Nuremberg*

Etiquette: Usually comedy of manners; *Educating Rita, My Fair Lady*

Evil Doctors: Don't go to these guys for a checkup *Malice, Dead Ringers*, and *Doctor X*

*Exploding Fish Tanks: Aquariums go crash, fish go splash

Exploitation: Rigged to take advantage of viewer, including historic treats like *Reefer Madness* and more recent ventures such as *Sleazemania*

Explorers: Going boldly where no man or woman has regularly gone before

Extraordinary Pairings: *Jesse James meets Frankenstein's Daughter*

Eyeballs!: Unnerving scenes involving pupils, irises, lids, and occasionally, lashes

Fairs & Expositions: Short term amusement parks: *State Fair*

Family Ties: Blood runs deep *Back to the Future, Five Easy Pieces, The Godfather, Homeward Bound, Lorenzo's Oil, The Mosquito Coast, Rocket Gibraltar*

Fantasy: Tales of the imagination, including *Alice* and her looking glass, *E.T., Ladyhawke, My Stepmother Is an Alien*

Fast Cars: *Eat My Dust*; racing in the street or on the track; *The Last American Hero*

Feds: Men and women of the Bureau, the Agency, or any national police organization with an acronym and a dress code

Female Bonding: Women get together, usually to the men's dismay; *Waiting to Exhale*

Femme Fatale: She done him and him and him wrong

Fencing: En garde, dude

Film & Film History: *America at the Movies;* includes movies important to film history

Film Noir: Dark and moody or tributes to dark and moody-*Farewell, My Lovely, The Postman Always Ring Twice, The Third Man, Who Framed Roger Rabbit?*

Film Stars: Movies or bios about cinema celebs, real or make-believe *Bogie, Chaplin, Sinatra*

Filmmaking: The making of a film within a film: *The Player*

Firemen: *Backdraft, Fahrenheit 451*, and other tales of brave people with hoses

Fires: *Frankenstein, Quest for Fire, Pyrates*

Flashback: Why I remember like it was yesterday. It all started when...*The Usual Suspects, Casablanca*

Flatulence: Embarrassing gaseous emissions

*Floods: Water, water everywhere

Flower Children: The sixties are still alive at *Alice's Restaurant*–reflect on*The Big Chill, The Doors*, and *Woodstock*; we all live in a *Yellow Submarine*

Folklore & Mythology: Age-old adult tales covering Atlantis, little people, Hercules, Ulysses

Football: Everything from terrorist attacks on the Superbowl (*Black Sunday*) to prison competition (*The Longest Yard*) plus *Diner*

Foreign Intrigue: Overseas mystery, with emphasis on accent and location

Frame-ups: Someone's set up to take the rap: *My Cousin Vinny* to *Consenting Adults*

France: From *Dirty Rotten Scoundrels* to *The Moderns* to *Gigi* to *The Last Metro* to *Killer Tomatoes Eat France*

Front Page: *Citizen Kane, All the President's Men, The Philadelphia Story*, and other journalistic stories

Fugitives: Running from the law; *Breathless, Nowhere to Hide, Posse*

Funerals: The final good-bye *Four Weddings and a Funeral, Gardens of Stone, The Big Chill*

Gambling: *Aces and Eights, The Color of Money, Eight Men Out, Honeymoon in Vegas*

Game Shows: *The Running Man* and *Queen for a Day*

Gangs: Criminally enterprising teens and adults running in packs: *State of Grace, Miller's Crossing, Public Enemy, The Wanderers*

Gays: Gay themes *Kiss of the Spider Woman, The Hunger*

Gender Bending: *The Crying Game, La Cage aux Folles, Her Life as a Man* and other instances of boys becoming girls and vice versa

Generation X: Slacking in the '90s *Reality Bites, Singles*

Genetics: Fooling with the double helix *The Fly*

Genies: *Aladdin* finds magic lamp filled with compressed Robin Williams

Genre Spoofs: Wacky takes on serious films, starting with the granddaddy of them all:*Airplane!*

Germany: *The Blue Angel, Wings of Desire*

Ghosts, Ghouls, & Goblins: *Ghostbusters, Topper, Poltergeist*

Giants: *The Amazing Colossal Man* visits *Village of the Giants*

Gifted Children: Kids show amazing talents that astound adults, from *Rookie of the Year* to *Little Man Tate*

Gigolos: Men try the oldest profession in the world, working around biological limitations

Go Fish: Casting a line in the river that runs through it; *Man of Aran, A Fish Called Wanda, Captains Courageous*

Going Native: Outsiders try to blend in; *Dances with Wolves, The Swiss Family Robinson*

Golf: Slow boring game best experienced on screen ('Be the ball, Danny')

Good Earth: Ecology, environment, nature, sod

Grand Hotel: Checkout time is noon; *Blame It on the Bellboy*

Great Britain: Thwarted royals (*Charles & Diana: A Palace Divided, Edward and Mrs. Simpson*), kings (*King Ralph*), queens (*The Naked Civil Servant*), class distinctions (*The Ruling Class*), vanished empires (*Cromwell, A Man for All Seasons*), criminals (*The Krays, The Long Good Friday*) plus multiple stiff upper lips, the Brontes, and Dickens

Great Death Scenes: Signing off with style or elaboration; *Buffy the Vampire Killer, Bonnie and Clyde, Breaker Morant*

Great Depression: The era, not the state of mind *Bound for Glory, Of Mice and Men, The Grapes of Wrath, Rambling Rose*

Great Escapes: Seizing the day for freedom *The Big Doll House, Escape from Alcatraz, Papillon*

Growing Older: *On Golden Pond, *batteries not included, Cocoon, Driving Miss Daisy, The Shootist, The Wild Bunch*

Guys in Kilts: Celtic hunks like *Rob Roy* in plaid skirts

Gymnastics: Human pretzels like *Nadia*

*Hackers: Computer whiz kids cause havoc–or just change their grades

Happy Hookers: Prostitution with a rosy glow; *The Happy Hooker Goes to Hollywood* and meets *Pretty Woman*

Hard Knock Life: Poverty and bad luck; *City of Joy, The Match Factory Girl*

Hearts!: Unnerving scenes involving human hearts, generally seen by the audience andalmost always still pumping

Hawaii: The 50th state, fun in the sun, if the volcanoes are behaving.

Heaven Sent: Visits or returns from the place where good souls and all dogs go *Field of Dreams* to *Made in Heaven* to *Oh God!*

Heists: The big lift

Hell High School: Place where adolescents gather against their will; also known as *Rock 'n' Roll High School*

*The Help: Female: Maids, nannies, governesses, cooks, housekeepers

*The Help: Male: Butlers, chauffeurs, manservants, valets

*High School Reunions: Adults gather to impress other adults they didn't like as adolescents

Hispanic America: Dominant Hispanic American themes (*Salsa, Mi Vida Loca*)

Historical Drama: Usually at least loosely based on a real incident or personality

Hit Men: Boys and girls armed with silencers; *Prizzi's Honor, Romeo is Bleeding*

Hockey: *Slap Shot* and other icy tales of passing the puck

Holidays: Easter, Thanksgiving, New Year's, Halloween, but generally not Christmas

Holocaust: *Playing for Time, Schindler's List*

Home Alone: Kids find themselves without adult supervision *Adventures in Babysitting* to *Young Sherlock Holmes*

*The Homefront: U.S./Canada: The war at home during WWII–looking for spies, rationing, waiting for word about 'the boys.'

*The Homefront: England: Air raids, stiff upper lips, they were a lot closer to the action, and were just as worried about their sons and husbands.

Homeless: Street people with no homes

Horrible Holidays: Holidays with a ghoulish twist *Bloody New Year, Halloween, My Bloody Valentine, Silent Night, Bloody Night*

Horror: Modern cut 'em up scare theater

Horror Anthologies: More than one scarefest on a cassette

Horror Comedy: Tongue-in-bloody cheek *The Fearless Vampire Killers, Piranha, Sorority Babes in the Slimeball Bowl-A-Rama*

Horses: Can you say *Black Beauty?*

Hospitals & Medicine: Dysfunctional institutional health care *Article 99, The Hospital, One Flew Over the Cuckoo's Nest, Young Doctors in Love*

Hostage!: People held against their will for bargaining purposes

Houston: That big city in Texas where J.R. didn't live, but Roger Clemens did.

Hunted!: Humans tracking humans for trophy purposes

Hunting: Where's dat wascally wabbit? *Caddyshack, The Bear, White Hunter, Black Heart*

Hurling: What goes down sometimes comes back up *The Exorcist, Parenthood*

I Love Detroit: The Motor City, home of Motown, lots of cars, and VideoHound

Identity: Who am I? Who are you? Who are we? Why do you ask so many questions?

Immigration: Melting pot stories *Avalon, Far and Away, Living on Tokyo Time*

Incest: Implied or actual relationships among family members *The Grifters, Spanking the Monkey*

India: On the road to *Bombay*

Interviews: When asked questions, people talk

Inventors & Inventions: Those wacky folks and their newfangled machines; *ChittyChitty Bang Bang*

*Invisibility: Now you see 'em, now you don't

Interracial Affairs: Couple from different racial backgrounds cause trauma for family and friends *Mississippi Masala, Jungle Fever*

Ireland: Aye, make that a pint for take away; *The Field, Cal, The Playboys*

Islam: Religious themes

Island Fare: Thin, isolated stretch of land surrounded by water notorious for encouraging natural appetites in men and women

Israel: *Cast a Giant Shadow, Exodus*

Italy: Passion, vino, lust, vino, Sophia Loren

*It's a Conspiracy, Man!: Just because you're paranoid doesn't mean they're not out to get you

Japan: *Land of the Rising Sun, Godzilla, Hiroshima, Mon Amour*

Japanimation: Animated cartoons from Japan with cult following

Judaism: *Fiddler on the Roof* meets *Funny Girl*

Jungle Stories: Tarzan, tribes, trees, treasure, temperature, temptresses, tigers

Justice Prevails?: The verdict's in, but is it fair? *And Justice for All, In the Name of the Father, Presumed Innocent*

Kidnapped!: Held for ransom or just for the heck of it *A Perfect World, Raising Arizona*

Killer Apes: *King Kong* lives on *The Planet of the Apes*

Killer Appliances: Defrosted refrigerator goes on killing binge

Killer Beasts: Cloned dinosaurs run amuck in backyard, destroying patio

Killer Brains: Literally has a mind of its own, i.e., *The Brain That Wouldn't Die*

Killer Bugs: Giant and/or miserably mean spiders, ants, bees, worms, flies, slugs, tarantulas, wasps, and other creepy things

Killer Cars: You should have changed *Christine's* oil

Killer Dogs: Fido takes a walk on the wild side *Cujo*, baby

Killer Dreams: More like nightmares on elm street

Killer Kats: Kitties with a killer instinct

Killer Pigs: Evil swine

Killer Plants: Too much fertilizer produces killer tomatoes (stewed)

Killer Rodents: Nasty mice, rats, bats, and shrews

Killer Toys: Demented play things develop homicidal urges; why hello, Chucky

Kindness of Strangers: Baffling altruistic behavior

King of Beasts (Dogs): Need we say more?

Korean War: *M*A*S*H* and friends

L.A.: Smoggy city in California also known as Los Angeles or the City of Angels; includes Hollywood & Beverly Hills

Labor & Unions: *Hoffa* and other working stiffs

Late Bloomin' Love: Better late than not blooming at all

Law & Lawyers: Tom Cruise joins *The Firm* and other realistic legal adventures

*Leprechauns: The wee mischievous people of Irish lore who carry around pots o' gold

Lesbians: Lesbian themes *Lianna, Bar Girls*

Libraries & Librarians: Important things happen where you can't talk–sometimes people even read!

Life Imitates Art: Kids, don't try this at home. (They did.)

Lifeguards: Rescuers of the swimming-challenged

London: City in merry old England, home to many generations of the most famous royals

Loner Cops: *Dirty Harry* Syndrome

Lost Worlds: From *Brigadoon* to *The People That Time Forgot*

*Lottery Winners: Ordinary schmoes get rich quick. Be careful what you wish for...

Lovable Loonies: Crazy, but not Norman Bates crazy; *Crazy People, Benny & Joon*

Lovers on the Lam: Couple commit crimes and find themselves on the run *Badlands, Natural Born Killers, True Romance*

Macho Men: Ah-nuld, The Duke, Van Damme, Stallone, Burt, Clint, Norris, Seagal, and many more cases of excessive testosterone

Mad Scientists: *The Brain That Wouldn't Die* spends an evening with *Frankenhooker*

Magic: Hocus pocus, often with evil intent

Magic Carpet Rides: *Aladdin* joins *Sinbad the Sailor* for *The Golden Voyage of Sinbad*

Marriage: Wedding bells, honeymoons, affairs, divorce, and growing old together, as well as the occasional unfortunate marital union with a blood-sucking vampire or knife-wielding satanist

Martial Arts: Fists of Aluminum Foil; much head-kicking, rib-crunching, chop-socky action

Martyred Pop Icons: For us, they gave their all; Buddy Holly, Elvis, Marilyn, James Dean, *Stardust Memories*

Mass Media: From *Network* to *Broadcast News* to *My Favorite Year*

May-December Romance: Older people meet younger people and the romantic sparks fly; *Harold and Maude* visit *Atlantic City*.

The Meaning of Life: The search for the elusive answer *My Life, The Remains of the Day, Shadowlands*

Medieval Romps: Dirty peasants, deodorized and glorified kings and queens, splendid knights in shining armor, and one for all and all for one

Meltdown: Or how I learned to stop worrying and love the bomb; also bad wiring at local nuclear plants

Men: What is man? Is he neither fish nor fowl? Or perhaps linoleum?

Men in Prison: Working on a chain gang; what we have here is a failure to communicate

Mental Retardation: *Bill, Charly, Dominick, Lenny, Raymond* (definitely)

Metamorphosis: Ch-ch-ch-changes From *The Fly* to *Wolf*

*Meteors & Comets: Chunks of stuff wizzing through space, sometimes they land andcause problems

Mexico: *South of Sante Fe* and *Against All Odds*

Miami: Extremely warm coastal city in southern Florida

Middle East: Desert fare and camel close-ups ranging from *Ishtar* to *Lawrence of Arabia* to *The Jewel of the Nile*

*Military: Air Force: Flyboys fight America's aerial battles

*Military: Army: GIs, Grunts, Dogfaces

Military Comedy: Marching to a different drummer, including *Stripes, M*A*S*H* and *No Time for Sergeants*

*Military: Foreign: Armed forces of other nations are the focus

*Military: Marines: Jarheads. The first ones in and the last ones out.

*Military: Navy: Fighting on the high seas and in the air

Miners & Mining: Helmets with the little flashlights are nifty; *Matewan* and *McCabe & Mrs. Miller*

Minnesota: Northern state that makes Michigan seem like the tropics. Home of theTwin cities and Prince, eh?

Missing Persons: People who disappear for a variety of reasons, sometimes because other people have taken them away

Missionaries: On a mission from God to save native populations

Misspelled Titles: Not proper Anglish

Mistaken Identity: You mean to say you're not the King of France?

Modern Cowboys: Fun-lovin' rascals adept at riding horses through busy city streets or with a yen to experience mid-life crisis by doing a rodeo

Moms: Maternal figures have a prominent role

Monkeyshines: Critters from the jungle, sometimes cute and fluffy, often wreaking havoc *Congo, Monkey Trouble, Outbreak*

Monster Moms: Loving on the outside, evil on the inside- *Mommie Dearest, Serial Mom*

Monsters, General: Not killer beasts, bugs, plants, appliances, aliens, toys, giants, vampires, werewolves, or politicians

Montreal: Cosmopolitan city of francophones currently in Canada

Moscow: City in Russia (the country formerly known as USSR)

Motor Vehicle Dept.: *Chitty Chitty Bang Bang* at the *Car Wash*, plus *Tucker, Herbie*, and the *Repo Man*

Mountaineering: *Cliffhanger*s

Movie & TV Trailers: Snippets of stuff

Mummies: Dead guys with leather-like skin, often wrapped in sheets

Murderous Children: *Children of the Corn* hang out on the outskirts of the *Village of the Damned*...isn't that near the 7-Eleven of Doom?

Music: *Amadeus* meets *The Fabulous Baker Boys* and *The Commitments* by way of *Mo' Better Blues* at *The Cotton Club*

Musical Comedy: Laughter, singing, and dancing

Musical Drama: Singing and dancing, less laughter, more tension

Musical Fantasy: Singing and dancing in a figment of someone's imagination

Musicals: High-energy singing and dancing, often for no particular reason

Musician Biopics: Real-life musicians get the Hollywood treatment

Mutiny: Gang of disgruntled sailors takes over the ship

Mystery & Suspense: Edge-of-the-couch thrillers and whodunits

*Nannies & Governesses: Musically-inclined women raise kids for rich people too busy to do it themselves

Nashville: Tennessee city that country music and Robert Altman made famous

Nashville Narratives: *Honkytonk Man* elopes with the *Coal Miner's Daughter*

Native America: Dancing with the wolves on *Pow Wow Highway*

Nazis & Other Paramilitary Slugs: *The Boys from Brazil* and *The Dirty Dozen* plus *SS she-wolf Ilsa* and modern David Duke adaptations

Negative Utopia: Things seemed so perfect until...

New Black Cinema: Spike is Godfather

New York, New York: It's a hell of a town...

New Orleans: City in Louisiana that boasts the Mardi Gras and cajun cookin'

New Year's Eve: Stay up late, count down with Dick Clark, drink too much, greet the New Year feeling like...

*Niagara Falls: Little upstate New York border town where honeymooners and barrel riders gather. Oh yeah, they have some water thing there, too...

Nifty '50s: *Grease, La Bamba, The Man in the Moon, Peggy Sue Got Married, School Ties* and 60 more from the Eisenhower era

Nightclubs: *Casablanca*, of course

No-Exit Motel: Sleazy motels with extremely lenient late-checkout policies

Not-So-True Identity: People pass themselves off as something else; *Soul Man, Gentleman's Agreement*

Nuns & Priests: Collars and habits; *Agnes of God, The Cardinal, Going My Way, Nuns on the Run, Sister Act*

Nuns With Guns: Sister Mary Margaret has traded up from the ol' yardstick. Better practice that penmanship.

Nursploitation!: *Night Call Nurses* offer *Tender Loving Care* in *The Hospital of Terror*

Obsessive Love: You like me. You really, really, *really* like me.

Occult: Witches, warlocks, devil worshipers, spell makers, spell breakers, haunted houses, and so on

*Office Surprise: Office supplies used as weapons

Oldest Profession: It's not accounting

The Olympics: *Chariots of Fire* and other tales of athletic discipline

On the Rocks: Alcoholism, alcohol, barflies, moonshining, Prohibition *Arthur, Days of Wine and Roses, Papa's Delicate Condition, My Favorite Year*

Only the Lonely: 50 ways to play solitaire *The Cemetery Club, The Heart Is a Lonely Hunter, Sleepless in Seattle*

Opera: Shouting in a melodic way while in costume

Order in the Court: Courtroom tales, including *The Accused, And Justice for All, A Few Good Men, Witness for the Prosecution*

Organized Crime: Gangsters with Franklin Planners

Otherwise Engaged: Couple buys ring, sets date, and gets ready to march down the aisle, sometimes with a new fiancee *Moonstruck, Only You, Sleepless in Seattle*

Outtakes & Bloopers: Inadvertent laugh riots

Overlooked Gems: No box office to speak of, but worth a rent

Pacific Islands: Hawaii, Tahiti, Philippines, etc.

Paperboys: Kids who toss papers everywhere but your front porch

Parades & Festivals: *Animal House* and *Ferris Bueller's Day Off*

Parallel Universes: There's a whole other world out there *Cool World, Who Framed Roger Rabbit?*

Parenthood: Moms, dads, substitutes *Dutch, Ma Barker's Killer Brood, Father of the Bride, Three Men and a Baby, Yours, Mine, and Ours, Raising Arizona*

Paris: Ze city in France with rude occupants and ze Eiffel Tower

Party Hell: *Psycho Girls* have fun at a sleepover until *Monsters Crash the Pajama Party* and it becomes *The Slumber Party Massacre*

Patriotism & Paranoia: Run the flag up the pole and salute it *Rambo, Patton, Norris,* etc.

Peace: *Friendly Persuasion, Gandhi*

Period Piece: Costume epics or evocative of a certain time and place *Bugsy, Cleopatra, Doctor Zhivago, The French Lieutenant's Woman, Swing Kids*

Persian Gulf War: Smart bombs away

Phobias!: Eeeeeeeeeeeeeeeek!

Phone Sex: Is it really the next best thing to being there?

Phone Terror: *Don't Answer the Phone*

Physical Problems: *My Left Foot, Coming Home, The Elephant Man, The Other Side of the Mountain, Untamed Heart, The Waterdance*

Pigs: Loveable swine *Gordy, Babe the Gallant Pig*

Pill Poppin': Life with a drugstore cowboy; consumption of drugs, mostly illegal or in extra-large dosages

Pirates: Avast, ye scurvy dogs! *Captain Blood* drops in on *Treasure Island*

Pittsburgh: City in western Pennsylvania, home of sports teams fond of the colors black and yellow.

Poetry: Not exactly a booming category, but think of *Poetic Justice*

Poisons: *Arsenic and Old Lace* and *D.O.A.*

Political Conspiracy: *All the President's Men* present a *Clear and Present Danger* to the Constitution

Politics: *Bob Roberts, Mandela, Whoops Apocalypse*

Pool: *The Hustler*

Pornography: *Hardcore, Body Double*

Post Apocalypse: No more convenience stores

Postwar: After effects of war, generally WWI or WWII but sometimes the Civil War, the War of 1812, the ' Revolutionary War, and the Ohio Automobile Dealers War

POW/MIA: Captured by the enemy

Pregnant Men: Ahh-nuld fails the *Rabbit Test*

Pregnant Pauses: Humorous takes on pregnancy and birth *Nine Months, She's Having a Baby*

Presidency: Mr. Lincoln, *JFK*, LBJ, FDR, and, of course, *Dave*

Price of Fame: What goes up...

Production Problems: When bad things happen to good (*The Crow*) and bad (*Vampire in Brooklyn*) movies

Propaganda: Deliberately stretching the truth in order to persuade

Protests: Hell no, we won't go (to bad movies)! Make popcorn, not war!

Psycho-Thriller: It's all in your mind *Bad Influence,·House of Games, The Silence of the Lambs*

Psychotics/Sociopaths: *Killer Inside Me, Reservoir Dogs, The Stepfather*

Puppets: Usually with strings, but also muppets

Pure Ego Vehicles: Big stars doing their big star thing- *Hudson Hawk, Harlem Nights, Yes, Giorgio*

Race Against Time: Tick, tock, tick, tock *China Syndrome, Lorenzo's Oil*

Radio: Over the airwaves *Choose Me, The Fisher King, Radio Days, Sleepless in Seattle*

Rags to Riches: Grit, determination, and hustling (or just pure dumb luck) lead to fortune *Trading Places, Working Girls*

Rape: Victims and often their revenge

Rebel With a Cause: Bucking the establishment for a reason

Rebel Without a Cause: Bucking the establishment just because it's the establishment

***The Red Cross:** Organization that helps those in need of blood, disaster relief, and war relief; also monitors treatment of POWs

Red Scare: Cold War and Communism *The Commies Are Coming, The Commies Are Coming, Reds*

Religion: *Witness, The Last Temptation of Christ*

Religious Epics: Charlton Heston parts the Red Sea religion on a really big scale

Renegade Body Parts: Hands, fingers, eyes, brains with a life of their own

Repressed Men: Often British (*see* Anthony Hopkins or Hugh Grant), always with plenty of stiffness in upper lip and little elsewhere

Rescue Missions: I'll save you *The Searcher, Free Willy*

Rescue Missions Involving Time Travel: I'll save you in another dimension *Back to the Future*

The Resistance: WWII rebels with an anti-Nazi cause

Revenge: A key motivating factor *Cape Fear, Death Wish, Hamlet*

Revolutionary War: Fought over tea

Rio: As in de Janeiro–that swingin' South American party town.

Road Trip: Escapism courtesy of two- and four-wheel vehicles *Easy Rider, Coupe de Ville, Pee Wee's Big Adventure, Wild at Heart*

Roaring '20s: Flappers, prohibition, bobbed hair

Robots/Androids: Mechanical but fascinating; *Blade Runner* and *The Terminator*

Rock Stars on Film: But can they act? Prince (Symbol), Sting, Elvis, Lennon, The Monkees, Whitney, and so on

Rodeos: Rope tricks with steers

Role Reversal: Vice versa; empathy test *Freaky Friday, My Fair Lady, Switch, Soul Man*

Roll Over Beethoven: Plot revolves around the music-meister, or he makes an appearance *Bill & Ted's Excellent Adventure, Immortal Beloved*

Romantic Adventures: Love among the chases and explosions *The African Queen, Romancing the Stone*

Romantic Comedy: Falling in love has its hilarious moments *French Kiss, Crossing Delancey, Modern Romance, Much Ado About Nothing*

Romantic Drama: Love thing leads to tension and anxiety- *Cyrano de Bergerac, Far and Away, Sommersby, Tender Mercies*

Romantic Triangles: Three where there's only room for two *The Age of Innocence, Casablanca, Three of Hearts*

Roommates from Hell: Sometimes they won't do the dishes, sometimes they're homicidal *Single White Female*

Royalty: Emperors, kings, queens, princes, princesses, crowns, scepters

Royalty, British: Emperors, kings, queens, etc in Merry Olde England

Royalty, Russian: Emperors, czars, and czarinas who ran things in Moscow till those mean old Bolsheviks showed up

Running: Jogging, panting, collapsing

Russia: Back in what used to be the USSR

Sail Away: Vessels on the water *Mutiny on the Bounty, Erik the Viking, Mister Roberts*

Saints: *Bernadette, Saint Joan, A Time for Miracles*

Salespeople: Have I got a deal for you...

***Salvation Army:** Paramilitary charity with Santa Clauses on every corner

San Francisco: Set in the Northern California city known for hills and sourdough bread

Sanity Check: Inmates running the asylum; also deviant mental states

Satanism: *Speak of the Devil*

Satire & Parody: Biting social commentary or genre spoofs, including *Being There, Airplane!, Down and Out in Beverly Hills, I'm Gonna Git You Sucka, Monty Python's The Meaning of Life, The Player*

Savants: Half-minded geniuses; *Rain Man, Forrest Gump*

Scams, Stings & Cons: The hustle *The Billionaire Boys Club, The Color of Money, A Fish Called Wanda, The Grifters, The Sting*

***Scared 'Chuteless:** Jumping out of airplanes without the proper equipment. Good candidates for a bad case of cement poisoning

School Daze: Education, school, and teachers, generally grammar school days *Lean on Me, Dead Poet's Society, To Sir, with Love, Teachers*

Sci Fi: Imagination fueled by science and a vision of the future

Science & Scientists: *Altered States, Darkman, Them, They, Son of Flubber, The Story of Louis Pasteur*

Scotland: Lush hills, thick brogues, kilts, bagpipes, and *Whiskey Galore*

Screwball Comedy: Snappy repartee between a man and a woman dealing with an impossibly silly situation

Scuba: Wet suits, including *The Abyss, Navy SEALS*

***Sculptors:** Artists who like to work with clay, rock, hammers, and chisels

Sea Critter Attack: Monsters from the deep (and not so deep) surface and surprise! *Jaws, Orca, Moby Dick*

Sea Disasters: We've sprung a leak *The Poseidon Adventure*

Seattle: Showcases the city in Washington state where it rains a lot; the home of grunge rock

Serial Killers: They just won't stop *Henry: Portrait of a Serial Killer, The Rosary Murders*

Serials: Segmented adventures; Heyday was in the 1930s *The Adventures of Red Ryder, The Little Rascals, Flash Gordon*

Sex & Sexuality: Focus is on lust, for better or worse *Alfie, Barbarella, Emmanuelle, Looking for Mr. Goodbar, Rambling Rose, She's Gotta Have It*

Sex on the Beach: Flashing the fish and getting sand in the darndest places; the most famous couple was in *From Here to Eternity* and *Airplane!* lost no time making fun of them

Sexploitation: Softcore epics usually lacking in plot but not skin *The Erotic Adventures of Pinocchio*

Sexual Abuse: Victims and their stories *Twin Peaks, Fire Walk with Me*

Sexual Harassment: When I say no, I mean it

Shipwrecked: Stranded on an island when your boat sinks

Showbiz Comedies: Laughter behind the scenes in Hollywood or on Broadway

Showbiz Dramas: Tension behind the scenes in Hollywood or on Broadway

Showbiz Musicals: Singing and dancing behind the scenes in Hollywood or on Broadway

Showbiz Thrillers: Screaming behind the scenes in Hollywood or on Broadway

Shrinks: Psychiatry or equivalent, with *The Prince of Tides, One Flew Over the Cuckoo's Nest*

Shutterbugs: Photographers and their pictures *The Public Eye, The Eyes of Laura Mars, Peeping Tom*

Silent Films: No small talk/no big talk/no talk talk

Silent Horror/Fantasy Classics: Silent screams, expressions of terror

***Single Parents:** Divorced or widowed, they're doing the work of two–and they're back in the dating scene, usually assisted by match-making kids

Singles: Not always swinging but still solidly single *About Last Night, Singles, When Harry Met Sally*

Skateboarding: Teens on wheels *Gleaming the Cube*

Skating: Roller and ice, including *The Cutting Edge, Xanadu*

Skiing: Slap on a couple of waxed boards and off you go *Downhill Racer, Swinging Ski Girls*

Skinheads: Nazi wannabes wreak havok and cause trouble

Skydiving: Jumping from a plane with a polyester slip

Slapstick Comedy: Humor of the physical sort, including Abbott and Costello, the Marx Brothers, sports comedies, Ernest, Pink Panther, Home Alone, the Three Stooges

Slavery: *Roots, Spartacus*

Slice of Life: Charming small stories of life the way it might be *The Bicycle Thief, Fried Green Tomatoes, Marty*

Snakes: Slithering creatures who frighten many *Raiders of the Lost Ark*

Soccer: Known as football outside of the USA *Victory, Ladybugs*

South America: Right below North America *Aguirre, the Wrath of God, The Mission*

Southern Belles: Southern gals ooze charm *Blaze, Driving Miss Daisy, Steel Magnolias*

Space Operas: Going where no spam has gone before *Alien, Star Trek, 2001: A Space Odyssey, Apollo 13*

Spaghetti Western: Clint with a squint, *A Fistful of Dollars, My Name is Nobody, Once Upon a Time in the West*

Spain: *Siesta*

Speculation: In search of...

Spies & Espionage: Trench coats, dark glasses, Bond, *North by Northwest*

Sports Comedies: Humorous athletic tales, generally not based on a true story

Sports Dramas: Intense athletic tales, often based on a true story

Spousal Abuse: *The Burning Bed, What's Love Got to Do With It?*

Stagestruck: Stories of the theatre; *Broadway Melody* sung at the *Stage Door* by *The Dolly Sisters*

Stalked: No, I do not want to switch to MCI

Star Gazing: Not Hollywood stars, astrology/astronomy type stars

Stepparents: New spouse hiding either alien origins or sociopathic tendencies greets existing clan

Stewardesses: *Three Guys Named Mike* go to *Stewardess School* and meet *Blazing Stewardesses*

Stolen from Asia: American remakes of Asian classics—usually Kurosawa's; *Seven Samurai* becomes *The Magnificent Seven*

Stolen from Europe: American remakes of European fare; *A Walk in the Clouds, The Vanishing, Scent of a Woman*

Stolen From France: Hollywood goes to its favorite remake well; *Diabolique, Cousins, Nine Months, Three Men and a Baby*

Storytelling: *Amazing Stories, Grim Prairie Tales*

Strained Suburbia: Neighborhood is not what it seems *Dennis the Menace, Neighbors, Edward Scissorhands*

Strippers: Take it off, take it all off

Struggling Musicians: Talented, but still reaching for the top

Stupid Is...: Stupidity on purpose *Billy Madison, Dumb and Dumber,* or dumbness as a plot device *Being There, Forrest Gump*

Submarines: Deep sea diving; *Das Boot, Up Periscope, Run Silent, Run Deep, Hunt for Red October*

Subways: A train for shorter trips *Speed, The Taking of Pelham One Two Three*

Suicide: Premature ends *The Big Chill, Scent of a Woman, Romeo and Juliet*

Summer Camp: Where children go to misbehave, including *Meatballs* and *Sleepaway Camp*

Super Heroes: Men and women of extraordinary strength and abilities wearing silly-looking costumes

Supernatural Comedies: *Beetlejuice* marries *She-Devil* and they take *The Ghost Train* to their *Haunted Honeymoon*

Supernatural Cop Thrillers: *Angel Heart, Maniac Cop, Wolfen*

Supernatural Horror: Forces from beyond terrorize those who are here

Supernatural Martial Arts: Kung fu *From Beyond the Grave*

Supernatural Westerns: Forces from beyond terrorize cowboys in the Old West

Surfing: Awesome wave, dude! *Mad Wax, The Surf Movie, Surf Nazis Must Die, Endless Summer*

Survival: *Alive, The Bridge over the River Kwai, Testament*

Suspended Animation: Frozen in time *Coma, Late for Dinner*

Swashbucklers: Crossed swords and rope swinging, including *Robin Hood, Zorro,* various Musketeers, *Captain Blood, The Three Amigos*

Swimming: Ranging from *Gremlins* to *Jaws* to *The Swimmer* to *Cocoon*

Swingers: *Bob & Carol & Ted & Alice* try *Group Marriage* and *Carol and Alice* become *Swinging Wives*

Sword & Sandal: *See* Arnold Schwarzenegger's early career

Tattoos: *The Illustrated Man* visits *Cape Fear* to do battle with *Cyber Bandits*

Team Efforts: Working together pays off *Hoosiers, Memphis Belle, Renaissance Man*

Tearjerkers: Crying fests *Love Story, Steel Magnolias, Old Yeller*

Technology Rampant: Machines that wreak havoc *Metropolis, Death Ray 2000, Blade Runner*

Teen Angst: Adolescent anxieties, including *Baby It's You* and almost everything produced or directed by John Hughes

Tennis: Anyone?

*Terminal Confusion: Luggage gets mixed up at the airport, bus station, etc. Trouble usually follows

Terror in Tall Buildings: From *Die Hard* to *Speed* to *The Towering Inferno*

Terrorism: Love affairs with hidden bombs

*Thanksgiving: Huge dinner, football, familial angst, turkey coma, Christmas shopping may now commence

This Is Your Life: Biography and autobiography, including *The Babe Ruth Story, Amazing Howard Hughes, Amadeus, Catherine the Great, Great Balls of Fire, Raging Bull, What's Love Got to Do With It?*

3-D Flicks: Bring your special glasses

Thumbs Up: Hitchin' a ride *Even Cowgirls Get the Blues, The Hitcher*

Time Travel: Fast forward or reverse with Bill and Ted, *Dr. Who, Back to the Future,* and *Peggy Sue Got Married*

*Time Warped: You wake up in an era not your own; *Austin Powers,* the Bradys and the Cleavers coping with the '90s

*Titanic: The unsinkable ship that hit an iceberg its first time out...and sunk. It was in all the papers

Tokyo: Crowded city in Japan terrorized by Godzilla

Torn in Two (or More): *Sybil* and Dr. Jekyll and Mr. Hyde are *Raising Cain* leading *Separate Lives* on the *Edge of Sanity*

Torrid Love Scenes: Steamy and/or sticky *Angel Heart, Bull Durham, From Here to Eternity, Risky Business, The Unbearable Lightness of Being*

Toys: *Babes in Toyland, The Toy, Toys*

Tragedy: The fate of humankind, magnified *King Lear, Madame Bovary, Tess, The World According to Garp*

Trains: Rhythm of the clackity clack *Romance on the Orient Express, Throw Momma from the Train, Running Scared, The Silver Streak*

Trapped with a Killer!: And there's no escape *Dead Calm, Misery, The Shining*

Treasure Hunt: Looking for hidden riches *Klondike Fever, Treasure of Sierra Madre, Romancing the Stone*

Trees & Forests: Can't see one for the other, that wilderness paradox includes *Mr. Sycamore* and *The Wizard of Oz*

True Crime: Based on fact, including *The Boston Strangler, The Executioner's Song, Helter Skelter*

True Stories: Approximations of real-life events often significantly fictionalized for the screen, including *All The President's Men, Chariots of Fire, Cry Freedom, Heart Like a Wheel, The Killing Fields, Silkwood*

TV Movies: First shown on broadcast, cable, or foreign television (BBC, etc.) *Adam, Autobiography of Miss Jane Pittman, Barbarians at the Gate, I Claudius, Longtime Companion, The Day After*

TV Pilot Movies: Some became series; some did not

TV Series: Collections, anthologies, and individual episodes of memorable shows *I Love Lucy, Star Trek, The Fugitive*

Twins: *Double Trouble, Double Vision, Mirror Images*

Twister!: The big wind not caused by Mexican food that picks up heavy things (houses, cows, trucks) and deposits them elsewhere

Unexplained Phenomena: No apparent reason for an event

Up All Night: Movie takes place mostly after the sun goes down and *Before Sunrise*

Urban Drama: *American Me* to *Boyz N the Hood* to *Grand Canyon* to *Zebrahead*

*The USO: Entertained the troops through two world wars and a variety of police actions—with Bob Hope usually leading the way

Vacations: From *City Slickers* to *Deliverance* to *Fraternity Vacation*

Vampire Babes: Blood sucking dames *The Brides of Dracula*

Vampire Spoof: Comedic blood suckers, including *Buffy, Andy Warhol's Dracula,Dracula Sucks*

Vampires: More serious vein of blood sucking varmint, including *Dracula* in his many manifestations

Variety: Little bit of everything

Venice: Italian city of gondolas

Veterans: Retired fighting men (and women) *Alamo Bay* to *Who'll Stop the Rain*

Vietnam War: *Platoon, Hamburger Hill, Apocalypse Now, Good Morning, Vietnam*

Vigilantes: Individuals take the law into their own hands *Death Wish, The Outlaw Josie Wales*

Viva Las Vegas!: Celebrating America's tackiest city *Honeymoon in Vegas, Sister Act*

Volcanoes: Mountain blowing off steam, including *Joe Versus the Volcano*

Volleyball: *Side Out* used to be the only one till we remembered the barechested boys from *Top Gun*

Voodoo: From *Angel Heart* to *How to Stuff a Wild Bikini* to *Weekend at Bernie's 2*

Waitresses: *Alice Doesn't Live Here Anymore,* she went to *Atlantic City* to get some *Mystic Pizza*

War Between the Sexes: Men and women battle for supremacy *It Happened One Night, The King and I, He Said, She Said, Romancing the Stone, When Harry Met Sally, The War of the Roses, Thelma & Louise*

War, General: Generally any conflict that defies other classification *The Alamo, Gunga Din, The Last of the Mohicans*

Wedding Bells: Memorable weddings; *Father of the Bride, Four Weddings and a Funeral, Sixteen Candles, The Wedding*

Wedding Hell: Horror-filled or anxiety-ridden weddings; *The Blood Spattered Bride, The Brides Wore Blood, The Graduate, Wedding Banquet*

Werewolves: Full moon wonders, like *Wolf*

Western Comedy: Gags and horses *Ballad of Cable Hogue, Blazing Saddles, Rancho Deluxe, Support Your Local Sheriff*

Westerns: Cowboys, cowgirls, horses and jingle jangling spurs on the frontier

Westrogens: The Old West through women's eyes

Whitewater Rafting: Wild ride down a raging river, often in the company of a psycho

Wild Kingdom: Animals on their own and interacting with confused humans, including *The Bear, Dumbo, Born Free, Free Willy, Never Cry Wolf*

Wilderness: More trees than a forest, plus wild critters *The Life and Times of Grizzly Adams*

Witchcraft: From *Hocus Pocus* to *Three Sovereigns for Sarah* to *The Wizard of Oz*

Women: Impressive women, less than impressive women, and issues concerning women *Crimes of the Heart*, *My Brilliant Career*, *Passion Fish*, *Working Girls*

Women Cops: Female officers of the law

Women in Prison: The things that go on in the big doll house

*Women in War: Nurses, WACs, WAVES, USO performers, sometimes prisoners–they also served...

Wonder Women: *Attack of the 50-Foot Woman*, *Ripley*, *La Femme Nikita*, *Supergirl*

World War I: The First Big One, including *African Queen*, *Gallipoli*, *Grand Illusion*

World War II: The Last Big One, including *A Bridge Too Far*, *Guadalcanal Diary*, *The Guns of Navarone*, *Hope and Glory*, *Memphis Belle*, *Tora! Tora! Tora!*

Wrestling: Choreographed sport involving men and women *No Holds Barred*, *All the Marbles*, *Wrestling Women vs. the Aztec Ape*

Writers: Tortured souls who put pen to paper when they're not putting bottle to lips. Does not include the ink-stained wretches of the journalistic trade

Wrong Side of the Tracks: Often involves relationship with someone on the right side *Cannery Row*, *The Flamingo Kid*, *Pretty in Pink*, *White Palace*

You Lose, You Die: Sports goes nuts only the winner survives; *Arena*, *Rollerball*, *Tron*

Yuppie Nightmares: Young adults find best-laid plans for attaining wealth and privilege going astray *Baby Boom*, *Desperately Seeking Susan*, *The Mighty Ducks*, *Pacific Heights*, *Something Wild*, *Wall Street*

Zombie Soldiers: Recently undead in the army *They Saved Hitler's Brain*

Zombies: Recently undead everywhere *I Walked with a Zombie*, *Night of the Living Dead*

Category Index

T he **Category Index** includes subject terms ranging from straight genre descriptions (Drama, Comedy, etc.) to more off-the-wall themes (Nuns with Guns, Eyeballs!). These terms can help you identify unifying themes (Baseball, Heists), settings (Miami, Nifty '50s), events (The Great Depression, World War II), occupations (Clowns, Cops, Doctors & Nurses), or suddenly animate objects (Killer Appliances, Killer Cars). Category definitions and cross-references precede the index; category terms are listed alphabetically. **A tipped triangle indicates a video rated three bones or higher.**

Action

Pattern for Plunder
Pay or Die
Payback
Peacemaker
Pentathlon
Perfect Crime
The Perfect Weapon
The Perils of Pauline
Perils of the Darkest Jungle
The Persuaders
Phantom Express
The Phantom Flyer
Phantom of the Air
Phoenix
P.I. Private Investigations
Picasso Trigger
Pink Cadillac
Pirate Ship
Pirate Warrior
Pirates of the Coast
Pirates of the Seven Seas
Platoon the Warriors
Platypus Cove
Pocahontas: The Legend
Point Break
Point of Impact
The Polar Bear King
The Port of Missing Girls
The P.O.W. Escape
Powder Keg
Pray for Death
Prayer of the Rollerboys
The President's Plane is Missing
President's Target
Presumed Guilty
Prettykill
Prey for the Hunter
Primary Target
Prime Risk
Prince Valiant
Prison Planet
Prisoner of Zenda▸
Prisoner of Zenda
Private Life of Don Juan
Private Road: No Trespassing
Private War
Private Wars
The Professional
Professionals
Project A: Part 2
Project: Eliminator
Project: Shadowchaser
Protector
Provoked
Psychopath
Public Enemies
Pucker Up and Bark Like a Dog
Punch the Clock
The Punisher
Pure Danger
Python Wolf
Q & A
Queen of Diamonds
Queen of the Amazons
Queen of the Jungle
Queen of the Road
The Quest
Quest for Fire▸
Quest of the Delta Knights
Quick
Quiet Cool
Quiet Fire
Quiet Thunder
Quo Vadis
The Racers
Radar Patrol vs. Spy King
Radar Secret Service
Rage of Honor
Rage to Kill
Raiders of Atlantis
Raiders of Ghost City
Raiders of the Sun
Rainbow Drive
The Rainbow Gang
Rambo: First Blood, Part 2
Rambo 3
Ransom Money
Ranson's Folly
Rapa Nui

The Rape of the Sabines
Rapid Fire
Ravenhawk
Raw Deal
Raw Justice
The Razor: Sword of Justice
Real Bullets
The Real McCoy
Reason to Die
Rebel Storm
Red Ball Express
Red Dawn
Red Dust▸
The Red Fury
Red Heat
Red Line
Red Scorpion
Red Scorpion 2
Red Signals
Red Snow
Red Tent▸
Relentless 2: Dead On
Rent-A-Cop
Repo Jake
Rescue Force
Retrievers
Return Fire
The Return of Casey Jones
Return of Chandu
The Return of Eliot Ness
The Return of Grey Wolf
Return of Superfly
Return of the Dragon
Return of the Man from
   U.N.C.L.E.
Return of the Tiger
Return to Africa
Return to Fantasy Island
Return to Macon County
Return to the Lost World
Revenge of the Barbarians
Revenge of the Ninja
The Revenger
Revolt of the Barbarians
Revolver
Ricco
The Riddle of the Sands
Riding High
Ring of Steel
Rip-Off
The Rip Off
Rip Roarin' Buckaroo
River of Death
River of Diamonds
River of Evil
Road House
Road Kill USA
The Road Killers
The Road Warrior▸
Roadkill
Robbers of the Sacred Mountain
Robby
Robin Hood▸
Robin Hood...The Legend:
   Herne's Son
Robin Hood...The Legend:
   Robin Hood and the Sorcerer
Robin Hood...The Legend: The
   Swords of Wayland
Robin Hood...The Legend: The
   Time of the Wolf
Robinson Crusoe
Robinson Crusoe & the Tiger
Robinson Crusoe of Clipper
   Island
Robinson Crusoe of Mystery
   Island
RoboCop 2
RoboCop 3
The Rock▸
Rock House
The Rocketeer▸
Rocketship X-M
Rogue Lion
Rogue Male
Roller Blade Warriors: Taken By
   Force
Rollercoaster
Rolling Vengeance

The Rookie
Rosebud
R.O.T.O.R.
Rough Cut
Roughnecks
The Rousters
Royce
Ruckus
Rudyard Kipling's the Second
   Jungle Book: Mowgli and
   Baloo
Rulers of the City
Rumble in the Streets
Run
Run, Angel, Run!
Run, Rebecca, Run
Runaway
The Runaway Barge
Runaway Nightmare
Running Blind
Running Cool
Running Hot
The Running Man
Running Scared
Rush
The Russian Terminator
The Rutanga Tapes
Safari 3000
Saga of the Vagabond
Sahara▸
Sahara
Saigon Commandos
Saints and Sinners
Salty
Salvador▸
Samar
Samson Against the Sheik
Samurai 1: Musashi Miyamoto▸
Samurai 2: Duel at Ichijoji
   Temple▸
Samurai 3: Duel at Ganryu
   Island▸
Sands of Sacrifice
Sanjuro▸
S.A.S. San Salvador
The Satan Killer
Satan's Sadists
Savage!
Savage Beach
Savage Dawn
Savage Drums
Savage Fury
The Savage Girl
Savage Instinct
Savage Island
Scarface▸
The Scarlet & the Black
Scorpion Spring
Sea Devils
Sea Hound
Sea of Sand
Sea Prince and the Fire Child
The Sea Wolf▸
The Sea Wolf
Search and Destroy
Second Chance
Secret Agent Super Dragon
The Secret Code
Secret Mission
The Secret of El Zorro
Secret of the Ice Cave
Serpent Island
Sesame Street Presents: Follow
   That Bird
Set It Off
Seven Blows of the Dragon
Seven Magnificent Gladiators
Seven Sinners▸
The Seven-Ups
The Seventh Coin
The Seventh Voyage of Sinbad▸
Sex, Love and Cold Hard Cash
Shadow Man
Shadow of Chikara
Shadow of the Eagle
Shadow of the Wolf
Shadowhunter
Shaft in Africa
Shaft's Big Score

Shakedown
Shaker Run
Shamus
Shaolin Ex-Monk
Shaolin Vengence
Shark Hunter
Shark River
Sharks' Treasure
Sharky's Machine
Sharpe's Battle
Sharpe's Company
Sharpe's Eagle
Sharpe's Enemy
Sharpe's Gold
Sharpe's Honour
Sharpe's Mission
Sharpe's Regiment
Sharpe's Rifles
Sharpe's Siege
Sharpe's Sword
S*H*E
She Devils in Chains
Sheba, Baby
Sheena
The Sheik▸
Shep Comes Home
Ships in the Night
Shipwrecked
Shogun's Ninja
Shoot
Shoot the Sun Down
Showdown at the Equator
Sidekicks
Sidewinder One
The Sign of Zorro
Silent Hunter
Silk 2
Silk Degrees
Sinbad and the Eye of the Tiger
Sinbad of the Seven Seas
Sinbad, the Sailor▸
633 Squadron
Sixteen Fathoms Deep
The Skateboard Kid
Skeleton Coast
Ski Bum
Ski Troop Attack
Skull: A Night of Terror
Skull & Crown
Sky Hei$t
Sky High
Sky Pirates
Skyscraper
Slate, Wyn & Me
Slaughter
Slaughter's Big Ripoff
Slave of the Cannibal God
Sloane
Slow Burn
Smokey & the Hotwire Gang
Smuggler's Cove
SnakeEater
SnakeEater 2: The Drug Buster
SnakeEater 3: His Law
Soldier Boyz
Soldier's Fortune
Solo
Solo Voyage: The Revenge
Son of Captain Blood
Son of Fury▸
Son of Kong
The Son of Monte Cristo
Son of Samson
Son of Sinbad
Son of Zorro
S.O.S. Coast Guard
Sourdough
South Beach
South of Pago Pago
South Seas Massacre
Southern Comfort▸
Space Mutiny
Space Raiders
Space Riders
Spacehunter: Adventures in the
   Forbidden Zone
The Spanish Main
Spartacus▸
Spawn▸

Special Investigator
Speed 2: Cruise Control
Speeding Up Time
Speedtrap
Spiderman: The Deadly Dust
Spiders▸
The Spirit of Youth
Spitfire
The Spoilers
Spy
Spy in Black▸
Spy Smasher
Spy Smasher Returns
The Spy Who Loved Me
Stalking Danger
Stamp Day for Superman
Stand and Deliver
Star Quest
Starbird and Sweet William
Starchaser: The Legend of Orin
Starflight One
Stargate
Steel
Steel Arena
Steel Dawn
Stone Cold
Storm and Sorrow
Stormquest
The Story of Dr. Wassell
The Story of Robin Hood & His
   Merrie Men▸
Straight Line
The Stranger
Street Asylum
Street Fighter
Street Hawk
Street Knight
Street Law
Street Soldiers
Street Wars
Strike Back
Strike Commando
Striking Point
Stunt Pilot
Stunts
The Substitute
Subway
Sudden Death
Sudden Impact
Suicide Battalion/Hell Squad
Suicide Patrol
Summerdog
Sunshine Run
Super Mario Bros.
Superargo
Superbug Super Agent
Superchick
Supercop
Superfly T.N.T.
Supergirl
Superman: The Movie▸
Superman 2▸
Superman 3
Superman 4: The Quest for
   Peace
Superman & the Mole Men
Supersonic Man
Supervixens
Surprise Attack
Survival Quest
Surviving the Game
Suspicious Agenda
Swamp Fire
Swamp Women
Swashbuckler
The Sweeper
Sweet Justice
Sweet Revenge
Sweet Sugar
Sweet Trash
Swift Justice
The Switch
Switchblade Sisters
The Sword & the Rose
The Sword of El Cid
Sword of Gideon
Sword of Lancelot
Sword of Monte Cristo
Sword of Sherwood Forest

Adolescence

see Coming of Age; Hell High School; Summer Camp; Teen Angst

Adoption & Orphans

see also Hard Knock Life; Only the Lonely

Made for Love
Mandela≯
Mandela and de Klerk
Manhattan Baby
Manhunt in the African Jungle
March or Die
The Mark of the Hawk≯
Master Harold and the Boys≯
Men of Two Worlds
Mercenary Fighters
Mighty Joe Young
Mines of Kilimanjaro
Mister Johnson≯
Mr. Kingstreet's War
Mogambo≯
Monster from Green Hell
Mountains of the Moon≯
My African Adventure
Nairobi Affair
The Naked Prey≯
Night of the Sorcerers
Notes for an African Orestes
Oddball Hall
One Step to Hell
Options
Out of Africa≯
Over Indulgence
Overseas: Three Women with
    Man Trouble≯
The Passenger≯
Pepe Le Moko≯
Place of Weeping
Quartier Mozart
Red Scorpion
Return to Africa
Rhodes
Rogue Lion
Sanders of the River≯
Sarafina!≯
Satan's Harvest
Secret Obsession
Shaft in Africa
Shaka Zulu≯
The Sheltering Sky≯
Simba≯
Skeleton Coast
The Snows of Kilimanjaro≯
Something of Value≯
Song of Freedom
Sundown
Tilai
Time to Kill
Tobruk
Touki Bouki
Trader Horn
The Treasure of Bengal
Tuxedo Warrior
Warriors from Hell
We are the Children
Wend Kuuni
White Cargo
White Hunter, Black Heart≯
White Mischief≯
Wild Geese
A World Apart≯
Yankee Zulu
Zulu
Zulu Dawn≯

African America

see also **New Black**
Cinema

Aaron Loves Angela
Above the Rim
The Affair
America's Dream≯
Ashes and Embers
Assault at West Point: The
    Court-Martial of Johnson
    Whittaker
The Autobiography of Miss Jane
    Pittman≯
B.A.P.'s
Bebe's Kids
Beware
The Big Dis
Bingo Long Traveling All-Stars &
    Motor Kings≯

Bird≯
Black Brigade
Black Godfather
The Black King
Black Like Me
Black Sister's Revenge
Blue Collar
Boardinghouse Blues
Body and Soul
Boyz N the Hood≯
Broken Strings
Bronze Buckaroo
The Brother from Another
    Planet≯
Brother John≯
Bucktown
Bush Mama
Cabin in the Sky≯
Carmen Jones≯
CB4: The Movie
Charlotte Forten's Mission:
    Experiment in Freedom≯
The Cherokee Kid
Chuck Berry: Hail! Hail! Rock 'n'
    Roll≯
Class Act
Clockers≯
The Color Purple≯
Conrack≯
Cooley High≯
Cosmic Slop
Cotton Comes to Harlem≯
The Court Martial of Jackie
    Robinson≯
Crooklyn≯
Darktown Strutters
Daughters of the Dust≯
Dead Presidents
The Defiant Ones≯
Devil in a Blue Dress≯
The Devil's Daughter
Dirty Gertie from Harlem U.S.A.
Disorderlies
Do the Right Thing≯
Don't Be a Menace to South
    Central While Drinking Your
    Juice in the Hood
Don't Look Back: The Story of
    Leroy "Satchel" Paige
Double Deal
A Dream for Christmas≯
DROP Squad
Drums O'Voodoo
Dutchman≯
Dynamite Chicken
The Ernest Green Story
A Family Thing≯
Fear of a Black Hat
Final Comedown
Firehouse
The Five Heartbeats≯
Fly by Night
For Us, the Living≯
48 Hrs.≯
Foxy Brown
Fresh
Friday
Gang in Blue
The George McKenna Story
Get On the Bus≯
Ghosts of Mississippi
Girl from Chicago
The Glass Shield
Glory≯
Go Down Death
Go Tell It On the Mountain
The Golden Child
A Good Day to Die
Graffiti Bridge
Greased Lightning
The Great White Hope
The Greatest
Green Pastures≯
Guess Who's Coming to
    Dinner≯
The Guy from Harlem
Half Slave, Half Free
Hallelujah!≯
Hangin' with the Homeboys

Hank Aaron: Chasing the
    Dream≯
Harlem Nights
Harlem on the Prairie
A Hero Ain't Nothin' But a
    Sandwich
Hi-De-Ho
Higher Learning
Hollywood Shuffle
Home of the Brave≯
Hoodlum
Hoop Dreams≯
House Party≯
House Party 2: The Pajama Jam
House Party 3
How U Like Me Now?≯
I Know Why the Caged Bird
    Sings≯
Identity Crisis
I'm Gonna Git You Sucka≯
Imitation of Life≯
In the Heat of the Night≯
The Inkwell
Intruder in the Dust≯
The Jackie Robinson Story≯
Jason's Lyric
J.D.'s Revenge
The Jesse Owens Story
Jo Jo Dancer, Your Life is
    Calling
The Joe Louis Story
Joe's Bed-Stuy Barbershop: We
    Cut Heads
Joey Breaker≯
The Josephine Baker Story≯
Juice
Juke Joint
Just Another Girl on the I.R.T.
Kansas City≯
Keep Punching
Killer Diller
Killing Floor
King≯
The Klansman
Krush Groove
Lady Sings the Blues
The Last Dragon
Laurel Avenue
Lean on Me≯
The Learning Tree
Let's Do It Again
Lilies of the Field≯
Lily in Winter
Livin' Large
The Long Walk Home≯
Look Out Sister≯
Losing Isaiah≯
Lost Boundaries
Lotto Land
Love Jones≯
Love Your Mama
A Low Down Dirty Shame
Lying Lips
Machine Gun Blues
Mahogany
Malcolm X≯
Mama, There's a Man in Your
    Bed≯
A Man Called Adam
Mandela and de Klerk
Menace II Society≯
Miracle in Harlem
Miss Evers' Boys
Miss Melody Jones
Mississippi Burning≯
Mississippi Masala≯
Mr. & Mrs. Loving≯
Mister Johnson≯
Mo' Better Blues≯
Mo' Money
Moon over Harlem
Murder on Lenox Avenue
Native Son
New Jack City
New Jersey Drive
Nightjohn
No Way Back
Nothing But a Man

Once Upon a Time ... When We
    Were Colored≯
One False Move≯
Original Gangstas
Out of Sync
Panther
Paris Is Burning≯
Pastime≯
A Patch of Blue≯
Paul Robeson
Penitentiary
Perfume
Phat Beach
The Piano Lesson≯
Pinky≯
Poetic Justice
The Preacher's Wife
Purple Rain
Putney Swope≯
Quartier Mozart
Quiet Fire
Race to Freedom: The Story of
    the Underground Railroad
A Rage in Harlem≯
A Raisin in the Sun≯
Rappin'
Rebound: The Legend of Earl
    "The Goat" Manigault
Return of Superfly
Ricochet≯
The River Niger
Rockwell: A Legend of the Wild
    West
Roll of Thunder, Hear My Cry
Roots≯
Roots: The Gift
Roots: The Next Generation≯
Rosewood≯
Rude
Scar of Shame
School Daze≯
Separate But Equal≯
Sepia Cinderella
Sergeant Rutledge≯
Set It Off
Shadows≯
Shaft≯
Shaft's Big Score
Shanty Tramp
Sheba, Baby
She's Gotta Have It≯
The Show
Six Degrees of Separation
Small Time
A Soldier's Story≯
Sophisticated Gents≯
Soul of the Game≯
Soul Vengeance
Sounder≯
South Central
Sparkle
Sprung
Straight Out of Brooklyn
Strapped
Sudie & Simpson≯
Sugar Hill
Sun Ra & His Intergalactic Solar
    Arkestra: Space Is the Place
Superfly
Superfly T.N.T.
Sweet Love, Bitter
Sweet Sweetback's Baadasssss
    Song≯
Tales from the Hood
Tap
A Thin Line Between Love and
    Hate
Three the Hard Way
A Time to Kill≯
To Sir, with Love
To Sleep with Anger≯
Tougher than Leather
Truck Turner
The Tuskegee Airmen≯
Tyson
Uncle Tom's Cabin
Uptown Angel
Waiting to Exhale≯
The Walking Dead

Watermelon Man
Way Down South
What's Love Got to Do with It?
When We Were Kings
White Man's Burden
White Men Can't Jump
The Wiz
The Women of Brewster Place≯
Words by Heart
You Must Remember This
You So Crazy
Zebrahead≯
Zooman≯
Zora Is My Name!

AIDS

see also **Disease of the**
Week

Amazing Grace
And the Band Played On≯
As Is
Blue
Boys on the Side
Common Threads: Stories from
    the Quilt
The Cure
An Early Frost≯
Forrest Gump≯
Heaven's a Drag
In the Gloaming≯
Intimate Contact≯
It's My Party
Jeffrey
Joey Breaker≯
Kids
Les Nuits Fauves≯
Longtime Companion≯
Love! Valour! Compassion!
Love Without Fear
Men in Love
A Mother's Prayer
Our Sons
Parting Glances≯
Peter's Friends
Philadelphia≯
A Place for Annie
Postcards from America
Via Appia
Zero Patience

Air Disasters

see also **Airborne; Disaster**
Flicks; Sea Disasters

Air Force One≯
Airport≯
Airport '75
Airport '77
Alaska
Alive
Apollo 13≯
Broken Arrow
The Buddy Holly Story≯
Con Air≯
The Concorde: Airport '79
The Crash of Flight 401
Die Hard 2: Die Harder≯
Executive Decision
Fearless≯
Fire and Rain
Flight to Fury
Get Shorty≯
Heaven's Prisoners
Hero≯
The Hindenburg
Jet Over the Atlantic
Madam Satan
Mercy Mission
Operation Intercept
Ordeal in the Arctic
Sole Survivor
Survivor
Tailspin: Behind the Korean
    Airline Tragedy
A Thousand Heroes
Tragedy of Flight 103: The
    Inside Story≯

Berlin

Bicycling

Big Battles

Big Budget Stinkers

Big Daddies

Big Digs

Big Ideas

Classic Horror

see also Horror; Horror Anthologies

Cloning Around

Clowns

see also Carnivals & Circuses

Cockroaches

see also Killer Bugs

Cold Spots

Cold War

see Red Scare

Comedy

see also Black Comedy; Comedy Drama; Comic Adventure; Horror Comedy; Military Comedy; Musical Comedy; Romantic Comedy; Satire & Parody; Screwball Comedy; Slapstick Comedy; Sports Comedies; Western Comedy

Comedy

Going Undercover
Gold of the Amazon Women
The Gold Rush▸
Golden Earrings
Gone are the Days
Gone Fishin'
Good Girls Don't
Goodbye Love
Goon Movie
Gordy
Gotcha!
Grad Night
The Grass is Always Greener
 Over the Septic Tank
Greased Lightning
The Great American Sex
 Scandal
Great Bank Hoax
Great Bikini Off-Road Adventure
The Great Impostor
The Great Muppet Caper▸
The Great Outdoors
The Great Rupert▸
The Great St. Trinian's Train
 Robbery
Greedy
Green Grow the Rushes
Green Pastures▸
Grosse Fatigue▸
Group Marriage
Grumpier Old Men
Guarding Tess
The Guardsman
Guest Wife
A Guide for the Married Woman
Gumball Rally
The Gun in Betty Lou's Handbag
Gung Ho
Hail Caesar
Halloween with the Addams
 Family
Hamburger...The Motion Picture
Hanging on a Star
The Happiest Days of Your Life▸
Happy Birthday, Gemini
Happy Gilmore
The Happy Hooker
The Happy Hooker Goes
 Hollywood
The Happy Hooker Goes to
 Washington
Happy Hour
A Happy New Year!
Happy New Year
Hardbodies
Hardbodies 2
Harper Valley P.T.A.
Harry and the Hendersons
Harry & Walter Go to New York
Harry's War
Have Rocket Will Travel
Hawmps!
Head Office
Heading for Heaven
Headline Woman
Heart and Souls
Heartbreak Hotel
Heaven Help Us
The Heavenly Kid
Heavy Traffic▸
Heavyweights
Hello Again
Hell's Belles
Help Wanted: Male
Her Life as a Man
Herbie Goes Bananas
Herbie Rides Again
Here Comes Cookie
Hero at Large
Hi-Di-Hi
Hiding Out
High School USA
High Strung
Hijazo de Mi Vidaza
Hillbilly Blitzkrieg
His Girl Friday▸
His Picture in the Papers
Hit the Ice

The Hoboken Chicken
 Emergency
Hocus Pocus
Hog Wild
Hold 'Em Jail
Holiday Hotel
Holiday Rhythm
Hollywood Zap
Holy Matrimony
Home Is Where the Hart Is
Home Remedy
Homer Comes Home
Hometown Boy Makes Good
Hometown U.S.A.
Homeward Bound 2: Lost in San
 Francisco
Homo Eroticus/Man of the Year
Honey, I Blew Up the Kid
The Honeymoon Machine
Honky Tonk Freeway
Hooch
Hootch Country Boys
Hopscotch▸
The Horse in the Gray Flannel
 Suit
The Horse's Mouth▸
Hostage for a Day
Hot Millions▸
Hot Pursuit
Hot Resort
Hot Stuff
Hot Summer in Barefoot County
Hot T-Shirts
Hot Touch
Hot Under the Collar
Hot Wire
Hotel Paradiso
H.O.T.S.
House Arrest
House of Errors
House Party▸
House Party 2: The Pajama Jam
House Party 3
Houseguest
Housemaster
How Come Nobody's On Our
 Side?
How Funny Can Sex Be?
How I Won the War
How to Be a Perfect Person in
 Just Three Days
How to Beat the High Cost of
 Living
How to Break Up a Happy
 Divorce
How to Commit Marriage
How to Frame a Figg
How to Kill 400 Duponts
How to Make a Doll
How to Murder Your Wife▸
How to Pick Up Girls
How to Seduce a Woman
How to Succeed with Girls
Huckleberry Finn
Hullabaloo Over Georgie &
 Bonnie's Pictures
Hunk
I Love Lucy
I Wanna Hold Your Hand
I Was a Male War Bride▸
I Was a Teenage TV Terrorist
I Wonder Who's Killing Her
 Now?
Identity Crisis
If I Were Rich
If It's Tuesday, This Must Be
 Belgium▸
If You Don't Stop It...You'll Go
 Blind
Illegally Yours
I'm No Angel▸
The Immigrant▸
Immortal Bachelor
Importance of Being Earnest▸
The Imported Bridegroom
The Impossible Years
Improper Channels
The In-Laws▸
In the Army Now

In the Money
In the Spirit
Inn of Temptation
Innocent Sorcerers
The Innocents Abroad
Innocents in Paris
Inside the Law
The Inspector General▸
Intervista▸
Into the Sun
Invasion of the Space Preachers
The Invisible Kid
Invisible Mom
The Invisible Woman▸
Irish Luck
Irreconcilable Differences
Is This Goodbye, Charlie
 Brown?
It Could Happen to You
It Happens Every Spring▸
It Takes Two
It Was a Short Summer, Charlie
 Brown
The Italian Job
It's A Gift▸
It's a Great Life
It's a Joke, Son!
It's Not the Size That Counts
It's Pat: The Movie
Izzy & Moe
Jabberwalk
Jack
Jack and His Friends
The Jackpot
Jeeves & Wooster: Jeeves'
 Arrival
The Jerky Boys
Jimmy the Kid
Jinxed
Jocks
Joe's Apartment
Johnny Stecchino▸
Jokes My Folks Never Told Me
Jonah Who Will Be 25 in the
 Year 2000▸
Josh and S.A.M.
Jumpin' Jack Flash
Jungle 2 Jungle
Junior
Jury Duty
Just One of the Guys
Just William's Luck
Just Your Luck
K-9
Keaton's Cop
Kelly the Second
Kid from Brooklyn
A Kid in King Arthur's Court
Kid Sister
The Kid with the 200 I.Q.
Kidco
Kika
Kill My Wife...Please!
Killer Dill
King of the Airwaves
Kingpin
A Kink in the Picasso
Kiss Me, Stupid!
Kisses for My President
Kitty and the Bagman
Klondike Annie
The Knack▸
Konrad
La Boum
La Cage aux Folles▸
La Cage aux Folles 2
La Cage aux Folles 3: The
 Wedding
La Grande Bouffe▸
La Grande Vadrouille▸
La Vie est Belle
Ladies Who Do
Lady Godiva Rides
Lady Killer▸
Lady of the Evening
L'Anne Sainte
Larger Than Life
Las Vegas Hillbillys
Las Vegas Weekend

Last Night at the Alamo▸
Last of the Red Hot Lovers
The Last Porno Flick
Last Resort
The Lavender Hill Mob▸
Law of Desire▸
Le Bonheur Est Dans le Pre
Le Cavaleur
Le Gendarme de Saint-Tropez
Le Gentleman D'Epsom
Le Sex Shop▸
Leader of the Band
The League of Gentlemen▸
Leap Year
Leave It to Beaver
The Lemon Drop Kid
Leningrad Cowboys Go America
Leon the Pig Farmer
Les Aventuriers
Les Comperes▸
Les Patterson Saves the World
L'Escorte
Lesson in Love
Let It Ride
Let's Do It Again
Let's Get Tough
Liar Liar
License to Drive
Lie Down with Dogs
The Life & Times of the
 Chocolate Killer
Life Is a Long Quiet River▸
Life with Father▸
Life with Mikey
Like Father, Like Son
Li'l Abner
Listen, Darling
Little Big League
Little Darlings
Little Giants
Little Indian, Big City
Little Miss Marker▸
Little Miss Marker
Little Miss Millions
The Little Rascals
Little World of Don Camillo▸
Livin' Large
Living in Oblivion▸
Living on Tokyo Time
Lobster for Breakfast
Lonely Wives
The Longest Yard
Look Who's Laughing
Look Who's Talking Now
Lookin' to Get Out
Loose Cannons
Lost Diamond
Lost Honeymoon
Lost in America▸
Love and Other Catastrophes
The Love Boat
The Love God?
Love Nest
Lucky Jim
Luggage of the Gods
Luna e L'Altra
Lupo
Luv
Ma and Pa Kettle at Home
Ma and Pa Kettle on Vacation
Mabel & Fatty
Macaroni
Mack Sennett Comedies: Vol. 1
Mack Sennett Comedies: Vol. 2
Mad About You
Mad Miss Manton
The Magic Christian▸
Maid to Order
Major League
Major League 2
Major Payne
Make a Million
Make Me an Offer
Making the Grade
Malcolm
The Malibu Beach Vampires
Mallrats
The Man from Left Field
Man from Nowhere

Man in the Silk Hat
Man of Destiny
The Man on the Box
The Man with the Perfect Swing
The Mandarin Mystery
Manhandled
Manhattan Murder Mystery▸
Mapp & Lucia
Marriage Is Alive and Well
Married to It
Martians Go Home!
Master Minds
Matilda▸
A Matter of Degrees
Max
Maxie
Maybe...Maybe Not
McHale's Navy
Me and the Kid
Me and the Mob
Medicine Man
Meet the Hollowheads
Meet the Mob
Meet the Parents
Meet Wally Sparks
Melvin and Howard▸
Men at Work
Merton of the Movies
Mexican Spitfire at Sea
Mexican Spitfire/Smartest Girl in
 Town
Mickey the Great
Midnight▸
A Midwinter's Tale
Mighty Aphrodite
Mille Bolle Blu
Million Dollar Duck
Million Dollar Mystery
A Million to Juan
Milo Milo
The Misadventures of Mr. Wilt
Misbehaving Husbands
Miss Firecracker▸
Miss Grant Takes Richmond
The Missing Corpse
Missing Pieces
Mrs. Doubtfire
Mistaken Identity
Mr. Baseball
Mr. Blandings Builds His Dream
 House▸
Mr. Hobbs Takes a Vacation▸
Mr. Mike's Mondo Video
Mr. Nice Guy
Mr. Peek-A-Boo
Mr. Reliable: A True Story
Mister Roberts▸
Mr. Skitch
Mr. Walkie Talkie
Mr. Wise Guy
Mr. Wrong
Mistress
Mixed Nuts
Modern Problems
Mon Oncle▸
Mon Oncle D'Amerique▸
Monsieur Beaucaire▸
Mother Goose Rock 'n' Rhyme
Motorama
Movie ... In Your Face
Movie Maker
Moving
Moving Violations
Multiplicity
Mutant Video
My Blue Heaven
My Cousin Vinny
My Father Is Coming
My Father the Hero
My Favorite Blonde▸
My Favorite Year▸
My Fellow Americans
My Geisha
My Lady of Whims
My Life's in Turnaround
My Little Chickadee▸
My Pleasure Is My Business
My Summer Story
My Sweet Little Village

Mystery of the Leaping Fish/
    Chess Fever
The Naked Truth
National Lampoon Goes to the
    Movies
National Lampoon's Attack of
    the 5 Ft. 2 Women
National Lampoon's Class
    Reunion
National Lampoon's Last Resort
National Lampoon's Senior Trip
Nature's Playmates
Naughty Knights
Near Misses
Necessary Roughness
Neighbors
Never a Dull Moment
Never on Tuesday
Never Say Goodbye
Never Wave at a WAC
Never Weaken/Why Worry?►
New Pastures
New York Stories
New York's Finest
Next Door
Nickel & Dime
Night After Night
The Night Before
A Night in the Life of Jimmy
    Reardon
A Night of Love
Night of the Comet
Night of the Living Babes
Night Partners
Night Shift
The Night They Raided
    Minsky's►
The Night They Robbed Big
    Bertha's
Nine Ages of Nakedness
Nine Lives of Fritz the Cat
Nine Months
9 to 5
1941
Ninja Academy
No Dessert Dad, 'Til You Mow
    the Lawn
Nobody's Perfect
Nobody's Perfekt
Norman Loves Rose
Norman's Awesome Experience
Northern Extremes
The Nostradamus Kid
Nothing to Lose
Now You See Him, Now You
    Don't
Nudity Required
Nudo di Donna►
The Nut
Nutcase
The Nutt House
The Nutty Professor►
O.C. and Stiggs
Ocean Drive Weekend
Ocean's 11
The Odd Couple►
The Odd Squad
Oddballs
Off the Mark
Oh, God!
Oh, God! Book 2
Oh, God! You Devil
Oh, Heavenly Dog!
Oh, Mr. Porter
Oklahoma Bound
Old Enough
Old Spanish Custom
Oldest Profession
On the Air Live with Captain
    Midnight
On the Fiddle
On the Right Track
On Top of the Whale
Once Upon a Crime
Once Upon a Honeymoon
Once Upon a Scoundrel
The One and Only
One Body Too Many
One Cooks, the Other Doesn't

One Crazy Night
One Crazy Summer
101 Dalmatians
One More Saturday Night
One of Our Dinosaurs Is Missing
One-Punch O'Day
One Wish Too Many
Only Two You Can Play►
Open All Hours
Operation Dames
Operation Petticoat►
Opportunity Knocks
Options
The Other Side of Sunday
Our Gang
Our Gang Comedies
Our Gang Comedy Festival
Our Gang Comedy Festival 2
Our Hospitality►
The Out-of-Towners►
Out on a Limb
Out to Sea
The Outlaws is Coming!
Outtakes
Packin' It In
Palombella Rossa
Pals
Panic Button
Papa's Delicate Condition►
The Paper Brigade
Paper Lion
Paper Moon►
Parade►
Paradise Motel
Paradise Park
Paradisio
Pardon Mon Affaire, Too!
The Parent Trap
Park Avenue Logger
Parlor, Bedroom and Bath
Party Animal
Party Camp
Party Favors
Party Girl
Party Incorporated
Party! Party!
Party Plane
Pas Tres Catholique
Passionate Thief
Passport to Pimlico
Paternity
Paths to Paradise►
Pauline at the Beach►
Peck's Bad Boy
Peck's Bad Boy with the Circus
The Pee Wee Herman Show
Pee Wee's Big Adventure►
Pee Wee's Playhouse Festival
    of Fun
People Are Funny
People's Choice
Pepper and His Wacky Taxi
Perfect Furlough
A Perfect Little Murder
The Perfect Marriage
Personal Exemptions
The Pest
Pet Shop
Petit Con
Phat Beach
Pick a Star
Pick-Up Summer
The Pickwick Papers
Piece of the Action
A Pig's Tale
Pink Motel
Pizza Man
Plain Clothes
Planes, Trains & Automobiles
Playing Away
Playing Dead
Playing for Keeps
Playmates
Plaza Suite►
Please Don't Eat My Mother
Please Don't Eat the Daisies
A Pleasure Doing Business
The Plot Against Harry►
Poison Ivy

Poker Alice
A Polish Vampire in Burbank
Pom Pom Girls
Pop Goes the Cork
The Pope Must Diet
Porky's
Porky's 2: The Next Day
Porky's Revenge
Porridge
Portrait of a White Marriage
Pot O' Gold
Pouvoir Intime
Pre-Madonnas: Rebels Without
    a Clue
Preacherman
Prehistoric Bimbos in
    Armageddon City
Prehysteria 3
Prep School
Preppies
Pretty Smart
The Primitive Lover
Prince of Pennsylvania
Princess Academy
Princess Caraboo
Private Affairs
The Private Eyes
Private Lessons
Private Parts
Private School
The Private Secretary
Prize Fighter
The Projectionist►
The Promoter►
The Pure Hell of St. Trinian's
Pure Luck
Purlie Victorious
Pygmalion►
Pyrates
Quartier Mozart
Queen for a Day
Rabbit Test
Radio Days►
Rascal Dazzle
Ratings Game
Rave Review
Ravishing Idiot
Real Genius►
Real Life►
Really Weird Tales
Rebel High
Record of a Tenement
    Gentleman
Reg'lar Fellers
The Reluctant Agent
The Reluctant Astronaut
Remote
Remote Control
Renaissance Man
Rendez-Moi Ma Peau
Rent-A-Kid
Rented Lips
The Return of Our Gang
Return of the Tall Blond Man
    With One Black Shoe
Return to Mayberry
Revenge of the Cheerleaders
Revenge of the Nerds
Revenge of the Nerds 2: Nerds
    in Paradise
Revenge of the Nerds 3: The
    Next Generation
Revenge of the Nerds 4: Nerds
    in Love
Revenge of the Teenage Vixens
    from Outer Space
Rhinestone
Rich Hall's Vanishing America
Richie Rich
Riders of the Storm
Riding on Air
Rikky and Pete
Ring of the Musketeers
Rink/Immigrant
Ripping Yarns
Risky Business►
Rita, Sue & Bob Too►
Road Show
The Road to Wellville

Robin of Locksley
Robot in the Family
Rock & the Money-Hungry Party
    Girls
Rockula
Roller Boogie
Romy and Michele's High
    School Reunion
Rookie of the Year
Rosebud Beach Hotel
Rosencrantz & Guildenstern Are
    Dead►
Rubberface
Ruddigore
Ruggles of Red Gap►
The Runaway Bus
The Russians are Coming, the
    Russians are Coming►
Ruthless People►
Ryder P.I.
Sabrina the Teenage Witch
Sailor-Made Man/Grandma's
    Boy►
St. Benny the Dip
The St. Tammany Miracle
Sally of the Sawdust
Salut l'Artiste►
Samantha
Sammy, the Way-Out Seal
The Sandlot►
Santa Claus Conquers the
    Martians
The Santa Clause
Santa with Muscles
The Saphead
Sawmill/The Dome Doctor
Say Yes!
Scandalous
Scared Stiff►
Scavenger Hunt
School Daze►
The Scout
Screwball Academy
The Search for One-Eyed Jimmy
Second Sight
The Secret Agent Club
The Secret Life of Walter Mitty►
The Secret War of Harry Frigg
Senior Trip
The Seniors
Sensations
Sgt. Bilko
Seven Chances►
Sex and Buttered Popcorn
Sex and the Other Man
Sex on the Run
Sexpot
The Sexual Life of the Belgians
The Shaggy D.A.
The Shaggy Dog
Shake Hands with Murder
She Couldn't Say No
The Sheep Has Five Legs
She's Out of Control
Shooting Elizabeth
Short Circuit 2
The Show-Off
Side By Side
Silence of the Hams
Silk n' Sabotage
Silver Bears
Simple Men►
A Simple Wish
The Sin of Harold Diddlebock
Singleton's Pluck►
Sinners
Sirens
Sister Act
Sister Act 2: Back in the Habit
Sitting Ducks►
Six of a Kind►
The Sixth Man
Ski School 2
Skinner's Dress Suit
Skyline►
Slam Dunk Ernest
The Slap
The Sleazy Uncle
Sleeping with Strangers

A Slightly Pregnant Man
Slumber Party '57
Small Change►
Small Hotel
Smart Money
Snapshot
Snowball Express
Snowballing
Snuffy Smith, Yard Bird
So Fine
So This Is Washington
Social Error
Soggy Bottom U.S.A.
Solid Gold Cadillac►
Son-in-Law
Sorority House Party
Sorrowful Jones
Sotto, Sotto►
South Beach Academy
Speak Easily
Splitting Heirs
Splitz
Spy Hard
Squeeze Play
Stalag Luft
Stephano Quantestorie
The Stoned Age
Story of William S. Hart/Sad
    Clowns
The Strange Case of the End of
    Civilization as We Know It
The Stranger
Strike It Rich
Stuart Saves His Family
The Sucker
The Summer House
Summer Rental
Summer School
Sunset Park
The Super
Super Seal
The Sure Thing►
Surf 2
Susan Slept Here
Sweet Liberty
Swimsuit: The Movie
Swindle
Swingers►
A Swingin' Summer
Switch►
Sylvia and the Phantom►
Tabloid!
Taking Care of Business
Talkin' Dirty After Dark
Talking About Sex
Tall Story
Tampopo►
Tattle Tale
Tax Season
Teen Wolf
Teen Wolf Too
The Telephone
Teresa's Tattoo
That Darn Cat
That Gang of Mine
That's Entertainment, Part 2
There Goes the Neighborhood
These Girls Won't Talk
A Thin Line Between Love and
    Hate
Things Happen at Night
Think Dirty
Three Men on a Horse►
Three Nuts in Search of a Bolt
Three O'Clock High
Three Stooges in Orbit
Three's Trouble
The Thrill of It All!
To Grandmother's House We
    Go
To Wong Foo, Thanks for
    Everything, Julie Newmar
Tommy Boy
Tonight for Sure
Too Much Sun
Topper►
Topper Returns►
Topper Takes a Trip►
The Toy

Comedy

Toy Story▶
Trading Places
Traffic
Traffic Jam
Trapped in Paradise
Tromeo & Juliet
Troop Beverly Hills
The Trouble with Angels
True Identity
Trusting Beatrice
The Tunnel of Love
Turner and Hooch
The Tuttles of Tahiti▶
Twelve Chairs▶
Twentieth Century▶
Twinsitters
Two Bits & Pepper
200 Motels
The Ugly Dachshund
Un Air de Famille
Uncle Buck▶
Under the Yum-Yum Tree
Undercover Blues
Undergrads▶
Unfaithfully Yours▶
Unfaithfully Yours
Unidentified Flying Oddball
Used Cars▶
Varieties on Parade
Vasectomy: A Delicate Matter
Vegas Vacation
Vermont Is for Lovers
A Very Brady Christmas
A Very Brady Sequel
Virgin High
Visitants
The Visitors
Volere Volare
Volunteers
The Wacky World of Wills & Burke
Walking and Talking
Water
Wayne's World▶
Wayne's World 2
A Wedding
Wedding Band
Wedding Rehearsal
Weekend Warriors
Weekend with the Babysitter
Weird Science
Welcome to 18
Welcome to the Dollhouse
We're in the Legion Now
We're in the Navy Now
We're Talkin' Serious Money
Western
Wet and Wild Summer
What About Bob?▶
What Did You Do in the War, Daddy?
What Do You Say to a Naked Lady?
What's Up Front
The Wheeler Dealers▶
When Knights were Bold
When's Your Birthday?
Where Angels Go, Trouble Follows
Where There's Life
Where's Willie?
Whiffs
Whiskey Galore▶
Who Done It?
Who Framed Roger Rabbit▶
Wholly Moses!
Who's Got the Action?
Who's Harry Crumb?
Who's Minding the Mint?▶
Who's the Man?
The Wild Life
Wild West
Will Success Spoil Rock Hunter?
Win, Place, or Steal
Window to Paris
Wings of Fame
Wish Me Luck
Women's Club
Woof!

Working Winnie/Oh So Simple
The Wrong Guys
Yankee Zulu
You Can't Hurry Love
You So Crazy
You Talkin' to Me?
Young Einstein
Young Love—Lemon Popsicle 7
Zazie dans le Metro▶
Zebra in the Kitchen
Zero to Sixty

Comedy Anthologies

***see also** Comedy*

The Adventures of Hairbreadth Harry
All Night Long/Smile Please
Amazon Women on the Moon
And Now for Something Completely Different▶
The Best of Chaplin
Best of Eddie Murphy
Best of Ernie Kovacs
The Best of John Candy on SCTV
The Best of the Kenny Everett Video Show
The Best of the Kids in the Hall
The Best of the Two Ronnies
Best of W.C. Fields
Boccaccio '70
Charlie Chaplin: The Early Years, Vol. 1
Charlie Chaplin: The Early Years, Vol. 2
Charlie Chaplin: The Early Years, Vol. 3
Charlie Chaplin: The Early Years, Vol. 4
Daffy Duck's Quackbusters
Desperate Scoundrel/The Pride of Pikeville
Early Cinema Vol. 1
Everything You Always Wanted to Know about Sex (But Were Afraid to Ask)▶
A Few Moments with Buster Keaton and Laurel and Hardy▶
The Flintstones
The Floorwalker/By the Sea
For Auld Lang Syne: The Marx Brothers
Foreplay
Going to Congress/Don't Park There
Golden Age of Comedy
Great Chase
The Groove Tube
His Prehistoric Past/The Bank
His Royal Slyness/Haunted Spooks
Hollywood Boulevard
Hot Foot/A Happy Married Couple
Hot Water/Safety Last
I'm on My Way/The Non-Stop Kid
Kentucky Fried Movie▶
Kid 'n' Hollywood and Polly Tix in Washington
Kid's Auto Race/Mabel's Married Life
Kings, Queens, Jokers
The Knockout/Dough and Dynamite▶
Laugh with Linder!
Laughfest
Laurel & Hardy and the Family
Laurel & Hardy: At Work
Laurel & Hardy Comedy Classics, Vol. 1
Laurel & Hardy Comedy Classics, Vol. 2
Laurel & Hardy Comedy Classics, Vol. 3
Laurel & Hardy Comedy Classics, Vol. 4

Laurel & Hardy Comedy Classics, Vol. 5
Laurel & Hardy Comedy Classics, Vol. 6
Laurel & Hardy Comedy Classics, Vol. 7
Laurel & Hardy Comedy Classics, Vol. 8
Laurel & Hardy Comedy Classics, Vol. 9
Laurel & Hardy On the Lam
Laurel & Hardy Special
Laurel & Hardy Spooktacular
Laurel & Hardy: Stan "Helps" Ollie
Little Rascals, Book 1
Little Rascals, Vol. 1
Little Rascals, Vol. 2
The Lizzies of Mack Sennett
Looney Looney Looney Bugs Bunny Movie▶
The Lost Stooges
Love Notes
Mack & Carole
The Marx Brothers in a Nutshell▶
MGM's The Big Parade of Comedy
Monty Python's Parrot Sketch Not Included
Monty Python's The Meaning of Life▶
National Lampoon Goes to the Movies
National Lampoon's Favorite Deadly Sins
Never Weaken/Why Worry?▶
New York Stories▶
Oldest Profession
Our Gang
Our Gang Comedies
Our Gang Comedy Festival
Our Gang Comedy Festival 2
Outtakes
Parade▶
Plaza Suite▶
Pop Goes the Cork
Queen for a Day
Rascal Dazzle
Really Weird Tales
The Return of Our Gang
Rink/Immigrant
Ripping Yarns
Sailor-Made Man/Grandma's Boy▶
Sawmill/The Dome Doctor
Sex and Buttered Popcorn
Shirley Temple Festival
Silent Laugh Makers, No. 1▶
Silent Laugh Makers, No. 2▶
Silent Laugh Makers, No. 3
Silent Movies...Just For the Fun of It!
Slapstick
Stan without Ollie, Vol. 1
Stooges Shorts Festival
The Stooges Story▶
Stop! Look! and Laugh!
Three Stooges Comedy Capers: Vol. 1
Three Stooges Comedy Classics
Three Stooges: Cookoo Cavaliers and Other Nyuks
Three Stooges Festival
Three Stooges: From Nurse to Worse and Other Nyuks
The Three Stooges: Half-Wit's Holiday and Other Nyuks
The Three Stooges: Idiots Deluxe and Other Nyuks
The Three Stooges: Nutty but Nice and Other Nyuks
The Three Stooges: They Stooge to Conga and Other Nyuks
Tigers in Lipstick
To See Such Fun
A Tribute to the Boys
Tunnelvision

Uncensored
When Comedy was King
Woman Times Seven
The World of Abbott & Costello
The Young Ones
Yours, Mine & Ours

Comedy Drama

***see also** Black Comedy; Comedy*

Adventure
Alice Doesn't Live Here Anymore
Alice's Restaurant
All I Want for Christmas
All My Good Countrymen
All Screwed Up▶
An Almost Perfect Affair
Aloha Summer
Always▶
Amarcord▶
American Boyfriends
American Graffiti▶
And Baby Makes Six
Androcles and the Lion
Andy Hardy Gets Spring Fever
Andy Hardy's Double Life
Andy Hardy's Private Secretary
Angel in a Taxi
Angie
Antonia's Line
The Apprenticeship of Duddy Kravitz▶
Arabian Nights▶
Arizona Dream
Armistead Maupin's Tales of the City
Article 99
Author! Author!
Autumn Marathon
Avalon▶
Awakenings▶
Ay, Carmela!▶
Babette's Feast▶
Baby It's You▶
The Baby-Sitters Club
Baby, Take a Bow
Back Roads
Bad Behavior
Bail Jumper
The Baker's Wife▶
The Ballad of Paul Bunyan
Band of Outsiders
Barcelona▶
Bartleby
Baxter
Beautiful Girls
Beautiful Thing▶
Being Human
Being Two Isn't Easy
The Bells of St. Mary's▶
Benji▶
The Best Way
Bhaji on the Beach
Big▶
The Big Chill▶
Big Girls Don't Cry...They Get Even
Big Night
Big Wednesday
Billy Liar▶
The Bishop's Wife▶
The Black King
Blueberry Hill
Blues Busters
Blume in Love▶
Bogus
Born to Win
Borsalino▶
The Boys Next Door
The Breakfast Club▶
Breaking Away▶
Breaking the Rules
Breaking Up Is Hard to Do
The Bretts▶
Bright Eyes
Brighton Beach Memoirs
Broadcast News▶

Bud and Lou
The Buddha of Suburbia▶
The Buddy System
Buddy's Song
Buffalo Bill
Bulldog Drummond's Revenge
A Bunny's Tale
Bureau of Missing Persons
Butterflies Are Free▶
Cadillac Ranch
Caesar and Cleopatra
Cafe Express
Calendar Girl
Candy Mountain
Cannery Row
Captain Newman, M.D.
Carbon Copy
Carnal Knowledge▶
Carnival in Flanders▶
Caro Diario▶
Carried Away
Casey's Shadow
Celestial Clockwork
Cesar▶
Cesar & Rosalie▶
The Challengers
Charles et Lucie▶
Charlie and the Great Balloon Chase
Cheaper to Keep Her
A Chef in Love
Children of the Revolution
Chimes at Midnight▶
China, My Sorrow
Chips, the War Dog
Chloe in the Afternoon▶
Choose Me▶
A Chorus of Disapproval
The Christmas Wife
Chungking Express▶
City Lights▶
City of Women
Claire's Knee▶
Clara's Heart
Class Reunion
Cleo from 5 to 7▶
Clipped Wings
Clown
Coast to Coast
Cocoon: The Return
Combination Platter
Come to the Stable▶
Commandments
Comment Ca Va?
Conspiracy of Terror
Cooperstown
Corvette Summer
Country Life
Coupe de Ville
The Courtship of Eddie's Father▶
Cousin, Cousine▶
Cousins▶
Crazy from the Heart▶
Crimes & Misdemeanors▶
Crooklyn▶
Danny Boy
David Holzman's Diary▶
The Decameron▶
The Decline of the American Empire▶
Der Purimshpiler
Desperate Teenage Lovedolls
Destiny Turns on the Radio
Details of a Duel: A Question of Honor
Detour to Danger
The Devil & Daniel Webster▶
Devil on Horseback
The Devil's Eye
Diary of a Chambermaid▶
Diary of a Mad Housewife▶
Diary of a Young Comic
Diary of Forbidden Dreams▶
Different for Girls▶
Digger
Dim Sum: A Little Bit of Heart▶
The Dining Room
Dinner at Eight▶

Comedy

She Must Be Seeing Things
Shirley Valentine▸
A Shock to the System▸
Shooters
Short Cuts▸
Side Out
Signs of Life
Simon, King of the Witches
A Simple Twist of Fate
Single Bars, Single Women
Six in Paris
Six Weeks
Skin Game▸
Slap Shot▸
Slaves of New York
Slightly Honorable
The Slingshot▸
The Slugger's Wife
Smart Alecks
Smugglers' Cove▸
The Snapper▸
Snoopy, Come Home▸
Soldier in the Rain
Some Kind of Hero
Some Kind of Wonderful
Someone Else's America▸
Something in Common
Something Special
Something to Talk About
Song of the Thin Man
Soul Man
Spencer's Mountain
Spike of Bensonhurst
Spitfire▸
Splash
Spoiled Children
Spook Busters
The Sprinter
Stage Door▸
Star of Midnight
Star Spangled Girl
Stardust Memories
Starlight Hotel
The Stars Fell on Henrietta
Starting Over▸
Staying Together
Stealing Beauty
Steamboat Bill, Jr.▸
Stoogemania
Storm in a Teacup
The Story of Seabiscuit
Stranger than Paradise▸
Strawberry Blonde▸
Street Music
Striptease
Strong Man▸
Stroszek▸
Stuck on You
Student Confidential
Sugarbaby▸
The Sugarland Express▸
Summer Fantasy
Summer Snow
The Sunshine Boys▸
Suppose They Gave a War and
　Nobody Came?
Swedenhelms
Sweet Adeline
Sweet Hearts Dance
Sweet Lorraine▸
Sweet William▸
Sweetie▸
Swept Away...▸
Swing Shift
Sylvia Scarlett
T Bone N Weasel
Table Settings
Take Down
Take This Job & Shove It
Take Your Best Shot
A Tale of Springtime
Tales of Manhattan▸
Talk
Talking Walls
Taxi Blues▸
A Taxing Woman▸
Teachers
Teacher's Pet▸
Teddy at the Throttle

Teddy at the Throttle/Speeding
　Along
10
Teresa Venerdi▸
Texasville
That Thing You Do!▸
That's Life!
That's My Baby!
There Goes My Baby
They Might Be Giants▸
The Thin Man Goes Home
Things Change▸
This Is My Life
Those Lips, Those Eyes
A Thousand Clowns▸
Three for the Road
Three in the Attic
Three Men and a Baby▸
Three Men and a Cradle▸
Three Men and a Little Lady
Thunder in the City▸
Thursday's Child
Thursday's Game▸
A Tiger's Tale
The Time of Your Life▸
Timepiece
Tin Men
The Tip-Off
Tito and Me▸
To Please a Lady
To Sleep with Anger▸
Toby Tyler▸
Tom Brown's School Days
Tom Brown's School Days▸
Tom Sawyer▸
Tony Draws a Horse
Too Pretty to Be Honest
Tootsie▸
Topaze▸
Torch Song Trilogy
Toys
Trading Hearts
The Tragedy of a Ridiculous
　Man
Train to Hollywood▸
Traveller▸
Travels with My Aunt
Trouble Along the Way
Trouble in the Glen
True Love▸
Truly, Madly, Deeply▸
Trust
Truth About Women
Tunes of Glory/Horse's Mouth
Turk 182!
Turkish Delights
Twenty Bucks▸
Twenty-One
29th Street
Twister
Two for the Road▸
Two for the Seesaw▸
Twogether
Ugetsu▸
Under the Biltmore Clock
Under the Boardwalk
Underworld
An Unfinished Piece for a Player
　Piano▸
Up the Down Staircase▸
Up the Sandbox
Used People
The Vals
The Van▸
Venice, Venice
Very Close Quarters
The Virgin Soldiers
Volpone▸
Wait Until Spring, Bandini
Walls of Glass
We Think the World of You▸
Weekend at the Waldorf▸
Welcome Home, Roxy
　Carmichael
We're No Angels
Whatever Happened to Susan
　Jane?
When Your Lover Leaves
Where the Heart Is

Whitcomb's War
The Whole Shootin' Match▸
Who's Who
Whose Life Is It Anyway?▸
Widow's Peak
The Wife
Wild in the Streets
Willie & Phil
Wings of Eagles
Winter Kills▸
Wired
Wise Blood▸
Wish You Were Here▸
With Honors
The Wizard
The Women▸
The World According to Garp▸
The World of Henry Orient▸
WR: Mysteries of the Organism▸
The Wrong Arm of the Law▸
A Yank in Australia
A Year in Provence▸
The Year My Voice Broke▸
Yesterday, Today and
　Tomorrow▸
The Young in Heart▸
You're a Big Boy Now▸
A Zed & Two Noughts▸

Comedy Mystery

see also Black Comedy;
Comedy; Comedy Drama;
Genre Spoofs; Horror;
Horror Comedy; Satire &
Parody

Charade▸
Clubhouse Detectives
Clue
Curse of the Pink Panther
Deathtrap
High Anxiety
Lady On a Train▸
Murder by Death
Off and Running
The Pink Panther▸
The Pink Panther Strikes Again▸
The Princess Comes Across▸
Return of the Pink Panther
Revenge of the Pink Panther
A Shot in the Dark▸
Trail of the Pink Panther
Whistling in Brooklyn
Whistling in Dixie
Whistling in the Dark▸

Comedy Performance

see Concert Films

Comedy Sci-fi

see also Comedy; Comic
Adventure; Genre Spoofs;
Satire & Parody; Sci Fi

The Absent-Minded Professor▸
Coneheads
Honey, I Shrunk the Kids
Honey, We Shrunk Ourselves
Ice Pirates
Men in Black▸
My Uncle: The Alien
Out There
Sleeper▸
Son of Flubber
Spaceballs
Theodore Rex

Comic Adventure

see also Action Adventure;
Comedy

Adventures Beyond Belief
Adventures in Babysitting
Adventures in Spying
Adventures of a Private Eye

Adventures of a Taxi Driver
The Adventures of Bullwhip
　Griffin
Air America
Alien from L.A.
All the Lovin' Kinfolk
All the Way, Boys
The Amazing Dobermans
The Ambushers
The Americano
Andy and the Airwave Rangers
Angel of H.E.A.T.
Angels Hard as They Come
Another 48 Hrs.
Another Stakeout
The Armour of God
Avenging Disco Godfather
Baby on Board
Back Roads
Back to the Future▸
Back to the Future, Part 2
Back to the Future, Part 3▸
Bad Guys
Bagdad Cafe▸
The Balloonatic/One Week
The Baltimore Bullet
Bananas Boat
Behind the Front
Beverly Hills Cop
Beverly Hills Cop 2
Beverly Hills Cop 3
The Big Slice
Big Zapper
Bingo
Bird on a Wire
Bloodstone
Blue Iguana
Body Trouble
Boris and Natasha: The Movie
Brink's Job▸
Brothers O'Toole
Burglar
Butler's Dilemma
California Straight Ahead
Campus Knights
Cannibal Women in the Avocado
　Jungle of Death
Cannonball Run▸
Cannonball Run 2
The Captain from Koepenick
Captain Swagger
Cartouche▸
Chan Is Missing▸
Chasers
Chu Chu & the Philly Flash
City Heat
Club Med
Collision Course
The Concrete Cowboys
Crocodile Dundee▸
Crocodile Dundee 2
Dirt Bike Kid
Doctor Detroit
Dog Pound Shuffle▸
Dolemite 2: Human Tornado
The Double O Kid
Down to Earth▸
Every Girl Should Have One
Explosion
Fast Getaway
Feds
The Fifth Musketeer
Fifty/Fifty
The Fighting American
Flatfoot
Flipper▸
Flirting with Fate▸
Forever Young
48 Hrs.▸
Foul Play▸
Free Ride
The Further Adventures of
　Tennessee Buck
Ghostbusters▸
Ghostbusters 2
Go for It
The Golden Child
The Gumshoe Kid
Gunmen

Hambone & Hillie
Harriet the Spy
Having Wonderful Time/Carnival
　Boat
Hawthorne of the USA
Here We Go Again!
High Road to China
High Voltage
Highpoint
Hudson Hawk
In Like Flint
In 'n Out
It's in the Bag
Jake Speed
Jane & the Lost City
The Jewel of the Nile
Just Tell Me You Love Me
Kazaam
Kindergarten Cop
King Kung Fu
Kiss My Grits
Kuffs
Landlord Blues
Last Action Hero
Leonard Part 6
A Low Down Dirty Shame
Lucky Devil
Lunch Wagon
Lust in the Dust▸
Mad About Money
Mademoiselle Striptease
Madigan's Millions
Magic Island
Magic Kid
A Man Called Sarge
The Man in the Raincoat
The Man Who Wasn't There
The Man with One Red Shoe
Master Mind
The Masters of Menace
Memoirs of an Invisible Man
Miami Supercops
Midnight Madness
Midnight Run▸
Miracles
Mr. Billion
Mr. Nanny
Mr. Robinson Crusoe
Mr. Superinvisible
Mitchell
Mo' Money
Mob Story
Mom and Dad Save the World
The Money
Monkey Hustle
Monkey's Uncle
Muppet Treasure Island
Mutants In Paradise
My African Adventure
My Breakfast with Blassie
My Dog, the Thief
My Science Project
The Naked Sword of Zorro
No Deposit, No Return
Oddball Hall
Odds and Evens
Operation Dumbo Drop
Our Man Flint
Over the Hill
Palookaville▸
Pippi Goes on Board
Pippi in the South Seas
Pippi Longstocking
Pippi on the Run
Pirates
Prehysteria
The Prince of Thieves
Red Lion
Reggie Mixes In▸
The Reivers▸
Rescue Me
The Return of the Musketeers
Return of the Rebels
Riff-Raff
Romancing the Stone▸
Round Trip to Heaven
Royal Flash▸
Rumble in the Bronx
Running Scared

Mill of the Stone Women
Ms. 45►
Missile to the Moon
Mom & Dad
Mommie Dearest
Mondo Trasho
Monsieur Verdoux►
Monty Python and the Holy
  Grail►
Monty Python's Life of Brian►
Motel Hell
Motor Psycho
Multiple Maniacs
The Mummy►
The Muppet Movie►
My Darling Clementine►
Naked Kiss
Nasty Rabbit
Never Give a Sucker an Even
  Break►
The Night of the Hunter►
Night of the Living Dead►
Oh Dad, Poor Dad (Momma's
  Hung You in the Closet & I'm
  Feeling So Sad)
Orgy of the Dead
Out of the Past►
The Outlaw
Peeping Tom►
Performance►
Petulia►
Phantasm
Phantom of the Paradise
Pink Flamingos
Plan 9 from Outer Space
Please Don't Eat My Mother
The Plot Against Harry►
Private Parts
The Producers►
The Projectionist►
Psycho►
Quadrophenia►
Queen of Outer Space
The Rain People►
Rancho Deluxe►
Re-Animator►
Rebel Without a Cause►
Reefer Madness
Repo Man►
Return of the Killer Tomatoes!
Ride the High Country►
The Road Warrior►
Roadkill
Robot Monster
Rock 'n' Roll High School►
The Rocky Horror Picture
  Show►
Satan's Sadists
Schlock
Sebastiane►
Sid & Nancy►
The Slumber Party Massacre
Sorority Babes in the Slimeball
  Bowl-A-Rama
Spider Baby
Start the Revolution Without
  Me►
Stoogemania
Strange Cargo
Surf Nazis Must Die
Sweet Movie
Tales from the Gimli Hospital
The Tall T
10th Victim►
Them!►
There's Nothing Out There
The Thing►
Thunder Road►
The Toxic Avenger
The Toxic Avenger, Part 2
Trash
Twin Peaks
Twin Peaks: Fire Walk with Me
Twister
2000 Maniacs
2001: A Space Odyssey►
The Undertaker and His Pals
Vanishing Point
Vortex

Wanderers►
The Warriors
The Wasp Woman
What Have I Done to Deserve
  This?►
Where the Boys Are
Where's Poppa?►
White Heat►
Wild Rapture
Wild Women of Wongo
The Wild World of Batwoman
Willy Wonka & the Chocolate
  Factory►
The Wizard of Oz►
Zachariah
Zardoz
Zontar, the Thing from Venus

Cult Items—New
see also Cult Items
The Adventures of Baron
  Munchausen►
Airplane!►
Better Off Dead
Bill & Ted's Excellent Adventure
The Blues Brothers
The Brady Bunch Movie►
The Breakfast Club►
Caddyshack►
Fast Times at Ridgemont High►
Ferris Bueller's Day Off►
A Fish Called Wanda►
Grease►
Heathers►
I Shot Andy Warhol►
Joe's Apartment
Mystery Science Theater 3000:
  The Movie
National Lampoon's Animal
  House►
Pretty in Pink
Real Genius►
St. Elmo's Fire
Saturday Night Fever
Sixteen Candles►
The Sure Thing►
This Is Spinal Tap►
The Untold Story
Wayne's World►

Cults
see also Occult; Satanism
Bad Dreams
The Believers
Beware! Children at Play
Blinded by the Light
Blood Clan
Bloodbath
Burial of the Rats
Children of the Corn 2: The Final
  Sacrifice
Cobra Woman
Cult of the Cobra
The Dark Secret of Harvest
  Home
Deadly Blessing
Death of an Angel
The Deceivers
Divided by Hate
Fatal Passion
Force: Five
Forever Evil
The Guyana Tragedy: The Story
  of Jim Jones
Helter Skelter
The House on Todville Road
In the Line of Duty: Ambush in
  Waco
The Lightning Incident
Lord of Illusions
The Mephisto Waltz►
Mind, Body & Soul
Next One
The Night God Screamed
Night of the Death Cult
Putney Swope►

The Pyx►
Raging Angels
The Reincarnate
Rest In Pieces
Revenge
Sabaka
Safe►
Servants of Twilight
Shock 'Em Dead
Shocking Asia
The Snake Hunter Strangler
The Snake People
The Spellbinder
Split Image►
Steps from Hell
Suicide Cult
Thou Shalt Not Kill...Except
Ticket to Heaven►
Treasure of the Four Crowns
Withnail and I►

Cyberpunk
Arcade
Blade Runner►
The Crow 2: City of Angels
Cyborg
Cyborg 2
Cyborg Cop
Cyborg Soldier
Demolition Man
Escape from L.A.
Escape from New York
The Fifth Element
Freejack
Ghost in the Shell
Hackers
Johnny Mnemonic
The Lawnmower Man
Lawnmower Man 2: Beyond
  Cyberspace
Mad Max►
Mad Max: Beyond
  Thunderdome
Megaville
Nemesis
Overdrawn at the Memory Bank
The Road Warrior►
RoboCop►
RoboCop 2
RoboCop 3
Tank Girl
TekWar
The Terminator►
Terminator 2: Judgment Day►
Tetsuo: The Iron Man
Total Recall►
Tron
Universal Soldier
Virtual Combat
Virtuosity

Dads
*see also Bad Dads; Moms;
  Monster Moms; Parenthood*
Address Unknown
The Adventures of Pinocchio
The Brady Bunch Movie►
Broken English
Bye Bye, Love
Carpool
Eat Drink Man Woman►
Eden Valley►
Father of the Bride►
Father's Day
The Favorite Son►
Fear
Getting Even with Dad
Ghost Dad
A Goofy Movie
Honey, We Shrunk Ourselves
House Arrest
Imaginary Crimes►
In the Gloaming►
Indiana Jones and the Last
  Crusade►
Jingle All the Way

Jungle 2 Jungle
Kolya►
Liar Liar
Life with Father►
Lone Star►
Magic in the Water
Memories of Me
Mr. Mom►
Mom and Dad Save the World
My Father Is Coming
My Father the Hero
National Lampoon's Christmas
  Vacation
National Lampoon's European
  Vacation
National Lampoon's Vacation►
Nick of Time
Parenthood►
Raising Arizona►
The Run of the Country►
She's the One
A Simple Wish
Sleepless in Seattle►
So I Married an Axe Murderer
The Stupids
The Sum of Us►
Superdad
Three Men and a Baby►
Three Men and a Cradle►
Three Men and a Little Lady
A Time to Kill►
To Gillian on Her 37th Birthday
A Very Brady Sequel
Wait Till Your Mother Gets
  Home
The War at Home

Dance Fever
*see also Ballet; Disco
  Musicals*
All That Jazz►
An American in Paris►
Anchors Aweigh►
April In Paris
Babes in Arms
The Bacchantes
The Band Wagon►
The Barefoot Contessa►
The Barkleys of Broadway►
Beat Street
The Belle of New York
Bert Rigby, You're a Fool
The Best of the Kenny Everett
  Video Show
Billy Rose's Jumbo►
Black Orpheus►
Blood Wedding►
Body Moves
Body Rock
Born to Dance
Breakin'
Breakin' 2: Electric Boogaloo
Breakin' Through
Broadway Melody of 1940
Cabin in the Sky►
Can-Can
Captain January
Carefree►
Carmen►
Charleston►
A Chorus Line
Chu Chu & the Philly Flash
Cover Girl►
Curdled
Daddy Long Legs►
Dames►
Dance or Die
Dancing Lady
Danzon►
Deadly Dancer
Delightfully Dangerous
Delivery Boys
Dirty Dancing►
The Discovery Program
Doll Face
The Eighties
El Amor Brujo►
Everybody's Dancin'

Everyone Says I Love You►
Faith
Fame►
Fass Black
Fast Forward
Faster Pussycat! Kill! Kill!
Femmes de Paris
Flashdance
Flower Drum Song
Flying Down to Rio
Follies Girl
Follow the Fleet►
Footlight Parade►
Footloose
The Forbidden Dance
42nd Street►
French Can-Can►
The Gay Divorcee►
Ginger & Fred►
Girl in Gold Boots
Girls Just Want to Have Fun
Give a Girl a Break
The Glass Slipper
Gold Diggers of 1933►
Gold Diggers of 1935►
Gotta Dance, Gotta Sing
Grease►
Grease 2
The Harvey Girls►
Heavenly Bodies
Hit the Deck
Holiday in Havana
Idiot's Delight►
The In Crowd
Isadora►
It Started in Naples►
Kiss Me Kate►
Lambada
Last Dance
The Last Dance
Le Bal►
Legs
Les Girls
Let's Dance
Liquid Dreams
Little Ballerina
Mad Youth
Manhattan Merengue!
Mantis in Lace
Meet Me in Las Vegas
Michael
Midnight Dancer
Minsky's Follies
Music in My Heart
Neurotic Cabaret
No Time for Romance
Nutcracker: The Motion Picture
Orgy of the Dead
Out to Sea
Paris Is Burning►
Party Girl►
Pennies From Heaven►
Pilot
The Pirate►
Portrait of a Showgirl
Portrait of a Stripper
Queen of the Stardust
  Ballroom►
Risky Business►
Roberta►
Romance in Manhattan
Rooftops
Roseland►
Salome, Where She Danced
Salsa
Saturday Night Fever
Scent of a Woman►
Second Chorus
Seven Brides for Seven
  Brothers►
Shag: The Movie►
Shall We Dance►
Showgirls
Silk Stockings►
Singin' in the Rain►
Slashdance
So This Is Paris►
Spirit of '76
Staying Alive

Stepping Out✦
The Story of Vernon and Irene
  Castle✦
Strictly Ballroom✦
Stripped to Kill II: Live Girls
Summer Stock✦
Sunset Strip
Sweet Charity✦
Swing Kids
Swing Time✦
Take Me Out to the Ball Game
Tango
Tango Bar
Tap
Taxi Dancers
Teen Wolf
Thank God It's Friday
That's Dancing!
That's Entertainment, Part 2
That's Entertainment, Part 3
They Shoot Horses, Don't
  They?✦
Those Lips, Those Eyes
Top Hat✦
The Turning Point
Urban Cowboy
What's the Matter with Helen?
Words and Music
Yankee Doodle Dandy✦
You Were Never Lovelier✦
You'll Never Get Rich✦
Ziegfeld Follies
Ziegfeld Girl✦
Zou Zou

Dates From Hell

see also Singles

After Hours✦
Blind Date
Bye Bye, Love
Ed's Next Move
Harold and Maude✦
Night of the Creeps
Reality Bites
Singles✦
Something Wild
Walking and Talking
What Happened Was...

A Day in the Life...

see also Up All Night

Before Sunrise
The Breakfast Club✦
The Daytrippers
Groundhog Day✦
Love and Other Catastrophes
Nothing Personal✦
Nowhere
One Fine Day
Sunday
12:01
Working Girls✦

Deafness

see also Physical Problems

Amy
Bridge to Silence
Children of a Lesser God✦
Copland✦
Crazy Moon
Dead Silence
For the First Time
Hear No Evil
The Heart is a Lonely Hunter✦
Immortal Beloved
Johnny Belinda✦
Johnny Belinda
Mandy✦
The Miracle Worker✦
Mr. Holland's Opus✦
Murderer's Keep
Psych-Out
Secret of Yolanda
See No Evil, Hear No Evil

Silent Victory: The Kitty O'Neil
  Story✦
Sincerely Yours
The Sound and the Silence
Sound of Love
The Sphinx
The Story of Alexander Graham
  Bell✦
A Summer to Remember
Suspect
Tin Man

Death & the Afterlife

*see also Angels; Funerals;
Ghosts, Ghouls, & Goblins;
Great Death Scenes;
Heaven Sent; Occult;
Suicide*

The Alchemist
All of Me
All That Jazz✦
Always
The Amityville Horror
Amityville 2: The Possession
Amityville 3: The Demon
Amityville 4
The Amityville Curse
Amityville 1992: It's About Time
Angel Heart
Angel on My Shoulder✦
Angel on My Shoulder
Another Chance
The Asphyx✦
Audrey Rose
Avanti!
Baby Girl Scott
Backwoods
Beetlejuice✦
Beyond Tomorrow
Bill & Ted's Bogus Journey
Black Force 2
Black Magic
Bliss✦
Blithe Spirit✦
Blood of the Vampire
Bloody New Year
The Bone Yard
Bowery at Midnight
Boys on the Side
The Bramble Bush
Breaking the Rules
Bulletproof Heart✦
Burnt Offerings
The Canterville Ghost
Carnival of Souls✦
Carousel✦
Carry Me Back
Castle of the Creeping Flesh
The Cat and the Canary✦
Cathy's Curse
Cemetery Man
The Chair
Chances Are✦
The Changeling
A Christmas Carol✦
A Christmas Carol
A Christmas Carol✦
Cold Heaven
The Corridor: Death
Courage Under Fire✦
The Crow
The Crow 2: City of Angels
Curse of the Cat People✦
Curse of the Living Corpse
Da
Daddy's Dyin'...Who's Got the
  Will?
Dark of the Night
Dark Tower
Dark Victory✦
Daughter of Horror
The Day It Came to Earth
Dead Heat
Dead Mate
Death Be Not Proud✦
Death Becomes Her✦
The Death Curse of Tartu

Death Row Diner
Defending Your Life✦
Deja Vu
The Devil & Max Devlin
Devil Kiss
The Diabolical Dr. Z
Diary of the Dead
Digging Up Business
D.O.A.✦
D.O.A.
Dr. Death, Seeker of Souls
Dr. Hackenstein
Doctor Phibes Rises Again
Dominique Is Dead
Dona Flor and Her Two
  Husbands✦
Donkey Skin✦
Donovan's Brain✦
Don't Go in the House
Doomed Love
The Duellists✦
Dying Young
Early Days
Earthling
Eleni
Emerald of Artama
Encounter with the Unknown
The End✦
The English Patient✦
Enrapture
The Entertainer✦
Epitaph
Estate of Insanity
Evil Spirits
Executive Suite✦
The Eyes, the Mouth
Fearless✦
The Fig Tree
Flatliners
Fluke
The Forgotten One
Friendly Fire✦
Frightmare
Frisk
From the Dead of Night✦
The Funeral✦
Funeral Home
Garbo Talks
Gates of Hell
The Ghost
Ghost✦
The Ghost and Mrs. Muir✦
Ghost Writer
Ghosts Can Do It
Ghosts Can't Do It
Ghosts of Berkeley Square
Go Down Death
Gotham✦
The Granny
Grave Secrets
The Green Room
Griffin and Phoenix: A Love
  Story
Hawks
Heart and Souls
Heart Condition
Heaven
Heaven Can Wait✦
The Heavenly Kid
Heaven's a Drag
Hello Again
Hercules the Legendary
  Journeys, Vol. 4: In the
  Underworld
Here Comes Mr. Jordan✦
Hideaway
High Plains Drifter
High Spirits
Highway 61
Hocus Pocus
Hold That Ghost✦
Hollow Gate
Homeward Bound
I Bury the Living✦
I Married a Witch✦
I Walked with a Zombie✦
Impure Thoughts
In an Old Manor House
In Between

In the Gloaming✦
The Indestructible Man
Infinity
Into the West✦
Intruso
It Came Upon a Midnight Clear
It Could Happen to You
It's a Wonderful Life✦
It's My Party
Jacob's Ladder
Judge & Jury
The Kid with the Broken Halo
Kill and Go Hide
Killing Grandpa
Kiss Me Goodbye
Kiss of Death
Kissed
La Vie Continue
The Lady in White✦
The Last Best Year
Last Light
The Legend of Hell House✦
Lightning Over Water
Liliom✦
Loot...Give Me Money, Honey!
The Loved One✦
Macbeth✦
Macbeth
Made in Heaven
The Man with Two Lives
Mannequin
Marvin's Room
Mausoleum
Maxie
Medea
The Midnight Hour
The Miracle of the Bells
Mr. Corbett's Ghost
Mister Halpren & Mister Johnson
Moonlight and Valentino
Mortuary Academy
A Mother's Prayer
My Life
Necropolis
The Newlydeads
Night of the Death Cult
Night of the Demons
Night of the Demons 2
Night of the Living Dead✦
Night of the Living Dead
Night Shift
The Nightcomers
Nightmare Castle
Oh Dad, Poor Dad (Momma's
  Hung You in the Closet & I'm
  Feeling So Sad)
Oh, Heavenly Dog!
On Borrowed Time✦
One Minute Before Death
The Oracle
Our Sons
Out of the Rain
Passed Away
The Peanut Butter Solution
Pet Sematary
Phantasm
Phantasm II
Phantasm III: Lord of the Dead
The Phantom Chariot
Phantom of the Ritz
The Plague
Playroom
Poltergeist✦
Poltergeist 2: The Other Side
Poltergeist 3
Ponette
Portrait of Jennie✦
The Possessed
Postmark for Danger/Quicksand
Premonition
The Premonition
Prison
Promises in the Dark
The Prophecy
The Psychic
Psychomania
The Reincarnation of Peter
  Proud

Resurrection of Zachary
  Wheeler
Retribution
Return
Revenge of the Dead
Riders to the Sea
Rimfire
The Rue Morgue Massacres
Savage Hearts
Scared Stiff✦
School Spirit
Scrooge✦
Scrooge
Scrooged
The Seventh Seal✦
Shadow Play
She Waits
Shock Waves
Sibling Rivalry
Silence Like Glass
The Sixth Man
Sole Survivor
Sometimes They Come Back
Somewhere Tomorrow
Soultaker
Spawn✦
Stand By Me✦
Star Trek 3: The Search for
  Spock
Stealing Beauty
Stones of Death
Strangers of the Evening
The Substitute Wife
Supernatural
Tell Me a Riddle
Terror Eyes
They Watch
Things to Do In Denver When
  You're Dead✦
13 Ghosts
Time Flies When You're Alive
To Dance with the White Dog✦
To Forget Venice
To Gillian on Her 37th Birthday
Tomb of Torture
Topper✦
Topper Returns✦
Topper Takes a Trip✦
Trick or Treat
Truly, Madly, Deeply✦
Truth or Dare?
Twice Dead
The Twilight Zone
Two of a Kind
The Unnamable
Unnatural
Unstrung Heroes
The Vacillations of Poppy Carew
The Vampire's Ghost
Vengeance
Visitor from the Grave
The Visitors
Weekend at Bernie's✦
Weekend at Bernie's 2
Welcome Back Mr. Fox
Where the Lilies Bloom✦
Whispers
White Light
The Widow
Wings of Fame
A Woman's Tale✦
A Zed & Two Noughts✦
Zone of the Dead

Death Row

*see also Men in Prison;
Women in Prison*

Angels with Dirty Faces✦
Beyond the Call
The Chamber
Crime of the Century
Daniel
A Dark Adapted Eye✦
Dead Man Out✦
Dead Man Walking✦
The Detective✦
The Executioner's Song
I Want to Live!✦

Curse of the Pink Panther
Cyberstalker
The Dain Curse
Dancing with Danger
Dark Corner▲
The Dark Hour
Dark Side of Midnight
Dead Again▲
Dead Connection
Dead Men Don't Wear Plaid
Dead Pigeon on Beethoven Street
Deadly Force
Deadly Illusion
Deadly Passion
Deadly Sins
Death from a Distance
Death on the Nile
Death Train
Deathmask
The Detective▲
Detective Sadie & Son
Detective School Dropouts
Detective Story▲
Devil in a Blue Dress▲
The Devil's Cargo
The Devlin Connection
Dick Barton, Special Agent
Dick Barton Strikes Back
Dick Tracy▲
Dick Tracy, Detective▲
Dick Tracy, Detective/The Corpse Vanishes
Dick Tracy Double Feature #1
Dick Tracy Double Feature #2
Dick Tracy Meets Gruesome
Dick Tracy Returns▲
Dick Tracy: The Original Serial, Vol. 1▲
Dick Tracy: The Original Serial, Vol. 2▲
Dick Tracy: The Spider Strikes
Dick Tracy vs. Crime Inc.
Dick Tracy vs. Cueball
Dick Tracy's Dilemma
Dirkham Detective Agency
Dragnet
Dressed to Kill
The Drowning Pool
Edge of Darkness
The Element of Crime
Emil and the Detectives
The Empty Beach
Endangered Species
The Enforcer
Entangled
Escape Clause
Everybody Wins
Evil under the Sun
Ex-Mrs. Bradford▲
The Falcon in Hollywood
The Falcon in Mexico
The Falcon Takes Over/Strange Bargain
The Falcon's Adventure/ Armored Car Robbery
The Falcon's Brother
Falling Down
False Witness
Farewell, My Lovely▲
Fearless
Fiction Makers
Final Notice
Finessing the King
Fletch
Fletch Lives
Follow Me Quietly▲
Footsteps in the Dark
The Force
The Foreigner
Fourth Story▲
The French Detective▲
From Hollywood to Deadwood
Fugitive Among Us
Ginger
Girl Hunters
The Glass Key▲
The Gore-Gore Girls
Gotham▲

Great K & A Train Robbery
The Great Mouse Detective▲
Green Eyes
Green for Danger
Guardian Angel
Gumshoe
The Gumshoe Kid
Hands of a Murderer
Hands of a Stranger
Hard-Boiled Mahoney
Hat Box Mystery
Heart Condition
Heat▲
The Hollywood Detective
Hollywood Harry
Hollywood Stadium Mystery
The Hound of the Baskervilles▲
The Hound of the Baskervilles
Hour of Decision
House of Fear
The House of Lurking Death
House of Mystery
The House of the Arrow▲
How to Kill 400 Duponts
The Human Monster
The Hunt for the Night Stalker
The Hustle
I Killed That Man
I, the Jury
In the Deep Woods
Infamous Crimes
The Inner Circle
Innocent Lies
Inspector Hornleigh
The Invisible Avenger
The Invisible Killer
Irish Luck
The Jade Mask
Jigsaw
Just Another Pretty Face
K-9
The Kennel Murder Case
The Kill
Kill Me Again
Killing 'em Softly
The King Murder
Kiss Me Deadly▲
Kojak: The Belarus File
La Rupture
Lady in Cement
Lady in the Lake
The Late Show▲
Laura▲
Little Miss Millions
The Long Goodbye▲
The Long Kiss Goodnight
Long Time Gone
Loose Cannons
Lord of Illusions
Love at Large▲
Love Happy
A Low Down Dirty Shame
Lure of the Islands
Lying Lips
The Mad Bomber
Magnum Force
Magnum P.I.: Don't Eat the Snow in Hawaii
The Maltese Falcon▲
Man from Cairo
The Man in the Mist
Man on the Eiffel Tower▲
The Man Who Would Not Die
The Man with Bogart's Face
The Mandarin Mystery
Manhattan Murder Mystery▲
Margin for Murder
Marlowe
Masks of Death
Master Mind
Meet Sexton Blake
Meeting at Midnight
Messenger of Death
Miami Vice 2: The Prodigal Son
Midnight 2: Sex, Death, and Videotape
Midnight Limited
A Mind to Murder
Mirage

Missing Pieces
Mr. Arkadin▲
Mr. Moto's Last Warning▲
Mr. Wong, Detective
Mr. Wong in Chinatown
Moonlighting
More! Police Squad
Mortal Sins
Murder Ahoy
Murder at the Baskervilles
Murder at the Gallop▲
Murder at the Vanities
Murder by Death
Murder by Decree▲
Murder by the Book
Murder in the Doll House
A Murder Is Announced
Murder Most Foul▲
Murder, My Sweet▲
Murder on Approval
Murder on the Orient Express▲
Murder over New York
Murder She Said
Murderous Vision
My Favorite Brunette
My New Partner
Mystery Island
Mystery Liner
Mystery of Mr. Wong
The Naked Gun: From the Files of Police Squad▲
Naked Gun 33 1/3: The Final Insult
Nancy Drew, Reporter
Nature's Playmates
New Orleans After Dark
Newman's Law
Nick Knight
Night Moves▲
Night School
Night Stalker
No Way to Treat a Lady▲
Nocturne
Number One with a Bullet
No. 17▲
On Dangerous Ground▲
One Body Too Many
One Good Cop
One of My Wives Is Missing
One Shoe Makes It Murder
Operation Julie
The Organization▲
Out of the Darkness▲
Out of the Past▲
Out of the Shadows
The Panther's Claw
Pas Tres Catholique
The Pearl of Death
Peter Gunn
The Phantom Light
Phantom of Chinatown
The Phantom of Soho
Pier 23
The Pink Chiquitas
The Pink Panther▲
The Pink Panther Strikes Again▲
Play Nice
Police Squad! Help Wanted!
Postmark for Danger
Powder Burn
The Presidio
Prettykill
Prime Suspect 5: Errors of Judgment▲
Prime Suspect: The Scent of Darkness▲
The Private Eyes
Private Hell 36
The Private Life of Sherlock Holmes▲
Pure Luck
Pursuit to Algiers
Radioactive Dreams
Red Barry
The Red Raven Kiss-Off
Relentless 3
Relentless 4
Remington Steele, Vol. 1: License to Steele

Rentadick
The Return of Boston Blackie
The Return of Dr. Mabuse
Return of Frank Cannon
Return of Superfly
Return of the Pink Panther
Revenge of the Pink Panther
Roaring City
The Rockford Files: Backlash of the Hunter
The Rose and the Jackal
Rough Cut
Ryder P.I.
The Saint
The Saint in London
The Saint in New York
The Saint Strikes Back
The Saint Takes Over
The Saint's Double Trouble
The Saint's Vacation/The Narrow Margin
Sapphire▲
Satan Met a Lady
Satan's Harvest
Scalp Merchant
Scarlet Claw▲
The Scarlet Clue
Sea of Love▲
Second Sight
Seven▲
Seven Doors to Death
The Seven-Per-Cent Solution▲
The Seven-Ups
Sexton Blake and the Hooded Terror
Shadow of the Thin Man▲
The Shadow Strikes
Shadows of the Orient
Shaft in Africa
Shaft's Big Score
Shamus
The Shanghai Cobra
Sheba, Baby
Sherlock Holmes and the Deadly Necklace
Sherlock Holmes and the Incident at Victoria Falls
Sherlock Holmes and the Secret Weapon▲
Sherlock Holmes Faces Death▲
Sherlock Holmes in Washington
Sherlock Holmes: The Master Blackmailer
Sherlock Holmes: The Sign of Four
Sherlock Holmes: The Silver Blaze
Sherlock Holmes: The Voice of Terror
Sherlock's Rivals & Where's My Wife
Shoot to Kill▲
Shooting Stars
A Shot in the Dark
A Shot in the Dark▲
The Sign of Four
The Silent Mr. Sherlock Holmes
The Silent Passenger
Silk
Slow Burn
Smart-Aleck Kill
Smile, Jenny, You're Dead
Soft Deceit
The Soft Kill
Someone to Watch Over Me▲
Song of the Thin Man
South Beach
The Speckled Band▲
Speedtrap
Spenser: Ceremony
Spenser: Pale Kings & Princes
Spider Woman▲
The Squeeze
Stakeout
Star of Midnight
Station
Stolen Kisses▲
The Strange Case of the End of Civilization as We Know It

Strange Shadows in an Empty Room
Stray Dog▲
Strike a Pose
A Study in Scarlet
A Study in Terror▲
Sunset Grill
Sweet Lies
Tales from the Crypt Presents Bordello of Blood
TekWar
Terror by Night
Terror by Night/Meeting at Midnight
They All Laughed
They Might Be Giants▲
The Thin Man▲
The Thin Man Goes Home
Third Degree Burn
The Third Key
13th Guest
To Catch a Killer▲
Tomorrow at Seven
Tony Rome
Top Dog
Trail of the Pink Panther
TripleCross
The Triumph of Sherlock Holmes
The Two Jakes
Ulterior Motives
The Unbreakable Alibi
Under Suspicion
Uneasy Terms
Unsuitable Job for a Woman
Vegas
Vertigo▲
V.I. Warshawski
Victim of Desire
Video Murders
Violated
Vortex
Waikiki
Web of Deception
Whistling in Brooklyn
Whistling in Dixie
Whistling in the Dark▲
Who Done It?
Who Framed Roger Rabbit▲
Who Is the Black Dahlia?▲
Who's Harry Crumb?
Witch Hunt
Without a Clue
Witness▲
The Woman in Green
World of the Depraved
X Marks the Spot
Young Sherlock Holmes

Detroit

see I Love Detroit

Devils

Beauty and the Devil
The Craft
Dark Angel: The Ascent
The Devil & Max Devlin
The Devils▲
Faust▲
Gates of Hell 2: Dead Awakening
God, Man and Devil
Guardian of the Abyss
Haunted Symphony
Hell's Belles
High Strung
Highway to Hell
Judgment Day
Legend
Les Visiteurs du Soir▲
The Mangler
Mr. Frost
Mother Joan of the Angels▲
Needful Things
The Prophecy
Second Time Lucky

The Sorrows of Satan►
Stephen King's The Stand
Tales from the Hood

Devil's Island

see also Great Escapes; Men in Prison

Papillon►
Passage to Marseilles►
We're No Angels

Dinosaurs

see also Killer Beasts

Adventures in Dinosaur City
At the Earth's Core
Baby ... Secret of the Lost Legend
Carnosaur
Carnosaur 2
Carnosaur 3: Primal Species
Caveman
Clifford
The Crater Lake Monster
Dennis the Menace: Dinosaur Hunter
Dinosaur Island
Dinosaurus!
Ganjasaurus Rex
Josh Kirby...Time Warrior: Chapter 1, Planet of the Dino-Knights
Jurassic Park►
King Dinosaur
The Land Before Time►
The Land Before Time 2: The Great Valley Adventure
The Land Before Time 3: The Time of the Great Giving
The Land Before Time 4: Journey Through the Mists
The Land that Time Forgot
The Land Unknown
The Lost Continent
The Lost World
The Lost World: Jurassic Park 2
Massacre in Dinosaur Valley
My Science Project
A Nymphoid Barbarian in Dinosaur Hell
One Million B.C.
One Million Years B.C.
One of Our Dinosaurs Is Missing
The People That Time Forgot
Planet of Dinosaurs
Prehysteria
Prehysteria 2
Prehysteria 3
Return to the Lost World
Sound of Horror
Super Mario Bros.
Tammy and the T-Rex
Teenage Caveman
Theodore Rex
Toy Story►
Two Lost Worlds
Unknown Island
The Valley of Gwangi►
We're Back! A Dinosaur's Story
When Dinosaurs Ruled the Earth

Disaster Flicks

see also Action Adventure; Air Disasters; Meltdown; Sea Disasters

Accident
After the Shock
Airport►
Airport '75
Airport '77
Alive
Assignment Outer Space
Avalanche
Avalanche Express
Beyond the Poseidon Adventure

The Big Bus
The Cassandra Crossing
The China Syndrome►
City on Fire
The Concorde: Airport '79
The Crash of Flight 401
Dante's Peak
The Day the Sky Exploded
Daylight
Dead Ahead: The Exxon Valdez Disaster►
The Doomsday Flight
Earthquake
Final Warning
Fire
Fire and Rain
Firestorm: 72 Hours in Oakland
Flood!
Gray Lady Down
The Hindenburg
The Hurricane►
Hurricane
In Old Chicago►
Independence Day►
Last Days of Pompeii
The Last Voyage
The Last Woman on Earth
The Lost Missile
Meteor
A Night to Remember►
Planet on the Prowl
The Poseidon Adventure
The Rains Came
Raise the Titanic
Red Alert
St. Helen's, Killer Volcano
Snowball
S.O.S. Titanic
Space: 1999—Alien Attack►
The Survivalist
Survivor
Tailspin: Behind the Korean Airline Tragedy
Terror on the 40th Floor
Tidal Wave
The Towering Inferno
Tragedy of Flight 103: The Inside Story►
Twister
Two Minute Warning
Volcano
When Time Ran Out
White Squall

Disco Musicals

see also Musicals

Can't Stop the Music
Car Wash
KISS Meets the Phantom of the Park
Pirate Movie
The Rocky Horror Picture Show►
Saturday Night Fever
Thank God It's Friday
The Wiz
Xanadu

Disease of the Week

see also AIDS; Emerging Viruses

The Affair►
The Ann Jillian Story
Bang the Drum Slowly
Beaches►
The Best Little Girl in the World►
Between Two Women
Bobby Deerfield
The Boy in the Plastic Bubble
Brian's Song►
Camille►
The Carrier
The Cassandra Crossing
Champions
Checking Out

Children of the Corn 4: The Gathering
C.H.U.D.
Cleo from 5 to 7►
Cries and Whispers►
Crystal Heart
The Curse
Damien: The Leper Priest
Daybreak
Dead Man Walking
Dead Space
Dick Barton, Special Agent
The Doctor
A Dream of Kings►
Duet for One
Dying Young
An Early Frost►
East of Kilimanjaro
The End►
Eric►
The First Deadly Sin
Fourth Wish
Gaby: A True Story►
Germicide
Glory Enough for All: The Discovery of Insulin
Griffin and Phoenix: A Love Story
Incredible Melting Man
Interrupted Melody►
Intimate Contact►
Isle of the Dead
Jack
Jericho Fever
Killer on Board
L.A. Bad
The Last Best Year
The Last Man on Earth
Lightning Over Water
Lorenzo's Oil►
Love Affair: The Eleanor & Lou Gehrig Story►
Love Story►
Mad Death
Marvin's Room
A Matter of WHO
Miles to Go
Miss Evers' Boys
A Mother's Prayer
My Father's House
My Life
Nasty Rabbit
On Her Majesty's Secret Service►
Panic in Echo Park
Parting Glances►
Philadelphia►
Pilgrim, Farewell
The Plague
The Plague Dogs
The Pride of the Yankees►
Princes in Exile
Project: Alien
Promises in the Dark
The Proud Ones
Quarantine
Question of Faith
A Quiet Duel
Rabid
Rasputin: Dark Servant of Destiny►
Reborn
Right of Way
The Road to Galveston►
The Road to Wellville
The Shadow Box►
Shadowlands►
A Shining Season►
Silence Like Glass
The Silver Streak
Six Weeks
Stigma
Sunchaser
Terms of Endearment►
Terror Creatures from the Grave
A Time to Live
Walking Through the Fire
The Wedding Gift►
When the Time Comes

When Wolves Cry
The White Legion
Xtro

Disorganized Crime

see also Crime & Criminals; Organized Crime

Ace Crawford, Private Eye
Airheads
Albino Alligator
Amos and Andrew
The Apple Dumpling Gang
The Apple Dumpling Gang Rides Again
Armed and Dangerous
Baby on Board
Baby's Day Out
Bottle Rocket
Cop and a Half
Crackers
Dr. Otto & the Riddle of the Gloom Beam
8 Heads in a Duffel Bag
Ernest Goes to Jail
Fargo►
Finders Keepers
A Fine Mess
Get Shorty►
Glitch!
Gridlock'd►
The Gun in Betty Lou's Handbag
Happy New Year
Headless Body in Topless Bar
Her Alibi
Herbie Goes Bananas
Home Alone►
Home Alone 2: Lost in New York
I Wonder Who's Killing Her Now?
Inside the Law
The Italian Job
The Jerky Boys
Keys to Tulsa
Killing Zoe
The League of Gentlemen►
Leather Jackets
Lunch Wagon
Mad Dog and Glory►
A Man, a Woman, and a Bank
Man of the House
Menage►
Mexican Hayride
Milo Milo
Miss Grant Takes Richmond
Mixed Nuts
Mutant on the Bounty
The Night They Robbed Big Bertha's
Ocean's 11
Once Upon a Crime
101 Dalmatians
Oscar
Out on a Limb
Palookaville►
Pouvoir Intime
Quick Change
Ransom Money
Reservoir Dogs►
Round Trip to Heaven
Ruthless People►
St. Benny the Dip
See No Evil, Hear No Evil
Shake Hands with Murder
The Shot
Silver Bears
Sister Act
Sitting Ducks►
Stop! or My Mom Will Shoot
Stop That Cab
The Super
Super Soul Brother
Survivors
Tall, Tan and Terrific
The Thief Who Came to Dinner
Things to Do In Denver When You're Dead►
Three Kinds of Heat
Thrilled to Death

Too Many Crooks
Trapped In Paradise
Truth or Consequences, N.M.
Two If by Sea
We're Talkin' Serious Money
The Wrong Arm of the Law►
The Young in Heart►

Divorce

see also Marriage; Single

The Accidental Tourist►
All I Want for Christmas
Alpha Beta
The Awful Truth►
Between Friends
A Bill of Divorcement
Breaking Up
Breaking Up Is Hard to Do
Bye Bye, Love
California Suite►
Can She Bake a Cherry Pie?
Cheaper to Keep Her
Children of Divorce
Clara's Heart
Cold Heat
A Conspiracy of Love
Cross My Heart
Desert Hearts►
Divorce American Style
Divorce His, Divorce Hers
Divorce—Italian Style►
The Divorcee
Early Frost
Edie & Pen
Escapade►
E.T.: The Extra-Terrestrial►
Every Other Weekend►
The Ex
Face the Music
Faces►
Falling Down
Family Pictures►
Father Figure
Fergie & Andrew: Behind Palace Doors
A Fight for Jenny
The First Wives Club
Found Alive
The Good Father►
The Good Mother
Goodbye Love
Hard Promises
Heartburn►
High Society►
History is Made at Night►
Hollow Reed►
House Arrest
How to Break Up a Happy Divorce
How to Commit Marriage
Husbands and Wives►
Interiors►
Irreconcilable Differences
Kramer vs. Kramer►
Let's Make It Legal
Liar Liar
The Liberation of L.B. Jones
Love and Hate: A Marriage Made in Hell
Love Matters
Marie►
The Marrying Kind
Melanie
Misbehaving Husbands
The Misfits►
Mrs. Doubtfire
Mr. Skeffington►
Mr. Wonderful
Mother
Nadine
Naked Paradise
Necessary Parties
Never Say Goodbye
A New Life
Night Life in Reno
Nothing in Common
Now and Then
The Odd Couple►

The Odd Job
One Cooks, the Other Doesn't
Patti Rocks▶
Peggy Sue Got Married
The Personals
Petulia▶
Pilgrim, Farewell
Play It Again, Sam▶
The Prize Pulitzer
Rich in Love
Rich Kids
Riptide▶
Scenes from a Marriage▶
Second Chance
See You in the Morning
Sex and the Single Parent
Shattered Silence
The Solitary Man
Starting Over▶
Strange Bedfellows
Sweet Revenge
Table for Five
Tattle Tale
Tell It to the Judge
Tell Me That You Love Me
Tenth Month
That Old Feeling
Till Murder Do Us Part
Twister
An Unmarried Woman▶
Valentino Returns
Wanted: The Perfect Guy
The War of the Roses▶
Without Anesthesia

Doctors & Nurses

see also AIDS; Dental Mayhem; Disease of the Week; Emerging Viruses; Evil Doctors; Hospitals & Medicine; Nursploitation!; Sanity Check; Shrinks

All Creatures Great and Small▶
Alone in the Dark
And the Band Played On▶
The Android Affair
Arrowsmith
Ashanti, Land of No Mercy
The Asphyx▶
Autopsy
Awakenings▶
Baby Girl Scott
Bad Medicine
Battle Circus
Bethune
Between Wars
The Black Dragons
Black Friday
Blind Justice
Bliss
Blood Mania
Bloodlink
Body Parts
Botany Bay
The Bramble Bush
Bramwell
Broken Glass
The Broken Mask
Calling Paul Temple
Candy Stripe Nurses
Carry On Doctor▶
Castle of the Creeping Flesh
Caught▶
Century
Children of Rage
Children of the Corn 4: The Gathering
China Beach▶
The Citadel▶
Circus of Horrors
City of Joy
The Clonus Horror
Club Havana
Coma▶
Corregidor
Corridors of Blood
Courageous Dr. Christian

Crimes & Misdemeanors▶
Crossover
Dead Ringers▶
Dead Sleep
Death Becomes Her▶
Death by Prescription
Death Nurse
The Devil's Web
Doc Hollywood
The Doctor
Dr. Alien
The Doctor and the Devils
Doctor at Large
Doctor at Sea
Dr. Bethune
Dr. Black, Mr. Hyde
Doctor Blood's Coffin
Doctor Butcher M.D.
Dr. Caligari
Dr. Christian Meets the Women
Dr. Cyclops
Dr. Death, Seeker of Souls
Doctor Detroit
Doctor Dolittle
Doctor Faustus
Dr. Frankenstein's Castle of Freaks
Dr. Hackenstein
Dr. Heckyl and Mr. Hype
Doctor in Distress
Doctor in the House▶
Dr. Jack/For Heaven's Sake
Dr. Jekyll and Mr. Hyde
Dr. Kildare's Strange Case
Dr. Mabuse, Parts 1 & 2▶
Dr. Mabuse vs. Scotland Yard
Dr. Petiot
Doctor Quinn, Medicine Woman
Doctor Satan's Robot
Doctor Takes a Wife▶
Dr. Tarr's Torture Dungeon
Dr. Terror's House of Horrors
Doctor Who
Doctor X
Doctors and Nurses
Doctors' Wives
Donor Unknown
Don't Cry, It's Only Thunder▶
Don't Look in the Basement
Drunken Angel▶
East of Borneo
The Egyptian
The Elephant Man▶
Emmanuelle in the Country
The English Patient▶
ER
Extreme Measures
False Faces
Fantastic Voyage▶
Flatliners
Flesh Feast
Foreign Body
The Fortune Cookie▶
The Fugitive▶
Glory Enough for All: The Discovery of Insulin
The Great Moment
Gross Anatomy
Guest in the House
Halloween 2: The Nightmare Isn't Over!
Hands Up▶
Healer
High Heels
Holy Terror
The Horrible Dr. Hichcock
The Horror Chamber of Dr. Faustus▶
Horror Hospital
The Hospital▶
Hospital of Terror
House Calls▶
I Love My...Wife
I Never Promised You a Rose Garden▶
The In-Laws▶
In Love and War
The Incredible Journey of Dr. Meg Laurel▶

An Indecent Obsession
Internes Can't Take Money
The Interns
Invasion
Jesse
Johnny Belinda▶
Johnny Belinda
Junior
Kidnapping of Baby John Doe
Korczak▶
The Last Angry Man▶
The Lazarus Syndrome
Le Cas du Dr. Laurent▶
Lie Down with Lions
Life Is a Long Quiet River▶
The Light in the Jungle
Like Father, Like Son
Love Is a Many-Splendored Thing
Lover's Knot
Mad Love▶
The Mad Monster
The Madness of King George▶
Make-Up
Malice
Mania
Marvin's Room
M*A*S*H▶
M*A*S*H: Goodbye, Farewell & Amen▶
M*A*S*H: The Collector's Edition
The Mask of Fu Manchu
A Matter of Life and Death
Meet Dr. Christian
Memories of Me
Men of Ireland
Metamorphosis: The Alien Factor
The Millionairess
Miss Evers' Boys
Mr. North
Monty Python's The Meaning of Life▶
Murder in Texas▶
Murder Once Removed
Murder or Mercy
My Father's Nurse
Nell
Night Call Nurses
Night Monster
Night Nurse▶
Night Nurse
Nightbreaker▶
Nine Months
Nomads
Not as a Stranger
Not of This Earth
Nurse
The Nurse
Nurse Edith Cavell▶
Nurse Marjorie
Nurse on Call
Old Swimmin' Hole
One Flew Over the Cuckoo's Nest▶
The Ordeal of Dr. Mudd▶
Outbreak▶
Panic in Echo Park
Panic in the Streets▶
Paper Mask
People Will Talk▶
Persona▶
Petulia
A Place for Annie
The Plague
Praying Mantis
Private Duty Nurses
Promises in the Dark
Purple Hearts
A Quiet Duel
The Raven▶
Reckless Disregard
Red Beard▶
Restoration▶
Riot Squad
The Road to Wellville
Roommates
Sawbones

Say Goodbye, Maggie Cole
Scalpel
Sister Dora
Sister Kenny▶
Skeezer
Slaughter Hotel
Sprague
State of Emergency
Stigma
Stitches
The Story of Dr. Wassell
The Student Nurses
Sunchaser
The Surgeon
Teenage Frankenstein
Tender Loving Care
Torture Ship
Tundra
The Unbearable Lightness of Being▶
The Vicious Circle
Vital Signs
We are the Children
Welcome Stranger
When the Bullet Hits the Bone
White Dwarf
Women of Valor
Young Doctors in Love
The Young Nurses

Docudrama

see also Documentary
Above Us the Waves▶
Adam▶
After the Shock
Al Capone▶
All You Need Is Cash▶
The Amy Fisher Story
And the Band Played On▶
Babyfever
The Battle of Algiers▶
Blind Ambition
Bob Roberts▶
The Boston Strangler
Bound for Glory▶
Call Northside 777▶
Casualties of Love: The "Long Island Lolita" Story
Christian the Lion
Close to Home
Cocaine: One Man's Seduction
Conspiracy: The Trial of the Chicago Eight▶
Countdown
The Courtesans of Bombay▶
Cruel Sea▶
A Cry in the Dark▶
Edge of the World▶
8-A
The Flaming Teen-Age
Free, White, and 21
The General Line▶
Glen or Glenda: Confessions of Ed Wood
H
Henry: Portrait of a Serial Killer▶
Hiroshima
The History of White People in America
The History of White People in America: Vol. 2
Hostages▶
Immortal Battalion▶
In Cold Blood▶
In Cold Blood
Inside the Third Reich
Iron & Silk
James Dean
The Jayne Mansfield Story
JFK: Reckless Youth
Journey Through Rosebud
Kamikaze Hearts
Kids
King▶
The Last Polka▶
Lethal Lolita—Amy Fisher: My Story
The Lion Has Wings

Looking for Richard▶
Mandela and de Klerk
Miss Evers' Boys
Murder in Texas▶
The Naked City▶
Panther
Pickpocket▶
The Poppy Is Also a Flower
Prince of the City▶
Qui Etes Vous, Mr. Sorge?
Real Life▶
The Red Menace
The Rise of Louis XIV▶
Shaka Zulu▶
S.O.S. Titanic
Soviet Spy
Special Bulletin▶
The Spy Who Came in from the Cold▶
Tailspin: Behind the Korean Airline Tragedy
Take the Money and Run▶
Teenage Devil Dolls
Ten Days That Shook the World▶
That's Adequate
The Thin Blue Line▶
32 Short Films about Glenn Gould▶
This Is Spinal Tap▶
Times of Harvey Milk
The Wild Aces
Women in Prison
Working Girls▶
Zelig▶

Documentary

see also Docudrama
Alive: 20 Years Later
American Fabulous
The American Gangster
Assassination of Trotsky
The Atomic Cafe▶
Baseball
Battle of China
The Battle of Russia
The Battle of San Pietro
Bob Dylan: Don't Look Back▶
Born to Boogie
A Brief History of Time▶
Brother's Keeper▶
Bruce Lee: Curse of the Dragon▶
Burden of Dreams
Caravaggio▶
The Celluloid Closet▶
A Century of Women
The Children of Theatre Street
Chuck Amuck: The Movie
Chuck Berry: Hail! Hail! Rock 'n' Roll▶
Ciao Federico! Fellini Directs Satyricon
The Civil War, Episode 1: The Cause—1861▶
The Civil War, Episode 2: A Very Bloody Affair—1862▶
The Civil War, Episode 3: Forever Free—1862▶
The Civil War, Episode 4: Simply Murder—1863▶
The Civil War, Episode 5: The Universe of Battle—1863▶
The Civil War, Episode 6: Valley of the Shadow of Death—1864▶
The Civil War, Episode 7: Most Hallowed Ground—1864▶
The Civil War, Episode 8: War is All Hell—1865▶
The Civil War, Episode 9: The Better Angels of Our Nature—1865▶
The Clowns▶
Common Threads: Stories from the Quilt
Crumb▶
Dance Hall Racket

Drama

Drama

Drama

Rebel Without a Cause►
Reborn
The Reckless Way
The Rector's Wife
The Red and the White►
The Red Badge of Courage►
Red Beard►
The Red Desert►
The Red Half-Breed
Red Hot
Red Line 7000
The Red Menace
Red Nightmare
Red Nights
The Red Pony►
Red Shoe Diaries
Red Shoe Diaries 2: Double Dare
Red Shoe Diaries 3: Another Woman's Lipstick
Red Shoe Diaries 4: Auto Erotica
Red Shoe Diaries 5: Weekend Pass
Red Shoe Diaries 6: How I Met My Husband
The Red Stallion
Red Surf
Red, White & Busted
Reds►
Redwood Curtain
Reefer Madness
The Reflecting Skin
Reflections in a Golden Eye
Reflections in the Dark
Reform School Girl
Reform School Girls
Regarding Henry►
The Reincarnation of Golden Lotus►
The Remains of the Day►
Rembrandt►
Rembrandt—1669
Rendez-vous►
Requiem for Dominic►
Reservoir Dogs►
The Respectful Prostitute
Resurrection►
Return to Earth
Return to Peyton Place
Reunion►
Revenge of a Kabuki Actor
Reversal of Fortune►
The Revolt of Job►
Rhapsody in August
Rhodes
Rhythm Thief
Rich Kids
Rich Man, Poor Man►
Richard III►
Richard Petty Story
Richard's Things
Riddance►
Ride a Wild Pony►
Ride in a Pink Car
Ridicule►
Riel
Riff Raff
Rift
The Right Hand Man
Right of Way
The Right to Remain Silent
The Ring
Ring of Bright Water►
Ringside
Riot
Riot Squad
Riptide►
Rising Son►
Risky Business
Rita Hayworth: The Love Goddess
The Rite
Rivals
The River►
The River
River Beat
The River Niger

River of Grass
River of Unrest
The River Rat
A River Runs Through It►
Riverbend
River's Edge►
The Road Home
Road House
Road Racers
The Road to Galveston►
The Road to Life
Roadhouse Girl
Roadhouse 66
Roadside Prophets
Roaring Roads
Roaring Speedboats
Robert Kennedy and His Times
Robot Pilot
Rocco and His Brothers►
Rock All Night
Rock, Pretty Baby
Rocket to the Moon
The Rocking Horse Winner
Rocky►
Rocky 2
Rocky 3
Rocky 4
Rocky 5
Rodrigo D.: No Future
Roe vs. Wade►
RoGoPaG
Roll of Thunder, Hear My Cry
Rolling Home
Rolling Thunder
Rollover
Rome '78
Romero
Ronnie and Julie
The Roof
The Room
Rooster: Spurs of Death!
Roosters
Rosa Luxemburg
The Rose and the Jackal
The Rose Garden
Roseanne: An Unauthorized Biography
Roseland►
Rosie: The Rosemary Clooney Story
Roswell: The U.F.O. Cover-Up
Round Midnight►
The Round Up
R.P.M.* (*Revolutions Per Minute)
Ruby
Ruby Gentry
Ruby in Paradise►
Ruby Jean and Joe
Ruby's Dream
Rudy
Rumble Fish►
The Rumor Mill
A Rumor of War►
Rumpole of the Bailey: Rumpole's Return►
Run for the Roses
Run Silent, Run Deep►
Runaway
Runaway Father
The Runaways
The Runner Stumbles
Running Brave
Running Free
Running Mates►
Running on Empty►
Rush►
The Russia House
Rusty's Birthday
The Rutherford County Line
Sabre Jet
The Sacrifice►
Sacrilege
Sadat
Safe►
Safe Passage
Saigon: Year of the Cat
St. Elmo's Fire
St. Ives

Saint Jack►
The Saint of Fort Washington
Sakharov►
Salaam Bombay!►
Salammbo
Salmonberries
Salo, or the 120 Days of Sodom
Salome
Salome/Queen Elizabeth
Salome, Where She Danced
Salt of the Earth►
Salute John Citizen►
Samaritan: The Mitch Snyder Story►
Sam's Son
Samson and Delilah►
Samson and Delilah
Sandakan No. 8►
Sandra of a Thousand Delights
Sanshiro Sugata►
Sansho the Bailiff►
Santa Sangre►
Sara Dane
Satan Met a Lady
Satan's Brew
Satan's Harvest
Saturday Night and Sunday Morning►
Savage Attraction
Savage Is Loose
Savage Run►
The Savage Seven
The Savage Woman
Savages from Hell
Savannah Smiles
Save the Lady
Save the Tiger►
Sawdust & Tinsel►
Say Goodbye, Maggie Cole
Scandal
Scandal►
Scandal in a Small Town
The Scar
Scarecrow
Scarface Mob
The Scarlet Letter
The Scarlet Letter►
The Scarlet Pimpernel►
Scarred
Scenes from a Marriage►
Scent of a Woman►
The Scent of Green Papaya►
Schindler's List►
School Ties►
The Scorpion Woman
Scott Turow's The Burden of Proof
Scout's Honor
Scrooge►
Scrubbers
Scruples
Scum►
Sea Lion
Sea Racketeers
The Seagull►
The Search►
The Search for Bridey Murphy
Searching for Bobby Fischer►
Season for Assassins
Season of Change
Sebastian
Second Best►
Second Chance
Second Coming of Suzanne
Second Victory
The Secret
The Secret Agent
Secret File of Hollywood
The Secret Four
The Secret Garden►
The Secret Garden
The Secret Garden►
The Secret Garden
Secret Honor►
The Secret of Roan Inish►
The Secret of the Loch
Secret Places
The Secret Rapture
A Secret Space

Secret Weapons
Secrets
Secrets and Lies
Secrets of a Soul
Seduce Me: Pamela Principle 2
The Seducers
The Seduction of Joe Tynan
Seduction: The Cruel Woman
See How She Runs►
Seize the Day►
A Sense of Freedom►
Sensual Partners
Sensuous Summer
The Sensuous Teenager
A Separate Peace
Separate Tables►
Separate Tables
Separate Ways
September
September 30, 1955
Sergeant Matlovich vs. the U.S. Air Force
Sergeant Ryker
The Serpent's Egg
Serpico►
The Servant►
Sessions
The Set-Up►
Seven Days in May►
Seven Deadly Sins►
Seven Miles from Alcatraz/Flight from Glory
The Seventeenth Bride
The 7th Commandment
The Seventh Cross►
The Seventh Seal►
The Seventh Veil►
Severance
Sex and the College Girl
Sex, Drugs, and Rock-n-Roll
sex, lies and videotape►
Sex Through a Window
S.F.W.
Shack Out on 101►
The Shadow Box►
Shadow Dancing►
Shadow of Angels
Shadow on the Sun
A Shadow You Soon Will Be
Shadowlands►
Shadows
Shadows►
Shadows of the Orient
Shadows Over Shanghai
Shake Hands with the Devil►
Shakespeare Wallah►
Shaking the Tree
Shame►
The Shame►
Shameless
The Shaming
Shanghai Express►
The Shanghai Gesture
Shanghai Triad►
Shanty Tramp
Sharma & Beyond
Shattered►
Shattered
Shattered Dreams
Shattered Spirits
Shattered Vows
The Shawshank Redemption►
She and He
She-Devils on Wheels
Sheer Madness►
She'll Be Wearing Pink Pajamas
The Shell Seekers
The Sheltering Sky►
She's So Lovely
Shifting Sands
Shiloh
Shine►
Shiokari Pass
Ship of Fools►
Shock Corridor►
The Shoes of the Fisherman
Shoeshine►
Shogun►
Shoot It Black, Shoot It Blue

Shoot the Moon
Shoot to Kill
Shooting
The Shooting Party
The Shooting Party►
The Shop on Main Street►
Shopping
Short Eyes►
Short Fuse
Showgirls
The Shrieking
Shy People►
Siberiade►
Sicilian Connection
The Sicilian Connection►
Sid & Nancy►
Sidewalks of London►
Signal 7
Signs of Life
Silas Marner►
The Silence►
Silence
Silence Like Glass
Silence of the Heart►
Silence of the North
The Silences of the Palace►
The Silent One
Silent Rebellion
The Silent Touch
Silent Victim
Silent Victory: The Kitty O'Neil Story►
Silent Witness
Silkwood►
The Silver Chalice
Silver Dream Racer
The Silver Streak
Simba►
Simon Bolivar
Simple Justice
A Simple Story►
Sin of Adam & Eve
Sin You Sinners
Sinatra
Sinbad
Sing Sing Nights
The Singing Blacksmith
The Singing Nun
Singing the Blues in Red►
Single Room Furnished
The Single Standard
Sinners in Paradise
Sins
Sins of Jezebel
Sirocco
Sister Kenny►
Sister My Sister
The Sisters►
Sisters of Gion►
Six Degrees of Separation
Sixteen
'68
Sizzle
Skag►
Skateboard
Skeezer
Skier's Dream
Skin
Skin Art
Skin Game
Skinheads: The Second Coming of Hate
Skullduggery
The Sky Pilot
Skylark
Skyscraper Souls►
Slacker►
Slash
Slashed Dreams
Slaughterday
Slavers
Sleepers
Sleeping Dogs
The Sleeping Tiger
The Slender Thread►
Sling Blade►
The Small Back Room►
A Small Circle of Friends
Small Faces►

Drama

Witness to the Execution
Wittgenstein
Wives Under Suspicion
The Wizard of Loneliness
Wolf Lake
Wolf Trap
The Wolves▲
A Woman and a Woman
A Woman, Her Men and Her Futon
Woman in Brown
A Woman in Flames▲
Woman in the Dunes▲
Woman in the Shadows
The Woman Inside
A Woman Named Jackie
A Woman Obsessed
A Woman of Rome
A Woman Rebels
A Woman Under the Influence▲
The Woman Who Willed a Miracle
Woman With a Past
A Woman's Secret
A Woman's Tale▲
A Woman's World▲
Women & Men: In Love There Are No Rules
Women & Men: Stories of Seduction
Women From the Lake of Scented Souls
Women in Cell Block 7
Women in Love▲
The Women of Brewster Place▲
Women of Valor
Women Unchained
Wonsan Operation
The Wooden Gun
The Wooden Man's Bride
Words by Heart
Workin' for Peanuts
Working Girls
A World Apart▲
The World Gone Mad
The World of Apu▲
A World of Strangers▲
World War II: When Lions Roared
The Worldly Madonna
Woyzeck▲
The Wrestler
Wrestling Ernest Hemingway
The Wrong Move
The Wrong Road
X Marks the Spot
Xica▲
Yanco
A Yank in the R.A.F.
Year of the Dragon
Year of the Gun
The Yearling
Yellow Cargo
Yellow Earth
Yol▲
You Must Remember This
You Only Live Once
The Young Americans
Young Aphrodites
Young Charlie Chaplin
The Young Graduates
The Young in Heart▲
The Young Lions▲
Young Love, First Love
The Young Nurses
The Young One
The Young Philadelphians▲
Young Tom Edison
Young Winston▲
Youngblood
Your Ticket Is No Longer Valid
Youth Aflame
You've Ruined Me, Eddie
Yuri Nosenko, KGB
Zabriskie Point▲
Zalmen or the Madness of God
Zandalee
Zelly & Me▲
Zero Degrees Kelvin

The Zoo Gang
Zooman▲
Zora Is My Name!
Zorba the Greek▲
Zvenigora▲

Dream Girls

see also Beauty Pageants

A la Mode
Alien Women
Barb Wire
The Barbarians
Baywatch the Movie: Forbidden Paradise
Beauties of the Night
Beautiful Girls
Beauty School
Beverly Hills Knockouts
Bikini Bistro
The Bikini Car Wash Company
The Bikini Car Wash Company 2
Bikini Drive-In
Bikini Island
Bikini Summer
Blondes Have More Guns
Bluebeard
Bolero
Burial of the Rats
Calendar Girl Murders
California Girls
Cannonball Run
Cannonball Run 2
Cheerleader Camp
City of Women
Cover Girl Models
Cover Me
Creatures the World Forgot
Cupid
Cycle Vixens
Daddy-O
Day of the Warrior
Deadly Weapons
Desperate Cargo
Desperate Moves
Devil Girl from Mars
The Devil's Hand
Diamonds Are Forever▲
Divine Nymph
Do or Die
Dr. Alien
Dr. Goldfoot and the Bikini Machine
Dr. No▲
The Doll
The Doll Squad
The Dolls
Domino
Downhill Willie
Dracula: Dead and Loving It
Dream Trap
Dreaming of Rita
Dumb & Dumber
Emmanuelle
Emmanuelle 4
Emmanuelle & Joanna
Emmanuelle in the Country
Emmanuelle on Taboo Island
Emmanuelle, the Joys of a Woman
Emmanuelle, the Queen
Emmanuelle's Daughter
Enchanted Island
Evil Toons
Exotica▲
Fair Game
Fate
Femme Fontaine: Killer Babe for the C.I.A.
Fire Maidens from Outer Space
Fireballs
Forbidden Planet▲
Forbidden Zone: Alien Abduction
Gamera vs. Guiron
Gator Bait
Ghosts Can't Do It
Girl Shy▲
Gold of the Amazon Women

Goldeneye▲
The Grace Kelly Story
Great Bikini Off-Road Adventure
Guns
Hard Hunted
Helen of Troy
Hell's Belles
Hercules and the Princess of Troy
Hired to Kill
Hollywood Boulevard 2
Hollywood or Bust
How I Learned to Love Women
How to Succeed with Girls
I Married a Centerfold
I Posed for Playboy
It Takes a Thief
Jokes My Folks Never Told Me
Kiss and Kill
La Collectionneuse
Last Dance
Les Girls
Les Mistons▲
The Lion of Thebes▲
The Loves of Hercules
Malibu Hot Summer
A Man with a Maid
Masseuse
The Mermaids of Tiburon
Mirror Images
Mirror Images 2
Mirror Mirror 3
Missile to the Moon
Mysterious Island of Beautiful Women
Mystery Date
Naked Souls
Naked Warriors
National Lampoon's Vacation▲
Never Say Never Again
Nine Ages of Nakedness
A Nymphoid Barbarian in Dinosaur Hell
Obsession: A Taste for Fear
Oxford Blues
Panther Squad
Party Incorporated
Phat Beach
Pin-Up Girl
Posed for Murder
Priceless Beauty
Princess Daisy
Private Affairs
Queen of Outer Space
Queen of the Jungle
The Reckless Way
Revenge of the Cheerleaders
Round Trip to Heaven
Savage Beach
Seduce Me: Pamela Principle 2
The Seven Year Itch▲
She Gods of Shark Reef
She's Dressed to Kill
Sidekicks
Silk n' Sabotage
Ski School 2
The Slumber Party Massacre
Some Like It Hot▲
Sorceress
Soup for One
South Beach Academy
Spinout
The Spring
Star Crash
The Story of a Love Story
Strawberry Blonde▲
The Sure Thing▲
Swimsuit: The Movie
The Swinging Cheerleaders
Tammy and the Doctor
Tanya's Island
Tarzan, the Ape Man
10
Thieves of Fortune
Thunder & Mud
To the Limit
Too Shy to Try
Total Exposure
Undercover

Underground Aces
Vampire Vixens from Venus
Vampire's Kiss▲
Vice Academy 3
Voyage to the Planet of Prehistoric Women
Wayne's World▲
Wayne's World 2
Weird Science
Wet and Wild Summer
When Dinosaurs Ruled the Earth
Will Success Spoil Rock Hunter?
Wish Me Luck
Wishful Thinking
The Woman in Red
You Only Live Twice
Young Nurses in Love

Drugs

see Pill Poppin'

Earthquakes

see also Disaster Flicks; L.A.; San Francisco

After the Shock
Black Scorpion 2: Ground Zero
Earthquake
Escape from L.A.
The Great Los Angeles Earthquake
Life and Nothing More ...
Marshal Law
Quake
The Rains Came

Eating

see Cannibalism; Edibles

Eco-Vengeance!

see also Killer Bugs

Alligator▲
Anaconda
Ants
The Applegates
Arachnophobia
Ben
Body Snatchers
The Crawlers
Day of the Animals
Deadly Harvest
Fangs
The Fire Next Time
Food of the Gods
Frogs
Grizzly
Idaho Transfer
Jaws▲
Jaws 2
Jaws 3
Jaws: The Revenge
Jurassic Park▲
Kingdom of the Spiders
Last Days of Planet Earth
Magic in the Water
On Deadly Ground
Phantom 2040 Movie: The Ghost Who Walks
Piranha
Piranha 2: The Spawning
Prophecy
Savage Capitalism
Squirm
The Swarm
Thunder Bay▲
Ticks
The Toxic Avenger
Virus
Willard

Edibles

see also Cannibalism

The Age of Innocence▲
Babette's Feast▲
Big Night
Bikini Bistro
Blood Diner
A Chef in Love
Combination Platter
Consuming Passions
The Cook, the Thief, His Wife & Her Lover▲
Dim Sum: A Little Bit of Heart▲
The Duchess of Duke Street▲
Eat a Bowl of Tea▲
Eat Drink Man Woman▲
Eat the Rich
Gabriela
The Godfather▲
The Godfather, Part 2▲
The Godfather, Part 3▲
Goodfellas▲
Grave Indiscretions
Hamburger...The Motion Picture
Hot Chocolate
Ice Cream Man
Just Your Luck
La Grande Bouffe▲
The Last Supper
Life Is Sweet▲
Like Water for Chocolate▲
Love Is All There Is
Monty Python's The Meaning of Life▲
9 1/2 Weeks
Of Cooks and Kung-Fu
The Spitfire Grill
The Story of Boys & Girls▲
Tampopo▲
301, 302
Tom Jones▲
The Untold Story
The Van▲
Who Is Killing the Great Chefs of Europe?▲
Willy Wonka & the Chocolate Factory▲

Elephants

see also Carnivals & Circuses; Wild Kingdom

Babar: The Movie
Billy Rose's Jumbo▲
Dumbo▲
Ele, My Friend
Elephant Boy▲
Elephant Walk
Fantasia▲
George of the Jungle
Jupiter's Darling
Larger Than Life
Maya
Operation Dumbo Drop
Pardon My Trunk
Smokey and the Bandit, Part 2
White Hunter, Black Heart▲

Elevators

see also Terror in Tall Buildings

Basic Instinct
The Client
Die Hard▲
Fatal Attraction▲
In the Line of Fire▲
The Lift
The Man with Two Brains▲
Mixed Nuts
Nick of Time
The Omen
Pretty Woman▲
The Secret of My Success
The Silence of the Lambs▲
Sleepless in Seattle▲
Speed▲

Fantasy

Atlas
Atlas in the Land of the Cyclops
Ator the Fighting Eagle
Babe▶
Baby ... Secret of the Lost
  Legend
Barbarella
Barbarian Queen
Baron Munchausen▶
Batman▶
Batman and Robin
Batman Forever▶
Batman Returns
*batteries not included
Beanstalk
Beastmaster
Beastmaster 2: Through the
  Portal of Time
Beastmaster 3: The Eye of
  Braxus
Beauties of the Night
Beauty and the Beast, Episode
  1: Once Upon a Time in New
  York
Beauty and the Beast: Though
  Lovers Be Lost
Beauty and the Devil
Benji's Very Own Christmas
  Story
Bernard and the Genie
Between Heaven and Earth
Beyond Atlantis
Beyond Tomorrow
Big▶
Big Top Pee Wee
Biggles
Bill and Coo
Bill & Ted's Excellent Adventure
The Bishop's Wife▶
Blithe Spirit
The Blood of a Poet
The Blue Bird▶
Blue Monkey
Blue Paradise
The Borrowers▶
The Boy God
The Boy Who Could Fly▶
The Boy Who Loved Trolls
Bridge to Terabithia
Brothers Lionheart
Cabin Boy
The Canterville Ghost
The Cat from Outer Space
Celine and Julie Go Boating
The Challenge
Charleston▶
Charley and the Angel
The Children of Noisy Village
Child's Christmas in Wales
The Christmas That Almost
  Wasn't
The Chronicles of Narnia
Cinderella 2000
Circus Angel
The City of Lost Children▶
The Clan of the Cave Bear
Clarence
Clash of the Titans
Cocoon▶
Cocoon: The Return
The Company of Wolves▶
Conan the Barbarian▶
Conan the Destroyer
A Connecticut Yankee
A Connecticut Yankee in King
  Arthur's Court
Conquest
Conquest of Mycene
Coriolanus, Man without a
  Country
The Crazy Ray▶
Crossworlds
The Crow
The Crow 2: City of Angels
Curse of the Cat People▶
Darby O'Gill & the Little People▶
The Dark Crystal▶
The Day the Earth Froze
Deathstalker

Deathstalker 2: Duel of the
  Titans
Deathstalker 3
Deathstalker 4: Match of Titans
Desperate Living
The Devil & Max Devlin
Devil of the Desert Against the
  Son of Hercules
Diary of Forbidden Dreams▶
Digby, the Biggest Dog in the
  World
Donkey Skin▶
Dos Cruces en Danger Pass▶
Dragonheart
Dragonslayer▶
Dragonworld
Dream a Little Dream
Dream a Little Dream 2
Dreamchild▶
Dreamscape
Dungeonmaster
Edward Scissorhands▶
Emmanuelle 4
The Enchanted Cottage
The Enchantress
Endgame
Eraserhead▶
Erotic Escape
Erotic Touch of Hot Skin
Escapes
E.T.: The Extra-Terrestrial▶
Eternal Return
The Ewok Adventure
The Ewoks: Battle for Endor
Excalibur▶
Explorers
Falcon
Fantasy Island
Faraway, So Close!
Field of Dreams▶
The Final Programme
Fire and Ice
Flight of Dragons
Flight of the Navigator
Fluke
Francis Goes to the Races
Francis the Talking Mule▶
Frankenstein and Me
Freddie the Frog
French Quarter
Frogs!
From the Earth to the Moon
Galgameth
George's Island▶
The Ghost and Mrs. Muir▶
Ghost Chase
Ghost Writer
Ghosts Can't Do It
Ghostwarrior
The Giants of Thessaly
Gladiators 7
The Glass Slipper
The Gnome-Mobile
Golden Voyage of Sinbad
The Golem▶
Goliath Against the Giants
Goliath and the Barbarians
Goliath and the Dragon
Goliath and the Sins of Babylon
Gor
The Great Land of Small
Greenstone
Grendel, Grendel, Grendel
Gryphon
Gulliver's Travels
A Guy Named Joe
The Hanged Man
Harvey▶
Hawk the Slayer
Heartbreak Hotel
Hearts & Armour
Heaven Can Wait▶
Hector's Bunyip
Helen of Troy
Herbie Rides Again
Hercules
Hercules and the Captive
  Women

Hercules and the Princess of
  Troy
Hercules in the Haunted World
Hercules, Prisoner of Evil
Hercules Unchained
Here Come the Littles: The
  Movie
Here Comes Mr. Jordan▶
Hey There, It's Yogi Bear
Highlander 2: The Quickening
Highlander: The Final Dimension
His Majesty, the Scarecrow of
  Oz/The Magic Cloak of Oz
The Hobbit▶
Hobgoblins
The Holes
Hook
Hoppity Goes to Town
Horrors of the Red Planet
A Hungarian Fairy Tale▶
Hyper-Sapien: People from
  Another Star
I Married a Witch▶
The Incredible Mr. Limpet
The Indian in the Cupboard
Indiana Jones and the Last
  Crusade▶
Inhibition
The Invasion of Carol Enders
The Invincible Gladiator
Invisible Agent
The Invisible Kid
Invisible: The Chronicles of
  Benjamin Knight
Irish Cinderella
The Iron Crown
Iron Warrior
Ironmaster
The Island of Nevawuz
It's a Wonderful Life▶
Jack the Giant Killer▶
James and the Giant Peach▶
Jason and the Argonauts▶
Jimmy, the Boy Wonder
Jonathan Livingston Seagull
Josh Kirby...Time Warrior:
  Chapter 1, Planet of the Dino-
  Knights
Josh Kirby...Time Warrior:
  Chapter 2, The Human Pets
Josh Kirby...Time Warrior:
  Chapter 3, Trapped on
  Toyworld
Josh Kirby...Time Warrior:
  Chapter 4, Eggs from 70
  Million B.C.
Josh Kirby...Time Warrior:
  Chapter 5, Journey to the
  Magic Cavern
Journey Beneath the Desert
Journey to the Center of the
  Earth▶
Journey to the Center of the
  Earth
Journey to the Lost City
Julia and Julia
Julia Has Two Lovers
Jumanji
The Jungle Book
Jungle Hell
Kazaam
A Kid for Two Farthings
Kids of the Round Table
King Kong▶
King Kong
Kiss Me Goodbye
Kriemhilde's Revenge▶
Krull
Kull the Conqueror
La Merveilleuse Visite
L.A. Story▶
Labyrinth▶
Ladyhawke
Land of Doom
The Land of Faraway
The Last Days of Pompeii
The Last Unicorn
Le Magnifique
Leapin' Leprechauns

Legend
The Legend of Suram Fortress
Legion of Iron
Leprechaun 2
Les Visiteurs du Soir▶
Like Father, Like Son
The Lion of Thebes▶
The Little Mermaid
Little Monsters
Little Nemo: Adventures in
  Slumberland
Little Red Riding Hood
Logan's Run
The Lord of the Rings
Lords of Magick
The Lost Continent
Love Notes
The Loves of Hercules
Maciste in Hell
Made in Heaven
The Magic Fountain
Magic in the Mirror: Fowl Play
Magic in the Water
Magic Island
Magic Serpent▶
The Magic Voyage of Sinbad
Magical Wonderland
The Magician▶
Making Contact
The Man in the Santa Claus Suit
The Man Who Could Work
  Miracles▶
The Man Who Wagged His Tail
Mannequin 2: On the Move
Marco Polo, Jr.
The Martian Chronicles: Part 1
The Martian Chronicles: Part 2
The Martian Chronicles: Part 3
Master of the World
Masters of the Universe
Max Headroom, the Original
  Story
Maxie
Mazes and Monsters
Medusa Against the Son of
  Hercules
Merlin
Merlin and the Sword
Merlin of the Crystal Cave
Messalina vs. the Son of
  Hercules
Michael
A Midsummer Night's Dream▶
Mighty Joe Young
Mighty Morphin Power Rangers:
  The Movie
Million Dollar Duck
Miracle Beach
Miracle in Milan▶
Mr. Destiny
Mr. Sycamore
Mole Men against the Son of
  Hercules
The Moon Stallion
Mortal Kombat 1: The Movie
Mouse and His Child
Munchie
My Friend Walter
My Neighbor Totoro
My Science Project
My Stepmother Is an Alien
The Mysterious Stranger
Mystery Island
Natas...The Reflection
The Navigator▶
Neutron vs. the Amazing Dr.
  Caronte
Neutron vs. the Death Robots
Neutron vs. the Maniac
The NeverEnding Story▶
NeverEnding Story 2: The Next
  Chapter
The Neverending Story 3:
  escape from Fantasia
Night Tide
The Nightmare Before
  Christmas▶
Nine Lives of Fritz the Cat
Nutcracker: The Motion Picture

Once a Hero
Once Upon a Time
One Magic Christmas
1001 Arabian Nights
One Wish Too Many
The Original Fabulous
  Adventures of Baron
  Munchausen
Orpheus
Outlaw of Gor
The Pagemaster
Pandora and the Flying
  Dutchman
Paperhouse▶
Patchwork Girl of Oz
The Peanut Butter Solution
Peter Pan▶
Pete's Dragon
The Phantom Chariot
Phantom Tollbooth
The Phoenix and the Magic
  Carpet
The Plague Dogs
The Point
The Polar Bear King
Powder
Prancer
Prehistoric Bimbos in
  Armageddon City
Prehistoric Women
Prehysteria
Prehysteria 2
Prehysteria 3
Prelude to a Kiss
The Princess and the Swineherd
Private Passions
The Puppetoon Movie
Quest for the Mighty Sword
Quest of the Delta Knights
Radio Flyer
Ratboy
Real Men
Reckless
The Red Balloon▶
Red Sonja
The Reluctant Dragon
Renoir Shorts▶
The Rescuers Down Under
Return from Witch Mountain
The Return of Jafar
The Return of Peter Grimm
The Return of the Borrowers▶
The Return of the Fly
The Return of the King
Return to Fantasy Island
Return to Oz
Return to the Lost World
Revolt of the Barbarians
The Rise & Rise of Daniel
  Rocket
Rock & Rule
Roland the Mighty
Rookie of the Year
Rudolph & Frosty's Christmas in
  July
Salome's Last Dance
Samson
Samson Against the Sheik
Samson and His Mighty
  Challenge
Samson and the 7 Miracles of
  the World
Santa Claus
Santa Claus Conquers the
  Martians
Santa Claus: The Movie
The Saragossa Manuscript
Saturday Night Serials
Saturday Night Sleazies, Vol. 1
The Scalawag Bunch
Sea of Dreams
The Sea Serpent
Search for the Gods
The Secret of NIMH▶
The Secret of Roan Inish▶
Serpent Island
7 Faces of Dr. Lao▶
Seven Magnificent Gladiators
The Seventh Voyage of Sinbad▶

Farming
see Crop Dusters

Fast Cars
see also Motor Vehicle
   Dept.

Feds
see also Detectives; Spies
   & Espionage

Female Bonding
see also Women; Wonder
   Women

Feminism
see Women; Wonder
   Women

Femme Fatale
see also Wonder Women

Filmmaking *(continued)*

Marilyn & Bobby: Her Final Affair
Merton of the Movies
My Favorite Year▸
My Wicked, Wicked Ways
Norma Jean and Marilyn
The Perils of Pauline
Queenie
Rainbow
Rascal Dazzle
Rita Hayworth: The Love Goddess
Rock Hudson's Home Movies
Sinatra
Sophia Loren: Her Own Story
Superstar: The Life and Times of Andy Warhol▸
That's Entertainment
That's Entertainment, Part 2
That's Entertainment, Part 3
Thursday's Child
Valentino
Veronika Voss▸
W.C. Fields: Flask of Fields
What Ever Happened to Baby Jane?▸
White Hot: The Mysterious Murder of Thelma Todd
Wild, Wild World of Jayne Mansfield

Filmmaking

see also At the Movies; Behind the Scenes

Abbott and Costello Meet the Keystone Kops
The Adjuster
An Almost Perfect Affair
...And God Spoke
Barton Fink▸
Big Show
Black Cat
Bloodbath in Psycho Town
Body Chemistry 3: Point of Seduction
Bombay Talkie
Cannes Man
Cass
Children Shouldn't Play with Dead Things
Chuck Amuck: The Movie
Ciao Federico! Fellini Directs Satyricon
Comment Ca Va?
Contempt▸
The Cool Surface
Dangerous Game
David Holzman's Diary▸
Day for Night▸
Dead Silence
Drifting
Dubeat-E-O
Ed Wood▸
Ed Wood: Look Back in Angora
84 Charlie Mopic▸
Elsa, Elsa
Elvis in Hollywood▸
F/X 2: The Deadly Art of Illusion
Final Cut
Finnegan's Wake
Frankenstein: A Cinematic Scrapbook
Get Shorty▸
Good Morning, Babylon▸
Hearts of Darkness: A Filmmaker's Apocalypse▸
Hi, Mom!▸
Hollywood Chaos
Hollywood Mystery
The House of Seven Corpses
How to Make a Monster
I'll Do Anything
In a Moment of Passion
Intervista▸
Invasion Force
Iron Cowboy
Island of Blood
It's All True
Jacquot

Kamikaze Hearts
The King of the Kickboxers
The Last Porno Flick
Les Violons du Bal
Living in Oblivion▸
Loaded
A Man, a Woman and a Killer
A Man Like Eva▸
The Mirror Crack'd
Mistress
Movies Money Murder
Mute Witness
My Dream Is Yours
My Life's in Turnaround
Nightmare in Blood
Nightmare in Wax
Notes for an African Orestes
Nudity Required
On an Island with You
Once in Paris...
The Pickle
Pictures
The Player▸
The Red Raven Kiss-Off
Secret File of Hollywood
She Must Be Seeing Things
Silent Motive
A Slave of Love▸
Special Effects
Stand-In
The Stunt Man▸
Sullivan's Travels▸
The Swap
Sweet Liberty
Swimming with Sharks▸
Two Weeks in Another Town
Ulysses' Gaze
Understudy: The Graveyard Shift 2
Venice, Venice
Visions of Light: The Art of Cinematography▸
Wes Craven's New Nightmare▸
White Hunter, Black Heart▸
The Wizard of Speed and Time
The Wonderful, Horrible Life of Leni Riefenstahl
You Must Remember This

Firemen

see also Fires

Always
Backdraft
Backfire!
Club Paradise
Fahrenheit 451▸
Fire Alarm
Fireballs
Firehouse
The Fireman
The Firemen's Ball▸
Hellfighters
Inferno in Paradise
Roxanne▸
Trespass
Turk 182!

Fires

see also Boom!; Disaster Flicks; Firemen

Always
Backdraft
Burning Rage
City on Fire
The Cremators
Dinosaurus!
Don't Go in the House
Endless Love
Erendira
Fire
Fire Alarm
Firehead
The Fireman
Firestarter
Firestorm: 72 Hours in Oakland
The Flaming Urge

Flashfire
Frankenstein▸
In Old Chicago▸
Island of the Burning Doomed
The Michigan Kid
Mighty Joe Young
Nice Girls Don't Explode
Oil
Pretty Poison▸
Pyrates
A Pyromaniac's Love Story
Quest for Fire▸
Rosewood▸
Save the Tiger▸
Sounds of Silence
Specimen
Speeding Up Time
Spontaneous Combustion
Terror on the 40th Floor
Ticks
The Towering Inferno
The Triangle Factory Fire Scandal
Twin Town
Volcano
Wilder Napalm

Flashback

Antonia's Line
Back of Beyond
Being at Home with Claude
Betrayal
Boys
Broken Harvest
Carried Away
Casablanca▸
Citizen Kane▸
The Confessional
Courage Under Fire▸
Dogfight▸
Dolores Claiborne▸
Edward Scissorhands▸
Exotica▸
A Family Thing▸
The Forbidden Quest
Frankie Starlight
Helas Pour Moi
Hellraiser 4: Bloodline
I Shot a Man in Vegas
Jacob's Ladder
Johnny Dangerously
Kicking and Screaming▸
Leave Her to Heaven▸
Les Voleurs▸
Liebestraum
Lone Star▸
The Marrying Kind
Mother Night▸
The Neon Bible
Nina Takes a Lover
The Ninth Configuration▸
Now and Then
Passage to Marseilles▸
Passenger▸
The Razor's Edge▸
The Razor's Edge
Reservoir Dogs▸
Sergeant Rutledge▸
Shattered
Shining Through
The Silences of the Palace▸
Stealing Home
Stephen King's It
Sweet Nothing▸
T-Men▸
301, 302
Total Eclipse
The Underneath▸
The Usual Suspects▸
Valentino
Walkabout▸
Wild Bill
The Wild Bunch▸

Flatulence

Blazing Saddles▸

Dumb & Dumber
Ed
Grumpier Old Men
National Lampoon's Senior Trip
The Nutty Professor▸
The Road to Wellville

Flight

see Airborne

Flood

see also Disaster Flicks

Flood!
Heroes of the Heart
The Last Wave▸
The Rains Came
The River
Waterworld
William Faulkner's Old Man

Flower Children

see also Boomer Reunions

Adam at 6 a.m.
Alice's Restaurant
American Blue Note
Angels Hard as They Come
Awakenings of the Beast
Best Enemies
Best Revenge
The Big Chill▸
The Big Fix▸
Blast-Off Girls
Bob & Carol & Ted & Alice
Born on the Fourth of July▸
Children Shouldn't Play with Dead Things
The Compleat Beatles▸
Conspiracy: The Trial of the Chicago Eight▸
The Crimson Cult
Dogfight▸
The Doors
Dynamite Chicken
Easy Rider▸
Even Cowgirls Get the Blues
Flashback▸
Four Friends▸
Free Grass
Fritz the Cat▸
Gimme Shelter
The Glory Stompers
Grace of My Heart
Greetings▸
Hair▸
Head▸
Help Wanted Female
High Hopes▸
I Drink Your Blood
I Love You, Alice B. Toklas!
Mantis in Lace
Married to It
The Mod Squad
More
More American Graffiti
Off Limits
Out
Petit Con
Psych-Out
Rainbow Bridge
The Rebel Set
R.P.M.* (*Revolutions Per Minute)
Rude Awakening
The Sandpiper
Satan's Sadists
Sea Devils
Second Thoughts
Slashed Dreams
A Small Circle of Friends
The Snake People
The Speed Lovers
The Stoned Age
The Strawberry Statement
There Goes My Baby
There's a Girl in My Soup

Thumb Tripping
The Trip
Where Angels Go, Trouble Follows
Where the Eagle Flies
Who'll Stop the Rain?▸
Wild in the Streets
Woodstock▸
Yellow Submarine▸

Flying Saucers

see Alien Beings—Benign; Alien Beings—Vicious; Space Operas

Folklore & Mythology

see also Storytelling

Antonio Das Mortes
Atlantis, the Lost Continent
Atlas in the Land of the Cyclops
The Ballad of Paul Bunyan
Beauty and the Devil
Black Orpheus▸
Candyman
Candyman 2: Farewell to the Flesh
Clash of the Titans
Colossus and the Amazon Queen
Crossroads
Darby O'Gill & the Little People▸
Disney's Storybook Classics
Donkey Skin▸
Down to Earth
Erik the Viking
Faust▸
The Fool Killer
Force on Thunder Mountain
The Fury of Hercules
The Giant of Marathon
The Giant of Metropolis
The Giants of Thessaly
Golden Voyage of Sinbad
Goliath Against the Giants
Goliath and the Barbarians
Goliath and the Dragon
Goliath and the Sins of Babylon
The Gorgon
Grendel, Grendel, Grendel
Helen of Troy
Hercules
Hercules▸
Hercules 2
Hercules Against the Moon Men
Hercules and the Captive Women
Hercules in the Haunted World
Hercules the Legendary Journeys, Vol. 1: And the Amazon Women
Hercules the Legendary Journeys, Vol. 2: The Lost Kingdom
Hercules the Legendary Journeys, Vol. 3: The Circle of Fire
Hercules the Legendary Journeys, Vol. 4: In the Underworld
Hercules Unchained
Into the West▸
Invincible Gladiators
Invitation to the Dance
Iphigenia
Jason and the Argonauts▸
Johnny Appleseed
Kismet▸
Kriemhilde's Revenge▸
Leapin' Leprechauns
The Legend of Gator Face
The Legend of Sleepy Hollow
The Legend of Suram Fortress
Leprechaun 2
Life on a String
The Loves of Hercules

Total Eclipse
Tropic of Cancer▶
True Colors
Uncertain Glory
Until September
Uranus▶
Valmont▶
Waterloo
Western
What Price Glory?▶
Window to Paris
A Year in Provence▶

Friendship

see Buddies

Front Page

see also Mass Media;
Shutterbugs

Absence of Malice
Act of Passion: The Lost Honor
of Kathryn Beck
Action in Arabia
The Adventures of Nellie Bly
Alice in the Cities▶
All the President's Men▶
American Autobahn
AngKor: Cambodia Express
Another Time, Another Place
Anzio
The Average Woman
The Barcelona Kill
The Beniker Gang
Between the Lines▶
The Big Hurt
Big News
Big Town
Big Town After Dark
Blessed Event▶
Boca
Boeing Boeing
Brenda Starr
Broadway Melody of 1936▶
Bulldog Edition
A Bunny's Tale
Call Northside 777▶
Caroline at Midnight
Circumstantial Evidence
Citizen Kane▶
City in Fear▶
Cobb▶
Concrete Beat
Continental Divide
Cover Story
Criminal Act
Cry Freedom
Cut and Run
Dark Side of Genius
Dead Air
Dead Connection
Deadline
Deadly Exposure
Defense of the Realm▶
The Devil's Commandment
Diamond Trail
Double Cross
Double Edge
Double Exposure
Down Came a Blackbird
Everything Happens at Night▶
Eyes Behind the Stars
Eyes of a Stranger
A Face in the Fog
Far East
Fast Money
Father Hood
Fatherland
Fever Pitch'
Final Extra
Finnegan Begin Again
Fit for a King
A Flash of Green
Fletch
Fletch Lives
The Forbidden Quest
Foreign Correspondent▶

Francis Covers the Big Town▶
Freeze Frame
The Front Page▶
The Front Page
Fun
Gentleman's Agreement▶
The Ghost and Mr. Chicken
The Great Muppet Caper▶
Grown Ups
Headline Woman
Heads
Heat Wave▶
Her Life as a Man
Hero▶
His Girl Friday▶
Hit the Ice
Hour of Decision
The Hudsucker Proxy▶
Hue and Cry▶
Hustling▶
I Cover the Waterfront▶
I Love Trouble
The Image
An Inconvenient Woman
The Infiltrator
Invasion of Privacy
Istanbul
Johnny Come Lately
Journey for Margaret▶
Just One of the Guys
Keeper of the City
Keeper of the Flame
Kid from Not-So-Big
Kill Slade
The Killing Beach
The Killing Device
The Killing Fields▶
Killing Stone
La Dolce Vita▶
Lana in Love
The Last Word
Late Extra
Let 'er Go Gallegher
Lethal Charm
Libeled Lady▶
Lip Service▶
L'Odeur des Fauves
Lonelyhearts
Love Is a Many-Splendored
Thing
The Love Machine
Malarek
The Man Inside
Man of Iron▶
Mean Season
Meet John Doe▶
Midnight Edition
Midnight Warrior
Mrs. Parker and the Vicious
Circle
Murder on the Campus
Murrow
Mystic Circle Murder
Natas...The Reflection
News at Eleven
Newsfront▶
Newsies
Night Hunter
The Nightmare Years
Nina Takes a Lover
No Time to Die
Not for Publication
Nothing Sacred▶
Novel Desires
November Conspiracy
The Odessa File
One Fine Day
One Man Out
The Other Woman
The Outlaws is Coming!
The Paper▶
Paper Lion
Paralyzed
The Payoff
The Pelican Brief
Perfect
The Philadelphia Story▶
Platinum Blonde▶
The Ploughman's Lunch▶

Primary Motive
Private Investigations
Profile
Qui Etes Vous, Mr. Sorge?
Reckless Disregard
Resurrection of Zachary
Wheeler
Revenge of the Radioactive
Reporter
Riding on Air
Roman Holiday▶
Roxie Hart
The Rumor Mill
Safari 3000
Salome, Where She Danced
Salvador▶
Savage Capitalism
Scandal
The Secrets of Wu Sin
Sex and the Single Girl
Sex Through a Window
The Shadow Conspiracy
Shock Corridor▶
Short Fuse
Shriek in the Night
Shy People▶
The Sixth Man
Somewhere I'll Find You▶
Soul Patrol
Special Bulletin▶
Speed Reporter
Star Reporter
Stavisky▶
Stay Tuned for Murder
Straight Talk
The Strange Love of Molly
Louvain
Stranger on the Third Floor▶
Street Smart
Sucker Money
Superman: The Movie▶
Sweet Rosie O'Grady
Sweet Smell of Success▶
Switching Channels
Tainted Blood
Tarnished Angels▶
Teacher's Pet▶
That Certain Age
That Lucky Touch
They All Kissed the Bride
They Got Me Covered
The Thirteenth Man
Thirteenth Reunion
Those Glory, Glory Days
Three O'Clock High
Tomorrow at Seven
Too Hot to Handle▶
Tough Assignment
Trahir▶
Transylvania 6-5000
Traps
Under Fire▶
The Underworld Story
Unexplained Laughter
Up to a Certain Point
Up Your Alley
Virgin Machine
The Wharf Rat
Where the Buffalo Roam
While the City Sleeps▶
Whispering City▶
Without Love
Woman Condemned
Woman of the Year▶
A World Apart▶
The World Gone Mad
The Year of Living
Dangerously▶

Fugitives

see also Lovers on the
Lam

Agent on Ice
Bad Girls
Bail Jumper
Ball of Fire▶
Ballad of Gregorio Cortez▶
Bandits of Orgosolo

Bed & Breakfast
The Big Fix▶
Bobbie Jo and the Outlaw
The Boldest Job in the West
A Boy Called Hate
Boys on the Side
Brannigan
Breathless
Bushwhacked
Butch and Sundance: The Early
Days
Butch Cassidy and the
Sundance Kid▶
Cadillac Ranch
Captured in Chinatown
Chain Reaction
The Chase
Cyber-Tracker 2
Danger: Diabolik
Dead Easy
The Deserters
Desperate
Desperate Measures▶
The Desperate Trail
Eddie Macon's Run
Eight on the Lam
Escape 2000
Father Hood
Fled
Frank and Jesse
Free Grass
The Fugitive▶
Fugitive Among Us
The Fugitive: Premiere Episode
The Fugitive: The Final Episode
Good Girls Don't
The Great Texas Dynamite
Chase
Gridlock'd▶
Hard Knocks
Hiding Out
Hold Me, Thrill Me, Kiss Me
Hollow Point
I Died a Thousand Times
I Met a Murderer
The Jesus Trip
Jungle Inferno
Keeping Track
Kiss of Death▶
Klondike Annie
Le Doulos▶
Leather Jackets
Liberators
Loners
Long Pants▶
The Love Flower
The Man Upstairs
Manhunt
Marked Man
Miami Cops
Miles from Home
Moving Target
Moving Violation
North by Northwest▶
Northwest Trail
Nowhere to Hide
On the Run
One Away
The Outlaw and His Wife
Outlaw Riders
Paris Express
A Perfect World
Posse▶
The Pursuit of D.B. Cooper
The Red Half-Breed
Rider on the Rain▶
Rough Cut
The Savage Woman
Scorpion Spring
Sea Devils
The Secret Agent
Shallow Grave
Shoot to Kill▶
Simple Men▶
Slate, Wyn & Me
Sonny and Jed
The Spy Within
Stray Dog▶
Strike Back

Suspect Device
Teenage Bonnie & Klepto Clyde
Three Days of the Condor▶
Three Fugitives
Thunder County
Time is Running Out
Truth or Consequences, N.M.
Twilight Man
The Walls of Malapaga
The Way Out
Woman With a Past
The Wrong Man

Funerals

see also Death & the
Afterlife
The Addams Family
The Big Chill▶
Blackwater Trail
City Hall▶
Dangerous Ground
The Evening Star
First Knight
Four Weddings and a Funeral▶
The Funeral▶
Funeral Home
Gardens of Stone
Harold and Maude▶
Heathers▶
Jack and Sarah
Kissed
Mr. Saturday Night
My Girl
My Girl 2
Only the Lonely
The Pallbearer
Roommates
Sleepless in Seattle▶
Steel Magnolias▶
Terms of Endearment▶
Tom and Huck▶
What's Eating Gilbert Grape▶

Future Cop

see also Cops
Apprentice to Murder
The Believers
The Dying Truth
The Fifth Element
The First Power
God Told Me To
Maniac Cop
Maniac Cop 2
Maniac Cop 3: Badge of Silence
Split Second
Wolfen▶

Gambling

see also Viva Las Vegas!
Aces and Eights
Action for Slander
Any Number Can Play
Atlantic City▶
Back to the Future, Part 2
A Big Hand for the Little Lady
Big Town
A Billion for Boris
Birds & the Bees
Bitter Sweet
Bob le Flambeur▶
Bugsy▶
Casino
Casino▶
Catch Me...If You Can
The Cheaters
The Cincinnati Kid
Cockfighter▶
The Color of Money▶
The Dark Dealer
Dead Lucky
Deadly Impact
Diamonds Are Forever▶
Diggstown
Dona Flor and Her Two
Husbands▶

Category Index

Punk Vacation
Quatorze Juliet
The Racket
The Racketeer
Rapid Fire
Renegades
Return of the Dragon
Return of the Rebels
Return of the Tiger
Revenge
Revenge of the Ninja
Ricco
Riot Squad
The Rise and Fall of Legs Diamond
The Ritz
The Roaring Twenties
Robin and the 7 Hoods
Rooftops
Rumble Fish
Rumble in the Bronx
The St. Valentine's Day Massacre
Satan's Sadists
The Savage Seven
Scared Stiff
Scarface
The Sea Serpent
Second Chance
The Set-Up
Sexton Blake and the Hooded Terror
Shaft
Shark Hunter
She's Back
Shining Star
Shoot the Piano Player
Showdown
Showdown in Little Tokyo
Sidewalks of New York
Small Faces
Smart Alecks
SnakeEater 3: His Law
Sno-Line
Some Like It Hot
South Central
Speedy
Spike of Bensonhurst
Spook Busters
Star Reporter
Stavisky
Steel
Sticky Fingers
Stingray
Stone Cold
Straight Line
Street Crimes
Street Hitz
Street Knight
Street Soldiers
Street Warriors
Street Warriors, Part 2
The Street with No Name
The Streets of L.A.
The Substitute
Sunnyside
The Sun's Burial
T-Bird Gang
Tattoo Connection
Tattooed Hit Man
Teenage Gang Debs
Teenage Wolfpack
This Time I'll Make You Rich
Timber Queen
The Tin Soldier
The Tip-Off
Tongs: An American Nightmare
Too Late for Tears
Topaze
Tough Assignment
Tough Kid
Tough to Handle
Tropical Snow
Trouble in Store
Truck Stop Women
True Believer
True Blood
Tuff Turf
Two to Tango

Underground Terror
The Underworld Story
Urban Crossfire
Variety
Vengeance
Verne Miller
Vietnam, Texas
Violent Professionals
The Violent Years
The Virginia Hill Story
Wanderers
The Warriors
West Side Story
When Gangland Strikes
The Wild One
Wilding
The Wolves
Wonder Man
Wonderland
The Wrong Arm of the Law
The Yakuza
Year of the Dragon
Young Warriors
Zooman

Gays

see also Bisexuality; Gender Bending; Lesbians

Abuse
Amazing Grace
American Fabulous
And the Band Played On
Another Country
Apart from Hugh
Arabian Nights
Armistead Maupin's Tales of the City
As Is
Beautiful Thing
The Best Way
The Birdcage
Blue
Boys in Love
The Boys in the Band
Boys Life
Breaking the Code
Carrington
The Celluloid Closet
City in Panic
Colonel Redl
The Conformist
Consenting Adult
Cruising
The Crying Game
Curse of the Queerwolf
Dear Boys
Death in Venice
The Detective
Different Story
Drifting
An Early Frost
Eclipse
Edward II
El Diputado
An Empty Bed
Entertaining Mr. Sloane
Ernesto
The Everlasting Secret Family
Flipping
Flirt
For a Lost Soldier
Forbidden Passion: The Oscar Wilde Movie
Fortune and Men's Eyes
Four Weddings and a Funeral
Fox and His Friends
Frisk
Fun Down There
The Garden
Go Fish
Grief
Happy Together
Hearing Voices
Heaven's a Drag
Hollow Reed
The Hours and Times
I Can't Sleep
It's My Party

Jeffrey
Joey Breaker
Kiss of the Spider Woman
La Cage aux Folles
La Cage aux Folles 2
La Cage aux Folles 3: The Wedding
Les Nuits Fauves
L'Escorte
L'Homme Blesse
Lie Down with Dogs
Like It Never Was Before
Lilies
The Living End
Longtime Companion
The Lost Language of Cranes
Love and Human Remains
Love! Valour! Compassion!
Madagascar Skin
Making Love
A Man of No Importance
Maurice
Maybe...Maybe Not
Men in Love
Menage
Midnight Cowboy
Midnight Dancers
Mouth to Mouth
The Music Lovers
My Beautiful Laundrette
My Best Friend's Wedding
My Father Is Coming
My Own Private Idaho
The Naked Civil Servant
Naked Lunch
Nerolio
Nijinsky
Norman, Is That You?
Nowhere
Okoge
Our Sons
Paris Is Burning
Parting Glances
Partners
Pedale Douce
Philadelphia
The Pillow Book
Prick Up Your Ears
Priest
Querelle
Ready to Wear
Reflections in a Golden Eye
The Ritz
Rock Hudson's Home Movies
The Rocky Horror Picture Show
Rope
Rude
Sand and Blood
Satan's Brew
Sergeant Matlovich vs. the U.S. Air Force
Smoke
The Sprinter
Stonewall
Straight for the Heart
Strawberry and Chocolate
The Sum of Us
Sunday, Bloody Sunday
Swoon
Taxi zum Klo
The Third Sex
This Special Friendship
Threesome
Tidy Endings
Times of Harvey Milk
To Forget Venice
To Play or To Die
Too Much Sun
Torch Song Trilogy
Total Eclipse
Totally F***ed Up
The Twilight of the Golds
A Very Natural Thing
Via Appia
Victim
Victor/Victoria
Vive L'Amour
We Think the World of You

The Wedding Banquet
Wild Reeds
Withnail and I
Wittgenstein
Wonderland
World and Time Enough
Zero Patience

Gender Bending

see also Gays; Lesbians; Role Reversal

Abroad with Two Yanks
The Adventures of Priscilla, Queen of the Desert
Anything for Love
At War with the Army
Auntie
Blue Murder at St. Trinian's
Boy! What a Girl
The Crying Game
The Damned
Desperate Living
Different for Girls
Divine
Dr. Jekyll and Ms. Hyde
Dressed to Kill
Ed Wood
Forever Mary
Glen or Glenda: Confessions of Ed Wood
Hairspray
Happily Ever After
Her Life as a Man
He's My Girl
I Like It Like That
I Shot Andy Warhol
I Wanna Be a Beauty Queen
I Want What I Want
I Was a Male War Bride
In a Year of 13 Moons
It's Pat: The Movie
Just Like a Woman
Just One of the Girls
La Cage aux Folles
La Cage aux Folles 2
La Cage aux Folles 3: The Wedding
Law of Desire
Le Sexe des Etoiles
Lilies
Lust in the Dust
M. Butterfly
Mascara
Mrs. Doubtfire
Mixed Nuts
Mutant on the Bounty
My Son, the Vampire
Myra Breckinridge
The Mystery of Alexina
The Newlydeads
Nobody's Perfect
Nowhere
Nuns on the Run
Old Mother Riley's Ghosts
Outrageous!
Paris Is Burning
Pink Flamingos
Polyester
Prime Suspect 3
Psycho
The Rocky Horror Picture Show
Shadey
The Silence of the Lambs
Some Like It Hot
Sonny Boy
Stonewall
Switch
To Wong Foo, Thanks for Everything, Julie Newmar
Tootsie
Torch Song Trilogy
Trash
Twelfth Night
Vegas in Space
Victor/Victoria
Wigstock: The Movie
Wild Party

Wild, Wild World of Jayne Mansfield
The Woman Inside
The World According to Garp
The Year of Living Dangerously
Yentl
Zazie dans le Metro

Generation X

Beautiful Girls
Before Sunrise
Bodies, Rest & Motion
Bottle Rocket
Chasing Amy
Clerks
Don't Do It
Ed's Next Move
Empire Records
Floundering
Keys to Tulsa
Kicking and Screaming
A Little Stiff
Live Bait
Loaded
Love and Other Catastrophes
The Low Life
Mallrats
Nowhere
omaha (the movie)
Party Girl
Reality Bites
S.F.W.
Singles
Slacker
Sleep with Me
subUrbia
When the Party's Over

Genetics

see also Mad Scientists; Metamorphosis

Biohazard: The Alien Force
The Boys from Brazil
Ed's Next Move
The Fly
The Fly
The Fly 2
Forbidden World
The Island of Dr. Moreau
Metamorphosis: The Alien Factor
Mimic
Rats
Tomcat: Dangerous Desires
The Twilight of the Golds
Wes Craven Presents Mind Ripper

Genies

see also Magic Carpet Rides

Aladdin
Aladdin and His Wonderful Lamp
Aladdin and the King of Thieves
Bernard and the Genie
Kazaam
Miracle Beach
The Outing
Priceless Beauty
The Return of Jafar
The Thief of Bagdad
The Thief of Baghdad
The Thief of Baghdad
A Thousand and One Nights
Three Wishes
Wildest Dreams
Wish Me Luck
Wishman
The Wonders of Aladdin

Historical

The Rise of Louis XIV➤
Road to Yesterday/The Yankee
  Clipper
Roanoak
Rob Roy—The Highland Rogue
The Robe
Robin and Marian
Roots
Roots: The Gift
Roots: The Next Generation➤
Rosewood➤
A Royal Scandal
Saint Joan
Salome
Samson and Delilah
Samurai Reincarnation
Scarlet Empress➤
The Scarlet Letter
The Scarlet Pimpernel➤
Sebastiane➤
The Seekers
Senso➤
Separate But Equal➤
Shaka Zulu➤
Shenandoah➤
Shin Heike Monogatari➤
The Sicilian
The Sign of the Cross
The Silk Road
Sins of Rome
Six Wives of Henry VIII➤
Soldier in Love
Soldier of Orange➤
Soul of the Game➤
Spartacus➤
Spy of Napoleon
Sunrise at Campobello➤
Surviving Picasso
The Sword of El Cid
Tai-Pan
A Tale of Two Cities➤
Tale of Two Cities/In the Switch
  Tower
Tamango
The Ten Commandments
The Ten Commandments➤
Ten Days That Shook the
  World➤
Ten Who Dared
Tharus Son of Attila
That Hamilton Woman➤
Therese➤
They Died with Their Boots On➤
'38: Vienna Before the Fall
This England
The Thorn Birds➤
Three Sovereigns for Sarah
The Tower of London
Tower of London
Tower of Screaming Virgins
The Triangle Factory Fire
  Scandal
Uncle Tom's Cabin
Uranus➤
Vanina Vanini➤
Victoria Regina
The Virgin Queen➤
Viva Zapata!➤
The Wannsee Conference➤
The War Lord
The Warriors
Waterloo
Where the Sky Begins
White Mischief➤
The White Rose➤
Who Has Seen the Wind?
The Winds of Kitty Hawk
The Wolf at the Door
A Woman Called Golda➤
A Woman Called Moses➤
Young Bess➤
Young Catherine➤
Young Mr. Lincoln➤

Hit Men

see also Assassinations

African Rage
Amateur➤

Assassins
Back to Back
Baja
Body Count
The Bodyguard
Breakaway
Bulletproof Heart➤
Cold Sweat
Confessions of a Hit Man
DaVinci's War
Deja Vu
Desperado➤
Diary of a Hitman
Direct Hit
Dumb & Dumber
8 Heads in a Duffel Bag
El Mariachi➤
Escape Clause
Faithful
The Family
Fatal Chase
Fatal Justice
Fight to the Death
Final Mission
Firepower
The Funeral➤
Grosse Pointe Blank➤
Hard-Boiled
The Hit List
Hit Woman: The Double Edge
Honor and Glory
The Killer➤
La Femme Nikita➤
The Last Hit
Lethal Panther
Little Odessa
Man with a Gun
The Manchurian Candidate➤
Mean Johnny Barrows
The Mechanic
Mr. Nice Guy
The Naked City➤
Night of the Running Man
The Outside Man
Over the Wire
Paid to Kill
Perfect Killer
Point of No Return
Portrait of a Hitman
The Positively True Adventures
  of the Alleged Texas
  Cheerleader-Murdering
  Mom➤
Prizzi's Honor➤
The Professional
The Professional: Golgo 13
Project: Kill!
Pulp Fiction➤
Quick
Red King, White Knight
Red Rock West➤
Savage Hearts
Season for Assassins
The Shadow Conspiracy
Sleepers
The Specialist
Stiletto
Strangers on a Train➤
Suddenly➤
Things to Do In Denver When
  You're Dead➤
Two Days in the Valley

Hockey

see also Skating

Accident
The Cutting Edge
D3: The Mighty Ducks
D2: The Mighty Ducks
Dutch Girls
Happy Gilmore
Hockey Night
Lethal Weapon 3
Love Story➤
The Mighty Ducks
Miracle on Ice
Mystery of the Million Dollar
  Hockey Puck

Paperback Hero
Slap Shot➤
Sudden Death
Touch and Go
Youngblood

Holidays

see also Christmas;
  Horrible Holidays

Bloody New Year
Carry On Behind
Clown Murders
Double Double Toil and Trouble
Easter Parade➤
Fourth Wise Man
Frankenstein and Me
Frankenstein Sings...The Movie
Groundhog Day➤
A Happy New Year!
Happy New Year, Charlie Brown
The Hoboken Chicken
  Emergency
Hocus Pocus
It's the Great Pumpkin, Charlie
  Brown
Jack-O
The Legend of Sleepy Hollow
Mrs. Wiggs of the Cabbage
  Patch
New Year's Evil
Night of the Demons 2
Spaced Invaders
Strange Days➤
Turumba➤
Two Weeks with Love
The White Balloon➤

The Holocaust

see also Germany;
  *Judaism; Nazis & Other
  Paramilitary Slugs; World
  War II*

Alan & Naomi
The Assault➤
The Assisi Underground
The Attic: The Hiding of Anne
  Frank
Au Revoir Les Enfants➤
The Boxer and Death➤
Charlie Grant's War
Christabel
Cold Days
David➤
A Day in October
Diamonds of the Night➤
The Diary of Anne Frank➤
Enemies, a Love Story➤
Era Notte a Roma➤
Europa, Europa➤
The Execution
Forced March
The Garden of the Finzi-
  Continis➤
Genghis Cohn
Getting Away With Murder
Good Evening, Mr. Wallenberg
Hanna's War
The Hiding Place
Hitler
The Holcroft Covenant
Holocaust➤
Holocaust
  Survivors...Remembrance of
  Love
In a Glass Cage
In the Presence of Mine
  Enemies
Kanal➤
Kapo➤
Korczak➤
The Last Butterfly
The Last Metro➤
Les Miserables
Les Violons du Bal
Max and Helen

Murderers Among Us: The
  Simon Wiesenthal Story➤
Murderers Are Among Us
Never Forget
Passenger➤
The Pawnbroker➤
Playing for Time➤
Reunion➤
The Revolt of Job➤
The Rose Garden
Schindler's List➤
The Shop on Main Street➤
Sophie's Choice➤
The Substance of Fire
Transport from Paradise
Triumph of the Spirit➤
The Wannsee Conference➤
War & Love
The White Rose➤

Home Alone

see also Childhood Visions

Adventures in Babysitting
And You Thought Your Parents
  Were Weird!
Anything for a Thrill
The Apple Dumpling Gang
Baby's Day Out
Blank Check
Bless the Beasts and Children
The Blue Lagoon
Camp Nowhere
Cloak & Dagger
Cohen and Tate
Courage Mountain
Cross My Heart
Dirkham Detective Agency
Dirt Bike Kid
Don't Tell Mom the Babysitter's
  Dead
Explorers
Famous Five Get into Trouble
A Far Off Place
Fatal Skies
Four Rooms
Gleaming the Cube
The Goonies
He is My Brother
Home Alone➤
Home Alone 2: Lost in New York
Honey, I Shrunk the Kids
Honey, We Shrunk Ourselves
Hook
The Horse Without a Head
House Arrest
Invaders from Mars
Island Trader
Just William's Luck
Legend of Billie Jean
The Littlest Horse Thieves
Lord of the Flies➤
Lord of the Flies
Mr. Wise Guy
Monkey Trouble
The Monster Squad➤
Paradise
The Rescue
Return to the Blue Lagoon
Scream➤
Shipwrecked
Snow Treasure
3 Ninjas
3 Ninjas Kick Back
A Waltz Through the Hills
The Window➤
Young Sherlock Holmes

The Homefront: England

see also World War II

The Affair
And a Nightingale Sang
Hope and Glory➤
Mrs. Miniver➤
The Weaker Sex
The White Cliffs of Dover➤

The Homefront: U.S./Canada

see also World War II

Bye Bye Blues
Come See the Paradise➤
For the Moment
The Human Comedy➤
In Love and War
In the Mood
A League of Their Own➤
The More the Merrier➤
1941
Racing with the Moon➤
Raggedy Man➤
Saboteur➤
Since You Went Away➤
The Summer of My German
  Soldier➤
Swing Shift
Wedding in White

Homeless

see also Great Depression;
  *Hard Knock Life; Yuppie
  Nightmares*

Accatone!➤
All Mine to Give
The Billion Dollar Hobo
Billy: Portrait of a Street Kid
Bums
Caught
Children of Sanchez
City Lights➤
Curly Sue
Distant Thunder➤
Dodes 'ka-den➤
Down, Out and Dangerous
Emanon
The Fisher King➤
God Bless the Child➤
The Grapes of Wrath➤
Home for Christmas
Home of Angels
Homecoming
Into the West➤
Kanal➤
The Kid➤
The Kid/Idle Class➤
Life Stinks
Los Olvidados➤
The Lower Depths➤
The Man from Left Field
Midnight Cowboy➤
None But the Lonely Heart➤
Oliver!➤
Oliver Twist➤
Oliver Twist
Oliver Twist➤
Oliver Twist
Original Intent
An Orphan Boy of Vienna
Pardon My Trunk
The Prince of Central Park➤
The Saint of Fort Washington
Salaam Bombay!➤
Samaritan: The Mitch Snyder
  Story➤
Scarecrow
Silas Marner➤
Sounder➤
Streetwise➤
Sullivan's Travels➤
Summer Magic
They Shall Have Music
Times Square
Up Your Alley
The Vagrant
Where the Day Takes You
With Honors

Horror

Horror

The Witch's Mirror
WitchTrap
The Wizard of Gore
Wolf
Wolf Blood
Wolfen►
The Wolfman
Woodchipper Massacre
The Worm Eaters
Wrestling Women vs. the Aztec Ape
Wrestling Women vs. the Aztec Mummy
Zoltan...Hound of Dracula
Zombie
The Zombie Army
Zombie High
Zombie Island Massacre
Zombie Lake
Zombie Nightmare
Zombies of Moratau
Zombiethon
Zone of the Dead

Horror Anthologies

see also Horror

Alien Massacre
Asylum
Body Bags
Creepshow
Creepshow 2
The Dark Dealer
Dead of Night►
Dead of Night
Deadtime Stories
Dr. Terror's House of Horrors
Escapes
Ghost Stories: Graveyard Thriller
Grim Prairie Tales
The Hitchhiker
Hitchhiker 2
Hitchhiker 3
Hitchhiker 4
The House that Dripped Blood
H.P. Lovecraft's Necronomicon: Book of the Dead
The Monster Club
Night Gallery►
Nightmares
The Offspring
Once Upon a Midnight Scary
Screamtime
Spirits of the Dead►
Tales from the Crypt►
Tales from the Crypt, Vol. 3
Tales from the Darkside: The Movie
Tales from the Hood
Tales That Witness Madness
Things
Trilogy of Terror
Trilogy of Terror 2
Twice-Told Tales►
Twilight Zone: The Movie
Two Evil Eyes
The Uncanny
Vault of Horror
The Willies

Horror Comedy

see also Horror

Adventures of Eliza Fraser
Andy Warhol's Dracula►
Andy Warhol's Frankenstein
April Fool's Day
Arachnophobia
Army of Darkness►
Attack of the Killer Refrigerator
Attack of the Killer Tomatoes
Attack of the Robots
Auntie Lee's Meat Pies
Autopsy of a Ghost
Bad Channels
Bad Taste►
Beauty on the Beach

Beetlejuice►
Bela Lugosi Meets a Brooklyn Gorilla
Beverly Hills Bodysnatchers
Big Meat Eater
Billy the Kid Versus Dracula
Black Magic
Blood & Donuts
Blood Beach
Blood Hook
Bloodbath at the House of Death
Body Bags
The Bone Yard
Bowery Boys Meet the Monsters
Brain Damage
Bride of Re-Animator
A Bucket of Blood►
Bugged!
Carry On Screaming
C.H.U.D.
C.H.U.D. 2: Bud the Chud
The Comedy of Terrors►
Creature from the Haunted Sea
Critters
Critters 2: The Main Course
Critters 3
Critters 4
Curse of the Queerwolf
Cutting Class
Dead Heat
Dr. Jekyll and Sister Hyde
Dolls
Doom Asylum
Dracula & Son
Dracula Blows His Cool
Dracula: Dead and Loving It
Dracula: Up in Harlem
Eat and Run
Ed and His Dead Mother
Elvira, Mistress of the Dark
Evil Spawn
Face of the Screaming Werewolf
The Fearless Vampire Killers►
Frankenhooker
Frankenstein Sings...The Movie
Frankenstein's Great Aunt Tillie
The Frighteners
From Beyond►
Funnyman
The Ghost Breakers►
Ghoulies
Ghoulies 2
Ghoulies 3: Ghoulies Go to College
Ghoulies 4
Goblin
Gore-Met Zombie Chef From Hell
The Granny
Gremlins►
Gremlins 2: The New Batch►
Hard to Die
Head of the Family
Highway to Hell
Hillbillies in a Haunted House
The Horror of Frankenstein
House 2: The Second Story
House of the Long Shadows
Human Beasts
Hysterical
I Married a Vampire
I Was a Teenage Zombie
Incredibly Strange Creatures Who Stopped Living and Became Mixed-Up Zombies
The Invisible Maniac
It Came from Hollywood
Killer Klowns from Outer Space
Killer Tomatoes Eat France
Killer Tomatoes Strike Back
The Kingdom
Little Shop of Horrors►
Mama Dracula
A Man with a Maid
The Mask►
Matinee
Microwave Massacre
Mindkiller

Mom
Monster in the Closet
Motel Hell
Munchies
My Boyfriend's Back
My Demon Lover
My Grandpa is a Vampire
My Mom's a Werewolf
My Son, the Vampire
Near Dark►
Night of a Thousand Cats
Night of the Creeps
Night of the Laughing Dead
Nightlife
Nocturna
Nothing But Trouble
The Old Dark House►
Old Mother Riley's Ghosts
Once Bitten
Out of the Dark
Phantom Brother
Phantom Empire
Piranha
Piranha 2: The Spawning
Psycho Girls
Psychos in Love
Q (The Winged Serpent)►
Rabid Grannies
Re-Animator►
Redneck Zombies
The Refrigerator
Return of the Killer Tomatoes!
Return of the Living Dead
Return of the Living Dead 2
Return of the Living Dead 3
Revenge of the Red Baron
Saturday the 14th
Saturday the 14th Strikes Back
Schlock
Shrunken Heads
Son of Ingagi
Sorority Babes in the Slimeball Bowl-A-Rama
Speak of the Devil
Spider Baby
Spooks Run Wild
Strangers of the Evening
Street Trash
Student Bodies
The Stuff
Tales from the Crypt Presents Bordello of Blood
Tales from the Crypt Presents Demon Knight
Teenage Exorcist
Terrorvision
Theatre of Blood►
There's Nothing Out There
The Thrill Killers
The Toxic Avenger
The Toxic Avenger, Part 2
The Toxic Avenger, Part 3: The Last Temptation of Toxie
Treasure of Fear
Tremors
Tremors 2: Aftershocks
The Undertaker and His Pals
Vamp
The Vampire Happening
Vampire in Brooklyn
Zombies on Broadway

Horse Racing

see Gambling; Horses

Horses

The Adventures of Gallant Bess
The Appaloosa
Archer's Adventure
The Bashful Bachelor
Bells of San Angelo
Bite the Bullet
Black Beauty
Black Beauty►
Black Beauty/Courage of Black Beauty

The Black Stallion►
The Black Stallion Returns
Blue Fire Lady
Boots Malone
Broadway Bill►
Call of the Forest
Casey's Shadow
Champions
Chino
City Slickers 2: The Legend of Curly's Gold
Cold Feet
Come On Tarzan
Courage of Black Beauty
Courage of the North
Danielle Steel's Palomino
Danny
Dark Horse
A Day at the Races►
Day the Bookies Wept
Devil Horse
Devil on Horseback
The Devil's Cargo
Duke of the Derby
Eagle's Wing
Eden Valley►
The Electric Horseman
Equus
Ex-Mrs. Bradford►
Far North
The Fighting Stallion►
A Fine Mess
Flame of Araby
The Flying Deuces►
Forbidden Trails
Francis Goes to the Races
A Girl in Every Port
Glory
The Golden Stallion
Great Dan Patch
The Great Mike
Gypsy Colt
Heart of the Rockies
Hell's Hinges
Hit the Saddle
A Horse for Danny
The Horse in the Gray Flannel Suit
Horsemasters
The Horsemen
Hot to Trot!
In Pursuit of Honor
Indian Paint
International Velvet
Into the West►
Italian Straw Hat►
It's a Great Life
Justin Morgan Had a Horse
Kentucky Blue Streak
King of the Sierras
King of the Stallions
King of the Wild Horses►
King of the Wind
Law of the Wild
Le Gentleman D'Epsom
The Lemon Drop Kid
The Lighthorsemen►
Lightning: The White Stallion
The Littlest Horse Thieves
The Littlest Outlaw
The Longshot
Lotna
Lucky Luke
Ma and Pa Kettle at the Fair
The Man from Snowy River
Marshal of Cedar Rock
Meet Wally Sparks
The Miracle of the White Stallions
The Misfits►
Misty
My Friend Flicka►
My Old Man
My Pal Trigger
National Lampoon's Animal House►
National Velvet►
Off and Running
On the Right Track

Phar Lap
Prince and the Great Race
The Quiet Man►
Racing Luck
A Rare Breed
The Red Fury
The Red Pony►
The Red Stallion
Return of Wildfire
Return to Snowy River►
Ride a Wild Pony►
Ride Him, Cowboy►
Riding High
Rolling Home
The Rounders
Run for the Roses
Running Wild
Saddle Buster
Saratoga
Silver Stallion
The Silver Stallion: King of the Wild Brumbies
Something to Talk About
Speedy►
The Story of Seabiscuit
Sundown Saunders
Sylvester
Tennessee Stallion
Texas to Bataan
Thoroughbreds Don't Cry
Three Men on a Horse►
Turf Boy
Two Bits & Pepper
The Undefeated
Western Double Feature 16
When the West Was Young
White Mane►
Wild Hearts Can't Be Broken►
Wild Horse Hank
Wild Horses
Wild Pony
Win, Place, or Steal
Winds of the Wasteland
Wings of the Morning

Hospitals & Medicine

see also Disease of the Week; Doctors & Nurses; Emerging Viruses; Sanity Check; Shrinks

Article 99
B.O.R.N.
Britannia Hospital
Carry On Nurse
A Child is Waiting
China Beach►
City of Joy
The Clonus Horror
Coma►
Come to the Stable►
Critical Condition
Dead Ringers►
Desperate Measures►
Disorderlies
Disorderly Orderly
Doctor at Large
Dr. Kildare's Strange Case
Doctors' Wives
East of Kilimanjaro
The Egyptian
ER
Extreme Measures
Frankenstein General Hospital
The Fugitive►
Green for Danger
Gross Anatomy
Halloween 2: The Nightmare Isn't Over!
Hard-Boiled
The Hasty Heart
Horror Hospital
The Hospital►
Hospital Massacre
Hospital of Terror
In for Treatment►
In Love and War
The Interns

The Walls of Malapaga
What Did You Do in the War, Daddy?
Where Angels Fear to Tread▸
Women in Prison
Year of the Gun

It's a Conspiracy, Man!

see also Capitol Capers; Mystery & Suspense

Absolute Power
All the President's Men▸
The Arrival
Chain Reaction
City Hall▸
Company Business
Conspiracy Theory▸
Copland▸
Eraser
Executive Action
Flashpoint
The Fourth Protocol▸
JFK▸
Looking for Richard▸
The Manchurian Candidate▸
Mulholland Falls
Murder at 1600
Nixon▸
No Way Out▸
November Conspiracy
The Package
The Parallax View▸
Seven Days in May▸
The Shadow Conspiracy
Sneakers
The Star Chamber
They Live
Three Days of the Condor▸
Winter Kills▸

Jail

see Great Escapes; Men in Prison; Women in Prison

Japan

see also Asia; Tokyo

Akira
The Ballad of Narayama▸
Barbarian and the Geisha
Battle of China
The Battle of the Japan Sea
Behind the Rising Sun
Black Rain▸
Black Rain
Blood on the Sun
Captive Hearts
Cold Fever
The Cruel Story of Youth▸
Destination Tokyo
Dodes 'ka-den▸
The Eel▸
Eijanaika▸
Enjo
Escapade in Japan
Flirt
47 Ronin, Part 1▸
47 Ronin, Part 2▸
The Geisha Boy
Geisha Girl
Girls of the White Orchid
Gung Ho
Heaven & Earth▸
Hiroshima▸
Hiroshima Maiden
Hiroshima, Mon Amour▸
The Hunted
The Idiot▸
The Imperial Japanese Empire
Imperial Navy
Journey of Honor
King's Ransom
Life of Oharu▸
Love and Faith▸

MacArthur's Children▸
Madame Butterfly
A Majority of One
The Makioka Sisters▸
The Men Who Tread on the Tiger's Tail
Midway
Minbo—Or the Gentle Art of Japanese Extortion
Mishima: A Life in Four Chapters▸
Mr. Baseball
Mother▸
No Regrets for Our Youth▸
Nomugi Pass
Objective, Burma!▸
Okoge
Osaka Elegy
The Pillow Book
Prisoners of the Sun▸
Professional Killers 1
Ran▸
Rashomon▸
Red Beard▸
Revenge of a Kabuki Actor
Rikyu▸
Rising Sun▸
Saga of the Vagabond
Samurai Cowboy
Samurai Reincarnation
Sansho the Bailiff▸
Sayonara▸
Seven Samurai▸
She and He
Shin Heike Monogatari▸
Shogun▸
Shogun's Ninja
Showdown in Little Tokyo
Snow Country
The Sun's Burial▸
Sword of Fury II
Thirty Seconds Over Tokyo▸
3 Ninjas Kick Back
Tokyo Decadence
Tokyo-Ga▸
Tokyo Pop
Tora! Tora! Tora!
Traffic Jam
Twenty-Four Eyes▸
Ugetsu▸
Utamaro and His Five Women
Walk, Don't Run
What's Up, Tiger Lily?▸
The Wolves▸
The Yakuza
You Only Live Twice
Zatoichi vs. Yojimbo▸

Japanimation

see also Animation & Cartoons

Akira
Alakazam the Great!
Arcadia of My Youth
The Dagger of Kamui
Demon City Shinjuku
Ghost in the Shell
GUY: Awakening of the Devil
Lensman
My Neighbor Totoro
Otaku no Video
Planet Busters
The Professional: Golgo 13
Project A-ko
Starvengers
Toward the Terra
Twilight of the Cockroaches
Urotsukidoj 1: Legend of the Overfiend
Urotsukidoj 2: Legend of the Demon Womb
Urusei Yatsura Movie 1: Only You
Urusei Yatsura Movie 2: Beautiful Dreamer
Urusei Yatsura Movie 3: Remember My Love

Urusei Yatsura Movie 4: Lum the Forever
Urusei Yatsura Movie 5: The Final Chapter
Urusei Yatsura Movie 6: Always My Darling
A Wind Named Amnesia

Journalism

see Front Page

Judaism

see also The Holocaust; Israel

American Matchmaker
Angry Harvest▸
The Apprenticeship of Duddy Kravitz▸
The Assisi Underground
Atalia
The Attic: The Hiding of Anne Frank
Au Revoir Les Enfants▸
The Blum Affair
A Brivele der Mamen▸
Broken Glass
Brussels Transit▸
The Cantor's Son
Charlie Grant's War
The Chosen▸
Commissar▸
Conspiracy of Hearts
The Corridor: Death
Crossfire
Crossing Delancey▸
David▸
David
A Day in October
The Diary of Anne Frank▸
Drifting
The Dunera Boys▸
The Dybbuk▸
East and West▸
Eli Eli
Enemies, a Love Story▸
Every Time We Say Goodbye
Exodus▸
Fiddler on the Roof▸
The Fixer▸
Freud Leaving Home
A Friendship in Vienna
The Frisco Kid
Funny Girl▸
The Garden of the Finzi-Continis▸
Gentleman's Agreement▸
God, Man and Devil
The Golem▸
Good Evening, Mr. Wallenberg
Goodbye, New York
Green Fields
Hamsin▸
Hanna's War
Hester Street▸
Hill 24 Doesn't Answer▸
Holocaust▸
Homicide▸
The House on Chelouche Street
I Love You, Alice B. Toklas!
I Love You Rosa
In the Presence of Mine Enemies
The Infiltrator
Ivan and Abraham
The Jazz Singer
Jud Suess▸
King David
Kuni Lemel in Tel Aviv
The Last Metro▸
The Last Winter
Leon the Pig Farmer
Les Violons du Bal
Lies My Father Told Me▸
The Light Ahead
Madman

The Man Who Captured Eichmann
Martha and I▸
Masada▸
Me and the Colonel
Miracle at Moreaux
Miss Rose White▸
Mr. Emmanuel
Moses
My Michael▸
No Way to Treat a Lady▸
Noa at Seventeen▸
The Only Way
Outside Chance of Maximillian Glick
Over the Brooklyn Bridge
The Pawnbroker▸
Power
The Proprietor
The Quarrel
Radio Days▸
The Revolt of Job▸
Sallah▸
Schindler's List▸
School Ties▸
A Secret Space
The Serpent's Egg
The Shop on Main Street▸
Sofie
The Sorrow and the Pity▸
A Stranger Among Us
The Substance of Fire
The Summer of Aviya
The Summer of My German Soldier▸
Table Settings
Tevye
They Were Ten
'38: Vienna Before the Fall
Transport from Paradise
The Twilight of the Golds
The Two of Us▸
Uncle Moses
Under the Domim Tree
Under the Earth▸
Unsettled Land
Unstrung Heroes
Used People
Voyage of the Damned▸
Wandering Jew
War & Love
Where Is My Child?
Where's Poppa?▸
The Wooden Gun
Yentl
Zalmen or the Madness of God

Jungle Stories

see also Monkeyshines; Treasure Hunt

Ace Ventura: When Nature Calls
Africa Screams
Aguirre, the Wrath of God▸
All the Way, Boys
Amazon
Amazon Jail
Anaconda
At Play in the Fields of the Lord▸
Baby ... Secret of the Lost Legend
Back from Eternity
Bat 21
Bela Lugosi Meets a Brooklyn Gorilla
Beyond Rangoon
Beyond the Carribean
Black Cobra 3: The Manila Connection
The Black Devils of Kali
Blonde Savage
Brenda Starr
Bride of the Gorilla
Cannibal Women in the Avocado Jungle of Death
Cobra Woman
Codename: Terminate
The Colombian Connection
Commando Invasion

Congo
Death in the Garden
Delta Force Commando
Diplomatic Immunity
Dr. Cyclops
East of Borneo
Elephant Boy▸
Elephant Walk
The Emerald Forest▸
Emerald Jungle
Emmanuelle 6
Enemy Unseen
Escape from Hell
Escape to Burma
Escape 2000
Farewell to the King
Fatal Mission
Field of Fire
Field of Honor
Final Mission
Firehawk
Firewalker
Fitzcarraldo▸
Five Came Back
Flight from Singapore
Found Alive
The Further Adventures of Tennessee Buck
Fury
George of the Jungle
Gold of the Amazon Women
Gold Raiders
Goliathon
Gorillas in the Mist▸
Green Fire
Green Inferno
Green Mansions
Greystoke: The Legend of Tarzan, Lord of the Apes
Harry Black and the Tiger
Heart of Darkness
Hell's Headquarters
How Tasty Was My Little Frenchman
Indio
Indio 2: The Revolt
Invincible Barbarian
Jacare
Jane & the Lost City
Jumanji
Jungle
The Jungle Book
The Jungle Book▸
Jungle Bride
Jungle Drums of Africa
Jungle Goddess
Jungle Heat
Jungle Hell
Jungle Inferno
Jungle Master
Jungle Patrol
Jungle Raiders
Jungle Siren
The Jungle Trap
Jungle Warriors
Killers
Killing Heat
King of the Kongo
King Solomon's Treasure
The Land Unknown
Law of the Jungle
Liana, Jungle Goddess
The Lion King▸
The Lion Man
Lion Man
The Lost City
Lost City of the Jungle
The Lost Continent
The Lost Jungle
The Lost Tribe
Lure of the Islands
Medicine Man
Merrill's Marauders
Mighty Jungle
Miracles
Missing in Action
The Mission▸
Mistress of the Apes
Mogambo▸

Justice Prevails...?

Kidnapped!

Killer Apes

Killer Appliances

Killer Beasts

The Great American Sex
  Scandal
Guilty as Sin
Honor Thy Father and Mother:
  The True Story of the
  Menendez Brothers
I Am the Law➤
Illegal
I'm No Angel➤
In the Name of the Father➤
The Incident➤
The Island of Dr. Moreau
JAG
The Jagged Edge
Judge Dredd
Judge Priest➤
Judicial Consent
The Juror
Jury Duty
Just Cause
Justice
Kavanagh Q.C.
King and Country➤
L.A. Law➤
Last Dance
The Last Innocent Man
Legal Eagles
Legend of Billie Jean
Let Freedom Ring
Let's Kill All the Lawyers
Liar Liar
Life & Times of Judge Roy Bean
Losing Isaiah➤
Love Crimes
Madame X
The Magnificent Yankee➤
Man from Colorado
Man of the House
Manhattan Melodrama➤
Marked Woman➤
Minbo—Or the Gentle Art of
  Japanese Extortion
Misbehaving Husbands
Mr. & Mrs. Loving➤
Murder In the First
My Cousin Vinny➤
The Narrow Margin➤
Night and the City➤
Night Falls on Manhattan➤
Nixon➤
North
Ordeal by Innocence
Original Intent
The Paper Chase➤
The Pelican Brief
Penthouse➤
The People vs. Larry Flynt➤
Perfect Witness
Perry Mason Returns➤
Philadelphia➤
Physical Evidence
Pinocchio's Revenge
Portraits of a Killer
Power of Attorney
Presumed Innocent➤
Primal Fear
Promised a Miracle
Reet, Petite and Gone➤
Regarding Henry➤
Road Agent
Roxie Hart
Rumpole of the Bailey
Rumpole of the Bailey:
  Rumpole's Return➤
Runaway Father
Rustler's Valley
Scandal
Scott Turow's The Burden of
  Proof
Sharon's Secret
Shoot to Kill
A Simple Twist of Fate
Sleepers
Slightly Honorable
The Star Chamber
State's Attorney
Stephen King's Thinner➤
The Summer of Ben Tyler

The Sun Shines Bright
The Sweet Hereafter➤
Swoon➤
A Time to Kill➤
To Kill a Mockingbird➤
Too Young to Die
The Trial
Trial & Error
Trial and Error
Trial by Jury
Trois Couleurs: Rouge➤
True Believer
True Colors
Truth or Die
Twelve Angry Men➤
The Verdict➤
Victim➤
Web of Deceit
The Winslow Boy➤
The Wistful Widow of Wagon
  Gap
Woman of Desire
The World's Oldest Living
  Bridesmaid
The Young Philadelphians➤

Leprechauns

Darby O'Gill & the Little People➤
Finian's Rainbow➤
Leprechaun
Leprechaun 2
Leprechaun 3
Spellbreaker: Secret of the
  Leprechauns

Lesbians

see also Bisexuality; Gays;
    Gender Bending
Alien Prey
Another Way➤
Bar Girls
The Berlin Affair
The Bitter Tears of Petra von
  Kant
Black Cobra
The Blood Spattered Bride
Bound
Boys on the Side
Butterfly Kiss
Carmilla
The Celluloid Closet➤
Chasing Amy
The Children's Hour
Claire of the Moon
Crocodiles in Amsterdam
Daughters of Darkness➤
Desert Hearts➤
Desperate Remedies
Different Story
Double Face
Entre-Nous➤
Even Cowgirls Get the Blues
Extramuros
Fanci's Persuasion
Foxfire
French Twist
Higher Learning
The Hunger
The Incredibly True Adventure of
  Two Girls in Love
I've Heard the Mermaids
  Singing➤
Kamikaze Hearts
The Killing of Sister George
Law of Desire➤
Les Voleurs➤
Lianna➤
Listen
Love and Other Catastrophes
Maedchen in Uniform➤
My Father Is Coming
My Sister, My Love
Nadja➤
Nowhere
Only the Brave
Oranges Are Not the Only Fruit

Personal Best➤
A Question of Love➤
The Rainbow➤
The Scorpion Woman
Seducers
Set It Off
She Must Be Seeing Things
The Silence➤
Sugar Cookies
Therese & Isabelle
These Three➤
Three of Hearts
Totally F***ed Up
The Vampire Lovers
Vampyres
A Village Affair
Virgin Machine
Walk on the Wild Side
When Night is Falling➤
Wild Side
Windows
X, Y & Zee

Libraries and Librarians

Adventure
The Breakfast Club➤
Desk Set➤
Foul Play➤
Ghostbusters➤
Good News
Goodbye Columbus➤
The Gun in Betty Lou's Handbag
Hard-Boiled
Kicking and Screaming➤
Mr. Sycamore
The Music Man➤
The Name of the Rose
No Man of Her Own
Off Beat
Only Two Can Play➤
The Pagemaster
Party Girl
7 Faces of Dr. Lao➤
The Shawshank Redemption➤
Something Wicked This Way
  Comes
With Honors

Life Imitates Art

The Deer Hunter➤
Menace II Society➤
Money Train
The Program
Taxi Driver➤

Lifeguards

see also Beach Blanket
    Bingo; Swimming
Baywatch the Movie: Forbidden
  Paradise
Caddyshack➤
Fun in Acapulco
Lifeguard
That Summer of White Roses
Wet and Wild Summer

London

see also Great Britain;
    Royalty
Abbott and Costello Meet Dr.
  Jekyll and Mr. Hyde
Alfie➤
American Roulette
An American Werewolf in
  London➤
Annie: A Royal Adventure
The Assassination Bureau➤
Autobiography of a Princess
Bad Behavior
Beautiful Thing➤
Bedlam➤
Broken Blossoms➤

The Buddha of Suburbia➤
Carpet of Horror
Century
Chicago Joe & the Showgirl
Claudia
Curse of the Yellow Snake
Danger UXB
Dick Barton, Special Agent
Different for Girls➤
Double Vision
Dracula's Daughter➤
Dream Street
The Duchess of Duke Street➤
The Elephant Man➤
11 Harrowhouse➤
Fanny Hill: Memoirs of a Woman
  of Pleasure
Fierce Creatures
Foreign Affairs➤
Foreign Correspondent➤
Forever and a Day➤
Frenzy➤
The Frightened City
Full Moon in Paris
The Gambler & the Lady
Gaslight➤
The Gay Lady
Great Expectations
The Great Muppet Caper➤
Hands of a Murderer
Heaven's a Drag
Hope and Glory➤
The Horse's Mouth➤
The House of Eliott
In the Name of the Father➤
Journey for Margaret➤
Just Like a Woman
The Knack➤
The Krays➤
Lady L
Lamb
The Little Princess➤
The Long Good Friday➤
The Lost Language of Cranes➤
Mary Poppins➤
Mary Reilly
Midnight Lace
The Missionary
Mrs. 'Arris Goes to Paris
Moll Flanders
Murder on Line One
My Beautiful Laundrette➤
My Friend Walter
The Mysterious Magician
Naked➤
National Lampoon's European
  Vacation
Night and the City➤
Nil by Mouth
The Old Curiosity Shop
101 Dalmatians
One Wish Too Many
Phantom Fiend
Priest
Prime Suspect 2➤
Quatermass and the Pit
Rough Cut
Royal Wedding➤
Sabotage➤
Sammy & Rosie Get Laid➤
Say Hello to Yesterday
The Secret Adversary
The Secret Agent
Secrets and Lies
Sherlock Holmes: The Master
  Blackmailer
Shine➤
Solitaire for 2
Split Second
Strange Bedfellows
Strapless
Tale of a Vampire
The Tall Guy➤
The Three Penny Opera➤
Time After Time➤
To Sir, with Love
Turtle Diary➤
Water Babies
Waterloo Bridge➤

Werewolf of London
Wild West
A Woman's Guide to Adultery
The Young Americans
The Young Poisoner's
  Handbook➤
Young Sherlock Holmes

Loneliness

see Only the Lonely

Loner Cops

see also Cops
Above the Law
Action Jackson
Bad Attitude
Bad Lieutenant➤
The Blue Knight
Code of Silence
The Cop & the Girl
Cop in Blue Jeans
Dead Bang
The Dead Pool
Deadly Dancer
Die Hard➤
Die Hard 2: Die Harder➤
Die Hard: With a Vengeance
Dirty Harry➤
The Enforcer
Excessive Force
Force of One
Heat
Heat➤
In the Heat of the Night➤
Judge Dredd
Klute➤
Magnum Force
McQ
Nightstick
Northwest Trail
One Good Cop
One Man Jury
Rent-A-Cop
RoboCop➤
Serpico➤
Sharky's Machine
SnakeEater
SnakeEater 2: The Drug Buster
SnakeEater 3: His Law
Speed➤
Stick
Stone Cold
Sudden Impact
Ten to Midnight
Year of the Dragon

Lost Worlds

see also Parallel Universes
At the Earth's Core
Beyond Atlantis
Brigadoon➤
Creatures the World Forgot
Gold of the Amazon Women
Jane & the Lost City
Journey to the Center of the
  Earth➤
Jumanji
The Land that Time Forgot
The Land Unknown
The Lost Continent
Lost Horizon➤
The Lost World
Mysterious Island➤
Mysterious Island of Beautiful
  Women
The People That Time Forgot
Warriors of Virtue
What Waits Below
When Dinosaurs Ruled the
  Earth
Where Time Began

Lottery Winners

Babette's Feast➤

Marriage

Martyred Pop Icons

see also *Rock Stars on Film*

Mass Media

see also *Front Page; Radio*

May-December Romance

see also *Coming of Age; Growing Older; Romantic Adventures; Romantic Comedy; Romantic Drama*

The Meaning of Life

Medieval Romps

see also *Camelot (Old); Historical Drama; Period Piece; Swashbucklers*

Fire and Sword
First Knight
The Flame & the Arrow►
Flesh and Blood
Galgameth
Hawk and Castle
Hawk the Slayer
Inquisition
Ivanhoe►
Ivanhoe
Ivanhoe►
Jabberwocky
Jack the Giant Killer►
The Juniper Tree
King Arthur, the Young Warlord
Knights of the Round Table
Kojiro►
Ladyhawke
The Lady's Not for Burning
Lancelot of the Lake
Legend
Leonor
The Lion in Winter►
Lionheart
Magdalene
Magic Serpent►
The Magic Sword
Mark of the Devil
Mark of the Devil 2
The Mongols
Monty Python and the Holy Grail►
The Name of the Rose
Naughty Knights
The Navigator►
Onibaba►
Pippin►
The Prince of Thieves
Ran►
Rashomon►
The Return of Martin Guerre►
Rikyu►
Robin and Marian
Robin Hood►
Robin Hood: Men in Tights
Robin Hood: Prince of Thieves
Robin Hood...The Legend: Herne's Son
Robin Hood...The Legend: Robin Hood and the Sorcerer
Robin Hood...The Legend: The Swords of Wayland
Robin Hood...The Legend: The Time of the Wolf
The Scalawag Bunch
The Secret of El Zorro
Seven Samurai►
The Seventh Seal►
Skullduggery
Star Knight
Stealing Heaven
Sword & the Dragon
Sword & the Sorcerer
The Sword in the Stone►
Sword of Lancelot
Sword of Sherwood Forest
Sword of the Valiant
Tales of Robin Hood
Tharus Son of Attila
Time Bandits
Time Trackers
Tor
The Undead
Unidentified Flying Oddball
The Vikings
The Warrior & the Sorceress
When Knights were Bold
Wholly Moses!
Wizards of the Demon Sword
Wizards of the Lost Kingdom
Young Ivanhoe
Young Warlord
The Zany Adventures of Robin Hood

Meltdown

see also Disaster Flicks

Above and Beyond►

Access Code
Amazing Grace & Chuck
Atomic Attack
The Atomic Cafe►
The Atomic Kid
Black Rain►
Bloodfist 6: Ground Zero
Bombs Away!
Broken Arrow
Chain Reaction
The China Syndrome►
Cloak and Dagger
Control
Crimson Tide►
Cyclotrode "X"
The Day After►
The Day the Earth Caught Fire►
The Death Merchant
Desert Bloom►
Dick Barton Strikes Back
Disaster at Silo 7
Dr. Strangelove, or: How I Learned to Stop Worrying and Love the Bomb►
Enola Gay: The Men, the Mission, the Atomic Bomb
Fail-Safe►
Fat Man and Little Boy
Final Sanction
First Spaceship on Venus►
First Strike
First Yank into Tokyo
Flight of Black Angel
The Fourth Protocol►
Full Fathom Five
Future Kill
Geisha Girl
Glen and Randa
Ground Zero►
H-Man
Hiroshima
Hiroshima Maiden
Hiroshima: Out of the Ashes►
I Live in Fear►
In the King of Prussia
Invasion U.S.A.
Jackie Chan's First Strike►
A Man Called Rage
The Manhattan Project
Massive Retaliation
Miracle Mile►
Modern Problems
Night Siege Project: Shadowchaser 2
Nuclear Conspiracy
A Nymphoid Barbarian in Dinosaur Hell
Omega Man
On the Beach►
One Night Stand►
Panic in the Year Zero!
The Patriot
Plutonium Incident
Prisoner in the Middle
Radioactive Dreams
Rats
Reactor
The Reflecting Skin
Rhapsody in August
Rocket Attack U.S.A.
The Sacrifice►
Seven Days in May►
The Shoes of the Fisherman
Silkwood►
Slugs
Special Bulletin►
Split Second
The Spy Who Loved Me
State of Things►
Superman 4: The Quest for Peace
TC 2000
Testament►
This Is Not a Test
Threads►
True Lies
The 27 Day
Unknown World
Utopia

Voyage to the Bottom of the Sea►
WarGames
Warhead
When the Wind Blows►
Young Lady Chatterly 2

Men

see also Dads; Macho Men; Repressed Men; War Between the Sexes

Bachelor Apartment
Carnal Knowledge►
City Hall►
City Slickers►
The Full Monty►
Good Luck
In the Company of Men
The Incredible Shrinking Man►
La Grande Bouffe►
The Men's Club
Mr. Mom►
90 Days►
Patti Rocks►
Planet of the Apes►
Raging Bull►
Rate It X
The Saint of Fort Washington
Swingers►
Three Men and a Baby►
Three Men and a Cradle►
Thursday's Game►
Truth or Die
Up to a Certain Point
Watch It►
The Young Poisoner's Handbook►

Men in Prison

see also Fugitives; Great Escapes; POW/MIA; Women in Prison

Against the Wall►
Alias, La Gringa
American Me►
Andersonville►
Angels with Dirty Faces►
Appointment with Crime
Attica►
Baba►
Bad Boys►
Band of the Hand
Behind Prison Walls
Beyond the Call
Beyond the Walls
Birdman of Alcatraz►
Black Lemons
Blind Faith
Bloodsport 2: The Next Kumite
Botany Bay
Boy's Reformatory
Breaker Morant►
Breakout
The Brig►
Broken Melody
Brubaker►
Buried Alive
Buy & Cell
The Cable Guy
Caged Heat 2: Stripped of Freedom
Caged in Paradiso
Call Northside 777►
Captives
Chain Gang Killings
The Chair
The Chamber
City Without Men
Club Fed
Colonel Chabert
Coming Out of the Ice►
Con Air►
Convict Cowboy
Cool Hand Luke►
The Count of Monte Cristo
The Count of Monte Cristo►

The Count of Monte Cristo
Crashout
Criminal Code
Cry Danger►
Das Testament des Dr. Mabuse►
Dead Man Out►
Dead Right
Deadlock
Deadlock 2
Death House
Death Warrant
Deathrow Gameshow
The Defiant Ones►
Devil's Canyon
The Devil's Cargo
The Dirty Dozen►
The Dirty Dozen: The Deadly Mission
The Dirty Dozen: The Fatal Mission
The Dirty Dozen: The Next Mission
Doin' Time
The Domino Principle
Double Team
Down by Law►
Each Dawn I Die
Eagles Attack at Dawn
Embassy
Empire of the Sun►
Ernest Goes to Jail
Escape from Alcatraz►
Escape from Death Row
Escape from DS-3
Escape from El Diablo
Escape from New York
Execution of Raymond Graham
The Executioner's Song
Face/Off►
Fast Walking
The Fence
Fled
Fortress
Framed
Gang Busters
Gideon's Trumpet
The Glass House►
The Grave
Gulag
Hangfire
Hard Frame
Hard Justice
Hold 'Em Jail
House Across the Bay
I Am a Fugitive from a Chain Gang►
In Hot Pursuit
In the Name of the Father►
An Innocent Man
Inside►
Invasion
The Invisible Strangler
Jailbreakin'
Jailhouse Rock►
The Jericho Mile
Johnny Handsome►
Kansas City Confidential►
Killer: A Journal of Murder
King of the Damned
Kiss of the Spider Woman►
L'Addition
The Last Detail►
The Last Mile
Les Miserables
The Life of Emile Zola►
Lilies
The Line
Little Red Schoolhouse
Live! From Death Row
Lock Up
The Longest Yard►
Lost Highway
A Man Escaped►
Man of La Mancha
The Man Who Broke 1,000 Chains
Maximum Security
McKenzie Break►

McVicar
Mean Frank and Crazy Tony
Midnight Express►
Mrs. Soffel
Mr. Frost
Moon 44
Murder In the First
Mutiny in the Big House
My Boys Are Good Boys
New Crime City: Los Angeles 2020
New Eden
The Night Visitor
984: Prisoner of the Future
No Escape
Off the Wall
On the Yard
Papillon►
Pardon Us
Payback
Penitentiary
Penitentiary 2
Penitentiary 3
Phantom Empire
Pressure Point►
Prison
Prison Break
Prison Planet
Prison Train
The Pursuit of Happiness
Real Bullets
Riot
Riot in Cell Block 11►
The Rock►
Runaway Train►
Samar
Scum►
A Sense of Freedom►
The Shawshank Redemption►
Shoeshine►
Short Eyes►
Slaughterhouse Rock
Some Mother's Son►
Soul Vengeance
Space Rage
Stir Crazy
Taking Care of Business
Tank
Terminal Island
Terror of the Bloodhunters
Terror on Alcatraz
There was a Crooked Man►
They Never Come Back
They Went That-a-Way & That-a-Way
Tomb of the Undead
Torture Ship
Triumph of the Spirit►
Truth or Die
Two-Way Stretch
Ulee's Gold►
Weeds►
William Faulkner's Old Man
Without Evidence
Women's Prison Massacre
Yol►

Mental Retardation

see also Physical Problems; Savants

Bill►
Bill: On His Own►
Charly►
A Child is Waiting►
A Dangerous Woman
Dark Night of the Scarecrow
A Day in the Death of Joe Egg►
Dominick & Eugene►
The Eighth Day
Family Pictures►
Heart of Dragon
Homer and Eddie
Larry
L'Enfant d'Eau
Lovey: A Circle of Children 2
Malcolm
Of Mice and Men►
Rain Man►

The Bridges at Toko-Ri
Chasers
Crimson Tide
Down Periscope
Enemy Below
A Few Good Men
Fighting Seabees
The Fighting Sullivans
Francis in the Navy
Hellcats of the Navy
Here Come the Waves
The Hunt for Red October
In Love and War
The Last Detail
McHale's Navy
Mission of the Shark
Mister Roberts
Navy Blue and Gold
The Navy Comes Through
Navy SEALS
Navy vs. the Night Monsters
Navy Way
No Way Out
An Officer and a Gentleman
On the Town
Operation Petticoat
PT 109
Run Silent, Run Deep
Skirts Ahoy!
They Were Expendable
Top Gun
Under Siege

Miners & Mining

Act of Vengeance
The Adventures of Bullwhip Griffin
Angels Die Hard
Backlash: Oblivion 2
Ballad of Cable Hogue
The Big Man: Crossing the Line
Black Fury
Brassed Off
Burning Rage
Cannibal! The Musical
Challenge to White Fang
The Christmas Coal Mine Miracle
Eureka Stockade
Fighting Cowboy
Fighting Valley
Flaming Frontiers
Gangster's Den
Gangsters of the Frontier
Germinal
Ghost Town Renegades
Girl Rush
Grand Canyon Trail
Green Fire
The Hallelujah Trail
Haunted Gold
Hills of Utah
How Green Was My Valley
Human Hearts
Kameradschaft
King Solomon's Mines
Little Church Around the Corner
The Man from Music Mountain
Margaret's Museum
Matewan
McCabe & Mrs. Miller
Molly Maguires
My Darlin' Clementine
'Neath Canadian Skies
No Man's Law
North Star
North to Alaska
Paint Your Wagon
Pale Rider
Phantom Gold
Poldark
Poldark 2
Precious Find
The Rainbow Gang
Red Earth
Rider from Tucson
The Ruthless Four

Salt of the Earth
Sands of Sacrifice
Silver Bandit
Smilla's Sense of Snow
The Spoilers
The Stars Look Down
The Strangeness
The War Wagon
Way Out West
Where the Green Ants Dream
Where Trails End
Wildrose
Within the Rock
Xica

Minnesota

see also America's Heartland

Beautiful Girls
D2: The Mighty Ducks
The Emigrants
Far North
Fargo
Feeling Minnesota
The Good Son
The Great Northfield Minnesota Raid
Grumpier Old Men
Grumpy Old Men
The Heartbreak Kid
Ice Castles
Iron Will
Little Big League
The Long Riders
The Mighty Ducks
The New Land
Patti Rocks
The Personals
Purple Rain
Slaughterhouse Five
That Was Then...This Is Now
Untamed Heart
Wildrose

Missing Persons

see also Hostage!; Kidnapped!

Adam
Agatha
Almost Human
American Nightmare
Anastasia
Anastasia: The Mystery of Anna
AngKor: Cambodia Express
Big Jake
Breakdown
Bureau of Missing Persons
Cavalcade of the West
Christina
Coming Out Alive
Curse of the Pink Panther
Disappearance
Dying Room Only
The Emerald Forest
Empire State
The Empty Beach
Equinox
Escapade in Japan
Experiment in Terror
Eye Witness
Final Cut
Foxtrap
Frantic
From Hollywood to Deadwood
Girl Hunters
Grayeagle
Green Eyes
Grievous Bodily Harm
Harem
Harper
Heading for Heaven
Hell Squad
Hide in Plain Sight
High Road to China
The Hit List
Hollywood Chaos

Home Is Where the Hart Is
Hurricane Smith
In the Mouth of Madness
Into Thin Air
The Island at the Top of the World
Jungle Goddess
Kentucky Jubilee
Kidnap Syndicate
The Lady Vanishes
The Lady Vanishes
The Last Winter
Little Miss Millions
A Low Down Dirty Shame
Midnight Warning
Misery
Missing
The Missing Corpse
Murder, My Sweet
Nickel & Dime
Night of the Cyclone
Norseman
Old Gringo
Picnic at Hanging Rock
The Port of Missing Girls
Prisoner of Zenda
The Professionals
Psych-Out
Psycho from Texas
Pure Luck
Raising Arizona
Romancing the Stone
Scandalous
Seance on a Wet Afternoon
The Search for One-Eyed Jimmy
The Searchers
Skull: A Night of Terror
Stark
Street Girls
Street Justice
Surfacing
Tarzan the Fearless
Terminal Force
Tokyo Joe
Tony Rome
The Vanishing
Wanted: Babysitter
Where Are the Children?
Where's Piccone?
White Fire
The Wicker Man
Without a Trace

Missionaries

see also Nuns & Priests; Religion; Religious Epics

The African Queen
At Play in the Fields of the Lord
Beyond the Next Mountain
Black Robe
Ethan
Hawaii
The Inn of the Sixth Happiness
The Keys of the Kingdom
The Mission
Mission to Glory
The Missionary

Misspelled Titles

Boyz N the Hood
The 'Burbs
Charly
Cheech and Chong: Still Smokin'
C.H.O.M.P.S.
Class of Nuke 'Em High
Class of Nuke 'Em High 2: Subhumanoid Meltdown
The Concentratin' Kid
Doin' Time
Doin' Time on Planet Earth
Feelin' Up
Fightin' Ranch
Fyre
Git Along Little Dogies
Gridlock'd

Hittin' the Trail
I Dood It
I Live with Me Dad
I Wanna Be a Beauty Queen
Lightnin' Carson Rides Again
Li'l Abner
Livin' Large
Lock 'n' Load
Menace II Society
The Mirror Crack'd
Mo' Better Blues
Mo' Money
'Neath Canadian Skies
Nobody's Perfekt
Old Swimmin' Hole
Packin' It In
Peddlin' in Society
Pete 'n' Tillie
Pudd'nhead Wilson
Puss 'n Boots
Rappin'
Rat Pfink a Boo-Boo
Reg'lar Fellers
Ride 'Em Cowgirl
Ridin' on a Rainbow
Ridin' the California Trail
Ridin' the Trail
Roamin' Wild
Roarin' Lead
Rockin' Road Trip
Rootin' Tootin' Rhythm
Singin' in the Rain
Six Shootin' Sheriff
Smilin' Through
Snowballin'
Spittin' Image
Straight Shootin'
Streetwalkin'
Sweet Sweetback's Baadasssss Song
Thrashin'
Tol'able David
We're Talkin' Serious Money
Workin' for Peanuts

Mistaken Identity

see also Amnesia; Gender Bending; Role Reversal

Across the Bridge
The Adventurer
The Adventures of Bullwhip Griffin
Along Came Jones
Alvin Rides Again
American Cop
Amore!
Amos and Andrew
Another You
As Good as Dead
As You Desire Me
As You Like It
As Young As You Feel
The Associate
Bachelor Mother
The Ballad of Little Jo
The Beautician and the Beast
The Beautiful Blonde from Bashful Bend
Being There
Betrayed
Big Mouth
Billy the Kid Returns
Bittersweet Love
Black Glove
Blackjack
Blame It on the Bellboy
Blind Justice
Blondie Knows Best
Body Snatchers
Borderline
Boy's Reformatory
Brighton Strangler
Broadway Limited
Broken Melody
Bullets or Ballots
Bullseye!
Bundle of Joy
Buona Sera, Mrs. Campbell

Bushwhacked
Butler's Dilemma
Camp Cucamonga: How I Spent My Summer Vacation
The Capture
Caroline?
Carry On Admiral
A Case of Deadly Force
CB4: The Movie
Center of the Web
The Challengers
Chameleon Street
Charade
Charley's Aunt
The Chase
Colonel Chabert
Convicted
Convicts at Large
Cornbread, Earl & Me
A Couch in New York
The Couch Trip
Counterblast
Court Jester
Dave
Deadwood
Deconstructing Sarah
The Desert Song
Don Juan DeMarco
Don't Tell Her It's Me
Double Play
Double Vision
El Mariachi
Ernest Goes to Jail
Erotic Touch of Hot Skin
Evergreen
Every Man's Law
Execution of Raymond Graham
F/X 2: The Deadly Art of Illusion
Family Reunion
Fargo Express
Fatal Exposure
Father
Feet First
Fighting Parson
Five Graves to Cairo
Gangway
The Gay Divorcee
Generale Della Rovere
Gentleman Bandit
Get That Man
The Glass Bottom Boat
Good Neighbor Sam
The Great Dictator
Grosse Fatigue
The Gun in Betty Lou's Handbag
Gunfire
Gunsmoke Trail
Hell on Frisco Bay
Her Life as a Man
Hero
High & Low
High Lonesome
Highway 13
His Brother's Ghost
His Wife's Lover
Hittin' the Trail
Hollywood Chaos
Hometown Boy Makes Good
Honolulu
A House in the Hills
Houseguest
I Love You
I Want to Live!
I Will, I Will for Now
If Looks Could Kill
The Imposter
In Person
In Society
The Inspector General
Instant Kung-Fu Man
Invasion of the Body Snatchers
It Started with Eve
It Takes Two
It! The Terror from Beyond Space
Jade
Johnny Handsome
Johnny Stecchino
Kansas City Confidential

Keaton's Cop
Killer Dill
The Killing Time
A Kiss Before Dying
Landslide
The Last Contract
The Last Winter
Laughing at Danger
Laurel & Hardy: The Hoose-Gow
Law of the Underworld
Le Bonheur Est Dans le Pre
Life Is a Long Quiet River➤
Lisa
The Little Drummer Girl➤
Little Sister
The Lookalike
Lost Highway
Love at Large
Lucky Cisco Kid
Mad About Music➤
Made in America
Maid's Night Out
The Man in the Raincoat
The Man on the Box
Man on the Run
The Man with One Red Shoe
Manhandled
The Mark of Zorro➤
Meet the Mob
Mexican Spitfire/Smartest Girl in
   Town
Miami Hustle
The Misadventures of Mr. Wilt
Mississippi Mermaid➤
Mistaken Identity
Mr. Klein➤
Monsignor Quixote
The Monster
Monte Carlo Nights
My Geisha
My Man Godfrey➤
My Outlaw Brother
My Twentieth Century➤
Mystery Date
Naked Tango
Naughty Marietta
Never a Dull Moment
Next of Kin
The Night We Never Met
Nightfall➤
Nobody's Perfect
North by Northwest➤
The Nutt House
The Obsessed
Obsession
One Body Too Many
Only You
Opportunity Knocks
Oscar
Out of Bounds
Out on a Limb
Paper Mask
Pardon My Sarong
The Passenger➤
Phantom Fiend
Phantom Killer
Picture Perfect
Pier 23
The Player➤
The Pope Must Diet
Prelude to a Kiss
The Princess Comes Across➤
Private Life of Don Juan
The Private Secretary
Profile
Purple Noon➤
Ranson's Folly
Rattler Kid
Red Firecracker, Green
   Firecracker
The Red Half-Breed
Red Heat
Red Rock West➤
The Reluctant Agent
The Reluctant Astronaut
Return of Jesse James
The Return of Martin Guerre➤
Return of the Tall Blond Man
   With One Black Shoe

River Beat
Romance on the High Seas➤
Running Hot
Ruyblas
St. Benny the Dip
The Santa Clause
Santa with Muscles
The Scar
Scream of Fear➤
Seconds➤
The Secret of My Success
The 7th Commandment
She Must Be Seeing Things
The Sinister Invasion
Sister Act
Sister Act 2: Back in the Habit
Six Gun Gospel
Six of a Kind➤
Small Kill
Smokey and the Bandit, Part 3
Social Error
Soldat Duroc...Ca Va Etre Ta
   Fete!
Someone at the Door
Splitting Heirs
Stolen Identity
A Stolen Life
Straight Talk
The Stupids
The Suitors
Sunday
Supergrass
Support Your Local Gunfighter➤
Suture
Switched at Birth
Tattle Tale
10 Rillington Place➤
The Tenth Man
Texas Carnival
Texas Cyclone
They Knew What They Wanted➤
The Thin Blue Line➤
Things Change➤
The 39 Steps➤
Tombstone Terror
Top Hat➤
Toto le Heros➤
True Identity
The Truth About Cats and
   Dogs➤
Twelfth Night
Two Much
The Unholy Three➤
The Well➤
We're No Angels
West of the Pecos
While You Were Sleeping➤
White Eagle
White of the Eye➤
Who's Harry Crumb?
Wings of the Morning
Withnail and I➤
The Worldly Madonna
The Wrong Guys
Young Master
Zertigo Diamond Caper

Modern Cowboys

see also Western Comedy;
   Westerns
Another Pair of Aces: Three of a
   Kind➤
Barbarosa➤
Bronco Billy
City Slickers➤
City Slickers 2: The Legend of
   Curly's Gold
Coogan's Bluff➤
The Cowboy Way
Dudes
8 Seconds
The Electric Horseman
Fool for Love
The Last of the Dogmen
Lonely Are the Brave➤
My Heroes Have Always Been
   Cowboys
Rhinestone

Ruby Jean and Joe
Samurai Cowboy
Sweet Creek County War
Toy Story➤
True West➤
Wild Horses

Moms

see also Bad Dads; Dads;
   Monster Moms; Parenthood
Amazing Grace
Aurora
Baby Boom
Bastard out of Carolina
Bogus
The Brady Bunch Movie➤
Children of the Revolution
The Daytrippers
Dead Ahead
Every Other Weekend➤
House Arrest
I Remember Mama➤
In the Gloaming➤
The Incredible Shrinking Woman
Invisible Mom
Little Women➤
Made in America
Manny & Lo➤
Mermaids➤
Mrs. Winterbourne
Mom and Dad Save the World
Mother
A Mother's Prayer
Nightmare
On My Own
Only the Lonely
Our Sons
Postcards from the Edge➤
The River Wild
Rumpelstiltskin
She-Devil
She's Having a Baby
So I Married an Axe Murderer
Some Mother's Son➤
Spanking the Monkey➤
Stop! or My Mom Will Shoot
Striptease
Throw Momma from the Train➤
To See Paris and Die
Trading Mom
Troop Beverly Hills
A Very Brady Sequel
The War at Home

Monkeyshines

see also Jungle Stories;
   Wild Kingdom
Born to Be Wild
Buddy
Congo
Dunston Checks In
Ed
George of the Jungle
King Kong➤
King Kong
Monkey Shines
Monkey Trouble
Outbreak➤

Monster Moms

see also Bad Dads; Dads;
   Moms; Parenthood
The Anniversary
The Baby
Bad Boy Bubby
Bellissima➤
Beyond the Door
Big Bad Mama
Big Bad Mama 2
Carrie➤
Deadly Advice
Die! Die! My Darling!
Flesh Eating Mothers
Gorgo
The Grifters➤

Gypsy
Invaders from Mars
Ma Barker's Killer Brood
Mad Youth
Mom
Mommie Dearest
Mommy
Mommy 2: Mommy's Day
Mother
Mother's Day
Parents➤
The Positively True Adventures
   of the Alleged Texas
   Cheerleader-Murdering
   Mom➤
Psycho➤
Psycho 2
Psycho 3
Public Enemies
Serial Mom➤
Sleepwalkers
Small Sacrifices
Spanking the Monkey➤
The Stepmother
Sybil➤
Trilogy of Terror 2

Monsters, General

see also Ghosts, Ghouls, &
   Goblins; Giants; Killer
   Beasts; Killer Bugs; Killer
   Plants; Killer Toys; Mad
   Scientists; Robots &
   Androids; Sea Critter
   Attack; Vampires;
   Werewolves; Zombies
The Astounding She-Monster
Atlas in the Land of the Cyclops
Barn of the Naked Dead
Basket Case➤
Basket Case 2
Basket Case 3: The Progeny
The Beast from Haunted Cave
Beast in the Cellar
Beast of the Yellow Night
The Beast of Yucca Flats
The Beast Within
The Being
Bio Hazard
Black Roses
Blackenstein
The Blob
The Blob➤
Blood Tide
Boggy Creek II
Bowery Boys Meet the Monsters
The Boy Who Loved Trolls
Brain of Blood
The Brainiac
The Bride
Bride of the Gorilla
Bride of the Monster
Brides of the Beast
Cameron's Closet
The Capture of Bigfoot
Carry On Screaming
Cast a Deadly Spell➤
Castle of Evil
The Cellar
The Channeler
C.H.U.D.
C.H.U.D. 2: Bud the Chud
The Crater Lake Monster
Creature of Destruction
Creeping Terror
Creepozoids
Creepshow
The Curse
Curse 2: The Bite
Curse 3: Blood Sacrifice
Curse of the Swamp Creature
Dagora, the Space Monster
The Dark
The Daughter of Dr. Jekyll
Deepstar Six
The Demon
Demon of Paradise

Demons
Demons of Ludlow
Demonstone
Demonwarp
Destroy All Monsters
Devil Kiss
Devil Monster
Devil Rider
Dr. Orloff's Invisible Horror
Dr. Orloff's Monster
Don't Be Afraid of the Dark
Dragonworld
Equinox➤
Evil Dead
Evil Dead 2: Dead by Dawn
The Evil of Frankenstein
Evil Town
The Evil Within
Fiend Without a Face
Fire Maidens from Outer Space
Fire Monsters Against the Son of
   Hercules
Forbidden Planet➤
Frankenstein➤
Frankenstein
Frankenstein: A Cinematic
   Scrapbook
Frankenstein '80
Frankenstein General Hospital
Frankenstein Meets the
   Wolfman➤
Frankenstein Unbound➤
Frankenstein's Daughter
Galgameth
Gamera, the Invincible
Gamera vs. Barugon
Gamera vs. Gaos
Gamera vs. Guiron
Gamera vs. Zigra
Gappa the Trifibian Monster
Gargoyles, The Movie: The
   Heroes Awaken
Gate 2
Geek Maggot Bingo
Ghidrah the Three Headed
   Monster
The Giant Claw
Godzilla, King of the Monsters
Godzilla 1985
Godzilla on Monster Island
Godzilla Raids Again
Godzilla vs. Biollante
Godzilla vs. Megalon
Godzilla vs. Monster Zero
Godzilla vs. Mothra
Godzilla vs. the Cosmic Monster
Godzilla vs. the Smog Monster
Godzilla's Revenge
Gorgo
Half Human
Hideous Sun Demon
Horror Express
Horror of Party Beach
House of Dracula
Howling 6: The Freaks
I Was a Teenage Zombie
The Incredible Two-Headed
   Transplant
Infra-Man
Intruder Within
Invasion of the Animal People
The Invisible Monster
Island of Dr. Moreau
It's Alive!
Jungle Heat
The Killer Shrews
The Kindred
King of Kong Island
Labyrinth➤
Lady Frankenstein
Legend of Boggy Creek
The Legend of Gator Face
Little Monsters
Loch Ness
Mad Doctor of Blood Island
The Mad Monster
Mad Monster Party
Man Beast

Man Made Monster
The Manster
Mary Shelley's Frankenstein
Maxim Xul
Meteor Monster
The Milpitas Monster
Mirror, Mirror
The Monolith Monsters
The Monster of Piedras Blancas
Monster on the Campus
The Monster Squad
The Monster That Challenged
   the World
Monsters Crash the Pajama
   Party
Mutant
Mutants In Paradise
My Demon Lover
The Odyssey
The People Under the Stairs
The Phantom Creeps
The Phantom from 10,000
   Leagues
The Prey
The Quatermass Experiment⸽
The Quest
Rana: The Legend of Shadow
   Lake
Rawhead Rex
The Return of Swamp Thing
Return to Boggy Creek
Revenge of Doctor X
Revolt of the Zombies
Samson in the Wax Museum
Saturday the 14th Strikes Back
Science Crazed
Scream Dream
The Screaming Dead
The Secret of the Loch
Seven Doors of Death
Shadow Creature
Shadowzone
Silent Night, Deadly Night 5: The
   Toymaker
The Slayer
The Slime People
The Snake Hunter Strangler
The Snow Creature
Sons of Hercules in the Land of
   Darkness
Space Monster
Squirm
Stay Awake
Stepmonster
The Strangeness
Subspecies
Swamp of the Lost Monster
Tales from the Darkside: The
   Movie
Terror Beneath the Sea
Terror in the Swamp
Terror of Mechagodzilla
Terror of Rome Against the Son
   of Hercules
The Terror Within
The Terror Within 2
Things
Tomb of Torture
Track of the Moonbeast
Transmutations
20 Million Miles to Earth
Varan the Unbelievable
The Video Dead
Voodoo Woman
Voyage to the Planet of
   Prehistoric Women
War of the Gargantuas
Watchers
Watchers 2
Yog, Monster from Space
Yongkari Monster of the Deep

Montreal

***see also** Canada*
The Apprenticeship of Duddy
   Kravitz⸽
Being at Home with Claude
Eliza's Horoscope

Jesus of Montreal⸽
L'Escorte
Love and Human Remains⸽
Malarek
Mystery of the Million Dollar
   Hockey Puck
Night Zoo
The Quarrel
Straight for the Heart
The Victory

Moscow

***see also** Russia/USSR*
American Cop
Back in the USSR
The Battle of Russia
Black Eyes
Comrade X
An Englishman Abroad⸽
Gorky Park
Luna Park
Moscow Does Not Believe in
   Tears⸽
Moscow Parade
Mute Witness
Police Academy: Mission to
   Moscow
Red Heat
The Russia House
The Saint
Taxi Blues⸽
Very Close Quarters

Motor Vehicle Dept.

***see also** Bikers; Fast Cars;
   Killer Cars*
Action Jackson
American Graffiti⸽
Back to the Future⸽
Bail Out
Belle Americaine
The Betsy
Black Moon Rising
The Blues Brothers
Cadillac Man
Car Trouble
Car Wash
Carpool
The Chase
Chitty Chitty Bang Bang
Comic Cabby
Corvette Summer
Coupe de Ville
Crash
Cry Panic
Dangerous Curves
Dark of the Night
D.C. Cab
Deadline Auto Theft
Dream Machine
Drive-In
Drive-In Massacre
The Driver
Driving Me Crazy
Duel⸽
Dumb & Dumber
Ferris Bueller's Day Off⸽
Firebird 2015 A.D.
Follow That Car
Ford: The Man & the Machine
Free Ride
Freedom
Freeway
Great American Traffic Jam
Gung Ho
The Hearse
Herbie Rides Again
High Rolling in a Hot Corvette
Highway Patrolman
Hometown U.S.A.
Hot Wire
How I Learned to Love Women
Jade
Killing Cars
License to Drive
The Love Bug

Maximum Overdrive
Moonshine Highway
Motorama
Moving Violations
My Chauffeur
National Lampoon's Vacation⸽
Night on Earth⸽
One Deadly Owner
Pepper and His Wacky Taxi
Pie in the Sky
Repo Jake
Repo Man⸽
Roger & Me⸽
Silkwood⸽
Smokey & the Hotwire Gang
Steel Arena
Stephen King's Thinner
Stingray
The Sucker
Sunset Limousine
Superbug Super Agent
This Man Must Die⸽
Tomboy
Traffic
Tucker: The Man and His
   Dream⸽
Used Cars⸽
The Van
Vanishing Point
Wheels of Terror
Zero to Sixty

Mountaineering

Alpine Fire
The Ascent
Bushwhacked
The Challenge⸽
Cliffhanger⸽
The Climb
Courage Mountain
The Eiger Sanction
Five Days One Summer
God's Bloody Acre
Heidi
K2: The Ultimate High
The Mountain
My Side of the Mountain
Storm and Sorrow
Third Man on the Mountain
The White Tower⸽

Movie & TV Trailers

Bikers, Blondes, and Blood
Cowboys of the Saturday
   Matinee
Frankenstein: A Cinematic
   Scrapbook
Hollywood Uncensored
It Came from Hollywood
Loose Shoes
The Professor
To See Such Fun

Mummies

***see also** Horror; Zombies*
Abbott and Costello Meet the
   Mummy
Attack of the Mayan Mummy
The Awakening
Castle of the Living Dead
The Curse of the Aztec Mummy
Curse of the Aztec Mummy/
   Robot vs. the Aztec Mummy
Dawn of the Mummy
The Monster Squad
The Mummy⸽
Mummy & Curse of the Jackal
The Mummy's Curse
The Mummy's Ghost
The Mummy's Hand
The Mummy's Revenge
The Mummy's Tomb
The Robot vs. the Aztec Mummy
Sphinx

Wrestling Women vs. the Aztec
   Mummy

Murderous Children

***see also** Childhood Visions*
The Bad Seed
Before and After
The Children
Children of the Corn
Children of the Corn 2: The Final
   Sacrifice
Children of the Corn 3: Urban
   Harvest
Children of the Damned
Daddy's Girl
Damien: Omen 2
Don't Go to Sleep
The Good Son
The Little Girl Who Lives Down
   the Lane
The Omen
The Other⸽
Relative Fear
Village of the Damned⸽
Village of the Damned

Music

***see also** Martyred Pop
   Icons; Musician Biopics;
   Nashville Narratives; Rock
   Stars on Film; Roll Over
   Beethoven; Struggling
   Musicians*
The Accompanist
Airheads
Alexander's Ragtime Band⸽
All You Need Is Cash⸽
Allegro Non Troppo⸽
Almost Blue
Amadeus⸽
American Blue Note
Americathon
The Apple
Bach: Mass in B Minor
Backbeat⸽
Ballad in Blue
Basileus Quartet⸽
Beat Street
The Beatniks
Beethoven
Beethoven Lives Upstairs
Beethoven's Nephew
The Benny Goodman Story
The Best of the Kenny Everett
   Video Show
Big Business Girl
Bird⸽
Bix
Blame It on the Night
Blink
Bloodhounds of Broadway
Blueberry Hill
Bob Dylan: Don't Look Back⸽
The Bodyguard
Born to Boogie
Bound for Glory⸽
Brassed Off
Broken Strings
Brother of Sleep⸽
Buddy's Song
Bummer
Burglar⸽
Camilla
Captain January
Carmen⸽
CB4: The Movie
The Challengers
Coal Miner's Daughter⸽
Comeback
The Commitments⸽
The Competition⸽
The Compleat Beatles⸽
Concrete Angels
The Conductor
Cool As Ice
Cool Mikado

The Cotton Club⸽
The Courier
Crossroads
Dead Girls
Death Drug
Death Games
Deception⸽
Decline of Western Civilization
   1⸽
Decline of Western Civilization
   2: The Metal Years
Diner⸽
Dingo
Disorderlies
Diva⸽
The Doors
The Doors: Soft Parade, a
   Retrospective
Double Trouble
Dreaming Lips
Dubeat-E-O
Duet for One
The Duke is Tops
Dutch Treat
Eddie and the Cruisers
Eddie and the Cruisers 2: Eddie
   Lives!
The Eddy Duchin Story
Edie in Ciao! Manhattan
Elvis and Me
Elvis: The Movie
Empire Records
Encounter at Raven's Gate
Escape Me Never
The Eternal Waltz
Eubie!
The Fabulous Baker Boys⸽
The Fabulous Dorseys
Face the Music
Fantasia⸽
Fastest Guitar Alive
Fear of a Black Hat
The Fighting Legion
Fighting Mad
Fingers⸽
Five Easy Pieces⸽
The Five Heartbeats⸽
The Five Pennies
Fly by Night
FM
Follow Me, Boys!⸽
Follow That Dream
For Those About to Rock:
   Monsters in Moscow
Forget Mozart
Frankie and Johnny
Friday
Fugitive Valley
The Gay Ranchero
The Gene Krupa Story
Georgia⸽
Get Crazy
Getting Over
Giant Steps
The Gig
Gimme Shelter
Give My Regards to Broad
   Street
The Glenn Miller Story⸽
Good Morning, Vietnam⸽
Gotta Dance, Gotta Sing
Grace of My Heart
Great Balls of Fire
The Great Waltz⸽
Green Card
Hail Caesar
Hard Core Logo
A Hard Day's Night⸽
Haunted Symphony
Hear My Song⸽
Heartbreak Hotel
Hearts of Fire
Heaven Tonight
Hi-De-Ho
Home Sweet Home
House Party⸽
House Party 2: The Pajama Jam
House Party 3
Humoresque⸽

Musicals

That's Entertainment, Part 2
That's Entertainment, Part 3
That's Singing: The Best of
  Broadway
Thousands Cheer
Three Little Words
The Threepenny Opera
Thrill of a Romance
Till the Clouds Roll By
Tin Pan Alley
The Toast of New Orleans
Tonight and Every Night
The Trouble with Girls (and How
  To Get Into It)►
Under the Cherry Moon
Vagabond Lover
The Vampyr
Velnio Nuotaka
Viva Las Vegas
Week-End In Havana
Welcome Stranger
Wigstock: The Movie
Window Shopping
Wintertime
Words and Music
Yes, Sir, Mr. Bones
Young People

Musician Biopics

see also *Nashville*
Narratives; Roll Over
Beethoven
Amadeus►
Bird►
The Buddy Holly Story►
Coal Miner's Daughter►
The Doors
Elvis: The Movie
The Gene Krupa Story
The Glenn Miller Story►
Great Balls of Fire
Immortal Beloved
John & Yoko: A Love Story
La Bamba►
Lady Sings the Blues
Living Proof: The Hank Williams
  Jr. Story
The Magic Bow
Nico Icon►
Selena
Shine►
Sweet Dreams
Whale Music
What's Love Got to Do with It?

Mutiny

see also *Deep Blue; Sail*
Away; Sea Disasters;
Shipwrecked
The Bounty►
Crimson Tide►
The Legend of the Sea Wolf
Mutiny
The Mutiny of the Elsinore
Mutiny on the Bounty►
Mutiny on the Bounty
Pirate Ship
The Sea Wolf►
The Sea Wolf

Mystery & Suspense

see also *Psycho-Thriller*
Abduction of St. Anne
Above Suspicion►
Above Suspicion
Absolution
Accidental Meeting
Accidents
Accomplice
Accused
Ace Crawford, Private Eye
Ace Drummond
Ace of Hearts
Across the Bridge
Across the Pacific►

Acting on Impulse
Address Unknown
Adrift
Adventures of a Private Eye
The Adventures of Sherlock
  Holmes
The Adventures of Sherlock
  Holmes: Hound of the
  Baskervilles
An Affair in Mind
The Affair of the Pink Pearl
African Rage
After Dark, My Sweet►
After Pilkington
After the Thin Man►
Agatha
Agatha Christie's Miss Marple
Alias John Preston
All-American Murder
All the Kind Strangers
Alligator Eyes
Almost Partners
The Alphabet Murders
Alphaville►
The Amateur
Amazing Mr. Blunden
The Amazing Mr. X
The Ambassador
The American Friend►
American Gigolo
Amsterdamned
And Soon the Darkness
And Then There Were None►
The Anderson Tapes►
Android
The Andromeda Strain
Angel Dust
Angel Heart
Animal Instincts
Animal Instincts 2
Another Thin Man
Any Man's Death
Apology
Appointment with Death
Appointment with Fear
Apprentice to Murder
Arabesque
Are You in the House Alone?
Arizona Stagecoach
The Arsenal Stadium Mystery
The Art of Crime
As Good as Dead
Assassin
The Assassination Run
Assault
At Close Range►
The Atomic City
Autopsy
The Avenging Hand
The Baby Doll Murders
The Babysitter
Back from Eternity
Back to Hannibal: The Return of
  Tom Sawyer and Huckleberry
  Finn
Back to the Wall
Backfire
Backstab
Backstreet Justice
Backtrack►
B.A.D. Cats
Bad Company
Bad Influence
Bad Ronald►
The Banker
The Barcelona Kill
Basic Instinct
The Bat Whispers
Battle Shock
Bedford Incident
Bedroom Eyes
Bedroom Eyes 2
The Bedroom Window
Before Morning
Behind Locked Doors
Bell from Hell
Bellamy
Benefit of the Doubt
Berlin Express►

Berserk!
The Best of Cracker Mysteries►
The Best of Lovejoy Mysteries
Best Seller►
Betrayal of the Dove
Betrayed
Beyond a Reasonable Doubt
Beyond the Bermuda Triangle
Beyond the Silhouette
Big Deadly Game
The Big Easy►
The Big Fix►
The Big Heat►
The Big Hurt
Big News
The Big Sleep►
The Big Sleep
The Big Switch
Big Town After Dark
Bikini Island
The Bird with the Crystal
  Plumage
Birgitt Haas Must Be Killed
Bitter Harvest
Bitter Vengeance
The Black Abbot
Black Bird
Black Box Affair
The Black Cat
Black Cobra
Black Glove
Black Gold
The Black Hand►
Black Hand
Black Ice
Black Limelight
Black Magic Woman
Black Panther
Black Rainbow►
The Black Raven
Black Sunday
Black Tide
Black Tower
A Black Veil for Lisa
Black Water
Black Widow►
The Black Windmill
Blackmail►
Blackout
Blackwater Trail
Blind Date
Blind Fear
Blind Justice
Blind Man's Bluff
Blind Side
Blind Vision
Blind Witness
Blindfold: Acts of Obsession
Blindside
Blindsided
Blink
Blonde Blackmailer
Blood Frenzy
Blood on the Sun
Blood Relations
Blood Relatives
Blood Simple►
Bloodhounds
Bloodhounds 2
Bloody Avenger
Blow Up►
Blown Away
Blue City
The Blue Dahlia►
Blue Desert►
Blue Ice
Blue Steel
Blue Tornado
Blue Velvet►
Bodily Harm
Body Chemistry
Body Chemistry 3: Point of
  Seduction
Body Double►
Body Heat►
The Body in the Library
Body Language
Body of Influence
Body Parts

Body Shot
The Body Vanished
Boomerang►
Borderline
B.O.R.N.
Born to Kill►
The Boston Strangler
Bounty Hunters
The Bourne Identity►
Bowery at Midnight/Dick Tracy
  vs. Cueball
The Boys from Brazil
Brass Target
Breakdown►
Breakheart Pass
Breaking All the Rules
The Bride Wore Black►
Bright Smiler
Brighton Strangler
The Brighton Strangler/Before
  Dawn
Broken Trust
Broken Vows
Brother Cadfael
Brother Cadfael 2
Brotherly Love
Bulldog Drummond
Bulldog Drummond at Bay
Bulldog Drummond Comes Back
Bulldog Drummond in Africa/
  Arrest Bulldog Drummond
Bulldog Drummond's Bride
Bulldog Drummond's Peril
Bulldog Drummond's Revenge
Bulldog Drummond's Revenge/
  Bulldog Drummond's Peril
Bulldog Drummond's Secret
  Police
Bullet to Beijing
Bulletproof Heart►
Bums
Burndown
Buying Time
By Dawn's Early Light
By the Blood of Others►
Calendar Girl Murders
The Caller
Calling Paul Temple
Candles at Nine
Caper of the Golden Bulls
Cardiac Arrest
Caribe
Carnival Lady
Caroline at Midnight
A Case for Murder
Case of the Baby Sitter
The Case of the Lucky Legs
The Case of the Missing Lady
Cast a Dark Shadow►
Cast a Deadly Spell►
Castle in the Desert
Cat and Mouse►
The Cat and the Canary►
The Cat and the Canary
Cat Chaser
The Cat o' Nine Tails
Catacombs
The Catamount Killing
Catch Me a Spy
Caught in the Act
Cause for Alarm
Center of the Web
The Centerfold Girls
Chain of Desire
Challenge of McKenna
Charlie Chan and the Curse of
  the Dragon Queen
Charlie Chan at the Opera
Charlie Chan at the Wax
  Museum
Charlie Chan in Paris
Charlie Chan in Rio
Charlie Chan in the Secret
  Service
Charlie Chan's Secret
Child in the Night
Child of Glass
Chill Factor
The China Lake Murders

China Moon
Chinatown►
The Chinese Cat
Choice of Arms
Christina
City in Panic
City Killer
City of Blood
City of Shadows
City on Fire
The Clay Pigeon
The Clergyman's Daughter
A Climate for Killing
Cloak and Dagger
The Clouded Yellow►
Clouds Over Europe►
Clown Murders
The Clutching Hand
The Cobra Strikes
The Cobweb
Code Name Alpha
Code Name: Diamond Head
Codename: Foxfire
Codename: Icarus
Cohen and Tate
Cold Comfort
Cold Eyes of Fear
Cold Sweat
The Colony
Color Me Dead
Color of Night
Columbo: Murder By the Book
Columbo: Prescription Murder
Coma►
Coming Out Alive
Compromising Positions
Concealed Weapon
Concrete Beat
The Confession
Confessions of a Hit Man
Confidentially Yours►
Consenting Adults
The Conversation►
Convicted
The Corpse Vanishes
Cosmo Jones, Crime Smasher
Counter Punch
The Cover Girl Murders
Cover Me
Cover Story
Crack-Up
The Crackler
The Cradle Will Fall
Crime Broker
Criminal Court
Criminal Law
Criminals Within
Criss Cross►
Cross Country
Crow Hollow
The Crucifer of Blood
The Crude Oasis
Cruise into Terror
Cruise Missile
Cruising
Cry Danger►
A Cry in the Night
The Cry of the Owl
Cry Panic
Cry Terror
Cry Wolf
The Crying Child
Curiosity Kills
Curse of the Yellow Snake
Cutter's Way
Cycle Psycho
Dagger Eyes
The Dain Curse
Damned River
Dance Macabre
Dance with Death
Dancing with Danger
Danger Man
Danger of Love
Danger on the Air
Danger Zone
The Dangerous
Dangerous Appointment
Dangerous Game

Mystery

Mythology

Nannies & Governesses

Nashville

Nashville Narratives

Native America

The Last of the Mohicans
The Last of the Mohicans♦
The Last of the Redmen
Legend of Walks Far Woman
The Legend of Wolf Mountain
The Light in the Forest
Little Big Man♦
Lost Legacy: A Girl Called Hatter Fox
The Magic Stone
A Man Called Horse♦
Man of the House
The Manitou
Map of the Human Heart
Mission to Glory
A Mormon Maid
Naked in the Sun
Natas...The Reflection
Northern Passage
On Top of the Whale
The Pathfinder
Pocahontas♦
Pocahontas: The Legend
Poltergeist 2: The Other Side
Powwow Highway♦
The Prophecy
Ravenhawk
The Red Fury
The Red Half-Breed
Renegades
Requiem for a Heavyweight♦
Roanoak
Running Brave
Savage Sam
The Savage Seven
Savage Wilderness
The Secret of Navajo Cave
Shadow of the Wolf
Shadowhunter
Silent Tongue
Sioux City
The Slayer/The Scalps
Smith!
Spirit Rider♦
Squanto: A Warrior's Tale♦
Sunchaser
Tecumseh: The Last Warrior
Tell Them Willie Boy Is Here♦
Terror in the Jungle
Texas John Slaughter: Geronimo's Revenge
3 Ninjas Knuckle Up
Three Warriors
Thunder Warrior
Thunder Warrior 2
Thunderheart♦
Tonka
Track of the Moonbeast
Unconquered
Uninvited
The Villain
Wagon Wheels
Walk the Proud Land
War Party
Where the Spirit Lives
White Fang 2: The Myth of the White Wolf
Windrunner
Windwalker♦

Nazis & Other Paramilitary Slugs

see also Germany; The Holocaust; Judaism; World War II
All Through the Night♦
Angel of Death
Angel with the Trumpet
Angry Harvest♦
Any Man's Death
Ark of the Sun God
The Assisi Underground
Background to Danger♦
Bedknobs and Broomsticks
The Berlin Affair
Berlin Express♦
Betrayed♦

The Black Klansman
The Boxer and Death♦
The Boys from Brazil
Brady's Escape
Broken Glass
Cabaret♦
Cabo Blanco
Casablanca♦
Casablanca Express
Charlie Grant's War
Clipped Wings
Closet Land
Cold Days
Commandos Strike at Dawn
The Conformist♦
Cottage to Let
Counterblast
The Counterfeit Traitor♦
The Coward
The Cut Throats
Dam Busters♦
Dawn Express
A Day in October
Dead Bang
Death Is Called Engelchen♦
The Death of Adolf Hitler
Descending Angel♦
Desert Commandos
The Desert Fox♦
Despair♦
The Devil's Brigade
The Diary of Anne Frank♦
The Dirty Dozen♦
The Dirty Dozen: The Deadly Mission
The Dirty Dozen: The Fatal Mission
The Dirty Dozen: The Next Mission
Dirty Heroes
Edge of Darkness♦
Elves
Enemy of Women
Enigma Secret
Equalizer 2000
Escape from Sobibor♦
Europa, Europa♦
The Execution
Eye of the Needle
The Fallen Sparrow♦
Father
Fatherland
Firewalker
Five Fingers♦
Five Graves to Cairo♦
Flesh Feast
Forbidden
Force 10 from Navarone
Foreign Correspondent♦
The Forty-Ninth Parallel♦
Four Bags Full
The Four Horsemen of the Apocalypse
A Friendship in Vienna
Genghis Cohn
Getting Away With Murder
Ghost on the Loose
Goldengirl
Good Evening, Mr. Wallenberg
The Great Dictator♦
The Great Escape♦
Hanna's War
Hanussen♦
He Lives: The Search for the Evil One
Hell Commandos
Hell Hunters
Hell River
Hell Squad
Heroes in Hell
The Heroes of Telemark
The Hiding Place
Higher Learning
Hitler
Hitler: Dead or Alive
Hitler's Daughter
Holocaust♦
Hornet's Nest

Hotel Reserve♦
The House on Carroll Street
The House on Garibaldi Street
House on 92nd Street♦
Ilsa, Harem Keeper of the Oil Sheiks
Ilsa, She-Wolf of the SS
In a Glass Cage
In the Presence of Mine Enemies
The Incredible Mr. Limpet
Indiana Jones and the Last Crusade♦
Indiana Jones and the Temple of Doom♦
The Infiltrator
Inside Out
Inside the Third Reich
Into the Homeland
Invisible Agent
Jenny's War
Judgment at Nuremberg♦
Julia♦
Jungle Siren
Kanal♦
Kapo♦
The Keep
The Key to Rebecca
The Klansman
Kojak: The Belarus File
Korczak♦
La Passante♦
Lassiter
The Last Butterfly
The Last Five Days
The Last Metro♦
The Last Train
Law of the Jungle
Les Miserables
Les Violons du Bal
Lifeboat♦
The Long Island Four
The Longest Day♦
The Lucifer Complex
Madame Rosa♦
A Man Escaped♦
The Man in the Glass Booth♦
The Man Who Captured Eichmann
Marathon Man♦
Martha and I
Massacre in Rome
Master Key
Master Race
Me and the Colonel
The Mediterranean in Flames
Mein Kampf: Hitler's Rise and Fall
Mephisto♦
Miracle at Moreaux
Mission Corbari
Mr. Klein♦
The Mortal Storm♦
Mother Night♦
Music Box
The Nasty Girl♦
Night Ambush
A Night in Casablanca♦
Night of the Fox
Night of the Generals♦
The Night Porter
Night Train to Munich♦
Night Train to Venice
No Dead Heroes
The North Star♦
Northern Pursuit
Notorious♦
Oasis of the Zombies
The Odessa File
Old Gun♦
Once Upon a Honeymoon
One of Our Aircraft Is Missing♦
The Only Way
Open City♦
Operation Amsterdam
Operation Crossbow♦
O.S.S.♦
Passage to Marseilles♦
The Pedestrian♦

Pimpernel Smith
A Prayer for Katarina Horovitzova♦
Prayer of the Rollerboys
Pressure Point♦
Puppet Master 3: Toulon's Revenge
The Quiller Memorandum♦
Raid on Rommel
Raiders of the Lost Ark♦
Reunion in France
The Revolt of Job♦
Richard III♦
Rio Rita
River of Death
River of Diamonds
The Rocketeer♦
The Rose Garden
The Salzburg Connection
Savage Attraction
The Scarlet & the Black
Schindler's List♦
Schtonk
Scream and Scream Again♦
Sea of Sand
The Secret Code
Secret Mission
The Secret War of Harry Frigg
Seven Miles from Alcatraz/Flight from Glory
The Seventh Cross♦
Severed Ties
She Demons
Shining Through
Shock Waves
Silent Scream
633 Squadron
Skinheads: The Second Coming of Hate
Snow Treasure
So Ends Our Night♦
Soldier of Orange♦
A Soldier's Tale
Son of Lassie
The Sorrow and the Pity♦
The Sound of Music♦
S.S. Experiment Camp 2
S.S. Love Camp No. 27
Stalag 17♦
Stalag Luft
The Stranger♦
Strangers in Paradise
Sundown
Surf Nazis Must Die
Sweet Light in a Dark Room♦
Swing Kids
A Taxing Woman's Return♦
That Summer of White Roses
They Saved Hitler's Brain
13 Rue Madeleine♦
'38: Vienna Before the Fall
This Land is Mine♦
Tiger Fangs
Tigershark
To Be or Not to Be♦
To Be or Not to Be
To Catch a King
Top Dog
Top Secret!♦
The Tormentors
Transport from Paradise
Triumph of the Spirit♦
Triumph of the Will
True Colors
U-Boat Prisoner
Uranus♦
War & Love
War & Remembrance, Part 1
War & Remembrance, Part 2
War & Remembrance: The Final Chapter, Part 8
War & Remembrance: The Final Chapter, Part 9
Watch on the Rhine♦
Waterfront
Where Eagles Dare♦
Where Trails End
Wild Geese 2
The Winds of War

Wings Over the Pacific
Wizards
A Woman at War
Wooden Horse♦
Yank in Libya
The Yesterday Machine
Zentropa
Zombie Lake
Zone Troopers

Negative Utopia

see also Post Apocalypse; Technology-Rampant
Alphaville♦
Animal Farm♦
Brazil♦
El Norte♦
Futureworld
Metropolis♦
Moonraker
The Mosquito Coast
984: Prisoner of the Future
1984♦
The Prisoner: Arrival
Rollerball
Soylent Green
10th Victim♦
THX 1138♦
Whodunit
Zardoz

New Black Cinema

see also African America; Blaxploitation
Boyz N the Hood♦
Clockers♦
Crooklyn♦
Do the Right Thing♦
The Five Heartbeats♦
Get On the Bus♦
Girl 6
Hangin' with the Homeboys♦
Hollywood Shuffle
I'm Gonna Git You Sucka♦
Joe's Bed-Stuy Barbershop: We Cut Heads
Jungle Fever♦
Just Another Girl on the I.R.T.
Livin' Large
Menace II Society♦
The Meteor Man
Mo' Better Blues
Poetic Justice
Posse♦
A Rage in Harlem♦
School Daze♦
Set It Off
She's Gotta Have It♦
Straight Out of Brooklyn
To Sleep with Anger♦

New Orleans

see also American South
Albino Alligator
Angel Heart
Band of Angels
The Big Easy♦
Birth of the Blues
Boxcar Blues
Candyman 2: Farewell to the Flesh
Child of Glass
Cry of the Werewolf
The Cure
The Dangerous
The Dark Side of Love
Dead Man Walking♦
Dixie: Changing Habits♦
Easy Rider♦
End of August
False Witness
The Family
French Quarter
French Quarter Undercover
French Silk

Hard Target
Heaven's Prisoners
Hotel
Interview with the Vampire
The Invisible Avenger
It Happened in New Orleans
J.D.'s Revenge
King Creole
Mardi Gras for the Devil
Mardi Gras Massacre
Mirrors
My Forbidden Past
New Orleans After Dark
Night of the Strangler
Panic in the Streets ►
Pretty Baby ►
Saratoga Trunk
The Savage Bees
Storyville
A Streetcar Named Desire ►
Suddenly, Last Summer ►
Thunderground
Tightrope ►
Toys in the Attic
Tune in Tomorrow
Undercover Blues
The Unholy
Walk on the Wild Side

New Year's Eve

*see also Christmas;
Holidays; Horrible Holidays*
About Last Night... ►
Bloody New Year
Century
Doctor Who
The Enforcer
Gridlock'd ►
Happy New Year ►
A Happy New Year!
Happy New Year
The Hudsucker Proxy ►
The January Man
New Year's Day ►
New Year's Evil
The Poseidon Adventure
Strange Days ►
Virtual Seduction
Waiting to Exhale ►
When Harry Met Sally... ►

New York, New York

*see also The Empire State
Building*
Across 110th Street
Addicted to Love
The Addiction
An Affair to Remember
After Hours ►
Alice ►
All About Eve ►
All That Jazz ►
All the Vermeers in New York ►
Alphabet City
Angelo My Love ►
Angels with Dirty Faces ►
Annie
Annie Hall ►
Another Woman ►
The Apartment ►
Arthur ►
Arthur 2: On the Rocks
Awakenings ►
Bad Lieutenant ►
Barefoot in the Park ►
The Basketball Diaries
Basquiat ►
The Beautician and the Beast
Bed of Roses
Big ►
The Big Bus
Big Business
Big Night
Big Street
Blackboard Jungle ►

Blade
Blink
Blue in the Face
Blue Skies ►
The Bonfire of the Vanities ►
Booty Call
Born to Win
The Bostonians
Breakfast at Tiffany's ►
Breathing Room
Bright Lights, Big City
Brighton Beach Memoirs
Broadway Bound
Broadway Danny Rose ►
The Broadway Drifter
Broadway Limited
Broadway Melody
Broadway Melody of 1936 ►
Broadway Melody of 1938
Broadway Melody of 1940
Broadway Rhythm
Broadway Serenade
The Bronx Executioner
A Bronx Tale ►
The Bronx War
The Brother from Another
    Planet ►
A Brother's Kiss
Bullet
Bullets Over Broadway ►
Carlito's Way ►
Carnal Knowledge ►
Cat People
A Chorus Line
City Hall ►
City Slickers ►
Clockers ►
Cocktail
The Cocoanuts
Coming to America ►
Compromising Positions
Conspiracy Theory ►
Coogan's Bluff ►
The Cotton Club ►
A Couch in New York
The Cowboy Way
Crimes & Misdemeanors ►
Crocodile Dundee ►
Crocodile Dundee 2
Crooklyn ►
Crossing Delancey ►
The Crowd ►
Cruising
Daylight
The Daytrippers
Dead Funny
Dead Presidents
Desolation Angels
Desperate Characters ►
Desperately Seeking Susan
Detective Story ►
The Devil's Own ►
Die Hard: With a Vengeance ►
Do the Right Thing ►
Dog Day Afternoon ►
Donnie Brasco ►
The Dream Team
Dressed to Kill
Drunks
Eddie
Ed's Next Move
Escape from New York
Everyone Says I Love You ►
Eyes of Laura Mars
Eyewitness
F/X ►
Falling in Love
Fame ►
Fatal Attraction ►
Fear, Anxiety and Depression
The Fifth Element
Fingers ►
First Love
The First Wives Club
The Fisher King ►
Fleshpot on 42nd Street
Flirt
For Love or Money
The Foreigner

Fort Apache, the Bronx ►
42nd Street ►
Frankie and Johnny ►
The French Connection ►
The Freshman
The Funeral ►
Funny Girl ►
Ghost ►
Ghostbusters ►
Ghostbusters 2
The Godfather ►
The Godfather, Part 2 ►
The Godfather, Part 3 ►
The Goodbye Girl ►
Goodbye, New York
Goodfellas ►
Gotti
Grace of My Heart ►
The Great Gatsby
Green Card
Greetings ►
The Guardian
Guys and Dolls ►
Hair ►
Hangin' with the Homeboys ►
Hannah and Her Sisters ►
Harlem Nights
Harry and Tonto ►
Headless Body in Topless Bar
Heartburn ►
Heartstrings
Heaven Help Us
Hello Again
Hester Street ►
Hi, Mom! ►
Highlander ►
His Butler's Sister
His Girl Friday ►
Home Alone 2: Lost in New York
Hoodlum
The Hunger
Hurricane Streets
Husbands and Wives ►
I'm Not Rappaport
It Could Happen to You
It Happened in Brooklyn
It Should Happen to You ►
It's My Turn
The January Man
Jeffrey
Joe
Joe's Apartment
Joe's Bed-Stuy Barbershop: We
    Cut Heads
Johnny Suede
Juice ►
Jungle Fever ►
Jungle 2 Jungle
Key Exchange
Kids
King Kong ►
King of Comedy ►
King of New York ►
King of the Gypsies
Kramer vs. Kramer ►
Lady On a Train ►
Last Exit to Brooklyn ►
The Last Seduction ►
Laws of Gravity ►
Legal Eagles
A Life of Her Own
Light Sleeper ►
Liquid Sky ►
Little Miss Marker ►
Living in Oblivion ►
Lonely in America
The Long Island Four
Look Who's Talking, Too
Looking for Richard ►
The Lords of Flatbush ►
Lost in Yonkers
Lotto Land
Love Affair
Love at First Bite
Love Is Better Than Ever
Love Story ►
Lullaby of Broadway
Ma and Pa Kettle Go to Town
Mad Dog and Glory ►

Malcolm X ►
The Manchurian Candidate ►
Manhattan ►
Manhattan Melodrama ►
Manhattan Merengue!
Manhattan Merry-Go-Round
Manhattan Murder Mystery ►
Marathon Man ►
Marty ►
Maximum Risk
Mean Streets ►
Metropolitan ►
Midnight Cowboy ►
Mighty Aphrodite ►
Mimic ►
Miracle on 34th Street ►
Miracle on 34th Street
The Mirror Has Two Faces
Mirrors
Misery ►
Mrs. Santa Claus
Mr. Blandings Builds His Dream
    House ►
Mo' Better Blues ►
Money Train
Morning Glory
Mortal Thoughts
Moscow on the Hudson ►
The Muppets Take Manhattan ►
My Favorite Year ►
My Man Godfrey ►
My Sister Eileen ►
Nadja ►
The Naked City ►
Naked in New York
The Natural ►
Network ►
New Jack City
New York Cop
New York, New York ►
New York Nights
New York Ripper
New York Stories ►
New York's Finest
News from Home
Next Stop, Greenwich Village ►
Nico Icon ►
Night and the City ►
Night Falls on Manhattan ►
Night on Earth ►
The Night They Raided
    Minsky's ►
The Night We Never Met
9 1/2 Weeks ►
1931: Once Upon a Time in New
    York
Nueba Yol
The Odd Couple ►
Off Beat
Oliver & Company ►
On the Town ►
On the Waterfront ►
Once Upon a Time in America ►
One Fine Day
Only When I Laugh ►
The Out-of-Towners ►
Outrageous! ►
Panic in Needle Park ►
The Paper ►
Paradise Alley
Paradise in Harlem
Paris Is Burning ►
The Park is Mine
Party Girl
Permanent Vacation
The Phantom
The Pick-Up Artist
Pillow Talk ►
Plaza Suite ►
The Pompatus of Love
Portrait of Jennie ►
Postcards from America
The Prince of Central Park ►
Prince of the City ►
The Prince of Tides ►
Prisoner of Second Avenue
Private Parts
The Public Eye ►
The Quest

Quick Change
Radio Days ►
A Rage in Harlem ►
Raging Bull ►
Ragtime ►
A Raisin in the Sun ►
Ransom ►
The Rat Race ►
Ready to Wear
Rear Window ►
Rift
Risk ►
The Roaring Twenties ►
Rosemary's Baby ►
Rumble in the Bronx
Saturday Night Fever
Scent of a Woman ►
Scrooged
Searching for Bobby Fischer ►
Serpico ►
Seven ►
The Seven-Ups
The Seven Year Itch ►
Shadows and Fog
ShadowZone: The Undead
    Express
She-Devil
She's Gotta Have It ►
She's the One
Shining Star
Single White Female
Six Degrees of Separation
Slaves of New York
Sleepers
Sliver
Smithereens
Someone Else's America ►
Something Short of Paradise
Something Wild
Sophie's Choice ►
Speedy ►
Splash
Stage Door ►
State of Grace ►
Staying Alive
Stepping Out ►
Still of the Night
Stonewall ►
Straight Out of Brooklyn
Stranger than Paradise ►
Street Scene ►
Street Smart
Street Trash
The Substance of Fire
Sugar Hill
Sunday
Sunset Park
The Super
Superfly
Sweet Charity ►
Sweet Nothing ►
Sweet Smell of Success ►
The Taking of Pelham One Two
    Three ►
Talk to Me
Tarzan's New York Adventure
Taxi Driver ►
They Call It Sin
Three Days of the Condor ►
Three Men and a Baby ►
Through the Eyes of a Killer
Times Square
Tootsie ►
Torch Song Trilogy
Trash
A Tree Grows in Brooklyn ►
A Troll in Central Park
29th Street
Underground U.S.A.
An Unmarried Woman ►
Untamed Heart
Unzipped ►
Uptown New York
Vampire in Brooklyn
A Very Natural Thing
Walking and Talking
Wall Street ►
Walls of Glass
The Way We Were ►

Category Index

1068

Two or Three Things I Know
About Her
Under the Roofs of Paris➤
Until September
Victor/Victoria➤
Victory
Window Shopping
Zazie dans le Metro➤

Party Hell

see also Horror

April Fool's Day
Carrie➤
The Club
Happy Birthday to Me
Hell Night
Hello Mary Lou: Prom Night 2
Killer Party
Meet Wally Sparks
Monsters Crash the Pajama
Party
Night of the Demons
Prom Night
Prom Night 3: The Last Kiss
Prom Night 4: Deliver Us From
Evil
Psycho Girls
Rabid Grannies
The Slumber Party Massacre
Slumber Party Massacre 2
Slumber Party Massacre 3
Twilight Zone: The Movie

Patriotism & Paranoia

see also Propaganda

Amber Waves
Born on the Fourth of July➤
The Chase
The Commies are Coming, the
Commies are Coming
The Cosmic Man
Death of a Bureaucrat➤
Delta Force
Dress Gray➤
FX➤
Fellow Traveler➤
Firefox
First Blood
Guilty by Suspicion
Harry's War
Heroes for Sale➤
Ivan the Terrible, Part 1➤
Ivan the Terrible, Part 2➤
Keeper of the Flame
Missing in Action
Mom & Dad
Murrow
Nixon➤
Panama Patrol
Paris Belongs to Us
Patton➤
The Prisoner➤
Radar Patrol vs. Spy King
Rambo: First Blood, Part 2
Rambo 3
Red Dawn
The Red Menace
Red Nightmare
Reunion in France
The Sea Hawk➤
The Secret Four
Skinheads: The Second Coming
of Hate
Sky High
So Proudly We Hail➤
The Spider's Stratagem➤
Strictly G.I.
Taps
Thirty Seconds Over Tokyo➤
The 27 Day

Peace

The Day the Earth Stood Still➤
The Deserters

Destry Rides Again➤
Diplomaniacs
Firehead
Friendly Persuasion➤
Gandhi➤
Sadat
War and Peace
War and Peace➤

Peculiar Partners

see also Buddies; Buddy Cops; Cops

Alien Nation
Alien Nation: Dark Horizon
The Beautician and the Beast
Cop and a Half
Dead Heat
Dollman
The Glimmer Man
Gridlock'd➤
The Hard Way➤
The Hidden
The Hidden 2
Judge Dredd
K-9
Stop! or My Mom Will Shoot
Theodore Rex
Top Dog
Turner and Hooch

Period Piece

see also Historical Drama; Medieval Romps; Royalty

A la Mode
Abbott and Costello Meet the
Keystone Kops
Acla's Descent into Floristella
Adventures of Don Juan➤
The Adventures of Marco Polo
The Adventures of Mark Twain➤
The Advocate➤
The Age of Innocence➤
Al Capone➤
All the Brothers Were Valiant
All Things Fair
Allonsanfan➤
Alone Against Rome
Amadeus➤
American Friends
American Graffiti➤
An American Story
America's Dream➤
The Amorous Adventures of Moll
Flanders
Angels and Insects➤
Anna and the King of Siam➤
Anna Karenina
Anne of Avonlea➤
Anne of Green Gables➤
Anthony Adverse
The Assassination Bureau➤
Assault at West Point: The
Court-Martial of Johnson
Whittaker
At Sword's Point
August
The Avenging Angel
The Awful Dr. Orloff
The Babe
The Bachelor➤
Back Home
Back to Hannibal: The Return of
Tom Sawyer and Huckleberry
Finn
Backbeat➤
The Ballad of Little Jo
Balto
Band of Angels
The Barbary Coast
The Barretts of Wimpole Street➤
Barry Lyndon➤
Barton Fink➤
Batman: Mask of the Phantasm
Battle of Valiant
The Bay Boy
Beau Brummel

Beautiful Dreamers
Beauty and the Beast➤
Becoming Colette
Belizaire the Cajun
Belle Epoque➤
Belle of the Nineties
Ben-Hur➤
The Best Intentions➤
Beulah Land
Billy Bathgate
Bix
The Black Castle
Black Robe➤
The Black Velvet Gown
Blacksnake!
Blanche Fury
Bleak House
Blood Clan
Blood Red
The Blue Kite➤
Blue Sky➤
Bopha!➤
The Bostonians
Botany Bay
Boxcar Bertha
Bram Stoker's Dracula➤
Bramwell
Brenda Starr
The Bretts➤
The Bridges of Madison
County➤
Broadway Bound
The Broken Chain
Broken Glass
A Bronx Tale➤
Brother Cadfael
Brother Cadfael 2
Brother of Sleep➤
Brothers Lionheart
Brutal Glory
The Buccaneers➤
Buffalo Girls
Bugsy➤
Burnt by the Sun➤
By the Light of the Silvery Moon
By Way of the Stars
Bye Bye Blues
Calendar Girl
Call of the Wild
The Canterbury Tales
Captain Boycott
Carlito's Way➤
Carnival in Flanders➤
Carrington
Carthage in Flames
Cartouche➤
Casanova➤
Casanova's Big Night
Casino➤
Casque d'Or➤
The Castilian
Catherine the Great
Century
Cesare Borgia
The Charge of the Light
Brigade➤
The Charge of the Light Brigade
The Charmer
Cheaper by the Dozen➤
Cheech and Chong's The
Corsican Brothers
Chinatown➤
Chips, the War Dog
The Chosen➤
A Christmas Carol➤
A Christmas Carol
Christopher Columbus
Christy
The Cisco Kid
City Boy➤
The Clan of the Cave Bear
Cleopatra
Cobb➤
Cold Comfort Farm➤
Cold Sassy Tree➤
Colonel Chabert
Colonel Redl➤
Color of a Brisk and Leaping
Day

The Color of Pomegranates➤
Coming Through
Conduct Unbecoming
Confessing to Laura
The Conqueror Worm➤
Conquest➤
Conquest of Cochise
Corrina, Corrina
Country Life
Courage Mountain
The Covered Wagon
Crime of the Century
Crooklyn➤
Crossing the Bridge
The Crucible➤
Cry of the Banshee
Daens➤
Daisy Miller
Damn the Defiant➤
Dangerous Liaisons➤
A Dangerous Man: Lawrence
after Arabia➤
Dante's Inferno: Life of Dante
Gabriel Rossetti
Danton➤
A Dark Adapted Eye➤
The Dark Angel➤
Dark of the Sun
Daughters of the Dust➤
Dazed and Confused➤
Dead Beat
Dead Man
Dead Presidents
Decameron Nights
The Deceivers
December Bride
Deja Vu
Delta of Venus
The Deluge
Delusion
Delusions of Grandeur
Demons of the Mind
Desiree
Desperate Remedies
Devil in a Blue Dress➤
The Devils➤
Dillinger
Dillinger and Capone
Diner➤
The Disappearance of Aimee➤
Disraeli➤
Dr. Bethune➤
Doctor Zhivago➤
The Dollmaker
A Doll's House
A Doll's House➤
The Dolly Sisters
DuBarry Was a Lady
Duel of Champions
Duel of Hearts
The Dwelling Place
East of Elephant Rock
Edvard Munch
Effi Briest➤
Eight Men Out➤
1860
Eijanaika➤
El Cid➤
Ele, My Friend
The Elegant Criminal
The Elephant Man➤
Elizabeth of Ladymead➤
Elizabeth, the Queen
The Emigrants➤
Emma
Emma➤
Emma's Shadow➤
Empire of the Sun➤
Enchanted April
End of Desire
The Englishman Who Went Up a
Hill But Came Down a
Mountain➤
The Ernest Green Story
Ernesto
Ethan Frome
The Europeans➤
Every Day's a Holiday
Fabiola➤

The Fall of the Roman Empire➤
Fall Time
Family Prayers
Fanny and Alexander➤
Fanny Hill: Memoirs of a Woman
of Pleasure
Far and Away
Far from the Madding Crowd➤
The Far Pavilions
Farewell, My Lovely➤
Farinelli
The Farmer Takes a Wife
Fatherland
Feast of July
Fiddler on the Roof➤
The Field➤
The Fifteen Streets
55 Days at Peking➤
The Fighting Kentuckian
Fiorile➤
Fire and Sword
First Knight
The First Olympics: Athens 1896
F.I.S.T.
Five Corners➤
Five Weeks in a Balloon
The Fixer➤
Flambards
The Flame Is Love
The Flame Trees of Thika➤
Flight of the Eagle
Flowers of Reverie
Follow the River
Fools of Fortune
For a Lost Soldier
The Forbidden Quest
Forest of Little Bear
Forever Amber
Forget Mozart
Fort Saganne
Fortunes of War➤
The Four Feathers➤
The Four Feathers
The Four Musketeers➤
Francesco
The Franchise Affair
Frankenstein
Frankie and Johnny
Freedom Road
The French Lieutenant's
Woman➤
The Front Page
Fulfillment
The Funeral➤
A Funny Thing Happened on the
Way to the Forum➤
The Gambling Man
Gaslight➤
Gate of Hell➤
George Washington
George Washington: The
Forging of a Nation
Germinal➤
Geronimo➤
Geronimo: An American Legend
Gervaise➤
The Getting of Wisdom
Gettysburg➤
Ghost in the Noonday Sun
The Glass Virgin
Glory➤
The Go-Between➤
Go Tell It On the Mountain
Gold Diggers of 1933➤
Golden Gate
Good Evening, Mr. Wallenberg
Good Morning, Babylon➤
The Good Old Boys
Goodbye, Miss 4th of July
The Gorgeous Hussy
Gothic➤
Grand Isle
The Grass Harp
Great Expectations➤
Great Expectations
Great Expectations➤
Great Expectations: The Untold
Story
The Great Gatsby

Midnight Run►
Mob Story
More
The Muppet Movie►
The Music of Chance
My Fellow Americans
My Own Private Idaho►
National Lampoon's Vacation►
Natural Born Killers
Neon City
Never on Tuesday
Night on Earth►
No Place to Run
The Odyssey
omaha (the movie)
One Way Out
Out
Over the Hill
Paper Moon►
The Passing of Evil
Patti Rocks►
Pee Wee's Big Adventure►
Phat Beach
Pierrot le Fou►
Pink Cadillac
Planes, Trains & Automobiles
Pontiac Moon
Powwow Highway►
Prime Target
Prison Train
The Raffle
Rain Man►
The Rain People►
Rainbow Bridge
Reckless
The Reivers►
Rescue Me
Rich Hall's Vanishing America
Ride in the Whirlwind
Road Games
Road Kill USA
The Road Killers
The Road to Bali►
The Road to Galveston►
The Road to Hong Kong
The Road to Lebanon
The Road to Morocco►
The Road to Rio►
The Road to Singapore
The Road to Utopia►
The Road to Zanzibar►
The Road Warrior►
Roadie
Roadkill
Roadside Prophets
Rockin' Road Trip
Rough Magic
Round Trip to Heaven
Rubin & Ed
The Runaway Bus
Running Hot
Running Wild
The Saragossa Manuscript
Sawdust & Tinsel►
Scarecrow
September Gun
A Shadow You Soon Will Be
Sincerely Charlotte►
Six of a Kind►
Slither►
Something Wild
Sorcerer
Spies Like Us
Starlight Hotel
Starman►
Stay As You Are
Summer City
Sunchaser
The Sure Thing►
Thelma & Louise►
Those Magnificent Men in Their
    Flying Machines►
Three for the Road
Thumb Tripping
Tilt
To Wong Foo, Thanks for
    Everything, Julie Newmar
Tokyo Pop
Traveling Man

Trouble Bound
True Romance
Truth or Consequences, N.M.
Twentieth Century►
Two for the Road►
Until The End of The World►
Wagons East
The Way West
Wedding Bell Blues
Weekend►
Western
Where the Eagle Flies
White Line Fever
Wild America►
Wild at Heart►
The Wizard of Oz►
The Wrong Man

Roaring '20s

Bare Knees
Bullets Over Broadway►
The Cotton Club►
Eight Men Out►
The Great Gatsby
Hoodlum
The Jazz Singer
Jazzman►
Killer: A Journal of Murder
Mapp & Lucia
Mrs. Parker and the Vicious
    Circle
The Moderns►
The Quest
The Roaring Twenties►
Rosewood
Temptress Moon
Theremin: An Electronic
    Odyssey►
Thoroughly Modern Millie
Underworld►
The Untouchables►

Robots & Androids

see also Technology-
    Rampant
Alien►
Alien Chaser
Aliens►
American Cyborg: Steel Warrior
And You Thought Your Parents
    Were Weird!
Android
The Android Affair
A.P.E.X.
Assassin
The Astro-Zombies
Automatic
Bill & Ted's Bogus Journey
The Black Hole
Blade Runner►
Chopping Mall
Circuit Breaker
Circuitry Man
Class of 1999
Class of 1999 2: The Substitute
The Companion
The Creation of the Humanoids
Cyber-Tracker
Cyber-Tracker 2
Cyberzone
Cyborg
Cyborg 2
Cyborg 3: The Recycler
Cyborg Cop
Cyborg Soldier
Daleks—Invasion Earth 2150
    A.D.
D.A.R.Y.L.
The Day the Earth Stood Still►
Devil Girl from Mars
Digital Man
Dr. Goldfoot and the Bikini
    Machine
Doctor Satan's Robot
Doctor Who: An Unearthly Child
Doctor Who and the Daleks

Downdraft
Edward Scissorhands►
The Eliminators
The Empire Strikes Back►
Eve of Destruction
Evolver
The Fifth Element
Forbidden Planet►
Future Cop
Ghost in the Shell
Heatseeker
The Hitchhiker's Guide to the
    Galaxy
How to Make a Doll
The Human Duplicators
Humanoid Defender
The Invisible Boy
K-9000
Knights
Kronos
Light Years
Mac and Me
Mandroid
Megaville
Metropolis►
Mystery Science Theater 3000:
    The Movie
Nemesis
Nemesis 2: Nebula
Nemesis 3: Time Lapse
Night Siege Project:
    Shadowchaser 2
Not Quite Human
Not Quite Human 2
Omega Doom
Planet Busters
Planets Against Us
Plughead Rewired: Circuitry
    Man 2
Programmed to Kill
Project: Shadowchaser
Project Shadowchaser 3000
Prototype►
Prototype X29A
Return of the Jedi►
RoboCop►
RoboCop 2
RoboCop 3
RoboCop the Series: The Future
    of Law Enforcement
Roboman
Robot Holocaust
Robot in the Family
Robot Jox
Robot Monster
The Robot vs. the Aztec Mummy
Robot Wars
R.O.T.O.R.
Runaway
Running Delilah
Shadow Warriors
Short Circuit
Short Circuit 2
Silent Running►
Solo
Star Crash
Star Wars►
Starship
Steel and Lace
Still Not Quite Human
Suspect Device
T-Force
TC 2000
The Terminator►
Terminator 2: Judgment Day►
Terror of Mechagodzilla
Tobor the Great
The Vindicator
Voyage of the Rock Aliens
War of the Robots
Westworld►

Rock Stars on Film

see also Concert Films;
    Martyred Pop Icons; Pure
    Ego Vehicles
Absolute Beginners
All You Need Is Cash►

Backbeat►
Bill & Ted's Excellent Adventure
Blow-Up►
Blue Hawaii
The Bodyguard
Breaking Glass
The Bride
Carny►
Caveman
Charro!
Chuck Berry: Hail! Hail! Rock 'n'
    Roll►
Clambake
Coal Miner's Daughter►
The Crossing Guard►
Double Trouble
Dune
Easy Come, Easy Go
End of the Line
Flaming Star►
Follow That Dream
Frankie and Johnny
Freddy's Dead: The Final
    Nightmare
Fun in Acapulco
G.I. Blues
The Girl Can't Help It
Girl Happy
Girls! Girls! Girls!
Give My Regards to Broad
    Street
Go, Johnny Go!
A Hard Day's Night►
The Harder They Come
Harum Scarum
Head►
Heat►
Help!►
How I Won the War
The Hunger
It Happened at the World's Fair
Jailhouse Rock►
Johnny Mnemonic
Kid Galahad
King Creole
KISS Meets the Phantom of the
    Park
Kissin' Cousins
La Bamba►
The Last Temptation of Christ►
The Legacy
Let It Be
Lisztomania
Live a Little, Love a Little
Love Me Tender
Loving You
The Magic Christian►
Magical Mystery Tour
The Man Who Fell to Earth►
McVicar
Merry Christmas, Mr.
    Lawrence►
Mrs. Brown, You've Got a Lovely
    Daughter
Monster Dog
Nomads
One Trick Pony
Paradise, Hawaiian Style
Pat Garrett & Billy the Kid►
Performance►
Pink Floyd: The Wall
Poetic Justice
The Preacher's Wife
Quadrophenia►
Rock 'n' Roll High School►
Roustabout
Sgt. Pepper's Lonely Hearts
    Club Band
Speedway
Spinout
Stay Away, Joe
That'll Be the Day
This Is Elvis
Tickle Me
Tommy
Traveller►
The Trouble with Girls (and How
    To Get Into It)►
Under the Cherry Moon

Viva Las Vegas
Waiting to Exhale►
Wild in the Country
Woodstock►
Yellow Submarine►

Rodeos

see also Westerns
The Adventures of Gallant Bess
Arizona Cowboy
Born Reckless
Convict Cowboy
The Cowboy Way
Desert Trail
8 Seconds
Feud of the West
Girl from Calgary
Goldenrod
Junior Bonner►
Kid from Gower Gulch
Lady Takes a Chance►
The Last Ride
Lights of Old Santa Fe
The Lusty Men►
Luzia
Man from Utah
The Misfits►
My Heroes Have Always Been
    Cowboys
Never a Dull Moment
Oklahoma Cyclone
Painted Hero
Rhythm on the Range
Rider from Tucson
Rodeo Girl
Rolling Home
Ruby Jean and Joe
Saddle Buster
Stir Crazy
Trouble in Texas
Western Double Feature 5
Wild Horse
Wild Horse Rodeo

Role Reversal

see also Gender Bending;
    Identity
Age Isn't Everything
All of Me
Anastasia►
Anastasia: The Mystery of Anna
Angel
Angel on My Shoulder►
Angel on My Shoulder
Babe►
Bad Manners
The Bank Dick►
Before Morning
Belfast Assassin
Big►
Biggles
Billy Madison
Blood of Dracula
Bloodlink
The Captain from Koepenick
Captive Heart►
Cheech and Chong's The
    Corsican Brothers
Christmas in Connecticut►
Cinderfella
Clambake
Class Act
Cleo/Leo
Coming to America►
Condorman
The Couch Trip
Courage►
Dave►
The Deputy Drummer
Desperately Seeking Susan
Devil's Canyon
Dr. Black, Mr. Hyde
Doctor Detroit
Doctor Dolittle
Dr. Heckyl and Mr. Hype
Dr. Jekyll and Mr. Hyde►

Romantic

Romantic

Young Catherine ►

Running

Across the Tracks
Billie
Chariots of Fire ►
College ►
Finish Line
Forrest Gump ►
The Four Minute Mile
Go for the Gold
The Gold & Glory
Goldengirl ►
The Jericho Mile
The Jesse Owens Story
Jim Thorpe: All American
The Loneliest Runner
The Loneliness of the Long
    Distance Runner ►
Marathon
Marathon Man ►
Off the Mark
On the Edge
Prefontaine
Raw Courage
Run for the Dream: The Gail
    Devers Story
Running Brave
Sam's Son
See How She Runs ►
A Shining Season ►
The Sprinter
The Terry Fox Story ►

Russia/USSR

   see also Moscow; Red
            Scare
American Cop
Anastasia ►
Anastasia: The Mystery of Anna
Anna Karenina ►
Anna Karenina
Assassination of Trotsky
Back in the USSR
Balalaika
Baltic Deputy ►
The Battle of Russia
The Battleship Potemkin ►
The Brothers Karamazov ►
Burglar ►
Burnt by the Sun ►
Children of the Revolution
Citizen X ►
Come and See ►
Coming Out of the Ice ►
The Commies are Coming, the
    Commies are Coming
Commissar ►
Comrade X
Creation of Adam
Crimson Tide ►
Days of Glory
Dersu Uzala ►
Doctor Zhivago ►
Don't Drink the Water
Drums of Jeopardy
The Eagle ►
The End of St. Petersburg ►
The Extraordinary Adventures of
    Mr. West in the Land of the
    Bolsheviks
Final Assignment
Final Warning
First Strike
The Fixer ►
For Those About to Rock:
    Monsters in Moscow
Freeze-Die-Come to Life ►
The Girl from Petrovka
Goldeneye ►
Gorky Park ►
Gulag
The Hunt for Red October ►
I Killed Rasputin
The Ice Runner
The Inner Circle ►

Ivan the Terrible, Part 1 ►
Ivan the Terrible, Part 2 ►
Kindergarten ►
Laser Mission
Last Command ►
Leo Tolstoy's Anna Karenina
The Light Ahead
Little Vera ►
Love and Death ►
The Man with a Movie Camera ►
The Mirror ►
Moscow Does Not Believe in
    Tears ►
Mother ►
The Music Lovers
Mute Witness
My Family Treasure
My Name is Ivan ►
Never Let Me Go
Nicholas and Alexandra
Nostalgia ►
One Day in the Life of Ivan
    Denisovich ►
One Russian Summer
Peter the Great ►
Prisoner of the Mountains ►
Rasputin ►
Rasputin and the Empress ►
Rasputin the Mad Monk
The Red and the White ►
Red Heat
Red Hot
Reds ►
The Road to Life
The Russia House
Russian Roulette
The Saint
Sakharov ►
Scarlet Dawn
Scarlet Empress ►
The Seagull ►
Siberiade ►
Sideburns
A Slave of Love ►
Solo Voyage: The Revenge
Stalin
Stalingrad
Taxi Blues ►
Terminal Velocity
Theremin: An Electronic
    Odyssey ►
The Three Sisters
The Ultimate Imposter
War and Peace
War and Peace ►
We the Living
White Nights
Window to Paris
World War III
Young Catherine ►

Sail Away

   see also Deep Blue; Go
   Fish; Mutiny; Scuba; Sea
         Critter Attack;
   Shipwrecked; Submarines
Abandon Ship
Adrift
Adventure Island
The Adventures of Huckleberry
    Finn ►
An Affair to Remember
The African Queen ►
All the Brothers Were Valiant
And the Ship Sails On ►
Anna Christie
Annapolis
Assault on a Queen
Away All Boats
The Baby and the Battleship
The Battleship Potemkin ►
Beat the Devil ►
Beyond the Poseidon Adventure
The Big Broadcast of 1938
The Big Broadcast of 1938
Billy Budd ►
Bitter Moon

Blood Voyage
The Boatniks
Botany Bay
The Bounty ►
Boy in Blue
Cabin Boy
The Caine Mutiny ►
The Caine Mutiny Court Martial ►
Captain Caution
Captain Horatio Hornblower ►
Captain Ron
Captains Courageous ►
Captains Courageous
Captain's Paradise ►
The Captain's Table
Carry On Admiral
Carry On Cruising
China Seas ►
Christopher Columbus
The Coast Patrol
Convoy
A Countess from Hong Kong
The Crew
Crimson Tide ►
Cruise into Terror
Damn the Defiant ►
Dangerous Charter
Dangerous Passage
Dark Tide
Das Boot ►
Day of the Assassin
The Day Will Dawn ►
Dead Ahead: The Exxon Valdez
    Disaster ►
Dead Calm ►
Dead Reckoning
Dead Tides
Deadly Voyage
Death Cruise
Death Ship
Death Tide
The Deep
Destroyer ►
Die Hard: With a Vengeance
Disney's Storybook Classics
Dixie Jamboree
Doctor at Sea
Don Winslow of the Coast Guard
The Dove
Down Periscope
Down to the Sea in Ships
Ensign Pulver
Erik, the Viking
The Evil Below
Far from Home: The Adventures
    of Yellow Dog
Feet First
Ferry to Hong Kong
The Fighting Sullivans ►
The Final Countdown ►
Flat Top
Flight of the Intruder
Flipper ►
Francis in the Navy
Friday the 13th, Part 8: Jason
    Takes Manhattan
Gangway
Geheimakte WB1
Ghost Ship
The Gift Horse
A Girl in Every Port
Give Me a Sailor
Going Overboard
Going Under
Golden Rendezvous
Goliath Awaits
Gone Fishin'
Gray Lady Down
The Great Lover
Gun Cargo
The Hairy Ape
Haunted Harbor
Hawaii Calls
He is My Brother
Hell-Ship Morgan
History is Made at Night ►
Horror of the Zombies
The Hunt for Red October ►
I Conquer the Sea

In Which We Serve ►
The Incredible Mr. Limpet
The Incredible Petrified World
Ironclads
Isle of Forgotten Sins
JAG
Jaws ►
Jaws 2
The Jewel of the Nile
John Paul Jones
Juggernaut ►
Kill Cruise
Killer on Board
King Kelly of the U.S.A.
Knife in the Water ►
The Last of Sheila
The Last Voyage
Law of the Sea
Le Crabe Tambour ►
The Legend of Sea Wolf
The Legend of the Sea Wolf
Lifeboat ►
Light at the Edge of the World
The Lightship
Live and Let Die
Loch Ness
Long John Silver
The Long Ships
The Long Voyage Home ►
Lord Jim ►
Love Affair ►
The Magic Stone
A Majority of One
Manfish
The Mermaids of Tiburon
Mister Roberts ►
Monkey Business ►
Moon in Scorpio
Moran of the Lady Letty
Muppet Treasure Island
Murder on the High Seas
Mutiny
The Mutiny of the Elsinore
Mutiny on the Bounty ►
Mutiny on the Bounty
Mystery Liner
The Mystery of the Mary Celeste
The Navigator ►
The Navy Comes Through
New Moon
A Night to Remember ►
The Odyssey
Old Ironsides ►
Operation Petticoat ►
Out to Sea
Oxford Blues
Passenger ►
Pirate Ship
The Port of Missing Girls
The Poseidon Adventure
The Princess Comes Across ►
PT 109
Pueblo Affair ►
Pursuit of the Graf Spee
Rainbow Warrior
Reaching for the Moon
Reap the Wild Wind
Rich and Strange
Roaring Speedboats
Romancing the Stone ►
Run Silent, Run Deep ►
The Sand Pebbles ►
Save the Lady
Sea Chase
Sea Devils
Sea Racketeers
The Sea Wolf ►
The Sea Wolf
Sharks' Treasure
She Shall Have Music
Ship Ahoy
Ship of Fools ►
Ships in the Night
Shout at the Devil
Sinbad, the Sailor ►
Sink the Bismarck ►
Souls at Sea
South Seas Massacre
Speed 2: Cruise Control

Steamboat Bill, Jr. ►
Submarine Seahawk
Swashbuckler
Tamango
Task Force
Temptation
Tentacles of the North
They Were Expendable ►
Three Daring Daughters
Thunder in Paradise
Till There was You
Titanic ►
Titanic
To Gillian on Her 37th Birthday
To Have & Have Not ►
Today We Live
Torpedo Run
Transatlantic Merry-Go-Round
Treacherous Crossing
The Treasure of Jamaica Reef
U-Boat Prisoner
Under Siege
The Unsinkable Molly Brown ►
Up the Creek
Voyage
Voyage of Terror: The Achille
    Lauro Affair
Voyage of the Damned ►
Wake of the Red Witch
Waterworld
We're Not Dressing ►
White Squall
Wild Orchids
Wind
Windjammer
Windrider
Witch Who Came from the Sea
Woman of Desire
Wonderland Cove
The World in His Arms
The Wreck of the Mary Deare
Yankee Clipper

Saints

   see also Religion
Augustine of Hippo ►
Bernadette
Brother Sun, Sister Moon
The Flowers of St. Francis ►
Francesco
Joan of Arc
The Messenger of the Blessed
    Virgin
Miracle in Rome
Miracle of Our Lady of Fatima
The Passion of Joan of Arc ►
The Proprietor
Saint Joan
Sebastiane ►
The Song of Bernadette ►
Therese ►
A Time for Miracles

Salespeople

   see also Corporate
          Shenanigans
Adventures in Babysitting
Cadillac Man
Death of a Salesman ►
The Fan
Glengarry Glen Ross ►
Jingle All the Way
Miss Rose White ►
The Music Man ►
Pennies From Heaven ►
The Rainmaker ►
Tin Men

The Salvation Army

Guys and Dolls ►
Major Barbara ►

Science & Scientists

*see also Genetics;
Inventors & Inventions;
Mad Scientists*

Dream Man
Georgia►
The Hitman
It Happened at the World's Fair
Little Buddha
My Own Private Idaho►
Singles►
Sleepless in Seattle►
The Slender Thread►
Stakeout
Streetwise►

Serial Killers

**see also Crime &
Criminals; Crime Sprees**
Addams Family Values
Ambition
American Strays
Amsterdamned
Angel Dust
Aroused
The Awful Dr. Orloff
The Baby Doll Murders
Band of Gold►
The Banker
Blackwater Trail
Blondes Have More Guns
Bloodhounds 2
Bluebeard►
Body Parts
The Boston Strangler
Breaking Point
Broken Mirrors
Bums
Butterfly Kiss
The China Lake Murders
Citizen X►
Cold Front
Cold Light of Day
Con Air►
Confessions of a Serial Killer
Cop
Copycat
Cosh Boy
Crimetime
Curdled
Cyberstalker
Dancing with Danger
Dangerous Love
The Dark Ride
Dead Certain
Dead Girls
Dead on Sight
Dead to Rights
Deadly Force
Deadly Games
Deadly Neighbor
The Deliberate Stranger►
A Demon in My View
Desire
Destroyer
Dirty Harry►
The Element of Crime
Evil Laugh
Evil Obsession
Exorcist 3: Legion
Eyes of a Stranger
Eyes of Laura Mars
Eyes of the Beholder
Fatal Charm
Fathers and Sons
Fear
Final Notice
The First Power
Freeway
The Freeway Maniac
The Frighteners
Ghost in the Machine
The Glimmer Man
The Hawk
Henry: Portrait of a Serial Killer►
Henry: Portrait of a Serial Killer
2: Mask of Sanity
Hidden Obsession
Hideaway
The Hillside Strangler
Honeymoon Killers►
The Horror Show

The Hunt for the Night Stalker
I Can't Sleep
Impulse
In the Deep Woods
Inn on the River
The Invisible Strangler
Jack the Ripper
Jack the Ripper►
The January Man
Jennifer 8
Kalifornia
L.A. Crackdown 2
Lady in Waiting
Laser Moon
The Laughing Policeman
The Limbic Region
Listen
Love and Human Remains►
M►
The Mad Executioners
Man Bites Dog
Maniac Cop
A Mind to Kill
Mr. Frost
Mixed Nuts
The Monster
Mortal Sins
Natural Born Killers
Nature of the Beast
Never Talk to Strangers
Night Shadow
Night Stalker
Nightscare
No Way to Treat a Lady►
The Paint Job
Pale Blood
Portraits of a Killer
Power 98
Prey of the Chameleon
Prime Suspect►
Prime Suspect: The Scent of
Darkness►
Probable Cause
Profile for Murder
Psychic
The Rain Killer
Relentless 3
Relentless 4
The Rosary Murders
The Satan Killer
Scream►
Serial Killer
Serial Mom►
Seven►
The Silence of the Lambs►
Slaughter of the Innocents
Sleepstalker: The Sandman's
Last Rites
Snapdragon
So I Married an Axe Murderer
Split Second
Stagefright
Stamp of a Killer
Star Time
Still Life
Stranger by Night
Strangler of Blackmoor Castle
Striking Distance
Tails You Live, Heads You're
Dead
10 Rillington Place►
Ten to Midnight
Terror at London Bridge
To Catch a Killer►
True Crime
Tunnel Vision
Turbulence
Undefeatable
When the Bough Breaks
While the City Sleeps►
Without Warning
Writer's Block
Zipperface

Serials

Ace Drummond

The Adventures of Captain
Marvel
The Adventures of Frank and
Jesse James
Adventures of Red Ryder
The Adventures of Rex & Rinty
Adventures of Smilin' Jack
The Adventures of Tarzan
The Adventures of the Flying
Cadets
The Adventures of the Masked
Phantom
Amazing Stories
Atom Man vs. Superman
Battling with Buffalo Bill
The Black Coin
The Black Widow
Blake of Scotland Yard
Bugs Bunny Superstar
Burn 'Em Up Barnes
Canadian Mounties vs. Atomic
Invaders
Captain America
Casey Jones and Fury (Brave
Stallion)
Cheyenne Rides Again
The Clutching Hand
Custer's Last Stand
Cyclotrode "X"
D-Day on Mars
Daredevils of the Red Circle
Darkest Africa
Daughter of Don Q
Destination Saturn
Devil Horse
Dick Tracy
Dick Tracy Returns
Dick Tracy: The Original Serial,
Vol. 1►
Dick Tracy: The Original Serial,
Vol. 2►
Dick Tracy vs. Crime Inc.
Doctor Satan's Robot
Don Daredevil Rides Again
Don Winslow of the Coast Guard
Don Winslow of the Navy
Drums of Fu Manchu►
East Side Kids/The Lost City
Federal Agents vs. Underworld,
Inc.
Federal Operator 99
Fighting Devil Dogs
Fighting Marines
Fighting with Kit Carson
Flaming Frontiers
Flash Gordon Conquers the
Universe
Flash Gordon: Mars Attacks the
World
Flash Gordon: Vol. 1
G-Men Never Forget
G-Men vs. the Black Dragon
The Galloping Ghost
Genie of Darkness
Government Agents vs.
Phantom Legion
Green Archer
The Green Hornet
Haunted Harbor
Hawk of the Wilderness
Heroes of the West
Holt of the Secret Service
Hurricane Express
In Old New Mexico
The Invisible Monster
Jesse James Rides Again
Jungle Drums of Africa
Junior G-Men
Junior G-Men of the Air
King of the Congo
King of the Forest Rangers
King of the Kongo
King of the Rocketmen
King of the Texas Rangers
Last Frontier
The Last of the Mohicans
Law of the Wild
A Lawman Is Born►
Lightning Warrior

The Lone Defender
The Lone Ranger
Lone Ranger
The Lost City
Lost City of the Jungle
The Lost Jungle
Lost Planet Airmen
Manhunt in the African Jungle
Manhunt of Mystery Island
Mansfield Park
The Masked Marvel
Master Key
Masters of Venus
The Miracle Rider
Mission: Monte Carlo
The Monster Demolisher
Mysterious Doctor Satan
Mystery Mountain
Mystery of the Riverboat
Mystery Squadron
Mystery Trooper
The New Adventures of Tarzan
Nyoka and the Tigermen
Oregon Trail
The Original Flash Gordon
Collection
Overland Mail
The Painted Stallion
The Perils of Pauline
Perils of the Darkest Jungle
The Phantom Creeps
The Phantom Empire
Phantom of the Air
Phantom of the West
The Phantom Rider
Pirates of the High Seas
The Purple Monster Strikes
Queen of the Jungle
Radar Men from the Moon
Radar Patrol vs. Spy King
Radio Patrol
Raiders of Ghost City
Red Barry
Return of Chandu
Riders of Death Valley
Robinson Crusoe of Clipper
Island
Robinson Crusoe of Mystery
Island
Rustlers of Red Dog
Saturday Night Serials
Savage Fury
Sea Hound
The Secret Code
Shadow of Chinatown
Shadow of the Eagle
Son of Zorro
S.O.S. Coast Guard
Space Soldiers Conquer the
Universe
Spy Smasher
Spy Smasher Returns
Stone Cold Dead
Sunset on the Desert
Superman: The Serial, Vol. 1
Tailspin Tommy
Tarzan the Tiger
Texas to Bataan
The Three Musketeers
Tim Tyler's Luck
Tom Mix Compilation 1
Tom Mix Compilation 2
Trader Tom of the China Seas
Trail of the Silver Spurs
Trail Riders
Tumbledown Ranch in Arizona
Undersea Kingdom
Vanishing Legion
The Vigilantes are Coming
Whispering Shadow
Winners of the West
Wolf Dog
Woman in Grey
Zombies of the Stratosphere
Zorro Rides Again
Zorro's Black Whip
Zorro's Fighting Legion

Sex & Sexuality

**see also Crimes of
Passion; Erotic Thrillers;
Pornography; Sex on the
Beach; Sexploitation**
ABC's of Love & Sex, Australia
Style
Accident
Acting on Impulse
The Adjuster
The Adultress
Adventures of a Private Eye
Adventures of a Taxi Driver
The Adventures of Sadie
The Advocate►
Alfie►
All Things Fair
The Allnighter
Almost Pregnant
Alpine Fire
Alvin Purple
Alvin Rides Again
The Amazing Transplant
American Gigolo
The Amorous Adventures of Mo
Flanders
The Amy Fisher Story
And God Created Woman
Andy Warhol's Dracula►
Andy Warhol's Frankenstein
Angel Heart
Angel of H.E.A.T.
Angels and Insects►
Animal Instincts
Animal Instincts 2
Animal Instincts 3: The
Seductress
Any Wednesday
The Apartment►
Armistead Maupin's Tales of the
City
The Arousers
Arrivederci, Baby!
Art for Teachers of Children
Assault
Baby Doll►
The Baby Doll Murders
Baby Face
Baby Love
The Baby Maker
The Bachelor►
Bachelor in Paradise
Bachelor Party
Bad Company
Bad Girls from Mars
Bad Lieutenant►
Bank Robber
Barbarella
Basic Training
Baton Rouge
The Bawdy Adventures of Tom
Jones
Beach Girls
Becoming Colette
Bedroom Eyes
Bedroom Eyes 2
Before Sunrise
Being at Home with Claude
Belle de Jour►
Belle Epoque►
Belle of the Nineties
Beneath the Valley of the Ultra-
Vixens
The Best Little Whorehouse in
Texas
Betrayal
Betty Blue►
Beverly Hills Madam
Beyond Erotica
Beyond the Silhouette
The Big Bet
The Big Dis
Bilitis
The Bitch
Bitter Harvest
Bitter Moon
Bitter Rice►
The Black Room

Sexual Abuse

Sexual Harrassment

Ships

Shipwrecked

Showbiz Comedies

Showbiz Dramas

Showbiz Musicals

Showbiz Thrillers

Silent Horror/ Fantasy Classics

see also Silent Films

Single Parents

see also Bringing Up Baby; Parenthood

Singles

see also Dates From Hell

Sports

see Baseball; Basketball; Bicycling; Boxing; Football; Golf; Hockey; The Olympics; Running; Scuba; Skating; Skiing; Skydiving; Soccer; Sports Comedies; Sports Dramas; Surfing; Swimming; Tennis; Volleyball

Sports Comedies

Sports

Little Big League
Little Giants
The Longest Yard
The Longshot
Major League
Major League 2
The Man with the Perfect Swing
The Mighty Ducks
Mr. Baseball
Monty Python's The Meaning of Life⋗
Necessary Roughness
North Dallas Forty⋗
Off the Mark
The One and Only
One-Punch O'Day
Paper Lion
Pat and Mike⋗
Prehysteria 3
Prize Fighter
Rookie of the Year
The St. Tammany Miracle
The Sandlot⋗
The Scout
Semi-Tough
The Sixth Man
Ski School
Slam Dunk Ernest
Slap Shot⋗
Space Jam
Splitz
Spring Fever
Squeeze Play
Sunset Park
Swim Team
Tin Cup⋗
Trading Hearts
White Men Can't Jump
Wildcats
The World's Greatest Athlete

Sports Dramas

Above the Rim
Airborne
Alex
All the Right Moves
American Anthem
American Flyers
American Kickboxer 1
Babe!⋗
The Babe
Babe Ruth Story
Bang the Drum Slowly
Bang the Drum Slowly⋗
The Big Blue
Big Mo
Billyboy
Blades of Courage
Blue Chips
Body and Soul⋗
Body & Soul
Boy in Blue
The Break
Breaking Away⋗
Breaking Free
Brian's Song⋗
Brutal Glory
Challenge of a Lifetime
Champion⋗
Champions
Chariots of Fire⋗
Chasing Dreams
The Club⋗
Coach
Cobb⋗
The Color of Money⋗
Crossbar
The Cutting Edge
Dawn!
Days of Thunder
Dempsey
Diving In
Don't Look Back: The Story of Leroy "Satchel" Paige
Downhill Racer
Dream to Believe
Dreamer
Dynamite Dan

Eight Men Out⋗
8 Seconds
The Fan
Fat City⋗
Field of Dreams⋗
Fight for the Title
Final Shot: The Hank Gathers Story
Finish Line
The First Olympics: Athens 1896
The Four Minute Mile
Gentleman Jim⋗
Gladiator
Go for the Gold
Going for the Gold: The Bill Johnson Story
The Gold & Glory
Goldengirl
Grambling's White Tiger
Heart Like a Wheel
Heaven is a Playground
The Hero
Hockey Night
Honeyboy
Hoosiers⋗
Hot Shot
The Hustler⋗
Ice Castles
Ice Pawn
International Velvet
The Jericho Mile
The Jesse Owens Story
Jim Thorpe: All American
The Joe Louis Story
Kid Galahad⋗
Knute Rockne: All American⋗
The Last American Hero⋗
The Last Fight
Last Time Out
The Loneliest Runner
Long Gone
Marciano
A Matter of Honor
Miracle on Ice
My Champion
Nadia
The Natural⋗
On the Edge
One in a Million: The Ron LeFlore Story
One Last Run
One on One
Over the Top
Paperback Hero
Pastime⋗
Personal Best⋗
Pistol: The Birth of a Legend
Players
Prefontaine
Pride of St. Louis
The Pride of the Yankees⋗
The Program
Pulsebeat
Raging Bull⋗
Rebound: The Legend of Earl "The Goat" Manigault
Red Line 7000
Red Surf
Requiem for a Heavyweight⋗
Rocky⋗
Rocky 2
Rocky 3
Rocky 4
Rocky 5
Rudy
Run for the Dream: The Gail Devers Story
Running Brave
Side Out
Skier's Dream
Soul of the Game⋗
The Spirit of West Point
The Stratton Story⋗
Talent for the Game
That Championship Season
This Sporting Life⋗
Tiger Town
Touch and Go
21 Hours at Munich⋗

Victory
Vision Quest
Wilma
Wind
A Winner Never Quits
The Winning Team
Youngblood

Spousal Abuse

see also Sexual Abuse

The Burning Bed⋗
Dangerous Game
Falling Down
Far Cry from Home
Independence Day
Intimate Strangers
Mesmerized
Mortal Thoughts
Nil by Mouth
Olivia
Remember Me
Shattered Dreams
Sleeping with the Enemy
This Boy's Life⋗
What's Love Got to Do with It?
Woman Undone
Woman With a Past

Stagestruck

see also Showbiz Comedies;
Showbiz Dramas; Showbiz
Thrillers

All About Eve⋗
Broadway Danny Rose⋗
Broadway Limited
Broadway Melody
Broadway Rhythm
Bullets Over Broadway⋗
The Dolly Sisters
Fame⋗
Gypsy⋗
Gypsy
Let's Make Love
A Midwinter's Tale
Morning Glory
Stage Door⋗
Stage Struck
Stagefright
Tea for Two⋗

Stalked!

see also Horror; Obsessive
Love

Addicted to Love
Backwoods
Breach of Conduct
The Cable Guy
Copycat
Dying Game
Evil Obsession
The Fan
Fatal Attraction⋗
A Kiss Goodnight
Mr. Wrong
Number One Fan
The Seduction
Stalking Laura
Taxi Driver⋗
Twilight Man

Star Gazing

The Arrival
Eliza's Horoscope
The Fish that Saved Pittsburgh
How Come Nobody's On Our Side?
Lamp at Midnight
Local Hero⋗

Stepparents

see also Family Ties;
Parenthood

The Adventures of Rusty
Big Girls Don't Cry...They Get Even
Cinderella⋗
Cinderella
Electra
Ellie
Everyone Says I Love You⋗
Fear
Hard Frame
Lassie
Lost
Night of the Twisters
The Orphan
Out on a Limb
Private Passions
Rivals
The Stepfather⋗
Stepfather 2: Make Room for Daddy
Stepfather 3: Father's Day
The Stepmother
A Summer to Remember⋗
This Boy's Life⋗

Stewardesses

see also Airborne

Airplane!⋗
Blazing Stewardesses
Boeing Boeing
Executive Decision
Passenger 57
Stewardess School
Three Guys Named Mike
Turbulence

Stolen from Asia

A Fistful of Dollars⋗
Last Man Standing
The Magnificent Seven⋗
Reservoir Dogs⋗
Star Wars⋗

Stolen from Europe

Kiss Me Goodbye
Last House on the Left
Scent of a Woman⋗
The Vanishing
A Walk in the Clouds

Stolen from France

The Associate
The Birdcage⋗
Blame It on Rio
Breathless
Buddy Buddy
Cousins⋗
Diabolique
Down and Out in Beverly Hills
Father's Day
Happy New Year
Jungle 2 Jungle
The Man Who Loved Women
The Man with One Red Shoe
Men Don't Leave
The Mirror Has Two Faces
Mixed Nuts
My Father the Hero
Nine Months
Paradise⋗
Point of No Return
Pure Luck
Quick Change
Scenes from the Class Struggle in Beverly Hills
Sommersby
Sorcerer
Three Fugitives
Three Men and a Baby⋗
The Toy

12 Monkeys⋗
The Woman in Red

Storytelling

Babyfever
The Company of Wolves⋗
Grim Prairie Tales
Monster in a Box⋗
My Dinner with Andre⋗
The Neverending Story 3: escape from Fantasia
Paper Tiger
The Princess Bride⋗
The Story Lady
The Willies
Windwalker⋗

Strained Suburbia

see also Yuppie Nightmares

Adventures in Spying
The Amityville Horror
Amongst Friends
Amos and Andrew
Beavis and Butt-Head Do America
Blue Velvet⋗
The Brady Bunch Movie⋗
The 'Burbs
Clown House
Coneheads
Consenting Adults
The Crude Oasis
Deadly Neighbor
Dennis the Menace
Desperate Hours⋗
Desperate Hours
Don't Talk to Strangers
Don't Tell Mom the Babysitter's Dead
Edward Scissorhands⋗
Faithful
The Graduate⋗
Grand Canyon⋗
The Grass is Always Greener Over the Septic Tank
Hocus Pocus
Home Alone⋗
House⋗
How to Beat the High Cost of Living
Hush Little Baby, Don't You Cry
I Love My...Wife
Jaws⋗
Jaws 2
Madhouse
Marked for Death
The Meal
Mr. Blandings Builds His Dream House⋗
The Money Pit
My Blue Heaven
My New Gun
Neighbors
1941
Opportunity Knocks
The Osterman Weekend
Over the Edge⋗
Parents⋗
The People Next Door
Please Don't Eat the Daisies
The Positively True Adventures of the Alleged Texas Cheerleader-Murdering Mom⋗
Return of the Living Dead 2
Revenge of the Stepford Wives
Serial Mom⋗
Shattered Spirits
Short Cuts⋗
The Stranger⋗
The Swimmer⋗
Terrorvision
Three Wishes
The Trigger Effect
Twice in a Lifetime⋗
The Underworld Story

Tattoos

Down Periscope
Escape from L.A.
Foxfire
The Illustrated Man▸
Lust in the Dust▸
The Night of the Hunter▸
Son-in-Law
Tattoo
Teresa's Tattoo
Waterworld
The Yakuza

Team Efforts

The Alamo▸
The Bad News Bears Go to Japan
The Bad News Bears in Breaking Training
Breaking Away▸
The Club▸
Coach
Codename: Foxfire
Codename: Wildgeese
Crossfire
The Cutting Edge
The Dirty Dozen▸
The Dirty Dozen: The Deadly Mission
The Dirty Dozen: The Fatal Mission
The Dirty Dozen: The Next Mission
Dirty Hands
The Doll Squad
D3: The Mighty Ducks
D2: The Mighty Ducks
Eddie
Finger on the Trigger
Force Five
Force 10 from Navarone
The Guns of Navarone▸
Hoosiers▸
Kill and Kill Again
Ladybugs
Let's Get Harry
The Losers
The Magnificent Seven▸
Memphis Belle▸
The Mighty Ducks
Miracle on Ice
Necessary Roughness
Race the Sun
Renaissance Man
Seven Magnificent Gladiators
Seven Samurai▸
Silverado▸
The Sixth Man
Soldier Boyz
Space Jam
Steel
Sunset Park
That Thing You Do!▸
Three the Hard Way
Twister
Uncommon Valor
The Untouchables▸
Victory
White Squall
Wild Geese
Wild Geese 2
Wind

Tearjerkers

Acorn People
An Affair to Remember
After the Promise
All Dogs Go to Heaven
All Fall Down
All Mine to Give
Another Time, Another Place
Baby Face
Back Street
Balboa
Ballad in Blue
Bang the Drum Slowly
Bang the Drum Slowly▸

Beaches▸
Big Bluff
Bittersweet Love
Black Eyes
Blind Spot
Blood of Jesus
Blossoms in the Dust
Bonjour Tristesse▸
Bouquet of Barbed Wire
Breaking the Rules
Brian's Song▸
The Cabin in the Cotton
Camille
Carrie▸
Carry On Cruising
Cast the First Stone
The Champ▸
The Champ
Chantilly Lace
The Cheat▸
Chinatown After Dark
Choices
Christmas Comes to Willow Creek
City That Never Sleeps
City Without Men
Claudia
Coquette
The Country Kid▸
The Courtney Affair
Craig's Wife▸
Crawlspace
Curly Sue
Dance Fools Dance▸
Dead Wrong
Death Be Not Proud▸
Dedee d'Anvers
Delinquent Parents
A Different Kind of Love
A Dog of Flanders
Dog Pound Shuffle▸
An Early Frost▸
Easy Sue
The Eddy Duchin Story
Eric▸
Escape Me Never
The Evening Star
Fine Things
Fire Down Below
Flamingo Road▸
The Forbidden City
Fortune's Fool
Found Alive
Fourth Wish
Free Willy
Fulfillment
Gangs, Inc.
The Garden of Allah▸
The Gathering
The Gathering: Part 2
Ghost▸
Girl from Chicago
The Girl Who Had Everything
Goodbye, Mr. Chips▸
Goodbye, My Lady
Great Day
The Greatest Question
Griffin and Phoenix: A Love Story
Harlow
Hearts of Humanity
Heaven and Earth
Heaven's a Drag
Hell-Ship Morgan
Her Silent Sacrifice
High Gear
A Home of Our Own
Honky Tonk▸
Hot Spell
Human Desire
Human Hearts
I Conquer the Sea
I Sent a Letter to My Love▸
Ice Castles
If Ever I See You Again
In This Our Life
Inside Daisy Clover
Intermezzo▸
Jack the Bear

Johnny Belinda▸
Johnny Belinda
Johnny Eager▸
Journey for Margaret▸
Keep Punching
The Kid with the Broken Halo
La Bete Humaine▸
La Chienne▸
Lady Caroline Lamb
The Lady Without Camelias
The Last Best Year
Le Jour Se Leve▸
Legends of the Fall
Leopard in the Snow
Leper
Letter from an Unknown Woman▸
The Little Match Girl
The Little Princess▸
A Little Princess▸
Look Who's Talking Now
Love Affair▸
Love Affair
Love Affair: The Eleanor & Lou Gehrig Story▸
Love Butcher
The Love Flower
Love Has Many Faces
Love in the Present Tense
Love Songs
Love Story▸
Lovers of Their Time
Loving
Lure of the Sila
Madame Butterfly
Madame X
Magnificent Obsession
Man of Evil
The Manxman
Marvin's Room
Matters of the Heart
Mayerling
Mildred Pierce▸
Miles to Go
Millie
Mimi
The Miniver Story
Miss Julie
Mrs. Silly
Mr. Holland's Opus▸
Mr. Skeffington▸
Mistress
Moment in Time
Moon over Harlem
A Mormon Maid
Mother and Son
Murder on Lenox Avenue
The Nest
The Night Cry
Night Life in Reno
Nomads of the North
Now, Voyager▸
Old Yeller▸
Only Angels Have Wings▸
An Orphan Boy of Vienna
The Other Side of the Mountain▸
The Other Side of the Mountain, Part 2
Our Sons
Our Time
Paradise Road
The Passing of the Third Floor Back
Pattes Blanches
Peg O' My Heart
Penny Serenade▸
A Place in the Sun▸
The Pride of the Yankees▸
The Promise
Question of Faith
A Question of Guilt
Quicksand
The Racket▸
Rage of Angels
The Rains Came
Random Harvest▸
Rebecca of Sunnybrook Farm
Red Kimono
Remolina de Pasiones

Rikisha-Man▸
The Road to Ruin
Romola
Scar of Shame
Secrets of a Married Man
Seizure: The Story of Kathy Morris
Sex
Shadowlands▸
She Goes to War
A Shining Season▸
The Shock
Shopworn Angel▸
Silent Night, Lonely Night
The Sin of Madelon Claudet▸
Since You Went Away▸
Six Weeks
Smilin' Through▸
Sommersby
Sooner or Later
Sparrows▸
Steel Magnolias▸
Stella
Stella Dallas▸
Stella Maris▸
Stolen Hours
The Story of Esther Costello
Strangers: The Story of a Mother and Daughter▸
Stromboli
Struggle
Suds
Summer and Smoke
A Summer Place
Sunny
Sunny Skies
Susan Lenox: Her Fall and Rise
Tango
Tell Me That You Love Me
Tender Comrade
Terms of Endearment▸
Test Tube Babies
That Certain Woman
They Drive by Night▸
Things in Their Season
This Boy's Life▸
Three Secrets
Thursday's Child
Tiefland
A Time to Live
To Gillian on Her 37th Birthday
Tomorrow's Children
The Tong Man
Torch Song
Toute Une Nuit▸
Traffic in Souls▸
Trapped by the Mormons
Under the Roofs of Paris▸
The Underdog
The Unholy Three▸
Untamed Heart
Uptown New York
Walk on the Wild Side
Walpurgis Night▸
Waterfront
Waterloo Bridge▸
Way Down East▸
The Weaker Sex
Welcome Home
West-Bound Limited
West of Zanzibar
When Wolves Cry
Where East Is East
Where the Red Fern Grows
The White Cliffs of Dover▸
The White Rose▸
Wide Sargasso Sea
Winter Meeting
Without a Trace
A Woman of Affairs
The World Accuses
The World is Full of Married Men
The World Owes Me a Living
Written on the Wind▸
X, Y & Zee
The Yearling▸

Technology-Rampant

see also Computers; Killer Appliances; Robots & Androids

A Nous la Liberte▸
The Android Affair
Armageddon: The Final Challenge
Assassin
Attack of the Killer Refrigerator
Attack of the Robots
Baby Girl Scott
Back to the Future▸
Batman Forever▸
Best Defense
The Bionic Woman
Black Cobra 3: The Manila Connection
The Black Hole
Blade Runner▸
Blades
Bloodlust
Brainscan
Chandu the Magician
Charly▸
Chopping Mall
Circuitry Man
Colossus: The Forbin Project▸
The Companion
Computer Beach Party
Computer Wizard
The Corporation
Crash and Burn
The Creation of the Humanoids
Cyber Bandits
Cyber-Tracker 2
Death Ray 2000
Defense Play
Demon Seed▸
Denise Calls Up
Detonator 2: Night Watch
Diamonds Are Forever▸
Digital Man
Dr. Goldfoot and the Bikini Machine
Downdraft
Dungeonmaster
Duplicates
Electric Dreams
The Eliminators
Eve of Destruction
Evolver
Fail-Safe▸
Fair Game
Family Viewing▸
The Fifth Element
Final Mission
The Final Programme
The Fly▸
The Fly▸
The Fly 2
Future Cop
Futureworld
Geheimakte WB1
Ghost in the Machine
Goldeneye▸
Hackers
Hide and Seek
Hologram Man
Improper Channels
Interface
Johnny Mnemonic
A Joke of Destiny, Lying in Wait Around the Corner Like a Bandit
Judge Dredd
A King in New York
Lawnmower Man 2: Beyond Cyberspace
The Lift
Live Wire: Human Timebomb
Lost Legacy: A Girl Called Hatter Fox
Maximum Overdrive
Metropolis▸
Microwave Massacre
Modern Times▸

Motorcycle Gang
Mouchette⚓
Murder in New Hampshire: The Pamela Smart Story
Muscle Beach Party
My American Cousin⚓
My Antonia
My Best Friend Is a Vampire
My Boyfriend's Back
My Boys Are Good Boys
My Father, My Rival
My Father the Hero
My Girl 2
My Own Private Idaho⚓
My Science Project
My Uncle: The Alien
Mystery Date
Mystic Pizza⚓
Naked Youth
National Lampoon's Senior Trip
The Neon Bible
New Jersey Drive
The Next Karate Kid
Nice Girls Don't Explode
Nickel Mountain
The Night Before
Night Breed
Night Friend
A Night in the Life of Jimmy Reardon
Night Life
Night of Evil
Night of the Twisters
A Nightmare on Elm Street 2: Freddy's Revenge
A Nightmare on Elm Street 3: Dream Warriors
A Nightmare on Elm Street 4: Dream Master
A Nightmare on Elm Street 5: Dream Child
1969⚓
Ninja Supremo
No Big Deal
Nobody's Perfect
Not My Kid
Now and Then
Nowhere
Nowhere to Run
O.C. and Stiggs
Odd Birds
On My Own
On the Edge: The Survival of Dana
One Crazy Night
One Crazy Summer
One Dark Night
Only the Brave
Only the Strong
Ordinary Magic
The Other Side of Sunday
Our Time
Outside Chance of Maximilian Glick
The Outsiders
Over the Edge⚓
Over the Summer
Pajama Party
Palm Springs Weekend
The Paper Brigade
Paradise Motel
Parenthood⚓
Party! Party!
Pathfinder⚓
Peggy Sue Got Married
The People Next Door
Peppermint Soda⚓
Phantom 2040 Movie: The Ghost Who Walks
Phat Beach
A Pig's Tale
Pin
Pippin⚓
Platypus Cove
Playing for Keeps
Playing with Fire
Poison Ivy
Pom Pom Girls
Porky's

Porky's 2: The Next Day
The Positively True Adventures of the Alleged Texas Cheerleader-Murdering Mom⚓
Pot, Parents, and Police
Powder
The Power Within
Prayer of the Rollerboys
Pretty in Pink
Pretty Smart
The Prime of Miss Jean Brodie⚓
The Prime Time
Princes in Exile
Prison for Children
Puberty Blues
Pump Up the Volume
Quadrophenia⚓
Quarterback Princess
Race the Sun
Racing with the Moon⚓
Rad
Rambling Rose⚓
Rebel Without a Cause⚓
Reckless
Red Kiss⚓
Return to Horror High
Return to the Blue Lagoon
Revenge of the Living Zombies
River's Edge⚓
Roadhouse 66
Robin of Locksley
Rock 'n' Roll High School Forever
Rock, Rock, Rock
Rockula
Rodrigo D.: No Future
Romeo and Juliet
Romeo and Juliet⚓
Ronnie and Julie
Rooftops
Roustabout
Ruby Jean and Joe
The Run of the Country⚓
Running Mates⚓
Sabrina the Teenage Witch
Say Anything⚓
Scarred
Scream⚓
Scream for Help
Screen Test
Screwballs
Season of Change
Secret Admirer
Secrets of Sweet Sixteen
Seizure: The Story of Kathy Morris
Senior Trip
Seven Minutes in Heaven
The Seventh Coin
S.F.W.
ShadowZone: The Undead Express
Shag: The Movie⚓
Shake, Rattle and Rock
Shao Lin Popeye
Sharma & Beyond
Sharon's Secret
She's Out of Control
Shine⚓
Shooting
Shout
Silence of the Heart⚓
The Silent One
Sing
Sixteen Candles⚓
Skateboard
Sleepers
Small Faces⚓
Smokey Bites the Dust
Smugglers' Cove⚓
Snowballing
Solarbabies
Some Kind of Wonderful
Something Special
Sooner or Later
The Spell
Spetters⚓
Spirit Rider⚓

Splendor in the Grass⚓
Spring Fever
Stand and Deliver⚓
Starchaser: The Legend of Orin
Stealing Beauty
Sticky Fingers
Still Not Quite Human
Stones of Death
Straight Out of Brooklyn
Straight Up
Strange Illusion
Streets
The Stripper
Student Bodies
Suburbia
Summer Camp Nightmare
Summer Holiday
Summer of '42⚓
The Summer of My German Soldier⚓
Summer School
Sunchaser
Sunnyside
Swap Meet
Sweet 16
Swim Team
Swing Kids
A Swingin' Summer
Tainted Blood
Tammy and the T-Rex
Tearaway
Teen Wolf
Teenage
Teenage Bad Girl
Teenage Bonnie & Klepto Clyde
Teenage Caveman
Teenage Crime Wave
Teenage Mother
Teenage Mutant Ninja Turtles 2: The Secret of the Ooze
Teenage Strangler
Teenage Wolfpack
Teenager
Teenagers from Outer Space
The Tender Age
Terminal Bliss
Tex
That Certain Age
That Darn Cat
That Night
That Thing You Do!⚓
That Was Then...This Is Now
There Goes My Baby
They Made Me a Criminal
36 Fillete⚓
This Boy's Life⚓
This Special Friendship
Thrashin'
3:15—The Moment of Truth
Three O'Clock High
Tiger Heart
Time Stands Still⚓
Times Square
To Die For⚓
To Gillian on Her 37th Birthday
To Play or To Die
Tom Brown's School Days⚓
Too Young to Die
Totally F***ed Up
Toughlove
Toy Soldiers
Treasure Island
Troop Beverly Hills
The Trouble with Angels
True Crime
Trust
Twirl
Twist & Shout⚓
Twisted
Twisted Love
Uncle Buck⚓
Under the Boardwalk
Under the Domim Tree
Unfinished Business
Unstrung Heroes
Up Against the Wall
Uptown Angel
Urusei Yatsura Movie 1: Only You

Urusei Yatsura Movie 2: Beautiful Dreamer
Urusei Yatsura Movie 3: Remember My Love
Valley Girl
The Vals
The Van
A Very Brady Sequel
Village of the Giants
Virgin High
Vision Quest
The Voyage of the Yes
Walking Back
Wanderers⚓
Warriors of Virtue
Weird Science
Welcome Home, Roxy Carmichael
Welcome to 18
Where Angels Go, Trouble Follows
Where the Boys Are '84
Where the Day Takes You
White Squall
White Wolves 2: Legend of the Wild
The Wild Life
Wild Ones on Wheels
Wild Pony
William Shakespeare's Romeo and Juliet⚓
Windrunner
Wish You Were Here⚓
The Wooden Gun
The Year My Voice Broke⚓
A Young Connecticut Yankee in King Arthur's Court
The Young Graduates
Young Guns
Young Love, First Love
The Young Poisoner's Handbook⚓
Youngblood
Youth Aflame
Youth on Parole
You've Ruined Me, Eddie
Zebrahead⚓
Zero Boys
Zombie Nightmare
The Zoo Gang

Television

see **Mass Media; TV Movies; TV Pilot Movies; TV Series**

Tennis

The Break
Jocks
Nobody's Perfect
Players
Racquet
Spring Fever

Terminal Confusion

Dumb & Dumber
8 Heads in a Duffel Bag
Wait Until Dark⚓
What's Up, Doc?⚓

Terror in Tall Buildings

see also **Elevators; Mystery & Suspense**

Blackout
Die Hard⚓
Hard to Die
Project: Shadowchaser
Skyscraper
Speed⚓
Terror on the 40th Floor
Tower of Terror

The Towering Inferno

Terrorism

see also **Crime & Criminals; Foreign Intrigue; Spies & Espionage**

Act of Passion: The Lost Honor of Kathryn Beck
Act of Piracy
Air Force One⚓
Airheads
The Amateur
Angel of Fury
The Applegates
The Assassination Run
Assignment Skybolt
Barcelona⚓
Belfast Assassin
Black Cobra 2
Black Cobra 3: The Manila Connection
Black Sunday
Black Terrorist
Blast
Blink of an Eye
Blood on the Badge
Bloodfist 6: Ground Zero
Blown Away
Captain America 2: Death Too Soon
Captive
Captive Rage
The Cassandra Crossing
Children of Rage
C.I.A. 2: Target Alexa
Circle of Deceit
Codename: Vengeance
Commando⚓
Could It Happen Here?
Cover-Up
Covert Assassin
Crash and Burn
Crash Dive
Cry of the Innocent⚓
The Crying Game⚓
Dark Rider
Deadline
Deadly Heroes
Deadly Outbreak
Death Before Dishonor
The Death Merchant
Death of the Incredible Hulk
Death Ray
Delta Force
Delta Force 3: The Killing Game
Delta Force Commando
Delta Force Commando 2
Demolition High
The Devil's Own⚓
Dick Barton, Special Agent
Die Hard⚓
Die Hard 2: Die Harder⚓
Die Hard: With a Vengeance
Dirty Games
Dr. Otto & the Riddle of the Gloom Beam
Dog Day Afternoon⚓
The Dogfighters
Double Team
The Enforcer
Eraser
The Evil That Men Do
Executive Decision
Exposed
Face/Off⚓
Fast Kill
A Father's Revenge
ffolkes
The Final Cut
The Final Option
Flashpoint Africa
Fortress of Amerikka
48 Hours to Live
French Quarter Undercover
Full Fathom Five
Galyon

Tragedy

Tragedy of Flight 103: The Inside Story♪
Trois Couleurs: Bleu♪
Trojan Women
Turkish Delights
Variety♪
A Very Private Affair
The Virgin Spring♪
Voyager♪
The Walls of Malapaga
The Wedding Gift♪
Where Angels Fear to Tread♪
The White Cliffs of Dover♪
White Mile
The White Sister♪
William Shakespeare's Romeo and Juliet♪
A Woman at Her Window
The Woman Next Door♪
The Wooden Man's Bride
The World According to Garp♪

Trains

see also Subways

Across the Bridge
Alberto Express
Avalanche Express
Before Sunrise
Berlin Express♪
Blood and Steel
Boxcar Bertha
The Brain
Breakheart Pass
Broken Arrow
Cafe Express
The Cassandra Crossing
Chattanooga Choo Choo
Closely Watched Trains♪
Color of a Brisk and Leaping Day
Courage Under Fire♪
Dakota
Danger Lights
Death Train
The Denver & Rio Grande
Detonator
The Dirty Dozen: The Fatal Mission
End of the Line
Express to Terror
Finders Keepers
Flame Over India♪
The Flying Scotsman
From Russia with Love♪
The Fugitive♪
The General♪
The Ghost and the Darkness
The Ghost Train
The Glory Trail
Go Kill and Come Back
Great K & A Train Robbery
The Great Locomotive Chase
The Great Train Robbery♪
The Grey Fox♪
Grit of the Girl Telegrapher/In the Switch Tower
The Harvey Girls♪
Horror Express
Hot Lead & Cold Feet
The Illusion Travels by Streetcar♪
Indiscretion of an American Wife
Inner Sanctum
Interrupted Journey
Jesse James at Bay
The Journey of Natty Gann♪
La Bete Humaine♪
The Lady Eve♪
Lady On a Train♪
The Lady Vanishes♪
The Lady Vanishes
Malcolm
Man Who Loved Cat Dancing
Man Without a Star♪
Midnight Limited
Mrs. Winterbourne
Mouvements du Desir
Murder on the Midnight Express

Murder on the Orient Express♪
My Twentieth Century♪
Mystery Mountain
Narrow Margin
Night Train to Munich♪
Night Train to Terror
Night Train to Venice
No. 17♪
The Odyssey of the Pacific
Oh, Mr. Porter
Once Upon a Time in the West♪
Panic on the 5:22
Paris Express
Phantom Express
Plunder Road
Prison Train
Railroaded
Railrodder♪
Red Signals
The Return of Casey Jones
Rhythm on the Range
The Road Home
The Road to Yesterday
Robbery
Romance on the Orient Express
Runaway Train♪
Running Scared
The Saint's Vacation/The Narrow Margin
Saratoga Trunk
Shanghai Express♪
The Silver Streak
Silver Streak♪
The Sleeping Car
Sleeping Car to Trieste
Some Like It Hot♪
Strangers on a Train♪
Subway
A Tale of Winter
Terror Train
Three for Bedroom C
3:10 to Yuma♪
Throw Momma from the Train♪
Thunder Over Texas
Torture Train
Tough Guys
Tracks
Trading Places
The Train♪
The Train Killer
Train Robbers
Train to Tombstone
Two Weeks to Live
Under Siege 2: Dark Territory
Union Pacific♪
Von Ryan's Express♪
Warm Nights on a Slow-Moving Train
Wild Engine/Mistaken Orders
Without Reservations
Zentropa

Transvestites & Transsexuals

see Gender Bending

Trapped with a Killer!

see also Psychotics/Sociopaths

Adrift
Air Force One♪
Alien Terminator
Blind Witness
Blink
Blood at Sundown
Blood Bride
Con Air♪
Copycat
Dead Calm♪
Deadbolt
Extremities
Eye of the Needle
Eyes of the Beholder
Fatal Attraction♪

Headless Body in Topless Bar
Hider in the House
Kalifornia
Lifepod
The Maddening
Manhunter♪
Misery♪
Mute Witness
Narrow Margin
Pacific Heights♪
The Penthouse
The Shining
The Silence of the Lambs♪
Slaughter of the Innocents
The Terror
Through the Eyes of a Killer
The Tie that Binds
Tracks of a Killer
Turbulence
Undertow
Unveiled
Voyage
Wait Until Dark♪
What's the Matter with Helen?
When a Stranger Calls
When a Stranger Calls Back

Treasure Hunt

Abbott and Costello Meet the Mummy
Adventure of the Action Hunters
The Adventurers
All the Brothers Were Valiant
Big Mouth
Blue Jeans and Dynamite
Cabo Blanco
Call of the Wild
City Slickers 2: The Legend of Curly's Gold
Comin' Round the Mountain
Curse of the Crystal Eye
Cutthroat Island
Enemy Gold
Ernest Rides Again
Finger on the Trigger
Girls in Prison
Gold Diggers: The Secret of Bear Mountain
The Goonies
The Grave
Greedy
Green Fire
Hear No Evil
Hunters of the Golden Cobra
Inside Out
The Jewel of the Nile
Kelly's Heroes
Klondike Fever
Kull the Conqueror
Legends of the North
Les Aventuriers
Lust in the Dust♪
Max is Missing
The Mermaids of Tiburon
Missing Pieces
Muppet Treasure Island
My Family Treasure
One-Eyed Soldiers
Operation Golden Phoenix
Pattern for Plunder
The Phantom of the Range
Romancing the Stone♪
Rudyard Kipling's The Jungle Book
The Secret of the Golden Eagle
Secret of the Ice Cave
Shadow of Chikara
Tarzan's Secret Treasure
Terror on Alcatraz
That Man from Rio
There Goes the Neighborhood
Thieves of Fortune
Tom and Huck♪
Treasure Island♪
Treasure Island
The Treasure of Jamaica Reef
The Treasure of Matecumbe
The Treasure of the Amazon

Treasure of the Four Crowns
Treasure of the Golden Condor
Treasure of the Sierra Madre♪
Treasure of the Yankee Zephyr
The Treasure Seekers
Trespass
Uninvited
Warrior Spirit
Whistling in Dixie
The Wrong Road

Trees & Forests

see also Good Earth; Wilderness

Big Trees♪
The Burning Season♪
Crosscut
Dr. Tarr's Torture Dungeon
Equinox♪
Evil Dead
Fatal Passion
5 Dark Souls
Forest Warrior
Himatsuri♪
Hole in the Sky
The Ice Flood
King of the Forest Rangers
Lassie: Adventures of Neeka
Les Grandes Gueules
Lunatic
The Many Adventures of Winnie the Pooh
Mr. Sycamore
The Night Brings Charlie
The Passion of Darkly Noon
Redwood Curtain
Redwood Forest Trail
Return of the Jedi♪
Surfacing
Where the Rivers Flow North
The Wizard of Oz♪

True Crime

see also Crime & Criminals; This is Your Life; True Stories

At Close Range♪
Ballad of Gregorio Cortez♪
Beyond Reasonable Doubt
Billionaire Boys Club
Black Oak Conspiracy
Black Panther
Blanche Fury
Bluebeard♪
Boomerang♪
The Boston Strangler
Chicago Joe & the Showgirl
Citizen X♪
Compulsion♪
Crime of the Century
Danger of Love
Deadly Voyage
Death Scream
The Deliberate Stranger♪
Dick Turpin
Dillinger
Dr. Petiot
Double-Crossed
Echoes in the Darkness
The Elegant Criminal
The Executioner's Song
The Falcon and the Snowman♪
Final Appeal
Getting Gotti
Gotti
Great Gold Swindle
The Great St. Louis Bank Robbery
Headless Body in Topless Bar
Helter Skelter
The Hillside Strangler
Honor Thy Father and Mother: The True Story of the Menendez Brothers
I Can't Sleep
In Cold Blood

Johnny 100 Pesos
Killer: A Journal of Murder
L'Appat
Mad Dog Morgan
The Man from the Pru
The Man in the Attic
McVicar
Mrs. Soffel
Money Movers
Murder in Coweta County
Murder in New Hampshire: The Pamela Smart Story
Murder in Texas♪
Murder So Sweet
Murph the Surf
Normal Life
Nowhere to Run
The O.J. Simpson Story
The Onion Field♪
The People vs. Jean Harris♪
The Preppie Murder
Prince of the City♪
The Pursuit of D.B. Cooper
Rainbow Warrior
Rampage
Rule #3
Sister My Sister
Squizzy Taylor
Stalking Laura
Stand Off
Swoon♪
Till Murder Do Us Part
Too Young to Die
Triple Cross♪
Undercover Cop
The Untouchables♪
Verne Miller
Without Evidence
The Zodiac Killer

True Stories

see also This is Your Life; True Crime

The Abduction of Kari Swenson
Above and Beyond♪
The Accused♪
Act of Vengeance
Adam♪
The Adventures of Nellie Bly
After the Promise
After the Shock
Afterburn♪
Against the Wall♪
Al Capone♪
The Alamo♪
Alamo Bay
Alive
All Mine to Give
All the President's Men♪
Alvarez Kelly
The Ambush Murders
Amelia Earhart: The Final Flight
An American Story
The Amityville Horror
Amor Bandido
The Amy Fisher Story
And I Alone Survived
And the Band Played On♪
Andersonville♪
Andre
The Ann Jillian Story
Anna and the King of Siam♪
Apollo 13♪
Apprentice to Murder
Archer's Adventure
Art for Teachers of Children
The Ascent
Assault at West Point: The Court-Martial of Johnson Whittaker
The Assisi Underground
At Close Range♪
The Attic: The Hiding of Anne Frank
Attica♪
Au Revoir Les Enfants♪
Awakening of Candra
Awakenings♪

Double Trouble
Double Vision
Dual Alibi
Equinox
The Eyes, the Mouth
Here Come the Waves►
Hotel de Love
How the West was Fun
Instant Kung-Fu Man
Invitation au Voyage
It Takes Two►
The Krays►
Lies of the Twins
Lost Honeymoon
Love! Valour! Compassion!
The Man in the Iron Mask►
Man with a Gun
Maximum Risk
Mirror Images
Mirror Images 2
Mother Lode
Nukie
The Nutt House
The Other►
Out on a Limb
The Parent Trap
Raising Cain
The Reluctant Agent
Sisters►
The Sphinx
Start the Revolution Without Me►
Steal Big, Steal Little
A Stolen Life
Thicker Than Water
To Grandmother's House We Go
Twin Sisters
Twin Town
Twins
Twins of Evil
Twinsanity
Twinsitters
Two Much
Wagon's Westward
The Worldly Madonna

Twister!

see also Disaster Flicks
Night of the Twisters
Places in the Heart►
Tornado!
Twister
The Wizard of Oz
The Wizard of Oz►

UFOs

see Alien Beings—Benign; Alien Beings—Vicious; Space Operas

Underground

see Avant-Garde

Unexplained Phenomena

The Adventures of Sherlock Holmes: Hound of the Baskervilles
The Amityville Curse
Angel Baby
Beyond the Bermuda Triangle
Black Rainbow►
Blue Monday
The Carpathian Eagle
The Carpenter
Carrie►
Catacombs
Daffy Duck's Quackbusters
Dead Again►
Dead Zone►
Delusion
Destiny Turns on the Radio

Die, Monster, Die!
Dream a Little Dream 2
Dying to Remember
Encounter with the Unknown
Endgame
The Entity
Escapes
E.S.P.
Eternal Evil
The Evil Mind
Eyes of Laura Mars
Fire in the Sky
Firestarter
The 4D Man
The Fury
Ghost Chasers
Ghost Town
The Ghosts of Hanley House
Grandma's House
Hangar 18
The Haunting Passion
The House of Seven Corpses
Lisa and the Devil
Lurkers
Maximum Overdrive
Michael
Miracle in Rome
Miracle of Our Lady of Fatima
Mondo Balardo
Murphy's Fault
A Name for Evil
The Night Stalker: Two Tales of Terror
Nomads
Out There
Phenomenon
Psychic
The Psychotronic Man
Retribution
Return from Witch Mountain
Roswell: The U.F.O. Cover-Up
Salem's Lot
Scared Stiff►
Shattered Silence
The Sleeping Car
Spook Busters
The Stranger
Things Happen at Night
The Three Lives of Thomasina►
The Tin Drum►
Truly, Madly, Deeply►
Twin Peaks
The Undead
Visions
Visions of Evil
Waiting for the Light
Wavelength
Web of the Spider
The X-Files: Pilot Episode/Deep Throat
X: The Man with X-Ray Eyes►

Up All Night

see also Vampire Babes; Vampires
After Hours►
Albino Alligator
American Graffiti►
Batman►
Before Sunrise
Blade Runner►
Dazed and Confused►
Escape from New York
From Dusk Till Dawn
Hocus Pocus
Into the Night
Judgment Night
Little Nemo: Adventures in Slumberland
Mannequin
Swingers►

Urban Drama

Above the Rim
American Heart►
American Me►

The Asphalt Jungle►
Bad Attitude
Bad Lieutenant►
Boston Kickout
Boyz N the Hood►
The Bronx War
A Brother's Kiss
Bullet
Carlito's Way►
City Hall►
Crossing the Bridge
Cry, the Beloved Country►
Curtis's Charm
Dangerous Minds
Dead Boyz Can't Fly
Do the Right Thing►
The Fence
Fly by Night
Fresh
The George McKenna Story
Grand Canyon►
Heaven is a Playground
Jason's Lyric
Juice
Jungleground
Just Another Girl on the I.R.T.
Love Your Mama
Menace II Society►
Mi Vida Loca
Money for Nothing
Naked►
New Jack City
New Jersey Drive
Night Falls on Manhattan►
Once Were Warriors►
Original Gangstas
Out of Sync
Poetic Justice
Rude
South Central
Straight Out of Brooklyn
Strange Days►
Strapped
Street Wars
Sugar Hill
Urban Crossfire
White Man's Burden
Zebrahead►
Zooman►

The USO

see also World War II
China Beach►
For the Boys
Hollywood Goes to War
Stage Door Canteen

Vacations

American Gothic
The American Scream
An American Werewolf in London►
Backwoods
Beyond the Door 3
Blame It on Rio
Blondie Takes a Vacation
Body Trouble
Cabin Boy
California Suite►
Camilla
Cancel My Reservation
Captain Ron
Casual Sex?
City Slickers►
Claire's Knee►
Cold Fever
Come September
Crackerjack
Dangerous Prey
Dead Cold
Deadly Intruder
Death Stalk
Death Weekend
Deliverance►
Demon Lust
Devil Wears White

Dirty Dancing►
Don't Drink the Water
8 Heads in a Duffel Bag
Enchanted April
Far from Home
A Far Off Place
The Fatal Image
A Fatal Inversion
Frantic►
Fraternity Vacation
Gidget Goes Hawaiian
Gidget Goes to Rome
Grotesque
Harry and the Hendersons
The Hills Have Eyes
Home Alone►
Home Alone 2: Lost in New York
Hot Pursuit
The Inkwell
Judgment Day
Killing at Hell's Gate
La Collectionneuse
Last Summer In the Hamptons►
Lena's Holiday
Lie Down with Dogs
Like It Never Was Before
Little Bigfoot
The Long, Long Trailer
Love! Valour! Compassion!
The Lunatic
Magic in the Water
Magic Kid
The Man Who Knew Too Much►
The Man Who Knew Too Much
Mr. Hobbs Takes a Vacation►
Mr. Hulot's Holiday►
A Month by the Lake
My Father the Hero
My Grandpa is a Vampire
National Lampoon's Christmas Vacation
National Lampoon's European Vacation
National Lampoon's Vacation►
Nightmare at Bittercreek
Ollie Hopnoodle's Haven of Bliss
The Out-of-Towners►
Pauline at the Beach►
Poor White Trash 2
Ring of Fire 3: Lion Strike
The River Wild
Russian Roulette
The Slayer/The Scalps
Spellbreaker: Secret of the Leprechauns
Spring Break
Stealing Beauty
The Sucker
Summer Rental
A Tale of Winter
Target
Terror at Red Wolf Inn
Terror at Tenkiller
Tracks of a Killer
Twitch of the Death Nerve
The Two Faces of Evil
Two If by Sea
Uncivilized
Unlawful Passage
Vegas Vacation
Week-End In Havana
Weekend at Bernie's
A Weekend in the Country
Welcome to Spring Break
Where the Boys Are '84
The Wild Life
Witchery

Vampire Babes

see also Up All Night; Vampires
The Addiction
The Brides of Dracula
Buffy the Vampire Slayer►
Captain Kronos: Vampire Hunter►
The Craving
Crypt of the Living Dead

Daughters of Darkness►
Demon Queen
Dracula's Daughter►
Fangs of the Living Dead
The Fearless Vampire Killers►
Fright Night
From Dusk Till Dawn
The Girl with the Hungry Eyes
Interview with the Vampire
The Kiss
Lemora, Lady Dracula
Lust for a Vampire
Mary, Mary, Bloody Mary
Nadja►
Night of the Sorcerers
Nightlife
Once Bitten
Tales from the Crypt Presents Bordello of Blood
Twins of Evil
Vamp
The Vampire Lovers
Vampyres
The Velvet Vampire

Vampire Spoof

see also Horror Comedy; Vampires
Andy Warhol's Dracula►
Beverly Hills Vamp
Buffy the Vampire Slayer►
Dracula & Son
Dracula Blows His Cool
Dracula: Dead and Loving It
Dracula Sucks
Dracula: Up in Harlem
Dracula vs. Frankenstein
The Fearless Vampire Killers►
Gore-Met Zombie Chef From Hell
I Married a Vampire
Love at First Bite
The Malibu Beach Vampires
My Best Friend Is a Vampire
My Grandpa is a Vampire
Near Dark►
Once Bitten
A Polish Vampire in Burbank
Rockula
Teen Vamp
Vamp
The Vampire Happening

Vampires

see also Up All Night; Vampire Babes; Vampire Spoof
The Addiction
Alien Massacre
The Bat People
Beast of Morocco
Billy the Kid Versus Dracula
Black Sabbath►
Black Vampire
Blacula
Blood & Donuts
Blood and Roses
Blood Freak
Blood of Dracula's Castle
Blood of the Vampire
The Blood Spattered Bride
Blood Thirst
Blood Ties
Bloodlust: Subspecies 3
Bloodstone: Subspecies 2
The Bloodsuckers
Bloodsuckers from Outer Space
The Bloody Vampire
Body Snatcher from Hell
Bram Stoker's Dracula
The Brides of Dracula
Bring Me the Vampire
Buffy the Vampire Slayer►
Captain Kronos: Vampire Hunter►
Carmilla

Barb Wire
Battle Hell
The Battle of Algiers⬧
The Battle of Austerlitz
The Beast
Beau Geste⬧
Before the Rain⬧
Behind the Front
Behold a Pale Horse
The Bitter Tea of General Yen⬧
Braveheart⬧
The Buccaneer
Bugles in the Afternoon
A Bullet for the General
By Dawn's Early Light
Captain Caution
Captain Horatio Hornblower⬧
Carthage in Flames
Cast a Giant Shadow
Cavalry Command
Chapayev⬧
The Charge of the Light
    Brigade⬧
The Charge of the Light Brigade
Civilization⬧
Codename: Terminate
Colonel Chabert
Colonel Wolodyjowski
The Conqueror
Conquest of the Normans
Coup de Grace
The Court Martial of Billy
    Mitchell⬧
Cromwell
Cup Final
Danton⬧
Days of Hell
Deadline
The Deluge
The Desert of the Tartars
Devil Wears White
Distant Drums
Doctor Zhivago⬧
Dragon Seed
Eagles Attack at Dawn
1860
El Cid⬧
El Paso Stampede
Elizabeth of Ladymead⬧
Emissary
The Enchanted Cottage
The End of St. Petersburg⬧
The Expendables
The Fall of the Roman Empire⬧
Field of Honor
The Fighter⬧
Fighting Marines
Fighting Pilot
The Fighting Prince of Donegal
The Finest Hour
Fire Over England⬧
The Firing Line
Flor Silvestre
Flowers of Reverie
For Whom the Bell Tolls⬧
Forever and a Day⬧
Fort Apache⬧
Forty Days of Musa Dagh
The Four Feathers⬧
The Four Feathers
F.P. 1
Funny, Dirty Little War⬧
Guerilla Brigade
Gunga Din⬧
Guns at Batasi
Hail the Conquering Hero⬧
Harry's War
Hawkeye: Premiere Episode
Heart of a Nation⬧
Heartbreak Ridge⬧
Hearts & Armour
Heaven & Earth⬧
Hell in the Pacific⬧
Hell on the Battleground
Hell Raiders
Henry V⬧
Hero Bunker
The Hidden Fortress⬧
Hill 24 Doesn't Answer⬧

Holy Terror
Homecoming⬧
How I Won the War
In the Name of the Pope-King⬧
The Informer⬧
The Invincible Gladiator
Johnny Got His Gun⬧
Judith of Bethulia⬧
Khartoum
Killers
Kolberg
La Marseillaise⬧
La Nuit de Varennes⬧
Land and Freedom⬧
The Last Command
The Last of the Mohicans
The Last of the Mohicans⬧
The Last Valley
Late Summer Blues
Latino
Laughing at Life
Legion of Missing Men
The Life and Death of Colonel
    Blimp⬧
Lion of the Desert⬧
Lipstick On Your Collar
The Longest Day⬧
The Lost Command
The Lost Idol/Shock Troop
Mademoiselle Fifi
Man from the Alamo⬧
Man with a Cross
Massive Retaliation
Megaforce
Mercenary Fighters
Mission to Glory
Mission to Kill
The Mongols
The Moonraker
Mother⬧
The Mouse That Roared⬧
Napoleon⬧
An Occurrence at Owl Creek
    Bridge/Coup de Grace
Old Gringo
One Night Stand⬧
Orphans of the Storm⬧
The Phantom Planet
Prehistoric Bimbos in
    Armageddon City
The Pride and the Passion
Prisoner of the Mountains⬧
Project: Alien
Rage to Kill
The Rape of the Sabines
The Real Glory⬧
A Reason to Live, A Reason to
    Die
The Red and the Black⬧
The Red and the White⬧
Red Dawn
Reds⬧
Reign of Terror
Revenge of the Barbarians
Rhodes
Richard III⬧
Ride to Glory
River of Unrest
Ryan's Daughter
Saga of the Vagabond
Salome, Where She Danced
Sanders of the River⬧
Scarlet Dawn
Senso⬧
The Seventeenth Bride
Shake Hands with the Devil⬧
The Shame⬧
Sharpe's Battle
Sharpe's Company
Sharpe's Eagle
Sharpe's Enemy
Sharpe's Gold
Sharpe's Honour
Sharpe's Mission
Sharpe's Regiment
Sharpe's Rifles
Sharpe's Siege
Sharpe's Sword
She Wore a Yellow Ribbon⬧

Simon Bolivar
Sinai Commandos
Smugglers
Something of Value⬧
Storm over Asia⬧
Striker
Surprise Attack
The Tempest/The Eagle⬧
This England
This Island Earth
The 317th Platoon⬧
Tiger Joe
Time to Kill
The Torch
Treasure of the Lost Desert
The Ugly American
Ulysses' Gaze
Under Fire⬧
The Uprising⬧
Vera Cruz
Villa Rides
Walker
War and Peace
War and Peace⬧
War Bus Commando
Warbirds
Waterloo
Weekend War
White Dwarf
Wild Geese 2
The World Owes Me a Living
World War III
Yank in Libya
Young Winston⬧
Zulu Dawn⬧

Washington, DC

see Capitol Capers

Wedding Bells

see also Marriage;
Otherwise Engaged;
Wedding Hell

Aladdin and the King of Thieves
Betsy's Wedding
Blind Date
The Bride Came C.O.D.
The Bride Walks Out
Date Bait
Easy Money
8 Seconds
Emma⬧
Everyone Says I Love You⬧
Fanci's Persuasion
Father of the Bride⬧
Father of the Bride
Foolin' Around
For Better and For Worse
Forget Paris
Four Weddings and a Funeral⬧
Full of Life
Give Me a Sailor
Hard Promises
Holy Matrimony
Honeymoon in Vegas
House Party 3
Housesitter
It Started with Eve⬧
Jack and Sarah
Jerry Maguire⬧
The Jewel of the Nile
Lovers and Other Strangers⬧
The Marrying Man
Miami Rhapsody
The Mirror Has Two Faces
Mrs. Winterbourne
Moonstruck⬧
Murders in the Rue Morgue
Muriel's Wedding⬧
My Best Friend's Wedding
My Favorite Wife⬧
Nine Months
Only You
The Philadelphia Story⬧
Prelude to a Kiss

Revenge of the Nerds 4: Nerds
    in Love
Rhythm on the Range
Roommates
Royal Wedding⬧
She's Having a Baby
Sixteen Candles⬧
The Summer House
That Old Feeling
The 30-Foot Bride of Candy
    Rock
Three Smart Girls Grow Up⬧
Waikiki Wedding⬧
A Wedding
Wedding Band
Wedding Bell Blues
The Wedding March⬧
The Wedding Party
Wedding Rehearsal
When Harry Met Sally...⬧
Where There's Life
The World's Oldest Living
    Bridesmaid

Wedding Hell

see also Marriage;
Otherwise Engaged;
Wedding Bells

Black Vampire
Blood Bride
The Blood Spattered Bride
The Bride
The Bride & the Beast
The Bride of Frankenstein⬧
Bride of Killer Nerd
Bride of Re-Animator
Bride of the Gorilla
Bride of the Monster
The Bride with White Hair
The Bride Wore Black⬧
Brides of the Beast
The Catered Affair⬧
Cheatin' Hearts
Feeling Minnesota
The Graduate⬧
He Knows You're Alone
Highway to Hell
Honeymoon
Honeymoon Horror
Honeymoon Killers⬧
I Married a Monster from Outer
    Space
My New Gun
The Newlydeads
Niagara
The Perfect Bride
That Old Feeling
True Love⬧
The Wedding Banquet⬧
Wedding in Blood⬧
Wedding in White

Werewolves

see also Metamorphosis

An American Werewolf in
    London⬧
Bad Moon
Black Werewolf
Blood of Dracula's Castle
Bride of the Gorilla
Children of the Full Moon
The Company of Wolves⬧
The Craving
Cry of the Werewolf
Curse of the Devil
Curse of the Queerwolf
The Curse of the Werewolf
Deathmoon
Dr. Jekyll and the Wolfman
Dr. Jekyll vs. the Werewolf
Dr. Terror's House of Horrors
Dracula vs. Frankenstein
Face of the Screaming Werewolf
Frankenstein Meets the
    Wolfman⬧
Full Eclipse

The Fury of the Wolfman
Hercules, Prisoner of Evil
House of Frankenstein
The Howling⬧
Howling 2: Your Sister Is a
    Werewolf
Howling 3: The Marsupials
Howling 4: The Original
    Nightmare
Howling 6: The Freaks
The Howling: New Moon Rising
I Was a Teenage Werewolf
Legend of the Werewolf
The Legend of the Wolf Woman
Lone Wolf
The Mad Monster
Meridian: Kiss of the Beast
Monster Dog
The Monster Squad
Moon of the Wolf
My Mom's a Werewolf
Night of the Howling Beast
Orgy of the Dead
Project Metalbeast: DNA
    Overload
The Rats are Coming! The
    Werewolves are Here!
Return of the Vampire
Silver Bullet
Teen Wolf
Teen Wolf Too
The Undying Monster
Werewolf
Werewolf in a Girl's Dormitory
Werewolf of London
Werewolf of Washington
The Werewolf vs. the Vampire
    Woman
Werewolves on Wheels
Wolf
Wolf Blood
The Wolf Man⬧
Wolfen⬧
The Wolfman

Western Comedy

see also Comedy; Westerns

Adios Amigo
Alias Jesse James
Along Came Jones⬧
The Apple Dumpling Gang
The Apple Dumpling Gang
    Rides Again
Bad Man's River
Ballad of Cable Hogue⬧
Bang Bang Kid
The Beautiful Blonde from
    Bashful Bend
Beyond the Trail
Blazing Saddles⬧
Bordello
Border Phantom
Boss
Bowery Buckaroos
Branded Men
Bronco Billy
Bus Stop⬧
Carry On Cowboy
Cat Ballou⬧
Catlow
Check & Double Check
The Cherokee Kid
The Cheyenne Social Club
The Cisco Kid
City Slickers⬧
City Slickers 2: The Legend of
    Curly's Gold
Cold Feet
The Cowboy Way
Desperate Women
Destry Rides Again⬧
The Duchess and the Dirtwater
    Fox
El Diablo Rides
Four Eyes and Six Guns
Four for Texas
The Frisco Kid
From Noon Till Three

Love Desperados
Lucky Cisco Kid
Lucky Luke: The Ballad of the Daltons
Lucky Terror
Lucky Texan
Lust for Gold
The Lusty Men▶
Macho Callahan
MacKenna's Gold
Madron
The Magnificent Seven▶
Major Dundee
A Man Alone
Man & Boy
A Man Called Horse▶
A Man Called Sledge
Man from Button Willow
Man from Cheyenne
Man from Colorado
The Man from Gun Town
The Man from Hell
Man from Hell's Edges
The Man from Laramie▶
Man from Montana
Man from Monterey
The Man from Music Mountain
The Man from Painted Post
The Man from Snowy River
Man from Texas
Man from the Alamo▶
Man from Thunder River
Man from Utah
Man in the Saddle
Man of Action
Man of the Forest
Man of the West
Man or Gun
Man Who Loved Cat Dancing
The Man Who Shot Liberty Valance▶
Man Without a Star▶
Manchurian Avenger
The Manhunt
Man's Country
Man's Land
Mark of the Spur
Marked for Murder
Marked Trails
Marshal of Cedar Rock
Marshal of Heldorado
The Marshal's Daughter
The Masked Rider
Mason of the Mounted
The Maverick Queen
Maverick: The Collector's Edition
McCabe & Mrs. Miller▶
The McMasters
The Meanest Men in the West
Melody of the Plains
Melody Ranch
Melody Trail
Mesquite Buckaroo
Minnesota Clay
Miracle in the Wilderness
The Miracle Rider
Missouri Breaks
Missourians
Mr. Horn
Mohawk
Molly & Lawless John
Montana
Montana Belle
Monte Walsh▶
Mosby's Marauders
Mountain Justice
The Mountain Men
Murder on the Yukon
My Darling Clementine▶
My Heroes Have Always Been Cowboys
My Outlaw Brother
My Pal, The King
My Pal Trigger
Mysterious Desperado
Mysterious Desperado/Rider From Tucson
The Mysterious Rider
Mystery Man

Mystery Mountain
Mystery of the Hooded Horseman
Mystery Ranch
Mystery Trooper
Naked Hills
Naked in the Sun
The Naked Spur▶
Narrow Trail▶
Navajo Joe
Near the Rainbow's End
'Neath Canadian Skies
'Neath the Arizona Skies
Ned Kelly
Nevada
Nevada City
Nevada Smith
The Nevadan
The New Frontier
Night of the Grizzly
Night Rider
Night Riders of Montana
Night Stage to Galveston
Night Time in Nevada
The Nine Lives of Elfego Baca
No Man's Law
No Man's Range
No Name On the Bullet▶
North of the Border
North of the Great Divide
Northern Passage
Oath of Vengeance
Oblivion
Oh Susannah
Oklahoma Annie
Oklahoma Badlands
Oklahoma Cyclone
The Oklahoman
Old Barn Dance
Old Corral
On the Night Stage
On the Old Spanish Trail
On Top of Old Smoky
One-Eyed Jacks▶
100 Rifles
One Little Indian
Only the Valiant
Oregon Trail
The Outcast
Outcasts of the Trail
The Outlaw
Outlaw Country
The Outlaw Deputy
Outlaw Express
Outlaw Fury
Outlaw Gang
The Outlaw Josey Wales▶
Outlaw Justice
Outlaw of the Plains
Outlaw Roundup
Outlaw Rule
The Outlaw Tamer
Outlaw Trail
Outlaw Women
Outlaws of Sonora
Outlaws of the Desert
Outlaws of the Range
Outlaw's Paradise
Overland Mail
Overland Stage Raiders▶
The Ox-Bow Incident▶
Painted Desert
The Painted Stallion
Pair of Aces
Pale Rider▶
Pals of the Range
Pals of the Saddle
Panamint's Bad Man
Pancho Villa
Pancho Villa Returns
Pardon My Gun
Paroled to Die
Partners of the Trail
Passion
Pat Garrett & Billy the Kid▶
Pecos Kid
Peter Lundy and the Medicine Hat Stallion
The Phantom Bullet

The Phantom Empire
Phantom Gold
The Phantom of the Range
Phantom of the West
Phantom Patrol
Phantom Rancher
Phantom Ranger
The Phantom Rider
Phantom Thunderbolt
Pinto Canyon
Pinto Rustlers
Pioneer Marshal
Pioneer Woman
The Pioneers
Pistoleros Asesinos
A Place Called Glory
The Plainsman
The Pocatello Kid
The Pony Express
Pony Express▶
Pony Express Rider▶
Pony Post
Posse▶
Powdersmoke Range
Prairie Badmen
The Prairie King
Prairie Moon
Prairie Pals
The Prairie Pirate
Prescott Kid
The Professionals▶
The Proud and the Damned
Proud Men
Proud Rebel▶
Public Cowboy No. 1
Purple Vigilantes
Pursued▶
The Quick and the Dead
Quigley Down Under
Racketeers of the Range
Rage at Dawn
Raiders of Red Gap
Raiders of Sunset Pass
Raiders of the Border
Rainbow Ranch
Rainbow's End
Ramrod
The Ramrodder
Rancho Notorious▶
Randy Rides Alone
Range Busters
Range Feud
The Range Feud/Two Fisted Law
Range Law
Range Renegades
Range Rider
Range Riders
Rangeland Empire
Rangeland Racket
Ranger and the Lady
Ranger's Roundup
The Rangers Step In
Rangers Take Over
The Rare Breed
Rattler Kid
Rawhide
Rawhide▶
Rawhide Romance
A Reason to Live, A Reason to Die
Red Desert
Red Garters
Red Headed Stranger
Red River▶
Red River Valley
Red Rock Outlaw
The Red Rope
Red Sun
The Redhead from Wyoming
Redwood Forest Trail
Renegade Girl
Renegade Ranger/Scarlet River
Renegade Trail
Renfrew of the Royal Mounted
Renfrew on the Great White Trail
The Restless Breed

The Return of a Man Called Horse
Return of Draw Egan
Return of Frank James▶
Return of Jesse James
The Return of Josey Wales▶
Return of the Bad Men
Return of the Lash
Return of the Seven
Return of Wildfire
Return to Lonesome Dove
Return to Snowy River▶
Revenge of the Virgins
The Revenge Rider
Ride 'Em Cowgirl
Ride Him, Cowboy▶
Ride in the Whirlwind
Ride Lonesome
Ride, Ranger, Ride
Ride the High Country▶
Ride the Man Down
Ride the Wind
Ride to Glory
Rider from Tucson
Rider of the Law
Riders of Death Valley
Riders of Destiny
Riders of Pasco Basin
Riders of the Desert
Riders of the Purple Sage
Riders of the Range
Riders of the Range/Storm Over Wyoming
Riders of the Rockies
Riders of the Timberline
Riders of the West
Riders of the Whistling Pines
Riders of the Whistling Skull
Ridin' Down the Canyon
Ridin' on a Rainbow
Ridin' the California Trail
Ridin' the Lone Trail
Ridin' the Trail
Ridin' Thru
The Riding Avenger
Riding On
Riding Speed
Riding the Sunset Trail▶
The Riding Tornado
Rim of the Canyon
Rimfire
Rin Tin Tin, Hero of the West
Rio Bravo▶
Rio Conchos▶
Rio Diablo
Rio Grande▶
Rio Grande Raiders
Rio Lobo
Rio Rattler
River of No Return
Road Agent
The Roamin' Cowboy
Roamin' Wild
Roarin' Lead
Roaring Guns
Roaring Ranch
Roaring Six Guns
Robbery Under Arms
Robin Hood of Texas
Robin Hood of the Pecos
Rock River Renegades
Rockwell: A Legend of the Wild West
Rocky Mountain Rangers
Rodeo Girl
Rogue of the Range
Rogue of the Rio Grande
Roll Along Cowboy
Roll on Texas Moon
Roll, Wagons, Roll
Rollin' Plains
Romance on the Range
Rooster Cogburn
Rootin' Tootin' Rhythm
Rose of Rio Grande
Rough Night in Jericho
Rough Riders of Cheyenne
Rough Riders' Roundup
Rough Ridin' Rhythm

Rough Riding Rangers
Round-Up Time in Texas
Rounding Up the Law
Run of the Arrow
Running Wild
Rustler's Hideout
Rustlers of Red Dog
Rustler's Paradise
Rustler's Roundup
Rustler's Valley
The Sacketts
Sacred Ground
Saddle Buster
Saddle Mountain Round-Up
Saga of Death Valley
Sagebrush Law
Sagebrush Trail▶
Salute to the "King of the Cowboys," Roy Rogers
San Antonio
San Fernando Valley
Sandflow
Santa Fe
Santa Fe Bound
Santa Fe Marshal
Santa Fe Stampede
Santa Fe Trail
Santa Fe Uprising
Santee
Sartana's Here...Trade Your Pistol for a Coffin
Savage Journey
Savage Land
Savage Wilderness
Scalps
The Searchers▶
Sergeant Rutledge▶
Seven Cities of Gold
Seventh Cavalry
The Shadow Riders
Shadows of Death
Shalako
Shane▶
She Wore a Yellow Ribbon▶
Sheriff of Tombstone
Shine on, Harvest Moon
Shoot the Living, Pray for the Dead
Shoot the Sun Down
The Shooting
The Shootist▶
Shotgun
The Showdown
Showdown
Showdown at Boot Hill
Showdown at Williams Creek
Silent Code
Silent Tongue
Silent Valley
Silver Bandit
The Silver Bullet
Silver City Bonanza
Silver City Kid
Silver Lode
Silver Queen
Silver River
Silver Spurs
Silver Stallion
Silver Star
Silverado▶
Sing, Cowboy, Sing
Singing Buckaroo
Singing Cowboys, Vol. 2
The Singing Cowgirl
Siringo
Six Gun Gospel
Six Gun Rhythm
Six Shootin' Sheriff
Sky Bandits
Sky High
Slaughter Trail
Smoke in the Wind
Smokey Smith
Sodbusters
Soldier Blue
The Sombrero Kid
Somewhere in Sonora
Son of a Gun
Son of God's Country

Creature of the Walking Dead
The Curse of the Aztec Mummy
Dawn of the Dead ➤
Dawn of the Mummy
Day of the Dead
Dead Alive
The Dead Don't Die
Dead Heat
Dead Men Don't Die
The Dead Next Door
Dead Pit
Death Becomes Her ➤
The Death Curse of Tartu
Deathdream
Demon Wind
Destroyer
Devil Kiss
Ed and His Dead Mother
Evil Town
The Ghost Brigade
The Ghoul
The Granny
The Hanging Woman
Haunting Fear
Hellgate
Horror of the Zombies
Horror Rises from the Tomb
The House of Seven Corpses
House of the Dead
I Eat Your Skin
I Walked with a Zombie ➤
Invisible Invaders
Isle of the Dead
The Jitters
King of the Zombies
Kiss Daddy Goodbye
The Mad Ghoul
Messiah of Evil
The Mummy ➤
Mummy & Curse of the Jackal
The Mummy's Revenge
My Boyfriend's Back
Neon Maniacs
Night Life
Night of Horror
Night of the Comet
Night of the Creeps
Night of the Death Cult
Night of the Ghouls
Night of the Living Babes
Night of the Living Dead ➤
Night of the Living Dead
Night of the Living Dead, 25th
    Anniversary Documentary
Nightmare Weekend
Oasis of the Zombies
Orgy of the Dead
The Outing
Pet Sematary 2
Phantasm III: Lord of the Dead
Plague of the Zombies
Plan 9 from Outer Space
Prison
Quatermass 2 ➤
Re-Animator ➤
Redneck Zombies
Return of the Evil Dead
Return of the Living Dead
Return of the Living Dead 2
Return of the Living Dead 3
Revenge of the Dead
Revenge of the Living Zombies
Revenge of the Zombies
Revolt of the Zombies
The Robot vs. the Aztec Mummy
Seedpeople
Seven Doors of Death
Shock Waves
Sole Survivor
Steps from Hell
The Stuff
Svengali ➤
Teenage Zombies
Tomb of the Undead
Tombs of the Blind Dead
Torture Chamber of Baron Blood
The Vampire's Ghost
Vengeance of the Zombies
Virgin Among the Living Dead

Voodoo Dawn
Voodoo Woman
The White Zombie ➤
Winterbeast
Zombie
The Zombie Army
Zombie High
Zombie Island Massacre
Zombie Lake
Zombie Nightmare
Zombies of Moratau
Zombies of the Stratosphere
Zombies on Broadway
Zombiethon

Kibbles and Series List

The **Kibbles** and **Series** indexes have been combined into one index. This is where you'll find info on where your favorite movies came from—literary, theatrical, cartoon, and television adaptations to name a few, as well as the behind the scenes talents that make movies possible, such as producers and special effects wizards. Another important feature of this index is the quality check it provides with categories like **Woofs!**, **4 Bones**, and **Top Grossing Films** by year. This index also provides information on recurring characters like James Bond or Mike Hammer, as well as notable screen partnerships. Some examples include Abbott & Costello, Hope & Crosby, and De Niro & Scorsese. **A tipped triangle denotes a three-bone or higher rating.** The categories are as follows, with an asterisk (*) denoting a new category:

Abbott & Costello

Adapted from:
a Book
a Cartoon
a Fairy Tale
a Game
a Play or Musical
a Poem
a Song
a Story
an Article
an Opera
Comics
Memoirs or Diaries
Television
the Radio

Alien and Rip-Offs
Allen & Farrow
Allen & Keaton
Amy Fisher
Andy Hardy
Astaire & Rogers
B/W & Color Combos
Basic Instinct and Rip-Offs
BBC TV Productions
Beach Party
Billy the Kid
Blondie
Bogart & Bacall

Books to Film:
Louisa May Alcott
Eric Ambler
Kingsley Amis
Hans Christian Andersen
Maya Angelou
Isaac Asimov
Jane Austen
Clive Barker
J.M. Barrie
Ambrose Bierce
Maeve Binchy
Robert Bloch

Judy Blume
Ray Bradbury
Barbara Taylor Bradford
Pearl S. Buck
Frances Hodgson Burnett
Edgar Rice Burroughs
William Burroughs
James M. Cain
Truman Capote
Barbara Cartland
Willa Cather
Raymond Chandler
Paddy Chayefsky
John Cheever
Anton Chechov
Agatha Christie
Tom Clancy
Mary Higgins Clark
Arthur C. Clarke
James Clavell
Jackie Collins
Richard Condon
Joseph Conrad
Pat Conroy
Robin Cook
Catherine Cookson
James Fenimore Cooper
Stephen Crane
Michael Crichton
Clive Cussler
Roald Dahl
Miguel de Cervantes
Guy de Maupassant
Daniel Defoe
Phillip K. Dick
Charles Dickens
E.L. Doctorow
Sir Arthur Conan Doyle
Daphne Du Maurier
Alexandre Dumas
Dominick Dunne
George Eliot
Bret Easton Ellis

Howard Fast
Edna Ferber
Henry Fielding
F. Scott Fitzgerald
Gustov Flaubert
Ian Fleming
Ken Follett
E.M. Forster
Frederick Forsyth
Rumer Godden
Nikolai Gogol
William Goldman
David Goodis
Elizabeth Goudge
Kenneth Grahame
Graham Greene
Zane Grey
John Grisham
H. Rider Haggard
Arthur Hailey
Alex Haley
Dashiell Hammett
Thomas Hardy
Harlequin Romances
Jim Harrison
Nathaniel Hawthorne
Ernest Hemingway
O. Henry
*Patricia Highsmith
James Hilton
S.E. Hinton
Victor Hugo
Fanny Hurst
John Irving
Washington Irving
Susan Isaacs
Rona Jaffe
John Jakes
Henry James
James Jones
James Joyce
Franz Kafka
Stephen King

Rudyard Kipling
Dean R. Koontz
Judith Krantz
Louis L'Amour
D.H. Lawrence
John Le Carre
Harper Lee
Elmore Leonard
Sinclair Lewis
Astrid Lindgren
Jack London
H.P. Lovecraft
Robert Ludlum
Peter Maas
Alistair MacLean
Norman Mailer
W. Somerset Maugham
Colleen McCullough
*Ian McEwan
Larry McMurtry
Herman Melville
James Michener
L.M. Montgomery
Vladimir Nabakov
Joyce Carol Oates
Marcel Pagnol
Nicholas Pileggi
Edgar Allan Poe
Katherine Ann Porter
Mario Puzo
*Ruth Rendell
Anne Rice
Harold Robbins
Sir Walter Scott
Sidney Sheldon
Mary Shelley
Danielle Steel
John Steinbeck
Stendahl
Robert Louis Stevenson
Bram Stoker
Harriet Beecher Stowe
Jacqueline Susann

Jonathan Swift
Paul Theroux
Jim Thompson
James Thurber
J.R.R. Tolkien
Leo Tolstoy
Scott Turow
Mark Twain
John Updike
Leon Uris
Jules Verne
Kurt Vonnegut
Alice Walker
Edgar Wallace
Joseph Wambaugh
Evelyn Waugh
H.G. Wells
Edith Wharton
William Wharton
Oscar Wilde
Thornton Wilder
Virginia Woolf
Cornell Woolrich
Herman Wouk

The Bowery Boys
Bulldog Drummond
Burton & Taylor
*Carpenter & Russell
Carry On
Charlie Brown and the
  Peanuts Gang
Charlie Chan
Cheech & Chong
Classics
Corman's Mama
Dirty Harry
Disney Animated Movies
Disney Family Movies
Dr. Christian
Dr. Mabuse
Dracula
Eddy & McDonald
Elvisfilm

Kibbles and Series Index

Recurrent characters, cinematic collaborations, various adaptations, and important behind-the-scenes personnel information is the focus of the **Kibbles and Series Index**. These categories are listed alphabetically. **A tipped triangle indicates a video rated three bones or higher.**

Adapted

Adapted

Adapted

The Return of the Native
Return of the Soldier➤
Return to Earth
Return to Oz
Reuben, Reuben➤
Reunion➤
Revenge
Reversal of Fortune➤
Rhapsody
Rhapsody in August
Rich in Love
Rich Man, Poor Man➤
The Riddle of the Sands
Ride a Wild Pony➤
Riders of the Purple Sage
The Right Stuff➤
Ring of Bright Water➤
Rip van Winkle
Rising Sun➤
The River Pirates
A River Runs Through It➤
The Robe
Robert Kennedy and His
    Times
Robin Hood➤
Robinson Crusoe
Rogue Male
Roll Along Cowboy
Roll of Thunder, Hear My Cry
Room at the Top➤
Room Service
A Room with a View➤
Roommates
Roots➤
Roots: The Gift
Roots: The Next Generation➤
The Rosary Murders
Rosebud
Rosemary's Baby➤
Roswell: The U.F.O. Cover-
    Up
Rough Magic
Roxanne➤
Royal Flash➤
Rudyard Kipling's The Jungle
    Book
Rudyard Kipling's the Second
    Jungle Book: Mowgli and
    Baloo
Rumble Fish➤
The Rumor Mill
A Rumor of War➤
Rumpole of the Bailey
Runaway
Running Against Time
The Running Man
Rush➤
The Russia House
The Russians are Coming,
    the Russians are Coming➤
Ruyblas
Sabotage➤
The Sacketts
Sadie Thompson➤
Safe Passage
The Sailor Who Fell from
    Grace with the Sea
The Saint
Saint Jack➤
Salo, or the 120 Days of
    Sodom
Salome
The Salzburg Connection
Sanctuary of Fear
Santa Fe
The Saragossa Manuscript
Sarah, Plain and Tall➤
Saratoga Trunk
Satan Met a Lady
Saturday Night and Sunday
    Morning➤
Savage Wilderness
Sayonara➤

The Scar
The Scarlet & the Black
Scarlet Dawn
The Scarlet Letter
The Scarlet Letter➤
The Scarlet Letter
The Scarlet Pimpernel➤
Scarlett
Schindler's List➤
Scott Turow's The Burden of
    Proof
Scrooge➤
Scrooge
Scruples
The Sea Wolf➤
The Sea Wolf
The Search for Bridey Murphy
Searching for Bobby Fischer➤
Second Best➤
Second Victory
Seconds➤
The Secret Adversary
The Secret Agent
The Secret Four
The Secret Garden
The Secret Garden
The Secret Garden➤
The Secret Garden
The Secret of NIMH➤
The Secret of Roan Inish➤
Seduced by Evil
Seduction: The Cruel Woman
The Seekers
Seize the Day➤
Sense & Sensibility
Sense and Sensibility➤
A Sense of Freedom➤
A Separate Peace
The Separation
Sergeant Rutledge➤
The Serpent and the Rainbow
Serpico➤
The Servant➤
Servants of Twilight
The Set Up
Seven Blows of the Dragon
7 Faces of Dr. Lao➤
The Seven-Per-Cent
    Solution➤
Seven Thieves➤
The Seventh Cross➤
S.F.W.
Shadow of China➤
Shadow of the Thin Man➤
Shadow of the Wolf
The Shadow Riders
ShadowZone: The Undead
    Express
Shaft➤
Shalako
Shane➤
Sharky's Machine
Sharpe's Battle
Sharpe's Company
Sharpe's Eagle
Sharpe's Enemy
Sharpe's Gold
Sharpe's Honour
Sharpe's Mission
Sharpe's Regiment
Sharpe's Rifles
Sharpe's Siege
Sharpe's Sword
Shattered Vows
She
She Came to the Valley
She-Devil
The Shell Seekers
The Sheltering Sky➤
Sherlock Holmes: The Silver
    Blaze
Sherlock Holmes: The Voice
    of Terror

Sherlock Hound: Tales of
    Mystery
Shiloh
The Shining
Shining Through
Ship of Fools➤
Shipwrecked
A Shock to the System➤
The Shoes of the Fisherman
Shogun➤
Shoot the Piano Player➤
The Shooting Party➤
The Shootist➤
The Shout➤
Shout at the Devil
Sidney Sheldon's Bloodline
Silas Marner➤
The Silence of the Lambs➤
The Silk Road
Silver Bears
Silver Bullet
The Silver Chalice
The Silver Horde
Silver River
The Silver Stallion: King of the
    Wild Brumbies
A Simple Twist of Fate
Single White Female
The Sins of Dorian Gray
The Sisters➤
Ski Bum
Skyscraper Souls➤
Slapstick of Another Kind
Slaughterhouse Five
Slaves of New York
Sleepers
Sleepy Eyes of Death: The
    Chinese Jade
Slightly Honorable
Slightly Scarlet
The Slingshot➤
Sliver
Slow Burn
A Small Killing
Smart-Aleck Kill
Smilla's Sense of Snow
Smith!
The Snake Pit➤
SnakeEater 3: His Law
The Snapper➤
Snow Country
Snow Treasure
Sofie
Solaris
Soldier Blue
Soldier in the Rain
Solo
Solomon and Sheba
Something of Value➤
Something Wicked This Way
    Comes
Sometimes a Great Notion➤
Somewhere in Sonora
Son of Fury➤
Son of the Morning Star➤
Sophie's Choice➤
Sounder➤
South Central
South Pacific➤
South Riding
The Spanish Gardener➤
Special Investigator
Spencer's Mountain
Spenser: Ceremony
Spenser: Pale Kings &
    Princes
Spirit Lost
Spirit Rider➤
Spirits of the Dead➤
The Spoilers➤
The Spook Who Sat By the
    Door
Spy in Black➤

Spy of Napoleon
Spy Story
The Spy Who Came in from
    the Cold➤
The Squeaker
Stars and Bars
Stars in My Crown➤
The Stars Look Down➤
State Fair➤
State Fair
Staying On
Steaming
Stella
Stella Dallas➤
Stephen King's It
Stephen King's The
    Langoliers
Stephen King's The Stand
Stephen King's The
    Tommyknockers
Stephen King's Thinner
Steppenwolf
Stick
Stiletto
Stonewall➤
Stopover Tokyo
Storm and Sorrow
The Story of a Three Day
    Pass
The Story of Dr. Wassell
The Story of Esther Costello
The Story of O
The Story of Qui Ju➤
Straight Time➤
Strange Case of Dr. Jekyll &
    Mr. Hyde
Strange Fruit
Strange Tales/Ray Bradbury
    Theatre
The Stranger Wore a Gun
Strangers on a Train➤
Strangers When We Meet
The Streets of San
    Francisco➤
Striptease
Stuart Saves His Family
Studs Lonigan
The Stunt Man➤
The Stupids
Sudden Fear➤
Sudie & Simpson➤
Sugartime
Summer Heat
The Summer House
Summer of Fear
The Summer of My German
    Soldier➤
A Summer Place
The Sundowners➤
Surviving Picasso
Suzy
Svengali➤
Svengali
Swann in Love
The Sweet Hereafter➤
Sweet Hostage
Sweet Killing
Sweet Love, Bitter
The Swiss Family Robinson➤
Sword of Gideon
Tai-Pan
A Tale of Two Cities➤
A Tale of Two Cities
A Tale of Two Cities➤
Tall Story
Taras Bulba
Tarnished Angels➤
Tarzan, the Ape Man➤
Tarzan, the Ape Man
Tecumseh: The Last Warrior
TekWar
Temptation of a Monk

Ten Days That Shook the
    World➤
Ten Days Wonder
Ten Little Indians
Ten North Frederick
The Tenant➤
Tender Is the Night
The Tenth Man
10th Victim
The Terminal Man
Terror Is a Man
Terror Stalks the Class
    Reunion
Tess➤
Tex
Texas
The Texas Rangers
That Darn Cat
That Eye, The Sky
That Forsyte Woman
That Night
That Obscure Object of
    Desire➤
That Uncertain Feeling
That Was Then...This Is No
They Call It Sin
They Came to Cordura
They Live by Night➤
They Won't Forget➤
Thicker Than Water
The Thief Who Came to
    Dinner
Thieves Like Us➤
The Thing➤
Things to Come➤
The Third Man➤
Third Man on the Mountain
This Gun for Hire
This Sweet Sickness
The Thorn Birds➤
Those Calloways
Three Came Home➤
Three Comrades➤
Three Days of the Condor➤
The Three Musketeers
The Three Musketeers➤
The Three Musketeers
The Three Musketeers➤
3:10 to Yuma➤
The Three Worlds of Gullive
Thumbelina
Thunder Mountain
Thunder Pass
Till Death Do Us Part
Till the End of Time
Tim
The Time Machine➤
Time Machine
Time of Indifference
A Time to Kill➤
A Time to Love & a Time to
    Die
The Tin Drum➤
To Catch a Thief➤
To Dance with the White
    Dog➤
To Die For➤
To Have & Have Not➤
To Hell and Back
To Kill a Mockingbird➤
To Play the King
To Sir, with Love
To the Devil, A Daughter➤
To the Last Man
To the Lighthouse
Tokyo Decadence
Tom and Huck
Tom Brown's School Days
Tom Brown's School Days➤
Tom Jones➤
Tom Sawyer
Tomb
Topaz➤

Adapted

Les Visiteurs du Soir►
The Little Match Girl
The Little Mermaid
The Little Mermaid►
Little Red Riding Hood
The Magic Fountain
The Magic Sword
Magical Wonderland
March of the Wooden
 Soldiers►
Mother Goose Rock 'n'
 Rhyme
The NeverEnding Story►
The Neverending Story 3:
 escape from Fantasia
The Nightingale
The Nutcracker Prince
Nutcracker: The Motion
 Picture
Once Upon a Brothers Grimm
Peter Pan►
The Pied Piper of Hamelin
Pinocchio►
Pinocchio
Pinocchio's Storybook
 Adventures
The Princess and the Pea
The Princess and the
 Swineherd
The Princess Bride►
Princess Cinderella
The Princess Who Never
 Laughed
Puss 'n Boots
Rapunzel
Red Riding Hood
Rip van Winkle
Rumpelstiltskin
The Scalawag Bunch
Sleeping Beauty►
Sleeping Beauty
The Snow Queen
Snow White
Snow White and the Seven
 Dwarfs
Snow White and the Three
 Stooges
The Swan►
The Swan Princess
The Tale of the Frog Prince►
The Three Little Pigs
Thumbelina
The Tin Soldier
Tom Thumb
Who Slew Auntie Roo?
The Wishmaker
The Witches►
The Wonderful World of the
 Brothers Grimm
The Wonders of Aladdin

Adapted from a Game

Clue
Double Dragon
Mortal Kombat 1: The Movie
Street Fighter
Super Mario Bros.
Tag: The Assassination
 Game

Adapted from a Play or Musical

Abe Lincoln in Illinois►
The Adventures of Robin
 Hood►
Aelita: Queen of Mars
Age Old Friends►
Agnes of God
Ah, Wilderness!►
Alfie►

Alice
All My Sons►
Amadeus►
American Buffalo
Anastasia►
Animal Crackers►
The Animal Kingdom►
Anna Christie►
Anna Christie
Annie
The Anniversary►
Another Country
Any Wednesday
Arsenic and Old Lace►
As Is
As You Desire Me►
August
The Avenger
The Awful Truth►
Babes in Arms
Babes in Toyland
Baby Doll►
Baby, the Rain Must Fall
The Bacchantes
The Bad Seed
The Balcony►
The Ballad of the Sad Cafe
Bar Girls
Barefoot in the Park►
Beatlemania! The Movie
Beau Brummel
Beau Brummel►
Beautiful Thing►
Becket►
Becky Sharp►
Being at Home with Claude►
Bells are Ringing►
Best Foot Forward
The Best Little Whorehouse in
 Texas
The Best Man►
Betrayal
Beyond Therapy
The Big Knife►
Big News
Billie
Biloxi Blues
The Birth of a Nation►
Bitter Sweet
Black Limelight
Black Lizard
Black Orpheus►
Blessed Event►
Blithe Spirit►
Blood Wedding
Bluebeard's Eighth Wife
Bodies, Rest & Motion
Bopha!►
Born Yesterday►
Born Yesterday
Boy Meets Girl►
The Boys in the Band
The Boys Next Door
Breaking the Code
Breath of Scandal
The Brig►
Brigadoon►
Brighton Beach Memoirs
Broadway Bound
Broken Glass
A Bronx Tale►
A Brother's Kiss
The Browning Version►
The Browning Version
Bus Stop►
Butterflies Are Free►
Bye, Bye, Birdie►
Cabaret►
Cactus Flower
Caesar and Cleopatra
California Suite►
Can-Can
Casablanca►

Casanova Brown
Cast a Dark Shadow►
Casual Sex?►
Cat on a Hot Tin Roof►
Cat on a Hot Tin Roof
Cavalcade►
Cease Fire
Ceiling Zero►
The Chalk Garden►
Chapter Two
Charm of La Boheme
The Chase
The Cheap Detective►
Children of a Lesser God►
The Children's Hour
Chimes at Midnight►
China
The Chocolate Soldier►
A Chorus Line
A Chorus of Disapproval
Circle of Love
Clarence Darrow►
Clarence, the Cross-eyed
 Lion►
Clash by Night►
The Climax
Columbo: Prescription Murder
Come Back, Little Sheba►
Come Back to the Five &
 Dime Jimmy Dean, Jimmy
 Dean►
Come Blow Your Horn►
Command Decision
Conduct Unbecoming
Cool Mikado
Coquette
The Corn is Green►
Cosi►
The Count of the Old Town
Country Girl►
County Fair
Craig's Wife►
Crimes of the Heart►
The Crucible►
Curse of the Starving Class
Cyrano de Bergerac►
Cyrano de Bergerac►
Da
Daddy's Dyin'...Who's Got the
 Will?
Damn Yankees►
A Day in the Death of Joe
 Egg►
Day of Wrath►
Daybreak
Dead End►
Death and the Maiden►
Death of a Salesman►
Deathtrap
The Desert Song
The Designated Mourner
Desire Under the Elms►
Desk Set►
Desperate Hours►
Detective Story►
Devil Girl from Mars
The Devil's Brother
The Devil's Disciple►
Dial "M" for Murder►
Diary of a Hitman
The Dining Room
Dinner at Eight►
Disraeli►
The Divorce of Lady X
The Doctor and the Devils
Doll Face
A Doll's House►
A Doll's House
Don't Drink the Water
Double Wedding►
The Dresser►
Driving Miss Daisy►

Drunks
DuBarry Was a Lady
Duet for One
Dumb Waiter
Dutchman►
The Eagle Has Two Heads►
Easy Virtue
Educating Rita►
Edward II
The Effect of Gamma Rays on
 Man-in-the-Moon
 Marigolds►
Emperor Jones
Emperor Jones/Paul
 Robeson: Tribute to an
 Artist
Employees' Entrance►
The Enchanted Cottage
Ensign Pulver
The Entertainer►
Entertaining Mr. Sloane
Equus
Escapade►
Escape Me Never
Everybody Wins
Evita►
Faithful
The Farmer Takes a Wife►
The Farmer's Wife
A Few Good Men►
Fiddler on the Roof►
The Field►
A Fine Romance
Finian's Rainbow►
Five Graves to Cairo►
Flower Drum Song
Follies in Concert
Fool for Love
Footlight Serenade
Footsteps in the Dark►
Forbidden Planet►
Forever Female►
Fortune and Men's Eyes►
Forty Carats
Foxfire►
Frankenstein Sings...The
 Movie
Frankie and Johnny►
The Front Page►
The Fugitive Kind
Fun
A Funny Thing Happened on
 the Way to the Forum►
Fury is a Woman►
Futz
Gaslight►
The Gay Divorcee►
The Gazebo►
Generation
Gentlemen Prefer Blondes►
George Washington Slept
 Here►
George White's Scandals
Getting Out
The Ghost Breakers►
Give Me a Sailor
The Glass Menagerie►
Glengarry Glen Ross►
Golden Boy►
The Golden Coach►
Gone are the Days
The Goodbye Girl►
The Gorilla
Grease►
Grease 2
The Great White Hope►
Green Pastures►
Grown Ups
The Guardsman►
Gypsy►
Gypsy
Hair►
The Hairy Ape

Hamlet
Hamlet
Hamlet►
The Happiest Days of Your
 Life►
Happy Birthday, Gemini
Harriet Craig►
He Who Gets Slapped►
Heartbreak House
Heaven Can Wait►
Hedda
The Heidi Chronicles
Hello, Dolly!
Henry IV
Henry V►
His Double Life
His Girl Friday►
Hit the Deck
Holiday►
Homage
The Honey Pot
Hotel Paradiso
The Hound of London
I Confess
I Do! I Do!
I Married an Angel
I Never Sang For My Father►
I Ought to Be in Pictures
I Remember Mama►
Idiot's Delight►
Illicit
Illusions
I'm Not Rappaport
The Impossible Years
In Celebration►
In Search of the Castaways►
In the Good Old
 Summertime►
Indiscreet
Inherit the Wind►
Iphigenia
Irma La Douce
Italian Straw Hat►
Jacknife►
Jeffrey
Jesus Christ, Superstar►
Joan of Arc
Johnny Belinda
Jubal
Julius Caesar►
Julius Caesar
Key Exchange
Key Largo►
The Killing of Sister George►
King and Country►
The King and I►
King Lear►
King Lear
Kiss Me Kate►
Kiss Me, Stupid!
The Knack►
K2: The Ultimate High
La Cage aux Folles►
La Cage aux Folles 2
La Cage aux Folles 3: The
 Wedding
La Ronde►
Ladies They Talk About
Lady Be Good
The Lady's Not for Burning
The Last of Mrs. Cheyney►
Last of the Red Hot Lovers
Laughing Sinners
Lenny►
Les Enfants Terrible►
A Life in the Theater
Li'l Abner
Lilies►
Lily Dale
The Lion in Winter►
The Little Foxes►
Little Johnny Jones
Little Murders►

Adapted

Legend of Tom Dooley
Love Potion #9
My Darlin' Clementine
The Night the Lights Went Out in Georgia
Ode to Billy Joe
Purple People Eater
Single Bars, Single Women
Take This Job & Shove It
Yellow Submarine►
You Light Up My Life

Adapted from a Story

ABC Stage 67: Truman Capote's A Christmas Memory
The Adventures of Ichabod and Mr. Toad►
The Affair of the Pink Pearl
Alice in Wonderland►
Alice in Wonderland
Amanda and the Alien
Ambassador Bill
America's Dream►
Androcles and the Lion
The Android Affair
Angels in the Outfield►
Angels with Dirty Faces►
Appointment with Crime
Arizona Bushwackers
As Young As You Feel►
Ashik Kerib►
The Assassination Bureau►
Ava's Magical Adventure
Babette's Feast►
The Babysitter
The Ballad of the Sad Cafe
Bartleby
The Beast from 20,000 Fathoms
Benefit of the Doubt
Big Business Girl
The Big Stampede
Billy the Kid
The Birds►
The Black Abbot
Blackmail►
Boots of Destiny
Border Caballero
Boss of Bullion City
A Boy and His Dog
Boys
Boys' Night Out►
Breakfast at Tiffany's►
Brief Encounter►
Brigham Young: Frontiersman
Bright Angel
Burial of the Rats
Burning Daylight
Bury Me Not on the Lone Prairie
By the Light of the Silvery Moon
Call of the Wild
Candyman
Candyman 2: Farewell to the Flesh
The Canterville Ghost
Carmilla
Casanova's Big Night
Cat's Eye
Caught in the Draft►
Celine and Julie Go Boating
Charade►
Cinderella
Cinderella 2000
The Cisco Kid
College Swing
Comanche Territory
Come to the Stable►
Comrade X
Cosmic Slop

Crash Dive
Creature from the Black Lagoon►
Creature with the Blue Hand
Cricket on the Hearth
Cult of the Cobra
Curtis's Charm
Dark Eyes►
Daughter of the Dragon
David and Bathsheba►
A Day in the Country►
The Day the Earth Stood Still►
The Dead►
The Decameron►
Decameron Nights
Department Store
The Desperadoes
Detonator 2: Night Watch
The Devil & Daniel Webster►
Diary of a Madman
Die, Monster, Die!
Dive Bomber►
Doomed at Sundown
Door with the Seven Locks
Double Trouble
Double Vision
D.P.
Drift Fence
DROP Squad
The Dropkick►
Eat a Bowl of Tea►
The Eyes of the Amaryllis
Eyes of the Panther
A Face in the Crowd►
Face to Face
Fallen Angels 1►
Fallen Angels 2►
Feud Maker
The Fig Tree
The Fighter►
Fighting Caravans
First Love
Five Days One Summer
The 5000 Fingers of Dr. T►
Flirtation Walk
Forger of London
Frontier Uprising
Galloping Romeo
Gangway
A Gentle Woman
The Ghost of Frankenstein
Ghost Valley
The Gift of Love
The Girl with the Hungry Eyes
The Glass House►
The Go-Between►
Great Adventure
The Great Man's Lady
Gunfight at the O.K. Corral►
Guys and Dolls►
Halfmoon
Hands Across the Table►
The Hard Way►
Haunting Fear
The Haunting of Morella
Highlander►
Hills of Oklahoma
Hole in the Sky
Home for the Holidays
Homecoming
Hondo►
Hostile Guns
The House of Usher
How the Grinch Stole Christmas►
How to Steal a Million►
H.P. Lovecraft's Necronomicon: Book of the Dead
I Don't Want to Talk About It
I'm the One You're Looking For
Importance of Being Earnest►

In Memoriam
In Old Chicago►
In the Gloaming►
The Incredible Sarah
The Indian Scarf
Internes Can't Take Money
Invasion U.S.A.
Inventing the Abbotts
The Invisible Boy
The Invisible Woman►
Isle of Forgotten Sins
It Came from Outer Space 2
It Started with Eve►
It's a Date
It's a Dog's Life
Jigsaw►
Johnny Eager►
Johnny Mnemonic
Johnny Reno
Jonathan Livingston Seagull
Judgment Night
The Jungle Book
The Juniper Tree
Kaos►
Key to the City
The Kill-Off
Kim►
Kissed
Kull the Conqueror
Kurt Vonnegut's Harrison Bergeron
Kurt Vonnegut's Monkey House
La Chute de la Maison Usher►
La Merveilleuse Visite
The Ladies of the Bois de Bologne
The Lady Eve►
Lady Killer►
Lady On a Train►
The Lady with the Dog►
The Land Unknown
Late Chrysanthemums
The Lawnmower Man
The Lawrenceville Stories
Le Plaisir
The Leech Woman
Legends of the North
L'Eleve
Life on a String
Little Miss Marker
The Little Prince
Lone Star
Lord of Illusions
The Lost World
Love on the Run
Loyalties
Lurking Fear
The Magic Fountain
The Magnificent Dope
Main Street to Broadway
Manfish
The Mangler
Mapp & Lucia
Margaret's Museum►
The Masked Rider
Masque of the Red Death►
Masque of the Red Death
Maximum Overdrive
Menace II Society►
Midnight►
A Million to Juan
Miracle in Rome
Mr. Reeder in Room 13
A Month by the Lake
The Most Dangerous Game►
The Mummy's Curse
The Mummy's Tomb
Murders in the Rue Morgue
The Murders in the Rue Morgue►
My Apprenticeship►

My Childhood►
My Favorite Blonde►
My Lucky Star
My Mother's Castle►
My Sister Eileen►
My Universities►
The Mysterious Magician
Mystic Circle Murder
Naked Jungle►
The Naked Maja
Nevada
Never Say Goodbye
Nightfall
Nightflyers
No Comebacks
Noir et Blanc
Noon Wine►
Now and Forever
Objective, Burma!►
The Oblong Box
O.C. and Stiggs
An Occurrence at Owl Creek Bridge/Coup de Grace
Of Human Hearts
On Moonlight Bay
100 Men and a Girl►
Our Modern Maidens
Our Relations►
The Outlaw Deputy
The Oval Portrait
Peck's Bad Boy
The Pied Piper of Hamelin
The Pit and the Pendulum►
The Pit & the Pendulum
Pittsburgh
Play Misty for Me►
Pocketful of Miracles►
The Possessed►
Premature Burial
The Prince and the Pauper
The Princess and the Swineherd
Pudd'nhead Wilson
The Purchase Price
The Quarrel
The Queen of Spades►
Quest for Love
Rawhead Rex
Re-Animator►
Rear Window►
Red Balloon/Occurrence at Owl Creek Bridge►
The Red Shoes►
The Redhead from Wyoming
The Reluctant Dragon
The Report on the Party and the Guests►
Return to Paradise
Return to the Lost World
Revenge of the Creature
Ride Him, Cowboy►
Ridin' Down the Canyon
Ridin' the Lone Trail
Robbers of the Sacred Mountain
Rocket to the Moon
The Rocking Horse Winner
Roman Holiday►
Roommate
Rough Ridin' Rhythm
Ruggles of Red Gap►
Rumpelstiltskin
Salome
Santa Fe
Saturday Night Fever
Screamers
Secret of the Black Trunk
Seven Brides for Seven Brothers►
The Seven Hills of Rome
Shadow of a Doubt►
Shanghai Express►

The Shawshank Redemption►
Sherlock Holmes: The Mast Blackmailer
Shinbone Alley
The Shooting Party
Shopworn Angel►
Short Cuts►
The Skull
Sleep of Death
Sleeping Car to Trieste
Smooth Talk►
The Snow Queen
Snow White and the Seven Dwarfs►
The Snows of Kilimanjaro►
Somewhere I'll Find You►
Song of the Thin Man
Sorrows of Gin
Sorry, Wrong Number►
The Southerner►
The Spectre of Edgar Allen Poe
Stagecoach►
Station West►
The Strange Countess
The Strange Door
Strawberry and Chocolate►
A Summer Story►
A Summer to Remember
Sunset Boulevard►
The Swimmer►
Tails You Live, Heads You're Dead
Tales from Avonlea, Vol. 1: The Journey Begins
Tales from the Darkside: The Movie
Tales of Terror
Tales of the Klondike: In a Fa Country
Tales of the Klondike: Race for Number One
Tales of the Klondike: The Scorn of Women
Tales of the Klondike: The Unexpected
The Tell-Tale Heart
Tennessee's Partner
They Met in Bombay
They Watch
The Thin Man►
The Thin Man Goes Home
The Thing
Three Brothers►
Three Cases of Murder►
The Three Little Pigs
Three Smart Girls►
Through the Eyes of a Killer
Thunder Pass
The Tin Soldier
Today We Live
Tomb of Ligeia►
Tomorrow►
Tonto Basin Outlaws
Too Far to Go►
The Topeka Terror
Torture Garden
Torture Ship
Trailin'
Transmutations
Trapped in Space
Tribute to a Bad Man►
Trio►
Tropical Heat
Trumps
Twelve Chairs►
12:01
Two by Forsyth
Two Evil Eyes
Uncertain Glory
An Unforgettable Summer
Vanina Vanini►

Death on the Nile
Endless Night
Evil under the Sun
Finessing the King
The House of Lurking Death
Love from a Stranger
The Man in the Mist
The Mirror Crack'd
Murder Ahoy
Murder at the Gallop⚫
A Murder Is Announced
Murder Most Foul⚫
Murder on the Orient
  Express⚫
Murder She Said
Ordeal by Innocence
A Pocketful of Rye
The Secret Adversary
Ten Little Indians
The Unbreakable Alibi
Witness for the Prosecution⚫

Books to Film: Tom Clancy

Clear and Present Danger
The Hunt for Red October⚫
Patriot Games⚫

Books to Film: Mary Higgins Clark

The Cradle Will Fall
A Cry in the Night
Double Vision
Terror Stalks the Class
  Reunion

Books to Film: Arthur C. Clarke

Trapped in Space
2001: A Space Odyssey⚫
2010: The Year We Make
  Contact⚫

Books to Film: James Clavell

King Rat
Noble House
Shogun⚫
Tai-Pan

Books to Film: Jackie Collins

The Bitch
The World is Full of Married
  Men
Yesterday's Hero

Books to Film: Richard Condon

Gun Crazy
The Manchurian Candidate⚫
Prizzi's Honor⚫
Winter Kills⚫

Books to Film: Joseph Conrad

Apocalypse Now⚫
The Duellists⚫
Face to Face
Heart of Darkness
Lord Jim⚫
Nostromo
Sabotage⚫
The Secret Agent

Books to Film: Pat Conroy

Conrack⚫
The Great Santini⚫
The Lords of Discipline
The Prince of Tides⚫

Books to Film: Robin Cook

Coma⚫
Sphinx

Books to Film: Catherine Cookson

The Black Velvet Gown
The Cinder Path
The Dwelling Place
The Fifteen Streets
The Gambling Man
The Glass Virgin
The Man Who Cried

Books to Film: James Fenimore Cooper

The Deerslayer
The Last of the Mohicans⚫
The Last of the Mohicans
The Last of the Mohicans⚫
The Last of the Redmen
The Pathfinder

Books to Film: Stephen Crane

Face to Face
The Red Badge of Courage⚫

Books to Film: Michael Crichton

The Andromeda Strain
Congo
The Great Train Robbery⚫
Jurassic Park⚫
The Lost World: Jurassic Park
  2
Rising Sun⚫
The Terminal Man
Westworld⚫

Books to Film: Clive Cussler

Raise the Titanic

Books to Film: Roald Dahl

James and the Giant Peach⚫
Matilda⚫
Willy Wonka & the Chocolate
  Factory⚫
The Witches⚫

Books to Film: Miguel de Cervantes

Don Quixote⚫
Man of La Mancha

Books to Film: Guy de Maupassant

A Day in the Country⚫
Diary of a Madman
Le Plaisir
The Private Affairs of Bel
  Ami⚫
A Woman Without Love⚫

Books to Film: Daniel Defoe

The Amorous Adventures of
  Moll Flanders
Crusoe
Man Friday
Moll Flanders
Robinson Crusoe
Robinson Crusoe on Mars

Books to Film: Phillip K. Dick

Barjo
Blade Runner⚫
Screamers
Total Recall⚫

Books to Film: Charles Dickens

An American Christmas Carol
Bleak House
A Christmas Carol⚫
A Christmas Carol
A Christmas Carol⚫
Cricket on the Hearth
David Copperfield⚫
David Copperfield
Great Expectations⚫
Great Expectations
Great Expectations⚫
Great Expectations: The
  Untold Story
The Life and Adventures of
  Nicholas Nickleby⚫
Little Dorrit, Film 1: Nobody's
  Fault⚫
Little Dorrit, Film 2: Little
  Dorrit's Story⚫
Martin Chuzzlewit
The Muppet Christmas Carol
The Mystery of Edwin Drood
Nicholas Nickleby⚫
The Old Curiosity Shop
Oliver!⚫
Oliver & Company
Oliver Twist⚫
Oliver Twist
Oliver Twist⚫
Oliver Twist
The Pickwick Papers
Scrooge⚫
Scrooge
A Tale of Two Cities⚫
A Tale of Two Cities
A Tale of Two Cities⚫
Tale of Two Cities/In the
  Switch Tower

Books to Film: E.L. Doctorow

Billy Bathgate
Daniel
Ragtime⚫

Books to Film: Fyodor Dostoyevski

The Brothers Karamazov⚫
Crime and Punishment⚫
Crime and Punishment
A Gentle Woman
La Vengeance d'une Femme
L'Idiot
White Nights⚫

Books to Film: Sir Arthur Conan Doyle

The Adventures of Sherlock
  Holmes

The Adventures of Sherlock
  Holmes: Hound of the
  Baskervilles
The Crucifer of Blood
Dressed to Kill
The Hound of the
  Baskervilles⚫
The Hound of the Baskervilles
House of Fear
The Lost World
Masks of Death
Murder at the Baskervilles
The Pearl of Death
Return to the Lost World
Robbers of the Sacred
  Mountain
Scarlet Claw⚫
Sherlock Holmes and the
  Deadly Necklace
Sherlock Holmes and the
  Secret Weapon⚫
Sherlock Holmes: The Master
  Blackmailer
Sherlock Hound: Tales of
  Mystery
The Sign of Four
The Silent Mr. Sherlock
  Holmes
Tales from the Darkside: The
  Movie
The Triumph of Sherlock
  Holmes
The Woman in Green

Books to Film: Daphne Du Maurier

The Birds⚫
Don't Look Now⚫
Jamaica Inn⚫
Rebecca⚫

Books to Film: Alexandre Dumas

At Sword's Point
Black Magic
Camille⚫
Camille
The Corsican Brothers⚫
The Count of Monte Cristo⚫
The Count of Monte Cristo⚫
The Count of Monte Cristo
The Four Musketeers⚫
The Iron Mask
The Man in the Iron Mask⚫
The Prince of Thieves
Queen Margot⚫
The Return of the Musketeers
Robin Hood⚫
Sword of Monte Cristo
The Three Musketeers⚫
The Three Musketeers⚫
The Three Musketeers
The Three Musketeers⚫

Books to Film: Dominick Dunne

An Inconvenient Woman

Books to Film: George Eliot

Middlemarch⚫
The Mill on the Floss
Silas Marner⚫
A Simple Twist of Fate

Books to Film: Bret Easton Ellis

Less Than Zero

Books to Film: Howard Fast

Freedom Road

Books to Film: William Faulkner

Intruder in the Dust⚫
The Long, Hot Summer⚫
The Reivers⚫
Tarnished Angels⚫
Today We Live
Tomorrow⚫
William Faulkner's Old Man

Books to Film: Edna Ferber

Cimarron
Dinner at Eight⚫
Dinner at Eight
Giant⚫
Saratoga Trunk
Show Boat⚫
Show Boat
Stage Door⚫

Books to Film: Henry Fielding

Joseph Andrews
Tom Jones⚫

Books to Film: F. Scott Fitzgerald

The Great Gatsby
The Last Time I Saw Paris
The Last Tycoon⚫
Tender Is the Night

Books to Film: Gustov Flaubert

Madame Bovary⚫
Salammbo

Books to Film: Ian Fleming

Casino Royale
Chitty Chitty Bang Bang
Diamonds Are Forever⚫
Dr. No⚫
For Your Eyes Only⚫
From Russia with Love⚫
Goldfinger⚫
License to Kill⚫
Live and Let Die
The Living Daylights⚫
The Man with the Golden Gun
Moonraker
Never Say Never Again
Octopussy
On Her Majesty's Secret
  Service⚫
The Poppy Is Also a Flower
The Spy Who Loved Me
Thunderball
A View to a Kill
You Only Live Twice

Books to Film: Ken Follett

Capricorn One⚫
Eye of the Needle
The Key to Rebecca
Lie Down with Lions

Books to Film: E.M. Forster

Howard's End⚫
Maurice⚫

Books

The Russia House
The Spy Who Came in from the Cold►

Books to Film: Harper Lee

To Kill a Mockingbird►

Books to Film: Elmore Leonard

The Ambassador
Cat Chaser
52 Pick-Up
Get Shorty►
Glitz
Hombre►
Last Stand at Saber River
Stick
3:10 to Yuma►
Touch
Valdez is Coming

Books to Film: Sinclair Lewis

Ann Vickers
Arrowsmith
Dodsworth►
Elmer Gantry►

Books to Film: Astrid Lindgren

The Land of Faraway
The New Adventures of Pippi Longstocking
Pippi Goes on Board
Pippi in the South Seas
Pippi Longstocking
Pippi on the Run

Books to Film: Jack London

The Assassination Bureau►
Burning Daylight
Call of the Wild
The Fighter
Great Adventure
The Legend of Sea Wolf
The Legend of the Sea Wolf
Legends of the North
The Mutiny of the Elsinore
The Sea Wolf►
The Sea Wolf
Tales of the Klondike: In a Far Country
Tales of the Klondike: Race for Number One
Tales of the Klondike: The Scorn of Women
Tales of the Klondike: The Unexpected
Torture Ship
White Fang►
White Fang and the Hunter
Wolf Call

Books to Film: H.P. Lovecraft

Blood Island
Bride of Re-Animator
Cthulhu Mansion
The Curse
Die, Monster, Die!
The Dunwich Horror
From Beyond►
The Haunted Palace
H.P. Lovecraft's Necronomicon: Book of the Dead

Lurking Fear
Re-Animator►
The Resurrected
The Sinister Invasion
The Unnamable
The Unnamable 2: The Statement of Randolph Carter

Books to Film: Robert Ludlum

The Bourne Identity►
The Holcroft Covenant
The Osterman Weekend

Books to Film: Peter Maas

King of the Gypsies
Marie►
Serpico►

Books to Film: Alistair MacLean

Bear Island
Breakheart Pass
Caravan to Vaccares
Detonator
Detonator 2: Night Watch
Force 10 from Navarone
Golden Rendezvous
The Guns of Navarone►
Ice Station Zebra
Puppet on a Chain
River of Death
Where Eagles Dare►

Books to Film: Norman Mailer

The Executioner's Song
Marilyn: The Untold Story►
The Naked and the Dead
Pursuit►
Tough Guys Don't Dance

Books to Film: W. Somerset Maugham

Adorable Julia
Beachcomber
Dirty Gertie from Harlem U.S.A.
Encore►
The Letter►
Miss Sadie Thompson►
The Moon and Sixpence►
Of Human Bondage►
Of Human Bondage
Overnight Sensation
The Painted Veil
Rain
The Razor's Edge►
The Razor's Edge
Sadie Thompson►
Trio►

Books to Film: Colleen McCullough

An Indecent Obsession
The Thorn Birds►
Tim

Books to Film: Ian McEwan

The Cement Garden
The Comfort of Strangers►
The Innocent

Books to Film: Larry McMurtry

The Best Little Whorehouse in Texas
Hud►
Larry McMurtry's Dead Man's Walk
The Last Picture Show►
Lonesome Dove►
Terms of Endearment►
Texasville

Books to Film: Herman Melville

Bartleby
Enchanted Island
Moby Dick►

Books to Film: James Michener

The Bridges at Toko-Ri►
Dynasty
Hawaii►
Return to Paradise
Sayonara►
Texas
Until They Sail

Books to Film: L.M. Montgomery

Anne of Avonlea►
Anne of Green Gables►
Lantern Hill
Tales from Avonlea, Vol. 1: The Journey Begins

Books to Film: Vladimir Nabokov

Despair►
Lolita►

Books to Film: Joyce Carol Oates

Foxfire
Smooth Talk►

Books to Film: Marcel Pagnol

The Baker's Wife►
Fanny►
Jean de Florette►
Manon of the Spring►
Marius►
My Father's Glory►
My Mother's Castle►
Topaze►

Books to Film: Nicholas Pileggi

Casino►
Goodfellas►

Books to Film: Edgar Allan Poe

The Black Cat►
The Black Cat
Dr. Tarr's Torture Dungeon
The Fall of the House of Usher
The Fall of the House of Usher►
The Fall of the House of Usher
The Haunted Palace
Haunting Fear
The Haunting of Morella
The House of Usher

Jaws of Justice
La Chute de la Maison Usher►
The Living Coffin
Manfish
Masque of the Red Death►
Masque of the Red Death
Murders in the Rue Morgue
The Murders in the Rue Morgue►
The Oblong Box
The Oval Portrait
The Pit and the Pendulum►
The Pit & the Pendulum
Premature Burial
The Raven►
The Raven
The Spectre of Edgar Allen Poe
Spirits of the Dead►
Tales of Terror
The Tell-Tale Heart
Tomb of Ligeia►
The Torture Chamber of Dr. Sadism
Two Evil Eyes
Web of the Spider

Books to Film: Katherine Anne Porter

Noon Wine►
Ship of Fools►

Books to Film: Mario Puzo

The Godfather►
The Godfather, Part 2►
The Godfather, Part 3►
The Last Don
The Sicilian

Books to Film: Ruth Rendell

A Dark Adapted Eye►
A Fatal Inversion►
Gallowglass►
La Ceremonie►

Books to Film: Anne Rice

Exit to Eden
Interview with the Vampire

Books to Film: Harold Robbins

The Adventurers
The Betsy
The Carpetbaggers
King Creole
The Lonely Lady
Nevada Smith
Never Love a Stranger
Stiletto
Where Love Has Gone

Books to Film: Sir Walter Scott

Ivanhoe►
Ivanhoe
Ivanhoe►
King Richard and the Crusaders

Books to Film: Sidney Sheldon

The Naked Face
The Other Side of Midnight

Rage of Angels
Rage of Angels: The Story Continues
Sidney Sheldon's Bloodline
Windmills of the Gods

Books to Film: Mary Shelley

The Bride of Frankenstein►
Frankenstein►
Frankenstein
Frankenstein Unbound►
Mary Shelley's Frankenstein

Books to Film: Danielle Steel

Danielle Steel's Changes
Danielle Steel's "Daddy"
Danielle Steel's Heartbeat
Danielle Steel's Kaleidoscope
Danielle Steel's Palomino
Danielle Steel's Star
Fine Things
Now and Forever
The Promise

Books to Film: John Steinbeck

Cannery Row
East of Eden►
East of Eden
The Grapes of Wrath►
Lifeboat►
Of Mice and Men►
The Pearl►
The Red Pony►
Tortilla Flat►

Books to Film: Stendhal

La Chartreuse de Parme
The Red and the Black►
Vanina Vanini►

Books to Film: Robert Louis Stevenson

Abbott and Costello Meet Dr. Jekyll and Mr. Hyde
Adventure Island
Black Arrow►
The Body Snatcher►
Dr. Jekyll and Mr. Hyde►
Dr. Jekyll and Mr. Hyde
Dr. Jekyll and Sister Hyde
Jekyll and Hyde
Jekyll & Hyde...Together Again
Kidnapped
Man with Two Heads
The Master of Ballantrae
Muppet Treasure Island
Strange Case of Dr. Jekyll & Mr. Hyde
The Strange Door
Treasure Island►
Treasure Island
The Wrong Box►

Books to Film: Bram Stoker

Bram Stoker's Dracula
Burial of the Rats
Count Dracula
Dracula►
Dracula
Dracula (Spanish Version)
The Horror of Dracula►

Books

The Lair of the White Worm⚬
Nosferatu⚬
Tomb

Books to Film: Harriet Beecher Stowe

Uncle Tom's Cabin

Books to Film: Jacqueline Susann

The Love Machine
Once is Not Enough

Books to Film: Jonathan Swift

Gulliver's Travels
The Three Worlds of Gulliver

Books to Film: Paul Theroux

Half Moon Street
The Mosquito Coast
Saint Jack⚬

Books to Film: Jim Thompson

After Dark, My Sweet⚬
Coup de Torchon⚬
The Getaway
The Grifters⚬
The Kill-Off

Books to Film: James Thurber

The Battle of the Sexes⚬
Billy Liar⚬
The Secret Life of Walter
   Mitty⚬

Books to Film: J.R.R. Tolkien

The Hobbit⚬
The Lord of the Rings
The Return of the King

Books to Film: Leo Tolstoy

Leo Tolstoy's Anna Karenina
Prisoner of the Mountains⚬
War and Peace⚬

Books to Film: Scott Turow

Presumed Innocent⚬

Books to Film: Mark Twain

The Adventures of Huck
   Finn⚬
The Adventures of
   Huckleberry Finn⚬
The Adventures of
   Huckleberry Finn
The Adventures of Tom
   Sawyer⚬
The Adventures of Tom
   Sawyer
Ava's Magical Adventure
A Connecticut Yankee
A Connecticut Yankee in King
   Arthur's Court
Huck and the King of Hearts
Huckleberry Finn
The Innocents Abroad
A Kid in King Arthur's Court

A Million to Juan
The Mysterious Stranger
The Prince and the Pauper⚬
The Prince and the Pauper
The Private History of a
   Campaign That Failed
Pudd'nhead Wilson
Tom and Huck⚬
Tom Sawyer⚬
Tom Sawyer
Unidentified Flying Oddball
A Young Connecticut Yankee
   in King Arthur's Court

Books to Film: John Updike

Roommate
Too Far to Go⚬
The Witches of Eastwick

Books to Film: Leon Uris

Battle Cry⚬
Exodus⚬
QB VII⚬
Topaz⚬

Books to Film: Jules Verne

Around the World in a Daze
Around the World in 80 Days⚬
Around the World in 80 Days
800 Leagues Down the
   Amazon
Five Weeks in a Balloon
From the Earth to the Moon
In Search of the Castaways⚬
Journey to the Center of the
   Earth⚬
Journey to the Center of the
   Earth
Light at the Edge of the World
Master of the World
Mysterious Island⚬
On the Comet⚬
Those Fantastic Flying Fools
20,000 Leagues Under the
   Sea⚬
Where Time Began

Books to Film: Kurt Vonnegut

D.P.
Kurt Vonnegut's Harrison
   Bergeron
Mother Night⚬
Slapstick of Another Kind
Slaughterhouse Five
Who Am I This Time?⚬

Books to Film: Alice Walker

The Color Purple⚬

Books to Film: Edgar Wallace

The Black Abbot
Chamber of Horrors
Creature with the Blue Hand
Curse of the Yellow Snake
Dead Eyes of London
Door with the Seven Locks
Forger of London
The Human Monster
The Indian Scarf
Mr. Reeder in Room 13
The Mysterious Magician
The Secret Four

Secret of the Black Trunk
The Squeaker
The Strange Countess
The Terror

Books to Film: Joseph Wambaugh

The Black Marble⚬
The Choirboys
Echoes in the Darkness
The Glitter Dome
The New Centurions
The Onion Field⚬

Books to Film: Evelyn Waugh

Brideshead Revisited⚬
A Handful of Dust⚬
The Loved One⚬

Books to Film: H.G. Wells

Empire of the Ants
First Men in the Moon
Food of the Gods
Food of the Gods: Part 2
Half a Sixpence
The Invisible Man⚬
The Invisible Man's Revenge
Island of Dr. Moreau
The Island of Dr. Moreau
Kipps⚬
La Merveilleuse Visite
The Man Who Could Work
   Miracles⚬
The New Invisible Man
Terror Is a Man
Things to Come⚬
The Time Machine⚬
Time Machine
Village of the Giants
The War of the Worlds⚬

Books to Film: Edith Wharton

The Age of Innocence⚬
The Buccaneers⚬
The Children
Ethan Frome
The Old Maid⚬

Books to Film: William Wharton

Birdy⚬
Dad
A Midnight Clear⚬

Books to Film: Oscar Wilde

The Canterville Ghost
Dorian Gray
Importance of Being Earnest⚬
Lady Windermere's Fan
Picture of Dorian Gray⚬
Salome
The Sins of Dorian Gray

Books to Film: Thornton Wilder

The Bridge of San Luis Rey⚬
Hello, Dolly!
The Matchmaker⚬
Mr. North
Our Town⚬
Our Town

Books to Film: Virginia Woolf

To the Lighthouse

Books to Film: Cornell Woolrich

The Bride Wore Black⚬
Mississippi Mermaid⚬
Mrs. Winterbourne
Rear Window⚬
The Window⚬

Books to Film: Herman Wouk

The Caine Mutiny⚬
The Caine Mutiny Court
   Martial⚬
Marjorie Morningstar
War & Remembrance, Part 1
War & Remembrance, Part 2
War & Remembrance, Part 3
War & Remembrance, Part 4
War & Remembrance, Part 5
War & Remembrance, Part 6
War & Remembrance, Part 7
War & Remembrance: The
   Final Chapter, Part 8
War & Remembrance: The
   Final Chapter, Part 9
War & Remembrance: The
   Final Chapter, Part 10
War & Remembrance: The
   Final Chapter, Part 11
War & Remembrance: The
   Final Chapter, Part 12
The Winds of War

The Bowery Boys

Angels with Dirty Faces⚬
Blues Busters
Bowery Blitzkrieg
Bowery Boys Meet the
   Monsters
Bowery Buckaroos
Boys of the City
Clipped Wings
Dead End⚬
East Side Kids
East Side Kids/The Lost City
Flying Wild
Follow the Leader
Ghost Chasers
Ghost on the Loose
Hard-Boiled Mahoney
Here Come the Marines
Kid Dynamite
Let's Get Tough
Little Tough Guys
Master Minds
Million Dollar Kid
Mr. Wise Guy
'Neath Brooklyn Bridge
Pride of the Bowery
Smart Alecks
Smugglers' Cove⚬
Spook Busters
Spooks Run Wild
That Gang of Mine
They Made Me a Criminal

Bulldog Drummond

Arrest Bulldog Drummond
Bulldog Drummond
Bulldog Drummond at Bay
Bulldog Drummond Comes
   Back
Bulldog Drummond Escapes
Bulldog Drummond in Africa/
   Arrest Bulldog Drummond
Bulldog Drummond's Bride

Bulldog Drummond's Peril
Bulldog Drummond's
   Revenge
Bulldog Drummond's
   Revenge/Bulldog
   Drummond's Peril
Bulldog Drummond's Secret
   Police
Bulldog Jack⚬

Burton & Taylor

Cleopatra
The Comedians
Divorce His, Divorce Hers
Doctor Faustus
Hammersmith is Out
The Sandpiper
The Taming of the Shrew⚬
Under Milk Wood
The V.I.P.'s⚬
Who's Afraid of Virginia
   Woolf?⚬

Carpenter & Russell

Big Trouble in Little China
Elvis: The Movie
Escape from L.A.
Escape from New York
The Thing

Carry On

Carry On at Your
   Convenience
Carry On Behind
Carry On Camping
Carry On Cleo
Carry On Cowboy
Carry On Cruising
Carry On Dick
Carry On Doctor⚬
Carry On Emmanuelle
Carry On England
Carry On Henry VIII
Carry On Nurse
Carry On 'Round the Bend
Carry On Screaming
Follow That Camel

Charlie Brown and the Peanuts Gang

Be My Valentine, Charlie
   Brown
Bon Voyage, Charlie Brown⚬
A Boy Named Charlie Brown⚬
A Charlie Brown Celebration
A Charlie Brown Christmas
A Charlie Brown Thanksgiving
Charlie Brown's All-Stars
He's Your Dog, Charlie
   Brown!
It Was a Short Summer,
   Charlie Brown
It's a Mystery, Charlie Brown
It's Arbor Day, Charlie Brown
It's Magic, Charlie Brown/
   Charlie Brown's All Star
It's the Great Pumpkin,
   Charlie Brown
Play It Again, Charlie Brown
Race for Your Life, Charlie
   Brown
Snoopy, Come Home⚬
Snoopy's Getting Married,
   Charlie Brown
Someday You'll Find Her,
   Charlie Brown
There's No Time for Love,
   Charlie Brown
You're a Good Man, Charlie
   Brown

Classics

Family

Three Godfathers▸
Wings of Eagles

4 Bones

A Nous la Liberte▸
Abe Lincoln in Illinois▸
Adam's Rib▸
The Adventures of Robin
    Hood▸
The African Queen▸
All About Eve▸
All Quiet on the Western
    Front▸
All the King's Men▸
An American in Paris▸
Anatomy of a Murder▸
Andrei Rublev▸
An Angel at My Table▸
Angels with Dirty Faces▸
Annie Hall▸
Apocalypse Now▸
The Asphalt Jungle▸
Au Revoir Les Enfants▸
The Awful Truth▸
The Ballad of Narayama▸
Bambi▸
The Bank Dick▸
The Battleship Potemkin▸
Beauty and the Beast▸
Ben-Hur▸
The Best Years of Our Lives▸
The Bicycle Thief▸
The Big Parade▸
The Big Sleep▸
The Birth of a Nation▸
The Blue Angel▸
The Boys of St. Vincent▸
Breathless▸
Brian's Song▸
The Bride of Frankenstein▸
The Bridge on the River
    Kwai▸
Brief Encounter▸
Bringing Up Baby▸
The Burmese Harp▸
Butch Cassidy and the
    Sundance Kid▸
The Cabinet of Dr. Caligari▸
The Caine Mutiny▸
The Cameraman▸
Casablanca▸
Cesar▸
Children of Paradise▸
Chimes at Midnight▸
Chinatown▸
Christ Stopped at Eboli▸
A Christmas Carol▸
Citizen Kane▸
City Lights▸
The Civil War, Episode 1: The
    Cause—1861▸
The Civil War, Episode 2: A
    Very Bloody Affair—1862▸
The Civil War, Episode 3:
    Forever Free—1862▸
The Civil War, Episode 4:
    Simply Murder—1863▸
The Civil War, Episode 5: The
    Universe of Battle—1863▸
The Civil War, Episode 6:
    Valley of the Shadow of
    Death—1864▸
The Civil War, Episode 7:
    Most Hallowed Ground—
    1864▸
The Civil War, Episode 8: War
    is All Hell—1865▸
The Civil War, Episode 9: The
    Better Angels of Our
    Nature—1865▸
A Clockwork Orange▸

Close Encounters of the Third
    Kind▸
Colonel Redl▸
Come and See▸
Commissar▸
The Conformist▸
Crime and Punishment▸
The Crowd▸
Cyrano de Bergerac▸
Danton▸
Das Boot▸
David Copperfield▸
Day for Night▸
Day of Wrath▸
Dead of Night▸
The Deer Hunter▸
Deliverance▸
Destry Rides Again▸
Diamonds of the Night▸
Dinner at Eight▸
The Discreet Charm of the
    Bourgeoisie▸
Dr. Strangelove, or: How I
    Learned to Stop Worrying
    and Love the Bomb▸
Don Quixote▸
Double Indemnity▸
Duck Soup▸
Dumbo▸
The Earrings of Madame
    De...▸
Earth▸
East of Eden▸
8 1/2▸
El Norte▸
The Elephant Man▸
The Empire Strikes Back▸
E.T.: The Extra-Terrestrial▸
Every Man for Himself & God
    Against All▸
Fanny▸
Fanny and Alexander▸
Fantasia▸
Fitzcarraldo▸
Five Easy Pieces▸
Forbidden Games▸
Foreign Correspondent▸
Forever and a Day▸
Forrest Gump▸
42nd Street▸
The Four Feathers▸
The 400 Blows▸
Frankenstein▸
The Freshman▸
From Here to Eternity▸
The Fugitive▸
Gallipoli▸
The Garden of the Finzi-
    Continis▸
The General▸
The General Line▸
Gigi▸
The Godfather▸
The Godfather 1902-1959:
    The Complete Epic▸
The Godfather, Part 2▸
The Gold Rush▸
Gone with the Wind▸
Goodfellas▸
The Gospel According to St.
    Matthew▸
The Graduate▸
Grand Illusion▸
The Great Dictator▸
Great Expectations▸
Greed▸
Gunga Din▸
Hamlet▸
Harold and Maude▸
Harvest▸
Hearts of Darkness: A
    Filmmaker's Apocalypse▸
Henry V▸

Henry: Portrait of a Serial
    Killer▸
Here Comes Mr. Jordan▸
High Noon▸
Hiroshima, Mon Amour▸
His Girl Friday▸
Hollywood Canteen▸
Hoop Dreams▸
How Green Was My Valley▸
Howard's End▸
Hud▸
The Hunchback of Notre
    Dame▸
The Hustler▸
I Am a Fugitive from a Chain
    Gang▸
The Idiot▸
If...▸
Ikiru▸
The Informer▸
Intolerance▸
The Invisible Man▸
Isn't Life Wonderful▸
It Happened One Night▸
It's a Wonderful Life▸
Ivan the Terrible, Part 1▸
Ju Dou▸
Judgment at Nuremberg▸
Jules and Jim▸
The King and I▸
King Kong▸
Knife in the Water▸
Koyaanisqatsi▸
Kriemhilde's Revenge▸
Kwaidan▸
La Chienne▸
La Dolce Vita▸
La Strada▸
Lady and the Tramp▸
The Lady Eve▸
The Lady Vanishes▸
L'Age D'Or▸
Last Command▸
The Last Detail▸
The Last Emperor▸
The Last Picture Show▸
The Last Seduction▸
Late Spring▸
Laura▸
Lawrence of Arabia▸
Les Miserables▸
The Letter▸
A Letter to Three Wives▸
The Life and Death of Colonel
    Blimp▸
The Lion in Winter▸
The Lion King▸
Little Women▸
The Lives of a Bengal
    Lancer▸
Local Hero▸
Lola Montes▸
Long Day's Journey into
    Night▸
Lost Horizon▸
The Lost Weekend▸
M▸
The Magnificent Ambersons▸
The Magnificent Seven▸
Male and Female▸
The Maltese Falcon▸
A Man for All Seasons▸
The Man Who Would Be
    King▸
The Manchurian Candidate▸
Manhattan▸
Marius▸
The Marriage of Maria Braun▸
M*A*S*H▸
McCabe & Mrs. Miller▸
Mean Streets▸
Metropolis▸
Miracle of Morgan's Creek▸

Miracle on 34th Street▸
Mrs. Miniver▸
Mr. & Mrs. Bridge▸
Mister Roberts▸
Mr. Smith Goes to
    Washington▸
Modern Times▸
Mon Oncle▸
The Music Man▸
Mutiny on the Bounty▸
My Left Foot▸
My Life As a Dog▸
My Life to Live▸
My Man Godfrey▸
Napoleon▸
Nashville▸
National Velvet▸
A Night at the Opera▸
The Night of the Hunter▸
The Night of the Shooting
    Stars▸
North by Northwest▸
Nosferatu▸
Notorious▸
O Lucky Man!▸
Objective, Burma!▸
Of Mice and Men▸
Oliver Twist▸
On the Waterfront▸
One Flew Over the Cuckoo's
    Nest▸
Only Angels Have Wings▸
Open City▸
Our Hospitality▸
The Ox-Bow Incident▸
Pandora's Box▸
The Passion of Joan of Arc▸
Pather Panchali▸
Paths of Glory▸
Pelle the Conqueror▸
Persona▸
Petulia▸
The Philadelphia Story▸
Pinocchio▸
Pixote▸
Poltergeist▸
The Private Life of Henry VIII▸
Psycho▸
Pulp Fiction▸
The Quiet Man▸
Quiz Show▸
Raging Bull▸
Raiders of the Lost Ark▸
A Raisin in the Sun▸
Ran▸
Rashomon▸
Rear Window▸
Rebecca▸
Rebel Without a Cause▸
Red River▸
The Red Shoes▸
The Reincarnation of Golden
    Lotus▸
The Report on the Party and
    the Guests▸
Ride the High Country▸
The River▸
A Room with a View▸
Roots▸
Rosemary's Baby▸
Ruggles of Red Gap▸
The Rules of the Game▸
Sansho the Bailiff▸
Scenes from a Marriage▸
Schindler's List▸
The Searchers▸
Sergeant York▸
Seven Beauties▸
Seven Samurai▸
The Seventh Seal▸
Shane▸
Shin Heike Monogatari▸
Shoeshine▸

Shoot the Piano Player▸
The Shop on Main Street▸
Show Boat▸
Siegfried▸
Singin' in the Rain▸
Small Change▸
Snow White and the Seven
    Dwarfs▸
Some Like It Hot▸
The Sound of Music▸
Sounder▸
The Southerner▸
Spartacus▸
Stagecoach▸
Stalag 17▸
Star Wars▸
Storm over Asia▸
Strangers on a Train▸
A Streetcar Named Desire▸
The Stunt Man▸
Sullivan's Travels▸
Sunrise▸
A Tale of Two Cities▸
The Third Man▸
The 39 Steps▸
Throne of Blood▸
The Tin Drum▸
To Kill a Mockingbird▸
To Live▸
Tokyo Story▸
Tom Jones▸
Tootsie▸
Top Hat▸
Touch of Evil▸
The Train▸
Treasure of the Sierra Madre▸
Tristana▸
Twelve Angry Men▸
Twentieth Century▸
2001: A Space Odyssey▸
Two Women▸
Umberto D▸
Un Chien Andalou▸
Vampyr▸
Variety▸
Vertigo▸
Viridiana▸
Viva Zapata!▸
Wages of Fear▸
The Wedding March▸
Who's Afraid of Virginia
    Woolf?▸
The Wild Bunch▸
Wild Strawberries▸
The Wind▸
The Wizard of Oz▸
Woman in the Dunes▸
Woman of the Year▸
Woodstock▸
The World of Apu▸
Wuthering Heights▸
Yankee Doodle Dandy▸
Yojimbo▸
Young Frankenstein▸
Z▸
Zero for Conduct▸
Zvenigora▸

Francis the Talking Mule

Francis Covers the Big Town
Francis Goes to the Races
Francis Goes to West Point
Francis in the Haunted House
Francis in the Navy
Francis Joins the WACs
Francis the Talking Mule▸

Frankenstein

Abbott and Costello Meet
    Frankenstein▸

Andy Warhol's Frankenstein
Blackenstein
The Bride
The Bride of Frankenstein▶
The Curse of Frankenstein
Dr. Frankenstein's Castle of
 Freaks
Dracula vs. Frankenstein
The Evil of Frankenstein
Frankenstein▶
Frankenstein
Frankenstein: A Cinematic
 Scrapbook
Frankenstein and Me
Frankenstein and the Monster
 from Hell
Frankenstein '80
Frankenstein General
 Hospital
Frankenstein Island
Frankenstein Meets the
 Space Monster
Frankenstein Meets the
 Wolfman▶
Frankenstein Sings...The
 Movie
Frankenstein Unbound▶
Frankenstein's Daughter
Frankenstein's Great Aunt
 Tillie
Frankenweenie
The Ghost of Frankenstein
Gothic▶
The Horror of Frankenstein
House of Frankenstein
Jesse James Meets
 Frankenstein's Daughter
Lady Frankenstein
Mary Shelley's Frankenstein
Mr. Stitch
The Munsters' Revenge
Nosferatu▶
Prototype▶
The Revenge of Frankenstein
The Screaming Dead
Son of Frankenstein▶
Teenage Frankenstein
The Vindicator
Young Frankenstein▶

Gable & Crawford

Chained
Dance Fools Dance▶
Dancing Lady
Forsaking All Others
Laughing Sinners
Love on the Run
Possessed
Strange Cargo

Garland & Rooney

Andy Hardy Meets Debutante
Babes in Arms
Babes on Broadway
Girl Crazy▶
Life Begins for Andy Hardy▶
Love Finds Andy Hardy▶
Strike Up the Band
Thoroughbreds Don't Cry
Thousands Cheer
Words and Music

Garson & Pidgeon

Blossoms in the Dust
Julia Misbehaves▶
Madame Curie▶
The Miniver Story
Mrs. Miniver▶
Mrs. Parkington
That Forsyte Woman

Gibson & Glover

Lethal Weapon▶
Lethal Weapon 2▶
Lethal Weapon 3
Maverick

Godzilla and Friends

Dagora, the Space Monster
Destroy All Monsters
Destroy All Planets
Gamera, the Invincible
Gamera vs. Barugon
Gamera vs. Gaos
Gamera vs. Guiron
Gamera vs. Zigra
Gappa the Trifibian Monster
Ghidrah the Three Headed
 Monster
Godzilla, King of the Monsters
Godzilla 1985
Godzilla on Monster Island
Godzilla Raids Again
Godzilla vs. Biollante
Godzilla vs. Megalon
Godzilla vs. Monster Zero
Godzilla vs. Mothra
Godzilla vs. the Cosmic
 Monster
Godzilla vs. the Sea Monster
Godzilla vs. the Smog
 Monster
Godzilla's Revenge
King Kong vs. Godzilla
Mothra▶
Rodan
Son of Godzilla
Terror of Mechagodzilla
Varan the Unbelievable
War of the Gargantuas
X from Outer Space
Yog, Monster from Space

"Gremlins" & Rip-Offs

Critters
Critters 2: The Main Course
Critters 3
Critters 4
Ghoulies
Ghoulies 2
Ghoulies 3: Ghoulies Go to
 College
Ghoulies 4
Gremlins▶
Gremlins 2: The New Batch▶
Munchie
Munchies
Spookies

Hallmark Hall of Fame

An American Story
Blind Spot
The Boys Next Door
Breathing Lessons
Calm at Sunset
Caroline?▶
Decoration Day▶
Foxfire▶
Harvest of Fire
Journey
Miss Rose White▶
O Pioneers!
One Against the Wind▶
The Piano Lesson▶
A Place for Annie
Redwood Curtain
The Return of the Native
Sarah, Plain and Tall▶
The Secret Garden▶

The Shell Seekers
Skylark
The Summer of Ben Tyler
To Dance with the White
 Dog▶
William Faulkner's Old Man

Hammer Films: Horror

Asylum
Blood of the Vampire
The Blood on Satan's Claw▶
The Brides of Dracula
Captain Kronos: Vampire
 Hunter▶
Count Dracula's Great Love
The Creeping Flesh
The Curse of Frankenstein
The Curse of the Werewolf
Die Screaming, Marianne
Dr. Jekyll and Sister Hyde
Dracula Has Risen from the
 Grave
Dracula, Prince of Darkness
The Evil of Frankenstein
Frankenstein and the Monster
 from Hell
The Ghoul
The Gorgon
Hands of the Ripper
The Horror of Dracula▶
The Horror of Frankenstein
The Hound of the Baskervilles
Hysteria
Kiss of the Vampire
Lust for a Vampire
Maniac
The Mummy▶
The Nanny
Nightmare
Paranoiac
The Phantom of the Opera
Plague of the Zombies
Rasputin the Mad Monk
The Reptile
The Revenge of Frankenstein
The Satanic Rites of Dracula
The Scars of Dracula
The 7 Brothers Meet Dracula
Tales from the Crypt▶
Tales That Witness Madness
Taste the Blood of Dracula
Theatre of Blood▶
To the Devil, A Daughter
Twins of Evil
The Two Faces of Dr. Jekyll
Vampire Circus
The Vampire Lovers
Vault of Horror

Hammer Films: Sci Fi & Fantasy

Creatures the World Forgot
Four Sided Triangle
Men of Sherwood Forest
One Million Years B.C.
Quatermass 2▶
Quatermass and the Pit
The Quatermass Experiment▶
Spaceways
Sword of Sherwood Forest
When Dinosaurs Ruled the
 Earth

Hawks & Wayne

El Dorado
Hatari!▶
Red River▶
Rio Bravo▶
Rio Lobo

Hepburn & Grant

Bringing Up Baby▶
Holiday▶
The Philadelphia Story▶
Sylvia Scarlett

Hepburn & Tracy

Adam's Rib▶
Desk Set▶
Guess Who's Coming to
 Dinner▶
Pat and Mike▶
State of the Union▶
Without Love
Woman of the Year▶

Hercules

Conquest of Mycene
The Fury of Hercules
Hercules
Hercules▶
Hercules 2
Hercules Against the Moon
 Men
Hercules and the Captive
 Women
Hercules in New York
Hercules in the Haunted
 World
Hercules, Prisoner of Evil
Hercules the Legendary
 Journeys, Vol. 1: And the
 Amazon Women
Hercules the Legendary
 Journeys, Vol. 2: The Lost
 Kingdom
Hercules the Legendary
 Journeys, Vol. 3: The
 Circle of Fire
Hercules the Legendary
 Journeys, Vol. 4: In the
 Underworld
Hercules Unchained
Jason and the Argonauts▶
The Loves of Hercules
Samson and His Mighty
 Challenge
The Three Stooges Meet
 Hercules

Hopalong Cassidy

Bar-20
Border Patrol
Border Vigilantes
Colt Comrades
Doomed Caravan▶
False Colors
The Frontiersmen
Hopalong Cassidy▶
Hopalong Cassidy: Borrowed
 Trouble
Hopalong Cassidy:
 Dangerous Venture
Hopalong Cassidy: False
 Paradise
Hopalong Cassidy: Hoppy's
 Holiday
Hopalong Cassidy: Renegade
 Trail
Hopalong Cassidy: Riders of
 the Deadline
Hopalong Cassidy: Silent
 Conflict
Hopalong Cassidy: Sinister
 Journey
Hopalong Cassidy: The Dead
 Don't Dream
Hopalong Cassidy: The
 Devil's Playground

Hopalong Cassidy: The
 Marauders
Hopalong Cassidy:
 Unexpected Guest
Hoppy Serves a Writ
In Old Colorado
Law of the Pampas
Leather Burners
Lost Canyon
Mystery Man
Outlaws of the Desert
Renegade Trail
Riders of the Timberline
Rustler's Valley
Santa Fe Marshal
The Showdown
Texas Masquerade
Twilight on the Trail
Undercover Man

Hope & Crosby

Cancel My Reservation
My Favorite Blonde▶
My Favorite Brunette
The Princess and the Pirate▶
The Road to Bali▶
The Road to Hong Kong
The Road to Morocco▶
The Road to Rio▶
The Road to Singapore
The Road to Utopia▶
The Road to Zanzibar▶
Scared Stiff▶
Star Spangled Rhythm▶

Jack the Ripper

Blade of the Ripper
Cosh Boy
Deadly Advice
Hands of the Ripper
He Kills Night After Night After
 Night
Jack the Ripper
Jack the Ripper▶
Jack's Back▶
The Monster of London City
Murder by Decree▶
Night Ripper
Phantom Fiend
The Ripper
Room to Let
A Study in Terror▶
Terror at London Bridge
Terror in the Wax Museum
Time After Time▶

James Bond

Diamonds Are Forever▶
Dr. No▶
For Your Eyes Only▶
From Russia with Love▶
Goldeneye▶
Goldfinger▶
License to Kill▶
Live and Let Die
The Living Daylights▶
The Man with the Golden Gun
Moonraker
Never Say Never Again
Octopussy
On Her Majesty's Secret
 Service▶
The Spy Who Loved Me
Thunderball
A View to a Kill
You Only Live Twice

James Bond Spoofs

The Ambushers

Lemmon & Matthau

Buddy Buddy
The Fortune Cookie
The Front Page
Grumpier Old Men
Grumpy Old Men
JFK
The Odd Couple
Out to Sea

Live Action/Animation Combos

Alice
Alice in Wonderland
Anchors Aweigh
Bedknobs and Broomsticks
Butterfly Ball
Cool World
Dangerous When Wet
Fabulous Adventures of
    Baron Munchausen
Fun & Fancy Free
Hollywood Party
The Incredible Mr. Limpet
James and the Giant Peach
Mary Poppins
The Pagemaster
Pete's Dragon
So Dear to My Heart
Space Jam
Tank Girl
The Three Caballeros
Tron
Volere Volare
Who Framed Roger Rabbit
Xanadu

The Lone Rider

Border Roundup
Death Rides the Plains
Law of the Saddle
The Lone Rider in Cheyenne
The Lone Rider in Ghost
    Town
Raiders of Red Gap
Rangeland Racket

Loy & Powell

After the Thin Man
Another Thin Man
Double Wedding
Evelyn Prentice
The Great Ziegfeld
I Love You Again
Libeled Lady
Love Crazy
Manhattan Melodrama
Shadow of the Thin Man
Song of the Thin Man
The Thin Man
The Thin Man Goes Home

Ma and Pa Kettle

Egg and I
The Kettles in the Ozarks
The Kettles on Old
    MacDonald's Farm
Ma and Pa Kettle
Ma and Pa Kettle at Home
Ma and Pa Kettle at the Fair
Ma and Pa Kettle at Waikiki
Ma and Pa Kettle Back On the
    Farm
Ma and Pa Kettle Go to Town
Ma and Pa Kettle on Vacation

Martin & Lewis

Artists and Models
At War with the Army

The Caddy
Hollywood or Bust
Jumping Jacks
My Friend Irma
Pardners
The Road to Bali
Scared Stiff
The Stooge

The Marx Brothers

Animal Crackers
At the Circus
Big Store
The Cocoanuts
A Day at the Races
Duck Soup
Go West
Horse Feathers
Love Happy
The Marx Brothers in a
    Nutshell
Monkey Business
A Night at the Opera
A Night in Casablanca
Room Service

MGM Musicals

An American in Paris
Anchors Aweigh
Athena
The Band Wagon
The Barkleys of Broadway
Because You're Mine
Bells are Ringing
Big Store
Born to Dance
Broadway Melody
Broadway Melody of 1936
Broadway Melody of 1938
Broadway Melody of 1940
Broadway Rhythm
Broadway Serenade
The Chocolate Soldier
Dancing Lady
Deep in My Heart
Double Trouble
The Duchess of Idaho
Easter Parade
Easy to Love
Everybody Sing
The Firefly
For Me and My Gal
Gigi
Girl of the Golden West
Give a Girl a Break
Going Hollywood
Good News
Goodbye, Mr. Chips
The Great Ziegfeld
Harum Scarum
Holiday in Mexico
Honolulu
I Love Melvin
I Married an Angel
In the Good Old
    Summertime
It Happened at the World's
    Fair
It Happened in Brooklyn
Lady Be Good
Les Girls
Little Nellie Kelly
Live a Little, Love a Little
Love Me or Leave Me
Lovely to Look At
Madam Satan
Maytime
Meet Me in Las Vegas
Meet Me in St. Louis
The Merry Widow
The Merry Widow

Million Dollar Mermaid
Mrs. Brown, You've Got a
    Lovely Daughter
On an Island with You
On the Town
Pagan Love Song
Rich, Young and Pretty
Rosalie
Rose Marie
Royal Wedding
Seven Brides for Seven
    Brothers
Ship Ahoy
Show Boat
Singin' in the Rain
Skirts Ahoy!
Small Town Girl
Spinout
Stay Away, Joe
Strike Up the Band
The Student Prince
Summer Stock
Sweethearts
Take Me Out to the Ball
    Game
Texas Carnival
That Midnight Kiss
That's Dancing!
That's Entertainment
That's Entertainment, Part 2
That's Entertainment, Part 3
Three Little Words
Thrill of a Romance
Till the Clouds Roll By
Till the Clouds Roll By/A Star
    Is Born
The Toast of New Orleans
The Trouble with Girls (and
    How To Get Into It)
The Unsinkable Molly Brown
Viva Las Vegas
The Wizard of Oz
Words and Music
Yankee Doodle Dandy
Yolanda and the Thief
Ziegfeld Follies
Ziegfeld Girl

Mike Hammer

Girl Hunters
I, the Jury
Kiss Me Deadly
Margin for Murder

Mr. Wong

Doomed to Die
The Fatal Hour
Mr. Wong, Detective
Mr. Wong in Chinatown
Mysterious Mr. Wong
Mystery of Mr. Wong
Phantom of Chinatown

Modern Shakespeare

Chimes at Midnight
A Double Life
Forbidden Planet
Fury is a Woman
The Godfather
The Godfather, Part 2
The Godfather, Part 3
Jubal
King Lear
Kiss Me Kate
Looking for Richard
Love Is All There Is
Men Are Not Gods
Men of Respect
A Midsummer Night's Sex
    Comedy
My Own Private Idaho

Otello
Prospero's Books
Ran
Richard III
Ring of Fire
Ronnie and Julie
Rosencrantz & Guildenstern
    Are Dead
Shakespeare Wallah
Throne of Blood
West Side Story
William Shakespeare's
    Romeo and Juliet

Monty Python

The Adventures of Baron
    Munchausen
All You Need Is Cash
And Now for Something
    Completely Different
Brazil
Clockwise
Consuming Passions
Down Among the Z Men
Erik the Viking
A Fish Called Wanda
The Fisher King
Jabberwocky
The Missionary
Monty Python and the Holy
    Grail
Monty Python Live at the
    Hollywood Bowl
Monty Python's Life of Brian
Monty Python's Parrot Sketch
    Not Included
Monty Python's The Meaning
    of Life
Nuns on the Run
The Odd Job
Personal Services
A Private Function
Privates on Parade
Rentadick
Ripping Yarns
Romance with a Double
    Bass
The Secret Policeman's Other
    Ball
Secret Policeman's Private
    Parts
Time Bandits
Whoops Apocalypse
Yellowbeard

The Muppets

The Adventures of a Gnome
    Named Gnorm
The Great Muppet Caper
Labyrinth
The Muppet Christmas Carol
The Muppet Movie
Muppet Treasure Island
The Muppets Take
    Manhattan
Sesame Street Presents:
    Follow That Bird

National Lampoon

National Lampoon's Animal
    House
National Lampoon's Attack of
    the 5 Ft. 2 Women
National Lampoon's
    Christmas Vacation
National Lampoon's Class of
    '86
National Lampoon's Class
    Reunion
National Lampoon's
    European Vacation

National Lampoon's Favorite
    Deadly Sins
National Lampoon's Last
    Resort
National Lampoon's Loaded
    Weapon 1
National Lampoon's Senior
    Trip
National Lampoon's
    Vacation

A Night at the Movies

Auntie Mame
Battle Cry
Days of Wine and Roses
Dial "M" for Murder
Fanny
Ocean's 11
The Prince and the Showgirl
PT 109
The Wrong Man
The Young Philadelphians

Our Gang

General Spanky
The Little Rascals
Little Rascals, Book 1
Little Rascals Christmas
    Special
Little Rascals, Vol. 1
Little Rascals, Vol. 2
Our Gang
Our Gang Comedies
Our Gang Comedy Festival
Our Gang Comedy Festival 2
Rascal Dazzle
The Return of Our Gang

The Pink Panther

Curse of the Pink Panther
The Pink Panther
The Pink Panther Strikes
    Again
Return of the Pink Panther
Revenge of the Pink Panther
A Shot in the Dark
Son of the Pink Panther
Trail of the Pink Panther

The Planet of the Apes

Battle for the Planet of the
    Apes
Beneath the Planet of the
    Apes
Conquest of the Planet of the
    Apes
Escape from the Planet of the
    Apes
Planet of the Apes

Plays to Film: Horton Foote

Baby, the Rain Must Fall
The Chase
Courtship
Lily Dale
1918
The Trip to Bountiful

Plays to Film: Beth Henley

Crimes of the Heart
Miss Firecracker
Nobody's Fool
True Stories

Rangebusters

Top Grossing Films of 1958

Auntie Mame
Cat on a Hot Tin Roof
Gigi
No Time for Sergeants
South Pacific

Top Grossing Films of 1959

Ben-Hur
Darby O'Gill & the Little People
Operation Petticoat
The Shaggy Dog
Sleeping Beauty

Top Grossing Films of 1960

The Alamo
Exodus
Psycho
Spartacus
The Swiss Family Robinson

Top Grossing Films of 1961

The Absent-Minded Professor
El Cid
The Guns of Navarone
West Side Story

Top Grossing Films of 1962

How the West Was Won
In Search of the Castaways
Lawrence of Arabia
The Longest Day
The Music Man

Top Grossing Films of 1963

Cleopatra
Irma La Douce
It's a Mad, Mad, Mad, Mad World
The Sword in the Stone
Tom Jones

Top Grossing Films of 1964

The Carpetbaggers
From Russia with Love
Goldfinger
Mary Poppins
My Fair Lady

Top Grossing Films of 1965

Doctor Zhivago
The Sound of Music
That Darn Cat
Those Magnificent Men in Their Flying Machines
Thunderball

Top Grossing Films of 1966

The Bible...In the Beginning
Hawaii
Lt. Robin Crusoe, U.S.N.
A Man for All Seasons
Who's Afraid of Virginia Woolf?

Top Grossing Films of 1967

Bonnie & Clyde
The Dirty Dozen
The Graduate
Guess Who's Coming to Dinner
The Jungle Book

Top Grossing Films of 1968

Bullitt
Funny Girl
The Odd Couple
Romeo and Juliet
2001: A Space Odyssey

Top Grossing Films of 1969

Butch Cassidy and the Sundance Kid
Easy Rider
Hello, Dolly!
The Love Bug
Midnight Cowboy

Top Grossing Films of 1970

Airport
Love Story
M*A*S*H
Patton

Top Grossing Films of 1971

Billy Jack
Diamonds Are Forever
Fiddler on the Roof
The French Connection
Summer of '42

Top Grossing Films of 1972

Deliverance
The Godfather
Jeremiah Johnson
The Poseidon Adventure
What's Up, Doc?

Top Grossing Films of 1973

American Graffiti
The Exorcist
Papillon
The Sting
The Way We Were

Top Grossing Films of 1974

Blazing Saddles
Earthquake
The Towering Inferno
The Trial of Billy Jack
Young Frankenstein

Top Grossing Films of 1975

Dog Day Afternoon
Jaws
One Flew Over the Cuckoo's Nest

Top Grossing Films of 1976

All the President's Men
King Kong

Rocky
Silver Streak
A Star is Born

Top Grossing Films of 1977

Close Encounters of the Third Kind
The Goodbye Girl
Saturday Night Fever
Smokey and the Bandit
Star Wars

Top Grossing Films of 1978

Every Which Way But Loose
Grease
Jaws 2
National Lampoon's Animal House
Superman: The Movie

Top Grossing Films of 1979

Alien
The Jerk
Kramer vs. Kramer
Rocky 2
Star Trek: The Motion Picture

Top Grossing Films of 1980

Airplane!
Any Which Way You Can
The Empire Strikes Back
9 to 5
Stir Crazy

Top Grossing Films of 1981

Arthur
Cannonball Run
On Golden Pond
Raiders of the Lost Ark
Stripes
Superman 2

Top Grossing Films of 1982

E.T.: The Extra-Terrestrial
An Officer and a Gentleman
Porky's
Rocky 3

Top Grossing Films of 1983

Return of the Jedi
Superman 3
Terms of Endearment
Trading Places
WarGames

Top Grossing Films of 1984

Beverly Hills Cop
Ghostbusters
Gremlins
Indiana Jones and the Temple of Doom
The Karate Kid

Top Grossing Films of 1985

Back to the Future
The Color Purple
Out of Africa

Rambo: First Blood, Part 2
Rocky 4

Top Grossing Films of 1986

Crocodile Dundee
The Karate Kid: Part 2
Platoon
Star Trek 4: The Voyage Home
Top Gun

Top Grossing Films of 1987

Beverly Hills Cop 2
Fatal Attraction
Good Morning, Vietnam
Lethal Weapon
Three Men and a Baby
The Untouchables

Top Grossing Films of 1988

Coming to America
Crocodile Dundee 2
Die Hard
Rain Man
Twins
Who Framed Roger Rabbit

Top Grossing Films of 1989

Batman
Driving Miss Daisy
Ghostbusters 2
Honey, I Shrunk the Kids
Indiana Jones and the Last Crusade
Lethal Weapon 2

Top Grossing Films of 1990

Dances with Wolves
Dick Tracy
Die Hard 2: Die Harder
Ghost
Home Alone
The Hunt for Red October
Pretty Woman
Teenage Mutant Ninja Turtles: The Movie
Total Recall

Top Grossing Films of 1991

The Addams Family
Backdraft
Boyz N the Hood
City Slickers
Doc Hollywood
Dying Young
Hot Shots!
Naked Gun 2 1/2: The Smell of Fear
New Jack City
101 Dalmatians
Robin Hood: Prince of Thieves
The Rocketeer
The Silence of the Lambs
Sleeping with the Enemy
Teenage Mutant Ninja Turtles 2: The Secret of the Ooze
Terminator 2: Judgment Day
What About Bob?

Top Grossing Films of 1992

Aladdin
Alien 3
Basic Instinct
Batman Returns
The Bodyguard
Boomerang
Bram Stoker's Dracula
Fried Green Tomatoes
The Hand that Rocks the Cradle
Home Alone 2: Lost in New York
The Last of the Mohicans
A League of Their Own
Lethal Weapon 3
Patriot Games
Sister Act
Under Siege
Unforgiven
Wayne's World
White Men Can't Jump

Top Grossing Films of 1993

Aladdin
Cliffhanger
A Few Good Men
The Firm
Free Willy
The Fugitive
In the Line of Fire
Indecent Proposal
Jurassic Park
Sleepless in Seattle

Top Grossing Films of 1994

Ace Ventura: Pet Detective
Clear and Present Danger
The Client
The Flintstones
Forrest Gump
The Lion King
The Mask
Maverick
Speed
True Lies

Top Grossing Films of 1995

Ace Ventura: When Nature Calls
Apollo 13
Batman Forever
Casper
Die Hard: With a Vengeance
Goldeneye
Jumanji
Pocahontas
Seven
Toy Story

Top Grossing Movies of 1996

The Birdcage
Broken Arrow
The Cable Guy
Courage Under Fire
Eraser
The First Wives Club
The Hunchback of Notre Dame
Independence Day
Jack
Jerry Maguire
Mission: Impossible
The Nutty Professor
101 Dalmatians

Phenomenon
Ransom➤
The Rock➤
Space Jam
Star Trek: First Contact➤
A Time to Kill➤
Twister

The Trail Blazers

Arizona Whirlwind
Death Valley Rangers
The Law Rides Again
Outlaw Trail

Trash

The Adventurers
The Alien Factor
Alien Massacre
Alien Prey
All the Lovin' Kinfolk
The Allnighter
Alone in the T-Shirt Zone
Amazon Women on the Moon
America
American Tickler
Andy Warhol's Bad➤
Andy Warhol's Dracula➤
Andy Warhol's Frankenstein
Angel of H.E.A.T.
Assassin of Youth
Assault of the Killer Bimbos
The Astounding She-Monster
The Astro-Zombies
Attack of the Beast Creatures
Attack of the Giant Leeches
Attack of the Killer Tomatoes
Bad Girls Go to Hell
Barn of the Naked Dead
The Beast of Yucca Flats
The Beast that Killed Women
The Beautiful, the Bloody and
  the Bare
Bela Lugosi Meets a Brooklyn
  Gorilla
The Bellboy and the Playgirls
Best Buns on the Beach
Beverly Hills Bodysnatchers
Beverly Hills Knockouts
The Big Gag
Bikini Drive-In
The Bitch
Black Venus
Blazing Stewardesses
Blood Freak
Blood of Ghastly Horror
Bloodlust
Bloodsucking Freaks
Body of Evidence
Bottoms Up
Brain of Blood
Candy Tangerine Man
The Carpetbaggers
The Castle of Fu Manchu
Cheerleader Camp
Cocaine Fiends
The Commies are Coming,
  the Commies are Coming
The Conqueror
The Corpse Grinders
Corruption
The Crater Lake Monster
Creature of Destruction
Creeping Terror
Crypt of the Living Dead
Curse of the Blue Lights
Curse of the Living Dead
Cyborg
Cycle Vixens
Dead Aim
The Dead Next Door
Delinquent School Girls

Demons
Desperate Living
Desperate Teenage Lovedolls
Detour to Danger
Dolemite
Dolemite 2: Human Tornado
Dracula vs. Frankenstein
Drop Dead Fred
Drum
Drums O'Voodoo
Dungeon of Harrow
Eegah!
Escape from Planet Earth
Fat Guy Goes Nutzoid
Female Trouble
The Fifth Floor
Film House Fever
Five Minutes to Love
Flesh and Blood Show
Frankenstein '80
Frankenstein Meets the
  Space Monster
Frostbiter: Wrath of the
  Wendigo
Fun Down There
Galactic Gigolo
Ghoul School
Glen or Glenda: Confessions
  of Ed Wood
Gore-Met Zombie Chef From
  Hell
Gun Cargo
Heartstopper
Hitchhikers
Hold Me, Thrill Me, Kiss Me
Hollywood After Dark
Hollywood Chainsaw Hookers
The Hollywood Strangler
  Meets the Skid Row
  Slasher
Honkytonk Nights
Horror of Party Beach
The House of Usher
I Spit on Your Grave
I Was a Zombie for the FBI
Ilsa, Harem Keeper of the Oil
  Sheiks
Ilsa, She-Wolf of the SS
Ilsa, the Tigress of Siberia
Impulse
In the Cold of the Night
Incredibly Strange Creatures
  Who Stopped Living and
  Became Mixed-Up
  Zombies
Infra-Man
Invasion of the Bee Girls➤
Island of Lost Girls
It's Not the Size That Counts
Jail Bait
Jungle Master
Killer Tomatoes Eat France
Killer Tomatoes Strike Back
Lady Godiva Rides
The Last Season
The Lonely Lady
Lost, Lonely, and Vicious
A Man Called Rage
Man with Two Heads
Manos, the Hands of Fate
Master Blaster
Microwave Massacre
Midnight 2: Sex, Death, and
  Videotape
Mind Trap
Mondo Balardo
Mondo Trasho
Motel Hell
Multiple Maniacs
The Naked Flame
A Night in Heaven
Night of the Cobra Woman
Night of the Demon

Night of the Ghouls
Nightmare
A Nymphoid Barbarian in
  Dinosaur Hell
Oasis of the Zombies
On the Edge: The Survival of
  Dana
Once is Not Enough
One Down, Two to Go!
One More Saturday Night
Orgy of the Dead
Out of the Body
The Outcast
Pagan Island
The Perverse Countess
Phantasm
Pink Flamingos
Plan 9 from Outer Space
Please Don't Eat My Mother
Pot, Parents, and Police
The Power
The Psychic
Queen of Outer Space
Rabid Grannies
Rat Pfink a Boo-Boo
The Rats are Coming! The
  Werewolves are Here!
Reform School Girl
Return of the Family Man
Return of the Killer Tomatoes!
Return to the Blue Lagoon
Revenge of the Virgins
Robot Monster
Rush
Satan in High Heels
Satan's Cheerleaders
Saturday the 14th Strikes
  Back
Savage Intruder
Screen Test
She Demons
She-Devils on Wheels
The Sinister Invasion
The Sinister Urge
Slaves in Bondage
Sleazemania III: The Good,
  the Bad & the Sleazy
Some Call It Loving
Sorority Girl
Space Monster
The Speed Lovers
Streetfight
Sweet Georgia
Sweet Trash
Tarzan, the Ape Man
Teenage Gang Debs
Teenage Mother
Teenage Strangler
Teenagers from Outer Space
Terror in the Jungle
Texas Layover
They Saved Hitler's Brain
Tomboy
Torture Dungeon
Train Station Pickups
The Trial of Billy Jack
Troma's War
Unholy Rollers
Valley of the Dolls
Vampire Vixens from Venus
Vegas in Space
Violated
The Violent Years
White Pongo
Wild Ones on Wheels
Wild Women of Wongo
Winterbeast
World of the Depraved
Youth Aflame
You've Ruined Me, Eddie
The Zombie Army

Troma Films

Beware! Children at Play
Blades
Blondes Have More Guns
Bloodsucking Freaks
Bugged!
Cannibal! The Musical
Chopper Chicks in
  Zombietown
Class of Nuke 'Em High
Class of Nuke 'Em High 2:
  Subhumanoid Meltdown
Class of Nuke 'Em High 3:
  The Good, the Bad and
  the Subhumanoid
Combat Shock
Cry Uncle
Deadly Daphne's Revenge
Evil Clutch
Fat Guy Goes Nutzoid
Ferocious Female Freedom
  Fighters
Frostbiter: Wrath of the
  Wendigo
Girls School Screamers
I Married a Vampire
I Was a Teenage TV Terrorist
Malibu Hot Summer
Monster in the Closet
A Nymphoid Barbarian in
  Dinosaur Hell
Preacherman
Rabid Grannies
Redneck Zombies
Splatter University
Squeeze Play
Stuck on You
Student Confidential
Surf Nazis Must Die
The Toxic Avenger
The Toxic Avenger, Part 2
The Toxic Avenger, Part 3:
  The Last Temptation of
  Toxie
Troma's War
Tromeo & Juliet
Vegas in Space
Wizards of the Demon Sword
Zombie Island Massacre

Turner & Douglas

The Jewel of the Nile
Romancing the Stone➤
The War of the Roses➤

20 Highest Grossing Films of All Time

Aladdin➤
Back to the Future➤
Batman➤
Beverly Hills Cop
The Empire Strikes Back➤
E.T.: The Extra-Terrestrial➤
Forrest Gump➤
Ghost➤
Ghostbusters➤
Gone with the Wind➤
Home Alone➤
Indiana Jones and the Last
  Crusade➤
Jaws➤
Jurassic Park➤
The Lion King➤
Mrs. Doubtfire
Raiders of the Lost Ark➤
Return of the Jedi➤
Star Wars➤
Terminator 2: Judgment Day➤

Universal Studios' Classic Horror

Abbott and Costello Meet Dr.
  Jekyll and Mr. Hyde
Abbott and Costello Meet
  Frankenstein➤
Abbott and Costello Meet the
  Killer, Boris Karloff
The Black Cat➤
The Bride of Frankenstein➤
Creature from the Black
  Lagoon➤
The Creature Walks Among
  Us
Dracula➤
Dracula (Spanish Version)
Dracula's Daughter➤
Frankenstein➤
Frankenstein Meets the
  Wolfman➤
The Ghost of Frankenstein➤
House of Dracula
House of Frankenstein
The Hunchback of Notre
  Dame➤
Invisible Agent
The Invisible Man➤
The Invisible Man Returns➤
The Invisible Woman➤
Island of Lost Souls➤
The Mummy➤
The Mummy's Curse
The Mummy's Ghost
The Mummy's Hand
The Mummy's Tomb
Murders in the Rue Morgue
The Phantom of the Opera➤
The Raven➤
Revenge of the Creature
Son of Dracula➤
Son of Frankenstein➤
Werewolf of London
The Wolf Man➤

Wilder & Pryor

Another You
See No Evil, Hear No Evil
Silver Streak➤
Stir Crazy

Wonderworks Family Movies

African Journey
Almost Partners
And the Children Shall Lead
Anne of Avonlea➤
Anne of Green Gables➤
The Boy Who Loved Trolls
Bridge to Terabithia
Brother Future
The Canterville Ghost
The Chronicles of Narnia
City Boy➤
Clowning Around
Clowning Around 2
Daniel and the Towers
The Fig Tree
Frog
Frogs!
A Girl of the Limberlost
Gryphon
The Haunting of Barney
  Palmer
Hector's Bunyip
Hiroshima Maiden
The Hoboken Chicken
  Emergency
Home at Last
The House of Dies Drear
How to Be a Perfect Person in
  Just Three Days

Wonderworks

Jacob Have I Loved
Konrad
Lantern Hill
The Little Princess
Lone Star Kid
Looking for Miracles
Maricela
The Mighty Pawns
Miracle at Moreaux
My Friend Walter
Necessary Parties
Runaway
Spirit Rider▸
Sweet 15
Walking on Air
A Waltz Through the Hills
Words by Heart
You Must Remember This

Woofs!

The Adventurers
Adventures of a Taxi Driver
The Adventures of Ford
    Fairlane
The Adventurous Knights
After the Fall of New York
Albino
The Alchemist
Alien Contamination
Alien from L.A.
Alien Massacre
Alien Predators
Alien Warrior
Almost Human
The Amazing Transparent
    Man
The Amazing Transplant
The Ambushers
American Gothic
American Ninja 3: Blood Hunt
American Ninja 4: The
    Annihilation
Americathon
Amin: The Rise and Fall
Amityville 2: The Possession
The Amityville Curse
Angel 3: The Final Chapter
Angel of Death
Angel of H.E.A.T.
Angels' Wild Women
The Annihilators
A*P*E*
The Appointment
The Astounding She-Monster
The Astro-Zombies
Atlas in the Land of the
    Cyclops
Atom Age Vampire
The Atomic Brain
Ator the Fighting Eagle
Attack of the Beast Creatures
Attack of the Killer
    Refrigerator
Attack of the Killer Tomatoes
Attack of the Mayan Mummy
Attack of the Swamp Creature
Auntie
Avenging Angel
Awakening of Candra
Baby Love
Bad Charleston Charlie
Bad Girls Do Cry
Bad Girls from Mars
Bad Girls Go to Hell
Bad Medicine
Balboa
Bananas Boat
Barn of the Naked Dead
Barracuda
Basic Training
Battle of the Bullies
Beaks: The Movie

Beast of the Yellow Night
The Beast of Yucca Flats
The Bees
Bela Lugosi Meets a Brooklyn
    Gorilla
The Bellboy and the Playgirls
Best Buns on the Beach
Beyond Atlantis
Beyond Evil
Beyond the Door
Beyond the Door 3
The Big Bust Out
Big Foot
The Bikini Car Wash
    Company
The Birds 2: Land's End
The Bitch
The Black Cat
Black Cobra
The Black Cobra
Black Gestapo
Black Magic Woman
The Black Maid
Black Shampoo
Black Venus
Blackenstein
Blade of the Ripper
Blastfighter
Blazing Stewardesses
Blockhouse
Blood Beach
Blood Diner
Blood Freak
Blood Games
Blood of Ghastly Horror
Blood Orgy of the She-Devils
Blood Rage
Blood Screams
Blood Sisters
Blood Voyage
Bloodmoon
Bloodstalkers
Bloodsuckers from Outer
    Space
Bloodsucking Freaks
Bloodsucking Pharoahs of
    Pittsburgh
The Bloody Brood
Bloody Moon
The Blue Lagoon
Blue Movies
Blue Paradise
The Body Beneath
Body of Evidence
Body Rock
The Body Shop
Bolero
Boogey Man 2
Boom in the Moon
Border Radio
Boss Foreman
Bottoms Up
Brain of Blood
The Bride & the Beast
Bride of the Monster
Brides of the Beast
Bug
Bullies
Bummer
Cabin Boy
Caged Terror
California Casanova
Caligula
Can I Do It...Till I Need
    Glasses?
Can't Stop the Music
Cartel
Castle of Evil
Castle of the Creeping Flesh
Cave Girl
Cave of the Living Dead
Cellar Dweller
The Centerfold Girls

Chain Gang Women
Chained for Life
Challenge
Cheaper to Keep Her
Cheech and Chong's The
    Corsican Brothers
Cheering Section
Cheerleader Camp
The Cheerleaders
Cheerleaders' Wild Weekend
Cherry Hill High
The Children
Child's Play 2
The Chilling
The Chosen
Chu Chu & the Philly Flash
C.H.U.D.
C.H.U.D. 2: Bud the Chud
City on Fire
Clash of the Titans
Class of 1984
Class of Nuke 'Em High 3:
    The Good, the Bad and
    the Subhumanoid
Class Reunion
Class Reunion Massacre
Claws
Clifford
Color Me Blood Red
Comic Cabby
Condemned to Hell
Confidential
The Conqueror
Conqueror & the Empress
Copkillers
The Corpse Grinders
Corruption
Cosh Boy
Cosmos: War of the Planets
The Cradle Will Fall
The Crater Lake Monster
The Crawling Hand
Crazed
Crazy Fat Ethel II
The Creation of the
    Humanoids
Creatures the World Forgot
Creeping Terror
The Cremators
Crocodile
Crucible of Terror
Cruise into Terror
Crypt of the Living Dead
Cthulhu Mansion
The Curse of the Aztec
    Mummy
Curse of the Aztec Mummy/
    Robot vs. the Aztec
    Mummy
Curse of the Blue Lights
Curse of the Stone Hand
Curtains
Cycle Psycho
Cycle Vixens
Dagora, the Space Monster
Dance of Death
Danger Zone
Dangerous Love
Dark Sanity
Dawn of the Mummy
The Day It Came to Earth
Dead Aim
Dead Pit
Dead Women in Lingerie
Deadly Darling
Deadly Embrace
Deadly Encounter
Deadly Prey
Deadly Sanctuary
Deadly Twins
The Death Curse of Tartu
Death Ray
Death Spa

Death Wish 2
Death Wish 5: The Face of
    Death
Deathstalker
Delinquent School Girls
Delirium
The Demon Lover
Demon of Paradise
Demonwarp
Detour to Danger
Devil Woman
Devil's Gift
Devil's Son-in-Law
Devil's Wedding Night
Die Laughing
Digging Up Business
Dirty Laundry
Dirty Mind of Young Sally
Doctor Butcher M.D.
Dr. Orloff's Monster
Dr. Tarr's Torture Dungeon
The Dolls
Don't Go in the Woods
Don't Look in the Attic
Don't Open the Door!
Don't Open Till Christmas
Doom Asylum
Dorm That Dripped Blood
Dracula: Up in Harlem
Dracula vs. Frankenstein
Dracula's Great Love
Dracula's Last Rites
Driller Killer
Drive-In
Drive-In Massacre
Driver's Seat
Drop Dead Fred
Drum
Drums O'Voodoo
Dutch Girls
Ecstasy
Eegah!
Emily
End of the World
Endless Descent
Erotic Images
Escape from Hell
Escape from Safehaven
Escape from the KGB
Escape 2000
Escapist
Eve of Destruction
The Evictors
Evil Laugh
The Evil Within
Evilspeak
Exterminators in the Year
    3000
Eyeball
Eyes of a Stranger
Fade to Black
Fair Game
Fanny Hill: Memoirs of a
    Woman of Pleasure
Fantasies
Far Out Man
Fat Guy Goes Nutzoid
Fatal Pulse
The Fear Chamber
Feelin' Up
The Female Bunch
Fever Pitch
Fiend
The Fiendish Plot of Dr. Fu
    Manchu
The Fifth Floor
Final Exam
Flesh Feast
Flight to Nowhere
Food of the Gods
Food of the Gods: Part 2
The Forbidden Dance
Forbidden World

Foreplay
Fowl Play
Frankenstein '80
Frankenstein General
    Hospital
Frankenstein Island
Frankenstein Meets the
    Space Monster
Frankenstein's Great Aunt
    Tillie
Friday the 13th, Part 2
Friday the 13th, Part 3
Friday the 13th, Part 4: The
    Final Chapter
Friday the 13th, Part 5: A New
    Beginning
Friday the 13th, Part 6: Jason
    Lives
Friday the 13th, Part 7: The
    New Blood
Frostbiter: Wrath of the
    Wendigo
Fun Down There
Galactic Gigolo
The Gamma People
Gangster's Law
The Garbage Pail Kids Movie
Gas
Gates of Hell
The Ghastly Ones
Ghost Fever
Ghost in the Noonday Sun
Ghoulies 3: Ghoulies Go to
    College
Giant from the Unknown
Giants of Rome
Gimme an F
The Girl in Room 2A
Girl on a Chain Gang
Glen or Glenda: Confessions
    of Ed Wood
The Glory Stompers
Goblin
God's Bloody Acre
Godzilla vs. the Sea Monster
Goliath and the Dragon
Goliathon
Goof Balls
Gore-Met Zombie Chef From
    Hell
Gorp
The Green Berets
The Green Slime
Grotesque
Grunt! The Wrestling Movie
Guess What We Learned in
    School Today?
H-Bomb
H-Man
Halloween with the Addams
    Family
Hallucination
Hands of Steel
Hangmen
Hardbodies 2
Hawmps!
The Hearse
Heavenly Bodies
Hell Night
Hell Up in Harlem
Hellcats
Hellgate
Hellriders
Hell's Brigade: The Final
    Assault
Hillbillies in a Haunted House
The Hills Have Eyes
His Name was King
Hitchhikers
The Hollywood Strangler
    Meets the Skid Row
    Slasher
Hollywood Zap

Woofs

The Uninvited
Unknown Powers
Vampire Raiders—Ninja
   Queen
Vasectomy: A Delicate Matter
Vegas in Space
Vengeance Is Mine
Venom
Vice Academy 3
Vice Squad
The Video Dead
Video Wars
Vigilante
Violated
Violent Ones
The Violent Years
Viva Knievel
Voyage to the Planet of
   Prehistoric Women
Vulcan God of Fire
Wacko
Waitress
Wanted: Babysitter
Warlords from Hell
Warrior of the Lost World
Warriors of the Apocalypse
Warriors of the Wasteland
Weekend with the Babysitter
Werewolves on Wheels
Wet and Wild Summer
When Lightning Strikes
When Nature Calls
Where the Boys Are '84
White Gorilla
White Pongo
Wholly Moses!
The Wild Beasts
Wild Guitar
Wild Ones on Wheels
Wild Orchid 2: Two Shades of
   Blue
Wild Riders
Wild Wheels
Wired to Kill
Witchcraft
The Witching
Woman Hunt
Women in Cell Block 7
Women in Fury
Women of the Prehistoric
   Planet
Women Unchained
Women's Prison Massacre
Woodchipper Massacre
The World is Full of Married
   Men
The Worm Eaters
Wrestling Women vs. the
   Aztec Ape
Wrestling Women vs. the
   Aztec Mummy
Xanadu
Xtro
The Yesterday Machine
You Light Up My Life
Youth Aflame
Zandalee
Zero Boys
Zombie Nightmare
Zombies of Moratau

Wyatt Earp

Cheyenne Autumn
Four Eyes and Six Guns
Gunfight at the O.K. Corral➤
Hour of the Gun
My Darling Clementine➤
Sunset
Tombstone➤
Wyatt Earp
Wyatt Earp: Return to
   Tombstone

Zucker/Abrahams/ Zucker

Airplane!➤
Kentucky Fried Movie➤
More! Police Squad
The Naked Gun: From the
   Files of Police Squad➤
Naked Gun 33 1/3: The Final
   Insult
Naked Gun 2 1/2: The Smell
   of Fear
Police Squad! Help Wanted!
Top Secret!➤

Awards Index

[T]he **Awards Index** lists films honored (or dishonored, in some [cas]es) by over 20 national and inter[nat]ional award bodies, representing [ove]r 100 categories of recognition. [Thi]s information can also be found in [the] reviews, following the credits. [No]minations have been added with [thi]s edition, increasing the use[ful]ness (and size) of this index. **Only [fea]tures available on video and re[vie]wed in the main section are list[ed] in this index; movies not yet re[lea]sed on video are not covered [he]re.** As award-winning and nomi[na]ted films find their way to video, [the]y will be added to the review sec[tio]n and covered in this index. The [aw]ards covered include:

Academy Awards
Australia Film Institute
British Academy of Film and
 Television Arts
Broadcast Film Critics Awards
Cannes Film Festival
Cesar Awards (French)
Directors Guild of America
Genie Awards (Canadian)
Golden Globe
Golden Raspberries
Independent Spirit Awards

Los Angeles Film Critics
 Association Awards
Montreal Film Festival
MTV Movie Awards
National Board of Review Awards
National Society of Film Critics
 Awards
New York Film Critics Awards
Screen Actors Guild Awards
Sundance Film Festival
Toronto-City Awards
Writers Guild of America

ACADEMY AWARDS

ACTOR

1928
★ Emil Jannings/*Last Command*
Charlie Chaplin/*The Circus*

1930
★ George Arliss/*Disraeli*
Wallace Beery/*The Big House*
Ronald Colman/*Bulldog Drummond*

1931
★ Lionel Barrymore/*A Free Soul*
Richard Dix/*Cimarron*
Adolphe Menjou/*The Front Page*

1932
★ Wallace Beery/*The Champ*
Fredric March/*Dr. Jekyll and Mr. Hyde*
Alfred Lunt/*The Guardsman*

1933
★ Charles Laughton/*The Private Life of Henry VIII*
Paul Muni/*I Am a Fugitive from a Chain Gang*

1934
★ Clark Gable/*It Happened One Night*

William Powell/*The Thin Man*

1935
★ Victor McLaglen/*The Informer*
Clark Gable/*Mutiny on the Bounty*
Charles Laughton/*Mutiny on the Bounty*
Franchot Tone/*Mutiny on the Bounty*

1936
★ Paul Muni/*The Story of Louis Pasteur*
Gary Cooper/*Mr. Deeds Goes to Town*
Walter Huston/*Dodsworth*
William Powell/*My Man Godfrey*
Spencer Tracy/*San Francisco*

1937
★ Spencer Tracy/*Captains Courageous*
Charles Boyer/*Conquest*
Fredric March/*A Star is Born*
Paul Muni/*The Life of Emile Zola*

1938
★ Spencer Tracy/*Boys Town*
Charles Boyer/*Algiers*
James Cagney/*Angels with Dirty Faces*
Robert Donat/*The Citadel*
Leslie Howard/*Pygmalion*

1939
★ Robert Donat/*Goodbye, Mr. Chips*
Clark Gable/*Gone with the Wind*
Laurence Olivier/*Wuthering Heights*
Mickey Rooney/*Babes in Arms*
James Stewart/*Mr. Smith Goes to Washington*

1940
★ James Stewart/*The Philadelphia Story*
Charlie Chaplin/*The Great Dictator*
Henry Fonda/*The Grapes of Wrath*
Raymond Massey/*Abe Lincoln in Illinois*
Laurence Olivier/*Rebecca*

1941
★ Gary Cooper/*Sergeant York*
Cary Grant/*Penny Serenade*
Walter Huston/*The Devil & Daniel Webster*
Robert Montgomery/*Here Comes Mr. Jordan*
Orson Welles/*Citizen Kane*

1942
★ James Cagney/*Yankee Doodle Dandy*
Ronald Colman/*Random Harvest*
Gary Cooper/*The Pride of the Yankees*

1939 Walter Pidgeon/*Mrs. Miniver*

1943
★ Paul Lukas/*Watch on the Rhine*
Humphrey Bogart/*Casablanca*
Gary Cooper/*For Whom the Bell Tolls*
Walter Pidgeon/*Madame Curie*
Mickey Rooney/*The Human Comedy*

1944
★ Bing Crosby/*Going My Way*
Charles Boyer/*Gaslight*
Barry Fitzgerald/*Going My Way*
Cary Grant/*None But the Lonely Heart*
Alexander Knox/*Wilson*

1945
★ Ray Milland/*The Lost Weekend*
Bing Crosby/*The Bells of St. Mary's*
Gene Kelly/*Anchors Aweigh*
Gregory Peck/*The Keys of the Kingdom*
Cornel Wilde/*A Song to Remember*

1946
★ Fredric March/*The Best Years of Our Lives*
Laurence Olivier/*Henry V*
Larry Parks/*The Jolson Story*

Gregory Peck/*The Yearling*
James Stewart/*It's a Wonderful Life*

1947
★ Ronald Colman/*A Double Life*
John Garfield/*Body and Soul*
Gregory Peck/*Gentleman's Agreement*
William Powell/*Life with Father*

1948
★ Laurence Olivier/*Hamlet*
Lew Ayres/*Johnny Belinda*
Montgomery Clift/*The Search*

1949
★ Broderick Crawford/*All the King's Men*
Kirk Douglas/*Champion*
Gregory Peck/*Twelve O'Clock High*
John Wayne/*Sands of Iwo Jima*

1950
★ Jose Ferrer/*Cyrano de Bergerac*
Louis Calhern/*The Magnificent Yankee*
William Holden/*Sunset Boulevard*
James Stewart/*Harvey*
Spencer Tracy/*Father of the Bride*

ACTOR ₋cont.

1951
- ★ **Humphrey Bogart/**The African Queen
- **Marlon Brando/**A Streetcar Named Desire
- **Montgomery Clift/**A Place in the Sun

1952
- ★ **Gary Cooper/**High Noon
- **Marlon Brando/**Viva Zapata!
- **Kirk Douglas/**The Bad and the Beautiful
- **Jose Ferrer/**Moulin Rouge
- **Alec Guinness/**The Lavender Hill Mob

1953
- ★ **William Holden/**Stalag 17
- **Marlon Brando/**Julius Caesar
- **Richard Burton/**The Robe
- **Montgomery Clift/**From Here to Eternity
- **Burt Lancaster/**From Here to Eternity

1954
- ★ **Marlon Brando/**On the Waterfront
- **Humphrey Bogart/**The Caine Mutiny
- **Bing Crosby/**Country Girl
- **James Mason/**A Star is Born

1955
- ★ **Ernest Borgnine/**Marty
- **James Cagney/**Love Me or Leave Me
- **James Dean/**East of Eden
- **Frank Sinatra/**The Man with the Golden Arm
- **Spencer Tracy/**Bad Day at Black Rock

1956
- ★ **Yul Brynner/**The King and I
- **James Dean/**Giant
- **Kirk Douglas/**Lust for Life
- **Rock Hudson/**Giant
- **Laurence Olivier/**Richard III

1957
- ★ **Alec Guinness/**The Bridge on the River Kwai
- **Marlon Brando/**Sayonara
- **Charles Laughton/**Witness for the Prosecution

1958
- ★ **David Niven/**Separate Tables
- **Tony Curtis/**The Defiant Ones
- **Paul Newman/**Cat on a Hot Tin Roof
- **Sidney Poitier/**The Defiant Ones

1959
- ★ **Charlton Heston/**Ben-Hur

Laurence Harvey/Room at the Top
Jack Lemmon/Some Like It Hot
Paul Muni/The Last Angry Man
James Stewart/Anatomy of a Murder

1960
- ★ **Burt Lancaster/**Elmer Gantry
- **Jack Lemmon/**The Apartment
- **Laurence Olivier/**The Entertainer
- **Spencer Tracy/**Inherit the Wind

1961
- ★ **Maximilian Schell/**Judgment at Nuremberg
- **Charles Boyer/**Fanny
- **Paul Newman/**The Hustler
- **Spencer Tracy/**Judgment at Nuremberg
- **Stuart Whitman/**The Mark

1962
- ★ **Gregory Peck/**To Kill a Mockingbird
- **Burt Lancaster/**Birdman of Alcatraz
- **Jack Lemmon/**Days of Wine and Roses
- **Marcello Mastroianni/**Divorce—Italian Style
- **Peter O'Toole/**Lawrence of Arabia

1963
- ★ **Sidney Poitier/**Lilies of the Field
- **Albert Finney/**Tom Jones
- **Richard Harris/**This Sporting Life
- **Rex Harrison/**Cleopatra
- **Paul Newman/**Hud

1964
- ★ **Rex Harrison/**My Fair Lady
- **Richard Burton/**Becket
- **Peter O'Toole/**Becket
- **Anthony Quinn/**Zorba the Greek
- **Peter Sellers/**Dr. Strangelove, or: How I Learned to Stop Worrying and Love the Bomb

1965
- ★ **Lee Marvin/**Cat Ballou
- **Richard Burton/**The Spy Who Came in from the Cold
- **Laurence Olivier/**Othello
- **Rod Steiger/**The Pawnbroker
- **Oskar Werner/**Ship of Fools

1966
- ★ **Paul Scofield/**A Man for All Seasons
- **Alan Arkin/**The Russians are Coming, the Russians are Coming
- **Richard Burton/**Who's Afraid of Virginia Woolf?

Michael Caine/Alfie
Steve McQueen/The Sand Pebbles

1967
- ★ **Rod Steiger/**In the Heat of the Night
- **Warren Beatty/**Bonnie & Clyde
- **Dustin Hoffman/**The Graduate
- **Paul Newman/**Cool Hand Luke
- **Spencer Tracy/**Guess Who's Coming to Dinner

1968
- ★ **Cliff Robertson/**Charly
- **Alan Arkin/**The Heart is a Lonely Hunter
- **Alan Bates/**The Fixer
- **Ron Moody/**Oliver!
- **Peter O'Toole/**The Lion in Winter

1969
- ★ **John Wayne/**True Grit
- **Richard Burton/**Anne of the Thousand Days
- **Dustin Hoffman/**Midnight Cowboy
- **Peter O'Toole/**Goodbye, Mr. Chips
- **Jon Voight/**Midnight Cowboy

1970
- ★ **George C. Scott/**Patton
- **Melvyn Douglas/**I Never Sang For My Father
- **James Earl Jones/**The Great White Hope
- **Jack Nicholson/**Five Easy Pieces
- **Ryan O'Neal/**Love Story

1971
- ★ **Gene Hackman/**The French Connection
- **Peter Finch/**Sunday, Bloody Sunday
- **Walter Matthau/**Kotch
- **George C. Scott/**The Hospital
- **Chaim Topol/**Fiddler on the Roof

1972
- ★ **Marlon Brando/**The Godfather
- **Michael Caine/**Sleuth
- **Peter O'Toole/**The Ruling Class
- **Laurence Olivier/**Sleuth
- **Paul Winfield/**Sounder

1973
- ★ **Jack Lemmon/**Save the Tiger
- **Marlon Brando/**Last Tango in Paris
- **Jack Nicholson/**The Last Detail
- **Al Pacino/**Serpico
- **Robert Redford/**The Sting

1974
- ★ **Art Carney/**Harry and Tonto
- **Albert Finney/**Murder on the Orient Express
- **Dustin Hoffman/**Lenny

Jack Nicholson/Chinatown
Al Pacino/The Godfather, Part 2

1975
- ★ **Jack Nicholson/**One Flew Over the Cuckoo's Nest
- **Walter Matthau/**The Sunshine Boys
- **Al Pacino/**Dog Day Afternoon
- **Maximilian Schell/**The Man in the Glass Booth
- **James Whitmore/**Give 'Em Hell, Harry!

1976
- ★ **Peter Finch/**Network
- **Robert De Niro/**Taxi Driver
- **Giancarlo Giannini/**Seven Beauties
- **William Holden/**Network
- **Sylvester Stallone/**Rocky

1977
- ★ **Richard Dreyfuss/**The Goodbye Girl
- **Woody Allen/**Annie Hall
- **Richard Burton/**Equus
- **Marcello Mastroianni/**A Special Day
- **John Travolta/**Saturday Night Fever

1978
- ★ **Jon Voight/**Coming Home
- **Warren Beatty/**Heaven Can Wait
- **Gary Busey/**The Buddy Holly Story
- **Robert De Niro/**The Deer Hunter
- **Laurence Olivier/**The Boys from Brazil

1979
- ★ **Dustin Hoffman/**Kramer vs. Kramer
- **Jack Lemmon/**The China Syndrome
- **Al Pacino/**And Justice for All
- **Roy Scheider/**All That Jazz
- **Peter Sellers/**Being There

1980
- ★ **Robert De Niro/**Raging Bull
- **Robert Duvall/**The Great Santini
- **John Hurt/**The Elephant Man
- **Jack Lemmon/**Tribute
- **Peter O'Toole/**The Stunt Man

1981
- ★ **Henry Fonda/**On Golden Pond
- **Warren Beatty/**Reds
- **Burt Lancaster/**Atlantic City
- **Dudley Moore/**Arthur
- **Paul Newman/**Absence of Malice

1982
- ★ **Ben Kingsley/**Gandhi
- **Dustin Hoffman/**Tootsie
- **Jack Lemmon/**Missing

Paul Newman/The Verdict
Peter O'Toole/My Favorite Year

1983
- ★ **Robert Duvall/**Tender Mercies
- **Michael Caine/**Educating Rita
- **Tom Conti/**Reuben, Reuben
- **Tom Courtenay/**The Dresser
- **Albert Finney/**The Dresser

1984
- ★ **F. Murray Abraham/**Amadeus
- **Jeff Bridges/**Starman
- **Albert Finney/**Under the Volcano
- **Tom Hulce/**Amadeus
- **Sam Waterston/**The Killing Fields

1985
- ★ **William Hurt/**Kiss of the Spider Woman
- **Harrison Ford/**Witness
- **James Garner/**Murphy's Romance
- **Jack Nicholson/**Prizzi's Honor
- **Jon Voight/**Runaway Train

1986
- ★ **Paul Newman/**The Color of Money
- **Dexter Gordon/**Round Midnight
- **Bob Hoskins/**Mona Lisa
- **William Hurt/**Children of a Lesser God
- **James Woods/**Salvador

1987
- ★ **Michael Douglas/**Wall Street
- **William Hurt/**Broadcast News
- **Marcello Mastroianni/**Dark Eyes
- **Jack Nicholson/**Ironweed
- **Robin Williams/**Good Morning, Vietnam

1988
- ★ **Dustin Hoffman/**Rain Man
- **Gene Hackman/**Mississippi Burning
- **Tom Hanks/**Big
- **Edward James Olmos/**Stand and Deliver
- **Max von Sydow/**Pelle the Conqueror

1989
- ★ **Daniel Day-Lewis/**My Left Foot
- **Kenneth Branagh/**Henry V
- **Tom Cruise/**Born on the Fourth of July
- **Morgan Freeman/**Driving Miss Daisy
- **Robin Williams/**Dead Poets Society

1990

Jeremy Irons/*Reversal of Fortune*
Kevin Costner/*Dances with Wolves*
Robert De Niro/*Awakenings*
Gerard Depardieu/*Cyrano de Bergerac*
Richard Harris/*The Field*

1991

★ Anthony Hopkins/*The Silence of the Lambs*
Warren Beatty/*Bugsy*
Robert De Niro/*Cape Fear*
Nick Nolte/*The Prince of Tides*
Robin Williams/*The Fisher King*

1992

★ Al Pacino/*Scent of a Woman*
Robert Downey, Jr./*Chaplin*
Clint Eastwood/*Unforgiven*
Stephen Rea/*The Crying Game*
Denzel Washington/*Malcolm X*

1993

★ Tom Hanks/*Philadelphia*
Daniel Day-Lewis/*In the Name of the Father*
Laurence "Larry" Fishburne/*What's Love Got to Do with It?*
Anthony Hopkins/*The Remains of the Day*
Liam Neeson/*Schindler's List*

1994

★ Tom Hanks/*Forrest Gump*
Morgan Freeman/*The Shawshank Redemption*
Nigel Hawthorne/*The Madness of King George*
Paul Newman/*Nobody's Fool*
John Travolta/*Pulp Fiction*

1995

★ Nicolas Cage/*Leaving Las Vegas*
Richard Dreyfuss/*Mr. Holland's Opus*
Anthony Hopkins/*Nixon*
Sean Penn/*Dead Man Walking*
Massimo Troisi/*The Postman*

1996

★ Geoffrey Rush/*Shine*
Tom Cruise/*Jerry Maguire*
Ralph Fiennes/*The English Patient*
Woody Harrelson/*The People vs. Larry Flynt*
Billy Bob Thornton/*Sling Blade*

ACTOR—SUPPORTING

1936

★ Walter Brennan/*Come and Get It*
Mischa Auer/*My Man Godfrey*
Stuart Erwin/*Pigskin Parade*
Basil Rathbone/*Romeo and Juliet*
Akim Tamiroff/*The General Died at Dawn*

1937

★ Joseph Schildkraut/*The Life of Emile Zola*
Ralph Bellamy/*The Awful Truth*
Thomas Mitchell/*The Hurricane*
H.B. Warner/*Lost Horizon*
Roland Young/*Topper*

1938

John Garfield/*Four Daughters*
Gene Lockhart/*Algiers*
Robert Morley/*Marie Antoinette*

1939

★ Thomas Mitchell/*Stagecoach*
Brian Aherne/*Juarez*
Harry Carey, Sr./*Mr. Smith Goes to Washington*
Brian Donlevy/*Beau Geste*
Claude Rains/*Mr. Smith Goes to Washington*

1940

★ Walter Brennan/*The Westerner*
Albert Basserman/*Foreign Correspondent*
William Gargan/*They Knew What They Wanted*
Jack Oakie/*The Great Dictator*
James Stephenson/*The Letter*

1941

★ Donald Crisp/*How Green Was My Valley*
Walter Brennan/*Sergeant York*
Charles Coburn/*The Devil & Miss Jones*
James Gleason/*Here Comes Mr. Jordan*
Sydney Greenstreet/*The Maltese Falcon*

1942

★ Van Heflin/*Johnny Eager*
William Bendix/*Wake Island*
Walter Huston/*Yankee Doodle Dandy*
Frank Morgan/*Tortilla Flat*
Henry Travers/*Mrs. Miniver*

1943

★ Charles Coburn/*The More the Merrier*

Charles Bickford/*The Song of Bernadette*
J. Carrol Naish/*Sahara*
Claude Rains/*Casablanca*
Akim Tamiroff/*For Whom the Bell Tolls*

1944

★ Barry Fitzgerald/*Going My Way*
Hume Cronyn/*The Seventh Cross*
Claude Rains/*Mr. Skeffington*
Clifton Webb/*Laura*
Monty Woolley/*Since You Went Away*

1945

★ James Dunn/*A Tree Grows in Brooklyn*
Michael Chekhov/*Spellbound*
John Dall/*The Corn is Green*

1946

★ Harold Russell/*The Best Years of Our Lives*
William Demarest/*The Jolson Story*
Claude Rains/*Notorious*
Clifton Webb/*The Razor's Edge*

1947

★ Edmund Gwenn/*Miracle on 34th Street*
Charles Bickford/*The Farmer's Daughter*
Robert Ryan/*Crossfire*
Richard Widmark/*Kiss of Death*

1948

★ Walter Huston/*Treasure of the Sierra Madre*
Charles Bickford/*Johnny Belinda*
Jose Ferrer/*Joan of Arc*
Oscar Homolka/*I Remember Mama*

1949

★ Dean Jagger/*Twelve O'Clock High*
John Ireland/*All the King's Men*
Arthur Kennedy/*Champion*
Ralph Richardson/*The Heiress*
James Whitmore/*Battleground*

1950

★ George Sanders/*All About Eve*
Jeff Chandler/*Broken Arrow*
Sam Jaffe/*The Asphalt Jungle*
Erich von Stroheim/*Sunset Boulevard*

1951

★ Karl Malden/*A Streetcar Named Desire*
Leo Genn/*Quo Vadis*
Peter Ustinov/*Quo Vadis*

1952

★ Anthony Quinn/*Viva Zapata!*
Arthur Hunnicutt/*The Big Sky*
Victor McLaglen/*The Quiet Man*
Jack Palance/*Sudden Fear*

1953

★ Frank Sinatra/*From Here to Eternity*
Eddie Albert/*Roman Holiday*
Jack Palance/*Shane*
Robert Strauss/*Stalag 17*
Brandon de Wilde/*Shane*

1954

★ Edmond O'Brien/*The Barefoot Contessa*
Lee J. Cobb/*On the Waterfront*
Karl Malden/*On the Waterfront*
Rod Steiger/*On the Waterfront*
Tom Tully/*The Caine Mutiny*

1955

★ Jack Lemmon/*Mister Roberts*
Joe Mantell/*Marty*
Sal Mineo/*Rebel Without a Cause*
Arthur O'Connell/*Picnic*

1956

★ Anthony Quinn/*Lust for Life*
Don Murray/*Bus Stop*
Anthony Perkins/*Friendly Persuasion*
Robert Stack/*Written on the Wind*

1957

★ Red Buttons/*Sayonara*
Sessue Hayakawa/*The Bridge on the River Kwai*
Arthur Kennedy/*Peyton Place*
Russ Tamblyn/*Peyton Place*

1958

★ Burl Ives/*The Big Country*
Theodore Bikel/*The Defiant Ones*
Lee J. Cobb/*The Brothers Karamazov*
Arthur Kennedy/*Some Came Running*
Gig Young/*Teacher's Pet*

1959

★ Hugh Griffith/*Ben-Hur*
Arthur O'Connell/*Anatomy of a Murder*
George C. Scott/*Anatomy of a Murder*
Robert Vaughn/*The Young Philadelphians*
Ed Wynn/*The Diary of Anne Frank*

1960

★ Peter Ustinov/*Spartacus*

Jack Kruschen/*The Apartment*
Sal Mineo/*Exodus*
Chill Wills/*The Alamo*

1961

★ George Chakiris/*West Side Story*
Montgomery Clift/*Judgment at Nuremberg*
Peter Falk/*Pocketful of Miracles*
Jackie Gleason/*The Hustler*
George C. Scott/*The Hustler*

1962

★ Ed Begley, Sr./*Sweet Bird of Youth*
Victor Buono/*What Ever Happened to Baby Jane?*
Telly Savalas/*Birdman of Alcatraz*
Omar Sharif/*Lawrence of Arabia*
Terence Stamp/*Billy Budd*

1963

★ Melvyn Douglas/*Hud*
Bobby Darin/*Captain Newman, M.D.*
Hugh Griffith/*Tom Jones*
John Huston/*The Cardinal*

1964

★ Peter Ustinov/*Topkapi*
John Gielgud/*Becket*
Stanley Holloway/*My Fair Lady*
Edmond O'Brien/*Seven Days in May*
Lee Tracy/*The Best Man*

1965

★ Martin Balsam/*A Thousand Clowns*
Ian Bannen/*The Flight of the Phoenix*
Tom Courtenay/*Doctor Zhivago*
Michael Dunn/*Ship of Fools*
Frank Finlay/*Othello*

1966

★ Walter Matthau/*The Fortune Cookie*
Mako/*The Sand Pebbles*
James Mason/*Georgy Girl*
George Segal/*Who's Afraid of Virginia Woolf?*
Robert Shaw/*A Man for All Seasons*

1967

★ George Kennedy/*Cool Hand Luke*
John Cassavetes/*The Dirty Dozen*
Gene Hackman/*Bonnie & Clyde*
Cecil Kellaway/*Guess Who's Coming to Dinner*
Michael J. Pollard/*Bonnie & Clyde*

1968

Seymour Cassel/*Faces*

Greer Garson/*Goodbye, Mr. Chips*

940

Ginger Rogers/*Kitty Foyle*
Bette Davis/*The Letter*
Joan Fontaine/*Rebecca*
Katharine Hepburn/*The Philadelphia Story*
Martha Scott/*Our Town*

941

Joan Fontaine/*Suspicion*
Bette Davis/*The Little Foxes*
Greer Garson/*Blossoms in the Dust*
Barbara Stanwyck/*Ball of Fire*

942

★ Greer Garson/*Mrs. Miniver*
Bette Davis/*Now, Voyager*
Katharine Hepburn/*Woman of the Year*
Teresa Wright/*The Pride of the Yankees*

1943

★ Jennifer Jones/*The Song of Bernadette*
Jean Arthur/*The More the Merrier*
Ingrid Bergman/*For Whom the Bell Tolls*
Greer Garson/*Madame Curie*

1944

★ Ingrid Bergman/*Gaslight*
Claudette Colbert/*Since You Went Away*
Bette Davis/*Mr. Skeffington*
Greer Garson/*Mrs. Parkington*
Barbara Stanwyck/*Double Indemnity*

1945

★ Joan Crawford/*Mildred Pierce*
Ingrid Bergman/*The Bells of St. Mary's*
Greer Garson/*The Valley of Decision*
Gene Tierney/*Leave Her to Heaven*

1946

Celia Johnson/*Brief Encounter*
Jennifer Jones/*Duel in the Sun*
Rosalind Russell/*Sister Kenny*
Jane Wyman/*The Yearling*

1947

★ Loretta Young/*The Farmer's Daughter*
Joan Crawford/*The Possessed*
Susan Hayward/*Smash-Up: The Story of a Woman*
Dorothy McGuire/*Gentleman's Agreement*

1948

★ Jane Wyman/*Johnny Belinda*
Ingrid Bergman/*Joan of Arc*
Irene Dunne/*I Remember Mama*
Barbara Stanwyck/*Sorry, Wrong Number*
Olivia de Havilland/*The Snake Pit*

1949

★ Olivia de Havilland/*The Heiress*
Jeanne Crain/*Pinky*
Loretta Young/*Come to the Stable*

1950

★ Judy Holliday/*Born Yesterday*
Anne Baxter/*All About Eve*
Bette Davis/*All About Eve*
Gloria Swanson/*Sunset Boulevard*

1951

★ Vivien Leigh/*A Streetcar Named Desire*
Katharine Hepburn/*The African Queen*
Eleanor Parker/*Detective Story*
Shelley Winters/*A Place in the Sun*

1952

★ Shirley Booth/*Come Back, Little Sheba*
Joan Crawford/*Sudden Fear*
Julie Harris/*The Member of the Wedding*

1953

★ Audrey Hepburn/*Roman Holiday*
Leslie Caron/*Lili*
Ava Gardner/*Mogambo*
Deborah Kerr/*From Here to Eternity*
Maggie McNamara/*The Moon Is Blue*

1954

★ Grace Kelly/*Country Girl*
Dorothy Dandridge/*Carmen Jones*
Judy Garland/*A Star is Born*
Audrey Hepburn/*Sabrina*
Jane Wyman/*Magnificent Obsession*

1955

★ Anna Magnani/*The Rose Tattoo*
Susan Hayward/*I'll Cry Tomorrow*
Katharine Hepburn/*Summertime*
Jennifer Jones/*Love Is a Many-Splendored Thing*
Eleanor Parker/*Interrupted Melody*

1956

★ Ingrid Bergman/*Anastasia*
Carroll Baker/*Baby Doll*

Katharine Hepburn/*The Rainmaker*
Nancy Kelly/*The Bad Seed*
Deborah Kerr/*The King and I*

1957

★ Joanne Woodward/*The Three Faces of Eve*
Deborah Kerr/*Heaven Knows, Mr. Allison*
Elizabeth Taylor/*Raintree County*
Lana Turner/*Peyton Place*

1958

★ Susan Hayward/*I Want to Live!*
Deborah Kerr/*Separate Tables*
Shirley MacLaine/*Some Came Running*
Rosalind Russell/*Auntie Mame*
Elizabeth Taylor/*Cat on a Hot Tin Roof*

1959

★ Simone Signoret/*Room at the Top*
Doris Day/*Pillow Talk*
Audrey Hepburn/*The Nun's Story*
Katharine Hepburn/*Suddenly, Last Summer*
Elizabeth Taylor/*Suddenly, Last Summer*

1960

★ Elizabeth Taylor/*Butterfield 8*
Greer Garson/*Sunrise at Campobello*
Deborah Kerr/*The Sundowners*
Shirley MacLaine/*The Apartment*
Melina Mercouri/*Never on Sunday*

1961

★ Sophia Loren/*Two Women*
Audrey Hepburn/*Breakfast at Tiffany's*
Piper Laurie/*The Hustler*
Geraldine Page/*Summer and Smoke*
Natalie Wood/*Splendor in the Grass*

1962

★ Anne Bancroft/*The Miracle Worker*
Bette Davis/*What Ever Happened to Baby Jane?*
Katharine Hepburn/*Long Day's Journey into Night*
Geraldine Page/*Sweet Bird of Youth*
Lee Remick/*Days of Wine and Roses*

1963

★ Patricia Neal/*Hud*
Shirley MacLaine/*Irma La Douce*
Rachel Roberts/*This Sporting Life*

Natalie Wood/*Love with the Proper Stranger*

1964

★ Julie Andrews/*Mary Poppins*
Anne Bancroft/*The Pumpkin Eater*
Sophia Loren/*Marriage Italian Style*
Debbie Reynolds/*The Unsinkable Molly Brown*
Kim Stanley/*Seance on a Wet Afternoon*

1965

★ Julie Christie/*Darling*
Julie Andrews/*The Sound of Music*
Samantha Eggar/*The Collector*
Elizabeth Hartman/*A Patch of Blue*
Simone Signoret/*Ship of Fools*

1966

★ Elizabeth Taylor/*Who's Afraid of Virginia Woolf?*
Anouk Aimee/*A Man and a Woman*
Ida Kaminska/*The Shop on Main Street*
Lynn Redgrave/*Georgy Girl*
Vanessa Redgrave/*Morgan!*

1967

★ Katharine Hepburn/*Guess Who's Coming to Dinner*
Anne Bancroft/*The Graduate*
Faye Dunaway/*Bonnie & Clyde*
Audrey Hepburn/*Wait Until Dark*

1968

★ Katharine Hepburn/*The Lion in Winter*
★ Barbra Streisand/*Funny Girl*
Vanessa Redgrave/*Isadora*
Joanne Woodward/*Rachel, Rachel*

1969

★ Maggie Smith/*The Prime of Miss Jean Brodie*
Genevieve Bujold/*Anne of the Thousand Days*
Jane Fonda/*They Shoot Horses, Don't They?*
Liza Minnelli/*The Sterile Cuckoo*
Jean Simmons/*The Happy Ending*

1970

★ Glenda Jackson/*Women in Love*
Jane Alexander/*The Great White Hope*
Ali MacGraw/*Love Story*
Sarah Miles/*Ryan's Daughter*
Carrie Snodgress/*Diary of a Mad Housewife*

1971

★ Jane Fonda/*Klute*
Julie Christie/*McCabe & Mrs. Miller*
Glenda Jackson/*Sunday, Bloody Sunday*
Janet Suzman/*Nicholas and Alexandra*

1972

★ Liza Minnelli/*Cabaret*
Diana Ross/*Lady Sings the Blues*
Maggie Smith/*Travels with My Aunt*
Cicely Tyson/*Sounder*
Liv Ullmann/*The Emigrants*

1973

★ Glenda Jackson/*A Touch of Class*
Ellen Burstyn/*The Exorcist*
Marsha Mason/*Cinderella Liberty*
Barbra Streisand/*The Way We Were*
Joanne Woodward/*Summer Wishes, Winter Dreams*

1974

★ Ellen Burstyn/*Alice Doesn't Live Here Anymore*
Faye Dunaway/*Chinatown*
Valerie Perrine/*Lenny*
Gena Rowlands/*A Woman Under the Influence*

1975

★ Louise Fletcher/*One Flew Over the Cuckoo's Nest*
Isabelle Adjani/*Story of Adele H.*
Ann-Margret/*Tommy*
Glenda Jackson/*Hedda*
Carol Kane/*Hester Street*

1976

★ Faye Dunaway/*Network*
Marie-Christine Barrault/*Cousin, Cousine*
Talia Shire/*Rocky*
Sissy Spacek/*Carrie*
Liv Ullmann/*Face to Face*

1977

★ Diane Keaton/*Annie Hall*
Anne Bancroft/*The Turning Point*
Jane Fonda/*Julia*
Shirley MacLaine/*The Turning Point*
Marsha Mason/*The Goodbye Girl*

1978

★ Jane Fonda/*Coming Home*
Ingrid Bergman/*Autumn Sonata*
Ellen Burstyn/*Same Time, Next Year*
Jill Clayburgh/*An Unmarried Woman*
Geraldine Page/*Interiors*

ACTRESS ▸cont.

1979

★ **Sally Field**/*Norma Rae*
Jill Clayburgh/*Starting Over*
Jane Fonda/*The China Syndrome*
Marsha Mason/*Chapter Two*
Bette Midler/*The Rose*

1980

★ **Sissy Spacek**/*Coal Miner's Daughter*
Ellen Burstyn/*Resurrection*
Goldie Hawn/*Private Benjamin*
Mary Tyler Moore/*Ordinary People*
Gena Rowlands/*Gloria*

1981

★ **Katharine Hepburn**/*On Golden Pond*
Diane Keaton/*Reds*
Marsha Mason/*Only When I Laugh*
Susan Sarandon/*Atlantic City*
Meryl Streep/*The French Lieutenant's Woman*

1982

★ **Meryl Streep**/*Sophie's Choice*
Julie Andrews/*Victor/Victoria*
Jessica Lange/*Frances*
Sissy Spacek/*Missing*
Debra Winger/*An Officer and a Gentleman*

1983

★ **Shirley MacLaine**/*Terms of Endearment*
Jane Alexander/*Testament*
Meryl Streep/*Silkwood*
Julie Walters/*Educating Rita*
Debra Winger/*Terms of Endearment*

1984

★ **Sally Field**/*Places in the Heart*
Judy Davis/*A Passage to India*
Jessica Lange/*Country*
Vanessa Redgrave/*The Bostonians*
Sissy Spacek/*The River*

1985

★ **Geraldine Page**/*The Trip to Bountiful*
Anne Bancroft/*Agnes of God*
Whoopi Goldberg/*The Color Purple*
Jessica Lange/*Sweet Dreams*
Meryl Streep/*Out of Africa*

1986

★ **Marlee Matlin**/*Children of a Lesser God*
Jane Fonda/*The Morning After*

Sissy Spacek/*Crimes of the Heart*
Kathleen Turner/*Peggy Sue Got Married*
Sigourney Weaver/*Aliens*

1987

★ **Cher**/*Moonstruck*
Glenn Close/*Fatal Attraction*
Holly Hunter/*Broadcast News*
Sally Kirkland/*Anna*
Meryl Streep/*Ironweed*

1988

★ **Jodie Foster**/*The Accused*
Glenn Close/*Dangerous Liaisons*
Melanie Griffith/*Working Girl*
Meryl Streep/*A Cry in the Dark*
Sigourney Weaver/*Gorillas in the Mist*

1989

★ **Jessica Tandy**/*Driving Miss Daisy*
Isabelle Adjani/*Camille Claudel*
Pauline Collins/*Shirley Valentine*
Jessica Lange/*Music Box*
Michelle Pfeiffer/*The Fabulous Baker Boys*

1990

★ **Kathy Bates**/*Misery*
Anjelica Huston/*The Grifters*
Julia Roberts/*Pretty Woman*
Meryl Streep/*Postcards from the Edge*
Joanne Woodward/*Mr. & Mrs. Bridge*

1991

★ **Jodie Foster**/*The Silence of the Lambs*
Geena Davis/*Thelma & Louise*
Laura Dern/*Rambling Rose*
Bette Midler/*For the Boys*
Susan Sarandon/*Thelma & Louise*

1992

★ **Emma Thompson**/*Howard's End*
Catherine Deneuve/*Indochine*
Mary McDonnell/*Passion Fish*
Michelle Pfeiffer/*Love Field*
Susan Sarandon/*Lorenzo's Oil*

1993

★ **Holly Hunter**/*The Piano*
Angela Bassett/*What's Love Got to Do with It?*
Stockard Channing/*Six Degrees of Separation*
Emma Thompson/*The Remains of the Day*
Debra Winger/*Shadowlands*

1994

★ **Jessica Lange**/*Blue Sky*
Jodie Foster/*Nell*
Miranda Richardson/*Tom & Viv*
Winona Ryder/*Little Women*
Susan Sarandon/*The Client*

1995

★ **Susan Sarandon**/*Dead Man Walking*
Elisabeth Shue/*Leaving Las Vegas*
Sharon Stone/*Casino*
Meryl Streep/*The Bridges of Madison County*
Emma Thompson/*Sense and Sensibility*

1996

★ **Frances McDormand**/*Fargo*
Brenda Blethyn/*Secrets and Lies*
Diane Keaton/*Marvin's Room*
Kristin Scott Thomas/*The English Patient*
Emily Watson/*Breaking the Waves*

ACTRESS— SUPPORTING

1936

★ **Gale Sondergaard**/*Anthony Adverse*
Beulah Bondi/*The Gorgeous Hussy*
Alice Brady/*My Man Godfrey*
Bonita Granville/*These Three*
Maria Ouspenskaya/*Dodsworth*

1937

★ **Alice Brady**/*In Old Chicago*
Andrea Leeds/*Stage Door*
Anne Shirley/*Stella Dallas*
Claire Trevor/*Dead End*

1938

★ **Fay Bainter**/*Jezebel*
Beulah Bondi/*Of Human Hearts*
Spring Byington/*You Can't Take It with You*
Milza Korjus/*The Great Waltz*

1939

★ **Hattie McDaniel**/*Gone with the Wind*
Geraldine Fitzgerald/*Wuthering Heights*
Edna May Oliver/*Drums Along the Mohawk*
Maria Ouspenskaya/*Love Affair*
Olivia de Havilland/*Gone with the Wind*

1940

★ **Jane Darwell**/*The Grapes of Wrath*

Judith Anderson/*Rebecca*
Ruth Hussey/*The Philadelphia Story*
Barbara O'Neil/*All This and Heaven Too*
Marjorie Rambeau/*Primrose Path*

1941

★ **Mary Astor**/*The Great Lie*
Sara Allgood/*How Green Was My Valley*
Patricia Collinge/*The Little Foxes*
Teresa Wright/*The Little Foxes*
Margaret Wycherly/*Sergeant York*

1942

★ **Teresa Wright**/*Mrs. Miniver*
Gladys Cooper/*Now, Voyager*
Agnes Moorehead/*The Magnificent Ambersons*
Susan Peters/*Random Harvest*
May Whitty/*Mrs. Miniver*

1943

★ **Katina Paxinou**/*For Whom the Bell Tolls*
Gladys Cooper/*The Song of Bernadette*
Paulette Goddard/*So Proudly We Hail*
Anne Revere/*The Song of Bernadette*
Lucile Watson/*Watch on the Rhine*

1944

★ **Ethel Barrymore**/*None But the Lonely Heart*
Jennifer Jones/*Since You Went Away*
Angela Lansbury/*Gaslight*
Aline MacMahon/*Dragon Seed*
Agnes Moorehead/*Mrs. Parkington*

1945

★ **Anne Revere**/*National Velvet*
Eve Arden/*Mildred Pierce*
Ann Blyth/*Mildred Pierce*
Angela Lansbury/*Picture of Dorian Gray*
Joan Lorring/*The Corn is Green*

1946

★ **Anne Baxter**/*The Razor's Edge*
Ethel Barrymore/*The Spiral Staircase*
Lillian Gish/*Duel in the Sun*
Flora Robson/*Saratoga Trunk*
Gale Sondergaard/*Anna and the King of Siam*

1947

★ **Celeste Holm**/*Gentleman's Agreement*
Ethel Barrymore/*The Paradine Case*
Gloria Grahame/*Crossfire*

Marjorie Main/*Egg and I*
Anne Revere/*Gentleman's Agreement*

1948

★ **Claire Trevor**/*Key Largo*
Barbara Bel Geddes/*Remember Mama*
Ellen Corby/*I Remember Mama*
Agnes Moorehead/*Johnny Belinda*
Jean Simmons/*Hamlet*

1949

★ **Mercedes McCambridge**/*All the King's Men*
Ethel Barrymore/*Pinky*
Celeste Holm/*Come to the Stable*
Elsa Lanchester/*Come the Stable*
Ethel Waters/*Pinky*

1950

★ **Josephine Hull**/*Harvey*
Celeste Holm/*All About Eve*
Nancy Olson/*Sunset Boulevard*
Thelma Ritter/*All About Eve*

1951

★ **Kim Hunter**/*A Streetcar Named Desire*
Lee Grant/*Detective Sto*

1952

★ **Gloria Grahame**/*The Ba and the Beautiful*
Jean Hagen/*Singin' in th Rain*
Colette Marchand/*Moul Rouge*
Terry Moore/*Come Back Little Sheba*

1953

★ **Donna Reed**/*From Here Eternity*
Grace Kelly/*Mogambo*
Marjorie Rambeau/*Torc Song*
Thelma Ritter/*Pickup on South Street*

1954

★ **Eva Marie Saint**/*On the Waterfront*
Nina Foch/*Executive Suite*
Katy Jurado/*Broken Lance*

1955

★ **Jo Van Fleet**/*East of Ede*
Betsy Blair/*Marty*
Peggy Lee/*Pete Kelly's Blues*
Marisa Pavan/*The Rose Tattoo*
Natalie Wood/*Rebel Without a Cause*

1956

★ **Dorothy Malone**/*Written on the Wind*
Mildred Dunnock/*Baby Doll*
Eileen Heckart/*The Bad Seed*

Mercedes McCambridge/*Giant*
Patty McCormack/*The Bad Seed*

1957
★ Miyoshi Umeki/*Sayonara*
Elsa Lanchester/*Witness for the Prosecution*
Hope Lange/*Peyton Place*
Diane Varsi/*Peyton Place*

1958
★ Wendy Hiller/*Separate Tables*
Peggy Cass/*Auntie Mame*
Martha Hyer/*Some Came Running*
Maureen Stapleton/*Lonelyhearts*
Cara Williams/*The Defiant Ones*

1959
★ Shelley Winters/*The Diary of Anne Frank*
Hermione Baddeley/*Room at the Top*
Susan Kohner/*Imitation of Life*
Juanita Moore/*Imitation of Life*
Thelma Ritter/*Pillow Talk*

1960
★ Shirley Jones/*Elmer Gantry*
Glynis Johns/*The Sundowners*
Janet Leigh/*Psycho*

1961
★ Rita Moreno/*West Side Story*
Fay Bainter/*The Children's Hour*
Judy Garland/*Judgment at Nuremberg*
Lotte Lenya/*Roman Spring of Mrs. Stone*
Una Merkel/*Summer and Smoke*

1962
★ Patty Duke/*The Miracle Worker*
Mary Badham/*To Kill a Mockingbird*
Shirley Knight/*Sweet Bird of Youth*
Angela Lansbury/*The Manchurian Candidate*
Thelma Ritter/*Birdman of Alcatraz*

1963
★ Margaret Rutherford/*The V.I.P.'s*
Diane Cilento/*Tom Jones*
Edith Evans/*Tom Jones*
Joyce Redman/*Tom Jones*
Lilia Skala/*Lilies of the Field*

1964
★ Lila Kedrova/*Zorba the Greek*
Gladys Cooper/*My Fair Lady*
Edith Evans/*The Chalk Garden*

Grayson Hall/*The Night of the Iguana*
Agnes Moorehead/*Hush, Hush, Sweet Charlotte*

1965
★ Shelley Winters/*A Patch of Blue*
Ruth Gordon/*Inside Daisy Clover*
Joyce Redman/*Othello*
Maggie Smith/*Othello*
Peggy Wood/*The Sound of Music*

1966
★ Sandy Dennis/*Who's Afraid of Virginia Woolf?*
Wendy Hiller/*A Man for All Seasons*
Jocelyn Lagarde/*Hawaii*
Vivien Merchant/*Alfie*
Geraldine Page/*You're a Big Boy Now*

1967
★ Estelle Parsons/*Bonnie & Clyde*
Carol Channing/*Thoroughly Modern Millie*
Mildred Natwick/*Barefoot in the Park*
Beah Richards/*Guess Who's Coming to Dinner*
Katharine Ross/*The Graduate*

1968
★ Ruth Gordon/*Rosemary's Baby*
Lynn Carlin/*Faces*
Sondra Locke/*The Heart is a Lonely Hunter*
Kay Medford/*Funny Girl*
Estelle Parsons/*Rachel, Rachel*

1969
★ Goldie Hawn/*Cactus Flower*
Cathy Burns/*Last Summer*
Dyan Cannon/*Bob & Carol & Ted & Alice*
Sylvia Miles/*Midnight Cowboy*
Susannah York/*They Shoot Horses, Don't They?*

1970
★ Helen Hayes/*Airport*
Karen Black/*Five Easy Pieces*
Sally Kellerman/*M*A*S*H*
Maureen Stapleton/*Airport*

1971
★ Cloris Leachman/*The Last Picture Show*
Ann-Margret/*Carnal Knowledge*
Ellen Burstyn/*The Last Picture Show*
Margaret Leighton/*The Go-Between*

1972
★ Eileen Heckart/*Butterflies Are Free*

Jeannie Berlin/*The Heartbreak Kid*
Geraldine Page/*Pete 'n' Tillie*
Susan Tyrrell/*Fat City*
Shelley Winters/*The Poseidon Adventure*

1973
★ Tatum O'Neal/*Paper Moon*
Linda Blair/*The Exorcist*
Candy Clark/*American Graffiti*
Madeline Kahn/*Paper Moon*
Sylvia Sidney/*Summer Wishes, Winter Dreams*

1974
★ Ingrid Bergman/*Murder on the Orient Express*
Valentina Cortese/*Day for Night*
Madeline Kahn/*Blazing Saddles*
Diane Ladd/*Alice Doesn't Live Here Anymore*
Talia Shire/*The Godfather, Part 2*

1975
★ Lee Grant/*Shampoo*
Ronee Blakley/*Nashville*
Sylvia Miles/*Farewell, My Lovely*
Lily Tomlin/*Nashville*
Brenda Vaccaro/*Once is Not Enough*

1976
★ Beatrice Straight/*Network*
Jane Alexander/*All the President's Men*
Jodie Foster/*Taxi Driver*
Lee Grant/*Voyage of the Damned*
Piper Laurie/*Carrie*

1977
★ Vanessa Redgrave/*Julia*
Leslie Browne/*The Turning Point*
Quinn Cummings/*The Goodbye Girl*
Melinda Dillon/*Close Encounters of the Third Kind*
Tuesday Weld/*Looking for Mr. Goodbar*

1978
★ Maggie Smith/*California Suite*
Dyan Cannon/*Heaven Can Wait*
Penelope Milford/*Coming Home*
Maureen Stapleton/*Interiors*
Meryl Streep/*The Deer Hunter*

1979
★ Meryl Streep/*Kramer vs. Kramer*
Jane Alexander/*Kramer vs. Kramer*
Barbara Barrie/*Breaking Away*
Candice Bergen/*Starting Over*

Mariel Hemingway/*Manhattan*

1980
★ Mary Steenburgen/*Melvin and Howard*
Eileen Brennan/*Private Benjamin*
Eva LeGallienne/*Resurrection*
Cathy Moriarty/*Raging Bull*
Diana Scarwid/*Inside Moves*

1981
★ Maureen Stapleton/*Reds*
Melinda Dillon/*Absence of Malice*
Jane Fonda/*On Golden Pond*
Joan Hackett/*Only When I Laugh*
Elizabeth McGovern/*Ragtime*

1982
★ Jessica Lange/*Tootsie*
Glenn Close/*The World According to Garp*
Teri Garr/*Tootsie*
Kim Stanley/*Frances*
Lesley Ann Warren/*Victor/Victoria*

1983
★ Linda Hunt/*The Year of Living Dangerously*
Cher/*Silkwood*
Glenn Close/*The Big Chill*
Amy Irving/*Yentl*
Alfre Woodard/*Cross Creek*

1984
★ Peggy Ashcroft/*A Passage to India*
Glenn Close/*The Natural*
Lindsay Crouse/*Places in the Heart*
Christine Lahti/*Swing Shift*
Geraldine Page/*The Pope of Greenwich Village*

1985
★ Anjelica Huston/*Prizzi's Honor*
Margaret Avery/*The Color Purple*
Amy Madigan/*Twice in a Lifetime*
Meg Tilly/*Agnes of God*
Oprah Winfrey/*The Color Purple*

1986
★ Dianne Wiest/*Hannah and Her Sisters*
Tess Harper/*Crimes of the Heart*
Piper Laurie/*Children of a Lesser God*
Mary Elizabeth Mastrantonio/*The Color of Money*
Maggie Smith/*A Room with a View*

1987
★ Olympia Dukakis/*Moonstruck*

Norma Aleandro/*Gaby: A True Story*
Anne Archer/*Fatal Attraction*
Anne Ramsey/*Throw Momma from the Train*
Ann Sothern/*The Whales of August*

1988
★ Geena Davis/*The Accidental Tourist*
Joan Cusack/*Working Girl*
Frances McDormand/*Mississippi Burning*
Michelle Pfeiffer/*Dangerous Liaisons*
Sigourney Weaver/*Working Girl*

1989
★ Brenda Fricker/*My Left Foot*
Anjelica Huston/*Enemies, a Love Story*
Lena Olin/*Enemies, a Love Story*
Julia Roberts/*Steel Magnolias*
Dianne Wiest/*Parenthood*

1990
★ Whoopi Goldberg/*Ghost*
Annette Bening/*The Grifters*
Lorraine Bracco/*Goodfellas*
Diane Ladd/*Wild at Heart*
Mary McDonnell/*Dances with Wolves*

1991
★ Mercedes Ruehl/*The Fisher King*
Diane Ladd/*Rambling Rose*
Juliette Lewis/*Cape Fear*
Kate Nelligan/*The Prince of Tides*
Jessica Tandy/*Fried Green Tomatoes*

1992
★ Marisa Tomei/*My Cousin Vinny*
Judy Davis/*Husbands and Wives*
Joan Plowright/*Enchanted April*
Vanessa Redgrave/*Howard's End*
Miranda Richardson/*Damage*

1993
★ Anna Paquin/*The Piano*
Holly Hunter/*The Firm*
Rosie Perez/*Fearless*
Winona Ryder/*The Age of Innocence*
Emma Thompson/*In the Name of the Father*

1994
★ Dianne Wiest/*Bullets Over Broadway*
Rosemary Harris/*Tom & Viv*
Helen Mirren/*The Madness of King George*

DIRECTOR

1928

Charlie Chaplin/*The Circus*
King Vidor/*The Crowd*
Ted Wilde/*Speedy*

1929

Harry Beaumont/*Broadway Melody*

1930

★ Lewis Milestone/*All Quiet on the Western Front*
Clarence Brown/*Anna Christie*
Clarence Brown/*Romance*
Robert Z. Leonard/*The Divorcee*
King Vidor/*Hallelujah!*

1931

Clarence Brown/*A Free Soul*
Lewis Milestone/*The Front Page*
Wesley Ruggles/*Cimarron*
Josef von Sternberg/*Morocco*

1932

King Vidor/*The Champ*
Josef von Sternberg/*Shanghai Express*

1933

★ Frank Lloyd/*Cavalcade*
Frank Capra/*Lady for a Day*
George Cukor/*Little Women*

1934

★ Frank Capra/*It Happened One Night*
Victor Schertzinger/*One Night of Love*
Woodbridge S. Van Dyke/*The Thin Man*

1935

★ John Ford/*The Informer*
Henry Hathaway/*The Lives of a Bengal Lancer*
Frank Lloyd/*Mutiny on the Bounty*

1936

★ Frank Capra/*Mr. Deeds Goes to Town*
Gregory La Cava/*My Man Godfrey*
Robert Z. Leonard/*The Great Ziegfeld*
Woodbridge S. Van Dyke/*San Francisco*
William Wyler/*Dodsworth*

1937

★ Leo McCarey/*The Awful Truth*
William Dieterle/*The Life of Emile Zola*
Sidney Franklin/*The Good Earth*
Gregory La Cava/*Stage Door*

William A. Wellman/*A Star is Born*

1938

★ Frank Capra/*You Can't Take It with You*
Michael Curtiz/*Angels with Dirty Faces*
Michael Curtiz/*Four Daughters*
Norman Taurog/*Boys Town*
King Vidor/*The Citadel*

1939

★ Victor Fleming/*Gone with the Wind*
Frank Capra/*Mr. Smith Goes to Washington*
John Ford/*Stagecoach*
Sam Wood/*Goodbye, Mr. Chips*
William Wyler/*Wuthering Heights*

1940

★ John Ford/*The Grapes of Wrath*
George Cukor/*The Philadelphia Story*
Alfred Hitchcock/*Rebecca*
Sam Wood/*Kitty Foyle*
William Wyler/*The Letter*

1941

★ John Ford/*How Green Was My Valley*
Alexander Hall/*Here Comes Mr. Jordan*
Howard Hawks/*Sergeant York*
Orson Welles/*Citizen Kane*
William Wyler/*The Little Foxes*

1942

★ William Wyler/*Mrs. Miniver*
Michael Curtiz/*Yankee Doodle Dandy*
John Farrow/*Wake Island*
Mervyn LeRoy/*Random Harvest*
Sam Wood/*Kings Row*

1943

★ Michael Curtiz/*Casablanca*
Clarence Brown/*The Human Comedy*
Henry King/*The Song of Bernadette*
Ernst Lubitsch/*Heaven Can Wait*
George Stevens/*The More the Merrier*

1944

★ Leo McCarey/*Going My Way*
Alfred Hitchcock/*Lifeboat*
Henry King/*Wilson*
Otto Preminger/*Laura*
Billy Wilder/*Double Indemnity*

1945

★ Billy Wilder/*The Lost Weekend*
Clarence Brown/*National Velvet*

Alfred Hitchcock/*Spellbound*
Leo McCarey/*The Bells of St. Mary's*
Jean Renoir/*The Southerner*

1946

★ William Wyler/*The Best Years of Our Lives*
Clarence Brown/*The Yearling*
Frank Capra/*It's a Wonderful Life*
David Lean/*Brief Encounter*

1947

★ Elia Kazan/*Gentleman's Agreement*
George Cukor/*A Double Life*
Edward Dmytryk/*Crossfire*
Henry Koster/*The Bishop's Wife*
David Lean/*Great Expectations*

1948

★ John Huston/*Treasure of the Sierra Madre*
Anatole Litvak/*The Snake Pit*
Jean Negulesco/*Johnny Belinda*
Laurence Olivier/*Hamlet*
Fred Zinnemann/*The Search*

1949

★ Joseph L. Mankiewicz/*A Letter to Three Wives*
Carol Reed/*The Fallen Idol*
Robert Rossen/*All the King's Men*
William A. Wellman/*Battleground*
William Wyler/*The Heiress*

1950

★ Joseph L. Mankiewicz/*All About Eve*
George Cukor/*Born Yesterday*
John Huston/*The Asphalt Jungle*
Carol Reed/*The Third Man*
Billy Wilder/*Sunset Boulevard*

1951

★ George Stevens/*A Place in the Sun*
John Huston/*The African Queen*
Elia Kazan/*A Streetcar Named Desire*
Vincente Minnelli/*An American in Paris*
William Wyler/*Detective Story*

1952

★ John Ford/*The Quiet Man*
Cecil B. DeMille/*The Greatest Show on Earth*
John Huston/*Moulin Rouge*

Joseph L. Mankiewicz/*Five Fingers*
Fred Zinnemann/*High Noon*

1953

★ Fred Zinnemann/*From Here to Eternity*
George Stevens/*Shane*
Charles Walters/*Lili*
Billy Wilder/*Stalag 17*
William Wyler/*Roman Holiday*

1954

★ Elia Kazan/*On the Waterfront*
Alfred Hitchcock/*Rear Window*
George Seaton/*Country Girl*
Billy Wilder/*Sabrina*

1955

★ Delbert Mann/*Marty*
Elia Kazan/*East of Eden*
David Lean/*Summertime*
Joshua Logan/*Picnic*
John Sturges/*Bad Day at Black Rock*

1956

★ George Stevens/*Giant*
Michael Anderson, Sr./*Around the World in 80 Days*
Walter Lang/*The King and I*
King Vidor/*War and Peace*
William Wyler/*Friendly Persuasion*

1957

★ David Lean/*The Bridge on the River Kwai*
Joshua Logan/*Sayonara*
Sidney Lumet/*Twelve Angry Men*
Mark Robson/*Peyton Place*
Billy Wilder/*Witness for the Prosecution*

1958

★ Vincente Minnelli/*Gigi*
Richard Brooks/*Cat on a Hot Tin Roof*
Stanley Kramer/*The Defiant Ones*
Mark Robson/*The Inn of the Sixth Happiness*
Robert Wise/*I Want to Live!*

1959

★ William Wyler/*Ben-Hur*
Jack Clayton/*Room at the Top*
George Stevens/*The Diary of Anne Frank*
Billy Wilder/*Some Like It Hot*
Fred Zinnemann/*The Nun's Story*

1960

★ Billy Wilder/*The Apartment*
Cecil B. DeMille/*The Greatest Show on Earth*
Jules Dassin/*Never on Sunday*
Alfred Hitchcock/*Psycho*

Fred Zinnemann/*The Sundowners*

1961

★ Robert Wise/*West Side Story*
Federico Fellini/*La Dolce Vita*
Stanley Kramer/*Judgment at Nuremberg*
Robert Rossen/*The Hustler*
J. Lee Thompson/*The Guns of Navarone*

1962

★ David Lean/*Lawrence of Arabia*
Pietro Germi/*Divorce—Italian Style*
Robert Mulligan/*To Kill a Mockingbird*
Arthur Penn/*The Miracle Worker*
Frank Perry/*David and Lisa*

1963

★ Tony Richardson/*Tom Jones*
Federico Fellini/*8 1/2*
Otto Preminger/*The Cardinal*
Martin Ritt/*Hud*

1964

★ George Cukor/*My Fair Lady*
Michael Cacoyannis/*Zorba the Greek*
Peter Glenville/*Becket*
Stanley Kubrick/*Dr. Strangelove, or: How I Learned to Stop Worrying and Love the Bomb*
Robert Stevenson/*Mary Poppins*

1965

★ Robert Wise/*The Sound of Music*
David Lean/*Doctor Zhivago*
John Schlesinger/*Darling*
Hiroshi Teshigahara/*Woman in the Dunes*
William Wyler/*The Collector*

1966

★ Fred Zinnemann/*A Man for All Seasons*
Michelangelo Antonioni/*Blow-Up*
Richard Brooks/*The Professionals*
Claude Lelouch/*A Man and a Woman*
Mike Nichols/*Who's Afraid of Virginia Woolf?*

1967

★ Mike Nichols/*The Graduate*
Richard Brooks/*In Cold Blood*
Norman Jewison/*In the Heat of the Night*
Stanley Kramer/*Guess Who's Coming to Dinner*
Arthur Penn/*Bonnie & Clyde*

FILM ►cont.

The Awful Truth
The Good Earth

1938
★ You Can't Take It with You
Alexander's Ragtime Band
Boys Town
Four Daughters
Grand Illusion
Jezebel
Pygmalion
Test Pilot
The Adventures of Robin
Hood
The Citadel

1939
★ Gone with the Wind
Mr. Smith Goes to
Washington
Dark Victory
Goodbye, Mr. Chips
Love Affair
Ninotchka
Of Mice and Men
Stagecoach
The Wizard of Oz
Wuthering Heights

1940
★ Rebecca
All This and Heaven Too
Foreign Correspondent
Kitty Foyle
Our Town
The Grapes of Wrath
The Great Dictator
The Letter
The Long Voyage Home
The Philadelphia Story

1941
★ How Green Was My Valley
Blossoms in the Dust
Citizen Kane
Here Comes Mr. Jordan
Sergeant York
Suspicion
The Little Foxes
The Maltese Falcon

1942
★ Mrs. Miniver
Kings Row
Random Harvest
Talk of the Town
The Magnificent
Ambersons
The Pride of the Yankees
Wake Island
Yankee Doodle Dandy

1943
★ Casablanca
For Whom the Bell Tolls
Heaven Can Wait
In Which We Serve
Madame Curie
The Human Comedy
The More the Merrier
The Ox-Bow Incident
The Song of Bernadette
Watch on the Rhine

1944
★ Going My Way
Double Indemnity
Gaslight
Since You Went Away

Wilson

1945
★ The Lost Weekend
Anchors Aweigh
Mildred Pierce
Spellbound
The Bells of St. Mary's

1946
★ The Best Years of Our
Lives
Henry V
It's a Wonderful Life
The Razor's Edge
The Yearling

1947
★ Gentleman's Agreement
Crossfire
Great Expectations
Miracle on 34th Street
The Bishop's Wife

1948
★ Hamlet
Johnny Belinda
The Red Shoes
The Snake Pit
Treasure of the Sierra
Madre

1949
★ All the King's Men
A Letter to Three Wives
Battleground
The Heiress
Twelve O'Clock High

1950
★ All About Eve
Born Yesterday
Father of the Bride
King Solomon's Mines
Sunset Boulevard

1951
★ An American in Paris
A Place in the Sun
A Streetcar Named Desire
Quo Vadis

1952
★ The Greatest Show on
Earth
High Noon
Ivanhoe
Moulin Rouge
The Quiet Man

1953
★ From Here to Eternity
Julius Caesar
Roman Holiday
Shane
The Robe

1954
★ On the Waterfront
Country Girl
Seven Brides for Seven
Brothers
The Caine Mutiny
Three Coins in the
Fountain

1955
★ Marty
Love Is a Many-
Splendored Thing
Mister Roberts
Picnic
The Rose Tattoo

1956
★ Around the World in 80
Days
Friendly Persuasion
Giant
The King and I
The Ten Commandments

1957
★ The Bridge on the River
Kwai
Peyton Place
Sayonara
Twelve Angry Men
Witness for the
Prosecution

1958
★ Gigi
Auntie Mame
Cat on a Hot Tin Roof
Separate Tables
The Defiant Ones

1959
★ Ben-Hur
Anatomy of a Murder
Room at the Top
The Diary of Anne Frank
The Nun's Story

1960
★ The Apartment
Elmer Gantry
The Alamo
The Sundowners

1961
★ West Side Story
Fanny
Judgment at Nuremberg
The Guns of Navarone
The Hustler

1962
★ Lawrence of Arabia
Mutiny on the Bounty
The Longest Day
The Music Man
To Kill a Mockingbird

1963
★ Tom Jones
Cleopatra
How the West Was Won
Lilies of the Field

1964
★ My Fair Lady
Dr. Strangelove, or: How I
Learned to Stop
Worrying and Love the
Bomb
Becket
Mary Poppins
Zorba the Greek

1965
★ The Sound of Music
A Thousand Clowns
Darling
Doctor Zhivago
Ship of Fools

1966
★ A Man for All Seasons
Alfie
The Russians are Coming,
the Russians are
Coming
The Sand Pebbles

Who's Afraid of Virginia
Woolf?

1967
★ In the Heat of the Night
Bonnie & Clyde
Doctor Dolittle
Guess Who's Coming to
Dinner
The Graduate

1968
★ Oliver!
Funny Girl
Rachel, Rachel
Romeo and Juliet
The Lion in Winter

1969
★ Midnight Cowboy
Anne of the Thousand
Days
Butch Cassidy and the
Sundance Kid
Hello, Dolly!
Z

1970
★ Patton
Airport
Five Easy Pieces
Love Story
M*A*S*H

1971
★ The French Connection
A Clockwork Orange
Fiddler on the Roof
Nicholas and Alexandra
The Last Picture Show

1972
★ The Godfather
Cabaret
Deliverance
Sounder
The Emigrants

1973
★ The Sting
A Touch of Class
American Graffiti
Cries and Whispers
The Exorcist

1974
★ The Godfather, Part 2
Chinatown
Lenny
The Conversation
The Towering Inferno

1975
★ One Flew Over the
Cuckoo's Nest
Barry Lyndon
Dog Day Afternoon
Jaws
Nashville

1976
★ Rocky
All the President's Men
Bound for Glory
Network
Taxi Driver

1977
★ Annie Hall
Julia
Star Wars
The Goodbye Girl
The Turning Point

1978
★ The Deer Hunter
An Unmarried Woman
Coming Home
Heaven Can Wait
Midnight Express

1979
★ Kramer vs. Kramer
All That Jazz
Apocalypse Now
Breaking Away
Norma Rae

1980
★ Ordinary People
Coal Miner's Daughter
Raging Bull
Tess
The Elephant Man

1981
★ Chariots of Fire
Atlantic City
On Golden Pond
Raiders of the Lost Ark
Reds

1982
★ Gandhi
E.T.: The Extra-Terrestrial
Missing
The Verdict
Tootsie

1983
★ Terms of Endearment
Tender Mercies
The Big Chill
The Dresser
The Right Stuff

1984
★ Amadeus
A Passage to India
A Soldier's Story
Places in the Heart
The Killing Fields

1985
★ Out of Africa
Kiss of the Spider Woman
Prizzi's Honor
The Color Purple
Witness

1986
★ Platoon
A Room with a View
Children of a Lesser God
Hannah and Her Sisters
The Mission

1987
★ The Last Emperor
Broadcast News
Fatal Attraction
Hope and Glory
Moonstruck

1988
★ Rain Man
Dangerous Liaisons
Mississippi Burning
The Accidental Tourist
Working Girl

1989
★ Driving Miss Daisy
Born on the Fourth of July
Dead Poets Society
Field of Dreams

FILM EDITING
►*cont.*

1976
★ Rocky
  All the President's Men
  Bound for Glory
  Network
  Two Minute Warning

1977
★ Star Wars
  Close Encounters of the
    Third Kind
  Julia
  Smokey and the Bandit
  The Turning Point

1978
★ The Deer Hunter
  Superman: The Movie
  Coming Home
  Midnight Express
  The Boys from Brazil

1979
★ All That Jazz
  Apocalypse Now
  Kramer vs. Kramer
  The Black Stallion
  The Rose

1980
★ Raging Bull
  Coal Miner's Daughter
  Fame
  The Competition
  The Elephant Man

1981
★ Raiders of the Lost Ark
  Chariots of Fire
  On Golden Pond
  Reds
  The French Lieutenant's
    Woman

1982
★ Gandhi
  An Officer and a
    Gentleman
  Das Boot
  E.T.: The Extra-Terrestrial
  Tootsie

1983
★ The Right Stuff
  Blue Thunder
  Flashdance
  Silkwood
  Terms of Endearment

1984
★ The Killing Fields
  A Passage to India
  Amadeus
  Romancing the Stone
  The Cotton Club

1985
★ Witness
  A Chorus Line
  Out of Africa
  Prizzi's Honor
  Runaway Train

1986
★ Platoon
  Aliens
  Hannah and Her Sisters
  The Mission

Top Gun

1987
★ The Last Emperor
  RoboCop
  Broadcast News
  Empire of the Sun
  Fatal Attraction

1988
★ Who Framed Roger Rabbit
  Die Hard
  Gorillas in the Mist
  Mississippi Burning
  Rain Man

1989
★ Born on the Fourth of July
  Driving Miss Daisy
  Glory
  The Bear
  The Fabulous Baker Boys

1990
★ Dances with Wolves
  Ghost
  Goodfellas
  The Godfather, Part 3
  The Hunt for Red October

1991
★ JFK
  Terminator 2: Judgment
    Day
  The Commitments
  The Silence of the Lambs
  Thelma & Louise

1992
★ Unforgiven
  A Few Good Men
  Basic Instinct
  The Crying Game
  The Player

1993
★ Schindler's List
  In the Line of Fire
  In the Name of the Father
  The Fugitive
  The Piano

1994
★ Forrest Gump
  Hoop Dreams
  Pulp Fiction
  Speed
  The Shawshank
    Redemption

1995
★ Apollo 13
  Babe
  Braveheart
  Crimson Tide
  Seven

1996
★ The English Patient
  Evita
  Fargo
  Jerry Maguire
  Shine

FILM—FOREIGN LANGUAGE

1948
★ Monsieur Vincent

1949
★ The Bicycle Thief

1950
★ The Walls of Malapaga

1951
★ Rashomon

1952
★ Forbidden Games

1954
★ Gate of Hell

1955
★ Samurai 1: Musashi
    Miyamoto

1956
★ La Strada
  Gervaise
  The Burmese Harp

1957
★ Nights of Cabiria

1958
★ Mon Oncle
  Big Deal on Madonna
    Street

1959
★ Black Orpheus
  Cousin, Cousine
  The Bridge
  The Great War

1960
★ The Virgin Spring
  Kapo

1961
★ Through a Glass Darkly

1962
★ Sundays & Cybele

1963
★ 8 1/2
  Knife in the Water

1964
★ Yesterday, Today and
    Tomorrow
  Sallah

1965
★ The Shop on Main Street
  Kwaidan
  Umbrellas of Cherbourg
  Woman in the Dunes

1966
★ A Man and a Woman
  Loves of a Blonde
  The Battle of Algiers

1967
★ Closely Watched Trains

1968
★ War and Peace
  Stolen Kisses
  The Firemen's Ball

1969
★ Z
  Battle of Neretva

1970
  First Love
  My Night at Maud's
  Tristana

1971
★ The Garden of the Finzi-
    Continis
  Dodes 'ka-den
  Tchaikovsky

1972
★ The Discreet Charm of the
    Bourgeoisie
  I Love You Rosa

1973
★ Day for Night
  The Deluge
  The House on Chelouche
    Street
  The Pedestrian
  Turkish Delights

1974
★ Amarcord
  Cat's Play

1975
★ Dersu Uzala
  Land of Promise
  Sandakan No. 8
  The Scent of a Woman

1976
★ Black and White in Color
  Cousin, Cousine
  Nights and Days
  Seven Beauties

1977
★ Madame Rosa
  A Special Day
  Iphigenia
  Operation Thunderbolt
  That Obscure Object of
    Desire

1978
★ Get Out Your
    Handkerchiefs

1979
★ The Tin Drum
  A Simple Story
  Maids of Wilko
  Mama Turns a Hundred
  To Forget Venice

1980
★ Moscow Does Not Believe
    in Tears
  Kagemusha
  The Last Metro
  The Nest

1981
★ Mephisto
  Man of Iron
  The Boat is Full
  Three Brothers

1982
  Alsino and the Condor
  Coup de Torchon
  Flight of the Eagle
  Private Life

1983
★ Fanny and Alexander
  Carmen
  Entre-Nous
  Le Bal

1984
★ Dangerous Moves
  Beyond the Walls

Camila

1985
★ The Official Story
  Angry Harvest
  Colonel Redl
  Three Men and a Cradle
  When Father was Away
    on Business

1986
★ The Assault
  Betty Blue
  My Sweet Little Village
  The Decline of the
    American Empire

1987
★ Babette's Feast
  Au Revoir Les Enfants
  Pathfinder
  The Family

1988
★ Pelle the Conqueror
  Hanussen
  Salaam Bombay!
  The Music Teacher
  Women on the Verge of a
    Nervous Breakdown

1989
★ Cinema Paradiso
  Camille Claudel
  Jesus of Montreal

1990
★ Journey of Hope
  Cyrano de Bergerac
  Ju Dou
  Open Doors
  The Nasty Girl

1991
★ Mediterraneo
  Raise the Red Lantern
  Sweetie
  The Elementary School
  The Ox

1992
★ Indochine
  Children of Nature
  Close to Eden
  Daens
  Schtonk

1993
★ Belle Epoque
  Farewell My Concubine
  Hedd Wyn
  The Scent of Green
    Papaya
  The Wedding Banquet

1994
★ Burnt by the Sun
  Before the Rain
  Eat Drink Man Woman
  Farinelli
  Strawberry and Chocolate

1995
★ Antonia's Line
  All Things Fair
  O Quatrilho
  The Star Maker

1996
★ Kolya
  A Chef in Love
  Prisoner of the Mountains
  Ridicule

The Other Side of Sunday

MAKEUP

1981
- ★ *An American Werewolf in London*
- *Heartbeeps*

1982
- ★ *Quest for Fire*
- *Gandhi*

1984
- ★ *Amadeus*
- *2010: The Year We Make Contact*
- *Greystoke: The Legend of Tarzan, Lord of the Apes*

1985
- ★ *Mask*
- *Remo Williams: The Adventure Begins*
- *The Color Purple*

1986
- ★ *The Fly*
- *Legend*
- *The Clan of the Cave Bear*

1987
- ★ *Harry and the Hendersons*
- *Happy New Year*

1988
- ★ *Beetlejuice*

1989
- ★ *Driving Miss Daisy*
- *Dad*
- *The Adventures of Baron Munchausen*

1990
- ★ *Dick Tracy*
- *Cyrano de Bergerac*
- *Edward Scissorhands*

1991
- ★ *Terminator 2: Judgment Day*
- *Hook*
- *Star Trek 6: The Undiscovered Country*

1992
- ★ *Bram Stoker's Dracula*
- *Batman Returns*
- *Hoffa*

1993
- ★ *Mrs. Doubtfire*
- *Philadelphia*
- *Schindler's List*

1994
- ★ *Ed Wood*
- *Forrest Gump*
- *Mary Shelley's Frankenstein*

1995
- ★ *Braveheart*
- *My Family*
- *Roommates*

1996
- ★ *The Nutty Professor*
- *Ghosts of Mississippi*
- *Star Trek: First Contact*

ADAPTED SCORE

1962
- ★ *The Music Man*
- *Billy Rose's Jumbo*
- *Gypsy*
- *The Wonderful World of the Brothers Grimm*

1963
- ★ *Irma La Douce*
- *A New Kind of Love*
- *Bye, Bye, Birdie*
- *Sundays & Cybele*
- *The Sword in the Stone*

1964
- ★ *My Fair Lady*
- *A Hard Day's Night*
- *Robin and the 7 Hoods*
- *The Unsinkable Molly Brown*

1965
- ★ *The Sound of Music*
- *A Thousand Clowns*
- *Cat Ballou*

1966
- ★ *A Funny Thing Happened on the Way to the Forum*
- *Return of the Seven*
- *The Gospel According to St. Matthew*
- *The Singing Nun*

1967
- ★ *Camelot*
- *Guess Who's Coming to Dinner*
- *Valley of the Dolls*

1968
- ★ *Oliver!*
- *Star!*

ORIGINAL DRAMATIC/ COMEDY SCORE

1941
- ★ *The Devil & Daniel Webster*
- *Dr. Jekyll and Mr. Hyde*
- *Ball of Fire*
- *Cheers for Miss Bishop*
- *Citizen Kane*
- *How Green Was My Valley*
- *King of the Zombies*
- *Lydia*
- *Sergeant York*
- *So Ends Our Night*
- *Sundown*
- *Suspicion*
- *Tanks a Million*
- *That Uncertain Feeling*
- *The Little Foxes*

1942
- ★ *Now, Voyager*
- *Arabian Nights*
- *Bambi*
- *Flying Tigers*
- *I Married a Witch*
- *Joan of Paris*
- *Random Harvest*
- *Silver Queen*
- *Talk of the Town*
- *The Black Swan*
- *The Corsican Brothers*
- *The Jungle Book*

The Pride of the Yankees
The Shanghai Gesture
To Be or Not to Be

1943
- ★ *The Song of Bernadette*
- *Casablanca*
- *Commandos Strike at Dawn*
- *For Whom the Bell Tolls*
- *Hi Diddle Diddle*
- *Johnny Come Lately*
- *Lady of Burlesque*
- *Madame Curie*
- *The Fallen Sparrow*
- *The Kansan*
- *The Moon and Sixpence*
- *The North Star*
- *War of the Wildcats*

1944
- ★ *Cover Girl*
- ★ *Since You Went Away*
- *Casanova Brown*
- *Double Indemnity*
- *Fighting Seabees*
- *Higher and Higher*
- *Jack London*
- *None But the Lonely Heart*
- *The Adventures of Mark Twain*
- *The Bridge of San Luis Rey*
- *The Hairy Ape*
- *The Princess and the Pirate*
- *The Woman of the Town*
- *Wilson*

1945
- ★ *Spellbound*
- *A Song to Remember*
- *Brewster's Millions*
- *Captain Kidd*
- *Flame of the Barbary Coast*
- *Guest Wife*
- *Guest in the House*
- *Objective, Burma!*
- *The Bells of St. Mary's*
- *The Enchanted Cottage*
- *The Keys of the Kingdom*
- *The Lost Weekend*
- *The Southerner*
- *The Valley of Decision*
- *Woman in the Window*

1946
- ★ *The Best Years of Our Lives*
- *Anna and the King of Siam*
- *Henry V*
- *Humoresque*

1947
- ★ *A Double Life*
- *Captain from Castile*
- *Fiesta*
- *Forever Amber*
- *Life with Father*
- *The Bishop's Wife*
- *The Road to Rio*

1948
- ★ *The Red Shoes*
- *Hamlet*
- *Joan of Arc*
- *Johnny Belinda*
- *The Snake Pit*

1949
- ★ *The Heiress*
- *Beyond the Forest*

Champion

1950
- ★ *Sunset Boulevard*
- *All About Eve*
- *Samson and Delilah*
- *The Flame & the Arrow*

1951
- ★ *A Place in the Sun*
- *A Streetcar Named Desire*
- *David and Bathsheba*
- *Quo Vadis*

1952
- ★ *High Noon*
- *Ivanhoe*
- *Miracle of Our Lady of Fatima*
- *The Thief*
- *Viva Zapata!*

1953
- ★ *Lili*
- *Above and Beyond*
- *From Here to Eternity*
- *Julius Caesar*

1954
- *Genevieve*
- *On the Waterfront*
- *The Caine Mutiny*
- *The Silver Chalice*

1955
- ★ *Love Is a Many- Splendored Thing*
- *Battle Cry*
- *Picnic*
- *The Man with the Golden Arm*
- *The Rose Tattoo*

1956
- ★ *Around the World in 80 Days*
- *Anastasia*
- *Between Heaven and Hell*
- *Giant*
- *The Rainmaker*

1958
- *Separate Tables*
- *The Big Country*
- *The Young Lions*

1959
- ★ *Ben-Hur*
- *On the Beach*
- *Pillow Talk*
- *The Diary of Anne Frank*
- *The Nun's Story*

1960
- ★ *Exodus*
- *Elmer Gantry*
- *Spartacus*
- *The Alamo*
- *The Magnificent Seven*

1961
- ★ *Breakfast at Tiffany's*
- *El Cid*
- *Fanny*
- *Summer and Smoke*
- *The Guns of Navarone*

1971
- ★ *Summer of '42*
- *Nicholas and Alexandra*
- *Shaft*
- *Straw Dogs*

1972
- *Napoleon and Samantha*
- *Sleuth*
- *The Poseidon Adventure*

1973
- ★ *The Way We Were*
- *A Touch of Class*
- *Cinderella Liberty*
- *Papillon*
- *The Day of the Dolphin*

1974
- ★ *The Godfather, Part 2*
- *Chinatown*
- *Murder on the Orient Express*
- *The Towering Inferno*

1995
- ★ *The Postman*
- *Apollo 13*
- *Braveheart*
- *Nixon*
- *Sense and Sensibility*

1996
- ★ *The English Patient*
- *Hamlet*
- *Michael Collins*
- *Shine*
- *Sleepers*

ORIGINAL SCORE

1938
- ★ *The Adventures of Robin Hood*
- *Breaking the Ice*
- *Marie Antoinette*
- *The Cowboy and the Lady*
- *The Young in Heart*

1939
- ★ *The Wizard of Oz*
- *Dark Victory*
- *Eternally Yours*
- *Golden Boy*
- *Gone with the Wind*
- *Gulliver's Travels*
- *Nurse Edith Cavell*
- *Of Mice and Men*
- *The Man in the Iron Mask*
- *The Rains Came*
- *Wuthering Heights*

1940
- ★ *Pinocchio*
- *Arizona*
- *Dark Command*
- *My Favorite Wife*
- *One Million B.C.*
- *Rebecca*
- *The Grapes of Wrath*
- *The Great Dictator*
- *The Howards of Virginia*
- *The Letter*
- *The Long Voyage Home*
- *The Mark of Zorro*
- *The Thief of Bagdad*
- *Waterloo Bridge*

1962
- ★ *Lawrence of Arabia*
- *Mutiny on the Bounty*
- *Taras Bulba*
- *To Kill a Mockingbird*

1963
- ★ *Tom Jones*
- *55 Days at Peking*
- *Cleopatra*

The Three Caballeros
Tonight and Every Night
Wonder Man

1946

★ *The Jolson Story*
Blue Skies
Night and Day
The Harvey Girls

1948

★ *Easter Parade*
Emperor Waltz
Romance on the High
Seas
The Pirate

1949

★ *On the Town*
Jolson Sings Again
Look for the Silver Lining

1950

Cinderella
The West Point Story
Three Little Words

1951

★ *An American in Paris*
Alice in Wonderland
Show Boat
The Great Caruso

1952

Hans Christian Andersen
Singin' in the Rain
The Medium

1953

Calamity Jane
Kiss Me Kate
The 5000 Fingers of Dr. T
The Band Wagon

1954

★ *Seven Brides for Seven*
Brothers
A Star is Born
Carmen Jones
The Glenn Miller Story
There's No Business Like
Show Business

1955

★ *Oklahoma!*
Daddy Long Legs
Guys and Dolls
It's Always Fair Weather
Love Me or Leave Me

1956

★ *The King and I*
High Society
Meet Me in Las Vegas
The Eddy Duchin Story

1958

★ *Gigi*
Damn Yankees
South Pacific

1959

Li'l Abner
Sleeping Beauty
The Five Pennies

1960

★ *Song Without End*
Bells are Ringing
Can-Can
Let's Make Love

1961

★ *West Side Story*
Babes in Toyland
Flower Drum Song
Paris Blues

1968

Finian's Rainbow
Funny Girl

1969

★ *Hello, Dolly!*
Goodbye, Mr. Chips
Paint Your Wagon
Sweet Charity
They Shoot Horses, Don't
They?

SONG

1934

★ "The Continental"/*The Gay Divorcee*
"Carioca"/*Flying Down to Rio*

1935

★ "Lullaby of Broadway"/*Gold Diggers of 1935*
"Cheek to Cheek"/*Top Hat*
"Lovely to Look At"/*Roberta*

1936

★ "The Way You Look Tonight"/*Swing Time*
"Did I Remember"/*Suzy*
"I've Got You Under My Skin"/*Born to Dance*
"My Own"/*That Certain Age*

1937

★ "Sweet Leilani"/*Waikiki Wedding*
"That Old Feeling"/*Vogues of 1938*
"They Can't Take That Away From Me"/*Shall We Dance*

1938

★ "Thanks for the Memories"/*The Big Broadcast of 1938*
★ "Thanks for the Memories"/*The Big Broadcast of 1938*
"Always and Always"/*Mannequin*
"Change Partners and Dance with Me"/*Carefree*
"Now It Can Be Told"/*Alexander's Ragtime Band*
"The Cowboy and the Lady"/*The Cowboy and the Lady*

1939

★ "Over the Rainbow"/*The Wizard of Oz*
"Faithful Forever"/*Gulliver's Travels*
"I Poured My Heart Into Song"/*Second Fiddle*
"Wishing"/*Love Affair*

1940

★ "When You Wish Upon a Star"/*Pinocchio*
"Down Argentine Way"/*Down Argentine Way*
"I'd Know You Anywhere"/*You'll Find Out*
"It's a Blue World"/*Music in My Heart*
"Love of My Life"/*Second Chorus*
"Only Forever"/*Rhythm on the River*
"Our Love Affair"/*Strike Up the Band*

1941

★ "The Last Time I Saw Paris"/*Lady Be Good*
"Baby Mine"/*Dumbo*
"Be Honest With Me"/*Ridin' on a Rainbow*
"Boogie Woogie Bugle Boy of Company B"/*Buck Privates*
"Chattanooga Choo Choo"/*Sun Valley Serenade*
"Since I Kissed My Baby Goodbye"/*You'll Never Get Rich*

1942

★ "White Christmas"/*Holiday Inn*
"Dearly Beloved"/*You Were Never Lovelier*
"How About You?"/*Babes on Broadway*
"I've Got a Gal in Kalamazoo"/*Orchestra Wives*
"Love Is a Song"/*Bambi*

1943

★ "You'll Never Know"/*Hello, Frisco, Hello*
"Happiness Is a Thing Called Joe"/*Cabin in the Sky*
"My Shining Hour"/*The Sky's the Limit*
"That Old Black Magic"/*Star Spangled Rhythm*
"They're Either Too Young or Too Old"/*Thank Your Lucky Stars*
"We Mustn't Say Goodbye"/*Stage Door Canteen*

1944

★ "Swinging on a Star"/*Going My Way*
"I Couldn't Sleep A Wink Last Night"/*Higher and Higher*
"I'll Walk Alone"/*Follow the Boys*
"Long Ago and Far Away"/*Cover Girl*
"Now I Know"/*Up in Arms*
"Sweet Dreams Sweetheart"/*Hollywood Canteen*
"The Trolley Song"/*Meet Me in St. Louis*

1945

★ "It Might as Well Be Spring"/*State Fair*
"Accentuate the Positive"/*Here Come the Waves*
"Anywhere"/*Tonight and Every Night*
"Aren't You Glad You're You"/*The Bells of St. Mary's*
"I Fall in Love Too Easily"/*Anchors Aweigh*
"More and More"/*Can't Help Singing*
"So in Love"/*Wonder Man*
"Some Sunday Morning"/*San Antonio*

1946

★ "On the Atchison, Topeka and Santa Fe"/*The Harvey Girls*
"I Can't Begin to Tell You"/*The Dolly Sisters*
"You Keep Coming Back Like a Song"/*Blue Skies*

1947

"I Wish I Didn't Love You So"/*The Perils of Pauline*
"Pass That Peace Pipe"/*Good News*

1948

★ "Buttons and Bows"/*The Paleface*
"It's Magic"/*Romance on the High Seas*

1949

★ "Baby It's Cold Outside"/*Neptune's Daughter*
"It's a Great Feeling"/*It's a Great Feeling*
"Lavender Blue"/*So Dear to My Heart*
"Through a Long and Sleepless Night"/*Come to the Stable*

1950

"Be My Love"/*The Toast of New Orleans*
"Bibbidy-Bobbidi-Boo"/*Cinderella*

1951

★ "In the Cool, Cool, Cool of the Evening"/*Here Comes the Groom*
"Too Late Now"/*Royal Wedding*
"Wonder Why"/*Rich, Young and Pretty*

1952

★ "High Noon (Do Not Forsake Me, Oh My Darlin')"/*High Noon*
"Am I in Love"/*Son of Paleface*
"Because You're Mine"/*Because You're Mine*
"Thumbelina"/*Hans Christian Andersen*

"Zing a Little Zong"/*Just for You*

1953

★ "Secret Love"/*Calamity Jane*
"My Flaming Heart"/*Small Town Girl*
"Sadie Thompson's Song (Blue Pacific Blues)"/*Miss Sadie Thompson*
"That's Amore"/*The Caddy*
"The Moon is Blue"/*The Moon Is Blue*

1954

★ "Three Coins in the Fountain"/*Three Coins in the Fountain*
"Count Your Blessings Instead of Sheep"/*White Christmas*
"Hold My Hand"/*Susan Slept Here*
"The Man That Got Away"/*A Star is Born*

1955

★ "Love Is a Many-Splendored Thing"/*Love Is a Many-Splendored Thing*
"(Love Is) The Tender Trap"/*The Tender Trap*
"I'll Never Stop Loving You"/*Love Me or Leave Me*
"Something's Gotta Give"/*Daddy Long Legs*

1956

★ "Que Sera, Sera"/*The Man Who Knew Too Much*
"Friendly Persuasion (Thee I Love)"/*Friendly Persuasion*
"True Love"/*High Society*
"Written on the Wind"/*Written on the Wind*

1957

"An Affair to Remember"/*An Affair to Remember*
"Tammy"/*Tammy and the Bachelor*

1958

★ "Gigi"/*Gigi*
"A Very Precious Love"/*Marjorie Morningstar*
"Almost in Your Arms (Love Song from Houseboat)"/*Houseboat*
"To Love and Be Loved"/*Some Came Running*

1959

★ "High Hopes"/*A Hole in the Head*
"Strange Are the Ways of Love"/*The Young Land*
"The Best of Everything"/*The Best of Everything*
"The Five Pennies"/*The Five Pennies*

"The Day I Fall in Love"/
Beethoven's 2nd

1994

★ "Can You Feel the Love
Tonight"/The Lion King
"Circle of Life"/The Lion
King
"Hakuna Matata"/The
Lion King
"Look What Love Has
Done"/Junior
"Make Up Your Mind"/
The Paper

1995

★ "Colors of the Wind"/
Pocahontas
"Dead Man Walking"/
Dead Man Walking
"Have You Ever Really
Loved a Woman?"/
Don Juan DeMarco
"Moonlight"/Sabrina
"You've Got a Friend"/
Toy Story

1996

★ "You Must Love Me"/
Evita
"Because You Loved
Me"/Up Close and
Personal
"For the First Time"/One
Fine Day
"I've Finally Found
Someone"/The Mirror
Has Two Faces
"That Thing You Do!"/
That Thing You Do!

SOUND

1933

★ A Farewell to Arms
42nd Street
Gold Diggers of 1933
I Am a Fugitive from a
Chain Gang

1934

★ One Night of Love
Cleopatra
The Gay Divorcee
Viva Villa!

1935

★ Naughty Marietta
Captain Blood
I Dream Too Much
The Bride of Frankenstein
The Lives of a Bengal
Lancer

1936

★ San Francisco
Mr. Deeds Goes to Town
Dodsworth
General Spanky
That Girl from Paris
The Charge of the Light
Brigade
The Texas Rangers
Three Smart Girls

1937

★ The Hurricane
100 Men and a Girl
In Old Chicago
Lost Horizon
Maytime
The Girl Said No
The Life of Emile Zola

Topper

1938

★ The Cowboy and the Lady
Four Daughters
Sweethearts
That Certain Age
Vivacious Lady
You Can't Take It with You

1939

Mr. Smith Goes to
Washington
Balalaika
Gone with the Wind
Goodbye, Mr. Chips
Of Mice and Men
The Hunchback of Notre
Dame
The Private Lives of
Elizabeth & Essex
The Rains Came

1940

★ Strike Up the Band
Captain Caution
Kitty Foyle
Our Town
The Grapes of Wrath
The Howards of Virginia
The Sea Hawk

1941

★ That Hamilton Woman
Ball of Fire
Citizen Kane
How Green Was My
Valley
Sergeant York
The Chocolate Soldier
Topper Returns

1942

★ Yankee Doodle Dandy
Mrs. Miniver
Arabian Nights
Bambi
Flying Tigers
Once Upon a Honeymoon
The Pride of the Yankees
The Road to Morocco
You Were Never Lovelier

1943

★ This Land is Mine
Madame Curie
Sahara
So This Is Washington
The North Star
The Phantom of the Opera
The Song of Bernadette
This Is the Army
War of the Wildcats

1944

★ Wilson
Casanova Brown
Cover Girl
Double Indemnity
His Butler's Sister
Hollywood Canteen

1945

★ The Bells of St. Mary's
A Song to Remember
Flame of the Barbary
Coast
Lady On a Train
Leave Her to Heaven
Rhapsody in Blue
The Southerner
The Three Caballeros
They Were Expendable

Wonder Man

1946

★ The Jolson Story
It's a Wonderful Life
The Best Years of Our
Lives

1947

★ The Bishop's Wife
Green Dolphin Street
T-Men

1948

★ The Snake Pit
Johnny Belinda
Moonrise

1949

★ Twelve O'Clock High
Sands of Iwo Jima

1950

★ All About Eve
Cinderella
Trio

1951

★ The Great Caruso
A Streetcar Named Desire
Two Tickets to Broadway

1952

Hans Christian Andersen
The Promoter
The Quiet Man

1953

★ From Here to Eternity
Calamity Jane
Knights of the Round
Table
The War of the Worlds

1954

★ The Glenn Miller Story
Brigadoon
Rear Window
Susan Slept Here
The Caine Mutiny

1955

★ Oklahoma!
Love Is a Many-
Splendored Thing
Love Me or Leave Me
Mister Roberts
Not as a Stranger

1956

★ The King and I
Friendly Persuasion
The Brave One
The Eddy Duchin Story
The Ten Commandments

1957

★ Sayonara
Gunfight at the O.K. Corral
Les Girls
Pal Joey
Witness for the
Prosecution

1958

★ South Pacific
A Time to Love & a Time
to Die
I Want to Live!
The Young Lions
Vertigo

1959

★ Ben-Hur
Journey to the Center of
the Earth
The Nun's Story

1960

★ The Alamo
Cimarron
Sunrise at Campobello
The Apartment

1961

★ West Side Story
Flower Drum Song
The Children's Hour
The Guns of Navarone
The Parent Trap

1962

★ Lawrence of Arabia
Bon Voyage!
That Touch of Mink
The Music Man
What Ever Happened to
Baby Jane?

1963

★ How the West Was Won
Bye, Bye, Birdie
Captain Newman, M.D.
Cleopatra
It's a Mad, Mad, Mad, Mad
World

1964

★ My Fair Lady
Becket
Father Goose
Mary Poppins
The Unsinkable Molly
Brown

1965

★ The Sound of Music
Doctor Zhivago
Shenandoah
The Agony and the
Ecstasy
The Great Race

1966

★ Grand Prix
Gambit
Hawaii
The Sand Pebbles
Who's Afraid of Virginia
Woolf?

1967

★ In the Heat of the Night
Camelot
Doctor Dolittle
The Dirty Dozen
Thoroughly Modern Millie

1968

★ Oliver!
Bullitt
Finian's Rainbow
Funny Girl
Star!

1969

★ Hello, Dolly!
Anne of the Thousand
Days
Butch Cassidy and the
Sundance Kid
Marooned

1970

★ Patton
Airport
Ryan's Daughter
Tora! Tora! Tora!
Woodstock

1971

★ Fiddler on the Roof
Diamonds Are Forever
Kotch
The French Connection

1972

★ Cabaret
Butterflies Are Free
The Candidate
The Godfather
The Poseidon Adventure

1973

★ The Exorcist
Paper Moon
The Day of the Dolphin
The Paper Chase
The Sting

1974

★ Earthquake
Chinatown
The Conversation
The Towering Inferno
Young Frankenstein

1975

★ Jaws
Bite the Bullet
Funny Lady
The Hindenburg
The Wind and the Lion

1976

★ All the President's Men
A Star is Born
King Kong
Rocky
Silver Streak

1977

★ Star Wars
Close Encounters of the
Third Kind
Sorcerer
The Deep
The Turning Point

1978

★ The Deer Hunter
Superman: The Movie
Days of Heaven
Hooper
The Buddy Holly Story

1979

★ Apocalypse Now
1941
Meteor
The Electric Horseman
The Rose

1980

★ The Empire Strikes Back
Altered States
Coal Miner's Daughter
Fame
Raging Bull

1981

★ Raiders of the Lost Ark
On Golden Pond
Outland
Pennies From Heaven

SOUND ‚cont.

Reds

1982
- ★ Gandhi
- Das Boot
- E.T.: The Extra-Terrestrial
- Tootsie
- Tron

1983
- ★ The Right Stuff
- Never Cry Wolf
- Return of the Jedi
- Terms of Endearment
- WarGames

1984
- ★ Amadeus
- 2010: The Year We Make Contact
- A Passage to India
- Dune
- The River

1985
- ★ Out of Africa
- A Chorus Line
- Back to the Future
- Ladyhawke
- Silverado

1986
- ★ Platoon
- Aliens
- Heartbreak Ridge
- Star Trek 4: The Voyage Home
- Top Gun

1987
- ★ The Last Emperor
- RoboCop
- Empire of the Sun
- Lethal Weapon
- The Witches of Eastwick

1988
- ★ Bird
- Die Hard
- Gorillas in the Mist
- Mississippi Burning
- Who Framed Roger Rabbit

1989
- ★ Glory
- Black Rain
- Born on the Fourth of July
- Indiana Jones and the Last Crusade
- The Abyss

1990
- ★ Dances with Wolves
- Days of Thunder
- Dick Tracy
- The Hunt for Red October
- Total Recall

1991
- ★ Terminator 2: Judgment Day
- Backdraft
- Beauty and the Beast
- JFK
- The Silence of the Lambs

1992
- ★ The Last of the Mohicans

A Few Good Men
Aladdin
Under Siege
Unforgiven

1993
- ★ Jurassic Park
- Cliffhanger
- Geronimo: An American Legend
- Schindler's List
- The Fugitive

1994
- ★ Speed
- Clear and Present Danger
- Forrest Gump
- Legends of the Fall
- The Shawshank Redemption

1995
- ★ Apollo 13
- Batman Forever
- Braveheart
- Crimson Tide
- Waterworld

1996
- ★ The English Patient
- Evita
- Independence Day
- The Rock
- Twister

ADAPTED SCREENPLAY

1928

The Jazz Singer

1931
- ★ Cimarron
- Criminal Code
- Little Caesar

1932

Dr. Jekyll and Mr. Hyde
Arrowsmith

1933
- ★ Little Women
- Lady for a Day

1934
- ★ It Happened One Night
- The Thin Man
- Viva Villa!

1956
- ★ Around the World in 80 Days
- Baby Doll
- Friendly Persuasion
- Giant
- Lust for Life

1957
- ★ The Bridge on the River Kwai
- Heaven Knows, Mr. Allison
- Peyton Place
- Sayonara
- Twelve Angry Men

1958
- ★ Gigi
- Cat on a Hot Tin Roof
- I Want to Live!
- Separate Tables
- The Horse's Mouth

1959
- ★ Room at the Top
- Anatomy of a Murder
- Ben-Hur
- Some Like It Hot
- The Nun's Story

1960
- ★ Elmer Gantry
- Inherit the Wind
- The Sundowners
- Tunes of Glory

1961
- ★ Judgment at Nuremberg
- Breakfast at Tiffany's
- The Guns of Navarone
- The Hustler
- West Side Story

1962
- ★ To Kill a Mockingbird
- David and Lisa
- Lawrence of Arabia
- Lolita
- The Miracle Worker

1963
- ★ Tom Jones
- Captain Newman, M.D.
- Hud
- Lilies of the Field
- Sundays & Cybele

1964
- ★ Becket
- Dr. Strangelove, or: How I Learned to Stop Worrying and Love the Bomb
- Mary Poppins
- My Fair Lady
- Zorba the Greek

1965
- ★ Doctor Zhivago
- A Thousand Clowns
- Cat Ballou
- Ship of Fools
- The Collector

1966
- ★ A Man for All Seasons
- Alfie
- Cool Hand Luke
- The Professionals
- The Russians are Coming, the Russians are Coming
- Who's Afraid of Virginia Woolf?

1967
- ★ In the Heat of the Night
- In Cold Blood
- The Graduate
- Ulysses

1968
- ★ The Lion in Winter
- Oliver!
- Rachel, Rachel
- Rosemary's Baby
- The Odd Couple

1969
- ★ Midnight Cowboy
- Anne of the Thousand Days
- Goodbye Columbus
- They Shoot Horses, Don't They?

Z

1970
- ★ M*A*S*H
- Airport
- I Never Sang For My Father
- Lovers and Other Strangers
- Women in Love

1971
- ★ The French Connection
- A Clockwork Orange
- The Conformist
- The Garden of the Finzi-Continis
- The Last Picture Show

1972
- ★ The Godfather
- Cabaret
- Pete 'n' Tillie
- Sounder
- The Emigrants

1973
- ★ The Exorcist
- Paper Moon
- Serpico
- The Last Detail
- The Paper Chase

1974
- ★ The Godfather, Part 2
- Lenny
- Murder on the Orient Express
- The Apprenticeship of Duddy Kravitz
- Young Frankenstein

1975
- ★ One Flew Over the Cuckoo's Nest
- Barry Lyndon
- The Man Who Would Be King
- The Scent of a Woman
- The Sunshine Boys

1976
- ★ All the President's Men
- Bound for Glory
- The Seven-Per-Cent Solution
- Voyage of the Damned

1977
- ★ Julia
- Equus
- I Never Promised You a Rose Garden
- Oh, God!
- That Obscure Object of Desire

1978
- ★ Midnight Express
- Bloodbrothers
- California Suite
- Heaven Can Wait
- Same Time, Next Year

1979
- ★ Kramer vs. Kramer
- A Little Romance
- Apocalypse Now
- La Cage aux Folles
- Norma Rae

1980
- ★ Ordinary People

Breaker Morant
Coal Miner's Daughter
The Elephant Man
The Stunt Man

1981
- ★ On Golden Pond
- Pennies From Heaven
- Prince of the City
- Ragtime
- The French Lieutenant's Woman

1982
- ★ Missing
- Das Boot
- Sophie's Choice
- The Verdict
- Victor/Victoria

1983
- ★ Terms of Endearment
- Betrayal
- Educating Rita
- Reuben, Reuben
- The Dresser

1984
- ★ Amadeus
- A Passage to India
- A Soldier's Story
- Greystoke: The Legend of Tarzan, Lord of the Apes
- The Killing Fields

1985
- ★ Out of Africa
- Kiss of the Spider Woman
- Prizzi's Honor
- The Color Purple
- The Trip to Bountiful

1986
- ★ A Room with a View
- Children of a Lesser God
- Crimes of the Heart
- Stand By Me
- The Color of Money

1987
- ★ The Last Emperor
- Fatal Attraction
- Full Metal Jacket
- My Life As a Dog
- The Dead

1988
- ★ Dangerous Liaisons
- Gorillas in the Mist
- Little Dorrit, Film 1: Nobody's Fault
- The Accidental Tourist
- The Unbearable Lightness of Being

1989
- ★ Driving Miss Daisy
- Born on the Fourth of July
- Enemies, a Love Story
- Field of Dreams
- My Left Foot

1990
- ★ Dances with Wolves
- Awakenings
- Goodfellas
- Reversal of Fortune
- The Grifters

1991
- ★ The Silence of the Lambs
- Europa, Europa

Fried Green Tomatoes
JFK
The Prince of Tides

1992
★ Howard's End
A River Runs Through It
Enchanted April
Scent of a Woman
The Player

1993
★ Schindler's List
In the Name of the Father
Shadowlands
The Age of Innocence
The Remains of the Day

1994
★ Forrest Gump
Nobody's Fool
Quiz Show
The Madness of King
George
The Shawshank
Redemption

1995
★ Sense and Sensibility
Apollo 13
Babe
Leaving Las Vegas
The Postman

1996
★ Sling Blade
Hamlet
The Crucible
The English Patient
Trainspotting

ORIGINAL SCREENPLAY

1940
★ The Great McGinty
Angels Over Broadway
Foreign Correspondent
The Great Dictator

1941
★ Citizen Kane
Sergeant York
The Devil & Miss Jones

1942
★ Woman of the Year
One of Our Aircraft Is
Missing
The Road to Morocco
Wake Island

1943
Air Force
In Which We Serve
So Proudly We Hail
The North Star

1944
★ Wilson
A Wing and a Prayer
Hail the Conquering Hero
Miracle of Morgan's Creek
Two Girls and a Sailor

1945
Dillinger

1946
★ The Seventh Veil
Children of Paradise
Notorious
The Blue Dahlia

The Road to Utopia

1947
★ The Bachelor and the
Bobby-Soxer
A Double Life
Body and Soul
Monsieur Verdoux
Shoeshine

1956
★ The Red Balloon
La Strada
The Ladykillers

1974
★ Chinatown
Alice Doesn't Live Here
Anymore
Day for Night
Harry and Tonto
The Conversation

1975
★ Dog Day Afternoon
Amarcord
And Now My Love
Lies My Father Told Me
Shampoo

1976
★ Network
Cousin, Cousine
Rocky
Seven Beauties
The Front

1977
★ Annie Hall
Star Wars
The Goodbye Girl
The Late Show
The Turning Point

1978
★ Coming Home
An Unmarried Woman
Autumn Sonata
Interiors
The Deer Hunter

1979
★ Breaking Away
All That Jazz
And Justice for All
Manhattan
The China Syndrome

1980
★ Melvin and Howard
Brubaker
Fame
Mon Oncle D'Amerique
Private Benjamin

1981
★ Chariots of Fire
Absence of Malice
Arthur
Atlantic City
Reds

1982
★ Gandhi
An Officer and a
Gentleman
Diner
E.T.: The Extra-Terrestrial
Tootsie

1983
★ Tender Mercies
Fanny and Alexander

Silkwood
The Big Chill
WarGames

1984
★ Places in the Heart
Beverly Hills Cop
Broadway Danny Rose
El Norte
Splash

1985
★ Witness
Back to the Future
Brazil
The Official Story
The Purple Rose of Cairo

1986
★ Hannah and Her Sisters
Crocodile Dundee
My Beautiful Laundrette
Platoon
Salvador

1987
★ Moonstruck
Au Revoir Les Enfants
Broadcast News
Hope and Glory
Radio Days

1988
★ Rain Man
A Fish Called Wanda
Big
Bull Durham
Running on Empty

1989
★ Dead Poets Society
Crimes & Misdemeanors
Do the Right Thing
When Harry Met Sally...
sex, lies and videotape

1990
★ Ghost
Alice
Avalon
Green Card
Metropolitan

1991
★ Thelma & Louise
Boyz N the Hood
Bugsy
Grand Canyon
The Fisher King

1992
★ The Crying Game
Husbands and Wives
Lorenzo's Oil
Passion Fish
Unforgiven

1993
★ The Piano
Dave
In the Line of Fire
Philadelphia
Sleepless in Seattle

1994
★ Pulp Fiction
Bullets Over Broadway
Four Weddings and a
Funeral
Heavenly Creatures
Trois Couleurs: Rouge

1995
★ The Usual Suspects
Braveheart
Mighty Aphrodite
Nixon
Toy Story

1996
★ Fargo
Jerry Maguire
Lone Star
Secrets and Lies
Shine

SCREENPLAY

1935
★ The Informer
Mutiny on the Bounty
The Lives of a Bengal
Lancer

1936
Mr. Deeds Goes to Town
After the Thin Man
Dodsworth
My Man Godfrey

1937
★ The Life of Emile Zola
Captains Courageous
Stage Door
The Awful Truth

1938
★ Pygmalion
Four Daughters
The Citadel
You Can't Take It with You

1939
★ Gone with the Wind
Goodbye, Mr. Chips
Wuthering Heights

1940
★ The Philadelphia Story
Kitty Foyle
Rebecca
The Grapes of Wrath
The Long Voyage Home

1941
★ Here Comes Mr. Jordan
How Green Was My
Valley
The Little Foxes
The Maltese Falcon

1942
★ Mrs. Miniver
Random Harvest
Talk of the Town
The Forty-Ninth Parallel
The Pride of the Yankees

1943
★ Casablanca
The More the Merrier
The Song of Bernadette
Watch on the Rhine

1944
★ Going My Way
Double Indemnity
Gaslight
Laura
Meet Me in St. Louis

1945
★ The Lost Weekend
A Tree Grows in Brooklyn

Mildred Pierce

1946
★ The Best Years of Our
Lives
Anna and the King of Siam
Brief Encounter
Open City

1947
★ Miracle on 34th Street
Boomerang
Crossfire
Gentleman's Agreement
Great Expectations

1948
★ Treasure of the Sierra
Madre
Johnny Belinda
The Search
The Snake Pit

1949
★ A Letter to Three Wives
All the King's Men
Champion
The Bicycle Thief
The Fallen Idol

1950
★ All About Eve
Born Yesterday
Broken Arrow
Father of the Bride
The Asphalt Jungle

1951
★ A Place in the Sun
A Streetcar Named Desire
Detective Story
La Ronde
The African Queen

1952
★ The Bad and the Beautiful
Five Fingers
High Noon
The Man in the White Suit
The Quiet Man

1953
★ From Here to Eternity
Cruel Sea
Lili
Roman Holiday
Shane
Titanic

1954
★ Country Girl
Rear Window
Sabrina
Seven Brides for Seven
Brothers
The Caine Mutiny

1955
★ Marty
Bad Day at Black Rock
Blackboard Jungle
East of Eden
Interrupted Melody
Love Me or Leave Me

STORY

1928
★ Underworld
Last Command

1931
Public Enemy

STORY ↙cont.

1932
★ The Champ
  What Price Hollywood?

1933
  Rasputin and the Empress
  The Prizefighter and the
  Lady

1934
★ Manhattan Melodrama
  Hide-Out

1935
  Broadway Melody of 1936

1936
★ The Story of Louis Pasteur
  Fury
  San Francisco
  The Great Ziegfeld
  Three Smart Girls

1937
★ A Star is Born
  100 Men and a Girl
  In Old Chicago

1938
★ Boys Town
  Alexander's Ragtime Band
  Angels with Dirty Faces
  Mad About Music
  Test Pilot

1939
★ Mr. Smith Goes to
  Washington
  Bachelor Mother
  Love Affair
  Ninotchka
  Young Mr. Lincoln

1940
  Comrade X
  Edison the Man
  My Favorite Wife
  The Westerner

1941
★ Here Comes Mr. Jordan
  Ball of Fire
  Meet John Doe
  The Lady Eve
  Tom, Dick, and Harry

1942
★ The Forty-Ninth Parallel
  Holiday Inn
  Talk of the Town
  The Pride of the Yankees
  Yankee Doodle Dandy

1943
★ The Human Comedy
  Action in the North Atlantic
  Destination Tokyo
  Shadow of a Doubt
  The More the Merrier

1944
★ Going My Way
  A Guy Named Joe
  Lifeboat

1945
★ House on 92nd Street
  A Song to Remember
  Objective, Burma!

1946
  Dark Mirror
  The Strange Love of
    Martha Ivers
  The Stranger

1947
★ Miracle on 34th Street
  Kiss of Death
  Smash-Up: The Story of a
    Woman

1948
★ The Search
  Louisiana Story
  Red River
  The Naked City
  The Red Shoes

1949
★ The Stratton Story
  Come to the Stable
  It Happens Every Spring
  Sands of Iwo Jima
  White Heat

1950
★ Panic in the Streets
  Bitter Rice
  The Gunfighter

1951
  Bullfighter & the Lady
  Here Comes the Groom

1952
★ The Greatest Show on
    Earth
  Pride of St. Louis
  The Narrow Margin

1953
★ Roman Holiday
  Above and Beyond
  Captain's Paradise
  Hondo
  Titanic

1954
★ Broken Lance
  Forbidden Games
  There's No Business Like
    Show Business

1955
★ Love Me or Leave Me
  Rebel Without a Cause
  Strategic Air Command
  The Private War of Major
    Benson
  The Sheep Has Five Legs

1956
★ The Brave One
  High Society
  The Eddy Duchin Story
  The Proud Ones
  Umberto D

STORY & SCREENPLAY

1949
★ Battleground
  Jolson Sings Again
  Paisan
  Passport to Pimlico

1950
★ Sunset Boulevard
  Adam's Rib
  The Men

1951
★ An American in Paris
  David and Bathsheba
  Go for Broke!
  The Well

1952
★ The Lavender Hill Mob
  Pat and Mike
  The Atomic City
  Viva Zapata!

1953
★ Titanic
  The Band Wagon
  The Desert Rats
  The Naked Spur

1954
★ On the Waterfront
  Genevieve
  The Barefoot Contessa
  The Glenn Miller Story

1955
★ Interrupted Melody
  Mr. Hulot's Holiday
  It's Always Fair Weather
  The Court Martial of Billy
    Mitchell
  The Seven Little Foys

1957
★ Designing Woman
  Funny Face
  I Vitelloni
  Man of a Thousand Faces
  The Tin Star

1958
★ The Defiant Ones
  Houseboat
  Teacher's Pet
  The Goddess

1959
★ Pillow Talk
  North by Northwest
  Operation Petticoat
  The 400 Blows
  Wild Strawberries

1960
★ The Apartment
  Hiroshima, Mon Amour
  Never on Sunday
  The Facts of Life

1961
★ Splendor in the Grass
  Ballad of a Soldier
  La Dolce Vita
  Lover Come Back

1962
★ Divorce—Italian Style
  Last Year at Marienbad
  That Touch of Mink
  Through a Glass Darkly

1963
★ How the West Was Won
  8 1/2
  Love with the Proper
    Stranger

1964
★ Father Goose
  That Man from Rio
  Alun Owen/A Hard Day's
    Night

1965
★ Darling
  Casanova '70
  The Train
  Those Magnificent Men in
    Their Flying Machines
  Umbrellas of Cherbourg

1966
★ A Man and a Woman
  Blow-Up
  Khartoum
  The Fortune Cookie
  The Naked Prey

1967
★ Guess Who's Coming to
    Dinner
  Bonnie & Clyde
  Divorce American Style
  Two for the Road

1968
★ The Producers
  2001: A Space Odyssey
  Faces
  Hot Millions
  The Battle of Algiers

1969
★ Butch Cassidy and the
    Sundance Kid
  Bob & Carol & Ted & Alice
  Easy Rider
  The Damned
  The Wild Bunch

1970
★ Patton
  Five Easy Pieces
  Joe
  Love Story
  My Night at Maud's

1971
★ The Hospital
  Klute
  Summer of '42
  Sunday, Bloody Sunday

1972
★ The Candidate
  Lady Sings the Blues
  Murmur of the Heart
  The Discreet Charm of the
    Bourgeoisie
  Young Winston

1973
★ The Sting
  A Touch of Class
  American Graffiti
  Cries and Whispers
  Save the Tiger

WRITING

1929
  Our Dancing Daughters
  The Leatherneck

1930
★ The Big House
  All Quiet on the Western
    Front
  Disraeli
  The Divorcee

AUSTRALIAN FILM INSTITUTE

ACTOR

1974
★ **Jack Thompson**/Sunday
    Too Far Away

1975
★ **John Meillon**/Fourth Wish

1976
★ **Simon Burke**/The Devil's
    Playground
★ **Nick Tate**/The Devil's
    Playground

1978
★ **Bill Hunter**/Newsfront

1979
★ **Mel Gibson**/Tim

1980
★ **Jack Thompson**/Breaker
    Morant

1981
★ **Mel Gibson**/Gallipoli

1983
★ **Norman Kaye**/Man of
    Flowers

1984
★ **John Hargreaves**/My First
    Wife

1986
★ **Colin Friels**/Malcolm

1987
★ **Leo McKern**/Travelling
    North

1989
★ **Sam Neill**/A Cry in the
    Dark

1990
★ **Max von Sydow**/Father

1991
★ **Hugo Weaving**/Proof

1992
★ **Russell Crowe**/Romper
    Stomper

1993
★ **Harvey Keitel**/The Piano

1994
★ **Nicholas Hope**/Bad Boy
    Bubby
  Terence Stamp/The
    Adventures of Priscilla,
    Queen of the Desert
  Hugo Weaving/The
    Adventures of Priscilla,
    Queen of the Desert

1995
★ **John Lynch**/Angel Baby

1996
★ **Geoffrey Rush**/Shine
  Noah Taylor/Shine

ACTOR—SUPPORTING

1991
★ **Russell Crowe/**Proof

1992
★ **Barry Otto/**Strictly Ballroom
Bill Hunter/The Last Days of Chez Nous

1994
Bill Hunter/Muriel's Wedding
John Polson/The Sum of Us

1995
★ **Ray Barrett/**Sorrento Beach

1996
★ **Armin Mueller-Stahl/**Shine
Barry Otto/Cosi

ACTRESS

1977
★ **Pat Bishop/**Don's Party

1980
★ **Tracey Mann/**Hard Knocks

1981
★ **Judy Davis/**The Winter of Our Dreams

1982
★ **Noni Hazlehurst/**Monkey Grip

1983
★ **Wendy Hughes/**Careful, He Might Hear You

1985
★ **Noni Hazlehurst/**Fran

1986
★ **Judy Davis/**Kangaroo

1987
★ **Judy Davis/**High Tide

1989
★ **Meryl Streep/**A Cry in the Dark

1990
★ **Julia Blake/**Father

1991
★ **Sheila Florence/**A Woman's Tale

1992
★ **Lisa Harrow/**The Last Days of Chez Nous

1993
★ **Holly Hunter/**The Piano

1994
★ **Toni Collette/**Muriel's Wedding

1995
★ **Jacqueline McKenzie/**Angel Baby

Caroline Gillmer/Sorrento Beach
Caroline Goodall/Sorrento Beach
Lisa Harrow/That Eye, The Sky

1996
★ **Judy Davis/**Children of the Revolution
Frances O'Connor/Love and Other Catastrophes

ACTRESS—SUPPORTING

1992
★ **Pat Thomsen/**Strictly Ballroom

1994
★ **Rachel Griffiths/**Muriel's Wedding
Jeanie Drynan/Muriel's Wedding
Deborah Kennedy/The Sum of Us

1995
★ **Toni Collette/**Lilian's Story
★ **Amanda Douge/**That Eye, The Sky

1996
★ **Toni Collette/**Cosi
Alice Garner/Love and Other Catastrophes
Annete Shun-Wah/Floating Life

ART DIRECTION

1996
★ **Children of the Revolution**

CINEMATOGRAPHY

1988
★ The Navigator

1992
★ Black Robe

1993
★ The Piano

1994
Bad Boy Bubby
The Adventures of Priscilla, Queen of the Desert

1995
★ Angel Baby

1996
★ Shine

COSTUME DESIGN

1992
★ Strictly Ballroom

1993
★ The Piano

1994
★ The Adventures of Priscilla, Queen of the Desert

1996
★ Children of the Revolution

DIRECTOR

1988
★ **Vincent Ward/**The Navigator

1991
★ **Jocelyn Moorhouse/**Proof

1992
★ **Baz Luhrmann/**Strictly Ballroom
Gillian Armstrong/The Last Days of Chez Nous

1993
★ **Jane Campion/**The Piano

1994
★ **Rolf de Heer/**Bad Boy Bubby
Stephan Elliott/The Adventures of Priscilla, Queen of the Desert
P.J. Hogan/Muriel's Wedding

1995
★ **Michael Rymer/**Angel Baby
Richard Franklin/Sorrento Beach
John Ruane/That Eye, The Sky

1996
★ **Scott Hicks/**Shine
Peter Duncan/Children of the Revolution
Clara Law/Floating Life

FILM

1974
★ Sunday Too Far Away

1976
★ The Devil's Playground

1978
★ Newsfront

1979
★ My Brilliant Career

1980
★ Breaker Morant

1981
★ Gallipoli

1982
★ Lonely Hearts

1983
★ Careful, He Might Hear You

1984
★ A Test of Love

1985
★ Bliss

1986
★ Malcolm

1987
★ The Year My Voice Broke

1988
★ The Navigator

1989
★ A Cry in the Dark

1990
★ Flirting

1991
★ Proof

1992
★ Strictly Ballroom
The Last Days of Chez Nous

1993
★ The Piano

1994
★ Muriel's Wedding
Bad Boy Bubby
The Adventures of Priscilla, Queen of the Desert
The Sum of Us

1995
★ Angel Baby
Sorrento Beach
That Eye, The Sky

1996
★ Shine
Mr. Reliable: A True Story
Children of the Revolution
Love and Other Catastrophes

FILM EDITING

1991
★ Proof

1992
★ Strictly Ballroom

1993
★ The Piano

1994
★ Bad Boy Bubby

1995
★ Angel Baby

1996
★ Shine

SCORE

1992
★ Romper Stomper

1993
★ The Piano

1996
★ Shine

SOUND

1992
★ Romper Stomper

1993
★ The Piano

1994
★ Muriel's Wedding

1996
★ Shine

ADAPTED SCREENPLAY

1994
★ The Sum of Us

1995
★ Sorrento Beach

1996
★ Cosi

ORIGINAL SCREENPLAY

1994
★ Bad Boy Bubby
Muriel's Wedding
The Adventures of Priscilla, Queen of the Desert

1995
★ Angel Baby

1996
★ Shine

SCREENPLAY

1991
★ Proof

1992
★ Strictly Ballroom

1993
★ The Piano

FILM—FOREIGN LANGUAGE

1992
★ Truly, Madly, Deeply

1993
★ The Crying Game

1994
★ Four Weddings and a Funeral

1995
★ Once Were Warriors
Heavenly Creatures
Priest
Pulp Fiction

1996
★ Fargo
Burnt by the Sun
Dead Man Walking
Trainspotting

BRITISH ACADEMY OF FILM AND TELEVISION ARTS

ACTOR

1952
★ **Marlon Brando/**Viva Zapata!

ACTOR ▶cont.

1953
- ★ Marlon Brando/*Julius Caesar*
- ★ John Gielgud/*Julius Caesar*

1954
- ★ Marlon Brando/*On the Waterfront*
- ★ Kenneth More/*Doctor in the House*

1955
- ★ Ernest Borgnine/*Marty*
- ★ Laurence Olivier/*Richard III*

1956
- ★ Francois Perier/*Gervaise*

1957
- ★ Henry Fonda/*Twelve Angry Men*
- ★ Alec Guinness/*The Bridge on the River Kwai*

1958
- ★ Trevor Howard/*The Key*
- ★ Sidney Poitier/*The Defiant Ones*

1959
- ★ Jack Lemmon/*Some Like It Hot*
- ★ Peter Sellers/*I'm All Right Jack*

1960
- ★ Jack Lemmon/*The Apartment*

1961
- ★ Peter Finch/*No Love for Johnnie*
- ★ Paul Newman/*The Hustler*

1962
- ★ Burt Lancaster/*Birdman of Alcatraz*
- ★ Peter O'Toole/*Lawrence of Arabia*

1963
- ★ Dirk Bogarde/*The Servant*
- ★ Marcello Mastroianni/*Divorce—Italian Style*

1964
- ★ Richard Attenborough/*Seance on a Wet Afternoon*
- ★ Marcello Mastroianni/*Yesterday, Today and Tomorrow*

1965
- ★ Dirk Bogarde/*Darling*
- ★ Lee Marvin/*Cat Ballou*

1966
- ★ Richard Burton/*Who's Afraid of Virginia Woolf?*
- ★ Rod Steiger/*The Pawnbroker*

1967
- ★ Paul Scofield/*A Man for All Seasons*
- ★ Rod Steiger/*In the Heat of the Night*

1968
- ★ Spencer Tracy/*Guess Who's Coming to Dinner*

1969
- ★ Dustin Hoffman/*Midnight Cowboy*

1970
- ★ Robert Redford/*Butch Cassidy and the Sundance Kid*

1971
- ★ Peter Finch/*Sunday, Bloody Sunday*

1972
- ★ Gene Hackman/*The French Connection*

1973
- ★ Walter Matthau/*Pete 'n' Tillie*

1974
- ★ Jack Nicholson/*Chinatown*
- ★ Jack Nicholson/*The Last Detail*

1975
- ★ Al Pacino/*Dog Day Afternoon*

1976
- ★ Jack Nicholson/*One Flew Over the Cuckoo's Nest*

1977
- ★ Peter Finch/*Network*

1978
- ★ Richard Dreyfuss/*The Goodbye Girl*

1979
- ★ Jack Lemmon/*The China Syndrome*

1980
- ★ John Hurt/*The Elephant Man*

1981
- ★ Burt Lancaster/*Atlantic City*

1982
- ★ Ben Kingsley/*Gandhi*

1983
- ★ Michael Caine/*Educating Rita*
- ★ Dustin Hoffman/*Tootsie*

1984
- ★ Haing S. Ngor/*The Killing Fields*

1985
- ★ William Hurt/*Kiss of the Spider Woman*

1986
- ★ Bob Hoskins/*Mona Lisa*

1987
- ★ Sean Connery/*The Name of the Rose*

1988
- ★ John Cleese/*A Fish Called Wanda*

1989
- ★ Daniel Day-Lewis/*My Left Foot*

1990
- ★ Philippe Noiret/*Cinema Paradiso*

1991
- ★ Anthony Hopkins/*The Silence of the Lambs*

1992
- ★ Robert Downey, Jr./*Chaplin*

1993
- ★ Anthony Hopkins/*The Remains of the Day*
  Daniel Day-Lewis/*In the Name of the Father*

1994
- ★ Hugh Grant/*Four Weddings and a Funeral*
  Anthony Hopkins/*Shadowlands*
  Liam Neeson/*Schindler's List*

1995
- ★ Nigel Hawthorne/*The Madness of King George*
  Nicolas Cage/*Leaving Las Vegas*
  Jonathan Pryce/*Carrington*
  Massimo Troisi/*The Postman*

1996
- ★ Geoffrey Rush/*Shine*
  Ralph Fiennes/*The English Patient*
  Ian McKellen/*Richard III*
  Timothy Spall/*Secrets and Lies*

ACTOR—SUPPORTING

1971
- ★ Edward Fox/*The Go-Between*

1972
- ★ Ben Johnson/*The Last Picture Show*

1973
- ★ Arthur Lowe/*O Lucky Man!*

1974
- ★ John Gielgud/*Murder on the Orient Express*

1975
- ★ Fred Astaire/*The Towering Inferno*

1976
- ★ Brad Dourif/*One Flew Over the Cuckoo's Nest*

1977
- ★ Edward Fox/*A Bridge Too Far*

1978
- ★ John Hurt/*Midnight Express*

1979
- ★ Robert Duvall/*Apocalypse Now*

1981
- ★ Ian Holm/*Chariots of Fire*

1982
- ★ Jack Nicholson/*Reds*

1983
- ★ Denholm Elliott/*Trading Places*

1984
- ★ Denholm Elliott/*A Private Function*

1985
- ★ Denholm Elliott/*Defense of the Realm*

1986
- ★ Ray McAnally/*The Mission*

1987
- ★ Daniel Auteuil/*Jean de Florette*

1988
- ★ Michael Palin/*A Fish Called Wanda*

1989
- ★ Ray McAnally/*My Left Foot*

1990
- ★ Salvatore Cascio/*Cinema Paradiso*

1991
- ★ Alan Rickman/*Robin Hood: Prince of Thieves*

1992
- ★ Gene Hackman/*Unforgiven*

1993
- ★ Ralph Fiennes/*Schindler's List*
  Tommy Lee Jones/*The Fugitive*
  John Malkovich/*In the Line of Fire*

1994
- ★ Samuel L. Jackson/*Pulp Fiction*
  Ben Kingsley/*Schindler's List*

1995
- ★ Tim Roth/*Rob Roy*
  Ian Holm/*The Madness of King George*
  Martin Landau/*Ed Wood*
  Alan Rickman/*Sense and Sensibility*

1996
- ★ Paul Scofield/*The Crucible*
  John Gielgud/*Shine*
  Edward Norton/*Primal Fear*
  Alan Rickman/*Michael Collins*

ACTRESS

1952
- ★ Vivien Leigh/*A Streetcar Named Desire*

1953
- ★ Leslie Caron/*Lili*
- ★ Audrey Hepburn/*Roman Holiday*

1955
- ★ Betsy Blair/*Marty*
- ★ Katie Johnson/*The Ladykillers*

1956
- ★ Anna Magnani/*The Rose Tattoo*

1958
- ★ Simone Signoret/*Room at the Top*

1959
- ★ Audrey Hepburn/*The Nun's Story*
- ★ Shirley MacLaine/*Ask Any Girl*

1960
- ★ Shirley MacLaine/*The Apartment*
- ★ Rachel Roberts/*Saturday Night and Sunday Morning*

1961
- ★ Sophia Loren/*Two Women*

1962
- ★ Anne Bancroft/*The Miracle Worker*

1963
- ★ Patricia Neal/*Hud*
- ★ Rachel Roberts/*This Sporting Life*

1964
- ★ Audrey Hepburn/*Charade*

1965
- ★ Julie Christie/*Darling*
- ★ Patricia Neal/*In Harm's Way*

1966
- ★ Elizabeth Taylor/*Who's Afraid of Virginia Woolf?*

1967
- ★ Anouk Aimee/*A Man and a Woman*

1968
- ★ Katharine Hepburn/*Guess Who's Coming to Dinner*

1969
★ Maggie Smith/*The Prime of Miss Jean Brodie*

1970
★ Katharine Ross/*Butch Cassidy and the Sundance Kid*

1971
★ Glenda Jackson/*Sunday, Bloody Sunday*

1972
★ Liza Minnelli/*Cabaret*

1973
★ Delphine Seyrig/*The Discreet Charm of the Bourgeoisie*

1974
★ Joanne Woodward/*Summer Wishes, Winter Dreams*

1975
★ Ellen Burstyn/*Alice Doesn't Live Here Anymore*

1976
★ Louise Fletcher/*One Flew Over the Cuckoo's Nest*

1977
★ Diane Keaton/*Annie Hall*

1978
★ Jane Fonda/*Julia*

1979
★ Jane Fonda/*The China Syndrome*

1980
★ Judy Davis/*My Brilliant Career*

1981
★ Meryl Streep/*The French Lieutenant's Woman*

1982
★ Katharine Hepburn/*On Golden Pond*

1983
★ Julie Walters/*Educating Rita*

1984
★ Maggie Smith/*A Private Function*

1985
★ Peggy Ashcroft/*A Passage to India*

1986
★ Maggie Smith/*A Room with a View*

1987
★ Anne Bancroft/*84 Charing Cross Road*

1988
★ Maggie Smith/*The Lonely Passion of Judith Hearne*

1989
★ Pauline Collins/*Shirley Valentine*

1990
★ Jessica Tandy/*Driving Miss Daisy*

1991
★ Jodie Foster/*The Silence of the Lambs*

1992
★ Emma Thompson/*Howard's End*

1993
★ Holly Hunter/*The Piano*
Miranda Richardson/*Tom & Viv*

1994
★ Susan Sarandon/*The Client*
Emma Thompson/*The Remains of the Day*
Debra Winger/*Shadowlands*

1995
★ Emma Thompson/*Sense and Sensibility*
Nicole Kidman/*To Die For*
Helen Mirren/*The Madness of King George*
Elisabeth Shue/*Leaving Las Vegas*

1996
★ Brenda Blethyn/*Secrets and Lies*
Frances McDormand/*Fargo*
Kristin Scott Thomas/*The English Patient*
Emily Watson/*Breaking the Waves*

ACTRESS—SUPPORTING

1961
★ Dora Bryan/*A Taste of Honey*

1969
★ Celia Johnson/*The Prime of Miss Jean Brodie*

1970
★ Susannah York/*They Shoot Horses, Don't They?*

1971
★ Margaret Leighton/*The Go-Between*

1972
★ Cloris Leachman/*The Last Picture Show*

1973
★ Valentina Cortese/*Day for Night*

1974
★ Ingrid Bergman/*Murder on the Orient Express*

1975
★ Diane Ladd/*Alice Doesn't Live Here Anymore*

1976
★ Jodie Foster/*Taxi Driver*

1977
★ Jenny Agutter/*Equus*

1978
★ Geraldine Page/*Interiors*
★ Vanessa Redgrave/*Julia*

1979
★ Rachel Roberts/*Yanks*

1982
★ Rohini Hattangady/*Gandhi*
★ Maureen Stapleton/*Reds*

1983
★ Jamie Lee Curtis/*Trading Places*

1984
★ Liz Smith/*A Private Function*

1985
★ Rosanna Arquette/*Desperately Seeking Susan*

1986
★ Judi Dench/*A Room with a View*

1987
★ Susan Wooldridge/*Hope and Glory*

1988
★ Judi Dench/*A Handful of Dust*

1989
★ Michelle Pfeiffer/*Dangerous Liaisons*

1990
★ Whoopi Goldberg/*Ghost*

1991
★ Kate Nelligan/*Frankie and Johnny*

1992
★ Miranda Richardson/*Damage*

1993
★ Miriam Margolyes/*The Age of Innocence*
Holly Hunter/*The Firm*
Maggie Smith/*The Secret Garden*

1994
★ Kristin Scott Thomas/*Four Weddings and a Funeral*
Winona Ryder/*The Age of Innocence*

1995
★ Kate Winslet/*Sense and Sensibility*
Joan Allen/*Nixon*
Mira Sorvino/*Mighty Aphrodite*

Elizabeth Spriggs/*Sense and Sensibility*

1996
★ Juliette Binoche/*The English Patient*
Lauren Bacall/*The Mirror Has Two Faces*
Marianne Jean-Baptiste/*Secrets and Lies*
Lynn Redgrave/*Shine*

CINEMATOGRAPHY

1995
★ *Braveheart*
Apollo 13
Sense and Sensibility
The Madness of King George

1996
★ *The English Patient*

DIRECTOR

1955
★ Laurence Olivier/*Richard III*

1968
★ Mike Nichols/*The Graduate*

1969
★ John Schlesinger/*Midnight Cowboy*

1970
★ George Roy Hill/*Butch Cassidy and the Sundance Kid*

1971
★ John Schlesinger/*Sunday, Bloody Sunday*

1972
★ Bob Fosse/*Cabaret*

1973
★ Francois Truffaut/*Day for Night*

1974
★ Roman Polanski/*Chinatown*

1975
★ Stanley Kubrick/*Barry Lyndon*

1976
★ Milos Forman/*One Flew Over the Cuckoo's Nest*

1977
★ Woody Allen/*Annie Hall*

1978
★ Alan Parker/*Midnight Express*

1979
★ Francis Ford Coppola/*Apocalypse Now*

1980
★ Akira Kurosawa/*Kagemusha*

1981
★ Louis Malle/*Atlantic City*

1982
★ Richard Attenborough/*Gandhi*

1983
★ Bill Forsyth/*Local Hero*

1984
★ Wim Wenders/*Paris, Texas*

1986
★ Woody Allen/*Hannah and Her Sisters*

1987
★ Oliver Stone/*Platoon*

1988
★ Louis Malle/*Au Revoir Les Enfants*

1989
★ Kenneth Branagh/*Henry V*

1990
★ Martin Scorsese/*Goodfellas*

1991
★ Alan Parker/*The Commitments*

1992
★ Clint Eastwood/*Unforgiven*

1993
★ Steven Spielberg/*Schindler's List*

1994
★ Mike Newell/*Four Weddings and a Funeral*
Richard Attenborough/*Shadowlands*
Jane Campion/*The Piano*
James Ivory/*The Remains of the Day*

1995
★ Michael Radford/*The Postman*
Mel Gibson/*Braveheart*
Nicholas Hytner/*The Madness of King George*
Ang Lee/*Sense and Sensibility*

1996
★ Joel Coen/*Fargo*
Scott Hicks/*Shine*
Mike Leigh/*Secrets and Lies*
Anthony Minghella/*The English Patient*

FILM

1947
★ *Odd Man Out*
★ *The Best Years of Our Lives*

1948
★ *Hamlet*
★ *The Fallen Idol*

1949
★ *The Bicycle Thief*

FILM ►cont.

★ The Third Man

1950
★ All About Eve
★ The Blue Lamp

1951
★ La Ronde
★ The Lavender Hill Mob

1953
★ Forbidden Games
★ Genevieve

1954
★ Hobson's Choice
★ Wages of Fear

1955
★ Richard III

1956
★ Gervaise
★ Reach for the Sky

1957
★ The Bridge on the River Kwai

1958
★ Room at the Top

1959
★ Ben-Hur
★ Sapphire

1960
★ Saturday Night and Sunday Morning
★ The Apartment

1961
★ A Taste of Honey
★ Ballad of a Soldier
★ The Hustler

1962
★ Lawrence of Arabia

1963
★ Tom Jones

1964
★ Dr. Strangelove, or: How I Learned to Stop Worrying and Love the Bomb

1965
★ My Fair Lady
★ The Ipcress File

1966
★ The Spy Who Came in from the Cold
★ Who's Afraid of Virginia Woolf?

1967
★ A Man for All Seasons

1968
★ The Graduate

1969
★ Midnight Cowboy

1970
★ Butch Cassidy and the Sundance Kid

1971
★ Sunday, Bloody Sunday

1972
★ Cabaret

1973
★ Day for Night

1975
★ Alice Doesn't Live Here Anymore

1976
★ One Flew Over the Cuckoo's Nest

1977
★ Annie Hall

1978
★ Julia

1979
★ Manhattan

1980
★ The Elephant Man

1981
★ Chariots of Fire

1982
★ Gandhi

1983
★ Educating Rita

1984
★ The Killing Fields

1985
★ The Purple Rose of Cairo

1986
★ A Room with a View

1987
★ Hope and Glory
★ Jean de Florette

1988
★ The Last Emperor

1989
★ Dead Poets Society

1990
★ Goodfellas

1991
★ The Commitments

1992
★ Unforgiven

1993
★ Schindler's List
★ Shadowlands
  Naked
  Raining Stones
  Tom & Viv

1994
★ Four Weddings and a Funeral
  The Piano
  The Remains of the Day

1970
★ Butch Cassidy and the Sundance Kid
  Babe
  Carrington
  Land and Freedom
  The Madness of King George
  The Usual Suspects
  Trainspotting

1996
★ The English Patient
  Fargo
  Secrets and Lies
  Shine

FILM—FOREIGN LANGUAGE

1996
★ Ridicule
  Kolya

SCORE

1993
  Sleepless in Seattle

1994
  Schindler's List
  The Piano

1995
★ The Postman
  Braveheart
  Sense and Sensibility
  The Madness of King George

1996
★ The English Patient

ADAPTED SCREENPLAY

1983
★ Heat and Dust

1984
★ The Killing Fields

1985
★ Prizzi's Honor

1986
★ Out of Africa

1987
★ Jean de Florette

1988
★ The Unbearable Lightness of Being

1989
★ Dangerous Liaisons

1990
★ Goodfellas

1991
★ The Commitments

1992
★ The Player

1993
★ Schindler's List
  In the Name of the Father
  Scent of a Woman

1994
★ Quiz Show
  Schindler's List
  Shadowlands
  The Remains of the Day

1995
★ Trainspotting
  Babe
  Leaving Las Vegas
  Sense and Sensibility
  The Madness of King George
  The Postman

1996
★ The English Patient
  Evita
  Richard III
  The Crucible

ORIGINAL SCREENPLAY

1983
★ King of Comedy

1984
★ Broadway Danny Rose

1985
★ The Purple Rose of Cairo

1986
★ Hannah and Her Sisters

1987
★ Wish You Were Here

1988
★ A World Apart

1989
★ When Harry Met Sally...

1990
★ Cinema Paradiso

1991
★ Truly, Madly, Deeply

1992
★ Husbands and Wives

1993
★ Groundhog Day
  In the Line of Fire
  Sleepless in Seattle

1994
★ Pulp Fiction
  The Piano

1995
★ The Usual Suspects
  Bullets Over Broadway
  Muriel's Wedding
  Seven

1996
★ Secrets and Lies
  Brassed Off
  Fargo
  Lone Star
  Shine

SCREENPLAY

1955
★ The Ladykillers

1956
★ The Man Who Never Was

1957
★ The Bridge on the River Kwai

1959
★ I'm All Right Jack

1961
★ The Day the Earth Caught Fire

1962
★ A Taste of Honey
★ Lawrence of Arabia

1963
★ Tom Jones

1964
★ The Pumpkin Eater

1965
★ Darling

1966
★ Morgan!

1967
★ A Man for All Seasons

1968
★ The Graduate

1969
★ Midnight Cowboy

1970
★ Butch Cassidy and the Sundance Kid

1971
★ The Go-Between

1972
★ The Hospital
★ The Last Picture Show

1973
★ The Discreet Charm of the Bourgeoisie

1974
★ Chinatown
★ The Last Detail

1975
★ Alice Doesn't Live Here Anymore

1976
★ Bugsy Malone

1977
★ Annie Hall

1978
★ Julia

1979
★ Manhattan

1981
★ Gregory's Girl

1982
★ Missing

1991
* John Turturro/*Barton Fink*

1992
* Tim Robbins/*The Player*

1993
* David Thewlis/*Naked*

1994
* Ge You/*To Live*

1995
* Jonathan Pryce/*Carrington*

1996
* Daniel Auteuil/*The Eighth Day*
* Pascal Duquenne/*The Eighth Day*

1997
* Sean Penn/*She's So Lovely*

ACTRESS

1946
* Michele Morgan/*La Symphonie Pastorale*

1951
* Bette Davis/*All About Eve*

1952
* Lee Grant/*Detective Story*

1953
* Shirley Booth/*Come Back, Little Sheba*

1956
* Susan Hayward/*I'll Cry Tomorrow*

1957
* Giulietta Masina/*Nights of Cabiria*

1958
* Bibi Andersson/*Brink of Life*
* Eva Dahlbeck/*Brink of Life*
* Ingrid Thulin/*Brink of Life*

1959
* Simone Signoret/*Room at the Top*

1960
* Melina Mercouri/*Never on Sunday*

1961
* Sophia Loren/*Two Women*

1962
* Katharine Hepburn/*Long Day's Journey into Night*
* Rita Tushingham/*A Taste of Honey*

1965
* Samantha Eggar/*The Collector*

1966
* Vanessa Redgrave/*Morgan!*

1967
* Pia Degermark/*Elvira Madigan*

1969
* Vanessa Redgrave/*Isadora*

1971
* Kitty Winn/*Panic in Needle Park*

1973
* Joanne Woodward/*The Effect of Gamma Rays on Man-in-the-Moon Marigolds*

1974
* Marie-Jose Nat/*Les Violons du Bal*

1975
* Valerie Perrine/*Lenny*

1976
* Dominique Sanda/*The Inheritance*

1978
* Jill Clayburgh/*An Unmarried Woman*
* Isabelle Huppert/*Violette*

1979
* Sally Field/*Norma Rae*

1981
* Isabelle Adjani/*Quartet*

1982
* Jadwiga Jankowska Cieslak/*Another Way*

1984
* Helen Mirren/*Cal*

1985
* Norma Aleandro/*The Official Story*
* Cher/*Mask*

1986
* Barbara Sukowa/*Rosa Luxemburg*

1987
* Barbara Hershey/*Shy People*

1988
* Barbara Hershey/*A World Apart*
* Jodhi May/*A World Apart*
* Linda Mvusi/*A World Apart*

1989
* Meryl Streep/*A Cry in the Dark*

1991
* Irene Jacob/*The Double Life of Veronique*

1992
* Pernilla August/*The Best Intentions*

1993
* Holly Hunter/*The Piano*

1994
* Virna Lisi/*Queen Margot*

1995
* Helen Mirren/*The Madness of King George*

1996
* Brenda Blethyn/*Secrets and Lies*

1997
* Kathy Burke/*Nil by Mouth*

DIRECTOR

1951
* Luis Bunuel/*Los Olvidados*

1952
* Christian-Jaque/*Fanfan la Tulipe*

1955
* Jules Dassin/*Rififi*

1957
* Robert Bresson/*A Man Escaped*

1958
* Ingmar Bergman/*Brink of Life*

1959
* Francois Truffaut/*The 400 Blows*

1969
* Vojtech Jasny/*All My Good Countrymen*

1976
* Ettore Scola/*Down & Dirty*

1978
* Nagisa Oshima/*The Empire of Passion*

1979
* Terence Malick/*Days of Heaven*

1982
* Werner Herzog/*Fitzcarraldo*

1983
* Robert Bresson/*L'Argent*

1984
* Bertrand Tavernier/*A Sunday in the Country*

1985
* Andre Techine/*Rendez-vous*

1986
* Martin Scorsese/*After Hours*

1989
* Emir Kusturica/*Time of the Gypsies*

1990
* Pavel Lounguine/*Taxi Blues*

1991
* Joel Coen/*Barton Fink*

1992
* Robert Altman/*The Player*

1993
* Mike Leigh/*Naked*

1994
* Nanni Moretti/*Caro Diario*

1995
* Mathieu Kassovitz/*Hate*

1996
* Joel Coen/*Fargo*

1997
* Wong Kar-Wai/*Happy Together*

FILM

1946
* *The Lost Weekend*

1949
* *The Third Man*

1951
* *Los Olvidados*
* *Miracle in Milan*
* *Miss Julie*

1952
* *Othello*
* *White Mane*

1953
* *Wages of Fear*

1954
* *Gate of Hell*

1957
* *Friendly Persuasion*

1958
* *The Cranes Are Flying*

1959
* *Black Orpheus*

1960
* *La Dolce Vita*

1961
* *Viridiana*

1964
* *Umbrellas of Cherbourg*

1966
* *A Man and a Woman*

1967
* *Blow-Up*
* *Dutchman*

1969
* *If...*
  Z

1970
* *M*A*S*H*

1971
* *The Go-Between*

1973
* *Scarecrow*

1974
* *The Conversation*

1976
* *Taxi Driver*

1977
* *Padre Padrone*

1978
* *The Tree of Wooden Clogs*

1979
* *Apocalypse Now*
* *The Tin Drum*

1980
* *All That Jazz*
* *Kagemusha*

1981
* *Man of Iron*

1982
* *Missing*
* *Yol*

1983
* *The Ballad of Narayama*

1984
* *Paris, Texas*

1985
* *Dance with a Stranger*
* *When Father was Away on Business*

1986
* *The Mission*

1987
* *Under Satan's Sun*

1988
* *Pelle the Conqueror*

1989
* *sex, lies and videotape*

1990
* *Overseas: Three Women with Man Trouble*
* *Wild at Heart*

1991
* *Barton Fink*

1992
* *My New Gun*
* *The Best Intentions*

1993
* *Farewell My Concubine*
* *The Piano*

1994
* *Pulp Fiction*

1995
* *Underground*

1996
* *Secrets and Lies*

Claire Nadeau/*Nelly et Monsieur Arnaud*

ART DIRECTION

1978
★ *Providence*

1981
★ *The Last Metro*

1984
★ *Moon in the Gutter*

1985
★ *Swann in Love*

1986
★ *Subway*

1987
★ *Pirates*

1988
★ *Au Revoir Les Enfants*

1989
★ *Camille Claudel*

1990
★ *Valmont*

1991
★ *Cyrano de Bergerac*

1992
★ *Delicatessen*

1993
★ *Indochine*

1994
★ *Smoking/No Smoking*

1995
★ *Farinelli*

1996
★ *The City of Lost Children*
  The Horseman on the Roof

CINEMATOGRAPHY

1978
★ *Le Crabe Tambour*

1980
★ *Tess*

1981
★ *The Last Metro*

1982
★ *Diva*

1983
★ *La Truite*

1984
★ *Tchao Pantin*

1985
★ *A Sunday in the Country*

1987
★ *Therese*

1988
★ *Au Revoir Les Enfants*

1989
★ *Camille Claudel*

1991
★ *Cyrano de Bergerac*

1992
★ *Tous les Matins du Monde*

1993
★ *Indochine*

1994
★ *Germinal*

1995
★ *Queen Margot*

1996
★ *The Horseman on the Roof*
  Hate
  The City of Lost Children

COSTUME DESIGN

1985
★ *Swann in Love*

1987
★ *Pirates*

1988
★ *Beatrice*

1989
★ *Camille Claudel*

1990
★ *Valmont*

1991
★ *Cyrano de Bergerac*

1994
★ *Germinal*

1995
★ *Queen Margot*

1996
  The City of Lost Children
  The Horseman on the Roof

DIRECTOR

1978
★ **Alain Resnais/***Providence*

1980
★ **Roman Polanski/***Tess*

1981
★ **Francois Truffaut/***The Last Metro*

1983
★ **Andrzej Wajda/***Danton*

1984
★ **Ettore Scola/***Le Bal*

1986
★ **Michel DeVille/***Peril*

1987
★ **Alain Cavalier/***Therese*

1988
★ **Louis Malle/***Au Revoir Les Enfants*

1990
★ **Bertrand Blier/***Too Beautiful for You*

1991
★ **Jean-Paul Rappeneau/***Cyrano de Bergerac*

1992
★ **Alain Corneau/***Tous les Matins du Monde*

1993
★ **Claude Sautet/***Un Coeur en Hiver*

1994
★ **Alain Resnais/***Smoking/No Smoking*
  Luc Besson/*The Professional*
  Krzysztof Kieslowski/*Trois Couleurs: Rouge*

1995
★ **Andre Techine/***Wild Reeds*
  Etienne Chatiliez/*Le Bonheur Est Dans le Pre*
  Patrice Chereau/*Queen Margot*
  Nicole Garcia/*The Favorite Son*

1996
★ **Claude Sautet/***Nelly et Monsieur Arnaud*
  Josiane Balasko/*French Twist*
  Claude Chabrol/*La Ceremonie*
  Mathieu Kassovitz/*Hate*
  Jean-Paul Rappeneau/*The Horseman on the Roof*

1997
★ **Patrice Leconte/***Ridicule*
★ **Bertrand Tavernier/***Captain Conan*
  Cedric Klapisch/*Un Air de Famille*
  Andre Techine/*Les Voleurs*

FILM

1978
★ *Providence*

1980
★ *Tess*

1981
★ *The Last Metro*

1983
★ *La Balance*

1984
★ *Le Bal*

1986
★ *Three Men and a Cradle*

1987
★ *Therese*

1988
★ *Au Revoir Les Enfants*

1989
★ *Camille Claudel*

1990
★ *Too Beautiful for You*

1991
★ *Cyrano de Bergerac*

1992
★ *Tous les Matins du Monde*

1993
★ *Les Nuits Fauves*

1994
★ *Smoking/No Smoking*
  The Professional
  Trois Couleurs: Rouge

1995
★ *Wild Reeds*
  Le Bonheur Est Dans le Pre
  Queen Margot
  The Favorite Son

1996
★ *Hate*
  French Twist
  La Ceremonie
  Nelly et Monsieur Arnaud
  The Horseman on the Roof

1997
★ *Captain Conan*
★ *Ridicule*
  Les Voleurs
  Microcosmos
  Pedale Douce
  Un Air de Famille

FILM EDITING

1994
★ *Trois Couleurs: Bleu*

1996
★ *Hate*
  Nelly et Monsieur Arnaud
  The Horseman on the Roof

SCORE

1977
★ *The Judge and the Assassin*

1978
★ *Providence*

1979
★ *Get Out Your Handkerchiefs*

1980
★ *Love on the Run*

1981
★ *The Last Metro*

1982
★ *Diva*

1983
★ *The Return of Martin Guerre*

1984
★ *Le Bal*

1988
★ *Field of Honor*

1989
★ *The Big Blue*

1990
★ *Life and Nothing But*

1991
★ *Cyrano de Bergerac*

1992
★ *Tous les Matins du Monde*

1993
★ *The Lover*

1994
★ *Trois Couleurs: Rouge*

1995
★ *Elisa*

1996
  Nelly et Monsieur Arnaud
  The City of Lost Children
  The Horseman on the Roof

SOUND

1977
★ *Mado*

1978
★ *Providence*

1979
★ *L'Etat Sauvage*

1981
★ *The Last Metro*

1982
★ *Diva*

1983
★ *La Passante*

1984
★ *Tchao Pantin*

1986
★ *Subway*

1988
★ *Au Revoir Les Enfants*

1989
★ *The Big Blue*

1990
★ *Monsieur Hire*

1991
★ *Cyrano de Bergerac*

1993
★ *Indochine*

1994
★ *Trois Couleurs: Bleu*

1995
★ *Farinelli*

1996
★ *The Horseman on the Roof*
  Hate
  Nelly et Monsieur Arnaud

WRITING

1977
★ The Judge and the Assassin

1978
★ Providence

1980
★ Buffet Froid

1981
★ The Last Metro

1983
★ The Return of Martin Guerre

1984
★ L'Homme Blesse
★ One Deadly Summer

1985
★ A Sunday in the Country

1986
★ Three Men and a Cradle

1987
★ Therese

1988
★ Au Revoir Les Enfants

1989
★ Life Is a Long Quiet River

1990
★ Too Beautiful for You

1991
★ La Discrete

1992
★ Delicatessen

1994
★ Smoking/No Smoking

1995
★ Wild Reeds
  Le Bonheur Est Dans le Pre

1996
★ French Twist
  Hate
  La Ceremonie
  Nelly et Monsieur Arnaud

FILM—FOREIGN LANGUAGE

1980
★ Manhattan

1981
★ Kagemusha

1982
★ The Elephant Man

1983
★ Victor/Victoria

1984
★ Fanny and Alexander

1985
★ Amadeus

1986
★ The Purple Rose of Cairo

1987
★ The Name of the Rose

1988
★ The Last Emperor

1989
★ Bagdad Cafe

1990
★ Dangerous Liaisons

1991
★ Dead Poets Society
★ Toto le Heros

1993
★ High Heels

1996
★ Land and Freedom

1997
★ Breaking the Waves
  Fargo
  Secrets and Lies
  The Postman

DIRECTORS GUILD OF AMERICA

DIRECTOR

1948
★ Joseph L. Mankiewicz/A Letter to Three Wives

1949
★ Carol Reed/The Third Man

1950
★ Joseph L. Mankiewicz/All About Eve

1951
★ George Stevens/A Place in the Sun

1952
★ John Ford/The Quiet Man

1953
★ Fred Zinnemann/From Here to Eternity

1954
★ Elia Kazan/On the Waterfront
★ Billy Wilder/Sabrina

1955
★ Delbert Mann/Marty

1956
★ George Stevens/Giant

1957
★ David Lean/The Bridge on the River Kwai

1958
★ Vincente Minnelli/Gigi

1959
★ William Wyler/Ben-Hur

1960
★ Billy Wilder/The Apartment

1961
★ Jerome Robbins/West Side Story
★ Robert Wise/West Side Story

1962
★ David Lean/Lawrence of Arabia

1963
★ Tony Richardson/Tom Jones

1964
★ George Cukor/My Fair Lady

1965
★ Robert Wise/The Sound of Music

1966
★ Fred Zinnemann/A Man for All Seasons

1967
★ Mike Nichols/The Graduate

1968
★ Anthony Harvey/The Lion in Winter

1969
★ John Schlesinger/Midnight Cowboy

1970
★ Charles Jarrott/Anne of the Thousand Days
★ Franklin J. Schaffner/Patton

1971
★ William Friedkin/The French Connection

1972
★ Francis Ford Coppola/The Godfather

1973
★ George Roy Hill/The Sting

1974
★ Francis Ford Coppola/The Godfather, Part 2

1975
★ Milos Forman/One Flew Over the Cuckoo's Nest

1976
★ John G. Avildsen/Rocky

1977
★ Woody Allen/Annie Hall

1978
★ Michael Cimino/The Deer Hunter

1979
★ Robert Benton/Kramer vs. Kramer

1980
★ Robert Redford/Ordinary People

1981
★ Warren Beatty/Reds

1982
★ Richard Attenborough/Gandhi

1983
★ James L. Brooks/Terms of Endearment

1984
★ Milos Forman/Amadeus

1985
★ Steven Spielberg/The Color Purple

1986
★ Oliver Stone/Platoon

1987
★ Bernardo Bertolucci/The Last Emperor

1988
★ Barry Levinson/Rain Man

1989
★ Oliver Stone/Born on the Fourth of July

1990
★ Kevin Costner/Dances with Wolves

1991
★ Jonathan Demme/The Silence of the Lambs

1992
★ Clint Eastwood/Unforgiven

1993
★ Steven Spielberg/Schindler's List
  Jane Campion/The Piano
  Andrew Davis/The Fugitive
  James Ivory/The Remains of the Day
  Martin Scorsese/The Age of Innocence

1994
★ Robert Zemeckis/Forrest Gump
  Frank Darabont/The Shawshank Redemption
  Mike Newell/Four Weddings and a Funeral
  Robert Redford/Quiz Show
  Quentin Tarantino/Pulp Fiction

1995
★ Ron Howard/Apollo 13
  Mike Figgis/Leaving Las Vegas
  Mel Gibson/Braveheart
  Ang Lee/Sense and Sensibility
  Michael Radford/The Postman

1996
★ Anthony Minghella/The English Patient
  Joel Coen/Fargo
  Cameron Crowe/Jerry Maguire
  Scott Hicks/Shine
  Mike Leigh/Secrets and Lies

FEATURE DOCUMENTARY

1992
★ Joe Berlinger/Brother's Keeper
★ Bruce Sinofsky/Brother's Keeper

1995
★ Steve James/Hoop Dreams
★ Terry Zwigoff/Crumb

1996
★ Al Pacino/Looking for Richard

GOLDEN GLOBE AWARDS

ACTOR—DRAMA

1944
★ Paul Lukas/Watch on the Rhine

1945
★ Alexander Knox/Wilson

1946
★ Ray Milland/The Lost Weekend

1947
★ Gregory Peck/The Yearling

1948
★ Ronald Colman/A Double Life

1949
★ Laurence Olivier/Hamlet

1950
★ Broderick Crawford/All the King's Men

1951
★ Jose Ferrer/Cyrano de Bergerac

1953
★ Gary Cooper/High Noon

1955
★ Marlon Brando/On the Waterfront

1956
★ Ernest Borgnine/Marty

1957
★ Kirk Douglas/Lust for Life

1958
★ Alec Guinness/The Bridge on the River Kwai

1959

★ David Niven/*Separate Tables*

1960

★ Anthony (Tony) Franciosa/*Career*

1961

★ Burt Lancaster/*Elmer Gantry*

1962

★ Maximilian Schell/ *Judgment at Nuremberg*

1963

★ Gregory Peck/*To Kill a Mockingbird*

1964

★ Sidney Poitier/*Lilies of the Field*

1965

★ Peter O'Toole/*Becket*

1966

★ Omar Sharif/*Doctor Zhivago*

1967

★ Paul Scofield/*A Man for All Seasons*

1968

★ Rod Steiger/*In the Heat of the Night*

1969

★ Peter O'Toole/*The Lion in Winter*

1970

★ John Wayne/*True Grit*

1971

★ George C. Scott/*Patton*

1972

★ Gene Hackman/*The French Connection*

1973

★ Marlon Brando/*The Godfather*

1974

★ Al Pacino/*Serpico*

1975

★ Jack Nicholson/ *Chinatown*

1976

★ Jack Nicholson/*One Flew Over the Cuckoo's Nest*

1977

★ Peter Finch/*Network*

1978

★ Richard Burton/*Equus*

1979

★ Jon Voight/*Coming Home*

1980

★ Dustin Hoffman/*Kramer vs. Kramer*

1981

★ Robert De Niro/*Raging Bull*

1982

★ Henry Fonda/*On Golden Pond*

1983

★ Robert Duvall/*Tender Mercies*

★ Ben Kingsley/*Gandhi*

1984

★ Tom Courtenay/*The Dresser*

1985

★ F. Murray Abraham/ *Amadeus*

1986

★ Jon Voight/*Runaway Train*

1987

★ Bob Hoskins/*Mona Lisa*

1988

★ Michael Douglas/*Wall Street*

1989

★ Dustin Hoffman/*Rain Man*

1990

★ Tom Cruise/*Born on the Fourth of July*

1991

★ Jeremy Irons/*Reversal of Fortune*

1992

★ Nick Nolte/*The Prince of Tides*

1993

★ Al Pacino/*Scent of a Woman*

1994

★ Tom Hanks/*Philadelphia*
Daniel Day-Lewis/*In the Name of the Father*
Harrison Ford/*The Fugitive*
Anthony Hopkins/*The Remains of the Day*
Liam Neeson/*Schindler's List*

1995

★ Tom Hanks/*Forrest Gump*
Richard Dreyfuss/*Mr. Holland's Opus*
Morgan Freeman/*The Shawshank Redemption*
Paul Newman/*Nobody's Fool*
Brad Pitt/*Legends of the Fall*
John Travolta/*Pulp Fiction*

1996

★ Nicolas Cage/*Leaving Las Vegas*
Anthony Hopkins/*Nixon*
Ian McKellen/*Richard III*

Sean Penn/*Dead Man Walking*

1997

★ Geoffrey Rush/*Shine*
Ralph Fiennes/*The English Patient*
Mel Gibson/*Ransom*
Woody Harrelson/*The People vs. Larry Flynt*
Liam Neeson/*Michael Collins*

ACTOR—MUSICAL/ COMEDY

1951

★ Fred Astaire/*Three Little Words*

1953

★ Donald O'Connor/*Singin' in the Rain*

1954

★ David Niven/*The Moon Is Blue*

1955

★ James Mason/*A Star is Born*

1956

★ Tom Ewell/*The Seven Year Itch*

1957

★ Cantinflas/*Around the World in 80 Days*

1958

★ Frank Sinatra/*Pal Joey*

1960

★ Jack Lemmon/*Some Like It Hot*

1961

★ Jack Lemmon/*The Apartment*

1962

★ Glenn Ford/*Pocketful of Miracles*

1963

★ Marcello Mastroianni/ *Divorce—Italian Style*

1965

★ Rex Harrison/*My Fair Lady*

1966

★ Lee Marvin/*Cat Ballou*

1967

★ Alan Arkin/*The Russians are Coming, the Russians are Coming*

1968

★ Richard Harris/*Camelot*

1969

★ Ron Moody/*Oliver!*

1970

★ Peter O'Toole/*Goodbye, Mr. Chips*

1971

★ Albert Finney/*Scrooge*

1972

★ Chaim Topol/*Fiddler on the Roof*

1974

★ George Segal/*A Touch of Class*

1975

★ Art Carney/*Harry and Tonto*

1976

★ Walter Matthau/*The Sunshine Boys*

1977

★ Kris Kristofferson/*A Star is Born*

1978

★ Richard Dreyfuss/*The Goodbye Girl*

1979

★ Warren Beatty/*Heaven Can Wait*

1980

★ Peter Sellers/*Being There*

1981

★ Ray Sharkey/*Idolmaker*

1982

★ Dudley Moore/*Arthur*

1983

★ Dustin Hoffman/*Tootsie*

1984

★ Michael Caine/*Educating Rita*

1985

★ Dudley Moore/*Micki & Maude*

1986

★ Jack Nicholson/*Prizzi's Honor*

1987

★ Paul Hogan/*Crocodile Dundee*

1988

★ Robin Williams/*Good Morning, Vietnam*

1989

★ Tom Hanks/*Big*

1990

★ Morgan Freeman/*Driving Miss Daisy*

1991

★ Gerard Depardieu/*Green Card*

1992

★ Robin Williams/*The Fisher King*

1993

★ Tim Robbins/*The Player*

1994

★ Robin Williams/*Mrs. Doubtfire*

Johnny Depp/*Benny & Joon*
Tom Hanks/*Sleepless in Seattle*
Kevin Kline/*Dave*
Colm Meaney/*The Snapper*

1995

★ Hugh Grant/*Four Weddings and a Funeral*
Jim Carrey/*The Mask*
Johnny Depp/*Ed Wood*
Arnold Schwarzenegger/ *Junior*
Terence Stamp/*The Adventures of Priscilla, Queen of the Desert*

1996

★ John Travolta/*Get Shorty*
Michael Douglas/*The American President*
Harrison Ford/*Sabrina*
Steve Martin/*Father of the Bride Part II*
Patrick Swayze/*To Wong Foo, Thanks for Everything, Julie Newmar*

1997

★ Tom Cruise/*Jerry Maguire*
Antonio Banderas/*Evita*
Kevin Costner/*Tin Cup*
Tom Cruise/*Jerry Maguire*
Nathan Lane/*The Birdcage*
Eddie Murphy/*The Nutty Professor*

ACTOR—SUPPORTING

1945

★ Barry Fitzgerald/*Going My Way*

1947

★ Clifton Webb/*The Razor's Edge*

1948

★ Edmund Gwenn/*Miracle on 34th Street*

1949

★ Walter Huston/*Treasure of the Sierra Madre*

1950

★ James Whitmore/ *Battleground*

1952

★ Peter Ustinov/*Quo Vadis*

1954

★ Frank Sinatra/*From Here to Eternity*

1955

★ Edmond O'Brien/*The Barefoot Contessa*

1957

★ Earl Holliman/*The Rainmaker*

1958

★ Red Buttons/*Sayonara*

ACTOR— SUPPORTING ‣cont.

1959
★ Burl Ives/*The Big Country*

1960
★ Stephen Boyd/*Ben-Hur*

1961
★ Sal Mineo/*Exodus*

1962
★ George Chakiris/*West Side Story*

1963
★ Omar Sharif/*Lawrence of Arabia*

1964
★ John Huston/*The Cardinal*

1965
★ Edmond O'Brien/*Seven Days in May*

1966
★ Oskar Werner/*The Spy Who Came in from the Cold*

1967
★ Richard Attenborough/*The Sand Pebbles*

1968
★ David Attenborough/*Doctor Dolittle*

1970
★ Gig Young/*They Shoot Horses, Don't They?*

1971
★ John Mills/*Ryan's Daughter*

1972
★ Ben Johnson/*The Last Picture Show*

1973
★ Joel Grey/*Cabaret*

1974
★ John Houseman/*The Paper Chase*

1975
★ Fred Astaire/*The Towering Inferno*

1976
★ Richard Benjamin/*The Sunshine Boys*

1977
★ Laurence Olivier/*Marathon Man*

1978
★ Peter Firth/*Equus*

1979
★ John Hurt/*Midnight Express*

1980
★ Melvyn Douglas/*Being There*
★ Robert Duvall/*Apocalypse Now*

1981
★ Timothy Hutton/*Ordinary People*

1982
★ John Gielgud/*Arthur*

1983
★ Louis Gossett, Jr./*An Officer and a Gentleman*

1984
★ Jack Nicholson/*Terms of Endearment*

1985
★ Haing S. Ngor/*The Killing Fields*

1986
★ Klaus Maria Brandauer/*Out of Africa*

1987
★ Tom Berenger/*Platoon*

1988
★ Sean Connery/*The Untouchables*

1989
★ Martin Landau/*Tucker: The Man and His Dream*

1990
★ Denzel Washington/*Glory*
Joe Pesci/*Goodfellas*

1991
★ Bruce Davison/*Longtime Companion*

1992
★ Jack Palance/*City Slickers*

1993
★ Gene Hackman/*Unforgiven*

1994
★ Tommy Lee Jones/*The Fugitive*
Leonardo DiCaprio/*What's Eating Gilbert Grape*
Ralph Fiennes/*Schindler's List*
John Malkovich/*In the Line of Fire*
Sean Penn/*Carlito's Way*

1995
★ Martin Landau/*Ed Wood*
Kevin Bacon/*The River Wild*
Samuel L. Jackson/*Pulp Fiction*
Gary Sinise/*Forrest Gump*
John Turturro/*Quiz Show*

1996
★ Brad Pitt/*12 Monkeys*
Ed Harris/*Apollo 13*

John Leguizamo/*To Wong Foo, Thanks for Everything, Julie Newmar*
Tim Roth/*Rob Roy*
Kevin Spacey/*The Usual Suspects*

1997
★ Edward Norton/*Primal Fear*
Cuba Gooding, Jr./*Jerry Maguire*
Samuel L. Jackson/*A Time to Kill*
Paul Scofield/*The Crucible*
James Woods/*Ghosts of Mississippi*

ACTRESS—DRAMA

1944
★ Jennifer Jones/*The Song of Bernadette*

1945
★ Ingrid Bergman/*Gaslight*

1946
★ Ingrid Bergman/*The Bells of St. Mary's*

1947
★ Rosalind Russell/*Sister Kenny*

1949
★ Jane Wyman/*Johnny Belinda*

1950
★ Olivia de Havilland/*The Heiress*

1951
★ Gloria Swanson/*Sunset Boulevard*

1953
★ Shirley Booth/*Come Back, Little Sheba*

1954
★ Audrey Hepburn/*Roman Holiday*

1955
★ Grace Kelly/*Country Girl*

1956
★ Anna Magnani/*The Rose Tattoo*

1957
★ Ingrid Bergman/*Anastasia*

1958
★ Joanne Woodward/*The Three Faces of Eve*

1959
★ Susan Hayward/*I Want to Live!*

1960
★ Elizabeth Taylor/*Suddenly, Last Summer*

1961
★ Greer Garson/*Sunrise at Campobello*

1962
★ Geraldine Page/*Summer and Smoke*

1963
★ Geraldine Page/*Sweet Bird of Youth*

1966
★ Samantha Eggar/*The Collector*

1967
★ Anouk Aimee/*A Man and a Woman*

1969
★ Joanne Woodward/*Rachel, Rachel*

1970
★ Genevieve Bujold/*Anne of the Thousand Days*

1971
★ Ali MacGraw/*Love Story*

1972
★ Jane Fonda/*Klute*

1974
★ Marsha Mason/*Cinderella Liberty*

1975
★ Gena Rowlands/*A Woman Under the Influence*

1976
★ Louise Fletcher/*One Flew Over the Cuckoo's Nest*

1977
★ Faye Dunaway/*Network*

1978
★ Jane Fonda/*Julia*

1979
★ Jane Fonda/*Coming Home*

1980
★ Sally Field/*Norma Rae*

1981
★ Mary Tyler Moore/*Ordinary People*

1982
★ Meryl Streep/*The French Lieutenant's Woman*

1983
★ Meryl Streep/*Sophie's Choice*

1984
★ Shirley MacLaine/*Terms of Endearment*

1985
★ Sally Field/*Places in the Heart*

1986
★ Whoopi Goldberg/*The Color Purple*

1987
★ Marlee Matlin/*Children of a Lesser God*

1988
★ Sally Kirkland/*Anna*
★ Sigourney Weaver/*Gorillas in the Mist*

1989
★ Jodie Foster/*The Accused*
★ Shirley MacLaine/*Madame Sousatzka*

1990
★ Michelle Pfeiffer/*The Fabulous Baker Boys*

1991
★ Kathy Bates/*Misery*

1992
★ Jodie Foster/*The Silence of the Lambs*

1993
★ Emma Thompson/*Howard's End*

1994
★ Holly Hunter/*The Piano*
★ Debra Winger/*A Dangerous Woman*
Juliette Binoche/*Trois Couleurs: Bleu*
Michelle Pfeiffer/*The Age of Innocence*
Emma Thompson/*The Remains of the Day*

1995
★ Jessica Lange/*Blue Sky*
Jodie Foster/*Nell*
Jennifer Jason Leigh/*Mrs. Parker and the Vicious Circle*
Miranda Richardson/*Tom & Viv*
Meryl Streep/*The River Wild*

1996
★ Sharon Stone/*Casino*
Susan Sarandon/*Dead Man Walking*
Elisabeth Shue/*Leaving Las Vegas*
Meryl Streep/*The Bridges of Madison County*
Emma Thompson/*Sense and Sensibility*

1997
★ Brenda Blethyn/*Secrets and Lies*
Courtney Love/*The People vs. Larry Flynt*
Kristin Scott Thomas/*The English Patient*
Meryl Streep/*Marvin's Room*
Emily Watson/*Breaking the Waves*

ACTRESS—MUSICAL/ COMEDY

1951
★ Judy Holliday/*Born Yesterday*

1955
★ Judy Garland/*A Star is Born*

1956
★ Jean Simmons/*Guys and Dolls*

1957
★ Deborah Kerr/*The King and I*

1958
★ Kay Kendall/*Les Girls*

1959
★ Rosalind Russell/*Auntie Mame*

1960
★ Marilyn Monroe/*Some Like It Hot*

1961
★ Shirley MacLaine/*The Apartment*

1963
★ Rosalind Russell/*Gypsy*

1964
★ Shirley MacLaine/*Irma La Douce*

1965
★ Julie Andrews/*Mary Poppins*

1966
★ Julie Andrews/*The Sound of Music*

1967
★ Lynn Redgrave/*Georgy Girl*

1968
★ Anne Bancroft/*The Graduate*

1969
★ Barbra Streisand/*Funny Girl*

1971
★ Carrie Snodgress/*Diary of a Mad Housewife*

1972
★ Twiggy/*The Boy Friend*

1973
★ Liza Minnelli/*Cabaret*

1974
★ Glenda Jackson/*A Touch of Class*

1975
★ Raquel Welch/*The Three Musketeers*

1976
★ Ann-Margret/*Tommy*

1977
★ Barbra Streisand/*A Star is Born*

1978
★ Diane Keaton/*Annie Hall*

★ Marsha Mason/*The Goodbye Girl*

1979
★ Ellen Burstyn/*Same Time, Next Year*
★ Maggie Smith/*California Suite*

1980
★ Bette Midler/*The Rose*

1981
★ Sissy Spacek/*Coal Miner's Daughter*

1982
★ Bernadette Peters/*Pennies From Heaven*

1983
★ Julie Andrews/*Victor/ Victoria*

1984
★ Julie Walters/*Educating Rita*

1985
★ Kathleen Turner/*Romancing the Stone*

1986
★ Kathleen Turner/*Prizzi's Honor*

1987
★ Sissy Spacek/*Crimes of the Heart*

1988
★ Cher/*Moonstruck*

1989
★ Melanie Griffith/*Working Girl*

1990
★ Jessica Tandy/*Driving Miss Daisy*

1991
★ Julia Roberts/*Pretty Woman*
Andie MacDowell/*Green Card*

1992
★ Bette Midler/*For the Boys*

1993
★ Miranda Richardson/*Enchanted April*

1994
★ Angela Bassett/*What's Love Got to Do with It?*
Stockard Channing/*Six Degrees of Separation*
Anjelica Huston/*Addams Family Values*
Diane Keaton/*Manhattan Murder Mystery*
Meg Ryan/*Sleepless in Seattle*

1995
★ Jamie Lee Curtis/*True Lies*
Geena Davis/*Speechless*
Andie MacDowell/*Four Weddings and a Funeral*

Shirley MacLaine/*Guarding Tess*
Emma Thompson/*Junior*

1996
★ Nicole Kidman/*To Die For*
Annette Bening/*The American President*
Sandra Bullock/*While You Were Sleeping*
Toni Collette/*Muriel's Wedding*
Vanessa Redgrave/*A Month by the Lake*

1997
★ Madonna/*Evita*
Glenn Close/*101 Dalmatians*
Frances McDormand/*Fargo*
Debbie Reynolds/*Mother*
Barbra Streisand/*The Mirror Has Two Faces*

ACTRESS— SUPPORTING

1945
★ Agnes Moorehead/*Mrs. Parkington*

1946
★ Angela Lansbury/*Picture of Dorian Gray*

1947
★ Anne Baxter/*The Razor's Edge*

1948
★ Celeste Holm/*Gentleman's Agreement*

1949
★ Ellen Corby/*I Remember Mama*

1950
★ Mercedes McCambridge/*All the King's Men*

1951
★ Josephine Hull/*Harvey*

1952
★ Kim Hunter/*A Streetcar Named Desire*

1953
★ Katy Jurado/*High Noon*

1954
★ Grace Kelly/*Mogambo*

1956
★ Marisa Pavan/*The Rose Tattoo*

1957
★ Eileen Heckart/*The Bad Seed*

1958
★ Elsa Lanchester/*Witness for the Prosecution*

1959
★ Hermione Gingold/*Gigi*

1960
★ Susan Kohner/*Imitation of Life*

1961
★ Janet Leigh/*Psycho*

1962
★ Rita Moreno/*West Side Story*

1963
★ Angela Lansbury/*The Manchurian Candidate*

1964
★ Margaret Rutherford/*The V.I.P.'s*

1965
★ Agnes Moorehead/*Hush, Hush, Sweet Charlotte*

1966
★ Ruth Gordon/*Inside Daisy Clover*

1967
★ Jocelyn Lagarde/*Hawaii*

1968
★ Carol Channing/*Thoroughly Modern Millie*

1969
★ Ruth Gordon/*Rosemary's Baby*

1970
★ Goldie Hawn/*Cactus Flower*

1971
★ Karen Black/*Five Easy Pieces*
★ Maureen Stapleton/*Airport*

1972
★ Ann-Margret/*Carnal Knowledge*

1973
★ Shelley Winters/*The Poseidon Adventure*

1974
★ Linda Blair/*The Exorcist*

1975
★ Karen Black/*The Great Gatsby*

1976
★ Brenda Vaccaro/*Once is Not Enough*

1977
★ Katharine Ross/*Voyage of the Damned*

1978
★ Vanessa Redgrave/*Julia*

1979
★ Dyan Cannon/*Heaven Can Wait*

1980
★ Meryl Streep/*Kramer vs. Kramer*

1981
★ Mary Steenburgen/*Melvin and Howard*

1982
★ Joan Hackett/*Only When I Laugh*

1983
★ Jessica Lange/*Tootsie*

1984
★ Cher/*Silkwood*

1985
★ Peggy Ashcroft/*A Passage to India*

1986
★ Meg Tilly/*Agnes of God*

1987
★ Maggie Smith/*A Room with a View*

1988
★ Olympia Dukakis/*Moonstruck*

1989
★ Sigourney Weaver/*Working Girl*

1990
★ Julia Roberts/*Steel Magnolias*
Lorraine Bracco/*Goodfellas*

1991
★ Whoopi Goldberg/*Ghost*
Nicole Kidman/*Billy Bathgate*

1992
★ Mercedes Ruehl/*The Fisher King*

1993
★ Joan Plowright/*Enchanted April*

1994
★ Winona Ryder/*The Age of Innocence*
Penelope Ann Miller/*Carlito's Way*
Anna Paquin/*The Piano*
Rosie Perez/*Fearless*
Emma Thompson/*In the Name of the Father*

1995
★ Dianne Wiest/*Bullets Over Broadway*
Kirsten Dunst/*Interview with the Vampire*
Sophia Loren/*Ready to Wear*
Uma Thurman/*Pulp Fiction*
Robin Wright/*Forrest Gump*

1996
★ Mira Sorvino/*Mighty Aphrodite*
Anjelica Huston/*The Crossing Guard*
Kathleen Quinlan/*Apollo 13*
Kyra Sedgwick/*Something to Talk About*
Kate Winslet/*Sense and Sensibility*

ACTRESS—SUPPORTING
‚cont.

1997
★ **Lauren Bacall**/*The Mirror Has Two Faces*
  Joan Allen/*The Crucible*
  Juliette Binoche/*The English Patient*
  Barbara Hershey/*Portrait of a Lady*
  Marianne Jean-Baptiste/*Secrets and Lies*
  Marion Ross/*The Evening Star*

BEST FILM—DRAMA

1944
★ *The Song of Bernadette*

1945
★ *Going My Way*

1946
★ *The Lost Weekend*

1947
★ *The Best Years of Our Lives*

1948
★ *Gentleman's Agreement*

1949
★ *Johnny Belinda*
★ *Treasure of the Sierra Madre*

1950
★ *All the King's Men*

1951
★ *Sunset Boulevard*

1952
★ *A Place in the Sun*

1953
★ *The Greatest Show on Earth*

1954
★ *The Robe*

1955
★ *On the Waterfront*

1956
★ *East of Eden*

1957
★ *Around the World in 80 Days*

1958
★ *The Bridge on the River Kwai*

1959
★ *The Defiant Ones*

1960
★ *Ben-Hur*

1961
★ *Spartacus*

1962
★ *The Guns of Navarone*

1963
★ *Lawrence of Arabia*

1964
★ *The Cardinal*

1965
★ *Becket*

1966
★ *Doctor Zhivago*

1967
★ *A Man for All Seasons*

1968
★ *In the Heat of the Night*

1969
★ *The Lion in Winter*

1970
★ *Anne of the Thousand Days*

1971
★ *Love Story*

1972
★ *The French Connection*

1973
★ *The Godfather*

1974
★ *The Exorcist*

1975
★ *Chinatown*

1976
★ *One Flew Over the Cuckoo's Nest*

1977
★ *Rocky*

1978
★ *The Turning Point*

1979
★ *Midnight Express*

1980
★ *Kramer vs. Kramer*

1981
★ *Ordinary People*

1982
★ *On Golden Pond*

1983
★ *E.T.: The Extra-Terrestrial*

1984
★ *Terms of Endearment*

1985
★ *Amadeus*

1986
★ *Out of Africa*

1987
★ *Platoon*

1988
★ *The Last Emperor*

1989
★ *Rain Man*

1990
★ *Born on the Fourth of July*
  Goodfellas

1991
★ *Dances with Wolves*

1992
★ *Bugsy*

1993
★ *Scent of a Woman*

1994
★ *Schindler's List*
  In the Name of the Father
  The Age of Innocence
  The Piano
  The Remains of the Day

1995
★ *Forrest Gump*
  Legends of the Fall
  Nell
  Pulp Fiction
  Quiz Show

1996
★ *Sense and Sensibility*
  Apollo 13
  Braveheart
  Leaving Las Vegas
  The Bridges of Madison County

1997
★ *The English Patient*
  Breaking the Waves
  Secrets and Lies
  Shine
  The People vs. Larry Flynt

BEST FILM—MUSICAL/COMEDY

1952
★ *An American in Paris*

1955
★ *Carmen Jones*

1956
★ *Guys and Dolls*

1957
★ *The King and I*

1958
★ *Les Girls*

1959
★ *Gigi*

1960
★ *Some Like It Hot*

1961
★ *Song Without End*
★ *The Apartment*

1962
★ *West Side Story*

1963
★ *That Touch of Mink*
★ *The Music Man*

1964
★ *Tom Jones*

1965
★ *My Fair Lady*

1966
★ *The Sound of Music*

1967
★ *The Russians are Coming, the Russians are Coming*

1968
★ *The Graduate*

1969
★ *Oliver!*

1971
★ *M*A*S*H*

1972
★ *Fiddler on the Roof*

1973
★ *Cabaret*

1974
★ *American Graffiti*

1975
★ *The Longest Yard*

1976
★ *The Sunshine Boys*

1977
★ *A Star is Born*

1978
★ *The Goodbye Girl*

1979
★ *Heaven Can Wait*

1980
★ *Breaking Away*

1981
★ *Coal Miner's Daughter*

1982
★ *Arthur*

1983
★ *Tootsie*

1984
★ *Yentl*

1985
★ *Romancing the Stone*

1986
★ *Prizzi's Honor*

1987
★ *Hannah and Her Sisters*

1988
★ *Hope and Glory*

1989
★ *Working Girl*

1990
★ *Driving Miss Daisy*

1991
★ *Green Card*

1992
★ *Beauty and the Beast*

1993
★ *The Player*

1994
★ *Mrs. Doubtfire*
  Dave
  Much Ado about Nothing
  Sleepless in Seattle
  Strictly Ballroom

1995
★ *The Lion King*
  Ed Wood
  Four Weddings and a Funeral
  Ready to Wear
  The Adventures of Priscilla, Queen of the Desert

1996
★ *Babe*
  Get Shorty
  Sabrina
  The American President
  Toy Story

1997
★ *Evita*
  Everyone Says I Love You
  Fargo
  Jerry Maguire
  The Birdcage

DIRECTOR

1944
★ **Henry King**/*The Song of Bernadette*

1945
★ **Leo McCarey**/*Going My Way*

1946
★ **Billy Wilder**/*The Lost Weekend*

1947
★ **Frank Capra**/*It's a Wonderful Life*

1948
★ **Elia Kazan**/*Gentleman's Agreement*

1949
★ **John Huston**/*Treasure of the Sierra Madre*

1950
★ **Robert Rossen**/*All the King's Men*

1951
★ **Billy Wilder**/*Sunset Boulevard*

1953
★ **Cecil B. DeMille**/*The Greatest Show on Earth*

1954
  Fred Zinnemann/*From Here to Eternity*

1955
★ **Elia Kazan**/*On the Waterfront*

1956
★ **Joshua Logan**/*Picnic*

1957
★ Elia Kazan/*Baby Doll*

1958
★ David Lean/*The Bridge on the River Kwai*

1959
★ Vincente Minnelli/*Gigi*

1960
★ William Wyler/*Ben-Hur*

1962
★ Stanley Kramer/*Judgment at Nuremberg*

1963
★ David Lean/*Lawrence of Arabia*

1965
★ George Cukor/*My Fair Lady*

1966
★ David Lean/*Doctor Zhivago*

1967
★ Fred Zinnemann/*A Man for All Seasons*

1968
★ Mike Nichols/*The Graduate*

1969
★ Paul Newman/*Rachel, Rachel*

1970
★ Charles Jarrott/*Anne of the Thousand Days*

1971
★ Arthur Hiller/*Love Story*

1972
★ William Friedkin/*The French Connection*

1973
★ Francis Ford Coppola/*The Godfather*

1974
★ William Friedkin/*The Exorcist*

1975
★ Roman Polanski/*Chinatown*

1976
★ Milos Forman/*One Flew Over the Cuckoo's Nest*

1977
★ Sidney Lumet/*Network*

1978
★ Herbert Ross/*The Turning Point*

1979
★ Michael Cimino/*The Deer Hunter*

1980
★ Francis Ford Coppola/*Apocalypse Now*

1981
★ Robert Redford/*Ordinary People*

1982
★ Warren Beatty/*Reds*

1983
★ Richard Attenborough/*Gandhi*

1984
★ Barbra Streisand/*Yentl*

1985
★ Milos Forman/*Amadeus*

1986
★ John Huston/*Prizzi's Honor*

1987
★ Oliver Stone/*Platoon*

1988
★ Bernardo Bertolucci/*The Last Emperor*

1989
★ Clint Eastwood/*Bird*

1990
★ Oliver Stone/*Born on the Fourth of July*
Martin Scorsese/*Goodfellas*

1991
★ Kevin Costner/*Dances with Wolves*

1992
★ Oliver Stone/*JFK*

1993
★ Clint Eastwood/*Unforgiven*

1994
★ Steven Spielberg/*Schindler's List*
Jane Campion/*The Piano*
Andrew Davis/*The Fugitive*
James Ivory/*The Remains of the Day*
Martin Scorsese/*The Age of Innocence*

1995
★ Robert Zemeckis/*Forrest Gump*
Robert Redford/*Quiz Show*
Oliver Stone/*Natural Born Killers*
Quentin Tarantino/*Pulp Fiction*
Edward Zwick/*Legends of the Fall*

1996
★ Mel Gibson/*Braveheart*
Mike Figgis/*Leaving Las Vegas*
Ron Howard/*Apollo 13*
Ang Lee/*Sense and Sensibility*
Rob Reiner/*The American President*
Martin Scorsese/*Casino*

1997
★ Milos Forman/*The People vs. Larry Flynt*
Joel Coen/*Fargo*
Scott Hicks/*Shine*
Anthony Minghella/*The English Patient*
Alan Parker/*Evita*

FILM—FOREIGN LANGUAGE

1996
Brother of Sleep

1997
★ Kolya
Luna e L'Altra

SCORE

1948
★ Life with Father

1949
★ The Red Shoes

1950
★ The Inspector General

1951
★ Sunset Boulevard

1952
★ September Affair

1953
★ High Noon

1960
★ On the Beach

1961
★ The Alamo

1962
★ The Guns of Navarone

1963
★ To Kill a Mockingbird

1965
★ The Fall of the Roman Empire

1966
★ Doctor Zhivago

1967
★ Hawaii

1968
★ Camelot

1969
★ The Shoes of the Fisherman

1970
★ Butch Cassidy and the Sundance Kid

1971
★ Love Story

1972
★ Shaft

1973
★ The Godfather

1974
★ Jonathan Livingston Seagull

1975
★ The Little Prince

1976
★ Jaws

1977
★ A Star is Born

1978
★ Star Wars

1979
★ Midnight Express

1980
★ Apocalypse Now

1981
★ The Stunt Man

1983
★ E.T.: The Extra-Terrestrial

1984
★ Flashdance

1985
★ A Passage to India

1986
★ Out of Africa

1987
★ The Mission

1988
★ The Last Emperor

1989
★ Gorillas in the Mist

1990
★ The Little Mermaid

1991
★ The Sheltering Sky

1993
★ Aladdin

1994
★ Heaven and Earth
Schindler's List
The Nightmare Before Christmas
The Piano
Trois Couleurs: Bleu

1995
★ The Lion King
Forrest Gump
Interview with the Vampire
Legends of the Fall
Nell

1996
★ A Walk in the Clouds
Braveheart
Don Juan DeMarco
Pocahontas
Sense and Sensibility

1997
★ The English Patient
Michael Collins
Shine

The Hunchback of Notre Dame
The Mirror Has Two Faces

SONG

1965
★ "Circus World"/*Circus World*

1968
★ "If Ever I Should Leave You"/*Camelot*

1969
★ "The Windmills of Your Mind"/*The Thomas Crown Affair*

1970
★ "Jean"/*The Prime of Miss Jean Brodie*

1971
★ "Whistling Away the Dark"/*Darling Lili*

1972
★ "Life Is What You Make It"/*Kotch*

1973
★ "Ben"/*Ben*

1974
★ "The Way We Were"/*The Way We Were*

1975
★ "I Feel Love"/*Benji*

1976
★ "I'm Easy"/*Nashville*

1977
★ "Evergreen"/*A Star is Born*

1978
★ "You Light Up My Life"/*You Light Up My Life*

1980
★ "The Rose"/*The Rose*

1981
★ "Fame"/*Fame*

1982
★ "Arthur's Theme"/*Arthur*

1983
★ "Up Where We Belong"/*An Officer and a Gentleman*

1984
★ "Flashdance...What a Feeling"/*Flashdance*

1985
★ "I Just Called to Say I Love You"/*The Woman in Red*

1986
★ "Say You, Say Me"/*White Nights*

1987
★ "Take My Breath Away"/*Top Gun*

SONG ▸cont.

1988
★ "(I've Had) the Time of My Life"/Dirty Dancing

1989
★ "Let the River Run"/ Working Girl

1990
★ "Under the Sea"/The Little Mermaid

1991
★ "Blaze of Glory"/Young Guns 2

1993
★ "A Whole New World"/ Aladdin

1994
★ "Streets of Philadelphia"/ Philadelphia
  "(You Made Me the) Thief of Your Heart"/In the Name of the Father
  "Again"/Poetic Justice
  "Stay"/Faraway, So Close!
  "The Day I Fall in Love"/ Beethoven's 2nd

1995
★ "Can You Feel the Love Tonight?"/The Lion King
  "Circle of Life"/The Lion King
  "Far Longer than Forever"/The Swan Princess
  "I'll Remember"/With Honors
  "Look What Love Has Done"/Junior
  "The Color of the Night"/ Color of Night

1996
★ "Colors of the Wind"/ Pocahontas
  "Have You Ever Really Loved a Woman?"/ Don Juan DeMarco
  "Hold Me, Thrill Me, Kiss Me, Kill Me"/Batman Forever
  "Moonlight"/Sabrina
  "You Got a Friend in Me"/Toy Story

1997
★ "You Must Love Me"/ Evita
  "Because You Loved Me"/Up Close and Personal
  "For the First Time"/One Fine Day
  "I've Finally Found Someone"/The Mirror Has Two Faces
  "That Thing You Do!"/ That Thing You Do!

SCREENPLAY

1948
★ Miracle on 34th Street

1949
★ The Search

1950
★ Battleground

1951
★ All About Eve

1953
★ Five Fingers

1954
★ Lili

1955
★ Sabrina

1966
★ Doctor Zhivago

1967
★ A Man for All Seasons

1968
★ In the Heat of the Night

1969
★ Charly

1970
★ Anne of the Thousand Days

1971
★ Love Story

1972
★ The Hospital

1973
★ The Godfather

1974
★ The Exorcist

1975
★ Chinatown

1976
★ One Flew Over the Cuckoo's Nest

1977
★ Network

1978
★ The Goodbye Girl

1979
★ Midnight Express

1980
★ Kramer vs. Kramer

1981
★ The Ninth Configuration

1982
★ On Golden Pond

1983
★ Gandhi

1984
★ Terms of Endearment

1985
★ Amadeus

1986
★ The Purple Rose of Cairo

1987
★ The Mission

1988
★ The Last Emperor

1989
★ Running on Empty

1990
★ Born on the Fourth of July Goodfellas

1991
★ Dances with Wolves

1993
★ Scent of a Woman

1994
★ Schindler's List Philadelphia Short Cuts The Piano The Remains of the Day

1995
★ Pulp Fiction Mr. Holland's Opus Forrest Gump Four Weddings and a Funeral Quiz Show The Shawshank Redemption

1996
★ Sense and Sensibility Braveheart Dead Man Walking Get Shorty The American President

1997
★ The People vs. Larry Flynt Fargo Lone Star Shine The English Patient

FILM—FOREIGN LANGUAGE

1950
★ The Bicycle Thief

1955
★ Genevieve

1956
★ Ordet

1957
★ Richard III
★ War and Peace

1959
★ A Night to Remember

1960
★ Black Orpheus
★ Odd Obsession
★ Wild Strawberries

1961
★ The Virgin Spring

1962
★ Two Women

1963
★ Divorce—Italian Style

1964
★ Tom Jones

1965
★ Marriage Italian Style
★ Sallah

1966
★ Darling

1967
★ A Man and a Woman
★ Alfie

1969
★ Romeo and Juliet
★ War and Peace

1970
★ Z

1971
★ Rider on the Rain
★ Women in Love

1972
★ Sunday, Bloody Sunday

1973
★ Young Winston

1974
★ The Pedestrian

1975
★ Scenes from a Marriage

1976
★ Lies My Father Told Me

1977
★ Face to Face

1978
★ A Special Day

1979
★ Autumn Sonata

1980
★ La Cage aux Folles

1981
★ Tess

1982
★ Chariots of Fire

1983
★ Gandhi

1984
★ Fanny and Alexander

1985
★ A Passage to India

1986
★ The Official Story

1987
★ The Assault

1988
★ My Life As a Dog

1989
★ Pelle the Conqueror

1990
★ Cinema Paradiso

1991
★ Cyrano de Bergerac

1992
★ Europa, Europa

1993
★ Indochine

1994
★ Farewell My Concubine Flight of the Innocent The Wedding Banquet Trois Couleurs: Bleu

1995
★ Farinelli Eat Drink Man Woman Queen Margot To Live Trois Couleurs: Rouge

1996
★ Les Miserables French Twist Shanghai Triad

1997
  Prisoner of the Mountains Ridicule The Eighth Day

INDEPENDENT SPIRIT AWARDS
ACTOR

1986
★ M. Emmet Walsh/Blood Simple

1987
★ James Woods/Salvador

1988
★ Dennis Quaid/The Big Easy

1989
★ Edward James Olmos/ Stand and Deliver

1990
★ Matt Dillon/Drugstore Cowboy

1991
★ Danny Glover/To Sleep with Anger

1992
★ River Phoenix/My Own Private Idaho

1993
★ Harvey Keitel/Bad Lieutenant

1994
★ Jeff Bridges/American Heart
  Vincent D'Onofrio/ Household Saints
  Mitchell Lichtenstein/ The Wedding Banquet
  Matthew Modine/Equinox

Tyrin Turner/*Menace II
Society*

1995
★ **Samuel L. Jackson**/*Pulp
Fiction*
Sihung Lung/*Eat Drink
Man Woman*
William H. Macy/*Oleanna*
Campbell Scott/*Mrs.
Parker and the Vicious
Circle*
Jon Seda/*I Like It Like
That*

1996
★ **Sean Penn**/*Dead Man
Walking*
Nicolas Cage/*Leaving
Las Vegas*
Tim Roth/*Little Odessa*
Jimmy Smits/*My Family*
Kevin Spacey/*Swimming
with Sharks*

1997
★ **William H. Macy**/*Fargo*
Chris Cooper/*Lone Star*
Christopher Penn/*The
Funeral*

ACTOR—SUPPORTING

1988
★ **Morgan Freeman**/*Street
Smart*

1989
★ **Lou Diamond Phillips**/
Stand and Deliver

1990
★ **Max Perlich**/*Drugstore
Cowboy*

1991
★ **Bruce Davison**/*Longtime
Companion*

1992
★ **David Strathairn**/*City of
Hope*

1993
★ **Steve Buscemi**/*Reservoir
Dogs*

1994
★ **Christopher Lloyd**/
Twenty Bucks
David Chung/
Combination Platter
Tate Donovan/*Inside
Monkey Zetterland*
Todd Field/*Ruby in
Paradise*
Edward Furlong/
American Heart

1995
★ **Chazz Palminteri**/*Bullets
Over Broadway*
Giancarlo Esposito/
Fresh
Larry Pine/*Vanya on 42nd
Street*
Eric Stoltz/*Pulp Fiction*
Nicholas Turturro/
Federal Hill

1996
★ **Benicio Del Toro**/*The
Usual Suspects*

James LeGros/*Living in
Oblivion*
David Morse/*The
Crossing Guard*
Max Perlich/*Georgia*
Harold Perrineau, Jr./
Smoke

1997
★ **Benicio Del Toro**/
Basquiat
Kevin Corrigan/*Walking
and Talking*
Matthew Faber/*Welcome
to the Dollhouse*
Gary Farmer/*Dead Man*
Richard Jenkins/*Flirting
with Disaster*

ACTRESS

1986
★ **Geraldine Page**/*The Trip
to Bountiful*

1987
★ **Isabella Rossellini**/*Blue
Velvet*

1988
★ **Sally Kirkland**/*Anna*

1989
★ **Jodie Foster**/*Five Corners*

1990
★ **Andie MacDowell**/*sex,
lies and videotape*

1991
★ **Anjelica Huston**/*The
Grifters*

1992
★ **Judy Davis**/*Impromptu*

1993
★ **Fairuza Balk**/*Gas Food
Lodging*

1994
★ **Ashley Judd**/*Ruby in
Paradise*
Suzy Amis/*The Ballad of
Little Jo*
May Chin/*The Wedding
Banquet*
Ariyan Johnson/*Just
Another Girl on the
I.R.T.*
Emma Thompson/*Much
Ado about Nothing*

1995
★ **Linda Fiorentino**/*The
Last Seduction*
Jennifer Jason Leigh/
*Mrs. Parker and the
Vicious Circle*
Karen Sillas/*What
Happened Was...*
Lauren Velez/*I Like It Like
That*
Chien-Lien Wu/*Eat Drink
Man Woman*

1996
★ **Elisabeth Shue**/*Leaving
Las Vegas*
Jennifer Jason Leigh/
Georgia
Elina Lowensohn/*Nadja*
Julianne Moore/*Safe*

Lili Taylor/*The Addiction*

1997
★ **Frances McDormand**/
Fargo
Maria Conchita Alonso/
Caught
Scarlett Johansson/
Manny & Lo
Catherine Keener/
Walking and Talking
Renee Zellweger/*The
Whole Wide World*

ACTRESS—SUPPORTING

1988
★ **Anjelica Huston**/*The
Dead*

1989
★ **Rosana De Soto**/*Stand
and Deliver*

1990
★ **Laura San Giacomo**/*sex,
lies and videotape*

1991
★ **Sheryl Lee Ralph**/*To
Sleep with Anger*

1992
★ **Diane Ladd**/*Rambling
Rose*

1993
★ **Alfre Woodard**/*Passion
Fish*

1994
★ **Lili Taylor**/*Household
Saints*
Lara Flynn Boyle/
Equinox
Ah-Leh Gua/*The
Wedding Banquet*
Lucinda Jenney/
American Heart
Julianne Moore/*Short
Cuts*

1995
★ **Dianne Wiest**/*Bullets
Over Broadway*
V.S. Brodie/*Go Fish*
Carla Gallo/*Spanking the
Monkey*
Kelly Lynch/*Forbidden
Choices*
Brooke Smith/*Vanya on
42nd Street*

1996
★ **Mare Winningham**/
Georgia
Jennifer Lopez/*My
Family*
Vanessa Redgrave/*Little
Odessa*
Chloe Sevigny/*Kids*
Celia Weston/*Dead Man
Walking*

1997
★ **Elizabeth Pena**/*Lone Star*
Mary Kay Place/*Manny &
Lo*
Queen Latifah/*Set It Off*
Lili Taylor/*Girls Town*
Lily Tomlin/*Flirting with
Disaster*

CINEMATOGRAPHY

1986
★ *Trouble in Mind*

1987
★ *Platoon*

1988
★ *Matewan*

1989
★ *The Unbearable Lightness
of Being*

1990
★ *Drugstore Cowboy*

1991
★ *Wild at Heart*

1992
★ *Kafka*

1993
★ *Night on Earth*

1994
★ *Menace II Society*
American Heart
Chain of Desire
Equinox
Ruby in Paradise

1995
★ *Barcelona*
Eat Drink Man Woman
Forbidden Choices
I Like It Like That
Suture

1996
★ *Leaving Las Vegas*
Little Odessa
Nadja
The Underneath
The Usual Suspects

1997
★ *Fargo*
Bound
*Color of a Brisk and
Leaping Day*
Dead Man
The Funeral

DIRECTOR

1986
★ **Joel Coen**/*Blood Simple*
★ **Martin Scorsese**/*After
Hours*

1987
★ **Oliver Stone**/*Platoon*

1988
★ **John Huston**/*The Dead*

1989
★ **Ramon Menendez**/*Stand
and Deliver*

1990
★ **Steven Soderbergh**/*sex,
lies and videotape*

1991
★ **Charles Burnett**/*To Sleep
with Anger*

1992
★ **Martha Coolidge**/
Rambling Rose

1993
★ **Carl Franklin**/*One False
Move*

1994
★ **Robert Altman**/*Short Cuts*
Ang Lee/*The Wedding
Banquet*
Victor Nunez/*Ruby in
Paradise*
Robert Rodriguez/*El
Mariachi*
John Turturro/*Mac*

1995
★ **Quentin Tarantino**/*Pulp
Fiction*
John Dahl/*Red Rock
West*
Ang Lee/*Eat Drink Man
Woman*
Roman Polanski/*Death
and the Maiden*
Alan Rudolph/*Mrs.
Parker and the Vicious
Circle*

1996
★ **Mike Figgis**/*Leaving Las
Vegas*
Michael Almereyda/
Nadja
Ulu Grosbard/*Georgia*
Todd Haynes/*Safe*
John Sayles/*The Secret
of Roan Inish*

1997
★ **Joel Coen**/*Fargo*
Abel Ferrara/*The Funeral*
David O. Russell/*Flirting
with Disaster*
Todd Solondz/*Welcome
to the Dollhouse*
Robert M. Young/*Caught*

FILM

1986
★ *After Hours*

1987
★ *Platoon*

1988
★ *River's Edge*

1989
★ *Stand and Deliver*

1990
★ *sex, lies and videotape*

1991
★ *The Grifters*

1992
★ *Rambling Rose*

1993
★ *The Player*

1994
★ *Short Cuts*
Equinox
Much Ado about Nothing
Ruby in Paradise
The Wedding Banquet

FILM ▸cont.

1995
- ★ Pulp Fiction
  Mrs. Parker and the
    Vicious Circle
  Bullets Over Broadway
  Eat Drink Man Woman
  Wes Craven's New
    Nightmare

1996
- ★ Leaving Las Vegas
  Living in Oblivion
  Safe
  The Addiction
  The Secret of Roan Inish

1997
- ★ Fargo
  Dead Man
  Lone Star
  The Funeral
  Welcome to the Dollhouse

FIRST FEATURE

1987
- ★ She's Gotta Have It

1988
- ★ Dirty Dancing

1989
- ★ Mystic Pizza

1990
- ★ Heathers

1991
- ★ Metropolitan

1992
- ★ Straight Out of Brooklyn

1993
- ★ The Waterdance

1994
- ★ El Mariachi
  American Heart
  Combination Platter
  Mac
  Menace II Society

1995
- ★ Spanking the Monkey
  Clean, Shaven
  Clerks
  I Like It Like That
  Suture

1996
- ★ The Brothers McMullen
  Kids
  Little Odessa
  Picture Bride
  River of Grass

1997
- ★ Sling Blade
  Big Night
  I Shot Andy Warhol
  Manny & Lo
  Tree's Lounge

SCREENPLAY

1986
- ★ The Trip to Bountiful

1987
- ★ Platoon

1988
- ★ River's Edge

1989
- ★ Stand and Deliver

1990
- ★ Drugstore Cowboy

1991
- ★ To Sleep with Anger

1992
- ★ My Own Private Idaho

1993
- ★ The Waterdance

1994
- ★ Short Cuts
  Combination Platter
  Household Saints
  Ruby in Paradise
  The Wedding Banquet

1995
- ★ Pulp Fiction
  Mrs. Parker and the
    Vicious Circle
  Bullets Over Broadway
  Eat Drink Man Woman
  Red Rock West

1996
- ★ The Usual Suspects
  Leaving Las Vegas
  Living in Oblivion
  Safe
  The Secret of Roan Inish

1997
- ★ Fargo
  Dead Man
  Flirting with Disaster
  Lone Star
  The Funeral

DEBUT PERFORMANCE

1995
- ★ Sean Nelson/Fresh
  Jeff Anderson/Clerks
  Jeremy Davies/Spanking
    the Monkey
  Alicia Witt/Fun
  Renee Zellweger/Love
    and a .45

1996
- ★ Justin Pierce/Kids
  Jason Andrews/Rhythm
    Thief
  Lisa Bowman/River of
    Grass
  Gabriel Casseus/New
    Jersey Drive
  Rose McGowan/The
    Doom Generation

1997
- ★ Heather Matarazzo/
    Welcome to the
    Dollhouse
  Jena Malone/Bastard out
    of Carolina
  Brendan Sexton, III/
    Welcome to the
    Dollhouse

Arie Verveen/Caught
Jeffrey Wright/Basquiat

FILM—FOREIGN LANGUAGE

1986
- ★ Kiss of the Spider Woman

1987
- ★ A Room with a View

1988
- ★ My Life As a Dog

1989
- ★ Wings of Desire

1990
- ★ My Left Foot

1992
- ★ An Angel at My Table

1993
- ★ The Crying Game

1994
- ★ The Piano
  Like Water for Chocolate
  Naked
  Orlando
  The Story of Qui Ju

1995
- ★ Trois Couleurs: Rouge
  32 Short Films about
    Glenn Gould
  Ladybird, Ladybird
  The Blue Kite
  The Boys of St. Vincent

1996
- ★ Before the Rain
  Exotica
  I Am Cuba
  The City of Lost Children
  Through the Olive Trees

1997
  Breaking the Waves
  Chungking Express
  Lamerica
  Secrets and Lies
  Trainspotting

LOS ANGELES FILM CRITICS ASSOCIATION AWARDS

ACTOR

1976
- ★ Robert De Niro/Taxi
    Driver

1977
- ★ Richard Dreyfuss/The
    Goodbye Girl

1978
- ★ Jon Voight/Coming Home

1979
- ★ Dustin Hoffman/Kramer
    vs. Kramer

1980
- ★ Robert De Niro/Raging
    Bull

1981
- ★ Burt Lancaster/Atlantic
    City

1982
- ★ Ben Kingsley/Gandhi

1983
- ★ Robert Duvall/Tender
    Mercies

1984
- ★ Albert Finney/Under the
    Volcano
  F. Murray Abraham/
    Amadeus

1985
- ★ William Hurt/Kiss of the
    Spider Woman

1986
- ★ Bob Hoskins/Mona Lisa

1987
- ★ Steve Martin/Roxanne
- ★ Jack Nicholson/Ironweed
- ★ Jack Nicholson/The
    Witches of Eastwick

1988
- ★ Tom Hanks/Big
- ★ Tom Hanks/Punchline

1989
- ★ Daniel Day-Lewis/My Left
    Foot

1990
- ★ Jeremy Irons/Reversal of
    Fortune

1991
- ★ Nick Nolte/The Prince of
    Tides

1992
- ★ Clint Eastwood/
    Unforgiven

1993
- ★ Anthony Hopkins/
    Shadowlands
- ★ Anthony Hopkins/The
    Remains of the Day

1994
- ★ John Travolta/Pulp
    Fiction

1995
- ★ Nicolas Cage/Leaving Las
    Vegas

1996
- ★ Geoffrey Rush/Shine

ACTOR—SUPPORTING

1977
- ★ Jason Robards, Jr./Julia

1978
- ★ Robert Morley/Who Is
    Killing the Great Chefs
    of Europe?

1979
- ★ Melvyn Douglas/Being
    There
- ★ Melvyn Douglas/The
    Seduction of Joe Tynan

1980
- ★ Timothy Hutton/Ordinary
    People

1981
- ★ John Gielgud/Arthur

1982
- ★ John Lithgow/The World
    According to Garp

1983
- ★ Jack Nicholson/Terms of
    Endearment

1984
- ★ Adolph Caesar/A
    Soldier's Story

1985
- ★ John Gielgud/Plenty
- ★ John Gielgud/The
    Shooting Party

1986
- ★ Dennis Hopper/Blue
    Velvet
- ★ Dennis Hopper/Hoosiers

1987
- ★ Morgan Freeman/Street
    Smart

1988
- ★ Alec Guinness/Little
    Dorrit, Film 1: Nobody's
    Fault
- ★ Alec Guinness/Little
    Dorrit, Film 2: Little
    Dorrit's Story

1989
- ★ Danny Aiello/Do the Right
    Thing

1990
- ★ Joe Pesci/Goodfellas

1991
- ★ Michael Lerner/Barton
    Fink

1992
- ★ Gene Hackman/
    Unforgiven

1993
- ★ Tommy Lee Jones/The
    Fugitive

1994
- ★ Martin Landau/Ed Wood

1995
- ★ Don Cheadle/Devil in a
    Blue Dress

1996
- ★ Edward Norton/Everyone
    Says I Love You
- ★ Edward Norton/Primal
    Fear
- ★ Edward Norton/The
    People vs. Larry Flynt

ACTRESS

1976
- ★ Liv Ullmann/Face to Face

1978
★ Jane Fonda/*Coming Home*

1979
★ Sally Field/*Norma Rae*

1980
★ Sissy Spacek/*Coal Miner's Daughter*

1981
★ Meryl Streep/*The French Lieutenant's Woman*

1982
★ Meryl Streep/*Sophie's Choice*

1983
★ Shirley MacLaine/*Terms of Endearment*

1984
★ Kathleen Turner/*Crimes of Passion*
★ Kathleen Turner/*Romancing the Stone*

1985
★ Meryl Streep/*Out of Africa*

1986
★ Sandrine Bonnaire/*Vagabond*

1987
★ Holly Hunter/*Broadcast News*
★ Sally Kirkland/*Anna*

1988
★ Christine Lahti/*Running on Empty*

1989
★ Andie MacDowell/*sex, lies and videotape*
★ Michelle Pfeiffer/*The Fabulous Baker Boys*

1990
★ Anjelica Huston/*The Grifters*
★ Anjelica Huston/*The Witches*

1991
★ Mercedes Ruehl/*The Fisher King*

1992
★ Emma Thompson/*Howard's End*

1993
★ Holly Hunter/*The Piano*

1994
★ Jessica Lange/*Blue Sky*

1995
★ Elisabeth Shue/*Leaving Las Vegas*

1996
★ Brenda Blethyn/*Secrets and Lies*

ACTRESS— SUPPORTING

1977
★ Vanessa Redgrave/*Julia*

1978
★ Maureen Stapleton/*Interiors*
★ Mona Washbourne/*Stevie*

1979
★ Meryl Streep/*Kramer vs. Kramer*
★ Meryl Streep/*Manhattan*
★ Meryl Streep/*The Seduction of Joe Tynan*

1980
★ Mary Steenburgen/*Melvin and Howard*

1981
★ Maureen Stapleton/*Reds*

1982
★ Glenn Close/*The World According to Garp*

1983
★ Linda Hunt/*The Year of Living Dangerously*

1984
★ Peggy Ashcroft/*A Passage to India*

1985
★ Anjelica Huston/*Prizzi's Honor*

1986
★ Cathy Tyson/*Mona Lisa*
★ Dianne Wiest/*Hannah and Her Sisters*

1987
★ Olympia Dukakis/*Moonstruck*

1988
★ Genevieve Bujold/*Dead Ringers*
★ Genevieve Bujold/*The Moderns*

1989
★ Brenda Fricker/*My Left Foot*

1990
★ Lorraine Bracco/*Goodfellas*

1991
★ Jane Horrocks/*Life Is Sweet*

1992
★ Judy Davis/*Husbands and Wives*

1993
★ Anna Paquin/*The Piano*
★ Rosie Perez/*Fearless*

1994
★ Dianne Wiest/*Bullets Over Broadway*

1995
★ Joan Allen/*Nixon*

1996
★ Barbara Hershey/*Portrait of a Lady*

CINEMATOGRAPHY

1975
★ Barry Lyndon

1976
★ Bound for Glory

1977
★ Julia

1978
★ Days of Heaven

1979
★ The Black Stallion

1980
★ Tess

1981
★ Reds

1982
★ Blade Runner

1983
★ Fanny and Alexander

1984
★ The Killing Fields

1985
★ Out of Africa

1986
★ The Mission

1987
★ The Last Emperor

1988
★ Wings of Desire

1989
★ The Fabulous Baker Boys

1990
★ Goodfellas

1991
★ Barton Fink

1992
★ Raise the Red Lantern

1993
★ Schindler's List
★ The Piano

1994
★ Ed Wood

1996
★ Michael Collins
★ The English Patient

DIRECTOR

1976
★ Sidney Lumet/*Network*

1977
★ Herbert Ross/*The Turning Point*

1978
★ Michael Cimino/*The Deer Hunter*

1979
★ Robert Benton/*Kramer vs. Kramer*

1980
★ Roman Polanski/*Tess*

1981
★ Warren Beatty/*Reds*

1982
★ Steven Spielberg/*E.T.: The Extra-Terrestrial*

1983
★ James L. Brooks/*Terms of Endearment*

1984
★ Milos Forman/*Amadeus*
Milos Forman/*Amadeus*

1985
★ Terry Gilliam/*Brazil*

1986
★ David Lynch/*Blue Velvet*

1987
★ John Boorman/*Hope and Glory*

1988
★ David Cronenberg/*Dead Ringers*

1989
★ Spike Lee/*Do the Right Thing*

1990
★ Martin Scorsese/*Goodfellas*

1991
★ Barry Levinson/*Bugsy*

1992
★ Clint Eastwood/*Unforgiven*

1993
★ Jane Campion/*The Piano*

1994
★ Quentin Tarantino/*Pulp Fiction*

1995
★ Mike Figgis/*Leaving Las Vegas*

1996
★ Mike Leigh/*Secrets and Lies*

FILM

1976
★ Network
★ Rocky

1977
★ Star Wars

1978
★ Coming Home

1979
★ Kramer vs. Kramer

1980
★ Raging Bull

1981
★ Atlantic City

1982
★ E.T.: The Extra-Terrestrial

1983
★ Terms of Endearment

1984
★ Amadeus

1985
★ Brazil

1986
★ Hannah and Her Sisters

1987
★ Hope and Glory

1988
★ Little Dorrit, Film 1: Nobody's Fault
★ Little Dorrit, Film 2: Little Dorrit's Story

1989
★ Do the Right Thing

1990
★ Goodfellas

1991
★ Bugsy

1992
★ Unforgiven

1993
★ Schindler's List

1994
★ Pulp Fiction

1995
★ Leaving Las Vegas

1996
★ Secrets and Lies

FEATURE DOCUMENTARY

1994
★ Hoop Dreams

SCORE

1983
★ Koyaanisqatsi

1992
★ Damage

1993
★ Olivier, Olivier
★ The Secret Garden
★ Trois Couleurs: Bleu

1994
★ Ed Wood

SCREENPLAY

1977
★ Annie Hall

Clueless
Dangerous Minds

1997

★ Scream
Independence Day
Jerry Maguire
The Rock
William Shakespeare's
Romeo and Juliet

KISS

1992

★ Macaulay Culkin/Anna
Chlumsky/My Girl

1993

★ Christian Slater/Marisa
Tomei/Untamed Heart

1994

★ Demi Moore/Woody
Harrelson/Indecent
Proposal
Christian Slater/Patricia
Arquette/True
Romance
Dana Carvey/Kim
Basinger/Wayne's
World 2
Ethan Hawke/Winona
Ryder/Reality Bites
Jason James Richter/
Willy/Free Willy

1995

★ Jim Carrey/Lauren Holly/
Dumb & Dumber
Arnold Schwarzenegger/
Jamie Lee Curtis/True
Lies
Ethan Hawke/Julie
Delpy/Before Sunrise
Keanu Reeves/Sandra
Bullock/Speed
Woody Harrelson/
Juliette Lewis/Natural
Born Killers

1996

★ Natasha Henstridge/
Anthony Guidera/
Species
Antonio Banderas/Salma
Hayek/Desperado
Jim Carrey/Sophie
Okonedo/Ace Ventura:
When Nature Calls
Keanu Reeves/Aitana
Sanchez-Gijon/A Walk
in the Clouds
Winona Ryder/Dermot
Mulroney/How to Make
an American Quilt

1997

★ Vivica A. Fox/Will Smith/
Independence Day
Christopher Daniel
Barnes/Christine
Taylor/A Very Brady
Sequel
Jennifer Tilly/Gina
Gershon/Bound
John Travolta/Kyra
Sedgwick/
Phenomenon
Leonardo DiCaprio/
Claire Danes/William
Shakespeare's Romeo
and Juliet

MOST DESIRABLE FEMALE

1992

★ Linda Hamilton/
Terminator 2: Judgment
Day

1993

★ Sharon Stone/Basic
Instinct

1994

★ Janet Jackson/Poetic
Justice
Kim Basinger/The
Getaway
Demi Moore/Indecent
Proposal
Sharon Stone/Sliver

1995

★ Sandra Bullock/Speed
Halle Berry/The
Flintstones
Cameron Diaz/The Mask
Demi Moore/Disclosure
Sharon Stone/The
Specialist

1996

★ Alicia Silverstone/
Clueless
Sandra Bullock/While
You Were Sleeping
Nicole Kidman/To Die
For
Michelle Pfeiffer/
Dangerous Minds

MOST DESIRABLE MALE

1992

★ Keanu Reeves/Point
Break

1993

★ Christian Slater/Untamed
Heart

1994

★ William Baldwin/Sliver
Tom Cruise/The Firm
Val Kilmer/Tombstone
Jean-Claude Van
Damme/Hard Target
Denzel Washington/The
Pelican Brief

1995

★ Brad Pitt/Interview with
the Vampire
Tom Cruise/Interview with
the Vampire
Andy Garcia/When a Man
Loves a Woman
Keanu Reeves/Speed
Christian Slater/Interview
with the Vampire

1996

★ Brad Pitt/Seven
Antonio Banderas/
Desperado
Mel Gibson/Braveheart
Val Kilmer/Batman
Forever
Keanu Reeves/A Walk in
the Clouds

NEW FILMMAKER

1992

★ John Singleton/Boyz N
the Hood

1993

★ Carl Franklin/One False
Move

1994

★ Steven Zaillian/Searching
for Bobby Fischer

1995

★ Steve James/Hoop
Dreams

1996

★ Wes Anderson/Bottle
Rocket

1997

★ Doug Liman/Swingers

ON-SCREEN DUO

1992

★ Mike Myers/Dana
Carvey/Wayne's World

1993

★ Mel Gibson/Danny
Glover/Lethal Weapon
3

1994

★ Harrison Ford/Tommy
Lee Jones/The Fugitive
Johnny Depp/Mary
Stuart Masterson/
Benny & Joon
Mike Myers/Dana
Carvey/Wayne's World
2
Tom Hanks/Denzel
Washington/
Philadelphia
Tom Hanks/Meg Ryan/
Sleepless in Seattle

1995

★ Keanu Reeves/Sandra
Bullock/Speed
Jim Carrey/Jeff Daniels/
Dumb & Dumber
John Travolta/Samuel L.
Jackson/Pulp Fiction
Tom Cruise/Brad Pitt/
Interview with the
Vampire
Woody Harrelson/
Juliette Lewis/Natural
Born Killers

1996

★ Chris Farley/David
Spade/Tommy Boy
Brad Pitt/Morgan
Freeman/Seven
Chris Tucker/Ice Cube/
Friday
Martin Lawrence/Will
Smith/Bad Boys
Tom Hanks/Tim Allen/
Toy Story

1997

★ Sean Connery/Nicolas
Cage/The Rock

Beavis/Butt-head/Beavis
and Butt-Head Do
America
Leonardo DiCaprio/Clare
Danes/William
Shakespeare's Romeo
and Juliet
Peter Stormare/Steve
Buscemi/Fargo
Robin Williams/Nathan
Lane/The Birdcage

SONG

1992

★ "(Everything I Do) I Do
for You"/Robin Hood:
Prince of Thieves

1993

★ "I Will Always Love
You"/The Bodyguard

1994

★ "Will You Be There"/Free
Willy
"All for Love"/The Three
Musketeers
"I Can't Help Falling in
Love"/Sliver
"I'm Gonna Be 500
Miles"/Benny & Joon
"Streets of
Philadelphia"/
Philadelphia
"When I Fall in Love"/
Sleepless in Seattle

1995

★ "Big Empty"/The Crow
"Can You Feel the Love
Tonight"/The Lion King
"Girl, You'll Be A
Woman Soon"/Pulp
Fiction
"I'll Remember"/With
Honors
"Regulate"/Above the
Rim

1996

★ "Sittin' Up in My Room"/
Waiting to Exhale
"Exhale (Shoop
Shoop)"/Waiting to
Exhale
"Gangsta's Paradise"/
Dangerous Minds
"Hold Me, Thrill Me, Kiss
Me, Kill Me"/Batman
Forever
"I Believe I Can Fly"/
Space Jam
"Kiss from a Rose"/
Batman Forever

1997

★ "Machinehead"/Fear
"#1 Crush"/William
Shakespeare's Romeo
and Juliet
"Change the World"/
Phenomenon
"Don't Cry for Me
Argentina"/Evita

VILLAIN

1992

★ Rebecca DeMornay/The
Hand that Rocks the
Cradle

1993

★ Jennifer Jason Leigh/
Single White Female

1994

★ Alicia Silverstone/The
Crush
T-Rex/Jurassic Park
Macaulay Culkin/The
Good Son
John Malkovich/In the
Line of Fire
Wesley Snipes/
Demolition Man

1995

★ Dennis Hopper/Speed
Tom Cruise/Interview with
the Vampire
Jeremy Irons/The Lion
King
Tommy Lee Jones/Blown
Away
Demi Moore/Disclosure

1996

★ Kevin Spacey/Seven
Jim Carrey/Batman
Forever
Tommy Lee Jones/
Batman Forever
Joe Pesci/Casino
John Travolta/Broken
Arrow

1997

★ Jim Carrey/The Cable
Guy
Robert De Niro/The Fan
Edward Norton/Primal
Fear
Kiefer Sutherland/A Time
to Kill
Mark Wahlberg/Fear

BEST DANCE SEQUENCE

1995

★ John Travolta/Uma
Thurman/Pulp Fiction
Arnold Schwarzenegger/
Tia Carrere/True Lies
Jim Carrey/Cameron
Diaz/The Mask
The Brady Kids/The
Brady Bunch Movie

BEST MALE PERFORMANCE

1992

★ Arnold Schwarzenegger/
Terminator 2: Judgment
Day

1993

★ Denzel Washington/
Malcolm X

1994

★ Tom Hanks/Philadelphia
Tom Cruise/The Firm
Harrison Ford/The
Fugitive
Val Kilmer/Tombstone
Robin Williams/Mrs.
Doubtfire

1995

★ Brad Pitt/Interview with
the Vampire

DIRECTOR ⸝cont.

1963
★ Tony Richardson/*Tom Jones*

1965
★ John Schlesinger/*Darling*

1966
★ Fred Zinnemann/*A Man for All Seasons*

1967
★ Richard Brooks/*In Cold Blood*

1968
★ Franco Zeffirelli/*Romeo and Juliet*

1969
★ Alfred Hitchcock/*Topaz*

1970
★ Francois Truffaut/*The Wild Child*

1971
★ Ken Russell/*The Devils*

1972
★ Bob Fosse/*Cabaret*

1973
★ Ingmar Bergman/*Cries and Whispers*

1974
★ Francis Ford Coppola/*The Conversation*

1975
★ Robert Altman/*Nashville*
★ Stanley Kubrick/*Barry Lyndon*

1976
★ Alan J. Pakula/*All the President's Men*

1977
★ Luis Bunuel/*That Obscure Object of Desire*

1978
★ Ingmar Bergman/*Autumn Sonata*

1979
★ John Schlesinger/*Yanks*

1980
★ Robert Redford/*Ordinary People*

1981
★ Warren Beatty/*Reds*

1982
★ Sidney Lumet/*The Verdict*

1983
★ James L. Brooks/*Terms of Endearment*

1984
★ David Lean/*A Passage to India*

1985
★ Akira Kurosawa/*Ran*

1986
★ Woody Allen/*Hannah and Her Sisters*

1987
★ Steven Spielberg/*Empire of the Sun*

1988
★ Alan Parker/*Mississippi Burning*

1989
★ Kenneth Branagh/*Henry V*

1990
★ Kevin Costner/*Dances with Wolves*

1991
★ Jonathan Demme/*The Silence of the Lambs*

1992
★ James Ivory/*Howard's End*

1993
★ Martin Scorsese/*The Age of Innocence*

1994
★ Quentin Tarantino/*Pulp Fiction*

1995
★ Ang Lee/*Sense and Sensibility*

1996
★ Joel Coen/*Fargo*

FILM

1991
★ *The Silence of the Lambs*

1992
★ *Howard's End*

1993
★ *Schindler's List*

1994
★ *Forrest Gump*
★ *Pulp Fiction*

1995
★ *Sense and Sensibility*

1996
★ *Shine*

FEATURE DOCUMENTARY

1991
★ *Hearts of Darkness: A Filmmaker's Apocalypse*

1992
★ *Brother's Keeper*

1993
★ *The War Room*

1994
★ *Hoop Dreams*

FILM—FOREIGN LANGUAGE

1991
★ *Europa, Europa*

1992
★ *Indochine*

1993
★ *Farewell My Concubine*

1994
★ *Eat Drink Man Woman*

NATIONAL SOCIETY OF FILM CRITICS AWARDS

ACTOR

1966
★ Michael Caine/*Alfie*

1967
★ Rod Steiger/*In the Heat of the Night*

1968
★ Per Oscarsson/*Hunger*

1969
★ Jon Voight/*Midnight Cowboy*

1970
★ George C. Scott/*Patton*

1971
★ Peter Finch/*Sunday, Bloody Sunday*

1972
★ Al Pacino/*The Godfather*

1973
★ Marlon Brando/*Last Tango in Paris*

1974
★ Jack Nicholson/*Chinatown*
★ Jack Nicholson/*The Last Detail*

1975
★ Jack Nicholson/*One Flew Over the Cuckoo's Nest*

1976
★ Robert De Niro/*Taxi Driver*

1977
★ Art Carney/*The Late Show*

1978
★ Gary Busey/*The Buddy Holly Story*

1979
★ Dustin Hoffman/*Kramer vs. Kramer*

1980
★ Peter O'Toole/*The Stunt Man*

1981
★ Burt Lancaster/*Atlantic City*

1982
★ Dustin Hoffman/*Tootsie*

1983
★ Gerard Depardieu/*The Return of Martin Guerre*

1984
★ Steve Martin/*All of Me*

1985
★ Jack Nicholson/*Prizzi's Honor*

1986
★ Bob Hoskins/*Mona Lisa*

1987
★ Steve Martin/*Roxanne*

1988
★ Michael Keaton/*Beetlejuice*
★ Michael Keaton/*Clean and Sober*

1989
★ Daniel Day-Lewis/*My Left Foot*

1990
★ Robert De Niro/*Awakenings*
★ Jeremy Irons/*Reversal of Fortune*

1991
★ River Phoenix/*My Own Private Idaho*

1992
★ Stephen Rea/*The Crying Game*

1993
★ David Thewlis/*Naked*

1994
★ Paul Newman/*Nobody's Fool*

1995
★ Nicolas Cage/*Leaving Las Vegas*

1996
★ Eddie Murphy/*The Nutty Professor*

ACTOR—SUPPORTING

1967
★ Gene Hackman/*Bonnie & Clyde*

1968
★ Seymour Cassel/*Faces*

1969
★ Jack Nicholson/*Easy Rider*

1970
★ Chief Dan George/*Little Big Man*

1972
★ Eddie Albert/*The Heartbreak Kid*
★ Joel Grey/*Cabaret*

1973
★ Robert De Niro/*Mean Streets*

1975
★ Henry Gibson/*Nashville*

1976
★ Jason Robards, Jr./*All the President's Men*

1977
★ Edward Fox/*A Bridge Too Far*

1978
★ Richard Farnsworth/*Comes a Horseman*

1979
★ Frederic Forrest/*Apocalypse Now*
★ Frederic Forrest/*The Rose*

1980
★ Joe Pesci/*Raging Bull*

1981
★ Robert Preston/*S.O.B.*

1982
★ Mickey Rourke/*Diner*

1983
★ Jack Nicholson/*Terms of Endearment*

1984
★ John Malkovich/*Places in the Heart*

1985
★ John Gielgud/*Plenty*
★ John Gielgud/*The Shooting Party*

1986
★ Dennis Hopper/*Blue Velvet*

1987
★ Morgan Freeman/*Street Smart*

1988
★ Dean Stockwell/*Married to the Mob*

1989
★ Beau Bridges/*The Fabulous Baker Boys*

1990
★ Bruce Davison/*Longtime Companion*

1991
★ Harvey Keitel/*Mortal Thoughts*
★ Harvey Keitel/*Thelma & Louise*

1992
★ Gene Hackman/*Unforgiven*

1993
★ Ralph Fiennes/*Schindler's List*

1994
★ Martin Landau/*Ed Wood*

1995
★ Don Cheadle/*Devil in a Blue Dress*

1996
★ Martin Donovan/*Portrait of a Lady*
★ Tony Shalhoub/*Big Night*

ACTRESS

1967
★ Bibi Andersson/*Persona*

1968
★ Liv Ullmann/*The Shame*

1969
★ Vanessa Redgrave/*Isadora*

1970
★ Glenda Jackson/*Women in Love*

1971
★ Jane Fonda/*Klute*

1972
★ Cicely Tyson/*Sounder*

1973
★ Liv Ullmann/*The New Land*

1974
★ Liv Ullmann/*Scenes from a Marriage*

1975
★ Isabelle Adjani/*Story of Adele H.*

1976
★ Sissy Spacek/*Carrie*

1977
★ Diane Keaton/*Annie Hall*

1978
★ Ingrid Bergman/*Autumn Sonata*

1979
★ Sally Field/*Norma Rae*

1980
★ Sissy Spacek/*Coal Miner's Daughter*

1981
★ Marilia Pera/*Pixote*

1982
★ Meryl Streep/*Sophie's Choice*

1983
★ Debra Winger/*Terms of Endearment*

1984
★ Vanessa Redgrave/*The Bostonians*

1985
★ Vanessa Redgrave/*Wetherby*

1986
★ Chloe Webb/*Sid & Nancy*

1987
★ Emily Lloyd/*Wish You Were Here*

1988
★ Judy Davis/*High Tide*

1989
★ Michelle Pfeiffer/*The Fabulous Baker Boys*

1990
★ Anjelica Huston/*The Grifters*
★ Anjelica Huston/*The Witches*

1991
★ Alison Steadman/*Life Is Sweet*

1992
★ Emma Thompson/*Howard's End*

1993
★ Holly Hunter/*The Piano*

1994
★ Jennifer Jason Leigh/*Mrs. Parker and the Vicious Circle*

1995
★ Elisabeth Shue/*Leaving Las Vegas*

1996
★ Emily Watson/*Breaking the Waves*

ACTRESS— SUPPORTING

1969
★ Sian Phillips/*Goodbye, Mr. Chips*

1970
★ Lois Smith/*Five Easy Pieces*

1971
★ Ellen Burstyn/*The Last Picture Show*

1972
★ Jeannie Berlin/*The Heartbreak Kid*

1973
★ Valentina Cortese/*Day for Night*

1974
★ Bibi Andersson/*Scenes from a Marriage*

1975
★ Lily Tomlin/*Nashville*

1976
★ Jodie Foster/*Taxi Driver*

1977
★ Ann Wedgeworth/*Citizens Band*

1978
★ Meryl Streep/*The Deer Hunter*

1979
★ Meryl Streep/*Kramer vs. Kramer*
★ Meryl Streep/*Manhattan*
★ Meryl Streep/*The Seduction of Joe Tynan*

1980
★ Mary Steenburgen/*Melvin and Howard*

1981
★ Maureen Stapleton/*Reds*

1982
★ Jessica Lange/*Tootsie*

1983
★ Sandra Bernhard/*King of Comedy*

1984
★ Melanie Griffith/*Body Double*

1985
★ Anjelica Huston/*Prizzi's Honor*

1986
★ Dianne Wiest/*Hannah and Her Sisters*

1987
★ Kathy Baker/*Street Smart*

1988
★ Mercedes Ruehl/*Married to the Mob*

1989
★ Anjelica Huston/*Enemies, a Love Story*

1990
★ Annette Bening/*The Grifters*

1991
★ Jane Horrocks/*Life Is Sweet*

1992
★ Judy Davis/*Husbands and Wives*

1993
★ Madeleine Stowe/*Short Cuts*

1994
★ Dianne Wiest/*Bullets Over Broadway*

1995
★ Joan Allen/*Nixon*

1996
★ Barbara Hershey/*Portrait of a Lady*

CINEMATOGRAPHY

1967
★ In the Heat of the Night

1968
★ Bullitt

1969
★ The Wild Bunch

1970
★ My Night at Maud's
★ The Wild Child

1971
★ Vittorio Storaro/*The Conformist*

1972
★ Cries and Whispers

1973
★ The Long Goodbye

1974
★ The Parallax View
The Godfather, Part 2

1975
★ Barry Lyndon

1976
★ Bound for Glory

1977
★ Aguirre, the Wrath of God

1978
★ Days of Heaven

1979
★ Being There
★ The Black Stallion

1980
★ Raging Bull

1981
★ Pennies From Heaven

1982
★ Diva

1983
★ Never Cry Wolf

1984
★ Comfort and Joy
★ The Killing Fields

1985
★ Ran

1986
★ Blue Velvet

1987
★ Hope and Glory

1988
★ Wings of Desire

1989
★ The Fabulous Baker Boys

1990
★ Where the Heart Is

1991
★ Barton Fink

1992
★ Raise the Red Lantern

1993
★ Schindler's List

1994
★ Ed Wood

1995
★ Devil in a Blue Dress

1996
★ Breaking the Waves
★ Dead Man

DIRECTOR

1966
★ Michelangelo Antonioni/*Blow-Up*

1967
★ Ingmar Bergman/*Persona*

1968
★ Ingmar Bergman/*Hour of the Wolf*
★ Ingmar Bergman/*The Shame*

1969
★ Francois Truffaut/*Stolen Kisses*

1970
★ Ingmar Bergman/*The Passion of Anna*

1971
★ Bernardo Bertolucci/*The Conformist*

1972
★ Luis Bunuel/*The Discreet Charm of the Bourgeoisie*

1973
★ Francois Truffaut/*Day for Night*

1974
★ Francis Ford Coppola/*The Conversation*
★ Francis Ford Coppola/*The Godfather, Part 2*

1975
★ Robert Altman/*Nashville*

1976
★ Martin Scorsese/*Taxi Driver*

1977
★ Luis Bunuel/*That Obscure Object of Desire*

1978
★ Terence Malick/*Days of Heaven*

1979
★ Woody Allen/*Manhattan*
★ Robert Benton/*Kramer vs. Kramer*

1980
★ Martin Scorsese/*Raging Bull*

1981
★ Louis Malle/*Atlantic City*

DIRECTOR ▸cont.

1982
★ Steven Spielberg/*E.T.: The Extra-Terrestrial*

1983
★ Paolo Taviani/*The Night of the Shooting Stars*
★ Vittorio Taviani/*The Night of the Shooting Stars*

1984
★ Robert Bresson/*L'Argent*

1985
★ John Huston/*Prizzi's Honor*

1986
★ David Lynch/*Blue Velvet*

1987
★ John Boorman/*Hope and Glory*

1988
★ Philip Kaufman/*The Unbearable Lightness of Being*

1989
★ Gus Van Sant/*Drugstore Cowboy*

1990
★ Martin Scorsese/ *Goodfellas*

1991
★ David Cronenberg/*Naked Lunch*

1992
★ Clint Eastwood/ *Unforgiven*

1993
★ Steven Spielberg/ *Schindler's List*

1994
★ Quentin Tarantino/*Pulp Fiction*

1995
★ Mike Figgis/*Leaving Las Vegas*

1996
★ Lars von Trier/*Breaking the Waves*

FILM

1966
★ *Blow-Up*

1967
★ *Persona*

1968
★ *The Shame*

1969
★ *Z*

1970
★ *M*A*S*H*

1971
★ *Claire's Knee*

1972
★ *The Discreet Charm of the Bourgeoisie*

1973
★ *Day for Night*

1974
★ *Scenes from a Marriage*

1975
★ *Nashville*

1976
★ *All the President's Men*

1977
★ *Annie Hall*

1978
★ *Days of Heaven*
★ *Get Out Your Handkerchiefs*

1979
★ *Breaking Away*

1980
★ *Melvin and Howard*

1981
★ *Atlantic City*

1982
★ *Tootsie*

1983
★ *The Night of the Shooting Stars*

1984
★ *Stranger than Paradise*

1985
★ *Ran*

1986
★ *Blue Velvet*

1987
★ *Hope and Glory*
★ *The Dead*

1988
★ *The Unbearable Lightness of Being*

1989
★ *Drugstore Cowboy*

1990
★ *Goodfellas*

1991
★ *Life Is Sweet*

1992
★ *Unforgiven*

1993
★ *Schindler's List*

1994
★ *Pulp Fiction*

1995
★ *Babe*

1996
★ *Breaking the Waves*

FEATURE DOCUMENTARY

1991
★ *Paris Is Burning*

1993
★ *Visions of Light: The Art of Cinematography*

1994
★ *Hoop Dreams*

1995
★ *Crumb*

SCREENPLAY

1967
★ *Bonnie & Clyde*

1968
★ *Faces*

1969
★ *Bob & Carol & Ted & Alice*

1970
★ *My Night at Maud's*

1971
★ *Sunday, Bloody Sunday*

1972
★ *Cries and Whispers*

1973
★ *American Graffiti*

1974
★ *Scenes from a Marriage*

1975
★ *Shampoo*

1976
★ *Jonah Who Will Be 25 in the Year 2000*

1977
★ *Annie Hall*

1978
★ *An Unmarried Woman*

1979
★ *Breaking Away*

1980
★ *Melvin and Howard*

1981
★ *Atlantic City*

1982
★ *Tootsie*

1983
★ *Local Hero*

1984
★ *Splash*

1985
★ *Lost in America*

1986
★ *My Beautiful Laundrette*

1987
★ *Hope and Glory*

1988
★ *Bull Durham*

1989
★ *Drugstore Cowboy*

1990
★ *To Sleep with Anger*

1991
★ *Naked Lunch*

1992
★ *Unforgiven*

1993
★ *The Piano*

1994
★ *Pulp Fiction*

1995
★ *Clueless*

1996
★ *Mother*

FILM—FOREIGN LANGUAGE

1990
★ *Ariel*

1991
★ *The Double Life of Veronique*

1992
★ *Raise the Red Lantern*

1993
★ *The Story of Qui Ju*

1994
★ *Trois Couleurs: Rouge*

1995
★ *Wild Reeds*

1996
★ *La Ceremonie*

NEW YORK FILM CRITICS AWARDS

ACTOR

1935
★ Charles Laughton/*Mutiny on the Bounty*
★ Charles Laughton/ *Ruggles of Red Gap*

1936
★ Walter Huston/*Dodsworth*

1937
★ Paul Muni/*The Life of Emile Zola*

1938
★ James Cagney/*Angels with Dirty Faces*

1939
★ James Stewart/*Mr. Smith Goes to Washington*

1940
★ Charlie Chaplin/*The Great Dictator*

1941
★ Gary Cooper/*Sergeant York*

1942
★ James Cagney/*Yankee Doodle Dandy*

1943
★ Paul Lukas/*Watch on the Rhine*

1944
★ Barry Fitzgerald/*Going My Way*

1945
★ Ray Milland/*The Lost Weekend*

1946
★ Laurence Olivier/*Henry V*

1947
★ William Powell/*Life with Father*
★ William Powell/*The Senator was Indiscreet*

1948
★ Laurence Olivier/*Hamlet*

1949
★ Broderick Crawford/*All the King's Men*

1950
  Gregory Peck/*Twelve O'Clock High*

1953
★ Burt Lancaster/*From Here to Eternity*

1954
★ Marlon Brando/*On the Waterfront*

1955
★ Ernest Borgnine/*Marty*

1956
★ Kirk Douglas/*Lust for Life*

1957
★ Alec Guinness/*The Bridge on the River Kwai*

1958
★ David Niven/*Separate Tables*

1959
★ James Stewart/*Anatomy of a Murder*

1960
★ Burt Lancaster/*Elmer Gantry*

1961
★ Maximilian Schell/ *Judgment at Nuremberg*

1963
★ Albert Finney/*Tom Jones*

ACTRESS ,cont.

1978
★ Ingrid Bergman/*Autumn Sonata*

1979
★ Sally Field/*Norma Rae*

1980
★ Sissy Spacek/*Coal Miner's Daughter*

1982
★ Meryl Streep/*Sophie's Choice*

1983
★ Shirley MacLaine/*Terms of Endearment*

1984
★ Peggy Ashcroft/*A Passage to India*

1985
★ Norma Aleandro/*The Official Story*

1986
★ Sissy Spacek/*Crimes of the Heart*

1987
★ Holly Hunter/*Broadcast News*

1988
★ Meryl Streep/*A Cry in the Dark*

1989
★ Michelle Pfeiffer/*The Fabulous Baker Boys*

1990
★ Joanne Woodward/*Mr. & Mrs. Bridge*

1991
★ Jodie Foster/*The Silence of the Lambs*

1992
★ Emma Thompson/*Howard's End*

1993
★ Holly Hunter/*The Piano*

1994
★ Linda Fiorentino/*The Last Seduction*

1995
★ Jennifer Jason Leigh/*Georgia*

1996
★ Emily Watson/*Breaking the Waves*

ACTRESS— SUPPORTING

1969
★ Dyan Cannon/*Bob & Carol & Ted & Alice*

1970
★ Karen Black/*Five Easy Pieces*

1971
★ Ellen Burstyn/*The Last Picture Show*

1972
★ Jeannie Berlin/*The Heartbreak Kid*

1973
★ Valentina Cortese/*Day for Night*

1974
★ Valerie Perrine/*Lenny*

1975
★ Lily Tomlin/*Nashville*

1976
★ Talia Shire/*Rocky*

1978
★ Mona Washbourne/*Stevie*

1979
★ Meryl Streep/*Kramer vs. Kramer*
★ Meryl Streep/*Manhattan*
★ Meryl Streep/*The Seduction of Joe Tynan*

1980
★ Mary Steenburgen/*Melvin and Howard*

1982
★ Jessica Lange/*Tootsie*

1983
★ Linda Hunt/*The Year of Living Dangerously*

1984
★ Christine Lahti/*Swing Shift*

1985
★ Anjelica Huston/*Prizzi's Honor*

1986
★ Dianne Wiest/*Hannah and Her Sisters*

1987
★ Vanessa Redgrave/*Prick Up Your Ears*

1988
★ Diane Venora/*Bird*

1989
★ Jennifer Jason Leigh/*Last Exit to Brooklyn*
★ Lena Olin/*Enemies, a Love Story*

1990
★ Jennifer Jason Leigh/*Miami Blues*

1991
★ Judy Davis/*Barton Fink*
★ Judy Davis/*Naked Lunch*

1992
★ Miranda Richardson/*The Crying Game*

1993
★ Gong Li/*Farewell My Concubine*

1994
★ Dianne Wiest/*Bullets Over Broadway*

1995
★ Mira Sorvino/*Mighty Aphrodite*

1996
★ Courtney Love/*The People vs. Larry Flynt*

CINEMATOGRAPHY

1980
★ *Tess*

1981
★ *Chariots of Fire*

1982
★ *Sophie's Choice*

1983
★ *Zelig*

1984
★ *The Killing Fields*

1985
★ *Out of Africa*

1986
★ *A Room with a View*

1987
★ *The Last Emperor*

1988
★ *Wings of Desire*

1989
★ *Do the Right Thing*

1990
★ *The Sheltering Sky*

1991
★ *Barton Fink*

1992
★ *The Player*

1993
★ *Schindler's List*

1994
★ *Ed Wood*

1996
★ *Breaking the Waves*
★ *Dead Man*

DIRECTOR

1935
★ John Ford/*The Informer*

1937
★ Gregory La Cava/*Stage Door*

1938
★ Alfred Hitchcock/*The Lady Vanishes*

1939
★ John Ford/*Stagecoach*

1940
★ John Ford/*The Grapes of Wrath*
★ John Ford/*The Long Voyage Home*

1941
★ John Ford/*How Green Was My Valley*

1942
★ John Farrow/*Wake Island*

1943
★ George Stevens/*The More the Merrier*

1944
★ Leo McCarey/*Going My Way*

1945
★ Billy Wilder/*The Lost Weekend*

1946
★ William Wyler/*The Best Years of Our Lives*

1947
★ Elia Kazan/*Gentleman's Agreement*

1948
★ John Huston/*Treasure of the Sierra Madre*

1949
★ Carol Reed/*The Fallen Idol*

1950
★ Joseph L. Mankiewicz/*All About Eve*

1951
★ Elia Kazan/*A Streetcar Named Desire*

1952
★ Fred Zinnemann/*High Noon*

1953
★ Fred Zinnemann/*From Here to Eternity*

1954
★ Elia Kazan/*On the Waterfront*

1955
★ David Lean/*Summertime*

1956
★ John Huston/*Moby Dick*

1957
★ David Lean/*The Bridge on the River Kwai*

1958
★ Stanley Kramer/*The Defiant Ones*

1959
★ Fred Zinnemann/*The Nun's Story*

1960
★ Billy Wilder/*The Apartment*

1961
★ Robert Rossen/*The Hustler*

1963
★ Tony Richardson/*Tom Jones*

1964
★ Stanley Kubrick/*Dr. Strangelove, or: How I Learned to Stop Worrying and Love the Bomb*

1965
★ John Schlesinger/*Darling*

1966
★ Fred Zinnemann/*A Man for All Seasons*

1967
★ Mike Nichols/*In the Heat of the Night*
★ Mike Nichols/*The Graduate*

1968
★ Paul Newman/*Rachel, Rachel*

1969
★ Constantin Costa-Gavras/*Z*

1970
★ Bob Rafelson/*Five Easy Pieces*

1971
★ Stanley Kubrick/*A Clockwork Orange*

1972
★ Ingmar Bergman/*Cries and Whispers*

1973
★ Francois Truffaut/*Day for Night*

1974
★ Federico Fellini/*Amarcord*

1975
★ Robert Altman/*Nashville*

1976
★ Alan J. Pakula/*All the President's Men*

1977
★ Woody Allen/*Annie Hall*

1978
★ Terence Malick/*Days of Heaven*

1979
★ Woody Allen/*Manhattan*

1980
★ Jonathan Demme/*Melvin and Howard*

1981
★ Sidney Lumet/*Prince of the City*

1982
★ Sydney Pollack/*Tootsie*

1983
★ Ingmar Bergman/*Fanny and Alexander*

1984
★ David Lean/*A Passage to India*

1985
★ John Huston/*Prizzi's Honor*

1986
★ Woody Allen/*Hannah and Her Sisters*

1987
★ James L. Brooks/*Broadcast News*

1988
★ Chris Menges/*A World Apart*

1989
★ Paul Mazursky/*Enemies, a Love Story*

1990
★ Martin Scorsese/*Goodfellas*
★ Whit Stillman/*Metropolitan*

1991
★ Jonathan Demme/*The Silence of the Lambs*

1992
★ Robert Altman/*The Player*

1993
★ Jane Campion/*The Piano*

1994
★ Quentin Tarantino/*Pulp Fiction*

1995
★ Ang Lee/*Sense and Sensibility*

1996
★ Lars von Trier/*Breaking the Waves*

FILM

1935
★ *The Informer*

1936
★ *Mr. Deeds Goes to Town*

1937
★ *The Life of Emile Zola*

1938
★ *The Citadel*

1939
★ *Wuthering Heights*

1940
★ *The Grapes of Wrath*

1941
★ *Citizen Kane*

1942
★ *In Which We Serve*

1943
★ *Watch on the Rhine*

1944
★ *Going My Way*

1945
★ *The Lost Weekend*

1946
★ *The Best Years of Our Lives*

1947
★ *Gentleman's Agreement*

1948
★ *Treasure of the Sierra Madre*

1949
★ *All the King's Men*

1950
★ *All About Eve*

1951
★ *A Streetcar Named Desire*

1952
★ *High Noon*

1953
★ *From Here to Eternity*

1954
★ *On the Waterfront*

1955
★ *Marty*

1956
★ *Around the World in 80 Days*

1957
★ *The Bridge on the River Kwai*

1958
★ *The Defiant Ones*

1959
★ *Ben-Hur*

1960
★ *The Apartment*

1961
★ *West Side Story*

1963
★ *Tom Jones*

1964
★ *My Fair Lady*

1965
★ *Darling*

1966
★ *A Man for All Seasons*

1967
★ *In the Heat of the Night*

1968
★ *The Lion in Winter*

1969
★ *Z*

1970
★ *Five Easy Pieces*

1971
★ *A Clockwork Orange*

1972
★ *Cries and Whispers*

1973
★ *Day for Night*

1974
★ *Amarcord*

1975
★ *Nashville*

1976
★ *All the President's Men*

1977
★ *Annie Hall*

1978
★ *The Deer Hunter*

1979
★ *Kramer vs. Kramer*

1980
★ *Ordinary People*

1981
★ *Reds*

1982
★ *Gandhi*

1983
★ *Terms of Endearment*

1984
★ *A Passage to India*

1985
★ *Prizzi's Honor*

1986
★ *Hannah and Her Sisters*

1987
★ *Broadcast News*

1988
★ *The Accidental Tourist*

1989
★ *My Left Foot*

1990
★ *Goodfellas*

1991
★ *The Silence of the Lambs*

1992
★ *The Player*

1993
★ *Schindler's List*

1994
★ *Quiz Show*

1995
★ *Leaving Las Vegas*

1996
★ *Fargo*

FEATURE DOCUMENTARY

1992
★ *Brother's Keeper*

1993
★ *Visions of Light: The Art of Cinematography*

1994
★ *Hoop Dreams*

SCREENPLAY

1956
★ *Around the World in 80 Days*

1958
★ *The Defiant Ones*

1959
★ *Anatomy of a Murder*

1960
★ *The Apartment*

1961
★ *Judgment at Nuremberg*

1963
★ *Hud*

1964
★ *The Servant*

1966
★ *A Man for All Seasons*

1967
★ *Bonnie & Clyde*

1968
★ *Pretty Poison*

1969
★ *Bob & Carol & Ted & Alice*

1970
★ *My Night at Maud's*

1971
★ *Sunday, Bloody Sunday*
★ *The Last Picture Show*

1972
★ *Cries and Whispers*

1973
★ *American Graffiti*

1974
★ *Scenes from a Marriage*

1975
★ *Story of Adele H.*

1976
★ *Network*

1977
★ *Annie Hall*

1978
★ *An Unmarried Woman*

1979
★ *Breaking Away*

1980
★ *Melvin and Howard*

1981
★ *Atlantic City*

1982
★ *Tootsie*

1983
★ *Local Hero*

1984
★ *Places in the Heart*

1985
★ *The Purple Rose of Cairo*

1986
★ *My Beautiful Laundrette*

1987
★ *Broadcast News*

1988
★ *Bull Durham*

1989
★ *Drugstore Cowboy*

1990
★ *Mr. & Mrs. Bridge*

1991
★ *Naked Lunch*

1992
★ *The Crying Game*

1993
★ *The Piano*

1994
★ *Pulp Fiction*

1996
★ *Mother*

FILM—FOREIGN LANGUAGE

1936
★ *Carnival in Flanders*

1937
★ *Mayerling*

1938
★ *Grand Illusion*

1939
★ *Harvest*

1940
★ *The Baker's Wife*

1946
★ *Open City*

1948
★ *Paisan*

1989
★ True Love

1990
★ Chameleon Street

1991
★ Paris Is Burning
★ Poison

1992
★ In the Soup

1993
★ Public Access
★ Ruby in Paradise

1994
★ What Happened Was...

1995
★ Crumb
★ The Brothers McMullen

1996
★ Welcome to the Dollhouse

1997
★ Sunday

SPECIAL JURY PRIZE

1987
★ River's Edge

1990
★ To Sleep with Anger

1991
★ Straight Out of Brooklyn

1992
★ The Hours and Times

1993
★ Just Another Girl on the I.R.T.

1994
★ Fresh

1995
★ Heavy
★ Rhythm Thief

TORONTO-CITY AWARD

CANADIAN FEATURE FILM

1985
★ Canada's Sweetheart: The Saga of Hal C. Banks

1986
★ The Decline of the American Empire

1987
★ Family Viewing

1988
★ Outside Chance of Maximillian Glick

1989
★ Roadkill

1990
★ H

1991
★ The Adjuster

1994
★ Exotica

1995
★ Live Bait

1996
★ Long Day's Journey Into Night

WRITERS GUILD OF AMERICA

ADAPTED SCREENPLAY

1968
★ Goodbye Columbus

1969
★ Butch Cassidy and the Sundance Kid
★ Midnight Cowboy

1970
★ I Never Sang For My Father
★ M*A*S*H

1971
★ Kotch
★ The French Connection

1972
★ Cabaret
★ The Godfather

1973
★ Paper Moon
★ Serpico

1974
★ The Apprenticeship of Duddy Kravitz
★ The Godfather, Part 2

1975
★ One Flew Over the Cuckoo's Nest
★ The Sunshine Boys

1976
★ All the President's Men
★ The Pink Panther Strikes Again

1977
★ Julia
★ Oh, God!

1978
★ Heaven Can Wait
★ Midnight Express

1979
★ Being There
★ Kramer vs. Kramer

1980
★ Airplane!
★ Ordinary People

1981
★ On Golden Pond
★ Rich and Famous

1982
★ Missing
★ Victor/Victoria

1983
★ Reuben, Reuben
★ Terms of Endearment

1984
★ The Killing Fields

1985
★ Prizzi's Honor

1986
★ A Room with a View

1987
★ Roxanne

1988
★ Dangerous Liaisons

1989
★ Driving Miss Daisy

1990
★ Dances with Wolves

1991
★ The Silence of the Lambs

1992
★ The Player

1993
★ Schindler's List
   In the Name of the Father
   The Fugitive
   The Joy Luck Club
   The Remains of the Day

1994
★ Forrest Gump
   Little Women
   Quiz Show
   The Madness of King George
   The Shawshank Redemption

1995
★ Sense and Sensibility
   Apollo 13
   Babe
   Get Shorty
   Leaving Las Vegas

1996
★ Sling Blade
   Emma
   The Birdcage
   The English Patient
   Trainspotting

ORIGINAL SCREENPLAY

1967
★ Bonnie & Clyde

1968
★ The Producers

1969
★ Bob & Carol & Ted & Alice

1970
★ Patton
★ The Out-of-Towners

1971
★ Sunday, Bloody Sunday
★ The Hospital

1972
★ The Candidate
★ What's Up, Doc?

1973
★ A Touch of Class
★ Save the Tiger

1974
★ Blazing Saddles
★ Chinatown

1975
★ Dog Day Afternoon
★ Shampoo

1976
★ Network
★ The Bad News Bears

1977
★ Annie Hall
★ The Turning Point

1978
★ Coming Home
★ Movie, Movie

1979
★ Breaking Away
★ The China Syndrome

1980
★ Melvin and Howard
★ Private Benjamin

1981
★ Arthur
★ Reds

1982
★ E.T.: The Extra-Terrestrial
★ Tootsie

1983
★ Tender Mercies
★ The Big Chill

1984
★ Broadway Danny Rose

1985
★ Witness

1986
★ Hannah and Her Sisters

1987
★ Moonstruck

1988
★ Bull Durham

1989
★ Crimes & Misdemeanors

1990
★ Avalon

1991
★ Thelma & Louise

1992
★ The Crying Game

1993
★ The Piano
   Dave
   In the Line of Fire
   Philadelphia
   Sleepless in Seattle

1994
★ Four Weddings and a Funeral
   Bullets Over Broadway
   Ed Wood
   Heavenly Creatures
   The Adventures of Priscilla, Queen of the Desert

1995
★ Braveheart
   Clueless
   Mighty Aphrodite
   Muriel's Wedding
   The American President

1996
★ Fargo
   Jerry Maguire
   Lone Star
   Secrets and Lies
   Shine

GOLDEN RASPBERRY AWARDS

WORST PICTURE

1980
★ Can't Stop the Music

1981
★ Mommie Dearest

1983
★ The Lonely Lady

1984
★ Bolero

1985
★ Rambo: First Blood, Part 2

1986
★ Howard the Duck
★ Under the Cherry Moon

1987
★ Leonard Part 6

1988
★ Cocktail

1989
★ Star Trek 5: The Final Frontier

1990
★ Ghosts Can't Do It
★ The Adventures of Ford Fairlane

1991
★ Hudson Hawk

1992
★ Shining Through

1993
★ Indecent Proposal

1994
★ Color of Night
   North
   On Deadly Ground
   The Specialist
   Wyatt Earp

WORST PICTURE
cont.

1995
★ *Showgirls*
Congo
It's Pat: The Movie
Waterworld

1996
★ *Striptease*
Barb Wire
Ed
The Island of Dr. Moreau
The Stupids

WORST REMAKE/ SEQUEL

1994
★ *Wyatt Earp*
The Flintstones

1995
★ *The Scarlet Letter*

WORST ACTOR

1980
★ Neil Diamond/*The Jazz Singer*

1981
★ Klinton Spilsbury/*Legend of the Lone Ranger*

1983
★ Christopher Atkins/*A Night in Heaven*

1984
★ Sylvester Stallone/*Rhinestone*

1985
★ Sylvester Stallone/*Rambo: First Blood, Part 2*
★ Sylvester Stallone/*Rocky 4*

1986
★ Prince/*Under the Cherry Moon*

1987
★ Bill Cosby/*Leonard Part 6*

1988
★ Sylvester Stallone/*Rambo 3*

1989
★ William Shatner/*Star Trek 5: The Final Frontier*

1990
★ Andrew Dice Clay/*The Adventures of Ford Fairlane*

1991
★ Kevin Costner/*Robin Hood: Prince of Thieves*

1992
★ Sylvester Stallone/*Stop! or My Mom Will Shoot*

1993
★ Burt Reynolds/*Cop and a Half*

1994
★ Kevin Costner/*Wyatt Earp*
Macaulay Culkin/*Getting Even with Dad*
Macaulay Culkin/*Richie Rich*
Macaulay Culkin/*The Pagemaster*
Bruce Willis/*Color of Night*
Bruce Willis/*North*

1995
★ Pauly Shore/*Jury Duty*
Kevin Costner/ *Waterworld*
Kyle MacLachlan/ *Showgirls*
Sylvester Stallone/ *Assassins*
Sylvester Stallone/*Judge Dredd*

1996
★ Tom Arnold/*Big Bully*
★ Tom Arnold/*Carpool*
★ Tom Arnold/*The Stupids*
★ Pauly Shore/*Bio-Dome*
Keanu Reeves/*Chain Reaction*
Adam Sandler/*Bulletproof*
Adam Sandler/*Happy Gilmore*
Sylvester Stallone/ *Daylight*

WORST ACTRESS

1980
★ Brooke Shields/*The Blue Lagoon*

1981
★ Bo Derek/*Tarzan, the Ape Man*
★ Faye Dunaway/*Mommie Dearest*

1982
★ Pia Zadora/*Butterfly*

1983
★ Pia Zadora/*The Lonely Lady*

1984
★ Bo Derek/*Bolero*

1985
★ Linda Blair/*Night Patrol*
★ Linda Blair/*Savage Island*
★ Linda Blair/*Savage Streets*

1986
★ Madonna/*Shanghai Surprise*

1987
★ Madonna/*Who's That Girl?*
★ Liza Minnelli/*Arthur 2: On the Rocks*

1988
★ Liza Minnelli/*Rent-A-Cop*

1990
★ Bo Derek/*Ghosts Can't Do It*

1991
★ Sean Young/*A Kiss Before Dying*

1992
★ Melanie Griffith/*A Stranger Among Us*
★ Melanie Griffith/*Shining Through*

1993
★ Madonna/*Body of Evidence*

1994
★ Sharon Stone/*Intersection*
★ Sharon Stone/*The Specialist*
Uma Thurman/*Even Cowgirls Get the Blues*

1995
★ Elizabeth Berkley/ *Showgirls*

1996
★ Demi Moore/*Striptease*
Whoopi Goldberg/*Bogus*
Whoopi Goldberg/*Eddie*
Whoopi Goldberg/ *Theodore Rex*
Melanie Griffith/*Two Much*
Demi Moore/*The Juror*
Julia Roberts/*Mary Reilly*

WORST SUPPORTING ACTOR

1980
★ John Adams/*Gloria*
★ Laurence Olivier/*The Jazz Singer*

1981
★ Steve Forrest/*Mommie Dearest*

1982
★ Ed McMahon/*Butterfly*

1983
★ Jim Nabors/*Stroker Ace*

1985
★ Rob Lowe/*St. Elmo's Fire*

1986
★ Jerome Benton/*Under the Cherry Moon*

1987
★ David Mendenhall/*Over the Top*

1988
★ Dan Aykroyd/*Caddyshack 2*

1989
★ Christopher Atkins/*Listen to Me*

1991
★ Dan Aykroyd/*Nothing But Trouble*

1990
★ Bo Derek/*Ghosts Can't Do It*

1991
★ Sean Young/*A Kiss Before Dying*

1992
★ Melanie Griffith/*A Stranger Among Us*
★ Melanie Griffith/*Shining Through*

1992
★ Tom Selleck/*Christopher Columbus: The Discovery*

1993
★ Woody Harrelson/ *Indecent Proposal*

1994
★ O.J. Simpson/*Naked Gun 33 1/3: The Final Insult*

1995
★ Dennis Hopper/ *Waterworld*
Robert Davi/*Showgirls*

1996
★ Marlon Brando/*The Island of Dr. Moreau*
Val Kilmer/*The Ghost and the Darkness*
Val Kilmer/*The Island of Dr. Moreau*
Burt Reynolds/*Striptease*
Steven Seagal/*Executive Decision*
Quentin Tarantino/*From Dusk Till Dawn*

WORST SUPPORTING ACTRESS

1980
★ Amy Irving/*Honeysuckle Rose*

1981
★ Diana Scarwid/*Mommie Dearest*

1982
★ Aileen Quinn/*Annie*

1983
★ Sybil Danning/*Chained Heat*
★ Sybil Danning/*Hercules*

1984
★ Lynn-Holly Johnson/ *Where the Boys Are '84*

1985
★ Brigitte Nielsen/*Rocky 4*

1987
★ Daryl Hannah/*Wall Street*

1988
★ Kristy McNichol/*Two Moon Junction*

1989
★ Brooke Shields/*Speed Zone*

1990
★ Sofia Coppola/*The Godfather, Part 3*

1991
★ Sean Young/*A Kiss Before Dying*

1992
★ Estelle Getty/*Stop! or My Mom Will Shoot*

1993
★ Faye Dunaway/*The Temp*

1994
★ Rosie O'Donnell/*Car 54, Where Are You?*
★ Rosie O'Donnell/*Exit to Eden*
★ Rosie O'Donnell/*The Flintstones*
Elizabeth Taylor/*The Flintstones*

1995
★ Madonna/*Four Rooms*
Gina Gershon/*Showgirls*

1996
★ Melanie Griffith/ *Mulholland Falls*
Faye Dunaway/*Dunston Checks In*
Faye Dunaway/*The Chamber*
Jami Gertz/*Twister*
Daryl Hannah/*Two Much*
Teri Hatcher/*Heaven's Prisoners*
Teri Hatcher/*Two Days in the Valley*

WORST DIRECTOR

1980
★ Robert Greenwald/ *Xanadu*

1981
★ Michael Cimino/*Heaven's Gate*

1982
★ Ken Annakin/*Pirate Movie*

1983
★ Peter Sasdy/*The Lonely Lady*

1984
★ John Derek/*Bolero*

1985
★ Sylvester Stallone/*Rocky 4*

1986
★ Prince/*Under the Cherry Moon*

1987
★ Norman Mailer/*Tough Guys Don't Dance*
★ Elaine May/*Ishtar*

1988
★ Blake Edwards/*Sunset*
★ Stewart Raffill/*Mac and Me*

1989
★ William Shatner/*Star Trek 5: The Final Frontier*

1990
★ John Derek/*Ghosts Can't Do It*

1991
★ Michael Lehmann/ *Hudson Hawk*

1992
★ David Seltzer/*Shining Through*

1993

★ Jennifer Lynch/*Boxing Helena*

1994

★ Steven Seagal/*On Deadly Ground*

1995

★ Paul Verhoeven/*Showgirls*

1996

★ Andrew Bergman/*Striptease*
 John Frankenheimer/*The Island of Dr. Moreau*
 Stephen Frears/*Mary Reilly*
 John Landis/*The Stupids*
 Brian Levant/*Jingle All the Way*

WORST SCREENPLAY

1980

★ *Can't Stop the Music*

1981

★ *Mommie Dearest*

1983

★ *The Lonely Lady*

1984

★ *Bolero*

1985

★ *Rambo: First Blood, Part 2*
★ *Rocky 4*

1986

★ *Howard the Duck*

1987

★ *Leonard Part 6*

1988

★ *Cocktail*

1989

★ *Harlem Nights*

1990

★ *The Adventures of Ford Fairlane*

1991

★ *Hudson Hawk*

1992

★ *Stop! or My Mom Will Shoot*

1993

★ *Indecent Proposal*

1994

★ *The Flintstones*

1995

★ *Showgirls*

1996

★ *Striptease*
 Barb Wire
 Ed
 The Island of Dr. Moreau
 The Stupids

WORST SONG

1980

★ "The Man with Bogart's Face"/*The Man with Bogart's Face*

1981

★ "Baby Talk"/*Paternity*

1982

★ "Pumpin' and Blowin'"/*Pirate Movie*

1983

★ "The Way You Do It"/*The Lonely Lady*

1984

★ "Drinkenstein"/*Rhinestone*

1985

★ "Peace In Our Life"/*Rambo: First Blood, Part 2*

1986

★ "Love or Money"/*Under the Cherry Moon*

1987

★ "I Want Your Sex"/*Beverly Hills Cop 2*

1988

★ "Jack Fresh"/*Caddyshack 2*

1989

★ "Bring Your Daughter to the Slaughter"/*A Nightmare on Elm Street 5: Dream Child*

1990

★ "He's Comin' Back (The Devil!)"/*Repossessed*

1991

★ "Addams Groove"/*The Addams Family*

1992

★ "High Times, Hard Times"/*Newsies*

1993

★ "WHOOMP! There It Is"/*Addams Family Values*

1994

★ "Marry the Mole"/*Thumbelina*

1995

★ "Walk into the Wind"/*Showgirls*

1996

★ "Pussy, Pussy, Pussy (Whose Kitty Cat Are You?)"/*Striptease*
 "Welcome to Planet Boom!"/*Barb Wire*
 "Whenever There is Love"/*Daylight*

WORST NEW STAR

1981

★ Klinton Spilsbury/*Legend of the Lone Ranger*

1982

★ Pia Zadora/*Butterfly*

1983

★ Lou Ferrigno/*Hercules*

1984

★ Olivia D'Abo/*Bolero*
★ Olivia D'Abo/*Conan the Destroyer*

1985

★ Brigitte Nielsen/*Red Sonja*
★ Brigitte Nielsen/*Rocky 4*

1987

★ David Mendenhall/*Over the Top*

1990

★ Sofia Coppola/*The Godfather, Part 3*

1991

★ Vanilla Ice/*Cool As Ice*

1992

★ Pauly Shore/*Encino Man*

1993

★ Janet Jackson/*Poetic Justice*

1994

★ Anna Nicole Smith/*Naked Gun 33 1/3: The Final Insult*

1995

★ Elizabeth Berkley/*Showgirls*
 David Caruso/*Kiss of Death*
 Cindy Crawford/*Fair Game*
 Julia Sweeney/*It's Pat: The Movie*

1996

★ Pamela Anderson Lee/*Barb Wire*
 Ellen DeGeneres/*Mr. Wrong*

Foreign Film Index

The **Foreign Film Index** classifies movies by the country of [re]cord in which they were produced. Since a film may be financed or produced in more than [o]ne country, some videos will appear with more than one country of [o]rigin. The codes appear in the [re]view, immediately following the [co]lor/black and white designation [b]efore the credits. In this index, [m]ovies are listed alphabetically by [co]untry. **A tipped triangle indi[c]ates a video rated three bones [o]r higher**.

Key to Country Origination Tags

AL Algerian	**DK** Danish	**IR** Irish	**PT** Portuguese
AR Argentinian	**NL** Dutch	**IS** Israeli	**RU** Russian
AT Austrian	**PH** Filipino	**IT** Italian	**SA** South African
AU Australian	**FI** Finnish	**JP** Japanese	**SP** Spanish
BE Belgian	**FR** French	**KO** Korean	**SW** Swedish
BR Brazilian	**GE** German	**LI** Lithuanian	**SI** Swiss
GB British	**GR** Greek	**MA** Macedonian	**TU** Turkish
CA Canadian	**HK** Hong Kong	**MX** Mexican	**TW** Taiwanese
CH Chinese	**HU** Hungarian	**NZ** New Zealand	**VT** Vietnamese
CL Colombian	**IC** Icelandic	**NI** Nicaraguan	**VZ** Venezuelan
CU Cuban	**IN** Indian	**NO** Norwegian	**YU** Yugoslavian
CZ Czech	**IA** Iranian	**PL** Polish	

Algerian

The Battle of Algiers▸

Argentinean

Camila▸
The Curious Dr. Humpp
The Devil's Possessed
The Enchanted Forest
Eversmile New Jersey
Far Away and Long Ago
Fridays of Eternity
Funny, Dirty Little War
I Don't Want to Talk About It
Killing Grandpa
La Boca del Lobo
Made in Argentina
Man Facing Southeast▸
Miss Mary
The Official Story▸
A Place in the World▸
A Shadow You Soon Will Be
The Stranger▸
Tango Bar
Time for Revenge
Times to Come▸
Two to Tango
Veronico Cruz

Australian

ABC's of Love & Sex,
    Australia Style
The Adventures of Priscilla,
    Queen of the Desert▸
Air Hawk
Alex
Alice to Nowhere
Alison's Birthday
All the Rivers Run

...Almost
Alvin Purple
Alvin Rides Again
American Roulette
Angel Baby▸
Anzacs: The War Down
    Under▸
Archer's Adventure
Around the World in 80 Ways
Attack Force Z
Babe▸
Back of Beyond
Backlash
Bad Boy Bubby
Barnaby and Me
Barry McKenzie Holds His
    Own
Between Wars
The Big Hurt
Black Robe▸
Blackwater Trail
Bliss▸
Blood Money
Bloodmoon
Blue Fin
Body Melt
Boulevard of Broken Dreams
Breaker Morant▸
Breakfast in Paris
Burke & Wills
Cactus
Caddie
Camel Boy
Careful, He Might Hear You▸
Carry Me Back
The Cars That Ate Paris▸
Celia: Child Of Terror
Children of the Revolution
The City's Edge
Clowning Around
Clowning Around 2
The Club▸
The Coca-Cola Kid▸

Color Me Dead
Contagion
Cosi▸
Country Life
Crocodile Dundee▸
The Crossing
A Cry in the Dark▸
The Custodian
Dangerous Summer
Dark Age
Dark Forces
Dead Calm▸
Dead Easy
Dead End Drive-In
Deadly Possession
Death in Brunswick
Death of a Soldier
Demonstrator
Desperate Prey
The Devil's Playground▸
Dingo
Dogs in Space
Don's Party▸
The Dunera Boys▸
Dusty
Earthling
East and West▸
Echo Park
Echoes of Paradise
The Efficiency Expert
The Empty Beach
Endplay
Escape 2000
Eureka Stockade
The Everlasting Secret Family
Fair Game
Fantasy Man
Fast Talking
Father
Fatty Finn
The Fire in the Stone
Fists of Blood
Flirting▸

Floating Life
For Love Alone
Fortress
Forty Thousand Horsemen
Fran
Frenchman's Farm
The Fringe Dwellers
Gallagher's Travels
Gallipoli▸
Georgia
The Getting of Wisdom
The Good Wife
Grendel, Grendel, Grendel
Gross Misconduct
Ground Zero▸
Hard Knocks
Heatwave▸
Heaven Tonight
High Rolling in a Hot Corvette
High Tide▸
The Highest Honor
Hotel de Love
Howling 3: The Marsupials
I Live with Me Dad
In Search of Anna
An Indecent Obsession
Inn of the Damned
Innocent Prey
The Irishman
Kangaroo▸
The Killing Beach
Killing of Angel Street
Kitty and the Bagman
The Last Bastion
The Last Days of Chez Nous
The Last Wave▸
The Lighthorsemen▸
Lilian's Story
Little Boy Lost
Lonely Hearts▸
Long John Silver
The Long Weekend
Love and Other Catastrophes

Mad Dog Morgan
Mad Max: Beyond
    Thunderdome
Magee and the Lady
Malcolm
The Man from Snowy River
Man of Flowers
The Mango Tree
Mesmerized
Midnight Dancer
Miracle Down Under
Mr. Reliable: A True Story
Money Movers
Monkey Grip▸
Moving Targets
Muriel's Wedding▸
My Brilliant Career▸
My First Wife
The Naked Country
Napoleon
Nevil Shute's The Far Country
Newsfront▸
Next of Kin
No Room to Run
Norman Loves Rose
Now and Forever
The Odd Angry Shot
One Crazy Night
Only the Brave
Overlanders▸
Palm Beach
Panic Station
Paperback Romance
Patrick
Phar Lap
The Piano▸
Picnic at Hanging Rock▸
Plumber
Poor Girl, A Ghost Story
Prince and the Great Race
Prisoner Cell Block H
Prisoners of the Sun▸
Proof▸

Puberty Blues
Puzzle
Queen of the Road
The Quest
Quigley Down Under
Razorback
Rebel
Reckless Kelly
Return of Captain Invincible
Return to Snowy River
Ride a Wild Pony
The Right Hand Man
Rikky and Pete
Road Games
Romper Stomper
Run, Rebecca, Run
Sara Dane
Savage Attraction
Second Time Lucky
Shame
Shine
Silver City
The Silver Stallion: King of the Wild Brumbies
Sirens
Sky Pirates
Smuggler's Cove
Snowy River, the MacGregor Saga: The Race
Sorrento Beach
Squizzy Taylor
Starstruck
Strangers
Stranglehold
Strictly Ballroom
The Sum of Us
Summer City
Sunday Too Far Away
Survivor
Sweet Talker
Sweetie
The Tale of Ruby Rose
Talk
Tearaway
A Test of Love
That Eye, The Sky
Three's Trouble
Thundering Forest
Tim
Touch & Go
A Town Like Alice
Traps
Travelling North
Treasure of the Yankee Zephyr
Tunnel Vision
Typhoon Treasure
Under Capricorn
Vincent: The Life and Death of Vincent van Gogh
The Wacky World of Wills & Burke
Walk into Hell
Walkabout
Warm Nights on a Slow-Moving Train
Waterfront
We of the Never Never
Who Killed Baby Azaria?
Wide Sargasso Sea
The Wild Duck
Windrider
The Winds of Jarrah
The Winter of Our Dreams
A Woman's Tale
A Yank in Australia
The Year My Voice Broke
The Year of Living Dangerously
Young Einstein

Austrian

The Hands of Orlac
Heidi
Time Troopers
Wandering Jew

Belgian

Between Heaven and Earth
A Couch in New York
Daens
Daughters of Darkness
The Devil's Nightmare
Dust
The Eighth Day
Farinelli
Les Rendez-vous D'Anna
Man Bites Dog
Mascara
The Music Teacher
Night and Day
One Sings, the Other Doesn't
The Passion of Darkly Noon
Rabid Grannies
The Sexual Life of the Belgians
Suite 16
Toute Une Nuit
A Wedding in Galilee

Brazilian

Amor Bandido
Antonio Das Mortes
At Midnight, I'll Take Your Soul
Awakenings of the Beast
Black God & White Devil
Black Orpheus
Bye Bye Brazil
The Dolphin
Dona Flor and Her Two Husbands
Earth Entranced
Gabriela
Hallucinations of a Deranged Mind
Happily Ever After
The Hour of the Star
How Tasty Was My Little Frenchman
I Love You
Killer Fish
Kiss of the Spider Woman
Lady on the Bus
Luzia
O Quatrilho
Opera do Malandro
Pixote
Quilombo
Savage Capitalism
The Story of Fausta
Strange World of Coffin Joe
Subway to the Stars
Via Appia
Women in Fury
Xica

British

Abandon Ship
Abdulla the Great
Abigail's Party
The Abominable Dr. Phibes
Above Us the Waves
Absolute Beginners
Absolutely Fabulous: The Last Shout
Absolution

Accident
Accused
Across the Bridge
Action for Slander
The Adventurers
Adventures of a Private Eye
Adventures of a Taxi Driver
The Adventures of Sadie
The Adventures of Sherlock Holmes: Hound of the Baskervilles
The Adventures of Tartu
The Advocate
The Affair
An Affair in Mind
The Affair of the Pink Pearl
The African Queen
After Darkness
After Julius
After Pilkington
After the Fox
Afterward
Agatha Christie's Miss Marple
Alamut Ambush
Alfie
Alias John Preston
Alice
Alice's Adventures in Wonderland
Alien Women
All Creatures Great and Small
American Friends
American Roulette
And Nothing But the Truth
And Now for Something Completely Different
And Now the Screaming Starts
And Soon the Darkness
Angel with the Trumpet
Angels and Insects
Anna Karenina
The Anniversary
Another Country
Another Time, Another Place
Another Time, Another Place
Antonia and Jane
Apartment Zero
Appointment with Crime
Aria
Armistead Maupin's Tales of the City
The Arsenal Stadium Mystery
As You Like It
The Asphyx
The Assassination Bureau
Assassination of Trotsky
The Assassination Run
Assault
Assault on Agathon
Asylum
At the Earth's Core
The Atomic Man
August
An Awfully Big Adventure
The Baby and the Battleship
Baby Love
Bachelor of Hearts
Backbeat
Bad Behavior
Ballad in Blue
The Ballad of the Sad Cafe
Ballet Shoes
Bananas Boat
Band of Gold
Bandit Queen
Battle Beneath the Earth
Battle Hell
The Battle of the Sexes
The Bawdy Adventures of Tom Jones
Beachcomber

Beast in the Cellar
Beast of Morocco
Beat Girl
Beautiful Thing
Bedazzled
Before the Rain
The Belles of St. Trinian's
Bellman and True
The Belly of an Architect
Benny Hill's Crazy World
Bernard and the Genie
Best Enemies
The Best of Cracker Mysteries
The Best of Lovejoy Mysteries
The Best of the Two Ronnies
Betrayal
Bewitched
Bhaji on the Beach
The Big Man: Crossing the Line
Big Zapper
Biggles
Billy Budd
Billy Liar
The Bitch
Bitter Sweet
Black Beauty
The Black Cat
Black Eyes
Black Limelight
Black Narcissus
The Black Velvet Gown
Black Werewolf
Blackmail
Blackout
Blake's Seven
Blanche Fury
Bleak House
Bleak Moments
The Bliss of Mrs. Blossom
Blithe Spirit
Blockhouse
Blonde Blackmailer
Blood Beast Terror
Blood Island
Blood of the Vampire
The Blood on Satan's Claw
Bloodbath at the House of Death
The Bloodsuckers
Blow-Up
Blue
Blue Blood
The Blue Lamp
Blue Money
Blue Murder at St. Trinian's
Bobo
Body & Soul
The Body in the Library
The Body Vanished
Bonnie Prince Charlie
The Borrowers
Boston Kickout
The Boy Friend
The Brain
Bramwell
Brassed Off
Brazil
Breaking Glass
Breaking the Code
The Bretts
The Brides of Dracula
Brideshead Revisited
The Bridge on the River Kwai
A Bridge Too Far
Brief Encounter
Bright Smiler
Brighton Rock
Brimstone & Treacle
Britannia Hospital
Broken Melody

Brother Cadfael
Brother Cadfael 2
Brothers in Law
The Browning Version
The Buccaneers
The Buddha of Suburbia
Buddy's Song
Bugsy Malone
Bulldog Drummond at Bay
Bulldog Jack
Bullet to Beijing
Bullshot
Burn Witch, Burn!
Burning Secret
Buster
Butler's Dilemma
Butterflies
Butterfly Ball
Butterfly Kiss
Caesar and Cleopatra
Call Him Mr. Shatter
Calling Paul Temple
Candles at Nine
A Canterbury Tale
Captain Boycott
Captain Horatio Hornblower
Captain Kronos: Vampire Hunter
Captain's Paradise
The Captain's Table
Captive Heart
Captives
Car Trouble
Caravaggio
Carlton Browne of the F.O.
Carrington
Carrington, V.C.
Carry On Admiral
Carry On at Your Convenience
Carry On Behind
Carry On Camping
Carry On Cleo
Carry On Cowboy
Carry On Dick
Carry On Doctor
Carry On Emmanuelle
Carry On England
Carry On Henry VIII
Carry On Nurse
Carry On 'Round the Bend
Carry On Screaming
The Case of the Frightened Lady
The Case of the Missing Lady
The Case of the Mukkinese Battle Horn
The Cassandra Crossing
Cast a Dark Shadow
The Castle of Fu Manchu
The Cat and the Canary
Catch Me a Spy
Catherine the Great
The Cement Garden
Century
The Chalk Garden
Chamber of Horrors
Champagne
Champions
Chaplin
The Charge of the Light Brigade
Chariots of Fire
Charlemagne
Charlie Grant's War
The Charmer
Chasing the Deer
Chicago Joe & the Showgirl
The Children
Children of Rage
Children of the Damned
Children of the Full Moon
Chinese Boxes

Thirteenth Day of Christmas
30 Is a Dangerous Age,
    Cynthia
The 39 Steps⏵
The Thirty-Nine Steps
This England
This Happy Breed⏵
This Lightning Always Strikes
    Twice
This Sporting Life⏵
Those Daring Young Men in
    Their Jaunty Jalopies
Those Fantastic Flying Fools
Those Glory, Glory Days
Those Magnificent Men in
    Their Flying Machines⏵
Threads⏵
Three Cases of Murder⏵
Three Stops to Murder
The Three Weird Sisters
Thunder in the City⏵
Thunderball
Thursday's Child
Ticket of Leave Man
Tiger Bay⏵
Time Bandits
Time Lock
Time Without Pity
Tintorera...Tiger Shark
To Play the King⏵
To See Such Fun
To Sir, with Love
Tom & Viv⏵
Tom Brown's School Days
Tom Brown's School Days⏵
Tom Jones⏵
Tom Thumb⏵
Tomb of Ligeia⏵
Tomb of the Undead
Too Many Crooks
Torture Garden
Touch Me Not
Tough Guy
Tower of Evil
Tower of Terror
A Town Called Hell
Traffik⏵
Trainspotting⏵
Transatlantic Tunnel
Transmutations
Trap
Treasure Island
Treasure of Monte Cristo
Trial & Error
The Trials of Oscar Wilde⏵
Triple Cross⏵
Triple Echo
The Triumph of Sherlock
    Holmes
Trouble in Store
Trouble in the Glen
Truth About Women
Tunes of Glory⏵
Turtle Diary⏵
Twelfth Night
21 Days
Twin Town
Twins of Evil
Twinsanity
Two Deaths
The Two Faces of Dr. Jekyll
Two for the Road⏵
2001: A Space Odyssey⏵
Two-Way Stretch
The Unbreakable Alibi
The Uncanny
Under Capricorn
Under Milk Wood
Under Suspicion
Under the Red Robe
The Unearthly Stranger
Uneasy Terms
Unexplained Laughter

Unholy Four
Unicorn
Unmasked Part 25
Unmasking the Idol
Unnatural Pursuits
The Unstoppable Man
Unsuitable Job for a Woman
Up the Creek
Utz
The Vacillations of Poppy
    Carew
Valentino
Valley of the Eagles
Vampire Circus
The Vampire Lovers
The Vampyr
Vampyres
The Van⏵
Vanity Fair
Vault of Horror
Vendetta for the Saint
Venom
Venus in Furs
Veronico Cruz
A Very British Coup⏵
The Very Edge
The Vicious Circle
Victim⏵
A View to a Kill
A Village Affair
Village of the Damned⏵
The V.I.P.'s⏵
The Virgin and the Gypsy
The Virgin Soldiers
The Virgin Witch
The Vision
A Voyage' Round My Father⏵
Wagner: The Complete Epic
Wagner: The Movie
Waltz of the Toreadors⏵
War Lover
The Warriors
Water
Water Babies
Watership Down
Wavelength
The Way Out
We Dive at Dawn⏵
We Think the World of You⏵
The Weaker Sex
The Wedding Gift⏵
Wetherby⏵
What a Carve-Up!
What's Good for the Goose
When Dinosaurs Ruled the
    Earth
When the Whales Came
When the Wind Blows⏵
When Thief Meets Thief
Where Angels Fear to Tread⏵
Where the Bullets Fly
While I Live
Whiskey Galore⏵
The Whistle Blower⏵
Whistle Down the Wind⏵
White Fire
White Huntress
Who Done It?
Whoops Apocalypse
Who's Who
The Wicked Lady
Wild Geese
Wild Geese 2
Wild West
Windom's Way⏵
Wings of Danger
Wings of the Morning
Winner Takes All
The Winslow Boy⏵
Winter Flight
Wish You Were Here⏵
Withnail and I⏵
Without a Clue

Wittgenstein
Woman in Black
The Woman in Question
A Woman's Guide to Adultery
Wombling Free
Women in Love⏵
Wonderland⏵
Wonderwall: The Movie
A World Apart⏵
The World is Full of Married
    Men
The World of Suzie Wong
The World Owes Me a Living
The Wreck of the Mary Deare
The Wrong Arm of the Law⏵
The Wrong Box⏵
Wuthering Heights
Xtro
A Year in Provence⏵
Yellow Submarine⏵
Yesterday's Hero
You Only Live Twice
The Young Americans
Young and Innocent⏵
The Young Ones
The Young Poisoner's
    Handbook⏵
Young Winston⏵
Yuri Nosenko, KGB
A Zed & Two Noughts⏵
Zeppelin

Canadian

Abducted
The Adjuster
The Agency
American Boyfriends
The Amityville Curse
And Then You Die⏵
Angel Square
Angela
Anne of Avonlea⏵
Anne of Green Gables⏵
The Apprenticeship of Duddy
    Kravitz⏵
Atlantic City⏵
Babar: The Movie
The Bay Boy
Beautiful Dreamers
Being at Home with Claude
The Best of the Kids in the
    Hall
Beyond the Silhouette
The Big Crimewave
Big Meat Eater
Black Christmas
Black Robe⏵
Blades of Courage
Blood & Donuts
Blood Relations
Blood Relatives
The Bloody Brood
Boy in Blue
The Boys Club
The Boys of St. Vincent⏵
Breaking All the Rules
The Brood
Buffalo Jump⏵
Bullies
Busted Up
By Design
By Way of the Stars
Bye Bye Blues
Cafe Romeo
Calendar⏵
Canada's Sweetheart: The
    Saga of Hal C. Banks
Candy Mountain
Cathy's Curse
The Changeling
Christina

Circle of Two
City Boy⏵
City on Fire
Class of 1984
Clearcut
Close to Home
Cold Comfort
Cold Front
Concrete Angels
The Confessional
Confidential
Covergirl
Crash
Cross Country
Curtains
Curtis's Charm
Dan Candy's Law
Dance Me Outside
Dancing in the Dark
Daughter of Death
Dead Ringers⏵
Death Ship
Death Weekend
Deathdream
The Decline of the American
    Empire⏵
Deranged⏵
Dirty Tricks
Disappearance
Distant Thunder
Dr. Bethune⏵
Doctor Who
Dog Pound Shuffle⏵
The Dog Who Stopped the
    War
A Doll's House⏵
Double Happiness⏵
Double Identity
The Double Negative
Drying Up the Streets
Eclipse
Eddie and the Cruisers 2:
    Eddie Lives!
Eliza's Horoscope
Exotica⏵
Family Viewing⏵
Fatal Attraction
Fight for Your Life
Final Assignment
Find the Lady
First Degree
Fish Hawk
Flesh Gordon 2: Flesh
    Gordon Meets the Cosmic
    Cheerleaders
For the Moment
Frankenstein and Me
Friends, Lovers & Lunatics
Full Circle
Funeral Home
The Funny Farm
Gas
The Girl in Blue
Girls on the Road
Glory Enough for All: The
    Discovery of Insulin
The Godsend
Going Berserk
Goldenrod
The Great American Sex
    Scandal
The Grey Fox⏵
The Groundstar Conspiracy⏵
The Gunfighters
The Gunrunner
H
Happy Birthday to Me
Hard Core Logo
Harry Tracy
Heads
Heartaches⏵
Heaven on Earth
Heavenly Bodies

Heavy Metal⏵
Henry & Verlin
High Ballin'
High Country
Highpoint
Hiroshima⏵
Hockey Night
Hog Wild
The Hound of London
The Housekeeper
Humongous
Iceman⏵
If You Could See What I Hear
In Celebration⏵
In Praise of Older Women
In Trouble
Incubus
Into the Fire
Iron Eagle 2
Iron Eagle 4
I've Heard the Mermaids
    Singing⏵
Jesus of Montreal⏵
John and the Missus
Joshua Then and Now⏵
Journey
Journey into Fear
Keeper
The Kidnapping of the
    President
Kids of the Round Table
Killing 'em Softly
King of the Airwaves
King Solomon's Treasure
Kissed
Ladies of the Lotus
Lantern Hill
Last Chase
The Last Place on Earth
The Last Winter
Le Polygraphe
Le Sexe des Etoiles
L'Enfant d'Eau
Leolo
Les Bons Debarras
L'Escorte
Lies My Father Told Me⏵
Lilies
The Little Girl Who Lives
    Down the Lane
The Little Kidnappers
Live Bait
Long Day's Journey Into
    Night⏵
Loose Screws
Lost
Lost in the Barrens
The Lotus Eaters
Love and Human Remains⏵
Love Songs
Loyalties
A Man, a Woman, and a Bank
A Man in Uniform
The Man Inside
Margaret's Museum⏵
Maria Chapdelaine
Martin's Day
Masala
The Mask
Mazes and Monsters
Meatballs
Melanie
Middle Age Crazy
Mindfield
Mon Amie Max
Mon Oncle Antoine⏵
Mouvements du Desir
Murder by Decree⏵
Murder by Phone
My American Cousin⏵
My Bloody Valentine
My Pleasure Is My Business
My Side of the Mountain

German

Faust▲
Fight for Gold
First Love
First Spaceship on Venus▲
Fitzcarraldo
Flatfoot
Flirt
For Your Love Only
Forger of London
Forget Mozart
Fortune's Fool
Fox and His Friends▲
F.P. 1
F.P. 1 Doesn't Answer
Frankenstein '80
Frozen Alive
Full Hearts & Empty Pockets
Geheimakte WB1
Germany in Autumn
The Goalie's Anxiety at the
  Penalty Kick▲
Gods of the Plague▲
The Golem▲
Halfmoon
Hanussen▲
The Head
Heart of Glass▲
Heidi▲
Heimat 1
Heimat 2
Homecoming▲
Horrors of Spider Island
The House of 1000 Dolls
I Only Want You to Love Me
In a Year of 13 Moons
The Indian Scarf
The Inheritors
Inn on the River
The Innocent
Invisible Adversaries
The Invisible Dr. Mabuse▲
Journey to the Lost City
Joyless Street▲
Jud Suess▲
The Jumper
Jungle Warriors
Just a Gigolo
Kameradschaft▲
Kamikaze '89▲
Kaspar Hauser
King, Queen, Knave▲
Kings of the Road—In the
  Course of Time▲
Knife in the Head
Kolberg
Kriemhilde's Revenge▲
La Passante▲
The Lacemaker▲
Land and Freedom▲
The Last Five Days
The Last Laugh▲
The Last Tomahawk
Les Miserables▲
Les Rendez-vous D'Anna
Let It Rock
Lethal Obsession
Liebelei
The Lost Honor of Katharina
  Blum▲
The Lost One
A Love in Germany
M▲
The Mad Executioners
Maedchen in Uniform▲
Malou
The Man Inside
A Man Like Eva▲
Marianne and Juliane▲
Mark of the Devil
Mark of the Devil 2
The Marriage of Maria Braun▲
Martha and I▲
Master Touch

Maybe...Maybe Not
Me and Him
Men...▲
Menschenfrauen
Metropolis▲
Mission Stardust
Mr. Superinvisible
The Monster of London City
Moon 44
Mother Kusters Goes to
  Heaven▲
Mozart: A Childhood
  Chronicle▲
Murderers Are Among Us
My Father Is Coming
The Mysterious Magician
Naked in the Night
The Name of the Rose
The Nasty Girl▲
Nelly et Monsieur Arnaud▲
Nico Icon▲
Night Flight from Moscow
1900▲
99 Women
No Survivors, Please
Nosferatu▲
The Odessa File
Oldest Profession
One Arabian Night▲
The Oppermann Family
An Orphan Boy of Vienna
Othello
Out of Order
Pandora's Box▲
Paris, Texas▲
Passion
The Passion of Darkly Noon
The Pedestrian▲
The Phantom of Soho
Possession
The Practice of Love
The Princess and the
  Swineherd
The Promise
Q Ships
Querelle
Requiem for Dominic▲
The Return of Dr. Mabuse
Reunion▲
The Revolt of Job▲
Roboman
Rosa Luxemburg
Rosalie Goes Shopping▲
Sacred Mountain/White
  Flame▲
Salmonberries
Satan's Brew
Savage Attraction
The Scarlet Letter▲
Schnelles Geld
Schtonk
The Scorpion Woman
Secret Agent Super Dragon
Secret of the Black Trunk
Secrets of a Soul
The Seducers
Seduction: The Cruel Woman
The Serpent's Egg
Shadow of Angels
Shattered▲
Sheer Madness▲
Sherlock Holmes and the
  Deadly Necklace
Shocking Asia
Siegfried▲
Signs of Life
Singing the Blues in Red▲
Slavers
Smilla's Sense of Snow
Someone Else's America▲
Spiders▲
Spies▲
Spring Symphony

The Squeaker
Stalingrad
State of Things▲
The Stationmaster's Wife
The Strange Countess
Stranger than Paradise▲
Strangler of Blackmoor Castle
The Street
Stroszek▲
Student of Prague▲
A Study in Terror▲
Sugarbaby▲
The Surgeon
Swann in Love
Swiss Conspiracy
Symphony in the Mountains
Taxi zum Klo▲
Teenage Wolfpack
Therese & Isabelle
They Were So Young
'38: Vienna Before the Fall
The Thousand Eyes of Dr.
  Mabuse▲
The Three Penny Opera▲
Tiefland
The Tin Drum▲
Tonio Kroger
The Torture Chamber of Dr.
  Sadism
Tower of Screaming Virgins
Traenen in Florenz
Triumph of the Will
Tromba, the Tiger Man
Uncle Tom's Cabin
Underground▲
Utz
The Vampire Happening
Vampyr▲
Variety▲
Veronika Voss▲
Via Appia
Virgin Machine
Voyager▲
The Wannsee Conference▲
Warning Shadows▲
Waxworks▲
Web of the Spider
The Werewolf vs. the Vampire
  Woman
Westfront 1918▲
Where the Green Ants Dream
The White Rose▲
Why Does Herr R. Run
  Amok?
Wings of Desire▲
A Woman in Flames▲
Woman in the Moon
The Wonderful, Horrible Life
  of Leni Riefenstahl
Woyzeck▲
The Wrong Move
Year of the Quiet Sun▲
Zentropa

Greek

The Brave Bunch
A Dream of Passion
Emmanuelle's Daughter
The Enchantress
Girl in Black
Iphigenia
Landscape in the Mist▲
A Matter of Dignity
The Mediterranean in Flames
Never on Sunday▲
Phaedra
Restless
Stella
Torpedo Attack
Ulysses' Gaze
When the Greeks

Young Aphrodites

Hong Kong

The Amsterdam Connection
The Amsterdam Kill
Autumn Moon
A Better Tomorrow, Part 2
A Better Tomorrow, Part 3
The Bride with White Hair
The Bride with White Hair 2
A Bullet in the Head▲
Chungking Express▲
Clash of the Ninja
Crack Shadow Boxers
Crime Story
The Day the Sun Turned
  Cold▲
The Executioners
Farewell My Concubine
Full Contact
Goliathon
Green Snake
Happy Together
Hard-Boiled
Heart of Dragon
The Heroic Trio
Infra-Man
Jackie Chan's First Strike▲
Jackie Chan's Police Force
Just Like Weather▲
The Killer▲
Last Hurrah for Chivalry
Lethal Panther
A Mongolian Tale
Ninja Champion
Ninja Destroyer
Ninja Exterminators
Ninja Fantasy
Ninja Hunt
Organized Crime & Triad
  Bureau
Red Firecracker, Green
  Firecracker
The Reincarnation of Golden
  Lotus▲
Rumble in the Bronx
Summer Snow
Supercop
Tai Chi 2
Temptress Moon
The Untold Story
Wicked City
Wing Chun
Young Master

Hungarian

Adoption▲
After the Revolution
Almanac of Fall
Another Way▲
Bad Guys
Brady's Escape
Cat's Play
Cold Days
Colonel Redl▲
Father▲
The Fifth Seal
Flowers of Reverie
The Girl▲
Hanussen▲
A Happy New Year!
A Hungarian Fairy Tale▲
Hungarian Rhapsody▲
Lily in Love
The Little Valentino
Love▲
Love Film
Mephisto▲
The Midas Touch

My Twentieth Century▲
Nice Neighbor▲
Nobody's Daughter
Oh, Bloody Life!
The Princess and the Goblin
The Red and the White▲
Red Earth
The Revolt of Job▲
Riddance▲
The Round Up
Sinbad
Stand Off
Sunday Daughters▲
Time Stands Still▲
25 Fireman's Street▲
Underground▲
Wagner: The Complete Epic
Wagner: The Movie
Where

Icelandic

Children of Nature
Cold Fever
The Juniper Tree
Remote Control

Indian

The Adversary
Aparajito▲
Bandit Queen
Bombay Talkie
Days and Nights in the Forest
Deadly Thief
The Deceivers
Devi▲
Distant Thunder▲
The Home and the World▲
The Householder
In Custody
Kama Sutra: A Tale of Love
Pather Panchali▲
Salaam Bombay!▲
Spices▲
The Stranger
Two Daughters▲
The World of Apu▲

Iranian

Life and Nothing More ...
The Taste of the Cherry
Through the Olive Trees▲
Where is My Friend's House?
The White Balloon▲

Irish

Broken Harvest
Broth of a Boy
Cal▲
The Commitments▲
The Courier
The Crying Game▲
Danny Boy▲
December Bride
Eat the Peach
Frankie Starlight
In the Name of the Father▲
Into the West▲
Lamb
Men of Ireland
My Left Foot▲
Nothing Personal▲
Paddy
Playboy of the Western World
Quackser Fortune Has a
  Cousin in the Bronx▲
The Snapper▲

Italian

The Last Man on Earth
Last Tango in Paris▸
The Last Tomahawk
Last Year at Marienbad▸
L'Avventura
Le Bal
The Legend of Blood Castle
The Legend of the Wolf Woman
Leon Morin, Priest
Leonor
Les Carabiniers▸
Les Miserables
Life of Verdi
Lightning Bolt
The Lion of Thebes▸
Lisa and the Devil
Little World of Don Camillo▸
Lobster for Breakfast
Lola
Love and Anarchy▸
Love in the City
Love Meetings
Lovers and Liars
Loves & Times of Scaramouche
The Loves of Hercules
Lucky Luciano
L'Udienza
Luna e L'Altra
Lunatics & Lovers
Lure of the Sila
Macaroni
Machine to Kill Bad People
Maciste in Hell
The Mad Butcher
Malicious
Mamma Roma▸
A Man Called Rage
Man from Cairo
Man from Deep River
Man of Legend
The Man Who Wagged His Tail
Man with a Cross
Manhattan Baby
Manhunt
Marauder
Marriage Italian Style▸
Master Touch
Mean Frank and Crazy Tony
Medea
Mediterraneo▸
Medusa Against the Son of Hercules
Messalina vs. the Son of Hercules
The Messiah▸
Miami Cops
Miami Horror
Mill of the Stone Women
Mille Bolle Blu
Millions
Minnesota Clay
A Minute to Pray, A Second to Die
The Miracle▸
Miracle in Milan▸
Mission Stardust
Mississippi Mermaid▸
Mister Mean
Mr. Superinvisible
Mole Men against the Son of Hercules
Mondo Cane
Mondo Cane 2
The Mongols
The Monster
Moon in the Gutter
Morgan the Pirate
Moving Target
Muriel▸
My Wonderful Life

The Name of the Rose
Nana
Navajo Joe
Nefertiti, Queen of the Nile
Nelly et Monsieur Arnaud▸
Nerolio
The New Gladiators
New Mafia Boss
New York Ripper
The Night After Halloween
The Night Evelyn Came Out of the Grave
Night Flight from Moscow
A Night Full of Rain
The Night of the Shooting Stars▸
Night of the Zombies
The Night Porter
Nightmare Castle
Nights of Cabiria▸
1900▸
1990: The Bronx Warriors
99 Women
Nostalgia
Nudo di Donna▸
Odds and Evens
Oedipus Rex▸
Oldest Profession
Once Upon a Time in the West▸
Open City▸
Open Doors▸
The Opponent
Orgy of the Vampires
Ossessione▸
Otello▸
Other Hell
Padre Padrone▸
Pain in the A—▸
Paisan▸
Palombella Rossa
Panic Button
Paranoia
Pardon My Trunk
Partner▸
The Passenger▸
Passion of Love▸
Passionate Thief
Peddlin' in Society
Phantom of Death
Phenomenal and the Treasure of Tutankamen
Pieces
Pierrot le Fou▸
Planet of the Vampires
Planet on the Prowl
Planets Against Us
Pool Hustlers
Porcile
The Postman▸
Private Affairs
The Puma Man
A Pure Formality
Quo Vadis
The Rape of the Sabines
The Red Desert▸
Red Sun
Redneck
Regina
The Return of Dr. Mabuse
Revenge of the Dead
Revolt of the Barbarians
Ricco
Rocco and His Brothers▸
RoGoPaG
Roland the Mighty
Romeo and Juliet
Romeo and Juliet▸
The Roof
Rorret
Rough Justice
Rush
The Ruthless Four

Sacrilege
Salammbo
Salo, or the 120 Days of Sodom
Samson
Samson Against the Sheik
Samson and His Mighty Challenge
Samson and the 7 Miracles of the World
Sandra of a Thousand Delights
Santa Sangre▸
Sardinia Kidnapped
Satanik
Savage Island
The Scalawag Bunch
Scenes from a Murder
The Scent of a Woman
The Scorpion's Tail
Secret Agent 00
Secret Agent Super Dragon
Seduced and Abandoned▸
Seduction of Mimi▸
Senso▸
The Sensuous Nurse
Seven Beauties▸
Seven Deadly Sins▸
Seven Deaths in the Cat's Eye
Seven Doors of Death
Sex with a Smile
The She-Beast
Shoeshine▸
Shoot Loud, Louder, I Don't Understand!
Sicilian Connection
Sinbad of the Seven Seas
Sins of Rome
The Slaughter of the Vampires
Slave of the Cannibal God
The Sleazy Uncle
Smugglers
Sodom and Gomorrah
Son of Captain Blood
Son of Samson
Sonny and Jed
Sonny Boy
Sotto, Sotto
Spaghetti House
A Special Day▸
The Spider's Stratagem▸
Spirits of the Dead▸
The Squeeze
Star Crash
The Star Maker
Stateline Motel
The Station
Stealing Beauty
Stephano Quantestorie
The Stolen Children▸
The Story of Boys & Girls▸
Stranger in Paso Bravo
Stromboli
Submission
Summer Affair
Summer Night
Summer Night with Greek Profile, Almond Eyes & Scent of Basil
Superargo
Suspiria▸
Swept Away...▸
The Swindle
The Sword of El Cid
The Taming of the Shrew▸
The Tempter
Tentacles
10th Victim▸
Teorema
Teresa Venerdi▸
Terranova

Terror Creatures from the Grave
Terror of Rome Against the Son of Hercules
Terror of the Steppes
That Man from Rio
They Call Me Trinity
Thief of Baghdad
Third Solution
Three Brothers▸
Throne of Fire
Thunder Warrior 2
Tiger of the Seven Seas
Tigers in Lipstick
Till Marriage Do Us Part
Time of Indifference
Time Out for Love
'Tis a Pity She's a Whore
To Forget Venice
Together?
Torso
Torture Chamber of Baron Blood
The Tragedy of a Ridiculous Man
Tramplers
The Tree of Wooden Clogs▸
Trinity is Still My Name
Tristana▸
Triumph of the Son of Hercules
12 Plus 1▸
Twitch of the Death Nerve
Two Evil Eyes
Two Nights with Cleopatra
2020 Texas Gladiators
Two Women▸
Tyrant of Lydia Against the Son of Hercules
Ulysses
Ulysses' Gaze
Umberto D▸
Uncle Tom's Cabin
Unsane
Ursus in the Valley of the Lions
Utz
Vanina Vanini▸
Variety Lights▸
Venus Against the Son of Hercules
Verdi
A Very Old Man with Enormous Wings
Viking Massacre
Violent Breed
Violent Professionals
The Virgin of Nuremberg
Viva Maria!
Volere Volare
Vulcan God of Fire
The Walls of Malapaga
War Bus Commando
The Warning
Warriors of the Wasteland
Watch Me When I Kill
Waterloo
The Wayward Wife
We All Loved Each Other So Much▸
We the Living
Web of the Spider
Wedding in Blood▸
Weekend▸
Werewolf in a Girl's Dormitory
When Women Had Tails
When Women Lost Their Tails
Where the Hot Wind Blows
Where's Piccone▸
White Nights▸
Wifemistress
Wild, Wild Planet

The Witch
A Woman of Rome
Woman Times Seven
Women in Cell Block 7
Women in Prison
Women's Prison Massacre
The Wonders of Aladdin
Yesterday, Today and Tomorrow▸
Yor, the Hunter from the Future
Zombie

Japanese

An Actor's Revenge
The Adventures of Milo & Otis▸
Akira
Akira Kurosawa's Dreams
Angel Dust
Antarctica
Arcadia of My Youth
Attack of the Mushroom People
Attack Squadron
An Autumn Afternoon▸
Baby Cart 1: Lend a Child...Lend an Arm
Baby Cart 4: Heart of a Parent...Heart of a Child
Baby Cart at the River Styx
Baby Cart to Hades
The Bad Sleep Well▸
The Ballad of Narayama▸
The Battle of the Japan Sea
Being Two Isn't Easy
Black Lizard
Black Magic Terror
Black Rain▸
Body Snatcher from Hell
The Burmese Harp▸
The Bushido Blade
The Castle of Cagliostro
The Crucified Lovers▸
The Cruel Story of Youth▸
Cyber Ninja
The Dagger of Kamui
Dagora, the Space Monster
The Day and the Hour
Demon City Shinjuku
Dersu Uzala▸
Destroy All Monsters
Destroy All Planets
Dodes 'ka-den▸
Double Suicide▸
Drifting Weeds▸
Drunken Angel▸
Early Summer▸
The Eel▸
Eijanaika▸
The Empire of Passion▸
Enjo
Equinox Flower
Face of Another
The Family Game▸
Fires on the Plain▸
Flirt
Forest of Little Bear
47 Ronin, Part 1▸
47 Ronin, Part 2▸
The Funeral
The Gambling Samurai
Gamera, the Invincible
Gamera vs. Barugon
Gamera vs. Gaos
Gamera vs. Guiron
Gamera vs. Zigra
Gappa the Trifibian Monster
Gate of Hell▸
A Geisha▸

Polish

The Deluge
Der Purimshpiler
The Double Life of Veronique
The Dybbuk
Enigma Secret
Family Life
Fever
First Spaceship on Venus►
Foul Play
A Generation►
Greta►
Hands Up►
Hero of the Year
Illumination
In an Old Manor House
In Desert and Wilderness
Innocent Sorcerers
The Interrogation►
Kanal►
Karate Polish Style
Knife in the Water►
Korczak►
Land of Promise
Leper
Lotna
Maids of Wilko
Mamele
Man of Iron►
Man of Marble►
Moonlighting►
Mother Joan of the Angels►
Mother of Kings
Nights and Days
No End
Paper Marriage
Passenger►
Pharaoh
Provincial Actors
The Saragossa Manuscript
The Silent Touch
The Singing Blacksmith
The Structure of Crystals
Train to Hollywood►
Trois Couleurs: Blanc►
Trois Couleurs: Rouge►
The Unapproachable
Without Anesthesia
Without Love
A Woman and a Woman
Year of the Quiet Sun►
Yidl Mitn Fidl

Portuguese

Black Orpheus►
The Convent
In the White City►
Life Is Beautiful
Return of the Evil Dead
Tombs of the Blind Dead

Romanian

The Oak
Trahir►
An Unforgettable Summer

Russian

Adomas Nori Buti Zmogumi
Aelita: Queen of Mars
Alexander Nevsky►
The Amphibian Man
Andrei Rublev►
Arsenal►
Ashik Kerib►
Autumn Marathon
Ballad of a Soldier►
Baltic Deputy►
The Battleship Potemkin►

Bed and Sofa►
Burglar►
Burnt by the Sun►
Chapayev►
The Children of Theatre Street
The Cigarette Girl of Mosselprom
Close to Eden
The Color of Pomegranates►
Come and See►
Commissar►
The Cranes Are Flying►
Creation of Adam
Crime and Punishment
The Day the Earth Froze
Dersu Uzala►
Don Quixote►
Earth►
The Errors of Youth
A Forgotten Tune for the Flute►
Freedom Is Paradise►
Freeze-Die-Come to Life►
Fury is a Woman►
The General Line►
The Girl with the Hat Box
Guerilla Brigade
Happiness
I Am Cuba
The Inspector General
Ivan the Terrible, Part 1►
Ivan the Terrible, Part 2►
Jazzman►
Kindergarten►
Kino Pravda/Enthusiasm
The Lady with the Dog►
The Legend of Suram Fortress
Little Vera►
Luna Park
The Magic Voyage of Sinbad
The Man with a Movie Camera►
The Mirror►
Moscow Does Not Believe in Tears►
Moscow Parade
Mother►
My Apprenticeship►
My Childhood►
My Name is Ivan►
My Universities►
No Greater Love
Oblomov►
Orphans►
The Overcoat►
The Patriots►
Peter the First: Part 1
Peter the First: Part 2
Planet Burg
Prisoner of the Mountains►
Private Life
Que Viva Mexico►
Rasputin►
Repentance►
The Road to Life
Shadows of Forgotten Ancestors►
The Shooting Party
Siberiade►
Sideburns
A Slave of Love►
Solaris
Solo Voyage: The Revenge
Stalker►
Storm over Asia►
Strike►
A Summer to Remember►
Sword & the Dragon
Taxi Blues►
Tchaikovsky

Ten Days That Shook the World►
The Theme►
To See Paris and Die
The Tsar's Bride►
An Unfinished Piece for a Player Piano►
War and Peace►
Waterloo
Window to Paris
Zvenigora►

South African

African Rage
City of Blood
Cry, the Beloved Country►
Deadly Passion
Emissary
The Evil Below
House of the Living Dead
Kill Slade
Place of Weeping
Stay Awake
Yankee Zulu

Spanish

Against the Wind
Anguish
Any Gun Can Play
Attack of the Robots
Autopsy of a Ghost
Ay, Carmela!►
Bad Man's River
Baton Rouge
Belle Epoque►
Between Heaven and Earth
Black Beauty
The Blood Spattered Bride
Blood Wedding►
Bullet for Sandoval
Butterfly Wings
Cabeza de Vaca►
Camila►
Carmen►
The Castle of Fu Manchu
Cauldron of Blood
Chimes at Midnight►
The Christmas Kid
The City and the Dogs►
City of the Walking Dead
Conquest
Count Dracula
Cria►
The Criminal Life of Archibaldo de la Cruz►
Curse of the Devil
Danzon►
Dark Habits
Demons in the Garden►
Desperados
Details of a Duel: A Question of Honor
The Devil's Possessed
The Diabolical Dr. Z
Dr. Jekyll and the Wolfman
Dr. Orloff's Monster
Don Juan, My Love►
Don Quixote►
Don Segundo Sombra
Dracula vs. Frankenstein
Dracula's Great Love
Duel of Champions
El Barbaro
El Cochecito►
El Condor
El Diputado►
El Muerto
El Norte►
El Super►

El: This Strange Passion►
Elisa, Vida Mia
Endless Descent
Escape from El Diablo
Exorcism's Daughter
The Exterminating Angel►
Exterminators in the Year 3000
Extramuros
The Fable of the Beautiful Pigeon Fancier
Fangs of the Living Dead
The Flower of My Secret►
Frida
From Hell to Victory
The Fury of the Wolfman
The Garden of Delights►
Garringo
Gladiators 7
Goliath Against the Giants
Grandes Amigos
Graveyard of Horror
Great Adventure
The Green Wall►
Half of Heaven►
The Hanging Woman
Hatchet for the Honeymoon
Hellbenders
High Heels►
The Holy Innocents►
Honey
Horror Express
Horror of the Zombies
Horror Rises from the Tomb
The House of 1000 Dolls
House of Psychotic Women
Human Beasts
The Hunt►
I, the Worst of All
I'm the One You're Looking For
In a Glass Cage
In Memoriam
Inquisition
Intruso►
The Invincible Gladiator
It Happened at Nightmare Inn
Jamon, Jamon►
Jornada de Muerte
Kashmiri Run
Kika
Killing Grandpa
King of Kong Island
Labyrinth of Passion
Land and Freedom►
Last Day of the War
Law of Desire►
Lazarillo
The Legend of Blood Castle
Leonor
Lightning Bolt
The Lion's Share
Lovers: A True Story►
Mama Turns a Hundred►
Man of Legend
The Man Who Wagged His Tail
Matador
Mayalunta
Miracle in Rome
Mission Stardust
Mr. Superinvisible
Mouth to Mouth
The Mummy's Revenge
Murder Mansion
Navajo Joe
The Nest
Night of the Death Cult
Night of the Howling Beast
Night of the Zombies
99 Women
Oasis of the Zombies
On the Line

Orgy of the Vampires
Outrage
Padre Nuestro
Pancho Villa
Passion for Power
Pepi, Luci, Bom and Other Girls on the Heap
Pieces
Pistoleros Asesinos
The Plague
Princess Cinderella
Pulsebeat
The Red Squirrel
Red Sun
Remolina de Pasiones
Return of the Evil Dead
The Return of the Musketeers
Ricco
The Rue Morgue Massacres
The Saga of the Draculas
Satanik
Savage Island
The Scarlet Letter►
The Scorpion's Tail
The Screaming Dead
The Sea Serpent
Sex Is Crazy
Skyline►
Son of Captain Blood
Sound of Horror
Spirit of the Beehive►
Star Knight
The Stilts►
Stormquest
The Summer of Miss Forbes
Superargo
Supersonic Man
The Sword of El Cid
Target Eagle
That Obscure Object of Desire►
Tie Me Up! Tie Me Down!
Tombs of the Blind Dead
A Town Called Hell
Trahir►
Treasure of the Four Crowns
Tristana►
Under the Earth►
The Uprising►
Ursus in the Valley of the Lions
Vengeance of the Zombies
A Very Old Man with Enormous Wings
Virgin Among the Living Dead
Viridiana►
Web of Deception
The Werewolf vs. the Vampire Woman
When the Screaming Stops
A Witch Without a Broom
Women on the Verge of a Nervous Breakdown
Yellow Hair & the Fortress of Gold
Zombie Lake

Swedish

The Adventures of Picasso
After the Rehearsal►
All Things Fair
The Assignment
The Atonement of Gosta Berling►
Autumn Sonata►
The Best Intentions►
Brink of Life
The Children of Noisy Village
The Count of the Old Town
Cries and Whispers►
The Devil's Eye

Devil's Wanton
The Doll
Dollar
Dreaming of Rita
Dreams
Elvira Madigan➤
The Emigrants➤
Evil Ed
Face to Face➤
Fanny and Alexander➤
Flight of the Eagle
Freud Leaving Home
From the Life of the
   Marionettes➤
Good Evening, Mr.
   Wallenberg
Gorilla
The Great Adventure➤
Hour of the Wolf➤
House of Angels
I Am Curious (Yellow)
The Inside Man
Intermezzo➤
Invasion of the Animal People
Istanbul
Jerusalem
June Night
Killing Heat
The Last Dance
Lesson in Love
Like It Never Was Before
The Magic Flute➤
The Magician➤
The Match Factory Girl➤
Miss Julie
Monika
Montenegro➤
The Mozart Brothers➤
My Life As a Dog➤
The New Land➤
Night Is My Future
Ninja Mission
Only One Night
The Outlaw and His Wife
The Ox
The Passion of Anna➤
Pelle the Conqueror➤
Persona➤
The Phantom Chariot
Pippi Goes on Board
Pippi in the South Seas
Pippi Longstocking
Pippi on the Run
Port of Call➤
The Rite
The Sacrifice➤
Sawdust & Tinsel➤
Scenes from a Marriage➤
Secrets of Women➤
The Seventh Seal➤
The Shame➤
The Silence➤
The Slingshot➤
Smiles of a Summer Night➤
Smilla's Sense of Snow
Sofie
Summer Interlude➤
Sunday's Children➤
Swedenhielms
Thomas Graal's Best Film➤
Three Strange Loves➤
Through a Glass Darkly➤
To Joy➤
Torment➤
The Touch
Treasure of Arne
The Virgin Spring➤
The Visitors
Walpurgis Night➤
Wardogs
Wild Strawberries➤
The Winter Light➤
Witchcraft Through the Ages➤

A Woman's Face➤

Swiss

After Darkness
Alpine Fire
Big Bluff
The Boat is Full➤
Candy Mountain
The Castle➤
Chimes at Midnight➤
Dangerous Moves➤
Drachenfutter➤
A Dream of Passion
First Love
Foxtrot
Hail Mary
Heidi
Helas Pour Moi
In the White City➤
Jonah Who Will Be 25 in the
   Year 2000➤
Journey of Hope➤
King Lear
La Salamandre
The Lacemaker➤
Messidor
Mouvements du Desir
Night and Day➤
Nouvelle Vague
The Pedestrian➤
Steppenwolf
Trahir➤
Trois Couleurs: Blanc➤
Trois Couleurs: Rouge➤

Taiwanese

The Association
Eat Drink Man Woman➤
The Outcasts➤
Vive L'Amour
The Wedding Banquet➤

Turkish

Baba➤
The Horse➤
Istanbul
The Wall➤
Yol➤

Venezuelan

Shoot to Kill

Vietnamese

The Scent of Green Papaya➤

Yugoslavian

The Battle of Austerlitz
Battle of Neretva
Battleforce
Cave of the Living Dead
Hey, Babu Riba
Innocence Unprotected
Kapo➤
The Love Affair, or The Case
   of the Missing Switchboard
   Operator➤
Man Is Not a Bird
One-Eyed Soldiers
Operation Cross Eagles
Romance of a Horsethief
The She-Beast
Son of Samson

Stealing Heaven
Sweet Movie
Time of the Gypsies➤
Tito and Me➤
Track of the Vampire
Uncle Tom's Cabin
Vukovar➤
Ward Six
When Father was Away on
   Business➤

The **Cast Index** provides a complete videography for cast members with more than one appearance on video. The listings for the actor names follow an alphabetical sort by last name (although the names appear in a first name last name format). The videographies are listed chronologically, from most recent film to earliest appearance, making it easier to trace the development of your favorite actor's career. When a cast member appears in more than one film in the same year, these movies are listed alphabetically within the year.

The Three Musketeers '39
The Great Waltz '38
Three Comrades '38
High Command '37
The Wrong Road '37
Captain Blood '35
Beggars in Ermine '34
Murders in the Zoo '33
Mystery of the Wax Museum '33
The Sphinx '33
Doctor X '32
The Vampire Bat '32

Anat Atzman
Double Edge '92
Every Time We Say Goodbye '86
Dead End Street '83

Rene Auberjonois
The Ballad of Little Jo '93
Lone Justice '93
Star Trek Deep Space Nine: Emissary '93
Wildcard '92
The Feud '90
Once Upon a Midnight Scary '90
A Connecticut Yankee in King Arthur's Court '89
Gore Vidal's Billy the Kid '89
My Best Friend Is a Vampire '88
Police Academy 5: Assignment Miami Beach '88
Walker '87
A Smoky Mountain Christmas '86
3:15—The Moment of Truth '86
Wild, Wild West Revisited '79
The Dark Secret of Harvest Home '78
Eyes of Laura Mars '78
King Kong '76
Pete 'n' Tillie '72
McCabe & Mrs. Miller '71
Brewster McCloud '70
M*A*S*H '70
Petulia '68

Lenore Aubert
Abbott and Costello Meet the Killer, Boris Karloff '49
Abbott and Costello Meet Frankenstein '48
Having Wonderful Crime '45
Action in Arabia '44

James Aubrey
Riders of the Storm '88
Forever Young '85
Home Before Midnight '84
The Terror '79
Bouquet of Barbed Wire '76
Lord of the Flies '63

Jimmy Aubrey
Legion of Missing Men '37
Aces and Eights '36
Courage of the North '35
Go-Get-'Em-Haines '35

Juliet Aubrey
Jacob '94
Middlemarch '93

Danielle Aubry
Operation C.I.A. '65
Bikini Beach '64

Jacques Aubuchon
Thunder Road '58
Gun Glory '57

Michel Auclair
Swashbuckler '84
The Story of a Love Story '73
Murder at 45 R.P.M. '65
Manon '50
Beauty and the Beast '46

Maxine Audley
Peeping Tom '60
The Trials of Oscar Wilde '60
A King in New York '57

Stephane Audran
Maximum Risk '96
Betty '92
The Turn of the Screw '92
Babette's Feast '87
Poor Little Rich Girl: The Barbara Hutton Story '87
La Cage aux Folles 3: The Wedding '86

The Blood of Others '84
Brideshead Revisited '81
Coup de Torchon '81
The Big Red One '80
Eagle's Wing '79
Silver Bears '78
Violette '78
Blood Relatives '77
Twist '76
Vincent, Francois, Paul and the Others '76
Black Bird '75
Ten Little Indians '75
Wedding in Blood '74
The Discreet Charm of the Bourgeoisie '72
La Rupture '70
Le Boucher '69
Les Biches '68
Six in Paris '68
Les Bonnes Femmes '60

Mischa Auer
Arrivederci, Baby! '66
The Christmas That Almost Wasn't '66
Sputnik '61
Mr. Arkadin '55
And Then There Were None '45
Brewster's Millions '45
Around the World '43
Hold That Ghost '41
Seven Sinners '40
Destry Rides Again '39
The Rage of Paris '38
Sweethearts '38
You Can't Take It with You '38
100 Men and a Girl '37
Pick a Star '37
Vogues of 1938 '37
My Man Godfrey '36
The Princess Comes Across '36
That Girl from Paris '36
Three Smart Girls '36
Condemned to Live '35
The Crusades '35
I Dream Too Much '35
Sucker Money '34
Flaming Signal '33
Woman Condemned '33
The Monster Walks '32
Drums of Jeopardy '31
Inside the Lines '30

Claudine Auger
Secret Places '85
Lobster for Breakfast '82
The Associate '79
Ricco '74
Head of the Family '71
Twitch of the Death Nerve '71
The Killing Game '67
Triple Cross '67
Thunderball '65
The Road to Lebanon '60

Lance August
Stripteaser '95
Terror Eyes '87

Pernilla August
Jerusalem '96
The Best Intentions '92

Robert August
The Endless Summer 2 '94
The Endless Summer '66

Ewa Aulin
The Legend of Blood Castle '72
Start the Revolution Without Me '70

Jean-Pierre Aumont
The Proprietor '96
Jefferson in Paris '94
Becoming Colette '92
A Tale of Two Cities '91
Windmills of the Gods '88
Sweet Country '87
The Blood of Others '84
Nana '82
Don't Look in the Attic '81
A Time for Miracles '80
Something Short of Paradise '79
Blackout '78
Cat and Mouse '78
Catherine & Co. '76
The Happy Hooker '75
Mahogany '75
Day for Night '73

Cauldron of Blood '67
The Horse Without a Head '63
The Devil at 4 O'Clock '61
John Paul Jones '59
Napoleon '55
Lili '53
Heartbeat '46
Maria Chapdelaine '34

Michel Aumont
Alberto Express '92
One Woman or Two '85
Grain of Sand '84
A Sunday in the Country '84
Les Comperes '83
La Vie Continue '82
Hothead '78
Spoiled Children '77

Tina Aumont
A Matter of Time '76
Lifespan '75
La Grande Bourgeoise '74
Malicious '74
Torso '73
Man of Legend '71
Partner '68
Texas Across the River '66

Marcus Aurelius
Suspect Device '95
A.P.E.X. '94

Albert Austin
Three Charlies and One Phoney! '18
Charlie Chaplin: The Early Years, Vol. 2 '17
The Cure '17
Charlie Chaplin: The Early Years, Vol. 3 '16
Charlie Chaplin: The Early Years, Vol. 4 '16
The Vagabond '16

Charlotte Austin
The Bride & the Beast '58
Daddy Long Legs '55

Julie Austin
Fatal Exposure '90
Elves '89

Karen Austin
When a Stranger Calls Back '93
When the Time Comes '91
A Girl to Kill For '90
Far from Home '89
Assassin '86
The Ladies Club '86
The Jagged Edge '85
Summer Rental '85

Terri Austin
False Witness '89
The Vindicator '85

William Austin
The Private Life of Henry VIII '33
Suds '20

Daniel Auteuil
Les Voleurs '96
The Eighth Day '95
Queen Margot '94
The Separation '94
Ma Saison Preferee '93
Un Coeur en Hiver '93
The Elegant Criminal '92
Mama, There's a Man in Your Bed '92
Jean de Florette '87
Manon of the Spring '87
Le Sex Shop '73

Alan Autry
Proud Men '87
At Close Range '86
Blue De Ville '86

Gene Autry
Bad Girls in the Movies '86
Cowboys of the Saturday Matinee '84
Gene Autry Matinee Double Feature #1 '53
Gene Autry Matinee Double Feature #2 '53
Gene Autry Matinee Double Feature #3 '53
Last of the Pony Riders '53
On Top of Old Smoky '53
Winning of the West '53
Blue Canadian Rockies '52

Night Stage to Galveston '52
Hills of Utah '51
Valley of Fire '51
Cow Town '50
The Big Sombrero '49
Riders of the Whistling Pines '49
Rim of the Canyon '49
Loaded Pistols '48
Robin Hood of Texas '47
Sioux City Sue '46
Western Double Feature 16 '46
Call of the Canyon '42
Heart of the Rio Grande '42
Down Mexico Way '41
Ridin' on a Rainbow '41
Twilight on the Rio Grande '41
Melody Ranch '40
Saturday Night Serials '40
Singing Cowboys, Vol. 2 '30s
South of the Border '39
The Man from Music Mountain '38
Oh Susannah '38
Old Barn Dance '38
Prairie Moon '38
Rootin' Tootin' Rhythm '38
Western Double Feature 1 '38
Big Show '37
Boots & Saddles '37
Git Along Little Dogies '37
Manhattan Merry-Go-Round '37
Public Cowboy No. 1 '37
Round-Up Time in Texas '37
Springtime in the Rockies '37
Western Double Feature 4 '37
Western Double Feature 5: Rogers & Autry '37
Yodelin' Kid From Pine Ridge '37
Old Corral '36
Red River Valley '36
Ride, Ranger, Ride '36
Melody Trail '35
The Phantom Empire '35
In Old Santa Fe '34
Mystery Mountain '34

Frankie Avalon
Back to the Beach '87
Blood Song '82
Grease '78
Dr. Goldfoot and the Bikini Machine '65
Beach Blanket Bingo '65
How to Stuff a Wild Bikini '65
I'll Take Sweden '65
Bikini Beach '64
Muscle Beach Party '64
Beach Party '63
The Castilian '63
Panic in the Year Zero! '62
Voyage to the Bottom of the Sea '61
The Alamo '60

Phillip Avalon
The Cursed Mountain Mystery '93
Summer City '77

Luis Avalos
Jungle 2 Jungle '96
Lone Justice 3: Showdown at Plum Creek '96
Lone Justice '93
Lone Justice 2 '93
Ghost Fever '87

Erik Avari
Stargate '94
The Beast '94

Loren Avedon
Virtual Combat '95
Operation Golden Phoenix '94
The King of the Kickboxers '91
No Retreat, No Surrender 3: Blood Brothers '91
No Retreat, No Surrender 2 '89

Brian Avery
Forced to Kill '93
The Graduate '67

James Avery
Spirit Lost '96
Beastmaster 2: Through the Portal of Time '91
Kicks '85

Linda Avery
Hitchhikers '72
Noon Sunday '71

Margaret Avery
White Man's Burden '95
Mardi Gras for the Devil '93
The Jacksons: An American Dream '92
Heat Wave '90
Return of Superfly '90
Riverbend '89
Blueberry Hill '88
For Us, the Living '88
The Color Purple '85
Lathe of Heaven '80
The Fish that Saved Pittsburgh '79
Which Way Is Up? '77
Hell Up in Harlem '73
Terror at Red Wolf Inn '72

Val Avery
Courage '86
Choices '81
The Chosen '81
Continental Divide '81
Black Caesar '73
Firehouse '72
A Dream of Kings '69
Faces '68

Angel Aviles
Scorpion Spring '96
Mi Vida Loca '93
Chain of Desire '93

Rick Aviles
Stephen King's The Stand '94
The Saint of Fort Washington '93
Ghost '90
Mystery Train '89
Spike of Bensonhurst '88

Mili Avital
Invasion of Privacy '96
Dead Man '95
Stargate '94

Chikage Awashima
The Human Condition: No Greater Love '58
Early Summer '51

Eddie Axberg
The New Land '73
The Emigrants '72

Nina Axelrod
Cross Country '83
Motel Hell '80

Hanne Axman
Five Fingers '52
The Red Menace '49

Hoyt Axton
Kingfish: A Story of Huey P. Long '95
Number One Fan '94
Season of Change '94
Buried Alive '90
The Rousters '90
Disorganized Crime '89
We're No Angels '89
Dixie Lanes '88
Retribution '88
Christmas Comes to Willow Creek '87
Guilty of Innocence '87
Act of Vengeance '86
Gremlins '84
Deadline Auto Theft '83
Goldilocks & the Three Bears '83
Heart Like a Wheel '83
Endangered Species '82
The Junkman '82

Ann Ayars
Fiesta '47
Reunion in France '42

Dan Aykroyd
Grosse Pointe Blank '97
Celtic Pride '96
Feeling Minnesota '96
Getting Away With Murder '96
My Fellow Americans '96
Sgt. Bilko '95
Tommy Boy '95
Exit to Eden '94

Marie '85
The Hotel New Hampshire '84
Look Back in Anger '80

Joy Bang
Messiah of Evil '74
Night of the Cobra Woman '72
Play It Again, Sam '72

Tallulah Bankhead
Die! Die! My Darling! '65
Lifeboat '44
Stage Door Canteen '43

Aaron Banks
Fist of Fear, Touch of Death '77
The Bodyguard '76

Jonathan Banks
Dark Breed '96
Flipper '96
Last Man Standing '95
Marilyn & Bobby: Her Final Affair '94
Walker: Texas Ranger: Deadly Reunion '94
Body Shot '93
Boiling Point '93
Freejack '92
There Goes the Neighborhood '92
Nightmare '91
Cold Steel '88
Armed and Dangerous '86
Assassin '86
Beverly Hills Cop '84
Nadia '84

Leslie Banks
Madeleine '50
Eye Witness '49
Henry V '44
Cottage to Let '41
Chamber of Horrors '40
The Arsenal Stadium Mystery '39
Jamaica Inn '39
Fire Over England '37
21 Days '39
Wings of the Morning '37
Sanders of the River '35
Transatlantic Tunnel '35
The Man Who Knew Too Much '34
The Most Dangerous Game '32

Vilma Banky
Blood and Sand/Son of the Sheik '26
Son of the Sheik '26
The Eagle '25

Ian Bannen
The Sound and the Silence '93
Blue Ice '92
Damage '92
The Big Man: Crossing the Line '91
George's Island '91
The Fifteen Streets '90
Ghost Dad '90
The Courier '88
Hope and Glory '87
Defense of the Realm '85
Lamb '85
The Prodigal '83
Eye of the Needle '81
The Watcher in the Woods '81
Bite the Bullet '75
The Gathering Storm '74
Driver's Seat '73
From Beyond the Grave '73
Mackintosh Man '73
The Offence '73
Doomwatch '72
Fright '71
Ride to Glory '71
Too Late the Hero '70
The Flight of the Phoenix '65
Carlton Browne of the F.O. '59
A Tale of Two Cities '58
The Third Key '57

Jill Banner
Hard Frame '70
Spider Baby '64

John Banner
Togetherness '70
Guilty of Treason '50
The Fallen Sparrow '43

Reggie Bannister
Phantasm III: Lord of the Dead '94
Silent Night, Deadly Night 4: Initiation '90
Survival Quest '89
Phantasm II '88
Phantasm '79

Jack Bannon
DaVinci's War '92
Miracle of the Heart: A Boys Town Story '86
Take Your Best Shot '82

Jim Bannon
Unknown World '51
The Fighting Redhead '50
Man from Colorado '49

Ildiko Bansagi
Meeting Venus '91
Mephisto '81

Li Bao-Tian
Shanghai Triad '95
Ju Dou '90

Nina Bara
Missile to the Moon '59
Black Hills '48

Theda Bara
The Love Goddesses '65
The Unchastened Woman '25
A Fool There Was '14

John Baragrey
Gamera, the Invincible '66
Pardners '56

Christine Baranski
The Birdcage '95
New Jersey Drive '95
The War '94
Addams Family Values '93
The Night We Never Met '93
The Ref '93
To Dance with the White Dog '93
Reversal of Fortune '90
9 1/2 Weeks '86
Crackers '84

Olivia Barash
Grave Secrets '89
Dr. Alien '88
Tuff Turf '85
Repo Man '83
Child of Glass '78

Richie Barathy
Body Trouble '92
Caged Fury '90

Luca Barbareschi
Private Affairs '89
Bye Bye Baby '88

Adrienne Barbeau
Burial of the Rats '95
Silk Degrees '94
Scott Turow's The Burden of Proof '92
Double-Crossed '91
Two Evil Eyes '90
Cannibal Women in the Avocado Jungle of Death '89
Back to School '86
Open House '86
Seduced '85
Terror at London Bridge '85
Next One '84
Charlie and the Great Balloon Chase '82
Creepshow '82
Swamp Thing '82
Cannonball Run '81
Escape from New York '81
Magic on Love Island '80
The Crash of Flight 401 '78
The Fog '78
Red Alert '77
Return to Fantasy Island '77

Ellen Barber
Blood Bride
Born Beautiful '82
The Premonition '75

Frances Barber
A Royal Scandal '96
We Think the World of You '88
A Zed & Two Noughts '88

Castaway '87
Prick Up Your Ears '87
Sammy & Rosie Get Laid '87
Pete Townshend: White City '85
Home Sweet Home '82

Gillian Barber
In Cold Blood '96
Maternal Instincts '96

Glynis Barber
Edge of Sanity '89
The Wicked Lady '83
Yesterday's Hero '79

Katie Barberi
Not Quite Human 2 '89
The Garbage Pail Kids Movie '87

Urbano Barberini
Torrents of Spring '90
Gor '88
Terror at the Opera '88
Outlaw of Gor '87
Demons '86

George Barbier
The Man Who Came to Dinner '41
Week-End In Havana '41
The Adventures of Marco Polo '38
Little Miss Broadway '38
My Lucky Star '38
On the Avenue '37
Waikiki Wedding '37
The Princess Comes Across '36
Wife Versus Secretary '36
The Crusades '35
Here Comes Cookie '35
The Merry Widow '34

Paula Barbieri
The Dangerous '95
Night Eyes 4: Fatal Passion '95
Red Shoe Diaries 5: Weekend Pass '95

Don Barclay
Outlaw Express '38
Thunder in the Desert '38
Border Phantom '37
Sweetheart of the Navy '37

Joan Barclay
The Shanghai Cobra '45
Sagebrush Law '43
The Black Dragons '42
The Corpse Vanishes '42
Flying Wild '41
Outlaw's Paradise '39
Lightnin' Carson Rides Again '38
Whirlwind Horseman '38
Blake of Scotland Yard '36
The Glory Trail '36
Phantom Patrol '36
Prison Shadows '36
Shadow of Chinatown '36
West of Nevada '36
Feud of the West '35
Finishing School '33

Roy Barcroft
Billy the Kid Versus Dracula '66
The Kettles on Old MacDonald's Farm '57
The Last Hunt '56
Marshal of Cedar Rock '53
Hoodlum Empire '52
Radar Men from the Moon '52
Don Daredevil Rides Again '51
North of the Great Divide '50
The Vanishing Westerner '50
Don Amigo/Stage to Chino '40s
Arizona Cowboy '50
Down Dakota Way '49
Federal Agents vs. Underworld, Inc. '49
Outcasts of the Trail '49
Eyes of Texas '48
G-Men Never Forget '48
Jesse James Rides Again '47
Son of Zorro '47
Stagecoach to Denver '46
Vigilantes of Boom Town '46
Bells of Rosarita '45
D-Day on Mars '45
Manhunt of Mystery Island '45
The Purple Monster Strikes '45
Sunset in El Dorado '45
The Topeka Terror '45

Haunted Harbor '44
Calling Wild Bill Elliott '43
Hoppy Serves a Writ '43
Raiders of Sunset Pass '43
Sagebrush Law '43
Six Gun Gospel '43
Below the Border '42
Dawn on the Great Divide '42
Sunset on the Desert '42
The Showdown '40
Hopalong Cassidy: Renegade Trail '39
Renegade Trail '39
The Frontiersmen '38

Javier Bardem
Mouth to Mouth '95
Jamon, Jamon '93

Trevor Bardette
Thunder Road '58
The Monolith Monsters '57
Hills of Oklahoma '50
Gun Crazy '49
Omoo Omoo, the Shark God '49
The Secret Code '42
Doomed Caravan '41

Aleksander Bardini
The Silent Touch '94
Trois Couleurs: Blanc '94
The Double Life of Veronique '91
No End '84

Brigitte Bardot
Legend of Frenchie King '71
Shalako '68
Spirits of the Dead '68
A Coeur Joie '67
Head Over Heels '67
Dear Brigitte '65
Viva Maria! '65
Contempt '64
Ravishing Idiot '64
Le Repos du Guerrier '62
A Very Private Affair '62
Voulez-Vous Danser Avec Moi? '59
The Bride Is Much Too Beautiful '58
That Naughty Girl '58
And God Created Woman '57
Mademoiselle Striptease '57
Doctor at Sea '56
Helen of Troy '56
Les Grandes Manoeuvres '55
Crazy for Love '52

Edda Barends
Broken Mirrors '85
Question of Silence '83

Lynn Bari
Trauma '62
Abbott and Costello Meet the Keystone Kops '54
Francis Joins the WACs '54
I Dream of Jeannie '52
I'd Climb the Highest Mountain '51
The Amazing Mr. X '48
Nocturne '46
Shock! '46
The Bridge of San Luis Rey '44
Hello, Frisco, Hello '43
The Magnificent Dope '42
Orchestra Wives '42
Sun Valley Serenade '41
Kit Carson '40

Sophie Barjac
Alice '86
Holiday Hotel '77

Jess Barker
Kentucky Rifle '55
Dragonfly Squadron '54

Lex Barker
The Torture Chamber of Dr. Sadism '69
Woman Times Seven '67
A Place Called Glory '66
Apaches Last Battle '64
Executioner of Venice '63
The Invisible Dr. Mabuse '62
Pirates of the Coast '61
The Return of Dr. Mabuse '61
La Dolce Vita '60
Mission in Morocco '59
Strange Awakening '58

Girl in Black Stockings '57
Away All Boats '56
The Black Devils of Kali '55
Mr. Blandings Builds His Dream House '48
Velvet Touch '48
The Farmer's Daughter '47

Ronnie Barker
Porridge '91
Open All Hours '83
The Best of the Two Ronnies '70s
Robin and Marian '76
The Man Outside '68

Steve Barkett
Bikini Drive-In '94
Dark Universe '93
Dinosaur Island '93
Aftermath '85

Ellen Barkin
The Fan '96
Trigger Happy '96
Wild Bill '95
Bad Company '94
Mac '93
This Boy's Life '93
Into the West '92
Man Trouble '92
Switch '91
Johnny Handsome '89
Sea of Love '89
Blood Money: The Story of Clinton and Nadine '88
The Big Easy '87
Siesta '87
Act of Vengeance '86
Desert Bloom '86
Down by Law '86
Terminal Choice '85
The Adventures of Buckaroo Banzai Across the Eighth Dimension '84
Harry & Son '84
The Princess Who Never Laughed '84
Daniel '83
Eddie and the Cruisers '83
Enormous Changes '83
Tender Mercies '83
Trumps '83
Diner '82
Kent State '81

Peter Barkworth
Champions '84
The Littlest Horse Thieves '76

Ivor Barnard
Beat the Devil '53
Madeleine '50

Binnie Barnes
Forty Carats '73
Where Angels Go, Trouble Follows '68
The Trouble with Angels '66
Decameron Nights '53
The Time of Their Lives '46
It's in the Bag '45
The Spanish Main '45
Call Out the Marines '42
I Married an Angel '42
In Old California '42
Melody Master '41
The Three Musketeers '39
The Adventures of Marco Polo '38
The Divorce of Lady X '38
Holiday '38
Broadway Melody of 1938 '37
The Last of the Mohicans '36
Three Smart Girls '36
Private Life of Don Juan '34
The Private Life of Henry VIII '33

Christopher Barnes
Angel of Fury '93
Battle of the Bullies '85
Tut & Tuttle '82

Christopher Daniel Barnes
A Very Brady Sequel '96
The Brady Bunch Movie '95
Murder without Motive '92

Joanna Barnes
Kill My Wife...Please!

Grand Hotel '32
Mata Hari '32
A Free Soul '31
Sadie Thompson '28
West of Zanzibar '28
America '24
America/The Fall of Babylon '24

Paul Bartel

Basquiat '96
The Death Artist '95
The Jerky Boys '95
The Usual Suspects '95
Number One Fan '94
Acting on Impulse '93
Desire and Hell at Sunset Motel '92
Liquid Dreams '92
Mortuary Academy '91
The Pope Must Diet '91
Far Out Man '89
Pucker Up and Bark Like a Dog '89
Scenes from the Class Struggle in Beverly Hills '89
Out of the Dark '88
Amazon Women on the Moon '87
Chopping Mall '86
Killer Party '86
Frankenweenie '84
Eating Raoul '82
Rock 'n' Roll High School '79
Piranha '78
Hollywood Boulevard '76

Eddie Barth

Mr. Write '92
Twenty Dollar Star '92
Thunder and Lightning '77

Richard Barthelmess

The Spoilers '42
Only Angels Have Wings '39
Spy of Napoleon '36
Heroes for Sale '33
The Cabin in the Cotton '32
The Dropkick '27
Just Suppose '26
Ranson's Folly '26
Shore Leave '25
Soul-Fire '25
Tol'able David '21
The Idol Dancer '20
The Love Flower '20
Way Down East '20
Broken Blossoms '19

Freddie Bartholomew

St. Benny the Dip '51
Sepia Cinderella '47
Tom Brown's School Days '40
Listen, Darling '38
Captains Courageous '37
Little Lord Fauntleroy '36
Lloyds of London '36
Anna Karenina '35
David Copperfield '35

Bennie Bartlett

Bowery Boys Meet the Monsters '54
Clipped Wings '53
Master Minds '49

Bonnie Bartlett

Shiloh '97
Dave '93
Dead to Rights '93
Twins '88
The Deliberate Stranger '86
Dempsey '83
Love Letters '83
A Long Way Home '81
Rape and Marriage: The Rideout Case '80

Robin Bartlett

Honey, We Shrunk Ourselves '97
Dangerous Minds '95
Fallen Angels 1 '93
Deceived '91
If Looks Could Kill '91
Regarding Henry '91
Alice '90
Lean on Me '89
Baby Boom '87

Eva Bartok

Blood and Black Lace '64
Operation Amsterdam '60
S.O.S. Pacific '60
Naked in the Night '58
The Gamma People '56
Norman Conquest '53
Spaceways '53
Crimson Pirate '52

Luciano Bartoli

Bizarre '87
Henry IV '85

Buzz Barton

The Riding Avenger '36
Feud of the West '35
Powdersmoke Range '35
The Tonto Kid '35
The Lone Defender '32
Mystery Trooper '32
Apache Kid's Escape '30

Diana Barton

Body of Influence '93
Sexual Malice '93

Gregg Barton

Silver City Bonanza '51
West to Glory '47

James Barton

The Misfits '61
Naked Hills '56
Here Comes the Groom '51
The Time of Your Life '48

Peter Barton

Friday the 13th, Part 4: The Final Chapter '84
Hell Night '81

Billy Barty

Ace Crawford, Private Eye
Wishful Thinking '92
Digging Up Business '91
Life Stinks '91
Lobster Man from Mars '89
Snow White '89
Willow '88
Body Slam '87
Masters of the Universe '87
Legend '86
Rumpelstiltskin '86
Tough Guys '86
Night Patrol '85
Under the Rainbow '81
Foul Play '78
The Amazing Dobermans '76
The Day of the Locust '75
Harum Scarum '65
Roustabout '64
The Undead '57
Mickey the Great '39
A Midsummer Night's Dream '35

Mikhail Baryshnikov

Company Business '91
Dancers '87
That's Dancing! '85
White Nights '85
The Turning Point '77

Gary Basaraba

A Horse for Danny '95
The War '94
Fried Green Tomatoes '91
Midnight Murders '91
One Magic Christmas '85

Richard Basehart

Marilyn: The Untold Story '80
Being There '79
The Rebels '79
Great Bank Hoax '78
Island of Dr. Moreau '77
Flood! '76
The Bounty Man '72
Rage '72
Chato's Land '71
The Andersonville Trial '70
Hans Brinker '69
Hitler '62
Portrait in Black '60
The Brothers Karamazov '58
Moby Dick '56
The Swindle '55
La Strada '54
Titanic '53
Reign of Terror '49
He Walked by Night '48
Cry Wolf '47

Count Basie

Sex and the Single Girl '64
Cinderfella '60

Toni Basil

Eating '90
Rockula '90
Angel 3: The Final Chapter '88
Slaughterhouse Rock '88
Mother, Jugs and Speed '76
Easy Rider '69
Pajama Party '64

Kim Basinger

Ready to Wear '94
The Getaway '93
The Real McCoy '93
Wayne's World 2 '93
Cool World '92
Final Analysis '92
The Marrying Man '91
Batman '89
My Stepmother Is an Alien '88
Blind Date '87
Nadine '87
Fool for Love '86
9 1/2 Weeks '86
No Mercy '86
The Natural '84
The Man Who Loved Women '83
Never Say Never Again '83
Mother Lode '82
Hard Country '81
Killjoy '81
From Here to Eternity '79

Elya Baskin

Spy Trap '92
Enemies, a Love Story '89
The Name of the Rose '86
Moscow on the Hudson '84

Marianne Basler

A Soldier's Tale '91
Overseas: Three Women with Man Trouble '90

Lena Basquette

Paradise Park '90s
Heroes of the Heart '94
A Night for Crime '42
Rose of Rio Grande '38
Hello Trouble '32
Hard Hombre '31
Pleasure '31

Alfie Bass

The Fearless Vampire Killers '67
The Lavender Hill Mob '51
Man on the Run '49

Albert Basserman

The Red Shoes '48
The Private Affairs of Bel Ami '47
Rhapsody in Blue '45
Since You Went Away '44
Madame Curie '43
The Moon and Sixpence '43
Invisible Agent '42
Reunion in France '42
The Shanghai Gesture '42
Melody Master '41
A Woman's Face '41
Foreign Correspondent '40

Angela Bassett

Contact '97
Strange Days '95
Vampire in Brooklyn '95
Waiting to Exhale '95
What's Love Got to Do with It? '93
The Jacksons: An American Dream '92
Malcolm X '92
Passion Fish '92
Boyz N the Hood '91
City of Hope '91
Critters 4 '91
The Heroes of Desert Storm '91

Linda Bassett

Mary Reilly '95
Waiting for the Moon '87

Alexandra Bastedo

Draw! '81
Find the Lady '75
The Ghoul '75
The Blood Spattered Bride '72

Kashmiri Run '69

Michal Bat-Adam

The Impossible Spy '87
Atalia '85
The House on Chelouche Street '73
I Love You Rosa '72

Sylvia Bataille

A Day in the Country '46
The Crime of Monsieur Lange '36

Alexei Batalov

Moscow Does Not Believe in Tears '80
The Lady with the Dog '59
The Cranes Are Flying '57

Nikolai Batalov

The Road to Life '31
Bed and Sofa '27
Mother '26
Aelita: Queen of Mars '24

Pierre Batcheff

Un Chien Andalou '28
Napoleon '27

Anthony Bate

Prime Suspect: Inner Circles '95
Philby, Burgess and MacLean: Spy Scandal of the Century '84
Madhouse Mansion '74

Jason Bateman

Breaking the Rules '92
A Taste for Killing '92
Necessary Roughness '91
Teen Wolf Too '87
Can You Feel Me Dancing? '85

Justine Bateman

A Century of Women '94
The Night We Never Met '93
Deadbolt '92
Primary Motive '92
The Closer '91
The Fatal Image '90
Satisfaction '88
Can You Feel Me Dancing? '85

Alan Bates

Grave Indiscretions '96
Silent Tongue '92
Unnatural Pursuits '91
Hamlet '90
Club Extinction '89
Mr. Frost '89
A Voyage' Round My Father '89
We Think the World of You '88
Prayer for the Dying '87
Duet for One '86
Trespasser '85
An Englishman Abroad '83
Separate Tables '83
The Wicked Lady '83
Britannia Hospital '82
Return of the Soldier '82
Quartet '81
Nijinsky '80
The Rose '79
The Shout '78
An Unmarried Woman '78
In Celebration '75
Royal Flash '75
The Story of a Love Story '73
A Day in the Death of Joe Egg '71
The Go-Between '71
Women in Love '70
The Fixer '68
Far from the Madding Crowd '67
Georgy Girl '66
The King of Hearts '66
Zorba the Greek '64
A Kind of Loving '62
Whistle Down the Wind '62
The Entertainer '60

Barbara Bates

Rhapsody '54
The Caddy '53
I'd Climb the Highest Mountain '51
Let's Make It Legal '51
Cheaper by the Dozen '50
The Inspector General '49
June Bride '48

Florence Bates

Lullaby of Broadway '51
The Judge Steps Out '49
A Letter to Three Wives '49
My Dear Secretary '49
I Remember Mama '48
Portrait of Jennie '48
Winter Meeting '48
The Secret Life of Walter Mitty '47
Diary of a Chambermaid '46
San Antonio '45
Saratoga Trunk '45
His Butler's Sister '44
Since You Went Away '44
Heaven Can Wait '43
Mr. Lucky '43
The Moon and Sixpence '43
Mexican Spitfire at Sea '42
The Tuttles of Tahiti '42
The Chocolate Soldier '41
Love Crazy '41
Road Show '41
The Son of Monte Cristo '41
Rebecca '40

Granville Bates

The Great Man Votes '38
Next Time I Marry '38
Waikiki Wedding '37

Jeanne Bates

Mom '89
Eraserhead '78
The Strangler '64
Sabaka '55
The Mask of Dijon '46

Kathy Bates

Diabolique '96
The Late Shift '96
The War at Home '96
Angus '95
Curse of the Starving Class '94
Dolores Claiborne '94
North '94
A Home of Our Own '93
Hostages '92
Prelude to a Kiss '92
Shadows and Fog '92
Used People '92
At Play in the Fields of the Lord '91
Fried Green Tomatoes '91
Dick Tracy '90
Misery '90
White Palace '90
High Stakes '89
Men Don't Leave '89
Roe vs. Wade '89
Signs of Life '89
Murder Ordained '87
Summer Heat '87
The Morning After '86
Come Back to the Five & Dime Jimmy Dean, Jimmy Dean '82
Straight Time '78

Michael Bates

A Clockwork Orange '71
Patton '70
Bedazzled '67

Paul Bates

The Preacher's Wife '96
Crazy People '90
Coming to America '88

Ralph Bates

Letters to an Unknown Lover '84
Second Chance '80
I Don't Want to Be Born '75
Poldark '75
Poldark 2 '75
The Graveyard '74
Murder Motel '74
Dynasty of Fear '72
Dr. Jekyll and Sister Hyde '71
Lust for a Vampire '71
The Horror of Frankenstein '70
Taste the Blood of Dracula '70

R.C. Bates

Werewolf '95
...And God Spoke '94

Timothy Bateson

Joseph '95
Heart of Darkness '93
The Mouse That Roared '59
The Guinea Pig '48

Chained Heat '83
Savage Streets '83
Hell Night '81
Ruckus '81
Roller Boogie '79
Wild Horse Hank '79
Summer of Fear '78
The Exorcist 2: The Heretic '77
Airport '75 '75
Sweet Hostage '75
Born Innocent '74
The Exorcist '73
The Sporting Club '72

Nicky Blair
The Crossing Guard '94
Viva Las Vegas '63

Tom Blair
Sure Fire '90
The Game '89

Deborah Blaisdell
Wildest Dreams '90
Student Affairs '88
Wimps '87

Amanda Blake
The Boost '88
B.O.R.N. '88
Gunsmoke: Return to Dodge '87
Betrayal '74
The Glass Slipper '55
Sabre Jet '53
The Duchess of Idaho '50
Stars in My Crown '50

Andre B. Blake
Philadelphia '93
Who's the Man? '93

Geoffrey Blake
The War at Home '96
Dominion '94
Marilyn & Bobby: Her Final Affair '94
Philadelphia Experiment 2 '93
Fatal Exposure '91
The Abduction of Kari Swenson '87

Jon Blake
The Lighthorsemen '87
Anzacs: The War Down Under '85
Early Frost '84
Freedom '81

Julia Blake
Hotel de Love '96
Father '90
Georgia '87
Travelling North '87
Man of Flowers '84
Lonely Hearts '82
Under Capricorn '82

Marie Blake
Sensations of 1945 '44
Love Finds Andy Hardy '38

Pamela Blake
Border Rangers '50
Gunfire '50
Sky Liner '49
Highway 13 '48
Rolling Home '48
Son of God's Country '48
Case of the Baby Sitter '47
Hat Box Mystery '47
Sea Hound '47
Kid Dynamite '43

Robert (Bobby) Blake
Lost Highway '96
Money Train '95
Heart of a Champion: The Ray Mancini Story '85
Of Mice and Men '81
Coast to Coast '80
Busting '74
Electra Glide in Blue '73
Counter Punch '71
Tell Them Willie Boy Is Here '69
In Cold Blood '67
This Property is Condemned '66
PT 109 '63
Pork Chop Hill '59
Treasure of the Golden Condor '52
Our Gang Comedies '40s
Western Double Feature 13 '40s

Western Double Feature 21 '40s
Treasure of the Sierra Madre '48
The Adventures of Rin Tin Tin '47
Homesteaders of Paradise Valley '47
Humoresque '46
Santa Fe Sunrise '46
Stagecoach to Denver '46
Vigilantes of Boom Town '46
Western Double Feature 12 '44
Woman in the Window '44
Andy Hardy's Double Life '42

Colin Blakely
Operation Julie '85
Loophole '83
Evil under the Sun '82
The Dogs of War '81
Little Lord Fauntleroy '80
Nijinsky '80
The Big Sleep '78
Equus '77
The Pink Panther Strikes Again '76
Love Among the Ruins '75
Murder on the Orient Express '74
Shattered '72
The Private Life of Sherlock Holmes '70
This Sporting Life '63

Donald Blakely
In the Shadow of Kilimanjaro '86
Short Eyes '79
Strike Force '75

Susan Blakely
Honor Thy Father and Mother: The True Story of the Menendez Brothers '94
Russian Roulette '93
Intruders '92
Blackmail '91
Wildflower '91
Dead Reckoning '89
The Incident '89
My Mom's a Werewolf '89
Out of Sight, Out of Her Mind '89
Broken Angel '89
Hiroshima Maiden '88
Ladykillers '88
The Survivalist '87
Over the Top '86
A Cry for Love '80
Make Me an Offer '80
The Concorde: Airport '79 '79
Dreamer '79
Secrets '77
Rich Man, Poor Man '76
The Lords of Flatbush '74
Report to the Commissioner '74
The Towering Inferno '74
Savages '72

Olive Blakeney
Billy the Kid '41
Gangway '37

Ronee Blakley
Murder by Numbers '89
Return to Salem's Lot '87
Someone to Love '87
Student Confidential '87
A Nightmare on Elm Street '84
The Baltimore Bullet '80
Lightning Over Water '80
Desperate Women '78
The Driver '78
The Private Files of J. Edgar Hoover '77
She Came to the Valley '77
Nashville '75

Dominique Blanc
Total Eclipse '95
Queen Margot '94
Indochine '92
May Fools '90

Erika Blanc
Sweet Spirits '80s
Mark of the Devil 2 '72
The Devil's Nightmare '71
The Night Evelyn Came Out of the Grave '71
Sartana's Here...Trade Your Pistol for a Coffin '70
Special Forces '68
Kill, Baby, Kill '66

Mel Blanc
Kiss Me, Stupid! '64
Neptune's Daughter '49

Michel Blanc
The Monster '96
Grosse Fatigue '94
Ready to Wear '94
The Favor, the Watch, & the Very Big Fish '92
Prospero's Books '91
Uranus '91
Monsieur Hire '89
Menage '86
French Fried Vacation '79

Jewel Blanch
Against A Crooked Sky '75
Baffled '72

Pierre Blanchar
La Symphonie Pastorale '46
Man from Nowhere '37
Crime and Punishment '35

Jarred Blanchard
The Boys Club '96
The Yearling '94

Mari Blanchard
Son of Sinbad '55
Abbott and Costello Go to Mars '53

Rachel Blanchard
Iron Eagle 4 '95
Young Ivanhoe '95

Susan Blanchard
She's in the Army Now '81
President's Mistress '78

Dorothee Blanck
Umbrellas of Cherbourg '64
Cleo from 5 to 7 '61

Sandrine Blancke
The Son of the Shark '93
Toto le Heros '91

Peter Bland
Tearaway '87
Dangerous Orphans '86
Came a Hot Friday '85

Clara Blandick
Dead Man's Eyes/Pillow of Death '44
Infamous Crimes '47
It Started with Eve '41
Dreaming Out Loud '40
The Wizard of Oz '39
The Adventures of Tom Sawyer '38
Small Town Boy '37
The Girl from Missouri '34
The Bitter Tea of General Yen '33
Murder at Midnight '31
Romance '30

Sally Blane
Fighting Mad '39
The Story of Alexander Graham Bell '39
Way Down South '39
Law of the Sea '38
The Silver Streak '34
Heritage of the Desert '33
Night of Terror '33
Cross Examination '32
Phantom Express '32
Probation '32
When the West Was Young '32
Vagabond Lover '29

Mark Blankfield
The Great American Sex Scandal '94
Robin Hood: Men in Tights '93
Angel 3: The Final Chapter '88
Frankenstein General Hospital '88
The Midnight Hour '86
Jack & the Beanstalk '83
Jekyll & Hyde...Together Again '82

Billy Blanks
Balance of Power '96
Expect No Mercy '95
Back in Action '94
Tough and Deadly '94
Showdown '93

TC 2000 '93
Talons of the Eagle '92
The King of the Kickboxers '91
Timebomb '91
Bloodfist '89

Arell Blanton
Assault of the Killer Bimbos '88
House of Terror '87
Wild Riders '71

Hans-Christian Blech
Colonel Redl '84
The Wrong Move '78
Dirty Hands '76
The Scarlet Letter '73
The Blum Affair '48

Jonah Blechman
Fall Time '94
This Boy's Life '93

Debra Blee
Malibu Bikini Shop '86
Sloane '84
Savage Streets '83
Beach Girls '82

Brian Blessed
Hamlet '96
Kidnapped '95
Chasing the Deer '94
Much Ado about Nothing '93
Back in the USSR '92
I, Claudius, Vol. 1: A Touch of Murder/Family Affairs '91
Prisoner of Honor '91
Robin Hood: Prince of Thieves '91
Henry V '89
High Road to China '83
The Hound of the Baskervilles '83
Flash Gordon '80
I, Claudius, Vol. 2: Waiting in the Wings/What Shall We Do With Claudius? '80
I, Claudius, Vol. 3: Poison is Queen/Some Justice '80
King Arthur, the Young Warlord '75
Young Warlord '75
Man of La Mancha '72
Trojan Women '71

Billy Bletcher
God's Country and the Man '37
Branded Men '31

Brenda Blethyn
Secrets and Lies '95
The Buddha of Suburbia '92
A River Runs Through It '92
The Witches '90
Grown Ups '80

Jason Blicker
African Journey '89
American Boyfriends '89

Bernard Blier
Buffet Froid '79
The Daydreamer '75
The Tall Blond Man with One Black Shoe '72
Catch Me a Spy '71
Casanova '70 '65
Les Miserables '57
The Man in the Raincoat '57
Dedee d'Anvers '49
Passion for Life '48
Jenny Lamour '47

Hunt Block
The Dirty Dozen: The Fatal Mission '87
Secret Weapons '85

Dan Blocker
Lady in Cement '68
Ride the Wind '66
Bonanza '64
The Errand Boy '61

Dirk Blocker
Night of the Scarecrow '95
Bonanza: The Return '93
Trouble in Mind '86

Michael Blodgett
The Ultimate Thrill '74
The Velvet Vampire '71

Joan Blondell
The Baron '88

The Woman Inside '83
The Champ '79
The Rebels '79
The Glove '78
Opening Night '77
The Dead Don't Die '75
Death at Love House '75
Support Your Local Gunfighter '71
Stay Away, Joe '68
Waterhole #3 '67
The Cincinnati Kid '65
Angel Baby '61
Hollywood Bloopers '50s
Desk Set '57
This Could Be the Night '57
Will Success Spoil Rock Hunter? '57
The Opposite Sex '56
Adventure '45
A Tree Grows in Brooklyn '45
Lady for a Night '42
Topper Returns '41
Bullets or Ballots '38
Stand-In '37
Three Men on a Horse '36
Dames '34
Footlight Parade '33
Gold Diggers of 1933 '33
Three Broadway Girls '32
Three on a Match '32
Big Business Girl '31
Blonde Crazy '31
Illicit '31
Millie '31
Night Nurse '31
Public Enemy '31

Anne Bloom
That's Adequate '90
Dirt Bike Kid '86

Brian Bloom
At Home with the Webbers '94
Voyage of Terror: The Achille Lauro Affair '90
Walls of Glass '85

Claire Bloom
Daylight '96
Mighty Aphrodite '95
A Village Affair '95
Shameless '94
Crimes & Misdemeanors '89
A Doll's House '89
Shadow on the Sun '88
Intimate Contact '87
Queenie '87
Sammy & Rosie Get Laid '87
Anastasia: The Mystery of Anna '86
Shadowlands '85
This Lightning Always Strikes Twice '85
Deja Vu '84
Ghostwriter '84
Separate Tables '83
Brideshead Revisited '81
Clash of the Titans '81
Islands in the Stream '76
The Illustrated Man '69
Charly '68
Soldier in Love '67
The Spy Who Came in from the Cold '65
The Haunting '63
The Wonderful World of the Brothers Grimm '62
The Brothers Karamazov '58
The Buccaneer '58
Look Back in Anger '58
Alexander the Great '55
Richard III '55
Innocents in Paris '53
Limelight '52

John Bloom
Casino '95
Bachelor Party '84
The Hills Have Eyes, Part 2 '84
Brain of Blood '71
Dracula vs. Frankenstein '71
The Incredible Two-Headed Transplant '71

Lindsay Bloom
French Quarter '78
Hughes & Harlow: Angels in Hell '77

Guns of Diablo '64
Four for Texas '63
The Great Escape '63
Kid Galahad '62
Master of the World '61
The Magnificent Seven '60
Never So Few '59
Machine Gun Kelly '58
Showdown at Boot Hill '58
When Hell Broke Loose '58
Jubal '56
Run of the Arrow '56
Drum Beat '54
House of Wax '53
Miss Sadie Thompson '53
Vera Cruz '53
Pat and Mike '52

Lillian Bronson
Spencer's Mountain '63
The Next Voice You Hear '50

Claudio Brook
Cronos '94
The Bees '78
Dr. Tarr's Torture Dungeon '75
Sisters of Satan '75
The Peking Blond '68
Simon of the Desert '66
Viva Maria! '65
Samson in the Wax Museum '63
Neutron and the Black Mask '61
The Young One '61
Daniel Boone: Trail Blazer '56

Clive Brook
On Approval '44
Convoy '40
Action for Slander '38
Cavalcade '33
Shanghai Express '32
Hula '28
Underworld '27

Faith Brook
Bloodbath
Eye of the Needle '81
After Julius '78
To Sir, with Love '67
Uneasy Terms '48

Irina Brook
Captive '87
The Girl in the Picture '86
Transmutations '85

Jayne Brook
Ed '96
Last Dance '96
Clean Slate '94
Kindergarten Cop '90

Lyndon Brook
Invasion '65
The Spanish Gardener '57
Above Us the Waves '56

Elwyn Brook-Jones
Rogue's Yarn '56
The Gilded Cage '54
Bonnie Prince Charlie '48

Hillary Brooke
The Man Who Knew Too Much '56
Heat Wave '54
Abbott and Costello Meet Captain Kidd '52
Never Wave at a WAC '52
The Lost Continent '51
Africa Screams '49
Big Town '47
Big Town After Dark '47
Underworld Scandal '47
The Road to Utopia '46
The Strange Woman '46
The Enchanted Cottage '45
The Woman in Green '45
Jane Eyre '44
Sherlock Holmes Faces Death '43
Sherlock Holmes: The Voice of Terror '42
To the Shores of Tripoli '42
Rangeland Racket '41
The Philadelphia Story '40

Sandy Brooke
Crazed Cop '88
Miami Vendetta '87
Star Slammer '87
Terror on Alcatraz '86

Walter Brooke
The Return of Count Yorga '71
Conquest of Space '55

Richard Brooker
Deathstalker '83
Friday the 13th, Part 3 '82

Jacqueline Brookes
Naked Gun 2 1/2: The Smell of Fear '91
Silent Witness '85
Hardhat & Legs '80
Rodeo Girl '80

Aimee Brooks
Critters 3 '91
Say Anything '89

Albert Brooks
Mother '96
The Scout '94
I'll Do Anything '93
Defending Your Life '91
Broadcast News '87
Lost in America '85
Unfaithfully Yours '84
Twilight Zone: The Movie '83
Modern Romance '81
Private Benjamin '80
Real Life '79
Taxi Driver '76

Avery Brooks
Spenser: Pale Kings & Princes '94
The Ernest Green Story '93
Spenser: Ceremony '93
Star Trek Deep Space Nine: Emissary '93
Roots: The Gift '88
Uncle Tom's Cabin '87
Half Slave, Half Free '85

Clarence Brooks
Bronze Buckaroo '39
Harlem Rides the Range '39

Conrad Brooks
Bikini Drive-In '94
Plan 9 from Outer Space '56

David Brooks
Magic in the Mirror: Fowl Play '96
Scream for Help '86

Elisabeth Brooks
The Forgotten One '89
The Howling '81

Foster Brooks
Oddballs '84
Cracking Up '83
The Villain '79
Super Seal '77

Geraldine Brooks
Johnny Tiger '66
The Green Glove '52
Challenge to Lassie '49
Reckless Moment '49
Cry Wolf '47
The Possessed '47

Hildy Brooks
Forbidden Love '82
The Chosen '81

Jean Brooks
Boss of Big Town '43
The Leopard Man '43
The Seventh Victim '43
Boot Hill Bandits '42

Joel Brooks
The Man Who Captured Eichmann '96
Indecent Proposal '93
Are You Lonesome Tonight '92

Leslie Brooks
The Cobra Strikes '48
Romance on the High Seas '48
The Scar '48
Tonight and Every Night '45
City Without Men '43
You Were Never Lovelier '42

Louise Brooks
Overland Stage Raiders '38
Prix de Beaute '30
Diary of a Lost Girl '29
Pandora's Box '28
It's the Old Army Game '26

Love 'Em and Leave 'Em '26

Mel Brooks
Dracula: Dead and Loving It '95
Robin Hood: Men in Tights '93
Life Stinks '91
Spaceballs '87
To Be or Not to Be '83
History of the World: Part 1 '81
High Anxiety '77
Silent Movie '76
Blazing Saddles '74
Twelve Chairs '70
Putney Swope '69

Phyllis Brooks
Dangerous Passage '44
Silver Spurs '43
The Shanghai Gesture '42
Slightly Honorable '40
Little Miss Broadway '38
Rebecca of Sunnybrook Farm '38
In Old Chicago '37

Rand Brooks
Comanche Station '60
The Vanishing Westerner '50
Ladies of the Chorus '49
Hopalong Cassidy: Borrowed Trouble '48
Hopalong Cassidy: Dangerous Venture '48
Hopalong Cassidy: False Paradise '48
Hopalong Cassidy: Silent Conflict '48
Hopalong Cassidy: Sinister Journey '48
Hopalong Cassidy: The Dead Don't Dream '48
Hopalong Cassidy: Hoppy's Holiday '47
Hopalong Cassidy: The Marauders '47
Hopalong Cassidy: Unexpected Guest '47
Hopalong Cassidy: The Devil's Playground '46
The Sombrero Kid '42
Gone with the Wind '39

Randi Brooks
Colors '88
Cop '88
Hamburger...The Motion Picture '86
Tightrope '84
Forbidden Love '82

Randy Brooks
Black Snow '93
Reservoir Dogs '92

Ray Brooks
Office Romances '86
House of Whipcord '75
Tiffany Jones '75
Flesh and Blood Show '73
Daleks—Invasion Earth 2150 A.D. '66
The Knack '65

Richard Brooks
The Crow 3: City of Angels '96
The Substitute '96
Machine Gun Blues '95

Richard Brooks
Memphis '91
To Sleep with Anger '90
84 Charlie Mopic '89
Shocker '89
Shakedown '88
Short Fuse '88
The Hidden '87

Edward Brophy
Last Hurrah '58
Roaring City '51
Renegade Girl '46
Swing Parade of 1946 '46
Cover Girl '44
The Thin Man Goes Home '44
Destroyer '43
Dance, Girl, Dance '40
The Invisible Woman '40
Great Guy '36
Kelly the Second '36
Mad Love '35
Show Them No Mercy '35
Evelyn Prentice '34

Hide-Out '34
What! No Beer? '33
The Champ '32
Speak Easily '32
Doughboys '30
The Cameraman '28

Kevin Brophy
Delos Adventure '86
The Seduction '82
Hell Night '81

Pierce Brosnan
Dante's Peak '97
Mars Attacks! '96
The Mirror Has Two Faces '96
Detonator 2: Night Watch '95
Goldeneye '95
Don't Talk to Strangers '94
Love Affair '94
The Broken Chain '93
Detonator '93
Entangled '93
Mrs. Doubtfire '93
The Lawnmower Man '92
Live Wire '92
Mister Johnson '91
Murder 101 '91
Victim of Love '91
Around the World in 80 Days '89
The Heist '89
The Deceivers '88
Noble House '88
Taffin '88
The Fourth Protocol '87
Nomads '86
Remington Steele, Vol. 1: License to Steele '82
The Carpathian Eagle '81
The Manions of America '81
The Long Good Friday '80
The Mirror Crack'd '80

Collette Brosset
Belle Americaine '61
Femmes de Paris '53

Dr. Joyce Brothers
The Lonely Guy '84
Desperate Lives '82
Embryo '76

Liliane Brousse
Maniac '63
Paranoiac '63

Amelda Brown
Little Dorrit, Film 1: Nobody's Fault '88
Little Dorrit, Film 2: Little Dorrit's Story '88

Barbara Brown
My Sister Eileen '55
Ma and Pa Kettle on Vacation '53
Home Town Story '51
Ma and Pa Kettle Back On the Farm '51
Ma and Pa Kettle Go to Town '50
Hollywood Canteen '44
The Fighting Sullivans '42

Barry Brown
He Who Walks Alone '78
The Disappearance of Aimee '76
The Ultimate Thrill '74
Bad Company '72

Blair Brown
The Day My Parents Ran Away '93
Passed Away '92
Strapless '90
Stealing Home '88
Hands of a Stranger '87
The Bad Seed '85
A Flash of Green '85
Kennedy '83
Continental Divide '81
Altered States '80
One Trick Pony '80
And I Alone Survived '78
The Choirboys '77

Bobby Brown
A Thin Line Between Love and Hate '96
Mother Goose Rock 'n' Rhyme '90

Bryan Brown
Full Body Massage '95
The Last Hit '93
Blame It on the Bellboy '92
Devlin '92
Dead in the Water '91
F/X 2: The Deadly Art of Illusion '91
Prisoners of the Sun '91
Sweet Talker '91
Cocktail '88
Gorillas in the Mist '88
F/X '86
The Good Wife '86
Tai-Pan '86
The Empty Beach '85
Far East '85
Rebel '85
A Town Like Alice '85
Give My Regards to Broad Street '84
Kim '84
Parker '84
The Thorn Birds '83
The Winter of Our Dreams '82
Blood Money '80
Breaker Morant '80
Palm Beach '79
The Irishman '78
Money Movers '78
Newsfront '78

Charles D. Brown
Follow Me Quietly '49
Merton of the Movies '47
Brother Orchid '40
Old Swimmin' Hole '40
Shopworn Angel '38
Dance of Life '29

Clancy Brown
Donor Unknown '95
The Shawshank Redemption '94
Last Light '93
Past Midnight '92
Pet Sematary 2 '92
Ambition '91
Cast a Deadly Spell '91
Love, Lies and Murder '91
Blue Steel '90
Season of Fear '89
Shoot to Kill '88
Highlander '86
The Bride '85
Bad Boys '83

David G. Brown
Chasing Dreams '81
Deadly Harvest '72

D.W. Brown
Mischief '85
Weekend Pass '84

Dwier Brown
Deconstructing Sarah '94
Lily in Winter '94
The Cutting Edge '92
Galaxies Are Colliding '92
Mom and Dad Save the World '92
The Guardian '90

Eric Brown
Video Murders '87
They're Playing with Fire '84
Private Lessons '81

Gary Brown
Invasion of the Space Preachers '90
The Glory Boys '84

Georg Stanford Brown
Tyson '95
Ava's Magical Adventure '94
Murder without Motive '92
House Party 2: The Pajama Jam '91
Alone in the Neon Jungle '87
North and South Book 1 '85
The Jesse Owens Story '84
The Kid with the Broken Halo '82
The Night the City Screamed '80
Roots: The Next Generation '79
Colossus: The Forbin Project '70
Dayton's Devils '68

Georgia Brown
Victim of Love '91

Brown ▸cont.

Love at Stake '87
Actor: The Paul Muni Story '78
Tales That Witness Madness '73
Nothing But the Night '72
Long Ago Tomorrow '71
The Fixer '68

Henry Brown
Uncaged '91
The Man in the Glass Booth '75

James Brown
Courage of Rin Tin Tin '83
Doctor Detroit '83
The Blues Brothers '80
Adios Amigo '75
Targets '68
Rin Tin Tin, Hero of the West '55
Objective, Burma! '45

Jim Brown
Mars Attacks! '96
Original Gangstas '96
The Divine Enforcer '91
Crack House '89
L.A. Vice '89
Twisted Justice '89
I'm Gonna Git You Sucka '88
L.A. Heat '88
Pacific Inferno '85
One Down, Two to Go! '82
Fingers '78
Kid Vengeance '75
Take a Hard Ride '75
Three the Hard Way '74
Slaughter's Big Ripoff '73
Slaughter '72
El Condor '70
The Passing of Evil '70
100 Rifles '69
Riot '69
Dark of the Sun '68
Ice Station Zebra '68
The Dirty Dozen '67
Rio Conchos '64

Joe E. Brown
The Comedy of Terrors '64
It's a Mad, Mad, Mad, Mad World '63
Some Like It Hot '59
Around the World in 80 Days '56
Show Boat '51
The Tender Years '47
Pin-Up Girl '44
The Gladiator '38
Wide Open Faces '38
Fit for a King '37
Riding on Air '37
When's Your Birthday? '37
Earthworm Tractors '36
A Midsummer Night's Dream '35
Lottery Bride '30

Johnny Mack Brown
Apache Uprising '66
Border Bandits '46
Gentleman from Texas '46
The Stranger from Pecos '45
Lawmen '44
Partners of the Trail '44
Raiders of the Border '44
Range Law '44
Ghost Rider '43
Six Gun Gospel '43
Texas Kid '43
Ride 'Em Cowboy '42
Boss of Bullion City '41
Bury Me Not on the Lone Prairie '41
Man from Montana '41
The Masked Rider '41
Pony Post '40
Riders of Pasco Basin '40
Oregon Trail '39
Fire Alarm '38
Flaming Frontiers '38
Boothill Brigade '37
The Gambling Terror '37
Guns in the Dark '37
A Lawman Is Born '37
Crooked Trail '36
Desert Phantom '36
Rogue of the Range '36
Undercover Man '36
Valley of the Lawless '36

Western Double Feature 3 '36
Between Men '35
Branded a Coward '35
Courageous Avenger '35
Every Man's Law '35
Rustlers of Red Dog '35
Belle of the Nineties '34
Female '33
Fighting with Kit Carson '33
Coquette '29
The Single Standard '29
Annapolis '28
Our Dancing Daughters '28
A Woman of Affairs '28

Juanita Brown
Black Starlet '74
Caged Heat '74

Judy Brown
The Manhandlers '73
The Big Doll House '71

Julie Brown
Clueless '95
Fist of the North Star '95
Out There '95
National Lampoon's Attack of the 5 Ft. 2 Women '94
Nervous Ticks '93
The Opposite Sex and How to Live With Them '93
Raining Stones '93
Shakes the Clown '92
Spirit of '76 '91
Earth Girls Are Easy '89
Bloody Birthday '80

Lou Brown
Death Games '82
Alison's Birthday '79
The Irishman '78

Pamela Brown
Wuthering Heights '70
Secret Ceremony '69
Cleopatra '63
Victoria Regina '61
Lust for Life '56
Alice in Wonderland '50
I Know Where I'm Going '45
One of Our Aircraft Is Missing '41

Paul Brown
Butterfly Kiss '94
Anne of Green Gables '85
Morons from Outer Space '85
Transmutations '85

Peter Brown
The Aurora Encounter '85
The Concrete Jungle '82
Act of Vengeance '74
Eagles Attack at Dawn '74
Memory of Us '74
Slashed Dreams '74
Chrome and Hot Leather '71
Hard Frame '70
Ride the Wild Surf '64
A Tiger Walks '64
Merrill's Marauders '62
Red Nightmare '62
Darby's Rangers '58
The Commies are Coming, the Commies are Coming '57

Phil Brown
Tropic of Cancer '70
Operation Cross Eagles '69
The Hidden Room '49
Without Reservations '46

Philip Brown
Wild Zone '89
Eye of the Needle '81
Special Olympics '78

Ralph Brown
Ivanhoe '97
Wayne's World 2 '93
Alien 3 '92
The Crying Game '92
Impromptu '90
Buster '88
Withnail and I '87

Reb Brown
Last Flight to Hell
Cage 2: The Arena of Death '94
The Firing Line '91
Street Hunter '90
The Cage '89

Mercenary Fighters '88
Space Mutiny '88
White Ghost '88
Strike Commando '87
Death of a Soldier '85
Howling 2: Your Sister Is a Werewolf '85
Uncommon Valor '83
Yor, the Hunter from the Future '83
Captain America '79
Captain America 2: Death Too Soon '79

Ritza Brown
The McGuffin '85
Ator the Fighting Eagle '83

Robert Brown
The Living Daylights '87
Pilgrim, Farewell '82
One Million Years B.C. '66
Tower of London '62
Shake Hands with the Devil '59

Roger Brown
Tall Tale: The Unbelievable Adventures of Pecos Bill '95
Don't Cry, It's Only Thunder '82
Paper Lion '68
Venus Against the Son of Hercules '62

Ron Brown
The Legend of Black Thunder Mountain '79
Charlie, the Lonesome Cougar '67

Sara Suzanne Brown
Killer Looks '94
Secret Games 2: The Escort '93
Test Tube Teens from the Year 2000 '93

Stephen Brown
Beyond Darkness '92
Metamorphosis '90

Thomas Wilson Brown
Diggstown '92
Honey, I Shrunk the Kids '89
Welcome Home '89

Tim Brown
Pacific Inferno '85
Code Name: Zebra '84
A Place Called Today '72

Timothy Brown
The Dynamite Brothers '74
Girls Are for Loving '73
Sweet Sugar '72

Tom Brown
The Choppers '61
Operation Haylift '50
Ringside '49
Buck Privates Come Home '47
Adventures of Smilin' Jack '43
The Payoff '43
In Old Chicago '37
Maytime '37
Navy Blue and Gold '37
I'd Give My Life '36
Anne of Green Gables '34

Vanessa Brown
Witch Who Came from the Sea '76
The Fighter '52
Three Husbands '50
The Ghost and Mrs. Muir '47

W. Earl Brown
Scream '96
Dead Air '94
Excessive Force '93

Wally Brown
Girl Rush '44
Zombies on Broadway '44

Woody Brown
Animal Instincts 2 '94
Dominion '94
Secret Games 3 '94
Alligator 2: The Mutation '90
The Rain Killer '90
The Accused '88

Charles A. Browne
Federal Agent '36
Tailspin Tommy '34

Coral Browne
Dreamchild '85
American Dreamer '84
An Englishman Abroad '83
Eleanor: First Lady of the World '82
The Ruling Class '72
The Killing of Sister George '69
Auntie Mame '58
The Courtney Affair '47

Leslie Browne
Dancers '87
Nijinsky '80
The Turning Point '77

Lucille Browne
Cheyenne Rides Again '38
Texas Terror '35
Western Frontier '35
Brand of Hate '34
Law of the Wild '34
The Devil's Brother '33
Mystery Squadron '33

Roscoe Lee Browne
Dear God '96
Last Summer In the Hamptons '96
The Pompatus of Love '95
Naked in New York '93
The Mambo Kings '92
Moon 44 '90
For Us, the Living '88
Legal Eagles '86
Haunting of Harrington House '82
Nothing Personal '80
Unknown Powers '80
King '78
Twilight's Last Gleaming '77
Logan's Run '76
Superfly T.N.T. '73
The World's Greatest Athlete '73
The Cowboys '72
The Liberation of L.B. Jones '70
Black Like Me '64
The Connection '61

Suzanne Browne
The Bikini Car Wash Company 2 '92
The Bikini Car Wash Company '90

Ricou Browning
Flipper's New Adventure '64
Creature from the Black Lagoon '54

Brenda Bruce
Splitting Heirs '93
Antonia and Jane '91
December Bride '91
Back Home '90
The Tenth Man '88
That'll Be the Day '73
Nightmare '63
Peeping Tom '60

Cheryl Lynn Bruce
Daughters of the Dust '91
Victimless Crimes '90
Music Box '89

Colin Bruce
Chicago Joe & the Showgirl '90
Crusoe '89
Gotham '88

David Bruce
Jungle Hell '55
Pier 23 '51
Calling Dr. Death/Strange Confession '43
Can't Help Singing '45
Lady On a Train '45
Salome, Where She Danced '45
The Mad Ghoul '43
The Sea Wolf '41

Kate Bruce
Struggle '31
The Idol Dancer '20
Judith of Bethulia '14

Lenny Bruce
Dynamite Chicken '70
Dance Hall Racket '58

Nigel Bruce
Limelight '52
Julia Misbehaves '48

The Two Mrs. Carrolls '47
Dressed to Kill '46
Terror by Night '46
Terror by Night/Meeting at Midnight '46
The Corn is Green '45
House of Fear '45
Pursuit to Algiers '45
Son of Lassie '45
The Woman in Green '45
The Pearl of Death '44
Scarlet Claw '44
Spider Woman '44
Lassie, Come Home '43
Sherlock Holmes Faces Death '43
Sherlock Holmes in Washington '43
Journey for Margaret '42
Roxie Hart '42
Sherlock Holmes and the Secret Weapon '42
Sherlock Holmes: The Voice of Terror '42
The Chocolate Soldier '41
Suspicion '41
The Blue Bird '40
Rebecca '40
Susan and God '40
The Adventures of Sherlock Holmes '39
The Hound of the Baskervilles '39
The Rains Came '39
The Last of Mrs. Cheyney '37
Thunder in the City '37
The Charge of the Light Brigade '36
Becky Sharp '35
She '35
The Scarlet Pimpernel '34
Stand Up and Cheer '34
Treasure Island '34

Virginia Bruce
Strangers When We Meet '60
State Department File 649 '49
Action in Arabia '44
Pardon My Sarong '42
The Invisible Woman '40
Let Freedom Ring '39
Born to Dance '36
The Great Ziegfeld '36
Let 'Em Have It '35
Jane Eyre '34

Patrick Bruel
Sabrina '95
Secret Obsession '88
Bandits '86

Eddie Brugman
Broken Mirrors '85
Keetje Tippel '75

Beau Brummel
Three Bullets for a Long Gun '73
Village of the Giants '65

Bo Brundin
Headless Eyes '83
Shoot the Sun Down '81
Russian Roulette '75

Fernando Bruno
Time Out for Love '61
Two Nights with Cleopatra '54

Philip Bruns
The Opposite Sex and How to Live With Them '93
Dead Men Don't Die '91
Return of the Living Dead 2 '88
The Stunt Man '80

Dora Bryan
Screamtime '83
The Great St. Trinian's Train Robbery '66
A Taste of Honey '61
Small Hotel '57
My Son, the Vampire '52
No Trace '50
The Fallen Idol '49

Jane Bryan
Each Dawn I Die '39
The Old Maid '39
The Sisters '38
Kid Galahad '37
Marked Woman '37

Jim Byrnes
Bloodhounds 2 '96
Suspicious Agenda '94
Dirty Work '92

Josephine Byrnes
Frauds '93
Brides of Christ '91

David Byron
Fade to Black '93
My Brother's Wife '89

Jeffrey Byron
Dungeonmaster '83
Metalstorm: The Destruction of Jared Syn '83
The Seniors '78

Kathleen Byron
Twins of Evil '71
Burn Witch, Burn! '62
Profile '54
Young Bess '53
The Gambler & the Lady '52
The Small Back Room '49
Black Narcissus '47

Marion Byron
Breed of the Border '33
Steamboat Bill, Jr. '28

Walter Byron
Mr. Boggs Steps Out '38
The Savage Girl '32
Vanity Fair '32
Queen Kelly '29

Susan Byun
Deadly Target '94
Crime Lords '91

James Caan
Bulletproof '96
Eraser '96
North Star '96
Bottle Rocket '95
Flesh and Bone '93
The Program '93
Honeymoon in Vegas '92
The Dark Backward '91
For the Boys '91
Dick Tracy '90
Misery '90
Alien Nation '88
Gardens of Stone '87
Bolero '82
Kiss Me Goodbye '82
The Godfather 1902-1959: The Complete Epic '81
Thief '81
Hide in Plain Sight '80
Chapter Two '79
Comes a Horseman '78
Little Moon & Jud McGraw '78
Another Man, Another Chance '77
A Bridge Too Far '77
Harry & Walter Go to New York '76
Silent Movie '76
Funny Lady '75
The Killer Elite '75
Rollerball '75
Freebie & the Bean '74
The Gambler '74
The Godfather, Part 2 '74
Cinderella Liberty '73
Slither '73
The Godfather '72
Gone with the West '72
Brian's Song '71
The Rain People '69
Countdown '68
El Dorado '67
Red Line 7000 '65
Lady in a Cage '64

Scott Caan
Nowhere '96
A Boy Called Hate '95

Katia Caballero
Sharpe's Eagle '93
Beyond Innocence '87

Bruce Cabot
Diamonds Are Forever '71
Chisum '70
The Undefeated '69
Hellfighters '68
The War Wagon '67
In Harm's Way '65

McLintock! '63
Hatari! '62
The Comancheros '61
Goliath and the Dragon '61
Goliath and the Barbarians '60
John Paul Jones '59
Lost in Alaska '52
Best of the Badmen '50
Fancy Pants '50
Sorrowful Jones '49
Angel and the Badman '47
Silver Queen '42
Sundown '41
Captain Caution '40
Susan and God '40
Dodge City '39
Renegade Ranger/Scarlet River '38
Sinners in Paradise '38
Fury '36
The Last of the Mohicans '36
Let 'Em Have It '35
Show Them No Mercy '35
Ann Vickers '33
Finishing School '33
King Kong '33

Sebastian Cabot
Family Jewels '65
Twice-Told Tales '63
The Time Machine '60
Johnny Tremain & the Sons of Liberty '58
Terror in a Texas Town '58
Omar Khayyam '57
Westward Ho, the Wagons! '56
Romeo and Juliet '54
Captain's Paradise '53
Dick Barton Strikes Back '48
Dual Alibi '47

Susan Cabot
The Wasp Woman '59
Machine Gun Kelly '58
Carnival Rock '57
Sorority Girl '57
Duel at Silver Creek '52
Son of Ali Baba '52
Flame of Araby '51

Jean Cadell
The Obsessed '51
Madeleine '50
Pygmalion '38
Love from a Stranger '37

Jason Cadieux
Lilies '96
Iron Eagle 4 '95

Michael Cadman
Poldark 2 '75
If... '69

Adolph Caesar
Club Paradise '86
Fortune Dane '86
The Color Purple '85
A Soldier's Story '84
The Hitter '79
Fist of Fear, Touch of Death '77

Harry Caesar
Ghetto Blaster '89
The Offspring '87

Sid Caesar
Cannon Movie Tales: The Emperor's New Clothes '89
Side By Side '88
Stoogemania '85
Cannonball Run 2 '84
Over the Brooklyn Bridge '83
Grease 2 '82
History of the World: Part 1 '81
The Munsters' Revenge '81
The Fiendish Plot of Dr. Fu Manchu '80
The Cheap Detective '78
Grease '78
Barnaby and Me '77
Curse of the Black Widow '77
Silent Movie '76
Airport '75 '75
It's a Mad, Mad, Mad, Mad World '63

Cheri Caffaro
Too Hot to Handle '76
Girls Are for Loving '73
The Abductors '72
Ginger '72

A Place Called Today '72

Stephen Caffrey
The Babe '92
Longtime Companion '90
Hard Rain-The Tet 1968 '89
Tour of Duty '87

Andrea Cagan
Teenager '74
Hot Box '72

Nicolas Cage
Con Air '97
Face/Off '97
The Rock '96
Leaving Las Vegas '95
Guarding Tess '94
It Could Happen to You '94
Kiss of Death '94
Trapped In Paradise '94
Amos and Andrew '93
Deadfall '93
Red Rock West '93
Honeymoon in Vegas '92
Zandalee '91
Fire Birds '90
Time to Kill '89
Vampire's Kiss '88
Moonstruck '87
Raising Arizona '87
Boy in Blue '86
Peggy Sue Got Married '86
Birdy '84
The Cotton Club '84
Racing with the Moon '84
Rumble Fish '83
Valley Girl '83

James Cagney
Ragtime '81
One, Two, Three '61
The Gallant Hours '60
Never Steal Anything Small '59
Shake Hands with the Devil '59
Man of a Thousand Faces '57
Tribute to a Bad Man '56
Love Me or Leave Me '55
Mister Roberts '55
The Seven Little Foys '55
A Lion Is in the Streets '53
What Price Glory? '52
Kiss Tomorrow Goodbye '50
The West Point Story '50
White Heat '49
The Time of Your Life '48
13 Rue Madeleine '46
Blood on the Sun '45
Johnny Come Lately '43
Captains of the Clouds '42
Yankee Doodle Dandy '42
The Bride Came C.O.D. '41
Strawberry Blonde '41
City for Conquest '40
The Fighting 69th '40
Each Dawn I Die '39
Oklahoma Kid '39
The Roaring Twenties '39
Angels with Dirty Faces '38
Boy Meets Girl '38
Great Guy '36
Something to Sing About '36
Ceiling Zero '35
Devil Dogs of the Air '35
"G" Men '35
A Midsummer Night's Dream '35
Footlight Parade '33
Lady Killer '33
Blonde Crazy '31
Public Enemy '31

Jeanne Cagney
Postmark for Danger/Quicksand '56
Kentucky Rifle '55
A Lion Is in the Streets '53
Don't Bother to Knock '52
Quicksand '50
The Time of Your Life '48
Yankee Doodle Dandy '42

William Cagney
Palooka '34
Ace of Aces '33

Howard Caine
Watermelon Man '70
Pressure Point '62

Michael Caine
Mandela and de Klerk '97
Blood & Wine '96
Bullet to Beijing '95
On Deadly Ground '94
World War II: When Lions Roared '94
Blue Ice '92
Death Becomes Her '92
The Muppet Christmas Carol '92
Noises Off '92
Bullseye! '90
Jekyll and Hyde '90
Mr. Destiny '90
A Shock to the System '90
Dirty Rotten Scoundrels '88
Jack the Ripper '88
Without a Clue '88
The Fourth Protocol '87
Jaws: The Revenge '87
Surrender '87
The Whistle Blower '87
Half Moon Street '86
Hannah and Her Sisters '86
Mona Lisa '86
Sweet Liberty '86
The Holcroft Covenant '85
Water '85
Blame It on Rio '84
The Jigsaw Man '84
Beyond the Limit '83
Educating Rita '83
Deathtrap '82
The Hand '81
Victory '81
Dressed to Kill '80
The Island '80
Ashanti, Land of No Mercy '79
Beyond the Poseidon Adventure '79
California Suite '78
Silver Bears '78
The Swarm '78
A Bridge Too Far '77
The Eagle Has Landed '77
Harry & Walter Go to New York '76
The Man Who Would Be King '75
Romantic Englishwoman '75
The Wilby Conspiracy '75
The Black Windmill '74
The Destructors '74
Pulp '72
Sleuth '72
X, Y & Zee '72
The Last Valley '71
Too Late the Hero '70
Battle of Britain '69
The Italian Job '69
Woman Times Seven '67
Alfie '66
Funeral in Berlin '66
Gambit '66
The Wrong Box '66
The Ipcress File '65
Zulu '64
Room 43 '58

John Cairney
Mania '60
A Night to Remember '58

David Calder
Bramwell '95
A Question of Attribution '91

Anna Calder-Marshall
The Two Faces of Evil '82
Wuthering Heights '70

Sergio Calderon
Men in Black '97
Border Shootout '90
Old Gringo '89

Paul Calderone
Sweet Nothing '96
The Addiction '95
Condition Red '95
Four Rooms '95
Lotto Land '95
Bad Lieutenant '92
Crisscross '92
Q & A '90

L. Scott Caldwell
Twilight Man '96

Down Came a Blackbird '94
God Bless the Child '88

Zoe Caldwell
Lantern Hill '90
The Purple Rose of Cairo '85
Medea '59

Don Calfa
H.P. Lovecraft's Necronomicon: Book of the Dead '93
Me, Myself & I '92
Chopper Chicks in Zombietown '91
Weekend at Bernie's '89
Treasure of the Moon Goddess '88
Return of the Living Dead '85
E. Nick: A Legend in His Own Mind '84
The Rainbow Gang '73

Louis Calhern
Forever Darling '56
High Society '56
Blackboard Jungle '55
The Prodigal '55
Athena '54
Betrayed '54
Executive Suite '54
Men of the Fighting Lady '54
Rhapsody '54
The Student Prince '54
Julius Caesar '53
Latin Lovers '53
Prisoner of Zenda '52
We're Not Married '52
The Asphalt Jungle '50
A Life of Her Own '50
The Magnificent Yankee '50
Nancy Goes to Rio '50
Two Weeks with Love '50
The Red Pony '49
Arch of Triumph '48
Notorious '46
The Bridge of San Luis Rey '44
Up in Arms '44
Heaven Can Wait '43
The Gorgeous Hussy '36
Last Days of Pompeii '35
Sweet Adeline '35
The Count of Monte Cristo '34
Duck Soup '33
The World Gone Mad '33
Night After Night '32
They Call It Sin '32
Blonde Crazy '31
The Blot '21
Too Wise Wives '21

Alice Calhoun
Tentacles of the North '26
The Man on the Box '25

Rory Calhoun
Pure Country '92
Roller Blade Warriors: Taken By Force '90
Bad Jim '89
Hell Comes to Frogtown '88
Avenging Angel '85
Angel '84
Mission to Glory '80
Motel Hell '80
Flatbed Annie and Sweetiepie: Lady Truckers '79
The Rebels '79
Midnight Auto Supply '78
Operation Cross Eagles '69
Dayton's Devils '68
Emerald of Artama '67
Apache Uprising '66
Finger on the Trigger '65
Hard Drivin' '60
Treasure of Pancho Villa '55
A Bullet Is Waiting '54
River of No Return '54
I'd Climb the Highest Mountain '51
Ticket to Tomahawk '50
Adventure Island '47
The Red House '47

Joseph Cali
The Lonely Lady '83
The Competition '80

Brandon Call
For the Boys '91
The Adventures of Ford Fairlane '90

Cassavetes ➤cont.

Mrs. Parker and the Vicious
  Circle '94
Twogether '94
Body of Influence '93
Broken Trust '93
Class of 1999 2: The Substitute
  '93
Sins of the Night '93
Sins of Desire '93
Delta Force 3: The Killing Game
  '91
Backstreet Dreams '90
Blind Fury '90
Assault of the Killer Bimbos '88
The Wraith '87

Jean-Pierre Cassel
La Ceremonie '95
Ready to Wear '94
Between Heaven and Earth '93
The Favor, the Watch, & the
  Very Big Fish '92
The Fatal Image '90
The Maid '90
The Phantom of the Opera '90
Mr. Frost '89
The Return of the Musketeers
  '89
Alice '86
La Truite '82
Nudo di Donna '83
La Vie Continue '82
From Hell to Victory '79
Les Rendez-vous D'Anna '78
Who Is Killing the Great Chefs of
  Europe? '78
The Killing of a Chinese Bookie
  '76
Twist '76
The Four Musketeers '75
That Lucky Touch '75
Murder on the Orient Express
  '74
The Three Musketeers '74
The Discreet Charm of the
  Bourgeoisie '72
La Rupture '70
The Killing Game '67
Is Paris Burning? '66
Those Magnificent Men in Their
  Flying Machines '65
The Elusive Corporal '62

Seymour Cassel
Cannes Man '96
Tree's Lounge '96
Bad Love '95
Dark Side of Genius '94
Imaginary Crimes '94
It Could Happen to You '94
Tollbooth '94
Boiling Point '93
Chain of Desire '93
Hand Gun '93
Indecent Proposal '93
Adventures in Spying '92
Honeymoon in Vegas '92
In the Soup '92
There Goes My Baby '92
Trouble Bound '92
Diary of a Hitman '91
White Fang '91
Dick Tracy '90
Sweet Bird of Youth '89
Wicked Stepmother '89
Johnny Be Good '88
Plain Clothes '88
Track 29 '88
Best Seller '87
Survival Game '87
Tin Men '87
Eye of the Tiger '86
Love Streams '84
Double Exposure '82
The Mountain Men '80
California Dreaming '79
Black Oak Conspiracy '77
Seducers '77
Valentino '77
Faces '68

Vincent Cassel
Hate '95
L'Eleve '95

Cafe au Lait '94

Alan Cassell
Squizzy Taylor '84
The Club '81
Money Movers '78

Wally Cassell
Until They Sail '57
Breakdown '53

Andrew Cassese
Revenge of the Nerds 2: Nerds
  in Paradise '87
Revenge of the Nerds '84

Gabriel Casseus
Get On the Bus '96
Nightjohn '96
New Jersey Drive '95

David Cassidy
Spirit of '76 '91
Instant Karma '90
The Night the City Screamed '80

Edward Cassidy
Buffalo Bill Rides Again '47
Son of Zorro '47
Devil Riders '44
Frontier Outlaws '44
Rustler's Hideout '44
Wild Horse Phantom '44
Sagebrush Law '43
Aces Wild '37
Boothill Brigade '37
Boots of Destiny '37
Roaring Six Guns '37
Santa Fe Bound '37
A Face in the Fog '36
Feud of the West '36
Toll of the Desert '35

Jack Cassidy
The Eiger Sanction '75
Columbo: Murder By the Book
  '71
The Andersonville Trial '70

Joanna Cassidy
Chain Reaction '96
Barbarians at the Gate '93
Stephen King's The
  Tommyknockers '93
Landslide '92
Live! From Death Row '92
Perfect Family '92
All-American Murder '91
Don't Tell Mom the Babysitter's
  Dead '91
Lonely Hearts '91
Nightmare at Bittercreek '91
A Girl of the Limberlost '90
May Wine '90
Wheels of Terror '90
Where the Heart Is '90
1969 '89
The Package '89
A Father's Revenge '88
Who Framed Roger Rabbit '88
The Fourth Protocol '87
The Children of Times Square
  '86
Club Paradise '86
Codename: Foxfire '85
Invitation to Hell '84
Under Fire '83
Blade Runner '82
Night Games '80
The Glove '79
The Late Show '77
Stunts '77
Bank Shot '74

Patrick Cassidy
How the West was Fun '95
Hitler's Daughter '90
Longtime Companion '90
Love at Stake '87
Dress Gray '86
Something in Common '86
Fever Pitch '85
Nickel Mountain '85
Just the Way You Are '84
Off the Wall '82

Shaun Cassidy
Texas Guns '90
Roots: The Gift '88

Ted Cassidy
Women's Prison Escape

Halloween with the Addams
  Family '79
Sunshine Run '79
Goin' Coconuts '78
Planet Earth '74
Thunder County '74
Poor Pretty Eddie '73
Butch Cassidy and the
  Sundance Kid '69
MacKenna's Gold '69
The Addams Family '64

Claudio Cassinelli
The New Gladiators '87
Hands of Steel '86
Hercules 2 '85
Slave of the Cannibal God '79
Allonsanfan '73

Nadia Cassini
Star Crash '78
Pulp '72

John Cassisi
Man's Best Friend '93
Bugsy Malone '76

Jean-Pierre Castaldi
A Fine Romance '92
La Merveilleuse Visite '74

Lou Castel
Rorret '87
The Eyes, the Mouth '83
The Scarlet Letter '73
Beware of a Holy Whore '70
Paranoia '69
A Bullet for the General '68

Dan Castellaneta
The War of the Roses '89
Nothing in Common '86

Richard Castellano
The Godfather 1902-1959: The
  Complete Epic '81
Night of the Juggler '80
Honor Thy Father '73
The Godfather '72
Lovers and Other Strangers '70

Vincent Castellanos
Anaconda '96
The Crow 2: City of Angels '96

Sergio Castellitto
The Star Maker '95
Alberto Express '92
The Big Blue '88

Willy Castello
Confessions of a Vice Baron '42
Mad Youth '40

Nino Castelnuovo
The English Patient '96
Umbrellas of Cherbourg '64

Christopher Castile
Beethoven's 2nd '93
Beethoven '92

Enrique Castillo
My Family '94
Blood in ... Blood Out: Bound by
  Honor '93

Gloria Castillo
Invasion of the Saucer Men '57
Meteor Monster '57
Reform School Girl '57

Don Castle
Motor Patrol '50
Who Killed Doc Robbin? '48

John Castle
The Crucifer of Blood '91
RoboCop 3 '91
The Bretts '88
Lillie '79
Man of La Mancha '72
The Lion in Winter '68

Peggy Castle
The Seven Hills of Rome '58
Beginning of the End '57
The Finger Man '55
The White Orchid '54
Invasion U.S.A. '52

Roy Castle
Alice Through the Looking Glass
  '66
Doctor Who and the Daleks '65

William Castle
Bug '75

Shampoo '75
Rosemary's Baby '68

Georgina Cates
Frankie Starlight '95
An Awfully Big Adventure '94

Helen Cates
The Whole Wide World '96
The Underneath '95
A Taste for Killing '92

Phoebe Cates
Princess Caraboo '94
Bodies, Rest & Motion '93
Drop Dead Fred '91
Gremlins 2: The New Batch '90
The Heart of Dixie '89
Shag: The Movie '89
Bright Lights, Big City '88
Date with an Angel '87
Gremlins '84
Private School '83
Fast Times at Ridgemont High
  '82
Paradise '82

Reg E. Cathey
Seven '95
Tank Girl '94

Brigitte Catillon
Un Coeur en Hiver '93
La Lectrice '88

Walter Catlett
The Inspector General '49
His Butler's Sister '44
They Got Me Covered '43
Yankee Doodle Dandy '42
It Started with Eve '41
Pop Always Pays '40
Remedy for Riches '40
Every Day's a Holiday '38
On the Avenue '37
Mr. Deeds Goes to Town '36
A Tale of Two Cities '36
Rain '32
The Front Page '31

Victoria Catlin
Howling 5: The Rebirth '89
Mutant on the Bounty '89

Juliette Caton
Courage Mountain '89
The Last Temptation of Christ
  '88

Christine Cattall
Bedroom Eyes '86
Screwball Academy '86

Kim Cattrall
Unforgettable '96
Where Truth Lies '96
Above Suspicion '95
The Heidi Chronicles '95
Live Nude Girls '95
Breaking Point '94
Running Delilah '93
Wild Palms '93
Double Vision '92
Split Second '92
Miracle in the Wilderness '91
Star Trek 6: The Undiscovered
  Country '91
The Bonfire of the Vanities '90
Honeymoon Academy '90
Smokescreen '90
Goodnight, Michelangelo '89
The Return of the Musketeers
  '89
Masquerade '88
Palais Royale '88
Mannequin '87
Midnight Crossing '87
Big Trouble in Little China '86
City Limits '85
Turk 182! '85
Police Academy '84
Porky's '82
Ticket to Heaven '81
Scruples '80
Tribute '80
The Rebels '79
The Bastard '78
Rosebud '75
Deadly Harvest '72

Philippe Caubere
My Father's Glory '91

My Mother's Castle '91

Daniel Cauchy
Bob le Flambeur '55
Grisbi '53

Lane Caudell
Archer: The Fugitive from the
  Empire '81
Hanging on a Star '78

Joan Caulfield
Pony Express Rider '76
Daring Dobermans '73
Buckskin '68
The Lady Says No '51
Dear Wife '49
Welcome Stranger '47
Blue Skies '46
Monsieur Beaucaire '46

Maxwell Caulfield
Backlash: Oblivion 2 '95
Empire Records '95
Alien Intruder '93
Gettysburg '93
In a Moment of Passion '93
Midnight Witness '93
No Escape, No Return '93
Animal Instincts '92
Dance with Death '91
Sundown '91
Exiled in America '90
Mind Games '89
Project: Alien '89
The Supernaturals '86
The Boys Next Door '85
Electric Dreams '84
Grease 2 '82

Valeria Cavalli
Double Team '97
Joseph '95
Everybody's Fine '90

Victor Cavallo
Dial Help '88
The Tragedy of a Ridiculous
  Man '81

Megan Cavanagh
Robin Hood: Men in Tights '93
A League of Their Own '92

Paul Cavanagh
Francis in the Haunted House
  '56
The Prodigal '55
Charade '53
House of Wax '53
Bride of the Gorilla '51
The Strange Door '51
Hi-Jacked '50
Black Arrow '48
Humoresque '46
House of Fear '45
The Woman in Green '45
Captains of the Clouds '42
Shadows on the Stairs '41
Goin' to Town '35
Tarzan and His Mate '34
A Bill of Divorcement '32

Tom Cavanagh
Bloodhounds 2 '96
A Vow to Kill '94

Hobart Cavanaugh
The Magnificent Dope '42
Rose of Washington Square '39
Wife Versus Secretary '36
I Cover the Waterfront '33

Elise Cavanna
The Barber Shop '33
Best of W.C. Fields '33
The Dentist '32
Pharmacist '32
W.C. Fields: Flask of Fields '30

Lumi Cavazos
Last Stand at Saber River '96
Bottle Rocket '96
Manhattan Merenque! '95
Like Water for Chocolate '93

Ingrid Caven
Malou '83
In a Year of 13 Moons '78
Mother Kusters Goes to Heaven
  '76
Satan's Brew '76
Shadow of Angels '76
Beware of a Holy Whore '70

Female '33

Daniel Chatto
Little Dorrit, Film 1: Nobody's
Fault '88
Little Dorrit, Film 2: Little Dorrit's
Story '88

Francois Chau
Beverly Hills Ninja '96
Teenage Mutant Ninja Turtles 2:
The Secret of the Ooze '91
Vietnam War Story 3 '89

Emmanuelle Chaulet
All the Vermeers in New York
'91
Boyfriends & Girlfriends '88

Lilyan Chauvin
Tyson '95
Silent Night, Deadly Night '84
Bloodlust '59
Lost, Lonely, and Vicious '59

Richard Chaves
Night Eyes 2 '91
Predator '87

Maury Chaykin
The Sweet Hereafter '96
Cutthroat Island '95
Devil in a Blue Dress '95
Sugartime '95
Unstrung Heroes '95
Camilla '94
Whale Music '94
Money for Nothing '93
Northern Extremes '93
Sommersby '93
Hero '92
Leaving Normal '92
The Adjuster '91
George's Island '91
Cold Comfort '90
Dances with Wolves '90
Mr. Destiny '90
Breaking In '89
Millennium '89
Higher Education '88
Iron Eagle 2 '88
Stars and Bars '88
Wild Thing '87
Canada's Sweetheart: The Saga
of Hal C. Banks '85
Def-Con 4 '85
Mrs. Soffel '84
July Group '70s

Mariann Chazel
The Visitors '95
Next Year If All Goes Well '83
French Fried Vacation '79

Don Cheadle
Volcano '97
Rebound: The Legend of Earl
"The Goat" Manigault '96
Rosewood '96
Devil in a Blue Dress '95
Lush Life '94
Colors '88
Hamburger Hill '87

Andrea Checchi
The Invaders '63
Black Sunday '60
The Walls of Malapaga '49

Micheline Cheirel
Cornered '45
Carnival in Flanders '35

Michael Chekhov
Rhapsody '54
Spectre of the Rose '46
Spellbound '45

Tsilla Chelton
Tatie Danielle '91
Peppermint Soda '77

Joan Chen
Precious Find '96
Judge Dredd '95
Wild Side '95
The Hunted '94
On Deadly Ground '94
Temptation of a Monk '94
Golden Gate '93
Heaven and Earth '93
The Killing Beach '92
Deadlock '91
Strangers '91

Twin Peaks '90
Twin Peaks '90
The Blood of Heroes '89
The Last Emperor '87
Night Stalker '87
Tai-Pan '86
Dim Sum: A Little Bit of Heart
'85

Tina Chen
Lady from Yesterday '85
Paper Man '71

Jacky Cheng
Of Cooks and Kung-Fu '80s
Ninja Exterminators '81

Cher
If These Walls Could Talk '96
Faithful '95
Mermaids '90
Moonstruck '87
Suspect '87
The Witches of Eastwick '87
Mask '85
Silkwood '83
Come Back to the Five & Dime
Jimmy Dean, Jimmy Dean '82

Patrice Chereau
The Last of the Mohicans '92
Danton '83

Nikolai Cherkassov
Don Quixote '57
Ivan the Terrible, Part 2 '46
Ivan the Terrible, Part 1 '44
Alexander Nevsky '38
Baltic Deputy '37

Virginia Cherrill
Late Extra '35
City Lights '31

George Chesebro
Check Your Guns '48
Stage to Mesa City '48
Cheyenne Takes Over '47
Fighting Vigilantes '47
Return of the Lash '47
Devil Riders '44
Holt of the Secret Service '42
Trigger Men '41
Red River Valley '36
Roamin' Wild '36
Laramie Kid '35
The Miracle Rider '35
In Old Santa Fe '34
The Silver Bullet '34
Fighting Champ '33
Wolf Blood '25

Craig Chester
I Shot Andy Warhol '96
Frisk '95
Grief '94
Swoon '91

Vanessa Lee Chester
The Lost World: Jurassic Park 2
'97
Harriet the Spy '96
A Little Princess '95

Morris Chestnut
Under Siege 2: Dark Territory
'95
The Ernest Green Story '93
Boyz N the Hood '91

Jacky Cheung
Wicked City '92
A Bullet in the Head '90

Leslie Cheung
Happy Together '96
Temptress Moon '96
The Bride with White Hair '93
The Bride with White Hair 2 '93
Farewell My Concubine '93
A Better Tomorrow, Part 2 '88
A Better Tomorrow '86

Maggie Cheung
The Executioners '93
Green Snake '93
The Heroic Trio '93
Supercop '92
Song of the Exile '90
Paper Marriage '88
Project A: Part 2 '87
Jackie Chan's Police Force '85

**Kevin Timothy
Chevalia**
Homeward Bound 2: Lost in San
Francisco '96
Homeward Bound: The
Incredible Journey '93
Folks! '92

Maurice Chevalier
Monkeys, Go Home! '66
A New Kind of Love '63
In Search of the Castaways '62
Panic Button '62
Fanny '61
Breath of Scandal '60
Can-Can '60
Gigi '58
Love in the Afternoon '57
The Merry Widow '34

Richard Chevolleau
Rude '96
Indian Summer '93

Laureen Chew
Dim Sum: A Little Bit of Heart
'85
Chan Is Missing '82

Yuen Man Chi
Bruce's Deadly Fingers '80
Young Dragon '77

Sun Chia-Lin
The Hot, the Cool, and the
Vicious '80s
Eighteen Jade Arhats '84

Liu Chia-Yung
Challenge of the Masters '89
Two Graves to Kung-Fu '82

Minoru Chiaki
Godzilla Raids Again '59
The Human Condition: Road to
Eternity '59
The Hidden Fortress '58
Throne of Blood '57
Seven Samurai '54

Dominic Chianese
The Night We Never Met '93
The Public Eye '92

David Chiang
Duel of Fists '89
Seven Blows of the Dragon '73
Duel of the Iron Fist '72

Roy Chiao
Summer Snow '94
Bloodsport '89

Walter Chiari
Girl Under the Sheet '60s
Husband Hunting '60s
Bonjour Tristesse '57

Sofiko Chiaureli
Ashik Kerib '88
The Color of Pomegranates '69

Sonny Chiba
Body Count '95
Immortal Combat '94
Aces: Iron Eagle 3 '92
Shogun's Ninja '82
Virus '82
Hunter in the Dark '80
Dragon Princess '70s
Karate Warriors '70s
Return of the Street Fighter '70s
Assassin '79
The Street Fighter's Last
Revenge '79
Kowloon Assignment '77
The Bodyguard '76
The Street Fighter '75
Terror Beneath the Sea '66

Etienne Chicot
36 Fillete '88
Osa '85

Linden Chiles
Deadline Assault '90
To Heal a Nation '88
Forbidden World '82
Red Flag: The Ultimate Game
'81
Death Be Not Proud '75
Who Is the Black Dahlia? '75
Texas Across the River '66

Lois Chiles
Speed 2: Cruise Control '97
Bliss '96
The Babysitter '95
Curdled '95
Lush Life '94
Diary of a Hitman '91
Twister '89
Broadcast News '87
Creepshow 2 '87
Raw Courage '84
Moonraker '79
Coma '78
Death on the Nile '78

Simon Chilvers
Ground Zero '88
The Big Hurt '87
Windrider '86
The Dunera Boys '85

Joey Chin
King of New York '90
China Girl '87

Tsai Chin
The Joy Luck Club '93
Enter the Panther '79
The Virgin Soldiers '69
The Castle of Fu Manchu '68
Kiss and Kill '68
You Only Live Twice '67
Invasion '65

William Ching
Terror in the Haunted House '58
Give a Girl a Break '53
Never Wave at a WAC '52
Pat and Mike '52
D.O.A. '49
The Wistful Widow of Wagon
Gap '47

Kieu Chinh
The Joy Luck Club '93
The Girl Who Spelled Freedom
'86
The Children of An Lac '80
Operation C.I.A. '65

Nicholas Chinlund
A Brother's Kiss '97
Con Air '97
Eraser '96
Letter to My Killer '95
Unveiled '94
Red Shoe Diaries 4: Auto
Erotica '93
The Ambulance '90

Anna Chlumsky
Gold Diggers: The Secret of
Bear Mountain '95
My Girl 2 '94
Trading Mom '94
My Girl '91

Margaret Cho
Face/Off '97
It's My Party '95

Tim Choate
Live Nude Girls '95
Blind Witness '89
Spy '89
Def-Con 4 '85
First Time '82

Jun Chong
Street Soldiers '91
Silent Assassins '88
Ninja Turf '86

Rae Dawn Chong
Mask of Death '97
The Break '95
Boca '94
Boulevard '94
Hideaway '94
Power of Attorney '94
Dangerous Relations '93
Time Runner '92
Common Bonds '91
Denial: The Dark Side of
Passion '91
Prison Stories: Women on the
Inside '91
When the Party's Over '91
Amazon '90
Curiosity Kills '90
Tales from the Darkside: The
Movie '90
The Borrower '89

Far Out Man '89
The Principal '87
The Squeeze '87
Running Out of Luck '86
Soul Man '86
American Flyers '85
Badge of the Assassin '85
City Limits '85
The Color Purple '85
Commando '85
Fear City '85
Beat Street '84
Cheech and Chong's The
Corsican Brothers '84
Choose Me '84
Quest for Fire '82

Thomas Chong
McHale's Navy '97
National Lampoon's Senior Trip
'95
Spirit of '76 '91
Far Out Man '89
Tripwire '89
Cheech and Chong's The
Corsican Brothers '84
Cheech and Chong: Still
Smokin' '83
Yellowbeard '83
Cheech and Chong: Things Are
Tough All Over '82
Cheech and Chong's Nice
Dreams '81
Cheech and Chong's Next
Movie '80
Cheech and Chong's Up in
Smoke '79

Sarita Choudhury
Kama Sutra: A Tale of Love '96
Down Came a Blackbird '94
The House of the Spirits '93
Wild West '93
Mississippi Masala '92

Etchika Choureau
Darby's Rangers '58
Lafayette Escadrille '58

Navin Chowdhry
The Seventh Coin '92
Madame Sousatzka '88

Ranjit Chowdhry
The Night We Never Met '93
Mississippi Masala '92
Lonely in America '90

Joseph Chrest
The Underneath '95
King of the Hill '93

Claudia Christian
The Adventures of a Gnome
Named Gnorm '93
Hexed '93
The Dark Backward '91
Strays '91
Mad About You '90
Maniac Cop 2 '90
Arena '89
Mom '89
Tale of Two Sisters '89
Clean and Sober '88
Never on Tuesday '88
The Hidden '87

John Christian
The Outfit '93
Comrades in Arms '91
Covert Action '88
Mob War '88

Linda Christian
Full Hearts & Empty Pockets '63
The V.I.P.'s '63
The Devil's Hand '61
Athena '54

Michael Christian
Hard Knocks
Private Obsession '94
Mid Knight Rider '84
The Legend of Frank Woods '77
Poor Pretty Eddie '73

Paul Christian
Journey to the Lost City '58
The Beast from 20,000 Fathoms
'53
Bagdad '49

Wings of Desire '88

Angelica Domrose
The Scorpion Woman '89
Girls Riot '88

Linda Dona
Delta Heat '92
Final Embrace '92

Elinor Donahue
The Invaders '95
Freddy's Dead: The Final
　Nightmare '91
Pretty Woman '90
High School USA '84
Girls' Town '59
Love Is Better Than Ever '52
Three Daring Daughters '48

Troy Donahue
South Seas Massacre
Showdown '93
Deadly Diamonds '91
The Pamela Principle '91
Sounds of Silence '91
Cry-Baby '90
Nudity Required '90
Omega Cop '90
Shock 'Em Dead '90
Assault of the Party Nerds '89
The Chilling '89
Deadly Spygames '89
Dr. Alien '89
Hawkeye '88
Sexpot '88
Terminal Force '88
A Woman Obsessed '88
Cyclone '87
Deadly Prey '87
Hollywood Cop '87
Grandview U.S.A. '84
Tin Man '83
The Godfather 1902-1959: The
　Complete Epic '81
The Legend of Frank Woods '77
Cockfighter '74
The Godfather, Part 2 '74
Love Thrill Murders '71
Those Fantastic Flying Fools '67
Palm Springs Weekend '63
Rome Adventure '62
Parrish '61
Imitation of Life '59
Monster on the Campus '59
A Summer Place '59
Tarnished Angels '57

James Donald
The Big Sleep '78
Cast a Giant Shadow '66
King Rat '65
The Great Escape '63
Victoria Regina '61
Third Man on the Mountain '59
The Vikings '58
The Bridge on the River Kwai
　'57
Lust for Life '56
Beau Brummel '54
The Pickwick Papers '54
The Gay Lady '49
Immortal Battalion '44
In Which We Serve '43

Norma Donaldson
Poetic Justice '93
The Five Heartbeats '91
Staying Alive '83
9 to 5 '80

Peter Donaldson
Escape Clause '96
Long Day's Journey Into Night
　'96
The Sweet Hereafter '96

Ted Donaldson
Rusty's Birthday '49
The Red Stallion '47
Son of Rusty '47
The Adventures of Rusty '45
A Tree Grows in Brooklyn '45

Peter Donat
The Babe '92
School Ties '92
The War of the Roses '89
Tucker: The Man and His Dream
　'88
Honeymoon '87
The Bay Boy '85

Massive Retaliation '85
Mazes and Monsters '82
The China Syndrome '79
Different Story '78
F.I.S.T. '78
Mirrors '78
Return Engagement '78

Robert Donat
The Inn of the Sixth Happiness
　'58
The Winslow Boy '48
Captain Boycott '47
The Adventures of Tartu '43
Goodbye, Mr. Chips '39
The Citadel '38
Knight Without Armour '37
The Ghost Goes West '36
The 39 Steps '35
The Count of Monte Cristo '34
If I Were Rich '33
The Private Life of Henry VIII '33

Ludwig Donath
The Lovable Cheat '49
The Jolson Story '46
The Secret Code '42

Manuel Donde
Swamp of the Lost Monster '65
Savage Wilderness '55

Yolande Donlan
The Adventurers '70
The Devil Bat '41

Brian Donlevy
Arizona Bushwackers '67
Five Golden Dragons '67
Gamera, the Invincible '66
How to Stuff a Wild Bikini '65
The Errand Boy '61
Cowboy '58
Quatermass 2 '57
The Quatermass Experiment '56
Big Combo '55
Ride the Man Down '53
Hoodlum Empire '52
Slaughter Trail '51
Impact '49
Command Decision '48
A Southern Yankee '48
Kiss of Death '47
The Virginian '46
Miracle of Morgan's Creek '44
The Glass Key '42
The Great Man's Lady '42
Wake Island '42
Billy the Kid '41
Birth of the Blues '41
Brigham Young: Frontiersman
　'40
The Great McGinty '40
Allegheny Uprising '39
Beau Geste '39
Destry Rides Again '39
Jesse James '39
Union Pacific '39
In Old Chicago '37
Barbary Coast '35

Steve Donmyer
Terminal Exposure '89
Glitch! '88

**Barnard Pierre
Donnadieu**
Beatrice '88
The Vanishing '88
The Return of Martin Guerre '83

Jeff Donnell
Gidget Goes to Rome '63
My Man Godfrey '57
Because You're Mine '52
Three Guys Named Mike '51
The Fuller Brush Girl '50
In a Lonely Place '50
Redwood Forest Trail '50
Walk Softly, Stranger '50
Outcasts of the Trail '49

Donal Donnelly
Squanto: A Warrior's Tale '94
The Godfather, Part 3 '90
The Dead '87
Waterloo '71
The Knack '65

Ruth Donnelly
A Lawless Street '55

I'd Climb the Highest Mountain
　'51
The Affairs of Annabel '38
Annabel Takes a Tour/Maid's
　Night Out '38
Holiday '38
Mr. Deeds Goes to Town '36
Hands Across the Table '35
Bureau of Missing Persons '33
Female '33
Footlight Parade '33
Ladies They Talk About '33
Blessed Event '32

Tim Donnelly
The Clonus Horror '79
The Toolbox Murders '78

Robert Donner
Lassie: Well of Love '90
Under the Rainbow '81
Man Who Loved Cat Dancing
　'73
Vanishing Point '71

Vincent D'Onofrio
Men in Black '97
Feeling Minnesota '96
Good Luck '96
The Whole Wide World '96
Strange Days '95
Being Human '94
Ed Wood '94
Imaginary Crimes '94
Stuart Saves His Family '94
Desire '93
Household Saints '93
Mr. Wonderful '93
The Player '92
Crooked Hearts '91
Dying Young '91
Fires Within '91
JFK '91
Naked Tango '91
The Blood of Heroes '89
Signs of Life '89
Mystic Pizza '88
Adventures in Babysitting '87
Full Metal Jacket '87
First Turn On! '83

Amanda Donohoe
Liar Liar '97
The Madness of King George
　'94
The Substitute '93
A Woman's Guide to Adultery
　'93
Double Cross '92
Shame '92
Paper Mask '91
Dark Obsession '90
An Affair in Mind '89
The Rainbow '89
The Lair of the White Worm '88
Castaway '87
Foreign Body '86

Donovan
Bob Dylan: Don't Look Back '91
Aliens from Spaceship Earth '77

King Donovan
The Hanging Tree '59
Cowboy '58
Invasion of the Body Snatchers
　'56
Easy to Love '53
Forever Female '53
The Merry Widow '52
Singin' in the Rain '52
The Enforcer '51

Martin Donovan
Portrait of a Lady '96
Flirt '95
Hollow Reed '95
Nadja '95
Amateur '94
Quick '93
Simple Men '92
Surviving Desire '91
Trust '91

Tate Donovan
Murder at 1600 '97
America's Dream '95
Holy Matrimony '94
Equinox '93
Inside Monkey Zetterland '93
Ethan Frome '92

Love Potion #9 '92
Little Noises '91
Memphis Belle '90
Dead Bang '89
Clean and Sober '88
Dangerous Curves '88
Vietnam War Story 2 '88
Into Thin Air '85
Not My Kid '85

Terence Donovan
The Winds of Jarrah '83
The Man from Snowy River '82
Money Movers '78

Alison Doody
Major League 2 '94
Temptation '94
Ring of the Musketeers '93
Duel of Hearts '92
Indiana Jones and the Last
　Crusade '89
Taffin '88
Prayer for the Dying '87

James Doohan
Storybook '95
Star Trek Generations '94
Amore! '93
Double Trouble '91
Star Trek 6: The Undiscovered
　Country '91
Star Trek 5: The Final Frontier
　'89
Star Trek 4: The Voyage Home
　'86
Star Trek 3: The Search for
　Spock '84
Star Trek 2: The Wrath of Khan
　'82
Star Trek: The Motion Picture
　'80
Man in the Wilderness '71
Star Trek Bloopers '69

Paul Dooley
Out There '95
The Underneath '95
Evolver '94
State of Emergency '94
Armistead Maupin's Tales of the
　City '93
Cooperstown '93
A Dangerous Woman '93
My Boyfriend's Back '93
Shakes the Clown '92
White Hot: The Mysterious
　Murder of Thelma Todd '91
The Court Martial of Jackie
　Robinson '90
Flashback '89
When He's Not a Stranger '89
Last Rites '88
Lip Service '88
The Murder of Mary Phagan '87
O.C. and Stiggs '87
Big Trouble '86
Sixteen Candles '84
Going Berserk '83
Strange Brew '83
Endangered Species '82
Hansel and Gretel '82
Kiss Me Goodbye '82
Rumpelstiltskin '82
Paternity '81
Popeye '80
Breaking Away '79
Rich Kids '79
A Wedding '78

Lucinda Dooling
Lovely ... But Deadly '82
The Alchemist '81
Miracle on Ice '81

Patric Doonan
Blackout '50
The Blue Lamp '49
Train of Events '49

Robert DoQui
Original Intent '91
Miracle Mile '89
Short Fuse '88
RoboCop '87
Nashville '75
Coffy '73
A Dream for Christmas '73

Karin Dor
Prisoner in the Middle '74

Die Screaming, Marianne '73
Dracula vs. Frankenstein '69
Topaz '69
The Torture Chamber of Dr.
　Sadism '69
You Only Live Twice '67
The Last Tomahawk '65
Carpet of Horror '64
Strangler of Blackmoor Castle
　'63
The Invisible Dr. Mabuse '62
Forger of London '61

Ann Doran
It! The Terror from Beyond
　Space '58
Rebel Without a Cause '55
Love Is Better Than Ever '52
The Painted Hills '51
Never a Dull Moment '50
Holiday in Havana '49
Rusty's Birthday '49
The Accused '48
Pitfall '48
Fear in the Night '47
Here Come the Waves '45
The More the Merrier '43
Mr. Wise Guy '42
Criminals Within '41
Meet John Doe '41
Blondie '38
Little Red Schoolhouse '36

Jesse Doran
Street Asylum '90
Heart '87

Mary Doran
Sing Sing Nights '35
The Strange Love of Molly
　Louvain '32
Criminal Code '31
The Divorcee '30
Broadway Melody '29

Edna Dore
Nil by Mouth '96
High Hopes '88

Johnny Dorelli
The Odd Squad '86
Bread and Chocolate '74
How to Kill 400 Duponts '65

Stephen Dorff
Blood & Wine '96
City of Industry '96
I Shot Andy Warhol '96
Innocent Lies '95
Reckless '95
Backbeat '94
S.F.W. '94
Judgment Night '93
Rescue Me '93
The Power of One '92
The Gate '87

Pierre Doris
Overseas: Three Women with
　Man Trouble '90
The Story of a Three Day Pass
　'68

Francoise Dorleac
Cul de Sac '66
The Soft Skin '64
That Man from Rio '64

Dolores Dorn
Truck Stop Women '74
Underworld, U.S.A. '60
Lucky Me '54

Michael Dorn
Star Trek: First Contact '96
Amanda and the Alien '95
Timemaster '95
Star Trek Generations '94
Star Trek the Next Generation,
　the Final Episode: All Good
　Things... '94
Star Trek 6: The Undiscovered
　Country '91
Star Trek the Next Generation:
　Encounter at Farpoint '87
The Jagged Edge '85

Philip Dorn
The Fighting Kentuckian '49
I've Always Loved You '46
Random Harvest '42
Reunion in France '42
Tarzan's Secret Treasure '41

Valerie Gaunt
The Horror of Dracula '58
The Curse of Frankenstein '57

Mikkel Gaup
Breaking the Waves '95
Pathfinder '87

Dan Gauthier
Excessive Force 2: Force on
Force '95
Illegal in Blue '95
Son-in-Law '93
Shame '92
Teen Witch '89

Dick Gautier
Get Smart, Again! '89
Glitch! '88
Marathon '80
Divorce American Style '67

Jean-Yves Gautier
A Chef in Love '96
The Promise '94

John Gavin
House of Shadows '83
History of the World: Part 1 '81
Sophia Loren: Her Own Story
'80
Jennifer '78
Murder for Sale '70
The Madwoman of Chaillot '69
Thoroughly Modern Millie '67
Back Street '61
Breath of Scandal '60
Midnight Lace '60
Psycho '60
Spartacus '60
Imitation of Life '59
A Time to Love & a Time to Die
'58

Cassandra Gaviola
The Black Room '82
Conan the Barbarian '82

William Gaxton
Best Foot Forward '43
The Heat's On '43
It's the Old Army Game '26

Gregory Gay
Seven Doors to Death '44
The Secret Code '42

Ramon Gay
The Curse of the Aztec Mummy
'59
Curse of the Aztec Mummy/
Robot vs. the Aztec Mummy
'59
The Robot vs. the Aztec Mummy
'59

Howard Gaye
Dante's Inferno '24
Flirting with Fate '16

Lisa Gaye
Class of Nuke 'Em High 3: The
Good, the Bad and the
Subhumanoid '94
Class of Nuke 'Em High 2:
Subhumanoid Meltdown '91
The Toxic Avenger, Part 3: The
Last Temptation of Toxie '89
Castle of Evil '66
Night of Evil '62
The Sign of Zorro '60
Shake, Rattle and Rock '57

Jackie Gayle
Mr. Saturday Night '92
Bert Rigby, You're a Fool '89
Plain Clothes '88
Tin Men '87
Pepper and His Wacky Taxi '72

Monica Gayle
Nashville Girl '76
Switchblade Sisters '75

Mitch Gaylord
Animal Instincts '92
American Tiger '89
American Anthem '86

George Gaynes
The Crucible '96
Police Academy: Mission to
Moscow '94
Vanya on 42nd Street '94
Stepmonster '92

Police Academy 6: City Under
Siege '89
Police Academy 5: Assignment
Miami Beach '88
Police Academy 4: Citizens on
Patrol '87
Police Academy 3: Back in
Training '86
Police Academy 2: Their First
Assignment '85
It Came Upon a Midnight Clear
'84
Micki & Maude '84
Police Academy '84
Dead Men Don't Wear Plaid '82
Tootsie '82
Breaking Up Is Hard to Do '79

Janet Gaynor
Till the Clouds Roll By/A Star Is
Born '46
The Young in Heart '38
A Star is Born '37
The Farmer Takes a Wife '35
Sunrise '27

Mitzi Gaynor
For Love or Money '63
South Pacific '58
Les Girls '57
Birds & the Bees '56
There's No Business Like Show
Business '54
We're Not Married '52

Eunice Gayson
From Russia with Love '63
Dr. No '62
The Revenge of Frankenstein
'58
Carry On Admiral '57

Wendy Gazelle
The Net '95
Triumph of the Spirit '89
Understudy: The Graveyard
Shift 2 '88
Hot Pursuit '87
Sammy & Rosie Get Laid '87

Ben Gazzara
Farmer & Chase '96
The Shadow Conspiracy '96
Convict Cowboy '95
The Dogfighters '95
Parallel Lives '94
Blindsided '93
Lies Before Kisses '92
Road House '89
Quicker Than the Eye '88
Secret Obsession '88
Control '87
An Early Frost '85
Tales of Ordinary Madness '83
They All Laughed '81
Question of Honor '80
Saint Jack '79
Sidney Sheldon's Bloodline '79
Opening Night '77
The Trial of Lee Harvey Oswald
'77
The Death of Richie '76
High Velocity '76
The Killing of a Chinese Bookie
'76
Voyage of the Damned '76
QB VII '74
Sicilian Connection '74
Neptune Factor '73
Fireball Forward '72
Pursuit '72
Shattered Silence '71
The Bridge at Remagen '69
Passionate Thief '60
Anatomy of a Murder '59

Michael V. Gazzo
Cookie '89
The Godfather 1902-1959: The
Complete Epic '81
Kill Castro '80
The Mercenaries '80
Gangsters '79
Love and Bullets '79
Fingers '78
King of the Gypsies '78
Black Sunday '77
The Godfather, Part 2 '74

Anthony Geary
Scorchers '92

Night of the Warrior '91
High Desert Kill '90
Crack House '89
UHF '89
Pass the Ammo '88
You Can't Hurry Love '88
Dangerous Love '87
Penitentiary 3 '87
Kicks '85
The Imposter '84

Bud Geary
D-Day on Mars '45
The Topeka Terror '45

Cynthia Geary
8 Seconds '94
To Grandmother's House We
Go '94

Jason Gedrick
The Last Don '97
Power 98 '96
The Force '94
Crossing the Bridge '92
Still Life '92
Backdraft '91
Rooftops '89
Promised Land '88
Stacking '87
Iron Eagle '86
The Heavenly Kid '85
Massive Retaliation '85
The Zoo Gang '85

Prunella Gee
Witching Time '84
Never Say Never Again '83
The Wilby Conspiracy '75

Ellen Geer
Hard Traveling '85
Bloody Birthday '80
A Shining Season '79
Babe! '75
Memory of Us '74
Silence '73
Harold and Maude '71

Will Geer
Bunco '83
Unknown Powers '80
The Billion Dollar Hobo '78
My Sister, My Love '78
A Woman Called Moses '78
Moving Violation '76
The Hanged Man '74
Hurricane '74
Memory of Us '74
Executive Action '73
Silence '73
The Waltons: A Thanksgiving
Story '73
Dear Dead Delilah '72
Jeremiah Johnson '72
Napoleon and Samantha '72
Brother John '70
The Reivers '69
Bandolero! '68
The President's Analyst '67
Seconds '66
Black Like Me '64
Salt of the Earth '54
Broken Arrow '50
Comanche Territory '50
To Please a Lady '50
Winchester '73 '50
Lust for Gold '49

Judy Geeson
Danger UXB '81
Horror Planet '80
Adventures of a Taxi Driver '76
Carry On England '76
Poldark '75
Poldark 2 '75
Murder on the Midnight Express
'74
Doomwatch '72
Dynasty of Fear '72
10 Rillington Place '71
The Executioner '70
It Happened at Nightmare Inn
'70
Twinsanity '70
Berserk! '67
To Sir, with Love '67

Sally Geeson
Cry of the Banshee '70
The Oblong Box '69

What's Good for the Goose '69

Martha Gehman
Threesome '94
Unveiled '94
Father of the Bride '91
A Kiss Before Dying '91
F/X '86
The Flamingo Kid '84

Bob Geldof
Pink Floyd: The Wall '82
The Secret Policeman's Other
Ball '82

Daniel Gelin
Iran: Days of Crisis '91
Life Is a Long Quiet River '88
Murmur of the Heart '71
Is Paris Burning? '66
The Testament of Orpheus '59
Mademoiselle Striptease '57
The Man Who Knew Too Much
'56
A Woman of Rome '56
La Ronde '51

Larry Gelman
Chatterbox '76
Slumber Party '57 '76

Grant Gelt
Mutant Species '95
Avalon '90

Giuliano Gemma
Blood at Sundown '88
Unsane '82
The Warning '80
Corleone '79
Battleforce '78
Smugglers '75
Master Touch '74
Erik, the Viking '72
Goliath and the Sins of Babylon
'64

Laura Gemser
Fury '80s
Women's Prison Massacre '85
Caged Women '84
Ator the Fighting Eagle '83
Black Cobra '83
Emmanuelle's Daughter '79
Crime Busters '78
Emmanuelle in the Country '78
Naked Paradise '78
Emmanuelle on Taboo Island
'76
Love Camp '76
Emmanuelle, the Queen '75

**Francois-Eric
Gendron**
Boyfriends & Girlfriends '88
Cloud Waltzing '87

Bryan Genesse
Terminal Virus '96
Live Wire: Human Timebomb '95
Terminal Impact '95
Night Siege Project:
Shadowchaser 2 '94
California Casanova '89
Loose Screws '85

Leo Genn
Mackintosh Man '73
Strange Case of Dr. Jekyll & Mr.
Hyde '68
Circus of Fear '67
The Longest Day '62
Moby Dick '56
Lady Chatterley's Lover '55
The Miniver Story '50
Wooden Horse '50
The Snake Pit '48
Velvet Touch '48
Green for Danger '47
Henry V '44
When Thief Meets Thief '37

Minnie Gentry
Def by Temptation '90
Georgia, Georgia '72

Roger Gentry
Alien Massacre '67
Horrors of the Red Planet '64

Carrie Genzel
Virtual Seduction '96
Caged Hearts '95

Paul Geoffrey
Flame to the Phoenix '85
Excalibur '81

Stephen Geoffreys
Moon 44 '90
976-EVIL '88
The Chair '87
Fraternity Vacation '85
Fright Night '85

Chief Dan George
Americathon '79
The Outlaw Josey Wales '76
The Bears & I '74
Harry and Tonto '74
Dan Candy's Law '73
Cancel My Reservation '72
Little Big Man '70

Christopher George
Gates of Hell '83
Pieces '83
AngKor: Cambodia Express '81
Enter the Ninja '81
Graduation Day '81
Mortuary '81
Exterminator '80
Cruise into Terror '78
Day of the Animals '77
Whiskey Mountain '77
Dixie Dynamite '76
Grizzly '76
Midway '76
Train Robbers '73
Man on a String '71
Chisum '70
El Dorado '67

Gladys George
Detective Story '51
Lullaby of Broadway '51
Flamingo Road '49
The Best Years of Our Lives '46
The Maltese Falcon '41
House Across the Bay '40
The Roaring Twenties '39
Marie Antoinette '38
Madame X '37

Goetz George
Schtonk '92
Out of Order '84

Heinrich George
Kolberg '45
Jud Suess '40
Metropolis '26

Lynda Day George
Pieces '83
Young Warriors '83
The Junkman '82
Mortuary '81
Beyond Evil '80
Casino '80
Racquet '79
Cruise into Terror '78
Aliens from Spaceship Earth '77
Ants '77
Day of the Animals '77
Roots '77
The Barbary Coast '74
Panic on the 5:22 '74

Maude George
The Wedding March '28
Foolish Wives '22

Rita George
On the Run '81
Hollywood Boulevard '76

Susan George
That Summer of White Roses
'90
Jack the Ripper '88
Lightning: The White Stallion '86
The Jigsaw Man '84
Pajama Tops '83
House Where Evil Dwells '82
Kiss My Grits '82
Venom '82
Enter the Ninja '81
Tintorera...Tiger Shark '78
Tomorrow Never Comes '77
A Small Town in Texas '76
Mandingo '75
Mission: Monte Carlo '75
Out of Season '75
Dirty Mary Crazy Larry '74
Die Screaming, Marianne '71

Gould ➤cont.

Kenny Rogers as the Gambler, Part 2: The Adventure Continues '83
Help Wanted: Male '82
Kenny Rogers as the Gambler '80
Seems Like Old Times '80
Better Late Than Never '79
Actor: The Paul Muni Story '78
The One and Only '78
How to Break Up a Happy Divorce '76
Love and Death '75
The Sting '73

Jason Gould
The Prince of Tides '91
The Big Picture '89
Say Anything '89

William Gould
Man from Montana '41
Tanks a Million '41
Rio Rattler '35
Phantom Thunderbolt '33
The Phantom '31

Robert Goulet
Mr. Wrong '95
Based on an Untrue Story '93
Naked Gun 2 1/2: The Smell of Fear '91
Scrooged '88

Gibson Gowland
Gun Cargo '49
The Secret of the Loch '34
Without Honors '32
Hell Harbor '30
The Phantom of the Opera '25
Greed '24

Patrick Goyette
Le Polygraphe '96
The Confessional '95

Harry Goz
Rappin' '85
Bill: On His Own '83
Bill '81
Mommie Dearest '81

Jody Graber
Edward II '92
The Garden '90

Betty Grable
The Worst of Hollywood: Vol. 3 '90
Gotta Dance, Gotta Sing '84
The Love Goddesses '65
Hollywood Goes to War '54
The Farmer Takes a Wife '53
How to Marry a Millionaire '53
The Beautiful Blonde from Bashful Bend '49
The Dolly Sisters '46
Pin-Up Girl '44
Strictly G.I. '44
Sweet Rosie O'Grady '43
Footlight Serenade '42
Song of the Islands '42
Springtime in the Rockies '42
I Wake Up Screaming '41
Moon over Miami '41
A Yank in the R.A.F. '41
Down Argentine Way '40
Tin Pan Alley '40
Day the Bookies Wept '39
College Swing '38
Give Me a Sailor '38
Follow the Fleet '36
Pigskin Parade '36
The Gay Divorcee '34
Hold 'Em Jail '32
Probation '32
Whoopee! '30

Sofie Graboel
The Silent Touch '94
The Wolf at the Door '87

Nickolas Grace
The Final Cut '95
Tom & Viv '94
Two Deaths '94
The Green Man '91
Diamond's Edge '88

Salome's Last Dance '88
Max Headroom, the Original Story '87
Robin Hood...The Legend: Herne's Son '85
Robin Hood...The Legend: The Time of the Wolf '85
Robin Hood...The Legend: Robin Hood and the Sorcerer '83
Robin Hood...The Legend: The Swords of Wayland '83
Heat and Dust '82

Wayne Grace
The Lazarus Man '96
My Summer Story '94
Fallen Angels 2 '93
Heroes Stand Alone '89

Elizabeth Gracen
The Expert '95
Discretion Assured '93
Final Mission '93
Lower Level '91
Death of the Incredible Hulk '90

Paulo Gracindo
Amor Bandido '79
Earth Entranced '66

Paul Graetz
Heart's Desire '37
Bulldog Jack '35
Mimi '35
Power '34

David Graf
Citizen Ruth '96
The Brady Bunch Movie '95
Father and Scout '94
Police Academy: Mission to Moscow '94
Roseanne: An Unauthorized Biography '94
Suture '93
Police Academy 6: City Under Siege '89
Police Academy 5: Assignment Miami Beach '88
Police Academy 4: Citizens on Patrol '87
Police Academy 3: Back in Training '86
Police Academy 2: Their First Assignment '85

Ilene Graff
The Great American Sex Scandal '84
Ladybugs '92

Todd Graff
The Beautician and the Beast '97
City of Hope '91
Framed '90
Opportunity Knocks '90
The Abyss '89
Vietnam War Story 3 '89
Dominick & Eugene '88
Five Corners '88
Sweet Lorraine '87

Wilton Graff
Bloodlust '59
Compulsion '59
The West Point Story '50
The Mozart Story '48

Aimee Graham
Amos and Andrew '93
Fallen Angels 1 '93

Bill Graham
Bugsy '91
The Doors '91
Gardens of Stone '87

Billy Graham
Bugged! '96
The Prodigal '83

Fred Graham
The Last Hunt '56
Trader Tom of the China Seas '54
Escape from Fort Bravo '53
Heart of the Rockies '51
The Fuller Brush Girl '50

Gary Graham
Alien Nation: Dark Horizon '94
Robot Jox '90

The Last Warrior '89
The Dirty Dozen: The Deadly Mission '87
No Place to Hide '81

Gerrit Graham
Philadelphia Experiment 2 '93
This Boy's Life '93
Frozen Assets '92
Child's Play 2 '90
Martians Go Home! '90
Night of the Cyclone '90
C.H.U.D. 2: Bud the Chud '89
It's Alive 3: Island of the Alive '87
Terrorvision '86
The Annihilators '85
The Man with One Red Shoe '85
Ratings Game '84
National Lampoon's Class Reunion '82
Soup for One '82
Spaceship '81
Used Cars '80
Home Movies '79
Demon Seed '77
Cannonball '76
Special Delivery '76
Tunnelvision '76
Phantom of the Paradise '74
Son of Blob '72
Hi, Mom! '70
Greetings '68

Heather Graham
Nowhere '96
Swingers '96
Don't Do It '94
Terrified '94
The Ballad of Little Jo '93
Six Degrees of Separation '93
Diggstown '92
Guilty as Charged '92
O Pioneers! '91
Shout '91
I Love You to Death '90
Drugstore Cowboy '89

Morland Graham
Bonnie Prince Charlie '48
Tower of Terror '42
Night Train to Munich '40
The Scarlet Pimpernel '34

Ronny Graham
The Substance of Fire '96
Ratings Game '84
World's Greatest Lover '77
New Faces of 1952 '54

Gloria Grahame
The Nesting '80
Autopsy '70s
The Big Scam '79
Chilly Scenes of Winter '79
Mama's Dirty Girls '74
Loners '72
The Todd Killings '71
Odds Against Tomorrow '59
The Cobweb '55
The Man Who Never Was '55
Not as a Stranger '55
Oklahoma! '55
Human Desire '54
The Big Heat '53
The Bad and the Beautiful '52
Macao '52
Sudden Fear '52
In a Lonely Place '50
A Woman's Secret '49
Crossfire '47
It Happened in Brooklyn '47
Merton of the Movies '47
Song of the Thin Man '47
It's a Wonderful Life '46

Margot Grahame
Fabulous Joe '47
The Informer '35
The Three Musketeers '35
Broken Melody '34

Kelsey Grammer
Down Periscope '96
Galaxies Are Colliding '92

Sam Grana
The Boys of St. Vincent '93
90 Days '86

Alexander Granach
The Seventh Cross '44

Joan of Paris '42
Kameradschaft '31
Dracula/Garden of Eden '28
Nosferatu '22

Daisy Granados
A Very Old Man with Enormous Wings '88
Portrait of Teresa '79
Memories of Underdevelopment '68

Rosario Granados
A Woman Without Love '51
The Great Madcap '49

Bjorn Granath
The Ox '91
Pelle the Conqueror '88

Pippa Grandison
Hotel de Love '96
Over the Hill '93

Dorothy Granger
Killer Dill '47
The Flustered Comedy of Leon Errol '39
W.C. Fields Comedy Bag '33
Fighting Fool '32

Farley Granger
Sweet Spirits '80s
Imagemaker '86
Very Close Quarters '84
The Prowler '81
The Widow '76
The Slasher '74
Arnold '73
Night Flight from Moscow '73
They Call Me Trinity '72
Deathmask '69
Senso '54
Small Town Girl '53
Behave Yourself! '52
Hans Christian Andersen '52
Strangers on a Train '51
They Live by Night '49
Rope '48
The Purple Heart '44
The North Star '43

Stewart Granger
Fine Gold '88
Hell Hunters '87
Wild Geese '78
Code Name Alpha '67
The Last Safari '67
Target for Killing '66
Sodom and Gomorrah '62
North to Alaska '60
Harry Black and the Tiger '58
Gun Glory '57
Bhowani Junction '56
The Last Hunt '56
Green Fire '55
Moonfleet '55
Beau Brummel '54
All the Brothers Were Valiant '53
Salome '53
Young Bess '53
Prisoner of Zenda '52
Scaramouche '52
King Solomon's Mines '50
Woman Hater '48
Blanche Fury '48
Man of Evil '48
Captain Boycott '47
The Magic Bow '47
Caesar and Cleopatra '46
The Man in Grey '45
Thursday's Child '43
Secret Mission '42
Convoy '47

Nils T. Granlund
Take It Big '44
Rhythm Parade '43

William Grannell
The Abductors '72
Ginger '72

Beth Grant
Speed '94
White Sands '92
The Dark Half '91
Love Field '91
Rain Man '88

Cary Grant
Walk, Don't Run '66
Father Goose '64

Charade '63
That Touch of Mink '62
The Grass is Greener '61
North by Northwest '59
Operation Petticoat '59
Houseboat '58
Indiscreet '58
An Affair to Remember '57
The Pride and the Passion '57
To Catch a Thief '55
Monkey Business '52
People Will Talk '51
I Was a Male War Bride '49
Every Girl Should Be Married '48
Mr. Blandings Builds His Dream House '48
The Bachelor and the Bobby-Soxer '47
The Bishop's Wife '47
Night and Day '46
Notorious '46
Arsenic and Old Lace '44
None But the Lonely Heart '44
Destination Tokyo '43
Mr. Lucky '43
Once Upon a Honeymoon '42
Talk of the Town '42
Penny Serenade '41
Suspicion '41
His Girl Friday '40
The Howards of Virginia '40
My Favorite Wife '40
The Philadelphia Story '40
Gunga Din '39
In Name Only '39
Only Angels Have Wings '39
Bringing Up Baby '38
Holiday '38
Amazing Adventure '37
The Awful Truth '37
Toast of New York '37
Topper '37
Suzy '36
Sylvia Scarlett '35
The Eagle and the Hawk '33
I'm No Angel '33
She Done Him Wrong '33
Blonde Venus '32

Charles Grant
Playback '95
Lady in Waiting '94

David Marshall Grant
The Chamber '96
The Lazarus Man '96
Three Wishes '95
Forever Young '92
Through the Eyes of a Killer '92
Air America '90
Bat 21 '88
American Flyers '85
Sessions '83
End of August '82
Happy Birthday, Gemini '80

Faye Grant
Vibrations '94
Omen 4: The Awakening '91
V '83
Senior Trip '81

Frances Grant
Oh Susannah '38
Cavalry '36
Red River Valley '36

Hugh Grant
Extreme Measures '96
The Englishman Who Went Up a Hill But Came Down a Mountain '95
Nine Months '95
Sense and Sensibility '95
An Awfully Big Adventure '94
Four Weddings and a Funeral '94
Restoration '94
Sirens '94
Night Train to Venice '93
The Remains of the Day '93
Bitter Moon '92
The Big Man: Crossing the Line '91
Our Sons '91
Impromptu '91
The Lady and the Highwayman '89
The Dawning '88

Gross ►cont.

Sometimes They Come
Back...Again '96
Tremors 2: Aftershocks '96
In the Heat of Passion 2:
Unfaithful '94
Firestorm: 72 Hours in Oakland
'93
Alan & Naomi '92
Cool As Ice '91
Midnight Murders '91
A Connecticut Yankee in King
Arthur's Court '89
Tremors '89
Big Business '88
In the Line of Duty: The FBI
Murders '88
Summer Fantasy '84

Paul Gross
Whale Music '94
Armistead Maupin's Tales of the
City '93
Aspen Extreme '93
Northern Extremes '93
Buffalo Jump '90

Brigitte Grothum
Inn on the River '62
The Strange Countess '61

Deborah Grover
Mania '80s
The Christmas Wife '88

Robert Grubb
Mad Max: Beyond
Thunderdome '85
Remember Me '85
Gallipoli '81

Gary Grubbs
Gone Fishin' '97
The Ernest Green Story '93
Without Warning: The James
Brady Story '91
Foxfire '87

Franz Gruber
X from Outer Space '67
Terror Beneath the Sea '66
Deutschland im Jahre Null '47

Gustav Grundgens
Liebelei '32
M '31

Olivier Gruner
Mercenary '96
Savage '96
The Fighter '95
Automatic '94
Nemesis '93
Angel Town '89

Ilka Gruning
Desperate '47
Joyless Street '25

Ah-Leh Gua
Eat Drink Man Woman '94
The Wedding Banquet '93

Dominic Guard
Absolution '81
Picnic at Hanging Rock '75
The Go-Between '71

Kit Guard
El Diablo Rides '39
Fighting Champ '33

Pippa Guard
Scarlett '94
Unsuitable Job for a Woman '82

Harry Guardino
Fist of Honor '92
The Neon Empire '89
Any Which Way You Can '80
Goldengirl '79
Matilda '78
Rollercoaster '77
The Enforcer '76
St. Ives '76
Whiffs '75
Get Christie Love! '74
They Only Kill Their Masters '72
Dirty Harry '71
Octaman '71
Lovers and Other Strangers '70
Madigan '68

The Adventures of Bullwhip
Griffin '66
Hell is for Heroes '62
The Five Pennies '59
Pork Chop Hill '59
Houseboat '58

Irina Gubanova
Private Life '82
War and Peace '68

Blanca Guerra
Danzon '91
Santa Sangre '90

Evelyn Guerrero
Cheech and Chong: Things Are
Tough All Over '82
Cheech and Chong's Nice
Dreams '81
Cheech and Chong's Next
Movie '80
The Toolbox Murders '78

Franco Guerrero
Deathfight '93
The Kick Fighter '91
Warriors of the Apocalypse '85
American Commandos '84
One Armed Executioner '80

Monica Guerritore
The Endless Game '89
Together? '79

Fausto Guerzoni
Black Orpheus '58
The Bicycle Thief '48

Christopher Guest
Waiting for Guffman '96
A Few Good Men '92
The Return of Spinal Tap '92
Sticky Fingers '88
The Princess Bride '87
Beyond Therapy '86
Little Shop of Horrors '86
This Is Spinal Tap '84
A Piano for Mrs. Cimino '82
Heartbeeps '81
The Last Word '80
The Long Riders '80
Girlfriends '78

Lance Guest
The Wizard of Loneliness '88
Jaws: The Revenge '87
My Father, My Rival '85
Just the Way You Are '84
The Last Starfighter '84
Roommate '84
I Ought to Be in Pictures '82
Halloween 2: The Nightmare
Isn't Over! '81

Nicholas Guest
Night Hunter '95
Kickboxer 4: The Aggressor '94
Puppet Master 5: The Final
Chapter '94
My Daughter's Keeper '93
Nemesis '93
Chrome Soldiers '92
Forever: A Ghost of a Love
Story '92
Grand Tour: Disaster in Time '92
Dollman '90
Assassin '89
National Lampoon's Christmas
Vacation '89
Strange Case of Dr. Jekyll & Mr.
Hyde '89
Criminal Act '88
The Long Riders '80

Carla Gugino
The War at Home '96
Wedding Bell Blues '96
The Buccaneers '95
Miami Rhapsody '95
Red Hot '95
Son-in-Law '93
This Boy's Life '93
Murder without Motive '92

Wandisa Guida
Gladiator of Rome '63
The Devil's Commandment '56

Giovanni Guidelli
Fiorile '93
Where Angels Fear to Tread '91

Anthony Guidera
Red Shoe Diaries 7: Burning Up
'96
Undercover '94

Nancy Guild
Francis Covers the Big Town '53
Abbott and Costello Meet the
Invisible Man '51
Black Magic '49

Paul Guilfoyle
Ransom '96
Manny & Lo '96
Extreme Measures '96
Celtic Pride '96
A Couch in New York '95
Amelia Earhart: The Final Flight
'94
Little Odessa '94
Mother's Boys '94
Fallen Angels 2 '93
Class of '61 '92
Dead Ahead: The Exxon Valdez
Disaster '92
Final Analysis '92
Cadillac Man '90
Curiosity Kills '90
Billy Galvin '86
Actors and Sin '52

Paul Guilfoyle
Follow Me Quietly '49
The Judge '49
The Missing Corpse '45
The Saint Takes Over '40
Law of the Underworld '38
The Crime of Dr. Crespi '35

Robert Guillaume
You Must Remember This '90s
First Kid '96
Run for the Dream: The Gail
Devers Story '96
A Good Day to Die '95
Cosmic Slop '94
The Meteor Man '93
The Penthouse '92
Death Warrant '90
Fire and Rain '89
Lean on Me '89
They Still Call Me Bruce '86
Wanted Dead or Alive '86
North and South Book 1 '85
The Kid with the 200 I.Q. '83
Prince Jack '83
The Kid with the Broken Halo '82
Seems Like Old Times '80
The Kid from Left Field '79
The Best of Soap: Who Killed
Peter? '77
Superfly T.N.T. '73

Fernando Guillen
Mouth to Mouth '95
Women on the Verge of a
Nervous Breakdown '88

Tim Guinee
Courage Under Fire '96
Lily Dale '96
Black Day Blue Night '95
Follow the River '95
How to Make an American Quilt
'95
The Pompatus of Love '95
Breathing Lessons '94
Men of War '94
Chain of Desire '93
The Night We Never Met '93
Once Around '91
American Blue Note '89
Vietnam War Story 2 '88
Tai-Pan '86

Rick Guinn
Mountain Charlie '80
Buffalo Rider '78

Alec Guinness
A Foreign Field '93
Kafka '91
Monsignor Quixote '91
A Handful of Dust '88
Little Dorrit, Film 1: Nobody's
Fault '88
Little Dorrit, Film 2: Little Dorrit's
Story '88
A Passage to India '84
From "Star Wars" to "Jedi": The
Making of a Saga '83

Lovesick '83
To See Such Fun '81
The Empire Strikes Back '80
Little Lord Fauntleroy '80
Raise the Titanic '80
Star Wars '77
Murder by Death '76
Brother Sun, Sister Moon '73
Hitler: The Last Ten Days '73
Cromwell '70
Scrooge '70
The Comedians '67
Hotel Paradiso '66
The Quiller Memorandum '66
Doctor Zhivago '65
The Fall of the Roman Empire
'64
Damn the Defiant '62
Lawrence of Arabia '62
Tunes of Glory '60
Tunes of Glory/Horse's Mouth
'60
The Horse's Mouth '58
The Bridge on the River Kwai
'57
A Majority of One '56
The Swan '56
The Ladykillers '55
The Prisoner '55
To Paris with Love '55
The Detective '54
Captain's Paradise '53
Malta Story '53
The Promoter '52
The Lavender Hill Mob '51
The Man in the White Suit '51
Last Holiday '50
Kind Hearts and Coronets '49
Oliver Twist '48
Great Expectations '46

Julien Guiomar
Leolo '92
My New Partner '84
Swashbuckler '84

Tom Guiry
Lassie '94
The Sandlot '93

Tito Guizar
On the Old Spanish Trail '47
The Gay Ranchero '42

Clu Gulager
The Killing Device '92
My Heroes Have Always Been
Cowboys '91
Tapeheads '89
I'm Gonna Git You Sucka '88
Teen Vamp '88
The Uninvited '88
The Hidden '87
Hunter's Blood '87
The Offspring '87
Into the Night '85
A Nightmare on Elm Street 2:
Freddy's Revenge '85
Return of the Living Dead '85
Chattanooga Choo Choo '84
The Initiation '84
Kenny Rogers as the Gambler,
Part 2: The Adventure
Continues '83
Lies '83
Living Proof: The Hank Williams
Jr. Story '83
Kenny Rogers as the Gambler
'80
Touched by Love '80
Force of One '79
Willa '79
He Who Walks Alone '78
A Question of Love '78
Snowblind '78
The Other Side of Midnight '77
Wonderland Cove '75
Hit Lady '74
McQ '74
Smile, Jenny, You're Dead '74
The Glass House '72
The Last Picture Show '71
Winning '69
And Now Miguel '66
The Killers '64

Dorothy Gulliver
Faces '68
The Fighting Marshal '32

Outlaw Justice '32
Shadow of the Eagle '32
The Galloping Ghost '31
Under Montana Skies '30

Leo Gullotta
La Scorta '94
Sinbad of the Seven Seas '89

David Gulpilil
Dark Age '88
Crocodile Dundee '86
The Last Wave '77
Mad Dog Morgan '76

Janet Gunn
The Nurse '97
Carnosaur 3: Primal Species '96
The Quest '96

Moses Gunn
Memphis '91
Perfect Harmony '91
The Women of Brewster Place
'89
The House of Dies Drear '88
Heartbreak Ridge '86
Certain Fury '85
Charlotte Forten's Mission:
Experiment in Freedom '85
Killing Floor '85
Firestarter '84
The NeverEnding Story '84
Amityville 2: The Possession '82
Ragtime '81
Aaron Loves Angela '75
Cornbread, Earl & Me '75
Rollerball '75
Amazing Grace '74
Haunts of the Very Rich '72
Shaft's Big Score '72
Shaft '71
Wild Rovers '71
The Great White Hope '70
The Hot Rock '70

Bob Gunton
Changing Habits '96
The Glimmer Man '96
Ace Ventura: When Nature Calls
'95
Broken Arrow '95
In Pursuit of Honor '95
Kingfish: A Story of Huey P.
Long '95
Roswell: The U.F.O. Cover-Up
'94
The Shawshank Redemption '94
Demolition Man '93
Father Hood '93
Lone Justice '93
Wild Palms '93
Dead Ahead: The Exxon Valdez
Disaster '92
Sinatra '92
Mission of the Shark '91
Judgment '90
Cookie '89
Glory '89
Matewan '87
Static '87
Lois Gibbs and the Love Canal
'82
Rollover '81

Alizia Gur
Beast of Morocco '66
From Russia with Love '63

Sigrid Gurie
Enemy of Women '44
Three Faces West '40
The Adventures of Marco Polo
'38
Algiers '38

Jennifer Gurney
Paradise Park '90s
Heroes of the Heart '94

Eric Gurry
Something Special '86
The Zoo Gang '85
Bad Boys '83
Mystery at Fire Island '81

Louis Guss
The Cemetery Club '93
American Blue Note '89
Nitti: The Enforcer '88
Moonstruck '87
Willie & Phil '80

Cast Index

The Double Life of Veronique '91
Au Revoir Les Enfants '87

Derek Jacobi
Hamlet '96
Breaking the Code '95
Brother Cadfael 2 '95
Brother Cadfael '94
Circle of Deceit '94
Dead Again '91
I, Claudius, Vol. 1: A Touch of Murder/Family Affairs '91
Henry V '89
Little Dorrit, Film 1: Nobody's Fault '88
Little Dorrit, Film 2: Little Dorrit's Story '88
The Tenth Man '88
The Secret Garden '87
Cyrano de Bergerac '85
Philby, Burgess and MacLean: Spy Scandal of the Century '84
Enigma '82
The Hunchback of Notre Dame '82
Inside the Third Reich '82
I, Claudius, Vol. 2: Waiting in the Wings/What Shall We Do With Claudius? '80
I, Claudius, Vol. 3: Poison is Queen/Some Justice '80
I, Claudius, Vol. 4: Queen of Heaven/Reign of Terror '80
I, Claudius, Vol. 5: Zeus, By Jove!/Hail Who? '80
I, Claudius, Vol. 6: Fool's Luck/A God in Colchester '80
I, Claudius, Vol. 7: Old King Log '80
The Human Factor '79
The Medusa Touch '78
The Odessa File '74
Blue Blood '73
The Day of the Jackal '73
Othello '65

Lou Jacobi
I.Q. '94
I Don't Buy Kisses Anymore '92
Avalon '90
Amazon Women on the Moon '87
The Boss' Wife '86
My Favorite Year '82
Arthur '81
Chu Chu & the Philly Flash '81
Off Your Rocker '80
Better Late Than Never '79
The Magician of Lublin '79
Roseland '77
Next Stop, Greenwich Village '76
Everything You Always Wanted to Know about Sex (But Were Afraid to Ask) '72
Little Murders '71
Cotton Comes to Harlem '70
Song Without End '60
The Diary of Anne Frank '59

Andre Jacobs
Curse of the Crystal Eye '93
Prey for the Hunter '92
Pursuit '90
Emissary '89

Lawrence-Hilton Jacobs
Indecent Behavior '93
The Jacksons: An American Dream '92
Quiet Fire '91
Angels of the City '89
Chance '89
East L.A. Warriors '89
Killcrazy '89
L.A. Vice '89
L.A. Heat '88
Paramedics '88
The Annihilators '85
For the Love of It '80
Cooley High '78

Manny Jacobs
The Seventh Sign '88
Battle of the Bullies '85

Steve Jacobs
Father '90
Alice to Nowhere '86
Echoes of Paradise '86

Ulla Jacobsson
Fox and His Friends '75
The Heroes of Telemark '65
Smiles of a Summer Night '55

Billy Jacoby
Dr. Alien '88
Party Camp '87
Just One of the Guys '85
Beastmaster '82
Bloody Birthday '80

Bobby Jacoby
Night of the Demons 2 '94
The Day My Parents Ran Away '93
The Applegates '89
Tremors '89
Wizards of the Lost Kingdom 2 '89
Iron Eagle '86

Dale Jacoby
Guardian Angel '94
Ring of Fire 2: Blood and Steel '92
Bloodmatch '91
Ring of Fire '91

Scott Jacoby
To Die for 2: Son of Darkness '91
To Die for '89
Return to Horror High '87
Midnight Auto Supply '78
The Little Girl Who Lives Down the Lane '76
Bad Ronald '74
Rivals '72

Hattie Jacques
Carry On 'Round the Bend '72
Make Mine Mink '60
Carry On Nurse '59
A Christmas Carol '51

Richard Jaeckel
Martial Outlaw '93
The King of the Kickboxers '91
Delta Force 2: Operation Stranglehold '90
Ghetto Blaster '89
Black Moon Rising '86
The Dirty Dozen: The Next Mission '85
Pacific Inferno '85
The Fix '84
Starman '84
Blood Song '82
...All the Marbles '81
Awakening of Candra '81
Cold River '81
The $5.20 an Hour Dream '80
Herbie Goes Bananas '80
The Dark '79
Speedtrap '78
Day of the Animals '77
Twilight's Last Gleaming '77
Grizzly '76
Jaws of Death '76
The Drowning Pool '75
Surabaya Conspiracy '75
Walking Tall: Part 2 '75
Born Innocent '74
The Kill '73
Pat Garrett & Billy the Kid '73
Firehouse '72
Ulzana's Raid '72
Sometimes a Great Notion '71
Chisum '70
The Devil's Brigade '68
The Green Slime '68
The Dirty Dozen '67
Once Before I Die '65
Flaming Star '60
The Gallant Hours '60
Platinum High School '60
Cowboy '58
When Hell Broke Loose '58
3:10 to Yuma '57
Come Back, Little Sheba '52
Hoodlum Empire '52
Battleground '49
Sands of Iwo Jima '49
Jungle Patrol '48

A Wing and a Prayer '44
Guadalcanal Diary '43

Frederick Jaeger
Nijinsky '80
Slaughterday '77

Chapelle Jaffe
Confidential '86
One Night Stand '77

Sam Jaffe
On the Line '83
Battle Beyond the Stars '80
Gideon's Trumpet '80
Bedknobs and Broomsticks '71
The Dunwich Horror '70
Night Gallery '69
Ben-Hur '59
Barbarian and the Geisha '58
The Day the Earth Stood Still '51
The Asphalt Jungle '50
The Accused '48
13 Rue Madeleine '46
Gunga Din '39
Lost Horizon '37
Scarlet Empress '34

Seth Jaffe
Scorned 2 '96
Beverly Hills Bodysnatchers '89
Stark '85

Madhur Jaffrey
Vanya on 42nd Street '94
Heat and Dust '82
Autobiography of a Princess '75
Shakespeare Wallah '65

Saeed Jaffrey
Masala '91
The Deceivers '88
The Courtesans of Bombay '85
My Beautiful Laundrette '85
The Razor's Edge '84
Gandhi '82
Hullabaloo Over Georgie & Bonnie's Pictures '78
The Man Who Would Be King '75
The Wilby Conspiracy '75

Dean Jagger
Evil Town '87
Alligator '80
Gideon's Trumpet '80
Game of Death '79
End of the World '76
The Lindbergh Kidnapping Case '76
Hootch Country Boys '75
The Hanged Man '74
I Heard the Owl Call My Name '73
The Stranger '73
Visions of Evil '73
The Glass House '72
Vanishing Point '71
Firecreek '68
Billy Rose's Jumbo '62
The Honeymoon Machine '61
Parrish '61
Cash McCall '60
Elmer Gantry '60
The Nun's Story '59
King Creole '58
Proud Rebel '58
It's a Dog's Life '55
Bad Day at Black Rock '54
Executive Suite '54
White Christmas '54
The Robe '53
The Denver & Rio Grande '51
Rawhide '50
The C-Man '49
Twelve O'Clock High '49
Pursued '47
I Live in Grosvenor Square '46
Sister Kenny '46
The North Star '43
Valley of the Sun '42
Western Union '41
Brigham Young: Frontiersman '40
Exiled to Shanghai '37
Revolt of the Zombies '36

Mick Jagger
Freejack '92
Running Out of Luck '86
The Nightingale '83

Burden of Dreams '82
The Compleat Beatles '82
All You Need Is Cash '78
Gimme Shelter '70
Ned Kelly '70
Performance '70
Sympathy for the Devil '70

Henry Jaglom
Last Summer In the Hamptons '96
Venice, Venice '92
New Year's Day '89
Someone to Love '87
Always '85
Sitting Ducks '80
Psych-Out '68

Lisa Jakub
The Beautician and the Beast '97
The Story Lady '93
Matinee '92
Rambling Rose '91
The Phone Call '89

Anthony James
Unforgiven '92
Slow Burn '90
The Teacher '74
Columbo: Prescription Murder '67
The Last Days of Dolwyn '49

Brion James
American Strays '96
Evil Obsession '96
The Killing Jar '96
The Lazarus Man '96
Precious Find '96
Virtual Assassin '95
Cabin Boy '94
The Companion '94
The Dark '94
Dominion '94
Hong Kong '97 '94
The Last Ride '94
Nature of the Beast '94
Radioland Murders '94
Savage Land '94
Scanner Cop '94
Sketch Artist 2: Hands That See '94
The Soft Kill '94
Steel Frontier '94
Future Shock '94
Rio Diablo '93
Striking Distance '93
Wishman '93
Black Magic '92
The Player '92
Time Runner '92
Ultimate Desires '91
Another 48 Hrs. '90
Beyond the Silhouette '90
Mutator '90
Street Asylum '90
The Horror Show '89
Mom '89
Red Scorpion '89
Tango and Cash '89
Dead Man Walking '88
Nightmare at Noon '87
Steel Dawn '87
Armed and Dangerous '86
Crimewave '85
Enemy Mine '85
Flesh and Blood '85
A Breed Apart '84
Ballad of Gregorio Cortez '83
Blade Runner '82
48 Hrs. '82
Southern Comfort '81

Clifton James
The Summer of Ben Tyler '96
Lone Star '95
Carolina Skeletons '92
The Bonfire of the Vanities '90
Eight Men Out '88
Where Are the Children? '85
Talk to Me '82
The Bad News Bears in Breaking Training '77
Rancho Deluxe '75
Sniper '75
Bank Shot '74
Buster and Billie '74

The Man with the Golden Gun '74
The Last Detail '73
Live and Let Die '73
Werewolf of Washington '73
Will Penny '67
Black Like Me '64
David and Lisa '62

Dalton James
My Father the Hero '93
The Substitute '93

Etta James
Tap '89
Chuck Berry: Hail! Hail! Rock 'n' Roll '87

Gennie James
The River Pirates '94
Broadcast News '87
The Secret Garden '87
A Smoky Mountain Christmas '86

Geraldine James
Rebecca '97
Moll Flanders '96
Band of Gold '95
If Looks Could Kill '91
The Tall Guy '89
The Jewel in the Crown '84

Gladden James
Paradise Island '30
The Social Secretary '16

Godfrey James
Magic in the Mirror: Fowl Play '96
Spellbreaker: Secret of the Leprechauns '96
Leapin' Leprechauns '95
At the Earth's Core '76
The Land that Time Forgot '75

Harry James
The Benny Goodman Story '55
Strictly G.I. '44
Two Girls and a Sailor '44
Best Foot Forward '43
Private Buckaroo '42

Hawthorne James
Heaven's Prisoners '95
Speed '94
The Five Heartbeats '91

Ida James
The Devil's Daughter '39
Hi-De-Ho '35

Jessica James
Immediate Family '89
I, the Jury '82

John James
Secret Passions '78
Lonesome Trail '55
Range Renegades '48
The Devil Bat's Daughter '46
Man from Thunder River '43

Julie James
Terror Beach '80s
Night of the Death Cult '75

Ken James
Landslide '92
Switching Channels '88

Lee James
The Taking of Beverly Hills '91
Cassandra '87

Michael James
Commando Invasion '87
Warriors of the Apocalypse '85

Ron James
Ernest Rides Again '93
The Boogey Man '80
Swinging Wives '79

Sidney James
Carry On Behind '75
Carry On Dick '75
Carry On 'Round the Bend '72
Carry On at Your Convenience '71
Carry On Camping '71
Carry On Henry VIII '71
Carry On Cowboy '66
Carry On Cleo '65
Carry On Cruising '62
What a Carve-Up! '62

The Missing Corpse '45
The Phantom of 42nd Street '45
The Falcon in Hollywood '44
His Butler's Sister '44
Rogue's Gallery '44
Shake Hands with Murder '44
Zombies on Broadway '44
Corregidor '43
The Navy Comes Through '42
His Girl Friday '40
First Love '39
That Girl from Paris '36

Si Jenks
Captain January '36
Fighting Shadows '35
The Outlaw Deputy '35
Rawhide Romance '34

Michael Jenn
Dance with a Stranger '85
Another Country '84

Bruce Jenner
Grambling's White Tiger '81
Can't Stop the Music '80

Lucinda Jenney
Stephen King's Thinner '96
Next Door '94
American Heart '92
Matinee '92
Thelma & Louise '91
Wired '89
Rain Man '88
Verne Miller '88

Brent Jennings
Children of the Corn 4: The
   Gathering '96
Soul of the Game '96
Nervous Ticks '93

Claudia Jennings
Death Sport '78
Fast Company '78
Moonshine County Express '77
The Great Texas Dynamite
   Chase '76
Sisters of Death '76
Truck Stop Women '74
Gator Bait '74
Group Marriage '72
Unholy Rollers '72
Jud '71
The Love Machine '71
The Stepmother '71

DeWitt Jennings
Kelly the Second '36
Criminal Code '31
The Bat Whispers '30
The Big House '30
The Little American '17

Juanita Jennings
Spirit Lost '96
Laurel Avenue '93

Tom Jennings
Stones of Death '88
Night Master '87

Waylon Jennings
Stagecoach '86
Sesame Street Presents: Follow
   That Bird '85

Rita Jenrette
End of the Line '88
Malibu Bikini Shop '86
Zombie Island Massacre '84

Salome Jens
Diary of the Dead '80s
The Grace Kelly Story '83
Tomorrow's Child '82
A Matter of Life and Death '81
Savages '72
Seconds '66
The Fool Killer '65
Angel Baby '61

David Jensen
The Underneath '95
King of the Hill '93

Karen Jensen
Deadly Blessing '81
The Salzburg Connection '72

Maren Jensen
Deadly Blessing '81
Battlestar Galactica '78

Sasha Jensen
Dazed and Confused '93
Dream Trap '90
A Girl to Kill For '90

Todd Jensen
Alien Chaser '96
Armageddon: The Final
   Challenge '94
Never Say Die '94
Cyborg Cop '93
Prey for the Hunter '92

Roy Jenson
Bandits '73
Crossfire '67

Adele Jergens
Girls in Prison '56
The Cobweb '55
Day the World Ended '55
Big Chase '54
Abbott and Costello Meet the
   Invisible Man '51
Armored Car Robbery '50
Blues Busters '50
The Falcon's Adventure/
   Armored Car Robbery '50
Radar Secret Service '50
Treasure of Monte Cristo '50
The Dark Past '49
Ladies of the Chorus '49
Pirate Ship '49
The Fuller Brush Man '48
The Prince of Thieves '48
Down to Earth '47
A Thousand and One Nights '45

Mary Jerrold
The Queen of Spades '49
Woman Hater '49

George Jessel
Diary of a Young Comic '79
Valley of the Dolls '67

Michael Jeter
Air Bud '97
The Boys Next Door '96
Mrs. Santa Claus '96
Waterworld '95
Drop Zone '94
Bank Robber '93
Gypsy '93
Sister Act 2: Back in the Habit
   '93
The Fisher King '91
Dead Bang '89

Joan Jett
Light of Day '87
Dubeat-E-O '84

Jimmy Jewel
The Krays '90
Arthur's Hallowed Ground '84

Isabel Jewell
The Arousers '70
The Leopard Man '43
The Seventh Victim '43
Gone with the Wind '39
Lost Horizon '37
Marked Woman '37
Swing It, Sailor! '37
Go West, Young Man '36
A Tale of Two Cities '36
Ceiling Zero '35
Evelyn Prentice '34
Manhattan Melodrama '34
Blessed Event '32

Penn Jillette
Hackers '95
Penn and Teller Get Killed '90
Tough Guys Don't Dance '87
Miami Vice 2: The Prodigal Son
   '85

Ann Jillian
Little White Lies '89
The Ann Jillian Story '88
Convicted: A Mother's Story '87
Girls of the White Orchid '85
Mae West '84
Mr. Mom '83
Gypsy '62

Joyce Jillson
Slumber Party '57 '76
Superchick '71

Yolanda Jilot
JFK: Reckless Youth '93

Diving In '90

Jose Luis Jimenez
Spiritism '61
The Vampire '57

Ma Jingwu
The Day the Sun Turned Cold
   '94
Raise the Red Lantern '91

Marlene Jobert
Swashbuckler '84
Ten Days Wonder '72
Catch Me a Spy '71
Rider on the Rain '70
Masculine Feminine '66

Zita Johann
The Mummy '32
Struggle '31

David Johansen
Car 54, Where Are You? '94
Mr. Nanny '93
Desire and Hell at Sunset Motel
   '92
Freejack '92
Tales from the Darkside: The
   Movie '90
Let It Ride '89
Married to the Mob '88
Scrooged '88

Paul Johansson
Midnight Witness '93
Martial Law 2: Undercover '91
Soapdish '91

I.S. Johar
Maya '66
Flame Over India '60

Elton John
Tommy '75
Born to Boogie '72

Gottfried John
Goldeneye '95
Abraham '94
Mata Hari '85
Berlin Alexanderplatz '80
The Marriage of Maria Braun '79
In a Year of 13 Moons '78
Mother Kusters Goes to Heaven
   '76

Karl John
The Mysterious Magician '65
The Lost One '51

Rosamund John
Fame Is the Spur '47
Spitfire '42

Glynis Johns
While You Were Sleeping '95
Nukie '93
The Ref '93
Zelly & Me '88
Sprague '84
Under Milk Wood '73
Vault of Horror '73
Dear Brigitte '65
Mary Poppins '64
Papa's Delicate Condition '63
The Sundowners '60
Shake Hands with the Devil '59
Another Time, Another Place '58
All Mine to Give '56
Court Jester '56
Land of Fury '55
Rob Roy—The Highland Rogue
   '53
The Sword & the Rose '53
Encore '52
The Promoter '52
No Highway in the Sky '51
Frieda '47
The Adventures of Tartu '43
The Forty-Ninth Parallel '41
South Riding '37

Mervyn Johns
Day of the Triffids '63
No Love for Johnnie '60
Romeo and Juliet '54
The Master of Ballantrae '53
A Christmas Carol '51
Tony Draws a Horse '51
Counterblast '48
Captain Boycott '47
Captive Heart '47
San Demetrio, London '47

Dead of Night '45
Pink String and Sealing Wax '45

Stratford Johns
Splitting Heirs '93
The Strange Case of the End of
   Civilization as We Know It '93
A Demon in My View '92
The Lair of the White Worm '88
Salome's Last Dance '88
Dance with a Stranger '85
Great Expectations '81

Tracy C. Johns
New Jack City '91
Mo' Better Blues '90
She's Gotta Have It '86

A.J. Johnson
B.A.P.'s '97
Double Trouble '91
House Party '90

Amy Jo Johnson
Turbo: A Power Rangers Movie
   '96
Mighty Morphin Power Rangers:
   The Movie '95

Anne-Marie Johnson
Dream Date '93
True Identity '91
Robot Jox '90
I'm Gonna Git You Sucka '88
Hollywood Shuffle '87

Arnold Johnson
My Demon Lover '87
Putney Swope '69

Arte Johnson
Assault of the Party Nerds 2:
   Heavy Petting Detective '95
Munchie '91
Evil Spirits '91
Evil Toons '90
The Red Raven Kiss-Off '90
Tax Season '90
What Comes Around '85
Bunco '83
If Things Were Different '79
Love at First Bite '79
Bud and Lou '78
Charge of the Model T's '76

Ben Johnson
The Evening Star '96
Ruby Jean and Joe '96
Angels in the Outfield '94
Bonanza: The Return '93
Radio Flyer '92
The Chase '91
My Heroes Have Always Been
   Cowboys '91
Back to Back '90
Dark Before Dawn '89
Cherry 2000 '88
Let's Get Harry '87
Trespasses '86
Champions '84
Red Dawn '84
Soggy Bottom U.S.A. '84
Wild Horses '84
The Shadow Riders '82
Tex '82
Ruckus '81
Terror Train '80
The Sacketts '79
Wild Times '79
The Swarm '78
Grayeagle '77
Breakheart Pass '76
The Red Pony '76
The Savage Bees '76
Town that Dreaded Sundown '76
Bite the Bullet '75
The Sugarland Express '74
Dillinger '73
Train Robbers '73
The Getaway '72
Junior Bonner '72
The Last Picture Show '71
Chisum '70
The Undefeated '69
The Wild Bunch '69
Will Penny '67
The Rare Breed '66
Major Dundee '65
One-Eyed Jacks '61
Tomboy & the Champ '58
Shane '53

Rio Grande '50
Wagon Master '50
Mighty Joe Young '49
She Wore a Yellow Ribbon '49
Three Godfathers '48

Beverly Johnson
The Cover Girl Murders '93
Ashanti, Land of No Mercy '79

Brad Johnson
Lone Justice 3: Showdown at
   Plum Creek '96
The Birds 2: Land's End '94
Dominion '94
'Siringo '94
Lone Justice 2 '93
Philadelphia Experiment 2 '93
An American Story '92
Flight of the Intruder '90
Always '89
Nam Angels '88
The Losers '70

Candy Johnson
Bikini Beach '64
Muscle Beach Party '64
Pajama Party '64
Beach Party '63

Celia Johnson
Unicorn '83
The Hostage Tower '80
Staying On '80
Les Miserables '78
The Prime of Miss Jean Brodie
   '69
Captain's Paradise '53
This Happy Breed '47
Brief Encounter '46
In Which We Serve '43

Chic Johnson
All Over Town '37
Country Gentlemen '36

Clark Johnson
Rude '96
Final Round '93
The Finishing Touch '92
Personals '90

Don Johnson
Tin Cup '96
In Pursuit of Honor '95
Born Yesterday '93
Guilty as Sin '93
Harley Davidson and the
   Marlboro Man '91
Paradise '91
Tales of the Unexpected '91
The Hot Spot '90
Dead Bang '89
Sweet Hearts Dance '88
The Long, Hot Summer '86
Cease Fire '85
Miami Vice 2: The Prodigal Son
   '85
Miami Vice '84
Soggy Bottom U.S.A. '84
Melanie '82
Beulah Land '80
Revenge of the Stepford Wives
   '80
The Rebels '79
Snowblind '78
The City '76
Law of the Land '76
A Boy and His Dog '75
Return to Macon County '75
Harrad Experiment '73
Zachariah '70

Dots Johnson
Paisan '46
Tall, Tan and Terrific '46

Georgann Johnson
Twilight Man '96
Murphy's Romance '85

Helen Johnson
Vice Squad '31
The Divorcee '30
Sin Takes a Holiday '30

Jill Johnson
Party Plane '90
Wildest Dreams '90

Joey Johnson
Courier of Death '84
Grad Night '81

Kimberley Kates
Bad Blood '94
Chained Heat 2 '92

Kazuo Kato
Hiroshima '95
Body Snatcher from Hell '69

Massaya Kato
Crime Broker '94
The Seventh Floor '93

Rosanne Katon
She Devils in Chains
Bachelor Party '84
Zapped! '82
Lunch Wagon '81
Chesty Anderson USN '76
The Muthers '76

Shintaro Katsu
The Razor: Sword of Justice '72
Zatoichi vs. Yojimbo '70
Zatoichi: The Blind Swordsman
  and the Fugitives '68
Zatoichi: The Blind Swordsman's
  Vengeance '66
Zatoichi: The Blind Swordsman
  and the Chess Expert '65
Zatoichi: Master Ichi and a
  Chest of Gold '64
Zatoichi: Zatoichi's Flashing
  Sword '64
Zatoichi: The Life and Opinion of
  Masseur Ichi '62

Andreas Katsulas
Star Trek the Next Generation,
  the Final Episode: All Good
  Things... '94
The Fugitive '93
Blame It on the Bellboy '92
Communion '89
Next of Kin '89
Someone to Watch Over Me '87

Nicky Katt
subUrbia '96
The Babysitter '95

William Katt
Daddy's Girl '96
Rattled '96
Piranha '95
American Cop '94
The Paperboy '94
Stranger by Night '94
Tollbooth '94
Desperate Motives '92
House 4: Home Deadly Home
  '91
Naked Obsession '91
The Defense Never Rests '90
Last Call '90
Swimsuit: The Movie '89
Wedding Band '89
White Ghost '88
Perry Mason: The Case of the
  Lost Love '87
House '86
Baby ... Secret of the Lost
  Legend '85
Perry Mason Returns '85
Thumbelina '82
Pippin '81
Butch and Sundance: The Early
  Days '79
Big Wednesday '78
First Love '77
Carrie '76

Omri Katz
Hocus Pocus '93
Adventures in Dinosaur City '92
Matinee '92

Yftach Katzur
Young Love—Lemon Popsicle 7
  '87
Atalia '85
Hot Bubblegum '81

Andy Kaufman
My Breakfast with Blassie '83
Heartbeeps '81

David Kaufman
Invisible: The Chronicles of
  Benjamin Knight '93
The Last Prostitute '91

Maurice Kaufman
Next Victim '74

Fright '71
The Hero '71
Die! Die! My Darling! '65

Christine Kaufmann
Bagdad Cafe '88
Welcome to 18 '87
Murders in the Rue Morgue '71
Taras Bulba '62
The Last Days of Pompeii '60

Joseph Kaufmann
Jud '71
Private Duty Nurses '71

Caroline Kava
Born on the Fourth of July '89
Little Nikita '88

Christine Kavanagh
The Glass Virgin '90s
Monkey Boy '90

John Kavanagh
Sharpe's Sword '94
Widow's Peak '94
Bellman and True '88
Cal '84

Julie Kavner
Forget Paris '95
I'll Do Anything '93
Shadows and Fog '92
This Is My Life '92
Alice '90
Awakenings '90
New York Stories '89
Radio Days '87
Surrender '87
Hannah and Her Sisters '86
Bad Medicine '85
Revenge of the Stepford Wives
  '80
Katherine '75

Hiroyuki Kawase
Godzilla vs. Megalon '76
Godzilla vs. the Smog Monster
  '72

Seizaburo Kawazu
Yojimbo '61
A Geisha '53

Yusuke Kawazu
The Human Condition: A
  Soldier's Prayer '61
The Cruel Story of Youth '60
The Human Condition: Road to
  Eternity '59

Dianne Kay
Andy and the Airwave Rangers
  '89
Portrait of a Showgirl '82

Jody Kay
Death Screams '83
House of Death '82
One Armed Executioner '80

Mary Ellen Kay
Thunder Pass '54
Colorado Sundown '52
Government Agents vs.
  Phantom Legion '51
Silver City Bonanza '51
Thunder in God's Country '51

Melody Kay
Camp Nowhere '94
The Neverending Story 3:
  escape from Fantasia '94

Yuzo Kayama
Zero '84
Red Beard '65

Caren Kaye
Satan's Princess '90
Poison Ivy '85
Help Wanted: Male '82
My Tutor '82
Kill Castro '80
The Mercenaries '80

Celia Kaye
Final Comedown '72
Island of the Blue Dolphins '64

Danny Kaye
Pinocchio '76
The Madwoman of Chaillot '69
The Five Pennies '59
Me and the Colonel '58
Court Jester '56

White Christmas '54
Hans Christian Andersen '52
The Inspector General '49
It's a Great Feeling '49
A Song is Born '48
The Secret Life of Walter Mitty
  '47
Kid from Brooklyn '46
Wonder Man '45
Up in Arms '44
Chasing Those Depression
  Blues '35

Lila Kaye
Dragonworld '94
Mrs. 'Arris Goes to Paris '92
Antonia and Jane '91
Nuns on the Run '90

Norman Kaye
Bad Boy Bubby '93
The Killing Beach '92
A Woman's Tale '92
Frenchman's Farm '87
Warm Nights on a Slow-Moving
  Train '87
Cactus '86
Man of Flowers '84
Where the Green Ants Dream
  '84
Lonely Hearts '82

Stubby Kaye
Who Framed Roger Rabbit '88
Minsky's Follies '83
The Big Push '75
The Way West '67
Cat Ballou '65
Cool Mikado '63
40 Pounds of Trouble '62
Li'l Abner '59
Guys and Dolls '55

Elia Kazan
The Arrangement '69
City for Conquest '40

Lainie Kazan
Love Is All There Is '96
Movies Money Murder '96
The Cemetery Club '93
I Don't Buy Kisses Anymore '92
29th Street '91
Eternity '90
Beaches '88
Out of the Dark '88
Harry and the Hendersons '87
Delta Force '86
The Journey of Natty Gann '85
Lust in the Dust '85
Obsessive Love '84
Pinocchio '83
Sunset Limousine '83
My Favorite Year '82
One from the Heart '82
A Cry for Love '80
Love Affair: The Eleanor & Lou
  Gehrig Story '77
Romance of a Horsethief '71
Dayton's Devils '68
Lady in Cement '68

Tim Kazurinsky
Shakes the Clown '92
A Billion for Boris '90
Best of Eddie Murphy '89
Dinner at Eight '89
Wedding Band '89
Hot to Trot! '88
Police Academy 4: Citizens on
  Patrol '87
Police Academy 3: Back in
  Training '86
The Princess and the Pea '83
Continental Divide '81

James Keach
The Dance Goes On '92
The Experts '89
Options '88
Evil Town '87
Film House Fever '86
Wildcats '86
Moving Violations '85
Stand Alone '85
The Razor's Edge '84
Love Letters '83
National Lampoon's Vacation
  '83
The Long Riders '80
Hurricane '79

Smokey & the Hotwire Gang '79
Slashed Dreams '74
Till Death Do Us Part '72

Stacy Keach
Legend of the Lost Tomb '97
Escape from L.A. '96
Amanda and the Alien '95
Young Ivanhoe '95
New Crime City: Los Angeles
  2020 '94
The Pathfinder '94
Texas '94
Body Bags '93
Raw Justice '93
Rio Diablo '93
Sunset Grill '92
Mission of the Shark '91
Class of 1999 '90
False Identity '90
The Forgotten '89
The Blue and the Gray '85
Mistral's Daughter '84
Princess Daisy '83
Butterfly '82
Dynasty '81
That Championship Season '82
Cheech and Chong's Nice
  Dreams '81
Road Games '81
The Long Riders '80
A Rumor of War '80
Cheech and Chong's Up in
  Smoke '79
Diary of a Young Comic '79
The Ninth Configuration '79
Slave of the Cannibal God '79
Battleforce '78
Ants '77
Gray Lady Down '77
The Squeeze '77
Killer Inside Me '76
Street People '76
Conduct Unbecoming '75
All the Kind Strangers '74
Luther '74
Man of Destiny '73
Watched '73
Fat City '72
Life & Times of Judge Roy Bean
  '72
The New Centurions '72
Brewster McCloud '70
End of the Road '70
The Heart is a Lonely Hunter '68

Marie Kean
The Dead '87
The Lonely Passion of Judith
  Hearne '87
Danny Boy '84

Staci Keanan
Downhill Willie '96
Lisa '90

Edward Keane
Rogue's Gallery '44
Midnight Limited '40
Heroes in Blue '39

Kerrie Keane
Malarek '89
Distant Thunder '88
Obsessed '88
Nightstick '87
Kung Fu: The Movie '86
Hot Pursuit '84
Incubus '82

Robert Emmett Keane
Hills of Oklahoma '50
Susanna Pass '49
Fear in the Night '47
Born to Be Wild '38

Stephen Kearney
The Nutt House '95
Rikky and Pete '88

Billy Kearns
The Day and the Hour '63
Purple Noon '60

Charles Keating
The Bodyguard '92
Brideshead Revisited '81

Fred Keating
Tin Pan Alley '40
Prison Train '38

I Live My Life '35

Larry Keating
The Incredible Mr. Limpet '64
Daddy Long Legs '55
Gypsy Colt '54
Above and Beyond '53
Give a Girl a Break '53
A Lion Is in the Streets '53
Monkey Business '52
Francis Goes to the Races '51
When Worlds Collide '51

Buster Keaton
Man in the Silk Hat '83
A Funny Thing Happened on the
  Way to the Forum '66
Beach Blanket Bingo '65
Buster Keaton Rides Again/The
  Railrodder '65
How to Stuff a Wild Bikini '65
Railrodder '65
A Few Moments with Buster
  Keaton and Laurel and Hardy
  '63
Great Chase '63
It's a Mad, Mad, Mad, Mad
  World '63
Days of Thrills and Laughter '61
The Adventures of Huckleberry
  Finn '60
When Comedy was King '59
Limelight '52
Sunset Boulevard '50
In the Good Old Summertime
  '49
Boom in the Moon '46
God's Country '46
Forever and a Day '43
The Villain Still Pursued Her '41
Li'l Abner '40
New Moon '40
Slapstick '30s
Old Spanish Custom '36
What! No Beer? '33
Speak Easily '32
Parlor, Bedroom and Bath '31
Sidewalks of New York '31
Doughboys '30
Free and Easy '30
Story of William S. Hart/Sad
  Clowns '20s
Spite Marriage '29
The Cameraman '28
Steamboat Bill, Jr. '28
College '27
The General '27
Battling Butler '26
Seven Chances '25
The Navigator '24
The Balloonatic/One Week '23
The Blacksmith/The Balloonatic
  '23
Our Hospitality '23
Three Ages '23
The Blacksmith/The Cops '22
Cops/One Week '22
The Saphead '21

Diane Keaton
The First Wives Club '96
Marvin's Room '96
Father of the Bride Part II '95
Amelia Earhart: The Final Flight
  '94
Manhattan Murder Mystery '93
Running Mates '92
Father of the Bride '91
The Godfather, Part 3 '90
The Lemon Sisters '90
The Good Mother '88
Baby Boom '87
Radio Days '87
Crimes of the Heart '86
The Little Drummer Girl '84
Mrs. Soffel '84
Shoot the Moon '82
The Godfather 1902-1959: The
  Complete Epic '81
Reds '81
Manhattan '79
Interiors '78
Annie Hall '77
Looking for Mr. Goodbar '77
Harry & Walter Go to New York
  '76
I Will, I Will for Now '76
Love and Death '75

The Godfather, Part 2 '74
Sleeper '73
The Godfather '72
Play It Again, Sam '72
Lovers and Other Strangers '70

Joe Keaton
The General '27
Our Hospitality '23

Michael Keaton
Desperate Measures '97
Multiplicity '96
The Paper '94
Speechless '94
Much Ado about Nothing '93
My Life '93
Batman Returns '92
One Good Cop '91
Pacific Heights '90
Batman '89
The Dream Team '89
Beetlejuice '88
Clean and Sober '88
The Squeeze '87
Touch and Go '86
Gung Ho '85
Johnny Dangerously '84
Mr. Mom '83
Night Shift '82

Ele Keats
White Dwarf '95
Mother '94
White Wolves 2: Legend of the Wild '94
Lipstick Camera '93

Steven Keats
Eternity '90
The Spring '89
In Dangerous Company '88
Badge of the Assassin '85
The Executioner's Song '82
Silent Rage '82
For Ladies Only '81
Mysterious Island of Beautiful Women '79
Black Sunday '77
Hester Street '75

Hugh Keays-Byrne
Kangaroo '86
Mad Max '80
Death Train '79

Lila Kedrova
Some Girls '88
Sword of the Valiant '83
Tell Me a Riddle '80
Le Cavaleur '78
Widow's Nest '77
Escape to the Sun '72
Torn Curtain '66
Zorba the Greek '64
Modigliani '58

James Kee
Double Standard '88
Shadow Dancing '88

Cornelius Keefe
The Trigger Trio '37
Death from a Distance '36
Hong Kong Nights '35
Mystery Liner '34
The Adorable Cheat '28
Man from Headquarters '28

Howard Keel
Irving Berlin's America '86
Arizona Bushwackers '67
The War Wagon '67
Day of the Triffids '63
Armored Command '61
Jupiter's Darling '55
Kismet '55
Deep in My Heart '54
Rose Marie '54
Seven Brides for Seven Brothers '54
Calamity Jane '53
I Love Melvin '53
Kiss Me Kate '53
Lovely to Look At '52
Show Boat '51
Texas Carnival '51
Three Guys Named Mike '51
Pagan Love Song '50

Ruby Keeler
That's Dancing! '85

Dames '34
Flirtation Walk '34
Footlight Parade '33
42nd Street '33
Gold Diggers of 1933 '33

Geoffrey Keen
The Living Daylights '87
Amin: The Rise and Fall '82
For Your Eyes Only '81
Moonraker '79
Number 1 of the Secret Service '77
The Spy Who Loved Me '77
Sacco & Vanzetti '71
Taste the Blood of Dracula '69
Dr. Syn, Alias the Scarecrow '64
A Matter of WHO '62
Sink the Bismarck '60
The Third Key '57
Postmark for Danger '56
The Man Who Never Was '55
Angels One Five '54
Doctor in the House '53
Genevieve '53
The Clouded Yellow '51
Cry, the Beloved Country '51
The Fallen Idol '49

Tom Keene
Plan 9 from Outer Space '56
Trail of Robin Hood '50
Arizona Roundup '42
Lone Star Law Men '42
Western Mail '42
Where Trails End '42
The Driftin' Kid '41
Dynamite Canyon '41
Riding the Sunset Trail '41
Renegade Ranger/Scarlet River '38
God's Country and the Man '37
Where Trails Divide '37
Desert Gold '36
Drift Fence '36
The Glory Trail '36
Hong Kong Nights '35
Our Daily Bread '34
Cheyenne Kid '33
Beyond the Rockies '32
Come On Danger! '32
Ghost Valley '32
Saddle Buster '32

Catherine Keener
If These Walls Could Talk '96
Walking and Talking '96
Living in Oblivion '94
Johnny Suede '92
Survival Quest '89

Matt Keeslar
Waiting for Guffman '96
The Run of the Country '95
The Stupids '95
Safe Passage '94

Jack Kehler
Lost Highway '96
My Fellow Americans '96
The Shot '96
The Invaders '95
Blindsided '93
Casualties of Love: The "Long Island Lolita" Story '93
Bloodstone '88

Jack Kehoe
Falling Down '93
Servants of Twilight '91
Young Guns 2 '90
The Untouchables '87
A Winner Never Quits '86
On the Nickel '80
The Fish that Saved Pittsburgh '79
Law and Disorder '74
Serpico '73

Andrew Keir
Rob Roy '95
Dragonworld '94
Absolution '82
The Thirty-Nine Steps '79
Zeppelin '71
The Night Visitor '70
Daleks—Invasion Earth 2150 A.D. '66
Dracula, Prince of Darkness '66
The Fighting Prince of Donegal '66

Lord Jim '65
Cleopatra '63
Suspended Alibi '56

Harvey Keitel
Copland '97
City of Industry '96
Blue in the Face '95
Clockers '95
From Dusk Till Dawn '95
Smoke '95
Ulysses' Gaze '95
Imaginary Crimes '94
Monkey Trouble '94
Pulp Fiction '94
Somebody to Love '94
Dangerous Game '93
The Piano '93
Point of No Return '93
Rising Sun '93
The Young Americans '93
Bad Lieutenant '92
Reservoir Dogs '92
Sister Act '92
Bugsy '91
Mortal Thoughts '91
Thelma & Louise '91
Two Evil Eyes '90
The Two Jakes '90
The January Man '89
Blindside '88
The Last Temptation of Christ '88
The Inquiry '87
The Pick-Up Artist '87
The Men's Club '86
Off Beat '86
Camorra: The Naples Connection '85
Star Knight '85
Corrupt '84
Falling in Love '84
Exposed '83
The Border '82
La Nuit de Varennes '82
Death Watch '80
Saturn 3 '80
Eagle's Wing '79
Blue Collar '78
Fingers '78
The Duellists '77
Welcome to L.A. '77
Buffalo Bill & the Indians '76
Mother, Jugs and Speed '76
Taxi Driver '76
The Virginia Hill Story '76
Shining Star '75
Alice Doesn't Live Here Anymore '74
Mean Streets '73
Who's That Knocking at My Door? '68

Brian Keith
National Lampoon's Favorite Deadly Sins '95
Picture Windows '95
The Gambler Returns: The Luck of the Draw '93
Escape '90
Bull of the West '89
Welcome Home '89
Young Guns '88
The Alamo: Thirteen Days to Glory '87
Death Before Dishonor '87
World War III '86
Charlie Chan and the Curse of the Dragon Queen '81
Sharky's Machine '81
The Mountain Men '80
The Chisholms '79
Meteor '79
The Seekers '79
Hooper '78
Joe Panther '76
The Loneliest Runner '76
The Longest Drive '76
The Wind and the Lion '75
The Yakuza '75
Scandalous John '71
McKenzie Break '70
Suppose They Gave a War and Nobody Came? '70
With Six You Get Eggroll '68
Reflections in a Golden Eye '67
Nevada Smith '66
The Rare Breed '66

The Russians are Coming, the Russians are Coming '66
The Hallelujah Trail '65
Those Calloways '65
A Tiger Walks '64
The Fugitive: Premiere Episode '63
Johnny Shiloh '63
Savage Sam '63
Moon Pilot '62
Deadly Companions '61
The Parent Trap '61
Ten Who Dared '60
The Young Philadelphians '59
Dino '57
Nightfall '56
Run of the Arrow '56
The Violent Men '55
Arrowhead '53

David Keith
Invasion of Privacy '96
Judge & Jury '96
Born Wild '95
Deadly Sins '95
Gold Diggers: The Secret of Bear Mountain '95
Major League 2 '94
Temptation '94
Texas '94
Till the End of the Night '94
Raw Justice '93
Caged Fear '92
Desperate Motives '92
Liar's Edge '92
Off and Running '90
The Two Jakes '90
The Further Adventures of Tennessee Buck '88
Heartbreak Hotel '88
White of the Eye '88
The Curse '87
Gulag '85
Firestarter '84
Independence Day '83
The Lords of Discipline '83
An Officer and a Gentleman '82
Back Roads '81
Take This Job & Shove It '81
Brubaker '80
The Great Santini '80
The Rose '79

Donald Keith
Outlaw Justice '32
Branded Men '31
Bare Knees '28
Dancing Mothers '26
Free to Love '25
My Lady of Whims '25

Ian Keith
It Came from Beneath the Sea '55
Dick Tracy's Dilemma '47
Scared to Death/Dick Tracy's Dilemma '47
Song of Old Wyoming '45
The Chinese Cat '44
Corregidor '43
Man from Thunder River '43
The Payoff '43
Mary of Scotland '36
The White Legion '36
The Crusades '35
The Three Musketeers '35
Queen Christina '33
The Sign of the Cross '33
Manhandled '24

Penelope Keith
The Norman Conquests, Part 1: Table Manners '80
The Norman Conquests, Part 2: Living Together '80
The Norman Conquests, Part 3: Round and Round the Garden '80
Madhouse Mansion '74

Robert Keith
Cimarron '60
Men in War '57
My Man Godfrey '57
Between Heaven and Hell '56
Written on the Wind '56
Love Me or Leave Me '55
Drum Beat '54
The Wild One '54

Young at Heart '54
Battle Circus '53
Devil's Canyon '53
Small Town Girl '53
Here Comes the Groom '51
Boomerang '47

Rosalind Keith
Bad Boy '39
Theodora Goes Wild '36

Sheila Keith
House of the Long Shadows '82
The Comeback '77
The Confessional '75
Frightmare '74

Robert Kellard
Gentleman from Dixie '41
Drums of Fu Manchu '40

Cecil Kellaway
Quick, Let's Get Married '71
Getting Straight '70
Guess Who's Coming to Dinner '67
Spinout '66
The Cardinal '63
Zotz! '62
Interrupted Melody '55
The Prodigal '55
The Beast from 20,000 Fathoms '53
Young Bess '53
Francis Goes to the Races '51
Harvey '50
Kim '50
Portrait of Jennie '48
Unconquered '47
Monsieur Beaucaire '46
The Postman Always Rings Twice '46
I Married a Witch '42
Birth of the Blues '41
Brother Orchid '40
The Letter '40
The Mummy's Hand '40
Gunga Din '39
Wuthering Heights '39
Maid's Night Out '38

Tina Kellegher
Scarlett '94
The Snapper '93

Hiram Keller
Countryman '83
Lifespan '75
Ciao Federico! Fellini Directs Satyricon '69
Fellini Satyricon '69

Marthe Keller
Mon Amie Max '94
Young Catherine '91
The Nightmare Years '89
Dark Eyes '87
Red Kiss '85
The Amateur '82
The Formula '80
Black Sunday '77
Bobby Deerfield '77
Marathon Man '76
And Now My Love '74

Mary Page Keller
Any Place But Home '97
The Colony '95
Ulterior Motives '92
Scared Stiff '87

Barbara Kellerman
The Chronicles of Narnia '89
Quatermass Conclusion '79

Sally Kellerman
Mirror, Mirror 2: Raven Dance '94
Ready to Wear '94
Younger & Younger '94
Boris and Natasha: The Movie '92
Victim of Beauty '91
Doppelganger: The Evil Within '90
All's Fair '89
Secret of the Ice Cave '89
You Can't Hurry Love '88
Meatballs 3 '87
Someone to Love '87
Three for the Road '87
Back to School '86

Kerry ⟶cont.

The Hunchback of Notre Dame
'23
Merry-Go-Round '23

Brian Kerwin
Getting Away With Murder '96
Jack '96
Gold Diggers: The Secret of
Bear Mountain '95
It Came from Outer Space 2 '95
Hard Promises '91
Love Field '91
Switched at Birth '91
Code Name: Chaos '90
Torch Song Trilogy '88
King Kong Lives '86
Murphy's Romance '85
Nickel Mountain '85
Wet Gold '84
Miss All-American Beauty '82
Getting Wasted '80
Hometown U.S.A. '79
A Real American Hero '78

Lance Kerwin
Enemy Mine '85
Fourth Wise Man '85
Side Show '84
The Snow Queen '83
The Mysterious Stranger '82
Shooting '82
Children of Divorce '80
Salem's Lot '79
The Loneliest Runner '76
Reflections of Murder '74

Maureen Kerwin
Reunion '88
The Destructors '74

Jillian Kesner
Roots of Evil '91
Starhops '78
Firecracker '71

Quin Kessler
Wishman '93
She '83

Sara Kestelman
Lady Jane '85
Lisztomania '75
Zardoz '73

Evelyn Keyes
Wicked Stepmother '89
Return to Salem's Lot '87
The Seven Year Itch '55
Prowler '51
The Jolson Story '46
A Thousand and One Nights '45
The Desperadoes '43
Here Comes Mr. Jordan '41
Before I Hang '40
The Lady in Question '40
Slightly Honorable '40
Gone with the Wind '39
Union Pacific '39

Irwin Keyes
Backlash: Oblivion 2 '95
The Flintstones '94
Frankenstein General Hospital
'88

Mark Keyloun
Separate Vacations '86
Gimme an F '85
Mike's Murder '84

The Keystone Cops
Golden Age of Comedy '58
Desperate Scoundrel/The Pride of
Pikeville '22
The Knockout/Dough and
Dynamite '14

Persis Khambatta
Deadly Intent '88
Phoenix the Warrior '88
First Strike '85
Warrior of the Lost World '84
Megaforce '82
Nighthawks '81
Star Trek: The Motion Picture
'80
Conduct Unbecoming '75
The Wilby Conspiracy '75

Arsinee Khanjian
The Sweet Hereafter '96
Exotica '94
Calendar '93
The Adjuster '91
Speaking Parts '89
Family Viewing '87

Leleti Khumalo
Cry, the Beloved Country '95
Sarafina! '92

Guy Kibbee
Three Godfathers '48
The Horn Blows at Midnight '45
Dixie Jamboree '44
Miss Annie Rooney '42
Whistling in Dixie '42
It Started with Eve '41
Our Town '40
Babes in Arms '39
Let Freedom Ring '39
Mr. Smith Goes to Washington
'39
Joy of Living '38
Of Human Hearts '38
Three Comrades '38
Captain January '36
Earthworm Tractors '36
Little Lord Fauntleroy '36
Three Men on a Horse '36
Captain Blood '35
Dames '34
Footlight Parade '33
42nd Street '33
Gold Diggers of 1933 '33
Lady for a Day '33
Rain '32
Scarlet Dawn '32
The Strange Love of Molly
Louvain '32
Laughing Sinners '31

Michael Kidd
Smile '75
It's Always Fair Weather '55

Margot Kidder
Bloodknot '95
Young Ivanhoe '95
Beanstalk '94
Henry & Verlin '94
Windrunner '94
To Catch a Killer '92
Mob Story '90
Vanishing Act '88
Louisiana '87
Superman 4: The Quest for
Peace '87
Keeping Track '86
Hitchhiker 2 '85
Little Treasure '85
The Glitter Dome '84
Superman 3 '83
Trenchcoat '83
Heartaches '82
Some Kind of Hero '82
Miss Right '81
Shoot the Sun Down '81
Superman 2 '80
Willie & Phil '80
The Amityville Horror '79
Mr. Mike's Mondo Video '79
Superman: The Movie '78
92 in the Shade '76
Black Christmas '75
The Great Waldo Pepper '75
The Reincarnation of Peter
Proud '75
Quiet Day In Belfast '74
Sisters '73
The Bounty Man '72
Quackser Fortune Has a Cousin
in the Bronx '70

Nicole Kidman
Portrait of a Lady '96
Batman Forever '95
To Die For '95
Malice '93
My Life '93
Far and Away '92
Billy Bathgate '91
Days of Thunder '90
Flirting '89
Night Master '87
Windrider '86
Archer's Adventure '85

BMX Bandits '83
Prince and the Great Race '83

Richard Kiel
Happy Gilmore '96
Think Big '90
Pale Rider '85
Mad Mission 3 '84
Hysterical '83
So Fine '81
War of the Wizards '81
Moonraker '79
Force 10 from Navarone '78
They Went That-a-Way & That-
a-Way '78
The Spy Who Loved Me '77
Silver Streak '76
Flash & Firecat '75
The Longest Yard '74
The Human Duplicators '64
Roustabout '64
Eegah! '62
The Phantom Planet '61

Sue Kiel
Survivor '87
Red Heat '85

Udo Kier
The Adventures of Pinocchio '96
Barb Wire '96
Red Shoe Diaries 7: Burning Up
'96
Breaking the Waves '95
Johnny Mnemonic '95
The Kingdom '95
For Love or Money '93
Zentropa '92
My Own Private Idaho '91
Seduction: The Cruel Woman
'89
The Stationmaster's Wife '77
Suspiria '77
The House on Straw Hill '76
Andy Warhol's Dracula '74
Andy Warhol's Frankenstein '74
Mark of the Devil '69

Robbie Kiger
Welcome Home, Roxy
Carmichael '90
Children of the Corn '84
Table for Five '83

Susan Kiger
Death Screams '83
House of Death '82
The Return '80
H.O.T.S. '79
Seven '79

Percy Kilbride
Ma and Pa Kettle at Waikiki '55
Ma and Pa Kettle at Home '54
Ma and Pa Kettle on Vacation
'53
Ma and Pa Kettle at the Fair '52
Ma and Pa Kettle Back On the
Farm '51
Ma and Pa Kettle Go to Town
'50
Riding High '50
Ma and Pa Kettle '49
Egg and I '47
Riff-Raff '47
Welcome Stranger '47
The Southerner '45
State Fair '45
The Adventures of Mark Twain
'44
The Woman of the Town '44
George Washington Slept Here
'42
Keeper of the Flame '42

Terence Kilburn
Lolita '62
Fiend Without a Face '58
National Velvet '44
They Shall Have Music '39
A Christmas Carol '38

Richard Kiley
Phenomenon '96
The Canterville Ghost '91
Separate But Equal '91
The Final Days '89
The Adventures of Huckleberry
Finn '85
The Bad Seed '85
George Washington '84

The Thorn Birds '83
Pray TV '82
Endless Love '81
Angel on My Shoulder '80
Looking for Mr. Goodbar '77
The Little Prince '74
Jigsaw '71
Murder Once Removed '71
Pendulum '69
Blackboard Jungle '55
Pickup on South Street '53

Victor Kilian
One Too Many '51
Unknown World '51
Rimfire '49
Dangerous Passage '44
Dr. Cyclops '40
Young Tom Edison '40
The Adventures of Tom Sawyer
'38
Lady from Nowhere '36
Riff Raff '35

Val Kilmer
The Saint '97
The Ghost and the Darkness '96
The Island of Dr. Moreau '96
Batman Forever '95
Heat '95
The Real McCoy '93
Tombstone '93
True Romance '93
Thunderheart '92
The Doors '91
Gore Vidal's Billy the Kid '89
Kill Me Again '89
Willow '88
The Man Who Broke 1,000
Chains '87
The Murders in the Rue Morgue
'86
Top Gun '86
Real Genius '85
Top Secret! '84

Lincoln Kilpatrick
Piranha '95
Fortress '93
Prison '88
Deadly Force '83

Patrick Kilpatrick
Free Willy 3 '97
Last Stand at Saber River '96
Riot '96
Beastmaster 2: The Eye of
Braxus '95
Open Fire '94
Scanner Cop 2: Volkin's
Revenge '94
Scanners: The Showdown '94
Showdown '93
3 Ninjas Knuckle Up '92
The Cellar '90
Class of 1999 '90
Death Warrant '90
Roanoak '86

Bobby Kim
Kill Line '91
Manchurian Avenger '84

Joon Kim
Gang Justice '94
Street Soldiers '91

Charles Kimbrough
The Good Mother '88
Switching Channels '88
Sunday in the Park with George
'86

Clinton Kimbrough
Night Call Nurses '72
Bloody Mama '70

Bruce Kimmel
Spaceship '81
The First Nudie Musical '75

Dana Kimmell
Friday the 13th, Part 3 '82
Sweet 16 '81

Kenneth Kimmins
My Best Friend Is a Vampire '88
Eleanor: First Lady of the World
'82

Isao Kimura
Black Lizard '68
Stray Dog '49

Aron Kincaid
The Proud and the Damned '72
Creature of Destruction '67

Kevin Kindlan
Heartstopper '92
Revenge of the Living Zombies
'88
The Majorettes '87

Adrienne King
Friday the 13th, Part 2 '81
Friday the 13th '80

Alan King
Casino '95
The Infiltrator '95
Night and the City '92
The Bonfire of the Vanities '90
Enemies, a Love Story '89
Memories of Me '88
Cat's Eye '85
Author! Author! '82
I, the Jury '82
Just Tell Me What You Want '80
Pleasure Palace '80
How to Pick Up Girls '78
The Anderson Tapes '71

Andrea King
Blackenstein '73
House of the Black Death '65
Band of Angels '57
Red Planet Mars '52
The World in His Arms '52
The Lemon Drop Kid '51
Mr. Peabody & the Mermaid '48
The Beast with Five Fingers '46
The Man I Love '46

Atlas King
The Thrill Killers '65
Incredibly Strange Creatures
Who Stopped Living and
Became Mixed-Up Zombies
'63

Brad King
Outlaws of the Desert '41
Riders of the Timberline '41
Twilight on the Trail '41

Charles King
The Silver Bullet '34
Broadway Melody '29

Charles "Blackie" King
Ambush Trail '46
The Caravan Trail '46
Colorado Serenade '46
Outlaw of the Plains '46
Border Badmen '45
Gangster's Den '45
His Brother's Ghost '45
Three in the Saddle '45
Devil Riders '44
Frontier Outlaws '44
Oath of Vengeance '44
Rustler's Hideout '44
Wild Horse Phantom '44
Texas Kid '43
Along the Sundown Trail '42
Arizona Stagecoach '42
Below the Border '42
Prairie Pals '42
Trail Riders '42
Where Trails End '42
Dead or Alive '41
Trigger Men '41
Death Rides the Range '40
Down the Wyoming Trail '39
Mesquite Buckaroo '39
Trigger Pals '39
Wild Horse Canyon '39
Gun Packer '38
The Phantom of the Range '38
Songs and Bullets '38
Thunder in the Desert '38
The Gambling Terror '37
God's Country and the Man '37
Hittin' the Trail '37
A Lawman Is Born '37
Lightning Bill Crandall '37
Mystery of the Hooded
Horseman '37
The Red Rope '37
Riders of the Rockies '37
Ridin' the Lone Trail '37
Santa Fe Bound '37

Andy Hardy's Double Life '42
The Fighting 69th '40
Three Smart Girls Grow Up '39
Danger on the Air '38
Wives Under Suspicion '38

Vic Lundin
Robinson Crusoe on Mars '64
Two for the Seesaw '62
Ma Barker's Killer Brood '60

Steve Lundquist
Killer Tomatoes Eat France '91
Killer Tomatoes Strike Back '90
Return of the Killer Tomatoes! '88

Jessica Lundy
The Stupids '95
Madhouse '90
Caddyshack 2 '88

Sihung Lung
Eat Drink Man Woman '94
The Wedding Banquet '93
Pushing Hands '92

Suma Wah Lung
Kick of Death: The Prodigal Boxer '80s
Prodigal Boxer: The Kick of Death '73

Ti Lung
Duel of Fists '89
A Better Tomorrow '86
Revenge of the Zombies '81
Duel of the Iron Fist '72

Cherie Lunghi
The Canterville Ghost '96
The Buccaneers '95
Jack and Sarah '95
Mary Shelley's Frankenstein '94
Intrigue '88
To Kill a Priest '89
The Lady's Not for Burning '87
Tales of the Klondike: The Unexpected '87
Harem '86
The Mission '86
King David '85
Letters to an Unknown Lover '84
Praying Mantis '83
The Sign of Four '83
Oliver Twist '82
Excalibur '81

Roldano Lupi
The Giant of Metropolis '61
The Mongols '60

Ida Lupino
My Boys Are Good Boys '78
Food of the Gods '76
Devil's Rain '75
Junior Bonner '72
While the City Sleeps '56
The Big Knife '55
Private Hell 36 '54
The Bigamist '53
Beware, My Lovely '52
On Dangerous Ground '51
Lust for Gold '49
Road House '48
Escape Me Never '47
The Man I Love '46
Hollywood Canteen '44
Forever and a Day '43
Thank Your Lucky Stars '43
High Sierra '41
The Sea Wolf '41
They Drive by Night '40
The Adventures of Sherlock Holmes '39
Sea Devils '37
One Rainy Afternoon '36
The Ghost Camera '33

Alberto Lupo
Django Shoots First '74
The Agony and the Ecstasy '65
Coriolanus, Man without a Country '64
The Bacchantes '63
Atom Age Vampire '61
The Giant of Marathon '60
Herod the Great '60

Patti LuPone
Song Spinner '95
The Water Engine '92
Family Prayers '91

Driving Miss Daisy '89
LBJ: The Early Years '88
Wise Guys '86
Witness '85
Fighting Back '82
1941 '79

Federico Luppi
A Place in the World '95
Cronos '94
Killing Grandpa '91
Mayalunta '86
Funny, Dirty Little War '83
Time for Revenge '82

John Lupton
Jesse James Meets Frankenstein's Daughter '65
The Rebel Set '59
Diane '55
All the Brothers Were Valiant '53
Escape from Fort Bravo '53

Peter Lupus
Acting on Impulse '93
Think Big '90
Pulsebeat '85
Escapist '83
More! Police Squad '82
Mission Impossible '66
Muscle Beach Party '64

Evan Lurie
Hologram Man '95
Shadow Warriors '95
T-Force '94
American Kickboxer 2: To the Death '93
Martial Law 2: Undercover '91

John Lurie
The Last Temptation of Christ '88
Down by Law '86
Permanent Vacation '84
Stranger than Paradise '84

Jaques Lussier
Norman's Awesome Experience '88
Pouvoir Intime '87

Aaron Lustig
Pinocchio's Revenge '96
Bad Channels '92

Franc Luz
Ghost Town '88
The Nest '88
Ecstasy '84

Jimmy Lydon
The Magnificent Yankee '50
Life with Father '47
Strange Illusion '45
Little Men '40
Tom Brown's School Days '40
Back Door to Heaven '39

Reg Lye
Freedom '81
Walk into Hell '57

Dorothy Lyman
Ruby in Paradise '93
Camp Cucamonga: How I Spent My Summer Vacation '90
Ollie Hopnoodle's Haven of Bliss '88
Summer Fantasy '84

Alfred Lynch
The Krays '90
Bewitched '85
Blockhouse '73
On the Fiddle '61

David Lynch
Twin Peaks: Fire Walk with Me '92
Zelly & Me '88

Helen Lynch
Smouldering Fires '25
The Return of Grey Wolf '22

John Lynch
Moll Flanders '96
Some Mother's Son '96
Angel Baby '95
Nothing Personal '95
Princess Caraboo '94
The Secret of Roan Inish '94
In the Name of the Father '93
The Secret Garden '93

Edward II '92
The Railway Station Man '92
Hardware '90
Monkey Boy '90
Cal '84

John Carroll Lynch
Face/Off '97
Volcano '97
Fargo '96

Kate Lynch
Lethal Lolita—Amy Fisher: My Story '92
Def-Con 4 '85
Reckless Disregard '84
Summer's Children '84
Meatballs '79

Kelly Lynch
Heaven's Prisoners '95
Virtuosity '95
White Man's Burden '95
Forbidden Choices '94
Imaginary Crimes '94
Three of Hearts '93
For Better and For Worse '92
Curly Sue '91
Desperate Hours '90
Drugstore Cowboy '89
Road House '89
Warm Summer Rain '89
Cocktail '88
Osa '85

Ken Lynch
My Pleasure Is My Business '74
Legend of Tom Dooley '59
I Married a Monster from Outer Space '58
Jet Attack/Paratroop Command '58

Richard Lynch
The Proposition '96
Terminal Virus '96
Warrior of Justice '96
Cyborg 3: The Recycler '95
Dragon Fury '95
Midnight Confessions '95
Werewolf '95
Scanner Cop '94
H.P. Lovecraft's Necronomicon: Book of the Dead '93
Showdown '93
Double Threat '92
Inside Edge '92
Maximum Force '92
Merlin '92
The Forbidden Dance '90
Invasion Force '90
Lockdown '90
Puppet Master 3: Toulon's Revenge '90
Trancers 2: The Return of Jack Deth '90
High Stakes '89
One Man Force '89
Aftershock '88
Bad Dreams '88
The Baron '88
Little Nikita '88
The Barbarians '87
Nightforce '86
Invasion U.S.A. '85
Savage Dawn '84
Sword & the Sorcerer '82
Sizzle '81
The Formula '80
Steel '80
Death Sport '78
Delta Fox '77
God Told Me To '76
The Premonition '75
Scarecrow '73

Susan Lynch
Ivanhoe '97
A Royal Scandal '96
The Secret of Roan Inish '94
The Best of Cracker Mysteries '93

Paul Lynde
The Villain '79
Rabbit Test '78
How Sweet It Is! '68
The Glass Bottom Boat '66
Beach Blanket Bingo '65
Send Me No Flowers '64
Bye, Bye, Birdie '63

Son of Flubber '63
Under the Yum-Yum Tree '63
New Faces of 1952 '54

Nicholas Lyndhurst
Stalag Luft
Gulliver's Travels '95

Carol Lynley
Howling 6: The Freaks '90
Spirits '90
Blackout '88
Dark Tower '87
Vigilante '83
Balboa '82
The Cat and the Canary '79
Bad Georgia Road '77
Washington Affair '77
Fantasy Island '76
Flood! '76
Four Deuces '75
If It's a Man, Hang Up '75
Death Stalk '74
Cotter '72
The Poseidon Adventure '72
Son of Blob '72
Blood Island '68
The Cardinal '63
The Stripper '63
Under the Yum-Yum Tree '63
Return to Peyton Place '61
The Light in the Forest '58

Ann Lynn
Estate of Insanity '70
Baby Love '69

Betty Lynn
Return to Mayberry '85
Texas John Slaughter: Geronimo's Revenge '60
Meet Me in Las Vegas '56
Cheaper by the Dozen '50
Father Was a Fullback '49
June Bride '48

Cheryl Lynn
Fate '90
Emanon '86
Thunder Run '86

Diana Lynn
The Annapolis Story '55
The Kentuckian '55
Bedtime for Bonzo '51
My Friend Irma '49
Every Girl Should Be Married '48
Miracle of Morgan's Creek '44

Emmett Lynn
The Fighting Redhead '50
The Caravan Trail '46
Song of Old Wyoming '45
Frontier Outlaws '44

Fonda Lynn
Ninja Brothers of Blood '89
Deadly Darling '85

Jeffrey Lynn
Tony Rome '67
Home Town Story '51
A Letter to Three Wives '49
All This and Heaven Too '40
The Fighting 69th '40
The Roaring Twenties '39
Four Daughters '38

Mara Lynn
G.I. Jane '51
Leave It to the Marines '51
Sky High '51
Prehistoric Women '50

Peter George Lynn
Mr. Wong in Chinatown '39
Mystery Plane '39
Wolf Call '39

Rebecca Lynn
Thrilled to Death '88
Sensations '87

Ben Lyon
Crimson Romance '34
I Cover the Waterfront '33
The Crooked Circle '32
Indiscreet '31
Night Nurse '31
Hell's Angels '30
Mad About Money '37

Richard Lyon
The Tender Years '47
Anna and the King of Siam '46

Sue Lyon
End of the World '76
The Invisible Strangler '76
Evel Knievel '72
Four Rode Out '69
Flim-Flam Man '67
Tony Rome '67
The Night of the Iguana '64
Lolita '62

Wendy Lyon
Hello Mary Lou: Prom Night 2 '87
Anne of Green Gables '85

Bruce Lyons
The Navigator '88
Model Behavior '82

James Lyons
I Shot Andy Warhol '96
Frisk '95
Postcards from America '95
Poison '91

Robert F. Lyons
American Eagle '90
Platoon Leader '87
Murphy's Law '86
Cease Fire '85
Black Oak Conspiracy '77
The Todd Killings '71
Getting Straight '70

Susan Lyons
Ebbtide '94
The Winds of Jarrah '83

Tzi Ma
Dante's Peak '97
Chain Reaction '96
Golden Gate '93
Rapid Fire '92

Byron Mabe
The Doberman Gang '72
The Defilers '65

Kate Maberly
Gulliver's Travels '95
Stephen King's The Langoliers '95
The Secret Garden '93

Eric Mabius
I Shot Andy Warhol '96
Welcome to the Dollhouse '95

Moms Mabley
Amazing Grace '74
Boardinghouse Blues '48
Killer Diller '48

Bernie Mac
Booty Call '96
Get On the Bus '96
Friday '95
Above the Rim '94
House Party 3 '94

Anne MacAdams
Don't Look in the Basement '73
Common Law Wife '63

James MacArthur
Hang 'Em High '67
Mosby's Marauders '66
Bedford Incident '65
Cry of Battle '63
Spencer's Mountain '63
The Interns '62
Kidnapped '60
The Swiss Family Robinson '60
Third Man on the Mountain '59
The Light in the Forest '58

Marc Macaulay
Cop and a Half '93
Hidden Fears '93

Donald MacBride
Meet Danny Wilson '52
Holiday Rhythm '50
Buck Privates Come Home '47
Egg and I '47
A Night to Remember '42
The Invisible Woman '40
Murder over New York '40
The Saint's Double Trouble '40
Blondie Takes a Vacation '39
The Great Man Votes '38
Room Service '38

Ralph Macchio
Naked in New York '93

E.T.: The Extra-Terrestrial '82

Patrick Macnee
Thunder in Paradise 2 '94
The Gambler Returns: The Luck of the Draw '93
The Hound of London '93
Thunder in Paradise '93
Sherlock Holmes and the Incident at Victoria Falls '91
Chill Factor '90
Around the World in 80 Days '89
Cult People '89
Lobster Man from Mars '89
Masque of the Red Death '89
Sorry, Wrong Number '89
Transformations '88
Waxwork '88
Shadey '87
Down Under '86
A View to a Kill '85
This Is Spinal Tap '84
Return of the Man from U.N.C.L.E. '83
Rehearsal for Murder '82
Young Doctors in Love '82
The Howling '81
Sea Wolves '81
Spaceship '81
Sweet 16 '81
Battlestar Galactica '78
Dead of Night '77
King Solomon's Treasure '76
The Bloodsuckers '70
Les Girls '57
A Christmas Carol '51
The Elusive Pimpernel '50

Peter MacNeill
Crash '95
A Vow to Kill '94

Peter MacNicol
Dracula: Dead and Loving It '95
Roswell: The U.F.O. Cover-Up '94
Addams Family Values '93
Hard Promises '92
Housesitter '92
American Blue Note '89
Ghostbusters 2 '89
Heat '87
Sophie's Choice '82
The Boy Who Left Home to Find Out About the Shivers '81
Dragonslayer '81

Elle Macpherson
Batman and Robin '97
Jane Eyre '96
The Mirror Has Two Faces '96
If Lucy Fell '95
Sirens '94
Alice '90

George MacQuarrie
The Idol Dancer '20
The Love Flower '20

Gordon MacRae
Danger in the Skies '79
Carousel '56
Oklahoma! '55
By the Light of the Silvery Moon '53
The Desert Song '53
On Moonlight Bay '51
Tea for Two '50
The West Point Story '50
Look for the Silver Lining '49

Heather MacRae
Secrets of Three Hungry Wives '78
Bang the Drum Slowly '73
The Connection '73

Meredith MacRae
Husbands, Wives, Money, and Murder '86
Vultures '84
Sketches of a Strangler '78
Bikini Beach '64

Michael MacRae
Madhouse '81
Isle of Secret Passion '85
Dear Detective '78
Great Ride '78
Greedy Terror '78

George Macready
The Return of Count Yorga '71
Tora! Tora! Tora! '70
The Great Race '65
The Human Duplicators '64
Where Love Has Gone '64
Taras Bulba '62
Two Weeks in Another Town '62
Paths of Glory '57
I Beheld His Glory '53
Julius Caesar '53
The Stranger Wore a Gun '53
Vera Cruz '53
The Green Glove '52
Detective Story '51
The Nevadan '50
The Doolins of Oklahoma '49
Knock on Any Door '49
The Big Clock '48
Black Arrow '48
Coroner Creek '48
Down to Earth '47
Gilda '46
The Seventh Cross '44

Bill Macy
Murder in the First '95
Me, Myself & I '92
The Doctor '91
Sibling Rivalry '90
Bad Medicine '85
Casey at the Bat '85
Movers and Shakers '85
My Favorite Year '82
Serial '80
Diary of a Young Comic '79
The Jerk '79
The Late Show '77
Oh! Calcutta! '72

William H. Macy
Down Periscope '96
Fargo '96
Ghosts of Mississippi '96
Andersonville '95
Mr. Holland's Opus '95
Being Human '94
Dead on Sight '94
ER '94
Oleanna '94
Benny & Joon '93
Searching for Bobby Fischer '93
Twenty Bucks '93
A Private Matter '92
The Water Engine '92
Homicide '91

Ciaran Madden
Ivanhoe '97
Fortunes of War '87
A Married Man '84

John Madden
Little Giants '94
P.K. and the Kid '85

Victor Maddern
I'm All Right Jack '59
Blood of the Vampire '58
Abandon Ship '57

Amy Madigan
Riders of the Purple Sage '96
The Dark Half '91
Field of Dreams '89
Roe vs. Wade '89
Uncle Buck '89
Prince of Pennsylvania '88
Nowhere to Hide '87
Alamo Bay '85
Twice in a Lifetime '85
Places in the Heart '84
Streets of Fire '84
Love Letters '83
The Ambush Murders '82
Love Child '82

James Madio
The Basketball Diaries '94
Hero '92

Guy Madison
Computer Wizard '77
Where's Willie? '77
Hell Commandos '69
Special Forces '68
Bang Bang Kid '67
Superargo '67
Five Giants from Texas '66
The Snake Hunter Strangler '66
Cold Steel for Tortuga '65

Place in Hell '65
Apaches Last Battle '64
Conqueror & the Empress '64
Executioner of Venice '63
Jet Over the Atlantic '59
Bullwhip '58
Savage Wilderness '55
Drums in the Deep South '51
Till the End of Time '46
Since You Went Away '44

Noel Madison
Footsteps in the Dark '41
Sailing Along '38
Gangway '37
The House of Secrets '37
A Nation Aflame '37
Cocaine Fiends '36

Rock Madison
Creature of the Walking Dead '60
Man Beast '55

Philip Madoc
A Mind to Kill '95
Space: 1999—Alien Attack '79

Madonna
Evita '96
Girl 6 '96
Blue in the Face '95
Four Rooms '95
Dangerous Game '93
Body of Evidence '92
A League of Their Own '92
Shadows and Fog '92
Truth or Dare '91
Dick Tracy '90
Bloodhounds of Broadway '89
Who's That Girl? '87
Shanghai Surprise '86
Desperately Seeking Susan '85
Certain Sacrifice '80

Michael Madsen
Donnie Brasco '96
Red Line '96
Free Willy 2: The Adventure Home '95
Man with a Gun '95
Mulholland Falls '95
Species '95
Dead Connection '94
Season of Change '94
Wyatt Earp '94
Almost Blue '93
Free Willy '93
The Getaway '93
A House in the Hills '93
Money for Nothing '93
Beyond the Law '92
Fatal Instinct '92
Inside Edge '92
Reservoir Dogs '92
Straight Talk '92
Trouble Bound '92
The Doors '91
Thelma & Louise '91
The End of Innocence '90
Kill Me Again '89
Shadows in the Storm '88
The Natural '84
Racing with the Moon '84

Virginia Madsen
Ghosts of Mississippi '96
Just Your Luck '96
The Prophecy '95
Bitter Vengeance '94
Blue Tiger '94
Caroline at Midnight '93
Linda '93
Becoming Colette '92
Candyman '92
Highlander 2: The Quickening '91
Love Kills '91
Victim of Love '91
The Hot Spot '90
Ironclads '90
The Heart of Dixie '89
Third Degree Burn '89
Gotham '88
Hot to Trot '88
Mr. North '88
Long Gone '87
Slamdance '87
Zombie High '87
Fire with Fire '86

Modern Girls '86
Creator '85
The Hearst and Davies Affair '85
Dune '84
Electric Dreams '84

Roma Maffia
The Heidi Chronicles '95
Nick of Time '95
Disclosure '94

Macha Magal
S.S. Experiment Camp 2 '86
SS Girls '78

Patrick Magee
The Monster Club '85
The Black Cat '81
Chariots of Fire '81
Rough Cut '80
Sleep of Death '79
Telefon '77
Barry Lyndon '75
A Killer in Every Corner '74
Luther '74
And Now the Screaming Starts '73
The Final Programme '73
Asylum '72
Demons of the Mind '72
Young Winston '72
A Clockwork Orange '71
The Fiend '71
King Lear '71
Trojan Women '71
Cromwell '70
Anzio '68
Marat/Sade '66
Portrait in Terror '66
Die, Monster, Die! '65
Masque of the Red Death '65
Masque of the Red Death/Premature Burial '65
The Skull '65
Seance on a Wet Afternoon '64
Dementia 13 '63
The Very Edge '63

Brandon Maggart
Running Mates '92
Terror in Toyland '85
The World According to Garp '82
Dressed to Kill '80

Benoit Magimel
Les Voleurs '96
Life Is a Long Quiet River '88

Anna Magnani
Mamma Roma '62
The Fugitive Kind '60
Passionate Thief '60
The Rose Tattoo '55
The Golden Coach '52
Bellissima '51
Amore '48
The Miracle '48
Peddlin' in Society '47
Open City '45

Ann Magnuson
Before and After '95
Cabin Boy '94
Checking Out '89
Heavy Petting '89
Love at Large '89
A Night in the Life of Jimmy Reardon '88
Sleepwalk '88
Tequila Sunrise '88
Making Mr. Right '86
Desperately Seeking Susan '85
Perfect Strangers '84
The Hunger '83
Vortex '81

Gerard Maguire
Prisoner Cell Block H '80
Demonstrator '71

Valerie Mahaffey
Jungle 2 Jungle '96
National Lampoon's Senior Trip '95
Witch Hunt '94
They Watch '93
Mr. Bill's Real Life Adventures '86
The Rise & Rise of Daniel Rocket '86
Women of Valor '86

George Maharis
Sword & the Sorcerer '82
The Crash of Flight 401 '78
Return to Fantasy Island '77
Murder on Flight 502 '75
Desperados '69
Land Raiders '69
Last Day of the War '69
Exodus '60

Bill Maher
Pizza Man '91
Cannibal Women in the Avocado Jungle of Death '89
House 2: The Second Story '87

Joseph Maher
Surviving Picasso '96
Bulletproof Heart '95
I.Q. '94
Sister Act '92
Funny Farm '88
My Stepmother Is an Alien '88
The Evil That Men Do '84
Under the Rainbow '81

Grace Mahlaba
Being Human '94
Bopha! '93

Bruce Mahler
Funland '89
Police Academy 6: City Under Siege '89

Shiek Mahmud-Bey
Joe's Apartment '96
Night Falls on Manhattan '96

Michael Mahonen
Giant Steps
By Way of the Stars '92

Jock Mahoney
Bad Bunch '76
The Glory Stompers '67
A Time to Love & a Time to Die '58
Battle Hymn '57
The Land Unknown '57
Range Rider '52
Cow Town '50
The Nevadan '50
Rim of the Canyon '49

John Mahoney
Primal Fear '96
She's the One '96
The American President '95
Reality Bites '94
The Hudsucker Proxy '93
In the Line of Fire '93
Striking Distance '93
Article 99 '92
The Secret Passion of Robert Clayton '92
The Water Engine '92
Barton Fink '91
Love Hurts '91
The Ten Million Dollar Getaway '91
Unnatural Pursuits '91
The Russia House '90
Dinner at Eight '89
The Image '89
Say Anything '89
Betrayed '88
Eight Men Out '88
Frantic '88
Moonstruck '87
Suspect '87
Tin Men '87
The Manhattan Project '86
Trapped in Silence '86

Tim Maier
Turnaround '87
Raw Courage '84

Marjorie Main
The Kettles on Old MacDonald's Farm '57
Friendly Persuasion '56
The Kettles in the Ozarks '56
Ma and Pa Kettle at Waikiki '55
The Long, Long Trailer '54
Ma and Pa Kettle at Home '54
Rose Marie '54
Ma and Pa Kettle on Vacation '53
The Belle of New York '52
Ma and Pa Kettle at the Fair '52

Harriet Hilliard Nelson
The Kid with the 200 I.Q. '83
The Adventures of Ozzie & Harriet '50s
Take It Big '44
Follow the Fleet '36

Herbert Nelson
Future Cop '76
When the North Wind Blows '74

John Allen Nelson
Deathstalker 3 '89
Killer Klowns from Outer Space '88
Saigon Commandos '88
Hunk '87

Judd Nelson
Steel '97
Blackwater Trail '95
Circumstances Unknown '95
Airheads '94
Blindfold: Acts of Obsession '94
Flinch '94
Hail Caesar '94
Caroline at Midnight '93
Entangled '93
Every Breath '93
Conflict of Interest '92
Primary Motive '92
The Dark Backward '91
New Jack City '91
Hiroshima: Out of the Ashes '90
Far Out Man '89
Relentless '89
Billionaire Boys Club '87
Blue City '86
From the Hip '86
The Breakfast Club '85
Fandango '85
St. Elmo's Fire '85
Making the Grade '84

Lloyd Nelson
The Wild World of Batwoman '66
Curse of the Stone Hand '64
The Incredible Petrified World '58
Man Beast '55

Lori Nelson
The Pied Piper of Hamelin '57
Hot Rod Girl '56
Mohawk '56
Pardners '56
Day the World Ended '55
I Died a Thousand Times '55
Ma and Pa Kettle at Waikiki '55
Revenge of the Creature '55
Francis Goes to West Point '52
Ma and Pa Kettle at the Fair '52

Margaret Nelson
Scalp Merchant '77
Picnic at Hanging Rock '75

Ozzie Nelson
The Impossible Years '68
The Adventures of Ozzie & Harriet '50s
People Are Funny '46
Take It Big '44
Big Street '42

Peter Nelson
Eye of the Eagle 3 '91
Sounds of Silence '91
The Expendables '89
Silk 2 '89
Crime Zone '88
V '83

Ricky Nelson
Wackiest Ship in the Army '61
The Adventures of Ozzie & Harriet '50s
Rio Bravo '59

Ruth Nelson
The Haunting Passion '83
A Christmas Without Snow '80
Humoresque '46
Wilson '44

Sandra Nelson
The Halfback of Notre Dame '96
Maternal Instincts '96

Sean Nelson
American Buffalo '95
Fresh '94

Tracy Nelson
The Game of Love '90
Down and Out in Beverly Hills '86
Maria's Lovers '84
Yours, Mine & Ours '68

Willie Nelson
Gone Fishin' '97
Another Pair of Aces: Three of a Kind '91
Pair of Aces '90
Texas Guns '90
Dynamite and Gold '88
Baja Oklahoma '87
Red Headed Stranger '87
Amazons '86
Last Days of Frank & Jesse James '86
Stagecoach '86
Songwriter '84
Hell's Angels Forever '83
Barbarosa '82
Coming Out of the Ice '82
Thief '81
Honeysuckle Rose '80
The Electric Horseman '79

Corin "Corky" Nemec
The War at Home '96
Operation Dumbo Drop '95
Drop Zone '94
Stephen King's The Stand '94
White Wolves 2: Legend of the Wild '94
Solar Crisis '92
Tucker: The Man and His Dream '88

Francesca Neri
Flight of the Innocent '93
Outrage '93

Rosalba (Sara Bay) Neri
Devil's Wedding Night '73
Naked Warriors '73
Lady Frankenstein '72
Slaughter Hotel '71
The Seducers '70
The Castle of Fu Manchu '68
Conquest of Mycene '63

David Nerman
Witchboard 3: The Possession '95
The Scorpio Factor '90

Franco Nero
David '97
Young Catherine '91
Die Hard 2: Die Harder '90
Magdalene '88
Windmills of the Gods '88
Sweet Country '87
Challenge to White Fang '86
The Girl '86
Wagner: The Movie '85
Day of the Cobra '84
Shark Hunter '84
Querelle '83
The Salamander '82
Enter the Ninja '82
The Man with Bogart's Face '80
Street Law '79
Force 10 from Navarone '78
Last Four Days '77
Submission '77
21 Hours at Munich '76
Legend of Valentino '75
Sardinia Kidnapped '75
Blood Brothers '74
Falcon '74
High Crime '73
Redneck '73
Confessions of a Police Captain '72
Fifth Day of Peace '72
Ring of Death '72
Devil's Crude '71
Tristana '70
The Virgin and the Gypsy '70
Battle of Neretva '69
Spaghetti Western '69
Django '68
Camelot '67
The Bible '66
The Bible...In the Beginning '66

Wild, Wild Planet '65

Toni Nero
No Dead Heroes '87
Silent Night, Deadly Night '84

Cathleen Nesbitt
Promise Her Anything '66
Separate Tables '58
An Affair to Remember '57
Desiree '54
Man of Evil '48
Men of Two Worlds '46
Nicholas Nickleby '46
Pygmalion '38
The Passing of the Third Floor Back '36

Derren Nesbitt
Funny Money '82
Horrors of Burke & Hare '71
Victim '61

Lois Nettleton
Mirror, Mirror 2: Raven Dance '94
Manhunt for Claude Dallas '86
Brass '85
Soggy Bottom U.S.A. '84
The Best Little Whorehouse in Texas '82
Butterfly '82
Deadly Blessing '81
The Man in the Glass Booth '75
The Good Guys and the Bad Guys '69
The Bamboo Saucer '68
Period of Adjustment '62

Martin Neufeld
Relative Fear '95
H '90

Jenny Neumann
Delos Adventure '86
Stage Fright '83
Hell Night '81
Mistress of the Apes '79
Swim Team '79

Bebe Neuwirth
The Adventures of Pinocchio '96
The Associate '96
Jumanji '95
Malice '93
The Paint Job '93
Wild Palms '93
Bugsy '91
Green Card '90
Say Anything '89

Aaron Neville
The Last Ride '94
Zandalee '91

John Neville
Swann '96
Song Spinner '95
Baby's Day Out '94
Little Women '94
The Road to Wellville '94
The Adventures of Baron Munchausen '89
A Study in Terror '66
The Unearthly Stranger '64
Billy Budd '62

Robyn Nevin
Angel Baby '95
Careful, He Might Hear You '84
The Irishman '78
Fourth Wish '77

Claudette Nevins
Child of Darkness, Child of Light '91
Sleeping with the Enemy '91
Take Your Best Shot '82
The Possessed '77
The Mask '61

Derek Newark
Bellman and True '88
The Offence '73

George Newbern
The Evening Star '96
Father of the Bride Part II '95
Witness to the Execution '94
Father of the Bride '91
Doppelganger: The Evil Within '90
It Takes Two '88
Paramedics '88

Switching Channels '88
Adventures in Babysitting '87
My Little Girl '87

Anthony Newcastle
Metallica '85
Captive Planet '78

William Newell
Escape from Fort Bravo '53
Doctor Satan's Robot '40
The Invisible Killer '40
The Mandarin Mystery '37

Bob Newhart
First Family '80
Little Miss Marker '80
Marathon '80
Thursday's Game '74
Cold Turkey '71
Catch-22 '70
On a Clear Day You Can See Forever '70
Hot Millions '68
Hell is for Heroes '62

James Newill
Boss of Rawhide '44
Guns of the Law '44
Outlaw Roundup '44
Fighting Valley '43
Rangers Take Over '43
The Great American Broadcast '41
Danger Ahead '40
Murder on the Yukon '40
Sky Bandits '40
Yukon Flight '40
Fighting Mad '39
Renfrew on the Great White Trail '38
Renfrew of the Royal Mounted '37

Anthony Newlands
Scream and Scream Again '70
Circus of Fear '67

Anthony Newley
Boris and Natasha: The Movie '92
The Garbage Pail Kids Movie '87
Outrage! '86
Stagecoach '86
Blade in Hong Kong '85
The Old Curiosity Shop '75
Doctor Dolittle '67
Let's Get Married '63
Fire Down Below '57
Above Us the Waves '56
Oliver Twist '48
Little Ballerina '47

Barry Newman
Daylight '96
Fatal Vision '84
Having It All '82
Amy '81
Deadline '81
City on Fire '78
The Salzburg Connection '72
Vanishing Point '71

Danny Newman
The Return of the Borrowers '96
Shopping '93

Laraine Newman
Jingle All the Way '96
Coneheads '93
Revenge of the Red Baron '93
Witchboard 2: The Devil's Doorway '93
Problem Child 2 '91
Invaders from Mars '86
Perfect '85
Her Life as a Man '83
Wholly Moses! '80
Saturday Night Live '70s
Mr. Mike's Mondo Video '79
Tunnelvision '76

Nanette Newman
The Mystery of Edwin Drood '93
Long Ago Tomorrow '71
The Madwoman of Chaillot '69
The Wrong Arm of the Law '63

Paul Newman
Nobody's Fool '94
The Hudsucker Proxy '93
Mr. & Mrs. Bridge '90

Blaze '89
Fat Man and Little Boy '89
The Color of Money '86
Harry & Son '84
The Verdict '82
Absence of Malice '81
Fort Apache, the Bronx '81
When Time Ran Out '80
Quintet '79
Slap Shot '77
Buffalo Bill & the Indians '76
Silent Movie '76
The Drowning Pool '75
The Towering Inferno '74
Mackintosh Man '73
The Sting '73
Life & Times of Judge Roy Bean '72
Pocket Money '72
Sometimes a Great Notion '71
Butch Cassidy and the Sundance Kid '69
Winning '69
The Secret War of Harry Frigg '68
Cool Hand Luke '67
Hombre '67
Harper '66
Tom Curtain '66
Lady L '65
Hud '63
A New Kind of Love '63
The Prize '63
Sweet Bird of Youth '62
The Hustler '61
Paris Blues '61
Exodus '60
From the Terrace '59
The Young Philadelphians '59
Cat on a Hot Tin Roof '58
The Left-Handed Gun '58
The Long, Hot Summer '58
Until They Sail '57
Bang the Drum Slowly '56
Somebody Up There Likes Me '56
The Silver Chalice '54

Phyllis Newman
The Beautician and the Beast '97
A Secret Space '88
Follies in Concert '85
Picnic '55

Stephen D. Newman
Yuri Nosenko, KGB '86
Sophie's Choice '82

Julie Newmar
Backlash: Oblivion 2 '95
Oblivion '94
Nudity Required '90
Deep Space '87
Evils of the Night '85
Streetwalkin' '85
Ecstasy '84
Hysterical '83
Terraces '77
MacKenna's Gold '69
For Love or Money '63
Li'l Abner '59
Seven Brides for Seven Brothers '54

John Haymes Newton
Alive '93
Desert Kickboxer '92

Margit Evelyn Newton
Night of the Zombies '83
The Last Hunter '80

Robert Newton
Around the World in 80 Days '56
The Desert Rats '53
Long John Silver '53
Androcles and the Lion '52
Blackbeard the Pirate '52
Tom Brown's School Days '51
Treasure Island '50
The Hidden Room '49
Oliver Twist '48
Odd Man Out '47
This Happy Breed '47
Henry V '44
Gaslight '40
Jamaica Inn '39
Beachcomber '38

Newton ⏴cont.

21 Days '37

Thandie Newton
Gridlock'd '96
The Journey of August King '95
Jefferson in Paris '94
Loaded '94
The Young Americans '93
Flirting '89

Theodore Newton
Ace of Aces '33
The Sphinx '33

Wayne Newton
Vegas Vacation '96
Best of the Best 2 '93
The Dark Backward '91
The Adventures of Ford Fairlane '90
License to Kill '89

Olivia Newton-John
It's My Party '95
Two of a Kind '83
Xanadu '80
Grease '78

Richard Ney
Premature Burial '62
The Lovable Cheat '49
Mrs. Miniver '42

Marina Neyelova
Autumn Marathon '79
The Errors of Youth '78

Haing S. Ngor
Fortunes of War '93
Heaven and Earth '93
My Life '93
Ambition '91
In Love and War '91
Last Flight Out: A True Story '90
Vietnam, Texas '90
The Iron Triangle '89
The Killing Fields '84

Dustin Nguyen
3 Ninjas Kick Back '94
Heaven and Earth '93
No Escape, No Return '93
Rapid Fire '92

Michelle Nicastro
When Harry Met Sally... '89
Bad Guys '86
Body Rock '84

Maurizio Nichetti
Luna e L'Altra '96
Stephano Quantestorie '93
Volere Volare '92
The Icicle Thief '89
Allegro Non Troppo '76

Angela Nicholas
Alien Space Avenger '91
Galactic Gigolo '87

Denise Nicholas
Ghost Dad '90
And the Children Shall Lead '85
Sophisticated Gents '81
Piece of the Action '77
Let's Do It Again '75
Blacula '72

Harold Nicholas
The Five Heartbeats '91
Tap '89
Fass Black '77

Paul Nicholas
Alice '86
Nutcracker Sweet '84
The World is Full of Married Men '80
Yesterday's Hero '79
Lisztomania '75
Tommy '75
Invitation to the Wedding '73

Thomas Ian Nicholas
A Kid in King Arthur's Court '95
Rookie of the Year '93
The Fear Inside '92

Nicholas Brothers
The Pirate '48
Stormy Weather '43

Anthony Nicholls
If... '69
Othello '65
Burn Witch, Burn! '62
Victim '61
The Franchise Affair '52

George Nicholls, Jr.
Finishing School '33
White Gold '28
The Eagle '25
The Country Kid '23
The Greatest Question '19

Phoebe Nicholls
Gulliver's Travels '95
Persuasion '95
Heart of Darkness '93
Deep Cover '88
Maurice '87

Barbara Nichols
The Human Duplicators '64
Scarface Mob '62
Sweet Smell of Success '57
Beyond a Reasonable Doubt '56
The King and Four Queens '56
Manfish '56

Britt Nichols
The Demons '74
Virgin Among the Living Dead '71

Conrad Nichols
Days of Hell '84
A Man Called Rage '84
Rush '84

Dandy Nichols
Ladies Who Do '63
Leather Boys '63
The Fallen Idol '49

Nichelle Nichols
Star Trek 6: The Undiscovered Country '91
Star Trek 5: The Final Frontier '89
Star Trek 4: The Voyage Home '86
The Supernaturals '86
Star Trek 3: The Search for Spock '84
Star Trek 2: The Wrath of Khan '82
Star Trek: The Motion Picture '80
Truck Turner '74
Say Goodbye, Maggie Cole '72
Star Trek Bloopers '69

Stephen Nichols
The Glass Cage '96
Phoenix '95
Soapdish '91
Witchboard '87

Taylor Nichols
Headless Body in Topless Bar '96
Norma Jean and Marilyn '95
Serpent's Lair '95
Barcelona '94
Metropolitan '90

Jack Nicholson
Blood & Wine '96
Mars Attacks! '96
The Crossing Guard '94
Wolf '94
A Few Good Men '92
Hoffa '92
Man Trouble '92
The Two Jakes '90
Batman '89
Broadcast News '87
Ironweed '87
The Witches of Eastwick '87
Heartburn '86
Prizzi's Honor '85
Terms of Endearment '83
The Border '82
The Postman Always Rings Twice '81
Reds '81
The Shining '80
Goin' South '78
The Last Tycoon '76
Missouri Breaks '76
One Flew Over the Cuckoo's Nest '75

The Passenger '75
Tommy '75
Chinatown '74
The Last Detail '73
The King of Marvin Gardens '72
Carnal Knowledge '71
Five Easy Pieces '70
On a Clear Day You Can See Forever '70
Easy Rider '69
Rebel Rousers '69
Psych-Out '68
Hell's Angels on Wheels '67
Ride in the Whirlwind '67
Flight to Fury '66
The Shooting '66
Ensign Pulver '64
The Raven '63
The Terror '63
Little Shop of Horrors '60
Studs Lonigan '60
The Wild Ride '60

Nick Nicholson
Fist of Steel '93
Triple Impact '92

Denise Nickerson
Zero to Sixty '78
Smile '75
Willy Wonka & the Chocolate Factory '71

Michael A. Nickles
Baja '95
Hamburger Hill '87

Julia Nickson-Soul
White Tiger '95
Double Dragon '94
Amityville: A New Generation '93
Sidekicks '93
K2: The Ultimate High '92
China Cry '91
Around the World in 80 Days '89
Glitch! '88
Noble House '88
Rambo: First Blood, Part 2 '85

Alex Nicol
A*P*E* '76
A Matter of WHO '62
The Screaming Skull '58
Stranger in Town '57
Great Day in the Morning '56
The Man from Laramie '55
Black Glove '54
The Gilded Cage '54
Heat Wave '54
The Redhead from Wyoming '53
Meet Danny Wilson '52
Red Ball Express '52

Daria Nicolodi
Terror at the Opera '88
Creepers '85
Macaroni '85
Unsane '82
Beyond the Door 2 '79
Deep Red: Hatchet Murders '75

Michael Nicolosi
Dream a Little Dream 2 '94
Sketch Artist 2: Hands That See '94

Brigitte Nielsen
Body Count '95
Galaxis '95
Chained Heat 2 '92
The Double O Kid '92
Mission of Justice '92
Murder by Moonlight '91
Bye Bye Baby '88
Domino '88
Beverly Hills Cop 2 '87
Cobra '86
Red Sonja '85
Rocky 4 '85

Hans Nielsen
The Monster of London City '64
Sherlock Holmes and the Deadly Necklace '62

Leslie Nielsen
Spy Hard '96
Dracula: Dead and Loving It '95
Rent-A-Kid '95
Digger '94
Naked Gun 33 1/3: The Final Insult '94

Surf Ninjas '93
All I Want for Christmas '91
Naked Gun 2 1/2: The Smell of Fear '91
Repossessed '90
Dangerous Curves '88
Home Is Where the Hart Is '88
The Naked Gun: From the Files of Police Squad '88
Nightstick '87
Nuts '87
Striker's Mountain '87
The Patriot '86
Soul Man '86
Blade in Hong Kong '85
Reckless Disregard '84
Creepshow '82
Foxfire Light '82
More! Police Squad '82
Police Squad! Help Wanted! '82
Wrong is Right '82
Spaceship '81
Airplane! '80
Prom Night '80
Riel '79
The Amsterdam Kill '78
City on Fire '78
Day of the Animals '77
Project: Kill! '77
Viva Knievel '77
Snatched '72
Resurrection of Zachary Wheeler '71
Four Rode Out '69
How to Commit Marriage '69
Dayton's Devils '68
The Reluctant Astronaut '67
Harlow '65
Tammy and the Bachelor '57
Forbidden Planet '56
The Opposite Sex '56

Lisa Niemi
Super Force '90
Steel Dawn '87

Jane Nigh
Motor Patrol '50
Operation Haylift '50

Bill Nighy
Antonia and Jane '91
The Phantom of the Opera '89

Miho Nikaido
Flirt '95
Tokyo Decadence '91

Jan Niklas
The House of the Spirits '93
Club Extinction '89
The Rose Garden '89
Anastasia: The Mystery of Anna '86
Colonel Redl '84

Anna Q. Nilsson
Fighting Father Dunne '48
Riders of the Timberline '41
Toll Gate '20
Seven Keys to Baldpate '17
Grit of the Girl Telegrapher/In the Switch Tower '15
Regeneration '15

Inger Nilsson
Pippi Goes on Board '75
Pippi in the South Seas '74
Pippi Longstocking '73

Maj-Britt Nilsson
Secrets of Women '52
Summer Interlude '50

Rob Nilsson
Heat and Sunlight '87
Northern Lights '79

Leonard Nimoy
David '97
Never Forget '91
Star Trek 6: The Undiscovered Country '91
Star Trek 5: The Final Frontier '89
Star Trek 4: The Voyage Home '86
Aladdin and His Wonderful Lamp '84
Star Trek 3: The Search for Spock '84

Seizure: The Story of Kathy Morris '82
Star Trek 2: The Wrath of Khan '82
A Woman Called Golda '82
Star Trek: The Motion Picture '80
Invasion of the Body Snatchers '78
Baffled '72
Catlow '71
Star Trek Bloopers '69
Star Trek: The Cage '65
The Man from U.N.C.L.E. '64
The Balcony '63
The Brain Eaters '58
Zombies of the Stratosphere '52

Annabelle Ninchi
Time Out for Love '61
La Dolce Vita '60

Yvette Nipar
Twilight Man '96
Doctor Mordrid: Master of the Unknown '90
Ski Patrol '89
Run If You Can '87

John Nishio
Overkill '86
Dim Sum: A Little Bit of Heart '85

Greta Nissen
Melody Cruise '32
Ambassador Bill '31

David Niven
Better Late Than Never '83
Curse of the Pink Panther '83
Trail of the Pink Panther '82
Sea Wolves '81
Rough Cut '80
The Big Scam '79
Escape to Athena '79
Candleshoe '78
Death on the Nile '78
Murder by Death '76
No Deposit, No Return '76
Paper Tiger '74
King, Queen, Knave '72
The Statue '71
The Brain '69
The Impossible Years '68
Casino Royale '67
Lady L '65
The Pink Panther '64
Bedtime Story '63
55 Days at Peking '63
The Guns of Navarone '61
Please Don't Eat the Daisies '60
Ask Any Girl '59
Separate Tables '58
Bonjour Tristesse '57
My Man Godfrey '57
Around the World in 80 Days '56
Birds & the Bees '56
The King's Thief '55
Carrington, V.C. '54
The Moon Is Blue '53
Happy Go Lovely '51
The Lady Says No '51
The Elusive Pimpernel '50
The Toast of New Orleans '50
Bonnie Prince Charlie '48
The Bishop's Wife '47
The Perfect Marriage '46
Immortal Battalion '44
Spitfire '42
Bachelor Mother '39
Eternally Yours '39
The Real Glory '39
Wuthering Heights '39
Bluebeard's Eighth Wife '38
Dawn Patrol '38
Dinner at the Ritz '37
Prisoner of Zenda '37
Beloved Enemy '36
The Charge of the Light Brigade '36
Dodsworth '36
Rose Marie '36
Barbary Coast '35

Kip Niven
New Year's Evil '78
Magnum Force '73

Allan Nixon
Mesa of Lost Women '52

The Hound of the Baskervilles '83
The Sign of Four '83
Whoops Apocalypse '83
A Midsummer Night's Dream '68
Marat/Sade '66

Jack Richardson
Trigger Tricks '30
Marked Money '28
Dynamite Dan '24
Toll Gate '20

Jay Richardson
Fugitive Rage '96
Wizards of the Demon Sword '94
Teenage Exorcist '93
Mind, Body & Soul '92
Sins of Desire '92
Original Intent '91
Vice Academy 3 '91
Bad Girls from Mars '90
Vice Academy 2 '90
Alienator '89
The Channeler '89
Slashdance '89
Death Row Diner '88
Hollywood Chainsaw Hookers '88
The Newlydeads '87

Joely Richardson
Event Horizon '97
101 Dalmatians '96
Hollow Reed '95
Loch Ness '95
Sister My Sister '94
I'll Do Anything '93
Shining Through '92
King Ralph '91
Drowning by Numbers '87
Wetherby '85

John Richardson
Cosmos: War of the Planets '80
Frankenstein '80 '79
Eyeball '78
Torso '73
One Million Years B.C. '66
Black Sunday '60

Latanya Richardson
Losing Isaiah '94
When a Man Loves a Woman '94

Lee Richardson
Skylark '93
A Stranger Among Us '92
Q & A '90
The Fly 2 '89
The Believers '87
Sweet Lorraine '87
Tiger Warsaw '87
Prizzi's Honor '85

Miranda Richardson
The Designated Mourner '97
The Evening Star '96
Swann '96
Kansas City '95
Century '94
Fatherland '94
Tom & Viv '94
The Bachelor '93
The Crying Game '92
Damage '92
Enchanted April '92
Twisted Obsession '90
After Pilkington '88
Empire of the Sun '87
Dance with a Stranger '85
Transmutations '85

Natasha Richardson
Nell '94
Widow's Peak '94
Hostages '93
The Favor, the Watch, & the Very Big Fish '92
Past Midnight '92
The Comfort of Strangers '91
The Handmaid's Tale '90
Fat Man and Little Boy '89
Patty Hearst '88
Gothic '87
A Month in the Country '87

Patricia Richardson
Ulee's Gold '97
In Country '89

Ralph Richardson
A Doll's House '89
Wagner: The Complete Epic '85
Give My Regards to Broad Street '84
Greystoke: The Legend of Tarzan, Lord of the Apes '84
Dragonslayer '81
Early Days '81
Time Bandits '81
The Man in the Iron Mask '77
Invitation to the Wedding '73
Lady Caroline Lamb '73
O Lucky Man! '73
Alice's Adventures in Wonderland '72
Tales from the Crypt '72
Who Slew Auntie Roo? '71
Battle of Britain '69
The Looking Glass War '69
Khartoum '66
The Wrong Box '66
Doctor Zhivago '65
Long Day's Journey into Night '62
Exodus '60
Richard III '55
The Fallen Idol '49
The Heiress '49
Anna Karenina '48
The Day Will Dawn '42
The Lion Has Wings '40
Clouds Over Europe '39
The Four Feathers '39
The Citadel '38
The Divorce of Lady X '38
Amazing Adventure '37
The Man Who Could Work Miracles '37
South Riding '37
Thunder in the City '37
Things to Come '36
Bulldog Jack '35
Java Head '35
The Ghoul '34

Regina Richardson
Nine Deaths of the Ninja '85
Tightrope '84

Salli Richardson
The Great White Hype '96
Soul of the Game '96
Lily in Winter '94
A Low Down Dirty Shame '94
Sioux City '94
Posse '93
How U Like Me Now? '92
Up Against the Wall '91

Sy Richardson
Floundering '94
Ring of Fire 2: Blood and Steel '92
Street Asylum '90
Backtrack '89
Dead Man Walking '88
They Live '88
Straight to Hell '87
Repo Man '83
Fairy Tales '76

Peter Mark Richman
Naked Gun 2 1/2: The Smell of Fear '91
Friday the 13th, Part 8: Jason Takes Manhattan '89
Judgment Day '88
City Killer '87
Dempsey '83
PSI Factor '80
Black Orchid '59

Anthony Richmond
One Wish Too Many '55
Devil Girl from Mars '54

Branscombe Richmond
To the Limit '95
Jericho Fever '93
Christopher Columbus: The Discovery '92
DaVinci's War '92
Inside Edge '92
The Taking of Beverly Hills '91

Fiona Richmond
Eat the Rich '87
The House on Straw Hill '76

Kane Richmond
Behind the Mask '46
Haunted Harbor '44
Spy Smasher '42
Spy Smasher Returns '42
Anything for a Thrill '37
Devil Diamond '37
Motorcycle Squad '37
Tough to Handle '37
The Reckless Way '36
The Adventures of Rex & Rinty '35
Confidential '35
East Side Kids/The Lost City '35
The Lost City '34
Cavalier of the West '31

Warner Richmond
Colorado Serenade '46
Wild West '46
Wild Horse Canyon '39
Doomed at Sundown '37
A Lawman Is Born '37
Where Trails Divide '37
Headin' for the Rio Grande '36
Song of the Gringo '36
The New Frontier '35
Rainbow's End '35
The Lost Jungle '34
Big News '29
The Speed Spook '24

Deborah Richter
The Banker '89
Cyborg '89
Promised Land '88
Square Dance '87
Hot Moves '84
Twirl '81
The Rebels '79
Swap Meet '79

Jason James Richter
Free Willy 3 '97
Free Willy 2: The Adventure Home '95
Cops and Robbersons '94
The Neverending Story 3: escape from Fantasia '94
Free Willy '93

Paul Richter
Kriemhilde's Revenge '24
Siegfried '24
Dr. Mabuse, Parts 1 & 2 '22

Tony Rickards
Castaway '87
Robbery '85
Great Gold Swindle '84
Waterfront '83

Don Rickles
Casino '95
Innocent Blood '92
Keaton's Cop '90
For the Love of It '80
Kelly's Heroes '70
Enter Laughing '67
Beach Blanket Bingo '65
Bikini Beach '64
Muscle Beach Party '64
X: The Man with X-Ray Eyes '63
The Rat Race '60
Run Silent, Run Deep '58

Alan Rickman
Michael Collins '96
Rasputin: Dark Servant of Destiny '96
Sense and Sensibility '95
An Awfully Big Adventure '94
Fallen Angels 1 '93
Bob Roberts '92
Close My Eyes '91
Robin Hood: Prince of Thieves '91
Truly, Madly, Deeply '91
Closet Land '90
Quigley Down Under '90
The January Man '89
Die Hard '88

Allen Rickman
I Was a Teenage Zombie '87
Shock! Shock! Shock! '87

John Ridgely
Cavalry Charge '51
Task Force '49
Cry Wolf '47

The Possessed '47
The Big Sleep '46
The Man I Love '46
Arsenic and Old Lace '44
Air Force '43
Destination Tokyo '43

Robert Ridgely
Philadelphia '93
Rosie: The Rosemary Clooney Story '82
Who Am I This Time? '82

Stanley Ridges
Task Force '49
The Possessed '47
Mr. Ace '46
Master Race '44
The Story of Dr. Wassell '44
Wilson '44
The Lady is Willing '42
The Sea Wolf '41
Sergeant York '41
Black Friday '40
Each Dawn I Die '39
Union Pacific '39
Internes Can't Take Money '37

Leni Riefenstahl
Tiefland '44
The Blue Light '32
Sacred Mountain/White Flame '31

Peter Riegert
Infinity '96
The Infiltrator '95
Pie In the Sky '95
Coldblooded '94
The Mask '94
Barbarians at the Gate '93
Gypsy '93
Utz '93
Passed Away '92
The Object of Beauty '91
Oscar '91
The Runestone '91
A Shock to the System '90
That's Adequate '90
Crossing Delancey '88
A Man in Love '87
The Stranger '87
News at Eleven '86
Local Hero '83
Americathon '79
Chilly Scenes of Winter '79
National Lampoon's Animal House '78

Richard Riehle
Dominion '94
Holy Matrimony '94
Lightning Jack '94
A Dangerous Woman '93
Lone Justice 2 '93
Body of Evidence '92
Hero '92
Of Mice and Men '92
The Public Eye '92

Ron Rifkin
I'm Not Rappaport '96
Last Summer In the Hamptons '96
The Substance of Fire '96
Norma Jean and Marilyn '95
Wolf '94
Manhattan Murder Mystery '93
Courage '86
The Chosen '81
Mrs. R's Daughter '79
Silent Running '71

Jorge Rigaud
Black Box Affair '66
The Castilian '63
Quatorze Juliet '32

Cathy Rigby
Challenge of a Lifetime '85
The Great Wallendas '78

Edward Rigby
The Happiest Days of Your Life '50
Convoy '40
Young and Innocent '37
Lorna Doone '34

Diana Rigg
Rebecca '97
Moll Flanders '96
Samson and Delilah '96
A Good Man in Africa '94
Genghis Cohn '93
Running Delilah '93
Mrs. 'Arris Goes to Paris '92
Snow White '89
Unexplained Laughter '89
The Worst Witch '86
Bleak House '85
Evil under the Sun '82
The Great Muppet Caper '81
A Little Night Music '77
In This House of Brede '75
Theatre of Blood '73
The Hospital '71
Julius Caesar '70
The Assassination Bureau '69
On Her Majesty's Secret Service '69
A Midsummer Night's Dream '68

Rebecca Rigg
Tunnel Vision '95
The Efficiency Expert '92
The Hunting '92
Fortress '85
Doctors and Nurses '82

Brad Rijn
Special Effects '85
Perfect Strangers '84

Robin Riker
Stepmonster '92
Body Chemistry 2: Voice of a Stranger '91
Alligator '80

Elaine Riley
Clipped Wings '53
Rider from Tucson '50
Hopalong Cassidy: Borrowed Trouble '49
Hopalong Cassidy: The Devil's Playground '46

Jack Riley
Portrait of a White Marriage '88
Night Patrol '85
Attack of the Killer Tomatoes '77
McCabe & Mrs. Miller '71

Jeannine Riley
Wackiest Wagon Train in the West '77
Electra Glide in Blue '73
The Comic '69
Big Mouth '67

Larry Riley
Dead Solid Perfect '88
Crackers '84
A Soldier's Story '84

Michael Riley
French Kiss '95
Heck's Way Home '95
...And God Spoke '94
Race to Freedom: The Story of the Underground Railroad '94
To Catch a Killer '92
Perfectly Normal '91

Walter Rilla
Frozen Alive '64
The Gamma People '56
The Golden Salamander '51
Mr. Emmanuel '44
House of Mystery '41
Black Eyes '39
The Scarlet Pimpernel '34

Shane Rimmer
Crusoe '89
Dreamchild '85
Out of Africa '85
The People That Time Forgot '77
S*P*Y*S '74

Molly Ringwald
Baja '95
Malicious '95
Stephen King's The Stand '94
Face the Music '92
Betsy's Wedding '90
Strike It Rich '90
Women & Men: Stories of Seduction '90
For Keeps '88

Savage ►cont.

Maria's Lovers '84
The Tender Age '84
The Amateur '82
Coming Out of the Ice '82
Inside Moves '80
Soldier's Revenge '70s
Hair '79
The Onion Field '79
The Deer Hunter '78
Eric '75
All the Kind Strangers '74
The Sister-in-Law '74
The Killing Kind '73
Steelyard Blues '73
Bad Company '72

Rick Savage
Ex-Cop '93
Sensations '87

Dany Saval
Boeing Boeing '65
Moon Pilot '62

Telly Savalas
Mind Twister '93
The Hollywood Detective '89
The Dirty Dozen: The Fatal
    Mission '88
The Dirty Dozen: The Deadly
    Mission '87
Kojak: The Belarus File '85
Cannonball Run 2 '84
Cartier Affair '84
Fake Out '82
Silent Rebellion '82
Beyond the Poseidon Adventure
    '79
Escape to Athena '79
Capricorn One '78
Beyond Reason '77
Inside Out '75
Killer Force '75
Lisa and the Devil '75
The Family '73
A Reason to Live, A Reason to
    Die '73
Redneck '73
Sonny and Jed '73
Horror Express '72
New Mafia Boss '72
Pancho Villa '72
Scenes from a Murder '72
A Town Called Hell '72
Kelly's Heroes '70
The Assassination Bureau '69
Crooks & Coronets '69
Land Raiders '69
MacKenna's Gold '69
On Her Majesty's Secret Service
    '69
Buona Sera, Mrs. Campbell '68
The Scalphunters '68
The Dirty Dozen '67
Battle of the Bulge '65
The Greatest Story Ever Told
    '65
The Slender Thread '65
Birdman of Alcatraz '62
The Interns '62
Cape Fear '61

Doug Savant
Maniac Cop 3: Badge of Silence
    '93
Shaking the Tree '92
Red Surf '90
Paint It Black '89
Masquerade '88

Lyudmila Savelyeva
The Seagull '71
War and Peace '68

John Savident
Othello '95
Middlemarch '93
Brain Donors '92
Mrs. 'Arris Goes to Paris '92
Impromptu '90
Mountains of the Moon '90

Tom Savini
From Dusk Till Dawn '95
Heartstopper '92
Creepshow 2 '87
Knightriders '81

Maniac '80

Camille Saviola
Sunset Park '96
Nightlife '90

Suzanne Savoy
The Man with the Perfect Swing
    '95
The Cellar '90

Devon Sawa
Wild America '97
The Boys Club '96
Night of the Twisters '95
Robin of Locksley '95
Little Giants '94

Julia Sawalha
A Midwinter's Tale '95
Pride and Prejudice '95
Martin Chuzzlewit '94

Joseph Sawyer
The Kettles in the Ozarks '56
The Killing '56
Mr. Walkie Talkie '52
As You Were '51
Comin' Round the Mountain '51
Indian Uprising '51
Fighting Father Dunne '48
The Naughty Nineties '45
Tanks a Million '41
The Border Legion '40
Lucky Cisco Kid '40
Melody Ranch '40
Special Investigator '36
The Informer '35
Ace of Aces '33

John Saxon
From Dusk Till Dawn '95
Beverly Hills Cop 3 '94
Killing Obsession '94
Wes Craven's New Nightmare
    '94
No Escape, No Return '93
Animal Instincts '92
The Baby Doll Murders '92
Hellmaster '92
Maximum Force '92
Blackmail '91
Deadly Conspiracy '91
Payoff '91
The Arrival '90
Blood Salvage '90
Crossing the Line '90
The Last Samurai '90
The Final Alliance '89
My Mom's a Werewolf '89
Aftershock '88
Criminal Act '88
Death House '88
Welcome to Spring Break '88
A Nightmare on Elm Street 3:
    Dream Warriors '87
Hands of Steel '86
Fever Pitch '85
Half Slave, Half Free '85
A Nightmare on Elm Street '84
Prisoners of the Lost Universe
    '84
Big Score '83
Invasion of the Flesh Hunters
    '82
Scorpion with Two Tails '82
Unsane '82
Wrong is Right '82
Blood Beach '81
Battle Beyond the Stars '80
Beyond Evil '80
The Electric Horseman '79
Running Scared '79
The Bees '78
Deadly Thief '78
Fast Company '78
The Glove '78
Moonshine County Express '77
Raid on Entebbe '77
Strange Shadows in an Empty
    Room '76
Black Christmas '75
Mitchell '75
Strange New World '75
Planet Earth '74
Enter the Dragon '73
Joe Kidd '72
Snatched '72
Mr. Kingstreet's War '71
Death of a Gunfighter '69

The Appaloosa '66
The Doomsday Flight '66
Night Caller from Outer Space
    '66
Planet of Blood '66
The Cardinal '63
Mr. Hobbs Takes a Vacation '62
Portrait in Black '60
The Unforgiven '60
The Reluctant Debutante '58
This Happy Feeling '58
Rock, Pretty Baby '56

Philip Sayer
Slayground '84
Green Horizon '83
Xtro '83

Alexei Sayle
Deadly Currents '93
Reckless Kelly '93
The Young Ones '88
Siesta '87
Whoops Apocalypse '83

John Sayles
Gridlock'd '96
Matinee '92
Straight Talk '92
City of Hope '91
Little Vegas '90
Eight Men Out '88
Unnatural Causes '86
Hard Choices '84

Syd Saylor
Ambush Trail '46
Harvest Melody '43
Arizona Days '37
Forlorn River '37
Sea Racketeers '37
Headin' for the Rio Grande '36
Kelly of the Secret Service '36
Kelly the Second '36
Prison Shadows '36
The Lost Jungle '34
When a Man Sees Red '34
The Light of Western Stars '30

Raphael Sbarge
The Hidden 2 '94
Carnosaur '93
Prison for Children '93
Murder 101 '91
Back to Hannibal: The Return of
    Tom Sawyer and Huckleberry
    Finn '90
Billionaire Boys Club '87
My Man Adam '86
My Science Project '85
Risky Business '83
Abuse '82

Mattia Sbragia
Year of the Gun '91
Dial Help '88

Greta Scacchi
The Odyssey '97
Emma '96
Rasputin: Dark Servant of
    Destiny '96
Country Life '95
The Browning Version '94
Jefferson in Paris '94
Desire '93
The Killing Beach '92
The Player '92
Fires Within '91
Shattered '91
Presumed Innocent '90
White Mischief '88
Good Morning, Babylon '87
A Man in Love '87
Ebony Tower '86
Burke & Wills '85
Defense of the Realm '85
The Coca-Cola Kid '84
Waterfront '83
Heat and Dust '82

Gia Scala
The Tunnel of Love '58
Don't Go Near the Water '57

Prunella Scales
Emma '97
Breaking the Code '96
An Awfully Big Adventure '94
The Rector's Wife '94
Second Best '94
Wolf '94

My Friend Walter '93
Howard's End '92
A Question of Attribution '91
A Chorus of Disapproval '89
Consuming Passions '88
The Lonely Passion of Judith
    Hearne '87
Mapp & Lucia '85
The Wicked Lady '83
Fawlty Towers '77
Room at the Top '59

Jack Scalia
Dark Breed '96
The Silencers '95
Storybook '95
Tall, Dark and Deadly '95
T-Force '94
Amore! '93
Casualties of Love: The "Long
    Island Lolita" Story '93
Shattered Image '93
Deadly Desire '91
Illicit Behavior '91
Runaway Father '91
After the Shock '90
Endless Descent '90
Fear City '85
The Amazons '84
The Devlin Connection '82

Carlo Scandiuzzi
Killing Zoe '94
Red Snow '91
Shredder Orpheus '89

Sean Scanlan
A Mind to Murder '94
A Sense of Freedom '78

Kevin Scannell
Backfield in Motion '91
Shoot to Kill '88

Michelle Scarabelli
The Colony '95
Alien Nation: Dark Horizon '94
Deadbolt '92
Age Old Friends '89
SnakeEater 2: The Drug Buster
    '89
Perfect Timing '84

Don Scardino
He Knows You're Alone '80
Squirm '76

Hal Scardino
Marvin's Room '96
The Indian in the Cupboard '95

Alan Scarfe
Once a Thief '96
Heart of Darkness '93
Jericho Fever '93
The Deserters '80s
Iron Eagle 2 '88
Python Wolf '88
Keeping Track '86
The Bay Boy '85
Joshua Then and Now '85
Cathy's Curse '77

Renato Scarpa
The Postman '94
Volere Volare '92
The Icicle Thief '89

Diana Scarwid
Bastard out of Carolina '96
If These Walls Could Talk '96
The Cure '95
Gold Diggers: The Secret of
    Bear Mountain '95
The Neon Bible '95
Truman '95
JFK: Reckless Youth '93
After the Promise '87
Brenda Starr '86
Extremities '86
The Ladies Club '86
Psycho 3 '86
A Bunny's Tale '85
Rumble Fish '83
Silkwood '83
Strange Invaders '83
Desperate Lives '82
Mommie Dearest '81
Inside Moves '80
Forever '78
Pretty Baby '78
The Possessed '77

Wendy Schaal
Out There '95
Going Under '91
When the Time Comes '91
Innerspace '87
Creature '85
Where the Boys Are '84 '84

Sam Schacht
Heart of Midnight '89
A Secret Space '88

Johnathon Schaech
Invasion of Privacy '96
That Thing You Do! '96
The Doom Generation '96
How to Make an American Quilt
    '95
Poison Ivy 2: Lily '95

Laura Schaefer
Curse 4: The Ultimate Sacrifice
    '90
Catacombs '89
Ghost Town '88

Eric Schaeffer
If Lucy Fell '95
My Life's in Turnaround '94

Rebecca Schaeffer
The End of Innocence '90
Voyage of Terror: The Achille
    Lauro Affair '90
Scenes from the Class Struggle
    in Beverly Hills '89

Natalie Schafer
Gilligan's Island: Meet the Crew
    '64
Forever Darling '56
Caught '49
The Time of Your Life '48

William Schallert
Held Hostage '91
House Party 2: The Pajama Jam
    '91
The Incident '89
War & Remembrance: The Final
    Chapter, Part 8 '89
War & Remembrance, Part 1 '88
Innerspace '87
The Grace Kelly Story '83
Twilight Zone: The Movie '83
Death Sentence '74
Trial of the Catonsville Nine '72
Man on a String '71
Colossus: The Forbin Project '70
The Computer Wore Tennis
    Shoes '69
Speedway '68
Tarnished Angels '57
Sword of Venus '53

Sabrina Scharf
Hunter '73
Easy Rider '69
Hell's Angels on Wheels '67

Roy Scheider
Covert Assassin '94
Romeo Is Bleeding '93
Naked Lunch '91
The Fourth War '90
The Russia House '90
Somebody Has to Shoot the
    Picture '90
Listen to Me '89
Night Game '89
Cohen and Tate '88
52 Pick-Up '86
The Men's Club '86
2010: The Year We Make
    Contact '84
Blue Thunder '83
Tiger Town '83
Still of the Night '83
All That Jazz '79
Last Embrace '79
Jaws 2 '78
Sorcerer '77
Marathon Man '76
Jaws '75
The Outside Man '73
The Seven-Ups '73
The French Connection '71
Klute '71
Stiletto '69
Paper Lion '68
Curse of the Living Corpse '64

Schwimmer ✏cont.

Jason Goes to Hell: The Final
    Friday '93
Lone Justice 2 '93

Hanna Schygulla
Dead Again '91
The Summer of Miss Forbes '88
Casanova '87
Forever, Lulu '87
Barnum '86
Delta Force '86
A Love in Germany '84
Sheer Madness '84
La Nuit de Varennes '82
Berlin Alexanderplatz '80
The Marriage of Maria Braun '79
The Wrong Move '78
Effi Briest '74
The Bitter Tears of Petra von
    Kant '72
The Merchant of Four Seasons
    '71
Beware of a Holy Whore '70
Gods of the Plague '69
Why Does Herr R. Run Amok?
    '69

Annabella Sciorra
Copland '97
The Funeral '96
Underworld '96
The Addiction '95
The Cure '95
National Lampoon's Favorite
    Deadly Sins '95
Mr. Wonderful '93
The Night We Never Met '93
Romeo Is Bleeding '93
The Hand that Rocks the Cradle
    '92
Whispers in the Dark '92
The Hard Way '91
Jungle Fever '91
Prison Stories: Women on the
    Inside '91
Cadillac Man '90
Internal Affairs '90
Reversal of Fortune '90
True Love '89

Edith Scob
The Milky Way '68
The Burning Court '62
The Horror Chamber of Dr.
    Faustus '59

Dean Scofield
Prehysteria 2 '94
Eden 3 '93
Eden 4 '93

Paul Scofield
The Crucible '96
Martin Chuzzlewit '94
Quiz Show '94
Utz '93
Hamlet '90
Mr. Corbett's Ghost '90
Henry V '89
When the Whales Came '89
The Attic: The Hiding of Anne
    Frank '88
Anna Karenina '85
Scorpio '73
King Lear '71
Bartleby '70
A Man for All Seasons '66
The Train '65
Carve Her Name with Pride '58

Tracy Scoggins
The Great American Sex
    Scandal '94
Alien Intruder '93
Dead On '93
Dollman vs Demonic Toys '93
Play Murder for Me '91
Timebomb '91
Ultimate Desires '91
Beyond the Silhouette '90
Demonic Toys '90
The Red Raven Kiss-Off '90
Watchers 2 '90
The Gumshoe Kid '89
One Last Run '89
In Dangerous Company '88

Toy Soldiers '84
Twirl '81

Peter Scolari
That Thing You Do! '96
Camp Nowhere '94
Fallen Angels 2 '93
Ticks '93
Perfect Harmony '91
Corporate Affairs '90
Mr. Bill's Real Life Adventures
    '86
Rosebud Beach Hotel '85
Bosom Buddies '80

Zvee Scooler
Trumps '83
Uncle Moses '32

Martin Scorsese
Quiz Show '94
Guilty by Suspicion '91
Akira Kurosawa's Dreams '90
Round Midnight '86

Nicollete Scorsese
Aspen Extreme '93
Boxing Helena '93

Alex Scott
Peter's Friends '92
Next of Kin '82
Space: 1999 '75
The Asphyx '72
The Abominable Dr. Phibes '71
The Persuaders '71

Bainbridge Scott
Death Chase '87
Hell Squad '85

Brenda Scott
Simon, King of the Witches '71
Johnny Tiger '66

Campbell Scott
The Daytrippers '96
Big Night '95
Mrs. Parker and the Vicious
    Circle '94
The Innocent '93
Singles '92
Dead Again '91
Dying Young '91
Longtime Companion '90
The Sheltering Sky '90
The Ghost of Fletcher Ridge
    '80s

Carey Scott
Diving In '90
Making the Grade '84

Debralee Scott
Police Academy '84
Just Tell Me You Love Me '80
Deathmoon '78
Our Time '74

Donovan Scott
Sheena '84
Goldilocks & the Three Bears
    '83
Savannah Smiles '82

Eric Scott
A Day for Thanks on Walton's
    Mountain '82
The Waltons: The Christmas
    Carol '80
The Waltons: A Thanksgiving
    Story '73

Fred Scott
Ridin' the Trail '40
Code of the Fearless '39
In Old Montana '39
Ranger's Roundup '38
Songs and Bullets '38
Melody of the Plains '37
The Roamin' Cowboy '37
Singing Buckaroo '37
Two-Gun Troubador '37

Geoffrey Scott
The Morning After '86
First & Ten '85
First & Ten: The Team Scores
    Again '85

George C. Scott
Titanic '96
Angus '95
Prince Brat and the Whipping
    Boy '95

Tyson '95
Deadly Currents '93
Malice '93
Descending Angel '90
Exorcist 3: Legion '90
Pals '87
Choices '86
The Last Days of Patton '86
The Murders in the Rue Morgue
    '86
Firestarter '84
Oliver Twist '82
Taps '81
The Changeling '80
The Formula '80
Hardcore '79
Movie, Movie '78
The Prince and the Pauper '78
Islands in the Stream '77
The Hindenburg '75
Bank Shot '74
Savage Is Loose '74
The Day of the Dolphin '73
Oklahoma Crude '73
The New Centurions '72
Rage '72
The Hospital '71
They Might Be Giants '71
Patton '70
Petulia '68
Flim-Flam Man '67
The Bible '66
The Bible...In the Beginning '66
Dr. Strangelove, or: How I
    Learned to Stop Worrying
    and Love the Bomb '64
The List of Adrian Messenger
    '63
The Hustler '61
Anatomy of a Murder '59
The Hanging Tree '59

Gordon Scott
Death Ray
Tramplers '66
Hercules and the Princess of
    Troy '65
Marauder '65
Coriolanus, Man without a
    Country '64
Conquest of Mycene '63
Gladiator of Rome '63
Hero of Rome '63
Tyrant of Lydia Against the Son
    of Hercules '63
Samson and the 7 Miracles of
    the World '62
Tarzan and the Trappers '58

Jacqueline Scott
Empire of the Ants '77
The Outer Limits: Galaxy Being
    '63

Janet Scott
Day of the Triffids '63
The Devil's Disciple '59

Janette Scott
Paranoiac '62
Helen of Troy '56

Jay Scott
All the Lovin' Kinfolk '89
The Cut Throats '69
Grave of the Vampire '72

John Scott
Horror of Party Beach '64
The Tell-Tale Heart '62

Kathryn Leigh Scott
The Last Days of Patton '86
Murrow '86
Visitor from the Grave '81
Witches' Brew '79
House of Dark Shadows '70
Dark Shadows '67

Kimberly Scott
Flatliners '90
The Abyss '89

Larry B. Scott
Fear of a Black Hat '94
Revenge of the Nerds 4: Nerds
    in Love '94
Super Force '90
SnakeEater 2: The Drug Buster
    '89
Revenge of the Nerds 2: Nerds
    in Paradise '87

The Children of Times Square
    '86
Iron Eagle '86
My Man Adam '86
That Was Then...This Is Now '85
Revenge of the Nerds '84
A Hero Ain't Nothin' But a
    Sandwich '78

Lizabeth Scott
Pulp '72
Loving You '57
Silver Lode '54
Scared Stiff '53
A Stolen Face '52
The Racket '51
Easy Living '49
Killer Bait '49
Too Late for Tears '49
Pitfall '48
Dead Reckoning '47
The Strange Love of Martha
    Ivers '46

Margaretta Scott
Calling Paul Temple '48
Counterblast '48
Man of Evil '48
Action for Slander '38
Things to Come '36

Martha Scott
Adam '83
Father Figure '80
The Turning Point '77
Ben-Hur '59
Sayonara '57
The Ten Commandments '56
Desperate Hours '55
The Falcon Takes Over/Strange
    Bargain '49
Hi Diddle Diddle '43
War of the Wildcats '43
Cheers for Miss Bishop '41
The Howards of Virginia '40
Our Town '40

Pippa Scott
Bad Ronald '74
Cold Turkey '71
Petulia '68

Randolph Scott
Ride the High Country '62
Comanche Station '60
Ride Lonesome '59
The Tall T '57
Seventh Cavalry '56
A Lawless Street '55
Rage at Dawn '55
Ten Wanted Men '54
The Stranger Wore a Gun '53
Hangman's Knot '52
Man in the Saddle '51
Santa Fe '51
The Cariboo Trail '50
The Nevadan '50
The Doolins of Oklahoma '49
Coroner Creek '48
Return of the Bad Men '48
Trail Street '47
Abilene Town '46
Badman's Territory '46
Captain Kidd '45
China Sky '44
Bombardier '43
The Desperadoes '43
Gung Ho! '43
Pittsburgh '42
The Spoilers '42
To the Shores of Tripoli '42
Western Union '41
My Favorite Wife '40
Virginia City '40
Jesse James '39
Susannah of the Mounties '39
Rebecca of Sunnybrook Farm
    '38
The Texans '38
Follow the Fleet '36
Go West, Young Man '36
The Last of the Mohicans '36
The Fighting Westerner '35
Roberta '35
She '35
Wagon Wheels '34
Buffalo Stampede '33
Heritage of the Desert '33
Man of the Forest '33

Murders in the Zoo '33
Supernatural '33
To the Last Man '33
When the West Was Young '32

Susan Scott
Student Confidential '87
Trap Them & Kill Them '84
Day of the Maniac '77
The Slasher '74

Timothy Scott
Lone Justice '93
Return to Lonesome Dove '93
Fried Green Tomatoes '91
Inside Out '91
Love Me Deadly '76

Tom Everett Scott
Dead Man on Campus '97
That Thing You Do! '96

Zachary Scott
The Young One '61
Flame of the Islands '55
Shotgun '55
Appointment in Honduras '53
Wings of Danger '52
Let's Make It Legal '51
Born to Be Bad '50
Flamingo Road '49
South of St. Louis '48
Cass Timberlane '47
Mildred Pierce '45
The Southerner '45

Kristin Scott Thomas
The English Patient '96
Angels and Insects '95
The Confessional '95
Gulliver's Travels '95
The Pompatus of Love '95
Richard III '95
Four Weddings and a Funeral
    '94
An Unforgettable Summer '94
The Bachelor '93
Body & Soul '93
Weep No More My Lady '93
Bitter Moon '92
Framed '90
Spymaker: The Secret Life of
    Ian Fleming '90
The Endless Game '89
A Handful of Dust '88
The Tenth Man '88
Under the Cherry Moon '86

Serena Scott Thomas
Nostromo '96
Diana: Her True Story '93
Harnessing Peacocks '92

Vito Scotti
I Wonder Who's Killing Her
    Now? '76
Caper of the Golden Bulls '67
What Did You Do in the War,
    Daddy? '66
Von Ryan's Express '65
Two Weeks in Another Town '62

Alexander Scourby
Me and the Colonel '58
The Big Heat '53
The Redhead from Wyoming '53
Affair in Trinidad '52

Angus Scrimm
Phantasm III: Lord of the Dead
    '94
Mindwarp '91
Subspecies '90
Transylvania Twist '89
Phantasm II '88
The Lost Empire '83
Phantasm '79

Sandra Seacat
The New Age '94
Promised Land '88

Susan Seaforth Hayes
Dream Machine '91
Billie '65

Steven Seagal
Executive Decision '96
The Glimmer Man '96
Under Siege 2: Dark Territory
    '95
On Deadly Ground '94
Under Siege '92
Out for Justice '91

Never Let Me Go '53
Night and the City '50
The Ghost and Mrs. Muir '47
The Razor's Edge '46
Leave Her to Heaven '45
Laura '44
Heaven Can Wait '43
The Shanghai Gesture '42
Son of Fury '42
Sundown '41
Return of Frank James '40

Jacob Tierney
The Neon Bible '95
Josh and S.A.M. '93

Lawrence Tierney
A Kiss Goodnight '94
Wizards of the Demon Sword '94
Casualties of Love: The "Long Island Lolita" Story '93
Reservoir Dogs '92
City of Hope '91
The Death Merchant '91
Why Me? '90
The Offspring '87
Tough Guys Don't Dance '87
Murphy's Law '86
Prizzi's Honor '85
Midnight '81
The Prowler '81
Never Pick up a Stranger '79
Abduction '75
The Female Jungle '56
The Bushwackers '52
The Greatest Show on Earth '52
The Hoodlum '51
Best of the Badmen '50
Born to Kill '47
The Devil Thumbs a Ride '47
The Devil Thumbs a Ride/ Having Wonderful Crime '47
Back to Bataan '45
Dillinger '45
Those Endearing Young Charms '45

Maura Tierney
Liar Liar '96
Primal Fear '96
Fly by Night '93
The Temp '93
White Sands '92
Dead Women in Lingerie '90

Angelo Tiffe
Sword of Honor '94
3 Ninjas Kick Back '94

Jerry Tiffe
Sword of Honor '94
Hollywood in Trouble '87

Pamela Tiffin
Viva Max '69
The Hallelujah Trail '65
State Fair '62
Summer and Smoke '61

Marie Tifo
Pouvoir Intime '87
Les Bons Debarras '81

Ken Tigar
Little Bigfoot '96
Rage '95

Kevin Tighe
In Cold Blood '96
Race the Sun '96
The Avenging Angel '95
Better Off Dead '94
Double Cross '94
Men of War '94
Caught in the Act '93
Geronimo: An American Legend '93
A Man in Uniform '93
What's Eating Gilbert Grape '93
Newsies '92
School Ties '92
Bright Angel '91
City of Hope '91
Another 48 Hrs. '90
Tales from the Crypt, Vol. 3 '90
K-9 '89
Lost Angels '89
Road House '89
Eight Men Out '88
Matewan '87

Zeffie Tilbury
The Grapes of Wrath '40
The Single Standard '29

Nadja Tiller
Wanted: Babysitter '75
Tonio Kroger '65
The Burning Court '62

Mel Tillis
Uphill All the Way '85
The Villain '79

Grant Tilly
Treasure of the Yankee Zephyr '83
Carry Me Back '82
Beyond Reasonable Doubt '80

Jennifer Tilly
American Strays '96
Bound '96
House Arrest '96
Liar Liar '96
Bird of Prey '95
Edie & Pen '95
Man with a Gun '95
The Pompatus of Love '95
At Home with the Webbers '94
Bullets Over Broadway '94
Double Cross '94
The Getaway '93
Heads '93
Made in America '93
Scorchers '92
Shadow of the Wolf '92
Inside Out '91
The Fabulous Baker Boys '89
Far from Home '89
Let It Ride '89
High Spirits '88
Remote Control '88
Rented Lips '88
He's My Girl '87
Moving Violations '85
No Small Affair '84

Meg Tilly
Journey '95
Primal Secrets '94
Sleep with Me '94
Body Snatchers '93
Fallen Angels 2 '93
Leaving Normal '92
The Two Jakes '90
Carmilla '89
The Girl in a Swing '89
Valmont '89
Masquerade '88
Off Beat '86
Agnes of God '85
Impulse '84
The Big Chill '83
Psycho 2 '83
One Dark Night '82
Tex '82

Charlene Tilton
Silence of the Hams '94
Center of the Web '92
Deadly Bet '91
Problem Child 2 '91
Border Shootout '90
Ragin' Cajun '90
Diary of a Teenage Hitchhiker '82
The Fall of the House of Usher '80
Sweater Girls '78

Martha Tilton
The Benny Goodman Story '55
Sunny '41

Cali Timmins
Hard Evidence '94
The Takeover '94

Patrick Timsit
Pedale Douce '96
Little Indian, Big City '95

Charles Tingwell
A Cry in the Dark '88
Miracle Down Under '87
Malcolm '86
Windrider '86
All the Rivers Run '84
Money Movers '78
Gone to Ground '76
Endplay '75
Dracula, Prince of Darkness '66

Murder Most Foul '65
Murder Ahoy '64
Murder at the Gallop '63
Murder She Said '62
The Desert Rats '53

Gabriele Tinti
Caged Women '84
Trap Them & Kill Them '84
Emmanuelle's Daughter '79
Delusions of Grandeur '76
Love Camp '76
Web of Deception '71
Journey Beneath the Desert '61

Jamie Tirelli
Lotto Land '95
Sudden Death '85

Kenneth Tobey
Honey, I Blew Up the Kid '92
Single White Female '92
Freeway '88
Innerspace '87
The Lost Empire '83
Strange Invaders '83
Rage '72
Gunfight at the O.K. Corral '57
Wings of Eagles '57
The Great Locomotive Chase '56
The Man in the Gray Flannel Suit '56
The Search for Bridey Murphy '56
Davy Crockett, King of the Wild Frontier '55
It Came from Beneath the Sea '55
The Beast from 20,000 Fathoms '53
The Bigamist '53
The Thing '51
I Was a Male War Bride '49

George Tobias
A New Kind of Love '63
Silk Stockings '57
The Seven Little Foys '55
Rawhide '50
The Judge Steps Out '49
The Set-Up '49
Sinbad, the Sailor '47
Objective, Burma! '45
Passage to Marseilles '44
Air Force '43
This Is the Army '43
Captains of the Clouds '42
Yankee Doodle Dandy '42
The Bride Came C.O.D. '41
Sergeant York '41
Strawberry Blonde '41
City for Conquest '40
Music in My Heart '40
The Hunchback of Notre Dame '39

Oliver Tobias
Mata Hari '85
Operation 'Nam '85
The Wicked Lady '83
The Big Scam '79
The Stud '78
King Arthur, the Young Warlord '75
Young Warlord '75
'Tis a Pity She's a Whore '73
Romance of a Horsethief '71

Dan Tobin
The Last Angry Man '59
The Big Clock '48
Velvet Touch '48
Woman of the Year '42
Black Limelight '38

Vivian Tobin
The Flustered Comedy of Leon Errol '39
The World Accuses '35

Stephen Tobolowsky
The Glimmer Man '96
Power 98 '96
Dr. Jekyll and Ms. Hyde '95
Murder In the First '95
Radioland Murders '94
Calendar Girl '93
Groundhog Day '93
Josh and S.A.M. '93
Basic Instinct '92

Hero '92
Memoirs of an Invisible Man '92
Single White Female '92
Sneakers '92
Where the Day Takes You '92
Deadlock '91
Thelma & Louise '91
Bird on a Wire '90
Funny About Love '90
Tagget '90
Breaking In '89
Great Balls of Fire '89
Roe vs. Wade '89
Mississippi Burning '88
Spaceballs '87
Nobody's Fool '86
Keep My Grave Open '80

Brian Tochi
Stitches '85
Revenge of the Nerds '84

Ann Todd
The Trouble with Father '50
Three Daring Daughters '48
How Green Was My Valley '41
Intermezzo '39

Ann Todd
The Human Factor '79
The Fiend '71
Son of Captain Blood '62
Scream of Fear '61
Time Without Pity '57
Madeleine '50
The Paradine Case '47
The Seventh Veil '46
Action for Slander '38
South Riding '37

Beverly Todd
Class of '61 '92
Lean on Me '89
Clara's Heart '88
The Ladies Club '86
Don't Look Back: The Story of Leroy "Satchel" Paige '81
Brother John '70

James Todd
High School Confidential '58
Trapped '49

Lisa Todd
Blood Hook '86
Imposters '84
Woman Hunt '72

Mabel Todd
The Ghost and the Guest '43
The Cowboy and the Lady '38

Richard Todd
Bloodbath
House of the Long Shadows '82
The Big Sleep '78
Number 1 of the Secret Service '77
Dorian Gray '70
Subterfuge '68
The Very Edge '63
The Longest Day '62
Never Let Go '60
Saint Joan '57
Battle Hell '56
D-Day, the Sixth of June '56
Dam Busters '55
A Man Called Peter '55
The Virgin Queen '55
Rob Roy—The Highland Rogue '53
The Sword & the Rose '53
The Story of Robin Hood & His Merrie Men '52
Interrupted Journey '49

Russell Todd
Sweet Murder '93
Border Shootout '90
One Last Run '89
Chopping Mall '86

Saira Todd
Bad Behavior '92
A Fatal Inversion '92

Thelma Todd
Swiss Miss '38
Way Out West '37
Bohemian Girl '36
Cockeyed Cavaliers '34
Hips, Hips, Hooray '34
Palooka '34

The Devil's Brother '33
Horse Feathers '32
Laurel & Hardy Comedy Classics, Vol. 4 '32
Speak Easily '32
Corsair '31
The Maltese Falcon '31
Monkey Business '31
Nevada '27

Tony Todd
The Rock '96
Beastmaster 3: The Eye of Braxus '95
Black Fox: Blood Horse '94
Black Fox: Good Men and Bad '94
Black Fox: The Price of Peace '94
Candyman 2: Farewell to the Flesh '94
The Crow '93
Excessive Force '93
Candyman '92
Keeper of the City '92
Criminal Justice '90
Ivory Hunters '90
Night of the Living Dead '90
Voodoo Dawn '89

Ricardo Tognazzi
Aurora '84
The Tragedy of a Ridiculous Man '81

Ugo Tognazzi
La Cage aux Folles 3: The Wedding '86
A Joke of Destiny, Lying in Wait Around the Corner Like a Bandit '84
La Cage aux Folles 2 '81
The Tragedy of a Ridiculous Man '81
La Cage aux Folles '78
La Grande Bouffe '73
Head of the Family '71
L'Udienza '71
Porcile '69
RoGoPaG '62
Love in the City '53

Niall Toibin
Frankie Starlight '95
Eat the Peach '86
Lovespell '79

Marilyn Tokuda
The Cage '89
Farewell to the King '89
The Jitters '88
My Tutor '82

Henriette Tol
Broken Mirrors '85
Question of Silence '83

Michael Tolan
Presumed Innocent '90
Half Slave, Half Free '85
Night Terror '76

Sidney Toler
Terror by Night/Meeting at Midnight '46
The Jade Mask '45
The Scarlet Clue '45
The Shanghai Cobra '45
Charlie Chan in the Secret Service '44
The Chinese Cat '44
Meeting at Midnight '44
Mr. Moto's Last Warning/ Meeting at Midnight '44
Adventures of Smilin' Jack '43
Isle of Forgotten Sins '43
Castle in the Desert '42
A Night to Remember '42
Charlie Chan in Rio '41
Charlie Chan at the Wax Museum '40
Murder over New York '40
Law of the Pampas '39
The Mysterious Rider '38
Wide Open Faces '38
Double Wedding '37
Our Relations '36
Champagne for Breakfast '35
Spitfire '34
Blonde Venus '32
Speak Easily '32

Monaco Forever '83

Monique Van De Ven
The Man Inside '90
Paint It Black '89
Amsterdamned '88
The Assault '86
Keetje Tippel '75
Turkish Delights '73

Sylvie van den Elsen
La Vie de Boheme '93
L'Argent '83

Nadine Van Der Velde
After Midnight '89
Shadow Dancing '88
Munchies '87
Critters '86

Diana Van Der Vlis
Lovespell '79
The Incident '67
X: The Man with X-Ray Eyes '63
Girl in Black Stockings '57

Trish Van Devere
Deadly Currents '93
Messenger of Death '88
Hollywood Vice Squad '86
Uphill All the Way '85
All God's Children '80
The Changeling '80
The Hearse '80
Movie, Movie '78
Stalk the Wild Child '76
Savage Is Loose '74
The Day of the Dolphin '73
Where's Poppa? '70

Mamie Van Doren
Voyage to the Planet of
   Prehistoric Women '68
Las Vegas Hillbillys '66
Navy vs. the Night Monsters '66
Three Nuts in Search of a Bolt
   '64
Born Reckless '59
Girls' Town '59
High School Confidential '58
Teacher's Pet '58
Girl in Black Stockings '57
Francis Joins the WACs '54

Granville Van Dusen
The Rose and the Jackal '90
Hotline '82
The Wild and the Free '80
Breaking Up '78
War Between the Tates '76

Barry Van Dyke
Foxfire Light '82
Ants '77

Conny Van Dyke
Framed '75
Hell's Angels '69 '69

Dick Van Dyke
Dick Tracy '90
Country Girl '82
The Runner Stumbles '79
Cold Turkey '71
The Comic '69
Chitty Chitty Bang Bang '68
Never a Dull Moment '68
Divorce American Style '67
Lt. Robin Crusoe, U.S.N. '66
Mary Poppins '64
Bye, Bye, Birdie '63

Jerry Van Dyke
Death Blow '87
Run If You Can '87
McLintock! '63
The Courtship of Eddie's Father
   '62

Peter Van Eyck
The Spy Who Came in from the
   Cold '65
Dr. Mabuse vs. Scotland Yard
   '64
The Brain '62
The Thousand Eyes of Dr.
   Mabuse '60
Wages of Fear '55
Five Graves to Cairo '43

John Van Eyssen
The Horror of Dracula '58
Men of Sherwood Forest '57

Quatermass 2 '57
Four Sided Triangle '53

Jo Van Fleet
The Tenant '76
Satan's School for Girls '73
I Love You, Alice B. Toklas! '68
Cool Hand Luke '67
Gunfight at the O.K. Corral '57
The King and Four Queens '56
I'll Cry Tomorrow '55
The Rose Tattoo '55
East of Eden '54

Kevin Van Hentenryck
Basket Case 3: The Progeny '92
Basket Case 2 '90
Basket Case '82

Merete Van Kamp
Lethal Woman '88
Princess Daisy '83

Peter Van Norden
Casualties of Love: The "Long
   Island Lolita" Story '93
The Accused '88
Scandal in a Small Town '88

Nina Van Pallandt
Jungle Warriors '84
Sword & the Sorcerer '82
Cutter's Way '81
Diary of a Young Comic '79
Quintet '79
A Wedding '78
Assault on Agathon '75
The Long Goodbye '73

Dick Van Patten
Love Is All There Is '96
Demolition High '95
A Dangerous Place '94
Robin Hood: Men in Tights '93
Body Trouble '92
Final Embrace '92
The New Adventures of Pippi
   Longstocking '88
Spaceballs '87
The Midnight Hour '86
The Hoboken Chicken
   Emergency '84
Diary of a Teenage Hitchhiker
   '82
High Anxiety '77
Freaky Friday '76
Gus '76
Superdad '73
Westworld '73
Joe Kidd '72
Son of Blob '72
Zachariah '70
Charly '68
Psychomania '63

James Van Patten
Twisted Justice '89
The Dirty Dozen: The Deadly
   Mission '87
Nightforce '86
Young Warriors '83
Roller Boogie '79
Tennessee Stallion '78

Joyce Van Patten
Breathing Lessons '94
Trust Me '89
Monkey Shines '88
Billy Galvin '86
Crawlspace '86
The Rumor Mill '86
The Falcon and the Snowman
   '85
St. Elmo's Fire '85
Eleanor: First Lady of the World
   '82
The Bad News Bears '76
Mame '74
The Stranger Within '74
Housewife '72
Thumb Tripping '72
The Trouble with Girls (and How
   To Get Into It) '69
I Love You, Alice B. Toklas! '68

Nels Van Patten
Mirror Images '91
One Last Run '89
Grotesque '87
Summer School '87

Timothy Van Patten
Curse 4: The Ultimate Sacrifice
   '90
Catacombs '89
The Wrong Guys '88
Dress Gray '86
Zone Troopers '84
Escape from El Diablo '83
Class of 1984 '82
Master Ninja '78
The White Shadow, Vol. 1 '78

Vincent Van Patten
The Break '95
Payback '90
The Victory '88
The Dirty Dozen: The Deadly
   Mission '87
Rooster: Spurs of Death! '83
Hell Night '81
Survival Run '80
Rock 'n' Roll High School '79
Chino '75
Charley and the Angel '73

Mario Van Peebles
Gang in Blue '96
Solo '96
Panther '95
Highlander: The Final Dimension
   '94
Urban Crossfire '94
Full Eclipse '93
Gunmen '93
Posse '93
New Jack City '91
Identity Crisis '90
Jaws: The Revenge '87
Heartbreak Ridge '86
Hot Shot '86
Rappin' '85
South Bronx Heroes '85
Delivery Boys '84
Exterminator 2 '84

Melvin Van Peebles
Calm at Sunset '96
Gang in Blue '96
Fist of the North Star '95
Terminal Velocity '94
Boomerang '92
O.C. and Stiggs '87
Sophisticated Gents '81
Sweet Sweetback's Baadasssss
   Song '71

Edward Van Sloan
The Mask of Dijon '46
Before I Hang '40
Danger on the Air '38
Dracula's Daughter '36
A Shot in the Dark '35
Manhattan Melodrama '34
The Death Kiss '33
Deluge '33
The Mummy '32
Dracula '31
Frankenstein '31

Deborah Van Valkenburgh
Erik '90
One Man Out '89
Phantom of the Ritz '88
Python Wolf '88
Rampage '87
A Bunny's Tale '85
Going for the Gold: The Bill
   Johnson Story '85
Streets of Fire '84
King of the Mountain '81
The Warriors '79

Monique Van Vooren
Sugar Cookies '77
Andy Warhol's Frankenstein '74
Ash Wednesday '73

Philip Van Zandt
Clipped Wings '53
Ghost Chasers '51
Woman in Brown '48
A Thousand and One Nights '45
Sherlock Holmes and the Secret
   Weapon '42
Citizen Kane '41

Courtney B. Vance
The Boys Next Door '96
The Last Supper '96

The Preacher's Wife '96
The Affair '95
Dangerous Minds '95
Panther '95
The Tuskegee Airmen '95
Holy Matrimony '94
The Piano Lesson '94
Race to Freedom: The Story of
   the Underground Railroad '94
The Adventures of Huck Finn '93
Percy & Thunder '93
Beyond the Law '92
The Hunt for Red October '90
Hamburger Hill '87

Danitra Vance
Jumpin' at the Boneyard '92
Little Man Tate '91
Limit Up '89
The War of the Roses '89
Sticky Fingers '88

Jim Vance
Blood Cult '85
How to Make a Doll '68

Joe Vance
Deadly Breed '89
L.A. Crackdown 2 '88

Musetta Vander
Backlash: Oblivion 2 '95
Project Shadowchaser 3000 '95
Under the Hula Moon '95

Alexandra Vandernoot
Blood of the Hunter '94
Highlander: The Gathering '93

Titos Vandis
Piece of the Action '77
Once Upon a Scoundrel '73
Never on Sunday '60

Pierre Vaneck
The Proprietor '96
Othello '95
Sweet Country '87
Is Paris Burning? '66

Charles Vanel
Three Brothers '80
Death in the Garden '56
Diabolique '55
To Catch a Thief '55
Wages of Fear '55

Vanilla Ice
Cool As Ice '91
Teenage Mutant Ninja Turtles 2:
   The Secret of the Ooze '91

Vanity
Highlander: The Gathering '93
DaVinci's War '92
South Beach '92
Neon City '91
Memories of Murder '90
Action Jackson '88
Deadly Illusion '87
52 Pick-Up '86
Never Too Young to Die '86
The Last Dragon '85
Tanya's Island '81
Terror Train '80

Renata Vanni
Wait Until Spring, Bandini '90
The Lady in White '88
Westward the Women '51

Joanne Vannicola
Iron Eagle 4 '95
Love and Human Remains '93

Luigi Vannucchi
Lovers Like Us '75
Red Tent '69

Victor Varconi
Unconquered '47
For Whom the Bell Tolls '43
My Favorite Blonde '42
Dancing Pirate '36
King of Kings '27

Evelyn Varden
The Bad Seed '56
The Night of the Hunter '55
Athena '54

Norma Varden
The Sound of Music '65
Jupiter's Darling '55

Fancy Pants '50
Forever Amber '47
National Velvet '44
The White Cliffs of Dover '44

Antonio Vargas
Strictly Ballroom '92
Whore '91

Jacob Vargas
Romy and Michele's High
   School Reunion '97
Selena '96
Mi Vida Loca '94
My Family '94
Gas Food Lodging '92

John Vargas
Seduced by Evil '94
Unnatural Causes '86

Valentina Vargas
Hellraiser 4: Bloodline '95
Dirty Games '93
The Tigress '93

Beatrice Varley
Room at the Top '59
Death Goes to School '53
Great Day '46
Young and Innocent '37

Jim Varney
The Expert '95
Slam Dunk Ernest '95
Ernest Goes to School '94
The Beverly Hillbillies '93
Ernest Rides Again '93
Wilder Napalm '93
Ernest Scared Stupid '91
Ernest Goes to Jail '90
The Rousters '90
Fast Food '89
Ernest Saves Christmas '88
Ernest Goes to Camp '87
Dr. Otto & the Riddle of the
   Gloom Beam '86

Diane Varsi
I Never Promised You a Rose
   Garden '77
Johnny Got His Gun '71
The People '71
Bloody Mama '70
Wild in the Streets '68
Sweet Love, Bitter '67
Compulsion '59
Ten North Frederick '58
Peyton Place '57

Michael Vartan
The Pallbearer '95
Fiorile '93

Razvan Vasilescu
The Oak '93
Trahir '93

Roberta Vasquez
Fit to Kill '93
Hard Hunted '92
Do or Die '91
The Rookie '90
Street Asylum '90
Easy Wheels '89
Picasso Trigger '89

Robert Vattier
Letters from My Windmill '54
The Baker's Wife '33

Frankie Vaughan
Let's Make Love '60
Dangerous Youth '58

Paris Vaughan
Buffy the Vampire Slayer '92
Heat Wave '90

Peter Vaughan
The Crucible '96
The Secret Agent '96
Circle of Deceit '94
Fatherland '94
Heart of Darkness '93
The Remains of the Day '93
Codename Kyril '91
Porridge '91
Prisoner of Honor '91
Mountains of the Moon '90
Haunted Honeymoon '86
Bleak House '85
Brazil '85
Forbidden '85
The Razor's Edge '84

The Thorn Birds '83
Dead Men Don't Wear Plaid '82
Night School '81
Sharky's Machine '81

Richard Ward
Mandingo '75
Across 110th Street '72

Robin Ward
Mark of Cain '84
Thrillkill '84
When Angels Fly '82

Roger Ward
Quigley Down Under '90
Mad Max '80

Sandy Ward
Blue Desert '91
Delta Force 3: The Killing Game '91
Tank '83
The Velvet Vampire '71

Sela Ward
My Fellow Americans '96
The Fugitive '93
Double Jeopardy '92
Child of Darkness, Child of Light '91
Rainbow Drive '90
Haunting of Sarah Hardy '89
Hello Again '87
Steele Justice '87
Nothing in Common '86

Simon Ward
The Monster Club '85
Supergirl '84
Deadly Strangers '82
Dominique Is Dead '79
Zulu Dawn '79
The Four Feathers '78
The Chosen '77
Children of Rage '75
The Four Musketeers '75
All Creatures Great and Small '74
The Three Musketeers '74
Dracula '73
Hitler: The Last Ten Days '73
Young Winston '72

Sophie Ward
A Village Affair '95
A Dark Adapted Eye '93
Class of '61 '92
A Demon in My View '92
The Shell Seekers '89
Little Dorrit, Film 1: Nobody's Fault '88
Little Dorrit, Film 2: Little Dorrit's Story '88
A Summer Story '88
Casanova '87
Young Sherlock Holmes '85

Wally Ward
The Chocolate War '88
The Invisible Kid '88
Thunder Run '86

Warwick Ward
The Informer '29
Variety '25

Zack Ward
Ed '96
The Club '94

Jennifer Ward-Leeland
Desperate Remedies '93
Dangerous Orphans '86

Anthony Warde
The Black Widow '47
King of the Forest Rangers '46
There Goes Kelly '45

Jack Warden
Ed '96
Mighty Aphrodite '95
Things to Do In Denver When You're Dead '95
While You Were Sleeping '95
Bullets Over Broadway '94
Guilty as Sin '93
Night and the City '92
Passed Away '92
Problem Child 2 '91
Everybody Wins '90
Judgment '90

Problem Child '90
Robert Kennedy and His Times '90
Dead Solid Perfect '88
The Presidio '88
September '88
The Aviator '85
Crackers '84
Hobson's Choice '83
The Verdict '82
Carbon Copy '81
Chu Chu & the Philly Flash '81
So Fine '81
Used Cars '80
And Justice for All '79
Being There '79
Beyond the Poseidon Adventure '79
The Champ '79
Dreamer '79
Death on the Nile '78
Heaven Can Wait '78
Raid on Entebbe '77
The White Buffalo '77
Shampoo '75
The Apprenticeship of Duddy Kravitz '74
Billy Two Hats '74
Man Who Loved Cat Dancing '73
The Sporting Club '72
Brian's Song '71
Man on a String '71
Summertree '71
Donovan's Reef '63
Darby's Rangers '58
Run Silent, Run Deep '58
Twelve Angry Men '57
Justice '55
From Here to Eternity '53

Herta Ware
Top Dog '95
Crazy in Love '92
Dakota '88
Cocoon '85

Irene Ware
The Dark Hour '36
Federal Agent '36
The Raven '35
King Kelly of the U.S.A. '34
Chandu the Magician '32

Chris Warfield
Diary of a Madman '63
Dangerous Charter '62

Emily Warfield
Bonanza: The Return '93
Calendar Girl '93
The Man in the Moon '91
Pair of Aces '90

Marsha Warfield
Mask '85
D.C. Cab '84

William Warfield
Old Explorers '90
Show Boat '51

Andy Warhol
Cocaine Cowboys '79
Driver's Seat '73

Todd Waring
Sinatra '92
Love & Murder '91

Billy Warlock
Honor Thy Father and Mother: The True Story of the Menendez Brothers '94
Society '92
Swimsuit: The Movie '89
Hot Shot '86

Gordon Warnecke
A Fatal Inversion '92
London Kills Me '91
My Beautiful Laundrette '85

David Warner
Rasputin: Dark Servant of Destiny '96
Beastmaster 3: The Eye of Braxus '95
Final Equinox '95
Ice Cream Man '95
In the Mouth of Madness '95
Naked Souls '95
Inner Sanctum 2 '94

Tryst '94
Body Bags '93
H.P. Lovecraft's Necronomicon: Book of the Dead '93
Quest of the Delta Knights '93
Return to the Lost World '93
Wild Palms '93
The Lost World '92
The Unnamable 2: The Statement of Randolph Carter '92
Cast a Deadly Spell '91
Star Trek 6: The Undiscovered Country '91
Teenage Mutant Ninja Turtles 2: The Secret of the Ooze '91
Blue Tornado '90
Code Name: Chaos '90
Mortal Passions '90
Spymaker: The Secret Life of Ian Fleming '90
Grave Secrets '89
Star Trek 5: The Final Frontier '89
Tripwire '89
Hanna's War '88
Hostile Takeover '88
Magdalene '88
Mr. North '88
My Best Friend Is a Vampire '88
Waxwork '88
The Company of Wolves '85
The Man with Two Brains '83
Frankenstein '82
Tron '82
The Boy Who Left Home to Find Out About the Shivers '81
Disappearance '81
Masada '81
Time Bandits '81
The Island '80
The Concorde: Airport '79 '79
Nightwing '79
S.O.S. Titanic '79
The Thirty-Nine Steps '79
Time After Time '79
Holocaust '78
Silver Bears '78
Providence '77
Cross of Iron '76
The Omen '76
The Old Curiosity Shop '75
A Doll's House '73
From Beyond the Grave '73
Straw Dogs '72
Ballad of Cable Hogue '70
The Fixer '68
A Midsummer Night's Dream '68
Morgan! '66
Tom Jones '63

H.B. Warner
The Ten Commandments '56
The Judge Steps Out '49
It's a Wonderful Life '46
Action in Arabia '44
Enemy of Women '44
Rogue's Gallery '44
Boss of Big Town '43
Hitler's Children '43
The Corsican Brothers '42
Yank in Libya '42
The Devil & Daniel Webster '41
Topper Returns '41
Bulldog Drummond's Bride '39
Bulldog Drummond's Secret Police '39
Let Freedom Ring '39
Mr. Smith Goes to Washington '39
The Rains Came '39
The Adventures of Marco Polo '38
Arrest Bulldog Drummond '38
Bulldog Drummond in Africa/ Arrest Bulldog Drummond '38
You Can't Take It with You '38
Lost Horizon '37
Mr. Deeds Goes to Town '36
A Tale of Two Cities '36
Supernatural '33
Cross Examination '32
King of Kings '27
Big Stakes '22

Jack Warner
The Quatermass Experiment '56
The Ladykillers '55

A Christmas Carol '51
Valley of the Eagles '51
The Blue Lamp '49
Train of Events '49
Against the Wind '48
Captive Heart '47
Dear Murderer '47
Hue and Cry '47
The Dummy Talks '43

Julie Warner
Wedding Bell Blues '96
Tommy Boy '95
The Puppet Masters '94
Indian Summer '93
Mr. Saturday Night '92
Doc Hollywood '91

Malcolm Jamal Warner
The Tuskegee Airmen '95
Tyson '95
Drop Zone '94
The Father Clements Story '87

E. Alyn Warren
Get That Man '35
Tarzan the Fearless '33
Abraham Lincoln '30
Medicine Man '30

Jennifer Warren
The Amazons '84
Mutant '83
The Choice '81
Intruder Within '81
Angel City '80
Ice Castles '78
Steel Cowboy '78
Another Man, Another Chance '77
Slap Shot '77
Night Moves '75
The Swap '71

Jennifer Leigh Warren
Grace of My Heart '96
The Crossing Guard '94

Lesley Ann Warren
Natural Enemy '96
Bird of Prey '95
Joseph '95
Color of Night '94
Pure Country '92
Life Stinks '91
A Fight for Jenny '90
Worth Winning '89
Cop '88
Baja Oklahoma '87
Burglar '87
Apology '86
Clue '85
Choose Me '84
The Dancing Princesses '84
Songwriter '84
A Night in Heaven '83
Treasure of the Yankee Zephyr '83
Portrait of a Showgirl '82
Victor/Victoria '82
Beulah Land '80
Portrait of a Stripper '79
Betrayal '78
Harry & Walter Go to New York '76
Legend of Valentino '75
Where the Eagle Flies '72
The One and Only, Genuine, Original Family Band '68
The Happiest Millionaire '67
Cinderella '64

Michael Warren
A Passion to Kill '94
Storyville '92
Heaven is a Playground '91
The Kid Who Loved Christmas '90
Hill Street Blues, Vol. 1: Hill Street Station '81
Norman, Is That You? '76

Harold Warrender
Pandora and the Flying Dutchman '51
Conspirator '49
Mimi '35

Ruth Warrick
Deathmask '69
One Too Many '50
Let's Dance '50
Three Husbands '50
Great Dan Patch '49
Guest in the House '45
China Sky '44
Mr. Winkle Goes to War '44
The Iron Major '43
The Corsican Brothers '42
Citizen Kane '41

David Warrilow
Barton Fink '91
Strong Medicine '84

James Warwick
The Affair of the Pink Pearl '84
The Clergyman's Daughter '84
The Crackler '84
Finessing the King '84
The House of Lurking Death '84
The Case of the Missing Lady '83
The Man in the Mist '83
The Secret Adversary '83
The Unbreakable Alibi '83

John Warwick
While I Live '47
The Face at the Window '39
Ticket of Leave Man '37

Robert Warwick
It Started with a Kiss '59
I Married a Witch '42
Sullivan's Travels '41
A Woman's Face '41
The Awful Truth '37
The Trigger Trio '37
The Bold Caballero '36
Bulldog Edition '36
Hopalong Cassidy '35
A Shot in the Dark '35
Whispering Shadow '33
The Secrets of Wu Sin '32
The Royal Bed '31
A Girl's Folly '17

Mona Washbourne
December Flower
Brideshead Revisited '81
Stevie '78
Driver's Seat '73
O Lucky Man! '73
If... '69
Mrs. Brown, You've Got a Lovely Daughter '68
The Collector '65
My Fair Lady '64
The Brides of Dracula '60
Stranger in Town '57
Cast a Dark Shadow '55

Beverly Washburn
When the Line Goes Through '71
Spider Baby '64
Old Yeller '57

Bryant Washburn
The Throwback '35
Drifting Souls '32
Kept Husbands '31
The Wizard of Oz '25

Rick Washburne
The Outfit '93
Comrades in Arms '91
Covert Action '88
Hangmen '87

Denzel Washington
Courage Under Fire '96
The Preacher's Wife '96
Crimson Tide '95
Devil in a Blue Dress '95
Virtuosity '95
Much Ado about Nothing '93
The Pelican Brief '93
Philadelphia '93
Malcolm X '92
Mississippi Masala '92
Ricochet '91
Heart Condition '90
Mo' Better Blues '90
Glory '89
The Mighty Quinn '89
Cry Freedom '87
The George McKenna Story '86

Zouzou
S*P*Y*S '74
Chloe in the Afternoon '72
Rod Zuanic
Fast Talking '86
Mad Max: Beyond
    Thunderdome '85
George Zucco
David and Bathsheba '51
Madame Bovary '49
The Pirate '48
The Devil Thumbs a Ride/
    Having Wonderful Crime '47
Scared to Death '47
Scared to Death/Dick Tracy's
    Dilemma '47
Where There's Life '47
Fog Island '45
Having Wonderful Crime '45
House of Frankenstein '44
The Mummy's Ghost '44
Return of the Ape Man '44
The Seventh Cross '44
The Black Raven '43
Dead Men Walk '43
The Mad Ghoul '43
Sherlock Holmes in Washington
    '43
The Black Swan '42
The Mad Monster '42
The Mummy's Tomb '42
My Favorite Blonde '42
The Monster and the Girl '41
A Woman's Face '41
The Mummy's Hand '40
The Adventures of Sherlock
    Holmes '39
The Hunchback of Notre Dame
    '39
Arrest Bulldog Drummond '38
Bulldog Drummond in Africa/
    Arrest Bulldog Drummond '38
Marie Antoinette '38
Three Comrades '38
The Bride Wore Red '37
The Firefly '37
Saratoga '37
Souls at Sea '37
Alex Zuckerman
Freaked '93
Me and the Kid '93
Daphne Zuniga
Charlie's Ghost: The Secret of
    Coronado '94
800 Leagues Down the Amazon
    '93
Prey of the Chameleon '91
Eyes of the Panther '90
The Fly 2 '89
Gross Anatomy '89
Staying Together '89
Last Rites '88
Spaceballs '87
Modern Girls '86
Quarterback Princess '85
The Sure Thing '85
Vision Quest '85
The Initiation '84
Jose Zuniga
Con Air '97
Hurricane Streets '96
Ransom '96
Crooklyn '94
Dianik Zurakowska
Orgy of the Vampires '73
Cauldron of Blood '67
Jahi JJ Zuri
Omega Doom '96
Nemesis 2: Nebula '94
Yoshitaka Zushi
Akira Kurosawa's Dreams '90
Dodes 'ka-den '70
Brad Zutaut
Knock Outs '92
Nudity Required '90
Hardbodies 2 '86
Noam Zylberman
Love and Hate: A Marriage
    Made in Hell '90
Outside Chance of Maximillian
    Glick '88

Elsa Zylberstein
Farinelli '94
Mina Tannenbaum '93

Director Index

T he **Director Index** provides a complete videography for any director with a video credit. The listings for the director names follow an alphabetical sort by last name (although the names appear in a first name last name format). The videographies are listed chronologically, from most recent film to directorial debut. If a director helmed more than one film in the same year, these movies are listed alphabetically within the year. Use this index in conjunction with the **Cast** (immediately preceding this index), **Writer**, and **Cinematographer** indexes (immediately following) to see where some of today's hottest directors got their starts.

Paul Aaron
In Love and War '91
Imperial Navy '80s
Maxie '85
Deadly Force '83
Force of One '79
The Miracle Worker '79
Different Story '78

Dodo Abashidze
Ashik Kerib '88

Charles Abbott
The Adventures of the Masked Phantom '38

George Abbott
Damn Yankees '58
The Pajama Game '57
Too Many Girls '40

Alan Abel
Is There Sex After Death? '71

Jeanne Abel
Is There Sex After Death? '71

Lewis Abernathy
House 4: Home Deadly Home '91

Derwin Abrahams
Northwest Trail '46
Border Vigilantes '41

Jim Abrahams
Hot Shots! Part Deux '93
Hot Shots! '91
Welcome Home, Roxy Carmichael '90
Big Business '88
Ruthless People '86
Top Secret! '84
Police Squad! Help Wanted! '82
Airplane! '80

Ivan Abramson
East and West '24

Tengiz Abuladze
Repentance '87

Jon Acevski
Freddie the Frog '92

Jovan Acin
Hey, Babu Riba '88

Robert Ackerman
Safe Passage '94

Rodney Ackland
Thursday's Child '43

David Acomba
Night Life '90

Catlin Adams
Sticky Fingers '88

Daniel Adams
Primary Motive '92
A Fool and His Money '88

Doug Adams
Blackout '88

Al Adamson
Cinderella 2000 '78
Hospital of Terror '78
Kill Factor '78
Black Samurai '77
Blazing Stewardesses '75
Jessie's Girls '75
Texas Layover '75
The Dynamite Brothers '74
I Spit on Your Corpse '74
Angels' Wild Women '72
Blood of Ghastly Horror '72
Brain of Blood '71
Dracula vs. Frankenstein '71
Horror of the Blood Monsters '70
Blood of Dracula's Castle '69
The Female Bunch '69
Gun Riders '69
Satan's Sadists '69

Victor Adamson
Boss Cowboy '35
Rawhide Romance '34
Fighting Cowboy '33

Gilbert Adler
Tales from the Crypt Presents Bordello of Blood '96

Joseph Adler
Scream, Baby, Scream '69
Sex and the College Girl '64

Lou Adler
Cheech and Chong's Up in Smoke '79

Percy Adlon
Younger & Younger '94
Salmonberries '91
Rosalie Goes Shopping '89
Bagdad Cafe '88
Sugarbaby '85
The Last Five Days '82
Celeste '81

Ed Adlum
Invasion of the Blood Farmers '72

Edvin Adolphson
The Count of the Old Town '34

Gabriel Aghion
Pedale Douce '96

Frank Agrama
Dawn of the Mummy '82

Joseph Louis Agraz
Treasure of the Moon Goddess '88

Javier Aguirre
The Rue Morgue Massacres '73
Dracula's Great Love '72

Agust Agustsson
Maya '82

Charlie Ahearn
Wild Style '83

Mac Ahlberg
Gangsters '79

Faruque Ahmed
Warlords 3000 '93

John Ainsworth
Pattern for Plunder '62

Chantal Akerman
A Couch in New York '95
Akermania, Vol. 1 '92
Night and Day '91
Window Shopping '86
The Eighties '83
Toute Une Nuit '82
Les Rendez-vous D'Anna '78
News from Home '76
Je Tu Il Elle '74

Moustapha Akkad
Lion of the Desert '81

Mohammed: Messenger of God '77

Jordan Alan
Terminal Bliss '91

Benito Alazraki
Invasion of the Zombies '61
Spiritism '61

Rafael Morena Alba
Exorcism's Daughter '74

Jean-Gabriel Albicocco
The Wanderer '67

Hans Albin
No Survivors, Please '63

Carlton J. Albright
Luther the Geek '90

Alan Alda
Betsy's Wedding '90
A New Life '88
Sweet Liberty '86
The Four Seasons '81

Thomas Alderman
The Severed Arm '73

Will Aldis
Stealing Home '88

Adell Aldrich
The Kid from Left Field '79

Robert Aldrich
...All the Marbles '81
The Frisco Kid '79
The Choirboys '77
Twilight's Last Gleaming '77
The Hustle '75
The Longest Yard '74
Ulzana's Raid '72
The Grissom Gang '71
Too Late the Hero '70
The Killing of Sister George '69
The Dirty Dozen '67
The Flight of the Phoenix '65
Hush, Hush, Sweet Charlotte '65
Four for Texas '63
Sodom and Gomorrah '62
What Ever Happened to Baby Jane? '62
Autumn Leaves '56

The Big Knife '55
Kiss Me Deadly '55
Apache '54
Vera Cruz '53

Goffredo Alessandrini
We the Living '42

Ottavio Alessi
The Seducers '70

Bill Alexander
Tartuffe '90

Jason Alexander
For Better or Worse '95

Tom Alexander
The Dark Dealer '95

Grigori Alexandrov
Que Viva Mexico '32
Ten Days That Shook the World '27

James Algar
Vanishing Prairie '54
The Adventures of Ichabod and Mr. Toad '49
The Legend of Sleepy Hollow '49

Sidney Algier
Wild Horse '31

Dan Algrant
Naked in New York '93

Marcello Aliprandi
Vatican Conspiracy '81

Howard Alk
Janis: A Film '74

Don Allan
Jungleground '95

Marc Allegret
Sois Belle et Tais-Toi '58
Mademoiselle Striptease '57
Lady Chatterley's Lover '55
The Love of Three Queens '54
Blanche Fury '48
Zou Zou '34
Fanny '32

Director Index

American Cyborg: Steel Warrior
'94
Solar Force '94
Going Bananas '88
Salsa '88
Dutch Treat '86
Last American Virgin '82
Hospital Massacre '81

Gordon Davidson
The Trial of Lee Harvey Oswald
'77
Trial of the Catonsville Nine '72

John Davidson
The Hanging Woman '72

John-Paul Davidson
Grave Indiscretions '96

Martin Davidson
Follow the River '95
Hard Promises '92
The Heart of Dixie '89
Long Gone '87
Eddie and the Cruisers '83
Hero at Large '80
The Lords of Flatbush '74

Gareth Davies
A Mind to Murder '96

Howard Davies
The Secret Rapture '94

John Davies
Devices and Desires '91
Kim '84
A Married Man '84

Terence Davies
The Neon Bible '95
The Long Day Closes '92
Distant Voices, Still Lives '88

Valentine Davies
The Benny Goodman Story '55

Andrew Davis
Chain Reaction '96
The Fugitive '93
Under Siege '92
The Package '89
Above the Law '88
Code of Silence '85
The Final Terror '83

Andy Davis
Steal Big, Steal Little '95

Beau Davis
Laser Mission '90

B.J. Davis
White Ghost '88

Charles Davis
Die Watching '93

Desmond Davis
Ordeal by Innocence '84
The Sign of Four '83
Clash of the Titans '81
Nice Girl Like Me '69

Eddie Davis
Color Me Dead '69

Gary Davis
Conflict of Interest '92

Julie Davis
Witchcraft 6: The Devil's
Mistress '94

Michael Paul Davis
Beanstalk '94

Ossie Davis
Gordon's War '73
Cotton Comes to Harlem '70

Philip Davis
Prime Suspect 5: Errors of
Judgment '96

Roy Davis
Surabaya Conspiracy '75

Tamra Davis
Billy Madison '94
CB4: The Movie '93
Guncrazy '92

Norman Dawn
Two Lost Worlds '50
Orphans of the North '40
Tundra '36

Vincent Dawn
Strike Commando '87

Caged Women '84
Rats '83

**Anthony (Antonio
Margheriti) Dawson**
Indio '90
Jungle Raiders '85
Tiger Joe '85
Codename: Wildgeese '84
Tornado '83
Yor, the Hunter from the Future
'83
Ark of the Sun God '82
Hunters of the Golden Cobra '82
Invasion of the Flesh Hunters
'82
The Last Hunter '80
The Squeeze '80
Killer Fish '79
The Rip Off '78
Death Rage '77
The Stranger and the Gunfighter
'76
Take a Hard Ride '75
Mr. Superinvisible '73
Seven Deaths in the Cat's Eye
'72
Web of the Spider '70
Lightning Bolt '67
Planet on the Prowl '65
The Virgin of Nuremberg '65
Wild, Wild Planet '65
Castle of Blood '64
Hercules, Prisoner of Evil '64
Assignment Outer Space '61
Battle of the Worlds '61

Ernest Day
Waltz Across Texas '83
Green Ice '81

Robert Day
The Quick and the Dead '87
Lady from Yesterday '85
Your Place or Mine '83
Peter and Paul '81
The Man with Bogart's Face '80
Walking Through the Fire '80
Murder by Natural Causes '79
The Grass is Always Greener
Over the Septic Tank '78
Initiation of Sarah '78
Death Stalk '74
Two-Way Stretch '60
First Man into Space '59
Corridors of Blood '58
The Haunted Strangler '58

Lyman Dayton
The Avenging '92
Dream Machine '91
Baker's Hawk '76

Jaime de Arminan
The Nest '80

**Jacques de
Baroncelli**
The French Way '40

Jan De Bont
Speed 2: Cruise Control '97
Twister '96
Speed '94

Philippe de Broca
The Green House '96
Louisiana '87
Jupiter's Thigh '81
Le Cavaleur '78
Dear Detective '77
Oldest Profession '67
The King of Hearts '66
That Man from Rio '64
Cartouche '62

Pierre de Celles
Pound Puppies and the Legend
of Big Paw '88

Ennio de Concini
Hitler: The Last Ten Days '73

Fred de Cordova
Frankie and Johnny '65
I'll Take Sweden '65
Bedtime for Bonzo '51

Paul de Cruccio
Desert Snow '89

Frank de Felitta
Scissors '91

Dark Night of the Scarecrow '81
The Two Worlds of Jenny Logan
'79

Eduardo de Filippo
Shoot Loud, Louder, I Don't
Understand! '66
Seven Deadly Sins '53

Michael de Gaetano
The Haunted '79
UFO: Target Earth '74

Rolf de Heer
Bad Boy Bubby '93
Dingo '90
Encounter at Raven's Gate '88

Ate De Jong
Highway to Hell '92
Drop Dead Fred '91
A Flight of Rainbirds '81

**Paula de
Koenigsberg**
Rate It X '86

**Hubert de la
Bouillerie**
The Right to Remain Silent '95

Eloy De La Iglesia
El Diputado '78

**Jose Antonio De La
Loma**
Street Warriors '87
Street Warriors, Part 2 '87
The Barcelona Kill '77

Robert De Lacy
Pardon My Gun '30

Charles De Latour
Impulse '55
The Limping Man '53

**Gerardo (Gerry) De
Leon**
Mad Doctor of Blood Island '69
Brides of the Beast '68
The Vampire People '66
Terror Is a Man '59

Marcus De Leon
The Big Squeeze '96
Kiss Me a Killer '91

Paul de Lussanet
Mysteries '84
Dear Boys '80

Alberto De Martino
Bloodlink '82
The Puma Man '80
The Chosen '77
The Tempter '74
New Mafia Boss '72
Scenes from a Murder '72
Dirty Heroes '71
Secret Agent 00 '67

Pierre De Moro
Hellhole '85
Savannah Smiles '82

Robert De Niro
A Bronx Tale '93

Manoel de Oliveira
The Convent '95

Oswald De Oliveira
Amazon Jail '85

Armando de Ossorio
Night of the Death Cult '75
People Who Own the Dark '75
Return of the Evil Dead '75
Horror of the Zombies '74
When the Screaming Stops '73
Tombs of the Blind Dead '72
Night of the Sorcerers '70
Fangs of the Living Dead '68

Frank De Palma
Private War '90

Guiseppe de Santis
Bitter Rice '49

Vittorio de Seta
Bandits of Orgosolo '61

Vittorio De Sica
The Garden of the Finzi-Continis
'71
Woman Times Seven '67

After the Fox '66
Marriage Italian Style '64
Yesterday, Today and Tomorrow
'64
Boccaccio '70 '62
Two Women '61
It Happened in the Park '56
The Roof '56
Umberto D '55
The Gold of Naples '54
Indiscretion of an American Wife
'54
Miracle in Milan '51
The Bicycle Thief '48
Shoeshine '47
The Children Are Watching Us
'44
Teresa Venerdi '41

Tom De Simone
Angel 3: The Final Chapter '88
Reform School Girls '86
The Concrete Jungle '82
Hell Night '81
Chatterbox '76
Terror in the Jungle '68

Steven E. de Souza
Street Fighter '94

Andre de Toth
The Mongols '60
Morgan the Pirate '60
The Indian Fighter '55
House of Wax '53
The Stranger Wore a Gun '53
Last of the Comanches '52
Springfield Rifle '52
Man in the Saddle '51
Pitfall '48
Ramrod '47
Dark Waters '44

Ralph De Vito
Family Enforcer '76

Elmo De Witt
Enemy Unseen '91

Basil Dean
21 Days '37
Lorna Doone '34

Charles Deane
Blonde Blackmailer '58

William Dear
Wild America '97
Angels in the Outfield '94
If Looks Could Kill '91
Harry and the Hendersons '87
Timerider '83

Basil Dearden
Mission: Monte Carlo '75
The Persuaders '71
The Man Who Haunted Himself
'70
The Assassination Bureau '69
Khartoum '66
Victim '61
The League of Gentlemen '60
Sapphire '59
The Smallest Show on Earth '57
Who Done It? '56
The Blue Lamp '49
Train of Events '49 ·
Captive Heart '47
Frieda '47
Dead of Night '45

James Dearden
A Kiss Before Dying '91
Pascali's Island '88
Cold Room '84

Frank Deasy
The Courier '88

John DeBello
Killer Tomatoes Eat France '91
Killer Tomatoes Strike Back '90
Return of the Killer Tomatoes!
'88
Happy Hour '87
Attack of the Killer Tomatoes '77

Gianfranco DeBosio
Moses '76

Tom DeCerchio
Celtic Pride '96

James D. Deck
Ravager '97

Henri Decoin
License to Kill '64

David DeCoteau
Puppet Master 3: Toulon's
Revenge '91
Lady Avenger '89
Dr. Alien '88
Creepozoids '87
Nightmare Sisters '87
Sorority Babes in the Slimeball
Bowl-A-Rama '87

Miles Deem
Jungle Master '56

**Allessandro
DeGaetano**
Project Metalbeast: DNA
Overload '94
Bloodbath in Psycho Town '89

Andre Degas
American Autobahn '84

Joseph DeGrasse
The Scarlet Car '17

Philip DeGuere
Misfits of Science '85
Dr. Strange '78

Jamil Dehlavi
Born of Fire '87

Mark Deimel
Perfect Match '88

Edward Dein
Curse of the Undead '59
The Leech Woman '59
Shack Out on 101 '55

Donna Deitch
Prison Stories: Women on the
Inside '91
The Women of Brewster Place
'89
Desert Hearts '86

Steve DeJarnatt
Miracle Mile '89
Cherry 2000 '88

Fred Dekker
RoboCop 3 '91
The Monster Squad '87
Night of the Creeps '86

Jack Del
A Session with the Committee
'69
The Committee '68

Peter Del Monte
Julia and Julia '87
Invitation au Voyage '82

Deborah Del Prete
Simple Justice '89

Roy Del Ruth
On Moonlight Bay '51
The West Point Story '50
Babe Ruth Story '48
Broadway Rhythm '44
DuBarry Was a Lady '43
The Chocolate Soldier '41
Topper Returns '41
Happy Landing '38
My Lucky Star '38
Broadway Melody of 1938 '37
On the Avenue '37
Born to Dance '36
Broadway Melody of 1936 '35
Kid Millions '34
Bureau of Missing Persons '33
Employees' Entrance '33
Lady Killer '33
Blessed Event '32
Blonde Crazy '31
The Maltese Falcon '31

Guillermo del Toro
Mimic '97
Cronos '94

Jean Delannoy
Bernadette '90
Imperial Venus '71
This Special Friendship '67
Love and the Frenchwoman '60
The Hunchback of Notre Dame
'57
La Symphonie Pastorale '46
Eternal Return '43

G.L. Eastman
Metamorphosis '90

Clint Eastwood
Absolute Power '97
The Bridges of Madison County '95
A Perfect World '93
Unforgiven '92
The Rookie '90
White Hunter, Black Heart '90
Bird '88
Heartbreak Ridge '86
Pale Rider '85
Sudden Impact '83
Firefox '82
Honkytonk Man '82
Bronco Billy '80
The Gauntlet '77
The Outlaw Josey Wales '76
The Eiger Sanction '75
High Plains Drifter '73
Play Misty for Me '71

Thom Eberhardt
Captain Ron '92
Gross Anatomy '89
The Night Before '88
Without a Clue '88
Night of the Comet '84
Sole Survivor '84

P. David Ebersole
Boys in Love '95

Ghasem Ebrahimian
The Suitors '88

Desire Ecare
Faces of Women '85

Nicolas Echevarria
Cabeza de Vaca '90

John L'Ecuyer
Curtis's Charm '96

Uli Edel
Rasputin: Dark Servant of Destiny '96
Tyson '95
Body of Evidence '92
Last Exit to Brooklyn '90
Christiane F. '82

Gustaf Edgren
Walpurgis Night '41

Don Edmunds
Terror on Tour '83
Bare Knuckles '77
Ilsa, She-Wolf of the SS '74
Tender Loving Care '73

Blake Edwards
Son of the Pink Panther '93
Switch '91
Peter Gunn '89
Skin Deep '89
Sunset '88
Blind Date '87
A Fine Mess '86
That's Life! '86
Micki & Maude '84
Curse of the Pink Panther '83
The Man Who Loved Women '83
Trail of the Pink Panther '82
Victor/Victoria '82
S.O.B. '81
10 '79
Revenge of the Pink Panther '78
The Pink Panther Strikes Again '76
Return of the Pink Panther '74
The Tamarind Seed '74
Wild Rovers '71
Darling Lili '70
The Party '68
What Did You Do in the War, Daddy? '66
The Great Race '65
The Pink Panther '64
A Shot in the Dark '64
Days of Wine and Roses '62
Experiment in Terror '62
Breakfast at Tiffany's '61
Operation Petticoat '59
Perfect Furlough '59
This Happy Feeling '58

Charles Edwards
The Flaming Teen-Age '56

Don Edwards
Black Cobra 3: The Manila Connection '90

George Edwards
The Attic '80

Harry Edwards
Baby Face Harry Langdon '26

Henry Edwards
The Private Secretary '35
Scrooge '35

Peter Edwards
A Mind to Kill '95

Robert Edwards
Thunder in the Pines '49

Christine Edzard
Little Dorrit, Film 1: Nobody's Fault '88
Little Dorrit, Film 2: Little Dorrit's Story '88

Arthur Egeli
Maxim Xul '91

Mark Egerton
The Winds of Jarrah '83

Colin Eggleston
The Wicked '89
Innocent Prey '88
Cassandra '87
Sky Pirates '87
Bellamy '80

Jan Egleson
The Last Hit '93
A Shock to the System '90
Roanoak '86
The Tender Age '84

Oleg Egorov
Osa '85

Atom Egoyan
The Sweet Hereafter '96
Exotica '94
Calendar '93
The Adjuster '91
Speaking Parts '89
Family Viewing '87
Next of Kin '84

Richard Eichberg
Night Birds '31

Franz Eichhorn
The Violent Years '56

Rafael Eisenman
Red Shoe Diaries 7: Burning Up '96
Red Shoe Diaries 3: Another Woman's Lipstick '93
Lake Consequence '92

Sergei Eisenstein
Ivan the Terrible, Part 2 '46
Ivan the Terrible, Part 1 '44
Alexander Nevsky '38
Que Viva Mexico '32
The General Line '29
Ten Days That Shook the World '27
The Battleship Potemkin '25
Strike '24

Nicolai Ekk
The Road to Life '31

George Elanjian, Jr.
Syngenor '90

Judit Elek
Maria's Day '84

Clifford S. Elfelt
Big Stakes '22

Richard Elfman
Shrunken Heads '94
Forbidden Zone '80

Michael Elias
Lush Life '94

Jan Eliasberg
Past Midnight '92

Larry Elikann
An Unexpected Family '96
Blue River '95
A Mother's Prayer '95
Tecumseh: The Last Warrior '95
Kiss of a Killer '93
The Story Lady '93

Fever '91
The Great Los Angeles Earthquake '91
One Against the Wind '91
Disaster at Silo 7 '88
God Bless the Child '88
Hands of a Stranger '87
Stamp of a Killer '87
Poison Ivy '85
Spraggue '84
Charlie and the Great Balloon Chase '82
The Great Wallendas '78

Harrison Ellenshaw
Dead Silence '90

Doug Ellin
Phat Beach '96

B. Ron Elliott
The Acid Eaters '67

Lang Elliott
Cage 2: The Arena of Death '94
The Private Eyes '80

Stephan Elliott
The Adventures of Priscilla, Queen of the Desert '94

Paul Elliotts
Great Adventure '75

Bob Ellis
The Nostradamus Kid '92
Warm Nights on a Slow-Moving Train '87

David R. Ellis
Homeward Bound 2: Lost in San Francisco '96

Joseph Ellison
Don't Go in the House '80

Javier Elorrieta
Blood and Sand '89

Maurice Elvey
The Obsessed '51
Beware of Pity '46
Phantom Fiend '35
Transatlantic Tunnel '35
The Evil Mind '34
Lily of Killarney '34

Cassian Elwes
Blue Flame '93

Tony Elwood
Road Kill USA '93

John Emerson
The Americano/Variety '25
Mystery of the Leaping Fish/ Chess Fever '25
The Americano '17
Down to Earth '17
Reaching for the Moon '17
His Picture in the Papers '16
The Social Secretary '16

Dick Emery
Yellow Submarine '68

Robert Emery
Ride in a Pink Car '74
Scream Bloody Murder '72

Ian Emes
Knights & Emeralds '87

Roland Emmerich
Independence Day '96
Stargate '94
Universal Soldier '92
Moon 44 '90
Ghost Chase '88
Making Contact '86

Robert Enders
Stevie '78

Cy Endfield
Zulu '64
Mysterious Island '61
Try and Get Me '50
The Underworld Story '50

Erich Engel
The Blum Affair '48

David Engelbach
America 3000 '86

Harrison Engle
Indomitable Teddy Roosevelt '83

John English
Hills of Utah '51
Valley of Fire '51
Cow Town '50
Riders of the Whistling Pines '49
Rim of the Canyon '49
Loaded Pistols '48
Utah '45
Captain America '44
Death Valley Manhunt '43
Man from Thunder River '43
Raiders of Sunset Pass '43
King of the Texas Rangers '41
Doctor Satan's Robot '40
Drums of Fu Manchu '40
Zorro's Fighting Legion '39
Daredevils of the Red Circle '38
Fighting Devil Dogs '38
The Lone Ranger '38
Arizona Days '37
Dick Tracy '37
Zorro Rides Again '37
Whistling Bullets '36

George Englund
Dixie: Changing Habits '85
The Vegas Strip Wars '84
A Christmas to Remember '78
Zachariah '70
The Ugly American '63

Robert Englund
976-EVIL '88

Robert Enrico
Old Gun '76
Le Secret '74
Jailbird's Vacation '65
Les Grandes Gueules '65
An Occurrence at Owl Creek Bridge/Coup de Grace '62
Red Balloon/Occurrence at Owl Creek Bridge '62

Ray Enright
Man from Cairo '54
Coroner Creek '48
Return of the Bad Men '48
South of St. Louis '48
Trail Street '47
China Sky '44
Gung Ho! '43
The Iron Major '43
The Spoilers '42
Earthworm Tractors '36
Dames '34
Tomorrow at Seven '33

Ildiko Enyedi
My Twentieth Century '90

Nora Ephron
Michael '96
Mixed Nuts '94
Sleepless in Seattle '93
This Is My Life '92

Jean Epstein
La Chute de la Maison Usher '28

Marcelo Epstein
Body Rock '84

Robert Epstein
The Celluloid Closet '95
Common Threads: Stories from the Quilt '89
Times of Harvey Milk '83

Rene Eram
Voodoo '95

Richard Erdman
Brothers O'Toole '73

Victor Erice
Spirit of the Beehive '73

A.F. Erickson
The Lone Star Ranger '30

Gordon Eriksen
The Big Dis '89

Charles Erman
Just Me & You '78

John Erman
The Boys Next Door '96
Breathing Lessons '94
Scarlett '94
Carolina Skeletons '92
Our Sons '91
When the Time Comes '91
The Last Best Year '90

Stella '89
The Attic: The Hiding of Anne Frank '88
An Early Frost '85
A Streetcar Named Desire '84
Eleanor: First Lady of the World '82
My Old Man '79
Child of Glass '78
Alexander: The Other Side of Dawn '77
Green Eyes '76

Frederic Ermler
No Greater Love '43

George Erschbamer
Flinch '93
Final Round '93
SnakeEater 3: His Law '92
SnakeEater '89
SnakeEater 2: The Drug Buster '89

Jack Ersgard
Invisible: The Chronicles of Benjamin Knight '93

Joakim Ersgard
Mandroid '93
The Visitors '89

Chester Erskine
Androcles and the Lion '52
A Girl in Every Port '52
Egg and I '47
Frankie and Johnny '36
Midnight '34

Dwain Esper
The Worst of Hollywood: Vol. 1 '90
Marihuana '36
Maniac '34

Jett C. Espirtu
P.O.W. Deathcamp '89

Joe Esposito
South Beach Academy '96

Harry Essex
The Cremators '72
Octaman '71

Emilio Estevez
The War at Home '96
Men at Work '90
Wisdom '87

Alexander Esway
Mauvaise Graine '33

Ray Etheridge
The Vernonia Incident '89

Corey Michael Eubanks
Two Bits & Pepper '95
Bigfoot: The Unforgettable Encounter '94

Bruce A. Evans
Kuffs '92

David Mickey Evans
First Kid '96
The Sandlot '93

John Evans
Blackjack '78
Black Godfather '74

Marc Evans
Thicker Than Water '93

Roger Evans
Jet Benny Show '86

D.S. Everett
Running Brave '83

Tim Everitt
Fatally Yours '95

Valie Export
The Practice of Love '84
Menschenfrauen '80
Invisible Adversaries '77

Richard Eyre
Loose Connections '87
Singleton's Pluck '84
The Ploughman's Lunch '83

John Eyres
Judge & Jury '96
Project Shadowchaser 3000 '95
Night Siege Project: Shadowchaser 2 '94

Fred Gallo
Machine Gun Blues '95
Lady in Waiting '94
Dracula Rising '93
The Finishing Touch '92
Dead Space '90

George Gallo
Trapped In Paradise '94
29th Street '91

Carmine Gallone
Carthage in Flames '60

Samuel Gallu
The Man Outside '68
Theatre of Death '67

Abel Gance
The Battle of Austerlitz '60
J'Accuse '37
Napoleon '27
The Torture of Silence '17

Pierre Gang
Sous Sol '96

Albert C. Gannaway
Man or Gun '58
Daniel Boone: Trail Blazer '56
Hidden Guns '56

Christophe Gans
H.P. Lovecraft's Necronomicon:
Book of the Dead '93

Armand Garabidian
Silk Degrees '94

David Garcia
Sex Crimes '92

Michael Garcia
Armageddon: The Final
Challenge '94

Nicole Garcia
The Favorite Son '94
Every Other Weekend '91

Bud Gardner
Model Behavior '82

Herb Gardner
I'm Not Rappaport '96
The Goodbye People '83

Richard Harding Gardner
Sherlock: Undercover Dog '94

Leo Garen
The Shrieking '73

Patrick Garland
A Doll's House '89

Lee Garmes
Actors and Sin '52
Angels Over Broadway '40
Dreaming Lips '37

Tay Garnett
Challenge To Be Free '76
The Big Push '75
Main Street to Broadway '53
One Minute to Zero '52
Cause for Alarm '51
A Connecticut Yankee in King
Arthur's Court '49
The Postman Always Rings
Twice '46
The Valley of Decision '45
Mrs. Parkington '44
Bataan '43
Cheers for Miss Bishop '41
Seven Sinners '40
Slightly Honorable '40
Eternally Yours '39
Joy of Living '38
Stand-In '37
China Seas '35
The Flying Fool '29

Tony Garnett
Deep in the Heart '83

Lila Garrett
Terraces '77

Otis Garrett
Danger on the Air '38

Roy Garrett
White Slave '86
Eyes Behind the Stars '72

Mick Garris
Stephen King's The Stand '94

Sleepwalkers '92
Psycho 4: The Beginning '90
Critters 2: The Main Course '88

Andrew Garroni
Body of Influence '93

Harry Garson
The Worldly Madonna '22
Mid-Channel '20

John Garwood
Violent Zone '89

Jerome Gary
Traxx '87
Stripper '86

Louis Gasnier
Murder on the Yukon '40
Reefer Madness '38
Topaze '33
Kismet '20

Mark Gasper
An Empty Bed '90

Leon Gast
When We Were Kings '96

Mae Gaston
Seven Keys to Baldpate '17

Nils Gaup
North Star '96
Shipwrecked '90
Pathfinder '87

Roberto Gavaldon
The Littlest Outlaw '54

Eleanor Gaver
Slipping into Darkness '88

Victor Gaviria
Rodrigo D.: No Future '91

Joe Gayton
Wes Craven Presents Mind
Ripper '95
Warm Summer Rain '89

Armand Gazarian
Prison Planet '92
Game of Survival '89

Gyula Gazdag
Stand Off '89
A Hungarian Fairy Tale '87

Glenn Gebhard
Desert Steel '94
One Last Run '89

Dieter Geissler
Deadly Game '83

Bruce Geller
The Savage Bees '76

Augusto Genina
Prix de Beaute '30
Cyrano de Bergerac '25

Arnaldo Genoino
Herod the Great '60

John Gentil
Battle of Valiant '63

Giacomo Gentilomo
Hercules Against the Moon Men
'64

George W. George
James Dean Story '57

Jim George
Rover Dangerfield '91

Matthew George
Under the Gun '95

Peter George
Surf Nazis Must Die '87

Terry George
Some Mother's Son '96

Maurice Geraghty
Sword of Monte Cristo '51

Fred Gerber
Rent-A-Kid '95

Haile Gerima
Ashes and Embers '82
Bush Mama '76

Marion Gering
Thunder in the City '37

Pietro Germi
Alfredo, Alfredo '72
Seduced and Abandoned '64

Divorce—Italian Style '62
Four Ways Out '57

Chris Gerolmo
Citizen X '95

Clyde Geronomi
101 Dalmatians '61
Sleeping Beauty '59
Alice in Wonderland '51
The Adventures of Ichabod and
Mr. Toad '49
The Legend of Sleepy Hollow
'49

Peter Gerretsen
Night Friend '87

Theodore Gershuny
Silent Night, Bloody Night '73

Nicolas Gessner
Black Water '94
Quicker Than the Eye '88
It Rained All Night the Day I Left
'78
The Little Girl Who Lives Down
the Lane '76
Someone Behind the Door '71
12 Plus 1 '70
The Peking Blond '68

Steven Gethers
The Hillside Strangler '89
Jenny's War '85
Jacqueline Bouvier Kennedy '81
Damien: The Leper Priest '80
Billy: Portrait of a Street Kid '77

Francis Giacobetti
Emmanuelle 4 '84
Emmanuelle, the Joys of a
Woman '76

David Giancola
Time Chasers '95

Alfredo Gianelli
Mother Doesn't Always Know
Best '60s

Duncan Gibbins
A Case for Murder '93
Eve of Destruction '90
Fire with Fire '86

Pamela Gibbons
Midnight Dancer '87

Rodney Gibbons
The Neighbor '93

Alan Gibson
The Charmer '89
Martin's Day '85
Silent Scream '84
The Two Faces of Evil '82
A Woman Called Golda '82
The Satanic Rites of Dracula '73
Twinsanity '70

Brian Gibson
The Juror '96
What's Love Got to Do with It?
'93
The Josephine Baker Story '90
Murderers Among Us: The
Simon Wiesenthal Story '89
Poltergeist 2: The Other Side '86
Breaking Glass '80

Mel Gibson
Braveheart '95
The Man Without a Face '93

Robert Gibson
Snow: The Movie '83

Tom Gibson
Singing Buckaroo '37

Gregory Gieras
The Whispering '94

Brian Gilbert
Tom & Viv '94
Not Without My Daughter '90
Vice Versa '88
The French Lesson '86
Sharma & Beyond '84

Lewis Gilbert
Haunted '95
Stepping Out '91
Shirley Valentine '89
Not Quite Paradise '86
Educating Rita '83
Moonraker '79

The Spy Who Loved Me '77
Paul and Michelle '74
Friends '71
The Adventurers '70
You Only Live Twice '67
Alfie '66
Damn the Defiant '62
Sink the Bismarck '60
Ferry to Hong Kong '59
A Cry from the Streets '57
Reach for the Sky '56
Cast a Dark Shadow '55
The Sea Shall Not Have Them
'55
Tough Guy '53

David Giler
Black Bird '75

David Giles
A Murder Is Announced '87
Mansfield Park '85
Vanity Fair '67

Tom Giles
Journey Through Rosebud '72

Joseph Gilford
Max '79

Mark Gilhuis
Bloody Wednesday '87

Tony Jiti Gill
Murder-in-Law '92

Stuart Gillard
Poltergeist: The Legacy '96
The Outer Limits: Sandkings '95
Teenage Mutant Ninja Turtles 3
'93
A Man Called Sarge '90
Paradise '82

Jeff Gillen
Deranged '74

Terry Gilliam
12 Monkeys '95
The Fisher King '91
The Adventures of Baron
Munchausen '89
Brazil '85
Time Bandits '81
Jabberwocky '77
Monty Python and the Holy Grail
'75

Sidney Gilliat
Endless Night '71
The Great St. Trinian's Train
Robbery '66
Only Two Can Play '62
Green for Danger '47

John Gilling
Night Caller from Outer Space
'66
Plague of the Zombies '66
The Reptile '66
Where the Bullets Fly '66
Mania '60
It Takes a Thief '59
The Gamma People '56
The Gilded Cage '54
White Fire '53
My Son, the Vampire '52
No Trace '50

Stuart Gilmore
The Half-Breed '51
Hot Lead '51
The Virginian '46

Frank D. Gilroy
The Gig '85
Once in Paris... '79
From Noon Till Three '76
Desperate Characters '71

Milton Moses Ginsberg
Werewolf of Washington '73

Brad F. Ginter
Flesh Feast '69

Robert Ginty
Vietnam, Texas '90
Bounty Hunters '89

Christian Gion
Here Comes Santa Claus '84

Jose Giovanni
Boomerang '76
Gypsy '75

Marita Giovanni
Bar Girls '95

Buddy Giovinazzo
Combat Shock '84

Bob Giraldi
Hiding Out '87
Club Med '83

Franco Giraldi
A Minute to Pray, A Second to
Die '67

Andre Girard
Qui Etes Vous, Mr. Sorge? '61

Bernard Girard
Little Moon & Jud McGraw '78
Mind Snatchers '72
Hard Frame '70
A Name for Evil '70
Dead Heat on a Merry-Go-
Round '66

Francois Girard
32 Short Films about Glenn
Gould '93

Michael Paul Girard
Witchcraft 9: Bitter Flesh '96
Witchcraft 7: Judgement Hour
'95

Bernard Giraudeau
Gone with the West '72

William Girdler
The Manitou '78
Day of the Animals '77
Grizzly '76
Sheba, Baby '75
Asylum of Satan '72
Three on a Meathook '72

Francois Girod
The Elegant Criminal '92
L'Etat Sauvage '78
Infernal Trio '74

Marcel Gisler
The Blue Hour '91

Wyndham Gittens
Tim Tyler's Luck '37

Paul Michael Glaser
Kazaam '96
The Air Up There '94
The Cutting Edge '92
The Running Man '87
Band of the Hand '86
The Amazons '84

Arnold Glassman
Visions of Light: The Art of
Cinematography '93

Leslie Linka Glatter
Now and Then '95
State of Emergency '94
Into the Homeland '87

Richard Glatzer
Grief '94

Michie Gleason
Summer Heat '87

John Glen
Aces: Iron Eagle 3 '92
Christopher Columbus: The
Discovery '92
License to Kill '89
The Living Daylights '87
A View to a Kill '85
Octopussy '83
For Your Eyes Only '81

John Glenister
After Julius '78

Bert Glennon
South of Santa Fe '32
Paradise Island '30

Peter Glenville
The Comedians '67
Hotel Paradiso '66
Becket '64
Summer and Smoke '61
Me and the Colonel '58
The Prisoner '55

James Glickenhaus
Timemaster '95
Slaughter of the Innocents '93
McBain '91
Shakedown '88

Man from Texas '39
Roll, Wagons, Roll '39
Renfrew on the Great White
Trail '38
Rollin' Plains '38
Utah Trail '38
Valley of Terror '38
Renfrew of the Royal Mounted
'37
Gun Play '36
Outlaws of the Range '36
Cowboy & the Bandit '35
Western Frontier '35
Whispering Shadow '33
Beyond the Trail '26

Jean Herman
Butterfly Affair '71
Honor Among Thieves '68

Mark Herman
Brassed Off '96
Blame It on the Bellboy '92

Charles Herman-Wurmfeld
Fanci's Persuasion '95

Jaime Humberto Hermosillo
The Summer of Miss Forbes '88
Dona Herlinda & Her Son '86

Miguel Hermoso
Marbella '85

Tibor Hernadi
Felix the Cat: The Movie '91

Denis Heroux
Naked Massacre '80s
The Uncanny '78

Mark Herrier
Popcorn '89

Rowdy Herrington
Striking Distance '93
Gladiator '92
Road House '89
Jack's Back '87

W. Blake Herron
Skin Art '93

Joel Hershman
Hold Me, Thrill Me, Kiss Me '93

Marshall Herskovitz
Jack the Bear '93

Gene Hertel
Showgirl Murders '95

Michael Herz
The Toxic Avenger, Part 2 '89
The Toxic Avenger, Part 3: The
Last Temptation of Toxie '89
Troma's War '88
The Toxic Avenger '86
Stuck on You '84
First Turn On '83
Sugar Cookies '77

John Herzfeld
Two Days in the Valley '96
Casualties of Love: The "Long
Island Lolita" Story '93
The Preppie Murder '89
A Father's Revenge '89
Two of a Kind '83

Werner Herzog
Where the Green Ants Dream
'84
Fitzcarraldo '82
Woyzeck '78
Stroszek '77
Every Man for Himself & God
Against All '75
Heart of Glass '74
Aguirre, the Wrath of God '72
Signs of Life '68

David Hess
To All a Goodnight '80

Eugene Hess
Don't Do It '94

Jon Hess
Excessive Force '93
Assassin '89
The Lawless Land '88
Watchers '88

Gordon Hessler
Journey of Honor '91
Tales of the Unexpected '91
The Girl in a Swing '89
Out on Bail '89
The Misfit Brigade '87
Rage of Honor '87
Pray for Death '85
Escape from El Diablo '83
KISS Meets the Phantom of the
Park '78
Puzzle '78
Secrets of Three Hungry Wives
'78
Betrayal '74
Medusa '74
Golden Voyage of Sinbad '73
Embassy '72
Murders in the Rue Morgue '71
Cry of the Banshee '70
Scream and Scream Again '70
The Oblong Box '69

Charlton Heston
A Man for All Seasons '88
Mother Lode '82
Antony and Cleopatra '73

Fraser Heston
Alaska '96
Needful Things '93
The Crucifer of Blood '91
Treasure Island '89

Neil Hetherington
Black Terrorist '85

David L. Hewitt
The Lucifer Complex '78
Alien Massacre '67
Journey to the Center of Time
'67
Monsters Crash the Pajama
Party '65
Horrors of the Red Planet '64

Jean Hewitt
Blood of Dracula's Castle '69

Pete Hewitt
Tom and Huck '95
Wild Palms '93
Bill & Ted's Bogus Journey '91

Rod Hewitt
The Dangerous '95
Verne Miller '88

Douglas Heyes
Powder Keg '70

Laurent Heynemann
The Old Lady Who Walked in
the Sea '91
Birgitt Haas Must Be Killed '83

Jesse Hibbs
Walk the Proud Land '56
To Hell and Back '55

Winston Hibler
Charlie, the Lonesome Cougar
'67

Jochen Hick
Via Appia '92

George Hickenlooper
The Low Life '95
The Ghost Brigade '93
Hearts of Darkness: A
Filmmaker's Apocalypse '91

Anthony Hickox
Invasion of Privacy '96
Payback '94
Full Eclipse '93
Warlock: The Armageddon '93
Hellraiser 3: Hell on Earth '92
Sundown '91
Waxwork 2: Lost in Time '91
Waxwork '88

Douglas Hickox
Blackout '85
Sins '85
Mistral's Daughter '84
The Hound of the Baskervilles
'83
Zulu Dawn '79
Sky Riders '76
Brannigan '75
Theatre of Blood '73

Entertaining Mr. Sloane '70

James D.R. Hickox
Children of the Corn 3: Urban
Harvest '95

Scott Hicks
Shine '95

Howard Higgin
Hell's House '32
Painted Desert '31
High Voltage '29
The Racketeer '29
Power '28

Colin Higgins
The Best Little Whorehouse in
Texas '82
9 to 5 '80
Foul Play '78

Nat Hiken
The Love God? '70
Car 54, Where Are You? '61

Claudio Guerin Hill
Bell from Hell '74

George Hill
The Big House '30

George Roy Hill
Funny Farm '88
The Little Drummer Girl '84
The World According to Garp '82
A Little Romance '79
Slap Shot '77
The Great Waldo Pepper '75
The Sting '73
Slaughterhouse Five '72
Butch Cassidy and the
Sundance Kid '69
Thoroughly Modern Millie '67
Hawaii '66
The World of Henry Orient '64
Toys in the Attic '63
Period of Adjustment '62
Min & Bill '30

Jack Hill
Switchblade Sisters '75
Foxy Brown '74
The Swinging Cheerleaders '74
Coffy '73
The Big Bird Cage '72
The Big Doll House '71
The Fear Chamber '68
Portrait in Terror '66
Track of the Vampire '66
Spider Baby '64

James Hill
The Wild and the Free '80
The Belstone Fox '73
Black Beauty '71
The Corrupt Ones '67
Born Free '66
A Study in Terror '66
Seaside Swingers '65
Trial & Error '62

Robert F. "Bob" Hill
East Side Kids '40
Wild Horse Canyon '39
Cheyenne Rides Again '38
Flash Gordon: Mars Attacks the
World '38
Man's Country '38
The Phantom of the Range '38
Whirlwind Horseman '38
Feud of the Trail '37
The Roamin' Cowboy '37
Blake of Scotland Yard '36
A Face in the Fog '36
Kelly of the Secret Service '36
Prison Shadows '36
Rip Roarin' Buckaroo '36
Rogue's Gallery '36
Danger Trails '35
Queen of the Jungle '35
Tarzan the Fearless '33
Come On Danger! '32

Sinclair Hill
Greek Street '30

Terence Hill
Lucky Luke '94

Walter Hill
Last Man Standing '96
Wild Bill '95
Geronimo: An American Legend
'93

Trespass '92
Another 48 Hrs. '90
Tales from the Crypt, Vol. 3 '90
Johnny Handsome '89
Tales from the Crypt '89
Red Heat '88
Extreme Prejudice '87
Crossroads '86
Brewster's Millions '85
Streets of Fire '84
48 Hrs. '82
Southern Comfort '81
The Long Riders '80
The Warriors '79
The Driver '78
Hard Times '75

Arthur Hiller
Carpool '96
Married to It '93
The Babe '92
Taking Care of Business '90
See No Evil, Hear No Evil '89
Outrageous Fortune '87
The Lonely Guy '84
Teachers '84
Romantic Comedy '83
Author! Author! '82
Making Love '82
The In-Laws '79
Nightwing '79
Silver Streak '76
The Man in the Glass Booth '75
Man of La Mancha '72
The Hospital '71
Plaza Suite '71
Love Story '70
The Out-of-Towners '70
Popi '69
Promise Her Anything '66
Tobruk '66
The Americanization of Emily '64
The Miracle of the White
Stallions '63
The Wheeler Dealers '63

Richard Hilliard
Psychomania '63

David Michael Hillman
The Strangeness '85

William B. Hillman
Ragin' Cajun '90
Double Exposure '82
Photographer '75

David Hills
Quest for the Mighty Sword '90
Blade Master '84
Ator the Fighting Eagle '83

Paul Hills
Boston Kickout '95

Lambert Hillyer
Range Renegades '48
Sundown Riders '48
Hat Box Mystery '47
Land of the Lawless '47
Border Bandits '46
Gentleman from Texas '46
South of the Rio Grande '45
The Stranger from Pecos '45
Partners of the Trail '44
Range Law '44
Six Gun Gospel '43
Texas Kid '43
Gang Bullets '38
Dracula's Daughter '36
The Invisible Ray '36
Fighting Fool '32
Hello Trouble '32
White Eagle '32
The Shock '23
Three Word Brand '21
Toll Gate '20
Wagon Tracks '19

Arthur Hilton
Cat Women of the Moon '53
Return of Jesse James '50

Howard Himelstein
Power of Attorney '94

Charles Hines
The Speed Spook '24

Bill Hinzman
Revenge of the Living Zombies
'88

Alexander Gregory Hippolyte
Animal Instincts 3: The
Seductress '96
Object of Obsession '95
Animal Instincts 2 '94
Secret Games 3 '94
Undercover '94
Mirror Images 2 '93
Secret Games 2: The Escort '93
Animal Instincts '92
Night Rhythms '92
Secret Games '92
Carnal Crimes '91
Mirror Images '91

Bettina Hirsch
Munchies '87

Ray Hirschman
Plutonium Baby '87

Leslie Hiscott
Department Store '35
The Triumph of Sherlock
Holmes '35

Alfred Hitchcock
Family Plot '76
Frenzy '72
Topaz '69
Torn Curtain '66
Marnie '64
The Birds '63
Psycho '60
North by Northwest '59
Vertigo '58
The Man Who Knew Too Much
'56
The Wrong Man '56
To Catch a Thief '55
The Trouble with Harry '55
Dial "M" for Murder '54
Rear Window '54
I Confess '53
Strangers on a Train '51
Stage Fright '50
Under Capricorn '49
Rope '48
The Paradine Case '47
Notorious '46
Spellbound '45
Alfred Hitchcock's Aventure
Malgache '44
Alfred Hitchcock's Bon Voyage
'44
Lifeboat '44
Shadow of a Doubt '43
Saboteur '42
Mr. & Mrs. Smith '41
Suspicion '41
Foreign Correspondent '40
Rebecca '40
Jamaica Inn '39
The Lady Vanishes '38
Young and Innocent '37
Sabotage '36
The Secret Agent '36
The 39 Steps '35
The Man Who Knew Too Much
'34
No. 17 '32
Rich and Strange '32
Skin Game '31
Juno and the Paycock '30
Murder '30
Blackmail '29
The Manxman '29
Champagne '28
The Farmer's Wife '28
Three by Hitchcock '28
Easy Virtue '27
The Ring '27
The Lodger '26

Carl K. Hittleman
Kentucky Rifle '55

Rupert Hitzig
Backstreet Dreams '90
Night Visitor '89

Jack B. Hively
California Gold Rush '81
The Adventures of Huckleberry
Finn '78
Starbird and Sweet William '73
Lassie: Adventures of Neeka '68

David Irving
Night of the Cyclone '90
Cannon Movie Tales: Sleeping
　Beauty '89
Cannon Movie Tales: The
　Emperor's New Clothes '89
C.H.U.D. 2: Bud the Chud '89
Rumpelstiltskin '86
Goodbye Cruel World '82

Richard Irving
The Jesse Owens Story '84
The Art of Crime '75
Columbo: Prescription Murder
　'67

James Isaac
The Horror Show '89

Ronnie Isaacs
Warriors from Hell '90

Antonio Isasi
Vengeance '86
Ricco '74

Robert Iscove
Mission of the Shark '91
The Lawrenceville Stories '80s
The Little Mermaid '84
Puss 'n Boots '84

Gerald I. Isenberg
Seizure: The Story of Kathy
　Morris '82

Wayne Isham
For Those About to Rock:
　Monsters in Moscow '91

Sogo Ishii
Angel Dust '96

Neal Israel
Surf Ninjas '93
Breaking the Rules '92
Combat Academy '86
Moving Violations '85
Bachelor Party '84
Americathon '79
Tunnelvision '76

Peter Israelson
Side Out '90

Juzo Itami
Minbo—Or the Gentle Art of
　Japanese Extortion '92
A Taxing Woman's Return '88
A Taxing Woman '87
Tampopo '86
The Funeral '84

Kenneth Ives
Poldark '75

James Ivory
Surviving Picasso '96
Jefferson in Paris '94
The Remains of the Day '93
Howard's End '92
Mr. & Mrs. Bridge '90
Slaves of New York '89
Maurice '87
A Room with a View '86
The Courtesans of Bombay '85
The Bostonians '84
Heat and Dust '82
Quartet '81
Jane Austen in Manhattan '80
The Europeans '79
Hullabaloo Over Georgie &
　Bonnie's Pictures '78
Roseland '77
Autobiography of a Princess '75
Wild Party '74
Savages '72
Bombay Talkie '70
Shakespeare Wallah '65
The Householder '63

David Jablin
National Lampoon's Favorite
　Deadly Sins '95

Arnaldo Jabor
I Love You '81

Fred Jackman
No Man's Law '27
King of the Wild Horses '24

David S. Jackson
Detonator 2: Night Watch '95
Detonator '93

Donald G. Jackson
Return to Frogtown '92
Roller Blade '85
The Demon Lover '77

Douglas Jackson
Natural Enemy '96
The Paperboy '94
Stalked '94
Deadbolt '92
Whispers '89

G. Philip Jackson
Replikator: Cloned to Kill '94

George Jackson
House Party 2: The Pajama Jam
　'91

Horace Jackson
The Bus Is Coming '72

Jalil Jackson
Lady Terminator '89

Larry Jackson
Bugs Bunny Superstar '75

Lewis Jackson
Terror in Toyland '85

Mick Jackson
Volcano '97
Indictment: The McMartin Trial
　'95
Clean Slate '94
The Bodyguard '92
L.A. Story '91
Chattahoochee '89
Yuri Nosenko, KGB '86
Threads '85

Mike Jackson
Blood Tracks '86

Pat Jackson
King Arthur, the Young Warlord
　'75
What a Carve-Up! '62
Encore '52

Peter Jackson
The Frighteners '96
Heavenly Creatures '94
Dead Alive '93
Meet the Feebles '89
Bad Taste '88

Philip Jackson
Project: Genesis '93

Wilfred Jackson
Cinderella '50

Alan Jacobs
Nina Takes a Lover '94

Harry Jacobs
Rebel High '88

Jerry P. Jacobs
A Dangerous Place '94

John Jacobs
Rocket to the Moon '86

Jon Jacobs
The Girl with the Hungry Eyes
　'94

**Lawrence-Hilton
Jacobs**
Quiet Fire '91
Angels of the City '89

Nicholas A.E. Jacobs
The Refrigerator '91

Werner Jacobs
Heidi '65

Rick Jacobson
Night Hunter '95
Shadow Warriors '95
Suspect Device '95
Bloodfist 6: Ground Zero '94
Ring of Fire 3: Lion Strike '94
Star Quest '94
The Unborn 2 '94
Full Contact '93

Anders Jacobsson
Evil Ed '96

Irving Jacoby
Snow Treasure '67

Joseph Jacoby
Great Bank Hoax '78
Hurry Up or I'll Be Thirty '73

Gualtiero Jacopetti
Mondo Cane 2 '64
Mondo Cane '63

Just Jaeckin
The Perils of Gwendoline '84
Lady Chatterley's Lover '81
The French Woman '79
The Story of O '75
Emmanuelle '74

Stanley R. Jaffe
Without a Trace '83

Henry Jaglom
Last Summer In the Hamptons
　'96
Babyfever '94
Venice, Venice '92
Eating '90
New Year's Day '89
Someone to Love '87
Always '85
Can She Bake a Cherry Pie? '83
National Lampoon Goes to the
　Movies '81
Sitting Ducks '80
Tracks '76

Sam Jaimes
Good Grief, Charlie Brown '83
Happy New Year, Charlie Brown
　'82

Patrick Jamain
Honeymoon '87

Alan James
Red Barry '38
Lucky Terror '36
When a Man Sees Red '34
Phantom Thunderbolt '33
Fargo Express '32
The Phantom '31
Backfire '22

Bob James
Alien Seed '89

Pedr James
Martin Chuzzlewit '94

Steve James
Prefontaine '96
Hoop Dreams '94

Jerry Jameson
Fire and Rain '89
The Cowboy & the Ballerina '84
Starflight One '83
Hotline '82
Killing at Hell's Gate '81
High Noon: Part 2 '80
Raise the Titanic '80
Sniper '75
The Bat People '74
Hurricane '74
Terror on the 40th Floor '74
Dirt Gang '71

Miklos Jancso
Hungarian Rhapsody '78
The Red and the White '68
The Round Up '66

Gerhard Janda
Tea For Three '84

Conrad Janis
November Conspiracy '96

Annabel Jankel
Super Mario Bros. '93
D.O.A. '88

Stole Jankovic
Hell River '75

Victor Janos
Last House on Dead End Street
　'77

Derek Jarman
Blue '93
Wittgenstein '93
Edward II '92
The Garden '90
Aria '88
The Last of England '87
Caravaggio '86
Sebastiane '79

Jim Jarmusch
Dead Man '95
Night on Earth '91
Mystery Train '89
Down by Law '86

Permanent Vacation '84
Stranger than Paradise '84

Charles Jarrott
Danielle Steel's Changes '91
Lucy and Desi: Before the
　Laughter '91
Night of the Fox '90
The Woman He Loved '88
Poor Little Rich Girl: The
　Barbara Hutton Story '87
Boy in Blue '86
The Amateur '82
Condorman '81
The Last Flight of Noah's Ark '80
The Other Side of Midnight '77
The Littlest Horse Thieves '76
The Dove '74
Anne of the Thousand Days '69
Strange Case of Dr. Jekyll & Mr.
　Hyde '68

Ilkka Jarvilaturi
City Unplugged '95

Vojtech Jasny
The Great Land of Small '86
All My Good Countrymen '68

Leigh Jason
The Choppers '61
Lost Honeymoon '47
Out of the Blue '47
Lady for a Night '42
Mad Miss Manton '38
The Bride Walks Out '36
That Girl from Paris '36
High Gear '33

Will Jason
Everybody's Dancin' '50

Vadim Jean
Leon the Pig Farmer '93
Nightscare '91

Roland S. Jefferson
Perfume '91

Tom Jeffrey
The Odd Angry Shot '79
Weekend of Shadows '77

Herbert Jeffries
World of the Depraved '67

Lionel Jeffries
Water Babies '79
Wombling Free '77
Amazing Mr. Blunden '72
The Railway Children '70

Richard Jeffries
Blood Tide '82

Andras Jeles
The Little Valentino '79

Bunker Jenkins
Space Ninja: Sword of the
　Space Ark '81

Michael Jenkins
Sweet Talker '91
Rebel '85

Patrick Jenkins
The Gambler & the Lady '52

Roger Jenkins
Poldark 2 '75

**Astrid Henning
Jensen**
Boy of Two Worlds '70

Johnny E. Jensen
The Lazarus Man '96

Leopold Jessner
Backstairs '21

Alain Jessua
The Killing Game '67

Jean-Marie Jeunet
The City of Lost Children '95
Delicatessen '92

Norman Jewison
Bogus '96
Only You '94
Other People's Money '91
In Country '89
Moonstruck '87
Agnes of God '85
A Soldier's Story '84
Best Friends '82
And Justice for All '79

F.I.S.T. '78
Rollerball '75
Jesus Christ, Superstar '73
Fiddler on the Roof '71
The Thomas Crown Affair '68
In the Heat of the Night '67
The Russians are Coming, the
　Russians are Coming '66
The Cincinnati Kid '65
Send Me No Flowers '64
The Thrill of It All! '63
40 Pounds of Trouble '62

**Ruth Prawer
Jhabvala**
The Courtesans of Bombay '8?

Huang Jianxin
The Wooden Man's Bride '94

Neal Jimenez
The Waterdance '91

Orlando Jiminez-Le:
8-A '92

Robert Jiras
I Am the Cheese '83

Duan Jishun
The Go-Masters '82

Mike Jittlov
The Wizard of Speed and Time
　'88

Leo Joannon
Utopia '51

Phil Joanou
Heaven's Prisoners '95
Fallen Angels 2 '93
Wild Palms '93
Final Analysis '92
State of Grace '90
Three O'Clock High '87

Dickie Jobson
Countryman '83

**Alejandro
Jodorowsky**
Santa Sangre '90

Steve Jodrell
Shame '87

Michael Joens
My Little Pony: The Movie '86

Arthur Joffe
Alberto Express '92
Harem '85

Mark Joffe
Cosi '95
The Efficiency Expert '92
Grievous Bodily Harm '89
Night Master '87

Roland Joffe
The Scarlet Letter '95
City of Joy '92
Fat Man and Little Boy '89
The Mission '86
The Killing Fields '84

Alan Johnson
Solarbabies '86
To Be or Not to Be '83

Cindy Lou Johnson
Trusting Beatrice '92

David Johnson
DROP Squad '94

Emory Johnson
Phantom Express '32

Irvin Johnson
Blood Ring '93
Fist of Steel '93

Jed Johnson
Andy Warhol's Bad '77

John H. Johnson
Curse of the Blue Lights '88

Kenneth Johnson
Steel '97
Alien Nation: Dark Horizon '94
Short Circuit 2 '88
V '83
Senior Trip '81
The Incredible Hulk '77

Lamont Johnson
The Broken Chain '93

Jerry Lewis
Cracking Up '83
Hardly Working '81
Which Way to the Front? '70
Big Mouth '67
Family Jewels '65
The Patsy '64
The Nutty Professor '63
The Errand Boy '61
The Ladies' Man '61
The Bellboy '60

Joseph H. Lewis
Terror in a Texas Town '58
Seventh Cavalry '56
Big Combo '55
A Lawless Street '55
Retreat, Hell! '52
Gun Crazy '49
Criminals Within '41
The Invisible Ghost '41
Pride of the Bowery '41
Boys of the City '40
That Gang of Mine '40

Mark Lewis
Gordy '95

Richard J. Lewis
Whale Music '94

Robert Lewis
The Crying Child '96
Circumstances Unknown '95
Don't Talk to Strangers '94
Memories of Murder '90
Dead Reckoning '89
Ladykillers '88
City Killer '87
Embassy '85
A Summer to Remember '84
Desperate Lives '82
Child Bride of Short Creek '81
Fallen Angel '81
If Things Were Different '79
S*H*E '79
No Room to Run '78
Pray for the Wildcats '74

Stanley Lewis
Punk Vacation '90

Denis Lewiston
Hot Target '85

Bruce Li
Counter Attack '84

Liu Chia Liang
Master Killer '84

Howard Libov
Midnight Edition '93

Carlo Liconti
Goodnight, Michelangelo '89

Jeff Lieberman
Remote Control '88
Just Before Dawn '80
Blue Sunshine '78
Squirm '76

Robert Lieberman
D3: The Mighty Ducks '96
Titanic '96

Ron Lieberman
All I Want for Christmas '91

Robert Liebmann
Fire in the Sky '93
Table for Five '83
Will: G. Gordon Liddy '82

Jimmy Lifton
Mirror, Mirror 2: Raven Dance '94

Mike Light
Flesh Gordon '72

Peter Lilienthal
The Uprising '81
David '79

Kevin Lima
A Goofy Movie '94

Walter Lima, Jr.
The Dolphin '87

Doug Liman
Swingers '96
Getting In '94

Fred J. Lincoln
Wild Man '89

Per Lindberg
June Night '40

Mitchell Linden
The American Scream '80s

Maud Linder
Man in the Silk Hat '15

Max Linder
Early Cinema Vol. 1 '19

Lance Lindsay
Real Bullets '90
Star Crystal '85

Michael Lindsay-Hogg
Frankie Starlight '95
Running Mates '92
The Habitation of Dragons '91
Murder by Moonlight '91
The Object of Beauty '91
Strange Case of Dr. Jekyll & Mr. Hyde '89
Annie Oakley '85
As Is '85
Master Harold and the Boys '84
Thumbelina '82
Brideshead Revisited '81
Nasty Habits '77
Let It Be '70

Jon Lindstrom
Dreaming of Rita '94

Leopold Lindtberg
Four in a Jeep '51
The Last Chance '45

John F. Link
Call of the Forest '49
The Devil's Cargo '48

Ron Link
Zombie High '87

Richard Linklater
subUrbia '96
Before Sunrise '94
Dazed and Confused '93
Slacker '91

Art Linson
The Wild Life '84
Where the Buffalo Roam '80

Aaron Lipstadt
Pair of Aces '90
City Limits '85
Android '82
The Slumber Party Massacre '82

Steven Lisberger
Slipstream '89
Hot Pursuit '87
Tron '82

David Lister
The Rutanga Tapes '90
Hunted '88

Peter MacKenzie Litten
Heaven's a Drag '94

Miguel Littin
Alsino and the Condor '82

Dwight Little
Murder at 1600 '97
Free Willy 2: The Adventure Home '95
Rapid Fire '92
Marked for Death '90
The Phantom of the Opera '89
Bloodstone '88
Halloween 4: The Return of Michael Myers '88
Getting Even '86

Lynne Littman
Testament '83

Anatole Litvak
Night of the Generals '67
Goodbye Again '61
Anastasia '56
The Snake Pit '48
Sorry, Wrong Number '48
All This and Heaven Too '40
City for Conquest '40
The Sisters '38
Mayerling '36

Gerry Lively
Body Moves '90

Jennie Livingston
Paris Is Burning '91

Carlo Lizzani
House of the Yellow Carpet '84
Last Four Days '77
Love in the City '53

Luis Llosa
Anaconda '96
The Specialist '94
800 Leagues Down the Amazon '93
Sniper '93
Crime Zone '88
Hour of the Assassin '86

Frank Lloyd
The Last Command '55
Blood on the Sun '45
Forever and a Day '43
The Howards of Virginia '40
Mutiny on the Bounty '35
Cavalcade '33
Oliver Twist '22

Harold Lloyd
His Royal Slyness/Haunted Spooks '20
Early Cinema Vol. 1 '19
I'm on My Way/The Non-Stop Kid '18

Norman Lloyd
Tales of the Unexpected '91

Ken Loach
Land and Freedom '95
Ladybird, Ladybird '93
Raining Stones '93
Riff Raff '93
Hidden Agenda '90
Singing the Blues in Red '87
Family Life '71

Moctezuma Lobato
I Like to Play Games '95

Tony LoBianco
Too Scared to Scream '85

Victor Lobl
Eden 3 '93
Eden '92

Sondra Locke
Impulse '90
Ratboy '86

Roy Lockwood
The Mutiny of the Elsinore '39

Norman Loftis
Small Time '91

Bob Logan
Meatballs 4 '92
Repossessed '90
Up Your Alley '89

Bruce Logan
Vendetta '85

Joshua Logan
Paint Your Wagon '69
Camelot '67
Ensign Pulver '64
Fanny '61
Tall Story '60
South Pacific '58
Sayonara '57
Bus Stop '56
Picnic '55

Stanley Logan
The Falcon's Brother '42

Tom Logan
Dream Trap '90
The Night Brings Charlie '90

Dimitri Logothetis
Body Shot '93
The Closer '91
Slaughterhouse Rock '88
Pretty Smart '87

J. Anthony Loma
A Man of Passion '90s
Fine Gold '88
Counterforce '87
Target Eagle '84

Joseph Loman
Surprise Attack '70s
The Boldest Job in the West '71

Francisco J. Lombardi
La Boca del Lobo '89

Lou Lombardo
P.K. and the Kid '85
Russian Roulette '75

Ulli Lommel
The Big Sweat '90
Cold Heat '90
Warbirds '88
Overkill '86
Strangers in Paradise '86
Devonsville Terror '83
Olivia '83
Brainwaves '82
The Boogey Man '80
Cocaine Cowboys '79

Richard Loncraine
Richard III '95
The Wedding Gift '93
Bellman and True '88
Deep Cover '88
Brimstone & Treacle '82
The Missionary '82
Full Circle '77

Jerry London
Victim of Love '91
Haunting of Sarah Hardy '89
Kiss Shot '89
Rent-A-Cop '88
Manhunt for Claude Dallas '86
Chiefs '83
The Scarlet & the Black '83
Father Figure '80
Shogun '80

Roy London
Diary of a Hitman '91

Stanley Long
Adventures of a Private Eye '87
Adventures of a Taxi Driver '76

Robert Longo
Johnny Mnemonic '95

Harry S. Longstreet
The Perfect Daughter '96
A Vow to Kill '94
Sex, Love and Cold Hard Cash '93

Temistocles Lopez
Bird of Prey '95
Chain of Desire '93
Exquisite Corpses '88

Del Lord
Vengeance '37

Jean-Claude Lord
Landslide '92
Eddie and the Cruisers 2: Eddie Lives! '89
Mindfield '89
Toby McTeague '87
The Vindicator '85
Covergirl '83
Visiting Hours '82

Ken Loring
Combat Killers '80

Peter Lorre
The Lost One '51

Vere Lorrimer
Blake's Seven '78

Joseph Losey
Steaming '86
La Truite '83
Roads to the South '78
Mr. Klein '75
Romantic Englishwoman '75
A Doll's House '73
Assassination of Trotsky '72
The Go-Between '71
Secret Ceremony '69
Accident '67
King and Country '64
The Servant '63
Time Without Pity '57
The Sleeping Tiger '54
Prowler '51
The Boy with the Green Hair '48

Emil Loteanu
The Shooting Party '77

Eb Lottimer
Twisted Love '95

Love Matters '93

Patrick Loubert
125 Rooms of Comfort '83

Pavel Lounguine
Luna Park '91
Taxi Blues '90

John Lounsbery
The Rescuers '77

Eugene Lourie
Gorgo '61
The Beast from 20,000 Fathoms '53

Eric Louzil
Class of Nuke 'Em High 3: The Good, the Bad and the Subhumanoid '94
Class of Nuke 'Em High 2: Subhumanoid Meltdown '91
Wilding '90
Lust for Freedom '87

Horace Love
Playing Away '87

Charles Loventhal
Mr. Write '92
My Demon Lover '87
First Time '82

Otho Lovering
Drift Fence '36

Bert Lovitt
Prince Jack '83

Robert Lovy
Plughead Rewired: Circuitry Man 2 '94

Steven Lovy
Plughead Rewired: Circuitry Man 2 '94
Circuitry Man '90

Lucas Lowe
American Shaolin: King of the Kickboxers 2 '92
The King of the Kickboxers '91

William Lowe
Slaughter in San Francisco '81

Richard Lowenstein
Dogs in Space '87
Pete Townshend: White City '85

Dick Lowry
Last Stand at Saber River '96
A Horse for Danny '95
Urban Crossfire '94
The Gambler Returns: The Luck of the Draw '93
In the Line of Duty: Ambush in Waco '93
Till Murder Do Us Part '92
Midnight Murders '91
In the Line of Duty: A Cop for the Killing '90
In the Line of Duty: The FBI Murders '88
Kenny Rogers as the Gambler, Part 3: The Legend Continues '87
Wet Gold '84
Wild Horses '84
Kenny Rogers as the Gambler, Part 2: The Adventure Continues '83
Living Proof: The Hank Williams Jr. Story '83
Smokey and the Bandit, Part 3 '83
Coward of the County '81
The Jayne Mansfield Story '80
Kenny Rogers as the Gambler '80

David Loxton
Lathe of Heaven '80

Nanni Loy
Where's Piccone '84
Cafe Express '83
Head of the Family '71

Arthur Lubin
The Incredible Mr. Limpet '64
Thief of Baghdad '61
Escapade in Japan '57
Francis in the Navy '55
Lady Godiva '55
Francis Joins the WACs '54

James Mallon
Mystery Science Theater 3000:
   The Movie '96
Blood Hook '86

Bruce Malmuth
Pentathlon '94
Hard to Kill '89
Where Are the Children? '85
The Man Who Wasn't There '83
Nighthawks '81
Foreplay '75

Mark Malone
Bulletproof Heart '95

William Malone
Creature '85
Scared to Death '80

Paul Maloney
I Live with Me Dad '86

**Djibril Diop
Mambety**
Touki Bouki '73

David Mamet
Oleanna '94
Homicide '91
Things Change '88
House of Games '87

Yuri Mamin
Window to Paris '95
Sideburns '91

Oshii Mamoru
Urusei Yatsura Movie 2:
   Beautiful Dreamer '92

Rouben Mamoulian
Silk Stockings '57
Summer Holiday '48
Blood and Sand '41
The Mark of Zorro '40
Golden Boy '39
Becky Sharp '35
Queen Christina '33
Dr. Jekyll and Mr. Hyde '32
Applause '29

Janine Manatis
Tales of the Klondike: In a Far
   Country '87

Milcho Manchevski
Before the Rain '94

Mario Mancini
Frankenstein '80 '79

Kevin Mancuso
2020 Texas Gladiators '85

Jeffrey Mandel
Elves '89
Robo-Chic '89

Robert Mandel
The Substitute '96
The X-Files: Pilot Episode/Deep
   Throat '93
School Ties '92
Perfect Witness '89
Big Shots '87
F/X '86
Touch and Go '86
Independence Day '83

Luis Mandoki
When a Man Loves a Woman
   '94
Born Yesterday '93
White Palace '90
Gaby: A True Story '87

Dharan Mandrayar
Ele, My Friend '93

Joseph Manduke
The Gumshoe Kid '89
Omega Syndrome '87
Beatlemania! The Movie '81
Cornbread, Earl & Me '75
Kid Vengeance '75

Gianni Manera
Fear in the City '81

Nino Manfredi
Nudo di Donna '81

Joseph Mangine
Neon Maniacs '86

James Mangold
Copland '97
Heavy '94

Francis Mankiewicz
Love and Hate: A Marriage
   Made in Hell '91
And Then You Die '88
Les Bons Debarras '81

Joseph L. Mankiewicz
Sleuth '72
There was a Crooked Man '70
The Honey Pot '67
Cleopatra '63
Suddenly, Last Summer '59
Guys and Dolls '55
The Barefoot Contessa '54
Julius Caesar '53
Five Fingers '52
People Will Talk '51
All About Eve '50
House of Strangers '49
A Letter to Three Wives '49
The Ghost and Mrs. Muir '47

Tom Mankiewicz
Taking the Heat '93
Delirious '91
Dragnet '87

Henry Mankiewirk
Hell's Brigade: The Final Assault
   '80

Abby Mann
King '78

Anthony Mann
Dandy in Aspic '68
The Heroes of Telemark '65
The Fall of the Roman Empire
   '64
El Cid '61
Cimarron '60
God's Little Acre '58
Man of the West '58
Men in War '57
The Tin Star '57
Far Country '55
The Man from Laramie '55
Savage Wilderness '55
Strategic Air Command '55
The Glenn Miller Story '54
The Naked Spur '53
Thunder Bay '53
Bend of the River '52
Winchester '73 '50
Reign of Terror '49
He Walked by Night '48
Raw Deal '48
Desperate '47
Railroaded '47
T-Men '47
Great Flamarion '45

Daniel Mann
The Man Who Broke 1,000
   Chains '87
Playing for Time '80
Matilda '78
Journey into Fear '74
Big Mo '73
Interval '73
Willard '71
A Dream of Kings '69
For Love of Ivy '68
Our Man Flint '66
Who's Got the Action? '63
Butterfield 8 '60
The Mountain Road '60
The Last Angry Man '59
Hot Spell '58
The Teahouse of the August
   Moon '56
I'll Cry Tomorrow '55
The Rose Tattoo '55
Come Back, Little Sheba '52

Delbert Mann
Lily in Winter '94
Ironclads '90
The Last Days of Patton '86
Love Leads the Way '84
The Member of the Wedding '83
Night Crossing '81
All Quiet on the Western Front
   '79
Home to Stay '79
Torn Between Two Lovers '79
The Birch Interval '78
Breaking Up '78
Francis Gary Powers: The True
   Story of the U-2 Spy '76

No Place to Run '72
She Waits '71
David Copperfield '70
Heidi '67
A Gathering of Eagles '63
That Touch of Mink '62
Lover Come Back '61
Desire Under the Elms '58
Separate Tables '58
Marty '55

Edward Mann
Hooch '76
Cauldron of Blood '67
Hallucination '67

Farhad Mann
Lawnmower Man 2: Beyond
   Cyberspace '95
Return to Two Moon Junction
   '93

Michael Mann
Heat '95
The Last of the Mohicans '92
Manhunter '86
The Keep '83
Thief '81
The Jericho Mile '79

Kim Manners
K-9000 '89

Michelle Manning
Blue City '86

Peter Manoogian
Seedpeople '92
Demonic Toys '90
Arena '89
Enemy Territory '87
The Eliminators '86
Dungeonmaster '83

Mark Manos
Josh Kirby...Time Warrior:
   Chapter 4, Eggs from 70
   Million B.C. '95
Liquid Dreams '92

**Manoussos
Manoussakis**
The Enchantress '85

Duncan Mansfield
Sweetheart of the Navy '37

Scott Mansfield
Deadly Games '80

Joe Mantello
Love! Valour! Compassion! '96

Guido Manuli
Volere Volare '92

Ray Manzarek
The Doors: Soft Parade, a
   Retrospective '69

Rene Manzor
Warrior Spirit '94

Robert Marcarelli
I Don't Buy Kisses Anymore '92
Original Intent '91

Terry Marcel
Jane & the Lost City '87
Prisoners of the Lost Universe
   '84
Hawk the Slayer '81

Siro Marcellini
Gangster's Law '86

Alex March
Master Mind '73
Firehouse '72
Paper Lion '68

**Rafael Romero
Marchent**
Garringo '69

David Marconi
The Harvest '92

G.D. Marcum
Gates of Hell 2: Dead
   Awakening '96

Adam Marcus
Jason Goes to Hell: The Final
   Friday '93

James Marcus
Double Cross '92

Mitch Marcus
A Boy Called Hate '95

Paul Marcus
Prime Suspect: The Scent of
   Darkness '95

Philip Marcus
Terror on Alcatraz '86

Andreas Marfori
Desperate Crimes '93
Evil Clutch '89

Stuart Margolin
How the West was Fun '95
Medicine River '94
Paramedics '88
The Glitter Dome '84
A Shining Season '79

Jeff Margolis
Oscar's Greatest Moments:
   1971-1991 '92

Edwin L. Marin
The Cariboo Trail '50
Abilene Town '46
Mr. Ace '46
Nocturne '46
Johnny Angel '45
Show Business '44
Tall in the Saddle '44
Invisible Agent '42
Miss Annie Rooney '42
A Christmas Carol '38
Everybody Sing '38
Listen, Darling '38
I'd Give My Life '36
The Death Kiss '33
A Study in Scarlet '33

**Richard "Cheech"
Marin**
Born in East L.A. '87

Lex Marinos
An Indecent Obsession '85
Remember Me '85

Peter Maris
Diplomatic Immunity '91
Hangfire '91
True Blood '89
Viper '88
Terror Squad '87
Land of Doom '84
Delirium '77

Chris Marker
Sans Soleil '82
Le Joli Mai '62

Russ Marker
The Yesterday Machine '63

Anthony Markes
Bikini Island '91
Last Dance '91

David Markey
1991: The Year Punk Broke '92
Desperate Teenage Lovedolls
   '84

Monte Markham
Neon City '91
Defense Play '88

Kelly Markin
Tiger Claws '91

Gabriel Markiw
Mob Story '90

Jancarlo Markiw
Mob Story '90

Fletcher Markle
The Incredible Journey '63
Jigsaw '49

Peter Markle
White Dwarf '95
Wagons East '94
Through the Eyes of a Killer '92
El Diablo '90
Nightbreaker '89
Bat 21 '88
Youngblood '86
Hot Dog...The Movie! '83
The Personals '83

Goran Markovic
Tito and Me '92

Murray Markowitz
Left for Dead '78

Robert Markowitz
David '97
The Tuskegee Airmen '95
Afterburn '92
Love, Lies and Murder '91
Decoration Day '90
Too Young to Die '90
Kojak: The Belarus File '85
My Mother's Secret Life '84
Pray TV '82
A Long Way Home '81

Arthur Marks
Monkey Hustle '77
J.D.'s Revenge '76
Bucktown '75
Friday Foster '75
Bonnie's Kids '73
Detroit 9000 '73
Togetherness '70

Ross Kagen Marks
The Twilight of the Golds '97
Homage '95

Morley Markson
Off Your Rocker '80

Brad Marlowe
At Home with the Webbers '94

**Malcolm
Marmorstein**
Dead Men Don't Die '91

Richard Marquand
Hearts of Fire '87
The Jagged Edge '85
Until September '84
Return of the Jedi '83
Eye of the Needle '81
The Legacy '79

Jacques Marquette
Meteor Monster '57

Leon Marr
Dancing in the Dark '86

Roberto Marrtero
Thirty-Six Hours of Hell '77

David Marsh
Stormswept '95
Lords of Magick '88

Ray Marsh
The Last Porno Flick '74

Philip Marshak
Cataclysm '81
Dracula Sucks '79

Frank Marshall
Congo '95
Alive '93
Arachnophobia '90

Garry Marshall
Dear God '96
Exit to Eden '94
Frankie and Johnny '91
Pretty Woman '90
Beaches '88
Overboard '87
Nothing in Common '86
The Flamingo Kid '84
Young Doctors in Love '82

George Marshall
Eight on the Lam '67
Boy, Did I Get a Wrong Number!
   '66
How the West Was Won '63
Papa's Delicate Condition '63
The Gazebo '59
It Started with a Kiss '59
The Mating Game '59
The Sad Sack '57
Red Garters '54
Houdini '53
Off Limits '53
Scared Stiff '53
Fancy Pants '50
Never a Dull Moment '50
My Friend Irma '49
The Perils of Pauline '47
The Blue Dahlia '46
Monsieur Beaucaire '46
Star Spangled Rhythm '42
Valley of the Sun '42
Pot O' Gold '41
Texas '41
The Ghost Breakers '40

Mark Mullin
Cool Blue '88
Claude Mulot
Black Venus '83
Christopher Munch
Color of a Brisk and Leaping
  Day '95
The Hours and Times '92
**Richard W.
Munchkin**
Evil Obsession '96
Texas Payback '95
Guardian Angel '94
Out for Blood '93
Ring of Fire 2: Blood and Steel
  '92
Deadly Bet '91
Ring of Fire '91
Dance or Die '87
Jag Mundhra
Irresistible Impulse '95
Improper Conduct '94
Eyewitness to Murder '93
Sexual Malice '93
Tropical Heat '93
L.A. Goddess '92
The Other Woman '92
Wild Cactus '92
Last Call '90
Legal Tender '90
Jigsaw Murders '89
Hack O'Lantern '87
Open House '86
Ian Mune
The Bridge to Nowhere '86
Came a Hot Friday '85
Chris Munger
Kiss of the Tarantula '75
Black Starlet '74
Angel Muniz
Nueba Yol '95
Andrzej Munk
Passenger '61
Cynthia Munroe
The Wedding Party '69
Jimmy T. Murakami
When the Wind Blows '86
Battle Beyond the Stars '80
Ryu Murakami
Tokyo Decadence '91
Toru Murakawa
New York Cop '94
Distant Justice '92
Walter Murch
Return to Oz '85
Fredi M. Murer
Alpine Fire '89
John Murlowski
Santa with Muscles '96
The Secret Agent Club '96
Automatic '94
Amityville: A New Generation '93
Return of the Family Man '89
F.W. Murnau
Tabu: A Story of the South Seas
  '31
City Girl '30
Sunrise '27
Faust '26
The Last Laugh '24
Nosferatu '22
The Haunted Castle '21
Jim Muro
Street Trash '87
Brianne Murphy
Mortal Danger '94
Dudley Murphy
One Third of a Nation '39
Emperor Jones '33
Emperor Jones/Paul Robeson:
  Tribute to an Artist '33
Eddie Murphy
Harlem Nights '89
Edward Murphy
Heated Vengeance '87
Raw Force '81

Geoff Murphy
Don't Look Back '96
Under Siege 2: Dark Territory
  '95
Blind Side '93
The Last Outlaw '93
Freejack '92
Never Say Die '90
Young Guns 2 '90
Red King, White Knight '89
The Quiet Earth '85
Utu '83
Goodbye Pork Pie '81
Maurice Murphy
Wet and Wild Summer '92
Fatty Finn '84
Doctors and Nurses '82
Ralph Murphy
The Black Devils of Kali '55
Mickey '48
The Spirit of West Point '47
Richard Murphy
Wackiest Ship in the Army '61
Tab Murphy
The Last of the Dogmen '95
Bill Murray
Quick Change '90
Don Murray
The Cross & the Switchblade '72
Katrina Murray
The Secret Garden '84
Robin Murray
Season of Change '94
Dance '90
Scott Murray
Beyond Innocence '87
William Murray
Primal Scream '87
John Musker
Hercules '97
Aladdin '92
The Little Mermaid '89
The Great Mouse Detective '86
Floyd Mutrux
There Goes My Baby '92
Aloha, Bobby and Rose '74
Nagangura Mweze
La Vie est Belle '87
Frank Myers
Lost, Lonely, and Vicious '59
Zion Myers
Sidewalks of New York '31
Alan Myerson
Police Academy 5: Assignment
  Miami Beach '88
Private Lessons '81
Steelyard Blues '73
John Myhers
Terror in Beverly Hills '90
Bruce Myles
Ground Zero '88
Arthur Nadel
Clambake '67
Michael Nader
The Great Escape 2: The Untold
  Story '88
Ivan Nagy
Skinner '93
Jane Doe '83
A Gun in the House '81
Captain America 2: Death Too
  Soon '79
Deadly Hero '75
Bad Charleston Charlie '73
Philippe Nahoun
A Girl on Her Own '76
Mira Nair
Kama Sutra: A Tale of Love '96
The Perez Family '94
Mississippi Masala '92
Salaam Bombay! '88
Sadao Nakajima
Renegade Ninja '83
Takehiro Nakajima
Okoge '93

Novuru Nakamuru
Shiokari Pass '77
Desmond Nakano
White Man's Burden '95
Key-Nam Nam
Dragon Force '82
**Lisandro Duque
Naranjo**
Miracle in Rome '88
Don Nardo
Stuff Stephanie in the Incinerator
  '89
In Deadly Heat '87
James Nares
Rome '78 '78
Silvio Narizzano
Bloodbath
The Body in the Library '87
Why Shoot the Teacher '79
The Class of Miss MacMichael
  '78
Redneck '73
Loot...Give Me Money, Honey!
  '70
Blue '68
Georgy Girl '66
Die! Die! My Darling! '65
24 Hours in a Woman's Life '61
Mikio Naruse
When a Woman Ascends the
  Stairs '60
Late Chrysanthemums '54
Mother '52
Paul Naschy
Human Beasts '80
Inquisition '76
Alan Nathanson
Playing with Fire '70s
Bill Naud
Ricky 1 '88
Whodunit '82
Gregory Nava
Selena '96
My Family '94
A Time of Destiny '88
El Norte '83
Tony Navarro
Widow's Nest '77
Erastheo J. Navda
The Boy God '86
Ray Nazarro
Dog Eat Dog '64
Kansas Pacific '53
Indian Uprising '51
Blazing Across the Pecos '48
Ronald Neame
Foreign Body '86
First Monday in October '81
Hopscotch '80
Meteor '79
The Odessa File '74
The Poseidon Adventure '72
Scrooge '70
The Prime of Miss Jean Brodie
  '69
Gambit '66
The Chalk Garden '64
I Could Go on Singing '63
Tunes of Glory '60
Tunes of Glory/Horse's Mouth
  '60
The Horse's Mouth '58
Windom's Way '57
The Man Who Never Was '55
The Promoter '52
The Golden Salamander '51
Hal Needham
Body Slam '87
Rad '86
Cannonball Run 2 '84
Stroker Ace '83
Megaforce '82
Cannonball Run '81
Smokey and the Bandit, Part 2
  '80
The Villain '79
Hooper '78
Smokey and the Bandit '77

Thomas L. Neff
Running Mates '86
Alberto Negrin
Voyage of Terror: The Achille
  Lauro Affair '90
Mussolini & I '85
Jean Negulesco
The Invincible Six '68
The Best of Everything '59
Daddy Long Legs '55
Three Coins in the Fountain '54
A Woman's World '54
How to Marry a Millionaire '53
Titanic '53
Phone Call from a Stranger '52
Three Came Home '50
Johnny Belinda '48
Road House '48
Humoresque '46
Marshall Neilan
Swing It, Professor '37
Vagabond Lover '29
Stella Maris '18
Rebecca of Sunnybrook Farm
  '17
Roy William Neill
Dressed to Kill '46
Terror by Night '46
Terror by Night/Meeting at
  Midnight '46
House of Fear '45
Pursuit to Algiers '45
The Woman in Green '45
The Pearl of Death '44
Scarlet Claw '44
Spider Woman '44
Sherlock Holmes Faces Death
  '43
Sherlock Holmes in Washington
  '43
Frankenstein Meets the
  Wolfman '42
Sherlock Holmes and the Secret
  Weapon '42
Dr. Syn '37
The Black Room '35
James Neilson
The First Time '69
Where Angels Go, Trouble
  Follows '68
Gentle Giant '67
The Adventures of Bullwhip
  Griffin '66
Dr. Syn, Alias the Scarecrow '64
The Moon-Spinners '64
Johnny Shiloh '63
Summer Magic '63
Bon Voyage! '62
Moon Pilot '62
Mooncussers '62
L.E. Neiman
Time Troopers '89
Daniel Neira
Immortal Combat '94
Frans Nel
American Kickboxer 1 '91
Lights! Camera! Murder! '89
David Nelson
Last Plane Out '83
A Rare Breed '81
Confessions of Tom Harris '72
Dusty Nelson
Necromancer: Satan's Servant
  '88
White Phantom: Enemy of
  Darkness '87
Gary Nelson
Revolver '92
The Lookalike '90
Get Smart, Again! '89
Allan Quatermain and the Lost
  City of Gold '86
The Baron and the Kid '84
Murder in Coweta County '83
Jimmy the Kid '82
Pride of Jesse Hallum '81
The Black Hole '79
Freaky Friday '76
Santee '73
Molly & Lawless John '72

Gene Nelson
Harum Scarum '65
Kissin' Cousins '64
Jessie Nelson
Corrina, Corrina '94
Ozzie Nelson
The Adventures of Ozzie &
  Harriet '50s
Ralph Nelson
Christmas Lilies of the Field '84
A Hero Ain't Nothin' But a
  Sandwich '78
Lady of the House '78
Embryo '76
The Wilby Conspiracy '75
Soldier Blue '70
Charly '68
Duel at Diablo '66
Father Goose '64
Lilies of the Field '63
Soldier in the Rain '63
Requiem for a Heavyweight '56
Sam Nelson
Sagebrush Law '43
Jan Nemec
The Report on the Party and the
  Guests '66
Diamonds of the Night '64
Luis Nepomuceno
Stickfighter '89
Efrain Lopez Neris
A Life of Sin '92
Berit Nesheim
The Other Side of Sunday '96
Avi Nesher
Savage '96
Timebomb '91
Doppelganger: The Evil Within
  '90
She '83
Max Neufeld
An Orphan Boy of Vienna '37
Kurt Neumann
The Fly '58
Kronos '57
Mohawk '56
They Were So Young '55
Carnival Story '54
The Ring '52
Rocketship X-M '50
Return of the Vampire '43
Bad Boy '39
Wide Open Faces '38
Make a Wish '37
Let's Sing Again '36
My Pal, The King '32
Peter Newbrook
The Asphyx '72
Chris Newby
Madagascar Skin '95
Mike Newell
Donnie Brasco '96
An Awfully Big Adventure '94
Four Weddings and a Funeral
  '94
Enchanted April '92
Into the West '92
Amazing Grace & Chuck '87
Bad Blood '87
The Good Father '87
Dance with a Stranger '85
The Awakening '80
The Man in the Iron Mask '77
Sam Newfield
Outlaw Women '52
Scotland Yard Inspector '52
Fingerprints Don't Lie '51
The Lost Continent '51
Western Pacific Agent '51
Three Desperate Men '50
State Department File 649 '49
Wild Weed '49
Adventure Island '47
Money Madness '47
Outlaw of the Plains '46
Border Badmen '45
Gangster's Den '45
His Brother's Ghost '45
The Lady Confesses '45
Lightning Raiders '45

George Ogilvie
Mad Max: Beyond
Thunderdome '85

Jorgo Ognenovski
Warrior of Justice '96

Gerry O'Hara
The Bitch '79
Leopard in the Snow '78
Maroc 7 '67

Terrence O'Hara
The Perfect Bride '91
Darkroom '90

Michael O'Herlihy
Cry of the Innocent '80
A Time for Miracles '80
The Flame Is Love '79
Peter Lundy and the Medicine
Hat Stallion '77
Smith! '69
The One and Only, Genuine,
Original Family Band '68
The Fighting Prince of Donegal
'66
Mosby's Marauders '66

Don Ohlmeyer
The Heroes of Desert Storm '91

Kazuki Ohmori
Godzilla vs. Biollante '89

Tom O'Horgan
Futz '69

Kihachi Okamoto
Zatoichi vs. Yojimbo '70
Red Lion '69
Sword of Doom '67

Steven Okazaki
Living on Tokyo Time '87

Kazuyoshi Okuyama
The Mystery of Rampo '94

Sidney Olcott
The Claw '27
Ranson's Folly '26
Monsieur Beaucaire '24
From the Manger to the Cross
'15

Gary Oldman
Nil by Mouth '96

Enrico Oldoini
Bye Bye Baby '88

Ronan O'Leary
Riders to the Sea '88

Joel Oliansky
The Competition '80

Ken Olin
In Pursuit of Honor '95
White Fang 2: The Myth of the
White Wolf '94

David Oliver
Cave Girl '85

Richard Oliver
A Girl to Kill For '90

Robert Oliver
Dr. Frankenstein's Castle of
Freaks '74

Ron Oliver
Liar's Edge '96
Prom Night 3: The Last Kiss '89

Ruby L. Oliver
Love Your Mama '89

Hector Olivera
A Shadow You Soon Will Be '94
Play Murder for Me '91
Two to Tango '88
Cocaine Wars '86
Barbarian Queen '85
Wizards of the Lost Kingdom '85
Funny, Dirty Little War '83
Fridays of Eternity '81
El Muerto '75

Laurence Olivier
The Prince and the Showgirl '57
Richard III '55
Hamlet '48
Henry V '44

Marty Ollstein
Dangerous Love '87

Ermanno Olmi
The Tree of Wooden Clogs '78
Fiances '63

Edward James Olmos
American Me '92

William Olsen
Return to Eden '89
Getting It On '83

David O'Malley
Easy Wheels '89
Kid Colter '85
Mountain Man '77

Carlo Ombra
Dracula Blows His Cool '82

Ron O'Neal
Up Against the Wall '91
Superfly T.N.T. '73

Douglas F. Oneans
Sno-Line '85

Robert Vincent O'Neil
Avenging Angel '85
Angel '84
Paco '75
The Deadly and the Beautiful '73
Blood Mania '70

Marcel Ophuls
The Sorrow and the Pity '71

Max Ophuls
Lola Montes '55
The Earrings of Madame De...
'54
Le Plaisir '52
La Ronde '51
Caught '49
Reckless Moment '49
Letter from an Unknown Woman
'48
De Mayerling a Sarajevo '40
La Signora di Tutti '34
Liebelei '32

Peer J. Oppenheimer
Terror in Paradise '90

Charlie Ordonez
Forgotten Warrior '86
Wolf '86

Wyott Ordung
Monster from the Ocean Floor
'54

Mario Orfini
Fair Game '89

Valery Orgorodnikov
Burglar '87

Dominic Orlando
Knights of the City '85

Susan Orlikoff-Simon
Image of Passion '86

Stuart Orme
Ivanhoe '97
The Puppet Masters '94
Hands of a Murderer '90
The Heist '89

James Ormerod
Frankenstein '82
Next Victim '74

Ron Ormond
The Girl from Tobacco Row '66
The Black Lash '52
Mesa of Lost Women '52
King of the Bullwhip '51
Yes, Sir, Mr. Bones '51

Peter Ormrod
Eat the Peach '86

Alan Ormsby
Deranged '74

Bruce Ornstein
Jack and His Friends '92

Gary Orona
Stripshow '95
Great Bikini Off-Road Adventure
'94
The Bikini Car Wash Company 2
'92

James Orr
Man of the House '95
Mr. Destiny '90

Breaking All the Rules '85

Valintino Orsini
Smugglers '75

Kenny Ortega
Hocus Pocus '93
Newsies '92

Aaron Osborne
Zarkorr! The Invader '96

Kent Osborne
Women Unchained '70s

Mamoru Oshii
Ghost in the Shell '95

Nagisa Oshima
Max, Mon Amour '86
Merry Christmas, Mr. Lawrence
'83
In the Realm of Passion '80
The Empire of Passion '79
In the Realm of the Senses '76
Violence at Noon '66
The Cruel Story of Youth '60
The Sun's Burial '60

Cliff Osmond
The Penitent '88

Jaime Osorio Gomez
Confessing to Laura '90

Sam O'Steen
The Best Little Girl in the World
'81
Sparkle '76
Brand New Life '72

Suzanne Osten
The Mozart Brothers '86

Thaddeus O'Sullivan
Nothing Personal '95
December Bride '91

Gerd Oswald
Crime of Passion '57
Paris Holiday '57

Richard Oswald
The Lovable Cheat '49
My Song Goes Round the World
'34
Cesare Borgia '23

Dominique Othenin-Girard
Beyond Desire '94
Private Lessons, Another Story
'94
Omen 4: The Awakening '91
Night Angel '90
Halloween 5: The Revenge of
Michael Myers '89
After Darkness '85

Katsuhiro Otomo
Akira '89

Matteo Ottaviano
Single Room Furnished '68

Henry Otto
Dante's Inferno '24

Filippo Ottoni
Detective School Dropouts '85

Lar Henrik Ottoson
Gorilla '56

Idrissa Ouedraogo
Tilai '90

Jean-Paul Ouellette
The Unnamable 2: The
Statement of Randolph Carter
'92
Chinatown Connection '90
The Unnamable '88

Gerard Oury
Delusions of Grandeur '76
The Brain '69
La Grande Vadrouille '66
The Sucker '65

Cliff Owen
The Bawdy Adventures of Tom
Jones '76
The Wrong Arm of the Law '63

Don Owen
Unfinished Business '89

Richard Owens
Killer Likes Candy '78

Earl Owensby
Manhunter '83

Jan Oxenberg
Thank You & Good Night '91

Frank Oz
The Indian in the Cupboard '95
Housesitter '92
What About Bob? '91
Dirty Rotten Scoundrels '88
Little Shop of Horrors '86
The Muppets Take Manhattan
'84
The Dark Crystal '82

Sakae Ozawa
The Street Fighter's Last
Revenge '79
The Street Fighter '75

Fedor Ozep
Whispering City '47

Ali Ozgenturk
The Horse '82

Yasujiro Ozu
An Autumn Afternoon '62
Drifting Weeds '59
Equinox Flower '58
Tokyo Story '53
Early Summer '51
Late Spring '49
Record of a Tenement
Gentleman '47

G.W. Pabst
Don Quixote '35
Kameradschaft '31
The Threepenny Opera '31
Westfront 1918 '30
Diary of a Lost Girl '29
Pandora's Box '28
Joyless Street '25
Secrets of a Soul '25

Al Pacino
Looking for Richard '96

Frank Packard
In Your Face '77

Calvin Jackson Padget
The Battle of El Alamein '68
Secret Agent Super Dragon '66

Anthony Page
Middlemarch '93
Final Warning '90
The Nightmare Years '89
Scandal in a Small Town '88
Heartbreak House '86
Monte Carlo '86
Forbidden '81
Bill: On His Own '83
The Grace Kelly Story '83
Johnny Belinda '82
Absolution '81
Bill '81
The Lady Vanishes '79
I Never Promised You a Rose
Garden '77
F. Scott Fitzgerald in Hollywood
'76
Missiles of October '74
Alpha Beta '73
Pueblo Affair '73

Teddy Page
Blood Debts '83

Marcel Pagliero
The Respectful Prostitute '52

Marcel Pagnol
Letters from My Windmill '54
Topaze '51
Well-Digger's Daughter '46
Le Schpountz '38
Harvest '37
Cesar '36
Angele '34
The Baker's Wife '33

John Paizs
The Big Crimewave '86

Alan J. Pakula
The Devil's Own '96
The Pelican Brief '93
Consenting Adults '92
Presumed Innocent '90
See You in the Morning '89

Orphans '87
Dream Lover '85
Sophie's Choice '82
Rollover '81
Starting Over '79
Comes a Horseman '78
All the President's Men '76
The Parallax View '74
Klute '71
The Sterile Cuckoo '69

George Pal
7 Faces of Dr. Lao '63
The Wonderful World of the
Brothers Grimm '62
Atlantis, the Lost Continent '61
The Time Machine '60
Tom Thumb '58

Laszlo Pal
Journey to Spirit Island '92

Tom Palazzolo
Caligari's Cure '82

Euzhan Palcy
A Dry White Season '89
Sugar Cane Alley '83

Larry Pall
Off Your Rocker '80

Jean Marie Pallardy
Truck Stop

Rospo Pallenberg
Cutting Class '89

Anders Palm
Dead Certain '92
Murder on Line One '90
Unmasked Part 25 '88

Thomas Palmer, Jr.
Forever: A Ghost of a Love
Story '92

Tony Palmer
The Children '90
Wagner: The Complete Epic '85
Wagner: The Movie '85

Conrad Palmisano
Busted Up '86
Space Rage '86

Bruce Paltrow
A Little Sex '82

Herve Palud
Little Indian, Big City '95

Rick Pamplin
Provoked '89

George Pan-Andreas
Crime Killer '85

Jafar Panahi
The White Balloon '95

Norman Panama
Barnaby and Me '77
I Will, I Will for Now '76
How to Commit Marriage '69
The Road to Hong Kong '62
The Trap '59
Court Jester '56
Above and Beyond '53

Gleb Panfilov
The Theme '79

Domenico Paolella
Pirates of the Coast '61

Deno Paoli
The Legend of Frank Woods '77

Phedon Papamichael
Dark Side of Genius '94
Sketch Artist '92

Michael Papas
The Lifetaker '89

Lakis Papastathis
When the Greeks '81

Giullo Paradisi
Spaghetti House '82
The Visitor '80

Sergei Paradjanov
Ashik Kerib '88
The Legend of Suram Fortress
'85
The Color of Pomegranates '69
Shadows of Forgotten Ancestors
'64

John Paragon
Twinsitters '95
Ring of the Musketeers '93
Double Trouble '91

Paul S. Parco
Pucker Up and Bark Like a Dog '89
Deadly Alliance '78

Chuck Parello
Henry: Portrait of a Serial Killer 2: Mask of Sanity '96

Domonic Paris
Splitz '84
Dracula's Last Rites '79

Jerry Paris
Police Academy 3: Back in Training '86
Police Academy 2: Their First Assignment '85
Make Me an Offer '80
How to Break Up a Happy Divorce '76
Only with Married Men '74
Star Spangled Girl '71
The Passing of Evil '70
Viva Max '69
Don't Raise the Bridge, Lower the River '68
How Sweet It Is! '68
Never a Dull Moment '68

Dean Parisot
Framed '90

Chul-Soo Park
301, 302 '94

Richard W. Park
American Chinatown '96
Gang Justice '94

Alan Parker
Evita '96
The Road to Wellville '94
The Commitments '91
Come See the Paradise '90
Mississippi Burning '88
Angel Heart '87
Birdy '84
Pink Floyd: The Wall '82
Shoot the Moon '82
Fame '80
Midnight Express '78
Bugsy Malone '76

Albert Parker
Late Extra '35
The Black Pirate '26

Ben Parker
The Invisible Avenger '58

Cary Parker
The Girl in the Picture '86

John Parker
Daughter of Horror '55

Norton S. Parker
The Road to Ruin '28

Oliver Parker
Othello '95

Percy G. Parker
Castle of the Creeping Flesh '68

Rocky Parker
Ava's Magical Adventure '94

Trey Parker
Cannibal! The Musical '96

Eric Parkinson
Future Shock '93

Tom Parkinson
Disciple of Death '72

Gordon Parks
Half Slave, Half Free '85
Three the Hard Way '74
Shaft's Big Score '72
Shaft '71
The Learning Tree '69

Gordon Parks, Jr.
Aaron Loves Angela '75
Superfly '72

Hugh Parks
Shoot '92
King's Ransom '91
Dream Trap '90
Shakma '89

Deadly Innocence '88
Michael Parks
The Return of Josey Wales '86

Billy Parolini
Igor & the Lunatics '85

Gianfranco Parolini
The Fury of Hercules '61
Samson '61

John H. Parr
Prey for the Hunter '92
Pursuit '90

Larry Parr
A Soldier's Tale '91

James D. Parriott
Heart Condition '90

Robert Parrish
The Destructors '74
A Town Called Hell '72
Journey to the Far Side of the Sun '69
Bobo '67
Casino Royale '67
Fire Down Below '57
Cry Danger '51

James Parrott
Pardon Us '31

Gordon Parry
Innocents in Paris '53
Tom Brown's School Days '51

John Parsons
Watched '73

Gabriel Pascal
Caesar and Cleopatra '46
Major Barbara '41

Michael Paseornek
Vibrations '94

Goran Paskalyevic
Someone Else's America '96

Pier Paolo Pasolini
Salo, or the 120 Days of Sodom '75
Arabian Nights '74
The Canterbury Tales '71
The Decameron '70
Medea '70
Notes for an African Orestes '70
Porcile '69
Teorema '68
The Hawks & the Sparrows '67
Oedipus Rex '67
The Gospel According to St. Matthew '64
Love Meetings '64
Mamma Roma '62
RoGoPaG '62
Accatone! '61

John Pasquin
Jungle 2 Jungle '96
The Santa Clause '94
Nightmare '91

Ivan Passer
Kidnapped '95
Stalin '92
Fourth Story '90
Haunted Summer '88
Creator '85
The Nightingale '83
Cutter's Way '81
Silver Bears '78
Crime & Passion '75
Law and Disorder '74
Born to Win '71

Giovanni Pastrone
Cabiria '14
Salammbo '14

Franca Pasut
Flashdance '83

Tom Patchett
Best Legs in the 8th Grade '84

Jonas Pate
The Grave '95

Michael Pate
Tim '79

Raju Patel
In the Shadow of Kilimanjaro '86

Sharad Patel
Amin: The Rise and Fall '82

Stuart Paton
Chinatown After Dark '31
20,000 Leagues Under the Sea '16

Matthew Patrick
Tainted Blood '93

Michael Patrick
Hider in the House '90

Nigel Patrick
Johnny Nobody '61

Robert Patrick
Road to Nashville '67

Frank Patterson
Black Snow '93

John D. Patterson
Grave Secrets: The Legacy of Hilltop Drive '92
The Spring '89
Taken Away '89
Deadly Innocence '88
Legend of Earl Durand '74

Pat Patterson
The Body Shop '72

Ray Patterson
The Good, the Bad, and Huckleberry Hound '88

Richard Patterson
J-Men Forever! '79

Willi Patterson
Dreams Lost, Dreams Found '87

Michael Pattinson
The Limbic Region '96
One Crazy Night '93
...Almost '90
Ground Zero '88
Moving Out '83

Peter Patzak
Midnight Cop '88
Lethal Obsession '87
Slaughterday '77

Byron Paul
Lt. Robin Crusoe, U.S.N. '66

Steven Paul
Eternity '89
Slapstick of Another Kind '84
Falling in Love Again '80

Stuart Paul
Fate '90
Emanon '86

David Paulsen
Schizoid '80

George Pavlou
Rawhead Rex '87
Transmutations '85

Yuri Pavlov
Creation of Adam '93

Michael Pavone
Chameleon '95

Clark Paylow
Ring of Terror '62

Alexander Payne
Citizen Ruth '96

Dave Payne
Alien Terminator '95
Criminal Hearts '95
Concealed Weapon '94

John Payson
Joe's Apartment '96

Barry Peak
The Big Hurt '87

Michael Pearce
James Joyce's Women '85

Richard Pearce
A Family Thing '96
Leap of Faith '92
Dead Man Out '89
The Final Days '89
The Long Walk Home '89
No Mercy '86
Country '84
Sessions '83
Threshold '83
Heartland '81

Steven Pearl
At First Sight '95

Robert E. Pearso
Devil & Leroy Basset '73

George Pearson
Midnight at the Wax Museum '36
A Shot in the Dark '33

Peter Pearson
Tales of the Klondike: The Unexpected '87
Paperback Hero '73

Max Pecas
The Sensuous Teenager '70
Erotic Touch of Hot Skin '65
Sweet Ecstasy '60

Brian Peck
The Willies '90

Ron Peck
Empire State '87

Sam Peckinpah
The Osterman Weekend '83
Convoy '78
Cross of Iron '76
The Killer Elite '75
Bring Me the Head of Alfredo Garcia '74
Pat Garrett & Billy the Kid '73
The Getaway '72
Junior Bonner '72
Straw Dogs '72
Ballad of Cable Hogue '70
The Wild Bunch '69
Major Dundee '65
Ride the High Country '62
Deadly Companions '61

Larry Peerce
Prison for Children '93
A Woman Named Jackie '91
The Court Martial of Jackie Robinson '90
The Neon Empire '89
Wired '89
Elvis and Me '88
Queenie '87
Hard to Hold '84
Love Child '82
The Bell Jar '79
The Other Side of the Mountain, Part 2 '78
Two Minute Warning '76
The Other Side of the Mountain '75
The Stranger Who Looks Like Me '74
Ash Wednesday '73
A Separate Peace '73
The Sporting Club '72
Goodbye Columbus '69
The Incident '67

Barbara Peeters
Humanoids from the Deep '80
Starhops '78
Summer School Teachers '75
Bury Me an Angel '71

Antonio Pelaez
Crystalstone '88

Anthony Pelissier
Encore '52
The Rocking Horse Winner '49

Scott Pembroke
Medicine Man '30

Nettie Pena
Home Sweet Home '80

Maurice Penczner
I Was a Zombie for the FBI '82

Sze Ma Peng
Venus the Ninja '80s

Chang Peng-I
Shaolin Kung Fu Mystagogue '84

Arthur Penn
Inside '96
The Portrait '93
Penn and Teller Get Killed '90
Dead of Winter '87
Target '85
Four Friends '81
Missouri Breaks '76
Night Moves '75
Little Big Man '70
Alice's Restaurant '69

Bonnie & Clyde '67
The Chase '66
Mickey One '65
The Miracle Worker '62
The Left-Handed Gun '58

Leonard Penn
Judgment in Berlin '88
The Dark Secret of Harvest Home '78
A Man Called Adam '66

Sean Penn
The Crossing Guard '94
The Indian Runner '91

D.A. Pennebaker
The War Room '93
Bob Dylan: Don't Look Back '91

Eagle Pennell
Ice House '89
Last Night at the Alamo '83
The Whole Shootin' Match '79

C.M. Pennington-Richards
Ladies Who Do '63
Hour of Decision '57

David Peoples
The Blood of Heroes '89

Richard Pepin
Dark Breed '96
Hologram Man '95
The Silencers '95
T-Force '94
Cyber-Tracker '93
Fist of Honor '92

Clare Peploe
Rough Magic '95
High Season '88

Mark Peploe
Afraid of the Dark '92

Frank Peregini
Scar of Shame '27

Miguel Pereira
Veronico Cruz '87

Hope Perello
Pet Shop '94
Howling 6: The Freaks '90

Marie Perennou
Microcosmos '96

Antonio Perez
The 13th Mission '91

Jack Perez
America's Deadliest Home Video '91

Severo Perez
... And the Earth Did Not Swallow Him '94

Virginia Perfili
Mirror Mirror 3 '96

Etienne Perier
Investigation '79
Zeppelin '71
The Hot Line '69
Murder at 45 R.P.M. '65

Paco Perinan
Against the Wind '90

Zoran Perisic
The Phoenix and the Magic Carpet '95

Anthony Perkins
Lucky Stiff '88
Psycho 3 '86

Harold Perkins
Help Wanted Female '68

Paul Perri
Revenge of the Virgins '62

Frank Perry
Hello Again '87
Compromising Positions '85
Monsignor '82
Mommie Dearest '81
Skag '79
Rancho Deluxe '75
Diary of a Mad Housewife '70
Last Summer '69
The Swimmer '68
ABC Stage 67: Truman Capote's A Christmas Memory '66

Frank Rainone
Me and the Mob '94

Alvin Rakoff
A Voyage' Round My Father '89
The First Olympics: Athens 1896 '84
Mister Halpren & Mister Johnson '83
Dirty Tricks '81
Death Ship '80
City on Fire '78
King Solomon's Treasure '76
Say Hello to Yesterday '71
Room 43 '58

Alexander Ramati
The Assisi Underground '84

Victor Rambaldi
Decoy '95

Vittoria Rambaldi
Primal Rage '90

Harold Ramis
Multiplicity '96
Stuart Saves His Family '94
Groundhog Day '93
Club Paradise '86
National Lampoon's Vacation '83
Caddyshack '80

Patrick Rand
Mom '89

Addison Randall
The Killing Zone '90
Chance '89
East L.A. Warriors '89

Tony Randel
Rattled '96
Fist of the North Star '95
One Good Turn '95
Ticks '93
Amityville 1992: It's About Time '92
Children of the Night '92
Hellbound: Hellraiser 2 '88

Arthur Rankin, Jr.
Flight of Dragons '82
The Return of the King '80
The Hobbit '78
The Ballad of Paul Bunyan '72
Santa Claus Is Coming to Town '70

Lazlo Ranody
Nobody's Daughter '76

Mort Ransen
Margaret's Museum '95

Whitney Ransick
Hand Gun '93

Krishna Rao
Crossworlds '96

Frederic Raphael
Women & Men: Stories of Seduction '90

Joel Rapp
The Battle of Blood Island '60

Mark Rappaport
From the Journals of Jean Seberg '95
Rock Hudson's Home Movies '92

Jean-Paul Rappeneau
The Horseman on the Roof '95
Cyrano de Bergerac '90
Swashbuckler '84
Lovers Like Us '75

Irving Rapper
Born Again '78
Joseph & His Brethren '60
Marjorie Morningstar '58
The Brave One '56
Forever Female '53
Deception '46
The Corn is Green '45
Rhapsody in Blue '45
The Adventures of Mark Twain '44
Now, Voyager '42

Steve Rash
Eddie '96

Son-in-Law '93
Queens Logic '91
Can't Buy Me Love '87
Rich Hall's Vanishing America '86
Under the Rainbow '81
The Buddy Holly Story '78

Jay Raskin
I Married a Vampire '87

Daniel Raskov
A Kiss Goodnight '94
The Masters of Menace '90
Wedding Band '89

Lars Rasmussen
The Littlest Viking '94

Tina Rathborne
Zelly & Me '88

Gregory Ratoff
Abdulla the Great '56
Black Magic '49
The Heat's On '43
The Corsican Brothers '42
Footlight Serenade '42
Adam Had Four Sons '41
Intermezzo '39
Rose of Washington Square '39

Jans Rautenbach
No One Cries Forever '85

Max Raven
The Abomination '88

Ousama Rawi
The Housekeeper '86

John Rawlins
Shark River '53
Dick Tracy Meets Gruesome '47
Dick Tracy's Dilemma '47
Arabian Nights '42
Sherlock Holmes: The Voice of Terror '42

Albert Ray
Undercover Man '36
Dancing Man '33
Shriek in the Night '33
13th Guest '32

Bernard B. Ray
Movie Stuntmen '53
Buffalo Bill Rides Again '47
House of Errors '42
Broken Strings '40
Roamin' Wild '36
Speed Reporter '36
Texas Jack '35
The Silver Bullet '34

Fred Olen Ray
Fugitive Rage '96
Invisible Mom '96
Attack of the 60-Foot Centerfold '95
Bikini Drive-In '95
Inner Sanctum 2 '94
Wizards of the Demon Sword '94
Dinosaur Island '93
Mind Twister '93
Possessed by the Night '93
Haunting Fear '91
Inner Sanctum '91
Bad Girls from Mars '90
Evil Toons '90
Mob Boss '90
Spirits '90
Alienator '89
Beverly Hills Vamp '88
Hollywood Chainsaw Hookers '88
Terminal Force '88
Warlords '88
Commando Squad '87
Cyclone '87
Deep Space '87
Phantom Empire '87
Star Slammer '87
Armed Response '86
Tomb '86
Alien Dead '85
Bio Hazard '85

Nicholas Ray
55 Days at Peking '63
The King of Kings '61
Party Girl '58
Rebel Without a Cause '55

Johnny Guitar '53
The Lusty Men '52
Flying Leathernecks '51
On Dangerous Ground '51
Born to Be Bad '50
In a Lonely Place '50
Knock on Any Door '49
They Live by Night '49
A Woman's Secret '49

Satyajit Ray
The Stranger '92
The Home and the World '84
Distant Thunder '73
The Adversary '71
Days and Nights in the Forest '70
Two Daughters '61
Devi '60
The World of Apu '59
Aparajito '58
Pather Panchali '54

Herman C. Raymaker
The Night Cry '26

Jack Raymond
The Speckled Band '31

Tom Raymonth
Battle of the Eagles '81

Spiro Razatos
Class of 1999 2: The Substitute '93
Fast Getaway '91

Daniel Reardon
White Cargo '96

Bill Rebane
The Capture of Bigfoot '79
The Alpha Incident '76
The Giant Spider Invasion '75

Ito Rebane
They '77

Robert Rector
Don't Change My World '83

Eric Red
Bad Moon '96
Undertow '95
Body Parts '91
Cohen and Tate '88

Robert Redford
Quiz Show '94
A River Runs Through It '92
The Milagro Beanfield War '88
Ordinary People '80

Carol Reed
Unicorn '83
Oliver! '68
The Agony and the Ecstasy '65
The Key '58
Trapeze '56
The Fallen Idol '49
The Third Man '49
Odd Man Out '47
Immortal Battalion '44
Kipps '41
Night Train to Munich '40
The Stars Look Down '39

James Reed
Mission Phantom '79

Jerry Reed
What Comes Around '85

Joel M. Reed
Night of the Zombies '81
Bloodsucking Freaks '75
G.I. Executioner '71

Luther Reed
Dixiana '30

Roland D. Reed
The House of Secrets '37
Red Lights Ahead '36

Theodore Reed
The Nut '21

William Reed
Scorpion '86

Clive Rees
When the Whales Came '89
Blockhouse '73

Jerry Rees
The Marrying Man '91

Christopher Reeve
In the Gloaming '97

Geoffrey Reeve
Souvenir '88
Caravan to Vaccares '74
Puppet on a Chain '72

Matt Reeves
The Pallbearer '95
Future Shock '93

Michael Reeves
The Conqueror Worm '68
The She-Beast '65

Thomas G. Reeves
Angry Joe Bass '76

Patrick Regan
Kiss Daddy Goodbye '81

Godfrey Reggio
Powaqqatsi: Life in Transformation '88
Koyaanisqatsi '83

Francisco Regueiro
Padre Nuestro '85

Kelly Reichardt
River of Grass '94

Mark Reichart
Union City '81

Alastair Reid
Nostromo '96
Armistead Maupin's Tales of the City '93
Teamster Boss: The Jackie Presser Story '92
Traffik '90
Shattered '72
Baby Love '69

Dorothy Davenport Reid
Sucker Money '34
Linda '29

Max Reid
Wild Thing '87

Tim Reid
Once Upon a Time ... When We Were Colored '95
The Little Mermaid '78

William Reilly
Men of Respect '91

Carl Reiner
That Old Feeling '96
Fatal Instinct '93
Sibling Rivalry '90
Bert Rigby, You're a Fool '89
Summer School '87
Summer Rental '85
All of Me '84
The Man with Two Brains '83
Dead Men Don't Wear Plaid '82
The Jerk '79
The One and Only '78
Oh, God! '77
Where's Poppa? '70
The Comic '69
Enter Laughing '67

Jeff Reiner
Serpent's Lair '95
Trouble Bound '92
Blood & Concrete: A Love Story '90

Lucas Reiner
Spirit of '76 '91

Rob Reiner
Ghosts of Mississippi '96
The American President '95
North '94
A Few Good Men '92
Misery '90
When Harry Met Sally... '89
The Princess Bride '87
Stand By Me '86
The Sure Thing '85
This Is Spinal Tap '84

Gottfried Reinhardt
Betrayed '54

John Reinhardt
Open Secret '48

Max Reinhardt
A Midsummer Night's Dream '35

Deborah Reinisch
Caught in the Act '93

Harald Reinl
Fight for Gold '86
Hell Hounds of Alaska '73
The Torture Chamber of Dr. Sadism '69
The Invisible Dr. Mabuse '62
Forger of London '61
The Return of Dr. Mabuse '61

Irving Reis
Three Husbands '50
The Falcon Takes Over/Strange Bargain '49
The Bachelor and the Bobby-Soxer '47
Crack-Up '46
Big Street '42

Walter Reisch
Men Are Not Gods '37

Allen Reisner
All Mine to Give '56

Charles F. Reisner
Train to Tombstone '50
The Cobra Strikes '48
The Man on the Box '25

Karel Reisz
Everybody Wins '90
Sweet Dreams '85
The French Lieutenant's Woman '81
Who'll Stop the Rain? '78
The Gambler '74
Isadora '68
Morgan! '66
Saturday Night and Sunday Morning '60

Wolfgang Reitherman
The Rescuers '77
Robin Hood '73
The Aristocats '70
The Jungle Book '67
The Sword in the Stone '63
101 Dalmatians '61
Sleeping Beauty '59

Ivan Reitman
Father's Day '96
Junior '94
Dave '94
Kindergarten Cop '90
Twins '88
Legal Eagles '86
Ghostbusters '84
Stripes '81
Meatballs '79

Edgar Reitz
Heimat 2 '80s
Heimat 1 '84
Germany in Autumn '78

Sheldon Renan
Akira '89

Norman Rene
Reckless '95
Prelude to a Kiss '92
Longtime Companion '90

Jean Renoir
Zero for Conduct/Taris/A Propos de Nice '21
The Little Theatre of Jean Renoir '71
The Elusive Corporal '62
Picnic on the Grass '59
The Testament of Dr. Cordelier '59
Elena and Her Men '56
French Can-Can '55
The Golden Coach '52
The River '51
A Day in the Country '46
Diary of a Chambermaid '46
The Southerner '45
This Land is Mine '43
The Rules of the Game '39
La Bete Humaine '38
Grand Illusion '37
La Marseillaise '37
The Crime of Monsieur Lange '36
The Lower Depths '36

Valerio Zurlini
The Girl with a Suitcase *'60*
John Zuru
The Mad Butcher *'72*
Martin Zweiback
Cactus in the Snow *'72*
Edward Zwick
Courage Under Fire *'96*
Legends of the Fall *'94*
Leaving Normal *'92*
Glory *'89*
About Last Night... *'86*
Special Bulletin *'83*
Having It All *'82*
Joel Zwick
Second Sight *'89*
Karl Zwicky
Vicious *'88*
Contagion *'87*
Terry Zwigoff
Crumb *'94*

Writer Index

The **Writer Index** provides a videography for any writer with a video credit. The listings for the writer names follow an alphabetical sort by last name (although the names appear in a first name last name format). The videographies are listed chronologically, from most recent film to their first. If a writer wrote (or script doctored) more than one film in the same year, these movies are listed alphabetically within the year. Used in conjunction with the **Cast** index, this index will let you find actors and actresses who wrote themselves juicy parts (with varying degrees of success). Directors also tend to show up here, either before their directorial ambitions surfaced, or after they'd gained enough clout to get one of their scripts to the screen.

Dough Aarniokoski
Puppet Master 4 '93

Paul Aaron
Laurel Avenue '93
Octagon '80

Scott Abbott
Breach of Conduct '94

Shepard Abbott
C.H.U.D. '84

Lewis Abernathy
Deepstar Six '89

Anthony Able
Project: Alien '89

Jim Abrahams
Hot Shots! Part Deux '93
Hot Shots! '91
The Naked Gun: From the Files of Police Squad '88
Top Secret! '84
Police Squad! Help Wanted! '82
Airplane! '80
Kentucky Fried Movie '77

Jerry Abrahamson
Wagons East '94

Jack Abramoff
Red Scorpion '89

Robert Abramoff
Red Scorpion '89

Celia Abrams
Easy Wheels '89

Ian Abrams
Undercover Blues '93

Jeffrey Abrams
Gone Fishin' '97
Forever Young '92
Regarding Henry '91
Taking Care of Business '90

Tom Abrams
The Desperate Trail '94

Jon Acevski
Freddie the Frog '92

Jovan Acin
Hey, Babu Riba '88

Rodney Ackland
Thursday's Child '43
The Forty-Ninth Parallel '41

Allen Actor
Dungeonmaster '83

Alfred Adam
Belle Americaine '61

Catlin Adams
Sticky Fingers '88

Daniel Adams
Primary Motive '92
A Fool and His Money '88

Gerald Drayson Adams
Duel at Silver Creek '52
Flame of Araby '51

Mikhaila Max Adams
Excess Baggage '96

Ewart Adamson
Circumstantial Evidence '35

Richard Adcock
Hyper-Sapien: People from Another Star '86

Alan J. Adler
Metalstorm: The Destruction of Jared Syn '83
The Concrete Jungle '82
Parasite '82
The Alchemist '81

Gilbert Adler
Tales from the Crypt Presents Bordello of Blood '96
Children of the Corn 2: The Final Sacrifice '92

Eleonore Adlon
Rosalie Goes Shopping '89
Bagdad Cafe '88

Felix Adlon
Younger & Younger '94
Salmonberries '91

Percy Adlon
Younger & Younger '94
Salmonberries '91
Rosalie Goes Shopping '89

Bagdad Cafe '88
Sugarbaby '85
Celeste '81

Nelly Adnil
Silent Victim '92

Gilles Adrien
The City of Lost Children '95
Delicatessen '92

James Agee
The Night of the Hunter '55
The African Queen '51

Gabriel Aghion
Pedale Douce '96

Faruque Ahmed
Warlords 3000 '93

Kamal Ahmed
The Jerky Boys '95

Chantal Akerman
A Couch in New York '95
Night and Day '91
Window Shopping '86
The Eighties '83
Les Rendez-vous D'Anna '78
News from Home '76

Andra Akers
Toute Une Nuit '82

William M. Akers
Ernest Rides Again '93

Norman Aladjem
Firewalker '86

Jordan Alan
Terminal Bliss '91

Jeff Albert
Danger Zone '95
Live Wire: Human Timebomb '95
Never Say Die '94

Marvin H. Albert
Rough Night in Jericho '67

Luis Alcoriza
Death in the Garden '56
El '52

Alan Alda
Betsy's Wedding '90
A New Life '88

Sweet Liberty '86
The Four Seasons '81
The Seduction of Joe Tynan '79

Robert Alden
Uncaged '91
Streetwalkin' '85

Steve Alden
Fall Time '94

Phillip Alderton
The Expendables '89

Will Aldis
Clifford '92
Stealing Home '88
The Couch Trip '87
Back to School '86

David Alexander
Dead Ahead '96

Kurt Alexander
De Mayerling a Sarajevo '40

Ronald Alexander
Billie '65

Scott Alexander
The People vs. Larry Flynt '96
That Darn Cat '96
Ed Wood '94
Problem Child 2 '91
Problem Child '90

Scott Lawrence Alexander
Spaced Invaders '90

Michel Alexandre
L.627 '92

Richard Alfieri
Harvest of Fire '95
A Friendship in Vienna '88
Echoes '83
Children of Rage '75

Dan Algrant
Naked in New York '93

Arif Aliev
Prisoner of the Mountains '96

Ranald Allan
The Crossing '92

Ted Allan
Dr. Bethune '90
Love Streams '84
Falling in Love Again '80
Lies My Father Told Me '75

Pat Allee
Bums '93

Chris Allen
The Last Remake of Beau Geste '77

Corey Allen
Avalanche '78

Curt Allen
Alligator 2: The Mutation '90
Blind Vengeance '90
Bloodstone '88
Hollywood Harry '86
Walking the Edge '83

Irwin Allen
Five Weeks in a Balloon '62
Voyage to the Bottom of the Sea '61

Janis Allen
The Double Negative '80
Meatballs '79

Jay Presson Allen
Year of the Gun '91
Deathtrap '82
Prince of the City '81
Just Tell Me What You Want '80
Funny Lady '75
Forty Carats '73
Cabaret '72
Travels with My Aunt '72
The Prime of Miss Jean Brodie '69
Marnie '64

Jim Allen
Land and Freedom '95
Raining Stones '93
Hidden Agenda '90

J.T. Allen
The Good Old Boys '95
Geronimo '93

Kevin Allen
Twin Town '97

Writer Index

1597

Harry Basil
Meet Wally Sparks '97
Kim Bass
A Thin Line Between Love and
Hate '96
Ronald Bass
My Best Friend's Wedding '97
Dangerous Minds '95
Waiting to Exhale '95
The Enemy Within '94
When a Man Loves a Woman
'94
The Joy Luck Club '93
Sleeping with the Enemy '91
Rain Man '88
Black Widow '87
Gardens of Stone '87
Code Name: Emerald '85
Seth Bass
The Twilight of the Golds '97
Lawrence Bassoff
Hunk '87
Weekend Pass '84
William Bast
The Betsy '78
James Dean '76
The Valley of Gwangi '69
Janet Scott Batchler
Batman Forever '95
Lee Batchler
Batman Forever '95
Kent Bateman
Headless Eyes '83
Alan Bates
The Story of a Love Story '73
Cary Bates
Christopher Columbus: The
Discovery '92
Djalma Batista
Savage Capitalism '93
Joe Batteer
Blown Away '94
Chasers '94
Curiosity Kills '90
Bradley Battersby
Blue Desert '91
Lloyd Battista
Treasure of the Four Crowns '82
Murray Battle
Stand Off '93
Fred Bauer
Under the Rainbow '81
Hans Bauer
Anaconda '96
Thomas Baum
Witness to the Execution '94
The Manhattan Project '86
The Sender '82
Carny '80
Simon '80
Hugo the Hippo '76
Noah Baumbach
Kicking and Screaming '95
Lamberto Bava
Demons 2 '87
Beyond the Door 2 '79
George L. Baxt
Circus of Horrors '60
Horror Hotel '60
John Baxter
The Time Guardian '87
Sergio Bazzini
Husbands and Lovers '91
Wayne Beach
Murder at 1600 '97
The Shadow Conspiracy '96
Peter S. Beagle
The Last Unicorn '82
The Lord of the Rings '78
The Dove '74
David Beaird
Scorchers '92
My Chauffeur '86
Party Animal '83
Octavia '82

Henry Bean
Desperate Measures '97
Deep Cover '92
Internal Affairs '90
Running Brave '83
**Douglas Carter
Beane**
To Wong Foo, Thanks for
Everything, Julie Newmar '95
Winston Beard
Cyber Bandits '94
Nicholas Beardsley
Savage Island '85
Richard Beattie
Cold Sweat '93
Warren Beatty
Love Affair '94
Reds '81
Reds '81
Heaven Can Wait '78
Shampoo '75
D.D. Beauchamp
Alias Jesse James '59
Abbott and Costello Go to Mars
'53
Simon Beaufoy
The Full Monty '96
Marcel Beaulieu
Farinelli '94
Trace Beaulieu
Mystery Science Theater 3000:
The Movie '96
Phil Beauman
Don't Be a Menace to South
Central While Drinking Your
Juice in the Hood '95
Gorman Bechard
Cemetery High '89
Jacques Becker
Modigliani '58
Ali Baba and the 40 Thieves '54
Grisbi '53
Casque d'Or '52
Jean Becker
Elisa '94
Josh Becker
Lunatics: A Love Story '92
Thou Shalt Not Kill...Except '87
Barry Beckerman
St. Ives '76
Shamus '73
**Michael Frost
Beckner**
Sniper '92
Dick Beebe
The Lazarus Man '96
Into the Badlands '92
Prison Stories: Women on the
Inside '91
Ford Beebe
Riders of Pasco Basin '40
Prescott Kid '36
Fighting Shadows '35
John Beech
Warlords of the 21st Century '82
Jeff Begun
Saturday the 14th '81
Marc Behm
Nana '82
Hospital Massacre '81
The Peking Blond '68
Help! '65
Harry Behn
Hell's Angels '30
Jack Behr
Birdy '84
S.N. Behrman
Me and the Colonel '58
A Tale of Two Cities '36
Hallelujah, I'm a Bum '33
Albert Beich
Girls in Chains '43
Jean-Jacques Beineix
Betty Blue '86

Moon in the Gutter '83
Diva '82
William Bekkala
Silent Motive '91
Dan Bell
The Shot '96
Elisa Bell
Vegas Vacation '96
Dancing with Danger '93
Treacherous Crossing '92
Writer's Block '91
Jeffrey Bell
Radio Inside '94
Neal Bell
Two Small Bodies '93
Terminal Choice '85
Robert Bell
Free Ride '86
Ross Bell
To Die Standing '91
James Warner Bellah
Sergeant Rutledge '60
Bruce Belland
Weekend Warriors '86
Michelle Bellerose
Replikator: Cloned to Kill '94
Donald P. Bellisario
JAG '95
Last Rites '88
Magnum P.I.: Don't Eat the
Snow in Hawaii '80
Stephen F. Bello
Circle of Power '81
Marco Bellocchio
Devil in the Flesh '87
Henry IV '85
The Eyes, the Mouth '83
Peter Bellwood
Highlander 2: The Quickening
'91
Highlander '86
Phobia '80
Vera Belmont
Red Kiss '85
Edmund Beloin
Lady On a Train '45
Jerry Belson
Always '89
Surrender '87
Jekyll & Hyde...Together Again
'82
Smokey and the Bandit, Part 2
'80
The End '78
Fun with Dick and Jane '77
Smile '75
How Sweet It Is! '68
James Belushi
Number One with a Bullet '87
Birthday Boy '85
Remy Belvaux
Man Bites Dog '91
**Maria-Luisa
Bemberg**
I Don't Want to Talk About It '94
I, the Worst of All '90
Miss Mary '86
Jean-Marie Benard
L'Amour en Herbe '77
Peter Benchley
The Island '80
The Deep '77
Jaws '75
Robert Benchley
Foreign Correspondent '40
**Alessandro
Bencivenni**
Ciao, Professore! '94
Lawrence Bender
Intruder '88
Barbara Benedek
Sabrina '95
Immediate Family '89
Men Don't Leave '89
The Big Chill '83

Tom Benedek
The Adventures of Pinocchio '96
Zeus and Roxanne '96
Cocoon '85
Robert Benedetto
The Canterville Ghost '96
Aloha Summer '88
Glenn Benest
Deadly Blessing '81
Roberto Benigni
The Monster '96
Johnny Stecchino '92
Tomas Benitez
Salsa '88
Jeff Benjamin
American Anthem '86
Richard Benner
Happy Birthday, Gemini '80
Rick Bennet
Balance of Power '96
Alan Bennett
The Madness of King George
'94
A Question of Attribution '91
Prick Up Your Ears '87
A Private Function '84
An Englishman Abroad '83
Bill Bennett
Backlash '86
Charles Bennett
Five Weeks in a Balloon '62
Voyage to the Bottom of the Sea
'61
Curse of the Demon '57
Dangerous Mission '54
The Green Glove '52
Black Magic '49
Unconquered '47
The Story of Dr. Wassell '44
Forever and a Day '43
Joan of Paris '42
Foreign Correspondent '40
Balalaika '39
The Young in Heart '38
Young and Innocent '37
King of the Damned '36
Sabotage '36
The Secret Agent '36
The 39 Steps '35
The Evil Mind '34
The Man Who Knew Too Much
'34
Blackmail '29
Edward Bennett
A Woman at War '94
Gary Bennett
Rain Without Thunder '93
Harve Bennett
Star Trek 4: The Voyage Home
'86
Star Trek 3: The Search for
Spock '84
Parker Bennett
Super Mario Bros. '93
Mystery Date '91
Valerie Bennett
The Companion '94
Wallace C. Bennett
Rage of Honor '87
Silent Scream '80
George! '70
Jean-Louis Benoit
A Couch in New York '95
Robby Benson
Betrayal of the Dove '92
Modern Love '90
Die Laughing '80
One on One '77
Sally Benson
Come to the Stable '49
Conspirator '49
Anna and the King of Siam '46
Shadow of a Doubt '43
Trevor Bentham
A Month by the Lake '95
Robert Bentley
Shanghai Surprise '86

Robert Benton
Nobody's Fool '94
Nadine '87
Places in the Heart '84
Still of the Night '82
Kramer vs. Kramer '79
Superman: The Movie '78
The Late Show '77
Bad Company '72
What's Up, Doc? '72
There was a Crooked Man '70
Bonnie & Clyde '67
David Benullo
Cupid '96
Leo Benvenuti
Ciao, Professore! '94
The Santa Clause '94
Luc Beraud
The Accompanist '93
This Sweet Sickness '77
The Best Way '76
Luca Bercovici
The Granny '94
Rockula '90
Ghoulies '84
Geza Beremenyi
The Midas Touch '89
Bruce Beresford
Paradise Road '97
Curse of the Starving Class '94
Mister Johnson '91
The Fringe Dwellers '86
Breaker Morant '80
Money Movers '78
Barry McKenzie Holds His Own
'74
Rhoisin Beresford
The Fringe Dwellers '86
James Berg
A Very Brady Sequel '96
John Berger
La Salamandre '71
Pamela Berger
The Magic Stone '95
The Imported Bridegroom '89
Sorceress '88
Robert Berger
Final Analysis '92
Stephen Berger
Children of the Corn 4: The
Gathering '96
Andrew Bergman
Striptease '96
It Could Happen to You '94
The Scout '94
Honeymoon in Vegas '92
Soapdish '91
The Freshman '90
Big Trouble '86
Fletch '85
Oh, God! You Devil '84
So Fine '81
The In-Laws '79
Blazing Saddles '74
Ingmar Bergman
Sunday's Children '94
The Best Intentions '92
After the Rehearsal '84
Fanny and Alexander '83
From the Life of the Marionettes
'80
Autumn Sonata '78
The Serpent's Egg '78
Face to Face '76
Scenes from a Marriage '73
Cries and Whispers '72
The Touch '71
The Passion of Anna '70
The Rite '69
Hour of the Wolf '68
The Shame '68
Persona '66
The Silence '63
The Winter Light '62
Through a Glass Darkly '61
The Devil's Eye '60
The Magician '58
Wild Strawberries '57
The Seventh Seal '56
Dreams '55

Blum ✒cont.

Heavy Metal '81
Stripes '81
Meatballs '79

John Blumenthal
Short Time '90

Don Bluth
Thumbelina '94
All Dogs Go to Heaven '89
The Secret of NIMH '82

Jeffrey Boam
The Phantom '96
Lethal Weapon 3 '92
Indiana Jones and the Last
Crusade '89
Lethal Weapon 2 '89
Funny Farm '88
Innerspace '87
The Lost Boys '87
Dead Zone '83
Straight Time '78

Al Boasberg
A Night at the Opera '35

Sam Bobrick
Jimmy the Kid '82
Norman, Is That You? '76

Steven Bochco
Columbo: Murder By the Book
'71
Silent Running '71

Sally Bochner
Strangers in Good Company '91

Sergei Bodrov
Prisoner of the Mountains '96
Somebody to Love '94

Sydney Boehm
Rough Night in Jericho '67

Michael Boekner
Psycho Girls '86

Knut Boeser
Nostradamus '93

Yurek Bogayevicz
Anna '87

Peter Bogdanovich
Texasville '90
They All Laughed '81
Saint Jack '79
The Last Picture Show '71
Targets '68
The Wild Angels '66

Michael Bogert
Dead End City '88

Willy Bogner
Fire and Ice '83

Eric Bogosian
subUrbia '96
Sex, Drugs, Rock & Roll: Eric
Bogosian '91
Talk Radio '88

Endre Bohem
Twenty Bucks '93

Leslie Bohem
Dante's Peak '97
Daylight '96
Nowhere to Run '93
Twenty Bucks '93
The Horror Show '89
A Nightmare on Elm Street 5:
Dream Child '89

Charles F. Bohl
He's My Girl '87

Dan Bohlinger
The Killing Time '87

Michael Derek Bohusz
Uninvited '93

Jerome Boivin
Barjo '93
Baxter '89

Bridget Boland
Gaslight '40

Chris Bold
Hard Justice '95

Heinrich Boll
Germany in Autumn '78

Joseph Bologna
Love Is All There Is '96
Lovers and Other Strangers '70

Craig Bolotin
That Night '93
Straight Talk '92
Black Rain '89

Troy Bolotnick
Cyborg 3: The Recycler '95
Red Scorpion 2 '94

Max Bolt
The Big Sweat '90

Robert Bolt
Without Warning: The James
Brady Story '91
The Mission '86
The Bounty '84
Lady Caroline Lamb '73
Ryan's Daughter '70
A Man for All Seasons '66
Doctor Zhivago '65
Lawrence of Arabia '62

Guy Bolton
Weekend at the Waldorf '45
Angel '37

Edward Bond
Walkabout '71

James Bond, III
Def by Temptation '90

Jonathan Bond
Santa with Muscles '96

Julian Bond
Lie Down with Lions '94
The Whistle Blower '87
The Shooting Party '85
The Duchess of Duke Street '78
Choice of Weapons '76

Timothy Bond
Happy Birthday to Me '81

Sergei Bondarchuk
Waterloo '71

Vittorio Bonicelli
Moses '76
The Bible '66

Mike Bonifer
Lipstick Camera '93

Pascal Bonitzer
Night and Day '91

Bob Bonney
The Night the Lights Went Out in
Georgia '81

Andre Bonzel
Man Bites Dog '91

J.R. Bookwalter
The Dead Next Door '89

John Boorman
Where the Heart Is '90
Hope and Glory '87
Excalibur '81
Zardoz '73

Telsche Boorman
French Twist '95
Where the Heart Is '90

Jon Boorstin
Dream Lover '85

Paul Boorstin
Fire with Fire '86

Sharon Boorstin
Fire with Fire '86

Charles G. Booth
House on 92nd Street '45

Connie Booth
Fawlty Towers '77

James Booth
American Ninja 2: The
Confrontation '87
Avenging Force '86
Pray for Death '85
Sunburn '79

Jason Booth
Out on Bail '89

Jose Luis Borau
On the Line '83

Ethel B. Borden
I Live My Life '35

Lizzie Borden
Erotique '94
Working Girls '87
Born in Flames '83

Allen Boretz
Where There's Life '47

Alvin Boretz
Brass Target '78

Robert Boris
Frank and Jesse '94
Extreme Justice '93
Steele Justice '87
Oxford Blues '84
Doctor Detroit '83
Some Kind of Hero '82
Electra Glide in Blue '73

Herb Borkland
Honor and Glory '92

Jim Borrelli
Cat Chaser '90

Clay Borris
Quiet Cool '86

Phillip Borsos
Far from Home: The Adventures
of Yellow Dog '94

Terry Borst
Private War '90

Chris Borthwick
A Test of Love '84

Michael Bortman
Chain Reaction '96
Crooked Hearts '91
The Good Mother '88

Aida Bortnik
Old Gringo '89
The Official Story '85

Roselyne Bosch
1492: Conquest of Paradise '92

John Boskovich
Inside Monkey Zetterland '93

James Bosley
Fun '94

Pierre Bost
Forbidden Games '52
The Red Inn '51
The Walls of Malapaga '49

Parker Bostwick
Dragon Fury 2 '96

Nancy Trite Botkin
Race to Freedom: The Story of
the Underground Railroad '94

Michel Marc Bouchard
Lilies '96

Sylvie Bouchard
King of the Airwaves '94

Jean Boudin
Being at Home with Claude '92

Roy Boulting
Carlton Browne of the F.O. '59
Brothers in Law '57
The Guinea Pig '48

Nouri Bouzid
The Silences of the Palace '94

Susan Bowen
The Power Within '95
Storybook '95

William Bowers
Support Your Local Sheriff '69
Alias Jesse James '59
My Man Godfrey '57
Split Second '53

Douglas Bowie
Boy in Blue '86

Mike Bowler
Things '93

Craig Bowlsby
The Hound of London '93

Alan Bowne
Spike of Bensonhurst '88

Kenneth Bowser
In a Shallow Grave '88

Frank Cottrell Boyce
Butterfly Kiss '94
A Woman's Guide to Adultery
'93

Daniel Boyd
Heroes of the Heart '94
Invasion of the Space Preachers
'90
Chillers '88

Don Boyd
Twenty-One '91
East of Elephant Rock '76

William Boyd
A Good Man in Africa '94
Chaplin '92
Mister Johnson '91
Tune in Tomorrow '90
Stars and Bars '88

Francois Boyer
Forbidden Games '52

Richard Boyle
Salvador '86

Bill Bozzone
Ivory Hunters '90
Full Moon in Blue Water '88

Gerard Brach
Bitter Moon '92
The Lover '92
The Bear '89
Frantic '88
Jean de Florette '87
Manon of the Spring '87
Shy People '87
The Name of the Rose '86
Pirates '86
Maria's Lovers '84
My Best Friend's Girl '84
Quest for Fire '82
I Sent a Letter to My Love '81
Tess '80
The Tenant '76
Diary of Forbidden Dreams '73
The Fearless Vampire Killers '67
Cul de Sac '66
Repulsion '65

Charles Brackett
Titanic '53
Sunset Boulevard '50
Emperor Waltz '48
The Lost Weekend '45
Five Graves to Cairo '43
Ball of Fire '41
Midnight '39
Bluebeard's Eighth Wife '38

Leigh Brackett
The Empire Strikes Back '80
The Long Goodbye '73
The Big Sleep '46

Jacob Brackman
Times Square '80
The King of Marvin Gardens '72

Malcolm Bradbury
Cold Comfort Farm '94
The Green Man '91

Ray Bradbury
Something Wicked This Way
Comes '83
Moby Dick '56
It Came From Outer Space '53

Robert North Bradbury
Valley of the Lawless '36
The Gallant Fool '33
Texas Buddies '32

Reb Braddock
Curdled '95

Al Bradley
Iron Warrior '87

Pat Bradley
Under the Rainbow '81

John Bradshaw
The Big Slice '90

Jim Brady
Boy Meets Girl '84

Brannon Braga
Star Trek: First Contact '96
Star Trek Generations '94
Star Trek the Next Generation,
the Final Episode: All Good
Things... '94

Melvin Bragg
Jesus Christ, Superstar '73
The Music Lovers '71
Isadora '68

Diana Braithwaite
Race to Freedom: The Story of
the Underground Railroad '9

Malcolm Braly
On the Yard '79

Bill Brame
Miss Melody Jones '73

Kenneth Branagh
Hamlet '96
Much Ado about Nothing '93
Henry V '89

Chris Brancato
Hoodlum '96

John Brancato
The Net '95
Interceptor '92
Into the Sun '92
Femme Fatale '90

Larry Brand
Till the End of the Night '94
Overexposed '90
Masque of the Red Death '89
Backfire '88
The Drifter '88

Max Brand
Uncertain Glory '44

Millen Brand
The Snake Pit '48

David Brandes
The Quarrel '93
Dirt Bike Kid '86

Richard Brandes
The Nurse '97
Dead Cold '96
Martial Law 2: Undercover '91
Martial Law '90
Party Line '88

Gary Brandner
Cameron's Closet '89
Howling 2: Your Sister Is a
Werewolf '85

Clark Brandon
Skeeter '93
Fast Food '89

John F. Brascia
The Baltimore Bullet '80

Marie Brassard
Le Polygraphe '96

Caliope Brattlestreet
Showdown in Little Tokyo '91

Asher Brauner
Deadly Exposure '93

Irving Brecher
Bye, Bye, Birdie '63
Best Foot Forward '43
DuBarry Was a Lady '43
Ship Ahoy '43

Andy Breckman
Sgt. Bilko '95
I.Q. '94
True Identity '91
Arthur 2: On the Rocks '88
Moving '88

Don Bredos
Where the Rivers Flow North '93

Philip M. Breen
Sword of the Valiant '83

Richard L. Breen
Titanic '53

Catherine Breillat
Police '85

Stephen Breimer
Night Warning '82

Michael Carreras
Creatures the World Forgot '70
Unholy Four '54
Jim Carrey
Ace Ventura: Pet Detective '93
Jean-Claude Carriere
The Horseman on the Roof '95
Circle of Deceit '81
At Play in the Fields of the Lord '91
Cyrano de Bergerac '90
May Fools '90
The Mahabharata '89
Valmont '89
The Unbearable Lightness of Being '88
Max, Mon Amour '86
Swann in Love '84
The Return of Martin Guerre '83
Danton '82
The Associate '79
The Tin Drum '79
That Obscure Object of Desire '77
Phantom of Liberty '74
The Discreet Charm of the Bourgeoisie '72
Borsalino '70
The Milky Way '68
Belle de Jour '67
Attack of the Robots '66
Hotel Paradiso '66
Viva Maria! '65
Diary of a Chambermaid '64
Matthieu Carriere
Beethoven's Nephew '88
James Carrington
Fluke '95
Joseph '95
Robert B. Carrington
Venom '82
Wait Until Dark '67
J. Larry Carroll
Day Time Ended '80
Sidney Carroll
Three Cases of Murder '55
Tod Carroll
Clean and Sober '88
Willard Carroll
The Runestone '91
Bob Carruthers
Chasing the Deer '94
L.M. Kit Carson
Texas Chainsaw Massacre, Part 2 '86
Chinese Boxes '84
Breathless '83
Paris, Texas '83
The Last Word '80
David Holzman's Diary '67
Robert Carson
Just for You '52
The Desperadoes '43
Angela Carter
The Company of Wolves '85
Bill Carter
The Late Shift '96
Chris Carter
The X-Files: Pilot Episode/Deep Throat '93
Ken Carter, Jr.
Magic in the Mirror: Fowl Play '96
Robert Carter
Traps '93
Ruth Carter
Coming Up Roses '87
Sara Flanigan Carter
Sudie & Simpson '90
Dee Caruso
Doin' Time '85
The World's Greatest Athlete '73
Which Way to the Front? '70
Steve Carver
Bulletproof '88
Denise Casano
Girls Town '95

David Casci
The Pagemaster '94
Marty Casella
One Night Stand '95
Richard Casey
Hellbent '90
Horror House on Highway 5 '86
Jim Cash
Anaconda '96
Dick Tracy '90
Turner and Hooch '89
The Secret of My Success '87
Legal Eagles '86
Top Gun '86
John Cassavetes
She's So Lovely '97
Opening Night '77
The Killing of a Chinese Bookie '76
A Woman Under the Influence '74
Faces '68
Nick Cassavetes
Unhook the Stars '96
Shaun Cassidy
Strays '91
Alexander Cassini
Star Time '92
James C. Cassity
Man or Gun '58
Alan Castle
Stranded '87
Alien Castle
Jailbait '93
Desire and Hell at Sunset Motel '92
Nick Castle
Hook '91
Tap '89
The Boy Who Could Fly '86
Tag: The Assassination Game '82
Escape from New York '81
Pray TV '82
Kiss Me, Kill Me '69
William Castle
Bug '75
Robert Caswell
A Far Off Place '93
Over the Hill '93
The Doctor '91
A Cry in the Dark '88
Don Catchlove
Mr. Reliable: A True Story '95
Alain Cavalier
Therese '86
Liliana Cavani
Francesco '93
Frank Cavett
Going My Way '44
James Cawthorn
The Land that Time Forgot '75
Jennifer Cecil
Cadillac Ranch '96
Stephanie Cedar
Downhill Willie '96
Jeff Celentano
Under the Hula Moon '95
Maria Elene Cellino
No Retreat, No Surrender 2 '89
Vincenzo Cerami
The Monster '96
Johnny Stecchino '92
Chris Ceraso
The Turning '92
Janus Cercone
Leap of Faith '92
Ginny Cerrella
Tainted Blood '93
Sister, Sister '87
Claude Chabrol
La Ceremonie '95
L'Enfer '93
Betty '92
The Cry of the Owl '92

Madame Bovary '91
The Story of Women '88
Blood Relatives '77
La Rupture '70
Le Boucher '69
Les Biches '68
Six in Paris '68
The Cousins '59
Le Beau Serge '58
Ilene Chaiken
Barb Wire '96
Kitty Chalmers
Deceit '93
Cyborg '89
Journey to the Center of the Earth '88
John C. Champion
The Texican '66
Eric Champnella
Eddie '96
Jackie Chan
Project A: Part 2 '87
Pauline Chan
Traps '93
Tony Chan
Combination Platter '93
Harry Chandlee
The Adventures of Mark Twain '44
Sergeant York '41
Robert Chandlee
Killer Inside Me '76
Elizabeth Chandler
A Little Princess '95
Afterburn '92
Evan Chandler
Robin Hood: Men in Tights '93
Raymond Chandler
Strangers on a Train '51
The Blue Dahlia '46
Double Indemnity '44
Tom Chaney
Mosquito '95
Frostbiter: Wrath of the Wendigo '94
Robert Chapin
Ring of Steel '94
Charlie Chaplin
A Countess from Hong Kong '67
Monsieur Verdoux '47
The Great Dictator '40
Modern Times '36
Three Charlies and One Phoney! '18
Charlie Chaplin: Night at the Show '15
Paul Chaplin
Mystery Science Theater 3000: The Movie '96
Graham Chapman
Monty Python's The Meaning of Life '83
Yellowbeard '83
Monty Python's Life of Brian '79
Monty Python and the Holy Grail '75
And Now for Something Completely Different '72
Rentadick '72
John T. Chapman
Satan in High Heels '62
Leigh Chapman
Impulse '90
Storm and Sorrow '90
Octagon '80
Steel '80
Dirty Mary Crazy Larry '74
Truck Turner '74
How Come Nobody's On Our Side? '73
A Swingin' Summer '65
Matthew Chapman
Color of Night '94
Consenting Adults '92
Heart of Midnight '89
Slow Burn '86
Strangers Kiss '83
Hussy '80

Priscilla Chapman
The Fan '81
Richard Chapman
My Fellow Americans '96
Robin Chapman
Force 10 from Navarone '78
Triple Echo '77
Rebecca Charles
Nemesis '93
Borden Chase
Lone Star '52
The World in His Arms '52
Red River '48
David Chase
Kounterfeit '96
David Chaskin
Midnight's Child '93
I, Madman '89
The Curse '87
A Nightmare on Elm Street 2: Freddy's Revenge '85
Etienne Chatiliez
Tatie Danielle '91
Life Is a Long Quiet River '88
Paddy Chayefsky
Altered States '80
Network '76
The Hospital '71
Paint Your Wagon '69
The Americanization of Emily '64
The Goddess '58
Marty '55
As Young As You Feel '51
Peter Chelsom
Funny Bones '94
Hear My Song '91
Chenal
Crime and Punishment '35
Zhang Chengzhi
A Mongolian Tale '94
Cynthia A. Cherbak
The Kissing Place '90
Patrice Chereau
Queen Margot '94
John R. Cherry, III
Slam Dunk Ernest '95
Ernest Rides Again '93
Ernest Scared Stupid '91
Ernest Goes to Camp '87
Lionel Chetwynd
Kissinger and Nixon '96
The Man Who Captured Eichmann '96
Moses '96
Joseph '95
Doomsday Gun '94
Jacob '93
The Heroes of Desert Storm '91
To Heal a Nation '88
Hanoi Hilton '87
Quintet '79
The Apprenticeship of Duddy Kravitz '74
Francois Chevallier
Daens '92
Peter Cheyney
Uneasy Terms '48
Andrew Chiaramonte
Twogether '94
Billy Chicago
Netherworld '90
Deven Chierighino
The Wizard of Speed and Time '88
Helen Childress
Reality Bites '94
Charles Chiodo
Killer Klowns from Outer Space '88
Stephen Chiodo
Killer Klowns from Outer Space '88
David Chisholm
Dead Man's Revenge '93
The Wizard '89

Jerome Chodorov
All Over Town '37
Michele S. Chodos
Police Academy: Mission to Moscow '94
Rae Dawn Chong
Boulevard '94
Thomas Chong
Far Out Man '89
Cheech and Chong's The Corsican Brothers '84
Cheech and Chong: Still Smokin' '83
Cheech and Chong: Things Are Tough All Over '82
Cheech and Chong's Nice Dreams '81
Cheech and Chong's Next Movie '80
Cheech and Chong's Up in Smoke '79
Michael Choquette
Stitches '85
Christian-Jaque
Fanfan la Tulipe '51
Nathaniel Christian
California Casanova '89
Roger Christian
King of the Mountain '81
Dick Chudnow
Spy Hard '96
Gene Church
Snapdragon '93
John Cianetti
Judge & Jury '96
Gerard Ciccoritti
Skull: A Night of Terror '88
A Whisper to a Scream '88
Psycho Girls '86
Cynthia Cidre
The Mambo Kings '92
Fires Within '91
In Country '89
Matt Cimber
Yellow Hair & the Fortress of Gold '84
Butterfly '82
Michael Cimino
Year of the Dragon '85
Heaven's Gate '81
The Deer Hunter '78
Thunderbolt & Lightfoot '74
Magnum Force '73
Silent Running '71
Tony Cinciripini
Confessions of a Hit Man '94
The Lawless Land '88
Paul Ciotti
Ted & Venus '91
Cindy Cirile
Rapid Fire '92
Patrick Cirillo
The Surgeon '94
Dangerous Heart '94
Homer and Eddie '89
Tom Citrano
Night Eyes '90
Rene Clair
Les Grandes Manoeuvres '55
Beauties of the Night '52
Beauty and the Devil '50
A Nous la Liberte '31
Wes Claridge
Deadly Game '91
B.D. Clark
Galaxy of Terror '81
Bob (Benjamin) Clark
My Summer Story '94
Loose Cannons '90
From the Hip '86
A Christmas Story '83
Porky's 2: The Next Day '83
Porky's '82
Children Shouldn't Play with Dead Things '72

Rupert Walters
Restoration '94

Fred Walton
When a Stranger Calls Back '93
Trapped '89
The Rosary Murders '87
Hadley's Rebellion '84

Hui-Ling Wang
Eat Drink Man Woman '94

Peter Wang
The Laserman '90
A Great Wall '86

Wayne Wang
Blue in the Face '95
Chan Is Missing '82

Orville Wanzer
The Devil's Mistress '68

David S. Ward
The Program '93
Sleepless in Seattle '93
King Ralph '91
Major League '89
The Milagro Beanfield War '88
Saving Grace '86
The Sting 2 '83
Cannery Row '82
Steelyard Blues '73
The Sting '73

Donal Lardner Ward
My Life's in Turnaround '94

Edmund Ward
Prayer for the Dying '87
Twinsanity '70

Kelly Ward
All Dogs Go to Heaven 2 '95
Once Upon a Forest '93

Morgan Ward
A Pyromaniac's Love Story '95

Stephen Ward
Backbeat '94

Vincent Ward
Map of the Human Heart '93
The Navigator '88
Vigil '84

David Warfield
Kiss of a Killer '93
Kill Me Again '89
Private Investigations '87

Regis Wargnier
Indochine '92

Charles Marquis Warren
Charro! '69

Hal P. Warren
Manos, the Hands of Fate '66

Jerry Warren
Terror of the Bloodhunters '62

John Warren
Flashfire '94
Girl in the Cadillac '94
Naked in New York '93

Joyce Warren
The Ice Runner '93

Deric Washburn
Extreme Prejudice '87
The Border '82
The Deer Hunter '78
Silent Running '71

Art Washington
Percy & Thunder '93

Wendy Wasserstein
The Heidi Chronicles '95

Remi Waterhouse
Ridicule '96

Daniel Waters
Demolition Man '93
Batman Returns '92
Hudson Hawk '91
The Adventures of Ford Fairlane '90
Heathers '89

John Waters
Serial Mom '94
Cry-Baby '90
Hairspray '88

Polyester '81
Desperate Living '77
Female Trouble '74
Pink Flamingos '72
Mondo Trasho '69

Peter Watkins
Edvard Munch '74

John Watson
Robin Hood: Prince of Thieves '91
The Zoo Gang '85

Keoni Waxman
I Shot a Man in Vegas '96

Damon Wayans
Major Payne '95
Blankman '94
Mo' Money '92

Keenen Ivory Wayans
A Low Down Dirty Shame '94
The Five Heartbeats '91
I'm Gonna Git You Sucka '88
Hollywood Shuffle '87

Marlon Wayans
Don't Be a Menace to South Central While Drinking Your Juice in the Hood '95

Shawn Wayans
Don't Be a Menace to South Central While Drinking Your Juice in the Hood '95

April Wayne
Dead On '93

Frank Wead
Dive Bomber '41
Ceiling Zero '35

Julian Weaver
Demon Possessed '93

Arthur Webb
Trained to Kill '88

James R. Webb
How the West Was Won '63

Weaver Webb
Courage Mountain '89

David Wechter
Malibu Bikini Shop '86
Midnight Madness '80

Lu Wei
To Live '94
Farewell My Concubine '93

Robert B. Weide
Mother Night '96

John Weidner
Midnight Kiss '93
Private Wars '93

Herschel Weingrod
Pure Luck '91
Kindergarten Cop '90
My Stepmother Is an Alien '88
Twins '88
Brewster's Millions '85
Trading Places '83
Cheaper to Keep Her '80

Peter Weir
Green Card '90
The Year of Living Dangerously '82
Gallipoli '81
Plumber '79
The Last Wave '77
The Cars That Ate Paris '74

Brenda Weisberg
Rusty's Birthday '49
The Mummy's Ghost '44
The Mad Ghoul '43

David Weisberg
Holy Matrimony '94

Joe Weisenfeld
Anne of Green Gables '85

Stanley Weiser
Fatherland '94
Project X '87
Wall Street '87

David A. Weiss
Rock-a-Doodle '92
All Dogs Go to Heaven '89

Jiri Weiss
Martha and I '91
Murder Czech Style '66

Marie Weiss
The Ref '93

Rob Weiss
Amongst Friends '93

David Weissman
Dream a Little Dream 2 '94

Peter Welbeck
Bullet to Beijing '95
The Mangler '94

Sandy Welch
A Dark Adapted Eye '93
A Fatal Inversion '92

Colin Welland
War of the Buttons '95
A Dry White Season '89
Twice in a Lifetime '85
Chariots of Fire '81
Yanks '79

Michael Weller
Lost Angels '89
Ragtime '81
Hair '79

Halsted Welles
The Hanging Tree '59

Orson Welles
Treasure Island '72
Chimes at Midnight '67
Touch of Evil '58
The Lady from Shanghai '48
The Magnificent Ambersons '42
Citizen Kane '41

David Wellington
A Man in Uniform '93

Peter Wellington
The Boys Club '96

William A. Wellman
A Star is Born '37

Audrey Wells
George of the Jungle '97

George Wells
The Impossible Years '68
The Horizontal Lieutenant '62
The Gazebo '59
Designing Woman '57
Don't Go Near the Water '57
Angels in the Outfield '51
Merton of the Movies '47
The Show-Off '46

John Wells
Princess Caraboo '94

Peter Wells
Desperate Remedies '93

Wim Wenders
Faraway, So Close! '93
Until The End of The World '91
Wings of Desire '88
Tokyo-Ga '85
Lightning Over Water '80
The American Friend '77
Kings of the Road—In the Course of Time '76
Alice in the Cities '74

Gina Wendkos
Jersey Girl '92
Ginger Ale Afternoon '89

Mike Werb
Face/Off '97
Darkman 3: Die Darkman Die '95
The Mask '94
Machine Gun Kelly '58

Lina Wertmuller
Ciao, Professore! '94
Summer Night with Greek Profile, Almond Eyes & Scent of Basil '87
Camorra: The Naples Connection '85
Sotto, Sotto '85
A Joke of Destiny, Lying in Wait Around the Corner Like a Bandit '84
Blood Feud '79
A Night Full of Rain '78
Seven Beauties '76

Swept Away... '75
All Screwed Up '74
Love and Anarchy '73
Seduction of Mimi '72

Quentin Werty
Dark of the Sun '68

Richard Wesley
Mandela and de Klerk '97
Native Son '86
Fast Forward '84
Let's Do It Again '75
Uptown Saturday Night '74

Claudine West
Mrs. Miniver '42
The Mortal Storm '40

Jessamyn West
Stolen Hours '63

Joseph West
Man Made Monster '41

Mae West
Every Day's a Holiday '38
Go West, Young Man '36
Klondike Annie '36
Goin' to Town '35
Belle of the Nineties '34
I'm No Angel '33
Night After Night '32

Roland West
The Bat Whispers '30
The Bat '26

Robert Westerby
Sea of Sand '58

Donald E. Westlake
The Grifters '90
Why Me? '90
The Stepfather '87
Hot Stuff '80
Cops and Robbers '73

Ellen Weston
Lies Before Kisses '92

Eric Weston
Marvin & Tige '84

Garnett Weston
Blackmail '29

Fulvio Wetzl
Rorret '87

Gerald Wexler
Margaret's Museum '95

Haskell Wexler
Latino '85
Medium Cool '69

John Wexley
Footsteps in the Dark '41
Angels with Dirty Faces '38

Joseph Whaley
Bodily Harm '95

Jim Wheat
Rattled '96
It Came from Outer Space 2 '95
The Birds 2: Land's End '94
The Fly 2 '89
Silent Scream '80

Ken Wheat
Rattled '96
It Came from Outer Space 2 '95
The Birds 2: Land's End '94
The Fly 2 '89
Silent Scream '80

Joss Whedon
Toy Story '95
Buffy the Vampire Slayer '92

Anne Wheeler
Bye Bye Blues '89

Paul Wheeler
Poldark '75

Rene Wheeler
Fanfan la Tulipe '51

Graeme Whifler
Dr. Giggles '92
Sonny Boy '87

Denis Whitburn
The Cursed Mountain Mystery '93

Cynthia Whitcomb
Buffalo Girls '95

Elizabeth White
Foxfire '96

Garry Michael White
The Promise '79
Sky Riders '76

James Gordon White
Hell's Belles '69

Robb White
The Tingler '59

Wally White
Lie Down with Dogs '95

Hugh Whitemore
Jane Eyre '96
Breaking the Code '95
The Rector's Wife '94
Elizabeth R '72

Steve Whitestone
The Pebble and the Penguin '94

Diane Whitley
Boston Kickout '95

Preston A. Whitmore, II
Fled '96
The Walking Dead '94

David Wickes
Frankenstein '93
Jekyll and Hyde '90
Jack the Ripper '88

Bernhard Wicki
The Longest Day '62

Gregory Widen
The Prophecy '95
Backdraft '91
Highlander '86

Bo Widerberg
All Things Fair '95
Elvira Madigan '67

Ken Wiederhorn
A House in the Hills '93

David Michael Wieger
Wild America '97

John Wierick
Bopha! '93

Joe Wiesenfeld
The Yearling '94

Crane Wilbur
Yellow Cargo '36

Billy Wilder
Buddy Buddy '81
The Front Page '74
Avanti! '72
The Private Life of Sherlock Holmes '70
The Fortune Cookie '66
Kiss Me, Stupid! '64
Irma La Douce '63
One, Two, Three '61
The Apartment '60
Some Like It Hot '59
Love in the Afternoon '57
Spirit of St. Louis '57
Witness for the Prosecution '57
The Seven Year Itch '55
Sabrina '54
Stalag 17 '53
Sunset Boulevard '50
Emperor Waltz '48
The Lost Weekend '45
Double Indemnity '44
Five Graves to Cairo '43
Ball of Fire '41
Midnight '39
Ninotchka '39
Bluebeard's Eighth Wife '38
Mauvaise Graine '33

Gene Wilder
See No Evil, Hear No Evil '89
Haunted Honeymoon '86
The Woman in Red '84
The Adventures of Sherlock Holmes' Smarter Brother '78
World's Greatest Lover '77
Young Frankenstein '74

John Wilder
Return to Lonesome Dove '93
Breaking Home Ties '87

Cinematographer Index

The **Cinematographer Index** provides a videography for any cinematographer, or Director of Photography, as they are also known, with a video credit. The listings for the cinematographer names follow an alphabetical sort by last name (although the names appear in a first name last name format). The videographies are listed chronologically, from most recent film to the first. If a cinematographer lensed more than one film in the same year, these movies are listed alphabetically within the year. Many of today's top directors started as cinematographers, the people responsible for the "look" of a movie.

Miguel Abal
Killing Grandpa '91

Thomas Ackerman
George of the Jungle '97
Jumanji '95
Baby's Day Out '94
Dennis the Menace '93
National Lampoon's Christmas Vacation '89
Beetlejuice '88
Back to School '86
Girls Just Want to Have Fun '85
Frankenweenie '84
Roadhouse 66 '84
Foxfire Light '82

Barry Ackroyd
Land and Freedom '95
Ladybird, Ladybird '93
Raining Stones '93

Remi Adefarasin
Hollow Reed '95
Captives '94
Bitter Harvest '93
The Wedding Gift '93
The Lost Language of Cranes '92
Truly, Madly, Deeply '91

Matthew Aeberhard
The Leopard Son '96

Lloyd Ahern
Last Man Standing '96
Turbulence '96
Wild Bill '95
Geronimo: An American Legend '93
Trespass '92

Mac Ahlberg
The Late Shift '96
A Very Brady Sequel '96
The Brady Bunch Movie '95
Beverly Hills Cop 3 '94
My Boyfriend's Back '93
Innocent Blood '92
Oscar '91
Robot Jox '90
The Horror Show '89
Prison '88
House 2: The Second Story '87

Ghostwarrior '86
House '86
Ghoulies '84
Prime Risk '84
Re-Animator '84
Zone Troopers '84
Chained Heat '83
Metalstorm: The Destruction of Jared Syn '83
Young Warriors '83
My Tutor '82
Parasite '82
The Seduction '82
Hell Night '81
Nocturna '79

Pierre Aim
Hate '95
Cafe au Lait '94

Robert Alazraki
My Father's Glory '91
The Old Lady Who Walked in the Sea '91
Love Songs '85

Arthur Albert
Beverly Hills Ninja '96
Happy Gilmore '96
One Night Stand '95
You So Crazy '94
By the Sword '93
Surf Ninjas '93
Passed Away '92
Heart Condition '90
Miss Firecracker '89
The Principal '87
The Squeeze '87
Streets of Gold '86
The Boys Next Door '85
Odd Jobs '85
Night of the Comet '84

Maryse Alberti
Zebrahead '92
Poison '91

Jose Luis Alcaine
Two Much '96
Ay, Carmela! '90
Tie Me Up! Tie Me Down! '90
Twisted Obsession '90
Women on the Verge of a Nervous Breakdown '88

Rustler's Rhapsody '85
Demons in the Garden '82

John Alcott
Beastmaster '82
The Shining '80
Zontar, the Thing from Venus '66

Henri Alekan
Wings of Desire '88
Mayerling '68
Forbidden Fruit '52

Nestor Almendros
Billy Bathgate '91
New York Stories '89
Nadine '87
Heartburn '86
Places in the Heart '84
Confidentially Yours '83
Pauline at the Beach '83
Sophie's Choice '82
Still of the Night '82
The Blue Lagoon '80
The Last Metro '80
Kramer vs. Kramer '79
Days of Heaven '78
Goin' South '78
The Green Room '78
Love on the Run '78
Madame Rosa '77
The Man Who Loved Women '77
Maitresse '76
Story of Adele H. '75
Cockfighter '74
Chloe in the Afternoon '72
Two English Girls '72
The Valley Obscured by the Clouds '72
Claire's Knee '71
The Wild Child '70
More '69
My Night at Maud's '69
Six in Paris '68
La Collectionneuse '67

Alan Almond
Loaded '94

John A. Alonzo
The Grass Harp '95
Star Trek Generations '94

World War II: When Lions Roared '94
The Meteor Man '93
Clifford '92
Cool World '92
Housesitter '92
The Guardian '90
Internal Affairs '90
Navy SEALS '90
Physical Evidence '89
Steel Magnolias '89
Roots: The Gift '88
Overboard '87
Real Men '87
Jo Jo Dancer, Your Life is Calling '86
Nothing in Common '86
The Hit '85
Out of Control '85
No Small Affair '84
Runaway '84
Blue Thunder '83
Cross Creek '83
Scarface '83
Back Roads '81
Zorro, the Gay Blade '81
Tom Horn '80
Norma Rae '79
Casey's Shadow '78
The Cheap Detective '78
Beyond Reason '77
Black Sunday '77
Which Way Is Up? '77
The Bad News Bears '76
I Will, I Will for Now '76
Farewell, My Lovely '75
Once is Not Enough '75
Chinatown '74
Conrack '74
Lady Sings the Blues '72
Pete 'n' Tillie '72
Sounder '72
Harold and Maude '71
Vanishing Point '71
Bloody Mama '70

John Alton
Elmer Gantry '60
The Brothers Karamazov '58
Designing Woman '57
The Catered Affair '56

Tea and Sympathy '56
The Teahouse of the August Moon '56
Big Combo '55
Battle Circus '53
An American in Paris '51
Father of the Bride '50
Reign of Terror '49
He Walked by Night '48
Raw Deal '48
T-Men '47
Courageous Dr. Christian '40

Juan Amoros
Mouth to Mouth '95

Jamie Anderson
Grosse Pointe Blank '97
The Juror '96
Man of the House '95
What's Love Got to Do with It? '93
Unlawful Entry '92
Malibu Beach '78
Piranha '78
Hollywood Boulevard '76

Oslo Anderson
omaha (the movie) '95

Shohei Ando
Hiroshima '95

Yves Angelo
Germinal '93
Tous les Matins du Monde '92

Philippe Angers
Rendez-vous '85

Gregg Araki
Totally F***ed Up '94
The Living End '92

Thierry Arbogast
The Fifth Element '97
She's So Lovely '97
Ridicule '96
The Horseman on the Roof '95
The Professional '94
Ma Saison Preferee '93
La Femme Nikita '91

Fernando Arguelles
Wes Craven Presents Mind Ripper '95

Rick Lamb
Hell's Belles '95
John Lambert
Hourglass '95
Giuseppe Lanci
Nostalgia '83
Charles Lang, Jr.
The Facts of Life '60
Some Like It Hot '59
Souls at Sea '37
Charles B(ryant) Lang
Forty Carats '73
Butterflies Are Free '72
The Love Machine '71
Doctors' Wives '70
Walk in the Spring Rain '70
Bob & Carol & Ted & Alice '69
Cactus Flower '69
Flim-Flam Man '67
Hotel '67
Wait Until Dark '67
How to Steal a Million '66
Inside Daisy Clover '65
Father Goose '64
Sex and the Single Girl '64
Charade '63
How the West Was Won '63
One-Eyed Jacks '61
Summer and Smoke '61
The Magnificent Seven '60
Strangers When We Meet '60
Last Train from Gun Hill '59
The Matchmaker '58
Separate Tables '58
Gunfight at the O.K. Corral '57
Autumn Leaves '56
The Rainmaker '56
Solid Gold Cadillac '56
The Man from Laramie '55
Queen Bee '55
It Should Happen to You '54
Phffft! '54
Sabrina '54
The Big Heat '53
Salome '53
Sudden Fear '52
Fancy Pants '50
September Affair '50
The Ghost and Mrs. Muir '47
Blue Skies '46
The Uninvited '44
Sundown '41
The Ghost Breakers '40
Midnight '39
Angel '37
The Lives of a Bengal Lancer '35
She Done Him Wrong '33
A Farewell to Arms '32
Vice Squad '31
Tom Sawyer '30
Roger Lanser
A Midwinter's Tale '95
Much Ado about Nothing '93
Jeanne Lapoirie
Les Voleurs '96
Wild Reeds '94
Stevan Larner
Forbidden Choices '94
Joseph LaShelle
Barefoot in the Park '67
The Fortune Cookie '66
Kiss Me, Stupid! '64
The Apartment '60
Career '59
The Long, Hot Summer '58
The Naked and the Dead '58
Crime of Passion '57
The Conqueror '56
Marty '55
River of No Return '54
Les Miserables '52
The Jackpot '50
Come to the Stable '49
Laura '44
Walter Lassally
The Ballad of the Sad Cafe '91
The Deceivers '88
The Bostonians '84
Private School '83
Heat and Dust '82

Danger in the Skies '79
Great Bank Hoax '78
Hullabaloo Over Georgie & Bonnie's Pictures '78
Wild Party '74
Run, Stranger, Run '73
Savages '72
Something for Everyone '70
Zorba the Greek '64
Tom Jones '63
The Loneliness of the Long Distance Runner '62
A Taste of Honey '61
Andrew Laszlo
The Owl and the Pussycat '70
Ernest Laszlo
Logan's Run '76
Showdown '73
Airport '70
Daddy's Gone A-Hunting '69
Star! '68
Luv '67
Fantastic Voyage '66
Ship of Fools '65
Baby, the Rain Must Fall '64
Four for Texas '63
It's a Mad, Mad, Mad, Mad World '63
Judgment at Nuremberg '61
Inherit the Wind '60
While the City Sleeps '56
The Big Knife '55
The Kentuckian '55
Kiss Me Deadly '55
Apache '54
Naked Jungle '54
The Moon Is Blue '53
Stalag 17 '53
Vera Cruz '53
The Well '51
D.O.A. '49
Impact '49
The Road to Rio '47
Paul Laufer
Frankie Starlight '95
Charles Lawton, Jr.
Comanche Station '60
Cowboy '58
Gunman's Walk '58
Vernon Layton
The Englishman Who Went Up a Hill But Came Down a Mountain '95
Robert Le Febvre
Casque d'Or '52
Jean-Yves Le Mener
The Visitors '95
Robert Leacock
Looking for Richard '96
John Leatherbarrow
The Thief and the Cobbler '96
Sam Leavitt
The Man in the Glass Booth '75
Star Spangled Girl '71
The Passing of Evil '70
Desperados '69
Guess Who's Coming to Dinner '67
Major Dundee '65
Advise and Consent '62
Diamond Head '62
Cape Fear '61
Seven Thieves '60
Anatomy of a Murder '59
Pork Chop Hill '59
The Defiant Ones '58
The Court Martial of Billy Mitchell '55
The Man with the Golden Arm '55
Carmen Jones '54
A Star is Born '54
The Thief '52
Pavel Lebeshev
Prisoner of the Mountains '96
Philip Lee
Galaxies Are Colliding '92
Jacques Lefrancois
Robert et Robert '78
Claude Lelouch
Les Miserables '95

Denis Lenoir
The Secret Agent '96
Carrington '95
The Separation '94
Dingo '90
Dean Lent
Acting on Impulse '93
Gas Food Lodging '92
John R. Leonetti
Spy Hard '96
Matthew F. Leonetti
Fled '96
Star Trek: First Contact '96
Strange Days '95
Weird Science '85
Jean Lepine
Beyond the Call '96
The Player '92
Andrew Lesnie
Babe '95
Two If by Sea '95
Temptation of a Monk '94
Pierre Letarte
Dangerous Minds '95
Sugartime '95
The Boys of St. Vincent '93
Richard Letterman
The Ex '96
Charles Levey
The Search for One-Eyed Jimmy '96
Moshe Levin
Hard Justice '95
Peter Levy
The War at Home '96
Broken Arrow '95
Cutthroat Island '95
David Lewis
The Proposition '96
The Set Up '95
Denis Lewiston
The Canterville Ghost '96
Nightmare '91
Stephen Lighthill
The Crying Child '96
Open Season '95
Doug Liman
Swingers '96
Jong Lin
Eat Drink Man Woman '94
Pushing Hands '92
Lionel Linden
O.S.S. '46
Karl Walter Lindenlaub
Independence Day '96
Up Close and Personal '96
The Last of the Dogmen '95
Rob Roy '95
John Lindley
Michael '96
Money Train '95
I Love Trouble '94
The Good Son '93
Sneakers '92
Father of the Bride '91
Lionel Lindon
Generation '69
Pendulum '69
Dead Heat on a Merry-Go-Round '66
Grand Prix '66
The Trouble with Angels '66
All Fall Down '62
The Manchurian Candidate '62
Alias Jesse James '59
I Want to Live! '58
Lonely Man '57
Around the World in 80 Days '56
Conquest of Space '55
A Man Alone '55
Casanova's Big Night '54
Destination Moon '50
Only the Valiant '50
My Favorite Brunette '47
Welcome Stranger '47
The Blue Dahlia '46
Monsieur Beaucaire '46

The Road to Utopia '46
Going My Way '44
Philip Linzey
Bloodknot '95
Jerzy Lipman
Lotna '64
Harold Lipstein
No Name On the Bullet '59
Walk the Proud Land '56
The Private War of Major Benson '55
Gerry Lively
Children of the Corn 3: Urban Harvest '95
Friday '95
Hellraiser 4: Bloodline '95
Without Mercy '95
H.P. Lovecraft's Necronomicon: Book of the Dead '93
Walt Lloyd
Feeling Minnesota '96
Private Parts '96
Empire Records '95
Frank and Jesse '94
Short Cuts '93
Kafka '91
To Sleep with Anger '90
Down Twisted '89
sex, lies and videotape '89
The Wash '88
Dangerously Close '86
Dietrich Lohmann
A Couch in New York '95
Chris Lombardi
Theremin: An Electronic Odyssey '95
Gordon C. Lonsdale
The Last Don '97
Pierre Lorraine
Little Indian, Big City '95
Emmanuel Lubezki
The Birdcage '95
A Little Princess '95
A Walk in the Clouds '95
Twenty Bucks '93
William Lubtchansky
Every Other Weekend '91
Yang Lun
Red Firecracker, Green Firecracker '93
Bernard Lutic
Colonel Chabert '94
Jingle Ma
Jackie Chan's First Strike '96
Rumble in the Bronx '96
Julio Macat
My Fellow Americans '96
The Nutty Professor '96
Moonlight and Valentino '95
Joe MacDonald
Will Success Spoil Rock Hunter? '57
Thierry Machado
Microcosmos '96
Kenneth Macmillan
Inventing the Abbotts '97
Mr. & Mrs. Loving '96
Glen MacPherson
Doctor Who '96
Captains Courageous '95
First Degree '95
Yonezo Maeda
Minbo—Or the Gentle Art of Japanese Extortion '92
Paul Maibaum
Tornado! '96
Stephen King's The Langoliers '95
David Makin
Kids In the Hall: Brain Candy '96
Michael Maley
Farmer & Chase '96
Denis Maloney
Baja '95
Witchcraft 7: Judgement Hour '95
Natural Causes '94

Teodoro Maniaci
Clean, Shaven '93
Isidore Mankofsky
The Heidi Chronicles '95
Second Coming of Suzanne '80
Bahram Manocheri
Bleak Moments '71
Mauro Marchetti
Cemetery Man '95
William Margulies
How to Frame a Figg '71
The Love God? '70
The Ghost and Mr. Chicken '66
Francis Marin
The Texican '66
Barry Markowitz
Sling Blade '96
Jack Marta
Earth vs. the Spider '58
Otello Martelli
Anna '51
Arthur Martinelli
Supernatural '33
Mario Masini
Padre Padrone '77
Steve Mason
Buddy '97
That Old Feeling '96
John Mathieson
Twin Town '97
Bye-Bye '96
Christian Matras
Fanfan la Tulipe '51
L'Idiot '46
Thomas Mauch
Signs of Life '68
Joe C. Maxwell
Zarkorr! The Invader '96
Bradford May
Darkman 2: The Return of Durant '94
Mike Mayers
Changing Habits '96
Denise Calls Up '95
Donald McAlpine
William Shakespeare's Romeo and Juliet '96
Nine Months '95
Don's Party '76
Barry McCann
Prime Suspect 5: Errors of Judgment '96
A Fatal Inversion '92
J. Michael McClary
The Turning '92
Gregory McClatchy
Blown Away '94
Seamus McGarvey
Butterfly Kiss '94
John McGlashan
The Buddha of Suburbia '92
Martin McGrath
Children of the Revolution '95
Teresa Medina
Reflections in the Dark '94
Phil Meheux
The Saint '97
Goldeneye '95
Ruby '92
Highlander 2: The Quickening '91
Renegades '89
The Fourth Protocol '87
Morons from Outer Space '85
Beyond the Limit '83
Experience Preferred... But Not Essential '83
The Final Option '82
The Final Conflict '81
The Long Good Friday '80
Ashok Mehta
Bandit Queen '94

Composer Index

The **Composer Index** provides a videography for any composer, arranger, lyricist, or band that has provided an original music score for a film now on video. The listings for the composer names follow an alphabetical sort by last name (although the names appear in a first name last name format). The videographies are listed chronologically, from most recent film to the first. If a composer provided music for more than one film in the same year, these movies are listed alphabetically within the year.

Michael Abene
Goodbye, New York '85
Barron Abramovitch
Profile for Murder '96
Tracks of a Killer '95
Hard Evidence '94
Jack Ackerman
Faces '68
Barry Adamson
Gas Food Lodging '92
Delusion '91
Richard Addinsell
A Christmas Carol '51
Blithe Spirit '45
Gaslight '40
South Riding '37
John Addison
The Phantom of the Opera '90
Something in Common '86
Code Name: Emerald '85
Grace Quigley '84
Eleanor: First Lady of the
   World '82
Love's Savage Fury '79
The Bastard '78
A Bridge Too Far '77
Joseph Andrews '77
The Seven-Per-Cent Solution
   '76
Swashbuckler '76
Ride a Wild Pony '75
Luther '74
Sleuth '72
Cry of the Penguins '71
Start the Revolution Without
   Me '70
The Charge of the Light
   Brigade '68
The Honey Pot '67
A Fine Madness '66
Torn Curtain '66

The Amorous Adventures of
   Moll Flanders '65
The Loved One '65
Guns at Batasi '64
Tom Jones '63
The Loneliness of the Long
   Distance Runner '62
A Taste of Honey '61
The Entertainer '60
Carlton Browne of the F.O.
   '59
Look Back in Anger '58
Lucky Jim '58
Reach for the Sky '56
Larry Adler
King and Country '64
Great Chase '63
A Cry from the Streets '57
Genevieve '53
Mark Adler
Decoy '95
Slam Dunk Ernest '95
Eat a Bowl of Tea '89
The Unbearable Lightness of
   Being '88
Heat and Sunlight '87
Yashushi Akutagawa
An Actor's Revenge '63
Robert Alcivar
Blind Witness '89
Naked Lie '89
Hysterical '83
One from the Heart '82
Olly Olly Oxen Free '78
Butterflies Are Free '72
Jeff Alexander
Gun Glory '57
Westward the Women '51
Van Alexander
Strait-Jacket '64
Platinum High School '60
Girls' Town '59

Jaguar '56
When Gangland Strikes '56
The Atomic Kid '54
Eric Allaman
Down Twisted '89
Angel 3: The Final Chapter
   '88
The Battleship Potemkin '25
Cameron Allan
Jericho Fever '93
JFK: Reckless Youth '93
The Good Wife '86
Midnite Spares '85
Billy Allen
The Acid Eaters '67
Dave Allen
The Harvest '92
Eric Allen
Bleak Moments '71
Peter Allen
Crackerjack '94
Woody Allen
Sleeper '73
Byron Allred
Don't Answer the Phone '80
Gerald Alters
Your Place or Mine '83
John Altman
A Royal Scandal '96
Bhaji on the Beach '94
Funny Bones '94
Bad Behavior '92
Hear My Song '91
Ed Alton
My Demon Lover '87
Minette Alton
Devlin '92
Children of Divorce '80
Dave Alvin
Border Radio '88

William Alwyn
Madeleine '50
Captain Boycott '47
Daniele Amfitheatrof
The Last Hunt '56
Singapore '47
O.S.S. '46
The Virginian '46
David Amram
The Arrangement '69
The Manchurian Candidate
   '62
Splendor in the Grass '61
Anastasia
Before the Rain '94
Laurie Anderson
Monster in a Box '92
Swimming to Cambodia '87
Something Wild '86
Pete Anderson
Chasers '94
Pascal Andreacchio
Le Bonheur Est Dans le Pre
   '95
Dwight Andrews
The Piano Lesson '94
Gerard Anfosso
Blue Country '77
Cousin, Cousine '76
**Antonio Ramirez
Angel**
The Awful Dr. Orloff '62
Scott Angley
Clerks '94
George Antheil
Actors and Sin '52
Paul Antonelli
China O'Brien '88
Out of the Dark '88
Princess Academy '87

Women's Club '87
Avenging Angel '85
Louis Applebaum
Lost Boundaries '49
Philip Appleby
Nothing Personal '95
Maria's Child '93
Shimon Arama
Bigfoot: The Unforgettable
   Encounter '94
Sebastian Argol
Yol '82
Eddie Arkin
Pretty Smart '87
Hardbodies 2 '86
Modern Girls '86
Harold Arlen
Last Summer In the
   Hamptons '96
Gay Purr-ee '62
Cabin in the Sky '43
Martin Armiger
The Crossing '92
Sweetie '89
Young Einstein '89
Michael Armstrong
Silent Night, Deadly Night 2
   '87
David Arnold
Independence Day '96
The Last of the Dogmen '95
The Young Americans '93
Malcolm Arnold
David Copperfield '70
Africa Texas Style '67
The Great St. Trinian's Train
   Robbery '66
The Heroes of Telemark '65
The Chalk Garden '64
Whistle Down the Wind '62
On the Fiddle '61

Pedale Douce '96

Bob Christianson
Vibrations '94

Frank Churchill
Bambi '42
Dumbo '41
Snow White and the Seven Dwarfs '37

Chuck Cirino
Inner Sanctum 2 '94

Eric Clapton
Nil by Mouth '96
The Van '95
Lethal Weapon 3 '92
Rush '91
Communion '89
Lethal Weapon 2 '89
Homeboy '88
Lethal Weapon '87
Edge of Darkness '86
The Hit '85
Wonderwall: The Movie '69

Stanley Clarke
B.A.P.'s '97
The Cherokee Kid '96
Dangerous Ground '96
Eddie '96
The Road to Galveston '96
Sprung '96
Panther '95
Poetic Justice '93
Watch It '93
What's Love Got to Do with It? '93
Passenger 57 '92
Book of Love '91
Boyz N the Hood '91
Cool As Ice '91
The Five Heartbeats '91

George Clinton
Austin Powers: International Man of Mystery '97

George S. Clinton
Beverly Hills Ninja '96
Beyond the Call '96
Delta of Venus '95
The Viking Sagas '95
Amelia Earhart: The Final Flight '94
Brainscan '94
Mother's Boys '94
Hard Promises '92
Lake Consequence '92
Through the Eyes of a Killer '92
American Ninja 3: Blood Hunt '89
Gotham '88
The Lion of Africa '87
Platoon Leader '87
Wild Thing '87
Avenging Force '86
The Boys Next Door '85
Cheech and Chong: Still Smokin' '83

Rene Cloerec
The Red Inn '51

Robert Cobert
Trilogy of Terror 2 '96

Tom Cochrane
Skier's Dream '88

Harvey R. Cohen
Ghost Town '88

Leonard Cohen
McCabe & Mrs. Miller '71

Stephen Cohen
Blood & Wine '96

Gardner Cole
Femme Fontaine: Killer Babe for the C.I.A. '95

Lionel Cole
Spirit Lost '96

Cy Coleman
Family Business '89
Power '86
Garbo Talks '84
Sweet Charity '69
Father Goose '64

Graeme Coleman
Breach of Trust '95
Bulletproof Heart '95
Malicious '95
White Tiger '95
Breaking Point '94
Dream Man '94
Final Round '93
Common Bonds '91

Jim Coleman
The Unbelievable Truth '90

Michel Colombier
Meet Wally Sparks '97
Barb Wire '96
Foxfire '96
Major League 2 '94
Posse '93
The Program '93
Deep Cover '92
Folks! '92
Diary of a Hitman '91
New Jack City '91
Strictly Business '91
Buried Alive '90
Impulse '90
Midnight Cabaret '90
Backtrack '89
Loverboy '89
Out Cold '89
Who's Harry Crumb? '89
Cop '88
Satisfaction '88
The Wizard of Loneliness '88
The Couch Trip '87
Florida Straits '87
Surrender '87
The Golden Child '86
The Money Pit '86
Ruthless People '86
White Nights '85
Against All Odds '84
Purple Rain '84
Steel '80
Paul and Michelle '74
Les Assassins de L'Ordre '71
Colossus: The Forbin Project '70

Shawn Colvin
Edie & Pen '95

Combustible Edison
Four Rooms '95

Betty Comden
On the Town '91
It's Always Fair Weather '55

Joseph Conlan
Silver Strand '95

Harry Connick, Jr.
When Harry Met Sally... '89

Rick Conrad
Watchers 2 '90
Amityville 4 '89
Crime Zone '88
The Drifter '88
The Nest '88
The Terror Within '88

Jean Constantin
The 400 Blows '59

Paolo Conte
A Couch in New York '95

Bill Conti
Napoleon '96
Spy Hard '96

Bushwhacked '95
8 Seconds '94
The Next Karate Kid '94
The Scout '94
The Adventures of Huck Finn '93
Blood In ... Blood Out: Bound by Honor '93
By the Sword '93
Rookie of the Year '93
A Captive in the Land '91
Necessary Roughness '91
Year of the Gun '91
Backstreet Dreams '90
The Fourth War '90
Rocky 5 '90
The Bear '89
The Karate Kid: Part 3 '89
Lean on Me '89
Lock Up '89
Murderers Among Us: The Simon Wiesenthal Story '89
The Big Blue '88
Cohen and Tate '88
For Keeps '88
A Night in the Life of Jimmy Reardon '88
Baby Boom '87
Broadcast News '87
Happy New Year '87
I Love N.Y. '87
Masters of the Universe '87
Prayer for the Dying '87
Big Trouble '86
The Boss' Wife '86
F/X '86
The Karate Kid: Part 2 '86
Nomads '86
North and South Book 2 '86
Beer '85
Gotcha! '85
North and South Book 1 '85
The Karate Kid '84
Mass Appeal '84
Unfaithfully Yours '84
Bad Boys '83
The Right Stuff '83
The Terry Fox Story '83
I, the Jury '82
Rocky 3 '82
Split Image '82
That Championship Season '82
Carbon Copy '81
For Your Eyes Only '81
Neighbors '81
Victory '81
The Formula '80
Gloria '80
Private Benjamin '80
Dreamer '79
Goldengirl '79
A Man, a Woman, and a Bank '79
Rocky 2 '79
The Seduction of Joe Tynan '79
The Big Fix '78
F.I.S.T. '78
Paradise Alley '78
An Unmarried Woman '78
Citizens Band '77
Next Stop, Greenwich Village '76
Rocky '76
Harry and Tonto '74
Blume in Love '73

Michael Convertino
Jungle 2 Jungle '96
Mother Night '96
Bed of Roses '95

Things to Do In Denver When You're Dead '95
Guarding Tess '94
Milk Money '94
The Santa Clause '94
Aspen Extreme '93
Bodies, Rest & Motion '93
Wrestling Ernest Hemingway '93
The Doctor '91
The Waterdance '91
The End of Innocence '90
Queen of Hearts '89
Bull Durham '88
The Hidden '87
Mistress '87
Children of a Lesser God '86
Hollywood Vice Squad '86

Ry Cooder
Last Man Standing '96
Geronimo: An American Legend '93
Trespass '92
Johnny Handsome '89
Tales from the Crypt '89
Blue City '86
Crossroads '86
Alamo Bay '85
Brewster's Millions '85
Streets of Fire '84
Paris, Texas '83
The Border '82
Southern Comfort '81
The Long Riders '80

David Cope
Out '88

Stewart Copeland
Gridlock'd '96
The Leopard Son '96
Boys '95
The Pallbearer '95
Tyson '95
White Dwarf '95
Silent Fall '94
Surviving the Game '94
Airborne '93
Bank Robber '93
Raining Stones '93
Rapa Nui '93
Riff Raff '92
Wide Sargasso Sea '92
Highlander 2: The Quickening '91
Hidden Agenda '90
The First Power '89
See No Evil, Hear No Evil '89
She's Having a Baby '88
Talk Radio '88
Wall Street '87
Out of Bounds '86
Rumble Fish '83

Aaron Copland
The Heiress '49
The Red Pony '49
The North Star '43
Our Town '40
Of Mice and Men '39

Carmine Coppola
The Godfather, Part 3 '90
New York Stories '89
Tucker: The Man and His Dream '88
Gardens of Stone '87
The Outsiders '83
Apocalypse Now '79
The Black Stallion '79
The Godfather, Part 2 '74
The People '71
Tonight for Sure '61
Napoleon '27

Normand Corbeil

Frankenstein and Me '96
Kids of the Round Table '96
Screamers '96

Chick Corea
Cat Chaser '90

Vladimir Cosma
The Favor, the Watch, & the Very Big Fish '92
My Father's Glory '91
My Mother's Castle '91
The Nightmare Years '89
Just the Way You Are '84
Mistral's Daughter '84
Les Comperes '83
Diva '82
Le Bal '82
La Boum '81
La Chevre '81
Pardon Mon Affaire, Too! '77
Dracula & Son '76
Pardon Mon Affaire '76
The Daydreamer '75
Return of the Tall Blond Man With One Black Shoe '74
Salut l'Artiste '74
The Tall Blond Man with One Black Shoe '72

Elvis Costello
The Courier '91
Party! Party! '83

Bruno Coulais
Microcosmos '96
The Son of the Shark '93

Charles Court
The Green House '96

James Covell
Santa with Muscles '96

Michael Covertino
Pie In the Sky '95

Noel Coward
This Happy Breed '47
In Which We Serve '43

Rick Cox
Inside Monkey Zetterland '93

Jonathan Crayford
Dark of the Night '85

Xavier Cugat
Bathing Beauty '44
The White Zombie '32

Miriam Cutler
Witchcraft 7: Judgement Hour '95

Carlos D'Alessi
Delicatessen '92

Zhang Dalong
The Wooden Man's Bride '96

John D'Andrea
Boiling Point '93
Beyond the Law '92
Child's Play 3 '91
Swimsuit: The Movie '89
Body Slam '87
Savage Streets '83
Grambling's White Tiger '81

Oswald D'Andrea
Captain Conan '96
Every Other Weekend '91

Charlie Daniels
Lone Star Kid '88

John Dankworth
Saturday Night and Sunday Morning '60

Jeff Danna
The Big Slice '90

Mychael Danna
Kama Sutra: A Tale of Love '96
Lilies '96

Horner *cont.*

Off Beat '86
Where the River Runs Black '86
Cocoon '85
Commando '85
Heaven Help Us '85
The Journey of Natty Gann '85
P.K. and the Kid '85
Volunteers '85
Star Trek 3: The Search for Spock '84
The Stone Boy '84
Between Friends '83
Brainstorm '83
The Dresser '83
Gorky Park '83
Krull '83
Something Wicked This Way Comes '83
Testament '83
Uncommon Valor '83
48 Hrs. '82
A Piano for Mrs. Cimino '82
Star Trek 2: The Wrath of Khan '82
Deadly Blessing '81
The Hand '81
The Pursuit of D.B. Cooper '81
Wolfen '81
Battle Beyond the Stars '80
Humanoids from the Deep '80
Lady in Red '79
Up from the Depths '79

Richard Horowitz
Broken Trust '95
Lakota Woman: Siege at Wounded Knee '94
The Sheltering Sky '90

Vladimir Horunzhy
Original Gangstas '96
Stephen King's The Langoliers '95

James Newton Howard
My Best Friend's Wedding '97
Father's Day '96
The Juror '96
One Fine Day '96
Primal Fear '96
Space Jam '96
The Trigger Effect '96
An Eye for an Eye '95
French Kiss '95
Waterworld '95
Junior '94
Just Cause '94
Outbreak '94
Restoration '94
Wyatt Earp '94
Alive '93
Dave '93
Falling Down '93
The Fugitive '93
Intersection '93
The Saint of Fort Washington '93
American Heart '92
Diggstown '92
Glengarry Glen Ross '92
Night and the City '92
Grand Canyon '91
Guilty by Suspicion '91
King Ralph '91
My Girl '91
The Prince of Tides '91
Coupe de Ville '90

Flatliners '90
Pretty Woman '90
Three Men and a Little Lady '90
The Image '89
Major League '89
The Package '89
Tap '89
Everybody's All American '88
Five Corners '88
Promised Land '88
Some Girls '88
Campus Man '87
Off Limits '87
Russkies '87
Head Office '86
Never Too Young to Die '86
Nobody's Fool '86
Tough Guys '86
Wildcats '86
8 Million Ways to Die '85

Ken Howard
Foreign Body '86

Tom Howard
Tryst '94

Alan Howarth
Halloween 6: The Curse of Michael Myers '95
Arcade '93
They Live '88
Big Trouble in Little China '86
Christine '84

Eugene Huddleston
World and Time Enough '95

Steven Hufsteter
Unhook the Stars '96

David A. Hughes
Solitaire for 2 '94

Steve Hunter
Cyber Bandits '94

Gottfried Huppertz
Metropolis '26

Walter Hus
Suite 16 '94

Zakir Hussain
In Custody '94

Dick Hyman
Everyone Says I Love You '96
Mighty Aphrodite '95
Alan & Naomi '92
Leader of the Band '87
The Purple Rose of Cairo '85

Jacques Ibert
Don Quixote '35

Abdullah Ibrahim
No Fear, No Die '90

Ice-T
Return of Superfly '90

Akira Ifukube
A Quiet Duel '49

Alberto Iglesias
The Flower of My Secret '95
The Red Squirrel '93

Shinichiro Ikebe
The Eel '96
Akira Kurosawa's Dreams '90

Paul Inder
The Girl with the Hungry Eyes '94

Tassos Ioannides
The Silver Stallion: King of the Wild Brumbies '93

Ernest Irving
Kind Hearts and Coronets '49

Ashley Irwin
The Expert '95
Stranger by Night '94

Secret Games 2: The Escort '93
Deadly Rivals '92

Pat Irwin
Breathing Room '96
My New Gun '92

Bjorn Isfalt
What's Eating Gilbert Grape '93

Mark Isham
Fly Away Home '96
Gotti '96
Last Dance '96
Night Falls on Manhattan '96
Home for the Holidays '95
Miami Rhapsody '95
The Net '95
The Browning Version '94
Losing Isaiah '94
Mrs. Parker and the Vicious Circle '94
Quiz Show '94
Safe Passage '94
Fire in the Sky '93
The Getaway '93
Made in America '93
Nowhere to Run '93
Romeo Is Bleeding '93
Short Cuts '93
A Midnight Clear '92
A River Runs Through It '92
Billy Bathgate '91
Little Man Tate '91
Mortal Thoughts '91
Point Break '91
The Beast '88
The Moderns '88
Made in Heaven '87
The Hitcher '86
Trouble in Mind '86
Mrs. Soffel '84

Howard Jackson
Merrill's Marauders '62
Sergeant Rutledge '60

Joe Jackson
Queens Logic '91
Tucker: The Man and His Dream '88
Party! Party! '83

Leos Janacek
The Unbearable Lightness of Being '88

Chaz Jankel
The Rachel Papers '89
D.O.A. '88

Alaric Jans
Things Change '88
House of Games '87

Pierre Jansen
La Rupture '70
Les Bonnes Femmes '60

Maurice Jarre
Sunchaser '96
Fearless '93
Mr. Jones '93
School Ties '92
Solar Crisis '92
Only the Lonely '91
After Dark, My Sweet '90
Ghost '90
Jacob's Ladder '90
Chances Are '89
Dead Poets Society '89
Enemies, a Love Story '89
Prancer '89
Distant Thunder '88
Gorillas in the Mist '88
Moon over Parador '88
Wildfire '88
Fatal Attraction '87
Gaby: A True Story '87

Julia and Julia '87
The Murder of Mary Phagan '87
No Way Out '87
Apology '86
The Mosquito Coast '86
Solarbabies '86
Tai-Pan '86
The Bride '85
Enemy Mine '85
Mad Max: Beyond Thunderdome '85
Witness '85
Dreamscape '84
A Passage to India '84
Samson and Delilah '84
Top Secret! '84
Coming Out of the Ice '82
Don't Cry, It's Only Thunder '82
Firefox '82
The Year of Living Dangerously '82
Young Doctors in Love '82
Lion of the Desert '81
Taps '81
Enola Gay: The Men, the Mission, the Atomic Bomb '80
The Last Flight of Noah's Ark '80
Resurrection '80
Shogun '80
The Black Marble '79
The Magician of Lublin '79
The Tin Drum '79
Winter Kills '79
The Prince and the Pauper '78
Users '78
Jesus of Nazareth '77
March or Die '77
Mohammed: Messenger of God '77
The Last Tycoon '76
Shout at the Devil '76
The Man Who Would Be King '75
Mandingo '75
Posse '75
The Island at the Top of the World '74
Mr. Sycamore '74
Ash Wednesday '73
Mackintosh Man '73
Life & Times of Judge Roy Bean '72
Plaza Suite '71
Red Sun '71
El Condor '70
Ryan's Daughter '70
The Damned '69
Topaz '69
Five Card Stud '68
The Fixer '68
Isadora '68
Villa Rides '68
Night of the Generals '67
Gambit '66
Grand Prix '66
Is Paris Burning? '66
The Professionals '66
The Collector '65
Doctor Zhivago '65
The Train '65
Behold a Pale Horse '64
Judex '64
Lawrence of Arabia '62
The Longest Day '62
Sundays & Cybele '62
The Horror Chamber of Dr. Faustus '59

Maurice Jaubert
The Man Who Loved Women '77
Small Change '76

Simon Jeffes
Malcolm '86

Peter Jermyn
The Climb '87

Zhao Jiping
Temptress Moon '96
To Live '94
Farewell My Concubine '93
The Story of Qui Ju '91

Antonio Carlos Jobim
Black Orpheus '58

David Johansen
Mr. Nanny '93

Elton John
The Lion King '94
Friends '71

Arthur Johnson
Sidewalks of London '38

Laurie Johnson
Dr. Strangelove, or: How I Learned to Stop Worrying and Love the Bomb '64
Tiger Bay '59

Adrian Johnston
Jude '96

Freedy Johnston
Kingpin '96

Philip Johnston
The Music of Chance '93

Alain Jomy
The Accompanist '93
The Little Thief '89
The Best Way '76

Darryl Jones
Love Jones '96

David Allen Jones
House Party 3 '94

John Paul Jones
Risk '94

Mick Jones
Amongst Friends '93

Quincy Jones
The Color Purple '85
The Wiz '78
Roots '77
The Getaway '72
The New Centurions '72
The Anderson Tapes '71
Dollars '71
Honky '71
Man & Boy '71
Brother John '70
The Hot Rock '70
They Call Me Mr. Tibbs! '70
Bob & Carol & Ted & Alice '69
Cactus Flower '69
The Italian Job '69
MacKenna's Gold '69
Dandy in Aspic '68
For Love of Ivy '68
Enter Laughing '67
In Cold Blood '67
In the Heat of the Night '67
Mirage '66
Walk, Don't Run '66
The Pawnbroker '65
The Slender Thread '65

Trevor Jones
Desperate Measures '97
Brassed Off '96
Gulliver's Travels '95
Loch Ness '95
Richard III '95
Hideaway '94
Kiss of Death '94

How to Commit Marriage '69
Hal Lindes
Band of Gold '95
The Infiltrator '95
Mort Lindsay
40 Pounds of Trouble '62
Christopher Lindsey
Sioux City '94
Michael Linn
American Ninja '85
Wang Liping
Women From the Lake of Scented Souls '94
Michael Lipton
Heroes of the Heart '94
Zdenek Liska
Murder Czech Style '66
Jay Livingston
Red Garters '54
Joseph Lo Duca
Hercules the Legendary Journeys, Vol. 1: And the Amazon Women '94
Hercules the Legendary Journeys, Vol. 2: The Lost Kingdom '94
Hercules the Legendary Journeys, Vol. 3: The Circle of Fire '94
Hercules the Legendary Journeys, Vol. 4: In the Underworld '94
H.P. Lovecraft's Necronomicon: Book of the Dead '93
Army of Darkness '92
Lunatics: A Love Story '92
Evil Dead 2: Dead by Dawn '87
Thou Shalt Not Kill...Except '87
Robert Lockhart
Cold Comfort Farm '94
Frank Loesser
How to Succeed in Business without Really Trying '67
Guys and Dolls '55
Hans Christian Andersen '52
The Perils of Pauline '47
Hoppity Goes to Town '41
Frederick Loewe
The Little Prince '74
Paint Your Wagon '69
Camelot '67
My Fair Lady '64
Gigi '58
Brigadoon '54
Nils Lofgren
Every Breath '93
Frank London
A Brother's Kiss '97
Diane Louie
Latino '85
Jacques Loussier
Dark of the Sun '68
Richard Lowry
Mommy 2: Mommy's Day '96
Mommy '95
Marcos Loya
... And the Earth Did Not Swallow Him '94
Dario Lucantoni
Acla's Descent into Floristella '87
Lydia Lunch
Vortex '81
Donal Lunny
Eat the Peach '86

Jun Lupito
Raw Target '95
Evan Lurie
The Monster '96
Tree's Lounge '96
The Night We Never Met '93
Johnny Stecchino '92
John Lurie
Manny & Lo '96
Get Shorty '95
Mystery Train '89
Down by Law '86
Permanent Vacation '84
Stranger than Paradise '84
Elisabeth Lutyens
Paranoiac '62
Allen Lynch
Mosquito '95
Rain Without Thunder '93
Randall Lynch
Mosquito '95
Rain Without Thunder '93
Jens Lysdal
A Day in October '92
Egisto Macchi
The Rose Garden '89
Padre Padrone '77
Don MacDonald
Kissed '96
Mader
Eat Drink Man Woman '94
In the Soup '92
Gustav Mahler
Death in Venice '71
Stefano Mainetti
Hidden Assassin '94
Hans-Martin Majewski
The Bridge '59
Curzio Malaparte
The Forbidden Christ '50
Gary Remal Malkin
Thousand Pieces of Gold '91
Manuel Malou
French Twist '95
Nikos Mamangakis
Kaspar Hauser '93
Yuri Mamin
Window to Paris '95
Mark Mancina
Con Air '97
Speed 2: Cruise Control '97
Moll Flanders '96
Twister '96
Assassins '95
Fair Game '95
Man of the House '95
Money Train '95
Monkey Trouble '94
Speed '94
Henry Mancini
Married to It '93
Son of the Pink Panther '93
Tom and Jerry: The Movie '93
Never Forget '91
Switch '91
Fear '90
Ghost Dad '90
Peter Gunn '89
Physical Evidence '89
Skin Deep '89
Welcome Home '89
Sunset '88
Without a Clue '88
Blind Date '87
The Glass Menagerie '87
A Fine Mess '86

The Great Mouse Detective '86
That's Life! '86
Lifeforce '85
Santa Claus: The Movie '85
That's Dancing! '85
Harry & Son '84
Better Late Than Never '83
Curse of the Pink Panther '83
The Man Who Loved Women '83
Second Thoughts '83
The Thorn Birds '83
Trail of the Pink Panther '82
Victor/Victoria '82
Back Roads '81
Condorman '81
Mommie Dearest '81
S.O.B. '81
A Change of Seasons '80
Little Miss Marker '80
The Shadow Box '80
Nightwing '79
Prisoner of Zenda '79
10 '79
Family Upside Down '78
House Calls '78
Revenge of the Pink Panther '78
Who Is Killing the Great Chefs of Europe? '78
Angela '77
The Pink Panther Strikes Again '76
Silver Streak '76
The Great Waldo Pepper '75
Once is Not Enough '75
The White Dawn '75
The Girl from Petrovka '74
99 & 44/100 Dead '74
Return of the Pink Panther '74
That's Entertainment '74
Oklahoma Crude '73
The Thief Who Came to Dinner '73
Sometimes a Great Notion '71
Darling Lili '70
Molly Maguires '70
The Night Visitor '70
Bachelor in Paradise '69
The Party '68
Two for the Road '67
Wait Until Dark '67
Arabesque '66
What Did You Do in the War, Daddy? '66
The Great Race '65
The Pink Panther '64
A Shot in the Dark '64
Charade '63
Man's Favorite Sport? '63
Soldier in the Rain '63
Days of Wine and Roses '62
Experiment in Terror '62
Hatari! '62
Mr. Hobbs Takes a Vacation '62
Breakfast at Tiffany's '61
The Great Impostor '61
Never Steal Anything Small '59
Touch of Evil '58
The Land Unknown '57
Rock, Pretty Baby '56
The Benny Goodman Story '55
Far Country '55
Abbott and Costello Meet the Keystone Kops '54
The Glenn Miller Story '54
Horizons West '52
Lost in Alaska '52

Johnny Mandel
The Last Detail '73
M*A*S*H '70
I Want to Live! '58
Harry Manfredini
Dead on Sight '94
Jason Goes to Hell: The Final Friday '93
House '86
Chuck Mangione
Children of Sanchez '79
Barry Manilow
The Pebble and the Penguin '94
Thumbelina '94
Barry Mann
All Dogs Go to Heaven 2 '95
Hummie Mann
Dracula: Dead and Loving It '95
Benefit of the Doubt '93
Robin Hood: Men in Tights '93
Year of the Comet '92
In Gold We Trust '91
Stoogemania '85
Shelley Manne
T-Bird Gang '59
David Mansfield
A Streetcar Named Desire '95
Truman '95
The Ballad of Little Jo '93
Me & Veronica '93
Miss Firecracker '89
Club Paradise '86
Bevan Manson
The Magic Stone '95
Jim Manzie
Night of the Scarecrow '95
Lurking Fear '94
Night of the Demons 2 '94
Anthony Marinelli
Two Days in the Valley '96
Underworld '96
One Man's Justice '95
Young Guns '88
Yannis Markopolous
Cactus '86
Rick Marotta
The Cover Girl Murders '93
Branford Marsalis
Mr. & Mrs. Loving '96
Sneakers '92
Mo' Better Blues '90
Wynton Marsalis
Tune in Tomorrow '90
Phil Marshall
Trial and Error '96
Kicking and Screaming '95
Noises Off '92
Full Moon in Blue Water '88
Philip Martell
The Anniversary '68
George Martin
Live and Let Die '73
Yellow Submarine '68
Hugh Martin
Athena '54
Cliff Martinez
The Underneath '95
King of the Hill '93
Kafka '91
sex, lies and videotape '89
Rick Marvin
Dead Men Can't Dance '97
Escape Clause '96
Galgameth '96
3 Ninjas Kick Back '94
Save Me '93

3 Ninjas '92
J. Mascis
Gas Food Lodging '92
Herve Masini
Pedale Douce '96
Harvey W. Mason
Only the Strong '93
Nick Mason
White of the Eye '88
Roger Mason
Crime Broker '94
Ted Mason
Robot in the Family '94
John Massari
The Big Sweat '90
Killer Klowns from Outer Space '88
The Wizard of Speed and Time '88
Greg Mathieson
American Flyers '85
Muir Mathieson
This Happy Breed '47
Peter Matz
Stepping Out '91
Torch Song Trilogy '88
Lust in the Dust '85
Brian May
Dr. Giggles '92
Bloodmoon '90
Cloak & Dagger '84
Stage Fright '83
Treasure of the Yankee Zephyr '83
The Road Warrior '82
Escape 2000 '81
Killing of Angel Street '81
Road Games '81
Mad Max '80
Survivor '80
Patrick '78
Curtis Mayfield
Return of Superfly '90
Piece of the Action '77
Sparkle '76
Superfly '72
Doug Maynard
Patti Rocks '88
Lyle Mays
The Falcon and the Snowman '85
Toshiro Mayuzumi
The Bible '66
Jim McBride
Great Balls of Fire '89
John McCallum
Little Heroes '91
Dennis McCarthy
McHale's Navy '97
Star Trek Generations '94
John McCarthy
Paris, France '94
Paul McCartney
Le Bal '82
John McCulloch
Careful '94
Garry McDonald
Official Denial '93
John McEuen
The Good Old Boys '95
David McHugh
Changing Habits '96
The Hidden 2 '94
Daddy's Dyin'...Who's Got the Will? '90
The Dream Team '89
Mr. North '88
Mystic Pizza '88

Formats Index
Digital

The **Digital Formats Index** lists videos that are available in formats that take advantage of the new digital technologies. The oldest and most well-known, Laserdisc, often provides bonuses such as extra footage, interviews with cast members, or the original theater trailer. CD-I enjoyed a brief stint as "the next big thing" and serves mainly as a historical bridge to the newest format, DVD (Digital Video Disc). DVDs are the size of regular audio CDs, but hold twice the amount of information as Laserdisc. This index contains comprehensive lists of movies for all three formats.

CD-I

Apocalypse Now
The Firm
A Hard Day's Night
Indecent Proposal
Patriot Games
Salt of the Earth
Sliver
Star Trek 6: The Undiscovered Country

Digital Videodisc

Absolute Power
The Arrival
Bad Boys
Basic Instinct
Batman
Batman Forever
Beetlejuice
The Birdcage
Blade Runner
Blazing Saddles
The Bodyguard
Bonnie & Clyde
Bram Stoker's Dracula
The Bridges of Madison County
Brigadoon
The Cable Guy
Caddyshack
Chariots of Fire
The Color Purple
Cool Hand Luke
The Craft
Cutthroat Island
Dead Man Walking
Desperado
Dirty Dancing
The Doors
Dumb & Dumber
Eraser
The Exorcist
Fargo
First Knight
Fly Away Home
Forbidden Planet
Four Weddings and a Funeral
The Fugitive
Get Shorty

Ghost in the Shell
The Glimmer Man
Goldeneye
Goodfellas
Grumpy Old Men
In the Line of Fire
Interview with the Vampire
Jerry Maguire
JFK
Jumanji
A League of Their Own
Legends of the Fall
Lethal Weapon
Little Women
Mars Attacks!
Mask
Matilda
Michael
Michael Collins
Midnight Cowboy
Mortal Kombat 1: The Movie
My Fellow Americans
Outbreak
The Pelican Brief
The Player
Poltergeist
Portrait of a Lady
Purple Rain
Raging Bull
Rain Man
Red Heat
Reservoir Dogs
The Right Stuff
The Road Warrior
Rocky
Rumble in the Bronx
Sense and Sensibility
Seven
Shine
Singin' in the Rain
Sleepers
Sleepless in Seattle
Space Jam
Species
Stargate
Strangers on a Train
A Streetcar Named Desire
The Substitute
Taxi Driver
10
Terminator 2: Judgment Day

A Time to Kill
Total Recall
Truth or Dare
Turbulence
Twister
Unforgiven
The Usual Suspects
The Wild Bunch
The Wizard of Oz
Zeus and Roxanne

Laserdisc

A la Mode
A Nos Amours
Abbott and Costello Meet Captain Kidd
Abbott and Costello Meet Frankenstein
Abbott and Costello Meet the Killer, Boris Karloff
The Abominable Dr. Phibes
About Last Night...
Above the Law
Above the Rim
Abraham Lincoln
Absence of Malice
The Absent-Minded Professor
Absolute Beginners
Absolute Power
Absolution
The Abyss
The Accidental Tourist
The Accused
Ace Ventura: Pet Detective
Ace Ventura: When Nature Calls
Aces: Iron Eagle 3
Aces Wild
Act of Piracy
Action Jackson
Actors and Sin
Adam's Rib
The Addams Family
Addams Family Values
Adios Amigo
Adrenalin: Fear the Rush
Adventures in Babysitting
Adventures in Dinosaur City
The Adventures of Baron Munchausen

The Adventures of Buckaroo Banzai Across the Eighth Dimension
The Adventures of Captain Marvel
Adventures of Don Juan
Adventures of Eliza Fraser
The Adventures of Ford Fairlane
The Adventures of Huck Finn
The Adventures of Ichabod and Mr. Toad
The Adventures of Mark Twain
The Adventures of Milo & Otis
The Adventures of Pinocchio
The Adventures of Priscilla, Queen of the Desert
The Adventures of Robin Hood
The Adventures of the Wilderness Family
The Adventures of Tom Sawyer
The Adventurous Knights
The Advocate
Aelita: Queen of Mars
Affair in Trinidad
An Affair to Remember
The Affairs of Annabel
Afraid of the Dark
Africa Screams
An African Dream
The African Queen
After Dark, My Sweet
After Hours
Afterburn
Against All Flags
Against All Odds
Against the Wall
The Age of Innocence
Agnes of God
The Agony and the Ecstasy
Air America
The Air Up There
Airborne
Airheads
Airplane!
Airplane 2: The Sequel
Airport
Airport '77
Akira
Akira Kurosawa's Dreams
Aladdin
The Alamo

Alamo Bay
Alan & Naomi
Alaska
Albino Alligator
Alex
Alexander Nevsky
Alexander the Great
Alice
Alice Adams
Alice Doesn't Live Here Anymore
Alice in Wonderland
Alien
Alien 3
Alien Chaser
Alien from L.A.
Alien Intruder
Alien Nation
Alienator
Aliens
Alive
Alive: 20 Years Later
All About Eve
All-American Murder
All Dogs Go to Heaven
All Dogs Go to Heaven 2
All I Want for Christmas
All of Me
All Quiet on the Western Front
All That Jazz
All the King's Men
...All the Marbles
All the President's Men
All the Right Moves
All the Vermeers in New York
All You Need Is Cash
Allegheny Uprising
Allegro Non Troppo
Alligator 2: The Mutation
All's Fair
...Almost
Almost an Angel
Almost Blue
Almost Pregnant
Aloha Summer
Alpine Fire
Alsino and the Condor
Altered States
Alvin Purple
Always
Amadeus

Digital Formats Index

1677

Summer

Summer Lovers
Summer of '42
The Summer of Miss Forbes
A Summer Place
Summer Rental
Summer School
Summer Stock
Summertime
Sunday, Bloody Sunday
Sunday in the Park with George
Sundown Riders
The Sundowners
Sunset
Sunset Boulevard
Sunset Park
Sunset Strip
The Sunshine Boys
Super Force
Super Mario Bros.
Supercop
Supergirl
Superman: The Movie
Superman 2
Superman 3
Superman 4: The Quest for Peace
Support Your Local Sheriff
Suppose They Gave a War and Nobody Came?
The Sure Thing
Surf Ninjas
Surrender
The Survivalist
Surviving Picasso
Surviving the Game
Survivor
Survivors
Susan Slept Here
Suspect
Suspicion
Suspiria
Swamp Thing
The Swan
Swashbuckler
Swedenhielms
Sweeney Todd: The Demon Barber of Fleet Street
Sweet Bird of Youth
Sweet Charity
Sweet Country
Sweet Dreams
Sweet Hearts Dance
Sweet Liberty
Sweet Smell of Success
Sweet Talker
Sweethearts
Sweetie
The Swimmer
Swimming to Cambodia
Swimming with Sharks
The Swindle
Swing Kids
Swing Shift
Swing Time
Swingers
The Swiss Family Robinson
Switch
Switching Channels
Swoon
The Sword & the Rose
Sword & the Sorcerer
The Sword in the Stone
Sword of Honor
The Swordsman
Sworn Enemies
Sylvester
Sylvia Scarlett
T Bone N Weasel
T-Force
T-Men
Table for Five
Taffin
Tai-Pan
Tailspin: Behind the Korean Airline Tragedy
Take Me Out to the Ball Game
Take the Money and Run
Take Two
Taken Away
The Takeover
Taking Care of Business
The Taking of Beverly Hills
The Taking of Flight 847: The Uli Derickson Story
The Tale of the Frog Prince
Talent for the Game
Tales from the Crypt

Tales from the Crypt Presents Bordello of Blood
Tales from the Crypt Presents Demon Knight
Tales from the Darkside
Tales from the Darkside: The Movie
The Tales of Hoffmann
Tales of Robin Hood
Tales of the Unexpected
Talk of the Town
Talk Radio
The Tall Guy
Tall in the Saddle
Tall Lie
Tall Story
Tall Tale: The Unbelievable Adventures of Pecos Bill
Tall Texan
Talons of the Eagle
The Taming of the Shrew
Tammy and the T-Rex
Tampopo
Tango and Cash
Tank
Tank Girl
Tanner '88
Tap
Tapeheads
Taras Bulba
Target
Tartuffe
Tarzan and His Mate
Tarzan, the Ape Man
A Taste for Killing
Tatie Danielle
Tattle Tale
Taxi Dancers
Taxi Driver
A Taxing Woman
A Taxing Woman's Return
TC 2000
Tea and Sympathy
The Teacher
Teachers
The Teahouse of the August Moon
Teamster Boss: The Jackie Presser Story
Teen Wolf
Teenage Exorcist
Teenage Mutant Ninja Turtles: The Movie
Teenage Mutant Ninja Turtles 3
The Telephone
Tell Them Willie Boy Is Here
The Temp
The Tempest
Temptation
10
The Ten Commandments
Ten Days That Shook the World
Ten Little Indians
10 Rillington Place
Ten to Midnight
Ten Wanted Men
Tender Mercies
The Tender Trap
The Tenth Man
Tequila Sunrise
Terminal Bliss
Terminal Exposure
Terminal Force
Terminal Impact
Terminal Velocity
The Terminator
Terminator 2: Judgment Day
Terms of Endearment
Terror by Night
Terror in Beverly Hills
Terror in the Swamp
Terror Street
Terror Train
Tess
Test Tube Teens from the Year 2000
Testament
Tex
Texas
Texas Across the River
The Texas Chainsaw Massacre
Texas Chainsaw Massacre, Part 2
Texas Guns
Texasville
Thank Your Lucky Stars
That Darn Cat

That Hamilton Woman
That Night
That Obscure Object of Desire
That Sinking Feeling
That Summer of White Roses
That Thing You Do!
That Touch of Mink
That Was Then...This Is Now
That'll Be the Day
That's Dancing!
That's Entertainment
That's Entertainment, Part 2
That's Entertainment, Part 3
That's Life!
That's Singing: The Best of Broadway
Theatre of Blood
Thelma & Louise
Them!
Theodore Rex
There Goes My Baby
Theremin: An Electronic Odyssey
There's No Business Like Show Business
There's Nothing Out There
These Three
They All Laughed
They Came to Cordura
They Got Me Covered
They Live
They Live by Night
They Made Me a Criminal
They Never Come Back
They Shoot Horses, Don't They?
They Were So Young
They Won't Believe Me
The Thief
Thief
The Thief of Bagdad
The Thief of Baghdad
Thief of Hearts
Thieves of Fortune
The Thin Blue Line
A Thin Line Between Love and Hate
The Thin Man
The Thing
The Thing Called Love
Things Change
The Things of Life
Things to Do In Denver When You're Dead
Think Big
Third Degree Burn
The Third Man
Third Solution
32 Short Films about Glenn Gould
'38: Vienna Before the Fall
The 39 Steps
This Boy's Life
This Could Be the Night
This Gun for Hire
This is Spinal Tap
This Island Earth
This Land is Mine
This Property is Condemned
Thompson's Last Run
Thoroughly Modern Millie
Those Daring Young Men in Their Jaunty Jalopies
Those Magnificent Men in Their Flying Machines
A Thousand Heroes
Thousand Pieces of Gold
Thousands Cheer
Three Amigos
The Three Caballeros
Three Days of the Condor
Three Days to a Kill
The Three Faces of Eve
Three for the Road
Three Fugitives
The 317th Platoon
Three Legionnaires
Three Men and a Baby
Three Men and a Cradle
Three Men and a Little Lady
The Three Musketeers
3 Ninjas
3 Ninjas Kick Back
3 Ninjas Knuckle Up
Three O'Clock High
Three of Hearts
The Three Penny Opera
3:10 to Yuma

Three Wishes
The Three Worlds of Gulliver
Threesome
Throne of Blood
Throw Momma from the Train
Thumbelina
Thunder & Mud
Thunder in Paradise
Thunder in the Pines
Thunderball
Thunderbolt & Lightfoot
Thunderground
Thunderheart
Thursday's Game
THX 1138
Ticks
Tie Me Up! Tie Me Down!
The Tie that Binds
Tiger Claws
Tiger Warsaw
A Tiger's Tale
Tightrope
The Tigress
Till Marriage Do Us Part
Till the Clouds Roll By
Till the End of Time
Tillie's Punctured Romance
Time After Time
Time Bandits
The Time Guardian
The Time Machine
A Time of Destiny
Time of the Gypsies
Time Runner
A Time to Die
Time to Kill
A Time to Kill
Timebomb
Timecop
Timemaster
Timerider
Times of Harvey Milk
Tin Cup
Tin Men
Tiny Toon Adventures: How I Spent My Vacation
To Be or Not to Be
To Catch a Killer
To Catch a Thief
To Die for
To Die For
To Die Standing
To Gillian on Her 37th Birthday
To Have & Have Not
To Joy
To Kill a Mockingbird
To Kill a Priest
To Live
To Live & Die in L.A.
To the Death
To Wong Foo, Thanks for Everything, Julie Newmar
Toast of New York
Tobor the Great
Toby McTeague
Togetherness
Tokyo Decadence
Tokyo Joe
Tokyo Olympiad
Tokyo Pop
Toll of the Desert
Tollbooth
Tom & Viv
Tom, Dick, and Harry
Tom Jones
Tom Sawyer
Tom Thumb
Tomb of Ligeia
Tombstone
Tomcat: Dangerous Desires
Tommy
Too Many Girls
Too Much Sun
Tootsie
Top Dog
Top Gun
Top Hat
Top Secret!
Topaz
Topaze
Topper Returns
Tora! Tora! Tora!
Torch Song
Torch Song Trilogy
Torchlight
Torn Curtain
Tornado!

Torrents of Spring
Torture Garden
Total Exposure
Total Recall
Toto le Heros
Touch and Go
Touch of Evil
Tough Assignment
Tough Guys
Tough Guys Don't Dance
Tour of Duty
Tourist Trap
Tous les Matins du Monde
The Towering Inferno
The Toxic Avenger
The Toxic Avenger, Part 2
The Toy
Toy Soldiers
Toy Story
Traces of Red
Tracks of a Killer
Trade Off
Trading Hearts
Trading Mom
Trading Places
Trail of Terror
Trail of the Mounties
Trail of the Pink Panther
The Train
Train Robbers
Train to Tombstone
Trained to Kill
Trainspotting
Trancers
Trancers 2: The Return of Jack Deth
Trancers 3: Deth Lives
Transformations
Transmutations
Transylvania 6-5000
Trap on Cougar Mountain
Trapeze
Trapped In Paradise
Trapper County War
Travels with My Aunt
Treasure Island
Treasure of Monte Cristo
Treasure of the Sierra Madre
A Tree Grows in Brooklyn
The Tree of Wooden Clogs
Tremors
Tremors 2: Aftershocks
Trespass
The Trial
Trial by Jury
Tribute
Tricks of the Trade
The Trigger Effect
Trinity is Still My Name
The Trip to Bountiful
Triple Impact
Tripods: The White Mountains
Tripwire
Triumph of the Spirit
Trois Couleurs: Bleu
Trois Couleurs: Rouge
Troll
A Troll in Central Park
Tron
Troop Beverly Hills
Tropical Snow
Trouble Bound
Trouble in Mind
The Trouble with Angels
The Trouble with Harry
True Believer
True Blood
True Colors
True Confessions
True Grit
True Lies
True Love
True Romance
True Stories
Trust
Trust Me
The Truth About Cats and Dogs
Truth or Dare
Truth or Die
Tucker: The Man and His Dream
Tuff Turf
Tumbleweeds
Tune in Tomorrow
Tunes of Glory
The Tunnel
The Tunnel of Love
The Turn of the Screw

Young

Young Guns
Young Guns 2
Young Lady Chatterly 2
The Young Lions
Young Man with a Horn
Young Master
Young Mr. Lincoln
Young Nurses in Love
Young Sherlock Holmes
Youngblood
Younger & Younger
Yours, Mine & Ours
Z
Zabriskie Point
Zandalee
Zapped!
Zapped Again
Zardoz
Zarkorr! The Invader
Zebrahead
Zelig
Zelly & Me
Zentropa
Zeppelin
Zero Tolerance
Ziegfeld Follies
Ziegfeld Girl
Zipperface
Zombie
Zombies of the Stratosphere
Zombies on Broadway
Zoot Suit
Zora Is My Name!
Zorba the Greek
Zorro's Black Whip
Zorro's Fighting Legion
Zou Zou
Zulu
Zulu Dawn

AAE—A & E Home Video
ABC—ABC Video
ACA—Academy Entertainment
ACD—Academy Videos
ACE—Ace Video
ACN—Acorn Video
ADL—Anti-Defamation League of B'nai B'rith
AEE—American Electronics & Entertainment Corporation
AEL—Atlantic Entertainment Ltd.
AFE—Amazing Fantasy Entertainment
AFR—Afro-Am Distributing Company
AHV—Active Home Video
AIM—AIMS Multimedia
AIP—A.I.P. Home Video, Inc.
ALD—Alden Films
ALL—Allied Artists
AMB—Ambrose Video Publishing, Inc.
ANI—AnimEigo Inc. (R)
AOV—Admit One Video
APD—Applause Productions, Inc. (R)
APP—Applause Theatre and Cinema
APX—A-PIX Entertainment Inc.
ATL—Atlas Entertainment Corporation
ATM—Atomic Pictures
ATS—Acorn Media Publishing
ATV—Atlantic Video
AUD—Audio-Forum
AVE—WarnerVision
AVI—Arrow Video, Inc.
BAR—Barr Films
BBE—Blockbuster Entertainment Corporation
BBF—Bonnie Business Forms
BFA—Phoenix/BFA Films & Video (R)
BFV—Best Film & Video Corporation (W)
BIJ—Bijou Video

BMG—BMG
BMV—Bennett Marine Video
BPG—Bridgestone Multimedia
BST—ETD
BSV—Bosko Video
BTV—Baker & Taylor Video
BUL—Bullfrog Films, Inc.
CAB—Cable Films & Video
CAF—Cabin Fever Entertainment
CAL—California Newsreel
CAN—Cannon Video
CCB—Critics' Choice Video, Inc.
CCC—Cyclops Communications Corp.
CCN—Cinevista
CCP—Cambridge Educational (R)
CDV—Television International
CEL—Celebrity Home Entertainment (W)
CFV—Carousel Film & Video
CHF—Churchill Media
CHI—Center for Humanities, Inc.
CIC—Cinema International Canada
CIG—The Cinema Guild
CMB—Columbia House Video Library
CMR—Camera Three Productions, Inc.
CNG—Congress Entertainment, Inc. (R)
CNM—Cinemacabre Video
COL—Columbia Tristar Home Video (W)
CPM—Central Park Media/U.S. Manga Corps
CRC—Criterion Collection
CRV—Crown Video
CRY—Crystal Productions
CSM—Coliseum Video
CTC—Coast to Coast Video
CTD—Coast to Coast Home Video
CTH—Corinth Video

CTL—Capitol Entertainment and Home Video (W)
CVC—Connoisseur Video Collection
CVD—Consumer Video Distributers
DIS—Walt Disney Home Video
DMP—Ariztical Entertainment
DSN—Disney Educational Productions
DVT—Discount Video Tapes, Inc./Hollywood's Attic (W)
EAG—Eagle Entertainment
EAI—Electronic Arts Intermix
ECU—EcuFilm
EDV—EDDE Entertainment
EEL—Englewood Entertainment LLC
ELE—Electric Productions
ELV—Electric Video
EMI—EMI Video
EPC—Epic Records
EPE—Epic Entertainment
ERG—Ergo Media Inc. (R)
EVD—European Video Distributor
EVE—Evergreen Entertainment
EXP—Expanded Entertainment
FAF—Fast Forward
FCT—Facets Multimedia, Inc.
FEI—FM Entertainment, Inc.
FFC—Family Films/Concordia
FFM—Flower Films (R)
FGF—Military/Combat Stock Footage Library
FHE—Family Home Entertainment
FHS—Films for the Humanities & Sciences
FHV—Foothill Video
FLI—Films Inc. Video
FLL—Filmakers Library, Inc.
FLL—Full Moon Home Video
FMT—Format International
FOX—CBS/Fox Video
FRA—Video France
FRF—First Run Features

FRG—Fright Video
FRH—Fries Home Video
FRV—First Run Video
FST—Festival Films (R)
FUS—Fusion Video
FXL—Fox/Lorber Home Video
FXV—FoxVideo
GEM—Video Gems
GFV—Vision Video/Gateway Films
GHV—Genesis Home Video
GKK—Goodtimes Entertainment
GLV—German Language Video Center
GNS—21st Genesis Home Video
GPV—Grapevine Video
GRE—Greycat Films (W)
GRG—Gorgon Video
GVV—Glenn Video Vistas, Ltd. (R)
HBO—HBO Home Video (W)
HCV—Henwood Cinema Video (R)
HEG—Horizon Entertainment
HHE—Hollywood Home Entertainment
HHT—Hollywood Home Theatre
HMD—Hemdale Home Video
HMK—Hallmark Home Entertainment
HMV—Home Vision Cinema
HPH—Hollywood Pictures Home Video
HSE—High/Scope Educational Research Foundation
HTV—Hen's Tooth Video (W)
HVF—Home Video Films
HVL—Home Video Library
ICA—First Run/Icarus Films
IGP—Ignatius Press
IHF—International Historic Films, Inc. (IHF)
IME—Image Entertainment
IMP—Imperial Entertainment Corp.

INC—Increase/SilverMine Video (W)
ING—Ingram Entertainment Inc. (W)
INT—Interama, Inc. (R)
IPI—Intrepid Productions Inc.
ITC—ITC
IUF—Pentrex (R)
IVY—Ivy Film/Video
JAF—James Agee Film Project
JEF—JEF Films, Inc.
JFK—Just for Kids Home Video (W)
JHV—Jim Henson Productions
JTC—J2 Communications
KAR—Karol Video (R)
KEP—Keep the Faith Inc.
KID—Kid Vision
KIT—Kit Parker Video
KIV—Kino on Video (W)
KUI—Knowledge Unlimited, Inc.
KUL—Kultur Video (W)
LBD—LB Distributors, Inc.
LCA—Modern Curriculum Press - MCP
LEO—Leo Films (W)
LIV—Live Entertainment
LME—Lucerne Media (R)
LOO—Loonic Video
LRP—Light Rain Productions
LSV—LSVideo, Inc.
LTY—Lightyear Entertainment
LUM—Lumivision Corporation
MAD—Madera Cinevideo
MAS—Mastervision, Inc. (R)
MAX—Miramax Pictures Home Video
MCG—Management Company Entertainment Group (MCEG), Inc.
MED—Media Home Entertainment
MET—Metromedia Entertainment
MFI—Meridian Films, Inc.
MFV—Mystic Fire Video (R)
MGI—Monarch Group, Inc.

MGM—MGM Home Entertainment
MHF—Magic Hour Films
MIL—Milestone Film & Video
MLB—Mike LeBell's Video (R)
MLT—Music for Little People
MNC—Monarch Home Video
MON—Monterey Home Video (W)
MOR—Morris Video
MOV—Movies Unlimited (R)
MPI—MPI Home Video
MRV—Moore Video
MSP—Modern Sound Pictures, Inc.
MTH—MTI Home Video (W)
MTI—Coronet/MTI Film & Video
MTM—MTM Home Video
MTP—Maryland Public Television
MTX—MNTEX Entertainment, Inc.
MVC—Moviecraft, Inc.
MVD—Music Video Distributors
MWF—Monday/Wednesday/Friday Video
NCJ—National Center for Jewish Film
NEW—New Video Group
NFB—National Film Board of Canada
NHO—New Horizons Home Video
NJN—New Jersey Network
NLC—New Line Home Video
NMD—Neville Meyer Distribution (NMD)
NOS—Nostalgia Family Video
NWV—New World Entertainment
NYF—New Yorker Video
NYR—Not Yet Released
NYS—New York State Education Department
ORI—Orion Home Video
ORP—Orphan Entertainment
PAR—Paramount Home Video
PAU—Paulist Productions
PBC—Princeton Book Co. Publishers
PBS—PBS Home Video
PEN—Pentrex Video
PGV—Polygram Video (PV)
PIC—Videos.com, Inc.
PME—Public Media Video
PMH—PM Entertainment Group, Inc.
PMR—Premiere Home Video
PMS—Professional Media Service Corp.
PPI—Planet Pictures, Inc.
PRD—Peter Pan Industries, Inc. (PPI) (W)
PRE—Prestige Video
PRS—Proscenium Entertainment
PRV—Prime Video
PSM—Prism Entertainment
PSV—Powersports Millennium
PTB—Proud To Be...A Black Video Collection
PYR—Pyramid Film & Video
QHV—Questar Video, Inc.
QVD—Quality Video
RAP—RAP Entertainment Inc.
RDG—Reader's Digest Home Video
REP—Republic Pictures Home Video
RHI—Rhino Home Video
RHP—Rhapsody Films, Inc.
RHU—Random House Media
RHV—Television Representatives, Inc. (W)
RMF—RM Films International, Inc. (R)
ROC—Rocket Pictures
RXM—Rex #Miller
SCH—Schoolmasters Video (R)

SCP—Screen Pix Home Video
SDE—Stardance Entertainment
SGE—Amsell Entertainment
SHL—Media Home Entertainment (R)
SHO—Shokus Video
SHR—Shanachie Entertainment
SHV—Strand Home Video
SIG—Signals
SIM—Simitar Entertainment
SLI—Silver Lake International
SMV—Sony Music Video Enterprises
SMW—Something Weird Video
SNC—Sinister Cinema
SPC—Spectrum Films, Inc.
STP—Streamline Pictures
STS—Stagestep
STV—Studio Video Productions
SUN—Sun Video (W)
SVE—Society for Visual Education, Inc. (SVE)
SWC—Simon Wiesenthal Center
SWI—ScreenWorks Inc.
TAI—Tai Seng Video Marketing
TCE—Third Coast Entertainment
TCF—20th Century Fox Film Corporation
TEM—Tempe Video
THA—3M Audio Visual Division
THV—Trimark Home Video
TIM—Timeless Video Inc.
TLF—Time-Life Video and Television
TOU—Buena Vista Home Video
TPI—Thomson Productions, Inc.
TPV—Tapeworm Video Distributors
TRI—Triboro Entertainment Group
TSR—Three Star Releasing
TTC—Turner Home Entertainment Company
TTV—Troma Team Video
TVC—The Video Catalog
TWE—Trans-World Entertainment
TWV—Time Warner Viewer's Edge
UAV—UAV Corporation
UND—Uni Distribution/June Morishita
UNI—Unicorn Video, Inc.
UNT—Unity Productions
USH—Universal Studios Home Video
UWA—University of Washington Educational Media Collection
VAI—Video Artists International, Inc.
VAN—Vantage Communications, Inc.
VBL—Video Bible Library, Inc.
VCD—Video City Productions/Distributing
VCI—VCI Home Video
VCN—Video Connection
VCO—Video Collectibles
VDA—Video Action (W)
VDC—Vidcrest
VDM—Video Dimensions (W)
VEC—Valencia Entertainment Corp.
VES—Vestron Video
VGR—Videograf
VHE—VCII Home Entertainment, Inc.
VIF—The VideoFinders Collection
VIP—VIP Video
VLL—Video Learning Library (R)
VRS—Video Resources
VSE—Vista Street Entertainment (W)
VSM—Video Search of Miami
VTR—Anchor Bay

VYY—Video Yesteryear
WAC—World Artists Home Video
WAR—Warner Home Video, Inc.
WAX—Waxworks/Videoworks, Inc.
WBF—Water Bearer Films
WEA—Warner/Elektra/Atlantic (WEA) Corporation
WFV—Western Media Systems
WLA—Western L.A. Film Productions, Inc.
WLF—Wolfe Video
WME—Warren Miller Entertainment
WMI—Wellspring Media, Inc.
WNE—WNET/Thirteen Non-Broadcast
WOM—Wombat Film and Video
WOV—Worldvision Home Video, Inc.
WRV—Warner Reprise Video (R)
WSH—Wishing Well Distributing
WST—White Star
WVE—World Video Enterprises, Inc.
XVC—Xenon
YHV—York Home Video
YOC—Yankee-Oriole Co. (W)
ZGI—Zeitgeist Films Ltd.

The **Distributor Guide** provides full contact information, including address, phone, fax and toll-free numbers, for over 340 distributors. The distributors are listed alphabetically within Wholesale or Retail sections. Some distributors sell to both markets, or have not stated which market they serve. These distributors will appear alphabetically at the beginning of this guide. Each video in the main section has at least one and as many as three distributor codes located at the end of the entry. The key to these codes, preceding this guide, will lead you to the appropriate distributor. Those reviews with the code **OM** are on moratorium, meaning that they were distributed at one time, but aren't currently. Since it was once available, an On Moratorium title may show up at your local video store. If the distributor for a movie is not known, the code **NO** will follow the review. New theatrical releases that haven't made it to video at press time have the designation **NYR** (not yet released). These are titles that we expect will be released on video before our next edition. **Warning!** From year to year, a small minority of distributors move without telling anyone, or just plain go out of business. **Warning! Warning!** Studio distributors do not sell to the general public, they generally act as wholesalers, selling only to retail outlets. Many video stores provide an ordering service. If your local video store doesn't have a title you want, you can ask them to order it for you.

A-PIX ENTERTAINMENT INC.*(APX)*
500 5th Ave., 46th Fl.
New York, NY 10110
212-764-7171

A & E HOME VIDEO *(AAE)*
c/o New Video Group
126 5th Ave., 15th Fl.
New York, NY 10011
212-206-8600
800-423-1212
Fax: 212-206-9001

ABC VIDEO *(ABC)*
1200 High Ridge Rd.
Stamford, CT 06905
203-968-9100
Fax: 203-329-6464

ACADEMY ENTERTAINMENT *(ACA)*
9250 Wilshire Blvd., Ste. 400
Beverly Hills, CA 90212
Fax: 310-275-2195

ACADEMY VIDEOS *(ACD)*
Box 5224
Sherman Oaks, CA 91423-5224
818-788-6662
800-423-2397
Fax: 818-788-1580

ACE VIDEO *(ACE)*
19749 Dearborn St.
Chatsworth, CA 91311
818-718-1116
800-727-2229
Fax: 818-718-9109

ACORN MEDIA PUBLISHING *(ATS)*
7910 Woodmont Ave., Ste. 350
Bethesda, MD 20814
301-907-0030
800-999-0212
Fax: 301-907-9049
Email: acorn1@ix.netcom.com

ACORN VIDEO *(ACN)*
c/o Academy Entertainment
9250 Wilshire Blvd., Ste. 400
Beverly Hills, CA 90212

ACTIVE HOME VIDEO *(AHV)*
12121 Wilshire Blvd., No. 401
Los Angeles, CA 90025
310-447-6131
800-824-6109
Fax: 310-207-0411

ADMIT ONE VIDEO *(AOV)*
PO Box 66, Sta. O
Toronto, ON, Canada M4A 2M8
416-463-5714
Fax: 416-463-5714

AFRO-AM DISTRIBUTING COMPANY *(AFR)*
1909 W. 95th St.
Chicago, IL 60643-1105
312-235-4504

AIMS MULTIMEDIA *(AIM)*
9710 DeSoto Ave.
Chatsworth, CA 91311-4409
818-773-4300
800-367-2467
Fax: 818-341-6700
Email:
infa@aims.multimedia.com

A.I.P. HOME VIDEO, INC. *(AIP)*
10726 McCune Ave.
Los Angeles, CA 90034
310-559-8089
Fax: 213-559-8849

ALDEN FILMS *(ALD)*
PO Box 449
Clarksburg, NJ 08510
908-462-3522
Fax: 908-294-0330

ALLIED ARTISTS *(ALL)*
3415 S. Sepulveda Blvd., Ste. 630
Los Angeles, CA 90034
310-390-6161
Fax: 310-390-6031

AMAZING FANTASY ENTERTAINMENT *(AFE)*
3061 Fletcher Dr.
Los Angeles, CA 90065
213-550-4530

AMBROSE VIDEO PUBLISHING, INC. *(AMB)*
28 W. 44th St.
New York, NY 10036
212-768-7373
800-526-4663
Fax: 212-768-9292
Email: ambrose.com

AMERICAN ELECTRONICS & ENTERTAINMENT CORPORATION *(AEE)*
7074 Commerce Circle, Ste. D
Pleasanton, CA 94588
510-416-1259
Fax: 510-416-1279

AMSELL ENTERTAINMENT *(SGE)*
12001 Ventura Pl., 4th Fl., Ste. 404
Studio City, CA 91604
818-766-8500
Fax: 818-766-7873

ANCHOR BAY *(VTR)*
500 Kirts Blvd.
Troy, MI 48084
810-362-9660
800-786-8777
Fax: 810-362-4454

ANTI-DEFAMATION LEAGUE OF B'NAI B'RITH *(ADL)*
Audio-Visual Dept.
823 United Nations Plaza
New York, NY 10017
212-490-2525
Fax: 212-867-0779

APPLAUSE THEATRE AND CINEMA *(APP)*
211 W. 71st St.
New York, NY 10023

212-496-7511
Fax: 212-721-2856

ARIZTICAL ENTERTAINMENT *(DMP)*
405 E. Wetmore, Ste. 117-516
Tucson, AZ 85705
800-356-4386

ARROW VIDEO, INC. *(AVI)*
135 W. 50th St., Ste. 1925
New York, NY 10020
212-258-2200
Fax: 212-245-1252

ATLANTIC ENTERTAINMENT LTD. *(AEL)*
1111 Rte. 110, Ste. 324
E. Farmingdale, NY 11735
Fax: 516-249-1690

ATLANTIC VIDEO *(ATV)*
75 Rockefeller Plaza
New York, NY 10019
212-275-2000

ATLAS ENTERTAINMENT CORPORATION *(ATL)*
1 Jocama Blvd., Ste. 2E
Old Bridge, NJ 08857
908-591-1155
Fax: 908-591-0660

ATOMIC PICTURES *(ATM)*
PO Box 15824
North Hollywood, CA 91615-5824

AUDIO-FORUM *(AUD)*
96 Broad St.
Guilford, CT 06437
203-453-9794
800-243-1234
Fax: 203-453-9774
Email:
74537.550@compuserve.com

BAKER & TAYLOR VIDEO *(BTV)*
501 S. Gladiolus
Momence, IL 60954

815-472-2444
800-775-2300
Fax: 800-775-3500

BARR FILMS *(BAR)*
12801 Schabarum
Irwindale, CA 91706
818-338-7878
800-234-7878
Fax: 818-814-2672

BENNETT MARINE VIDEO *(BMV)*
8436 W. 3rd St., Ste. 740
Los Angeles, CA 90048
213-951-7570
800-733-8862
Fax: 213-957—595

BIJOU VIDEO *(BIJ)*
1349 N. Wells
Chicago, IL 60610
312-943-5397
800-932-7111
Fax: 312-337-1270

BLOCKBUSTER ENTERTAINMENT CORPORATION *(BBE)*
12655 N. Central Expwy., Ste. 600
Dallas, TX 75243
214-866-2200
800-733-3000
Fax: 214-866-2250

BMG *(BMG)*
6363 Sunset Blvd., 6th Fl.
Hollywood, CA 90028-7318

BONNIE BUSINESS FORMS *(BBF)*
2691 Freewood
Dallas, TX 75220
214-357-3956
Fax: 214-357-4512

BOSKO VIDEO *(BSV)*
3802 E. Cudahy Ave.
Cudahy, WI 53110-1234

BRIDGESTONE MULTIMEDIA(BPG)
300 N. McKemy Ave.
Chandler, AZ 85226
602-940-5771
800-523-0988
Fax: 602-940-8924

BUENA VISTA HOME VIDEO(TOU)
350 S. Buena Vista St.
Burbank, CA 91521-7145
818-562-3568

BULLFROG FILMS, INC.(BUL)
PO Box 149
Oley, PA 19547
610-779-8226
800-543-3764
Fax: 610-370-1978
Email: bullfrog@igc.org
HomePage: http://bullfrogfilms.com

CABIN FEVER ENTERTAINMENT(CAF)
100 W. Putnam Ave.
Greenwich, CT 06830
203-661-1100
Fax: 203-863-5258

CABLE FILMS & VIDEO(CAB)
Country Club Sta.
PO Box 7171
Kansas City, MO 64113
816-362-2804
800-514-2804
Fax: 816-341-7365

CALIFORNIA NEWSREEL(CAL)
149 9th St., Ste. 420
San Francisco, CA 94103
415-621-6196
Fax: 415-621-6522
Email:
newsreel@ix.netcom.com

CAMERA THREE PRODUCTIONS, INC.(CMR)
PO Box 739
Kent, CT 06757
860-868-1771
Fax: 860-868-9999

CANNON VIDEO(CAN)
PO Box 17198
Beverly Hills, CA 90290
310-772-7765

CAROUSEL FILM & VIDEO(CFV)
260 5th Ave., Rm. 905
New York, NY 10001
212-683-1660
800-683-1660
Fax: 212-683-1662
Email: carousel@pipeline.com

CBS/FOX VIDEO(FOX)
PO Box 900
Beverly Hills, CA 90213
562-373-4800
800-800-2369
Fax: 562-373-4803

CENTER FOR HUMANITIES, INC.(CHI)
Box 1000
Mount Kisco, NY 10549
914-666-4100
800-431-1242
Fax: 914-666-5319
Email: gavideoi@aol.com

CENTRAL PARK MEDIA/U.S. MANGA CORPS(CPM)
250 W. 57th St., Ste. 317
New York, NY 10107
212-977-7456
800-833-7456
Fax: 212-977-8709

CHURCHILL MEDIA(CHF)
6901 Woodley Ave.
Van Nuys, CA 91406

818-778-1978
800-334-7830
Fax: 818-778-1994

THE CINEMA GUILD(CIG)
1697 Broadway, Ste. 506
New York, NY 10019
212-246-5522
800—723-5522
Fax: 212-246-5525
Email: thecinema@aol.com

CINEMA INTERNATIONAL CANADA(CIC)
8275 Mayrand
Montreal, PQ, Canada H4P 2C8
514-342-2340
Fax: 514-342-1922

CINEMACABRE VIDEO(CNM)
PO Box 10005-D
Baltimore, MD 21285-0005

CINEVISTA(CCN)
560 W. 43rd, No. 8J
New York, NY 10036
212-947-4373
800-341-CINE
Fax: 212-947-0644

COAST TO COAST HOME VIDEO(CTD)
1766 Griffith Park Blvd., Apt. 4
Los Angeles, CA 90226-1060

COAST TO COAST VIDEO(CTC)
148 Lafayette St., 5th Fl.
New York, NY 10013
212-431-3890
800-221-3420

COLISEUM VIDEO(CSM)
430 W. 54th St.
New York, NY 10019
212-489-8130
800-288-8130
Fax: 212-582-5690

COLUMBIA HOUSE VIDEO LIBRARY(CMB)
PO Box 1112
Terre Haute, IN 47811
812-262-2001
800-538-7766

CONNOISSEUR VIDEO COLLECTION(CVC)
1575 Westwood Blvd., Ste. 305
Los Angeles, CA 90024
310-231-1350
800-529-2300
Fax: 310-231-1359
Email: Eurocine@aol.com or 76460.1327@compuserve.com
HomePage: http://www.meridianvideo.com

CONSUMER VIDEO DISTRIBUTERS(CVD)
1427 Woodhurst St.
Bowling Green, KY 42104
502-843-8300
Fax: 502-843-8300

CORINTH VIDEO(CTH)
34 Gansevoort St.
New York, NY 10014
212-463-0305
800-221-4720
Fax: 212-929-0010

CORONET/MTI FILM & VIDEO(MTI)
4350 Equity Dr.
PO Box 2649
Columbus, OH 43216
614-876-0371
800-777-8100
Fax: 614-771-5841

CRITERION COLLECTION(CRC)
c/o The Voyager Company
1 Bridge St.
Irvington, NY 10533-1543

CRITICS' CHOICE VIDEO, INC.(CCB)
900 N. Rohlwing Rd.
Itasca, IL 60143
708-775-3300
800-367-7765
Fax: 708-775-3340

CROWN VIDEO(CRV)
225 Park Ave., S.
New York, NY 10003

CRYSTAL PRODUCTIONS(CRY)
1812 Johns Dr.
Box 2159
Glenview, IL 60025
708-657-8144
800-255-8629
Fax: 708-657-8149

CYCLOPS COMMUNICATIONS CORP.(CCC)
44 Gibson Ave.
Toronto, ON, Canada M5R 1T5
416-926-8981
Fax: 416-926-9878

DISNEY EDUCATIONAL PRODUCTIONS(DSN)
4350 Equity
Columbus, OH 43228
800-621-2131
Fax: 614-771-7362

EAGLE ENTERTAINMENT(EAG)
3800 S. Ocean Dr.
Hollywood, FL 33019

ECUFILM(ECU)
810 12th Ave. S.
Nashville, TN 37203
615-242-6277
800-251-4091
Fax: 615-742-5125

EDDE ENTERTAINMENT(EDV)
19749 Dearborn St.
Chatsworth, CA 91311
818-718-1116
800-727-2229
Fax: 818-718-9026

ELECTRIC PRODUCTIONS(ELE)
10010 Canoga Ave., No. B-8
Chatsworth, CA 91311-6734

ELECTRIC VIDEO(ELV)
PO Box 784
Tiffin, OH 44883
419-447-0110

ELECTRONIC ARTS INTERMIX(EAI)
536 Broadway, 9th Fl.
New York, NY 10012
212-966-4605
Fax: 212-941-6118
Email: eai@interport.net

EMI VIDEO(EMI)
1290 Ave. of the Americas, 42nd Fl.
New York, NY 10104
212-492-1200

ENGLEWOOD ENTERTAINMENT LLC(EEL)
10917 Winner Rd.
Independence, MO 64052
816-252-4288
Fax: 816-836-3400
Email: moss@enterwaynet
HomePage: http://www.englewd.com

EPIC ENTERTAINMENT(EPE)
2321 W. Olive Ave., Ste. D
Burbank, CA 91506
818-841-9550
800-663-7061
Fax: 818-841-0889

EPIC RECORDS(EPC)
550 Madison Ave.

New York, NY 10022-3297
212-833-7442
Fax: 212-833-5719

ETD(BST)
1221 Profit Dr.
Dallas, TX 75247-3919
214-634-7883
800-541-1008
Fax: 214-634-9747

EUROPEAN VIDEO DISTRIBUTOR(EVD)
2402 W. Olive Ave.
Burbank, CA 91506
818-848-5902
800-423-6752
Fax: 818-848-1965

EVERGREEN ENTERTAINMENT(EVE)
6100 Wilshire Blvd., Ste. 1400
Los Angeles, CA 90048

EXPANDED ENTERTAINMENT(EXP)
28024 Dorothy Dr.
Agoura Hills, CA 91301-2635
818-991-2884
800-996-TOON
Fax: 818-991-3773

FACETS MULTIMEDIA, INC.(FCT)
1517 W. Fullerton Ave.
Chicago, IL 60614
312-281-9075
800-331-6197
Fax: 312-929-5437

FAMILY FILMS/ CONCORDIA(FFC)
3558 S. Jefferson Ave.
St. Louis, MO 63118-3968
314-268-1000
800-325-3040
Fax: 314-268-1329

FAMILY HOME ENTERTAINMENT(FHE)
c/o Live Home Video
15400 Sherman Way
PO Box 10124
Van Nuys, CA 91410-0124
818-908-0303
800-677-0789
Fax: 818-778-3259

FAST FORWARD(FAF)
3420 Ocean Park Blvd., Ste. 3075
Santa Monica, CA 90405
310-396-4434
Fax: 310-396-2292

FILMAKERS LIBRARY, INC.(FLL)
124 E. 40th
New York, NY 10016
212-808-4980
800-555-9815
Fax: 212-808-4983
Email: info@filmakers.com

FILMS FOR THE HUMANITIES & SCIENCES(FHS)
PO Box 2053
Princeton, NJ 08543-2053
609-275-1400
800-257-5126
Fax: 609-275-3767

FILMS INC. VIDEO(FLI)
5547 N. Ravenswood Ave.
Chicago, IL 60640-1199
312-878-2600
800-323-4222
Fax: 312-878-0416

FIRST RUN FEATURES(FRF)
153 Waverly Pl.
New York, NY 10014
212-243-0600
Fax: 212-989-7649

FIRST RUN/ICARUS FILMS(ICA)
153 Waverly Pl.
New York, NY 10014
212-727-1711
800-876-1710
Fax: 212-989-7649
Email: frif@echonyc.com

FIRST RUN VIDEO(FRV)
622 N. Alpine Dr.
Beverly Hills, CA 90210-3304
Fax: 310-246-9606

FM ENTERTAINMENT, INC.(FEI)
10551 W. Pico Blvd.
Los Angeles, CA 90064
310-441-4417
Fax: 310-446-9791

FOOTHILL VIDEO(FHV)
PO Box 547
Tujunga, CA 91043
818-353-8591
Fax: 818-353-7242

FORMAT INTERNATIONAL(FMT)
2421 E. Washington St.
Indianapolis, IN 46201-4123

FOX/LORBER HOME VIDEO(FXL)
419 Park Ave., S., 20th Fl.
New York, NY 10016
212-532-3392
Fax: 212-685-2625

FOXVIDEO(FXV)
2121 Avenue of the Stars, 25th Fl.
Los Angeles, CA 90067
310-369-3900
800-800-2FOX
Fax: 310-369-5811

FRIES HOME VIDEO(FRH)
6922 Hollywood Blvd., 12th Fl.
Hollywood, CA 90028
213-466-2266
Fax: 213-466-2126

FRIGHT VIDEO(FRG)
P.O. Box 277
North Billerica, MA 01862

FULL MOON HOME VIDEO(FLL)
8721 Santa Monica Blvd., Ste. 526
W. Hollywood, CA 90069
213-341-5959

FUSION VIDEO(FUS)
100 Fusion Way
Country Club Hills, IL 60478
708-799-2073
Fax: 708-799-8375

GENESIS HOME VIDEO(GHV)
15820 Arminta St.
Van Nuys, CA 91406

GERMAN LANGUAGE VIDEO CENTER(GLV)
7625 Pendleton Pike
Indianapolis, IN 46226-5298
317-547-1257
800-252-1957
Fax: 317-547-1263

GOODTIMES ENTERTAINMENT(GKK)
16 E. 40th St., 8th Fl.
New York, NY 10016-0113
212-951-3000
Fax: 212-213-9319

GORGON VIDEO(GRG)
10750 W. 161st
Orland Park, IL 60462
708-873-3131
800-367-3845
Fax: 708-873-3135

GRAPEVINE VIDEO(GPV)
PO Box 46161
Phoenix, AZ 85063
602-973-3661
Fax: 602-973-0060

**HALLMARK HOME
ENTERTAINMENT**(HMK)
6100 Wilshire Blvd., Ste. 1400
Los Angeles, CA 90048
213-634-3000
Fax: 213-549-3760

HEMDALE HOME VIDEO(HMD)
7966 Beverly Blvd.
Los Angeles, CA 90048
213-966-3700
Fax: 213-653-5452

**HIGH/SCOPE EDUCATIONAL
RESEARCH
FOUNDATION**(HSE)
600 N. River St.
Ypsilanti, MI 48198-2898
313-485-2000
800-40-PRESS
Fax: 313-485-0704

**HOLLYWOOD HOME
ENTERTAINMENT**(HHE)
6165 Crooked Creek Rd., Ste. B
Norcross, GA 30092-3105

**HOLLYWOOD HOME
THEATRE**(HHT)
9830 Charlieville Blvd.
Beverly Hills, CA 90212
310-203-9868

**HOLLYWOOD PICTURES
HOME VIDEO**(HPH)
Fairmont Bldg. 526
500 S. Buena Vista St.
Burbank, CA 91505-9842

HOME VIDEO FILMS(HVF)
3213 Florida, No. 200
Kenner, LA 70065
504-464-6671

HOME VIDEO LIBRARY(HVL)
Better Homes & Gardens Books
PO Box 10670
Des Moines, IA 50336
800-678-2665
Fax: 515-237-4765

HOME VISION CINEMA(HMV)
5547 N. Ravenswood Ave.
Chicago, IL 60640-1199
312-878-2600
800-826-3456

**HORIZON
ENTERTAINMENT**(HEG)
45030 Trevor Ave.
Lancaster, CA 93534
805-940-1040
800-323-2061
Fax: 805-940-8511

IGNATIUS PRESS(IGP)
33 Oakland Ave.
Harrison, NY 10528-9974
914-835-4216
Fax: 914-835-8406

IMAGE ENTERTAINMENT(IME)
9333 Oso Ave.
Chatsworth, CA 91311
818-407-9100
800-473-3475
Fax: 818-407-9111

**IMPERIAL ENTERTAINMENT
CORP.**(IMP)
11846 Ventura Blvd., Ste.300
Studio City, CA 91604
818-762-0005
Fax: 818-762-0006

**INTERNATIONAL HISTORIC
FILMS, INC. (IHF)**(IHF)
PO Box 29035
Chicago, IL 60629

773-927-2900
Fax: 773-927-9211
HomePage: http://
www.IHFfilm.com

**INTREPID PRODUCTIONS
INC.**(IPI)
203 - 2130 W. 3rd Ave.
Vancouver, BC, Canada V6K
1L1
604-737-0530

ITC(ITC)
13515 Dulles Technology Dr.
Herndon, VA 22071-3416
703-713-3335
800-638-3757
Fax: 703-713-0065

IVY FILM/VIDEO(IVY)
PO Box 18376
Asheville, NC 28814
704-285-9995
800-669-4057
Fax: 704-285-9997
Email: cryspic@aol.com

**JAMES AGEE FILM
PROJECT**(JAF)
316 1/2 E. Main St.
Johnson City, TN 37601
615-926-8637
800-352-5111
Fax: 615-971-2921

JEF FILMS, INC.(JEF)
Film House
143 Hickory Hill Circle
Osterville, MA 02655-1322
508-428-7198
Fax: 508-428-7198
Email: finchleyrd@aol.com

**JIM HENSON
PRODUCTIONS**(JHV)
5358 Melrose Ave., Ste. 300W
Los Angeles, CA 90038
818-953-3030

J2 COMMUNICATIONS(JTC)
10850 Wilshire Blvd., Ste. 1000
Los Angeles, CA 90024
310-474-5252
800-521-8273
Fax: 310-474-1219

KEEP THE FAITH INC.(KEP)
PO Box 10544
10 Audrey Pl.
Fairfield, NJ 07004
201-244-1990
Fax: 201-244-1990

KID VISION(KID)
75 Rockefeller Plaza
New York, NY 10019
212-275-2900
800-3KID-VID
Fax: 212-765-0899

KIT PARKER VIDEO(KIT)
c/o Central Park Media
250 W, 57th St., Ste. 317
New York, NY 10107
212-977-7456
Fax: 212-977-8709

**KNOWLEDGE UNLIMITED,
INC.**(KUI)
Box 52
Madison, WI 53701-0052
608-836-6660
800-356-2303
Fax: 608-831-1570
HomePage: http://www.ku.com

LB DISTRIBUTORS, INC.(LBD)
3200 Doolittle Dr.
Northbrook, IL 60062
708-564-8820
800-950-0255
Fax: 800-564-8656

**LIGHT RAIN
PRODUCTIONS**(LRP)
1927 NW Kearney

Portland, OR 97209
503-224-4080
Fax: 503-224-4180

**LIGHTYEAR
ENTERTAINMENT**(LTY)
350 5th Ave., Ste. 5101
New York, NY 10118
212-563-4610
800-229-7867
Fax: 212-563-1932
Email:
lightworks@lightworksav.com
HomePage: http://
lightworksav.com

LIVE ENTERTAINMENT(LIV)
15400 Sherman Way
PO Box 10124
Van Nuys, CA 91410-0124
818-988-5060

LOONIC VIDEO(LOO)
2022 Taraval St., Ste. 6427
San Francisco, CA 94116
510-526-5681

LSVIDEO, INC.(LSV)
PO Box 415
Carmel, IN 46032

**LUMIVISION
CORPORATION**(LUM)
877 Federal Blvd.
Denver, CO 80204-3212
303-446-0400
800-776-LUMI
Fax: 303-446-0101

MADERA CINEVIDEO(MAD)
525 E. Yosemite Ave.
Madera, CA 93638
209-661-6000
Fax: 209-674-3650

MAGIC HOUR FILMS(MHF)
114 Vine St.
Seattle, WA 98121
206-443-9818
Fax: 206-443-1453
Email: magichour@msn.com
HomePage: http://
www.magichour.com

**MANAGEMENT COMPANY
ENTERTAINMENT GROUP
(MCEG), INC.**(MCG)
1888 Century Park, E., Ste.
1777
Los Angeles, CA 90067-1721
310-282-0871
Fax: 310-282-8303

**MARYLAND PUBLIC
TELEVISION**(MTP)
11767 Owings Mills Blvd.
Owings Mills, MD 21117-1499
410-356-5600
800-873-6154
Fax: 410-581-0980

**MEDIA HOME
ENTERTAINMENT**(MED)
510 W. 6th St., Ste. 1032
Los Angeles, CA 90014
213-236-1336
Fax: 213-236-1346

MERIDIAN FILMS, INC.(MFI)
Box 5917
Columbia, SC 29250
803-988-1028
800-THE-FIRM
Fax: 803-988-1023

**METROMEDIA
ENTERTAINMENT**(MET)
1888 Century Park E., Ste. 700
Los Angeles, CA 90067
310-282-0550
Fax: 310-201-0798

**MGM HOME
ENTERTAINMENT**(MGM)
2500 Broadway
Santa Monica, CA 90404-6061

310-449-3000
Fax: 310-449-3100

**MILESTONE FILM &
VIDEO**(MIL)
275 W. 96th St., Ste 28C
New York, NY 10025
212-865-7449
Fax: 212-222-8952
Email: milesfilm@aol.com

**MILITARY/COMBAT STOCK
FOOTAGE LIBRARY**(FGF)
PO Box 399
Union Washington
Union, WA 98592
206-898-8080
Fax: 206-898-8081

REX MILLER(RXM)
Rte. 1, Box 457-D
East Prairie, MO 63845
314-649-5048

**MIRAMAX PICTURES HOME
VIDEO**(MAX)
500 S. Buena Vista St.
Burbank, CA 91521

**MNTEX ENTERTAINMENT,
INC.**(MTX)
500 Kirts Dr.
Troy, MI 48084-5225

**MODERN CURRICULUM
PRESS - MCP**(LCA)
PO Box 70935
108 Wilmot Rd.
Chicago, IL 60673-0933
800-777-8100

**MODERN SOUND PICTURES,
INC.**(MSP)
1402 Howard St.
Omaha, NE 68102
402-341-8476
800-228-9584
Fax: 402-341-8487

**MONARCH HOME
VIDEO**(MNC)
Two Ingram Blvd.
La Vergne, TN 37086-7006
615-287-4632
Fax: 615-287-4992

MONARCH GROUP, INC.(MGI)
2550 Corporate Pl., Ste. C103
Monterey Park, CA 91754
213-268-2288
800-700-8998
Fax: 213-268-2233

**MONDAY/WEDNESDAY/
FRIDAY VIDEO**(MWF)
123 Scribner Ave.
Staten Island, NY 10301
718-447-1347

MOORE VIDEO(MRV)
PO Box 5703
Richmond, VA 23220-0703
804-745-9785
Fax: 804-745-9785

MORRIS VIDEO(MOR)
2707 Plaza Del Amo, Ste. 601
Torrance, CA 90503
310-533-4800
800-843-3606
Fax: 310-533-1993

MOVIECRAFT, INC.(MVC)
PO Box 438
Orland Park, IL 60462
708-460-9082
Fax: 708-460-9099
Email: larryu@moviecraft.com

MPI HOME VIDEO(MPI)
16101 S. 108th Ave.
Orland Park, IL 60462
708-460-0555
Fax: 708-873-3177

MTM HOME VIDEO(MTM)
2200 Carolina Place

Fort Mill, SC 29715
803-548-7300
Fax: 803-548-3335

**MUSIC FOR LITTLE
PEOPLE**(MLT)
Box 1460
Redway, CA 95560
707-923-3991
800-346-4445
Fax: 707-923-3241

**MUSIC VIDEO
DISTRIBUTORS**(MVD)
O'Neill Industrial Center
1210 Standbridge St.
Norristown, PA 19401
610-272-7771
800-888-0486
Fax: 610-272-6074

**NATIONAL CENTER FOR
JEWISH FILM**(NCJ)
Brandeis University
Lown Bldg. 102
Waltham, MA 02254-9110
617-899-7044
Fax: 617-736-2070
Email:
ncjf@logos.cc.branders.eu

**NATIONAL FILM BOARD OF
CANADA**(NFB)
1251 Avenue of the Americas,
16th Fl.
New York, NY 10020-1173
212-596-1770
800-542-2164
Fax: 212-596-1779

**NEVILLE MEYER
DISTRIBUTION (NMD)**(NMD)
65 High Ridge Road, Ste. 304
Stamford, CT 06905
203-968-8905
Fax: 203-968-2953

**NEW HORIZONS HOME
VIDEO**(NHO)
2951 Flowers Rd., S., Ste. 237
Atlanta, GA 30341
404-458-3488
800-854-3323
Fax: 404-458-2679

NEW JERSEY NETWORK(NJN)
CN-777
Trenton, NJ 08625-0777
609-777-5000
800-792-8645
Fax: 609-633-2920

NEW LINE HOME VIDEO(NLC)
116 N. Robertson Blvd.
Los Angeles, CA 90048
310-967-6670
Fax: 310-854-0602

NEW VIDEO GROUP(NEW)
126 5th Ave., 15th Fl.
New York, NY 10011
212-206-8600
800-423-1212
Fax: 212-206-9001

**NEW WORLD
ENTERTAINMENT**(NWV)
1440 S. Sepulveda Blvd.
Los Angeles, CA 90025
310-444-8100
Fax: 310-444-8101

**NEW YORK STATE
EDUCATION
DEPARTMENT**(NYS)
Media Distribution Network
Rm. C-7 - CEC
Empire State Plaza
Albany, NY 12230
518-474-3168

NEW YORKER VIDEO(NYF)
16 W. 61st St., 11th Fl.
New York, NY 10023

212-247-6110
800-447-0196
Fax: 212-307-7855

NOSTALGIA FAMILY VIDEO*(NOS)*
PO Box 606
Baker City, OR 97814
503-523-9034
800-784-8362
Fax: 503-523-7115

ORION HOME VIDEO*(ORI)*
1888 Century Park E.
Los Angeles, CA 90067
310-282-0550
Fax: 310-282-9902

ORPHAN ENTERTAINMENT*(ORP)*
6930 Sunset Blvd.
Hollywood, CA 90028
213-962-6280

PARAMOUNT HOME VIDEO*(PAR)*
Bluhdorn Bldg.
5555 Melrose Ave.
Los Angeles, CA 90038
213-956-3952

PAULIST PRODUCTIONS*(PAU)*
PO Box 1057
Pacific Palisades, CA 90272
310-454-0688
800-624-8613
Fax: 310-459-6549
Email: paulistpro.aol.com

PBS HOME VIDEO*(PBS)*
Catalog Fulfillment Center
PO Box 4030
Santa Monica, CA 90411
800-531-4727
800-645-4PBS

PENTREX VIDEO*(PEN)*
PO Box 94911
Pasadena, CA 91107
818-793-3400
800-950-9333
Fax: 818-793-3797

PLANET PICTURES, INC.*(PPI)*
PO Box 1151, Old Chelsea Sta.
New York, NY 10011
212-779-0660
Fax: 212-779-9129

PM ENTERTAINMENT GROUP, INC.*(PMH)*
9450 Chivers Ave.
Sun Valley, CA 91352
818-504-6332
800-934-2111
Fax: 818-504-6380

POLYGRAM VIDEO (PV)*(PGV)*
825 8th Ave.
New York, NY 10019
212-333-8000
800-825-7781
Fax: 212-603-7960

POWERSPORTS MILLENNIUM*(PSV)*
18226 Ventura Blvd., Ste. 102
Tarzana, CA 91356-4229
818-708-9995
Fax: 818-708-0598
Email: intl@ps-mill.com
HomePage: http://www.ps-mill.com

PREMIERE HOME VIDEO*(PMR)*
755 N. Highland
Hollywood, CA 90038
213-934-8903
Fax: 213-934-8910

PRESTIGE VIDEO*(PRE)*
4501 Van Nuys Blvd., Ste. 215
Sherman Oaks, CA 91403
818-503-0280
Fax: 818-503-8289

PRIME VIDEO*(PRV)*
19749 Dearborn St.
Chatsworth, CA 91311-6510
818-718-1116
800-727-2229
Fax: 818-718-9026

PRINCETON BOOK CO. PUBLISHERS*(PBC)*
PO Box 57
Pennington, NJ 08534
609-737-8177
800-220-7149
Fax: 609-737-1869

PRISM ENTERTAINMENT*(PSM)*
1888 Century Park, E., Ste. 350
Los Angeles, CA 90067
310-277-3270
Fax: 310-203-8036

PROFESSIONAL MEDIA SERVICE CORP.*(PMS)*
19122 S. Vermont Ave.
Gardena, CA 90248
310-532-9024
800-223-7672
Fax: 800-253-8853
Email: promedia@class.org

PROSCENIUM ENTERTAINMENT*(PRS)*
PO Box 909
Hightstown, NJ 08520
800-222-6260
Fax: 609-448-9499

PROUD TO BE...A BLACK VIDEO COLLECTION*(PTB)*
1235-E East Blvd., Ste. 209
Charlotte, NC 28203
704-523-2227

PUBLIC MEDIA VIDEO*(PME)*
5547 N. Ravenswood Ave.
Chicago, IL 60640-1199
312-878-2600
800-826-3456
Fax: 312-878-8406

PYRAMID FILM & VIDEO*(PYR)*
P.O. Box 1048 .
Santa Monica, CA 90406-1048
310-828-7577
800-421-2304
Fax: 310-453-9083
Email: info@pyramedia.com
HomePage: http://www.pyramidmedia.com

QUALITY VIDEO*(QVD)*
7399 Bush Lake Rd.
Minneapolis, MN 55439-2027
612-893-0903
Fax: 612-893-1585
Email: email@qualitydino.com

QUESTAR VIDEO, INC.*(QHV)*
PO Box 11345
Chicago, IL 60611
312-266-9400
800-544-8422
Fax: 312-266-9523

RANDOM HOUSE MEDIA*(RHU)*
400 Hahn Rd.
Westminster, MD 21157
410-848-1900
800-726-0600
Fax: 800-632-9242

RAP ENTERTAINMENT INC.*(RAP)*
100-707 15th Ave. SW
Calgary, AB, Canada T2R 0R8
403-244-7000
800-565-7777
Fax: 403-245-0511

READER'S DIGEST HOME VIDEO*(RDG)*
Reader's Digest Rd.
Pleasantville, NY 10570

REPUBLIC PICTURES HOME VIDEO*(REP)*
5700 Wilshire Blvd., Ste. 525 North
Los Angeles, CA 90036-3659
213-965-6900
Fax: 213-965-6963

RHAPSODY FILMS, INC.*(RHP)*
46-2 Becket Hill Rd.
Lyme, CT 06371
860-434-3610
Fax: 860-434-6201

RHINO HOME VIDEO*(RHI)*
10635 Santa Monica Blvd., 2nd Fl.
Los Angeles, CA 90025-4900
310-828-1980
800-843-3670
Fax: 310-453-5529

ROCKET PICTURES*(ROC)*
9536 Wilshire Blvd., Ste. 410
Beverly Hills, CA 90212
310-550-3300

SCREEN PIX HOME VIDEO*(SCP)*
1219 1/2 W. El Segundo Blvd.
Gardena, CA 90247-1521
213-242-8880
800-906-4749
Fax: 213-756-1207
Email: spix1@loop.net
HomePage: http://www.screenpix.com

SCREENWORKS INC.*(SWI)*
8019 1/2 Melrose Ave., Ste. 6
Los Angeles, CA 90046
213-782-3865
Fax: 213-782-3868

SHANACHIE ENTERTAINMENT*(SHR)*
13 Laight St.
New York, NY 10013
212-334-0284
Fax: 212-334-5207
Email: shanach@shaven.ios.com

SHOKUS VIDEO*(SHO)*
PO Box 3125
Chatsworth, CA 91313
818-704-0400
Fax: 818-701-0560

SIGNALS*(SIG)*
7000 Westgate Dr.
St. Paul, MN 55114
612-659-3700
800-669-5225
Fax: 612-659-0083
Email: kyle@rivertrade.com

SILVER LAKE INTERNATIONAL*(SLI)*
18840 Ventura Blvd., Ste. 210
Tarzana, CA 91356
818-757-0007
Fax: 818-757-0038

SIMITAR ENTERTAINMENT*(SIM)*
3850 Annapolis Ln., Ste. 140
Plymouth, MN 55447
612-559-6660
800-486-TAPE
Fax: 612-559-0210

SIMON WIESENTHAL CENTER*(SWC)*
9760 W. Pico Blvd.
Los Angeles, CA 90035-4792
310-553-9036
Fax: 310-553-8007

SINISTER CINEMA*(SNC)*
PO Box 4369
Medford, OR 97501-0168
503-773-6860
Fax: 503-779-8650

SOCIETY FOR VISUAL EDUCATION, INC. (SVE)*(SVE)*
6677 N. NW Hwy.
Chicago, IL 60631
312-775-9550
800-829-1900
Fax: 312-775-5091

SOMETHING WEIRD VIDEO*(SMW)*
c/o Mike Vraney
PO Box 33664
Seattle, WA 98133
206-361-3759
206-364-7526

SONY MUSIC VIDEO ENTERPRISES*(SMV)*
550 Madison Ave.
New York, NY 10022
212-833-7095

SPECTRUM FILMS, INC.*(SPC)*
Box 801
Carlsbad, CA 92018
619-434-6191

STAGESTEP*(STS)*
2000 Hamilton St.
Ste. C200
Philadelphia, PA 19130
215-636-9000
800-877-3342
Fax: 215-829-0508
Email: stagestep@juno.com

STARDANCE ENTERTAINMENT*(SDE)*
11101 Washington Blvd., Ste. 101
Culver, CA 90232
800-959-8985
Fax: 310-559-8987

STRAND HOME VIDEO*(SHV)*
225 Santa Monica Blvd., Ste. 810
Santa Monica, CA 90401
310-395-5002

STREAMLINE PICTURES*(STP)*
2908 Nebraska Avenue
Santa Monica, CA 90404-4109
310-998-0070
800-846-1453
Fax: 310-998-1145

STUDIO VIDEO PRODUCTIONS*(STV)*
793 Foothills Blvd., Ste. A
San Luis Obispo, CA 93405
805-543-0707
800-541-1843
Fax: 805-549-0352

TAI SENG VIDEO MARKETING*(TAI)*
170 S. Spruce Ave., Ste. 200
San Francisco, CA 94080
415-871-8118
800-888-3836
Fax: 415-871-2392
Email: webstaff@taiseng.com
HomePage: http://www.taiseng.com

TAPEWORM VIDEO DISTRIBUTORS*(TPV)*
27833 Hopkins Ave., Unit 6
Valencia, CA 91355
805-257-4904
Fax: 805-257-4820
Email: tapewo01interserv.com

TELEVISION INTERNATIONAL*(CDV)*
c/o Jason Films
2825 Wilcrest, Ste. 407
Houston, TX 77042
713-266-3097
Fax: 713-266-3148

TEMPE VIDEO*(TEM)*
Box 6573
Akron, OH 44312

216-628-1950
Fax: 216-628-4316

THIRD COAST ENTERTAINMENT*(TCE)*
12750 Ventura Blvd., Ste. 102
Studio City, CA 91604
818-769-9986

THOMSON PRODUCTIONS, INC.*(TPI)*
PO Box 1225
Orem, UT 84059
801-226-0155
Fax: 801-226-0166

THREE STAR RELEASING*(TSR)*
15745 Stagg St.
Van Nuys, CA 91406

3M AUDIO VISUAL DIVISION*(THA)*
6801 Riverplace Blvd.
Austin, TX 78726-9000
800-328-1371

TIME-LIFE VIDEO AND TELEVISION*(TLF)*
1450 E. Parham Rd.
Richmond, VA 23280
804-266-6330
800-621-7026

TIME WARNER VIEWER'S EDGE*(TWV)*
PO Box 85098
Richmond, VA 23285-5098
800-947-3928
Fax: 203-699-9586

TIMELESS VIDEO INC.*(TIM)*
9943 Canoga Ave., Ste. B2
Chatsworth, CA 91311
818-773-0284
800-478-6734
Fax: 818-773-0176

TRANS-WORLD ENTERTAINMENT*(TWE)*
8899 Beverly Blvd., 8th Fl.
Los Angeles, CA 90048-2412

TRIBORO ENTERTAINMENT GROUP*(TRI)*
12 W. 27th St., 15th Fl.
New York, NY 10001
212-686-6116
Fax: 212-686-6178

TRIMARK HOME VIDEO*(THV)*
2644 30th St.
Santa Monica, CA 90405-3009
310-314-2000
Fax: 310-392-0252

TROMA TEAM VIDEO*(TTV)*
1501 Broadway, Ste. 2605
New York, NY 10036
212-997-0595
Fax: 212-997-0968

TURNER HOME ENTERTAINMENT COMPANY*(TTC)*
Box 105366
Atlanta, GA 35366
404-827-3066
800-523-0823
Fax: 404-827-3266

20TH CENTURY FOX FILM CORPORATION*(TCF)*
PO Box 900
Beverly Hills, CA 90213
310-369-1000
Fax: 310-369-3318

21ST GENESIS HOME VIDEO*(GNS)*
15820 Arminta St.
Van Nuys, CA 91406

UAV CORPORATION*(UAV)*
PO Box 5497
Fort Mill, SC 29715

803-548-7300
800-486-6782
Fax: 803-548-3335

UNI DISTRIBUTION/JUNE MORISHITA(UND)
10 Universal City Plaza, Ste. 400
Universal City, CA 91608
318-777-4400
Fax: 818-866-0306

UNICORN VIDEO, INC.(UNI)
9025 Eton Ave., Ste. D.
Canoga Park, CA 91304
818-407-1333
800-528-4336
Fax: 818-407-8246

UNITY PRODUCTIONS(UNT)
4007 Willowwood Ln.
Aberdeen, SD 57401-9544

UNIVERSAL STUDIOS HOME VIDEO(USH)
100 Universal City Plaza
Universal City, CA 91608-9955
818-777-1000
Fax: 818-866-1483

UNIVERSITY OF WASHINGTON EDUCATIONAL MEDIA COLLECTION(UWA)
Kane Hall
Box 353090
Seattle, WA 98195
206-543-9909
Fax: 206-685-7892

VALENCIA ENTERTAINMENT CORP.(VEC)
45030 Trevor Ave.
Lancaster, CA 93534-2648
805-940-1040
800-323-2061
Fax: 805-940-8511

VANTAGE COMMUNICATIONS, INC.(VAN)
PO Box 546-G
Nyack, NY 10960
914-268-0715
800-872-0068
Fax: 914-268-3429

VCI HOME VIDEO(VCI)
11333 E. 60th Pl.
Tulsa, OK 74146
918-254-6337
800-331-4077
Fax: 918-254-6117
Email:
    vcihomevideo@mail.webter.com

VCII HOME ENTERTAINMENT, INC.(VHE)
13418 Wyandotte St.
North Hollywood, CA 91605
818-764-1777
800-350-1931
Fax: 818-764-0231

VESTRON VIDEO(VES)
c/o Live Home Video
15400 Sherman Way
PO Box 10124
Van Nuys, CA 91410-0124
818-988-0303
800-367-7765
Fax: 818-778-3194
Email: cust_serv@live-
    entertainment.com

VIDCREST(VDC)
PO Box 69642
Los Angeles, CA 90069
213-650-7310
Fax: 213-654-4810

VIDEO ARTISTS INTERNATIONAL, INC.(VAI)
158 Linwood Plaza, Ste. 301
Fort Lee, NJ 07024
201-944-0099
800-477-7146
Fax: 201-947-8850

VIDEO BIBLE LIBRARY, INC.(VBL)
Box 17515
Portland, OR 97217
360-892-7707
Fax: 360-254-8318

THE VIDEO CATALOG(TVC)
7000 Westgate Dr.
Saint Paul, MN 55114
612-659-3700
800-733-6656
Fax: 612-659-0083
Email: kyle@rivertrade.com

VIDEO CITY PRODUCTIONS/ DISTRIBUTING(VCD)
4266 Broadway
Oakland, CA 94611
510-428-0202
Fax: 510-654-7802

VIDEO COLLECTIBLES(VCO)
1500 Clinton St.
Buffalo, NY 14206-9911
800-268-3891
Fax: 800-269-8877
Email:
info@collectablesdirect.com
HomePage: http://
www.collectablesdirect.com

VIDEO CONNECTION(VCN)
3123 W. Sylvania Ave.
Toledo, OH 43613
419-472-7727
800-365-0449
Fax: 419-472-2655

VIDEO FRANCE(FRA)
4822 St. Elmo Ave.
Bethesda, MD 20814
301-654-2224
Fax: 301-229-0621
Email: france@wizard.net

VIDEO GEMS(GEM)
12228 Venice Blvd., No. 504
Los Angeles, CA 90066

VIDEO RESOURCES(VRS)
220 W. 71st St.
New York, NY 10023
212-724-7055
800-442-7055
Fax: 212-595-0189

VIDEO SEARCH OF MIAMI(VSM)
PO Box 161917
Miami, FL 33116
305-279-9773
Fax: 305-598-2665

VIDEO YESTERYEAR(VYY)
Box C
Sandy Hook, CT 06482
800-243-0987
Fax: 203-797-0819
Email: video@yesteryear.com

THE VIDEOFINDERS COLLECTION(VIF)
National Fulfillment Center
PO Box 27054
Glendale, CA 91225
800-799-1199
Fax: 818-637-5276

VIDEOGRAF(VGR)
144 W. 27th St.
New York, NY 10001
212-242-7871
Fax: 212-206-6986

VIDEOS.COM, INC.(PIC)
202 S. Pearl St., Ste. 4
Charlotte, MI 48813
517-541-1630
800-670-9282
Fax: 517-541-1631
Email: steve@videos.com
HomePage: http://
www.videos.com

VIP VIDEO(VIP)
c/o JEF Films
Film House
143 Hickory Hill Circle
Osterville, MA 02655-1322
508-428-7198
Fax: 508-428-7198

VISION VIDEO/GATEWAY FILMS(GFV)
2030 Wentz Church Rd.
Box 540
Worcester, PA 19490-0540
610-584-1893
800-523-0226
Fax: 610-584-4610
Email: visionvideo@aol.com

WALT DISNEY HOME VIDEO(DIS)
500 S. Buena Vista St.
Burbank, CA 91521
818-562-3560

WARNER/ELEKTRA/ ATLANTIC (WEA) CORPORATION(WEA)
9451 LBJ Fwy., Ste. 107
Dallas, TX 75243
214-234-6200
Fax: 214-699-9343

WARNER HOME VIDEO, INC.(WAR)
4000 Warner Blvd.
Burbank, CA 91522
818-954-6000

WARNERVISION(AVE)
A Time Warner Company
75 Rockefeller Plaza
New York, NY 10019
212-275-2900
800-95-WARNER
Fax: 212-765-0899

WARREN MILLER ENTERTAINMENT(WME)
2540 Frontier Ave., Ste. 104
Boulder, CO 80301
303-442-3430
800-523-7117
Fax: 303-442-3402
Email: robd@wmfilms.com

WATER BEARER FILMS(WBF)
48 W. 21st St., No. 301
New York, NY 10010
212-242-8686
800-551-8304
Fax: 212-242-4560
Email: wbf.com

WAXWORKS/VIDEOWORKS, INC.(WAX)
325 E. 3rd St.
Owensboro, KY 42303
502-926-0008
800-825-8558
Fax: 502-685-0563

WELLSPRING MEDIA, INC.(WMI)
65 Bleecker St.
New York, NY 10012
800-538-5856
Fax: 212-475-1790

WESTERN L.A. FILM PRODUCTIONS, INC.(WLA)
7425 Clinton St.
Los Angeles, CA 90036-5703

WESTERN MEDIA SYSTEMS(WFV)
30941 W. Agoura Rd., Ste. 302
Westlake Village, CA 91361
818-889-7350
Fax: 818-889-7350

WHITE STAR(WST)
195 Hwy. 36
West Long Branch, NJ 07764
908-229-2343
800-458-5887
Fax: 908-229-0066

WISHING WELL DISTRIBUTING(WSH)
PO Box 1008
Silver Lake, WI 53170
414-889-8501
800-888-9355
Fax: 414-889-8591

WNET/THIRTEEN NON-BROADCAST(WNE)
356 W. 58th St.
New York, NY 10019
212-560-2000
Fax: 212-582-3297

WOLFE VIDEO(WLF)
PO Box 64
New Almaden, CA 95042
408-268-6782
800-438-9653
Fax: 408-268-9449
Email: maria@wolfevideo.com
    HomePage: http://
    www.wolfevideo.com

WOMBAT FILM AND VIDEO(WOM)
1560 Sherman Ave., Ste. 100
Evanston, IL 60201
708-328-6700
800-323-9084
Fax: 708-328-6706

WORLD ARTISTS HOME VIDEO(WAC)
5150 Wilshire Blvd., Ste. 506
Los Angeles, CA 90036
213-933-7057
800-821-1205
Fax: 213-933-2356
Email: world@worldfists.com
    HomePage: http://
    www.worldartist.com/world

WORLD VIDEO ENTERPRISES, INC.(WVE)
150 Executive Park Blvd., No. 1600
San Francisco, CA 94134-3303
415-468-6218
Fax: 415-468-1381

WORLDVISION HOME VIDEO, INC.(WOV)
1700 Broadway
New York, NY 10019-5905
212-261-2700
Fax: 212-261-2950

XENON(XVC)
211 Arizona Ave.
Santa Monica, CA 90401

YORK HOME VIDEO(YHV)
4733 Lankershim Blvd.
North Hollywood, CA 91602
310-278-1034
800-84-MOVIE
Fax: 818-505-8290

ZEITGEIST FILMS LTD.(ZGI)
247 Centre St., 2nd Fl.
New York, NY 10013
212-274-1989
Fax: 212-274-1644
Email: mail@zeitgeistfilm.com

RETAIL

ANIMEIGO INC.(ANI)
PO Box 989
Wilmington, NC 28402-0989
910-251-1850
800-242-6463
Fax: 910-763-2376
Email:
    treborassistantanimeigo@

APPLAUSE PRODUCTIONS, INC.(APD)
85 Longview Rd.
Port Washington, NY 11050

516-883-2825
800-278-7326
Fax: 516-883-7460
Email: apptora@aol.com

CAMBRIDGE EDUCATIONAL(CCP)
PO Box 2153
Charleston, WV 25328-2153
304-744-9323
800-468-4227
Fax: 304-744-9351

CONGRESS ENTERTAINMENT, INC.(CNG)
P.O. Box 845
Tannersville, PA 18372-0845
717-420-8551
800-847-8273
Fax: 717-420-8554
Email: karolyn28@acx.com

ERGO MEDIA INC.(ERG)
668 American Legion Dr.
PO Box 2037
Teaneck, NJ 07666
201-692-0404
800-695-3746
Fax: 201-692-0663
Email: ergo@intec.com

FESTIVAL FILMS(FST)
6115 Chestnut Terr.
Excelsior, MN 55331-8107
612-470-2172
800-798-6083
Fax: 612-470-2172
Email: fesfilms@aol.com

FLOWER FILMS(FFM)
10341 San Pablo Ave.
El Cerrito, CA 94530
510-525-0942
800-572-7618
Fax: 510-525-1204
Email: blankfilm@aol.com

GLENN VIDEO VISTAS, LTD.(GVV)
6924 Canby Ave., Ste. 103
Reseda, CA 91335
818-881-8110
Fax: 818-981-5506
Email: mglass@worldnet.att.net

HENWOOD CINEMA VIDEO(HCV)
PO Box 376
Jamison, PA 18929-0376
215-552-8584
Fax: 215-788-7186
Email: Cinema376@aol.com

INTERAMA, INC.(INT)
301 W. 53rd St., Ste. 19E
New York, NY 10019
212-977-4830
Fax: 212-581-6582
Email: InteramaNY@aol.com

KAROL VIDEO(KAR)
PO Box 7600
350 N. Pennsylvania Ave.
Wilkes Barre, PA 18773
717-822-8899
Fax: 717-822-8226
Email: karolm@epix.net

LUCERNE MEDIA(LME)
37 Ground Pine Rd.
Morris Plains, NJ 07950
201-538-1401
800-341-2293
Fax: 201-538-0855
Email:
    lucernemedia@worldnet.att.net

MASTERVISION, INC.(MAS)
969 Park Ave.
New York, NY 10028
212-879-0448

MEDIA HOME ENTERTAINMENT(SHL)
11 Appaloosa Lane
Bell Canyon, CA 91307-1002

RETALL ▸cont.

Fax: 818-992-6520
Email: bellcanyon@aol.com

MIKE LEBELL'S VIDEO(MLB)
75 Freemont Pl.
Los Angeles, CA 90005
213-938-3333
Fax: 213-938-3334
Email: mlvideo@aol.com

MOVIES UNLIMITED(MOV)
3015 Darnell Rd.
Philadelphia, PA 19154
215-637-4444
800-466-8437
Fax: 215-637-2350
Email:
movies@moviesunlimited.com

MYSTIC FIRE VIDEO(MFV)
524 Broadway, Ste. 604
New York, NY 10012
212-941-0999
800-292-9001
Fax: 212-941-1443
HomePage: http://
www.mysticfire.com

PENTREX(IUF)
PO Box 94911
Pasadena, CA 91109-4911
818-793-3400
800-950-9333
Fax: 818-793-3797
Email: pentrex@aol.com

PHOENIX/BFA FILMS &
VIDEO(BFA)
2349 Chaffee Dr.
St. Louis, MO 63146
314-569-0211
800-221-1274
Fax: 314-569-2834
Email:
BFAEduc@worldnet.att.net
Phoenix
films@worldnet.att.net

RM FILMS INTERNATIONAL,
INC.(RMF)
PO Box 3748
Los Angeles, CA 90078
213-466-7791
Fax: 213-461-4152
Email: 103234.1546@

SCHOOLMASTERS
VIDEO(SCH)
745 State Circle
PO Box 1941
Ann Arbor, MI 48106
313-761-5175
800-521-2832
Fax: 313-761-8711
Email: kidvideis@aol.com
HomePage: http://
www.schoolmasters.com

VIDEO LEARNING
LIBRARY(VLL)
15838 N. 62nd St., Ste. 100
Scottsdale, AZ 85254
602-596-9970
800-383-8811
Fax: 602-596-9973
Email: video2@goodnet.com

WARNER REPRISE
VIDEO(WRV)
3300 Warner Blvd.
Burbank, CA 91505-4694
818-846-9090
Fax: 818-953-3329

WHOLESALE

BEST FILM & VIDEO
CORPORATION(BFV)
108 New South Rd.
Hicksville, NY 11802-9025

516-931-6969
800-527-2189
Fax: 516-931-5959

CAPITOL ENTERTAINMENT
AND HOME VIDEO(CTL)
6205 Adelaide Dr.
Betthesda, MD 20817
301-564-9700
Fax: 301-564-0797
Email: capent@erols.com
HomePage: http://
www.capitolent.com

CELEBRITY HOME
ENTERTAINMENT(CEL)
22025 Ventura Blvd., Ste. 200
PO Box 4112
Woodland Hills, CA 91365-4112
818-595-0666
Fax: 818-716-0168

COLUMBIA TRISTAR HOME
VIDEO(COL)
Sony Pictures Plaza
10202 W. Washington Blvd.
Culver City, CA 90232
310-280-5418
Fax: 310-280-2485
HomePage: http://
www.spe.sony.com

DISCOUNT VIDEO TAPES,
INC./HOLLYWOOD'S
ATTIC(DVT)
PO Box 7122
Burbank, CA 91510
818-843-3366
Fax: 818-843-3821

GREYCAT FILMS(GRE)
3829 Delaware Lane
Las Vegas, NV 89109
702-737-0670
Fax: 702-734-3628
Email: greycat@aol.com

HBO HOME VIDEO(HBO)
1100 6th Ave.
New York, NY 10036
212-512-7400
Fax: 212-512-7498
HomePage: http://
www.hbohomevideo.com

HEN'S TOOTH VIDEO(HTV)
2805 E. State Blvd.
Fort Wayne, IN 46805
219-471-4332
Fax: 219-471-4449

INCREASE/SILVERMINE
VIDEO(INC)
6860 Canby Ave., Ste. 118
Reseda, CA 91335
818-342-2880
800-233-2880
Fax: 818-342-4029
Email: quksil@aol.com

INGRAM ENTERTAINMENT
INC.(ING)
2 Ingram Blvd.
La Vergne, TN 37086-7006
615-287-4000
800-759-5000
Fax: 615-287-4992
HomePage: http://
www.ingramentertainment.com

JUST FOR KIDS HOME
VIDEO(JFK)
22025 Ventura Blvd., Ste. 200
PO Box 4112
Woodland Hills, CA 91365-0549
818-595-0666
Fax: 818-716-0168

KINO ON VIDEO(KIV)
333 W. 39th St., Ste. 503
New York, NY 10018
212-629-6880
800-562-3330
Fax: 212-714-0871
Email: kinoint@infunnse.com

KULTUR VIDEO(KUL)
195 Hwy. No. 36
West Long Branch, NJ 07764
908-229-2343
800-458-5887
Fax: 908-229-0066
Email: kultur@monmouth.com

LEO FILMS(LEO)
1509 N. Hoover, Ste. 1/2
Los Angeles, CA 90027
213-666-7140
Fax: 213-666-7414
Email: LUSTGAR@IDT.NET
HomePage: http://movies-
online.com

MONTEREY HOME
VIDEO(MON)
28038 Dorothy Dr., Ste. 1
Agoura Hills, CA 91301
818-597-0047
800-424-2593
Fax: 818-597-0105

MTI HOME VIDEO(MTH)
14216 SW 136th St.
Miami, FL 33186
305-255-8684
800-821-7461
Fax: 305-233-6943
Email: mti@mtivideo.com

PETER PAN INDUSTRIES,
INC. (PPI)(PRD)
88 St. Francis St.
Newark, NJ 07105
201-344-4214
Fax: 201-344-0465
Email: PPIGROUP@aol.com
HomePage: http://
www.peterpan.com

SUN VIDEO(SUN)
15 Donnybrook
Demarest, NJ 07627
201-784-0662
Fax: 201-784-0665
Email:
hs@methodsworkshop.com

TELEVISION
REPRESENTATIVES,
INC.(RHV)
9911 W. Pico Blvd.
Suite PH-E
Los Angeles, CA 90035
310-552-2660
Fax: 310-552-9039

VIDEO ACTION(VDA)
708 W. 1st St.
Los Angeles, CA 90012
213-687-8262
800-422-2241
Fax: 213-687-8425

VIDEO DIMENSIONS(VDM)
322 8th Ave., 1701
New York, NY 10001
212-929-6135
Fax: 212-929-6135
Email: video@cultvideo.com
HomePage: http://
www.cultvideo.com/
video.html

VISTA STREET
ENTERTAINMENT(VSE)
9831 W. Pico Blvd., Ste. 4
Los Angeles, CA 90035
310-556-3074
Fax: 310-556-8815

YANKEE-ORIOLE CO.(YOC)
398 Ogden Ave.
Jersey City, NJ 07307-1115
201-656-4348
Fax: 201-656-4348

Suddenly, the Internet has become an important resource for movie information, appreciation, and (especially) obsession. For your web surfing enjoyment, we have compiled a comprehensive list of many of the top entertainment websites that will expand your knowledge of either a particular movie, actor, director, or Hollywood studio. If you're looking for information on how to make your own film, there are sites for that, too. The

guide is divided into six categories: actors and actresses (ranges from Cher to Elijah Wood); cult movie resources; directors; film magazines; film studios; filmmaker resources; film reviews; general entertainment; individual movies; and video outlets. The sites are listed alphabetically within each category, and each site includes name and URL address information. Actors, directors, and movies may have more than one URL, as they are likely to have more

than one site devoted to them. These sites have no description because the name of the website is self-explanatory. The general information websites briefly describe what you can expect to find. Just as you can spend hours flipping through *Videohound*, you can spend hours cruising the web with the sites listed below since a majority of these homepages can link you to other sites on the web.

ACTORS AND ACTRESSES

Kevin Bacon (The Oracle of)
http://www.cs.virginia.edu/~bct7m/bacon.html

Alec Baldwin
http://sailor.saturn.simplenet.com/alec.html

Stephen Baldwin
http://www.li.net/~yesnet/Opening_Page/Opening_page.htm

Antonio Banderas
http://www.sju.edu/~delvalle/antonio.html

Drew Barrymore
http://www.wfu.edu/~david/drew/

Halle Berry
http://www.contrib.andrew.cmu.edu/~jack/halle.html

Kenneth Branagh
http://sfbox.vt.edu:10021/T/tpower/ken.html

Matthew Broderick
http://www.ccn.cs.dal.ca/~ag249//matt.html

Pierce Bronson
http://www.mcs.net/~klast/www/brosnan.html

Sandra Bullock
http://www.dancopublishing.com/sandra.htm

Nicholas Cage
http://members.aol.com/ToniGrrl/cage/main.htm

Bruce Campbell
http://spage.com/bruce/

Jim Carrey
http://www.inforamp.net/~petroff/

Cher
http://www.inch.com/~harbur/cher/index.html

Jackie Chan
http://www.pitt.edu/~oren/jackie/jackie.html

Jean Claude Van Damme
http://www.anaheim.quik.com/tseo/van.htm

George Clooney
http://copper.ucs.indiana.edu/~mtsai/george_clooney.html

Sean Connery
http://www.wsu.edu:8080/~dock/

Kevin Costner
http://www.geocities.com/Hollywood/7555/

Courtney Cox
http://www.azstarnet.com/~polska/cox/ccox.html

Tom Cruise
http://www.thezone.pair.com/cruise/

Maucaulay Culkin
http://www.axe.net./culkin/

Jamie Lee Curtis
http:http://www.geocities.com/Hollywood/Hills/5752/index.htm

John Cusack
http://www.unm.edu/~matts/John_Cusack.html

Geena Davis
http://www.mv.com/users/dld/geena/

Judy Davis
http://elycion.geology.ualberta.ca/~tpreston/judy.html

Daniel Day Lewis
http://www.well.com/user/dkscully/index.htm

James Dean
http://www.americanlegends.com/jamesdean

Rebecca DeMornay
http://web-star.com/rebecca/rebecca.html

Robert DeNiro
http://www.cs.bc.edu/~kawashim/deniro.html

Johnny Depp
http://mastrangelo.polito.it/jonydepp/index.htm
http://www.wigout.com/depp/johnny.html

Cameron Diaz
http://www.cs.uit.no/~haakonb/diaz.html

Web Site Guide

Leonardo DiCaprio
http://meadow.greenwing.com/leo/

Michael Douglas
http://www.texas/net/users/mikedoug/

Clint Eastwood
http://www.powernet.net/~cal/eastwood.html

Chris Farley
http://pantheon.cis.yale.edu/~odonnell/farley/farley.html

Ralph Fiennes
http://student-www.uchicago.edu/users/cceccare/Fiennes.html

Harrison Ford
http://www.smartlink.net/~deej7/ford.html

Jodie Foster
http://www.tcp.com/~mary/foster.html

Mel Gibson
http://ourworld.compuserve.com/homepages/melward/gibson.htm
http://www.geocities.com/Hollywood/7505/

Whoopi Goldberg
http://www.tu-berlin.de/~gruhlke/forum/whoopi/index.html

Tom Hanks
http://www.wsu.edu:8080/~jtwillia/hanks.html

Ed Harris
http://www.wenet.net/~mhoopes/edharris.html

Teri Hatcher
http://www.escape.ca/~hazlitt/teri/thind.htm

Dustin Hoffman
http://www.sky.net/~emily/dustin.html

Sir Anthony Hopkins
http://www.mit.edu:8001/people/douglas/sirtony.html

Nicole Kidman
http://www-personal.umich.edu/~rkmead/kidman.html

Val Kilmer
http://www.eskimo.com/~kilmer

Brandon Lee
http://europa.cs.mun.ca/~loreilly/brandon.htm

Bruce Lee
http://www.infi.net/~danaj/bruce.html

Juliette Lewis
http://www.solace.mh.se/~alpha/jlwp/jl.htm

Marcello Mastroianni
http://www.dolcevita.com

Steve Martin
http://qlink.queensu.ca/~4kgd/steve/

Bette Milder
http://www.interactive8.com/bette/

Marilyn Monroe
http://www.ionet.net/~jellenc/marilyn.html

Demi Moore
http://www.diskriter.com/demi/

Sam Neill
http://kevin.net/~erika/sn.html

Gary Oldman
http://www.csh.rit.edu/~halle/oldman.html

Al Pacino
http://pubweb.acns.nwu.edu/~apoorman/pacino.html

Bill Paxton
http://qlink.queensu.ca/~3bjw6/

Michelle Pfeiffer
http://www.geocities.com/Paris/1032/pfeiffer.html

Brad Pitt
http://www.geocities.com/Hollywood/Hills/4932/Brad_Pitt.html

Keanu Reeves
http://www.empirenet.com/~rdaeley/skc/

Julia Roberts
http://studentweb.tulane.edu/~sbuckle/

Tim Roth
http://weber.u.washington.edu/~jenhwolf/

Meg Ryan
http://web.cs.ualberta.ca/~davidw/MegRyan/meg.cgi

Winona Ryder
http://www.duc.auburn.edu/~harshec/WWW/Winona.html

Susan Sarandon
http://zen.sunderland.ac.uk/~aa1gha/susan.html

Alicia Silverstone
http://homegrohn.com/alicia/

Kevin Spacey
http://www.duke.edu/~jlg1/kevin-spacey.html

Jimmy Stewart
http://www.jimmy.org
http://www.jimmy.org/films/tph.html

Uma Thurman
http://users.why.net/cfish/uma/uma.html

Marisa Tomei
http://www.vuse.vanderbilt.edu/~burketrd/tomei.htm

John Travolta
http://www.auburn.edu/~proppka/travolta.htm

Christopher Walken
http://www.ior.com/~cmohney/walken/walken.html

John Wayne
http://www.napanet.net~donc/

Sigourney Weaver
http://www.pt.hk-r.se/student/di94vno/ripley.html

Bruce Willis
http://www.accsyst.com/writers/bruno.htm

Kate Winslet
http://www2.cibola.net/~michaela/kate

Elijah Wood
http://www.elijahwood.com/

CULT MOVIE RESOURCES

AnimEigo
http://www.animeigo.com
Gives extensive history on this rapidly growing Japanese export of animation.

Anime Resources and Info
http://www.best.com:80/~gaxiola/Anime/
Informs users of upcoming anime features and background information on the genre itself.

The Cult Shop
http://lasarto.cnde.iastate.edu/Movies/CultShop
Gives the latest information on your favorite cult movie stars like Bruce Campbell and Steve Buscemi. Also offers links to other movie sites.

The Gamera Home Page
http://tswww.cc.emory.edu/~kgowen/gamera.html
A home page devoted to that Japanese superstar turtle, Gamera. Showcases, in depth, all nine of his films from Gamera *to* Gamera vs. Legion.

Hong Kong Movies Home Page
http://egret0.stanford.edu/hk/index.html
An interest in Hong Kong films has significantly increased due to the sudden rise of Jackie Chan and action director John Woo. This comprehensive site offers much information on the Hong

Kong film industry. Includes an update of new Hong Kong films, filmographies, interviews, reviews, and a searchable database on Hong Kong actors and actresses.

Mad Prof. Mike's Headbanger Movie Reviews
http://www.dnai.com/~ochobbit/topten.html
Witness the lunatic rantings of Professor Headbanger as he raves about such schlock classics as Teenagers from Outer Space *and* This Island Earth.

Manga Video
http://www.manga.com/manga
A spin-off of anime, video retailer offering comic books, sound-tracks, and fan club information.

Mel's Godzilla Page
http://www.ama.caltech.edu/users/mrm/godzilla.html
Designed to give glory to Japan's most favorite export. Features updated reports on an upcoming Godzilla movie in the states, photos of Godzilla in action and a listing of FAQ's about this creature and its movies.

No Place for a Woman: The Family in Film Noir
http://www.obs.net:80/Noir/
Reports on the implications that film noir has had on society. The author, John Blaser, pinpoints the role that women and family have in this genre. Subtopics include, "Pro-family Messages in Film Noir" and "Women's Anti-Family Function in Film Noir."

Professor Neon's TV and Movie Mania
http://www.vortex.com/ProfNeon.html
Covers a gamut of information on film, television, radio and cable industry. When it comes to films, the Professor leans more to sci-fi, cult and weird stuff.

Reel Talk
http://www.reellife.com/PFE/index.html
Allows you to talk amongst yourselves about recent or past cult film releases.

The Vampyre's Haven
http://www.wam.umd.edu/~mcarter/
A listing of most, not all, vampire films made, including the most obscure ones like Bloedverwatnen *(from the Netherlands) and* Wanda Does Transylvania.

DIRECTORS

Woody Allen
http://www.idt.unit.no/~torp/woody

Allison Anders
http://home.earthlink.net/~kristinm/aahome.html

Roger Avary
http://www.avary.com/

Ingmar Bergman
www.voyagerco.com/CC/gh/featured/p.bergman.htm;
Not a homepage, but a Criterion Collection site for famed director.

James Cameron
http://www.soton.ac.uk/~pdc194/cameron/

Joel and Ethan Coen
http://lasarto.cnde.iastate.edu/Movies/CultShop/Movies/coen.html

Frederico Fellini
http://www.conexis.es/ddc/

Terry Gilliam
http://www.ionsys.com/~gurney/terry.html
http://gladstone.uoregon.edu/~chrismcg/gilliam.html

Alfred Hitchcock
http://nextch.mty.itesm.mx/~plopezg/Kaplan/Hitchcock.html
http://www.primenet.com/~mwc/

Stanley Kubrick
http://pages.prodigy.com/Other/kubrick/
http://www.lehigh.edu/~pj12/kubrick.html

Akira Kurosawa
http://www.voyagerco.com/CC/ghgraphics/kurosawa.html

David Lynch
http://web.city.ac.uk/~cb157/Dave.html
http://www.4w.com/pages/mdunn/dltp.htm

Rob Reiner
http://zen.sunderland.ac.uk/~aa4dhu/rob.html

Martin Scorsese
http://www.afionline.org/Scorsese

Oliver Stone
http://www.geocities.com/Hollywood/2682

Quentin Tarantino
http://www.GANet.Net/~pg0/quentin/greatbig.htm
http://osiris.sunderland.ac.uk/~ca5sli/home.htm
http://www.xs4all.nl/~mrblond/
http://www.blarg.net/~kbilly/
http://www.calweb.com/~gerrit01/qtshrine/
http://www.tarantino.com/top.shtml

Francios Truffault
http://www.inxpress.net/~avatar/truffaut.html

John Waters
http://www.hotwired.com/retina.95/29/waters/index.html
http://www.reed.edu/~mfagan/dreamland.html
http://blackrock.sametz.com/dreamland/
http://www.northcoast.com/~shojo/Waters/

Orson Welles
http://www.voyagerc.com/CC/gh/welles/intro.html
Not a homepage. Part of the Criterion Collection series.

John Woo
http://www.voyagerco.com/movies/directors/woo/

Ed Wood
http://hem2.passagen.se/mwrang/edwood.htm

FILM FESTIVALS

AFI Los Angeles International Film Festival (USA)
http://www.afionline.org/afihomes/aaa.home.html
Features attractions from this huge film festival held every October. Also lists synposes of the films featured.

Berlin Film Festivals
http://www.b.shuttle.de/forum-ifb/
Lists production information on all the films featured in this festival.

Cannes Film Festival
http://www.filmscouts.com
Official site gives you a rundown of all the films running in the competition and an icon called "guest book" so that you can go starchasing in cyberspace.

Chicago International Film Festival
http://www.chicago.ddbn.com/filmfest/menu.html
Answers questions in the area of awards, entries, juries and transportation.

Chicago Lesbian and Gay International Film Festival
http://videos.com/outspoken/gllist.htm
Offers a rundown of films featured in this alternative film festival.

Denver International Film Festival
http://www2.csn.net/DenverFilm/
Besides information on the entries, this site offers insight into the Denver Film Society, supporters, new media and workshops.

London Film Festival
http://www.ibmpcug.co.uk/lff.html
Lists the star attendees and has a program diary which records all the relevant action at this film festival.

Montreal World Film Festival
http://www.ffm-montreal.org/home-f.htm
Offers a rundown of the festival in both English and French.

Santa Clarita International Film Festival
http://www.smartlink.net/~director/scviff
Acknowledges the only film festival in Santa Clarita, California specializing in family films.

Seattle International Film Festival
http://www.seattlefilm.com/
Enables you to look at some photo stills from the festival, read audio speeches and check out some internet broadcasts.

Sundance Film Festival
http://www.sundancefilm.com
Official site may not be as exciting as actually rubbing elbows among the hot talent but it does come close. Sections include a daily report, listings of films competing and a guide for getting around. Also has an archive for past festivals.

Toronto International Film Festival
http://www.bell.ca/toronto/filmfest/
Includes cine-bytes and a feature to browse the poster gallery and check out the paparazzi.

Venice Film Festival
http://www.portve.interbusiness.it/wetvenice/biennale/binfoe.html
Includes information on the film festival, as well as news on other cultural activities happening in Venice.

FILM MAGAZINES

Box Office
http://www.boxoff.com
One of the first trade publications to go online, reporting the latest on current films and films in production.

CinemaSpace
http://cinemaspace.berkeley.edu/
Journal dedicated to all aspects of cinema and new media. Covers such areas as film theory, criticism, multimedia lectures and the film program at UC Berkeley.

Film Threat
http://www.filmthreat.com/
The irreverrent film magazine may be out of circulation, but this site is the next best thing.

FilmMaker
http://found.cs.nyu.edu/CAT/affiliates/filmmaker/filmmaker.html
Quarterly publication that showcases independent film and filmmakers.

Millennium Film Journal
http://www.sva.edu/MFJ/
Published articles about independent, experimental, and avant-garde cinema, video, and, more recently, works that use the newer technologies. Also has an archive for past issues.

Premiere
http://www.premieremag.com/
On-line version of the leading entertainment magazine with various segments including a chat circle called schmoozing and a trivia game.

Time Out
http://www.timeout.co.uk./
Provides a rundown of many cultural and art events happening around the world.

FILM STUDIOS

A-Pix Entertainment
http://www.panix.com/~1weston/virtual_combat.shtml
Showcases its most recent releases to home video with plot synopsis, cast information and production tidbits.

Fine Line Features
http://www.flf.com/

The leading studio of independent films presents information on upcoming releases and offers enlightenment to budding filmmakers.

Gramercy Pictures
http://spider.media.philips.com/polygram/PolyGram.html
http://www.reelife.com
A division of Polygram, where you can jump to various sites dealing with their movies and music.

October Films
http://www.octoberfilms.com
A bevy of recently released independent films are covered here.

MCA/Universal Cyberwalk
http://www.mca.com
Take a stroll through MCA's family tree of entertainment companies which includes Universal Studios, MCA Home Video, MCA Records and Spencer's Gifts. Links you to coming attractions and to a screening room with current video releases.

MGM Lion's Den
http://www.mgmua.com/
Home of the revamped ShowGirls site, also has coverage on the huge distributor's large slate of theatrical releases. Divided into MGM's niches, such as MGM television and home video.

The Miramax Cafe
http://www.miramax.com/
Walk into a smorgasbord of Miramax delectables. Includes chances to win a trip to premieres and Miramax clothing. Click on their week's specials and get a glimpse into their upcoming and current releases.

MPI Home Video
http://www.mpimedia.com
Answers questions on availibility for MPI video releases.

New Line Cinema
http://www.newline.com
Displays their current and upcoming releases.

Paramount Pictures
http://www.paramount.com
Click on any icon from the movies shown and receive information on production and cast.

Republic Pictures
http://www.republic-pictures.com
Includes countless bits of information on this golden oldie studio, with synopses, reviews, and director information. Also lists its entire film library.

Sony Classics
http://www.spe.sony.com/Pictures/SonyClassics
Focuses on Sony's independent releases and offers links to other sites.

Sony Pictures Entertainment
http://www.spe.sony.com/Pictures/SonyMovies/index.html
Sony (which includes Columbia and TriStar) gives you the latest on their crop of films. Along with film and studio information, you can enter their contests to win movie t-shirts or trips to a Hollywood premiere.

Trimark Pictures
http://www.trimarkpictures.com/
Takes you behind the scenes of their latest releases and gives you a glimpse of future films.

Troma
http://www.troma.com/home
With its #1 citizen Toxie welcoming you, indulge in the finest camp cinema that Troma brought to new heights, or lows. Features information on such classics as Toxic Avenger, Class of Nuke'em High and their latest, Sgt. Kabukiman NYPD.

Twentieth Century Fox Home Entertainment
http://www.tcfhe.com
Promotes the studio's library of films which includes such mega hits as the Star Wars and Die Hard trilogies on video. Divided

into a time line enabling you to browse through their collection, beginning with the 1920's and continuing right on to the present.

United International Pictures
http://www.uip.com/
Comes in a variety of languages and has materials on their films which can be downloaded.

Walt Disney Studios
http://www.disney.com
Divided into nine categories where you can find the latest on Disney books, home video, movies, music, shopping, software, television, theater and theme parks.

Warner Brothers
http://www.movies.warnerbros.com/
Get the latest on WB's films, tv programs, music, merchandise, DC comics and kid's programming.

FILMMAKER RESOURCES

American Film Institute
http://www.afionline.org/
The American Film Institute created this site to further its cause of finding talent that will prolong the life of art and film. The site reveals the various courses, studies facilities and grants that this non-profit organziation offers.

American Film Marketing Asssn.(AFMA)
http://www.afma.com
Set up for those who exclusively license, distribute and produce independent films.

Assn. of Independent Video and Filmmakers (AIVF)
http://www.virtualfilm.com/aivf/
Resource that offers information on festivals and self distribution.

Cyber Film School
http://www.cyberfilmschool.com/
Want to become the next Quentin or Spike, but can't afford film school? Try this informative and entertaining venue that teaches the tricks of the trade in areas such as screenwriting, cinematography and producing.

Film Finances
http://www.primenet.com/~ffi/ffihome.html
Check out this site provided by the world leader of financial supplements to film, television and CD-ROM productions if you're looking for financing for a film project.

Filmmakers Foundations (FF)
http://www.filmfound.org
A base for information, training and networking for the novice filmmaker.

Independent Film and Video Makers Internet Resource Guide
http://www.echonyc.com/~mvidal/Indi-Film+Video.html
Questions on funding and film festivals are answered and changes in film and video production are documented on this site.

Mandy's Film and Television Production Directory
http://www.mandy.com/
An international geographical listing of film technicans, facilities and producers. Helpful site for anyone looking for a film crew.

Screenwriter's Online
http://www.screenwriter.com/insider/news.html
Welcomes novice screenwriters to interact with those who are in the business.

Screenwriter's Resources Pages
http://www.teleport.com/~cdeemer/Screenwriters.html
A screenwriter's one-stop resource site. Learn about the format and structure of scripts, how to market your script, network among your peers, receive tips from the pros and become informed of the latest events and seminars.

FILM REVIEWS

Critics Roost
http://moviereviews.com/coc-roost.html
The home of a circle of film critics with their individual slant on film. Women's Lip, The Movie Avenger, The Movie Assassin and J-Man offer their personal perspective on film.

Doug Y's Movie Reviews
http://www.bway.net/~dougy/movies.html
This snappy reviewer includes such categories as Òlf I Were Rex Reed I Would Say.Ó

Film.com
http://www.film.com/film/
Bringing a casual spin on film criticism from self-made critics around the country. Also has a calendar noting upcoming film releases.

The Man Who Viewed Too Much
pages.nyu.edu/~mqd8478/
A New York screenwriting student with a soft touch for the art house fluff and mediocre gems, like Joe Versus the Volcano.

Mandel & Patrick's Movie Corner!
http://www.fyi.net/~andre/mand&pat.htm
Two teenaged boys, using a star system, review current releases as well as video releases.

The Movie Mom's Guide to Movies and Videos for Families
http://pages.prodigy.com/VA/rcpj55a/moviemom.html
Created by movie critic and mother, Nell Minow, who gives critiques and advice on how to get children to watch movies that aren't doused in violence.

The Movie Pit
http://www.geocities.com/Athens/9200/index.htm
Offers film reviews of cheesy movies such as Ice-T's and Rutger Hauer's Surviving the Game and Cat from Outer Space.

Movie Reviews by Ellis: The Art and Craft of Cultural Context
http://movie.infocom.net/
Film critic Joan Ellis puts her acerbic and astute observations on the Internet as she examines the cultural innuendoes in current film.

Movie Reviews by Matt and Kenny
http://www.winternet.com/~nudnik/reviews/
Gives skeletal reviews of films but offers a link to information regarding Lucasfilm's THX sound system.

Movie Review Query Engine
http://www.cinema.pgh.pa.us/movie/reviews
Allows you to search on any movie and find all available reviews appearing in the Usernet group rec.arts.movies. reviews.

Mr. Cranky Rates the Movies
http://internet-plaza.net/zone/mrcranky/
The joke here is that this guy doesn't like any movie, hence Cranky. His rating scale is based on bombs and his followers (code names Lizard, and Philm Pham, just to name a few) are as nutty as his reviews.

Out Magazine Movie Reviews
http://www.out.com/out/entertainment/movies.html
On-line version of the gay magazine that includes movie reviews and commentary on gay and lesbian cinema.

Reviews in Rhyme
http://www.datasync.com/~booda/rir/movies.html
Unique, if not juvenile, way of reviewing films that involves poetry done by ÒMs. Dana's 7th Grade English Class.Ó Samples for Speed: ÒDon't go below fifty/The flying bus looks nifty.Ó

Roger Ebert
http://www.suntimes.com/ebert
Newspapers, books, television, now the web. Offers his newspaper film reviews, with an archive that goes back to 1985.

Skew
http://www.ot.com/skew/

Targeted for the teenage crowd, includes adolescent criticisms on films and popular culture.

Teen Movie Critic
http://www.dreamagic.com/roger/teencritic.html
Seventeen year old movie buff from Minnesota offers his thoughts on current theatrical releases. Also has a link to a listing of many video rental stores around America.

The Third Thumb
http://www.ganesa.com/ganesa/~pat/movies/movrev2.html
Gives brief film reviews and has a searchable database.

The Tripper's Multimedia Movie Reviews
http://www.execpc.com/~tripper/movies.html
Offers film clips, music samples and audio clips.

Uncle Bill's Shack O'Movies
http://www.tmsonline.com/movies/
Funny guide takes on such movies as Bound and includes animation (courtesy of Java) to help get his point across.

VideoHound
http://www.videohound.com
Our home page. Includes reviews of current and highlighted video releases, as well as information on other VIP titles.

Women Studies Film Reviews
http://www.inform.umd.edu:8080/EdRes/Topic/womensStudies/FilmReviews/
Movie reviews with a feminist angle written by Florida radio personality Linda Lopez McAlister and film scholar Cynthia Fuchs.

GENERAL ENTERTAINMENT

Absolut
http://www.absolutvodka.com
Devoted to the annual animation festival that the vodka maker sponsors.

Academy of Motion Picture Arts and Sciences
http://www.oscars.org/ampas/
Site proves that the AMPAS does more than just hand out gold statuettes every year. This homepage reveals this organization's dedication to spreading the love of film around the world. Includes information on AMPAS's varous fellowships, educational and historical activities.

The alt.sex.movies Page
http://www.xmission.com/~legalize/asm/asm.html
Includes miscellanous facts on famous porn stars and essays on pornography and censorship.

American Memory
http://lcweb2.loc.gov/papr/mpixhome.html
Collection of historical film stock that can be downloaded from the Library of Congress. Time frame is from 1897 to 1916 and includes such archival footage as President William McKinley's funeral and "actuality films" showing panoramic views of old San Francisco policemen and firemen in action.

Beatrice's Web Guide
http://www.bguide.com
Female based site that links you to the Barbra Striesand museum.

Belles of the Nineties
http://www.netlink.co.uk/user/michael/belle.html
French contemporary actresses (Emmanuelle Beart and Isabelle Huppert to name a few) are showcased with photos, vital statistics and sound clips.

Big Bad Barbarian
http://pages.ripco.com:8080/~bbb/movies.html
There are many popular scripts on the Internet, such as ,Star Wars and Alien, and the barabarian can lead you to them.

The Black Film Center/Archive
http://www.indiana.edu/~bfca/index.html

An academic reference devoted to sharing resources on black cinema.

Black Rebel
http://www.blackrebel.com
Created by the screenwriter of Eraser, Tony Puryear, who sets his site from the rest by offering ÒfunkierÓ viewpoints on film, with added information on music.

Blockbuster Entertainment
http://pwr.com/blockbuster/
Explores all the goodies the chain has to offer from their many stores and the latest contests or sweepstakes going on.

The Cabinet of Dr. Casey
http://www.cat.pdx.edu/~caseyh/horror/index.html
Immense site that includes interviews from artists and actors in horror films and graphics from famous horror movies. Links you to other horror sites such as "The Ooga Booga Page" and "The Page That Dripped Blood".

CelebSite
http://www.celebsite.com
Spinoff of the very popular Mr. Showbiz site that centers on bio, daily news and links on more than 500 celebrities.

Cine Fantom
http://www.sunsite.cs.msu.su/wwwart/cine/
Exposes Russian experimental films and videos.

Cinemedia
http://www.gu.edu.au/gwis/cinemedia/CineMedia.cinema.html
An index which allows you to begin your own search for other entertainment web sites.

Crazy Movie Credits
http://www.cis.ohio-state.edu/hypertext/faq/usenet/movies/crazy-credits/faq.html
If you think that a movie ends when the credits roll, then you're wrong, at least for some movies. This site showcases the end credits of quirky movies that go out of their way to leave the best for last.

Cybersleaze
http://metaverse.com/vibe/sleaze/index.html
Created by former MTV veejay Adam Curry, this site dishes out the dirt on the celebrities, but in a playful way.

Cyber Sightings
http://www.cyberpages.com/cybersightings
Create your own rumors for others to read and perhaps spread. Stumble onto this site, you may very well be convinced that Babe the pig actually can talk but the government is trying to cover it up.

The Darkside of the Web
http://www.cascade.net/darkweb.html
Specializes in shedding light on the bizarre and creepy.

Dermatology in the Cinema
http://www.itsa.ucsf.edu/~vcr/Dermcin.html
Proof that anything can go on the Web. Exposes how skin afflictions are handled in films. Broken down in three categories: ÒRepresentation of Evil;Ó ÒActors with Skin Findings;Ó and Realistic and Sympathetic Portrayals.Ó Informative and healthy.

Drew's Scripts-o-Rama
http://www.script-o-rama.com
Provides links to pages where transcripts or manuscripts of movie, television, and anime scripts can be found.

The Drudge Report
http://www.lainet.com/~drudge
If you get past the political reports and the weather forecasts that smother this site, you can find some interesting gossip from an anonymous insider from Hollywood.

E! Online
http://www.eonline.com/Hot/Oscar
A fun site to visit come Oscar time. Involves games at the expense of stars not nominated to partake in the festivites.

Each Movie
http://www.eachmovie.com

Recommends films you would like based on ratings you have
given five similar films. Call it the SAT approach to video viewing.

The Electronic Urban Report
http://www.EURweb.com/
Supports the positive images of African Americans in film and
offers the latest celebrity news on the top black stars.

The Envelope Please
http://garbo.virtualize.com/
The official site for the Oscars which provides eye catching graphics, an expansive Oscar trivia game and information on production
of the award show. Noteworthy feature involves video clips from
nominated films which can be downloaded.

Film and Video Resources
http://http2.sils.umich.edu/Public/fvl/film.html
Created by the folks at the University of Michigan School of
Information and Library Studies, this site leads you to many of the
textual resources available that deal with film and video.
Organized according to reviews, filmographies, discussions and
other databases.

Film Forum
http://www.filmforum.com/
Showcases the latest releases in New York's leading independent
movie house. Offers premiere information on independent features and reportory programming.

Film 100
http://www.film100.com
Ranks Hollywood's top visionaries in filmmaking and film business.
Such visionaries include a wide range like John Cassavetes and
actor Joseph Cotton.

Filmzone
http://www.Filmzone.com/
Offers information on independent films, including long lost gems
and interviews with filmmakers and actors suchs as the Coen
Brothers and Jackie Chan. Also gives visitors the current trends in
mulitplexes.

Foresight New Media
http://www.foresight.co.uk/ents/
European company that makes web site pages has its own site
that can link you to other movie sites.

The Gigaplex
http://www.gigaplex.com/
This site has information divided into 15 plexes that include film,
tv, music, theater, books, photos, art, golf, yoga, food, sex, love ,
travel, puzzles and top ten listings from every spectrum of popular
culture.

Girls on Film
http://www.girlsonfilm.com
Four girls talk about pop culture and films.

The GRAFICS Server
http://grafics.histart.umontreal.ca/default-eng.html
Sponsored by a French-Canadian research group that specalizes
in the early cinema of Quebec. Much of the information is in
French, but you can dowload many documents and articles on this
province's early cinema.

Hollywood Online
http://www.hollywood.com
Packaged like a row of slot machines in Vegas, try your luck at
movie trailers, movie trivia, movie chat, vote on the latest contest
or check out some real estate in California.

Hollywood Sign
http://www.rfx.com/hollywood/
Shows snapshots of the famous Hollywood sign from various
angles.

IndieFilms
http://www.indiefilms.com
An easy, inexpensive way to distribute any feature, short or documentary film you made. Allows independent filmmakers to make
contact with potential investors and distributors.

The Internet Entertainment Network
http://www.hollywoodnetwork.com/dealmaking/index.html
Enables you to become a member of the Screenwriters,
Producers or Writers Network. Divided into such sites as deal-
making, box office, in- production and script sales.

The Internet Movie Database
http://www.msstate.edu/Movies
The mother of all entertainment databases. Users can frequently
update the information and submit their own film reviews. With
thousands of movies stored in its database, you can search by
title, actor, director, country and even by character name.

The Internet Movie Institute
http://www.dkdigital.com/Netties/
Involves information on movies and awards.

James Bond
http://www.mcs.net/~klast/www/bond.html
With the arrival and success of Goldeneye, the phenomenon of
Bond has invaded cyberspace with his own homepage. Includes
a rundown of all Bond villains and their famous lines, and trivia on
every Bond film ever made.

Kino on Video
http://www.kino.com/
Kino International showcases a breadth of films from world cinema.

Kinema Club
Includes reviews of Japanese films and dedicated to the exposure of
contemporay Japanese films.

The Left-Wing Film Guide
http://ccme-mac4.bsd.uchicago.edu/DSADocs/Films.html
Helpful guide for any social and political group planning their next
movie themed rally. Pick any movie from any of their categories
that include feminism, race relations and anti-authoritian struggles.

Library of Congress Archive
http://lcweb2.loc.gov/papr/mpixhome.html
Allows you to download historical film images from the early
1900's.

Local Movie Listings
http://www.actwin.com/movies/other.html
Includes movie theater showtimes from Canada, England and
South Africa as well as American cities.

Lucy Lipps
http://www.lucylipps.com/
Includes a Kiss & Tell section which brings you the latest scoop on
celebrities and the buzz around Tinseltown.

Movies.com
http://www.movies.com/
Displays the latest films and allows celebrities to welcome visitors
onto the site.

The Movie Cliches List
http://www.like.it/vertigo/cliches.html
A vast list of common stereotypes and instances that stifle logic
found in film. Divided into over fifty topics including bodily functions, minorities, teenagers and wood. A growing site since people can submit their own materials.

Moviefinder.com
http://www.moviefinder.com/
Presented by ElOnline, it's an all in one site that enables you to
find, buy or rent a movie. Includes among other things, search
engine, archive of film reviews, and listings for local theaters.

MovieLink
http://www.movielink.com/?TP:National
On-line movie guide with listings of local movie theaters in the 22
most populated cities in the country. Features include a section
for users to cast their votes for "The American Moviegoer Awards"
and a place called the "cafe" for users to chit chat.

Movie Mania
http://www.clicked.com/moviemania/

Find out what's new and what's hot on the video scene. Also keeps you informed of the latest free software available on the Web.

MovieNet
http://www.movienet.com/
A consulting firm used by Hollywood execs seeking information on the latest film projects in production, up and coming directors, acting talent and news on the acquistions of remakes.

The Movie Posters Archive
http://anubis.science.unitn.it/services/movies/index.html
An on-line vault of old movie posters from the sci-fi, horror, animation and classic genres.

Movie Poster Web Page
http://www.musicman.com/mp/mp.html
No, you're not seeing double. This one is a catalog of movie posters available for sale. Includes foreign films.

Movie Snapshot
http://www.moviesnapshot.com/'
Reviews, photographs, celebrity interviews, biographies, games and awards.

The Movie Sound Page
http://www.moviesounds.com.html
Download various sound bites from famous flicks and link to other sites.

Movie Recommendation System
http://www.labs.bt.com/innovate/multimed/morse/morse.htm
Your votes count with this site that enables you to rate movies you have seen and based on your rating, will recommend movies you might like. This is not a game, but a service.

Movies at MSN
http://207.68.142.34/movies.movies
Companion piece to Microsoft's Cinemania CD-ROM.

MovieWEB
http://movieweb.com/movie/movie.html
Groups all film studios in to one site and offers production information and still photos of their new releases. Also offers the latest box office statistics.

Mr. Showbiz
http://www.mrshowbiz.com/showbiz/
Bundles the latest entertainment gossip and news with movie and music reviews. Includes an in-depth volume of knowledge on the history of the Academy Awards.

The Muse
http://www.hyperlink.com/muse
Dedicated to the Greek mythology figure who spawned the arts. Among its links for books, music, theater and dance, includes one for cinema where it will showcase such directors as Roman Polanski and Martin Scorsese.

The Obituary Page
http://catless.ncl.ac.uk/Obituary/movies.html
A listing of the latest celebrity deaths in Hollywood.

OscarNet
http://www.dkdigital.com/Netties/
Encourages visitors to vote for nominees and for alternative nominations called the "Netty Awards". Visitors can vote for the" Golden Raspberry Awards "for the year's worst performances.

Our Secret Century: Revelations from The Prelinger Archive
gopher://gopher.well.sf.ca.us:70/11/Art/Experimental.Film.and.Video/secret.century
Contains footage and information on films from The Prelinger Archives which is a collection of instititional films made from Ô30's to the early Ô60's. Some of these clips can been seen on The Late Show with David Letterman.

Pathfinder
http://www.pathfinder.com
Created by Time Warner, site links to their magazines that check the pulse of popular culture such as People, Vibe, Groove and Entertainment Weekly.

The Phantasmagoria Graveyard Web Page
http://libstaff.lib.lehigh.edu
Audio website that features the theme music from such horror films as Halloween *and* The Shining.

Planet Earth
http://www.demon.co.uk/elpasso/planet-earth/index.htm
If you're looking for film and tv memorablilia from such popular movies and series as Alien *or* Space 1999, *this is the place to order such merchandise. An on-line catalog for costumes, model kits, back issues of specialized magazines and trading cards. You can even post any items you might want to sell.*

Popcornq
http://www.popcornq.com
Dedicated to showcasing films dealing with gays and lesbians.

Reel Talk
http://www.reellife.com/PFE/index.html
If you're a movie buff, then join the crowd as you talk amongst yourselves about the latest releases.

Science Fiction Contiuum
http://www.webcreations.com/sjvideo/
A guide to a diverse collection of sci-fi and horror films as well as animation, television and UFO documentaries on video and laser disc.

ScreenSite
http://www.sa.ua.edu/Screesite/
Primarily wants to encourage the teaching and researching of film and television.

Silent Movies
http://www.cs.monash.edu.au/~pringle/silent/
Information on silent films. Includes a listing for many silent film screening and bios on many of the era's top stars such as Charlie Chaplin, Buster Keaton and Lillian Gish.

The Top 25
http://movieweb.com/movie/top25.html
Anxious to see if a certain movie has broken any box office records during its opening week? This site provides the box office ranking of all current releases. Updated every Thursday.

U.C. Berkeley Film Studies Science Fiction Page
http://remarque.berkeley.edu:8001/~xcohen/Resources/localres.html
For avid SciFi film buffs, site has separate pages for such classics as Blade Runner, Star Trek, Alien, Star Wars *and other genre related sites.*

UFO Diaries
http://www.ufo-diaries.com
Learn about new sci-fi releases from Republic Pictures.

Wiretap Archive
gopher://wiretap.spies.com:70/11/Library/Media/Film
Very straightforward and diverse listing of special interest movies. Categories include: films with rape scenes, film noir listing, railway movies, Japanese monster guide, naval related movies and vampires in movies.

INDIVIDUAL MOVIE SITES

Addicted to Love
http://www.addictedtolove.com/main.html

The Adventures of Buckaroo Banzai
http://bbs.annex.com/relayer/bbanzai.htm

Air Force One
www.spe.sony.com/Pictures/SonyMovies/soon/index.html

Airplane
http://www.d.umn.edu/~elindsko/Airplane/airplane.html

ALIEN Saga
http://found.cs.nyu.edu/michael/alien/

Alien Resurrection
http://www.alien-resurrection.com

The American President
http://www.americanpresident.com

Anaconda
www.spe.sony.com/Pictures/SonyMovies/movies/Anaconda/entry.html

Apocalypse Now
http://www.luhsd.k12.ca.us/~nc670597/apocnow.html

Apollo 13
http://www.mca.com/universal_pictures/apollo13/index.html

Batman and Robin
http://www.batman-robin.com/
http://home.revealed.net/riddler/batrob.htm

Blade Runner
http://kzsu.stanford.edu/uwi/br/off-world.html

Braveheart
http://www.aloha.net/~brvhrt/index.html

Brazil
http://www.cis.ohio-state.edu/hypertext/faq/usenet/movies/brazil-faq.html

Buddy
http://us.imdb.com/M/title-exact?Buddy%20%281997%29
http://www.spe.sony.com/Pictures/SonyMovies/movies/Buddy/index2.html

The Cable Guy
http://www.thecableguy.com

A Christmas Story
http://www.easttexas.com/pdlg/c-story/

Clueless
http://www.paramount.com/Clueless.html

Con Air
http://www.movies.com/conair/

Crash
www.flf.com/crash

Death Race 2000
http://www.mcn.net/~netrencher/dr2k.html

Desperate Measures
www.spe.sony.com/Pictures/SonyMovies/movies/Desperate/intro.html

The Doom Generation
http://www.filmzone.com/doom

Dragonheart
http://www.mca.com/universal_pictures/dragonheart/

Eraserhead
http://users.aol.com/RayWolf1/eraser.htm

Event Horizon
www.islandnet.com/~corona/films/details/eventhorizon.html

The Evil Dead
http://www.daze.com/exit13/evil/

Fast Times at Ridgemont High
http://wizvax.net/tuegger/fast-times.html

The Fifth Element
http://www.cinema1.com/movies97/fifthelement/us.html

From Dusk Till Dawn
http://www.hooked.net/users/cpatubo/fdtd.html

George of the Jungle
http://wwwdisney.com/DisneyPictures/George_of_the_Jungle/index.html
http:movi[web.com/movie/georgejungle/index.html

Get Shorty
http://www.uip.com/getshorty/

Ghostbusters
http://www.nwdc.com/~vostok/ghostbusters.html

The Godfather Trilogy
http://www.exit109.com/~jgeoff/godfathr.html

Goldeneye
http://www.mgmua.com/bond/index.html

Gone Fishin'
http://www.movies.com/gonefishin/

Gone With the Wind
http://users.aol.com/axlrose75/gone.htm

Halloween
http://www.wavenet.com/~gbernard/

Head Above Water
http://bluedevil.com/bz/haw.htm

Hercules:The Legendary Journeys
http://www.disney.com/DisneyPictures/Hercules/index.html

Indiana Jones
http://www.smartlink.net/~deej7/indiana_jones.html

Independence Day
http://www.id4.com/

Jade
http://www.paramount.com/jade/index.html

Jaws
http://www.winternet.com/~tandj04/jaws.html

The Jerk
http://www.hirons.com/~lburgess/jerk.html

Jurassic Park
http://uslink.net/~warrior/

Kull the Conqueror
http://hub.islandnet.com/~corona/films/details/kull.html

Leave It To Beaver
http://www.mca.com/universal_pictures/ComingIndex.html

The Lost World: Jurassic Park
http://www.powerup.com.au/~stott/LWindex.html
http://wwwo.lost-world.com/
http://nac.net/~users/splat/lw/

Love!Valour!Compassion!
http://www.flf.com/lvc/index.html

Men In Black
http://www.meninblack.com/

Mission Impossible
http://www.missionimpossible.com.

Monty Python's Holy Grail
http://bucket.ualr.edu/holygrail

Mortal Kombat
http://www.newline.com/nlc_releases/nlc_releases.html
http://www.nclpub.com/Relsched/mortal.html
http://www.mortalkombat.com/newsite/index.html

My Best Friend's Wedding
http://www.spe.sony.com/Pictures/SonyMovies/movies/Bestfriend/intro.html

Night Falls on Manhattan
http://us.imdb.com/cache/urls/title+72876

Nowhere
http://www.flf.com/nowhere/index.html

101 Dalmations
http://www.101.com

Out to Sea
http://www.metronet.com/~shreck/ca/Ots.html

The People vs. Larry Flynt
www.spe.com/sony

Phantasm
http://www.phantasm.com/

Plan 9 From Outer Space
http://www.eng2.uconn.edu/~jstrip/plan9/

Psycho
http://www.geocities.com/Hollywood/1645/index.html

Reservoir Dogs
http://www.foresight.co.uk/ents/dogs/

Return of the Texas Chainsaw Massacre
http://chainsaw.crimson.com/rtcm/

Rob Roy
http://www.mgmua.com/robroy/index.html

Rocky Horror Picture Show
http://www-scf.usc.edu/~proulx/RHPS.html
http://www.insv.com/rhps/

Scarface
http://pubweb.acns.nwu.edu/~apoorman/scarface.html

Seven
http://www.filmzone.com/seven

Shaft
http://users.aol.com/PizarroD/shaft.html
http://www.rapidcity.com

Shall We Dance
http://www.cinema1.com/movies97/shallwedance/us.html

The Shining
http://pubweb.acns.nwu.edu/~mdk899/overlook.html

Showgirls
http://www.mgmua.com/showgirls/index.html

Silence of the Lambs
http://www.pitt.edu/~elkst2/silence.html

Spawn
http://www.spawn.com/film.html

Speed 2
http://www.speed2-cruisecontrol.com/site/index_new.htm

Sprung
http://www.cinema1.com/movies97/sprung/us.html

Star Trek (Trek Reviews Archive)
http://www.mcs.net/~forbes/trek-reviews/

Star Trek: First Contact
http://www.first-contact.com

Steel
http://www.globalserve.net/~ejdylan/steel2.html

Sunday
http://www.sundancechannel.com/festival97.webcast/s-19438675097.
html

Superfly
http://student-www.uchicago.edu/users/bra9/fly.html

Terminator (1 &2)
http://www.maths.tcd.ie/pub/films/terminator/

Tetsuo II: Body Hammer
http://wwwwp.com.com/69031/home/html
movienet.culnet.fi/mondonet/movies/tesuo.htm (not in english)

This Is Spinal Tap
http://www.spinaltap.com/

Titanic
http://bluedevil.com/bz/tita.htm
http://www.titancimovie.com/
http://www.geocities.com/Hollywood/9251/titanic.html

Trial and Error
http://www.trialanderror.com/

Toy Story
http://www.disney.com/ToyStory/?GL=H

Truck Turner
http://www.castle.net/~dcentury/truck.html

Twister
http://www.indirect.com/www/storm5/twisterhomepage.html

2001: A Space Odyssey
http://www.lehigh.edu/~pj12/films/2001.html

The Usual Suspects
http://www.spectra.net/~funkman/spacey/usual/usual/html

The Van
http://www.filmscouts.com/films/van.html

Virtuosity
http://www.paramount.com/virtuosity/index.html

Wild America
http://us.imdb.com/M/title-exact?Wild%20America%20

VIDEO OUTLETS

Adventures in Video
http://www.tds.net/aiv/htm
Offers a wide assortment of video titles from self-help to study aides.

Art and Trash Video
http://www.io.org/~imp/athome.htm
An outlet of over 7,500 titles in the art and trash genre that are hard to find.

Best Video
http://www.bestvideo.com
With over 24,000 titles, you can search their inventory via various topics and subject categories. Also includes brief monthly reviews of current releases.

Big Lizard Video
http://www.well.com/user/bigliz/
Order through the mail the most obscure and bizarre films ever made.

Blockbuster
http://pwr.com/blockbuster/
Find video releases, movie merchandise, movie reviews and news here. Ordering is only done through e-mail.

Carpel Video
http://www.peakcom.com/carpel/
If you're only interested in purchasing blank and recycled video tapes, then you've hit the jackpot with this site.

CINEVISTA Video
http://www.gayweb.com/112/112home.html
Deals mainly in the distribution of independent gay films and videos.

Family Home Video
http://www.iea.com/~fhv/
On-line ordering service for over 25,000 titles that are also linked to the Internet Movie Database.

Flicks on Disc
http://www.teleport.com/~gilbert/flicks/public_html/index.html
Exclusive to the laser disc market with an expansive list of titles and news of upcoming releases.

HBO Home Video Online
http://hbohomevideo.com/
Along with information of their productions released on video, this site includes sounds, video clips, and celebrity photos.

Ken Crane's Laser Disc Super Store
http://www.kencranes.com/laserdiscs/
Largest retailer of laser discs that can be ordered either through the mail or on-line.

Moovies Online
http://www.bnt.com/moovies/index.html
National video chain based in South Carolina that doesn't merely advertise its products but provides an entertaining and informative site.

The Movie Show Video

http://www.movieshow.com/

Three-store chain in Dallas advertises its entire stock and gives links to other sites.

Movies Unlimited

http://www.moviesunlimited.com

The world's largest video retailer breaks down its huge selection into some interesting sections, such as Fast Forward, which includes information on upcoming releases; Let's Go to the Lobby, has the latest news from Hollywood; and the Studio Tour, which links you to other related sites.

Picture Palace

http://www.ids.net/picpal/index.html

Enormous on-line catalog that has a comprehensive and searchable database for its 36,000+ titles. Also has special features including a magazine rack and a place for international cinema.

Rocket Video

http://www.rocketvideo.com/

"A virtual video store" that carries over 12,000 VHS titles and 500 laser discs. Has features which include "staff picks" and "coming soon".

World Artists Home Video

http://www.worldartists.com/world

Get up-to-date information on upcoming releases from this underground outlet.